Thoma

EUROPEAN RAIL TIMETABLE

INDEPENDENT TRAVELLER'S EDITION

Winter 2007/8

Thomas Cook
Publishing

Published by
Thomas Cook Publishing,
P. O. Box 227
The Thomas Cook Business Park
Coningsby Road
Peterborough PE3 8SB
United Kingdom

ISBN 978-1-84157-838-5

Head of Travel Books : John Sadler

Editor : Brendan Fox

Editorial team : Kevin Flynn, John Potter, David Turpie, Chris Woodcock

Telephone (Sales) +44 (0)1733 416477 (Editorial) +44 (0)1733 416322
Fax +44 (0)1733 416688

e-mail (Sales): publishing-sales@thomascook.com
e-mail (Editorial): timetables@thomascook.com

Website and on-line bookshop : www.thomascookpublishing.com

Front cover photograph:

The narrow gauge Brunig Line, Switzerland
A train about to depart Giswil for Luzern (Table 561)
© Reinhard Reiss www.reissweb.net

Printed in Great Britain by William Clowes Ltd, Beccles, Suffolk

INTRODUCTION

This **Independent Traveller's Edition** is a specially enlarged version of the monthly **European Rail Timetable**, published by Thomas Cook for over 130 years and recognised throughout the world as the indispensable compendium of European rail schedules. The Independent Traveller's Edition appears twice yearly in Winter and Summer versions based on the December and June editions of the European Rail Timetable.

The much-loved red **Thomas Cook European Rail Timetable** has for years been the travelling companion of the dedicated European rail-based tourist and business traveller. For travel further afield you need the blue **Thomas Cook Overseas Timetable** covering North and South America, Asia, Africa and Australasia.

The intention of this special **Independent Traveller's Edition** is to make the timetable more widely available to the increasing numbers of holidaymakers who are touring Europe by train, whether using InterRail, Eurail or one of the other popular European rail passes, or simply travelling point to point. It includes additional information of use to rail travellers, especially those trying this kind of holiday for the first time.

Our feature on **Rail Passes** (pages v to xi) includes full details of the InterRail Global Pass and InterRail One Country Pass schemes (for European residents), as well as latest details of the various Eurail passes for those resident outside Europe. Many other passes are also featured, including a selection of citywide tickets and visitor cards for those visiting major European cities.

The **Country-by-Country** section (pages xii to xxxii) is packed with useful information about each country, and there is a chart of visa requirements on page xxxii. In the main body of the timetable, **Newslines** on page 3 has information about the latest changes and about the particular contents of this edition. Pages 10 to 11 help you make vital preparations for your journey, whilst a little time spent reading the notes on pages 4 to 9, explaining how to read the timetable, will be amply repaid when you get down to the task of planning your travels.

Whether you intend to travel only in one or two countries, or are attempting a spectacular grand tour of Europe, the timetables in this book will cover most of the routes you will need and will enable you to pre-plan your journey, which is often half the fun. Rail timetables are, however, always liable to change and you are recommended to consult the latest monthly edition of the European Rail Timetable or local information before travelling.

ACCOMMODATION

Hotels:

Europe offers an excellent choice, from five-star hotels to room only. Your main problem may lie in finding something to suit your budget. Rooms in private houses are often a good, inexpensive and friendly option (local tourist offices often have lists), but you may be expected to stay for more than one night. The quality of cheaper hotels in Eastern Europe may still be less than inspiring and you may do better with a private room. Local tourist offices are almost always your best starting point if you haven't pre-booked. If they don't handle bookings themselves (there's usually a small charge), they will re-direct you to someone who does and/or supply you with the information to do it yourself – tell them your price horizons.

Hostels:

For those on a tight budget, the best bet is to join **HI** (Hostelling International); there's no age limit. Membership of a national association will entitle you to use over 5000 HI hostels in 60 different countries and, apart from camping, they often provide the cheapest accommodation. The norm is dormitory-style, but many hostels also have single and family rooms.

Many offer excellent-value dining and many have self-catering and/or laundry facilities. Some hostels are open 24 hours, but most have lock-out times and reception's hours are usually limited; advise them if you are arriving out of hours. Reservation is advisable – many hostels fill well in advance and even those with space are likely to limit your stay to three nights if you just turn up without booking. In winter (except around Christmas) you may be able to get special price deals.

Buy the HI's directory Europe, which lists hostel addresses, contact numbers, locations and facilities; the HI website is *www.iyhf.org.*

Camping:

This is obviously the cheapest accommodation if you're prepared to carry the equipment. There are campsites right across Europe, from basic (just toilets and showers) to luxury family-oriented sites with dining-rooms, swimming pools and complexes of permanent tents. The drawback is that sites are often miles from the city centres. There's no really good pan-European guide to campsites, but most tourist offices can provide a directory for their country.

WHAT TO TAKE WITH YOU

Luggage:

Backpack (not more than 50 litres for women or 60 litres for men) plus day sack; sort your luggage into see-through polythene bags (makes fishing out your socks from the backpack much easier), plus take plastic bags for dirty clothes etc, and elastic bands for sealing them.

Clothing:

Lightweight clothing, preferably of a type that doesn't need ironing; smart casual clothes for evening wear, swimsuit, sun hat, long-sleeved garment to cover shoulders (essential in some churches/temples; women may need head scarves); non-slip foot-wear – and don't forget underwear! All-purpose hiking boots (useful for big walks around cities) or rubber sandals with chunky soles are good when it's hot; flip flops for the shower etc.

First Aid/Medical:

Insect repellent and antihistamine cream, sun-screen cream, after-sun lotion, water-sterilising tablets, something for headaches and tummy troubles, antiseptic spray or cream, medicated wet-wipes, plasters for blisters, bandage, contraceptives and tampons (especially if visiting Eastern Europe, where they can be sometimes difficult to get – or try the luxury shop in the city's biggest hotel). Spare spectacles/contact lenses and a copy of your prescription.

Overnight Equipment:

Lightweight sleeping-bag (optional), sheet liner (for hostelling), inflatable travel pillow, earplugs, and eyemask.

Documents:

Passport, tickets, photocopies of passport/visas (helps if you lose the passport itself) and travel insurance, travellers' cheques counterfoil, passport photos, student card, numbers of credit cards and where to phone if you lose them.

Other items:

A couple of lightweight towels, small bar of soap, water-bottle, pocket knife, torch (flashlight), sewing kit, padlock and chain (for anchoring your luggage), safety matches, mug and basic cutlery, toothbrush, travel wash, string (for a washing-line), travel adapter, universal bath plug (often missing from wash-basins), sunglasses, alarm clock, note-pad and pen, pocket calculator (to convert money), a money-belt and a good book/game (for long journeys).

EUROPEAN RAIL PASSES

Rail passes represent excellent value for train travellers who are touring around Europe (or parts of it) or making a number of journeys within a short period. They can offer substantial savings over point-to-point tickets, as well as greater flexibility.

Passes may cover most of Europe (e.g. InterRail or Eurail), a specific group of countries, single countries, or just a certain area. InterRail passes are only available to European residents, whereas Eurail passes are only for non-European residents. Most passes cannot be used in your country of residence.

Passes either cover a specified number of consecutive days, or are of the flexi type where you get so many 'travel days' within a specified period (you write each date of use in a box on the pass). Free travel will mean the use of a travel day, whereas discounted travel may not. Many passes are available from appointed agents or their websites, whereas some may be purchased from principal railway stations. Your passport may be required for identification, also one or two passport-size photos.

Passes generally cover the ordinary services of the national rail companies, but supplements often have to be paid for travel on express and high-speed services and on 'global price' trains. 'Private' railways may not accept passes but may give discounts to passholders. Extra charges always apply for travel in sleeping cars or couchettes.

In this feature USD = US dollars, € = euros, £ = pounds sterling.

InterRail

InterRail Global Pass

Area of validity

The *InterRail Global Pass* is valid for unlimited travel on the national railways of 30 European countries, namely Austria, Belgium, Bosnia-Herzegovina, Bulgaria, Croatia, Czech Republic, Denmark, Finland, France, Germany, Great Britain, Greece, Hungary, Republic of Ireland, Italy, Luxembourg, Republic of Macedonia, Montenegro, the Netherlands, Norway, Poland, Portugal, Romania, Serbia, Slovakia, Slovenia, Spain, Sweden, Switzerland and Turkey, also on ferry services between Italy and Greece operated by Attica (i.e. SuperFast Ferries and Blue Star Ferries). Passes are **not** valid in the purchaser's country of residence. Note that passes are no longer valid in Morocco or Northern Ireland.

Who can buy the pass?

The pass can be purchased by anyone who has lived for at least six months in one of the European countries where the pass is valid, or is a national of that country and holds a valid passport. Those resident for at least six months in other European countries (including Russia) are also entitled to purchase the pass, and can do so in any of the participating countries - others have to buy it in their country of residence. Passes can be purchased up to three months before travel begins.

Periods of validity and prices

- Any 5 days within 10 days (flexi): adult 1st class €329/£241, adult 2nd class €249/£182, youth 2nd class €159/£117.
- Any 10 days within 22 days (flexi): adult 1st class €489/£357, adult 2nd class €359/£263, youth 2nd class €239/£175.
- 22 days (continuous): adult 1st class €629/£460, adult 2nd class €469/£343, youth 2nd class €309/£226.
- 1 month (continuous): adult 1st class €809/£591, adult 2nd class €599/£438, youth 2nd class €399/£292.

Youth prices are available to those aged 25 or under on the first day for which the pass is valid. Child fares for ages 4 to 11 are available at approximately half the price of the adult pass.

Note that under the new scheme there are no 'zonal' InterRail passes.

Supplements payable

Supplements are payable for certain types of express or high-speed train, including: *Alaris, Altaria, Arco, AVE, Euromed, Talgo* (Spain), *Alfa Pendular* (Portugal), *ES* (Eurostar Italia), *S220* (Finnish Pendolino), *TGV, Téoz* (France), *X2000 (Sweden), Cisalpino* (Switzerland - Italy), also *Icity* and *IcityE* trains in Greece. Discounted 'passholder' fares apply on *Eurostar* and *Thalys* trains, also on *Elipsos* (night trains France/Italy - Spain), Artesia (France - Italy), Lyria (*TGV* service France - Switzerland) and on certain other 'global price' routes. Passholders now travel free on German *ICE* services. The official website www.interrailnet.com gives further details.

Sleeping car and couchette supplements are not included. Seat reservation fees are also excluded - these can sometimes be compulsory, for example on all main-line trains in Spain (€6 in tourist class, €10 on *AVE* and *Talgo 200* trains), on German *Nachtzüge* night trains, French *TGV* trains and express trains in Norway and Sweden.

Note that on the Greece - Italy ferry services (SuperFast and Blue Star), you will need to pay port taxes, also fuel and high-season surcharges. Upgrades to cabin accommodation or reclining seats are extra.

Discount in country of residence

Although the pass is not valid in the country of residence, passholders can obtain a reduction for one return ticket to the border of 25% - 50%, except in Great Britain, Poland or Romania (children pay half this reduced fare).

Validity on other railways

InterRail passes are valid on the principal railway companies in each country, but may not be valid on 'private' or locally run railways (some give discounts). Selected details are as follows (some require reservations): **Denmark**: 50% discount on Hjørring - Hirtshals and Frederikshavn - Skagen. **France**: 25% discount on CP (Nice - Digne), 50% on railways in Corsica. **Hungary**: GySEV services are included. **Norway**: the Myrdal - Flåm line is treated as a 'private' line and gives 30% discount. **Spain**: FGC railways give 50% discount. **Sweden**: the Arlanda Express and Inlandsbanan are included, as are services operated by Veolia, which includes the night trains to the north. **Switzerland**: free travel on certain railways including BLS, FART/SSIF, MOB, RhB, SOB, THURBO. Many others offer 50% discount, including CJ, LSE, Rigibahnen, Pilatusbahn. The MGB (Disentis - Brig - Zermatt and Göschenen - Andermatt) and Gornergratbahn offer 50% to under-26s only. No discounts are available on the BRB or the narrow gauge railways in the Jungfrau area (BOB, JB, WAB). Information is subject to change and it's best to check before travelling.

Discounts on other ferry services

Reductions of between 20% and 50% are available on various ferry services, many of which are shown below (details are subject to alteration). Ferry discounts usually exclude cabin accommodation, and other restrictions (such as compulsory reservation) may apply:

Color Line day sailings 50%; DFDS 25% on certain services; Fjord Line special prices; Flaggruten 50%; Fylkesbaatane 40%; Grimaldi 20%; Hellenic Mediterranean 50% (summer); Irish Ferries 50%; Iscomar 30% (not high summer); Minoan Lines special prices; Sea France 50%; Silja Line 50% (restrictions apply); Stena 30% (25% on *Lynx* Fishguard - Rosslare); Superfast Rosyth - Zeebrugge 25%; Tallink Rostock - Helsinki special prices; Viking Line 50%. No discount on SNCM to Corsica.

Note that passes are valid on Austrian lake services operated by ÖBB, and discounts are available on certain Swiss lake steamers. For further details of discounts see the InterRail website www.interrailnet.com.

Other discounts

DDSG offer 20% on Melk - Krems river cruises. Certain bus services in Norway offer a 50% discount. Some railway museums offer free or discounted entry and a limited number of tourist attractions, hotels, hostels and cycle hire outlets offer discounts.

InterRail One Country Pass

This new pass replaced the EuroDomino scheme from April 1, 2007.

Area of validity

The *InterRail One Country Pass* is valid for travel in any **one** of the participating countries above, with the exception of Bosnia- Herzegovina and Montenegro. It is **not** available for travel in the purchaser's country of residence. Note that Benelux (Belgium, Luxembourg and the Netherlands) counts as one country. There are two passes for Greece - the *Greece Plus* variant includes ferry services between Italy and Greece operated by Attica (i.e. SuperFast Ferries and Blue Star Ferries).

Periods of validity and prices

All passes are flexi passes, valid for 3, 4, 6 or 8 days within 1 month. Prices shown are for adult 1st class, adult 2nd class and youth (under 26) respectively, and are in euros (for approx £ prices multiply by 0.73). Eligibility / supplements / discounts are as for the *InterRail Global Pass*.

- Price level 1 - France, Germany, Great Britain, Norway, Sweden: 3 days €255/189/125, 4 days €285/209/139, 6 days €363/269/175, 8 days €404/299/194.
- Price level 2 - Austria, Benelux, Finland, Greece 'Plus', Republic of Ireland, Italy, Spain, Switzerland: 3 days €147/109/71, 4 days €188/139/90, 6 days €255/189/123, 8 days €309/229/149.
- Price level 3 - Croatia, Denmark, Greece, Hungary, Poland, Portugal, Romania: 3 days €93/69/45, 4 days €120/89/58, 6 days €161/119/77, 8 days €188/139/90.
- Price level 4 - Bulgaria, Czech Republic, Republic of Macedonia, Serbia, Slovakia, Slovenia, Turkey: 3 days €66/49/32, 4 days €93/69/45, 6 days €134/99/64, 8 days €161/119/77.

Eurail

Eurail Global Pass

Area of validity

The *Eurail Global Pass* is valid for unlimited travel on the national railways of 18 European countries, namely Austria, Belgium, Denmark, Finland, France, Germany, Greece, Hungary, the Republic of Ireland, Italy, Luxembourg, the Netherlands, Norway, Portugal, Romania, Spain, Sweden and Switzerland. New for 2008 will be Croatia and Slovenia.

Note that additional countries participate in the *Eurail Select Pass*, *Eurail Regional Pass* and *Eurail National Pass* (see below).

Who can buy the pass?

The pass can be purchased by anyone resident outside Europe (but excluding residents of the former USSR or Turkey). Passes are sold through official Eurail Sales Agents and can also be bought directly from Eurail through www.Eurail.com.

The option exists to buy the passes after arrival in Europe but it is much cheaper to buy them beforehand, and since you can buy them up to six months in advance, there is no point in waiting until the last minute. Pass validity cannot be changed once in Europe, and passes must be validated before first use.

Periods of validity and prices

Adult *Eurail Global Passes* are valid for first class travel (naturally you can also travel in second class), wheras the under-26 Youth version is for 2nd class travel only:

- 15 days: adult 675 USD, youth 439 USD.
- 21 days: adult 879 USD, youth 569 USD.
- 1 month: adult 1,089 USD, youth 709 USD.
- 2 months: adult 1,539 USD, youth 999 USD.
- 3 months: adult 1,899 USD, youth 1,235 USD.
- 10 days within 2 months: adult 799 USD, youth 519 USD.
- 15 days within 2 months: adult 1,049 USD, youth 679 USD.

Children aged 4 - 11 pay half fare, and children under 4 travel free (except if a reservation for a separate seat or bed is required).

Two or more people travelling together are eligible for the *Saver* rate, giving a reduction of 15% on the adult fare (there is no youth *Saver*, children aged 4 - 11 in the group pay half the *Saver* rate).

Supplements payable

Supplements are not required for *EC*, *IC*, *ICE* trains. *Thalys* charge a special passholder rate, as do other 'global price' trains (including many night trains). French *TGV* and *Téoz* require the reservation fee only. In Spain most long-distance trains have a supplement/reservation fee (sample rates: regional trains €4, long-distance €6.50, *AVE* Turista class €10; on services where meal provided in 1st/Preferente class €23.50). Supplements are also payable on *ICE Sprinter*, *Cisalpino* (€5), *Eurostar Italia* (€20), *X2000* (€7-17) and *IcityE* in Greece. As with all passes, sleeper/couchette supplements and seat reservations are extra.

Validity on other railways

Eurail passes are valid on the principal railway companies in each country, but may not be valid on 'private' or locally run railways (some give discounts). Selected details are as follows (some require reservations): **Denmark**: 50% discount on Hjørring - Hirtshals and Frederikshavn - Skagen. **France**: valid on RER in Paris (obtain a voucher), 25% discount on CP (Nice - Digne), 50% on railways in Corsica, 50% on the Vivarais Railway. **Hungary**: GySEV services are included, 50% discount on 'nostalgia' steam trips and the train to the railway museum. **Norway**: the Myrdal - Flåm line is treated as a 'private' line and gives 30% discount. **Spain**: FGC railways give 50% discount. **Sweden**: the Arlanda Express and services operated by Veolia (including the night trains to the north) are included. **Switzerland**: free travel on many railways including BLS, CJ, FART/SSIF, MOB, RhB, SOB, SZU, THURBO, TMR, TPC, ZB. There is 50% discount on Vitznau-Rigi, the Pilatus line (and cable car) offers 30%, and there is a 25% discount on railways in the Jungfrau region (BOB, JB, WAB), the MGB (Disentis-Brig- Zermatt), and the Gornergratbahn. There are reductions on some cable cars as well. A list of bonuses is included in the Traveler's Guide issued with your pass. Note that *Eurostar* also offer special prices.

Ferry services

Free passage or fare reductions are available on various ferry services; the main ones are shown below. Ferry discounts usually exclude cabin accommodation, and other restrictions (such as compulsory reservation) may apply:

Color Line day sailings 50%; DFDS 25% (restricted availability); Flaggruten 50%; Grimaldi 20%, Hellenic Mediterranean 50% (summer); Irish Ferries 30%; Minoan Lines free deck passage if pass valid in Italy and Greece (summer surcharges €16-26); Sea France 50%; Silja Line free passage if pass valid in Sweden and Finland, 30% on Rostock - Helsinki (port taxes extra); Stena Line 30%; Superfast/Blue Star free passage if pass valid in Italy and Greece (summer surcharge €15-30, port tax €6, fuel surcharge €10); Superfast Zeebrugge-Rosyth 25%.

Most boat services on the Swiss lakes are included in the pass, as are Austrian lake services operated by ÖBB. Bodensee ferries operated by BSB, SBS, ÖBB give 50% discount. There are also reductions on some river cruises (e.g. certain DDSG sailings); KD Line give free travel on their scheduled Rhine and Mosel boats.

Other discounts

The Europabus services in our Table **927** give 60% reduction, and certain bus services in Norway offer a 50% discount. Some railway museums offer free or discounted entry and a limited number of tourist attractions, hotels and hostels offer discounts. If in doubt, ask!

Note regarding flexi passes: free travel requires the use of a 'travel day', wheras discounted travel does not, provided it is within the overall validity of the pass. For free overnight travel by ferry you can enter either the day of departure or day of arrival. A direct overnight train leaving after 1900 hrs requires only the following day to be used as a 'travel day'.

International journeys using *Select*, *Regional* or *National Eurail* passes (below): the pass must be valid in both the country of departure and arrival to obtain free travel, but in only one of these for discounted travel.

Eurail Select Pass

A *Eurail Select Pass* allows unlimited travel in 3, 4 or 5 adjoining countries from the following (some are grouped together and count as one):

- Austria • Bulgaria/Montenegro/Serbia
- Benelux (Belgium/Netherlands/Luxembourg) • Croatia/Slovenia
- Denmark • Finland • France • Germany • Greece • Hungary
- Republic of Ireland • Italy • Norway • Portugal • Romania
- Spain • Sweden • Switzerland.

'Adjoining' means linked by a direct train (not through another country) or shipping line included in the Eurail scheme; for example Italy's links include Spain and Greece, and France can be linked with Ireland.

The Select Pass is available for 5, 6, 8 or 10 travel days within a two-month period (the 5-country pass is also available for 15 days). The 5-day adult pass costs 429/479/529 USD for 3/4/5 countries respectively; 6 days costs 469/519/569 USD, 8 days 559/609/659 USD, 10 days 649/699/749 USD, and the 5-country 15-day pass costs 949 USD. The *Saver* pass for 2 or more people travelling together gives 15% reduction.

The Youth (under 26) pass is priced at 65% of the adult price and children aged 4 to 11 travel at half the adult fare. As with the *Eurail Global Pass*, the adult version gives 1st class travel, the youth version 2nd class. Eligibility, supplements, discounts etc are as for the *Global Pass* above.

Eurail Regional Pass

A *Eurail Regional Pass* allows unlimited travel in two European countries (or country combinations) as listed below. Conditions vary but all are available for 5, 6, 8 or 10 days within 2 months, and some also for 4, 7 or 9 days (Portugal-Spain also for 3 days). All are available in adult and saver 1st class versions (most also in 2nd class), and there is a youth 2nd class version for all except Portugal-Spain. Passes must be obtained before travelling to Europe, but those shown with the symbol § are also for sale in the countries where the pass is valid (but not to European residents). For current prices and further information see www.eurail.com. Eligibility, supplements, discounts etc are generally as for the *Global Pass* above.

- Austria-Croatia/Slovenia § • Austria-Czech Republic
- Austria-Germany • Austria-Hungary § • Austria-Switzerland
- Benelux-France • Benelux-Germany • Croatia/Slovenia-Hungary §
- Czech Republic-Germany • Denmark-Germany • France-Germany
- France-Italy • France-Spain • France-Switzerland
- Germany-Poland • Germany-Switzerland • Greece-Italy §
- Hungary-Romania § • Italy - Spain • Portugal - Spain

New 2008: • Finland-Sweden • Denmark-Sweden • Norway-Sweden

Sample prices: France-Spain 4 days 1st/2nd 349/305 USD, 10 days 589/509 USD. Hungary-Romania 1st class 5/10 days 249/369 USD.

Eurail One Country Passes (National Pass)

A *Eurail National Pass* allows unlimited travel in a single European country (or country combination) as listed below. Each pass has its own characteristics regarding class of travel, number of travel days, and availability of saver, youth and child versions. A few also have discounts for seniors. For prices and further information see www.eurail.com.

- Benelux • Croatia § • Denmark • Finland • Greece §
- Holland § • Hungary § • Ireland § • Italy § • Norway • Poland
- Portugal § • Romania § • Spain • Sweden. (§ - for sale in Europe)

New for 2008: • Austria • Czech Republic • Slovenia • Scandinavia (Denmark, Finland, Norway, Sweden. 2nd class only. Youth 25% off).

Sample prices: Benelux 5 days in 1 month adult 315/209 USD 1st/2nd. Spain 3-10 days 255-535 USD 1st class, 199-429 USD 2nd class.

ScanRail

Area of validity

The *Scanrail Pass* is valid for unlimited standard class travel on the national railways of Sweden, Norway, Denmark and Finland.

Who can buy the pass?

Available to anyone, but stricter conditions apply if it is purchased inside Scandinavia (see below). The pass is to be withdrawn from Jan. 1, 2008.

Periods of validity and approximate prices

- 5 days within 2 months: adult £168, senior £149, youth £109.
- 8 days within 2 months: adult £214, senior £188, youth £147.
- 10 days within 2 months: adult £237, senior £209, youth £164.
- 21 consecutive days: adult £273, senior £240, youth £191.

Senior prices apply to those aged 60+; youth prices are for ages 12-25; child fares (4-11) are half the adult fare. If purchased inside Scandinavia, only 3 travel days are allowed in the country of purchase, and only the 5 and 21 day passes are available (the 5 days have to be used in 15 days).

Arlanda Express, Arriva (Denmark) and certain bus routes are included. Extra charges (which include seat reservations) apply on *X2000* (€7), Connex night trains (€10-18 in seats), Finnish *Pendolino* (€7-13 in 2nd class), Finnish *IC* (€3-7 in 2nd class). In Norway seat reservations (€6-9) are compulsory on most trains. The Flåm Railway gives 30% discount; Nabotåget (Östersund - Trondheim) 50%. Inlandsbanan: 25% on Inlandsbane card but not on point to point tickets. Various ferry discounts.

BritRail

Britrail is a pass for overseas visitors to Great Britain, allowing unlimited travel on the national rail network in England, Scotland and Wales. It is not available to residents of Great Britain, Northern Ireland, the Isle of Man or the Channel Islands. It is best to buy the pass before arriving in Britain. Prices shown are the US prices for 2007. Further information: www.britrail.com.

BritRail Consecutive Pass

Allows travel for a certain number of consecutive days, in either first or standard class. Children (5-15) travel at half the adult fare.

(USD prices)	Adult 1st class	Adult Standard	Senior (60+) 1st class	Youth (16-25) Standard §
4 days	349	232	296	185
8 days	499	332	425	265
15 days	748	499	636	400
22 days	950	631	808	505
1 month	1124	748	956	599

BritRail FlexiPass

The FlexiPass version gives 4, 8 or 15 days travel within a two-month period.

(USD prices)	Adult 1st class	Adult Standard	Senior (60+) 1st class	Youth (16-25) Standard §
4 days in 2 months	436	293	370	235
8 days in 2 months	638	425	542	340
15 days in 2 months	960	644	816	515

§ – First-class youth passes are also available (at 80% of the adult 1st rates).

Britrail England Pass

Excludes Wales and Scotland. Prices are 20% cheaper than those shown above. Available in both the Consecutive and Flexi versions.

Discounts

Reductions are available on adult passes as follows, but only one type of discount can be used (this includes youth and senior discounts):

Off-Peak Discount: all adult/child prices above are reduced by 20% for travel between November 1 and February 28.

Party Discount: for 3 to 9 adults travelling in a group. Passengers 3 to 9 receive a 50% discount on the cost of their passes. The passes must be of the same type and duration and the party must travel together.

Family Discount: if you purchase any adult or senior pass, one accompanying child (aged 5–15) receives a free pass of the same type and duration. Any further children travelling receive a 50% discount. All children under 5 travel free.

Guest Pass Discount: a friend or relative who is a UK resident may accompany the pass holder. Both get 25% off the adult fare and must travel together at all times. The guest must carry proof of UK residence.

Two additional passes are available covering larger or smaller areas:

BritRail Pass + Ireland

Adds Northern Ireland and the Republic of Ireland, plus a return ferry crossing (Stena Line/Irish Ferries). 5 days within one month costs 636 USD first class, 462 USD standard. 10 days within one month: 1040/733 USD first/standard. Not available to residents of the Republic of Ireland.

BritRail London Plus Pass

This 'flexi' pass allows unlimited rail travel in London and the surrounding area. You can visit such places as Canterbury, Salisbury, Oxford, Cambridge, Kings Lynn, the whole coast from Colchester to Weymouth, and even get as far as Worcester. Children aged 5–15 pay 50% of the adult fare. No youth or senior discount available.

(USD prices)	Adult 1st class	Adult Standard
2 days within 8 days	113	74
4 days within 8 days	187	140
7 days within 15 days	249	187

Other International Passes

BALKAN FLEXIPASS

Unlimited 1st class travel in Bulgaria, Greece, Macedonia, Montenegro, Romania, Serbia and Turkey for any 5/10/15 days in one month. Available in the countries above (but not for residents of those countries), also in the USA (e.g. Rail Europe) and the UK (e.g. Railchoice). Typical UK prices: adults £119/204/244, youth (12-25) £69/119/145, senior (60+) £94/162/194. Children half adult fare. Supplements for *IC* trains.

BENELUX PASS

Unlimited rail travel throughout Belgium, Luxembourg, Netherlands for any 5 days in a month. Available in UK (e.g. International Rail) and USA, and from stations in Belgium/Luxembourg, but not Netherlands. 1st class £141, 2nd class £94, under 26 (2nd class) £71. Not valid on *Thalys*.

EUREGIO-BODENSEE TAGESKARTE

One day's unlimited travel in border region Austria/Germany/Switzerland surrounding Lake Constance. Includes buses and ferries. In Germany valid only on DB local trains. Adult 43 CHF/€28, family 75 CHF/€50. Zonal versions also available for smaller areas.

EUREGIO MAAS-RHEIN

One days unlimited travel in border region Belgium/Netherlands/Germany by rail and bus (covers Liège, Hasselt, Maastricht, Heerlen, Aachen, Düren). In Germany covers only local trains and buses. Price €14. At weekends/public holidays valid as a family ticket (2 adults plus 3 children under 12). Further information: www.euregio-ticket.com

EUROPEAN EAST PASS

Available to non-European residents; offers unlimited rail travel throughout Austria, Czech Republic, Hungary, Poland and Slovakia for any 5 days within a month. 1st class 284 USD, 2nd class 199 USD (up to 5 extra days 34/26 USD per day). Children aged 4-11 half price. Discounts available on river cruises, steam trips in Hungary, Children's Railway etc.

ÖRESUND RUNDT

Two days unlimited travel on trains in the København, Malmö and Helsingborg area, 199 SEK/179 DKK. A larger area extending further into Sweden (Ystad, Kristianstad) is also available for 249 SEK/229 DKK. Children 7-15 half price. The Öresund can only be crossed by rail in one direction; ferry (included) must be used in the other direction.

SAAR-LOR-LUX TICKET

One day's unlimited 2nd class travel on Saturday or Sunday throughout Saarland (i.e. Saarbrücken area of Germany, local trains only), Lorraine (i.e. Metz, Nancy, Épinal area of France) and all of Luxembourg. Price €18. For groups of 2-5 people add €9 per extra person.

Railplus

Railplus cards are valid for one year and offer a discount of 25% on cross-border rail travel (excluding supplements) between the participating countries, which are Austria, Belgium, Bulgaria, Croatia, Czech Republic, Denmark, Finland, France, Germany, Great Britain, Greece, Hungary, Republic of Ireland, Italy, Latvia, Lithuania, Luxembourg, Macedonia, Montenegro, Netherlands, Norway, Poland, Portugal, Romania, Serbia, Slovakia, Slovenia, Spain, Sweden, Switzerland and Ukraine. France, Norway, Spain and Sweden only grant discounts to youth (12-25) and seniors (60+), and Ireland only to seniors. Cards are not available for sale in all participating countries, and you may be required to hold a national railcard for the country where you buy the pass, in addition to the Railplus card. Note that Rail Europe in the UK, who used to sell the Railplus Senior Card, no longer do so, although they do sell the SNCF Carte Senior, giving 25% off cross-border journeys.

Passes for Domestic Travel

Every effort has been made to show latest prices, but some may have changed. Most cities offer day tickets valid on public transport (some include local trains), and larger cities often have Visitor Cards, available from airports and tourist information offices (often also hotels and online).

AUSTRIA

European residents: see InterRail Global Pass and One Country Pass. Non-European residents: see Eurail Global Pass, Eurail Select/Regional Passes, European East Pass. See also Euregio-Bodensee Tageskarte.

Austrian Railpass: for non-Europeans, must be purchased outside Europe. 3 to 8 days out of 15, 208/142 USD 1st/2nd class for 3 days plus 28/26 USD per extra day. Children aged 6-11 half price. Also valid on certain 'private' railways, e.g. Wiener Lokalbahn, Steiermärkische Landesbahnen, Graz-Koeflacher Bahn, Montafonerbahn, Salzburger Lokalbahn. Discounts on selected river trips by DDSG, Wurm & Köck.

Einfach-Raus-Ticket: one day's 2nd class travel on regional trains for groups of 2 to 5 people, €28. On Mons to Fris not valid before 0900 hrs.

Discounts on ÖBB point to point tickets: **1-PLUS-Freizeitticket** discount of 25-40% for the 2nd to 5th people in a group travelling together, and bicycles may be taken free. **Gruppenticket** for groups of 6 or more, discounts of 30% up to 100km and 40% over 100km. **Vorteilscard** annual cards giving 50% discount; the *Classic* version is available to all but there are cheaper cards for families, seniors and those under 26.

Wien-Karte: unlimited travel on local transport in Vienna plus discounted museum entry, 72 hours €18.50. One child up to age 15 free.

Wien metro/tram/bus: 24 hours €5.70; 72 hours €13.60; 8 days €27.20; buy additional zone (€1.70) to include airport. Off-peak (after 0900 Mon-Fri) weekly ticket also available €14.00.

Other visitor cards giving local travel plus museum/sights discounts for 24/48/72 hours: **Salzburg Card** €23/31/36 (reduced by €2 outside June to Oct period); **Innsbruck Card** €24/29/34. Children half price.

BELARUS

There are no rail passes that we are aware of that are valid in Belarus.

Minsk: 10-day public transport passes are available from metro stations.

BELGIUM

European residents: see InterRail Global Pass and One Country Pass. Non-European residents: see Eurail Global Pass, Eurail Select/Regional/National Passes. See also Benelux Tourrail, Euregio Ticket.

Discounts on SNCB point to point tickets: **Go Pass** (under 26) and **Rail Pass** (26+) allow 10 single journeys between two specified stations for €45 (2nd class) and €106/69 (1st/2nd) respectively, valid 1 year. Various discounts are available for return journeys at weekends.

Carte Jump d'un Jour valid on all public transport in greater Brussels (including SNCB rail services), 1 day €4 (valid for 2 people Sats/Suns/holidays). **Carte 3 Jours** gives 3 days on local transport (STIB only) for €9. Cards for 5 or 10 journeys also available. **Brussels Card** public transport (STIB) plus museums, 24 hrs €20, 48 hrs €28, 72 hrs, €33.

BOSNIA-HERZEGOVINA

European residents: see InterRail Global Pass.

BULGARIA

European residents: see InterRail Global Pass and One Country Pass. Non-European residents: see Eurail Select Pass.
See also Balkan Flexipass.

Sofiya: all SKGT local transport, 1 day 3 BGN, 5 days 12 BGN.

CROATIA

European residents: see InterRail Global Pass and One Country Pass. Non-European residents: see Eurail Select/Regional/National Passes.

Zagreb: a day ticket for all trams and buses in zone 1 is available.

CZECH REPUBLIC

European residents: see InterRail Global Pass and One Country Pass. Non-European residents: see Eurail Regional Pass, European East.

Kilometrická banka 2000 (KMB): 2000 km of 2nd class travel within 6 months, 1400 CZK. Some restrictions apply.

SONE+: one day's travel on Sat or Sun for up to 5 people (max 2 adults), 2nd class, 130 CZK local trains, 390 CZK all trains except EC, IC, SC. Regional variants including border areas of adjacent countries.

Network tickets: one week 1053/810 1st/2nd class, one month 3,240/2,700. Reductions: under 15s, ISIC student card.

Praha: all public transport including ČD trains, extending up to 50 km from the centre: 24 hrs 80 CZK, 3 days 220 CZK, 7 days 280 CZK, 15 days 320 CZK. **Prague Card**: 4-day admission card with 3-day transport add-on as above 960 CZK (students 710 CZK).

DENMARK

European residents: see InterRail Global Pass and One Country Pass. Non-European residents: see Eurail Global Pass, Eurail Select/National Passes. See also Scanrail, Öresund Rundt.

Fares based on national zonal system. **Pendlerkort**: 30 day all-zone 2nd class ticket max fare 4,060 DKK, photocard required. 10-journey tickets also available. **DSB WildCard**: discount card for 16-25 year olds, giving 50% off (25% on Fris/Suns), 200 DKK.

København: **24-Hour Ticket** valid on bus, metro and DSB trains in greater København, 110 DKK. **Flexcard 7-Days** is a 7 day zonal card from 195 DKK for 2 zones to 540 DKK for all 7 zones in København.

Copenhagen Card (CPH Card) gives public transport plus free entry to 60 attractions, 24 hrs 199 DKK (child 129), 72 hrs 429 DKK (child 249).

ESTONIA

There are no rail passes that we are aware of that are valid in Estonia.

Tallinn Card: free city transport, sightseeing tours, many museums etc 6 hrs €8, 24 hrs €22.5, 48 hrs €26, 72 hrs €29. Under 14s half price

FINLAND

European residents: see InterRail Global Pass and One Country Pass Non-European residents: see Eurail Global Pass, Eurail Select/Nationa Passes. See also Scanrail.

Finnrailpass: unlimited rail travel for 3/5/10 days in any 1 month; 1st class €188/251/340, 2nd class €126/168/227. Ages 6-16 half price Seat reservation fees required for Pendolino trains. Available to non-Finnish residents. Can be purchased at main stations in Finland.

Helsinki Tourist Ticket: bus/tram/metro/local trains 1/3/5 days for €6/12/18 (children 7-16 half price); regional area also available.
Helsinki Card: public transport plus free entry to over 50 attractions €33/43/53 for 24/48/72 hours (children 7-16: €11/14/17).

FRANCE

European residents: see InterRail Global Pass and One Country Pass Non-European residents: see Eurail Global Pass, Eurail Select/Regional/National Passes.

France Railpass: now only available to non-European residents, valid for 3 to 9 days within one month. Adult 3 days 278/237 USD 1st/2nd class plus 41/35 USD per extra day; Youth (12-25) 206/175 USD plus 29/26 USD per day; Senior (60+, 1st class only) 254 USD for 3 days plus 36 USD per day. Saver version for 2-5 people (must include at least 2 adults) gives around 15% discount. Children pay 50% of the adult (or Saver) fare Special Passholder fare payable on Eurostar, Thalys, Artesia, night trains etc. Reservation fee payable on TGV and Téoz. 50% discount on CP Corsica, Vivarais Railway, Sea France. Various attraction discounts.

Discounts on point to point tickets: **Découverte Séjour**: 25% discount (15%-35% on *TGV* and *Corail Téoz*), blue periods only, min 200 km return trip, Sat night away. **Prem's** and **iDTGV** are low-cost advance purchase tickets; book online for best deals.

Carte 12-25 and **Carte Sénior**: young person's railcard for those aged 12 - 25 (€49) and senior railcard for those over 60 (€53). Valid 1 year. Both give at least 25% discount (up to 50% for journeys purchased in advance). **Carte Escapades**: railcard for ages 26 - 59 giving at least 25% discount (min 200 km return, must spend Sat night away), €85.

Regional Tickets: several regions offer day tickets or discounted fares on TER (local) trains at weekends and holidays. Conditions vary and some only valid in Summer. Details generally available on TER website www.ter-sncf.com.

Paris Visite: public transport within greater Paris, plus free or discounted entry to 20 attractions: zones 1–3: €8.50/13.95/18.60/27.20 for 1/2/3/5 days. Zones 1–6 (includes airports): €17.05/27.15/38.10/46.60 Children 4-11 half price. **Mobilis**: Paris one-day ticket (not available at airports), €5.60 (zones 1–2) to €15.90 (zones 1–6).

Lyon day ticket €4.40, covers all TCL tram/bus/metro/funicular.
Lille day ticket €3.50; similar tickets in most cities.

GERMANY

European residents: see InterRail Global Pass and One Country Pass Non-European residents: see Eurail Global Pass, Eurail Select/Regiona Passes. See also Euregio-Bodensee, Euregio Ticket, Sar-Lor-Lux Ticket

German Rail Pass: for people resident outside Europe; 4 to 10 days unlimited travel within 1 month. 4 days 316/244 USD 1st/2nd class; add 44/29 USD per extra day. Also **Youth Pass** for those under 26 (2nd class only) - 4 days 201 USD, add 15 USD for each extra day. **Twin Pass** also available giving up to 50% for second adult. Certain versions also available from Deutsche Bahn London and certain German stations, but not available to European residents. No supplements on *ICE, IC, EC* 60% discount on Romantische Strasse and Burgenstrasse buses.

Schönes-Wochenende-Ticket: one day's unlimited travel on Saturday or Sunday (to 0300 following day) on local trains (IRE/RE/RB/SB), 2nd class. Price €33 from machines, €35 from ticket offices, €36 on train Valid for up to 5 people, buy on the day. Also valid on trams/buses in certain areas, and on certain rail lines in Poland and Czech Republic.

Regional tickets (Länder-Tickets): one day's unlimited travel for up to 5 people on DB local trains (not before 0900 on Mon-Fri, valid to 0300 nex day). **Baden-Württemberg** €18 for one person, €27 for 2-5 people. **Bayern** €19 for one person, €27 for 2-5 people. **Brandenburg-Berlin** €26. **Hessen** (includes most buses) €29. **Mecklenburg-Vorpommern** €24. **Niedersachsen** €18 for one person, €26 for 2-5 people. **Nordrhein-Westfalen** (SchönerTagTicket) one person €22, 2-5 people €29.50. **Rheinland-Pfalz** €18 for one person, €25 for 2-5 people. **Saarland** €18 for one person, €25 for 2-5 people. **Sachsen** €18 for one person, €26 for 2-5 people. **Sachsen-Anhalt** €18 for one person, €26 for 2-5 people. **Schleswig-Holstein** €29 (includes all public transport in Hamburg). **Thüringen** €18 for one person, €26 for 2-5 people. Buy on the day from machines (some cost €2 more if purchased from travel centres).

Bahncard 25/50: valid for 1 year, giving discounts of 25% or 50% on all national daytime DB trains for €53 or €212, 2nd class, passport photo required (1st class €106/424). With Bahncard 50, travel companions get 50% and children under 15 travel free. Both cards give 25% discount on journeys between Germany and Austria or Switzerland. Bahncards available at discounted prices to young people, families, seniors, disabled persons. **Mobility Bahncard 100** gives unlimited travel for 1 year, €3,400 (1st class €5,700). Bahncards also available from DB London.

Sparpreis 25/50: advance purchase tickets giving 25% or 50% discount, also 50% off for up to 4 travel companions. Weekend restrictions apply to 50% version. Group versions (6+) available giving 50% to 70% off.

Harz: HSB narrow gauge railway 3/5 days €40/45, child 6-11 50%.

Tageskarte (day ticket): most urban areas offer 24/48/72 hour tickets valid on most public transport; generally a zonal system operates.

Welcome Tickets: most public transport in selected cities, also includes free or reduced entry to many museums and visitor attractions. Buy from Tourist Information, main stations, some airports and hotels. Examples:

Berlin Welcome Card: one adult and up to 3 children under 14; 48 hours €16, 72 hours €21. Covers zones A, B and C and includes DB trains.

Dresden City Card: 48 hours €21, includes some Elbe river trips.

Frankfurt Card: 1 day €8; 2 days €12, all transport, includes airport.

Hamburg Card: Day Ticket (valid from 1800 hrs previous day) €8. Also 3 days €18, 5 days €33. Group version also available.

Hannover Card: 1 day €9, 3 days €15, group (up to 5) €17/29.

Köln Welcome Card: 24/48/72 hours €9/14/19, family (2 adults plus 2 children up to 14) €18/28/38, group (3 adults) €18/28/38.

Leipzig Card: 1 day €7.90, 3 days €16.50, 3 day group (2 adults and up to 3 children under 14) €29.

Nürnberg Card: 2 days €19, children up to age 12 free.

GREAT BRITAIN

European residents: see InterRail Global Pass and One Country Pass. See also Britrail.

All-Line Rail Rover: covers whole National Rail network, 1st/standard class £565/£375 (7 days), £860/£565 (14 days). 34% discount for children aged 5-15 and holders of Senior and Disabled Persons railcards, and (standard class only) Young Persons railcard. Not valid on Eurostar, Heathrow Express/Connect, London Underground, private railways.

Freedom of Scotland Travelpass: all rail services in Scotland (includes Carlisle and Berwick) plus Caledonian MacBrayne ferry services and some buses. Standard class only. Valid 4 out of 8 days (£100) or 8 out of 15 days (£135); not before 0915 Mon to Fri (except on Glasgow - Oban/Mallaig services and north of Inverness). 34% discount with Young Persons/Senior/Disabled railcard; 50% discount for children (5-15). 20% discount on Northlink Ferries to Orkney and Shetland; 10% off sleeper fares to/from Scotland. Smaller areas also available: **Highland Rover**, 4 days out of 8 £65; **Central Scotland Rover** 3 days out of 7 £30.

Freedom of Wales Flexi Pass: gives 8 consecutive days travel on most buses in Wales, plus standard-class rail travel on any 4 days out of the 8 (not before 0915 Mon to Fri), price £65, children half price, railcard holders (Young Persons/Senior/Disabled) £42.90. Includes Ffestiniog and Welsh Highland Railways, with discounts on other tourist railways and attractions. Tickets available online and at most staffed stations. Smaller areas cover South Wales (£45) or North and Mid Wales (£45).

A range of **Rover** and **Flexi Rover** tickets is available covering various areas. Many are flexi passes, some are for consecutive days. Most are not valid before 0900 on Monday to Friday. Examples: Anglia Plus, Coast and Peaks, Devon & Cornwall, East Midlands, Heart of England, Kent, North Country, North East, North West, Settle & Carlisle Line, Severn & Solent, Shakespeare Country, South West. **Ranger** day tickets also available, for example Cheshire, Cornwall, Cumbrian Coast, Derbyshire, Devon, East Midlands, Fylde Coast, Lincolnshire, Tees, Tyne Valley, Valley Lines, West Midlands, Wolds Coast. Details: nationalrail.co.uk.

Railcards: annual cards giving 34% discount on most rail fares; Young Persons (16-25), Family, Senior, all £20. Disabled Persons £18. Network Railcard gives off-peak discount in South East England, £20.

London: Day Travelcards covers almost all transport (Underground/bus/rail) in the London area; peak version from £6.60 (central London, zones 1–2) to £13.20 (all zones), off-peak version (not before 0930 Mon–Fri) from £5.10 to £6.70. 3-day Travelcards cost £16.40 (zones 1–2) or £39.60 (all zones); off-peak all-zones version costs £20.10. Travelcard holders may take up to four children aged 5-15 for £1 each off-peak (otherwise half fare). 7 day tickets from £23.20 (central zones) to £43 (all zones). Best value fares are with stored-value Oyster cards; Visitor Oyster card costs £12 preloaded with £10 credit (also available online from www.visitlondon.com); can be topped up at numerous outlets.

All-day tickets (some off-peak) covering rail and bus are also available in Glasgow, Greater Manchester, Derbyshire, Merseyside, South Yorkshire, West Yorkshire, Tyneside and West Midlands. Most large bus companies have day and weekly tickets. 'Plus Bus' add-on tickets are available with many rail fares, giving bus travel in the specified city.

GREECE

European residents: see InterRail Global Pass and One Country Pass. Non-European residents: see Eurail Global Pass, Eurail Regional/National Passes. See also Balkan Flexipass.

Multiple journey card: unlimited journeys for 10 (€48.10), 20 (€72.20) or 30 (€96.30) days in 2nd class. Discounts available for up to 5 persons travelling together. Supplements not included.

Greek Flexipass: 3 days 1st class rail travel within one month €112, 5 days €172 (youth version age 12-26 €94/146, child €82/127). Available to visitors resident outside Greece, but not widely available through agents. **Rail 'n Fly** version gives 3 days train travel within one month plus a one-way or return flight to the Greek islands.

Vergina Flexipass gives 3, 5 or 10 days rail travel within one month (two months for the 10 day pass), with extras such as accommodation and excursions. 1st class €328/398/520 for 3/5/10 days, 2nd class €308/394 for 5/10 days. Up to 10% discount for youth (under 26), 10-20% for children under 12. Available to visitors resident outside Greece.

Athens: 24-hour ticket valid on metro (including ISAP), trams and buses €3, but excludes airport (weekly ticket €10). A return to airport is €10.

HUNGARY

European residents: see InterRail Global Pass and One Country Pass. Non-European residents: see Eurail Global Pass, Eurail Select/Regional/National Passes, European East.

Balaton Mix: unlimited travel on MÁV trains around Lake Balaton, also valid on boats. May 18 - Sept. 16 only. 1 day HUF 2,100, 2 days HUF 4,000, 3 days HUF 5,500 (children aged 6-16 HUF 1,200/2,100/2,650). Families (2 adults, 2 children) HUF 4,500/8,500/11,500.

Budapest: BKV tram/metro/bus, 1 day HUF 1,350, 3 days HUF 3,100, 7 day travelcard HUF 3,600. 14 day and 1 month passes also available. Weekend family ticket HUF 2,200. **Budapest Card** also includes museums and discounts: 48 hours HUF 6,450, 72 hours HUF 7,950; 1 child up to 14 years old goes free. The **BKSZ bérlet** includes local rail services and is aimed at commuters.

IRELAND

REPUBLIC OF IRELAND ONLY:

European residents: see InterRail Global Pass and One Country Pass. Non-European residents: see Eurail Global/Select/National Passes.

Irish Explorer: any 5 days in 15 on IÉ rail services, €138 (child €70), standard class only.

Irish Explorer Rail and Bus: IÉ rail plus Bus Éireann services, any 8 days in 15, €210 (child €133).

Open Road passes; flexi passes giving 3 to 15 days travel on Bus Éireann services, €47 to €209.

Dublin area: bus and suburban rail 'short hop' (excludes Airlink): 1 day €8.80, family (2 adults + 4 under 16s) €13.50, 3 days €17.30, 7 days €30. Medium/long/giant hop cover Dublin hinterland Sun-Sat (photo-card required). Rambler (bus only, includes Airlink): 1 day €6, family €8.50, 7 days €21, pack of 5 one-day tickets €18.30. Bus+LUAS (tram) 1 day €6.50, 7 day €25 (must validate on bus before using tram).

REPUBLIC OF IRELAND AND NORTHERN IRELAND:

See also Britrail + Ireland.

Emerald Card Rail and Bus: All rail and all Bus Eireann and Ulsterbus services in the Republic of Ireland and Northern Ireland. Any 8 days in 15 €236 (child €118); any 15 days in 30 €406 (child €202). There is also an **Irish Rover Bus Only** pass.

Irish Rover: any 5 days in 15 on IÉ and NIR rail services, standard class only, €171/£118, children half price.

NORTHERN IRELAND ONLY:

Freedom of Northern Ireland: valid for 1 day (£14), 3 out of 8 days (£34) or 7 consecutive days (£50) on all Translink services (Northern Ireland Railways, Ulsterbus, Belfast Citybus). Children: 50% reduction. The one day ticket is now available from bus drivers and train conductors.

ITALY

European residents: see InterRail Global Pass and One Country Pass.

Passes for Domestic Travel

Non-European residents: see Eurail Global Pass, Eurail Select/ Regional/National Passes.

Roma: Roma Pass is a new 3 day museum/transport pass, €20. Biglietto Integrato Giornaliero (BIG) covers rail/metro/bus in urban area for one day, €4 (excludes Fiumicino airport, restrictions on rail/metro). Biglietto Turistico Integrato (BTI) valid 3 days €11, weekly ticket (CIS) €16. Roma & Lazio day ticket (BIRG) covers wider area in 6 zones (max €10.50), also 3 day ticket (BTR) max €28.50.

Milano: 24 hour ticket (abbonamento) on ATM city services (including local rail) €3.00, 48 hrs €5.50.

Napoli: 'Campania > artecard' ia a museum/transport visitors card, with two types of 3 day ticket (€13 or €25, youth aged 18-25 pay €8 or €18) and a 7 day ticket (€28, youth €21).

Venice Card: blue version - public transport (including waterbuses) with other discounts €18.50/34/56 for 12 hrs/48 hrs/7 days (add €23 to include airport). Orange version adds free museum entry €30/55/82. *Junior* discounts for under 29s.

Day tickets available in other major cities.

LATVIA

There are no rail passes that we are aware of that are valid in Latvia.

Riga: there are no day tickets on local trams/buses, but fares are cheap. Monthly tickets are available.

LITHUANIA

There are no rail passes that we are aware of that are valid in Lithuania.

Vilnius: 24 hr ticket on local buses 6 LTL, 72 hrs 14 LTL, 10 days 27 LTL.

LUXEMBOURG

European residents: see InterRail Global Pass and One Country Pass. Non-European residents: see Eurail Global Pass, Eurail Select/ Regional/National Passes. See also Benelux Tourrail, Sar-Lor-Lux Ticket.

Billet Réseau: day ticket €4.00, unlimited 2nd-class travel on all public transport throughout the country; not valid to border stations; valid to 0800 hrs following morning. Carnet of 5 cards €16.00; one month (Oeko Pass) €45; from CFL offices.

Luxembourg Card: unlimited travel on trains and buses throughout the country, plus free entry to many attractions. 1 day €10; any 2 days €17, any 3 days €24 (the 2/3 day tickets must be used within a year). Family pass for 2-5 people (max. 3 adults) at twice one person rate.

MACEDONIA

European residents: see InterRail Global Pass and One Country Pass. See also Balkan Flexipass.

MONTENEGRO

European residents: see InterRail Global Pass. Non-European residents: see Eurail Select Pass. See also Balkan Flexipass.

NETHERLANDS

European residents: see InterRail Global Pass and One Country Pass. Non-European residents: see Eurail Global Pass, Eurail Select/ Regional/National Passes. See also Benelux Tourrail, Euregio Ticket.

Holland Pass: 3 or 5 days unlimited travel on Netherlands Railways within 1 month. Not valid on *Thalys* trains. Available in the UK from SimplyRail.com (cannot be purchased in the Netherlands). 3 days £60 1st class, £41 2nd class; 5 days £96 1st class, £65 2nd class. Youth fare (2nd class) 3 days £31, 5 days £49. This pass will be discontinued at the end of 2007, but will still be available as a Eurail National Pass.

NS Day Card (Dagkaart) allows unlimited travel on Netherlands Railways for one day: €68.40 1st class, €40.30 2nd class, available at stations. **OV Dagkaart** costs €5 extra and includes buses, trams and metro throughout the country. Five NS Day Cards can be purchased in one transaction as a 5-Dagkaart (price is five times the above). Monthly and yearly versions also available, with or without OV add-on. Avalable from booking offices and ticket automats.

Railrunner: Up to 3 children (aged 4–11) may accompany an adult (aged 19+) for a flat rate of €2 per day. Excludes *Thalys*.

Zomertoer: 2 days' unlimited travel within any 7 day period between July 1 and Sept. 6. 2nd class only, €59 for 2 people, €79 for 3 people. **Zomertoer Plus** includes bus / tram / metro: €69 for 2, €95 for 3.

Amsterdam Dagkaart: tram/bus/metro. 24 hrs €6.50, 48 hrs €10.50, 72 hrs €13.50, 96 hrs €16.50 (over 65s and children 4-11 get discount only on 24 hr ticket, €4.50). **I amsterdam Card**: tram/bus/metro/canal boat tour, plus free museum admission and discounts at various tourist attractions, 24/48/72 hrs: €33/43/53.

NORWAY

European residents: see InterRail Global Pass and One Country Pass. Non-European residents: see Eurail Global Pass, Eurail Select/National Passes. See also Scanrail.

Eurail Norway Pass: for non-Europeans: 3 to 8 days 2nd class travel within one month, 245 USD for 3 days, add approx 44 USD per extra day Seniors (60+) get 15% reduction; youth (under 26) get 25% reduction; children aged 4-15 half price. 30% discount on Flåm Railway, various ferry discounts; not valid on Oslo Airport Express.

Oslo: 24 hour ticket for all public transport (Dagskort) 60 NOK, 7 days (7 dagers kort) 210 NOK, children 4-16 half price. **Oslo Pass**: unlimited travel on buses, trams, underground and NSB local trains (up to Zone 4), free entry to attractions, discounts on sightseeing buses/boats: 24/48/72 hours 210/300/390 NOK (children 90/110/140 NOK).

Bergen Card: local buses plus attractions, 24/48 hrs: 170/250 NOK (children aged 3-15, 70/100 NOK).

POLAND

European residents: see InterRail Global Pass and One Country Pass. Non-European residents: see Eurail Select/Regional/National Passes. European East.

Bilet Weekendowy (weekend ticket): unlimited travel on *Ex/IC/EC* trains (except Berlin-Warszawa-Express) 1800 Fri to 2400 Sun and on public holidays, 149 PLZ 1st class, 99 PLZ 2nd class. Available from over 660 stations equipped with KURS reservation system.

Bilet Turystyczny (tourist ticket): unlimited travel on PKP local trains 1800 Friday to 0600 Monday, 60 PLZ 2nd class, 80 PLZ 1st class.

PORTUGAL

European residents: see InterRail Global Pass and One Country Pass. Non-European residents: see Eurail Global Pass, Eurail Select/ Regional/National Passes.

Bilhete Turístico: unlimited travel on CP network in 1st and 2nd class: 7 days €132; 14 days €226; 21 days €330. Under 12s and over 65s pay half fare. Available from major stations in Portugal only.

Intra-Rail: zonal (4 zones) pass for ages 12-30, 3 days (Fri-Sun) €55 (€49 with Youth Card), 10 days (starting Mon-Thurs) €185/159. Includes nights at youth hostels. Not valid on Alfa. Buy at major stations.

Lisboa: Carris tram/bus and metro - one-day ticket (bilhete 1 dia) €3.35, 5 days €13.50. **Lisboa Card** (includes tourist attractions): 24/48/72 hrs for €14.85/25.50/31 (children 5-11 €7.50/12.75/15.50).

Train and Bus Tourist Ticket: day ticket valid on the CP Sintra and Cascais lines (also suburban trains Alcântara to Oriente), also on Scotturb bus network, €12. Buy from main stations in the area.

Coimbra: day ticket on local buses €2.80.

Porto: metro+STCP bus+local rail, all zones, 1 day €4, 3 days €9.

ROMANIA

European residents: see InterRail Global Pass and One Country Pass. Non-European residents: see Eurail Global Pass, Eurail Select/ Regional/National Passes. See also Balkan Flexipass.

Bucureşti: day ticket for urban tram/bus network 7 RON, 7 days 15 RON, 15 days 22 RON.

RUSSIA

Moskva: bus/tram tickets available from kiosks in strips of 10/20. Separate 10-trip tickets available for metro. Monthly *yediniy bilyet* covers bus/tram/metro. No tourist tickets. **St Peterburg**: bus/tram tickets available in packs of 10; multi-journey cards can be bought for the metro.

SERBIA

European residents: see InterRail Global Pass and One Country Pass. Non-European residents: see Eurail Select Pass. See Balkan Flexipass.

Beograd: urban transport seems to use single tickets; no day tickets.

SLOVAKIA

European residents: see InterRail Global Pass and One Country Pass. Non-European residents: see European East.

Kilometrica Banka : 2000 km of travel (2000 SKK); minimum journey 100 km; valid in 1st/2nd class.

Bratislava: urban tram/bus network, 24 hrs 90 SKK, 48 hrs 170 SKK, 3 days 210 SKK, 7 days 310 SKK. **Bratislava City Card** includes walking tour and many discounts, 1 day €6/200 SKK, 2 days €9/300 SKK, 3 days €11/370 SKK, available from tourist offices.

SLOVENIA

European residents: see InterRail Global Pass and One Country Pass. Non-European residents: see Eurail Select/Regional Passes.

Slovenian Railpass: for those resident outside Slovenia; 3 to 8 days in one month; prices for 3 days 1st class €42, 2nd class €30, for each extra day add €6 for 1st class, €5 for 2nd class. Supplement payable on *ICS* trains (1050 SIT 1st, 450 SIT 2nd). Only available from Ljubljana, Maribor, Celje and Koper stations.

Passes for Domestic Travel

jubljana Card: city buses, museums and discounts, 72 hrs €12.50.

;PAIN

uropean residents: see InterRail Global Pass and One Country Pass. on-European residents: see Eurail Global Pass, Eurail Select/ Regional/National Passes.

'urail Spain Pass: this pass for people resident outside Europe gives nlimited travel on RENFE main-line services for 3 to 10 days within a eriod of 2 months. 3 days: 255 USD 1st class, 199 USD 2nd class. Each xtra day 40 USD 1st class, 30-35 USD 2nd class. Children aged 4-11 alf fare. Supplements payable on *AVE/Talgo 200/Trenhotel.*

arcelona T-Dia ticket: valid 1 day on all public transport (TMB, FGC, am, local rail), from €5.25 (1 zone) to €15.00 (all 6 zones). 2 day avelcard €9.60, 3 days €13.70, 4 days €17.50, 5 days €20.80. **arcelona Card** adds various discounts 2/3/4/5 days €23/28/31/34.

ladrid: Abono Turístico gives all public transport in Zone A, 1/2/3 days :3.80/6.80/9.00, also 5/7 days €14.20/19.80, children half fare. Also vailable for wider area (zone T) at double the price. **Madrid Card** adds ee or reduced entry to various attractions, 24/48/72 hrs €39/49/59.

evilla Card: public transport plus free entry to most museums, 24 hrs :50, 48 hrs €60, 72 hrs €65. Tourist cards also available for Burgos, órdoba, Zaragoza.

;WEDEN

uropean residents: see InterRail Global Pass and One Country Pass. on-European residents: see Eurail Global Pass, Eurail Select/National asses. See also Scanrail, Öresund Rundt.

J Sommarkort: a new pass giving 5 days 2nd class travel out of 30 ays during the period June 17 to Aug. 19, 1750 SEK. Also valid to Oslo nd København. Available from main stations.

tockholm: all SL public transport in Greater Stockholm, 24 hours 90 EK, 72 hours 190 SEK, 7 days 230 SEK, 30 days 620 SEK; reductions f 40-50% for under 20s and over 65s. Annual cards also available. **tockholm Card** includes free entry to museums, 290/420/540 SEK for 4/48/72 hours (children aged 7-17 120/160/190 SEK).

;WITZERLAND

'uropean residents: see InterRail Global Pass and One Country Pass. on-European residents: see Eurail Global Pass, Eurail Select/Regional 'asses. See also Euregio-Bodensee.

wiss Pass: available to all non-Swiss residents. Consecutive days on wiss Railways, boats and most alpine postbuses and city buses. Valid r 4, 8, 15, 22 days or 1 month. 1st class £162/234/283 for 4/8/15 ays, £326/360 for 22 days/1 month. 2nd class £108/156/189 for 4/8/ 5 days, £218/240 for 22 days/1 month. Free upgrade to 1st class on 4 nd 8 day passes if travelling Oct. 1-Dec. 23 2007. Youth Pass gives 5% reduction for under 26s. All versions give 50% reduction on many inicular and mountain railways. Also acts as a Museum Pass - free entrance to 400 sites. Children aged 6-15 travel free with a Family Card (issued free by Switzerland Tourism, London) if accompanied by a parent (not other relatives), otherwise half fare.

Swiss Flexi Pass: as above but valid for 3, 4, 5, 6 or 8 days within 1 month. Prices 1st/2nd class £155/103 (3 days), £188/125 (4 days), £217/145 (5 days), £247/165 (6 days), £289/193 (8 days). No Youth discount.

Saver Program: applies to the Swiss Pass or Flexi Pass (not Youth Pass) - 15% reduction per person for 2-5 adults travelling together.

Swiss Transfer Ticket: return ticket from any airport/border station to any other Swiss station; use within 1 month. Each journey must be completed on day of validation. 1st class £80, 2nd class £52. Family Card valid, see above. Cannot be obtained in Switzerland.

Swiss Card: as Swiss Transfer Ticket but also offers unlimited half-fare tickets for 1 month and 50% reduction on many private railways. 1st class £106, 2nd class £75. Family card valid, see above under Swiss Pass.

Swiss Half Fare Card: 50% off most public transport, price £42, valid one month. Annual cards also available.

Note that the above passes are available from Switzerland Tourism, London, tel. 02074 204900, also online. Also available (except Swiss Transfer ticket) at major Swiss stations; Swiss Card only at border/airport stations. None of the above passes are available to Swiss residents.

Regional Passes: several areas available, e.g. Bernese Oberland for 7 days (3 days unlimited 2nd class travel plus 4 at 50% discount) 224 CHF, or 15 days (5 plus 10), 270 CHF, available May to October. Other passes include Adventure Card Wallis, and Graubünden Summer Holiday Pass. Not available from the UK, obtain locally in Switzerland.

Bern: day ticket, all transport in city (zones 10/11) 20/12 CHF 1st/2nd class, wider area (zones 70/71) 18/11 CHF, all zones in region 60/36 CHF. **Bern Card** gives all transport in zones 10/11 plus free museum admission, 24/48/72 hours: 20/31/38 CHF.

Genève: Day ticket (Carte 24 Heures) includes buses, trams, trains and boats: 10 CHF, or 7 CHF after 0900 hrs. Valid for 2 people at weekends.

Zürich: Tageskarte gives 24 hours on all transport including SBB trains, 13/7.80 CHF 1st/2nd class (central zone only); all zones in Canton 50.40/30.40 CHF. Off-peak version is 9-Uhr Tagespass, all zones, not before 0900 Mon-Fri, 38/23 CHF (also available for use on 6 different days 204/124 CHF; monthly version also available). **Zürich Card** includes visitor attractions: 24 hours 17 CHF, 72 hours 34 CHF (children 12/24 CHF), includes airport.

TURKEY

European residents: see InterRail Global Pass and One Country Pass.

UKRAINE

There are no rail passes that we are aware of that are valid in Ukraine.

Kyïv: a monthly travelcard is available but there are no tourist tickets.

Where to Buy your Pass

ources of rail passes include the following. Many can also provide point) point tickets and further information about rail travel.

N THE UNITED KINGDOM

:ail Pass Direct
hase House, Gilbert Street, Ropley, Hampshire SO24 0BY
) 08700 84 14 13 fax 0870 751 5005 www.railpassdirect.co.uk

eutsche Bahn UK (German Railways)
'K Booking Centre, PO Box 687a, Surbiton KT6 6UB
' 08718 80 80 66 (8p per minute) fax 08718 80 80 65
ww.deutsche-bahn.co.uk

uropean Rail Ltd
avistock House North, Tavistock Square, London WC1H 3HR
) 020 7387 0444 fax 0207 387 0888 www.europeanrail.co.uk

festiniog Travel
arbour Station, Porthmadog, Gwynedd, Wales LL49 9NF
) 01766 512 400 fax 01766 514 715 www.festtravel.co.uk

:ail Canterbury
) Palace Street, Canterbury, Kent CT1 2DZ
) 01227 45 00 88 fax 01227 47 00 72 www.rail-canterbury.co.uk

:ailChoice
5 Colman House, Empire Square, High Street, London SE20 7EX
y appointment only).
' 0870 165 7300 fax 0208 659 7466 www.railchoice.co.uk

Rail Europe
178 Piccadilly, London W1V 0BA
✆ 08705 848 848 www.raileurope.co.uk

Stephen Walker Travel
Assembly Rooms, Market Place, Boston, Lincs PE21 6LY
✆ 08707 466 400 fax 01205 35 23 23.

Trainseurope
4 Station Approach, March, Cambs PE15 8SJ
Also at Cambridge Station
✆ 08717 00 77 22 fax 01354 660 444 www.trainseurope.co.uk

Ultima Travel
424 Chester Road, Little Sutton, South Wirral CH66 3RB
✆ 0151 339 6171 fax 0151 339 9199.

IN THE USA

Rail Europe Inc.
Toll-free ✆ 1-800-4EURAIL, 1-888-BRITRAIL or 1-800-EUROSTAR
www.raileurope.com

See also **Rick Steve's** comprehensive website: www.ricksteves.com

In other European countries passes are often available from the travel centres at major stations.

AUSTRIA

CAPITAL
Vienna (Wien).

CLIMATE
Moderate Continental climate. Warm summer; high snowfall in winter.

CURRENCY
Euro (EUR / €). 1 euro = 100 cent. For exchange rates see page 11.

EMBASSIES IN VIENNA
Australia: Mattiellistraße 2, ✆ 01 506 740. **Canada**: Laurenzerberg 2, ✆ 01 531 383 000. **New Zealand** (Consulate): Salesianergasse 15/3, ✆ 013 188 505. **UK**: Jaurèsgasse 12, ✆ 01 716 130. **USA**: Boltzmanngasse 16, ✆ 01 313 390.

EMBASSIES OVERSEAS
Australia: 12 Talbot St, Forrest, Canberra ACT 2603, ✆ 0 262 951 533. **Canada**: 445 Wilbrod St, Ottawa ON, KIN 6M7, ✆ 6 137 891 444. **UK**: 18 Belgrave Mews West, London SW1X 8HU, ✆ 02 073 443 250. **USA**: 3524 International Court NW, Washington DC 20008, ✆ 2 028 956 700.

LANGUAGE
German; English is widely spoken in tourist areas.

OPENING HOURS
Banks: mostly Mon, Tues, Wed, Fri 0800–1230 and 1330–1500, Thur 0800–1230 and 1330–1730. **Shops**: Mon–Fri 0800–1830 (some closing for a 1- or 2-hour lunch), Sat 0800–1200/1300 (in larger towns often until 1700). **Museums**: check locally.

POST OFFICES
Indicated by golden horn symbol; all handle poste restante (*postlagernde Briefe*). Open mostly Mon–Fri 0800–1200 and 1400–1800. Main and station post offices in larger cities open 24 hrs. Stamps (*Briefmarke*) also sold at Tabak/Trafik shops.

PUBLIC HOLIDAYS
Jan 1, Jan 6 (Epiphany), Easter Mon, May 1, Ascension Day, Whit Mon, Corpus Christi, Aug 15 (Assumption), Oct 26 (National Day), Nov 1 (All Saints), Dec 8 (Imm. Conception), Dec 25, Dec 26. For dates of movable holidays see page 2.

PUBLIC TRANSPORT
Most long-distance travel is by rail (see below). Inter-urban buses operated by ÖBB-Postbus (www.postbus.at); usually based by rail stations or post offices. City transport is efficient with integrated ticketing; buy tickets from machines or Tabak/Trafik booths. Wien has an extensive metro and tram system; for day tickets see Passes section. Other cities with tram networks include Graz, Innsbruck and Linz. Taxis are metered; extra charges for luggage (fixed charges in smaller towns).

RAIL TRAVEL
See Tables **950 - 999**. Operated by Österreichische Bundesbahnen (ÖBB) (www.oebb.at). Mostly electrified; fast and reliable; ÖIC or IC trains every 1–2 hrs with connecting regional trains. Other fast trains: ICE, ÖEC and EC (with stops only in larger cities); D (ordinary express trains); REX (semi-fast/local trains). Most overnight trains convey sleeping-cars (up to three berths), couchettes (four/six berths) and 2nd-class seats. Seat reservations available on long-distance services. Most stations have left luggage facilities.

TELEPHONES
Dial in: ✆ +43 then number (omit initial 0). Outgoing: ✆ 00. Long-distance calls are cheapest 2000–0600 and on public holidays. Operator assistance / enquiries: ✆ 1611 (national); ✆ 1613 (rest of Europe); ✆ 1614 (rest of world). Emergency: ✆ 112. Police: ✆ 133. Fire: ✆ 122. Ambulance: ✆ 144.

TIPPING
Hotels, restaurants, cafés and bars: service charge of 10–15% but tip of around 10% still expected. Taxis 10%.

TOURIST INFORMATION
Austrian National Tourist Office (www.austria.info). Staff invariably speak some English. Tourist office opening times vary widely, particularly restricted at weekends in smaller places. Usually called *Fremdenverkehrsbüro*; look for green 'i' sign. Main tourist office in Vienna: Albertinaplatz / Maysedergasse, ✆ 01 24 555.

TOURIST OFFICES OVERSEAS
Australia: 1st Floor, 36 Carrington St, Sydney NSW 2000, ✆ 0 292 993 621, info@antosyd.org.au. **Canada**: 2 Bloor St W, Suite 400, Toronto ON, M4W 3E2, ✆ 4 169 674 967, antotor@sympatico.ca. **UK**: 13-14 Cork Street, London W1S 3NS, ✆ 02 076 290 461, tourism@austria.org.uk. **USA**: Box 1142, New York NY 10108, ✆ 2 129 446 880, travel@austria.info.

VISAS
See page xxxii for visa requirements.

BELGIUM

CAPITAL
Brussels (Bruxelles/Brussel).

CLIMATE
Rain prevalent at any time; warm summers, cold winters (often with snow).

CURRENCY
Euro (EUR / €). 1 euro = 100 cent. For exchange rates see page 11.

EMBASSIES IN BRUSSELS
Australia: rue Guimard 6-8, ✆ 022 860 500. **Canada**: Avenue de Tervueren 2, ✆ 027 410 611. **New Zealand**: square de Meeûs 1, ✆ 025 121 040. **UK**: rue d'Arlon 85, ✆ 022 876 211. **USA**: Regentlaan 27 Boulevard du Régent, ✆ 025 082 111.

EMBASSIES OVERSEAS
Australia: 19 Arkana St, Yarralumla, ACT 2600, Canberra, ✆ 0 262 732 501. **Canada**: 360 Albert St, Suite 820, Ottawa ON, K1R 7X7, ✆ 6 132 367 267. **UK**: 17 Grosvenor Crescent, London SW1X 7EE, ✆ 02 074 703 700. **USA**: 33302 Garfield St NW, Washington DC 20008, ✆ 2 023 336 900.

LANGUAGE
Dutch (north), French (south) and German (east). Many speak both French and Dutch, plus often English and/or German.

OPENING HOURS
Many establishments close 1200–1400. **Banks**: Mon–Fri 0900–1600. **Shops**: Mon–Sat 0900/1000–1800/1900 (often later Fri). **Museums**: vary, but most open six days a week: 1000–1700 (usually Tues–Sun, Wed–Mon or Thur–Tues).

POST OFFICES
Postes / Posterijen / De Post open Mon–Fri 0900–1700 (very few open Sat morning). Stamps are also sold at newsagents.

PUBLIC HOLIDAYS
Jan 1, Easter Mon, May 1, Ascension Day, Whit Mon, July 21 (National Day), Aug 15 (Assumption), Nov 1 (All Saints), Nov 11 (Armistice), Dec 25. For dates of movable holidays see page 2. Transport and places that open usually keep Sunday times on public holidays.

PUBLIC TRANSPORT
National bus companies: De Lijn (Flanders), TEC (Wallonia, i.e. the French-speaking areas); few long-distance buses. Brussels has extensive metro / tram / bus system operated by STIB with integrated

ticketing; tickets can be purchased from tram / bus driver but it's cheaper to buy in advance from machines at metro stations or special kiosks (also offices labelled *Bootik*). For day tickets see Passes section. Some tram and bus stops are request stops – raise your hand. Taxis seldom stop in the street, so find a rank or phone; double rates outside city limits.

RAIL TRAVEL

See Tables **400 - 449**. Operated by NMBS (in Dutch) / SNCB (in French) (www.b-rail.be). Rail information offices: 'B' in an oval logo. Seat reservations available for international journeys only. Refreshments are not always available. Some platforms serve more than one train at a time; check carefully. Left luggage and cycle hire at many stations. Timetables usually in two sets: Mondays to Fridays and weekends/holidays.

TELEPHONES

Dial in: ✆ +32 then number (omit initial 0). Outgoing: ✆ 00. Phonecards are sold at rail stations, post offices, bookshops, some tobacconists. Some public phones accept credit cards. Most international calls are cheaper Mon–Sat 2000–0800, all day Sun. Emergency: ✆ 112. Police: ✆ 101. Fire, ambulance: ✆ 100.

TIPPING

Tipping in cafés, bars, restaurants and taxis is not the norm, as service is supposed to be included in the price, but is starting to be expected in places where staff are used to serving people from the international community (who often leave generous tips): 10 to 15%. Tip hairwashers in salons, delivery men, cloakroom / toilet attendants.

TOURIST INFORMATION

Toerisme Vlaanderen (www.toervl.be). Office de Promotion du Tourisme Wallonie - Bruxelles (www.belgium-tourism.net). Dutch: *Dienst voor Toerisme*. French: *Office de Tourisme*. German: *Verkehrsamt*. Brussels tourist office: Hôtel de Ville, Grand Place, ✆ 025 138 940. Most tourist offices have English-speaking staff and free English-language literature, but charge for walking itineraries and good street maps. Opening hours, especially in small places and off-season, are flexible.

TOURIST OFFICES OVERSEAS

UK: Tourism Flanders - Brussels, 31 Pepper St, London E14 9RW; Belgian Tourist Office 217 Marsh Wall, London E14 9FJ. ✆ 09 063 020 245 (premium rate), ✆ 08 009 545 245 (to order brochures), info@belgiumtheplaceto.be. **USA / Canada**: 220 East 42nd St, Suite 3402, New York NY 10017, ✆ 2 127 588 130, info@visitbelgium.com

VISAS

See page xxxii for visa requirements.

BULGARIA

CAPITAL

Sofia (Sofiya).

CLIMATE

Hot summers; wet spring and autumn; snow in winter (skiing popular).

CURRENCY

Lev (BGN or Lv.); 1 lev = 100 stotinki (st). Tied to euro. For exchange rates, see page 11. Credit cards are increasingly accepted.

EMBASSIES IN SOFIA

Australia (Consulate): ulitsa Trakia 37, ✆ 029 461 334. **Canada**: *refer to Canadian Embassy in Romania*. **UK**: ulitsa Moskovska 9, ✆ 029 339 222. **USA**: ulitsa Kozyak 16, ✆ 029 375 100.

EMBASSIES OVERSEAS

Australia: 33 Culgoa Circuit, O'Malley, ACT 2606 Canberra, ✆ 0 262 869 711. **Canada**: 325 Steward St, Ottawa ON, K1N 6K5, ✆ 6 137 893 215. **UK**: 186 Queen's Gate, London SW7 5HL, ✆ 02 078 700 602 350. **USA**: 1621 22nd St NW, Washington DC 20008, ✆ 2 023 877 969.

LANGUAGE

Bulgarian (written in the Cyrillic alphabet); English, German, Russian and French in tourist areas. Nodding the head indicates 'no' (*ne*); shaking it means 'yes' (*da*).

OPENING HOURS

Banks: Mon–Fri 0900–1500. Some exchange offices open longer hours and weekends. **Shops**: Mon–Fri 0800–2000, closed 1200–1400 outside major towns, Sat open 1000–1200. **Museums**: vary widely, but often 0800–1200, 1400–1830. Many close Mon or Tues.

POST OFFICES

Stamps (*marki*) are sold only at post offices (*poshta*), usually open Mon–Sat 0800–1730. Some close 1200–1400.

PUBLIC HOLIDAYS

Jan 1, Mar. 3 (National Day), Orthodox Easter Mon, May 1, May 24 (Education), Sept 6 (Union), Sept 22 (Independence), Nov. 1 (Spiritual Leaders), Dec 24, 25, 26. For dates of movable holidays see page 2.

PUBLIC TRANSPORT

There is an extensive bus network but quality is variable. They are slightly more expensive than trains but both are very cheap for hard-currency travellers. In Sofia buses and trams use the same ticket; punch it at the machine after boarding, get a new ticket if you change. For day tickets see Passes section.

RAIL TRAVEL

See Tables **1500 - 1599**. Bulgarian State Railways (BDZ), (www.bdz.bg) run express, fast and stopping trains. Often crowded; reservations are recommended (obligatory for express trains). Most long-distance trains provide a limited buffet service; certain services also convey a restaurant car. Overnight trains convey 1st- and 2nd-class sleeping cars and seats (also 2nd-class couchettes on certain trains between Sofia and Black Sea resorts). One platform may serve two tracks, platforms and tracks are both numbered. Signs at stations are in Cyrillic.

TELEPHONES

Dial in: ✆ + 359 then number (omit initial 0). Outgoing: ✆ 00. Use central telephone offices in major towns for long-distance calls. Police: ✆ 166. Fire: ✆ 160. Ambulance: ✆ 150.

TIPPING

Waiters and taxi drivers expect a tip of about 10%.

TOURIST INFORMATION

Bulgarian Tourism Authority (www.bulgariatravel.org). Main tourist office: 1 Sveta Nedelia Sq., 1040 Sofia, ✆ 029 335 845. There are tourist offices in all main cities and resorts.

TOURIST OFFICES OVERSEAS

UK: Tourism Section, Bulgarian Embassy, 186–188, Queen's Gate, London SW7 5HL, ✆ 02 075 849 400, bgtourism@btcon-nect.com. **USA**: Bulgarian Tourist Information Center, 545 W 59th St, New York NY 10019, ✆ 2 128 225 900.

VISAS

See page xxxii for visa requirements. Passports must have 3 months validity remaining. Visitors staying with friends or family (i.e. not in paid accommodation) need to register on arrival.

CROATIA

CAPITAL

Zagreb.

CLIMATE

Continental on the Adriatic coast, with very warm summers.

CURRENCY

Kuna (HRK or kn); 1 kuna = 100 lipa. For exchange rates, see page 11. Credit cards are widely accepted.

EMBASSIES IN ZAGREB

Australia: Centar Kaptol, 3rd Floor, Nova Ves 11, ✆ 014 891 200. **Canada**: Prilaz Gjure Dezelica 4, ✆ 014 881 211. **New Zealand** (Consulate): Vlaska ulica 50A, ✆ 014 612 060. **UK**: Ivana Lucica 4, ✆ 016 009 100. **USA**: Ulica Thomasa Jeffersona 2, ✆ 016 612 200.

EMBASSIES OVERSEAS

Australia: 14 Jindalee Crescent, O'Malley, Canberra ACT 2606, ✆ 0 262 866 988. **Canada**: 229 Chapel St, Ottawa ON, K1N 7Y6, ✆ 6 135 627 820. **New Zealand** (consulate): 131 Lincoln Rd, Henderson, PO Box 83-200, Edmonton, Auckland, ✆ 098 365 581. **UK**: 21 Conway St, London, W1T 6BN, ✆ 02 073 872 022. **USA**: 2343 Massachusetts Ave. NW, Washington DC 20008-2803, ✆ 2 025 885 899.

LANGUAGE

Croatian. English, German and Italian spoken in tourist areas.

OPENING HOURS

Banks: Mon–Fri 0700–1900, Sat 0700–1300, but may vary, some banks may open Sun in larger cities. Most **shops**: Mon–Fri 0800–2000, Sat 0800–1400/1500; many shops also open Sun, especially in summer. Some shops close 1200–1600. Most open-air **markets** daily, mornings only. **Museums**: vary.

POST OFFICES

Usual hours: Mon–Fri 0700–1900 (some post offices in larger cities open until 2200), Sat 0700–1300. Stamps (*markice*) are sold at newsstands and tobacconists (*trafika*), Post boxes are yellow.

PUBLIC HOLIDAYS

Jan 1, Jan 6 (Epiphany), Easter Mon, May 1, Corpus Christi, June 22 (Antifascist Struggle), Aug. 5 (Nat. Thanksgiving), Aug. 15 (Assumption), Oct 8 (Independence), Nov 1 (All Saints), Dec. 25, 26. For dates of movable holidays see page 2. Many local Saints' holidays.

PUBLIC TRANSPORT

Buses and trams are cheap, regular and efficient. Zagreb and Osijek have tram networks. Jadrolinija maintains most domestic ferry lines; main office in Rijeka, ✆ +385 51 666 111.

RAIL TRAVEL

See Tables **1300 - 1359**. National railway company: Hrvatske željeznice (HŽ) (www.hznet.hr). Zagreb is a major hub for international trains. Efficient services but there is a limited network and services can be infrequent. Daytime trains on the Zagreb - Split line are operated by modern tilting diesel trains. Station amenities: generally left luggage, a bar, newsstand and WCs.

TELEPHONES

Dial in: ✆ +385 then number (omit initial 0). Outgoing: ✆ 00. Post offices (*HPT*) have telephone booths – pay the assistant after the call. Other public phones accept phonecards only (sold at post offices, newsstands and tobacconists). Police: ✆ 92. Fire: ✆ 93. Ambulance: ✆ 94.

TIPPING

Leave 10% for good service in a restaurant. It's not necessary to tip in bars.

TOURIST INFORMATION

Croatian National Tourist Board (www.croatia.hr). Main office: Iblerov trg 10/4, 10000 Zagreb, ✆ 014 699 333, info@htz.hr.

TOURIST OFFICES OVERSEAS

UK: 2 Lanchesters, 162-164 Fulham Palace Rd, London, W6 9ER, ✆ 02 085 637 979, info@cnto.freeserve.co.uk **USA**: 350 Fifth Ave., Suite 4003, New York NY 10118, ✆ 2 122 798 672, cntony@earthlink.net

VISAS

See page xxxii for visa requirements.

CZECH REPUBLIC

CAPITAL

Prague (Praha).

CLIMATE

Mild summers and very cold winters.

CURRENCY

Czech crown or koruna (CZK or Kč); 1 koruna = 100 haléřu. For exchange rates, see page 11. Credit cards are widely accepted.

EMBASSIES IN PRAGUE

Australia (Consulate): 6th Floor, Solitaire Building, ulica Klimentska 10, ✆ 296 578 350. **Canada**: Muchova 6, ✆ 272 101 800. **New Zealand** (Consulate): Dykova 19, ✆ 222 514 672. **UK**: Thunovská 14, ✆ 257 402 111. **USA**: Tržíště 15, ✆ 257 022 000.

EMBASSIES OVERSEAS

Australia: 8 Culgoa Circuit, O'Malley, ACT 2606, Canberra, ✆ 0 262 901 386. **Canada**: 251 Cooper St., Ottawa ON, K2P 0G2, ✆ 6 135 623 875. **UK**: 26 Kensington Palace Gardens, London W8 4QY, ✆ 02 072 431 115. **USA**: 3900 Spring of Freedom St NW, Washington DC 20008, ✆ 2 022 749 100.

LANGUAGE

Czech. Czech and Slovak are closely related Slavic tongues. English, German and Russian are widely understood, but Russian is less popular.

OPENING HOURS

Banks: Mon–Fri 0800–1800. **Shops**: Mon–Fri 0900–1800, Sat 0900–1200 (often longer in Prague Sat–Sun). **Food shops**: usually open earlier plus on Sun. **Museums**: (usually) Tues–Sun 1000–1800. Most castles close Nov–Mar.

POST OFFICES

Usual opening hours are 0800–1900. Stamps also available from newsagents and tobacconists. Post boxes: orange and blue.

PUBLIC HOLIDAYS

Jan 1, Easter Mon, May 1, May 8 (Liberation), July 5 (Cyril & Methodius), July 6 (Jan Hus), Sept 28 (Statehood), Oct 28 (Founding), Nov. 17 (Freedom & Democracy), Dec 24, 25, 26. For dates of movable holidays see page 2.

PUBLIC TRANSPORT

Extensive long-distance bus network competing with the railways, run by ČSAD or increasingly by private companies. In Prague the long-distance bus station is close to Florenc metro station. If boarding at a bus station with a ticket window, buy your ticket in advance, otherwise pay the driver. Good urban networks with integrated ticketing. Prague (Praha) has metro and tram system - see Passes feature for day tickets. Other cities with trams include Brno, Ostrava, Plzeň, Olomouc, Liberec.

RAIL TRAVEL

See Tables **1100 - 1169**. National rail company is České Dráhy (ČD) (www.cd.cz). An extensive network with many branch lines, cheap fares, sometimes crowded trains. Main line trains: *IC*, *EC* and express; supplements payable on *IC*, *EC* but not for passholders. Fastest Praha - Ostrava trains are classified *SC PENDOLINO* (*SC* means SuperCity) and operated by tilting trains - special tickets available; passholders pay a supplement. Other trains: spešný (semi-fast), osobný (very slow). A handful of branch lines are now operated by private companies. Some trains convey dining cars; sleepers and couchettes. Seats for express trains may be reserved at least one hour before departure at the counter marked R at stations.

TELEPHONES

Dial in: ✆ +420 then number. Outgoing: ✆ 00. Police: ✆ 158. Fire: ✆ 150. Ambulance: ✆ 155.

TIPPING

You should tip at pubs and restaurants, in hotels and taxis and hairdressers. In general, round up the nearest CZK 10 unless you are somewhere upmarket, when you should tip 10%.

TOURIST INFORMATION

Czech Tourism (www.czechtourism.com). Main office: Vinohradska 46, PO Box 32, 120 41 Praha 2, Vinohrady, ✆ 221 580 111. Prague Information Service (www.pis.cz), Information centre, Old Town Hall, Staromestská námesti 1, Praha 1.

TOURIST OFFICES OVERSEAS

Canada: 401 Bay St, Suite 1510, Toronto ON, M5H 2Y4, ✆ 4 163 639 928, ctacanada@iprimus.ca **UK**: Suite 29–31, Morley House, 320 Regent Street, London W1B 3BG, ✆ 02 076 310 427, info-uk@czechtourism.com **USA**: 1109 Madison Ave., New York NY 10028, ✆ 2 122 880 830, info@czechcenter.com

VISAS

See page xxxii for visa requirements.

DENMARK

CAPITAL

Copenhagen (København).

CLIMATE

Maritime climate. July–Aug is warmest, May–June often very pleasant, but rainier; Oct–Mar is wettest, with periods of frost.

CURRENCY

Danish crown or krone, DKK or kr; 1 krone = 100 øre. For exchange rates, see page 11.

EMBASSIES IN COPENHAGEN

Australia: 2nd floor, Dampfaergevej 26, ✆ 70 263 676. **Canada**: Kristen Bernikowsgade 1, ✆ 33 483 200.
New Zealand (Consulate): Store Strandstraede 21, ✆ 33 377 702. **UK**: Kastelsvej 36-40, ✆ 35 445 200. **USA**: Dag Hammarskjölds Allé 24, ✆ 33 417 100.

EMBASSIES OVERSEAS

Australia (Consulate): Gold Fields House, 1 Alfred St, Circular Quay, Sydney NSW 2000, ✆ 0 292 472 224. **Canada**: 47 Clarence St, Suite 450, Ottawa ON, K1N 9K1, ✆ 6 135 621 811. **New Zealand** (Consulate): 273 Bleakhouse Rd, Howick, PO Box 619, Auckland 1015, ✆ 095 373 099. **UK**: 55 Sloane St, London SW1X 9SR, ✆ 02 073 330 200. **USA**: 3200 Whitehaven St NW, Washington DC 20008-3683, ✆ 2 022 344 300.

LANGUAGE

Danish. English is almost universally spoken.

OPENING HOURS

Banks (Copenhagen): Mon–Fri 0930–1600 (some until 1700; most until 1800 on Thur). Vary elsewhere. **Shops**: (mostly) Mon–Thur 0930–1730, Fri 0930–1900/2000, Sat 0900–1300/1400, though many in Copenhagen open until 1700 and may also open Sun. **Museums**: (mostly) daily 1000/1100–1600/1700. In winter, hours shorter and museums usually close Mon.

POST OFFICES

Mostly Mon–Fri 0900/1000–1700/1800, Sat 0900–1200 (but opening times vary greatly). Stamps also sold at newsagents.

PUBLIC HOLIDAYS

Jan 1, Maundy Thurs, Good Fri, Easter Sun/Mon, Common Prayer Day (4th Fri after Easter), Ascension, Whit Monday, June 5 (Constitution Day), Dec. 25, 26. For dates of movable holidays see page 2.

PUBLIC TRANSPORT

Long-distance travel is easiest by train (see below). Excellent regional and city bus services, many connecting with trains. Expanding modern and efficient metro (www.m.dk) and suburban rail network in and around the capital; see Passes feature for day tickets. No trams in København; bus network can be tricky to fathom. Bridges or ferries link all the big islands. Taxis: green *Fri* sign when available; metered, and most accept major credit cards. Many cycle paths and bike hire shops; free use of City Bikes in Copenhagen central area.

RAIL TRAVEL

See Tables **700 - 729**. Operator: Danske Statsbaner (DSB); (www.dsb.dk). Some independent lines, and certain former DSB services are now operated by private company ArrivaTog. *IC* trains reach up to 200 km/h. *Re* (regionaltog) trains are frequent, but slower. Refreshment trolleys available on most *IC* trains. Reservations are recommended (not compulsory) on *IC* and *Lyn* trains - DKK 20 in standard class; reservation included in business class. Reservations close 15 minutes before a train leaves its originating station. Nationwide reservations ✆ 70 13 14 15. Baggage lockers at most stations, usually DKK 20 per 24 hrs. Usually free trolleys, but you may need a (returnable) coin.

TELEPHONES

Dial in: ✆ +45 then number. Outgoing: ✆ 00. Most operators speak English. Phonecards (DKK 30–100) are available from DSB kiosks, post offices and newsstands. Directory enquiries: ✆ 118. International operator/directory: ✆ 14. Emergency services: ✆ 112.

TIPPING

At least DKK 20 in restaurants. Elsewhere (taxis, cafés, bars, hotels etc) tipping is not expected.

TOURIST INFORMATION

Danish Tourist Board (www.visitdenmark.com). Nearly every decent-sized town in Denmark has a tourist office (*turistbureau*), normally found in the town hall or central square; they distribute maps, information and advice. Some will also book accommodation for a small fee, and change money.

TOURIST OFFICES OVERSEAS

UK: 55 Sloane St, London SW1X 9SY, ✆ 02 072 595 959, dtb.london@dt.dk **USA/Canada**: 655 Third Ave., 18th Floor, New York NY 10017, ✆ 2 128 859 700, info@goscandinavia.com

VISAS

See page xxxii for visa requirements.

ESTONIA

CAPITAL

Tallinn.

CLIMATE

Warm summers, cold, snowy winters; rain all year, heaviest in August.

CURRENCY

Estonian crown or kroon (EEK or kr); 1 kroon = 100 senti. For exchange rates, see page 11. Currency exchange facilities are limited, though cash machines (ATMs) are plentiful, especially in Tallinn.

EMBASSIES IN TALLINN

Australia: *refer to Australian Embassy in Sweden.* **Canada**: *refer to Canadian Embassy in Latvia.* **New Zealand**: *refer to NZ Embassy in Poland.* **UK**: Wismari 6, ✆ 6 674 700. **USA**: Kentmanni 20, ✆ 6 688 100.

EMBASSIES OVERSEAS

Australia (Consulate): 86 Louisa Rd, Birchgrove, Sydney NSW 2041, ✆ 0 298 107 468. **Canada**: 260 Dalhousie St, Suite 210, Ottawa ON, K1N 7E4, ✆ 16 137 894 222. **UK**: 16 Hyde Park Gate, London SW7 5DG, ✆ 02 075 893 428. **USA**: 2131 Massachusetts Ave. NW, Washington DC 20008, ✆ 12 025 880 101.

LANGUAGE

Estonian. Some Finnish is useful, plus Russian in Tallinn and the north-east.

OPENING HOURS

Banks: Mon–Fri 0900–1600. **Shops**: Mon–Fri 0900/1000–1800/1900, Sat 0900/1000–1500/1700; many also open Sun. **Museums**: days vary (usually closed Mon and/or Tues); hours commonly 1100–1600.

POST OFFICES

Post offices *(Eesti Post)* are generally open 0900–1800 Mon–Fri, 0930–1500 Sat. The central post office in Tallinn is located at Narva 1. Stamps are also sold at large hotels, newsstands, and tourist offices.

PUBLIC HOLIDAYS

Jan 1, Feb 24 (Independence), Good Friday, Easter Mon (unofficial), May 1, June 23 (Victory), June 24 (Midsummer), Aug 20 (Restoration of Independence), Dec 25, 26. For dates of movable holidays see page 2.

PUBLIC TRANSPORT

Long-distance bus services are often quicker, cleaner, and more efficient than rail, but getting pricier. The main operator is Eurolines (www.eurolines.ee). Book international journeys in advance at bus stations; pay the driver on rural and local services. Tallinn has a tram network.

RAIL TRAVEL

See Tables **1800 - 1899**. Local rail services are operated by Edelaraudtee (www.edel.ee), international services by GoRail (www.gorail.ee). Comfortable overnight trains to Russia; best to take berth in 2nd-class coupé (4-berth compartments); 1st-class *luxe* compartments (2-berth) also available. Reservations are compulsory for all sleepers; entry visa to Russia may need to be shown when booking. Very little English spoken at stations.

TELEPHONES

Dial in: ✆ +372 then number. Outgoing: ✆ 00. Pay phones take phonecards (from hotels, Tourist Offices, post offices, newsstands). Police: ✆ 110. Fire, ambulance: ✆ 112.

TIPPING

Not necessary to tip at the bar or counter, but tip 10% if served at your table. Round up taxi fares to a maximum of 10%.

TOURIST INFORMATION

Welcome to Estonia (visitestonia.com). Information: Niguliste 2/ Kullassepa 4, 10146 Tallinn, ✆ 6457 777, turismiinfo@tallinnlv.ee. Ekspress Hotline (www.1182.ee), is an English-speaking information service covering all Estonian towns: ✆ 1 182 (available only within Estonia).

TOURIST OFFICES OVERSEAS

Germany: Baltikum Tourismus Zentrale, Katharinenstraße 19-20, 10711 Berlin, ✆ 03 089 009 091, info@baltikuminfo.de.

VISAS

See page xxxii for visa requirements.

FINLAND

CAPITAL

Helsinki (Helsingfors).

CLIMATE

Extremely long summer days; spring and autumn curtailed further north; continuous daylight for 70 days north of 70th parallel. Late June to mid-August best for far north, mid-May to September for south. Ski season: mid-January to mid-April.

CURRENCY

Euro (EUR/€). 1 euro = 100 cent. For exchange rates see page 11.

EMBASSIES IN HELSINKI

Australia: *refer to Australian Embassy in Sweden.*
Canada: Pohjoisesplanadi 25B, ✆ 09 228 530.
New Zealand (Consulate): Johannesbrinken 2, ✆ 024 701 818.
UK: Itäinen Puistotie 17, ✆ 0 922 865 100.
USA: Itäinen Puistotie 14B, ✆ 09 616 250.

EMBASSIES OVERSEAS

Australia: 12 Darwin Ave., Yarralumla, ACT 2600, Canberra ✆ 0 262 733 800. **Canada**: 55 Metcalfe St, Suite 850, Ottawa ON, K1P 6L5, ✆ 6 132 882 233. **UK**: 38 Chesham Place, London SW1X 8HW, ✆ 02 078 386 200. **USA**: 3301 Massachusetts Ave. NW, Washington DC 20008, ✆ 2 022 985 800.

LANGUAGE

Finnish, and, in the north, Lapp/Sami. Swedish, the second language, often appears on signs after the Finnish. English is widely spoken, especially in Helsinki. German is reasonably widespread.

OPENING HOURS

Banks: Mon–Fri 0915–1615, with regional variations. **Shops**: Mon–Fri 0900–2000, Sat 0900–1500, though many shops open Mon–Fri 0700–2100, Sat 0900–1800; many shops also open Sun, June–Aug. **Stores/food shops**: Mon–Sat 0900–1800/2000. **Museums**: usually close Mon, hours vary. Many close in winter.

POST OFFICES

Most *posti* open at least Mon–Fri 0900–1700. Stamps also sold at shops, hotels and bus and train stations. Yellow postboxes.

PUBLIC HOLIDAYS

Jan 1, Jan 6 (Epiphany), Good Friday, Easter Mon, May 1, Ascension, Midsummer (Sat falling June 20–26), All Saints (Sat falling Oct 31 - Nov 6), Dec 6 (Independence), Dec 24, 25, 26. For dates of movable holidays see page 2.

PUBLIC TRANSPORT

The national timetable book *Aikataulut/Tidtabeller* (in Finnish and Swedish, from bookshops, €29) covers trains, buses, and boats in detail. Bus stations (*Linja-autoasema*) have restaurants and shops. There are more than 300 bus services daily from Helsinki to all parts of the country. The main long-distance bus operators are Matkahuolto (www.matkahuolto.fi) and the Expressbus consortium (www.expressbus.com). It is usually cheaper to buy tickets in advance. Bus stop signs show a black bus on a yellow background (local services) or a white bus on a blue background (long distance). Helsinki has metro/tram/bus network with integrated ticketing. Taxis can be hailed in the street: they are for hire when the yellow *taksi* sign is lit.

RAIL TRAVEL

See Tables **790 - 799**. National rail company: VR (www.vr.fi); tilting Pendolinos (up to 220 km/h) run on certain lines. Fares depend upon train type - those for *S220* (Pendolino), *IC* (InterCity) and *P* (express) trains include a seat reservation. Sleeping-cars: two or three berths per compartment (2nd class), single compartment (1st class). In winter sleeping accommodation generally costs less on Mondays to Thursdays. Rail station: *Rautatieasema* or *Järnvägsstation*; virtually all have baggage lockers.

TELEPHONES

Dial in: ✆ + 358 then number (omit initial 0). Outgoing: ✆ 00. Phonecards are sold by *R-kiosk* newsstands, tourist offices, *Tele* offices, and some post offices. Emergency services: ✆ 112. Police: ✆ 10022.

TIPPING

Service charge included in hotel and restaurant bills but leave coins for good service. Hotel and restaurant porters and sauna attendants expect a euro or two. Taxi drivers and hairdressers do not expect a tip.

TOURIST INFORMATION

Finnish Tourist Board (www.visitfinland.com). PO Box 625, Töölönkatu 11, 00101 Helsinki, ✆ 010 60 58 000, mek@mek.fi. Every Finnish town has a tourist office *(Matkailutoimistot)* where staff speak English. English literature, mostly free.

TOURIST OFFICES OVERSEAS

Canada: 1200 Bay St, Suite 604, Toronto ON, M5R 2A5, ✆ 4 169 649 159. **UK**: 3rd Floor, 30-35 Pall Mall, London SW1Y 5LP, ✆ 02 078 394 048, mek.loon@mek.fi. **USA**: PO Box 4649, Grand Central Station, New York NY 10163-4649, ✆ 2 129 492 333, mek.usa@mek.fi.

VISAS

See page xxxii for visa requirements.

FRANCE

CAPITAL

Paris, divided into *arrondissements* 1 to 20 (1[er], 2[e] etc).

CLIMATE

Cool–cold winters, mild–hot summers; south coast best Oct–Mar, Alps and Pyrenees, June and early July. Paris best spring and autumn.

CURRENCY

Euro (EUR / €). 1 euro = 100 cent. For exchange rates see page 11.

EMBASSIES IN PARIS

Australia: 4 rue Jean Rey, ✆ 0 140 593 300. **Canada**: 35 avenue Montaigne, ✆ 0 144 432 900. **New Zealand**: 7 ter rue Léonard de Vinci, ✆ 0 145 014 343. **UK**: 35 rue du Faubourg St Honoré, ✆ 0 144 513 100. **USA**: 2 avenue Gabriel, ✆ 0 143 122 222.

EMBASSIES OVERSEAS

Australia: 6 Perth Ave., Yarralumla ACT 2600, Canberra, ✆ 0 262 160 100. **Canada**: 42 Sussex Drive, Ottawa ON, K1M 2C9, ✆ 6 137 891 795. **New Zealand**: 34-42 Manners St, Wellington, ✆ 043 842 555. **UK**: 58 Knightsbridge, London SW1X 7JT, ✆ 02 070 731 000. **USA**: 4101 Reservoir Rd, NW, Washington DC 20007, ✆ 2 029 446 090.

LANGUAGE

French; many people can speak a little English, particularly in Paris.

OPENING HOURS

Paris and major towns: shops, banks and post offices are generally open 0900/1000–1700/1900 Mon-Fri, plus often Sat am / all day. Small shops can be open Sun am but closed Mon. **Provinces**: weekly closing is mostly Sun pm / all day and Mon; both shops and services generally close 1200–1400; services may have restricted opening times. Most **super/hypermarkets** open unti; 2100/2200. **Museums**: (mostly) 0900–1700, closing Mon and/or Tues; longer hours in summer; often free or discount rate on Sun. **Restaurants** serve 1200–1400 and 1900–2100 at least. Public holidays: services closed, food shops open am in general; check times with individual museums and tourist sights.

POST OFFICES

Called *La Poste*. Letter boxes are small, wall or pedestal-mounted, and yellow. Basic rate postage stamps (*timbres*) can also be bought from tobacconists (*Tabacs* or *Café-Tabacs*).

PUBLIC HOLIDAYS

Jan 1, Easter Mon, Whit Mon, May 1, May 8 (Victory), Ascension Day, July 14 (National Day), Aug 15 (Assumption), Nov 1 (All Saints), Nov 11 (Armistice), Dec 25. For dates of movable holidays see page 2. If a holiday falls on a Tuesday or Thursday, many businesses close additionally on the Monday or Friday.

PUBLIC TRANSPORT

In Paris, use the Métro where possible: clean, fast, cheap and easy. For urban and suburban transport, *carnets* (sets of 10 tickets) are cheaper than individual tickets; for day tickets see Passes feature. Bus and train timetable leaflets (free) are available from tourist offices, bus and rail stations. Many cities have modern tram / light rail networks; Lyon, Marseille and Toulouse also have metro systems. Bus services are infrequent after 2030 and on Sundays. Sparse public transport in rural areas, and few long-distance bus services. Licensed taxis (avoid others) are metered; white roof-lights when free; surcharges for luggage, extra passengers, and journeys beyond the centre.

RAIL TRAVEL

See Tables **250 - 399**. Société Nationale des Chemins de fer Français (SNCF) (www.sncf.com), ✆ 0 892 353535 (premium rate, in French). Excellent network from Paris to major cities with *TGV* trains using dedicated high-speed lines (up to 320 km/h on the new *Est Européen* line to eastern France) as well as conventional track. However, some cross-country journeys can be slow and infrequent. Trains can get very full at peak times, so to avoid having to spend the journey standing, book a seat. Prior reservation is compulsory on *TGV* high-speed trains and the charge is included in the ticket price; rail pass holders will have to pay at least the reservation fee. Tickets can cost more at busy times. Long distance trains on several non-TGV routes are branded *Corail Téoz* using refurbished rolling stock - reservation is compulsory. Reservation is also compulsory on all overnight trains: most convey couchettes and reclining seats, only a few have sleeping cars. Sleeping-car cabins are single-sex unless booked by a couple or family. A certain number of couchette compartments are reserved for women only or those with small children; otherwise, couchette accommodation is mixed. There is a minimal bar/trolley service on most long-distance trains. Larger stations have 24-hour coin-operated left-luggage lockers, and possibly pay-showers.

TELEPHONES

Dial in: ✆ + 33 then number (omit initial 0). Outgoing: ✆ 00. Most payphones have English instructions. Few accept coins; some take credit cards. Phonecards (*télécartes*) are sold by post offices, some tobacconists and certain Tourist Offices. Many post offices have metered phones: pay when you've finished. Restaurants etc have (more expensive) pay phones; avoid calling from your hotel. Emergency: ✆ 112. Police: ✆ 17. Fire: ✆ 18. Ambulance: ✆ 15.

TIPPING

Not necessary to tip in bars or cafés although it is common practise to round up the price. In restaurants there is no obligation to tip, but if you wish to do so, leave €1–2.

TOURIST INFORMATION

Maison de la France (www.franceguide.com). Main office: 20 avenue de l'Opéra, 75041 Paris, ✆ 0 142 967 000. Local tourist offices: look for *Syndicat d'Initiative* or *Office de Tourisme.* Staff generally speak English. Many sell passes for local tourist sights or services and can organise accommodation (for a fee). Opening times are seasonal.

TOURIST OFFICES OVERSEAS

Australia: Level 20, 25 Bligh St, Sydney NSW 2000, ✆ 0 292 315 244, info.au@franceguide.com. **Canada**: 1981 avenue McGill College, suite 490, Montréal QC, H3A 2W9, ✆ 5 142 882 026, canada@franceguide.com. **UK**: 178 Piccadilly, London W1J 9AL, ✆ 09 068 244 123 (premium rate), info.uk@franceguide.com. **USA**: 444 Madison Ave., New York NY 10022, ✆ 4 102 868 310, info.us@franceguide.com. Also in Beverley Hills and Chicago.

VISAS
See page xxxii for visa requirements.

GERMANY

CAPITAL
Berlin.

CURRENCY
Euro (EUR/€). 1 euro = 100 cent. For exchange rates see page 11.

EMBASSIES IN BERLIN
Australia: Wallstraße 76-79, ✆ 0 308 800 880.
Canada: Leipziger Platz 17, ✆ 030 203 120.
New Zealand: Friedrichstraße 60, ✆ 030 206 210.
UK: Wilhelmstraße 70, ✆ 030 204 570.
USA: Neustädtische Kirchstraße 4-5, ✆ 0 302 385 174.

EMBASSIES OVERSEAS
Australia: 119 Empire Circuit, Yarralumla, Canberra ACT 2600, ✆ 0 262 701 911. **Canada**: 1 Waverley St, Ottawa ON, K2P 0T8, ✆ 6 132 321 101. **New Zealand**: 90-92 Hobson St, Thorndon, Wellington, ✆ 044 736 063. **UK**: Embassy, 23 Belgrave Sq., London SW1X 8PZ, ✆ 02 078 241 300. **USA**: 4645 Reservoir Rd NW, Washington DC, 20007-1998, ✆ 2 022 984 000.

LANGUAGE
German; English and French widely spoken in the west, especially by young people, less so in the east.

OPENING HOURS
Vary; rule of thumb: **Banks**: Mon–Fri 0830–1300 and 1430–1600 (until 1730 Thur). **Shops**: Mon–Fri 0900–1830 (large department stores may open 0830/0900–2000) and Sat 0900–1600. **Museums**: Tues–Sun 0900–1700 (until 2100 Thur).

POST OFFICES
Mon–Fri 0800–1800, Sat 0800–1200. Main post offices have poste restante (*Postlagernd*).

PUBLIC HOLIDAYS
Jan 1, Jan 6*, Good Fri, Easter Mon, May 1, Ascension Day, Whit Mon, Corpus Christi*, Aug 15*, Oct 3 (German Unity), Nov 1* (All Saints), Dec 24 (afternoon); Dec 25, Dec 26. For dates of movable holidays see page 2.
* Catholic feastdays, celebrated only in the south (see p. 363).

PUBLIC TRANSPORT
Most large cities have U-Bahn (U) underground railway and S-Bahn (S) urban rail service, many have trams. City travel passes cover these and other public transport, including local ferries in some cities (e.g. Hamburg). International passes usually cover S-Bahn. Single fares are expensive; a day card (*Tagesnetzkarte*) or multi-ride ticket (*Mehrfahrkarte*) pays for itself if you take more than three rides (see Passes feature for selected day tickets). Long-distance buses are not common.

RAIL TRAVEL
See Tables **800 - 949**. Deutsche Bahn (DB) (www.bahn.de). ✆ 11 861 (premium rate) for timetable and fares information, ticket purchase and reservations. Timetable freephone (automated): ✆ 0800 1507090. UK booking centre ✆ 08718 80 80 66 (8p per minute). Discounts of 25% or 50% are available on long-distance tickets if purchased at least 3 days in advance - 50% tickets have restrictions. Long-distance trains: *ICE* (modern high-speed trains; up to 300km/h; higher fares but no extra charge for InterRail holders), *IC, EC, EN, CNL, D*. Regional trains: *IRE, RE, RB* (modern, comfortable, link with long-distance network). Frequent local S-Bahn services operate in major cities. Some local services now operated by private railways. Overnight services convey sleeping-cars (up to three berths) and/or couchettes (up to six berths), also reclining seats - reservation is generally compulsory. Most long-distance trains convey a bistro or restaurant car. Seat reservations possible on long-distance trains. Stations are well staffed, often with left luggage and bicycle hire. *Hbf.* (Hauptbahnhof) means main (central) station; *Bf.* (Bahnhof) means station.

TELEPHONES
Dial in: ✆ +49 then number (omit initial 0). Outgoing: ✆ 00. *Kartentelefon* boxes take phonecards only (available from news-agents, tobacconists, some kiosks). National directory enquiries: ✆ 11833 (11837 in English). International directory enquiries: ✆ 11834. Emergency: ✆ 112. Police: ✆ 110. Fire: ✆ 112. Ambulance: ✆ 115.

TIPPING
Not a must but customary for good service. Small sums are rounded up, while for larger sums you could add a tip of EUR 1, or up to 10% of the bill.

TOURIST INFORMATION
German National Tourist Office (www.germany-tourism.de). Main office: Beethovenstraße 69, 60325 Frankfurt am Main, ✆ 069 974 640, info@d-z-t.com Tourist offices are usually near rail stations. English is widely spoken; English-language maps and leaflets available. Most offer a room-finding service.

TOURIST OFFICES OVERSEAS
Australia: PO Box 1461, Sydney NSW 2001, ✆ 0 282 960 488, gnto@germany.org.au. **Canada**: 480 University Ave., Suite 1410, Toronto ON, M5G 1V2, ✆ 4 169 681 685, info@-gnto.ca. **UK**: PO Box 2695, London W1A 3TN, ✆ 02 073 170 908, gntolon@d-z-t.com. **USA**: 122 East 42nd St, 52nd Floor, New York NY 10168, ✆ 2 126 617 200, gntonyc@d-z-t.com. Also in Chicago and Los Angeles.

VISAS
See page xxxii for visa requirements.

GREECE

CAPITAL
Athens (Athína).

CLIMATE
Uncomfortably hot in June–Aug; often better to travel in spring or autumn.

CURRENCY
Euro (EUR/€). 1 euro = 100 cent. For exchange rates see page 11.

EMBASSIES IN ATHENS
Australia: Level 6, Thon Building, Kifisias/Alexandras, Ambe-lokipi, ✆ 2 108 704 000. **Canada**: Ioannou Ghennadiou 4, ✆ 2 107 273 400. **New Zealand** (Consulate): Kifissias 76, Ambelokipi, ✆ 2 106 924 136. **UK**: Ploutarchou 1, ✆ 2 107 272 600. **USA**: Vassilissis Sofias 91, ✆ 2 107 212 951.

EMBASSIES OVERSEAS
Australia: 9 Turrana St, Yarralumla, Canberra ACT 2600, ✆ 0 262 733 011. **Canada**: 76-80 MacLaren St, Ottawa ON, K2P 0K6, ✆ 6 132 386 271. **UK**: 1A Holland Park, London W11 3TP, ✆ 02 072 216 467. **USA**: 2221 Massachusetts Ave. NW, Washington DC 20008, ✆ 2 029 391 300.

LANGUAGE
Greek; English widely spoken in Athens and tourist areas (some German, French or Italian), less so in remote mainland areas.

OPENING HOURS
Banks: (usually) Mon–Thur 0800–1400, Fri 0830–1330, longer hours in peak holiday season. **Shops**: vary; in summer most close midday and reopen in the evening (Tue, Thu, Fri) 1700–2000. **Sites and museums**: mostly 0830–1500; Athens sites and other major archaeological sites open until 1900 or open until sunset in summer.

POST OFFICES

Normally Mon–Fri 0800–1300, Sat 0800–1200; money exchange, travellers cheques, Eurocheques. Stamps sold from vending machines outside post offices, street kiosks.

PUBLIC HOLIDAYS

Jan 1, Jan 6 (Epiphany), Shrove Monday (48 days before Easter*), Mar 25 (Independence), Good Friday*, Easter Monday*, May 1, Whit Monday*, Aug 15 (Assumption), Oct 28 (National Day), Dec 25, 26. Everything closes for Easter. Holidays related to Easter are according to the Orthodox calendar – dates usually differ from those of Western Easter (see page 2).

PUBLIC TRANSPORT

KTEL buses: fast, punctual, fairly comfortable long-distance services; well-organised stations in most towns (tickets available from bus terminals), website: www.ktel.org. Islands connected by ferries and hydrofoils; see Thomas Cook guide *Greek Island Hopping* (order form at the back of this edition). City transport: bus or (in Athens) trolleybus, tram and metro; services may be crowded. Outside Athens, taxis are plentiful and good value.

RAIL TRAVEL

See Tables **1400 - 1499**. Operator: Hellenic Railways (Organismós Sidiródromon Éllados; OSE) (www.ose.gr). Call centre for reservations and information (24-hour, english spoken): ✆ 1110. Limited rail network, especially north of Athens. Reservations are essential on most express trains. *ICity* and *ICityE* trains (supplement payable) are fast and fairly punctual, higher supplement applies on *ICityE* trains. There is a new line from Athens Airport and Athens to Kórinthos. Stations: often no left luggage or English-speaking staff, but many have bars.

TELEPHONES

Dial in: ✆ +30 then number. Outgoing: ✆ 00. Payphones take phonecards only (on sale at most shops, street kiosks). Bars, restaurants, and kiosks often have privately owned metered phones: pay after making the call. Emergency: ✆ 112. Police: ✆ 100. Fire: ✆ 199. Ambulance: ✆ 166. Tourist police (24 hrs, English-speaking): ✆ 171.

TIPPING

Not necessary for restaurants or taxis.

TOURIST INFORMATION

Greek National Tourist Organisation (www.gnto.gr). Main office: Tsoha 7, 11521 Athens, ✆ 2 108 707 000. Athens information desk: Amalias 26, ✆ 2 103 310 392. Tourist offices provide sightseeing information, fact sheets, local and regional transport schedules.

TOURIST OFFICES OVERSEAS

Australia: 51-57 Pitt St, Sydney NSW 2000, ✆ 0 292 411 663, hto@tpg.com.au. **Canada**: 1300 Bay St, Main Level, Toronto ON, M5R 3K8, ✆ 4 169 682 220, grnto.tor@sympatico.ca. **UK**: 4 Conduit St, London W1S 2DJ, ✆ 02 074 959 300, info@gnto.co.uk. **USA**: Olympic Tower, 645 Fifth Ave., New York NY 10022, ✆ 2 124 215 777, gnto@greektourism.com.

VISAS

See page xxxii for visa requirements.

HUNGARY

CAPITAL

Budapest.

CURRENCY

Forint (HUF or Ft). For exchange rates see page 11. You can buy your currency at banks and official bureaux. Credit cards and small denomination travellers cheques are widely accepted. Euros are more useful than dollars or sterling.

EMBASSIES IN BUDAPEST

Australia: Királyhágó tér 8–9, ✆ 0 614 579 777. **Canada**: Ganz u. 12-14, ✆ 0 613 923 360. **New Zealand** (Consulate): Nagymazö utca 50, ✆ 013 022 484. **UK**: Harmincad utca 6, ✆ 12 662 888. **USA**: Szabadság tér 12, ✆ 0 614 754 400.

EMBASSIES OVERSEAS

Australia: 17 Beale Crescent, Deakin ACT 2600, Canberra, ✆ 0 262 823 226. **Canada**: 299 Waverley St, Ottawa ON, K2P 0V9, ✆ 6 132 302 717. **UK**: 35 Eaton Place, London SW1X 8BY, ✆ 02 072 355 218. **USA**: 3910 Shoemaker St NW, Washington DC 20008, ✆ 2 023 626 730.

LANGUAGE

Hungarian. English and German are both widely understood.

OPENING HOURS

Food/tourist shops, markets, malls open Sun. **Banks**: commercial banks Mon–Thur 0800–1500, Fri 0800–1300. **Food shops**: Mon–Fri 0700–1900, others: 1000–1800 (Thur until 1900); shops close for lunch and half-day on Sat (1300). **Museums**: usually Tues–Sun 1000–1800, free one day a week, closed public holidays.

POST OFFICES

Mostly 0800–1800 Mon–Fri, 0800–1200 Sat. Stamps also sold at tobacconists. Major post offices cash Eurocheques and change western currency; all give cash for Visa Eurocard/Mastercard, Visa Electron and Maestro cards.

PUBLIC HOLIDAYS

Jan 1, Mar 15 (Revolution), Easter Sun/Mon, May 1, Whit Monday, Aug 20 (Constitution), Oct 23 (Republic), Dec 25, 26. For dates of movable holidays see page 2.

PUBLIC TRANSPORT

Long-distance buses: *Volánbusz* (www.volanbusz.hu), ✆ +36 1 382 0888. Extensive metro / tram / bus system in Budapest with integrated tickets; for day tickets see Passes section. Debrecen, Miskolc and Szeged also have trams. Ferry and hydrofoil services operate on the Danube.

RAIL TRAVEL

See Tables **1200 - 1299**. A comprehensive network operated by Hungarian State Railways (MÁV) (www.mav.hu) connects most towns and cities. Express services link Budapest to major centres and Lake Balaton: *IC* trains require compulsory reservation and supplement. InterPici (*IP*) trains are fast railcars connecting with *IC* trains, also with compulsory reservation. Most *EC* trains require a supplement but not reservation (for exceptions see page 485). Other trains include *gyorsvonat* (fast trains) and *sebesvonat* (semi-fast). Local trains (*személyvonat*) are very slow. Book sleepers well in advance.

TELEPHONES

Dial in: ✆ +36 then number (omit initial 06). Outgoing: ✆ 00. Phonecards are on sale at newsstands, tobacconists, post offices, supermarkets. Payphones take HUF 10, 20, and 50 coins. International directory assistance: ✆ 199. Emergency: ✆ 112. Police: ✆ 107. Fire: ✆ 105. Ambulance: ✆ 104.

TIPPING

Round up by 5–15% for restaurants and taxis. People do not generally leave coins on the table; instead the usual practise is to make it clear that you are rounding up the sum. Service is included in some upmarket restaurants.

TOURIST INFORMATION

Hungarian National Tourist Office (www.hungarytourism.hu). Tourinform ✆ 06 80 630 800, info@hungarytourism.hu *Tourinform* branches throughout Hungary. English-speaking staff. The *Hungarian Tourist Card* (www.hungarycard.hu), giving various discounts, costs HUF 5520 (± EUR 22, USD 31).

TOURIST OFFICES OVERSEAS

UK: 46 Eaton Place, London SW1X 8AL, ✆ 02 078 231 459, htlondon@hungarytourism.hu
USA: 150 E 58th St, 33rd Floor, New York NY 10155, ✆ 2 123 550 240, htnewyork@hungarytourism.hu

VISAS

See page xxxii for visa requirements.

IRELAND

CAPITAL

Dublin. For Northern Ireland see under United Kingdom.

CLIMATE

Cool, wet winters, mild spring and autumn. Intermittent rain is a common feature of the Irish weather.

CURRENCY

Euro (EUR/€). 1 euro = 100 cent. For exchange rates see page 11.

EMBASSIES IN DUBLIN

Australia: 7th Floor, Fitzwilton House, Wilton Terrace, ✆ 016 645 300. **Canada**: 7-8 Wilton Terrace, ✆ 014 174 100. **New Zealand** (Consulate): 37 Leeson Park, ✆ 016 604 233. **UK**: 29 Merrion Road, Ballsbridge,
✆ 012 053 700. **USA**: 42 Elgin Road, ✆ 016 688 777.

EMBASSIES OVERSEAS

Australia: 20 Arkana St, Yarralumla ACT 2600, Canberra, ✆ 0 262 733 022. **Canada**: Suite 1105, 130 Albert St, Ottawa ON, K1P 5G4, ✆ 6 132 336 281. **UK**: 17 Grosvenor Place, London SW1X 7HR, ✆ 02 072 352 171. **USA**: 2234 Massachusetts Ave. NW, Washington DC 20008-2849, ✆ 2 024 623 939.

LANGUAGE

Most people speak English. The Irish language (Gaeilge) is spoken in several areas (known as the Gaeltacht) scattered over seven counties and four provinces, mostly along the western seaboard. Official documents use both languages.

OPENING HOURS

Shops generally open Mon - Sat 0900 - 1730; most shopping centres stay open until 2000 on Thurs and Fri. Some shops open on Sunday, 1200 - 1800.

POST OFFICES

Postal service: *An Post*, www.anpost.ie. Most communities have a post office, usually open Mon-Fri 0900 - 1730 or 1800, Sat 0900 - 1300; often closed one hour at lunchtime (except main offices). Sub post offices often close at 1300 one day per week.

PUBLIC HOLIDAYS

January 1 (New Year's Day), March 17 (St Patrick's Day), Good Friday (bank holiday only), Easter Monday, first Monday in May, first Monday in June, first Monday in August, last Monday in October, December 25 (Christmas Day), December 26 (St Stephen's Day). Holidays falling at the weekend are transferred to the next following weekday.

PUBLIC TRANSPORT

A modern tramway system in Dublin called *Luas* (www.luas.ie) has two unconnected lines; the red line is the most useful for visitors as it connects Connolly and Heuston stations. Dublin Bus operates an extensive network throughout the capital, but journeys can be very slow in rush-hour traffic. Almost all bus services outside Dublin are operated by Bus Éireann (www.buseireann.ie), ✆ 01 836 6111 (daily 0830–1900). Long distance services leave from the Dublin bus station (*Busáras*) in Store St, near Connolly rail station.

RAIL TRAVEL

See Tables **230 - 249**. Rail services are operated by Iarnród Éireann (IÉ) (www.irishrail.ie). Timetable and fares enquiries: ✆ 01 836 6222 (0900–1800 Mon-Sat, 1000–1800 Sun). The *Enterprise* express service Dublin - Belfast is operated jointly with Northern Ireland Railways. Local IÉ north-south electric line in Dublin is called DART.

TELEPHONES

Dial in: ✆ +353 then number (omit initial 0). Outgoing: ✆ 00 (048 for Northern Ireland). Most payphones take cards only. Operator assistance: ✆ 100. Emergency services: ✆ 112 or 999.

TIPPING

A tip of 12 - 15% is expected in restaurants. Taxis 10%.

TOURIST INFORMATION

Fáilte Ireland (www.ireland.ie). Main office: Baggot St Bridge, Baggot St, Dublin 2, ✆ 016 024 000. Tourist offices offer a wide range of information, also accommodation bookings.

TOURIST OFFICES OVERSEAS

Australia: 36 Carrington St, 5th Level, Sydney NSW 2000, ✆ 0 292 996 177. **Canada**: 2 Bloor St W, Suite 1501, Toronto ON, M4W 3E2, ✆ 8 002 236 470. **UK**: 150 New Bond St, London W1Y 0AQ, ✆ 02 074 933 201. **USA**: 345 Park Ave., New York NY 10154, ✆ 2 124 180 800.

VISAS

See page xxxii for visa requirements.

ITALY

CAPITAL

Rome (Roma).

CLIMATE

Very hot in July and Aug. May, June, and Sept are best for sightseeing. Holiday season ends mid Sept or Oct. Rome is crowded at Easter.

CURRENCY

Euro (EUR/€). 1 euro = 100 cent. For exchange rates see page 11.

EMBASSIES IN ROME

Australia: Via Antonio Bosio 5, ✆ 06 852 721. **Canada**: Via Zara 30, ✆ 06 854 441. **New Zealand**: Via Zara 28, ✆ 064 417 171. **UK**: Via XX Settembre 80a, ✆ 0 642 200 001. **USA**: Via Vittorio Veneto 121, ✆ 0 646 741.

EMBASSIES OVERSEAS

Australia: 12 Grey St, Deakin, Canberra ACT 2600, ✆ 0 262 733 333. **Canada**: 275 Slater St, 21st Floor, Ottawa ON, K1P 5H9, ✆ 6 132 322 401. **New Zealand**: 34-38 Grant Rd, Thorndon, Wellington, ✆ 044 947 170. **UK**: 14 Three Kings Yard, London W1K 4EH, ✆ (020) 7312 2200. **USA**: 3000 Whitehaven St NW, Washington DC 20008, ✆ 2 026 124 400.

LANGUAGE

Italian; standard Italian is spoken across the country though there are marked regional pronunciation differences. Some dialects in more remote areas. Many speak English in cities and tourist areas. In the south and Sicily, French is often more useful than English.

OPENING HOURS

Banks: Mon–Fri 0830–1330, 1430–1630. **Shops**: (usually) Mon–Sat 0830/0900–1230, 1530/1600–1900/1930; closed Mon am/Sat pm July/Aug. **Museums/sites**: usually Tues–Sun 0930–1900; last Sun of month free; most refuse entry within an hour of closing. Churches often close at lunchtime.

POST OFFICES

Mostly Mon–Fri 0830–1330/1350, Sat 0830–1150. Some counters (registered mail and telegrams) may differ; in main cities some open in the afternoon. Send anything urgent via express. *Posta prioritaria* stamps also guarantee a faster delivery. Stamps (*francobolli*) are available from tobacconists (*tabacchi*). Poste restante (*Fermo posta*) at most post offices.

PUBLIC HOLIDAYS

All over the country: Jan 1, Jan 6 (Epiphany), Easter Mon, Apr 25 (Liberation), May 1, June 2 (Republic), Aug 15 (Assumption, virtually nothing opens), Nov 1 (All Saints), Dec 8 (Immaculate Conception), Dec 25, Dec 26. For dates of movable holidays see page 2. Regional Saints' days: Apr 25 in Venice, June 24 in Florence, Genoa and Turin, June 29 in Rome, July 11 in Palermo, Sept 19 in Naples, Oct 4 in Bologna, Dec 6 in Bari, Dec 7 in Milan.

PUBLIC TRANSPORT

Buses are often crowded, but regular, and serve many areas inaccessible by rail. Services may be drastically reduced at weekends; this is not always made clear in timetables. Roma, Milano and Napoli have metro systems; most major cities have trams. Taxis (metered) can be expensive; steer clear of unofficial ones.

RAIL TRAVEL

See Tables **580 - 649**. The national operator is Trenitalia, a division of Ferrovie dello Stato (FS) (website www.trenitalia.it). National rail information ✆ 892 021 (from within Italy only). High-speed express services operate between major cities. 'Alta Velocità' (*AV*) are premium fare services using high-speed lines. 'Eurostar Italia' (*ES*) and 'Eurostar City' (*ESc*) trains also require payment of a higher fare. InterCity Plus (*ICp*) uses refurbished *IC* stock. Reservation is compulsory on *AV*, *ES*, *ESc* and *ICp* trains. Reservation is also possible on *IC*, *EC* and *ICN* (InterCityNight) trains. *TrenOK* are low-cost high-speed services with tickets only available via the internet, a special call-centre, and self-service ticket machines. Other services are classified *Espresso* (long-distance domestic train, stopping only at main stations) and *Regionale* (stops at most stations). Services are reasonably punctual. Some long-distance trains do not carry passengers short distances. Sleepers: single or double berths in 1st class, three (occasionally doubles) in 2nd. Couchettes: four berths in 1st class, six in 2nd. Refreshments on most long-distance trains. There are often long queues at stations; buy tickets and make reservations at travel agencies (look for FS symbol).

TELEPHONES

Dial in: ✆ +39 then number. Outgoing: ✆ 00. Public phones take coins or phonecards *(carte telefoniche)*, available from newsstands and post offices. Metered phones (*scatti*) are common in bars and restaurants; pay the attendant after use. English-speaking assistance for international calls: ✆ 15 for European countries; ✆ 170 for rest of the world. Police: ✆ 113. Fire: ✆ 115. Ambulance: ✆ 118.

TIPPING

In restaurants you need to look at the menu to see if service charge is included. If not, a tip of 10% is fine depending on how generous you feel like being. The same percentage applies to taxi drivers. A helpful porter can expect up to €2.50.

TOURIST INFORMATION

Italian State Tourist Board (www.enit.it). Main office: Via Marghera 2/6, 00185 Roma, ✆ 0 649 711, sedecentrale@enit.it. Most towns and resorts have an *Azienda Autonoma di Soggiorno e Turismo* (AAST), many with their own websites, or *Pro Loco* (local tourist board).

TOURIST OFFICES OVERSEAS

Australia: Level 4, 46 Market St, Sydney NSW 2000, ✆ 0 292 621 666, italia@italiantourism.com.au. **Canada**: 175 Bloor St E, Suite 907, South Tower, Toronto ON, M4W 3R8, ✆ 4 169 254 882, enit.canada@on.aibn.com. **UK**: 1 Princes St, London W1B 2AY, ✆ 02 074 081 254, italy@italiantouristboard.co.uk.
USA: 630 Fifth Ave., Suite 1565, New York NY 10111, ✆ 2 122 455 618, enitny@italiantourism.com. Also in Chicago and Los Angeles.

VISAS

See page xxxii for visa requirements.

LATVIA

CAPITAL

Riga.

CLIMATE

Warm summers, cold, snowy winters; rain all year, heaviest in August.

CURRENCY

Lats (LVL or Ls) 1 lats = 100 santimu. For exchange rates, see page 11.

EMBASSIES IN RIGA

Australia: *refer to Australian Embassy in Sweden.* **Canada**: 6th floor, Baznicas iela 20/22, ✆ 87 813 945. **New Zealand**: *refer to NZ Embassy in Poland.* **UK**: Alunana iela 5, ✆ 07 774 700.
USA: Raiņa bulvaris 7, ✆ 87 036 200.

EMBASSIES OVERSEAS

Australia (Consulate): 2 Mackennel Street, East Ivanhoe VIC 3079, ✆ 0 394 996 920. **Canada**: 350 Sparks St, Suite 1200, Ottawa ON, K1R 7S8, ✆ 6 132 386014. **UK**: 45 Nottingham Place, London W1U 5LY, ✆ 02 073 120 040. **USA**: 2306 Massachusetts Ave. NW, Washington DC 20008, ✆ 2 023 282 840.

LANGUAGE

Latvian is the majority language. Russian is the first language of around 30% and is widely understood. English and German can often be of use, especially in the larger towns.

OPENING HOURS

Banks: mainly Mon–Fri 0900–1700, some Sat 0900–1300. **Shops**: Mon–Fri 0900/1000–1800/1900 and Sat 0900/1000–1700. Many close on Mon. **Museums**: days vary, but usually open Tues/Wed–Sun 1100–1700.

POST OFFICES

Mon–Fri 0900–1800, Sat 0900–1300. The main post office in Riga, at Brivibas bulvaris 19, is open 24 hrs. Postboxes are yellow.

PUBLIC HOLIDAYS

Jan 1, Good Friday, Easter Mon, May 1, June 23 (Ligo Day), June 24 (Saint John), Nov 18 (Republic), Dec 25, 26, 31. For dates of movable holidays see page 2.

PUBLIC TRANSPORT

Very cheap for Westerners. Taxis generally affordable (agree fare first if not metered). Beware of pickpockets on crowded buses and trams. Long-distance bus network preferred to slow domestic train service.

RAIL TRAVEL

See Table **1800 - 1899**. Comfortable overnight trains; best to take berth in 2nd-class coupé (4-berth compartment); 1st-class *luxe* compartments (2-berth) are also available on trains to Moscow etc. Reservation is compulsory for all sleepers; Russian-bound ones may require proof of entry visa when booking. Very little English spoken at stations.

TELEPHONES

Dial in: ✆ +371 then number (omit initial 8). Outgoing: ✆ 00. Phonecards for LVL 2, 5, or 10 are sold at post offices, shops and kiosks. Police: ✆ 110. Fire and ambulance: ✆ 112.

TIPPING

Not necessary to tip at the bar or counter, but tip 10% if served at your table. Round up taxi fares to a maximum of 10%.

TOURIST INFORMATION

Latvian Tourism Development Agency (www.latviatourism.lv). Main office: Pils Lauk 4, 1050 Riga, ✆ 87 229 945, info@latviatourism.lv.

TOURIST OFFICES OVERSEAS

Finland: Latvian Tourism Information Centre, Mariankatu 8B, 00170 Helsinki, ✆ 092 784 774, latviatravel@kolumbus.fi.
Germany: Baltische Tourismus Zentrale, Salzmannstraße 152, 48159 Münster, ✆ 02 512 150 742, info@baltic-info.de.

VISAS

See page xxxii for visa requirements. Applications may take up to 30 days; confirmed hotel reservations are required. Visas may also be valid for Estonia and Lithuania. Passports must be valid for at least 3 months following the stay. Visas issued on arrival at the airport (not train border crossings) are valid 10 days.

LITHUANIA

CAPITAL

Vilnius.

CLIMATE

Warm summers, cold, snowy winters; rain all year, heaviest in August.

CURRENCY

Litas (LTL or Lt); 1 litas = 100 centu (ct), singular centas. Travellers cheques and credit cards are widely accepted. For exchange rates see page 11.

EMBASSIES IN VILNIUS

Australia: *refer to Australian Embassy in Sweden.* **Canada**: *refer to Canadian Embassy in Latvia.* **New Zealand**: *refer to NZ Embassy in Poland.* **UK**: Antakalnio 2, ✆ 0 52 462 900.
USA: Akmenu gatve 6, ✆ 852 665 500.

EMBASSIES OVERSEAS

Australia (Consulate): 40B Fiddens Wharf Rd, Killara NSW 2071, Sydney, ✆ 0 294 982 571. **Canada**: 130 Albert St, Suite 204, Ottawa ON, K1P 5G4, ✆ 6 135 675 458. **UK**: 84 Gloucester Pl., London W1U 6AU, ✆ 02 074 866 401. **USA**: 4590 MacArthur Blvd. NW, Suite 200, Washington DC 20007, ✆ 2 022 345 860.

LANGUAGE

Lithuanian. Russian is the first language of around 10% of the population. English and German can often be of use, especially in the larger towns.

OPENING HOURS

Banks: mostly Mon–Thur 0900–1600, Fri 0900–1500. **Shops**: (large shops) Mon–Fri 1000/1100–1900; many also open Sat until 1600. Some close for lunch 1400–1500 and also on Sun and Mon. **Museums**: days vary, most close Mon and sometimes Tues and open at least Wed and Fri; often free on Wed; hours usually at least 1100–1700, check locally.

POST OFFICES

All towns have post offices *(Lietuvos Paštas)* with an international telephone service. Offices are generally open 0800–1830 Mon–Fri and 0800–1400 Sat. Smaller offices often close for an hour at midday.

PUBLIC HOLIDAYS

Jan 1, Feb 16 (Independence Day), Mar 11 (Restoration of Statehood), Easter Mon, May 1 (not banks), July 6 (King Mindaugas), Aug. 15 (Assumption), Nov 1 (All Saints), Dec 25, 26. For dates of movable holidays see page 2.

PUBLIC TRANSPORT

Similar to Latvia (see above).

RAIL TRAVEL

See Tables **1800 - 1899**. Major routes are to St Petersburg, Moscow and Kaliningrad (Russia), Warsaw (Poland), and Minsk (Belarus). Warsaw trains have standard European couchettes and sleepers. Other overnight trains have 54-bunk open coaches (P), 4-bed compartments (K) and (on Moscow trains only) 2-bed compartments (M-2).

TELEPHONES

Dial in: ✆ +370 then number (omit initial 8). Outgoing: ✆ 00. Phonecards are sold at newsstands. Police: ✆ 02. Fire: ✆ 01. Ambulance: ✆ 03.

TIPPING

Not necessary to tip at the bar or counter, but tip 10% if served at your table. Round up taxi fares to a maximum of 10%.

TOURIST INFORMATION

Lithuania State Department of Tourism (www.tourism.lt and www.travel.lt). Main tourist office in Vilnius: Didzioji 31, LT-2001 Vilnius, ✆ 526 264 70, turizm.info@vilnius.lt. There are tourist offices in most towns.

TOURIST OFFICES OVERSEAS

Germany: Baltische Tourismus Zentrale, Salzmannstraße 152, 48159 Münster, ✆ 02 512 150 742, info@baltic-info.de.

VISAS

See page xxxii for visa requirements.

LUXEMBOURG

CAPITAL

Luxembourg City (Ville de Luxembourg).

CLIMATE

Rain prevalent at any time; warm summers, cold winters (often with snow).

CURRENCY

Euro (EUR/€). 1 euro = 100 cent. For exchange rates see page 11.

EMBASSIES IN LUXEMBOURG

Australia: *refer to Australian Embassy in Belgium.* **Canada**: *refer to Canadian Embassy in Belgium.* **New Zealand**: *refer to NZ Embassy in Belgium.* **UK**: 5 Boulevard Joseph II, ✆ 229 864. **USA**: 22 Boulevard Emmanuel Servais, ✆ 460 123.

EMBASSIES OVERSEAS

Australia (Consulate): Level 4 Quay West 111, Harrington Street, Sydney NSW 2000, ✆ 0 292 534 708. **UK**: 27 Wilton Crescent, London SW1X 8SD, ✆ 02 072 356 961. **USA/Canada**: 2200 Massachusetts Ave. NW, Washington DC 20008, ✆ 2 022 654 171.

LANGUAGE

Luxembourgish is the national tongue, but almost everybody also speaks fluent French and/or German, plus often at least some English.

OPENING HOURS

Many establishments take long lunch breaks. **Banks**: usually Mon–Fri 0830–1200 and 1400–1630 or later. **Shops**: Mon 1300/1400–1800; Tues–Sat 0800/0900–1800. **Museums**: most open six days a week (usually Tues–Sun).

POST OFFICES

Usually open Mon–Fri 0800–1200 and 1400–1700.

PUBLIC HOLIDAYS

Jan 1, Carnival (Monday before Shrove Tuesday), Easter Mon, May 1, Ascension, Whit Mon, Corpus Christi, June 23 (National Day), Aug 15 (Assumption), Nov 1 (All Saints), Dec 25, 26. For dates of movable holidays see page 2. When a holiday falls on a Sunday, the next working day becomes a substitute holiday.

PUBLIC TRANSPORT

Good bus network between most towns. Taxis not allowed to pick up passengers in the street; most stations have ranks.

RAIL TRAVEL

See Table **445** for local services. Operator: Société Nationale des Chemins de fer Luxembourgeois (CFL) (www.cfl.lu), ✆ 49 904 990. Frequent rail services converge on Luxembourg City. Inexpensive multi-ride passes (good for one hour or up to 24 hours) are valid on trains and local buses. Most rail stations are small with few facilities.

TELEPHONES

Dial in: ✆ +352 then number. Outgoing: ✆ 00. Phonecards (*Telekaarten*) are available from post offices and stations. Police: ✆ 113. Fire and ambulance: ✆ 112.

TIPPING

In restaurants, cafés and bars service charge is usually included (round up bill to the next euro). Taxi drivers EUR 2–5; porters EUR 1–2; hairdressers EUR 2; cloakroom attendants EUR 0.50; toilet attendants EUR 0.25.

TOURIST INFORMATION

Office National du Tourisme (www.ont.lu). Gare Centrale, PO Box 1001, L-1010 Luxembourg, ✆ 4 282 821. Information and hotel bookings: Luxembourg City Tourist Office, Place d'Armes, PO Box 181, L-2011 Luxembourg, ✆ 222 809, touristinfo@lcto.lu (www.lcto.lu),

TOURIST OFFICES OVERSEAS

UK: 122 Regent St, London W1B 5SA, ✆ 02 074 342 800, tourism@luxembourg.co.uk. **USA**: 17 Beekman Place, New York NY 10022, ✆ 2 129 358 888, luxnto@aol.com.

VISAS

See page xxxii for visa requirements.

NETHERLANDS

CAPITAL

Amsterdam is the capital city. The Hague (Den Haag) is the seat of government.

CLIMATE

Can be cold in winter; rain prevalent all year. Many attractions close Oct–Easter, while Apr–May is tulip time and the country is crowded; June–Sept can be pleasantly warm and is busy with tourists.

CURRENCY

Euro (EUR/€). 1 euro = 100 cent. For exchange rates see page 11.

EMBASSIES IN THE HAGUE

Australia: Carnegielaan 4, ✆ 0 703 108 200. **Canada**: Sophialaan 7, ✆ 0 703 111 600. **New Zealand**: Eisenhowerlaan 77, ✆ 0 703 469 324. **UK**: Lange Voorhout 10, ✆ 0 704 270 427. **USA**: Lange Voorhout 102, ✆ 0 703 102 209.

EMBASSIES OVERSEAS

Australia: 120 Empire Circuit, Yarralumla, Canberra ACT 2600, ✆ 0 262 209 400. **Canada**: Constitution Square Building, 350 Albert St, Suite 2020, Ottawa ON, K1R 1A4, ✆ 6 132 375 030. **New Zealand**: Investment House, 10th floor, cnr Ballance & Featherston Streets, Wellington, ✆ 044 716 390. **UK**: 38 Hyde Park Gate, London SW7 5DP, ✆ 02 075 903 200. **USA**: 4200 Linnean Ave. NW, Washington DC 20008, ✆ 18 733 882 443.

LANGUAGE

Dutch; English is very widely spoken.

OPENING HOURS

Banks: Mon–Fri 0900–1600/1700 (later Thur or Fri). **Shops**: Mon–Fri 0900/0930–1730/1800 (until 2100 Thur or Fri), Sat 0900/0930–1600/1700. Many close Mon morning. **Museums**: vary, but usually Mon–Sat 1000–1700, Sun 1100–1700 (some close Mon). In winter many have shorter hours.

POST OFFICES

Post offices *(TPG Post)* are generally open Mon–Fri 0830–1700; some also open on Sat 0830–1200. Many shops selling postcards also sell stamps. Post international mail in the left slot, marked *overige* (other), of the red *TPG* mailboxes.

PUBLIC HOLIDAYS

Jan 1, Good Fri, Easter Mon, Apr 30 (Queen's Birthday), May 5 (Liberation Day), Ascension Day, Whit Mon, Dec 25, Dec 26. For dates of movable holidays see page 2.

PUBLIC TRANSPORT

Premium rate number for all rail and bus enquiries (computerised, fast and accurate): ✆ 09 009 292 (www.9292ov.nl). Taxis are best boarded at ranks or ordered by phone as they seldom stop in the street. In many cities (not Amsterdam), shared *Treintaxis* have ranks at stations and yellow roof signs (€4.20 for anywhere within city limits; tickets from rail ticket offices). *Strippenkaarten* (from stations, city transport offices, post offices and sometimes VVV) are strip tickets, valid nation-wide on metros, buses, trams and some trains (2nd class) within city limits; zones apply; validate on boarding; valid one hour; change of transport allowed.

RAIL TRAVEL

See Tables **450 - 499**. National rail company Nederlandse Spoorwegen (NS) (www.ns.nl) provides most services, though private operators run local train services in some parts of the north and east. Through tickets can be purchased between all stations in the Netherlands, regardless of operator. Credit cards are not accepted, though larger stations usually have ATM machines from which cash can be obtained. Cycle hire and cycle and baggage storage are usually available at larger stations. Smaller stations are usually unstaffed, but all stations have ticket vending machines. Undated tickets must be validated before travel in one of the ticket stamping machines located at platform entrances. Travellers found to have boarded a train without a valid ticket must pay a fine of €35 plus the cost of their fare. Seat reservations are not available except for international journeys. The fastest domestic trains, calling at principal stations only, are classified *Intercity*. *Stoptreinen* call at all stations. Between these two categories are *sneltreinen* (fast trains) which miss out the less important stations.

TELEPHONES

Dial in: ✆ +31 then number (omit initial 0). Outgoing: ✆ 00. Booths (green) have instructions in English and take only phonecards (*telefoonkaarten*), available from post offices, tourist offices (VVV), rail stations (NS), telecom shops (Primafoon) and some other shops (some booths also take credit cards). International calls are cheapest Mon–Fri evenings and all day Sat, Sun. Most information-line numbers are prefixed 0900 and are at premium rates. Operator: ✆ 118. International enquiries: ✆ 09 008 418. National enquiries: ✆ 09 008 008. Emergency services: ✆ 112.

TIPPING

Although service charges are included, it is customary in restaurants, bars and cafés to leave a tip of 5–10% if you are satisfied. Taxi drivers expect a 10% tip.

TOURIST INFORMATION

Vereniging voor Vreemdelingenverkeer (VVV: signs show a triangle with three Vs) (www.holland.com). Tourist bureaux are all open at least Mon–Fri 0900–1700, Sat 1000–1200. The *Museumkaart* (EUR 25, under 25s EUR 12.50) obtainable from VVV and participating museums, is valid for one year and gives free entry to over 400 museums nationwide.

TOURIST OFFICES OVERSEAS

Netherlands Board of Tourism (www.goholland.com). **Canada**: 25 Adelaide St E., Suite 710, Toronto ON, M5C 1Y2, ✆ 4 163 631 577, info@goholland.com. **UK**: PO Box 30783, London WC2B 6DH, ✆ 02 075 397 950, information@nbt.org.uk. **USA**: 355 Lexington Ave., 21st Floor, New York NY 10017, ✆ 2 123 707 360, info@goholland.com. Also in Chicago and Los Angeles.

VISAS

See page xxxii for visa requirements.

NORWAY

CAPITAL

Oslo.

CLIMATE

Surprisingly mild considering it's so far north; can be very warm in summer, particularly inland; the coast is appreciably cooler. May and June are driest months, but quite cool; summer gets warmer and wetter as it progresses, and the western fjords have high rainfall year-round. Days are very long in summer: the sun never sets in high summer in the far north. July and Aug is the busiest period; Sept can be delightful. Winter is the time to see the Northern Lights (*Aurora Borealis*). Excellent snow for skiing Dec–Apr.

CURRENCY

Norwegian crown or krone (NOK or kr); 1 krone = 100 øre. For exchange rates see page 11. On slot machines, *femkrone* means a NOK 5 coin and *tikrone* a NOK 10 coin.

EMBASSIES IN OSLO

Australia (Consulate): Wilh. Wilhelmsen ASA, Strandveien 20, Lysaker, ✆ 67 584 848. **Canada**: 4th floor, Wergelandsveien 7, ✆ 22 995 300. **New Zealand** (Consulate): C/o Halfdan Ditlev-Simonsen & Co AS, Strandveien 50, Lysaker. ✆ 67 110 033. **UK**: Thomas Heftyesgate 8, ✆ 23 132 700. **USA**: Henrik Ibsens gate 48, ✆ 22 448 550.

EMBASSIES OVERSEAS

Australia: 17 Hunter St, Yarralumla, Canberra ACT 2600, ✆ 0 262 733 444. **Canada**: 90 Sparks St, Suite 532, Ottawa ON, K1P 5B4, ✆ 6 132 386 571. **UK**: 25 Belgrave Sq., London, SW1X 8QD, ✆ 02 075 915 500. **USA**: 2720 34th St NW, Washington D.C. 20008, ✆ 2 023 336 000.

LANGUAGE

Norwegian, which has two official versions: *Nynorsk* and *Bokmål*. Norwegian has three additional vowels: æ, ø, å, which (in that order) follow z. Almost everyone speaks English; if not, try German.

OPENING HOURS

Banks: Mon–Wed and Fri 0815–1500 (1530 in winter), Thur 0815–1700. In Oslo, some open later, in the country some close earlier. Many have minibank machines that accept Visa, MasterCard (Eurocard) and Cirrus. **Shops**: Mon–Fri 0900–1600/1700 (Thur 0900–1800/2000), Sat 0900–1300/1500, many open later, especially in Oslo. **Museums**: usually Tues–Sun 1000–1500/1600. Some open Mon, longer in summer and/or close completely in winter.

POST OFFICES

Usually Mon–Fri 0800/0830–1700, Sat 0830–1300. Yellow postboxes with red crown-and-posthorn symbol are for local mail; red boxes with yellow symbol for all other destinations.

PUBLIC HOLIDAYS

Jan 1, Maundy Thur, Good Fri, Easter Mon, May 1, Ascension Day, May 17 (Constitution Day), Whit Mon, Dec 25, 26. For dates of movable holidays see page 2.

PUBLIC TRANSPORT

Train, boat and bus schedules are linked to provide good connections. It is often worth using buses or boats to connect two dead-end rail lines (e.g. Bergen and Stavanger), rather than retracing your route. Rail passes sometimes offer good discounts, even free travel, on linking services. NorWay Bussekspress (www.nor-way.no), Karl Johans gate 2, N-0154 Oslo, ✆ 82 021 300 (premium rate) has the largest bus network with routes going as far north as Kirkenes. Long-distance buses are comfortable, with reclining seats, ample leg room. Tickets: buy on board or reserve, ✆ 81 544 444 (premium-rate). Taxis: metered, can be picked up at ranks or by phoning; treat independent taxis with caution.

RAIL TRAVEL

See Tables **770 - 789**. Operated by: Norges Statsbaner (NSB) (www.nsb.no). All trains convey 2nd-class seating. Most medium- and long-distance trains also convey *NSB Komfort* accommodation, a dedicated area with complimentary tea/coffee and newspapers (supplement payable). Sleeping cars have one-, two and three-berth compartments (passengers may reserve a berth in any category with a 2nd-class ticket). Long-distance trains convey refreshments. Reservation possible on all long-distance trains, ✆ (within Norway) 81 500 888, then dial 4 for an english speaking operator. Reserved seats not marked, but your confirmation specifies carriage and seat/berth numbers. Carriage numbers shown by the doors, berth numbers outside compartments, seat numbers on seat-backs or luggage racks. Stations: most have baggage lockers, larger stations have baggage trolleys. Narvesen chain (at most stations; open long hours) sells English-language publications and a good range of snacks.

TELEPHONES

Dial in: ✆ +47 then number. Outgoing: ✆ 00. *Telekort* (phonecards) are available from Narvesen newsstands and post offices. Card phones (green) are spreading fast; some accept credit cards. Coin and card phones are usually grouped together. Overseas calls are cheapest 2200–0800 and at weekends. Directory enquiries: ✆ 180 (Nordic countries), ✆ 181 (other countries). Local operator: ✆ 117. International operator: ✆ 115. Operators speak English. These are all premium-rate. Police: ✆ 112. Fire: ✆ 110. Ambulance: ✆ 113.

TIPPING

Tip 10% in restaurants (but not bars/cafés) if you are satisfied with the food, service etc. Not necessary for taxis.

TOURIST INFORMATION

Norwegian Tourist Board (www.visitnorway.com). Main office: Stortorvet 10, N-0155 Oslo, ✆ 2414 4600. Tourist offices (*Turistkontorer*) and bureaux (*Reiselivslag / Turistinformasjon*) exist in almost all towns and provide free maps, brochures, etc.

TOURIST OFFICES OVERSEAS

UK: Charles House, 5 Regent St, London SW1Y 4LR, ✆ 02 078 396 255, greatbritain@nortra.no. **USA**: 655 Third Ave., New York NY 10017, ✆ 2 128 859 710, usa@ntr.no.

VISAS

See page xxxii for visa requirements.

POLAND

CAPITAL

Warsaw (Warszawa).

CLIMATE

Temperate, with warm summers and cold winters; rain falls throughout year.

CURRENCY

Złoty (PLN or zł), divided into 100 groszy. For exchange rates see page 11. British pounds, American dollars and (especially) euros are useful. *Kantor* exchange offices sometimes give better rates than banks and opening hours are longer. Credit cards are increasingly accepted but not universal.

EMBASSIES IN WARSAW

Australia: Ulica Nowogrodzka 11, ✆ 0 225 213 444. **Canada**: Ulica Jana Matejki 1/5, ✆ 0 225 843 100. **New Zealand**: Dom Dochodawy, Level 5, Aleje Ujazdowskie 51, ✆ 0 225 210 500. **UK**: Aleje Róz 1, ✆ 0 223 110 000. **USA**: Aleje Ujazdowskie 29/31, ✆ 0 225 042 000.

EMBASSIES OVERSEAS

Australia: 7 Turrana St, Yarralumla, Canberra ACT 2600, ✆ 0 262 721 000. **Canada**: 443 Daly Ave., Ottawa ON, K1N 6H3,

✆ 6 137 890 468. **New Zealand**: 17 Upland Rd, Kelburn, Wellington, ✆ 044 759 453. **UK**: 47 Portland Place, London W1N 3AG, ✆ 08 707 742 700. **USA**: 2640 16th St NW, Washington DC 20009, ✆ 2 022 343 800.

LANGUAGE

Polish. Many older Poles speak German; younger Poles, particularly students, are likely to understand English. Russian is widely understood, but unpopular.

OPENING HOURS

Banks: Mon–Fri 0800–1600/1800, Sat 0800–1300. **Shops**: Mon–Fri 0800/1100–1900, Sat 0900–1300. **Food shops**: Mon–Fri 0600–1900, Sat 0600–1600. **Museums**: usually Tues–Sun 1000–1600; often closed public holidays and following day.

POST OFFICES

Known as *Poczta*; Mon–Fri 0700/0800–1800/2000, Sat 0800–1400 (main offices). City post offices are numbered (main office is always 1); number should be included in the post restante address. Post boxes: green (local mail), red (long-distance).

PUBLIC HOLIDAYS

Jan 1, Easter Mon, May 1, May 3 (Constitution), Corpus Christi, Aug 15 (Assumption), Nov 1 (All Saints), Nov 11 (Independence), Dec 25, 26. For dates of movable holidays see page 2.

PUBLIC TRANSPORT

PKS buses: cheap and sometimes more practical than trains. Main long-distance bus station in Warszawa is adjacent to the Zachodnia (western) station. Tickets normally include seat reservations (seat number is on back), bookable from bus station. In rural areas, bus drivers will often halt between official stops if you flag them down. Extensive tram networks in Warszawa and most other cities; Warszawa also has a modern north-south metro line.

RAIL TRAVEL

See Tables **1000 - 1099**. Cheap and punctual, run by Polskie Koleje Państwowe (PKP), www.pkp.pl. At stations, departures (*odjazdy*) are shown on yellow paper, arrivals (*przyjazdy*) on white. IC, IC+, express (*ekspres* or Ex) and semi-express trains (*pospieszny*) are printed in red (all bookable). *Osobowy* trains are the slowest. Fares are about 50% higher for 1st class, but still cheap by western standards and probably worth it. Overnight trains usually have 1st/2nd-class sleepers, plus 2nd-class couchettes and seats. *TLK* are low cost, long distance trains on day and night services. Most long-distance trains have refreshments. Left luggage and refreshments in major stations. Few ticket clerks speak English.

TELEPHONES

Dial in: ✆ +48 then number (omit initial 0). Outgoing: ✆ 0*0 *(wait for tone after first 0)*. Older public phones take tokens (*żetony* – from post offices, hotels and Ruch kiosks). Newer phones accept phonecards. English-speaking operator: ✆ 903. Police: ✆ 997. Fire: ✆ 998. Ambulance: ✆ 999.

TIPPING

An older system of rounding up has now been largely superseded by a flat rate 10% for table service in bars and restaurants, also for hairdressers, taxis and guides.

TOURIST INFORMATION

Polish National Tourist Office (www.visitpoland.org and www.polandtour.org). IT tourist information office can usually help with accommodation. Also Orbis offices, for tourist information, excursions and accommodation.

TOURIST OFFICES OVERSEAS

UK: Level 3, Westec House, West Gate, London W5 1YY, ✆ 08 700 675 010, info@visitpoland.org. **USA**: 5 Marine View Plaza, Hoboken NJ 07030, ✆ 2 014 209 910, pntonyc@polandtour.org

VISAS

See page xxxii for visa requirements. For travellers in Germany, visas are obtainable from the Polish consulate in Leipzig (Trufanow-Str. 25, 04105 Leipzig, ✆ (0341) 5623300, www.botschaft-polen.de); open Mon, Tues, Thur and Fri, 0900–1200.

PORTUGAL

CAPITAL

Lisbon (Lisboa).

CLIMATE

Hotter and drier as you go south; southern inland parts very hot in summer; spring and autumn milder, but wetter. Mountains are very cold in winter.

CURRENCY

Euro (EUR/€). 1 euro = 100 cent. For exchange rates see page 11.

EMBASSIES IN LISBON

Australia: 2nd floor, Avenida da Liberdade 200, ✆ 213 101 500. **Canada**: 3rd Floor, Avenida da Liberdade 198/200, ✆ 213 164 600. **New Zealand**: (Consulate) Rua do Periquito. Lote A-13, ✆ 213 705 779. **UK**: Rua de São Bernado 33, ✆ 213 924 000. **USA**: Avenida das Forças Armadas, ✆ 217 273 300.

EMBASSIES OVERSEAS

Australia: 23 Culgoa Circuit, Deakin, Canberra ACT 2600, ✆ 0 262 901 733. **Canada**: 645 Island Park Dr., Ottawa ON, K1Y OB8, ✆ 6 137 290 883. **New Zealand**: (Consulate) NZ Suite 1, 1st floor, 21 Marion Street, Wellington ✆ 443 827 655. **UK**: 11 Belgrave Sq., London SW1X 8PP, ✆ 02 072 355 331. **USA**: 2012 Massachusetts Ave. NW, Washington DC 20036, ✆ 2 023 288 610.

LANGUAGE

Portuguese. Older people often speak French as second language, young people Spanish and/or English. English, French, and German in some tourist areas.

OPENING HOURS

Banks: Mon–Fri 0830–1445/1500. **Shops**: Mon–Fri 0900/1000–1300 and 1500–1900, Sat 0900–1300. City shopping centres often daily 1000–2300 or later. **Museums**: Tues–Sun 1000–1700/1800; some close for lunch and some are free on Sun. Palaces and castles usually close on Wed.

POST OFFICES

Post offices (*Correios*) are open Mon–Fri 0900–1800. The main offices in larger towns and at airports also open on Sat 0900–1300. Stamps (*selos*) can also be bought wherever you see the *Correios* symbol: a red-and-white horseback rider.

PUBLIC HOLIDAYS

Jan 1, Shrove Tues (47 days before Easter), Good Fri, Apr 25 (Freedom), May 1, Corpus Christi, June 10 (National Day), Aug 15 (Assumption), Oct 5 (Republic), Nov 1 (All Saints), Dec 1 (Independence), Dec 8 (Immaculate Conception), Dec 25. Many local saints' holidays. For dates of movable holidays see page 2.

PUBLIC TRANSPORT

Usually buy long-distance bus tickets before boarding. Bus stops: *paragem;* extend your arm to stop a bus. Taxis: black with green roofs or beige; illuminated signs; cheap, metered in cities, elsewhere fares negotiable; drivers may ask you to pay for their return journey; surcharges for luggage over 30 kg and night travel; 10% tip. City transport: single tickets can be bought as you board, but books of tickets or passes are cheaper; on boarding, insert 1–3 tickets (according to length of journey) in the machine behind the driver.

RAIL TRAVEL

See Tables **690 - 699**. Operator: Comboios de Portugal (CP) (www.cp.pt). Cheap and generally punctual; 1st/2nd class on long-distance. Fastest trains are *IC* and *AP* (Alfa Pendular), modern, fast; supplement payable; seat reservations compulsory, buffet cars. CP information line, ✆ 808 208 208. Left-luggage lockers in most stations.

TELEPHONES

Dial in: ✆ +351 then number. Outgoing: ✆ 00. Payphones take coins, phonecards (from post offices, newsstands, and most hotels), and occasionally credit cards. Higher charges are made for phones in hotels etc. International calls are best made at post offices; pay after the call. Operator: ✆ 118. Emergency services: ✆ 112.

TIPPING

Not necessary in hotels; customary to round up taxi fares and bills in cafeś/bars, though not essential. Tip 10% in restaurants.

TOURIST INFORMATION

Portuguese National Tourist Office (www.portugal.org). Portuguese Tourism Institute (www.visitportugal.com). info@visitportugal.com, ✆ 808 781 212

TOURIST OFFICES OVERSEAS

Canada: 60 Bloor St W, Suite 1005, Toronto ON, M4W 3B8, ✆ 4 169 217 376. **UK**: 22-25A Sackville St, London W1S 3LY, ✆ 02 074 945 720, tourism@portugaloffice.org.uk. **USA**: 590 Fifth Ave., 4th Floor, New York NY 10036, ✆ 2 123 544 403.

VISAS

See page xxxii for visa requirements.

ROMANIA

CAPITAL

Bucharest (Bucureşti).

CLIMATE

Hot inland in summer, coast cooled by breezes; milder in winter, snow inland, especially in the mountains.

CURRENCY

Leu (plural: lei). 1 leu = 100 bani. For exchange rates see page 11. Carry pounds, euros or, ideally, dollars, in small denominations, plus traveller's cheques; change cash (commission-free) at exchange kiosks or banks; as rates can vary it's wise to check a few places first. Keep hold of your exchange vouchers; avoid black market exchange (risk of theft). Credit cards are needed for car rental, and are accepted in better hotels and restaurants. *Bancomats* (automatic cash dispensers; accept most cards at good rates) in most cities.

EMBASSIES IN BUCHAREST

Australia (Consulate): World Trade Center, F, Regus Centre 10, Montreal Sq., ✆ 0 213 167 558. **Canada**: 1-3 Tuberozelor St, ✆ 0 213 075 000. **UK**: Jules Michelet 24, ✆ 0 212 017 200. **USA**: Tudor Arghezi 7–9, ✆ 0 212 003 300.

EMBASSIES OVERSEAS

Australia: 4 Dalman Crescent, O'Malley, Canberra ACT 2606, ✆ 061 262 862 343. **Canada**: 655 Rideau St, Ottawa ON, K1N 6A3, ✆ 6 137 893 709. **UK**: Arundel House, 4 Palace Green, London W8 4QD, ✆ 02 079 379 666. **USA**: 1607 23rd St NW, Washington DC, 20008, ✆ 2 023 324 846.

LANGUAGE

Romanian. English is understood by younger people, plus some German, and Hungarian throughout Transylvania.

OPENING HOURS

Banks: Mon–Fri 0900–1200/1300; private exchange counters open longer. **Shops**: usually 0800/0900–1800/2000, plus Sat morning or all day; often close 1300–1500. Local food shops often 0600–late. Few except in Bucharest open Sun. **Museums**: usually 0900/1000–1700/1800; open weekends, closed Mon (and maybe Tues).

POST OFFICES

There are post offices *(Posta Romana)* in all towns, open 0700-1900 Mon–Fri and until 1300 Sat. Postboxes are red. Mail usually takes five days to reach western Europe and up to two weeks to reach the US.

PUBLIC HOLIDAYS

Jan 1, Jan 2, Easter Mon (Orthodox), May 1, Dec 1 (National Unity Day), Dec 25, 26. For dates of movable holidays see page 2.

PUBLIC TRANSPORT

Buy bus/tram/metro tickets in advance from kiosks (as a rule) and cancel on entry. Taxis are inexpensive; if the meter not in use agree a price first and always pay in lei, not foreign currency. Trains are best for long-distance travel, although bus routes are expanding and connect important towns and cities.

RAIL TRAVEL

See Tables **1600 - 1699**. Compania Naţională de Căi Ferate (CFR) operates an extensive network linking all major towns. Most main lines are electrified and quite fast, but branch lines services are very slow. Trains are fairly punctual and very cheap. Buy tickets in advance from Agenţia de Voiaj CFR, or at the station from one hour before departure. Except for local trains, reserve and pay a speed supplement in advance (tickets issued abroad include the supplement): cheapest are *tren de persoane* (very slow), then *accelerat* (still cheap), *rapid*, and finally *IC* trains (prices approaching Western levels). Food is normally available only on *IC* trains and some *rapids*; drinks are sold on other trains. Couchette (*cuşeta*) or sleeper (*vagon de dormit*) accommodation is inexpensive.

TELEPHONES

Dial in: ✆ +40 then number (omit initial 0). Outgoing: ✆ 00. Operator-connected calls from hotels and post offices: pay after making the call. Blue public phones accept coins only, oranges ones take phonecards (ROL 50,000 or 100,000) available from post offices and newsstands. Police: ✆ 955. Fire: ✆ 981. Ambulance: ✆ 961.

TIPPING

Small tips are appreciated for good service at restaurants, hotels and in taxis. Only tip 10% at top-notch restaurants.

TOURIST INFORMATION

Romanian National Tourist Office (www.romaniatourism.com). Main office in Bucharest: ✆ 0 213 149 957. Regional tourist information offices in all major centres.

TOURIST OFFICES OVERSEAS

UK: 22 New Cavendish St, London W1M 7LH, ✆ 02 072 243 692, infouk@romaniatourism.com. **USA**: 355 Lexington Ave., 19th Floor, New York NY 10017, ✆ 2 125 458 484, infous@romaniatourism.com.

VISAS

See page xxxii for visa requirements. Make sure you keep your visa papers when you enter – you'll pay a large fine if you don't have them when you leave Romania.

SLOVAKIA

CAPITAL

Bratislava.

CLIMATE

Mild summers and very cold winters.

CURRENCY

Slovak crown or koruna (SKK or Sk); 1 koruna = 100 halier. For exchange rates, see page 11.

EMBASSIES IN BRATISLAVA

Australia: *refer to Australian Embassy in Austria.* **Canada**: *refer to Canadian Embassy in the Czech Republic.* **New Zealand**: *refer to NZ Embassy in Germany.* **UK**: Panská 16, ✆ 0 259 982 000. **USA**: Hviezdoslavovo námestie 4, ✆ 0 254 433 338.

EMBASSIES OVERSEAS

Australia/New Zealand: 47 Culgoa Circuit, O'Malley, Canberra ACT

2606, ✆ 0 262 901 516. **Canada**: 50 Rideau Terrace, Ottawa ON, K1M 2A1, ✆ 6 137 494 442. **UK**: 25 Kensington Palace Gardens, London W8 4QY, ✆ 02 073 136 470. **USA**: 3523 International Court NW, Washington DC 20008, ✆ 2 022 371 054.

LANGUAGE

Slovak, a Slavic tongue closely related to Czech. Some Russian (unpopular), German, Hungarian (especially in the south), plus a little English and French.

OPENING HOURS

Banks: Mon–Fri 0800–1800. **Shops**: Mon–Fri 0900–1800, Sat 0800–1200. **Food shops** usually open 0800 and Sun.
Museums: (usually) Tues–Sun 1000–1700. Most **castles** close on national holidays and Nov–Mar.

POST OFFICES

Usual post office hours: 0800–1900. Stamps are also available from newsagents and tobacconists. Post boxes are orange.

PUBLIC HOLIDAYS

Jan 1, Jan 6 (Epiphany), Good Fri, Easter Mon, May 1, July 5 (Cyril & Methodius), Aug 29 (National Day), Sept 1 (Constitution), Sept 15 (Virgin Mary), Nov 1 (All Saints), Nov 17 (Freedom and Democracy), Dec 24, 25, 26. For dates of movable holidays, see page 2.

PUBLIC TRANSPORT

There is a comprehensive long-distance bus network, often more direct than rail in upland areas. Buy tickets from the driver; priority is given to those with bookings.

RAIL TRAVEL

See Tables **1170 - 1199**. The national rail operator is Železničná spoločnosť (ŽSSK), running on the network of ŽSR. Trains are cheap, but often crowded. Apart from a small number of *EC* and *IC* trains (for which higher fares apply), the fastest trains are *expresný* (*Ex*) and *Rýchlik* (*R*). Cheaper are *zrýchlený* (semi-fast) and *osobný* (very slow). At stations, departures (*odjezdy*) are shown on yellow posters, arrivals (*prijezdy*) on white. Sleeping cars/couchettes (reserve at all main stations, well in advance in summer) are provided on most overnight trains. Seat reservations (at station counters marked R) are recommended for express trains. Reservation agency: MTA, Páričkova 29, Bratislava, ✆ 0 255 969 343.

TELEPHONES

Dial in: ✆ +421 then number (omit initial 0). Outgoing: ✆ 00. Public phones take coins or phonecards (cheapest SKK 150, available from post offices and selected newsstands).
Information: ✆ 120 (national), ✆ 0149 (international). Police: ✆ 158. Fire: ✆ 150. Ambulance: ✆ 155.

TIPPING

Tipping is expected at hotels, hairdressers, in eateries and taxis. In general, round up to the next SKK 10, unless you are somewhere very upmarket, where you should tip 10%.

TOURIST INFORMATION

Slovak Tourist Board (www.sacr.sk). Main office: Namestie L. Stura 1, PO Box 35, 974 05 Banska Bystrica, ✆ 0 484 136 146. Bratislava Information Service (www.bratislava.sk), Klobucnicka 2, 814 28 Bratislava, ✆ 0 254 433 715, info@bkis.sk. Staff speak English and can arrange accommodation.

TOURIST OFFICES OVERSEAS

USA: Czech & Slovak Service Center, 1511 K St NW, Suite 1030, Washington DC 20005, ✆ 2 023 377 242.

VISAS

See page xxxii for visa requirements.

SLOVENIA

CAPITAL

Ljubljana.

CLIMATE

Warm summers, cold winters; Mediterranean climate along coast; snow in the mountains in winter.

CURRENCY

Euro (EUR/€). 1 euro = 100 cent. For exchange rates see page 11.

EMBASSIES IN LJUBLJANA

Australia (Consulate): 12th floor, Trg Republike 3/XII, ✆ 014 254 252. **Canada**: *refer to Canadian Embassy in Hungary.*
New Zealand: (Consulate) Lek d.d., Verovskova 57, ✆ 015 803 055.
UK: 4th floor, Trg Rep-ublike 3, ✆ 012 003 910.
USA: Prešernova 31, ✆ 012 005 500.

EMBASSIES OVERSEAS

Australia: Level 6, 60 Marcus Clarke St, Canberra ACT 2601, ✆ 0 262 434 830. **Canada**: 4300 Village Centre Courts, Mississauga, ON, L4Z 1S2, ✆ 6 135 655 781. **UK**: 10 Little College St, London SW1P 3SJ, ✆ 02 072 225 400. **USA**: 1525 New Hampshire Ave. NW, Washington DC 20036, ✆ 2 026 675 363.

LANGUAGE

Slovenian. English, German and Italian are often spoken in tourist areas.

OPENING HOURS

Banks: vary, but mostly Mon–Fri 0830–1230 and 1400–1630, Sat 0830–1200. **Shops**: mostly Mon–Fri 0800–1900, Sat 0830–1200.
Museums: larger ones 1000–1800, many smaller ones 1000–1400; some close Mon.

POST OFFICES

Mon–Fri 0800–1800, Sat 0800–1200. Main post offices in larger centres may open evenings and on Sun. Ljubljana's main post office in Trg Osvobodilne Fronte 5, by the railway station, is open 24 hrs.

PUBLIC HOLIDAYS

Jan 1, 2, Feb 8 (Culture), Easter Sun/Mon, Apr 27 (Resistance), May 1, 2, June 25 (Statehood), Aug 15 (Assumption), Oct 31 (Reformation), Nov 1 (All Saints), Dec 25, 26. For dates of movable holidays, see page 2.

PUBLIC TRANSPORT

Long-distance bus services are frequent and inexpensive; normally, buy your ticket on boarding. Information: Trg Osvobodilne Fronte 5, next to Ljubljana station, ✆ 012 344 606. On city buses pay by dropping the exact flat fare or a cheaper token (available from newsstands and post offices) into the farebox next to the driver. Daily and weekly passes are available in the main cities.

RAIL TRAVEL

See Tables **1300 - 1359**. Operator: Slovenske železnice (SŽ) (website www.slo-zeleznice.si). Information: ✆ 012 913 332. Efficient network, but fewer services on Saturdays. Reserve for *ICS* trains; supplements are payable on other express services. Tickets available from stations or from agents such as Mladi Turist, Salendrova 4, Ljubljana, ✆ 014 259 260.

TELEPHONES

Dial in: ✆ +386 then number (omit initial 0). Outgoing: ✆ 00. International calls are best made in post offices (pay afterwards). Phone booths: buy phonecards from post offices or tokens from post offices/newsstands. Police: ✆ 113. Fire and ambulance: ✆ 112.

TIPPING

No need to tip bar staff or taxi drivers, although you can round sums up as you wish. In restaurants add 10%.

TOURIST INFORMATION

Slovenian Tourist Board (www.slovenia.info). Main office: Krekov trg 10, SI-1000 Ljubljana, ✆ 01 306 45 75, stic@ljubljana-tourism.si

TOURIST OFFICES OVERSEAS

UK: New Barn Farm, Tadlow Rd, Royston, Herts SG8 0EP, ✆ 08 702 255 305, info@slovenian-tourism.co.uk.
USA: 345 East 12th St, New York NY 10003, ✆ 2 123 589 686, info@sloveniatravel.com

VISAS

See page xxxii for visa requirements.

SPAIN

CAPITAL

Madrid.

CURRENCY

Euro (EUR/€). 1 euro = 100 cent. For exchange rates see page 11.

EMBASSIES IN MADRID

Australia: Plaza del Descubridor Diego de Ordás 3, ✆ 913 536 600. **Canada:** Núñez de Balboa 35, ✆ 914 233 250. **New Zealand**: 3rd floor, Calle de Pinar 7, ✆ 915 230 226. **UK**: Fernando el Santo 16, ✆ 917 008 200. **USA**: Serrano 75, ✆ 915 872 200.

EMBASSIES OVERSEAS

Australia: 15 Arkana St, Yarralumla, Canberra ACT 2600, ✆ 0 262 733 555. **Canada**: 74 Stanley Avenue, Ottawa ON, K1M 1P4, ✆ 6 137 472 252. **UK**: 39 Chesham Place, London SW1X 8SB, ✆ 02 072 355 555. **USA**: 2375 Pennsylvania Ave. NW, Washington DC 20037, ✆ 23 754 520 100.

LANGUAGE

Castilian Spanish is the most widely spoken language. There are three other official languages: Catalan in the east; Galician (*Galego*) in the north-west, and Basque (*Euskera*) in the Basque country and parts of Navarre. English is fairly widely spoken in tourist areas. Note that in Spanish listings *Ch* often comes after the *C*'s, *Ll* after the *L*'s, and *Ñ* after the *N*'s.

OPENING HOURS

Banks: Mon–Thur 0930–1630; Fri 0830–1400; Sat 0830–1300 (winter); Mon–Fri 0830–1400 (summer). **Shops**: Mon–Sat 0930/1000–1400 and 1700–2000/2030; major stores do not close for lunch, food shops often open Sun. **Museums**: vary, mostly open 0900/1000, close any time from 1400 to 2030. Few open Mon and some also close (or open half day) Sun. Expect to find most places closed 1300–1500/1600, especially in the south.

POST OFFICES

Most *Oficinas de Correos* are open 0830–1430 Mon–Fri, 0930–1300 Sat, although the main offices in large cities often stay open until around 2100 on Mon–Fri. Main offices offer poste restante *(lista de correos)*. Stamps *(sellos)* are also sold at tobacconists (estancos). Post overseas mail in the slot marked *Extranjero*.

PUBLIC HOLIDAYS

Jan 1, Jan 6 (Epiphany), several days at Easter, May 1, July 25, Aug 15 (Assumption), Oct 12 (National Day); Nov 1 (All Saints), Dec 6 (Constitution), Dec 8 (Immaculate Conception) and several days at Christmas. Not all of these are official holidays, but many places close anyway. Each region has at least four more public holidays, usually local saints' days (e.g. Andalucia Feb 28, Galacia July 25, Catalonia Sept 11). For the dates of movable holidays, see page 2.

PUBLIC TRANSPORT

Numerous regional bus companies provide a fairly comprehensive and cheap (if sometimes confusing) service. The three largest bus operating groups are ALSA Enatcar (www.alsa.es), Auto-Res (www.auto-res.net and www.lasepulvedana.es), and Continental-Auto Alsina Graells (www.continental-auto.es). City buses are efficient and there are metro systems in Madrid, Barcelona, València and Bilbao.

RAIL TRAVEL

See Tables **650 - 689**. National rail company: Red Nacional de los Ferrocarriles Españoles (RENFE) (www.renfe.es). FEVE and a number of regionally-controlled railways operate lines in coastal regions. General information: RENFE ✆ 902 240 202; FEVE ✆ 902 100 818; AVE (high-speed): ✆ 915 066 329; Grandes Líneas (other long-distance): ✆ 902 105 205; international: ✆ 934 901 122. RENFE offer money back if their AVE trains on the Sevilla line arrive more than 5 minutes late! Premier Grandes Líneas services include *Talgo* (light articulated train), *Euromed*, *Alaris* (Madrid–Valencia), and IC expresses. *Diurno*: ordinary long-distance day train. *Estrella*: night train (including sleeper and/or couchette cars). A pricier alternative for night travel is the *Trenhotel* (hotel train), offering sleeping compartments with their own shower and WC. All convey 1st- and 2nd-class accommodation (*Preferente* and *Turista*; AVE also have a 'super-first' class: *Club*) and require advance reservation. *Regionales*: local stopping service; *Cercanías*: suburban trains. In remoter parts of country, services may be very infrequent. Reservation is compulsory on all services for which a train category (*Talgo, IC* etc) is shown in the timing column of this timetable.

TELEPHONES

Dial in: ✆ +34 then number. Outgoing: ✆ 00. Public phones usually have English instructions and accept credit cards, coins, or *Teletarjeta* (phonecard, sold in tobacconists, post offices, some shops). There is at least one *Telefónica* office (the former state telephone company) in every large town: use a booth to make a call and pay the clerk afterwards. Payphones in bars are usually more expensive. General emergency number (police/fire/ambulance): ✆ 112.

TIPPING

Not necessary to tip in bars and taxis; tipping is more common in restaurants but by no means obligatory. If you want to tip for good service, add around 5%.

TOURIST INFORMATION

Spanish Tourist Office / Turespaña (USA: www.okspain.org, www.spain.info, UK: www.tourspain.co.uk). Local *Oficinas de Turismo* can provide maps and information on accommodation and sightseeing, and generally have English-speaking staff. Regional offices stock information for the whole region, municipal offices cover only that city; larger towns have both types of office.

TOURIST OFFICES OVERSEAS

UK: PO Box 4009, London W1A 6NB, ✆ 02 074 868 077, londres@tourspain.es. **USA**: 666 Fifth Ave., 35th Floor, New York NY 10103, ✆ 2 122 658 822, oetny@tourspain.es. Also in Chicago, Los Angeles, and Miami.

VISAS

See page xxxii for visa requirements.

SWEDEN

CAPITAL

Stockholm.

CLIMATE

Often warm (especially in summer; continuous daylight in far north). Huge range between north and south; it can be mild in Skåne (far south) in Feb, but spring comes late May in the north. Winter generally very cold everywhere.

CURRENCY

Swedish crown or krona (SEK, kr, or Skr); 1 krona = 100 öre. For exchange rates see page 11. *Växlare* machines give change. The best exchange rate is obtained from Forex, which has branches at many stations. Keep receipts so that you can reconvert at no extra cost.

EMBASSIES IN STOCKHOLM

Australia: 11th floor, Sergels Torg 12, ✆ 086 132 900. **Canada**: 7th floor, Tegelbacken 4, ✆ 084 533 000. **New Zealand** (Consulate): Norrlandsgatan 15, ✆ 085 063 200. **UK**: Skarpögatan 6–8, ✆ 086 713 000. **USA**: Dag Hammarskjölds Väg 31, ✆ 087 835 300.

EMBASSIES OVERSEAS

Australia: 5 Turrana St, Yarralumla, Canberra ACT 2600, ✆ 0 262 702 700. **Canada**: 377 Dalhousie St, Ottawa ON, K1N 9N8, ✆ 6 132 448 200. **New Zealand** (Consulate): Level 7, Molesworth House, 101 Molesworth Street, Wellington, ✆ 044 999 895. **UK**: 11 Montagu Pl., London W1H 2AL, ✆ 02 079 176 400. **USA**: 901 30th. Street NW, Washington DC 20007, ✆ 2 024 672 600.

LANGUAGE

Swedish. English is widely spoken. Useful rail / bus / ferry words include *daglig* (daily), *vardagar* (Mon–Sat), and *helgdagar* (Sundays and holidays).

OPENING HOURS

Banks: Mon–Fri 0930–1500 (Thur, and Mon–Fri in some cities, until 1730). Some, especially at transport terminals, have longer hours. **Shops**: mostly Mon–Fri 0900/0930–1700/1800, Sat 0900/0930–1300/1600. In larger towns department stores open until 2000/2200; also some on Sun 1200–1600. **Museums**: vary widely. In winter, many attractions close Mon and some close altogether.

POST OFFICES

Generally Mon–Fri 0900–1800, Sat 1000–1300, but there are local variations. Stamps are also sold at newsagents and tobacconists. Post boxes: yellow (overseas), blue (local).

PUBLIC HOLIDAYS

Jan 1, Jan 6 (Epiphany), Good Friday, Easter Mon, May 1, Ascension Day, Whit Sun/Mon, June 6 (National Day), Midsummer Day (Sat falling June 20–26) plus Midsummer Eve (previous day), All Saints Day (Sat falling Oct 31 - Nov 6), Dec 24, 25, 26. Many places close early the previous day, or Fri if it's a long weekend. For dates of movable holidays, see page 2.

PUBLIC TRANSPORT

The transport system is highly efficient; ferries are covered (in whole or part) by rail passes and city transport cards. Swebus (www.swebus.se), ✆ 0 854 630 000, is the biggest operator of long-distance buses. Advance booking is required on some routes and always advisable in summer; bus terminals usually adjoin rail stations.

RAIL TRAVEL

See Tables **730 - 769**. National rail company: Statens Järnvägar (SJ) (www.sj.se). Some local lines are run by regional authorities or private companies such as Veolia Transport (formerly called Connex), who operate services to the far north. SJ information and sales line, ✆ (0) 771 757575, Veolia ✆ (0) 771 260 000. Supplements are required on *X2000* trains (up to 200 km/h); lower supplements for *CityExpress* trains. Sleeping-cars: one or two berths in 2nd class; couchettes: six berths; female-only compartment available. 1st-class sleeping-cars (en-suite shower and WC) on many overnight services; 2nd-class have wash-basins, shower and WC are at the end of the carriage. Long-distance trains have a refreshment service. Many trains have a family coach with a playroom, and facilities for the disabled. Seat reservations are compulsory on *X2000* and night trains. *X2000* services operate between Sweden and Copenhagen via the Öresund bridge and tunnel but it is better to use the frequent local trains for short journeys. 'C' (for Central) in timetables etc. means the town's main station. Large, detailed timetables are displayed for long-distance trains: yellow for departures, white for arrivals. *Biljetter* indicates the station ticket office. *Pressbyrån* kiosks (at most stations) sell snacks and English-language publications.

TELEPHONES

Dial in: ✆ +46 then number (omit initial 0). Outgoing: ✆ 00. Coin-operated phones are decreasing in number; most card phones accept credit cards and *Telia* phonecards (*telefonkor-ten*), from most newsagents, tobacconists, and *Pressbyrån* kiosks). Emergency services (police, fire, ambulance): ✆ 112.

TIPPING

Restaurants include a service charge but a tip of 10–15% is appreciated. Taxis 10%. Tip hotel staff, porters, cloakroom attendants etc. at your discretion.

TOURIST INFORMATION

Swedish Travel & Tourism Council (www.visitsweden.com). Tourist offices, of which there are 400 throughout the country, are called *Turistbyråer*. Stockholm City Tourist Centre: Sverigehuset, Hamngatan 27, 10327 Stockholm, ✆ 085 0828508, info@svb.stockholm.se.

TOURIST OFFICES OVERSEAS

UK: 5 Upper Montagu St, London W1H 2AG, ✆ 02 078 705 609, info@swetourism.org.uk. **USA**: 655 Third Ave., Suite 1810, New York NY 10017, ✆ 2 128 859 700, info@swetourism.com.

VISAS

See page xxxii for visa requirements.

SWITZERLAND

CAPITAL

Berne (Bern).

CLIMATE

Rainfall spread throughout the year. May–Sept are best in the mountains. June or early July best for the wild flowers. Snow at high altitudes even in midsummer. Season in the lakes: Apr–Oct. July and Aug get very busy.

CURRENCY

Swiss franc (CHF or Sfr.); 1 franc = 100 centimes. For exchange rates, see page 11.

EMBASSIES IN BERNE

Australia (Consulate in Geneva): 2 Chemin des Fins, Geneva, ✆ 0 227 999 100. **Canada**: Kirchenfeldstrasse 88, ✆ 0 313 573 200. **New Zealand** (Consulate in Geneva): 2 Chemin des Fins, Geneva, ✆ 0 229 290 350. **UK**: Thunstrasse 50, ✆ 0 313 597 700. **USA**: Jubiläumsstrasse 93, ✆ 0 313 577 011.

EMBASSIES OVERSEAS

Australia: 7 Melbourne Avenue, Forrest, Canberra ACT 2603, ✆ 0 261 628 400. **Canada**: 5 Marlborough Avenue, Ottawa ON, K1N 8E6, ✆ 6 132 351 837. **UK**: 16-18 Montagu Place, London W1H 2BQ, ✆ 02 076 166 000. **USA**: 2900 Cathedral Ave. NW, Washington DC 20008, ✆ 2 027 457 900.

LANGUAGE

German, French, Italian, and Romansch are all official languages. Most Swiss people are at least bilingual. English is widespread.

OPENING HOURS

Banks: Mon–Fri 0800–1200 and 1400–1700. Money change desks in most rail stations, open longer hours. **Shops**: Mon–Fri 0800–1200 and 1330–1830, Sat 0800–1200 and 1330–1600. Many close Mon morning. In stations, shops open longer hours and on Sun. **Museums**: usually close Mon. Hours vary.

POST OFFICES

Usually Mon–Fri 0730–1200 and 1345–1830, Sat 0730–1100; longer in cities. Poste restante (*Postlagernd*) facilities are available at most post offices.

PUBLIC HOLIDAYS

Jan 1, Jan. 2, Good Fri, Easter Mon, Ascension Day, Whit Mon, Aug 1 (National Day), Dec 25, 26. Also May 1 and Corpus Christi in some areas. For dates of movable holidays see page 2.

PUBLIC TRANSPORT

Swiss buses are famously punctual. Yellow postbuses call at rail stations; free timetables from post offices. Swiss Pass valid (see Passes feature), surcharge for some scenic routes. The best way to get around centres is often on foot. Most cities have efficient tram and bus networks with integrated ticketing.

RAIL TRAVEL

See Tables **500 - 579**. The principal rail carrier is Swiss Federal Railways (SBB / CFF / FFS) (www.sbb.ch). Information: ✆ 0 900 300 300 (English-speaking operator). There are also many small, local lines. Services are fast and punctual, trains spotlessly clean. Some international trains have sleepers (3 berths) and/or couchettes (up to 6 people). Sleepers can be booked up to 3 months in advance, couchettes/seats up to 2 months ahead. Reservations are required on some sightseeing trains (e.g. Glacier Express, Bernina-Express). All main stations have information offices (and usually tourist offices), shopping and eating facilities. Bicycle hire at most stations.

TELEPHONES

Dial in: ✆ +41 then number (omit initial 0). Outgoing: ✆ 00. Phonecards (*taxcard*) are available from Swisscom offices, post offices, newsagents and most rail stations in denominations of CHF 5, 10, 20, and 50. Press button L on public phones to choose the language display. Some payphones accept Euros. National enquiries: ✆ 111. International operator: ✆ 1141. All operators speak English. Police: ✆ 117. Fire: ✆ 118. Ambulance: ✆ 144.

TIPPING

Not necessary or expected in restaurants or taxis.

TOURIST INFORMATION

Switzerland Tourism (www.myswitzerland.com). Main office: Tödistrasse 7, CH-8002 Zürich, ✆ 044 288 11 11. International toll-free ✆ 080 010 020 030 (information, reservations, etc.). There are Tourist Offices in almost every town and village. The standard of information is excellent.

TOURIST OFFICES OVERSEAS

Canada: 926 The East Mall. Toronto ON, M9B 6K1, ✆ 4 166 592 090, info.caen@switzerlandtourism.ch. **UK**: 1st Floor, 30 Bedford St, London WC2E 9ED, ✆ 02 074 204 900, info.uk@switzerland.com. **USA**: 608 Fifth Ave., New York NY 10020, ✆ 2 127 575 944, info.usa@switzerlandtourism.ch.

VISAS

See page xxxii for visa requirements.

TURKEY

CAPITAL

Ankara.

CLIMATE

Very hot summers, more manageable in spring or autumn. Cool Nov–Mar.

CURRENCY

New Turkish lira (TRY or YTL). 1 lira = 100 kuruş. For exchange rates, see page 11. Credit cards are widely accepted.

CONSULATES IN ISTANBUL

Australia: 2nd Floor, Suzer Plaza, Askerocaği Caddesi No 15, Elmadağ 34367, ✆ 02 122 431 333. **New Zealand**: (Embassy in Ankara) Level 4, Iran Caddesi 13, Kavaklidere, Ankara. **UK**: Mesrutiyet Caddesi No 34, Tepebasi Beyoglu, ✆ 02 123 346 400. **USA**: İstinye Mahallesi, Kaplıcalar Mekvii No 2, İstinye 34460, ✆ 02 123 359 000.

EMBASSIES OVERSEAS

Australia: 60 Mugga Way, Red Hill, Canberra ACT 2603, ✆ 0 262 950 227. **Canada**: 197 Wurtemburg St., Ottawa ON, K1N 8L9, ✆ 6 137 894 044. **UK**: 43 Belgrave Sq., London SW1X 8PA, ✆ 02 073 930 202. **USA**: 2525 Massachusetts Ave, NW, Washington, DC 20008, ✆ 2 026 126 700.

LANGUAGE

Turkish, which is written using the Latin alphabet. English and German are often understood.

OPENING HOURS

Banks: 0830–1200, 1300–1700, Mon–Fri (some private banks are open at lunchtime). Shops 0930–1900; until around 2400 in tourist areas. **Government offices**: 0830–1230, 1300–1700 (closed Sat and Sun). In Aegean and Mediterranean regions, many establishments stay open very late in summer. **Museums**: many close on Mon.

POST OFFICES

Post offices have PTT signs. Major offices: Airport, Beyoğlu and Sirkeci open 24 hrs all week (limited services at night). Small offices: 0830–1700 (some close 1230–1300).

PUBLIC HOLIDAYS

Jan 1, Apr 23, May 19, Aug 30, Oct 29. Religious festivals have movable dates and can affect travel arrangements and business opening times over an extended period. The main festival periods are *Kurban Bayrami* (Dec 20 - 23 in 2007, Dec 8 - 11 in 2008) and *Seker Bayrami* (Sept. 30 - Oct. 2 in 2008).

PUBLIC TRANSPORT

An excellent long-distance bus system, run by competing companies (the best are Varan and Ulusoy), generally provides quicker journies than rail. *Dolmuş* minibuses that pick up passengers like a taxi, but at much cheaper rates and operating along set routes, can be used for shorter journies. Istanbul has a modern metro line, as well as a light-rail and tram route. TML (Turkish Maritime Lines) operates passenger ferries.

RAIL TRAVEL

See Table **1550** – for journeys in Asian Turkey beyond Istanbul, consult the *Thomas Cook Overseas Timetable*. Operator: TCDD (Turkish State Railways) (www.tcdd.gov.tr). Routes are tortuous and journeys slow, but a new high-speed route is under construction between Istanbul and Ankara.

TELEPHONES

Dial in: ✆ +90 then number (omit initial 0). Outgoing: ✆ 00. Payphones take *Türk Telekom* phonecards (*Telekart*, available in 30, 60, and 100 units from post offices, shops and kiosks) and are the best way to make calls. Hotels often charge very high rates. International operator: ✆ 115. Emergency: ✆ 112. Police: ✆ 155. Fire: ✆ 110.

TIPPING

A 10% tip is usual in restaurants, unless service is included. Do not tip barmen directly. 10–20% is customary at hair salons. Do not tip taxi drivers.

TOURIST INFORMATION

Turkish National Tourist Office (www.tourismturkey.org). Istanbul directorate: Mesrutiyet Caddesi 57, Kat 7, Beyoglu, ✆ 02 122 433 472.

TOURIST OFFICES OVERSEAS

UK: 170-173 Piccadilly, London W1J 9EJ, ✆ 02 076 297 771, info@gototurkey.co.uk. **USA**: 821 United Nations Plaza, New York NY 10017, ✆ 2 126 872 194, ny@tourismturkey.org.

VISAS

See page xxxii for visa requirements.

UNITED KINGDOM

CAPITAL
London.

CLIMATE
Cool, wet winters, mild spring and autumn, winter can be more extreme. Wetter in the west. Aug and Bank Holiday weekends busiest in tourist areas.

CURRENCY
Pounds Sterling (GBP or £). £1 = 100 pence (p). For exchange rates, see page 11.

EMBASSIES IN LONDON
Australia (High Commission): Australia House, The Strand, ✆ 02 073 794 334. **Canada** (High Commission) Canada House, Trafalgar Square, ✆ 02 072 586 600. **New Zealand** (High Commission): New Zealand House, 80 Haymarket, ✆ 02 079 308 422.
USA: 24 Grosvenor Square, ✆ 02 074 999 000.

EMBASSIES OVERSEAS
Australia (High Commission): Commonwealth Ave, Yarralumla, Canberra ACT 2600, ✆ 0 262 706 666. **Canada** (High Commission): 80 Elgin St, Ottawa ON, K1P 5K7, ✆ 6 132 371 530. **New Zealand** (High Commission): 44 Hill St, Wellington, ✆ 049 242 888.
USA: 3100 Massachusetts Ave. NW, Washington DC 20008, ✆ 2 025 886 500.

LANGUAGE
English, plus Welsh in Wales and Gaelic in parts of Scotland.

OPENING HOURS
Banks: Mon–Fri 0930–1530 (or later); some open Sat morning. **Shops**: Mon–Sat 0900–1730. Many supermarkets and some small shops open longer, plus Sunday 1000–1600. **Museums**: usually Mon–Sat 0900/1000–1730/1800, half-day Sun.

POST OFFICES
Usually Mon–Fri 0930–1730, Sat 0930–1300; stamps sold in newsagents etc.

PUBLIC HOLIDAYS
Jan 1, Good Fri, Easter Mon *(not Scotland)*, Early May Bank Holiday (first Mon in May), Spring Bank Holiday (last Mon in May), Summer Bank Holiday (last Mon in August) *(not Scotland)*, Dec 25, 26.
Scotland: *also* Jan 2, Summer Bank Holiday (first Monday in August). Northern Ireland: *also* Mar 17 (St Patrick), July 12 (Orangemen).
Holidays falling at the weekend are transferred to the following weekday. For the dates of movable holidays, see page 2.

PUBLIC TRANSPORT
Intercity express bus services (coaches) are generally cheaper, but slower, than trains, and mostly require prebooking. The main long-distance coach operator in England and Wales is National Express (www.nationalexpress.com), or Citylink (www.citylink.co.uk) in Scotland. Comprehensive local bus network; most companies belong to large groups such as Stagecoach, First or Arriva. Bus stations are rarely adjacent to railway stations. Traveline (www.traveline.org.uk) is an on-line and telephone service for all UK timetables:
✆ 0871 200 22 23 (10p per minute). Extensive 'Underground' railway network in London operated by Transport for London (www.tfl.gov.uk) who also control the bus service using private companies.
In Northern Ireland, Ulsterbus (www.ulsterbus.co.uk) is the principal bus operator.

RAIL TRAVEL
See Tables **100 - 234**. Passenger services in Great Britain are provided by a number of train operating companies, working together as National Rail (www.nationalrail.co.uk). Through tickets are available to all stations in the country. If asked, booking-office staff will quote the cheapest fare regardless of operator (time period restrictions apply to the very cheapest fares). National Rail enquiries: ✆ 08457 48 49 50. Fast trains, comfortable and frequent, have first and standard class. Other long- and medium-distance regional services are often standard-class only. Refreshments are often available on board. Sleepers: cabins are two-berth or (higher charge) single. Advance reservation (essential for sleepers) is available for most long-distance services and is normally free of charge. Travel between Saturday evening and Sunday afternoon is sometimes interrupted by engineering works and buses may replace trains.
In Northern Ireland, trains are operated by Northern Ireland Railways (NIR), part of Translink. NIR enquiries: ✆ 028 90 666 630.

TELEPHONES
Dial in: ✆ +44 then number (omit initial 0). Outgoing: ✆ 00. Payphones take coins, phonecards (sold at newsagents) or credit cards. Emergency services: ✆ 999 or 112.

TIPPING
Tip 10% in restaurants, except where service is included (becoming increasingly common), but not in pubs, self-service restaurants or bars. Tip taxis (10%) hailed in the street.

TOURIST INFORMATION
VisitBritain (www.visitbritain.com). Britain and London Visitor Centre: 1 Regent Street, London SW1Y 4XT, ✆ 020 8846 9000, blvcinfo@visitbritain.org. There are local tourist offices in most towns and cities.

TOURIST OFFICES OVERSEAS
Australia: Level 2, 15 Blue St, North Sydney NSW 2060, ✆ 0 290 214 400, visitbritainaus@visitbritain.org. **Canada**: 5915 Airport Rd, Suite 120, Mississauga ON, L4V 1T1, ✆ 9 054 051 720, britinfo@visitbritain.org. **New Zealand**: Level 17, 151 Queen St, Auckland 1, ✆ 093 031 446, newzealand@visitbritain.org.
USA: 551 Fifth Ave., Suite 701, New York NY 10176-0799, ✆ 2 129 862 266, travelinfo@visitbritain.org.

VISAS
See below for visa requirements.

Visa Requirements

The table below shows whether nationals from selected countries (shown in columns) need visas to visit countries in Europe (shown in rows) - the symbol ▲ indicates that a visa **is** required. This information applies to tourist trips for up to 30 days - different requirements may apply for longer trips or for visits for other purposes, also if you are resident in a country other than your own.

The first row and column, labeled **Schengen area**, apply to the 15 European countries which have signed the Schengen Agreement whereby border controls between the member countries have been abolished. It is possible to obtain a single Schengen visa to cover all these countries, which are:

Austria, Belgium, Denmark, Finland, France, Germany, Greece, Iceland, Italy, Luxembourg, the Netherlands, Norway, Portugal, Spain, and Sweden.

Nine new countries will join the Schengen area from December 21, 2007 (March 30, 2008 for air travel). These are Czech Republic, Estonia, Hungary, Latvia, Lithuania, Malta, Poland, Slovakia and Slovenia.

Visas should generally be applied for in advance from an Embassy or Consulate of the country you are visiting, although sometimes they are available on arrival. Transit visas may be available for those travelling through a country in order to reach another, but these may also need to be purchased in advance. The information show below is given as a guide only - entry requirements may be subject to change.

NATIONALS OF →

▲ VISA REQUIRED

TRAVELLING TO ↓	Schengen area	Albania	Belarus	Bosnia-Herzegovina	Bulgaria	Croatia	Cyprus	Czech Republic	Estonia	Hungary	Latvia	Lithuania	Macedonia	Malta	Moldova	Poland	Romania	Russia	Serbia / Montenegro	Slovakia	Slovenia	Switzerland	Turkey	UK / Ireland	Ukraine	Australia	Canada	Japan	New Zealand	USA
Schengen area	–	▲	▲	▲									▲		▲			▲	▲				▲		▲					
Albania		–	▲	▲									▲		▲			▲	▲						▲					
Belarus	▲	▲	–	▲	▲	▲	▲	▲	▲	▲	▲	▲		▲			▲			▲	▲	▲	▲	▲		▲	▲	▲	▲	▲
Bosnia-Herzegovina		▲	▲	–	▲		▲	▲	▲	▲	▲	▲			▲	▲				▲					▲					
Bulgaria		▲	▲	▲	–										▲			▲	▲				▲		▲					
Croatia		▲	▲			–									▲			▲							▲					
Cyprus		▲	▲	▲			–						▲		▲			▲	▲				▲		▲					
Czech Republic		▲	▲	▲				–					▲		▲			▲	▲				▲		▲					
Estonia		▲	▲	▲					–				▲		▲			▲	▲				▲		▲					
Hungary		▲	▲							–			▲		▲			▲	▲				▲		▲					
Latvia		▲	▲	▲							–		▲		▲			▲	▲				▲		▲					
Lithuania		▲	▲	▲								–	▲		▲			▲	▲				▲		▲					
Macedonia		▲	▲[1]										–		▲		▲	▲[1]							▲[1]	▲	▲			
Malta		▲	▲	▲									▲	–	▲			▲	▲				▲		▲					
Moldova		▲		▲	▲										–				▲				▲			▲			▲	
Poland		▲	▲	▲									▲		▲	–		▲	▲				▲		▲					
Romania		▲	▲	▲									▲				–	▲	▲				▲		▲	▲			▲	
Russia	▲	▲		▲	▲	▲	▲	▲	▲	▲	▲	▲	▲	▲		▲	▲	–	▲	▲	▲	▲	▲	▲		▲	▲	▲	▲	▲
Serbia / Montenegro		▲[2]		▲[2]									▲[2]		▲		▲	▲[2]	–				▲		▲[2]					
Slovakia		▲	▲	▲									▲		▲			▲	▲	–			▲		▲					
Slovenia		▲	▲	▲									▲		▲			▲	▲		–		▲		▲					
Switzerland		▲	▲	▲									▲		▲			▲	▲			–	▲		▲					
Turkey	▲[3]	●	●		●		●	▲	●	●	●	●		●	●	●	●	●	●	●	▲		–	●	●	●	●			●
UK / Ireland		▲	▲	▲		▲							▲		▲			▲	▲				▲	–	▲					
Ukraine	▲	▲		▲		▲							▲		▲							▲	▲		–	▲			▲	

NOTES

▲ – Visa required (see also general notes above table).

▲[1] – Visa required except for organized tourist visits.

▲[2] – Visa required for Serbia but not for Montenegro.

▲[3] – ● applies to nationals of Austria, Belgium, Italy, Netherlands, Norway, Portugal and Spain.

● – Sticker-type entry visas must be purchased on entering the country (prices vary according to nationality, e.g. UK citizens pay GBP 10 per person, payable in £10 notes only).

ISSN 0952-620X
Published Monthly

Thomas Cook

December 2007
Valid from Dec. 9

EUROPEAN RAIL TIMETABLE

CONTENTS

TABLE DES MATIÈRES *INDICE DELLE MATERIE* *INHALTSVERZEICHNIS* *ÍNDICE DE MATERIAS*

INFORMATION

Thomas Cook Publishing	*Head of Travel Books: John Sadler*	
Editor	Brendan Fox	+44 (0)1733 416322
Editorial Team	Kevin Flynn	+44 (0)1733 417357
	John Potter	+44 (0)1733 417354
	David Turpie	+44 (0)1733 417155
	Chris Woodcock	+44 (0)1733 416408
Commercial Manager	Lisa Bass	+44 (0)1733 402003
Subscriptions	Gemma Slater	+44 (0)1733 402002
Sales enquiries		+44 (0)1733 416477
Advertising		+44 (0)1733 416322
Fax		+44 (0)1733 416688
Rail Pass Direct		08700 841 413
e-mail (Sales)		publishing-sales@thomascook.com
e-mail (Editorial)		timetables@thomascook.com
Publishing homepage:		www.thomascookpublishing.com
Thomas Cook homepage:		www.thomascook.com

Thomas Cook Publishing, P.O. Box 227
Coningsby Road, Peterborough PE3 8SB, UK
A division of Thomas Cook Tour Operations Ltd
Company Registration No. 1450464 England

Thomas Cook

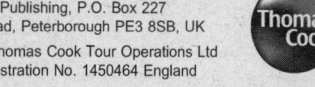

Cover picture (monthly edition): a northbound local from Brig heads towards the Lötschberg Tunnel © Philip Wormald

Printed in Great Britain by William Clowes Ltd, Beccles, Suffolk

RAIL – INTERNATIONAL

Selected summer timings from June 15, 2008 will appear from the February edition

RAIL – COUNTRY BY COUNTRY

SHIPPING

SPECIAL FEATURES

will appear in alternate editions as follows:

January **Sample Fares**, *March* **Cruise Trains and Rail Holidays**, *May* **Rail Passes**, *July* **Tourist Railways**, *September* **High-Speed Trains**, *November* **Night Trains**

CALENDAR

CALENDRIER CALENDARIO KALENDER CALENDARIO

2007

JULY

M	T	W	T	F	S	S
①	②	③	④	⑤	⑥	⑦
30	31	–	–	–	–	1
2	3	4	5	6	7	8
9	10	11	12	13	14	15
16	17	18	19	20	21	22
23	24	25	26	27	28	29

AUGUST

M	T	W	T	F	S	S
①	②	③	④	⑤	⑥	⑦
–	–	1	2	3	4	5
6	7	8	9	10	11	12
13	14	15	16	17	18	19
20	21	22	23	24	25	26
27	28	29	30	31	–	–

SEPTEMBER

M	T	W	T	F	S	S
①	②	③	④	⑤	⑥	⑦
–	–	–	–	–	1	2
3	4	5	6	7	8	9
10	11	12	13	14	15	16
17	18	19	20	21	22	23
24	25	26	27	28	29	30

OCTOBER

M	T	W	T	F	S	S
①	②	③	④	⑤	⑥	⑦
1	2	3	4	5	6	7
8	9	10	11	12	13	14
15	16	17	18	19	20	21
22	23	24	25	26	27	28
29	30	31	–	–	–	–

NOVEMBER

M	T	W	T	F	S	S
①	②	③	④	⑤	⑥	⑦
–	–	–	1	2	3	4
5	6	7	8	9	10	11
12	13	14	15	16	17	18
19	20	21	22	23	24	25
26	27	28	29	30	–	–

DECEMBER

M	T	W	T	F	S	S
①	②	③	④	⑤	⑥	⑦
31	–	–	–	–	1	2
3	4	5	6	7	8	9
10	11	12	13	14	15	16
17	18	19	20	21	22	23
24	25	26	27	28	29	30

2008

JANUARY

M	T	W	T	F	S	S
①	②	③	④	⑤	⑥	⑦
–	1	2	3	4	5	6
7	8	9	10	11	12	13
14	15	16	17	18	19	20
21	22	23	24	25	26	27
28	29	30	31	–	–	–

FEBRUARY

M	T	W	T	F	S	S
①	②	③	④	⑤	⑥	⑦
–	–	–	–	1	2	3
4	5	6	7	8	9	10
11	12	13	14	15	16	17
18	19	20	21	22	23	24
25	26	27	28	29	–	–

MARCH

M	T	W	T	F	S	S
①	②	③	④	⑤	⑥	⑦
31	–	–	–	–	1	2
3	4	5	6	7	8	9
10	11	12	13	14	15	16
17	18	19	20	21	22	23
24	25	26	27	28	29	30

APRIL

M	T	W	T	F	S	S
①	②	③	④	⑤	⑥	⑦
–	1	2	3	4	5	6
7	8	9	10	11	12	13
14	15	16	17	18	19	20
21	22	23	24	25	26	27
28	29	30	–	–	–	–

MAY

M	T	W	T	F	S	S
①	②	③	④	⑤	⑥	⑦
–	–	–	1	2	3	4
5	6	7	8	9	10	11
12	13	14	15	16	17	18
19	20	21	22	23	24	25
26	27	28	29	30	31	–

JUNE

M	T	W	T	F	S	S
①	②	③	④	⑤	⑥	⑦
30	–	–	–	–	–	1
2	3	4	5	6	7	8
9	10	11	12	13	14	15
16	17	18	19	20	21	22
23	24	25	26	27	28	29

JULY

M	T	W	T	F	S	S
①	②	③	④	⑤	⑥	⑦
–	1	2	3	4	5	6
7	8	9	10	11	12	13
14	15	16	17	18	19	20
21	22	23	24	25	26	27
28	29	30	31	–	–	–

AUGUST

M	T	W	T	F	S	S
①	②	③	④	⑤	⑥	⑦
–	–	–	–	1	2	3
4	5	6	7	8	9	10
11	12	13	14	15	16	17
18	19	20	21	22	23	24
25	26	27	28	29	30	31

SEPTEMBER

M	T	W	T	F	S	S
①	②	③	④	⑤	⑥	⑦
1	2	3	4	5	6	7
8	9	10	11	12	13	14
15	16	17	18	19	20	21
22	23	24	25	26	27	28
29	30	–	–	–	–	–

OCTOBER

M	T	W	T	F	S	S
①	②	③	④	⑤	⑥	⑦
–	–	1	2	3	4	5
6	7	8	9	10	11	12
13	14	15	16	17	18	19
20	21	22	23	24	25	26
27	28	29	30	31	–	–

NOVEMBER

M	T	W	T	F	S	S
①	②	③	④	⑤	⑥	⑦
–	–	–	–	–	1	2
3	4	5	6	7	8	9
10	11	12	13	14	15	16
17	18	19	20	21	22	23
24	25	26	27	28	29	30

DECEMBER

M	T	W	T	F	S	S
①	②	③	④	⑤	⑥	⑦
1	2	3	4	5	6	7
8	9	10	11	12	13	14
15	16	17	18	19	20	21
22	23	24	25	26	27	28
29	30	31	–	–	–	–

PUBLIC HOLIDAYS December 2007 - December 2008

JOURS FÉRIÉS GIORNI FESTIVI FEIERTAGE DÍAS FESTIVOS

The dates given below are those of national public holidays (other than those which fall on a Sunday). They do not include regional or half-day holidays Passengers intending to travel on public holidays, or on days immediately preceding or following them, are strongly recommended to reserve seats and tc confirm timings locally. Further information regarding special transport conditions applying on holiday dates may be found in the introduction to each country

Austria : Dec. 8, 25, 26, Jan. 1, Mar. 24, May 1, 12, 22, Aug. 15, Nov. 1, Dec. 8, 25, 26.

Belarus : Dec. 25, Jan. 1, 7, Mar. 8, 15, Apr. 2, May 1, 6, 9, July 3, Nov. 2, Dec. 25.

Belgium : Dec. 25, Jan. 1, Mar. 24, May 1, 12, July 21, Aug. 15, Nov. 1, 11, Dec. 25.

Bulgaria : Dec. 24, 25, 26, Jan. 1, Mar. 3, Apr. 28, May 1, 6, 24, Sept. 6, 22, Nov. 1, Dec. 24, 25, 26.

Croatia : Dec. 25, 26, Jan. 1, Mar. 24, May 1, 22, June 25, Aug. 5, 15, Oct. 8, Nov. 1, Dec. 25, 26.

Czech Republic : Dec. 24, 25, 26, Jan. 1, Mar. 24, May 1, 8, July 5, Oct. 28, Nov. 17, Dec. 24, 25, 26.

Denmark : Dec. 24, 25, 26, Jan. 1, Mar. 20, 21, 24, Apr. 18, May 1, 12, June 5, Dec. 24, 25, 26.

Estonia : Dec. 24, 25, Jan. 1, Mar. 21, May 1, June 23, 24, Aug. 20, Dec. 24, 25.

Finland : Dec. 6, 24, 25, 26, Jan. 1, Mar. 21, 24, May 1, 17, June 21, Nov. 1, Dec. 6, 24, 25, 26.

France : Dec. 25, Jan. 1, Mar. 24, May 1, 8, 12, July 14, Aug. 15, Nov. 1, 11, Dec. 25.

Germany : Dec. 25, 26, Jan. 1, Mar. 21, 24, May 1, 12, Oct. 3, Dec. 25, 26.

Great Britain : *England & Wales*: Dec. 25, 26, Jan. 1, Mar. 21, 24, May 5, 26, Aug. 25, Dec. 25, 26; *Scotland*: Dec. 25, 26, Jan. 1, 2, Mar. 21, May 5, 26, Aug. 4, Dec. 1, 25, 26.

Greece : Dec. 25, 26, Jan. 1, Mar. 10, 25, Apr. 25, 28, May 1, June 16, Aug. 15, Oct. 28, Dec. 25, 26.

Hungary : Dec. 25, 26, Jan. 1, Mar. 15, 24, May 1, 12, Aug. 20, Oct. 23, Nov. 1, Dec. 25, 26.

Ireland (Northern) : Dec. 25, 26, Jan. 1, Mar. 17, 21, 24, May 5, 26, July 14, Aug. 25, Dec. 25, 26.

Ireland (Republic) : Dec. 25, 26, Jan. 1, Mar. 17, 24, May 5, June 2, Aug. 4, Oct. 27, Dec. 25, 26.

Italy : Dec. 8, 25, 26, Jan. 1, Mar. 24, Apr. 25, May 1, June 2, Aug. 15, Nov. 1, Dec. 8, 25, 26.

Latvia : Dec. 25, 26, 31, Jan. 1, Mar. 21, 24, May 1, June 23, 24, Nov. 18, Dec. 25, 26, 31.

Lithuania : Dec. 25, 26, Jan. 1, Feb. 16, Mar. 11, 24, May 1, June 24, Aug. 15, Nov. 1, Dec. 25, 26.

Luxembourg : Dec. 25, 26, Jan. 1, Feb. 4, Mar. 24, May 1, 12, June 23, Aug. 15, Nov. 1, Dec. 25, 26.

Macedonia : Dec. 8, Jan. 1, 2, 7, Apr. 28, May 1, 24, Aug. 2, Sept. 8, Oct. 11, Dec. 8.

Moldova : Jan. 1, 7, 8, Mar. 8, Apr. 28, May 1, 9, Aug. 27.

Netherlands : Dec. 25, 26, Jan. 1, Mar. 21, 24, Apr. 30, May 1, 12, Dec. 25, 26.

Norway : Dec. 25, 26, Jan. 1, Mar. 20, 21, 24, May 1, 12, 17, Dec. 25, 26.

Poland : Dec. 25, 26, Jan. 1, Mar. 24, May 1, 3, 12, 22, Aug. 15, Nov. 1, 11, Dec. 25, 26.

Portugal : Dec. 1, 8, 25, Jan. 1, Mar. 21, 24, May 1, 22, June 10, Aug. 15, Nov. 1, Dec. 1, 8, 25.

Romania : Dec. 1, 25, 26, Jan. 1, Apr. 28, May 1, Dec. 1, 25, 26.

Russia : Jan. 1, 2, 3, 4, 5, 7, Feb. 23, Mar. 8. May 1, 9 June 12, Nov. 4.

Slovakia : Dec. 24, 25, 26, Jan. 1, Mar. 21, 24, May 1 8, July 5, Aug. 29, Sept. 1, 15, Nov. 1, 17, Dec. 24 25, 26.

Slovenia : Dec. 25, 26, Jan. 1, 2, Feb. 8, Mar. 24, May 1, 2, June 25, Aug. 15, Oct. 31, Nov. 1, Dec. 25, 26

Spain : Dec. 6, 8, 25, Jan. 1, Mar. 21, May 1, Aug. 15 Nov. 1, Dec. 6, 8, 25.

Sweden : Dec. 25, 26, Jan. 1, Mar. 21, 24, May 1, June 6, 21, Nov. 1, Dec. 25, 26.

Switzerland : Dec. 25, 26, Jan. 1, 2, Mar. 21, 24, Ma 1, 12, Aug. 1, Dec. 25, 26.

Ukraine : Jan. 1, 7, Mar. 8, 10, Apr. 28, May 1, 2, 9, June 16, 28, 30, Aug. 24, 25.

MOVABLE HOLIDAYS

Fêtes mobiles – Feste mobile
Bewegliche Feste – Fiestas movibles

	2007	2008
Good Friday	April 6	Mar 21*
Easter Monday	April 9	Mar 24*
Ascension Day	May 17	May 1*
Whit Monday (Pentecost)	May 28	May 12*
Corpus Christi	June 7	May 22

** 5 weeks later in the Orthodox calendar*

TIME COMPARISON

COMPARAISON DES HEURES COMPARAZIONE DELLE ORE ZEITVERGLEICH COMPARACIÓN DE LAS HORAS

West European Time	*WINTER: GMT* *SUMMER: GMT +1*	Canaries, Faroes, Ireland, Portugal, United Kingdom, Iceland *(GMT all year)*
Central European Time	*WINTER: GMT +1* *SUMMER: GMT +2*	Albania, Austria, Belgium, Bosnia, Croatia, Czech Rep., Denmark, France, Germany, Hungary, Italy, Luxembourg, Macedonia, Malta, Montenegro, Netherlands, Norway, Poland, Serbia, Slovakia, Slovenia, Spain, Sweden, Switzerland
East European Time	*WINTER: GMT +2* *SUMMER: GMT +3*	Belarus, Bulgaria, Cyprus, Estonia, Finland, Greece, Kaliningrad, Latvia, Lithuania, Moldova, Romania, Turkey, Ukraine
Moskva Time	*WINTER: GMT +3* *SUMMER: GMT +4*	Western Russia *(except Kaliningrad)*

In 2008 clocks are advanced by one hour in all countries (except Iceland) between 0100 GMT on Mar. 30 and 0100 GMT on Oct. 26 *(GMT = Greenwich Mean Time = UT*

What's new this month

The team here at Thomas Cook has worked hard to bring you the new schedules from **December 9**, which affect almost all countries throughout Europe. Despite several railways sending their information later than normal, there is very little information which is missing in this edition. There are, however, two countries where only partial information had been received as we went to press, these being Italy (see below) and Serbia. As our main edition is published monthly, we will of course be updating our tables at the earliest opportunity.

Almost every timing in this edition has changed. In some areas the pattern of service remains similar, but with timings typically changed by a few minutes. In many other areas, the railways have taken the opportunity to rewrite their timetables from scratch. The changes are far too many to detail here in 'Newslines', and we can only highlight a few of the key changes. For services to December 8, please continue to use our November edition.

INTERNATIONAL

Regular readers who have been following our Winter International Supplements in the September, October and November editions will already be aware of the principal changes to international services. We are repeating the summary of these changes, updated to reflect the latest information, on pages 40 and 41. For further details of the new *City Night Line* branding (incorporating former *NZ* and *UEx* trains) please see page 10.

GREAT BRITAIN

As mentioned last month, changes to the structure of a number of passenger rail franchises in November have seen the departure of train operating companies Central Trains, Midland Mainline, and Silverlink, and the arrival of three new operators. **CrossCountry** have taken over most of Virgin Trains' routes which do not run to and from London Euston, as well as a number of Central's longer-distance services. **East Midlands Trains** has inherited all of the Midland Mainline network and most of Central's routes east of the main line from London to Manchester. **London Midland** is the company that has taken over most of the western half of the Central Trains 'empire' as well as the Silverlink County routes.

The general timetable change on December 9 sees another new operator, **National Express East Coast**, taking over from GNER on the East Coast Main Line.

IRELAND

Irish Rail also has a revised timetable from December 9. On the Dublin - Cork route (Table **245**) there is an increase in restaurant car provision and also an extra Sunday morning train each way. The weekday service between Limerick Junction and Waterford (Table **239**) is increased from three to four trains. From January 21 the Dublin - Sligo service (Table **236**) will be recast with additional trains, and the new timetable will be found on page 541.

FRANCE

Major changes in France are usually related to the opening of new high-speed lines, as happened in June 2007 in eastern France. However, French Railways has taken the unusual step of rewriting many of their timetables for the south-eastern region, with local trains in the Lyon area in particular bearing no resemblance to the old timetable. Indeed, certain lines have moved towards regular-interval working with departures at the same minutes past each hour. The changes have required a number of our tables to be renumbered, notably in the range **341** to **348**. The changes also affect *TGV Méditerranée* (Table **350**) where new stopping patterns see more trains calling at Aix en Provence TGV, whereas Valence TGV is mainly served by Montpellier trains. Paris - Clermont Ferrand (Table **330**) is also completely recast.

Elsewhere in France, the Paris - St Malo line sees a new early-morning *TGV* train, with also a later train back to Paris at weekends. From March 31, the Strasbourg - Bordeaux *TGV* service (introduced in June) will be increased from one to three trains each way, and there will also be an extra train between Strasbourg and Nantes (Table **391**).

The next phase of track renewal in Corsica sees a revised timetable from November 19 with bus substitution Corte - Ajaccio and Ponte Leccia - Calvi (Table **379**).

BELGIUM, LUXEMBOURG, NETHERLANDS

The new timetable includes changes on most lines. The hoped-for provisional Amsterdam - Rotterdam service via the new *HSL Zuid* high-speed line is not ready to start and an announcement is awaited.

SWITZERLAND

The December 9 timetable change brings major revisions to services as a result of the full opening of the new 34.6km Lötschsberg Base Tunnel between Frutigen and Raron near Visp. The new route is served by hourly Romanshorn - Zürich - Bern - Brig trains, and a two-hourly Basel - Bern - Brig service (four trains of which are *Cisalpino* tilting units to Milano) shown in a restructured Table **560**. All trains call at Visp, where there are connections for the Rhône Valley and Zermatt. The traditional route via the Lötschberg Pass is served by hourly Spiez - Brig trains, some of which are extended to Bern (Table **562**).

The *Matterhorn Gotthard Bahn* (MGB) has taken advantage of the increased potential of Visp as an interchange and has recast timetables. Journeys between Brig and Göschenen all now require a change of train at Andermatt as the direct services have been withdrawn. To create the extra space required for service expansion, our Swiss lakes tables have been combined into summary format as Table **506**. For the first time the Zürichsee is also included.

ITALY

Our tables have been updated as far as possible from the incomplete information received from *Trenitalia*, but readers should be aware that numerous train schedules were missing from the data supplied, including many high-speed, long distance, overnight and local services. Days and dates of running are also affected, and travellers are strongly advised to check locally before commencing their journey. Readers are also welcome to check the latest situation by contacting our editorial office (see page 1).

SPAIN

The latest additions to Spain's high-speed rail network are due to be inaugurated on December 23 and 24. They are the first stage, as far as Valladolid, of the new northwestern high-speed line from Madrid, and the final section, south of Antequera - Santa Ana station, of the high-speed route from Madrid to Málaga. The proposed new timetables will be found at the back of this edition on page 540.

Opening of the northwestern route will not only permit *Alta Velocidad Española (AVE)* trains to reach Valladolid, but will mean the acceleration of all long-distance trains between the capital and Asturias, Cantabria, and the Basque Country, as these services will in future be provided by high-speed *Alvia* units, which can run on both the new international-gauge line and the 'classic' Iberian-gauge lines north of Valladolid. As a result, journey times to Gijón, Santander, and Bilbao will be cut by at least an hour. In Andalucía too, gauge-changing trains, in this case known as *Altaria*, are able to use the high-speed network for most of their journeys to Algeciras and Granada – and completion of the high-speed line to Málaga will enable faster *AVE* services to run direct to Málaga, cutting the fastest journey time from 3 h. 47 to 2 h. 30.

A third opening – of the final stretch of the high-speed line between Tarragona and Barcelona – was also due to take place just before Christmas. However, geological problems encountered on the approaches to Spain's second city have put back the completion of tunnelling work and this section is not now expected to open before the end of February at the earliest.

PORTUGAL

Portugal is one of the few countries not affected by the December timetable change. However, a date of February 16 has finally been announced for the reopening of Rossio station for services to Sintra, and other changes are predicted for March 2008.

DENMARK and NORWAY

The current timetables in both these countries are valid to January 5, and we expect to show the new timetables in our January edition.

SWEDEN and FINLAND

Until now, Sweden and Finland have not changed their timetables on the December date adopted by most countries, preferring instead to change in early January along with the rest of Scandinavia. From this year, however, both railways are making a general timetable change on December 9. The Swedish timetable is valid to June 14, whereas that for Finland, which contains fairly extensive changes, comes to an end on May 31.

CONTINUED ON PAGE 40

EXPLANATION OF STANDARD SYMBOLS

	EXPLANATION OF SYMBOLS	*EXPLICATION DES SIGNES*	*DELUCIDAZIONE DEI SEGNI*	*ZEICHENERKLÄRUNG*	*EXPLICACIÓN DE LOS SIGNOS*
	SERVICES	**SERVICES**	**SERVIZI**	**DIENSTE**	**SERVICIOS**
12	Through service (1st and 2nd class seats)	Relation directe (places assises 1re et 2e classe)	Relazione diretta (con posti di 1a e 2a classe)	Direkte Verbindung (Sitzplätze 1. und 2. Klasse)	Relación directa (con asientos de 1a y 2a clase)
🛏	Sleeping car	Voiture-lits	Carrozza letti	Schlafwagen	Coche-camas
━	Couchette car	Voiture-couchettes	Carrozza cuccette	Liegewagen	Coche-literas
✕	Restaurant car	Voiture-restaurant	Carrozza ristorante	Speisewagen	Coche-restaurante
🍸	Snacks and drinks available *(see page 10)*	Voiture-bar ou vente ambulante *(voir page 10)*	Carrozza bar o servizio di buffet *(vedere pagina 10)*	Imbiss und Getränke im Zug *(siehe Seite 10)*	Servicio de cafetería o bar móvil *(véase pág. 10)*
2	Second class only	Uniquement deuxième classe	Sola seconda classe	Nur zweite Klasse	Sólo segunda clase
🚌	Bus or coach service	Service routier	Servizio automobilistico	Buslinie	Servicio de autobuses
⛴	Shipping service	Service maritime	Servizio marittimo	Schifffahrtslinie	Servicio marítimo
	DAYS OF RUNNING	**JOURS DE CIRCULATION**	**GIORNI DI EFFETTUAZIONE**	**VERKEHRSTAGE**	**DÍAS DE CIRCULACIÓN**
⚒	Mondays to Saturdays except holidays*	Du lundi au samedi, sauf les fêtes*	Dal lunedì al sabato, salvo i giorni festivi*	Montag bis Samstag außer Feiertage*	De lunes a sábado, excepto festivos*
Ⓐ	Mondays to Fridays except holidays*	Du lundi au vendredi, sauf les fêtes*	Dal lunedì al venerdì, salvo i giorni festivi*	Montag bis Freitag außer Feiertage*	De lunes a viernes, excepto festivos*
Ⓑ	Daily except Saturdays	Tous les jours sauf les samedis	Giornalmente, salvo il sabato	Täglich außer Samstag	Diario excepto sábados
Ⓒ	Saturdays, Sundays and holidays*	Les samedis, dimanches et fêtes*	Sabato, domenica e giorni festivi*	Samstage, Sonn- und Feiertage*	Sábados, domingos y festivos*
†	Sundays and holidays*	Les dimanches et fêtes*	Domenica e giorni festivi*	Sonn- und Feiertage*	Domingos y festivos*
①②	Mondays, Tuesdays	Les lundis, mardis	Lunedì, martedì	Montag, Dienstag	Lunes, martes
③④	Wednesdays, Thurdays	Les mercredis, jeudis	Mercoledì, giovedì	Mittwoch, Donnerstag	Miércoles, jueves
⑤⑥	Fridays, Saturdays	Les vendredis, samedis	Venerdì, sabato	Freitag, Samstag	Viernes, sábados
⑦	Sundays	Les dimanches	Domenica	Sonntag	Domingos
①–④	Mondays to Thursdays	Des lundis aux jeudis	Dal lunedì al giovedì	Montag bis Donnerstag	De lunes a jueves
	OTHER SYMBOLS	**AUTRES SIGNES**	**ALTRI SIMBOLI**	**SONSTIGE SYMBOLE**	**OTROS SÍMBOLOS**
IC **29**	Train number (**bold figures** above train times)	Numéro du train (en **caractères gras** au-dessus de l'horaire du train)	Numero del treno (in **neretto** sopra gli orari del treno)	Zugnummer (über den Fahrplanzeiten in **fetter Schrift** gesetzt)	Número del tren (figura en **negrita** encima del horario del tren)
♦	See footnotes (listed by train number)	Renvoi aux notes données en bas de page (dans l'ordre numérique des trains)	Vedi in calce alla pagina l'annotazione corrispondente al numero del treno	Siehe die nach Zugnummern geordneten Fußnoten	Véase al pie de la página la nota correspondiente al número del tren
Ⓡ	Reservation compulsory	Réservation obligatoire	Prenotazione obbligatoria	Reservierung erforderlich	Reserva obligatoria
🏛	Frontier station	Gare frontalière	Stazione di frontiera	Grenzbahnhof	Estación fronteriza
✈	Airport	Aéroport	Aeroporto	Flughafen	Aeropuerto
|	Train does not stop	Sans arrêt	Il treno non ferma qui	Zug hält nicht	El tren no para aquí
━━	Separates two trains in the same column between which no connection is possible	Sépare deux trains de la même colonne qui ne sont pas en correspondance	Separa due treni della stessa colonna che non sono in coincidenza	Trennt zwei in derselben Spalte angegebene Züge, zwischen denen kein Anschluß besteht	Separa dos trenes de la misma columna entre los cuales no hay enlace
→	Continued in later column	Suite dans une colonne à droite	Continuazione più avanti a destra	Fortsetzung weiter rechts	Continuación a la derecha
←	Continued from earlier column	Suite d'une colonne à gauche	Seguito di una colonna a sinistra	Fortsetzung von links	Continuación desde la izquierda
v.v.	Vice versa	Vice versa	Viceversa	Umgekehrt	A la inversa
	** Public holiday dates for each country are given on page 2.* *Other, special symbols are explained in table footnotes or in the introduction to each country.*	** Les dates des fêtes légales nationales sont données en page 2.* *D'autres signes particuliers sont expliqués dans les notes ou bien dans l'avant-propos relatif à chaque pays.*	** Per le date dei giorni festivi civili nei diversi paesi vedere pagina 2.* *Altri segni particolari vengono spiegati nelle note in calce ai quadri o nella introduzione attinente a ogni paese.*	** Gesetzlichen Feiertage der jeweiligen Länder finden Sie auf Seite 2.* *Besondere Symbole sind in den Fußnoten bzw. in der Einleitung zu den einzelnen Ländern erklärt.*	** Las fechas de los días festivos en cada país figuran en la página 2.* *La explicación de otros signos particulares se da en las notas o en el preámbulo correspondiente a cada país.*

What is the European Rail Timetable?

The Thomas Cook European Rail Timetable is a concise guide to rail and ferry schedules throughout Europe. Needless to say, it cannot be comprehensive (it would run into thousands of pages), but through our knowledge and experience, together with valuable feedback from our readers, we can select those services which we believe will satisfy the needs of most travellers.

When do the services change?

There is a major annual timetable change in mid-December affecting almost all European countries, with a second change in mid-June affecting most, although the British summer timetable now starts in late May once again. The winter timetable in Denmark and Norway comes into effect in January rather than December, and Sweden has a further change in August. Russia and the other CIS countries have their main change at the end of May. Many holiday areas also have separate timetables for the high-summer period. In fact, changes can happen at any time of year, and railways issue amendments either on set dates or as and when necessary. Engineering work also causes frequent changes. Shipping schedules can change at any time, although many companies issue their timetables on a calendar year or seasonal basis.

Why do I need a subscription?

Apart from getting the latest available schedules, you will also be benefitting from advance information for the following season in relevant editions (see below) and also special features in alternate editions, covering the following topics: *January* **Sample Fares**, *March* **Cruise Trains and Rail Holidays**, *May* **Rail Passes**, *July* **Tourist Railways**, *September* **High-Speed Trains**, and *November* **Night Trains**. You may wish to keep a year's worth of timetables on your bookshelf so that you can refer to these features. Note that the Rail Passes feature also appears in the quarterly *Independent Travellers Edition*.

What about forthcoming schedule changes?

A major benefit of a full subscription is obtaining the latest available details of forthcoming changes to International services. Advance summer timings start in our February edition with an 18-page Summer Supplement, which is expanded to 34 pages in March and the full 50 pages in April and May. These summer versions of our international tables are corrected and updated as the information comes in. Winter Supplements appear in our September, October and November editions, leading up to the new schedules from mid-December.

How are the trains selected for inclusion?

People travel for many reasons, whether for leisure, business, sightseeing, visiting friends or relations, or just for the fun of it, and there are no hard and fast rules for selecting the services that we show. Naturally, major towns and inter-city services are shown as a matter of course, but the level of smaller places and local trains shown will depend on the country and even the area. It's surprising just how many minor lines we manage to squeeze in! Generally we will show a greater number of local trains in areas which are popular tourist destinations or where other services are sparse.

It is not possible to show suburban trains within cities or conurbations, or most outer-suburban routes to places close to large cities. However, where there are places of particular interest or importance in this category we do try to show brief details of frequency and journey time.

When should I use the International section?

The rail tables are divided into two sections - International (Tables **10** to **99**) and Country by Country (Tables **100** to **1999**). The International section contains most international routes, but for some services between adjacent countries (for example Stockholm - Oslo or Hamburg - Århus) it is necessary to use the relevant Country tables - the index or maps will guide you. Local trains which cross international frontiers will usually only be found in the Country sections.

Most international trains also carry passengers internally within each country and will therefore be found in the Country tables as well as the International section. Some services are primarily for international travel and will therefore only be found in the International section - this includes *Eurostar* trains (London - Paris / Brussels) and *Thalys* services between Paris and Brussels, as well as certain long-distance night trains.

What about places outside Europe?

No problem. Our sister publication in the blue cover, the **Thomas Cook Overseas Timetable**, is packed with rail, bus and ferry schedules for everywhere you can think of outside Europe, and plenty of other places you have probably never heard of! It is published six times per year and further details can be found on the order form at the back of this timetable.

Our on-line bookstore at www.thomascookpublishing.com has all of our publications, and there is a 10% discount for timetable orders.

New readers start here ...

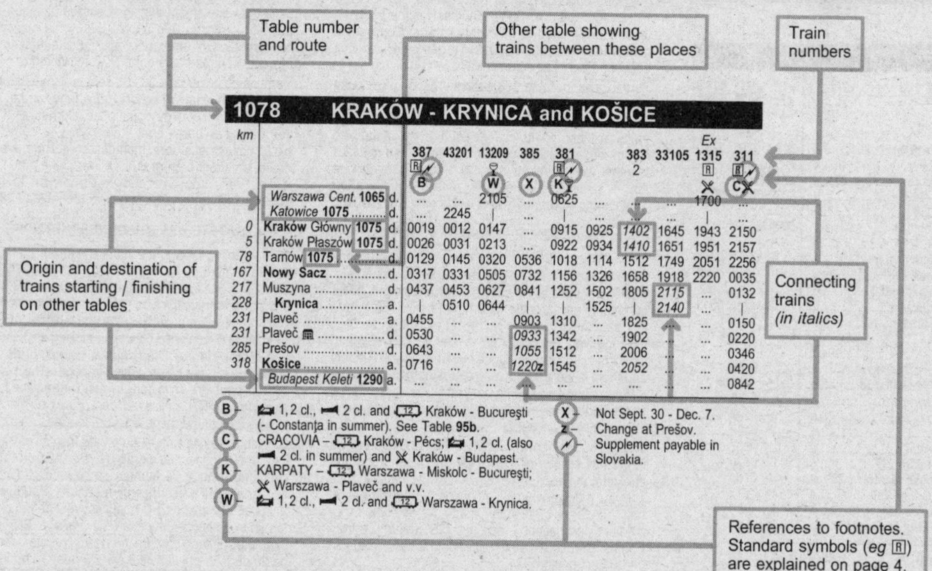

1078 KRAKÓW - KRYNICA and KOŠICE

km		387	43201	13209	385	381		383	33105	1315	311
		® B		W	X	® K		2		Ex ® ✕	® C ✕
	Warszawa Cent. **1065** d.	...	...	2105	...	0625	...	...	...	1700	...
	Katowice **1075** d.	...	2245	|	...	|	...	...	...	|	...
0	**Kraków** Główny **1075** d.	0019	0012	0147	...	0915	0925	*1402*	1645	1943	2150
5	Kraków Płaszów **1075** d.	0026	0031	0213	...	0922	0934	*1410*	1651	1951	2157
78	Tarnów **1075** d.	0129	0145	0320	0536	1018	1114	1512	1749	2051	2256
167	**Nowy Sacz** d.	0317	0331	0505	0732	1156	1326	1658	1918	2220	0035
217	Muszyna d.	0437	0453	0627	0841	1252	1502	1805	*2115*	...	0132
228	**Krynica** a.	|	0510	0644	|	|	1525	|	*2140*	...	|
231	Plaveč a.	0455	...	...	0903	1310	...	1825	...	...	0150
231	Plaveč d.	0530	...	...	*0933*	1342	...	1902	...	...	0220
285	Prešov d.	0643	...	...	*1055*	1512	...	2006	...	...	0346
318	**Košice** a.	0716	...	...	*1220*z	1545	...	*2052*	...	...	0420
	Budapest Keleti **1290** a.	...	...	...	...	...	...	...	...	...	0842

B – 1, 2 cl., 2 cl. and (12) Kraków - Bucureşti (- Constanţa in summer). See Table **95b**.
C – CRACOVIA – (12) Kraków - Pécs; 1, 2 cl. (also 2 cl. in summer) and ✕ Kraków - Budapest.
K – KARPATY – (12) Warszawa - Miskolc - Bucureşti; ✕ Warszawa - Plaveč and v.v.
W – 1, 2 cl., 2 cl. and (12) Warszawa - Krynica.
X – Not Sept. 30 - Dec. 7.
z – Change at Prešov.
Supplement payable in Slovakia.

– *use the maps and index to find the tables you need*
– *trains run daily unless shown otherwise by a symbol or footnote*
– *always read the footnotes!*
– *for more detailed advice on how to use the timetable,* *see pages 6 to 9*

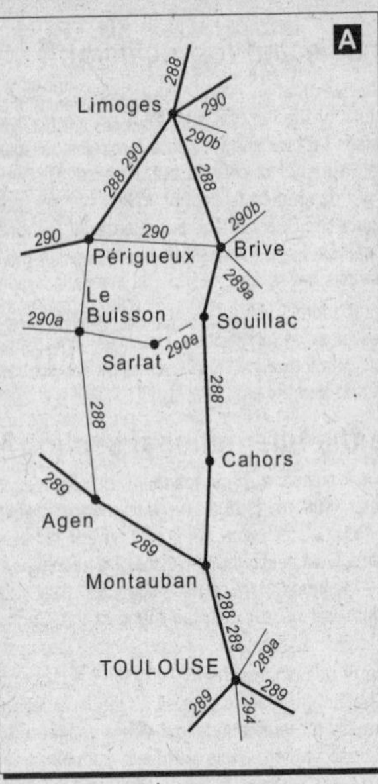

B

Agen, 288, 289
Brive la Gaillarde, 48, 288b, 289a, 290, 290b
Cahors, 288
Le Buisson, 288, 290a
Limoges, 288, 290, 290b
Montauban, 288, 289
Périgueux, 288, 290
Sarlat, 290a
Souillac, 288, 290a
TOULOUSE
- Aurillac, 289a
- Avignon, 313
- Bordeaux, 289
- *etc.*

288

km	**C**	473 ♦	4425 ♦	4425 4423 Q
0	**Paris Austerlitz 291** ....d.	2139	2256	2256
	Orléans ....d.	*2237*	*2350*	*2350*
119	Les Aubrais-Orléans **291**..d.	2246	0004	0004
200	Vierzon **291** ....d.	2329	0055	0055
236	Issoudun ....d.	|	|	|
263	Châteauroux........d.	0004	0132	0132
341	La Souterraine........d.	|	|	|
400	**Limoges** ....a.	0116	0254	0254
400	**Limoges 290** ....d.	0120	0259	0312
499	Périgueux **290** ....d.	|	|	0450
539	Les Eyzies........d.	|	|	0519
556	Le Buisson........d.	|	|	0537
651	**Agen** ....a.	|	|	0705
459	Uzerche ....d.	|	|	...
499	**Brive la Gaillarde**........a.	0222	0408	...
499	**Brive la Gaillarde**........d.	0225	0421	...
536	Souillac ....d.	|	0449	...
559	Gourdon........d.	|	0507	...
600	Cahors ....d.	|	0538	...
639	Caussade........d.	|	0607	...
662	Montauban **289** ....d.	0411	0628	...
713	**Toulouse Matabiau 289**..a.	0440	0700	...
	Narbonne **289**........a.	0644	...	...
	Portbou **289**........a.	0842	...	...
	La Tour de Carol **294** ...a.	0758	...	...

♦ – **NOTES** (LISTED BY TRAIN NUMBER):

473 – PARIS - CÔTE VERMEILLE – [couchette] 1, 2 cl. (T2), [sleeper] 1, 2 cl. and [2] Paris - Portbou. Conveys, except when train **4415** runs, [2] and [sleeper] 1, 2 cl. Paris - La Tour de Carol.

4425 – ⑤⑦ (also Dec. 25, Jan. 1, Apr. 8, May 15; not Dec. 24, 31, Apr. 7, May 17): [12] and [sleeper] 2 cl. Paris - Toulouse (also [sleeper] 1, 2 cl. on ⑤**f**).

Q – ⑤ (also May 15; not May 17): [sleeper] 1, 2 cl. and [2] Paris - Agen.

f – Also May 15; not May 17.

FINDING YOUR TRAIN

USING THE MAPS

The maps included in the timetable (see extract **A**, left) provide a diagrammatic index to services. Showing major places, line termini and junctions, they are the quickest way – if you already know the geographical location of the start and end points of your journey – of finding the table numbers you require, as indicated by the figures appearing beside each route.

The maps will also help you to work out routes and changing-points for journeys between places not connected by through services. For example, for a journey from Périgueux to Toulouse you will need to consult either Tables **290** and **288** (via Brive) or Tables **288** and **289** (via Agen).

Where services along a section of line appear in more than one table, then more than one number is shown alongside that section. An example in **A** is Limoges - Périgueux: trains (not necessarily the same ones) running on this section appear in Tables **288** and **290**.

A broken line (e.g. Sarlat - Souillac in **A**) indicates a bus link.

USING THE ALPHABETICAL INDEX

If you cannot find the start and end points of your journey on the maps (and many places are, of course, too small to feature), the alphabetical index on pages 13–28 lists all the places included in the timetable and the numbers of the tables in which those places appear. Extract **B** shows the list of places appearing in map **A**. In the case of major centres (see the entry for Toulouse) there are separate sub-entries for principal destinations reachable from that place.

Look up the two places between which you are travelling. If they have no table number in common, use the numbers given, together with the maps, to work out your route, and where you may need to change trains. It can often be helpful to start your search from the *smaller* of the two locations.

READING THE TABLES

THE STATION COLUMN

Services from Paris to Toulouse via Limoges appear in Table **288**, and an extract from that table is shown in **C**, left. As will be seen from the map, the stations shown between Périgueux and Agen inclusive lie on a branch from the main route of the table. This is indicated in the table by the fact that these station names are indented.

Just as the map showed that services between Limoges and Périgueux appear in two tables, so the same fact is indicated in the tables themselves: here, by the figures **290** printed to the right of the station names concerned. Similarly, Table **291** gives other services between Paris, Les Aubrais and Vierzon.

Some trains in Table **288** continue beyond Toulouse to Narbonne and Portbou and/or La Tour de Carol. For your convenience, the times of arrival of through trains at these points are included in the table. The names of the stations concerned are printed *in italics* together with a table number in **bold**, e.g. *Narbonne* **289** – meaning that for fuller details of trains from Toulouse to Narbonne you should consult Table **289**.

TRAIN NUMBERS AND HEADNOTES

At the head of the columns containing train timings there appear, when appropriate, the train number (e.g. **473**) – preceded in the case of special-category trains by letters indicating the train type (e.g. *EC* **69**) – and any standard symbols (⚒, 🍷 ...) or letters (**A**, **B**...) referring you to footnotes. A key to the standard symbols used throughout the book appears on page 4 and there is more information about footnotes on page 8. Train numbers may be omitted in the case of local trains without reservable seats or in countries where train numbers are not announced.

When a train is shown with more than one number, as in the last column of extract **C**, this means that the service changes its number during the course of its journey. It does not imply a change of train. However, trains in Europe are often made up of portions for different destinations – see the 2256 departure from Paris shown here – and you should take care to join the correct portion.

DAYS OF RUNNING

Unless otherwise shown, days and dates of running given are those that apply at the station (referred to in a footnote if not shown in the table itself) where the train *starts* its journey. Thus the last train in extract **C** leaves Paris on *Friday* evening (⑤ in the footnotes) and, having travelled through the night, arrives at Agen on *Saturday* morning.

Continued on page 8 ▶

COMMENT TROUVER VOTRE TRAIN

EN UTILISANT LES CARTES

Les cartes (voir l'extrait **A** à gauche) donnent un répertoire schématique des relations reprises dans l'indicateur. Leur consultation – si vous savez déjà la location géographique de vos points de départ et d'arrivée – est le moyen le plus rapide de repérer les numéros des tableaux relatifs à votre parcours. Les chiffres à côté du tracé de chaque ligne renvoient aux tableaux correspondants. Les cartes vous aiderez aussi à établir votre itinéraire et, là où il n'y a pas de service direct, vos gares de changement. Pour un voyage entre Périgueux et Toulouse, par exemple, il faut consulter ou les tableaux **290** et **288** (en passant par Brive) ou bien le **288** et le **289** (par Agen).

Parfois l'ensemble des trains desservant une section sera reparti entre deux ou plusieurs tableaux. On notera dans l'extrait **A** l'exemple de la ligne Limoges - Périgueux: il circule entre ces deux villes des trains (pas forcément les mêmes) repris dans les deux tableaux **288** et **290**. Les traits pointillés (Sarlac - Souillac sur la carte **A**) indiquent des liaisons routières.

EN UTILISANT LE RÉPERTOIRE DES VILLES

Si vous ne savez pas localiser les points de départ et d'arrivée de votre itinéraire sur les cartes, ou s'ils sont trop petits pour y figurer, le répertoire des villes (pages 13 à 28) donne pour chaque localité mentionnée dans l'indicateur les numéros des tableaux qui s'y rapportent. Dans l'extrait **B** vous verrez la liste de toutes les villes de la carte **A**. Pour quelques grands nœuds ferroviaires (p.ex. Toulouse) les numéros des tableaux sont présentés selon les destinations.

Cherchez les deux bouts du parcours désiré sur la liste des villes. S'il n'y a aucun numéro de tableau en commun, recourez aux cartes pour établir votre itinéraire et les éventuels points de correspondance en se servant des numéros indiqués. Commencer par la ville de moindre importance peut faciliter la tâche.

COMMENT LIRE LES TABLEAUX

LA COLONNE DES GARES

Les trains de Paris à Toulouse par Limoges figurent sur le tableau **288**, dont un extrait apparaît sous la lettre **C** à gauche. En examinant la carte on verra que les gares comprises entre Périgueux et Agen sont situées sur une ligne d'embranchement. La mise en retrait sur le tableau des noms de ces gares indique la même circonstance.

Tout comme la carte a montré que les trains entre Limoges et Périgueux sont repris dans deux tableaux, ce fait est également témoigné sur les tableaux eux-mêmes: ici par le **290** à côté des noms des gares concernées. On remarquera aussi que le tableau **291** reprend d'autres trains entre Paris et Vierzon.

Certains trains du tableau **288** sont prolongés au-delà de Toulouse jusqu'à Narbonne, Portbou, ou La Tour de Carol. Par souci de commodité, les heures d'arrivée dans ces gares sont indiquées. Les noms des gares concernées sont imprimés en *italique* avec, à droite, un numéro en **gras** p.ex. *Narbonne* **289**. C'est à dire: vous trouverez des précisions sur le trajet Toulouse - Narbonne en consultant le tableau **289**.

L'EN-TÊTE DES COLONNES HORAIRES

À l'en-tête de la colonne horaire figurent, selon les cas, le numéro du train (p.ex. **473**) – précédé éventuellement d'une indication de catégorie (p.ex. *EC* **69**) – des signes conventionnels (⚒, 🍷 ...) et/ou une lettre vous renvoyant aux notes en bas du tableau (**A**, **B**...). L'explication de signes conventionnels, d'application à tout l'indicateur, paraît en page 4. Pour d'autres commentaires sur les notes, voyez la page 8. Le numéro du train peut être omis dans le cas d'une liaison locale sans possibilité de réserver des places ou dans les pays où les numéros de train ne sont pas annoncés.

L'indication de plus d'un numéro de train à l'en-tête (la dernière colonne de l'extrait **C**) signifie que le train concerné change de numéro au cours du trajet: elle ne signale pas un changement de train. Pourtant, les trains en Europe se composant souvent de tranches à terminus distincts (le départ de Paris à 2256, par exemple), il faut prendre garde de monter dans la partie du train qui convient à votre destination.

JOURS DE CIRCULATION

Sauf indication contraire, les jours et les dates de circulation mentionnés sont ceux applicables à la *gare d'origine* du train (mentionnée si elle ne figure pas sur le tableau même dans les notes). Ainsi le dernier train de l'extrait **C** part de Paris les *vendredis* (⑤ dans les notes), arrive pourtant à Agen le *samedi*, le parcours s'achevant après minuit.

Suite à la page 8 ▶

COME TROVARE IL VOSTRO TRENO

USANDO LE CARTINE

Le cartine incluse nell'orario (vedi l'esempio **A**, a sinistra) forniscono un indice diagrammatico dei servizi. Sono il modo più rapido per trovare i numeri quadri-orario di cui avete bisogno - come indicato dai numeri che compaiono a fianco di ogni linea - se conoscete già la collocazione geografica dei punti di inizio e conclusione del vostro viaggio, perché indicano i luoghi principali, le stazioni terminali delle linee e i nodi ferroviari. Le cartine vi aiuteranno anche a studiare i percorsi e le stazioni dove cambiare per viaggi tra località non collegate da servizi diretti. Per esempio, per un viaggio da Périgueux a Toulouse dovrete consultare anche le tavole **290** e **288** (via Brive) oppure le tavole **288** e **289** (via Agen).

Nel caso in cui i servizi lungo la sezione di una linea appaiano in più di un quadro, allora a lato di quella sezione vengono indicati più numeri. Un caso nell'esempio **A** è Limoges - Périgueux: i treni (non necessariamente gli stessi) che percorrono questa linea compaiono nei quadri **288** e **290**. Una linea interrotta (per es. in **A** Sarlat - Souillac) indica un collegamento con autobus.

USANDO L'INDICE ALFABETICO

Se non riuscite a trovare sulle cartine i punti di partenza e di arrivo (e molte destinazioni sono naturalmente troppo piccole per essere indicate) l'indice alfabetico delle pagine 13–28 elenca le località incluse nell'orario e i numeri dei quadri in cui compaiono tali località. L'essempio **B** mostra la lista dei luoghi che compaiono nella cartina **A**, nel caso di centri maggiori (per esempio la voce Toulouse) ci sono delle voci separate per le principali destinazioni raggiungibili da quella località.

Se le due località tra le quali avete intenzione di viaggiare non hanno numeri di quadri in comune, usate i numeri dati, insieme alle cartine, per elaborare il vostro percorso, considerando che potreste dover cambiare treno. Spesso può essere di aiuto iniziare la ricerca dalle località più piccole.

COME LEGGERE I QUADRI ORARIO

LA COLONNA DEI STAZIONI

I servizi da Paris a Toulouse via Limoges compaiono nella tavola **288** e trovate un estratto del quadro **C**, a sinistra. Come si può vedere dalla cartina le stazioni tra Périgueux e Agen inclusa si trovano su una diramazione del percorso principale della tavola. Ciò è indicato nella tavola dal fatto che i nomi di queste stazioni sono rientrati.

Esattamente come la cartina mostra che i servizi tra Limoges e Périgueux appaiono in due quadri così lo stesso fatto è anche indicato nei quadri-orario. In questo caso accanto al numero **290** stampato sulla destra dei nomi delle stazioni interessate. In modo simile il quadro **291** riferisce altri servizi tra Paris, Les Aubrais e Vierzon.

Alcuni treni del quadro **288** proseguono oltre Toulouse verso Narbonne e Portbou e/o La Tour de Carol. Per vostra comodità gli orari di arrivo dei treni diretti con queste destinazioni sono inclusi nel quadro. I nomi delle stazioni interessate sono stampati *in corsivo* insieme con un numero di quadro in **grassetto**, per es. *Narbonne* **289**, il che significa che per ulteriori dettagli sui treni da Toulouse a Narbonne bisogna consultare il quadro **289**.

NUMERI DEI TRENI E NOTE DI TESTATA

In cima alla colonna che riporta l'orario del treno compare, dove necessario, il numero del treno (per es. **473**) – preceduto in caso di treni di categoria speciale dalle lettere indicanti il tipo di treno (per es. *EC* **69**) – e ogni altro simbolo standard (⚒, 🍸 ...) o lettera (**A**, **B**...) che si riferiscono alle note a piè di pagina. Una legenda dei simboli standard usati in tutto il volume compare a pagina 4 e trovate ulteriori informazioni sulle note a piè di pagina a pagina 9. I numeri dei treni possono essere omessi nel caso di treni locali senza possibilità di posti riservati o di paesi dove i numeri dei treni non vengono indicati.

Quando un treno è contrassegnato da più di un numero, come nell'ultima colonna dell'esempio **C**, significa che il servizio cambia numero nel corso del viaggio. Questo non implica comunque un cambio di treno. In Europa spesso i treni sono costituiti da sezioni con destinazioni diverse - come il treno in partenza da Paris alle 2256 qui mostrato - e bisogna fare attenzione a salire sui vagoni giusti.

GIORNI DI CIRCOLAZIONE

Salvo casi in cui sia diversamente indicato, i giorni e le date di circolazione si riferiscono alla stazione dove il treno inizia il suo viaggio (come viene riportato in una nota a piè di pagina se non nel quadro stesso). Così l'ultimo treno nell'esempio **C** lascia Paris il *venerdì* sera (⑤ nella nota a piè di pagina) e, viaggiando tutta la notte, arriva a Agen il *sabato* mattina.

Continua a pagina 9 ▶

WIE FINDE ICH MEINEN ZUG?

MIT HILFE DER ÜBERSICHTSKARTEN

Kennen Sie die geographische Lage der Ausgangs- und Bestimmungsorte Ihrer Reise, dann empfehlen wir einen Blick in die im Kursbuch eingeschlossene Übersichtskarte (siehe den Auszug **A** links). Sie zeigen nicht nur die wichtigsten Orte, Endstationen und Knotenpunkte an, sondern neben den Strecken die Nummern der entsprechenden Fahrplantabellen. Die Karten helfen auch beim Aussuchen Ihres Reisewegs und der zweckmäßigen Anschlussstationen wenn Sie eine Reise ohne Direktverbindungen machen wollen. Möchten Sie, zum Beispiel, von Périgueux nach Toulouse, schlagen Sie entweder in den Tabellen **290** und **288** (Reiseweg über Brive) oder in den Tabellen **288** und **289** (über Agen) nach.

Manchmal ist der Gesamtverkehr einer bestimmten Strecke in keiner einzigen Tabelle zu finden. In solchen Fällen sind zwei oder mehrere Nummern angegeben. Ein Beispiel aus **A** ist Limoges - Périgueux: über diese Strecke verkehren Züge (nicht unbedingt dieselben), die in den Tabellen **280** und **290** dargestellt sind.

MIT HILFE DES ORTSVERZEICHNISSES

Können Sie Ihre Ausgangs- und Bestimmmungsorte auf den Karten nicht ermitteln (und natürlich sind viele kleine Orte ausgelassen), dann schlagen Sie in dem alphabetischen Ortsverzeichnis nach. Hier finden Sie alle die im Kursbuch erwähnten Orte mit den entsprechenden Fahrplannummern. Im Auszug **B** sehen Sie die Liste der in **A** dargestellten Orte. Für größere Knotenpunkte (z.B. Toulouse) sind die Tabellnummern nach den daraus erreichbaren Hauptbestimmungen getrennt. Suchen Sie Ihre Start- und Endbahnhöfe im Ortsverzeichnis nach. Haben diese keine gemeinsame Nummer, so ziehen Sie die Karten heran und wenden Sie die angegebenen Nummern an, um Ihre Reiseroute, sowie eventuell notwendige Umsteigeorte, herauszuarbeiten. Dazu empfehlen wir, Ihre Suche aus der Richtung des *kleineren* Ortes aufzunehmen.

WIE LESE ICH DIE FAHRPLÄNE?

DIE BAHNHOFSSPALTE

In der Tabelle **288** stehen Züge von Paris nach Toulouse über Limoges. Einen Auszug aus dieser Tabelle sehen Sie links (Abbildung **C**). Die Bahnhöfe zwischen Périgueux und Agen liegen – das sieht man in der Übersichtskarte – auf einer Nebenstrecke. Der gleiche Umstand ist in der Tabelle wegen des eingezogenen Drucks der betreffenden Bahnhofsnamen auch erkennbar.

In der Karte sehen wir, wie der Gesamtverkehr zwischen Limoges und Périgueux in zwei Tabellen steht. Dasselbe ist in der Tabelle angezeigt: hier durch die Nummer **290** neben den betreffenden Bahnhofsnamen. Gleicherweise ist das Vorhandsein anderer in der Tabelle **291** stehenden Züge zwischen Paris und Vierzon angezeigt. Einige Züge der Tabelle **288** fahren jenseits Toulouse fort, nach Narbonne, Portbou oder La Tour de Carol. Aus Übersichtlichkeitsgründe schließen wir die Ankunftzeiten dieser Züge auf ihren Endbahnhöfe in der Tabelle ein. Die betreffende Bahnhofsnamen sind *kursiv* gedruckt zusammen mit einer **fett** gedruckten Fahrplannummer (z.B. *Narbonne* **289**). Das bedeutet: Näheres über den Zugdienst Toulouse - Narbonne finden Sie in der Tabelle **289**.

ZUGNUMMERN UND KOPFNOTEN

Im Kopf der Zugspalte stehen, nach Bedarf: die Zugnummer (z.B. **473**), gelegentlich mit einem vorangehenden Hinweis auf die Zuggattung (z.B. *EC* **69**); Standard-Symbole (⚒, 🍸 ...); und möglicherweise ein buchstablicher Hinweis auf die Fußnoten (**A**, **B**...). Eine Erklärung der überall in dem Kursbuch verwendeten konventionellen Zeichen finden Sie auf Seite 4, sowie auf Seite 9 Näheres zum Thema Fußnoten. In einigen Fällen – Nahverkehrzüge ohne Reservierungsmöglichkeiten, Länder wo die Nummern nicht bekanntgemacht sind – können die Zugnummern ausgelassen werden.

Die Angabe von zwei Zugnummern, z.B. in der letzten Spalte des Auszugs **C**, bedeutet, dass die Nummer im Laufe der Reise wechselt, besagt aber keinen Umsteigebedarf. Merken Sie, jedoch, dass Züge in Europa oft aus Teilen mit verschiedenen Bestimmungen bestehen – siehe zum Beispiel die Abfahrt von Paris um 2256. Bemühen Sie sich darum, in den richtigen Teil des Zuges einzusteigen.

VERKEHRSTAGE

Die erwähnten Tage und Zeitabschnitte für Züge, die nicht täglich verkehren, gelten für den Ausgangsbahnhof des Zuges (wenn dieser nicht in der Tabelle steht, ist er in einer Fußnote erwähnt). Demgemäß fährt der letzte Zug des Auszugs **C** an *Freitag* ab (⑤ in den Noten), kommt aber an *Samstag* in Agen an, weil der Zug die Nacht über fährt.

Fortsetzung auf Seite 9 ▶

COMO BUSCAR SU TREN

SIRVIÉNDOSE DE LOS MAPAS

Los mapas (véase el ejemplo **A** a la izquierda) ofrecen un índice esquemático de las relaciones presentadas en esta guía. Indican los centros principales, los puntos terminales y de empalme de cada línea, y señalan al lado de los trayectos los números de los cuadros horarios correspondientes. Por eso constituyen – si ya sabe localizar en ellos los puntos de inicio y conclusión de su viaje – el modo más rápido de encontrar los números de los cuadros que debe consultar. Los mapas le ayudarán también a estudiar su itinerario y, caso de que no haya servicio directo, sus puntos de enlace óptimos. La figura **A** demuestra, por ejemplo, que si propone viajar entre Périgueux y Toulouse debe consultar o los cuadros **290** y **288** (viaje por Brive) o bien el **288** y el **289** (por Agen).

A veces no se recoge en un solo cuadro todos los trenes recorriendo un determinado tramo de línea. Un ejemplo en el mapa **A** es la línea Limoges - Périgueux, recorrida por trenes (normalmente distintos) incluidos en los dos cuadros **288** y **290**. Se indica con una línea interrumpida (p.ej. Sarlat - Souillac) un servicio de autobuses.

SIRVIÉNDOSE DEL ÍNDICE ALFABÉTICO

Si no consigue localizar en los mapas los puntos de inicio y conclusión de su viaje (y muchos destinos, naturalmente, son demasiado pequeños para constar), acuda al índice alfabético en las páginas 13–28 donde encontrará el elenco de todos los lugares incluidos en la guía con los números de los cuadros horarios correspondientes. El ejemplo **B** da la lista de las localidades que constan en el mapa **A**. Verá que para los nodos mayores, como Toulouse, se señalan aparte los destinos principales. Si las dos localidades entre las cuales desea viajar carecen de número de cuadro en común, utilice los números facilitados, conjuntamente con los mapas, para establecer su itinerario y los puntos de éste en que pueda ser necesario que cambie de tren. Le puede resultar más fácil iniciar su búsqueda empezando con el lugar de *menor* importancia.

COMO LEER LOS CUADROS

LA COLUMNA DE LAS ESTACIONES

Los trenes de Paris a Toulouse por Limoges aparecen el el cuadro **288** y en la figura **C** a la izquierda se presenta un trozo de este cuadro. Como ya vimos en el mapa las estaciones entre Périgueux y Agen están situadas en un ramal de la línea principal, hecho representado en el cuadro por la impresión sangrada de los nombres de estas estaciones.

El mapa señala que los servicios entre Limoges y Périgueux figuran en dos cuadros horarios. Esto se evidencia también en el cuadro mismo: por la impresión del número **290** a la derecha de los nombres de las estaciones interesadas. De modo igual, se indica que en el cuadro **291** constan otros trenes entre Paris, Les Aubrais y Vierzon. Algunos trenes del cuadro **288** prosiguen más allá de Toulouse, hasta Narbonne o La Tour de Carol, y sus horas de llegada en estas localidades están incluidas en el cuadro. Se imprimen *en cursiva* los nombres de tales estaciones con, a la derecha, un número **en negrita** (p. ej. *Narbonne* **289**) – lo cual quiere decir que en el cuadro **289** encontrará detalles más amplios sobre el servicio de trenes entre Toulouse y Narbonne.

LAS NOTAS DEL ENCABEZAMIENTO

En el encabezamiento de cada columna horaria se dan, según los casos: el número del tren (p.ej. **473**), precedido eventualmente de letras indicando su tipo (p.ej. *EC* **69**), los signos convencionales (⚒, 🍸 ...) y/o letras (**A**, **B**...) le remitiendo a las notas al pie del cuadro. Encontrará en la página 4 una explicación de los signos convencionales de uso corriente en la guía, y se informa más ampliamente sobre las notas en la página 9. En algunos casos – trenes locales sin posibilidad de reservar plazas, o en países donde no se los comunican – se omiten los números de los trenes.

La indicación de más de un número de tren (véase la última columna del ejemplo **C**) quiere decir que el servicio cambia de número en el curso de su recorrido: no supone ningún cambio de tren. Sin embargo los trenes europeos se componen a menudo de secciones a destinos distintos – véase en el ejemplo el tren con salida de Paris a las 2256 – y conviene asegurarse de que suba en el coche justo.

DÍAS DE CIRCULACÍON

Salvo indicación contraria los días y las fechas de circulación son aquéllos aplicables en la estación de *origen* del tren (mencionada, si no figura en el cuadro mismo, en una nota). Así el último tren del ejemplo **C**, aunque sale de Paris por la noche del *viernes* (símbolo ⑤ en las notas), como acaba su viaje después de medianoche, llega a Agen por la mañana del *sábado*.

Sigue en la página 9 ▶

289

D

	TGV 8503 ⚒k 🍷		162 163 ♦ ✕
Paris Montparnasse **286** ....d.	0705	...	...
Paris Austerlitz **286 288** ....d.	|	...	...
Nantes **284** ....d.	|	...	...
Bordeaux St Jean ....d.	1005	1015	1115
Marmande ....d.	|	1059	|
Agen ....d.	1106	1129	|
Montauban **288** ....d.	1142	▬	|
Hendaye 287 ....d.	|	...	|
St Jean de Luz **287** ....d.	|	...	|
Biarritz **287** ....d.	|	...	|
Bayonne **287** ....d.	|	...	|
Puyoô ....d.	|	...	|
Pau **287** ....d.	|	...	|
Lourdes **287** ....d.	|	...	|
Tarbes 287 ....d.	|	...	|
Lannemezan ....d.	|	...	|
Montréjeau ....d.	|	...	|
Boussens ....d.	|	...	|
Toulouse Matabiau 288 ....a.	1209	⚒	1312
Toulouse Matabiau ....d.	...	1220	1316
Castelnaudary ....d.	...	1255	|
Carcassonne ....d.	...	1317	|
Lézignan ....d.	...	...	|
Narbonne ....a.	...	...	|
Marseille **313** ....a.	...	...	1642**z**
Nice **314** ....a.	...	...	1910**z**
Lyon Part Dieu **301** ....a.	...	...	...
Genève **309** ....a.	...	...	...
Perpignan **313** ....a.	...	...	...
Port Bou **313** ....a.	...	...	...

♦ – **NOTES** (LISTED BY TRAIN NUMBER):

162/3 – LE GRAND SUD – (12) and ✕ Bordeaux - Nice.

k – Also Nov. 1, 11, May 16.

z – Arrives 10–12 minutes earlier from Mar. 10.

290

E

	6390 V		P	6380
Bordeaux St Jean ....d.	0747	0747	...	1051
Libourne ....d.	0809	0809	...	1112
Coutras ....d.	0821	0821	...	|
Périgueux ....a.	0910	0910	...	1206
Périgueux **288** ....d.	0912	0912	0933	1211
Brive la Gaillarde ....a.	1005	1005	|	|
Clermont Ferrand **290b** ..a.	1344	...	|	|
Limoges 288 ....a.	|	...	1041	1311
Limoges ....d.	|	...	...	1313
Guéret ....d.	|	...	...	1410
Montluçon ....d.	|	...	...	1505
Gannat ....d.	|	...	...	1608
St Germain des Fossés ......d.	1447	...	...	1627
Roanne ....d.	1530	...	...	1708
Lyon Part Dieu ....a.	1650	...	...	1824
Lyon Perrache ....a.	1700	...	...	1834

P – ①-⑥ (not Dec. 25, Jan. 1, Apr. 8).

V – LE VENTADOUR – ⑤ (also Oct. 26 - Nov. 5, Dec. 19 - Jan. 7, ⑥⑦ Feb. 17 - Mar. 17, Apr. 6, 8, 13, 14, 20, 21, 27, 28, May 1, 3, 8, 10, 15, 19, 24; not May 17, 31).

The timetable extracts shown here are for purposes of illustration only.

Consult the full tables in this book for the latest information on the services mentioned.

Train services in Europe, and with them the tables in this book, are constantly evolving – which is why the Thomas Cook European Rail Timetable is published monthly.

▶ **Continued from page 6**

TRAIN TIMINGS

Timings are given in the 24-hour system – from 0000 hours (midnight departure) to 2400 hours (midnight arrival) – and are always expressed in local time at the place concerned (for time zones, see page 2). The station list indicates for each timing whether it is a departure (d.) or an arrival time (a.). Note, however, that the timing given for the *first* appearance of a train in a table is always a *departure* time, that for its *last* appearance is always an *arrival* time.

THROUGH TRAINS AND CONNECTIONS

Timings in normal (roman) type indicate a through service. Thus, in extract **D**, train **8503**, originating in Paris, runs from Bordeaux to Toulouse, calling at Agen and Montauban en route. The train does not stop at Marmande or, of course, at any of the stations on the branch from Hendaye: this is shown by the symbol | in the centre of the column against the names of the stations concerned.

As just seen, train **8503** does not call at Marmande; passengers travelling from Paris by this service can, however, reach Marmande by changing at Bordeaux to the train, shown in the following column, which leaves there at 1015.

Similarly, while train **8503** completes its journey at Toulouse, passengers wishing to continue to Castelnaudary or Carcassonne have a connecting train at 1220 on ⚒.

Note that, although shown in the same column, the services leaving Bordeaux at 1015 and Toulouse at 1220 are two different trains which do not connect with each other: this is confirmed by the symbol ▬ separating them.

Where timings are *in italics* they refer to a *connecting service* involving a change of trains. Thus, in extract **C** on page 6, train **473** from Paris does not call at Orléans, which is situated – as the indentation shows – on a branch from the main line. However, passengers from Orléans can take a connecting service at *2237* to the main-line station at Les Aubrais-Orléans and change there to train **473**. *Italic* timings always imply a *change of train*.

Warning! While the connections shown in the timetable are believed, on the basis of experience and operators' advice, to be feasible, it cannot be guaranteed that they will always be maintained in such cases as late running. Bear in mind, too, that at large city stations transfer between trains can involve a long walk with change of levels. You should judge for yourself how much time you wish to allow for making a connection 'comfortably'.

FOOTNOTES

When more information about a train needs to be given than can be expressed entirely in standard symbols at the head of the timing column, you will be referred to a footnote.

The symbol ♦ in the headnotes means: refer to the footnote with the corresponding train number. A letter (**A**, **B** ...) means: refer to the footnote with that letter. As will be seen from the timetable extracts, footnotes give much important information about such things as days of running, train composition and through carriages, and you should always consult them when planning your journey.

A letter (**b**, **c** ...) beside a particular timing refers only to that timing. In extract **D**, for example, the **z** beside the last two timings for train **162/163** refers you to a note explaining that arrival times will be earlier from March 10 (but only at Marseille and Nice).

Note that where no days or dates are given, the train runs *daily*. Thus, in extract **E**, a train bearing the name *Le Ventadour* leaves Bordeaux at 0747 and runs via Brive to Lyon – but only on the dates shown in note **V**. Nevertheless, there is a service from Bordeaux to Brive at 0747 *daily* (shown in the following column). In other words, even when the Bordeaux - Lyon train does not run there is still a Bordeaux - Brive train at 0747.

If no other indication is given, trains convey both 1st and 2nd classes of accommodation. Trains conveying 2nd-class accommodation only are distinguished by '2' in the headnotes, by (2), ⟞ 2 cl., etc. in the footnotes, or by '2nd class' in the table heading.

WHERE ELSE TO LOOK IN THE TIMETABLE

Page 10 gives general information about travelling by train in Europe. You are also strongly advised to consult the introduction to each national section. Here you will find important information concerning each country's transport services, such as train categories, catering, the payability or otherwise of supplements, reservation requirements, etc.

▶ **Suite de la page 6**

LES HORAIRES DES TRAINS

Toutes les indications horaires sont donnés en heures locales (voir tableau de comparaison des heures à la page 2). Le départ à minuit est indiqué par 0000, l'arrivée à minuit par 2400. Il est précisé dans la colonne des gares s'il s'agit d'une heure de départ (d.) ou d'arrivée (a.). À noter, pourtant, que pour chaque train la *première* mention est toujours une heure de *départ*, la *dernière* toujours une heure d'*arrivée*.

TRAINS DIRECTS ET CORRESPONDANCES

Les heures en caractère droit indiquent des relations directes. Prenons l'exemple, dans l'extrait **D**, du train **8503** qui (ayant pour origine Paris) circule sur le parcours Bordeaux - Toulouse en effectuant des arrêts à Agen et à Montauban. Ce train ne dessert pas Marmande ni, bien sûr, aucune des gares de l'embranchement Hendaye - Toulouse: c'est le sens du symbole | placé au milieu de la colonne en face des noms de ces gares.

On notera que malgré la non desserte de Marmande par le train **8503**, cette ville est toujours accessible aux voyageurs venant de Paris: moyennant un changement vers le train, mentionné dans la colonne suivante, qui quitte Bordeaux à 1015.

Les voyageurs à destination de Castelnaudary et de Carcassonne ont également la possibilité de prendre à Toulouse les jours ouvrables (⚒) le train en correspondance qui part à 1220.

À noter pourtant le fait – comme en témoigne le symbole ▬ placé entre les deux trains de la deuxième colonne horaire – qu'il n'y a aucune correspondance *entre ces deux trains-là*.

Les heures en *italique* indiquent une *correspondance* et supposent dans tous les cas un changement de train. Ainsi, dans l'extrait **C** (page 6), on verra que le train **473** de Paris ne dessert pas Orléans, situé – comme l'indique la mise en retrait du son nom – sur une ligne d'embranchement. Les passagers en provenance d'Orléans ont pourtant la possibilité d'y prendre à *2237* un train en correspondance qui leur permettra de rejoindre le train **473** aux Aubrais-Orléans.

Attention! Nous nous sommes efforcés de ne mentionner dans l'indicateur que les correspondances réellement faisables, tenant compte surtout des conseils des compagnies exploitantes. Aucune correspondance n'est garantie pourtant. N'oubliez pas non plus que dans les grandes gares les changements peuvent entrainer une longue marche et l'emprunt d'escaliers. À vous de juger combien de temps vous voulez vous permettre pour effectuer un changement 'en tout confort'.

LES NOTES EN BAS DU TABLEAU

Parfois les signes conventionnels placés à l'en-tête de la colonne horaire ne suffisent pas à donner tous les renseignements nécessaires. Dans ces cas-là, il y a un renvoi aux notes en bas du tableau.

Le symbole ♦ à l'en-tête d'une colonne signifie qu'il faut consulter le note portant le numéro du train concerné. Les lettres (**A**, **B** ...) sont également expliquées en bas du tableau. Vu l'importance des précisions données dans les notes – jours de circulation, composition des trains, voitures directes, etc. – il faut toujours les consulter en préparant votre itinéraire.

Une lettre (**b**, **c** ...) placée après une heure de départ ou d'arrivée n'a rapport qu'à l'heure concernée. Ainsi, dans l'extrait **D**, le **z** des indications 1642**z** et 1910**z** du train **162/163** signifie qu'à partir du 10 mars les heures d'arrivée du train (à Marseille et à Nice exclusivement) seront avancées.

À noter que dans l'absence d'une mention particulière les trains circulent tous les jours. Dans l'extrait **E**, par exemple, *Le Ventadour* (départ de Bordeaux à 0747 pour Lyon par Brive) ne circule que les jours précisés dans le note **V**. La relation Bordeaux - Brive à 0747 est néanmoins *quotidienne*. Comme l'indique la deuxième colonne, il y a un train de Bordeaux à Brive à 0747 même les jours où *le Ventadour* ne circule pas.

Sauf indication contraire, les trains ont des places de 1re et de 2e classe. Les trains n'ayant que des places de 2e classe sont distingués par les mentions '2' à l'en-tête de la colonne, (2), ⟞ 2 cl., etc. dans les notes, ou '2nd class' à l'en-tête du tableau.

AUTRES PAGES À CONSULTER

Vous trouverez à la page 10 des renseignements d'application générale au sujet des voyages par train en Europe. Il vous est fortement recommandé de consulter aussi l'introduction à chaque section nationale: vous y trouverez des précisions concernant la classification des trains, les prestations offertes à bord des trains, les suppléments, la réservation des places, etc.

COME SI CONSULTA L'ORARIO – II

▶ Seguito della pagina 7

GLI ORARI DEI TRENI

Gli orari vengono forniti in base al sistema delle 24 ore - dalle 0000 (partenza di mezzanotte) alle 2400 (arrivo di mezzanotte) - e sono sempre espressi in ora locale (per i fusi orari vedere pagina 2). La lista delle stazioni indica per ogni orario se si tratta di un orario di partenza (d.) o di arrivo (a.). Notate, comunque, che l'orario che compare per *primo* in una tavola è sempre un orario di *partenza*, mentre quello che compare per *ultimo* è sempre un orario di *arrivo*.

TRENI DIRETTI E COINCIDENZE

L'orario in caratteri normali indica un servizio diretto. Così nell'esempio **D** il treno **8503**, che ha origine a Paris va da Bordeaux a Toulouse fermando lungo il percorso a Agen e Montauban. Il treno non ferma invece a Marmande né, naturalmente, in nessuna delle stazioni sulla diramazione di Hendaye: il che è indicato dal simbolo | nel centro della colonna accanto ai nomi delle stazioni interessate.

Come si è appena visto, il treno **8503** non passa da Marmande; i passeggeri che viaggiano da Paris con questo servizio possono comunque raggiungere Marmande cambiando a Bordeaux con il treno, mostrato nella colonna successiva, che parte alle 1015.

Allo stesso modo, dal momento che il treno **8503** termina il suo viaggio a Toulouse, i passeggeri che desiderano proseguire per Castelnaudary o Carcassonne hanno nei giorni feriali (⚒) un treno in coincidenza alle ore 1220.

Notate che, sebbene siano segnati nella stessa colonna, i servizi che lasciano Bordeaux alle 1015 e Toulouse alle 1220 sono due treni differenti che non hanno coincidenze: il che è indicato dal simbolo ▬ che li separa.

Dove gli orari sono *in corsivo* si riferiscono a un servizio *in coincidenza* che implica un cambio di treno. Perciò nell'essempio **C** a pagina 6 il treno **473** da Paris non ferma ad Orléans, che è situata - come mostra il rientro di riga - su una diramazione della linea a principale. Comunque, i passeggeri provenienti da Orléans possono prendere un treno in coincidenza alle *2237* per la stazione principale della linea a Les Aubrais-Orléans e prendere lì il treno **473**. L'orario scritto *in corsivo* implica sempre un *cambio di treno*.

Attenzione! Mentre le coincidenze indicate nell'orario sono quelle ritenute realmente fattibili sulla base dell'esperienza e delle indicazioni delle amministrazioni ferroviarie, non può essere garantito che siano mantenute in caso di ritardi. Ricordate anche che nelle stazioni delle grandi città il trasferimento tra due treni può significare un lungo tratto da percorrere a piedi e con l'uso di scale. Dovrete giudicare da voi quanto tempo vi occorre per cambiare comodamente treno.

NOTE A PIÈ DI PAGINA

Quando sarà necessario dare maggiori informazioni su di un treno di quante possano essere interamente espresse in simboli standard, in cima alla colonna degli orari ci sarà un rimando a una nota a piè di pagina.

Il simbolo ♦ nelle note di testa significa: fate riferimento a una nota a piè di pagina con il numero corrispondente. Una lettera (**A**, **B**...) significa: fate riferimento alla nota con quella lettera. Come si vede dall'esempio **E** le note hanno molte informazioni importanti come giorni di percorrenza, composizione dei treni e carrozze dirette, e occorre sempre consultarle quando programmate il vostro viaggio.

Una lettera (**b**, **c**...) accanto ad un particolare orario si riferisce soltanto a quell'orario. Nell'esempio **D** la lettera **z** accanto agli ultimi due orari per i treni **162**/**163** vi rimanda ad una nota che spiega che l'orario di arrivo sarà anticipato dal 10 di marzo (ma soltanto a Marseille e Nice).

Notate che quando non ci sono giorni e date il treno viaggia *ogni giorno*. Perciò nell'esempio **E** il treno chiamato *Le Ventadour* lascia Bordeaux alle 0747 e va via Brive a Lyon - ma solo nei giorni indicati nella nota **V**. Tuttavia c'è un servizio quotidiano da Bordeaux a Brive alle 0747 (indicato nella colonna successiva), in altre parole anche quando il treno Bordeaux - Lyon non fa servizio c'è comunque il treno Bordeaux - Brive alle 0747.

Se non ci sono altre indicazioni i treni hanno sia la prima sia la seconda classe. I treni con sole carrozze di seconda classe sono identificabili dal '2' nelle note di testata, nei simboli delle carrozze, nelle note a piè di pagina o dall'indicazione '2nd class' nell'intestazione del quadro.

ALTRE PAGINE DA CONSULTARE

A pagina 10 trovate delle informazioni generali sui viaggi in treno in Europa. Vi consigliamo vivamente di consultare anche l'introduzione a ciascuna sezione dedicata ad una nazione. Vi troverete importanti informazioni riguardanti i servizi di trasporto di ciascun paese, così come le categorie dei treni, la ristorazione, il pagamento di supplementi, le necessità di prenotazione, ecc.

BENUTZUNGSHINWEISE – II

▶ Fortsetzung der Seite 7

FAHRZEITANGABEN

Die Abfahrtzeit um Mitternacht ist 0000, die Ankunftzeit um Mitternacht ist 2400. Fahrzeiten sind immer in der jeweiligen Landeszeit angegeben (eine Zeitvergleichstabelle finden Sie auf Seite 2). Die Buchstaben d. (ab) und a. (an) nach den Ortsnamen in der Bahnhofsspalte kennzeichnen Abfahrt- bzw. Ankunftzeiten. Bermerken Sie jedoch, dass es sich stets bei der ersten für einen Zug angegebenen Zeit um eine Abfahrtzeit, bei der letzten um eine Ankunftzeit, handelt.

DIREKTE ZÜGE UND ANSCHLÜSSE

Normal (in gerader Schrift) gedruckte Zeitangaben verweisen auf direkte Verbindungen. Eine solche sieht man in dem Auszug **D**. Der Zug **8503** aus Paris verkehrt von Bordeaux nach Toulouse, hält auf den Bahnhöfen Agen und Montauban, fährt aber bei Marmande durch. Die auf die Seitenstrecken von Hendaye liegende Bahnhöfe bedient er natürlich auch nicht. Dies wird von dem in der Mitte der Zugspalte stehenden Symbol | gekennzeichnet.

Wie soeben erläutert: der Zug **8503** hält in Marmande nicht. Reisende aus Paris können Marmande trotzdem erreichen, mittels Umsteigen in Bordeaux in den in der nächsten Spalte angegebenen Zug (Abfahrt von Bordeaux um 1015).

Gleicherweise, obwohl der Zug **8503** nicht weiter als Toulouse fährt, haben die Passagiere, die ihre Reise bis Castelnaudary oder Carcassonne verlängern wollen, an Werktagen (⚒) einen Anschlusszug dennoch um 1220.

Merken Sie sich, dass die Züge mit den Abfahrtzeiten Bordeaux 1015 bzw. Toulouse 1220 verschiedene Züge und keine Anschlusszüge sind. Das Zeichen ▬ zwischen den beiden Zügen deutet dies an.

Kursiv gedruckte Zeitangaben weisen auf *Anschlussverbindungen* hin und bedeuten Umsteigen. Der Zug **473** in der Abbildung **C** (Seite 6), zum Beispiel, bedient Orléans nicht, weil diese Stadt auf einer Nebenstrecke liegt. Reisende aus Orléans haben jedoch die Möglichkeit, um *2237* einen Anschlusszug zu benutzen, also auf dem Hauptstreckenbahnhof Les Aubrais-Orléans in dem Zug **473** umzusteigen. *Kursiv* gedruckte Zeitangaben weisen immer auf das Umsteigen hin.

Achtung! Alle die im Kursbuch angezeigten Anschlussmöglichkeiten sind nach unserem besten Wissen und den Meldungen der Verkehrsbetriebe erreichbar. Anschlussversäumnisse durch Verspätung oder Ausfall von Zügen sind aber immer möglich. Merken Sie sich auch, dass man auf Großstadtbahnhöfe oft einen langen Umweg zu Fuß machen und Treppe benutzen muss. Beurteilen Sie bitte selbst, wieviel Zeit zum Umsteigen Sie benötigen.

FUSSNOTEN

Manchmal ist es nötig, Ergänzungsinformationen zu vermitteln, für welche die Standard-Symbole nicht genügen. In diesen Fällen wird es auf eine unter der Fahrplantabelle stehenden Fußnote hingewiesen.

Das Zeichen ♦ im Kopf der Zugspalte bedeutet: schlagen Sie die Note mit der Nummer des betreffenden Zuges nach. Ein Buchstabe (**A**, **B**...) weist auf die mit demselben Buchstaben bezeichneten Note hin. Die Fußnoten enthalten – so sieht man das in den Auszügen – viele wichtige Auskünfte: über Verkehrstage, Zugbildung, Kurswagen und so weiter. Lesen Sie immer die Fußnote bei der Planung Ihrer Reise

Ein Buchstabe (**b**, **c**...) neben einer bestimmten Zeitangabe gilt nur für diese Angabe. Das **z** hinter die zwei letzten Zeitangaben des Zuges **162**/**163** (im Auszug **D**), zum Beispiel, deutet auf das vom 10. Mai frühere Einlaufen dieses Zuges in Marseille und in Nice hin (aber *nur* dorthin).

Sofern nicht anders angemeldet, verkehren die Züge *täglich*. In dem Auszug **E**, fährt der Zug *Le Ventadour* von Bordeaux um 0747 ab und verkehrt nach Lyon über Brive – aber nur in dem in der Note **V** angegebenen Zeitabschnitt. Es ist jedoch in der nächsten Spalte ein Zug auch mit Abfahrt von Bordeaux um 0747 angegeben, diesmal aber ohne Hinweis auf eine bestimmte Verkehrsperiode. Das heißt, dass man *täglich* um 0747 von Bordeaux nach Brive fahren kann, auch wenn *Le Ventadour* nicht verkehrt.

Im Allgemeinen führen die Züge die 1. und 2. Wagenklasse. Abweichungen (das heißt, Züge mit nur 2. Klasse) sind durch die Erwähnungen '2' im Kopf der Zugspalte, (2), ⟝ 2 cl., usw. in der Noten, bzw. '2nd class' in der Tabellenüberschrift, erkennbar.

AUCH ZUM LESEN

Auf Seite 10 erscheinen allgemeine Auskünfte über das Thema Reisen mit der Bahn in Europa. Es ist auch sehr zu empfehlen, die Einleitungen zu jedem einzelnen Land zu lesen. Darin werden Sie wichtige Informationen über die Besonderheiten jedes Landes finden: Zugcharakterisierung, Services an Bord der Züge, Zuschlagpflicht, Reservierungsbedingungen usw.

MODO DE EMPLEO – II

▶ Continuación de la página 7

LAS INDICACIONES HORARIAS

Éstas se exprimen siempre en la hora del país interesado (véase el cuadro de comparación horaria en la página 2). Por 0000 se entiende una salida de medianoche, por 2400 una llegada a la misma hora. En la lista de las estaciones se aclara para todo horario si se trata de una salida (d.) o de una llegada (a.). Nótese sin embargo que en todos los casos el *primer* horario indicado para un tren determinado en las columnas es un horario de *salida*, el *último* un horario de *llegada*.

TRENES DIRECTOS Y ENLACES

Los horarios en caracteres normales representan servicios directos. Así, en el ejemplo **D**, el tren **8503**, naciendo en Paris, circula de Bordeaux a Toulouse, haciendo escala en Agen y Montauban. No para en Marmande ni, claro, en ninguna de las estaciones del ramal de Hendaye, lo cual está indicado por la presencia del símbolo | en el centro de la columna enfrente de los nombres de estas estaciones.

Como acabamos de ver, el tren **8503** no hace escala en Marmande. Sin embargo los pasajeros que vienen de Paris pueden llegar a esta localidad mediante un cambio de tren en Bordeaux, de donde pueden tomar el tren, indicado en la columna siguiente, que sale de Bordeaux a las 1015. Del mismo modo, los pasajeros del tren **8503** – si bien que acaba su recorrido en Toulouse – deseosos de llegar a Castelnaudary o a Carcassonne tienen a su disposición los días laborables (⚒) un tren de enlace a las 1220. Nótese que los trenes saliendo respectivamente de Bordeaux a las 1015 y de Toulouse a las 1220, si bien que están señalados en la misma columna, son dos trenes distintos entre los cuales no hay enlace, lo cual está indicado por el símbolo ▬ que los separa.

Se refiere, en el caso de horarios imprimidos en *cursivo*, a correspondencias, es decir servicios de enlace que suponen un *cambio de tren*. Así, en el ejemplo **C** de la página 6, el tren **473** de Paris no hace escala en Orléans, estación situada, como lo indica la impresión sangrada de su nombre, en un ramal. Sin embargo existe para los pasajeros deseando iniciar su viaje en Orléans un tren, saliendo de allí a las *2237*, que enlaza en la estación de la línea principal de Les Aubrais-Orléans con el tren **473**.

¡Ojo! Bien que creemos, apoyándonos en las indicaciones suministradas por las administraciones, que todos los enlaces indicados en la guía son factibles, no podemos garantizar que las correspondencias serán respectadas en la práctica, sobre todo en el caso de retrasos. Hay que ser consciente también que el transbordo en las estaciones de las grandes ciudades puede suponer un desplazamiento bastante largo a pie y el uso de escaleras. A usted de decidir cuánto tiempo le conviene para efectuar cómodamente los cambios de tren.

LAS NOTAS AL PIE DEL CUADRO

Cuando los signos convencionales no bastan para expresar toda la información que hay que comunicar acerca de un tren, entonces se remite el lector a una nota al pie del cuadro.

El símbolo ♦ en el encabezamiento de la columna quiere decir: consulte la nota que lleva el número del tren interesado. Una letra (**A**, **B**...) significa que hay que consultar la nota que lleva esta letra. Come se ve en los ejemplos, las notas comunican datos muy importantes como días de circulación, composición de los trenes, coches directos, y es imprescindible consultarlas cuando prepara su viaje. Una minúscula (**b**, **c**...) al lado de un horario determinado se refiere únicamente a ese horario. Por ejemplo, en **D**, la **z** al lado de los dos últimos horarios del tren **162**/**163** le remite a una nota que le explica que las llegadas serán anticipadas a partir del día 10 de marzo (pero *solo* en Marseille y Nice).

Nótese que en los casos donde no se comunica ningún día ni fecha la circulación del tren es *diaria*. Así, en el ejemplo **E**, el tren *Le Ventadour* sale de Bordeaux a las 0747 para Lyon por vía de Brive – pero sólo en los días indicados en la nota **V**. En la columna siguiente, sin embargo, se indica un servicio diario de Bordeaux a Brive. Es decir que hay una salida de Bordeaux para Brive a las 0747 aun cuando no circula *Le Ventadour*.

Salvo indicación contraria los trenes llevan coches de primera y de segunda clase. Los trenes que llevan exclusivamente coches de segunda clase están distinguidos o por la cifra '2' el la parte superior de la columna, por (2), ⟝ 2 cl., etc. en las notas, o por la mención '2nd class' en el encabezamiento general del cuadro.

OTRAS PÁGINAS QUE CONSULTAR

En la página 10 encontrará otras informaciones generales sobre el tema de los viajes por tren en Europa. Se le recomienda vivamente que consulte también los preámbulos al comienzo de cada sección nacional: le proporcionarán datos importantes sobre las particularidades de cada país: tipos de trenes, restauración, pago de suplementos, necesidades de reservación anticipada, etc.

The following is designed to be a concise guide to travelling in Europe by train. For more details of accommodation available, catering, supplements etc., see the introduction to each country.

BUYING YOUR TICKET

Train tickets must be purchased before travelling, either from travel agents or at the station ticket office (or machine). Where a station has neither a ticket office nor a ticket machine, the ticket may usually be purchased on the train.

Tickets which are not dated when purchased (for example in France, Italy and the Netherlands) must be validated before travel in one of the machines at the entrance to the platform.

In certain Eastern European countries foreign nationals may have to buy international rail tickets at the office of the state tourist board concerned and not at the railway station. The tickets can sometimes only be purchased in Western currency and buying tickets can take a long time.

All countries in Europe (except Albania) offer two classes of rail accommodation, usually 1st and 2nd class. 1st class is more comfortable and therefore more expensive than 2nd class. Local trains are often 2nd class only. In Southern and Eastern Europe, 1st class travel is advisable for visitors as fares are reasonable and 2nd class can be very overcrowded.

RESERVATIONS

Many express trains in Europe are restricted to passengers holding advance seat reservations, particularly in France, Sweden and Spain. This is shown by the symbol 🅁 in the tables, or by notes in the introduction to each country. All *TGV*, *Eurostar* and *Pendolino* trains require a reservation, as do all long-distance trains in Spain.

Reservations can usually be made up to two months in advance. A small fee is charged, but where a supplement is payable the reservation fee is often included. Reservations can often be made on other long-distance services and this is recommended at busy times.

SUPPLEMENTS

Many countries have faster or more luxurious train services for which an extra charge is made. This supplement is payable when the ticket is purchased and often includes the price of a seat reservation. The supplement can sometimes be paid on the train, but usually at extra cost. The introduction to each country gives further information. On certain high-speed services, the first class fare includes the provision of a meal.

RAIL PASSES

Tickets are available which give unlimited travel on all trains in a given area. These rail passes range from Eurail and InterRail passes which cover the whole of Western Europe for up to one month, to local passes which cover limited areas for 1 day. Passports may need to be shown when purchasing such tickets. A special feature on rail passes appears each year in our May edition and also in the quarterly Independent Travellers Edition.

FINDING YOUR TRAIN

At most stations departures are listed on large paper sheets (often yellow), and/or on electronic departure indicators. These list trains by departure, giving principal stops, and indicate from which platform they leave.

On each platform of principal European stations, a display board can be found giving details of the main trains calling at that platform. This includes the location of individual coaches, together with their destinations and the type of accommodation provided.

A sign may be carried on the side of the carriage indicating the train name, principal stops and destination and a label or sign near the door will indicate the number allocated to the carriage, which is shown on reservation tickets. 1st class accommodation is usually indicated by a yellow band above the windows and doors and/or a figure 1 near the door or on the windows

A sign above the compartment door will indicate seat numbers and which seats are reserved. In non-compartment trains, reserved seats have labels on their headrests. In some countries, notably Sweden and Yugoslavia, reserved seats are not marked and occupants will be asked to move when the passenger who has reserved the seat boards the train.

✕ CATERING 🍷

Many higher quality and long-distance trains in Europe have restaurant cars serving full meals, usually with waiter service, or serve meals at the passenger's seat. Such trains are identified with the symbol ✕ in the tables. Full meals may only be available at set times, sometimes with separate sittings, and may only be available to passengers holding first class tickets. However, the restaurant car is often supplemented by a counter or trolley service offering light snacks and drinks.

Other types of catering are shown with the symbol 🍷. This varies from a self-service buffet car serving light meals (sometimes called bistro or café) to a trolley which is wheeled through the train, serving only drinks and sandwiches. Where possible, the introduction to each country gives further information on the level of catering to be expected on particular types of train.

The catering shown may not be available throughout the journey and may be suspended or altered at weekends or on holidays.

SLEEPING CARS 🛏

Sleeping cars are shown as 🛏 in the timetables. Standard sleeping car types have bedroom style compartments with limited washing facilities and full bedding. Toilets are located at one or both ends of the coach. An attendant travels with each car or pair of cars and will serve drinks and continental breakfast at an extra charge. 1st class sleeping compartments have one or two berths (in Britain and Norway, and in older Swedish sleeping cars, two berth compartments require only 2nd class tickets) and 2nd class compartments have three berths. Some trains convey special T2 cabins, shown as 🛏 (T2) in the tables, with one berth in 1st class and two berths in 2nd class

Compartments are allocated for occupation exclusively by men or by women except when married couples or families occupy all berths. Children travelling alone, or who cannot be accommodated in the same compartment as their family, are placed in women's compartments. In Russia and other countries of the former USSR, however, berths are allocated in strict order of booking and men and women often share the same compartments.

Some trains have communicating doors between sleeping compartments which can be opened to create a larger room if both compartments are occupied by the same family group. Berths can be reserved up to 2 months (3 months on certain trains) before the date of travel and early reservation is recommended as space is limited, especially on French ski trains and in Eastern Europe. Berths must be claimed within 15 minutes of boarding the train or they may be resold.

HOTEL TRAINS

A new generation of overnight trains known collectively as Hotel trains are now running on a selection of national and international routes. The facilities are of a higher standard than those offered in conventional sleeping cars, and special fares are payable. The trains fall into the following categories:

City Night Line: Most night trains radiating from Germany, as well as domestic overnight trains within Germany, now come under the *City Night Line* banner. They operate on around 30 routes serving nine countries, and are shown as *CNL* in our tables. *De Luxe* class consists of one or two berth cabins, with one or two moveable armchairs, a table and an en suite washroom containing toilet, washbasin and shower. *Comfort* compartments have two berths, the upper of which folds away against the cabin wall, and the lower becomes a seat for day use. There are also four berth family compartments as well as couchettes and reclining seats (sleeperettes). A first class ticket is required for *De Luxe* compartments (but no longer for single occupancy of a *Comfort* compartment). A new rule on *CNL* trains is that only entire compartments can be booked, so people travelling alone must book a single compartment rather than sharing with others.

Trenhotel (Spain). These trains, of the *Talgo* type, run on the international routes from Madrid to Paris and Lisboa, and from Barcelona to Paris, Zürich and Milano. They also run on internal routes within Spain, from Barcelona to A Coruña, Vigo, Málaga and Sevilla and v.v., and Madrid to A Coruña and Vigo and v.v. The highest class of accommodation is known as *Gran Clase*, which has shower and toilet facilities in each compartment and can be used for single or double occupancy.

Compartments with showers can also now be found on a number of services in Sweden, Norway and Italy, and other international routes include Wien to Zürich and Roma, the Brussels - Warszawa *Jan Kiepura* and the *Berlin Night Express* running between Berlin and Malmö. Further details of sleeper services are shown in our Night Trains feature in the November edition.

COUCHETTES ▬

Couchettes (▬) are a more basic form of overnight accommodation consisting of simple bunk beds with a sheet, blanket and pillow. The couchettes are converted from ordinary seating cars for the night, and there are usually 4 berths per compartment in 1st class, 6 berths in 2nd class. On certain trains (e.g. in Austria and Italy), 4 berth compartments are available to 2nd class passengers, at a higher supplement. Washing and toilet facilities are provided at the ends of each coach. Men and women are booked into the same compartments and are expected to sleep in daytime clothes. A small number of trains in Germany, however, have women-only couchette compartments.

WHEELCHAIR ACCESS ♿

High-quality main line and international trains are now often equipped to accommodate passengers in wheelchairs. Access ramps are available at many stations and some trains are fitted with special lifts. The following trains have at least one wheelchair space, often with accessible toilets:

International: all Eurostar trains, many EC and other trains. CityNightLine trains have a special compartment. *Austria:* many IC/EC trains. *Denmark:* IC and Lyn trains. *France:* all TGV trains and many other long distance services. *Germany:* all EC, ICE, IC and IR trains. *Italy:* all Pendolino and many EC or IC trains. *Netherlands:* most trains. *Sweden:* X2000 and most IC and IR trains, some sleeping cars. *Switzerland:* All IC, most EC and some regional trains. *Austria, Great Britain, Ireland, Poland:* certain trains only.

Most of these railways publish guides to accessibility, and some countries, for example France, provide special staff to help disabled travellers. Wheelchair users normally need to reserve in advance, stating their requirements. The Editor would welcome information for countries not listed.

CAR-SLEEPERS

Trains which convey motor cars operate throughout much of Europe and are shown in Table **1** for international services and Table **2** for other services. The motor cars are conveyed in special wagons while passengers travel in sleeping cars or couchettes, usually (but not always) in the same train.

LUGGAGE & BICYCLES

Luggage may be registered at many larger stations and sent separately by rail to your destination. In some countries, bicycles may also be registered in advance and certain local and some express trains will convey bicycles (there may be a charge). The relevant railways will advise exact details on request.

HEALTH REQUIREMENTS

It is not mandatory for visitors to Europe to be vaccinated against infectious diseases unless they are travelling from endemic areas. For travellers' peace of mind, however, protection against the following diseases should be considered:

AIDS	Cholera
Hepatitis A	Hepatitis B
Polio	Rabies
Tetanus	Typhoid

Full information is available from the manual published by the World Health Organisation, and travellers should seek advice from their Travel Agent.

WATER: Tap water is usually safe to drink in most parts of Europe. Those travelling in some southern countries, or who doubt the purity of the tap water, are recommended to boil it, to use sterilisation tablets, or to drink bottled water. The water in washrooms or toilets on trains is not suitable for drinking.

CLIMATE

Most of Europe lies within the temperate zone but there can be considerable differences between North and South, East and West, as illustrated in the table below. Local temperatures are also affected by altitude and the difference between summer and winter temperatures tends to be less marked in coastal regions than in areas far removed from the sea.

	Bucureşti	Dublin	Madrid	Moskva
JANUARY				
Highest	2°	8°	10°	−6°
Lowest	−6°	3°	3°	−12°
Rain days	6	13	9	11
APRIL				
Highest	18°	11°	18°	10°
Lowest	6°	4°	7°	2°
Rain days	7	10	11	9
JULY				
Highest	29°	19°	31°	23°
Lowest	16°	11°	18°	14°
Rain days	7	9	3	12
OCTOBER				
Highest	18°	14°	19°	8°
Lowest	6°	8°	10°	2°
Rain days	5	11	9	10

Highest = Average highest daily temperature in °C
Lowest = Average lowest daily temperature in °C
Rain days = Average number of days with recorded precipitation

Source : World Weather Information Service

PASSPORTS AND VISAS

Nationals of one country intending to travel to or pass through another country normally require a valid passport and will also require a visa unless a special visa-abolition agreement has been made between the countries concerned. The limit of stay permitted in each country is usually 3 months.

Applications for visas must be made on special consular forms, and in most cases one or more passport-size photographs are also required. Consuls usually make a charge for issuing a visa. Before issuing a transit visa, a consul normally requires to see the visa of the country of destination.

Applications for visas should be made well in advance of the date of travel to the local consulate of the country concerned.

The possession of a valid passport or visa does not necessarily grant the holder automatic access to all areas of the country to be visited. Certain countries have zones which are restricted or prohibited to foreign nationals.

CURRENCY CONVERSION

The information shown below is intended to be indicative only. Rates fluctuate from day to day and commercial exchange rates normally include a commission element.

Country	unit	1 EUR =	1 GBP =	1 USD =	100 JPY =
Euro zone (‡)	**euro**	**1.00**	**1.39**	**0.68**	**0.62**
Albania	lek	121.00	168.00	81.80	75.60
Belarus	rubl	3 190.00	4 430.00	2 150.00	1 990.00
Bosnia	marka	1.95	2.71	1.32	1.22
Bulgaria	lev	1.95	2.71	1.32	1.22
Croatia	kuna	7.33	10.20	4.95	4.58
Cyprus	pound	0.58	0.81	0.39	0.36
Czech Republic	koruna	26.70	37.20	18.10	16.70
Denmark	krone	7.45	10.40	5.04	4.66
Estonia	kroon	15.60	21.80	10.60	9.77
Hungary	forint	257.00	358.00	174.00	161.00
Iceland	krona	92.90	129.00	62.80	58.10
Latvia	lats	0.70	0.97	0.47	0.44
Lithuania	litas	3.45	4.80	2.33	2.16
Macedonia	denar	61.30	85.30	41.50	38.30
Malta §	lira	0.43	0.59	0.29	0.27
Moldova	leu	16.60	23.10	11.20	10.40
Norway	krone	8.05	11.20	5.44	5.03
Poland	złoty	3.69	5.13	2.49	2.30
Romania	leu nou	3.62	5.04	2.45	2.26
Russia	rubl	36.00	50.10	24.40	22.50
Serbia	dinar	81.00	113.00	54.80	50.60
Slovakia	koruna	33.60	46.70	22.70	21.00
Sweden	krona	9.32	13.00	6.30	5.83
Switzerland	franc	1.63	2.27	1.10	1.02
Turkey	yeni lira	1.77	2.47	1.20	1.11
Ukraine	hryvnya	7.47	10.40	5.05	4.67
United Kingdom	pound	0.72	1.00	0.49	0.45

‡ – Austria, Belgium, Finland, France, Germany, Greece, Ireland, Italy, Luxembourg, the Netherlands, Portugal, Slovenia, and Spain.
The euro is also legal tender in Andorra, Kosovo, Monaco, Montenegro, San Marino, and the Vatican City.

§ – Malta will adopt the euro from January 1, 2008.

METRIC CONVERSION TABLES

The Celsius system of temperature measurement, the metric system of distance measurement and the twenty-four hour clock are used throughout this book. The tables below give Fahrenheit, mile and twelve-hour clock equivalents.

TEMPERATURE

°C	°F
−20	−4
−15	5
−10	14
−5	23
0	32
5	41
10	50
15	59
20	68
25	77
30	86
35	95
40	104

Conversion formulae :
(°C x 9 / 5) + 32 = °F
(°F – 32) x 5 / 9 = °C

DISTANCE

km	miles	km	miles	km	miles
1	0.62	45	27.96	300	186.41
2	1.24	50	31.07	400	248.55
3	1.86	55	34.18	500	310.69
4	2.49	60	37.28	600	372.82
5	3.11	65	40.39	700	434.96
6	3.73	70	43.50	800	497.10
7	4.35	75	46.60	900	559.23
8	4.97	80	49.71	1000	621.37
9	5.59	85	52.82	1100	683.51
10	6.21	90	55.92	1200	745.65
15	9.32	95	59.03	1300	807.78
20	12.43	100	62.14	1400	869.92
25	15.53	125	77.67	1500	932.06
30	18.64	150	93.21	2000	1242.74
35	21.75	175	108.74	3000	1864.11
40	24.85	200	124.27	4000	2485.48

TIME

Midnight depart	=	0000
1 am	=	0100
5 am	=	0500
5.30 am	=	0530
11 am	=	1100
12 noon	=	1200
1 pm	=	1300
3.45 pm	=	1545
Midnight arrive	=	2400

GLOSSARY

🔑	FRANÇAIS	ITALIANO	DEUTSCH	ESPAÑOL
additional trains	d'autres trains	ulteriori treni	weitere Züge	otros trenes
also	[circule] aussi	[si effettua] anche	[verkehrt] auch	[circula] también
alteration	modification	variazione	Änderung	modificación
approximately	environ	circa	ungefähr	aproximadamente
arrival, arrives (a.)	arrivée, arrive	arrivo, arriva	Ankunft, kommt an	llegada, llega
and at the same minutes past each hour until	puis toutes les heures aux mêmes minutes jusqu'à	poi ai stessi minuti di ogni ora fino a	und so weiter im Takt bis	luego a los mismos minutos de cada hora hasta
calls at	s'arrête à	ferma a	hält in	efectúa parada en
certain	déterminé	certo	bestimmt	determinado
change at	changer à	cambiare a	umsteigen in	cambiar en
composition	composition	composizione	Zugbildung	composición
confirmation	confirmation	conferma	Bestätigung	confirmación
connection	correspondance, relation	coincidenza, relazione	Anschluss, Verbindung	correspondencia, enlace
conveys	comporte, achemine	ha in composizione	befördert, führt	lleva
daily	tous les jours	giornalmente	täglich	diariamente
delay	retard	ritardo	Verspätung	retraso
departure, departs (d.)	départ, part	partenza, parte	Abfahrt, fährt ab	salida, sale
earlier	plus tôt	più presto	früher	más temprano
engineering work	travaux de voie	lavori sul binario	Bauarbeiten	obras de vía
even / uneven dates	jours pairs / impairs	giorni pari / dispari	gerade / ungerade Daten	fechas pares / impares
every 30 minutes	toutes les 30 minutes	ogni 30 minuti	alle 30 Minuten	cada 30 minutos
except	sauf	escluso	außer	excepto
fast(er)	(plus) rapide	(più) rapido	schnell(er)	(más) rápido
for	pour	per	für	para
from Rennes	(en provenance) de Rennes	(proviene) da Rennes	von Rennes	(procede) de Rennes
from Jan. 15	à partir du 15 janvier	dal 15 di gennaio	vom 15. Januar (an)	desde el 15 de enero
hourly	toutes les heures	ogni ora	stündlich	cada hora
hours (hrs)	heures	ore	Stunden	horas
journey	voyage, trajet	viaggio, percorso	Reise	viaje, trayecto
journey time	temps de parcours	tempo di tragitto	Reisezeit	duración del recorrido
later	plus tard	più tardi	später	más tarde
may	peut, peuvent	può, possono	kann, können	puede(n)
minutes (mins)	minutes	minuti	Minuten	minutos
not	ne [circule] pas	non [si effettua]	[verkehrt] nicht	no [circula]
not available	pas disponible	non disponibile	nicht erhältlich	no disponible
on the dates shown in Table **81**	les jours indiqués dans le tableau **81**	nei giorni indicati nel quadro **81**	an den in der Tabelle **81** angegebene Daten	los días indicados en el cuadro **81**
only	seulement	esclusivamente	nur	sólo
operator	entreprise de transports	azienda di trasporto	Verkehrsunternehmen	empresa de transportes
other	autre	altro	andere	otros
runs	circule	circola, si effettua	verkehrt	circula
sailing	traversée	traversata	Überfahrt	travesía
ship	bateau, navire	nave, battello	Schiff	barco
stopping trains	trains omnibus	treni regionali	Nahverkehrszüge	trenes regionales
stops	s'arrête	ferma	hält	efectúa parada
subject to	sous réserve de	soggetto a	vorbehaltlich	sujeto a
summer	été	estate	Sommer	verano
supplement payable	avec supplément	con pagamento di supplemento	zuschlagpflichtig	con pago de suplemento
then	puis	poi	dann	luego
through train	train direct	treno diretto	durchgehender Zug	tren directo
timings	horaires	orari	Zeitangaben	horarios
to York	vers, à destination de York	(diretto) a York	nach York	(continúa) a York
to / until July 23	jusqu'au 23 juillet	fino al 23 di luglio	bis zum 23. Juli	hasta el día 23 de julio
to pick up	pour laisser monter	per viaggiatori in partenza	zum Zusteigen	para recoger viajeros
to set down	pour laisser descendre	per viaggiatori in arrivo	zum Aussteigen	para dejar viajeros
unless otherwise shown	sauf indication contraire	salvo indicazione contraria	sofern nicht anders angezeigt	salvo indicación contraria
valid	valable	valido	gültig	válido
when train **44** runs	lors de la circulation du train **44**	quando circola il treno **44**	beim Verkehren des Zuges **44**	cuando circula el tren **44**
winter	hiver	inverno	Winter	invierno

PICTOGRAMS

Information
Information
Renseignements
Información

Ticket office
Fahrkartenschalter
Guichet
Despacho de billetes

Luggage office
Gepäckaufbewahrung
Consigne
Consigna

Luggage lockers
Gepäckschließfächer
Consigne automatique
Taquillas de equipaje

Ladies
Damen
Dames
Señoras

Gentlemen
Herren
Hommes
Caballeros

Lost property
Fundbüro
Objets trouvés
Objetos perdidos

Bureau de change
Geldwechsel
Bureau de change
Cambio

Post office
Postamt
Poste
Correos

Telephone
Telefon
Téléphone
Teléfono

Restaurant
Restaurant
Restaurant
Restaurante

Buffet
Buffet
Buffet
Comedor

Meeting point
Treffpunkt
Point de rencontre
Lugar de reunión

Entrance
Eingang
Entrée
Entrada

Exit
Ausgang
Sortie
Salida

Bus
Bus
Autobus
Autobús

Boat
Schiff
Bateau
Barco

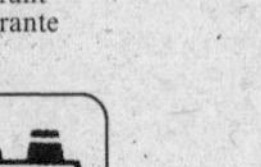

Tram
Straßenbahn
Tramway
Tranvía

INDEX OF PLACES

by table number

🚆 Connection by train from the nearest station shown in this timetable.
⛴ Connection by boat from the nearest station shown in this timetable.
🚌 Connection by bus from the nearest station shown in this timetable.
10/355 Consult both indicated tables to find the best connecting services.

CRUISE TRAINS

The services shown in the European Rail Timetable are the regular scheduled services of the railway companies concerned. However, a number of specialised operators also run luxurious cruise trains taking several days to complete their journey. Overnight accommodation is provided either on the train or in hotels. Cruise trains are bookable only through the operating company or its appointed agents and normal rail tickets are not valid on these trains. A selection of operators is shown below.

Al Andalús Expreso: 4-day luxury train journeys through Andalucía. UK agents: Cox and Kings Travel Ltd, Gordon House, 10 Greencoat Place, London SW1P 1PH; ✆ +44 (0) 20 7873 5000, fax +44 (0) 20 7630 6038. Also: Mundi Color Holidays, 276 Vauxhall Bridge Rd, London SW1V 1BE, ✆ +44 (0) 20 7828 6021, fax +44 (0) 20 7963 4430. Website: www.alandalusexpreso.com.

The Royal Scotsman: luxury tours of Scotland starting from Edinburgh. Operator: The Royal Scotsman, 46a Constitution St., Edinburgh EH6 6RS, UK; ✆ (enquiries) +44 (0) 131 555 1344, (reservations) +44 (0) 131 555 1021, fax +44 (0) 131 555 1345. Website: www.royalscotsman.com

El Transcantábrico: 1000-km 8-day rail cruise along Spain's northern coast. Operator: El Transcantábrico, Plaza de los Ferroviarios, s/n. 33012 Oviedo, Spain. ✆ +34 985 981 711, fax +34 985 981 710. Website: www.transcantabrico.feve.es

Trans-Siberian Express: Tours by private hotel train along the Trans-Siberian Railway. Operator: The Trans-Siberian Express Company, GW Travel Ltd, Denzell House, Denzell Gardens, Dunham Road, Altrincham WA14 4QF, England. ✆ +44 (0)161 928 9410, fax +44 (0)161 941 6101. Website: www.gwtravel.co.uk. USA agent: MIR Corporation, 85 South Washington Street, Suite 210, Seattle, Washington 98104, USA; ✆ +1 (206) 624 7289, fax +1 (206) 624 7360. Website: www.mircorp.com/tsx.html

Venice Simplon-Orient-Express: This well-known luxury train runs once or twice weekly from late March to early November, mostly on its established London - Paris - Venezia route. Operator: Venice Simplon-Orient-Express Ltd, Sea Containers House, 20 Upper Ground, London SE1 9PF, United Kingdom; ✆ +44 (0) 20 7805 5060, fax +44 (0) 20 7805 5908.

For further details of these and other operators, see our annual Cruise Trains and Rail Holidays feature in the March edition

TOURIST AND HERITAGE RAILWAYS

A small number of the most popular lines are included in each edition of the timetable. However, for a much greater selection see the ***Tourist Railways*** feature which appears in our July edition each year. This includes operating dates, contact details, location, and in many cases a detailed timetable.

LIST OF ADVERTISERS

FFESTINIOG TRAVEL	inside back cover	INFORAIL	60, 142, 293
GREEK ISLAND HOPPING	522	THOMAS COOK PUBLISHING	543-544
HOSTELLING INTERNATIONAL	inside back cover	TRAINSEUROPE LIMITED	inside front cover

CITY
STATION LOCATION
PLANS

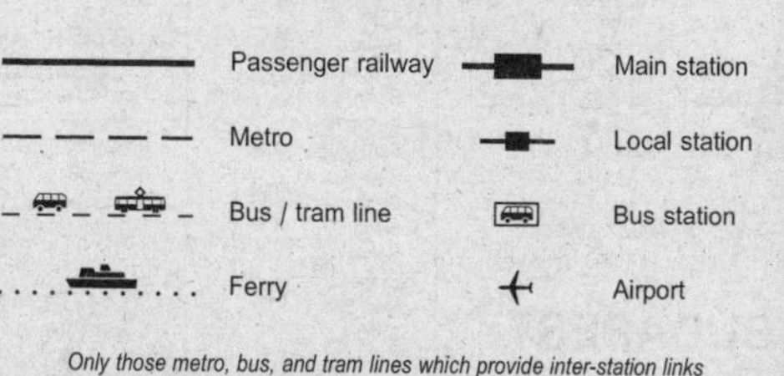
Passenger railway
Main station
Metro
Local station
Bus / tram line
Bus station
Ferry
Airport
Only those metro, bus, and tram lines which provide inter-station links or connect outlying main stations to the city centre are shown.

AMSTERDAM
1 km
Sloterdijk
CENTRAAL
Muiderpoort
Lelylaan
Amstel
14 km
Zuid WTC
RAI

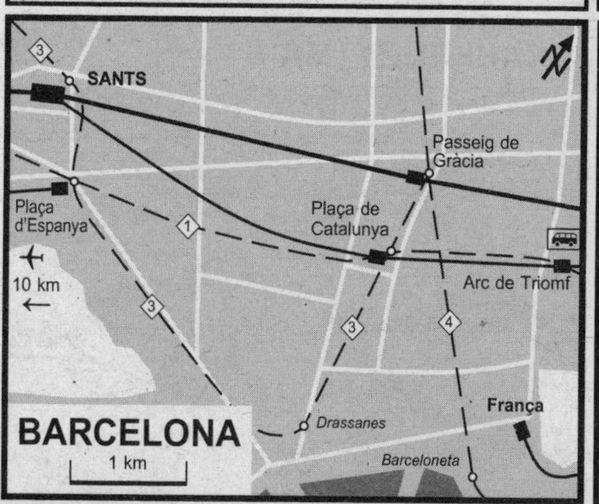
SANTS
Passeig de Gràcia
Plaça d'Espanya
Plaça de Catalunya
10 km
Arc de Triomf
Drassanes
França
BARCELONA
1 km
Barceloneta

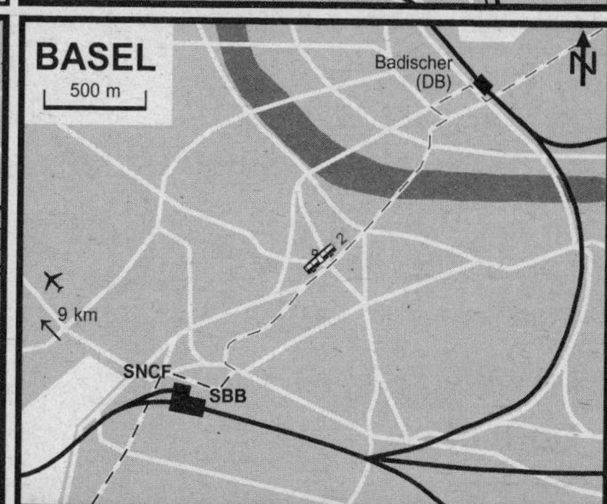
BASEL
500 m
Badischer (DB)
9 km
SNCF
SBB

BELFAST
250 m
Ferry Terminal
City
Laganside
International
26 km
City Hall
Europa
Great Victoria Street
CENTRAL
City Hospital
Botanic

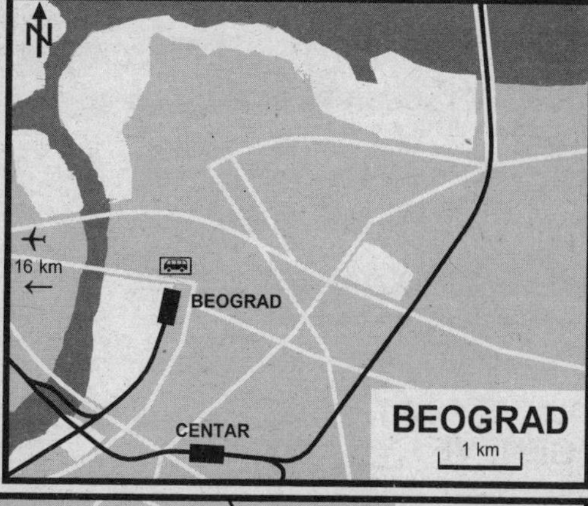
16 km
BEOGRAD
CENTAR
BEOGRAD
1 km

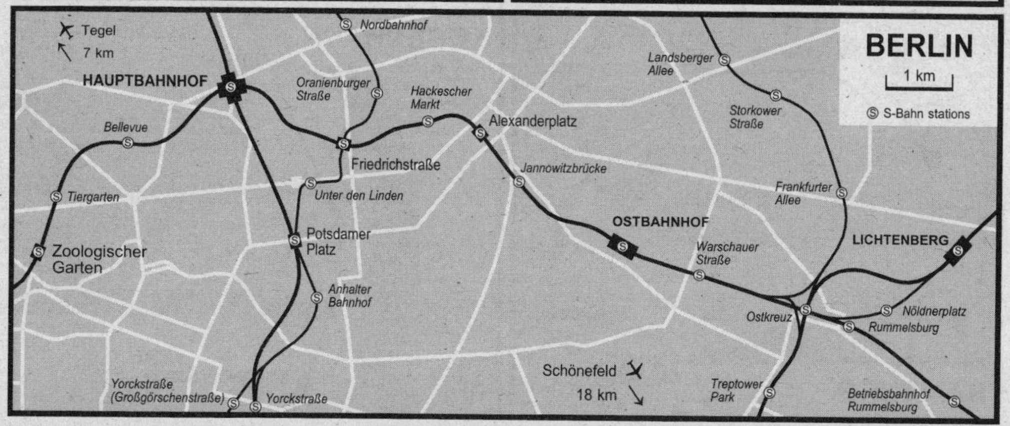
Tegel
7 km
HAUPTBAHNHOF
Nordbahnhof
Oranienburger Straße
Hackescher Markt
Alexanderplatz
Landsberger Allee
Storkower Straße
BERLIN
1 km
S-Bahn stations
Bellevue
Friedrichstraße
Jannowitzbrücke
Tiergarten
Unter den Linden
Frankfurter Allee
OSTBAHNHOF
Potsdamer Platz
Warschauer Straße
LICHTENBERG
Zoologischer Garten
Anhalter Bahnhof
Ostkreuz
Nöldnerplatz
Rummelsburg
Schönefeld
18 km
Yorckstraße (Großgörschenstraße)
Yorckstraße
Treptower Park
Betriebsbahnhof Rummelsburg

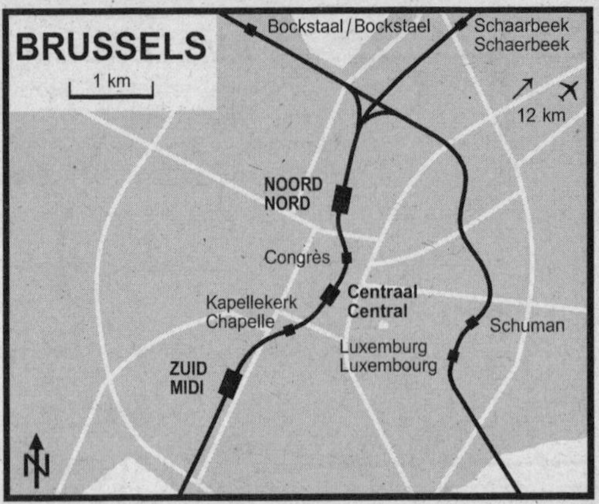
BRUSSELS
1 km
Bockstaal / Bockstael
Schaarbeek
Schaerbeek
12 km
NOORD
NORD
Congrès
Centraal
Central
Kapellekerk
Chapelle
Schuman
Luxemburg
Luxembourg
ZUID
MIDI

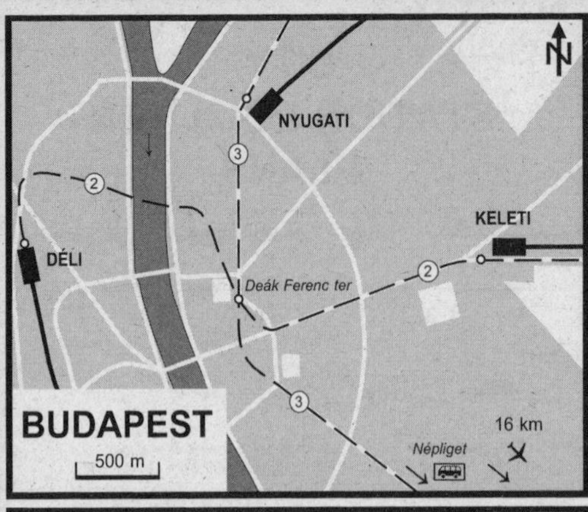
NYUGATI
KELETI
DÉLI
Deák Ferenc ter
BUDAPEST
500 m
16 km
Népliget

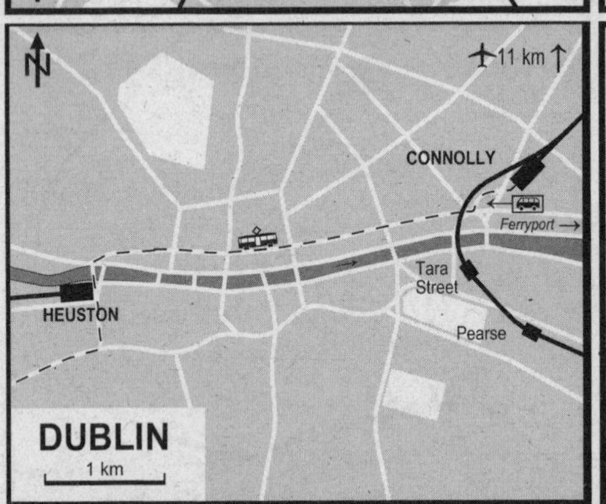
11 km
CONNOLLY
Ferryport
Tara
Street
HEUSTON
Pearse
DUBLIN
1 km

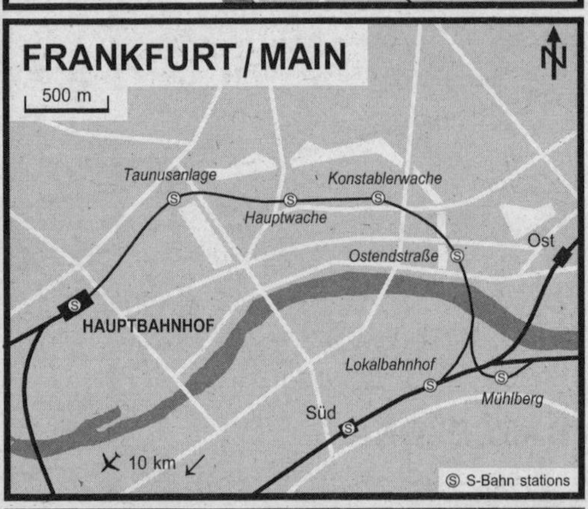
FRANKFURT / MAIN
500 m
Taunusanlage
Konstablerwache
Hauptwache
Ostendstraße
Ost
HAUPTBAHNHOF
Lokalbahnhof
Mühlberg
Süd
10 km
S-Bahn stations

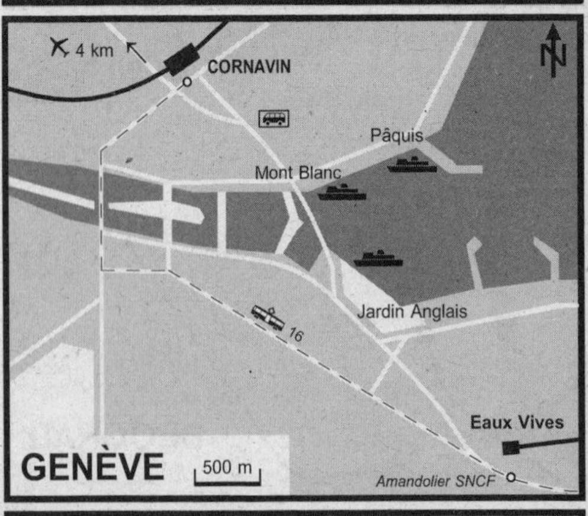
4 km
CORNAVIN
Pâquis
Mont Blanc
Jardin Anglais
16
Eaux Vives
GENÈVE
500 m
Amandolier SNCF

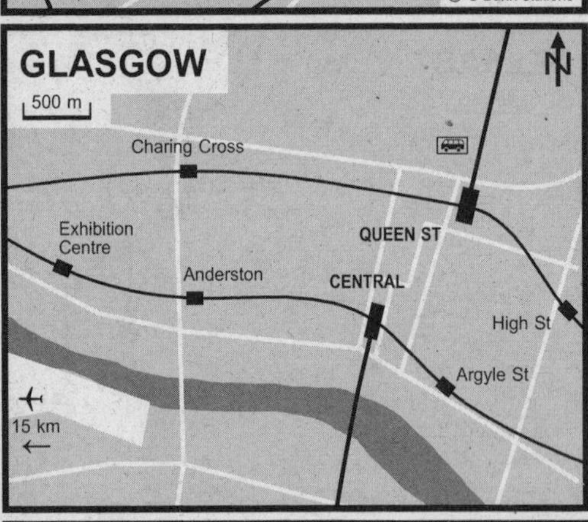
GLASGOW
500 m
Charing Cross
Exhibition
Centre
QUEEN ST
Anderston
CENTRAL
High St
Argyle St
15 km

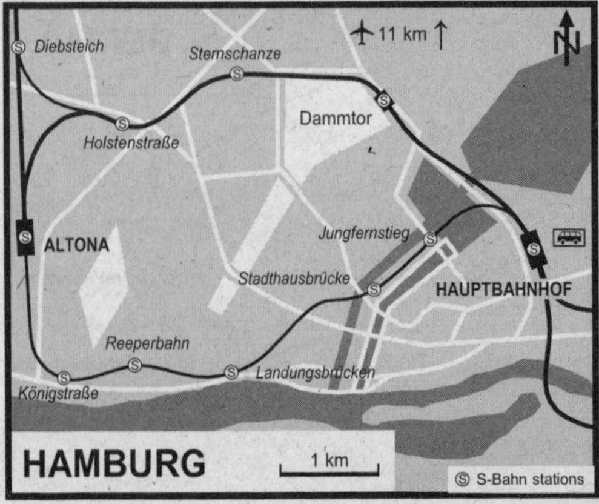
Diebsteich
Sternschanze
11 km
Dammtor
Holstenstraße
ALTONA
Jungfernstieg
Stadthausbrücke
HAUPTBAHNHOF
Reeperbahn
Landungsbrücken
Königstraße
HAMBURG
1 km
S-Bahn stations

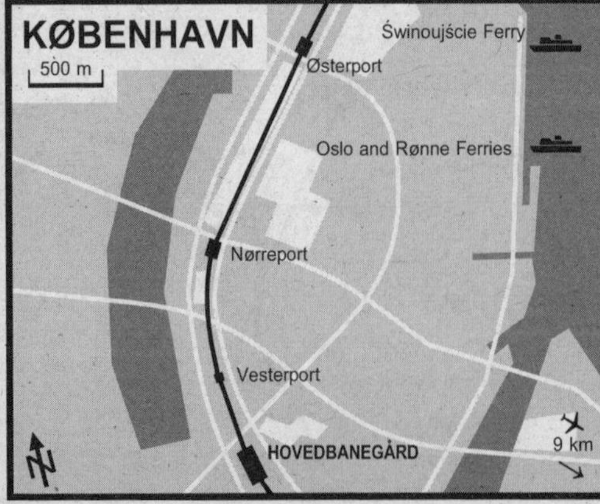
KØBENHAVN
500 m
Świnoujście Ferry
Østerport
Oslo and Rønne Ferries
Nørreport
Vesterport
HOVEDBANEGÅRD
9 km

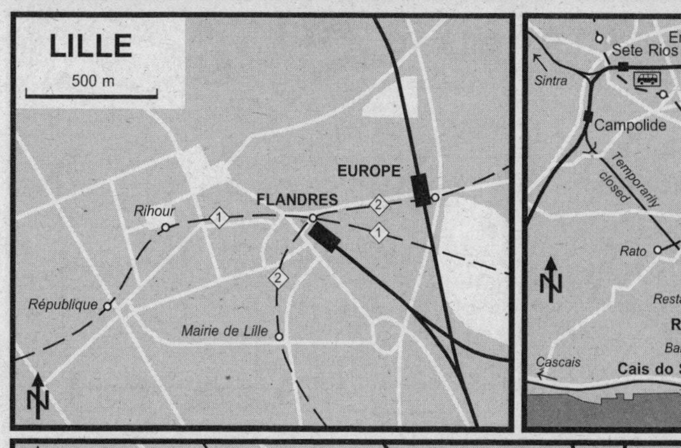
LILLE
500 m
EUROPE
FLANDRES
Rihour
République
Mairie de Lille

Entrecampos
Sete Rios
Areeiro
Roma-Areeiro
Sintra
Oriente
Roma
Campolide
Alameda
Temporarily closed
Oriente
Marquês de Pompal
Rato
Restauradores
Rossio
SANTA APOLÓNIA
Baixa-Chiado
Rossio
Cascais
Cais do Sodré
Terreiro do Paço
1 km
Barreiro
LISBOA

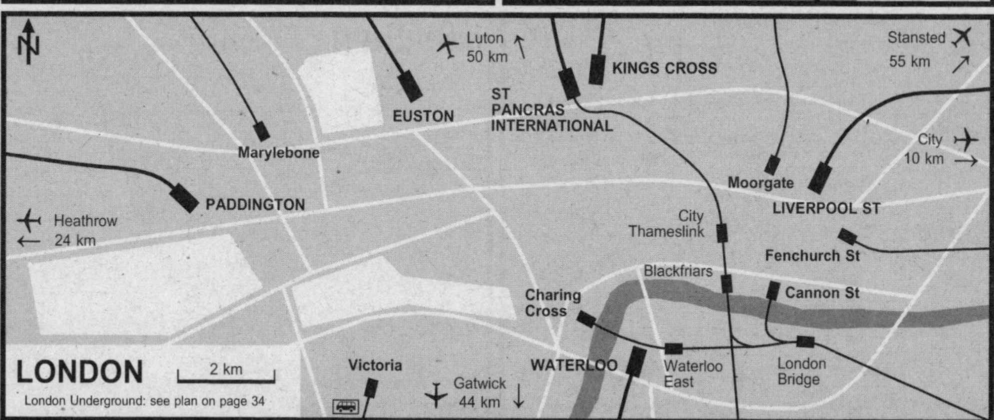
Luton 50 km
Stansted 55 km
KINGS CROSS
EUSTON
ST PANCRAS INTERNATIONAL
Marylebone
City 10 km
Moorgate
PADDINGTON
LIVERPOOL ST
Heathrow 24 km
City Thameslink
Fenchurch St
Blackfriars
Charing Cross
Cannon St
LONDON
2 km
Victoria
WATERLOO
Waterloo East
London Bridge
Gatwick 44 km
London Underground: see plan on page 34

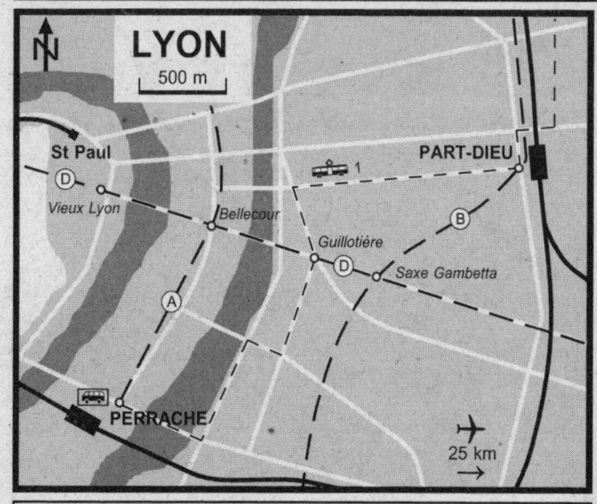
LYON
500 m
St Paul
PART-DIEU
Vieux Lyon
Bellecour
Guillotière
Saxe Gambetta
PERRACHE
25 km

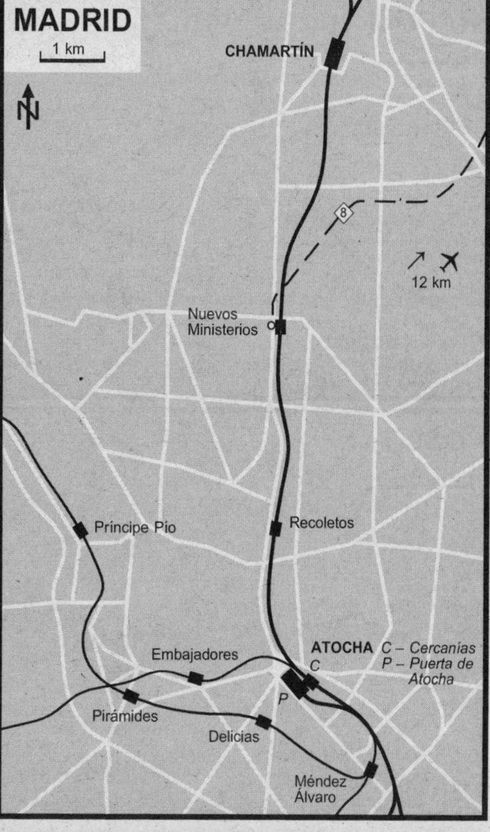
MADRID
1 km
CHAMARTÍN
12 km
Nuevos Ministerios
Principe Pio
Recoletos
ATOCHA
C – Cercanías
P – Puerta de Atocha
Embajadores
Pirámides
Delicias
Méndez Álvaro

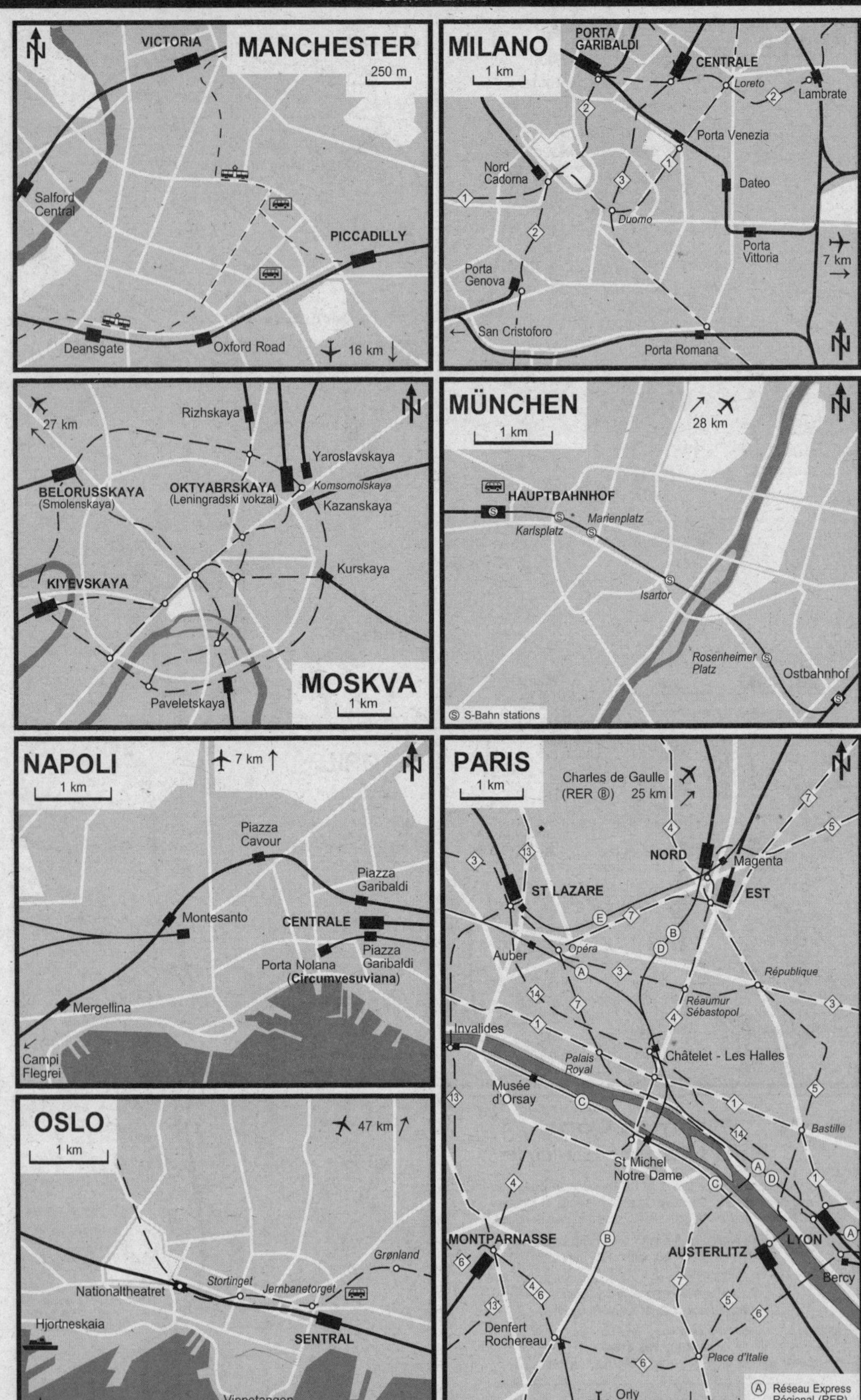
MANCHESTER
250 m
VICTORIA
Salford Central
PICCADILLY
Deansgate
Oxford Road
16 km
MILANO
1 km
PORTA GARIBALDI
CENTRALE
Loreto
Lambrate
Porta Venezia
Nord Cadorna
Dateo
Duomo
Porta Vittoria
7 km
Porta Genova
San Cristoforo
Porta Romana
27 km
Rizhskaya
Yaroslavskaya
Komsomolskaya
BELORUSSKAYA
(Smolenskaya)
OKTYABRSKAYA
(Leningradski vokzal)
Kazanskaya
Kurskaya
KIYEVSKAYA
Paveletskaya
MOSKVA
1 km
MÜNCHEN
1 km
28 km
HAUPTBAHNHOF
Marienplatz
Karlsplatz
Isartor
Rosenheimer Platz
Ostbahnhof
S-Bahn stations
NAPOLI
1 km
7 km
Piazza Cavour
Piazza Garibaldi
Montesanto
CENTRALE
Piazza Garibaldi
Porta Nolana
(Circumvesuviana)
Mergellina
Campi Flegrei
OSLO
1 km
47 km
Grønland
Stortinget
Jernbanetorget
Nationaltheatret
Hjortneskaia
SENTRAL
Vippetangen
PARIS
1 km
Charles de Gaulle
(RER B) 25 km
NORD
Magenta
ST LAZARE
EST
Opéra
Auber
République
Réaumur Sébastopol
Invalides
Palais Royal
Châtelet - Les Halles
Musée d'Orsay
Bastille
St Michel Notre Dame
MONTPARNASSE
AUSTERLITZ
LYON
Bercy
Denfert Rochereau
Place d'Italie
Orly
(RER B C)
15 km
Réseau Express Régional (RER)
Métro urbain
(selected lines)

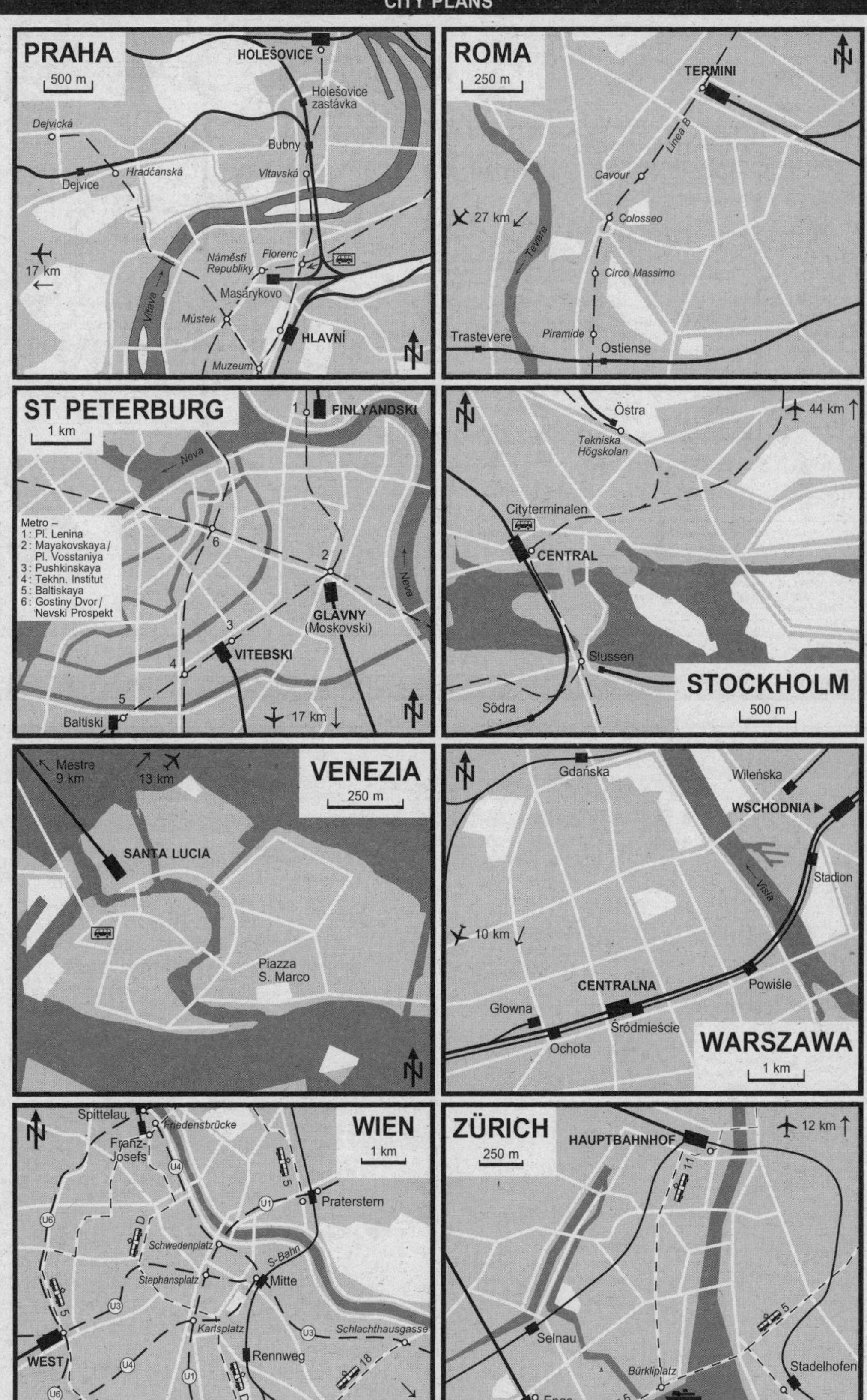
PRAHA
500 m
HOLEŠOVICE
Holešovice zastávka
Dejvická
Bubny
Hradčanská
Dejvice
Vltavská
17 km
Náměsti Republiky
Florenc
Masarykovo
Vltava
Můstek
HLAVNÍ
Muzeum
ROMA
250 m
TERMINI
Linea B
Cavour
27 km
Colosseo
Tevere
Circo Massimo
Trastevere
Piramide
Ostiense
ST PETERBURG
1 km
FINLYANDSKI
Neva
Metro –
1: Pl. Lenina
2: Mayakovskaya / Pl. Vosstaniya
3: Pushkinskaya
4: Tekhn. Institut
5: Baltiskaya
6: Gostiny Dvor / Nevski Prospekt
GLAVNY (Moskovski)
VITEBSKI
Baltiski
17 km
Östra
44 km
Tekniska Högskolan
Cityterminalen
CENTRAL
Slussen
Södra
STOCKHOLM
500 m
Mestre 9 km
13 km
VENEZIA
250 m
SANTA LUCIA
Piazza S. Marco
Gdańska
Wileńska
WSCHODNIA
Stadion
Wisła
10 km
CENTRALNA
Powiśle
Głowna
Śródmieście
Ochota
WARSZAWA
1 km
Spittelau
Friedensbrücke
Franz-Josefs
WIEN
1 km
U4
U1
Praterstern
U6
Schwedenplatz
S-Bahn
Stephansplatz
Mitte
U3
Karlsplatz
Schlachthausgasse
WEST
Rennweg
17 km
Südtiroler Platz
Längenfeldg.
SÜD
ZÜRICH
250 m
HAUPTBAHNHOF
12 km
Selnau
Bürkliplatz
Stadelhofen
Enge

LONDON UNDERGROUND

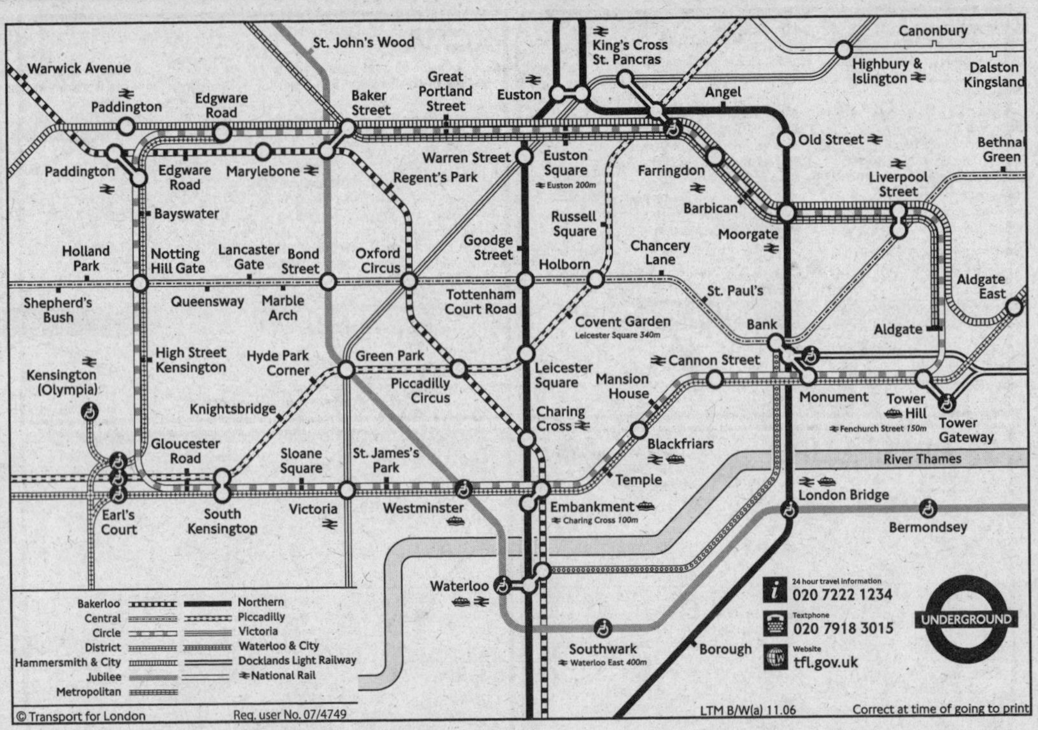

St. John's Wood
King's Cross St. Pancras
Canonbury
Warwick Avenue
Highbury & Islington
Dalston Kingsland
Paddington
Edgware Road
Baker Street
Great Portland Street
Euston
Angel
Old Street
Bethnal Green
Paddington
Edgware Road
Marylebone
Warren Street
Euston Square (Euston 200m)
Regent's Park
Farringdon
Liverpool Street
Barbican
Bayswater
Russell Square
Moorgate
Goodge Street
Chancery Lane
Holland Park
Notting Hill Gate
Lancaster Gate
Bond Street
Oxford Circus
Holborn
Aldgate East
St. Paul's
Shepherd's Bush
Queensway
Marble Arch
Tottenham Court Road
Covent Garden (Leicester Square 340m)
Bank
Aldgate
High Street Kensington
Hyde Park Corner
Green Park
Cannon Street
Kensington (Olympia)
Piccadilly Circus
Leicester Square
Mansion House
Monument
Tower Hill (Fenchurch Street 150m)
Tower Gateway
Knightsbridge
Charing Cross
Blackfriars
Gloucester Road
Sloane Square
St. James's Park
River Thames
Temple
London Bridge
Earl's Court
South Kensington
Victoria
Westminster
Embankment (Charing Cross 100m)
Bermondsey
Waterloo
Southwark (Waterloo East 400m)
Borough

Bakerloo
Central
Circle
District
Hammersmith & City
Jubilee
Metropolitan
Northern
Piccadilly
Victoria
Waterloo & City
Docklands Light Railway
National Rail

24 hour travel information 020 7222 1234
Textphone 020 7918 3015
Website tfl.gov.uk

UNDERGROUND

LTM B/W(a) 11.06
Correct at time of going to print

INTERNATIONAL CAR-CARRYING TRAIN TERMINALS

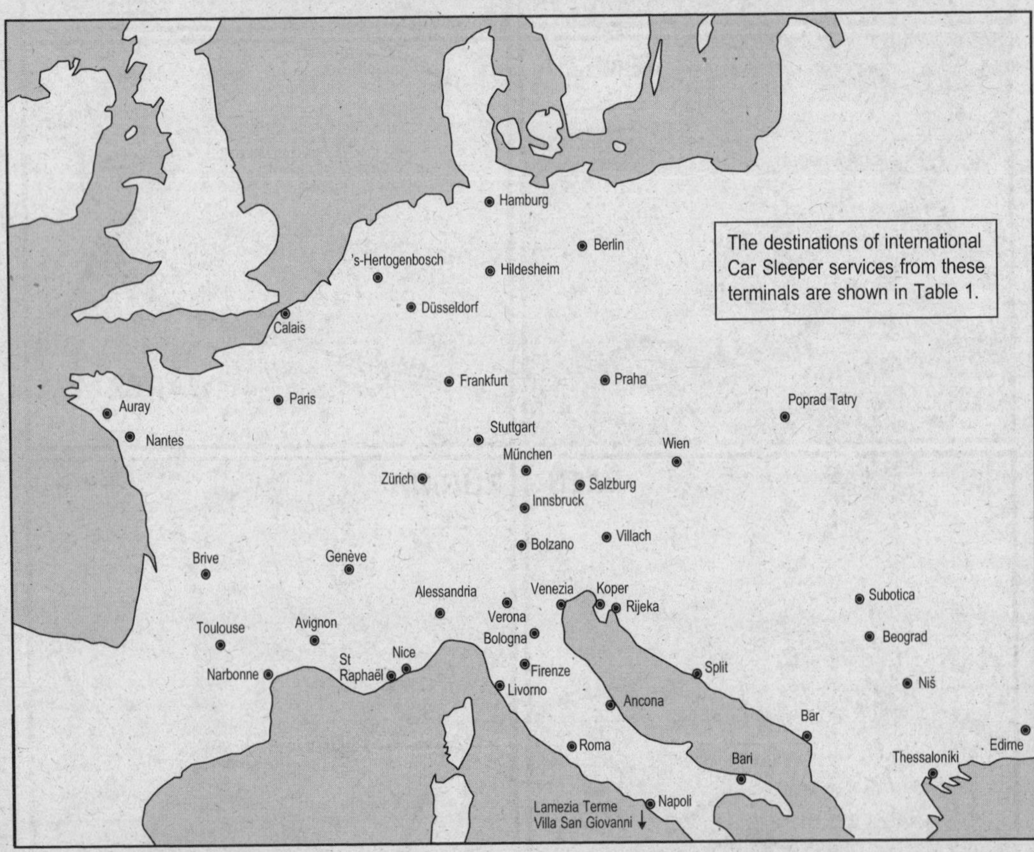

Hamburg
Berlin
's-Hertogenbosch
Hildesheim
Düsseldorf
Calais
Frankfurt
Praha
Poprad Tatry
Auray
Paris
Nantes
Stuttgart
Wien
München
Zürich
Salzburg
Innsbruck
Bolzano
Villach
Brive
Genève
Alessandria
Venezia
Koper
Rijeka
Subotica
Verona
Toulouse
Avignon
Bologna
Beograd
Nice
St Raphaël
Narbonne
Firenze
Split
Livorno
Niš
Ancona
Bar
Roma
Edirne
Bari
Thessaloniki
Napoli
Lamezia Terme
Villa San Giovanni ↓

The destinations of international Car Sleeper services from these terminals are shown in Table 1.

AUTO-TRAIN, AUTOREISEZÜGE, MOTORAIL

Car-carrying trains are composed of special wagons or vans for the conveyance of motorcars usually with sleeping cars and couchettes enabling the driver and passengers to travel overnight in comfort in the same train. Some services (particularly in France) convey vehicles separately allowing passengers a choice of trains for their own journey. Some shorter distance services run by day and convey seating coaches.

Cars are often loaded on the trains at separate stations from the passenger station and may be loaded some time before the passenger train departs. International car-carrying trains (including services from Calais) are shown in Table **1**, Domestic car-carrying trains (including services from Genève) in Table **2**. Some services also carry passengers without cars.

Details of Channel Tunnel shuttle services may be found on page 46. Austrian and Swiss alpine tunnel car-carrying trains are shown in the relevant country section - see pages 455 and 260 respectively for details.

Readers should be careful to check that dates refer to current schedules, as old dates may be left in the table until such time as current information is received. Loading and train times may vary on some dates, but will be confirmed by the agent when booking.

Full details of days and dates of running are shown only in the February, April, June, August, October and December editions of the European Rail Timetable. A summary of services is shown in other editions.

Some services shown in Table **1** are operated by organisations other than national railway companies. Contact details for these are:
Services from Belgium: The Train Company, Domplein 11, NL-3512 JD Utrecht; ✆ +31 (0)30 232 04 30, fax +31 (0)30 232 04 39. *Services will commence summer 2007.*
Services from Germany: DB AutoZug, (UK booking centre); ✆ 08718 80 80 66.
Services from Netherlands: Euro-Express-Traincharter, Singelstraat 1a, 2613 EM Delft; ✆ +31 (0)15 213 36 36.
Services from Calais: French Motorail (Rail Europe), 178 Piccadilly, London W1; ✆ 08702 415 415.
Certain Eastern European services (see table for details):

SEE MAP PAGE 34

INTERNATIONAL CAR-CARRYING TRAINS 1

ALESSANDRIA to

DÜSSELDORF: ① Mar. 17-31, 2008.
Alessandria loading time not advised, depart 1840, Düsseldorf Hbf arrive 0840.
Train **13378**: 🛏 1,2 cl., 🛌 2 cl. and ✖.

HAMBURG: ① Mar. 17-31, 2008.
Alessandria loading time not advised, depart 1840, Hamburg Altona arrive 1301.
Train **13378**: 🛏 1,2 cl., 🛌 2 cl. and ✖.

ANCONA to

WIEN: ⑥ June 2 - Sept. 8, 2007.
Ancona load 1530 - 1630, depart 1705, Wien Süd arrive 0801.
Train **1134**: 🛏 1,2 cl., 🛌 2 cl. and (12).

AVIGNON to

Loading at Avignon Sud (🚌 connection to Centre).

BERLIN: ① Apr. 9 - Oct. 29, 2007.
Timings not advised.
🛏 1,2 cl., 🛌 2 cl. and ✖.

CALAIS: ⑥ May 17 - July 19; ①⑥ July 21 - Aug. 25; ⑥ Aug. 30 - Sept. 13, 2008.
Avignon load 1730 - 2000, depart 2227, Calais arrive 0948.
🛌 and 🍸.
Operator: French Motorail (see table heading).

DÜSSELDORF: ① May 7 - Oct. 29, 2007.
Timings not advised.
🛏 1,2 cl., 🛌 2 cl. and ✖.

HAMBURG: ④ Apr. 12 - Oct. 18, 2007.
Timings not advised.
🛏 1,2 cl., 🛌 2 cl. and ✖.

's-HERTOGENBOSCH: ⑥ June 9 - Sept. 1, 2007.
Avignon Sud loading time not advised, depart 1911, s'-Hertogenbosch arrive 0802.
Train **1402/3**: 🛏 1,2 cl., 🛌 2 cl. and ✖.
Operator: Euro-Express-Traincharter (see table heading).

HILDESHEIM: ⑥ Apr. 7 - Oct. 27, 2007.
Timings not advised.
🛏 1,2 cl., 🛌 2 cl. and ✖.

BAR to

BEOGRAD: daily.
Bar loading times not advised, depart 2200, Beograd arrive 0650. *Also day train in summer.*
Train **9610**: 🛏 1,2 cl. and 🛌 1,2 cl.

SUBOTICA: June 21 - Sept. 2, 2008.
Timings not advised.
Train **436**: 🛌 2 cl. and ✖.

BARI to

ZÜRICH: ⑥ June 9 - Oct. 20, 2007.
Bari load 2005 - 2105, depart 2205, Zürich Altstetten arrive 1251.
Train **1388**: 🛏 1,2 cl., 🛌 2 cl. and (12).

BEOGRAD to

BAR: daily.
Beograd loading times not advised, depart 2310, Bar arrive 0831. *Also day train in summer.*
Train **9611**: 🛏 1,2 cl. and 🛌 1,2 cl.

BERLIN to

AVIGNON: ⑦ Apr. 8 - Oct. 28, 2007.
Timings not advised.
🛏 1,2 cl., 🛌 2 cl. and ✖.

BOLZANO: ⑤ Apr. 6 - Oct. 26; ⑤ Dec. 21, 2007 - Mar. 28, 2008.
Berlin Wannsee load 1840 - 1910, depart 2050, Bolzano arrive 0912.
Train **13305**: 🛏 1,2 cl., 🛌 2 cl. and ✖.

BERLIN (continued) to

INNSBRUCK: ⑤ Dec. 21, 2007 - Mar. 28, 2008.
Berlin Wannsee load 1910 - 2000, depart 2050, Innsbruck arrive 0629.
Train **13305**: 🛏 1,2 cl., 🛌 2 cl. and ✖.

NARBONNE: ⑦ Apr. 8 - Oct. 28, 2007.
Timings not advised.
🛏 1,2 cl., 🛌 2 cl. and ✖.

SALZBURG: ③ May 16 - Oct. 10; ⑤ Dec. 21, 2007 - Mar. 28, 2008.
Berlin Wannsee load 1915 - 1945, depart 2111, Salzburg Hbf arrive 0719.
Train **13395**: 🛏 1,2 cl., 🛌 2 cl. and ✖.

VERONA: ⑤ Apr. 6 - Oct. 26, 2007.
Timings not advised.
🛏 1,2 cl., 🛌 2 cl. and ✖.

VILLACH: ③ May 16 - Oct. 10, 2007.
Timings not advised.
🛏 1,2 cl., 🛌 2 cl. and ✖.

WIEN: daily until Mar. 31, 2008.
Berlin Wannsee load 1900 - 1930, depart 2029, Wien Westbf arrive 0906.
Train **429**: 🛏 1,2 cl. and 🛌 2 cl.

BOLOGNA to

's-HERTOGENBOSCH: ⑥ June 7 - Sept. 6, 2008.
Timings not advised.
🛏 1,2 cl., 🛌 2 cl. and ✖.
Operator: Euro-Express-Traincharter (see table heading).

BOLZANO to

German services may be bookable only in Germany.

BERLIN: ⑥ Apr. 7 - Oct. 27; ⑥ Dec. 22, 2007 - Mar. 29, 2008.
Bolzano load 1700 - 1745, depart 1905, Berlin Wannsee arrive 0852.
Train **13304**: 🛏 1,2 cl., 🛌 2 cl. and ✖.

DÜSSELDORF: ①④⑥ June 18 - Oct. 1; ⑥ Oct. 6 - 27; ⑥ Dec. 22, 2007 - Mar. 29, 2008 (also Oct. 8, 15, Dec. 27, Jan. 3).
Bolzano load 1500 - 1545, depart 1656, Düsseldorf Hbf arrive 0625.
Train **13324**: 🛏 1,2 cl., 🛌 2 cl. and ✖.

HAMBURG: ①④⑥ June 18 - Oct. 1; ⑥ Oct. 6 - 27; ⑥ Dec. 22, 2007 - Mar. 29, 2008 (also Oct. 8, 15; not Dec. 29).
Timings not advised.
🛏 1,2 cl., 🛌 2 cl. and ✖.

HILDESHEIM: ⑥ Apr. 7 - 28; ①⑥ May 5 - Oct. 20, 2007 (also Oct. 27).
Timings not advised.
🛏 1,2 cl., 🛌 2 cl. and ✖.

BRIVE to

CALAIS: ⑥ May 17 - July 19; ①⑥ July 21 - Aug. 25; ⑥ Aug. 30 - Sept. 13, 2008.
Brive load 1700 - 2100, depart 2250, Calais arrive 0735.
🛌 and 🍸.
Operator: French Motorail (see table heading).

CALAIS to

AVIGNON: ⑤ May 16 - July 18; ⑤⑦ July 20 - Aug. 24; ⑤ Aug. 29 - Sept. 12, 2008.
Calais load 1540 - 1740, depart 1805, Avignon arrive 0542.
🛌 and 🍸.
Operator: French Motorail (see table heading).

BRIVE: ⑤ May 16 - July 18; ⑤⑦ July 20 - Aug. 24; ⑤ Aug. 29 - Sept. 12, 2008.
Calais load 1815 - 2010, depart 2040, Brive arrive 0620.
🛌 and 🍸.
Operator: French Motorail (see table heading).

CALAIS (continued) to

NARBONNE: ⑤ May 16 - July 18; ⑤⑦ July 20 - Aug. 24; ⑤ Aug. 29 - Sept. 12, 2008.
Calais load 1815 - 2010, depart 2040, Narbonne arrive 1011.
🛌 and 🍸.
Operator: French Motorail (see table heading).

NICE: ⑤ May 16 - July 18; ⑤⑦ July 20 - Aug. 24; ⑤ Aug. 29 - Sept. 12, 2008.
Calais load 1540 - 1740, depart 1805, Nice arrive 0957.
🛌 and 🍸.
Operator: French Motorail (see table heading).

ST. RAPHAËL: ⑤ May 16 - July 18; ⑤⑦ July 20 - Aug. 24; ⑤ Aug. 29 - Sept. 12, 2008.
Calais load 1540 - 1740, depart 1805, St. Raphaël arrive 0909.
🛌 and 🍸.
Operator: French Motorail (see table heading).

TOULOUSE: ⑤ May 16 - July 18; ⑤⑦ July 20 - Aug. 24; ⑤ Aug. 29 - Sept. 12, 2008.
Calais load 1815 - 2010, depart 2040, Toulouse arrive 0833.
🛌 and 🍸.
Operator: French Motorail (see table heading).

DÜSSELDORF to

ALESSANDRIA: ⑦ Mar. 16 - 30, 2008.
Düsseldorf Hbf load 1640 - 1610, depart 1654, Alessandria 0745.
Train **13379**: 🛏 1,2 cl., 🛌 2 cl. and ✖.

AVIGNON: ⑦ May 6 - Oct. 28, 2007.
Timings not advised.
🛏 1,2 cl., 🛌 2 cl. and ✖.

BOLZANO: ⑤ Oct. 5 - 26; ⑤ Dec. 21, 2007 - Mar. 28, 2008 (also Oct. 7, 14, Dec. 19, 26, Jan. 2).
Düsseldorf Hbf load 1930 - 1950, depart 2102, Bolzano arrive 1000.
Train **13325**: 🛏 1,2 cl., 🛌 2 cl. and ✖.

INNSBRUCK: ③ May 2 - Oct. 17; ⑤ Dec. 21, 2007 - Mar. 28, 2008 (also Dec. 19, 26, Jan. 2).
Düsseldorf load 1950 - 2010, depart 2102, Innsbruck arrive 0720.
Train **13325**: 🛏 1,2 cl., 🛌 2 cl. and ✖.

LIVORNO: ⑦ May 6 - Oct. 7, 2007.
Timings not advised.
🛏 1,2 cl., 🛌 2 cl. and ✖.

NARBONNE: ③⑤ Apr. 6 - Oct. 19; Nov. 4, 18, Dec. 2, 16, 2007, Jan. 6, 20, Feb. 3, 17; ⑦ Mar. 2 - 30, 2008 (also Oct. 26).
Düsseldorf Hbf load 1440 - 1510, depart 1554, Narbonne arrive 1008.
Train **1211/1411**: 🛏 1,2 cl., 🛌 2 cl. and ✖.

RIJEKA: ⑤ Apr. 6 - Oct. 26, 2007.
Timings not advised.
🛏 1,2 cl., 🛌 2 cl. and ✖.

ST. RAPHAËL: ⑦ May 6 - Oct. 28, 2007.
Timings not advised.
🛏 1,2 cl., 🛌 2 cl. and ✖.

SALZBURG: ⑦ Apr. 1 - Oct. 14; ⑤ Dec. 21, 2007 - Mar. 28, 2008 (also Dec. 19, 26, Jan. 2).
Düsseldorf Hbf load 1750 - 1810, depart 1854, Salzburg Hbf arrive 0551.
Train **13315**: 🛏 1,2 cl., 🛌 2 cl. and ✖.

VERONA: ⑤ Apr. 6 - 27; ⑤⑦ May 4 - Oct. 14, 2007 (also Oct. 19, 26).
Timings not advised.
🛏 1,2 cl., 🛌 2 cl. and ✖.

DÜSSELDORF (continued) to

VILLACH: ⑤ Oct. 5 - 26; ⑤ Dec. 21, 2007 - Mar. 28, 2008 (also Dec. 19, 26, Jan. 2).
Düsseldorf Hbf load 1730 - 1750, depart 1854, Villach Ost arrive 0934.
Train **13315**: 🛏 1,2 cl., 🛌 2 cl. and 🍴.

WIEN: daily until Mar. 31, 2008.
Düsseldorf Hbf load 1900 - 1920, depart 2015, Wien Westbf arrive 0906.
Train **325/429**: 🛏 1,2 cl. and 🛌 2 cl.

EDIRNE to

VILLACH: ④ Apr. 26 - May 31; June 3, 7, 10, 17, 21, 24, 28, July 2, 4, 7, 8, 10, 13, 16, 18, 20, 22, 25, 27, 29, 30, Aug. 1, 2, 5, 9, 10, Aug. 12 - Sept. 14, Sept. 16, 17, 20, 21, 23, 24, 27, 28, 30; ①④ Oct. 1 - Nov. 26, 2007 (also Oct. 19, Nov. 30; not Oct. 18).
Timings vary. 🛌 2 cl. (also 🛏 1,2 cl. on some services). *Contact operator for further details.*
Operator: Optima Tours (see table heading).

FIRENZE to

WIEN: ⑥ Mar. 15 - Sept. 27, 2008.
Firenze Campo di Marte load 1825 - 1910, depart 2056, Wien Süd arrive 0839.
Train **1236**: 🛏 1,2 cl., 🛌 2 cl. and 🚗12.

FRANKFURT (NEU ISENBURG) to

LIVORNO: ⑤⑦ May 4 - Oct. 12; ⑤ Oct. 19 - 26, 2007 (also Apr. 20, 27).
Timings not advised.
🛏 1,2 cl., 🛌 2 cl. and 🍴.

NARBONNE: ③⑤⑦ Apr. 6 - Oct. 28; Nov. 4, 18, Dec. 2, 16, 2007, Jan. 6, 20, Feb. 3, 17; ⑦ Mar. 2 - 30, 2008 (not Oct. 24).
Frankfurt Neu Isenburg load 1850 - 1930, depart 2035 or 2102, Narbonne arrive 1008.
Train **1211/1391**: 🛏 1,2 cl., 🛌 2 cl. and 🍴.

RIJEKA: ⑦ May 6 - Sept. 30, 2007.
Frankfurt Neu Isenburg load 1730 - 1830, depart 1903, Rijeka arrive 1142.
Train **13493**: 🛏 1,2 cl., 🛌 2 cl. and 🍴.

VERONA: ⑦ May 6 - Oct. 14, 2007.
Timings not advised.
🛏 1,2 cl., 🛌 2 cl. and 🍴.

VILLACH: ⑤ Apr. 6 - 27; ③⑤ May 2 - Sept. 28; ⑤ Oct. 5 - 26, 2007.
Timings not advised.
🛏 1,2 cl., 🛌 2 cl. and 🍴.

FRÉJUS ST. RAPHAEL – see St. Raphael

GENÈVE – see Table 2

HAMBURG to

ALESSANDRIA: ⑦ Mar. 16 - 30, 2008.
Hamburg Altona load 1110 - 1140, depart 1213, Alessandria arrive 0745.
Train **13379**: 🛏 1,2 cl., 🛌 2 cl. and 🍴.

AVIGNON: ③ Apr. 11 - Oct. 17, 2007.
Timings not advised.
🛏 1,2 cl., 🛌 2 cl. and 🍴.

BOLZANO: ⑤ Oct. 5 - 26; ⑤ Dec. 21, 2007 - Mar. 28, 2008 (also Oct. 7, 14; not Dec. 28).
Hamburg Altona loading and departure times not advised, Bolzano arrive 1205.
Train **13385**: 🛏 1,2 cl., 🛌 2 cl. and 🍴.

INNSBRUCK: ⑤ Dec. 21, 2007 - Mar. 28, 2008 (not Dec. 28).
Hamburg Altona loading and departure times not advised, Innsbruck arrive 0940.
Train **13385**: 🛏 1,2 cl., 🛌 2 cl. and 🍴.

LIVORNO: ⑤ Apr. 20 - Oct. 26, 2007.
Timings not advised.
🛏 1,2 cl., 🛌 2 cl. and 🍴.

NARBONNE: ③⑤ Apr. 6 - Oct. 26; Nov. 4, 18, Dec. 2, 16, 2007, Jan. 6, 20, Feb. 3, 17; ⑦ Mar. 2 - 30, 2008 (not Oct. 24).
Hamburg Altona load 1220 - 1300, depart 1322, Narbonne arrive 1008.
Train **1391**: 🛏 1,2 cl., 🛌 2 cl. and 🍴.

RIJEKA: ⑤⑦ May 6 - Sept. 30; ⑤ Oct. 5 - 26, 2007.
Hamburg Altona load 1220 - 1245, depart 1320, Rijeka arrive 1142.
Train **13493**: 🛏 1,2 cl., 🛌 2 cl. and 🍴.

ST. RAPHAËL: ⑦ May 6 - Oct. 28, 2007.
Timings not advised.
🛏 1,2 cl., 🛌 2 cl. and 🍴.

HAMBURG (continued) to

SALZBURG: ⑦ May 13 - Oct. 28; ⑤ Dec. 21, 2007 - Mar. 28, 2008.
Hamburg Altona load 1620 - 1640, depart 1651, Salzburg Hbf arrive 0719.
Train **13395**: 🛏 1,2 cl., 🛌 2 cl. and 🍴.

VERONA: ⑤ Apr. 6 - 27; ⑤⑦ May 4 - June 17; ③⑤⑦ June 20 - Sept. 30; ⑤⑦ Oct. 5 - 14; ⑤ Oct. 19 - 26, 2007.
Timings not advised.
🛏 1,2 cl., 🛌 2 cl. and 🍴.

VILLACH: ⑤ Sept. 28 - Oct. 26; ⑤ Dec. 21, 2007 - Mar. 28, 2008 (also Oct. 30).
Hamburg Altona load 1600 - 1620, depart 1651, Villach Ost arrive 1055.
Train **13395**: 🛏 1,2 cl., 🛌 2 cl. and 🍴.

WIEN: daily until Mar. 31, 2008.
Hamburg Altona load 1930 - 1950, depart 2014, Wien Westbf arrive 0906.
Train **491**: 🛏 1,2 cl. and 🛌 2 cl.

's-HERTOGENBOSCH to

AVIGNON: ⑤ June 8 - Aug. 31, 2007.
s'-Hertogenbosch loading time not advised, depart 1813, Avignon Sud arrive 0730.
Train **1401/00**: 🛏 1,2 cl., 🛌 2 cl. and 🍴.
Operator: Euro-Express-Traincharter (see table heading).

BOLOGNA: ⑤ June 6 - Sept. 5, 2008.
Timings not advised.
🛏 1,2 cl., 🛌 2 cl. and 🍴.
Operator: Euro-Express-Traincharter (see table heading).

LIVORNO: ⑤ July 4 - Aug. 22, 2008.
Timings not advised.
🛏 1,2 cl., 🛌 2 cl. and 🍴.
Operator: Euro-Express-Traincharter (see table heading).

HILDESHEIM to

AVIGNON: ⑤ Apr. 6 - Oct. 26, 2007.
Timings not advised.
🛏 1,2 cl., 🛌 2 cl. and 🍴.

BOLZANO: ⑤ Apr. 6 - 27; ⑤⑦ May 4 - Oct. 19, 2007 (also Oct. 26).
Timings not advised.
🛏 1,2 cl., 🛌 2 cl. and 🍴.

INNSBRUCK: ⑤ Dec. 21, 2007 - Mar. 28, 2008 (not Dec. 28).
Hildesheim loading and departure times not advised, Innsbruck arrive 0940.
Train **13385**: 🛏 1,2 cl., 🛌 2 cl. and 🍴.

LIVORNO: ⑤ Apr. 20 - Oct. 26, 2007.
Timings not advised.
🛏 1,2 cl., 🛌 2 cl. and 🍴.

NARBONNE: ③⑤ Apr. 6 - Oct. 26; Nov. 4, 18, Dec. 2, 16, 2007, Jan. 6, 20, Feb. 3, 17; ⑦ Mar. 2 - 30, 2008 (not Oct. 24).
Hamburg Altona load 1220 - 1300, depart 1322, Narbonne arrive 1008.
Train **1391**: 🛏 1,2 cl., 🛌 2 cl. and 🍴.

SALZBURG: ③ June 6 - Sept. 19, 2007.
Timings not advised.
🛏 1,2 cl., 🛌 2 cl. and 🍴.

VILLACH: ⑤ May 11 - 25; ③⑤ June 1 - Sept. 21; ⑤ Sept. 28 - Oct. 26, 2007.
Timings not advised.
🛏 1,2 cl., 🛌 2 cl. and 🍴.

INNSBRUCK to

BERLIN: ⑥ Dec. 22, 2007 - Mar. 29, 2008.
Innsbruck load 2000 - 2050, depart 2120, Berlin Wannsee arrive 0852.
Train **13304**: 🛏 1,2 cl., 🛌 2 cl. and 🍴.

DÜSSELDORF: ④ May 3 - Oct. 18; ⑥ Dec. 22, 2007 - Mar. 29, 2008 (also Dec. 27, Jan. 3).
Innsbruck load 1750 - 1835 (1815 - 1900④), depart 1916 (1950④), Düsseldorf arrive 0625.
Train **13324**: 🛏 1,2 cl., 🛌 2 cl. and 🍴.

HAMBURG: ⑥ Dec. 22, 2007 - Mar. 29, 2008 (not Dec. 29).
Innsbruck load 1900 - 1930, depart 2030, Hamburg Altona arrival time not advised.
Train **13384**: 🛏 1,2 cl., 🛌 2 cl. and 🍴.

HILDESHEIM: ⑥ Dec. 22, 2007 - Mar. 29, 2008 (not Dec. 29).
Innsbruck load 1930 - 1950, depart 2030, Hildesheim arrival time not advised.
Train **13384**: 🛏 1,2 cl., 🛌 2 cl. and 🍴.

KOPER to

WIEN: ⑥ June 14 - Aug. 23, 2008.
Koper load 1945 - 2130, depart 2215, Wien Sud arrive 0720.
Train **1458**: 🛌 2 cl. and 🚗2.

KOŠICE

PRAHA: daily except Dec. 24, 31.
Košice depart 2218, Praha Hlavní arrive 0830.
Train **422**: 🛏 1,2 cl., 🛌 2 cl. and 🚗2.

LAMEZIA to

ZÜRICH: ① June 25 - Aug. 27, 2007.
Lamezia Terme load 1740 - 1840, depart 1935, Zürich Altstetten arrive 1502.
Train **1384**: 🛏 1,2 cl., 🛌 2 cl. and 🚗12.

LIVORNO to

German services may be bookable only in Germany.

DÜSSELDORF: ① May 7 - Oct. 8, 2007.
Timings not advised.
🛏 1,2 cl., 🛌 2 cl. and 🍴.

FRANKFURT: ①⑥ May 5 - Oct. 13; ⑥ Oct. 20 - 27, 2007 (also Apr. 21, 28).
Timings not advised.
🛏 1,2 cl., 🛌 2 cl. and 🍴.

HAMBURG: ⑥ Apr. 21 - Oct. 27, 2007.
Timings not advised.
🛏 1,2 cl., 🛌 2 cl. and 🍴.

's-HERTOGENBOSCH: ⑥ July 5 - Aug. 23, 2008.
Timings not advised.
🛏 1,2 cl., 🛌 2 cl. and 🍴.
Operator: Euro-Express-Traincharter (see table heading).

HILDESHEIM: ⑥ Apr. 21 - Oct. 27, 2007.
Timings not advised.
🛏 1,2 cl., 🛌 2 cl. and 🍴.

MÜNCHEN to

NAPOLI: ②④⑦ Apr. 29 - Oct. 14, 2007.
München Ost load 1930 - 2000, depart 2037, Napoli Centrale arrive 1023.
Train **287/1287**: 🛏 1,2 cl., 🛌 2 cl. and 🚗2.

NARBONNE: ① Apr. 2 - Oct. 29, 2007.
Timings not advised.
🛏 1,2 cl., 🛌 2 cl. and 🍴.

NAPOLI to

MÜNCHEN: ①③⑤ Apr. 27 - Oct. 12, 2007.
Napoli load 1630 - 1730, depart 1930, München Ost arrive 0905.
Train **286/1286**: 🛏 1,2 cl., 🛌 2 cl. and 🚗2.

NARBONNE to

Loading at Gare auto/train (🚌 connection)

BERLIN: ① Apr. 9 - Oct. 29, 2007.
Timings not advised.
🛏 1,2 cl., 🛌 2 cl. and 🍴.

CALAIS: ⑥ May 17 - July 19; ①⑥ July 21 - Aug. 25; ⑥ Aug. 30 - Sept. 13, 2008.
Narbonne load 1400 - 1700, depart 1822, Calais arrive 0735.
🛌 and 🍸.
Operator: French Motorail (see table heading).

DÜSSELDORF: ④⑥ Apr. 7 - Oct. 20; Nov. 5, 19, Dec. 3, 17, 2007, Jan. 7, 21, Feb. 4, 18; ① Mar. 3 - 31, 2008 (also Oct. 27).
Narbonne load 1500 - 1600, depart 1737, Düsseldorf Hbf arrive 1228.
Train **1392**: 🛏 1,2 cl., 🛌 2 cl. and 🍴.

FRANKFURT: ①④⑥ Apr. 7 - Oct. 29; Nov. 5, 19, Dec. 3, 17, 2007, Jan. 7, 21, Feb. 4, 18; ① Mar. 3 - 31, 2008 (not Oct. 25).
Narbonne load 1500 - 1600, depart 1737, Frankfurt Neu Isenburg 0721 or 0752.
Train **1392**: 🛏 1,2 cl., 🛌 2 cl. and 🍴.

HAMBURG: ④⑥ Apr. 7 - Oct. 27; Nov. 5, 19, Dec. 3, 17, 2007, Jan. 7, 21, Feb. 4, 18; ① Mar. 3 - 31, 2008 (not Oct. 25).
Narbonne load 1500 - 1600, depart 1737, Hamburg Altona arrive 1442.
Train **1392**: 🛏 1,2 cl., 🛌 2 cl. and 🍴.

HILDESHEIM: ④⑥ Apr. 7 - Oct. 27; Nov. 5, 19, Dec. 3, 17, 2007, Jan. 7, 21, Feb. 4, 18; ① Mar. 3 - 31, 2008 (not Oct. 25).
Narbonne load 1500 - 1600, depart 1737, Hildesheim Hbf arrive 1210.
Train **1392**: 🛏 1,2 cl., 🛌 2 cl. and 🍴.

MÜNCHEN: ② May 3 - Oct. 30, 2007.
Timings not advised.
🛏 1,2 cl., 🛌 2 cl. and 🍴.

SALZBURG: ② Apr. 3 - Oct. 30, 2007.
Timings not advised.
🛏 1,2 cl., 🛌 2 cl. and 🍴.

STUTTGART: ② Apr. 3 - Oct. 30, 2007.
Timings not advised.
🛏 1,2 cl., 🛌 2 cl. and 🍴.

NICE to

CALAIS: ⑥ May 17 - July 19; ①⑥ July 21 - Aug. 25; ⑥ Aug. 30 - Sept. 13, 2008.
Nice load 1400 - 1630, depart 1758, Calais arrive 0948.
🛌 and 🍸.
Operator: French Motorail (see table heading).

NIŠ

VILLACH: July 2, 16, 30, Aug. 3, 6, 9, 17, 24, 30, Sept. 3, 7, 2007.
Timings vary. 🛌 2 cl.
Contact operator for further details.
Operator: Optima Tours (see table heading).

POPRAD TATRY to

PRAHA: daily except Dec. 24, 31.
Poprad Tatry depart 2145, Praha Hlavni arrive 0630.
Train **424**: 🛏 1,2 cl., 🛌 2 cl. and (12).

PRAHA to

KOŠICE: daily except Dec. 24, 31.
Praha Hlavní depart 2002, Košice arrive 0648.
Train **423**: 🛏 1,2 cl., 🛌 2 cl. and (2).

POPRAD TATRY: daily except Dec. 24, 31.
Praha Hlavní depart 2207, Poprad Tatry arrive 0626
Train **225**: 🛏 1,2 cl., 🛌 2 cl. and (12).

SPLIT: June 20 - Sept. 5, 2008.
Praha Hlavní depart 0754, Split arrive 0554.
Train **1203/1200/1823**: 🛏 1,2 cl. and 🛌 2 cl.

RIJEKA to

DÜSSELDORF: ⑥ Apr. 7 - Oct. 27, 2007.
Timings not advised.
🛏 1,2 cl., 🛌 2 cl. and ✕.

FRANKFURT: ① May 7 - Oct. 1, 2007.
Timings not advised.
🛏 1,2 cl., 🛌 2 cl. and ✕.

HAMBURG: ①⑥ May 7 - Oct. 6; ⑥ Oct. 13 - 27, 2007.
Timings not advised.
🛏 1,2 cl., 🛌 2 cl. and ✕.

WIEN: ⑥ June 14 - Aug. 23, 2008.
Rijeka load 1900 - 2000, depart 2045, Wien Süd arrive 0720.
Train **480/1458**: 🛌 2 cl. and (2).

ROMA to

WIEN: ⑥ Mar. 15 - Sept. 27, 2008.
Roma Termini load 1505 - 1545, depart 1700, Wien Süd arrive 0839.
Train **1236**: 🛏 1,2 cl., 🛌 2 cl. and (12).

ST RAPHAËL to

CALAIS: ⑥ May 17 - July 19; ①⑥ July 21 - Aug. 25; ⑥ Aug. 30 - Sept. 13, 2008.
St Raphaël load 1600 - 1745, depart 1919, Calais arrive 0948.
🛌 and 🍸.
Operator: French Motorail (see table heading).

DÜSSELDORF: ① May 7 - Oct. 29, 2007.
Timings not advised.
🛏 1,2 cl., 🛌 2 cl. and ✕.

HAMBURG: ① May 7 - Oct. 29, 2007.
Timings not advised.
🛏 1,2 cl., 🛌 2 cl. and ✕.

SALZBURG to

BERLIN: ④ May 17 - Oct. 11; ⑥ Dec. 22, 2007 - Mar. 29, 2008.
Salzburg Hbf load 2025 - 2040, depart 2110, Berlin Wannsee arrive 0752.
Train **13394**: 🛏 1,2 cl., 🛌 2 cl. and ✕.

DÜSSELDORF: ① Apr. 2 - Oct. 15; ⑥ Dec. 22, 2007 - Mar. 29, 2008 (also Dec. 27, Jan. 3).
Salzburg Hbf load 2120 - 2140, depart 2209, Düsseldorf Hbf arrive 0801.
Train **13314**: 🛏 1,2 cl., 🛌 2 cl. and ✕.

HAMBURG: ③ May 9 - Oct. 31; ⑥ Dec. 22, 2007 - Mar. 29, 2008.
Salzburg Hbf load 2015 - 2025, depart 2110, Hamburg Altona arrive 1156.
Train **13394**: 🛏 1,2 cl., 🛌 2 cl. and ✕.

HILDESHEIM: ④ June 7 - Sept. 20, 2007.
Timings not advised.
🛏 1,2 cl., 🛌 2 cl. and ✕.

NARBONNE: ① Apr. 2 - Oct. 29, 2007.
Timings not advised.
🛏 1,2 cl., 🛌 2 cl. and ✕.

SPLIT to

PRAHA: June 21 - Sept. 6, 2008.
Split depart 2100, Praha arrive 2000.
Train **1822/783/1201/1202**: 🛏 1,2 cl. and 🛌 2 cl.

WIEN: ⑦ June 15 - Aug. 24, 2008.
Split load 2015 - 2045, depart 2222, Wien Süd arrive 1402.
Train **824/158**: 🛌 2 cl.

STUTTGART (KORNWESTHEIM) to

NARBONNE: ① Apr. 2 - Oct. 29, 2007.
Timings not advised.
🛏 1,2 cl., 🛌 2 cl. and ✕.

SUBOTICA to

BAR: June 20 - Sept. 1, 2008.
Timings not advised.
Train **437**: 🛌 2 cl. and ✕.

THESSALONÍKI to

VILLACH: July 2, 16, 30, Aug. 3, 6, 9, 17, 24, 30, Sept. 3, 7, 14, 21, 28, Oct. 19, 2007.
Timings vary. 🛌 2 cl.
Contact operator for further details.
Operator: Optima Tours (see table heading).

TOULOUSE to

CALAIS: ⑥ May 17 - July 19; ①⑥ July 21 - Aug. 25; ⑥ Aug. 30 - Sept. 13, 2008.
Toulouse load 1500 - 1830, depart 2019, Calais arrive 0735.
🛌 and 🍸.
Operator: French Motorail (see table heading).

VENEZIA to

WIEN: ⑥ June 2 - Sept. 8, 2007.
Venezia Mestre load 2145 - 2245, depart 0002⑦, Wien Süd arrive 0801.
Train **1134**: 🛏 1,2 cl., 🛌 2 cl. and (12).

VERONA to

German services may be bookable only in Germany.

BERLIN: ⑥ Apr. 7 - Oct. 27, 2007.
Timings not advised.
🛏 1,2 cl., 🛌 2 cl. and ✕.

DÜSSELDORF: ⑥ Apr. 7 - 28; ①⑥ May 5 - Oct. 20, 2007 (also Oct. 27).
Timings not advised.
🛏 1,2 cl., 🛌 2 cl. and ✕.

FRANKFURT: ① May 7 - Oct. 15, 2007.
Timings not advised.
🛏 1,2 cl., 🛌 2 cl. and ✕.

HAMBURG: ⑥ Apr. 7 - 28; ①⑥ May 5 - June 16; ①④⑥ June 18 - Sept. 29; ①⑥ Oct. 1 - 20, 2007 (also Oct. 27).
Timings not advised.
🛏 1,2 cl., 🛌 2 cl. and ✕.

VILLACH to

BERLIN: ④ May 17 - Oct. 11, 2007.
Timings not advised.
🛏 1,2 cl., 🛌 2 cl. and ✕.

DÜSSELDORF: ⑥ Oct. 6 - 27; ⑥ Dec. 22, 2007 - Mar. 29, 2008 (also Dec. 27, Jan. 3).
Villach Ost load 1715 - 1800, depart 1841, Düsseldorf Hbf arrive 0801.
Train **13314**: 🛏 1,2 cl., 🛌 2 cl. and ✕.

EDIRNE: Apr. 5, 10, 14, 17, 21, 24, 28, May 1, 5, 8, 12, 15, 19, 22, 26, 28, 29, June 1, 2, 4, 5, 8, 9, 11, 12, 15, 16, 18 - 20, 22, 23, 25 - 27, June 29 - Aug. 5, Aug. 7, 10, 11, 14, 18, 21, 25, 28, Sept. 1, 4, 8, 12, 15, 19, 22, 29, Oct. 6, 13, 27, Nov. 10, 21, 2007.
Timings vary. 🛌 2 cl. (also 🛏 1,2 cl. on some services).
Contact operator for further details.
Operator: Optima Tours (see table heading).

FRANKFURT: ⑥ Apr. 7 - 28; ④⑥ May 3 - Sept. 29; ⑥ Oct. 6 - 27, 2007.
Timings not advised.
🛏 1,2 cl., 🛌 2 cl. and ✕.

HAMBURG: ⑥ Sept. 29 - Oct. 27; ⑥ Dec. 22, 2007 - Mar. 29, 2008 (also Oct. 1).
Villach Ost load 1600 - 1645, depart 1729, Hamburg Altona arrive 1156.
Train **13394**: 🛏 1,2 cl., 🛌 2 cl. and ✕.

HILDESHEIM: ⑥ May 12 - 26; ④⑥ June 2 - Sept. 22; ⑥ Sept. 29 - Oct. 27, 2007.
Timings not advised.
🛏 1,2 cl., 🛌 2 cl. and ✕.

VILLACH (continued) to

NIŠ: ⑥ June 16 - Aug. 4, 2007 (also July 31, Aug. 7, 22).
Villach depart 0748 (1505 from Aug. 1), Thessaloníki arrive 1107 (1800 from Aug. 1). 🛌 2 cl.
Contact operator for further details.
Operator: Optima Tours (see table heading).

THESSALONÍKI: ⑥ June 16 - Aug. 4, 2007 (also July 31, Aug. 7, 15, 22, Sept. 1, 5).
Timings vary. 🛌 2 cl.
Contact operator for further details.
Operator: Optima Tours (see table heading).

VILLA SAN GIOVANNI to

ZÜRICH: ① June 25 - Aug. 27, 2007.
Villa San Giovanni load 1605 - 1705, depart 1755, Zürich Altstetten arrive 1502.
Train **1384**: 🛏 1,2 cl., 🛌 2 cl. and (12).

WIEN to

ANCONA: ⑤ June 1 - Sept. 7, 2007.
Wien Süd load 1945 - 2030, depart 2105, Ancona arrive 1005.
Train **1135**: 🛏 1,2 cl., 🛌 2 cl. and (12).

BERLIN: daily until Mar. 31, 2008.
Wien Westbf load 1905 - 1920, depart 1950, Berlin Wannsee arrive 0825.
Train **428**: 🛏 1,2 cl. and 🛌 2 cl.

DÜSSELDORF: daily until Mar. 31, 2008.
Wien Westbf load 1845 - 1900, depart 1950, Düsseldorf Hbf arrive 0706.
Train **428/324**: 🛏 1,2 cl. and 🛌 2 cl.

EDIRNE: ⑤ June 23 - Aug. 4; ⑥ Aug. 12 - 26, 2006.
Wien loading times not advised, depart 2247, Edirne arrive 0821. 🛌 2 cl. (also 🛏 1,2 cl. on some services).
Contact operator for further details.
Operator: Optima Tours (see table heading).

FIRENZE: ⑤ Mar. 14 - Sept. 26, 2008.
Wien Süd load 1845 - 1905, depart 2005, Firenze Campo di Marte arrive 0705.
Train **1237**: 🛏 1,2 cl., 🛌 2 cl. and (12).

HAMBURG: daily until Mar. 31, 2008.
Wien Westbf load 1925 - 1940, depart 1955, Hamburg Altona arrive 0806.
Train **490**: 🛏 1,2 cl. and 🛌 2 cl.

KOPER: ⑤ June 13 - Aug. 22, 2008.
Wien Süd load 2130 - 2150, depart 2205, Koper arrive 0642.
Train **1459**: 🛌 2 cl. and (2).

RIJEKA: ⑤ June 13 - Aug. 22, 2008.
Wien Süd load 2110 - 2130, depart 2205, Rijeka arrive 0851.
Train **1459/481**: 🛌 2 cl. and (2).

ROMA: ⑤ Mar. 14 - Sept. 26, 2008.
Wien Süd load 1910 - 1930, depart 2005, Roma Termini arrive 0957.
Train **1237**: 🛏 1,2 cl., 🛌 2 cl. and (12).

SPLIT: ⑥ June 14 - Aug. 23, 2008.
Wien Süd load 1500 - 1530, depart 1557, Split arrive 0653.
Train **159/825**: 🛌 2 cl.

VENEZIA: ⑤ June 1 - Sept. 7, 2007.
Wien Süd load 2015 - 2045, depart 2105, Venezia Mestre arrive 0446.
Train **1135**: 🛏 1,2 cl., 🛌 2 cl. and (12).

ZÜRICH to

BARI: ⑤ June 15 - Oct. 26, 2007.
Zürich Altstetten load 1730 - 1900, depart 1910, Bari arrive 0946.
Train **1389**: 🛏 1,2 cl., 🛌 2 cl. and (12).

LAMEZIA: ⑦ June 24 - Aug. 26, 2007.
Zürich Altstetten load 1500 - 1530, depart 1640, Lamezia arrive 1041.
Train **1385**: 🛏 1,2 cl., 🛌 2 cl. and (12).

VILLA SAN GIOVANNI: ⑦ June 24 - Aug. 26, 2007.
Zürich Altstetten load 1530 - 1600, depart 1640, Villa San Giovanni arrive 1220.
Train **1385**: 🛏 1,2 cl., 🛌 2 cl. and (12).

AUSTRIA

to 14/06/08

Feldkirch - Graz: daily (day and overnight trains).
Feldkirch - Wien: daily (day and overnight trains).
Feldkirch - Villach: daily.
Graz - Feldkirch: daily (day and overnight trains).
Innsbruck - Wien: daily (day train).
Salzburg - Wien: daily (day train).
Villach - Feldkirch: daily.
Villach - Wien: daily (1 – 3 day trains).
Wien - Feldkirch: daily (day and overnight trains).
Wien - Innsbruck: daily (day train).
Wien - Salzburg: daily (day train).
Wien - Villach: daily (1 – 3 day trains).

CROATIA

to 13/12/08

Split - Zagreb: daily. Also additional train in summer.
Zagreb - Split: daily. Also additional train in summer.

FINLAND

to 31/05/08

Subject to alteration on and around holiday dates.

Helsinki - Kemijärvi: ⑤ Feb. 29 - May 31 (also Mar. 19, 23).
Helsinki - Kolari: ③⑤⑥ Dec. 9 - Jan. 30; daily Jan. 31 - May 3.
Helsinki - Oulu: daily (not Dec. 24).
Helsinki - Rovaniemi: daily (not Dec. 24).
Kemijärvi - Helsinki: ⑥ Feb. 29 - May 31 (also Mar. 20, 24).
Kolari - Helsinki: ④⑥⑦ Dec. 9 - Jan. 30; daily Jan. 31 - May 3.
Kolari - Tampere: ④⑥⑦ Dec. 9 - Jan. 30; ①②③④⑥ Jan. 31 - May 3.
Kolari - Turku: Dec. 20 - 22, 26 - 30, Jan. 1, 4, 5; ⑥ Feb. 15 - Apr. 26 (also Mar. 20, 21, 23, 24).
Oulu - Helsinki: daily (not Dec. 24).
Rovaniemi - Helsinki: daily (not Dec. 24).
Rovaniemi - Tampere: daily (not Dec. 24).
Rovaniemi - Turku: daily (not Dec. 24).
Tampere - Kolari: ③⑤⑥ Dec. 9 - Jan. 30; ①②③⑤⑦ Jan. 31 - May 3.
Tampere - Rovaniemi: daily (not Dec. 24).
Turku - Kolari: Dec. 19 - 22, 26 - 30, Jan. 3, 4; ⑤ Feb. 15 - Apr. 26 (also Mar. 19, 20, 22, 23).
Turku - Rovaniemi: daily (not Dec. 24).

FRANCE

to 12/06/08

For services from Calais, see Table **1**.

Auray - Genève: *summer only.*
Auray - Lyon: *summer only.*
Auray - Metz: *summer only.*
Auray - Strasbourg: *summer only.*
Avignon - Metz: *summer only.*
Avignon - Paris▲: ②④⑥ Dec. 11 - Apr. 26; daily Apr. 27 - June 12 (not Dec. 25, Jan. 1).
Avignon - Seclin (Lille): *summer only.*
Avignon - Strasbourg: *summer only.*
Biarritz - Genève: *summer only.*
Biarritz - Metz: *summer only.*
Biarritz - Paris: ②④⑥ May 29 - June 12.
Biarritz - Strasbourg: *summer only.*
Bordeaux - Marseille: *summer only.*
Bordeaux - Metz: *summer only.*
Bordeaux - Paris▲: ②⑥ Dec. 11 - May 27; ②④⑥ May 29 - June 12 (also May 11; not Dec. 25, Jan. 1, Feb. 23, May 10).
Bordeaux - St. Raphaël▲: *summer only.*
Bordeaux - Strasbourg: *summer only.*
Briançon - Paris: *summer only.*
Brive - Paris▲: ②④⑥ May 29 - June 12.
Fréjus-St. Raphaël – see St. Raphaël.
Genève - Auray: *summer only.*
Genève - Biarritz: *summer only.*
Genève - Nantes: *summer only.*
Genève - Paris▲: *summer only.*
Lille – see Seclin (Lille).
Lyon - Auray: *summer only.*
Lyon - Nantes: *summer only.*
Lyon - Paris▲: ⑥ Dec. 15 - Apr. 26; ②④⑥ Apr. 29 - June 12.
Marseille - Bordeaux▲: *summer only.*
Marseille - Paris▲: ②④⑥ Dec. 11 - Apr. 26; daily Apr. 27 - June 12 (not Dec. 25, Jan. 1).
Metz - Auray: *summer only.*
Metz - Avignon: *summer only.*
Metz - Biarritz: *summer only.*
Metz - Bordeaux: *summer only.*
Metz - Nantes: *summer only.*
Metz - Narbonne: *summer only.*
Metz - St. Raphaël: *summer only.*
Mulhouse - Narbonne: *summer only.*
Nantes - Genève: *summer only.*
Nantes - Lyon: *summer only.*
Nantes - Metz: *summer only.*
Nantes - St. Raphaël: *summer only.*
Nantes - Strasbourg: *summer only.*
Narbonne - Metz: *summer only.*
Narbonne - Mulhouse: *summer only.*
Narbonne - Paris: ②⑥ Dec. 11 - May 27; ②④⑥ May 29 - June 12 (also May 11; not Dec. 25, Jan. 1, Feb. 23, May 10).
Narbonne - Seclin (Lille)▲: *summer only.*
Narbonne - Strasbourg: *summer only.*
Nice - Paris: ②④⑥ Dec. 11 - Apr. 26; daily Apr. 27 - June 12 (not Dec. 25, Jan. 1).
Paris - Avignon▲: ①③⑤ Dec. 10 - Apr. 25; daily Apr. 26 - June 12 (not Dec. 24, 31).
Paris - Biarritz: ①③⑤ May 28 - June 12.
Paris - Bordeaux▲: ①⑤ Dec. 10 - May 26; ①③⑤ May 28 - June 12 (also May 7; not Dec. 24, 31, Feb. 25, May 9).
Paris - Briançon: *summer only.*
Paris - Brive▲: ①③⑤ May 28 - June 12.
Paris - Genève▲: *summer only.*
Paris - Lyon▲: ⑤ Dec. 14 - Apr. 25; ①③⑤ Apr. 28 - June 12.
Paris - Marseille▲: ①③⑤ Dec. 10 - Apr. 25; daily Apr. 26 - June 12 (not Dec. 24, 31).
Paris - Narbonne: ①⑤ Dec. 10 - May 26; ①③⑤ May 28 - June 12 (also May 7; not Dec. 24, 31, Feb. 25, May 9).
Paris - Nice: ①③⑤ Dec. 10 - Apr. 25; daily Apr. 26 - June 12 (not Dec. 24, 31).
Paris - St. Raphaël: ①③⑤ Dec. 10 - Apr. 25; daily Apr. 26 - June 12 (not Dec. 24, 31).
Paris - Tarbes: ①③⑤ May 28 - June 12.
Paris - Toulon: ①③⑤ Dec. 10 - Apr. 25; daily Apr. 26 - June 12 (not Dec. 24, 31).
Paris - Toulouse: ①⑤ Dec. 10 - May 26; ①③⑤ May 28 - June 12 (also May 7; not Dec. 24, 31, Feb. 25, May 9).
St. Raphaël - Bordeaux▲: *summer only.*
St. Raphaël - Metz: *summer only.*
St. Raphaël - Nantes: *summer only.*
St. Raphaël - Paris: ②④⑥ Dec. 11 - Apr. 26; daily Apr. 27 - June 12 (not Dec. 25, Jan. 1).
St. Raphaël - Seclin (Lille)▲: *summer only.*
St. Raphaël - Strasbourg: *summer only.*
Seclin (Lille) - Avignon▲: *summer only.*
Seclin (Lille) - Narbonne▲: *summer only.*
Seclin (Lille) - St. Raphaël▲: *summer only.*
Strasbourg - Auray: *summer only.*
Strasbourg - Avignon: *summer only.*
Strasbourg - Biarritz: *summer only.*
Strasbourg - Bordeaux: *summer only.*
Strasbourg - Nantes: *summer only.*
Strasbourg - Narbonne: *summer only.*
Strasbourg - St. Raphaël: *summer only.*
Tarbes - Paris: ②④⑥ May 29 - June 12.
Toulon - Paris: ②④⑥ Dec. 11 - Apr. 26; daily Apr. 27 - June 12 (not Dec. 25, Jan. 1).
Toulouse - Paris: ②⑥ Dec. 11 - May 27; ②④⑥ May 29 - June 12 (also May 11; not Dec. 25, Jan. 1, Feb. 23, May 10).

▲ – These services offer the passenger a choice of departure times, usually including day and night trains.

GERMANY

to 31/03/08

Basel (Lörrach) - Hamburg Altona: ①②④⑤⑥⑦ Sept. 20 - Oct. 8; ⑤⑥⑦ Oct. 12-28; ⑥ Nov. 3 - Jan. 26; ①⑥ Feb. 2-16; ①④⑥ Feb. 18 - Mar. 31 (also Oct. 11, Dec. 16, 20, 21, 23, Jan. 1, 2, 3, 7; not Dec. 29).
Basel (Lörrach) - Hildesheim: ①②④⑤⑥⑦ Sept. 20 - Oct. 8; ⑤⑥⑦ Oct. 12-28; ⑥ Nov. 3 - Jan. 26; ①⑥ Feb. 2-16; ①④⑥ Feb. 18 - Mar. 31 (also Oct. 11, Dec. 16, 20, 21, 23, Jan. 1, 2, 3, 7; not Dec. 29).
Berlin Wannsee - München Ost: daily. [**NZ** train].
Düsseldorf - Lindau: *day train*: ⑥ Apr. 21-28, 2007.
Düsseldorf - München Ost: ③⑦ May 2 - Oct. 17.
Frankfurt Neu Isenburg - Niebüll: ⑦ Sept. 23 - Oct. 14.
Frankfurt Neu Isenburg - Rostock: ⑤ May 11 - Oct. 12.
Frankfurt Neu Isenburg - Sassnitz: ⑤ May 11 - Oct. 12.
Frankfurt Neu Isenburg - Westerland: ⑦ Sept. 23 - Oct. 14.
Hamburg Altona - Basel (Lörrach): ①③④⑤⑥⑦ Sept. 19 - Oct. 7; ⑤⑥⑦ Oct. 12-27; ⑤ Nov. 2 - Jan. 25; ⑤⑦ Feb. 1-17; ③⑤⑦ Feb. 20 - Mar. 30 (also Oct. 10, 11, Dec. 15, 19, 20, 22, 23, Jan. 1, 2, 6; not Dec. 28).
Hamburg Altona - München Ost: ①③⑤⑦ June 4 - Oct. 7; ⑤⑦ Oct. 12-28; ⑤ Dec. 14 - Feb. 1; ③⑤ Feb. 6-29; ③⑤⑦ Mar. 2-30 (also Oct. 10, Dec. 19, 20, 22, 23, Jan. 1, 2; not Dec. 28). Also daily **NZ** train.

Hildesheim - Basel (Lörrach): ①③④⑤⑥⑦ Sept. 19 - Oct. 7; ⑤⑥⑦ Oct. 12-27; ⑤ Nov. 2 - Jan. 25; ⑤⑦ Feb. 1-17; ③⑤⑦ Feb. 20 - Mar. 30 (also Oct. 10, 11, Dec. 15, 19, 20, 22, 23, Jan. 1, 2, 6; not Dec. 28).
Hildesheim - München Ost: ①③⑤⑦ June 4 - Oct. 7; ⑤⑦ Oct. 12-28; ⑤ Dec. 14 - Feb. 1; ③⑤ Feb. 6-29; ③⑤⑦ Mar. 2-30 (also Oct. 10, Dec. 19, 20, 22, 23, Jan. 1, 2; not Dec. 28).
Köln Troisdorf - Lindau: *day train*: ⑥ Apr. 21-28, 2007.
Köln Troisdorf - München Ost: ③⑦ May 2 - Oct. 17.
Lindau - Düsseldorf: *day train*: ⑥ Apr. 21-28, 2007.
Lindau - Köln Troisdorf: *day train*: ⑥ Apr. 21-28, 2007.
München Ost - Berlin Wannsee: daily. [**NZ** train].
München Ost - Düsseldorf: ①④ May 3 - Oct. 18.
München Ost - Hamburg Altona: ②③④⑥ June 5 - Oct. 6; ③⑥ Oct. 10-31; ⑥ Dec. 15 - Feb. 2; ④⑥ Feb. 7-28; ①④⑥ Mar. 1-31 (also Oct. 11, Dec. 15, 20, 21, 23, Jan. 1, 2, 3; not Dec. 29). Also daily **NZ** train.
München Ost - Hildesheim: ②③④⑥ June 5 - Oct. 6; ③⑥ Oct. 10-31; ⑥ Dec. 15 - Feb. 2; ④⑥ Feb. 7-28; ①④⑥ Mar. 1-31 (also Oct. 11, Dec. 20, 21, 23, Jan. 1, 2, 3; not Dec. 29).
München Ost - Köln Troisdorf: ①⑦ May 3 - Oct. 18.

Niebüll - Frankfurt Neu Isenburg: ① Sept. 17 - Oct. 15.
Niebüll - Stuttgart Kornwestheim: ① Sept. 17 - Oct. 15.
Niebüll - Westerland: Daily shuttle service; 18-28 per day in summer, 12-14 per day in winter.
Rostock - Frankfurt Neu Isenburg: ⑥ May 12 - Oct. 13.
Rostock - Stuttgart Kornwestheim: ⑥ May 12 - Oct. 13.
Sassnitz - Frankfurt Neu Isenburg: ⑥ May 12 - Oct. 13.
Sassnitz - Stuttgart Kornwestheim: ⑥ May 12 - Oct. 13.
Stuttgart Kornwestheim - Niebüll: ⑦ Sept. 23 - Oct. 14.
Stuttgart Kornwestheim - Rostock: ⑤ May 11 - Oct. 12.
Stuttgart Kornwestheim - Sassnitz: ⑤ May 11 - Oct. 12.
Stuttgart Kornwestheim - Westerland: ⑦ Sept. 23 - Oct. 14.
Westerland - Frankfurt Neu Isenburg: ① Sept. 17 - Oct. 15.
Westerland - Niebüll: Daily shuttle service; 18-28 per day in summer, 12-14 per day in winter.
Westerland - Stuttgart Kornwestheim: ① Sept. 17 - Oct. 15.

NZ – *DB NachtZug* (see page **10** for description).

GREECE

to 13/12/08

Athína - Thessaloníki: daily (day and night trains).

Thessaloníki - Athína: daily (day and night trains).

ITALY

to 08/12/07

Bari - Bolzano: ⑤ Dec. 22 - Mar. 16, June 8 - Sept. 7.
Bari - Milano: ②⑤⑦ June 5 - Sept. 16.
Bari - Torino: ⑦ Jan. 7 - Apr. 23; ①②③④⑤⑥ June 11 - Sept. 8; ⑦ Sept. 23 - Dec. 2 (also Dec. 10, 17, 23, 30, Apr. 9; not Apr. 8).
Bologna - Catania: daily.
Bologna - Lamezia: ③⑤ June 8 - Sept. 7.
Bologna - Villa San Giovanni: daily (also additional train ③⑤ June 8 - Sept. 7).
Bolzano - Bari: ⑥ Jan. 6 - Mar. 17, June 9 - Sept. 8 (also Dec. 26, Jan. 1).
Bolzano - Lamezia: ⑥ Dec. 16 - Mar. 24, June 2 - Sept. 8 (also Dec. 21, 28, Jan. 4, Apr. 6, 10).
Bolzano - Roma: Dec. 22, 23, 26-28, 30, Jan. 2, 3, 5; ⑥ Jan. 6 - Feb. 3; ⑥⑦ Feb. 10 - Mar. 25, June 16 - July 22; daily July 28 - Sept. 2 (also Jan. 7).
Bolzano - Villa San Giovanni: ⑥ Dec. 16 - Mar. 24, June 2 - Sept. 8 (also Dec. 21, 28, Jan. 4, Apr. 6, 10).
Brunico - Roma: Dec. 22, 23, 26-28, 30, Jan. 2, 3, 5; ⑥ Jan. 6 - Feb. 3; ⑥⑦ Feb. 10 - Mar. 25, June 16 - July 22; daily July 28 - Sept. 2 (also Jan. 7).
Calalzo - Roma: Dec. 22, 23, 26-28, 30, Jan. 2, 3, 5-7; ⑥ Jan. 13 - Mar. 24, June 16 - July 21; daily July 28 - Sept. 2.
Catania - Bologna: daily.
Catania - Milano: ①④ June 11 - Sept. 6.
Catania - Roma: ⑤ Dec. 15 - June 15; ①④⑥ June 18 - Sept. 8; ⑤ Sept. 14 - Dec. 7.
Catania - Torino: ②⑤ June 12 - Sept. 7.
Foggia - Torino: ⑦ June 10 - Sept. 16.
Lamezia - Bologna: ④⑥ June 9 - Sept. 8.
Lamezia - Bolzano: ⑤ Dec. 15 - Mar. 23, June 1 - Sept. 7 (also Dec. 20, 27, Jan. 3, Apr. 5, 9).
Lamezia - Milano: Dec. 18, 22, Jan. 1, 7; ③ Apr. 4 - May 2; ⑤⑦ June 8 - July 8; ②⑤⑦ July 10 - Sept. 11. Also additional train July 18, 24, 27, 30, Aug. 6, 15, 22, 29, Sept. 8.

Lamezia - Roma: ⑦ June 17 - Sept. 9.
Lamezia - Torino: Dec. 20, Jan. 5; ④ Apr. 5 - May 3; ④⑥ June 7 - July 7; ①④⑥ July 9 - Sept. 10. Also additional train July 12, 19, 26, 31, Aug. 2, 4, 7, 11, 18, 25, 28, Sept. 1, 4, 10.
Milano - Bari: ①④⑥ June 4 - Sept. 15.
Milano - Catania: ②⑤ June 12 - Sept. 7.
Milano - Lamezia: Dec. 19, 23, Jan. 2, 8; ④ Apr. 5 - May 3; ④⑥ June 9 - July 7; ①④⑥ July 9 - Sept. 13. Also additional train July 11, 17, 22, 25, 29, Aug. 1, 5, 8, 17, 21, 24, 28, 31, Sept. 5.
Milano - Milazzo: ②⑤ June 12 - Sept. 7.
Milano - Palermo: ②⑤ June 12 - Sept. 7.
Milano - Villa San Giovanni: Dec. 19, 23, Jan. 2, 8; ④ Apr. 5 - May 3; ④⑥ June 9 - July 7; ①④⑥ July 9 - Sept. 13. Also additional train July 11, 17, 22, 25, 29, Aug. 1, 5, 8, 17, 21, 24; 28, 31, Sept. 5.
Milazzo - Milano: ①④ June 11 - Sept. 6.
Milazzo - Torino: ②⑤ June 12 - Sept. 7.
Napoli - Torino: ⑦ (also Dec. 26, Jan. 1, Apr. 9, 25, May 1, Nov. 1; not Dec. 24, 31, Apr. 8).
Palermo - Milano: ①④ June 11 - Sept. 6.
Palermo - Roma: ①④⑥ June 18 - Sept. 8.
Palermo - Torino: ②⑤ June 12 - Sept. 7.
Roma - Bolzano: Dec. 21, 22, 25-27, 29, Jan. 1, 2, 4-6; ⑤ Jan. 12 - Feb. 2; ⑤⑥ Feb. 9 - Mar. 24, June 15 - July 21; daily July 27 - Sept. 1.
Roma - Brunico: Dec. 21, 22, 25-27, 29, Jan. 1, 2, 4-6; ⑤ Jan. 12 - Feb. 2; ⑤⑥ Feb. 9 - Mar. 24, June 15 - July 21; daily July 27 - Sept. 1.
Roma - Calalzo: Dec. 21, 22, 25-27, 29, Jan. 1, 2, 4-6; ⑤ Jan. 12 - Mar. 23, June 15 - July 20; daily July 27 - Sept. 1.
Roma - Catania: ⑦ Dec. 17 - June 17; ③⑤⑦ June 20 - Sept. 9; ⑦ Sept. 19 - Dec. 2.
Roma - Lamezia: ⑤ June 15 - Sept. 7.
Roma - Palermo: ③⑤⑦ June 20 - Sept. 9.
Roma - Torino: ⑦ (also Dec. 26, Jan. 1, Apr. 9, 25, May 1, Nov. 1; not Dec. 24, 31, Apr. 8).
Roma - Villa San Giovanni: ④⑥ Dec. 21 - Dec. 8.

Torino - Bari: ⑤ Dec. 15 - June 1; ①②③④⑥⑦ June 9 - Sept. 8; ⑤ Sept. 21 - Dec. 7 (not Nov. 2).
Torino - Catania: ③⑥ June 13 - Sept. 8.
Torino - Foggia: ⑤ June 8 - Sept. 14.
Torino - Lamezia: Dec. 21, Jan. 6; ⑤ Apr. 6 - May 4; ⑤⑦ June 8 - July 8; ②⑤⑦ July 10 - Sept. 11. Also additional train July 11, 18, 25, 30, Aug. 1, 3, 6, 10, 17, 24, 27, 31, Sept. 3, 8.
Torino - Milazzo: ③⑥ June 13 - Sept. 8.
Torino - Napoli: ⑤ (also Apr. 24, 30, Oct. 31).
Torino - Palermo: ③⑥ June 13 - Sept. 8.
Torino - Roma: ⑤ (also Apr. 24, 30, Oct. 31).
Torino - Villa San Giovanni:
Train 1: ⑤ Dec. 15 - June 1; ①⑤ June 8 - Sept. 14; ⑤ Sept. 21 - Dec. 7.
Train 2: ⑤ Apr. 6 - May 4; ⑤⑦ June 8 - July 8; ②⑤⑦ July 10 - Sept. 11.
Train 3: July 11, 18, 25, 30, Aug. 1, 3, 6, 10, 17, 24, 27, 31, Sept. 3, 8.
Venezia - Villa San Giovanni: ③⑤ June 8 - Sept. 7.
Villa San Giovanni - Bologna: daily (also additional train ④⑥ June 9 - Sept. 8).
Villa San Giovanni - Bolzano: ⑤ Dec. 15 - Mar. 23, June 1 - Sept. 7 (also Dec. 20, 27, Jan. 3, Apr. 5, 9).
Villa San Giovanni - Milano: Dec. 18, 22, Jan. 1, 7; ③ Apr. 4 - May 2; ⑤⑦ June 8 - July 8; ②⑤⑦ July 10 - Sept. 11. Also additional train July 18, 24, 27, 30, Aug. 6, 15, 22, 29, Sept. 8.
Villa San Giovanni - Roma: ⑤⑦ Dec. 22 - Dec. 7 (also Dec. 10).
Villa San Giovanni - Torino:
Train 1: ⑦ Dec. 17 - June 3; ②⑦ June 10 - Sept. 16; ⑦ Sept. 23 - Dec. 2.
Train 2: ④ Apr. 5 - May 3; ④⑥ June 7 - July 7; ①④⑥ July 9 - Sept. 10.
Train 3: July 12, 19, 26, 31, Aug. 2, 4, 7, 11, 18, 25, 28, Sept. 1, 4, 10.
Villa San Giovanni - Venezia: ④⑥ June 9 - Sept. 8.

GERMANY

One feature of the new timetable from December 9 is the rerouting of Essen - München *ICE* trains to call at Köln Messe/Deutz station instead of the main station. These particular trains provide the fastest ever link between Köln and Frankfurt, taking just 64 minutes. Regular S-Bahn and regional trains link the Hauptbahnhof and Messe/Deutz stations. Dresden and Nürnberg are linked by an enhanced hourly Regional Express service (Table **880**), running two-hourly via Bayreuth. Binz and Stralsund lose their daily overnight service to München and Köln.

There will be major engineering work in the Hamburg area between December 24 and January 1, particularly affecting services to Hannover and Bremen. Most Bremen line trains and *ICE* trains via Hannover will start from / terminate at Hamburg **Harburg** (situated to the south of Hamburg). Most *IC* trains will be suspended between Hannover and Hamburg, together with a number of early morning/late evening *ICE* trains. A limited number of services will continue to operate from / to Hamburg Hbf but with earlier departures / later arrivals. Trains to / from Kiel and Westerland will use a diversionary route calling at Hamburg Harburg. Please confirm timings before travelling during this period.

AUSTRIA

Amonst the changes here are a slight speeding up of services on the Wien - Salzburg *Westbahn*, which has seen significant infrastructure improvements over the last few years.

POLAND

There are extensive timetable changes throughout the country, and a small increase in *IC* trains. Inter City *Odra* Warszawa - Wrocław runs via Katowice instead of Poznań.

CZECH REPUBLIC

The biggest changes are on the main lines heading east from Praha, to Brno and Ostrava. An enhanced fast service to Brno (Table **1150**) means that slower trains are now shown in a separate section of the table, whereas trains via Havlickův Brod are in new Table **1151**. Similarly, it has been necessary to show the *SuperCity* and fast *IC* services to Ostrava in a separate section of Table **1160**, whilst the hourly Brno - Ostrava trains now have their own table (**1161**). New through trains from Praha to Luhačovice and Veseli nad Moravou in the south-eastern part of the country are shown in expanded Table **1162**, and we have also managed to find space in Table **1169** to mention some additional local services to places of tourist interest, namely Litomyšl, Kroměříž and Karlštejn.

HUNGARY

With the slight increase in the Budapest - Wien service, the main changes here are on the Budapest - Györ corridor and the various other routes shown in Table **1250**, where it has been necessary to split off slower trains into separate sections. Györ - Bratislava (now Table **1252**) only has one through train, but there are increased possibilities by changing at Rajka. The Budapest - Békéscsaba - Lökösháza line (Table **1280**) is also recast, and journeys to Gyula now require a change at Békéscsaba. The Budapest - Satu Mare train has reverted to running via Nyirábrány (Romanian table **1627**) rather than Mátészalka.

SLOVENIA, CROATIA, BOSNIA, SERBIA

The new timetables for Slovenia and Croatia are shown in our tables, and we also have information for Macedonia, parts of Bosnia, and international services in Serbia. Domestic routes in Serbia and Montenegro were not available as we went to press, however, and we continue to have difficulty obtaining information from that part of Bosnia Herzegovina known as the Federation.

BULGARIA and ROMANIA

The changes in Bulgaria are not extensive, whereas many Romanian trains have been significantly retimed, with some new links introduced (for example, a through Craiova - Braşov train, Table **1602**), and some trains running to slightly extended schedules.

NEXT MONTH

As well as further verification of the new timings, our January edition will include our **Sample Fares** feature, giving examples of fare levels in different countries across Europe.

Winter International Services from December 9

The following summary of changes to International trains refers to our International Section (Tables **9** to **99**).

Table 9 – The Rail Europe *Snow Train* runs from Paris Nord to Bourg St Maurice with a Eurostar connection from London St Pancras. There is also a connection from Ebbsfleet, replacing the Ashford stop. Eurostar ski services **9092** and **9095** to Bourg St Maurice run for two additional Saturdays in March and April. Further to last month's news, the additional Eurostar ski service, train **9095** from Bourg St Maurice, runs on Sundays April 6 and 13 instead of the reported Saturdays. *TGV* ski trains **5108 / 5178** Lille - St Gervais run via Annemasse instead of Aix les Bains.

Table 10 – Due to changes on the Calais - Boulogne - Paris line, the last rail - sea - rail connecting service from London to Paris is earlier on Mondays to Fridays, departing London Charing Cross at 1023 instead of 1153 and arriving Paris Nord one hour earlier at 2020.

The newly accelerated Eurostar service between London and Paris will benefit from additional departures from February 10.

Table 11 – Some retiming of services from / to western and southern France has occured. Train **5104 / 5186** Lille - Toulouse is extended to and from Brussels on Mondays to Fridays numbered **9804 / 9886**. Train **5162** from Perpignan and Montpellier to Lille (combined with **5144** from Marseille) terminates at Lille Flandres instead of Lille Europe. This also applies to train **9816** Bordeaux to Lille, creating a rather tight connection for passengers continuing to London.

Table 14 – The retiming of Paris - Genève services creates new journey opportunities, including a late-afternoon train from Genève at 1614 which arrives into Paris in time for a daily connection to London St Pancras, arriving at 2234.

Tables 15 and **18** – *Thalys* services on the Paris - Brussels - Amsterdam route call at Antwerpen Centraal instead of Antwerpen Berchem. Timings are recast in anticipation of the full opening of the *HSL Zuid* line north of Antwerpen, expected in late 2008.

The *Benelux* services (Brussels - Amsterdam) are also retimed and revert to a daily timetable, remaining unaltered at the weekend. The services have been given four figure train numbers, spaced four apart, presumably to accommodate any future increase in service. The retimings adversely affect Eurostar connections to and from London, as shown in Table **15**, however this will be a temporary situation until these services are able to use the high-speed line.

Table 17 – *Thalys* train **9499** Paris - Liège is retimed 30 minutes later (one hour later on Saturdays and Sundays).

Table 20 – A new later connection from London to Hamburg is now possible (depart 1300, arrive 0021) by changing at Brussels and Köln. The Paris - Hamburg night train **242 / 243** combines with **408 / 409** *CityNightLine* Zürich - Hamburg between Dortmund and Hamburg, resulting in the journey time being extended by two hours. The night trains which used to cease running between early November and mid-December will run all year in 2008, and will also run on December 24 and 31, 2007.

Table 22 – A through night train runs between Amsterdam and Praha, formed by diverting the current Hagen - Duisburg - Köln - Berlin - Praha train **378 / 379**. The train still runs via Köln, but no longer serves Essen. The Hagen - København portion is similarly rerouted to give a new Amsterdam - København night service.

Table 24 – To add to the revolution in Amsterdam's night train provision, the *Jan Kiepura* to Warszawa now runs from Amsterdam instead of Frankfurt (still via Köln), with through sleeping cars to Minsk and Moskva. Whilst over the last few years sleeping cars between Russia and western Europe have been on the decline, the new train features through sleepers from both Basel and München to Moskva, as well as couchette cars for Warszawa. These two portions also provide a direct service from Frankfurt, Mannheim and Nürnberg and full details have been squeezed into the table. Also shown is the new through sleeper from Paris to Moskva which we understand runs twice weekly from the start of the new timetable. An unusual feature of this service is a 7 hour stopover in Berlin, with a 12 hour stopover westbound!

Table 28 – Some Amsterdam - Köln - Frankfurt *ICE* services are retimed, while most have been renumbered. *ICE* **223 / 222** now runs only as far as Frankfurt (numbered *ICE* **121 / 120**) but connections are maintained to München at Frankfurt Flughafen in the same timings. *ICE* **121** runs on Mondays to Saturdays only and resumes calling at Köln Messe / Deutz instead of Köln Hbf, whilst the return *ICE* **120** does not run on Saturdays. The *Donau-Kurier* is extended to run Amsterdam - Köln - Frankfurt - Wien, giving Amsterdam yet another new sleeper service (restoring a facility withdrawn some years ago).

Table 30 – There are five *ICE* trains running Paris - Saarbrücken - Frankfurt, replacing the previous service of one to Frankfurt and two to Saarbrücken. These trains, of course, use the new high-speed line in eastern France (opened in June 2007) and complete the journey in three hours 45 minutes.

Table 32 – The three Paris - Strasbourg - Stuttgart *TGV* trains have been joined by a fourth train, which runs through to München taking six hours 15 minutes. A new pair of trains numbered *EC* **43 / 44** has been introduced between Wien and Budapest.

Table 40 – The Lötschberg Base Tunnel has opened fully for passenger trains, speeding up services between Basel and Brig. *EC* **90 / 91** *Vauban* runs from Brussels to / from Zürich instead of Interlaken Ost. A third *TGV* pair has been introduced between Paris and Zürich (1224 from Paris and 1802 from Zürich), and on Saturdays during the winter sports season the 0824 departure from Paris is extended to Chur, returning late afternoon.

Table 42 – The 1804 Paris to Bern *TGV* train (Fridays and Sundays only) has been withdrawn, as well as the 0623 Bern to Paris, which previously ran on Mondays and Saturdays.

Table 44 – There have been some timing changes to the Paris - Milano day services. In particular, the 0910 Milano - Paris train departs one hour earlier, thereby severing a number of overnight connections from southern Italy.

Table 46 – Thanks to the opening of the new stretch of high-speed line in Spain, from December 23 it will be possible to travel between London and Madrid in one day, without the use of a night train.

Tables 49 and **90** – The twice-weekly overnight train **5508 / 5506** from Nice to Cerbère (returning from Portbou) has been withdrawn, affecting connections from Barcelona and Milano.

Table 50 – The early-morning København - Hamburg train has been extended to Berlin, returning mid-afternoon, and is formed of *ICE* stock (the *ICE-TD* diesel variety). A second København - Hamburg train will change to *ICE* from January 6. The 1853 departure from København used to convey, uniquely, cars of three different night stock: *EN*, *NZ* and *CNL*, but is now purely *CNL*.

Table 51 – The Berlin - Poznań - Kaliningrad sleeping car in train **344 / 345** is running all year, bringing to an end the seasonal service via Szczecin to Kaliningrad and Ełk.

Table 56 – Train **345** from Berlin to Lviv, Kyïv, Odesa and Kraków departs from Berlin Lichtenberg station instead of Zoo and Hauptbahnhof. It now thus matches its westbound counterpart, train **344**, which already terminates at Lichtenberg. A new early-morning Poznań - Berlin *EC* train has been introduced on Mondays and Saturdays, returning on Friday and Sunday evenings. Services between Berlin and Warszawa are being diverted and retimed on certain dates and these are shown in a special table on page 75. A new Kraków - Warszawa - Moskva sleeping car has been introduced.

Table 57 – The service from Praha via Furth im Wald to München and Nürnberg has been recast and increased to four trains each way (two for each destination). All have names and the München - Praha trains are operated by Arriva Länderbahn Express (ALX). *CityNightLine* **363 / 362** *Orion* Praha - München has been withdrawn.

Table 58 – night train **353 / 352** Wiesbaden - Frankfurt Hbf - Praha now runs Basel - Frankfurt Süd - Praha Holešovice, but starts at Praha Hlavní for the return journey.

Tables 58, 60 – Night train **377 / 376** Dresden - Praha - Bratislava no longer starts in Germany, commencing instead at Františkovy Lázně and running to Praha via Cheb and Plzeň. The sleeping and couchette cars were previously conveyed between Bratislava and Budapest in the *Báthory* but since the latter train has been withdrawn, the whole train, now named *Galileo Galilei*, is extended to Budapest, running via Štúrovo instead of Györ. Departure from Budapest is at 1950, three hours later than in the previous timetable.

An additional Praha - Budapest facility is formed by the means of a 2nd class portion attached to *EC* **71** and *IC* **131**, returning in *IC* **130** / *EC* **70**. The sleepers and couchettes conveyed between Praha and Budapest in **375/374** *Pannonia* are extended to Lököshaza. Train *EC* **370/1** no longer runs through to Hamburg and Århus but is diverted at Berlin to run instead to Stralsund, extended to the Baltic resort of Binz on seasonal dates.

461 / 460 *Transbalkan* Budapest - Bucureşti - Sofiya - Thessaloníki is withdrawn, replaced on the Bucureşti - Sofiya - Thessaloníki stretch by train **463 / 462** *Romania* with couchettes and a restaurant car, also new sleeping cars Bucureşti - Athína. There are still sleeping cars from Budapest (conveyed Budapest - Bucureşti in the *Ister*) but these only go as far as Sofiya. Through couchettes Budapest - Thessaloníki will run in summer but these will be routed via Beograd.

Table 62 – Train **411 / 410** *Olympus* Ljubljana - Zagreb - Beograd - Skopje - Thessaloníki is reduced to run Ljubljana - Zagreb - Beograd and has lost its name. Trains **293** and **335** are no longer combined between Beograd and Niš, with **335** departing Beograd nearly two hours later at 2220, arriving Thessaloníki at 1307. The return train (**334**) departs Thessaloníki over 150 minutes earlier at 1615 arriving Beograd at 0521, enabling an earlier connection into *IC* **210** to München. There is a through seats car München - Rijeka in train **296 / 297**, joined by sleeping and couchette cars on certain dates.

Table 64 – Daytime services between Nürnberg and Wien are increased from four to six, running every two hours. Most have connections to and from Hamburg and Berlin, but *ICE* **91 / 90** Hamburg - Kassel - Wien has been withdrawn.

Table 65 – As the weekly Hamburg - Rijeka train is withdrawn and the weekly Hamburg - Bolzano train can be incorporated into Table **70**, the opportunity has been taken to create a München - Wien - Budapest table, particularly in view of the forthcoming ÖBB *railjet* services to be introduced on this route from December 2008.

Table 66 – Services on the Dortmund - Köln - Frankfurt - Wien - Budapest axis have been recast with the number of direct daytime Frankfurt - Wien services (operated by tilting *ICE* trains), doubling from three to six, running every two hours. *EC* **25 / 24** Dortmund - Wien - Budapest has been replaced by an *ICE* running between Dortmund and Wien, but with no services venturing beyond Wien to Budapest.

Table 68 – The weekly Dortmund - Rijeka train has been cut back to Villach.

Table 70 – Trains **287 / 286** *Capri* München - Roma - Napoli and **289 / 288** München - Firenze / Venezia have been combined to form new *City Night Line* train **389 / 388** with portions from München to Venezia and from München to Roma via Firenze. The München - Stuttgart - Basel - Chiasso - Milano night train (**260 / 301** and **300 / 260**) has been withdrawn.

Table 82 – *Cisalpino* services have been revised, with all four Basel - Bern - Milano trains being operated by tilting units. In conjunction with the new Lötschberg Base Tunnel this gives time savings of up to an hour. Certain Zürich - Milano services have the tilting *CIS* trains, but all services on the Genève - Milano and Basel - Luzern - Milano routes are operated using conventional trains, classified *EC*, at least until new *ETR 610* units are delivered during 2008.

The Basel - Bern - Roma portion of night train **313 / 314** *Luna* has been withdrawn, but the Zürich - Roma portion now runs via Bern to compensate. Passengers from Basel can join the train by using a local connection to Olten, and in the return direction there is a connection from Bern. The weekly *Freccia delle Puglie* between Zürich and Lecce no longer runs.

Table 89b – train *EC* **50 / 51** Venezia - Budapest is renumbered **60/61**.

Table 91 – train *IC* **200 / 201** *Kvarner* Budapest - Zagreb has been retimed to depart Budapest two hours earlier at 0605.

Table 95 – The Moskva - Bratislava sleeping car runs in the *Chopin* via Bohumín and Břeclav, and is extended to Budapest, giving Budapest two routes to Moskva once again. Note there is also a new Moskva - Košice sleeping car (Table **1750**) extended to Žilina on four days a week (Table **1180**). The Moskva - Wien cars run daily all year. The weekly St Peterburg - Budapest carriage has been withdrawn.

Table 96 – The sleeping car Wien - Bratislava - Košice - Lviv - Kyïv departs Wien seven hours earlier at 1228, thereby reducing the journey to one night, although it remains unchanged in the other direction.

Table 98 – The twice weekly service between Chişinău and Istanbul via Bucureşti has been withdrawn.

Table 99 – Train **336 / 337** *Báthory* Warszawa - Zwardoń - Žilina - Bratislava - Budapest has been withdrawn, but the cars run instead in **202 / 203** *Chopin*. Train **380 / 381** *Cracovia* Kraków - Košice - Bucureşti will run only in summer. A new *EuroCity* daytime service *EC* **382 / 383** *Jósef Bem* has been introduced between Warszawa and Budapest via Kraków and Košice.

5 AIRPORT → CITY CENTRE LINKS

City Plans are on pages 29–33

Airport code and name		City	Distance	Journey	Transport ‡	City terminal	Tabl
AAR	Aarhus	Århus	37 km	40 mins	🚌	Central train station	
ABZ	Aberdeen, Dyce	Aberdeen	11 km	40 mins	🚌 **27**, ①–⑥ every 30–40 mins, ⑦ 70 - 125 mins	Guild Street. Also taxis to Dyce rail station	
ALC	Alacant	Alacant	12 km	30 mins	🚌 **C6**, every 40 mins	Plaça del Mar	
AMS	Amsterdam, Schiphol	Amsterdam	17 km	20 mins	Train, every 10 mins (every hour 2400 - 0600)	Centraal rail station	45
		Rotterdam	65 km	45 mins	Train, every 30 mins	Centraal rail station	45
		Den Haag	43 km	30 mins	Train, every 30 mins	Centraal rail station	45
AOI	Ancona, Falconara	Ancona	16 km	30 mins	1) 🚌 **9**, 2) Train hourly at peak times: 17 mins	Main rail station	
ATH	Athína, Elefthérios Venizélos	Athína	35 km	28 mins	Train, hourly	Main rail station (Larissa)	
		Athína	27 km	41 mins	Metro (line **3**), every 30 mins	Syntagma	
		Pireás	41 km	90 mins	🚌 **E96**, every 15–20 mins	Platía Karaiskáki	
SOB	Balaton, Sármellék	Keszthely	12 km	20 mins	🚌, connects with Ryanair flights	Rail station. Also 🚌 to Budapest Déli (190 mins), Siófok and Székesfehérvár	
BCN	Barcelona, Aeroport del Prat	Barcelona	14 km	20 mins	Train, 2 per hour; 0600 - 2229	Sants. Also calls at Passeig de Gràcia and França rail stns.	66
BSL	Basel - Mulhouse - Freiburg	Basel	9 km	20 mins	🚌 **50**, 4 per hour	SBB rail station / Kannenfeldplatz	
		Mulhouse	22 km	30 mins	🚌 every 70 - 90 mins, 0645 - 2100	Rail station	
BFS	Belfast, International	Belfast	26 km	40 mins	🚌 *Airbus* **300**, Ⓐ every 10 mins; ⑥ every 20; ⑦ every 30	Europa Buscentre (adjacent to Great Victoria St rail station)	
BHD	Belfast, City	Belfast	2 km	15 mins	🚌 *Airlink* **600**, ①–⑥ every 20 mins; ⑦ every 40 mins	Europa Buscentre. Also train from Sydenham rail station.	
BEG	Beograd	Beograd	16 km	30 mins	🚌 connects with flights	JAT City Terminal, rail station	
SXF	Berlin, Schönefeld	Berlin	24 km	27 mins	Train *AirportExpress* **RE7/ RB14** 2 per hour 0631 - 2331	Berlin Ost, Alexanderplatz, Hbf and Zoo rail stations	84
TXL	Berlin, Tegel	Berlin	7 km	22 mins	🚌 *JetExpressBus TXL*, Ⓐ every 10 mins, Ⓒ every 20 mins	Berlin Hauptbahnhof rail station	
BIQ	Biarritz - Anglet - Bayonne	Biarritz	3 km	22 mins	🚌 *STAB* **6**, every hour approx.	Town centre	
		Bayonne	7 km	28 mins	🚌 *STAB* **6**, every hour approx.	Rail station	
BIO	Bilbao, Sondika	Bilbao	10 km	45 mins	🚌 Bizkaibus **A-3247**, every 30 mins 0630 - 2300	Plaza Moyúa (Metro station Moyúa)	
BHX	Birmingham, International	Birmingham	12 km	11 mins	Train, ①–⑥ ± 6 per hour, ⑦ 3 per hour	New Street rail station from International	129, 142, 14
FRL	Bologna, Forlì	Bologna	66 km	75 mins	🚌, connects with Ryanair flights	Centrale rail station, also 🚌 to Forlì rail station every 20 minute	
BLQ	Bologna, Guglielmo Marconi	Bologna	8 km	20 mins	🚌 *Aerobus* BLQ, every 30 mins 0530 - 2100	Centrale rail station	
BOD	Bordeaux, Mérignac	Bordeaux	12 km	45 mins	🚌, every 45 mins 0745 - 2245	St Jean rail station	
BTS	Bratislava, Milan Rastislav Štefánika	Bratislava	10 km	20 mins	🚌 **61**, ①–⑤ 3 - 6 per hour, ⑥⑦ 2 - 4 per hour	Main rail station (Hlavná stanica)	
BRE	Bremen	Bremen	3 km	20 mins	Tram **6**, ①–⑥ every 10 mins, ⑦ every 20 mins	Main rail station	
VBS	Brescia, Montichiari, Verona	Verona	50 km	45 mins	🚌, connects with Ryanair flights	Main rail station	
		Brescia	18 km	20 mins	🚌, connects with Ryanair flights	Main rail station	
BRS	Bristol, International	Bristol	13 km	30 mins	🚌 *International Flyer*, 2–3 per hour	Bus station, also Temple Meads rail station	
BRU	Brussels, National / Zaventem	Brussels	12 km	25 mins	Train, every 20 mins	Midi / Zuid rail station (also calls at Central and Nord)	40.
OTP	Bucureşti, Henri Coanda, Otopeni	Bucureşti	16 km	40 mins	🚌 **783**, ①–⑤ every 15 mins; ⑥⑦ every 30 mins	Piaţa Victoriei (800m from Nord station or 1 stop on subway)	
BUD	Budapest, Ferihegy	Budapest	16 km	40 mins	🚌 **200**, every 10 - 20 mins	Kőbánya-Kispest metro station (metro connection to city centre)	
	Terminal 1	Budapest	18 km	25 mins	Train, every 30 mins	Nyugati rail station. Ferihegy station is 200m from Terminal 1	
BZG	Bydgoszcz	Bydgoszcz	4 km	20 mins	🚌 **80**	Main rail station	
CCF	Carcassonne, Salvaza	Carcassonne	5 km	10 mins	🚌 CART **7**, 7 - 8 services daily	Place Gambetta and Carcassonne rail station	
CWL	Cardiff	Cardiff	19 km	40 mins	🚌 *Airbus Xpress* **X91**, ①–⑥ hourly, ⑦ every 2 hours	Central rail station, city centre	
		Cardiff	19 km	50 mins	🚌 to Rhoose then Train: ①–⑥ hourly, ⑦ every 2 hours	Central rail station	
CRL	Charleroi, Brussels	Brussels	55 km	60 mins	🚌, connects with Ryanair flights	Brussels Midi (corner of Rue de France / Rue de l'Instruction)	
		Charleroi		9 mins	🚌 *Line* **A**, ①–⑤ 2 per hour, ⑥⑦ hourly	Main rail station	
ORK	Cork	Cork	8 km	25 mins	🚌 **226**, hourly, additional services in peak periods	Parnell Place Bus Station, then 🚌 **5** to rail station	
DOL	Deauville, St Gatien	Deauville	7 km		Taxi's only, 25 euro's 20 mins.		
LDY	Derry (Londonderry)	Londonderry	11 km	30 mins	🚌 connects with flights	Foyle Street Bus Station	
DNR	Dinard - Pleurtuit - St-Malo	St Malo	10 km	30 mins	🚌 **991**, connects with Ryanair flights on ⚒ only	St Malo rail station via Dinard	
DSA	Doncaster - Sheffield	Doncaster	10 km	25 mins	🚌 **707** *Airport Arrow*, hourly	Rail station	
DTM	Dortmund, Wickede	Dortmund	10 km	25 mins	🚌 every hour, Stadtbahnlinie	Main rail station (Hbf). Also 🚌 to Holzwickede rail station.	
DRS	Dresden	Dresden	15 km	23 mins	Train (S-Bahn **S2**) every 30 mins	Main rail stations (Hauptbahnhof and Neustadt)	857
DUB	Dublin	Dublin	11 km	35 mins	🚌 *Airlink* **747**, every 10 mins (15 - 20 mins on ⑦)	Bus station (Busaras), O'Connell Street	
		Dublin	11 km	45 mins	🚌 *Airlink* **748**, every 30 mins	Heuston rail station, Bus station (Busaras), Connolly rail station	
		Belfast	157 km	130 mins	🚌 **001 / 200**, hourly 0620 - 2120	Europa Buscentre (adjacent to Great Victoria St rail station)	
DBV	Dubrovnik, Čilipi	Dubrovnik	24 km	30 mins	🚌 connects with flights	Bus station	
DUS	Düsseldorf, International	Düsseldorf	7 km	12 mins	Train (S - Bahn **S7**) Ⓐ every 20 mins, Ⓒ every 30 mins	Main rail station (Hauptbahnhof)	800, 802, 80
EMA	East Midlands, Nottingham - - Leicester - Derby	Nottingham	21 km	45 mins	🚌 *skylink*, every 30 mins 0405-2305; (60 mins 2305-0405)	Rail station, Market Square	
		Derby	19 km	31 mins	🚌 *Airline shuttle* hourly 0245 - 2300	Bus station	
		Loughborough	8 km	30 mins	🚌 *Airline shuttle* hourly 0355 - 0015	Rail station	
		Leicester	23 km	50 mins	🚌 *Skylink* hourly 0407 - 2317	St Margaret's Bus station	
EDI	Edinburgh, Turnhouse	Edinburgh	11 km	25 mins	🚌 *Airlink* **100**, every 10 mins. **N22** 2400-0600 every 30mins.	Haymarket rail station; Waverley Bridge (next to Waverley station	
ERF	Erfurt	Erfurt	6 km	22 mins	Tram, Line 4, Ⓐ every 10 mins, Ⓒ every 30 mins	Main rail station (Hauptbahnhof)	
EBJ	Esbjerg	Esbjerg	12 km	21 mins	🚌 **8**	Main rail station (Banegarden)	
FLR	Firenze, Amerigo Vespucci	Firenze	7 km	20 mins	🚌 Ataf *Vola in bus* **62**, every 30 mins	Santa Maria Novella rail station	
HHN	Frankfurt, Hahn	Frankfurt	120 km	105 mins	🚌, connects with Ryanair flights	Stuttgarter Straße, adjacent to main rail station (Hauptbahnhof)	
	Also 🚌 to Bingen, 60 mins; Heidelberg hbf, 140 mins; Koblenz, 70 mins; Köln hbf, 135 mins; Luxembourg, 105 mins; Mainz, 70 mins; Rüdesheim, 85 mins; Saarbrücken, 125 mins; Traben - Trarbach, 25 mins						
FRA	Frankfurt	Frankfurt	10 km	15 mins	Train (S-Bahn **S8** or **S9**), 4–6 times hourly	Main rail station (Hauptbahnhof)	917
FDH	Friedrichshafen	Friedrichshafen	4 km	7 mins	1–2 trains per hour	Main rail station (Stadt) or Harbour (Hafen)	93
GDN	Gdańsk, Lech Walesa	Gdańsk	10 km	26 mins	🚌 **110**, 1–2 per hour	Wrzeszcz rail station: 3 stops (every 15 mins) from Główny	
GVA	Genève	Genève	4 km	9 mins	Train, 4 times hourly	Cornavin rail station	500, 57
GOA	Genova, Cristoforo Colombo	Genova	7 km	30 mins	🚌 *Volabus* **100**, 2 per hour	Brignole and Principe rail stations / Piazza de Ferrari	
GRO	Girona	Girona	12 km	20 mins	🚌, connects with Ryanair flights	Rail / Bus station (Estación autobuses)	
		Barcelona	102 km	70 mins	🚌, connects with Ryanair flights	Estacio del Nord, corner of carrer Ali Bei 80 / Sicilia	
GLA	Glasgow, International	Glasgow	15 km	25 mins	🚌 **905**, every 30 mins (every 15 mins 0730 - 2000 daily)	Buchanan bus station	
PIK	Glasgow, Prestwick	Glasgow	61 km	45 mins	Train, ①–⑥ every 30 mins, ⑦ every 60 minutes	Central station	21
GSE	Göteborg, City	Göteborg	12 km	30 mins	🚌, connects with Ryanair flights	Nils Ericson Terminalen (bus station)	
GOT	Göteborg, Landvetter	Göteborg	25 km	30 mins	🚌, ①–⑤ every 20 mins, ⑥⑦ 20–30 mins	City Air Terminal / Central rail station	
GRZ	Graz	Graz	9 km	9 mins	1) Train ¶ 2) 🚌. 1) and 2) 15 - 19 services daily	1) Main rail station (Hauptbahnhof) 2) Jakominiplatz : 20 mins	
HAM	Hamburg, Fuhlsbüttel	Hamburg	11 km	25 mins	🚌 Jasper, every 15 mins	Main rail station (Hauptbahnhof) / Kirchenallee	
HAJ	Hannover, Langenhagen	Hannover	15 km	17 mins	Train (S-Bahn **S5**), every 30 mins	Main rail station (Hauptbahnhof)	80
HEL	Helsinki, Vantaa	Helsinki	19 km	30 mins	🚌 **615**, ①–⑤ every 12 mins, ⑥⑦ every 20–30 mins	Rail station (stop 10)	
		Tikkurila	7 km	22 mins	🚌 **61**, ①–⑤ every 15 mins, ⑥⑦ every 20 mins	Rail station for trains to Helsinki (20 mins; 16 km)	
IOM	Isle of Man, Ronaldsway	Douglas	16 km	30 mins	🚌 **1**, hourly (every 30 mins in peak periods)	Lord street	
IST	İstanbul, Atatürk	İstanbul	24 km	45 mins	🚌, ± hourly 0600 - 2300	City Terminal, Şişhane	
		İstanbul	24 km	60 mins	Metro to Zeytinburnu, then over bridge for Tram	Sirkeci rail station	
SAW	İstanbul, Sabiha Gökçen	İstanbul	32 km	60 mins	🚌, 1–2 per hour, 0540–2040	Bus station. Also Pendik rail station is 4km from airport.	
FKB	Karlsruhe - Baden-Baden	Baden-Baden	8 km	15 mins	🚌 **205**, connects with Ryanair flights	Rail station; also 🚌 to Karlsruhe Durlach rail station, 45min	
KTW	Katowice, Pyrzowice	Katowice	34 km	60 mins	🚌, 1144 Ⓐ, 1225 Ⓒ, 1245 Ⓐ, 1725 ⚒, 2350 ⚒	Main rail station	
KUN	Kaunas	Kaunas	13 km	40 mins	🚌 **120, 29**	City centre	
KLU	Klagenfurt	Klagenfurt	5 km	25 mins	🚌 **45**, to Annabichl rail station, then train or 🚌 **40**	Main rail station and bus station	
KOC	Knock	Charlestown	8 km	15 mins	🚌 **449A**, ①–⑥ 6 per day, ⑦ 5 per day	Rooney's public house.	
CPH	København, Kastrup	København	12 km	15 mins	Train, every 10 mins	Main rail station (Hovedbanegård)	70
		Malmö	36 km	22 mins	Train, every 20 mins	Central rail station	70
CGN	Köln / Bonn, Konrad Adenauer	Bonn	20 km	30 mins	🚌 **670**, ①–⑤ every 20–30 mins; ⑥⑦ every 30–60 mins	Main rail station (Hauptbahnhof)	
		Köln	15 km	16 mins	Train **S13**, ①–⑤ every 20 mins, ⑥⑦ every 30 mins	Main rail station (Hbf). Also to Mönchengladbach, Koblenz	80
KRK	Kraków, Balice	Kraków	12 km	15 mins	Train, every 30 mins	Kraków Główny. Balice rail station is 200m from air terminal.	
KBP	Kyïv, Boryspol	Kyïv	34 km	60 mins	🚌 *Polit*, every 30 mins	Main rail station	
LBA	Leeds - Bradford	Leeds	16 km	40 mins	🚌 **757**, every 30 mins	Leeds City Centre (Bus and Rail Stations)	
		Bradford	11 km	35 mins	🚌 **647, 651, 747**, every 60 mins	Bradford Interchange	
LEJ	Leipzig - Halle	Leipzig	20 km	14 mins	Train, every 30mins	Main rail station (Hauptbahnhof)	81
AOC	Leipzig, Altenburg-Nobitz	Leipzig	75 km	70 mins	🚌 **250** *ThüSac*, connects with Ryanair flights	Main rail station. Also stops at Altenburg rail station after 15 mins	

‡ – The frequencies shown apply during daytime on weekdays and are from the airport to the city centre. There may be fewer journeys in the evenings, at weekends and during the winter months. Extended 🚌 journey times could apply during peak hours.

¶ – Graz Airport - Feldkirchen rail station is located about 30 metres away from the airport.

City Plans are on pages 29–33

AIRPORT → CITY CENTRE LINKS

irport code and name	City	Distance	Journey	Transport ‡	City terminal	Table
NZ Linz, Blue Danube	Linz	12 km	19 mins	🚌, connects with Ryanair flights	Main rail station. Also free 🚌 to Hörsching rail station, 3 mins.	
IS Lisboa, Portela	Lisboa	7 km	45 mins	🚌 *Aero-Bus* **91**, every 20 mins 0740 - 2040	Cais do Sodré and Rossio rail stations	
PL Liverpool, John Lennon	Liverpool	11 km	45 mins	🚌 **500**, every 30 mins 0515-0015	Lime Street rail station, Norton St. coach station	
JU Ljubljana, Brnik	Ljubljana	26 km	45 mins	🚌, Ⓐ hourly 0500–2000; Ⓒ 0700, every 2 hours 1000–2000	Bus station (Avtobusna postaja)	
CJ Łódź, Lublinek	Łódź	6 km	20 mins	🚌 **65**	Kaliska rail station	
CY London, City	London	12 km	23 mins	Train (Docklands Light Railway), every 7–10 mins	Bank underground (tube) station	**140**
GW London, Gatwick	London	44 km	30 mins	Train *Gatwick Express*, every 15 minutes	Victoria rail station	**103, 140**
HR London, Heathrow	London	24 km	15 mins	Train *Heathrow Express*, every 15 minutes	Paddington rail station	**140**
	London	24 km	58 mins	Underground train (tube), every 4–10 mins	Kings Cross & St Pancras rail stations	**140**
TN London, Luton	London	50 km	35 mins	Frequent trains (🚌 between ✈ and rail station)	Kings Cross Thameslink and St Pancras rail stations	**103, 140**
TN London, Stansted	London	55 km	45 mins	Train *Stansted Express*, every 15 minutes	Liverpool Street rail station	**140**
BC Lübeck, Blankensee	Lübeck	8 km	30 mins	🚌 **6**, every 20 mins	Main bus station (bus stop 5) adjacent to rail station	
	Hamburg	59 km	75 mins	🚌, connects with Ryanair flights	Corner Adenauerallee / Brockesstrasse (ZOB) near main rail station	
UX Luxembourg, Findel	Luxembourg	7 km	25 mins	🚌 **16**, every 15 mins ①–⑤, every 20 mins ⑥	Central rail station	
WO Lviv, Sknilov	Lvov	10 km		🚌, Taxi-bus *Marshrutka*	City Centre	
YS Lyon, St Exupéry	Grenoble	91 km	65 mins	🚌 Satobus, hourly 0830 - 1930, 2030 Ⓑ, 2145, 2315	Bus station (gare routière), Place de la Résistance	
	Lyon	25 km	50 mins	🚌 *Navette Aéroport*, every 20 mins 0600 - 2320	Part Dieu (journey 35 mins) and Perrache (50 mins) rail stations	
	Chambéry	87 km	60 mins	🚌, 4–5 times daily	Bus station (gare routière)	
IAD Madrid, Barajas	Madrid	12 km	45 mins	1) Metro (Line **8**) every 4 - 5 mins; 2) 🚌 **89** ± every 10 mins	1) Nuevos Ministerios rail / metro station 2) Plaza Colón	
GP Málaga	Málaga	7 km	12 mins	Train, every 30 mins	Centro-Alameda and RENFE rail stations	**672**
IMX Malmö, Sturup	Malmö	30 km	45 mins	🚌 *flygbussarna*, connects with Ryanair flights	Central rail station	
	København	45 km	50 mins	🚌 **737** *graahundbus*, connects with Ryanair flights	Central rail station	
IAN Manchester	Manchester	16 km	14 mins	Train, up to 6 per hour (2 per hour through the night)	Piccadilly rail station	
IBX Maribor, Orehova vas	Maribor	9 km	15 mins	🚌, connects with Ryanair flights	Bus station, stand 6	
IRS Marseille, Provence	Marseille	28 km	25 mins	🚌, every 20 mins	St Charles rail station; also 🚌 to Aix TGV rail stn. every 30 mins.	
IN Milano, Linate	Milano	9 km	20 mins	1) 🚌 **73** every 10 mins; 2) 🚌 *Starfly*, every 30 mins	1) Piazza S. Babila; 2) Centrale rail station	
IXP Milano, Malpensa	Milano	45 km	40 mins	*Malpensa Express* train, every 30 mins	Cadorna and Bovisa rail stations	**583**
			60 mins	🚌 *Bus Express*, 2 per hour / *Shuttle Air* 3 per hour	Centrale rail station	
GY Milano, Orio al Serio, Bergamo	Milano	45 km	60 mins	🚌, every 30 - 60 mins	Centrale rail station (Air Terminal)	
	Bergamo	4 km	15 mins	🚌, 2 per hour	Rail station	
IME Moskva, Domodedovo	Moskva	35 km	40 mins	Train, every hour (every 30 mins peak times)	Moskva Paveletskaya	
VO Moskva, Sheremetyevo	Moskva	29 km	50 mins	1) 🚌 **817** 2) 🚌 **851** ; every 20 mins 0545 - 0030	1) Planernaya metro station 2) Rechnoi vokzal metro station	
KO Moskva, Vnukovo	Moskva	28 km	35 mins	Train, hourly	Kiyevskaya rail station	
IUC München, International	München	37 km	40 mins	Train (S-Bahn **S1**, **S8**), every 10 mins	Main rail station (Hauptbahnhof)	**892**
	Freising	6 km	24 mins	🚌 *MVV* **635**, every 20 mins	Rail station for connections to Regensburg, Passau	**878, 944**
ITE Nantes, Atlantique	Nantes	9 km	30 mins	🚌 *Tan Air*, ± hourly	Main rail station	
IAP Napoli, Capodichino	Napoli	7 km	20 mins	🚌 *ANM* **3S** line, every 10 mins	Piazza Garibaldi (Central rail station)	
ICL Newcastle, International	Newcastle	9 km	20 mins	Metro train, every 10 - 12 mins	Main rail station	
ICE Nice, Côte d'Azur	Nice	7 km	20 mins	🚌 **99**, every 30 mins 0800 - 2030. Also local 🚌.	SNCF rail station	
		8 km	6 mins	Train, from Nice St Augustin, 500m from Terminal 1	SNCF rail station	
IRN Niederrhein	Düsseldorf	70 km	75 mins	🚌, connects with Ryanair flights	Main rail station (Hauptbahnhof) Worringer Street	
	Düsseldorf	74 km	82 mins	🚌 **1**, to Weeze rail station, then train, Table **802**	Main rail station (Hauptbahnhof)	
NI Nîmes - Arles - Camargue	Nîmes	12 km	15 mins	🚌, connects with Ryanair flights	Rail station	
WI Norwich, International	Norwich	6 km	22 mins	🚌 **X5**, hourly	Bus Station (St Stephens Street)	
UE Nürnberg	Nürnberg	6 km	12 mins	Train, U-bahn **U2**, 4–6 per hour	Main rail station (Hauptbahnhof)	
SL Oslo, Gardermoen	Oslo	49 km	19 mins	Train, 2 - 4 per hour	Central rail station	
RF Oslo, Sandefjord Torp	Oslo	140 km	105 mins	🚌 Torp Express, connects with Ryanair flights	Bus terminal. Also 🚌 to Sandefjord for train to Oslo	
MO Palermo, Falcone-Borsellino	Palermo	24 km	45 mins	Train *Trinacria express*, hourly: xx40 from Punta Raisi	Centrale rail station	
MI Palma, Mallorca	Palma	11 km	30 mins	🚌 **1**, every 15 mins	Paseo de Mallorca, Plaça d'Espanya (for rail stations), the Port	
VA Paris, Beauvais	Paris	80 km	75 mins	🚌, connects with Ryanair flights	Porte Maillot, Metro (Line 1) for Châtelet Les Halles, Gare de Lyon	
DG Paris, Charles de Gaulle	Paris	25 km	35 mins	RER train, (Line B), every 7 - 15 mins	Nord, Châtelet Les Halles, and St Michel stations	**398**
RY Paris, Orly	Paris	15 km	35 mins	RER train, (Line C), every 15 mins	Austerlitz, St Michel, Musée d'Orsay, and Invalides stations	**398**
GF Perpignan, Rivesaltes	Perpignan	5 km	15 mins	🚌, connects with flights	Rail station, bus station	
SA Pisa, Galileo Galilei	Pisa	2 km	5 mins	1) Train, 1 - 2 per hour 2) 🚌 **3**, every 20 mins	Central rail station (some trains continue to Firenze)	**614**
PO Porto	Porto	17 km	30 mins	Train, 2 per hour	Campanhã rail station	
OZ Poznań, Ławica	Poznań	6 km	20 mins	🚌 **L** *MKP*, every hour	Rail station	
RG Praha, Ruzyně	Praha	17 km	60 mins	🚌 **119**, every 10 mins	Dejvická metro station, then Metro line A to muzeum (see City Plans)	
	Praha	16 km	40 mins	🚌 **AE** *Airport Express*, every 30 mins	Holešovice rail station	
UY Pula	Pula	6 km	15 mins	🚌, connects with Ryanair flights	Town centre	
ZE Rzeszów, Jasionka	Rzeszów	10 km	15 mins	🚌 **L**, departs 1150	Main rail station	
EF Reykjavík, Keflavík	Reykjavík	48 km	55 mins	🚌, connects with flights	Hótel Loftleidir	
IX Riga	Riga	13 km	30 mins	🚌 **22**, every 10–30 mins	Abrenes iela (street) next to rail station	
JK Rijeka	Rijeka	30 km	45 mins	🚌 Autotrolej	Bus station, Jelačić Square	
IA Roma, Ciampino	Roma	15 km	15 mins	🚌, to Ciampino station, for train to Roma	Termini rail station	**622**
CO Roma, Fiumicino	Roma	26 km	42 mins	Train, up to 4 per hour	Ostiense, Tiburtina, and Termini rail stations	**622**
(also known as Leonardo da Vinci)		26 km	31 mins	*Leonardo Express* rail service, every 30 mins	Roma Termini	**622**
TM Rotterdam	Rotterdam	5 km	20 mins	*Airport Shuttle* **33**, ①–⑤ every 10 mins, ⑥⑦ every 15 mins	Groot Handelsgebouw (adjacent to Centraal rail station).	
ED St Peterburg, Pulkovo II	St Peterburg	17 km	60 mins	🚌 **T-13**	Moskovskaya Metro station, Line 2 for Nevski Pr. (see City Plans)	
ZG Salzburg, W. A. Mozart	Salzburg	5 km	22 mins	🚌 **2**, ①–⑥ every 10 mins, ⑦ every 20 mins	Main rail station	
OF Sofiya, International	Sofiya	10 km	25 mins	🚌 **84**, every 10–20 mins	University	
OU Southampton	Southampton	8 km	8 mins	Train, 50 metres from terminal	Main rail station	**108, 126**
PU Split, Kaštela	Split	16 km	50 mins	🚌 **37**, ①–⑤ every 20 mins, ⑥⑦ every 30 mins	Departs 200m from Airport terminal. Arrives at bus station	
VG Stavanger, Sola	Stavanger	14 km	30 mins	🚌, ①–⑤ every 20 mins, ⑥ every 45 mins, ⑦ hourly	Atlantic Hotel / Fiskepiren	
RN Stockholm, Arlanda	Stockholm	44 km	20 mins	*Arlanda Express* train, every 15 mins	Central rail station	**747**
YO Stockholm, Skavsta	Stockholm	103 km	80 mins	🚌, connects with Ryanair flights	Cityterminal (bus station), also 🚌 to Nyköping train station	
ST Stockholm, Västerås	Stockholm	107 km	75 mins	🚌, connects with Ryanair flights	Cityterminal (bus station), also 🚌 **941** to Västerås train station	
XB Strasbourg, Entzheim	Strasbourg	12 km	20 mins	🚌, every 20–30 mins to Baggersee, then tram line **A**	Étoile / Homme de Fer / Central rail station	
			12 mins	Train from Entzheim (5 mins walk) infrequent service	Strasbourg	
TR Stuttgart, Echterdingen	Stuttgart	14 km	27 mins	Train (S-Bahn **S2**, **S3**), 2–4 times hourly 0508 - 0008	Main rail station (Hauptbahnhof)	**932**
ZZ Szczecin, Goleniów	Szczecin	38 km	60 mins	🚌, connects with Ryanair flights	Szczecin Główny. Also 🚌, 7km, to Goleniów train station.	
MP Tampere, Pirkkala	Tampere	18 km	25 mins	🚌, connects with Ryanair flights	City Centre (Rautatieasema)	
RN Torino, Caselle	Torino	16 km	20 mins	*SATTI* train every 30 mins	Torino Dora rail station, Piazza Baldissera	
	Torino	16 km	40 mins	🚌, every 30–45 minutes	Torino Porta Nuova and Porta Susa	
LS Toulouse, Blagnac	Toulouse	8 km	20 mins	🚌, every 20 minutes	Place Jeanne d'Arc / Matabiau rail / Bus station (gare routière)	
RS Trieste, Ronchi dei Legionari	Trieste	33 km	50 mins	🚌 **51**, 2 per hour	Bus station, next to rail station	
	Monfalcone	4 km	17 mins	🚌 **10**, ①–⑥ 2–3 per hour; ⑦ hourly	Rail station	
RD Trondheim, Værnes	Trondheim	33 km	37 mins	Train, ①–⑤ hourly, ⑥⑦ every two hours	Rail station	**787**
LC València	València	9 km	22 mins	Train, Lines **3**, **5**, Ⓐ every 6–9 mins; ⑥⑦ every 8–12 mins	Xátiva for Nord rail station	
CE Venezia, Marco Polo	Venezia	12 km	21 mins	🚌 **5**, ①–⑥ every 30 mins; ⑦ every 60 mins	Santa Lucia rail station	
	Venezia		60 mins	Waterbus ± every 60 mins	Lido / Piazza S. Marco	
SF Venezia, Treviso	Venezia	30 km	70 mins	🚌, connects with Ryanair flights	Piazzale Roma	
RN Verona, Villafranca	Verona	12 km	20 mins	🚌, every 20 mins 0635 - 2335	Rail station	
NO Vilnius	Vilnius	5 km	15 mins	🚌 **1** / **2**, every 10 - 15 mins	🚌 **1** : Rail station / 🚌 **2** : Lukiškiu square	
AW Warszawa, Frederic Chopin, Okęcie	Warszawa	10 km	30 mins	🚌 **175** *Airport-City*, ①–⑤ every 20 mins, ⑥⑦ every 30 mins	Centralna rail station	
IE Wien, Schwechat	Wien	21 km	16 mins	*CAT*, every 30 mins	Mitte rail station	**979**
	Wien	21 km	25 mins	S-bahn, every 30 mins	Mitte rail station	**979**
	Bratislava	45 km	70 mins	🚌 ÖBB-Bahn Bus / SAD Bratislava, hourly	AS Mlynské nivy (bus station)	**979**
RO Wrocław, Copernicus	Wrocław	10 km	30 mins	🚌 **406**, ①–⑥ 2–3 per hour; ⑦ every 40 mins	Rail station, bus station	
AG Zagreb	Zagreb	17 km	25 mins	🚌, every 30–60 mins	Bus station (Autobusni kolodvor), Avenija Marina Drzica	
RH Zürich	Zürich	10 km	13 mins	Train, 7 - 8 times per hour	Main rail station (**HB**)	**529**

‡ – The frequencies shown apply during daytime on weekdays and are from the airport to the city centre. There may be fewer journeys in the evenings, at weekends and during the winter months. Extended 🚌 journey times could apply during peak hours.

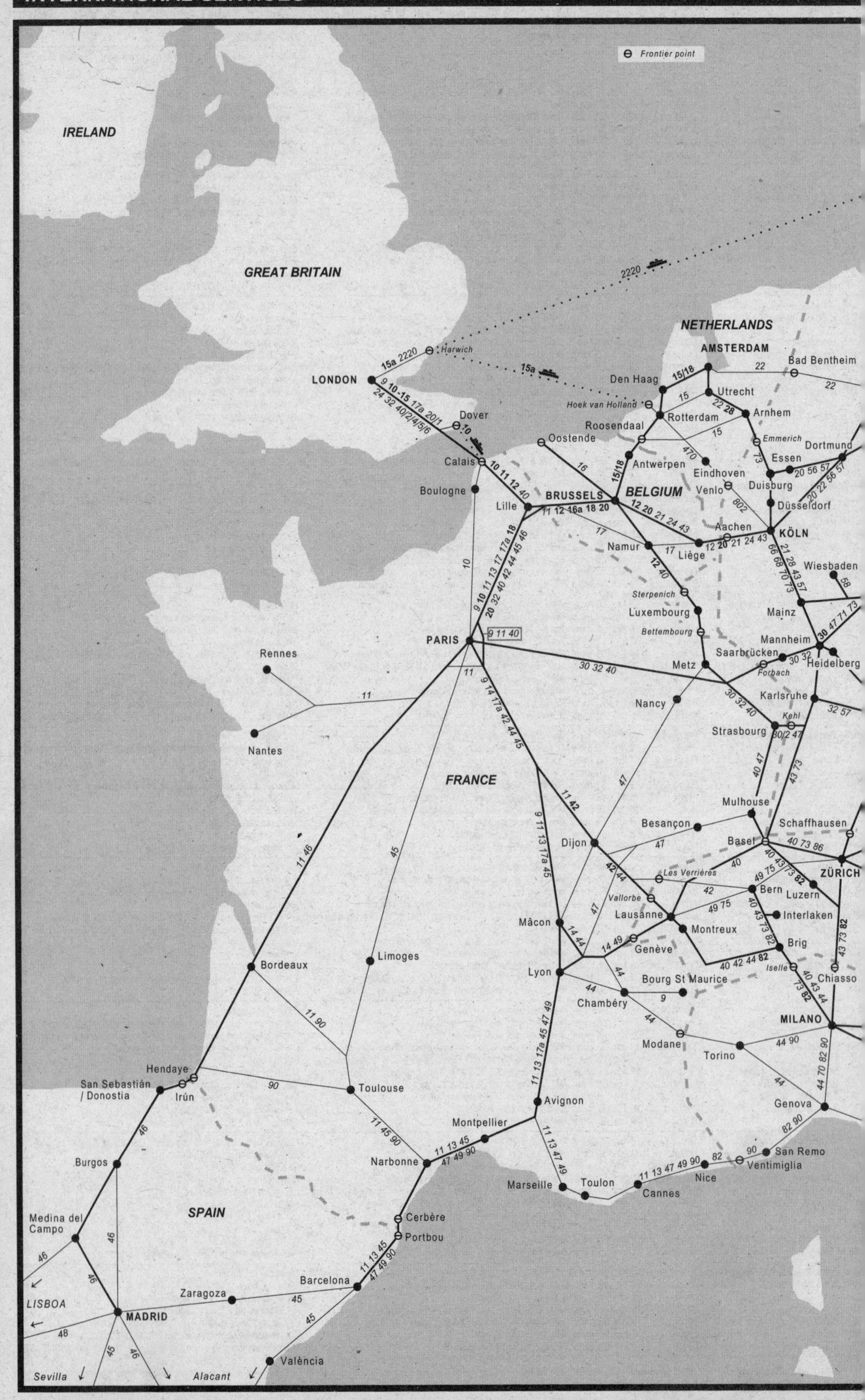
Frontier point
IRELAND
GREAT BRITAIN
NETHERLANDS
BELGIUM
FRANCE
SPAIN
LONDON
Harwich
Dover
Calais
Boulogne
Lille
Oostende
BRUSSELS
AMSTERDAM
Den Haag
Hoek van Holland
Rotterdam
Roosendaal
Antwerpen
Utrecht
Arnhem
Emmerich
Eindhoven
Venlo
Essen
Duisburg
Dortmund
Düsseldorf
KÖLN
Aachen
Liège
Namur
Bad Bentheim
Wiesbaden
Mainz
Mannheim
Heidelberg
Sterpenich
Luxembourg
Bettembourg
Metz
Saarbrücken
Forbach
Karlsruhe
Kehl
Strasbourg
Nancy
PARIS
Rennes
Nantes
Mulhouse
Basel
Schaffhausen
ZÜRICH
Luzern
Bern
Interlaken
Besançon
Dijon
Les Verrières
Vallorbe
Lausanne
Montreux
Brig
Iselle
Chiasso
Mâcon
Lyon
Genève
Bourg St Maurice
Chambéry
Modane
Torino
MILANO
Genova
San Remo
Ventimiglia
Nice
Cannes
Toulon
Marseille
Avignon
Montpellier
Narbonne
Cerbère
Portbou
Barcelona
Bordeaux
Limoges
Toulouse
Hendaye
Irún
San Sebastián / Donostia
Burgos
Medina del Campo
Zaragoza
MADRID
València
LISBOA
Sevilla
Alacant

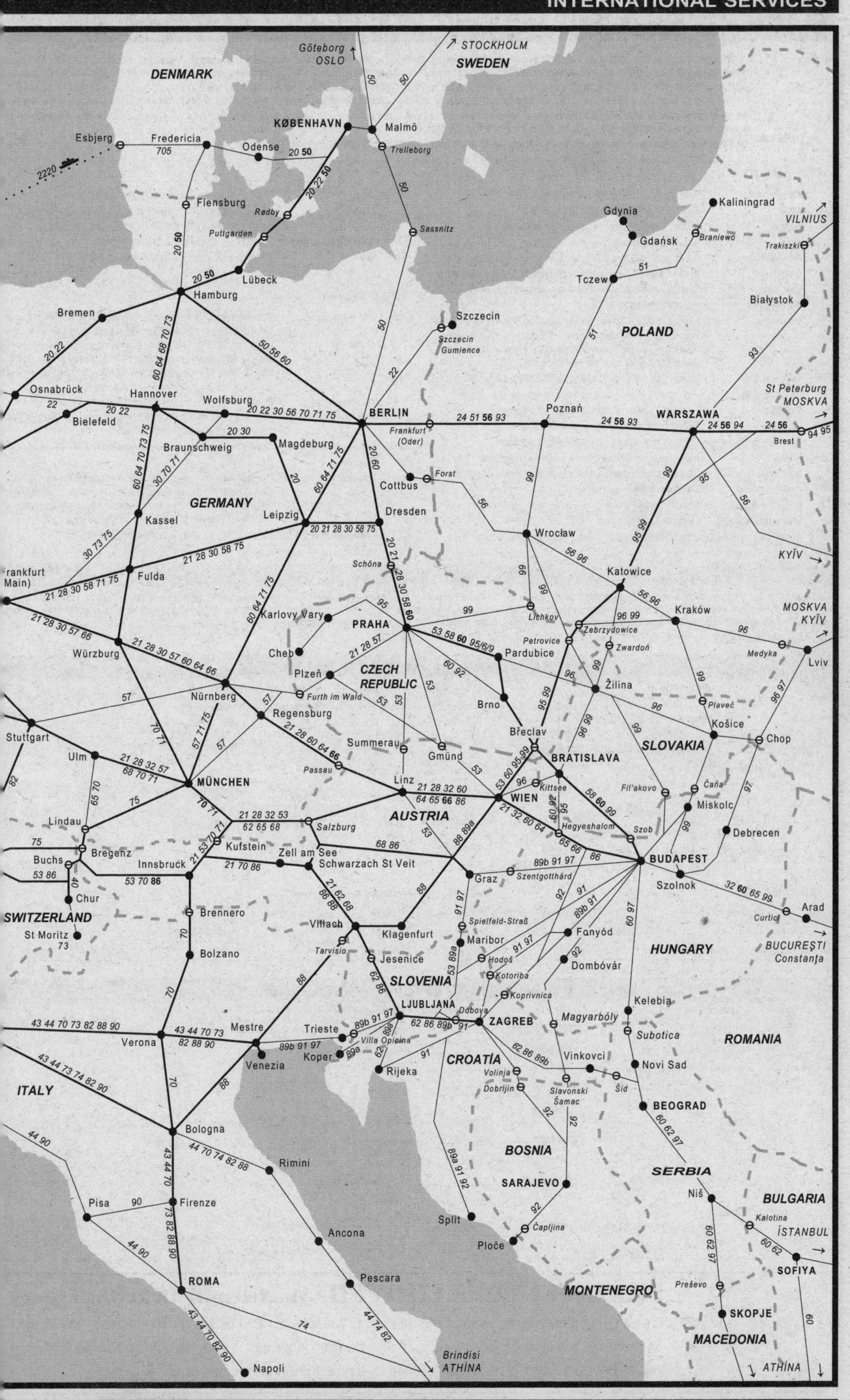
Göteborg
OSLO
STOCKHOLM
SWEDEN
DENMARK
KØBENHAVN
Malmö
Trelleborg
Esbjerg
Fredericia
Odense
Flensburg
Rødby
Puttgarden
Sassnitz
Lübeck
Hamburg
Bremen
Szczecin
Szczecin Gumience
Gdynia
Gdańsk
Kaliningrad
Braniewo
VILNIUS
Trakiszki
Tczew
Białystok
POLAND
Osnabrück
Hannover
Wolfsburg
Bielefeld
BERLIN
Poznań
WARSZAWA
St Peterburg
MOSKVA
Brest
Frankfurt (Oder)
Braunschweig
Magdeburg
Forst
Cottbus
GERMANY
Kassel
Leipzig
Dresden
Wrocław
KYÏV
Frankfurt (Main)
Fulda
Schöna
Katowice
Karlovy Vary
PRAHA
Lichkov
Kraków
MOSKVA
KYÏV
Cheb
Petrovice
Zebrzydowice
Zwardoń
Pardubice
Medyka
Lviv
Würzburg
Plzeň
CZECH REPUBLIC
Žilina
Nürnberg
Furth im Wald
Brno
Plaveč
Stuttgart
Regensburg
Břeclav
Košice
Chop
SLOVAKIA
Summerau
Gmünd
BRATISLAVA
Ulm
MÜNCHEN
Passau
Linz
Kittsee
Fil'akovo
Čaňa
WIEN
Miskolc
Lindau
AUSTRIA
Salzburg
Hegyeshalom
Szob
Debrecen
Bregenz
Kufstein
Zell am See
Schwarzach St Veit
BUDAPEST
Buchs
Innsbruck
Graz
Szentgotthárd
Szolnok
Chur
Curtici
Arad
SWITZERLAND
Brennero
Villach
Spielfeld-Straß
St Moritz
Tarvisio
Klagenfurt
Maribor
Fonyód
Jesenice
Hodoš
BUCUREŞTI
Constanţa
Bolzano
Kotoriba
Dombóvár
HUNGARY
SLOVENIA
Koprivnica
LJUBLJANA
Dobova
ZAGREB
Magyarbóly
Kelebia
Mestre
Trieste
Villa Opicina
Subotica
ROMANIA
Verona
Venezia
Koper
Rijeka
CROATIA
Vinkovci
Novi Sad
Volinja
Dobrljin
Šid
ITALY
Slavonski Šamac
BEOGRAD
Bologna
BOSNIA
SERBIA
Rimini
SARAJEVO
Niš
BULGARIA
Pisa
Firenze
Split
Kalotina
ISTANBUL
Čapljina
Ploče
Ancona
SOFIYA
Pescara
ROMA
MONTENEGRO
Preševo
SKOPJE
MACEDONIA
Napoli
Brindisi
ATHÍNA
ATHÍNA

INTERNATIONAL SERVICES

Services All trains convey first and second classes of seating accommodation unless otherwise noted. For information on types of sleeping car (🛏) and couchette car (▬) see page Restaurant (✕) and buffet (🍸) cars vary considerably from country to country in standard of service offered. The catering car may not be carried or open for the whole journ

Timings **Valid December 9, 2007 – June 14, 2008.** Services can change at short notice and passengers are advised to consult the latest Thomas Cook European Rail Timetable befo travelling. International trains are not normally affected by public holidays, but may alter at Christmas and Easter - these changes (where known) are shown in the tables.

Tickets **Seat reservations** are available for most international trains and are advisable as some trains can get very crowded. **Supplements** are payable on **EuroCity** (*EC*) trains in m countries and on most InterCity trains – consult the introduction at the start of each country to see which supplements apply.

Listed below is a selection of the different types of trains found in the International Section.

DAY SERVICES:

AP	**Alfa Pendular**	Portuguese high-quality tilting express train.
Alvia	**Alvia**	The newest Spanish high-speed trains.
Alta	**Altaria**	Spanish quality express using light, articulated stock.
Arco	**Arco**	Spanish quality express train.
AV	**Alta Velocità**	Italian premium fare **ETR 500** services using high-speed lines.
CIS	***Cisalpino***	Italian **ETR 470** international high-speed (200 km/h) tilting train.
EC	**EuroCity**	Quality International express. Supplement may be payable.
Em	***Euromed***	Spanish 200 km/h trains.
☆	**Eurostar**	High speed (300 km/h) service between London - Paris and Brussels. Special fares payable. Three classes of service: (Business Premier, Leisure Select and Standard). Minimum check-in time 30 minutes. Non–smoking.
ES	**Eurostar Italia**	Italian high speed **ETR 450 / 460 / 500** (250 - 300 km/h) service.
ESc	**Eurostar City**	High speed loco-hauled services, premium fares payable.
Ex	**Express**	Express between Czech Republic and Slovakia.
IC	**InterCity**	Express train. Supplement may be payable.
ICE	**InterCity Express**	German high speed (250 - 300 km/h) service.
ICp	**InterCity** Plus	Italian express formed of new coaches, supplement payable.
IR	**InterRegio**	Inter-regional express usually with refurbished coaches.
RX	**RegioExpress**	Swiss semi-fast regional train.
RB	**Regional Bahn**	German stopping train.
RE	**Regional Express**	German semi-fast train.
SC	**Super City**	Czech Pendolino **680** tilting train, supplement payable.
Talgo	**Talgo**	Spanish quality express using light, articulated stock.
⇌	***Thalys***	High-speed (300 km/h) international train Paris - Brussels - Amsterdam/Köln. Special fares apply. Non–smoking.
TGV	**Train à Grande Vitesse**	French high-speed (270 - 300 km/h) train.
X2000	**X2000**	Swedish high speed (210 km/h) tilting trains.

NIGHT SERVICES:

CNL	**City Night Line**	German brand name covering *CityNightLine*, DB NachtZug a UrlaubsExpress services. Facilities range from *Deluxe* sleepi cars (1 and 2 berth) with en-suite shower and WC, to modernis sleeper and couchette cars. Most trains convey shower faciliti and 🍸 (also ✕ on certain services). Special fares apply and reservation is compulsory on most services.
D	**Durchgangszug** or **Schnellzug**	Overnight or international express. Some may only convey passengers to international destinations and are likely to be compulsory reservation, marked 🄡.
EN	**EuroNight**	Quality international overnight express.
Estr	**Estrella**	Spanish night train.
Hotel	**Trenhotel**	Spanish international quality overnight train. Conveys Gran Clase / Grande Classe sleeping accommodation comprising *de luxe* (1 and 2 berth) compartments with en-suite shower a WC. Also conveys 1, 2 and 4 berth sleeping cars.
ICN	**InterCityNight**	Italian overnight train, supplement payable.

EUROTUNNEL

The frequent car-carrying service between Folkestone and Calais through the **Channel Tunnel** is operated by Eurotunnel. The service operates up to four times hourly (less frequently at night) a takes about 35 minutes. Passengers stay with their cars during the journey. Separate less-frequent trains operate for lorries, coaches, motorcycles, and cars with caravans. Reservations a advisable but passengers can buy tickets at the toll booths when they arrive at the terminal and board the next available shuttle.

Freephone customer information service: ✆ 080 00 96 99 92. Reservations: ✆ 08705 35 35 35.

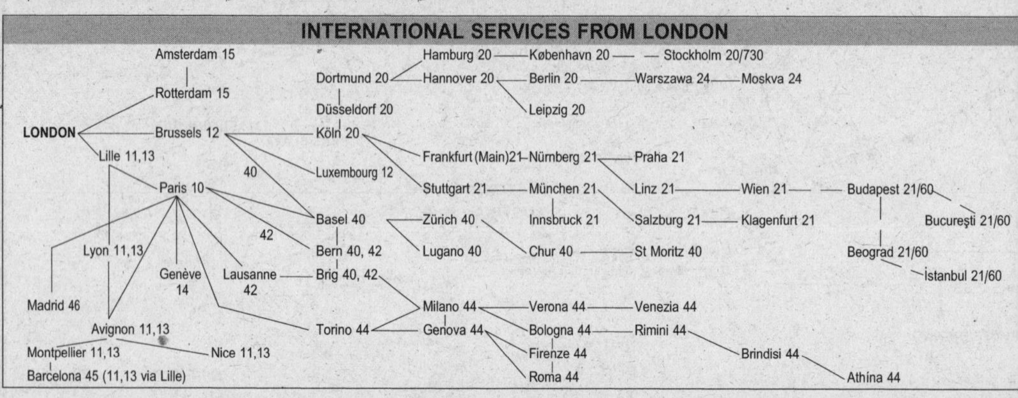

LONDON, BRUSSELS and LILLE - ST GERVAIS, BOURG ST MAURICE and BRIANÇON 9

Other connections are available by changing in Paris (or in Lille and Lyon). Supplements are payable on TGV trains

train type		TGV	⇌	TGV			⇌		☆		☆	☆			☆							TGV		
train number		5106	9904	5108			9920		9092		9046	9044	27050		9096		4800	4802		4804		5146		
train number		5107	9905	5109			9921		9093		[R]	[R]	27051		9066		4801	4803	18907	4805		5147		
notes		[R] 🍷	[R] 🍷	[R] 🍷	2		[R] 🍷		[R] 🍴		🍴	🍴	❖		[R] 🍴		⊡	⊡	2	⊡ ♣		[R] 🍷		
notes		K	Q	K			C		M		V ❖	V ❖	A		R ◐		X	G		T		H		
ondon St Pancras d.	...	...	...	...	...	...	...	...	1000	...	...	1730	...	...	2031	...	...	...	...	...	...	...	...	...
bbsfleet International d.	...	...	...	...	...	...	...	...	|	...	1815	|	...	...	|	...	...	...	...	...	...	...	...	...
shford International **11** d.	...	...	...	...	...	...	...	...	1046	...	|	|	...	...	2115	...	...	...	...	...	...	...	...	...
Amsterdam Centraal d.	...	...	...	...	...	...	0532	...	|	...	|	|	...	...	|	...	...	...	...	...	...	...	...	...
Schiphol ✈ d.	...	...	...	...	...	...	0551	...	|	...	|	|	...	...	|	...	...	...	...	...	...	...	...	...
Den Haag HS d.	...	...	...	...	...	...	0620	...	|	...	|	|	...	...	|	...	...	...	...	...	...	...	...	...
Rotterdam CS d.	...	...	...	...	...	...	0640	...	|	...	|	|	...	...	|	...	...	...	...	...	...	...	...	...
Antwerpen Centraal d.	...	...	...	...	...	...	0742	...	|	...	|	|	...	...	|	...	...	...	...	...	...	...	...	...
Brussels Midi / Zuid d.	...	...	0724	...	...	...	0826	...	|	...	|	|	...	...	|	...	...	...	...	...	...	...	...	...
Calais Ville d.	...	...	|	...	...	...	|	...	|	...	|	|	...	...	|	...	...	...	...	1801	...	...	...	...
Dunkerque d.	...	...	|	...	...	...	|	...	|	...	|	|	...	...	|	...	...	...	...	|	...	2147	...	...
ille Europe 11 d.	...	0651	|	0710	...	...	|	...	|	...	|	|	...	...	|	...	...	...	...	|	...	2225	...	...
ille Flandres d.	...	|	|	|	...	...	|	...	|	...	|	|	...	...	|	...	1741	1934	...	1919	...	|	...	...
ouai **11** d.	...	0717	|	|	...	...	|	...	|	...	|	|	...	...	|	...	1817	2005	...	1946	...	2249	...	...
rras **11** d.	...	0735	|	|	...	...	|	...	|	...	|	|	...	...	|	...	1839	2023	...	|	...	2308	...	...
Amiens d.	...	|	|	|	...	...	|	...	|	...	|	|	...	...	|	...	|	|	...	|	...	|	...	...
GV Haute Picardie **11** d.	...	0759	|	0739	...	...	|	...	|	...	|	|	...	...	|	...	|	|	...	|	...	2328	...	...
aris Charles de Gaulle ✈ **11** d.	...	0833	|	0812	...	...	|	...	|	...	|	|	...	...	|	...	|	|	...	|	...	0001	...	...
arne la Valleé Chessy § **11** d.	...	0848	|	0827	...	...	|	...	|	...	|	|	...	...	|	...	|	|	...	|	...	0017	...	...
aris Nord d.	...	|	|	|	...	...	|	...	|	...	2120	2050	2255	...	|	...	|	|	...	|	...	|	...	...
Aix les Bains a.	...	|	|	|	...	...	|	...	|	...	...	...	|	...	|	...	|	0414	...	|	...	|	...	...
Annecy a.	...	|	|	|	...	...	|	...	|	...	...	...	|	...	|	...	|	0515	...	|	...	|	...	...
La Roche sur Foron a.	...	|	|	|	...	...	|	...	|	...	...	...	|	...	|	...	|	0608	...	|	...	|	...	...
Cluses (Haute Savoie) a.	...	|	|	1301	...	...	|	...	|	...	...	...	|	...	|	...	|	0657	...	|	...	|	...	...
Salanches Megève a.	...	|	|	1323	...	...	|	...	|	...	...	...	|	...	|	...	|	0715	...	|	...	|	...	...
St Gervais a.	...	|	|	1328	1332	...	|	...	|	...	...	...	|	...	|	...	|	0724	0732	|	...	|	...	...
Chamonix a.	...	|	|	...	1411	...	|	...	|	...	...	...	|	...	|	...	|	...	0811	|	...	|	...	...
Gap a.	...	|	|	...	...	...	|	...	|	...	...	...	|	...	|	...	0757	...	...	|	...	|	...	...
Briançon a.	...	|	|	...	...	...	|	...	|	...	...	...	|	...	|	...	0948	...	...	|	...	|	...	...
hambéry a.	...	1148	1152	...	...	...	1236	...	|	...	...	...	0631	...	|	...	...	...	...	0445	...	0502	...	...
lbertville a.	...	1223	1246	...	...	...	1311	...	|	...	...	...	0718	...	|	...	...	...	...	0527	...	0547	...	...
oûtiers-Salins a.	...	1252	1317	...	...	...	1348	...	1730	...	...	...	0755	...	0537	...	...	...	...	0609	...	0626	...	...
ime la Plagne a.	...	1309	...	...	...	...	1409	...	1802	...	...	...	0816	...	0605	...	...	...	...	0634	...	0656	...	...
andry a.	...	1319	...	...	...	...	1419	...	|	...	...	...	0828	...	|	...	...	...	...	0646	...	0713	...	...
ourg St Maurice a.	...	1328	...	...	...	...	1429	...	1820	...	...	...	0838	...	0627	...	...	...	...	0702	...	0726	...	...

train type	☆	☆	TGV		⇌		TGV		TGV		⇌			☆	☆						☆	☆		
train number	9095	9095	5174		9963		5178		5182		9987		27052	9011	9015			4832	4828	4830	9099	9099		
train number	9094	9094	5175		9962	18922	5179		5183		9986		27053	[R] 🍴	[R] 🍴		18934	4833	4829	4831	9098	9098		
notes	[R] 🍴	[R] 🍴	[R] 🍷		[R] 🍷	2	[R] 🍷		[R] 🍷		[R] 🍷		❖	❖	❖		2	⊡ ♣	⊡	⊡ ♣	[R] 🍴	[R] 🍴		
notes	E	U	Y		N		K		K		D		B	W	W			Z	J	L	S ◧	P ◧		
ourg St Maurice d.	0932	0950	1017	...	...	...	...	...	1504	...	1543	...	1905	...	...	...	...	...	...	2028	2215	2215	...	...
andry d.	|	|	1028	...	...	...	...	...	1515	...	1553	...	1915	...	...	...	...	...	...	2036	|	|	...	...
ime la Plagne d.	|	|	1039	...	...	...	...	...	1527	...	1602	...	1925	...	...	...	...	...	...	2046	|	|	...	...
oûtiers-Salins d.	1019	1044	1101	...	1415	...	...	...	1543	...	1623	...	2002	...	...	...	...	...	...	2114	2309	2309	...	...
lbertville d.	|	|	1135	...	1448	...	...	...	1619	...	1658	...	2040	...	...	...	...	...	...	2155	|	|	...	...
hambéry d.	|	|	|	...	1530	...	...	...	1652	...	1732	...	2116	...	...	...	...	...	...	2239	|	|	...	...
Briançon d.	|	|	|	...	|	...	...	...	|	...	|	...	|	...	...	...	...	...	1905	|	|	|	...	...
Gap d.	|	|	|	...	|	...	...	...	|	...	|	...	|	...	...	...	...	...	2053	|	|	|	...	...
Chamonix d.	|	|	|	...	|	1439	...	...	|	...	|	...	|	...	...	...	1839	...	|	|	|	|	...	...
St Gervais d.	|	|	|	...	|	1520	1542	...	|	...	|	...	|	...	...	...	1920	1953	|	|	|	|	...	...
Salanches Megève d.	|	|	|	...	|	...	1552	...	|	...	|	...	|	...	...	...	...	2002	|	|	|	|	...	...
Cluses (Haute Savoie) d.	|	|	|	...	|	...	1608	...	|	...	|	...	|	...	...	...	...	2025	|	|	|	|	...	...
La Roche sur Foron d.	|	|	|	...	|	...	|	...	|	...	|	...	|	...	...	...	...	2104	|	|	|	|	...	...
Annecy d.	|	|	|	...	|	...	|	...	|	...	|	...	|	...	...	...	...	2141	|	|	|	|	...	...
Aix les Bains d.	|	|	|	...	|	...	|	...	|	...	|	...	|	...	...	...	...	2245	|	|	|	|	...	...
aris Nord a.	|	|	|	...	|	...	|	...	|	...	|	...	0600	0807	0913	...	...	|	|	|	|	|	...	...
arne la Vallée Chessy § **11** a.	|	|	1447	...	|	...	2032	...	1946	...	|	...	...	|	|	...	...	|	|	|	|	|	...	...
aris Charles de Gaulle ✈ **11** a.	|	|	1504	...	|	...	2048	...	2001	...	|	...	...	|	|	...	...	|	|	|	|	|	...	...
GV Haute Picardie **11** a.	|	|	1538	...	|	...	2119	...	2037	...	|	...	...	|	|	...	...	|	|	|	|	|	...	...
Amiens a.	|	|	|	...	|	...	|	...	|	...	|	...	...	|	|	...	...	|	|	|	|	|	...	...
rras **11** a.	|	|	1601	...	|	...	|	...	2057	...	|	...	...	|	|	...	...	0615	0726	|	|	|	...	...
ouai **11** a.	|	|	1617	...	|	...	|	...	2113	...	|	...	...	|	|	...	...	0632	0744	0800	|	|	...	...
lle Flandres a.	|	|	|	...	|	...	|	...	2137	...	|	...	...	|	|	...	...	0655	0807	0825	|	|	...	...
lle Europe 11 a.	|	|	1637	...	|	...	2147	...	...	...	|	...	...	|	|	...	...	...	...	|	|	|	...	...
Dunkerque a.	|	|	1711	...	|	...	...	...	...	...	|	...	...	|	|	...	...	...	...	|	|	|	...	...
Calais Ville a.	|	|	...	...	|	...	...	...	...	...	|	...	...	|	|	...	...	...	...	0950	|	|	...	...
Brussels Midi / Zuid a.	|	|	...	...	1951	...	...	...	...	...	2144	...	...	|	|	...	...	...	...	...	|	|	...	...
Antwerpen Centraal a.	|	|	...	...	...	...	...	...	...	...	2232	...	...	|	|	...	...	...	...	...	|	|	...	...
Rotterdam CS a.	|	|	...	...	...	...	...	...	...	...	2336	...	...	|	|	...	...	...	...	...	|	|	...	...
Den Haag HS a.	|	|	...	...	...	...	...	...	...	...	2356	...	...	|	|	...	...	...	...	...	|	|	...	...
Schiphol ✈ a.	|	|	...	...	...	...	...	...	...	...	0019	...	...	|	|	...	...	...	...	...	|	|	...	...
Amsterdam Centraal a.	|	|	...	...	...	...	...	...	...	...	0036	...	...	|	|	...	...	...	...	...	|	|	...	...
shford International **11** a.	1536	1536	...	...	...	...	...	...	...	...	...	...	...	|	|	...	...	...	...	...	0634	0734	...	...
bsfleet International a.	|	|	...	...	...	...	...	...	...	...	...	...	...	0918	|	...	...	...	...	...	|	|	...	...
ndon St Pancras a.	1611	1612	...	...	...	...	...	...	...	...	...	...	...	...	1038	...	...	...	...	...	0716	0812	...	...

– WHITE TRAIN – ⑤ Jan. 18, 2008 - Apr. 4: 🛏 2 cl. (6 berth), disco car and 🍷 Paris Nord - Bourg St Maurice.

– WHITE TRAIN – ⑥ Jan. 26, 2008 - Apr. 12: 🛏 2 cl. (6 berth), disco car and 🍷 Bourg St Maurice - Paris Nord.

– THALYS NEIGE – ⑥ Dec. 22, 2007 - Mar. 15, 2008: [12] and 🍷 Amsterdam - Bourg St Maurice; ⑥ Dec. 22, 2007 - Apr. 5, 2008: [12] and 🍷 Brussels - Bourg St Maurice.

– THALYS NEIGE – ⑥ Dec. 29, 2007 - Mar. 22, 2008: [12] and 🍷 Bourg St Maurice - Amsterdam; ⑥ Dec. 22, 2007 - Apr. 5, 2008: [12] and 🍷 Bourg St Maurice - Brussels. On Feb. 9, 16, 23, Mar. 1, 8 depart Bourg St Maurice 1532, Landry 1546, Aime la Plagne 1555, Moûtiers-Salins 1617, Albertville 1700, Chambéry 1734.

– Apr. 6, 13.

– Feb. 8, 15, 2008.

– ⑤ Dec. 14, 2007 - Mar. 28, 2008.

- Dec. 29, 2007, Jan. 5, Feb. 16, 23, 2008.

– ⑥ Dec. 15, 2007 - Apr. 26, 2008.

- ⑥ Dec. 22, 2007 - Feb. 23, 2008.

– ⑥ Dec. 22, 2007 - Apr. 5, 2008.

- Dec. 29, 2007, Feb. 9, 2008.

– Mar. 29, 2008.

Q – Dec. 22, 2007, Feb. 2, 2008.

R – ⑤ Dec. 28, 2007 - Mar. 21, 2008, (also Feb. 9 as Train **9066**).

S – ⑥ Jan. 5, 2007 - Mar. 22, 2008.

T – ⑤ Dec. 21, 2007 - Feb. 22, 2008.

U – ⑥ Dec. 29, 2007 - Mar. 29, 2008, (also Feb. 17 as Train **9081**).

V – ⑤ Jan. 18, 2008 - Apr. 4.

W – ⑦ Jan. 27, 2008 - Apr. 13.

X – Dec. 21, 28, 2007, Feb. 8, 15, 2008.

Y – ⑥ Dec. 15, 2007 - Mar. 29, 2008.

Z – Feb. 16, 2008.

⊡ – Conveys 🛏 1, 2 cl. only.

§ – Station for Disneyland, Paris.

⇌ – *Thalys* high-speed train [R] 🍷 Special fares payable.

◐ – 🍴 from Ashford. 🍷 2031–0100. 🍴 and 🍷 from 0500.

◧ – 🍴 from Moûtiers. 🍷 2215–0100. 🍴 and 🍷 from 0500.

❖ – Special fares payable. Tickets available only through Rail Europe Limited and its agents.

♣ – For connection to / from London by rail and sea, see Table **101** (London Charing Cross - Dover Priory and v.v.) and Table **2110** (⛴ Dover Eastern Docks - Calais Port and v.v.).

☆ – Eurostar train. Special fares payable. Minimum check-in time 30 minutes.

10 LONDON - LILLE - PARIS and BRUSSELS *by Eurostar*

Minimum check-in time is 30 minutes. Not available for London - Ebbsfleet - Ashford or v.v. Special fares payable that include three classes of service

All times shown are local times (France is one hour ahead of Great Britain). All Eurostar services are 🄡, non-smoking and convey ✗.

Service Dec. 9, 2007 – July 5, 2008

km	km	train number	9078	9106	9002	9002	9004	9110	9006	9114	9114	9010	9010	9074	9014	9120	9016	9018	9020	9022	9082	9024	9024	9132	9132	
		notes	①–⑤	①–⑤	⑥	①–⑤	①–⑥	①–⑥	①–⑥	⑦	①–⑥	⑦	①–⑥				⑥			⑤	⑦	①–⑤	⑥⑦	⑤⑦		
		notes												M			B				C				J	
0	0	**London St Pancras** d.	0527	0600	0627	0630	0655	0700	0730	0800	0805	0825	0832	0853	0926	1000	1000	1030	1105	1132	1202	1230	1230	1257	1300	...
35	35	Ebbsfleet International d.	0543	0615	0645	0645	|	0714	0745	0815	|	0841	|	|	0942	1015	|	|	|	|	|	1245	1245	1315	1315	...
90	90	Ashford International d.	|	|	|	|	0725	|	|	|	|	|	|	0926	|	|	|	1058	|	|	|	|	|	|	|	...
166	166	Calais Fréthun a.	|	|	|	|	|	|	0929	|	|	|	|	|	|	|	|	|	|	|	|	|	1429	|	|	...
267	267	Lille Europe a.	|	|	|	|	|	0924	|	|	|	|	|	1124	|	1224	|	|	|	|	|	|	|	1524	1524	...
	373	**Brussels Midi / Zuid** a.	|	0856	|	|	|	1003	|	1056	1056	|	|	...	|	1303	|	|	|	|	|	|	|	1603	1603	...
492		**Paris Nord** a.	0850	...	0950	0950	1017	...	1056	...	...	1147	1147	...	1247	...	1317	1353	1420	1447	1517	1550	1556	...	...	...

train number	9026	9030	9138	9036	9144	9040	9146	9148	9150	9044	9044	9046	9154	9048	9154	9050	9050	9050	9052	9158	9054	9054	9056		
notes	⑦				⑦		①–⑤	⑥⑦	①–⑤	①–⑤	⑥⑦	⑧	⑥⑦	①–⑤	①–⑤	⑥	⑦	①–⑤	⑤		⑦	①–⑤	⑦		
notes														D							E				
London St Pancras d.	1300	1404	1434	1530	1604	1625	1635	1655	1726	1730	1731	1800	1831	1832	1835	1900	1900	1905	1932	1934	2005	2005	2035	...	...
Ebbsfleet International d.	|	|	|	1545	|	|	|	1712	1745	|	|	1815	|	|	|	1915	|	|	|	|	|	|	|	...	...
Ashford International d.	|	|	|	|	|	1655	|	|	|	|	|	|	|	|	|	|	|	|	|	|	|	|	|	...	...
Calais Fréthun a.	|	|	|	1729	1802	|	|	|	|	|	1926	|	|	|	|	|	|	|	|	|	|	2159	|	...	...
Lille Europe a.	|	1624	1654	|	|	|	|	1921	1954	|	|	|	2051	|	|	|	|	|	|	2154	|	|	|	...	...
Brussels Midi / Zuid a.	|	|	1733	|	1903	|	1926	1959	2033	|	|	|	2133	|	2133	|	|	|	|	2233	|	|	|	...	...
Paris Nord a.	1617	1726	...	1856	...	1947	...	...	...	2050	2053	2120	...	2147	...	2220	2220	2220	2247	...	2320	2326	2350	...	...

train number	9109	9005	9007	9113	9113	9113	9009	9011	9117	9015	9015	9121	9019		9023	9127	9027	9031		9035	9141	9037			
notes	①–⑥	①–⑤	①–⑥	⑥	⑦	①–⑤	①–⑤		①–⑤	①–⑤	⑥⑦	⑥⑦			⑥⑦					⑤⑦		⑦			
notes							D													G					
Paris Nord d.	...	0643	0713	...	...	...	0743	0807	...	0907	0913	...	1013	...	1113	...	1213	1301	...	1413	...	1443	...	...	...
Brussels Midi / Zuid d.	0659	|	|	0759	0759	0805	|	|	0859	|	|	0959	|	...	|	1159	|	|	...	|	1459	|	...	...	...
Lille Europe d.	0735	|	|	|	0835	|	|	|	0935	1009	|	1035	|	...	|	1235	|	1403	...	|	1535	|	...	...	...
Calais Fréthun d.	|	|	|	0902	|	|	|	0934	|	|	|	|	|	...	|	|	|	1433	...	|	|	|	...	...	...
Ashford International a.	|	|	|	|	|	|	|	|	|	1006	1006	|	|	...	|	|	|	|	...	|	|	|	...	...	...
Ebbsfleet International a.	|	|	|	|	|	|	|	0918	0945	|	|	1045	|	...	|	1245	|	1418	...	|	|	|	...	...	...
London St Pancras a.	0755	0758	0828	0856	0856	0856	0859	0934	1003	1038	1038	1101	1128	...	1228	1303	1328	1434	...	1528	1556	1559	...	...	...

train number	9039	9039	9145	9043	9149	9149	9047	9049	9153	9051	9157	9053	9055	9057	9059	9059	9061	9165	9165	9063					
notes	①–⑤	⑥⑦	①–⑤		①–⑤	⑥⑦	⑧	⑧	⑧			①–⑤	⑧		①–⑤	⑥⑦	⑦	⑦	①–⑥						
notes							H							M											
Paris Nord d.	1513	1507	...	1613	...	...	1713	1743	...	1813	...	1843	1913	...	2013	2013	2043	...	...	2113	...	...	...	...	...
Brussels Midi / Zuid d.	|	|	1605	|	1701	1701	|	|	1759	|	1859	|	|	...	|	|	|	2059	2102	|	...	...	...	...	...
Lille Europe d.	|	|	|	|	1738	1738	|	|	1835	|	1935	|	|	2038	|	|	|	2135	2139	|	...	...	...	...	...
Calais Fréthun d.	|	1634	|	|	|	|	|	|	|	|	|	|	|	|	|	|	|	|	|	|	...	...	...	...	...
Ashford International a.	1606	1606	|	|	|	|	|	|	|	|	|	1936	|	2037	|	2106	|	|	|	|	...	...	...	...	...
Ebbsfleet International a.	|	|	1645	1718	|	1747	1818	|	1845	1918	|	|	|	|	2118	2125	|	2145	2148	2218	...	...	...	...	...
London St Pancras a.	1637	1637	1703	1734	1758	1803	1834	1859	1903	1934	1956	2007	2028	2113	2134	2142	2159	2203	2204	2234	...	...	...	...	...

B – ⑥ Feb. 10 - July 5.
C – ⑦ Feb. 10 - July 5.
D – ①–⑤ Feb. 10 - July 5.
E – ⑦ (⑥⑦ Feb. 10 - July 5).
G – ⑤⑦ (⑤⑥⑦ Feb. 10 - July 5).
H – ⑧ (daily Feb. 10 - July 5).
J – ①②③④⑥.
M – To / from Marne la Vallée - Chessy (see table below).

10 LONDON – PARIS *by rail – sea – rail*

Other services are available by taking normal service trains between London and Dover (Tables **100**, **101**), sailings between Dover and Calais (Table **2110**) and normal service trains betwee Calais and Paris (Tables **260**, **265**), passengers making their own way between stations and docks at Dover and Calais, allowing at least 1 hour for connections.

No service Dec. 25, 26.

French train number								2032					2038							2042					2044	
sea crossing (see below)		⛴	2			⛴	2				⛴	2					⛴	2	2				⛴	2		
notes	⑥	⑥	⑥		①–⑤	①–⑤	①–⑤			⑦	⑦	⑦	⑦			①–⑥	①–⑥	①–⑤	⑥			⑦	⑦	⑦	⑦	
			g		w		f			m		g	h		B	w		f	g			m		g	k	
London Charing Cross d.	0600	...	...	...	0700	...	...	...	...	0854	...	...	...	...	0954	1023	...	...	...	...	...	1154	...	...	...	...
Dover Priory ❖ a.	0756	...	...	...	0859	...	...	...	...	1041	...	...	...	...	1141	1210	...	...	...	...	...	1341	...	...	...	...
Dover Eastern Docks 🚌 ❖ d.	...	0925	...	...	...	1005	...	...	...	...	1215	...	...	...	...	...	1300	...	...	...	...	...	1425	...	...	...
Calais Port 🚌 ❖ a.	...	1155	...	...	...	1235	...	...	...	...	1445	...	...	...	...	...	1530	...	...	...	...	...	1655	...	...	...
Calais Ville ❖ d.	...	...	1305	...	...	...	1349	...	...	...	...	1552	...	...	...	...	...	1644	1652	...	...	...	...	1745	...	...
Boulogne Ville d.	...	...	1338	...	...	...	1423	1437	...	...	...	1626	1630	...	...	...	...	1721	1726	1742	...	...	...	1818	1832	...
Amiens a.	...	...	...	...	...	...	...	1602	...	...	...	...	1758	...	...	...	...	...	...	1858	...	...	...	...	2000	...
Paris Nord a.	...	...	...	...	...	...	...	1720	...	...	...	...	1920	...	...	...	...	...	...	2020	...	...	...	...	2123	...

French train number	2003				2007				TGV			2015							2025							
sea crossing (see below)		2	⛴			2	⛴	⛴	7229	⛴			2	2	⛴					2	⛴		2	⛴		
notes	①–⑥	①–⑥	①–⑥	①–⑥	⑦	⑦	⑦	⑦	⛴				⑦	①–⑥		⑥	①–⑤	⑦		①–⑤	①–⑤	①–⑤	⑥⑦	⑥⑦	⑦	⑥
	p	f		b	k	g		m	🄡A		e		g	f			w	m		f		w	g		m	
Paris Nord d.	0707	...	...	...	0804	...	...	...	0958	...	...	1007	...	...	...	...	...	...	1419	...	...	...	...	...	...	...
Amiens d.	0828	...	...	...	0925	...	...	...	|	...	...	1123	...	...	...	...	...	...	1535	...	...	...	...	...	...	...
Boulogne Ville d.	0944	0957	...	...	1041	1051	...	...	|	...	...	1248	1258	1335	...	...	...	...	1659	1703	...	...	1739	...	...	...
Calais Ville ❖ a.	...	1031	...	...	...	1122	...	...	1140	...	...	...	1333	1414	...	...	...	...	...	1739	...	...	1816	...	...	...
Calais Port 🚌 ❖ d.	...	...	1150	...	...	...	1235	...	...	1235	...	...	...	...	1525	...	...	...	...	...	1820	...	...	1945	...	...
Dover Eastern Dock 🚌 ❖ a.	...	...	1220	...	...	...	1305	...	...	1305	...	...	...	...	1555	...	...	...	...	...	1850	...	...	2015	...	...
Dover Priory ❖ d.	...	...	...	1333	...	...	...	1418	...	...	1350	...	...	...	...	1637	1640	1718	...	...	...	1950	...	...	2109	211
London Charing Cross a.	...	...	...	1506	...	...	...	1607	...	...	1536	...	...	...	...	1836	1837	1907	...	...	...	2148	...	...	2306	231

A – ①–⑥ (not Dec. 25, Jan. 1, Mar. 24, May 12).
B – Jan. 1, Mar. 21, 24, May 5, 26.
b – On Jan. 1, Mar. 21, 24, May 5, 26 depart Dover 1318, arrive London 1507.
e – On Jan. 1, Mar. 21, 24, May 5, 26 depart Dover 1418, arrive London 1607.
f – Not Dec. 25, Jan. 1, Mar. 24, May 1, 8, 12.
g – Also Dec. 25, Jan. 1, Mar. 24, May 1, 8, 12.
h – Also Dec. 25, Jan. 1, Mar. 24, May 12.
k – Also Dec. 25, Jan. 1, Mar. 24, May 12; not Mar. 23, May 11.
m – Also Jan. 1, Mar. 21, 24, May 5, 26.
p – Not Dec. 25, Jan. 1, Mar. 24, May 12.
w – Not Jan. 1, Mar. 21, 24, May 5, 26.
⛴ – Ship service, operated by P & O Ferries. One class only on ship. ✗ on ship. For additional ferry services see Table **2110**. Subject to confirmation from Jan. 1, 2008.
❖ – 🚌 service between Dover Priory and Dover Eastern Docks and v.v. (every 20 minutes approx, not a guaranteed connection). 🚌 service between Calais Port and Calais Ville and v.v. (every 20 minutes approx, not a guaranteed connection). Provisional timetable: Calais Port depart 1000, 1045, 1130, 1210, 1255, 1335, 1445, 1545, 1630, 1710, 1810, 1915. Calais Ville depart 1015, 1100, 1145, 1225, 1310, 1350, 1500, 1600 1645, 1725, 1830, 1930.

RAIL – SEA – RAIL SERVICE SEA CROSSING: Connections between Rail - Sea - Rail services are not guaranteed. Please note – London - Paris and v.v. Through Rail – Sea – Rail tickets are not now available. Separate tickets have to be purchased for each stage of the journey.

LONDON / BRUSSELS - LILLE - CHARLES DE GAULLE ✈ - WESTERN / SOUTHERN FRANCE 11

DAY TRAINS (FOR NIGHT TRAINS SEE TABLE 13). Supplements are payable on *TGV* trains. Connections at Lille are not guaranteed. Other connections available via Paris.

train type	*TGV*	*TGV*	*TGV*	*TGV*	*TGV*	*TGV*	*TGV*	*TGV*	*TGV*	*Talgo*	*TGV*	*TGV*	☆	☆	*TGV*	*TGV*	**TGV**	☆	*TGV*	*TGV*	*TGV*	*TGV*	*TGV*	*TGV*	
train number	**5102**	**9804**	**5104**	**5200**	**5110**	**9802**	**5212**	**8515**	**5112**	**71/70**	**5214**	**5214**	**9110**	**9084**	**9826**	**5164**	**5128**	**9074**	**9832**	**5114**	**5224**	**5227**	**5218**	**5221**	
train number	**5103**	**9805**	**5105**	**5201**	**5111**	**9803**	[R]	[R]	**5113**	[R]🍷	**5213**	**5215**	[R]	[R]	**9827**	[R]	**5129**	[R]	**9833**	**5115**	**5225**	[R]	**5219**	[R]	
notes	[R]🍷	[R]🍷	[R]🍷	[R]🍷	[R]🍷	[R]🍷	🍷	🍷	[R]🍷	/	[R]🍷	[R]🍷	✗	✗	[R]🍷	🍷	[R]🍷	✗	[R]	[R]🍷	[R]🍷	🍷	[R]🍷	🍷**z**	
		A	**B**	**r**						**N**	**y**		①–⑥	**P**			**W**		🍷			**t**	**z**	⑦**k**	
ndon St Pancras 12 .... d.	...	...	...	...	...	...	...	...	...	...	...	...	0700	0719	...	...	...	0853	...	...	...	...	...	...	...
osfleet International **12**..... d.	...	...	...	...	...	...	...	...	...	...	...	...	0714	|	...	...	...	|	...	...	...	...	...	...	...
nford International **12**....... d.	...	...	...	...	...	...	...	...	...	...	...	...	|	0755	...	...	...	0926	...	...	...	...	...	...	...
Brussels Midi / Zuid 12 ... d.	...	0540	...	...	...	0732	...	...	...	...	...	...	|	|	1021	...	...	|	1110	...	...	...	...	...	...
e Europe 12.................. a.	...	0615	...	...	...	|	...	...	...	...	...	...	0924	0952**s**	|	...	...	1124**s**	1146	...	...	...	...	...	...
e Europe......................... d.	0559	0625	0625	0558	0643**c**	|	0759	...	0828	...	0846	0846	...	|	|	1030	1113	|	1156	1156	1210	1210	1238**x**	1238**x**	...
uai....................................... d.	|	|	|	0628	0709	|	|	...	|	...	0908	0908	...	|	|	|	|	|	|	|	|	|	|	|	...
as .... d.	|	|	|	0647	0727	|	|	...	|	...	0927	0927	...	|	|	|	|	|	|	|	|	|	|	|	...
V Haute Picardie............. d.	|	0653	0653	0707	0746	|	|	...	|	...	0952	0952	...	|	|	1103	|	|	|	|	1244	1244	|	|	...
ris Charles de Gaulle ✈... a.	0649	0720	0720	0735	0816	0846	0851	...	0921	...	1022	1022	...	|	1137	1132	1202	|	1247	1246	1312	1312	1332	1332	...
ris Charles de Gaulle ✈... d.	0654	0725	0725	0739	0821	0856	0856	...	0925	...	1027	1027	...	|	1142	1142	1206	|	1258	1258	1316	1316	1337	1337	...
rne la Vallée §................ d.	0710	0740	0740	0756	0835	0910	0910	...	0940	...	1042	1042	...	|	1156	1156	1222	1227	1311	1311	1329	1329	1351	1351	...
Dijon............................. a.	|	|	|	|	|	|	|	...	|	...	|	|	...	|	|	|	|	...	|	|	|	|	|	|	...
Massy TGV........................ d.	|	|	|	0831	|	0946	0946	...	|	...	1117	1117	...	|	|	|	|	...	|	|	1401	1401	1431	1431	...
Le Mans.............................. a.	|	|	|	|	|	|	|	...	|	...	1207	1207	...	|	|	|	|	...	|	|	1450	1450	|	|	...
Rennes........................ a.	|	|	|	|	|	|	|	...	|	...	|	1327	...	|	|	|	|	...	|	|	1607	|	|	|	...
Angers St Laud............ a.	|	|	|	|	|	|	|	...	|	...	1251	...	...	|	|	|	|	...	|	|	▬	1539	|	|	...
Nantes .... a.	|	|	|	|	|	|	|	...	|	...	1333	...	...	|	|	|	|	...	|	|	...	1617	|	|	...
St Pierre des Corps .... a.	|	|	|	0921	|	1035	1035	...	|	...	...	...	...	|	|	|	|	...	|	|	...	...	1521	1521	...
Poitiers............................ a.	|	|	|	1011	|	1117	1117	...	|	...	...	...	...	|	|	|	|	...	|	|	...	...	1611	1611	...
Angoulême........................ a.	|	|	|	1059	|	1203	1203	...	|	...	...	...	...	|	|	|	|	...	|	|	...	...	1657	1657	...
Bordeaux .... a.	|	|	|	1200	|	1305	1305	1314	|	...	...	...	...	|	|	|	|	...	|	|	...	...	1803	1803	...
rún .... a.	|	|	|	1426**g**	|	▬	...	1540	|	...	...	...	...	|	|	|	|	...	|	|	...	...	|	2034	...
Creusot TGV .... a.	|	|	|	...	|	...	...	...	|	...	...	...	...	|	|	|	|	...	|	|	...	...	|	...	...
on Part Dieu.................... a.	0901	0931	0931	...	1031	...	...	...	1131	...	...	...	...	|	|	|	|	...	1501	1501	...	...	|	...	...
on Perrache..................... a.	|	|	|	...	|	...	...	...	|	...	...	...	...	|	|	|	|	...	|	|	...	...	|	...	...
Grenoble........................ a.	|	|	|	...	|	...	...	...	|	...	...	...	...	|	|	|	1514	...	|	|	...	...	|	...	...
lence TGV........................ a.	|	1011	1011	...	1112	...	...	...	1212	...	...	...	...	|	1403	1403	...	...	1541	|	...	...	|	...	...
gnon TGV......................... a.	1009	|	|	...	1146	...	...	...	|	...	...	...	...	1412**p**	1437	1437	...	...	|	|	...	...	|	...	...
Nîmes .... a.	|	1059	1059	...	|	...	...	...	1258	...	...	...	...	...	|	|	...	...	1629	|	...	...	|	...	...
Montpellier....................... a.	|	1129	1129	...	|	...	...	...	1342	1702	...	...	...	...	|	|	...	...	1657	|	...	...	|	...	...
Béziers............................... a.	|	1213	1213	...	|	...	...	...	...	1740	...	...	...	...	|	|	...	...	1751	|	...	...	|	...	...
Narbonne .... a.	|	1235	1235	...	|	...	...	...	...	1756	...	...	...	...	|	|	...	...	1807	|	...	...	|	...	...
Toulouse Matabiau...... a.	|	1356	1356	...	|	*TGV*	...	...	...	|	...	...	...	...	|	|	...	...	|	|	*TGV*	...	2016	...	...
Perpignan........................... a.	|	...	...	...	|	**5148**	...	...	...	1835	...	...	...	...	|	|	...	...	1844	|	**6818**	...	...	...	...
Portbou 🏛 .... a.	|	...	...	...	|	**5149**	...	...	...	1931	...	...	...	...	|	|	...	...	...	|	**6819**	...	...	...	...
Barcelona França .... a.	|	...	...	...	|	[R]	...	...	...	2145	...	...	...	...	|	|	...	...	...	|	[R]	...	...	...	...
en Provence TGV .... a.	1032	...	...	...	1210	🍷	...	...	...	...	...	...	...	...	|	|	...	...	...	1634	🍷	...	...	...	...
rseille St Charles .... a.	1047	...	...	...	1225	1301	...	...	...	...	...	...	...	...	1509	1509	...	...	..	1649	1729	...	...	...	...
ulon..................................... a.	1138	...	...	...	...	1342	...	...	...	...	...	...	...	...	1559	1559	...	...	...	...	1809	...	...	...	...
Raphaël - Valescure .... a.	1231	...	...	...	...	1437	...	...	...	...	...	...	...	...	1651	1651	...	...	...	...	1906	...	...	...	...
nnes.................................... a.	1255	...	...	...	...	1502	...	...	...	...	...	...	...	...	1714	1714	...	...	...	...	1932	...	...	...	...
ce .... a.	1325	...	...	...	...	1532	...	...	...	...	...	...	...	...	1749	1749	...	...	...	...	2006	...	...	...	...

train type	☆	*TGV*	*TGV*	*TGV*	*TGV*	*TGV*	*TGV*	*TGV*		☆	☆	*TGV*	*TGV*	*TGV*		☆	*TGV*		☆	*TGV*	*TGV*				
train number	**9120**	**9828**	**5117**	**5232**	**5216**	**5216**	**5232**	**5118**		**9132**	**9132**	**5222/3**	**9834**	**6181**		**9030**	**9836**		**9138**	**5236**	**5231**				
train number	[R]	**9829**	**5116**	**5233**	**5229**	[R]	**5205**	**5119**		[R]	[R]	[R]🍷	**9835**	[R]		[R]	**9837**		[R]	**5238**	[R]				
notes	✗	[R]🍷	🍷	[R]🍷	[R]🍷	🍷	[R]🍷	[R]🍷		✗	✗	⑤⑥**q**	[R]🍷	🍷		✗	[R]🍷		✗	[R]🍷	🍷				
				C	⑦**k**	⑦**k**	**D**			⑤⑦	**Q**	**b**								⑧**h**	⑧**h**				
ndon St Pancras 12 .... d.	1000	...	...	...	...	...	...	...	...	1257	1300	...	...	...	...	1404	...	...	1434	...	...	...	...	...	...
bsfleet International **12**..... d.	1015	...	...	...	...	...	...	...	...	1315	1315	...	...	...	...	|	...	...	|	...	...	...	...	...	...
nford International **12**....... d.	|	...	...	...	...	...	...	...	...	|	|	...	...	...	...	|	...	...	|	...	...	...	...	...	...
Brussels Midi / Zuid 12 ... d.	|	1210	...	...	...	...	...	...	...	|	|	...	1509	...	...	|	1609	...	|	...	...	...	...	...	...
le Europe 12.................. a.	1224	1245	...	...	...	...	...	...	...	1524	1524	...	1546	...	...	1624	1644	...	1654	...	...	...	...	...	...
le Europe........................ d.	...	1258	...	1447	1447	1447	1447	1458**v**	...	...	...	1541	1557	...	...	...	1654	...	...	1729	1729	...	...	...	...
uai....................................... d.	...	|	...	|	|	|	|	|	...	...	...	|	|	...	...	...	|	...	...	|	|	...	...	...	...
as .... d.	...	|	...	|	|	|	|	|	...	...	...	|	|	...	...	...	|	...	...	|	|	...	...	...	...
V Haute Picardie............. d.	...	|	...	|	|	|	|	|	...	...	...	|	|	...	...	...	|	...	...	|	|	...	...	...	...
ris Charles de Gaulle ✈... a.	...	1349	...	1538	1538	1538	1538	1548	...	...	...	1634	1647	...	...	...	1746	...	...	1820	1820	...	...	...	...
ris Charles de Gaulle ✈... d.	...	1354	...	1542	1542	1542	1542	1553	...	...	...	1638	1652	...	...	...	1751	...	...	1824	1824	...	...	...	...
rne la Vallée §................ d.	...	1409	...	1557	1557	1557	1557	1610	...	...	...	1653	1710	...	...	...	1810	...	...	1840	1840	...	...	...	...
Dijon............................. a.	...	|	...	|	|	|	|	|	...	...	...	|	|	...	...	...	|	...	...	|	|	...	...	...	...
Massy TGV........................ d.	...	|	...	1631	1631	1631	1636	|	...	...	...	1730	|	...	...	...	|	...	...	1916	1921	...	...	...	...
Le Mans.............................. a.	...	|	...	1720	|	|	|	|	...	...	...	|	|	...	...	...	|	...	...	2005	|	...	...	...	...
Rennes........................ a.	...	|	...	1836	|	|	|	|	...	...	...	|	|	...	...	...	|	...	...	2125	|	...	...	...	...
Angers St Laud............ a.	...	|	...	...	|	1813	|	|	...	...	...	|	|	...	...	...	|	...	...	...	2105	...	...	...	...
Nantes .... a.	...	|	...	...	|	1854	|	|	...	...	...	|	|	...	...	...	|	...	...	...	2147	...	...	...	...
St Pierre des Corps .... a.	...	|	...	...	1721	1721**f**	1727	|	...	...	...	1821	|	...	...	...	|	...	...	...	2011**f**	...	...	...	...
Poitiers............................ a.	...	|	...	...	1807	...	1809	|	...	...	...	1903	|	...	...	...	|	...	...	...	...	...	...	...	...
Angoulême........................ a.	...	|	...	...	...	...	1859	|	...	...	...	1949	|	...	...	...	|	...	...	...	...	...	...	...	...
Bordeaux .... a.	...	|	...	...	...	...	2000	|	...	...	...	2051	|	...	...	...	|	...	...	...	...	...	...	...	...
rún .... a.	...	|	...	...	...	...	...	|	...	...	...	...	|	...	...	...	|	...	...	...	...	...	...	...	...
Creusot TGV .... a.	...	|	...	...	...	...	...	|	...	...	...	...	|	...	...	...	|	...	...	...	...	...	...	...	...
on Part Dieu.................... a.	...	1601	1707	...	...	...	...	1801	...	...	...	...	1901	...	...	...	2001	...	...	...	...	...	...	...	...
on Perrache..................... a.	...	|	|	...	...	...	...	|	...	...	...	...	|	...	...	...	|	...	...	...	...	...	...	...	...
Grenoble........................ a.	...	|	|	...	...	...	...	|	...	...	...	...	|	...	...	...	|	...	...	...	...	...	...	...	...
lence TGV........................ a.	...	|	1742	...	...	...	...	|	...	...	...	...	|	...	...	...	2042	...	...	...	...	...	...	...	...
gnon TGV......................... a.	...	1709	|	...	...	...	...	|	...	...	...	...	2011	...	...	...	|	...	...	...	...	...	...	...	...
Nîmes .... a.	...	|	1829	...	...	...	...	1927	...	...	...	...	|	...	...	...	2127	...	...	...	...	...	...	...	...
Montpellier....................... a.	...	|	1856	...	...	...	...	1955	...	...	...	...	|	...	...	...	2155	...	...	...	...	...	...	...	...
Béziers............................... a.	...	|	1940	...	...	...	...	2044	...	...	...	...	|	...	...	...	2244**j**	...	...	...	...	...	...	...	...
Narbonne .... a.	...	|	1955	...	...	...	...	2101	...	...	...	...	|	...	...	...	2300**j**	...	...	...	...	...	...	...	...
Toulouse Matabiau...... a.	...	|	2112	...	...	...	...	|	...	...	...	...	|	...	...	...	|	...	...	...	...	...	...	...	...
Perpignan........................... a.	...	|	...	...	...	...	...	2135	...	...	...	...	|	...	...	...	2335**j**	...	...	...	...	...	...	...	...
Portbou 🏛 .... a.	...	|	...	...	...	...	...	...	...	...	...	...	|	...	...	...	...	...	...	...	...	...	...	...	...
Barcelona França .... a.	...	|	...	...	...	...	...	...	...	...	...	...	|	...	...	...	...	...	...	...	...	...	...	...	...
en Provence TGV .... a.	...	1733	...	...	...	...	...	...	...	...	...	...	2034	2045	...	...	...	...	...	...	...	...	...	...	...
rseille St Charles .... a.	...	1747	...	...	...	...	...	...	...	...	...	...	2049	|	...	...	...	...	...	...	...	...	...	...	...
ulon..................................... a.	...	...	...	...	...	...	...	...	...	...	...	...	2141**j**	2134	...	...	...	...	...	...	...	...	...	...	...
Raphaël - Valescure .... a.	...	...	...	...	...	...	...	...	...	...	...	...	...	2224	...	...	...	...	...	...	...	...	...	...	...
nnes.................................... a.	...	...	...	...	...	...	...	...	...	...	...	...	...	2248	...	...	...	...	...	...	...	...	...	...	...
ce .... a.	...	...	...	...	...	...	...	...	...	...	...	...	...	2317	...	...	...	...	...	...	...	...	...	...	...

– ①–⑤ (not Dec. 25, Jan. 1, Mar. 24, May 1, 8, 12).
– ⑥⑦ (also Dec. 25, Jan. 1, Mar. 24, May 1, 8, 12).
– ①–⑥ (not Dec. 25, Jan. 1, Mar. 24, May 12).
– ①–④ (also May 2; not Dec. 25, Jan. 1, Mar. 24, Apr. 30, May 7, 12).
– CATALÁN TALGO – (12) and ✗ Montpellier - Barcelona. Special fares payable.
– ⑥ July 12, 2008 - Sept. 6.
– ①②③④⑥.
– ⑥ Dec. 15, 2007 - Mar. 29, 2008.

b – To Hendaye, arrive 2308.
c – 0647 on ⑥.
f – Runs Massy TGV - St Pierre des Corps - Angers St Laud - Nantes.
g – ⑥ (also May 1, 8; not May 10).
h – Not May 1, 8.
j – ⑤⑦ (also Dec. 25, Jan. 1, Mar. 24, Apr. 30, May 7, 12; not May 2).
k – Also Dec. 25, Jan. 1, Mar. 24, May 12.

p – Avignon **Centre**.
q – Also Apr. 30, May 1, 7, 8; not May 2, 9, 10).
r – Calls at Futuroscope 0959.
s – Stops to set down only.
t – Not May 10, 11.
v – 1454 on ⑥⑦ (also Dec. 24, 25, 26, 31, Jan. 1, Mar. 24, May 1, 5, 8, 12, 26).
x – Lille **Flandres**, 500 metres from Lille Europe; see City Plan on page 31.
y – Not May 11.

z – Calls at Futuroscope 1558.
☆ – Eurostar train. Special fares payable. Minimum check-in time 30 minutes. Valid Dec. 9, 2007 - July 5, 2008.
§ – Marne la Vallée - Chessy (station for Disneyland).

11 LONDON / BRUSSELS - LILLE - CHARLES DE GAULLE ✈ - WESTERN / SOUTHERN FRANCE

DAY TRAINS (FOR NIGHT TRAINS SEE TABLE 13). Supplements payable on all *TGV* services. Connections at Lille are not guaranteed. Other connections available via Paris.

train type	☆	*TGV*	*TGV*	*TGV*	*TGV*	*TGV*	*TGV*	*TGV*	*TGV*	*TGV*	*TGV*	*TGV*		☆	*TGV*	*TGV*	*TGV*	*TGV*	*TGV*	*TGV*	*TGV*	
train number	**9138**	**5123**	**5126**	**5124**	**5240**	**5130**	**5132**	**5242**	**5142**	**5142**	**5136**	**5136**		**9148**	**5248**	**5248**	**5234**	**5138**	**5210**	**5210**	**9846**	
train number	[R]	[R]🍸	**5127**	**5125**	**5241**	**5131**	**5133**	**5243**	**5135**	**5143**	**5137**	**5137**		[R]	**5249**	**5245**	**5235**	**5139**	**5211**	**5247**	[R]	
notes	🍴	①–⑥	[R]🍸	[R]🍸	[R]🍸	[R]🍸	[R]🍸	[R]🍸	[R]🍸	[R]🍸	①–④	[R]🍸		🍴	[R]🍸	[R]🍸	[R]🍸	[R]🍸	[R]🍸	[R]🍸	🍸	
		k	⑦p	B	⑧g	m	⑦p	C	⑦p	⑦p	k	⑤⑥f		⑥⑦	⑥j	⑥y	G	⑦p	⑤⑦p	⑦p		
London St Pancras 12 d.	1434	...	...	...	...	...	...	...	...	...	...	...	...	1655	...	...	...	...	...	...	...	...
Ebbsfleet International **12** d.	|	...	...	...	...	...	...	...	...	...	...	...	...	1712	...	...	...	...	...	...	...	...
Ashford International **12** d.	|	...	...	...	...	...	...	...	...	...	...	...	...	|	...	...	...	...	...	...	...	...
Brussels Midi / Zuid 12 d.	|	...	...	...	...	...	...	...	...	...	...	...	...	|	...	...	...	...	...	...	2036	...
Lille Europe 12 a.	1654	...	...	...	...	...	...	...	...	...	...	...	...	1921	...	...	...	...	...	...	|	...
Lille Europe d.	...	1752	1752	1752	1809	1842e	1842e	1829	1931	1931	1915	1915	...	...	1939	1939	1939	2021e	2014	2014	|	...
Douai d.	...	|	|	|	|	|	|	|	|	|	1936	1936	...	...	|	|	|	2043	|	|	|	...
Arras d.	...	|	|	|	|	|	|	|	|	|	1952	1952	...	...	|	|	|	2059	|	|	|	...
TGV Haute Picardie d.	...	1823	1823	1823	1837	|	|	|	|	|	2015	2015	...	...	|	|	|	2119	|	|	|	...
Paris Charles de Gaulle ✈ a.	...	1850	1850	1850	1907	1936	1936	1921	2021	2021	2043	2043	...	...	2030	2030	2030	2146	2105	2105	2150	...
Paris Charles de Gaulle ✈ d.	...	1854	1854	1854	1911	1941	1941	1925	2026	2026	2048	2048	...	...	2034	2034	2034	2150	2109	2109	2154	...
Marne la Vallée § d.	...	1908	1908	1908	1927	2000	2008	1942	2040	2040	2103	2103	...	...	2050	2050	2050	2204	2125	2125	2206	...
Dijon a.	...	|	|	|	|	2139	|	|	|	|	|	|	...	...	|	|	|	|	|	|	...	...
Massy TGV d.	...	|	|	|	2000	...	|	2018	|	|	|	|	...	...	2134	2134	2131	|	2201	2201	...	...
Le Mans a.	...	|	|	|	|	...	|	|	|	|	|	|	...	...	2224	2224	2220	|	2250	2250	...	...
Rennes a.	...	|	|	|	|	...	|	|	|	|	|	|	...	...	2344	|	|	|	|	0010	...	...
Angers St Laud a.	...	|	|	|	|	...	|	|	|	|	|	|	...	...	...	2304	2301	|	2328	...	...	...
Nantes a.	...	|	|	|	|	...	|	|	|	|	|	|	...	...	...	2343	2338z	|	0007	...	...	...
St Pierre des Corps a.	...	|	|	|	|	...	|	2109	|	|	|	|	...	...	...	...	...	|	...	...	...	...
Poitiers a.	...	|	|	|	2123	...	|	2158	|	|	|	|	...	...	...	...	...	|	...	...	...	...
Angoulême a.	...	|	|	|	2210	...	|	2247	|	|	|	|	...	...	...	...	...	|	...	...	...	...
Bordeaux a.	...	|	|	|	2312	...	|	2352	|	|	|	|	...	...	...	...	...	|	...	...	...	...
Irún a.	...	|	|	|	...	...	|	...	|	|	|	|	...	...	...	...	...	|	...	...	...	...
Le Creusot TGV a.	...	|	|	|	...	...	|	...	|	|	2220	2220	...	...	...	...	...	2319	...	...	...	...
Lyon Part Dieu a.	...	2101	|	2101	...	...	2201	...	2231	2231	2259	2259	...	...	...	...	...	2358	...	...	...	...
Lyon Perrache a.	...	|	|	|	...	...	|	...	|	|	...	|	...	...	...	...	...	0013	...	...	...	...
Grenoble a.	...	2225	|	|	...	...	2317	...	|	|	...	|	...	...	...	...	...	...	...	...	...	...
Valence TGV a.	...	...	2114	|	...	...	...	...	2315	|	...	2341	...	...	...	...	...	...	...	...	...	...
Avignon TGV a.	...	...	2148	2208	...	...	...	...	|	2343	...	0018	...	...	...	...	...	...	...	...	...	...
Nîmes a.	...	...	|	|	...	...	...	...	0002	|	...	|	...	...	...	...	...	...	...	...	...	...
Montpellier a.	...	...	|	|	...	...	...	...	0030	|	...	|	...	...	...	...	...	...	...	...	...	...
Béziers a.	...	...	|	|	...	...	...	...	...	|	...	|	...	...	...	...	...	...	...	...	...	...
Narbonne a.	...	...	|	|	...	...	...	...	...	|	...	|	...	...	...	...	...	...	...	...	...	...
Toulouse Matabiau a.	...	...	|	|	...	...	...	...	...	|	...	|	...	...	...	...	...	...	...	...	...	...
Perpignan a.	...	...	|	|	...	...	...	...	...	|	...	|	...	...	...	...	...	...	...	...	...	...
Portbou 🏛 a.	...	...	|	|	...	...	...	...	...	|	...	|	...	...	...	...	...	...	...	...	...	...
Barcelona França a.	...	...	|	|	...	...	...	...	...	|	...	|	...	...	...	...	...	...	...	...	...	...
Aix en Provence TGV a.	...	...	|	2231	...	...	...	...	...	0006	...	0041	...	...	...	...	...	...	...	...	...	...
Marseille St Charles a.	...	...	2221	2245	...	...	...	...	...	0020	...	0055	...	...	...	...	...	...	...	...	...	...
Toulon a.	...	...	...	...	...	...	...	...	...	...	...	...	...	...	...	...	...	...	...	...	...	...
St Raphaël - Valescure a.	...	...	...	...	...	...	...	...	...	...	...	...	...	...	...	...	...	...	...	...	...	...
Cannes a.	...	...	...	...	...	...	...	...	...	...	...	...	...	...	...	...	...	...	...	...	...	...
Nice a.	...	...	...	...	...	...	...	...	...	...	...	...	...	...	...	...	...	...	...	...	...	...

train type or number	*TGV*	*TGV*	*TGV*	☆		*TGV*	☆		*TGV*	*TGV*	*TGV*	*TGV*	☆		*TGV*	*TGV*	*TGV*	*TGV*	*TGV*	*TGV*	☆	
train number	**9811**	**9807**	**5152**	**9117**		**5154**	**9015**		**5158**	**5160**	**5254**	**5252**	**9121**		**9854**	**5156**	**9856**	**5260**	**5260**	**5260**	**9127**	
train number	[R]	[R]	**5153**	[R]		**5155**	[R]		**5159**	**5161**	**5255**	[R]	[R]		**9855**	**5157**	**9857**	**5261**	**5261**	**5261**	[R]	
notes	🍸	🍸	[R]🍸	🍴		[R]🍸	🍴		[R]🍸	[R]🍸	[R]🍸	🍸	🍴		[R]🍸	[R]🍸	[R]🍸	[R]🍸	[R]🍸	[R]🍸	🍴	
	G		Gw	①–⑤		B	①–⑤		H	⑦p	B	B	⑥⑦		G	Kx	A	P	R	Q		
Nice d.	...	...	...	...	...	...	...	...	...	...	...	...	...	...	...	...	...	...	...	...	...	...
Cannes d.	...	...	...	...	...	...	...	...	...	...	...	...	...	...	...	...	...	...	...	...	...	...
St Raphaël - Valescure d.	...	...	...	...	...	...	...	...	...	...	...	...	...	...	...	...	...	...	...	...	...	...
Toulon d.	...	...	...	...	...	...	...	...	...	...	...	...	...	...	...	...	0517q	...	...	...	...	...
Marseille St Charles d.	...	...	...	...	...	...	...	...	0539	...	...	...	...	...	0539	...	0609	...	...	...	...	...
Aix en Provence TGV d.	...	...	...	...	...	...	...	...	0554	...	...	...	...	...	|	...	0624	...	...	...	...	...
Barcelona França d.	...	...	...	...	...	...	...	...	|	...	...	...	...	...	|	...	|	...	...	...	...	...
Cerbère 🏛 d.	...	...	...	...	...	...	...	...	|	...	...	...	...	...	|	...	|	...	...	...	...	...
Perpignan d.	...	...	...	...	...	...	...	...	|	...	...	...	...	...	|	...	|	...	...	...	...	...
Toulouse Matabiau d.	...	...	...	...	...	...	...	...	|	...	...	...	...	...	|	...	|	...	...	...	...	...
Narbonne d.	...	...	...	...	...	...	...	...	|	...	...	...	...	...	|	...	|	...	...	...	...	...
Béziers d.	...	...	...	...	...	...	...	...	|	...	...	...	...	...	|	...	|	...	...	...	...	...
Montpellier d.	...	...	...	...	...	...	...	...	|	...	...	...	...	...	|	...	|	...	...	...	...	...
Nîmes d.	...	...	...	...	...	...	...	...	|	...	...	...	...	...	|	...	|	...	...	...	...	...
Avignon TGV d.	...	...	...	...	...	...	...	...	0616	...	...	...	...	...	0611	...	0647	...	...	...	...	...
Valence TGV d.	...	...	...	...	...	...	...	...	0650	...	...	...	...	...	0645	...	|	...	...	...	...	...
Grenoble d.	...	...	...	...	...	0451	...	...	|	0540	...	...	...	...	|	...	|	...	...	...	...	...
Lyon Perrache d.	...	...	...	...	...	|	...	...	|	|	...	...	...	...	|	...	|	...	...	...	...	...
Lyon Part Dieu d.	...	...	...	...	...	0613	...	...	|	0700	...	...	...	...	0726	...	0756	...	...	...	...	...
Le Creusot TGV d.	...	...	...	...	...	0653	...	...	|	0742	...	...	...	...	|	...	|	...	...	...	...	...
Hendaye d.	...	...	...	...	...	|	...	...	|	|	...	...	...	...	|	...	|	...	...	...	...	...
Bordeaux d.	...	...	...	...	...	|	...	...	|	|	...	...	...	...	|	...	|	0535	0614	0634	...	...
Angoulême d.	...	...	...	...	...	|	...	...	|	|	...	...	...	...	|	...	|	0638	0714	0734	...	...
Poitiers d.	...	...	...	...	...	|	...	...	|	|	...	...	...	...	|	...	|	0724	0801	0821	...	...
St Pierre des Corps d.	...	...	...	...	...	|	...	...	|	|	...	...	...	...	|	...	|	0803	0841	0902	...	...
Nantes d.	...	...	...	...	...	|	...	...	|	|	...	0604	...	...	|	...	|	|	|	|	...	...
Angers St Laud d.	...	...	...	...	...	|	...	...	|	|	...	0643	...	...	|	...	|	|	|	|	...	...
Rennes d.	...	...	...	...	...	|	...	...	|	|	0610	|	...	...	|	...	|	|	|	|	...	...
Le Mans d.	...	...	...	...	...	|	...	...	|	|	0730	0730	...	...	|	...	|	|	|	|	...	...
Massy TGV d.	...	...	...	...	...	|	...	...	|	|	0821	0821	...	...	|	...	|	|	|	0958	...	...
Dijon d.	...	...	0632	...	...	|	...	...	|	|	|	|	...	...	|	0744	|	|	|	|	...	...
Marne la Vallée § d.	...	0729	0810	...	...	0817	...	...	0908	0902	0904	0904	...	...	0920	0922	0949	0932	1011	1041	...	...
Paris Charles de Gaulle ✈ a.	...	0740	0821	...	...	0827	...	...	0918	0912	0914	0914	...	...	0930	0933	0959	0942	1021	1050	...	...
Paris Charles de Gaulle ✈ d.	...	0744	0825	...	...	0839	...	...	...	0916	0918	0918	...	...	0940	0937	1009	0947	1027	1054	...	...
TGV Haute Picardie d.	...	|	|	...	...	0909	...	...	...	0949	|	|	...	...	|	|	|	1017	1101	1124	...	...
Arras a.	...	|	|	...	...	|	...	...	...	|	|	|	...	...	|	|	|	|	|	|	...	...
Douai a.	...	|	|	...	...	|	...	...	...	|	|	|	...	...	|	|	|	|	|	|	...	...
Lille Europe a.	...	|	0915	...	...	0937	...	...	...	1015	1009	1009	...	...	1028	1027	1100	1044	1128	1151	...	...
Lille Europe 12 d.	0729	|	...	0935	...	...	1009	...	...	...	...	...	1035	...	1041	...	1110	...	...	...	1235	...
Brussels Midi / Zuid 12 a.	0805	0859	...	|	...	...	|	...	...	...	...	...	|	...	1115	...	1144	...	...	...	|	...
Ashford International **12** a.	...	...	...	|	...	...	1006	...	...	...	...	...	|	...	...	...	...	...	...	...	|	...
Ebbsfleet International **12** a.	...	...	...	0945	...	...	|	...	...	...	...	...	1045	...	...	...	...	...	...	...	1245	...
London St Pancras 12 a.	...	...	...	1003	...	...	1038	...	...	...	...	...	1101	...	...	...	...	...	...	...	1303	...

A – ⑥⑦ (also Dec. 25, Jan. 1, Mar. 24, May 1, 8, 12).
B – ①–⑥ (not Dec. 25, Jan. 1, Mar. 24, May 12).
C – ⑤⑥⑦ (also Dec. 25, Jan. 1, Mar. 24, Apr. 30, May 1, 7, 8, 12; not May 2).
G – ①–④ (not Dec. 25, Jan. 1, Mar. 24, May 1, 8, 12).
H – ⑥ (also May 1, 8).
K – ⑥⑦ (also Dec. 25, Jan. 1, Mar. 24, May 12).
P – ①–⑥ Mar. 31 - June 9 (not May 9, 10, 12).
Q – Dec. 9 - Mar. 30.

R – ⑦ Apr. 6 - June 9 (also May 12; not May 11).
e – Lille **Flandres**, 500 metres from Lille Europe; see City Plan on page 31.
f – Also Apr. 30, May 1, 7, 8; not May 2.
g – Not May 1, 8.
j – Also May 1, 8.
k – Not Dec. 25, Jan. 1, Mar. 24, May 12.
m – To Besançon (arrive 2232).
p – Also Dec. 25, Jan. 1, Mar. 24, May 12.

q – ⑥ (also May 1, 8).
w – From Besançon depart 0540.
x – From Besançon depart 0652.
y – Not May 10.
z – 0110 Jan. 22 - Feb. 29.
§ – Marne la Vallée - Chessy. Station for Disneyland Paris.
☆ – Eurostar train. Special fares payable. Minimum check-in time 30 minutes. Valid Dec. 9, 2007 - July 5, 2008.

SOUTHERN / WESTERN FRANCE - CHARLES DE GAULLE ✈ - LILLE - BRUSSELS / LONDON 11

DAY TRAINS (FOR NIGHT TRAINS SEE TABLE 13). Supplements payable on all *TGV* services. Connections at Lille are not guaranteed. Other connections available via Paris.

train type or number	*TGV*	*TGV*	*TGV*	*TGV*	*TGV*	*TGV*	*TGV*	*TGV*	☆		*TGV*		*TGV*	*TGV*	☆	☆		*TGV*	*TGV*	☆			
train number	**5144**	**5162**	**5264**	**5268**	**5270**	**5272**	**9860**	**5166**	**9031**		**5276**	**17484**	**5368**	**9862**	**9149**	**9149**		**9864**	**9866**	**9153**			
train number	[R]	**5163**	**5265**	[R]	**5271**	[R]	[R]	[R] 🍷	[R]		**5277**		[R]	**9863**	[R]	[R]		**9865**	**9867**	[R]			
notes	🍷	[R] 🍷	[R] 🍷	🍷	[R] 🍷	🍷	🍷		🍴		[R] 🍷		🍷	[R] 🍷	🍴	🍴		[R]	[R] 🍷	🍴			
			x	Wx									E		①–⑤	⑥⑦		🍷		Ⓑ			
ice d.	...	...	...	...	...	...	...	...	...	...	...	0833q	...	...	...	...	...	1032q	...	...	...	...	...
annes d.	...	...	...	...	...	...	...	...	...	...	...	0904q	...	...	...	...	...	1101q	...	...	...	...	...
Raphaël - Valescure d.	...	...	...	...	...	...	...	...	...	...	...	0927	...	...	...	...	...	1125	...	...	...	...	...
oulon d.	...	...	...	...	...	...	0745e	...	...	...	...	1022	...	...	...	...	...	1218	...	...	...	...	...
arseille St Charles d.	0710	...	...	...	...	...	0839	...	...	...	...	1102	1133	...	...	...	...	1309	1340	...	...	...	...
x en Provence TGV d.	0725	...	...	...	...	...	0853	...	...	...	...	...	1147	...	...	...	...	|	1356	...	...	...	...
Barcelona França d.	|	...	...	...	...	...	|	...	...	...	...	...	|	...	...	...	...	|	|	...	...	...	...
Cerbère 🚆 d.	|	...	...	...	...	...	|	...	...	...	...	...	|	...	...	...	...	|	|	...	...	...	...
Perpignan d.	|	0505r	...	...	...	...	|	0642	...	...	...	...	|	...	...	...	...	|	|	...	...	...	...
Toulouse Matabiau d.	|	|	0527	...	...	...	|	|	...	...	...	...	|	...	...	...	...	|	|	...	...	...	...
Narbonne d.	|	0544r	|	...	...	...	|	0720	...	...	...	...	|	...	...	...	...	|	|	...	...	...	...
Béziers d.	|	0601r	|	...	...	...	|	0737	...	...	...	...	|	...	...	...	...	|	|	...	...	...	...
Montpellier d.	|	0652	|	...	...	...	|	0826	...	...	...	...	|	1156	...	...	...	|	|	...	...	...	...
Nîmes d.	|	0718	|	...	...	...	|	0853	...	...	...	...	|	1227	...	...	...	|	|	...	...	...	...
vignon TGV d.	0747	|	|	...	...	...	0916	|	...	...	...	...	1209	|	...	...	...	1339	1418	...	...	...	...
alence TGV d.	|	0810	|	...	...	...	|	0938	...	...	...	...	1243	|	...	...	...	1414	|	...	...	...	...
Grenoble d.	|	|	|	...	...	...	|	|	...	...	...	...	|	|	...	...	...	|	|	...	...	...	...
yon Perrache d.	|	|	|	...	...	...	|	|	...	...	...	...	|	|	...	...	...	|	|	...	...	...	...
yon Part Dieu d.	0856	0856	|	...	...	...	1026	1026	...	...	...	...	1320	1356	...	...	...	|	1526	...	...	...	...
e Creusot TGV d.	|	|	|	...	...	...	|	|	...	...	...	...	...	|	...	...	...	|	|	...	...	...	...
Hendaye d.	|	|	|	0529	...	...	|	|	...	...	0839y	...	...	|	...	...	...	|	|	...	...	...	...
Bordeaux d.	|	|	0750	0750	...	...	|	|	...	...	1100	...	...	|	...	...	...	|	|	...	...	...	...
Angoulême d.	|	|	0850	0850	...	...	|	|	...	...	1202	...	...	|	...	...	...	|	|	...	...	...	...
Poitiers d.	|	|	0935	0935	...	...	|	|	...	...	1250	...	...	|	...	...	...	|	|	...	...	...	...
St Pierre des Corps d.	|	|	1023	1023	...	...	|	|	...	...	1333	...	...	|	...	...	...	|	|	...	...	...	...
Nantes d.	|	|	|	|	0910h	...	|	|	...	...	|	...	...	|	...	...	...	|	|	...	...	...	...
Angers St Laud d.	|	|	|	|	0948h	...	|	|	...	...	|	...	...	|	...	...	...	|	|	...	...	...	...
Rennes d.	|	|	|	|	|	0915	|	|	...	...	|	...	...	|	...	...	...	|	|	...	...	...	...
Le Mans d.	|	|	|	|	1041	1041	|	|	...	...	|	...	...	|	...	...	...	|	|	...	...	...	...
Massy TGV d.	|	|	1115	1115	1141	1141	|	|	...	...	1427	...	...	|	...	...	...	|	|	...	...	...	...
Dijon d.	|	|	|	|	|	|	|	|	...	...	|	...	...	|	...	...	...	|	|	...	...	...	...
arne la Vallée § d.	1049	1049	1157	1157	1227	1227	1220	1220	...	...	1511	...	...	1549	...	...	...	1623	|	...	...	...	...
aris Charles de Gaulle ✈ a.	1059	1059	1207	1207	1237	1237	1230	1230	...	...	1521	...	...	1559	...	...	...	1633	1724	...	...	...	...
aris Charles de Gaulle ✈ d.	1109	1109	1212	1212	1242	1242	1235	1235	...	...	1525	...	...	1609	...	...	...	1639	1728	...	...	...	...
GV Haute Picardie d.	|	|	|	|	1313	1313	|	|	...	...	|	...	...	1640	...	...	...	1710	|	...	...	...	...
rras a.	1151	1151	|	|	|	|	|	|	...	...	|	...	...	|	...	...	...	|	|	...	...	...	...
ouai a.	1207	1207	|	|	|	|	|	|	...	...	|	...	...	|	...	...	...	|	|	...	...	...	...
lle Europe a.	1235p	1235p	1304	1304	1341	1341	1326	1326	...	...	1615	...	...	1707	...	...	...	1738	1820	...	...	...	...
lle Europe 12 d.	...	...	...	...	...	...	1336	...	1403	...	...	...	...	1719	1738	1738	...	1748	1835	1835	...	...	...
Brussels Midi / Zuid 12 a.	...	...	...	...	...	...	1412	...	|	...	...	...	...	1754	|	|	...	1822	1910	|	...	...	...
shford International **12** a.	...	...	...	...	...	...	...	...	|	...	...	...	...	...	|	|	...	...	...	|	...	...	...
bsfleet International **12** a.	...	...	...	...	...	...	...	...	1418	...	...	...	...	...	|	1747	...	...	...	1845	...	...	...
ondon St Pancras 12 a.	...	...	...	...	...	...	...	...	1434	...	...	...	...	...	1758	1803	...	...	...	1903	...	...	...

train type or number	*TGV*	*TGV*	☆	*Talgo*	*TGV*	*TGV*	*TGV*	☆	☆	☆	*TGV*	*TGV*	*TGV*	*TGV*	*TGV*	*TGV*	*TGV*	*TGV*	*TGV*	*TGV*	*TGV*		
train number	**5280**	**5278**	**9157**	**73/72**	**9868**	**9816**	**9816**	**9087**	**9057**	**9165**	**5192**	**5180**	**5180**	**5284**	**5176**	**5290**	**5288**	**5184**	**5187**	**5292/3**	**5294**		
train number	**5281**	[R]	[R]	[R] 🍷	**9869**	**9817**	**5279**	[R]	[R]	[R]	**5193**	**5181**	**5181**	**5285**	**5177**	[R]	**5289**	**5185**	**5186**	[R]	**5295**		
notes	[R] 🍷	🍷	🍴	⚡	[R]	[R] 🍷	[R] 🍷	🍴	🍴	🍴	[R] 🍷	[R] 🍷	[R] 🍷	[R] 🍷	[R] 🍷	🍷	[R]	[R]	[R] 🍷	🍷	[R] 🍷		
				N	🍷			X		⑦	A	A	C	⑧ f z	⑥ B		🍷	🍷		D	⑦ t		
ice d.	...	...	...	...	...	...	...	...	...	...	...	...	...	...	...	...	...	1531q	...	...	...	...	...
annes d.	...	...	...	...	...	...	...	...	...	...	...	...	...	...	...	...	...	1603q	...	...	...	...	...
Raphaël - Valescure d.	...	...	...	...	...	...	...	...	...	...	...	...	...	...	...	...	...	1628	...	...	...	...	...
oulon d.	...	...	...	...	...	...	...	...	...	...	...	...	...	...	...	...	...	1720	...	...	...	...	...
arseille St Charles d.	...	...	...	...	...	...	...	...	...	...	...	1709	1709	...	...	...	...	1810	...	...	...	...	...
x en Provence TGV d.	...	...	...	...	...	...	...	...	...	...	...	1723	1723	...	...	...	...	1824	...	...	...	...	...
Barcelona França d.	...	...	...	0845	...	...	...	...	...	...	...	|	|	...	...	...	...	|	...	...	...	...	...
Cerbère 🚆 d.	...	...	...	1114	...	...	...	...	...	...	...	|	|	...	...	...	...	|	...	...	...	...	...
Perpignan d.	...	...	...	1145	1240	...	...	...	...	...	...	|	|	...	...	...	...	|	...	...	...	...	...
Toulouse Matabiau d.	...	...	...	|	|	...	...	...	...	...	...	|	|	...	...	...	...	|	1608v	...	...	...	...
Narbonne d.	...	...	...	1221	1320	...	...	...	...	...	...	|	|	...	...	...	...	|	1728	...	...	...	...
Béziers d.	...	...	...	1239	1337	...	...	...	...	...	...	|	|	...	...	...	...	|	1745	...	...	...	...
Montpellier d.	...	...	...	1322	1430	...	...	...	...	...	...	|	|	...	...	...	...	|	1830	...	...	...	...
Nîmes d.	...	...	...	...	1457	...	...	...	...	...	...	|	|	...	...	...	...	|	1857	...	...	...	...
vignon TGV d.	...	...	...	...	|	...	...	1624c	...	...	...	|	|	...	...	...	...	1846	|	...	...	...	...
alence TGV d.	...	...	...	...	1544	...	...	|	...	...	...	1815	1815	...	...	...	...	|	1945	...	...	...	...
Grenoble d.	...	...	...	...	|	...	...	|	...	...	...	|	|	...	1806	...	...	|	|	...	...	...	...
yon Perrache d.	...	...	...	...	|	...	...	|	...	...	...	|	|	...	|	...	...	|	|	...	...	...	...
yon Part Dieu d.	...	...	...	...	1626	...	...	|	...	...	1756	1856	1856	...	|	...	...	1956	2026	...	...	...	...
e Creusot TGV d.	...	...	...	...	|	...	...	|	...	...	|	|	|	...	|	...	...	|	|	...	...	...	...
Hendaye d.	...	...	...	...	|	...	...	|	...	...	|	|	|	...	|	...	...	|	|	1625j	...	...	...
Bordeaux d.	...	...	...	...	|	1422	1422	|	...	...	|	|	|	1643	|	...	...	|	|	1841	...	...	...
Angoulême d.	...	...	...	...	|	1526	1526	|	...	...	|	|	|	1745	|	...	...	|	|	1946	...	...	...
Poitiers d.	...	...	...	...	|	1614	1614	|	...	...	|	|	|	1834	|	...	...	|	|	2040	...	...	...
St Pierre des Corps d.	...	...	...	...	|	1655	1655	|	...	...	|	|	|	1928	|	...	...	|	|	2127	...	...	...
Nantes d.	...	1435k	...	...	|	|	|	|	...	...	|	|	|	|	|	...	1835k	|	|	|	...	...	...
Angers St Laud d.	...	1513k	...	...	|	|	|	|	...	...	|	|	|	|	|	...	1912k	|	|	|	...	...	...
Rennes d.	1435	|	...	...	|	|	|	|	...	...	|	|	|	|	|	1840	|	|	|	|	2020	...	...
Le Mans d.	1557	1557	...	...	|	|	|	|	...	...	|	|	|	|	|	2000	2000	|	|	|	2138	...	...
Massy TGV d.	1651	1651	...	...	|	1749	1749	|	...	...	|	|	|	2021	|	2050	2050	|	|	2220	2230	...	...
Dijon d.	|	|	...	...	|	|	|	|	...	...	|	|	|	|	|	|	|	|	|	|	|	...	...
arne la Vallée § d.	1732	1732	...	...	1820	1831	1831	|	1935	...	1949	2049	2049	2103	2106	2134	2134	2149	2219	2256	2306	...	...
aris Charles de Gaulle ✈ a.	1741	1741	...	...	1830	1841	1841	|	|	...	1959	2103	2103	2112	2117	2146	2146	2159	2229	2306	2316	...	...
aris Charles de Gaulle ✈ d.	1745	1745	...	...	1840	1848	1845	|	|	...	2009	2108	2108	2116	2124	2150	2150	2209	2236	2310	2320	...	...
GV Haute Picardie d.	|	|	...	...	|	|	|	|	|	...	|	2140	2140	2150	|	2220	2220	|	2306	2341b	|	...	...
ras a.	|	|	...	...	|	|	1924	|	|	...	2050	|	2159	|	|	2238	2238	|	|	|	|	...	...
ouai a.	|	|	...	...	|	|	1940	|	|	...	2107	|	2214	|	|	2254	2254	|	|	|	|	...	...
lle Europe a.	1838p	1838p	...	...	1936	|	2003p	|	|	...	2128	2206	2238	2219	2215	2318	2318	2301	2332	0000	0010	...	...
lle Europe 12 d.	...	...	1935	...	1946	|	...	2032u	2038u	2135	...	...	...	...	...	...	...	...	...	...	...	...	...
Brussels Midi / Zuid 12 a.	...	...	|	...	2022	2003	...	|	|	|	...	...	...	...	...	...	...	...	...	...	...	...	...
shford International **12** a.	...	...	|	...	...	...	...	2033	2037	|	...	...	...	...	...	...	...	...	...	...	...	...	...
bsfleet International **12** a.	...	...	|	...	...	...	...	|	|	2145	...	...	...	...	...	...	...	...	...	...	...	...	...
ondon St Pancras 12 a.	...	...	1956	...	...	...	...	2110	2113	2203	...	...	...	...	...	...	...	...	...	...	...	...	...

– ①–⑤ (not Dec. 25, Jan. 1, Mar. 24, May 12).
– ⑥ Dec. 15 - Mar. 29.
– ⑥⑦ (also Dec. 25, Jan. 1, Mar. 24, May 12).
– ①–⑥ (not Dec. 25, Jan. 1, Mar. 24, May 1, 8, 9, 10, 12).
– ①–⑥ (not Dec. 25, Jan. 1, Mar. 24, May 12).
– CATALÁN TALGO – 🛏12 and 🍴 Barcelona - Montpellier. Special fares payable.
– ①⑥ (also Dec. 26, Jan. 2, Mar. 25, May 1, 8, 13; not Dec. 24, 31, Mar. 24, May 10, 12).
– ⑥ July 19, 2008 - Sept. 13, 2008.

b – Stops at TGV Haute Picardie on ⑤⑥ (also Apr. 30, May 1, 7, 8; not May 2, 9, 10), arrives Lille 0007.
c – Avignon **Centre**.
e – ⑥ (also May 1, 8).
f – Not May 1, 8, 9.
h – Not May 11.
j – ⑥ (also May 1, 8; not May 10).
k – Not May 10, 11.

p – Lille **Flandres**, 500 metres from Lille Europe; see City Plan on page 31.
q – Depart 7 mins earlier Jan. 3 - Feb. 22.
r – ①⑥ (also Dec. 26, Jan. 2, Mar. 25, May 1, 8, 13; not Dec. 24, 31, Mar. 24, May 12).
t – Also Dec. 25, Jan. 1, Mar. 24, May 12.
u – Stops to pick up only.
v – 1549, 1556, 1603 on certain dates.
x – Calls at Futuroscope 0946.

y – ⑦ (also Dec. 25, Jan. 1, Mar. 24, May 12; not May 11).
z – Calls at Futuroscope 1850.
☆ – Eurostar train. Special fares payable. Minimum check-in time 30 minutes. Valid Dec. 9, 2007 - July 5, 2008.
§ – Marne la Vallée - Chessy, Station for Disneyland Paris.
⚡ – Supplement payable.

12 LONDON - LILLE - BRUSSELS *by Eurostar*

All times shown are local times (France and Belgium are one hour ahead of Great Britain).

For the complete service London - Lille see Table 10. For other services Lille - Brussels (by TGV) see Table 16a.

Service Dec. 9, 2007 – July 5, 2008.

km	*train type*	☆			☆	⇌				☆	☆			*ICE*		☆	☆	⇌				☆	☆			
	train number	**9106**			**9110**	**9417**				**9114**	**9114**			**15**		**9074**	**9120**	**9429**				**9132**	**9132**			
	notes	①–⑤			①–⑥					⑦	①–⑥			★			①–⑥					⑤⑦	**A**			
0	**London St Pancras** . d.	0600	...	...	0700	...	...	...	...	0800	0805	...	...	...	...	0853	1000	...	...	...	...	1257	1300	...	...	...
35	Ebbsfleet International d.	0615	...	...	0714	...	...	...	...	0815	|	...	...	...	...	|	1015	...	...	...	...	1315	1315	...	...	...
90	Ashford International . d.	|	...	...	|	...	...	...	...	|	|	...	...	...	...	0926	|	...	...	...	...	|	|	...	...	...
267	Lille Europe .... a.	|	...	...	0924	...	...	...	...	|	|	...	...	...	...	1124	1224	...	...	...	...	1524	1524	...	...	...
373	**Brussels Midi / Zuid** . a.	0856	0936	0957	1003	1025	1032	1036	1057	1056	1056	1132	1136	1159	1157	...	1303	1325	1332	1336	1357	1603	1603	1632	1636	165
	Brugge .... a.	*0932*	|	|	...	|	1125	|	|	...	...	1225	|	|	|	...	...	|	1425	|	|	...	...	1726	|	|
	Leuven.............. a.	...	|	1025	...	|	...	|	1125	...	...	...	|	|	1225	...	...	|	...	|	1425	...	...	...	|	172
	Liège Guillemins. a.	...	|	1102	...	1111	...	|	1202	...	...	...	|	1250	1302	...	...	1411	...	|	1502	...	...	...	|	180
	Namur .... a.	...	1039	...	...	...	...	1139	...	...	...	...	1239	...	...	...	...	...	...	1439	...	...	...	...	1739	...
	Luxembourg.... a.	...	1236	...	...	...	...	1336	...	...	...	...	1436	...	...	...	...	...	...	1636	...	...	...	...	1936	...

train type	☆	*ICE*					☆	⇌					☆				☆	⇌				☆				
train number	**9138**	**17**			①–⑤		**9144**	**9453**					**9146**				**9148**	**9457**				**9150**				
notes		★			**f**		⑦						①–⑤				⑥⑦	Ⓑ **p**				①–⑤				
London St Pancras .. d.	1434	...	...	...	...	...	1604	...	...	...	...	...	1635	...	...	...	1655	...	...	...	...	1726	...	...	...	...
Ebbsfleet International .d.	|	...	...	...	...	...	|	...	...	...	...	...	|	...	...	...	1712	...	...	...	...	1745	...	...	...	...
Ashford International.. d.	|	...	...	...	...	...	|	...	...	...	...	...	|	...	...	...	|	...	...	...	...	|	...	...	...	...
Lille Europe .... a.	1654	...	...	...	...	...	|	...	...	...	...	...	|	...	...	...	1921	...	...	...	...	1954	...	...	...	...
Brussels Midi / Zuid.. a.	1733	1759	1757	1806	1809	1836	1903	1925	1928	1932	1936	...	1926	1957	2006	2036	1959	2025	2028	2032	2036	2033	2057	2106	2136	...
Brugge .... a.	...	|	|	1859	|	|	...	|	|	2025	|	...	...	|	2058	|	...	|	|	2125	|	...	|	2158	|	...
Leuven.............. a.	...	|	1825	...	|	|	...	|	1956	...	|	...	...	2025	...	|	...	|	2056	...	|	...	2125	...	|	...
Liège Guillemins . a.	...	1850	1902	...	|	|	...	2011	2054	...	|	...	...	2102	...	|	...	2111	2154	...	|	...	2202	...	|	...
Namur............ a.	...	...	...	...	1913	1939	...	...	...	...	2039	...	...	...	...	2139	...	...	...	...	2139	...	...	...	2239	...
Luxembourg .... a.	...	...	...	...	2059	2136	...	...	...	...	2236	...	...	...	...	2336	...	...	...	...	2336	...	...	...	0036	...

train type	☆	☆				☆				
train number	**9154**	**9154**				**9158**				
notes	⑥⑦	①–⑤							⑥⑦	
London St Pancras .. d.	1831	1835	...	...	...	1934	...	...	...	...
Ebbsfleet International .d.	|	|	...	...	...	|	...	...	...	...
Ashford International.. d.	|	|	...	...	...	|	...	...	...	...
Lille Europe .... a.	2051	|	...	...	...	2154	...	...	...	...
Brussels Midi / Zuid.. a.	2133	2133	2157	2206	2206	2233	2257	2306	2336	...
Brugge .... a.	...	...	|	2258	|	...	|	2358	|	...
Leuven.............. a.	...	...	2225	...	|	...	2325	...	|	...
Liège Guillemins . a.	...	...	2302	...	|	...	0011	...	|	...
Namur............ a.	...	...	...	...	2309	...	...	...	0045	...
Luxembourg .... a.	...	...	...	...	...	...	...	...	...	...

train type					☆				☆	☆	☆
train number		**2126**			**9109**		**2127**		**9113**	**9113**	**911**
notes	Ⓒ	Ⓐ		Ⓐ	①–⑥				⑥	⑦	①–(
Luxembourg .... d.	...	...	...	...	...	...	...	...	...	...	...
Namur.................. d.	0437	0521	...	...	...	...	0621	...	...	...	...
Liège Guillemins .... d.	|	|	...	0508	...	0555	|	...	...	...	...
Leuven .... d.	|	|	...	0600	...	0635	|	...	...	...	...
Brugge........................ d.	|	|	0529	|	...	|	|	0635	...	...	...
Brussels Midi / Zuid........ d.	0546	0624	0628	0632	0659	0703	0724	0728	0759	0759	080
Lille Europe .... d.	...	...	...	...	0735	...	...	...	|	0835	|
Ashford International........ a.	...	...	...	...	|	...	...	...	|	|	|
Ebbsfleet International ..... a.	...	...	...	...	|	...	...	...	|	|	|
London St Pancras........ a.	...	...	...	...	0755	...	...	...	0856	0856	085

train type				⇌	☆	☆				⇌	☆				☆					⇌	☆				☆	
train number		**2127**		**9412**	**9117**	**9015**		**2129**		**9416**	**9121**		**2131**		**9127**			**2134**		**9436**	**9141**		**2135**		**9145**	
notes		Ⓐ		①–⑥**q**	①–⑤	①–⑤				①–⑥**t**	⑥⑦														①–⑤	
Luxembourg .... d.	...	0524	...	...	...	...	...	0624	...	...	...	...	0824	...	...	...	...	1124	...	...	...	...	1224	...	...	...
Namur............ d.	...	0721	...	...	...	...	...	0821	...	...	...	...	1021	...	...	...	...	1321	...	...	...	...	1421	...	...	...
Liège Guillemins . d.	0628	|	...	0749	...	...	0758	|	...	0849	...	0958	|	...	...	...	1258	|	...	1349	...	1358	|	...	...	...
Leuven.............. d.	0733	|	...	|	...	...	0833	|	...	|	...	1033	|	...	...	...	1333	|	...	|	...	1433	|	...	...	...
Brugge .... d.	|	|	0735	|	...	...	|	|	0835	|	...	|	|	1035	...	...	|	|	1335	|	...	|	|	1435	...	...
Brussels Midi / Zuid.. d.	0805	0824	0828	0835	0859	...	0908	0924	0928	0935	0959	1107	1124	1128	1159	...	1407	1424	1428	1435	1459	1507	1524	1528	1605	...
Lille Europe .... d.	...	...	...	...	0935	1009	...	...	...	...	1035	...	...	...	1235	...	...	...	...	...	1535	...	...	...	|	...
Ashford International.. a.	...	...	...	...	|	1006	...	...	...	...	|	...	...	...	|	...	...	...	...	...	|	...	...	...	|	...
Ebbsfleet International a.	...	...	...	...	0945	|	...	...	...	...	1045	...	...	...	1245	...	...	...	...	...	|	...	...	...	1645	...
London St Pancras.. a.	...	...	...	...	1003	1038	...	...	...	...	1101	...	...	...	1303	...	...	...	...	...	1556	...	...	...	1703	...

train type				☆	☆		*ICE*				⇌	☆					☆	☆					⇌	☆	☆	
train number		**2136**		**9149**	**9149**		**14**		**2137**		**9448**	**9153**			**2138**		**9157**	**9057**			**2140**	**518**	**9460**	**9165**	**9165**	
notes				①–⑤	⑥⑦		★					Ⓑ												⑦	①–⑥	
Luxembourg .... d.	...	1324	...	...	...	...	...	...	1424	...	...	...	...	...	1524	...	...	...	...	...	1724	...	...	...	...	...
Namur............ d.	...	1521	...	...	...	...	...	...	1621	...	...	...	...	...	1721	...	...	...	...	...	1921	...	...	...	...	...
Liège Guillemins . d.	1458	|	...	...	...	...	1610	1558	|	...	1649	...	...	1658	|	...	...	...	...	1858	|	...	1949	...	...	...
Leuven.............. d.	1533	|	...	...	...	...	|	1633	|	...	|	...	...	1733	|	...	...	...	...	1933	|	...	|	...	...	...
Brugge .... d.	|	|	1535	...	...	...	|	|	|	1635	|	...	...	|	|	1735	...	...	...	|	|	1935	|	...	...	...
Brussels Midi / Zuid.. d.	1607	1624	1628	1701	1701	...	1701	1707	1724	1728	1735	1759	...	1807	1824	1828	1859	...	...	2007	2024	2028	2035	2059	2102	...
Lille Europe .... d.	...	...	...	1738	1738	...	...	...	...	...	...	1835	...	...	...	...	1935	2038	...	...	...	...	...	2135	2139	...
Ashford International.. a.	...	...	...	|	|	...	...	...	...	...	...	|	...	...	...	...	|	2037	...	...	...	...	...	|	|	...
Ebbsfleet International a.	...	...	...	|	1747	...	...	...	...	...	...	1845	...	...	...	...	|	|	...	...	...	...	...	2145	2148	...
London St Pancras.. a.	...	...	...	1758	1803	...	...	...	...	...	...	1903	...	...	...	...	1956	2113	...	...	...	...	...	2203	2204	...

A – ①②③④⑥.

f – Not Dec. 25, Jan. 1.

p – Not Dec. 24, 25, 31, Mar. 23, Apr. 30, May 1, 11.

q – Not Dec. 25, 26, Jan. 1, Mar. 24, May 1, 2, 12.

t – Not Dec. 25, Jan. 1, Mar. 24, May 1, 12.

⇌ – *Thalys* high-speed train 🅁 🍸 special fares payable (Paris - Brussels - Köln and v.v.).

☆ – Eurostar train 🅁 ✕, non-smoking. Special fares payable. Minimum check-in time 30 minutes. Valid Dec. 9, 2007 - July 5, 2008. Not available for London - Ebbsfleet - Ashford or v.v. journey

★ – *ICE 3* train 🍸 special fares payable.

INTERNATIONAL SERVICES FROM BRUSSELS

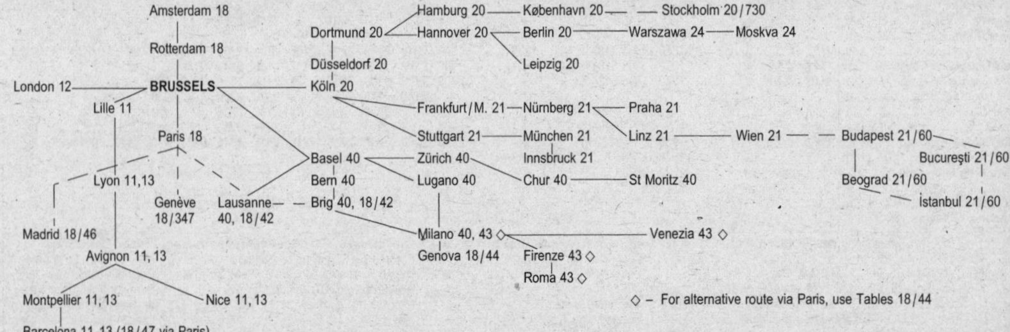

LONDON, CALAIS and LILLE - SOUTHERN FRANCE and BARCELONA 13

THROUGH NIGHT TRAINS. For day trains (via Charles de Gaulle ✈) see Table 11

Summer 2008 service (no service Winter 2007 / 2008 until Apr. 3)

train number	☆	☆					4208				
train number	**9148**	**9150**			**2042**	**2048**	**4209**			**76407**	**5090**
notes	[R] ✗	[R] ✗	①–⑤	⑥⑦		⑦	⊕			⊠	2
	⑥⑦	①–⑤				f	A	Ⓑ	⑥	2	
ndon St Pancras .... d.	1655	1726	...	...	...	...	...	...	...	...	...
bsfleet International . d.	1712	1745	...	...	...	...	...	...	...	...	...
hford International .... d.	|	|	...	...	...	...	...	...	...	...	...
Calais Ville .... d.	|	|	1827	1932	...	...	...	...	...	...	...
Hazebrouck .... d.	|	|	1922	2020	...	...	...	...	...	...	...
e Europe .... a.	1921	1954	|	|	...	...	...	...	...	...	...
e Flandres .... d.	...	...	2002	2058	...	...	2125	...	...	...	...
uai .... d.	...	...	...	...	...	...	2148	...	...	...	...
as .... d.	...	...	...	...	...	...	2205	...	...	...	...
Amiens .... d.	...	...	...	...	1909	2216	|	...	...	...	...
ngueau .... d.	...	...	...	...	1914	2222	2239	...	...	...	...
ignon Centre .... a.	...	...	...	...	...	...	0636	0655	0657	0726	...
es .... a.	...	...	...	...	...	...	|	0713	0714	|	...
Nîmes .... a.	...	...	...	...	...	...	|	...	...	0756	...
Montpellier .... a.	...	...	...	...	...	...	|	...	...	0829	...
Agde .... a.	...	...	...	...	...	...	|	...	...	0906	...
Béziers .... a.	...	...	...	...	...	...	|	...	...	0919	...
Narbonne .... a.	...	...	...	...	...	...	|	...	...	0941	...
Perpignan .... a.	...	...	...	...	...	...	|	...	...	1026	...
Argelès sur Mer .... a.	...	...	...	...	...	...	|	...	...	1103	...
Banyuls sur Mer .... a.	...	...	...	...	...	...	|	...	...	1118	...
Cerbère 🏛 .... a.	...	...	...	...	...	...	|	...	...	1126	❖
Portbou 🏛 .... a.	...	...	...	...	...	...	|	...	...	❖	1340
Barcelona Sants ..... a.	...	...	...	...	...	...	|	...	...	...	1546
rseille St Charles ... a.	...	...	...	...	...	...	0749	...	...	...	...
ulon .... a.	...	...	...	...	...	...	0850	...	...	...	...
Raphaël - Valescure . a.	...	...	...	...	...	...	0946	...	...	...	...
nnes .... a.	...	...	...	...	...	...	1012	...	...	...	...
tibes .... a.	...	...	...	...	...	...	1031	...	...	...	...
ce .... a.	...	...	...	...	...	...	1055	...	...	...	...

train number					4308					☆	☆	☆
train number		**76428**	**76434**		**4309**	**48703**	**48467**			**9117**	**9015**	**9121**
notes	2	g	Ⓑ		⊕	①–⑥	⑦	①–⑤	⑥⑦	[R] ✗	[R] ✗	[R] ✗
				C	B					①–⑤	①–⑤	⑥⑦
Nice .... d.	...	...	...	...	1911	...	...	...	...	...	...	...
Antibes .... d.	...	...	...	...	1933	...	...	...	...	...	...	...
Cannes .... d.	...	...	...	...	1948	...	...	...	...	...	...	...
St Raphaël - Valescure .. d.	...	...	...	...	2015	...	...	...	...	...	...	...
Toulon .... d.	...	...	...	...	2113	...	...	...	...	...	...	...
Marseille St Charles .... d.	...	...	...	...	2207	...	...	...	...	...	...	...
Barcelona Sants ...... d.	1125	...	...	...	|	...	...	...	...	...	...	...
Portbou 🏛 .... d.	1402	...	...	...	|	...	...	...	...	...	...	...
Cerbère 🏛 .... d.	1406	1542	1725	...	|	...	...	...	...	...	...	...
Banyuls sur Mer .... d.	▬	1550	1732	...	|	...	...	...	...	...	...	...
Argelès sur Mer .... d.	...	1608	1747	...	|	...	...	...	...	...	...	...
Perpignan .... d.	...	1628	1808	...	|	...	...	...	...	...	...	...
Narbonne .... d.	...	1713	1856	...	|	...	...	...	...	...	...	...
Béziers .... d.	...	1729	1911	...	|	...	...	...	...	...	...	...
Agde .... d.	...	1742	1924	...	|	...	...	...	...	...	...	...
Montpellier .... d.	...	1814	2000	...	|	...	...	...	...	...	...	...
Nîmes .... d.	Ⓑ	1846	2033	...	|	...	...	...	...	...	...	...
Arles .... d.	2019	|	|	2136	|	...	...	...	...	...	...	...
Avignon Centre .... d.	2036	1915	2102	2154	2308	...	...	...	...	...	...	...
Longueau .... a.	...	...	...	...	0656	0714	0904	...	...	...	...	...
Amiens .... a.	...	...	...	...	|	0719	0910	...	...	...	...	...
Arras .... a.	...	...	...	...	0738	...	...	...	...	...	...	...
Douai .... a.	...	...	...	...	0804	...	...	...	...	...	...	...
Lille Flandres .... a.	...	...	...	...	0835	...	...	0902	0922	...	...	...
Lille Europe .... d.	...	...	...	...	...	...	...	|	|	0935	1009	1035
Hazebrouck .... a.	...	...	...	...	...	...	...	0938	0955	|	|	|
Calais Ville .... a.	...	...	...	...	...	...	...	1018	1037	|	|	|
Ashford International ..... a.	...	...	...	...	...	...	...	...	...	|	1006	|
Ebbsfleet International .. a.	...	...	...	...	...	...	...	...	...	0945	|	1045
London St Pancras ..... a.	...	...	...	...	...	...	...	...	...	1003	1038	1101

- *CORAIL LUNÉA* – June 27, 2008 - Sept. 1 (also Apr. 4, 11, 18, 20, 30, May 7, 12): ▬ 1, 2 cl. and [2] (reclining) Lille Flandres - Nice.
- *CORAIL LUNÉA* – June 26, 2008 - Aug. 31 (also Apr. 3, 10, 12, 19, 29, May 3, 11): ▬ 1, 2 cl. and [2] (reclining) Nice - Lille Flandres.
- ①②③④⑥ (not Dec. 25, Jan. 1, Mar. 24, May 1, 8, 12).
- Also Dec. 25, Jan. 1, Mar. 24, May 12; not Mar. 23, May 11.

g – Not Mar. 22.
⊕ – Not available for local journeys.
☆ – Eurostar train. Special fares payable. Minimum check-in time 30 minutes. See Tables **10** and **12**. Valid Dec. 9, 2007 - July 5, 2008.
❖ – Passengers make their own way between Cerbère and Portbou.

LONDON - GENÈVE 14

For the full service Paris - Genève, see Table **341**

train type	☆	*TGV*	☆	☆	*TGV*	☆	*TGV*	☆	☆	☆	*TGV*	☆	*TGV*	☆	*TGV*	☆	☆	5595	5595		
train number	**9002**	**6569**	**9010**	**9010**	**6571**	**9018**	**6577**	**9024**	**9024**	**9026**	**6581**	**9030**	**6585**	**9036**	**6589**	**9044**	**9046**	**5594**	**5594**		
notes	[R]	♥	[R]	[R]	♥	[R]	♥	[R]	[R]	[R]	♥	[R]	♥	[R]	♥	[R]	[R]	🍷	🍷		
notes	✗		✗	✗	Ⓑj	✗		✗	✗	✗		✗		✗	⑤f	✗	✗	R	P	A	
	①–⑥		⑦	①–⑥				①–⑤	⑥⑦	⑦						⑥⑦	Ⓑ				
ndon St Pancras 10 .... d.	0630v	...	0825	0832	...	1030	...	1230	1230	1300	...	1404	...	1530	...	1731	1800	...	...	...	...
is Nord 10 .... a.	0950	...	1147	1147	...	1353	...	1550	1556	1617	...	1726	...	1856	...	2053	2120	...	...	...	...
is Gare de Lyon .... d.	...	1110	...	...	1310	...	1504	...	...	...	1810	...	1907	...	2010	...	...	...	...	...	...
is Austerlitz .... d.	...	|	...	...	|	...	|	...	...	...	|	...	|	...	|	...	...	2226	2246	...	...
con Loché TGV .... a.	...	|	...	...	|	...	1639	...	...	...	|	...	2044	...	|	...	...	|	|	...	...
Roche sur Foron .... a.	...	|	...	...	|	...	|	...	...	...	|	...	|	...	|	...	...	0733	0813	0918	...
nève Cornavin .... a.	...	1435	...	...	1635	...	1835	...	...	...	2132	...	2245	...	2335	...	...	...	...	|	...
nève Eaux Vives .... a.	...	...	...	...	...	...	...	...	...	...	...	...	...	...	...	...	...	...	...	0958	...

train type	*TGV*	☆	☆	*TGV*	☆	*TGV*	☆	☆	☆		*TGV*	☆	☆		*TGV*	☆			5596	☆	
train number	**6560**	**9023**	**9027**	**6564**	**9031**	**6568**	**9037**	**9039**	**9039**		**6572**	**9053**	**9055**		**6576**	**9063**			**5597**	**9011**	
notes	♥	[R]	[R]	♥	[R]	♥	[R]	[R]	[R]		♥	[R]	[R]		♥	[R]			🍷	[R]	
notes	A	✗	✗		✗		✗	✗	✗			✗	✗		D	✗		B	Q	✗	
		⑥⑦					⑦	⑥⑦	①–⑤			①–⑤	Ⓑ								
nève Eaux Vives .... d.	...	...	...	...	...	...	...	...	...	...	...	...	...	...	...	...	...	1702	...	...	...
nève Cornavin .... d.	0535	...	...	0717	...	0917	...	...	...	...	1317	...	...	...	1614	...	...	|	...	...	...
Roche sur Foron .... a.	|	...	...	|	...	|	...	...	...	...	|	...	...	...	|	...	...	1736	2158	...	...
con Loché TGV .... d.	|	...	...	|	...	|	...	...	...	...	|	...	...	...	1805	...	...	...	|	...	...
is Austerlitz .... ❖ a.	|	...	...	|	...	|	...	...	...	...	|	...	...	...	|	...	...	...	0636x	...	...
is Gare de Lyon .... ❖ a.	0903	...	...	1049	...	1249	...	...	...	...	1649	...	...	...	1943	...	...	...	...	...	...
is Nord 10 .... ❖ d.	...	1113	1213	...	1301	...	1443	1507	1513	...	...	1843	1913	...	...	2113	...	...	...	0807	...
ndon St Pancras 10 .... a.	...	1228	1328	...	1434	...	1559	1637	1637	...	...	2007	2028	...	...	2234	...	...	...	0934	...

- ①–⑤ (not Dec. 25, Jan. 1, Mar. 24, May 1, 12).
- ①–⑤ (not Dec. 25, Jan. 1, 2, Mar. 21, 24, May 1, 12).
- ①–⑤ (daily Dec. 9 - May 9) not May 1, 3, 4, 8, 12.
- *CORAIL LUNÉA* – ④⑤⑥ Dec. 20 - Mar. 29 (also Dec. 23, 25, 26, 30, Jan. 1, 2, Mar. 23); ⑤⑥⑦ Apr. 18 - May 11 (also Apr. 30, May 1, 7, 8; not May 2): [R] ▬ 1, 2 cl. and [2] (reclining) Paris - La Roche sur Foron - St Gervais.
- *CORAIL LUNÉA* – ⑤⑥⑦ Dec. 21 - Mar. 30 (also Dec. 26, 27, Jan. 2, 3); ③④⑤⑥⑦ Apr. 19 - May 11 (also May 12; not Apr. 23, 24, May 2): [R] ▬ 1, 2 cl. and [2] (reclining) St Gervais - La Roche sur Foron - Paris.
- *CORAIL LUNÉA* – ①②③⑦ Jan. 6 - Mar. 26 (also Dec. 9, 14, 15, 16; not Mar. 23); ⑤⑥⑦ Apr. 4–13; May 12; ⑤⑥⑦ May 16 - June 15: [R] ▬ 1, 2 cl. and [2] (reclining) Paris - La Roche sur Foron - St Gervais.

f – Also Apr. 30, May 7; not May 2, 9.
j – Not May 1, 8.
v – 0627 on ⑥.
x – 0620 on certain dates.
♥ – *TGV Lyria* service. [R] special fares payable.
❖ – 90 minutes (including Eurostar check-in time of 30 minutes) has been allowed from Paris **Lyon** and Paris **Austerlitz** to Paris **Nord**; additional Eurostar services are available, see Table **10**.
☆ – Eurostar train. Minimum check-in time 30 minutes. Special fares payable. Connections across Paris between *TGV* and Eurostar services are not guaranteed. See Table **10**. Valid Dec. 9, 2007 - July 5, 2008.

AIN NAMES: **6577** EUROCITY VERSAILLES **6569/6572** EUROCITY VOLTAIRE **6581/6568** EUROCITY HENRY DUNANT **6585/6564** EUROCITY J J ROUSSEAU

15 LONDON - ROTTERDAM - AMSTERDAM *by Eurostar*

Due to engineering works connected with the new High Speed Line between Amsterdam and Antwerpen, services may be affected until further notice.

train type	☆				☆	⇌	☆	☆					☆					☆	☆				
train number	**9106**	**9213**			**9110**	**9319**	**9114**	**9114**	**9221**				**9120**	**9233**				**9132**	**9132**	**9245**			
notes	①–⑤	🍷			①–⑥	C	⑦	①–⑥	🍷					🍷				⑤⑦	A	🍷			
London St Pancras 12 d.	0600	...	...	...	0700	...	0800	0805	...	...	...	...	1000	...	...	...	...	1257	1300	...	...	...	...
Ebbsfleet International **12** d.	0615	...	...	...	0714	...	0815	|	...	...	...	...	1015	...	...	...	...	1315	1315	...	...	...	...
Lille Europe **12** d.	|	...	...	...	0927	...	|	|	...	...	...	...	1227	...	...	...	...	1527	1527	...	...	...	...
Brussels Midi/Zuid 12 a.	0856	...	...	...	1003	...	1056	1056	...	...	...	...	1303	...	...	...	...	1603	1603	...	...	...	...
Brussels Midi/Zuid d.	...	0915	...	...	...	1052	...	...	1115	...	...	...	...	1415	...	...	...	...	...	1715	...	...	...
Brussels Nord/Noord d.	...	0924	...	...	...	|	...	...	1124	...	...	...	...	1424	...	...	...	...	...	1724	...	...	...
Mechelen a.	...	0940	...	...	...	|	...	...	1140	...	...	...	...	1440	...	...	...	...	...	1740	...	...	...
Antwerpen Berchem a.	...	|	...	...	...	|	...	...	|	...	...	...	...	|	...	...	...	...	...	|	...	...	...
Antwerpen Centraal a.	...	0957	...	...	...	1132	...	...	1157	...	...	...	...	1457	...	...	...	...	...	1757	...	...	...
Roosendaal 🚌 a.	...	1029	...	1051	...	|	...	...	1229	...	1251	...	...	1529	...	1551	...	...	...	1829	...	1851	...
Breda a.	...	|	...	1108	...	|	...	...	|	...	1308	...	...	|	...	1608	...	...	...	|	...	1908	...
Tilburg a.	...	|	...	1123	...	|	...	...	|	...	1323	...	...	|	...	1623	...	...	...	|	...	1923	...
's-Hertogenbosch a.	...	|	...	1142	...	|	...	...	|	...	1342	...	...	|	...	1642	...	...	...	|	...	1942	...
Nijmegen a.	...	|	...	1213	...	|	...	...	|	...	1413	...	...	|	...	1713	...	...	...	|	...	2013	...
Arnhem a.	...	|	...	1234	...	|	...	...	|	...	1434	...	...	|	...	1734	...	...	...	|	...	2034	...
Dordrecht a.	...	1053	...	...	...	|	...	...	1253	...	...	...	...	1553	...	...	...	...	...	1853	...	...	...
Rotterdam Centraal a.	...	1106	1117	...	...	1236	...	...	1306	1317	...	...	...	1606	1617	...	...	...	...	1906	1917	...	...
Utrecht Centraal a.	...	|	1156	...	...	|	...	...	|	1356	...	...	...	|	1656	...	...	...	...	|	1956	...	...
Den Haag HS a.	...	1125	...	...	...	1256	...	...	1325	...	...	...	...	1625	...	...	...	...	...	1925	...	...	...
Schiphol ✈ a.	...	1149	...	...	...	1319	...	...	1349	...	...	...	...	1649	...	...	...	...	...	1949	...	...	...
Amsterdam Centraal a.	...	1206	...	...	...	1336	...	...	1406	...	...	...	...	1706	...	...	...	...	...	2006	...	...	...

train type	☆	⇌					☆	☆	⇌				☆	☆	⇌	⇌				☆	☆		☆
train number	**9138**	**9347**		**9249**			**9144**	**9146**	**9355**	**9257**			**9148**	**9150**	**9359**	**9359**	**9261**			**9154**	**9154**	**9265**	**915**
notes		⑦**b**		🍷			⑦	①–⑤	**k**	🍷**k**			⑥⑦	①–⑤	**E**	**B**	🍷**k**			⑥⑦	⑦	⑥🍷	
London St Pancras 12 d.	1434	...	...	...	...	...	1604	1635	...	...	...	...	1655	1726	...	...	...	...	...	1831	1835	...	193
Ebbsfleet International **12** d.	|	...	...	...	...	...	|	|	...	...	...	...	1712	1745	...	...	...	...	...	|	|	...	|
Lille Europe **12** d.	1657	...	...	...	...	...	|	|	...	...	...	...	1924	1957	...	...	...	...	...	2054	|	...	215
Brussels Midi/Zuid 12 a.	1733	...	...	...	...	...	1903	1926	...	...	...	...	1959	2033	...	...	...	...	...	2133	2133	...	223
Brussels Midi/Zuid d.	...	1752	...	1815	...	...	...	...	1952	2015	...	...	...	...	2052	2052	2115	...	...	...	...	2215	...
Brussels Nord/Noord d.	...	|	...	1824	...	...	...	...	|	2024	...	...	...	...	|	|	2124	...	...	...	...	2224	...
Mechelen a.	...	|	...	1840	...	...	...	...	|	2040	...	...	...	...	|	|	2140	...	...	...	...	2240	...
Antwerpen Berchem a.	...	|	...	|	...	...	...	...	|	|	...	...	...	...	|	|	|	...	...	...	...	|	...
Antwerpen Centraal a.	...	1832	...	1857	...	...	...	...	2032	2057	...	...	...	...	2132	2132	2157	...	...	...	...	2257	...
Roosendaal 🚌 a.	...	|	...	1929	...	1951	...	...	|	2129	2151	...	...	...	|	...	2229	2251	...	...	...	2328	...
Breda a.	...	|	...	|	...	2008	...	...	|	|	2208	...	...	...	|	...	|	2308	...	...	...	|	...
Tilburg a.	...	|	...	|	...	2023	...	...	|	|	2223	...	...	...	|	...	|	2323	...	...	...	|	...
's-Hertogenbosch a.	...	|	...	|	...	2042	...	...	|	|	2242	...	...	...	|	...	|	2342	...	...	...	|	...
Nijmegen a.	...	|	...	|	...	2113	...	...	|	|	2313	...	...	...	|	...	|	0013	...	...	...	|	...
Arnhem a.	...	|	...	|	...	2134	...	...	|	|	2334	...	...	...	|	...	|	0035	...	...	...	|	...
Dordrecht a.	...	|	...	1953	...	...	...	...	|	2153	...	...	...	...	|	...	2253	...	...	...	...	2353	...
Rotterdam Centraal a.	...	1936	1947	2006	2032	...	...	...	2136	2206	...	2232	...	...	2236	...	2306	...	2332	...	...	0006	...
Utrecht Centraal a.	...	|	2026	|	2111	...	...	...	|	|	...	2311	...	...	|	...	|	...	0011	...	...	...	...
Den Haag HS a.	...	1956	...	2025**k**	...	...	...	...	2156	2225	...	...	...	...	2256	...	2325	...	...	...	...	...	...
Schiphol ✈ a.	...	2019	...	2049**k**	...	...	...	...	2219	2249	...	...	...	...	2319	...	2349	...	...	...	...	...	...
Amsterdam Centraal a.	...	2036	...	2106**k**	...	...	...	...	2236	2306	...	...	...	...	2336	...	0006	...	...	...	...	...	...

train type	**4527**	☆	**4527**	☆	☆	**4528**	☆	☆				☆					☆					☆	
train number	①–⑤	**9109**	⑥⑦	**9113**	**9113**	①–⑤	**9113**	**9117**	①–⑤	①–⑤	**9212**	**9121**	⑦	①–⑥	①–⑥	**9220**	**9127**	⑧	①–⑥		**9232**	**9141**	
notes	**q**	①–⑥	**g**	⑥	⑦	**q**	①–⑤	①–⑤	**q**	**q**	①–⑥	⑥⑦	**g**	**p**	**p**	🍷			**p**		🍷		
Amsterdam Centraal d.	...	...	...	...	...	...	...	...	...	...	0556	...	...	...	...	0756	...	...	...	...	1056	...	...
Schiphol ✈ △ d.	...	...	...	...	...	...	...	...	...	...	0612	...	...	...	...	0812	...	...	...	...	1112	...	...
Den Haag HS d.	...	...	...	...	...	...	...	...	...	...	0636	...	...	...	...	0836	...	...	...	...	1136	...	...
Utrecht Centraal d.	...	...	...	...	...	...	...	...	...	0603	|	...	0747	0803	...	|	...	1048	1103	...	|	...	...
Rotterdam Centraal d.	...	...	...	...	...	...	...	...	...	0642	0656	...	0838	0842	...	0856	...	1127	1142	...	1156	...	...
Dordrecht d.	...	...	...	...	...	...	...	...	...	...	0710	...	...	...	...	0910	...	...	...	...	1210	...	...
Arnhem d.	...	...	...	...	...	...	...	...	...	...	|	...	...	...	0728	|	...	...	...	1028	|	...	...
Nijmegen d.	...	...	...	...	...	...	...	...	...	...	|	...	...	...	0749	|	...	...	...	1049	|	...	...
's-Hertogenbosch d.	...	...	...	...	...	...	...	...	0620	...	|	...	...	...	0820	|	...	...	...	1120	|	...	...
Tilburg d.	...	...	...	...	...	...	...	...	0637	...	|	...	...	...	0837	|	...	...	...	1137	|	...	...
Breda d.	...	...	...	...	...	...	...	...	0652	...	|	...	...	...	0852	|	...	...	...	1152	|	...	...
Roosendaal 🚌 d.	...	...	...	...	...	...	...	...	0711	...	0734	...	...	...	0911	0934	...	...	...	1211	1234	...	...
Antwerpen Centraal d.	0550	...	0638	...	...	0650	...	...	...	...	0803	...	...	...	...	1003	...	...	...	...	1303	...	...
Antwerpen Berchem d.	0556	...	0644	...	...	0656	...	...	...	...	|	...	...	...	...	|	...	...	...	...	|	...	...
Mechelen d.	0610	...	0657	...	...	0710	...	...	...	...	0820	...	...	...	...	1020	...	...	...	...	1320	...	...
Brussels Nord/Noord a.	0626	...	0717	...	...	0726	...	...	...	...	0836	...	...	...	...	1036	...	...	...	...	1336	...	...
Brussels Midi/Zuid a.	0635	...	0726	...	...	0735	...	...	...	...	0845	...	...	...	...	1045	...	...	...	...	1345	...	...
Brussels Midi/Zuid 12 d.	...	0659	...	0759	0759	...	0805	0859	...	...	...	0959	...	...	...	...	1159	...	...	...	...	1459	...
Lille Europe **12** a.	...	0732	...	|	0832	...	|	0932	...	...	...	1032	...	...	...	...	1232	...	...	...	...	1532	...
Ebbsfleet International **12** a.	...	|	...	|	|	...	|	0945	...	...	...	1045	...	...	...	...	1245	...	...	...	...	|	...
London St Pancras 12 a.	...	0755	...	0856	0856	...	0856	1003	...	...	...	1101	...	...	...	...	1303	...	...	...	...	1556	...

train type				☆				☆	☆				☆				☆				☆	☆	
train number			**9236**	**9145**			**9240**	**9149**	**9149**			**9244**	**9153**			**9248**	**9157**			**9256**	**9165**	**9165**	
notes			🍷	①–⑤			🍷	①–⑤	⑥⑦			🍷	⑧			🍷				🍷**k**	⑦	①–⑥	
Amsterdam Centraal d.	...	...	1156	...	...	...	1256	...	...	...	...	1356	...	...	...	1456	...	...	...	1656	...	...	...
Schiphol ✈ △ d.	...	...	1212	...	...	...	1312	...	...	...	...	1412	...	...	...	1512	...	...	...	1712	...	...	...
Den Haag HS d.	...	...	1236	...	...	...	1336	...	...	...	...	1436	...	...	...	1536	...	...	...	1736	...	...	...
Utrecht Centraal d.	1203	...	|	...	1303	...	|	...	...	1403	...	|	...	1503	...	|	...	1703	...	|	...	...	...
Rotterdam Centraal d.	1242	...	1256	...	1342	...	1356	...	...	1442	...	1456	...	1542	...	1556	...	1742	...	1756	...	...	...
Dordrecht d.	...	...	1310	...	...	...	1410	...	...	...	...	1510	...	...	...	1610	...	...	...	1810	...	...	...
Arnhem d.	...	1128	|	...	...	1228	|	...	...	...	1328	|	...	...	1428	|	...	...	1628	|	...	...	...
Nijmegen d.	...	1149	|	...	...	1249	|	...	...	...	1349	|	...	...	1449	|	...	...	1649	|	...	...	...
's-Hertogenbosch d.	...	1220	|	...	...	1320	|	...	...	...	1420	|	...	...	1520	|	...	...	1720	|	...	...	...
Tilburg d.	...	1237	|	...	...	1337	|	...	...	...	1437	|	...	...	1537	|	...	...	1737	|	...	...	...
Breda d.	...	1252	|	...	...	1352	|	...	...	...	1452	|	...	...	1552	|	...	...	1752	|	...	...	...
Roosendaal 🚌 d.	...	1311	1334	...	...	1411	1434	...	...	...	1511	1534	...	...	1611	1634	...	...	1811	1834	...	...	...
Antwerpen Centraal d.	...	...	1403	...	...	...	1503	...	...	...	...	1603	...	...	...	1703	...	...	...	1903	...	...	...
Antwerpen Berchem d.	...	...	|	...	...	...	|	...	...	...	...	|	...	...	...	|	...	...	...	|	...	...	...
Mechelen d.	...	...	1420	...	...	...	1520	...	...	...	...	1620	...	...	...	1720	...	...	...	1920	...	...	...
Brussels Nord/Noord a.	...	...	1436	...	...	...	1536	...	...	...	...	1636	...	...	...	1736	...	...	...	1936	...	...	...
Brussels Midi/Zuid a.	...	...	1445	...	...	...	1545	...	...	...	...	1645	...	...	...	1745	...	...	...	1945	...	...	...
Brussels Midi/Zuid 12 d.	...	...	...	1605	...	...	...	1701	1701	...	...	...	1759	...	...	...	1859	...	...	...	2059	2102	...
Lille Europe **12** a.	...	...	...	|	...	...	...	1735	1735	...	...	...	1832	...	...	...	1932	...	...	...	2132	2136	...
Ebbsfleet International **12** a.	...	...	...	1645	...	...	...	|	1747	...	...	...	1845	...	...	...	|	...	...	...	2145	2148	...
London St Pancras 12 a.	...	...	...	1703	...	...	...	1758	1803	...	...	...	1903	...	...	...	1956	...	...	...	2203	2204	...

A – ①②③④⑥.
B – ①–④ (⑧ Dec. 9 - Mar. 28) not Dec. 25, Jan. 1, Mar. 24, May 1, 12.
C – ①–④ Dec. 10 - Mar. 27; ⑤⑦ Mar. 30 - June 14 (also May 12; not Dec. 25, Jan. 1, Mar. 24).
E – ⑤⑦ Mar. 30 - June 14 (also May 12).
b – Also Dec. 25, Jan. 1, Mar. 24, May 12.

g – Also Dec. 25, 26, Jan. 1, Mar. 24, May 12.
k – Not Dec. 31.
p – Not Dec. 25, 26, Jan. 1, Mar. 24, May 12.
q – Not Dec. 25, 26, Jan. 1, Mar. 24, Apr. 30, May 1, 12.

☆ – Eurostar train 🅁 ✕. Special fares payable. Minimum check-in time 30 minutes. Valid Dec. 9, 2007 - July 5, 2008. See Table **12**.

⇌ – *Thalys* high-speed train
🍷. Special fares payab
△ – Trains stop to pick up or

LONDON - AMSTERDAM *by rail–sea–rail via Harwich - Hoek van Holland* 15a

Service December 8 - May 17

notes	①–⑥	⑥	⑥	①–⑤	①–⑤	①–⑤	⑦	⑦	⛴ A					⑦
ondon Liverpool Street .. d.	...	...	0618	...	0625	...	...	...	...	...	...	...	...	...
Peterborough .... d.	...	...	│	...	│	...	...	...	...	...	...	...	...	1747
Cambridge .... d.	...	...	│	...	│	...	...	...	...	...	...	...	...	│
Norwich .... d.	...	0630	│	0625	│	...	0700	...	...	...	...	...	...	│
Ipswich .... d.	0700	0708	│	0708	│	...	0740	0745	...	...	...	...	...	1927
lanningtree .... d.	│	0718	0726	0718	0732	0735	...	│	...	...	...	...	...	...
larwich International 🏛 ..... d.	0725	...	0744	...	...	0751	...	0810	0900	...	...	...	...	...
loek van Holland Haven 🏛. a.	...	...	...	...	...	...	...	...	1615	1637	...	...	...	...
chiedam Centrum .... a.	...	...	...	...	...	...	...	...	...	1703	1716	...	...	...
otterdam Centraal .... a.	...	...	...	...	...	...	...	...	...	1708	│	1728	...	...
en Haag HS .... a.	...	...	...	...	...	...	...	...	...	...	1732	1744	...	...
chiphol ✈ .... a.	...	...	...	...	...	...	...	...	...	...	│	1817	...	...
msterdam Centraal .... a.	...	...	...	...	...	...	...	...	...	...	1822	1833	...	...

notes	⑦	⑦	⑦	①–⑥	①–⑥	⑥	①–⑤	①–⑥	①–⑥	⛴ B				
ondon Liverpool Street .. d.	...	...	2000	...	...	...	...	...	2038	...	...	...	...	...
Peterborough .... d.	...	...	│	1747	...	1818	1833	...	│	...	...	...	...	...
Cambridge .... d.	1912	...	│	│	...	1908	1929	1943	│	...	...	...	...	...
Norwich .... d.	│	2000	│	│	2000	...	...	│	│	...	...	...	...	...
Ipswich .... d.	2035	2042	│	1925	2040	...	...	2104	│	...	...	...	...	...
lanningtree .... d.	│	2052	2104	...	...	...	...	│	2146	...	...	...	...	...
larwich International 🏛 ..... d.	2102	...	2122	...	...	...	...	2128	2202	2345	...	...	...	...
loek van Holland Haven 🏛. a.	...	...	...	...	...	...	...	...	...	0745	0807	...	...	...
chiedam Centrum .... a.	...	...	...	...	...	...	...	...	...	...	0833	...	...	...
otterdam Centraal .... a.	...	...	...	...	...	...	...	...	...	...	0838	0858	...	...
en Haag HS .... a.	...	...	...	...	...	...	...	...	...	...	...	0914	...	...
chiphol ✈ .... a.	...	...	...	...	...	...	...	...	...	...	...	0947	...	...
msterdam Centraal .... a.	...	...	...	...	...	...	...	...	...	...	...	1003	...	...

notes			⛴ C	⑦	⑦	①–⑤	⑥	⑦	⑦	①–⑥	①–⑤	⑥		
msterdam Centraal .... d.	1156	...	...	...	...	...	...	...	...	...	...	...	...	1859
chiphol ✈ .... d.	1212	...	...	...	...	...	...	...	...	...	...	...	...	1915
en Haag HS .... d.	1236	...	...	...	...	...	...	...	...	...	...	...	...	1946
otterdam Centraal .... d.	1253	1313	...	...	...	...	...	...	...	...	...	...	...	2002
chiedam Centrum .... d.	...	1317	...	...	...	...	...	...	...	...	...	...	...	...
loek van Holland Haven 🏛. d.	...	1342	1430	...	...	...	...	...	...	...	...	...	...	...
larwich International 🏛 ..... a.	...	...	2000	2058	...	2106	2106	2110	...	2134	...	...	...	...
lanningtree .... a.	...	...	...	2114	2118	2122	2122	│	...	│	...	...	...	...
Ipswich .... a.	...	...	...	...	│	│	│	2137	2144	2200	2243	2246	...	...
Norwich .... a.	...	...	...	...	│	│	│	...	2229	...	2328	2332	...	...
Cambridge .... a.	...	...	...	...	│	│	│	...	...	...	...	...	...	...
Peterborough .... a.	...	...	...	...	│	│	│	...	...	...	...	...	...	...
ondon Liverpool Street .. a.	...	...	...	...	2242	2236	2238	...	...	...	...	...	...	...

notes			⛴ D	①–⑤	⑥	⑦	①–⑥	①–⑥	①–⑥	⑦	⑦	⑦		
msterdam Centraal .... d.	1910	...	...	...	...	...	...	...	...	...	...	...	...	...
chiphol ✈ .... d.	│	...	...	...	...	...	...	...	...	...	...	...	...	...
en Haag HS .... d.	2001	...	...	...	...	...	...	...	...	...	...	...	...	...
otterdam Centraal .... d.	2020	2043	...	...	...	...	...	...	...	...	...	...	...	...
chiedam Centrum .... d.	...	2047	...	...	...	...	...	...	...	...	...	...	...	...
loek van Holland Haven 🏛. d.	...	2112	2200	...	...	...	...	...	...	...	...	...	...	...
larwich International 🏛 ..... a.	...	...	0630	0710	0706	0725	0747	...	...	0830	...	...	...	...
lanningtree .... a.	...	...	...	0722	0722	0738	│	...	...	│	...	...	...	...
Ipswich .... a.	...	...	...	│	│	│	0815	...	0842	0855	0944	0955	...	...
Norwich .... a.	...	...	...	│	│	│	│	...	0927	│	1029	│	...	...
Cambridge .... a.	...	...	...	│	│	│	0939	1004	...	1024	...	│	...	...
Peterborough .... a.	...	...	...	│	│	│	...	1053	...	...	...	1141	...	...
ondon Liverpool Street .. a.	...	...	...	0848	0833	0859	...	...	...	...	...	...	...	...

– Not Dec. 24, 25, 26, Mar. 7–13. On Jan. 1 depart 1100, arrive 1815. **B** – Not Dec. 24, 25, 31, Mar. 15. **C** – Not Dec. 24, 25, 26, Mar. 15. **D** – Not Dec. 24, 25, 31, Mar. 6–12.

EA CROSSING (for rail / sea / rail journeys): ⛴ – Ship service, operated by Stena Line. 🅁 One class only on ship. ✕ on ship. A cabin berth is necessary on night sailings.

PARIS - BRUSSELS - OOSTENDE 16

For additional services change at Brussels Midi. Table **18** Paris - Brussels. Table **400 / 401** Brussels - Gent - Brugge. Table **400** Brussels - Oostende.

	⇄	⇄	⇄	⇄
	9313	**9329**	**9455**	**9363**
	⑥	⑦	①–⑤	⑦
	p	q	h	k
aris Nord 18 .... d.	0755	1155	1825	2025
russels Midi / Zuid 18 .... a.	0917	1317	1947	2147
russels Midi / Zuid .... d.	0926	1326	1959	2159
ent Sint-Pieters .... a.	0959	1359	2030	2230
rugge .... a.	1025	1425	2056	2256
ostende .... a.	1040	1440	2111	2311

	⇄	⇄	⇄	⇄
	9308	**9308**	**9450**	**9454**
	⑥	①–⑤	⑦	⑥
		b	q	p
Oostende .... d.	0610	0611	1650	1750
Brugge .... d.	0625	0626	1706	1805
Gent Sint-Pieters .... d.	0651	0653	1730	1830
Brussels Midi / Zuid .... a.	0722	0725	1801	1901
Brussels Midi / Zuid 18 .... d.	0743	0743	1813	1913
Paris Nord 18 .... a.	0905	0905	1935	2035

b – Not Dec. 26, Jan. 1, Mar. 24, May 2, 12.
h – Not Dec. 25, 31, Jan. 1, Mar. 24, May 1, 12.
k – Also Jan. 1, Mar. 24, May 12; not Mar. 23, May 11.
p – Also Dec. 25, May 1; not Feb. 2, 9.
q – Also Jan. 1, Mar. 24, May 12.
⇄ – *Thalys* high-speed train 🅁 🍷 special fares payable.

LILLE - BRUSSELS (Summary Table) 16a

train type		*TGV*		☆		*TGV*	*TGV*		☆	*TGV*		☆		☆	*TGV*	*TGV*	*TGV*	☆	*TGV*	☆	☆	☆	
train number		**9811**		**9110**		**9854/5**	**9856/7**		**9120**	**9860**		**9132**		**9138**	**9862/3**	**9864/5**	**9866/7**	**9148**	**9868/9**	**9150**	**9154**	**9160**	
notes		🅁 🍷		①–⑥		🅁 🍷	🅁 🍷			🅁 🍷					🅁 🍷	🅁 🍷	🅁 🍷	⑥⑦	🅁 🍷	①–⑤	⑥⑦		
notes		A				A	B																
ille Europe .... d.	...	0729	...	0928	...	1041	1110	...	1228	1336	...	1524	...	1658	1719	1748	1835	1925	1946	1958	2055	2158	...
russels Midi / Zuid .... a.	...	0805	...	1003	...	1115	1144	...	1303	1412	...	1603	...	1733	1754	1822	1910	1959	2022	2033	2133	2233	...

train type		*TGV*		☆		☆	☆	☆		*TGV*	☆	*TGV*		☆	*TGV*	*TGV*	☆	☆	☆		☆	☆	
train number		**9804/5**		**9109**		**9113**	**9117**	**9121**		**9832/3**	**9127**	**9828/9**		**9141**	**9834/5**	**9836/7**	**9149**	**9153**	**9157**		**9165**	**9165**	
notes		🅁 🍷		①–⑥		⑦	①–⑤	⑥⑦		🅁 🍷		🅁 🍷			🅁 🍷	🅁 🍷		Ⓑ			⑦	①–⑥	
notes		A																					
russels Midi / Zuid .... d.	...	0540	...	0659	...	0759	0859	0959	...	1110	1159	1210	...	1459	1509	1609	1701	1759	1859	...	2059	2102	...
lle Europe .... a.	...	0615	...	0731	...	0832	0935	1032	...	1146	1235	1245	...	1532	1546	1644	1735	1832	1935	...	2135	2139	...

– ①–⑤ (not Dec. 25, Jan. 1, Mar. 24, May 1, 8, 12).
– ⑥⑦ (also Dec. 25, Jan. 1, Mar. 24, May 1, 8, 12).

☆ – Eurostar train. 🅁 ✕ Minimum check-in time 30 minutes departing from Brussels. Special fares payable. Valid Dec. 9, 2007 - July 5, 2008.

PARIS - CHARLEROI - NAMUR - LIÈGE 17

km	*train type*	⇄	⇄
	train number	**9499**	**9499**
	notes	①–⑤	⑥⑦
	notes	p	q
0	**Paris Nord** .... ▲ d.	1943	2016
282	Mons .... a.	2101	2133
323	Charleroi Sud .... a.	2133	2201
359	**Namur** .... a.	2206	2234
419	**Liège Guillemins** .... ▲ a.	2245	2314

train type	⇄	⇄
train number	**9496**	**9496**
notes	①–⑤	⑥⑦
notes	p	q
Liège Guillemins .. ▲ d.	0640	0647
Namur .... d.	0720	0726
Charleroi Sud .... d.	0756	0759
Mons .... d.	0825	0826
Paris Nord .... ▲ a.	0944	0944

LONDON - ASHFORD - AVIGNON / MARNE LA VALLÉE 17a

train type	☆		☆
train number	**9084**		**9074**
train number	**9085**		
notes	P		R
London St Pancras .... d.	0719	...	0853
Ashford International .... d.	0755	...	0926
Lille Europe .... a.	0952s	...	1124s
Marne la Vallée § .... a.	│	...	1227
Avignon Centre .... a.	1412	...	...

train type	☆		☆
train number	**9057**		**9087**
train number			**9086**
notes	R		Q
Avignon Centre .... d.	...	...	1624
Marne la Vallée § .... d.	1935	...	│
Lille Europe .... d.	2038u	...	2032u
Ashford International . a.	2037	...	2033
London St Pancras . a.	2113	...	2110

OTES FOR TABLES 17 AND 17a

– ⑥ July 12, 2008 - Sept. 6, 2008.
– ⑥ July 19, 2008 - Sept. 13, 2008.
– Nov. 14, 2007 - Dec. 13, 2008.
– Not Dec. 25, Jan. 1, Mar. 24, May 1, 8, 12.

q – Also Dec. 25, Jan. 1, Mar. 24, May 1, 8, 12.
s – Stops to set down only.
u – Stops to pick up only.

☆ – Eurostar train. 🅁 ✕ Special fares payable. Minimum check-in time 30 minutes. See Table **10**.
▲ – For other trains Paris - Liège see Table **20**.
⇄ – *Thalys* high-speed train. Special fares payable. 🅁 🍷.
§ – Marne la Vallée - Chessy (station for Disneyland).

INTERNATIONAL SERVICES FROM AMSTERDAM

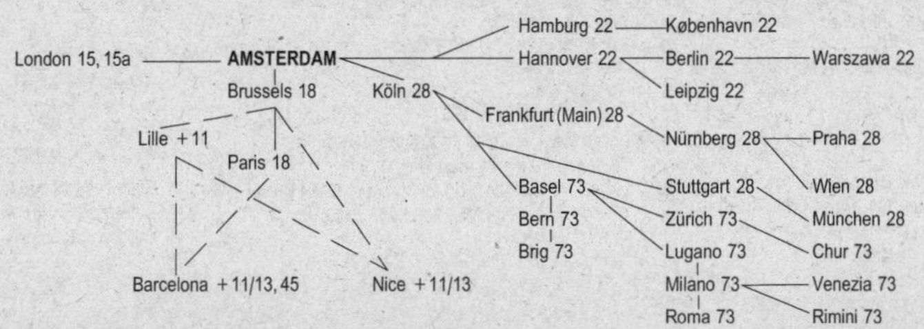

18 AMSTERDAM - BRUSSELS - PARIS

Brussels - Disneyland: see Table 11

km	km	train number	9304	4527	9306		9308	4528	9310	9310	9920/1	9412	9212	9314	9416	9216	9318	9418	9220	9322	9224	9326	9326	9428		
		train type	⇌		⇌		⇌		⇌	⇌	⇌	⇌		⇌	⇌		⇌	⇌		⇌		⇌	⇌	⇌		
		notes	R 🍷 J	K	R 🍷 K		R 🍷	K	R 🍷 ⑥b	R 🍷 H	R 🍷 A⊕	R 🍷	🍷 ①–⑥	R 🍷 U	R 🍷 ①–⑥	🍷	R 🍷 V	R 🍷 N	🍷	R 🍷	🍷	R 🍷 F	R 🍷	R 🍷		
0	0	**Amsterdam Centraal** d.	...	...	...	...	...	...	...	...	0532	...	0556	0626	...	0656	0726	...	0756	0826	0856	0926	...	...	...	...
17	17	Schiphol ✈ ⊕ d.	...	...	...	...	...	...	...	...	0551	...	0612	0642	...	0712	0742	...	0812	0842	0912	0942	...	...	...	...
60	60	Den Haag HS d.	...	...	...	...	...	...	...	...	0620	...	0636	0706	...	0736	0806	...	0836	0906	0936	1006	...	...	...	...
82	82	**Rotterdam Centraal** d.	...	...	...	...	...	...	...	...	0640	...	0656	0726	...	0756	0826	...	0856	0926	0956	1026	...	...	...	...
102	102	Dordrecht d.	...	...	...	...	...	...	...	...	|	...	0710	|	...	0810	|	...	0910	|	1010	|	...	...	...	...
140	140	Roosendaal 🏛 d.	...	...	...	...	...	...	...	...	|	...	0734	|	...	0834	|	...	0934	|	1034	|	...	...	...	...
184		**Antwerpen Centraal** d.	...	0550	0620	...	...	0650	0720	...	0742	...	0803	0828	...	0903	0928	...	1003	1028	1103	1128	...	...	...	...
187	182	Antwerpen Berchem d.	...	0556	|	...	...	0656	|	...	|	...	|	|	...	|	|	...	|	|	|	|	...	...	...	...
208	203	Mechelen d.	...	0610	|	...	...	0710	|	...	|	...	0820	|	...	0920	|	...	1020	|	1120	|	...	...	...	...
229	224	Brussels Nord / Noord a.	...	0626	|	...	...	0726	|	...	|	...	0836	|	...	0936	|	...	1036	|	1136	|	...	...	...	...
235	227	**Brussels Midi / Zuid** a.	...	0635	0701	...	...	0735	0801	...	|	...	0845	0908	...	0945	1008	...	1045	1108	1145	1208	...	...	...	...
235	227	**Brussels Midi / Zuid** d.	0643	...	0713	...	0743	...	0813	0813	0826	0843	...	0913	0943	...	1013	1013	...	1113	...	1213	1213	1243	...	...
547	540	**Paris Nord** a.	0805	...	0835	...	0905	...	0935	0935	...	1005	...	1035	1105	...	1135	1135	...	1235	...	1335	1335	1405	...	...

train number	9228	9330	9232		9436	9236	9338	9240	9342	9342	9344	9244	9346	9346	9448	9248	9350	9350	9352	9252	9354	9456	9256	9460		
train type		⇌			⇌		⇌		⇌	⇌	⇌		⇌	⇌	⇌		⇌	⇌	⇌		⇌	⇌		⇌		
notes	🍷	R 🍷 K	🍷		R 🍷	🍷	R 🍷 ⑧j	🍷	R 🍷 ⑥f	R 🍷 Z	R 🍷 ⑧t	🍷	R 🍷 O	R 🍷 ⑧j	R 🍷	🍷	R 🍷 L	R 🍷 ⑧t	R 🍷 ⑧q	🍷	R 🍷	R 🍷	🍷 p	R 🍷		
Amsterdam Centraal d.	0956	...	1056	...	...	1156	1226	1256	1326	...	...	1356	1426	...	...	1456	1526	...	...	1556	1626	...	1656	...	...	...
Schiphol ✈ ⊕ d.	1012	...	1112	...	...	1212	1242	1312	1342	...	...	1412	1442	...	...	1512	1542	...	...	1612	1642	...	1712	...	...	...
Den Haag HS d.	1036	...	1136	...	...	1236	1306	1336	1406	...	...	1436	1506	...	...	1536	1606	...	...	1636	1706	...	1736	...	...	...
Rotterdam Centraal d.	1056	...	1156	...	...	1256	1326	1356	1426	...	...	1456	1526	...	...	1556	1626	...	...	1656	1726	...	1756	...	...	...
Dordrecht d.	1110	...	1210	...	...	1310	|	1410	|	...	...	1510	|	...	...	1610	|	...	...	1710	|	...	1810	...	...	...
Roosendaal 🏛 d.	1134	...	1234	...	...	1334	|	1434	|	...	...	1534	|	...	...	1634	|	...	...	1734	|	...	1834	...	...	...
Antwerpen Centraal d.	1203	...	1303	...	...	1403	1428	1503	1528	...	...	1603	1628	...	...	1703	1728	...	...	1803	1828	...	1903	...	...	...
Antwerpen Berchem d.	|	...	|	...	...	|	|	|	|	...	...	|	|	...	...	|	|	...	...	|	|	...	|	...	...	...
Mechelen d.	1220	...	1320	...	...	1420	|	1520	|	...	...	1620	|	...	...	1720	|	...	...	1820	|	...	1920	...	...	...
Brussels Nord / Noord a.	1236	...	1336	...	...	1436	|	1536	|	...	...	1636	|	...	...	1736	|	...	...	1836	|	...	1936	...	...	...
Brussels Midi / Zuid a.	1245	...	1345	...	...	1445	1508	1545	1608	...	...	1645	1708	...	...	1745	1808	...	...	1845	1908	...	1945	...	...	...
Brussels Midi / Zuid d.	...	1313	...	...	1443	...	1513	...	1613	1613	1643	...	1713	1713	1743	...	1813	1813	1843	...	1913	1943	...	2043	...	...
Paris Nord a.	...	1435	...	...	1605	...	1635	...	1735	1735	1805	...	1835	1835	1905	...	1935	1935	2005	...	2035	2105	...	2205	...	...

train number	9260	9362	9364	9264	9366	9268	9272	9276	
train type		⇌	⇌		⇌				
notes	🍷 p	R 🍷 ⑧j	R 🍷 D	🍷 p	R 🍷 P	🍷 p	🍷 p	⑥	
Amsterdam Centraal d.	1756	1820	...	1856	...	1956	2056	2156	...
Schiphol ✈ ⊕ d.	1812	1842	...	1912	...	2012	2112	2212	...
Den Haag HS d.	1836	1906	...	1936	...	2036	2136	2236	...
Rotterdam Centraal d.	1856	1926	...	1956	...	2056	2156	2256	...
Dordrecht d.	1910	|	...	2010	...	2110	2210	2310	...
Roosendaal 🏛 d.	1934	|	...	2034	...	2134	2234	2334	...
Antwerpen Centraal d.	2003	2028	...	2103	...	2203	2303	0003	...
Antwerpen Berchem d.	|	|	...	|	...	|	|	|	...
Mechelen d.	2020	|	...	2120	...	2220	2320	0020	...
Brussels Nord / Noord a.	2036	|	...	2136	...	2236	2336	0036	...
Brussels Midi / Zuid a.	2045	2108	...	2145	...	2245	2345	0045	...
Brussels Midi / Zuid d.	...	2113	2143	...	2213	...	...	...	...
Paris Nord a.	...	2235	2305	...	2335	...	...	...	...

train number	9201		9205	9307	9209	9409	9311	9311	9213		
train type				⇌		⇌	⇌	⇌			
notes	①–⑥ 🍷 x		🍷	R 🍷 K	🍷	R 🍷	R 🍷 Q	R 🍷 ⑥f	🍷		
Paris Nord d.	...	...	...	0625	...	0655	0725	0725	...	...	...
Brussels Midi / Zuid a.	...	...	...	0747	...	0817	0847	0847	...	...	...
Brussels Midi / Zuid d.	0615	...	0715	0752	0815	...	...	0852	0915	...	...
Brussels Nord / Noord d.	0624	...	0724	|	0824	...	...	|	0924	...	...
Mechelen a.	0642	...	0740	|	0840	...	...	|	0940	...	...
Antwerpen Berchem a.	|	...	|	|	|	...	...	|	|	...	...
Antwerpen Centraal a.	0657	...	0757	0832	0857	...	...	0932	0957	...	...
Roosendaal 🏛 a.	0729	...	0829	|	0929	...	...	|	1029	...	...
Dordrecht a.	0753	...	0853	|	0953	...	...	|	1053	...	...
Rotterdam Centraal a.	0806	...	0906	0936	1006	...	...	1036	1106	...	...
Den Haag HS a.	0825	...	0925	0956	1025	...	...	1056	1125	...	...
Schiphol ✈ a.	0849	...	0949	1019	1049	...	...	1119	1149	...	...
Amsterdam Centraal a.	0906	...	1006	1036	1106	...	...	1136	1206	...	...

train number	9313	9315	9315	9217	9417	9319	9319	9221	9323	9323	9225	9425	9229	9429	9331	9233	9433	9237	9339	9339	9241	9343	9343	9245	9445	
train type	⇌	⇌	⇌		⇌	⇌	⇌		⇌	⇌		⇌		⇌	⇌		⇌		⇌	⇌		⇌	⇌		⇌	
notes	R 🍷 M	R 🍷	R 🍷 C	🍷	R 🍷	R 🍷	R 🍷 E	🍷	R 🍷	R 🍷 G	🍷	R 🍷 T	🍷	R 🍷	R 🍷	🍷	R 🍷	🍷	R 🍷	R 🍷 ⑦k	🍷	R 🍷	R 🍷 U	🍷	R 🍷	
Paris Nord d.	0755	0825	0825	...	0855	0925	0925	...	1025	1025	....	1055	...	1155	1225	...	1255	...	1425	1425	...	1525	1525	...	1555	...
Brussels Midi / Zuid a.	0917	0947	0947	...	1017	1047	1047	...	1147	1147	...	1217	...	1317	1347	...	1417	...	1547	1547	...	1647	1647	...	1717	...
Brussels Midi / Zuid d.	...	...	0952	1015	...	...	1052	1115	...	1152	1215	...	1315	...	1352	1415	...	1515	...	1552	1615	...	1652	1715	...	...
Brussels Nord / Noord d.	...	...	|	1024	...	...	|	1124	...	|	1224	...	1324	...	|	1424	...	1524	...	|	1624	...	|	1724	...	...
Mechelen a.	...	...	|	1040	...	...	|	1140	...	|	1240	...	1340	...	|	1440	...	1540	...	|	1640	...	|	1740	...	...
Antwerpen Berchem a.	...	...	|	|	...	...	|	|	...	|	|	...	|	...	|	|	...	|	...	|	|	...	|	|	...	...
Antwerpen Centraal a.	...	...	1032	1057	...	...	1132	1157	...	1232	1257	...	1357	...	1432	1457	...	1557	...	1632	1657	...	1732	1757	...	...
Roosendaal 🏛 a.	...	...	|	1129	...	...	|	1229	...	|	1329	...	1428	...	|	1529	...	1629	...	|	1729	...	|	1829	...	...
Dordrecht a.	...	...	|	1153	...	...	|	1253	...	|	1353	...	1453	...	|	1553	...	1653	...	|	1753	...	|	1853	...	...
Rotterdam Centraal a.	...	...	1136	1206	...	...	1236	1306	...	1336	1406	...	1506	...	1536	1606	...	1706	...	1736	1806	...	1836	1906	...	...
Den Haag HS a.	...	...	1156	1225	...	...	1256	1325	...	1356	1425	...	1525	...	1556	1625	...	1725	...	1756	1825	...	1856	1925	...	...
Schiphol ✈ a.	...	...	1219	1249	...	...	1319	1349	...	1419	1449	...	1549	...	1619	1649	...	1749	...	1819	1849	...	1919	1949	...	...
Amsterdam Centraal a.	...	...	1236	1306	...	...	1336	1406	...	1436	1506	...	1606	...	1636	1706	...	1806	...	1836	1906	...	1936	2006	...	...

train number	9347	9347	9249	9349	9351	9253	9453	9355	9355	9257	9457	9359	9359	9359	9261	9361	9986/7	9363	9265	9365	9367	9369	9371			
train type	⇌	⇌		⇌	⇌		⇌	⇌	⇌		⇌	⇌	⇌	⇌		⇌	⇌	⇌		⇌	⇌	⇌	⇌			
notes	R 🍷 ⑧q	R 🍷 ⑦k	🍷	R 🍷	R 🍷 J	🍷 p	R 🍷	R 🍷	R 🍷 p	🍷 p	R 🍷 W	R 🍷	R 🍷 Y	R 🍷 X	🍷 p	R 🍷 ⑤⑦y	R 🍷 B⊗	R 🍷 S	⑥	R 🍷 ⑤	R 🍷 ⑦y	R 🍷 M	R 🍷 ⑦h			
Paris Nord d.	1625	1625	...	1655	1725	...	1755	1825	1825	...	1855	1925	1925	1925	...	1955	...	2025	...	2055	2125	2155	2231	...	...	...
Brussels Midi / Zuid a.	1747	1747	...	1817	1847	...	1917	1947	1947	...	2017	2047	2047	2047	...	2117	2144	2147	...	2217	2247	2317	2353	...	...	...
Brussels Midi / Zuid d.	...	1752	1815	...	...	1915	...	...	1952	2015	...	...	2052	2052	2115	...	|	...	2215	...	...	...	...	...	...	...
Brussels Nord / Noord d.	...	|	1824	...	...	1924	...	...	|	2024	...	...	|	|	2124	...	|	...	2224	...	...	...	...	...	...	...
Mechelen a.	...	|	1840	...	...	1940	...	...	|	2040	...	...	|	|	2140	...	|	...	2240	...	...	...	...	...	...	...
Antwerpen Berchem a.	...	|	|	...	...	|	...	...	|	|	...	...	|	|	|	...	|	...	|	...	...	...	...	...	...	...
Antwerpen Centraal a.	...	1832	1857	...	...	1957	...	...	2032	2057	...	...	2132	2132	2157	...	2232	...	2257	...	...	...	...	...	...	...
Roosendaal 🏛 a.	...	|	1929	...	...	2029	...	...	|	2129	...	...	|	...	2229	...	|	...	2328	...	...	...	...	...	...	...
Dordrecht a.	...	|	1953	...	...	2053	...	...	|	2153	...	...	|	...	2253	...	|	...	2353	...	...	...	...	...	...	...
Rotterdam Centraal a.	...	1936	2006	...	...	2106	...	...	2136	2206	...	...	2236	...	2306	...	2336	...	0006	...	...	...	...	...	...	...
Den Haag HS a.	...	1956	2025p	...	...	2125	...	...	2156	2225	...	...	2256	...	2325	...	2356	...	...	...	...	...	...	...	...	...
Schiphol ✈ a.	...	2019	2049p	...	...	2149	...	...	2219	2249	...	...	2319	...	2349	...	0019	...	...	...	...	...	...	...	...	...
Amsterdam Centraal a.	...	2036	2106p	...	...	2206	...	...	2236	2306	...	...	2336	...	0006	...	0036	...	...	...	...	...	...	...	...	...

A – THALYS NEIGE – ⑥ Dec. 22, 2007 - Mar. 15, 2008: 🚃12 and 🍷 Amsterdam - Bourg St Maurice, Table **9** (Winter).
B – THALYS NEIGE – ⑥ Dec. 29, 2007 - Mar. 22, 2008: 🚃12 and 🍷 Bourg St Maurice - Amsterdam, Table **9** (Winter).
C – ⑤⑥⑦ Dec. 9 - Mar. 23; ①–⑥ Mar. 28 - June 14 (also Dec. 25, Jan. 1, Mar. 24; not May 12).
D – ①–④ (not Dec. 24–27, 31, Jan. 1–3, Mar. 24, May 1, 12).
E – ①–④ Dec. 10 - Mar. 27; ⑤⑦ Mar. 30 - June 14 (also May 12; not Dec. 25, Jan. 1, Mar. 24).
F – ⑤⑥⑦ Dec. 9 - Mar. 23; ①⑤⑥⑦ Mar. 28 - June 14 (also Dec. 25, Jan. 1, Mar. 24, May 1).
G – ⑤⑥⑦ (daily Mar. 31 - June 14) also Dec. 25, Jan. 1, Mar. 4.
H – ①–⑥ (not Dec. 24, 26–28, 31, Jan. 1–4, Mar. 24, May 12).
J – ①–⑤ (not Dec. 24–28, 31, Jan. 1–4, Mar. 24, May 1, 12).
K – ①–⑤ (not Dec. 25, Jan. 1, Mar. 24, May 1, 12).
L – ⑤ (⑤⑦ Mar. 30 - June 14) also May 12.
M – ①–⑥ (not Jan. 1, Mar. 24, May 12).
N – Not Dec. 24, 27, 28, 31, Jan. 2–4.
O – ⑦ (⑧ Mar. 31 - June 14) also Dec. 25, Jan. 1, Mar. 4, May 12; not May 1.
P – ⑤⑦ (also Jan. 1, May 12; not Dec. 28, Jan. 4, Mar. 23, May 11).
Q – ①–⑥ (not Dec. 24, 26, 27, 28, 31, Jan. 1–4, Mar. 24, May 12).
S – ①②③④⑥⑦.
T – Not Dec. 24–28, 31, Jan. 1–4.
U – ①–⑥ (not Dec. 25, Jan. 1, Mar. 24, May 12).
V – ⑥ Apr. 5 - June 14 (also May 1).
W – ①–⑥ (not Dec. 24, 31, Mar. 23, Apr. 30, May 11).
X – ①–④ (⑧ Dec. 9 - Mar. 28) not Dec. 25, Jan. 1, Mar. 24, May 1, 12).
Y – ⑤⑦ Mar. 30 - June 14 (also May 12).
Z – Not Dec. 24, 26, 27, 28, 31, Jan. 2, 3, 4.
b – Also Dec. 25, May 1.
f – Also May 1.
h – Also Jan. 1, Mar. 24, May 12; not Mar. 23, May 1.
j – Not May 1.
k – Also Dec. 25, Jan. 1, Mar. 24, May 12.
p – Not Dec. 31.
q – Not Dec. 24–28, 31, Jan. 2–4, May 1.
t – Not Dec. 25, May 1.
x – Not Dec. 25, 26, Jan. 1, Mar. 24, May 12.
y – Also Jan. 1, Mar. 24, May 12.
⇌ – *Thalys* high-speed train. Special fares payable.
⊗ – Calls to set down only.
⊕ – Calls to pick up only.

LONDON, PARIS and BRUSSELS - KÖLN, HAMBURG and BERLIN 20

For the full service London - Brussels and v.v. see Table **12**. For Paris - Brussels and v.v. see Table **18**. Connections at Brussels are not guaranteed.

train type	*ICE*	*IC*	*ICE*	*IC*	*ICE*	*EC*	*RE*	*ICE*	⇌	*IC*	*IC*	*ICE*	*RE*	*ICE*	*EC*	☆	⇌	*IC*	*ICE*	*IC*	*RE*	*ICE*	*IC*	*ICE*		
train number	**11**	**431**	**857**	**2141**	**1549**	**371**	**10115**	**928**	**9409**	**2116**	**2049**	**1641**	**11014**	**859**	**179**	**9110**	**9417**	**2114**	**37**	**2047**	**11018**	**951**	**2047**	**1643**		
notes	★	**331** 🍷	🍷	🍷	🍴	🍴		🍷	[R] 🍷	🍷	🍷	🍴		🍷	🍴	[R] 🍴 ①–⑥	[R] 🍷	🍷	[R] 🍷	🍷 ⑧ **j**		🍷	🍷	🍴 **h**		
ondon St Pancras .. d.	...	...	...	...	...	...	...	...	...	...	...	...	...	...	...	0700	...	...	...	...	...	...	...	...	...	...
bsfleet International d.	...	...	...	...	...	...	...	...	...	...	...	...	...	...	...	0714	...	...	...	...	...	...	...	...	...	...
shford International .. d.	...	...	...	...	...	...	...	...	...	...	...	...	...	...	...	|	...	...	...	...	...	...	...	...	...	...
le Europe .... d.	...	...	...	...	...	...	...	...	...	...	...	...	...	...	...	0928	...	...	...	...	...	...	...	...	...	...
Paris Nord .... d.	...	...	...	...	...	...	...	...	0655	...	...	...	...	...	...	|	0855	...	...	...	...	...	...	...	...	...
russels Midi/Zuid ... a.	...	...	...	...	...	...	...	...	0817	...	...	...	...	...	...	1003	1017	...	...	...	...	...	...	...	...	...
russels Midi/Zuid ... d.	0659	...	...	...	...	...	...	...	0825	...	...	...	...	...	...	...	1025	...	...	...	...	...	...	...	...	...
ège Guillemins .... a.	0750	...	...	...	...	...	...	...	0911	...	...	...	...	...	...	...	1111	...	...	...	...	...	...	...	...	...
ège Guillemins .... d.	0752	...	...	...	...	...	...	...	0913	...	...	...	...	...	...	...	1113	...	...	...	...	...	...	...	...	...
achen 🚌 .... a.	0836	...	...	...	...	...	...	...	0958n	...	...	...	...	...	...	...	1158n	...	...	...	...	...	...	...	...	...
öln Hbf .... a.	0915	...	...	...	...	...	...	...	1045	...	...	...	...	...	...	...	1245	...	...	...	...	...	...	...	...	...
öln Hbf .... d.	...	0948	0949	...	...	...	0951	1011	...	1111	1113	...	1131	1149	...	...	...	1311	...	1313	1331	1349	...	...	...	...
Wuppertal Hbf .... a.	...	|	1015	...	...	...	|	1041	...	|	1141	...	|	1215	...	...	...	|	...	1341	|	1415	...	...	...	...
Hagen Hbf .... a.	...	|	1033	...	...	...	|	1059	...	|	1159	...	|	1233	...	...	...	|	...	1359	|	1433	...	...	...	...
üsseldorf Hbf .... a.	...	1009	|	...	...	...	1021	|	...	1132	|	...	1200	|	...	...	...	1332	...	|	1400	|	...	...	...	...
uisburg Hbf .... a.	...	1023	|	...	...	...	1037	|	...	1145	|	...	1218	|	...	...	...	1345	...	|	1418	|	...	...	...	...
berhausen .... a.	...	1031	|	...	...	...	|	|	...	|	|	...	1226	|	...	...	...	|	...	|	1426	|	...	...	...	...
ssen Hbf .... a.	...	|	|	...	...	...	1051	|	...	1158	|	...	...	|	...	...	...	1358	...	|	...	|	...	...	...	...
chum Hbf .... a.	...	|	|	...	...	...	1103	|	...	1209	|	...	...	|	...	...	...	1409	...	|	...	|	...	...	...	...
rtmund Hbf .... a.	...	|	|	...	...	...	1115	1120	...	1221	1220	...	...	|	...	...	...	1421	...	1420	...	|	...	...	...	...
amm Hbf .... a.	...	|	1102	...	...	...	1145	|	...	|	1243	...	...	1302	...	...	...	|	...	1443	...	1502	...	...	...	...
Münster .... a.	...	1127	|	...	...	...	...	1155	...	1254	|	...	...	|	...	...	...	1454	...	|	...	|	...	...	...	...
Osnabrück Hbf ...... a.	...	...	|	...	...	...	...	1221	...	1321	|	...	...	|	...	...	...	1521	...	|	...	|	...	...	...	...
Bremen Hbf .... a.	...	...	|	...	...	...	...	1314	...	1414	|	...	...	|	...	...	...	1614	...	|	...	|	...	...	...	...
Hamburg Hbf .... a.	...	...	|	...	...	...	...	1412	...	1512	|	...	...	|	...	...	...	1712	1728	|	...	|	...	...	...	...
København H ⊙ a.	...	...	|	...	...	...	...	...	...	...	|	...	...	|	...	...	...	...	2209	|	...	|	...	...	...	...
elefeld Hbf .... a.	...	...	1135	...	...	...	...	...	...	...	1313	...	...	1335	...	...	...	...	...	1513	...	1535	...	...	...	...
annover Hbf .... a.	...	...	1228	1236	...	...	...	...	...	...	1418	...	...	1428	...	...	...	...	...	1618	...	1628	1636	...	...	...
Wolfsburg .... a.	...	...	1303	|	...	...	...	...	...	...	|	...	...	1503	...	...	...	...	...	|	...	1703	|	...	...	...
aunschweig Hbf ...... a.	...	...	|	1309	...	...	...	...	...	...	1509	...	...	|	...	...	...	...	...	1709	...	|	1709	...	...	...
agdeburg Hbf .... a.	...	...	|	1357p	...	...	...	...	...	...	1557p	...	...	|	...	...	...	...	...	1757p	...	|	1757p	...	...	...
Halle Hbf .... a.	...	...	|	1453	...	...	...	...	...	...	1653	...	...	|	...	...	...	...	...	1853	...	|	1853	...	...	...
Leipzig Hbf .... a.	...	...	|	1520	1551	...	...	...	...	...	1720	1751	...	|	...	...	...	...	...	1920	...	|	1920	1951	...	...
rlin Hbf .... a.	...	...	1410	...	|	1446	...	...	...	...	...	|	...	1610	1646	...	...	...	...	...	...	1810	...	|	...	...
rlin Ostbahnhof ... a.	...	...	1421	...	|	|	...	...	...	...	...	|	...	1621	|	...	...	...	...	...	...	1821	...	|	...	...
Dresden Hbf .... a.	...	...	...	...	1702	1710d	...	...	...	...	...	1902	...	...	1910d	...	...	...	...	...	...	...	...	2102	...	...
Bad Schandau 🚌 ... a.	...	...	...	...	...	1738	...	...	...	...	...	...	...	...	1936	...	...	...	...	...	...	...	...	...	...	...
Děčín .... a.	...	...	...	...	...	1757	...	...	...	...	...	...	...	...	1957	...	...	...	...	...	...	...	...	...	...	...
Praha Holešovice . a.	...	...	...	...	...	1918	...	...	...	...	...	...	...	...	2118	...	...	...	...	...	...	...	...	...	...	...
Praha Hlavní .... a.	...	...	...	...	...	1931	...	...	...	...	...	...	...	...	2132	...	...	...	...	...	...	...	...	...	...	...

train type	☆	☆	*ICE*	⇌	*ICE*	*RE*	*IC*	☆	☆	⇌	*IC*	*ICE*	*RE*	*ICE*	*IC*	*IC*	⇌	*EC*	*ICE*	☆	☆	⇌	*ICE*	*ICE*	*RE*	*ICE*
train number	**9114**	**9114**	**15**	**9323**	**651**	**10125**	**2112**	**9074**	**9120**	**9429**	**2026**	**518**	**11024**	**653**	**2135**	**2012**	**9433**	**100**	**945**	**9132**	**9132**	**9445**	**26**	**514**	**29738**	**120**
notes	[R] 🍴 ⑦	[R] 🍴 ①–⑥	★	[R] 🍷	🍷		🍷	[R] 🍴	[R] 🍴	[R] 🍷	🍷	🍷		🍷 **h**	🍷	🍷	[R] 🍷	**102** **B**	🍷	[R] 🍴 ⑤⑦	[R] 🍴 **J**	[R] 🍷	🍷	🍷		🍷 ⑧ **g**
ondon St Pancras .. d.	0800	0805	...	...	...	...	...	0853	1000	...	...	...	...	...	...	...	...	...	...	1257	1300	...	...	...	...	...
bsfleet International d.	0815	|	...	...	...	...	...	|	1015	...	...	...	...	...	...	...	...	...	...	1315	1315	...	...	...	...	...
shford International .. d.	|	|	...	...	...	...	...	0926	|	...	...	...	...	...	...	...	...	...	...	|	|	...	...	...	...	...
le Europe .... d.	|	|	...	...	...	...	...	1124	1228	...	...	...	...	...	...	...	...	...	...	1528	1528	...	...	...	...	...
Paris Nord .... d.	|	|	...	1025	...	...	...	▬	|	1155	...	...	...	...	...	...	1255	...	...	|	|	1555	...	...	...	...
russels Midi/Zuid ... a.	1056	1056	...	1147y	...	...	...	...	1303	1317	...	...	...	...	...	...	1417	...	...	1603	1603	1717	...	...	...	...
russels Midi/Zuid ... d.	...	...	1159	▬	...	...	...	...	▬	1325	...	...	...	...	...	...	1425	...	...	▬	▬	1725	...	...	...	...
ège Guillemins .... a.	...	...	1250	...	...	...	...	...	...	1411	...	...	...	...	...	...	1511	...	...	*ICE*	...	1811	...	...	...	...
ège Guillemins .... d.	...	...	1252	...	...	...	...	...	...	1413	...	...	...	...	...	...	1513	...	...	**955**	...	1813	...	...	...	...
achen 🚌 .... a.	...	...	1335	*RE*	...	...	...	...	...	1458n	...	...	...	...	...	...	1558n	...	...	⑧ **g**	...	1858n	...	...	...	...
öln Hbf .... a.	...	...	1415	**11020**	...	...	...	...	...	1545	...	...	...	...	...	...	1645	...	...	🍷	...	1945	...	...	...	...
öln Hbf .... d.	...	...	...	1431	1449	1451	1511	...	...	...	1611	1611	1631	1649	...	1648	...	1711	...	1749	...	...	2011	2011	2021	2048
Wuppertal Hbf .... a.	...	...	...	|	1515	|	|	...	...	...	1641	|	|	1715	...	|	...	|	...	1815	...	...	2041	|	2054	|
Hagen .... a.	...	...	...	|	1533	|	|	...	...	...	1659	|	|	1733	...	|	...	|	...	1833	...	...	2059	|	2119	|
isseldorf Hbf .... a.	...	...	...	1500	|	1521	1532	...	...	...	|	1632	1700	|	...	1712	...	1732	...	|	...	...	|	2032	|	2111
iisburg Hbf .... a.	...	...	...	1518	|	1537	1545	...	...	...	|	1645	1718	|	...	1725	...	1745	...	|	...	...	|	2045	|	2124
berhausen .... a.	...	...	...	1526	|	|	|	...	...	...	|	|	1726	|	...	|	...	|	...	|	...	...	|	|	|	2133
ssen Hbf .... a.	...	...	...	...	|	1551	1558	...	...	...	|	1657	...	|	...	1740	...	1758	...	|	...	...	|	2057	|	...
chum Hbf .... a.	...	...	...	...	|	1603	1609	...	...	...	|	1709	...	|	...	1751	...	1809	...	|	...	...	|	2109	|	...
rtmund Hbf .... a.	...	...	...	...	|	1615	1621	...	...	...	1720	1721	...	|	...	1805	...	1821	1848	|	...	...	2120	2121	|	...
amm .... a.	...	...	...	...	1602	1640	|	...	...	...	|	...	...	1802	...	1843	...	|	1906	1902	...	...	...	|	2157	...
Münster .... a.	...	...	...	...	|	...	1654	...	...	...	1754	...	...	|	...	|	...	1854	|	|	...	...	...	2157	2229	...
Osnabrück .... a.	...	...	...	...	|	...	1721	...	...	...	1821	...	...	|	...	|	...	1921	|	|	...	...	...	2225	...	...
Bremen Hbf .... a.	...	...	...	...	|	...	1814	...	...	...	1914	...	...	|	...	|	...	2014	|	|	*IC*	...	...	2320	...	...
Hamburg Hbf .... a.	...	...	...	...	|	...	1912	*IC*	...	...	2012	...	...	|	...	|	...	2112	|	|	**2012**	...	...	0021	...	...
København H ⊙ a.	...	...	...	...	|	...	...	**2133**	...	...	...	...	...	|	...	|	...	...	|	|	🍷	...	...	...	...	...
elefeld .... a.	...	...	...	...	1636	...	...	🍷	...	...	...	...	...	1836	...	1913	...	...	1935	1935	**v**	...	...	...	...	...
annover Hbf .... a.	...	...	...	...	1728	...	...	1736	...	...	...	...	...	1928	1936	2018	...	...	2028	2028	2036	...	...	...	...	...
Wolfsburg .... a.	...	...	...	...	|	...	...	|	*ICE*	...	...	...	...	|	|	|	...	...	2103	2103	|	...	...	...	...	...
aunschweig Hbf ..... a.	...	...	...	...	|	...	...	1808	**1655**	...	...	...	...	|	2008	2109v	...	...	|	|	2109	...	...	...	...	...
agdeburg Hbf .... a.	...	...	...	...	|	...	...	1858p	🍴	...	...	...	...	|	2058p	2157z	...	...	|	|	2157p	...	...	...	...	...
Halle .... a.	...	...	...	...	|	...	...	1951	⑧ **g**	...	...	...	...	|	2153	2256v	...	...	|	|	2256	...	...	...	...	...
Leipzig Hbf .... a.	...	...	...	...	|	...	...	2018	2051	...	...	...	...	|	2220	2323v	...	...	|	|	2323	...	...	...	...	...
rlin Hbf .... a.	...	...	...	...	1908	...	...	...	|	...	...	...	...	2108	|	...	...	...	2221	2221	...	...	...	...	...	...
rlin Ostbahnhof ... a.	...	...	...	...	1919	...	...	...	|	...	...	...	...	2119	|	...	...	...	2231	2231	...	...	...	...	...	...
Dresden Hbf .... a.	...	...	...	...	...	...	...	...	2202	...	...	...	...	...	*0039*k	...	...	...	...	...	...	...	...	...	...	...
Bad Schandau 🚌 ... a.	...	...	...	...	...	...	...	...	...	...	...	...	...	...	...	...	...	...	...	...	...	...	...	...	...	...
Děčín .... a.	...	...	...	...	...	...	...	...	...	...	...	...	...	...	...	...	...	...	...	...	...	...	...	...	...	...
Praha Holešovice . a.	...	...	...	...	...	...	...	...	...	...	...	...	...	...	...	...	...	...	...	...	...	...	...	...	...	...
Praha Hlavní .... a.	...	...	...	...	...	...	...	...	...	...	...	...	...	...	...	...	...	...	...	...	...	...	...	...	...	...

– [1] (panorama car), [12] and 🍴 Chur - Basel - Köln - Dortmund - Hamburg (- Kiel ⑦ also Dec. 26, Jan. 1, Mar. 24, May 12; not Dec. 23, 30, Mar. 23, May 11).

– ①②③④⑥.

– Departure time.

– Not Dec. 24, 25, 31, Mar. 21, 23, May 11.

– Not Dec. 24, 31.

- Also Dec. 29, Mar. 22, May 3; not Mar. 21, May 1.

– Not Dec. 25, Jan. 1.

n – Depart 8 minutes later.

p – Magdeburg **Buckau** from May 25.

v – ⑤⑦ (also Dec. 26, Jan. 1, Mar. 20, 24, Apr. 30, May 12; not Dec. 23, 30, Mar. 21, 23, May 2, 11).

y – Connects with train in previous column.

z – ⑤⑦ (also Dec. 26, Jan. 1, Mar. 20, 24, Apr. 30, May 12; not Dec. 23, 30, Mar. 21, 23, May 2, 11). Magdeburg **Buckau** from May 25.

⇌ – *Thalys* high-speed train. Special fares payable.

★ – *ICE 3* train 🍷 special fares payable.

☆ – Eurostar train. Special fares payable. Minimum check-in time 30 minutes. See Table **12**. Valid Dec. 9, 2007 - July 5, 2008.

⊙ – 🚌 between Hamburg and København is Rødby, see Table **720**.

For London - Esbjerg/København by rail and sea via Harwich, see DFDS Seaways Table 2220

20 LONDON, PARIS and BRUSSELS - KÖLN, HAMBURG and BERLIN

For the full service London - Brussels and v.v. see Table **12**. For Paris - Brussels and v.v. see Table **18**. Connections at Brussels are not guaranteed.

train type	☆	⇌	ICE	RE	EC	ICE	IC	☆	⇌	ICE	ICE	RE	CNL	CNL	IC	IC	☆	☆	⇌	☆	CNL	IC	ICE	CNL	EC*
train number	9138	9347	17	11032 11042	114	657	2318	9144	9453	24	512	29742	379	40347	2020	2243	9146	9148	9457	9158	243	2147	1543	237	33
notes	R✕	R🍷 ⑥h	★		🍷	🍷 ⑦v	🍷 ⑥g	R✕ ⑦	R🍷	🍷	🍷 z		C R	H R	w	Q	R✕ ①-⑤	R✕ ⑥⑦	R🍷 ⑥f	R✕	A R	🍷 P	✕	N R	R🍷 F
London St Pancras .. d.	1434	...	...	...	...	...	...	1604	...	...	...	...	...	...	...	...	1635	1655	...	1934	...	...	...	...	...
Ebbsfleet International d.	|	...	...	...	...	...	...	|	...	...	...	...	...	...	...	...	|	1712	...	|	...	...	...	...	...
Ashford International .. d.	|	...	...	...	...	...	...	|	...	...	...	...	...	...	...	...	|	|	...	|	...	...	...	...	...
Lille Europe .... d.	1658	...	...	...	...	...	...	|	...	...	...	...	...	...	...	...	|	1925	...	2158	...	...	...	...	...
Paris Nord .... d.	|	1625	...	...	...	...	...	|	1755	...	...	...	...	...	...	...	|	|	1855	|	2046x	...	...	2046x	...
Brussels Midi/Zuid ... a.	1733	1747	...	...	...	...	...	1903	1917	...	...	...	...	...	...	...	1926	1959	2017	2233	◐	...	...	◐	...
Brussels Midi/Zuid ... d.	...	...	1759	...	...	...	...	▬	1925	...	...	...	...	...	...	...	...	...	2025	...	2341u	...	...	2341u	...
Liège Guillemins .... a.	...	...	1850	...	...	...	...	...	2011	...	...	...	...	...	...	...	...	...	2111	...	|	...	...	|	...
Liège Guillemins .... d.	...	...	1852	...	...	...	...	ICE	2013	...	...	...	...	...	...	...	...	...	...	...	0052u	...	...	0052u	...
Aachen 🏛 .... a.	...	...	1935	...	...	...	...	502	2058n	...	...	...	...	...	...	...	...	...	...	...	|	...	...	|	...
Köln Hbf .... a.	...	...	2015	...	...	...	...	🍷	2145	...	...	...	...	...	...	...	...	...	...	...	|	...	...	|	...
Köln Hbf .... d.	...	...	...	2031	2045	2049	2111	2111	...	2211	2211	2221	2228	2228	0210	...	...	...	...	...	|	...	...	|	...
Wuppertal Hbf .... a.	...	...	...	|	|	2115	|	2141	...	2241	|	2254	2314u	2314u	|	...	...	...	...	...	|	...	...	|	...
Hagen Hbf .... a.	...	...	...	|	|	2133	|	2159	...	2259	|	2319	2334u	2334u	|	...	...	...	...	...	|	...	...	|	...
Düsseldorf Hbf .... a.	...	...	...	2100	2106	|	2132	|	...	|	2232	|	|	|	0232	...	...	...	...	...	|	...	...	|	...
Duisburg Hbf .... a.	...	...	...	2118	2128	|	2145	|	...	|	2245	|	|	|	0249	...	...	...	...	...	|	...	...	|	...
Oberhausen .... a.	...	...	...	2126	|	|	|	|	...	|	*2316*	|	|	|	|	...	...	...	...	...	|	...	...	|	...
Essen Hbf .... a.	...	...	...	...	2141	|	2158	|	...	|	2257	|	|	|	0304	...	...	...	...	...	|	...	...	|	...
Bochum Hbf .... a.	...	...	...	...	2152	|	2209	|	...	|	2309	|	|	|	0315	...	...	...	...	...	|	...	...	|	...
Dortmund Hbf .... a.	...	...	...	...	2205	|	2221	2220	...	2320	2321	|	2356u	2356u	0327	...	...	...	...	...	|	...	...	0515s	...
Hamm .... a.	...	...	...	...	...	2202	|	2248	...	...	|	2357	0014u	0014u	|	...	...	...	...	...	|	...	...	|	...
Münster .... a.	...	...	...	...	...	|	2254v	|	...	...	2357	0036d	|	|	0416	0538	...	...	...	...	|	...	...	0555s	...
Osnabrück Hbf .... a.	...	...	...	...	...	|	...	|	...	...	...	...	|	|	0445	0603	...	...	...	...	|	...	...	0622s	...
Bremen Hbf .... a.	...	...	...	...	...	|	...	|	...	...	...	...	|	|	0552	|	...	...	...	...	|	...	...	0722s	...
Hamburg Hbf .... a.	...	...	...	...	...	|	...	|	...	...	...	...	|	b	0651	|	...	...	...	...	|	...	...	0832	0928
København H ⊙ a.	...	...	...	...	...	|	...	|	...	...	...	...	|	0959	...	|	...	...	...	...	|	...	...	▬	1409
Bielefeld Hbf .... a.	...	...	...	...	...	2236	...	2318	...	...	...	...	0043u	...	...	|	...	...	...	...	0439s	...	...	...	...
Hannover Hbf .... a.	...	...	...	...	...	2328	...	0026	...	...	...	...	|	...	...	0718	...	...	...	...	0600s	0636	...	...	...
Wolfsburg .... a.	...	...	...	...	...	|	...	...	...	...	...	...	|	...	...	0754	...	...	...	...	0646s	...	...	...	...
Braunschweig Hbf ...... a.	...	...	...	...	...	|	...	...	...	...	...	...	|	...	...	|	...	...	...	...	|	0709	...	...	...
Magdeburg Hbf .... a.	...	...	...	...	...	|	...	...	...	...	...	...	|	...	...	|	...	...	...	...	|	0757p	...	...	...
Halle Hbf .... a.	...	...	...	...	...	|	...	...	...	...	...	...	|	...	...	|	...	...	...	...	|	0853	...	EC	...
Leipzig Hbf .... a.	...	...	...	...	...	|	...	...	...	...	...	...	|	...	...	|	...	...	...	...	|	0920	0951	173	...
Berlin Hbf .... a.	...	...	...	...	...	0111	...	...	...	...	...	...	0422	...	...	0921	...	...	...	...	0810	...	|	✕	...
Berlin Ostbahnhof ... a.	...	...	...	...	...	0122	...	...	...	...	...	...	0434	...	...	0932	...	...	...	...	0820	...	|	↗	...
Dresden Hbf .... a.	...	...	...	...	...	...	...	...	...	...	...	...	0705	...	...	...	...	...	...	...	...	...	1102	1110	...
Bad Schandau 🏛 ... a.	...	...	...	...	...	...	...	...	...	...	...	...	0736	...	...	...	...	...	...	...	...	...	...	1136	...
Děčín .... a.	...	...	...	...	...	...	...	...	...	...	...	...	0757	...	...	...	...	...	...	...	...	...	...	1157	...
Praha Holešovice . a.	...	...	...	...	...	...	...	...	...	...	...	...	0918	...	...	...	...	...	...	...	...	...	...	1318	...
Praha Hlavní .... a.	...	...	...	...	...	...	...	...	...	...	...	...	0933	...	...	...	...	...	...	...	...	...	...	...	...

train type	CNL	CNL	☆	☆	⇌	☆	☆	IC	CNL	CNL	RE		ICE	IC	⇌	☆	RE	EC	RE	⇌	☆
train number	236	242	9109	9113	9412	9117	9121	2021	40483	378	11103	29707	501	2319	9416	9121	10104	115	11005	9418	9127
notes	M R	A R	R✕ ①-⑥	R✕ ⑦	R🍷 U	R✕ ①-⑤	R✕ ⑥⑦		H R	C R	K	J	🍷 d	🍷 Q	R🍷 ①-⑥	R✕ ⑥⑦		🍷	J	R🍷 ⑦q	R✕
Praha Hlavní .... d.	...	...	...	...	...	...	...	...	...	1850	...	...	...	...	p	...	...	...	...	...	...
Praha Holešovice . d.	...	...	...	...	...	...	...	...	...	1902	...	...	...	...	...	...	...	...	...	...	...
Děčín .... d.	...	...	...	...	...	...	...	...	...	2038	...	...	...	...	...	...	...	...	...	...	...
Bad Schandau 🏛 ... d.	...	...	...	...	...	...	...	...	...	2056	...	...	...	...	...	...	...	...	...	...	...
Dresden Hbf .... d.	...	...	...	...	...	...	...	...	...	2123	...	...	...	...	...	...	...	...	...	...	...
Berlin Ostbahnhof ... d.	...	2117	...	...	...	...	...	...	...	0022	...	...	...	...	...	...	...	...	...	...	...
Berlin Hbf .... d.	...	2126u	...	...	...	...	...	...	...	0032	...	...	...	...	...	...	...	...	...	...	...
Leipzig Hbf .... d.	...	|	...	...	...	...	...	...	...	|	...	...	...	...	...	...	...	...	...	...	...
Halle Hbf .... d.	...	|	...	...	...	...	...	...	...	|	...	...	...	...	...	...	...	...	...	...	...
Magdeburg Hbf .... d.	...	|	...	...	...	...	...	...	...	|	...	...	...	...	...	...	...	...	...	...	...
Braunschweig Hbf ..... d.	...	|	...	...	...	...	...	...	...	|	...	...	...	...	...	...	...	...	...	...	...
Wolfsburg .... d.	...	2252u	...	...	...	...	...	...	...	|	...	...	...	...	...	...	...	...	...	...	...
Hannover Hbf .... d.	...	2331u	...	...	...	...	...	...	...	|	...	...	...	...	...	...	...	...	...	...	...
Bielefeld Hbf .... d.	...	0030u	...	...	...	...	...	...	...	0354s	...	...	...	...	...	...	...	...	...	...	...
København H ⊙ d.	...	|	...	...	...	...	...	...	1853	|	...	...	...	...	...	...	...	...	...	...	...
Hamburg Hbf .... d.	2024	|	...	...	...	...	...	2246	k	|	...	...	...	...	...	...	...	...	...	...	...
Bremen Hbf .... d.	2130u	|	...	...	...	...	...	2347	|	|	...	...	...	...	...	...	...	...	...	...	...
Osnabrück Hbf .... d.	2231u	|	...	...	...	...	...	0047	|	|	...	...	...	...	...	...	...	...	...	...	...
Münster .... d.	|	|	...	...	...	...	...	0115	|	|	...	...	...	0504c	...	...	...	...	...	...	...
Hamm .... d.	|	|	...	...	...	...	...	0137	0425s	0425s	...	0501	...	|	...	...	0516	...	...	...	...
Dortmund Hbf .... d.	|	|	...	...	...	...	...	0203	0448s	0448s	...	|	0537	0538	...	...	0545	0552	...	...	...
Bochum Hbf .... d.	|	|	...	...	...	...	...	0215	|	|	...	|	|	0549	...	...	0556	0605	...	...	...
Essen Hbf .... d.	|	|	...	...	...	...	...	0228	|	|	...	|	|	0600	...	...	0609	0616	...	...	...
Oberhausen .... d.	|	|	...	...	...	...	...	|	|	|	0534	|	|	|	...	...	|	|	0634	...	...
Duisburg Hbf .... d.	|	|	...	...	...	...	...	0241	|	|	0542	|	|	0613	...	...	0624	0632	0642	...	...
Düsseldorf Hbf .... d.	|	|	...	...	...	...	...	0302	|	|	0558	|	|	0627	...	...	0640	0650	0658	...	...
Hagen Hbf .... d.	|	|	...	...	...	...	...	|	0521s	0521s	|	0539	0557	|	...	...	|	|	|	...	...
Wuppertal Hbf .... d.	|	|	...	...	...	...	...	|	0539s	0539s	|	0604	0614	|	...	...	|	|	|	...	...
Köln Hbf .... a.	|	|	...	...	...	...	...	0336	0614	0614	0629	0638	0646	0649	...	...	0711	0714	0729	...	...
Köln Hbf .... d.	|	|	...	...	...	...	...	...	...	...	...	...	...	...	0714	...	...	...	...	0740	...
Aachen 🏛 .... d.	|	|	...	...	...	...	...	...	...	...	...	...	...	...	0802t	...	...	...	...	0818	...
Liège Guillemins .... a.	0454s	0454s	...	...	...	...	...	...	...	...	...	...	...	...	0847	...	...	...	...	0908	...
Liège Guillemins .... d.	...	...	...	...	0749	...	...	...	...	...	...	...	...	...	0849	...	...	...	...	0910	...
Brussels Midi/Zuid ... a.	0615s	0615s	...	...	0835	...	...	...	...	...	...	...	...	...	0935	...	...	...	...	1001	...
Brussels Midi/Zuid ... d.	◐	◐	0659	0759	0843	0859	0959	...	...	...	...	...	...	...	0943	0959	...	...	...	1013	1159
Paris Nord .... a.	0914	0914	|	|	1005	|	|	...	...	...	...	...	...	...	1105	|	...	...	...	1135	|
Lille Europe .... a.	...	...	0732	0832	...	0932	1032	...	...	...	...	...	...	...	...	1032	...	...	...	...	1232
Ashford International .. a.	...	...	|	|	...	|	|	...	...	...	...	...	...	...	...	|	...	...	...	...	|
Ebbsfleet International a.	...	...	|	|	...	0945	1045	...	...	...	...	...	...	...	...	1045	...	...	...	...	1245
London St Pancras .. a.	...	...	0755	0856	...	1003	1101	...	...	...	...	...	...	...	...	1101	...	...	...	...	1303

NOTES for pages 58 and 59

A – *City Night Line* 🛏 1, 2 cl., 🛋 2 cl. (including ladies only berths), (2) and ✕ Paris - Brussels - Berlin and v.v. R Special fares apply.
B – *ICE SPRINTER* – ①–④ (not Dec. 21 - Jan. 1, Mar. 24, May 1, 12, 22), supplement payable.
C – *City Night Line* KOPERNIKUS: 🛏 1, 2 cl., 🛋 2 cl., (2) and 🍷 Amsterdam - Köln - Berlin - Dresden - Praha and v.v. R Special fares apply.
F – (12) and 🍷 Hamburg - København and v.v.
H – *City Night Line* 🛏 1, 2 cl., 🛋 2 cl., (2) and ✕ Amsterdam - Köln - København and v.v. R Special fares apply.
J – ①–⑥ (not Dec. 25, 26, Jan. 1, Mar. 21, 24, May 1, 12, 22).
K – ①–⑤ (not Dec. 24, 25, 26, 31, Jan. 1, Mar. 21, 24, May 1, 12, 12).
L – ⑥ (not May 1).
M – *City Night Line* 🛏 1, 2 cl., 🛋 2 cl. (including ladies only berths), (2) and ✕ Hamburg Altona (depart 2008) - Hamburg Hbf - Brussels - Paris. R Special fares apply.
N – *City Night Line* 🛏 1, 2 cl., 🛋 2 cl. (including ladies only berths), (2) and ✕ Paris - Brussels - Hamburg Hbf - Hamburg Altona (arrive 0853). R Special fares apply.

P – ①–⑤ (not Dec. 24, 25, 26, 31, Jan. 1, Mar. 21, 24, May 12).
Q – ①–⑥ (not Dec. 25, 26, Jan. 1, Mar. 22, 24, May 12).
T – Dec. 9 - Jan. 5, Mar 15 - Oct. 27 (not Dec. 25, Jan. 1).
U – ①–⑥ (not Dec. 25, 26, Jan. 1, Mar. 24, May 1, 2, 12).

b – Via Flensburg (0546**s**), Padborg (0559**s**) and Odense (0820s
c – ① (also Dec. 27, Jan. 2, Mar. 25, May 13; not Dec. 24, 31, Ma 24, May 12).
d – Not Dec. 25, Jan. 1.
e – ①⑥ (also Dec. 27, Jan. 2, Mar. 21, 25, May 1, 13).
f – Not Dec. 24, 25, 31, Mar. 23, Apr. 30, May 1, 11.
g – Not Dec. 24, 25, 31, Mar. 21, 23, May 11.
h – Not Dec. 24–28, 31, Jan. 2–4, May 1.

NOTES CONTINUED ON NEXT PAGE →

BERLIN, HAMBURG and KÖLN - BRUSSELS, PARIS and LONDON 20

For the full service Brussels - London and v.v. see Table **12**. For Brussels - Paris and v.v. see Table **18**. Connections at Brussels are not guaranteed.

train type	ICE	ICE	RE	IC	ICE	ICE	RE	RE	ICE	ICE	ICE	⇌	IC	ICE	RE	IC	ICE	⇌	IC	ICE	IC	ICE	IC	ICE	⇌	☆
train number	25	513	10106	438	16	656	11009	29713	515	27	1034	9428	2013	654	11013	2025	517	9436	2027	1642	2046	952	434	14	9346	9153
notes	✕	🍷		🍷 Q	★	✕ P			✕	✕	® 🍷 B	® 🍷	🍷	✕		✕	✕	® 🍷	🍷	🍷 d	🍷 Q	✕	🍷	★	® 🍷 L	® ✕ ⑥
Praha Hlavní d.	...	...	...	...	...	...	...	...	...	...	...	...	...	...	...	...	...	...	...	...	...	...	...	...	...	...
Praha Holešovice d.	...	...	...	...	...	...	...	...	...	...	...	...	...	...	...	...	...	...	...	...	...	...	...	...	...	...
Děčín d.	...	...	...	...	...	...	...	...	...	...	...	...	...	...	...	...	...	...	...	...	...	...	...	...	...	...
Bad Schandau 🏛 d.	...	...	...	...	...	...	...	...	...	...	...	...	...	...	...	...	...	...	...	...	...	...	...	...	...	...
Dresden Hbf d.	...	...	...	...	...	...	...	...	...	...	...	...	...	...	...	...	...	...	...	0655	...	...	...	...	...	...
Berlin Ostbahnhof d.	...	...	...	...	...	0417	...	...	...	...	...	...	...	0640	...	...	...	...	...	|	...	0938	...	...	...	...
Berlin Hauptbahnhof d.	...	...	...	...	...	0428	...	...	...	...	...	...	...	0651	...	...	...	...	...	|	...	0948	...	...	...	...
Leipzig Hbf d.	...	...	...	...	...	|	...	...	...	...	...	...	0437e	|	...	...	...	...	...	0807	0840	|	...	...	...	...
Halle Hbf d.	...	...	...	...	...	|	...	...	...	...	...	...	0503e	|	...	...	...	...	...	▬	0906	|	...	...	...	...
Magdeburg Hbf d.	...	...	...	...	...	|	...	...	...	...	...	...	0600y	|	...	...	...	...	...	...	1000r	|	...	...	...	...
Braunschweig Hbf d.	...	...	...	...	...	|	...	...	...	...	...	...	0650y	|	...	...	...	...	...	...	1050	|	...	...	...	...
Wolfsburg d.	...	...	...	...	...	0546	...	...	...	...	...	...	|	|	...	...	...	...	...	...	|	1055	...	...	...	...
Hannover Hbf d.	...	...	...	...	...	0621	...	...	...	...	...	...	0740	0831	...	...	...	...	...	...	1123	1131	...	...	...	...
Bielefeld Hbf d.	...	...	...	...	...	0720	...	...	...	...	...	...	0842	0922	...	...	...	...	...	...	...	1222	...	...	...	...
København H ⊙ d.	...	...	...	...	...	|	...	...	...	...	...	...	|	|	...	...	...	...	...	...	...	|	...	...	...	...
Hamburg Hbf d.	...	...	...	...	...	|	...	...	0537	...	0611	...	|	|	...	0746	...	...	0946	...	...	|	...	...	...	...
Bremen Hbf d.	...	...	...	...	...	|	...	...	0637	...	|	...	|	|	...	0844	...	...	1044	...	...	|	...	...	...	...
Osnabrück Hbf d.	...	...	...	...	...	|	...	...	0732	...	|	...	|	|	...	0937	...	...	1137	ICE	...	|	...	...	...	...
Münster d.	...	0601	...	0631	...	|	...	0734	0801	...	|	...	|	|	...	1004	...	...	1204	**539**	...	|	1232	...	...	...
Hamm d.	...	|	0616	|	...	0754	...	0801	|	...	|	...	0914	0954	...	|	...	...	|	🍷	...	1254	|	...	...	...
Dortmund Hbf d.	0636	0638	0645	|	...	|	...	|	0837	0838	|	...	0952	|	...	1036	1038	...	1236	1238	...	|	|	...	...	...
Bochum Hbf d.	|	0649	0656	|	...	|	...	|	|	0849	|	...	1003	|	...	|	1049	...	|	1249	...	|	|	...	...	...
Essen Hbf d.	|	0700	0709	|	...	|	...	|	|	0900	0853s	...	1014	|	...	|	1100	...	|	1300	...	|	|	...	...	...
Oberhausen d.	|	|	|	0727	...	|	0834	|	|	|	|	...	|	|	1034	|	|	...	|	|	...	|	1328	...	...	...
Duisburg Hbf d.	|	0713	0724	0735	...	|	0842	|	|	0913	|	...	1032	|	1042	|	1113	...	|	1313	...	|	1335	...	...	...
Düsseldorf Hbf d.	|	0727	0740	0752	...	|	0858	|	|	0927	0915s	...	1050	|	1058	|	1127	...	|	1327	...	|	1349	...	...	...
Hagen Hbf d.	0657	|	|	|	...	0824	|	0839	0857	|	|	...	|	1024	|	1057	|	...	1257	|	...	1324	|	...	...	...
Wuppertal Hbf d.	0714	|	|	|	...	0841	|	0904	0914	|	|	...	|	1041	|	1114	|	...	1314	|	...	1341	|	...	...	...
Köln Hbf a.	0746	0749	0811	0815	...	0909	0929	0938	0946	0949	0941	...	1112	1109	1129	1146	1149	...	1346	1349	...	1409	1412	...	...	...
Köln Hbf d.	...	...	...	...	0844	▬	▬	...	...	...	...	1014	...	...	...	...	...	1214	▬	...	...	...	...	1444	...	...
Aachen 🏛 d.	...	...	...	...	0921	⇌	☆	...	...	...	...	1102t	...	...	...	...	...	1302t	☆	...	...	...	...	1521	...	...
Liège Guillemins a.	...	...	...	...	1008	**9322**	**9127**	...	...	...	...	1147	...	...	...	...	...	1347	**9141**	...	...	...	...	1608	...	...
Liège Guillemins d.	...	...	...	...	1010	®	®	...	...	...	...	1149	...	...	...	...	...	1349	®	...	...	...	...	1610	...	...
Brussels Midi/Zuid a.	...	...	...	...	1101	🍷	✕	...	...	...	...	1235	...	...	...	...	...	1435	✕	...	...	...	...	1701	...	...
Brussels Midi/Zuid d.	...	...	...	...	...	1113	1159	...	...	...	...	1243	...	...	...	...	...	1443	1459	...	...	...	...	...	1713	1759
Paris Nord a.	...	...	...	...	...	1235	|	...	...	...	...	1405	...	...	...	...	...	1605	|	...	...	...	...	...	1835	|
Lille Europe a.	...	...	...	...	...	...	1232	...	...	...	...	...	...	...	...	...	...	...	1532	...	...	...	...	...	...	1832
Ashford International a.	...	...	...	...	...	...	|	...	...	...	...	...	...	...	...	...	...	...	|	...	...	...	...	...	...	|
Ebbsfleet International a.	...	...	...	...	...	...	1245	...	...	...	...	...	...	...	...	...	...	...	|	...	...	...	...	...	...	1845
London St Pancras a.	...	...	...	...	...	...	1303	...	...	...	...	...	...	...	...	...	...	...	1556	...	...	...	...	...	...	1903

train type	RE	IC	IC	EC	ICE	IC	ICE	ICE	IC	IC	⇌	ICE	IC	ICE	ICE	ICE	⇌	EC	ICE	IC	IC	RE	ICE	IC	ICE	ICE
train number	11019	2046	2115	178	1640	2048	950	38	2311	2048	9456	1650	2038	558	927 / 1027	613	9460	176	1548	2140	2213	10130	1558	2036	556	10
notes		🍷 Q	🍷	✕✓	🍷	🍷	✕ z	® 🍷	🍷	🍷	® 🍷	🍷	🍷	✕ z	✕	🍷	® 🍷	✕	✕	🍷	🍷		🍷	🍷	✕	★
Praha Hlavní d.	...	...	...	0625	...	...	...	...	...	...	...	...	...	...	...	...	...	0825	...	...	...	...	...	...	...	...
Praha Holešovice d.	...	...	...	0636	...	...	...	...	...	...	...	...	...	...	...	...	...	0836	...	...	...	...	...	...	...	...
Děčín d.	...	...	...	0758	...	...	...	...	...	...	...	...	...	...	...	...	...	0958	...	...	...	...	...	...	...	...
Bad Schandau 🏛 d.	...	...	...	0818	...	...	...	...	...	...	...	...	...	...	...	...	...	1018	...	...	...	...	...	...	...	...
Dresden Hbf d.	...	...	...	0846	0855	...	...	...	...	...	...	0955	...	...	...	...	...	1046	1055	...	...	...	1155	...	...	...
Berlin Ostbahnhof d.	...	...	...	▬	|	...	1138	...	...	...	...	|	...	1240	...	...	...	▬	|	...	...	...	|	...	1440	...
Berlin Hauptbahnhof d.	...	...	...	...	|	...	1148	...	...	...	...	|	...	1251	...	...	...	...	|	...	...	...	|	...	1451	...
Leipzig Hbf d.	...	0840	...	...	1007	1040	|	...	...	...	...	1107	1142	|	...	...	...	...	1207	1240	...	...	1307	1342	|	...
Halle Hbf d.	...	0906	...	...	▬	1106	|	...	...	...	...	...	1208	|	...	...	...	...	▬	1306	...	...	...	1408	|	...
Magdeburg Hbf d.	...	1000r	...	...	...	1200r	|	...	...	...	...	...	1300r	|	...	...	...	...	...	1400r	...	...	...	1500r	|	...
Braunschweig Hbf d.	...	1050	...	...	...	1250	|	...	...	...	...	...	1351	|	...	...	...	...	...	1450	...	...	...	1551	|	...
Wolfsburg d.	...	|	...	...	...	|	1255	...	...	←	...	...	|	|	...	...	...	...	...	|	...	...	...	|	|	...
Hannover Hbf d.	...	1140	...	...	...	1323	1331	...	...	1340	...	...	1423	1431	...	...	...	...	...	1540	...	...	...	1623	1631	...
Bielefeld Hbf d.	...	1242	...	...	...	→	1422	...	...	1442	...	...	▬	1522	...	...	...	...	...	1642	...	...	...	▬	1722	...
København H ⊙ d.	...	|	...	...	...	▬	|	0745	...	|	...	...	...	|	...	...	...	...	...	|	...	...	...	...	|	...
Hamburg Hbf d.	...	|	1046	...	...	...	|	1216	1246	|	...	...	...	|	1346	...	...	...	...	|	1446	...	...	...	|	...
Bremen Hbf d.	...	|	1144	...	...	...	|	▬	1344	|	...	...	...	|	1444	...	...	...	...	|	1544	...	...	...	|	...
Osnabrück Hbf d.	...	|	1237	...	...	...	|	...	1437	|	...	...	...	|	1537	...	...	...	...	|	1637	...	...	...	|	...
Münster d.	...	|	1304	...	...	...	|	...	1504	|	...	...	...	|	1603	...	...	...	...	|	1704	...	...	...	|	...
Hamm d.	...	1314	|	...	...	...	1454	...	|	1514	...	...	...	1554	|	...	...	...	...	1714	|	1720	...	...	1754	...
Dortmund Hbf d.	...	1337	1338	...	...	...	|	...	1538	1537	...	...	...	|	1636	1638	...	...	...	1737	1738	1745	...	...	|	...
Bochum Hbf d.	...	|	1349	...	...	...	|	RE	1549	|	...	...	RE	|	|	1649	...	...	...	|	1749	1756	...	RE	|	...
Essen Hbf d.	...	|	1400	...	...	...	|	**11023**	1600	|	...	...	**11025**	|	|	1700	...	...	...	|	1800	1809	...	**11029**	|	...
Oberhausen d.	1334	|	|	...	...	...	|	1534	|	|	...	...	1634	|	|	|	...	...	...	|	|	|	...	1834	|	...
Duisburg Hbf d.	1342	|	1413	...	...	...	|	1542	1613	|	...	...	1642	|	|	1713	...	...	...	|	1813	1824	...	1842	|	...
Düsseldorf Hbf d.	1358	|	1427	⇌	...	...	|	1558	1627	|	...	...	1658	|	|	1727	...	...	...	|	1827	1840	...	1858	|	...
Hagen Hbf d.	|	1357	|	**9448**	...	...	1524	|	|	1557	...	...	|	1624	1657	|	...	...	...	1757	|	|	...	|	1824	...
Wuppertal Hbf d.	|	1414	|	®	...	...	1541	|	|	1614	...	...	|	1641	1714	|	...	...	...	1814	|	|	...	|	1841	...
Köln Hbf a.	1429	1445	1450	🍷	...	...	1609	1629	1649	1645	...	...	1729	1709	1746	1749	...	...	...	1845	1849	1911	...	1929	1909	...
Köln Hbf d.	...	...	...	1514	☆	...	...	...	...	...	1714	...	...	...	...	...	1814	...	...	...	...	...	...	...	...	1944
Aachen 🏛 d.	...	...	...	1602t	**9153**	☆	...	...	...	...	1802t	...	...	...	...	...	1902t	☆	☆	...	...	...	...	...	...	2021
Liège Guillemins a.	...	...	...	1647	®	**9157**	...	...	...	...	1847	...	...	...	...	...	1947	**9165**	**9165**	...	...	...	...	...	...	2108
Liège Guillemins d.	...	...	...	1649	✕	®	...	...	...	...	1849	...	...	...	...	...	1949	® ✕	® ✕	...	...	...	...	...	...	2110
Brussels Midi/Zuid a.	...	...	...	1735	⑥	✕	...	...	...	...	1935	...	...	...	...	...	2035	⑦	①-⑥	...	...	...	...	...	...	2201
Brussels Midi/Zuid d.	...	...	...	1743	1759	1859	...	...	...	...	1943	...	...	...	...	...	2043	2059	2102	...	...	...	...	...	...	...
Paris Nord a.	...	...	...	1905	|	|	...	...	...	...	2105	...	...	...	...	...	2205	|	|	...	...	...	...	...	...	...
Lille Europe a.	...	...	...	...	1832	1932	...	...	...	...	...	...	...	...	...	...	...	2132	2136	...	...	...	...	...	...	...
Ashford International a.	...	...	...	...	|	|	...	...	...	...	...	...	...	...	...	...	...	|	|	...	...	...	...	...	...	...
Ebbsfleet International a.	...	...	...	...	1845	|	...	...	...	...	...	...	...	...	...	...	...	2145	2148	...	...	...	...	...	...	...
London St Pancras a.	...	...	...	...	1903	1956	...	...	...	...	...	...	...	...	...	...	...	2203	2204	...	...	...	...	...	...	...

← NOTES CONTINUED FROM PREVIOUS PAGE

d – ⑦ only.
k – Via Odense (2023u), Padborg (2218u) and Flensburg (2232u).
m – Depart 8 minutes later.
o – Not Dec. 25, Jan. 1, Mar. 24, May 1, 12.
q – Also Dec. 25, 26, Jan. 1, Mar. 24, May 1, 12.
r – Magdeburg **Buckau** from May 25.
s – Stops to set down only.
t – Arrive 10 minutes earlier.

u – Stops to pick up only.
v – ⑦ (also Dec. 26, Jan. 1, Mar. 24, May 12).
w – Not Dec. 24, Jan. 2.
x – 2001 on Dec. 9, Apr. 12, 26, 27, May 3, 8.
y – ①-⑥ (not Dec. 25, 26, Jan. 1, Mar. 22, 24, May 12).
z – Not Dec. 24, 31.
* – *ICE* from Jan. 6.
◐ – 🏛 is Quévy.

★ – *ICE 3* train 🍷 special fares payable.
⇌ – *Thalys* high-speed train. Special fares payable.
☆ – Eurostar train. Special fares payable. Minimum check-in time: 30 minutes. See Table **12**. Valid Dec. 9, 2007 - July 5, 2008.
⊙ – 🏛 between Hamburg and København is Rødby (Table **720**).

For København/Esbjerg - London by rail and sea via Harwich, see DFDS Seaways Table 2220

21 LONDON and BRUSSELS - FRANKFURT, WIEN and MÜNCHEN

train type	ICE	ICE	RE	ICE	RE	IC	ICE	⇌	ICE	ICE	D	IC	EC	ICE	D	EC	IC	☆	⇌	ICE	ICE	IC	ICE	ICE	ALX
train number	11	621	453	515	30021	83	27	9409	105	595	1281	2299	189	27	347	101	2013	9110	9417	507	597	2113	123	629	457
notes	⊖	✕		⊖	30051	✕ ♣	✕ R	[R] 🍸	⊖	✕	G	🍸	✕ ♣	✕ R	✕ M	🍸	🍸	[R] ✕ ①–⑥	[R] 🍸	⊖	🍸	🍸	⊖	✕	🍸
London St Pancras .. d.	...	...	...	...	...	...	...	...	...	...	...	...	...	...	...	...	...	0700	...	...	...	...	...	...	...
Ebbsfleet International d.	...	...	...	...	...	...	...	...	...	...	...	...	...	...	...	...	...	0714	...	...	...	...	...	...	...
Ashford International .. d.	...	...	...	...	...	...	...	...	...	...	...	...	...	...	...	...	...	|	...	...	...	...	...	...	...
Lille Europe .... d.	...	...	...	...	...	...	...	...	...	...	...	...	...	...	...	...	...	0928	...	...	...	...	...	...	...
Paris Nord .... d.	...	...	...	...	...	...	...	0655	...	...	...	...	...	...	...	...	...	|	0855	...	...	...	...	...	...
Brussels Midi / Zuid .. a.	...	...	...	...	...	...	...	0817	...	...	...	...	...	...	...	...	...	1003	1017	...	...	...	...	...	...
Brussels Midi / Zuid .. d.	0659	...	...	...	...	...	...	0825	...	...	...	...	...	...	...	...	...	...	1025	...	...	...	...	...	...
Liège Guillemins .... a.	0750	...	...	...	...	...	...	0911	...	...	...	...	...	...	...	...	...	...	1111	...	...	...	...	...	...
Liège Guillemins .... d.	0752	...	...	...	...	...	...	0913	...	...	...	...	...	...	...	...	...	...	1113	...	...	...	...	...	...
Aachen Hbf 🏛 .... a.	0836	...	...	...	...	...	...	0958n	...	...	...	...	...	...	...	...	...	...	1158n	...	...	...	...	...	...
Köln Hbf .... a.	0915	...	...	...	...	...	...	1045	...	...	...	...	...	...	...	...	...	...	1245	...	...	...	...	...	...
Köln Hbf .... d.	0920	...	...	0954	...	...	0953	...	1054	...	...	...	...	...	...	1053	1118	...	...	1254	...	1253	1320	...	...
Bonn Hbf .... a.	|	...	...	|	...	...	1012	...	|	...	...	...	...	...	...	1112	1135	...	...	|	...	1312	|	...	...
Koblenz Hbf .... a.	|	...	...	|	...	...	1046	...	|	...	...	...	...	←	...	1146	1215	...	...	|	...	1346	|	...	...
Mainz Hbf .... a.	|	...	...	|	...	...	1138	...	|	...	...	...	...	1140	...	1237	1311	...	...	|	...	1437	|	...	...
Frankfurt Flughafen ✈ a.	1014	...	...	1051	...	...	→	...	1151	...	...	...	...	1159	...	|	|	...	...	1351	...	|	1414	...	...
Frankfurt (Main) Hbf. a.	1030	1054	...	|	...	...	...	...	|	...	...	...	...	1213	...	|	|	...	...	|	...	|	1430	1454	...
Würzburg Hbf .... a.	...	1203	...	|	...	...	...	...	|	...	...	...	...	1331	...	|	|	...	...	|	...	|	...	1603	...
Nürnberg Hbf .... a.	...	1259	1340	|	...	...	...	...	|	...	...	...	...	1428	...	|	|	...	...	|	...	|	...	1659	*1736*f
Regensburg Hbf ...... a.	...	|	|	|	...	...	...	...	|	...	...	...	...	1522	...	|	|	...	...	|	...	|	...	...	|
Praha Hlavní **57** .. a.	...	|	1845	|	...	...	...	...	|	...	...	...	...	|	...	|	|	...	...	|	...	|	...	...	2245
Mannheim Hbf .... a.	...	|	...	1124	...	...	...	...	1224	1231	...	...	...	|	...	1321	1352	...	...	1424	1431	1521	...	...	...
Stuttgart Hbf .... a.	...	|	...	1208	...	...	...	...	...	1308	...	1358	...	|	...	...	1446	...	...	...	1508	1622	...	...	...
Ulm Hbf .... a.	...	|	...	1306	...	...	...	...	...	1406	...	1453	...	|	...	...	1558	...	...	...	1606	...	...	...	...
Augsburg Hbf .... a.	...	|	...	1350	...	...	...	...	...	1450	...	1539	...	|	...	...	...	...	...	...	1650	...	...	...	...
München Hbf .... a.	...	1404	...	1431	1446	1530	...	...	...	1531	1600	1617	1731	|	...	...	...	...	...	...	1731	...	...	...	...
Salzburg .... a.	...	...	...	...	1647	|	...	...	...	...	|	1803	|	|	...	...	...	...	...	...	...	...	...	...	...
Kufstein 🏛 .... a.	...	...	...	...	...	1632	...	...	...	...	1711	...	1832	|	...	...	...	...	...	...	...	...	...	...	...
Wörgl .... a.	...	...	...	...	...	1643	...	...	...	...	1723	...	1843	|	...	...	...	...	...	...	...	...	...	...	...
Kitzbühel .... a.	...	...	...	...	...	|	...	...	...	...	1814	...	|	|	...	...	...	...	...	...	...	...	...	...	...
Zell am See .... a.	...	...	...	...	...	|	...	...	...	...	1906	...	|	|	...	...	...	...	...	...	...	...	...	...	...
Innsbruck .... a.	...	...	...	...	...	1720	...	...	...	...	...	...	1920	|	...	...	...	...	...	...	...	...	...	...	...
Bad Gastein .... a.	...	...	...	...	...	...	...	...	...	...	...	...	...	|	...	...	...	...	...	...	...	...	...	...	...
Villach .... a.	...	...	...	...	...	...	...	...	...	...	...	...	...	|	...	...	...	...	...	...	...	...	...	...	...
Klagenfurt .... a.	...	...	...	...	...	...	...	...	...	...	...	...	...	|	...	...	...	...	...	...	...	...	...	...	...
Passau 🏛 .... a.	...	...	...	...	...	...	...	...	...	...	...	...	...	1626	...	...	...	...	...	...	...	...	...	...	...
Linz .... a.	...	...	...	...	...	...	...	...	...	...	...	...	...	1745	...	...	...	...	...	...	...	...	...	...	...
Wien Westbahnhof. a.	...	...	...	...	...	...	...	...	...	...	...	...	...	1926	1948	...	...	...	...	...	...	...	...	...	...
Budapest Keleti ▲.. a.	...	...	...	...	...	...	...	...	...	...	...	...	...	...	2253	...	...	...	...	...	...	...	...	...	...

train type / number	☆	☆	⇌	ICE	ICE	ICE	ICE	ICE	IC	IC	☆	☆	⇌	ICE	CNL	ICE	IC	⇌	ICE	ICE	IC	IC	ICE	EN
train number	9114	9114	9323	15	721	509	109	229	391	2115	9074	9120	9429	611	389	725	2029	9433	601	691	2029	2311	727	269
notes	[R] ✕ ⑦	[R] ✕ ①–⑥	[R] 🍸	★	⊖	⊖	✕	🍸	🍸	🍸 w	[R] ✕	[R] ✕	[R] 🍸	⊖	D	⊖	🍸	[R] 🍸	⊖	⊖	🍸	🍸 w	⊖ ⑧y	✕ B
London St Pancras .. d.	0800	0805	...	...	...	...	...	...	...	...	0853	1000	...	...	...	...	...	...	...	...	...	...	...	...
Ebbsfleet International d.	0815	|	...	...	...	...	...	...	...	...	|	1015	...	...	...	...	...	...	...	...	...	...	...	...
Ashford International .. d.	|	|	...	...	...	...	...	...	...	...	0926	|	...	...	...	...	...	...	...	...	...	...	...	...
Lille Europe .... d.	|	|	...	...	...	...	...	...	...	...	1124	1228	...	...	...	...	...	...	...	...	...	...	...	...
Paris Nord .... d.	|	|	1025	...	...	...	...	...	...	...	...	|	1155	...	...	...	...	1255	...	...	...	...	...	...
Brussels Midi / Zuid .. a.	1056	1056	1147	...	...	...	...	...	...	...	...	1303	1317	...	...	...	...	1417	...	...	...	...	...	...
Brussels Midi / Zuid .. d.	...	...	...	1159	...	...	...	...	...	...	...	...	1325	...	...	...	...	1425	...	...	...	...	...	...
Liège Guillemins .... a.	...	...	...	1250	...	...	...	...	...	...	...	...	1411	...	...	...	...	1511	...	...	...	...	...	...
Liège Guillemins .... d.	...	...	...	1252	...	...	...	...	...	...	...	...	1413	...	...	...	...	1513	...	...	...	...	...	...
Aachen Hbf 🏛 .... a.	...	...	...	1335	...	...	...	...	...	...	...	...	1458n	...	...	...	...	1558n	...	...	...	...	...	...
Köln Hbf .... a.	...	...	...	1415	...	...	...	...	...	...	...	...	1545	...	...	...	...	1645	...	...	...	...	...	...
Köln Hbf .... d.	...	...	...	1420	1428	1454	...	...	...	1453	...	...	...	1554	...	...	1553	...	1654	...	...	1653	...	...
Bonn Hbf .... a.	...	...	...	|	|	|	...	...	...	1512	...	...	...	|	...	...	1612	...	|	...	...	1712	...	...
Koblenz Hbf .... a.	...	...	...	|	|	|	...	...	...	1546	...	...	...	|	...	...	1646	...	|	...	←	1746	...	...
Mainz Hbf .... a.	...	...	...	|	|	|	...	...	...	1637	...	...	...	|	...	...	1738	...	|	...	1740	1837	...	...
Frankfurt Flughafen ✈ a.	...	...	...	1522	1534	1551	...	...	...	|	...	...	...	1651	...	1737	→	...	1751	...	1759	...	1837	...
Frankfurt (Main) Hbf. a.	...	...	...	1540	1548	|	...	1621	1620	|	...	...	...	|	...	1748	...	...	|	...	1813	|	1848	...
Würzburg Hbf .... a.	...	...	...	...	1703	|	...	1731	|	|	...	...	...	|	...	1903	...	...	|	...	1931	|	2003	...
Nürnberg Hbf .... a.	...	...	...	...	1759	|	...	1828	|	|	...	...	...	|	...	1959	...	...	|	...	2028	|	2059	...
Regensburg Hbf ...... a.	...	...	...	...	|	|	...	1922	|	|	...	...	...	|	...	...	...	...	|	...	2131	|	...	...
Praha Hlavní **57** .. a.	...	...	...	...	|	|	...	|	|	|	...	...	...	|	...	...	...	...	|	...	|	|	...	...
Mannheim Hbf .... a.	...	...	...	...	|	1624	1631	|	|	1721	...	...	...	1724	...	...	...	...	1824	1831	|	1921	...	...
Stuttgart Hbf .... a.	...	...	...	...	|	...	1708	|	1753	1822	...	...	...	1808	...	...	...	...	...	1908	|	...	...	...
Ulm Hbf .... a.	...	...	...	...	|	...	1806	|	1852	...	...	...	...	1906	...	...	...	...	...	2006	|	...	...	...
Augsburg Hbf .... a.	...	...	...	...	|	...	1850	|	1939	...	...	...	...	1950	...	...	...	...	...	2050	|	...	...	...
München Hbf .... a.	...	...	...	...	1904	...	1931	|	2017	...	...	...	...	2031	2103	...	...	...	...	2134	|	...	...	2345
Salzburg .... a.	...	...	...	...	...	...	|	|	2209	...	...	...	...	...	|	...	...	...	...	...	|	...	...	0121
Kufstein 🏛 .... a.	...	...	...	...	...	...	2033	|	...	...	...	...	...	...	2207	...	...	...	...	...	|	...	...	|
Wörgl .... a.	...	...	...	...	...	...	2043	|	...	...	...	...	...	...	2218	...	...	...	...	...	|	...	...	|
Kitzbühel .... a.	...	...	...	...	...	...	|	|	...	...	...	...	...	...	|	...	...	...	...	...	|	...	...	|
Zell am See .... a.	...	...	...	...	...	...	|	|	...	...	...	...	...	...	|	...	...	...	...	...	|	...	...	|
Innsbruck .... a.	...	...	...	...	...	...	2120	|	...	...	...	...	...	...	2255	...	...	...	...	...	|	...	...	|
Bad Gastein .... a.	...	...	...	...	...	...	...	|	...	...	...	...	...	...	...	...	...	...	...	...	|	...	...	|
Villach .... a.	...	...	...	...	...	...	...	|	...	...	...	...	...	...	...	...	...	...	...	...	|	...	...	|
Klagenfurt .... a.	...	...	...	...	...	...	...	|	...	...	...	...	...	...	...	...	...	...	...	...	|	...	...	|
Passau 🏛 .... a.	...	...	...	...	...	...	...	2026	...	...	...	...	...	...	...	...	...	...	...	...	2242	...	...	|
Linz .... a.	...	...	...	...	...	...	...	2145	2342y	...	...	...	...	...	...	...	...	...	...	...	...	...	...	0340
Wien Westbahnhof. a.	...	...	...	...	...	...	...	2326	...	...	...	...	...	...	...	...	...	...	...	...	...	...	...	0555
Budapest Keleti ▲.. a.	...	...	...	...	...	...	...	...	...	...	...	...	...	...	...	...	...	...	...	...	...	...	...	0923

B – KÁLMÁN IMRE – 🛏 1,2 cl., 🛌 2 cl. and (2) München - Wien - Budapest. Conveys 🛏 1,2 cl. München - Wien - Budapest - Bucureşti.
D – *City Night Line* 🛏 1,2 cl., 🛌 2 cl., (2) and ✕ München - Innsbruck - Roma. [R] Special fares apply.
G – ⑥ Dec. 22 - Mar. 22 (also Jan. 2): GROSSGLOCKNER – (12) München - Kufstein 🏛 - Wörgl - Zell am See.
M – DACIA EXPRESS – (12) and ✕ Wien - Budapest. (See Table **65** for additional cars).
R – (12) and ✕ Dortmund - Köln - Nürnberg - Wien.
f – *1736* dep. Nürnberg, change at Schwandorf (arr. 1843, dep. 1856 *ALX* **457**) Table **57**.

n – Depart 8 minutes later.
y – ⑧ (not Dec. 24, 25, 31, Mar. 21, 23, May 11).
w – Not Dec. 24, 31.
⇌ – *Thalys* high-speed train. Special fares payable.
♣ – Special 'global' fares payable.
◐ – 🏛 is at Lindau and Bregenz.
▲ – 🏛 is at Hegyeshalom.

⊖ – *ICE 3* train 🍸, via high speed line, premium fares payable.
☆ – Eurostar train. Special fares payable. Minimum check-in time: 30 minutes. Valid Dec. 9, 2007 - July 5, 2008. See Table **12**.

OTHER TRAIN NAMES:
IC **83** PAGANINI
EC **189** VAL GARDENA / GRÖDNERTA

LONDON and BRUSSELS - FRANKFURT, WIEN and MÜNCHEN 21

train type	☆	☆	⇌	*ICE*	*ICE*	*CNL*	☆	*ICE*	*ICE*	*CNL*	*ICE*	*CNL*	*IC*	☆	⇌	*ICE*	*IC*	*ICE*	*CNL*	*IC*	*EC*	☆	☆	⇌	
train number	**9132**	**9132**	**9445**	**615**	**929**	**313**	**9138**	**17**	**929**	**353**	**675**	**313**	**2215** **2315**	**9144**	**9453**	**619**	**2321** **2121**	**1591**	**319**	**111**	**81**	**9146**	**9148**	**9457**	**13221**
notes	R ✗ ⑤⑦	R ✗ **J**	R 🍷	⊖ **k**	🍷	R **C**	R ✗	⊖	🍷	R **A**	⊖	R **C**		R ✗ ⑦	R 🍷	⊖	🍷	🍷 **g**	R **H**		✗ ♣ **G**	R ①–⑤	R ⑥⑦	R 🍷 ⑧**h**	R **P**
London St Pancras ....d.	1257	1300	...	...	...	...	1434	...	...	...	...	...	...	1604	...	...	...	...	...	...	...	1635	1655	...	...
Ebbsfleet International ..d.	1315	1315	...	...	...	...	|	...	...	...	...	...	...	|	...	...	...	...	...	...	...	|	1712	...	...
Ashford International....d.	|	|	...	...	...	...	|	...	...	...	...	...	...	|	...	...	...	...	...	...	...	|	|	...	...
Lille Europe ....d.	1528	1528	...	...	...	...	1658	...	...	...	...	...	...	|	...	...	...	...	...	...	...	|	1925	...	...
Paris Nord..............d.	|	|	1555	...	...	...	|	...	...	...	...	...	...	|	1755	...	...	...	...	...	...	|	|	1855	...
Brussels Midi / Zuid....a.	1603	1603	1717	...	...	...	1733	...	...	...	...	...	...	1903	1917	...	...	...	...	...	...	1926	1959	2017	...
Brussels Midi / Zuid....d.	...	...	1725	...	...	...	...	1759	...	...	...	...	...	...	1925	...	...	...	...	...	...	...	...	2025	2215
Liège Guillemins ....a.	...	...	1811	...	...	...	...	1850	...	...	...	...	...	...	2011	...	...	...	...	...	...	...	...	2111	|
Liège Guillemins ....d.	...	...	1813	...	...	...	...	1852	...	...	...	...	...	...	2013	...	...	...	...	...	...	...	...	...	2346
Aachen Hbf 🏛 ....a.	...	...	1858**n**	...	...	...	...	1935	...	...	...	...	...	...	2058**n**	...	...	...	...	...	...	...	...	...	|
Köln Hbf ....a.	...	...	1945	...	...	...	...	2015	...	...	...	...	...	...	2145	...	...	...	...	...	...	...	...	...	|
Köln Hbf ....d.	...	...	...	1954	1953	2006	...	2020	...	...	...	...	2053	...	...	2154	2153	...	2346	...	...	...	...	...	|
Bonn Hbf ....a.	...	...	...	|	2012	2035	...	|	...	...	...	...	2112	...	...	|	2212	...	0007**u**	...	...	...	...	...	|
Koblenz Hbf.................a.	...	...	...	|	2046	2115	...	|	...	...	...	←	2146	...	...	|	2246	...	0102**u**	...	...	...	...	...	|
Mainz Hbf.....................a.	...	...	...	|	2140	2209	...	|	...	...	...	2212	2238	...	...	|	2338	...	|	...	...	...	...	...	|
Frankfurt Flughafen ✈ .a.	...	...	...	2051	2159	→	...	2114	...	...	2120	|	2259	...	...	2256	2359	0028	|	...	...	...	...	...	|
Frankfurt (Main) Hbf...a.	...	...	...	*2114*	2213	...	...	2130	2218	2219**c**	|	2247	|	...	...	2310	0013	|	|	...	...	...	...	...	|
Würzburg Hbf...........a.	...	...	...	|	2341	...	...	...	2341	|	|	|	|	...	...	...	...	|	|	...	...	...	...	...	|
Nürnberg Hbf..........a.	...	...	...	|	0037	...	...	...	0037	|	|	|	|	...	...	...	...	|	|	...	...	...	...	...	|
Regensburg Hbf ....a.	...	...	...	|	...	...	...	...	...	|	|	|	|	...	...	...	...	|	|	...	...	...	...	...	|
Praha Hlavní **57**....a.	...	...	...	|	...	...	...	...	...	0818**y**	|	|	|	...	...	...	...	|	|	...	...	...	...	...	|
Mannheim Hbf ....a.	...	...	...	2124	...	...	...	...	...	...	2153	2332**d**	2336	...	...	...	...	0104	|	...	...	...	...	...	|
Stuttgart Hbf ....a.	...	...	...	2208	...	...	...	...	...	...	2248	|	0051	...	...	...	...	0236	0419**z**	...	...	...	...	...	|
Ulm Hbf ....a.	...	...	...	2306	...	...	...	...	...	...	...	|	▬	...	...	...	...	0335**f**	0542	...	...	...	...	...	|
Augsburg Hbf..............a.	...	...	...	2353	...	...	...	...	...	...	...	|	...	...	...	...	...	0424**f**	0634	...	...	...	...	...	|
München Hbf.............a.	...	...	...	0035	...	...	...	...	...	...	...	|	...	...	...	...	...	0505**f**	0716	0726	0730	...	...	...	0904**o**
Salzburg....................a.	...	...	...	...	...	...	...	...	...	...	...	0509	...	...	...	...	...	...	...	0858	|	...	...	...	|
Kufstein 🏛..................a.	...	...	...	...	...	...	...	...	...	...	...	|	...	...	...	...	...	...	...	|	0832	...	...	...	1013
Wörgl...........................a.	...	...	...	...	...	...	...	...	...	...	...	|	...	...	...	...	...	...	...	|	0843	...	...	...	1025
Kitzbühel......................a.	...	...	...	...	...	...	...	...	...	...	...	|	...	...	...	...	...	...	...	|	|	...	...	...	1113
Zell am See..................a.	...	...	...	...	...	...	...	...	...	...	...	|	...	...	...	...	...	...	...	|	|	...	...	...	1211
Innsbruck.................a.	...	...	...	...	...	...	...	...	...	...	...	|	...	...	...	...	...	...	...	|	0920	...	...	...	...
Bad Gastein..................a.	...	...	...	...	...	...	...	...	...	...	...	|	...	...	...	...	...	...	...	1040	...	...	...	...	...
Villach..........................a.	...	...	...	...	...	...	...	...	...	...	...	|	*IC*	...	...	...	...	...	...	1147	...	...	...	...	...
Klagenfurt ....a.	...	...	...	...	...	...	...	...	...	...	...	|	**345**	...	...	...	...	...	...	1220	...	...	...	...	...
Passau 🏛 ....a.	...	...	...	...	...	...	...	...	...	...	...	|	✗	...	...	...	...	...	...	...	...	...	...	...	...
Linz.............................a.	...	...	...	...	...	...	...	...	...	...	...	0644	**S**	...	...	...	...	...	...	...	...	...	...	...	...
Wien Westbahnhof...a.	...	...	...	...	...	...	...	...	...	...	...	0835	0952	...	...	...	...	...	...	...	...	...	...	...	...
Budapest Keleti ▲....a.	...	...	...	...	...	...	...	...	...	...	...	...	1253	...	...	...	...	...	...	...	...	...	...	...	...

train type	⇌	*EC*	*IC*	*CNL*	*ICE*	*IC*	⇌	☆	*ICE*	⇌	☆	*IC*	*IC*	*ICE*	*CNL*	*ICE*	⇌	*EC*	*CNL*	*ICE*	*ICE*	*ICE*	*ICE*	⇌	☆
train number	**9412**	**80**	**110**	**318**	**828**	**2212**	**9416**	**9121**	**826**	**9418**	**9127**	**1590**	**2120**	**616**	**352**	**16**	**9322**	**44**	**312**	**928**	**822**	**812**	**614**	**9428**	**9141**
notes	R 🍷	✗ ♣	✗	R	⊖		R 🍷	R ✗	⊖	R 🍷	R ✗	✗	**2320**	⊖	R	⊖	R	✗	R	🍷	⊖	⊖	⊖	R 🍷	R ✗
notes	**K**	**G**		**H**	**D**	**g**	①–⑥	⑥⑦		⑦**q**		**g**	🍷		**B**		🍷		**C**			⑧**b**			
Budapest Keleti ▲....d.	...	...	...	...	...	...	**p**	...	...	...	...	...	...	...	...	...	...	1710	...	...	...	...	...	...	...
Wien Westbahnhof ..d.	...	...	...	...	...	...	...	...	...	...	...	...	...	...	...	...	...	2008	2035	...	...	...	...	...	...
Linz...........................d.	...	...	...	...	...	...	...	...	...	...	...	...	...	...	...	...	...	▬	2220	...	...	...	...	...	...
Passau 🏛 ....d.	...	...	...	...	...	...	...	...	...	...	...	...	...	...	...	...	...	...	|	...	...	...	...	...	...
Klagenfurt ....d.	...	...	1726	...	...	...	...	...	...	...	...	...	...	...	...	...	...	...	|	...	...	...	...	...	...
Villach........................d.	...	...	1811	...	...	...	...	...	...	...	...	...	...	...	...	...	...	...	|	...	...	...	...	...	...
Bad Gastein.................d.	...	...	1918	...	...	...	...	...	...	...	...	...	...	...	...	...	...	...	|	...	...	...	...	...	...
Innsbruck.................d.	...	2037	|	...	...	...	...	...	...	...	...	...	...	...	...	...	...	...	|	...	...	...	...	...	...
Zell am See.................d.	...	|	|	...	...	...	...	...	...	...	...	...	...	...	...	...	...	...	|	...	...	...	...	...	...
Kitzbühel.....................d.	...	|	|	...	...	...	...	...	...	...	...	...	...	...	...	...	...	...	|	...	...	...	...	...	...
Wörgl..........................d.	...	2114	|	...	...	...	...	...	...	...	...	...	...	...	...	...	...	...	|	...	...	...	...	...	...
Kufstein 🏛.................d.	...	2125	|	...	...	...	...	...	...	...	...	...	...	...	...	...	...	...	|	...	...	...	...	...	...
Salzburg......................d.	...	|	2104	...	...	...	...	...	...	...	...	...	...	...	...	...	...	...	2342	...	...	...	...	...	...
München Hbf.............d.	...	2226	2232	2242	...	...	...	...	...	...	...	0033**f**	...	0317	...	...	...	...	|	...	...	...	0523	...	...
Augsburg Hbf..............d.	...	▬	▬	2318	...	...	...	...	...	...	...	0114**f**	...	0357	...	...	...	...	|	...	...	...	0604	...	...
Ulm Hbf.......................d.	...	...	...	0010	...	...	...	...	...	...	...	0202**f**	...	0440	...	...	...	...	|	...	...	...	0651	...	...
Stuttgart Hbf ....d.	...	...	...	0126**z**	...	...	...	...	...	...	...	0305	...	0551	...	...	...	...	|	...	...	...	0751	...	...
Mannheim Hbf ....d.	...	...	...	|	...	...	...	...	...	...	...	0440	...	0635	...	...	...	...	0515**a**	...	...	...	0835	...	...
Praha Hlavní **57**....d.	...	...	...	|	...	...	...	...	...	...	...	|	...	|	2025	...	...	...	|	...	...	...	|	...	...
Regensburg Hbf ....d.	...	...	...	|	...	...	...	...	...	...	...	|	...	|	|	...	...	...	|	...	...	...	|	...	...
Nürnberg Hbf..........d.	...	...	...	|	...	...	...	...	...	...	...	|	...	|	|	...	...	...	|	0530	0600	...	|	...	...
Würzburg Hbf............d.	...	...	...	|	...	...	...	...	...	...	...	|	...	|	|	...	...	...	|	0627	0656	...	|	...	...
Frankfurt (Main) Hbf..d.	...	...	...	|	0449	...	...	...	0548	...	...	|	0542	|	0654**j**	0728	...	...	0600	0742	0810	0816	|	...	...
Frankfurt Flughafen ✈..d.	...	...	...	|	0502	...	...	...	0607	...	...	0512	0558	0709	...	0743	...	...	|	0758	0824	0831	0909	...	...
Mainz Hbf.....................d.	...	...	...	|	|	...	...	...	|	...	...	...	0618	|	...	|	...	...	0632**a**	0820	|	|	|	...	...
Koblenz Hbf.................d.	...	...	...	0426**s**	|	0606	...	...	|	...	...	...	0712	|	...	|	...	...	0744**a**	0912	|	|	|	...	...
Bonn Hbf.......................d.	...	...	...	0521**s**	|	0644	...	...	|	...	...	...	0744	|	...	|	...	...	0817**a**	0944	|	|	|	...	...
Köln Hbf.....................a.	...	...	...	0545	0619**x**	0705	...	...	0714**x**	...	...	...	0805	0805	...	0840	...	...	0842	1005	0914**x**	0940	1005	...	...
Köln Hbf.....................d.	...	...	...	...	...	...	0714	...	...	0740	...	...	...	...	...	0844	...	...	...	...	...	...	...	1014	...
Aachen Hbf 🏛 ....d.	...	☆	☆	...	...	...	0802**t**	...	...	0818	...	...	...	...	...	0921	...	...	...	...	...	...	...	1102**t**	...
Liège Guillemins ....a.	...	**9117**	**9121**	...	...	...	0847	...	...	0908	...	...	...	...	...	1008	...	☆	...	...	...	...	...	1147	...
Liège Guillemins ....d.	0749	R ✗	R ✗	...	...	...	0849	...	...	0910	...	...	...	...	...	1010	...	**9127**	...	...	...	...	...	1149	...
Brussels Midi / Zuid....a.	0835	①–⑤	⑥⑦	...	...	...	0935	...	...	1001	...	...	...	...	...	1101	...	R ✗	...	...	...	...	...	1235	...
Brussels Midi / Zuid....d.	0843	0859	0959	...	...	...	0943	0959	...	1013	1159	...	...	...	...	...	1113	1159	...	...	...	...	...	1243	1459
Paris Nord...............d.	1005	|	|	...	...	...	1105	|	...	1135	|	...	...	...	...	...	1235	|	...	...	...	...	...	1405	|
Lille Europe ....a.	...	0932	1032	...	...	...	...	1032	...	...	1232	...	...	...	...	...	...	1232	...	...	...	...	...	...	1532
Ashford International....a.	...	|	|	...	...	...	...	|	...	...	|	...	...	...	...	...	...	|	...	...	...	...	...	...	|
Ebbsfleet International .a.	...	0945	1045	...	...	...	...	1045	...	...	1245	...	...	...	...	...	...	1245	...	...	...	...	...	...	|
London St Pancras....a.	...	1003	1101	...	...	...	...	1101	...	...	1303	...	...	...	...	...	...	1303	...	...	...	...	...	...	1556

– *City Night Line* JOHANNES KEPLER – 🛏 1,2 cl., ▬ 2 cl. and (2) Basel - Frankfurt (Main) **Süd** - Fulda - Děčín 🏛 - Praha Holešovice. ✗ Basel - Fulda. R Special fares apply.
– *City Night Line* JOHANNES KEPLER – 🛏 1,2 cl., ▬ 2 cl. and (2) Praha Hlavní - Praha Holešovice - Děčín 🏛 - Fulda - Frankfurt (Main) **Süd** - Basel. ✗ Fulda - Basel. R Special fares apply.
– *City Night Line* DONAU KURIER – 🛏 1, 2 cl., 🛏 1, 2 cl. (T4), ▬ 2 cl. (4, 6 berth), (2) and ✗ Amsterdam - Köln - Wien and v.v. R Special fares apply. For International journeys only.
– GARDA – (12) and 🍷 München - Innsbruck - Verona and v.v.
– *City Night Line* POLLUX – 🛏 1,2 cl., 🛏 1, 2 cl. (T4), ▬ 2 cl. (4, 6 berth), (2) (reclining) and ✗ Amsterdam - Köln - München and v.v. R Special fares apply.
– ①②③④⑥.
– ①–⑥ (not Dec. 25, 26, Jan. 1, Mar. 24, May 1, 2, 12).
– GO SNOW / TRESKI – Dec. 21, 28, Feb. 1, 8: ▬ 2 cl. and (2) Brussels - Leuven (depart 2250) - Verviers (0009) - Wörgl - Kirchberg in Tirol (arrive 1103) - Kitzbühel - St Johann in Tirol (1123) - Saalfelden (1159) - Zell am See. R special fares apply.
– AVALA – (12) and ✗ Wien - Budapest - Beograd and v.v.

– Arrival time.
– Not Dec. 24, 25, 31, Mar. 21, 23, May 11.
– Frankfurt (Main) **Süd**. Connection from *ICE* **17** departs Frankfurt (Main) **Hbf** 2142, arrives Frankfurt (Main) **Süd** 2146.
– Departure time.
– ① (also Dec. 27, Jan. 2, Mar. 25, May 13).

g – Not Dec. 25, Jan. 1.
h – Not Dec. 24, 25, 31, Mar. 23, Apr. 30, May 1, 11.
j – Frankfurt (Main) **Süd**. Connection to *ICE* **16** departs Frankfurt (Main) **Süd** 0706, arrives Frankfurt (Main) **Hbf** 0711.
k – Not Dec. 24, 31.
o – München **Ost**.
p – Not Dec. 25, Jan. 1, Mar. 24, May 1, 12.
q – Also Dec. 25, 26 Jan. 1, Mar. 24, May 1, 12.
s – Stops to set down only.
t – Arrive 10 minutes earlier.
u – Stops to pick up only.
x – Köln **Messe/Deutz**.
y – Praha **Holešovice**.
z – Not May 15 - Oct. 27.

☆ – Eurostar train. Special fares payable. Minimum check-in time 30 minutes. See Table **12**. Valid Dec. 9, 2007 - July 5, 2008.
⊖ – *ICE 3* train 🍷, via high speed line, premium fares payable.
⇌ – *Thalys* high-speed train. Special fares payable.
▲ – 🏛 is at Hegyeshalom.
♣ – Special 'global' fares payable.

21 MÜNCHEN, WIEN and FRANKFURT - BRUSSELS and LONDON

train type	ICE	EN	CNL	ICE	⇌	☆	ICE	IC	RE	ICE	ICE	IC	ICE	ICE	⇌	☆	IC	ICE	ICE	ICE	EC	D	ICE	ICE	⇌
train number	926	268	388	612	9436	9141	610	2028	450	722	14	2112	108	508	9448	9153	390	228	628	810	100	1280	596	506	9456
notes	1026	✖	♣	🍷	[R] 🍷	[R] ✖	⊖	🍷		⊖	⊖	🍷	✖	⊖	[R] 🍷	[R] ✖	🍷	🍷	⊖	⊖	102		✖	⊖	[R]
notes	⊖	K	C													Ⓑ						G			🍷
Budapest Keleti ▲ d.	...	2020	...	...	...	...	...	...	...	...	...	...	...	...	...	...	...	...	...	...	...	...	...	...	...
Wien Westbahnhof d.	...	2345	...	...	...	...	...	...	...	...	...	...	...	...	...	...	...	0640	...	...	...	...	...	...	...
Linz d.	...	0146	...	...	...	...	...	...	...	...	...	...	...	...	...	...	0626c	0816	...	...	...	...	...	...	...
Passau 🏛 d.	...	|	...	...	...	...	...	0719	...	...	...	...	...	...	...	...	|	0931	...	...	...	...	...	...	...
Klagenfurt d.	...	|	...	...	...	...	...	|	...	...	...	...	...	...	...	...	|	|	...	...	...	...	...	...	...
Villach d.	...	|	...	...	...	...	...	|	...	...	...	...	...	...	...	...	|	|	...	...	...	...	...	...	...
Bad Gastein d.	...	|	...	...	...	...	...	|	...	...	...	...	...	...	...	...	|	|	...	...	...	...	...	...	...
Innsbruck d.	...	|	0434	...	...	...	...	|	...	...	...	...	0824	...	...	...	|	|	...	...	...	...	...	...	...
Zell am See d.	...	|	|	...	...	...	...	|	...	...	...	...	|	...	...	...	|	|	...	...	...	0853	...	...	...
Kitzbühel d.	...	|	|	...	...	...	...	|	...	...	...	...	|	...	...	...	|	|	...	...	...	0944	...	...	...
Wörgl d.	...	|	0514	...	...	...	...	|	...	...	...	...	0858	...	...	...	|	|	...	...	...	1035	...	...	...
Kufstein 🏛 d.	...	|	0530	...	...	...	...	|	...	...	...	...	0909	...	...	...	|	|	...	...	...	1046	...	...	...
Salzburg d.	...	0428	|	...	...	...	...	|	...	...	...	...	|	...	...	...	0753c	|	...	...	...	|	...	...	...
München Hbf d.	...	0615	0630	0723	...	...	0923	|	...	0956	...	...	1023	...	...	...	0939	|	1156	...	...	1154	1223	...	...
Augsburg Hbf d.	...	▬	...	0804	...	...	1004	|	...	|	...	...	1104	...	...	...	1017	|	|	...	...	...	1304	...	...
Ulm Hbf d.	...	...	...	0851	...	...	1051	|	...	|	...	...	1151	...	...	...	1105	|	|	...	...	...	1351	...	...
Stuttgart Hbf d.	...	...	...	0951	...	...	1151	|	...	|	...	1137	1251	...	...	...	1205	|	|	...	...	...	1451	...	...
Mannheim Hbf d.	...	*ICE*	...	1035	...	...	1235	|	...	|	...	1239	1328	1335	...	...	|	|	|	...	1439	...	1528	1535	...
Praha Hlavni **57** d.	...	**728**	...	|	...	...	|	|	0516	|	...	|	...	|	...	...	|	|	|	...	|	...	...	|	...
Regensburg Hbf d.	...	⊖	...	|	...	...	|	0828	|	|	...	|	...	|	...	...	|	1033	|	...	|	...	...	|	...
Nürnberg Hbf d.	0729	0800	...	|	...	...	|	0928	1009	1101	...	|	...	|	...	...	|	1128	1301	...	|	...	...	|	...
Würzburg Hbf d.	0827	0856	...	|	...	...	|	1025	...	1156	...	|	...	|	...	...	|	1225	1356	...	|	...	...	|	...
Frankfurt (Main) Hbf d.	0942	1010	...	|	...	...	|	1144	...	1305	1328	|	...	|	...	...	1340	1340	1505	1517	|	...	...	|	...
Frankfurt Flughafen ✈ d.	0958	1021	...	1109	...	...	1309	1159	...	...	1343	|	...	1409	...	...	▬	...	...	1532	|	...	...	1609	...
Mainz Hbf d.	1020	|	...	|	...	...	|	1220	...	...	|	1320	...	|	...	...	...	...	...	|	1520	...	...	|	...
Koblenz Hbf d.	1112	|	...	|	...	...	|	1312	...	...	|	1412	...	|	...	...	...	...	...	|	1612	...	...	|	...
Bonn Hbf d.	1144	|	...	|	...	...	|	1344	...	...	|	1444	...	|	...	...	...	...	...	|	1644	...	...	|	...
Köln Hbf a.	1205	1140	...	1205	...	...	1405	1405	...	...	1440	1505	...	1505	...	...	...	...	...	1640	1705	...	...	1705	...
Köln Hbf d.	...	...	...	...	1214	...	...	...	...	...	1444	...	...	...	1514	...	...	...	...	...	...	...	...	...	1714
Aachen Hbf 🏛 d.	...	...	...	...	1302t	...	...	...	...	...	1521	...	...	...	1602t	...	☆	...	...	...	...	...	...	...	1802
Liège Guillemins a.	...	...	...	...	1347	...	...	...	...	...	1608	...	...	...	1647	...	**9157**	...	...	...	...	...	...	...	1847
Liège Guillemins d.	...	...	...	...	1349	...	...	...	...	...	1610	...	...	...	1649	...	[R]	...	...	...	...	...	...	...	1849
Brussels Midi/Zuid a.	...	...	...	...	1435	...	...	...	...	...	1701	...	...	...	1735	...	✖	...	...	...	...	...	...	...	1935
Brussels Midi/Zuid d.	...	...	...	...	1443	1459	...	...	...	...	...	...	...	...	1743	1759	1859	...	...	...	...	...	...	...	1943
Paris Nord a.	...	...	...	...	1605	|	...	...	...	...	...	...	...	...	1905	|	|	...	...	...	...	...	...	...	2105
Lille Europe a.	...	...	...	...	...	1535	...	...	...	...	...	...	...	...	...	1832	1932	...	...	...	...	...	...	...	...
Ashford International a.	...	...	...	...	...	|	...	...	...	...	...	...	...	...	...	|	|	...	...	...	...	...	...	...	...
Ebbsfleet International a.	...	...	...	...	...	|	...	...	...	...	...	...	...	...	...	1845	|	...	...	...	...	...	...	...	...
London St Pancras a.	...	...	...	...	...	1556	...	...	...	...	...	...	...	...	...	1903	1956	...	...	...	...	...	...	...	...

train type	ICE	IC	ICE	ICE	EC	ICE	⇌	☆	☆		IC	D	ALX	ICE	IC	EC	ICE	ICE	IC	ICE	ICE	ICE			
train number	28	2298	626	122	188	516	9460	9165	9165		118	346	454	26	2296	6	1090	504	88	622	10	26	13220		
notes	✖	🍷	⊖	⊖	✖	⊖	[R] 🍷	[R] ✖	[R] ✖		🍷	✖	🍷	✖	🍷	🍷	594	104	✖	⊖	⊖	✖	[R]		
notes					♣			⑦	①–⑥			M		R			✖	⊖	♣			R	P		
Budapest Keleti ▲ d.	...	...	...	...	...	...	...	...	...	...	...	0555	...	...	...	...	...	...	...	...	...	...	...	...	...
Wien Westbahnhof d.	0840	...	...	...	...	...	...	...	...	...	...	0857	...	1040	...	...	...	...	...	...	...	...	...	...	...
Linz d.	1016	...	...	...	...	...	...	...	...	...	...	...	...	1216	...	...	...	...	...	...	...	...	...	...	...
Passau 🏛 d.	1131	...	...	...	...	...	...	...	...	...	...	...	...	1331	...	...	...	...	...	...	...	...	...	...	...
Klagenfurt d.	|	...	...	...	...	...	...	...	...	...	...	...	...	|	...	...	...	...	...	...	...	...	...	...	...
Villach d.	|	...	...	...	...	...	...	...	...	...	...	...	...	|	...	...	...	...	...	...	...	...	...	...	...
Bad Gastein d.	|	...	...	...	...	...	...	...	...	...	...	...	...	|	...	...	...	...	...	...	...	...	...	...	...
Innsbruck d.	|	...	...	...	1037	...	...	...	...	...	0910	...	...	|	...	...	...	...	1237	...	...	...	...	...	...
Zell am See d.	|	...	...	...	|	...	...	...	...	...	|	...	...	|	...	...	...	...	|	...	...	...	2038	...	...
Kitzbühel d.	|	...	...	...	|	...	...	...	...	...	|	...	...	|	...	...	...	...	|	...	...	...	2137	...	...
Wörgl d.	|	...	...	...	1114	...	...	...	...	...	|	...	...	|	...	...	...	...	1314	...	...	...	2231	...	...
Kufstein 🏛 d.	|	...	...	...	1125	...	...	...	...	...	◐	...	...	|	...	...	...	...	1325	...	...	...	2242	...	...
Salzburg d.	|	0957	...	...	|	...	...	...	...	...	|	...	...	|	1153	...	...	...	|	...	...	...	|	...	...
München Hbf d.	|	1141	1255	...	1226	1323	...	...	...	...	|	...	...	|	1339	...	1423	...	1427	1455	...	...	2341o	...	...
Augsburg Hbf d.	|	1217	|	...	...	1404	...	...	...	...	|	...	...	|	1417	...	1504	...	...	|	...	...	|	...	...
Ulm Hbf d.	|	1305	|	...	...	1451	...	...	...	...	1356	...	...	|	1505	...	1551	...	...	|	...	...	|	...	...
Stuttgart Hbf d.	|	1405	|	...	...	1551	...	...	...	...	1512	...	...	|	1605	...	1651	...	...	|	...	...	|	...	...
Mannheim Hbf d.	|	|	|	...	...	1635	...	...	...	...	1608	...	...	|	|	1639	1731	1735	...	|	...	...	|	...	...
Praha Hlavní **57** d.	|	|	|	...	...	|	...	...	...	...	|	...	0916	|	|	|	|	|	...	|	...	...	|	...	...
Regensburg Hbf d.	1233	|	|	...	...	|	...	...	...	...	|	...	1337	1433	|	|	|	|	...	|	...	...	|	...	...
Nürnberg Hbf d.	1328	|	1400	...	...	|	...	...	...	...	|	...	...	1528	|	|	|	|	...	1600	...	...	|	...	...
Würzburg Hbf d.	1427	|	1456	...	...	|	...	...	...	...	|	...	...	1627	|	|	|	|	...	1656	...	...	|	...	...
Frankfurt (Main) Hbf d.	1536	1540	1610	1628	...	|	...	...	...	...	|	...	...	1742	1740	|	1808	|	...	1805	1828	←	|	...	...
Frankfurt Flughafen ✈ d.	...	...	1623	1643	...	1709	...	...	...	...	|	...	...	1755	...	|	...	1809	...	...	1843	1758	|	...	...
Mainz Hbf d.	...	...	|	|	...	|	...	...	...	...	1648	...	...	→	...	1720	...	|	...	...	|	1821	|	...	...
Koblenz Hbf d.	...	...	|	|	...	|	...	...	...	...	1743	...	...	...	...	1812	...	|	...	...	|	1912	|	...	...
Bonn Hbf d.	...	...	|	|	...	|	...	...	...	...	1822	...	...	...	...	1844	...	|	...	...	|	1945	|	...	...
Köln Hbf a.	...	...	1731	1740	...	1805	...	...	...	...	1842	...	...	...	...	1905	...	1905	...	...	1940	2005	|	...	...
Köln Hbf d.	...	...	...	...	...	...	1814	...	...	...	...	...	...	...	...	...	...	...	...	...	1944	...	|	...	...
Aachen Hbf 🏛 d.	...	...	...	...	...	...	1902t	...	...	...	...	...	...	...	...	...	...	...	...	...	2021	...	|	...	...
Liège Guillemins a.	...	...	...	...	...	...	1947	...	...	...	...	...	...	...	...	...	...	...	...	...	2108	...	0829	...	...
Liège Guillemins d.	...	...	...	...	...	...	1949	...	...	...	...	...	...	...	...	...	...	...	...	...	2110	...	|	...	...
Brussels Midi/Zuid a.	...	...	...	...	...	...	2035	...	...	...	...	...	...	...	...	...	...	...	...	...	2201	...	0947	...	...
Brussels Midi/Zuid d.	...	...	...	...	...	...	2043	2059	2102	...	...	...	...	...	...	...	...	...	...	...	...	...	...	...	...
Paris Nord d.	...	...	...	...	...	...	2205	|	|	...	...	...	...	...	...	...	...	...	...	...	...	...	...	...	...
Lille Europe a.	...	...	...	...	...	...	...	2132	2136	...	...	...	...	...	...	...	...	...	...	...	...	...	...	...	...
Ashford International a.	...	...	...	...	...	...	...	|	|	...	...	...	...	...	...	...	...	...	...	...	...	...	...	...	...
Ebbsfleet International a.	...	...	...	...	...	...	...	2145	2148	...	...	...	...	...	...	...	...	...	...	...	...	...	...	...	...
London St Pancras a.	...	...	...	...	...	...	...	2203	2204	...	...	...	...	...	...	...	...	...	...	...	...	...	...	...	...

C – *City Night Line* 🛏 1, 2 cl., 🛌 2 cl., (2) and ✖ Roma - Innsbruck - München. [R] Special fares apply. Table **70**.
D – VAL GARDENA / GRÖDNERTAL – (12) and 🍷 Verona - Bolzano / Bozen - München.
G – GROSSGLOCKNER – ⑥ Dec. 29 - Mar. 22 (also Jan. 6, Mar. 24): (12) Zell am See - Wörgl - Kufstein 🏛 - München.
K – KÁLMÁN IMRE – 🛏 1, 2 cl., 🛌 2 cl. and (2) Budapest - Wien - München. Conveys 🛏 1, 2 cl. Bucureşti - Budapest - Wien - München.
M – DACIA EXPRESS – (12) and ✖ Budapest - Wien. (See Table **65** for additional cars).

P – GO SNOW / TRESKI – Dec. 29, Jan. 5, Feb. 9, 16: 🛌 2 cl. and (2) Zell am See - Saalfelden (depart 2050) - St Johann in Tirol (2127) - Kitzbühel - Kirchberg in Tirol (2148) - Wörgl - Verviers (arrive 0808) - Leuven (0917) - Brussels. [R] special fares apply.
R – (12) and ✖ Wien - Nürnberg - Köln - Dortmund.
c – ①–⑥ (not Dec. 25, 26, Jan. 1, Mar. 22, 24, May 12).
o – München **Ost**.
t – Arrive 10 minutes earlier.
x – Köln **Messe/Deutz**.

▲ – 🏛 is at Hegyeshalom.
◐ – 🏛 is at Lindau and Bregenz.
♣ – Special 'global' fares payable.
⇌ – *Thalys* high-speed train. Special fares payabl
☆ – Eurostar train. Special fares payable. Minimu check-in time: 30 minutes. Valid Dec. 9, 2007 July 5, 2008. See Table **12**.
⊖ – *ICE 3* train 🍷, via high speed line, premium fares payable.

AMSTERDAM - HAMBURG and BERLIN — 22

train type		IC		IC		IC		IC	IC	ICE
train number		141		143		145		147	2024	645
notes	P	🍸		88100		🍸		🍸	🍸	🍴
				J						v
Schiphol ✈ a.	...	0648x	1048	...	...	1448	...	1648	...	...
Amsterdam Centraal d.	0657	|	|	1057	1457	|	1657	|	...	...
Amsterdam Zuid WTC d.	|	0658x	1057	|	|	1458	|	1658	...	...
Duivendrecht d.	|	0705x	1102	|	|	1504	|	1704	...	...
Amersfoort d.	0732	0741x	1132	1141	1532	1541	1732	1741	...	...
Deventer d.	...	0820x	▬	1220	▬	1620	▬	1820	...	...
Hengelo d.	...	0858x	*IC*	1258	*ICE*	1658	*IC*	1858	...	...
Bad Bentheim ▦ a.	...	0918x	**2120**	1318	**926**	1718	**2026**	1918	...	...
Rheine a.	...	0943x	**2320**	1343	**1026**	1743	🍸	1940	...	...
Osnabrück a.	...	1010x	1023	1410	1423	1810	1823	2007	2023	...
Minden a.	...	1047x	|	1447	|	1847	|	2047	|	...
Hannover Hbf a.	...	1118x	|	1518	|	1918	|	2118	|	2131
Bremen Hbf a.	...	|	1114	|	1514	|	1914	|	2114	|
Hamburg Hbf a.	...	|	1212	|	1612	|	2012	|	2212	|
Wolfsburg a.	...	1154	...	1554	...	1954	...	2154j	...	|
Stendal a.	...	1224	...	1624	...	2024	...	2224j	...	|
Berlin Spandau a.	...	1307	...	1707	...	2107	...	2307j	...	2253
Berlin Hauptbahnhof a.	...	1321	...	1717	...	2121	...	2321j	...	2308
Berlin Ostbahnhof a.	...	1332	...	|	...	2132	...	2332j	...	2319
Szczecin Gł. a.	...	...	...	1938p	...	...	...	...	...	...

train type	ICE	IC	IC	IC	ICE	IC	IC	IC	
train number	515	146	2027	88101	927	142	2121	140	
notes	🍴	🍸	🍸	144	1027	🍸	2321	🍸	
				J			🍸		
Szczecin Gł. d.	...	...	...	0611q	...	...	...	...	...
Berlin Ostbahnhof d.	...	...	...	|	...	1228	...	1628	...
Berlin Hauptbahnhof d.	...	...	...	0839	...	1238	...	1638	...
Berlin Spandau d.	...	...	...	0849	...	1252	...	1652	...
Stendal d.	...	...	...	0935	...	1335	...	1735	...
Wolfsburg d.	...	...	...	1005	...	1405	...	1805	...
Hamburg Hbf d.	0537	...	0946	|	1346	|	1746	|	...
Bremen Hbf d.	0637	...	1044	|	1444	|	1844	|	...
Hannover Hbf d.	|	0640	|	1040	|	1440	|	1840v	...
Minden d.	|	0712	|	1112	|	1512	|	1912v	...
Osnabrück d.	0730	0752	1135	1150	1535	1550	1935	1950v	...
Rheine d.	...	0820	▬	1217	▬	1617	▬	2017v	...
Bad Bentheim ▦ d.	...	0844	...	1244	...	1644	...	2044v	...
Hengelo a.	...	0904	...	1304	...	1704	...	2104v	...
Deventer a.	...	0942	...	1342	...	1742	...	2142v	...
Amersfoort a.	...	1023	1028	1423	1428	1821	1825	2223v	2228
Duivendrecht a.	...	1054	|	1454	|	|	1856	2254v	|
Amsterdam Zuid WTC a.	...	1101	|	1501	|	|	1901	2301v	|
Amsterdam Centraal a.	...	|	1101	|	1501	1901	|	|	2301
Schiphol ✈ a.	...	1108	...	1508	...	...	1908	2308v	...

Summary of Night Services AMSTERDAM - BERLIN, KØBENHAVN and PRAHA — 22

train type	CNL	CNL
train number	379	347
notes	A	482
	[R]	H [R]
Amsterdam Centraal d.	1903z	1903z
Köln Hbf d.	2228	2228
Dortmund Hbf d.	2356	2356
København 50 ⊡ a.	|	0959
Berlin Hauptbahnhof a.	0422	...
Berlin Ostbahnhof a.	0434	...
Dresden Hbf a.	0705	...
Praha Hlavní § a.	0933	...

train type	CNL	CNL
train number	483	378
notes	346	A
	H [R]	[R]
Praha Hlavní § d.	...	1850
Dresden Hbf d.	...	2123
Berlin Ostbahnhof d.	...	0022
Berlin Hauptbahnhof d.	...	0032
København 50 ⊡ d.	1853	|
Dortmund Hbf a.	0448	0448
Köln Hbf a.	0614	0614
Amsterdam Centraal a.	1027z	1027z

§ – ▦ is at Schöna.
⊡ – ▦ is at Flensburg and Padborg.

A – *City Night Line* 🛏 1, 2 cl., ━ 2 cl., (2) and 🍸 Amsterdam - Köln - Berlin - Dresden - Praha and v.v. [R] Special fares apply. On Jan. 11–14, Feb. 22–25 trains **378/379** are retimed Amsterdam - Köln - Berlin and v.v., see Table **24**.
H – *City Night Line* 🛏 1, 2 cl., ━ 2 cl. and (2) Amsterdam - Köln - København and v.v. (Table **50**). [R] Special fares apply.
J – (12) and 🍸 Amsterdam - Hannover - Berlin - ▦ Tantow (ticket point) - ▦ Szczecin Gumience - Szczecin and v.v.
j – ⑤⑦ (also Dec. 26, Jan. 1, Mar. 24, Apr. 30, May 12; not Dec. 23, 28, 30, Mar. 21, 23, May 11).
p – Not Dec. 23, 24, 25, 31, Mar. 22, 23.
q – Not Dec. 24, 25, 26, Jan. 1, Mar. 23, 24.
v – Not Dec. 24, 31.
x – Not Dec. 25, Jan. 1.
z – Not Apr. 30.

LONDON, PARIS and BRUSSELS - WARSZAWA and MOSKVA — 24

train type	☆	⇌	EN	EN	EN
train number	9138	9453	347	347	347
notes	[R] 🍴	[R] 🍸	A	C	E
notes			[R] ❖	[R]	[R]
London St Pancras d.	1434	...	...	...	...
Ebbsfleet International d.	|	...	...	...	...
Lille Europe **12** d.	1658	...	...	...	...
Paris Nord d.	|	1755	...	...	...
Brussels Midi / Zuid d.	1733	1925	...	...	...
Liège Guillemins d.	...	2013	...	...	...
Aachen ▦ d.	...	2106	...	...	...
Amsterdam Centraal d.	...	|	1903z	...	...
Duisburg d.	...	|	2147	...	...
Düsseldorf d.	...	|	2202	...	...
Köln Hbf d.	...	2145	2228	...	...
Solingen Hbf d.	...	...	2300	...	...
Wuppertal Hbf d.	...	...	2314	...	...
Hagen Hbf d.	...	...	2334	...	...
Dortmund Hbf d.	...	...	2356	...	...
Hamm d.	...	...	0014	...	...
Bielefeld d.	...	...	0043	...	...
Basel SBB ♥ d.	...	...	|	1804	...
München Hbf ♣ d.	...	...	|	|	1900x
Fulda d.	...	...	|	2340	2340
Hannover d.	...	...	|	|	|
Berlin Ostbahnhof d.	...	...	|	|	|
Frankfurt (Oder) ▦ d.	...	...	|	|	|
Rzepin a.	...	...	0601	0601	0601
Poznań Gł. a.	...	...	0739	0739	0739
Konin a.	...	...	0838	0838	0838
Kutno a.	...	...	0923	0923	0923
Warszawa Centralna a.	...	...	1040	1040	1040
Warszawa Wschodnia a.	...	...	1052	1052	1052
Warszawa Wschodnia d.	...	..	1208	1208	1208
Terespol a.	...	...	1525	1525	1525
Terespol d.	...	...	1555	1555	1555
Brest ▦ a.	...	...	1741	1741	1741
Brest ▦ d.	...	...	1945	1945	1945
Baranavichy a.	...	...	2151	2151	2151
Minsk a.	...	...	2333	2333	2333
Orsha Tsentralnaya a.	...	...	0220	0220	0220
Smolensk Tsentralny ▦ a.	...	...	0456	0456	0456
Vyazma a.	...	...	0705	0705	0705
Moskva Belorusskaya a.	...	...	1059	1059	1059

train type	EN
train number	347
notes	A
	[R] ❖
Amsterdam Centraal d.	1903z
Utrecht Centraal d.	1931
Arnhem d.	2008
Emmerich d.	2050
Oberhausen Hbf d.	2139
Düisburg Hbf d.	2147

train type	EN
train number	50353
notes	482
	347
	C
	[R]
Basel SBB d.	1804
Basel Bad. Bf ▦ d.	1817
Freiburg (Brsg) Hbf d.	1904
Offenburg d.	1937
Karlsruhe Hbf d.	2018
Mannheim Hbf d.	2116
Frankfurt (Main) Süd d.	2219
Fulda d.	2340

train type	EN
train number	50482
notes	347
	E
	[R]
München Hbf d.	1900x
Ingolstadt Hbf d.	1948x
Nürnberg Hbf d.	2135
Würzburg Hbf d.	2233
Fulda d.	2340

train type	EN	EN	EN	⇌	☆
train number	346	346	346	9416	9127
notes	F	D	B	[R] 🍸	[R] 🍴
notes	[R]	[R]	[R] ⊠	①–⑥	
Moskva Belorusskaya d.	2109	2109	2109	p	...
Vyazma d.	0034	0034	0034	...	...
Smolensk Tsentralny ▦ d.	0300	0300	0300	...	...
Orsha Tsentralnaya d.	0338	0338	0338	...	...
Minsk d.	0643	0643	0643	...	...
Baranavichy d.	0828	0828	0828	...	...
Brest ▦ a.	1030	1030	1030	...	...
Brest ▦ d.	1250	1250	1250	...	...
Terespol a.	1208	1208	1208	...	...
Terespol d.	1248	1248	1248	...	...
Warszawa Wschodnia a.	1611	1611	1611	...	...
Warszawa Wschodnia d.	1742	1742	1742	...	...
Warszawa Centralna d.	1755	1755	1755	...	...
Kutno d.	1913	1913	1913	...	...
Konin d.	1955	1955	1955	...	...
Poznań Gł. d.	2105	2105	2105	...	...
Rzepin d.	2244	2244	2244	...	...
Frankfurt (Oder) ▦ d.	|	|	|	...	...
Berlin Ostbahnhof a.	|	|	|	...	...
Hannover a.	|	|	|	...	...
Fulda a.	0450	0450	|	...	...
München Hbf ♣ a.	0857	|	|	...	...
Basel SBB ♥ a.	...	1037	|	...	...
Bielefeld a.	...	...	0354	...	...
Hamm a.	...	...	0425	...	...
Dortmund Hbf a.	...	...	0448	...	...
Hagen Hbf a.	...	...	0521	...	...
Wuppertal Hbf a.	...	...	0539	...	...
Solingen Hbf a.	...	...	|	...	...
Köln Hbf a.	...	...	0614	0714	...
Düsseldorf a.	...	...	0654	|	...
Duisburg a.	...	...	0715	|	☆
Amsterdam Centraal d.	...	...	1027z	|	**9127**
Aachen ▦ a.	...	...	...	0752	[R]
Liège Guillemins a.	...	...	...	0847	🍴
Brussels Midi / Zuid a.	...	...	...	0935	1159
Paris Nord a.	...	...	...	1105	|
Lille Europe **12** a.	...	...	...	...	1232
Ebbsfleet International a.	...	...	...	...	1245
London St Pancras a.	...	...	...	...	1303

train type	EN
train number	346
notes	B
	[R] ⊠
Düisburg Hbf a.	0715
Oberhausen Hbf a.	0732
Emmerich a.	0824
Arnhem a.	0922
Utrecht Centraal a.	0956
Amsterdam Centraal a.	1027z

train type	EN
train number	346
notes	483
	352
	[R]
	D
Fulda a.	0450
Frankfurt (Main) Süd a.	0654
Mannheim Hbf a.	0750
Karlsruhe Hbf a.	0818
Offenburg a.	0901
Freiburg (Brsg) Hbf a.	0939
Basel Bad. Bf ▦ a.	1027
Basel SBB a.	1037

train type	EN
train number	346
notes	483
	[R]
	F
Fulda a.	0450
Würzburg Hbf a.	0534
Nürnberg Hbf a.	0645
Ingolstadt Hbf a.	0807
München Hbf a.	0857

A – JAN KIEPURA – 🛏 1, 2 cl. Amsterdam (**347**) - Köln - Warszawa (**11013**) - Brest (**12**) - Moskva (journey 2 nights). 🛏 1, 2 cl., ━ 2 cl., (2) and 🍴 Amsterdam - Warszawa.
B – JAN KIEPURA – 🛏 1, 2 cl. Moskva (**11**) - Brest (**11014**) - Warszawa (**346**) - Köln - Amsterdam (journey 2 nights). 🛏 1, 2 cl., ━ 2 cl., (2) and 🍴 Warszawa (**346**) - Amsterdam.
C – 🛏 1, 2 cl. Basel (**50353**) - Frankfurt - Fulda (**482**) - Hannover (**347**) - Warszawa - Moskva (journey 2 nights). 🛏 1, 2 cl., ━ 2 cl. and 🍴 Basel - Warszawa.
D – 🛏 1, 2 cl. Moskva (**11**) - Warszawa (**346**) - Hannover (**483**) - Fulda (**352**) - Frankfurt - Basel (journey 2 nights). 🛏 1, 2 cl., ━ 2 cl. and 🍴 Warszawa - Basel.
E – 🛏 1, 2 cl. München (**50482**) - Nürnberg - Fulda - Hannover (**347**) - Warszawa - Moskva (journey 2 nights). 🛏 1, 2 cl., ━ 2 cl. and 🍴 München - Warszawa.
F – 🛏 1, 2 cl. Moskva (**11**) - Warszawa (**346**) - Hannover (**483**) - Fulda - Nürnberg - München (journey 2 nights). 🛏 1, 2 cl., ━ 2 cl. and 🍴 Warszawa - München.
p – Not Dec. 25, Jan. 1, Mar. 24, May 1, 12.
x – On ⑥⑦ (also Dec. 25, 26, Jan. 1, Mar. 21, 24, May 1, 12) depart München 1916, Ingolstadt 2011.
z – Not Apr. 30.
⊖ – *ICE 3* train 🍸 premium fares payable.
♥ – For intermediate stops Basel - Fulda see inset.
♣ – For intermediate stops München - Fulda see inset.

♠ – For intermediate stops Amsterdam - Düisburg see inset.
❖ – On Jan. 11, 12, Feb. 22, 23 departs Amsterdam 1802 (Train **349**) and runs 1 hour earlier until Rzepin.
⊠ – On Jan. 11, 12, 13, Feb. 22, 23, 24 arrives Bielefeld 0445 (Train **348**), runs 30–51 minutes later and arrives Amsterdam 1057.
☆ – Eurostar train. Special fares payable. Minimum check-in time 30 minutes. For additional services see Table **12**. Valid Dec. 9, 2007 - July 5, 2008.
⇌ – *Thalys* high-speed train. Special fares payable. For additional services see Tables **18**, **20**, **21**.

Through sleeper PARIS - MOSKVA 🛏 1, 2 cl. (journey 2 nights)

See Tables **20** *and* **56**	**243 / 247** ④⑥
Paris Nord d.	2046
Berlin Zoo a.	0803
Berlin Zoo d.	1513
Moskva Belorusskaya a.	2035

	246 / 242 ②④
Moska Belorusskaya d.	0800
Berlin Zoo a.	0910
Berlin Zoo d.	2134
Paris Nord a.	0914

28 AMSTERDAM - FRANKFURT, WIEN and MÜNCHEN

train type		ICE	ICE		ICE	ICE	ICE	ALX		ICE	ICE	ICE	ICE		ICE	ICE	ICE		ICE	ICE	ICE		ICE	ICE	ICE	CNL
train number		121	515		105	595	27	457		123	629	519	229		125	723	611		127	727	613		129	821	615	353
notes	⚒	⊖ G	🍷		⊖ J	🍷	✕	🍷		⊖	🍷	🍷	✕		⊖	🍷 Ⓑf	🍷		⊖ T	🍷 Ⓑf	🍷		⊖	🍷	🍷 g	P
Amsterdam Centraal d.	...	0704	...	...	0804	...	...	...	...	1034	...	...	...	...	1234	...	...	...	1434	...	...	...	1634	...	...	...
Rotterdam Centraal d.	0632	|	...	0732	|	...	...	...	1002	|	...	...	...	1202	|	...	...	1402	|	...	...	1602	|	...	...	...
Utrecht Centraal d.	0711	0732	...	0811	0832	...	...	...	1042	1100	...	...	...	1242	1300	...	...	1442	1500	...	...	1642	1700	...	...	...
Arnhem ◐ d.	...	0808	...	...	0908	...	...	...	...	1137	...	...	...	...	1337	...	...	...	1537	...	...	...	1737	...	...	...
Oberhausen ◐ a.	...	0858	...	...	0958	...	...	...	...	1224	...	...	...	...	1424	...	...	...	1624	...	...	...	1824	...	...	...
Duisburg a.	...	0906	...	...	1006	...	...	...	...	1232	...	...	...	...	1432	...	...	...	1632	...	...	...	1832	...	...	...
Düsseldorf Hbf a.	...	0920	...	...	1020	...	...	...	...	1246	...	...	...	...	1446	...	...	...	1646	...	...	...	1846	...	...	...
Köln Hbf a.	...	0943t	...	...	1045	...	...	...	...	1312	...	...	...	...	1512	...	...	...	1712	...	...	...	1912	...	...	...
Köln Hbf d.	...	0951t	...	...	1054	...	...	...	...	1320	...	...	...	...	1520	...	...	...	1720	...	...	...	1920	...	...	...
Bonn Hbf a.	...	|	...	...	|	...	...	...	...	|	...	...	...	...	|	...	...	...	|	...	...	...	|	...	...	...
Koblenz a.	...	|	...	...	|	...	...	...	...	|	...	...	...	...	|	...	...	...	|	...	...	...	|	...	...	...
Mainz a.	...	|	...	...	|	...	...	...	...	|	...	...	...	...	|	...	...	...	|	...	...	...	|	...	...	...
Frankfurt Flughafen ✈ a.	...	1043	1054	...	1151	...	1201	...	...	1414	...	1454	...	...	1614	...	1654	...	1814	...	1854	...	2014	...	2054	...
Frankfurt (Main) Hbf a.	...	1102	|	...	|	...	1213	...	...	1430	1454	|	1621	...	1630	1654	|	...	1830	1854	|	...	2030	2054	|	2219k
Würzburg a.	...	...	|	...	|	...	1331	...	...	...	1603	|	1731	...	...	1803	|	...	...	2003	|	...	...	2203	|	|
Nürnberg a.	...	...	|	...	|	...	1428	...	...	...	1659	|	1828	...	...	1859	|	...	...	2059	|	...	...	2259	|	|
Regensburg a.	...	...	|	...	|	...	1522	1821	...	...	|	|	1922	...	...	|	|	...	...	|	|	...	...	|	|	|
Praha Hlavní 58 a.	...	...	|	...	|	...	|	2245	...	...	|	|	|	...	...	|	|	...	...	|	|	...	...	|	|	0818y
Mannheim a.	...	...	1124	...	1224	1231	|	...	...	...	|	1524	|	...	...	|	1724	...	...	|	1924	...	...	|	2124	...
Stuttgart a.	...	...	1208	...	...	1308	|	...	...	...	|	1608	|	...	...	|	1808	...	...	|	2008	...	...	|	2208	...
Ulm a.	...	...	1306	...	...	1406	|	...	...	...	|	1706	|	...	...	|	1906	...	...	|	2106	...	...	|	2306	...
Augsburg a.	...	...	1350	...	...	1450	|	...	...	...	|	1750	|	...	...	|	1950	...	...	|	2150	...	...	|	2353	...
München Hbf a.	...	...	1431	...	...	1531	|	...	...	...	1804	1831	|	...	...	2004	2031	...	...	2208	2231	...	...	0005h	0035	...
Passau 🏛 a.	...	...	...	...	...	...	1626	...	...	...	...	...	2026	...	...	...	...	...	...	...	...	...	...	...	...	...
Linz a.	...	...	...	...	...	...	1745	...	...	...	...	...	2145	...	...	...	...	...	...	...	...	...	...	...	...	...
Wien Westbahnhof a.	...	...	...	...	...	...	1926	...	...	...	...	...	2326	...	...	...	...	...	...	...	...	...	...	...	...	...

train type	CNL		ICE	CNL	IC		CNL		CNL
train number	313		227	313	1591		379		319
notes	A		⊖	A	b		B Ⓡ		Ⓡ 🍷 F
Amsterdam Centraal d.	1703x	...	1834	...	...	...	1903x	...	2032x
Rotterdam Centraal d.	|	1802	|	...	...	1832	|	2002	|
Utrecht Centraal d.	1732	1841	1900	...	...	1911	1931	2041	2102
Arnhem ◐ d.	1808	...	1937	...	...	...	2008	...	2139
Oberhausen ◐ a.	|	...	2024	...	...	...	|	...	2248d
Duisburg a.	|	...	2032	...	...	...	2147d	...	2256d
Düsseldorf Hbf a.	1935d	...	2046	...	...	...	2202d	...	2312d
Köln Hbf a.	|	...	2112	...	...	...	|	...	|
Köln Hbf d.	2006	...	2120	...	...	...	2228	...	2346
Bonn Hbf a.	2035d	...	|	...	...	...	|	...	0007d
Koblenz a.	2115d	...	|	...	...	...	|	...	0102d
Mainz a.	2212d	...	|	...	...	...	|	...	|
Frankfurt Flughafen ✈ a.	|	...	2218	←	...	...	|	...	|
Frankfurt (Main) Hbf a.	2247d	...	2234	2247	0007	...	|	...	|
Würzburg a.	→	...	...	|	|	...	|	...	|
Nürnberg a.	...	...	...	|	|	...	|	...	|
Regensburg a.	...	...	...	|	|	...	|	...	|
Praha Hlavní 58 a.	...	...	...	|	|	...	0933	...	|
Mannheim a.	...	...	...	2332d	0104	...	...	...	|
Stuttgart a.	...	...	...	|	0236	...	...	...	0419z
Ulm a.	...	...	...	|	...	...	...	...	0542
Augsburg a.	...	...	...	|	...	...	...	...	0634
München Hbf a.	...	...	...	|	...	...	...	...	0716
Passau 🏛 a.	...	...	...	|	...	...	...	...	...
Linz a.	...	...	...	0644	...	...	...	...	...
Wien Westbahnhof a.	...	...	...	0835	...	...	...	...	...

train type	CNL	ICE	ICE	ICE	ICE	ICE	RE	ICE	ICE	ICE		
train number	352	616	226	614	820	128	4242	612	726	126		
notes	Q	🍷	⊖	🍷	🍷 R	⊖		🍷	🍷 S	⊖ T		
Wien Westbahnhof d.	...	...	...	...	...	...	...	...	...	...	...	...
Linz d.	...	...	...	...	...	...	...	...	...	...	...	...
Passau 🏛 d.	...	...	...	...	...	...	0549	...	...	...	...	...
München Hbf d.	...	0317	...	0523	0551	...	|	0723	0755	...	...	...
Augsburg d.	...	0357	...	0604	|	...	|	0804	|	...	...	...
Ulm d.	...	0440	...	0651	|	...	|	0851	|	...	...	...
Stuttgart d.	...	0551	...	0751	|	...	|	0951	|	...	...	...
Mannheim d.	...	0635	...	0835	|	...	|	1035	|	...	...	...
Praha Hlavní 57 d.	2025	|	...	|	|	...	|	|	|	...	...	...
Regensburg d.	|	|	...	|	*0541*	...	0720	|	|	...	...	...
Nürnberg d.	|	|	...	|	0701	...	0825	|	0900	...	...	...
Würzburg d.	|	|	...	|	0756	...	▬	|	0956	...	...	...
Frankfurt (Main) Hbf d.	0654k	|	0728	|	0905	0928	...	|	1105	1128	...	...
Frankfurt Flughafen ✈ d.	...	0706	0743	0906	▬	0943	...	1106	...	1143	...	...
Mainz d.	...	...	|	▬	...	|	...	...	...	|	...	...
Koblenz d.	...	...	|	...	...	|	...	...	...	|	...	...
Bonn Hbf d.	...	...	|	...	...	|	...	...	...	|	...	...
Köln Hbf a.	...	...	0840	...	...	1040	...	...	...	1240	...	...
Köln Hbf d.	...	...	0843	...	...	1048	...	...	...	1248	...	...
Düsseldorf Hbf d.	...	...	0915	...	...	1113	...	...	...	1314	...	...
Duisburg d.	...	...	0927	...	...	1126	...	...	...	1328	...	...
Oberhausen ◐ d.	...	...	0935	...	...	1135	...	...	...	1335	...	...
Arnhem ◐ a.	...	...	1023	G	...	1223	...	...	...	1423	...	...
Utrecht Centraal a.	...	...	1056	1103	1118	1256	1303	...	...	1456	1503	...
Rotterdam Centraal a.	...	...	|	1142	1157	|	1342	...	...	|	1542	...
Amsterdam Centraal a.	...	...	1125	...	...	1325	...	...	...	1525	...	...

train type	IC	ICE	RE	ICE	ICE	EC	ICE	ICE	ICE	ICE	ALX	ICE	ICE	ICE		ICE	ICE	ICE	CNL	CNL	ICE	ICE		CNL		
train number	2028	610	450	722	124	100	28	596	626	122	454	26	1090	104		514	620	120	318	378	1590	226		312		
notes	🍷	🍷		🍷	⊖	102 🍷	✕	🍷	🍷	⊖	🍷	🍷	594 ⊖	K ⊖		🍷	🍷 Ⓑf	⊖ Ⓑf	🍷 F	B Ⓡ	b	⊖		A		
Wien Westbahnhof d.	...	...	...	...	...	...	0840	...	...	...	...	1040	...	...	...	...	...	...	...	...	...	...	...	2035	...	...
Linz d.	...	...	...	...	...	...	1016	...	...	...	...	1216	...	...	...	...	...	...	...	...	...	...	...	2220	...	...
Passau 🏛 d.	0719	...	...	...	...	...	1131	...	...	...	...	1331	...	...	...	...	...	...	...	...	...	...	...	|	...	...
München Hbf d.	|	0923	...	0956	...	...	|	1223	1255	...	...	|	1423	...	...	1523	1556	...	2242	...	...	...	...	|	...	...
Augsburg d.	|	1004	...	|	...	...	|	1304	|	...	...	|	1504	...	...	1604	|	...	2318	...	...	...	...	|	...	...
Ulm d.	|	1051	...	|	...	...	|	1351	|	...	...	|	1551	...	...	1651	|	...	0010	...	...	...	...	|	...	...
Stuttgart d.	|	1151	...	|	...	...	|	1451	|	...	...	|	1651	...	...	1751	|	...	0126z	...	0305	...	...	|	...	...
Mannheim d.	|	1235	...	|	...	1439	|	1531	|	...	...	|	1728	1735	...	1835	|	...	|	...	0440	...	...	0515a	...	...
Praha Hlavní 58 d.	|	|	0516	|	...	|	|	|	|	...	0916	|	...	|	...	|	|	...	|	1850	|	...	...	|	...	...
Regensburg d.	0828	|	|	*0919*	...	|	1233	|	|	...	1337	1433	...	|	...	|	|	...	|	|	|	...	...	|	...	...
Nürnberg d.	0928	|	1009	1101	...	|	1328	|	1400	...	▬	1528	...	|	...	|	1701	...	|	|	|	...	...	|	...	...
Würzburg d.	1025	|	...	1156	...	|	1427	|	1456	...	...	1627	...	|	...	|	1756	...	|	|	|	...	...	|	...	...
Frankfurt (Main) Hbf d.	1144	|	...	1305	1328	|	1536	1608	1610	1628	...	1736	...	|	...	|	1905	1928	|	|	0535	0728	...	0600a	...	...
Frankfurt Flughafen ✈ d.	1159	1306	...	...	1343	|	...	...	...	1643	...	1755	...	1809	...	1906	...	1943	|	|	▬	0743	...	|	...	...
Mainz d.	1220	...	...	...	|	1520	...	...	...	|	...	...	...	|	...	...	...	|	|	|	...	|	...	0645a	...	...
Koblenz d.	1312	...	...	...	|	1612	...	...	...	|	...	...	...	|	...	...	...	|	0426a	|	...	|	...	0744a	...	...
Bonn Hbf d.	1344	...	...	...	|	1644	...	...	...	|	...	...	...	|	...	...	...	|	0512a	|	...	|	...	0817a	...	...
Köln Hbf a.	1405	...	...	...	1440	1705	...	...	...	1740	...	...	...	1905	...	...	...	2040	0545a	0614a	...	0840	...	0842	...	...
Köln Hbf d.	...	...	...	...	1448	▬	...	...	...	1748	...	...	...	1917	...	...	...	2048	|	|	...	0843	...	|	...	...
Düsseldorf Hbf d.	...	...	...	...	1514	...	...	...	...	1813	...	...	...	1940	...	...	...	2113	0613a	0654a	...	0915	...	0909a	...	...
Duisburg d.	...	...	...	...	1528	...	...	...	...	1826	...	...	...	1953	...	...	...	2126	0628a	0715a	...	0927	...	|	...	...
Oberhausen ◐ d.	...	...	...	...	1535	...	...	...	...	1835	...	...	...	2000	...	...	...	2135	0636a	|	...	0935	...	|	...	...
Arnhem ◐ a.	...	...	...	...	1623	...	...	...	...	1923	...	...	...	2052	...	...	...	2223	0752	0922	...	1023	...	1122	...	...
Utrecht Centraal a.	...	...	...	...	1656	1703	...	...	...	1956	2003	...	...	2126	2148	...	...	2256	0826	0956	1018	1056	1118	1156	...	...
Rotterdam Centraal a.	...	...	...	...	|	1742	...	...	...	|	2042	...	...	|	2227	...	...	*2357*	|	|	1057	|	1157	|	...	...
Amsterdam Centraal a.	...	...	...	...	1725	...	...	...	...	2025	...	...	...	2155	...	...	...	2325	0856x	1027x	...	1125	...	1227	...	...

A – *City Night Line* DONAU-KURIER – 🛏 1,2 cl., 🛏 1,2 cl. (T4), ▬ 2 cl. (4,6 berth), (2) and ✕: Amsterdam - Köln - Frankfurt - Salzburg 🏛 - Wien and v.v. Ⓡ Special fares apply. For international journeys only.
B – *City Night Line* 🛏 1,2 cl., ▬ 2 cl., (2) and 🍷 Amsterdam - Köln - Berlin - Dresden - Praha and v.v. Ⓡ Special fares apply. On Jan. 11–14, Feb. 22–25 trains **378/379** are retimed Amsterdam - Köln - Berlin, see Table **24**.
F – *City Night Line* POLLUX – 🛏 1,2 cl., 🛏 1,2 cl. (T4), ▬ 2 cl. (4,6 berth), (2) (reclining) and ✕ Amsterdam - München and v.v. Ⓡ Special fares apply. To/from Garmisch-Partenkirchen on dates in Table **895**.
G – ①–⑥ (not Dec. 25, 26, Jan. 1, Mar. 24, May 12).
J – (12) and 🍷 Amsterdam - Köln - Mannheim - Basel. Not Amsterdam - Köln on Dec. 25, Jan. 1.
K – (12) and 🍷 Basel - Mannheim - Köln - Amsterdam. Not Köln - Amsterdam on Dec. 24, 31.
P – *City Night Line* JOHANNES KEPLER – 🛏 1,2 cl., ▬ 2 cl. and (2) Basel - Frankfurt (Main) **Süd** - Fulda - Děčín 🏛 - Praha Holešovice. ✕ Basel - Fulda. Ⓡ Special fares apply.
Q – *City Night Line* JOHANNES KEPLER – 🛏 1,2 cl., ▬ 2 cl. and (2) Praha Hlavní - Praha Holešovice - Děčín 🏛 - Fulda - Frankfurt (Main) Süd - Basel. ✕ Fulda - Basel. Ⓡ Special fares apply.
R – ①–⑤ (not Dec. 24, 25, 26, 31, Jan. 1, Mar. 21, 24, May 12).
S – ①–⑥ (not Dec. 25, 26, Jan. 1, Mar. 22, 24, May 12).
T – Mar. 14 - Oct. 26.

a – Arrival time.
b – Not Dec. 25, Jan. 1.
d – Departure time.
f – Not Dec. 24, 25, 31, Mar. 21, 23, May 11.
g – Not Dec. 24, 31.
h – ①⑥ (also Dec. 27, Jan. 2, Mar. 21, 25, May 1, 13, 22; not Dec. 24, 31, Mar. 24, May 12).
j – Not Dec. 23, 24, 30, Apr. 4, 6, May 25.
k – Frankfurt (Main) **Süd**.
t – Köln **Messe / Deutz**.
x – Not Apr. 30.
y – Praha **Holešovice**.
z – Not May 15 - Oct. 27.
◐ – 🏛 between Arnhem and Oberhausen is Emmerich.
⊖ – *ICE 3* train 🍷, via high speed line, premium fares payable.

PARIS - FRANKFURT - BERLIN, LEIPZIG, DRESDEN and PRAHA 30

Alternative services Paris - Frankfurt are available via Brussels (Table **21**). Alternative services Paris - Berlin are available via Brussels (Table **20**).

train type	*ICE*	*ICE*	*ICE*	*EC*	*ICE*	*ICE*	*ICE*	*ICE*	*ICE*	*EC*	*ICE*	*ICE*	*ICE*	*ICE*	*ICE*	*ICE*	*ICE*	*ICE*	*CNL*	*ICE*
train number	**9551**	**278**	**1559**	**371**	**623**	**9553**	**9553**	**372**	**1651**	**179**	**627**	**9555**	**276**	**1655**	**725**	**9557**	**1659**	**929**	**353**	**9559**
notes	♣	✕	⊖	✕	🍷	♣	♣	✕	⊖	✕	🍷	♣	✕	⊖	🍷	♣	⊖	🍷		♣
notes	Q	L		K		⑦j	Q	L		D			L h	Ⓑg		Ⓑf	Ⓑk		B	
aris Est d.	0658	...	...	...	...	0901	0909	...	...	...	...	1309	...	...	...	1709	...	...	...	1905
›rbach 🏛 d.	0849	...	...	...	...	1049	|	...	...	...	...	|	...	...	...	|	...	...	...	2050
aarbrücken a.	0858	...	...	...	...	1058	1058	...	...	...	...	1458	...	...	...	1858	...	...	...	2058
aiserlautern a.	0935	...	...	...	...	1135	1135	...	...	...	...	1535	...	...	...	1935	...	...	...	2135
arlsruhe Hbf a.	|	...	...	...	...	|	|	...	...	...	...	|	...	...	...	|	...	...	...	|
lannheim a.	1016	...	...	...	...	1216	1216	...	...	...	...	1616	...	...	...	2016	...	...	...	2216
rankfurt (Main) Hbf a.	1058	...	...	...	...	1258	1258	...	...	...	...	1658	...	...	...	2058	...	...	...	2258
rankfurt (Main) Hbf d.	...	1113	1119	...	1154	...	...	1313	1319	...	1354	...	1713	1720	1754	...	2119	2218	2219q	...
Würzburg a.	...	|	|	...	1303	...	...	|	|	...	1503	...	|	|	1903	...	|	2341	|	...
Nürnberg a.	...	|	|	...	1359	...	...	|	|	...	1559	...	|	|	1959	...	|	0037	|	...
ılda a.	...	1209	1211	...	...	...	...	1409	1411	...	...	...	1809	1811	...	...	2211	...	0047u	...
furt a.	...	|	1332	...	...	...	...	|	1533	...	...	...	|	1932	...	...	2332	...	|	...
eipzig Hbf a.	...	|	1442	...	...	...	...	|	1642	...	...	...	|	2042	...	...	0046r	...	0425	...
resden Hbf a.	...	|	1602	1710	...	...	...	|	1802	1910	...	...	|	2202	...	...	...	...	0551	...
ěčín (🏛 = Schöna) a.	...	|	...	1757	...	...	...	|	...	1957	...	...	|	...	...	...	...	...	0653	...
aha Holešovice a.	...	|	...	1918	...	...	...	|	...	2118	...	...	|	...	...	...	...	...	0818	...
aha Hlavní a.	...	|	...	1931	...	...	...	|	...	2132	...	...	|	...	...	...	...	...	...	...
assel Wilhelmshöhe a.	...	1242	...	...	...	...	...	1442	...	...	...	...	1842	...	...	...	...	...	...	...
aunschweig a.	...	1358	...	...	...	...	...	1558	...	...	...	...	1958	...	...	...	...	...	...	...
olfsburg a.	...	1416	...	...	...	...	...	1616	...	...	...	...	2016	...	...	...	...	...	...	...
erlin Hauptbahnhof a.	...	1526	...	...	...	...	...	1725	...	...	...	...	2125	...	...	...	...	...	...	...
erlin Ostbahnhof a.	...	1537	...	...	...	...	...	1736	...	...	...	...	2136	...	...	...	...	...	...	...

train type	*CNL*	*ICE*	*ICE*	*EC*	*ICE*
train number	**261**	**972**	**1555**	**175**	**525**
notes	Ⓡ	🍷	⊖	✕	🍷
notes	A			F	p
aris Est d.	2245x	...	...	...	...
›rbach 🏛 d.	◧	...	...	...	...
aarbrücken a.	|	...	...	...	...
aiserlautern a.	|	...	...	...	...
arlsruhe Hbf a.	0455	0559	...	...	...
annheim a.	...	0622	...	...	...
rankfurt (Main) Hbf a.	...	0708	...	...	...
rankfurt (Main) Hbf d.	...	0713	0720	...	0754
Würzburg a.	...	|	|	...	0903
Nürnberg a.	...	|	|	...	0959
ılda a.	...	0809	0811	...	...
furt a.	...	|	0932	...	...
eipzig Hbf a.	...	|	1042	...	...
resden Hbf a.	...	|	1202	1310	...
ěčín (🏛 = Schöna) a.	...	|	...	1357	...
aha Holešovice a.	...	|	...	1518	...
aha Hlavní a.	...	|	...	...	...
assel Wilhelmshöhe a.	...	0842	...	...	...
aunschweig a.	...	0958	...	...	...
olfsburg a.	...	1016	...	...	...
erlin Hauptbahnhof a.	...	1125	...	...	...
erlin Ostbahnhof a.	...	1136	...	...	...

train type	*ICE*	*CNL*	*ICE*	*ICE*	*ICE*	*ICE*	*ICE*
train number	**9558**	**352**	**822**	**1656**	**375**	**9556**	**9556**
notes	♣		🍷	⊖	✕	♣	♣
notes	Q	C		S	P	Q	⑦j
Berlin Ostbahnhof d.	...	...	...	...	0422	...	...
Berlin Hauptbahnhof d.	...	...	...	...	0433	...	...
Wolfsburg d.	...	...	...	...	0540	...	...
Braunschweig d.	...	...	...	...	0558	...	...
Kassel Wilhelmshöhe d.	...	...	...	...	0715	...	...
Praha Hlavní d.	...	2025	...	...	|	...	...
Praha Holešovice d.	...	2036	...	...	|	...	...
Děčín (🏛 = Schöna) d.	...	2158	...	...	|	...	...
Dresden Hbf d.	...	2256	...	...	|	...	...
Leipzig Hbf d.	...	0054	...	0501	|	...	...
Erfurt d.	...	|	...	0618	|	...	...
Fulda d.	...	0423s	...	0744	0747	...	...
Nürnberg d.	...	|	0600	|	|	...	...
Würzburg d.	...	|	0656	|	|	...	...
Frankfurt (Main) Hbf a.	...	0654q	0805	0837	0844	...	...
Frankfurt (Main) Hbf d.	0600	...	...	...	...	0901	0901
Mannheim d.	0640	...	...	...	...	0941	0941
Karlsruhe Hbf d.	|	...	...	...	...	|	|
Kaiserlautern d.	0722	...	...	...	...	1022	1022
Saarbrücken d.	0800	...	...	...	...	1101	1101
Forbach 🏛 a.	0808	...	...	...	...	|	1109
Paris Est a.	0950	...	...	...	...	1249	1253

train type	*ICE*	*ICE*	*ICE*	*ICE*	*ICE*	*ICE*	*EC*	*ICE*	*ICE*	*ICE*	*EC*	*ICE*	*ICE*	*ICE*	*EC*	*ICE*	*ICE*	*ICE*	*CNL*
train number	**724**	**1652**	**875**	**9554**	**626**	**279**	**176**	**1558**	**9552**	**622**	**370**	**1556**	**879**	**9550**	**172**	**1542**	**524**	**971**	**260**
notes	🍷	⊖	✕	♣	🍷	✕	✕	⊖	♣	🍷	✕	⊖	✕	♣	✕	⊖	🍷	🍷	Ⓡ
notes						L	G				E			Ⓑf	J	Ⓑg			A
erlin Ostbahnhof d.	...	...	0821	...	...	1222	...	...	...	...	...	...	1422	...	...	...	...	1822	...
erlin Hauptbahnhof d.	...	...	0832	...	...	1233	...	...	...	...	...	...	1433	...	...	...	...	1833	...
olfsburg d.	...	...	0940	...	...	1340	...	...	...	...	...	...	1540	...	...	...	...	1940	...
aunschweig d.	...	...	0958	...	...	1358	...	...	...	...	...	...	1558	...	...	...	...	1958	...
assel Wilhelmshöhe d.	...	...	1115	...	...	1515	...	...	...	...	...	...	1715	...	...	...	...	2115	...
aha Hlavní d.	...	...	|	...	...	|	0825	...	...	...	...	...	|	...	...	...	...	|	...
aha Holešovice d.	...	...	|	...	...	|	0836	...	...	...	1036	...	|	...	1436	...	...	|	...
ěčín (🏛 = Schöna) d.	...	...	|	...	...	|	0958	...	...	...	1158	...	|	...	1558	...	...	|	...
resden Hbf d.	...	0755	|	...	...	|	1046	1155	...	...	1246	1355	|	...	1646	1655	...	|	...
eipzig Hbf d.	...	0916	|	...	...	|	...	1316	...	...	...	1516	|	...	...	1811	...	|	...
furt d.	...	1023	|	...	...	|	...	1423	...	...	...	1623	|	...	...	1923	...	|	...
ılda d.	...	1144	1147	...	...	1547	...	1544	...	...	...	1744	1747	...	...	2044	...	2147	...
Nürnberg d.	1000	|	|	...	1400	|	...	|	...	1600	...	|	|	...	...	|	2000	|	...
Würzburg d.	1056	|	|	...	1456	|	...	|	...	1656	...	|	|	...	...	|	2056	|	...
rankfurt (Main) Hbf a.	1205	1237	1244	...	1605	1644	...	1637	...	1805	...	1837	1844	...	...	2146	2205	2244	...
rankfurt (Main) Hbf d.	...	...	...	1301	...	...	...	...	1701	...	...	...	...	1901	...	...	...	2300	...
annheim d.	...	...	...	1341	...	...	...	...	1741	...	...	...	...	1941	...	...	...	2349	...
arlsruhe Hbf d.	...	...	...	|	...	...	...	...	|	...	...	...	...	|	...	...	...	0013	0054
aiserlautern d.	...	...	...	1422	...	...	...	...	1822	...	...	...	...	2022	...	...	...	...	|
aarbrücken d.	...	...	...	1501	...	...	...	...	1901	...	...	...	...	2101	...	...	...	...	|
›rbach 🏛 a.	...	...	...	|	...	...	...	...	1909	...	...	...	...	|	...	...	...	...	◧
aris Est a.	...	...	...	1650	...	...	...	...	2051t	...	...	...	...	2253	...	...	...	...	0646

– *City Night Line* 🛏 1,2 cl., ▬ 2 cl. (including ladies only compartment), ⟨2⟩ and ✕ Paris - Kehl 🏛 - Karlsruhe - München and v.v. Ⓡ Special fares apply. For direct Paris - Berlin service see Table **20**.

– *City Night Line* JOHANNES KEPLER – 🛏 1,2 cl., ▬ 2 cl. and ⟨2⟩ Basel - Frankfurt (Main) **Süd** - Fulda - Děčín 🏛 - Praha Holešovice. ⟨12⟩ Leipzig - Praha. ✕ Basel - Fulda. Ⓡ Special fares apply.

– *City Night Line* JOHANNES KEPLER – 🛏 1,2 cl., ▬ 2 cl. and ⟨2⟩ Praha Hlavní - Praha Holešovice - Děčín 🏛 - Fulda - Frankfurt (Main) **Süd** - Basel. ⟨12⟩ Praha - Leipzig. ✕ Fulda - Basel. Ⓡ Special fares apply.

– ⟨12⟩ and ✕ Berlin - Dresden - Praha and v.v.

– ⟨12⟩ and ✕ Wien - Praha - Dresden - Berlin - Stralsund. To Ostseebad Binz on dates in Table **60**.

– JAN JESENIUS – ⟨12⟩ and ✕ Hamburg - Berlin - Dresden - Praha - Budapest.

– ⟨12⟩ and ✕ Praha - Dresden - Berlin - Hamburg.

– VINDOBONA – ⟨12⟩ and ✕ Wien - Praha - Dresden - Berlin - Hamburg.

– ⟨12⟩ and ✕ Stralsund - Berlin - Dresden - Praha. From Ostseebad Binz on dates in Table **60**.

– ⟨12⟩ and 🍷 Interlaken Ost - Basel - Mannheim - Berlin and v.v.

– ①–⑤ (not Dec. 24, 25, 26, 31, Jan. 1, Mar. 21, 24, May 12).

– ①–⑥ (not Dec. 25, Jan. 1, Mar. 24, May 12).

– ①–⑥ (not Dec. 25, 26, Jan. 1, Mar. 22, 24, May 12).

Not Dec. 24, 31, Mar. 23, May 11.

g – Ⓑ (not Dec. 24, 25, 31, Mar. 21, 23, May 11).

h – Not Dec. 24, 25, 31, Mar. 23, May 11.

j – Also Dec. 25, Jan. 1, Mar. 24, May 12.

k – Ⓑ (not Dec. 23, 24, 25, 30, 31, Mar. 21, 23, May 11).

p – Not Dec. 25, Jan. 1.

q – Frankfurt (Main) **Süd**.

r – ①⑥ (also Dec. 27, Jan. 2, Mar. 21, 25, May 1, 13; not Dec. 24, 31, Mar. 22, 24, May 12).

s – Stops to set down only.

t – 2057 on ⑥ (also Dec. 24, 31, Mar. 23, May 11).

u – Stops to pick up only.

x – 2118 ①–⑤ Mar. 3 - Apr. 25 (not Mar. 24).

⊖ – *ICE-T* (tilting train) 🍷 premium fares payable.

♣ – Ⓡ (Paris - Saarbrücken and v.v.); supplement payable, 🍷.

◧ – 🏛 is Kehl.

32 LONDON - PARIS - MÜNCHEN - WIEN - BUDAPEST - BUCUREŞTI

Alternative services London - München and London - Wien - Budapest are available via Brussels (Table **21**)

train type	EC	EC	IC	EC	TGV	ICE	EC	D	☆	TGV	ICE	IC	IC	☆	TGV	☆	☆	TGV	ICE	EN
train number	**61**	**113**	**645**	**49**	**9571**	**1091**	**69**	**347**	**9004**	**9573**	**597**	**2391**	**747**	**9020**	**9575**	**9024**	**9024**	**9577**	**693**	**269**
train number/notes	✕	✕	🍷	✕		**593**	✕	✕	①–⑥		🍷	🍷	🍷			①–⑤	⑥⑦	⑧	🍷	✕
notes						🍷	**Z**	**M**				⑧ **k**						**p**		**E**
London St Pancras 10 d.	...	...	...	...	...	...	...	...	0655	...	...	...	...	1105	...	1230	1230	...	...	...
Paris Nord 10 a.	...	...	...	...	...	...	...	...	1017	...	...	...	...	1420	...	1550	1556	...	...	...
Paris Est d.	...	...	...	...	0724	...	...	...	...	1124	...	...	...	...	1524	...	...	1724	...	...
Strasbourg d.	0654	...	...	...	0947	...	...	...	...	1347	...	...	...	...	1747	...	...	1947	...	...
Kehl d.	0705	...	...	...	|	...	...	...	...	|	...	...	...	...	|	...	...	|	...	...
Baden Baden d.	0732	...	...	...	|	...	...	...	...	|	...	...	...	...	|	...	...	|	...	...
Karlsruhe Hbf d.	0806	...	...	...	1027	...	...	...	...	1427	...	...	...	...	1827	...	...	2027	...	...
Stuttgart Hbf d.	0853	...	...	...	1103	1112	...	...	...	1503	1512	1558	...	...	1919	...	...	2103	2112	...
Ulm Hbf d.	0955	...	...	...	...	1208	...	...	...	...	1608	1655	...	...	2017**p**	...	...	...	2208	...
Augsburg Hbf d.	1038	...	...	...	...	1252	...	...	...	...	1652	1741	...	...	2101**p**	...	...	...	2252	...
München Pasing a.	1107**s**	...	...	...	...	1321**s**	...	...	...	...	1721**s**	|	...	...	|	...	...	...	2321**s**	...
München Hbf a.	1117	...	...	...	...	1331	...	...	...	...	1731	1817	...	...	2140**p**	...	...	...	2331	...
München Hbf d.	...	1126	...	...	...	...	1526	...	...	...	...	1822	...	...	...	...	...	...	...	2345
Salzburg Hbf a.	...	1254	1308	...	...	...	1654	...	...	...	...	2003	2008	...	...	...	...	...	...	0121
Linz Hbf a.	...	...	1427	...	...	...	1804	...	...	...	...	...	2127	...	...	...	...	...	...	0340
St Pölten Hbf a.	...	...	1531	...	...	...	|	...	...	...	...	...	2231	...	...	...	...	...	...	0458
Wien Westbahnhof a.	...	...	1618	...	...	...	1935	...	...	...	...	...	2318	...	...	...	...	...	...	0555
Wien Westbahnhof d.	...	...	...	1752	...	...	...	1948	...	...	...	...	...	...	...	...	...	...	...	0625
Hegyeshalom a.	...	...	...	1854	...	...	...	2054	...	...	...	...	...	...	...	...	...	...	...	0727
Györ a.	...	...	...	1925	...	...	...	2125	...	...	...	...	...	...	...	...	...	...	...	0758
Budapest Keleti a.	...	...	...	2053	...	...	...	2253	...	...	...	...	...	...	...	...	...	...	...	0923
Bucureşti Nord a.	...	...	...	...	...	...	...	1402	...	...	...	...	...	...	...	...	...	...	...	2359

train type	☆	TGV	EN	IC	☆	☆	CNL	EC	EN
train number	**9030**	**2375**	**265**	**345**	**9044**	**9046**	**261**	**63**	**371**
train number/notes		**9219**	🍷	✕	⑥⑦	⑧	Ⓡ	✕	✕
notes			**A**	**C**			**G**	**S**	**R**
London St Pancras 10 d.	1404	...	...	...	1731	1800	...	...	...
Paris Nord 10 a.	1726	...	...	...	2053	2120	...	...	...
Paris Est d.	...	1924	...	...	...	...	2245**x**	...	...
Strasbourg d.	...	2143	2220	...	...	...	|	...	...
Kehl d.	...	...	2242	...	...	...	|	...	...
Baden Baden d.	...	...	2307	...	...	...	|	...	...
Karlsruhe Hbf d.	...	...	0022	...	...	...	0455**s**	...	...
Stuttgart Hbf d.	...	...	|	...	...	...	0611**s**	...	...
Ulm Hbf d.	...	...	|	...	...	...	0725**s**	...	...
Augsburg Hbf d.	...	...	|	...	...	...	0811**s**	...	...
München Pasing a.	...	...	|	...	...	...	|	...	...
München Hbf a.	...	...	0343**o**	...	...	...	0858	...	...
München Hbf d.	...	...	0345**o**	...	...	...	...	0927	...
Salzburg Hbf a.	...	...	0509	...	...	...	...	1054	...
Linz Hbf a.	...	...	0644	...	...	...	...	1204	...
St Pölten Hbf a.	...	...	0745	...	...	...	...	1256	...
Wien Westbahnhof a.	...	...	0835	...	...	...	...	1338	...
Wien Westbahnhof d.	...	...	...	0952	...	...	...	1352	...
Hegyeshalom a.	...	...	...	1054	...	...	...	1454	...
Györ a.	...	...	...	1125	...	...	...	1525	...
Budapest Keleti a.	...	...	...	1253	...	...	...	1653	1745
Bucureşti Nord a.	...	...	...	...	...	...	...	...	0843

train type	TGV	☆	EN	TGV	☆	IC	ICE	TGV	☆	☆
train number	**9578**	**9027**	**268**	**9576**	**9039**	**390**	**108**	**9574**	**9049**	**905**
train number/notes	①–⑥		✕			🍷	🍷		⑧	
notes	**q**		**K**							
Bucureşti Nord d.	...	...	0545	...	...	...	...	...	...	...
Budapest Keleti d.	...	...	2020	...	...	...	...	...	...	...
Györ d.	...	...	2147	...	...	...	...	...	...	...
Hegyeshalom d.	...	...	2216	...	...	...	...	...	...	...
Wien Westbahnhof a.	...	...	2322	...	...	...	...	...	...	...
Wien Westbahnhof d.	...	...	2345	...	...	...	...	...	...	...
St Pölten Hbf d.	...	...	0030	...	...	...	...	...	...	...
Linz Hbf d.	...	...	0146	...	...	0626**c**	...	...	...	...
Salzburg Hbf d.	...	...	0428	...	...	0753**c**	...	...	...	...
München Hbf a.	...	...	0615	...	...	0934**c**	...	...	...	...
München Hbf d.	...	...	...	0621**q**	...	0939	1023	...	...	...
München Pasing d.	...	...	...	|	...	|	1032**u**	...	...	...
Augsburg Hbf d.	...	...	...	0658**q**	...	1017	1104	...	...	...
Ulm Hbf d.	...	...	...	0743**q**	...	1105	1151	...	...	...
Stuttgart Hbf d.	0655	...	...	0855	...	1200	1247	1255	...	...
Karlsruhe Hbf d.	0732	...	...	0932	...	...	...	1332	...	...
Baden Baden d.	|	...	...	|	...	...	...	|	...	...
Kehl d.	|	...	...	|	...	...	...	|	...	...
Strasbourg a.	0811	...	...	1012	...	...	...	1411	...	...
Paris Est a.	1034	...	...	1234	...	...	...	1634	...	...
Paris Nord 10 d.	...	1213	...	...	1513	...	...	...	1743	181
London St Pancras 10 a.	...	1328	...	...	1637	...	...	...	1859	193

train type	EC	ICE	TGV	D	EC	EC	ICE	TGV	EC	EN	EC	CNL	☆	IC	EN	TGV	☆	☆
train number	**68**	**594**	**9572**	**346**	**162**	**114**	**592**	**9570**	**60**	**370**	**62**	**260**	**9011**	**344**	**264**	**2410**	**9023**	**9027**
train number/notes	✕	**1090**	⑥⑦	✕	✕	✕	🍷	①–⑤	✕	✕	✕	Ⓡ		✕	🍷	**2352**	⑥⑦	
notes	**Z**	🍷	**f**	**M**				**h**		**R**	**S**	**G**		**C**	**A**			
Bucureşti Nord d.	...	...	...	1645	...	...	...	...	...	1850	...	...	...	...	...	...	...	...
Budapest Keleti d.	...	...	...	0555	...	...	...	...	...	0717	1310	...	...	1510	...	...	...	...
Györ d.	...	...	...	0722	...	...	...	...	...	...	1437	...	...	1637	...	...	...	...
Hegyeshalom d.	...	...	...	0755	...	...	...	...	...	...	1506	...	...	1706	...	...	...	...
Wien Westbahnhof a.	...	...	...	0857	...	...	...	...	...	...	1608	...	...	1808	...	...	...	...
Wien Westbahnhof d.	0822	...	...	...	0940	...	...	...	...	...	1622	...	...	...	2035	...	...	...
St Pölten Hbf d.	|	...	...	...	1022	...	...	...	...	...	1704	...	...	...	2120	...	...	...
Linz Hbf d.	0953	...	...	...	1116	...	...	...	...	...	1754	...	...	...	2220	...	...	...
Salzburg Hbf d.	1103	...	...	...	1227	1302	...	...	...	...	1903	...	...	...	2342	...	...	...
München Hbf a.	1231	...	...	...	...	1430	...	...	...	...	2034	...	...	...	0108**o**	...	...	...
München Hbf d.	...	1423	...	...	...	...	1623	...	1642	...	...	2053	...	...	0110**o**	...	...	...
München Pasing d.	...	1431**u**	...	...	...	...	1631**u**	...	1650**u**	...	...	|	...	...	|	...	...	...
Augsburg Hbf d.	...	1504	...	...	...	...	1704	...	1722	...	...	2133**u**	...	...	|	...	...	...
Ulm Hbf d.	...	1551	...	...	...	...	1751	...	1805	...	...	2220**u**	...	...	|	...	...	...
Stuttgart Hbf d.	...	1647	1655	...	...	...	1847	1855	1911	...	...	2331**u**	...	...	|	...	...	...
Karlsruhe Hbf d.	...	...	1732	...	...	...	...	1932	2006	...	...	0054**u**	...	...	0532	...	...	...
Baden Baden d.	...	...	|	...	...	...	...	|	2024	...	...	|	...	...	0554	...	...	...
Kehl d.	...	...	|	...	...	...	...	|	2051	...	...	|	...	...	0635	...	...	...
Strasbourg a.	...	...	1811	...	...	...	...	2011	2101	...	...	|	...	...	0643	0715	...	...
Paris Est a.	...	...	2034	...	...	...	...	2231	...	...	...	0646	...	...	...	0934	...	...
Paris Nord 10 d.	...	...	...	...	...	...	...	...	...	...	...	...	0807	...	...	...	1113	1213
London St Pancras 10 a.	...	...	...	...	...	...	...	...	...	...	...	...	0934	...	...	...	1228	1328

A – ORIENT EXPRESS – [sleeper] 1,2 cl., [couchette] 2 cl. and [2] Strasbourg - Wien and v.v.

B – WIENER WALZER – [12] and ✕ Wien - Budapest and v.v. For additional cars see Table **86**.

C – AVALA – [12] and ✕ Wien - Budapest - Beograd and v.v.

E – KÁLMÁN IMRE – [sleeper] 1,2 cl., [couchette] 2 cl. and [2] München - Wien - Budapest. [sleeper] 1, 2 cl. München - Wien - Budapest (**730/47**) - Timişoara (**594**) - Bucureşti. [12] Wien - Budapest - Arad - Timişoara. ✕ Wien - Bucureşti.

G – *City Night Line* [sleeper] 1, 2 cl., [couchette] 2 cl. (including ladies only compartment), [2] and ✕ Paris - Kehl - Karlsruhe - München and v.v. Ⓡ Special fares apply.

K – KÁLMÁN IMRE – [sleeper] 1,2 cl., [couchette] 2 cl. and [2] Budapest - Wien - München. [sleeper] 1, 2 cl. Bucureşti (**591**) - Timişoara (**46/74**) - Budapest (**268**) - Wien - München. [12] Timişoara - Arad - Budapest - Wien. ✕ Bucureşti - Wien.

M – DACIA – [sleeper] 1, 2 cl., [couchette] 2 cl. and [2] Wien - Budapest - Bucureşti and v.v. [12] and ✕ Wien - Budapest and v.v. [2] and ✕ Budapest - Bucureşti and v.v.

R – *EuroNight* ISTER – [sleeper] 1, 2 cl., [couchette] 2 cl., [2] and ✕ Budapest - Bucureşti and v.v.

S – [12] and ✕ München - Wien - Budapest and v.v.

Z – MOZART – [12] and ✕ München - Wien and v.v.

c – ①–⑥ (not Dec. 25, 26, Jan. 1, Mar. 22, 24, May 12).

f – Also Dec. 25, Jan. 1, Mar. 24, May 1, 12.

k – Not Dec. 24, 25, 31, Mar. 21, 23, May 11.

h – Not Dec. 25, Jan. 1, Mar. 24, May 1, 12.

o – München **Ost**.

p – Not Dec. 24, 31, Mar. 23, May 11.

q – Not Dec. 25, Jan. 1, Mar. 24, May 12.

s – Calls to set down only.

u – Stops to pick up only.

x – 2118 ①–⑤ Mar. 3 - Apr. 25 (not Mar. 24).

☆ – Eurostar train. Ⓡ, ✕. Minimum check-in time 3 minutes. Special fares payable. Valid Dec. 9, 20 - July 5, 2008; additional Eurostar services are available, see Table **10**.

♣ – Ⓡ (Paris - Saarbrücken and v.v.); supplement payable, 🍷.

TGV – Ⓡ, supplement payable, 🍷.

LONDON, PARIS and BRUSSELS - BASEL - ZÜRICH, INTERLAKEN, BRIG and MILANO 40

For Brussels - Köln - Basel - Milano services see Table **43**.

train type/number	*TGV*	*ICE*	*IC*	*IC*	*TGV*	*IC*	*IC*	*ICN*	*EC*	*IC*	*IC*	*TGV*	*IR*	*TGV*	*ICE*	*ICN*	*IR*	*CIS*	*CIS*	*EC*	*IR*	*IC*		*ICN*	*ICN*	*EC*
train number	**9201**	**271**	**569**	**1069**	**9203**	**969**	**820**	**620**	**115**	**771**	**571**	**9211**	**775**	**9221**	**375**	**1622**	**2173**	**155**	**47**	**91**	**779**	**1077**		**628**	**1528**	**119**
notes	♥ h ①–⑤	🍷	🍷	🍷	♥ ⑥ t	🍴	🍴	🍴	🍷 [R] ¶		🍷	♥ b	🍷	♥ ⑥ f	🍷	🍴		[R] ⊕ 🍴	[R] ⊕ 🍴	V	🍷	🍷		🍴	🍴	🍷 [R] ¶
London St Pancras d.	...	...	...	...	...	...	...	...	...	...	...	...	...	...	...	...	...	...	...	...	...	...	...	...	...	...
Paris Nord a.	...	...	...	...	...	...	...	...	...	...	...	...	...	...	...	...	...	...	...	...	...	...	...	...	...	...
Paris Est d.	0624	...	...	...	0654	...	...	...	...	...	...	0824	...	0824	...	...	...	...	...	...	...	...	...	...	...	...
Brussels Midi/Zuid § d.	|	...	...	...	|	...	...	...	...	...	...	|	...	|	...	...	...	...	...	0733	...	...	...	...	...	...
Namur § d.	|	...	...	...	|	...	...	...	...	...	...	|	...	|	...	...	...	...	...	0842	...	...	...	...	...	...
Luxembourg 🏛 § d.	|	...	...	...	|	...	...	...	...	...	...	|	...	|	...	...	...	...	...	1046	...	...	...	...	...	...
Thionville d.	|	...	...	...	|	...	...	...	...	...	...	|	...	|	...	...	...	...	...	1111	...	...	...	...	...	...
Metz d.	|	...	...	...	|	...	...	...	...	...	...	|	...	|	...	...	...	...	...	1132	...	...	...	...	...	...
Strasbourg d.	0847	...	...	...	0917	...	...	...	...	...	...	1047	...	1047	...	...	...	...	...	1253	...	...	...	...	...	...
Mulhouse d.	0937	...	...	...	1006	...	...	...	...	...	...	1132	...	1132	...	...	...	...	...	1356	...	...	...	...	...	...
Basel SNCF 🏛 ▷ a.	0956	...	...	...	1025	...	...	...	...	...	...	1150	...	1150	...	...	...	...	...	1420	...	...	...	...	...	...
Basel SBB ▷ d.	...	1007	1022	1030	▬	1101	...	1103	1104	1107	1122	1207	...	1207	1201	1203	1204	...	1230	1440	...	1430	...	1503	...	1504
Zürich HB a.	...	1100	1126	|	...	|	...	|	|	1200	1226	1300	1312	1300	|	|	|	...	|	1540	1612	|	...	|	...	|
Sargans a.	...	...	1232	|	...	|	...	|	|	▬	1332	...	1419	1403	|	|	|	...	|	...	1719	|	...	|	...	|
Landquart a.	...	...	1241	|	...	|	...	|	|	...	1341	...	1432	1413	|	|	|	...	|	...	1732	|	...	|	...	|
Davos Platz a.	...	...	*1355*	|	...	|	...	|	|	...	*1455*	...	*1555*	|	|	|	|	...	|	...	*1855*	|	...	|	...	|
Chur a.	...	...	1252	|	...	|	...	|	|	...	1352	...	1443	1425	|	|	|	...	|	...	1743	|	...	|	...	|
St Moritz a.	...	...	*1458*	|	...	|	...	|	|	...	*1558*	...	*1658*	...	|	|	|	...	|	...	*1958*	|	...	|	...	|
Luzern a.	...	...	...	|	...	|	...	|	1214	...	...	...	...	...	|	|	1314	...	|	...	...	|	...	|	...	1614
Arth Goldau a.	...	...	...	|	...	|	...	|	1246	...	...	...	...	...	|	|	1346	1350	|	...	...	|	...	|	...	1646
Bellinzona a.	...	...	...	|	...	|	...	|	1436	...	...	...	...	...	|	|	1558	1524	|	...	...	|	...	|	...	1836
Locarno a.	...	...	...	|	...	|	...	|	*1506*	...	...	...	...	...	|	|	1619	|	|	...	...	|	...	|	...	|
Lugano a.	...	...	...	|	...	|	...	|	1503	...	...	...	...	...	|	|	▬	1547	|	...	...	|	...	|	...	1903
Chiasso 🏛 a.	...	...	...	|	...	|	...	|	1528	...	...	...	...	...	|	|	...	|	|	...	...	|	...	|	...	1928
Bern a.	...	...	...	1127	...	1156	1207	|	|	...	...	...	...	...	1256	|	...	|	1327	...	...	1527	...	|	...	|
Thun a.	...	...	...	1152	...	1221	1224	|	|	...	...	...	...	...	1321	|	...	|	1352	...	...	1552	...	|	...	|
Spiez a.	...	...	...	1202	1225	1231	1234	|	|	*ICN*	...	...	...	...	1331	|	*ICN*	|	1402	...	...	1602	1605	|	...	|
Interlaken West a.	...	...	...	|	1244	1251	|	|	|	**1520**	...	...	...	...	1351	|	**522**	|	|	...	...	|	1624	|	...	|
Interlaken Ost a.	...	...	...	|	1250	1257	|	|	|	🍴	...	...	...	...	1357	|	🍴	|	|	...	...	|	1629	|	...	|
Biel/Bienne a.	...	...	...	|	▬	...	|	1210	|	1216	...	...	...	...	...	1310	1319	|	|	...	...	|	▬	1610	1616	|
Neuchâtel a.	...	...	...	|	*EC*	...	|	1235	|	1232	...	...	...	...	...	1332	1335	|	|	...	...	|	*EC*	1635	1632	|
Lausanne a.	...	...	...	|	**125**	...	|	|	|	1315	...	...	...	...	...	1415	|	|	|	...	...	|	**127**	|	1715	|
Genève a.	...	...	...	|	[R] ¶	...	|	1346	|	...	...	...	...	...	...	...	1446	|	|	...	...	|	[R] ¶	1746	...	|
Brig a.	...	...	...	1240	1320	...	1311	...	|	...	...	...	...	...	...	...	...	|	1440	...	...	1640	1720	...	...	|
Como San Giovanni a.	...	...	...	...	◧	...	...	...	1552	...	...	...	...	...	...	...	...	|	◧	...	...	...	◧	...	...	1952
Milano a.	...	...	...	...	1535	...	...	...	1635	...	...	...	...	...	...	...	...	1642	1640	...	...	...	1935	...	...	2035

train type/number	☆	*TGV*	*IC*	*ICN*	*IR*	*EC*	*EC*	*IC*	☆	*EC*	*ICE*	*ICN*	*IR*	*EC*	*IR*	☆	*TGV*	*IC*	*IC*	*IC*	*IR*	*ICN*	☆	*TGV*	☆	*EC*
train number	**9006**	**9213**	**979**	**1630**	**2181**	**179**	**101**	**1081**	**9114**	**97**	**279**	**1640**	**2191**	**97**	**2293**	**9024**	**9217**	**999**	**3191**	**993**	**795**	**1644**	**9030**	**9219**	**9132**	**295**
notes	①–⑥	♥		🍴		🍷 [R] ¶	w 🍴	🍷	①–⑥	A	🍴	🍴		A			♥ ⑧							♥ ⑥		⑧ C
London St Pancras d.	0730	...	...	...	...	...	...	...	0805	...	...	...	...	...	...	1230	...	...	...	...	...	...	1404	...	1257	...
Paris Nord a.	1056	...	...	...	...	...	...	...	|	...	...	...	...	...	...	1550x	...	...	...	...	...	...	1726	...	|	...
Paris Est d.	...	1224	...	...	...	...	...	...	|	...	...	...	...	...	...	▬	1754	...	...	...	...	...	▬	1924	|	...
Brussels Midi/Zuid § d.	...	|	...	...	...	...	...	...	1056	1309	...	...	...	...	...	...	|	...	...	...	...	...	...	|	1603	1727
Namur § d.	...	|	...	...	...	...	...	...	▬	1414	...	...	...	...	...	...	|	...	...	...	...	...	...	|	▬	1835
Luxembourg 🏛 § d.	...	|	...	...	...	...	...	...	...	1603	...	...	...	...	...	...	|	...	...	...	...	...	...	|	...	2026
Thionville d.	...	|	...	...	...	...	...	...	...	1632	...	...	...	...	...	...	|	...	...	...	...	...	...	|	...	2051
Metz d.	...	|	...	...	...	...	...	...	*CIS*	1653	...	...	...	...	...	...	|	...	...	...	...	...	...	|	...	2115
Strasbourg d.	...	1447	...	...	...	...	...	...	**51**	1823	...	...	...	...	...	...	2015	...	...	...	...	...	...	2147	...	2253
Mulhouse d.	...	1533	...	...	...	...	...	...	[R] ⊕	1924	...	...	...	←	...	*IC*	2058	...	...	...	...	...	...	2237	*IC*	2351
Basel SNCF 🏛 ▷ a.	...	1551	...	...	...	...	...	...	🍴	1948	...	...	...	1948	...	**1091**	2115	...	...	...	...	...	...	2255	**995**	0013
Basel SBB ▷ d.	...	1607c	1601	1603	1604	...	1622	1630	1730	2007	2001	2003	2004	2007	...	2030	2120	2130	...	2201	...	2203	...	2301	2305	...
Zürich HB a.	...	1700c	|	|	|	...	1726	|	|	→	|	|	|	2100	2209	|	2214	|	...	|	2312	|	...	2356	|	...
Sargans a.	...	...	|	|	|	...	1832	|	|	...	|	|	|	2219	|	|	...	|	...	|	0024	|	...	...	|	...
Landquart a.	...	...	|	|	|	...	1841	|	|	...	|	|	|	2234	|	|	...	|	...	|	0039	|	...	...	|	...
Davos Platz a.	...	...	|	|	|	...	*1955*	|	|	...	|	|	|	|	|	|	...	|	...	|	|	|	...	...	|	...
Chur a.	...	...	|	|	|	...	1852	|	|	...	|	|	|	2245	|	|	...	|	...	|	0049	|	...	...	|	...
St Moritz a.	...	...	|	|	|	...	*2058*	|	|	...	|	|	|	...	|	|	...	|	...	|	...	|	...	...	|	...
Luzern a.	...	...	|	|	1714	...	...	|	|	...	|	|	2114	...	|	|	...	|	...	|	...	|	...	...	|	...
Arth Goldau a.	...	...	|	|	1746	1752	...	|	|	...	|	|	2146	...	2248	|	...	|	...	|	...	|	...	...	|	...
Bellinzona a.	...	...	|	|	1958	1936	...	|	|	...	|	|	▬	...	0037	|	...	|	...	|	...	|	...	...	|	...
Locarno a.	...	...	|	|	2019	|	...	|	|	...	|	|	...	...	*0106*	|	...	|	...	|	...	|	...	...	|	...
Lugano a.	...	...	|	|	▬	2003	...	|	|	...	|	|	...	...	0112	|	...	|	...	|	...	|	...	...	|	...
Chiasso 🏛 a.	...	...	|	|	...	2028	...	|	|	...	|	|	...	...	0146	|	...	|	...	|	...	|	...	...	|	...
Bern a.	...	...	1656	|	...	|	...	1727	1827	...	2056	|	...	...	...	2127	...	2227	2239	2256	...	|	...	...	2359	...
Thun a.	...	...	1721	|	...	|	...	1752	1852	...	2121	|	...	...	...	2152	...	...	2256	2326	...	|	...	...	...	...
Spiez a.	...	...	1731	|	*ICN*	|	...	1802	1902	...	2131	|	*ICN*	...	...	2202	...	...	2306	2336	...	|	*ICN*	...	...	...
Interlaken West a.	...	...	1751	|	**530**	|	...	|	|	...	2149	|	**1540**	...	...	|	...	...	|	2357	...	|	**1544**	...	...	...
Interlaken Ost a.	...	...	1757	|	🍴	|	...	|	|	...	2155	|	🍴	...	...	|	...	...	|	0003	...	|	🍴	...	...	...
Biel/Bienne a.	...	...	...	1710	1719	|	...	|	|	...	...	2110	2116	...	...	|	...	...	|	...	...	2310	2316	...	...	...
Neuchâtel a.	...	...	...	1732	1735	|	...	|	|	...	...	...	2132	...	...	|	...	...	|	...	...	...	2332	...	...	...
Lausanne a.	...	...	...	1815	|	|	...	|	|	...	...	...	2215	...	...	|	...	...	|	...	...	...	0015	...	...	...
Genève a.	...	...	...	...	1846	|	...	|	|	...	...	...	...	...	...	|	...	...	|	...	...	...	...	...	...	...
Brig a.	...	...	...	...	...	|	...	1840	1940	...	...	...	...	...	...	2239v	...	...	0012	...	...	...	...	...	...	...
Como San Giovanni a.	...	...	...	...	...	2052	...	...	◧	...	...	...	...	...	...	...	...	...	...	...	...	...	...	...	...	...
Milano a.	...	...	...	...	...	2135	...	...	2135	...	...	...	...	...	...	...	...	...	...	...	...	...	...	...	...	...

LONDON - LILLE - STRASBOURG - BASEL

			TGV	*TGV*			☆	*TGV*					☆	*TGV*	4					
			5400	**9211**			**9110**	**5402**	①–⑥	⑦			**9138**	**5416**	**295**					
							①–⑥		g	k					⑧					
London St Pancras d.	...	...	...	...	...	...	0700	...	...	...	...	...	1434	...	...	...	...	...	...	...
Lille Europe d.	...	...	0652	...	...	...	0924	1121	...	...	...	...	1654	1858	...	...	...	...	...	...
Strasbourg d.	...	...	1010	1047	...	...	...	1517	1553	1553	...	...	...	2217	2253	...	...	...	...	...
Basel SNCF a.	...	...	...	1150	...	...	...	...	1709	1716	...	...	...	...	0013	...	...	...	...	...

A – IRIS – (12) Brussels - Basel - Zürich - Chur. 🍷 Strasbourg - Basel.
C – JEAN MONNET – (12) Brussels - Basel.
V – VAUBAN – (12) Brussels - Basel - Zürich. 🍷 Metz - Basel.
b – On ⑦ **9211** departs Mulhouse 1138 and arrives Basel 1156. Connections at Basel to Trains **375, 1622, 2173** do not apply. Additional connections available 60 minutes later.
c – On ⑥ depart Basel 1558, arrive Zürich 1707.
f – Dec. 15 - Mar. 29.
g – Not Dec. 26, Mar. 21.
h – Not May 1, 8.
k – Also Dec. 26, Mar. 21.
t – Also May 1, 8.

v – 2301 on ⑦ (also Dec. 25, Jan. 1, Mar. 21, 24).
w – On ⑥ runs as *EC***103**, depart Basel 1607, arrive Zürich 1700, Sargans 1819, Landquart 1832, Chur 1843.
x – 6 minutes later on ⑥⑦.
◧ – 🏛 between Brig and Milano is Domodossola. Ticket point is **Iselle**.
§ – Additional services run Brussels - Namur - Luxembourg. (Table **430**).
¶ – Supplement payable in Italy (except with international tickets). *IC* in Italy.
♥ – *TGV Lyria* service. [R] 🍷 special fares payable.

⊕ – **ETR 470** *Cisalpino*. [R] and supplement payable for international journeys. [R] and *IC* supplement payable for internal journeys within Italy.
☆ – Eurostar train. [R] 🍴 Minimum check-in time 30 minutes. Special fares payable. Valid Dec. 9, 2007 - July 5, 2008. See Tables **10** and **12**.
▷ – Trains arrive at SNCF (French) platforms and depart from SBB (Swiss) platforms. Connections at Basel are not guaranteed.

OTHER TRAIN NAMES FOR TABLE 82:

EC **119** – CISALPINO TIZIANO
EC **115** – CISALPINO MEDIOLANUM
EC **125** – CISALPINO LEMANO
EC **127** – CISALPINO VALLESE
EC **179** – CISALPINO INSUBRIA

40 LONDON, PARIS and BRUSSELS - BASEL - ZÜRICH, INTERLAKEN, BRIG and MILANO

For Milano - Basel - Köln - Brussels services see Table 43.

train type	EC	ICE	ICN	ICN	IR	TGV		IR	ICN	ICN	IC	IC	IC	TGV	☆	CIS	IC	IC		IC	ICN	ICN	EC	☆	☆
train number	296	278	1511	611	758	9212		2166	1517	617	817	1066	566	9204	9043	40	968	570		672	523	1623	90	9165	9163
notes	B Ⓑ		✕	✕	🍷	♥	2		✕	✕		✕	🍷	♥		[R] ⊕ ✕		🍷	2		✕	✕	V	⑦	①–⑥
Milano d.	...	...	...	...	...	...	...	...	...	...	...	...	...	...	...	0725	...	...	...	...	...	...	...	...	...
Como San Giovanni d.	...	...	...	...	...	...	...	...	...	...	...	...	...	...	...	◧	...	...	...	...	...	...	...	...	...
Brig d.	...	...	...	...	...	...	...	...	...	...	0749	...	...	...	...	0920	...	...	...	...	...	...	...	...	...
Genève d.	...	...	...	...	...	...	...	...	...	0714	|	...	...	...	...	|	...	...	...	...	1014	...	...	...	...
Lausanne d.	...	...	0539	...	...	...	...	...	0745	|	|	...	...	...	...	|	...	...	...	...	|	1045	...	...	...
Neuchâtel d.	...	...	0624	...	...	...	...	...	0827	0824	|	...	...	...	...	|	...	...	...	...	1124	1127	...	...	...
Biel/Bienne d.	...	...	0640	0650	...	...	...	...	0843	0850	|	...	...	...	...	|	...	...	...	...	1140	1150	...	...	...
Interlaken Ost d.	...	0601	...	|	...	...	...	...	...	|	|	0831	...	...	...	|	1101	...	...	...	...	|	...	...	...
Interlaken West d.	...	0606	...	|	...	...	...	...	...	|	|	0836	...	...	...	|	1106	...	...	...	...	|	...	...	...
Spiez d.	...	0623	...	|	...	...	...	...	...	|	0825	0854	...	...	...	0954	1123	...	...	...	...	|	...	...	...
Thun d.	...	0634	...	|	...	...	...	...	...	|	0837	0905	...	...	...	1005	1134	...	...	...	...	|	...	...	...
Bern d.	...	0704	...	|	...	...	...	...	...	|	0855	0934	...	...	...	1034	1204	...	...	...	...	|	...	...	...
Chiasso 🏛 d.	...	|	...	|	...	...	...	...	...	|	...	|	...	...	...	|	|	...	...	0831	...	|	...	...	...
Lugano d.	...	|	...	|	...	...	...	...	...	|	...	|	...	...	...	|	|	...	...	0855	...	|	...	...	...
Locarno d.	...	|	...	|	...	...	0523	...	...	|	...	|	...	...	...	|	|	...	0853	|	...	|	...	...	...
Bellinzona d.	...	|	...	|	...	...	0548	0600	...	|	...	|	...	...	...	|	|	...	0918	0923	...	|	...	...	...
Arth Goldau d.	...	|	...	|	...	...	▬	0812	...	|	...	|	...	...	...	|	|	...	...	1112	...	|	...	...	...
Luzern d.	...	|	...	|	...	...	...	0845	...	|	...	|	...	...	...	|	|	...	...	1145	...	|	...	...	...
St Moritz d.	...	|	...	|	...	...	...	|	...	|	...	|	...	...	...	|	|	*0802*	...	|	...	|	...	...	...
Chur d.	...	|	...	|	0513	...	...	|	...	|	...	|	0809	...	...	|	|	1009	...	|	...	|	...	...	...
Davos Platz d.	...	|	...	|	|	...	...	|	...	|	...	|	*0702*	...	...	|	|	*0902*	...	|	...	|	...	...	...
Landquart d.	...	|	...	|	0523	...	...	|	...	|	...	|	0819	...	...	|	|	1019	...	|	...	|	...	...	...
Sargans d.	...	|	...	|	0539	...	...	|	...	|	...	|	0828	...	...	|	|	1028	...	|	...	|	...	...	...
Zürich HB d.	...	|	...	|	0647	0702	...	|	...	|	...	|	0934	...	...	|	|	1134	...	|	...	|	1136	...	...
Basel SBB ◁ a.	...	0754	...	0753	...	0756	...	0951	...	0953	...	1029	1038	...	...	1129	1254	1238	...	1251	...	1253	1248	...	...
Basel SNCF 🏛 ◁ d.	0648	▬	...	...	...	0804	...	...	...	...	...	...	...	1101	...	...	...	...	...	...	...	...	1307	...	...
Mulhouse a.	0710	...	...	...	...	0823	...	...	...	...	...	...	...	1120	...	...	...	...	...	...	...	...	1332	...	...
Strasbourg a.	0803	...	...	...	...	0910	...	...	...	...	...	...	...	1210	...	...	...	...	...	...	...	...	1433	...	...
Metz a.	0926	...	...	...	...	|	...	...	...	...	...	...	...	|	...	...	...	...	...	...	...	...	1554	...	...
Thionville a.	0950	...	...	...	...	|	...	...	...	...	...	...	...	|	...	...	...	...	...	...	...	...	1615	...	...
Luxembourg 🏛 § a.	1014	☆	...	...	...	|	...	...	...	...	...	...	...	|	...	...	...	...	...	...	...	...	1645	...	...
Namur § a.	1218	**9141**	...	...	...	|	...	...	...	...	...	...	...	|	...	...	...	...	...	...	...	...	1846	...	...
Brussels Midi/Zuid § a.	1327	1459	...	...	...	|	☆	...	...	...	...	...	...	|	...	...	...	...	...	...	...	...	1951	2059	2102
Paris Est a.	...	|	...	...	...	1134	**9031**	...	...	...	...	...	...	1434	...	...	...	...	...	...	...	...	...	|	|
Paris Nord d.	...	|	...	...	...	...	1301	...	...	...	...	...	...	...	1613	...	...	...	...	...	...	...	...	|	|
London St Pancras a.	...	1556	...	...	...	...	1434	...	...	...	...	...	...	...	1734	...	...	...	...	...	...	...	...	2203	2204

train type	IC	IC		EC	ICN	ICN	IC	TGV	☆	CIS	EC	CIS	IR	ICN	ICN	IC	EC	IC	IC	EC	ICN	ICN	IC	TGV	TGV
train number	827	974		106	527	1627	574	9216	9059	44	96	154	2178	1529	629	978	96	837	986	110	537	1637	582	9218	9222
notes		🍷		[R] 🍷	✕	✕	🍷	♥		[R] ⊕ ✕	A	[R] ⊕ ✕		✕	✕	🍷	A		🍷	[R] 🍷	✕	✕	🍷	♥	♥ ⑥j
Milano d.	...	...	...	0925	...	...	...	...	...	1120	...	1118	...	...	...	...	...	...	...	1325	...	...	...	...	...
Como San Giovanni d.	...	...	...	1007	...	...	...	...	...	◧	...	|	...	...	...	...	...	...	...	1407	...	...	...	...	...
Brig d.	1249	...	...	|	...	...	...	...	...	1320	...	|	...	...	...	...	...	1649	...	|	...	...	...	...	...
Genève d.	|	...	...	|	1214	...	...	...	...	|	...	|	...	...	1314	...	...	|	...	|	1614	...	...	...	...
Lausanne d.	|	...	...	|	|	1245	...	...	...	|	...	|	...	1345	|	...	...	|	...	|	|	1645	...	...	...
Neuchâtel d.	|	...	...	|	1324	1327	...	...	...	|	...	|	...	1427	1424	...	...	|	...	|	1724	1727	...	...	...
Biel/Bienne d.	|	...	...	|	1340	1350	...	...	...	|	...	|	...	1444	1450	...	...	|	...	|	1740	1750	...	...	...
Interlaken Ost d.	|	1301	...	|	...	|	...	...	...	|	...	|	...	...	|	1401	...	|	1701	|	...	|	...	...	...
Interlaken West d.	|	1306	...	|	...	|	...	...	...	|	...	|	...	...	|	1406	...	|	1706	|	...	|	...	...	...
Spiez d.	1325	1323	...	|	...	|	...	...	...	1354	...	|	...	...	|	1423	...	1725	1723	|	...	|	...	...	...
Thun d.	1337	1334	...	|	...	|	...	...	...	1405	...	|	...	...	|	1434	...	1737	1734	|	...	|	...	...	...
Bern d.	1355	1404	...	|	...	|	...	...	...	1434	...	|	...	...	|	1504	...	1755	1804	|	...	|	...	...	...
Chiasso 🏛 d.	...	|	...	1031	...	|	...	...	...	|	...	|	...	...	|	|	...	...	|	1431	...	|	...	...	...
Lugano d.	...	|	...	1055	...	|	...	...	...	|	...	1209	...	...	|	|	...	...	|	1455	...	|	...	...	...
Locarno d.	...	|	1053	|	...	|	...	...	...	|	...	|	1139	...	|	|	...	...	|	*1453*	...	|	...	...	...
Bellinzona d.	...	|	1118	1123	...	|	...	...	...	|	...	1234	1200	...	|	|	...	...	|	1523	...	|	...	...	...
Arth Goldau d.	...	|	...	1312	...	|	...	...	...	|	...	1408	1412	...	|	|	...	...	|	1712	...	|	...	...	...
Luzern d.	...	|	...	1345	...	|	...	...	...	|	...	...	1445	...	|	|	...	...	|	1745	...	|	...	...	...
St Moritz d.	...	|	...	|	...	|	*1002*	...	...	|	*1102*	...	|	...	|	|	...	...	|	|	...	|	*1402*	...	...
Chur d.	...	|	...	|	...	|	1209	...	...	|	1309	...	|	...	|	|	...	...	|	|	...	|	1609	...	1633
Davos Platz d.	...	|	...	|	...	|	*1102*	...	...	|	*1202*	...	|	...	|	|	...	...	|	|	...	|	*1502*	...	|
Landquart d.	...	|	...	|	...	|	1219	...	...	|	1319	...	|	...	|	|	...	...	|	|	...	|	1619	...	1645
Sargans d.	...	|	...	|	...	|	1228	...	...	|	1328	...	|	...	|	|	...	...	|	|	...	|	1628	...	1655
Zürich HB d.	...	|	...	|	...	|	1323	1402	...	|	1434	...	|	...	|	|	←	...	|	|	...	|	1747	1802	1802
Basel SBB ◁ a.	...	1454	...	1451	...	1453	...	1456	...	1529	1538	...	1551	...	1553	1554	1538	...	1854	1851	...	1853	...	1856	1856
Basel SNCF 🏛 ◁ d.	...	...	...	...	...	...	...	1504	...	...	1607	...	...	...	...	...	1607	...	...	...	...	...	...	1904	1904
Mulhouse a.	...	...	...	...	...	...	...	1523	...	...	→	...	...	...	...	...	1631	...	...	...	...	...	...	1922	1923
Strasbourg a.	...	...	...	...	...	...	...	1610	...	...	...	...	...	...	...	...	1732	...	...	...	...	...	...	2007	2012
Metz a.	...	...	...	...	...	...	...	|	...	...	...	...	...	...	...	...	1853	...	...	...	...	...	...	|	|
Thionville a.	...	...	...	...	...	...	...	|	...	...	...	...	...	...	...	...	1912	...	...	...	...	...	...	|	|
Luxembourg 🏛 § a.	...	...	...	...	...	...	...	|	...	...	...	...	...	...	...	...	1936	...	...	...	...	...	...	|	|
Namur § a.	...	...	...	...	...	...	...	|	...	...	...	...	...	...	...	...	2126	...	...	...	...	...	...	|	|
Brussels Midi/Zuid § a.	...	...	...	...	...	...	...	|	...	...	...	...	...	...	...	...	2233	...	...	...	...	...	...	|	|
Paris Est a.	...	...	...	...	...	...	...	1834	...	...	...	...	...	...	...	...	...	...	...	...	...	...	...	2234	2234
Paris Nord d.	...	...	...	...	...	...	...	...	2013	...	...	...	...	...	...	...	...	...	...	...	...	...	...	...	...
London St Pancras a.	...	...	...	...	...	...	...	...	2134z	...	...	...	...	...	...	...	...	...	...	...	...	...	...	...	...

BASEL - STRASBOURG - LILLE - LONDON

		TGV	☆	TGV	☆					TGV	☆	☆					TGV			
		5420	9015	5420	9121			⑦	①–⑥	5422	9149	9149			①–⑤	⑥⑦	5426			
		D	①–⑤	E	⑥⑦			f	w		①–⑤	⑥⑦			w	f				
Basel SNCF d.	...	...	...	...	...	...	...	1004	1018	...	...	...	...	...	1718	1718	...	...	...	...
Strasbourg d.	...	0611	...	0620	...	...	...	1134	1135	1206	...	...	...	...	1833	1842	1900	...	...	...
Lille Europe d.	...	0946	1009	0946	1035	...	...	...	...	1559	1738	1738	...	...	...	...	2223	...	...	...
London St Pancras a.	...	...	1038	...	1101	...	...	...	...	...	1758	1803	...	...	...	...	...	...	...	...

A – IRIS – 🚃12 Chur - Zürich - Basel - Brussels. 🍷 Chur - Zürich and 🍷 Basel - Metz.
B – JEAN MONNET – 🚃12 Basel - Brussels. 🍷 Strasbourg - Metz.
C – ⑥ (①–⑥ Dec. 10 - Mar. 23 and Apr. 7 - June 11) also Mar. 24.
D – ①–⑥ (not Dec. 25, Jan. 1, Mar. 24, May 12).
E – ⑦ (also Dec. 25, Jan. 1, Mar. 24, May 12).
V – VAUBAN – 🚃12 Zürich - Basel - Brussels.

f – Also Dec 26, Mar. 21.
j – Dec. 15 - Mar. 29.
w – Not Dec 26, Mar. 21.
z – 8 minutes later on ⑥⑦.

♥ – *TGV Lyria* service. [R] 🍷 special fares payable.
◧ – 🏛 between Brig and Milano is Domodossola. Ticket point is **Iselle**.

§ – Additional services run Luxembourg - Namur - Brussels. (Table **430**).
¶ – Supplement payable in Italy (except with international tickets).
☆ – Eurostar train. [R] ✕ Minimum check-in time 30 minutes. Special fares payable. See Tables **10** and **12**. Valid Dec. 9, 2007 - July 5, 2008.
⊕ – **ETR 470** *Cisalpino*. [R] and supplement payable for international journeys. [R] and *IC* supplement payable for internal journeys within Italy.
◁ – Trains arrive at SBB (Swiss) platforms and depart from SNCF (French) platforms. Connections at Basel are not guaranteed.

OTHER TRAIN NAMES:

EC **106** – CISALPINO TIZIANO
EC **110** – CISALPINO TICINO

LONDON and PARIS - BERN, LAUSANNE and BRIG — 42

train type	TGV	TGV	IR	IR	TGV	ICE	☆	☆	TGV	TGV	IR	☆	TGV	IR	EC	☆	TGV	TGV	IR	IR	TGV	ICE	TGV	☆	TGV	EN
train number	9261	9261	1725	1427	9281	375	9010	9010	9269	9269 9267	1737	9014	9271	1739	129	9020	9273	9273	1743	1445	9285	279	9287	9024	9277	311
notes	♥ 🍷	♥ 🍷 B			♥ 🍷 ⑧f	🍷	[R] 🍴 ⑦	[R] 🍴 ①–⑥	♥ 🍷	A♥		[R] 🍴	♥ 🍷 D		🍷 § m	[R] 🍴	♥ 🍷	♥ 🍷 C			♥ 🍷 ⑤j	🍷	♥ 🍷 H	[R] 🍴	♥ 🍷	
ondon St Pancras 10 d.	...	...	...	...	...	...	0825	0832	...	...	...	0926	...	...	...	1105	...	...	...	...	...	...	...	1230	...	...
aris Nord 10 a.	...	...	...	...	...	...	1147	1147	...	...	...	1247	...	...	...	1420	...	...	...	...	...	...	...	1550x	...	...
aris Gare de Lyon d.	0758	0758	...	...	0758	...	...	...	1258	1258	...	▬	1410	...	...	▬	1558	1558	...	...	1558	...	1658	▬	1758	...
ijon d.	0938	0938	...	...	0938	...	...	...	1440	1440	...	...	1550	...	...	...	1738	1738	...	...	1738	...	1846	...	1938	...
rasne a.	1056	1056	...	...	1056	...	...	...	1558	1558	...	...	1704	...	...	...	1827	1827	...	...	1827	...	1927	IC	2056	...
Pontarlier 🛃 a.	|	|	...	...	1110	...	...	...	|	|	...	...	|	...	...	...	|	|	...	...	1911	...	2021	3391	|	...
Neuchâtel a.	|	|	...	...	1157	...	...	...	|	|	...	...	|	...	...	...	|	|	...	...	1957	...	2107		|	...
Bern a.	|	|	...	...	1243	1304	...	...	|	|	...	...	|	...	...	...	|	|	...	...	2034	2104	2141	2204	|	...
Thun a.	|	|	...	...	...	1321	...	...	|	|	...	...	|	...	...	...	|	|	...	...	▬	2121	...	2221	|	...
Spiez a.	|	|	...	...	...	1331	...	...	|	|	...	...	|	...	...	...	|	|	...	...	...	2131	...	2231	|	...
Interlaken West a.	|	|	...	...	...	1351	...	...	|	|	...	...	|	...	...	...	|	|	...	...	...	2149	...	2249	|	...
Interlaken Ost a.	|	|	...	...	...	1357	...	...	|	|	...	IR	|	...	...	IR	|	|	...	...	...	2155	...	2255	|	...
allorbe 🛃 a.	1117	1117	...	...	...	...	...	...	1616	1616	...	1439	1722	...	...	1441	1917	1917	...	...	...	...	...	...	2114	...
ausanne a.	1152	1152	...	...	...	...	...	...	1652	1652	...		1758	...	...		1952	1952	...	...	...	...	...	...	2152	...
ausanne d.	...	1157	1220	1245	...	...	...	...	...	1657	1720	1745	...	1820	1846	1850	...	1957	2020	2045	...	...	...	...	...	2220
lontreux a.	...	1214	1239	1304	...	...	...	...	...	1714	1739	1804	...	1839	1904	1909	...	2014	2039	2104	...	...	...	...	...	2239
igle a.	...	1226	1250	1315	...	...	...	...	...	1727	1750	1815	...	1850	|	1920	...	2026	2050	2115	...	...	...	...	...	2250
ex a.	...	|	|	1323	...	...	...	...	...	...	|	1823	...	|	|	1928	...	|	2058	2123	...	...	...	...	...	2258
t Maurice a.	...	|	|	1327	...	...	...	...	...	...	|	1827	...	|	|	1931	...	|	2102	2127	...	...	...	...	...	2302
lartigny a.	...	1248	1307	▬	...	...	...	...	...	...	1807	▬	...	1907	|	▬	...	2044	2112	2127	...	...	...	...	...	2312
ion a.	...	1303	1322	...	...	...	...	...	...	...	1822	...	...	1922	1941	...	...	2100	2127	2153	...	...	...	...	...	2327
ierre a.	...	1315	1334	...	...	...	...	...	...	...	1834	...	...	1934	1952	...	...	2113	...	2205	...	...	...	...	...	2339
isp a.	...	1336	1352	1410	...	...	...	...	...	...	1852	1910	...	1952	|	2010	...	2136	...	2223	2240	...	...	...	...	2357
Zermatt a.	...	|	|	1514	...	...	...	...	...	...	|	2014	...	|	|	2114	...	|	...	|	2344	...	...	...	...	|
rig a.	...	1345	1402	...	...	...	...	...	...	...	1903	...	...	2002	2014	...	...	2147	...	2231	...	...	...	...	...	0005

train type	IR	IR	TGV		IR	TGV	IC	TGV	☆	EC		IR	TGV	TGV	☆		IR	TGV	IC	TGV	EC		IR	TGV	TGV	TGV
train number	1404	1706	9260		316	9264	956	9284	9039	120		1720	9268	9268	9053		1730	9272	982	9288	124		1432	9274	9274	9274
notes			♥ 🍷			♥ 🍷 E	🍴	♥ 🍷	[R] 🍴 ⑥⑦	🍷 § m			♥ 🍷	♥ 🍷 B	[R] 🍴 ①–⑤			♥ 🍷 ⑧f	🍷	♥ 🍷 ⑧f	🍷 § m			♥ 🍷 G	♥ 🍷 A	♥ 🍷 B
rig d.	0428	...	...	...	0657	...	...	...	...	1046	...	1057	...	1032	...	...	1557	...	...	...	1646	...	1729	...	...	1716
Zermatt d.	|	...	...	0539	|	...	...	...	...	|	0939	|	...	|	...	1439	|	...	...	...	|	1613	|	...	...	|
isp d.	0435	...	...	0647	0707	...	...	...	...	|	1047	1107	...	1040	...	1547	1607	...	...	...	|	1722	1736	...	...	1724
ierre d.	0454	...	...	▬	0726	...	...	...	...	1106	▬	1126	...	1110	...	▬	1626	...	...	...	1706	...	1754	...	...	1745
ion d.	0505	0532	...	...	0737	...	...	...	...	1117	...	1137	...	1129	...	...	1637	...	...	...	1717	...	1806	...	...	1759
lartigny d.	0519	0546	...	...	0751	...	...	...	...	|	...	1151	...	1145	...	...	1651	...	...	...	|	...	1820	...	...	1815
't Maurice d.	0531	0556	...	0731	|	...	...	...	...	|	1126	|	...	|	...	1631	|	...	...	...	|	...	1831	...	...	|
ex d.	0536	0601	...	0736	|	...	...	...	...	|	1131	|	...	|	...	1636	|	...	...	...	|	...	1836	...	...	|
igle d.	0543	0608	...	0743	0808	...	...	...	...	|	1138	1208	...	1214	...	1643	1708	...	...	...	|	...	1843	...	1836	1836
lontreux d.	0554	0619	...	0754	0819	...	...	...	...	1155	1149	1219	...	1226	...	1654	1719	...		...	1755	...	1854	...	1849	1849
ausanne a.	0615	0640	...	0815	0840	...	...	...	...	1214	1210	1240	...	1245	...	1715	1740	...	...	...	1814	...	1915	...	1908	1908
ausanne d.	...	...	0703	▬	...	0903	...	...	...	...	▬	...	1303	1303	...	▬	...	1803	...	...	...	...	...	1922	1922	1922
allorbe 🛃 d.	...	...	0740	...	...	0940	...	...	...	...	...	...	1342	1342	...	...	...	1840	...	...	...	...	...	2005	2005	2005
Interlaken Ost d.	...	...	|	...	...	|	0701	...	...	...	...	...	|	|	...	...	...	|	1601	...	...	...	...	|	|	|
Interlaken West d.	...	...	|	...	...	|	0706	...	...	...	...	...	|	|	...	...	...	|	1606	...	...	...	...	|	|	|
Spiez d.	...	...	|	...	...	|	0723	...	...	...	...	...	|	|	...	...	...	|	1623	...	...	...	...	|	|	|
Thun d.	...	...	|	...	...	|	0734	...	...	...	...	...	|	|	...	...	...	|	1634	...	...	...	...	|	|	|
Bern d.	...	...	|	...	...	|	0752	0817	...	...	...	...	|	|	...	...	...	|	1652	1717	...	...	...	|	|	|
Neuchâtel d.	...	...	|	...	...	|	...	0902	...	...	☆	...	|	|	...	...	...	|	...	1802	...	...	...	|	|	|
Pontarlier 🛃 d.	...	...	|	☆	...	|	...	0945	...	...	9039	...	|	|	...	☆	...	|	...	1845	...	...	...	|	|	|
rasne d.	...	...	0805	9031	...	1006	...	1006	...	...	[R]	...	1402	1402	...	9053	...	1906	...	1906	...	...	...	2025	2025	2025
ijon d.	...	...	0924	[R]	...	1125	...	1125	...	...	🍴	...	1515	1515	...	[R] 🍴	...	2020	...	2020	...	...	...	2144	2144	2144
aris Gare de Lyon a.	...	...	1103	🍴	...	1303	...	1303	...	...	①–⑤	...	1655	1655	...	⑥	...	2159	...	2159	...	...	...	2324	2324	2324
aris Nord 10 d.	...	...	...	1301	...	...	...	...	1507	...	1513	...	...	...	1843	1913	...	...	...	...	...	...	...	...	...	...
ondon St Pancras 10 a.	...	...	...	1434	...	...	...	...	1637	...	1637	...	...	...	2007	2028	...	...	...	...	...	...	...	...	...	...

– *TGV DES NEIGES* – ⑦ Dec. 16 - Mar. 30 (also Dec. 25, Jan. 1, Mar. 24).
– *TGV DES NEIGES* – ⑥ Dec. 15 - Mar. 29.
– *TGV DES NEIGES* – ⑤ Dec. 14 - Mar. 28.
– ⑦ (also Dec. 25, Jan. 1, Feb. 23, Mar. 1, 24, Apr. 30, May 7, 12).
– ①–⑥ (not Dec. 25, Jan. 1, Mar. 24, May 12).
– ⑤⑥⑦ (also Dec. 25, Jan. 1, Mar. 24, Apr. 30, May 1, 7, 8, 12; not May 2).
– ①②③④⑥⑦ (also May 2; not Apr. 30, May 7).

– Not May 1, 8.
– Also Apr. 30, May 7.
n – To/from Milano.
– 6 minutes later on ⑥⑦.

☆ – Eurostar train. Special fares payable. Minimum check-in time 30 minutes. See Table **10**. Valid Dec. 9, 2007 - July 5, 2008.
§ – Supplement payable in Italy (except with international tickets). *IC* in Italy.
♥ – *TGV Lyria* service. [R]. Special fares payable. Supplement payable.

TRAIN NAME:

EC **120** – CISALPINO VALLESE
EC **124** – CISALPINO BORROMEO
EC **129** – CISALPINO MONTE ROSA

BRUSSELS - KÖLN - MILANO, VENEZIA and ROMA — 43

For Eurostar and rail/sea connections from London see Table **12**.

train type	ICE	EC	ES	IC	⇌	CNL	AV	IC	
train number	503	117	9451	635	9445	301	9429	607	
notes	🍷 ⊖	🍷 §	[R] 🍴 ⚡	🍷 ⚡	🍷	[R] A	[R] 🍴 ⚡	🍷 ⚡	
russels Midi/Zuid d.	...	...	...	...	1725	...	...	...	...
achen 🛃 d.	...	...	...	...	1906	...	...	...	...
öln Hbf a.	...	...	...	...	1945	...	...	...	...
öln Hbf d.	0854	...	...	...	...	2006	...	...	...
rankfurt Flughafen ✈ d.	0954	...	...	...	...	|	...	...	...
rankfurt (Main) Hbf d.	|	...	...	...	...	2247	...	...	...
asel SNCF/SBB 🛃 d.	1247	1304	...	...	...	◐	...	...	...
hiasso 🛃 a.	...	1728	...	...	...	0631	...	...	...
ilano Centrale a.	...	1835	1900	1905	...	0745	0800	0805	...
Verona a.	...	...	|	2040	...	...	|	0940	...
Padova a.	...	...	|	2136	...	...	|	1036	...
Venezia Santa Lucia a.	...	...	|	2209	...	...	|	1109	...
ologna a.	...	...	2042	...	...	...	0942	...	...
irenze SMN a.	...	...	2144	...	...	...	1044	...	...
oma Termini a.	...	...	2330	...	...	...	1230	...	...
apoli Centrale a.	...	...	...	...	...	...	1412	...	...

train number	AV	IC	CNL	ICE	E		ESc	EC	ICE	ICE
train number	9444	626	300	16	1910		9700	106	504 104	10
notes	[R] 🍴 ⚡	🍷 ⚡	[R] A	⊖	B		[R] 🍴 C ⚡	🍷 §	🍷	⊖
Napoli Centrale d.	1348	...	...	...	2036	...	...	...	...	...
Roma Termini d.	1530	...	...	...	2300	...	...	...	...	...
Firenze SMN d.	1714	...	...	...	|	...	...	...	...	...
Bologna d.	1816	...	...	...	|	...	...	...	...	...
Venezia Santa Lucia d.	|	1751	...	...	|	0519	0630	...	...	...
Padova d.	|	1823	...	...	|	0551	0700	...	...	...
Verona d.	|	1918	...	...	|	0650	0743	...	...	...
Milano Centrale d.	2000	2055	2112c	...	0715	0850	0905	0925	...	...
Chiasso 🛃 d.	...	...	2221c	...	...	...	...	1031	...	...
Basel SBB/SNCF 🛃 a.	...	...	◐	...	...	...	...	1451	1512	...
Frankfurt (Main) Hbf a.	...	...	0600	0728	...	...	...	...	|	...
Frankfurt Flughafen ✈ a.	...	...	|	0740	...	...	...	...	1806	1843
Köln Hbf a.	...	...	0842e	0840	...	...	...	...	1905	1940
Köln Hbf d.	...	...	...	0844	...	...	...	...	...	1944
Aachen 🛃 a.	...	...	...	0916	...	...	...	...	...	2016
Brussels Midi/Zuid a.	...	...	...	1101	...	...	...	...	...	2201

– *City Night Line* 🛏 1, 2 cl., 🛏 2 cl. (4, 6 berth), [2] and 🍴 Amsterdam - Köln - Milano and v.v. [R] Special fares apply.
– 🛏 1,2 cl. (Excelsior), 🛏 1, 2 cl. (T2), 🛏 1,2 cl. and 🛏 2 cl. (4 berth) Napoli - Milano. 🛏 2 cl. and [2] Salerno - Napoli - Milano.
– ①–⑥ (Not Dec. 25, Jan. 1, Mar. 24).

– On ⑦ depart Milano 2055, Train **1300**, not stop at Chiasso.
– Connection from *NZ* **300** to *ICE* **16** is at Frankfurt (Main) Hbf.
– Change at Venezia **Mestre**, see Table **600**.

– Supplement payable in Italy (except with international tickets).
– *Thalys* high-speed train. Special fares payable.
– *ICE 3* train 🍷, via high speed line, premium fares payable.

⚡ – Supplement payable.
◐ – Frontier/ticketing point.

TRAIN NAMES:

EC **106** – CISALPINO TIZIANO
EC **117** – CISALPINO VERDI

44 LONDON - PARIS - TORINO - MILANO - VENEZIA and ROMA

train type		TGV	EC	ES	EC	IC	IC	AV	☆			TGV			E	ICN		☆		TGV	E	E		
train number	83505	9241	111	9419	159	533	595	9445	9014		83321	9247	2117	2199	901	785		9020	83329	9249	809	1911	10827	
notes		[R] ⊻ ♣	[R] ⊻ L ⚡	[R] ✕ ⚡	[R] ⊻ ⚡	⊻ ⚡	⚡	[R] ✕ ⚡			①-⑤ h	[R] ⊻ ♣			O	⚡ T			①-⑤ h	[R] ⊻ ♣x	Q	H	2	
London St Pancras 10 12 d.	...	...	...	...	...	...	...	...	0926	...	...	...	...	...	...	...	...	1105	...	...	...	...	...	...
Lille Europe 11 d.	...	...	...	...	...	...	...	...	|	...	...	...	...	...	...	...	...	|	...	...	...	...	...	...
Paris Nord 10 a.	...	...	...	...	...	...	...	...	1247	...	...	...	...	...	...	...	...	1420	...	...	...	...	...	...
Paris Gare de Lyon d.	...	0742	...	...	...	...	...	...	▬	...	...	1350	...	...	...	...	...	...	...	1524	...	...	...	...
Paris Gare de Bercy ✣ d.	...	|	...	...	...	...	...	...	...	...	...	|	...	...	...	...	...	...	...	|	...	...	...	...
Dijon d.	...	|	...	...	...	...	...	...	...	...	...	|	...	...	...	...	...	...	...	|	...	...	...	...
Lyon Perrache d.	...	|	...	...	...	...	...	...	...	...	...	|	...	...	...	...	...	...	...	|	...	...	...	...
Lyon Part Dieu d.	0915	|	...	...	...	...	...	...	...	...	1541	|	...	...	...	...	...	...	1651	|	...	...	...	...
Aix les Bains d.	|	|	...	...	...	...	...	...	...	...	|	|	...	...	...	...	...	...	|	|	...	...	...	...
Chambéry d.	1029	1045	...	...	...	...	...	...	...	...	1700	1711	...	...	...	...	...	...	1755	1839	...	...	...	...
Modane 🏛 d.	...	1155	...	...	...	...	...	...	...	...	...	1820	...	...	...	...	...	...	...	1945	...	...	...	...
Oulx ▲ a.	...	1228	...	...	...	...	...	...	*EC*	...	...	1855	...	...	...	...	...	...	...	2024	...	...	...	...
Torino Porta Nuova a.	...	|	...	...	...	1505	...	...	**175**	...	...	|	...	...	2105	...	...	...	...	|	2155	...	...	...
Torino Porta Susa a.	...	1317	...	...	...	|	...	...	[R] ⊻	...	...	1945	...	...	|	...	...	...	...	2116	|	...	...	...
Novara a.	...	|	...	...	...	|	...	...	M ⚡	...	...	2043	...	...	|	...	...	...	...	2212	|	...	...	...
Milano Centrale a.	...	1450	1505	1505	1510	|	1510	1600	1600	...	...	2120	2215	2225	|	2300	...	...	...	2250	|	2320	0025	...
Alessandria a.	...	...	|	|	|	1600	|	|	|	...	...	...	|	|	2204	|	...	...	...	...	2257	|	|	...
Genova Piazza Principe a.	...	...	|	|	1642	1649	|	|	1742	...	...	...	|	0020	|	|	...	...	...	...	2350	|	|	...
La Spezia a.	...	...	|	|	▬	1804	|	|	1917	...	...	...	|	...	|	|	...	...	...	...	0124	|	|	...
Viareggio a.	...	..	|	|	...	1838	|	|	1954	...	...	...	|	...	|	|	...	...	...	...	|	|	|	...
Pisa Centrale a.	...	...	|	|	...	1857	|	|	2012	...	...	...	|	...	|	|	...	...	...	...	0214	|	|	...
Livorno a.	...	...	|	|	...	1914	|	|	2030	...	...	...	|	...	|	|	...	...	...	...	0235	|	|	...
Grosseto a.	...	...	|	|	...	2032	|	|	...	...	...	...	|	...	|	|	...	...	...	...	0356	|	|	...
Brescia a.	...	...	1555	|	...	|	|	|	...	...	...	...	2321	...	|	|	...	...	...	...	|	|	0144	...
Verona Porta Nuova a.	...	...	1640	|	...	|	|	|	...	...	...	...	0007	...	|	|	...	...	...	...	|	|	0232	...
Vicenza a.	...	...	1718	|	...	|	|	|	...	...	...	...	...	...	|	|	...	...	...	...	|	|	...	...
Padova a.	...	...	1736	|	...	|	|	|	...	...	...	...	...	...	|	|	...	...	...	...	|	|	...	...
Venezia Mestre a.	...	...	1757	|	...	|	|	|	...	...	...	...	...	...	|	|	...	...	...	...	|	|	...	...
Venezia Santa Lucia a.	...	...	1809	|	...	|	|	|	...	...	...	...	...	...	|	|	...	...	...	...	|	|	...	...
Piacenza a.	...	...	...	|	...	|	1550	|	...	...	...	...	...	...	2312	2343	...	...	...	...	|	0008	...	...
Parma a.	...	...	...	|	...	|	1619	|	...	...	...	...	...	...	2349	0016	...	...	...	...	|	0059	...	...
Reggio Emilia a.	...	...	...	|	...	|	1634	|	...	...	...	...	...	...	0008	0036	...	...	...	...	|	|	...	...
Modena a.	...	...	...	|	...	|	1649	|	...	...	...	...	...	...	0025	0053	...	...	...	...	|	|	...	...
Bologna Centrale a.	...	...	...	1652	...	|	1711	1742	...	...	...	...	...	...	0054	0124	...	...	...	...	|	|	...	...
Rimini a.	...	...	...	1751	...	|	|	|	...	...	...	...	...	...	0200	0235	...	...	...	...	|	|	...	...
Ancona a.	...	...	...	1842	...	|	|	|	...	...	...	...	...	...	0257	0333	...	...	...	...	|	|	...	...
Pescara Centrale a.	...	...	...	1957	2	|	|	|	...	...	...	...	...	...	0422	0459	...	...	...	...	|	|	...	...
Bari Centrale a.	...	...	...	2304	2310	|	|	|	...	...	...	...	...	...	0749	0831	...	...	...	...	|	|	...	...
Athina ⊖ a.	...	...	...	⊖	|	|	|	|	...	...	...	...	...	...	⊖	⊖	...	...	...	...	|	|	...	...
Brindisi a.	...	...	...	...	0028	|	|	|	...	...	...	...	...	...	0929	...	...	...	...	...	|	|	...	...
Firenze SMN a.	...	...	...	...	...	|	1826j	1844	...	...	...	...	...	...	...	...	...	...	...	...	|	|	...	...
Roma Termini a.	...	...	...	...	...	2228	2106	2030	...	...	...	...	...	...	...	...	...	...	...	...	0558o	0715	...	...
Napoli Centrale a.	...	...	...	...	...	...	2336	2212	...	...	...	...	...	...	...	...	...	...	...	...	0911	1007	...	...

train type			☆	EN		ICp	IC			☆	EN	ES		ICp	ES	ICp	IC							
train number			9030	227	2121	501	583			9036	221	9458	2004	645	9751	585	553							
notes				⊠ A		[R] ⊻ ⚒ ⚡	⊻ ⚡				⊠ B	[R] ✕ ⚡		[R] ⚡	[R] ✕ ⚡	[R] ⚡	⊻ ⚡							
London St Pancras 10 12 d.	...	...	1404	...	...	...	...	...	...	1530	...	...	...	...	...	...	...	...	...	...	...	...	...	...
Lille Europe 11 d.	...	...	|	...	...	...	...	...	...	|	...	...	...	...	...	...	...	...	...	...	...	...	...	...
Paris Nord 10 a.	...	...	1726	...	...	...	...	...	...	1856	...	...	...	...	...	...	...	...	...	...	...	...	...	...
Paris Gare de Bercy ✣ d.	...	...	...	1859	...	...	...	...	...	...	1942	...	...	...	...	...	...	...	...	...	...	...	...	...
Dijon d.	...	...	...	2137	...	...	...	...	...	...	2237	...	...	...	...	...	...	...	...	...	...	...	...	...
Modane 🏛 d.	...	...	...	⊙	...	...	...	...	...	...	⊙	...	...	...	...	...	...	...	...	...	...	...	...	...
Milano Centrale a.	...	...	...	|	...	...	...	...	...	...	0538	...	0600	0610	0705	0710	0910	...	...	...	...	...	...	...
Novara a.	...	...	...	|	...	...	...	...	...	...	|	...	0643	|	|	|	|	...	...	...	...	...	...	...
Torino Porta Nuova a.	...	...	...	|	...	...	...	...	...	...	|	...	0800	|	|	|	|	...	...	...	...	...	...	...
Genova Piazza Principe a.	...	...	...	|	...	...	...	...	...	...	|	...	...	0744	|	|	|	...	...	...	...	...	...	...
La Spezia a.	...	...	...	|	...	...	...	...	...	...	|	...	...	0917	|	|	|	...	...	...	...	...	...	...
Viareggio a.	...	...	...	|	...	...	...	...	...	...	|	...	...	1000	|	|	|	...	...	...	...	...	...	...
Pisa Centrale a.	...	...	...	|	...	...	...	...	...	...	|	...	...	1018	|	|	|	...	...	...	...	...	...	...
Livorno a.	...	...	...	|	...	...	...	...	...	...	|	...	...	1038	|	|	|	...	...	...	...	...	...	...
Grosseto a.	...	...	...	|	...	...	...	...	...	...	|	...	...	...	|	|	|	...	...	...	...	...	...	...
Brescia a.	...	...	...	|	...	...	...	...	...	...	0643	0705	...	...	|	|	|	...	...	...	...	...	...	...
Verona Porta Nuova a.	...	...	...	|	...	...	...	...	...	...	0725	|	...	...	|	|	|	...	...	...	...	...	...	...
Vicenza a.	...	...	...	|	...	...	...	...	...	...	0826	|	...	...	|	|	|	...	...	...	...	...	...	...
Padova a.	...	...	...	|	...	...	...	...	...	...	0852	|	...	...	|	|	|	...	...	...	...	...	...	...
Venezia Mestre a.	...	...	...	|	...	...	...	...	...	...	0926	|	...	...	|	|	|	...	...	...	...	...	...	...
Venezia Santa Lucia a.	...	...	...	|	...	...	...	...	...	...	0939	|	...	...	|	|	|	...	...	...	...	...	...	...
Piacenza a.	...	...	...	0444	...	...	...	...	...	...	...	|	...	...	0742	0750	0951	...	...	...	...	...	...	...
Parma a.	...	...	...	0512	...	...	...	...	...	...	...	0818	...	...	|	0823	1019	...	...	...	...	...	...	...
Reggio Emilia a.	...	...	...	|	...	...	...	...	...	...	...	|	...	...	|	0840	1034	...	...	...	...	...	...	...
Modena a.	...	...	...	|	...	...	...	...	...	...	...	0848	...	...	|	0856	1050	...	...	...	...	...	...	...
Bologna Centrale a.	...	...	...	0558	0638	...	...	...	...	...	...	0916	...	...	0852	0922	1116	...	...	...	...	...	...	...
Rimini a.	...	...	...	|	0805	...	...	...	...	...	...	|	...	...	0951	|	1238	...	...	...	...	...	...	...
Ancona a.	...	...	...	|	0924	...	...	...	...	...	...	|	...	...	1050	|	1334	...	...	...	...	...	...	...
Pescara Centrale a.	...	...	...	|	...	...	...	...	...	...	...	|	...	...	1204	|	1509	...	...	...	...	...	...	...
Bari Centrale a.	...	...	...	|	...	...	...	...	...	...	...	|	...	...	1452	|	1847	...	...	...	...	...	...	...
Athina ⊖ a.	...	...	...	|	...	...	...	...	...	...	...	|	...	...	⊖	|	⊖	...	...	...	...	...	...	...
Brindisi a.	...	...	...	|	...	...	...	...	...	...	...	|	...	...	1558	|	...	...	...	...	...	...	...	...
Firenze SMN a.	...	...	...	0716f	...	...	...	...	...	...	...	1017j	...	...	...	1026j	...	...	...	...	...	...	...	...
Roma Termini a.	...	...	...	0950	...	1027	1128	...	...	...	...	1203	...	...	...	1303	...	...	...	...	...	...	...	...
Napoli Centrale a.	...	...	...	...	...	1236	1336	...	...	...	...	...	...	...	...	...	...	...	...	...	...	...	...	...

NOTES for pages 70 and 71

- **A** – PALATINO *Trainhotel Artesia* – 🛏 1, 2 cl., ▬ 2 cl. (6 berth, Comfort 4 berth and ladies only Comfort 4 berth) and ✕: Paris - Bologna - Firenze - Roma and v.v.
- **B** – STENDHAL *Trainhotel Artesia* – 🛏 1, 2 cl., ▬ 2 cl. (6 berth, Comfort 4 berth and ladies only Comfort 4 berth) and ✕: Paris - Milano - Venezia and v.v.
- **F** – CISALPINO CINQUE TERRE – 🚃 and ⊻ Livorno - Milano - Chiasso 🏛 - Zürich.
- **H** – 🛏 1, 2 cl. (Excelsior), 🛏 1, 2 cl. (T2), 🛏 1, 2 cl., and ▬ 2 cl. (4 berth) Milano - Napoli and v.v.
- **K** – FRECCIA SALENTINA – 🛏 1, 2 cl., 🛏 1, 2 cl. (T2), ▬ 2 cl. (4 berth) and 🚃 Lecce - Brindisi - Milano.
- **L** – CISALPINO SAN MARCO – 🚃 and ⊻ Basel - Milano - Venezia.
- **M** – CISALPINO CINQUE TERRE – 🚃 and ⊻ Schaffhausen - Zürich - Chiasso 🏛 - Milano - Livorno.
- **O** – FRECCIA ADRIATICA – 🛏 1, 2 cl. (T2), ▬ 2 cl. and 🚃 Torino - Brindisi - Lecce.
- **P** – ⑧ (daily Feb. 10 - July 5).
- **Q** – 🛏 1, 2 cl. (T2), ▬ 2 cl. (4 berth) and 🚃 Napoli - Roma - Torino.
- **T** – FRECCIA DEL LEVANTE – Not Dec. 24, 25, 31: 🛏 1, 2 cl., 🛏 1, 2 cl. (T2), ▬ 2 cl. and 🚃 Milano - Bari - Taranto.
- **V** – MONTE CARLO – 🛏 1, 2 cl. (Excelsior), 🛏 1, 2 cl. and ▬ 2 cl. (6, 4 berth) Roma - Torino.

- **f** – Firenze **Campo di Marte**.
- **g** – Napoli **Piazza Garibaldi**.
- **h** – Not Dec. 25, Jan. 1, Mar. 24, May 1, 8, 12.
- **j** – Firenze **Rifredi**.
- **k** – Calls at Lyon St Exupéry TGV ✈, arrive 2124.
- **o** – Roma **Ostiense**.
- **p** – Not Dec. 25, Jan. 1, Mar. 24, May 1, 8, 12.
- **q** – Also Dec. 25, Jan. 1, Mar. 24, May 1, 8, 12.
- **s** – Stops to set down only.
- **t** – Roma **Tiburtina**.
- **x** – Calls at Lyon St Exupéry TGV ✈, depart 1720.
- **z** – Arrive 2305.

NOTES CONTINUED ON NEXT PAGE →

ROMA and VENEZIA - MILANO - TORINO - PARIS - LONDON 44

train type		EN	TGV			☆	ICN	E			TGV				☆	☆	☆	IC	ES	AV	EC	ICp	ICp	TGV	
train number		366	9240	17568	83652	9043	780	1910	2718	2710	9242	17525	83160	17576	9047	9049	9051	582	9410	9434	176	614	516	9248	
notes		367	[R] 🍷			[R]	✓				[R] 🍷	①–⑥			[R] ✕	[R] ✕	✓ ✕	🍷	[R] ✕	[R] ✕	[R] ✕	[R]	[R] 🍷	[R] 🍷	
		V	♣			✕	K	H			♣	2h			P	Ⓑ		✓	✓	✓	F ✓	✓	✓	♣ k	
Napoli Centrale d.	...	...	...	...	...	...	...	2036	...	...	...	...	...	...	...	...	...	0624	...	0848	...		0730	...	...
Roma Termini d.	...	2116	...	...	...	...	...	2300	...	...	...	...	...	...	...	...	...	0855	...	1030	...	...	0946	...	...
Firenze SMN d.	...	2325f	...	...	...	...	...	|	...	...	...	...	...	...	...	...	...	1127f	...	1214	...	...	|	...	...
Brindisi d.	...	|	...	...	...	...	1930	|	...	...	...	...	...	...	...	...	...	|	*0406*	|	...	...	|	...	...
Athína ⊖ d.	...	|	...	...	...	...	⊖	|	...	...	...	...	...	...	...	...	...	|	⊖	|	...	...	|	...	...
Bari Centrale d.	...	|	...	...	...	...	2101	|	...	...	...	...	...	...	...	...	...	|	0653	|	...	...	|	...	...
Pescara Centrale d.	...	|	...	...	...	...	0028	|	...	...	...	...	...	...	...	...	...	|	0953	|	...	...	|	...	...
Ancona d.	...	|	...	...	...	...	0159	|	...	...	...	...	...	...	...	...	...	|	1116	|	...	...	|	...	...
Rimini d.	...	|	...	...	...	...	0256	|	...	...	...	...	...	...	...	...	...	|	1209	|	...	...	|	...	...
Bologna Centrale d.	...	|	...	...	...	...	0412	|	...	...	...	...	...	...	...	...	...	1244	1308	1316	...	...	|	...	...
Modena d.	...	|	...	...	...	...	0437	|	...	...	...	...	...	...	...	...	...	1305	|	|	...	...	|	...	...
Reggio Emilia d.	...	|	...	...	...	...	0455	|	...	...	...	...	...	...	...	...	...	1319	|	|	...	...	|	...	...
Parma d.	...	|	...	...	...	...	0514	|	...	...	...	...	...	...	...	...	...	1336	|	|	...	...	|	...	...
Piacenza d.	...	|	...	...	...	...	0554	|	...	...	...	...	...	...	...	...	...	1409	|	|	...	...	|	...	...
Venezia Santa Lucia d.	...	|	...	...	...	...	|	|	...	...	...	...	...	...	...	...	...	|	|	|	...	1252	|	...	...
Venezia Mestre d.	...	|	...	...	...	...	|	|	...	...	...	...	...	...	...	...	...	|	|	|	...	1304	|	...	...
Padova d.	...	|	...	...	...	...	|	|	...	...	...	...	...	...	...	...	...	|	|	|	...	1324	|	...	...
Vicenza d.	...	|	...	...	...	...	|	|	...	...	...	...	...	...	...	...	...	|	|	|	...	1342	|	...	...
Verona Porta Nuova d.	...	|	...	...	...	...	|	|	...	0610	...	...	...	...	...	...	...	|	|	|	...	1418	|	...	...
Brescia d.	...	|	...	...	...	...	|	|	...	0652	...	...	...	...	...	...	...	|	|	|	...	1505	|	...	...
Grosseto d.	...	|	...	...	...	...	|	|	...	|	...	...	...	...	...	...	...	|	|	|	...	|	1129	...	...
Livorno d.	...	|	...	...	...	...	|	|	...	|	...	...	...	...	...	...	...	|	|	|	1126	|	1242	...	...
Pisa Centrale d.	...	0038	...	...	...	...	|	|	...	|	...	...	...	...	...	...	...	|	|	|	1144	|	1300	...	...
Viareggio d.	...	|	...	...	...	...	|	|	...	|	...	...	...	...	...	...	...	|	|	|	1201	|	|	...	...
La Spezia d.	...	|	...	...	...	...	|	|	...	|	...	...	...	...	...	...	...	|	|	|	1240	|	1354	...	...
Genova Piazza Principe d.	...	0530	...	...	...	...	|	|	0545	|	...	...	...	...	...	...	...	|	|	|	1419	|	1512	...	...
Alessandria d.	...	0617s	...	...	...	...	|	|	|	|	...	...	...	...	...	...	...	|	|	|	|	|	1556	...	...
Milano Centrale d.	...	|	0640	...	...	...	0705	0715	0740	0755	0810	...	...	...	...	...	...	1450	1455	1500	1550	1555	|	1610	...
Novara d.	...	|	0714	...	...	...	...	...	...	...	0844	...	...	...	...	...	...	...	...	...	...	...	|	|	...
Torino Porta Susa d.	...	|	0811	...	...	...	...	...	...	...	0940	...	...	...	...	...	...	...	...	...	...	...	|	1735	...
Torino Porta Nuova d.	...	0720	|	...	...	...	...	...	...	...	|	...	...	...	...	...	...	...	...	...	...	...	1655	|	...
Oulx ▲ d.	...	...	0900	...	...	...	...	...	...	...	1030	...	...	...	...	...	...	...	...	...	...	...	...	1825	...
Modane 🏛 a.	...	...	0938	...	...	...	...	...	...	...	1105	...	...	...	...	...	...	...	...	...	...	...	...	1905	...
Chambéry a.	...	...	1052	1120	1228	...	...	...	...	...	1220	1321	1338	...	...	...	...	...	...	...	...	...	...	2022	...
Aix les Bains a.	...	...	|	|	1240	...	...	...	...	...	|	1332	1349	1400	...	...	...	...	...	...	...	...	...	|	...
Lyon Part Dieu a.	...	...	|	1239	...	...	...	...	...	...	|	...	...	1516	...	...	...	...	...	...	...	...	...	|	...
Lyon Perrache a.	...	...	|	...	...	...	...	...	...	...	|	...	...	1527	...	...	...	...	...	...	...	...	...	|	...
Dijon a.	...	...	|	...	...	...	...	...	...	...	|	...	...	...	...	...	...	...	...	...	...	...	...	|	...
Paris Gare de Bercy ✣ a.	...	...	|	...	...	...	...	...	...	...	|	...	...	...	...	...	...	...	...	...	...	...	...	|	...
Paris Gare de Lyon a.	...	...	1355	...	...	...	...	...	...	...	1515	...	...	...	...	...	...	...	...	...	...	...	...	2319	...
Paris Nord 10 d.	...	...	...	...	...	1613	...	...	...	...	...	...	...	...	1713	1743	1813	...	...	...	...	...	...	...	...
Lille Europe 11 d.	...	...	...	...	...	|	...	...	...	...	...	...	...	...	|	|	|	...	...	...	...	...	...	...	...
London St Pancras 10 12 a.	...	...	...	...	...	1734	...	...	...	...	...	...	...	...	1834	1859	1934	...	...	...	...	...	...	...	...

train type		IC	AV		IC	EC	ICp	ES	ES	EN	TGV	☆	☆	☆			EN	TGV	☆	☆	☆				
train number		568	9448	2029	538	147	592	9418	9460	220	5152	9117	9121	9019			226	5156	9127	9023	9027				
notes		🍷	[R] ✕		✓	148	[R]	[R] ✕	[R] ✕	⊠	[R] 🍷						⊠	[R] 🍷							
		✓	✓			[R] 🍷	✓	✓	✓	B	①–⑤	①–⑤	⑥⑦				A	⑥⑦		⑥⑦					
						✓					p							q							
Napoli Centrale d.	...	...	1548	...	...		...	...	...	...		...	...	...	...	...	...		...	...	...	...	...	...	...
Roma Termini d.	...	...	1730	...	1546	...	1655	...	1635	...	...	...	...	...	...	...	1836	...	...	...	...	...	...	...	...
Firenze SMN d.	...	...	1914	...	|	...	1931j	...	1821j	...	...	...	...	...	...	...	2053f	...	...	...	...	...	...	...	...
Brindisi d.	...	...	|	...	|	...	|	1400	|	...	...	...	...	...	...	...	|	...	...	...	...	...	...	...	...
Athína ⊖ d.	...	⊖	|	...	|	...	|	⊖	|	...	...	...	...	...	...	...	|	...	...	...	...	...	...	...	...
Bari Centrale d.	...	1112	|	...	|	...	|	1508	|	...	...	...	...	...	...	...	|	...	...	...	...	...	...	...	...
Pescara Centrale d.	...	1435	|	...	|	...	|	1748	|	...	...	...	...	...	...	...	|	...	...	...	...	...	...	...	...
Ancona d.	...	1620	|	...	|	...	|	1913	|	...	...	...	...	...	...	...	|	...	...	...	...	...	...	...	...
Rimini d.	...	1722	|	...	|	...	|	2009	|	...	...	...	...	...	...	...	|	...	...	...	...	...	...	...	...
Bologna Centrale d.	...	1844	2016	...	|	...	2050	2108	1923	...	...	...	...	...	...	...	2202	...	...	...	...	...	...	...	...
Modena d.	...	1904	|	...	|	...	2110	|	1947	...	...	...	...	...	...	...	|	...	...	...	...	...	...	...	...
Reggio Emilia d.	...	1919	|	...	|	...	2125	|	|	...	...	...	...	...	...	...	|	...	...	...	...	...	...	...	...
Parma d.	...	1936	|	...	|	...	2143	|	2015	...	...	...	...	...	...	...	2254	...	...	...	...	...	...	...	...
Piacenza d.	...	2009	|	...	|	...	2213	|	|	...	...	...	...	...	...	...	2328	...	...	...	...	...	...	...	...
Venezia Santa Lucia d.	...	|	|	...	|	...	|	|	|	2007	...	...	...	...	...	...	|	...	...	...	...	...	...	...	...
Venezia Mestre d.	...	|	|	...	|	...	|	|	|	2019	...	...	...	...	...	...	|	...	...	...	...	...	...	...	...
Padova d.	...	|	|	...	|	...	|	|	|	2040	...	...	...	...	...	...	|	...	...	...	...	...	...	...	...
Vicenza d.	...	|	|	...	|	...	|	|	|	2100	...	...	...	...	...	...	|	...	...	...	...	...	...	...	...
Verona Porta Nuova d.	...	|	|	...	|	...	|	|	|	2134	...	...	...	...	...	...	|	...	...	...	...	...	...	...	...
Brescia d.	...	|	|	...	|	...	|	|	2140	2213	...	...	...	...	...	...	|	...	...	...	...	...	...	...	...
Grosseto d.	...	|	|	...	1729	...	|	|	...	|	...	...	...	...	...	...	|	...	...	...	...	...	...	...	...
Livorno d.	...	|	|	...	1842	...	|	|	...	|	...	...	...	...	...	...	|	...	...	...	...	...	...	...	...
Pisa Centrale d.	...	|	|	...	1900	...	|	|	...	|	...	...	...	...	...	...	|	...	...	...	...	...	...	...	...
Viareggio d.	...	|	|	...	1917	...	|	|	...	|	...	...	...	...	...	...	|	...	...	...	...	...	...	...	...
La Spezia d.	...	|	|	...	1953	...	|	|	...	|	...	...	...	...	...	...	|	...	...	...	...	...	...	...	...
Genova Piazza Principe d.	...	|	|	...	2108	2119	|	|	...	|	...	...	...	...	...	...	|	...	...	...	...	...	...	...	...
Torino Porta Nuova d.	...	|	|	2050	...	|	|	|	...	|	...	...	...	...	...	...	|	...	...	...	...	...	...	...	...
Novara d.	...	|	|	2203	...	|	|	|	...	|	...	...	...	...	...	...	|	...	...	...	...	...	...	...	...
Milano Centrale d.	...	2050	2200	2245	...	2250	2255	2300	...	2335z	...	...	...	...	...	...	|	...	...	...	...	...	...	...	...
Modane 🏛 a.	...	...	...	...	...	...	...	...	...	⊙	...	...	...	...	...	...	⊙	...	...	...	...	...	...	...	...
Dijon a.	...	...	...	...	...	...	...	...	...	0609	0632	...	...	...	...	...	0633	0744	...	...	...	...	...	...	...
Paris Gare de Bercy ✣ a.	...	...	...	...	...	...	...	...	...	0847	|	...	...	...	...	...	0910	|	...	...	...	...	...	...	...
Paris Nord 10 d.	...	...	...	...	...	...	...	...	...	...	|	...	...	1013	...	...	...	|	...	1113	1213	...	...	...	...
Lille Europe 11 d.	...	...	...	...	...	...	...	...	...	...	0915	0935	1035	|	...	...	...	1027	1235	|	|	...	...	...	...
London St Pancras 10 12 a.	...	...	...	...	...	...	...	...	...	...	...	1003	1101	1128	...	...	...	...	1303	1228	1328	...	...	...	...

→ **NOTES CONTINUED FROM PREVIOUS PAGE**

✓ – Supplement payable.

♣ – Special 'global' fares payable.

▲ – Station for the resorts of Cesana, Claviere and Sestriere.

✣ – Paris **Gare de Bercy**, 1km from **Gare de Lyon**; see City Plan of Paris page 32.

⊠ – For use by passengers making international journeys only. Special fares payable.

⊖ – For connections to Athína (by 🚢 Ancona / Bari - Pátra), see Tables **74, 2715, 2755**.

☆ – Eurostar train. [R] ✕ Minimum check-in time 30 minutes. Special fares payable. See Tables **10** and **12**. Valid Dec. 9, 2007 - July 5, 2008.

⊙ – Frontier/ticketing points 🏛 are Vallorbe and Domodossola (via Switzerland, non–EU nationals may require transit visas). Ticket point for Domodossola is **Iselle**.

OTHER TRAIN NAMES: **147/148** – LIGUIRE **9242, 9247** – ALEXANDRE DUMAS **9241, 9248** – ALESSANDRO MANZONI **9240, 9249** – CARAVAGGIO

45 LONDON - PARIS - BARCELONA - ALACANT

train number	9010	9010	6211	70/71	373	9036	477/6	1598	1101	1619	9044	3731	3733	463/2		1638	
train type	☆	☆	TGV	Talgo		☆	Hotel	Alvia	Em	Alta	☆			Talgo		Alvia	
notes	⑦	①–⑥		T 🍷	W		J			F		G [R]	B	M 🍷	2		
London Waterloo 10 .. d.	0825	0832	...	...	...	1530	...	...	...	...	1730	...	...	...	...	...	...
Paris Nord 10 .... a.	1147	1147	...	...	...	1856	...	...	...	...	2053	...	...	...	...	...	...
Paris Austerlitz .... d.	...	...	...	...	...	...	2032	...	...	...	...	2156	2202	...	...	...	...
Paris Gare de Lyon ..... d.	...	...	1320	...	...	...	│	...	...	...	...	│	│	...	...	...	...
Les Aubrais-Orléans .. d.	...	...	│	...	...	...	2132	...	...	...	...	2257	2303	...	...	...	...
Limoges .... d.	...	...	│	...	...	...	2354	...	...	...	...	0117	0122	...	...	...	...
Montpellier .... d.	...	...	1645	1702	...	...	│	...	...	...	...	│	│	0726	...	...	...
Perpignan .... d.	...	...	...	1837	...	...	│	...	...	...	...	0722	0746	0856	...	...	...
Cerbère .... d.	...	...	...	1914	...	...	│	...	...	...	...	0817	0850	0931	...	...	...
Portbou 🏛 .... a.	...	...	...	1931	1940	...	│	...	...	...	...	0821	0854	0948	1014r	...	...
Figueres .... a.	...	...	...	1953	2004	...	0624	...	...	...	...	...	...	1012	1037r	...	...
Girona .... a.	...	...	...	2019	2037	...	0654	...	...	...	...	...	...	1040	1115	...	...
Barcelona França .... a.	...	...	...	2145	│	...	0824	...	...	...	...	...	...	│	│	...	...
Barcelona Sants .... a.	...	...	...	...	2202	...	...	0930	1000	1130	...	...	...	1146	1246	1330	...
Zaragoza Delicias .... a.	...	...	...	...	│	...	...	1157	│	1409	...	...	...	│	...	1557	...
Madrid Puerta de Atocha a.	...	...	...	...	0721c	...	...	1350	│	1600	...	...	...	│	...	1755	...
València Nord .... a.	...	...	...	...	...	...	...	...	1300	│	...	...	...	1515	...	...	...
Alacant Términal .... a.	...	...	...	...	...	...	...	...	1502	│	...	...	...	1724	...	...	...
Sevilla Santa Justa ...... a.	...	...	...	...	...	...	...	...	...	1934	...	...	...	...	...	...	...

train number	370		73/72	6212	9055	9059	1119	460/1		3730	3732	9019	1138	1162	475/4	9023	9027
train type			Talgo	TGV	☆	☆	Alvia	Talgo				☆	Alta	Em	Hotel	☆	☆
notes	W	2	T 🍷		⑧	⑥⑦		P 🍷	2	G [R]	A		H		J	⑥⑦	
Sevilla Santa Justa ...... d.	...	...	...	...	...	...	...	...	...	...	...	...	0925	...	...	...	...
Alacant Términal .... d.	...	...	...	...	...	...	...	1109	...	...	...	...	│	1420	...	...	...
València Nord .... d.	...	...	...	...	...	...	...	1308	...	...	...	...	│	1605	...	...	...
Madrid Puerta de Atocha d.	2200c	...	...	...	...	...	1145	│	...	...	...	...	1305	│	...	...	...
Zaragoza Delicias .... d.	│	...	...	...	...	...	1340	│	...	...	...	...	1450	│	...	...	...
Barcelona Sants .... d.	0752	0825	...	...	...	...	1613	1642	1725	...	...	...	1742	1910	...	...	...
Barcelona França .... d.	│	│	0845	...	...	...	...	│	│	...	...	...	...	...	2105	...	...
Girona .... d.	0925	1007	0955	...	...	...	...	1748	1858	...	...	...	...	...	2217	...	...
Figueres .... d.	0958	1045	1025	...	...	...	...	1815	1936	...	...	...	...	...	2247	...	...
Portbou .... d.	1025s	1109	1054	...	...	...	...	1844	2003	...	...	...	...	...	│	...	...
Cerbère 🏛 .... d.	1035	1113	1114	...	...	...	...	1906	2007	2121	21354	...	...	...	│	...	...
Perpignan .... d.	...	...	1145	...	...	...	...	1939	...	2214	2227	...	...	...	│	...	...
Montpellier .... a.	...	...	1322	1423	...	...	...	2109	...	│	│	...	...	...	│	...	...
Limoges .... a.	...	...	...	│	...	...	...	...	...	│	0436	...	...	...	0504	...	...
Les Aubrais-Orléans .. a.	...	...	...	│	...	...	...	...	...	0622	0704	...	...	...	0740	...	...
Paris Gare de Lyon ..... a.	...	...	...	1749	...	...	...	...	...	│	│	...	...	...	│	...	...
Paris Austerlitz .... a.	...	...	...	...	...	...	...	...	...	0727	0812	...	...	...	0900e	...	...
Paris Nord 10 .... d.	...	...	...	...	1913	2013	...	...	...	...	...	1013	...	...	...	1113	1213
London Waterloo 10 ... a.	...	...	...	...	2028	2142	...	...	...	...	...	1128	...	...	...	1228	1328

A – Dec. 25, Jan. 1, May 3, 12: ▬ 1, 2 cl. and [2] (reclining) Cerbère - Paris.
B – Dec. 21, 28, Apr. 30, May 7: ▬ 1, 2 cl., and [2] (reclining) Paris - Portbou.
F – [12] and 🍴 Barcelona - Zaragoza - Madrid - Córdoba - Sevilla - Cádiz (arrive 2126).
G – *CORAIL LUNÉA* – ▬ 1, 2 cl., [2] (reclining) and 🍷 Paris - Portbou and Cerbère - Paris. Not Dec. 24, 31.
H – [12] and 🍴 Cádiz (depart 0740) - Sevilla - Córdoba - Madrid - Zaragoza - Barcelona.
J – JOÁN MIRÓ *Trainhotel Elipsos* – 🛏 1, 2 cl., 🛏 1, 2 cl. (T4) [2] (reclining) and 🍴 Paris - Barcelona and v.v. [R] Special fares apply.
M – MARE NOSTRUM – [12] and 🍴 Montpellier - Portbou - Barcelona - Alacant - Cartagena (arrive 1952), [R] ✓ Special fares payable.
N – *Euromed* train. [R] 🍴 ✓.
P – MARE NOSTRUM – [12] and 🍴 Cartagena (depart 0835) - Alacant - Barcelona - Portbou - Montpellier, [R] ✓ Special fares payable.
T – CATALÁN TALGO – [12] and 🍴 Montpellier - Portbou - Barcelona and v.v. [R] ✓ Special fares payable.
W – COSTA BRAVA – 🛏 1, 2 cl., ▬ 2 cl., [12] and 🍴 Portbou - Barcelona - Zaragoza - Madrid and Madrid - Zaragoza - Barcelona - Cerbère.

c – Madrid **Chamartín**.
e – 0848 on ⑥⑦ (also Dec. 25, Jan. 1, Mar. 24, May 1, 8, 12).
r – 6–7 mins. later on ⑥.
s – Stops to set down only.
u – Stops to pick up only.
✓ – Supplement payable.
Arco – *Arco* [R] ✓ 🍷.
Alvia – *Alvia* [R] ✓ 🍷.
Alta – *Altaria* [R] ✓ 🍷.
TGV – *Train à Grande Vitesse* [R] 🍷 ✓.
☆ – Eurostar train. [R] 🍴. Minimum check-in time: 30 minutes. Valid Dec. 9, 2007 - July 5, 2008. Special fares payable.

46 LONDON - PARIS - LISBOA, PORTO and MADRID

train number	8505	413	60	9078	8515	610	9020	8543	313/312	521	523	204	1096	9030	409/8	1126	9044	9046	8587	4053	4086	202	78	8308	283
train type/number	TGV		Talgo	☆	TGV	Alta	☆	TGV		IC	IC		Alta	☆	Hotel	Alta	☆	☆	TGV		Alvia	IC	Alta		
notes	[R] ✓ 🍷 k	🍷 2	[R] ✓ 🍷	[R] 🍴 ①–⑤	[R] ✓ 🍷		[R] 🍴	[R] ✓ 🍷 p	[R] 🍴 A	①–⑥ [R] 🍷	[R] 🍷	[R] K 🍷	🍴	[R] 🍴	[R] 🍴 H	🍴	[R] 🍴 ⑥⑦	[R] 🍴 ⑧	[R] ✓ Q 🍷	[R] F	[R] ✓ S	[R] ✓ R	🍷	2	🍷 2
London Waterloo 10 ...... d.	...	...	...	0527	...	...	1105	...	...	...	...	...	...	1404	...	...	1731	1800	...	...	...	...	...	...	...
Paris Nord 10 .... a.	...	...	...	0850	...	...	1420	...	...	...	...	...	...	1726	...	...	2053	2120	...	...	...	...	...	...	...
Paris Montparnasse .... d.	0715	...	...	...	1010r	...	...	1550	...	...	...	...	...	...	...	...	...	...	2245	...	...	...	...	...	...
Paris Austerlitz .... d.	│	...	...	...	│	...	...	│	...	...	...	...	...	...	1943	...	...	...	│	2311	...	...	...	...	...
Blois .... d.	│	...	...	...	│	...	...	│	...	...	...	...	...	...	2108	...	...	...	│	│	...	...	...	...	...
Poitiers .... d.	│	...	...	...	│	...	...	│	...	...	...	...	...	...	2209	...	...	...	0103	│	...	...	...	...	...
Bordeaux St Jean .... d.	1025	...	...	...	1310	...	...	1855	...	...	...	...	...	...	│	...	...	...	│	│	...	...	...	...	...
Hendaye .... d.	1245	...	...	...	1532	...	...	2119	...	...	...	...	...	...	│	...	...	...	0621	0727	...	...	...	...	...
Irún 🏛 .... d.	1251	1320	...	...	1540	1705	...	2125	2200	...	...	2215	...	...	│	...	...	...	0626	0732	0815	0815	...	...	0845
San Sebastián / Donostia .... a.	...	1335	...	...	...	1720	...	...	2218	...	...	2235	...	...	│	...	...	...	...	...	0830	0830	...	...	0901
Vitoria / Gasteiz .... a.	...	1514	...	...	...	│	...	...	0014	...	...	0031	...	...	0405	...	...	...	...	...	1007	1007	...	...	1039
Burgos .... a.	...	1703	...	...	...	│	...	...	0157	...	...	0219	...	...	0520	...	...	...	...	...	1124	1124	...	...	1212
Valladolid Campo Grande a.	...	1811	1845	...	...	│	...	...	0318	...	...	0355	...	...	0622	...	...	...	...	...	1229	1229	1307	1353	...
Medina del Campo .... a.	...	1839	1906	...	...	│	...	...	0352	...	...	0430	...	...	│	...	...	...	...	...	│	1252	1327	1417	...
Salamanca .... a.	...	1933	│	...	...	│	...	...	0448	...	...	│	...	...	│	...	...	...	...	...	│	│	│	1516	...
Coimbra-B ⊙ .... a.	...	...	│	...	...	│	...	...	0849	0931	1134	│	...	...	│	...	...	...	...	...	│	│	│	...	...
Lisboa Santa Apolónia .. a.	...	...	│	...	...	│	...	...	1103	│	│	│	...	...	│	...	...	...	...	...	│	│	│	...	...
Porto Campanhã .... a.	...	...	│	...	...	│	...	...	...	1039	1239	│	...	...	│	...	...	...	...	...	│	│	│	...	...
Madrid Chamartín .... a.	...	...	2120	...	...	2244h	...	...	...	...	...	0735	0905	...	0913	1205	...	...	...	...	1353	1512	1540	...	...
Alacant Terminal .... a.	...	...	...	...	...	...	...	...	...	...	...	...	1245	...	...	1550	...	...	...	...	...	...	1957	...	...

train number	601	8558	9063	410	203	8584	1077	609	280	79	8306	209	4167	4052	9015	8592	1147	407/6	9019	528	310/311	1187	205	8524	9039
train type/number	Alta	TGV	☆		IC 🍷	TGV	Alta	Alta		Alta		IC ✓	Alvia		☆	TGV	Alta	Hotel	☆	IC		Alta		TGV	☆
notes	S	[R] ✓ 🍷	[R] 🍴	🍷 2	[R] ✓ ①–⑥	[R] ✓ p	🍴 ①–⑥	🍷 R	🍷 2	🍴	2	[R] ⑦ R	[R] ✓ S	[R] F	[R] 🍴	[R] ✓ Q 🍷	🍴	[R] 🍴 H	[R] 🍴	[R] 🍷	[R] 🍴 B	🍴	[R] K 🍷	[R] ✓ 🍷	[R] 🍴 ⑥⑦
Alacant Terminal .... d.	...	...	...	...	...	...	0705	...	...	1035	...	...	...	...	...	...	1405	...	...	...	...	1805	...	...	...
Madrid Chamartín .... d.	0715h	...	...	...	1000	...	1029g	1405h	...	1428	...	1442	1610	...	...	...	1746	1900	...	...	...	2143	2245	...	...
Porto Campanhã .... d.	│	...	...	...	│	...	...	│	...	...	...	│	│	...	...	...	▬	│	...	1652	...	...	│	...	...
Lisboa Santa Apolónia .... d.	│	...	...	...	│	...	...	│	...	...	...	│	│	...	...	...	...	│	...	│	1606	...	│	...	...
Coimbra-B ⊙ .... d.	│	...	...	...	│	...	...	│	...	...	...	│	│	...	...	...	...	│	...	1756	1826	...	│	...	...
Salamanca .... d.	│	...	...	1030	│	...	...	│	...	...	1350	│	│	...	...	...	...	│	...	...	0005	...	│	...	...
Medina del Campo .... d.	│	...	...	1120	1203	...	...	◐	...	...	1447	1652	│	...	...	...	...	│	...	...	0057	...	0110	...	...
Valladolid Campo Grande d.	│	...	...	1147	1225	...	...	│	...	...	1508	1714	1734	...	...	...	...	2120	...	...	0130	...	0142	...	...
Burgos .... d.	│	...	...	1300	1326	...	...	│	1644	...	...	1821	1835	...	...	...	...	2221	...	...	0254	...	0317	...	...
Vitoria / Gasteiz .... d.	│	...	...	1459	1440	...	...	│	1813	...	...	1937	1951	...	...	...	...	2339	...	...	0424	...	0456	...	...
San Sebastián / Donostia .... d.	1234s	...	...	1640	1625s	...	...	1924	2005	...	...	2123s	2130s	...	...	...	...	│	...	...	0634	...	0652s	...	...
Irún .... d.	1252s	...	...	1702	1650s	...	...	1941s	2027s	...	...	2146s	2154s	...	...	...	...	│	...	...	0658	...	0720	...	...
Hendaye 🏛 .... a.	1257	1411	...	1707	1656	1726	...	1946	2035	...	...	2151	2200	2219	...	2314	...	│	...	...	0710	...	0725	0758	...
Bordeaux St Jean .... a.	...	1630	...	...	...	1947	...	...	...	...	...	...	...	│	...	│	...	│	...	...	...	...	...	1021	...
Poitiers .... a.	...	│	...	...	...	2137	...	...	...	...	...	...	...	│	...	│	...	0558	...	...	...	...	...	1211	...
Blois .... a.	...	│	...	...	...	│	...	...	...	...	...	...	...	│	...	│	☆	0659	...	...	...	...	...	│	...
Paris Austerlitz .... a.	...	│	...	...	...	│	...	...	...	...	...	...	...	0710	...	│	**9011**	0827	...	...	...	...	...	│	...
Paris Montparnasse .... a.	...	1945	...	...	...	2320	...	...	...	...	...	...	...	...	...	0600	[R] 🍴	...	...	...	...	...	...	1345v	...
Paris Nord 10 .... d.	...	...	2113	...	...	...	...	...	...	...	...	...	...	...	0907	...	0807	...	1013	...	...	...	...	...	1507c
London Waterloo 10 ...... a.	...	...	2234	...	...	...	...	...	...	...	...	...	...	...	1038	...	0934	...	1128	...	...	...	...	...	1637

A – SUREX / SUD EXPRESSO – 🛏 1, 2 cl., ▬ 2 cl., [2] and 🍴 Irún - Vilar Formoso (**312**) - Lisboa.
B – SUD EXPRESSO / SUREX – 🛏 1, 2 cl., ▬ 2 cl., [2] and 🍴 Lisboa - Vilar Formoso (**310**) - Hendaye.
F – *CORAIL LUNÉA* – ▬ 1, 2 cl. and [2] (reclining) Paris - Irún and Hendaye - Paris. Not Dec. 24, 31.
H – FRANCISCO DE GOYA *Trainhotel Elipsos* – 🛏 1, 2 cl., 🛏 1, 2 cl. (T4), [2] (reclining) and 🍴 Paris - Madrid and v.v. [R] Special fares apply.
K – COSTA VASCA – 🛏 1, 2 cl., ▬ 2 cl. and [1] Irún - Madrid and Madrid - Hendaye.
Q – ⑤⑦ (also Dec. 25, Jan. 1, Mar. 24, Apr. 30, May 7, 12; not May 2).
R – Until Dec. 22.
S – From Dec. 23.

c – 1513 on ①–⑤.
g – Madrid **Atocha Cercanias** adjacent to Puerta de Atocha, see City Plans page 31.

h – Madrid **Puerta de Atocha**.
k – Not May 10, 11.
p – Not May 8, 9, 10.
r – 0955 on Ⓐ Jan. 7 - Feb. 20, Mar. 13 - 21.
s – Stops to set down only.
v – 1350, 1355 on certain dates.

✓ – Supplement payable.
⊙ – 🏛 at Fuentes de Oñoro.
◐ – Via Pamplona.

Alvia – *Alvia* [R] 🍷 ✓.
Alta – *Altaria*. [R] 🍷 ✓.
☆ – Eurostar train. Minimum check-in time 30 minutes. Special fares payable. Valid Dec. 9, 2007 - July 5, 2008. Additional services are shown on Table **10**.

KÖLN and FRANKFURT - BARCELONA and NICE 47

train type/ number	IC	4239	4248	ICE	ICE	87454	4293	Talgo	ICE	ICE	87460	4297
train number	432	4238	4249	611	279	31964	4248	463	691	601	31966	4296
notes	🍷	[R]	[R]	🍷	🍷	2	[R]	462	🍷	🍷	2	[R]
	Ⓑf	C	J				A	M🍷				P
Köln Hbf .... d.	1618	...	...	1554	...	...	...	...	...	1654	...	...
Luxembourg 🏛 .... d.	1934	1946	...	|	...	...	...	...	...	|	...	...
Metz .... d.	...	2044	2112	|	...	...	...	...	...	|	...	...
Nancy .... d.	...	2133	2200	|	...	...	...	...	...	|	...	...
rankfurt (Main) Hbf . d.	...	|	|	|	1650	...	...	...	1750	|	...	...
annheim .... d.	...	|	|	1724	1736	...	...	...	1828	1836	...	...
arlsruhe .... d.	...	|	|	...	1801	...	...	...	...	1901	...	...
ffenburg .... d.	...	|	|	...	1827	1834	...	...	...	1927	2004	...
ehl 🏛 .... d.	...	|	|	...	...	1852	...	...	...	...	2022	...
trasbourg .... d.	...	|	|	...	...	1904	2019	...	...	...	2034	2056
ulhouse .... d.	...	|	|	...	...	...	2134	...	...	...	▬	2207
esançon .... d.	...	|	|	...	...	...	2322	...	...	...	...	0001
jon .... d.	...	|	0116	...	...	...	0116	...	...	...	...	|
yon Part Dieu .... a.	...	|	|	...	...	...	|	...	...	...	...	|
vignon Centre .... a.	...	0412	|	...	...	...	|	...	...	...	...	0438
les .... a.	...	|	|	...	...	...	|	...	...	...	...	0507
Nîmes .... a.	...	|	0552	...	...	...	0552	...	...	...	...	|
Montpellier .... a.	...	|	0627	...	...	...	0627	0726	...	...	...	|
Béziers .... a.	...	|	0720	...	...	...	0720	0804	...	...	...	|
Narbonne .... a.	...	|	0739	...	...	...	0739	0820	...	...	...	|
Perpignan .... a.	...	|	0826	...	...	...	0826	0854	...	...	...	|
Cerbère .... a.	...	|	0916	...	...	...	0916	0921	...	...	2	|
Portbou 🏛 .... a.	...	|	0927	...	...	...	0927	0948	...	...	1014	|
Figueres .... a.	...	|	...	...	...	...	...	1012	...	...	1037	|
Girona .... a.	...	|	...	...	...	...	...	1040	...	...	1115	|
Barcelona Sants .... a.	...	|	...	...	...	...	...	1146	...	...	1246	|
arseille St Charles .. a.	...	0515	...	...	...	...	...	...	...	...	...	0556
oulon .... a.	...	0616	...	...	...	...	...	...	...	...	...	0707
es Arcs - Draguignan . a.	...	0656	...	...	...	...	...	...	...	...	...	0747
Raphaël - Valescure a.	...	0715	...	...	...	...	...	...	...	...	...	0805
annes .... a.	...	0744	...	...	...	...	...	...	...	...	...	0837
ntibes .... a.	...	0757	...	...	...	...	...	...	...	...	...	0851
ce .... a.	...	0820	...	...	...	...	...	...	...	...	...	0912

train type/ number	4394	4330		4348	4348	87417	ICE	ICE	
train number	4395	4331		4349	4393	31955	600	690	
notes	[R]	[R]	2	[R]	[R]	2	🍷	🍷	
	P	C		J	A				
Nice .... d.	1946q	2017q	...	...	...	...	...	...	...
Antibes .... d.	2007q	2034q	...	...	...	...	...	...	...
Cannes .... d.	2019q	2047q	...	...	...	...	...	...	...
St Raphaël - Valescure . d.	2045	2112	...	...	...	...	...	...	...
Les Arcs - Draguignan .. d.	2107	2132	...	...	...	...	...	...	...
Toulon .... d.	2154	2214	...	...	...	...	...	...	...
Marseille St Charles ... d.	2251	2310	...	...	...	...	...	...	...
Barcelona Sants ..... d.	|	|	1725	...	...	...	...	...	...
Girona .... d.	|	|	1858	...	...	...	...	...	...
Figueres .... d.	|	|	1936	...	...	...	...	...	...
Portbou .... d.	|	|	2003	...	...	...	...	...	...
Cerbère 🏛 .... d.	|	|	2007	2042	2042	...	...	...	...
Perpignan .... d.	|	|	▬	2133	2133	...	...	...	...
Narbonne .... d.	|	|	...	2213	2213	...	...	...	...
Béziers .... d.	|	|	...	2230	2230	...	...	...	...
Montpellier .... d.	|	|	...	2319	2319	...	...	...	...
Nîmes .... d.	|	|	...	2349	2349	...	...	...	...
Arles .... d.	2342	|	...	|	|	...	...	...	...
Avignon Centre .... d.	0014	0025	...	|	|	...	...	...	...
Lyon Part Dieu .... a.	|	|	...	|	|	...	...	...	...
Dijon .... a.	|	|	...	0407	0407	...	...	...	...
Besançon .... a.	0449	|	...	|	0530	...	...	...	...
Mulhouse .... a.	0640	|	...	|	0723	...	...	...	...
Strasbourg .... a.	0758	|	...	|	0834	0923	...	...	...
Kehl 🏛 .... a.	...	|	...	|	...	0933	...	...	...
Offenburg .... a.	...	|	...	|	...	0952	1030	...	...
Karlsruhe .... a.	...	|	...	|	...	...	1058	...	...
Mannheim .... a.	...	|	...	|	...	...	1123	1131	...
Frankfurt (Main) Hbf .. a.	...	|	*IC*	|	...	...	|	1208	...
Nancy .... a.	...	0655	**435**	0730	...	...	|	...	...
Metz .... a.	...	0745	🍷	0818	...	...	|	...	...
Luxembourg 🏛 .... a.	...	0845	1024	...	...	...	|	...	...
Köln Hbf .... a.	...	...	1342	...	...	...	1305	...	...

– *CORAIL LUNÉA* – ⑤⑦ (also Dec. 20–23, 25–30, Jan. 1–6, Feb. 9, 16, 23, Mar. 1, 8, 24, daily Apr. 4–27, also Apr. 30, daily May 7–12, June 6–14; not Mar. 23): 🛏 1, 2 cl. and [2] (reclining) Strasbourg - Portbou and Cerbère - Strasbourg.

– *CORAIL LUNÉA* – ⑤⑦ (also Dec. 19–23, 25–30, Jan. 1–6, daily Feb. 6 - Mar. 9, also Mar. 24, 25, daily Apr. 2 - May 2, also May 5, 6, 7, 10, 12, 13, daily June 7–14): 🛏 1, 2 cl. and [2] (reclining) Luxembourg - Nice and v.v.

– *CORAIL LUNÉA* – ⑤⑦ (also Dec. 20–23, 25–30, Jan. 1–6, Feb. 9, 16, 23, Mar. 1, 8, 24, daily Apr. 4–27, also Apr. 30, daily May 7–12, June 6–14; not Mar. 23): 🛏 1, 2 cl. and [2] (reclining) Metz - Portbou and Cerbère - Metz.

– *CORAIL LUNÉA* – ⑤⑦ (also Dec. 19–23, 25–30, Jan. 1–6, daily Feb. 6 - Mar. 9, also Mar. 24, 25, daily Apr. 2 - May 2, also May 5, 6, 7, 10, 12, 13, daily June 7–14): 🛏 1, 2 cl. and [2] (reclining) Strasbourg - Nice and v.v.

M – MARE NOSTRUM – [12] and ✕ Montpellier - Barcelona - Alacant - Cartagena (arrive 1952), [R] ⁄ Special fares payable.

f – Not Dec. 24, 25, 31, Mar. 21, 23, May 11.

q – Depart up to 7 mins earlier Jan. 3 - Feb. 22.

MADRID - LISBOA 48

train number		Hotel	
notes		332 [R]	
		✕A	
adrid Chamartín .... d.	...	2245	...
alavera de La Reina .... d.	...	0055	...
avalmoral de La Mata .... d.	...	0127	...
áceres .... d.	...	0316	...
an Vicente de Alcántara .... d.	...	0508	...
alencia de Alcántara .... 🏛 ES d.	...	0545	...
arvão Beirã .... 🏛 PT d.	...	0502	...
brantes .... a.	...	0617	...
ntroncamento .... a.	...	0637	...
sboa Oriente .... a.	...	0751	...
sboa Santa Apolónia .... a.	...	0800	...

train number		Hotel	
notes		335 [R]	
		✕A	
Lisboa Santa Apolónia ...... d.	...	2200	...
Lisboa Oriente .... d.	...	2209	...
Entroncamento .... d.	...	2317	...
Abrantes .... d.	...	2338	...
Marvão Beirãa .... 🏛 PT d.	...	0054	...
Valencia de Alcántara 🏛 ES d.	...	0230	...
San Vicente de Alcántara ..... d.	...	0247	...
Cáceres .... a.	...	0409	...
Navalmoral de La Mata .... a.	...	0538	...
Talavera de La Reina .... a.	...	0614	...
Madrid Chamartín .... a.	...	0843	...

A – LUSITANIA *Hotel Train* – 🛏 *Gran Clase* (1, 2 berths), 🛏 *Preferente* (1, 2 berths), 🛏 1, 2 cl. (T4), [2] (also [1] from Dec. 3) and ✕ Madrid - Lisboa and v.v. Special fares apply.

ES – Spain (Central European Time).

PT – Portugal (West European Time).

BARCELONA - MARSEILLE, NICE, LYON, GENÈVE and ZÜRICH 49

train type/number	Talgo	TGV	IC	4657		Talgo	4667		Hotel	
train number	73/2	6866/7	739	4656		460/1	4666		✕ *EN*	
notes	⁄[R]	⁄[R]	✕	🍷		⁄[R]	A		273/2	
	W🍷	🍷				M✕			[R] B	
arcelona Sants .... d.	...	...	...	...	...	1642	...	...	...	...
arcelona França .... d.	0845	...	...	...	...	|	...	...	2015	...
rona .... d.	0955	...	...	...	...	1748	...	...	2125	...
gueres .... d.	1025	...	...	...	...	1815	...	...	2154	...
ortbou .... d.	1054	...	...	...	...	1844	...	...	|	...
erbère 🏛 .... d.	1114	...	...	...	...	1906	...	...	|	...
erpignan .... a.	1143	...	...	...	...	1936	...	...	2318d	...
arbonne .... a.	1219	...	...	...	...	2013	...	...	|	...
ontpellier .... a.	1322	1356	...	1511	...	2109	2306	...	|	...
îmes .... a.	...	1421	...	|	...	...	2334	...	|	...
vignon Centre .... a.	...	|	...	|	...	...	|	...	|	...
Marseille St Charles .... a.	...	|	...	1639	...	...	0043	...	|	...
Nice .... a.	...	|	...	1923	...	...	...	...	|	...
alence Ville .... a.	...	1510v	...	...	...	...	...	...	|	...
Lyon Part Dieu .... a.	...	1550	...	...	...	...	...	...	|	...
enève 🏛 .... a.	...	1735	1745	...	...	...	...	...	0530	...
ausanne .... a.	...	...	1818	...	...	...	...	...	0654	...
ibourg .... a.	...	...	1903	...	...	...	...	...	0747	...
ern .... a.	...	...	1926	...	...	...	...	...	0849	...
irich HB .... a.	...	...	2028	...	...	...	...	...	1010	...

train type/number	Talgo		IC	TGV		4762	Talgo		Hotel	
train number	463/2		716	6816/7	17488	4763	70/71		✕ *EN*	
notes	⁄[R]		✕	⁄[R]	E	🍷	⁄[R]		274/5	
	M✕			🍷			W🍷		[R] C	
Zürich HB .... d.	...	...	0932	...	...	...	...	...	1927	...
Bern .... d.	...	...	1034	...	...	...	...	...	2051	...
Fribourg .... d.	...	...	1055	...	...	...	...	...	2145	...
Lausanne .... d.	...	...	1142	...	...	...	...	...	2242	...
Genève 🏛 .... d.	...	...	1215	1244	...	...	...	...	2325	...
Lyon Part Dieu .... d.	...	...	...	1437	...	...	...	...	|	...
Valence Ville .... d.	...	...	...	1516v	...	...	...	...	|	...
Nice .... d.	...	...	...	|	1112q	...	...	...	|	...
Marseille St Charles .... d.	...	...	...	|	1342	1500	...	...	|	...
Avignon Centre .... d.	...	...	...	|	...	|	...	...	|	...
Nîmes .... d.	...	...	...	1602	...	1612	...	...	|	...
Montpellier .... d.	0726	...	...	1626	...	1642	1702	...	|	...
Narbonne .... d.	0822	...	...	...	...	...	1758	...	|	...
Perpignan .... d.	0856	...	...	...	...	...	1837	...	0548a	...
Cerbère .... d.	0931	...	...	...	...	...	1914	...	|	...
Portbou 🏛 .... a.	0948	...	...	...	...	...	1931	...	|	...
Figueres .... a.	1012	...	...	...	...	...	1953	...	0709	...
Girona .... a.	1040	...	...	...	...	...	2019	...	0737	...
Barcelona França .... a.	|	...	...	...	...	...	2145	...	0901	...
Barcelona Sants .... a.	1146	...	...	...	...	...	...	...	...	...

– ⑤⑦ (also Dec. 24, Jan. 1, Mar. 24, Apr. 30, May 7, 12; not Mar. 23, May 2, 11).

– PAU CASALS *Trainhotel Elipsos* ②④⑦ Dec. 9 - June 15, 2008; daily June 17 - Sept. 2; ②④⑦ Sept. 4 - Dec. 13: 🛏 1, 2 cl., 🛏 1, 2 cl. (T4), [1] (reclining) and ✕ Barcelona - Zürich and v.v.

– PAU CASALS *Trainhotel Elipsos* ①③⑤ Dec. 9 - June 18, 2008; daily June 19 - Sept. 3; ①③⑤ Sept. 5 - Dec. 13: 🛏 1, 2 cl., 🛏 1, 2 cl. (T4), [1] (reclining) and ✕ Zürich - Barcelona and v.v.

– ①–⑤ (not Dec. 25, Jan. 1, Mar. 24, May 1, 8).

– MARE NOSTRUM – [12] and ✕ Cartagena - Alacant - Barcelona - Montpellier and v.v. Special fares payable.

– CATALÁN TALGO – [12] and ✕ Barcelona - Montpellier and v.v. Special fares payable.

a – Arrival time.

d – Departure time.

q – Depart up to 7 mins earlier Jan. 3 - Feb. 22.

v – Valence **TGV**.

⁄ – Supplement payable.

50 OSLO, STOCKHOLM and KØBENHAVN - HAMBURG - BERLIN

Services are subject to alteration around holidays, please refer to relevant countries for details.

train type / number	1		ICE			EC	IC	X2000		EC*	ICE		X2000		X2000			X2000		EC
train number	[R]		38	1039		36	2071	525	1057	32	703	391	529	1069	531	1075	393	489		30
notes	LG		[R]🍷	①–⑤		[R]🍷	🍷			[R]🍷	🍷	①–⑤			⑧	①–⑤	⑥k	429		[R]🍷
notes	⑧		c⟋			c⟋		d		c⟋	P	🍷h					🍷	⑧fy		Sc⟋
Oslo Sentral d.	...	...	...	...	...	...	...	...	...	...	...	0700	...	...	...	...	0900	...	...	...
Stockholm Central d.	2305	...	...	...	...	...	...	0820	...	...	...	|	1020	...	1120	...	|	...	...	...
Göteborg d.	|	...	...	0625	...	...	...	|	0940	...	...	1057	|	1140	|	1240	1256	1330	...	...
Malmö d.	0642	0702	...	1002	1002	...	...	1246	1302	...	...	...	1446	1502	1546	1602	...	1615	1642	...
København H. d.	...	0737	0745	1037	1037	1145	...	...	1337	1538	...	...	...	1537	...	1637	...	...	1717	1738
Malmö d.	...	...	|	...	...	|	...	...	...	|	...	...	...	...	...	...	...	...	...	|
Rødby Ferry ⛴ d.	...	...	0945	...	...	1335	...	...	...	1734	...	...	...	...	...	...	...	...	...	1945
Puttgarden ⛴ a.	...	...	1030	...	...	1435	...	...	...	1835	...	...	...	...	...	...	...	...	...	2030
Lübeck Hbf a.	...	...	1136	...	...	1536s	...	...	...	1936s	...	...	...	...	...	...	...	...	...	2136s
Odense d.	...	...	|	...	...	|	...	...	...	|	...	...	...	...	...	...	...	...	...	|
Padborg ⛴ d.	...	...	|	...	...	|	...	...	...	|	...	...	...	...	...	...	...	...	...	|
Flensburg ⛴ d.	...	...	|	...	...	|	...	...	...	|	...	...	...	...	...	...	...	...	...	|
Hamburg Hbf a.	...	...	1216	...	...	1616	1644	...	...	2016	2121	...	...	...	...	...	...	...	...	2216
Köln 20 800 a.	...	...	|	...	...	...	|	...	...	...	|	...	...	...	...	...	...	...	...	...
Amsterdam 22 a.	...	...	|	...	...	...	|	...	...	...	|	...	...	...	...	...	...	...	...	...
München Hbf 900 a.	...	...	|	...	...	...	|	...	...	...	|	...	...	...	...	...	...	...	...	...
Basel SBB 912 a.	...	...	|	...	...	...	|	...	...	...	|	...	...	...	...	...	...	...	...	...
Berlin Hauptbahnhof a.	...	...	1436	...	...	...	1843	...	...	...	2312	...	...	...	...	...	...	...	...	...

train type	X2000			CNL	CNL	CNL	X2000				EN
train number	533	1081		40483	483	50483	541	395	1105		211
notes								⑧p			[R]
notes				A	H	B	z	🍷	y		Db
Oslo Sentral d.	...	...	...	...	...	...	...	1300	...	...	...
Stockholm Central d.	1220	...	...	...	...	...	1620	|	...	...	...
Göteborg d.	|	1335	...	...	...	...	|	1656	1740	...	...
Malmö d.	1646	1702	1742	...	...	...	|	...	|	...	...
København H. d.	...	1737	1817	1853	1853	1853	|	...	|	2043	...
Malmö d.	...	...	...	|	|	|	2046	...	2052	2118	2132x
Rødby Ferry ⛴ d.	...	...	...	|	|	|	...	...	...	...	|
Puttgarden ⛴ a.	...	...	...	|	|	|	...	...	...	...	|
Lübeck Hbf a.	...	...	...	|	|	|	...	...	...	...	|
Odense d.	...	...	...	2023u	2023u	2023u	...	...	...	...	|
Padborg ⛴ d.	...	...	...	2218u	2218u	2218u	...	...	...	...	|
Flensburg ⛴ d.	...	...	...	2232u	2232u	2232u	...	...	...	...	|
Hamburg Hbf a.	...	...	...	|	|	|	...	...	...	...	|
Köln 20 800 a.	...	...	...	0614	|	|	...	...	...	...	|
Amsterdam 22 a.	...	...	...	1027	|	|	...	...	...	...	|
München Hbf 900 a.	...	...	...	...	0857	|	...	...	...	...	|
Basel SBB 912 a.	...	...	...	...	...	1037	...	...	...	...	|
Berlin Hauptbahnhof a.	...	...	...	...	...	...	...	...	...	...	0604

train type	ICE	EC				X2000	ICE	EC*		X2000	ICE	EC		X2000
train number	702	31	1050	396	398	538	1518	33	1062	542	1514	35	1086	550
notes	🍷	[R]🍷		⑥q	⑧g	518	708	[R]🍷			1714/24	[R]🍷		J
notes		Tc⟋		🍷	🍷	y	🍷	c⟋		z	🍷	c⟋	y	⑧
Berlin Hauptbahnhof d.	0518	...	...	...	...	...	0718	...	...	...	1118	...	...	...
Basel SBB 912 d.	|	...	...	...	...	...	|	...	...	...	|	...	...	...
München Hbf 900 d.	|	...	...	...	...	...	|	...	...	...	|	...	...	...
Amsterdam 22 d.	|	...	...	...	...	...	|	...	...	...	|	...	...	...
Köln 20 800 d.	|	...	...	...	...	...	|	...	...	...	|	...	...	...
Hamburg Hbf d.	0707	0725	...	...	...	...	0857	0928	...	...	1254	1328	...	...
Flensburg ⛴ a.	...	|	...	...	...	...	...	|	...	...	...	|	...	...
Padborg ⛴ a.	...	|	...	...	...	...	...	|	...	...	...	|	...	...
Odense a.	...	|	...	...	...	...	...	|	...	...	...	|	...	...
Lübeck Hbf d.	...	0807u	...	...	...	...	...	1007u	...	...	...	1407u	...	...
Puttgarden ⛴ d.	...	0910	...	...	...	...	...	1110	...	...	...	1510	...	...
Rødby Ferry ⛴ a.	...	1000	...	...	...	...	...	1200	...	...	...	1600	...	...
Malmö a.	...	|	...	...	...	...	...	|	...	...	...	|	...	...
København H. d.	...	1209	1223	...	...	1231	...	1409	1423	...	...	1809	1823	...
Malmö a.	...	...	1258	...	...	1314u	...	...	1458	1514	...	...	1858	1914
Göteborg a.	...	...	1615	1639	1745	|	...	...	1815	|	...	...	2220	|
Stockholm Central a.	...	...	...	|	|	1740t	...	...	...	1940	...	...	...	2340
Oslo Sentral a.	...	...	...	2045	2145	...	...	...	...	...	...	...	...	...

train type	ICE		2	EN				X2000	X2000	CNL	CNL	CNL		X2000		
train number	37		[R]	210		1026	394	528	530	40353	482	40347	1038	534	396	398
notes	[R]🍷		LG	[R]			⑧p								⑥j	⑧g
notes	c⟋		⑧	Cb			🍷	Q		B	H	A			🍷	🍷
Berlin Hauptbahnhof d.	1511	...	...	2316	...	...	...	...	...	...	...	...	...	...	...	...
Basel SBB 912 d.	|	...	...	|	...	...	...	...	...	1804	...	...	...	...	...	...
München Hbf 900 d.	|	...	...	|	...	...	...	...	...	|	1900e	...	...	...	...	...
Amsterdam 22 d.	|	...	...	|	...	...	...	...	...	|	|	1903r	...	...	...	...
Köln 20 800 d.	|	...	...	|	...	...	...	...	...	|	|	2228r	...	...	...	...
Hamburg Hbf d.	1728	...	...	|	...	...	...	...	...	|	|	|	...	...	...	...
Flensburg ⛴ a.	|	...	...	|	...	...	...	...	...	0546s	0546s	0546s	...	...	...	...
Padborg ⛴ a.	|	...	...	|	...	...	...	...	...	0559s	0559s	0559s	...	...	...	...
Odense a.	|	...	...	|	...	...	...	...	...	0820s	0820s	0820s	...	...	...	...
Lübeck Hbf d.	1807	...	...	|	...	...	...	...	...	|	|	|	...	...	...	...
Puttgarden ⛴ d.	1915	...	...	|	...	...	...	...	...	|	|	|	...	...	...	...
Rødby Ferry ⛴ a.	2000	...	...	|	...	...	...	...	...	|	|	|	...	...	...	...
Malmö a.	|	...	...	0801	0822	0908	...	0814	0914	|	|	|	...	...	...	...
København H. d.	2209	2223	...	...	0857	|	...	|	|	0959	0959	0959	1023	...	...	...
Malmö a.	...	2258	2308	...	...	|	...	|	|	...	...	...	1058	1114	...	...
Göteborg a.	...	...	|	...	...	1220	1245	|	|	...	...	...	1420	|	1639	1745
Stockholm Central a.	...	...	0555	...	...	...	|	1240	1340	...	...	...	...	1540	|	|
Oslo Sentral a.	...	...	...	...	...	...	1645	...	...	...	...	...	...	...	2045	2145

A – *City Night Line* 🛏 1, 2 cl., ▬ 2 cl., (2) and ✗ København - Köln - Amsterdam and v.v. [R] Special fares apply.
B – *City Night Line* AURORA – 🛏 1, 2 cl., ▬ 2 cl. (4, 6 berth), (2) and ✗ København - Frankfurt - Basel and v.v. [R] Special fares apply.
C – BERLIN NIGHT EXPRESS – Dec. 26, 29, Jan. 1; ②④⑥ Mar. 15 - Apr. 25 (also Mar. 23, 24; not Mar. 22); daily Apr. 26 - Aug. 24; ①④⑥ Aug. 25 - Sept. 23; ②④⑥ Sept. 24 - Oct. 11 (also Oct. 28, Nov. 1): 🛏 1, 2 cl. and ▬ 2 cl. Berlin - Malmö. [R] Special fares apply.
D – BERLIN NIGHT EXPRESS – Dec. 21, 28, 30; ③⑤⑦ Mar. 14 - Apr. 25 (also Mar. 20, 24; not Mar. 21); daily Apr. 26 - Aug. 24; ③⑤⑦ Aug. 25 - Oct. 11 (also Oct. 24, 29): 🛏 1, 2 cl. and ▬ 2 cl. Malmö - Berlin. [R] Special fares apply.
G – 🛏 1, 2 cl. and (2) Stockholm - Malmö and v.v.
H – *City Night Line* HANS CHRISTIAN ANDERSEN – 🛏 1, 2 cl., ▬ 2 cl., (2) and ✗ København - München and v.v. [R] Special fares apply.
J – Dec. 9–23, Jan. 6 - June 14.
L – Dec. 9–23, Jan. 6 - June 14 (also Feb. 16, 23, Mar. 1; not Mar. 21, 23, Apr. 30, June 6).
P – ①–⑥ (also Dec. 23, 30, Mar. 23, May 11; not Dec. 26, Jan. 1, Mar. 24, May 12).
Q – ①–⑥ (not Mar. 22).
S – Dec. 9 - Jan. 5, Mar. 14 - Oct. 26 (not Dec. 24, 31).
T – Dec. 9 - Jan. 5, Mar. 18 - Oct. 27 (not Dec. 25, Jan. 1).
b – Train is conveyed by train-ferry Trelleborg ⛴ - Sassnitz Fährhafen ⛴ (Mukran) and v.v.
c – Passengers to / from Rødby or Puttgarden should leave / board the train on board the ferry.
d – Not Dec. 25, Jan. 1.
e – 1916 on ⑥⑦ (also Dec. 25, 26, Jan. 1, Mar. 21, 24, May 1, 12).
f – Also Dec. 15, 22, 29, Jan. 5.
g – Also Mar. 22, May 17; not Dec. 25, Mar. 20.
h – Not Mar. 20, May 12.
j – Also Mar. 20; not Dec. 24, 31, Mar. 22, May 17, 31.
k – Also Mar. 20; not Mar. 22, May 17, 31.
p – Also Mar. 22, May 17; not Ma[r.] 20.
q – Also Mar. 20; not Dec. 24, 31, Mar. 22, May 17, 31.
r – On Jan. 11, 12, Feb. 22, 23 departs Amsterdam 1802, Köln 2133.
s – Stops to set down only.
t – 1735 on ⑦.
u – Calls to pick up only.
x – 2152 on Dec. 21, 28, 30.
y – Not Dec. 24.
z – Not Dec. 24, 31.
⟋ – Supplement payable.
* – *ICE* from Jan. 6.
X2000 – High speed train. [R] ✗ ⟋.

For explanation of standard symbols see page 4

BERLIN - ELK, GDAŃSK and KALININGRAD 51

train type			D		D			
train number			345		7/345			
notes			W		C			
Berlin Zoo d.	...	...	...	...	...	...	...	...
Berlin Hauptbahnhof d.	...	...	...	...	...	...	...	...
Berlin Ostbahnhof ◐ d.	...	...	...	...	...	...	...	...
Berlin Lichtenberg ◐ d.	...	...	2138	...	2138	...	...	...
Rzepin ◐ d.	...	...	2347	...	2347	...	...	...
Poznań Gł. d.	...	...	0240	...	0240	...	...	...
Tczew a.	...	...	0738	...	0738	...	...	...
Gdańsk Gł. a.	...	...	0812	...	|	...	...	...
Gdynia Gł. a.	...	...	0845	...	|	...	...	...
Malbork a.	...	...	...	...	0911	...	...	...
Malbork d.	...	...	...	...	0913	...	...	...
Elblag a.	...	...	...	...	0941	...	...	...
Olsztyn a.	...	...	...	...	|	...	...	...
Ełk a.	...	...	...	...	|	...	...	...
Braniewo ▥ a.	...	...	...	...	1038	...	...	...
Kaliningrad § a.	...	...	...	...	1516	...	...	...

train type			D		D			
train number			344		8/344			
notes			X		D			
Kaliningrad § d.	...	...	...	...	1844	...	...	...
Braniewo ▥ d.	...	...	...	...	1950	...	...	...
Ełk d.	...	...	...	...	|	...	...	...
Olsztyn d.	...	...	...	...	|	...	...	...
Elblag d.	...	...	...	...	2040	...	...	...
Malbork a.	...	...	...	...	2107	...	...	...
Malbork d.	...	...	...	...	2109	...	...	...
Gdynia Gł. d.	...	...	2114	...	|	...	...	...
Gdańsk Gł. d.	...	...	2144	...	|	...	...	...
Tczew d.	...	...	2222	...	2222	...	...	...
Poznań Gł. a.	...	...	0230	...	0230	...	...	...
Rzepin ◐ a.	...	...	0503	...	0503	...	...	...
Berlin Lichtenberg ◐ a.	...	...	0714	...	0714	...	...	...
Berlin Ostbahnhof ◐ a.	...	...	...	...	...	...	...	...
Berlin Hauptbahnhof a.	...	...	...	...	...	...	...	...
Berlin Zoo a.	...	...	...	...	...	...	...	...

C – 🛏 1, 2 cl. Berlin (**345**) - Frankfurt an der Oder ▥ - Poznan (**65200**) - Gniezno (**65201**) - Tczew (**55001**) - Braniewo ▥ (**7**) - Kaliningrad. (Table **1038**).
D – 🛏 1, 2 cl. Kaliningrad (**8**) - Braniewo ▥ (**55002**) - Tczew (**56200**) - Gniezno (**56201**) - Poznan (**344**) - Frankfurt an der Oder ▥ - Berlin. (Table **1038**).
W – 🛏 1, 2 cl. Berlin (**345**) - Poznań (**65200**) - Gniezno (**65201**) - Gdynia.
X – 🛏 1, 2 cl. Gdynia (**56200**) - Gniezno (**56201**) - Poznań (**344**) - Berlin.

◐ – ▥ is at Frankfurt (Oder).
§ – Moskva time (2 hours ahead of Polish time, 1 hour ahead of Kaliningrad time).

PRAHA - BŘECLAV - WIEN 53

train type	*EC*			•*EC*	*EC*						*EC*	*EC**	*EC**	*EC*	*D*	*EC*						*EC*	*EC*			
train number	**71**	**667**	**1761**	**101**	**162**	**631**	**363**	**665**	**633**	**1931**	**566**	**73**	**75**	**171**	**273**	**173**	**681**	**275**	**641**	**361**	**1933**	**768**	**177**	**207**	**225**	
notes	✕		**2119**	✕	✕					**1933**	✕	🍸	🍸	✕		✕				**2129**	**1937**	✕	✕	**466**	**203**	
		y	2y	A	T							⊙	⊙			V					k		G	B	P	
Cheb d.	...	...	...	...	...	...	...	...	...	...	...	...	...	...	...	...	...	...	...	...	...	...	...	...	...	...
Plzeň hlavní d.	...	0603	...	...	...	...	0803	1003	...	...	...	...	...	...	...	...	...	...	...	1603	...	...	...	...	...	...
Praha Holešovice d.	...	|	...	...	...	...	|	|	...	...	...	0823	1023	1133	...	1333	...	...	...	|	...	...	1733	...	...	...
Praha Hlavní d.	0500	|	...	0611	...	0711	|	|	0911	...	...	|	|	|	...	|	1553	...	1511	|	...	...	|	1711	2206	...
Tábor d.	|	|	...	0750	...	0858	|	|	1058	...	...	|	|	|	...	|	|	...	1658	|	...	...	|	1858	|	...
Veselí nad Lužnicí d.	|	|	...	0817	...	0929	|	|	1129	...	...	|	|	|	...	|	|	...	1729	|	...	...	|	1929	|	...
České Budějovice d.	|	0756	0801	0902	...	1004	1009	1156	1204	1209	...	|	•|	|	...	|	|	...	1804	1809	1811	...	|	2030	|	...
Brno Hlavní d.	0743	...	|	|	...	...	|	▬	...	|	...	1051	1251	1417	1438	1617	1934	1938	...	|	|	...	2017	|	0335	...
Břeclav ▥ d.	0823	...	|	|	...	...	|	...	...	|	...	1123	1323	1449	1525	1658	...	2025	...	|	|	...	2058	|	0457	...
Summerau ▥ d.	|	...	|	1010	...	...	|	...	...	1336	...	|	|	...	|	|	...	|	...	|	1933	...	|	2147	|	...
Linz Hbf a.	|	...	|	1106	1116	...	|	...	...	1443	1516	|	|	...	|	|	...	|	...	|	2045	2053	|	2244	|	...
Salzburg a.	|	...	|	|	1227	...	|	...	...	...	1627	|	|	...	|	|	...	|	...	|	...	2158	|	0014	|	...
Zürich HB a.	|	...	|	|	1820	...	|	...	...	...	...	|	|	...	|	|	...	|	...	|	...	...	|	0620	|	...
Graz a.	|	...	|	1400	...	...	|	**2121**	...	...	...	|	|	...	|	|	...	|	...	|	...	...	|	...	|	...
Ljubljana a.	|	...	|	1732	...	...	|	2	...	...	...	|	|	...	|	|	...	|	...	|	...	...	|	...	|	...
Gmünd NÖ ▥ a.	|	...	0902	...	...	...	1107	1113*	...	...	...	|	|	...	|	|	...	|	...	1905	...	...	|	...	|	...
Wien Franz-Josefs-Bf a.	|	...	1130	...	...	...	...	1330	...	...	...	|	|	...	|	|	...	|	...	2147	...	...	|	...	|	...
Wien Südbahnhof a.	0928	...	...	...	...	...	...	...	...	...	...	1228	1428	...	1630	1803	...	2130	...	...	...	...	2203	...	0603	...

train type	*EC*			*D*	*EC*		*EC*				*EC**		*EC**			*EC*	*EC*		*EC*							
train number	**370**	**2100**	**638**	**270**	**174**		**172**	**1930**	**646**	**664**	**72**		**74**			**163**	**100**	**2116**	**70**	**1936**	**1934**	**1836**	**202**	**467**		
notes	✕	**360**			✕		✕	**1934**			🍸		🍸	**2110**	**362**	✕	✕	**1760**	✕	**1932**	**1932**		**224**	**206**		
	E	2					V				⊙		⊙	2		T	A	2		Ⓒf	Ⓐf	f	Q	B		
Wien Südbahnhof d.	0608	...	...	0732	...	...	1004	...	...	...	1333	...	1533	...	...	...	...	...	1833	...	...	...	2233	...	...	...
Wien Franz-Josefs-Bf d.	|	0622	...	|	...	...	|	...	...	...	|	...	|	1429	...	...	...	1659	|	...	...	...	|	...	...	...
Gmünd NÖ ▥ d.	|	0850	...	|	...	...	|	...	...	...	|	...	|	1646	1655	...	...	1917	|	...	...	...	|	...	...	...
Ljubljana d.	|	|	...	|	...	...	|	...	...	...	|	...	|	...	|	...	1018	|	|	...	...	...	|	...	...	...
Graz d.	|	|	...	|	...	...	|	...	...	...	|	...	|	...	|	...	1349	|	|	...	...	...	|	...	...	...
Zürich HB d.	|	|	...	|	...	...	|	...	...	...	|	...	|	...	|	0940	|	|	|	...	...	...	|	2240	...	...
Salzburg d.	|	|	...	|	...	...	|	...	...	...	|	...	|	...	|	1534	|	|	|	...	...	...	|	0441	...	...
Linz Hbf d.	|	|	...	|	...	...	|	1308	...	...	|	...	|	...	|	1645	1654	|	|	1808	1830	...	|	0614	...	...
Summerau ▥ a.	|	|	...	|	...	...	|	1414	...	...	|	...	|	...	|	...	1749	|	|	1926	1932	...	|	0714	...	...
Břeclav ▥ d.	0717	|	...	0839	0908	...	1113	|	...	...	1435	...	1635	...	|	...	|	|	1950	|	|	...	0002	|	...	...
Brno Hlavní d.	0750	|	...	0917	0943	...	1146	|	...	...	1507	...	1707	...	|	...	|	|	2023	|	|	...	0038	|	...	...
České Budějovice a.	|	0949	0954	...	|	...	|	1549	1554	1602	|	...	|	...	1749	...	1854	2019	|	2100	2100	2105	|	0820	...	...
Veselí nad Lužnicí a.	|	|	1024	...	|	...	|	...	1624	|	|	...	|	...	|	...	1939	...	|	...	...	2145	|	0925	...	...
Tábor a.	|	|	1056	...	|	...	|	...	1656	|	|	...	|	...	|	...	2014	...	|	...	...	2215	|	0956	...	...
Praha Hlavní a.	|	|	1253	...	|	...	|	...	1853	|	|	...	|	...	|	...	2155	...	2310	...	...	2357	0621	1153	...	...
Praha Holešovice a.	1025	|	...	...	1225	...	1425	...	...	|	1732	...	1932	...	|	...	...	...	...	...	...	...	...	...	...	...
Plzeň hlavní a.	...	1158	...	...	...	...	...	...	...	1758	...	...	...	...	1958	...	...	...	...	...	...	...	...	...	...	...
Cheb a.	...	...	...	...	...	...	...	...	...	...	...	...	...	...	...	...	...	...	...	...	...	...	...	...	...	...

A – JÓŽE PLEČNIK - (12) and ✕ Praha - Linz - Graz - Spielfeld-Straß ▥ - Ljubljana and v.v. *Ex* in Czech Republic.
B – 🛏 1, 2 cl. and ▬ 2 cl. (4, 6 berth) Praha - Summerau ▥ - Linz - Buchs ▥ - Zürich and v.v. Table **86**. (12) Praha - Linz - Salzburg and v.v. ▬ 2 cl. Praha - Venezia and v.v.
E – (12) and ✕ Wien - Praha - Berlin - Stralsund. To Ostseebad Binz on dates in Table **60**.
G – (12) and ✕ Berlin - Dresden - Praha - Wien.
P – 🛏 1, 2 cl. Praha (**225**) - Přerov (**203**) - Brno - Břeclav - Wien.
Q – 🛏 1, 2 cl. Wien (**202**) - Břeclav - Brno - Přerov (**224**) - Praha.
T – TRANSALPIN – (1) (panorama car), (12) and ✕ Wien - Linz - Zürich - Basel and v.v. Table **86**.
V – VINDOBONA – (12) and ✕ Hamburg - Berlin - Praha - Wien and v.v.

f – Not Dec. 24, 25, 31.
k – Not Dec. 24, 31.
y – Not Dec. 25, Jan. 1.
⊙ – ČD 680 Pendolino (Czech Railways tilting train) Ⓡ supplement payable.
* – *SC* in Czech Republic.

OTHER TRAIN NAMES:

EC **70/71** – ANTONÍN DVOŘÁK
*EC** **72/73** – JOHANN GREGOR MENDEL
*EC** **74/75** – SMETANA

BERLIN - WARSZAWA 56

Service for Jan. 12, 13, Feb. 23, 24, Oct 18 - Nov. 30.

Due to engineering works on the above dates, services will be retimed and diverted as shown below.

train type		*EC*	*EC*	*EC*		*EC*		
train number		**441**	**445**	**447**		**449**		
notes		✕	✕	✕		✕		
notes		A E	A E	A E		B C		
Berlin Lichtenberg d.	...	0658	1150	1547	...	1850	...	...
Frankfurt (Oder) ▥ d.	...	|	|	|	...	|	...	...
Rzepin a.	...	0944	1404	1821	...	2109	...	...
Poznań Gł. a.	...	1108	1535	1948	...	2251	...	...
Konin a.	...	1207	1634	2053	...	...	...	...
Kutno **1020** a.	...	1257	1721	2140	...	...	...	...
Warszawa Centralna a.	...	1415	1845	2257	...	...	...	...
Warszawa Wschodnia a.	...	1427	1857	2307	...	...	...	...

train type		*EC*		*EC*	*EC*	*EC*			
train number		**448**		**446**	**444**	**440**			
notes		✕		✕	✕	✕			
notes		B D		A E	A E	A E			
Warszawa Wschodnia d.	...	...	...	0713	1113	1613	...	...	...
Warszawa Centralna d.	...	...	...	0725	1125	1625	...	...	...
Kutno **1020** d.	...	...	...	0842	1242	1742	...	...	...
Konin d.	...	...	...	0921	1321	1821	...	...	...
Poznań Gł. d.	...	0639	...	1020	1420	1920	...	...	...
Rzepin d.	...	0825	...	1147	1547	2047	...	...	...
Frankfurt (Oder) ▥ a.	...	|	...	|	|	|	...	...	...
Berlin Lichtenberg a.	...	1047	...	1402	1804	2303	...	...	...

A – BERLIN WARSZAWA EXPRESS – (12) and ✕ Berlin - Poznań - Warszawa and v.v. Ⓡ Special fares apply. Supplement payable in Poland.
B – BERLIN WARSZAWA EXPRESS – (12) and ✕ Berlin - Poznań and v.v. Ⓡ Special fares apply. Supplement payable in Poland.
C – Jan. 13, Feb. 24, also ⑤⑥ Oct 19 - Nov. 30.
D – Jan. 12, Feb. 23, also ①⑥ Oct 18 - Nov. 29.
E – Jan. 12, 13, Feb. 23, 24, Oct 18 - Nov. 30.

56 KÖLN - BERLIN - WARSZAWA - MOSKVA

train number	41	10	541	241	855	45	104	857	247	247	1249	859	47	951	49	953	345	345	345	345	345	347	12	12
train type/number	*EC*		*ICE*	*EC*	*ICE*	*EC*	11011	*ICE*				*ICE*	*EC*	*ICE*	*EC*❖	*ICE*						⊠		31110
notes	✗❖ Tp	11001 P	✗ Z	[R]⊡ Wg	✗ A	✗❖ Tq	132 V	✗ A	♣ M	♣ L	♣ D	✗ A	✗❖ Tq	✗ A	EE U✗	✗A CC	K	AA	G	S	2 Nh	[R] J	11013 X	11013 FF
Köln Hbf d.	...	...	0429	...	0749	...	...	0949	...	...	...	1149	...	1349	...	1549	...	...	...	...	...	2228	...	...
Düsseldorf Hbf d.	...	...	0453	...	0753z	...	...	0953z	...	...	...	1153z	...	1353z	...	1555z	...	...	...	...	...	2202	...	...
Dortmund Hbf d.	...	...	0548	...	0848z	...	...	1048z	...	...	...	1248z	...	1448z	...	1649z	...	...	...	...	...	2356	...	...
Bielefeld Hbf d.	...	...	0638	...	0937	...	...	1137	...	...	...	1337	...	1537	...	1737	...	...	...	...	...	0043	...	...
Hannover Hbf d.	...	...	0731	...	1031	...	...	1231	...	...	...	1431	...	1631	...	1831	...	...	...	...	...	|	...	...
Hamburg Hbf d.	...	...	|	0703y	|	...	...	|	...	...	...	|	...	|	...	|	...	...	...	...	...	|	...	...
Berlin Zoo d.	...	...	|	|	|	...	...	|	1513	1513	1513	|	...	|	...	|	...	...	...	...	...	|	...	...
Berlin Hauptbahnhof d.	0629	...	0908s	0940	1210s	1229	...	1410s	1522	1522	1522	1610s	1629	1810	1826	2010s	...	...	...	...	...	|	...	...
Berlin Ostbahnhof d.	0640u	...	0919	0949	1221	1240u	...	1421	1533	1533	1533	1621	1640u	1821	1838u	2021	...	...	...	...	...	|	...	...
Berlin Lichtenberg d.	|	...	...	|	...	|	...	▬	|	|	|	...	|	...	|	...	2138	2138	2138	2138	2138	|	...	...
Frankfurt (Oder) 🛃 d.	0739	...	...	|	...	1339	...	...	1711u	1711u	1711u	...	1739	...	1939	...	|	|	|	|	|	|	...	...
Rzepin a.	0755	...	...	|	...	1355	...	...	1753u	1753u	1753u	...	1755	...	1956	...	2347u	2347u	2347u	2347u	2347u	0601	...	...
Poznań Gł. a.	0932	...	...	|	...	1532	...	...	1937u	1937u	1937u	...	1932	...	2145	...	0138	0138	0138	0138	0138	0739	...	...
Cottbus ◧ a.	|	...	...	1112	...	|	...	...	|	|	|	...	|	...	...	...	|	|	|	|	|	|	...	...
Legnica ◧ a.	|	...	...	1414	...	|	...	**68**	|	|	|	...	|	...	...	...	|	|	|	|	|	|	...	...
Wrocław Gł. a.	|	...	...	1534	...	|	...	**22001**	|	|	|	...	|	...	...	...	|	|	|	|	0430	|	...	...
Katowice a.	|	...	...	1815	...	|	...	**13211**	|	|	|	...	|	...	...	...	|	|	|	|	0729	|	...	...
Kraków Gł. a.	|	...	...	1944	...	|	...	**C**	|	|	|	...	|	...	...	...	|	|	|	|	0858	|	...	0610
Warszawa Centralna a.	1235	1625	...	...	...	1835	2135	2130	2346u	2346u	2346u	...	2235	...	...	...	0550	0550	0550	0550	...	1040	...	1105
Warszawa Wschodnia a.	1247	1635d	...	...	...	1847	2050d	2147d	2358u	2358u	2358u	...	2247	...	...	...	0602	0602	0602	0602	...	1052	1208	1208
Terespol a.	...	1938	...	...	...	...	0003	|	0330u	0330u	0330u	...	...	...	...	...	|	|	|	|	...	1525	1525	1525
Brest 🛃 a.	...	2144	...	...	...	...	0222	|	0516	0516	0516	...	...	...	...	...	|	|	|	|	...	1741	1741	1741
Yahodyn 🛃 a.	...	|	...	...	...	...	|	0407	|	|	|	...	...	...	...	...	1242	1242	1242	1242	...	|	|	|
Lviv a.	...	|	...	...	...	...	|	|	|	|	|	...	...	...	...	...	|	0709	|	|	...	|	|	|
Kyïv a.	...	|	...	...	...	...	|	1621	|	|	|	...	...	...	...	...	2252	...	|	2252	...	|	|	|
Odesa a.	...	|	...	...	...	...	|	|	|	|	|	...	...	...	...	...	...	...	1110	|	...	|	|	|
Simferopol a.	...	|	...	...	...	...	|	1302	|	|	|	...	...	...	...	...	...	...	...	1607	...	|	|	|
Minsk a.	...	0251	...	...	...	...	0814	...	1046	1046	1114	...	...	...	...	...	...	...	...	...	...	2333	2333	2333
Orsha Tsentralnaya a.	...	0514	...	...	...	...	...	...	1330	1330n	1408	...	...	...	...	...	...	...	...	...	...	0220	0220	0220
St Peterburg Vitebski a.	...	|	...	...	...	...	...	...	|	0618	|	...	...	...	...	...	...	...	...	...	...	|	|	|
Smolensk Tsentralny 🛃 a.	...	0733	...	...	...	...	...	...	1601	...	1652	...	...	...	...	...	...	...	...	...	...	0456	0456	0456
Moskva Belorusskaya ‡ a.	...	1210	...	...	...	...	...	...	2035	...	...	...	...	...	...	...	...	...	...	...	...	1059	1059	1059

train number	1248	246	246	652	48	11008	22000	46	858	44	240	9	40	1502	11	11014	346	344	344	344	344	344	954	652
train type/number				*ICE*	*EC*❖	103	67	*EC*	*ICE*	*EC*	*EC*		*EC*	*ICE*		11	⊠						*ICE*	*ICE*
notes	♣ B	♣ Q	♣ F	✗ A	EE Y✗	132 V	31210 C	✗❖ Tq	✗ Ak	✗❖ Tq	[R]⊡ Wk	11002 P	✗❖ Tt	912 ✗k	11014 X	13110 GG	[R] E	O	R	H	BB	Nh	✗A DD	✗ A
Moskva Belorusskaya ‡ d.	...	...	0800	...	...	...	...	...	...	...	...	1920	...	...	2109	2109	2109	...	...	...	...	...	...	...
Smolensk Tsentralny 🛃 d.	1122	...	1223	...	...	...	...	...	...	...	...	2359	...	...	0300	0300	0300	...	...	...	...	...	...	...
St Peterburg Vitebski d.	|	2340	|	...	...	...	...	...	...	...	...	|	...	...	|	|	|	...	...	...	...	...	...	...
Orsha Tsentralnaya d.	1217	1250j	1250	...	...	...	...	...	...	...	...	0050	...	...	0338	0338	0338	...	...	...	...	...	...	...
Minsk d.	1503	1526	1526	...	...	2040	...	...	...	...	...	0332	...	...	0643	0643	0643	...	...	...	...	...	...	...
Simferopol d.	|	|	|	...	...	|	1525	...	...	...	...	|	...	...	|	|	|	1530	...	...	...	...	...	...
Odesa d.	|	|	|	...	...	|	|	...	...	...	...	|	...	...	|	|	|	|	...	1816	...	...	...	...
Kyïv d.	|	|	|	...	...	|	1230	...	...	...	...	|	...	...	|	|	|	0800	0800	|	...	...	...	...
Lviv d.	|	|	|	...	...	|	|	...	...	...	...	|	...	...	|	|	|	|	|	|	0048	...	...	...
Yahodyn 🛃 d.	|	|	|	...	...	|	0030	...	...	...	...	|	...	...	|	|	|	1833	1833	1833	1833	...	...	...
Brest 🛃 d.	2107f	2115f	2115f	...	...	0240	|	...	...	...	...	0837	...	...	1250	1250	1250	|	|	|	|	...	...	...
Terespol d.	2113	2113	2113	...	...	0238	|	...	...	...	...	0835	...	...	1248	1248	1248	|	|	|	|	...	...	...
Warszawa Wschodnia d.	0033s	0033s	0033s	...	...	0614a	0636a	0713	...	1113	...	1133a	1613	...	1611	1638	1742e	2317	2317	2317	2317	...	...	...
Warszawa Centralna d.	0045s	0045s	0045s	...	...	0625	0645	0725	...	1125	...	1145	1625	...	...	1650	1755	2330	2330	2330	2330	...	...	...
Kraków Gł. d.	|	|	|	...	...	...	...	|	...	|	0731	▬	|	...	...	2155	|	|	|	|	|	2005	...	...
Katowice d.	|	|	|	...	...	...	...	|	...	|	0854	...	|	...	...	...	|	|	|	|	|	2140	...	...
Wrocław Gł. d.	|	|	|	...	...	...	...	|	...	|	1136	...	|	...	...	...	|	|	|	|	|	0025	...	...
Legnica ◧ d.	|	|	|	...	...	...	...	|	...	|	1257	...	|	...	...	...	|	|	|	|	|	|	...	...
Cottbus ◧ d.	|	|	|	...	...	...	...	|	...	|	1559	...	|	...	...	...	|	|	|	|	|	|	...	...
Poznań Gł. d.	0420s	0420s	0420s	...	0601	...	...	1020	...	1420	|	*ICE*	1920	...	...	...	2105	0330	0330	0330	0330	0330	...	...
Rzepin d.	0613s	0613s	0613s	...	0754	...	...	1154	...	1554	|	**854**	2054	...	...	...	2244	0503s	0503s	0503s	0503s	0503s	...	...
Frankfurt (Oder) 🛃 a.	0658s	0658s	0658s	...	0813	...	...	1213	...	1613	|	✗	2112	...	...	...	|	|	|	|	|	|	...	...
Berlin Lichtenberg a.	|	|	|	...	|	...	...	|	...	|	|	**CC**	|	...	...	...	|	0714	0714	0714	0714	0714	...	...
Berlin Ostbahnhof a.	0822	0822	0822	0840	0915s	...	...	1315s	1338	1715s	1721	1738	2209s	...	...	...	|	...	...	...	...	...	0738	0840
Berlin Hauptbahnhof a.	0901	0901	0901	0851d	0926	...	...	1326	1348d	1726	1731	1748d	2220	2303	...	...	|	...	...	...	...	...	0748d	0851d
Berlin Zoo a.	0910	0910	0910	|	...	...	...	...	|	...	|	|	...	|	...	...	|	...	...	...	...	...	|	|
Hamburg Hbf a.	...	...	...	|	...	...	...	...	|	...	2027x	|	...	0036	...	...	|	...	...	...	...	...	|	|
Hannover Hbf a.	...	...	...	1028	...	...	...	...	1528	...	...	1928	...	...	...	...	|	...	...	...	...	...	0928	1028
Bielefeld Hbf a.	...	...	...	1120	...	...	...	...	1620	...	...	2020	...	...	...	...	0354	...	...	...	...	...	1020	1120
Dortmund Hbf a.	...	...	...	1209z	...	...	...	...	1709z	...	...	2109z	...	...	...	...	0448	...	...	...	...	...	1109z	1209z
Düsseldorf Hbf a.	...	...	...	1305z	...	...	...	...	1805z	...	...	2205z	...	...	...	...	0654	...	...	...	...	...	1205z	1305z
Köln Hbf a.	...	...	...	1309	...	...	...	...	1809	...	...	2209	...	...	...	...	0614	...	...	...	...	...	1209	1309

A – 🚃(12) and ✗ Köln - Wuppertal - Hamm - Berlin and Düsseldorf - Hamm - Berlin and v.v. Table **800**.
B – ④: 🛏 1, 2 cl. (1, 2, 4 berth) Saratov (**69**) (depart 1129) - Smolensk (depart ⑤) - Terespol (**1248**) - Berlin (arrive ⑥).
②: 🛏 2 cl. (3, 4 berth) Novosibirsk (**113**), also Rostov-na-Donu (**49**) (depart ④), Omsk ③ - Perm II ③ - Gorkii ④ - Minsk ⑤ - Terespol (**1248**) - Berlin (arrive ⑥). (Table **1980**).
C – KIEW EXPRESS – 🛏 1, 2 cl. Warszawa - Kyïv and v.v. ②⑥: 🛏 2 cl. Warszawa (**68**) - Kyïv (**72 / 71 / 67**) - Simferopol; ④⑦: 🛏 2 cl. Simferopol (**40 / 39**) - Kyïv (**67**) - Warszawa (journey two nights).
D – ⑥: 🛏 1, 2 cl. (1, 2, 4 berth) Berlin (**1249**) - Brest 🛃 (**70**) (arrive ⑦) - Smolensk ⑦ - Saratov ① (arrive 1519). ⑥: 🛏 2 cl. (3, 4 berth) Berlin (**1249**) - Brest 🛃 (**70**) - Minsk (**64**) -7 Gorkii (arrive ①) - Perm II ② - Omsk ③ - Novosibirsk ③, also Rostov-na-Donu ② (Table **1980**).
E – JAN KIEPURA – 🛏 1, 2 cl. Moskva (**11**) - Brest (**11014**) - Warszawa (**346**) - Köln - Amsterdam (journey 2 nights). 🛏 1, 2 cl., ▬ 2 cl., 🚃(2) and ✗ Warszawa (*EN* **346**) - Köln - Amsterdam. Table **24**.
F – MOSKVA EXPRESS – ②③④⑥ Dec. 9, 2007 - May 24, 2008 (not Jan. 12, Feb. 23); ①②③④⑥⑦ May 25 - Sept. 29: 🛏 1 cl. *Lux*, 🛏 1, 2 cl. Moskva (**13**) - Terespol (**246**) - Warszawa - Berlin. ✗ Moskva - Brest.
G – ①③⑤: 🛏 2 cl. Berlin - Dorohusk (**30**) - Kowel (**84 / 83**) - Odesa (journey 2 nights).
H – ①③⑥: 🛏 2 cl. Odesa (**84 / 83**) - Kowel (**29**) - Dorohusk (**344**) - Berlin (journey 2 nights).
J – JAN KIEPURA – 🛏 1, 2 cl. Amsterdam (**347**) - Köln - Warszawa (**11013**) - Brest (**12**) - Moskva (journey 2 nights). 🛏 1, 2 cl., ▬ 2 cl., 🚃(2) and ✗ Amsterdam (*EN* **347**) - Köln - Warszawa. Table **24**.
K – 🛏 1, 2 cl. and ▬ 2 cl. Berlin - Warszawa (not Jan. 11, 12, 13). 🛏 2 cl. Berlin - Dorohusk (**30**) - Kyïv. ✗ Warszawa - Kyïv. Conveys on ④⑦: 🛏 2 cl. Berlin - Kyïv (**116**) - Kharkiv (journey 2 nights). Also conveys 🛏 1, 2 cl. Berlin - Poznań - Gdynia / Kaliningrad.
L – ③④⑤⑦ Dec. 9, 2007 - May 23, 2008 (not Jan. 13, Feb. 24); ①②③④⑤⑦ May 25 - Oct. 3: 🛏 2 cl. Berlin (**247**) - Warszawa - Brest 🛃 (**14**) - Orsha (**20**) - St Peterburg (journey 2 nights).
M – MOSKVA EXPRESS – ③④⑤⑦ Dec. 9, 2007 - May 25, 2008 (not Jan. 13, Feb. 24); ①②③④⑤⑦ May 26 - Sept. 30: 🛏 1 cl. *Lux*, 🛏 1, 2 cl. Berlin (**247**) - Warszawa - Brest 🛃 (**14**) - Moskva. ✗ Brest - Moskva.
N – 🛏 1, 2 cl. and ▬ 2 cl. Berlin - Poznań (**83704**) - Kraków and Kraków (**38705**) - Poznań (**344**) - Berlin.
O – ④⑦: 🛏 2 cl. Simferopol (**40 / 39**) - Kyïv (**29**) - Berlin (journey 2 nights).
P – POLONEZ – 🛏 1, 2 cl. and ✗ Warszawa - Moskva and v.v.
Q – ②③④⑥ Dec. 9, 2007 - May 22, 2008 (not Jan. 12, Feb. 23); ①②③④⑥⑦ May 25 - Oct. 2: 🛏 2 cl. St Peterburg (**19**) - Orsha (**13**) - Terespol (**246**) - Warszawa - Berlin (journey 2 nights).
R – 🛏 1, 2 cl. and ▬ 2 cl. Warszawa - Berlin (not Jan. 11, 12). 🛏 2 cl. Kyïv (**29**) - Dorohusk (**344**) - Berlin. ✗ Kyïv - Warszawa. Conveys on ②⑤ 🛏 2 cl. Kharkiv (**343**) - Kyïv (**29**) - Berlin (journey 2 nights). Also conveys 🛏 1, 2 cl. Gdynia / Kaliningrad - Poznań - Berlin.
S – ②⑤: 🛏 2 cl. Berlin - Kyïv (**146 / 145**) - Simferopol (journey 2 nights).
T – BERLIN WARSZAWA EXPRESS – 🚃(12) and ✗ ❖ Berlin - Poznań - Warszawa and v.v. [R] Special fares apply. Supplement payable in Poland.

U – ⑤⑦ (also Jan. 1, Mar. 20, 24, Apr. 30, May 12; not Dec. 30, Jan. 13, Feb. 24, Mar. 21, 23, May 2, 11).❖
V – 🛏 1, 2 cl. Minsk - Warszawa and v.v.
W – WAWEL – 🚃(12) and 🍷 (Hamburg ①–⑥ **y** -) Berlin - Wrocław - Kraków and Kraków - Wrocław - Berlin (- Hamburg ⑧ **x**).
X – OST WEST – 🛏 1, 2 cl. Warszawa - Moskva and v.v.
Y – ①⑥ (also Jan. 2, Mar. 21, 25, May 1, 13; not Dec. 31, Jan. 12, Feb. 23, Mar. 22, 24, May 3, 12).
Z – ①–⑥ (not Dec. 24, 25, 26, 31, Jan. 1, Mar. 24, May 12).
AA – ⑥ (not Jan. 12): 🛏 2 cl. Berlin (**345**) - Dorohusk (**30**) - Kovel (**364**) - Zdolbunov (**13**) - Lviv (journey 2 nights).
BB – ④ (not Jan. 10: 🛏 2 cl. Lviv (**164**) - Zdolbunov (**363**) - Kovel (**29**) - Dorohusk (**344**) - Berlin (journey 2 nights).
CC – ⑧ (not Dec. 24, 25, 31, Mar. 21, 23, May 11).
DD – ①–⑥ (not Dec. 25, 26, Jan. 1, Mar. 22, 24, May 12).
EE – BERLIN WARSZAWA EXPRESS – 🚃(12) and ✗ ❖ Berlin - Poznań and v.v. [R] Special fares apply. Supplement payable in Poland.
FF – 🛏 1, 2 cl. Kraków - Moskva (not Dec. 22, 23, 25, 26, 29, Jan. 1, Mar. 20, 23)
GG – 🛏 1, 2 cl. Moskva - Kraków (not Dec. 23, 24, 26, 27, 30, Jan. 2, Mar. 21, 24)

a – Arrival time.
d – Departure time.
e – Arrive 1611.
f – Arrive 1855.
g – Not Dec. 25, 31.
h – Not Dec. 24.
j – Arrive 1046.
k – Not Dec. 24, 31.
n – Depart 1637.
p – Not Dec. 25, Jan. 12, 13, Feb. 23, 24.❖
q – Not Jan. 12, 13, Feb. 23, 24.❖
s – Stops to set down only.
t – Not Dec. 24, 25, 26, 31, Jan. 1, Mar. 24, May 12.
u – Stops to pick up only.
x – ⑧ (also Dec. 24, 25, 30, 31, Mar. 21, 23, May 11).
y – ①–⑥ (not Dec. 25, 26, 31, Jan. 1, Mar. 22, 24, May 12)
z – For train number, days of running and possible earlie timings of Düsseldorf portion see Table **800**.
⊡ – Supplement payable in Poland.

◧ – 🛃 between Cottbus and Legnica is Forst (also ticketing point) / Zasieki.
‡ – Also known as Moskva **Smolenskaya** station.
❖ – Services on Jan. 12, 13, Feb. 23, 24 are shown in special Table on page 75
⊠ – On Jan. 11, 12, Feb. 22, 23 Trains **346 / 347** are retimed. See Table **24**.
♣ – On Jan. 13, Feb. 24 from / to Berlin **Lichtenberg**, (a. 0858) and (d. 1509)

DORTMUND - FRANKFURT - NÜRNBERG - PRAHA 57

train type	RE	RE	ICE	ICE	RE	RE	ALX		IC	ICE	ICE	ALX	RE	IC	ICE		IC	ICE	RE	RE	ALX		ICE	CNL	
train number	**3690**	**451**	**21**	**523**	**19905**	**3583**	**455**		**2065**	**25**	**621**	**86008**	**453**	**2069**	**29**		**2025**	**629**	**19939**	**3599**	**457**		**17**	**353**	
notes			⊖	P ⊖			🍷		🍷	⊖	⊖	🍷		🍷	⊖		w ⊖	⊖	🍷		🍷		⊖	A	
ortmund Hbf d.	...	...	...	0401	...	...	...	...	...	0636	...	...	...	...	...	...	1036	...	...	...	...	...	...	...	...
öln Hbf d.	...	...	...	0518t	...	...	...	...	...	0753	0944t	...	...	...	...	...	1153	1344t	...	...	...	...	2020	...	...
onn Hbf d.	...	...	...	|	...	...	...	...	...	0814	|	...	...	...	...	...	1214	|	...	...	...	...	|	...	...
oblenz d.	...	...	...	|	...	...	...	...	...	0848	|	...	...	...	...	...	1248	|	...	...	...	...	|	...	...
ainz d.	...	...	...	|	...	...	...	...	...	0940	|	...	...	...	...	...	1340	|	...	...	...	...	|	...	...
rankfurt Flughafen ✈ d.	...	...	...	0637	...	...	...	...	...	1001	1037	...	...	...	...	...	1401	1437	...	...	...	...	2117	...	...
rankfurt (Main) Hbf d.	...	...	0622	0654	...	...	...	...	...	1021	1054	...		...	1416	...	1413	1454	...	...	...	...	2130	2219k	...
/ürzburg Hbf d.	...	...	0734	0805	...	...	...	...	...	1134	1205	...	...	...	1534	...	...	1605	...	...	...	...	...	|	...
Karlsruhe Hbf d.	...	...	|	|	...	...	...	...	0906	|	|	...	...	1306	|	...	...	|	...	...	...	...	...	|	...
Stuttgart Hbf d.	...	...	|	|	0640	...	...	...	1007	|	|	...	...	1407	|	...	...	|	1440	...	...	...	...	|	...
ünchen Hbf d.	...	...	|	|	|	...	0844	...	|	|	|	1244	...	|	|	...	...	|	|	...	1644	...	...	|	...
ürnberg Hbf d.	...	0540	0831	0859	0925	0936	|	...	1217	1228	1259	|	1340	1617	1631	...	...	1659	1725	1736	|	...	...	|	...
Regensburg d.	0623	|	0922	...	...	|	1021	...	...	...	...	1421	|	...	1722	...	...	...	...	|	1821	...	...	|	...
Schwandorf d.	0650	0655	...	...	...	1044	1056	...	...	...	...	1446	1456	...	...	...	...	...	...	1843	1856	...	...	|	...
Furth im Wald 🏛 d.	...	0749	...	...	...	...	1149	...	...	...	...	...	1549	...	...	...	...	...	...	...	1949	...	...	◧	...
lzeň Hlavní a.	...	0857	...	...	...	...	1257	...	...	...	...	...	1657	...	...	...	...	...	...	...	2057	...	...	|	...
raha Hlavní a.	...	1045	...	...	...	...	1445	...	...	...	...	...	1845	...	...	...	...	...	...	...	2245	...	...	0818y	...

train type	RE	ALX	RE	ICE	IC	IC		ALX	RE	RE	ICE	ICE	IC		RE	ALX	RE	ICE	ICE	ALX	RE		CNL	ICE	
train number	**450**	**86007**	**19932**	**722**	**2026**	**2068**		**454**	**3558**	**19948**	**624**	**26**	**2064**		**452**	**86015**	**19962**	**526**	**22**	**456**	**3574**		**352**	**16**	
notes		🍷	🍷	⊖	🍷	🍷		🍷		🍷	⊖	⊖	🍷			🍷		S ⊖	🍴	🍷			B	🍷	
raha Hlavní d.	0516	...	...	...	...	...	...	0916	...	...	...	...	...	...	1316	...	...	...	...	1716	...	...	2025	...	...
lzeň Hlavní d.	0700	...	...	...	...	...	...	1100	...	...	...	...	...	...	1500	...	...	...	...	1900	...	...	|	...	...
Furth im Wald 🏛 a.	0811	...	...	...	...	...	...	1211	...	...	...	...	...	...	1611	...	...	...	...	2011	...	...	◧	...	...
Schwandorf a.	0903	0907	...	...	...	...	...	1303	1309	...	...	...	...	...	1703	1709	...	...	...	2105	2113	...	|	...	...
Regensburg a.	|	0936	...	...	...	...	...	1337	|	...	...	1433	...	...	|	1736	...	...	...	2148	|	...	|	...	...
ürnberg Hbf a.	1009	|	1035	1101	...	1141	...	|	1421	1435	1501	1525	1541	...	1809	|	1835	1901	1928	|	2221	2335	|	...	...
ünchen Hbf a.	...	1116	|	|	...	|	...	1519	...	|	|	|	|	...	...	1919	|	|	|	2321	...	|	|	...	...
Stuttgart Hbf a.	...	...	1318	|	...	1353	...	...	...	1719	|	|	1753	...	...	...	2118	|	|	...	...	|	|	...	...
Karlsruhe a.	...	...	...	|	...	1453	...	...	...	...	|	|	1853	...	...	...	...	|	|	...	...	|	|	...	...
/ürzburg Hbf a.	...	...	...	1154	...	...	...	...	...	...	1554	1625	...	...	...	...	...	1954	2025	...	...	0056	|	...	...
rankfurt (Main) Hbf a.	...	...	...	1305	1344	...	...	...	...	...	1705	1736	...	...	...	...	...	2105	2136	...	...	...	0654k	0728	...
rankfurt Flughafen ✈ a.	...	...	...	1321	1356	...	...	...	...	...	1721	1755	...	...	...	...	...	2121	2157	...	...	...	...	0740	...
ainz a.	...	...	...	|	1416	...	...	...	...	...	|	1815	...	...	...	...	...	|	2217	...	...	...	...	|	...
oblenz a.	...	...	...	|	1510	...	...	...	...	...	|	1910	...	...	...	...	...	|	2310	...	...	...	...	|	...
onn Hbf a.	...	...	...	|	1542	...	...	...	...	...	|	1943	...	...	...	...	...	|	2342	...	...	...	...	|	...
öln Hbf a.	...	...	...	1414t	1605	...	...	...	...	...	1814t	2005	...	...	...	...	...	2219t	0005	...	...	...	...	0840	...
ortmund Hbf a.	...	...	...	-	1720	...	...	...	...	...	1929	2133	...	...	...	...	...	2336	0122f	...	...	...	...	...	...

– *City Night Line* JOHANNES KEPLER – 🛏 1,2 cl., 🛌 2 cl. and [2] Basel - Frankfurt (Main) **Süd** - Fulda - Děčín 🏛 - Praha Holešovice. 🍴 Basel - Fulda. Ⓡ Special fares apply.
– *City Night Line* JOHANNES KEPLER – 🛏 1,2 cl., 🛌 2 cl. and [2] Praha Hlavní - Praha Holešovice - Děčín 🏛 - Fulda - Frankfurt (Main) **Süd** - Basel. 🍴 Fulda - Basel. Ⓡ Special fares apply.
– ①–⑥ (not Dec. 25, 26, Jan. 1, Mar. 22, 24, May 12).
– ①–⑤ (not Dec. 24, 25, 26, 31, Jan. 1, Mar. 21, 24, May 12).

S – ⑧ (not Dec. 24, 25, 31, Mar. 21, 23, May 11).
f – Not Dec. 25, Jan. 1.
k – Frankfurt (Main) **Süd**.
t – Köln **Messe / Deutz**.
y – Praha **Holešovice**.

w – Not Dec. 25 - Jan. 1.
◧ – 🏛 is Děčín; Ticketing point is Schöna.
ALX – Arriva Länderbahn Express.
⊖ – *ICE 3* train 🍷, via high speed line, premium fares payable.

TRAIN NAMES *RE* **451 / 452** JAN HUS *RE* **453 / 450** KAREL CAPEK *ALX* **455 / 456** ALBERT EINSTEIN *ALX* **457 / 454** FRANZ KAFKA

FRANKFURT - LEIPZIG - DRESDEN - PRAHA 58

train type	CNL		CNL	IC	ICE	EC	ICE	ICE	EC		ICE	ICE	EC	ICE	EC	ICE	ICE	EC	ICE	ICE	EC		
train number	**353**	**379**	**459**	**61459**	**1741**	**171**	**1543**	**1543**	**173**		**1545**	**1745**	**175**	**1547**	**177**	**1559**	**1549**	**371**	**1651**	**1641**	**179**		
notes		2			Ⓡ 🍷	🍴	⊖	Ⓡ 🍷	🍴		⊖	⊖	🍴	⊖	🍴	Ⓡ 🍷	Ⓡ 🍷	🍴	Ⓡ 🍷	Ⓡ 🍷	🍴		
	A	L	G		N ⊖	B	N	⊖	C		N	⑦b	H		S	⊖	⊖	D	⊖	⊖	Q		
/iesbaden Hbf d.	...	...	...	...	...	...	...	...	...	...	...	...	...	...	...	1024	...	...	1224	...	...	...	...
rankfurt Flughafen ✈ d.	...	...	...	...	...	...	...	...	...	...	0811	...	...	1011	...	1102	1211	...	1302	1411	...	...	...
rankfurt (Main) Hbf d.	...	...	...	...	...	...	0618	...	...	...	|	0822	...	*1013*q	...	1119	*1213*q	...	1319	*1413*q	...	...	...
rankfurt (Main) Süd d.	2219	...	0055	...	...	...	|	...	...	...	0822	|	...	1022	...	|	1222	...	|	1422	...	...	...
ulda d.	0047	...	|	0341	...	...	0715	...	...	...	0915	0915	...	1115	...	1213	1315	...	1413	1515	...	...	...
rfurt Hbf d.	|	...	0523s	0525	...	...	0837	...	...	...	1037	1037	...	1237	...	1334	1437	...	1535	1637	...	...	...
/eimar d.	|	...	0540s	0542	...	...	0853	...	...	...	1053	1053	...	1253	...	1351	1453	...	1551	1653	...	...	...
eipzig d.	0425s	...	0641s	0651	0751	...	0951	0951	...	...	1151	1151	...	1351	...	1451	1551	...	1651	1751	...	...	...
resden Hbf d.	0551s	0710	0803	0803	0902	0910	1102	1102	1110	...	1302	1302	1310	1502	1510	1602	1702	1710	1802	1902	1910	...	...
ad Schandau 🏛 ◧ d.	0636s	0738	...	...	...	0940	...	...	1140	...	...	...	1340	...	1540	...	...	1740	...	...	1940	...	...
ěčín 🏛 ◧ d.	0653s	0759	...	...	...	0959	...	...	1159	...	...	...	1359	...	1559	...	...	1759	...	...	1959	...	...
raha Holešovice a.	0818	0918	...	...	...	1118	...	...	1318	...	...	...	1518	...	1718	...	...	1918	...	...	2118	...	...
raha Hlavní a.	...	0933	...	...	...	|	...	...	|	...	...	...	|	...	|	...	...	1931	...	...	2132	...	...
Wien Südbahnhof a.	...	...	...	...	...	|	...	...	1803	...	...	...	|	...	2203	...	...	...	...	...	...	...	...
Bratislava Hlavná a.	...	...	...	...	...	1542	...	...	...	...	...	...	1942	...	...	...	...	...	...	...	...	...	...
Budapest Keleti a.	...	...	...	...	...	1832	...	...	...	...	...	...	2232	...	...	...	...	...	...	...	...	...	...

train type	EC	ICE	EC	ICE	ICE	EC	ICE	ICE	EC	ICE	ICE	ICE	EC	ICE	EC	ICE	ICE	IC	CNL			CNL	
train number	**178**	**1640**	**176**	**1548**	**1558**	**370**	**1546**	**1556**	**174**	**1544**	**1744**	**1554**	**172**	**1542**	**170**	**1740**	**1554**	**61458**	**458**	**378**		**352**	
notes	🍴	⊖	🍴	Ⓡ 🍷	⊖	🍴	⊖	⊖	🍴	⊖	⊖	⊖	🍴	⊖	🍴	⊖	⊖			2	2		
	Q		P	⊖		F			H	M	⑦f	p	C	⑧j	B	⑧y	⑦f		G	L	p	E	
Budapest Keleti d.	...	...	...	...	...	...	...	...	0530	...	...	...	...	...	0930	...	...	...	...	...	...	...	...
Bratislava Hlavná d.	...	...	...	...	...	...	...	...	0815	...	...	...	...	...	1215	...	...	...	...	...	...	...	...
Wien Südbahnhof d.	...	...	...	...	...	0608	...	...	|	...	...	...	1004	...	|	...	...	...	...	...	...	...	...
raha Hlavní d.	0625	...	0825	...	...	|	...	...	|	...	...	...	|	...	|	...	...	...	...	1850	...	2025	...
raha Holešovice d.	0636	...	0836	...	...	1036	...	...	1236	...	...	...	1436	...	1636	...	...	...	...	1902	...	2036u	...
ěčín 🏛 ◧ d.	0758	...	0958	...	...	1158	...	...	1358	...	...	...	1558	...	1758	...	...	...	...	2038	...	2158u	...
ad Schandau 🏛 ◧ a.	0816	...	1016	...	...	1216	...	...	1418	...	...	...	1618	...	1818	...	...	...	...	2052	...	2215u	...
resden Hbf a.	0846	0855	1046	1055	1155	1246	1255	1355	1446	1455	1455	1555	1646	1655	1846	1855	1955	2054	2054	2121	2221	2256u	...
eipzig a.	...	1007	...	1207	1307	...	1407	1507	...	1607	1607	1707	...	1807	...	2004	2107	2208	2218u	...	0001	0054u	...
/eimar a.	...	1104	...	1304	1406	...	1504	1606	...	1704	1704	1806	...	1904	...	...	2207	2318	2320u	...	...	|	...
rfurt Hbf a.	...	1121	...	1321	1421	...	1521	1621	...	1721	1721	1822	...	1921	...	...	2223	2336	2338u	...	...	|	...
ulda a.	...	1242	...	1442	1542	...	1642	1742	...	1842	1842	1942	...	2042	...	...	2349	0137	|	...	...	0423s	...
rankfurt (Main) Süd a.	...	1335	...	1535	|	...	1735	|	...	|	1935	|	...	2137	...	...	0044	...	0359	...	...	0654	...
rankfurt (Main) Hbf a.	...	*1344*q	...	*1544*q	1637	...	*1744*q	1837	...	1940	*1944*q	2037	...	2146	...	...	0051	...	...	...	...	...	...
rankfurt Flughafen ✈ a.	...	1348	...	1548	1656	...	1748	1856	...	...	1948	2056	...	...	...	...	...	...	...	...	...	...	...
/iesbaden Hbf a.	...	...	...	...	1732t	...	...	1932	...	...	...	2132	...	...	...	...	...	...	...	...	...	...	...

– *City Night Line* JOHANNES KEPLER – 🛏 1,2 cl., 🛌 2 cl. and [2] Basel - Frankfurt (Main) **Süd** - Fulda - Děčín 🏛 - Praha Holešovice. [12] Leipzig - Praha. 🍴 Basel - Fulda. Ⓡ Special fares apply.
– HUNGARIA – [12] and 🍴 Berlin - Dresden - Praha - Budapest and v.v.
– VINDOBONA – [12] and 🍴 Hamburg - Berlin - Dresden - Praha - Wien and v.v. Not Hamburg - Berlin Dec. 25, Jan. 1; not Berlin - Hamburg Dec. 24, 31.
– [12] and 🍴 Stralsund - Berlin - Dresden - Praha. From Ostseebad Binz on dates in Table **60**.
– *City Night Line* JOHANNES KEPLER – 🛏 1,2 cl., 🛌 2 cl. and [2] Praha Hlavní - Praha Holešovice - Děčín 🏛 - Fulda - Frankfurt (Main) **Süd** - Basel. [12] Praha - Leipzig. 🍴 Fulda - Basel. Ⓡ Special fares apply.
– [12] and 🍴 Wien - Praha - Dresden - Berlin - Stralsund. To Ostseebad Binz on dates in Table **60**.
– *City Night Line* SEMPER – 🛏 1, 2 cl., 🛏 1, 2 cl. (T4), 🛌 2 cl. (4, 6 berth), [2] (reclining) and 🍴 Zürich - Basel - Frankfurt - Leipzig - Dresden and v.v. Ⓡ Special fares apply.
– JAN JESENIUS – [12] and 🍴 Hamburg - Berlin - Dresden - Praha - Budapest and v.v.

L – [2] Berlin - Dresden - Praha and v.v. Conveys 🛏 1, 2 cl., 🛌 2 cl. and [2] Amsterdam - Berlin - Dresden - Praha and v.v.
M – ①–⑥ (also Dec. 23, 30, Mar. 23, May 11; not Dec. 26, Jan. 1, Mar. 24, May 12).
N – ①–⑥ (not Dec. 25, 26, Jan. 1, Mar. 22, 24, May 12).
P – [12] and 🍴 Praha - Dresden - Berlin - Hamburg.
Q – [12] and 🍴 Berlin - Dresden - Praha and v.v.
S – [12] and 🍴 Berlin - Dresden - Praha - Wien.

b – Also Dec. 26, Mar. 22, 24, May 12.
f – Also Dec. 26, Jan. 1, Mar. 24, May 12; not Dec. 23, 30, Mar. 23, May 11.
j – Not Dec. 24, 25, 31, Mar. 21, 23, May 11.

p – Not Dec. 24, 31.
q – Change trains at Fulda.
s – Stops to set down only.
t – Not ⑥⑦ May 17 - June 14.
u – Stops to pick up only.
y – Not Dec. 23, 24, 25, 30, 31, Mar. 21, 23, May 11.

⊖ – *ICE - T* train Ⓡ 🍷 with premium fares payable.
◧ – Ticketing point is Schöna.

60 HAMBURG - BERLIN - PRAHA / WIEN - BUDAPEST - BUCUREŞTI and İSTANBUL

train type	EN	EN	IC345	EC	EC71	734	EC	EN	371	463	463	EC*		D	EC*	EC	D	EC		EC	347¶	491		347¶	383	
train number	491	429	794	71	IC/Ex	355¶	279	371	463	Ⓡ	491	73	277	60379	75	171	273	173	233	175	790	81031	391	738	4663	
notes	493	Ⓡ	✕	✕	131	626	✕	✕	Ⓡ🍷	AA	81031	🍷	1203	O	🍷	✕		🍷		✕	341	T	⚡			
	NN Ⓡ	M	J			C	P	R	F		Ⓡ	⊙			⊙			V			491		🍷	E	LL	
Hamburg Hbf d.	2033	...	...	...	...	...	...	...	...	...	KK	...	...	...	...	...	...	0640y	...	0844y	G	...	...	...	...	...
Berlin Hbf d.	|	2056	...	...	...	...	...	...	...	...	...	...	...	0453o	...	0646	...	0846	...	1046	...	...	...	...	...	...
Dresden Hbf d.	|	|	...	...	...	...	...	...	...	...	...	...	...	0710	...	0910	...	1110	...	1310	...	...	...	...	...	...
Bad Schandau 🏛 d.	◧	◧	...	...	...	...	...	...	...	...	...	...	...	0738	...	0940	...	1140	...	1340	...	...	...	...	...	...
Děčín d.	|	|	...	...	...	...	...	...	...	...	...	...	...	0759	...	0959	...	1159	...	1359	...	...	...	...	...	...
Praha Holešovice d.	|	|	...	...	...	...	0733	...	...	...	...	0823	...	0918a	1023	1133	...	1333	...	1533	...	...	...	...	...	...
Praha Hlavní d.	|	|	...	0500	0500	...	|	...	...	...	...	|	0753	0933	|	|	...	|	...	|	...	...	...	...	...	...
Pardubice d.	|	|	...	0605	0605	...	0836	...	...	...	...	0921	|	...	1121	1236	...	1436	...	1636	...	...	...	...	...	...
Brno Hlavní d.	|	|	...	0743	0743	...	1017	...	...	...	...	1051	1140	...	1251	1417	1438	1617	...	1817	...	...	...	...	...	...
Břeclav d.	|	|	...	0823	0833	...	1052	...	...	...	...	1123	1220	...	1323	1452	1525	1658e	1659	1852	...	...	...	...	...	...
Wien Südbahnhof a.	|	|	...	0928	|	...	|	...	...	...	...	1228	|	...	1428	|	1630	1803	|	|	...	...	...	...	...	...
Wien Westbahnhof d.	0902v	0908	0952	▬	|	...	|	...	...	...	...	...	|	...	...	|	...	...	|	|	1948	...	...	1948	...	...
Kúty 🏛 d.	...	...	|	...	0849	...	1106	...	...	...	...	...	1234	...	...	1506	...	...	1715	1906	|	...	...	|	...	...
Bratislava Hlavná d.	...	...	|	...	0940	...	1145	...	...	...	...	...	1318	...	...	1545	...	...	1759	1945	|	...	...	|	...	...
Rajka 🏛 a.	...	...	|	...	|	...	|	...	...	...	...	...	...	...	...	|	...	...	...	|	|	...	...	|	...	...
Štúrovo 🏛 d.	...	...	|	...	1109	...	1309	...	...	...	...	...	...	...	...	1709	...	...	...	2109	|	...	...	|	...	...
Hegyeshalom 🏛 a.	...	...	1054	...	|	...	|	...	...	...	...	...	...	...	...	|	...	...	...	|	2054	...	...	2054	...	...
Györ a.	...	...	1125	...	|	...	|	...	...	...	...	...	...	...	...	|	...	...	...	|	2125	...	...	2125	...	...
Budapest Nyugati a.	...	...	|	...	|	...	|	...	...	...	...	...	...	...	...	|	...	...	...	|	|	...	...	|	...	...
Budapest Keleti a.	...	...	1253	...	1232'	...	1432	...	...	...	...	...	...	...	...	1832	...	...	...	2232	2253	...	...	2253	...	...
Budapest Keleti d.	...	...	1320	...	▬	1245	▬	1745	1745	...	...	...	...	...	...	...	...	...	...	...	2325	...	...	2325	...	...
Lökösháza a.	...	...	|	...	...	1540	...	2040	2040	...	...	...	...	...	...	...	...	...	...	...	|	...	...	0220	...	...
Curtici 🏛 a.	...	...	|	...	...	1713	...	2213	2213	...	...	...	...	...	...	...	...	...	...	...	|	...	...	0352	...	...
Arad a.	...	...	|	...	...	1756	...	2246	2246	...	...	...	...	...	...	...	...	...	...	...	|	...	...	0425	...	...
Timişoara a.	...	...	|	...	...	|	...	|	|	...	...	...	...	...	...	...	...	...	...	...	|	...	...	|	...	...
Craiova a.	...	...	|	...	...	|	...	|	|	...	...	...	...	...	...	...	...	...	...	...	|	...	...	|	...	...
Braşov a.	...	...	|	...	...	0210	...	0535	0535	...	...	...	...	...	...	...	...	...	...	...	|	...	...	1114	...	...
Bucureşti Nord a.	...	...	|	...	...	0515	...	0843	0843	...	...	...	...	...	...	...	...	...	...	...	|	...	...	1402	...	...
Bucureşti Nord d.	...	...	|	...	...	...	...	...	1253	1253	1253	...	...	...	...	...	...	...	...	...	|	...	...	...	1953	...
Ruse 🏛 a.	...	...	|	...	...	...	...	...	1540	1540	1540	...	...	...	...	...	...	...	...	...	|	...	...	...	2230	...
Varna a.	...	...	|	...	...	...	...	...	|	|	|	...	...	...	...	...	...	...	...	...	|	...	...	...	|	...
Burgas a.	...	...	|	...	...	...	...	...	|	|	|	...	...	...	...	...	...	...	...	...	|	...	...	...	|	...
Subotica 🏛 a.	...	...	1701	**293**	**335**	...	...	...	|	|	|	...	...	...	...	...	...	...	...	...	0251	...	...	...	|	...
Novi Sad a.	...	...	1919	**W**	**K**	...	...	...	|	|	|	...	...	...	...	...	...	...	...	...	0514	...	...	...	|	...
Beograd a.	...	...	2043	2110	2220	...	...	...	|	|	|	...	...	...	...	...	...	...	...	...	0639	0840	1405	...	|	...
Niš a.	...	...	...	0133	0224	...	...	...	|	|	|	...	...	...	...	...	...	...	...	...	1236	1236	1800	...	|	...
Tabanovci 🏛 a.	...	...	...	|	0613	...	...	...	|	|	|	...	...	...	...	...	...	...	...	...	|	|	2120	...	|	...
Skopje a.	...	...	...	|	0729	...	...	...	|	|	|	...	...	...	...	...	...	...	...	...	|	|	2254	...	|	...
Idoméni 🏛 a.	...	...	...	|	1145	...	...	...	|	|	|	...	...	...	...	...	...	...	...	...	|	|	...	...	|	...
Dimitrovgrad 🏛 a.	...	...	...	0415	|	...	...	...	|	|	|	...	...	...	...	...	...	...	...	...	1534	1534	...	...	|	...
Kalotina Zapad 🏛 a.	...	...	...	0545	|	...	...	...	|	|	|	...	...	...	...	...	...	...	...	...	1704	1704	...	...	|	...
Sofiya a.	...	...	...	0755	|	...	...	...	2212	2212	|	...	...	...	...	...	...	...	...	...	1815	1815	...	...	0605	...
Svilengrad a.	...	...	...	...	|	...	*IC*	...	...	|	0025	...	...	...	...	...	...	...	...	...	...	0025	...	...	...	...
Kapikule 🏛 a.	...	...	...	...	|	...	**55**	...	...	|	0125	...	...	...	...	...	...	...	...	...	...	0135	...	...	...	...
İstanbul Sirkeci a.	...	...	...	...	|	...	🍷	...	...	|	0800	...	...	...	...	...	...	...	...	...	...	0800	...	...	...	...
Kulata 🏛 a.	...	...	...	...	|	...	⚡	...	...	0233	...	...	...	...	...	...	...	...	...	...	...	...	...	...	...	...
Thessaloníki a.	...	...	...	...	1307	...	1454	...	...	0541	...	...	...	...	...	...	...	...	...	...	...	...	...	...	...	...
Athína Lárisa a.	...	...	...	...	...	...	1949	...	...	1410	...	...	...	...	...	...	...	...	...	...	...	...	...	...	...	...

train type	EC	SC	EC	EC	375¶	269¶		EN	269¶		
train number	177	135	371	179	732	79/730	225	377	79/730		
notes	✕	⊙	✕	✕	🍷	594	203		594		
		N	H		A	Ⓡ✕	CC	SS	Ⓡ✕		
Hamburg Hbf d.	...	...	...	...	...	L	...	...	L	...	...
Berlin Hbf d.	1246	...	1446	1646	...	...	...	...	...	...	...
Dresden Hbf d.	1510	...	1710	1910	...	...	...	...	...	...	...
Bad Schandau 🏛 d.	1540	...	1740	1940	...	...	...	...	...	...	...
Děčín d.	1559	...	1759	1959	...	...	...	...	...	...	...
Praha Holešovice d.	1733	1823	1918a	2118a	...	...	...	...	...	...	...
Praha Hlavní d.	|	|	1931	2132	2153	...	2206	0030	...	...	...
Pardubice d.	1836	1921	...	...	|	...	2330	0146	...	...	...
Brno Hlavní d.	2017	2051	...	...	0135	...	|	0335	...	...	...
Břeclav d.	2058	2123	...	...	0224	...	0457	0450	...	...	...
Wien Südbahnhof a.	2203	|	...	...	|	...	0603	|	...	...	...
Wien Westbahnhof d.	...	|	...	...	|	0625	...	|	...	...	...
Kúty 🏛 d.	...	2137	...	...	0240	|	...	0504	...	...	...
Bratislava Hlavná d.	...	2213	...	...	0356	|	...	0544	...	...	...
Rajka 🏛 a.	...	...	...	...	0437	|	...	|	...	...	...
Štúrovo 🏛 d.	...	...	...	...	|	|	...	0709	...	...	...
Hegyeshalom 🏛 a.	...	...	...	...	0459	0727	...	|	...	...	...
Györ a.	...	...	...	...	0527	0758	...	|	...	...	...
Budapest Nyugati a.	...	...	...	...	|	|	...	|	←	...	...
Budapest Keleti a.	...	...	...	...	0703	0923	...	0832	0923	...	...
Budapest Keleti d.	...	...	...	...	0745	0945	...	...	0945	...	...
Lökösháza a.	...	...	...	...	1035	→	...	...	1240	...	...
Curtici 🏛 a.	...	...	...	...	1213	...	...	...	1413	...	...
Arad a.	...	...	...	...	1246	...	...	...	1446	...	...
Timişoara a.	...	...	...	...	|	...	...	...	1534	...	...
Craiova a.	...	...	...	...	|	...	...	...	2110	...	...
Braşov a.	...	...	...	...	2003	...	...	...	|	...	...
Bucureşti Nord a.	...	...	...	...	2316	...	...	...	2359	...	...
Bucureşti Nord d.	...	...	...	...	...	...	...	...	...	...	...
Ruse 🏛 a.	...	...	...	...	...	...	...	...	...	...	...
Varna a.	...	...	...	...	...	...	...	...	...	...	...
Burgas a.	...	...	...	...	...	...	...	...	...	...	...
Subotica 🏛 a.	...	...	...	...	...	...	...	...	...	...	...
Novi Sad a.	...	...	...	...	...	...	...	...	...	...	...
Beograd a.	...	...	...	...	...	...	...	...	...	...	...
Niš a.	...	...	...	...	...	...	...	...	...	...	...
Tabanovci 🏛 a.	...	...	...	...	...	...	...	...	...	...	...
Skopje a.	...	...	...	...	...	...	...	...	...	...	...
Idoméni 🏛 a.	...	...	...	...	...	...	...	...	...	...	...
Dimitrovgrad 🏛 a.	...	...	...	...	...	...	...	...	...	...	...
Kalotina Zapad 🏛 a.	...	...	...	...	...	...	...	...	...	...	...
Sofiya a.	...	...	...	...	...	...	...	...	...	...	...
Svilengrad a.	...	...	...	...	...	...	...	...	...	...	...
Kapikule 🏛 a.	...	...	...	...	...	...	...	...	...	...	...
İstanbul Sirkeci a.	...	...	...	...	...	...	...	...	...	...	...
Kulata 🏛 a.	...	...	...	...	...	...	...	...	...	...	...
Thessaloníki a.	...	...	...	...	...	...	...	...	...	...	...
Athína Lárisa a.	...	...	...	...	...	...	...	...	...	...	...

train type/number	EC	EC	4662	390		81032	D	EC	346	490	
train number	178	176	382	🍷	232	490	270	174	739	340	
notes	✕	✕	Ⓡ	⚡				✕		799	
			LL			T			E	346	
Athína Lárisa d.	...	...	...	...	...	...	...	...	...	G Ⓡ	...
Thessaloníki d.	...	...	...	...	...	...	...	...	...	...	...
Kulata 🏛 d.	...	...	...	...	...	...	...	...	...	...	...
İstanbul Sirkeci d.	...	...	...	...	...	2200	...	...	...	...	...
Kapikule 🏛 d.	...	...	...	...	...	0405	...	...	...	...	...
Svilengrad d.	...	...	...	...	...	0505	...	...	...	...	...
Sofiya d.	...	...	1930	...	...	1340	...	...	...	1240	...
Kalotina Zapad 🏛 d.	...	...	|	...	...	1346	...	...	...	1346	...
Dimitrovgrad 🏛 d.	...	...	|	...	...	1315	...	...	...	1315	...
Idomeni 🏛 d.	...	...	|	...	...	|	...	...	...	|	...
Skopje d.	...	...	|	0612	...	|	...	...	...	|	...
Tabanovci 🏛 d.	...	...	|	0724	...	|	...	...	...	|	...
Niš d.	...	...	|	1058	...	1604	...	...	...	1604	...
Beograd d.	...	...	|	1526	...	2012	...	...	...	2200	...
Novi Sad d.	...	...	|	...	...	▬	...	...	...	2328	...
Subotica 🏛 d.	...	...	|	...	...	...	...	...	...	0144	...
Burgas d.	...	...	|	...	...	...	...	...	...	|	...
Varna d.	...	...	|	...	...	...	...	...	...	|	...
Ruse 🏛 d.	...	...	0315	...	...	...	...	...	...	|	...
Bucureşti Nord a.	...	...	0605	...	...	...	...	...	...	|	...
Bucureşti Nord d.	...	...	...	...	...	...	...	...	1645	|	...
Braşov d.	...	...	...	...	...	...	...	...	1930	|	...
Craiova d.	...	...	...	...	...	...	...	...	|	|	...
Timişoara d.	...	...	...	...	...	...	...	...	|	|	...
Arad d.	...	...	...	...	...	...	...	...	0208	|	...
Curtici 🏛 d.	...	...	...	...	...	...	...	...	0253	|	...
Lököshaza d.	...	...	...	...	...	...	...	...	0225	|	...
Budapest Keleti a.	...	...	...	...	...	...	...	...	0517	0503	...
Budapest Keleti d.	...	...	...	...	...	...	...	0530	0555	0555	...
Budapest Nyugati d.	...	...	...	...	...	...	...	|	|	|	...
Györ d.	...	...	...	*SC*	...	...	...	|	0722	0722	...
Hegyeshalom 🏛 d.	...	...	...	**134**	...	...	...	|	0755	0755	...
Štúrovo 🏛 d.	...	...	...	⊙	...	...	...	0653	|	|	...
Rajka 🏛 d.	...	...	...	**N**	...	*EC*	...	|	|	|	...
Bratislava Hlavná d.	...	...	...	0542	0608	**370**	...	0815	|	|	...
Kúty 🏛 d.	...	...	...	0620	0654	✕	...	0853	|	|	...
Wien Westbahnhof a.	...	...	...	|	|	**Q**	...	|	0857	0857	...
Wien Südbahnhof d.	...	...	...	|	|	0608	0732	|	...	...	...
Břeclav d.	...	...	...	0635	0708	0717	0839	0908	...	...	...
Brno Hlavní d.	...	...	...	0707	...	0750	0917	0943	...	...	...
Pardubice d.	...	...	...	0834	...	0924	...	1122	...	...	...
Praha Hlavní d.	0625	0825	...	|	...	|	...	|	...	...	...
Praha Holešovice d.	0636	0836	...	0932	...	1036	...	1236	...	...	...
Děčín d.	0758	0958	...	...	...	1158	...	1358	...	...	...
Bad Schandau 🏛 a.	0816	1016	...	...	...	1216	...	1416	...	...	...
Dresden Hbf a.	0846	1046	...	...	...	1246	...	1446	...	...	...
Berlin Hbf a.	1113	1313	...	...	...	1513	...	1713	...	...	...
Hamburg Hbf a.	...	1518f	...	...	...	...	...	1918f	...	...	...

CONTINUED ON NEXT PAGE

İSTANBUL - BUCUREŞTI - BUDAPEST - WIEN / PRAHA - BERLIN - HAMBURG 60

train type/number	EC	81032	462	462	EN	EC	EC*	D		EC*	EC	IC/Ex	EC	IC			IC344	EN	EN	625	EN	733	202	591
train number	172	4644	Ⓡ	370	370	170	72	60378	276	74	278	130	70	52	334	292	793	490	428	354¶	376	374¶	224	78/731
notes	✕	462	AA	Ⓡ🍸	✕	✕	🍸		1202	🍸	✕	EC70	✕	Ⓡ✓			✕	492	X	735		🍸		268
	V	Ⓡ KK		F	R		⊙	S		⊙	P			✕	K	W	J	NN Ⓡ	Ⓡ	D	SS	B	CC	Ⓡ L
thína Lárisa d.	...	...	1651	...	...	...	...	...	...	...	...	...	...	1051	...	...	...	...	...	...	...	...	...	...
hessaloníki d.	...	...	0004	...	...	...	...	...	...	...	...	...	...	1546	1615	...	...	...	...	...	...	...	...	...
ulata 🏛 d.	...	...	0340	...	...	...	...	...	...	...	...	...	...	...	|	...	...	...	...	...	...	...	...	...
İstanbul Sirkeci d.	...	2200	|	...	...	...	...	...	...	...	...	...	...	...	|	...	...	...	...	...	...	...	...	...
Kapikule 🏛 d.	...	0405	|	...	...	...	...	...	...	...	...	...	...	...	|	...	...	...	...	...	...	...	...	...
Svilengrad d.	...	0505	|	...	...	...	...	...	...	...	...	...	...	...	|	...	...	...	...	...	...	...	...	...
ofiya d.	...	|	0818	0818	...	...	...	...	...	...	...	...	...	...	|	2220	...	...	...	...	...	...	...	...
alotina Zapad 🏛 d.	...	|	|	|	...	...	...	...	...	...	...	...	...	...	|	2331	...	...	...	...	...	...	...	...
imitrovgrad 🏛 d.	...	|	|	|	...	...	...	...	...	...	...	...	...	...	|	2259	...	...	...	...	...	...	...	...
Idoméni 🏛 d.	...	|	|	|	...	...	...	...	...	...	...	...	...	...	1740	|	...	...	...	...	...	...	...	...
Skopje d.	...	|	|	|	...	...	...	...	...	...	...	...	...	...	2006	|	...	...	...	...	...	...	...	...
Tabanovci 🏛 d.	...	|	|	|	...	...	...	...	...	...	...	...	...	...	2118	|	...	...	...	...	...	...	...	...
Niš d.	...	|	|	|	...	...	...	...	...	...	...	...	...	...	0105	0130	...	...	...	...	...	...	...	...
Beograd d.	...	|	|	|	...	...	...	...	...	...	...	...	...	...	0506	0545	0645	...	...	...	...	...	...	...
Novi Sad d.	...	|	|	|	...	...	...	...	...	...	...	...	...	...	...	...	0810	...	...	...	...	...	...	...
Subotica 🏛 d.	...	|	|	|	...	...	...	...	...	...	...	...	...	...	...	...	1044	...	...	...	...	...	...	...
Burgas d.	...	|	|	|	...	...	...	...	...	...	...	...	...	...	...	...	|	...	...	...	...	...	...	...
Varna d.	...	|	|	|	...	...	...	...	...	...	...	...	...	...	...	...	|	...	...	...	...	...	...	...
use 🏛 d.	...	1445	1445	1445	...	...	...	...	...	...	...	...	...	...	...	...	|	...	...	...	...	...	...	...
ucureşti Nord a.	...	1709	1709	1709	...	...	...	...	...	...	...	...	...	...	...	...	|	...	...	...	...	...	...	...
ucureşti Nord d.	...	...	...	1850	1850	...	...	...	...	...	...	...	...	...	...	...	|	...	...	2358	...	0630	...	0545
raşov d.	...	...	...	2135	2135	...	...	...	...	...	...	...	...	...	...	...	|	...	...	0304	...	0937	...	|
Craiova d.	...	...	...	|	|	...	...	...	...	...	...	...	...	...	...	...	|	...	...	|	...	|	...	0830
Timişoara d.	...	...	...	|	|	...	...	...	...	...	...	...	...	...	...	...	|	...	...	|	...	|	...	1600
rad d.	...	...	...	0416	0416	...	...	...	...	...	...	...	...	...	...	...	|	...	...	1103	...	1618	...	1648
urtici 🏛 d.	...	...	...	0448	0448	...	...	...	...	...	...	...	...	...	...	...	|	...	...	1148	...	1648	...	1718
ököshaza d.	...	...	...	0420	0420	...	...	...	...	...	...	...	...	...	...	...	|	...	...	1120	...	1620	...	1650
udapest Keleti a.	...	...	...	0717	0717	...	...	...	...	...	...	...	...	...	...	...	1409	...	...	1417	...	1917	...	1947
udapest Keleti d.	...	...	...	...	...	0930	...	...	...	...	1330	1530	...	...	...	...	1510	...	...	...	2000	1940	...	2020
udapest Nyugati d.	...	...	...	...	...	|	...	...	...	...	|	|	...	...	...	...	|	...	...	...	|	|	...	|
Györ d.	...	...	...	...	...	|	...	...	...	...	|	|	...	...	...	...	1637	...	...	...	|	2134	...	2147
egyeshalom 🏛 d.	...	...	...	...	...	|	...	...	...	...	|	|	...	...	...	...	1706	...	...	...	|	2208	...	2216
túrovo 🏛 d.	...	...	...	...	...	1053	...	...	...	...	1453	1657	...	...	...	...	|	...	...	...	2120	|	...	|
Rajka 🏛 d.	...	...	...	...	...	|	...	...	...	...	|	|	...	...	...	...	|	...	...	...	|	2235	...	|
ratislava Hlavná d.	...	...	...	...	...	1215	...	...	1444	...	1615	1840	...	...	...	...	|	...	...	...	2251	2344	...	|
úty 🏛 d.	...	...	...	...	...	1253	...	...	1530	...	1653	1921	...	...	...	...	|	...	...	...	2330	0102	...	|
ien Westbahnhof a.	...	...	...	...	...	|	...	...	|	...	|	|	...	...	...	...	1808	1957c	1952	...	|	|	...	2322
Wien Südbahnhof d.	1004	...	...	...	...	|	1333	...	|	1533	|	|	1833*	...	...	...	...	|	|	...	|	|	2233	...
řeclav d.	1113	...	...	...	...	1308	1435	...	1544	1635	1708	1950	1950	...	...	...	...	|	|	...	0002	0140	0005	...
rno Hlavní d.	1146	...	...	...	...	1343	1507	...	1624	1707	1743	2023	2023	...	...	...	...	|	|	...	0038	0225	|	...
ardubice d.	1322	...	...	...	...	1522	1634	...	|	1834	1922	2200	2200	...	...	...	...	|	|	...	0217	|	0454	...
raha Hlavní d.	|	...	...	...	...	|	|	1850	2004	|	2033	2310	2310	...	...	...	...	|	|	...	0332	0614	0621	...
raha Holešovice d.	1436	...	...	...	...	1636	1732	1902	...	1932	...	...	...	...	...	...	...	|	|	...	...	...	...	...
ěčín d.	1558	...	...	...	...	1758	...	2038	...	...	...	...	...	...	...	...	...	|	|	...	...	...	...	...
ad Schandau 🏛 a.	1616	...	...	...	...	1816	...	2054	...	...	...	...	...	...	...	...	...	◧	◧	...	...	...	...	...
resden Hbf a.	1646	...	...	...	...	1846	...	2121	...	...	...	...	...	...	...	...	...	|	|	...	...	...	...	...
erlin Hbf a.	1913	...	...	...	...	2112	...	2350o	...	...	...	...	...	...	...	...	...	|	0801	...	...	...	...	...
amburg Hbf a.	2120f	...	...	...	...	...	...	...	...	...	...	...	...	...	...	...	...	0750	...	...	...	...	...	...

– PANNONIA – 🛏 1,2 cl., ▬ 2 cl. and [12] Praha - Budapest - Lököshaza. [2] (also 🛏 1,2 cl. ②⑥, daily June 7 - Sept. 21) Praha - Bucureşti. [12] and ✕ Ⓡ Budapest - Bucureşti.

– PANNONIA – 🛏 1,2 cl., ▬ 2 cl. and [12] Lököshaza - Budapest - Praha. [2] (also 🛏 1,2 cl. ①⑤, daily June 6 - Sept. 20) Bucureşti - Praha. [12] and ✕ Ⓡ Bucureşti - Budapest.

– MAROS / MUREŞ – [12] Budapest (**734**) - Lökösháza (**355**) - Arad (**626**) - Targu Mureş. Conveys 🛏 1,2 cl. Venezia (**241**) - Budapest (**734**) - Lökösháza (**355**) - Arad (**626**) - Bucureşti (journey 2 nights) and conveys on ②③④⑥⑦ [2] Venezia - Budapest - Bucureşti.

– MUREŞ / MAROS – [12] Targu Mureş - Arad (**354**) - Lökösháza (**735**) - Budapest. Conveys 🛏 1,2 cl. Bucureşti (**625**) - Arad (**354**) - Lökösháza (**735**) - Budapest (**240**) - Venezia (journey 2 nights) and conveys on ①②④⑤⑦ [2] Bucureşti - Budapest - Venezia.

– DACIA EXPRESS – 🛏 1,2 cl., ▬ 2 cl. and [2] Wien - Budapest - Bucureşti and v.v. [12] and ✕ Wien - Budapest and v.v. [2] and ✕ Budapest - Bucureşti and v.v.

– 🛏 1,2 cl. Budapest (**371/370**) - Bucureşti - Sofiya and v.v.

– BEOGRAD – 🛏 1,2 cl. and ▬ 2 cl. Wien - Budapest - Beograd and v.v. 🛏 1,2 cl. Wien - Beograd - Sofiya and v.v. [2] Budapest - Beograd and v.v.

– [12] and ✕ Stralsund - Berlin - Praha, (from Ostseebad Binz, depart 1042, Dec. 22 - Jan. 6; ⑥⑦ Mar. 15 - June 14; also Mar. 21, 24, May 1, 2, 12).

– AVALA – [12] and ✕ Wien - Budapest - Beograd and v.v. Conveys 🛏 2 cl. Moskva - Budapest - Beograd and v.v. (journey 2 nights, Table **97**).

– HELLAS EXPRESS – 🛏 1,2 cl., ▬ 2 cl. and [12] Beograd - Thessaloníki and v.v. 🛏 1,2 cl., ▬ 2 cl. and [2] Beograd - Skopje and v.v.

– KÁLMÁN IMRE – [12] Wien - Budapest - Lökösháza - Arad - Timişoarã and v.v. 🛏 1,2 cl., ▬ 2 cl. and [2] München - Wien - Budapest and v.v. 🛏 1,2 cl. München - Wien - Budapest - Lökösháza - Timişoara - Bucureşti and v.v. ✕ Wien - Bucureşti and v.v.

– SPREE - DONAU - KURIER – 🛏 1,2 cl., ▬ 2 cl. and [2] Berlin **Zoo** (depart 2048) - Berlin **Hbf** - Berlin **Ost** (2106) - Berlin **Schönefeld** ✈ (2125) - Leipzig (2316) - Wien.

– SLOVENSKÁ STRELA – [12] and ✕ Praha - Bratislava and v.v.

– [2] Berlin - Dresden - Praha. Conveys 🛏 1,2 cl., ▬ 2 cl. and [2] *CNL* **379** Amsterdam - Köln - Berlin - Dresden - Praha. Ⓡ Special fares apply.

– JAROSLAV HAŠEK – [12] and ✕ Praha - Budapest and v.v.

– [12] and ✕ Wien - Praha - Berlin - Stralsund, (to Ostseebad Binz, arrive 1919, Dec. 21 - Jan. 5; ⑤⑥ Mar. 14 - June 14; also Mar. 20, 23, Apr. 30, May 1, 11).

– *EuroNight* ISTER – 🛏 1,2 cl., ▬ 2 cl., [2] and ✕ Budapest - Bucureşti and v.v.

– [2] Praha - Dresden - Berlin. Conveys 🛏 1,2 cl., ▬ 2 cl. and [2] *CNL* **378** Praha - Dresden - Berlin - Köln - Amsterdam. Ⓡ Special fares apply.

– BALKAN – 🛏 1,2 cl. Beograd - Sofiya - Svilengrad - İstanbul and v.v. [12] Beograd - Sofiya and v.v.

– VINDOBONA – [12] and ✕ Hamburg Altona - Hamburg Hbf - Berlin - Praha - Wien and v.v. Not Hamburg - Berlin Dec. 25, Jan. 1; not Berlin - Hamburg Dec. 24, 31.

– 🛏 1,2 cl., ▬ 2 cl. and [12] Beograd - Sofiya and v.v.

– DONAU - SPREE - KURIER – 🛏 1,2 cl., ▬ 2 cl. and [2] Wien - Leipzig (arrive 0529) - Berlin **Schönefeld** ✈ (0732) - Berlin **Ost** (0750) - Berlin **Hbf** - Berlin **Zoo** (0809).

AA – ROMANIA – ▬ 1,2 cl. and ✕ Bucureşti - Sofiya - Thessaloníki and v.v. 🛏 1,2 cl. Bucureşti - Athína and v.v. [2] Bucureşti - Sofiya and v.v.

CC – 🛏 1,2 cl. Praha - Přerov - Wien and v.v.

KK – 🛏 1,2 cl. and ▬ 2 cl. Bucureşti - İstanbul and v.v.

LL – BULGARIA EXPRESS – 🛏 1,2 cl. and [12] Bucureşti - Sofiya and v.v. Conveys 🛏 2 cl. Moskva, Lviv, Kyïv and Minsk - Sofiya and v.v. on dates shown in Table **98**.

NN – HANS ALBERS – 🛏 1,2 cl., ▬ 2 cl., [2] and 🍸 Hamburg - Passau 🏛 - Wien and v.v. Table **64**.

SS – GALILEO GALILEI – ▬ 2 cl. and [12] Františkovy Lázně - Praha - Brno - Břeclav - Bratislava - Budapest and v.v.

a – Arrival time.

c – Depart 1952 as **428** on certain dates, see Table **64**.

e – Arrive at 1649.

f – Arrive Hamburg **Altona** 16–21 minutes later.

n – Arrive 0804.

o – Berlin **Ostbahnhof**.

r – Depart 2020.

v – Arrive 0902. Also arrive 0908 as **429** on certain dates, see Table **64**.

x – Depart 2300.

y – Depart Hamburg **Altona** 18–24 minutes earlier.

⊙ – ČD 680 Pendolino (Czech Railways tilting train). Ⓡ supplement payable.

* – *SC* in Czech Republic.

◧ – Via Passau 🏛.

✓ – Supplement payable.

¶ – Train number for international bookings.

THER TRAIN NAMES: *EC* **70 / 71** – ANTONÍN DVOŘÁK *EC* **72 / 73** – JOHANN GREGOR MENDEL *EC* **74 / 75** – SMETANA *EC* **174 / 175** – JAN JESENIUS

62 MÜNCHEN - LJUBLJANA - ZAGREB - BEOGRAD - THESSALONÍKI

train type/number	IC111		EC113		EC	IC		EC	EC			241			297	297				IC			
train number	IC211	483	EC213		115	311	411	69	315	411	491	413	413	391	741	481	415	293	335	55			
notes	🍷▮		🍷▮		🍴			🍴	🍴▮				🍴	🍷	419					⚡			
	G	A	M		W		J	H	Y	J	D	R		⚡	L	C	F	P	E	🍴			
München Hbf d.	0726	...	1126	...	1327	...	...	1526	...	...	...	...	...	...	2345	2345	...	...	...	...	...	...	...
Salzburg Hbf 🏛 d.	0904	...	1304	...	1504	...	...	1654	1713	...	...	...	...	...	0138	0138	...	...	...	...	...	...	...
Bischofshofen d.	0953	...	1353	...	1553	...	...	...	1758	...	...	...	...	...	|	|	...	...	...	...	...	...	...
Schwarzach St Veit d.	1010	...	1410	...	1610	...	...	...	1813	...	...	...	...	...	0229	0229	0430	...	...	...	...	...	...
Bad Gastein d.	1042	...	1442	...	1642	...	...	...	1845	...	...	...	...	...	|	|	0502	...	...	...	...	...	...
Villach Hbf d.	1204	...	1555	...	1746	1804	...	...	1957	...	...	...	...	...	0408	0408	0626	...	...	...	...	...	...
Jesenice 🏛 a.	1241	...	1632	...	...	1842	...	...	2034	...	...	...	...	...	0445	0445	0707	...	...	...	...	...	...
Ljubljana a.	1353	1455	1742	...	...	1948	2105	...	2142	...	...	0200	...	...	0605	0605	0828	...	...	...	...	...	...
Rijeka a.	|	1725	|	...	...	...	|	...	|	...	...	|	...	...	|	0851	|	...	...	...	...	...	...
Dobova 🏛 a.	1547	...	1918	...	...	...	2245	...	2320	←	...	0334	...	...	0750	...	1009	...	...	...	...	...	...
Zagreb a.	1632	...	2004	...	...	...	2329	...	0003	2329	...	0418	...	...	0834	...	1053	...	...	...	...	...	...
Zagreb d.	1650	...	...	...	...	...	0015	...	...	0015	...	0603	0603	...	0900	...	1110	...	...	...	...	...	...
Vinkovci a.	1955	...	...	...	...	...	→	...	...	0320	...	0914	0914	...	1205	...	1422	...	...	...	...	...	...
Šid 🏛 a.	2052	...	...	...	...	...	...	...	...	0422	...	1014	1014	...	1327	...	1517	...	...	...	...	...	...
Beograd a.	2247	...	...	...	...	...	...	...	...	0623	0840	1212	1212	1405	1533	...	1725	2110	2220	...	...	...	...
Niš a.	...	...	...	...	...	...	...	...	...	...	1236	...	...	1800	...	...	...	0133	0214	...	...	...	...
Dimitrovgrad 🏛 a.	...	...	...	...	...	...	...	...	...	...	1534	...	...	|	...	...	...	0415	|	...	...	...	...
Kalotina Zapad 🏛 a.	...	...	...	...	...	...	...	...	...	...	1704	...	...	|	...	...	...	0545	|	...	...	...	...
Sofiya a.	...	...	...	...	...	...	...	...	...	...	1815	...	...	|	...	...	...	0755	|	...	...	...	...
Tabanovci 🏛 a.	...	...	...	...	...	...	...	...	...	...	...	...	...	2144	...	...	...	...	0613	...	...	...	...
Skopje a.	...	...	...	...	...	...	...	...	...	...	...	...	...	2254	...	...	...	...	0729	...	...	...	...
Idoméni 🏛 a.	...	...	...	...	...	...	...	...	...	...	...	...	...	...	...	...	...	...	1145	...	...	...	...
Thessaloníki a.	...	...	...	...	...	...	...	...	...	...	...	...	...	...	...	...	...	...	1307	1454	...	...	...
Athína Lárisa a.	...	...	...	...	...	...	...	...	...	...	...	...	...	...	...	...	...	...	...	1949	...	...	...

train type	IC				IC210			418	480				412				IC	EC	EC212		EC	IC	
train number	52	334	292	482	IC110		414	748	296		390	412	240		490	410	310	114	EC112		314	2290	
notes	🅁⚡				🍷▮			296			🍷							🍴	🍷▮		🍴▮	🍷	
	🍴	E	P	A	G		F	L	B			🍴	R		D	J		W	M		Y		
Athína Lárisa d.	1051	...	...	...	...	...	...	...	...	...	...	...	...	...	...	...	...	...	...	...	...	...	...
Thessaloníki d.	1546	1615	...	...	...	...	...	...	...	...	...	...	...	...	...	...	...	...	...	...	...	...	...
Idoméni 🏛 d.	...	1740	...	...	...	...	...	...	...	...	...	...	...	...	...	...	...	...	...	...	...	...	...
Skopje d.	...	2006	...	...	...	...	...	...	...	...	0612	...	...	...	...	...	...	...	...	...	...	...	...
Tabanovci 🏛 d.	...	2118	...	...	...	...	...	...	...	...	0710	...	...	...	...	...	...	...	...	...	...	...	...
Sofiya d.	...	|	2220	...	...	...	...	...	...	...	|	...	...	...	1235	...	...	...	...	...	...	...	...
Kalotina Zapad 🏛 d.	...	|	2331	...	...	...	...	...	...	...	|	...	...	...	1346	...	...	...	...	...	...	...	...
Dimitrovgrad 🏛 d.	...	|	2259	...	...	...	...	...	...	...	|	...	...	...	1315	...	...	...	...	...	...	...	...
Niš d.	...	0105	0130	...	...	...	...	...	...	...	1058	...	...	...	1605	...	...	...	...	...	...	...	...
Beograd d.	...	0506	0545	...	0620	...	1045	1320	...	...	1526	1545	1545	...	2012	2215	...	...	...	...	...	...	...
Šid 🏛 d.	...	...	...	...	0903	...	1334	1603	...	...	...	1828	1828	...	...	0102	...	...	...	...	...	...	...
Vinkovci d.	...	...	...	...	0958	...	1440	1725	...	...	...	1938	1938	...	...	0150	...	...	...	...	...	...	...
Zagreb a.	...	...	...	...	1304	...	1748	2050	...	...	...	2240	2240	...	...	0455	...	...	...	...	...	...	...
Zagreb d.	...	...	...	...	1315	...	1810	2105	...	...	...	...	2335	...	...	0530	...	...	0750	...	0944	...	...
Dobova 🏛 d.	...	...	...	...	1402	...	1856	2154	...	...	...	...	0040	...	...	0614	...	...	0836	...	1027	...	...
Rijeka d.	...	...	...	1257	|	...	|	|	2045	...	...	...	|	...	...	|	...	...	|	...	|	...	...
Ljubljana d.	...	...	...	1525	1600	...	2035	2350	2350	...	...	...	0212	...	...	0750	0805	...	1012	...	1205	...	...
Jesenice 🏛 d.	...	...	...	...	1722	...	2155	0054	0054	...	...	...	...	...	...	...	0923	...	1121	...	1316	...	...
Villach Hbf a.	...	...	...	...	1758	...	2231	0130	0130	...	...	...	...	...	...	...	1000	1011	1158	...	1352	...	...
Bad Gastein a.	...	...	...	...	1916	...	0012	|	|	...	...	...	...	...	...	...	...	1118	1316	...	1516	...	...
Schwarzach St Veit a.	...	...	...	...	1947	...	0042	0314	0314	...	...	...	...	...	...	...	...	1147	1347	...	1547	...	...
Bischofshofen a.	...	...	...	...	2007	...	...	|	|	...	...	...	...	...	...	...	...	1206	1406	...	1602	...	...
Salzburg Hbf 🏛 a.	...	...	...	...	2048	...	...	0405	0405	...	...	...	...	...	...	...	...	1255	1455	...	1648	1653	...
München Hbf a.	...	...	...	...	2232	...	...	0615	0615	...	...	...	...	...	...	...	...	1430	1632	...	...	1834	...

A – LJUBLJANA – [12] Ljubljana - Rijeka and v.v. Conveys [2] Wien - Ljubljana - Rijeka and v.v. Table **89a**.
B – [2] Rijeka - München (also 🛏 1, 2 cl. Apr. 30 - Sept. 19, also ▬ 2 cl. Dec. 9 - 20, Jan. 1 - 6, Mar. 14 - 29, Apr. 30 - Sept. 19); [12] Rijeka - Ljubljana.
C – [2] München - Rijeka (also 🛏 1, 2 cl. May 1 - Sept. 20, also ▬ 2 cl. Dec. 9 - 21, Jan. 2 - 7, Mar. 15 - 30, May 1 - Sept. 20); [12] Ljubljana - Rijeka.
D – BALKAN – 🛏 1, 2 cl. Beograd - Sofiya - Svilengrad - İstanbul and v.v. [12] Beograd - Sofiya and v.v.
E – HELLAS EXPRESS – 🛏 1, 2 cl., ▬ 2 cl. and [12] Beograd - Thessaloníki and v.v. 🛏 1, 2 cl., ▬ 2 cl. and [2] Beograd - Skopje and v.v.
F – [2] Zürich (**465**) - Schwarzach St Veit (**415**) - Zagreb - Beograd and Beograd (**414**) - Zagreb - Schwarzach St Veit (**464**) - Zürich. [12] and 🍴 Jesenice - Beograd and v.v. Table **86**.
G – [12] München - Villach - Jesenice 🏛 - Beograd and v.v. [2] and 🍴 Jesenice 🏛 - Beograd and v.v.
H – MOZART – [12] and 🍴 München - Salzburg - Linz - Wien and v.v.
J – 🛏 1, 2 cl. and [2] Ljubljana - Zagreb - Beograd and v.v. [12] Ljubljana - Zagreb and v.v.
L – LISINSKI – 🛏 1, 2 cl., ▬ 2 cl., and [2] München - Zagreb and v.v. [2] München - Zagreb - Beograd and v.v.
M – [12] München - Zagreb and v.v. 🍴 München - Villach and v.v.
P – 🛏 1, 2 cl., ▬ 2 cl. and [12] Beograd - Sofiya and v.v.
R – ▬ 2 cl. Venezia - Beograd and v.v.
W – WÖRTHERSEE [12] and 🍴 Dortmund - Klagenfurt and v.v.
Y – AGRAM – [12] and 🍴 Salzburg - Zagreb and v.v.
⚡ – Supplement payable.
▮ – Supplement payable: Jesenice 🏛 - Ljubljana - Zagreb - Beograd and v.v.

64 HAMBURG / BERLIN - WIEN - BUDAPEST

train type	ICE	EC	ICE	ICE	ICE	ICE	EC	ICE	ICE	ICE	EC	ICE	ICE	ICE	D	ICE	ICE	ICE	ICE	ICE	ICE	EN	EN	EN	IC
train number	21	63	1605	783	783	23	45	1727	785	25	49	1001	787	27	347	1003	789	29	1613	881	229	491	493	429	345
notes	🍴	🍴	🍴	🍴	🍴	🍴	🍴	1607	🍴	🍴	🍴	🍴	🍴	🍴	🍴	🍴	🍴	🍴	🍴	🍴	🍴	A J	429	B	🍴
			P	⑥f				🍴															A K		
Hamburg Altona d.	...	...	...	0551	*0551*x	...	...	...	0749	...	...	...	0946	...	...	...	1146	...	...	1346	...	2018	2018	...	...
Hamburg Hbf d.	...	...	...	0605	*0607*x	...	...	...	0803	...	...	...	1001	...	...	...	1201	...	...	1401	...	2033	2033	...	...
Hannover Hbf d.	...	...	...	0726	0726	...	...	...	0926	...	...	...	1126	...	...	...	1326	...	...	1526	...	2226	2226	...	...
Berlin Hbf d.	...	...	0549	|	|	...	...	0753	|	...	...	0953	|	...	...	1153	|	...	1353	|	...	|	|	2056	...
Leipzig Hbf d.	...	...	0711	|	|	...	...	0911	|	...	...	1111	|	...	...	1311	|	...	1511	|	...	|	|	2316	...
Nürnberg d.	0831	...	1020	1024	1024	1031	...	1220	1224	1231	...	1420	1424	1431	...	1620	1624	1631	1820	1824	1831	0319	0323	0323	...
Passau 🏛 d.	1035	...	...	...	...	1235	...	...	...	1435	...	...	...	1635	...	...	...	1835	...	...	2035	0525a	0532a	0532a	...
Linz Hbf a.	1145	...	...	...	...	1345	...	...	...	1545	...	...	...	1745	...	...	...	1945	...	...	2145	0650	0658	0658	...
Wien Westbahnhof a.	1326	1352	...	...	...	1526	1552	...	...	1726	1752	...	...	1926	1948	...	...	2126	...	...	2326	0902	0908	0908	0952
Budapest Keleti § a.	...	1653	...	...	...	...	1853	...	...	...	2053	...	...	...	2253	...	...	...	...	...	...	...	...	...	1253

train type	ICE	ICE	ICE	ICE	ICE	ICE	D	EC	ICE	ICE	ICE	EC	ICE	ICE	ICE	EC	ICE	ICE	ICE	EC	ICE	IC	EN	EN	EN
train number	228	880	1608	28	788	1000	346	42	26	786	1604	46	24	784	1602	48	22	782	1600	62	20	344	428	428	490
notes	🍴	🍴	🍴	🍴	🍴	1006	🍴	🍴	🍴	🍴	1704	🍴	🍴	🍴	🍴	🍴	🍴	🍴	🍴	🍴	🍴	🍴	B	492	A H
						🍴					🍴t				⑧j				⑤⑦y					A G	
Budapest Keleti § d.	...	...	...	...	...	...	0555	0710	...	...	...	0910	...	...	...	1110	...	...	...	1310	...	1510	...	...	...
Wien Westbahnhof d.	0640	...	...	0840	...	...	0857	1008	1040	...	...	1208	1240	...	...	1408	1440	...	...	1608	1640	1808	1952	1952	1957
Linz Hbf d.	0816	...	...	1016	...	...	...	...	1216	...	...	...	1416	...	...	...	1616	...	...	...	1816	...	2151	2151	2156
Passau 🏛 a.	1024	...	...	1124	...	...	...	...	1324	...	...	...	1524	...	...	...	1724	...	...	...	1924	...	2305d	2305d	2312d
Nürnberg a.	1125	1133	1137	1325	1333	1337	...	...	1525	1533	1537	...	1725	1734	1738	...	1925	1933	1937	...	2124	...	0117	0117	0121
Leipzig Hbf a.	...	|	1446	...	|	1646	...	...	...	|	1846	...	...	|	2046	...	...	|	2251	...	...	...	0529	|	|
Berlin Hbf a.	...	|	1606	...	|	1805	...	...	...	|	2005	...	...	|	2205	...	...	|	0010	...	...	...	0801	|	|
Hannover Hbf a.	...	1432	...	...	1632	...	...	...	...	1832	...	...	...	2032	...	...	...	2239	...	...	...	...	...	0613	0613
Hamburg Hbf a.	...	1554	...	...	1755	...	...	...	...	1954	...	...	...	2155	...	...	...	0003	...	...	...	...	...	0750	0750
Hamburg Altona a.	...	1608	...	...	1809	...	...	...	...	2009	...	...	...	2209	...	...	...	0018	...	...	...	...	...	0806	0806

A – HANS ALBERS – 🛏 1, 2 cl., ▬ 2 cl., [2] and 🍷 Hamburg - Passau 🏛 - Wien and v.v.
B – DONAU-SPREE-KURIER – 🛏 1, 2 cl., ▬ 2 cl. and [2] Berlin - Wien and v.v.
G – Daily Dec. 20 - Jan. 5, Mar. 13–29; ④⑤⑥ Apr. 3 - June 14 (also Apr. 29, 30, May 11, 20, 21).
H – Daily Dec. 9–19, Jan. 6 - Mar. 12; ①②③⑦ Mar. 30 - June 14 (not Apr. 29, 30, May 11, 20, 21).
J – Daily Dec. 21 - Jan. 6, Mar. 14–30; ⑤⑥⑦ Apr. 4 - June 22 (also Apr. 30, May 1, 12, 21, 22).
K – Daily Dec. 9–20, Jan. 7 - Mar. 13; ①②③④ Mar. 31 - June 26 (not Apr. 30, May 1, 12, 21, 22).
P – ①–⑥ (not Dec. 25, 26, Jan. 1, Mar. 22, 24, May 12).

a – Arrival time.
d – Departure time.
f – Also Mar. 21; not Dec. 29, Mar. 22.
j – Not Dec. 24, 25, 31, Mar. 21, 23, May 11.
t – Not Dec. 24, 31.
x – ①–⑤ (not Dec. 22 - Jan. 1, Mar. 21, 24, May 12).

y – Also Dec. 26, Jan. 1, Mar. 20, 24, Apr. 30, May 12, 21; not Dec. 23, 30, Mar. 21, 23, May 2, 11, 23.
§ – 🏛 is at Hegyeshalom.

MÜNCHEN - WIEN - BUDAPEST - BUCUREŞTI 65

train type	EC	EN	EC	EN	734	EN	IC	EC	EC	EN	EC	EC	IC	EC		EC	D		ICE	IC	IC	IC	
train number	43	269	41	467	355	265	345	47	63	371	45	113	645	49		69	347		117	2391	747	391	
notes	✕	✕	✕	✕	626	🍷	794	✕	✕	✕	✕	✕	🍷	✕		✕	✕		✕	🍷	🍷	🍷	
		A		W	C	P	T		S	R						Z	D			⑧k			
München Hbf d.	...	2345	...	...	...	0345o	...	...	0927	...	...	1126	...	...	...	1526	...	...	1723	1822	...	2024	...
Salzburg Hbf 🛃 d.	...	0218	...	...	...	0526	...	...	1100	...	...	1254	1308	...	...	1700	...	...	1904	2003	2008	2215e	...
Linz Hbf d.	...	0342	...	...	...	0647	...	...	1206	...	...	...	1430	...	...	1806	...	...	2010	...	2130	2342e	...
St Pölten Hbf d.	...	0500	...	...	...	0747	...	...	1258	...	...	...	1533	...	...	|	...	...	2102	...	2233	...	...
Wien Westbahnhof a.	...	0555	...	...	...	0835	...	...	1338	...	...	...	1618	...	...	1935	...	...	2142	...	2318	...	...
Wien Westbahnhof d.	0525	0625	0752	0825	...	...	0952	1152	1352	...	1552	...	...	1752	...	...	1948	...	...	...	...	...	...
Hegyeshalom 🛃 a.	0627	0727	0857	0927	...	...	1054	1254	1454	...	1654	...	...	1854	...	...	2054	...	...	...	...	...	...
Györ a.	0658	0758	0927	0958	...	...	1125	1325	1525	...	1725	...	...	1925	...	...	2125	...	...	...	...	...	...
Budapest Keleti a.	0823	0923	1053	1123	1245	...	1253	1453	1653	1745	1853	...	...	2053	...	...	2253	...	...	...	...	...	...
Bucureşti Nord a.	...	2340	...	...	0515	...	...	...	...	0843	...	...	...	...	...	...	1402	...	...	...	...	...	...
train type		D	EC	EC		EC	EN	EC	EC		EC	625	IC	EN	EC	EN	EC	EN	IC	ICE	EC		
train number		346	162	114		42	370	46	48		62	354	344	264	44	466	40	268	390	116	68		
notes		✕	✕	✕		✕	✕	✕	✕		✕	735	793	🍷	✕	✕	✕	✕	🍷	✕	✕		
		D					R				S	C	T	P		W		B	V		Z		
Bucureşti Nord d.	...	1645	...	...	...	...	1850	...	...	...	...	2358	...	...	...	...	...	0545	...	...	...	...	...
Budapest Keleti d.	...	0555	...	...	...	0710	0717	0910	1110	...	1310	1417	1510	...	1710	1805	1910	2020	...	...	...	...	...
Györ d.	...	0722	...	...	...	0837	...	1037	1237	...	1437	...	1637	...	1837	1932	2037	2147	...	...	...	...	...
Hegyeshalom 🛃 d.	...	0755	...	...	...	0906	...	1106	1306	...	1506	...	1706	...	1906	2003	2106	2216	...	...	...	...	...
Wien Westbahnhof a.	...	0857	...	...	...	1008	...	1208	1408	...	1608	...	1808	...	2008	2105	2208	2322	...	...	...	...	...
Wien Westbahnhof d.	...	...	0940	...	...	...	...	...	...	...	1622	...	...	2035	...	...	...	2345	...	0614	0822	...	...
St Pölten Hbf d.	...	...	1022	...	...	...	...	...	...	...	1704	...	...	2120	...	...	...	0030	...	0656	|	...	...
Linz Hbf d.	...	...	1116	...	...	...	...	...	...	...	1754	...	...	2220	...	...	...	0146	0626	0747	0953	...	...
Salzburg Hbf 🛃 d.	...	...	1227	1302	...	...	...	...	...	...	1903	...	...	2342	...	...	...	0428	0753	0903	1103	...	...
München Hbf a.	...	...	...	1430	...	...	...	...	...	...	2034	...	...	0108o	...	...	...	0615	0934	1031	1231	...	...

A – KÁLMÁN IMRE – sleeper 1,2 cl., couchette 2 cl. and [2] München - Wien - Budapest. sleeper 1,2 cl. München (**269**) - Wien - Budapest (**75/47**) - Timişoara (**594**) - Bucureşti. [12] Wien - Budapest - Arad - Timişoara. ✕ Wien - Bucureşti.
B – KÁLMÁN IMRE – sleeper 1,2 cl., couchette 2 cl. and [2] Budapest - Wien - München. sleeper 1,2 cl. Bucureşti (**591**) - Timişoara (**46/74**) - Budapest (**268**) - Wien - München. [12] Timişoara - Arad - Budapest - Wien. ✕ Bucureşti - Wien.
C – [12] Budapest - Bucureşti and v.v. Conveys sleeper 1,2 cl. Venezia - Budapest - Bucureşti and v.v. See Table **60**.
D – DACIA – sleeper 1,2 cl., couchette 2 cl. and [2] Wien - Budapest - Bucureşti and v.v. [12] and ✕ Wien - Budapest and v.v. [2] and ✕ Budapest - Bucureşti and v.v.
P – ORIENT EXPRESS – sleeper 1,2 cl., couchette 2 cl. and [2] and 🍷 Strasbourg - Wien and v.v.
R – *EuroNight* ISTER – sleeper 1,2 cl., couchette 2 cl., [2] and ✕ Budapest - Bucureşti and v.v.
S – [12] and ✕ München - Wien - Budapest and v.v.
T – AVALA – [12] and ✕ Wien - Budapest - Beograd and v.v.
V – ①–⑥ (not Dec. 25, 26, Jan. 1, Mar. 22, 24, May 12).
W – WIENER WALZER – [12] and ✕ Wien - Budapest and v.v.
Z – MOZART – [12] and ✕ München - Wien and v.v.
e – ⑧ (not Dec. 24, 25, 31, Mar. 21, 23, May 11).
k – Not Dec. 24, 25, 31, Mar. 21, 23, May 11.
o – München **Ost**.

DORTMUND - KÖLN - FRANKFURT - WIEN - BUDAPEST 66

train type	CNL	IC	ICE	EC	ICE	EC	ICE	EC	ICE	D	ICE	ICE
train number	313	345	21	63	23	45	25	49	27	347	29	229
notes	A	✕	✕	✕	✕	✕	✕	✕	✕	✕	✕	✕
Dortmund Hbf d.	...	...	...	...	0420c	...	0620	...	0838	...	...	...
Bochum Hbf d.	...	...	...	...	0444c	...	|	...	0849	...	...	...
Essen Hbf d.	...	...	...	...	0455c	...	⊙	...	0900	...	...	...
Duisburg Hbf d.	...	...	...	...	0508c	...	|	...	0913	...	...	...
Düsseldorf Hbf d.	1935	...	...	...	0523c	...	|	...	0927	...	...	...
Köln Hbf d.	2006	...	...	...	0553	...	0753	...	0953	...	...	...
Bonn Hbf d.	2035	...	...	...	0614	...	0814	...	1014	...	...	...
Koblenz d.	2115	...	...	...	0648	...	0848	...	1048	...	...	...
Mainz d.	2212	...	...	...	0740	...	0940	...	1140	...	...	...
Frankfurt Flug. ✈ d.	|	...	...	...	0801	...	1001	...	1201	...	...	...
Frankfurt (M) Hbf d.	2247	...	0622	...	0818	...	1021	...	1221	...	1416	1621
Würzburg d.	|	...	0734	...	0934	...	1134	...	1334	...	1534	1734
Nürnberg d.	△	...	0831	...	1031	...	1231	...	1431	...	1631	1831
Regensburg d.	|	...	0924	...	1124	...	1324	...	1524	...	1724	1924
Passau 🛃 d.	|	...	1035	...	1235	...	1435	...	1635	...	1835	2035
Salzburg 🛃 a.	0510	...	|	...	|	...	|	...	|	...	|	|
Linz a.	0644	...	1145	...	1345	...	1545	...	1745	...	1945	2145
Wien Westbf a.	0835	0952	1326	1352	1526	1552	1726	1752	1926	1948	2126	2326
Hegyeshalom 🛃 a.	...	1054	...	1454	...	1654	...	1854	...	2054	...	...
Budapest Keleti a.	...	1253	...	1653	...	1853	...	2053	...	2253	...	...

train type	ICE	ICE	EC	ICE	EC	ICE	EC	ICE	EC	ICE	EC	CNL
train number	228	28	42	26	46	24	48	22	62	20	44	312
notes	✕	✕	✕	✕	✕	✕	✕	✕	✕	✕	✕	A
Budapest Keleti d.	...	...	0710	...	0910	...	1110	...	1310	...	1710	...
Hegyeshalom 🛃 d.	...	...	0906	...	1106	...	1306	...	1506	...	1906	...
Wien Westbf d.	0640	0840	1008	1040	1208	1240	1408	1440	1608	1640	2008	2035
Linz d.	0816	1016	...	1216	...	1416	...	1616	...	1816	...	2220
Salzburg 🛃 d.	|	|	...	|	...	|	...	|	...	|	...	2342
Passau 🛃 a.	0924	1124	...	1324	...	1524	...	1724	...	1924	...	|
Regensburg a.	1031	1231	...	1431	...	1631	...	1831	...	2032	...	|
Nürnberg a.	1125	1325	...	1525	...	1725	...	1925	...	2124	...	△
Würzburg a.	1225	1425	...	1625	...	1825	...	2025	...	2227	...	|
Frankfurt (M) Hbf a.	1340	1536	...	1736	...	1936	...	2136	...	2339	...	0600
Frankfurt Flug. ✈ a.	...	...	...	1755	...	1955	...	2157	...	...	...	|
Mainz a.	...	...	...	1815	...	2016	...	2217	...	...	...	0632
Koblenz a.	...	...	...	1910	...	2110	...	2310	...	...	...	0744
Bonn Hbf a.	...	...	...	1943	...	2142	...	2342	...	...	...	0817
Köln Hbf a.	...	...	...	2005	...	2205	...	0005	...	...	...	0842
Düsseldorf Hbf a.	...	...	...	|	...	|	...	0034c	...	...	...	0909
Duisburg Hbf a.	...	...	...	|	...	|	...	0047c	...	...	...	...
Essen Hbf a.	...	...	...	⊙	...	⊙	...	0059c	...	...	...	...
Bochum Hbf a.	...	...	...	|	...	|	...	0109c	...	...	...	...
Dortmund Hbf a.	...	...	...	2120	...	2335	...	0122c	...	...	...	...

A – *City Night Line* DONAU-KURIER – sleeper 1,2 cl., sleeper 1,2 cl. (T4), couchette 2 cl. (4, 6 berth), [2] and ✕ Amsterdam - Köln - Frankfurt - Salzburg 🛃 - Wien and v.v. [R] Special fares payable. For International journeys only.
c – Not Dec. 25, Jan. 1.
△ – Via Mannheim (Table **28**).
⊙ – Via Hagen, Wuppertal (Table **800**).

DORTMUND - KÖLN - MÜNCHEN - GRAZ and KLAGENFURT 68

train type/number	CNL	IC	IC	EC	IC	CNL	CNL	CNL	EC	CNL	
train number	319	111	111	115	311	43315	13375	13365	790	43395	
notes	[R] 🍷	🍷	211	✕		[R]	13465	13465	✕	[R]	
	K	J	H 🍷	W		C	[R] A	[R] A		D	
Hamburg Altona d.	...	...	...	...	...	...	1724	...	...	1651	...
Dortmund Hbf d.	...	...	...	0552	...	1725	|	1952	...	|	...
Bochum Hbf d.	...	...	...	0605	...	|	|	2004	...	|	...
Essen Hbf d.	...	...	...	0616	...	1748	|	2016	...	|	...
Duisburg Hbf d.	2256	...	...	0632	...	1803	|	2029	...	|	...
Düsseldorf Hbf d.	2312	...	...	0650	...	1854	|	2051	...	|	...
Köln Hbf d.	2346	...	...	0718	...	1928	|	2122	...	|	...
Bonn Hbf d.	0007	...	...	0737	...	1956b	|	2144	...	|	...
Koblenz Hbf d.	0102	...	...	0817	...	|	|	2235	...	|	...
Mainz Hbf d.	|	...	...	0913	...	|	|	2344	...	|	...
Frankfurt (M) Hbf d.	|	...	...	|	...	2229z	|	0032z	...	|	...
Mannheim d.	|	...	...	0954	...	|	|	|	...	|	...
Heidelberg d.	|	...	...	1006	...	|	|	|	...	|	...
Stuttgart Hbf d.	0419x	...	...	1054	...	|	|	|	...	|	...
Ulm d.	0543s	...	...	1155	...	|	|	|	...	|	...
Augsburg d.	0634s	...	...	1238	...	|	|	|	...	|	...
München Hbf d.	0716	0726	0726	1327	...	|	|	|	...	|	...
Salzburg 🛃 a.	...	0858	0858	1454	...	0600	0626	0626	0704	0720	...
Bischofshofen a.	...	0951	0951	1551	...	0702	0723	0723	0751	0830	...
Selzthal a.	...	*1140*	|	*1740*	...	|	0926	0926	*0940*	|	...
Graz a.	...	*1325*	|	*1925*	...	|	...	...	*1125*	|	...
Schwarzach St Veit a.	...	1007	1007	1607	...	0723	...	...	0807	0849	...
Villach Hbf a.	...	1147	1147	1747	1804	0927	...	...	0948	1048	...
Klagenfurt a.	...	1220	|	1820	|	...	...	...	1020	...	...
Ljubljana a.	...	...	1353	...	1948	...	...	...	...	...	...
Rijeka a.	...	...	...	...	...	...	...	...	...	...	...

train type/number	IC	EC	IC	IC	CNL	EC	CNL	CNL	CNL	CNL	
train number	310	114	110	210	318	797	13464	13464	43394	43314	
notes		✕	🍷	110	[R] 🍷	✕	13364	13374	E	F	
		W	J	H 🍷	K		[R] B	[R] B	[R]	[R]	
Rijeka d.	...	...	...	...	...	...	...	...	...	...	...
Ljubljana d.	0805	...	...	1600	...	...	...	...	...	...	...
Klagenfurt d.	|	0936	1726	|	...	1936	...	...	...	...	...
Villach Hbf d.	1000	1011	1811	1811	...	2011	...	...	1735	1848	...
Schwarzach St Veit d.	...	1152	1953	1953	...	2148	...	...	1946	2050	...
Graz d.	...	*0835*	*1635*	|	...	*1835*	...	...	|	|	...
Selzthal d.	...	*1018*	*1818*	|	...	*2018*	2032	2032	|	|	...
Bischofshofen d.	...	1208	2009	2009	...	2202	2235	2235	2004	2108	...
Salzburg 🛃 d.	...	1302	2104	2104	...	...	2334	2334	2110	2209	...
München Hbf a.	...	1430	2232	2232	2242	...	|	|	|	|	...
Augsburg a.	...	1519	...	...	2320u	...	|	|	|	|	...
Ulm a.	...	1603	...	...	0010u	...	|	|	|	|	...
Stuttgart Hbf a.	...	1705	...	...	0126x	...	|	|	|	|	...
Heidelberg a.	...	1753	...	...	|	...	|	|	|	|	...
Mannheim a.	...	1806	...	...	|	...	|	|	|	|	...
Frankfurt (M) Hbf a.	...	|	...	...	|	...	0535z	|	|	0432z	...
Mainz Hbf a.	...	1846	...	...	|	...	0607	|	|	0500	...
Koblenz Hbf a.	...	1941	...	...	0426	...	0704	|	|	0556	...
Bonn Hbf a.	...	2020	...	...	0521	...	0748b	|	|	0655b	...
Köln Hbf a.	...	2042	...	...	0545	...	0816	|	|	0732	...
Düsseldorf Hbf a.	...	2106	...	...	0613	...	0901	|	|	0801	...
Duisburg Hbf a.	...	2128	...	...	0628	...	0921	|	|	0849	...
Essen Hbf a.	...	2141	...	...	...	...	0934	|	|	0902	...
Bochum Hbf a.	...	2152	...	...	...	...	0948	|	|	0913	...
Dortmund Hbf a.	...	2205	...	...	...	...	1001	|	|	0928	...
Hamburg Altona a.	...	...	...	...	...	...	...	1050	1156	...	...

A – ⑤ Jan. 4 - Mar. 28: couchette 2 cl. Dortmund/Hamburg - Selzthal.
B – ⑥ Jan. 5 - Mar. 29: couchette 2 cl. Selzthal - Dortmund/Hamburg.
C – ⑤ Dec. 21 - Mar. 28 (also Dec. 19, 26, Jan. 2): sleeper 1,2 cl., and couchette 2 cl. Dortmund - Villach.
D – ⑤ Dec. 21 - Mar. 28: sleeper 1,2 cl. and couchette 2 cl. Hamburg - Villach.
E – ⑥ Dec. 22 - Mar. 29: sleeper 1,2 cl. and couchette 2 cl. Villach - Hamburg.
F – ⑥ Dec. 22 - Mar. 29 (also Dec. 20, 27, Jan. 3): sleeper 1,2 cl. and couchette 2 cl. Villach - Dortmund.
H – [12] and 🍷 München - Villach - Ljubljana - Zagreb - Beograd and v.v.
J – [12] and 🍷 München - Villach - Klagenfurt and v.v.
K – *City Night Line* POLLUX – sleeper 1,2 cl. (T4), sleeper 1,2 cl., couchette 2 cl. (4, 6 berth), [2] (reclining) and ✕ Amsterdam - Duisburg - München and v.v. [R] Special fares apply. To/from Garmisch-Partenkirchen on dates in Table **895**.
W – WÖRTHERSEE – [12] and ✕ Dortmund - Klagenfurt and v.v.
b – Bonn **Beuel**.
s – Stops to set down only.
u – Stops to pick up only.
x – Not May 15 - Oct. 27.
z – Frankfurt (Main) **Süd**.

70 DORTMUND - MÜNCHEN - INNSBRUCK - VENEZIA and MILANO

train type	CNL	CNL	EC		ICE	ICE	EC	IC	ICE	EC	EC	ICE
train number	1289	319	81	1507	699	521	85	2021	525	61	87	529
notes	🄡	🄡	♣⊡	2	🍷	🍷	♣⊡		🍷	✕	♣⊡	🍷
	A	L	S🍷	♥		⊖	R✕		⊖f		V✕	⊖
Hamburg Altona d.	2202	...	...	...	...	...	...	2232	...	...	...	...
Berlin Hbf d.	│	...	...	...	...	...	...	│	...	...	...	...
Dortmund Hbf d.	│	...	...	...	...	...	...	0203	0523	...	...	0723p
Bochum Hbf d.	│	...	...	...	...	...	...	0215	0535	...	...	0735p
Essen Hbf d.	│	...	...	...	...	...	...	0228	0551	...	...	0753
Duisburg Hbf d.	│	2256	...	...	...	...	...	0241	0605	...	...	0808
Dusseldorf Hbf d.	│	2312u	...	...	...	...	...	0302	0622	...	...	0822
Köln Hbf d.	│	2346u	...	...	...	0420	...	0352	0644k	...	...	0844k
Bonn Hbf d.	│	0007u	...	...	...	│	...	│	│	...	...	│
Koblenz Hbf d.	│	0102u	...	...	...	│	...	0530	│	...	...	│
Mainz Hbf d.	│	│	...	...	...	│	...	0629	│	...	...	│
Frankfurt Flughafen ✈ d.	│	│	...	...	...	0535	...	0648	0737	...	...	0937
Frankfurt (Main) Hbf d.	│	│	...	...	...	0551	...	0702	0754	...	...	0954
Mannheim Hbf d.	│	│	...	...	...	│	...	—	│	...	...	│
Heidelberg Hbf d.	│	│	...	...	...	│	...	...	│	...	...	│
Stuttgart Hbf d.	│	0419z	...	...	0656	│	...	...	│	0853	...	│
Ulm Hbf d.	│	0543s	...	...	0755	│	...	...	│	0955	...	│
Lindau 🏛 a.	│	│	...	...	│	│	...	...	│	│	...	│
Bregenz a.	│	│	...	...	│	│	...	...	│	│	...	│
Bludenz a.	│	│	...	...	│	│	...	...	│	│	...	│
Langen am Arlberg a.	│	│	...	...	│	│	...	...	│	│	...	│
St Anton am Arlberg a.	│	│	...	...	│	│	...	...	│	│	...	│
Landeck-Zams a.	│	│	...	...	│	│	...	...	│	│	...	│
Augsburg Hbf d.	0622s	0634s	...	...	0839	│	...	*EC*	│	1038	...	│
München Hbf d.	0705	0716	0730	...	0921	0904	0932	**669**	1104	1117	1130	1304
München Ost ▲ d.	...	...	0740	...	—	...	0941	✕	—	—	1140	—
Kufstein 🏛 d.	...	...	0834	...	...	...	1035	♥	...	...	1234	**1511**
Wörgl d.	...	...	0845	0959	...	...	1046	1210	...	...	1245	1359
Kitzbühel a.	...	...	│	1028	...	...	│	1239	...	...	│	1428
St Johann in Tirol a.	...	...	│	1036	...	...	│	1247	...	...	│	1436
Saalfelden a.	...	...	│	1106	...	...	│	1317	...	...	│	1506
Zell am See a.	...	...	│	1116	...	...	│	1328	...	...	│	1516
Jenbach a.	...	...	0858	—	...	...	1059	—	...	...	1258	—
Innsbruck Hbf a.	...	...	0920	...	...	...	1121	...	...	...	1320	...
Innsbruck Hbf d.	...	...	0926	...	*EC*	...	1126	...	*EC*	...	1326	...
Brennero/Brenner 🏛 a.	...	...	1002	...	**114**	...	1202	*IC*	**173**	...	1402	*IC*
Bolzano/Bozen a.	...	...	1129	**2095**	🄡	...	1329	**618**	🄡	...	1529	**624**
Trento a.	...	...	1205		🍷⚡	...	1405	🍷⚡	✕⚡	...	1605	🍷⚡
Verona a.	...	...	1301	1307	1318	...	1501	1518	1543	*ES*	1701	1718
Venezia Santa Lucia a.	...	...	...	1449	│	...	│	│	1708	**9419**	1831	│
Milano Centrale a.	...	...	...	...	1455	...	│	1655	—	🄡⚡	...	1855
Genova Piazza Principe a.	...	...	...	...	*1642*	...	│	*1945*	*ICp*	✕	...	*2146*
Bologna Centrale a.	...	...	...	...	...	...	1645	...	**527**	1656	...	...
Firenze SMN a.	...	...	...	...	...	...	1753	...	🄡⚡	│	...	...
Roma Termini a.	...	...	...	...	...	...	2010	...	2027	│	...	...
Napoli Centrale a.	...	...	...	...	...	...	...	...	2236	│	...	...
Rimini a.	...	...	...	...	...	...	...	...	...	1751	...	...
Ancona a.	...	...	...	...	...	...	...	...	...	1842	...	...
Pescara Centrale a.	...	...	...	...	...	...	...	...	...	1957	...	...

train type	EC	EC 89	IC	ICE	IC	IC		D	IC	EC	ICE	ICE	EC
train number	115	EC 92‡	613	623	2369	83	1545	1281	119	101	517	627	189
notes	✕	♣⊡	🍷	🍷	🍷	♣⊡	2	H	🍷	103	🍷	🍷	♣⊡
	Q	G✕	♥	⊖		T✕			K	🍷	⊖	⊖	D✕
Hamburg Altona d.	...	...	...	...	...	...	...	...	...	...	...	...	...
Berlin Hbf d.	...	...	...	...	...	...	...	...	...	...	...	...	...
Dortmund Hbf d.	0552	...	...	...	...	...	...	...	...	...	1038	...	...
Bochum Hbf d.	0605	...	...	...	...	...	...	...	...	...	1049	...	...
Essen Hbf d.	0616	...	...	...	...	...	...	...	0823	...	1100	...	...
Duisburg Hbf d.	0632	...	...	...	...	...	...	...	0838	...	1113	...	...
Dusseldorf Hbf d.	0650	...	...	...	...	...	...	...	0852	...	1127	...	...
Köln Hbf d.	0718	...	...	1020	...	...	...	...	0918	...	1154	1220	...
Bonn Hbf d.	0737	...	...	│	...	...	...	...	0937	1114	│	│	...
Koblenz Hbf d.	0817	...	...	│	...	...	...	...	1017	1148	│	│	...
Mainz Hbf d.	0913	...	...	│	...	...	...	...	1113	1239	│	│	...
Frankfurt Flughafen ✈ d.	│	...	...	1130	...	...	...	...	│	│	1254	1330	...
Frankfurt (Main) Hbf d.	│	...	...	1154	...	...	...	...	│	│	│	1354	...
Mannheim Hbf d.	0954	...	...	│	...	...	...	...	1154	1321	1333	│	...
Heidelberg Hbf d.	1006	...	...	│	...	...	...	...	1206	—	│	│	...
Stuttgart Hbf d.	1054	...	...	│	1253	...	...	...	1257	...	1412	│	...
Ulm Hbf d.	1155	...	...	│	1355	...	...	...	1411	...	1508	│	...
Lindau 🏛 a.	│	...	...	│	│	...	...	...	1554	...	│	│	...
Bregenz a.	│	...	...	│	│	...	...	...	1614	...	│	│	...
Bludenz a.	│	...	...	│	│	...	...	...	1702	...	│	│	...
Langen am Arlberg a.	│	...	...	│	│	...	...	...	1736	...	│	│	...
St Anton am Arlberg a.	│	...	...	│	│	...	...	...	1746	...	│	│	...
Landeck-Zams a.	│	...	...	│	│	...	...	...	1809	...	│	│	...
Augsburg Hbf d.	1238	...	...	│	1438	...	...	...	│	...	1552	│	...
München Hbf d.	1317	1331	...	1504	1516	1530	...	1600	│	...	1631	1704	1731
München Ost ▲ d.	—	1341	...	—	...	1540	...	│	│	...	—	...	1741
Kufstein 🏛 d.	...	1435	...	...	...	1634	...	1714	│	...	...	...	1834
Wörgl d.	...	1446	1610	...	...	1645	1706	1735	│	...	...	...	1845
Kitzbühel a.	...	│	1639	...	...	│	1740	1814	│	...	...	...	*2034*
St Johann in Tirol a.	...	│	1647	...	...	│	1749	1823	│	...	...	...	*2042*
Saalfelden a.	...	│	1717	...	...	│	1826	1856	│	...	...	...	*2113*
Zell am See a.	...	│	1728	...	...	│	*1845*y	1906	│	...	...	...	*2125*
Jenbach a.	*ES*	1459	—	...	...	1658	—	—	│	...	*E*	...	1858
Innsbruck Hbf a.	**9313**	1521	...	...	...	1720	...	...	1856	*E*	**925**	...	1920
Innsbruck Hbf d.	🄡⚡	1526	...	...	...	1726	*ICp*	*IC*	...	**925**	**837**	...	1926
Brennero/Brenner 🏛 a.	✕	1602	...	...	...	1802	**632**	**639**	...	**E**	**F**	...	2002
Bolzano/Bozen a.	1618	1729	**2107**	...	...	1929	🄡	🄡⚡	...	2045	2045	...	2129
Trento a.	1652	1805		...	...	2005	🍷⚡	Ⓑg	...	2129	2129	...	2205
Verona a.	1750	1901	1915	...	...	2101	2111	2143	...	2234	2234	...	2301
Venezia Santa Lucia a.	│	│	2043	...	...	...	│	2309	...	│	│	...	...
Milano Centrale a.	│	2045	...	**2065**	...	...	2245	...	...	│	│	...	...
Genova Piazza Principe a.	│	*2242*	...	...	...	...	...	...	...	│	│	...	...
Bologna Centrale a.	1937	...	...	2038	...	...	...	...	...	0058	0058	...	...
Firenze SMN a.	2033	...	...	│	...	...	...	...	...	│	│	...	...
Roma Termini a.	2220	...	...	│	...	...	...	...	...	│	0609t	...	...
Napoli Centrale a.	...	...	...	│	...	...	...	...	...	│	0926	...	...
Rimini a.	...	...	...	2205	...	...	...	...	...	0243	...	...	...
Ancona a.	...	...	...	2324	...	...	...	...	...	0341	...	...	...
Pescara Centrale a.	...	...	...	...	...	...	...	...	...	0522	...	...	...

train type/number	ICE	ICE	ICE	CNL	CNL	CNL	CNL	CNL	CNL	CNL
train number	109	723	611	389	40389	43305	13365	13365	13375	13355
notes	✕	🍷	🍷	B	C	🄡	13375	🄡	🄡	🄡
	Y	Ⓑv	⊖			N	🄡O	AA	W	CC
Hamburg Altona d.	...	...	...	...	...	...	...	...	1724	1909
Berlin Hbf d.	...	...	...	...	...	2009	...	...	│	│
Dortmund Hbf d.	...	...	1438	...	...	│	1952	1952	│	│
Bochum Hbf d.	...	...	1449	...	...	│	2004	2004	│	│
Essen Hbf d.	...	...	1500	...	...	│	2016	2016	│	│
Duisburg Hbf d.	...	...	1513	...	...	│	2029	2029	│	│
Dusseldorf Hbf d.	...	...	1527	...	...	│	2051	2051	│	│
Köln Hbf d.	...	...	1554	...	...	│	2122	2122	│	│
Bonn Hbf d.	...	...	│	...	...	│	2144	2144	│	│
Koblenz Hbf d.	...	...	│	...	...	│	2235	2235	│	│
Mainz Hbf d.	...	...	│	...	...	│	2344	2344	│	│
Frankfurt Flughafen ✈ d.	...	...	1654	...	...	│	│	│	│	│
Frankfurt (Main) Hbf d.	1550	1654	│	...	...	│	0032e	0032e	│	│
Mannheim Hbf d.	1631	│	1733	...	...	│	│	│	│	│
Heidelberg Hbf d.	│	│	│	...	...	│	│	│	│	│
Stuttgart Hbf d.	1712	│	1812	...	...	│	│	│	│	│
Ulm Hbf d.	1808	│	1908	...	...	│	│	│	│	│
Lindau 🏛 a.	│	│	│	...	...	│	│	│	│	│
Bregenz a.	│	│	│	...	...	│	│	│	│	│
Bludenz a.	│	│	│	...	...	│	│	│	│	1032q
Langen am Arlberg a.	│	│	│	...	...	│	│	│	│	0950q
St Anton am Arlberg a.	│	│	│	...	...	│	│	│	│	0931q
Landeck-Zams a.	│	│	│	...	...	│	│	│	│	0849q
Augsburg Hbf d.	1852	│	1952	...	...	│	│	│	│	│
München Hbf d.	1936	2004	2031	2103	2103	│	│	│	│	│
München Ost ▲ d.	1945	—	...	│	│	│	│	│	│	│
Kufstein 🏛 d.	2035	2	...	2209	2209	0539	0600	│	0600	0627
Wörgl d.	2045	2208	...	2220	2220	0550	0615	0947c	0615	0642
Kitzbühel a.	│	2243	...	│	│	│	│	0913c	│	│
St Johann in Tirol a.	│	2251	...	│	│	│	│	0903c	│	│
Saalfelden a.	│	2322	...	│	│	│	│	0830c	│	│
Zell am See a.	│	...	...	│	│	│	│	0818c	│	│
Jenbach a.	2058	...	...	2233	2233	0605	0637	...	0637	0704
Innsbruck Hbf a.	2120	...	...	2255	2255	0629	0709	...	0709	0734q
Innsbruck Hbf d.	...	...	...	2304	2304	│	│	...	│	...
Brennero/Brenner 🏛 a.	...	...	...	2340	2340	0724	0759	...	0759	...
Bolzano/Bozen a.	...	...	...	0105	0105	0912	0939	...	0939	...
Trento a.	...	...	...	0138	0138	...	...	...	...	...
Verona a.	...	...	...	0235	0235	...	...	...	...	...
Venezia Santa Lucia a.	...	...	...	│	0737	...	...	...	...	...
Milano Centrale a.	...	...	...	│	...	...	...	...	...	...
Genova Piazza Principe a.	...	...	...	│	...	...	...	...	...	...
Bologna Centrale a.	...	...	...	0435	...	...	...	...	...	...
Firenze SMN a.	...	...	...	0618	...	...	...	...	...	...
Roma Termini a.	...	...	...	0905	...	...	...	...	...	...
Napoli Centrale a.	...	...	...	...	...	...	...	...	...	...
Rimini a.	...	...	...	...	...	...	...	...	...	...
Ancona a.	...	...	...	...	...	...	...	...	...	...
Pescara Centrale a.	...	...	...	...	...	...	...	...	...	...

train type		ICE		IC	D	EC	ICE	E	E	IC 93‡	EC
train number	1500	108	1502	118	1280	188	626	924	824	IC 88	114
notes	2	✕	2	🍷		♣⊡	🍷		924	♣⊡	✕
	♦	Y	♦	K	J	D✕	⊖	E	F	G✕	Q
Pescara Centrale d.	...	...	...	...	...	...	...	0000	...	...	...
Ancona d.	...	...	...	...	...	...	...	0132	...	...	...
Rimini d.	...	...	...	...	...	...	...	0230	...	...	...
Napoli Centrale d.	...	...	...	...	...	...	...	│	1845	...	...
Roma Termini d.	...	...	...	...	...	...	...	│	2207t	...	...
Firenze SMN d.	...	...	...	...	...	...	...	│	│	...	...
Bologna Centrale d.	...	...	...	...	...	...	...	0400	0400	...	...
Genova Piazza Principe d.	...	...	...	...	...	...	...	│	│	...	...
Milano Centrale d.	...	...	...	...	...	...	...	│	│	0705	...
Venezia Santa Lucia d.	...	...	...	...	...	...	...	│	│	*0651*h	...
Verona d.	...	...	...	...	...	0659	...	0620	0620	0859	...
Trento d.	...	...	...	...	...	0757	...	0739	0739	0957	...
Bolzano/Bozen d.	...	...	...	...	...	0831	...	0843	0843	1031	...
Brennero/Brenner 🏛 d.	...	*0737*	...	...	...	1000	...	—	—	1200	...
Innsbruck Hbf a.	...	*0816*	...	...	...	1035	...	**1504**	...	1233	...
Innsbruck Hbf d.	...	0824	...	0910	...	1037	...	2	...	1237	...
Jenbach d.	...	0843	...	│	...	1058	...	♦	...	1258	...
Zell am See d.	0620	│	0843	│	0853	│	...	1043	...	│	...
Saalfelden d.	0638	│	0852	│	0902	│	...	1052	...	│	...
St Johann in Tirol d.	0710	│	0921	│	0935	│	...	1121	...	│	...
Kitzbühel d.	0718	│	0929	│	0944	│	...	1129	...	│	...
Wörgl d.	0754	0858	0959	│	1035	1114	...	1159	*IC*	1314	...
Kufstein 🏛 a.	...	0907	—	│	1044	1123	...	...	**2296**	1323	...
München Ost ▲ a.	...	0956	...	│	│	1215	...	...		1415	...
München Hbf a.	...	1007	...	│	1154	1226	1255	...	1339	1427	1440
Augsburg Hbf a.	...	1102	...	│	...	...	│	...	1414	...	1519
Landeck-Zams d.	...	│	...	0957	...	...	│	...	│	...	│
St Anton am Arlberg d.	...	│	...	1020	...	...	│	...	│	...	│
Langen am Arlberg d.	...	│	...	1031	...	...	│	...	│	...	│
Bludenz d.	...	│	...	1057	...	...	│	...	│	...	│
Bregenz d.	...	│	...	1142	...	...	│	...	│	...	│
Lindau 🏛 d.	...	│	*ICE*	1205	...	...	│	...	│	...	│
Ulm Hbf a.	...	1149	**508**	1345	...	...	│	...	1503	...	1603
Stuttgart Hbf a.	...	1247	🍷	1458	...	...	│	...	1600	...	1705
Heidelberg Hbf a.	...	│	⊖	1553	...	...	│	...	1645	...	1753
Mannheim Hbf a.	...	1328	1335	1606	...	...	│	...	│	...	1806
Frankfurt (Main) Hbf a.	...	1408	│	│	...	...	1605	...	1740	...	│
Frankfurt Flughafen ✈ a.	...	...	1406	│	...	...	1621	...	...	...	│
Mainz Hbf a.	...	...	│	1646	...	...	│	...	...	...	1846
Koblenz Hbf a.	...	...	│	1741	...	...	│	...	...	...	1941
Bonn Hbf a.	...	...	│	1820	...	...	│	...	...	...	2020
Köln Hbf a.	...	...	1505	1842	...	...	1731	...	...	...	2042
Dusseldorf Hbf a.	...	...	...	1909	...	...	...	...	...	...	2106
Duisburg Hbf a.	...	...	...	1924	...	...	...	...	...	...	2128
Essen Hbf a.	...	...	...	1936	...	...	...	...	...	...	2141
Bochum Hbf a.	...	...	...	...	...	...	...	...	...	...	2152
Dortmund Hbf a.	...	...	...	...	...	...	...	...	...	...	2205
Berlin Hbf a.	...	...	...	...	...	...	...	...	...	...	...
Hamburg Altona a.	...	...	...	...	...	...	...	...	...	...	...

FOR NOTES SEE NEXT PAGE

MILANO and VENEZIA - INNSBRUCK - MÜNCHEN - DORTMUND 70

train type / number	IC	IC	ICp	EC	IC	EC	IC	ICE	ES	ICp	IC	ICE	ICE	EC	EC	CNL	CNL	CNL	CNL	CNL	CNL	CNL	CNL	CNL	ICE
train number	611	82	558	174	613	84	2290	524	9310	619	86	990	520	111	80	318	1288	43304	13354	13374	13374 13364	13364	388	40388	612
notes	🍷⚡	♣⊡ T✗	🍷⚡ Ⓡ	🍷⚡ Ⓡ	🍷⚡	♣⊡ R✗	⑧v 🍷	🍷 ⊖	Ⓡ⚡	Ⓡ⚡ 🍷	♣⊡ V✗	✗	🍷 M	Ⓡ⚡ 🍷	♣⊡ S🍷	Ⓡ L	Ⓡ A	Ⓡ U	Ⓡ DD	Ⓡ X	P	Ⓡ BB	B	C	🍷 ⊖
Pescara Centrale d.	...	...	0635	...	...	...	...	...	...	...	...	...	...	...	...	...	...	...	...	...	...	...	...	...	...
Ancona d.	...	...	0815	...	...	...	...	...	...	...	...	...	...	...	...	...	...	...	...	...	...	...	...	...	...
Rimini d.	...	...	0922	...	...	...	...	...	...	...	...	...	...	...	...	...	...	...	...	...	...	...	...	...	...
Napoli Centrale d.	...	...	|	...	...	...	...	...	*0630*	...	...	...	...	...	...	...	...	...	...	...	...	...	...	...	...
Roma Termini d.	...	...	|	...	...	0742	...	...	0900	...	...	...	...	...	...	...	...	...	...	...	...	...	1910	...	...
Firenze SMN d.	...	...	|	...	...	0957	...	...	1047	...	...	...	...	...	...	...	...	...	...	...	...	...	2153	...	...
Bologna Centrale d.	...	...	1031	...	...	1122	...	...	1201	...	...	...	...	...	...	...	...	...	...	...	...	...	2305	...	...
Genova Piazza Principe d.	*0719*	...	▬	...	*0919*	|	...	...	|	*1119*	...	...	...	*1319*	...	...	...	...	...	...	...	...	|	...	...
Milano Centrale d.	0905	...	...	...	1105	|	...	...	|	1305	...	...	...	1505	...	...	...	...	...	...	...	...	|	...	...
Venezia Santa Lucia d.	|	...	...	1051	|	|	...	...	|	|	1333	...	...	|	*1451*	...	...	...	...	...	...	...	|	2251	...
Verona d.	1040	1059	...	1215	1240	1259	...	...	1342	1440	1500	...	...	1640	1659	...	...	...	...	...	...	...	0101	0101	...
Trento d.	▬	1157	...	▬	▬	1357	...	...	1435	▬	1557	...	...	▬	1757	...	...	...	...	...	...	...	0155	0155	...
Bolzano / Bozen d.	...	1231	...	...	...	1431	...	...	1508	...	1631	...	...	...	1831	...	...	1905	...	2030	2030	...	0230	0230	...
Brennero / Brenner 🏛 d.	*IC*	1400	...	...	*EC*	1600	...	...	▬	...	1800	...	...	...	2000	...	...	2032	...	2211	2211	...	0356	0356	...
Innsbruck Hbf a.	**512**	1433	...	...	**668**	1633	...	...	...	**1510**	1833	...	...	**1512**	2033	...	...	|	...	|	|	...	0430	0430	...
Innsbruck Hbf d.	🍷	1437	...	...	✗	1637	...	...	...	2	1837	...	...	2	2037	...	...	2120	2125**q**	2255	2255	...	0434	0434	...
Jenbach d.	♦	1458	...	...	♦	1658	...	...	...	♦	1858	...	...	♦	2058	...	...	2142	2154	2321	2321	...	|	|	...
Zell am See d.	1232	|	...	...	1432	|	...	...	...	1643	|	...	...	1843	|	...	...	|	|	|	|	2120**c**	|	|	...
Saalfelden d.	1242	|	...	...	1442	|	...	...	...	1652	|	...	...	1852	|	...	...	|	|	|	|	2108**c**	|	|	...
St Johann in Tirol d.	1311	|	*ICE*	...	1511	|	...	...	*ICE*	1721	|	...	...	1921	|	...	...	|	|	|	|	2032**c**	|	|	...
Kitzbühel d.	1319	|	**528**	...	1519	|	...	...	**510**	1729	|	...	...	1929	|	...	...	|	|	|	|	2023**c**	|	|	...
Wörgl d.	1349	1514	**1828**	*EC*	1549	1714	...	...	**1810**	1759	1914	...	...	1959	2114	...	...	2158	2217	2338	2338	1948**c**	0514	0514	...
Kufstein 🏛 a.	...	1523	🍷	**60**	▬	1723	...	...	🍷	▬	1923	...	...	...	2123	...	...	2209	2230	2353	2353	|	0525	0525	...
München Ost ▲ a.	...	1615	⊖**n**	✗	...	1815	...	...	**x**	...	2015	...	...	...	2214	...	...	|	|	|	|	|	|	|	...
München Hbf a.	...	1626	1655	1642	...	1826	1839	1855	1923	...	2026	2039	2056	...	2226	2242	2254	|	|	|	|	|	0630	0630	0723
Augsburg Hbf a.	...	...	|	1720	...	...	1915	|	2002	...	...	2114	|	...	...	2318**u**	2339**u**	|	|	|	|	|	...	...	0802
Landeck - Zams d.	...	...	|	|	...	...	|	|	|	...	...	|	|	...	...	|	|	|	2025**q**	|	|	|	...	...	|
St Anton am Arlberg d.	...	...	|	|	...	...	|	|	|	...	...	|	|	...	...	|	|	|	1959**q**	|	|	|	...	...	|
Langen am Arlberg d.	...	...	|	|	...	...	|	|	|	...	...	|	|	...	...	|	|	|	1935**q**	|	|	|	...	...	|
Bludenz d.	...	...	|	|	*IC*	...	|	|	|	...	...	|	|	...	...	|	|	|	1904**q**	|	|	|	...	...	|
Bregenz d.	...	...	|	|	**2110**	...	|	|	|	...	...	|	|	...	...	|	|	|	|	|	|	|	...	...	|
Lindau 🏛 a.	...	...	|	|	🍷	...	|	|	|	...	...	|	|	...	...	|	|	|	|	|	|	|	...	...	|
Ulm Hbf a.	...	...	|	1803	⑧**v**	...	2003	|	2049	...	...	2202	|	...	...	0010**u**	|	|	|	|	|	|	...	...	0849
Stuttgart Hbf a.	...	...	|	1907	1937	...	2106	|	2147	...	...	2300	|	...	...	0126**z**	|	|	|	|	|	|	...	...	0947
Heidelberg Hbf a.	...	...	|	...	2023	...	...	|	|	*IC*	...	|	|	...	...	|	|	|	|	|	|	|	...	...	|
Mannheim Hbf a.	...	...	|	...	2037	...	...	|	2228	**2020**	...	2342	|	...	...	|	|	|	|	|	|	|	...	...	1026
Frankfurt (Main) Hbf a.	...	...	2005	...	|	...	...	2205	2325**r**		...	0042**r**	0012	...	...	|	|	|	|	|	0535**e**	0535**e**	...	...	|
Frankfurt Flughafen ✈ a.	...	...	2021	...	|	...	...	2221	2303**r**	2329	...	0023**r**	...	...	...	|	|	|	|	|	|	|	...	...	1106
Mainz Hbf a.	...	...	|	...	2118	...	...	|	...	2345	...	...	...	...	...	|	|	|	|	|	0607	0607	...	...	|
Koblenz Hbf a.	...	...	|	...	2210	...	...	|	...	0045	...	...	...	...	...	|	|	|	|	|	0704	0704	...	...	|
Bonn Hbf a.	...	...	|	...	2242	...	...	|	...	0140	...	...	...	...	...	0512**s**	|	|	|	|	0748**b**	0748**b**	...	...	|
Köln Hbf a.	...	...	2114**k**	...	...	...	...	2341**k**	...	...	...	...	...	...	...	0545**s**	|	|	|	|	0816	0816	...	...	1205
Dusseldorf Hbf a.	...	...	2137	...	...	...	...	0004	...	...	...	...	...	...	...	0613**s**	|	|	|	|	0901	0901	...	...	1232
Duisburg Hbf a.	...	...	2149	...	...	...	...	0017	...	...	...	...	...	...	...	0628	|	|	|	|	0921	0921	...	...	1245
Essen Hbf a.	...	...	2202	...	...	...	...	0029	...	...	...	...	...	...	...	...	|	|	|	|	0934	0934	...	...	1257
Bochum Hbf a.	...	...	2214	...	...	...	...	0040	...	...	...	...	...	...	...	...	|	|	|	|	0948	0948	...	...	1309
Dortmund Hbf a.	...	...	2242	...	...	...	...	0052	...	...	...	...	...	...	...	...	|	|	|	|	1001	1001	...	...	1321
Berlin Hbf a.	...	...	...	...	...	...	...	...	...	...	...	...	...	...	...	...	|	0922	|	|	...	...	...	...	...
Hamburg Altona a.	...	...	...	...	...	...	...	...	...	...	...	...	...	...	...	...	0755	...	0854	1050	...	...	...	...	...

A – *CNL* METEOR – 🛏 1, 2 cl., 🛌 2 cl., (2) (reclining) and ✗ Hamburg - München and v.v. Special fares payable. Talgo stock.
B – *CNL* – 🛏 1, 2 cl., 🛌 2 cl., (2) and ✗ München - Innsbruck - Roma and v.v. Special fares apply. Ⓡ for journeys to / from Italy.
C – *CNL* 🛏 1, 2 cl., 🛌 2 cl. and (2) München - Venezia and v.v.
D – VAL GARDENA / GRÖDNERTAL – (12) and 🍷 München - Verona and v.v.
E – ①②④⑤⑥⑦ (◧) from Bolzano; ①③④⑤⑥⑦ (◐) from Lecce: 🛏 1, 2 cl. (T2), 🛌 2 cl. (6, 4 berth) and (2) Bolzano - Bologna - Pescara - Lecce and v.v.
F – ①②④⑤⑥⑦ (◧) from Bolzano; ①③④⑤⑥⑦ (◐) from Napoli: 🛏 1, 2 cl., 🛌 2 cl. (4 berth) and (2) Bolzano - Bologna - Napoli and v.v.
G – LEONARDO DA VINCI – (12) and ✗ München - Milano and v.v.
H – GROSSGLOCKNER – ⑥ Dec. 22 - Mar. 22 (also Jan. 2): (12) München - Kufstein 🏛 - Wörgl - Zell am See.
J – GROSSGLOCKNER – ⑥ Dec. 29 - Mar. 22 (also Jan. 6, Mar. 24): (12) Zell am See - Wörgl - Kufstein 🏛 - München.
K – (12) and 🍷 Munster - Köln - Stuttgart - Lindau 🏛 - Innsbruck and v.v.
L – *CNL* POLLUX – 🛏 1, 2 cl., 🛏 1, 2 cl. (T4), 🛌 2 cl. (4, 6 berth), (2) (reclining) and ✗ Amsterdam - Duisburg - München and v.v. Ⓡ Special fares apply.
M – ①–⑥ (also Dec. 23, 30, Mar. 23, May 11; not Dec. 26, Jan. 1, Mar. 24, May 12).
N – *CNL* ⑤ Dec. 21 - Mar. 28: 🛏 1, 2 cl., and 🛌 2 cl. Berlin - Bolzano / Bozen.
O – *CNL* ⑤ Jan. 4 - Mar. 28: 🛏 1, 2 cl., 🛌 2 cl. and ✗ Dortmund - Bolzano / Bozen.
P – *CNL* ⑥ Jan. 5 - Mar. 29: 🛏 1, 2 cl., 🛌 2 cl. and ✗ Bolzano / Bozen - Dortmund.
Q – WÖRTHERSEE – (12) and ✗ Dortmund - München - Klagenfurt and v.v.
R – MICHELANGELO – (12) and ✗ München - Roma and v.v.
S – GARDA – (12) and 🍷 München - Verona and v.v.
T – PAGANINI – (12) and ✗ München - Verona and v.v.
U – *CNL* ⑥ Dec. 22 - Mar. 29: 🛏 1, 2 cl., and 🛌 2 cl. Bolzano / Bozen - Berlin.
V – TIEPOLO – (12) and ✗ München - Venezia and v.v.
W – *CNL* ⑤ Jan. 4 - Mar. 28: 🛌 2 cl. Hamburg - Bolzano / Bozen.

X – *CNL* ⑥ Jan. 5 - Mar. 29: 🛌 2 cl. Bolzano / Bozen - Hamburg.
Y – (12) and ✗ Berlin - Frankfurt - München - Innsbruck and v.v.
AA – *CNL* ⑤ Jan. 4 - Mar. 28: 🛌 2 cl. Dortmund - Wörgl.
BB – *CNL* ⑥ Jan. 5 - Mar. 29: 🛌 2 cl. Wörgl - Dortmund.
CC – *CNL* ⑤ Jan. 4 - Mar. 28: 🛌 2 cl. Hamburg - Bludenz.
DD – *CNL* ⑥ Jan. 5 - Mar. 29: 🛌 2 cl. Bludenz - Hamburg.

b – Bonn **Beuel**.
c – Note running order of train: Zell am See - Saalfelden - St Johann in Tirol - Kitzbühel - Wörgl and v.v.
e – Frankfurt (Main) **Süd**.
f – Not Dec. 25, Jan. 1.
g – Not Dec. 24, 25, 31, Mar. 23, Apr. 24, 30, June 1.
h – ①–⑥ (not Dec. 25, 26, Jan. 1, Mar. 24, Apr. 25, May 1, June 2).
k – Köln **Messe / Deutz**.
n – Not Dec. 24, 31.
p – ⑥⑦ (also Dec. 24, 25, 26, 31, Jan. 1, Mar. 21, 24, May 12).

q – Note running order of train: Innsbruck - Landeck - St Anton im Arlberg - Langen am Arlberg - Bludenz and v.v.
r – Train stops at Frankfurt Flughafen before Frankfurt (Main) Hbf.
s – Stops to set down only.
t – Roma **Tiburtina**.
u – Stops to pick up only.
v – ⑧ (not Dec. 24, 25, 31, Mar. 21, 23, May 11).
x – Not Dec. 25.
y – ①–⑥ (not Dec. 25, 31, Jan. 1, Mar. 24, May 12).
z – Not May 15 - Oct. 27.
◧ – Also Dec. 26, Jan. 2, Apr. 30; not Dec. 24, 25, 31, Apr. 29.
◐ – Also Jan. 1, Apr. 29; not Dec. 24, 31, Apr. 28.
‡ – Train number Milano - Verona and v.v.
♣ – Special 'global' fares payable.
⊖ – *ICE 3* train 🍷, via high speed line, premium fares payable.
⚡ – Supplement payable.
⊡ – Compulsory reservation to / from Italy.
▲ – Change here for München Airport (Table **892**).
♥ – Earlier connections available from Wörgl to certain stations on certain days. See Table **960** for details.
♦ – Later connections available to Wörgl from certain stations on certain days. See Table **960** for details.

BERLIN - INNSBRUCK 71

For other services from Berlin to Innsbruck, change at München (Tables **850** and **70**); for Dresden - München connections see Table **880**.

train type	CNL	ICE	ICE	ICE	ICE	ICE	ICE	ICE	ICE
train number	1201	1603	1505	1507	1509 1709	109	1511	109	1513
notes	✗Ⓡ B	✗⊖ Q	✗ ⊖	✗ ⊖	✗⊖	✗ A	✗ ⊖	✗ A	✗ ⊖
Berlin Hbf d.	2214	...	0652	0858**c**	1059	1137	1258	...	1458
Leipzig Hbf d.	|	0501	0816	1016	1216	|	1416	...	1616
Nürnberg Hbf d.	|	0823	1128	1328	1528	|	1728	←	1928
München Hbf a.	0642	0937	1239	1439	1639	1931	1840	1931	2039
	EC 81 🍷 E	*EC* 87 ✗ E	*EC* 89 ✗ E	*EC* 83 ✗ E	*EC* 189 ✗ E	|		|	*CNL* 389 ✗ E
München Hbf d.	0730	1130	1330	1530	1731	1936	...	1936	2103
Kufstein 🏛 a.	0832	1232	1433	1632	1832	→	...	2033	2207
Innsbruck a.	0920	1320	1521	1720	1920	...	...	2120	2255

train type	CNL	ICE	ICE	ICE	EC	EC	EC	EC	EC
train number	388	108	1508 1708	108	188	88	82	84	80
notes	✗ E	✗ A	✗⊖	✗ A	✗ E	✗ E	✗ E	✗ E	🍷 E
Innsbruck d.	0434	0824	...	...	1037	1237	1437	1637	2037
Kufstein 🏛 d.	0530	0909	...	←	1125	1325	1525	1725	2125
München Hbf a.	0630	1007	...	1007	1226	1427	1626	1826	2226
	ICE 1512 1712 ✗⊖	|		|	*ICE* 1506 1706 ✗⊖	*ICE* 1504 1702 ✗⊖	*ICE* 1502 1722 ✗⊖j	*ICE* 1500 ✗ ⊖f	*CNL* 1200 ✗Ⓡ C
München Hbf d.	0722	1023	1122	1023	1322	1522	1722	1922	2301
Nürnberg Hbf a.	0832	→	1232	|	1432	1632	1832	2032	|
Leipzig Hbf a.	1142	...	1542	|	1742	1942	2142	2348	|
Berlin Hbf a.	1300	...	1700	1819	1900	2101	2300	...	0748

A – (12) and ✗ Berlin - Frankfurt - Stuttgart - München - Kufstein 🏛 - Innsbruck and v.v.
B – *City Night Line* PLUTO – 🛏 1, 2 cl., 🛌 2 cl., (2) (reclining) and ✗ Berlin Lichtenberg (depart 2150) - Berlin Ostbahnhof (2204) - Berlin Hbf - Berlin Zoo (2221) - Berlin Wannsee (2253) - München. Special fares payable. Talgo stock.
C – *City Night Line* PLUTO – 🛏 1, 2 cl., 🛌 2 cl., (2) (reclining) and ✗ München - Berlin Wannsee (arrive 0715) - Berlin Zoo (0736) - Berlin Hbf - Berlin Ostbahnhof (0758) - Berlin Lichtenberg (0813). Special fares payable. Talgo stock.
E – See notes in Table **70** for details of this train.

Q – ①–⑥ (not Dec. 24, 25, 26, 31, Jan. 1, Mar. 21, 24, May 12).
c – ①–⑥ (not Dec. 25, 26, Jan. 1, Mar. 22, 24, May 12) see Table **851** for connections on ⑦.
f – Not Dec. 24, 31.
j – Not Dec. 24, 25, 31.
⊖ – *ICE - T* train with premium fares payable 🍷.

73 AMSTERDAM, BERLIN, DORTMUND and KÖLN - BASEL - ZÜRICH, MILANO and ROMA

For other connections Basel - Luzern - Chiasso see Table **550**, for Basel - Bern - Interlaken and Brig see Table **560**.

train type	ICE	ICE	IC	ICE	ICE	CNL	ICE	IC	IC	ICE	ICE	IR	ICE	ICE	EC	ICE	ICE	EC	ICE	EC	ICE	ICE	IR	IC	EC
train number	**521**	**5**	**2021**	**511**	**271**	**50483**	**501**	**969**	**2319**	**513**	**375**	**2173**	**503**	**71**	**117**	**121**	**515**	**7**	**277**	**7**	**105**	**73**	**779**	**977**	**119**
notes	⊖	🍷 **M**		🍷 ⊖	🍷	**C**	⊖ **g**	✕	✕ **J**	🍷 ⊖	✕	¶	⊖	✕	⊡ 🍷	⊖ **H**	🍷 ⊖**g**	✕ **B**	✕	✕ **B**	⊖ **R**	✕	🍷	🍷	⊡ 🍷
København H. d.	...	...	...	...	...	1853	...	...	...	...	...	...	...	...	...	...	...	...	...	...	...	...	...	...	...
Hamburg Hbf d.	...	0024e	2246	...	...	│	...	...	...	...	...	...	...	0619	...	...	...	0441v	...	...	...	0824	...	...	...
Bremen Hbf d.	...	│	2347	...	...	│	...	...	...	...	...	...	...	│	...	...	...	0540v	...	...	...	│	...	...	...
Berlin Hauptbahnhof d.	...	│	│	...	...	│	...	...	...	...	0433p	...	...	│	...	...	...	│	0633	...	...	│	...	...	...
Hannover Hbf d.	...	0150e	│	...	...	│	...	...	...	...	│	...	0540	0741	...	...	...	│	│	...	...	0941	...	...	...
Dortmund Hbf d.	...	│	0203	...	...	│	0537	...	...	0638	│	...	0737	│	...	...	0837	0738	│	...	...	│	...	...	...
Essen Hbf d.	...	│	0228	...	...	│	│	...	...	0700	│	...	│	│	...	...	│	0800	│	...	...	│	...	...	...
Amsterdam Centraal d.	...	│	│	...	...	│	│	...	...	│	│	...	│	│	...	0704	│	│	│	...	0804	│	...	...	...
Utrecht Centraal d.	...	│	│	...	...	│	│	...	...	│	│	...	│	│	...	0732	│	│	│	...	0832	│	...	...	...
Arnhem ⊙ d.	...	│	│	...	...	│	│	...	...	│	│	...	│	│	...	0808	│	│	│	...	0908	│	...	...	...
Duisburg Hbf d.	...	│	0241	...	...	│	h	...	...	0713	│	...	h	│	...	0908	h	0813	│	...	1008	│	...	...	...
Düsseldorf Hbf d.	...	│	0302	...	...	│	│	...	...	0727	│	...	│	│	...	0922	│	0827	│	...	1022	│	...	...	...
Köln Hbf d.	0420	│	0352	0554	...	│	0654	...	...	0754	│	...	0854	│	...	0951x	0954	0853	│	...	1054	│	...	...	...
Bonn Hbf d.	│	│	│	│	...	│	│	...	0714	│	│	...	│	│	...	│	│	0914	│	...	│	│	...	...	...
Koblenz Hbf d.	│	│	0530	│	...	│	│	...	0748	│	│	...	│	│	...	│	│	0948	│	...	│	│	...	...	...
Mainz Hbf d.	│	│	0629	│	...	│	│	...	0839	│	│	...	│	│	...	│	│	1039	│	...	│	│	...	...	...
Frankfurt Flughafen ✈ d.	0533	0555r	0646	0654	...	│	0754	...	│	0854	│	...	0954	│	...	1048	1054	│	│	...	1154	│	...	...	...
Frankfurt (Main) Hbf d.	...	0538r	▬	│	0650	0654j	│	...	│	│	0850	...	│	1005	...	1102	│	│	1050	...	│	1205	...	...	...
Mannheim Hbf d.	...	0627	...	0724	0736	0750s	0836	...	0921	0924	0936	...	1036	1044	...	▬	1124	1123	1136	...	1236	1244	...	...	...
Karlsruhe Hbf d.	...	0657	...	▬	0801	0818s	0901	...	▬	▬	1001	...	1101	1109	...	...	▬	1149	1201	...	1301	1309	...	...	...
Freiburg (Brsg) Hbf d.	...	0802	...	...	0901	0939s	1002	...	...	...	1101	...	1201	1210	...	...	...	1255	1302	...	1401	1410	...	...	...
Basel Bad Bf 🏛 a.	...	0837	...	...	0936	1027s	1037	...	...	...	1136	...	1236	1246	...	...	...	1329	1336	←	1436	1446	...	...	...
Basel SBB a.	...	0847	...	...	0947	1037	1047	...	...	...	1147	...	1247	1255	...	...	...	1337	1347	1337	1447	1455	...	...	...
	...	│	*IR* **767** 🍷	EC **111** ⊡ 🍷	│	▬	▬ *IC* **967**		*EC* **115** ⊡ 🍷	*IC* **571** 🍷	│		▬ *CIS* **47** ✕	▬		*IR* **777** 🍷	*IC* **973** 🍷	│	│	│	▬	│			
Basel SBB ★ d.	...	0901	0907	0904	1007	...	1001	1101	1104	1122	1201	1204	1230	...	1304	1307	1301	1407	1401	1407	...	1507	...	1501	1504
Bern a.	...	0956	│	│	│	...	1056	1156	│	│	1256	│	1327	...	│	│	1356	→	1456	│	...	│	...	1556	│
Spiez a.	...	1031	│	│	│	*EC*	1131	1231	│	│	1331	│	1402	...	│	│	1431	...	1537	│	*EC*	│	...	1631	│
Interlaken Ost a.	...	1057	│	│	│	**175**	1157	1257	│	│	1357	│	│	...	│	│	1457	...	1557	│	**177**	│	...	1657	│
Brig a.	...	*1111f*	│	│	│	✕ ⊡	*1211f*	*1311f*	│	│	*1411f*	│	1440	...	│	│	*1511f*	...	*1611f*	│	⊡	│	...	*1711f*	│
Domodossola 🏛 § a.	...	...	│	│	│	**P**	▬	...	│	│	▬	│	1512	...	│	│	▬	...	...	│	🍷	│	...	▬	│
Zürich HB a.	...	...	1000	│	1100	1109	...	...	│	1226	...	│	...	...	│	1400	...	...	...	1500	1509	1600	1612	...	│
Landquart a.	...	...	1132	│	*1232*	...	...	...	│	1341	...	│	...	...	│	1532	...	...	...	1632	│	▬	1732	...	│
Davos Platz a.	...	...	*1255*	│	│	...	...	...	│	*1455*	...	│	...	...	│	*1655*	...	...	...	*1755*	│	...	*1855*	...	│
Chur a.	...	...	1143	│	*1243*	...	...	...	│	1352	*CIS*	│	...	...	│	1543	...	...	...	1643	│	...	1743	...	│
St Moritz a.	...	...	*1358*	│	▬	...	...	...	│	*1558*	**155**	│	...	...	│	*1758*	...	...	...	*1858*	│	...	*1958*	...	│
Luzern a.	...	...	...	1014	...	│	...	...	1214	...	✕	1314	│	...	1414	▬	...	...	...	...	│	...	▬	...	1614
Arth-Goldau a.	...	...	...	1046	...	1148	...	...	1246	...	1350	1346y	│	...	1446	...	...	...	...	...	1548	...	...	...	1646
Bellinzona a.	...	...	...	1236	*ES*	1336	*AV*	...	1436	...	1524	1558	│	*AV*	1636	*ES*	*IC*	...	...	...	1736	*ES*	*IC*	...	1836
Lugano a.	...	...	...	1303	**9443**	1403	**9445**	...	1503	...	1547	...	│	**9447**	1703	**9451**	**635**	...	...	...	1803	**9453**	**639**	...	1903
Chiasso 🏛 a.	...	...	...	1328	🅁✕	1428	🅁✕	...	1528	...	│	...	│	🅁✕	1728	🅁✕	⚡	...	...	...	1828	🅁✕	⚡🍷	**2113**	1928
Como San Giovanni a.	...	...	...	1352	⚡	1452	⚡	...	1552	...	│	...	│	⚡	1752	⚡	...	...	...	...	1852	⚡	Ⓑ**m**	│	1952
Milano Centrale a.	...	...	...	1435	1500	1535	1600	...	1635	...	1642	...	1640	1700	1835	1900	1905	...	...	...	1935	2000	2005	2015	2035
Venezia Santa Lucia a.	...	...	...	1809	│	*1909*	│	...	...	...	...	...	*2008*	│	...	│	2209	...	...	...	...	│	2308	2340	...
Bologna Centrale a.	...	...	...	...	1642	...	1742	...	...	...	...	...	...	1842	...	2042	...	...	...	...	...	2142	...	...	...
Firenze SMN a.	...	...	...	...	1744	...	1844	...	...	...	...	...	...	1944	...	2144	...	...	...	...	...	2244	...	...	...
Roma Termini a.	...	...	...	...	1930	...	2030	...	...	...	...	...	...	2130	...	2330	...	...	...	...	...	...	...	...	...

train type	EC	ICE	ICE	EC	ICE	ICE	IR	IC	ICE	ICE	CIS	ICE	ICE	ICE	ICE	ICE	IC	ICE	ICE	ICE	ICE	ICE	IR	IC	EN
train number	**101**	**517**	**875**	**101**	**507**	**75**	**785**	**2113**	**123**	**519**	**51**	**373**	**109**	**509**	**77**	**125**	**2115**	**611**	**279**	**691**	**601**	**79**	**2193**	**1093**	**313**
notes	**103** **D**✕	🍷 ⊖	✕	**103** **D**✕	⊖	🍷		🍷	⊖	🍷 ⊖	✕	✕	✕	⊖	✕	⊖	🍷 **z**	🍷 ⊖	✕	✕	⊖	✕			⚡ **N**
København H. d.	...	...	...	...	...	...	...	...	...	...	...	...	...	...	...	...	...	...	...	...	...	...	...	...	...
Hamburg Hbf d.	0646	...	...	...	...	1024	...	...	...	...	...	...	...	...	1224	...	...	...	...	...	...	1424	...	...	...
Bremen Hbf d.	0744	...	...	...	...	│	...	...	...	...	...	...	...	...	│	...	...	...	...	...	...	│	...	...	...
Berlin Hauptbahnhof d.	│	...	0832	...	...	│	...	...	...	...	...	1033	1137	...	│	...	...	...	1233	1337	...	│	...	...	...
Hannover Hbf d.	│	...	│	...	...	1141	...	...	...	...	...	│	│	...	1341	...	...	...	│	│	...	1541	...	...	...
Dortmund Hbf d.	0938	1038	│	...	...	│	...	...	...	1238	...	│	│	...	│	...	...	1438	│	│	...	│	...	...	...
Essen Hbf d.	1000	1100	│	...	...	│	...	...	...	1300	...	│	│	...	│	...	...	1500	│	│	...	│	...	...	...
Amsterdam Centraal d.	│	│	│	...	...	│	...	...	1034	│	...	│	│	...	│	1234	...	│	│	│	...	│	...	...	...
Utrecht Centraal d.	│	│	│	...	...	│	...	...	1100	│	...	│	│	...	│	1300	...	│	│	│	...	│	...	...	...
Arnhem ⊙ d.	│	│	│	...	...	│	...	...	1137	│	...	│	│	...	│	1337	...	│	│	│	...	│	...	...	...
Duisburg Hbf d.	1013	1113	│	...	...	│	...	...	1235	1313	...	│	│	...	│	1434	...	1513	│	│	...	│	...	...	...
Düsseldorf Hbf d.	1027	1127	│	...	...	│	...	...	1248	1327	...	│	│	...	│	1448	...	1527	│	│	...	│	...	...	...
Köln Hbf d.	1053	1154	│	...	1254	│	...	...	1320	1354	...	│	│	1454	│	1520	...	1554	│	│	1654	│	...	...	...
Bonn Hbf d.	1114	│	│	...	│	│	...	1314	│	│	...	│	│	│	│	│	1514	│	│	│	│	│	...	...	...
Koblenz Hbf d.	1148	│	│	...	│	│	...	1348	│	│	...	│	│	│	│	│	1548	│	│	│	│	│	...	...	...
Mainz Hbf d.	1239	│	│	...	│	│	...	1439	│	│	...	│	│	│	│	│	1639	│	│	│	│	│	...	...	...
Frankfurt Flughafen ✈ d.	│	1254	│	...	1354	│	...	│	1417	1454	...	│	│	1554	│	1617	│	1654	│	│	1754	│	...	...	...
Frankfurt (Main) Hbf d.	│	│	1250	...	│	1405	...	│	1430	│	...	1450	1550	│	1605	1630	│	│	1650	1750	│	1805	...	...	...
Mannheim Hbf d.	1323	1324	1336	...	1436	1444	...	1521	▬	1524	...	1536	1628	1636	1644	▬	1721	1724	1736	1828	1836	1844	...	...	...
Karlsruhe Hbf d.	1349	▬	1401	...	1501	1509	...	▬	...	▬	...	1601	▬	1701	1709	...	▬	▬	1801	▬	1901	1909	...	...	...
Freiburg (Brsg) Hbf d.	1455	...	1501	...	1601	1610	...	...	...	...	...	1701	...	1801	1810	...	...	...	1901	...	2001	2010	...	...	...
Basel Bad Bf 🏛 a.	1529	...	1536	←	1636	1646	...	...	...	...	...	1736	...	1836	1846	...	...	...	1936	...	2036	2046	...	...	...
Basel SBB a.	1537	...	1547	1537	1647	1655	...	...	...	...	...	1747	...	1847	1855	...	...	...	1947	...	2047	2055	...	...	...
	│	*IC* **979**	▬ *IC* **830**	│	▬ *IR*¶ **2181**	│		*IC* **981** 🍷	*IC* **685**	*IC* **832**			*IC* **787**	▬ *IR* **2187**	│	*IR* **2189**		*ICE* **987** 🍷	│	*EC* **97**	▬	│			
Basel SBB ★ d.	1622k	1601	🍷	1622k	1604	1707	...	1701	1704	...	1730	1801	1807	1804	1907	1904	...	1901	2001	2007	...	2107	2104	2130	...
Bern a.	→	1656	1707	│	│	│	...	1756	│	1807	1827	1856	│	│	│	│	...	1956	2056	│	...	│	│	2227	2304
Spiez a.	...	1731	1734	│	│	│	...	1831	│	1834	1902	1931	│	│	│	│	...	2031	2131	│	...	│	│	*2306*	2334u
Interlaken Ost a.	...	1757	│	│	│	│	...	1857	│	│	│	1957	│	│	│	│	*IR*	2055	2155	│	...	│	│	│	│
Brig a.	...	...	1811	│	│	│	...	...	│	1911	1940	*2011f*	│	│	│	│	**789**	*2111f*	*2239‡*	│	*IR*	│	│	*0012*	0100d
Domodossola 🏛 § a.	...	...	...	│	│	│	...	...	│	...	2012	...	│	│	│	│	│	...	...	│	**793**	│	│	...	◐
Zürich HB a.	...	...	...	1726k	│	1800	1812	...	...	...	│	...	1900	│	2000	│	2012	...	...	2100	2212	2200y	│	...	│
Landquart a.	...	...	...	1841k	│	▬	1932	...	...	...	│	...	2034	│	▬	│	2134	...	...	2234	2334	...	│	...	│
Davos Platz a.	...	...	...	*1955*	│	*EC*	*2057*	...	...	...	│	...	*2157*	│	...	│	*2257*	...	...	...	...	...	│	...	│
Chur a.	...	...	...	1852k	│	**179**	1943	...	...	...	│	...	2045	│	*CIS*	│	2145	...	...	2245	2345	...	│	...	│
St Moritz a.	...	...	...	*2058*	│	⊡	*2159*	...	...	...	│	...	*2259*	│	**157**	│	⊗	...	...	...	...	...	│	...	│
Luzern a.	...	...	...	...	1714	│	...	...	1814	...	│	...	...	1914	✕	2014	▬	...	...	...	...	...	2214	...	│
Arth-Goldau a.	...	...	...	...	1746	1752	...	...	1846	...	│	...	...	1946	1950	2046	...	...	...	...	...	...	2246	...	│
Bellinzona a.	...	...	...	...	1958	1936	...	...	2036	...	│	...	...	2157	2124	2257	...	...	...	...	...	...	*0037*	...	│
Lugano a.	...	...	...	...	...	2003	...	...	2103	...	│	...	...	2226	2147	2326	*E*	...	...	...	...	...	*0112*	...	│
Chiasso 🏛 a.	...	...	...	...	...	2028	...	...	2128	...	│	...	...	2258	│	2358	**1911**	...	...	...	...	...	*0146*	...	│
Como San Giovanni a.	...	...	...	...	...	2052	...	...	...	...	│	...	...	...	2212	...	**E**	...	...	...	...	...	...	...	│
Milano Centrale a.	...	...	...	...	...	2135	...	...	...	...	2135	...	...	...	2247	...	2320	...	...	...	...	...	...	...	│
Venezia Santa Lucia a.	...	...	...	...	...	...	...	...	...	...	...	...	...	...	...	...	│	...	...	...	...	...	...	...	│
Bologna Centrale a.	...	...	...	...	...	...	...	...	...	...	...	...	...	...	...	...	│	...	...	...	...	...	...	...	0519
Firenze SMN a.	...	...	...	...	...	...	...	...	...	...	...	...	...	...	...	...	│	...	...	...	...	...	...	...	0646q
Roma Termini a.	...	...	...	...	...	...	...	...	...	...	...	...	...	...	...	...	0715	...	...	...	...	...	...	...	0912

CONTINUED ON NEXT PAGE

AMSTERDAM, BERLIN, DORTMUND and KÖLN - ZÜRICH, MILANO and ROMA 73

train type	IC	ICE	ICE	ICE	IR	IC	ICE	ICE	CNL	ICE	IC	IC	ICE	CNL	CNL	IC	IC	EC	IC	IC	CNL	IC	IR	CIS	IC
train number	2311	127	613	879	795	993	227	677	301	809	955	559	542	409	40319	561	959	109	810	60458	1242	961	2165	43	565
notes	🍷	⊖	🍷	✗			⊖	🍷	✗	🍷	🍷	🍷	🍷	✗	✗	🍷	🍷	🍷	🍷		[R]✗		¶	✗	🍷
notes	z	T	⊖						Q					K	A			⊡			G				
København H d.	...	...	...	...	...	...	...	...	...	...	...	...	...	...	...	...	...	...	...	...	...	...	...	...	...
Hamburg Hbf d.	...	...	...	...	...	...	...	1824	...	1946	...	...	...	2024	...	...	...	...	...	...	...	...	...	...	...
Bremen Hbf d.	...	...	...	...	...	...	...	|	...	2044	...	...	...	2130	...	...	...	...	...	...	...	...	...	...	...
Berlin Hauptbahnhof d.	...	...	...	1433	...	...	...	|	...	|	...	...	1851	|	...	...	...	...	...	...	2126	...	...	...	...
Hannover Hbf d.	...	...	...	|	...	...	...	1941	...	|	...	...	2031	|	...	...	...	...	...	...	2352	...	...	...	...
Dortmund Hbf d.	...	...	1638	|	...	...	...	|	...	2238	...	...	2212	2338	...	...	...	...	...	...	|	...	...	...	...
Essen Hbf d.	...	...	1700	|	...	...	...	|	...	2300	...	...	2236	|	...	...	...	...	...	...	|	...	...	...	...
Amsterdam Centraal d.	...	1434	|	|	...	...	1834	|	1703n	|	...	...	|	|	2032n	...	...	...	...	...	|	...	...	...	...
Utrecht Centraal d.	...	1500	|	|	...	...	1900	|	1732	|	...	...	|	|	2102u	...	...	...	...	...	|	...	...	...	...
Arnhem ⊙ d.	...	1537	|	|	...	...	1937	|	1808	|	...	...	|	|	2139u	...	...	...	...	...	|	...	...	...	...
Duisburg Hbf d.	...	1634	1713	|	...	...	2034	|	|	2313	...	...	2249	|	2255u	...	...	...	...	...	|	...	...	...	...
Düsseldorf Hbf d.	...	1648	1727	|	...	...	2048	|	1935	2327	...	...	2307	|	2311u	...	...	...	...	...	|	...	...	...	...
Köln Hbf d.	...	1720	1754	|	...	...	2120	|	2006	2353	...	...	2329	|	2346u	...	...	...	...	...	|	...	...	...	...
Bonn Hbf d.	1714	|	|	|	...	...	|	|	2035	0014	...	...	▬	|	0007u	...	...	...	...	...	|	...	...	...	...
Koblenz Hbf d.	1748	|	|	|	...	...	|	|	2115	0048	...	...	...	|	|	...	...	...	...	...	|	...	...	...	...
Mainz Hbf d.	1839	|	|	|	...	...	|	|	2212	0143	...	...	...	|	|	...	...	...	...	...	|	...	...	...	...
Frankfurt Flughafen ✈ d.	|	1817	1854	|	...	...	2221	|	|	0205	...	...	...	|	|	...	...	...	...	...	|	...	...	...	...
Frankfurt (Main) Hbf d.	|	1830	|	1850	...	...	2234	2200	2247	0222	...	...	...	|	|	...	...	...	...	0402b	0400j	...	...	...	...
Mannheim Hbf d.	1921	...	1924	1936	...	...	▬	...	2332	0302	...	...	...	|	|	...	...	...	...	0445	0443s	...	...	...	...
Karlsruhe Hbf d.	...	...	...	2001	...	...	...	...	0005	0337	...	...	...	0437s	0437s	...	...	...	...	0543	0540s	...	...	...	...
Freiburg (Brsg) Hbf d.	...	...	...	2101	...	...	...	...	|	0452	...	...	...	0556s	0556s	...	...	...	...	0655	0653s	...	...	...	...
Basel Bad Bf 🏛 a.	...	...	...	2136	...	...	...	...	◐	0537	...	...	...	0643s	0643s	...	...	...	...	0746	0746s	...	...	...	...
Basel SBB a.	...	...	...	2147	...	...	...	...	|	0548	...	...	...	0654s	0654s	...	...	...	...	0755	0755s	...	...	...	...
									|	▬			*CIS*	|	|					▬	|				
				IR			*IR*		|				41	|	|						|				
				1995			**2197**		|				✗	|	|						|				
Basel SBB ★ d.	...	...	...	2152	...	2201	2204	...	|	...	0601	0622	0630	|	|	...	0701	0704	...	...	|	0801	0804	0830	0822
Bern a.	...	...	...	|	...	2256	|	...	|	...	0656	|	0727	|	|	...	0756	|	0807	...	|	0856	|	0927	|
Spiez a.	...	...	...	|	...	2336	|	...	|	...	0731	|	0802	1047o	1047o	...	0831	|	0834	...	|	0931	|	1002	|
Interlaken Ost a.	...	...	...	|	...	0003	|	...	|	...	0757	|	|	|	|	...	0857	|	|	...	|	0957	|	|	|
Brig a.	...	...	...	|	...	...	|	...	|	...	*0811*f	|	0840	1200o	1200o	...	...	|	0911	...	|	*1011*f	|	1040	|
Domodossola 🏛 § a.	...	...	...	|	...	...	|	...	|	...	▬	|	0912	|	|	...	...	|	▬	...	|	...	|	1112	|
Zürich HB a.	...	...	...	2300	2312	...	|	...	|	...	...	0726	|	0822	0822	0837	...	|	...	...	0918	...	|	|	0937d
Landquart a.	...	...	...	...	0039	...	|	...	|	...	...	0841	|	▬	...	0941	...	|	...	...	...	...	|	|	1041
Davos Platz a.	...	...	...	...	|	...	|	...	|	...	...	*0955*	|	...	...	*1055*	...	|	...	...	...	...	|	|	*1155*
Chur a.	...	...	...	...	0049	...	|	...	|	...	...	0852	|	...	...	0952	...	|	...	...	...	...	|	|	1052
St Moritz a.	...	...	...	...	...	...	|	...	|	...	...	*1058*	|	...	...	*1158*	...	|	...	...	...	...	|	|	*1258*
Luzern a.	...	...	...	...	...	...	2317	...	|	...	...	...	|	...	...	...	...	0814	...	...	...	...	0914	|	▬
Arth-Goldau a.	...	...	...	...	...	...	*2351*	...	|	...	...	...	|	...	...	...	...	0846	...	...	...	...	0946	|	...
Bellinzona a.	...	...	...	...	...	...	...	...	0540	*AV*	*ICp*	...	|	*IC*	...	...	...	1036	*ESc*	*ES*	...	...	1158	|	*AV*
Lugano a.	...	...	...	...	...	...	...	...	0608	**9429**	**607**	...	|	**603**	...	...	...	1103	**9707**	**9439**	...	...	...	|	**9441**
Chiasso 🏛 a.	...	...	...	...	...	...	...	...	0631	[R]✗	[R]🍷	...	|		...	...	...	1128	[R]🍷	[R]✗	...	...	...	|	[R]✗
Como San Giovanni a.	...	...	...	...	...	...	...	...	0656	⚡	⚡	...	|	⚡	...	...	...	1147	⚡	⚡	...	...	...	|	⚡
Milano Centrale a.	...	...	...	...	...	...	...	...	0745	0800	0805	...	1035	1105	...	...	...	1235	1255	1300	...	...	...	1245	1400
Venezia Santa Lucia a.	...	...	...	...	...	...	...	...	...	|	1109	...	...	1410	...	...	...	...	1530	|	...	...	...	*1615*	|
Bologna Centrale a.	...	...	...	...	...	...	...	...	...	0942	...	...	...	...	...	...	...	...	...	1442	...	...	...	...	1542
Firenze SMN a.	...	...	...	...	...	...	...	...	...	1044	...	...	...	...	...	...	...	...	...	1544	...	...	...	...	1644
Roma Termini a.	...	...	...	...	...	...	...	...	...	1230	...	...	...	...	...	...	...	...	...	1730	...	...	...	...	1830

A – *City Night Line* PEGASUS – 🛏 1,2 cl., 🛏 1,2 cl. (T4), ═ 2 cl. (4,6 berth), (2) (reclining) and ✗ Amsterdam - Basel - Zürich (- Spiez - Brig ⑥ Dec. 22 - Mar. 29). [R] Special fares apply.
B – (12) and ✗ (Hamburg ①–⑥ **c** -) Dortmund - Köln - Basel - Zürich - Chur.
C – *City Night Line* AURORA – 🛏 1,2 cl., ═ 2 cl. (4,6 berth), (2) and ✗ København - Basel. [R] Special fares apply.
D – (12) and ✗ Hamburg - Dortmund - Köln - Basel - Zürich - Chur.
E – 🛏 1,2 cl., 🛏 1,2 cl. (Excelsior), 🛏 1,2 cl. (T2) and ═ 2 cl. Milano - Roma - Napoli.
G – *City Night Line* BERLINER – 🛏 1,2 cl., 🛏 1,2 cl. (T4), ═ 2 cl. (4,6 berth), (2) (reclining) and ✗ Berlin - Hannover - Basel - Zürich. [R] Special fares apply. Conveys *City Night Line* **458** SEMPER Dresden - Zürich, see Table **75**.
H – ①–⑥ (not Dec. 25, 26, Jan. 1, Mar. 24, Apr. 30, May 12).
J – ①–⑥ (not Dec. 25, 26, Jan. 1, Mar. 22, 24, May 12).
K – *City Night Line* KOMET – 🛏 1,2 cl., 🛏 1,2 cl. (T4), ═ 2 cl. (4,6 berth), (2) (reclining) and ✗ Hamburg - Hannover - Basel - Zürich (- Spiez - Brig ⑥ Dec. 22 - Mar. 29). [R] Special fares apply.
M – (12) and 🍷 (Hamburg ① **e**) - Frankfurt - Basel - Interlaken Ost.
N – ROMA – 🛏 1,2 cl. and ═ 2 cl. (6 berth) Zürich - Bern - Roma.
P – CISALPINO CINQUE TERRE – (12) and ✗ Schaffhausen - Zürich - Milano - Genova (arrive 1742) - Pisa (arrive 2012) - Livorno (2030).
Q – *City Night Line* 🛏 1,2 cl., ═ 2 cl. (4,6 berth), (2) and ✗ Amsterdam - Köln - Frankfurt - Milano and v.v. [R] Special fares apply.
R – (12) and 🍷 Amsterdam - Köln - Mannheim - Basel. Not Amsterdam - Köln on Dec. 25, Jan. 1.
T – Mar. 14 - Oct. 26.

b – Frankfurt (Main) **Süd**.
c – Not Dec. 25, 26, Jan. 1, Mar. 22, 24, May 12.
d – Departure time.
e – ① (also Jan. 2, Mar. 25, May 13; not Dec. 24, 31, Mar. 24, May 12).
f – Change at Bern.
g – Not Dec. 25, Jan. 1.
h – Via Hagen and Wuppertal.
j – Frankfurt (Main) **Süd**. Stops to set down only.

k – On ⑥ depart Basel 1607, arrive Zürich 1700, Landquart 1832, Chur 1843.
m – Not Dec. 24, 25, 31, Mar. 23, Apr. 24, 30, June 1.
n – Not Apr. 30.
o – ⑥ Dec. 22 - Mar. 29. Note train calls in following order: Basel - Zürich - Spiez - Brig.
p – ①–⑤ (not Dec. 24, 25, 26, 31, Jan. 1, Mar. 21, 24, May 12).
q – Firenze **Campo di Marte**.
r – Train stops at Frankfurt (Main) Hbf before Frankfurt Flughafen.
s – Stops to set down only.
t – Roma **Tiburtina**.
u – Stops to pick up only.
v – ①–⑥ (not Dec. 25, 26, Jan. 1, Mar. 24, May 12).
x – Köln **Messe / Deutz**.
y – Connects with train in previous column.
z – Not Dec. 24, 31.

CIS – **ETR 470** *Cisalpino*. [R], Supplement payable for international journeys. *IC* supplement payable for internal journeys within Italy.
⊠ – Change at Landquart for St Moritz. Landquart depart 2147, Klosters arrive 2228, change trains, depart 2230, St Moritz arrive 2346.
★ – Connections at Basel are not guaranteed.
⊖ – *ICE 3* train 🍷, via high speed line, premium fares payable.
‡ – Change at Bern. 2301 on ⑦ and holidays.
⊡ – Supplement payable in Italy (except with international tickets).

¶ – To Locarno.
⊙ – 🏛 is at Emmerich.
§ – Ticket point is **Iselle**.
◐ – Ticket point / frontier.
⚡ – Supplement payable.

OTHER TRAIN NAMES:

EC **109** – CISALPINO TICINO
EC **111** – CISALPINO SAN MARCO
EC **115** – CISALPINO MEDIOLANUM
EC **117** – CISALPINO VERDI
EC **119** – CISALPINO TIZIANO
EC **177** – CISALPINO MONTE CENERI
EC **179** – CISALPINO INSUBRIA

MILANO and ROMA - PATRAS - ATHÍNAI 74

train type	*ES*	*ICp*	*ES*			*ES*		*ICp*	*ES*	
train number	**9353**	**553**	**9415**			**9324**	**12110**	**557**	**9417**	
notes	[R]✗	[R]🍷	[R]✗	⛴		[R]✗	2	[R]🍷	[R]✗	⛴
	⚡	⚡	⚡	*SF*		⚡	⚒	⚡	⚡	*SF*
Milano Centrale d.	...	0910	1105	...	...	...	...	1200	1305	...
Bologna d.	...	1129	1256	...	...	...	...	1429	1456	...
Roma Termini d.	1338	|	|	...	...	0938	1135	|	|	...
Foligno d.	|	|	|	...	...	1111	1328	|	|	...
Ancona d.	|	1337	1444	...	...	1248	1538	1700	1641	...
Ancona Marittima d.	|	|	|	...	...	...	...	...	...	1900
Pescara Centrale d.	|	1518	1608	...	...	....	...	...	....	|
Caserta d.	1520	|	|	...	...	...	...	...	...	|
Foggia d.	1714	1730	1750	...	...	...	...	...	...	|
Bari Centrale a.	1815	1844	1853	...	...	...	...	...	...	|
Bari Marittima d.	...	...	...	2000	...	...	...	...	...	|
Patras a.	...	...	...	1230	...	...	...	...	...	1700
Athína Lárisa a.	...	...	...	❖	...	...	...	...	...	❖

train type		*ES*	*IC*	*ES*		*ES*	*IC*	*ICp*	*ES*	*ES*
train number		**9414**	**568**	**9354**		**9416**	**588**	**570**	**9418**	**9337**
notes	⛴	✗[R]	🍷	✗[R]	⛴	✗[R]	🍷	🍷[R]	✗[R]	🍷[R]
	SF	⚡	⚡	⚡	*SF*	⚡	⚡	⚡	⚡	⚡
Athína Lárisa d.	❖	...	...	...	❖	...	...	...	...	...
Patras d.	1800	...	...	...	2000	...	...	...	...	...
Bari Marittima a.	0830	...	...	...	|	...	...	...	...	...
Bari Centrale d.	...	1105	1113	1342	|	...	...	...	...	...
Foggia a.	...	1207	1224	1444	|	...	...	...	...	...
Caserta a.	...	|	|	1635	|	...	...	...	...	...
Pescara Centrale a.	...	1345	1432	|	|	...	...	...	...	...
Ancona Marittma a.	...	|	|	|	1600	...	...	...	...	...
Ancona a.	...	1515	1617	|	...	1715	...	1900	1913	1805
Foligno a.	...	|	|	|	...	|	...	|	|	1944
Roma Termini a.	...	|	|	1822	...	|	...	|	|	2120
Bologna a.	...	1704	1831	...	...	1904	1944	2129	2104	...
Milano Centrale a.	...	1855	2050	...	...	...	2150	2359	2300	...

❖ – For shipping operators' bus connections see Table **2770**; for rail service see Table **1450**.
SF – **Superfast Ferries**, for days of running see Tables **2715**, **2755**.
⚡ – Supplement payable.

73 ROMA, MILANO and ZÜRICH - KÖLN, DORTMUND, BERLIN and AMSTERDAM

For other connections Basel - Luzern - Chiasso see Table **550**, for Basel - Bern - Interlaken and Brig see Table **560**.

train type	ICE	IR	EN	TGV	ICE	IC	IC	IR	ICE	IC	IR	ICE	IC	IC	IR	ICE	CIS	IR	EC	CIS	ICE	IR	IC	ICE	IC	ICE
train number	**78**	**758**	**314**	**9212**	**278**	**664**	**956**	**760**	**76**	**562**	**2166**	**372**	**962**	**668**	**566**	**74**	**156**	**2170**	**100**	**40**	**272**	**770**	**672**	**72**	**968**	**122**
notes	🍷		🛏 **N**	🍷🛏	🍷				🍷			🍷				🍷	✕		**102** **G**✕	✕	✕	🍷		🍷		⊖
Roma Termini d.	...	...	1955	...	...	...	...	...	...	...	...	...	...	...	...	...	...	...	...	...	...	...	...	...	...	...
Firenze SMN d.	...	...	2200q	...	...	...	...	...	...	...	...	...	...	...	...	...	...	...	...	...	...	...	...	...	...	...
Bologna Centrale d.	...	...	2318	...	...	...	...	...	...	...	...	...	...	...	...	...	...	...	...	...	...	...	...	...	...	...
Venezia Santa Lucia d.	...	...	|	...	...	...	...	...	...	...	...	...	...	...	...	...	...	...	...	...	...	...	...	...	...	...
Milano Centrale d.	...	...	|	...	...	...	...	...	...	...	...	...	...	...	...	...	0710	...	...	0725	...	...	...	...	...	...
Como San Giovanni d.	...	...	|	...	...	...	...	...	...	...	...	...	...	...	...	...	0743	...	...	|	...	...	...	...	...	...
Chiasso 🛃 d.	...	...	|	...	...	...	...	...	...	...	...	...	...	0628	...	...	|	0658	...	|	...	...	0831	...	...	...
Lugano d.	...	...	|	...	...	...	...	...	...	...	...	...	...	0655	...	...	0809	0725	...	|	...	...	0855	...	...	...
Bellinzona d.	...	...	|	...	...	...	...	...	...	...	0600	...	...	0723	...	...	0834	0800	...	|	...	...	0923	...	...	...
Arth-Goldau d.	...	...	|	...	...	*0657*	...	...	...	...	0812	...	...	0912	...	...	1012	1012	...	|	...	...	1112	...	...	...
Luzern d.	...	...	|	...	...	0745	...	...	...	...	0845	...	...	0945	...	...	|	1045	...	|	...	...	1145	...	...	...
St Moritz d.	...	...	|	...	...	|	...	...	...	...	|	...	...	|	*0540*k	...	|	|	*0702*	|	...	*0802*	|	...	...	...
Chur d.	...	0513	|	...	...	|	...	0613	...	0709	|	...	...	|	0809	...	|	|	0916	|	...	1016	|	...	...	...
Davos Platz d.	...	|	|	...	...	|	...	|	...	*0550*	|	...	...	|	*0702*	...	|	|	*0802*	|	...	*0902*	|	...	...	...
Landquart d.	...	0523	|	...	...	|	...	0623	...	0719	|	...	...	|	0819	...	|	|	0926	|	...	1026	|	...	...	...
Zürich HB d.	0554	0647	|	0702	...	|	...	0747	0802	0834	|	...	...	|	0934	1002	1051	|	1102	|	...	1147	|	1202	...	...
Domodossola 🛃 § d.	|	▬	◐	|	...	|	...	▬	|	|	|	...	...	|	|	|	▬	|	|	0848	...	▬	|	|	...	...
Brig d.	|	...	0439a	|	*0547*f	|	*0649*f	...	|	|	|	*0749*f	*0849*f	|	|	|	...	|	|	0920	*0949*f	EC	|	|	*1049*f	...
Interlaken Ost d.	|	...	|	|	0601	|	0701	...	|	|	|	0801	0901	|	|	|	...	|	|	|	1001	**100/2**	|	|	1101	...
Spiez d.	|	...	0543s	|	0623	|	0723	...	|	|	|	0823	0923	|	|	|	...	|	|	0954	1023	**G**✕	|	|	1123	...
Bern d.	|	...	0620	|	0704	|	0804	...	|	|	|	0904	1004	|	|	|	...	|	|	1034	1104	←	|	|	1204	...
Basel SBB ★ a.	0658	...	...	0756	0754	0851	0854	...	0856	0938	0951	0954	1054	1051	1038	1056	...	1151	1156	1129	1154	1156	1251	1256	1254	...
	|	ICE 602 ⊖			|	▬	▬		|	▬ ICE⊖ 600		|	▬	▬	▬	|	ICE 508 ⊖	▬	|		|	|		|	ICE 506 ⊖	
Basel SBB d.	0704	0712	...	...	0812	ICE	...	...	0904	0912	...	1012	ICE	...	...	1104	1112	...	1218	...	1212	1218	...	1304	1312	...
Basel Bad Bf 🛃 d.	0713	0721	...	...	0822	**612**	ICE	IC	0913	0922	...	1022	**610**	...	IC	1113	1122	IC	→	...	1222	1227	...	1313	1322	...
Freiburg (Brsg) Hbf d.	0749	0756	...	...	0857	🍷	**126**	**2114**	0949	0957	...	1057	🍷	ICE	**2112**	1149	1157	**2012**	...	...	1257	1304	...	1349	1357	...
Karlsruhe Hbf d.	0851	0901	...	...	1000	⊖	⊖	🍷	1051	1100	...	1200	⊖	**124**	🍷	1251	1300	🍷	...	...	1400	1412	...	1451	1500	...
Mannheim Hbf a.	0914	0924	...	...	1022	1035	**T**	1039	1114	1123	...	1222	1235	⊖	1239	1314	1323	1408	...	...	1422	1437	...	1514	1523	...
Frankfurt (Main) Hbf a.	0953	|	...	...	1108	|	1128	|	1153	|	...	1308	|	1328	|	1353	|	|	...	...	1508	|	...	1553	|	1628
Frankfurt Flughafen ✈ a.	|	1006	...	...	|	1106	1140	|	|	1206	...	|	1306	1340	|	|	1406	|	...	...	|	|	...	|	1606	1640
Mainz Hbf a.	|	|	...	...	|	|	|	1118	|	|	...	|	|	|	1318	|	|	1446	...	...	|	1518	...	|	|	|
Koblenz Hbf a.	|	|	...	...	|	|	|	1210	|	|	...	|	|	|	1410	|	|	1541	...	...	|	1610	...	|	|	|
Bonn Hbf a.	|	|	...	...	|	|	|	1242	|	|	...	|	|	|	1442	|	|	1620	...	...	|	1642	...	|	|	|
Köln Hbf a.	|	1105	...	...	|	1205	1240	1305	|	1305	...	|	1405	1440	1505	|	1505	1642	...	...	|	1705	...	|	1705	1740
Düsseldorf Hbf a.	|	...	...	...	|	1232	1311	1332	|	...	...	|	1432	1511	1532	|	...	1712	...	...	|	1732	...	|	|	1811
Duisburg Hbf a.	|	...	...	...	|	1245	1326	1345	|	...	...	|	1445	1526	1545	|	...	1725	...	...	|	1745	...	|	h	1824
Arnhem ⊙ a.	|	...	...	...	|	|	1423	|	|	...	...	|	|	1623	|	|	...	|	...	...	|	|	...	|	|	1923
Utrecht Centraal a.	|	...	...	...	|	|	1456	|	|	...	...	|	|	1656	|	|	...	|	...	...	|	|	...	|	|	1956
Amsterdam Centraal a.	|	...	...	...	|	|	1525	|	|	...	...	|	|	1725	|	|	...	|	...	...	|	|	...	|	|	2025
Essen Hbf a.	|	...	...	...	|	1257	...	1358	|	...	...	|	1457	...	1558	|	...	1740	...	...	|	1758	...	|	|	...
Dortmund Hbf a.	|	...	...	...	|	1321	...	1421	|	...	...	|	1521	...	1621	|	...	1805	...	...	|	1821	...	|	1820	...
Hannover Hbf a.	1217	...	...	...	|	...	...	|	1417	...	...	|	...	...	|	1617	...	2018	...	...	|	|	...	1817	...	...
Berlin Hauptbahnhof a.	|	...	...	...	1526	...	...	|	|	...	...	1725	...	...	|	|	...	...	...	...	1925	|	...	|	...	...
Bremen Hbf a.	|	...	...	...	...	...	...	1614	|	...	...	...	...	...	1814	|	...	...	...	...	...	2014	...	|	...	...
Hamburg Hbf a.	1335	...	...	...	...	...	...	1712	1535	...	...	...	...	...	1912	1735	...	...	...	...	...	2112	...	1935	...	...
København H. a.	...	...	...	...	...	...	...	...	...	...	...	...	...	...	...	...	...	...	...	...	...	...	...	...	...	...

train type	EC	IC	EC	EC	IR	EC	IC	ESc	EC	IC	ES	CIS	CIS	IR	IC	ICE	IC	EC	ES	EC	ICE	ICE	IC	IC	EC	IR
train number	**120**	**1072**	**6**	**170**	**2174**	**6**	**574**	**9700**	**106**	**606**	**9426**	**44**	**154**	**2178**	**978**	**514**	**578**	**108**	**9428**	**122**	**374**	**502**	**1080**	**580**	**172**	**2182**
notes	🍷 ⊡	🍷	✕ **G**	🍷 ⊡	¶	✕ **G**	🍷	Ⓡ✕ 🛏	🍷 ⊡	🍷 🛏	Ⓡ✕ 🛏	✕	✕	¶	🍷	🍷 ⊖	🍷	🍷 ⊡	Ⓡ✕ 🛏	🍷 ⊡	🍷	⊖	🍷	🍷	🍷 ⊡	¶
Roma Termini d.	...	...	...	...	...	...	...	...	...	...	0630	...	...	...	...	...	...	...	0730	...	...	...	...	...	...	...
Firenze SMN d.	...	...	...	...	...	...	...	...	...	...	0814	...	...	...	...	...	...	...	0914	...	...	...	...	...	...	...
Bologna Centrale d.	...	...	...	...	...	...	...	...	...	...	0916	...	...	...	...	...	...	...	1016	...	...	...	...	...	...	...
Venezia Santa Lucia d.	...	...	...	...	...	...	...	0630	...	0752	|	...	0842t	...	...	...	...	...	|	...	...	...	...	...	...	...
Milano Centrale d.	0825	...	...	0825	...	...	...	0905	0925	1055	1100	1120	1118	...	...	...	...	1125	1200	1225	...	...	...	...	1225	...
Como San Giovanni d.	|	...	...	0907	...	...	...	▬	1007	▬	▬	|	|	...	...	...	...	1207	...	|	...	...	...	...	1307	...
Chiasso 🛃 d.	|	...	...	0931	...	...	...	...	1031	...	...	|	|	...	...	...	...	1231	...	|	...	...	...	...	1331	...
Lugano d.	|	...	...	0955	...	...	...	...	1055	...	...	|	1209	...	...	...	...	1255	...	|	...	...	...	...	1355	...
Bellinzona d.	|	...	...	1023	1000	...	...	...	1123	...	EC	|	1234	1200	...	...	...	1323	...	|	...	...	...	...	1423	1400
Arth-Goldau d.	|	...	...	1208	1212	...	...	...	1312	...	**96**	|	1408	1412	...	...	...	1512	...	|	...	...	...	...	1608	1612
Luzern d.	|	...	...	▬	1245	...	...	...	1345	...	🍷	|	...	1445	...	...	...	1545	...	|	...	...	...	...	▬	1645
St Moritz d.	|	...	*0902*	...	|	...	*1002*	...	|	...	*1102*	|	...	|	...	...	*1202*	|	...	|	...	...	...	*1302*	...	|
Chur d.	|	...	1116	...	|	...	1209	...	|	...	1309	|	...	|	...	...	1409	|	...	|	...	...	...	1509	...	|
Davos Platz d.	|	...	*1002*	...	|	...	*1102*	...	|	...	*1202*	|	...	|	...	...	*1302*	|	...	|	...	...	...	*1402*	...	|
Landquart d.	|	...	1126	ICE	|	...	1219	IC	|	...	1319	|	...	|	...	...	1419	|	...	|	...	...	...	1519	IC	|
Zürich HB d.	|	...	1302	**276**	|	...	1334	**874**	|	...	1434	|	...	|	...	...	1534	|	...	|	...	...	...	1634	**982**	|
Domodossola 🛃 § d.	1010	...	|	🍷	|	...	|	🍷	|	...	...	1248	...	|	...	...	|	|	...	1410	...	...	...	|	🍷	|
Brig d.	1040	1120	|	*1149*f	|	...	|	*1249*f	|	...	...	1320	...	|	*1349*f	...	|	|	...	1440	*1449*f	...	1520	|	*1549*f	|
Interlaken Ost d.	...	|	|	1201	|	...	|	1301	|	...	...	|	...	|	1401	...	|	|	...	...	1501	...	*1529*	|	1601	|
Spiez d.	...	1154	|	1223	|	...	|	1323	|	...	...	1354	...	|	1423	...	|	|	...	...	1523	...	1554	|	1623	|
Bern d.	...	1234	|	1304	|	←	|	1404	|	...	...	1434	...	|	1504	...	|	|	...	...	1604	...	1634	|	1704	|
Basel SBB ★ a.	...	1329	1356	1354	1351y	1356	1438	1454	1451	ICE	1538	1529	...	1551	1554	...	1638	1651	...	...	1654	...	1729	1738	1754	1751y
			|	|	▬	|			ICE 70 ✕	**104** ⊖ **B**					ICE 872 ✕		▬	▬			|		▬		CNL 40353 J	ICE 870/6 🍷
Basel SBB d.	...	...	1418	1412	ICE	1418	...	...	1504	1512	...	...	...	...	1612	...	...	IC	...	...	1704	1712	...	...	1804	1812
Basel Bad Bf 🛃 d.	...	...	→	1422	**516**	1427	...	...	1513	1522	...	...	...	...	1621	...	ICE	**2318**	...	...	1713	1721	ICE	...	1817u	1822
Freiburg (Brsg) Hbf d.	...	...	...	1457	🍷	1504	...	...	1549	1557	...	...	...	...	1656	...	**120**	🍷	...	...	1749	1756	**592**	...	1904u	1857
Karlsruhe Hbf d.	...	...	...	1600	⊖	1612	...	...	1651	1700	...	...	...	...	1801	...	⊖	**p**	...	...	1851	1901	✕	...	2018u	2000
Mannheim Hbf a.	...	...	...	1622	1635	1637	...	...	1714	1723	...	...	...	...	1823	1835	Ⓑe	1839	...	...	1914	1924	1931	...	2116u	2022
Frankfurt (Main) Hbf a.	...	...	...	1708	|	|	...	...	1753	|	...	...	...	...	1908	|	1928	|	...	...	1953	|	2008	...	2219b	2108
Frankfurt Flughafen ✈ a.	...	...	...	|	1706	|	...	...	|	1806	...	...	...	...	|	1906	1940	|	...	...	|	2006	|	...	|	...
Mainz Hbf a.	...	...	...	|	|	1718	...	...	|	|	...	...	...	...	|	|	|	1918	...	...	|	|	|	...	|	...
Koblenz Hbf a.	...	...	...	|	|	1810	...	...	|	|	...	...	...	...	|	|	|	2010	...	...	|	|	|	...	|	...
Bonn Hbf a.	...	...	...	|	|	1842	...	...	|	|	...	...	...	...	|	|	|	2042	...	...	|	|	|	...	|	...
Köln Hbf a.	...	...	...	|	1805	1905	...	...	|	1905	...	...	...	...	|	2005	2040	2105	...	...	|	2105	|	...	|	...
Düsseldorf Hbf a.	...	...	...	|	|	1932	...	...	|	1938	...	...	...	...	|	2032	2111	...	...	...	|	|	|	...	|	...
Duisburg Hbf a.	...	...	...	|	h	1945	...	...	|	1951	...	...	...	...	|	2045	2124	...	...	...	|	h	|	...	|	...
Arnhem ⊙ a.	...	...	...	|	|	|	...	...	|	2052	...	...	...	...	|	|	2223	...	...	...	|	|	|	...	|	...
Utrecht Centraal a.	...	...	...	|	|	|	...	...	|	2126	...	...	...	...	|	|	2256	...	...	...	|	|	|	...	|	...
Amsterdam Centraal a.	...	...	...	|	|	|	...	...	|	2155	...	...	...	...	|	|	2325	...	...	...	|	|	|	...	|	...
Essen Hbf a.	...	...	...	|	|	1958	...	...	|	...	...	...	...	...	|	2057	...	...	...	...	|	|	|	...	|	...
Dortmund Hbf a.	...	...	...	|	1920	2021	...	...	|	...	...	...	...	...	|	2121	...	...	...	...	|	2220	|	...	|	...
Hannover Hbf a.	...	...	...	|	...	...	...	...	2017	...	...	...	...	...	|	|	...	...	...	...	2217j	...	|	...	|	...
Berlin Hauptbahnhof a.	...	...	...	2125z	...	...	...	...	|	...	...	...	...	...	2325	|	...	...	...	...	|	...	0027	...	|	...
Bremen Hbf a.	...	...	...	...	...	2218e	...	...	|	...	...	...	...	...	...	2320	...	...	...	...	|	...	...	...	|	...
Hamburg Hbf a.	...	...	...	...	...	2314e	...	...	2138	...	...	...	...	...	...	0021	...	...	...	...	2345j	...	...	...	|	...
København H. a.	...	...	...	...	...	...	...	...	...	...	...	...	...	...	...	...	...	...	...	...	...	...	...	...	0959	...

CONTINUED ON NEXT PAGE

ROMA, MILANO and ZÜRICH - KÖLN, DORTMUND, BERLIN and AMSTERDAM 73

train type	IC	ES	ESc	EC	AV	EC	IC	AV	EC	IC		AV	ES	EC	IR	IR	CNL	CNL	IC	AV	CIS	IC	AV	CNL	CNL
train number	582	9430	9704	110	9432	174	988	9434	114	588		9436	9402	176	2192	792	408	40408	622	9440	48	694	9444	1300	300
notes	♀	[R]✕ ⁄	[R]✕ ⁄	♀ ⊡	[R]✕ ⁄	✕ ⊡	♀	[R]✕ ⁄	♀ ⊡	♀		[R]✕ ⁄	[R]✕ ⁄	✕	¶		✕ K	✕ A	♀⁄	[R]✕ ⁄	✕		[R]✕ ⁄	Q ⑦	Q ①–⑥
Roma Termini d.	...	0830	...	...	0930	...	...	1030	...	...	...	1130	...	...	...	...	...	...	...	1330	...	...	1530	...	...
Firenze SMN d.	...	1014	...	...	1114	...	...	1214	...	...	...	1314	...	...	...	...	...	...	...	1514	...	...	1714	...	...
Bologna Centrale d.	...	1116	...	...	1216	...	...	1316	...	...	...	1416	...	...	...	...	...	...	...	1616	...	...	1816	...	...
Venezia Santa Lucia d.	...	|	1030	...	|	1051	...	|	1151	...	...	|	1345	...	...	...	...	...	1451	|	...	...	|	*1730*	*1751*
Milano Centrale d.	...	1300	1305	1325	1400	1425	...	1500	1525	...	...	1600	1605	1625	...	...	...	...	1755	1800	1825	...	2000	2055	2112
Como San Giovanni d.	...	...	▬	1407	▬	1507	...	▬	1607	...	...	▬	▬	1707	...	...	...	...	...	...	|	...	▬	|	2156
Chiasso 🏛 d.	...	...	...	1431	...	1531	...	...	1631	...	...	...	...	1731	...	...	...	...	...	...	|	1831	...	|	2221
Lugano d.	...	...	...	1455	...	1555	...	...	1655	...	...	...	...	1755	...	...	...	...	...	...	|	1855	...	|	2244
Bellinzona d.	...	...	...	1523	*IR*	1623	...	...	1723	...	...	...	...	1823	1800	...	...	...	...	...	|	1923	...	|	2313
Arth-Goldau d.	...	...	...	1712	**788**	1812	...	...	1912	...	...	...	...	2008	2012	...	...	...	...	...	|	2112	...	|	|
Luzern d.	...	...	...	1745		|	...	...	1945	...	...	...	...	▬	2045	...	...	...	...	...	|	2145	...	|	|
St Moritz d.	*1402*	...	...	|	*1502*	|	...	...	|	*1602*	...	*CNL*	...	...	|	*1702*	...	...	...	...	|	|	...	|	|
Chur d.	1609	...	...	|	1716	|	...	*ICE*	|	1809	...	**1243**	...	...	|	1916	...	...	...	...	|	|	...	|	|
Davos Platz d.	*1502*	...	...	|	*1602*	|	...	**270**	|	*1702*	...	✕	...	...	|	*1802*	...	...	...	...	|	|	...	|	|
Landquart d.	1619	...	*IC*	|	1726	|	...	♀	|	1819	...	C	...	...	|	1926	...	...	...	...	|	|	...	|	|
Zürich HB d.	1734	...	**986**	|	1847	1851	...	1902	|	1934	*IC*	1944	*IC*	...	|	2102	2042	2042	...	...	|	|	...	|	|
Domodossola 🏛 § d.	|	...	♀	|	...	...	...	|	|	|	**990**	|	**992**	...	|	|	|	|	...	...	1948	|	*ICE*	|	|
Brig d.	|	...	*1649*f	|	...	...	*1749*f	|	|	|	*1849*f	|	*1949*f	...	|	|	1652r	1652r	...	...	2020	|	**994**	2340	|
Interlaken Ost d.	|	...	1701	|	...	...	1801	|	|	|	1901	|	2001	...	|	|	|	|	...	...	|	|	2101	|	|
Spiez d.	|	...	1723	|	...	...	1823	|	|	|	1923	|	2023	...	|	|	1813r	1813r	...	...	2054	|	2123	|	|
Bern d.	|	...	1804	|	...	...	1904	|	|	|	2004	|	2104	...	|	|	|	|	...	...	2134	|	2204	|	|
Basel SBB ★ a.	1838	...	1854	1851	...	...	1954	1956	2051	2038	2054	|	2154	...	2151	2156	|	|	...	...	2229	2251	2304	|	|
				ICE				|				|	▬				|	|					*ICE*	|	|
				500				|				|	*IC*				|	|					**808**	|	|
				⊖ p				|				|	**60459**				|	|					♀	|	|
Basel SBB d.	...	...	...	1912	...	...	...	2012	...	...	...	2107u	2107	*ICE*	...	...	2207u	2207u	...	...	...	...	2326	|	|
Basel Bad Bf 🏛 d.	...	...	...	1921	...	...	...	2022	...	...	...	2121u	2121	**990**	...	...	2219u	2219u	...	...	...	...	2334	◐	◐
Freiburg (Brsg) Hbf d.	...	...	...	1956	...	...	...	2057	...	...	...	2158u	2158	♀	...	...	2257u	2257u	...	...	...	...	0014	|	|
Karlsruhe Hbf d.	...	...	...	2101	...	...	...	2200	...	...	...	2305u	2305	d	...	...	0010u	0010u	...	...	...	...	0133	0426s	0426s
Mannheim Hbf a.	...	...	...	2124	...	...	...	2222	...	...	...	0005u	2346	2351	...	...	|	|	...	...	...	...	0222	0515s	0515s
Frankfurt (Main) Hbf a.	...	...	...	|	...	...	...	2315	...	...	...	0055b	...	0042	...	...	|	|	...	...	...	...	0308	0600s	0600s
Frankfurt Flughafen ✈ a.	...	...	...	2206	...	...	...	...	...	...	...	|	...	0023	...	...	|	|	...	...	...	...	0330	|	|
Mainz Hbf a.	...	...	...	|	...	...	...	...	...	...	...	|	...	...	...	...	|	|	...	...	...	...	0406	0632s	0645s
Koblenz Hbf a.	...	...	...	|	...	...	...	...	...	...	...	|	...	...	...	...	|	|	...	...	...	...	0501	0744s	0744s
Bonn Hbf a.	...	...	...	|	...	...	...	...	...	...	...	|	...	...	...	...	|	0521s	...	...	...	...	0534	0817s	0817s
Köln Hbf a.	...	...	...	2312	...	...	...	...	...	...	...	|	...	...	...	...	|	0545s	...	...	...	...	0605	0842s	0842s
Düsseldorf Hbf a.	...	...	...	2338	...	...	...	...	...	...	...	|	...	...	...	...	|	0613s	...	...	...	...	0631	0909s	0909s
Duisburg Hbf a.	...	...	...	2351	...	...	...	...	...	...	...	|	...	...	...	...	|	0628s	...	...	...	...	0644	|	|
Arnhem ⊙ a.	...	...	...	|	...	...	...	...	...	...	...	|	...	...	...	...	|	0752s	...	...	...	...	|	1122	1122
Utrecht Centraal a.	...	...	...	|	...	...	...	...	...	...	...	|	...	...	...	...	|	0826s	...	...	...	...	|	1156	1156
Amsterdam Centraal a.	...	...	...	|	...	...	...	...	...	...	...	|	...	...	...	...	|	0856x	...	...	...	...	|	1227	1227
Essen Hbf a.	...	...	...	0003	...	...	...	...	...	...	...	|	...	...	...	...	|	...	...	...	...	...	0658	...	...
Dortmund Hbf a.	...	...	...	0026	...	...	...	...	...	...	...	|	...	...	...	...	0515s	...	...	...	...	...	0721	...	...
Hannover Hbf a.	...	...	...	...	...	...	...	...	...	...	...	0537	...	...	...	...	|	...	...	...	...	...	|	...	...
Berlin Hauptbahnhof a.	...	...	...	...	...	...	...	...	...	...	...	0810	...	...	...	...	|	...	...	...	...	...	|	...	...
Bremen Hbf a.	...	...	...	...	...	...	...	...	...	...	...	...	...	...	...	...	0722	...	...	...	...	...	0914	...	...
Hamburg Hbf a.	...	...	...	...	...	...	...	...	...	...	...	...	...	...	...	...	0832	...	...	...	...	...	1012	...	...
København H. a.	...	...	...	...	...	...	...	...	...	...	...	...	...	...	...	...	...	...	...	...	...	...	...	...	...

A – *City Night Line* PEGASUS – 🛏 1,2 cl., 🛏 1,2 cl. (T4), 🛏 2 cl. (4,6 berth), [2] (reclining) and ✕ (⑥ Dec. 22 - Mar. 29 Brig - Spiez -) Zürich - Basel - Amsterdam. [R] Special fares apply.
B – [12] and ♀ Basel - Köln - Amsterdam. Not Köln - Amsterdam on Dec. 24, 31.
C – *City Night Line* BERLINER – 🛏 1,2 cl., 🛏 1,2 cl. (T4), 🛏 2 cl. (4,6 berth), [2] (reclining) and ✕ Zürich - Basel - Hannover - Berlin. [R] Special fares apply. Conveys *City Night Line* **459** SEMPER Zürich - Dresden, see Table **75**.
G – [12] and ✕ Chur - Basel - Köln - Dortmund - Hamburg.
J – *City Night Line* AURORA – 🛏 1,2 cl., 🛏 2 cl. (4,6 berth), [2] and ✕ Basel - København. [R] Special fares apply.
K – *City Night Line* KOMET – 🛏 1,2 cl., 🛏 1,2 cl. (T4), 🛏 2 cl. (4,6 berth), [2] (reclining) and ✕ (Brig - Spiez ⑥ Dec. 22 - Mar. 29 -) Zürich - Basel - Dortmund - Hamburg. [R] Special fares apply.
N – ROMA – 🛏 1,2 cl. and 🛏 2 cl. (6 berth) Roma - Bern - Zürich.
Q – *City Night Line* 🛏 1,2 cl., 🛏 2 cl. (4,6 berth), [2] and ✕ Milano - Frankfurt - Amsterdam. [R] Special fares apply.
T – Mar. 14 - Oct. 26.
a – Arrival time.
b – Frankfurt (Main) **Süd**. Stops to pick up only.
d – Train calls Mannheim - Frankfurt Flughafen ✈ - Frankfurt (Main) Hbf.
e – ⑧ (not Dec. 24, 25, 31, Mar. 21, 23, May 11).

f – Change trains at Bern.
h – Via Wuppertal, Hagen.
j – ⑤⑦ (also Jan. 1, Mar. 20, 24, Apr. 30, May 12, 21; not Dec. 23, 28, 30, Mar. 21, 23, May 2, 11, 23).
k – Depart 0557 on ⑦ (also Dec. 25, Jan. 1).
p – Not Dec. 24, 31.
q – Firenze **Campo di Marte**.
r – ⑥ Dec. 22 - Mar. 29. Note train calls in following order: Brig - Spiez - Zürich - Basel.
s – Stops to set down only.
t – Venezia **Mestre**.
u – Stops to pick up only.
x – Not Apr. 30.
y – Connects with train in previous column.
z – Not Dec. 24, 25, 31, Mar. 23, May 11.
CIS – **ETR 470** *Cisalpino*. Supplement payable for international journeys. *IC* supplement payable for internal journeys within Italy.
★ – Connections at Basel are not guaranteed.

⊖ – *ICE 3* train ♀, via high speed line, premium fares payable.
⊡ – Supplement payable in Italy.
¶ – From Locarno.
§ – Ticket point is **Iselle**.
◐ – Ticket point / frontier.
⁄ – Supplement payable.
⊙ – 🏛 is at Emmerich.

OTHER TRAIN NAMES:

EC **106** – CISALPINO TIZIANO
EC **108** – CISALPINO VERDI
EC **110** – CISALPINO TICINO
EC **114** – CISALPINO SAN MARCO
EC **120** – CISALPINO VALLESE
EC **122** – CISALPINO MONTE ROSA
EC **170** – CISALPINO MONTE CENERI
EC **172** – CISALPINO INSUBRIA
EC **174** – CISALPINO CANALETTO
EC **176** – CISALPINO CINQUE TERRE

For Table 74 see page 83

BERLIN - MÜNCHEN - ZÜRICH - BERN - GENÈVE 75

train type	CNL	CNL	CNL	EC	ICE	EC	ICE	EC	IC	ICE	EC
train number	1242	458	1201	196	1605	194	1001	192	2542	1003	190
notes	✕ A	✕ B	✕ D	✕ C	✕⊖ P	✕ C	✕ ⊖	✕ C		✕ ⊖	✕ C
Berlin Hbf d.	2126	...	2214	...	0549	...	0953	...	...	1153	...
Dresden Hbf d.	|	2054	|	...	|	...	|	...	...	|	...
Leipzig Hbf d.	|	2216	|	...	0711	...	1111	...	...	1311	...
Nürnberg Hbf d.	|	|	|	...	1023	...	1429	...	...	1629	...
München Hbf d.	|	|	0642	0712	1137	1234	1612	1632	...	1812	1834
Lindau 🏛 d.	|	|	...	0955	...	1456	...	1855	...	...	2056
Bregenz 🏛 d.	|	|	...	1006	...	1507	...	1906	...	...	2107
St Margrethen 🏛 a.	|	|	...	1018	...	1519	...	1918	...	...	2119
St Gallen a.	|	|	...	1041	...	1541	...	1941	...	...	2141
Winterthur a.	|	|	...	1117	...	1617	...	2017	...	...	2217
Basel SBB (🏛 = Bad) a.	0755	0755	...	|	...	|	...	|	...	...	|
Zürich Flughafen ✈ a.	|	|	...	1132	...	1632	...	2032	...	...	2232
Zürich HB a.	0918	0918	...	1144	...	1644	...	2044	...	...	2244
		IC		*IC*		*IC*					
		716		**722**		**732**		*IC*			*IC*
		✕		✕		♀		**942**			**846**
Zürich HB d.	...	0932	...	1232	...	1732	...	2100	...	...	2300
Bern a.	...	1029	...	1329	...	1829	...	2157	2204	...	0002
Lausanne a.	...	1140	...	1440	...	1940	...	...	2315	...	...
Genève a.	...	1215	...	1515	...	2015	...	...	0004	...	...
Genève Aéroport ✈ a.	...	1224	...	1524	...	2024	...	...	...	...	...

train type	IC	IC	IC	ICE	IC	IC	IC	IC	IC	CNL	CNL
train number	809	2515	815	1604 / 1704	2523	823	731	835	737	1243	459
notes	✕		✕	✕⊖		✕	♀	♀	✕	✕ A	✕ B
Genève Aéroport ✈ d.	...	...	...	...	1001	...	1436	...	1636	...	...
Genève d.	...	0556	...	...	1010	...	1445	...	1645	...	...
Lausanne d.	...	0645	...	...	1045	...	1520	...	1720	...	...
Bern d.	0602	0756	0802	...	1156	1202	1632	1702	1830	...	...
Zürich HB a.	0702	▬	0858	...	...	1258	1728	1758	1928	...	...
	EC		*EC*			*EC*	▬	*EC*	▬		
	191		**193**			**195**		**197**			
	✕ C		✕ C			✕ C		✕ C			
Zürich HB d.	0716	...	0916	...	...	1316	...	1816	...	1944	1944
Zürich Flughafen ✈ d.	0728	...	0928	...	...	1328	...	1828	...	|	|
Basel SBB (🏛 = Bad) d.	|	...	|	...	...	|	...	|	...	2107	2107
Winterthur d.	0742	*ICE*	0942	...	...	1342	...	1842	...	|	|
St Gallen d.	0819	**1506**	1019	...	...	1419	*ICE*	1919	*CNL*	|	|
St Margrethen 🏛 d.	0842	**1706**	1042	...	...	1442	**1500**	1942	**1200**	|	|
Bregenz 🏛 d.	0855	✕	1055	...	...	1455	✕	1955	✕	|	|
Lindau 🏛 a.	0905	⊖	1105	...	...	1505	⊖ f	2005	D	|	|
München Hbf a.	1128	1322	1328	1340	...	1728	1922	2245	2301	|	|
Nürnberg Hbf a.	...	1432	...	1523	...	...	2032	...	|	|	|
Leipzig Hbf a.	...	1742	...	1846	...	...	2348	...	|	|	0642
Dresden Hbf a.	...	|	...	|	...	...	...	...	|	|	0807
Berlin Hbf a.	...	1900	...	2005	...	...	...	...	0748	0811	...

A – *City Night Line* BERLINER – 🛏 1,2 cl., 🛏 1,2 cl. (T4), 🛏 2 cl. (4,6 berth), [2] (reclining) and ✕ Berlin - Hannover - Frankfurt - Basel - Zürich and v.v. [R] Special fares apply.
B – *City Night Line* SEMPER – 🛏 1,2 cl., 🛏 1,2 cl. (T4), 🛏 2 cl. (4,6 berth), [2] (reclining) and ✕ Dresden - Leipzig - Frankfurt - Basel - Zürich and v.v. [R] Special fares apply.
C – [12] and ✕ München - Zürich and v.v.
D – *City Night Line* PLUTO – 🛏 1,2 cl., 🛏 2 cl., [2] (reclining) and ✕ Berlin - München and v.v. [R] Special fares apply. Talgo stock
P – ①–⑥ (not Dec. 25, 26, Jan. 1, Mar. 22, 24, May 12).
f – Not Dec. 24, 31.
⊖ – *ICE 3*, premium fares.

82 GENÈVE, BASEL, STUTTGART, ZÜRICH and LUZERN - MILANO - VENEZIA and ROMA

train type	*CIS*	*IR*	*CIS*	*IC*	*EC*⚡	*ICp*	*EC*	*CIS*	*AV*	*EC*	*EC*	*CIS*	*ES*	*ES*	*IR*	*EC*	*EC*	*AV*	*EC*	*IR*	*EC*	*ES*	*ES*	*EC*⚡
train number	**41**	**2159**	**151**	**613**	**143**	**591**	**121**	**153**	**9437**	**171**	**109**	**43**	**9439**	**9417**	**2165**	**123**	**173**	**9441**	**173**	**2267**	**111**	**9443**	**9419**	**159**
notes	[R]✕ ⊕		[R]✕ ⊕	🍷⚡	**144** [R]🍷	🍷 ⚡	🍷 §	[R]✕ ⊕	[R]✕ ⚡	🍷 §	🍷 §	[R]✕ ⊕	[R]✕ ⚡y	[R]✕ ⚡		🍷 §	✕ §	[R]✕ ⚡	✕ §		🍷 §	[R]✕ ⚡	[R]✕ ⚡	**160** [R]🍷
Genève Aéroport ✈ d.	...	...	...	...	...	...	0658	...	...	...	...	...	...	...	...	...	...	...	...	...	...	...	...	...
Genève d.	...	...	...	...	...	...	0707	...	...	...	...	...	...	...	...	0907	...	...	...	...	...	...	...	...
Lausanne d.	...	...	...	...	...	...	0746	...	...	...	...	...	...	...	...	0946	...	...	...	...	...	...	...	...
Sion d.	...	...	...	...	...	...	0843	...	...	...	...	...	...	...	...	1043	...	...	...	...	...	...	...	...
Stuttgart Hbf d.	...	...	...	...	...	...	|	...	...	...	...	...	...	...	...	|	...	...	...	...	...	...	...	...
Singen d.	...	...	...	...	...	...	|	...	...	...	...	...	...	...	...	|	...	...	...	...	...	...	...	...
Schaffhausen 🏛 d.	...	...	...	...	...	...	|	...	...	...	...	...	...	...	...	|	0809	...	...	...	...	...	...	...
Zürich HB a.	...	...	...	...	...	...	|	...	...	...	...	...	...	...	...	|	0847	...	...	...	...	...	...	...
Zürich HB d.	...	...	0709	...	...	...	|	0742	...	0715	...	...	...	...	...	|	0909	...	...	1009	...	...	...	...
Basel SBB d.	0630	0604	|	...	...	...	|	|	...	|	0704	0830	...	...	0804	|	|	...	...	|	0904	...	...	...
Olten d.	0700	|	|	...	...	...	|	|	...	|	0733	0900	...	...	|	|	|	...	...	|	0933	...	...	...
Bern d.	0735	|	|	...	...	...	|	|	...	|	|	0935	...	...	|	|	|	...	...	|	|	...	...	...
Spiez d.	0805	|	|	...	...	...	|	|	...	|	|	1005	...	...	|	|	|	...	...	|	|	...	...	...
Luzern d.	|	0721	|	...	...	...	|	|	...	|	0821	|	...	...	0921	|	|	...	...	|	1021	...	...	...
Arth-Goldau d.	|	0746	0750	...	...	...	|	0834	...	0809	0852	|	...	...	0946	|	0952	...	...	1048	1052	...	...	...
Bellinzona d.	|	...	0925	...	...	...	|	1013	...	0954	1038	|	...	...	▬	|	1138	...	...	▬	1238	...	...	...
Lugano d.	|	...	0948	...	...	...	|	1037	...	1021	1105	|	...	...	...	|	1205	...	...	...	1305	...	...	...
Chiasso 🏛 d.	|	...	|	...	...	...	|	|	...	1105	1142	|	...	...	...	|	1248	...	...	...	1348	...	...	...
Como San Giovanni a.	|	...	1012	...	...	...	|	1103	...	1110	1147	|	...	...	...	|	1252	...	...	...	1352	...	...	...
Brig d.	0844	...	|	...	...	...	0920	|	...	|	|	1044	...	...	...	1120	|	...	...	...	|	...	...	...
Domodossola 🏛 ¶ a.	0912	...	|	...	...	...	0950	|	...	|	|	1112	...	...	...	1150	|	...	...	...	|	...	...	...
Stresa a.	|	...	|	...	...	...	1030	|	...	|	|	1138	...	...	...	1230	|	...	...	...	|	...	...	...
Arona a.	|	...	|	...	...	...	1044	|	...	|	|	|	...	...	...	1244	|	...	←	...	|	...	...	...
Milano Centrale a.	1035	...	1047	...	...	...	1135	1138	...	1150	1235	1245	...	...	...	1335	1335	...	1335	...	1435	...	...	...
	ES **9435** ✕⚡ [R]y		*ES* **9415** ✕⚡ [R]				|	|		▬ *ICp* **557** [R]⚡	*ES* **9707** [R]✕ ⚡				*ICp* **609** [R] 🍷⚡	*ES* **9403** [R]✕ ⚡	|		|	*ICp* **655** [R] 🍷⚡	|			
Milano Centrale d.	1100	...	1105	1105	1110	1110	1155	1150	1200	1200	1255	...	1300	1305	1310	1355	1405	1400	1405	1410	1505	1500	1505	1510
Genova PP ▲ a.	|	...	|	|	1242	|	|	*1342*	|	|	|	...	|	|	1442	|	→	|	|	1542	|	|	|	1642
Ventimiglia 🏛 a.	|	...	|	|	1507	|	|	|	|	|	|	...	|	|	1707	|	...	|	|	...	|	|	|	1907
Nice Ville a.	|	...	|	|	1601	|	|	|	|	|	|	...	|	|	*1848*	|	...	|	|	...	|	|	|	1958
Verona Porta Nuova a.	|	...	|	1240	...	|	1314	|	|	|	1414	...	|	|	...	|	...	|	1540	...	1640	|	|	...
Venezia Santa Lucia a.	|	...	|	1409	...	|	1430	|	|	|	1530	...	|	|	...	1615	...	|	1709	...	1809	|	|	...
Bologna Centrale a.	1242	...	1252	...	...	1311	...	1336	1342	1416	...	...	1442	1452	...	...	...	1542	...	...	...	1642	1652	...
Rimini a.	|	...	1351	...	...	|	...	|	|	1538	...	...	|	1551	...	...	...	|	...	...	...	|	1751	...
Ancona a.	|	...	1441	...	...	|	...	|	|	1700	...	...	|	1641	...	...	...	|	...	...	...	|	1842	...
Pescara Centrale a.	|	...	1605	...	...	|	...	|	|	...	...	...	|	1805	...	...	...	|	...	...	...	|	1957	...
Bari Centrale a.	|	...	1853	...	...	|	...	|	|	...	...	...	|	2055	...	...	...	|	...	...	...	|	2304	...
Brindisi a.	|	...	2002	...	...	|	...	|	|	...	...	...	|	...	...	...	...	|	...	...	...	|	...	...
Lecce a.	|	...	2030	...	...	|	...	|	|	...	...	...	|	...	...	...	...	|	...	...	...	|	...	...
Firenze SMN a.	1344	...	...	...	...	1424r	...	1432	1444	...	...	...	1544	...	...	...	...	1644	...	...	...	1744	...	...
Roma Termini a.	1530	...	...	...	...	1703	...	...	1630	...	...	...	1730	...	...	...	...	1830	...	...	...	1930	...	...
Napoli Centrale a.	...	...	...	...	...	1936	...	...	1812	...	...	...	...	...	...	...	...	...	...	...	...	...	...	...

train type	*IC*	*EC*	*IR*	*ICE*	*EC*	*AV*	*IR*	*EC*	*IR*	*CIS*	*ICE*	*CIS*	*AV*	*ICp*	*IR*	*EC*	*IR*	*ICE*	*EC*	*IC*	*EC*	*IC*	*ICp*	*E*
train number	**1069**	**125**	**2169**	**181**	**175**	**9445**	**2271**	**115**	**1427**	**47**	**183**	**155**	**9447**	**659**	**2275**	**117**	**2177**	**185**	**177**	**1077**	**127**	**639**	**665**	**923**
notes	🍷	🍷 §		[R]🍷 F⊖	✕§ Q	[R]✕ ⚡		🍷 §		[R]✕ ⊕	[R]🍷 ⊖	[R] C⊕	[R]✕ ⚡	[R] 🍷⚡		🍷 §		[R]✕ ⊖	🍷§		🍷 §	🍷⚡ ⑧m	[R] ⚡	Tz
Genève Aéroport ✈ d.	...	...	...	...	...	...	...	...	1147	...	...	...	...	...	...	...	...	...	...	...	1501	...	...	...
Genève d.	...	1107	...	...	...	...	...	...	1156	...	...	...	...	...	...	...	...	...	...	...	1510	...	...	...
Lausanne d.	...	1146	...	...	...	...	...	...	1245	...	...	...	...	...	...	...	...	...	...	...	1546	...	...	...
Sion d.	...	1243	...	...	...	...	...	...	1355	...	...	...	...	...	...	...	...	...	...	...	1643	...	...	...
Stuttgart Hbf d.	...	|	...	0804	...	...	...	...	|	...	1004	...	...	...	...	...	...	1204	...	...	|	...	...	...
Singen d.	...	|	...	0954	...	...	...	...	|	...	1154	...	...	...	...	...	...	1354	...	...	|	...	...	...
Schaffhausen 🏛 d.	...	|	...	1009	1016	...	...	...	|	...	1209	...	...	...	...	...	...	1409	...	...	|	...	...	...
Zürich HB a.	...	|	...	1048	1055	...	...	...	|	...	1248	...	...	...	...	...	...	1448	...	...	|	...	...	...
Zürich HB d.	...	|	...	...	1109	...	1209	...	|	...	...	1309	...	...	1409	...	...	▬	1509	...	|	...	...	...
Basel SBB d.	1030	|	1004	...	|	...	|	1104	|	1230	...	|	...	...	|	1304	1404	...	|	1430	|	...	...	...
Oltern d.	|	|	|	...	|	...	|	1133	|	1300	...	|	...	...	|	1333	|	...	|	|	|	...	...	...
Bern d.	1135	|	|	...	|	...	|	|	|	1335	...	|	...	...	|	|	|	...	|	1535	|	...	...	...
Spiez d.	1205	|	|	...	|	...	|	|	|	1405	...	|	...	...	|	|	|	...	|	1605	|	...	...	...
Luzern d.	|	|	1121	...	|	...	|	1221	|	|	...	|	...	...	|	1421	1521	...	|	|	|	...	...	...
Arth-Goldau d.	|	|	1146	...	1152	...	1248	1252	|	|	...	1350	...	...	1448	1452	1546	...	1552	|	|	...	...	...
Bellinzona d.	|	|	...	...	1338	...	▬	1438	|	|	...	1525	...	...	▬	1638	▬	...	1738	|	|	...	...	...
Lugano d.	|	|	...	...	1405	...	...	1505	|	|	...	1548	...	...	...	1705	...	...	1805	|	|	...	...	...
Chiasso 🏛 d.	|	|	...	...	1448	...	...	1548	|	|	...	|	...	...	...	1748	...	...	1848	|	|	...	...	...
Como San Giovanni a.	|	|	...	...	1452	...	...	1552	|	|	...	|	...	...	...	1752	...	...	1852	|	|	...	...	...
Brig d.	1240	1320	...	...	|	...	...	|	1431	1444	...	|	...	...	...	|	...	...	|	1640	1720	...	...	...
Domodossola 🏛 ¶ a.	...	1350	...	...	|	...	...	|	...	1512	...	|	...	...	...	|	...	...	|	...	1750	...	...	...
Stresa a.	...	1430	...	...	|	...	...	|	...	|	...	|	...	...	...	|	...	...	|	...	1830	...	...	...
Arona a.	...	1444	...	...	|	...	...	|	...	|	...	|	...	...	...	|	...	...	|	...	1844	...	...	...
Milano Centrale a.	...	1535	...	...	1535	...	...	1635	...	1640	...	1642	...	...	...	1835	...	...	1935	...	1935	...	...	...
					|		*IC* **625** 🍷 ⚡	▬ *ICp* **561** [R]⚡				|			*ICp* **563** [R] 🍷⚡	*ES* **9451** [R]✕ ⚡	*ICp* **663** [R] 🍷⚡	*IC* **635** 🍷 ⚡	▬ *ICp* **565** 🍷⚡		*ES* **9453** [R]✕ ⚡			
Milano Centrale d.	...	...	...	...	1600	1600	1605	1605	...	...	...	1655	1700	1700	1710	1900	1905	1905	1910	...	2000	2005	2010	2040
Genova PP ▲ a.	...	...	...	...	1742	|	|	|	...	...	...	|	|	1842	|	|	2042	|	|	...	|	|	2146	|
Ventimiglia 🏛 a.	...	...	...	...	...	|	|	|	...	...	...	|	|	2107	|	|	*2315*	|	|	...	|	|	*0104*	|
Nice Ville a.	...	...	...	...	...	|	|	|	...	...	...	|	|	*0021*	|	|	*0021*g	|	|	...	|	|	...	|
Verona Porta Nuova a.	...	...	...	...	...	|	1740	|	...	...	...	1814	|	...	|	|	...	2040	|	...	|	2140	...	|
Venezia Santa Lucia a.	...	...	...	...	...	|	1909	|	...	...	...	1918q	|	...	|	|	...	2209	|	...	|	2309	...	|
Bologna Centrale a.	...	...	...	...	...	1742	...	1816	...	...	...	...	1842	...	1916	2042	...	...	2120	...	2142	...	...	2310
Rimini a.	...	...	...	...	...	|	...	1938	...	...	...	...	|	...	2038	|	...	...	2238	...	|	...	...	0027
Ancona a.	...	...	...	...	...	|	...	2047	...	...	...	...	|	...	2141	|	...	...	2346	...	|	...	...	0135
Pescara Centrale a.	...	...	...	...	...	|	...	2225	...	...	...	...	|	...	2315	|	...	...	...	...	|	...	...	0257
Bari Centrale a.	...	...	...	...	...	|	...	...	...	...	...	...	|	...	...	|	...	...	...	...	|	...	...	0623
Brindisi a.	...	...	...	...	...	|	...	...	...	...	...	...	|	...	...	|	...	...	...	...	|	...	...	0743
Lecce a.	...	...	...	...	...	|	...	...	...	...	...	...	|	...	...	|	...	...	...	...	|	...	...	0814
Firenze SMN a.	...	...	...	...	...	1844	...	...	...	...	...	...	1944	...	...	2144	...	...	...	...	2244	...	...	...
Roma Termini a.	...	...	...	...	...	2030	...	...	...	...	...	...	2130	...	...	2330	...	...	...	...	...	...	...	...
Napoli Centrale a.	...	...	...	...	...	2212	...	...	...	...	...	...	2312	...	...	...	...	...	...	...	...	...	...	...

NOTES FOR PAGES 88 and 89

C – [12] and ✕ Zürich - Milano - Venezia Mestre - Trieste (arrive 2130).
D – LUNA – 🛏 1, 2 cl. and couchette 2 cl. (4, 6 berth) Genève Aéroport - Genève - Roma.
E – FRECCIA SALENTINA – 🛏 1, 2 cl., 🛏 1, 2 cl. (T2), couchette 2 cl. (4, 6 berth) and [12] Milano - Lecce and v.v.
F – [12] and 🍷 (Frankfurt, ①–⑥ not Dec. 24, 25, 31, Jan. 1, Mar. 24, May 12: depart 0618 -) Stuttgart - Zürich.
J – FRECCIA DEL LEVANTE – 🛏 1, 2 cl., 🛏 1, 2 cl. (T2), couchette 2 cl., [12] and 🍷 Milano - Bari and v.v.
K – ⑧: 🛏 1, 2 cl., 🛏 1, 2 cl. (Excelsior), 🛏 1, 2 cl. (T2) and couchette 2 cl. (4, 6 berth) Milano - Napoli and v.v.
Q – CISALPINO CINQUE TERRE – [12] and ✕ Schaffhausen - Zürich - Milano - Genova - Pisa (arrive 2012) - Livorno (2030).
S – LUNA – 🛏 1, 2 cl. and couchette 2 cl. (4, 6 berth) Zürich - Roma.
T – 🛏 1, 2 cl. (T2), couchette 2 cl. (4, 6 berth) and [2] Milano - Lecce and v.v.
U – [12] and 🍷 Trieste (depart 0630) - Venezia Mestre - Milano - Zürich - Schaffhausen.

b – Firenze **Campo di Marte**.
f – Not Dec. 25, Jan. 1, Mar. 24.
g – Change at Genova and Ventimiglia.
h – Venezia **Mestre**. Connection departs 0006 to arrive Venezia **Santa Lucia** 0016.
j – ①–⑤. Change at Ventimiglia and Genova.

NOTES CONTINUED ON PAGE 89 →
FOR OTHER TRAIN NAMES, SEE PAGE 91

GENÈVE, BASEL, STUTTGART, ZÜRICH and LUZERN - MILANO - VENEZIA and ROMA 82

train type	*IR*	*EC*	*ICp*	*ICE*	*IR*	*CIS*	*IR*	*EC*		*EC*	*ICN*	*IR*	*ICE*	*CIS*	*E*	*ICE*		*IC*	*EN*	*EN311*	*AV*	*ICE*		
train number	**2279**	**119**	**667**	**187**	**1439**	**51**	**2181**	**179**	**2199**	**129**	**785**	**2187**	**281**	**157**	**1911**	**283**		**1093**	**313**	**313**	**9425**	**285**		
notes		🍷	[R]	[R]🍷		[R]✕		🍷		🍷	[R]⚡		[R]🍷	[R]✕	**K**	[R]🍷			[R]⚡	[R]⚡	[R]✕	[R]🍷		
		[R] §	🍷⚡	⊖		⊕		[R] §		[R] §	**J z**		⊖	⊕		⊖			**S**	**D**	⚡	⊖		
Genève Aéroport ✈ d.	...	...	...	...	1647	...	...	...	...	1758	...	...	...	...	...	...	...	...	...	...	...	...	...	...
Genève d.	...	...	...	...	1656	...	...	...	...	1807	...	...	...	...	...	...	...	...	...	2136	...	...	...	...
Lausanne d.	...	...	...	...	1745	...	...	...	...	1846	...	...	...	...	...	...	...	...	...	2220	...	...	...	...
Sion d.	...	...	...	...	1855	...	...	...	...	1943	...	...	...	...	...	...	...	...	...	2329	...	...	...	...
Stuttgart Hbf d.	...	...	...	1404	|	...	...	...	...	|	...	...	1604	...	...	1804	...	...	...	|	...	2004	...	...
Singen d.	...	...	...	1554	|	...	...	...	...	|	...	...	1754	...	...	1954	...	...	...	|	...	2156	...	...
Schaffhausen 🏛 d.	...	...	...	1609	|	...	...	...	...	|	...	...	1809	1816	...	2009	...	...	...	|	...	2211	...	...
Zürich HB a.	...	...	...	1648	|	...	...	...	...	|	...	...	1848	1855	...	2048	...	...	...	|	...	2248	...	...
Zürich HB d.	1609	...	...	▬	|	...	...	1709	...	|	...	...	...	1909	...	...	...	...	2127	|	...	...	...	...
Basel SBB d.	|	1504	...	...	|	1730	1604	|	...	|	...	1804	...	|	...	...	...	2130	|	|	...	...	...	...
Olten d.	|	1533	...	...	|	1800	|	|	...	|	...	|	...	|	...	...	...	2158	2209	|	...	...	...	...
Bern d.	|	|	...	...	|	1835	|	|	...	|	...	|	...	|	...	...	...	2227	2304	|	...	...	...	...
Spiez d.	|	|	...	...	|	1905	|	|	...	|	...	|	...	|	...	...	...	...	2334	|	...	...	...	...
Luzern d.	|	1621	...	...	|	|	1721	|	...	|	...	1921	...	|	...	...	...	...	|	|	...	...	...	...
Arth-Goldau d.	1648	1652	...	...	|	|	1746	1752	...	|	...	1946	...	1950	...	...	...	...	|	|	...	...	...	...
Bellinzona d.	...	1838	...	...	|	|	...	1938	...	|	...	...	...	2125	...	...	...	...	|	|	...	...	...	...
Lugano d.	...	1905	...	...	|	|	...	2005	...	|	...	...	...	2148	...	...	...	...	|	|	...	...	...	...
Chiasso 🏛 d.	...	1948	...	...	|	|	...	2048	...	|	...	...	...	|	...	...	...	...	|	|	...	...	...	...
Como San Giovanni a.	...	1952	...	...	|	|	...	2052	...	|	...	...	...	2212	...	...	...	...	|	|	...	...	...	...
Brig d.	...	|	...	...	1931	1944	...	|	...	2020	...	...	...	|	...	...	...	...	0058	0058	...	...	...	...
Domodossola 🏛 ¶ a.	...	|	...	...	...	2012	...	|	...	2050	...	...	...	|	...	...	...	...	|	|	...	...	...	...
Stresa a.	...	|	...	...	...	|	...	|	...	2130	...	...	...	|	...	...	...	...	|	|	...	...	...	...
Arona a.	...	|	...	...	...	|	...	|	...	2144	...	...	...	|	...	...	...	...	|	|	...	...	...	...
Milano Centrale a.	...	2035	...	...	...	2135	...	2135	...	2235	...	...	...	2247	...	...	...	...	|	|	...	...	...	...
train type		*IC*		*ICN*															|	|				
train number		**641**		**781**															|	|				
notes				[R]⚡ **E**															|	|				
Milano Centrale d.	...	2105	2110	2120	...	...	...	...	2225	...	2300	...	...	...	2320	...	...	...	|	|	...	...	...	...
Genova PP ▲ a.	...	|	2242	|	...	...	...	...	0020	...	|	...	...	...	|	...	...	...	|	|	...	...	...	...
Ventimiglia 🏛 a.	...	|	0104	|	...	...	...	...	...	...	|	...	...	...	|	...	...	...	|	|	...	...	...	...
Nice Ville a.	...	|	...	|	...	...	...	...	...	...	|	...	...	...	|	...	...	...	|	|	...	...	...	...
Verona Porta Nuova a.	...	2240	...	|	...	...	...	...	...	...	|	...	...	...	|	...	...	...	|	|	...	...	...	...
Venezia Santa Lucia a.	...	2356**h**	...	|	...	...	...	...	...	...	|	...	...	...	|	...	...	...	|	|	...	...	...	...
Bologna Centrale a.	...	...	...	2352	...	...	...	...	...	...	0124	...	...	...	|	...	...	...	0519	0519	...	...	...	...
Rimini a.	...	...	...	0102	...	...	...	...	...	...	0235	...	...	...	|	...	...	...	|	|	...	...	...	...
Ancona a.	...	...	...	0201	...	...	...	...	...	...	0333	...	...	...	|	...	...	...	|	|	...	...	...	...
Pescara Centrale a.	...	...	...	0329	...	...	...	...	...	...	0459	...	...	...	|	...	...	...	|	|	...	...	...	...
Bari Centrale a.	...	...	...	0647	...	...	...	...	...	...	0831	...	...	...	|	...	...	...	|	|	...	...	...	...
Brindisi a.	...	...	...	0822	...	...	...	...	...	...	*1104*	...	...	...	|	...	...	...	|	|	...	...	...	...
Lecce a.	...	...	...	0850	...	...	...	...	...	...	*1205*	...	...	...	|	...	...	...	|	|	...	...	...	...
Firenze SMN a.	...	...	...	...	...	...	...	...	...	...	...	...	...	...	|	...	...	...	0646**b**	0646**b**	...	...	...	...
Roma Termini a.	...	...	...	...	...	...	...	...	...	...	...	...	...	...	0715	...	...	...	0912	0912	1045	...	...	...
Napoli Centrale a.	...	...	...	...	...	...	...	...	...	...	...	...	...	...	1007	...	...	...	...	...	1212	...	...	...

train type	*CIS*	*IR*	*ICE*	*CIS*	*E*	*ICN*			*ICE*	*EC*	*ICN*	*ICp*	*ESc*	*IR*	*E*	*ICp*	*ICp*	*ES*	*CIS*	*ICE*	*CIS*	*IR*	*EC*	*IR*
train number	**156**	**2170**	**280**	**40**	**1910**	**780**	**2178**	**2710**	**186**	**120**	**784**	**651**	**9700**	**2276**	**926**	**656**	**556**	**9426**	**154**	**184**	**44**	**1424**	**108**	**2280**
notes	[R]✕		[R]🍷	[R]✕	**K**	[R]⚡			[R]🍷	🍷	[R]⚡	[R]	[R]✕			[R]	[R]🍷	[R]✕	[R]✕	[R]🍷	[R]✕		🍷	
	⊕		⊖	⊕		**E**			⊖	§	**J z**	🍷⚡	⚡		**T z**	🍷⚡	⚡	⚡	**U** ⊕	⊖	⊕		§	
Napoli Centrale d.	...	...	...	...	2036	...	...	...	...	...	...	...	...	...	...	...	...	...	...	...	...	...	...	...
Roma Termini d.	...	...	...	...	2300	...	...	...	...	...	...	...	...	...	...	...	...	0630	...	...	...	...	...	...
Firenze SMN d.	...	...	...	...	|	...	...	...	...	...	...	...	...	...	...	...	...	0814	...	...	...	...	...	...
Lecce d.	...	...	...	...	|	1857	...	...	...	...	...	...	...	...	2200	...	...	|	...	...	...	...	...	...
Brindisi d.	...	...	...	...	|	1924	...	...	...	...	...	...	...	...	2231	...	...	|	...	...	...	...	...	...
Bari Centrale d.	...	...	...	...	|	2101	...	...	...	...	2259	...	...	...	2357	...	...	|	...	...	...	...	...	...
Pescara Centrale d.	...	...	...	...	|	0028	...	...	...	...	0204	...	...	...	0322	...	...	|	...	...	...	...	...	...
Ancona d.	...	...	...	...	|	0200	...	...	...	...	0330	...	...	...	0446	...	0620	|	...	...	...	...	...	...
Rimini d.	...	...	...	...	|	0256	...	...	...	...	0427	...	...	...	0542	...	0722	|	...	...	...	...	...	...
Bologna Centrale d.	...	...	...	...	|	0412	...	...	...	...	0548	...	...	...	0657	...	0837	0916	...	...	...	...	...	...
Venezia Santa Lucia d.	...	...	...	...	|	|	...	...	...	...	|	...	0630	...	|	...	|	|	0842**q**	...	...	...	...	...
Verona Porta Nuova d.	...	...	...	...	|	|	...	0610	...	...	|	...	0743	...	|	...	|	|	0945	...	...	...	...	...
Nice Ville d.	...	...	...	...	|	|	...	|	...	...	|	...	|	...	|	*0525*j	|	|	|	...	...	...	...	...
Ventimiglia 🏛 d.	...	...	...	...	|	|	...	|	...	...	|	0442	|	...	|	*0633*	|	|	|	...	...	...	...	...
Genova PP ▲ d.	...	...	...	...	|	|	0545	|	...	...	|	0719	|	...	|	0919	|	|	|	...	...	...	...	...
Milano Centrale a.	...	...	...	...	0715 ▬	0705	0740	0755	...	...	0820 ▬	0850 ▬	0905	...	0925	1050	1055	1100	1105	...	...	...	...	...
train type					*IR*			*EC*					*EC*						|					
train number					**1414**			**170**					**106**						|					
notes								🍷 §					🍷 §						|					
Milano Centrale d.	0710	...	...	0725	...	...	...	0825	...	0825	...	...	0925	...	...	...	...	...	1118	...	1120	...	1125	...
Arona d.	|	...	...	|	...	...	...	|	...	0916	*IC*	...	|	...	...	...	...	...	|	...	|	...	|	...
Stresa d.	|	...	...	|	...	...	...	|	...	0929	**1072**	...	|	...	...	...	...	...	|	...	|	...	|	...
Domodossola 🏛 ¶ d.	|	...	...	0848	...	...	...	|	...	1010	🍷	...	|	...	...	...	...	...	|	...	1248	...	|	...
Brig a.	|	...	...	0916	0929	...	...	|	...	1040	1120	...	|	...	...	...	...	...	|	...	1316	1329	|	...
Como San Giovanni d.	0743	...	...	|	|	...	...	0907	...	|	|	...	1007	...	...	...	...	...	|	...	|	|	1207	...
Chiasso 🏛 a.	|	...	...	|	|	...	...	0912	...	|	|	*IR*	1012	...	...	...	...	...	|	...	|	|	1212	...
Lugano a.	0808	...	...	|	|	...	...	0953	...	|	|	**2174**	1053	...	...	...	...	...	1208	...	|	|	1253	...
Bellinzona a.	0833	...	...	|	|	...	...	1021	...	|	|		1121	...	...	...	...	...	1233	...	|	|	1321	...
Arth-Goldau a.	1008	1012	...	|	|	...	...	1208	...	|	|	1212	1308	1312	...	...	...	...	1408	...	|	|	1508	1512
Luzern a.	|	1037	...	|	|	...	...	|	...	|	|	1237	1337	|	...	...	...	...	|	...	|	|	1537	|
Spiez a.	|	|	...	0953	|	...	...	|	...	|	1153	|	|	|	...	...	...	...	|	...	1353	|	|	|
Bern a.	|	|	...	1023	|	...	...	|	...	|	1223	|	|	|	...	...	...	...	|	...	1423	|	|	|
Olten a.	|	|	...	1100	|	...	...	|	...	|	|	|	1424	|	...	...	...	...	|	...	1500	|	1624	|
Basel SBB a.	|	1151	...	1129	|	...	...	|	...	|	1329	1351	1451	|	...	...	...	...	|	...	1529	|	1651	|
Zürich HB a.	1051	...	...	...	|	...	...	1251	...	|	...	...	...	1351	...	...	...	...	1451	...	...	|	...	1551
Zürich HB d.	...	...	1114	...	|	...	...	...	1314	|	...	...	...	...	...	...	...	...	1505	1514	...	|	...	...
Schaffhausen 🏛 a.	...	...	1150	...	|	...	...	...	1350	|	...	...	...	...	...	...	...	...	1547	1550	...	|	...	...
Singen a.	...	...	1205	...	|	...	...	...	1405	|	...	...	...	...	...	...	...	...	...	1605	...	|	...	...
Stuttgart Hbf a.	...	...	1356	...	|	...	...	...	1556	|	...	...	...	...	...	...	...	...	...	1756	...	|	...	...
Sion a.	...	...	...	...	1004	...	...	...	...	1115	...	...	...	...	...	...	...	...	...	...	...	1404	...	...
Lausanne a.	...	...	...	...	1115	...	...	...	...	1214	...	...	...	...	...	...	...	...	...	...	...	1515	...	...
Genève a.	...	...	...	...	1204	...	...	...	...	1250	...	...	...	...	...	...	...	...	...	...	...	1604	...	...
Genève Aéroport ✈ a.	...	...	...	...	1213	...	...	...	...	1259	...	...	...	...	...	...	...	...	...	...	...	1613	...	...

NOTES FOR PAGES 88 and 89 – CONTINUED

m – Not Dec. 24, 25, 31, Mar. 23, Apr. 24, 30, June 1. On ⑥ (also Dec. 24, 25, 31, Mar. 23, Apr. 24, 30, June 1) depart Milano 2015, arrive Verona 2207, Venezia 2340 (train **2113**).

q – Venezia **Mestre**.

r – Firenze **Rifredi**

t – Roma **Tiburtina**.

y – Not Dec. 25, Jan. 1.

z – Not Dec. 24, 25, 31.

⚡ – Supplement payable.

¶ – Ticket point is **Iselle**.

▲ – Genova **Piazza Principe**.

§ – Supplement payable in Italy (except with international tickets). *IC* in Italy.

⊕ – **ETR 470** *Cisalpino*. Supplement payable for international journeys. *IC* supplement payable for internal journeys within Italy.

⊖ – *ICE-T* train with 🍷 and premium fares payable.

FOR OTHER TRAIN NAMES SEE PAGE 91

82 ROMA, VENEZIA - MILANO - LUZERN, ZÜRICH, STUTTGART, BASEL and GENÈVE

train type	ES	IR	EC	ICp	ICp	ES	ESc	ICp	AV	EC	ICE	IR	EC	IC	EC⧸	ES	AV	EC	EC	AV	ES	EC	IR	ICp
train number	9428	2182	122	657/8	558	9430	9704	662	9432	174	180	2188	124	582	139 140	9410	9434	114	176	9436	9402	176	2192	627/8
notes	[R]✕ ⧸		🍷 §	[R] ⧸🍷	[R] ⧸🍷	[R]✕ ⧸	[R]✕ ⧸	[R] 🍷⧸	[R]✕ ⧸	✕ §	[R]🍷 F ⊖		🍷 §	⧸ 🍷	🍷[R]	[R]✕ ⧸	[R]✕ ⧸	🍷 §	✕§ E	[R]✕ ⧸	[R]🍷 ⧸	✕§ E		[R] ⧸
Napoli Centrale d.	...	...	...	...	...	...	...	...	0748	...	...	...	...	0624	...	...	0848	...	...	0948	...	...	...	...
Roma Termini d.	0730	...	...	...	...	0830	...	...	0930	...	...	...	...	0855	...	...	1030	...	...	1130	...	...	...	...
Firenze SMN d.	0914	...	...	...	...	1014	...	...	1114	...	...	...	...	1127f	...	...	1214	...	...	1314	...	...	...	...
Lecce d.	|	...	...	...	...	|	...	...	|	...	...	...	...	|	...	...	|	...	...	|	...	...	...	...
Brindisi d.	|	...	...	...	...	|	...	...	|	...	...	...	...	|	...	*0406*	|	...	...	|	...	...	...	...
Bari Centrale d.	|	...	...	...	...	|	...	...	|	...	...	...	...	|	...	0653	|	...	...	|	...	...	...	...
Pescara Centrale d.	|	...	...	...	0635	|	...	...	|	...	...	...	...	|	...	0953	|	...	...	|	...	...	...	...
Ancona d.	|	...	...	...	0815	|	...	...	|	...	...	...	...	|	...	1116	|	...	...	|	...	...	...	...
Rimini d.	|	...	...	...	0922	|	...	...	|	...	...	...	...	|	...	1209	|	...	...	|	...	...	...	...
Bologna Centrale d.	1016	...	...	...	1044	1116	...	...	1216	...	...	...	...	1244	...	1308	1316	...	...	1416	...	...	...	...
Venezia Santa Lucia d.	|	...	...	...	|	|	1030	...	|	1051	...	...	...	|	...	|	|	1151	...	|	1345	...	...	...
Verona Porta Nuova d.	|	...	...	...	|	|	1143	...	|	1217	...	...	...	|	...	|	|	1319	...	|	|	...	...	...
Nice Ville d.	|	...	...	*0751*j	|	|	|	...	|	|	...	...	...	|	1004	|	|	|	...	|	|	...	...	*1209*q
Ventimiglia 🏛 d.	|	...	...	0858	|	|	|	...	|	|	...	...	...	|	1058	|	|	|	...	|	|	...	...	1258
Genova PP ▲ d.	|	...	...	1119	|	|	|	1219	|	|	...	...	...	|	1319	|	|	|	1419	|	|	←	...	1519
Milano Centrale a.	1200	...	...	1250	1255	1300	1305	1350	1400	1355	...	...	...	1450	1450	1455	1500	1455	1550	1600	1605	1550	...	1650
	EC 172 🍷 §						*EC* 110 🍷 §														*EC* 126 🍷 §			
Milano Centrale d.	1225	...	1225	...	...	...	1325	...	...	1425	...	...	1425	...	...	...	...	1525	1625	...	1625	1625	...	...
Arona d.	|	...	1316	*IC*	...	...	|	...	...	|	...	...	1516	*IC*	...	...	...	|	→	...	1716	|	...	*IC*
Stresa d.	|	...	1329	**1080**	...	...	|	...	...	|	...	...	1529	**837**	...	...	...	|	▬	...	1729	|	...	**1090**
Domodossola 🏛 ¶ d.	|	...	1410	🍷	...	...	|	...	...	|	...	...	1610	...	...	...	...	|	...	...	1810	|	...	...
Brig a.	|	...	1440	1520	...	...	|	...	...	|	...	...	1640	1649	...	...	...	|	...	...	1840	|	...	1850
Como San Giovanni d.	1307	...	|	|	...	...	1407	...	...	1507	...	...	|	|	...	...	...	1607	...	...	|	1707	...	|
Chiasso 🏛 a.	1312	...	|	|	...	...	1412	*IR*	...	1512	...	...	|	|	...	...	...	1612	*IR*	...	|	1712	...	|
Lugano a.	1353	...	|	|	...	...	1453	**2286**	...	1553	...	...	|	|	...	...	...	1653	**2290**	...	|	1753	...	|
Bellinzona a.	1421	...	|	|	...	...	1521	...	...	1621	...	...	|	|	...	...	...	1721	...	...	|	1821	...	|
Arth-Goldau a.	1608	1612	|	|	...	...	1708	1712	...	1808	...	1812	|	|	*IC*	...	...	1908	1912	...	|	2008	2012	|
Luzern a.	|	1637	|	|	...	...	1737	|	...	|	...	1838	|	|	**983**	...	...	1937	|	...	|	|	2038	|
Spiez a.	|	|	|	1553	...	...	|	|	...	|	...	|	|	1724	...	...	...	|	|	...	|	|	|	1953
Bern a.	|	|	|	1623	*ICE*	...	|	|	...	|	...	|	|	1755	1804	...	...	|	|	...	|	|	|	2023
Olten a.	|	|	|	|	**182**	...	1824	|	...	|	...	|	|	...	|	...	...	2024	|	...	|	|	|	|
Basel SBB a.	|	1751	|	1729	[R]🍷	...	1851	|	...	|	...	1951	|	...	1854	...	...	2051	|	...	|	|	2151	2129
Zürich HB a.	1651	...	|	...	⊖	...	...	1751	...	1851	...	...	|	...	...	...	...	...	1951	...	|	2051	...	...
Zürich HB d.	...	...	|	...	1705	...	...	...	...	1905	1914	...	|	...	...	...	...	...	...	...	|	...	...	...
Schaffhausen 🏛 a.	...	...	|	...	1750	...	...	...	...	1950	1951	...	|	...	...	...	...	...	...	...	|	...	...	...
Singen a.	...	...	|	...	1805	...	...	...	...	...	2005	...	|	...	...	...	...	...	...	...	|	...	...	...
Stuttgart Hbf a.	...	...	|	...	1956	...	...	...	...	...	2156	...	|	...	...	...	...	...	...	...	|	...	...	...
Sion a.	...	...	1515	...	...	...	...	...	...	...	...	...	1715	...	...	...	...	...	...	...	1915	...	...	...
Lausanne a.	...	...	1614	...	...	...	...	...	...	...	...	...	1814	...	...	...	...	...	...	...	2014	...	...	...
Genève a.	...	...	1653	...	...	...	...	...	...	...	...	...	1853	...	...	...	...	...	...	...	2050	...	...	...
Genève Aéroport ✈ a.	...	...	1702	...	...	...	...	...	...	...	...	...	...	...	...	...	...	...	...	...	2059	...	...	...

train type/number	ESc	ES	ESc	ICp	IC	AV	IR	EC	CIS	EC⧸	ICp	ES	ES	EC	ICp	AV	CIS	CIS	IR	ICE	EN 314	EN	IC	ICE
train number	9752	9438	9708	664	622	9440	1440	116	150	145 146	586	9414	9442	128	666	9444	50✕	50✕	1444	284	316	314	1058	282
notes	[R]✕ ⧸	[R]✕ y⧸	[R]✕ ⧸	[R] 🍷⧸	🍷⧸	[R]✕ ⧸		🍷 §	[R]✕ ⊕	🍷[R]	[R] 🍷⧸	[R]✕ ⧸	[R]✕ ⧸	🍷 §	[R] 🍷⧸	[R]✕ ⧸	[R]⊕ ①–⑥	[R]⊕ ⑦		[R]🍷 ⊖	[R]⧸ R	[R]⧸ S	🍷	[R]🍷 ⊖
Napoli Centrale d.	...	...	...	...	...	1148	...	...	...	...	1024	...	...	...	...	1348	...	...	...	...	...	...	...	...
Roma Termini d.	...	1230	...	...	...	1330	...	...	...	...	1257	...	1430	...	...	1530	...	...	...	...	1955	1955	...	...
Firenze SMN d.	...	1414	...	...	...	1514	...	...	1528	...	1527f	...	1614	...	...	1714	...	...	...	...	2200f	2200f	...	...
Lecce d.	0700	|	...	...	...	|	...	...	|	...	|	...	|	...	...	|	...	...	...	...	|	|	...	...
Brindisi d.	0725	|	...	...	...	|	...	...	|	...	|	...	|	...	...	|	...	...	...	...	|	|	...	...
Bari Centrale d.	0836	|	...	...	...	|	...	...	|	...	|	1105	|	...	...	|	...	...	...	...	|	|	...	...
Pescara Centrale d.	1119	|	...	...	...	|	...	...	|	...	|	1348	|	...	...	|	...	...	...	...	|	|	...	...
Ancona d.	1241	|	...	...	...	|	...	...	|	...	|	1518	|	...	...	|	...	...	...	...	|	|	...	...
Rimini d.	1339	|	...	...	...	|	...	...	|	...	|	1609	|	...	...	|	...	...	...	...	|	|	...	...
Bologna Centrale d.	1508	1516	...	...	...	1616	...	...	1634	...	1644	1708	1716	...	...	1816	...	...	...	...	2318	2318	...	...
Venezia Santa Lucia d.	|	|	1430	...	1451	|	...	...	|	...	|	|	|	1630	...	|	...	...	...	...	|	|	...	...
Verona Porta Nuova d.	|	|	1543	...	1618	|	...	...	|	...	|	|	|	1745	...	|	...	...	...	...	|	|	...	...
Nice Ville d.	|	|	|	...	|	|	...	...	|	1405	|	|	|	|	...	|	...	...	...	...	|	|	...	...
Ventimiglia 🏛 d.	|	|	|	...	|	|	...	...	|	1458	|	|	|	|	...	|	...	...	...	...	|	|	...	...
Genova PP ▲ d.	|	|	|	1619	|	|	...	...	|	1719	|	|	|	|	1819	|	...	...	...	...	|	|	...	...
Milano Centrale a.	1655	1700	1705	1750	1755	1800	...	...	1830	1850	1850	1855	1900	1905	1950	2000	...	...	...	...	|	|	...	...
			CIS 152 [R]✕ ⊕			*CIS* 48 [R]✕ ⊕									*EC* 178 🍷 §									
Milano Centrale d.	...	...	1738	...	...	1825	...	1825	1843	...	...	...	...	1920	1925	...	2025	2025	...	...	|	|	...	...
Arona d.	...	...	|	...	...	|	...	|	|	...	...	...	...	2012	|	...	|	|	...	...	|	|	...	...
Stresa d.	...	...	|	...	...	1921	...	|	|	*EC*	...	...	...	2025	|	...	|	|	...	...	|	|	...	...
Domodossola 🏛 ¶ d.	...	...	|	...	...	1948	...	|	|	**116**	...	...	...	2110	|	...	2148	2148	...	...	|	|	...	...
Brig a.	...	...	|	...	...	2016	2029	|	|	🍷	...	...	...	2140	|	...	2216	2216	2229	...	0439	0439	...	...
Como San Giovanni d.	...	...	1813	...	...	|	|	1905	1917	§	...	...	...	|	1959	...	|	|	|	...	|	|	...	...
Chiasso 🏛 a.	...	...	|	*IC*	...	|	|	1910	|	←	...	...	...	|	2004	...	|	|	|	...	|	|	...	...
Lugano a.	...	...	1838	**694**	...	|	|	1942	1945	1948	...	...	...	|	2035	...	|	|	|	...	|	|	...	...
Bellinzona a.	...	...	1902		...	|	|	→	2008	2014	...	...	...	|	2102	...	|	|	|	...	|	|	...	...
Arth-Goldau a.	...	...	2043	2112	...	|	|	...	2146	2208	...	...	...	|	2248	...	|	|	|	...	|	|	...	...
Luzern a.	...	...	|	2138	...	|	|	...	|	2237	...	...	...	|	|	...	|	|	|	...	|	|	...	...
Spiez a.	...	...	|	|	...	2053	|	...	|	|	...	...	...	|	|	...	2253	2322	|	...	|	0543	...	...
Bern a.	...	...	|	|	...	2123	|	...	|	|	...	...	...	|	|	...	2323	2352	|	...	|	0620	0634	...
Olten a.	...	...	|	|	...	2200	|	...	|	2324	...	...	...	|	|	...	0000	0030	|	...	|	0740	|	...
Basel SBB a.	...	...	|	2251	...	2229	|	...	|	2351	...	...	...	|	|	..	0029	0058	|	...	|	|	0729	...
Zürich HB a.	...	...	2125	...	...	...	|	...	2229	...	...	...	...	|	2331	...	...	...	|	...	|	0834	...	...
Zürich HB d.	...	...	...	...	...	...	|	...	...	...	...	...	...	|	...	...	...	...	|	0714	|	...	...	0914
Schaffhausen 🏛 a.	...	...	...	...	...	...	|	...	...	...	...	...	...	|	...	...	...	...	|	0750	|	...	...	0950
Singen a.	...	...	...	...	...	...	|	...	...	...	...	...	...	|	...	...	...	...	|	0805	|	...	...	1005
Stuttgart Hbf a.	...	...	...	...	...	...	|	...	...	...	...	...	...	|	...	...	...	...	|	0956	|	...	...	1156
Sion a.	...	...	...	...	...	...	2104	...	...	...	...	...	...	2215	...	...	...	...	2304	...	0732	...	...	...
Lausanne a.	...	...	...	...	...	...	2215	...	...	...	...	...	...	2314	...	...	...	...	0015	...	0840	...	...	...
Genève a.	...	...	...	...	...	...	*2318*	...	...	...	...	...	...	2350	...	...	...	...	...	...	0924	...	...	...
Genève Aéroport ✈ a.	...	...	...	...	...	...	*2327*	...	...	...	...	...	...	2359	...	...	...	...	...	...	0933	...	...	...

A – ①–⑥ (not Dec. 25, Jan. 1, Mar. 24).

E – CISALPINO CINQUE TERRE – (12) and ✕ Livorno (depart 1126) - Pisa (1144) - Genova - Milano - Zürich.

F – (12) and 🍷 Zürich - Stuttgart - Frankfurt (arrive 2339).

R – LUNA – 🛏 1, 2 cl. and ▬ 2 cl. (4, 6 berth) Roma - Genève Aéroport.

S – LUNA – 🛏 1, 2 cl. and ▬ 2 cl. (4, 6 berth) Roma - Zürich.

f – Firenze **Campo di Marte**.

j – ①–⑥ (not Dec. 25, Jan. 1, Mar. 24, May 1, 8).

q – ①–⑥.

y – Not Dec. 24, 31.

⧸ – Supplement payable.

¶ – Ticket point is **Iselle**.

▲ – Genova **Piazza Principe**.

§ – Supplement payable in Italy (except with international tickets). *IC* in Italy.

⊕ – **ETR 470** *Cisalpino*. Supplement payable for international journeys. *IC* supplement payable for internal journeys within Italy.

⊖ – *ICE-T* train with 🍷 and premium fares payable.

FOR OTHER TRAIN NAMES SEE PAGE 91

ZÜRICH - INNSBRUCK - WIEN, ZAGREB and BUDAPEST — 86

train type/number	EC	IC	IC111	IR	IC	EC	EC	EC	EC	EC	D	IC	EC	IR	EC		EC	IC	EC	EC	IR	EN	EN	EN	IR	EN
train number	561	515	IC211	559	169	669	113	565	113	163	347	613	315	573	161	1515	110	615	101	165	591	465	465	15465	593	467
notes	✕	🍷		🍷		✕	213 🍷	✕	✕	✕ B	✕	🍷	✕	🍷	✕ M	2	🍷	🍷	581	✕ P	🍷	H	415 KT	415 KS		🍷 A
Basel SBB d.	...	...	...	0622	...	...	...	...	...	0814	...	...	...	1222	...	...	...	...	1622	...	2022	...	...	...	2122	...
Zürich HB d.	...	...	...	0726	0740	...	...	...	...	0940	...	...	...	1326	1340	...	...	...	1726	1740	2126	2140	2140	2140	2226	2240
Sargans d.	...	...	...	▬	0837	...	...	...	...	1037	...	...	...	▬	1437	...	...	...	▬	1837	▬	2237	2237	2237	▬	2337
Buchs 🏛 d.	...	...	...	...	0856	...	...	...	...	1102	...	...	...	...	1502	...	...	...	...	1902	...	2259	2259	2259	...	0005
Bregenz d.	0500	...	...	...	|	0841	...	...	...	|	...	...	...	...	|	...	...	...	...	|	...	|	|	|	...	|
Feldkirch a.	0522	...	...	...	0912	0920**d**	...	...	...	1118	...	...	...	...	1518	...	...	...	...	1918	...	2314	2314	2314	...	0020
Bludenz a.	0536	...	...	...	...	0932	...	...	...	1132	...	...	...	...	1532	...	...	...	...	1932	...	2345	2345	2359	...	0035
Langen am Arlberg a.	|	...	...	...	...	1001	...	...	...	1202	...	...	...	...	1601	...	...	...	...	2001	...	0019	0019	0034	...	|
St Anton am Arlberg a.	0611	...	...	...	...	1010	...	...	...	1212	...	...	...	...	1610	...	...	...	...	2010	...	0029	0029	0045	...	|
Landeck-Zams a.	0634	...	...	...	...	1033	...	...	...	1238	...	...	...	...	1633	...	...	...	...	2033	...	0053	0053	0108	...	|
Ötztal a.	0659	...	...	...	...	1057	...	...	...	1302	...	...	...	...	1657	...	...	...	...	2057	**1519**	|	|	|	...	|
Innsbruck Hbf a.	0726	0735	...	...	...	1121	...	1130	...	1326	...	1535	...	...	1721	1724	...	...	...	2121	2	0140	0140	0154	...	0224
Jenbach a.	0749	0754	...	...	...	1154	...	1149	...	1349	...	1554	...	...	1750	1745	...	...	...	2149		|	|	|	...	|
Wörgl a.	0803	0809	...	...	...	1209	...	1203	...	1403	...	1609	...	...	1804	1759	...	...	...	2203	2208	0216	0216	0233	...	|
Kitzbühel a.	|	0839	...	...	...	1239	...	|	...	|	...	1639	...	...	|	1829	...	...	...	|	2243	|	|	|	...	|
St Johann in Tirol a.	|	0847	...	...	...	1247	...	|	...	|	...	1647	...	...	|	1837	...	...	IC	|	2251	|	|	|	...	|
Saalfelden a.	|	0917	...	IC	...	1317	...	|	...	|	...	1717	...	...	|	1907	...	...	**692**	|	2322	|	|	|	...	|
Zell am See a.	|	0928	...	**111**	...	1328	...	|	...	|	...	1728	...	...	|	1918	...	...	🍷	|	...	|	|	|	...	|
Schwarzach St Veit a.	|	0958	1010	1010	...	1358	1410	|	1410	|	...	1758	1813	...	|	1950	1953	...	2010	|	...	0355	0355	0414	...	|
Bischofshofen a.	|	1011	|	|	...	1411	|	|	|	|	...	1811	|	**1712**	|	▬	2007	2013	|	|	...	0412	|	|	IC	|
Selzthal a.	|	1140	|	|	...	1540	|	|	|	|	...	1940	|	**4294**	|	...	...	2140	|	|	...	0539	|	|	**532**	|
Graz Hbf a.	|	1325	|	|	...	1725	|	|	|	|	...	2125	|	2	|	...	...	2325	|	|	...	0737	|	|	🍷	|
Villach Hbf a.	|	▬	1147	1147	...	...	1547	|	1547	|	...	▬	1949	1954	|	...	...	...	2149	|	...	...	0609	0609	0620	|
Klagenfurt a.	|	...	|	1220	...	...	|	|	1620	|	...	**411**	|	2027**y**	|	**411**	...	...	*2230*	|	...	...	|	|	0646	|
Jesenice 🏛 a.	|	...	1241	...	...	...	1632	|	▬	|	...	**E**	2034	...	|	**E**	...	...	...	|	...	...	0707	0707	...	|
Ljubljana ⊙ a.	|	...	1353	...	...	...	1742	|	...	|	...	2105	2142	...	|	←	...	...	...	|	...	...	0828	0828	...	|
Zagreb ⊙ a.	|	...	1632	...	...	...	2004	|	...	|	...	2329	0003	...	|	0015	...	...	...	|	...	...	1053	1053	...	|
Vinkovci ⊕ a.	|	...	1955	...	...	...	...	|	...	|	...	→	...	...	|	0320	...	...	...	|	...	...	1422	1422	...	|
Beograd ⊕ a.	|	...	2247	...	...	...	...	|	...	|	...	...	...	...	|	0623	...	...	...	|	...	...	1725	1725	...	|
Salzburg Hbf a.	0929	EC	...	...	...	...	...	1329	EC	1529	...	...	...	...	1929	...	...	...	...	2329	...	...	...	...	...	0424
Linz Hbf a.	1045	**63**	...	...	...	...	...	1445	**49**	1645	...	...	...	...	2045	...	...	...	...	...	...	...	...	...	...	0554
St Pölten a.	1141	✕	...	...	...	...	...	1541	✕	1741	...	...	...	...	2141	...	...	...	...	...	...	...	...	...	...	0707
Wien Westbahnhof a.	1228	1352	...	...	...	...	...	1628	1752	1828	1948	...	...	...	2228	...	...	...	...	...	...	...	...	...	...	0803
Hegyeshalom 🏛 a.	...	1454	...	...	...	...	...	...	1854	...	2054	...	...	...	...	...	...	...	...	...	...	...	...	...	...	0927
Győr a.	...	1525	...	...	...	...	...	...	1925	...	2125	...	...	...	...	...	...	...	...	...	...	...	...	...	...	0958
Budapest Keleti a.	...	1653	...	...	...	...	...	...	2053	...	2253	...	...	...	...	...	...	...	...	...	...	...	...	...	...	1123

train type/number		EC	IC		EC		IC	EC	D	EC	EC	EC	EC	EC	EC	EC	EC	IC	IC210	EC	EC	EN	EC	EN	EN	EN
train number	1500	164	693	1504	160	410	310	114	346	162	212	42	564	668	314	46	566	110	IC110	62	660	466	633	414	414	464
notes	2	✕ P	🍷	2	✕ M	E		✕	✕	✕ B	112 ✕	✕	✕	✕	✕	✕	✕			✕	✕	🍷 A		15464 KS	464 KT	H
Budapest Keleti d.	...	...	...	...	...	...	...	...	0555	...	...	0710	...	...	...	0910	...	...	...	1310	...	1805	...	...	...	...
Győr d.	...	...	...	...	...	...	...	...	0722	...	...	0837	...	...	...	1037	...	...	...	1437	...	1932	...	...	...	...
Hegyeshalom 🏛 d.	...	...	...	...	...	...	...	...	0755	...	...	0906	...	...	...	1106	...	...	...	1506	...	2003	...	...	...	...
Wien Westbahnhof d.	...	...	...	...	0740	...	...	...	0857	0940	...	1008	1140	...	...	1208	1340	...	...	1608	1740	2125	...	...	...	...
St Pölten d.	...	...	...	...	0822	...	...	...	▬	1022	...	▬	1222	...	...	▬	1422	...	...	▬	1822	2209	...	...	...	...
Linz Hbf d.	...	...	...	...	0916	...	...	...	...	1116	...	...	1316	...	...	...	1516	...	...	...	1916	2314	...	...	...	...
Salzburg Hbf d.	...	0622	...	...	1031	...	...	...	...	1231	...	...	1431	...	...	...	1631	...	...	...	2030	0044	...	...	...	...
Beograd ⊕ d.	...	|	...	...	|	2215	...	...	...	|	...	...	|	...	...	...	|	...	0620	...	|	|	...	1045	1045	...
Vinkovci ⊕ d.	...	|	...	...	|	0150	...	...	...	|	...	...	|	...	...	...	|	...	0958	...	|	|	...	1440	1440	...
Zagreb ⊙ d.	...	|	...	...	|	0530	...	...	...	|	0750	EC	|	...	0944	...	|	...	1315	...	|	|	...	1810	1810	...
Ljubljana ⊙ d.	...	|	...	...	|	0750	0805	...	...	|	1012	**112**	|	...	1205	...	|	...	1600	...	|	|	...	2035	2035	...
Jesenice 🏛 d.	...	|	...	...	|	▬	0923	...	IC	|	1121	✕	|	...	1316	...	|	...	1722	IC	|	|	...	2155	2155	...
Klagenfurt d.	...	|	0736	...	|	...	|	0936	**512**	|	|	1126	|	...	*1326*	...	|	1726	|	**610**	|	|	2215	|	|	...
Villach Hbf d.	...	|	0811	...	|	...	1000	1011	🍷	|	1211	1211	|	...	1411	...	|	1811	1811	🍷	|	|	2236	2300	2300	...
Graz Hbf d.	...	|	|	...	|	...	...	|	0835	|	|	|	|	1035	|	**1510**	|	|	|	1635	|	|	▬	|	|	2135
Selzthal d.	...	|	|	...	|	...	...	|	1018	|	|	|	|	1218	|	2	|	|	|	1818	|	|	...	|	|	2339
Bischofshofen d.	0521	|	|	*0921*	|	...	...	|	1149	|	|	|	|	1349	|		|	|	|	1949	|	|	...	|	|	0108
Schwarzach St Veit d.	0544	|	0947	1011	|	...	...	1147	1202	|	1347	1347	|	1402	1547	1611	|	1947	1947	2002	|	|	...	0101	0145	0145
Zell am See d.	0620	|	▬	1043	|	...	...	...	1232	|	...	...	|	1432	▬	1643	|	...	...	2032	|	|	...	|	|	|
Saalfelden d.	0638	|	...	1052	|	...	...	...	1242	|	...	...	|	1442	...	1652	|	...	...	2042	|	|	...	|	|	|
St Johann in Tirol d.	0710	|	...	1121	|	...	...	...	1311	|	...	...	|	1511	...	1721	|	...	...	2111	|	|	...	|	|	|
Kitzbühel d.	0718	|	...	1129	|	...	...	...	1319	|	...	...	|	1519	...	1729	|	...	...	2119	|	|	...	|	|	|
Wörgl d.	0755	0749	...	1200	1156	...	...	...	1350	1356	...	...	1556	1550	...	1800	1756	...	...	2150	2156	|	...	|	|	|
Jenbach d.	0812	0806	...	1215	1210	...	...	...	1405	1410	...	...	1610	1605	...	1815	1810	...	...	2205	2210	|	...	|	|	|
Innsbruck Hbf d.	0835	0839	...	1235	1239	...	...	...	1425	1439	...	...	1632	1639	...	1835	1839	...	...	2225	2233	0241	...	0345	0402	0402
Ötztal d.	...	0903	...	...	1303	...	...	...	...	1503	...	...	...	1703	...	▬	1903	...	...	...	2300	|	...	|	|	|
Landeck-Zams d.	...	0927	...	...	1327	...	...	...	...	1527	...	...	...	1727	...	...	1927	...	...	...	2323	|	...	0439	0453	0453
St Anton am Arlberg d.	...	0951	...	...	1351	...	...	...	...	1551	...	...	...	1751	IC	...	1951	...	...	...	2345	|	...	0505	0518	0518
Langen am Arlberg d.	...	1001	...	...	1401	...	...	...	...	1601	...	...	...	1801	**168**	...	2001	...	...	...	2356	|	...	0516	0529	0529
Bludenz d.	...	1028	...	...	1428	...	...	...	...	1628	...	...	...	1828		...	2028	...	...	...	0021	0427	...	0555	0615	0615
Feldkirch d.	...	1042	...	...	1442	...	...	...	...	1642	...	...	...	1844	1846	...	2042	...	...	...	0033	0446	...	0646	0646	0646
Bregenz a.	...	|	IR	...	|	IR	...	...	...	|	...	...	...	1915	|	IR	2105	...	...	...	0056	|	IR	|	|	|
Buchs 🏛 a.	...	1058	**572**	...	1458	**580**	...	...	...	1658	...	...	...	...	1902	**590**	...	...	...	...	...	0502	**558**	0702	0702	0702
Sargans a.	...	1122	🍷	...	1522	🍷	...	...	...	1722	...	...	...	...	1922		...	...	...	...	...	0522	🍷	0722	0722	0722
Zürich HB a.	...	1220	1234	...	1620	1634	...	...	...	1820	...	...	...	...	2020	2034	...	...	...	...	...	0620	0634	0820	0820	0820
Basel SBB a.	...	...	1338	...	...	1738	...	...	...	1948	...	...	...	...	...	2138	...	...	...	...	...	...	0738	*0938*	*0938*	*0938*

A – WIENER WALZER – 🛏 1, 2 cl., 🛏 1, 2 cl. (T4), ▬ 2 cl. (4, 6 berth), (2) and ✕ Zürich - Wien and v.v. Special fares payable. ▬ 2 cl. (4, 6 berth), (2) and ✕ Zürich - Wien - Budapest and v.v. (12) Wien - Budapest and v.v. 🛏 1, 2 cl. and ▬ 2 cl. (4, 6 berth) Zürich - Linz - Praha and v.v. Table **59**.

B – TRANSALPIN – (1) (panorama car), (12) and ✕ Basel - Wien and v.v.

E – 🛏 1, 2 cl. and (2) Ljubljana - Zagreb - Beograd and v.v. Table **62**.

H – ZÜRICHSEE – 🛏 1, 2 cl., ▬ 2 cl. (4, 6 berth) and (2) Zürich - Graz and v.v.

K – 🛏 1, 2 cl. and ▬ 2 cl. (4, 6 berth) Zürich - Zagreb and v.v. (2) Zürich - Beograd and v.v. (12) and ✕ Jesenice - Beograd and v.v.

M – VORARLBERG – (12) and ✕ Zürich - Wien and v.v.

P – KAISERIN ELISABETH – (12) and ✕ Zürich - Salzburg and v.v.

S – Daily Dec. 9 - Jan. 6; daily Mar. 13–25; ⑤⑥⑦ Mar. 28 - June 22; also Feb. 15, 16, 22, 23, May 1, 12, 21.

T – Daily except on dates in note **S**.

d – Departure time, arrive 0912.

y – 2022 on ⑦ (also Dec. 25, 26, Jan. 1, Mar. 24, May 1, 12, 22).

⊙ – 🏛 between Ljubljana and Zagreb is Dobova.

⊕ – 🏛 between Vinkovci and Beograd is Šid.

← NOTES FOR TABLE 82 (continued from page 90)

OTHER TRAIN NAMES FOR TABLE 82:

EC **106/119** – CISALPINO TIZIANO
EC **108/117** – CISALPINO VERDI
EC **109/110** – CISALPINO TICINO
EC **111/114** – CISALPINO SAN MARCO
EC **115/116** – CISALPINO MEDIOLANUM
EC **121/128** – CISALPINO MONTERVERDI
EC **123/124** – CISALPINO BORROMEO
EC **125/126** – CISALPINO LEMANO
EC **127/120** – CISALPINO VALLESE
EC **129/122** – CISALPINO MONTE ROSA
EC **170/177** – CISALPINO MONTE CENERI
EC **171/178** – CISALPINO TEODOLINDA
EC **173/174** – CISALPINO CANALETTO
EC **179/172** – CISALPINO INSUBRIA

88 WIEN - VENEZIA, MILANO, ROMA and ANCONA

train type/number		EC	EC	IC	IC	ES/	ICp	ES/	EC	EC	ICN		ICN	IC	IC	EN	EN235	EN	EN	EN	EN	ES/	ICp/	IC	IC	
train number	①–⑥	790	31	705	559	9402	618	9477	113	33	779	358	771	742	796	235	600	1239	1237	237	207	9467	703	608	1506	
notes	2 f	🍴	A	🍷/	/	🍴[R]	[R]/	🍴[R]	🍴	B	f		f	🍷	🍷	R/	W/	C/	P/	G/	T♣	🍴[R]	[R]🍷	J/	K/	
Wien Südbahnhof d.	...	...	0630	...	...	...	...	...	...	1257	...	...	...	...	...	1915	1915	2005	2005	2040r	...	...	...	...	...	...
Bruck an der Mur d.	...	...	0818	...	...	...	...	...	...	1501	...	...	...	...	...	2124	2124	2207	2207	|	...	...	...	...	...	...
Klagenfurt Hbf d.	...	...	1013	...	...	...	...	...	...	1713	...	...	...	...	...	2335	2335	0014	0014	|	...	...	...	...	...	...
Praha Hlavní d.	...	...	|	...	...	...	...	...	...	|	...	...	...	...	...	|	|	|	|	|	1711	...	...	...	...	...
Linz Hbf d.	0510	...	|	...	...	...	...	...	*1132*	|	...	...	...	1932	...	|	|	|	|	2232	2246	...	...	...	...	...
Salzburg Hbf d.	0648	0704	|	...	...	...	...	...	1304	|	...	...	...	2050	2104z	|	|	|	|	0138	0138	...	...	...	...	...
Villach Hbf d.	...	0948	1037	...	...	...	...	...	1547	1749	...	...	...	...	2347z	0003	0003	0045	0045	0423	0423	...	...	...	...	...
Tarvisio 🛂 a.	...	...	1059	...	...	...	...	...	...	1811	...	...	...	...	...	0026	0026	0108	0108	0446	0446	...	...	...	...	...
Udine a.	...	...	1203	...	...	...	...	...	...	1917	...	...	2150	...	...	|	|	0217	0217	0557	0557	...	...	...	...	...
Venezia Mestre a.	...	...	1318	1335	...	1356	1404	...	...	2048	2206	2304	2331	...	...	0252	0252h	0332	0332	0833	0833	0854	0921	0914	1003	...
Venezia Santa Lucia a.	...	...	1330	|	...	|	|	1443	...	2100	|	|	2343	...	...	|	|	|	|	0845	0845	|	|	|	|	...
Padova a.	...	...	...	1355	...	1412	1422	1509	...	...	2227	2325	0037	...	...	|	0622	0418	0418	▬	...	0909	0939	0931	1023	...
Verona Porta Nuova a.	...	...	...	|	...	|	1515	|	...	...	|	0025	|	...	...	|	0715	|	|	**2121**	...	|	|	1042	1119	...
Milano Centrale a.	...	...	...	|	...	1605	1655	|	...	...	|	...	|	...	...	|	0855	|	|		...	|	|	1255	1255	...
Bologna Centrale a.	...	...	...	1516	1529	...	...	1620	...	...	|	...	0217	...	...	0448	...	0541	0541	0638	...	1020	1116	...	...	...
Firenze SMN a.	...	...	...	1629e	|	...	...	1722	...	...	|	...	|	...	...	0618	...	0705e	0705e	|	...	1122	1229e	...	...	...
Roma Termini a.	...	...	...	1903	|	...	...	1908	...	...	|	...	0656t	...	...	0905	...	1045	0957	|	...	1308	1503	...	...	...
Ravenna a.	...	...	...	...	|	...	...	...	...	...	0028	...	...	...	...	...	...	...	...	|	...	...	...	...	...	...
Rimini a.	...	...	...	...	1638	...	...	...	...	...	0111	...	...	...	...	...	...	...	...	0805	...	...	...	...	...	...
Ancona a.	...	...	...	...	1747	...	...	...	...	...	0209	...	...	...	...	...	...	...	...	0924	...	...	...	...	...	...

train type/number	ICN	ICN		EC	EC	ES/	AV/	IC	EC	EC	IC	ES/	ES/	IC	ES	ICp	EN	EN	ES/			EN	641	IC	IC	
train number	774	776		32	112	9466	9432	714	121	30	110	9414	9478	629	9405	706	206	236	9418	1236	1238	234	EN234	791	547	
notes		f		B	🍴/	🍴[R]	🍴[R]	/	/	A	🍷/	🍴[R]	🍴[R]	/	[R]/	[R]	T♣	H/	🍴[R]	Q/	D/	R/	W/	🍷	🍷	
Ancona d.	...	0234	...	...	...	...	...	1020	...	...	...	1518	...	...	...	🍷/	...	...	1913	...	...	...	...	...	...	...
Rimini d.	...	0333	...	...	...	...	...	1122	...	...	...	1609	...	...	...	...	...	...	2009	...	...	...	...	...	...	...
Ravenna d.	...	0413	...	...	...	...	...	|	...	...	...	|	...	...	...	...	...	...	|	...	...	...	...	...	...	...
Roma Termini d.	2250t	|	...	...	...	0850	0930	|	...	...	...	|	1450	...	...	1457	...	...	|	1700	1720	1910	...	...	...	...
Firenze SMN d.	0147e	|	...	...	...	1038	1114	|	...	...	...	|	1638	...	...	1727e	...	...	|	2056e	2056e	2153	...	...	...	...
Bologna Centrale d.	0318	|	...	...	...	1140	1212	1248	...	...	...	1704	1740	...	...	1844	...	...	2104	2223	2223	2320	...	...	...	...
Milano Centrale d.	|	|	...	...	...	|	...	|	1155	...	...	▬	|	1705	1755	|	...	...	...	|	|	|	2105	...	...	...
Verona Porta Nuova d.	|	|	0604	...	...	|	...	|	1316	...	...	...	|	1843	|	|	...	...	...	|	|	|	2243	...	...	...
Padova d.	0452	0628	0721	...	...	1251	...	1410	1402	...	...	...	1851	1938	1948	2006	...	...	...	2349	2349	0041	2337	...	...	...
Venezia Santa Lucia d.	0601	|	|	0846	...	1317	...	|	|	1444	...	...	1917	|	|	|	2026	2026	...	|	|	|	|	...	...	...
Venezia Mestre d.	0613	0648	0746	0858	...	▬	...	1430	1418	1456	...	...	...	1956	2004	2026	2038	2038	...	0036	0036	0126	0126g	...	...	...
Udine d.	0804	...	...	1028	...	*IC*	...	...	...	1614	...	*ICE*	...	...	...	...	2304	2304	...	0157	0157	|	|	...	...	...
Tarvisio 🛂 d.	...	...	...	1140	...	**745**	...	...	...	1718	...	**661**	...	...	...	...	0020	0020	...	0319	0319	0352	0352	...	...	...
Villach Hbf a.	...	...	...	1202	1211	🍷	...	...	...	1740	1811	🍴	...	...	...	...	0042	0042	...	0341	0341	0415	0415	0609x	...	...
Salzburg Hbf a.	...	...	...	|	1455	1508	...	...	...	|	2048	2132	...	...	...	...	0405	0405	...	|	|	|	|	0855x	0908	...
Linz Hbf a.	...	...	...	|	...	1627	...	...	...	|	...	2241	...	...	...	...	0602	0627	...	|	|	|	|	...	1027	...
Praha Hlavní a.	...	...	...	|	...	...	...	...	...	|	...	...	...	...	...	...	1153	|	...	|	|	|	|	...	...	...
Klagenfurt Hbf a.	...	...	...	1246	...	...	...	...	...	1804	...	...	...	...	...	...	...	|	...	0413	0413	0438	0438	...	...	...
Bruck an der Mur a.	...	...	...	1459	...	...	...	...	...	1956	...	...	...	...	...	...	...	|	...	0624	0624	0639	0639	...	...	...
Wien Südbahnhof a.	...	...	...	1702	...	...	...	...	...	2144	...	...	...	...	...	...	...	0830r	...	0839	0855	0852	0852	...	...	...

A – ALLEGRO JOHANN STRAUSS – [12] and 🍴 [R] ♣ / Wien - Venezia and v.v.
B – ALLEGRO STRADIVARI – [12] and 🍷 [R] ♣ / Wien - Venezia and v.v.
C – ALLEGRO RIGOLETTO – Dec. 21, 23, 27, 28, 29, Jan. 1–5, Mar. 16, 23, Apr. 30, May 11, 21: 🛏 1, 2 cl., ▬ 2 cl. and [2] [R] Wien - Firenze - Roma.
D – ALLEGRO RIGOLETTO – Dec. 22, 25, 28, 29, 30, Jan. 2–6, Mar. 17, 24, May 1, 12, 22: 🛏 1, 2 cl., ▬ 2 cl. and [2] [R] Roma - Firenze - Wien.
G – ALLEGRO DON GIOVANNI – 🛏 1, 2 cl., ▬ 2 cl. and [2] Wien (**748**) - Salzburg (**297**) - Villach (**237**) - Udine (**238**) - Venezia.
H – ALLEGRO DON GIOVANNI – 🛏 1, 2 cl., ▬ 2 cl. and [2] Venezia (**239**) - Udine (**236**) - Villach (**296**) - Salzburg (**849**) - Wien.
J – ①–⑤ (not Dec. 25, 26, Jan. 1, Mar. 24, Apr. 25, May 1, June 2).
K – ⑥⑦ (also Dec. 25, 26, Jan. 1, Mar. 24, Apr. 25, May 1, June 2).
P – ALLEGRO ROSSINI ⑤ Mar. 14 - Sept. 26: 🛏 1, 2 cl., ▬ 2 cl. and [2] Wien - Firenze - Roma.
Q – ALLEGRO ROSSINI ⑥ Mar. 15 - Sept. 27: 🛏 1, 2 cl., ▬ 2 cl. and [2] Roma - Firenze - Wien.
R – ALLEGRO TOSCA – 🛏 1, 2 cl., ▬ 2 cl. (6, 4 berth) and [2] Wien - Roma and v.v.
T – ▬ 2 cl. Praha - Linz - Venezia and v.v.
W – 🛏 1, 2 cl. and ▬ 2 cl. (4 berth) Wien - Milano and v.v.
e – Firenze **Campo di Marte**.
f – Not Dec. 25, 26, Jan. 1, Mar. 24, May 1, 12, 22.
g – Arrive 2356.
h – Depart 0603.
r – Wien **Westbahnhof**.
t – Roma **Tiburtina**.
x – On ⑦ (also Dec. 25, 26, Jan. 1, Mar. 24, May 1, 12, 22) change trains at Schwarzach St Veit.
z – On ⑥ (also Dec. 24, 25, 31, Mar. 23, Apr. 30, May 11, 21) change trains at Schwarzach St Veit.
♣ – Special 'global' fares payable.
/ – Supplement payable.

89a WIEN - LJUBLJANA and ZAGREB

train type	IC	ICS	EC	EC	EC	EC	IC	ICS	EC	ICS		
train number	153	13	157	151	101	557	155	21	159	23		
notes	/	[R]	🍴/	483	🍴	🍴	/	[R]	🍴	[R]		
			Z	A	B	/		W	C/			
Wien Südbahnhof d.	...	...	0557	0757	...	1157	...	...	1557	...	...	...
Graz Hbf d.	0655	...	0836	1036	1402	1434	1540	...	1837	...	...	...
Spielfeld-Straß 🛂 d.	0740	...	0921	1121	1447	...	1626	...	1921	...	...	...
Maribor a.	0756	0822	0938	1139	1504	...	1647	1650	1938	1950	...	...
Pragersko a.	...	0834	1000	1205	1529	...	...	1702	2010	2002	...	...
Zidani Most a.	...	0925	|	1309	1634	...	...	1753	|	2053	...	...
Dobova 🛂 a.	...	|	1145	|	|	...	...	|	2149	|	...	...
Zagreb a.	...	|	1229	|	|	...	...	|	2233	|	...	...
Ljubljana a.	...	1010	...	1410	1732	...	...	1838	...	2138	...	...
Koper a.	...	...	...	|	...	...	...	...	...	...	...	...
Rijeka a.	...	...	...	1725	...	...	...	...	...	...	...	...
Split a.	...	...	...	...	...	...	...	...	...	...	...	...

train type/number	ICS	EC	EC	IC	EC	IC	EC	482	IC	IC	IC	
train number	14	158	100	154	558	506	156	EC	502	152	654	
notes	[R]	🍴	🍴	/	🍴		🍴/	150		/	🍷	
		C/	B				Z	A				
Split d.	...	...	...	...	...	...	...	...	...	...	...	...
Rijeka d.	...	...	...	...	...	...	...	1257	...	...	...	...
Koper d.	...	...	...	...	...	...	...	|	...	...	...	...
Ljubljana d.	0830	...	1018	...	...	1245	...	1600	1725	...	...	...
Zagreb d.	|	0725	|	...	...	|	1335	|	|	...	...	...
Dobova 🛂 d.	|	0808	|	...	...	|	1420	|	|	...	...	...
Zidani Most d.	0914	|	1113	...	...	1342	|	1654	1824	...	...	...
Pragersko d.	1004	0953	1218	...	...	1452	1601	1758	1935	...	...	...
Maribor d.	1016	1021	1242	1414	...	1508	1621	1819	1952	2015	...	...
Spielfeld-Straß 🛂 a.	...	1039	1300	1432	...	...	1638	1837	...	2032	...	...
Graz Hbf a.	...	1124	1347	1520	1526	...	1724	1922	...	2119	2126	...
Wien Südbahnhof a.	...	1402	...	...	1802	...	2002	2202	...	...	0002	...

A – EMONA – [12] and 🍴 Wien - Ljubljana and v.v. [2] Wien - Ljubljana - Rijeka and v.v. [12] Ljubljana - Rijeka and v.v.
B – JOŽE PLEČNIK - [12] and 🍴 Praha - Linz - Graz - Ljubljana and v.v.
C – CROATIA – [12] and 🍴 Wien - Zagreb and v.v.
W – ①–⑤ (not Dec. 25, Jan. 1, Mar. 24).
Z – ZAGREB – [12] and 🍴 Wien - Zagreb and v.v.
/ – Supplement payable.

89b VENEZIA – LJUBLJANA, ZAGREB, BEOGRAD and BUDAPEST

train type		IC		EC			EN	EN	
train number		211		61	411		241	241	
notes		🍴/		♣[R]				413	
		E		T	A		B	P	
Venezia Santa Lucia d.	...	...	...	1546	...	...	2127	2127	...
Venezia Mestre d.	...	...	...	1558	...	...	2140	2140	...
Trieste Centrale d.	...	...	...	|	...	...	|	|	...
Villa Opicina 🛂 d.	...	...	...	1750	...	...	2348	2348	...
Ljubljana ⊙ a.	...	1408	...	1932	2105	...	0151	0151	...
Zagreb ⊙ a.	...	1632	...	...	2329	...	0418	0418	...
Vinkovci ⊕ a.	...	1955	...	...	0320	...	◧	0914	...
Beograd ⊕ a.	...	2247	...	...	0623	...	|	1212	...
Budapest Keleti a.	...	...	...	...	...	...	1058	...	...

train type		EN	EN			EC		IC	
train number		240	240		410	60		210	
notes			412			♣[R]		🍴/	
		B	P		A	T		E	
Budapest Keleti d.	...	1700	...	...	...	...	...	...	...
Beograd ⊕ d.	...	|	1545	...	2215	...	...	0620	...
Vinkovci ⊕ d.	...	◧	1938	...	0150	...	...	0958	...
Zagreb ⊙ d.	...	2335	2335	...	0530	...	...	1315	...
Ljubljana ⊙ d.	...	0222	0222	...	0750	1035	...	1538	...
Villa Opicina 🛂 a.	...	0428	0428	...	...	1215	...	...	...
Trieste Centrale a.	...	|	|	...	...	|	...	...	...
Venezia Mestre a.	...	0704	0704	...	...	1409	...	...	...
Venezia Santa Lucia a.	...	0716	0716	...	...	1421	...	...	...

A – 🛏 1, 2 cl. and [2] Ljubljana - Beograd and v.v. [12] Ljubljana - Zagreb and v.v. Table **62**.
B – VENEZIA – ♣, [R], 🛏 1,2 cl., ▬ 2 cl. and [2] Venezia - Budapest and v.v. 🍴 Dobova - Zagreb - Budapest and v.v.
E – SAVA – [12] München - Villach - Ljubljana - Beograd and v.v. [2] and 🍴 Jesenice - Ljubljana - Beograd and v.v.
P – ♣ [R] ▬ 2 cl. Venezia - Zagreb - Beograd and v.v. [12] and 🍴 Zagreb - Beograd and v.v.
T – CASANOVA – [12] and 🍷 Venezia - Ljubljana and v.v.
♣ – Special fares payable for journeys to or from Italy.
/ – Supplement payable.
◧ – 🛂 is Koprivnica and Gyékényes.
⊙ – 🛂 between Ljubljana and Zagreb is Dobova.
⊕ – 🛂 between Vinkovci and Beograd is Šid.

BARCELONA, MARSEILLE and NICE - MILANO, ROMA and VENEZIA — 90

train type/number	4621	4620	EC	ICp	ICp	EC	IC	TGV	TGV	EC	EC	IC	IC	EC	ICp ⚡	ICN	Talgo	4657	EN	EN	AV	Hotel	ES	IC
train number	4620	4621	139	653	527	111	595	5301	5102	145	175	539	635	147	543	761	73/72	4656	369	369	9425	EN	9435	613
notes	🄡	🄡	140	🄡	🄡	🄡 🍷	🍷	🄡 🍷	🄡 🍷	146	🍴	540	🍷	148	🄡 🍷	🄡	🄡 ⚡	🄡	362	374	🄡 ⚡	371	⚡ 🄡	🍷
	B	C	T	🍷 ⚡	🍷 ⚡	⚡	⚡			T	⚡	🍷 ⚡	⚡	T	Ⓑ f	⚡	G 🍴	🍷	363	375	🍴	273	🍴	⚡
Hendaye d.	...	1853	...	...	...	...	...	...	...	...	...	...	...	...	...	...	...	...	E	F	...	11273	...	...
Bordeaux St Jean d.	2148	2148	...	...	...	...	...	...	...	...	...	...	...	...	...	...	...	1102n	...	...	...	A	...	...
Toulouse d.	0011	0011	...	...	...	...	...	0655r	...	...	...	...	...	...	...	...	...	1307	...	...	...	...	...	...
Barcelona França d.	|	|	...	...	...	...	...	|	...	...	...	...	...	...	...	...	0845	|	...	...	...	2015	...	...
Girona d.	|	|	...	...	...	...	...	|	...	...	...	...	...	...	...	...	0955	|	...	...	...	2125	...	...
Figueres d.	|	|	...	...	...	...	...	|	...	...	...	...	...	...	...	...	1025	|	...	...	...	2154	...	...
Cerbère 🏛 d.	|	|	...	...	...	...	...	|	...	...	...	...	...	...	...	...	1114	|	...	...	...	|	...	...
Perpignan d.	|	|	...	...	...	...	...	|	...	...	...	...	...	...	...	...	1145	|	...	...	...	2318	...	...
Narbonne d.	|	|	...	...	...	...	...	0812	...	...	...	...	...	...	...	...	1221	|	...	...	...	|	...	...
Montpellier d.	|	|	...	...	...	...	...	0915	...	...	...	...	...	...	...	...	1322	1511	...	...	...	|	...	...
Marseille St Charles d.	0557	0557	...	...	...	...	...	1040	1100	...	...	...	...	...	...	...	▬	1654	...	...	...	|	...	...
Toulon d.	0645	0645	...	...	...	...	...	...	1141	...	...	...	...	...	...	...	...	1740	...	...	...	|	...	...
Cannes d.	0805	0805	...	...	...	...	...	...	1258	...	...	...	...	...	...	...	...	1858	...	...	...	|	...	...
Nice d.	0837	0837	1004	...	...	...	...	...	1325	1405	...	...	...	1805	...	...	...	1923	2150	2150	...	|	...	...
Monaco - Monte Carlo d.	...	...	1021	...	...	...	...	...	...	1420	...	...	...	1820	...	...	...	...	2205	2205	...	|	...	...
Ventimiglia 🏛 d.	...	...	1058	...	...	...	...	...	...	1458	...	...	...	1858	...	...	...	...	2245	2245	...	|	...	...
San Remo a.	...	...	1113	...	...	...	...	...	...	1513	...	...	...	1913	...	...	...	...	2302	2302	...	|	...	...
Genova Piazza Principe a.	...	...	1306	1347	1452	...	...	...	...	1706	1748	1852	...	2106	2052	2240	**10827**	...	0107	0107	...	|	...	...
Torino Porta Susa a.	...	...	|	|	|	...	...	...	...	|	|	|	...	|	|	|		...	|	|	...	0812	...	...
Milano Centrale a.	...	...	1450	|	|	1505	1510	...	...	1850	|	|	1905	2250	|	|	0025	...	|	|	...	0959	1100	1105
Verona a.	...	...	...	|	|	1640	|	...	...	...	|	|	2040	...	|	|	0232	...	0511	|	...	...	|	1240
Venezia Santa Lucia a.	...	...	...	|	|	1809	|	...	...	...	|	|	2209	...	|	|	...	...	0737	|	...	...	|	1410
La Spezia a.	...	...	...	1518	1604	...	|	...	...	...	1917	2004	...	...	2210	2355	...	...	...	|	...	...	|	...
Pisa Centrale a.	...	...	...	...	1657	...	|	...	...	...	2012	2053	...	...	2310	0047	...	...	...	0525	...	...	|	...
Firenze **Rifredi** a.	...	...	...	...	|	...	1826	...	...	...	...	2200v	...	...	...	|	...	...	...	0653z	...	...	1344v	...
Roma Termini a.	...	...	...	...	2014	...	2106	...	...	...	...	...	...	...	...	|	...	...	...	0945	1045	...	1530	...
Napoli Centrale a.	...	...	...	...	2236	...	2336	...	...	...	...	...	...	...	...	0601y	...	...	...	...	1212	...	...	...

train type/number	EN	ICp	EN	4758	Talgo	ICp	EC	4764	IC	IC	EC	TGV	IC	EC	ICp	ICp	EC	4720	4720	AV	ES	EC	Hotel	
train number	358	598	366	4759	70/71	654	141	4765	606	505	143	6876	582	114	516	664	159	4721	4721	9440	9442	128	EN	
notes	359	🄡	367	🍷	🄡 ⚡	🄡	142	🄡	🍷	506	144	🄡		🄡 🍷	🄡	🄡	160	🄡	🄡	🄡 ⚡	🄡 ⚡	🍷	372	
	368	🍷 ⚡	368	🄡	G 🍴	🍷 ⚡	T	🍷	⚡	🍷 ⚡	T	🍷	🍷 ⚡	⚡	🍷 ⚡	🍷 ⚡	T	B	C	🍴	🍴	⚡	274	
Napoli Centrale d.	E	1824	F	...	...	...	...	...	...	...	...	...	0624	...	0730	...	...	...	...	1148	...	...	11274	...
Roma Termini d.	...	2033	2116	...	...	...	...	...	...	...	...	...	0855	...	0946	...	...	...	...	1330	1430	...	A	...
Firenze **Rifredi** d.	...	...	2325z	...	...	...	...	...	...	0751v	...	...	1136	...	|	...	...	...	...	1514	1614	...	...	...
Pisa Centrale d.	...	...	0038	...	...	0544	...	...	...	0902	...	...	|	...	1300	1344	...	...	...	|	|	...	...	...
La Spezia d.	...	...	|	...	...	0640	...	...	...	0953	...	...	|	...	1354	1440	...	...	...	|	|	...	...	...
Venezia Santa Lucia d.	2251	...	|	...	...	|	...	...	0752	|	...	...	|	1151	|	|	...	...	...	|	|	1630	...	...
Verona d.	0040	...	|	...	...	|	...	...	0918	|	...	...	|	1318	|	|	...	...	...	|	|	1745	...	...
Milano Centrale d.	|	...	|	...	...	|	0710	...	1055	|	1110	...	1450	1455	|	|	1510	...	...	1800	1900	1905	1947	...
Torino Porta Susa d.	|	...	|	...	...	|	|	...	...	|	|	...	...	...	|	|	|	...	...	...	...	...	2117	...
Genova Piazza Principe d.	0445	...	0445	...	...	0816	0855	...	...	1108	1255	...	...	...	1508	1616	1655	...	...	...	...	...	|	...
San Remo d.	0713	...	0713	...	...	...	1050	...	...	...	1450	...	...	...	...	...	1850	...	...	...	...	...	|	...
Ventimiglia 🏛 a.	0731	...	0731	...	...	...	1107	...	...	...	1507	...	...	...	...	...	1907	...	...	...	...	...	|	...
Monaco - Monte Carlo a.	0817	...	0817	...	...	...	1145	...	...	...	1545	...	...	...	...	...	1942	...	...	...	...	...	|	...
Nice a.	0840	...	0840	1008q	...	...	1201	1335q	...	...	1601	1725q	...	...	...	...	1958	2058q	2058q	...	...	...	|	...
Cannes a.	...	...	...	1033q	...	...	...	1359q	...	...	...	1754q	...	...	...	...	...	2127q	2127q	...	...	...	|	...
Toulon a.	...	...	...	1152	...	...	...	1519	...	...	...	1914	...	...	...	...	...	2305	2305	...	...	...	|	...
Marseille St Charles a.	...	...	...	1238	...	...	...	1604	...	...	...	1958	...	...	...	...	...	2350	2350	...	...	...	|	...
Montpellier a.	...	...	...	1420	1702	...	...	1745	...	...	...	...	...	...	...	...	...	|	|	...	...	...	|	...
Narbonne a.	...	...	...	|	1756	...	...	|	...	...	...	...	...	...	...	...	...	|	|	...	...	...	|	...
Perpignan a.	...	...	...	|	1835	...	...	|	...	...	...	...	...	...	...	...	...	|	|	...	...	...	0548	...
Portbou 🏛 a.	...	...	...	|	1931	...	...	|	...	...	...	...	...	...	...	...	...	|	|	...	...	...	|	...
Figueres a.	...	...	...	|	1953	...	...	|	...	...	...	...	...	...	...	...	...	|	|	...	...	...	0709	...
Girona a.	...	...	...	|	2019	...	...	|	...	...	...	...	...	...	...	...	...	|	|	...	...	...	0737	...
Barcelona França a.	...	...	...	|	2145	...	...	|	...	...	...	...	...	...	...	...	...	|	|	...	...	...	0901	...
Toulouse a.	...	...	...	1623	...	...	...	1951	...	...	...	...	...	...	...	...	...	0514	0514	...	...	...	...	...
Bordeaux St Jean a.	...	...	...	1829	...	...	...	2157	...	...	...	...	...	...	...	...	...	0810	0810	...	...	...	...	...
Irún a.	...	...	...	...	...	...	...	...	...	...	...	...	...	...	...	...	...	...	1057	...	...	...	...	...

A – SALVADOR DALÍ *Train-hotel Elipsos* ②④⑦ Dec. 9 - June 15, daily June 17 - Sept. 2, ②④⑦ Sept. 4 - Dec. 13 from Barcelona; ①③⑤ Dec. 9 - June 16, daily June 18 - Sept. 3, ①③⑤ Sept. 5 - Dec. 13 from Milano: 🛏 1, 2 cl., 🛏 1, 2 cl. (T4), (1) (reclining) and 🍴 Barcelona - Milano and v.v. 🄡 special fares apply.
B – *CORAIL LUNÉA* – ▬ 1, 2 cl. and (2) (reclining) Bordeaux - Nice and v.v.
C – ⑤⑦ (also Dec. 22, 25–30, Jan. 1–6, Feb. 8 - Mar. 9, Mar. 24, Apr. 4 - May 4, May 7–12; not Mar. 23): *CORAIL LUNÉA* – ▬ 1, 2 cl. and (2) (reclining) Hendaye - Nice and Nice - Irún.
E – MONTE CARLO – 🛏 1, 2 cl. and ▬ 2 cl. (4 berth) Nice - Venezia and v.v.
F – MONTE CARLO – 🛏 1, 2 cl. and ▬ 2 cl. (4 berth) Nice - Roma and v.v.
G – CATALÁN TALGO. (12) and 🍴 Barcelona - Montpellier and v.v. Special fares payable.
T – (12) and 🍷 🄡 ⚡ Nice - Milano and v.v.

f – Not Dec. 24, 25, 31, Mar. 23, Apr. 24, 30, June 1.
n – 1046, 1050, 1051, 1057 on certain dates.
q – Depart up to 7 minutes earlier Jan. 3 - Feb. 22.
r – 0650 Jan. 7 - Feb. 8.
v – Firenze **SMN**.
y – Napoli **Campi Flegrei**.
z – Firenze **Campo di Marte**.
⚡ – Supplement payable.

BUDAPEST - ZAGREB - LJUBLJANA - VENEZIA — 91

train type/number	EC	EC 50		IC			IC 955	1203	856	EN 240	
train number	212	♣ 🄡	2207	200	525	702	IC 246	1822	204	♣ 🄡	
notes		V		840			🄡 T	P	M R	A	
Budapest Keleti d.	...	...	...	0605	...	...	1250d	...	1500	1700	...
Székesfehérvár d.	...	...	...	0723	...	...	1400	...	1619	1818	...
Siófok d.	...	...	...	0804	...	...	|	...	1701	1901	...
Fonyód d.	...	...	...	0849	...	...	|	...	1754	1952	...
Nagykanizsa d.	...	...	...	0950	...	...	|	1840	1904	2051	...
Gyékényes d.	...	...	...	1030	...	...	|	1937	|	2134	...
Zalaegerszeg d.	...	...	...	|	...	...	1642	|	|	|	...
Hodoš 🏛 a.	...	...	...	|	...	...	1727	|	|	|	...
Kotoriba 🏛 a.	...	...	...	|	...	...	|	|	1942	|	...
Koprivnica 🏛 a.	...	...	...	1044	...	...	|	1951	|	2148	...
Zagreb a.	0750	...	...	1201	1522	1715	|	2119	2222	2305	...
Rijeka a.	|	...	...	...	|	2111	|	|	...	|	...
Split a.	|	...	...	...	2048	...	|	0554	...	|	...
Dobova 🏛 a.	0819	...	...	...	▬	...	|	...	...	0004	...
Ljubljana a.	1010	1028	...	...	...	...	2131	...	...	0212	...
Villa Opicina 🏛 a.	...	1215	...	...	**2215**	...	...	...	...	0428	...
Monfalcone a.	...	1255	1331	...	1950	...	...	...	...	0542	...
Trieste Centrale a.	...	|	1354	...	2013	...	...	...	...	|	...
Venezia Santa Lucia a.	...	1421	...	...	...	...	...	...	...	0716	...

train type/number	EN 241	1822	205	IC 247			IC		EC 51		
train number	♣ 🄡	1202	855	IC 954	703	2452	201	2218	♣ 🄡	411	
notes	A	Q	M R	🄡 T			841		V		
Venezia Santa Lucia d.	2104	...	...	...	...	...	...	...	1544	...	...
Trieste Centrale d.	|	...	...	...	...	0854	...	1547	|	...	...
Monfalcone d.	2247	...	...	...	...	0917	...	1610	1706	...	...
Villa Opicina 🏛 d.	2348	...	...	...	...	▬	...	...	1750	...	...
Ljubljana d.	0200	...	...	0740	...	...	...	...	1948	2105	...
Dobova 🏛 d.	0349	...	...	|	...	**520**	...	...	...	2300	...
Split d.	|	2056	...	|	...	0737	...	...	...	|	...
Rijeka d.	|	|	...	|	0545	|	...	...	...	|	...
Zagreb d.	0456	0659	0720	|	0941	1307	1546	...	...	2329	...
Koprivnica 🏛 d.	0611	0817	|	|	...	...	1701	...	...	...	...
Kotoriba 🏛 d.	|	|	1005	|	...	...	|	...	...	...	...
Hodoš 🏛 d.	|	|	|	1141	...	...	|	...	...	...	...
Zalaegerszeg a.	|	|	|	1226	...	...	|	...	...	...	...
Gyékényes a.	0624	0830	|	|	...	...	1714	...	...	...	...
Nagykanizsa a.	0710	0909	1045	|	...	...	1758	...	...	...	...
Fonyód a.	0811	...	1203	|	...	...	1909	...	...	...	...
Siófok a.	0901	...	1253	|	...	...	1954	...	...	...	...
Székesfehérvár a.	0941	...	1336	1515	...	...	2036	...	...	...	...
Budapest Keleti a.	1058	...	1458	1623d	...	...	2153	...	...	...	...

A – VENEZIA – 🛏 1, 2 cl., ▬ 2 cl. and (2) Budapest - Venezia and v.v. (12) and 🍴 Budapest - Gyékényes and v.v. 🛏 1, 2 cl. Bucureşti - Venezia and v.v. ②③④⑥⑦: (2) Venezia - Budapest - Bucureşti. ①②④⑤⑦: (2) Bucureşti - Budapest - Venezia. ▬ 2 cl. Beograd - Ljubljana - Venezia and v.v.
M – MAESTRAL – (12) 🄡 Budapest - Zagreb and v.v.
P – JADRAN – June 22 - Sept. 7: 🛏 1, 2 cl., ▬ 2 cl. and (2) Praha - Split. Table **92**.
Q – JADRAN – June 23 - Sept. 8: 🛏 1, 2 cl., ▬ 2 cl. and (2) Split - Praha. Table **92**.
R – Conveys on dates shown in Table **97**: 🛏 1, 2 cl. Zagreb - Budapest - Kyïv / Moskva and v.v.

T – CITADELLA – (12) 🄡 Budapest - Hodoš - Murska Sobota - Ljubljana and v.v.
V – CASANOVA – (12) and 🍷 Venezia - Ljubljana and v.v.

d – Budapest **Déli**.
m – June 8 - Sept. 16.

♣ – Special fares payable for journeys to or from Italy.

92 BUDAPEST / ZAGREB - SARAJEVO

train number		397	259		399	391
notes		A	C ®		B	
Ljubljana	d.	...	...	...	...	...
Dobova 🏛	d.	...	...	...	...	...
Zagreb	d.	0857	...	...	2049	...
Sunja	d.	1022	...	...	2222	...
Volinja 🏛	d.	1103	...	...	2308	...
Dobrljin 🏛	d.	1129	...	...	2335	...
Novi Grad §	d.	1144	...	...	2351	...
Banja Luka	d.	1315	...	...	0124	...
Budapest Keleti	d.	|	0930	...	|	...
Dombóvár	d.	|	1141	...	|	...
Pécs	d.	|	1240	...	|	...
Magyarbóly 🏛	d.	|	1340	...	|	...
Beli Manastir 🏛	d.	|	1422	...	|	...
Osijek	d.	|	1454	...	|	...
Slavonski Šamac 🏛	d.	|	1621	...	|	...
Šamac 🏛	d.	|	1648	...	|	...
Doboj	d.	1512	1814	...	0326	...
Zenica	d.	1647	1951	...	0502	...
Sarajevo	a.	1805	2109	...	0620	...
Sarajevo	d.	1818	...	...	...	0645
Mostar	d.	2043	...	...	...	0906
Ploče	d.	2216	...	...	...	1041

train number		258	396	390	398	
notes		F ®	A		B	
Ploče	d.	...	0605	1700	...	...
Mostar	d.	...	0738	1840	...	...
Sarajevo	a.	...	1002	2059	...	...
Sarajevo	d.	0714	1027	...	2120	...
Zenica	d.	0834	1147	...	2240	...
Doboj	d.	1017	1329	...	0032	...
Šamac 🏛	d.	1144	|	...	|	...
Slavonski Šamac 🏛	d.	1209	|	...	|	...
Osijek	d.	1315	|	...	|	...
Beli Manastir 🏛	d.	1410	|	...	|	...
Magyarbóly 🏛	a.	1423	|	...	|	...
Pécs	a.	1518	|	...	|	...
Dombóvár	a.	1641	|	...	|	...
Budapest Keleti	a.	1903	|	...	|	...
Banja Luka	d.	...	1529	...	0221	...
Novi Grad §	d.	...	1657	...	0348	...
Dobrljin 🏛	d.	...	1728	...	0420	...
Volinja 🏛	d.	...	1756	...	0452	...
Sunja	d.	...	1823	...	0519	...
Zagreb	a.	...	1947	...	0643	...
Dobova 🏛	a.	...	...	...	...	...
Ljubljana	a.	...	...	...	...	...

train number		1203
notes		P
Praha Hlavní	d.	...
Havlíčkův Brod	d.	...
Brno Hlavní	d.	...
Břeclav	d.	...
Kúty 🏛	d.	...
Bratislava Hlavná	d.	...
Rajka 🏛	a.	...
Győr	a.	...
Szombathely	a.	...
Nagykanizsa	a.	...
Gyékényes 🏛	a.	...
Koprivnica 🏛	a.	...
Zagreb	a.	...
Split	a.	...

train number		1202
notes		Q
Split	d.	...
Zagreb	d.	...
Koprivnica 🏛	d.	...
Gyékényes 🏛	d.	...
Nagykanizsa	d.	...
Szombathely	d.	...
Győr	d.	...
Rajka 🏛	d.	...
Bratislava Hlavná	a.	...
Kúty 🏛	a.	...
Břeclav	a.	...
Brno Hlavní	a.	...
Havlíčkův Brod	a.	...
Praha Hlavní	a.	...

A – (1,2 cl.) Zagreb - Sarajevo - Ploče and v.v.
B – 🛏 2 cl. and (2 cl.) Zagreb - Sarajevo and v.v.
C – (1,2 cl.) ® Budapest (**802**) - Pécs (**812**) - Magyarbóly (**259**) - Sarajevo. ✕ Budapest - Pécs.
F – (1,2 cl.) ® Sarajevo (**258**) - Magyarbóly (**813**) - Pécs (**803**) - Budapest. ✕ Pécs - Budapest.
P – Train runs Summer only.
Q – Train runs Summer only.

§ – Formerly Bosanski Novi.

93 BERLIN - WARSZAWA - VILNIUS

train number		🚌		345	91001	194	
train number		99928			910		
notes		D		A		2	
Berlin Lichtenberg	d.	...	...	2138	...	...	...
Warszawa Centralna	a.	...	...	0550	...	...	...
Warszawa Centralna	d.	2300	...	|	0720	...	...
Warszawa Wschodnia	d.	|	...	0602	0729	...	...
Białystok	d.	0200	...	...	1009	...	...
Suwałki	d.	|	...	...	1241	...	...
Šeštokai 🏛 §	a.	|	...	...	1448	1503	...
Kaunas	a.	0720	...	...	...	1634	...
Vilnius	a.	0900	...	...	...	1749	...

train number		193	91002	344		🚌	
train number		2	910			99927	
notes				A		E	
Vilnius	d.	1147	...	...	...	2200	...
Kaunas	d.	1303	...	...	...	2330	...
Šeštokai 🏛 §	d.	1438	1508	...	...	|	...
Suwałki	a.	...	1516	...	...	|	...
Białystok	a.	...	1748	...	...	0220	...
Warszawa Wschodnia	a.	...	2020	2317	...	|	...
Warszawa Centralna	a.	...	2030	|	...	0500	...
Warszawa Centralna	d.	...	...	2330	...	...	...
Berlin Lichtenberg	a.	...	...	0714	...	...	...

A – 🛏 1,2 cl. and ▬ 2 cl. Berlin - Warszawa and v.v.
D – ①③⑤ (daily June 14 - Sept. 13) 🚌 run by PKP InterCity.
E – ②④⑥ (daily June 15 - Sept. 14) 🚌 run by PKP InterCity.
§ – 🏛 at Trakiszki / Mockava.

94 MOSKVA / St PETERBURG - WARSZAWA

train number					103					
notes		246	246		11008		9		346	11
		G	N		T		R		P	Q
Moskva Belorusskaya	d.	...	0800	...	...	...	1920	...	2109	2109
Smolensk Tsentralny 🏛	d.	...	1223	...	...	...	2359	...	0300	0300
St Peterburg Vitebski	d.	2340	|	...	...	...	|	...	|	|
Orsha Tsentralnaya	d.	1250j	1250	...	...	...	0050	...	0338	0338
Minsk	d.	1526	1526	...	2036	...	0332	...	0643	0643
Brest 🏛	d.	2115	2115	...	0240	...	0837	...	1250	1250
Terespol	a.	2033	2033	...	0158	...	0755	...	1208	1208
Warszawa Wschodnia	a.	0033	0033	...	0614	...	1133	...	1611	1611
Warszawa Centralna	a.	0045	0045	...	0630	...	1145	...	1750	...

train number							11011			
notes		347	12		10		104		247	247
		P	Q		R		T		M	H
Warszawa Centralna	d.	1045	...	...	1625	...	2035	...	2346	2346
Warszawa Wschodnia	d.	1208	1208	...	1635	...	2050	...	2358	2358
Terespol	d.	1555	1555	...	2008	...	0036	...	0330	0330
Brest 🏛	a.	1741	1741	...	2144	...	0222	...	0516	0516
Minsk	a.	2333	2333	...	0251	...	0801	...	1045	1045
Orsha Tsentralnaya	a.	0220	0220	...	0514	...	...	...	1330	1330c
St Peterburg Vitebski	a.	|	|	...	|	...	...	...	|	0618
Smolensk Tsentralny 🏛	a.	0456	0456	...	0733	...	...	...	1601	...
Moskva Belorusskaya	a.	1059	1059	...	1210	...	...	...	2035	...

G – ②③④⑥ Dec. 9, 2007 - May 22, 2008; ①②③④⑥⑦ May 25 - Oct. 2 (not Jan. 12, Feb. 23): 🛏 2 cl. St Peterburg (**19**) - Orsha (**13**) - Terespol (**246**) - Warszawa - Berlin (journey 2 nights).
H – ③④⑤⑦ Dec. 9, 2007 - May 23, 2008; ①②③④⑤⑦ May 25 - Oct. 3 (not Jan. 13, Feb. 24): 🛏 2 cl. Berlin (**247**) - Warszawa - Brest 🏛 (**14**) - Orsha (**20**) - St Peterburg (journey 2 nights).
M – MOSKVA EXPRESS – ③④⑤⑦ Dec. 9 - May 23, 2008; ①②③④⑤⑦ May 25 - Oct. 3 (not Jan. 13, Feb. 24): 🛏 1 cl. *Lux*, 🛏 1,2 cl. Berlin (**247**) - Warszawa - Brest 🏛 (**14**) - Moskva. ✕ Brest - Moskva.
N – MOSKVA EXPRESS – ②③④⑥ Dec. 9, 2007 - May 22, 2008; ①②③④⑥⑦ May 25 - Oct. 2 (not Jan. 12, Feb. 23): 🛏 1 cl. *Lux*, 🛏 1,2 cl. Moskva (**13**) - Terespol (**246**) - Warszawa - Berlin. ✕ Moskva - Brest.
P – JAN KIEPURA – 🛏 1,2 cl. Moskva - Warszawa - Köln - Amsterdam and v.v. (journey 2 nights; for timings of Basel, Amsterdam and München cars see Table **24**).
Q – OST–WEST – 🛏 1,2 cl. Warszawa - Moskva and v.v.
R – POLONEZ – 🛏 1,2 cl. Warszawa - Moskva and v.v.
T – 🛏 1,2 cl. Minsk - Warszawa and v.v.
c – Depart 1637.
j – Arrive 1046.

95 MOSKVA / St PETERBURG - WIEN, BRATISLAVA, BUDAPEST and PRAHA

train number			208	208	208	208	208	
notes			B	V	J	C	F	
Moskva Belorusskaya	d.	...	...	2344	2344	2344	2344	...
Smolensk Tsentralny 🏛	d.	...	...	0508	0508	0508	0508	...
St Peterburg Vitebski	d.	...	1500	|	|	|	|	...
Orsha Tsentralnaya	d.	...	0123	0542	0542	0542	0542	...
Minsk	d.	...	0408	0824	0824	0824	0824	...
Brest 🏛	d.	...	1440x	1440z	1440z	1440z	1440z	...
Terespol	a.	...	1358	1358	1358	1358	1358	...
Katowice	a.	...	2230	2230	2230	2230	2230	...
Bohumín 🏛	a.	...	0015	0015	0015	0015	0015	...
Ostrava Hlavní	a.	...	0043	0043	0043	0222	0222	...
Břeclav	a.	...	|	|	|	0430	0430	...
Wien Südbahnhof	a.	...	|	|	|	0603	|	...
Bratislava Hlavná	a.	...	|	|	|	...	0541	...
Budapest Keleti	a.	...	|	|	|	...	0832	...
Olomouc	a.	...	0151	0151	0151	...	...	...
Pardubice	a.	...	0338	0338	0338	...	...	...
Praha Hlavní	a.	...	0503	0503	0503e	...	...	...
Karlovy Vary	a.	...	...	...	1047	...	...	...
Cheb	a.	...	...	...	1141	...	...	...

train number			209	209	209	209	209	
notes			G	H	K	W	D	
Cheb	d.	...	...	...	1615	...	...	...
Karlovy Vary	d.	...	...	...	1707	...	...	...
Praha Hlavní	d.	...	...	...	2256f	2256	2256	...
Pardubice	d.	...	...	...	0014	0014	0014	...
Olomouc	d.	...	...	...	0154	0154	0154	...
Budapest Keleti	d.	...	2000	...	|	|	|	...
Bratislava Hlavná	d.	...	2251	...	|	|	|	...
Wien Südbahnhof	d.	...	|	2233	|	|	|	...
Břeclav	d.	...	0005	0005	|	|	|	...
Ostrava Hlavní	d.	...	0204	0204	0300	0300	0300	...
Bohumín 🏛	d.	...	0333	0333	0333	0333	0333	...
Katowice	d.	...	0510	0510	0510	0510	0510	...
Terespol	d.	...	1318	1318	1318	1318	1318	...
Brest 🏛	a.	...	1504c	1504c	1504c	1504c	1504c	...
Minsk	a.	...	2102	2102	2102	2102	2102	...
Orsha Tsentralnaya	a.	...	2340	2340	2340	2340	2340	...
St Peterburg Vitebski	a.	...	|	|	|	|	1243	...
Smolensk Tsentralny 🏛	a.	...	0215	0215	0215	0215	...	...
Moskva Belorusskaya	a.	...	0824	0824	0824	0824	...	...

B – ③④ Dec. 9 - June 5; ①③④⑥ June 7 - Sept. 22; ③④ Sept. 24 - Dec. 13: 🛏 1,2 cl. St Peterburg (**49**) - Terespol (**208**) - Praha (journey 2 nights).
C – CHOPIN – 🛏 1,2 cl. Moskva (**21**) - Terespol (**208**) - Katowice - Bohumín (**203**) - Wien (journey 2 nights).
D – ⑤⑥ Dec. 9 - June 7; ①③⑤⑥ June 9 - Sept. 24; ⑤⑥ Sept. 26 - Dec. 13: 🛏 1,2 cl. Praha (**209**) - Brest (**22**) - Orsha (**61/62**) - St Peterburg (journey 2 nights).
F – 🛏 1,2 cl. Moskva (**21**) - Terespol (**208**) - Katowice - Bohumín (**203**) - Břeclav (**377**) - Bratislava - Budapest (journey 2 nights).
G – 🛏 1,2 cl. Budapest (**376**) - Bratislava - Břeclav (**202**) - Bohumín (**209**) - Katowice - Brest (**22**) - Moskva (journey 2 nights).
H – CHOPIN – 🛏 1,2 cl. Wien (**202**) - Bohumín (**209**) - Katowice - Brest (**22**) - Moskva (journey 2 nights).
J – 🛏 1,2 cl. Moskva - Praha (**604**) - Cheb (journey 2 nights). ✕ Moskva - Brest.
K – 🛏 1,2 cl. Cheb (**605**) - Praha - Moskva (journey 2 nights). ✕ Brest - Moskva.
V – VLTAVA – 🛏 1,2 cl. Moskva (**21**) - Terespol (**208**) - Praha (journey 2 nights). ✕ Moskva - Brest.
W – VLTAVA – 🛏 1,2 cl. Praha (**209**) - Brest (**22**) - Moskva (journey 2 nights). ✕ Brest - Moskva.

c – Depart 1707.
e – Depart 0725.
f – Arrive 2035.
x – Arrive 1242.
z – Arrive 1215.

PRAHA, WIEN and WROCŁAW - KYÏV — 96

train number	EC	609	609			73100/1	33011	
train number	121	8	8		201	51	35	
notes	✕	A	X		C	P	R✣	
Praha Hlavní d.	1106	...	...	...	2124	...	...	...
Pardubice d.	1219	...	...	...	2241	...	...	...
Česká Třebová d.	1300	...	...	...	2324	...	...	...
Olomouc d.	1357	...	...	...	0026	...	...	...
Wien Südbahnhof d.	|	1128	1128	...	|	...	...	...
Bratislava Hlavná d.	|	1347	1347	...	|	...	...	...
Žilina d.	1631	1640	1640	...	|	...	...	...
Košice a.	1921	1950	1950	...	|	...	...	...
Košice d.	...	2007	2007	...	|	...	...	...
Čierna nad Tisou ▣ a.	...	2156	2156	...	|	...	...	...
Chop ▣ a.	...	2306	2306	...	|	...	...	...
Bohumín ▣ d.	...	|	|	...	0307	...	...	...
Zebrzydowice ▣ d.	...	|	|	...	0331	...	...	...
Wrocław Główny d.	...	|	|	...	|	0915	...	...
Katowice d.	...	|	|	...	|	1215	...	...
Kraków Główny d.	...	|	|	...	1319e	1405	2128	...
Przemyśl a.	...	|	|	...	1705	1735	0050	...
Przemyśl d.	...	|	|	...	1925	1925	0120	...
Mostiska II ◐ d.	...	|	|	...	2222	2222	0327	...
Lviv a.	...	0859	0859	...	2346	2346	0448	...
Kyïv a.	...	2007	*2007*	...	1024	1024	1438	...

train number	33012	37100/1			7	7		
train number	36	51/52	200		422	422	422	
notes	S✣	Q	D		B	Y	E	
Kyïv d.	2241	2041	2041	...	2356	*2356*	...	...
Lviv d.	0835	0718	0718	...	1000	1000	...	...
Mostiska II ◐ d.	1028	0940	0940	...	|	|	...	...
Przemyśl a.	1003	0935	0935	...	|	|	...	...
Przemyśl d.	1038	1115	1158	...	|	|	...	...
Kraków Główny a.	1350	1445	1544c	...	|	|	...	...
Katowice a.	...	1636	|	...	|	|	...	...
Wrocław Główny a.	...	1925	|	...	|	|	...	...
Zebrzydowice ▣ a.	...	...	0047	...	|	|	...	...
Bohumín ▣ a.	...	...	0109	...	|	|	...	...
Chop ▣ d.	...	...	|	...	1850	1850	...	...
Čierna nad Tisou ▣ d.	...	...	|	...	2020	2020	...	...
Košice a.	...	...	|	...	2200	2200	...	...
Košice d.	...	...	|	...	2222	2222	2222	...
Žilina a.	...	...	|	...	0125	0125	0125	...
Bratislava Hlavná a.	...	...	|	...	0530	0530	|	...
Wien Südbahnhof a.	...	...	|	...	0658	0658	|	...
Olomouc a.	...	...	0337	...	...	...	0526	...
Česká Třebová a.	...	...	0441	...	...	...	0627	...
Pardubice a.	...	...	0526	...	...	...	0705	...
Praha Hlavní a.	...	...	0645	...	...	...	0829	...

A – ①②④⑤⑦: 🛏 1, 2 cl. Wien (**2520**) - Bratislava (**609**) - Košice (**8815**) - Čierna nad Tisou (**8860**) - Chop (**8**) - Kyïv.
B – ②③⑤⑥⑦: 🛏 1, 2 cl. Kyïv (**7**) - Chop (**8865**) - Čierna nad Tisou (**8814**) - Košice (**422**) - Žilina (**706**) - Bratislava (**2507**) - Wien (journey 2 nights).
C – 🛏 1, 2 cl. Praha (**201**) - Kraków (**7310**) - Przemyśl (**52**) - Kyïv (journey 2 nights). 🛏 1, 2 cl., ▬ 2 cl. and [12] Praha - Kraków.
D – 🛏 1, 2 cl. Kyïv (**51**) - Przemyśl (**3710**) - Kraków (**200**) - Praha (journey 2 nights). 🛏 1, 2 cl., ▬ 2 cl. and [12] Kraków - Praha.
E – CASSOVIA – 🛏 1, 2 cl., ▬ 2 cl. and [2] Košice - Žilina - Praha.
R – ✣ JÓZEF CHEŁMOŃSKI ③⑤⑦: 🛏 2 cl. Kraków - Kyïv.
S – ✣ JÓZEF CHEŁMOŃSKI ②④⑥: 🛏 2 cl. Kyïv - Kraków.
P – ①②④⑥⑦: 🛏 2 cl. Wrocław - Kyïv.
Q – ①②③⑤⑦: 🛏 2 cl. Kyïv - Wrocław.
X – ③⑥: 🛏 1, 2 cl. Wien - Lviv.
Y – ②⑤: 🛏 1, 2 cl. Lviv - Wien.
c – Depart 2225.
e – Arrive 0622.
◐ – ▣ at Medyka / Mostiska II (Table 1056).
✣ – A change of train may be necessary at the border.

MOSKVA - BUDAPEST, VENEZIA, BEOGRAD and ATHÍNAI — 97

train type/number	15	335	IC		15	15	15	EN 240
notes			55					R ✓
notes	A	M	✕✓		K	Y	Q	C
Moskva Kiyevskaya d.	2131	...	...	...	2131	...	2131	...
Minsk d.	|	...	...	...	|	...	|	...
Kyïv d.	0953	...	...	...	0953	0953	0953	...
Lviv d.	2030	...	...	...	2030	2030	2030	...
Chop ▣ d.	0500	...	...	...	0500	0500	0500	...
Debrecen a.	0647	...	...	...	0647	0647	0647	...
Szolnok a.	0819	...	...	...	0819	0819	0819	...
Budapest Keleti a.	0947	...	...	...	0947	0947	0947	...
Budapest Keleti d.	1320	...	...	...	1500	1500	1700	1700
Siófok a.	|	...	...	...	1659	1659	1858	1858
Zagreb a.	|	...	...	...	2232	2232	2305	2305
Ljubljana a.	|	...	...	...	...	...	0212	0212
Trieste Centrale a.	|	...	...	...	...	...	|	|
Venezia Santa Lucia a.	|	...	...	...	...	...	0716	0716
Subotica ▣ a.	1648	...	...	...	...	...	...	...
Novi Sad a.	1904	...	...	...	...	...	...	...
Beograd a.	2055	2220	...	...	...	...	...	...
Niš a.	...	0224	...	...	...	...	...	...
Skopje ⊖ a.	...	0729	...	...	...	...	...	...
Thessaloníki ⊡ a.	...	1307	1454	...	...	...	...	...
Athína Lárisa a.	...	...	1949	...	...	...	...	...

train type/number	EN241	16	16	16		IC	334	16	
notes	R ✓					52			
notes	C	R	L	Z		✕✓	M	B	
Athína Lárisa d.	...	...	...	...	...	1051	...	...	...
Thessaloníki ⊡ d.	...	...	...	...	...	1546	1615	...	...
Skopje ⊖ d.	...	...	...	...	...	...	2006	...	...
Niš d.	...	...	...	...	...	...	0105	...	...
Beograd d.	...	...	...	...	...	...	0506	0645	...
Novi Sad d.	...	...	...	...	...	...	...	0934	...
Subotica ▣ d.	...	...	...	...	...	...	...	1200	...
Venezia Santa Lucia d.	2104	2104	...	...	...	...	...	|	...
Trieste Centrale d.	|	|	...	...	...	...	...	|	...
Ljubljana d.	0200	0200	...	...	...	...	...	|	...
Zagreb d.	0456	0456	0720	0720	...	...	...	|	...
Siófok d.	0903	0903	1255	1255	...	...	...	|	...
Budapest Keleti a.	1058	1058	1458	1458	...	...	...	1409	...
Budapest Keleti d.	...	1815	1815	1815	...	...	...	1815	...
Szolnok d.	...	1939	1939	1939	...	...	...	1939	...
Debrecen d.	...	2105	2105	2105	...	...	...	2105	...
Chop ▣ a.	...	0058	0058	0058	...	...	...	0058	...
Lviv a.	...	0914	0914	0914	...	...	...	0914	...
Kyïv a.	...	2001	2001	2001	...	...	...	2001	...
Minsk a.	...	|	|	...	...	...	...	|	...
Moskva Kiyevskaya a.	...	1000	1000	...	...	...	...	1000	...

A – TISZA – 🛏 2 cl. Moskva (**15**) - Záhony (**629**) - Budapest (**794**) - Kelebia (**345**) - Beograd (journey 2 nights).
B – TISZA – 🛏 2 cl. Beograd (**344**) - Kelebia (**793**) - Budapest (**628**) - Chop (**16**) - Moskva (journey 2 nights).
C – VENEZIA – 🛏 1, 2 cl., ▬ 2 cl. and [2] Budapest - Ljubljana - Venezia and v.v.
K – ②④⑥: 🛏 1, 2 cl. Moskva - Kyïv - Chop - Budapest (**856**) - Murakeresztúr (**204**) - Zagreb (journey 2 nights).
L – ②⑤⑦: 🛏 1, 2 cl. Zagreb (**205**) - Murakeresztúr (**855**) - Budapest (**628**) - Chop (**16**) - Kyïv - Moskva (journey 2 nights).
M – HELLAS EXPRESS – 🛏 1, 2 cl., ▬ 2 cl. and [12] Beograd - Thessaloníki and v.v. 🛏 1, 2 cl., ▬ 2 cl. and [2] Beograd - Skopje and v.v.
Q – ⑦: 🛏 1, 2 cl. Moskva - Venezia. (3 nights).
R – ③: 🛏 1, 2 cl. Venezia - Moskva. (3 nights).
Y – ④: 🛏 1, 2 cl. Kyïv - Zagreb.
Z – ⑥: 🛏 1, 2 cl. Zagreb - Kyïv.
⊖ – ▣ at Preševo / Tabanovci.
⊡ – ▣ at Gevgelija / Idomeni.
✓ – R with supplement payable.

MOSKVA - BUCUREŞTI, SOFIYA and ISTANBUL — 98

train number	101		76	76	86			59	59	59
train number	1003	491	59	1183	383	383	383	1181	1183	383
notes	R	M	F	W	N	B	A	V	K	X
Moskva Kiyevskaya d.	...	...	...	...	...	2139	0025	0025	0025	0025
Minsk d.	1737	...	...	...	2050	|	|	|	|	|
Kyïv d.	|	...	...	...	1404	1540	1404	1404	1404	1404
Lviv d.	0657	...	2246	2246	|	|	|	|	|	|
Zhmerynka d.	|	...	|	|	|	|	|	|	|	|
Chernivtsi d.	1230	...	0704	0704	0704	0704	0704	0704	0704	0704
Vadul Siret ▣ d.	1530	...	1020	1020	1020	1020	1020	1020	1020	1020
Chişinău d.	|	...	|	|	|	|	|	|	|	|
Ungheni ▣ d.	|	...	|	|	|	|	|	|	|	|
Bucureşti Nord a.	0053	1253	1953	1953	1953	1953	1953	1953	1953	1953
Ruse ▣ a.	0430	1540	2230	2230	2230	2230	2230	2230	2230	2230
Varna a.	0920	|	|	|	|	|	|	0615	|	|
Burgas a.	...	|	|	0845	|	|	|	...	0845	|
Sofiya a.	...	|	0605	...	0605	0605	0605	...	...	0605
Thessaloníki a.	...	|	...	...	...	...	...	...	...	1530
Kapikule ▣ a.	...	0135	...	...	...	...	...	...	...	...
Istanbul Sirkeci a.	...	0800	...	...	...	...	...	...	...	...

train number	1004		1180	1182			382	382	1182	
train number	102	382	382	382	382	382	85	604	60	490
notes	Z	Y	Q	S	C	D	P	U	T	G
Istanbul Sirkeci d.	...	...	...	...	...	...	...	...	...	2200
Kapikule ▣ d.	...	...	...	...	...	...	...	...	...	0405
Thessaloníki d.	...	0753	...	...	...	...	...	...	...	|
Sofiya d.	...	1930	...	...	1930	1930	1930	1930	...	|
Burgas d.	...	|	...	1935	|	|	|	|	1935	|
Varna d.	2040	|	2240	|	|	|	|	|	|	|
Ruse ▣ d.	0105	0315	0315	0315	0315	0315	0315	0315	0315	1445
Bucureşti Nord d.	0403	0638	0638	0638	0638	0638	0638	0638	0638	1709
Ungheni ▣ a.	|	|	|	|	|	|	|	|	|	...
Chişinău a.	|	|	|	|	|	|	|	|	|	...
Vadul Siret ▣ a.	1305	1510	1510	1510	1510	1510	1510	1510	1510	...
Chernivtsi a.	1613	1816	1816	1816	1816	1816	1816	1816	1816	...
Zhmerynka a.	|	|	|	|	|	|	|	|	|	...
Lviv a.	2236	|	|	|	|	|	|	0805	0805	...
Kyïv a.	|	0928	0928	0928	0926	0942x	1818	...	...	...
Minsk a.	1158	|	|	|	|	|	0601	...	...	...
Moskva Kiyevskaya a.	...	2236	2236	2236	2236	0533	...	...	...	...

A – BULGARIA EXPRESS – June 5 - Sept 3: 🛏 1, 2 cl. Moskva (**59**) - Vadul Siret (**383**) - Bucureşti - Sofiya.
B – BULGARIA EXPRESS – Dec. 10 - June 3, Sept. 3 - Dec. 5: 🛏 1, 2 cl. Moskva (**3**) - Kyïv (**59**) - Vadul Siret (**383**) - Bucureşti - Ruse (**4663**) - Sofiya.
C – BULGARIA EXPRESS – June 7 - Sept. 5: 🛏 1, 2 cl. Sofiya (**382**) - Bucureşti - Vadul Siret (**60**) - Moskva.
D – BULGARIA EXPRESS – Dec. 10 - June 6, Sept. 6 - Dec. 8: 🛏 1, 2 cl. Sofiya (**60**) - Ruse (**382**) - Bucureşti - Vadul Siret (**60**) - Kyïv (**42**) - Moskva.
F – ①④⑥ Dec. 10 - June 4; Sept. 3 - Dec. 6: 🛏 2 cl. Lviv (**76**) - Chernivtsi (**59**) - Vadul Siret (**383**) - Bucureşti - Ruse ▣ (**4665**) - Sofiya.
G – 🛏 1, 2 cl. and ▬ 2 cl. Istanbul (**81032**) - Kapikule ▣ (**490**) - Ruse ▣ (**462**) - Bucureşti.
K – ④⑥ June 7 - Sept. 1: 🛏 2 cl. Moskva (**59**) - Vadul Siret (**383**) - Bucureşti - Ruse ▣ (**1183**) - Burgas.
M – 🛏 1, 2 cl. and ▬ 2 cl. Bucureşti (**463**) - Ruse ▣ (**491**) - Kapikule ▣ (**81031**) - Istanbul.
N – ⑥ (also ② June 2 - Sept. 4): 🛏 2 cl. Minsk (**86**) - Kyïv (**59**) - Sofiya.
P – ② (also ⑤ June 8 - Sept. 7): 🛏 2 cl. Sofiya (**382**) - Kyïv (**85**) - Minsk.
Q – ②③④⑤⑦ June 7 - Sept. 5: 🛏 2 cl. Varna (**1180**) - Ruse ▣ (**382**) - Bucureşti - Vadul Siret (**60**) - Moskva.
R – ③ June 13 - Sept. 19: 🛏 2 cl. Minsk - Varna.
S – ①⑥ June 9 - Sept. 3: 🛏 2 cl. Burgas (**1182**) - Ruse ▣ (**382**) - Bucureşti - Vadul Siret (**60**) - Moskva.
T – ①⑥ June 9 - Sept. 3: 🛏 2 cl. Burgas - Lviv.
U – ①③⑥ Dec. 10 - June 4; Sept. 8 - Dec. 8: 🛏 2 cl. Sofiya (**60**) - Ruse ▣ (**382**) - Bucureşti - Vadul Siret (**60**) - Chernivtsi (**604**) - Lviv.
V – ①②③⑤⑦ June 5 - Sept. 3: 🛏 2 cl. Moskva (**59**) - Vadul Siret (**383**) - Bucureşti - Ruse ▣ (**1181**) - Varna.
W – ④⑥ June 7 - Sept. 1: 🛏 2 cl. Lviv - Burgas.
X – ④ June 7 - Aug. 30: 🛏 2 cl. Moskva - Thessaloníki.
Y – ⑦ June 10 - Sept. 2: 🛏 2 cl. Thessaloníki - Moskva.
Z – ⑤ June 15 - Sept. 21: 🛏 2 cl. Varna - Minsk.
x – Depart 1430.

99 WARSZAWA, WROCŁAW, KRAKÓW - PRAHA, WIEN, BUDAPEST and BUCUREŞTI

train type/number	*EC*	*EC*	*EC*			*EC/Ex*		*EC*		*EC*	*EC*	*EC*		200								
train number	**108**	**108**	**103**	**277**	**624**	**383**	**38104**	**106**	**27100**	**105**	**175**	**142**	**4411**	**203**	**200**	**200**	**203**	**203**	**203**			
notes	[R]	**103**	[R]	**1203**	✕	✕	**38105**	[R]	**27101**	[R]	✕	✕	**333**	**377**	**203**		**377**	[R]	**200**			
notes	⊡	[R]⊡	✕⊡					✕⊡		✕⊡		⌿					[R]		[R]			
notes	**V**	**W**	**R**			**D**		**X**		**Y**			**p**	**A**	**E**	**S**	**B**	**C**	**Q**			
Warszawa Wschodnia d.	...	...	0548	...	...	0853	...	0858	...	1043	...	...	...	...	...	...	2053	2053	2053	...	...	...
Warszawa Centralna d.	...	...	0600	...	...	0905	...	0910	...	1100	...	...	...	...	...	...	2105	2105	2105	...	...	...
Wrocław Główny d.	...	...	|	...	...	|	...	|	...	|	...	...	...	...	...	...	|	|	|	...	...	...
Lichkov 🏛 d.	...	...	|	...	...	|	...	|	...	|	...	...	...	...	...	...	|	|	|	...	...	...
Kraków Gł. d.	0700	0700	|	...	...	1210	0953	|	1053	|	...	...	...	2225	2225	2225	|	|	|	...	...	...
Tarnów d.	|	|	|	...	...	1311	|	|	|	|	...	...	...	|	|	|	|	|	|	...	...	...
Katowice d.	|	|	0832	...	...	|	1136	1150	1236	1332	...	...	1510	|	|	|	2352	2352	2352	...	...	...
Zebrzydowice 🏛 d.	0919	0919	0943	...	...	|	...	1304	...	1443	...	...	|	0048	0048	0048	0103	0103	0103	...	...	...
Bohumín 🏛 a.	0938	0938	1002	...	...	|	...	1324	...	1502	...	...	|	0109	0109	0109	0121	0121	0121	...	...	...
Bohumín 🏛 d.	0950	1014	1014	...	...	|	...	1350	...	1514	...	...	|	0213	0213	0220	0213	0213	0220	...	...	...
Zwardoń 🏛 a.	|	|	|	...	...	|	...	|	...	|	...	...	1805	|	|	|	|	|	|	...	...	...
Skalité 🏛 a.	|	|	|	...	...	|	...	|	...	|	...	...	1838	|	|	|	|	|	|	...	...	...
Čadca 🏛 a.	|	|	|	...	...	|	...	|	...	|	...	...	1856	|	|	|	|	|	|	...	...	...
Žilina a.	|	|	|	...	...	|	...	|	...	|	...	...	1927	|	|	|	|	|	|	...	...	...
Ostrava Hlavní a.	0959	1022	1022	...	...	|	...	1359	...	1522	...	1601	...	0222	0222	0229	0222	0222	0229	...	...	...
Přerov a.	|	1111	1111	...	1143	|	...	|	...	1611	...	|	...	0315	0315	|	0315	0315	|	...	...	...
Olomouc a.	1104	|	|	...	1157	|	...	1504	...	|	...	1704	...	|	|	0337	|	|	0337	...	...	...
Pardubice a.	1241	|	|	...	1354	|	...	1641	...	|	...	1841	...	|	|	0526	|	|	0526	...	...	...
Praha Hlavní a.	1400	|	|	...	1519	|	...	1800	...	|	...	1959	...	|	|	0645	|	|	0645	...	...	...
Břeclav a.	...	1214	1214	1220	...	|	...	...	...	1714	1852	...	...	0430	0430	...	0430	0430	...	...	...	...
Wien Südbahnhof a.	...	1328	1328	|	...	|	...	...	...	1828	|	...	...	|	0603	...	|	0603	...	...	...	...
Kúty 🏛 a.	...	...	...	1232	...	|	...	...	...	...	1904	...	...	0502	...	...	0502	...	...	...	...	...
Bratislava Hlavná a.	...	...	...	1318	...	|	...	...	...	...	1942	...	...	0541	...	...	0541	...	...	...	...	...
Štúrovo 🏛 a.	...	...	...	...	...	|	...	...	...	...	2104	...	...	0704	...	...	0704	...	...	...	...	...
Plaveč 🏛 a.	...	...	...	...	...	1620	...	...	...	...	|	...	...	|	...	...	|	...	...	...	...	...
Košice a.	...	...	...	...	...	1800	...	...	...	...	|	...	...	|	...	...	|	...	...	...	...	...
Hidasnémeti 🏛 a.	...	...	...	...	...	1825	...	...	...	...	|	...	...	|	...	...	|	...	...	...	...	...
Miskolc a.	...	...	...	...	...	1926	...	...	...	...	|	...	...	|	...	...	|	...	...	...	...	...
Budapest Keleti a.	...	...	...	...	...	2127	...	...	...	...	2232	...	...	0832	...	...	0832	...	...	...	...	...
Budapest Nyugati a.	...	...	...	...	...	...	...	...	...	...	...	...	...	...	...	...	...	...	...	...	...	...
Szolnok a.	...	...	...	...	...	...	...	...	...	...	...	...	...	...	...	...	...	...	...	...	...	...
Curtici 🏛 a.	...	...	...	...	...	...	...	...	...	...	...	...	...	...	...	...	...	...	...	...	...	...
Arad a.	...	...	...	...	...	...	...	...	...	...	...	...	...	...	...	...	...	...	...	...	...	...
Bucureşti Nord a.	...	...	...	...	...	...	...	...	...	...	...	...	...	...	...	...	...	...	...	...	...	...
Varna a.	...	...	...	...	...	...	...	...	...	...	...	...	...	...	...	...	...	...	...	...	...	...
Burgas a.	...	...	...	...	...	...	...	...	...	...	...	...	...	...	...	...	...	...	...	...	...	...

train type/number		*EC*	*EC*	*EC*		*EC*		*EC/Ex*	*SC*		*EC*	*EC*	*EC*						376			
train number	**332**	**143**	**174**	**104**	**72100**	**107**	**83100**	**382**	**509**	**276**	**102**	**102**	**109**	**202**	**202**	**201**	**201**	**376**	**202**			
notes	**4412**	✕	✕	[R]	**72101**	[R]	**83101**	✕	✕	**1202**	[R]	**109**	[R]	[R]	**201**	**202**		**203**	**201**			
notes		⌿		✕⊡		✕⊡			⌿		✕⊡	[R]⊡	⊡			[R]						
notes	**q**			**Y**		**X**		**D**			**R**	**W**	**V**	**C**	**E**	**Q**	**S**	**B**	**F**			
Burgas d.	...	...	...	...	...	...	...	...	...	...	...	...	...	...	...	...	...	...	...	...	...	...
Varna d.	...	...	...	...	...	...	...	...	...	...	...	...	...	...	...	...	...	...	...	...	...	...
Bucureşti Nord d.	...	...	...	...	...	...	...	...	...	...	...	...	...	...	...	...	...	...	...	...	...	...
Arad d.	...	...	...	...	...	...	...	...	...	...	...	...	...	...	...	...	...	...	...	...	...	...
Curtici 🏛 d.	...	...	...	...	...	...	...	...	...	...	...	...	...	...	...	...	...	...	...	...	...	...
Szolnok d.	...	...	...	...	...	...	...	...	...	...	...	...	...	...	...	...	...	...	...	...	...	...
Budapest Nyugati d.	...	...	...	...	...	...	...	...	...	...	...	...	...	...	...	...	...	...	...	...	...	...
Budapest Keleti d.	...	...	0530	...	...	...	...	0835	...	...	...	...	...	...	...	...	...	2000	2000	...	...	...
Miskolc d.	...	...	|	...	...	...	...	1034	...	...	...	...	...	...	...	...	...	|	|	...	...	...
Hidasnémeti 🏛 d.	...	...	|	...	...	...	...	1132	...	...	...	...	...	...	...	...	...	|	|	...	...	...
Košice d.	...	...	|	...	...	...	...	1155	...	...	...	...	...	...	...	...	...	|	|	...	...	...
Plaveč 🏛 d.	...	...	|	...	...	...	...	1330	...	...	...	...	...	...	...	...	...	|	|	...	...	...
Štúrovo 🏛 d.	...	...	0653	...	...	...	...	|	...	...	...	...	...	...	...	...	...	2120	2120	...	...	...
Bratislava Hlavná d.	...	...	0815	...	...	...	...	|	...	1444	...	...	...	...	...	...	...	2251	2251	...	...	...
Kúty 🏛 d.	...	...	0853	...	...	...	...	|	...	1530	...	...	...	...	...	...	...	2330	2330	...	...	...
Wien Südbahnhof d.	...	...	|	0908	...	...	...	|	...	|	1433	1433	...	2233	2233	...	...	|	|	...	...	...
Břeclav d.	...	...	0905	1019	...	...	...	|	...	1542	1552	1552	...	0005	0005	...	...	0005	0005	...	...	...
Praha Hlavní d.	...	0806	...	|	...	1006	...	|	1323h	...	|	|	1406	|	|	2124	2124	|	|	...	...	...
Pardubice d.	...	0923	...	|	...	1123	...	|	1421	...	|	|	1519	|	|	2241	2241	|	|	...	...	...
Olomouc d.	...	1057	...	|	...	1257	...	|	1540	...	|	|	1657	|	|	0026	0026	|	|	...	...	...
Přerov d.	...	|	...	1120	...	|	...	|	|	...	1652	1652	|	0110	0110	|	|	0110	0110	...	...	...
Ostrava Hlavní d.	...	1200	...	1213	...	1404	...	|	1635	...	1747	1747	1802	0204	0204	0135	0135	0204	0204	...	...	...
Žilina d.	0850	|	...	|	...	|	...	|	...	...	|	|	|	|	|	|	|	|	|	...	...	...
Čadca 🏛 d.	0921	|	...	|	...	|	...	|	...	...	|	|	|	|	|	|	|	|	|	...	...	...
Skalité 🏛 a.	0938	|	...	|	...	|	...	|	...	...	|	|	|	|	|	|	|	|	|	...	...	...
Zwardoń 🏛 a.	0952	|	...	|	...	|	...	|	...	...	|	|	|	|	|	|	|	|	|	...	...	...
Bohumín 🏛 a.	|	1210	...	1221	...	1412	...	|	...	...	1755	1755	1810	0213	0213	0144	0144	0213	0213	...	...	...
Bohumín 🏛 d.	|	...	...	1234	...	1434	...	|	...	...	1813	1826	1826	0251	0307	0251	0307	0251	0307	...	...	...
Zebrzydowice 🏛 d.	|	...	...	1256	...	1456	...	|	...	...	1834	1848	1848	0315	0331	0315	0331	0315	0331	...	...	...
Katowice a.	1245	...	...	1355	1515	1556	1615	|	...	...	1932	|	|	0418	|	0418	|	0418	|	...	...	...
Tarnów a.	...	...	...	|	|	|	|	1645	...	...	|	|	|	|	|	|	|	|	|	...	...	...
Kraków Gł. a.	...	...	...	|	1655	|	1755	1745	...	...	|	2119	2119	|	0622	|	0622	|	0622	...	...	...
Lichkov 🏛 a.	...	...	...	|	...	|	...	|	...	...	|	...	...	|	...	|	...	|	...	...	...	...
Wrocław Główny a.	...	...	...	|	...	|	...	|	...	...	|	...	...	|	...	|	...	|	...	...	...	...
Warszawa Centralna a.	...	...	...	1640	...	1840	...	2049	...	...	2215	...	...	0705	...	0705	...	0705	...	...	...	...
Warszawa Wschodnia a.	...	...	...	1652	...	1852	...	2101	...	...	2227	...	...	0717	...	0717	...	0717	...	...	...	...

A – 🛏 1, 2 cl. and 🛌 2 cl. Kraków (**200**) - Petrovice (**203**) - Břeclav (**377**) - Budapest.

B – 🛏 1, 2 cl., 🛌 2 cl. and (2) Warszawa - Bratislava - Budapest and v.v. 🛏 1, 2 cl. Moskva - Budapest and v.v.

C – CHOPIN – 🛏 1, 2 cl., 🛌 2 cl. and (2) Warszawa - Wien and v.v. 🛏 1, 2 cl. Moskva - Wien and v.v..

D – JÓZEF BEM – (12) and ✕ Warszawa - Kraków - Košice - Budapest and v.v.

E – 🛏 1, 2 cl. (also 🛌 2 cl. Apr. 29 - Sept. 27 from Kraków; Apr. 30 - Sept. 28 from Wien) Kraków - Wien and v.v.

F – 🛏 1, 2 cl. and 🛌 2 cl. Budapest (**376**) - Břeclav (**202**) - Petrovice (**201**) - Kraków.

Q – 🛏 1, 2 cl., 🛌 2 cl. and (2) Warszawa - Praha and v.v.

R – POLONIA – (12) and ✕ Warszawa - Wien and v.v.

S – SILESIA – 🛏 1, 2 cl., 🛌 2 cl. and (12) Kraków - Praha and v.v.

V – COMENIUS – (12) and ✕ Kraków - Praha and v.v.

W – (2) and ✕ Kraków - Wien and v.v.

X – PRAHA – (12) and ✕ Warszawa - Praha and v.v.

Y – SOBIESKI – (12) and ✕ Warszawa - Wien and v.v.

h – Praha **Holešovice**.

p – Not Dec. 24, 25, 26, 31, Mar. 22, 23.

q – Not Dec. 24, 25, 26, Jan. 1, Mar. 22, 23.

◇ – Local train, second class only.

⊡ – Supplement payable in Poland.

GREAT BRITAIN

SEE MAP PAGES 98–99

Operators: Passenger services are provided by a number of private passenger train companies operating the **National Rail** network on lines owned by the British national railway infrastructure company **Network Rail**. The following Network Rail codes are used in the table headings to indicate the **principal** operators of trains in each table:

AW	Arriva Trains Wales	GR	National Express East Coast	LM	London Midland	SR	First ScotRail
CH	Chiltern Railways	GW	First Great Western	ME	Merseyrail	SW	South West Trains
EM	East Midlands Trains	HT	Hull Trains	NT	Northern Rail	TP	TransPennine Express
FC	First Capital Connect	IL	Island Line	SE	Southeastern	VT	Virgin Trains
GC	Grand Central Railway	LE	one	SN	Southern	XC	Arriva Cross Country

Timings: Except where indicated otherwise, timings are valid from **December 9, 2007**, until **May 17, 2008**. As service patterns at weekends (especially on ⑦) usually differ greatly from those applying on Mondays to Fridays, the timings in most tables are grouped by days of operation: Ⓐ = Mondays to Fridays; ⚒ = Mondays to Saturdays; ⑥ = Saturdays; ⑦ = Sundays. Track engineering work, affecting journey times, frequently takes place at weekends, so it is advisable to confirm your journey details locally if planning to travel in the period between the late evening of ⑥ and the late afternoon of ⑦. Confirm timings, too, if you intend travelling on public holidays (see page **2**) as there may be alterations to services at these times. Suburban and commuter services are the most likely to be affected; the majority of long-distance and cross-country trains marked Ⓐ and ⚒ run as normal on these dates. However, **no trains** (except limited Gatwick and Heathrow Express services) run on **December 25** and (in England and Wales) only a few London suburban services operate on **December 26**. In Scotland, no trains run on **January 1** except those connecting Edinburgh and Glasgow to stations in England.

Services: Unless indicated otherwise (by '2' in the train column or '2nd class' in the table heading), trains convey both **first** (1st) and **standard** (2nd) classes of seated accommodation. Light refreshments (snacks, hot and cold drinks) are available from a **buffet car** or a **mobile trolley service** on board those trains marked 🍷 and ✕: the latter also convey a **restaurant car** or serve meals to passengers at their seats (this service is in some cases available to first-class ticket holders only). Note that catering facilities may not be available for the whole of a train's journey. **Sleeping-cars** (🛏) have one berth per compartment in first class and two in standard class.

Reservations: Seats on most long-distance trains and berths in sleeping-cars can be reserved in advance when purchasing travel tickets at rail stations or directly from train operating companies (quote the departure time of the train and your destination). Seat reservation is normally free of charge.

SE — LONDON - CHATHAM - DOVER and RAMSGATE — 100

For London to Canterbury and Dover via Ashford, see Table **101**

km			②–⑤		Ⓐ	Ⓐ	Ⓐ	Ⓐ	Ⓐ	Ⓐ	Ⓐ	Ⓐ	Ⓐ	Ⓐ	Ⓐ	Ⓐ	Ⓐ	Ⓐ	Ⓐ	Ⓐ	Ⓐ	Ⓐ		Ⓐ	Ⓐ
0	**London** Victoria .... d.	Ⓐ	0003	...	...	...	0532	...	0616	...	0639	...	0733	...	0803	0803	0833	0833	0903	0903	0933	0933	and at the same minutes past each hour until	1403	1403
55	**Chatham** .... d.		0046	...	0536	...	0629	...	0717	...	0742	...	0819	...	0848	0848	0918	0918	0947	0947	1017	1017		1447	1447
72	Sittingbourne .... d.		0106	...	0554	...	0648	...	0735	...	0804	...	0837	...	0904	0904	0934	0934	1002	1002	1033	1033		1502	1502
84	Faversham .... d.		0116	...	0605	0613	0702	0704	0746	0753	0817	0819	0847	0849	0915	0918	0946	0948	1014	1016	1044	1047		1514	1516
99	Canterbury East ...... d.		|	...	0619	|	|	0718	|	0808	0832	|	|	0904	|	0932	|	1008	|	1028	|	1101		|	1528
124	**Dover** .... a.		|	...	0648	|	|	0745	|	0836	0900	|	|	0932	|	0952	|	1035	|	1045	|	1127		|	1544
119	Margate .... d.		0146	...	...	0645	0734	...	0818	...	...	0852	0920	...	0943	...	1019	...	1041	...	1115	...		1541	...
128	**Ramsgate** .... a.		0157	...	...	0656	0745	...	0829	...	...	0903	0930	...	0952	...	1030	...	1051	...	1127	...		1551	...

	Ⓐ	Ⓐ	Ⓐ	Ⓐ	Ⓐ	Ⓐ	Ⓐ	Ⓐ	Ⓐ	Ⓐ	Ⓐ	Ⓐ	Ⓐ	Ⓐ	Ⓐ	Ⓐ	Ⓐ	Ⓐ	Ⓐ	Ⓐ	Ⓐ	Ⓐ	Ⓐ	Ⓐ	Ⓐ	Ⓐ
London Victoria .... d.	1433	1433	1503	1503	1533	1533	1603	1603	1623	1623	1642	1708c	1709	1730c	1749	1750c	1804	1833	1833	1904	1904	1934	1934	2003	2003	2034
Chatham .... d.	1517	1517	1547	1547	1616	1616	1647	1647	1708	1708	1728	1749	1756	1814	1834	1838	1855	1917	1917	1948	1948	2019	2019	2047	2047	2118
Sittingbourne .... d.	1532	1532	1603	1603	1632	1632	1703	1703	1727	1727	1745	1808	1815	1831	1852	1855	1912	1935	1935	2005	2005	2036	2036	2102	2102	2134
Faversham .... d.	1544	1546	1615	1617	1644	1647	1715	1718	1741	1745	1803	1819	1834	1844	1911	1908	1932	1947	1949	2019	2021	2048	2052	2116	2118	2146
Canterbury East ..... d.	|	1600	|	1632	|	1701	|	1733	|	1800	1818	|	1849	|	1926	|	1947	|	2006	|	2036	|	2106	|	2132	|
Dover .... a.	|	1627	|	1659	|	1728	|	1803	|	1830	1848	|	1917	|	1955	|	2015	|	2033	|	2103	|	2133	|	2159	|
Margate .... d.	1615	...	1647	...	1716	...	1745	...	1813	...	...	1848	...	1916	...	1940	...	2020	...	2047	...	2119	...	2143	...	2218
Ramsgate .... a.	1626	...	1658	...	1727	...	1756	...	1826	...	...	1900	...	1928	...	1954	...	2032	...	2059	...	2130	...	2153	...	2229

	Ⓐ	Ⓐ	Ⓐ	Ⓐ	Ⓐ	Ⓐ			⑥		⑥	⑥	⑥	⑥	⑥	⑥	⑥	⑥	⑥		⑥	⑥	⑥	⑥	⑥
London Victoria .... d.	2034	2103	2103	2203	...	2303	...	⑥	0003	...	...	0539	...	0639	0639	0733	0733	0803	0803	and at the same minutes past each hour until	1803	1803	1833	1833	1903
Chatham .... d.	2118	2150	2150	2246	...	2349	...		0046	...	0546	0638	...	0738	0738	0817	0817	0847	0847		1847	1847	1917	1917	1949
Sittingbourne .... d.	2134	2205	2205	2301	...	0001	...		0103	...	0603	0655	...	0755	0755	0832	0832	0902	0902		1902	1902	1932	1932	2005
Faversham .... d.	2148	2217	2220	2311	2313	0012	...		0113	...	0615	0714	0716	0814	0816	0844	0846	0914	0916		1914	1916	1944	1946	2016
Canterbury East ..... d.	2203	|	2234	|	2327	|	...		|	...	0629	|	0730	0830	|	|	0900	|	0931		|	1931	|	2000	|
Dover .... a.	...	|	2301	|	2347	|	...		|	...	0656	|	0757	0857	|	|	0928	|	0946		|	1946	|	2028	|
Margate .... d.	...	2248	...	2342	...	0043	...		0143	...	...	0746	...	...	0848	0915	...	0941	...		1941	...	2015	...	2047
Ramsgate .... a.	...	2259	...	2353	...	0054	...		0154	...	...	0758	...	...	0859	0926	...	0951	...		1951	...	2026	...	2057

	⑥		⑥	⑥	⑥	⑥		⑥	⑥		⑥			⑦		⑦	⑦		⑦	⑦		⑦	⑦		⑦
London Victoria .... d.	1903	...	2003	2003	2103	2103	...	2203	2203	...	2303	...	⑦	0003	...	0803	0803	and at the same minutes past each hour until	2103	2103	...	2203	2203	...	2303
Chatham .... d.	1949	...	2049	2049	2149	2149	...	2249	2249	...	2349	...		0049	...	0847	0847		2147	2147	...	2247	2247	...	2347
Sittingbourne .... d.	2005	...	2105	2105	2205	2205	...	2305	2305	...	0005	...		0106	...	0902	0902		2202	2202	...	2302	2302	...	0002
Faversham .... d.	2018	...	2116	2118	2216	2218	...	2316	2318	...	0016	...		0116	...	0914	0917		2214	2217	...	2314	2316	...	0014
Canterbury East ..... d.	2033	...	|	2133	|	2233	...	|	2332	...	|	...		|	...	|	0931		|	2231	...	|	2329	...	|
Dover .... a.	2101	...	|	2201	|	2301	...	|	2347	...	|	...		|	...	|	0958		|	2258	...	|	2345	...	|
Margate .... d.	...	...	2147	...	2247	...	...	2347	...	...	0047	...		0147	...	0944	...		2244	...	...	2344	...	...	0044
Ramsgate .... a.	...	...	2157	...	2257	...	...	2357	...	...	0058	...		0158	...	0955	...		2255	...	...	2355	...	...	0055

		Ⓐ	Ⓐ	Ⓐ	Ⓐ	Ⓐ	Ⓐ	Ⓐ	Ⓐ	Ⓐ	Ⓐ	Ⓐ	Ⓐ	Ⓐ	Ⓐ	Ⓐ	Ⓐ	Ⓐ	Ⓐ	Ⓐ	Ⓐ	Ⓐ	Ⓐ	Ⓐ	Ⓐ	Ⓐ
Ramsgate .... d.	Ⓐ	0438	...	0504	...	0528	0546	...	0611	...	0630	...	0650	...	0711	0722	...	0752	...	0817	...	0850	...	0922	...	0959
Margate .... d.		0448	...	0514	...	0538	0557	...	0622	...	0640	...	0700	...	0722	0732	...	0802	...	0828	...	0902	...	0934	...	1008
Dover .... d.		|	0450	|	0512	|	|	0549	|	0624	|	0645	|	0709	|	|	0750	|	0817	|	0904	|	0922	|	1004	|
Canterbury East ..... d.		|	0517	|	0541	|	|	0617	|	0651	|	0713	|	0737	|	|	0818	|	0844	|	0921	|	0949	|	1021	|
Faversham .... d.		0519	0531	0543	0556	0610	0629	0632	0653	0706	0713	0728	0732	0750	0755	0804	0831	0834	0903	0903	0938	0938	1008	1008	1038	1038
Sittingbourne .... d.		0528	0541	0554	0604	0618	...	0643	0702	...	0724	...	0743	...	0805	0812	...	0843	0913	0913	0947	0947	1017	1017	1047	1047
Chatham .... a.		0546	0600	0613	0621	0635	...	0701	0719	...	0742	...	0801	...	0824	0828	...	0859	0929	0929	1003	1003	1033	1033	1103	1103
London Victoria .... a.		0630	0700	0712	0713c	0722	...	0752	0811	...	0834	...	0852	...	0916c	0926	...	0951	1017	1017	1047	1047	1117	1117	1147	1147

		Ⓐ	Ⓐ	Ⓐ	Ⓐ	Ⓐ	Ⓐ	Ⓐ	Ⓐ	Ⓐ	Ⓐ	Ⓐ	Ⓐ	Ⓐ	Ⓐ	Ⓐ	Ⓐ	Ⓐ	Ⓐ	Ⓐ	Ⓐ	Ⓐ	Ⓐ	Ⓐ	Ⓐ
Ramsgate .... d.	and at the same minutes past each hour until	...	1259	...	1322	...	1357	...	1421	...	1457	...	1521	...	1552	...	1620	...	1648	...	1722	...	1750	...	1821
Margate .... d.		...	1308	...	1334	...	1406	...	1432	...	1506	...	1532	...	1604	...	1632	...	1659	...	1734	...	1801	...	1832
Dover .... d.		1304	|	1322	|	1402	|	1420	|	1502	|	1520	|	1552	|	1620	|	1648	|	1722	|	1750	|	1821	|
Canterbury East ..... d.		1321	|	1349	|	1419	|	1447	|	1519	|	1547	|	1619	|	1647	|	1716	|	1749	|	1818	|	1849	|
Faversham .... d.		1338	1338	1408	1408	1436	1436	1506	1506	1536	1536	1606	1606	1638	1638	1706	1706	1735	1735	1808	1809	1837	1837	1908	1908
Sittingbourne .... d.		1347	1347	1417	1417	1445	1445	1515	1515	1545	1545	1615	1615	1647	1647	1715	1715	1743	1743	1817	1817	1845	1845	1917	1917
Chatham .... a.		1403	1403	1433	1433	1501	1501	1531	1531	1601	1601	1631	1631	1703	1703	1730	1730	1759	1759	1834	1834	1901	1901	1933	1933
London Victoria .... a.		1447	1447	1517	1517	1547	1547	1617	1617	1649	1649	1717	1717	1758	1758	1817	1817	1848	1848	1917	1917	1947	1947	2017	2017

	Ⓐ	Ⓐ	Ⓐ	Ⓐ	Ⓐ	Ⓐ		Ⓐ	Ⓐ	Ⓐ	Ⓐ	Ⓐ	Ⓐ			⑥	⑥	⑥	⑥	⑥		⑥	⑥	⑥	⑥
Ramsgate .... d.	1848	...	1948	...	2050	...	...	...	2155	2210	...	2253	...	...	⑥	0438	...	0522	...	0559	and at the same minutes past each hour until	...	1759	...	1822
Margate .... d.	1859	...	1959	...	2101	...	...	...	2206	2220	...	2304	...	...		0446	...	0534	...	0608		...	1808	...	1834
Dover .... d.	|	1854	|	1952	|	2052	...	2155	|	|	2301	|	...	...		|	0522	|	0604	|		1804	|	1822	|
Canterbury East ..... d.	|	1922	|	2019	|	2120	...	2222	|	|	2318	|	...	...		|	0549	|	0621	|		1821	|	1849	|
Faversham .... d.	1939	1939	2037	2037	2138	2138	...	2235	2238	2248	2330	2336	2342	...		0512	0608	0608	0638	0638		1838	1838	1908	1908
Sittingbourne .... d.	1947	1947	2045	2045	2147	2147	...	...	2247	2258	...	...	2352	...		0520	0617	0617	0647	0647		1847	1847	1917	1917
Chatham .... a.	2003	2003	2101	2101	2203	2203	...	...	2303	2316	...	...	0011	...		0536	0633	0633	0703	0703		1903	1903	1933	1933
London Victoria .... a.	2048	2048	2147	2147	2247	2247	...	...	2347	0018	...	...	0113	...		0632	0717	0717	0747	0747		1947	1947	2017	2017

	⑥	⑥		⑥	⑥	⑥	⑥		⑥	⑥	⑥	⑥	⑥			⑦	⑦		⑦	⑦		⑦	⑦	⑦	⑦
Ramsgate .... d.	...	1852	...	...	1952	...	2052	...	...	2152	...	2255	...	...	⑦	...	0622	...	...	0722	and at the same minutes past each hour until	...	2122	...	2155
Margate .... d.	...	1904	...	...	2004	...	2104	...	...	2204	...	2306	...	...		...	0634	...	...	0734		...	2134	...	2205
Dover .... d.	1852	|	...	1952	|	2052	|	...	2152	|	2304	|	...	...		...	|	...	0722	|		2122	|	2153	|
Canterbury East ..... d.	1919	|	...	2019	|	2119	|	...	2219	|	2322	|	...	...		...	|	...	0749	|		2149	|	2221	|
Faversham .... d.	1938	1938	...	2038	2038	2138	2138	...	2238	2238	2334	2338	2342	...		0615	0708	...	0808	0808		2208	2208	2234	2237
Sittingbourne .... d.	1947	1947	...	2047	2047	2147	2147	...	2247	2247	...	...	2352	...		0625	0717	...	0817	0817		2217	2217	...	2248
Chatham .... a.	2003	2003	...	2103	2103	2203	2203	...	2303	2303	...	...	0011	...		0643	0733	...	0833	0833		2233	2233	...	2306
London Victoria .... a.	2047	2047	...	2147	2147	2247	2247	...	2347	2347	...	...	0113	...		0748	0816	...	0916	0916		2316	2316	...	2349

c – London Cannon Street.

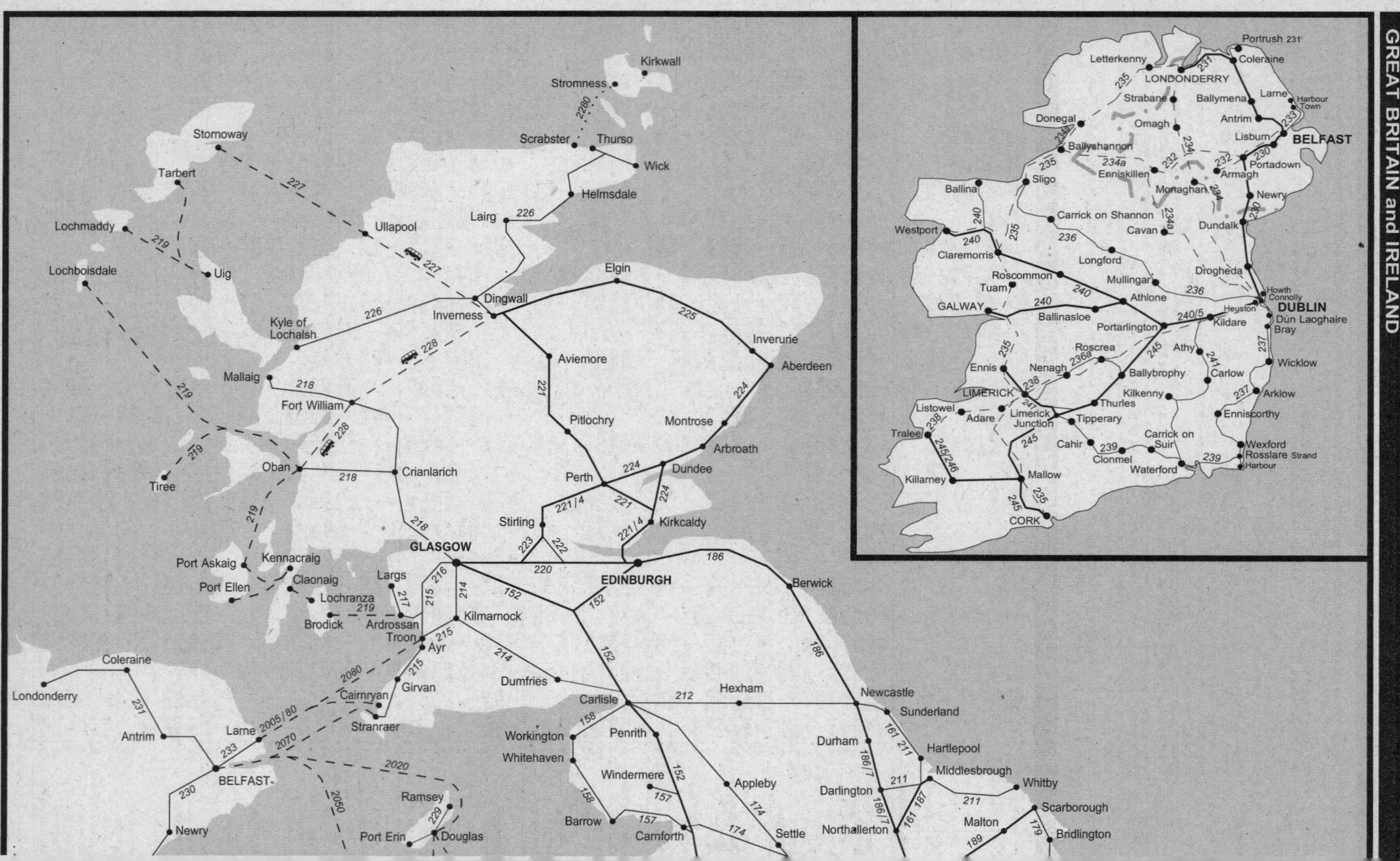
Kirkwall
Stromness
Scrabster
Thurso
Wick
Helmsdale
Lairg
Stornoway
Tarbert
Lochmaddy
Lochboisdale
Uig
Ullapool
Dingwall
Inverness
Elgin
Inverurie
Aberdeen
Kyle of Lochalsh
Mallaig
Fort William
Aviemore
Pitlochry
Montrose
Arbroath
Dundee
Perth
Kirkcaldy
Stirling
Oban
Crianlarich
Tiree
GLASGOW
EDINBURGH
Berwick
Port Askaig
Kennacraig
Port Ellen
Claonaig
Lochranza
Brodick
Largs
Ardrossan
Troon
Ayr
Kilmarnock
Girvan
Cairnryan
Stranraer
Dumfries
Carlisle
Hexham
Newcastle
Sunderland
Workington
Whitehaven
Penrith
Windermere
Barrow
Carnforth
Appleby
Settle
Durham
Hartlepool
Middlesbrough
Darlington
Northallerton
Whitby
Scarborough
Malton
Bridlington
Coleraine
Londonderry
Antrim
Larne
BELFAST
Newry
Ramsey
Port Erin
Douglas
Portrush
Letterkenny
LONDONDERRY
Strabane
Ballymena
Harbour
Town
Donegal
Omagh
Lisburn
Ballyshannon
Enniskillen
Portadown
Armagh
Monaghan
Sligo
Ballina
Carrick on Shannon
Cavan
Dundalk
Westport
Claremorris
Longford
Drogheda
Roscommon
Tuam
Mullingar
Athlone
Howth
Connolly
DUBLIN
Heuston
Dún Laoghaire
Bray
GALWAY
Ballinasloe
Portarlington
Kildare
Roscrea
Athy
Ennis
Nenagh
Ballybrophy
Carlow
Wicklow
LIMERICK
Kilkenny
Thurles
Arklow
Listowel
Adare
Limerick Junction
Tipperary
Enniscorthy
Tralee
Cahir
Carrick on Suir
Clonmel
Wexford
Rosslare Strand
Rosslare Harbour
Waterford
Killarney
Mallow
CORK

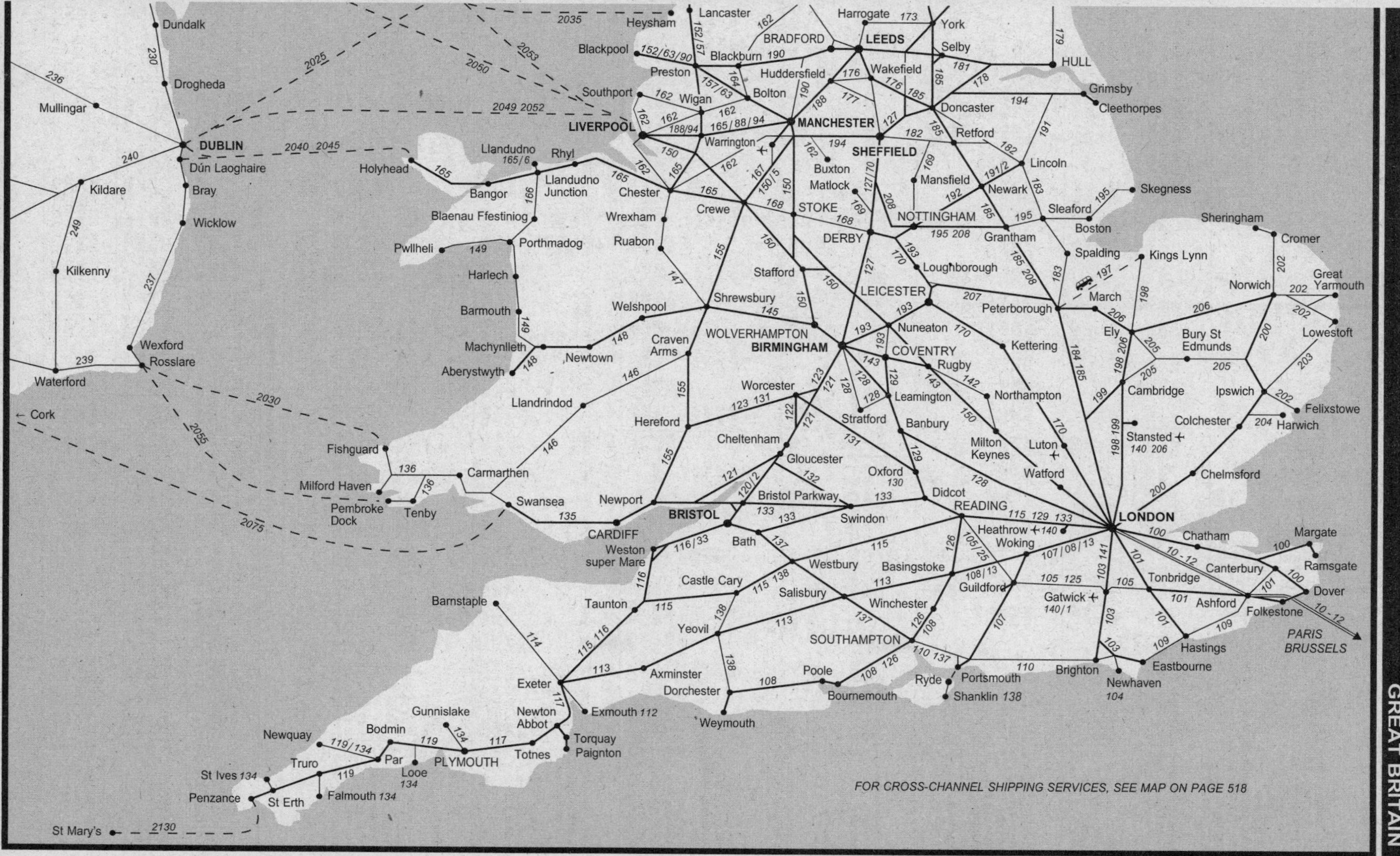

LONDON
BIRMINGHAM
MANCHESTER
LIVERPOOL
LEEDS
SHEFFIELD
BRADFORD
HULL
NOTTINGHAM
LEICESTER
COVENTRY
DERBY
STOKE
WOLVERHAMPTON
BRISTOL
CARDIFF
READING
SOUTHAMPTON
PLYMOUTH
DUBLIN
Lancaster
Heysham
Harrogate
York
Selby
Blackpool
Blackburn
Preston
Huddersfield
Wakefield
Southport
Wigan
Bolton
Doncaster
Grimsby
Cleethorpes
Warrington
Retford
Lincoln
Buxton
Matlock
Mansfield
Newark
Skegness
Sleaford
Boston
Grantham
Spalding
Kings Lynn
Loughborough
Peterborough
March
Ely
Sheringham
Cromer
Norwich
Great Yarmouth
Lowestoft
Bury St Edmunds
Ipswich
Felixstowe
Harwich
Colchester
Chelmsford
Cambridge
Stansted 140 206
Nuneaton
Kettering
Rugby
Northampton
Leamington
Stratford
Banbury
Milton Keynes
Luton
Watford
Oxford 130
Didcot
Swindon
Heathrow 140
Woking
Guildford
Gatwick 140/1
Chatham
Canterbury
Margate
Ramsgate
Dover
Tonbridge
Ashford
Folkestone
Hastings
Eastbourne
PARIS
BRUSSELS
Brighton
Newhaven 104
Portsmouth
Ryde
Shanklin 138
Basingstoke
Winchester
Bournemouth
Poole
Weymouth
Dorchester
Westbury
Salisbury
Bath
Bristol Parkway
Gloucester
Cheltenham
Worcester
Hereford
Shrewsbury
Stafford
Crewe
Chester
Wrexham
Ruabon
Welshpool
Craven Arms
Newtown
Llandrindod
Holyhead
Llandudno 165/6
Rhyl
Llandudno Junction
Bangor
Blaenau Ffestiniog
Porthmadog
Pwllheli
Harlech
Barmouth
Machynlleth
Aberystwyth
Fishguard
Milford Haven
Pembroke Dock
Tenby
Carmarthen
Swansea
Newport
Weston super Mare
Taunton
Castle Cary
Yeovil
Axminster
Barnstaple
Exeter
Exmouth 112
Newton Abbot
Torquay
Paignton
Totnes
Gunnislake
Bodmin
Newquay
Par
Looe 134
Truro
St Ives 134
Falmouth 134
Penzance
St Erth
St Mary's
Dundalk
Drogheda
Mullingar
Dún Laoghaire
Bray
Kildare
Wicklow
Kilkenny
Wexford
Rosslare
Waterford
← Cork
FOR CROSS-CHANNEL SHIPPING SERVICES, SEE MAP ON PAGE 518

101 LONDON - TONBRIDGE - HASTINGS and DOVER SE

For London to Canterbury and Dover via Chatham, see Table **100**

km			Ⓐ	Ⓐ	Ⓐ	Ⓐ	Ⓐ	Ⓐ	Ⓐ	Ⓐ	Ⓐ	Ⓐ	Ⓐ	Ⓐ		Ⓐ	Ⓐ	Ⓐ	Ⓐ	Ⓐ	Ⓐ	Ⓐ	Ⓐ	Ⓐ	Ⓐ
							A					A		A		A		A		A	A				
0	**London** Ch. Cross ⊕ d.	Ⓐ	0530	0625	0700	0745c	0752	0845c	0854	0858	0945	0953	1045	1053	and at the same minutes past each hour until	1353	1445	1453	1545	1553	1646	1700c	1734	1744c	1800
36	Sevenoaks d.		0611	0700	0736	0824	0830	0918	|	0936	1016	|	1116	|		|	1516	|	1620	|	|	1728	|	1812	|
48	**Tonbridge** d.		0622	0711	0749	0833	0840	0928	0935	0947	1025	1031	1125	1131		1431	1525	1531	1629	1633	1725	1739	1815	1821	|
55	Tunbridge Wells a.		*0654*	*0739*	|	0845	|	0939	|	|	1036	|	1135	|		|	1535	|	1639	|	|	1749	|	|	1847
100	**Hastings** a.		*0745*	*0827*	|	0937	|	1023	|	|	1117	|	1217	|		|	1619	|	1727	|	|	1841	|	|	1939
90	Ashford a.		0659	0752	0827	...	0917	...	1005	1025	...	1053	...	1153		1453	...	1553	...	1657	1757	...	1848	1852	...
113	**Canterbury** West a.		*0728*	|	*0854*	...	0942	...	|	1044	...	1123	...	1218		1518	...	1620	...	1723	1827	...	|	1917	...
113	Folkestone Central a.		0723	0815	0845	...	0935	...	1029	...	...	1118	...	1212		1512	...	1621	...	1723	1822	...	1915	...	...
124	**Dover** a.		0735	0827	0859	...	0946	...	1040	...	...	1130	...	1224		1524	...	1634	...	1735	1834	...	1927	...	...

	Ⓐ	Ⓐ	Ⓐ	Ⓐ	Ⓐ	Ⓐ	Ⓐ	Ⓐ	Ⓐ	Ⓐ	Ⓐ	Ⓐ	Ⓐ	Ⓐ	Ⓐ	Ⓐ		⑥	⑥	⑥	⑥	⑥	⑥	⑥	⑥	⑥
	A		A																			A				A
London Ch. Cross ⊕ d.	1830c	1850	1924	1945	2000	2030	2045	2100	2130	2145	2200	2230	2245	2300	2330	2337	⑥	0600	0700	0730	0745	0800	0830	0845	0945	0953
Sevenoaks d.	1858	1920	|	2020	2032	2104	2120	2134	2204	2220	2234	2304	2320	2334	0006	0010		0636	0736	0806	0820	0836	0906	0916	1016	|
Tonbridge d.	1907	1931	2003	2029	2043	2115	2129	2145	2215	2229	2245	2315	2329	2345	0017	0021		0647	0747	0815	0830	0847	0915	0926	1026	1031
Tunbridge Wells a.	|	1941	|	2042	|	|	2139	|	|	2239	|	|	2339	|	|	0031		*0710*	*0810*	|	0840	|	|	0937	1037	|
Hastings a.	|	2030	|	2121	|	|	2227	|	|	2327	|	|	0027	|	|	0119		*0758*	*0858*	|	0939	|	|	1017	1117	|
Ashford a.	1945	...	2036	...	2121	2152	...	2217	2252	...	2317	2352	...	0017	0054	...		0724	0824	0848	...	0926	0949	...	...	1052
Canterbury West a.	2014	...	2104	...	|	2216	...	|	2316	...	|	0016	...	*0118*	|	...		*0812*	*0912*	|	...	0953	|	...	...	1117
Folkestone Central a.	2011	...	2100	...	2144	...	...	2240	...	...	2340	...	...	0040	0118	...		0745	0845	0917	...	0947	1017	...	...	1117
Dover a.	2026	...	2112	...	2156	...	...	2252	...	...	2352	...	...	0052	0130	...		0756	0856	0929	...	0958	1028	...	...	1128

	⑥	⑥		⑥	⑥	⑥	⑥	⑥	⑥	⑥	⑥	⑥	⑥	⑥	⑥	⑥	⑥	⑥	⑥	⑥	⑥	⑥		⑦	⑦
		A			A																				A
London Ch. Cross ⊕ d.	1045	1053	and at the same minutes past each hour until	1745	1753	1823	1830	1845	1900	1930	1945	2000	2030	2045	2100	2130	2145	2200	2230	2245	2300	2330	⑦	0810	0824
Sevenoaks d.	1116	|		1816	|	|	1904	1917	1934	2004	2020	2034	2104	2120	2134	2204	2220	2236	2304	2320	2336	0004		0845	0859
Tonbridge d.	1126	1131		1826	1831	1903	1915	1926	1945	2015	2030	2045	2115	2130	2145	2215	2230	2247	2315	2330	2347	0018		0854	0910
Tunbridge Wells a.	1137	|		1837	|	|	|	1937	|	|	2040	|	|	2140	|	|	2240	|	|	2340	|	*0031*		0904	*0934*
Hastings a.	1217	|		1917	|	|	|	2017	|	|	2127	|	|	2227	|	|	2327	|	|	0027	|	*0118*		0951	*1011*
Ashford a.	...	1152		...	1852	1924	1948	...	2023	2048	...	2123	2148	...	2223	2248	...	2326	2348	...	0024	0055		...	0946
Canterbury West a.	...	1218		...	1922	|	2011	...	|	2111	...	|	2211	...	|	2311	...	|	0013	...	*0119*	|		...	1012
Folkestone Central a.	...	1211		...	1911	1947	...	...	2043	...	...	2143	...	...	2243	...	...	2348	...	...	0047	0116		...	1013
Dover a.	...	1223		...	1923	1958	...	...	2055	...	...	2155	...	...	2255	...	...	2359	...	...	0059	0127		...	1025

	⑦	⑦	⑦		⑦	⑦	⑦	⑦	⑦
London Ch. Cross ⊕ d.	0854	0910	0924	and at the same minutes past each hour until	2124	2154	2210	2224	2310
Sevenoaks d.	0933	0945	0959		2200	2229	2249	2300	2350
Tonbridge d.	0942	0954	1010		2211	2238	2257	2311	0001
Tunbridge Wells a.	|	1004	|		|	|	2307	|	0010
Hastings a.	|	1051	|		|	|	2354	|	0058
Ashford a.	1013	...	1046		2247	2309	...	2347	...
Canterbury West a.	|	...	1112		2312	|	...	|	...
Folkestone Central a.	1034	...	...		...	2330	...	0011	...
Dover a.	1045	...	...		...	2341	...	0022	...

		Ⓐ	Ⓐ	Ⓐ	Ⓐ	Ⓐ	Ⓐ	Ⓐ	Ⓐ	Ⓐ	Ⓐ
Dover d.	Ⓐ	0451	...	0524	...	...	0625	...	...	...	0705
Folkestone Central d.		0503	...	0537	...	...	0637	...	...	...	0717
Canterbury West d.		|	...	|	0542	...	|	0636	...	0656	|
Ashford d.		0524	...	0558	0607	...	0658	0702	...	0722	0738
Hastings d.		|	0516	|	|	0556	|	|	0642	|	|
Tunbridge Wells d.		|	0606	|	|	0642	|	|	0736	|	|
Tonbridge d.		0602	0618	0630	0645	0653	0736	0742	|	0758	0817
Sevenoaks a.		0612	0630	0639	0657	0703	0748	0752	|	0808	0829
London Ch. Cross ⊡ a.		0646	0705	0714	0732	0736c	0820c	0826	0828c	0841c	0901c

	Ⓐ	Ⓐ	Ⓐ	Ⓐ	Ⓐ	Ⓐ	Ⓐ		Ⓐ	Ⓐ	Ⓐ	Ⓐ	Ⓐ	Ⓐ	Ⓐ	Ⓐ	Ⓐ	Ⓐ	Ⓐ	Ⓐ	Ⓐ	Ⓐ	Ⓐ	Ⓐ	Ⓐ
					B		B		B		B		B			B		B						B	
Dover d.	0735	...	0810	...	0848	...	0950	and at the same minutes past each hour until	1350	...	1446	...	1540	...	...	1640	...	1708	...	...	1752	...	...	1852	...
Folkestone Central d.	0747	...	0821	...	0900	...	1001		1402	...	1458	...	1552	...	...	1652	...	1720	...	...	1804	...	...	1904	...
Canterbury West d.	*0747*	...	*0806*	...	0853	...	1006		1406	...	1502	...	1551	1611	...	1651	...	1711	1751	...	|	1827	...	1859	1927
Ashford d.	0810	...	0846	...	0921	...	1028		1428	...	1524	...	1619	1641	...	1719	...	1741	1816	...	1825	1851	...	1929	1951
Hastings d.	|	0750	|	0842	|	0931	|		|	1431	|	1535	|	|	1635	|	1711	|	|	1747	|	|	1847	|	|
Tunbridge Wells d.	|	0840	|	0936	|	1008	|		|	1508	|	1616	|	|	1730	|	1804	|	|	1840	|	|	1938	|	|
Tonbridge d.	0846	0900	0924	0946	0958	1018	1058		1458	1518	1554	1628	1651	1718	1740	1750	1816	1820	1846	1854	1911	1930	1948	2000	2031
Sevenoaks a.	0856	0909	0934	0955	|	1027	|		|	1527	1603	1637	1703	1730	1750	1802	1825	1829	1858	1904	|	1939	1957	2009	2040
London Ch. Cross ⊡ a.	0928c	0944	1007	1033	1036	1103	1136		1536	1603	1638	1719	1741	1807	1830	1837	1900	1907	1935	1942	1950	2018	2034	2048	2118

	Ⓐ	Ⓐ	Ⓐ	Ⓐ	Ⓐ	Ⓐ	Ⓐ	Ⓐ			⑥	⑥	⑥	⑥	⑥	⑥	⑥	⑥	⑥	⑥	⑥	⑥		⑥	⑥
															B			B	B		B			B	
Dover d.	...	1950	...	...	2056	...	...	2200	...	⑥	0444	...	0543	...	0618	0654	...	0723	0750	...	0850	...	and at the same minutes past each hour until	1550	...
Folkestone Central d.	...	2002	...	...	2108	...	...	2212	...		0456	...	0555	...	0629	0706	...	0735	0802	...	0902	...		1602	...
Canterbury West d.	...	|	2027	...	|	2127	...	|	...		|	...	|	...	0624	|	...	0724	0801	...	0906	...		1606	...
Ashford d.	...	2029	2051	...	2129	2151	...	2233	...		0521	...	0620	...	0652	0726	...	0752	0828	...	0928	...		1628	...
Hastings d.	1947	|	|	2047	|	|	2135	*2205*	...		|	0547	|	0616	|	|	0716	|	|	0818	|	0931		|	1631
Tunbridge Wells d.	2036	|	|	2136	|	|	2226	*2256*	...		|	0636	|	0706	|	|	0806	|	|	0906	|	1008		|	1708
Tonbridge d.	2048	2100	2130	2148	2200	2230	2242	2310	...		0600	0646	0659	0716	0731	0800	0816	0831	0857	0916	0957	1018		1657	1718
Sevenoaks a.	2057	2109	2139	2157	2209	2239	2251	2322	...		0612	0656	0711	0726	0743	0809	0826	0843	|	0926	|	1027		|	1727
London Ch. Cross ⊡ a.	2134	2148	2218	2234	2248	2318	2328	0001	...		0648	0734	0748	0805	0818	0848	0903	0918	0936	1003	1036	1103		1736	1803

	⑥	⑥	⑥	⑥	⑥	⑥	⑥	⑥	⑥	⑥	⑥	⑥	⑥	⑥	⑥			⑦	⑦	⑦		⑦	⑦	⑦	⑦
	B													B											B
Dover d.	1637	1719	...	...	1819	...	...	1919	...	...	2019	...	...	2115	2205	...	⑦	0718	...	...	and at the same minutes past each hour until	2018	...	...	2109
Folkestone Central d.	1649	1731	...	...	1831	...	...	1931	...	...	2031	...	...	2127	2216	...		0730	...	...		2030	...	...	2121
Canterbury West d.	1648	|	...	1804	|	...	1904	|	...	2004	|	...	2104	2113	*2159*	...		|	0752	...		|	2052	...	2113
Ashford d.	1709	1751	...	1828	1851	...	1928	1951	...	2028	2051	...	2128	2151	2236	...		0752	0815	...		2052	2115	...	2145
Hastings d.	|	|	1747	|	|	1847	|	|	1947	|	|	2047	|	|	*2207*	...		|	|	0808		|	|	2108	|
Tunbridge Wells d.	|	|	1836	|	|	1936	|	|	2036	|	|	2136	|	|	*2255*	...		|	|	0856		|	|	2156	|
Tonbridge d.	1748	1830	1846	1900	1930	1946	2000	2030	2046	2100	2130	2146	2200	2230	2313	...		0822	0851	0908		2122	2151	2206	2221
Sevenoaks a.	1800	1842	1856	1909	1942	1956	2009	2042	2056	2109	2142	2156	2209	2242	2325	...		0832	0902	0918		2132	2202	2216	2232
London Ch. Cross ⊡ a.	1836	1919	1934	1949	2019	2034	2049	2119	2134	2149	2219	2234	2249	2318	0001	...		0907	0937	0955		2207	2237	2253	2306

A – 12 London - Canterbury; 12 London - Dover.
B – 12 Dover - London; 12 Canterbury - London.
c – London Cannon Street.
⊕ – London Charing Cross; trains also call (3 minutes later) at London Waterloo (East).
⊡ – London Charing Cross; trains also call (3–5 minutes earlier) at London Waterloo (East).

London – Maidstone – Canterbury

km			Ⓐ	Ⓐ	Ⓐ	Ⓐ		Ⓐ	Ⓐ	Ⓐ	Ⓐ	Ⓐ	Ⓐ	Ⓐ	Ⓐ	Ⓐ	Ⓐ	Ⓐ		⑥	⑥	⑥	⑥		⑥	⑥
0	**London** Victoria d.	Ⓐ	...	0610	0719	0818	and hourly until	1318	1418	1518	1627	1722	1818	1918	2018	2109	2209	2311	⑥	...	0618	0718	0818	and hourly until	1518	1618
76	Maidstone East d.		0633	0723	0821	0917		1413	1521	1619	1734	1829	1925	2020	2121	2213	2313	0014		0619	0719	0819	0913		1613	1713
95	Ashford a.		0702	0752	0853	0946		1443	1554	1648	1805	1858	1955	2049	2150	2242	2342	0043		0648	0748	0848	0943		1643	1743
118	**Canterbury** West a.		0728	0817	0924	1012		1507	*1620*	*1721*	*1854*	*1941*	*2029*	*2130*	*2216*	*2316*	*0016*	0118		0714	0812	0912	1007		1707	*1817*

	⑥	⑥	⑥	⑥	⑥	⑥	⑥		⑦		⑦	⑦
London Victoria d.	1718	1818	1918	2018	2118	2218	2318	⑦	0818	and hourly until	2118	2218
Maidstone East d.	1813	1913	2019	2119	2219	2319	0019		0919		2219	2319
Ashford a.	1842	1942	2048	2148	2248	2348	0048		0948		2248	2348
Canterbury West a.	*1922*	*2011*	*2211*	*2311*	...	*0013*	0119		*1012*		*2312*	...

		Ⓐ	Ⓐ	Ⓐ	Ⓐ	Ⓐ	Ⓐ	Ⓐ		Ⓐ
Canterbury West d.	Ⓐ	...	*0542*	*0636*	0747	0820	0943	1024	and hourly until	1424
Ashford d.		0533	0612	0713	0814	0904	1005	1105		1503
Maidstone East d.		0603	0641	0742	0845	0933	1035	1134		1532
London Victoria a.		0708	0749	0853	0950	1032	1132	1232		1633

	Ⓐ	Ⓐ	Ⓐ	Ⓐ	Ⓐ	Ⓐ	Ⓐ		⑥	⑥	⑥	⑥	⑥		⑥	⑥	⑥	⑥	⑥	⑥			⑦	⑦		⑦
Canterbury West d.	1532	*1611*	*1711*	*1827*	1934	*2027*	*2127*	⑥	...	*0624*	*0724*	*0835*	0924	and hourly until	1624	1724	*1804*	*1904*	*2004*	*2123*	...	⑦	...	*0752*	and hourly until	*2052*
Ashford d.	1559	1658	1800	1900	1958	2058	2208		0601	0700	0805	0905	1005		1705	1800	1900	2000	2100	2200	...		0729	0829		2129
Maidstone East d.	1628	1728	1830	1929	2028	2128	2238		0630	0730	0834	0934	1034		1734	1830	1930	2030	2130	2230	...		0759	0859		2159
London Victoria a.	1731	1833	1931	2032	2129	2232	2345		0731	0832	0932	1032	1132		1832	1932	2032	2132	2232	2332	...		0901	1001		2301

SN, FC — LONDON - GATWICK ✈ - BRIGHTON and EASTBOURNE — 103

This table shows a selection of the fastest trains only. There are up to 4 trains per hour (2 per hour on ⑦) between London St Pancras and Brighton.
For details of the direct *Gatwick Express* service between London Victoria and Gatwick Airport, see Table **151**.

km		⚒	②–⑥	②–⑥	⚒		⚒	Ⓐ	⑥	⚒	Ⓐ	⑥	⚒	Ⓐ	⚒	⑥	Ⓐ	⑥	⑥	⚒	⚒	⑥	Ⓐ	⑥	Ⓐ
	London St Pancras d.		...	...	...	...	...	0425	0423	...	...	...	0534	...	0624	...	...	...	...	0717p	...	...	...	...	...
0	**London** Victoria d.		0005	0005	0100	...	0400	|	|	0502	0532	0532	|	0621	|	...	0647	0706	0736	|	0747	0806	0806	0817	0817
17	East Croydon d.		0025	0025	0122	...	0422	0502	0502	0522	0549	0548	0604	0639	0654	...	0703	0722	0752	0754	0803	0822	0822	0833	0833
43	**Gatwick** Airport ✈ d.		0043	0043	0147	...	0447	0522	0522	0549	0620	0621	0620	0704	0711	...	0719	|	|	0811	0819	|	|	0849	0849
61	Haywards Heath d.		0100	0102	|	...	|	0536	0542	0606r	0634	0641	0638	0721	0727	0733	0733	|	|	0827	0832	|	0851	0907	0913
82	**Brighton** a.		0114	|	0232	...	0516	0559	0607	0628r	|	0702	0659q	0742	0749	|	*0802*	0758	0828	0849	|	0858	0908	|	|
81	Lewes a.		...	0116	...	...	...	...	...	...	0649	...	*0743*	...	...	0748	0752	...	...	...	0852	...	...	0922	0928
106	**Eastbourne** a.		...	0138	...	...	...	...	...	...	0716	...	*0804*	...	...	0813	0814	...	...	...	0913	...	...	0944	0950

	⚒	⑥	⚒	Ⓐ	⚒	⚒	⚒	⚒	⚒		⚒	⚒	⚒	⚒	⚒	⚒	⑥	Ⓐ	⑥	Ⓐ	⚒	⑥	Ⓐ	Ⓐ
London St Pancras d.	...	0824	...	0820	...	...	...	0924d	...	and at the same minutes past each hour until	...	...	1524	...	...	...	...	...	1624	1627	...	...	...	...
London Victoria d.	0836	|	0847	|	0906	0917	0936	|	0947		1517	1536	|	1547	1606	1617	1636	1636	|	|	1647	1706	1707	1717
East Croydon d.	0852	0854	0903	0906	0922	0933	0952	0954	1003		1533	1552	1554	1603	1622	1633	1652	1652	1654	1700	1703	1722	1724	1733
Gatwick Airport ✈ d.	|	0911	0919	0923	|	0949	|	1011	1019		1549	|	1611	1619	|	1649	|	|	1711	1716	1720	|	|	|
Haywards Heath d.	|	0927	0934	0940	|	1007	|	1027	1034		1607	|	1627	1633	|	1706	|	1716	1727	1732	1734	|	1752	1803
Brighton a.	0930r	0949	|	0954	0958	|	1028	1051	|		|	1627	1649	|	1700	|	1727	1732	1749	1754	|	1758	1815	|
Lewes a.	...	...	0952	...	...	1022	...	...	1052		1622	...	...	1652r	...	1722	...	...	...	...	1754	...	...	1818
Eastbourne a.	...	...	1013	...	...	1044	...	...	1113		1644	...	...	1714	...	1748r	...	...	...	...	1816r	...	...	1853

	⑥	⑥	Ⓐ	⑥	⑥	Ⓐ	Ⓐ	⑥	Ⓐ	⚒	⑥	Ⓐ	⑥	⚒	Ⓐ	⑥	Ⓐ	⑥	Ⓐ	⚒	⑥	⚒	Ⓐ	⑥	Ⓐ
London St Pancras d.	...	...	...	1724	...	1735	...	...	...	...	...	...	1824	...	1839	...	...	...	...	...	1924	...	1939	...	...
London Victoria d.	1717	1736	1737	|	1747	|	1753	1806	1807	1817	1836	1832	|	1847	|	1906	1906	1917	1917	1936	|	1947	|	2006	2006
East Croydon d.	1735	1752	1754	1754	1803	1808	1810	1822	1824	1833	1852	1848	1854	1903	1910	1922	1922	1933	1933	1952	1954	2003	2014	2022	2022
Gatwick Airport ✈ d.	1750	|	|	1811	1819	1824	1829	|	|	1849	|	1904	1911	1919	1926	|	|	1949	1949	|	2011	2019	2031	|	|
Haywards Heath d.	1807	|	1820	1827	1834	1836	1841	|	1850	1905	|	1922	1927	1933	1940	|	1945	2007	2013	2015	2027	2036	2042	|	2047
Brighton a.	|	1827	1844	1849	|	1902	|	1858	1913	|	1927	1939	1949	|	2000	1958	2003	|	|	2033r	2049	|	2058	2058	2101
Lewes a.	1822	...	...	...	1852	...	1901	...	...	1924	...	...	...	1952	...	...	...	2022	2028	...	...	2055	...	...	...
Eastbourne a.	1844	...	...	...	1913	...	1923	...	...	1950v	...	...	...	2013	...	...	...	2048	2054	...	...	2115	...	...	...

	⚒	⚒	⚒	⚒	⚒	⚒	⚒	⚒	⚒	⚒	⚒	⚒	⚒	⚒	⚒	⚒	⑦	⑦	⑦	⑦		⑦	⑦	⑦	⑦
London St Pancras d.	...	...	2024	...	...	...	...	2124	...	...	...	2224	...	...	2254	...		...	...	...	...	...	...	...	...
London Victoria d.	2017	2036	|	2047	2106	2117	2136	|	2147	2206	2236	|	2247	2306	|	2332		0005	0005	0100	...	0400	0502	0547	0632
East Croydon d.	2033	2052	2054	2103	2122	2133	2152	2154	2203	2222	2252	2254	2303	2322	2324	2352		0025	0025	0122	...	0422	0523	0606	0652
Gatwick Airport ✈ d.	2049	|	2111	2119	|	2149	|	2211	2219	|	|	2311	2319	|	2341	0014		0043	0043	0147	...	0447	0546	0632	0719
Haywards Heath d.	2107	2115	2126	2137	2145	2208	2215	2226	2234	2245	2315	2326	2334	2345	2358	0030		0100	0102	|	...	|	0600	0647	0736
Brighton a.	|	2130	2148	|	2200	|	2230	2248	|	2300	2330	2348	|	2359	0020	0051		0114	|	0220	...	0520	0618	0708	0758
Lewes a.	2122	...	...	2154	...	2223	...	...	2251	...	...	...	2351	...	...	...		...	0116	...	...	...	...	*0758*	...
Eastbourne a.	2148	...	...	2215	...	2248	...	...	2314	...	...	...	0016	...	...	...		...	0138	...	...	...	...	*0819*	...

	⑦	⑦	⑦	⑦	⑦		⑦	⑦	⑦
London St Pancras d.	0654	...	0754	...	...	and at the same minutes past each hour until	...	2254	...
London Victoria d.	|	0732	|	0832	0847		2247	|	2332
East Croydon d.	0727	0752	0827	0852	0907		2307	2327	2353
Gatwick Airport ✈ d.	0750	0812	0850	0912	0929		2329	2350	0014
Haywards Heath d.	0803	0828	0903	0928	0941		2341	0003	0030
Brighton a.	0822	0850	0922	0950	|		|	0022	0051
Lewes a.	*0858*	...	...	...	0958		2358	...	...
Eastbourne a.	*0919*	...	...	...	1019		0020	...	...

	⚒	⚒	Ⓐ	⑥	⑥	Ⓐ	⑥	⑥	Ⓐ	Ⓐ
Eastbourne d.		...	...	0503	...	0508	...	...	0542	...
Lewes d.		...	...	0525	...	0529	...	...	0605	...
Brighton d.		0350	0509	|	0524	|	0550	0604	|	0609
Haywards Heath d.		0425	0530	0540	0545	0547	0611	0618	0627	0630
Gatwick Airport ✈ d.		0503	0546	...	0601	0559	0625	0631	0642	0646
East Croydon d.		0529	0602	...	0617	0615	0641	0647	0659	0702
London Victoria a.		0558	*0625*	...	*0644*	0633	0658	|	0714b	|
London St Pancras a.		...	0633	...	0645	...	...	0717	...	0732

	⑥	Ⓐ	⑥	Ⓐ	⑥	Ⓐ	⑥	Ⓐ	⑥	Ⓐ	⑥	Ⓐ	⑥	Ⓐ	Ⓐ	⑥	Ⓐ	⑥	⑥	⑥	Ⓐ	Ⓐ	⑥	Ⓐ	⑥
Eastbourne d.	...	...	*0550*	...	0624	0624	...	...	...	...	0658	0657	...	...	...	0731	0732	...	...	0758	0757	...	...	0818	0831
Lewes d.	...	...	*0610*	...	0650	0650	...	...	...	...	0720	0723	...	...	...	0750	0754	...	...	0820	0823	...	...	0847	0850
Brighton d.	0610	0620	0649	0647	|	|	0704	0700	0719	0716	|	|	0749	0747	0750	|	|	0804	0819	|	|	0845	0849	|	|
Haywards Heath d.	0639	0637	|	0708	0713	0713	0718	0723	|	0737	0743	0744	|	0806	0809	0813	0815	0818	|	0840	0844	0858	|	0906	0913
Gatwick Airport ✈ d.	0654	0652	|	0722	0725	0730	0731	0737	|	|	0755	|	|	|	0822	0825	|	0831	|	0855	0856	0911	|	0923	0925
East Croydon d.	0710	0716	0724	0738	0740	0747	0747	0754	0755	0804	0810	0815	0824	0834	0838	0840	0847	0847	0855	0910	0914	0926	0924	0939	0940
London Victoria a.	0727	0734	0740	0757	0757	0803b	|	|	0811	0822	0827	0833	0840	0852	|	0857	0907	|	0911	0927	0933	0944	0940	0958	0957
London St Pancras a.	...	...	...	...	...	...	0817	0833	...	...	...	...	...	...	0918	...	...	0918	...	...	...	...	...	...	...

	⚒	⚒	⚒	⚒	⚒	⚒	⚒	⚒	⚒	⚒	⚒	⚒	⚒	⚒	⚒		⚒	⚒	⚒	⚒	⚒	⑥	Ⓐ	⚒
Eastbourne d.	...	...	0856	...	0929	...	...	0956	...	1028j	...	...	1058	...	1431	and at the same minutes past each hour until	...	...	1458	...	1531	...	...	...
Lewes d.	...	...	0917j	...	0949	...	...	1020	...	1049	...	...	1120	...	1150		...	...	1519	...	1550	...	...	...
Brighton d.	0900j	0917	|	0949	|	1004	1019	|	1049	|	1104	1119	|	1149	|		1504	1519	|	1549	|	1604	1607	1619
Haywards Heath d.	0916	|	0943	|	1013r	1018	|	1043	|	1113	1118	|	1143	|	1213		1518	|	1543	|	1613	1618	1626	|
Gatwick Airport ✈ d.	0931	|	0955	|	1025r	1031	|	1055	|	1125	1131	|	1155	|	1225		1531	|	1555	|	1625	1631	1641	|
East Croydon d.	0947	0955	1010	1024	1038	1047	1055	1110	1124	1140	1147	1155	1210	1224	1240		1547	1555	1610	1624	1640	1647	1657	1655
London Victoria a.	|	1013	1028	1040	1058	|	1111	1127	1140	1158	|	1211	1228	1240	1257		|	1611	1629	1641	1658	|	|	1711
London St Pancras a.	1018	...	...	...	...	1118	...	...	...	...	1218	...	...	...	...		1618	...	...	...	...	1718	1735	...

	⚒	⚒	⚒	⚒	⚒	⚒	⚒	⚒	⚒	⚒	⚒	⚒	⚒	⚒	⚒	⚒	⚒	⚒	⚒	⚒	⚒	⚒	⚒	⚒	⚒
Eastbourne d.	1558	...	1631	...	...	1658	...	1731	...	...	1757	...	1831	...	...	1858	...	1932	...	...	...	2031	...	...	...
Lewes d.	1619	...	1650	...	...	1719	...	1750	...	...	1818	...	1850	...	...	1920	...	1951	...	...	...	2050	...	...	...
Brighton d.	|	1649	|	1703	1719	|	1749	|	1803	1819	|	1849	|	1907	1919	|	1949	|	2004	2019	2049	|	2119	2107	2149
Haywards Heath d.	1643	|	1713	1718	|	1743	|	1813	1818	|	1843	|	1913	1932	|	1943	|	2013	2018	|	|	2113	|	2132	|
Gatwick Airport ✈ d.	1655	|	1725	1731	|	1755	|	1825	1831	|	1855	|	1925	1946	|	1955	|	2025	2031	|	|	2125	|	2146	|
East Croydon d.	1710	1724	1740	1747	1755	1810	1824	1840	1847	1855	1910	1924	1940	2002	1955	2010	2024	2040	2047	2055	2124	2140	2155	2202	2224
London Victoria a.	1728	1743r	1758	|	1811	1828	1840	1859	|	1911	1929	1940	1959	|	2011	2028	2040	2059	|	2111	2140	2158	2211	|	2240
London St Pancras a.	...	...	...	1835c	...	...	...	...	1919	...	...	...	...	2033	...	...	...	...	2118	...	...	...	...	2233	...

	⚒	⚒	⚒	⚒	⚒	①–④	⑦	⑦	⑦	⑦	⑦	⑦	⑦	⑦	⑦	⑦		⑦	⑦	⑦	⑦	⑦	⑦
Eastbourne d.	2131	...	...	2215j	...	...	...	...	...	...	0654	...	...	0755	...	...	and at the same minutes past each hour until	2055	...	...	*2155*	...	*2255*
Lewes d.	2150	...	...	2240	...	...	...	...	...	...	0720	...	...	0816	...	...		2116	...	...	*2218*	...	*2318*
Brighton d.	|	2200	2207	|	2302	2337	0350	0544	0644	0700	|	0744	0800	|	0844	0900		|	2144	2200	2244	2302	2344
Haywards Heath d.	2212	2222	2232	2259	2324	2359	|	0601	0701	0721	0739	0801	0821	0839	0901	0921		2139	2201	2221	2301	2324	0001
Gatwick Airport ✈ d.	2225	2238	2246	2313	2353	0015	0503	0615	0715	0738	0753	0815	0838	0853	0915	0939		2153	2215	2238	2315	2347	0015
East Croydon d.	2240	2300	2302	2330	0017	0036	0528	0632	0732	0759	0810	0832	0905	0910	0932	0959		2210	2232	2259	2332	0017	0036
London Victoria a.	2258	2320r	|	2352	0037	|	0558	|	|	0818	0831	|	0921	0931	|	1018		2231	|	2320	|	0037	|
London St Pancras a.	...	...	2332	...	...	0107	...	0702	0801	...	...	0901	...	...	1001	...		...	2301	...	0002	...	0107

– London Bridge.
– 1818 on ⑥.
d – 0920 on Ⓐ (then hourly from 1024).
j – 3–4 minutes later on ⑥.
p – 0724 on ⑥.
q – 0651 on ⑥.
r – 3–4 minutes earlier on ⑥.
v – 1944 on ⑥.

SN — BRIGHTON - NEWHAVEN - SEAFORD — 104

From Brighton: (Lewes *13 km* 15 mins, Newhaven *23 km* 29 mins, Seaford *27 km* 37 mins)

: 0545, 0600 **L**, 0639, 0652, 0713, 0740, 0813, 0846, 0910, 0940 and every 30 minutes until 1740; then 1752 **L**, 1817, 1836, 1850 **L**, 1905, 1940, 2010, 2040, 2104, 2140, 2204, 2234, 2334.

: 0552, 0610, 0640 and every 30 minutes until until 2040; then 2104, 2140, 2204, 2234, 2334.

: 0715, 0750, 0809, 0850, 0909, 0939 and every 30 minutes until 2239.

– Change at Lewes.

From Seaford (and **Newhaven Town ▲** 7 minutes later):

Ⓐ: 0509, 0545, 0630, 0657 **L**, 0716, 0733, 0758, 0821 **L**, 0857, 0925, 0958 and at 25 and 58 minutes past each hour until 1825; then 1843, 1858, 1915, 1932, 1958, 2028, 2058, 2128, 2158, 2220, 2258, 2325.

⑥: 0505, 0628, 0658, 0728, 0758, 0825, 0858 and at 25 and 58 minutes past each hour until 1958; then 2028, 2058, 2128, 2158, 2220, 2258, 2325.

⑦: 0753, 0828, 0853 and at 28 and 53 minutes past each hour until 2253.

▲ – ± 500m from **Newhaven Harbour**; most trains also call at the Harbour station.

105 GATWICK ✈ - TONBRIDGE and READING — GW, SE

For long-distance services from Gatwick and Guildford to Reading, Birmingham and Manchester and v.v., see Table **125**

km			Ⓐ	Ⓐ	Ⓐ		Ⓐ	Ⓐ	Ⓐ		Ⓐ	Ⓐ		Ⓐ		Ⓐ	Ⓐ	Ⓐ	Ⓐ		Ⓐ	Ⓐ		Ⓐ
0	**Gatwick** Airport ✈ d.	Ⓐ	0531	0554	0557	...	*0637*	0659	*0713*	...	*0741*	0758	...	*0837*	...	0917	*0923*	0952	1003	and at	1553	1603	...	*1638*
10	Redhill d.		0544	0609	0614	...	0658	0711	0735	...	0805	0809	...	0859	...	0929	0944	1007	1014	the same	1607	1614	...	1707
42	**Tonbridge** a.		|	0642	|	...	0727	|	0806	...	0835	|	...	0928	...	|	1008	1037	|	minutes	1636	|	...	1736
43	Guildford d.		0612	...	0642	...	...	0742	...	...	...	0837	...	...	...	0957	...	...	1043	past each	...	1643	...	...
84	**Reading** a.		0658	...	0728	...	...	0828	...	...	...	0916	...	...	...	1027	...	...	1119	hour until	...	1719	...	...

	Ⓐ	Ⓐ		Ⓐ	Ⓐ		Ⓐ		Ⓐ	Ⓐ		Ⓐ	Ⓐ		Ⓐ	Ⓐ		Ⓐ		Ⓐ		Ⓐ		Ⓐ	Ⓐ
Gatwick Airport ✈ d.	1703	*1708*	...	1803	*1808*	...	*1838*	...	*1908*	1916	...	*1939*	2003	...	2053	2103	...	2153	...	2223	...	2253	...	2318	*2323*
Redhill d.	1714	1728	...	1814	1823	...	1855	...	1924	1927	...	2008	2014	...	2107	2114	...	2207	...	2233	...	2310	...	2329	2353
Tonbridge a.	|	1757	...	|	1852	...	1924	...	1956	|	...	2037	|	...	2137	|	...	2237	...	|	...	2339	...	|	0015
Guildford d.	1746	...	...	1849	...	...	...	...	...	1955	...	...	2043	...	...	2142	...	...	...	2314	...	...	...	0001	...
Reading a.	1828	...	...	1925	...	...	...	...	...	2037	...	...	2120	...	...	2219	...	...	...	0002	...	...	...	0038	...

		⑥	⑥	⑥	⑥		⑥	⑥	⑥	⑥	⑥	⑥			⑦		⑦	⑦		⑦	⑦		⑦
Gatwick Airport ✈ d.	⑥	0531	*0545*	0603	0653	and at	2103	2153	2222	2253	2318	*2323*	...	⑦	0607	...	0707	0756	and at	2155	2207	...	2307
Redhill d.		0543	0611	0614	0707	the same	2114	2207	2234	2311	2329	2354	...		0619	...	0719	0810	the same	2210	2219	...	2319
Tonbridge a.		|	0640	|	0736	minutes	|	2237	|	2337	|	0016	...		|	...	|	0840	minutes	2239	|	...	|
Guildford d.		0612	...	0643	...	past each	2143	...	2314	...	0001	...	...		0651	...	0756	...	past each	...	2255	...	2356
Reading a.		0702	...	0719	...	hour until	2219	...	2359	...	0042	...	...		0730	...	0835	...	hour until	...	2337	...	0036

		Ⓐ	Ⓐ	Ⓐ	Ⓐ	Ⓐ	Ⓐ	Ⓐ	Ⓐ	Ⓐ	Ⓐ	Ⓐ	Ⓐ	Ⓐ		Ⓐ	Ⓐ	Ⓐ	Ⓐ	Ⓐ	Ⓐ	Ⓐ	Ⓐ	Ⓐ
Reading d.	Ⓐ	...	0434	...	0534	...	0634	...	...	0734	...	0834	0934	...	and at	1434	...	...	1528	...	1634	...	...	1734
Guildford d.		...	0510	...	0610	...	0710	...	...	0818	...	0910	1011	...	the same	1510	...	...	1610	...	1710	...	...	1818
Tonbridge d.		0500	|	0600	|	0650	|	0738	0818	|	0908	|	|	1004	minutes	|	1504	1604	|	1629	|	1743	1821	|
Redhill a.		0531	0539	0630	0638	0720	0738	0808	0848	0851	0939	0941	1039	1040	past each	1538	1539	1639	1647	1659	1738	1813	1851	1852
Gatwick Airport ✈ a.		0542	0554	*0653*	0656	...	0754	*0839*	...	0902	0954	0959	1051	1055	hour until	1550	1556	1656	1700	*1732*	1750	*1832*	...	1907

	Ⓐ	Ⓐ	Ⓐ	Ⓐ	Ⓐ	Ⓐ	Ⓐ	Ⓐ	Ⓐ	Ⓐ	Ⓐ			⑥	⑥	⑥	⑥	⑥	⑥	⑥	⑥		⑥	⑥
Reading d.	1834	...	...	1934	...	2034	...	2134	...	2234	2334	...	⑥	0434	...	0534	...	0634	...	0734	...	and at	1734	...
Guildford d.	1910	...	...	2010	...	2110	...	2218	...	2318	0021	...		0510	...	0610	...	0710	...	0810	...	the same	1810	...
Tonbridge d.	|	1909	1953	|	2053	|	2153	|	2317	|	|	...		|	0552	|	0652	|	0734	|	0804	minutes	|	1804
Redhill a.	1938	1939	2024	2038	2124	2148	2223	2248	2348	2358	0049	...		0538	0623	0638	0723	0738	0804	0838	0839	past each	1838	1839
Gatwick Airport ✈ a.	1950	*1958*	2035	2050	2134	2204	2234	2304	...	0011	0101	...		0553	0635	0650	0734	0750	*0823*	0850	0855	hour until	1850	1855

	⑥	⑥	⑥	⑥	⑥	⑥	⑥	⑥	⑥	⑥	⑥			⑦	⑦	⑦	⑦		⑦	⑦	⑦	⑦	⑦	⑦
Reading d.	...	1834	...	1934	...	2034	...	2134	...	2234	2334	...	⑦	0604	...	0702	...	and at	2003	...	2100	2203	2234	2315
Guildford d.	...	1910	...	2010	...	2110	...	2218	...	2318	0021	...		0644	...	0742	...	the same	2043	...	2143	2243	2318	2355
Tonbridge d.	1852	|	1952	|	2052	|	2152	|	2315	|	|	...		|	0657	|	0754	minutes	|	2054	|	|	|	|
Redhill a.	1923	1938	2023	2038	2123	2144	2223	2252	2349	2358	0049	...		0717	0724	0817	0824	past each	2117	2125	2221	2317	2358	0030
Gatwick Airport ✈ a.	1934	1950	2034	2050	2134	2159	2234	2303	...	0010	0101	...		0730	0737	0830	0837	hour until	2130	2138	2239	2330	0010	0043

107 LONDON - GUILDFORD - PORTSMOUTH — SW

km			Ⓐ		Ⓐ	Ⓐ		Ⓐ	Ⓐ		Ⓐ	Ⓐ	Ⓐ	Ⓐ		Ⓐ	Ⓐ	Ⓐ	Ⓐ	Ⓐ	Ⓐ	Ⓐ	Ⓐ
0	**London** Waterloo d.	Ⓐ	...	...	0500	0520	...	0615	0645	...	0730	0800	0830	0900	and at	1500	1530	1600	1630	1700	1730	1800	1830
39	Woking d.		...	...	0551	0613	...	0643	0713	...	0755	0825	0855	0925	the same	1525	1555	1625	1655	1725	1756	|	1858
49	**Guildford** d.		0515	...	0600	0625	...	0655	0725	...	0804	0839	0904	0934	minutes	1534	1604	1634	1704	1737	1808	1833	1908
69	Haslemere d.		0530	...	0625	0655	...	0720	0755	...	0825	0855	0925	0950	past	1550	1624	1651	1724	1752	1826	1852	1926
107	Havant d.		0602	...	0658	0728	...	0752	0827	...	0850	0919	0950	1015	each	1615	1650	1716	1749	1819	1851	1917	1951
118	Portsmouth & Southsea a.		0618	...	0716	0746	...	0807	0843	...	0902	0932	1002	1027	hour	1627	1702	1728	1802	1832	1903	1929	2003
120	**Portsmouth** Harbour a.		0622	...	0720	...	...	0812	0848	...	0907	0937	1007	1032	until	1632	1707	1735	1809	1839	1910	1936	2010

	Ⓐ	Ⓐ	Ⓐ	Ⓐ	Ⓐ 🍷	Ⓐ 🍷	Ⓐ 🍷	Ⓐ	Ⓐ	Ⓐ	Ⓐ			⑥		⑥		⑥	⑥	⑥		⑥	⑥
London Waterloo d.	1900	1930	2000	2030	2100	2130	2200	2230	2245	2315	2345	...	⑥	...	...	*0530*	...	0645	0730	0800	and at	1930	2000
Woking d.	1925	1955	2025	2055	2125	2155	2225	2255	2313	2343	0013	...		...	...	0613	...	0713	0755	0825	the same	1955	2025
Guildford d.	1937	2004	2034	2104	2134	2204	2234	2305	2325	2352	0025	...		0515	...	0625	...	0725	0804	0834	minutes	2004	2034
Haslemere d.	1953	2022	2055	2122	2155	2225	2255	2325	2350	0013	0050	...		0529	...	0645	...	0745	0821	0850	past	2021	2050
Havant d.	2019	2049	2120	2146	2219	2249	2319	2349	0022	0037	0122	...		0601	...	0717	...	0817	0849	0915	each	2049	2115
Portsmouth & Southsea a.	2031	2102	2133	2158	2232	2303	2332	0002	0038	0050	0138	...		0621	...	0732	...	0832	0902	0927	hour	2102	2127
Portsmouth Harbour a.	2036	2107	2138	2202	2238	2308	2337	0007	...	0055	...	...		0626	...	0737	...	0837	0907	0932	until	2107	2132

	⑥	⑥	⑥	⑥	⑥	⑥	⑥	⑥			⑦		⑦	⑦		⑦	⑦		⑦	⑦		⑦	⑦
London Waterloo d.	2030	2100	2130	2200	2230	2245	2315	2345	...	⑦	...	...	0800	0830	...	0900	0930	...	1000	1030	and at	2300	2330
Woking d.	2055	2125	2155	2225	2255	2313	2343	0013	...		0732	...	0835	0904	...	0935	1004	...	1032	1102	the same	2332	0002
Guildford d.	2104	2134	2204	2234	2305	2325	2352	0025	...		0746	...	0846	0914	...	0946	1014	...	1046	1112	minutes	2346	0012
Haslemere d.	2121	2155	2225	2255	2325	2350	0013	0050	...		0812	...	0912	0929	...	1012	1029	...	1112	1127	past	0012	0027
Havant d.	2146	2219	2249	2319	2349	0022	0037	0122	...		0845	...	0945	0952	...	1045	1053	...	1145	1151	each	0045	0051
Portsmouth & Southsea a.	2158	2232	2302	2332	0002	0038	0050	0138	...		0859	...	0959	1005	...	1059	1105	...	1159	1204	hour	0059	0104
Portsmouth Harbour a.	2203	2236	2307	2337	0007	...	0055	...	...		0904	...	1004	1011	...	1104	1111	...	1204	1211	until	0104	0109

		Ⓐ	Ⓐ	Ⓐ	Ⓐ	Ⓐ	Ⓐ	Ⓐ	Ⓐ	Ⓐ	Ⓐ	Ⓐ		Ⓐ	Ⓐ	Ⓐ	Ⓐ	Ⓐ	Ⓐ	Ⓐ	Ⓐ	Ⓐ	Ⓐ
Portsmouth Harbour d.	Ⓐ	0430	0519	0550	0615	0642	0713	0745	0813	0845	0915	0945	and at	1445	1515	1545	1615	1645	1715	1745	1815	1845	1915
Portsmouth & Southsea d.		0435	0524	0555	0620	0647	0718	0750	0818	0850	0920	0950	the same	1450	1520	1550	1620	1650	1720	1750	1820	1850	1920
Havant d.		0451	0541	0611	0634	0700	0732	0803	0833	0904	0934	1004	minutes	1504	1534	1604	1634	1704	1734	1804	1834	1904	1934
Haslemere d.		0526	0616	0647	0702	0735	0800	0832	0902	0932	1002	1032	past	1532	1602	1637	1702	1737	1802	1832	1902	1932	2002
Guildford d.		0550	0631	0707	0717	0754	0815	0854	0917	0947	1017	1049	each	1547	1617	1700	1717	1800	1817	1855	1921	1947	2017
Woking a.		0600	0639	0715	0725	|	0826	*0911*	0927	0959	1025	1057	hour	1557	1625	1711	1725	1811	|	1903	1928	1957	2025
London Waterloo a.		0629	0712	0744	0754	0832	0855	0931	0955	1027	1051	1124	until	1623	1651	1743	1752	1843	1859	1929	1959	2023	2050

	Ⓐ	Ⓐ	Ⓐ	Ⓐ		Ⓐ		Ⓐ			⑥	⑥	⑥	⑥	⑥		⑥	⑥	⑥	⑥	⑥	⑥	⑥
Portsmouth Harbour d.	1945	2015	2045	2115	...	2217	...	2318	...	⑥	0443	0518	0618	0645	0715	and at	1615	1645	*1701*	1745	1815	1845	1915
Portsmouth & Southsea d.	1950	2020	2050	2124	...	2224	...	2324	...		0448	0524	0624	0650	0720	the same	1620	1650	1710	1750	1820	1850	1920
Havant d.	2004	2034	2104	2140	...	2240	...	2340	...		0504	0540	0640	0704	0734	minutes	1634	1704	1726	1804	1834	1904	1934
Haslemere d.	2032	2102	2132	2215	...	2315	...	0015	...		0539	0615	0715	0732	0802	past	1702	1732	1802	1832	1902	1932	2002
Guildford d.	2047	2117	2147	2239	...	2339	...	0037	...		0602	0632	0732	0747	0817	each	1717	1747	1817	1847	1917	1947	2017
Woking a.	2057	2125	2157	2249	...	2349	...	...	...		0611	0644	0744	0757	0826	hour	1726	1757	1825	1857	1925	1957	2025
London Waterloo a.	2127	2150	2227	2318	...	0029	...	...	...		0640	0713	0813	0823	0851	until	1751	1823	1851	1923	1950	2023	2050

	⑥	⑥	⑥	⑥	⑥	⑥			⑦	⑦	⑦	⑦	⑦	⑦	⑦	⑦	⑦	⑦	⑦		⑦	⑦	⑦
Portsmouth Harbour d.	1945	2015	2045	2117	2217	2318	...	⑦	0648	0732	0748	0832	0848	0932	0948	1032	1048	1132	1148	and at	2148	2232	2248
Portsmouth & Southsea d.	1950	2020	2050	2124	2224	2323	...		0653	0737	0753	0837	0853	0937	0953	1037	1053	1137	1153	the same	2153	2237	2253
Havant d.	2004	2034	2104	2146	2240	2341	...		0707	0750	0807	0850	0907	0950	1007	1050	1107	1150	1207	minutes	2207	2250	2307
Haslemere d.	2032	2102	2132	2215	2315	0015	...		0742	0817	0842	0917	0942	1017	1042	1117	1142	1217	1242	past	2242	2317	2342
Guildford d.	2049	2117	2149	2239	2339	0037	...		0805	0835	0905	0935	1005	1035	1105	1135	1205	1235	1305	each	2305	2335	0005
Woking a.	2057	2125	2157	2249	2349	...	...		0813	0842	0914	0942	1013	1042	1114	1142	1213	1242	1313	hour	2313	2342	0013
London Waterloo a.	2124	2150	2224	2318	0031	...	...		0849	0919	0949	1021	1049	1119	1149	1219	1247	1314	1344	until	2344	0014	...

☛ 🍷 conveyed by trains from London at 0730 and 0830–2200 on Ⓐ; at 0900–1930 on ⑥; and hourly 1130–2030 on ⑦.

☛ 🍷 conveyed by trains from Portsmouth at 0519 and 0615–1845 on Ⓐ; at 0645–1645 and 1745 on ⑥; and hourly 0932–1832 on ⑦.

SW LONDON - SOUTHAMPTON - WEYMOUTH 108

For other trains Basingstoke - Bournemouth and v.v., see Table **126**

km		✕	②–⑥		⑥	Ⓐ	✕	✕	⑥	Ⓐ	Ⓐ	⑥	✕	✕	⑥	Ⓐ	✕	✕♀		✕♀	✕♀		✕♀	✕♀
0	**London** Waterloo d.		0005	...	0105	0105	...	...	...	...	0530	0530	...	0630	...	...	0735	0805	...	0835	0905	and	1435	1505
39	Woking d.		0036	...	0142	0141	...	...	...	...	0601	0601	...	0657	...	...	0800	|	...	0900	|	at	1500	|
77	Basingstoke d.		0057	...	0205s	0211s	...	...	...	0540	0621	0621	...	0718	...	0730	0821	0850	...	|	0950	the	|	1550
107	Winchester d.		0113	...	0222s	0228s	...	...	...	0559	0638	0641	...	0734	...	0750	0838	0906	...	0933	1006	same	1533	1606
120	Southampton Airport d.		0127	...	0236s	0242s	...	...	...	0613	0653	0656	...	0748	...	0806	0851	0915	...	0942	1015	minutes	1542	1615
128	**Southampton Central** d.		0137	...	0246	0252	...	...	0625	0625	0701	0705	0718v	0759	0822	0819	0900	0924	...	0951	1024	past	1551	1624
149	Brockenhurst d.		0153s	...	...	...	...	0616	0644	0644	0718	0722	0744	0816	0844	0845	0916	0938	...	1005	1038	each	1605	1638
174	**Bournemouth** d.		0216	...	...	...	0611	0644	0711	0711	0749	0749	0811	0843	0911	0912	0943	1004	...	1024	1104	hour	1624	1704
183	Poole d.		...	...	...	...	0624	0657	0724	0724	0802	0802	0824	0856	0924	0925	0956	1014	...	1037	1114	until	1637	1714
219	Dorchester South d.		...	...	...	...	0658	0731	0758	0759	0836	0834	0858	0928	0958	0959	1027	1056c	...	1105	1149		1705	1749
230	**Weymouth** a.		...	...	...	...	0709	0742	0809	0810	0847	0845	0909	0940	1009	1010	1035	1107c	...	1113	1200		1713	1801

	✕♀	⑥♀	Ⓐ♀	✕♀	Ⓐ♀	⑥♀	Ⓐ♀	⑥♀	Ⓐ	Ⓐ♀	⑥♀	Ⓐ♀	⑥♀	✕♀	⑥♀	Ⓐ♀	✕	✕♀	✕♀	✕	✕♀	✕♀	✕	✕♀	✕♀
London Waterloo d.	1535	1605	1605	1635	1705	1705	1735	1735	1748	1805	1805	1835	1835	1905	1935	1935	1939	2005	2035	2039	2105	2135	2139	2205	2235
Woking d.	1600	|	|	1700	|	|	|	1800	1813	|	|	|	1900	|	2000	2000	|	|	2100	|	2132	2200	|	2232	2300
Basingstoke d.	|	1650	1650	|	|	1750	|	|	1833	|	1850	|	|	1950	|	|	2036	2050	|	2136	2153	|	2236	2253	|
Winchester d.	1633	1706	1706	1733	1801	1806	1831	1833	1850	1901	1906	1931	1933	2006	2033	2033	2052	2106	2133	2152	2209	2233	2255	2309	2333
Southampton Airport d.	1642	1715	1715	1742	1810	1815	1840	1842	1903	1910	1915	1940	1942	2015	2042	2042	2108	2115	2142	2208	2223	2242	2311	2323	2342
Southampton Central d.	1651	1724	1724	1751	1822	1824	1852	1851	1916	1919	1924	1952	1951	2024	2051	2051	2115	2124	2151	2215	2231	2251	2318	2331	2351
Brockenhurst d.	1708r	1738	1738	1808r	|	1838	|	1905	...	1936	1938	|	2005	2038	2105	2108	...	2143	2205	...	2250	2305	...	2350	0005
Bournemouth d.	1724	1804	1809	1824	1850	1904	1921	1924	...	2006	2004	2021	2024	2104	2124	2127	...	2210	2224	...	2318	2328	...	0018	0024
Poole d.	1737	1814	1819	1837	1903	1914	1934	1937	...	2019	2014	2034	2037	2114	2137	2139	...	2223	2237	...	2330	2340	...	0030	0036
Dorchester South d.	1805	1849	1853	1905	1937	1949	2002	2005	...	2053	2049	2102	2105	2147	2209	2212	...	...	2309	...	...	0013	...	...	...
Weymouth a.	1813	1900	1905	1917r	1950	2001	2015	2013	...	2106	2102	2113	2113	2158	2220	2223	...	...	2320	...	...	0024	...	...	...

	✕	✕	✕		⑦	⑦		⑦	⑦		⑦	⑦	⑦	⑦	⑦	⑦	⑦	⑦♀		⑦	⑦♀	⑦		⑦
London Waterloo d.	2239	2305	2339	...		0005	...	0105	...	...	...	...	0754	0835	0854	0935	0954	1035	and	2054	2135	2154	...	2254
Woking d.	|	2332	0008	...		0036	...	0141	...	...	...	...	0828	0908	0928	1008	1028	1107	at	2128	2207	2228	...	2328
Basingstoke d.	2334	2353	0036	...		0057	...	0211s	...	...	0748	...	0849	0929	0948	1029	1048	1128	the	2148	2228	2248	...	2348
Winchester d.	2351	0012	0053	...		0113	...	0228s	...	...	0808	...	0908	0945	1008	1045	1108	1144	same	2208	2244	2308	...	0008
Southampton Airport d.	0006	0025	0106	...		0127	...	0242s	...	...	0827	...	0927	0954	1027	1054	1127	1153	minutes	2227	2253	2327	...	0027
Southampton Central d.	0015	0036	0113	...		0137	...	0252	...	...	0835	0903	0935	1004	1035	1104	1135	1203	past	2235	2303	2335	...	0037
Brockenhurst d.	...	0052s	...	...		0153s	...	...	...	...	0857	0917	0957	1018	1057	1118	1157	1217	each	2257	2317	2354	...	0053s
Bournemouth d.	...	0116	...	...		0216	...	...	0840	...	0925	0940	1025	1040	1125	1140	1225	1240	hour	2325	2340	0022	...	0118
Poole d.	...	0129	...	...		...	...	...	0852	...	0934	0952	1034	1052	1134	1152	1234	1252	until	2334	2352	0035	...	0130
Dorchester South d.	...	...	...	...		...	...	...	0925	...	...	1025	...	1125	...	1225	...	1325		...	0025	...	...	...
Weymouth a.	...	...	...	...		...	...	...	0936	...	...	1036	...	1136	...	1236	...	1336		...	0036	...	...	...

	✕	Ⓐ	⑥		Ⓐ♀	⑥	⑥♀	Ⓐ♀	Ⓐ♀	⑥	⑥♀	Ⓐ♀	Ⓐ	⑥♀	Ⓐ♀	✕♀	Ⓐ♀	⑥♀	Ⓐ	✕♀	Ⓐ♀	⑥♀	Ⓐ		✕♀
Weymouth d.		...	...	...	...	...	...	...	...	...	...	0555	...	...	0625	0655	...	0720	0725	0755v	...	0820	0825	...	0903
Dorchester South d.		...	...	...	...	...	...	...	...	...	...	0607	...	...	0637	0707	...	0732	0737	0807v	...	0832	0837	...	0913
Poole d.		...	...	...	0500	...	0528	0545	0611	...	0628	0641	...	0706	0711	0741	0755	0806	0811	0840	0906	0906	0911	...	0940
Bournemouth d.		...	...	...	0515	...	0542	0557	0625	...	0642	0656	...	0721	0726	0759	0810	0821	0826	0859	0918	0921	0926	...	0955d
Brockenhurst d.		...	...	...	0538	...	0610	0614	|	...	0710	|	...	0744	|	0815	0841	0844	0853	0915	0941	0944	0953	...	1011d
Southampton Central d.		0455	0512	...	0555	0600	0630	0630	0700	0700	0730	0730	0738	0800	0800	0830	0900	0900	...	0930	1000	1000	1008	...	1030
Southampton Airport d.		0502	0520	...	0603	0608	0638	0638	0708	0708	0738	0738	0749	0808	0808	0838	0908	0908	...	0938	1008	1008	...	...	1038
Winchester d.		0518	0534	...	0618	0623	0652	0648	0718	0724	0748	0748	0806	0818	0818	0848	0918	0918	...	0948	1018	1018	...	...	1048
Basingstoke d.		0539	0554	...	0636	0640	0709	|	|	0742	|	|	0822	0836	0835	|	0936	0936	...	|	1036	1036	...	...	|
Woking a.		0605	0628	...	0654	0658	0727	|	|	0808	0821	|	*0848*	|	0853	0922r	0954	|	...	1020	|	|	...	...	1119
London Waterloo a.		0634	0706	...	0725	0731	0753	0746	0816	0838	0849	0848	*0917*	0920	0925	0953r	1023	1020	...	1049	1120	1120	...	...	1149

	✕♀		✕♀		✕♀	✕♀		✕♀	✕♀		✕♀	✕♀		✕♀	✕♀	✕	✕		✕	✕		✕		✕
Weymouth d.	0920	...	1003	and	1603	1620	...	1703	1720	...	1803	1820	...	1903	1920	...	2010	...	...	2110	...	2210	...	2310
Dorchester South d.	0932	...	1013	at	1613	1632	...	1713	1732	...	1813	1832	...	1913	1937r	...	2022	...	...	2122	...	2222	...	2322
Poole d.	1006	...	1040	the	1640	1706	...	1740	1806	...	1840	1906	...	1940	2009r	...	2054	...	...	2154	...	2254	...	2354
Bournemouth d.	1021	...	1059	same	1659	1721	...	1759	1821	...	1859	1921	...	1959	2021	...	2112	...	...	2212	...	2312	...	0003
Brockenhurst d.	1044	...	1115	minutes	1715	1744	...	1815	1844	...	1915	1944	...	2015	2044	...	2140	...	...	2240	...	2340	...	...
Southampton Central d.	1100	...	1130	past	1730	1800	...	1830	1900	...	1930	2000	...	2030	2100	2130	2200	...	2230	2300	...	0001	...	...
Southampton Airport d.	1108	...	1138	each	1738	1808	...	1838	1908	...	1938	2008	...	2038	2108	2138	2208	...	2238	2308	...	0012	...	...
Winchester d.	1118	...	1148	hour	1748	1818	...	1848	1918	...	1948	2018	...	2048	2118	2148	2218	...	2254	2324	...	*0030*j	...	...
Basingstoke d.	1136	...	|	until	|	1836	...	|	1936	...	|	2036	...	|	2136	|	2236	...	2312	2344	...	...	...	...
Woking a.	|	...	1219		1819	|	...	1924r	|	...	2019	|	...	2119	|	2219	2354	...	2332	0018	...	...	...	...
London Waterloo a.	1220	...	1249		1849	1920	...	1951	2020	...	2049	2122	...	2149	2222	2249	2323	...	0004q	0102	...	...	...	...

	⑦	⑦		⑦♀		⑦	⑦♀	⑦	⑦♀	⑦	⑦♀	⑦	⑦♀	⑦	⑦♀		⑦♀	⑦		⑦		⑦	⑦	⑦
Weymouth d.		...	...	...	...	...	0748	...	0848	...	0948	...	1048	...	1148		1848	...	...	1958	...	2058	2158	2258
Dorchester South d.		...	...	...	...	...	0800	...	0900	...	1000	...	1100	...	1200	and	1900	...	...	2010	...	2110	2210	2310
Poole d.		...	...	0650	...	0750	0832	0855	0932	0955	1032	1055	1132	1155	1232	at	1932	1955	...	2050	...	2150	2250	2350
Bournemouth d.		...	...	0706	...	0806	0850	0906	0950	1006	1050	1106	1150	1206	1250	the	1950	2006	...	2106	...	2206	2306	0003
Brockenhurst d.		...	...	0734	...	0834	0909	0934	1009	1034	1109	1134	1109	1234	1309	same	2009	2034	...	2134	...	2234	2334	...
Southampton Central d.		0655	...	0755	...	0855	0925	0955	1025	1055	1125	1155	1125	1255	1325	minutes	2025	2055	...	2155	...	2255	2353	...
Southampton Airport d.		0703	...	0803	...	0903	0933	1003	1033	1103	1133	1203	1133	1303	1333	past	2033	2103	...	2203	...	2303	...	...
Winchester d.		0723	...	0823	...	0923	0942	1023	1042	1123	1141	1223	1242	1323	1342	each	2042	2123	...	2223	...	2323	...	...
Basingstoke d.		0744	...	0844	...	0944	1000	1044	1100	1144	1200	1244	1300	1344	1400	hour	2100	2144	...	2244	...	2343	...	...
Woking a.		0802	...	0902	...	1002	1018	1102	1118	1202	1218	1302	1318	1402	1418	until	2118	2202	...	2302	...	0002	...	...
London Waterloo a.		0842	...	0942	...	1042	1054	1140	1152	1240	1252	1340	1349	1437	1449		2149	2237	...	2337	...	0033	...	...

– 7 minutes earlier on ⑥.
– 4 minutes later on ⑥.
j – Change at Eastleigh.
q – 0007 on ⑦.
r – 3–5 minutes earlier on ⑥.
s – Stops to set down only.
v – 6–8 minutes later on ⑥.

SN ASHFORD - HASTINGS - BRIGHTON 109

km		Ⓐ	Ⓐ	Ⓐ	Ⓐ	Ⓐ		Ⓐ	Ⓐ	Ⓐ		⑥	⑥		⑥		⑥	⑥	⑥		⑦	⑦	⑦		⑦	⑦
0	**Ashford** d.		0624	0730	0830	0930		2030	2130	2224	...		0623	...	0730		2030	2130	2224	...		0815	0921		2121	2220
25	Rye d.		0648	0754	0855	0954	and	2054	2157	2247	...		0648	...	0754	and	2054	2157	2247	...		0840	0945	and	2145	2243
42	**Hastings** d.		0712	0815	0913	1012	hourly	2112	2216	2309	...		0711	...	0812	hourly	2112	2216	2309	...		0903	1003	hourly	2203	2305
50	Bexhill a.		0721	0824	0922	1021	until	2121	2225	*2322*	...		0721	...	0821	until	2121	2225	*2322*	...		0912	1012	until	2212	*2327*
67	Eastbourne a.		0737	0840	0938	1037		2137	2241	*2343*	...		0737	...	0837		2137	2240	*2343*	...		0929	1029		2229	*2348*
93	Lewes a.		0807	0907	1007	1108		2207	2307	*0008*	...		0807	...	0907		2207	2307	*0008*	...		0959	1059		2259	...
106	**Brighton** a.		0820	0920	1020	1121		2220	2320	*0024*	...		0820	...	0920		2220	2320	*0024*	...		1012	1112		2312	...

	Ⓐ	Ⓐ	Ⓐ		Ⓐ	Ⓐ	Ⓐ		Ⓐ	Ⓐ	Ⓐ	Ⓐ		⑥	⑥	⑥		⑥	⑥		⑦	⑦		⑦		⑦
Brighton d.		...	*0530*	...	0632	0732	0832		1732	1830	1932	2032	...		*0530*	0632		1932	2032	...		*0709*	...	0820		2020
Lewes d.		...	*0541*	...	0644	0744	0844	and	1744	1842	1944	2044	...		*0541*	0644	and	1944	2044	...		*0725*	...	0832	and	2032
Eastbourne d.		0500	0604	...	0708	0808	0908	hourly	1808	1909	2008	2108	...		0605	0708	hourly	2008	2108	...		0758	...	0903	hourly	2103
Bexhill d.		*0514*	0618	...	0722	0825	0922	until	1823	1923	2022	2122	...		0618	0722	until	2022	2124	...		0811	...	0916	until	2116
Hastings d.		0530	0629	...	0734	0836	0934		1834	1934	2035	2134	...		0626	0729		2029	2134	...		0822	...	0927		2127
Rye d.		0547	0649	...	0754	0854	0954		1854	1954	2054	2157	...		0650	0754		2054	2157	...		0841	...	0946		2146
Ashford a.		0615	0711	...	0816	0916	1016		1916	2016	2116	2219	...		0713	0816		2116	2219	...		0903	...	1008		2208

☛ Additional trains operate Hastings - Eastbourne - Brighton and v.v.

110 BRIGHTON - PORTSMOUTH and SOUTHAMPTON SN

km		Ⓐ	Ⓐ	Ⓐ	Ⓐ	Ⓐ	Ⓐ	Ⓐ	Ⓐ	Ⓐ 2B	Ⓐ	Ⓐ		Ⓐ	Ⓐ	Ⓐ	Ⓐ	Ⓐ 2B	Ⓐ	Ⓐ	Ⓐ	Ⓐ	Ⓐ
0	**Brighton** d.	0530	0553	0633	0636	0706	0715	0730	0803	0900	0903	0933	and	1503	1533	1603	1633	1700	1703	1733	1808	1835	1903
2	Hove d.	0534	0557	0637	0640	0710	0719	0734	0807	0904	0907	0937	at	1507	1537	1607	1637	1704	1707	1737	1812	1839	1907
17	Worthing d.	0555	0609	0650	0657	0723	0736	0752	0820	0922	0926	0955	the	1525	1555	1625	1655	1722	1725	1755	1830	1901	1929
36	Barnham d.	0618	0624	0705	0720	0745	0753	0814	0842	0938	0945	1015	same	1547	1615	1647	1715	1738	1747	1815	1852	1917	1952
46	**Chichester** d.	0626	0632	0713	0728	0753	0801	0822	0850	0947	0953	1023	minutes	1555	1623	1655	1723	1747	1755	1823	1900	1925	2000
60	Havant d.	0640	0653	0731	0741	0804	0822	0837	0901	0959	1004	1037	past	1606	1637	1708	1737	1758	1813	1837	1911	1938	2011
71	Portsmouth & Southsea a.	|	0708	|	0753	|	0837	|	0916	|	1016	|	each	1619	|	1722	|	|	1825	|	1923	|	2023
73	**Portsmouth** Harbour a.	|	0712	|	0757	|	0841	|	0921	|	1020	|	hour	*1632*	|	*1735*	|	|	1831	|	1927	|	2027
76	Fareham a.	0659	...	0746	...	0824	...	0853	...	1013	...	1052	until	...	1652	...	1752	1812	...	1852	...	1952	...
100	**Southampton Central** a.	0726	...	0813	...	0856	...	0919	...	1038	...	1118		...	1719	...	1819	1838	...	1919	...	2018	...

	Ⓐ	Ⓐ	Ⓐ	Ⓐ	Ⓐ	Ⓐ	⑥	⑥	⑥	⑥	⑥	⑥	⑥	⑥ 2B	⑥	⑥		⑥	⑥	⑥ 2B	⑥	⑥	⑥
Brighton d.	1934	2003	2030	2103	2133	2203	0527	0601	0631	0703	0733	0803	0833	0900	0903	0933	and	1603	1633	1700	1703	1733	1803
Hove d.	1938	2007	2034	2107	2137	2207	0531	0605	0635	0707	0737	0807	0837	0904	0907	0937	at	1607	1637	1704	1707	1737	1807
Worthing d.	2000	2029	2056	2129	2159	2229	0553	0623	0653	0725	0755	0825	0855	0922	0925	0955	the	1625	1655	1722	1725	1755	1825
Barnham d.	2018	2051	2118	2151	2221	2251	0615	0645	0715	0745	0815	0845	0915	0941	0945	1015	same	1645	1715	1741	1745	1815	1845
Chichester d.	2026	2059	2126	2159	2229	2259	0623	0653	0723	0753	0823	0853	0923	0949	0953	1023	minutes	1653	1723	1749	1753	1823	1853
Havant d.	2037	2110	2137	2210	2243	2311	0637	0704	0737	0804	0837	0904	0937	1000	1004	1037	past	1704	1737	1800	1804	1837	1904
Portsmouth & Southsea a.	|	2123	|	2222	2256	2323	*0658*	0717	|	0818	|	0916	|	|	1016	|	each	1716	|	|	1816	|	1916
Portsmouth Harbour a.	|	2127	|	2226	2300	2327	*0702*	0721	|	0822	|	0920	|	|	1020	|	hour	1720	|	|	1820	|	1920
Fareham a.	2053	...	2152	*2242*v	...	...	0652	...	0752	...	0852	...	0952	1014	...	1052	until	...	1752	1814	...	1852	...
Southampton Central a.	2118	...	2217	*2307*v	...	...	0718	...	0818	...	0918	...	1018	1038	...	1118		...	1818	1838	...	1918	...

	⑥	⑥	⑥	⑥	⑥	⑥	⑥	⑥		⑦	⑦	⑦	⑦	⑦ 2C	⑦	⑦	⑦	⑦	⑦	⑦	⑦	⑦	⑦ 2B	⑦
Brighton d.	1833	1903	1927	1956	2030	2103	2133	2203	...	0715	0815	0917	*1017*	1110	*1117*	*1217*	1217	*1317*	1317	*1417*	1417	*1517*	1547	*1617*
Hove d.	1837	1907	1931	2000	2034	2107	2137	2207	...	0718	0818	0926	1024	1114	1124	1224	1226	1324	1326	1424	1426	1524	1551	1624
Worthing d.	1855	1929	1953	2022	2056	2129	2159	2229	...	0731	0831	0948	1040	1129	1140	1240	1248	1340	1348	1440	1448	1540	1608	1640
Barnham d.	1915	1951	2015	2044	2118	2151	2221	2251	...	0747	0847	1012	1055	1146	1155	1255	1312	1355	1412	1455	1512	1555	1625	1655
Chichester d.	1923	1959	2023	2052	2126	2159	2229	2259	...	0755	0855	1020	1103	1158	1203	1303	1320	1403	1420	1503	1520	1603	1634	1703
Havant d.	1937	2010	2037	2110	2137	2210	2243	2310	...	0809	0910	1041	1117	1210	1217	1317	1341	1417	1441	1517	1541	1617	1648	1717
Portsmouth & Southsea a.	|	2022	|	2122	|	2222	2255	2322	...	0822	0922	1054	1129	|	1229	1329	1354	1429	1454	1529	1554	1629	|	1729
Portsmouth Harbour a.	|	2026	|	2126	|	2226	2259	2326	...	0826	0926	1058	1135	|	1235	1335	1358	1435	1458	1535	1558	1635	|	1735
Fareham a.	1952	...	2052	...	2152	*2241*v	...	...	...	*0905*r	*0935*v	*1131*r	*1205*r	1231	*1305*r	*1405*r	*1431*r	*1505*r	*1531*r	*1605*r	*1631*r	...	1702	*1805*
Southampton Central a.	2018	...	2118	...	2218	*2305*v	...	...	...	*0940*r	*0959*v	*1153*r	*1240*r	1253	*1340*r	*1440*r	*1453*r	*1540*r	*1553*r	*1640*r	*1653*r	...	1724	*1840*

	⑦	⑦	⑦ 2B	⑦	⑦	⑦	⑦	⑦	⑦	⑦	⑦
Brighton d.	1617	*1717*	1747	*1817*	1817	*1917*	1917	*2017*	2017	*2117*	2117
Hove d.	1626	1724	1751	1824	1826	1924	1926	2024	2026	2124	2126
Worthing d.	1648	1740	1808	1840	1848	1940	1948	2040	2048	2140	2148
Barnham d.	1712	1755	1825	1855	1912	1955	2012	2055	2112	2155	2212
Chichester d.	1720	1803	1834	1903	1920	2003	2020	2103	2120	2203	2220
Havant d.	1741	1817	1848	1917	1941	2017	2041	2117	2141	2217	2241
Portsmouth & Southsea a.	1754	1829	|	1929	1954	2029	2054	2129	2154	2229	2254
Portsmouth Harbour a.	1758	1835	|	1935	1958	2035	2058	2135	2158	2235	2258
Fareham a.	*1831*r	...	1900	*2005*r	*2031*r	*2105*r	*2135*v	*2205*r	*2231*r	*2305*r	*2335*v
Southampton Central a.	*1853*r	...	1922	*2040*r	*2053*r	*2140*r	*2159*v	*2240*r	*2253*r	*2340*r	*2359*v

	Ⓐ	Ⓐ	Ⓐ	Ⓐ	Ⓐ	Ⓐ	Ⓐ	Ⓐ
Southampton Central d.	...	...	0610	...	*0621*r	0706	...	0736
Fareham d.	...	...	0634	...	*0658*r	0731	...	0800
Portsmouth Harbour d.	0534	0604	|	0701	0720	|	...	*0745*
Portsmouth & Southsea d.	0538	0608	|	0705	0724	|	...	*0750*
Havant d.	0554	0620	0653	0720	0736	0747	...	0815
Chichester d.	0615	0635	0708	0732	0747	0808	...	0830
Barnham d.	0623	0643	0716	0740	0755	0816	0820	0838
Worthing d.	0645	0708	0738	0800	0816	...	0842	0857
Hove a.	0706	0725	0755	0813	0834	...	0903	0914
Brighton a.	0710	0730	0800	0819	0838	...	0908	0919

	Ⓐ		Ⓐ	Ⓐ		Ⓐ	Ⓐ	Ⓐ 2B	Ⓐ	Ⓐ	Ⓐ	Ⓐ	Ⓐ	Ⓐ	Ⓐ	Ⓐ	Ⓐ	Ⓐ	Ⓐ	Ⓐ	Ⓐ	Ⓐ	Ⓐ	Ⓐ
Southampton Central d.	*0742*r	...	0836	...	and	1336	...	1434	...	1536	...	1636	...	1736	...	1827	...	1936	...	2036	...	*2111*v	*2123*v	*2212*
Fareham d.	*0806*r	...	0900	...	at	1400	...	1456	...	1600	...	1700	...	1800	...	1856	...	2000	...	2100	...	*2139*v	*2156*v	*2236*
Portsmouth Harbour d.	0826	...	|	0928	the	|	1428	|	1528	|	1628	|	1728	|	1828	|	1928	|	*2022*	|	*2054*	2140	2215	2244
Portsmouth & Southsea d.	0830	...	|	0932	same	|	1432	|	1532	|	1632	|	1732	|	1832	|	1932	|	2032	|	2115	2144	2219	2248
Havant d.	0845	...	0915	0945	minutes	1415	1445	1511	1545	1615	1645	1715	1745	1815	1845	1911	1945	2015	2045	2115	2131	2200	2235	2304
Chichester d.	0856	...	0930	0956	past	1430	1456	1522	1556	1630	1656	1730	1756	1826	1856	1922	1956	2026	2056	2126	2152	2211	2252	2317
Barnham d.	0904	...	0938	1004	each	1438	1504	1530	1604	1638	1704	1738	1804	1834	1904	1930	2004	2034	2104	2134	2200	2219	2300	2325
Worthing d.	0926	...	0956	1026	hour	1456	1526	1550	1626	1656	1726	1756	1826	1853	1923	1952	2022	2053	2122	2156	2222	2252	2322	2359
Hove a.	0943	...	1013	1043	until	1513	1543	1608	1643	1713	1743	1813	1847	1914	1944	2013	2043	2114	2143	2217	2243	2313	2343	0020
Brighton a.	0948		1018	1048		1518	1548	1614	1648	1718	1748	1818	1852	1918	1948	2018	2048	2118	2148	2222	2248	2318	2348	0025

	⑥	⑥	⑥	⑥		⑥	⑥	⑥ 2B	⑥	⑥	⑥	⑥	⑥	⑥	⑥	⑥	⑥	⑥	⑥	⑥	⑥	⑥	⑥
Southampton Central d.	...	...	0636	...	and	1336	...	1435	...	1536	...	1636	...	1736	...	1836	...	1936	...	2036	*2111*v	*2123*v	*2211*
Fareham d.	...	...	0700	...	at	1400	...	1456	...	1600	...	1700	...	1800	...	1900	...	2000	...	2100	*2139*v	*2155*v	*2239*
Portsmouth Harbour d.	0628	0648	|	0728	the	|	1428	|	1528	|	1628	|	1728	|	1828	|	1928	|	2028	|	2140	2215	2244
Portsmouth & Southsea d.	0632	0653	|	0732	same	|	1432	|	1532	|	1632	|	1732	|	1832	|	1932	|	2032	|	2144	2219	2248
Havant d.	0645	0710	0715	0745	minutes	1415	1445	1511	1545	1615	1645	1715	1745	1815	1845	1915	1945	2015	2045	2115	2200	2235	2304
Chichester d.	0656	0721	0730	0756	past	1430	1456	1522	1556	1630	1656	1730	1756	1830	1856	1930	1956	2026	2056	2126	2211	2252	2317
Barnham d.	0704	0729	0738	0804	each	1438	1504	1530	1604	1638	1704	1738	1804	1838	1904	1938	2004	2034	2104	2134	2219	2300	2325
Worthing d.	0726	0750	0756	0826	hour	1456	1526	1550	1626	1656	1726	1756	1826	1856	1926	1954	2026	2053	2126	2156	2252	2322	2359
Hove a.	0743	0807	0813	0843	until	1513	1543	1607	1643	1713	1743	1813	1843	1913	1943	2015	2043	2114	2143	2217	2313	2343	0020
Brighton a.	0748	0815	0818	0848		1518	1548	1614	1648	1718	1748	1818	1848	1918	1948	2020	2048	2118	2148	2222	2318	2348	0025

	⑦	⑦	⑦ 2	⑦	⑦	⑦	⑦	⑦	⑦	⑦	⑦ 2C	⑦	⑦	⑦	⑦ 2C	⑦	⑦	⑦	⑦	⑦	⑦ 2C	⑦	⑦	⑦
Southampton Central d.	*0635*r	*0735*r	0831	*0835*r	*0925*v	*0935*r	*1104*r	*1207*r	*1225*v	*1235*r	1312	*1359*r	*1425*v	*1435*r	1530	*1607*r	*1707*r	*1807*r	*1907*r	*1925*v	2007	...	*2033*r	*2101*
Fareham d.	*0710*r	*0810*r	0855	*0910*r	*0950*v	*1010*r	*1126*r	*1229*r	*1250*v	*1310*r	1334	*1421*r	*1450*v	*1510*r	1555	*1629*r	*1729*r	*1829*r	*1929*r	*1950*v	2029	...	*2055*r	*2123*
Portsmouth Harbour d.	0743	0843	|	0943	1014	1043	1143	1243	1314	1343	|	1443	1514	1543	|	1643	1743	1843	1943	2014	|	2043	2114	2143
Portsmouth & Southsea d.	0747	0847	|	0947	1018	1047	1147	1247	1318	1347	|	1447	1518	1547	|	1647	1747	1847	1947	2018	|	2047	2118	2147
Havant d.	0800	0900	0911	1000	1033	1100	1200	1300	1333	1400	1404	1500	1533	1600	1611	1700	1800	1900	2000	2033	2053	2100	2133	2200
Chichester d.	0814	0914	0922	1014	1053	1114	1214	1314	1353	1414	1419	1514	1553	1614	1622	1714	1814	1914	2014	2053	2104	2114	2153	2214
Barnham d.	0822	0922	0930	1022	1108	1122	1222	1322	1408	1422	1427	1522	1608	1622	1630	1722	1822	1922	2022	2108	2112	2122	2208	2222
Worthing d.	0841	0942	0945	1042	1130	1142	1242	1342	1430	1442	1445	1542	1630	1642	1645	1742	1842	1942	2042	2130	2134	2200	2230	2300
Hove a.	0853	0953	0959	1053	1151	1153	1253	1353	1451	1453	1459	1553	1651	1653	1657	1753	1853	1953	2053	2151	2155	2221	2251	2321
Brighton a.	*0900*	*1000*	1005	*1100*	1200	*1200*	*1300*	*1400*	1500	*1500*	1506	*1600*	1700	*1700*	1705	*1800*	*1900*	*2000*	*2100*	2155	2201	2226	2256	2325

B – To / from Bristol. C – To / from Cardiff. r – Change at Fratton. v – Change at Havant.

112 EXETER - EXMOUTH GW 2nd class

EXETER St Davids – Exeter Central – **EXMOUTH** *18 km*

Ⓐ: 0535, 0600, 0645, 0710, 0749, 0815, 0846, 0918, 0949, 1018, 1045, 1118, 1145, 1218, 1245, 1318, 1345, 1418, 1445, 1518, 1545, 1618, 1645, 1718, 1750, 1818, 1849, 1949, 2049, 2149, 2315.

⑥: 0535, 0645, 0714, 0746, 0815, 0846, 0918, 0945, 1018, 1045, 1118, 1145, 1218, 1245, 1318, 1418, 1445, 1518, 1545, 1618, 1645, 1718, 1750, 1849, 1949, 2049, 2145, 2310.

⑦: 1032, 1125, 1225, 1325, 1425, 1525, 1625, 1725, 1835, 1935, 2035, 2135, 2230, 2316. (Also 0825 and 0925 from Mar. 30).

EXMOUTH – Exeter Central – **EXETER** St Davids Journey time: ± 28 minutes

Ⓐ: 0605, 0648, 0715, 0750, 0820 and every 30 minutes until 1820; then 1854, 1920, 2020, 2120, 2220, 2345.

⑥: 0615, 0718, 0750, 0820 and every 30 minutes until 1820; then 1854, 1920, 2026, 2120, 2220, 2341.

⑦: 1110, 1205, 1305, 1409, 1510, 1610 and hourly until 2210; then 2301, 2347. (Also 0910 and 1000 from Mar. 30).

SW LONDON - SALISBURY - EXETER 113

km		⚒	⚒	Ⓐ	⑥	⚒	⚒	⚒ 🍷	Ⓐ 🍷	⑥ 🍷	⚒ 🍷	⚒ 🍷	⑥ 🍷	Ⓐ 🍷	⚒ 🍷 C	⚒ 🍷	⚒ 🍷	⚒ 🍷	⚒ 🍷	⚒ 🍷	⚒ 🍷	⑥ 🍷	Ⓐ 🍷	Ⓐ 🍷	⑥ 🍷	Ⓐ 🍷
0	**London** Waterloo d.		...	...	...	...	*0630*	0710	0820	0820	0920	1020	1120	1120	1220	1320	1350	1420	1450	1520	1550	1620	1620	1650	1720	1720
39	Woking d.		...	...	...	...	*0657*	0736	0846	0846	0946	1046	1146	1146	1246	1346	1416	1446	1516	1546	1616	1646	1646	1716u	1746	1746u
77	Basingstoke d.		...	...	...	...	0722	0757	0907	0907	1007	1107	1207	1207	1307	1407	1437	1507	1537	1607	1637	1707	1707	1737	1807	1807
107	Andover d.		...	...	...	...	0744	0819	0924	0924	1024	1124	1224	1224	1324	1424	1459	1524	1559	1624	1659	1724	1729	1759	1824	1829
134	**Salisbury** a.		...	...	...	...	0803	0840	0942	0942	1042	1142	1242	1242	1343	1442	1518	1542	1618	1642	1718	1742	1748	1818	1842	1848
134	**Salisbury** d.		...	0608	0615	0712	0808	0845	0948	0948	1048	1148	1248	1248	1348	1448	1523a	1548	—	1648	1723a	1748	1753	1823	1853	1853
169	Gillingham d.		...	0642	0642	0743	0841	0907	1013	1013	1113	1213	1310	1313	1413	1513	1544a	1613	...	1713	1747a	1813	1818	1848	1918	1918
190	Sherborne d.		...	0657	0657	0758	0856	0922	1028	1028	1128	1228	|	1328	1428	1528	—	1628	...	1728	—	1828	1833	1903	1933	1933
197	**Yeovil** Junction a.		...	0703	0703	0804	0902	0927	1033	1033	1133	1233	1327	1333	1433	1533	...	1633	...	1733	...	1833	1838	1910	1938	1938
197	**Yeovil** Junction d.		0615	0708	0708	—	...	0929	1035	1035	1135	1235	1328	...	1435	...	...	1635	...	—	...	1835	1840	...	...	1940
211	Crewkerne d.		0624	0717	0717	...	...	0938	1044	1044	|	1244	|	...	1444	...	...	1644	...	...	⚒	1844	1849	...	...	1949
233	Axminster d.		0655	0737	0737	⚒	...	0952	1104	1105	1155	1304	|	...	1504	...	⚒	1704	⑥	Ⓐ	1823	1904	1904	...	...	2003
249	Honiton d.		0715	0749	0749	0900	...	1004	1116	1130	1207	1316	1400	...	1516	...	1601	1716	1730	1730	1838	1930	1930	...	...	2015
276	Exeter Central a.		0731	0812	0820	0923	...	1029	1138	1151	1229r	1338	1419	...	1538	...	1623	1733	1752	1755	1900	1951	1956	...	...	2030
277	**Exeter** St Davids a.		0735d	0815	0830	0927	...	1033	1142	1156	1233r	1342	1423	...	1542	...	1627	1738	1757	1759	1904	1957	2003	...	...	2036
	Paignton **117** a.		...	...	0923	...	...	1131	...	...	|	...	1515	...	|	...	...	1840a	1850	...	...	...	...	...	...	...
	Plymouth **117** a.		...	...	...	...	...	...	...	...	1356d	...	...	...	1658	...	...	...	...	...	...	...	...	...	...	...

	Ⓐ 🍷	⚒ 🍷	①–④ 🍷 C	⑤⑥ 🍷 C	⑥ 🍷	Ⓐ 🍷	⑥ 🍷	Ⓐ 🍷	⚒ 🍷	⑦	⑦	⑦	⑦ 🍷	⑦ 🍷	⑦ 🍷	⑦ 🍷	⑦ 🍷 C	⑦ 🍷	⑦ 🍷	⑦ 🍷	⑦ 🍷	⑦ 🍷	⑦ 🍷 C	⑦ 🍷	⑦ 🍷	⑦ 🍷
London Waterloo d.	1750	1820	1920	1920	2020	2020	2120	2120	2335		...	...	0815	0915	1015	1115	1215	1315	1415	1515	1615	1715	1815	1915	2015	2115
Woking d.	*1813*	1846	1946	1946	2046	2049	2149	2149	0003		...	...	0847	0947	1046	1146	1246	1346	1446	1546	1646	1746	1846	1946	2046	2146
Basingstoke d.	1838	1907	2007	2007	2107	2110	2210	2210	0024		...	0809	0908	1008	1107	1207	1307	1407	1507	1607	1707	1807	1907	2007	2107	2207
Andover d.	1900	1929r	2029	2029v	2129	2132	2232	2232	0046		...	0831	0930	1025	1129	1224	1329	1424	1529	1624	1729	1824	1929	2024	2129	2224
Salisbury a.	1920	1948r	2049	2049v	2148	2151	2251	2255	0105		...	0850	0950	1041	1148	1240	1348	1440	1548	1640	1748	1840	1948	2042	2148	2244
Salisbury d.	1924	1953	2053	2053	2200	2206	2304	2304	...		0710	0854	0954	1050	1154	1248	1354	1448	1554	1654	1754	1848	1954	2054	2154	2248
Gillingham d.	1946	2018	2118	2118	2226	2231	2329s	2332s	...		0735	0919	1019	1115	1219	1315	1419	1515	1619	1719	1819	1915	2019	2119	2219	2315
Sherborne d.	2001	2033	2133	2133	2241	2246	2344s	2347s	...		0750	0934	1034	1130	1234	1330	1434	1530	1634	1734	1834	1930	2034	2134	2234	2330
Yeovil Junction a.	2011	2038	2138	2138	2246	2251	2350	2353	...		0755	0939	1039	1135	1239	1335	1439	1535	1639	1739	1840	1935	2039	2140	2239	2335
Yeovil Junction d.	...	2040	2140	2140	...	2253	...	...	...		0757	0941	1041	1140	...	1340	...	1540	...	1740	...	1940	...	2140	...	2337
Crewkerne d.	...	2049	2149	2149	...	2302	...	...	...		0806	0950	|	1149	...	1349	...	1549	...	1749	...	1949	...	2149	...	2346
Axminster d.	...	2111	2203	2203	...	2316	...	...	...		0820	1011	1101	1211	...	1411	...	1611	...	1811	...	2013	...	2211	...	2358
Honiton d.	...	2123	2214	2215	...	2328	...	...	...		0835	1023	1113	1223	...	1423	...	1623	...	1823	...	2025	...	2223	...	0010
Exeter Central a.	...	2147	...	2236	...	2349	...	...	...		0854	1044	1128	1244	...	1442	...	1642	...	1842	...	2044	...	2242	...	|
Exeter St Davids a.	...	2153	...	2241	...	2354	...	...	...		0859	1049	1132	1249	...	1446	...	1646	...	1846	...	2049	...	2246	...	0030
Paignton **117** a.	...	...	...	...	...	...	...	...	...		...	1142	...	1349	...	1538	...	1743	...	...	...	2138	...	...	...	...
Plymouth **117** a.	...	...	...	...	...	...	...	...	...		...	...	...	...	...	...	...	...	...	...	...	...	...	...	...	...

	⚒	⚒ 🍷	Ⓐ 🍷	Ⓐ 🍷	⑥ 🍷	Ⓐ 🍷	⑥ 🍷	⚒ 🍷	Ⓐ 🍷	⑥ 🍷	⚒ 🍷	⚒	⚒ 🍷 C	⚒ 🍷	⚒ 🍷	Ⓐ 🍷	⑥ 🍷	⚒ 🍷	⚒ 🍷	⚒ 🍷	⚒ 🍷	⚒ 🍷	⚒ 🍷 C	⑥ 🍷	Ⓐ 🍷	Ⓐ
Plymouth **117** d.		...	...	...	...	...	...	...	...	...	...	...	...	...	...	...	...	...	...	...	...	...	...	1450	1447	...
Paignton **117** d.		...	...	...	...	...	...	...	...	...	...	...	...	...	...	...	1012	...	...	1235	...	...	...	|	|	...
Exeter St Davids d.		...	...	...	...	0510	0510	...	...	...	0641	0805r	0825	...	1010	...	1108	1210	...	1335	1410	1529	...	1610	1610	1636
Exeter Central d.		...	...	...	...	0514	0514	...	...	...	0644	0808	0830	...	1014	...	1112	1214	...	1339	1414	1533	...	1614	1614	1643
Honiton d.		...	...	...	...	0538	0538	0620	...	...	0712	0831	0846	...	1040	...	1128	1238	...	1357	1438	1557	...	1638	1638	1707
Axminster d.		...	...	...	...	0549	0549	0631	...	...	0723	—	0857	...	1051	...	1139	1249	...	1408	1449	—	...	1649	1649	—
Crewkerne d.		...	...	...	...	0602	0602	0644	...	...	0736	⚒	0910	...	1104	...	1200	1303	...	|	1503	...	...	1703	1703	...
Yeovil Junction a.		...	...	...	...	0611	0611	0652	...	...	0745	🍷	0919	...	1113	...	1209	1312	...	1427	1512	...	...	1712	1712	...
Yeovil Junction d.		...	0515	0550	...	0620	0620	0654	0720	...	0750	0820	0920	1020	1120	1220	1220	1320	1350a	1428	1520	⚒	1620	1720	1720	...
Sherborne d.		...	0521	0556	...	0626	0626	0700	0726	...	0756	0826	0926	1026	1126	1226	1226	1326	1356a	|	1526	🍷	1626	1726	1726	...
Gillingham d.		...	0537	0612	...	0642	0642	0716	0744	...	0812	0842	0942	1042	1142	1242	1242	1342	1413a	1445	1545r	1615a	1642	1742	1748	⚒
Salisbury a.		...	0602	0639	...	0710	0710	0740	0809	...	0837	0914	1015	1115	1215	1315	1315	1415	1435a	1515	1615	1640a	1715	1815	1820	🍷
Salisbury d.		0515	0608	0645	0645	0715	0720	0745	0815	0820	0845	0920	1020	1120	1220	1320	1320	1420	1445	1520	1620	1645	1720	1820	1825	1845
Andover d.		0535	0628	0705	0704	0735	0737	0804	0835	0837	0904	0937	1037	1137	1237	1337	1337	1437	1504	1537	1637	1704	1737	1837	1842	1904
Basingstoke a.		0558	0651	0728	0727	0758	0754	0828	0858	0854	0927	0954	1055	1154	1254	1354	1354	1454	1527	1554	1656	1727	1754	1854	1859	1927
Woking a.		0618	0711	*0805*	0749	0818	0817	0849	0918	0915	0949	1015	1115	1215	1315	1415	1415	1515	1549	1615	1716	1749	1815	1915	1919	1949
London Waterloo a.		0649	0744	0814	0819	0846	0849	0919	0951	0949	1019	1049	1149	1249	1349	1449	1449	1549	1619	1649	1745d	1819	1845d	1949	1949	2019q

	⑥	⚒	⚒ 🍷	⚒ 🍷	⚒	⚒	⑥	Ⓐ	⑦	⑦ 🍷	⑦ 🍷	⑦ 🍷	⑦ 🍷	⑦ 🍷	⑦ 🍷	⑦ 🍷	⑦ 🍷	⑦ 🍷	⑦ 🍷 C	⑦ 🍷	⑦ 🍷	⑦ 🍷	⑦ 🍷	⑦	⑦	⑦
Plymouth **117** d.	...	...	...	1748v	...	...	...	...		...	...	...	...	...	...	...	...	...	...	...	...	...	...	...	...	...
Paignton **117** d.	1552	...	...	|	1910d	...	...	...		...	...	...	...	...	...	...	1225	...	...	1527	1610	...	1823	...	...	2210
Exeter St Davids d.	1640	1740	1810	1910	2015	2100	2257	2257		...	...	...	0920	...	1120	...	1318	...	1518	1633	1718	...	1920	...	2120	2310
Exeter Central d.	1644	1744	1814	1914	2019	2104	2301	2301		...	...	...	0924	...	1124	...	1322	...	1523	1637	1723	...	1924	...	2124	2314
Honiton d.	1707	1808	1838	1930	2046	2123	2328	2331		...	...	0846	0946	...	1146	...	1346	...	1546	1655	1746	...	1946	...	2146	2329s
Axminster d.	—	1818	1849	1941	2057	2145	2339	2342		...	...	0857	0957	...	1157	...	1357	...	1557	1706	1757	...	1957	...	2157	2340s
Crewkerne d.	⚒	...	1910v	2008z	2110	2208	2352	2355		...	...	0910	1010	...	1210	...	1410	...	1610	1719	1810	...	2010	...	2210	0004s
Yeovil Junction a.	🍷	...	1918v	2016z	2119	2217	0001	0005		...	...	0918	1018	...	1218	...	1418	...	1618	1728	1818	...	2018	...	2218	0013s
Yeovil Junction d.	1820	...	1920	2020	2120	2224	0002	0005		0732	...	0925	1025	1125	1225	1325	1425	1525	1625	1729	1825	1925	2025	2125	2225	|
Sherborne d.	1826	...	1926	2026	2126	2230	|	|		0738	...	0931	1031	1131	1231	1331	1431	1531	1631	1736	1831	1931	2031	2131	2231	|
Gillingham d.	1848v	...	1948v	2042	2142	2251v	|	|		0755	...	0947	1047	1147	1247	1347	1447	1547	1647	1751	1847	1947	2046	2147	2247	|
Salisbury a.	1921	...	2020	2120	2208	2315r	0036	0040		0820	...	1021	1117	1221	1317	1421	1517	1621	1721	1822	1917	2021	2121	2221	2317	0050
Salisbury d.	1925	...	2025	2125	2225	...	...	...		0826	0926	1026	1126	1226	1326	1426	1526	1626	1726	1826	1926	2026	2126	2226	...	...
Andover d.	1944	...	2044	2144	2244	...	...	...		0846	0943	1046	1143	1246	1343	1446	1543	1646	1743	1846	1943	2046	2143	2246	...	...
Basingstoke a.	2008	...	2108	2208	2307	...	...	...		0908	1000	1108	1200	1308	1400	1508	1600	1708	1800	1908	2000	2108	2200	2308	...	...
Woking a.	2029	...	2129	2228	*2332*	...	...	...		0930	1023	1130	1223	1330	1423	1530	1623	1730	1823	1930	2023	2130	2223	*2350*	...	...
London Waterloo a.	2100d	...	2204	2257	*0004*j	...	...	...		1008	1103	1203	1303	1404	1458	1604	1658	1804	1858	2004	2058	2204	2258	*0038*	...	...

London - Salisbury also at Ⓐ: 0750, 0850, 0950, 1050, 1150, 1250, 1850, 1950, 2220. ⑥: 0750, 0850, 0950, 1050, 1150, 1250, 1650, 1750, 1850, 1950, 2220. ⑦: 2215, 2335

Salisbury - London also at Ⓐ: 0542, 0945, 1045, 1145, 1245, 1345, 1545, 1745. ⑥: 0542, 0617, 0945, 1045, 1145, 1245, 1345, 1545, 1745. ⑦: 0645, 0726.

C – Conveys (12) London - Salisbury - Bristol and v.v.
a – Ⓐ only.
d – 3–4 minutes later on ⑥.
j – *0007* on ⑦.
q – 2026 on ⑥.
r – 3–4 minutes earlier on ⑥.
s – Stops to set down only.
u – Stops to pick up only.
v – 5–7 minutes earlier on ⑥.
z – 13–14 minutes earlier on ⑥.

GW 2nd class BARNSTAPLE - EXETER 114

km		⚒	⚒	⚒	Ⓐ	⑥	⚒	⚒	⚒	⚒	⑥	Ⓐ	⚒	⚒	⑥	Ⓐ		⑦	⑦	⑦	⑦	⑦	⑦		⑦
0	**Barnstaple** d.		0703	0841	1030	1040	1241	1435	1542	1648	1800	1806	1924	2022	2206	2209	...		1110	1319	1511	1717	1910	...	2130
28	Eggesford d.		0734	0907	1056	1106	1307	1503	1608	1716	1832	1837	1951	2048	2235	2238	...		1142	1346	1542	1749	1941	...	2158
51	Crediton d.		0800	0930	1119	1130	1329	1526	1630	1738	1856	1901	2013	2109	2258	2302	...		1209	1409	1608	1818	2006	...	2216
63	Exeter St Davids a.		0815	0940v	1132	1142	1340	1538v	1640v	1748	1907	1913	2026	2125r	2309	2313	...		1223	1422	1622	1833	2020	...	2229
64	**Exeter** Central a.		0820	0948	1138	1148	1348	1548	1648	1754	...	1926	2052	2152r	2313	2318	...		1228	1428	1628	1838	2038	...	2233

	⚒	⚒	⚒		Ⓐ	⑥	⑥	Ⓐ	⚒	⚒	⚒	⚒	⑥	Ⓐ	⚒	⚒		⑦	⑦		⑦	⑦	⑦	⑦	⑦
Exeter Central d.		...	...	...	0904	...	1114	1118	1314	1414	1514d	1632j	1745	1746	1850	2044z	...		0937b	...	1137	1329	1534	1734	1934
Exeter St Davids d.		0556	0651	...	0912	0918	1119	1127	1319	1426	1533	1636	1750	1755	1908	2055	...		0941	...	1155	1355	1554	1800	1949
Crediton d.		0605	0701	...	0930	0929	1130	1138	1329	1436	1544	1647	1803	1808	1922	2109	...		0957	...	1210	1410	1609	1814	2007
Eggesford d.		0630	0750z	...	0957	0956	1154	1202	1357	1504	1608	1718	1832	1836	1951	2137	...		1026	...	1237	1440	1639	1841	2037
Barnstaple a.		0658	0816	...	1021	1020	1220	1228	1425	1530	1635	1745	1901	1904	2019	2205	...		1055	...	1302	1509	1708	1906	2106

b – From Mar. 30.
d – 1531 on ⑥.
j – 1614 on ⑥.
r – 3–4 minutes earlier on ⑥.
v – 3–4 minutes later on ⑥.
z – 2050 on ⑥.

115 LONDON - READING - EXETER GW

Services on ⑥⑦ are subject to alteration from February 2

km		Ⓐ ✕	Ⓐ 🍷	Ⓐ 🍷	Ⓐ 🍷	Ⓐ P🍷	Ⓐ ✕	Ⓐ ✕	Ⓐ 🍷	Ⓐ 🍷	Ⓐ ✕	Ⓐ 🍷	Ⓐ 🍷	Ⓐ 🍷	Ⓐ 🍷	Ⓐ 🍷	Ⓐ 🍷	Ⓐ P🍷	Ⓐ ✕	Ⓐ 🍷	Ⓐ 🍷	Ⓐ 🍷	Ⓐ ✕
0	**London** Paddington **131 133** d.	0730	0818	0905	1005	1000	1105	1205	1218	1305	1405	1505	1605	1633	1703	1630	1706	1733	1803	1730	1806	1836	190
58	Reading **131 133** ‡ d.	0757	0847	0932	1032	1027	1132	1232	1247	1332	1432	1532	1632	1704	1732	1657	1737	1802	1832	1757	1836	1903	193
85	Newbury ‡ d.	|	0910	|	|	|	|	|	1310	|	|	|	|	1720	1748	|	1801	1818	|	|	1901	1919	194
154	Westbury **139** d.	|	1000	|	|	|	1222	|	1358	|	|	1622	|	1803	|	|	1852	1858	|	|	1952	2005	|
186	Castle Cary **139** d.	|	1016	|	|	|	1240	|	1422	|	|	1640	|	1821	|	|	...	1916	|	|	...	2022	|
	Bristol T. Meads **116 133** d.	0913	|	|	|	1146	|	|	|	|	|	|	|	|	|	1822	...	|	|	1916	...	|	|
230	Taunton **116** d.	0946	1038	1048	|	1229	1302	|	1445	1450	1548	1704	1748	1843	1853	1930	...	1938	1947	2027	...	2044	205
253	Tiverton Parkway **116** a.	|	1051	1101	|	|	1315	|	...	1503	1601	1717	1801	1856	1905	...	...	1950	*2028*	...	...	2057	*212*
279	**Exeter** St Davids **116** a.	1012	1111	1117	1210	1256	1332	1410	...	1520	1617	1733	1818	1918	1922	...	...	2007	2013	...	...	2115	212
	Plymouth **117** a.	1115	...	1222	1309	...	1436	1509	...	1627	1721	1839	1924	...	2025	...	...	...	2117	...	...	...	222
	Penzance **117** a.	1321	...	*1441*	1512	...	*1636*	1711	...	...	1937	2041	2130	...	2230	...	...	...	2310	...	...	...	003

	Ⓐ 🍷	Ⓐ 🍷	⚒ 🍷		⑤ Z🍷	①–④ Z🍷		⑥ 🍷	⑥ 🍷	⑥ 🍷	⑥ 🍷	⑥ 🍷	⑥ 🍷	⑥ 🍷	⑥ 🍷	⑥ 🍷	⑥ 🍷	⑥ 🍷	⑥ 🍷	⑥ P🍷	⑥ 🍷	⑥ 🍷	⑥ 🍷
London Paddington **131 133** d.	1945	2035	2145	...	2345b	2345b	...	0730	0818	0905	1005	1105	1205	1218	1305	1405	1505	1605	1705	1630	1805	1830	190
Reading **131 133** ‡ d.	2011	2102	2212	...	0037u	0037u	...	0757	0849	0932	1032	1132	1232	1249	1332	1432	1532	1621	1732	1657	1832	1857	193
Newbury ‡ d.	2026	2118	|	...	|	|	...	|	0912	|	|	|	|	1313	|	|	|	|	|	|	|	|	194
Westbury **139** d.	2107	2158	|	...	|	|	...	|	0956	|	|	|	|	1356	|	|	1622	|	1822	|	|	|	202
Castle Cary **139** d.	2124	2216	|	...	|	|	...	|	1013	|	|	|	|	1414	|	|	1640	|	1840	|	|	|	204
Bristol T. Meads **116 133** d.	|	|	2345	...	|	|	...	0917	|	|	|	|	|	|	|	|	|	|	|	1815	|	2015	|
Taunton **116** d.	2146	2259	0042s	...	0340	0355	...	0951	1035	1048	|	1302	|	1436	1448	1550	1703	1748	1902	1907	1947	2106	210
Tiverton Parkway **116** a.	2159	2319	0118s	...	|	|	...	*1028*	1047	1101	|	1315	|	...	1501	1603	1716	1801	1915	1920	*2028*	...	212
Exeter St Davids **116** a.	2216	2343	0145	...	0436	0444	...	1017	1106	1117	1210	1332	1410	...	1518	1620	1732	1818	1932	1937	2013	...	213
Plymouth **117** a.	2322	0047	...	...	0547	0547	...	1120	...	1223	1310	1436	1509	...	1625	1723	1839	1921	2036	...	2117	...	224
Penzance **117** a.	...	...	...	...	0800	0800	...	1323	...	*1446*	1513	*1636*	1711	...	...	1923	2041	2130	2245	...	2317	...	...

	⑥ 🍷	⑥ 🍷		⑦ 🍷	⑦ 🍷	⑦ 🍷	⑦ 🍷	⑦ P🍷	⑦ 🍷	⑦ 🍷	⑦ 🍷	⑦ 🍷	⑦ 🍷	⑦ 🍷	⑦ 🍷	⑦ 🍷	⑦ 🍷	⑦ 🍷	⑦ 🍷	⑦ 🍷	⑦ 🍷		⑦ Z🍷
London Paddington **131 133** d.	2005	2030	...	0800	0842	0957	1057	1118	1157	1207	1257	1357	1457	1507	1557	1657	1757	1857	1907	1957	2057	...	2350
Reading **131 133** ‡ d.	2032	2057	...	0843	0932	1034	1132	1153	1232	1242	1332	1434	1532	1542	1632	1732	1833	1932	1942	2034	2133	...	0037
Newbury ‡ d.	2046	|	...	|	0948	|	|	|	1248	|	|	1451	|	|	1648	|	1851	|	|	2051	|	...	|
Westbury **139** d.	2125	|	...	|	1028	|	|	1243	|	|	1419	*1430*	|	|	1729	|	1934	|	|	2131	|	...	|
Castle Cary **139** d.	2144	|	...	|	|	1137	|	1301	|	|	|	1536	|	|	1747	|	|	2029	|	2149	|	...	|
Bristol T. Meads **116 133** d.	|	2216	...	1003	|	|	|	|	|	1401	|	|	|	1702	|	|	|	|	2102	|	|	...	|
Taunton **116** d.	2205	2310	...	1036	1104	1157	1247	1323	1359	1435	1454	1558	1649	1753	1808	1849	2008	2051	2154	2209	2251s	...	|
Tiverton Parkway **116** a.	2219	2324	...	1050	1117	|	*1328*	1336	*1428*	|	1507	*1628*	1701	...	1821	1901	2022	2104	2206	2222	2304s	...	|
Exeter St Davids **116** a.	2236	2344	...	1107	1134	1226	1314	1353	1425	1502	1524	1625	1718	...	1838	1918	2039	2121	2224	2239	2323	...	0243
Plymouth **117** a.	2347	...	...	1215	1237	1334	1411	...	1530	1605	1628	1737	1821	...	1940	2021	2143	2230	...	2347	...	...	0537
Penzance **117** a.	...	...	...	1416	1440	...	1614	...	*1739*	...	1837	*1954*	2022	...	*2148*	2220	2343	...	...	...	...	...	0847

	① Z🍷	②–⑤ Z🍷	Ⓐ 🍷	Ⓐ 🍷	Ⓐ 🍷	Ⓐ ✕	Ⓐ 🍷	Ⓐ 🍷	Ⓐ 🍷	Ⓐ ✕	Ⓐ P🍷	Ⓐ ✕	Ⓐ ✕	Ⓐ 🍷	Ⓐ 🍷	Ⓐ 🍷	Ⓐ ✕	Ⓐ ✕	Ⓐ 🍷	Ⓐ P🍷	Ⓐ ✕	Ⓐ 🍷	Ⓐ 🍷
Penzance **117** d.	2115n	2200n	...	...	...	...	...	...	...	0505	...	0542	0643	0743	0845	...	1000	*1036*	...	*1140*	*1242*	1400	*145*
Plymouth **117** d.	2320n	0020	...	...	...	0524	0535	...	0600	0655	*0725*	0747	0855	0947	1045	...	1200	1255	...	*1333*	1500	1600	170
Exeter St Davids **116** d.	0207	0127	...	...	0547	0631	0639	0645	0655	0752	0840	0849	0957	1055	1140	1154	1302	1357	*1446*	1501	1602	1701	180
Tiverton Parkway **116** d.	|	|	...	...	0607	|	0654	0659	|	*0752*	|	0903	1011	1109	|	1208	1316	*1337*	*1500*	1515	1617	1716	181
Taunton **116** d.	|	0247	...	...	0621	0656	0707	0714	0719	0816	0904	0918	1026	1124	|	1223	1331	1422	1523	1530	1631	1730	183
Bristol T. Meads **116 133** a.	|	|	...	...	|	0757	|	0822	|	|	0955	|	|	1156	|	|	|	|	|	|	|	|	|
Castle Cary **139** d.	|	|	...	...	0643	|	0729	|	|	|	|	0939	|	|	|	1244	|	1443	1544	|	|	|	185
Westbury **139** d.	|	|	0608	0621	0705	|	0751	|	|	|	|	0958	1102	|	|	1303	|	1502	1601	|	|	|	191
Newbury ‡ a.	|	|	0649	0711	0746	|	0830	|	|	|	|	|	|	|	|	1349	|	|	1648	|	|	|	194
Reading **133** ‡ a.	0418s	0452s	0718	0741	0807	0914	0851	0944	0833	0934	1109	1051	1151	1309	1317	1415	1451	1551	1717	1651	1751	1851	200
London Paddington **131 133** a.	0511c	0542c	0752	0809	0838	0944	0922	1014	0900	1003	1142	1123	1223	1342	1345	1444	1523	1622	1753	1723	1819	1924	203

	Ⓐ 🍷	Ⓐ ✕	Ⓐ 🍷	Ⓐ 🍷	Ⓐ 🍷	⑥ Z🍷	⑥ 🍷	⑥ 🍷	⑥ 🍷	⑥ 🍷	⑥ P🍷	⑥ 🍷	⑥ 🍷	⑥ 🍷	⑥ 🍷	⑥ 🍷	⑥ 🍷	⑥ 🍷	⑥ 🍷	⑥ 🍷	⑥ 🍷	⑥ 🍷	⑥ 🍷
Penzance **117** d.	...	1600	*1644*	1735	...	2200n	...	...	...	...	...	...	0645	0803	0848	...	1000	1058	*1145*	...	*1250*	1400	...
Plymouth **117** d.	...	1802	*1843*	1935	...	0020	...	0540	...	0655	...	0754	0852	1005	1046	...	1200	1255	1400	...	1504	1600	1654
Exeter St Davids **116** d.	...	1904	1953	2037	...	0127	...	0641	0730	0753	0805	0856	0954	1106	1144	1154	1302	1357	1459	...	1606	1701	1753
Tiverton Parkway **116** d.	...	1918	2008	2052	...	|	...	0656	0745	|	0819	0911	1008	1121	|	1209	1316	*1337*	1513	...	1620	1716	*1737*
Taunton **116** d.	...	1933	2022	2106	2130	0240	0700	0710	0759	0818	0834	0925	1023	1135	|	1223	1331	1422	1528	1534	1635	1730	1817
Bristol T. Meads **116 133** a.	...	|	|	2139	2229	|	0758	|	0853	|	0920	|	|	|	|	|	|	|	|	|	|	|	|
Castle Cary **139** d.	...	|	2043	|	|	|	|	0732	|	|	|	0946	|	|	|	1244	|	1443	|	1600	|	|	1838
Westbury **139** d.	1917	|	2103	|	|	|	|	0754	|	|	|	|	1059	|	|	1303	|	1502	|	1619	|	|	1857
Newbury ‡ a.	2006	|	2141	|	|	|	|	0832	|	|	|	|	|	|	|	1349	|	|	|	1704	|	|	1931
Reading **131 133** ‡ a.	2033	2051	2200	2255	2352	0451s	0914	0852	1009	0935	1045	1051	1150	1253	1322	1419	1451	1551	1650	1734	1753	1848	1950
London Paddington **131 133** a.	2102	2122	2230	2336v	0032	0535c	0944	0922	1042	1008	1115	1124	1222	1323	1353	1446	1523	1622	1723	1809	1823	1924	2021

	⑥ 🍷	⑥ 🍷	⑥ 🍷		⑦ 🍷	⑦ 🍷	⑦ 🍷	⑦ 🍷	⑦ 🍷	⑦ 🍷	⑦ 🍷	⑦ 🍷	⑦ 🍷	⑦ 🍷	⑦ P🍷	⑦ 🍷	⑦ 🍷	⑦ 🍷	⑦ 🍷	⑦ 🍷	⑦ 🍷	⑦ 🍷	⑦ 🍷
Penzance **117** d.	1554	1735	...	...	...	...	...	0830	...	0950	1050	*1130*	1250	...	...	...	...	1446	...	*1508*	1615	1720	...
Plymouth **117** d.	1754	1935	...	...	...	0845	0950	1035	1050	1145	1250	1344	1450	1505	...	1545	1610	1650	...	1750	1810	1915	1955
Exeter St Davids **116** d.	1856	2037	...	...	0830	0951	1052	1136	1153	1250	1352	1447	1550	1607	1636	1646	1717	1752	...	1850	1915	2019	2055
Tiverton Parkway **116** d.	1910	2052	...	...	0844	|	1106	1152	1207	|	1405	*1437*	1605	1622	1651	1702	1732	1805	...	*1853*	1928	2035	2109
Taunton **116** d.	1925	2110	2130	...	0858	1016	1120	1205	1221	1315	1420	1511	1620	1636	1704	1715	1745	1820	1826	1915	1942	2047	2122
Bristol T. Meads **116 133** a.	|	2144	2228	...	|	|	1156	|	1255	|	|	|	|	1719	1758	|	1824	|	1925	|	|	|	2157
Castle Cary **139** d.	1946	|	|	...	0920	|	|	1227	|	|	|	1533	|	|	|	1737	|	|	|	|	2005	2110	|
Westbury **139** d.	2005	|	|	...	0939	1054	|	1245	|	|	|	1551	|	|	|	1757	|	|	|	|	2024	2131	|
Newbury ‡ a.	|	|	|	...	1016	1128	|	1324	|	|	|	1630	|	|	|	1834	|	|	|	2022	|	2210	|
Reading **131 133** ‡ a.	2056	2307	2352	...	1037	1147	1313	1342	1414	1438	1538	1648	1738	1844	1914	1853	1946	1938	2044	2040	2112	2229	2326
London Paddington **131 133** a.	2128	2338	0032	...	1121	1228	1355	1422	1454	1522	1621	1736	1821	1924	1958	1934	2024	2021	2126	2124	2153	2323	0017

P – To / from Paignton.
Z – Also conveys 🛏 1, 2 cl.
b – 🛏 may be occupied from 2230.
c – 🛏 may be occupied until 0730.
n – Previous day.
s – Stops to set down only.
u – Stops to pick up only.
v – 2329 on ⑤.
‡ – Additional local services operate Reading - Newbury and v.v.

116 BRISTOL - EXETER GW, XC

Services are subject to alteration from January 28

km		Ⓐ 2	Ⓐ 2	Ⓐ 2	Ⓐ 2	Ⓐ 🍷	Ⓐ 🍷 D	Ⓐ ✕	Ⓐ 🍷 D	Ⓐ 2	Ⓐ 🍷 L	Ⓐ 2	Ⓐ 🍷 N	Ⓐ 🍷 M	Ⓐ 🍷	Ⓐ 2	Ⓐ 🍷 E	Ⓐ 🍷 N	Ⓐ 🍷 M	Ⓐ 2	Ⓐ 🍷 U	Ⓐ 🍷 N	Ⓐ 🍷 M	Ⓐ 2
	London Paddington **115** d.	...	...	...	...	...	...	0730	...	...	...	...	...	...	1000	...	...	...	...	...	...	...	...	...
	Birmingham New St **120** d.	...	...	...	...	0610	0710	|	0810	...	0910	...	0940	1010	|	...	1110	1140	1210	...	1310	1340	1410	...
0	**Bristol** T. Meads **115 137** d.	0531	0619	0647	0719	0811	0844	0913	0944	0955	1044	1053	1114	1144	1146	1153	1244	1311	1344	1353	1444	1511	1544	1553
★	Weston super Mare d.	0552	0650	0710	0748	|	|	|	|	1024	|	1123	1142	|	1210	1223	|	|	|	1423	|	|	|	1625
54	Bridgwater d.	0610	0708	|	0807	|	|	|	|	1043	|	1142	|	|	|	1242	|	|	|	1442	|	|	|	1645
72	Taunton **115** d.	0625	0723	0738	0821	0843	0917	0946	1017	1059	1117	1159	1205	1217	1232	1259	1317	1350r	1417	1459	1517	1543	1617	1700
95	Tiverton Parkway **115** a.	0640	...	0753	...	|	0928	|	1028	...	1128	...	1216	1228	*1315*	...	1328	1401	1428	...	1528	1554	1628	...
122	**Exeter** St Davids **115** a.	0658	...	0811	...	0907	0943	1012	1043	...	1143	...	1231	1243	1258	...	1343	1416	1443	...	1543	1610	1643	...
	Paignton **117** a.	|	...	|	...	0947	|	|	|	...	|	...	1320	|	1350	...	|	1505	|	...	|	|	|	...
	Plymouth **117** a.	0815	...	0922	...	...	1048	1115	1148	...	1248	...	...	1348	...	...	1448	...	1548	...	1648	1715	1748	...
	Penzance **117** a.	1019	...	1124	...	...	...	1321	...	...	...	...	...	...	...	...	...	...	...	...	...	...	1949	...

D – From Derby.
E – From Edinburgh.
L – From Leeds.
M – From Manchester.
N – From Newcastle.
U – From Dundee.
r – Arrives 1342.
★ – Bristol - Weston: *31 km*. Weston - Bridgwater: *24 km*.

Services are subject to alteration from January 28

	Ⓐ 🍷 G	Ⓐ 🍷 N	Ⓐ 🍷 M	Ⓐ 2	Ⓐ 🍷 E	Ⓐ 🍷	Ⓐ 2	Ⓐ 🍷 M	Ⓐ 🍷	Ⓐ 2	Ⓐ E	Ⓐ 2	Ⓐ 🍷 M	Ⓐ 2		Ⓐ 2	Ⓐ 🍷		⑥	⑥ 2🍷	⑥ 2	⑥ 2🍷	⑥ 2		⑥ 🍷 D
London Paddington **115** d.	...	...	...	...	...	1630	...	...	1730	...	...	...	...	...	...	...	2145	...		...	...	...	...	...	...
Birmingham New St **120** d.	1510	1540	1610	...	1710	|	...	1810	|	...	1910	...	2010	...	...	...	|	...		...	...	...	...	...	0710
Bristol T. Meads **115 137** d.	1644	1711	1744	1753	1844	1822	1855	1944	1916	1955	2044	2055	2144	2155	...	2306	2345	...		0525	0620	0648	0717	...	0844
Weston super Mare d.	|	|	|	1828	|	1856	1930	|	1957a	2030	|	2130	|	2230	...	2341	|	...		0546	0649	0712	0747	...	|
Bridgwater d.	|	|	|	1847	|	1913	1949	|	2013	2049	|	2149	|	2249	...	2359	|	...		0605	0708	|	0805	...	|
Taunton **115** d.	1717	1744	1817	1901	1917	1930	2004	2017	2030	2104	2117	2203	2215s	2303	...	0014	0042s	...		0620	0722	0738	0821	...	0917
Tiverton Parkway **115** a.	1728	1755	1828	...	1928	*1950*	...	2028	*2057*	...	2128	*2319*	2245s	...	...	...	0118s	...		0635	...	0755	...	...	0928
Exeter St Davids **115** a.	1743	1810	1843	...	1943	*2007*	...	2043	*2115*	...	2143	*2343*	2310s	...	...	...	0145	...		0654	...	0817	...	...	0943
Paignton **117** a.	|	|	|	...	|	...	...	|	...	...	|	...	|	...	...	...	...	...		|	...	|	...	...	|
Plymouth **117** a.	1852	1920	1948	...	2048	...	...	2148	...	...	2248	...	0018	...	...	...	...	...		0811	...	0928	...	...	1048
Penzance **117** a.	2056	...	2147	...	...	...	...	...	...	...	...	...	...	...	...	...	...	...		1015	...	1126	...	...	...

	⑥ 🍷	⑥ 🍷		⑥ 🍷 L	⑥ 2	⑥ 🍷 Y	⑥ 🍷 M	⑥ 2	⑥ 🍷 E	⑥ 2	⑥ 🍷 M	⑥ 2	⑥ 🍷 E	⑥ 🍷 N	⑥ 🍷 M	⑥ 2	⑥ 🍷 G	⑥ 2	⑥ 🍷 M	⑥ 2	⑥ 🍷	⑥ 🍷 E	⑥ 2	⑥ 🍷 M	⑥ 2
London Paddington **115** d.	0730	...	...	...	...	...	...	...	...	...	...	...	...	...	...	...	...	...	...	...	1615	...	...	...	...
Birmingham New St **120** d.	|	0810	...	0910	...	0940	1010	...	1110	...	1210	...	1310	1340	1410	...	1510	...	1610	...	|	1710	...	1810	...
Bristol T. Meads **115 137** d.	0917	0944	...	1044	1053	1114	1144	1153	1244	1253	1344	1353	1444	1511	1544	1553	1644	1653	1744	1753	1816	1844	1853	1944	1953
Weston super Mare d.	|	|	...	|	1123	1142	|	1223	|	1323	|	1423	|	|	|	1623	|	1723	|	1823	1836	|	1925	|	2024
Bridgwater d.	|	|	...	|	1142	|	|	1242	|	1342	|	1442	|	|	|	1642	|	1742	|	1842	|	|	1944	|	2043
Taunton **115** d.	0951	1017	...	1117	1156	1205	1217	1256	1317	1356	1417	1456	1517	1543	1617	1656	1717	1756	1817	1856	1859	1917	1958	2017	2058
Tiverton Parkway **115** a.	|	1028	...	1128	...	1216	1228	*1315*	1328	...	1428	...	1528	1554	1628	...	1728	...	1828	...	1912	1928	...	2028	*2120*
Exeter St Davids **115** a.	1017	1043	...	1143	...	1231	1243	*1332*	1343	...	1443	...	1543	1610	1643	...	1743	...	1843	...	1929	1943	...	2043	*2138*
Paignton **117** a.	|	|	...	|	...	1320	|	...	|	...	|	...	|	|	|	...	|	...	|	...	2020	|	...	|	...
Plymouth **117** a.	1120	1148	...	1248	...	...	1348	...	1448	...	1548	...	1648	1715	1748	...	1848	...	1948	...	...	2048	...	2148	...
Penzance **117** a.	1323	...	...	...	...	...	...	...	...	...	...	...	...	...	1949	...	2059	...	2143	...	...	...	...	...	...

	⑥ 🍷	⑥ 🍷 E	⑥ 🍷	⑥ 2	⑥ 🍷 M	⑥ 2	⑥ 🍷		⑦	⑦ 2	⑦ 2	⑦ 2	⑦ 🍷	⑦ 2		⑦ 2	⑦ 🍷 M	⑦ 🍷 L		⑦ 🍷 M	⑦ 🍷	⑦ 🍷 N	⑦ 🍷 N	⑦ 🍷 M	⑦ 2
London Paddington **115** d.	1830	...	1900	...	...	...	2030	...		...	...	...	0800	...	...	...	...	...	...	...	1207	...	...	...	...
Birmingham New St **120** d.	|	1910	|	...	2010	...	|	...		...	...	...	|	...	...	...	1010	1110	...	1210	|	1310	1340	1410	...
Bristol T. Meads **115 137** d.	2015	2044	2049	2056	2144	2153	2216	...		0730	0815	0905	1003	1010	...	1110	1144	1244	...	1344	1401	1444	1511	1544	1550
Weston super Mare d.	2037	|	2115	2128	|	2227	2242	...		0750	0843	0932	|	1041	...	1142	1202	|	...	|	|	|	|	|	1627
Bridgwater d.	|	|	2131	2147	|	2246	2259	...		|	0902	0950	|	1059	...	1200	|	|	...	|	|	|	|	|	1646
Taunton **115** d.	2106	2117	2147	2202	2217	2301	2310	...		0818	0917	1003	1036	1116	...	1214	1224	1317	...	1417	1435	1517	1544	1617	1702
Tiverton Parkway **115** a.	...	2128	...	2217	2228	2316	2324	...		0833	0932	...	1048	|	...	...	|	1328	...	1428	|	1528	1555	1628	...
Exeter St Davids **115** a.	...	2143	...	2234	2249	2335	2344	...		0851	0950	...	1107	*1226*	...	...	1248	1343	...	1443	1502	1543	1611	1643	...
Paignton **117** a.	...	|	...	...	|	...	...	...		|	|	...	|	...	...	...	1337	|	...	|	|	|	|	|	...
Plymouth **117** a.	...	2255	...	...	2359	...	...	...		1002	1059	...	1215	...	...	...	...	1448	...	1548	1605	1648	1718	1755	...
Penzance **117** a.	...	...	...	...	...	...	...	...		1205	1303	...	1416	...	...	...	...	...	...	...	...	...	...	...	...

	⑦ 🍷 E	⑦ 🍷	⑦ 🍷 M	⑦ 2	⑦ 🍷 G		⑦ 🍷 M		⑦ 🍷 E	⑦ 🍷	⑦ 🍷 M
London Paddington **115** d.	...	1507	...	...	...	...	...	...	...	1907	...
Birmingham New St **120** d.	1510	|	1610	...	1710	...	1810	...	1910	|	2010
Bristol T. Meads **115 137** d.	1644	1702	1744	1810	1844	...	1944	...	2044	2102	2144
Weston super Mare d.	|	1731	|	1840	|	...	|	...	|	2132	|
Bridgwater d.	|	|	|	1858	|	...	|	...	|	|	|
Taunton **115** d.	1717	1753	1817	1911	1917	...	2017	...	2117	2154	2217
Tiverton Parkway **115** a.	1728	*1820*	1828	1925	1928	...	2028	...	2128	2206	2228
Exeter St Davids **115** a.	1743	*1838*	1843	1942	1945	...	2045	...	2143	2224	2245
Paignton **117** a.	|	...	|	...	|	...	|	...	|	...	|
Plymouth **117** a.	1855	...	1955	...	2051	...	2156	...	2248	...	2359
Penzance **117** a.	...	...	...	...	...	...	...	...	...	...	...

	Ⓐ	Ⓐ 2	Ⓐ 2	Ⓐ 2	Ⓐ 🍷 M	Ⓐ 🍴	Ⓐ 🍷	Ⓐ 🍷 E	Ⓐ 🍷 N
Penzance **117** d.		...	...	...	...	...	...	...	...
Plymouth **117** d.		...	...	...	...	0524	...	0625	0640
Paignton **117** d.		...	...	...	...	|	...	|	|
Exeter St Davids **115** d.		...	...	0600	0623	0631	0645	0723	0738
Tiverton Parkway **115** d.		...	...	0617	0637	|	0659	0737	0752
Taunton **115** d.		0530	0602	0634	0651	0656	0714	0751	0806
Bridgwater d.		0541	0614	0647	|	0707	0724	|	|
Weston super Mare d.		0602	0634	0708	|	0727	0750	|	0830
Bristol T. Meads **115 137** a.		0631	0709	0744	0725	0757	0822	0825	0850
Birmingham New St **120** a.		...	...	...	0857	|	|	0957	1026
London Paddington **115** a.		...	...	...	...	0944	1015	...	...

	Ⓐ 🍷 M	Ⓐ 🍷	Ⓐ 🍷 E	Ⓐ 2	Ⓐ 🍷 M	Ⓐ 🍷 N	Ⓐ 🍷	Ⓐ 🍷 U	Ⓐ 2	Ⓐ 🍷 M	Ⓐ 🍷 N	Ⓐ 🍷 G	Ⓐ 2	Ⓐ 🍷 M	Ⓐ 🍷 N	Ⓐ 2	Ⓐ 🍷 E	Ⓐ 2	Ⓐ 🍷 M	Ⓐ 🍷 N	Ⓐ 🍷 Y	Ⓐ 2		Ⓐ 🍷 M	Ⓐ 2
Penzance **117** d.	...	...	...	...	0730	...	0743	0830	...	0930	...	...	...	...	...	...	...	...	...	...	...	...	...	...	...
Plymouth **117** d.	0725	...	0825	...	0925	...	0945	1025	...	1125	1150	1225	...	1325	...	...	1425	...	1525	...	1625	...	...	1725	...
Paignton **117** d.	|	0738	|	...	|	1002	|	|	...	|	|	|	...	|	1403	...	|	...	|	1615	|	...	...	|	...
Exeter St Davids **115** d.	0823	0840	0923	...	1023	1048	1053	1123	...	1223	1248	1323	...	1423	1446	...	1523	...	1623	1653	1723	...	...	1823	...
Tiverton Parkway **115** d.	0837	|	0937	...	1037	1101	1107	1137	...	1237	1302	1337	...	1437	1500	...	1537	...	1637	1707	1737	...	...	1838	...
Taunton **115** d.	0851	0904	0951	1007	1051	1116	1122	1151	1207	1251	1316	1351	1407	1451	1514	1518	1551	1605	1651	1721	1751	1807	...	1852	1911
Bridgwater d.	|	|	|	1019	|	|	|	|	1219	|	|	|	1419	|	|	1530	|	1617	|	|	|	1819	...	|	1923
Weston super Mare d.	|	0927	|	1040	|	|	|	|	1242	|	|	|	1440	|	1536	|	|	1637	|	|	|	1840	...	|	1947
Bristol T. Meads **115 137** a.	0927	0955	1025	1111	1125	1153	1155	1225	1313	1325	1354	1425	1511	1525	1555	1615	1625	1708	1725	1755	1825	1915	...	1925	2017
Birmingham New St **120** a.	1057	|	1157	...	1257	1326	|	1357	...	1457	1526	1557	...	1657	1726	...	1757	...	1857	1926	1957	...	...	2057	...
London Paddington **115** a.	...	1141	...	...	...	...	1342	...	...	...	...	...	...	...	...	...	...	...	...	...	...	...	...	...	...

	Ⓐ 🍷 L	Ⓐ 2	Ⓐ 🍷	Ⓐ 🍷		Ⓐ 2	Ⓐ 2		⑥	⑥ 2		⑥ 2	⑥ 🍷 M	⑥ 🍷		⑥ 🍷 E	⑥ 🍷	⑥ 🍷 M		⑥ 🍷 E	⑥ 2	⑥ 🍷 M	⑥ 🍷 N	⑥ 🍷 U	⑥ 2
Penzance **117** d.	...	...	1735	...	...	...	...	...		...	...	...	...	...	...	...	...	...	...	...	...	0730	...	0830	...
Plymouth **117** d.	1825	...	1935	...	...	...	...	...		...	...	...	...	...	...	0625	...	0725	...	0825	...	0925	...	1025	...
Paignton **117** d.	|	...	|	...	...	...	...	...		...	...	...	...	...	...	|	0717	|	...	|	...	|	1005	|	...
Exeter St Davids **115** d.	1923	*1953*	2037	...	...	2126	...	...		...	...	0539	0610	...	...	0723	0805	0823	...	0923	...	1023	1048	1123	...
Tiverton Parkway **115** d.	1937	*2008*	2052	...	...	2142	...	...		...	...	0556	0624	...	...	0737	0819	0837	...	0937	...	1037	1101	1137	...
Taunton **115** d.	1951	2028	2106	2130	...	2220b	2245	...		0526	...	0613	0638	0700	...	0751	0834	0851	...	0951	1011	1051	1116	1151	1211
Bridgwater d.	|	2041	|	2140	...	|	2257	...		0537	...	0626	|	0710	...	|	|	|	...	|	1023	|	|	|	1222
Weston super Mare d.	|	2101	|	2159	...	2246	2318	...		0602r	...	0649	0700	0728	...	|	0900r	|	...	|	1043	|	|	|	1241
Bristol T. Meads **115 137** a.	2025	2136	2139	2228	...	2306	2354	...		0631	...	0724	0727	0757	...	0825	0920	0925	...	1025	1114	1125	1155	1225	1311
Birmingham New St **120** a.	2157	...	|	|	...	...	...	...		...	...	...	0857	|	...	0957	|	1058	...	1157	...	1257	1326	1357	...
London Paddington **115** a.	...	...	2336v	0032	...	...	...	...		...	...	...	...	0944	...	...	1115	...	...	...	...	...	...	...	...

	⑥ 🍷 M	⑥ 2	⑥ 🍷 G	⑥ 2	⑥ 🍷 M	⑥ 🍷 E	⑥ 🍷 N	⑥ 2	⑥ 🍷 M	⑥ 2	⑥ 🍷 Y	⑥ 2	⑥ 🍷 M	⑥ 2	⑥ 🍷 D	⑥ 2		⑥ 🍷		⑦	⑦ 2		⑦ 2	⑦ 🍷 M	⑦ 🍷 N
Penzance **117** d.	0930	...	...	...	...	...	...	...	...	...	...	...	...	...	...	...	...	...	...		...	...	...	...	...
Plymouth **117** d.	1125	...	1225	...	1325	...	1425	...	1525	...	1625	...	1725	...	1825	...	...	...	...		...	...	...	0925	...
Paignton **117** d.	|	...	|	...	|	1405	|	...	|	...	|	...	|	...	|	...	...	...	...		...	...	...	|	...
Exeter St Davids **115** d.	1223	...	1323	...	1423	1448	1523	...	1623	...	1723	...	1823	...	1923	...	...	...	...		0815	...	*0951*	1023	1048
Tiverton Parkway **115** d.	1237	...	1337	...	1437	1501	1537	...	1637	...	1737	...	1837	...	1937	...	...	...	...		0830	...	|	1037	1101
Taunton **115** d.	1251	1307	1351	1407	1451	1516	1551	1607	1651	1707	1751	1807	1851	1907	1951	2007	...	2130	...		0845	...	1022	1051	1116
Bridgwater d.	|	1318	|	1418	|	|	|	1618	|	1718	|	1819	|	1918	|	2018	...	2140	...		0856	...	1033	|	|
Weston super Mare d.	|	1339	|	1439	|	|	|	1639	|	1739	|	1840	|	1939	|	2040	...	2158	...		0914	...	1051	|	|
Bristol T. Meads **115 137** a.	1325	1409	1425	1509	1525	1555	1625	1642	1725	1809	1825	1911	1925	2009	2025	2114	...	2228	...		0945	...	1120	1125	1155
Birmingham New St **120** a.	1457	...	1557	...	1657	1726	1757	...	1857	...	1957	...	2057	...	2157	...	...	|	...		...	...	...	1251	1326
London Paddington **115** a.	...	...	...	...	...	...	...	...	...	...	...	...	...	...	...	...	...	0032	...		...	...	...	...	...

D – From / to Derby.
E – From / to Edinburgh.
G – From / to Glasgow.
L – From / to Leeds.
M – From / to Manchester.
N – From / to Newcastle.
U – To Dundee.
Y – From / to York.
a – Arrives 9–10 minutes earlier.
r – Arrives 6–8 minutes earlier.
s – Stops to set down only.
v – 2329 on ⑤.

116 EXETER - BRISTOL

GW, XC

Services are subject to alteration from January 28

	⑦ 🍷	⑦ 🍷 U	⑦ 🍷	⑦ 🍷 M	⑦ 2	⑦ 🍷 G		⑦ 🍷 M	⑦ 🍷 N	⑦ 2	⑦ 🍷 E	⑦ 🍷	⑦ 🍷 M	⑦ 🍷	⑦ 🍷	⑦ 🍷 Y	⑦ 🍷	⑦ 🍷 M	⑦ 2🍷		⑦ 🍷 L		⑦ 2	⑦ 🍷	⑦ 2
Penzance **117** .... d.	...	...	...	0930	...	1030	...	1130	...	...	...	...	...	...	...	...	...	...	1508	...	...	...	...	...	...
Plymouth **117** .... d.	0950	1025	1050	1125	...	1225	...	1325	...	...	1425	1505	1525	...	1610	1625	...	1725	1708	...	1825	...	...	1955	...
Paignton **117** .... d.	|	|	|	|	...	|	...	|	1359	...	|	|	|	1551	|	|	...	|	|	...	|	...	...	|	...
Exeter St Davids **115** .... d.	1052	1123	1153	1223	*1250*	1323	...	1423	1443	*1447*	1523	1607	1623	1636	1717	1723	*1752*	1823	1835	...	1923	...	...	2055	...
Tiverton Parkway **115** .... d.	1106	1137	1207	1237	|	1337	...	1437	|	|	1537	1622	1637	1651	1732	1737	*1805*	1837	1853	...	1937	...	...	2108	...
Taunton **115** .... d.	1120	1151	1221	1251	1320	1351	...	1451	1506	1521	1551	1636	1651	1704	1745	1751	1826	1851	1910	...	1951	...	2045	2122	2135
Bridgwater .... d.	|	|	|	|	1331	|	...	|	|	1532	|	|	|	|	|	|	1836	|	1922	...	|	...	2057	|	2146
Weston super Mare .... d.	|	|	|	|	1349	|	...	|	1529	1551	|	1658	|	1730	|	|	1854	|	1942	...	|	...	2119	|	2205
Bristol T. Meads **115 137** .... a.	1156	1225	1255	1325	1419	1425	...	1525	1550	1621	1625	1719	1725	1758	1824	1825	1925	1925	2011	...	2025	...	2152	2157	2233
Birmingham New St **120** ... a.	|	1351	|	1457	...	1551	...	1657	1726	...	1751	|	1857	|	|	1951	|	2057	...	...	2151	...	...	|	...
London Paddington **115** .... a.	1355	...	1454	...	...	...	...	...	...	...	...	1924	...	1958	2024	...	2126	...	...	...	...	...	...	0017	...

E – To Edinburgh.
G – To Glasgow.
L – To Leeds.
M – To Manchester.
N – To Newcastle.
U – To Dundee.
Y – To York.

117 EXETER - PAIGNTON and PLYMOUTH

GW, XC

Services on ⑥⑦ are subject to alteration from February 2

km			① 🍷 Z	②–⑤ 🍷 Z	Ⓐ 2	Ⓐ 2	Ⓐ 2	Ⓐ 2	Ⓐ 2	Ⓐ 2	Ⓐ 🍷 B	Ⓐ 2	Ⓐ 2	Ⓐ 🍷 D	Ⓐ ✕	Ⓐ 🍷 D	Ⓐ 🍷 W	Ⓐ 🍷	Ⓐ 🍷 L	Ⓐ 2	Ⓐ 🍷	Ⓐ 2	Ⓐ 🍷 N	Ⓐ 🍷 M	Ⓐ 🍷 W	Ⓐ 🍷
	London Padd. **115** .. d.	Ⓐ	2350n	2345n	...	...	...	...	...	...	...	...	...	...	0730	...	...	0905	...	...	1005	...	...	...	...	1000
	Bristol T. M. **116** ..... d.		|	|	...	0531	...	0647	...	...	0811	...	...	0844	0913	0944	...	|	1044	...	|	...	1114	1144	...	1146
0	**Exeter** St Davids ..... ‡d.		0437	0447	0615	0700	0748	0813	0829	...	0907	0856	0920	0945	1013	1045	1039	1118	1145	1151	1210	1215	1233	1245	1239	1257
20	Dawlish .... ‡d.		|	|	0635	0719	0808	0826	0842	...	|	0923	0933	|	|	|	1101	|	|	1211	|	1228	1245	|	1301	1310
24	Teignmouth .... ‡d.		|	|	0640	0724	0813	0831	0847	...	|	0928	0938	|	|	|	1106	|	|	1216	|	1233	1250	|	1306	1315
32	**Newton Abbot** .... ‡d.		0457	0509	0648	0731	0821	0838	0854	0902	|	0938	0946	1004	1034	1104	1114	1139	1204	1224	1231	1240	1257	1304	1313	1323
42	Torquay .... ‡a.		*0553*	*0553*	0658	|	0831	|	0905	|	0934	0948	|	|	*1052*	|	1123	|	|	1234	|	|	1307	|	|	1335
45	**Paignton** .... ‡a.		*0600*	*0600*	0705	|	0838	|	0913	|	0947	0955	|	|	*1059*	|	1131	|	|	1241	|	|	1320	|	|	1347
46	Totnes .... d.		|	|	...	0745	...	0851	...	0914	...	...	0959	1017	1047	1117	...	1152	1217	...	|	1252	...	1317	1326	...
84	**Plymouth** .... a.		0537	0547	...	0815	...	0922	...	0947	...	...	1030	1048	1115	1148	...	1222	1248	...	1309	1325	...	1348	1356	...
	Penzance **119** .... a.		0847	0800	...	1019	...	1124	...	...	...	...	1224	...	1321	...	...	...	...	...	1512	...	...	...	...	...

	Ⓐ ✕	Ⓐ 🍷 E	Ⓐ 2	Ⓐ ✕	Ⓐ 🍷 N	Ⓐ 🍷 M	Ⓐ 2	Ⓐ 🍷	Ⓐ 🍷 U	Ⓐ 🍷 W	Ⓐ 🍷 N	Ⓐ ✕	Ⓐ 2	Ⓐ 🍷 M	Ⓐ 2	Ⓐ 2	Ⓐ 🍷	Ⓐ 🍷 G	Ⓐ 🍷 W	Ⓐ 🍷 N	Ⓐ 🍷	Ⓐ 🍷 M	Ⓐ 🍷	Ⓐ 2	Ⓐ 🍷 E	Ⓐ ✕
London Padd. **115** .. d.	1105	...	...	1205	...	...	...	1305	...	...	...	1405	...	...	...	...	1505	...	...	...	1605	...	1703	...	...	1803
Bristol T. M. **116** ..... d.	|	1244	...	|	1311	1344	...	|	1444	...	1511	|	...	1544	...	...	|	1644	...	1711	|	1744	|	...	1844	|
Exeter St Davids ..... ‡d.	1333	1345	1351	1411	1418	1445	1450	1521	1545	1550	1612	1619	1623	1645	1651	...	1733	1745	1749	1812	1821	1845	1923	1928	1945	2015
Dawlish .... ‡d.	|	|	1411	|	1430	|	1510	|	|	1602	|	|	1643	|	1711	...	|	|	1808	1824	|	|	|	1948	|	|
Teignmouth .... ‡d.	|	|	1416	|	1435	|	1515	|	|	1607	|	|	1648	|	1716	...	|	|	1813	1829	|	|	|	1953	|	|
Newton Abbot .... ‡d.	1354	1404	1424	1432	1442	1504	1523	1542	1604	1614	1631	1640	1656	1704	1724	1729	1758	1809	1821	1836	1842	1904	1944	2008r	2004	2036
Torquay .... ‡a.	|	|	1434	|	1452	|	1533	|	*1618*	|	|	|	1706	|	1734	|	|	|	1832	|	|	*1919*	|	2018	*2018*	|
Paignton .... ‡a.	|	|	1442	|	1505	|	1540	|	*1624*	|	|	|	1713	|	1741	|	|	|	1840	|	|	*1926*	|	2025	*2025*	|
Totnes .... d.	1407	1417	...	|	...	1517	...	1556	1617	1626	1644	1653	...	1717	...	1741	1811	1822	...	1849	1856	1917	1958	...	2017	2049
Plymouth .... a.	1436	1448	...	1509	...	1548	...	1627	1648	1657	1715	1721	...	1748	...	1813	1839	1852	...	1920	1924	1948	2025	...	2048	2117
Penzance **119** .... a.	...	...	...	1711	...	...	...	...	...	...	...	1937	...	1949	...	...	2041	2056	...	...	2130	2147	2230	...	...	2310

	Ⓐ 🍷	Ⓐ 🍷 M	Ⓐ ✕	Ⓐ 2	Ⓐ 🍷 E	Ⓐ 🍷	Ⓐ 2	Ⓐ 🍷 M	Ⓐ 🍷		⑥ 🍷 Z	⑥ 2	⑥ 2	⑥ 2🍷	⑥ 2	⑥ 2🍷	⑥ S	⑥ 2🍷	⑥ 🍷 D	⑥ 2	⑥ 🍷	⑥ 🍷 B	⑥ 🍷 W	⑥ 🍷	⑥ 🍷 L	⑥ 2
London Padd. **115** .. d.	1733	...	1903	...	...	1945	...	...	2035	⑥	2345n	...	...	...	...	...	...	...	...	...	0730	...	...	0905	...	...
Bristol T. M. **116** ..... d.	|	1944	|	...	2044	|	...	2144	|		|	...	...	0525	...	0648	...	...	0844	...	0917	0944	...	|	1044	...
Exeter St Davids ..... ‡d.	2019	2045	2122	2128	2145	2217	2230	2313	2345		0447	0529	0614	0655	0748	0819	0837	0920	0945	0952	1018	1045	1038	1118	1145	1150
Dawlish .... ‡d.	2041	|	|	2148	|	|	2250	|	|		|	0549	0634	0715	0808	0832	0850	0933	|	1012	|	|	1101	|	|	1210
Teignmouth .... ‡d.	2046	|	|	2153	|	|	2255	|	|		|	0554	0639	0720	0813	0837	0855	0938	|	1017	|	|	1106	|	|	1215
Newton Abbot .... ‡d.	2054	2104	2143	2208r	2204	2238	2310r	2334	0006		0509	0602	0647	0727	0821	0844	0906	0946	1004	1025	1039	1104	1114	1139	1204	1223
Torquay .... ‡a.	2107	|	|	2219	*2219*	|	2321	|	|		|	0612	0657	*0747*	0831	|	0915	|	|	1035	|	|	1123	|	|	1237
Paignton .... ‡a.	2120	|	|	2226	*2226*	|	2328	|	|		|	0619	0704	*0755*	0838	|	0923	|	|	1042	|	|	1131	|	|	1244
Totnes .... d.	...	2117	2157	...	2217	2252	...	2347	0018		|	...	...	0741	...	0857	...	0959	1017	...	1052	1117	...	1152	1217	...
Plymouth .... a.	...	2148	2224	...	2248	2322	...	0018	0047		0547	...	...	0811	...	0928	...	1030	1048	...	1120	1148	...	1223	1248	...
Penzance **119** .... a.	...	...	0035	...	...	...	...	...	...		0800	...	...	1015	...	1126	...	1231	...	...	1323	...	...	...	...	...

	⑥ 🍷	⑥ 🍷 Y	⑥ 🍷 M	⑥ 🍷 W	⑥ 🍷	⑥ 🍷 E	⑥ 2	⑥ 🍷	⑥ 🍷 W	⑥ 🍷 M	⑥ 🍷	⑥ 🍷 E	⑥ 🍷 W	⑥ 2	⑥ 🍷 N	⑥ 🍷	⑥ 🍷 M	⑥ 2	⑥ 🍷	⑥ 🍷 G	⑥ 🍷 W	⑥ H	⑥ 🍷	⑥ 2	⑥ 🍷 M	⑥ 🍷
London Padd. **115** .. d.	1005	...	...	...	1105	...	...	1205	...	...	1305	...	...	...	...	1405	...	...	1505	...	...	...	1605	...	...	1705
Bristol T. M. **116** ..... d.	|	1114	1144	...	|	1244	...	|	...	1344	|	1444	...	...	1511	|	1544	...	|	1644	...	...	|	...	1744	|
Exeter St Davids ..... ‡d.	1210	1233	1245	1239	1333	1345	1351	1411	1428	1445	1519	1545	1551	1554	1612	1621	1645	1651	1733	1745	1744	1802	1819	1826	1845	1933
Dawlish .... ‡d.	|	1245	|	1304	|	|	1411	|	1443	|	|	|	1603	1614	|	|	|	1711	|	|	1806	1819	|	1846	|	|
Teignmouth .... ‡d.	|	1250	|	1309	|	|	1416	|	1448	|	|	|	1608	1619	|	|	|	1716	|	|	1811	1824	|	1851	|	|
Newton Abbot .... ‡d.	1231	1257	1304	1316	1354	1404	1424	1432	1456	1504	1540	1604	1615	1627	1631	1642	1704	1724	1758	1807	1820	1832	1839	1859	1904	1953
Torquay .... ‡a.	|	1307	|	|	|	|	1435	|	1507	|	|	|	|	1637	|	|	|	1734	|	|	|	1841	|	1910	|	|
Paignton .... ‡a.	|	1320	|	|	|	|	1442	|	1515	|	|	|	|	1644	|	|	|	1741	|	|	|	1850	|	1917	|	|
Totnes .... d.	|	...	1317	1328	1407	1417	...	|	...	1517	1554	1617	1627	...	1644	1655	1717	...	1811	1820	1832	...	1853	...	1917	2007
Plymouth .... a.	1310	...	1348	1359	1436	1448	...	1509	...	1548	1625	1648	1658	...	1715	1723	1748	...	1839	1848	1902	...	1921	...	1948	2036
Penzance **119** .... a.	1513	...	...	...	...	...	...	1711	...	...	...	...	...	...	...	1923	1949	...	2041	2059	2105	...	2130	...	2143	2245

	⑥ 🍷	⑥ 🍷 E	⑥ 2	⑥ 🍷	⑥ 🍷 M	⑥ 2	⑥ 🍷	⑥ 🍷 E	⑥ 🍷	⑥ 🍷 M		⑦ 2	⑦ 2	⑦ 2	⑦ 2	⑦ K	⑦ 🍷	⑦ 🍷	⑦ 🍷 W	⑦ 🍷	⑦ 2	⑦ 🍷 W	⑦ 🍷	⑦ 🍷 L	⑦ 🍷	⑦ 🍷
London Padd. **115** .. d.	1630	...	...	1805	...	...	1905	...	2005	...	⑦	...	...	...	...	...	0800	0842	...	0957	...	...	1057	...	1118	1157
Bristol T. M. **116** ..... d.	1815	1844	...	|	1944	...	|	2044	|	2144		0730	...	0815	...	...	1003	|	...	|	...	...	|	1244	|	|
Exeter St Davids ..... ‡d.	1938	1945	1954	2015	2045	2053	2139	2145	2237	2245		0853	0925	0952	1015	1056	1108	1135	1140	1227	1235	1255	1315	1345	1354	1425
Dawlish .... ‡d.	|	|	2015	|	|	2113	|	|	2249	|		0906	0945	1005	1035	1111	1121	|	|	|	1307	1312	|	|	1407	|
Teignmouth .... ‡d.	|	|	2020	|	|	2118	|	|	2255	|		0911	0950	1010	1040	1116	1127	|	|	|	1312	1320	|	|	1413	|
Newton Abbot .... ‡d.	1959	2004	2028	2036	2104	2126	2200	2207	2303	2312		0918	0958	1017	1048	1124	1134	1157	1202	1249	1321	1331	|	1404	1421	1447
Torquay .... ‡a.	2012	|	2038	|	|	2136	|	|	|	|		|	1008	|	1058	1134	*1152*	|	*1240*	|	1333	1341	|	|	1432	|
Paignton .... ‡a.	2023	|	2045	|	|	2143	|	|	|	|		|	1015	|	1105	1142	*1159*	|	*1247*	|	1340	1349	|	|	1440	|
Totnes .... d.	...	2017	...	2049	2117	...	2213	2222	2316	2327		0931	...	1030	...	...	1147	1209	1217	1301	...	...	|	1417	...	1500
Plymouth .... a.	...	2048	...	2117	2148	...	2243	2255	2347	2359		1002	...	1059	...	...	1215	1237	1247	1334	...	...	1411	1448	...	1530
Penzance **119** .... a.	...	...	...	2317	...	...	...	...	...	...		1205	...	1303	...	...	1416	1440	...	...	...	...	1614	...	...	...

B – From Birmingham.
D – From/ to Derby.
E – From/ to Edinburgh.
G – From/ to Glasgow.
H – From/ to Honiton.
K – From/ to Basingstoke.
L – From/ to Leeds.
M – From/ to Manchester.
N – From/ to Newcastle.
S – From/ to Salisbury.
U – To Dundee.
W – From/ to London Waterloo.
Y – From/ to York.
Z – Also conveys 🛏 1, 2 cl.
j – Arrives 10–11 minutes earlier.
n – Previous day.
r – Arrives 8–9 minutes earlier.
v – 2329 on ⑤.
‡ – Additional local trains serve these stations.

EXETER - PAIGNTON and PLYMOUTH

Services on ⑥⑦ are subject to alteration from February 2

	⑦ 🍷 M	⑦ 🍷 W	⑦ 🍷	⑦ 2	⑦ 🍷	⑦ 🍷 N	⑦ 2	⑦ 🍷	⑦ 🍷 M	⑦ 🍷 W	⑦ 🍷	⑦ 🍷 E	⑦ 2	⑦ 🍷	⑦ 🍷 M	⑦ 2	⑦ 🍷	⑦ 🍷 G	⑦ 2	⑦ 🍷	⑦ 🍷 M	⑦ 🍷 W	⑦ 🍷	⑦ 🍷 E	⑦ 2	⑦ 🍷
London Padd. **115** .. d.	...	...	1207	...	1257	...	...	1357	...	...	1457	...	...	1557	...	...	1657	...	...	1757	...	...	1857	...	...	1957
Bristol T. M. **116** ..... d.	1344	...	1401	...	|	1444	...	|	1544	...	|	1644	...	|	1744	...	|	1844	...	|	1944	...	|	2044	...	|
keter St Davids ..... ‡d.	1445	1452	1502	1510	1525	1545	1603	1625	1645	1657	1720	1745	1750	1838	1845	1852	1919	1948	2005	2039	2045	2055	2121	2145	2153	2239
awlish .... ‡d.	|	|	|	1530	|	|	1616	|	|	1710	|	|	1810	|	|	1912	|	|	2025	|	|	2108	|	|	2214	|
eignmouth .... ‡d.	|	|	|	1535	|	|	1621	|	|	1715	|	|	1815	|	|	1917	|	|	2030	|	|	2113	|	|	2219	|
ewton Abbot .... ‡d.	1504	1521	1524	1543	1545	1604	1638	1645	1704	1726	1740	1804	1823	1900	1904	1925	1939	2007	2038	2101	2108	2121	2148	2204	2227	2300
Torquay .... ‡a.	|	1530	|	1553	|	|	|	*1705*	|	1735	|	|	1833	|	|	1935	|	|	2048	|	|	2130	|	|	2238	|
Paignton .... ‡a.	|	1538	|	1601	|	|	|	*1712*	|	1743	|	|	1840	|	|	1942	|	|	2055	|	|	2138	|	|	2245	|
otnes .... d.	1517	...	|	...	1600	1617	1653	1701	1717	...	1754	1816	...	|	1917	...	1953	2020	...	2116	2124	...	2202	2217	...	2314
ymouth .... a.	1548	...	1605	...	1628	1648	1724	1737	1748	...	1821	1848	...	1940	1948	...	2021	2051	...	2143	2156	...	2230	2248	...	2347
Penzance **119** .... a.	...	...	...	...	1837	...	1929	...	1954	...	2022	2048	...	...	2148	...	2220	...	...	2343	...	...	...	...	...	...

	Ⓐ	②–⑤ 🍷 Z	Ⓐ 🍴	Ⓐ 🍷	Ⓐ 2	Ⓐ 🍷	Ⓐ 🍷 E	Ⓐ 2	Ⓐ 🍷 N	Ⓐ 🍴	Ⓐ 🍷 M	Ⓐ 🍷	Ⓐ 🍴	Ⓐ 🍷 E	Ⓐ 2	Ⓐ 🍴	Ⓐ 🍷 M	Ⓐ 🍷 N	Ⓐ 🍷	Ⓐ 2	Ⓐ 🍷 U	Ⓐ 🍷	Ⓐ 2	Ⓐ 🍷 M	Ⓐ 🍷 N	Ⓐ 🍴
Penzance **119** .... d.		2200n	...	...	...	...	...	...	...	0505	...	...	0542	...	...	0643	0730	...	0743	...	0830	0845	...	0930	...	1001
ymouth .... d.		0020	0524	0535	...	0600	0625	...	0640	0655	0725	...	0747	0825	...	0855	0925	...	0947	...	1025	1045	...	1125	1150	1200
otnes .... d.		0048	0551	0603	...	|	0650	...	0705	|	0750	...	0814	0850	...	0922	0950	...	1014	...	1050	|	...	1150	1215	1227
Paignton .... ‡d.		|	|	|	0607	|	*0642*	0642	|	*0709*	*0738*	0738	|	*0842*	0842	*0914*	|	1002	|	1025	|	|	1123	|	|	*1219*
Torquay .... ‡d.		|	|	|	0612	|	*0647*	0647	|	*0714*	*0744*	0744	|	*0847*	0847	*0919*	|	1008	|	1030	|	|	1128	|	|	*1224*
ewton Abbot .... ‡d.		0101	0604	0616	0625	0635	0703	0708j	0718	0730	0803	0806r	0827	0903	0907r	0935	1003	1019	1027	1043	1103	|	1141	1203	1228	1240
eignmouth .... ‡d.		|	0611	|	0632	|	|	0715	|	|	|	0813	|	|	0914	|	|	1026	1034	1050	|	|	1148	|	|	|
awlish .... ‡d.		|	0617	|	0637	|	|	0720	|	|	|	0819	|	|	0919	|	|	1031	1040	1055	|	|	1153	|	|	|
keter St Davids ..... ‡a.		0123	0629	0637	0702	0654	0721	0746	0736	0750	0821	0839	0847	0921	0939	0955	1021	1043	1053	1115	1121	1138	1214	1221	1246	1300
Bristol T. M. **116** ..... a.		|	0757	|	...	|	0825	...	0856	|	0927	0955	|	1025	...	|	1125	1153	1156	...	1225	|	...	1325	1354	|
London Padd. **115** .. a.		0542	0944	0922	...	0900	...	...	...	1003	...	1142	1123	...	...	1223	...	...	1342	...	...	1345	...	...	...	1523

	Ⓐ 🍷 W	Ⓐ 🍷 G	Ⓐ 🍴	Ⓐ 🍷 M	Ⓐ 2	Ⓐ 🍷 N	Ⓐ 🍷	Ⓐ 2	Ⓐ 🍷 E	Ⓐ 🍷 W	Ⓐ 🍴	Ⓐ 🍷 M	Ⓐ 🍷 N	Ⓐ 🍷	Ⓐ 2	Ⓐ 🍷 Y	Ⓐ 🍷	Ⓐ 2	Ⓐ 🍷 M	Ⓐ 2	Ⓐ 🍷 W	Ⓐ 🍴	Ⓐ 🍷 L	Ⓐ 2	Ⓐ K	Ⓐ 2
Penzance **119** .... d.	...	...	...	...	1140	...	...	...	...	...	...	...	...	1400	...	...	...	...	...	...	...	1600	...	1644	...	...
ymouth .... d.	...	1225	1255	1325	1333	...	...	...	1425	1447	1500	1525	...	1600	...	1625	1700	...	1725	...	1748	1802	1825	1843	...	...
otnes .... d.	...	1250	1322	1350	1402	...	...	...	1450	1516	1527	1550	...	1627	...	1650	1727	...	1750	...	1817	1829	1850	1912	...	...
Paignton .... ‡d.	1235	|	*1314*	|	|	1403	1415	1425	|	|	*1519*	*1543*	1615	|	1627	|	*1719*	1719	|	1750	|	*1821*	|	|	1910	1930
Torquay .... ‡d.	1241	|	*1319*	|	|	1409	1420	1430	|	|	*1524*	*1546*	1621	|	1632	|	*1724*	1724	|	1755	|	*1826*	|	|	1916	1935
ewton Abbot .... ‡d.	1253	1303	1335	1403	1415	1421	1433	1443	1503	1529	1540	1603	1633	1640	1644	1703	1740	1743r	1803	1808	1830	1842	1903	1925	1928	1948
eignmouth .... ‡d.	1300	|	|	|	|	1428	1440	1450	|	1536	|	|	|	|	1651	|	|	1750	|	1815	1837	|	|	|	1935	1955
awlish .... ‡d.	1305	|	|	|	|	1433	1446	1455	|	1541	|	|	|	|	1656	|	|	1755	|	1820	1842	|	|	|	1940	2000
keter St Davids ..... ‡a.	1327	1321	1355	1421	1438	1444	1459	1515	1521	1556	1600	1621	1651	1700	1716	1721	1800	1815	1821	1840	1857	1902	1921	1946	1959	2020
Bristol T. M. **116** ..... a.	...	1425	|	1525	...	1555	|	...	1625	...	|	1725	1755	|	...	1825	|	...	1925	...	...	|	2025	...	...	...
London Padd. **115** .. a.	...	...	1622	...	...	...	1723	...	...	...	1819	...	...	1924	...	...	2039	...	...	...	...	2122	...	...	...	...

	Ⓐ 🍷	Ⓐ 2	Ⓐ 2	Ⓐ 2	Ⓐ 2	⑥	⑥ 🍷 Z	⑥ 🍷	⑥ 2	⑥ 🍷 E	⑥ 🍷	⑥ 🍷	⑥ 🍷 M	⑥ 🍷	⑥ 🍷	⑥ 🍷 E	⑥ 🍷	⑥ 2	⑥ 🍷 M	⑥ 🍷 N	⑥ 🍷 W	⑥ 🍷	⑥ 🍷 U	⑥ 2	⑥ 🍷	⑥ 2
Penzance **119** .... d.	1735	...	1905	...	...		2200n	...	...	...	...	...	...	...	0604	...	0645	...	0730	...	...	0803	0830	...	0848	...
ymouth .... d.	1935	...	2113	...	...		0020	0540	...	0625	0655	...	0725	0754	0810	0825	0852	...	0925	...	...	1005	1025	...	1046	...
otnes .... d.	2002	...	2143	...	...		0048	0607	...	0650	|	...	0750	0821	0839	0850	0919	...	0950	...	...	1032	1050	...	|	...
Paignton .... ‡d.	|	2030	*2128*	2230	2332		|	|	0623	|	*0708*	0717	|	*0813*	|	|	*0911*	0911	|	1005	1012	|	|	1046	|	1117
Torquay .... ‡d.	|	2035	*2134*	2235	2337		|	|	0628	|	*0713*	0723	|	*0818*	|	|	*0916*	0916	|	1011	1018	|	|	1051	|	1122
ewton Abbot .... ‡d.	2015	2048	2155	2248	2350		0101	0620	0641	0703	0731	0737	0803	0834	0852	0903	0932	0938j	1003	1022	1031	1045	1103	1107	1122	1135
eignmouth .... ‡d.	|	2055	2202	2255	2357		|	|	0648	|	|	0744	|	|	|	|	|	0945	|	1029	1038	|	|	1114	|	1142
awlish .... ‡d.	|	2100	2207	2300	0002		|	|	0653	|	|	0750	|	|	|	|	|	0950	|	1034	1043	|	|	1119	|	1147
keter St Davids ..... ‡a.	2035	2120	2228	2320	0022		0123	0640	0711	0721	0751	0803	0821	0854	0916	0921	0952	1010	1021	1046	1058	1105	1121	1136	1142	1207
Bristol T. M. **116** ..... a.	2139	...	...	...	...		|	|	...	0825	|	0920	0925	|	...	1025	|	...	1125	1155	...	|	1225	...	|	...
London Padd. **115** .. a.	2336v	...	...	...	...		0535	0922	...	...	1008	1115	...	1124	...	...	1222	...	...	...	...	1323	...	...	1353	...

	⑥ 🍷 M	⑥ 🍷	⑥ 🍷 W	⑥ 🍷 G	⑥ 🍷	⑥ 🍷 M	⑥ 🍷 E	⑥ 🍷	⑥ 🍷 N	⑥ 2	⑥ 🍷 W	⑥ 🍷	⑥ 🍷 M	⑥ H	⑥ 🍷	⑥ 2	⑥ 🍷 Y	⑥ 🍷	⑥ 🍷 M	⑥ 2	⑥ W	⑥ 🍷	⑥ 🍷 D	⑥ 2	⑥ 🍷	⑥ K
Penzance **119** .... d.	0930	1000	...	...	1058	...	...	...	...	...	...	...	...	...	1400	...	...	...	...	...	...	1554	...	...	1640	...
ymouth .... d.	1125	1200	...	1225	1255	1325	...	1400	1425	...	1450	1504	1525	...	1600	...	1625	1654	1725	...	1742	1754	1825	...	1845	...
otnes .... d.	1150	1227	...	1250	1322	1350	...	|	1450	...	1519	1531	1550	...	1627	...	1650	|	1750	...	1811	1821	1850	...	1914	...
Paignton .... ‡d.	|	*1212*	1235	|	*1315*	|	1405	|	|	1453	|	|	|	1552	*1619*	1619	|	*1710*	|	1752	|	|	|	1852	|	1914
Torquay .... ‡d.	|	*1217*	1241	|	*1320*	|	1411	|	|	1458	|	|	|	1558	*1624*	1624	|	*1715*	|	1757	|	|	|	1857	|	1920
ewton Abbot .... ‡d.	1203	1240	1253	1303	1336	1403	1422	1437	1503	1511	1532	1544	1603	1610	1640	1643r	1703	1731	1803	1810	1824	1834	1903	1910	1926	1932
eignmouth .... ‡d.	|	|	1300	|	|	|	1429	|	|	1518	1539	|	|	1617	|	1650	|	|	|	1817	1831	|	|	1917	1933	1939
awlish .... ‡d.	|	|	1305	|	|	|	1434	|	|	1523	1544	|	|	1622	|	1655	|	|	|	1822	1836	|	|	1922	1938	1944
keter St Davids ..... ‡a.	1221	1300	1327	1321	1355	1421	1446	1457	1521	1542	1559	1604	1621	1635	1700	1715	1721	1751	1821	1842	1900	1854	1921	1942	1951	2003
Bristol T. M. **116** ..... a.	1325	|	...	1425	|	1525	1555	|	1625	...	...	|	1725	...	|	...	1825	|	1925	...	...	|	2025	...	...	...
London Padd. **115** .. a.	...	1523	...	...	1622	...	...	1723	...	...	...	1823	...	...	1924	...	...	2021	...	...	...	2128	...	...	...	...

	⑥ 🍷	⑥ 2	⑥	⑥ 2	⑥ 2 🍷	⑥ 2	⑦	⑦ 🍷	⑦ 🍷 M	⑦ 🍷	⑦ 2	⑦ 🍷 U	⑦ 🍷	⑦ 🍷	⑦ 🍷 M	⑦ 🍷	⑦ 🍷 W	⑦ 🍷 G	⑦ 2	⑦ 🍷	⑦ 🍷 M	⑦ 🍷	⑦ 2	⑦ 🍷 W	⑦ 🍷 E	⑦ 🍷
Penzance **119** .... d.	1735	...	...	...	1908	...		...	...	...	...	...	0830	...	0930	0950	...	1030	...	1050	1130	...	...	...	...	1250
ymouth .... d.	1935	...	...	...	2118	...		0845	0925	0950	...	1025	1035	1050	1125	1145	...	1225	...	1250	1325	1344	...	1406	1425	1450
otnes .... d.	2002	...	...	...	2147	...		0911	0950	1017	...	1050	1102	1118	1150	1215	...	1250	...	1317	1350	1410	...	1435	1450	1517
Paignton .... ‡d.	|	2006	2035	2107	|	2150		|	|	|	1025	|	|	*1104*	|	*1208*	1225	|	1255	|	|	|	1420	|	|	*1502*
Torquay .... ‡d.	|	2011	2041	2112	|	2155		|	|	|	1030	|	|	*1109*	|	*1213*	1231	|	1300	|	|	|	1425	|	|	*1507*
ewton Abbot .... ‡d.	2015	2024	2053	2125	2159	2208		0926	1003	1030	1043	1103	1115	1131	1203	1229	1244	1303	1313	1330	1403	1424	1438	1447	1503	1530
eignmouth .... ‡d.	|	2031	|	2132	2206	2215		0933	|	|	1050	|	|	|	|	|	1251	|	1320	|	|	|	1445	1454	|	|
awlish .... ‡d.	|	2036	|	2137	2211	2220		0938	|	|	1055	|	|	|	|	|	1258	|	1325	|	|	|	1450	1459	|	|
keter St Davids ..... ‡a.	2035	2056	2113	2157	2230	2240		0951	1021	1050	1115	1121	1135	1151	1221	1249	1313	1321	1346	1350	1421	1446	1510	1514	1521	1550
Bristol T. M. **116** ..... a.	2144	...	...	...	...	...		|	1125	1156	...	1225	|	1255	1325	|	...	1425	...	|	1525	|	...	...	1625	|
London Padd. **115** .. a.	2338	...	...	...	...	...		1228	...	1355	...	...	1422	1454	...	1522	...	...	...	1621	...	1736	...	...	...	1821

	⑦ 🍷	⑦ 🍷 W	⑦ 🍷 M	⑦ 🍷	⑦ 🍷	⑦ 🍷 W	⑦ 🍷 W	⑦ 🍷	⑦ 🍷 Y	⑦ 🍷	⑦ 2	⑦ 2🍷	⑦ 🍷 M	⑦ 🍷	⑦ 🍷 W	⑦ 🍷	⑦ 🍷	⑦ 2	⑦ 🍷	⑦ 2	⑦ 🍷	⑦ 2	⑦ 🍷	⑦ S	⑦ 2	⑦ 🍷 Z
Penzance **119** .... d.	...	...	...	...	...	...	1350	...	...	...	...	1508	...	...	...	...	...	...	1720	...	...	...	1900	...	...	2115
ymouth .... d.	1505	...	1525	...	1545	...	1602	1610	1625	1650	...	1708	1725	1750	...	1810	1825	...	1915	...	1955	...	2115	...	...	2320
otnes .... d.	1532	...	1550	...	1612	...	1631	1642	1650	1717	...	1739	1750	1816	...	1840	1850	...	1945	...	|	...	2142	...	...	2348
Paignton .... ‡d.	|	1527	|	1551	|	1610	|	*1631*	|	|	1720	|	|	|	1823	|	|	1855	|	1950	|	2100	|	2210	2300	|
Torquay .... ‡d.	|	1533	|	1556	|	1616	|	*1636*	|	|	1725	|	|	|	1829	|	|	1900	|	1955	|	2105	|	2216	2305	|
ewton Abbot .... ‡d.	1545	1549	1603	1608	1625	1632	1643	1655	1703	1730	1738	1752	1803	1829	1841	1852	1903	1913	1958	2008	2032	2118	2154	2228	2318	0001
eignmouth .... ‡d.	|	1556	|	1616	|	|	|	|	|	|	1745	1800	|	|	1848	|	|	1920	|	2015	|	2125	2201	2235	2325	|
awlish .... ‡d.	|	1601	|	1620	|	|	|	|	|	|	1750	1805	|	|	1853	|	|	1925	|	2020	|	2130	2206	2240	2330	|
keter St Davids ..... ‡a.	1605	1628	1621	1634	1645	1653	1705	1715	1722	1750	1810	1819	1822	1850	1908	1913	1921	1945	2018	2040	2053	2150	2221	2255	2350	0026
Bristol T. M. **116** ..... a.	1719	...	1725	1758	|	...	...	1824	1826	|	...	2011	1925	|	...	|	2030	...	|	...	2157	...	...	...	...	|
London Padd. **115** .. a.	1924	...	...	1958	1934	...	...	2024	...	2021	...	...	...	2124	...	2153	...	...	2323	...	0017	...	...	...	...	0511

◁ *FOR NOTES SEE FACING PAGE*

For explanation of standard symbols see page 4

119 PLYMOUTH - NEWQUAY and PENZANCE

GW, X

km		Ⓐ	②-⑤ 🍷 Z	②-⑤ 🍷	① 🍷 Z	Ⓐ	Ⓐ 2 B	Ⓐ 2	Ⓐ 2 B	Ⓐ 2	Ⓐ ✕	Ⓐ 2	Ⓐ ✕	Ⓐ 2	Ⓐ ✕	Ⓐ 2		Ⓐ ✕	Ⓐ 🍷 M	Ⓐ 2	Ⓐ 🍷	Ⓐ 🍷 G	Ⓐ 🍷	Ⓐ 🍷 M	Ⓐ 🍷
	London Padd. 115 d.		2345n	...	2350n	...	...	...	...	...	0730	*0905*	1005	*1105*	1205	...	...	1405	...	...	1505	...	1605	...	170
	Exeter St Davids 117 d.		0447	...	0437	...	0700	...	0813	0920	1013	*1118*	1210	*1333*	1411	*1445*	...	1619	1645	...	1733	1745	1820	1845	192
0	**Plymouth** d.		0550	0630	0630	0705	0819	0828	0923	1032	1117	1244	1310	1441	1511	1557	...	1725	1755	1812	1840	1900	1926	1950	202
7	Saltash d.		|	|	|	0718	0827	0838	|	1040	|	1252	|	|	|	1611	...	1735	|	1826	|	|	1936	|	|
29	Liskeard d.		0616	0653	0700	0737	0846	0901	0947	1057	1141	1311	1334	1505	1535	1632	...	1757	1818	1847	1904	1923	1955	2013	205
43	Bodmin Parkway d.		0630	0706	0714	0749	0858	|	0959	1109	1153	1323	1347	1517	1547	1644	...	1810	1831	1859	1916	1935	2007	2026	210
56	Par a.		0642	0717	0727	0801	0910	0924	1011	1119	1204	1335	1357	1527	1557	1655	...	1821	1840	1913	1926	1946	2017	2035	21
	Newquay 134 a.		|	|	|	|	|	1015	|	*1214*	|	|	*1450*	|	|	|	...	|	|	2023	*2023*	|	|	|	|
63	St Austell a.		0650	0723	0734	0808	0917	...	1019	1126	1211	1342	1404	1534	1604	1703	...	1828	1846	...	1934	1953	2025	2041	212
86	**Truro** a.		0709	0741	0753	0827	0935	...	1038	1144	1229	1400	1422	1552	1623	1720	...	1846	1904	...	1953	2010	2043	2059	214
101	Redruth a.		0722	0752	0809	0839	0949	...	1052	1157	1242	1413	1435	1606	1635	1734	...	1859	1916	...	2005	2021	2055	2113	215
107	Camborne a.		0730	0759	0816	0846	0955	...	1058	1203	1249	1419	1442	1612	1643	1742	...	1906	1923	...	2013	2028	2103	2120	220
119	St Erth 134 a.		0743	0811	0830	0859	1006	...	1109	1212	1302	1428	1455	1623	1653	1753	...	1919	1933	...	2023	2039	2116	2130	221
128	**Penzance** 134 a.		0800	0827	0847	0914	1019	...	1124	1224	1321	1441	1512	1636	1711	1806	...	1937	1949	...	2041	2056	2129	2147	223

	Ⓐ ✕	Ⓐ ✕		⑥ ▲	⑥ 2	⑥ 🍷 Z	⑥ 🍷		⑥ 2🍷 B	⑥ 2	⑥ 2🍷 B	⑥ 2🍷	⑥ 2🍷	⑥ 🍷	⑥ 2🍷	⑥ 🍷	⑥ 2	⑥ 🍷	⑥ 2🍷	⑥ 🍷	⑥ 2	⑥ 🍷 M	⑥ 2🍷	⑥ 🍷	⑥ G
London Padd. 115 d.	1803	1903	...		...	2345n	...	...	...	...	...	...	...	0718	*0905*	1005	*1105*	1205	...	1405	...	...	...	1505	
Exeter St Davids 117 d.	2015	2122	...		...	0447	...	...	0655	...	0819	...	0920	1018	*1118*	1210	*1333*	1411	*1445*	1621	...	1645	...	1733	174
Plymouth d.	2119	2226	...		...	0550	0630	...	0813	0825	0929	1000	1034	1123	1244	1310	1441	1511	1557	1725	1732	1755	1759	1840	19
Saltash d.	|	2236	...		...	|	|	...	0821	0836	|	1010	1043	|	1252	|	|	|	1605	|	1744	|	1813	|	|
Liskeard d.	2143	2255	...		...	0616	0653	...	0840	0855	0953	1031	1102	1146	1315	1334	1505	1535	1626	1749	1803	1819	1833	1904	192
Bodmin Parkway d.	2155	2307	...		...	0630	0706	...	0855	|	1005	1043	1114	1158	1327	1347	1517	1547	1638	1803	1817	1832	1845	1916	193
Par a.	2205	2319	...		0610	0642	0717	...	0907	0916	1017	1055	1124	1208	1339	1357	1529	1556	1650	1813	1829	1842	1857	1926	194
Newquay 134 a.	|	|	...		|	|	|	...	|	1011	|	|	*1220*	|	|	*1455*	|	|	|	|	1937	*1937*	|	|	|
St Austell a.	2213	2326	...		0617	0650	0723	...	0915	...	1024	1102	1131	1216	1347	1405	1536	1604	1656	1820	...	1848	1904	1933	19
Truro a.	2230	2344	...		0633	0709	0741	...	0932	...	1042	1119	1149	1233	1403	1422	1553	1623	1714	1838	...	1906	1921	1951	200
Redruth a.	2243	2357	...		0647	0722	0752	...	0946	...	1054	1133	1202	1246	1417	1435	1606	1634	1727	1851	...	1917	1934	2004	202
Camborne a.	|	0004	...		0653	0730	0759	...	0952	...	1100	1139	1208	1253	1423	1442	1612	1643	1733	1858	...	1924	1940	2011	202
St Erth 134 a.	|	0017	...		0704	0743	0811	...	1003	...	1110	1150	1217	1306	1434	1455	1623	1652	1745	1909	...	1934	1952	2022	203
Penzance 134 a.	2310	0035	...		0717	0800	0827	...	1015	...	1126	1202	1231	1323	1446	1512	1636	1711	1757	1923	...	1950	2004	2041	205

	⑥ 🍷	⑥ 🍷 M	⑥ 🍷	⑥		⑦ ▲	⑦ 🍷	⑦ 2🍷	⑦ 2 B	⑦ 2 B	⑦ 🍷	⑦ 🍷		⑦ 🍷		⑦ 2🍷	⑦ 🍷	⑦ 2	⑦ 🍷 M	⑦ 🍷	⑦ 🍷 E	⑦ 2	⑦ 🍷 M	⑦ 🍷	⑦ 🍷
London Padd. 115 d.	1605	...	1705	...	...		...	...	...	...	0800	0857	...	1057	...	...	1257	...	...	1457	...	...	...	1657	175
Exeter St Davids 117 d.	1819	1845	1933	...	...		...	...	0853	0952	1108	1135	...	1315	...	...	1525	1603	1645	1720	1745	...	1845	1919	203
Plymouth d.	1925	1950	2038	2147	...		0910	0930	1003	1100	1217	1240	...	1413	...	1536	1630	1725	1755	1823	1855	1925	1955	2023	214
Saltash d.	|	|	2049	|	...		|	|	1021	1109	|	|	...	|	...	|	|	1734	|	|	|	|	|	|	|
Liskeard d.	1950	2013	2107	2211	...		0933	0954	1035	1130	1241	1302	...	1437	...	1600	1657	1755	1824	1847	1918	1949	2018	2047	220
Bodmin Parkway d.	2005	2026	2120	2223	...		0945	1006	1047	1142	1253	1315	...	1450	...	1612	1709	1807	1837	1859	1931	2001	2031	2059	222
Par a.	2015	2035	2133	2233	...		0954	1018	1058	1154	1304	1325	...	|	...	1624	1721	1819	1846	1910	1940	2013	2040	2110	223
Newquay 134 a.	|	|	|	|	...		|	|	|	|	|	|	...	|	...	|	|	|	|	|	|	|	|	|	|
St Austell a.	2022	2041	2141	2240	...		1001	1025	1106	1201	1311	1332	...	1505	...	1631	1727	1826	1852	1917	1946	2020	2046	2117	223
Truro a.	2040	2058	2159	2257	...		1018	1043	1123	1219	1329	1351	...	1527	...	1649	1748	1844	1910	1935	2004	2038	2104	2135	225
Redruth a.	2052	2110	2211	2311	...		1029	1057	1137	1232	1341	1403	...	1539	...	1703	1800	1857	1921	1947	2015	2052	2115	2147	230
Camborne a.	2100	2116	2219	2317	...		1036	1103	1143	1239	1349	1411	...	1547	...	1709	1808	1904	1928	1955	2022	2058	2124	2155	231
St Erth 134 a.	2113	2126	2232	2326	...		1049	1114	1153	1250	1400	1422	...	1558	...	1720	1819	1915	1938	2008	2032	2109	2136	2206	232
Penzance 134 a.	2127	2143	2245	2339	...		1106	1132	1205	1303	1416	1440	...	1614	...	1739	1837	1929	1954	2021	2048	2129	2152	2220	234

	Ⓐ	Ⓐ ✕	Ⓐ 2	Ⓐ ✕	Ⓐ 2	Ⓐ ✕	Ⓐ 🍷 M	Ⓐ 🍷	Ⓐ 🍷 D	Ⓐ 🍷	Ⓐ 🍷 M	Ⓐ ✕	Ⓐ 2	Ⓐ 2	Ⓐ 2		Ⓐ 🍷	Ⓐ 2	Ⓐ 2		Ⓐ ✕	Ⓐ 2	Ⓐ 🍷		Ⓐ 2
Penzance 134 d.		0505	0523	0542	0604	0643	0730	0743	0830	0845	0930	1000	1036	1140	1242	...	1400	...	1450	...	1600	1644	1735	...	190
St Erth 134 d.		|	|	|	0612	0654	0738	0753	0838	0856	0938	1011	1044	1148	1250	...	1411	...	1458	...	1611	1652	1746	...	191
Camborne d.		|	0542	0602	0625	0707	0748	0808	0848	0908	0948	1022	1057	1201	1301	...	1422	...	1511	...	1622	1705	1759	...	192
Redruth d.		0526	0548	0609	0631	0714	0754	0815	0854	0915	0954	1029	1103	1207	1307	...	1429	...	1517	...	1629	1711	1806	...	193
Truro d.		0539	0558	0621	0643	0727	0806	0827	0906	0927	1006	1041	1115	1219	1319	...	1441	...	1528	...	1641	1723	1819	...	194
St Austell d.		0556	...	0639	0700	0744	0822	0845	0922	0945	1022	1059	1132	1236	1336	...	1459	...	1545	...	1659	1740	1836	...	200
Newquay 134 d.		|	...	|	|	|	|	|	|	|	|	*1018*	|	|	*1242*	...	|	1452	|	...	|	|	|	...	|
Par d.		|	...	0646	0707	0751	0829	|	0929	|	1029	1106	1139	1244	1344	...	1506	1540	1555	...	1706	1747	1843	...	200
Bodmin Parkway d.		0612	...	0659	0720	0758	0840	0901	0940	1001	1040	1117	1152	1255	1356	...	1517	|	1607	...	1722	1800	1855	...	202
Liskeard d.		0627	...	0712	0734	0817	0852	0914	0952	1014	1052	1130	1205	1308	1409	...	1530	|	1620	...	1735	1813	1908	...	203
Saltash d.		|	...	0734	0753	0839	|	0933	|	|	|	|	1224	|	1427	...	|	|	1640	...	|	1831	|	...	205
Plymouth a.		0652	...	0745	0809	0851	0914	0945	1018	1039	1117	1157	1237	1332	1438	...	1555	1625	1655	...	1759	1841	1933	...	210
Exeter St Davids 117 a.		0750	...	0847	*0921*	0955	1021	1053	1121	1138	1221	1300	*1355*	1438	*1556*	...	1700	...	*1800*	...	1902	1946	2035	...	222
London Padd. 115 a.		1002	...	1123	...	1223	...	1342	...	1345	...	1523	*1622*	*1722*	*1822*	...	1924	...	*2039*	...	2122	*2230*	2336d	...	...

	Ⓐ	Ⓐ	Ⓐ 🍷 Z		⑥ ▲	⑥ 2	⑥ 🍷	⑥ 2	⑥ 🍷	⑥ 🍷 M	⑥ 2🍷	⑥ 🍷	⑥ 🍷 D	⑥ 🍷	⑥ 🍷 M	⑥ 🍷	⑥ 2🍷	⑥ 🍷	⑥ 2🍷	⑥ 2🍷		⑥ 🍷	⑥ 2🍷	⑥ 🍷	⑥ 2🍷
Penzance 134 d.	2011	2055	2200	...		0530	0604	...	0645	0730	0743	0803	0830	0848	0930	1000	1036	1058	1145	1250	...	1400	1450	1554	164
St Erth 134 d.	2021	2103	2210	...		|	0612	...	0656	0738	0753	0814	0838	0859	0938	1011	1044	1109	1153	1258	...	1411	1458	1605	164
Camborne d.	2035	2116	2224	...		0547	0625	...	0709	0748	0806	0827	0848	0910	0948	1022	1057	1120	1206	1309	...	1422	1511	1616	170
Redruth d.	2042	2122	2232	...		0553	0631	...	0716	0754	0812	0834	0854	0917	0954	1029	1103	1127	1212	1315	...	1429	1517	1623	170
Truro d.	2055	2134	2244	...		0604	0643	...	0729	0806	0825	0847	0906	0929	1006	1041	1115	1139	1224	1327	...	1441	1530	1635	171
St Austell d.	2112	2150	2302	...		...	0700	...	0746	0822	0842	0904	0922	0947	1022	1059	1132	1157	1241	1344	...	1459	1547	1653	173
Newquay 134 d.	*2025*	|	|	...		...	|	...	|	|	|	|	|	|	|	*1013*	|	|	|	*1242*	...	|	*1510*	|	|
Par d.	2120	2157	2311	...		...	0707	0725	0753	0829	0849	0911	0931	0954	1029	1106	1139	|	1249	1352	...	1506	1603	1700	174
Bodmin Parkway d.	2133	2208	2326	...		...	0720	0738	0806	0840	0901	0923	0940	1005	1040	1117	1152	1213	1300	1403	...	1517	1616	1714	175
Liskeard d.	2146	2220	2341	...		...	0734	0751	0819	0852	0914	0936	0952	1018	1052	1130	1205	1226	1313	1416	...	1530	1629	1727	180
Saltash d.	2204	|	|	...		...	0753	|	|	|	0935	|	|	|	|	|	1224	|	|	1434	...	|	1652	|	183
Plymouth a.	2216	2251	0007	...		...	0809	0816	0844	0914	0948	1001	1019	1043	1116	1157	1237	1251	1338	1445	...	1555	1700	1752	183
Exeter St Davids 117 a.	...	...	0123	...		...	0916	...	0952	1021	...	1105	1121	1142	1221	1300	...	1355	*1457*	*1559*	...	1700	*1821*	1854	195
London Padd. 115 a.	...	...	0542c	...		...	...	...	1224	...	...	1323	...	1351	...	1521	...	1622	*1723*	*1825*	...	1922	...	2142	...

	⑥ 🍷	⑥ 2	⑥		⑦ ▲	⑦ 🍷	⑦ 🍷 E	⑦ 🍷	⑦ 🍷 M	⑦ 🍷	⑦ 🍷 M	⑦ 2		⑦ 🍷 W	⑦ 🍷	⑦ 2🍷 B		⑦ 🍷		⑦ 🍷		⑦ 2🍷	⑦ 2🍷	⑦	⑦ 🍷 Z
Penzance 134 d.	1908	...	2045	...		0830	0930	0950	1030	1050	1130	1225	...	1350	1446	1508	...	1615	...	1720	...	1900	2000	2055	211
St Erth 134 d.	1916	...	2053	...		0840	0938	1000	1038	1100	1138	1232	...	1400	1457	1517	...	1626	...	1730	...	1909	2009	|	212
Camborne d.	1929	...	2106	...		0854	0948	1012	1048	1112	1148	1244	...	1413	1508	1530	...	1637	...	1742	...	1921	2021	2111	213
Redruth d.	1935	...	2113	...		0900	0954	1018	1054	1118	1154	1250	...	1419	1515	1536	...	1644	...	1749	...	1927	2027	2117	214
Truro d.	1947	...	2124	...		0915	1006	1030	1106	1130	1206	1302	...	1431	1529	1548	...	1656	...	1800	...	1939	2040	2129	215
St Austell d.	2004	...	2140	...		0931	1022	1048	1122	1148	1222	1320	...	1448	1546	1605	...	1714	...	1819	...	1957	2057	2145	221
Newquay 134 d.	|	1957	|	...		|	|	|	|	|	|	|	...	|	|	|	...	|	...	|	...	|	|	|	|
Par d.	2012	2045	2148	...		0939	1029	1055	1129	1155	1229	1328	...	1456	1553	1613	...	1720	...	1825	...	2004	2104	2153	|
Bodmin Parkway d.	2025	2100	2159	...		0951	1040	1107	1140	1207	1240	1342	...	1508	1605	1625	...	1732	...	1837	...	2018	2115	2204	223
Liskeard d.	2038	2113	2211	...		1004	1052	1120	1152	1220	1252	1356	...	1522	1618	1638	...	1745	...	1850	...	2034	2128	2216	224
Saltash d.	2057	2133	|	...		1023	|	|	|	|	|	|	...	1544	|	1659	...	|	...	|	...	2055	|	|	|
Plymouth a.	2112	2142	2240	...		1032	1119	1145	1216	1247	1321	1420	...	1553	1643	1707	...	1810	...	1915	...	2104	2153	2245	231
Exeter St Davids 117 a.	*2220**	...	...	...		1135	1221	1249	1321	1350	1421	*1521*	...	1705	1750	1819	...	1913	...	2018	...	2221	...	...	002
London Padd. 115 a.	...	...	...	...		1422	...	1522	...	1621	*1736*	*1924*	...	...	2021	*2124*	...	2153	...	2323	...	...	...	...	051

B – From/to Bristol.
D – To Dundee.
E – To Edinburgh.
G – From Glasgow.
M – From/to Manchester.
W – To London Waterloo.
Z – Also conveys 🛏 1, 2 cl.
c – 0525 on ⑥.
d – 2329 on ⑤.
n – Previous day.
* – By 🚌.
▲ – Services on ⑥⑦ are subject to alteration from Feb. 2.

BIRMINGHAM - BRISTOL

m			Ⓐ 2	Ⓐ 🍷 T	Ⓐ 🍷 D	Ⓐ 🍷 D	Ⓐ 🍷 D	Ⓐ 🍷 Y	Ⓐ 🍷 L	Ⓐ 🍷 T	Ⓐ 🍷	Ⓐ 🍷	Ⓐ 🍷	Ⓐ 🍷 T	Ⓐ 🍷	Ⓐ 🍷	Ⓐ 🍷 U	Ⓐ 🍷	Ⓐ 🍷 P	Ⓐ 🍷	Ⓐ 🍷 GP	Ⓐ 🍷	Ⓐ 🍷 P	Ⓐ 🍷
	Edinburgh 127 d.	Ⓐ	...	...	...	...	...	...	...	...	...	...	0605	...	...	...	0813	...	...	...	1005	...	...	...
	Newcastle 127 d.		...	...	...	...	...	...	...	0619	...	0723	0744	0824	...	0935	0940	1025	...	1125	1140	1219	...	1333
	Manchester Piccadilly 150 d.		...	...	...	...	...	...	...	|	0824	|	|	|	1024	|	|	|	1224	|	|	|	1424	|
0	**Birmingham** New St 121 d.		0530	0610	0710	0740	0810	0840	0910	0940	1010	1040	1110	1140	1210	1240	1310	1340	1410	1440	1510	1540	1610	1640
73	Cheltenham 132 121 d.		0643	0722	0752	0822	0852	0922	0952	1022	1052	1122	1152	1222	1252	1322	1352	1422	1452	1522	1552	1622	1652	1722
84	Gloucester 132 121 a.		0652	0736	0823	0840	0921	0939	1021	1040	1121	1139	1221	1240	1321	1339	1421	1440	1521	1539	1624	1640	1723	1739
35	Bristol Parkway a.		0747	0754	0825	0854	0925	0954	1025	1054	1125	1154	1225	1254	1325	1354	1425	1454	1525	1554	1625	1654	1725	1754
45	**Bristol** Temple Meads a.		0800	0811	0841	0911	0941	1011	1041	1111	1141	1211	1241	1311	1341	1411	1441	1511	1541	1611	1641	1711	1741	1811
	Exeter St Davids 116 a.		...	0907	0943	...	1043	...	1143	1231	1243	...	1343	1416	1443	...	1543	1610	1643	...	1743	1810	1843	...
	Plymouth 117 a.		...	...	1048	...	1148	...	1248	...	1348	...	1448	...	1548	...	1648	1715	1748	...	1852	1920	1948	...

	Ⓐ 🍷	Ⓐ 🍷 C	Ⓐ 🍷	Ⓐ 🍷	Ⓐ 🍷	Ⓐ 🍷	Ⓐ 🍷	Ⓐ 🍷	Ⓐ 🍷			⑥ 2		⑥ 🍷 D	⑥ 2 D	⑥ 🍷	⑥ 🍷 L	⑥ 🍷 L	⑥ 🍷 YT	⑥ 🍷	⑥ 🍷	⑥ 🍷	⑥ 🍷	⑥ 🍷
Edinburgh 127 d.	1205	...	...	...	1405	...	...	1605	1705	...	⑥	...	...	...	...	...	...	...	...	...	...	0605	...	...
Newcastle 127 d.	1340	1422	...	1522	1540	1627	...	1740	1840	...		...	...	...	...	...	...	...	...	...	0650	0740	0824	...
Manchester Piccadilly 150 d.	|	|	1624	|	|	|	1824	|	|	...	▲	...	...	...	...	...	...	...	...	0824	|	|	|	1024
Birmingham New St 121 d.	1710	1740	1810	1840	1910	1940	2010	2110	2210	...		0530	...	0710	0730	0810	0840	0910	0940	1010	1040	1110	1140	1210
Cheltenham 132 121 d.	1752	1822	1852	1922	1952	2022	2052	2152	2252	...		0643	...	0752	0811	0852	0922	0952	1022	1052	1122	1152	1222	1252
Gloucester 132 121 a.	1829	1834	1923	1940	2010	2058	2112	2210	2313	...		0652	...	|	0820	0910	0939	1018*	1056	1110	1139	1221	|	1310
Bristol Parkway a.	1825	1905	1925	1954	2025	2054	2125	2223	2322	...		0815	...	0825	0919	0925	0957	1025	1056	1125	1156	1225	1256	1325
Bristol Temple Meads a.	1841	1922	1941	2011	2041	2111	2141	2237	2339	...		0834	...	0841	0935	0941	1013	1041	1113	1141	1213	1241	1313	1341
Exeter St Davids 116 a.	1943	...	2043	...	2143	...	2310	...	...	...		...	...	0943	...	1043	...	1143	1231	1243	...	1343	...	1443
Plymouth 117 a.	2048	...	2148	...	2248	...	0018	...	...	...		...	...	1048	...	1148	...	1248	...	1348	...	1448	...	1548

	⑥ 🍷	⑥ 🍷	⑥ 🍷	⑥ 🍷 P	⑥ 🍷	⑥ 🍷 GP	⑥ 🍷	⑥ 🍷 P	⑥ 🍷	⑥ 🍷	⑥ 🍷 C	⑥ 🍷	⑥ 🍷	⑥ 🍷	⑥ 🍷	⑥ 🍷			⑦ 🍷	⑦ 🍷 L	⑦ 🍷	⑦ 🍷 L	⑦ 🍷	⑦ 🍷
Edinburgh 127 d.	...	0805	...	...	...	1005	...	...	...	1205	...	...	...	1405	...	1605	...	⑦	...	...	...	...	...	0850
Newcastle 127 d.	0925	0940	1025	...	1125	1140	1217	...	1327	1340	1422	...	1522	1540	...	1740	...		...	...	...	...	...	1025
Manchester Piccadilly 150 d.	|	|	|	1224	|	|	|	1424	|	|	|	1624	|	|	1824	|	...	▲	0810	...	1024	...	1208	|
Birmingham New St 121 d.	1240	1310	1340	1410	1440	1510	1540	1610	1640	1710	1740	1810	1840	1910	2010	2110	...		1010	1110	1210	1310	1410	1510
Cheltenham 132 121 d.	1322	1352	1422	1452	1522	1552	1622	1652	1722	1752	1824	1852	1922	1952	2052	2152	...		1052	1152	1252	1352	1452	1552
Gloucester 132 121 a.	1339	1418*	1456	1510	1540	1618*	1656	1718*	1739	1818*	1835	1918*	1943	2018*	2112	2209	...		1121	1207	1324	1421	1510	1621
Bristol Parkway a.	1357	1425	1456	1525	1556	1625	1656	1725	1756	1825	1906	1925	1956	2025	2125	2225	...		1125	1225	1325	1425	1524	1625
Bristol Temple Meads a.	1413	1441	1511	1541	1613	1641	1713	1741	1813	1841	1924	1941	2013	2041	2141	2241	...		1138	1238	1338	1438	1538	1638
Exeter St Davids 116 a.	...	1543	1610	1643	...	1743	...	1843	...	1943	...	2049	...	2149	2249	...	...		1257	1350	1450	1550	1650	1750
Plymouth 117 a.	...	1652	1715	1748	...	1848	...	1948	...	2048	...	...	...	...	...	...	...		...	...	...	...	...	...

	⑦ 🍷 P	⑦ 🍷	⑦ 🍷	⑦ 🍷 G		⑦ 🍷		⑦ 🍷 A	⑦ 🍷
Edinburgh 127 d.	...	1050	...	1250	...	...	...	1450	1550
Newcastle 127 d.	...	1225	...	1425	...	...	...	1625	1725
Manchester Piccadilly 150 d.	1424	|	1624	|	...	1824	...	|	|
Birmingham New St 121 d.	1610	1710	1810	1910	...	2010	...	2110	2210
Cheltenham 132 121 d.	1652	1752	1852	1952	...	2052	...	2152	2252
Gloucester 132 121 a.	1712	1822	1925	2023	...	2112	...	2211	|
Bristol Parkway a.	1725	1825	1925	2025	...	2125	...	2225	2325
Bristol Temple Meads a.	1738	1838	1938	2038	...	2138	...	2241	2341
Exeter St Davids 116 a.	1850	1953	2050	2143	...	2253	...	...	...
Plymouth 117 a.	...	...	...	...	...	...	...	...	...

		Ⓐ 🍷	Ⓐ 🍷	Ⓐ 🍷	Ⓐ 🍷 C	Ⓐ 🍷	Ⓐ 🍷	Ⓐ 🍷	Ⓐ 🍷	Ⓐ 🍷
Plymouth 117 d.	Ⓐ	...	...	...	...	0625	0640	0725	...	0825
Exeter St Davids 116 d.		...	...	0623	...	0723	0738	0823	...	0923
Bristol Temple Meads d.		0615	0700	0730	0800	0830	0900	0930	1000	1030
Bristol Parkway d.		0625	0710	0740	0810	0840	0910	0940	1010	1040
Gloucester 132 121 d.		0702	0721	0754	0821	0850	|	0950	1021	1050
Cheltenham 132 121 d.		0712	0742	0812	0842	0912	0942	1012	1042	1112
Birmingham New St 121 a.		0757	0826	0857	0926	0957	1026	1058	1126	1157
Manchester P'dilly 150 a.		|	|	1102	|	|	|	1302	|	|
Newcastle 127 a.		1133	1154	...	1307	1334	1350	...	1457	1532
Edinburgh 127 a.		1316	...	...	...	1516	...	...	...	1716

	Ⓐ 🍷	Ⓐ 🍷 P	Ⓐ 🍷 T	Ⓐ 🍷 PU	Ⓐ 🍷	Ⓐ 🍷 P	Ⓐ 🍷	Ⓐ 🍷 G	Ⓐ 🍷	Ⓐ 🍷	Ⓐ 🍷 T	Ⓐ 🍷	Ⓐ 🍷	Ⓐ 🍷	Ⓐ 🍷 T	Ⓐ 🍷 Y	Ⓐ 🍷	Ⓐ 🍷		Ⓐ 2 N	Ⓐ 🍷 L	Ⓐ 2		Ⓐ
Plymouth 117 d.	...	0925	...	1025	...	1125	1150	1225	...	1325	...	1425	...	1525	...	1625	...	1725	...	...	1825	...	...	...
Exeter St Davids 116 d.	...	1023	1048	1123	...	1223	1248	1323	...	1423	1446	1523	...	1623	1653	1723	...	1823	...	...	1923	...	...	...
Bristol Temple Meads d.	1100	1130	1200	1230	1300	1330	1400	1430	1500	1530	1600	1630	1700	1730	1800	1830	1900	1930	...	1941	2030	2041	...	2200
Bristol Parkway d.	1110	1140	1210	1240	1310	1340	1410	1440	1510	1540	1610	1640	1710	1740	1810	1840	1910	1940	...	1952	2040	2052	...	2210
Gloucester 132 121 d.	1121	1150	|	1250	1321	1350	1421	1450	|	1550	1622	1650	1722	1754	1822	1850	1921	1954	...	2057	|	2146	...	2223
Cheltenham 132 121 d.	1142	1212	1242	1312	1342	1412	1442	1512	1542	1612	1642	1712	1742	1812	1842	1912	1942	2012	...	2107	2112	2157	...	2242
Birmingham New St 121 a.	1226	1257	1326	1357	1426	1457	1526	1557	1626	1700	1726	1757	1826	1859	1926	1957	2042	2057	...	2152	2157	2248	...	2343
Manchester Piccadilly 150 a.	|	1502	|	|	|	1702	|	|	|	1902	|	|	|	2102	|	...	2232	2302	...	...	...	...	...	...
Newcastle 127 a.	1600	...	1652	1728	1754	...	1856	1935	2004	...	2054	2142	2201	...	2300	...	...	...	...	...	...	...	...	...
Edinburgh 127 a.	...	...	...	1857	...	...	...	2108	...	...	...	2328	...	...	...	...	...	...	...	...	...	...	...	...

		⑥ 🍷	⑥ 🍷	⑥ 🍷	⑥ 🍷	⑥ 🍷	⑥ 🍷	⑥ 🍷 C	⑥ 🍷	⑥ 🍷	⑥ 🍷 P	⑥ 🍷 T	⑥ 🍷 PU	⑥ 🍷	⑥ 🍷 P	⑥ 🍷	⑥ 🍷 G	⑥ 🍷	⑥ 🍷	⑥ 🍷 T	⑥ 🍷	⑥ 🍷	⑥ 🍷	⑥ 🍷 Y
Plymouth 117 d.	⑥	...	...	...	0625	...	0725	...	0825	...	0925	...	1025	...	1125	...	1225	...	1325	...	1425	...	1525	...
Exeter St Davids 116 d.		...	0610	...	0723	...	0823	...	0923	...	1023	1048	1123	...	1223	...	1323	...	1423	1448	1523	...	1623	...
Bristol Temple Meads d.	▲	0615	0730	0800	0830	0900	0930	1000	1030	1100	1130	1200	1230	1300	1330	1400	1430	1500	1530	1600	1630	1700	1730	1800
Bristol Parkway d.		0625	0740	0810	0840	0910	0940	1010	1040	1110	1140	1210	1240	1310	1340	1410	1440	1510	1540	1610	1640	1710	1740	1810
Gloucester 132 121 d.		0701	0746	0822	0846	|	0946	1021	1046	1122	1146	|	1246	1321	1346	1421	1446	|	1546	1621	1646	1721	1746	1823
Cheltenham 132 121 d.		0712	0812	0842	0912	0942	1012	1042	1112	1142	1212	1242	1312	1342	1412	1442	1512	1542	1612	1642	1712	1742	1812	1842
Birmingham New St 121 a.		0757	0857	0926	0957	1026	1058	1126	1157	1226	1258	1326	1357	1426	1457	1527	1557	1626	1657	1726	1757	1826	1857	1927
Manchester Piccadilly 150 a.		|	1104	|	|	|	1304	|	|	|	1504	|	|	|	1702	|	|	|	1902	|	|	|	2102	...
Newcastle 127 a.		1136	...	1257	1335	1350	...	1454	1534	1555	...	1651	1734	1758	...	1856	1934	1953	...	2054	2141	2234	...	...
Edinburgh 127 a.		1313	...	...	1513	...	...	...	1714	...	...	...	1912	...	...	...	2113	...	...	2231	...	...	...	...

	⑥ 🍷 Y	⑥	⑥ 🍷	⑥ 2 N	⑥ 🍷 D	⑥ 2		⑦ 🍷	⑦ 🍷	⑦ 🍷	⑦ 🍷 G	⑦ 🍷	⑦ 🍷	⑦ 2 N	⑦ 🍷	⑦ 🍷	⑦ 2 N	⑦ 🍷	⑦ 🍷 L	⑦ 2 N	⑦ 🍷	⑦ 🍷 L	⑦ 2	⑦ 🍷
Plymouth 117 d.	1625	...	1725	...	1825	...	⑦	...	...	...	...	...	...	...	...	...	...	...	...	...	...	...	...	...
Exeter St Davids 116 d.	1723	...	1823	...	1923	...	▲	...	...	1020	1120	1220	1320	...	1420	1520	...	1620	1720	...	1820	1920	...	...
Bristol Temple Meads d.	1830	1900	1930	1941	2030	2041		0915	1030	1130	1230	1330	1430	1444	1530	1630	1644	1730	1830	1844	1930	2030	2044	2210
Bristol Parkway d.	1840	1910	1940	1952	2040	2052		0925	1040	1140	1240	1340	1440	1455	1540	1640	1655	1740	1840	1855	1940	2040	2055	2220
Gloucester 132 121 d.	1846	1921	1946	2057	|	2146		1000	1038	1144	1246	1344	1446	1546	1551	1646	1746	1751	1846	1946	|	2046	2146	|
Cheltenham 132 121 d.	1912	1942	2012	2107	2112	2157		1012	1112	1212	1312	1412	1512	1557	1612	1712	1757	1812	1912	1957	2012	2112	2157	2252
Birmingham New St 121 a.	1957	2031	2057	2152	2157	2302		1051	1151	1251	1351	1457	1551	1639	1657	1751	1845	1857	1951	2045	2057	2151	2245	2344
Manchester Piccadilly 150 a.	...	...	2302	...	...	...		1257	|	1457	|	1657	|	...	1857	|	...	2055	...	...	2257	...	...	...
Newcastle 127 a.	...	...	...	...	...	...		...	1635	...	1835	...	2036	...	...	2242	...	...	...	...	...	...	...	...
Edinburgh 127 a.	...	...	...	...	...	...		...	1814	...	2013	...	2222	...	...	...	...	...	...	...	...	...	...	...

– From Aberdeen.
– To/from Cardiff.
– From/to Derby.

G – From/to Glasgow.
L – From/to Leeds.
N – To Nottingham.

P – To/from Penzance.
T – To/from Paignton.
U – From/to Dundee.

Y – From/to York.
* – By 🚌.

▲ – Services on ⑥⑦ are subject to alteration from Feb. 2.

121 CARDIFF - GLOUCESTER - BIRMINGHAM

2nd class XC, AW

For other services Gloucester - Birmingham and v.v. changing at Cheltenham, see Table **120**

km		⚒ ▲	⑥	⚒ ◇	Ⓐ	⚒	⚒	Ⓐ ◇	⚒	⚒	⚒	⑥ ◇	⚒	⚒	⚒	⚒	⚒	⚒	⚒	⚒	⚒	⚒	⚒	⚒	Ⓐ
0	**Cardiff** Central ....d.		...	...	...	0612	...	0700	0712	0745	0845	0900	0912	0945	1012	1045	1145	1212	1245	1312	1345	1445	1512	1545	161
19	Newport........................d.		...	...	...	0627	...	0715	0727	0759	0859	0915	0927	0959	1027	1059	1159	1227	1259	1327	1359	1459	1527	1559	162
47	Chepstow ....d.		...	...	...	0649	...	|	0749	|	|	|	0949	|	1049	|	|	1249	|	1349	|	|	1549	|	165
91	**Gloucester**.......... **122** d.		0646	0701	0709	0721	0746	|	0821	0846	0946	|	1020	1046	1121	1146	1246	1321	1346	1421	1446	1546	1621	1646	172
101	Cheltenham .... **122** a.		0656	0710	0718	0734	0756	0840	0834	0855	0956	1040	1034	1055	1134	1156	1256	1334	1355	1434	1455	1556	1634	1655	173
113	Ashchurch §......... **122** a.		0704	|	0727	...	0804	|	...	|	1004	|	...	|	*1155*	|	|	*1358*	|	...	|	1604	...	1704	*175*
152	Bromsgrove ....a.		0723	|	0749	...	0823	|	...	0921	|	|	...	|	...	|	|	...	|	...	|	|	...	|	...
174	**Birmingham** New St ..a.		0745	0757	0818	...	0846	0926	...	0945	1045	1126	...	1145	...	1246	1345	...	1445	...	1545	1645	...	1745	...
	Nottingham **127** ....a.		0910	...	...	...	1005	...	...	1104	1206	...	...	1305	...	1405	1505	...	1605	...	1706	1806	...	1905	...

	⑥	⚒	⚒	⚒	⚒	⚒	⚒	⚒	Ⓐ	⑥ V	⚒	Ⓐ	⑥		⑦ ▲	⑦ ◇		⑦	⑦	⑦	⑦	⑦	⑦	⑦	⑦
Cardiff Central ....d.	1612	1645	1712	1745	1812	1845	2000	2015	2050	2050	2114	2320	2320	...		...	...	1030	1150	...	1230	1350	1430	1450	155
Newport.........................d.	1626	1659	1727	1759	1827	1859	2015	2030	2104	2104	2129	2339	2340	...		...	...	1045	1204	...	1245	1404	1445	1504	160
Chepstow ....d.	1647	|	1749	|	1849	|	|	2052	|	|	2151	0008	0008	...		...	...	1107	|	...	1307	|	1507	|	|
Gloucester........... **122** d.	1721	1746	1822	1846	1921	1946	2057	2123	2146	2146	2223	0039	0042	...		1000	...	1144	1246	1316	1344	1446	1538	1546	164
Cheltenham .... **122** a.	1734	1755	1834	1855	1934	1957	2107	2134	2156	2155	2236**a**	0052	...	...		1012	...	1204	1256	1327	1357	1455	1551	1555	165
Ashchurch §.......... **122** a.	...	1804	...	|	*1956***a**	2004	|	*2151*	|	|	...	...	...	...		|	...	...	|	|	...	1504	...	|	|
Bromsgrove ....a.	...	|	...	|	...	|	|	...	2220	|	...	...	...	...		|	...	...	|	|	...	|	...	|	|
Birmingham New St ...a.	...	1846	...	1946	...	2043	2152	...	2248	2302	...	...	...	...		1051	...	...	1340	1419	...	1544	...	1639	174
Nottingham **127** ....a.	...	2006**q**	...	2107**q**	...	2204**z**	2305	...	...	...	...	...	...	...		...	...	...	1502	...	...	1710	...	1804	191

	⑦	⑦	⑦	⑦	⑦	⑦	⑦	⑦	⑦ W	⑦
Cardiff Central ....d.	1630	1650	1750	1830	1850	1950	2030	...	2140	2230
Newport.........................d.	1645	1704	1804	1845	1904	2004	2045	...	2155	2249
Chepstow ....d.	1707	|	|	1907	|	|	2107	...	|	2317
Gloucester........... **122** d.	1738	1746	1846	1942	1946	2046	2137	2146	2244	2347
Cheltenham .... **122** a.	1751	1755	1855	1955	1957	2057	...	2157	2256	...
Ashchurch §.......... **122** a.	...	|	|	...	|	|	...	|	2303	...
Bromsgrove ....a.	...	|	|	...	|	|	...	2220	...	...
Birmingham New St ...a.	...	1845	1945	...	2045	2144	...	2245	...	...
Nottingham **127** ....a.	...	2000	2107	...	2207	...	...	...	...	...

	⚒ ▲	⚒	⚒ W	⚒ V	⚒	⚒	⚒	⚒	⚒	⚒
Nottingham **127** ....d.		...	...	...	...	...	...	0658	0800	...
Birmingham New St..........d.		...	...	0530	...	0730	...	0830	0930	...
Bromsgrove ....d.		...	...	|	...	|	...	|	|	...
Ashchurch § .... **122** d.		...	0555	0633	*0705***c**	|	...	|	*0921*	...
Cheltenham .... **122** d.		0537**b**	0604	0643	0745	0811	0845	0911	1011	104
Gloucester................. **122** d.		0550	0616	0700	0758	0825	0858	0922	1022	105
Chepstow.............................d.		0619	0644	0728	0827	|	0927	|	|	112
Newport ....a.		0642	0706	0750	0850	0907	0950	1009**r**	1110**r**	115
Cardiff Central.....................a.		0700	0727	0812	0910	0929	1010	1030**r**	1132**r**	121

	⚒	⚒	⚒	⚒	⚒	⚒	⚒	⚒		⚒	⚒	⚒	⚒	⚒	⚒ ◇	⚒	⚒	⚒	Ⓐ	⑥	⚒	⑥	Ⓐ		⑤ V
Nottingham **127** ....d.	0900	...	1002	1100	...	1202	...	1300	...	1400	...	1500	...	1600	...	...	1700	...	1800	1834	...	...	...	...	...
Birmingham New St ...d.	1030	...	1130	1230	...	1330	...	1430	...	1530	...	1630	...	1730	1740	...	1830	...	1930	2000	...	...	...	...	230
Bromsgrove ....d.	|	...	|	|	...	|	...	|	...	|	...	1651	...	1751	|	...	1851	...	|	|	...	...	...	...	232
Ashchurch §.......... **122** d.	|	*1121*	|	|	*1321*	|	...	|	...	1606	...	|	*1721*	1809	|	...	|	*1922***q**	2006	2036	*2124***a**	*2152*	...	...	235
Cheltenham .... **122** d.	1111	1145	1211	1311	1345	1411	1445	1511	...	1615	1645	1714	1745	1818	1822	1845	1914	1945	2015	2049	2145	*2201*	2245	...	000
Gloucester........... **122** d.	1122	1158	1222	1322	1358	1422	1458	1522	...	1626	1658	1725	1758	1829	1838	1858	1925	1958	2026	2101	2158	2258	2258	...	001
Chepstow ....d.	|	1227	|	|	1427	|	1527	|	...	|	1727	|	1827	|	|	1927	|	2027	|	...	2227	2327	2327	...	...
Newport.........................a.	1209**r**	1250	1309**r**	1410**r**	1452	1509**r**	1551	1609**r**	...	1709	1751	1809**d**	1850	1914	1959	1950	2010**d**	2050	2110	...	2257	2357	2359	...	...
Cardiff Central ....a.	1232**r**	1310	1334**c**	1432**r**	1511	1532**r**	1609	1632**r**	...	1732**r**	1810	1832**r**	1910	1936**d**	2019	2011	2029**d**	2110	2131	...	2318	0018	0022	...	...

	⑦ ▲	⑦ W	⑦	⑦		⑦	⑦ V	⑦		⑦	⑦	⑦		⑦	⑦	⑦		⑦	⑦	⑦		⑦	⑦	⑦	⑦
Nottingham **127** ....d.		...	...	...	...	...	...	...	...	1209	...	...	...	1401	...	1502	...	1609	...	1713	...	1806	...	1908	...
Birmingham New St ...d.		...	...	1030	...	...	1146	1230	...	1330	...	1430	...	1530	...	1630	...	1730	...	1830	...	1930	...	2030	...
Bromsgrove ....d.		...	...	|	...	...	1205	|	...	|	...	|	...	|	...	|	...	|	...	|	...	|	...	|	...
Ashchurch §.......... **122** d.		0949	...	|	...	...	|	|	...	|	...	1506	...	|	...	*1655*	...	|	...	|	...	|	...	2105	...
Cheltenham .... **122** d.		0958	...	1111	...	1216	1245	1312	...	1411	1416	1515	...	1612	1616	1715	...	1812	1816	1915	...	2012	2020	2114	*220*
Gloucester........... **122** d.		1011	1033	1122	...	1233	1255	1326	...	1422	1432	1526	...	1626	1633	1726	...	1823	1833	1926	...	2023	2033	2128	223
Chepstow ....d.		|	1102	|	...	1302	...	|	...	|	1501	|	...	|	1702	|	...	|	1902	|	...	...	2102	...	230
Newport.........................a.		1054	1125	1204	...	1325	...	1408	...	1504	1524	1608	...	1708	1727	1808	...	1905	1926	2012	...	...	2125	...	233
Cardiff Central ....a.		1113	1145	1225	...	1345	...	1429	...	1525	1545	1629	...	1729	1745	1826	...	1926	1945	2033	...	...	2146	...	235

V – Via Worcester.
W – To / from Worcester.

a – Ⓐ only.

b – *0530* on ⑥.
c – 9 minutes earlier on ⑥.
d – 3–4 minutes earlier on ⑥.
q – 4 minutes later on ⑥.

r – 5–7 minutes earlier on ⑥.
z – ⑥ only.

◇ – Conveys [12].

§ – Ashchurch for Tewkesbury.

▲ – Additional services operate Cardiff - Gloucester and v.v. on ⑥⑦. Services are subject to alteration from Feb. 2.

122 BRISTOL - GLOUCESTER - WORCESTER

GW

km		⚒ ▲	⑥	Ⓐ	⚒ E	Ⓐ	⚒		⚒	⚒	⚒	Ⓐ		⚒	⚒		⚒	⚒		Ⓐ	⚒		Ⓐ	Ⓐ
0	**Bristol** Temple Meads.... **120** d.		...	...	0615	...	0741	...	0841	0941	1041	1141	...	1241	1341	...	1441	1541	...	1641	1741	...	1841	194
9	Bristol Parkway.............. **120** d.		...	...	0625	...	0752	...	0852	0952	1052	1152	...	1252	1352	...	1452	1552	...	1652	1752	...	1852	195
62	**Gloucester**.............................a.		...	...	0655	...	0832	...	0929	1031	1130	1229	...	1329**z**	1431	...	1531	1632	...	1729	1832	...	1929	202
62	**Gloucester**.................... **121** d.		0550	0602	0701	0715	...	...	0938	...	1136	...	...	1338	...	...	1538	...	...	1738	...	...	1938	203
72	Cheltenham .... **120 121** d.		0600	0612	0710	0725	...	...	0948	...	1145	...	...	1349	...	...	1547	...	...	1749	...	...	1949	204
84	Ashchurch §.................... **121** d.		0608	0620	...	0733	...	...	0956	...	1153	...	...	1357	...	...	1555	...	...	1757	...	...	1957	...
108	**Worcester** Shrub Hill.............a.		0630	0640	...	0754	...	...	1014	...	1213	...	...	1420**v**	...	...	1622**r**	...	...	1817	...	...	2014	...

	⑥	⑥	⑥	Ⓐ	⑥ B	Ⓐ	⑥	Ⓐ		⑦ ▲	⑦ M	⑦		⑦		⑦		⑦		⑦		⑦		⑦ C
Bristol Temple Meads.... **120** d.	1940	*2030**	2041	2041	...	*2200**	2206	2210	...		0915	0944	...	1244	...	1444	...	1644	...	1844	...	2044	...	...
Bristol Parkway.............. **120** d.	1952	*2040**	2052	2052	...	*2210**	2218	2221	...		0925	0955	...	1255	...	1455	...	1655	...	1855	...	2055	...	...
Gloucester..............................a.	2031	|	2131	2129	...	|	2301	2301	...		0955	1035	...	1332	...	1537	...	1735	...	1934	...	2132	...	...
Gloucester..................... **121** d.	2038	2117	2134	2134	2146	2241	...	...	...		1000	1038	...	1336	...	1551	...	1751	...	1938	...	2136	...	224
Cheltenham .... **120 121** d.	2045	2127	2142	2144	2157	2252	...	...	...		1010	1049	...	1348	...	1601	...	1802	...	1948	...	2145	...	225
Ashchurch §..................... **121** d.	...	|	...	2152	|	|	...	...	...		...	...	...	1356	...	1610	...	1810	...	1956	...	...	...	230
Worcester Shrub Hill.............a.	...	2154	...	2210	2220	2315	...	...	...		...	...	...	1425	...	1629	...	1829	...	2014	...	...	...	232

	⚒ ▲	⚒ C	⚒	⚒ BC	Ⓐ	⑥	Ⓐ	⚒		⚒	⚒		⚒		⚒	⚒		⚒	⚒		⚒	⚒	⚒ N	⚒
Worcester Shrub Hill.............d.		0540	...	0617	...	0640	0649	...	...	0905	...	...	1105	...	...	1305	...	...	1505	...	...	1705	...	...
Ashchurch §..................... **121** d.		0555	...	0633	...	0656	0705	...	...	0921	...	...	1121	...	...	1321	...	...	1521	...	...	1721	...	...
Cheltenham .... **120 121** d.		0604	...	0643	0659	0706	0715	...	...	0931	...	...	1131	...	...	1331	...	...	1531	...	...	1731	1822	...
Gloucester..................... **121** a.		0615	...	0652	0709	0714	0725	...	...	0939	...	...	1139	...	...	1339	...	...	1540	...	...	1739	1835	...
Gloucester..............................d.		...	0621	...	0712	0740	0748	0842	...	0942	1042	...	1142	...	1242	1342	...	1442	1542	...	1642	1742	1838	184
Bristol Parkway.............. **120** a.		...	0700	...	0747	0815	0824	0919	...	1019	1119	...	1219	...	1319	1419	...	1519	1619	...	1719	1819	1906	191
Bristol Temple Meads.... **120** a.		...	0715	...	0800	0834	0836	0935	...	1035	1135	...	1235	...	1336	1434	...	1536	1634	...	1736	1835	1924	193

	Ⓐ	⑥		⚒	Ⓐ	⑥	Ⓐ	Ⓐ		⑤ B		⑦ ▲	⑦ C	⑦		⑦		⑦ B		⑦		⑦		⑦
Worcester Shrub Hill.............d.	1906	1910	...	...	2108	2134	...	2232	...	2344	...		0935	...	...	...	...	1224	...	1436	...	1639	...	203
Ashchurch §..................... **121** d.	1922	1926	...	...	2124	2152	...	2250	...	2358	...		0949	...	...	...	...	|	...	1452	...	1655	...	205
Cheltenham .... **120 121** d.	1932	1935	...	2102	2134	2201	2231	2300	...	0007	...		0958	1006	...	1157	...	1245	...	1501	...	1704	...	210
Gloucester..................... **121** a.	1940	1943	...	2112	2145	2209	2241	2313	...	0016	...		1008	1016	...	1207	...	1255	...	1510	...	1712	...	211
Gloucester..............................d.	1944	1944	...	2115	|	...	2249	...	...	...	...		...	1019	...	1211	...	...	...	1514	...	1717	...	211
Bristol Parkway.............. **120** a.	2019	2019	...	2151	2223*	...	2316	...	...	...	...		...	1055	...	1248	...	...	...	1549	...	1752	...	215
Bristol Temple Meads.... **120** a.	2034	2036	...	2204	2237*	...	2330	...	...	...	...		...	1107	...	1301	...	...	...	1610	...	1807	...	220

B – To / from Birmingham.
C – From / to Cardiff.
E – [12] to Edinburgh.

M – [12] to Manchester.
N – [12] Newcastle - Cardiff.

r – 1613 on ⑥.
v – 1426 on ⑥.
z – 1333 on ⑥.

* – Change at Cheltenham.
§ – Ashchurch for Tewkesbury.

▲ – Services on ⑥⑦ are subject to alteration from Feb. 2.

CT 2nd class — BIRMINGHAM - WORCESTER - HEREFORD — 123

Additional trains operate Birmingham Snow Hill - Droitwich - Worcester - Great Malvern and v.v. via Kidderminster.

km			Ⓐ	⚒ C	⑥	Ⓐ	⑥	Ⓐ	⚒	⚒	⚒	Ⓐ	⑥	Ⓐ	⚒	⚒	⑥	Ⓐ	⑥	Ⓐ	⚒	Ⓐ	⑥	Ⓐ	Ⓐ
0	**Birmingham** New St.... 121 d.	⚒	...	0530	...	0659	0659	0720	0759	0859	0959	1013‡	1059	1059	1159	1259	1359	1359	1459	1459	1559	1619	1659	1659	1719
21	Bromsgrove .... 121 d.		...	|	...	0723	0723	0747	0821	0921	1021	|	1121	1121	1221	1321	1421	1421	1521	1521	1621	|	1721	1721	1745
32	Droitwich .... d.		...	|	...	0733	0732	0757	0831	0931	1031	1100	1131	1131	1231	1331	1431	1431	1531	1531	1631	1649	1731	1731	1754
41	Worcester Shrub Hill.. 131 a.		0600	0611	0638	|	0740	0805	|	|	|	1108	|	|	|	|	|	|	|	|	|	1700	|	1738	1805
41	Worcester Foregate St.. 131 a.		0602	...	0640	0741	0746	0810	0839	0939	1039	*1116*	1139	1139	1239	1339	1439	1439	1539	1539	1639	1710	1739	1744	1811
54	Great Malvern .... 131 a.		0615	...	0652	0754	0758	0822	0852	0952	1052	*1129*	1152	1155	1252	1352	1452	1455	1552	1557	1652	1724	1752	1758	1823
65	Ledbury .... 131 a.		0627	...	0707	0812	0814	...	0906	1006	1106	*1142*	1206	...	1306	1406	1506	...	1606	1617	1706	...	1806	1820	1836
87	**Hereford** .... 131 a.		0650	...	0728	0833	0835	...	0928	1028	1128	*1205*	1228	...	1328	1428	1528	...	1628	1638	1728	...	1828	1841	1857

	Ⓐ	Ⓐ	⑥	Ⓐ	Ⓐ	Ⓐ	⑥	Ⓐ	⚒	Ⓐ	Ⓐ F			⑦	⑦ G		⑦		⑦		⑦	⑦	⑦		⑦
Birmingham New St.... 121 d.	1750	1759	1759	1819	1843‡	1919	1930	1927‡	2059	2159	2304	...	⑦	1018‡	1146	...	1345	...	1600	...	1800	1900	1918‡	...	2100
Bromsgrove .... 121 d.	|	1822	1821	1847	|	1940	1936	|	2121	2221	2323	...		|	1205	...	1405	...	1621	...	1821	1921	|	...	2121
Droitwich .... d.	1819	1835	1831	1856	1931	1950	1951	2019	2131	2231	2332	...		1104	1213	...	1415	...	1630	...	1830	1931	2008	...	2130
Worcester Shrub Hill.. 131 a.	1829	|	1840	1911	|	2001	2007	2026	2141r	2245	2345d	...		1111	1222	...	1422	...	1641	...	1838	1941	2015	...	2147
Worcester Foregate St.. 131 a.	...	1844	1852	...	1940	2014	2014	*2042*	2150	...	...	...		1128	*1311*	...	1430	...	1647	...	1844	*2011*	*2113*	...	2142
Great Malvern........ 131 a.	...	1857	1904	...	*2001*	2026	2026	*2056*	2202	...	...	...		1140	*1325*	...	1442	...	1702	...	1856	*2026*	*2127*	...	2154
Ledbury .... 131 a.	...	1910	1917	...	*2015*	2039	2040	*2110*	2215	...	...	...		*1234*	*1339*	...	1455	...	*1739*	...	1909	...	*2140*	...	2207
Hereford .... 131 a.	...	1933	1942	...	*2036*	2100	2100	*2131*	2236	...	...	...		*1253*	*1404*	...	1519	...	*1758*	...	1930	...	*2159*	...	2228

		Ⓐ	Ⓐ	⑥	Ⓐ	Ⓐ	⑥	Ⓐ	⑥	Ⓐ	⑥	Ⓐ	⚒	⚒	⚒	Ⓐ	⑥	⚒	⚒	⚒	Ⓐ	⑥	Ⓐ	⑥	⚒
Hereford .... 131 d.	⚒	...	...	...	*0542*	...	...	0709	0722	0735	0737	...	0850	0950	1050	...	1150	1250	*1323*r	1350	...	1450	1538	1550	1650
Ledbury .... 131 d.		...	...	...	*0600*	...	...	0726	0740	0751	0754	...	0907	1007	1107	...	1207	1307	*1339*	1407	...	1507	1555	1607	1707
Great Malvern........ 131 d.		0550	...	0620	0649	0705	...	0737	0752	0803	0806	0835	0918	1018	1118	1218	1218	1318	*1352*	1418	1514	1518	1610	1618	1718
Worcester Foregate St.. 131 d.		0603	...	0631	0659	0716	...	0749	0807	0819	0819	0846	0931	1031	1131	1231	1231	1331	1415	1431	1525	1531	1624	1631	1731
Worcester Shrub Hill .. 131 d.		|	0625	|	0706	0724	0733	0756	0810	|	0826	|	|	|	|	|	|	|	|	|	|	|	|	|	|
Droitwich .... d.		0612	0633	0640	0714	0734	0740	0805	...	0832	0834	0855	0940	1040	1140	1240	1240	1340	1424	1440	1534	1540	1634	1640	1740
Bromsgrove .... 121 d.		0621	0642	0650	0723	|	0750	|	...	0841	0843	|	0950	1050	1150	1250	1250	1350	|	1450	1544	1550	1644	1650	1749
Birmingham New St.... 121 a.		0645	0707	0716	0747	0809	0816	0837	...	0907	0914	0943	1024r	1123	1223	1318	1321	1423	1515‡	1521	1609	1621	1714	1721	1821

	Ⓐ	⑥	Ⓐ	⑥	Ⓐ	⑥		Ⓐ	⑥ C	⑥	Ⓐ	⑥			⑦		⑦	⑦		⑦		⑦	⑦		⑦
Hereford .... 131 d.	1740	1750	1852	*1904*	1950	1959	...	2130	...	*2133*	2243	2245	...	⑦	*1330*	...	*1430*	1546	...	*1630*	...	*1830*	2005	...	2240
Ledbury .... 131 d.	1756	1807	1911	*1920*	2017	2015	...	2147	...	*2149*	2259	2302	...		*1348*	...	*1457*	1602	...	*1647*	...	*1848*	2021	...	2256
Great Malvern........ 131 d.	1807	1818	1922	*1931*	2028	2026	...	2158	...	*2200*	2310	2314	...		1435	...	*1509*	1615	...	1716	...	*1908*	2032	...	2308
Worcester Foregate St.. 131 d.	1819	1831	1934	1950	2042	2038	...	2210	...	*2213*	2320	2325	...		1445	...	*1524*	1626	...	1727	...	*1923*	2044	...	2322
Worcester Shrub Hill .. 131 d.	1826	|	1954	|	|	2044	...	|	2222	2248	2325	2331	...		1451	...	1546	1633	...	1733	...	1956	2050	...	2324
Droitwich .... d.	1834	1840	2002	1959	2051	2052	...	2219	|	2256	...	...	...		1459	...	1554	1641	...	1741	...	2004	2058	...	...
Bromsgrove .... 121 d.	1842	1850	2010	|	2059	2100	...	2228	|	|	...	...	...		1509	...	|	1651	...	1751	...	2013	2108	...	...
Birmingham New St.... 121 a.	1912	1921	2044	2053‡	2127	2128	...	2257	2302	2337‡	...	...	...		1540	...	1635‡	1717	...	1812	...	2040	2145	...	...

C – From / to Cardiff. F – To Gloucester on ⑤. G – To Gloucester. d – 2342 on ⑤. r – 3 minutes earlier on ⑥. ‡ – Birmingham Snow Hill.

XC All trains convey 🍷 — (MANCHESTER -) READING - GATWICK ✈ — 125

Long-distance through services only. For other trains Reading - Gatwick and v.v., see Table **105**.

km		Ⓐ	⑥	⚒	⚒	⑦	Ⓐ	⑥	⑦	Ⓐ
	Manchester Piccadilly 157 d.	0754	...	1254a	1454a	...	1654	...	...	1754
	Birmingham New St 128 ...d.	0933	0933	1433	1633	1733	1833	1833	1833	1933
0	**Reading** .... d.	1108	1113	1611	1811	1912	2009	2013	2021	2106
41	Guildford .... d.	|	|	1659	|	1955	|	2100	2055	2143
	Kensington Olympia .... d.	1157	1157	|	1902	|	2052	|	|	|
84	**Gatwick Airport** ✈ .... a.	1233	1253	*1750*	1952	2043	2147	2147	2146	2232
121	Brighton .... a.	1315	1337	...	2030	2113	*2248*	*2248*	*2250*	*2348*

	⚒	Ⓐ	⑥	⑥	Ⓐ	⑦	⚒	⑥	Ⓐ
Brighton .... d.	*0350*	...	...	0915	0921	*0919*	1422	...	...
Gatwick Airport ✈ .... d.	0515	0545	0545	0947	0946	1011	1451v	*1703*	*1703*
Kensington Olympia .... d.	|	|	0650	1034	1037	1058	1536v	|	|
Guildford .... d.	0600	0651	|	|	|	|	|	1758	1757
Reading .... a.	0630v	0735	0735	1135	1135	1137	1636	1835	1838
Birmingham New St 128 ... a.	0818	0918	0918	1318	1318	1318	1818	2018	2018
Manchester Piccadilly 157 a.	1003	...	...	...	...	...	2002a	...	2202

a – Ⓐ only. v – 3–5 minutes later on ⑥. ☛ Services on ⑥⑦ are subject to alteration from Feb. 2.

XC All trains convey 🍷 — (BIRMINGHAM -) READING - BOURNEMOUTH — 126

For other trains Basingstoke - Bournemouth and v.v., see Table **108**

km			Ⓐ	⚒ C	⚒ S	⚒ M	⚒ N	⚒ M	⚒ G	⚒ M	⚒ U	⚒ M	⚒ A	⚒ M	⚒ E	⚒ M	⚒ E	⚒ M			⑦	⑦ D	⑦ M	⑦ L
	Birmingham New St 128 ..... d.	⚒ ▲	0603	0703	0803	0903	1003	1103	1203	1303	1403	1503	1603	1703	1803	1903	2003	2103	...	⑦ ▲	0903	1003	1103	1203
0	**Reading** .... d.		0745	0845	0945	1045	1145	1245	1345	1445	1545	1645	1745	1845	1945	2045	2145	2245	...		1050	1150	1250	1350
25	Basingstoke .... d.		0810	0910	1010	1110	1210	1310	1410	1510	1610	1710	1810	1910	2010	2110	2210	2310	...		1110	1210	1310	1410
55	Winchester .... d.		0825	0925	1025	1125	1225	1325	1425	1525	1625	1725	1825	1925	2025	2125	2225	2325	...		1125	1225	1325	1425
69	Southampton Airport ✈ .... a.		0833	0933	1033	1133	1233	1333	1433	1533	1633	1733	1833	1933	2033	2133	2233	2333	...		1133	1233	1333	1433
76	**Southampton** Central .... a.		0840	0940	1040	1140	1240	1342	1440	1540	1640	1740	1840	1940	2040	2141	2248	2347	...		1142	1242	1342	1442
97	Brockenhurst .... a.		0856	0956	1056	1156	1256	1356	1456	1556	1656	1756	1856	1956	2056	2156	*2304*v	*0004*v	...		1202	1302	1402	1502
122	**Bournemouth** .... a.		0915	1015	1115	1215	1315	1415	1515	1615	1715	1815	1915	2025	2126	2226	2323v	0022v	...		1232	1332	1432	1532

	⑦ M	⑦ N	⑦ M	⑦ E	⑦ M	⑦ G	⑦ M	⑦ E	⑦ M	
Birmingham New St 128 ..... d.	1303	1403	1503	1603	1703	1803	1903	2003	2103	...
Reading .... d.	1450	1550	1650	1750	1850	1950	2050	2153	2250	...
Basingstoke .... d.	1510	1610	1710	1810	1910	2010	2110	2210	2310	...
Winchester .... d.	1525	1625	1725	1825	1925	2025	2125	|	2325	...
Southampton Airport ✈ .... a.	1533	1633	1733	1833	1933	2033	2133	2318	2333	...
Southampton Central .... a.	1542	1642	1742	1842	1942	2042	2142	2331	2345	...
Brockenhurst .... a.	1602	1702	1802	1902	2002	2102	2202	*2316*r	*0053*s	...
Bournemouth .... a.	1632	1732	1832	1932	2032	2132	2232	*2335*r	*0116*	...

		Ⓐ M	⚒ E	⚒ M	⚒ A	⚒ M	⚒ E	⚒ M	⚒ G
Bournemouth .... d.	⚒ ▲	...	*0515*a	0630j	0730y	0845	0945	1045	1145
Brockenhurst .... d.		...	*0538*a	0648j	0747z	0900	1000	1100	1200
Southampton Central .... d.		0515	0615	0715	0815	0915	1015	1115	1215
Southampton Airport ✈ .... d.		0522	0622	0722	0822	0922	1022	1122	1222
Winchester .... d.		0531	0631	0731	0831	0931	1031	1131	1231
Basingstoke .... d.		0547	0647	0747	0847	0947	1047	1147	1247
Reading .... a.		0604	0704	0804	0904	1004	1104	1204	1304
Birmingham New St 128 .. a.		0745	0848	0945	1046	1145	1245	1345	1446

	⚒ M	⚒ E	⚒ E	⚒ N	⚒ M	⚒ L	⚒ M	⚒			⑦	⑦ M	⑦ U	⑦ M	⑦ G	⑦ M	⑦ E	⑦ M	⑦ Y	⑦ M	⑦ L	⑦ M	⑦ D	⑦
Bournemouth .... d.	1245	1345	1445	1545	1645	1745	1845	1945	...	⑦ ▲	0806	...	*0920**	1040	1140	1240	1340	1440	1540	1640	1740	1840	1940	2040
Brockenhurst .... d.	1300	1400	1500	1600	1700	1800	1900	2000	...		0834	...	*0934*	1057	1157	1257	1357	1457	1557	1657	1757	1857	1957	2057
Southampton Central .... d.	1315	1415	1515	1615	1715	1815	1915	2015	...		0855	0839	1015	1115	1215	1315	1415	1515	1615	1715	1815	1915	2015	2115
Southampton Airport ✈ .... d.	1322	1422	1522	1622	1722	1822	1922	2022	...		0903	0846	1022	1122	1222	1322	1422	1522	1622	1722	1822	1922	2022	2122
Winchester .... d.	1331	1431	1531	1631	1731	1831	1931	2031	...		0923	|	1031	1131	1231	1331	1431	1531	1631	1731	1831	1931	2031	2131
Basingstoke .... d.	1347	1447	1547	1647	1747	1847	1947	2047	...		0942	0947	1047	1147	1247	1347	1447	1547	1647	1747	1847	1947	2047	2147
Reading .... a.	1404	1504	1604	1704	1804	1904	2004	2104	...		...	1005	1105	1205	1305	1405	1505	1605	1705	1805	1905	2005	2105	2205
Birmingham New St 128 ...... a.	1545	1646	1745	1846	1945	2048d	2145	2252	...		...	1146	1246	1346	1446	1546	1646	1746	1846	1946	2046	2146	2258	2355

A – From / to Aberdeen.
C – From Crewe.
D – From / to Derby.
E – From / to Edinburgh.
G – From / to Glasgow.
L – To Leeds.
M – From / to Manchester.
N – From / to Newcastle.
S – From Sheffield (and Leeds on Ⓐ).
U – From / to Dundee.
Y – To York.
a – Ⓐ only.
d – 2045 on ⑥.
j – 6–7 minutes later on ⑥.
r – Change at Basingstoke.
s – Stops to set down only.
v – Change at Southampton Airport.
y – 0745 on ⑥.
z – 0800 on ⑥.
* – By 🚌.
▲ – Services on ⑥⑦ are subject to alteration from Feb. 2.

127 BIRMINGHAM - NOTTINGHAM, SHEFFIELD and YORK XC

Services on ⑥⑦ are subject to alteration from February 2

km			⚒ 🍷	⑥ 2	Ⓐ 2	⚒ 🍷	⚒ 🍷	Ⓐ 2	⑥ 2	⚒ 🍷	⑥ 🍷 L	Ⓐ 2	⑥ 2 U	Ⓐ 🍷	⑥ 🍷	⑥ 2	Ⓐ 2	Ⓐ 🍷	⑥ 🍷	⚒ 2 U	⚒ 🍷 S	⑥ 2	Ⓐ 2	Ⓐ 🍷
	Cardiff **121** d.	⚒	...	...	...	...	...	...	...	...	...	...	...	...	...	...	...	...	...	...	...	...	...	0700
	Bristol Temple Meads **120** d.		...	...	...	...	...	...	...	...	...	...	...	0615	0615	...	...	0700	...	...	...	...	...	0800
0	**Birmingham** New St d.		0600	0609	0609	0630	0703	0710	0710	0730	...	0749	0749	0803	0803	0813	0819	0830	0830	0849	0903	0913	0919	0930
28	Tamworth d.		0615	0631	0631	0647	0719	0730	0728	0747	...	0809	0810	0819	0819	0834	0836	0847	0847	0908	|	0930	0936	|
48	Burton on Trent d.		0625	0642	0642	0658	0729	0742	0739	0758	...	0820	0822	0829	0829	0846	0848	0858	0858	0920	|	0941	0947	|
67	**Derby 170** d.		0639	0706	0711	0714	0742	0803	0808	0814	0834	0839	0842	0842	0842	0906	0911	0914	0914	0940v	0942	1011	1011	1014
	Nottingham a.		|	0737	0734	*0753*a	|	0832	0832	*0845*a	|	0904	0910	|	|	0935	0941	|	|	1005	|	1037	1037	|
105	Chesterfield **170** a.		|	...	...	0732	0802	...	...	0832	0856	...	...	|	0901	...	...	0934	0932	...	|	...	...	1032
125	**Sheffield 170 177 178 194** a.		0709	...	...	0751	0817	...	...	0850r	0913	...	...	0918	0917	...	...	0950	0950	...	1015	...	...	1051
154	Doncaster **178 185 194** a.		|	...	...	0824	|	...	...	0921	0952	...	...	|	|	...	...	1015	1018	...	|	...	...	1115
171	Wakefield Westgate **185** a.		0736	...	...	|	0846	...	...	|	|	...	...	0946	0946	...	...	|	|	...	1046	...	...	|
187	**Leeds 177 185** a.		0752	...	...	|	0904	...	...	|	|	...	...	1002	1002	...	...	|	|	...	1102	...	...	|
199	**York 185** a.		0824	...	...	0849	0933	...	...	0948	1016	...	...	1029	1031	...	...	1040	1044	...	1129	...	...	1142
	Newcastle **186** a.		0926	...	...	1001	1035	...	...	1059	...	...	...	1133	1136	...	...	1154	1157	...	1237	...	...	1307
	Edinburgh **186** a.		1102	...	...	...	1213	...	...	...	...	...	...	1316	1313	...	...	...	...	...	1416r	...	...	...

	⑥ 🍷	⚒ 2🍷	⚒ 🍷 P	⚒ 2	⚒ 🍷 Q	⚒ 2🍷	⚒ 🍷 BA	⚒ 2	⚒ 🍷	⚒ 2🍷	⚒ 🍷 P	⚒ 2	⚒ 🍷	⚒ 2🍷	⚒ 🍷 B	⑥ 2	Ⓐ 2	⚒ 🍷 N	⚒ 2🍷	⚒ 🍷 ZD	Ⓐ 2	⑥ 2	⚒ 🍷	⚒ 2
Cardiff **121** d.	...	0745	...	...	...	0845	...	...	0900g	0945	...	...	...	1045	...	...	...	...	1145	...	...	...	...	1245
Bristol Temple Meads **120** d.	0800	|	0830	...	0900	|	...	...	1000	|	1030	...	1100	|	...	...	...	1200	|	1230	...	...	1300	|
Birmingham New St d.	0930	0949	1003	1013	1030	1049	1103	1113	1130	1149	1203	1213	1230	1249	1303	1313	1313	1330	1349	1403	1413	1413	1430	1449
Tamworth d.	|	1006	|	1033	1047	1106	|	1133	|	1207	|	1232	1247	1308	|	1330	1333	|	1406	|	1430	1433	1447	1508
Burton on Trent d.	|	1018	|	1044	1058	1119	|	1144	|	1219	|	1244	1258	1320	|	1342	1344	|	1418	|	1442	1446	1458	1520
Derby 170 d.	1014	1041	1042	1111	1114	1141	1142	1211	1214	1241	1242	1311	1314	1341	1342	1411	1411	1414	1441	1442	1511	1511	1514	1541
Nottingham a.	|	1104	|	1142	|	1206	|	1240	|	1305	|	1341	|	1405	|	1435	1439	|	1505	|	1541	1541	|	1605
Chesterfield **170** a.	1032	...	|	...	1132	...	|	...	1232	...	|	...	1332	...	|	...	...	1432	...	|	...	...	1532	...
Sheffield 170 177 178 194 a.	1050	...	1115	...	1151	...	1215	...	1251	...	1315	...	1351	...	1415	...	...	1450	...	1515	...	...	1550	...
Doncaster **178 185 194** a.	1116	...	|	...	1215	...	|	...	1322r	...	|	...	1418r	...	|	...	...	1515	...	|	...	...	1615	...
Wakefield Westgate **185** a.	|	...	1146	...	|	...	1246	...	|	...	1346	...	|	...	1446	...	...	|	...	1546	...	...	|	...
Leeds 177 185 a.	|	...	1202	...	|	...	1302	...	|	...	1402	...	|	...	1502	...	...	|	...	1602	...	...	|	...
York 185 a.	1145	...	1229	...	1243	...	1329	...	1346	...	1429	...	1445	...	1529	...	...	1540v	...	1629	...	...	1640v	...
Newcastle **186** a.	1257	...	1335	...	1350	...	1437	...	1457r	...	1534	...	1600r	...	1639r	...	...	1652	...	1728v	...	...	1754v	...
Edinburgh **186** a.	...	...	1516r	...	...	...	1616v	...	...	...	1716	...	...	...	1816	...	...	...	...	1857b	...	...	...	...

	⚒ 🍷 BG	⚒ 2	⚒ 🍷 Q	⚒ 2	⚒ 🍷 PG	⚒ 2	Ⓐ 🍷	⑥ 🍷	⚒ 2	⚒ 🍷 B	Ⓐ 2	⑥ 2	⑥ 🍷 N	Ⓐ 🍷 N	⑥ 🍷 L	Ⓐ 🍷 L	⚒ 2	⑥ 🍷 P	Ⓐ 🍷 P	⚒ 2	⑥ 🍷	Ⓐ 🍷	⑥ 🍷 L	⚒ 2
Cardiff **121** d.	...	...	...	1345	...	...	...	...	1445	...	...	...	...	...	...	...	1545	...	...	...	...	...	...	1645
Bristol Temple Meads **120** d.	...	...	1400	|	1430	...	1500	1500	|	...	...	...	1600	1600	...	...	|	1630	1630	...	1700	1700	...	|
Birmingham New St d.	1503	1513	1530	1549	1603	1619r	1630	1630	1649	1703	1709	1713	1730	1730	...	...	1749	1803	1803	1809v	1830	1830	...	1849
Tamworth d.	|	1533	|	1608	|	1635	|	1647	1708	|	1729	1735	|	|	...	...	1809	|	|	1836	1847	1847	...	1908
Burton on Trent d.	|	1544	|	1620	|	1646	|	1658	1720	|	1740	1747	|	|	...	...	1820	|	|	1848	1858	1858	...	1920
Derby 170 d.	1542	1611	1614	1641	1642	1710	1714	1714	1741	1742	1811	1811	1814	1814	1818	1836	1841	1842	1842	1912	1914	1914	1932	1941
Nottingham a.	|	1639r	|	1706	|	1740	|	|	1806	|	1837	1838	|	|	|	|	1905	|	|	1942	|	|	|	2006v
Chesterfield **170** a.	|	...	1632	...	|	...	1737	1732	...	|	...	...	1832	1834	1838	1856	...	1901	1902	...	1932	1932	1952	...
Sheffield 170 177 178 194 a.	1615	...	1651	...	1715	...	1750	1748	...	1817	...	...	1846	1850	1859	1913	...	1916	1917	...	1947	1947	2008	...
Doncaster **178 185 194** a.	|	...	1715v	...	|	...	1816	1821	...	|	...	...	1918	1917	1929	|	...	|	|	...	2016	2020	2036	...
Wakefield Westgate **185** a.	1646	...	|	...	1746	...	|	|	...	1846	...	...	|	|	1959	1944	...	1946	1949	...	|	|	2053	...
Leeds 177 185 a.	1704	...	|	...	1802	...	|	|	...	1902	...	...	|	|	2022	2006	...	2002	2006	...	|	|	2115	...
York 185 a.	1730	...	1740v	...	1829	...	1841	1846	...	1929v	...	...	1949	1944	...	...	...	2029	2033	...	2042	2046	...	...
Newcastle **186** a.	1837r	...	1856	...	1935	...	2004	1953	...	2037	...	...	2054	2054	...	...	...	2141	2142	...	2234	2201	...	...
Edinburgh **186** a.	2013	...	...	...	2108v	...	...	...	...	2224d	...	...	2231	...	...	...	...	...	2328	...	...	...	...	...

	⑥ 🍷 B	Ⓐ 🍷 B	Ⓐ 🍷 L	⑥ 🍷 L	Ⓐ 🍷 N	⑥ 🍷	Ⓐ 🍷 L	⚒ 2	⚒ 🍷 P	Ⓐ 🍷 L	⑥ 🍷 L	⑥ 2	Ⓐ 2	Ⓐ 🍷 B	⑥ 🍷 B	⚒ 2	⑥ 🍷 P	Ⓐ 🍷 P		⑦ 🍷 G	⑦ 🍷	⑦ 🍷 T	⑦ 🍷 A	⑦ 🍷
Cardiff **121** d.	...	...	...	...	...	...	...	1745	...	...	...	...	...	...	...	2000	...	...	⑦	...	...	...	...	...
Bristol Temple Meads **120** d.	...	...	...	...	1800	1800	...	|	1830	...	...	...	...	...	...	|	2030	2030		...	...	...	...	...
Birmingham New St d.	1903	1903	...	...	1930	1930	...	1949	2003	...	...	2044	2049	2103	2050	2154	2203	2203		0846	0903	...	1003	1103
Tamworth d.	|	|	...	...	1947	1947	...	2009	2019	...	...	2103	2109	2119	2123	2212	2219	2229		|	|	...	|	|
Burton on Trent d.	|	|	...	...	1958	1958	...	2020	2029	...	...	2114	2120	2129	2133	2223	2229	2249		0929	0958	...	1058	1158
Derby 170 d.	1942	1942	...	2011	2014	2011	2022	2040	2042	2113	2111	2141	2141	2142	2145	2241	2247	2308		0942	1014	1035	1114	1214
Nottingham a.	|	|	...	|	|	|	|	2107v	|	|	|	2204	2204	|	|	2305	*2337*	*0001*		*1037*	*1143*	|	|	
Chesterfield **170** a.	2000	2002	2018	2030	2032	2036	2043	...	2103	2133	2131	...	...	2202	2204	...	*0006**	2327		1001	1032	1055	1132	1232
Sheffield 170 177 178 194 a.	2018	2017	2033	2047	2048	2051	2059	...	2118	2149	2147	...	...	2217	2219	...	*0037**	2354		1017	1046	1109	1146	1246
Doncaster **178 185 194** a.	|	|	|	2113	|	|	2125	...	|	2212	2221	...	...	|	|	...	...	|		|	1116	1134	1216	1315
Wakefield Westgate **185** a.	2048	2053	2101	2134	|	|	2144	...	2149r	2230	2238	...	...	2246s	2246s	...	...	|		1044	1144	|	1244	1344
Leeds 177 185 a.	2105	2109	2121	2154	|	|	2205	...	2205r	2250	2300	...	...	2305	2309	...	...	0101		1101	1202	|	1301	1401
York 185 a.	2135	2134	...	...	2148	2154	...	...	2258y.	...	...	...	...	...	...	...	...	...		1133	1233	1157	1333	1432
Newcastle **186** a.	2311	2242	...	...	2300	...	...	...	...	...	...	...	...	...	...	...	...	...		1237	1336	...	1437	1542
Edinburgh **186** a.	...	...	...	...	...	...	...	...	...	...	...	...	...	...	...	...	...	...		1412	1521	...	1624	1718

	⑦ 🍷	⑦ 2	⑦ 🍷 SD	⑦ 2	⑦ 🍷 EG	⑦ 🍷 BG	⑦ 2	⑦ 🍷 E	⑦ 2	⑦ 🍷 B	⑦ 2	⑦ 🍷 E	⑦ 2	⑦ 🍷 B	⑦ 🍷 L	⑦ 2	⑦ 🍷 E	⑦ 🍷 L	⑦ 2	⑦ 🍷 B	⑦ 🍷 E	⑦ 2	⑦ 🍷 L	⑦ 🍷 B
Cardiff **121** d.	...	...	...	1150	...	...	1350		1450	...	1550	...	1650	...	...	1750	...	...	1850	...	...	...	...	...
Bristol Temple Meads **120** d.	1030	...	...	|	1230	...	|	1430	|	...	|	1630	|	...	...	|	1830	...	|	...	2030	...	...	...
Birmingham New St d.	1203	1212	1303	1349	1403	1503	1552	1603	1649	1703	1749	1803	1849	1903	...	1949	2003	...	2049	2103	2203	2220	...	2306
Tamworth d.	|	1233	|	1406	|	|	1612	|	1711	|	1809	|	1910	|	...	2009	|	...	2109	|	|	2240	...	|
Burton on Trent d.	1258	1216	1358	1418	1458	1558	1623	1658	1723	1758	1821	1858	1921	1958	...	2021	2039	...	2121	2139	2239	2253	...	2342
Derby 170 d.	1314	1306	1414	1434	1514	1614	1645	1714	1740	1814	1845	1914	1941	2014	2032	2041	2051	2138	2141	2152	2253	2315	2325	2359
Nottingham a.	|	1330	|	1502	|	|	1710	*1757*	1804	|	1911	|	2000	|	|	2107	*2143*	|	2207	*2306*	|	2340	|	...
Chesterfield **170** a.	1332	...	1433	...	1532	1632	...	1732	...	1832	...	1932	...	2032	2051	...	2110	2157	...	2211	2312	...	2345	...
Sheffield 170 177 178 194 a.	1346	...	1451	...	1550	1649	...	1747	...	1848	...	1948	...	2048	2110	...	2127	2213	...	2225	2326	...	2359	...
Doncaster **178 185 194** a.	1416	...	1516	...	1616	1715	...	1816	...	1916	...	2016	...	2116	2138	...	|	2238	...	|	|	...	|	...
Wakefield Westgate **185** a.	1444	...	1544	...	1644	1744	...	1844	...	1944	...	2044	...	2144	2201	...	2209	2256	...	2259s	2352s	...	0029	...
Leeds 177 185 a.	1501	...	1601	...	1701	1801	...	1901	...	2001	...	2101	...	2201	2222	...	2231	2317	...	2321	0034	...	0106	...
York 185 a.	1533	...	1633	...	1733	1833	...	1933	...	2033	...	2132	...	2236	...	...	...	...	...	...	...	...	...	...
Newcastle **186** a.	1635	...	1739	...	1835	1935	...	2036	...	2137	...	2242	...	...	...	...	...	...	...	...	...	...	...	...
Edinburgh **186** a.	1814	...	1910	...	2013	2113	...	2222	...	2318	...	...	...	...	...	...	...	...	...	...	...	...	...	...

A – To Aberdeen.
B – From Bournemouth.
D – To Dundee.
E – From Exeter.
G – To Glasgow.
L – From London St Pancras.

N – From Paignton.
P – From Plymouth.
Q – From Plymouth on Ⓐ.
S – From Southampton.
T – From Leicester.
U – From Gloucester.

Z – From Penzance.

a – Ⓐ only.
b – 1912 on ⑥.
d – 2213 on ⑥.
g – ⑥ only.

r – 3–6 minutes earlier on ⑥.
v – 3–6 minutes later on ⑥.

YORK, SHEFFIELD and NOTTINGHAM - BIRMINGHAM

Services on ⑥⑦ are subject to alteration from February 2

⚒	⚒ 🍷 P	⚒ 2	Ⓐ 🍷	⑥ 2	Ⓐ 2	⑥ 🍷 B	Ⓐ 🍷 B	⑥ 2🍷	Ⓐ 2🍷	⑥ 🍷	Ⓐ 🍷	Ⓐ ✖ L	⚒ 2	⑥ 🍷 P	Ⓐ 🍷 P	⚒ 2	⚒ 🍷 N	⑥ 🍷 L	Ⓐ 🍷 L	⚒ 2	⚒ 🍷 B	⚒ 2	⑥ 🍷
Edinburgh **186** d.	...	...	...	...	...	...	...	...	...	...	...	...	...	...	...	...	...	...	...	...	...	...	...
Newcastle **186** d.	...	...	...	...	...	...	...	...	...	...	...	...	...	...	...	...	0619a	...	...	...	0644n	...	*0700*
ork 185 d.	...	...	...	...	...	...	...	...	...	...	0616	...	...	...	...	...	0727	...	...	...	0744	...	0819
Leeds 177 185 d.	...	...	...	...	...	...	0600	...	...	0600	|	0614	...	0648	0705	...	|	0719	0726	...	0810	...	|
Wakefield Westgate **185** d.	...	...	...	...	...	...	0612	...	...	0612	|	0626	...	|	0719	...	|	0732	0738	...	0823	...	|
oncaster 178 185 194 d.	...	...	...	...	...	...	|	...	...	|	|	0645	...	0726	|	...	0752	0759	0759	...	|	...	|
heffield 170 177 178 194 d.	*0520*y	...	...	...	...	0601	0645	...	...	0648	0723	0727	...	0753	0753	...	0823	0827	0827	...	0853	...	0923
hesterfield 170 d.	*0533*y	...	...	...	...	0624	0657	...	...	0716	0735	0739	...	0805	0805	...	0835	0839	0840	...	...	...	0935
Nottingham d.	|	*0552*g	0555	0634	0638	|	|	0658	0700	|	|	...	0734	|	|	0800	|	|	|	0832	|	0900	|
erby 170 d.	0610	0634	0657	0706	0708	0717	0720	0738	0739	0757	0757	...	0805	0827	0827	0838	0857	0901	0901	0906	0924	0938	0957
urton on Trent a.	0619	0651	0706	0719	0719	0727	|	0751	0750	0807	|	...	0819	0836	0837	0851	|	...	...	0919	|	0951	1007
amworth a.	0630	0703	0717	0730	0730	0737	|	0802	0802	0818	|	...	0830	0847	0848	0903	|	...	...	0928v	|	1002	1017
irmingham New St a.	0651	0727	0736	0754	0757	0758	0758	0828	0825	0836	0836	...	0854	0906	0906	0927	0936	...	...	0954	0958	1027	1036
Bristol Temple Meads **120** a.	0841	|	0911	...	...	...	...	|	|	1013	1011	...	...	1041	1041	|	1113	...	...	...	...	|	1213
Cardiff **121** a.	...	0929	...	...	...	...	...	1025	1030	...	...	...	...	...	...	1132d	...	...	...	...	...	1232d	...

	Ⓐ 🍷	Ⓐ 🍷 L	⑥ 🍷 L	⚒ 2	⚒ 🍷 P	Ⓐ 2🍷	⑥ 2	⑥ 🍷	Ⓐ 🍷 N	⚒ 2	⚒ 🍷 GB	⚒ 2	⑥ 🍷	Ⓐ 🍷	⚒ 2	⑥ 🍷 P	Ⓐ 🍷 DP	⚒ 2	⚒ 🍷 P	⚒ 2	⚒ 🍷 DB	⚒ 2	⚒ 🍷	⚒ 2
Edinburgh **186** d.	...	...	...	...	0605	...	...	...	...	...	0705	...	...	...	...	0805	0813	...	...	...	0905	...	...	...
Newcastle **186** d.	0723	...	...	...	0744r	...	...	0824	0824	...	0840	...	0925	0935	...	0940	0940	...	1025	...	1040	...	1125	...
ork 185 d.	0827	...	...	...	0844	...	...	0927	0927	...	0944	...	1025	1034	...	1044	1044	...	1127	...	1144	...	1225	...
Leeds 177 185 d.	|	0828	0840	...	0910	...	...	|	|	...	1010	...	|	|	...	1110	1110	...	|	...	1210	...	|	...
Wakefield Westgate **185** d.	|	0839	0852	...	0923	...	...	|	|	...	1023	...	|	|	...	1123	1123	...	|	...	1223	...	|	...
oncaster 178 185 194 d.	0851	|	|	...	|	...	...	0951	0956	...	|	...	1053	1058	...	|	|	...	1154	...	|	...	1255r	...
heffield 170 177 178 194 d.	0923	0927	0927	...	0953	...	...	1023	1023	...	1053	...	1123	1123	...	1153	1153	...	1223	...	1253	...	1323	...
hesterfield 170 d.	0935	0940	0940	...	|	...	...	1035	1035	...	|	...	1135	1135	...	|	|	...	1235	...	...	...	1335	...
Nottingham d.	|	|	|	0934	|	1002	1002	|	|	1034	|	1100	|	|	1134	|	|	1202	|	1234	|	1300	|	1334
erby 170 d.	0957	1001	1002	1008	1024	1038	1038	1057	1057	1108	1124	1138	1157	1157	1208	1224	1224	1238	1257	1308	1324	1338	1357	1408
urton on Trent a.	1006	...	...	1021	|	1051	1053	|	|	1121	|	1151	1207	1206	1220	|	|	1251	|	1319	|	1351	1407	1421
amworth a.	1017	...	...	1033	|	1102	1105	|	|	1133r	|	1203	1217	1217	1231	|	|	1303	|	1330	|	1402	1417	1433
irmingham New St a.	1036	...	...	1055	1104	1127	1127	1136	1136	1154	1158	1227	1236	1236	1255	1304	1304	1327	1336	1354	1358	1436	1436	1454
Bristol Temple Meads **120** a.	1211	...	...	...	1241	|	|	1313	1311	...	...	|	1413	1411	...	1441	1441	|	1511	...	...	|	1613	...
Cardiff **121** a.	...	...	...	...	...	1334	1325	...	...	...	...	1432d	...	...	...	...	...	1532d	...	...	...	1632d	...	...

	⚒ 🍷 GZ	⚒ 2	⚒ 🍷 Q	⚒ 2	⚒ 🍷 AB	⚒ 2	⚒ 🍷	⚒ 2	⚒ 🍷 P	⚒ 2	⚒ 🍷	⚒ 2	⚒ 🍷 B	⚒ 2	⚒ 🍷	⚒ 2	⚒ 🍷 P	⚒ 2	⑥ 🍷	Ⓐ 🍷	⚒ 2 T	⚒ 🍷 S	⑥ 🍷 L	⚒ 🍷
Edinburgh **186** d.	1005	...	...	...	1105	...	...	...	1205	...	...	...	1305	...	...	...	1405	...	...	...	...	1505	...	...
Newcastle **186** d.	1140	...	1217	...	1240	...	1333r	...	1340	...	1422	...	1440	...	1522	...	1540	...	1620	1627	...	1640	...	1717
ork 185 d.	1244	...	1328	...	1344	...	1430	...	1444	...	1527	...	1544	...	1625	...	1644	...	1725	1734	...	1744	1749	1824
Leeds 177 185 d.	1310	...	|	...	1410	...	|	...	1510	...	|	...	1610	...	|	...	1710	...	|	|	...	1810	|	|
Wakefield Westgate **185** d.	1323	...	|	...	1422	...	|	...	1523	...	|	...	1623	...	|	...	1723	...	|	|	...	1823	|	|
oncaster 178 185 194 d.	|	...	1354	...	|	...	1455	...	|	...	1555	...	|	...	1653	...	|	...	1755	1758	...	|	1815	1851
heffield 170 177 178 194 d.	1353	...	1423	...	1453	...	1523	...	1553	...	1623	...	1653	...	1720	...	1753	...	1823	1823	...	1853	1907b	1923
hesterfield 170 d.	|	...	1435	...	|	...	1535	...	|	...	1635	...	|	...	1735	...	|	...	1835	1835	...	|	1919	1935
Nottingham d.	|	1400	|	1434	|	1500	|	1534	|	1600	|	1634	|	1700	|	1734	|	1800	|	|	1834	|	|	|
erby 170 d.	1424	1438	1457	1508	1524	1538	1557	1608	1624	1638	1657	1706	1724	1738	1757	1806	1824	1838	1857	1857	1906	1924	1942	1957
urton on Trent a.	|	1451	|	1519	|	1551	1607	1620	|	1651	|	1721	|	1751	1807	1820	|	1851	|	|	1921	|	...	2007
amworth a.	|	1502	|	1530	|	1603	1617	1633r	|	1703	|	1733	|	1803	1817	1832	|	1902	|	|	1933	|	...	2017
irmingham New St a.	1506	1527	1536	1554	1558	1627	1636	1654	1707r	1727	1736	1754	1758	1827	1836	1856	1908r	1927	1941	1936	1954	1958	...	2043
Bristol Temple Meads **120** a.	1641	|	1713	...	...	|	1813	...	1841	|	1924	...	...	|	2013	...	2041	|	...	2111	...	...	...	...
Cardiff **121** a.	...	1732d	...	...	...	1832d	...	...	...	1936r	2019	...	...	2029r	...	...	...	2131a	...	...	...	...	...	...

	Ⓐ 2	⑥ 2	⚒ 🍷	⑥ 2	Ⓐ 🍷	Ⓐ 2	Ⓐ 🍷	⑥ 🍷	Ⓐ 2	⑥ 2	⚒ 🍷	Ⓐ 🍷	⑦	⑦ 🍷 B		⑦ 🍷 E	⑦ 🍷 L		⑦ 🍷 B	⑦ 🍷 E	⑦ 🍷 L	⑦ 2	⑦ 🍷 B
Edinburgh **186** d.	...	...	1605	...	...	...	1705	...	...	...	1805	...		...	...	...	...	...	...	...	...	...	...
Newcastle **186** d.	...	...	1740	...	1820	...	1840	1840	...	...	1940v	2026		...	...	...	...	...	...	...	...	...	0928
ork 185 d.	...	...	1844	...	1929	...	1944	1944	...	...	2044	2124		...	...	...	...	...	...	...	...	...	1028
Leeds 177 185 d.	...	...	1910	...	|	...	2010	2010	...	...	2110	|		...	...	0845	0835	...	0920	1000	1025	...	1100
Wakefield Westgate **185** d.	...	...	1923	...	|	...	2023	2023	...	...	2123	|		...	...	0857	0847	...	0932	1012	1036	...	1112
oncaster 178 185 194 d.	...	...	|	...	1957	...	|	|	...	...	|	|		...	...	|	0907	...	0953	1050	|	...	1150
heffield 170 177 178 194 d.	...	...	1953	...	2023	...	2053	2053	...	...	2153	2227		...	...	0935	0940	...	1023	1123	1127	...	1223
hesterfield 170 d.	...	...	2005	...	2035	...	2105	2105	...	...	2205	2253		...	...	0947	0953	...	1035	1135	1140	...	1235
Nottingham d.	1934	1940	|	2011	|	2034	|	|	2136	2145	|	...		...	...	|	|	...	|	|	|	1209	|
erby 170 d.	2008	2007	2027	2040	2057	2109	2127	2127	2208	2217	2227	2315		0905	...	1009	1015	...	1057	1157	1201	1239	1257
urton on Trent a.	2019	2019	|	2052	|	2118	2137	2137	2219	2229	2237	2325		0915	...	1018	...	...	1107	1207	...	1250	1307
amworth a.	2030	2032	|	2104	|	2130	2148	2148	2230	2241	2248	2336		|	...	|	...	...	|	|	...	1302	|
irmingham New St a.	2058	2054	2104	2128	2144	2157	2208	2213	2254	2303	2321	2359		0955	...	1104	...	...	1153	1251	...	1324	1353
Bristol Temple Meads **120** a.	...	...	2237v	...	...	...	2339	...	...	...	...	...		...	...	1238	...	...	...	1438	...	|	...
Cardiff **121** a.	...	...	...	...	...	...	...	...	...	...	...	...		...	...	...	...	...	...	...	...	1525	...

	⑦ 🍷 E	⑦ 2	⑦ 🍷 B	⑦ 2	⑦ 🍷 E	⑦ 2	⑦ 🍷 GB		⑦ 2	⑦ 🍷 GE	⑦ 🍷 L	⑦ 2	⑦ 🍷 S		⑦ 2 U	⑦ 🍷 A	⑦ 2	⑦ 🍷	⑦ 🍷 G		⑦ 2	⑦ 🍷		⑦ 🍷
Edinburgh **186** d.	0850	...	0950	...	1050	...	1150	...	...	1250	...	...	1350	...	...	1450	...	1550	1650	...	...	1750	...	1850
Newcastle **186** d.	1025	...	1125	...	1225	...	1325	...	...	1425	...	...	1525	...	...	1625	...	1725	1825	...	...	1925	...	2025
ork 185 d.	1128	...	1228	...	1328	...	1428	...	...	1528	1640	...	1628	...	...	1728	...	1828	1928	...	...	2028	...	2126
Leeds 177 185 d.	1200	...	1300	...	1400	...	1500	...	...	1600	|	...	1700	...	...	1800	...	1900	2000	...	...	2100	...	|
Wakefield Westgate **185** d.	1212	...	1312	...	1412	...	1512	...	...	1612	|	...	1712	...	...	1812	...	1912	2012	...	...	2112	...	|
oncaster 178 185 194 d.	1250	...	1350	...	1450	...	1550	...	...	1650	1706	...	1750	...	...	1850	...	1950	|	...	...	|	...	2150
heffield 170 177 178 194 d.	1323	...	1423	...	1523	...	1623	...	...	1723	1733	...	1823	...	...	1923	...	2023	2048	...	...	2148	...	2223
hesterfield 170 d.	1335	...	1435	...	1535	...	1635	...	...	1735	1745	...	1835	...	...	1935	...	2035	2100	...	...	2202	...	2235
Nottingham d.	|	1401	|	1502	|	1609	|	...	1713	|	|	1806	|	...	1908	|	2008	|	|	...	2141	|	...	|
erby 170 d.	1357	1435	1457	1537	1557	1638	1657	...	1742	1757	...	1839	1857	...	1939	1957	2036	2057	2124	...	2209	2224	...	2257
urton on Trent a.	1407	1451	1507	1551	1607	1649	1708	...	1753	1807	...	1851	1907	...	1950	2007	2050	2107	2133	...	2221	2234	...	2307
amworth a.	|	1502	|	1604	|	1700	|	...	1804	|	...	1902	|	...	2001	|	2103	|	|	...	2233	|	...	|
irmingham New St a.	1451	1527	1553	1627	1651	1724	1753	...	1827	1851	...	1926	1953	...	2029	2053	2127	2153	2225	...	2255	2326	...	2352
Bristol Temple Meads **120** a.	1638	|	...	|	1838	|	...	...	|	2038	...	|	...	...	...	2241	...	2341	...	...	...	...	...	...
Cardiff **121** a.	...	1729	...	1826	...	1926	...	...	2033	...	...	2023	...	...	...	...	...	...	...	...	...	...	...	...

A – From Aberdeen.
B – To Bournemouth.
D – From Dundee.
E – To Exeter.
G – From Glasgow.
L – To London St Pancras.

N – To Paignton.
P – To Plymouth.
Q – To Plymouth on Ⓐ.
S – To Southampton.
T – To Gloucester on ⑥.
U – To Gloucester.

Z – To Penzance.

a – Ⓐ only.
b – Arrives 1845.
d – 7 minutes earlier on ⑥.
g – ⑥ only.

n – *0635* on ⑥.
r – 3–5 minutes earlier on ⑥.
s – Stops to set down only.
v – 4–5 minutes later on ⑥.
y – 20–21 minutes earlier on ⑥.

* – By 🚌.

128 LONDON - LEAMINGTON - STRATFORD and BIRMINGHAM

2nd class CH

km			Ⓐ	Ⓐ	Ⓐ	Ⓐ	Ⓐ	Ⓐ	Ⓐ	Ⓐ	Ⓐ	Ⓐ	Ⓐ	Ⓐ	Ⓐ	Ⓐ	Ⓐ	Ⓐ	Ⓐ	Ⓐ	Ⓐ	Ⓐ	Ⓐ	Ⓐ	Ⓐ
0	**London** Marylebone ‡d.	Ⓐ	...	...	...	...	...	...	...	0600	0650	0720	...	0750	0820	0850	0854	0920	0950	1020	1050	1054	1120	1150	1220
45	High Wycombe ‡d.		...	...	...	...	0610	...	...	0642	0720	0749	...	0819	0851	0920	0925	0950	1019	1051	|	1128	1150	|	1250
111	Banbury **129** ‡d.		...	...	...	...	0702	...	*0725*	0737	0805	0834	...	0856	0935	0956	1014	1035	1057	1135	1156	1217	1235	1255	1335
143	**Leamington Spa 129** d.		0548	0630	0655	0707	0722	0747	0803	*0810*	0824	0853	0904	0915	0954	1015	1034	1054	1116	1154	1215	1238	1254	1314	1354
146	Warwick d.		0552	0634	0658	0711	0726	0751	0807	...	0828	0857	0907	0920	0958	1020	1038	1059	1121	1159	1219	1242	1259	1319	1359
167	**Stratford upon Avon** a.		|	|	0730	|	|	|	|	...	|	|	0937	|	|	|	1108	|	|	|	|	1311	|	|	|
169	Solihull d.		0618	0700	...	0741	0751	0818	0836	...	0848	0921	...	0940	1023	1040	...	1119	1141	1223	1239	...	1321	1339	1423
180	**Birmingham** Snow Hill a.		0637	0721	...	0759	0811	0837	0851	...	0907	0941	...	1001	1041	1101	...	1140	1201	1242	1302	...	1340	1401	1442

	Ⓐ	Ⓐ	Ⓐ	Ⓐ	Ⓐ	Ⓐ	Ⓐ	Ⓐ	Ⓐ	Ⓐ	Ⓐ	Ⓐ	Ⓐ	Ⓐ	Ⓐ	Ⓐ	Ⓐ	Ⓐ	Ⓐ	Ⓐ	Ⓐ	Ⓐ	Ⓐ	Ⓐ	Ⓐ
London Marylebone ‡d.	1250	1254	1320	1350	1420	1450	1454	1520	1600	1630	1634	1700	1730	1741	1800	1830	1900	1930	1933	2000	2030	2100	2130	2210	2310
High Wycombe ‡d.	|	1328	1350	|	1450	|	1528	1550	|	|	1704	|	|	1815	|	|	|	|	2004	|	2100	|	2200	2243	2345
Banbury **129** ‡d.	1356	1417	1435	1456	1535	1556	1617	1635	1703	1734	1749	1803	1839	1858	1903	1936	2003	2038	2049	2106	2147	2208	2247	2329	0042
Leamington Spa 129 d.	1415	1438	1454	1515	1554	1614	1638	1654	1722	1752	1807	1823	1858	1916	1922	1954	2023	2056	2107	2125	2205	2227	2306	2348	...
Warwick d.	1419	1442	1459	1519	1559	1619	1642	1658	|	1757	|	|	1903	1920	|	1959	|	2100	2112	|	2210	|	2310	2353	...
Stratford upon Avon a.	|	1509	|	|	|	|	1712	|	|	|	1840	|	|	1951	|	|	|	|	2143	|	|	|	|	|	...
Solihull d.	1439	...	1521	1539	1623	1639	...	1721	1744	1819	...	1845	1927	...	1944	2023	2045	2125	...	2147	2236	2249	2330	0013	...
Birmingham Snow Hill a.	1502	...	1541	1601	1642	1701	...	1741	1812	1840	...	1901	1947	...	2001	2044	2103	2147	...	2204	2258	2305	2351	0031	...

	⑤			⑥	⑥	⑥	⑥	⑥	⑥	⑥	⑥	⑥	⑥	⑥	⑥	⑥	⑥	⑥	⑥	⑥	⑥	⑥	⑥	⑥	⑥
London Marylebone ‡d.	2354	...	⑥	...	...	...	0627	...	0723	0820	0823	0854	0918	0945	1018	1050	1053	1120	1150	1220	1250	1253	1320	1350	1420
High Wycombe ‡d.	0028	...		...	0612	...	0713	...	0808	0853	0908	0928	0951	1015	1048	|	1127	1150	|	1250	|	1327	1350	|	1450
Banbury **129** ‡d.	0117	...		...	0700	*0725*	0801	0840	0857	0939	0956	1017	1039	1058	1135	1158	1219	1235	1258	1335	1358	1419	1435	1458	1535
Leamington Spa 129 d.	0139	...		0628	0719	0755	0820	0900	0916	0958	1014	1038	1058	1116	1154	1217	1239	1254	1317	1354	1417	1439	1454	1517	1554
Warwick d.	...	...		0632	0724	0759	0824	0904	0922	1002	1018	1042	1102	1120	1159	1222	1243	1259	1322	1359	1422	1443	1459	1522	1559
Stratford upon Avon a.	...	...		|	|	|	|	0935	|	|	|	1112	|	|	|	|	1311	|	|	|	|	1510	|	|	|
Solihull d.	...	...		0656	0744	0827	0850	...	0944	1022	1044	...	1122	1141	1223	1242	...	1320	1342	1423	1442	...	1520	1542	1623
Birmingham Snow Hill a.	...	...		0715	0807	0848	0911	...	1004	1041	1103	...	1141	1201	1242	1301	...	1341	1401	1442	1501	...	1540	1601	1641

	⑥	⑥	⑥	⑥	⑥	⑥	⑥	⑥	⑥	⑥	⑥	⑥	⑥	⑥	⑥	⑥	⑥	⑥			⑦	⑦	⑦	⑦	⑦
London Marylebone ‡d.	1450	1453	1520	1550	1620	1650	1653	1720	1750	1820	1850	1853	1920	2000	2050	2140	2245	2345	...	⑦	0800	0915	1015	1050	1120
High Wycombe ‡d.	|	1527	1550	|	1650	|	1727	1750	|	1850	|	1927	1950	2030	2122	2214	2320	0020	...		0844	0949	1049	|	1154
Banbury **129** ‡d.	1558	1619	1635	1658	1735	1759	1819	1835	1903	1935	2003	2019	2037	2119	2207	2303	0014	0114	...	▲	0934	1036	1138	1202	1241
Leamington Spa 129 d.	1617	1639	1653	1717	1754	1818	1839	1854	1923	1954	2023	2039	2055	2139	2228	2324	...	...	...		0954	1057	1159	1222	1302
Warwick d.	1622	1643	1658	1722	1759	1823	1843	1859	1927	1959	2027	2043	2100	2143	2232	2328	...	...	...		0959	1101	1203	|	1306
Stratford upon Avon a.	|	1711	|	|	|	|	1913	|	|	|	|	2110	|	|	|	|	...	...	...		|	*1140**	|	|	*1345*
Solihull d.	1642	...	1723	1742	1823	1843	...	1924	1948	2023	2048	...	2125	2204	2252	2350	...	...	...		1021	1124	1224	1245	1328
Birmingham Snow Hill a.	1701	...	1741	1801	1841	1902	...	1941	2006	2042	2106	...	2143	2226	2310	0009	...	...	...		1040	1141	1243	1303	1349

	⑦	⑦	⑦	⑦	⑦	⑦	⑦	⑦	⑦	⑦	⑦	⑦	⑦	⑦	⑦	⑦	⑦	⑦	⑦	⑦	⑦	⑦	⑦	⑦	⑦
London Marylebone ‡d.	1150	1220	1250	1320	1333	1350	1420	1450	1520	1533	1550	1620	1657	1720	1735	1757	1820	1857	1922	1957	2020	2050	2140	2245	2345
High Wycombe ‡d.	|	1254	|	1354	1408	|	1454	|	1554	1608	|	1654	|	1754	1810	|	1854	|	1956	|	2054	2124	2214	2329	0030
Banbury **129** ‡d.	1305	1343	1402	1441	1501	1505	1541	1602	1640	1701	1705	1741	1809	1841	1901	1909	1941	2009	2044	2109	2141	2210	2301	0023	0123
Leamington Spa 129 d.	1326	1403	1422	1502	1520	1526	1602	1622	1701	1720	1726	1802	1829	1902	1920	1929	2002	2029	2104	2129	2202	2231	2322	...	...
Warwick d.	|	1407	|	1506	1524	|	1606	|	1706	1724	|	1806	|	1906	1924	|	2006	|	2109	|	2206	2235	2326	...	...
Stratford upon Avon a.	|	|	|	|	*1605**	|	|	|	|	*1805**	|	|	|	|	*2005**	|	|	|	|	|	|	|	|	...	...
Solihull d.	1348	1428	1445	1528	...	1548	1628	1645	1727	...	1748	1829	1852	1930	...	1952	2028	2052	2130	2152	2226	2259	2346	...	...
Birmingham Snow Hill a.	1406	1447	1503	1549	...	1606	1646	1703	1746	...	1807	1849	1910	1948	...	2010	2046	2110	2148	2210	2245	2318	0004	...	...

		Ⓐ	Ⓐ	Ⓐ	Ⓐ	Ⓐ	Ⓐ	Ⓐ	Ⓐ	Ⓐ	Ⓐ	Ⓐ	Ⓐ	Ⓐ	Ⓐ	Ⓐ	Ⓐ	Ⓐ	Ⓐ	Ⓐ	Ⓐ	Ⓐ	Ⓐ	Ⓐ	Ⓐ
Birmingham Snow Hill d.	Ⓐ	...	...	0543	...	0614	...	0650	0656	0713	...	0745	0812	0852	0912	...	0952	1012	1052	1112	...	1152	1212	1252	1312
Solihull d.		...	...	0556	...	0627	...	0704	0714	0726	...	0758	0825	0905	0925	...	1005	1025	1105	1125	...	1205	1225	1305	1325
Stratford upon Avon d.		...	...	|	0612	|	0646	|	|	|	0736	|	|	|	|	0941	|	|	|	|	1140	|	|	|	|
Warwick d.		...	...	0615	0638	|	0713	|	0737	0746	0805	0823	0845	0924	0949	1005	1025	1049	1124	1145	1203	1224	1249	1324	1345
Leamington Spa 129 d.		...	0545	0620	0645	0649	0718	0726	0744	0750	0809	0827	0849	0929	0954	1010	1029	1054	1129	1149	1208	1229	1254	1329	1349
Banbury **129** ‡d.		0524	0603	0638	...	0707	0736	0744	...	0808	0828	0845	0908	0947	1012	1028	1047	1113	1147	1209	1228	1247	1312	1347	1408
High Wycombe ‡a.		0612	|	|	...	|	|	|	...	|	0915	|	0943	|	1057	1115	|	1157	|	1253	1316	|	1357	|	1452
London Marylebone ‡a.		0650	0718	0752	...	0815	0850	0852	...	0923	0953	0959	1021	1059	1130	1155	1159	1230	1259	1328	1355	1359	1430	1459	1526

	Ⓐ	Ⓐ	Ⓐ	Ⓐ	Ⓐ	Ⓐ	Ⓐ	Ⓐ	Ⓐ	Ⓐ	Ⓐ	Ⓐ	Ⓐ	Ⓐ	Ⓐ	Ⓐ	Ⓐ	Ⓐ	Ⓐ	Ⓐ		Ⓐ	Ⓐ	Ⓐy	Ⓐ
Birmingham Snow Hill d.	...	1352	1412	1452	1512	...	1552	1612	1652	1710	...	1734	1752	1757	1812	1845	1912	...	...	2012	...	2115	2215	...	2330
Solihull d.	...	1405	1425	1505	1525	...	1605	1625	1705	1723	...	1754	1805	1815	1825	1904	1925	...	...	2025	...	2127	2232	...	2347
Stratford upon Avon d.	1339	|	|	|	|	1541	|	|	|	|	1742	|	|	|	|	|	|	1943	2000	|	...	|	|	2300	|
Warwick d.	1402	1424	1449	1524	1544	1604	1624	1649	1724	1748	1808	1819	1826	1840	1849	1927	1950	2009	2023	2050	...	2150	2256	2321	0011
Leamington Spa 129 d.	1407	1429	1454	1529	1549	1608	1629	1654	1729	1753	1812	1824	1830	1847	1854	1932	1954	2014	2033	2054	...	2155	2301	2325	0015
Banbury **129** ‡d.	1426	1447	1512	1547	1607	1627	1647	1712	1747	1811	1832	...	1849	...	1912	...	2011	2032	...	2112	...	2214	2323	2343	0038
High Wycombe ‡a.	1514	|	1557	|	1653	1718	|	1757	1830	1856	1919	...	1930	...	1958	...	2055	2120	...	2156	...	2304	...	...	...
London Marylebone ‡a.	1551	1559	1631	1701	1731	1755	1804	1833	1907	1933	1957	...	2006	...	2035	...	2138	2157	...	2232	...	2353	...	...	...

		⑥	⑥	⑥	⑥	⑥	⑥	⑥	⑥	⑥	⑥	⑥	⑥	⑥	⑥	⑥	⑥	⑥	⑥	⑥	⑥	⑥	⑥	⑥	⑥
Birmingham Snow Hill d.	⑥	...	...	0612	0637	0712	...	0752	0812	0852	0912	...	0952	1012	1052	1112	...	1152	1212	1252	1312	...	1352	1412	1452
Solihull d.		...	...	0625	0650	0725	...	0804	0825	0906	0925	...	1005	1025	1105	1125	...	1205	1225	1305	1325	...	1405	1425	1505
Stratford upon Avon d.		...	...	|	|	|	0735	|	|	|	|	0936	|	|	|	|	1138	|	|	|	|	1340	|	|	|
Warwick d.		...	...	0644	0709	0750	0803	0823	0848	0927	0946	1004	1026	1049	1126	1145	1207	1226	1248	1324	1345	1406	1424	1448	1524
Leamington Spa 129 d.		...	...	0649	0714	0754	0808	0829	0852	0932	0950	1008	1030	1054	1131	1149	1212	1230	1252	1329	1349	1411	1429	1452	1529
Banbury **129** ‡d.		0605	0634	0708	0733	0812	0827	0847	0912	0950	1010	1028	1048	1112	1149	1207	1227	1249	1311	1347	1407	1430	1447	1511	1547
High Wycombe ‡a.		0653	|	0752	|	0847	0916	|	0958	|	1057	1116	|	1157	|	1252	1318	|	1358	|	1452	1519	|	1558	|
London Marylebone ‡a.		0731	0747	0829	0847	0930	0955	1001	1032	1100	1131	1156	1159	1230	1301	1331	1358	1401	1433	1501	1530	1558	1601	1633	1659

	⑥	⑥	⑥	⑥	⑥	⑥	⑥	⑥	⑥	⑥	⑥	⑥	⑥		⑥		⑥			⑦	⑦	⑦	⑦	⑦	⑦
Birmingham Snow Hill d.	1512	...	1552	1612	1652	1712	...	1752	1812	1910	...	2010	2111	...	2215	...	2338	...	⑦	...	...	0910	0940	...	1010
Solihull d.	1525	...	1605	1625	1706	1725	...	1806	1825	1923	...	2023	2123	...	2232	...	2356	...		...	...	0922	0952	...	1022
Stratford upon Avon d.	|	1539	|	|	|	|	1736	|	|	|	1953	|	*2115*z	...	|	...	|	...	▲	...	...	|	|	*0945**	|
Warwick d.	1545	1604	1624	1645	1726	1746	1802	1825	1848	1947	2019	2048	2147	...	2256	...	0019	...		...	...	0942	|	1024	1041
Leamington Spa 129 d.	1549	1609	1629	1649	1730	1749	1807	1829	1852	1951	2023	2053	2152	...	2301	...	0024	...		...	...	0947	1016	1029	1047
Banbury **129** ‡d.	1607	1628	1647	1712	1749	1812	1826	1847	1912	2010	2042	2115	2215	...	2322	...	...	...		0900	0947	1006	1036	1048	1106
High Wycombe ‡a.	1652	1719	|	1756	1827	1857	1917	1928	2000	2059	2131	2201	2303	...	...	...	...	...		0947	1033	|	1123	1137	|
London Marylebone ‡a.	1729	1756	1759	1832	1902	1930	1954	2001	2037	2136	2221	2240	2346	...	...	...	...	...		1027	1110	1123	1200	1216	1222

	⑦	⑦	⑦	⑦	⑦	⑦	⑦	⑦	⑦	⑦	⑦	⑦	⑦	⑦	⑦	⑦	⑦	⑦	⑦	⑦	⑦	⑦	⑦		⑦
Birmingham Snow Hill d.	1040	1110	1140	...	1210	1240	1310	1340	...	1410	1440	1510	1540	...	1610	1640	1710	1740	...	1810	1840	1915	2015	...	2115
Solihull d.	1052	1122	1152	...	1222	1252	1323	1352	...	1422	1452	1522	1552	...	1622	1652	1722	1752	...	1822	1852	1927	2027	...	2127
Stratford upon Avon d.	|	|	|	*1145**	|	|	|	|	*1345**	|	|	|	|	*1545**	|	|	|	|	*1745**	|	|	|	*2000**	...	|
Warwick d.	|	1141	|	1224	1241	|	1342	|	1424	1441	|	1541	|	1624	1641	|	1741	|	1824	1841	|	1948	2048	...	2148
Leamington Spa 129 d.	1116	1147	1216	1229	1246	1316	1347	1416	1429	1447	1516	1547	1616	1629	1647	1716	1747	1816	1829	1847	1916	1953	2053	...	2153
Banbury **129** ‡d.	1136	1206	1236	1248	1306	1336	1406	1436	1448	1506	1536	1606	1636	1648	1706	1736	1806	1836	1848	1906	1935	2013	2113	...	2215
High Wycombe ‡a.	1223	|	1323	1337	|	1423	|	1523	1537	|	1623	|	1723	1737	|	1823	|	1923	1937	|	2023	2102	2202	...	2305
London Marylebone ‡a.	1300	1322	1400	1416	1422	1500	1522	1600	1616	1622	1700	1722	1800	1816	1821	1900	1922	2000	2016	2021	2100	2150	2250	...	2353

y – To Oxford (a. 0018).
z – Change at Hatton.
* – By 🚌.
‡ – Additional trains run London - Banbury and v.v.
▲ – Services on ⑦ are subject to alteration from Feb. 3.

Stratford upon Avon – Birmingham Snow Hill

2nd class LM

⚒: 0631 Ⓐ, 0654 Ⓐ, 0700 ⑥, 0723 Ⓐ, 0745, 0827, 0927, 1027, 1127, 1227, 1327, 1427, 1527, 1627, 1727, 1758 Ⓐ, 1807 ⑥, 1826 Ⓐ, 1846, 1927, 2027.

⑦ (by 🚌; journey time 2 hrs 1 min): 0805, 0905 and hourly until 1905.

☛ Trains also call at Birmingham Moor St. All trains and buses call at **Henley in Arden** (*13 km*, ± 13 mins by train, 21 mins by 🚌, from Stratford).

Birmingham Snow Hill – Stratford upon Avon

40 km Journey: ± 54 mins

⚒: 0558 Ⓐ, 0629 Ⓐ, 0643 Ⓐ, 0720 ⑥, 0725 Ⓐ, 0827, 0927, 1027, 1127, 1227, 1327, 1427, 1527, 1627, 1702 Ⓐ, 1707 ⑥, 1727 Ⓐ, 1747, 1827, 1927, 2027.

⑦ (by 🚌; journey time 2 hrs 11 mins): 0825, 0925 and hourly until 1825.

☛ Trains also call (3 mins later) at Birmingham Moor St. All trains and buses (except the 0558 Ⓐ) call at **Henley in Arden** (*27 km*, ± 38 mins by train, 99 mins by bus, from Birmingham).

(LONDON -) READING - LEAMINGTON - BIRMINGHAM 129

km		Ⓐ	Ⓐ 🍷 SM	Ⓐ 🍷 TM	Ⓐ 🍷 SE	Ⓐ 🍷 T	Ⓐ 🍷 BM	Ⓐ	Ⓐ 🍷 M	Ⓐ 🍷 BA	Ⓐ 🍷	Ⓐ 🍷 BM	Ⓐ 🍷 M	Ⓐ	Ⓐ 🍷 BE	Ⓐ 🍷 R	Ⓐ 🍷 BM	Ⓐ 🍷 M	Ⓐ	Ⓐ 🍷 BG	Ⓐ 🍷	Ⓐ 🍷 BM	Ⓐ 🍷 M
0	London Paddington 115 133 ‡ d.	...	0527	0542	0630	0700	0730	0751	0800	0830	0905	0930	1005	1021	1030	1105	1130	1205	1221	1230	1305	1330	1405
58	**Reading 115 133** d.	...	0610	0640	0710	0740	0810	0823	0840	0910	0940	1010	1040	1053	1110	1140	1210	1240	1253	1310	1340	1410	1440
02	Oxford ‡ d.	0545	0636	0707	0736	0807	0833	0853	0907	0936	1007	1036	1107	1123	1136	1207	1236	1307	1323	1336	1407	1436	1507
39	Banbury 128 d.	0614	0653	0725	0753	0825	0853	0922	0925	0953	1025	1053	1125	1151	1153	1225	1253	1325	1351	1353	1425	1453	1525
71	**Leamington Spa 128** d.	...	0711	0743	0811	0843	0911	...	0943	1011	1043	1111	1143	...	1211	1243	1311	1343	...	1411	1443	1511	1543
86	Coventry a.	...	0722	|	0822	|	0922	...	|	1022	|	1122	|	...	1222	|	1322	|	...	1422	|	1522	|
03	Birmingham International ✈ a.	...	0733	|	0833	|	0933	...	|	1033	|	1133	|	...	1233	|	1333	|	...	1433	|	1533	|
16	**Birmingham** New St a.	...	0745	0818	0848	0918	0945	...	1018	1046	1118	1145	1218	...	1245	1318	1345	1418	...	1445	1518	1545	1618

	Ⓐ 🍷 BE	Ⓐ 🍷 D	Ⓐ	Ⓐ 🍷 BM	Ⓐ 🍷 RM	Ⓐ 🍷 BN	Ⓐ 🍷	Ⓐ 🍷 BM	Ⓐ 🍷 FM	Ⓐ 🍷 BL	Ⓐ 🍷	Ⓐ 🍷 BM	Ⓐ	Ⓐ 🍷 B	Ⓐ	⑥ ▲	⑥ 🍷 TM	⑥ 🍷 SEy	⑥	⑥ 🍷 T	⑥ 🍷 BM	⑥ 🍷	⑥ 🍷 BAy	⑥ 🍷
ondon Paddington 115 133 ‡ d.	1430	1505	1521	1530	1605	1633	1703	1733	1803	1836	1903	1930	1951	2035	2148		0542	0630	0651	0700	0730	0800	0837	0905
eading 115 133 d.	1510	1540	1553	1610	1640	1710	1740	1810	1840	1910	1940	2010	2023	2110	2221		0640	0710	0723	0740	0810	0840	0910	0940
xford ‡ d.	1536	1607	1623	1636	1707	1736	1807	1836	1907	1936	2007	2036	2057	2136	2256		0707	0736	0753	0807	0836	0907	0936	1007
anbury 128 d.	1553	1625	1651	1653	1725	1753	1825	1853	1925	1953	2025	2053	2126	2153	2325		0725	0753	0821	0825	0853	0925	0953	1025
eamington Spa 128 d.	1611	1643	...	1711	1743	1811	1843	1911	1943	2011	2043	2111	2204	2211	...		0743	0811	...	0843	0911	0943	1011	1043
oventry a.	1622	|	...	1722	|	1822	|	1922	|	2022	|	2122	...	2222	...		|	0821	...	|	0921	|	1021	|
rmingham International ✈ a.	1633	|	...	1733	|	1833	|	1933	|	2033	|	2133	...	2233	...		|	0833	...	|	0933	|	1033	|
rmingham New St a.	1645	1718	...	1745	1818	1846	1918	1945	2018	2048	2118	2145	...	2252	...		0818	0846	...	0918	0945	1018	1045	1118

	⑥ 🍷 BM	⑥ 🍷	⑥ 🍷 BE	⑥ 🍷 R	⑥ 🍷 BM	⑥ 🍷	⑥ 🍷 BG	⑥ 🍷	⑥ 🍷 BM	⑥ 🍷	⑥ 🍷 BE	⑥ 🍷	⑥ 🍷 BM	⑥ 🍷 R	⑥ 🍷 BN	⑥ 🍷	⑥ 🍷 BM	⑥ 🍷 F	⑥ 🍷 BL	⑥ 🍷	⑥ 🍷 BM	⑥	⑥ 🍷 B	🚌
ondon Paddington 115 133 ‡ d.	0937	1005	1037	1105	1137	1205	1237	1305	1337	1405	1437	1505	1537	1605	1633	1705	1737	1805	1833	1905	1937	1951	2030	2151
eading 115 133 d.	1010	1040	1110	1140	1210	1240	1310	1340	1410	1440	1510	1540	1610	1640	1710	1740	1810	1840	1910	1940	2010	2023	2110	2223
xford ‡ d.	1036	1107	1136	1207	1235	1307	1336	1407	1436	1507	1536	1607	1636	1707	1736	1807	1836	1907	1936	2007	2036	2120	2136	2337
anbury 128 d.	1053	1125	1153	1225	1253	1325	1353	1425	1453	1525	1553	1625	1653	1725	1753	1825	1853	1925	1953	2025	2053	2148	2153	0037
eamington Spa 128 d.	1111	1143	1211	1243	1311	1343	1411	1443	1511	1543	1611	1643	1711	1743	1811	1843	1911	1943	2011	2043	2111	...	2211	...
oventry a.	1121	|	1221	|	1321	|	1421	|	1521	|	1621	|	1721	|	1821	|	1921	|	2021	|	2121	...	2221	...
rmingham International ✈ a.	1133	|	1233	|	1333	|	1433	|	1533	|	1633	|	1733	|	1833	|	1933	|	2033	|	2133	...	2233	...
rmingham New St a.	1145	1218	1245	1318	1345	1418	1446	1518	1545	1618	1646	1718	1745	1818	1845	1918	1945	2018	2045	2122	2145	...	2250	...

	⑦ ▲	⑦ 🍷 SM	⑦ 🍷 BU	⑦ 🍷 R	⑦ 🍷 BM	⑦ 🍷	⑦ 🍷 BG	⑦ 🍷	⑦ 🍷 BM	⑦ 🍷	⑦ 🍷 BE	⑦ 🍷	⑦ 🍷 BM	⑦ 🍷	⑦ 🍷 BY	⑦ 🍷	⑦ 🍷 BM	⑦ 🍷	⑦ 🍷 BL	⑦ 🍷 BM	⑦ 🍷 BD	⑦ 🍷 B		⑦ 🚌
ondon Paddington 115 133 ‡ d.		0927	1027	1057	1127	1157	1227	1257	1327	1357	1427	1457	1527	1557	1627	1657	1727	1757	1827	1927	2007	2107	...	2144
eading 115 133 d.		1010	1110	1139	1210	1240	1310	1340	1410	1440	1510	1540	1610	1640	1710	1740	1810	1840	1910	2010	2110	2210	...	2247
xford ‡ d.		1036	1136	1206	1236	1306	1336	1406	1436	1506	1536	1606	1636	1706	1736	1806	1836	1906	1936	2036	2136	2236	...	2337
anbury 128 d.		1053	1153	1225	1253	1325	1353	1425	1453	1525	1553	1625	1653	1725	1753	1825	1853	1925	1953	2053	2153	2253	...	0037
eamington Spa 128 d.		1111	1211	1243	1311	1343	1411	1443	1511	1543	1611	1643	1711	1743	1811	1843	1911	1943	2011	2111	2211	2311	...	...
oventry a.		1123	1223	1254	1323	1354	1423	1454	1523	1554	1623	1654	1723	1754	1823	1854	1923	1954	2023	2123	2223	2327	...	...
rmingham International ✈ a.		1135	1235	1304	1335	1404	1435	1504	1535	1604	1635	1704	1735	1804	1835	1904	1935	2004	2035	2135	2235	2338	...	...
rmingham New St a.		1146	1246	1318	1346	1418	1446	1518	1546	1618	1646	1718	1746	1818	1846	1918	1946	2021	2046	2146	2258	2355	...	...

	Ⓐ	Ⓐ	Ⓐ 🍷 B	Ⓐ 🍷	Ⓐ	Ⓐ 🍷 CB	Ⓐ 🍷	Ⓐ 🍷 LB	Ⓐ 🍷 M	Ⓐ 🍷 MB	Ⓐ 🍷 MR	Ⓐ 🍷 NB	Ⓐ 🍷 M	Ⓐ 🍷 MB	Ⓐ 🍷 M	Ⓐ 🍷 GB	Ⓐ 🍷 M	Ⓐ 🍷 MB	Ⓐ 🍷 M	Ⓐ 🍷 UB	Ⓐ 🍷 MF	Ⓐ 🍷 MB	Ⓐ 🍷 M	Ⓐ 🍷 AB
rmingham New St d.		...	0603	0633	...	0703	0733	0803	0833	0903	0933	1003	1033	1103	1133	1203	1233	1303	1333	1403	1433	1503	1533	1603
rmingham International ✈ d.		...	0615	|	...	0715	|	0815	|	0915	|	1015	|	1115	|	1215	|	1315	|	1415	|	1515	|	1615
oventry d.		...	0625	|	...	0725	|	0825	|	0925	|	1025	|	1125	|	1225	|	1325	|	1425	|	1525	|	1625
eamington Spa 128 d.		...	0638	0700	...	0738	0800	0838	0900	0938	1000	1038	1100	1138	1200	1238	1300	1338	1400	1438	1500	1538	1600	1638
anbury 128 d.		0608	0655	0719	0728	0755	0819	0855	0919	0955	1019	1055	1119	1155	1219	1255	1319	1355	1419	1455	1519	1555	1619	1655
xford ‡ a.		0636	0714	0741	0756	0814	0841	0914	0941	1014	1041	1114	1141	1214	1241	1314	1341	1414	1441	1514	1541	1614	1641	1714
eading 115 133 a.		0725	0739	0813	0835	0839	0913	0939	1013	1039	1108	1139	1213	1239	1313	1339	1413	1439	1513	1539	1611	1639	1713	1739
ondon Paddington 115 133 ‡ a.		0758	0814	0851	0909	0922	0947r	1027	1059	1123	1152	1223	1259	1326	1358	1422	1459	1523	1559	1622	1652	1722	1758	1822

	Ⓐ 🍷 MR	Ⓐ 🍷 MB	Ⓐ 🍷 M	Ⓐ 🍷 EB	Ⓐ	Ⓐ 🍷 MT	Ⓐ 🍷 MB	Ⓐ 🍷 MT	Ⓐ 🍷 ES		Ⓐ 🍷 MS		Ⓐ 2 Q	Ⓐ		⑥ ▲	⑥ 🍷	⑥	⑥ 🍷 CB	⑥ 🍷	⑥ 🍷 HB	⑥ 🍷	⑥ 🍷 MB	⑥ 🍷 R
rmingham New St d.	1633	1703	1733	1803	...	1833	1903	1933	2003	...	2103	...	...	...	...		0603	...	0703	0733	0803	0833	0903	0933
rmingham International ✈ d.	|	1715	|	1815	...	|	1915	|	2015	...	2115	...	...	...	...		0615	...	0715	|	0815	|	0915	|
oventry d.	|	1725	|	1825	...	|	1925	|	2025	...	2125	...	...	...	...		0625	...	0725	|	0825	|	0925	|
eamington Spa 128 d.	1700	1738	1800	1838	...	1900	1938	2000	2038	...	2138	...	2325	2325	...		0638	...	0738	0800	0838	0900	0938	1000
anbury 128 d.	1719	1755	1819	1855	1901	1919	1955	2019	2055	...	2155	...	2344	2350	...		0655	0702	0755	0819	0855	0919	0955	1019
xford ‡ a.	1741	1814	1841	1914	1928	1941	2014	2041	2114	...	2214	...	0018	0018	...		0714	0730	0814	0841	0914	0941	1014	1041
eading 115 133 a.	1811	1839	1913	1939	1954	2009	2039	2106	2139	...	2239	...	...	0058	...		0744	0759	0839	0913	0939	1013	1039	1113
ondon Paddington 115 133 ‡ a.	1853	1915	1959	2015	2028	2102	2122	2214	2215	...	2325	...	...	0148	...		0821	0836	0928	0957	1016	1100	1114	1156

	⑥ 🍷 NB	⑥ 🍷	⑥ 🍷 MB	⑥ 🍷	⑥ 🍷 GB	⑥ 🍷	⑥ 🍷 MB	⑥ 🍷	⑥ 🍷 UB	⑥ 🍷 F	⑥ 🍷 MB	⑥ 🍷	⑥ 🍷 AB	⑥ 🍷 R	⑥ 🍷 MB	⑥ 🍷	⑥ 🍷 EB	⑥ 🍷 T	⑥ 🍷 MB	⑥	⑥	⑥ 🍷 ES		⑥ 🍷 MS
rmingham New St d.	1003	1033	1103	1133	1203	1233	1303	1333	1403	1433	1503	1533	1603	1633	1703	1733	1803	1833	1903	...	...	2003	...	2103
rmingham International ✈ d.	1015	|	1115	|	1215	|	1315	|	1415	|	1515	|	1615	|	1715	|	1815	|	1915	...	...	2015	...	2115
oventry d.	1025	|	1125	|	1225	|	1325	|	1425	|	1525	|	1625	|	1725	|	1825	|	1925	...	...	2025	...	2125
eamington Spa 128 d.	1038	1100	1138	1200	1238	1300	1338	1400	1438	1500	1538	1600	1638	1700	1738	1800	1838	1900	1938	...	1951	2038	...	2138
anbury 128 d.	1055	1119	1155	1219	1255	1319	1355	1419	1455	1519	1555	1619	1655	1719	1755	1819	1855	1919	1955	2002	2038	2055	...	2155
xford ‡ a.	1114	1141	1214	1241	1314	1341	1414	1441	1514	1541	1614	1641	1714	1741	1814	1841	1914	1941	2014	2030	2106	2114	...	2214
eading 115 133 a.	1139	1213	1239	1313	1339	1413	1439	1513	1539	1658	1639	1713	1739	1813	1839	1913	1939	2013	2039	2128	...	2139	...	2241
ondon Paddington 115 133 ‡ a.	1224	1256	1323	1351	1413	1455	1521	1555	1618	1654	1714	1754	1825	1854	1922	1957	2022	2053	2122	2201	...	2219	...	2333

	⑦ ▲	⑦ 🍷 B	⑦ 🍷 DB	⑦ 🍷 C	⑦ 🍷 MB	⑦ 🍷	⑦ 🍷 LB	⑦ 🍷	⑦ 🍷 MB	⑦ 🍷	⑦ 🍷 NB	⑦ 🍷	⑦ 🍷 MB	⑦ 🍷	⑦ 🍷 EB	⑦ 🍷	⑦ 🍷 MB	⑦ 🍷 R	⑦ 🍷 GB	⑦ 🍷 T	⑦ 🍷 MB	⑦ 🍷 ES		⑦ 🍷 MS
rmingham New St d.		0903	1003	1033	1103	1133	1203	1233	1303	1333	1403	1433	1503	1533	1603	1633	1703	1733	1803	1833	1903	2003	...	2103
rmingham International ✈ d.		0915	1015	1045	1115	1145	1215	1245	1315	1345	1415	1445	1515	1545	1615	1645	1715	1745	1815	1845	1915	2015	...	2115
oventry d.		0925	1025	1054	1125	1156	1225	1256	1325	1356	1425	1456	1525	1556	1625	1656	1725	1756	1825	1856	1925	2025	...	2125
eamington Spa 128 d.		0938	1038	1107	1138	1209	1238	1309	1338	1409	1438	1509	1538	1609	1638	1709	1738	1809	1838	1909	1938	2038	...	2138
anbury 128 d.		0955	1055	1123	1155	1226	1255	1326	1355	1426	1455	1526	1555	1626	1655	1726	1755	1826	1855	1926	1955	2055	...	2155
xford ‡ a.		1014	1114	1143	1214	1253	1314	1345	1414	1445	1514	1553	1614	1653	1714	1753	1814	1845	1914	1953	2014	2114	...	2214
eading 115 133 a.		1044	1144	1215	1244	1328	1346	1422	1444	1522	1544	1628	1644	1728	1744	1828	1844	1911	1944	2019	2044	2144	...	2249
ondon Paddington 115 133 ‡ a.		1146	1230	1259	1329	1421	1444	1515	1530	1608	1655	1715	1736	1822	1901	1915	1934	2007	2102	2116	2140	2256	...	2351

– To/ from Aberdeen.
– From/ to Bournemouth.
– From Crewe.
– To/ from Derby.
– To/ from Edinburgh.
– From/ to Guidford.
G – To/ from Glasgow.
H – From Sheffield.
L – To/ from Leeds.
M – To/ from Manchester.
N – To/ from Newcastle.
Q – From Stratford upon Avon.
R – From/ to Brighton.
S – From/ to Southampton.
T – From/ to Gatwick.
U – To/ from Dundee.
Y – To York.
r – Change at Oxford.
‡ – For all fast trains Oxford - London and v.v., see Table **129**.
▲ – Services on ⑥⑦ are subject to alteration from Feb. 2.

130 LONDON - OXFORD GW

A frequent service operates on this route. Shown below is a selection of the faster connections, with journey times of between 53 and 79 minutes (average: 58 minutes).

102 km

London Paddington – Oxford:

Ⓐ: 0021, 0522, 0542, 0607, 0648, 0721, 0751 and every 30 minutes until 1951; then 2019, 2051, 2121, 2148, 2221, 2251, 2321.

⑥: 0021, 0512, 0542, 0621, 0651 and every 30 minutes until 2151.

⑦: 0806, 0842, 0942 and hourly until 2242; then 2337.

Oxford – London Paddington:

Ⓐ: 0008, 0550, 0630, 0657, 0730, 0807, 0850, 0906, 0938, 1000, 1030 and every 30 minutes until 1700; then 1738, 1800, 1900, 1930, 2030, 2138, 2221, 2305.

⑥: 0001, 0630, 0700, 0735, 0800, 0830, 0900, 0930, 0957, 1100, 1200, 1230 and every 30 minutes (except 1530, 1630) until 1930; then 2009, 2030, 2100, 2130, 2200, 2230.

⑦: 0838, 0938 and hourly until 2238.

131 LONDON - WORCESTER - HEREFORD GW

For London - Hereford and v.v. via Newport, see Tables **133** and **155**

km		Ⓐ	Ⓐ 🍷	Ⓐ 🍷	Ⓐ 🍷	Ⓐ 🍷	Ⓐ 🍷	Ⓐ 🍷	Ⓐ 🍷	Ⓐ 🍷	Ⓐ	Ⓐ 🍷	Ⓐ 🍷	Ⓐ 🍷	Ⓐ 🍷	Ⓐ 🍷	Ⓐ		⑥ 🍷	⑥ 🍷	⑥ 🍷	⑥ 🍷
0	**London** Paddington 115 133 d.	...	0542	0648j	0751	0851	0951	1151	1351	1551	1621	1721	1751	1821	1921	2019	2148	...	0542	0651	0751	0851
58	Reading 115 133 d.	...	0620	0723	0823	0923	1023	1223	1423	1623	1653	1750	1821	1850	1953	2053	2221	...	0614	0723	0823	0923
103	**Oxford** d.	...	0655	0802	0849	0956	1049	1256	1449	1649	1731	1816	1855	1919	2021	2119	2252	...	0648	0748	0848	0948
148	Moreton in Marsh d.	...	0731	0838	0925	1032	1125	1332	1525	1725	1815	1854	1937	1958	2057	2153	2327	...	0724	0827	0927	1027
172	Evesham a.	...	0750	0856	0944	1051	1144	1351	1544	1744	1833	1913	1954	2017	2116	2211	2346	...	0746	0845	0945	1045
172	Evesham d.	0611	0756	0902	1000	1052	1156	1352	1545	1746	1842	1921	1956	2019	2123	2212	2346	...	0758	0848	0957	1047
194	**Worcester** Shrub Hill 123 a.	0629	0815	0921	1022	1111	1220	1411	1614	1809	1910	1944	2022	2039	2141	2231	0007	...	0820	0907	1022	1106
195	**Worcester** Foregate St. 123 a.	0639	0820	0926	1026	1116	1226	1415	1617	1830	1915	1948	...	2042	2150	2234	...	...	0826	0911	1026	1111
208	Great Malvern 123 a.	0754	0852	0952	1042	1129	1252	1428	1634	1840	...	2001	...	2056	2202	2248	...	...	0837	0925	1039	1124
219	Ledbury 123 a.	0812	0906	1006	1106	1142	1306	1441	1706	1910q	...	2015	...	2110	2215	...	...	...	0906	1006	1106	1206
241	**Hereford** 123 a.	0833	0928	1028	1128	1205	1328	1504	1728	1933q	...	2036	...	2131	2236	...	...	...	0928	1028	1128	1228

Ⓐ ⑥ ▲

	⑥ 🍷	⑥ 🍷	⑥ 🍷	⑥ 🍷	⑥ 🍷	⑥ 🍷	⑥ 🍷	⑥ 🍷	⑥	⑥		⑦ 🍷	⑦ 🍷	⑦ 🍷	⑦ 🍷	⑦ 🍷	⑦ 🍷	⑦ 🍷	⑦ 🍷	⑦ 🍷	⑦ 🍷	⑦ 🍷	⑦ 🍷
London Paddington 115 133 d.	0951	1051	1151	1351	1451	1551	1651	1821	1951	2151	...	0803	0935	1042	1242	1342	1442	1542	1642	1742	1842	1942	2142
Reading 115 133 d.	1023	1123	1223	1423	1523	1623	1723	1853	2023	2223	...	0846	1013	1120	1320	1420	1520	1620	1720	1820	1920	2020	2220
Oxford d.	1048	1148	1248	1448	1548	1648	1748	1919	2049	2248	...	0915	1045	1150	1350	1450	1550	1650	1750	1850	1950	2049	2250
Moreton in Marsh d.	1127	1227	1327	1529	1627	1727	1829	1958	2124	2323	...	0956r	1123	1228	1429	1524	1628	1724	1828	1928	2029	2124	2327
Evesham a.	1145	1245	1345	1548	1645	1745	1847	2016	2143	2341	...	1013	1141	1247	1445	1544	1616	1744	1847	1947	2048	2141	2344
Evesham d.	1148	1248	1348	1557	1648	1748	1850	2019	2145	2343	...	1015	1144	1248	1447	1548	1649	1749	1849	1949	2050	2149	2346
Worcester Shrub Hill 123 a.	1206	1307	1406	1622	1707	1807	1914	2038	2204	0002	...	1033	1203	1307	1506	1607	1708	1808	1908	2006	2109	2207	0004
Worcester Foregate St. 123 a.	1210	1311	1410	1626	1711	1811	1918	2046	2208	...	...	1037	1207	1311	1510	1647	1712	1844	1912	2012	2113	2219	...
Great Malvern 123 a.	1221	1352	1421	1639	1725	1825	1932	2059	2221	...	...	1050	1220	1325	1521	1702	1725	1856	1926	2026	2127	2235	...
Ledbury 123 a.	1234	1406	1434	1706	1806	1917	1945	2113	...	...	...	...	1234	1339	1532	...	1739	1909	...	...	2140	...	...
Hereford 123 a.	1253	1428	1453	1728	1828	1942	2002	2132	...	...	...	...	1254	1404	1551	...	1758	1930	...	...	2159	...	...

⑦ ▲

	Ⓐ 🍷	Ⓐ 🍷	Ⓐ 🍷	Ⓐ	Ⓐ 🍷	Ⓐ 🍷	Ⓐ 🍷	Ⓐ 🍷	Ⓐ 🍷	Ⓐ 🍷	Ⓐ 🍷	Ⓐ 🍷	Ⓐ 🍷	Ⓐ	Ⓐ 🍷	Ⓐ 🍷		⑥	⑥ 🍷	⑥ 🍷	⑥ 🍷	⑥ 🍷
Hereford 123 d.	...	...	0542	...	0643	0735	0850	0950	...	1323	1519	1538	1740	...	1950	2130	...	...	...	0722	0737	0850
Ledbury 123 d.	...	...	0600	...	0700	0751	0907	1007	...	1341	1536	1555	1756	...	2017	2147	...	...	...	0740	0754	0907
Great Malvern 123 d.	...	0531	0613	...	0715	0803	0918	1106	1218	1353	1551	1706	1807	1854	2028	2220	...	0603	0708	0752	0908	0948
Worcester Foregate St. 123 d.	...	0542	0628	0652	0729	0837	0937	1126	1240	1408	1606	1721	1819	1927	2054	2235	...	0619	0723	0807	0921	1003
Worcester Shrub Hill 123 d.	...	0546	0632	0655	0734	0841	0940	1131	1244	1414	1610	1725	1854	1930	2058	2239	...	0623	0727	0817r	0927	1027
Evesham a.	...	0602	0649	0712	0752	0858	0956	1148	1301	1430	1633	1742	1917	1952	2115	2256	...	0639	0744	0839	0944	1044
Evesham d.	...	0603	0649	0712	0754	0900	0958	1149	1302	1444	1635	1748	1919	2021	2120	2257	...	0641	0754	0850	0953	1056
Moreton in Marsh d.	0550	0622	0709	0729	0814	0919	1018	1213	1321	1516v	1656	1820v	1935	2041	2139	2316	...	0700	0813	0909	1016	1116
Oxford a.	0628	0655	0748	0812	0848	0958	1058	1258	1358	1558	1736	1858	2024	2119	2219	2353	...	0736	0858	0955	1058	1158
Reading 115 133 a.	0657	0725	0822	0902	0914	1024	1125	1325	1425	1625	1803	1926	2055	2208	2245	0022	...	0808	0926	1021	1125	1225
London Paddington 115 133 a.	0729	0758	0851	0938c	0947	1059	1158	1358	1459	1659	1831	1959	2127	2251	2324	0102	...	0840	0958	1054	1158	1258

Ⓐ ⑥ ▲

	⑥ 🍷	⑥ 🍷	⑥ 🍷	⑥ 🍷	⑥ 🍷	⑥ 🍷	⑥ 🍷	⑥ 🍷		⑥		⑦ 🍷		⑦ 🍷	⑦ 🍷	⑦ 🍷	⑦ 🍷	⑦ 🍷	⑦ 🍷	⑦ 🍷	⑦ 🍷	⑦ 🍷	⑦ 🍷
Hereford 123 d.	0950	1050	1150	1320	1523	1550	1650	1750	...	2133	...	...	...	...	...	1330	1430	...	1630	...	1830	...	2005
Ledbury 123 d.	1007	1107	1207	1339	1540	1607	1707	1807	...	2149	...	...	...	...	...	1348	1457	...	1647	...	1848	...	2021
Great Malvern 123 d.	1105	1145	1218	1405v	1553	1708	1808	1845	...	2240	...	0901	...	1108	1306	1401	1509	...	1700	1716	1908	2008	2105
Worcester Foregate St. 123 d.	1122	1200	1322	1421	1606	1723	1823	1901	...	2251	...	0913	...	1119	1320	1416	1524	...	1721	1727	1923	2023	2123
Worcester Shrub Hill 123 d.	1126	1224d	1326	1428	1627z	1727	1827	1915v	...	2255	...	0917	...	1123	1324	1420	1529	1625	1726	1825	1927	2027	2127
Evesham a.	1143	1241	1343	1444	1643	1744	1844	1932	...	2312	...	0933	...	1139	1341	1439	1545	1641	1742	1843	1944	2044	2144
Evesham d.	1156	1256	1356	1454	1656	1756	1856	1934	...	...	...	0934	...	1146	1342	1451	1550	1650	1747	1849	1950	2051	2147
Moreton in Marsh d.	1216	1316	1416	1514	1716	1816	1926v	2016p	...	...	...	0953	...	1205	1401	1511	1609	1709	1806	1908	2009	2111	2206
Oxford a.	1258	1358	1458	1559	1758	1858	2007	2058	...	...	...	1027	...	1241	1437	1548	1646	1747	1840	1947	2046	2148	2238
Reading 115 133 a.	1327	1425	1525	1626	1825	1925	2033	2124	...	...	...	1106	...	1320	1504	1618	1718	1818	1906	2018	2119	2219	2307
London Paddington 115 133 a.	1359	1458	1558	1658	1858	1958	2106	2158	...	...	...	1146	...	1408	1543	1707	1808	1908	1952	2108	2203	2305	2353

⑦ ▲

c – Change at Oxford and Reading.
d – Arrives 21 minutes earlier.
j – Change at Oxford.
p – Arrives 1952.
q – Change at Worcester Shrub Hill and Great Malvern.
r – Arrives 6–7 minutes earlier.
v – Arrives 11–14 minutes earlier.
z – Arrives 1611.
▲ – Services on ⑥⑦ are subject to alteration from Feb. 2.

132 (LONDON -) SWINDON - GLOUCESTER - CHELTENHAM GW

km		Ⓐ 🍷	Ⓐ 2	Ⓐ 🍷	Ⓐ 2	Ⓐ 🍷	Ⓐ 2	Ⓐ 🍷	Ⓐ 2	Ⓐ 🍷	Ⓐ 2	Ⓐ 🍷	Ⓐ 2	Ⓐ 🍷	Ⓐ 🍷	Ⓐ 🍷	Ⓐ 2	Ⓐ 2		⑥ 2	⑥ 🍷	⑥ 2	⑥ 🍷
	London Paddington 133 d.	0534	0645	0748	0845	0948	1045	1148	1245	1348	1445	1548	1645	1748	1848	1948	2045	2215	...	...	0815	0900	1015
0	**Swindon** d.	0646	0752	0852	0952	1052	1152	1252	1352	1452	1552	1654	1752	1854	1954	2053	2152	2333	...	0716	0911	1011	1111
40	Stroud d.	0714	0820	0920	1020	1120	1220	1320	1420	1520	1620	1724	1821	1924	2024	2122	2220	0002	...	0745	0940	1040	1140
59	Gloucester 121 122 a.	0742	0842	0942	1041	1147	1241	1341	1441	1542	1642	1747	1844	1947	2044	2143	2243	0023	...	0806	1001	1101	1201
70	**Cheltenham** 121 122 a.	0802	0901	1003	1101	1203	1254	1403	1500	1602	1701	1803	1901	2003	2100	2201	2256	...	...	0823	1018	1118	1218

	⑥ 2	⑥ 🍷	⑥ 2	⑥ 🍷	⑥ 2	⑥ 🍷	⑥ 2	⑥ 🍷	⑥ 2	⑥ 🍷	⑥ 2		⑦ 🍷	⑦	⑦ 🍷	⑦ 🍷	⑦ 2	⑦ 🍷	⑦ 🍷	⑦ 2	⑦ 🍷	⑦ 2	⑦ 🍷	⑦ 2
London Paddington 133 d.	1100	1215	1300	1415	1500	1615	1700	1815	1845	2015	2045	...	0837	0937	1003	1203	1303	1403	1630	1703	1830	1903	2030	2137
Swindon d.	1211	1311	1411	1511	1611	1711	1811	1916	1955	2116	2235	...	0955	1045	1129	1329	1421	1529	1743	1821	1943	2027	2143	2257
Stroud d.	1240	1340	1440	1540	1640	1740	1840	1945	2024	2145	2304	...	1023	1114	1158	1358	1453	1558	1814	1849	2014	2056	2214	2326
Gloucester 121 122 a.	1301	1401	1501	1601	1701	1801	1901	2006	2045	2205	2325	...	1044	1135	1219	1419	1513	1619	1835	1911	2035	2116	2234	2347
Cheltenham 121 122 a.	1316	1418	1516	1618	1716	1818	1916	2022	2058	2222	...	...	1100	1148	1235	1436	1527	1635	1901	1949	2052	2130	2300	2359

	Ⓐ 2	Ⓐ 🍷	Ⓐ 🍷	Ⓐ 🍷	Ⓐ 🍷	Ⓐ 2	Ⓐ 🍷	Ⓐ 2	Ⓐ 🍷	Ⓐ 2	Ⓐ 🍷	Ⓐ 2	Ⓐ 🍷	Ⓐ 2	Ⓐ 🍷	Ⓐ 2	Ⓐ 🍷	Ⓐ 2		⑥ 2	⑥ 🍷	⑥ 🍷	⑥ 2
Cheltenham 121 122 d.	...	0540	0610	0715	0846	0946	1046	1146	1246	1346	1446	1535	1635	1728	1835	1946	2046	2200	...	0530	0729	0846	0946
Gloucester 121 122 d.	0529	0600	0630	0735	0902	1002	1102	1203	1302	1402	1502	1551	1651	1743	1851	2003	2102	2215	...	0543	0746	0902	1002
Stroud d.	0547	0619	0649	0754	0920	1020	1120	1220	1320	1420	1520	1609	1709	1800	1909	2020	2120	2231	...	0559	0804	0920	1020
Swindon a.	0616	0647	0717	0822	0949	1052	1149	1251	1349	1451	1549	1640	1738	1831	1938	2055	2150	2300	...	0630	0832	0949	1050
London Paddington 133 a.	0729	0752	0823	0926	1056	1202	1256	1402	1456	1602	1656	1802	1842	1941	2043	2215	2336z	0032	...	0741	0939	1055	1214

	⑥ 🍷	⑥ 2	⑥ 🍷	⑥ 2	⑥ 🍷	⑥ 2	⑥	⑥ 2	⑥ 🍷	⑥ 2	⑥ 2		⑦ 2		⑦ 🍷	⑦ 2	⑦ 🍷		⑦ 🍷	⑦ 2	⑦ 🍷	⑦ 2	⑦ 🍷	⑦ 2
Cheltenham 121 122 d.	1046	1146	1246	1346	1446	1546	1646	1746	1846	1946	2115	...	0935	...	1146	1235	1346	...	1546	1635	1740	1901	1946	2142
Gloucester 121 122 d.	1102	1200	1302	1400	1502	1600	1702	1800	1902	2001	2130	...	0949	...	1204	1249	1403	...	1604	1649	1757	1931	2003	2200
Stroud d.	1120	1219	1320	1419	1520	1619	1720	1819	1920	2019	2147	...	1006	...	1222	1306	1421	...	1622	1706	1815	1949	2021	2217
Swindon a.	1149	1248	1349	1448	1549	1648	1749	1848	1949	2049	2218	...	1035	...	1250	1336	1449	...	1650	1736	1849	2018	2102	2247
London Paddington 133 a.	1254	1426	1454	1614	1654	1814	1854	2014	2053	2216	2329	...	1200	...	1410	1500	1610	...	1805	1902	2005	2140	2210	...

r – Change at Gloucester.
z – 2329 on ⑤.
* – By 🚐.

GW LONDON - BRISTOL and CARDIFF 133

km			Ⓐ	Ⓐ	Ⓐ	Ⓐ	Ⓐ	Ⓐ	Ⓐ	Ⓐ	Ⓐ	Ⓐ	Ⓐ	Ⓐ	Ⓐ	Ⓐ	Ⓐ	Ⓐ	Ⓐ	Ⓐ	Ⓐ	Ⓐ	Ⓐ	Ⓐ
			🍷	🍷	2	🍷	🍷	🍷	🍷	✕	✕	🍷	🍷	🍷	🍷	🍷	🍷	🍷	🍷	✕	🍷	🍷	🍷	🍷
				C						Z		C									C	P		
0	**London** Paddington **115 131** d.	Ⓐ	0527	0530	...	0630	0645	0700	0715	0730	0745	0748	0800	0815	0830	0845	0900	0915	0930	0945	0948	1000	1015	1030
58	Reading **115 131** d.		0557	0607	...	0657	0711	0727	0741	0757	0811	0816	0827	0841	0857	0911	0927	0941	0957	1011	1016	1027	1041	1057
85	Didcot d.		|	0623	...	0712	|	0742	0756	|	|	0831	0842	0856	0912	|	|	0956	1012	|	1031	|	1056	1112
124	**Swindon** d.		0626	0642	...	0730	0740	0800	0815	0826	0840	0853	0901	0915	0931	0940	0956	1015	1031	1040	1053	1056	1115	1131
151	Chippenham a.		0640	...	...	0744	|	0815	|	0840	|	...	0915	|	0945	|	1010	|	1045	|	...	1110	|	1145
172	Bath **137** a.		0656	...	...	0759	|	0831	|	0855	|	...	0930	|	1000	|	1025	|	1100	|	...	1125	|	1200
180	Bristol Parkway d.		|	...	0739r	|	0807	|	0842	|	0907	...	|	0942	|	1007	|	1042	|	1107	...	|	1142	|
190	**Bristol** T. Meads **137** a.		0710	...	|	0817	*0836*	0845	|	0910	*0935*	...	0945	*1011*	1015	*1034*	1042	*1111*	1115	*1135*	...	1142	*1211*	1215
190	**Bristol** T. Meads **116** d.		0715	...	0719r	...	|	*0855*	|	*0925*	|	...	*0955*	|	*1025*	|	*1053*	|	*1125*	|	...	1146	|	*1225*
221	Weston super Mare **116** a.		*0825*	...	|	...	|	*0923*	|	*0959*	|	...	*1023*	|	*1059*	|	*1121*	*1132*	*1159*	|	...	1206	|	*1259*
215	Newport a.		0744	...	0808	...	0829	...	0904	...	0929	...	...	1004	...	1029	...	1104	...	1129	...	...	1204	...
234	**Cardiff** Central a.		0801	...	0828	...	0848	...	0923	...	0948	...	...	1023	...	1048	...	1123	...	1147	...	...	1223	...
	Swansea **135** a.		0856	...	...	...	0944	...	...	...	1045	...	...	...	...	1143	...	...	...	1245	...	...	...	...

	Ⓐ	Ⓐ	Ⓐ	Ⓐ	Ⓐ	Ⓐ	Ⓐ	Ⓐ	Ⓐ	Ⓐ	Ⓐ	Ⓐ	Ⓐ	Ⓐ	Ⓐ	Ⓐ	Ⓐ	Ⓐ	Ⓐ	Ⓐ	Ⓐ	Ⓐ	Ⓐ	Ⓐ
	✕	🍷	🍷	🍷	✕	🍷	🍷	🍷	🍷	✕	🍷	🍷	🍷	🍷	🍷	🍷	🍷	🍷	🍷	🍷	🍷	🍷	🍷	🍷
						C									C									C
London Paddington **115 131** d.	1045	1100	1115	1130	1145	1148	1200	1215	1230	1245	1300	1315	1330	1345	1348	1400	1415	1430	1445	1500	1515	1530	1545	1548
Reading **115 131** d.	1111	1127	1141	1156	1211	1216	1227	1241	1257	1311	1327	1341	1357	1411	1416	1427	1441	1457	1511	1527	1541	1557	1611	1616
Didcot d.	|	|	1156	1212	|	1231	|	1256	1312	|	|	1356	1412	|	1431	|	1456	1512	|	|	1556	1612	|	1632
Swindon d.	1140	1156	1215	1231	1240	1253	1256	1315	1331	1340	1356	1415	1431	1440	1453	1456	1515	1531	1540	1556	1615	1631	1640	1654
Chippenham a.	|	1210	|	1245	|	...	1310	|	1345	|	1410	|	1445	|	...	1510	|	1545	|	1610	|	1645	|	...
Bath **137** a.	|	1225	|	1300	|	...	1325	|	1400	|	1425	|	1500	|	...	1525	|	1600	|	1625	|	1700	|	...
Bristol Parkway d.	1207	|	1242	|	1307	...	|	1342	|	1407	|	1442	|	1507	...	|	1542	|	1607	|	1642	|	1707	...
Bristol T. Meads **137** a.	*1235*	1242	*1311*	1315	*1336*	...	1342	*1411*	1415	*1434*	1442	*1511*	1515	*1536*	...	1542	*1611*	1615	*1634*	1642	*1711*	1715	*1736*	...
Bristol T. Meads **116** d.	|	*1253*	|	*1325*	|	...	*1353*	|	*1425*	|	*1453*	|	*1525*	|	...	*1553*	|	1618	|	*1653*	|	1718	|	...
Weston super Mare **116** a.	|	*1321*	|	*1359*	|	...	*1421*	|	*1459*	|	*1522*	|	*1559*	|	...	*1625*	|	1648	|	*1725*	|	1751	|	...
Newport a.	1229	...	1304	...	1329	...	...	1405	...	1429	...	1504	...	1529	...	...	1604	...	1629	...	1704	...	1729	...
Cardiff Central a.	1248	...	1323	...	1348	...	...	1423	...	1449	...	1523	...	1548	...	...	1623	...	1649	...	1723	...	1748	...
Swansea **135** a.	1345	...	...	...	1445	...	...	...	...	1543	...	...	...	1645	...	...	...	...	1743	...	*1844*	...	1846	...

	Ⓐ	Ⓐ	Ⓐ	Ⓐ	Ⓐ	Ⓐ	Ⓐ	Ⓐ	Ⓐ	Ⓐ	Ⓐ	Ⓐ	Ⓐ	Ⓐ	Ⓐ	Ⓐ	Ⓐ	Ⓐ	Ⓐ	Ⓐ	Ⓐ	Ⓐ	Ⓐ	Ⓐ
	🍷	🍷	🍷	🍷	🍷	🍷	🍷	🍷	🍷	🍷	🍷	🍷	🍷	🍷	🍷	🍷	🍷	🍷	🍷	🍷	🍷	🍷	🍷	🍷
			T				T	N	A	N	C					C				C				
London Paddington **115 131** d.	1600	1615	1630	1645	1700	1715	1730	...	1745	...	1748	1800	1815	1830	1845	1848	1900	1915	1930	1948	2000	2015	2045	2115
Reading **115 131** d.	1627	1641	1657	1711	1727	1741	1757	...	1811	...	1816	1827	1841	1857	1911	1916	1927	1941	1957	2016	2027	2041	2112	2141
Didcot d.	|	1656	1712	1726	1742	1756	1812	...	|	...	1831	1842	1856	1912	|	1931	1942	1956	|	2031	2042	2056	2127	2200
Swindon d.	1656	1715	1731	1745	1801	1815	1831	...	1840	...	1853	1900	1915	1931	1940	1953	2001	2015	2026	2053	2101	2115	2146	2220
Chippenham a.	1710	|	1745	|	1815	|	1845	...	*1901*	...	...	1915	|	1945	|	...	2015	|	2040	...	2115	|	2200	|
Bath **137** a.	1725	|	1800	|	1830	|	1900	...	|	...	...	1930	|	2000	|	...	2030	|	2055	...	2130	|	2215	|
Bristol Parkway d.	|	1742	|	1813	|	1842	|	1906	1911	...	...	|	1942	|	2007	...	|	2042	|	...	|	2142	|	2246
Bristol T. Meads **137** a.	1742	*1811*	1815	*1834*	1845	|	1925	1922	*1936*	←	...	1945	*2011*	2015	*2034*	...	2045	|	2110	...	2145	*2202*	2230	*2330*
Bristol T. Meads **116** d.	*1753*	|	1822	|	*1855*	|	1925	1925	|	1925	...	*1955*	|	2016	|	...	*2055*	|	2113	...	*2155*	|	*2306*	|
Weston super Mare **116** a.	*1826*	|	1853	|	*1929*	|	1947	→	|	|	...	*2029*	*2039*	2053	|	...	*2128*	|	2144	...	*2228*	|	*2340*	|
Newport a.	...	1804	...	1836	...	1904	...	...	1934	1959	...	...	2004	...	2029	...	...	2104	...	...	...	2205	...	2315
Cardiff Central a.	...	1823	...	1853	...	1923	...	...	1950	2019	...	...	2021	...	2048	...	...	2122	...	...	...	2227	...	2337
Swansea **135** a.	...	1934	...	1948	...	2023	...	...	2046	...	...	...	2120	...	2142	...	...	2218	...	...	...	2331	...	0032

	Ⓐ	⑤	①–④	⑤	①–④		⑤	①–④			⑥		⑥	⑥	⑥	⑥	⑥	⑥	⑥	⑥	⑥	⑥	⑥	⑥
	🍷	🍷	🍷	🍷	🍷		🍷	🍷			🍷		🍷	2	🍷	🍷	🍷	🍷	🍷	🍷	🍷	🍷	🍷	🍷
	E															Z			C					
London Paddington **115 131** d.	2145	2215	2215	2245	2245	...	2330	2330	...	⑥	...	...	0630	...	0700	0730	0745	0800	0815	0830	0845	0900	0930	0945
Reading **115 131** d.	2212	2241	2249	2311	2318	...	0002	0006	...		...	...	0655	...	0727	0757	0811	0827	0841	0857	0911	0927	0957	1011
Didcot d.	2232	2300	2307	2330	2337	...	0020	0024	...	△	...	...	0712	...	|	0812	|	|	0856	0912	|	|	1012	|
Swindon d.	2252	2319	2326	2350	2356	...	0039	0043	...		...	...	0730	...	0756	0830	0840	0856	0915	0931	0940	0956	1031	1040
Chippenham a.	2312	2333	2340	|	|	...	0054	0058	...		...	...	0744	...	0810	0845	|	0910	...	0945	|	1010	1045	|
Bath **137** a.	2326	2348	2355	|	|	...	0109	0113	...		...	...	0800	0818	0824	0900	|	0924	...	1000	|	1025	1100	|
Bristol Parkway d.	|	|	|	0017	0022	...	|	|	...		0713r	...	|	|	|	|	0907	|	...	|	1007	|	|	1107
Bristol T. Meads **137** a.	2341	0005	0011	|	|	...	0125s	0129s	...		|	...	0815	0829	0840	0915	*0935*	0940	...	1015	*1035*	1042	1115	*1135*
Bristol T. Meads **116** d.	2345	...	...	|	|	...	|	|	...		0658r	...	*0825*	0854	*0853*	*0925*	|	...	...	*1025*	|	*1053*	*1125*	|
Weston super Mare **116** a.	0013	...	...	|	|	...	|	|	...		|	...	*0859*	|	*0921*	*0959*	|	...	...	*1059*	|	*1121*	*1159*	|
Newport a.	...	...	...	0048	0052	...	0215s	0212s	...		0734	...	...	0923	...	...	0930	...	...	...	1031	...	...	1129
Cardiff Central a.	...	...	...	0104	0112	...	0233	0233	...		0751	...	...	0940	...	...	0948	...	...	...	1048	...	...	1148
Swansea **135** a.	...	...	...	0210	0210	...	...	...	...		0848	...	...	...	...	...	1043	...	...	...	1143	...	...	1243

	⑥	⑥	⑥	⑥	⑥	⑥	⑥	⑥	⑥	⑥	⑥	⑥	⑥	⑥	⑥	⑥	⑥	⑥	⑥	⑥	⑥	⑥	⑥	⑥
	🍷	🍷	🍷	🍷	🍷	🍷	🍷	🍷	🍷	🍷	🍷	🍷	🍷	🍷	🍷	🍷	🍷	🍷	🍷	🍷	🍷	🍷	🍷	🍷
		C							C							C							C	P
London Paddington **115 131** d.	1000	1015	1030	1045	1100	1130	1145	1200	1215	1230	1245	1300	1330	1345	1400	1415	1430	1445	1500	1530	1545	1600	1615	1630
Reading **115 131** d.	1027	1041	1057	1111	1127	1157	1211	1227	1241	1258	1311	1327	1357	1411	1427	1441	1457	1511	1527	1557	1611	1627	1641	1657
Didcot d.	|	1056	1112	|	|	1212	|	|	1256	1315	|	|	1412	|	|	1456	1512	|	|	1612	|	|	1656	1712
Swindon d.	1056	1115	1131	1140	1156	1231	1240	1256	1315	1335	1340	1356	1431	1440	1456	1515	1531	1540	1556	1631	1640	1956	1715	1731
Chippenham a.	1110	...	1145	|	1210	1245	|	1310	...	1348	|	1410	1445	|	1510	...	1545	|	1610	1645	|	1710	...	1745
Bath **137** a.	1125	...	1200	|	1225	1300	|	1325	...	1402	|	1425	1500	|	1525	...	1600	|	1625	1700	|	1725	...	1800
Bristol Parkway d.	|	...	|	1207	|	|	1307	|	...	|	1407	|	|	1507	|	...	|	1607	|	|	1707	|	...	|
Bristol T. Meads **137** a.	1142	...	1215	*1235*	1242	1315	*1335*	1342	...	1417	*1434*	1442	1515	*1535*	1542	...	1615	*1634*	1642	1715	*1735*	1742	...	1815
Bristol T. Meads **116** d.	*1153*	...	*1225*	|	*1253*	*1325*	|	*1353*	...	...	|	*1453*	*1525*	|	*1553*	...	*1625*	|	*1653*	*1725*	|	*1753*	...	1815
Weston super Mare **116** a.	*1221*	...	*1259*	|	*1321*	*1359*	|	*1421*	...	...	|	*1521*	*1559*	|	*1621*	...	*1659*	|	*1721*	*1759*	|	*1821*	...	1835
Newport a.	...	...	...	1231	...	...	1329	...	...	...	1431	...	...	1529	...	...	...	1632	...	...	1729	...	...	...
Cardiff Central a.	...	...	...	1248	...	...	1348	...	...	...	1448	...	...	1548	...	...	...	1648	...	...	1747	...	...	...
Swansea **135** a.	...	...	...	1343	...	...	1443	...	...	...	1543	...	...	1643	...	...	...	1743	...	...	1846	...	...	...

	⑥	⑥	⑥	⑥	⑥	⑥	⑥	⑥	⑥	⑥	⑥	⑥	⑥	⑥	⑥	⑥	⑥	⑥		⑥	⑥	⑥		⑥
	🍷	🍷	🍷	🍷	🍷	🍷	🍷	🍷	🍷	🍷	🍷	🍷	🍷	🍷	🍷	🍷	🍷	🍷		🍷		🍷		🍷
				N	A	N		C	T		T					G	E							
London Paddington **115 131** d.	1645	1700	1730	...	1745	...	1800	1815	1830	1845	1900	1915	1930	1945	2000	2015	2030	2045	...	2130	2200	2230	...	2330
Reading **115 131** d.	1711	1727	1756	...	1811	...	1827	1841	1857	1911	1927	1941	1957	2011	2027	2041	2057	2111	...	2157	2227	2257	...	2359
Didcot d.	|	|	1812	...	|	...	|	1856	1912	|	|	1956	2012	|	2042	2056	2112	|	...	2212	2242	2316	...	0016
Swindon d.	1740	1756	1831	...	1840	...	1856	1915	1931	1940	1956	2015	2031	2040	2101	2115	2131	2146	...	2231	2301	2337	...	0036
Chippenham a.	|	1810	1845	...	|	...	1910	...	1945	|	2010	|	2045	|	2115	...	2144	|	...	2245	|	2350	...	0050
Bath **137** a.	|	1825	1900	...	|	...	1925	...	2000	|	2025	|	2100	|	2130	...	2159	|	...	2300	|	0005	...	0105
Bristol Parkway d.	1807	|	|	1908	1912	...	|	...	|	2007	|	2042	|	2106	|	...	|	2212	...	|	2329	|	...	|
Bristol T. Meads **137** a.	*1835*	1842	1915	1924	*1936*	←	1942	...	2015	*2029*	2042	*2113*	2115	*2141*	2147	...	2216	|	...	2315	|	0020	...	0121
Bristol T. Meads **116** d.	|	*1853*	1916	1924	|	1924	*1953*	...	2015	|	2049	|	*2153*	|	...	...	2216	|	...	...	|	...	...	...
Weston super Mare **116** a.	|	*1923*	1952	→	|	|	*2023*	...	2037	|	2113	|	*2225*	|	...	...	2241	|	...	...	|	...	...	...
Newport a.	1831	...	...	...	1935	1959	...	...	...	2031	...	2104	...	2131	...	...	...	2244	...	...	0001	...	...	...
Cardiff Central a.	1848	...	...	...	1952	2019	...	...	...	2048	...	2122	...	2147	...	...	...	2305	...	...	0023	...	...	...
Swansea **135** a.	1943	...	...	...	2048	...	...	...	...	2147	...	2218	...	2246	...	...	...	0001	...	...	...	...	...	...

A – To Carmarthen.
C – To Cheltenham.
E – To Exeter.
G – To Gloucester.
N – From Newcastle.
P – To Paignton.
T – To Taunton.
Z – To Penzance.
r – Service is routed Bristol Temple Meads - Bristol Parkway.
s – Stops to set down only.
△ – Timings on ⑥ are valid Dec. 22 - Jan. 26.

133 LONDON - BRISTOL and CARDIFF GW

		⑦ 🍷 E	⑦ 🍷	⑦ 🍷	⑦ 🍷		⑦ 🍷	⑦ 🍷	⑦ 🍷	⑦ 🍷	⑦ 🍷	⑦ 🍷 E	⑦ 🍷	⑦ 🍷	⑦ 🍷	⑦ 🍷		⑦ 🍷	⑦ 🍷	⑦ 🍷	⑦ 🍷 T	⑦ 🍷		⑦ 🍷
London Paddington **115 131** d.	⑦	0800	0827	0907	0927	...	1007	1027	1050	1107	1127	1207	1227	1250	1307	1327	...	1407	1427	1450	1507	1527	...	160
Reading **115 131** d.		0843	0904	0943	1003	...	1045	1105	1124	1144	1203	1242	1305	1325	1343	1403	...	1443	1505	1525	1543	1603	...	164
Didcot d.	▲	|	0921	|	|	...	|	1120	1140	|	|	|	1320	1339	|	|	...	|	1520	1539	|	|	...	|
Swindon ❖ d.		|	0942	|	1034	...	|	1139	1200	|	1232	|	1339	1414	|	1434	...	|	1539	1559	|	1632	...	|
Chippenham ❖ a.		|	|	|	|	...	|	|	...	|	|	|	|	...	|	|	...	|	|	...	|	|	...	|
Bath **137** ❖ a.		0948	|	1050	|	...	1150	|	...	1249	|	1348	|	...	1448	|	...	1549	|	...	1648	|	...	174
Bristol Parkway ❖ d.		|	|	|	|	...	|	|	...	|	|	|	|	...	|	|	...	|	|	...	|	|	...	|
Bristol T. Meads **137** a.		1002	|	1105	|	...	1206	|	...	1303	|	1402	|	...	1503	|	...	1603	|	...	1703	|	...	180
Bristol T. Meads **116** d.		*1110*	|	*1144*	|	...	1206	|	...	1305	|	...	|	...	*1516*	|	...	*1616*	|	...	1704	|	...	...
Weston super Mare **116** a.		*1140*	|	*1201*	|	...	1234	|	...	1332	|	...	|	...	*1549*	|	...	*1647*	|	...	1732	|	...	...
Newport ❖ a.		...	1114	...	1204	...	...	1312	...	...	1357	...	1510**b**	...	...	1606	...	...	1712	...	...	1807	...	...
Cardiff Central ❖ a.		...	1130	...	1229	...	...	1328	...	...	1428	...	1528	...	...	1628	...	...	1728	...	...	1830	...	...
Swansea **135** a.		...	1229	...	1327	...	...	1425	...	...	1527	...	1625	...	...	1725	...	...	1825	...	...	1930	...	...

	⑦ 🍷	⑦ 🍷	⑦ 🍷	⑦ 🍷		⑦ 🍷	⑦ 🍷	⑦ 🍷	⑦ 🍷 E	⑦ 🍷		⑦ 🍷	⑦	⑦	⑦	⑦ 🍷	⑦ 🍷	⑦ 🚌	⑦ 🍷	⑦ 🚌	⑦ 🍷	⑦ 🚌	⑦ 🍷	① 🚌
London Paddington **115 131** d.	1627	1650	1707	1727	...	1807	1827	1850	1907	1927	...	2007	2027	2107	2137	2142	2207	...	2237	...	2307	...	2345	...
Reading **115 131** d.	1705	1725	1743	1803	...	1843	1904	1925	1943	2003	...	2043	2105	2143	2213	2220	2244	2252	2315	2323	2348	2356	0024	003
Didcot d.	1720	1739	|	|	...	|	1920	1939	|	|	...	|	2120	|	|	2237	|	|	|	|	|	|	|	|
Swindon ❖ d.	1740	1759	|	1833	...	|	1939	1959	|	2033	...	|	2140	|	2248	*2352*j	|	2352	|	0028	|	0101**s**	|	0137
Chippenham ❖ a.	|	...	|	|	...	|	|	...	|	|	...	|	|	|	|	...	|	0032	|	|	|	0136	|	021
Bath **137** ❖ a.	|	...	1848	|	...	1957	|	...	2048	|	...	2154	|	2247	|	...	2349	...	|	|	0053**s**	...	0129**s**	...
Bristol Parkway ❖ a.	|	...	|	|	...	|	|	...	|	|	...	|	|	|	|	...	|	...	|	0123	|	...	|	...
Bristol T. Meads **137** a.	|	...	1902	|	...	2011	|	...	2102	|	...	2208	|	2303	|	...	0004	...	0030	...	0107	...	0143	...
Bristol T. Meads **116** d.	|	...	1904	|	...	*2025*	|	...	2104	|	...	*2230*	|	2303	|	...	...	...	...	...	...	...	...	...
Weston super Mare **116** a.	|	...	1931	|	...	*2053*	|	...	2130	|	...	*2303*	|	2332	|	...	...	...	...	...	...	...	...	...
Newport ❖ a.	1911	...	...	2005	...	...	2112	...	...	2209	...	...	2312	...	0019	...	...	...	...	...	...	...	...	...
Cardiff Central ❖ a.	1928	...	...	2028	...	...	2128	...	...	2227	...	...	2329	...	0035	...	...	...	...	...	...	...	...	...
Swansea **135** a.	2025	...	...	2128	...	...	2225	...	...	2325	...	...	0026	...	0133	...	...	...	...	...	...	...	...	...

		Ⓐ 🍷		Ⓐ 🍷	Ⓐ 🍷	Ⓐ 🍷	Ⓐ 🍷	Ⓐ 🍷 C	Ⓐ 🍷	Ⓐ 🍷	Ⓐ 🍷	Ⓐ 🍷 C	Ⓐ 🍷	Ⓐ 🍷	Ⓐ 🍴	Ⓐ 🍷 N	Ⓐ 🍴	Ⓐ 🍷 N	Ⓐ 🍷 C	Ⓐ 🍴 L	Ⓐ 🍷	Ⓐ 🍷 E	Ⓐ 🍷	Ⓐ 🍷 C
Swansea **135** d.	Ⓐ	...	...	...	0400	...	0458	...	...	...	0524	...	...	0559	...	...	0629	...	...	...	0659	...	0729	...
Cardiff Central d.		...	...	...	0515	...	0554	...	...	...	0620	...	...	0655	...	0700	0725	...	...	...	0755	...	0825	...
Newport d.		...	...	...	0533	...	0608	...	...	...	0634	...	...	0709	...	0715	0739	...	...	...	0809	...	0839	...
Weston super Mare **116** d.		...	...	...	|	...	|	...	...	...	|	...	0624	|	0648	|	|	←	...	0727	|	0750	|	...
Bristol T. Meads **116** a.		...	...	...	|	...	|	...	...	...	|	...	0657	|	0721	0753	|	0753	...	0757	|	0822	|	...
Bristol T. Meads **137** d.		0447	...	0530	|	0600	*0615*	...	0630	0640	|	...	0700	|	0730	→	*0741*	0800	...	0800	|	0830	*0841*	...
Bristol Parkway d.		0457**u**	...	|	0601	|	0631	...	|	|	0657	...	|	0732	|	...	0802	0808	...	|	0832	|	0902	...
Bath **137** d.		|	...	0543	|	0613	|	...	0643	0652	|	...	0713	|	0743	...	|	...	...	0813	|	0843	|	...
Chippenham d.		|	...	0555	|	0625	|	...	0655	0705	|	...	0725	*0730*	0755	...	|	...	...	0825	|	0855	|	...
Swindon d.		0523	...	0611	0628	0641	0658	0702	0711	0721	0725	0736	0741	0759	0811	...	0829	...	0833	0841	0859	0911	0929	093
Didcot a.		0541	...	0628	0645	0658	|	0719	0728	|	0742	0754	0800	0816	0828	...	0846	...	0852	0858	|	0928	|	095
Reading **115 131** a.		0557	...	0643	0702	0714	0729	0735	0744	|	0758	0812	0815	0832	0844	...	0901	...	0906	0914	0927	0944	0957	100
London Paddington **115 131** a.		0630	...	0716	0732	0742	0801	0806	0814	0818	0830	0841	0844	0906	0915	...	0929	...	0938	0944	0959	1015	1027	103

	Ⓐ 🍷	Ⓐ 🍴	Ⓐ 🍷	Ⓐ 🍴 A	Ⓐ 🍷 P	Ⓐ 🍷	Ⓐ 🍷	Ⓐ 🍷	Ⓐ 🍷 C	Ⓐ 🍷	Ⓐ 🍷	Ⓐ 🍷	Ⓐ 🍷	Ⓐ 🍷 Z	Ⓐ 🍷	Ⓐ 🍷	Ⓐ 🍴	Ⓐ 🍷 C	Ⓐ 🍷	Ⓐ 🍷	Ⓐ 🍷	Ⓐ 🍷	Ⓐ 🍷	Ⓐ 🍷
Swansea **135** d.	...	0759	...	0829	...	*0855*	...	0929	...	...	*0955*	...	1029	...	*1055*	...	1129	...	...	*1155*	...	1229	...	*125*
Cardiff Central d.	...	0855	...	0925	...	0955	...	1025	...	...	1055	...	1125	...	1155	...	1225	...	...	1255	...	1325	...	135
Newport d.	...	0910	...	0939	...	1009	...	1039	...	...	1109	...	1139	...	1209	...	1239	...	...	1309	...	1339	...	140
Weston super Mare **116** d.	*0830*	|	*0840*	|	0927	|	*0940*	|	...	*1010*	|	*1040*	|	*1110*	|	*1140*	|	...	*1210*	|	*1242*	|	*1310*	|
Bristol T. Meads **116** a.	*0850*	|	*0914*	|	0955	|	*1014*	|	...	*1044*	|	*1111*	|	*1144*	|	*1212*	|	...	*1244*	|	*1313*	|	*1344*	|
Bristol T. Meads **137** d.	0900	*0910*	0930	*0941*	1000	|	1030	*1041*	...	1100	|	1130	*1141*	1200	|	1230	*1241*	...	1300	|	1330	*1341*	1400	|
Bristol Parkway d.	|	0932	|	1002	|	1032	|	1102	...	|	1132	|	1202	|	1232	|	1302	...	|	1332	|	1402	|	143
Bath **137** d.	0913	|	0943	|	1013	|	1043	|	...	1113	|	1143	|	1213	|	1243	|	...	1313	|	1343	|	1413	|
Chippenham d.	0925	|	0955	|	1025	|	1055	|	...	1125	|	1155	|	1225	|	1255	|	...	1325	|	1355	|	1425	|
Swindon d.	0941	0959	1011	1029	1041	1059	1111	1129	1135	1141	1159	1211	1229	1241	1259	1311	1329	1335	1341	1359	1411	1429	1441	145
Didcot a.	|	1016	1028	1046	|	1116	1128	1146	1152	|	1216	1228	1246	|	1316	1328	1346	1352	|	1416	1428	1446	|	151
Reading **115 131** a.	1009	1032	1044	1101	1109	1132	1144	1201	1207	1209	1232	1244	1301	1309	1332	1344	1401	1407	1409	1432	1444	1501	1509	153
London Paddington **115 131** a.	1044	1102	1115	1132	1142	1202	1215	1232	1239	1242	1302	1315	1329	1342	1402	1415	1432	1439	1442	1502	1515	1530	1542	160

	Ⓐ 🍷	Ⓐ 🍷	Ⓐ 🍷 C	Ⓐ 🍷	Ⓐ 🍷	Ⓐ 🍷	Ⓐ 🍷	Ⓐ 🍷	Ⓐ 🍷	Ⓐ 🍷	Ⓐ 🍷	Ⓐ 🍷 C	Ⓐ 🍷	Ⓐ 🍷	Ⓐ 🍷	Ⓐ 🍷	Ⓐ 🍷	Ⓐ 🍷	Ⓐ 🍷	Ⓐ 🍷	Ⓐ 🍷 C		Ⓐ 🍷	Ⓐ 🍷
Swansea **135** d.	...	1329	...	...	*1355*	...	1429	...	*1455*	...	1529	...	...	*1555*	...	1629	...	*1655*	...	1729	...	...	...	182
Cardiff Central d.	...	1425	...	...	1455	...	1525	...	1555	...	1625	...	...	1655	...	1725	...	1755	...	1825	...	...	...	192
Newport d.	...	1439	...	...	1509	...	1539	...	1609	...	1639	...	...	1709	...	1739	...	1809	...	1839	...	...	...	193
Weston super Mare **116** d.	*1340*	|	...	*1410*	|	*1440*	|	*1510*	*1536*	...	|	...	*1610*	|	1708	|	*1714*	|	1809	|	...	...	*1840*	|
Bristol T. Meads **116** a.	*1411*	|	...	*1444*	|	*1511*	|	*1544*	|	...	|	...	*1644*	|	1729	|	*1744*	|	1829	|	...	...	*1915*	|
Bristol T. Meads **137** d.	1430	*1441*	...	1500	|	1530	*1541*	1600	|	1630	*1641*	...	1700	*1710*	1730	*1741*	1800	|	1831	*1841*	...	...	1930	*194*
Bristol Parkway d.	|	1502	...	|	1532	|	1602	|	1632	|	1702	...	|	1732	|	1802	|	1832	|	1902	...	...	|	200
Bath **137** d.	1443	|	...	1513	|	1543	|	1613	|	1643	|	...	1713	|	1743	|	1813	|	1843	|	...	...	1943	|
Chippenham d.	1455	|	...	1525	|	1555	|	1625	|	1655	|	...	1725	|	1755	|	1825	|	1855	|	...	...	1955	*200*
Swindon d.	1511	1529	1535	1541	1559	1611	1629	1641	1659	1711	1729	1735	1741	1759	1811	1829	1841	1859	1911	1929	1935	...	2011	202
Didcot a.	1528	1546	1552	|	1616	1628	1646	|	1716	1728	|	1752	|	1816	1828	1846	|	1916	1929	1946	1952	...	2028	204
Reading **115 131** a.	1544	1601	1607	1612	1632	1644	1701	1709	1732	1744	1757	1807	1813	1832	1844	1901	1909	1932	1945	2001	2012	...	2044	210
London Paddington **115 131** a.	1615	1630	1639	1644	1702	1715	1730	1742	1802	1815	1827	1839	1845	1902	1915	1932	1942	2002	2015	2030	2044	...	2115	213

	Ⓐ 🍷	Ⓐ 🍷		Ⓐ 🍷 Z	Ⓐ 🍷		Ⓐ 🍷 T			⑥ 🍷	⑥ 🍷		⑥ 🍷	⑥ 🍷	⑥ 🍷	⑥ 🍷	⑥ 🍷	⑥ 🍷	⑥ 🍷 C	⑥ 🍷 T	⑥ 🍷	⑥ 🍷	⑥ 🍷	⑥ 🍷 E
Swansea **135** d.	...	1929	...	...	2029	...	...	...	⑥	...	0400	...	0459	...	...	0559	...	0629	...	...	0659	...	0729	...
Cardiff Central d.	...	2025	...	...	2125	...	...	...		...	0455	...	0555	...	...	0655	...	0725	...	...	0755	...	0825	...
Newport d.	...	2039	...	...	2139	...	...	...	△	...	0509	...	0609	...	...	0709	...	0739	...	...	0809	...	0839	...
Weston super Mare **116** d.	*1948*	|	...	...	|	...	2200	...		...	|	...	|	...	0624	|	...	*0700*	...	0728	|	*0734*	|	082
Bristol T. Meads **116** a.	*2018*	|	...	...	|	...	2229	...		...	0553**z**	...	|	...	0653	|	...	|	...	0757	|	*0808*	|	085
Bristol T. Meads **137** d.	2030	*2041*	...	2140	|	...	2233	...		0530	0600	...	*0615*	0630	0700	|	0730	*0741*	...	0800	|	0830	*0841*	090
Bristol Parkway d.	|	2102	...	|	2202	...	|	...		|	0542**z**	...	0632	|	|	0732	|	0802	...	|	0832	|	0902	|
Bath **137** d.	2043	|	...	2156	|	...	2246	...		0543	0613	...	|	0643	0713	|	0743	|	...	0813	|	0843	|	091
Chippenham d.	2055	|	...	2208	|	...	2258	...		0555	0625	...	|	0655	0725	|	0755	|	...	0825	|	0855	|	092
Swindon d.	2111	2129	...	2224	2229	...	2314	..		0611	0641	...	0659	0711	0742	0759	0811	0829	0833	0841	0859	0911	0929	094
Didcot a.	2128	2150	...	|	2246	...	2331	...		0628	0658	...	0716	0728	0759	0816	0828	0846	0851	0858	0916	0928	0946	|
Reading **115 131** a.	2144	2215	...	2255	2306	...	2352	...		0643	0714	...	0732	0744	0814	0832	0844	0902	0907	0914	0933	0944	1001	100
London Paddington **115 131** a.	2215	2256**d**	...	2336**y**	2350**y**	...	0032	...		0714	0741	...	0801	0814	0845	0906	0915	0930	0936	0944	1001	1014	1031	104

A – From Carmarthen.
C – From Cheltenham.
E – To / from Exeter.
L – From Plymouth.

N – To Newcastle.
P – From Paignton.
T – To / from Taunton.
Z – From Penzance.

b – 1514 on Dec. 16.
d – 2251 on ⑤.
j – By 🚌.
s – Stops to set down only.

u – Stops to pick up only.
y – 7–8 minutes earlier on ⑤.
z – Service is routed Bristol Parkway - Bristol Temple Meads.

▲ – Timings on ⑦ are subject to alteration from Dec. 23.
△ – Timings on ⑥ are valid Dec. 22 - Jan. 26.

❖ – On ⑦, connecting 🚌 services operate Swindon - Chippenham - Bath and Swindon - Bristol Parkway.

❖ – On ⑦, additional trains leave Bristol Parkway for Newport and Cardiff at 1004, 1203, 1403, 1502, 1602, 1702, 1802, 1903, 2002, 2102, 2204, and 2302 (journey time: ± 43 minutes).

GW — CARDIFF and BRISTOL - LONDON — 133

	⑥ 🍷	⑥ 🍷 C	⑥ 🍷 P	⑥ 🍷 N	⑥ 🍷	⑥ 🍷 N	⑥ 🍷		⑥ 🍷	⑥ 🍷	⑥ 🍷	⑥ 🍷 C	⑥ 🍷	⑥ 🍷 A	⑥ 🍷		⑥ 🍷		⑥ 🍷 C	⑥ 🍷	⑥ 🍷	⑥ 🍷		⑥ 🍷
Swansea **135** d.	0759	...	...	...	0829	...	...	...	...	0929	...	...	...	1029	...	...	1129	...	...	...	1229	...	...	...
Cardiff Central d.	0855	...	...	0900	0925	...	...	...	...	1025	...	...	...	1125	...	...	1225	...	...	...	1325	...	...	...
Newport d.	0909	...	...	0915	0939	...	...	...	...	1039	...	...	...	1139	...	...	1239	...	...	...	1339	...	...	...
Weston super Mare **116** d.	|	...	0900	|	|	←	*0909*	...	*0940*	|	*1008*	...	*1043*	|	*1108*	...	|	...	...	*1241*	|	*1308*	...	*1339*
Bristol T. Meads **116** a.	|	...	0920	0951	|	0951	*0944*	...	*1010*	|	*1042*	...	*1114*	|	*1142*	...	|	...	...	*1311*	|	*1342*	...	*1409*
Bristol T. Meads **137** d.	|	...	0930	→	*0941*	1000	1000	...	1030	*1041*	1100	...	1130	|	1200	...	*1241*	...	...	1330	*1341*	1400	...	1430
Bristol Parkway d.	0932	...	|	...	1002	1008	|	...	|	1102	|	...	|	1202	|	...	1302	...	...	|	1402	|	...	|
Bath **137** d.	|	...	0943	...	|	...	1013	...	1043	|	1113	...	1143	|	1213	...	|	...	...	1343	|	1413	...	1443
Chippenham d.	*0930*	...	0955	...	|	...	1025	...	1055	|	1125	...	1155	|	1225	...	|	...	...	1355	|	1425	...	1455
Swindon d.	0959	1004	1011	...	1029	...	1041	...	1111	1129	1141	1204	1211	1229	1241	...	1329	...	1404	1411	1429	1441	...	1511
Didcot a.	1016	1021	1028	...	|	...	|	...	1128	1146	|	1221	1228	1246	|	...	1346	...	1421	1428	1446	|	...	1528
Reading **115 128** a.	1032	1037	1045	...	1059	...	1109	...	1144	1202	1209	1236	1244	1301	1309	...	1401	...	1436	1444	1501	1509	...	1544
London Paddington **115 128** a.	1059	1107	1115	...	1131	...	1142	...	1215	1232	1242	1306	1315	1336	1342	...	1430	...	1506	1515	1531	1542	...	1615

	⑥ 🍷		⑥ 🍷 C	⑥ 🍷	⑥ 🍷	⑥ 🍷	⑥ 🍷		⑥ 🍷 C	⑥ 🍷	⑥ 🍷	⑥ 🍷		⑥ 🍷	⑥ 🍷		⑥ 🍷 C	⑥ 🍷	⑥ 🍷		⑥ 🍷	⑥ 🍷		⑥ T
Swansea **135** d.	1329	...	...	...	...	...	1529	...	...	...	1629	...	...	...	1729	...	...	...	1829	...	...	1929	...	...
Cardiff Central d.	1425	...	...	...	...	...	1625	...	...	...	1725	...	...	...	1825	...	...	...	1925	...	...	2025	...	...
Newport d.	1439	...	...	...	...	...	1639	...	...	...	1739	...	...	...	1839	...	...	...	1939	...	...	2039	...	...
Weston super Mare **116** d.	|	...	...	*1439*	*1508*	*1539*	|	...	...	*1639*	|	*1708*	...	*1739*	|	...	...	*1840*	|	...	2010	|	...	2159
Bristol T. Meads **116** a.	|	...	...	*1509*	*1542*	*1609*	|	...	...	*1709*	|	*1742*	...	*1809*	|	...	...	*1911*	|	...	2030	|	...	2228
Bristol T. Meads **137** d.	*1441*	...	...	1530	1600	1630	*1641*	...	...	1730	*1741*	1800	...	1830	|	...	...	1930	*1940*	...	2033	*2041*	...	2233
Bristol Parkway d.	1502	...	...	|	|	|	1702	...	...	|	1802	|	...	|	1902	...	...	|	2002	...	|	2102	...	|
Bath **137** d.	|	...	...	1543	1613	1643	|	...	...	1743	|	1813	...	1843	|	...	...	1943	|	...	2046	|	...	2246
Chippenham d.	|	...	*1528*	1555	1625	1655	|	...	...	1755	|	1825	...	1855	|	...	...	1955	|	...	2058	|	...	2258
Swindon d.	1529	...	1604	1611	1641	1711	1729	...	1804	1811	1829	1841	...	1911	1929	...	2004	2011	2029	...	2114	2129	...	2314
Didcot a.	1546	...	1621	1628	|	1728	1746	...	1821	1828	1846	|	...	1928	1946	...	2021	2028	2046	...	2131	|	...	2331
Reading **115 128** a.	1601	...	1636	1644	1709	1744	1801	...	1836	1844	1901	1909	...	1944	2001	...	2038	2044	2103	...	2148	2158	...	2352
London Paddington **115 128** a.	1630	...	1706	1715	1742	1815	1831	...	1906	1915	1931	1942	...	2015	2031	...	2109	2115	2136	...	2216	2231	...	0032

		⑦ 🍷		⑦ 🍷	⑦ 🍷	⑦ 🍷		⑦ 🍷	⑦ 🍷	⑦ 🍷	⑦ 🍷	⑦ 🍷	⑦ 🍷	⑦ 🍷 E	⑦ 🍷		⑦ 🍷 E	⑦ 🍷		⑦ 🍷	⑦ 🍷		⑦ 🍷	⑦ 🍷
Swansea **135** d.	⑦	...	...	...	...	...	...	...	*0755*j	...	0905	...	...	...	1005	...	...	1105	...	...	1205	...	1305	...
Cardiff Central ❖ d.		...	...	...	0745	...	...	...	0905	...	1005	...	...	...	1105	...	...	1205	...	...	1305	...	1405	...
Newport ❖ d.	▲	...	...	...	0803	...	...	...	0920	...	1019	...	...	...	1119	...	...	1219	...	...	1319	...	1419	...
Weston super Mare **116** d.		...	...	...	|	0828	...	*0914*	|	...	|	1028	...	*1051*	|	...	...	|	...	1332	|	...	|	1428
Bristol T. Meads **116** a.		...	...	...	|	0855	...	*0945*	|	...	|	1055	...	*1120*	|	...	...	|	...	1356	|	...	|	1454
Bristol T. Meads **137** d.		0740	...	0810	|	0900	...	1000	|	1030	|	1100	...	1200	|	...	1300	|	...	1400	|	...	|	1500
Bristol Parkway ❖ d.		|	...	|	|	|	...	|	|	|	|	|	...	|	|	...	|	|	...	|	|	...	|	|
Bath **137** ❖ d.		0753	...	0823	|	0913	...	1013	|	1043	|	1113	...	1213	|	...	1313	|	...	1413	|	...	|	1513
Chippenham ❖ d.		|	...	|	|	|	...	|	|	|	|	|	*1140*j	|	|	...	|	|	...	|	|	...	|	|
Swindon ❖ d.		|	...	|	0923	|	...	|	1100	|	1146	|	1224	|	1301	...	|	1408	...	|	1502	...	1546	|
Didcot a.		|	...	|	|	|	...	|	|	|	|	|	|	|	|	...	|	|	...	|	|	...	|	|
Reading **115 128** a.		0859	...	0939	0954	1023	...	1119	1129	1154	1214	1220	1252	1319	1329	...	1419	1436	...	1519	1530	...	1614	1620
London Paddington **115 128** a.		0941	...	1014	1039	1058	...	1159	1208	1237	1252	1259	1329	1358	1408	...	1458	1522	...	1558	1608	...	1655	1705

	⑦ 🍷	⑦ 🍷	⑦ 🍷		⑦ 🍷	⑦ 🍷	⑦ 🍷	⑦ 🍷 E	⑦ 🍷	⑦ 🍷 P	⑦ 🍷 E	⑦ 🍷	⑦ 🍷	⑦ 🍷 T		⑦ 🍷	⑦ 🍷		⑦ 🍷	⑦		⑦ 🍷 E	⑦ 🍷	⑦ 🚌
Swansea **135** d.	...	1405	...	...	...	1505	...	...	1605	...	...	...	1705	...	...	...	1805	...	1905	...	...	...	2005	...
Cardiff Central ❖ d.	...	1505	...	...	...	1605	...	...	1705	...	...	...	1805	...	...	...	1905	...	2005	...	...	...	2105	...
Newport ❖ d.	...	1519	...	...	...	1619	...	...	1719	...	...	...	1819	...	...	...	1919	...	2019	...	...	...	2119	...
Weston super Mare **116** d.	...	|	...	...	*1615*	|	...	1658	|	1731	...	*1816*	|	1855	...	...	|	...	|	2038	...	*2119*	|	...
Bristol T. Meads **116** a.	...	|	...	...	*1649*	|	...	1719	|	1800	...	*1850*	|	1926	...	...	|	...	|	2058	...	*2152*	|	...
Bristol T. Meads **137** d.	1600	|	1630	...	1700	|	...	1730	|	1802	1830	1900	|	1930	...	2000	|	...	|	2100	...	2205	|	...
Bristol Parkway ❖ d.	|	|	|	...	|	|	...	|	|	|	|	|	|	|	...	|	|	...	|	|	...	|	|	...
Bath **137** ❖ d.	1613	|	1643	...	1712	|	...	1743	|	1815	1843	1913	|	1942	...	2013	|	...	|	2113	...	2218	|	...
Chippenham ❖ d.	|	|	|	...	|	|	*1740*j	|	|	|	|	|	|	|	...	|	|	...	|	|	...	|	|	2231
Swindon ❖ d.	|	1701	|	...	|	1808	1825	|	1901	|	|	|	2008	|	...	|	2100	...	2148	|	...	|	2255	2306
Didcot a.	|	|	|	...	|	|	|	|	|	|	|	|	|	|	...	|	|	...	|	|	...	|	|	|
Reading **115 128** a.	1719	1729	1749	...	1819	1836	1853	1859	1929	1927	1949	2019	2038	2047	...	2126	2129	...	2216	2235	...	2324	2331	0011
London Paddington **115 128** a.	1800	1813	1834	...	1901	1921	1938	1939	2007	2010	2028	2102	2122	2129	...	2208	2211	...	2256	2326	...	0016	0021	*0118*

A – From Carmarthen.
C – From Cheltenham.
E – From Exeter.
N – To Newcastle.
P – From Paignton.
T – From Taunton.
j – By 🚌.
▲ – Timings on ⑦ are subject to alteration from Dec. 23.
☛ Timings on ⑥ are valid Dec. 22 - Jan. 26.

❖ – On ⑦, connecting 🚌 services operate Bristol Parkway - Swindon and Bath - Chippenham - Swindon.

❖ – On ⑦, additional trains leave Cardiff for Newport and Bristol Parkway at 0805, 0909, 1009, 1109, 1209, 1309, 1409, 1509, 1609, 1709, 1809, 1909, 2009, 2009, and 2205 (journey time: ± 38 minutes).

GW 2nd class — CORNISH BRANCH LINES — 134

PLYMOUTH – GUNNISLAKE *24 km*

Ⓐ: 0642, 0934, 1130, 1333, 1635, 1816, 2124.
⑥: 0645, 0934, 1130, 1335, 1644, 1816, 2124.
⑦: 0935, 1140, 1345, 1545, 1745.

GUNNISLAKE – PLYMOUTH Journey time: ± 45 minutes

Ⓐ: 0734, 1023, 1219, 1424, 1724, 1907, 2215.
⑥: 0742, 1023, 1219, 1424, 1733, 1907.
⑦: 1025, 1245, 1445, 1655, 1837.

LISKEARD – LOOE *14 km*

Ⓐ: 0610, 0715, 0956, 1150, 1345, 1515, 1636, 1802, 1911.
⑥: 0612, 0715, 0956, 1210, 1345, 1515, 1631, 1757, 1911.

LOOE – LISKEARD Journey time: ± 26 minutes

Ⓐ: 0641, 0746, 1025, 1233, 1430, 1549, 1706, 1835, 1943.
⑥: 0645, 0746, 1025, 1240, 1430, 1549, 1710, 1830, 1943.

PAR – NEWQUAY *33 km*

Ⓐ: 0923, 1124, 1400, 1933.
⑥: 1128, 1403.

NEWQUAY – PAR Journey time: ± 53 minutes

Ⓐ: 1018, 1242, 1452, 2025.
⑥: 1013, 1242, 1510.

TRURO – FALMOUTH Docks *20 km*

Ⓐ: 0631, 0731, 0832, 0945, 1047, 1239, 1429, 1628, 1726, 1852, 2000, 2104.
⑥: 0625, 0730, 0830, 0943, 1125, 1247, 1435, 1558, 1651, 1802, 1956, 2104.
⑦: 1111, 1226, 1335, 1434, 1536 **A**, 1555 **B**, 1655, 1830, 1941 **C**, 1949 **D**, 2050, 2200.

FALMOUTH Docks – **TRURO** Journey time: ± 24 minutes

Ⓐ: 0657, 0757, 0857, 1011, 1147, 1327, 1457, 1653, 1822, 1916, 2026, 2130.
⑥: 0653, 0756, 0856, 1009, 1151, 1313, 1501, 1624, 1725, 1828, 2026, 2131.
⑦: 1137, 1252, 1401, 1500, 1604 **A**, 1624 **B**, 1721, 1900, 2007 **C**, 2015 **D**, 2120, 2226.

ST ERTH – ST IVES *7 km*

Ⓐ: 0645 **p**, 0724, 0817, 0910 **p**, 1011, 1041 and every 30 minutes until 1641; then 1712, 1759, 1836, 1940, 2030, 2135.
⑥: 0703 **p**, 0732, 0906 **p**, 1011, 1041 and every 30 minutes until 1641; then 1712, 1759, 1836, 1923, 2025, 2132.
⑦: 1200 **p**, 1302, 1401, 1506, 1612, 1646, 1732, 1826, 1920.

ST IVES – ST ERTH Journey time: ± 12 minutes

Ⓐ: 0708, 0738, 0835 **q**, 0927, 1025, 1055 and every 30 minutes until 1625; then 1657, 1727, 1817, 1855, 2000, 2046, 2151 **q**.
⑥: 0717, 0746, 0923, 1025, 1056 and at 25 and 56 minutes past each hour until 1625; then 1657, 1727, 1817, 1855, 2000, 2045, 2150 **q**.
⑦: 1230, 1330, 1430, 1539, 1630, 1702, 1740, 1845, 1940 **q**.

A – Until Mar. 23.
B – From Mar. 30.
C – Not Feb. 3 - Mar. 23.
D – Feb. 3 - Mar. 23 only.
p – 🚌(2) Penzance - St Ives (departs Penzance ± 10 minutes earlier).
q – 🚌(2) St Ives - Penzance (journey time St Ives - Penzance: ± 22 minutes).

135 CARDIFF - SWANSEA

AW, GW

km			①	②–⑤		Ⓐ 2🍷 A	Ⓐ 2	Ⓐ 2🍷 CA	Ⓐ 🍷	Ⓐ 2 S	Ⓐ 🍷	Ⓐ 2🍷 C	Ⓐ 2	Ⓐ ✕	Ⓐ 2🍷 MA	Ⓐ 🍷	Ⓐ 2🍷 M	Ⓐ 2	Ⓐ ✕	Ⓐ 2🍷 MA	Ⓐ ✕	Ⓐ 2🍷 M	Ⓐ 2	Ⓐ ✕	Ⓐ 2🍷 MA	Ⓐ ✕
	London Pad'ton **133** d.	Ⓐ	2137n	2245n	...	...	...	...	0527	...	0645	...	...	0745	...	0845	...	...	0945	...	1045	...	...	1145	...	1245
0	**Cardiff** Central d.		0038	0112	...	0540	0652	0758	0801	0809	0848	0904	0914	0948	1004	1048	1104	1114	1147	1204	1248	1304	1314	1348	1404	1449
32	Bridgend d.		0100	0158	...	0608	0712	0817	0822	0829	0909	0923	0934	1009	1023	1109	1123	1134	1208	1223	1309	1323	1334	1409	1423	1510
52	Port Talbot d.		0113	0211	...	0624	0728	0830	0835	0845	0922	0936	0950	1022	1036	1122	1136	1150	1221	1236	1322	1336	1350	1422	1436	1523
61	Neath d.		0121	0218	...	0635	0739	0837	0843	0856	0929	0943	1001	1029	1043	1130	1143	1201	1229	1243	1329	1343	1401	1429	1443	1529
74	**Swansea** a.		0133	0235	...	0652	0754	0849	0856	0913	0944	0956	1020	1045	1058	1143	1156	1220	1245	1256	1345	1356	1420	1445	1456	1543
	Carmarthen **136** a.		...	...	...	0742	0851	0947	...	*1040*	...	1051	...	...	1146	*1240*	1251	...	...	1346	...	1447	...	...	1549	*1640*

	Ⓐ 2🍷 M	Ⓐ 2	Ⓐ 🍷	Ⓐ 2🍷 MA	Ⓐ 🍷	Ⓐ 2🍷 M	Ⓐ 2	Ⓐ 🍷	Ⓐ 2🍷 MA	Ⓐ 🍷	Ⓐ 🍷	Ⓐ 2🍷 M	Ⓐ 🍷	Ⓐ 2	Ⓐ 🍷	Ⓐ 🍷	Ⓐ 🍷	Ⓐ 2🍷 MA	Ⓐ 🍷	Ⓐ 2🍷 M	Ⓐ 🍷	Ⓐ 2	Ⓐ 🍷		⑥	⑥ 2🍷 A
London Pad'ton **133** d.	...	...	1345	...	1445	...	*1515*	1545	...	1615	1645	...	1715	...	1745	1815	1845	...	1915	...	2015	...	2115	⑥ ▲	2245n	...
Cardiff Central d.	1504	1514	1548	1604	1649	1704	1738	1748	1804	1828	1853	1904	1924	1937	1950	2022	2048	2107	2122	2209	2235	2315	2337		0104	0540
Bridgend d.	1523	1534	1609	1623	1710	1725	1758	1809	1826	1853	1913	1923	1949	1956	2011	2042	2109	2128	2142	2228	2255	2342	2357		0128	0608
Port Talbot d.	1536	1550	1622	1636	1723	1739	1814	1822	1842	1906	1926	1935	2002	2012	2024	2057	2122	2143	2155	2241	2308	2359	0010		0141	0624
Neath d.	1543	1601	1629	1643	1729	1750	1825	1830	1849	1913	1934	1942	2009	2023	2032	2104	2129	2150	2203	2248	2315	0010	0018		0148	0635
Swansea a.	1556	1620	1645	1656	1743	1805	1844	1846	1901	1934	1948	1956	2023	2042	2046	2120	2142	2203	2218	2300	2331	0025	0032		0210	0651
Carmarthen **136** a.	1651	...	...	1752	*1840*	1900	...	...	1946	...	...	2046	...	...	2149	...	...	2311	*2311*	0003	*0025*	0137	*0137*		...	0742

	⑥ 2	⑥ 🍷	⑥ 2 CA	⑥ 2 S	⑥ 2 C	⑥ 2	⑥ 🍷	⑥ 2🍷 MA	⑥ 🍷	⑥ 2🍷 M	⑥ 2	⑥ 🍷	⑥ 2🍷 MA	⑥ 🍷	⑥ 2🍷 M	⑥ 2	⑥ 🍷	⑥ 2🍷 MA	⑥ 🍷	⑥ 2🍷 M	⑥ 2	⑥ 🍷	⑥ 2🍷 MA	⑥ 🍷	⑥ 2🍷 M	⑥ 🍷
London Pad'ton **133** d.	...	...	...	...	...	...	0700	...	0730	...	...	0837	...	0937	...	...	1037	...	1137	...	...	1237	...	1337	...	1437
Cardiff Central d.	0652	0753	0804	0809	0904	0914	0941	1004	1026	1104	1114	1126	1204	1226	1304	1314	1326	1404	1426	1504	1514	1526	1604	1628	1704	1730
Bridgend d.	0712	0813	0823	0829	0923	0934	1002	1023	1052	1123	1134	1152	1223	1252	1323	1334	1352	1423	1452	1523	1534	1552	1623	1652	1725	1752
Port Talbot d.	0728	0826	0836	0845	0936	0950	1015	1036	1105	1136	1150	1205	1236	1305	1336	1350	1405	1436	1505	1536	1550	1605	1636	1705	1740	1805
Neath d.	0739	0834	0843	0856	0943	1001	1022	1043	1112	1143	1201	1212	1243	1312	1343	1401	1412	1443	1512	1543	1601	1612	1643	1712	1751	1812
Swansea a.	0755	0848	0855	0913	0956	1020	1038	1101	1128	1156	1220	1228	1256	1328	1356	1420	1428	1456	1528	1556	1620	1628	1656	1728	1806	1828
Carmarthen **136** a.	0851	...	0947	*1040*	1051	...	...	1147	*1240*	1251	...	...	1346	...	1447	...	...	1549	*1640*	1651	...	...	1756	*1840*	1900	...

	⑥ 2	⑥ 2🍷 MA	⑥ 🍷	⑥ 2🍷 M	⑥ 🍷	⑥ 2	⑥ 2🍷 MA	⑥ 🍷	⑥ 2🍷 MD	⑥ 🍷	⑥ 2🍷 M	⑥ 🍷	⑥ 2	⑥ 🍷			⑦ 2 A	⑦ 2 HF	⑦ 🍷	⑦ 🍷	⑦ 🍷	⑦ 🍷 C	⑦ 🍷	⑦ 🍷	⑦ 2🍷 MA	⑦ 🍷
London Pad'ton **133** d.	...	...	1537	...	1633	...	...	1737	...	1833	...	1937	...	2045	...	⑦ ▲	...	...	0827	0927	1027	...	1127	1227	...	1327
Cardiff Central d.	1738	1802	1828	1904	1923	1938	2001	2028	2107	2122	2209	2228	2241	2334	...		0930	1120	1133	1231	1331	1403	1430	1531	1618	1629
Bridgend d.	1758	1821	1852	1923	1952	2007	2019	2052	2128	2142	2228	2248	2308	2357	...		0958	1140	1155	1254	1352	1424	1453	1552	1645	1653
Port Talbot d.	1814	1834	1905	1936	2005	2024	2032	2104	2143	2155	2241	2301	2324	0010	...		1014	1154	1208	1307	1406	1438	1506	1606	1659	1705
Neath d.	1825	1841	1912	1943	2012	2035	|	2111	2150	2203	2248	2309	2335	0017	...		1025	1202	1216	1315	1413	1446	1513	1613	1707	1713
Swansea a.	1844	1856	1926	1956	2028	2054	|	2126	2203	2218	2300	2325	2351	0033	...		1040	1214	1229	1327	1425	1458	1527	1625	1720	1725
Carmarthen **136** a.	...	1946	...	2046	...	...	2129	2222	2311	*2311*	0003	*0025*	0058	...	...		1137	1305	...	...	*1530**	1553	...	*1730**	1814	...

	⑦ 🍷	⑦ 2🍷 MB	⑦ 🍷	⑦ 🍷	⑦ 2🍷 MA	⑦ 🍷	⑦ 🍷	⑦ 2	⑦ 🍷	⑦ 2 F	⑦ 🍷
London Pad'ton **133** d.	1427	...	1527	1627	...	1727	1827	...	1927	...	2027
Cardiff Central d.	1731	1818	1829	1929	2022	2029	2129	2130	2229	2235	2330
Bridgend d.	1753	1838	1853	1952	2042	2053	2153	2157	2252	2254	2353
Port Talbot d.	1806	1852	1906	2005	2056	2106	2205	2212	2304	2307	0007
Neath d.	1814	1900	1913	2014	2104	2113	2214	2223	2313	2314	0014
Swansea a.	1825	1912	1928	2025	2116	2128	2225	2239	2325	2326	0026
Carmarthen **136** a.	*1930**	2002	...	...	2208	...	...	2334	...	0017	...

		Ⓐ 🍷	Ⓐ 🍷	Ⓐ 🍷	Ⓐ 2🍷 M	Ⓐ 🍷	Ⓐ ✕	Ⓐ 2 M	Ⓐ 🍷	Ⓐ 2
Carmarthen **136** d.	Ⓐ	*0244*	...	...	0504	...	...	0550	...	0618
Swansea d.		0355	0458	0524	|	0559	0629	0640	0659	0709
Neath d.		0407	0509	0536	|	0610	0640	0651	0710	0720
Port Talbot d.		0414	0517	0543	0601	0618	0648	0658	0718	0735
Bridgend d.		0427	0528	0555	0613	0629	0659	0717	0729	0750
Cardiff Central a.		0513	0551	0617	0641	0652	0722	0745	0752	0818
London Paddington **133** a.		0732	0801	0830	...	0906	0929	...	0959	...

	Ⓐ 🍷	Ⓐ 2🍷 AM	Ⓐ ✕	Ⓐ ✕	Ⓐ 2🍷 AM	Ⓐ 2 S	Ⓐ 🍷	Ⓐ 2🍷 M	Ⓐ 🍷	Ⓐ 2🍷 AM	Ⓐ 2	Ⓐ ✕	Ⓐ 2🍷 M	Ⓐ 🍷	Ⓐ 2🍷 AM	Ⓐ 2	Ⓐ 🍷	Ⓐ 2🍷 M	Ⓐ 🍷	Ⓐ 2🍷 AM	Ⓐ 2	Ⓐ 🍷	Ⓐ 2🍷 M	Ⓐ 🍷	Ⓐ 2🍷 AM	Ⓐ 2
Carmarthen **136** d.	...	0700	...	0730	0759	...	*0830*	0900	...	1005	...	*1030*	1105	...	1205	...	*1230*	1305	...	1405	...	*1434*	1505	...	1605	...
Swansea d.	0729	0745	0759	0829	0855	0910	0929	0955	1029	1055	1110	1129	1155	1229	1250	1310	1329	1355	1429	1455	1510	1529	1555	1629	1655	1710
Neath d.	0740	0756	0810	0840	0906	0925	0940	1006	1040	1106	1125	1140	1206	1240	1306	1325	1340	1406	1440	1506	1525	1540	1606	1640	1706	1725
Port Talbot d.	0748	0803	0818	0848	0913	0936	0948	1013	1048	1113	1136	1148	1213	1248	1313	1336	1348	1413	1448	1513	1536	1548	1613	1648	1713	1736
Bridgend d.	0759	0818	0829	0859	0925	0952	0959	1025	1059	1125	1154	1159	1225	1259	1325	1354	1359	1425	1459	1525	1554	1559	1625	1659	1725	1754
Cardiff Central a.	0822	0844	0852	0922	0947	1017	1022	1047	1122	1147	1217	1222	1247	1322	1347	1416	1422	1447	1522	1547	1618	1622	1647	1722	1747	1817
London Pad'ton **133** a.	1027	...	1102	1132	*1202*	...	1232	*1302*	1329	*1402*	...	1432	*1502*	1530	*1602*	...	1630	*1702*	1730	*1802*	...	1827	*1902*	1932	*2002*	...

	Ⓐ 🍷	Ⓐ 2🍷 M	Ⓐ 🍷	Ⓐ 2 M	Ⓐ 2	Ⓐ 🍷	Ⓐ 2🍷 E	Ⓐ 🍷	Ⓐ 2 AC	Ⓐ 2 B	Ⓐ 2	Ⓐ 2		⑥ 🍷	⑥ 🍷	⑥ 2🍷 M	⑥ 🍷	⑥ 🍷	⑥ 2 M	⑥ 2	⑥ 🍷	⑥ 2🍷 AM	⑥ 🍷	⑥ 2🍷 AM	⑥ 2 S	⑥ 🍷
Carmarthen **136** d.	*1631*	1701	...	...	...	*1830*	1910	...	2005	2036	2105	...	⑥ ▲	*0244*	...	0504	...		0550	0618	...	0700	...	0759	...	*0830*
Swansea d.	1729	1755	1829	1858	1910	1929	1955	2029	2055	2135	2155	2230		0400	0444	|	0559	0629	0640	0709	0729	0745	0829	0855	0910	0929
Neath d.	1740	1806	1840	1909	1925	1940	2006	2040	2106	2150	2206	2245		0411	0455	|	0610	0640	0651	0724	0740	0756	0840	0906	0925	0940
Port Talbot d.	1748	1813	1848	1916	1936	1948	2013	2048	2113	2201	2213	2256		0419	0503	0601	0618	0648	0658	0735	0748	0803	0848	0913	0936	0948
Bridgend d.	1759	1825	1859	1928	1954	1959	2025	2059	2125	2216	2225	2311		0430	0514	0613	0629	0659	0717	0750	0759	0818	0859	0925	0952	0959
Cardiff Central a.	1822	1848	1922	1950	2018	2022	2047	2122	2147	2239	2250	2336		0453	0537	0641	0652	0722	0745	0818	0822	0844	0922	0947	1017	1022
London Pad'ton **133** a.	2030	...	2130	...	...	2251	...	2350v	...	...	...	...		0757	0821	...	0947	1016	...	...	1114	...	1225	...	...	1325

	⑥ 2🍷 M	⑥ 🍷	⑥ 2🍷 AM	⑥ 2	⑥ 🍷	⑥ 2🍷 M	⑥ 🍷	⑥ 2🍷 AM	⑥ 2	⑥ 🍷	⑥ 2🍷 M	⑥ 2🍷 AM	⑥ 2	⑥ 🍷	⑥ 2🍷 M	⑥ 🍷	⑥ 2🍷 AM	⑥ 2	⑥ 🍷	⑥ 2🍷 M	⑥ 🍷	⑥ 2🍷 M	⑥ 2	⑥ 🍷	⑥ 2🍷 E	⑥ 2 AC
Carmarthen **136** d.	0900	0935	1005	...	*1030*	1105	...	1205	...	*1230*	1305	1405	...	*1434*	1505	...	1605	...	*1631*	1701	...	1807	...	*1830*	1910	2005
Swansea d.	0955	1029	1055	1110	1129	1155	1229	1250	1310	1329	1355	1455	1510	1529	1555	1629	1655	1710	1729	1755	1829	1855	1910	1929	1955	2055
Neath d.	1006	1040	1106	1125	1140	1206	1240	1306	1325	1340	1406	1506	1525	1540	1606	1640	1706	1725	1740	1806	1840	1906	1925	1940	2006	2106
Port Talbot d.	1013	1048	1113	1136	1148	1213	1248	1313	1336	1348	1413	1513	1536	1548	1613	1648	1713	1736	1748	1813	1848	1913	1936	1948	2013	2113
Bridgend d.	1025	1059	1125	1154	1159	1225	1259	1325	1354	1359	1426	1525	1554	1559	1626	1659	1725	1755	1759	1825	1859	1925	1953	1959	2025	2125
Cardiff Central a.	1047	1122	1147	1217	1222	1247	1322	1347	1416	1422	1447	1546	1617	1622	1647	1722	1747	1818	1822	1847	1922	1950	2017	2022	2047	2147
London Pad'ton **133** a.	...	1413	...	...	1523	...	1618	...	...	1714	...	...	...	1930	...	2022	...	...	2125	...	2219	...	...	2333	...	...

	⑥ 2	⑥ 2	⑥ 2		⑦ 2 F	⑦ 🚌	⑦ 🚌	⑦ 🍷	⑦ 🍷	⑦ 🍷	⑦ 2🍷 M	⑦ 🍷	⑦ 🍷	⑦ 2🍷 M	⑦ 🍷	⑦ 🍷	⑦ 2🍷 AM	⑦ 🍷	⑦ 🍷	⑦ 2🍷 AM	⑦ 🍷	⑦ 🍷	⑦ 2🍷 AC	⑦ 🍷	⑦ 2 BH	⑦ 2 A
Carmarthen **136** d.	*2035*	2105	...	⑦ ▲	0241	...	...	...	...	...	1030	...	...	1235	...	*1400*	1442	...	*1545**	1631	...	*1745**	1835	*1915j*	2035	2235
Swansea d.	2135	2155	2220		0325	0725	0755	0905	1005	1105	1122	1205	1305	1335	1405	1505	1530	1605	1705	1735	1805	1905	1935	2005	2135	2335
Neath d.	2150	2206	2235		0336	0743	|	0917	1017	1117	1137	1217	1317	1347	1417	1517	1541	1617	1717	1746	1817	1917	1946	2017	2150	2346
Port Talbot d.	2201	2213	2246		0343	0755	|	0924	1024	1124	1148	1224	1324	1355	1424	1524	1549	1624	1724	1754	1824	1924	1954	2024	2201	2354
Bridgend d.	2216	2225	2301		0355	0820	|	0936	1036	1136	1203	1236	1336	1408	1436	1536	1602	1636	1736	1807	1836	1936	2007	2036	2216	0007
Cardiff Central a.	2239	2250	2326		0444	0855	0855	1002	1102	1202	1231	1302	1402	1430	1502	1602	1628	1702	1802	1826	1902	2002	2029	2102	2244	0050
London Pad'ton **133** a.	...	...	...		...	...	*1208*	1252	1408	1522	...	1608	1655	...	1813	1921	...	2007	2122	...	2211	2256	...	0021	...	...

A – To / from Milford Haven.
B – To / from Pembroke Dock.
C – From / to Crewe.
D – To Haverfordwest.
E – To Chester.
F – To / from Fishguard.
H – From / to Hereford.
M – From / to Manchester.
S – To / from Shrewsbury.
j – By 🚌. Change at Port Talbot.
n – Previous day.
v – 2342 on ⑤.
* – By 🚌.
▲ – Services on ⑥⑦ are subject to alteration.

SWANSEA - SOUTH WEST WALES 136

AW 2nd class

Services are subject to alteration on ⑥⑦

km		⑥	②–⑥		⚒	⚒	⚒ S	⚒	⚒		⚒🍷		⚒🍷	⚒	⑥◇🍷	⚒🍷 C	⚒ S	⚒🍷	⚒ C		⚒🍷 M	⚒🍷	⚒🍷	⚒🍷 M
	Cardiff Central **135** ... d.	...	2315	...	...	...	...	...	...	...	0540	...	...	0652	...	0758p	0809	...	0904	...	1004	1055	...	1104
0	**Swansea** d.	0005	0045	...	...	...	0436	...	0550	...	0654	...	0750	0805	0813	0900	0915	0950	1005	...	1105	|	1150	1205
18	Llanelli d.	0023	0102s	...	...	...	0452	...	0608	...	0711	...	0808	0823	0834	0919	0931	1008	1024	...	1121	1158	1208	1221
51	**Carmarthen** a.	0059	0137	...	...	...	...	...	0640	...	0742	...	0840	0851	0908	0947	...	1040	1051	...	1146	|	1240	1251
51	**Carmarthen** d.	...	...	...	0455	0545	...	0605	0643	...	0742	...	0856	<<	...	0952	...	1056	<<	...	1152	|	1256	<<
74	Whitland d.	...	...	...	0511	0601	...	0620	0700	...	0800	...	0912	...	...	1014	...	1112	...	...	1214	1233	1312	...
99	Tenby a.	...	...	...	|	0627	...	|	0728	...	|	...	0938	...	...	|	...	1138	...	...	|	|	1338	...
118	**Pembroke Dock** a.	...	...	...	|	0704	...	|	0817	...	|	...	1017	...	...	|	...	1217	...	...	|	|	1417	...
101	Haverfordwest a.	...	...	...	0534	...	...	0641	...	...	0821	...	...	...	...	1035	...	...	...	...	1235	|	...	...
115	**Milford Haven** a.	...	...	...	0557	...	...	0704	...	...	0844	...	...	...	...	1058	...	...	...	...	1258	|	...	...
118	Fishguard a.	...	...	...	...	...	...	...	...	...	...	...	...	...	...	...	...	...	...	...	...	1314	...	...
	Rosslare ⛴ **2030** a.	...	...	...	...	...	...	...	...	...	...	...	...	...	...	...	...	...	...	...	...	*1800*	...	...

	⚒🍷 M	⚒ S	⚒🍷 M	⚒🍷		⚒🍷 M	⚒	⚒🍷 M		Ⓐ🍷 M	⑥🍷 M	⚒🍷	⚒🍷 M	⚒ S	⚒🍷 M		⚒🍷 M	⚒	⑥🍷 M	Ⓐ◇🍷 L	⑥◇🍷 L		⚒🍷 M	⚒🍷 M	⚒
Cardiff Central **135** ... d.	1204	...	1304	...	...	1404	*1449*z	1504	...	1604	1604	*1649*z	1704	...	1802	...	1904	...	2001	1950	2028	...	*2122*	2209	*2235*a
Swansea d.	1305	1316	1400	1405	...	1505	1550	1605	...	1705	1705	1750	1809	1821	1905	...	2000	2005	|	2100	2131	...	2225	2306	2345
Llanelli d.	1321	1332	1416	1424	...	1524	1608	1621	...	1723	1727	1808	1826	1837	1921	...	2016	2024	2104	2116	2150	...	2242	2328	0001
Carmarthen a.	1346	...	1447	1456	...	1549	1640	1651	...	1752	1756	1840	1900	...	1946	...	2046	2056	2129	2149	2222	...	2311	0003	0025
Carmarthen d.	1352	...	...	1459	...	1552	1656	<<	...	1755	1759	1905	<<	...	1952	...	...	2059	2204	...	...	...	2317	...	0027
Whitland d.	1407	...	...	1515	...	1616	1712	...	...	1814	1814	1921	...	...	2007	...	...	2115	2221	...	...	...	2332	...	0043
Tenby a.	|	...	...	1541	...	|	1738	...	...	|	|	1947	...	...	|	...	...	2143	|	...	...	...	|	...	|
Pembroke Dock a.	|	...	...	1617	...	|	1817	...	...	|	|	2022	...	...	|	...	...	2219	|	...	...	...	|	...	|
Haverfordwest a.	1428	...	...	...	...	1637	...	...	...	1835	1835	...	...	...	2028	...	...	...	2242	...	...	...	2353p	...	|
Milford Haven a.	1451	...	...	...	...	1700	...	...	...	1858	1858	...	...	...	2051	...	...	...	2305	...	...	...	0011y	...	|
Fishguard a.	...	...	...	...	...	...	...	...	...	...	...	...	...	...	...	...	...	...	...	...	...	...	...	...	0123
Rosslare ⛴ **2030** a.	...	...	...	...	...	...	...	...	...	...	...	...	...	...	...	...	...	...	...	...	...	...	...	...	*0615*

⑦	⑦		⑦	⑦	⑦ S		⑦ H	⑦	⑦	⑦ 🚌	⑦🍷 C	⑦	⑦ S	⑦	⑦ 🚌	⑦🍷 M	⑦ 🚌	⑦🍷 M	⑦ 🚌		⑦🍷 M		⑦	⑦
Cardiff Central **135** ... d.	2241n	...	0930	...	...	...	1120	...	...	*1331*	1403	...	...	...	*1531*	1618	*1731*	1818	...	...	2022	...	2130	2235
Swansea d.	0005	...	1043	...	1109	...	1217	...	...	1435	1506	...	1516	...	1635	1735	1835	1917	...	...	2119	...	2250	2330
Llanelli d.	0022s	...	1106	...	1127	...	1235	...	...	1450	1522	...	1534	...	1650	1743	1850	1935	...	...	2137	...	2306	2347
Carmarthen a.	0058	...	1137	...	...	...	1305	...	...	1530	1553	...	...	...	1730	1814	1930	2002	...	...	2208	...	2334	0017
Carmarthen d.	...	...	1205	...	...	...	1308	1405	1420	...	...	1605	...	1705	...	1816	...	2009	2030	...	2210	...	...	0019
Whitland d.	...	...	1224	1230	...	...	1324	1421	1436	...	...	1621	...	1721	...	1833	...	2034	2050	...	2227	...	...	0034
Tenby a.	...	...	|	1300	...	...	|	|	1504	...	...	|	...	1749	...	|	...	2101	|	...	|	...	...	|
Pembroke Dock a.	...	...	|	...	...	...	|	|	1553	...	...	|	...	1825	...	|	...	2140	|	...	|	...	...	|
Haverfordwest a.	...	...	1246	...	...	...	|	1444	...	...	...	1644	...	...	...	1854	...	...	2145	...	2248	...	...	|
Milford Haven a.	...	...	1306	...	...	...	|	1505	...	...	...	1705	...	...	...	1917	...	...	2210	...	2311	...	...	|
Fishguard a.	...	...	...	...	...	...	1400	...	...	...	...	...	...	...	...	...	...	...	...	...	...	...	...	0115
Rosslare ⛴ **2030** a.	...	...	...	...	...	...	*1800*	...	...	...	...	...	...	...	...	...	...	...	...	...	...	...	...	*0615*

	②–⑥		⚒		⚒🍷 M		⚒ M	⚒		⚒🍷 M	Ⓐ◇✕ L	⚒🍷 M	⚒ S	⚒🍷	⚒🍷 M	⑥◇✕ L	⚒🍷 M	⚒🍷	⚒🍷 M		⚒🍷 M	⚒ S	⚒🍷	⚒🍷 M
Rosslare ⛴ **2030** d.	...	...	*2115*n	...	...	...	...	...	...	...	...	...	...	...	...	...	...	...	...	...	...	...	...	...
Fishguard d.	...	...	0150	...	...	...	...	...	...	...	...	...	...	...	...	...	...	...	...	...	...	...	...	...
Milford Haven d.	0015	...	|	...	...	...	...	...	...	0605	...	0705	...	...	...	...	0910	...	...	...	1110	...	...	...
Haverfordwest d.	0030	...	|	...	...	...	...	...	...	0620	...	0720	...	...	...	...	0925	...	...	...	1125	...	...	...
Pembroke Dock d.	|	...	|	...	...	...	...	...	...	|	...	|	...	0705	...	...	|	0905	...	...	|	...	1105	...
Tenby d.	|	...	|	...	...	...	...	...	...	|	...	|	...	0740	...	...	|	0942	...	...	|	...	1142	...
Whitland d.	0050	...	0222	...	...	...	...	...	...	0640	...	0740	...	0808	...	...	0945	1009	...	...	1145	...	1209	...
Carmarthen a.	0112	...	0239	...	...	...	...	...	...	0656	...	0756	...	0827	...	...	1001	1026	...	...	1201	...	1226	...
Carmarthen d.	...	...	0244	...	0504	...	0550	0618	...	0700	0730	0759	...	0830	0900	0935	1005	1030	1105	...	1205	...	1230	1305
Llanelli d.	...	...	0306	...	0528	...	0618	0646	...	0724	0804	0827	0845	0900	0926	1003	1028	1100	1129	...	1229	1233	1300	1329
Swansea a.	...	...	0325	...	|	...	0635	0706	...	0743	0822	0848	0907	0922	0946	1021	1045	1122	1146	...	1246	1301	1322	1348
Cardiff Central **135** ... a.	...	...	*0513*q	...	0641	...	0745	0818	...	0844	0922	0947	1017	*1022*	1047	1122	1147	*1222*	1247	...	1347	*1416*	*1422*	1447

	⚒🍷 M	⚒	⚒🍷	⚒🍷 M		⚒🍷 M	⚒	⚒🍷 M	⚒ S		⚒🍷	⚒🍷	⚒🍷 E		⚒ D	⑥	Ⓐ	⚒	⚒ S	⚒	⚒		⚒		⚒
Rosslare ⛴ **2030** d.	...	*0900*	...	...	...	...	...	...	...	...	...	...	...	...	...	...	...	...	...	...	...	...	...	...	...
Fishguard d.	...	1334	...	...	...	...	...	...	...	...	...	...	...	...	...	...	...	...	...	...	...	...	...	...	...
Milford Haven d.	1310	|	...	...	...	1510	...	...	...	...	1710	...	...	...	1910	...	...	...	...	2120	...	...	...	...	2315
Haverfordwest d.	1325	|	...	...	...	1525	...	...	...	...	1725	...	...	...	1925	...	...	...	...	2135	...	...	...	...	2330
Pembroke Dock d.	|	|	1305	...	...	|	1505	...	...	...	|	1705	...	...	|	1916	1916	...	...	|	2111	...	2222	...	|
Tenby d.	|	|	1342	...	...	|	1544	...	...	...	|	1742	...	...	|	1947	1947	...	...	†	2145	...	2251	...	|
Whitland d.	1345	1406	1413	...	...	1545	1611	...	...	...	1745	1809	...	...	1945	2014	2016	...	...	2155	2214	...	2318	...	2357
Carmarthen a.	1401	|	1431	...	...	1601	1628	...	...	...	1801p	1826	...	...	2001	2033	2033	...	...	2216	2232	...	2340	...	0018
Carmarthen d.	1405	|	1434	1505	...	1605	1631	1701	...	...	1805	1830	1910	...	2005	2035	2036	2105	...	...	2235	...	...	...	...
Llanelli d.	1429	1443	1504	1529	...	1629	1701	1729	1736	...	1833	1900	1934	...	2029	2106	2110	2133	2144	...	2305	...	...	...	...
Swansea a.	1448	|	1522	1546	...	1648	1722	1746	1806	...	1852	1922	1951	...	2050	2124	2133	2152	2213	...	2329	...	...	...	...
Cardiff Central **135** ... a.	1547	1604	*1622*	1647	...	1747	*1822*	1848	*1922*	...	1950	*2022*	2047	...	2147	*2239*	2239	2250	*2336*j	...	...	...	...	...	...

⑦	⑦		⑦🍷 M		⑦🍷 M		⑦	⑦🍷 M	⑦ S	⑦	⑦ 🚌	⑦🍷 M	⑦	⑦ 🚌	⑦🍷 D	⑦ 🚌	⑦ S		⑦ H	⑦		⑦	⑦	⑦
Rosslare ⛴ **2030** d.	*2115*n	...	...	...	...	...	...	...	...	*0900*	...	...	...	...	...	...	...	...	...	...	...	...	...	...
Fishguard d.	0150	...	...	...	...	...	...	...	...	1430	...	...	...	...	...	...	...	...	...	...	...	...	...	...
Milford Haven d.	|	...	...	...	...	...	...	1335	...	|	...	1535	...	...	1735	...	...	...	...	1935	...	2135	...	2315
Haverfordwest d.	|	...	...	...	...	...	...	1350	...	|	...	1550	...	...	1750	...	...	...	...	1950	...	2150	...	2330
Pembroke Dock d.	|	...	...	...	...	...	...	|	...	|	...	|	1605	...	|	...	...	...	1905	|	...	|	2205	|
Tenby d.	|	...	...	...	...	...	1305	|	...	|	...	|	1635	...	|	...	...	...	1935	|	...	|	2235	|
Whitland d.	0222	...	...	...	...	...	1334	1411	...	1502	...	1610	1704	...	1811	...	...	...	2004	2012	...	2213	2304	2351
Carmarthen a.	0238	...	...	...	...	...	1352	1428	...	1520	...	1627	1725	...	1828	...	...	...	2021	2030	...	2230	2325	0007
Carmarthen d.	0241	...	1030	...	1235	...	1400	1442	...	...	1545	1631	...	1745	1835	1845	...	...	2035	<<	...	2235	...	...
Llanelli d.	0304	...	1058	...	1304	...	1430	1506	1545	...	1630	1659	...	1830	1903	1930	1952	...	2105	...	...	2305	...	...
Swansea a.	0321	...	1118	...	1321	...	1452	1525	1607	...	1655	1719	...	1855	1927	1955	2013	...	2126	...	...	2326	...	...
Cardiff Central **135** ... a.	0444	...	1231	...	1430	...	*1602*	1628	*1802*	...	...	1826	...	*2002*	2029	...	2130	...	2244	...	...	0050	...	...

C – From Crewe.
D – To Crewe.
E – To Chester.
L – From / to London.
H – From / to Hereford.
M – From / to Manchester.

S – To / from Shrewsbury.

a – *2228* on ⑥.
j – *2326* on ⑥.
n – Previous day.
p – 4–6 minutes later on ⑥.

q – *0453* on ⑥.
s – Stops to set down only.
v – Change at Swansea.
y – Not ⑦.
z – 21 minutes earlier on ⑥.

<< Connects with train in column to the left.

◇ – Also conveys 🛏.

137 CARDIFF - BRISTOL - SALISBURY - PORTSMOUTH

2nd class GW

km			Ⓐ	Ⓐ		Ⓐ 🍷	Ⓐ	Ⓐ		Ⓐ 🍷	Ⓐ	Ⓐ 🍷	Ⓐ W	Ⓐ ◇🍷	Ⓐ	Ⓐ 🍷	Ⓐ W	Ⓐ 🍷	Ⓐ	Ⓐ	Ⓐ 🍷	Ⓐ W	Ⓐ 🍷	Ⓐ
0	**Cardiff** Central ... d.	Ⓐ	...	...	...	...	...	...	...	0630	...	0730	...	...	0800	0830	...	0930	...	...	1030	...	1130	...
19	Newport ... d.		...	...	...	...	...	...	...	0644	...	0744	...	...	0815	0844	...	0944	...	...	1044	...	1144	...
61	**Bristol** Temple Meads ... d.		...	...	...	0545	...	0643	...	0722	0749	0822	0840	0850	0909	0922	0949	1022	...	1049	1122	1149	1222	1239
80	Bath ... d.		...	...	...	0602	...	0700	...	0736	0807	0836	0857	0905	0927	0935	1007	1036	...	1107	1136	1207	1236	1257
95	Bradford on Avon ... d.		...	...	...	0618	...	0715	...	0747	0823	0847	0912	0920	0938	|	1023	1047	...	1123	1147	1223	1247	1312
100	Trowbridge ... d.		...	...	...	0625	...	0721	...	0753	0829	0853	0918	0927	0944	0950	1029	1053	...	1129	1153	1229	1253	1318
107	**Westbury** ... d.		0526	0549	...	0635	0703	0730	...	0801	0836	0901	0925	0939r	0951	0958	1036	1101	1107	1136	1201	1236	1301	1327
114	Warminster ... d.		0534	0556	...	0643	0713	...	...	0808	...	0908	...	0946	...	1007	...	1108	1116	...	1208	...	1308	1336
146	**Salisbury** ... 113 d.		0558	0620	...	0711	0736	...	...	0832	...	0932	...	1020c	...	1030	...	1132	1139	...	1232	...	1332	1359
	London Waterloo ... 113 a.		0744	0814	...	0846	0917	...	...	1019	...	1119	...	1149	...	1219	...	|	1319	...	1419	...	1519	1549
173	Romsey ... d.		...	0638	...	0730	0756	...	...	0850	...	0950	...	...	...	1051	...	1150	1202	...	1250	...	1350	1419
184	**Southampton** Central ... a.		...	0649	...	0741	0809	...	...	0902	...	1002	...	...	...	1102	...	1202	1218	...	1302	...	1402	1432
208	Fareham ... a.		...	0714	...	0805	0859	...	...	0926	...	1026	...	...	...	1126	...	1226	1259	...	1326	...	1426	1455
	Brighton **110** ... a.		...	0919	...	0948a	1018	...	...	1118	...	1218	...	...	...	1318	...	|	1418	...	1518	...	1447	1614
225	Portsmouth & Southsea ... a.		...	0738	...	0824	0940	...	...	0947	...	1047	...	...	...	1147	...	1247	1340	...	1347	...	1452	1528z
226	**Portsmouth** Harbour ... a.		...	0745	...	0830	...	...	...	0952	...	1052	...	...	...	1152	...	1252	...	...	1352	...	...	1532z

	Ⓐ 🍷	Ⓐ	Ⓐ 🍷	Ⓐ W	Ⓐ 🍷	Ⓐ	Ⓐ ◇🍷	Ⓐ 🍷	Ⓐ W	Ⓐ	Ⓐ 🍷	Ⓐ W	Ⓐ	Ⓐ 🍷	Ⓐ	Ⓐ 🍷	Ⓐ	Ⓐ 🍷	Ⓐ W	Ⓐ 🍷	Ⓐ	Ⓐ ◇		Ⓐ
Cardiff Central ... d.	1230	...	1330	...	1430	...	...	1530	...	1600	1630	...	1700	1730	...	1830	...	1930	...	2030	2100	...	...	2200
Newport ... d.	1244	...	1344	...	1444	...	...	1544	...	1615	1644	...	1715	1744	...	1844	...	1944	...	2044	2114	...	...	2217
Bristol Temple Meads ... d.	1322	1349	1422	1449	1522	1543	1552	1622	1649	1707	1722	1749	1807	1822	1849	1922	1949	2022	2049	2122	2200r	2225	...	2316
Bath ... d.	1336	1407	1436	1507	1536	1601	1606	1636	1707	1714	1736	1807	1825	1836	1907	1936	2007	2036	2107	2136	2219	2238	...	2335
Bradford on Avon ... d.	1347	1423	1447	1523	1547	1615	1622	1647	1723	1741	|	1823	1841	1847	1923	1947	2023	2047	2123	2147	2233	2251	...	2351
Trowbridge ... d.	1353	1429	1453	1529	1553	1621	1628	1653	1729	1747	1753	1829	1847	1853	1929	1953	2029	2053	2129	2153	2239	2257	...	2357
Westbury ... d.	1401	1436	1501	1536	1601	1628	1639	1701	1736	1756	1801	1836	1856	1901	1937	2001	2036	2101	2136	2201	2247	2304	...	0004
Warminster ... d.	1408	...	1508	...	1608	...	1647	1708	...	...	1808	...	...	1908	1946	2008	...	2108	...	2208	...	2311	...	...
Salisbury ... 113 d.	1432	...	1532	...	1632	...	1720c	1732	...	...	1832	...	...	1933	2011	2032	...	2132	...	2232	...	2334	...	...
London Waterloo ... 113 a.	1619	...	1719	...	1817	...	1845	1919	...	...	2019	...	...	|	2204	2257	...	|	...	|	...	...	...	...
Romsey ... d.	1450	...	1550	...	1650	...	...	1750	...	...	1850	...	...	1951	2032	2049	...	2150	...	2250	...	...	...	...
Southampton Central ... a.	1502	...	1602	...	1702	...	...	1804	...	...	1901	...	...	2004	2045	2103	...	2204	...	2304	...	...	...	...
Fareham ... a.	1526	...	1626	...	1726	...	...	1826	...	...	1926	...	...	2026	...	2126	...	2239	...	2327	...	...	...	...
Brighton **110** ... a.	1718	...	1818	...	1918	...	...	2018	...	...	2118	...	...	2222	...	2318a	...	|	...	2347	...	...	...	...
Portsmouth & Southsea ... a.	1547	...	1651	...	1747	...	...	1851	...	...	1947	...	...	2051	...	2147	...	2300	...	2352	...	...	...	...
Portsmouth Harbour ... a.	1552	...	1657	...	1752	...	...	1857	...	...	1952	...	...	2057	...	2152	...	2304	...	...	...	...	...	...

		⑥	⑥	⑥		⑥	⑥	⑥ 🍷	⑥ W	⑥ ◇🍷	⑥ 🍷	⑥ W	⑥ 🍷	⑥	⑥	⑥ 🍷	⑥ W	⑥ 🍷	⑥		⑥ 🍷	⑥	⑥ 🍷	⑥ W🍷
Cardiff Central ... d.	⑥	...	...	0455	...	0630	...	0730	...	...	0830	...	0930	...	...	1030	...	1130	...	...	1230	...	1330	...
Newport ... d.		...	...	0509	...	0644	...	0744	...	...	0844	...	0944	...	...	1044	...	1144	...	...	1244	...	1344	...
Bristol Temple Meads ... d.		0545	...	0643	...	0724r	0749	0824r	0840	0850	0924r	0949	1024r	...	1049	1124r	1149	1224r	1239	...	1324r	1349	1424r	1449
Bath ... d.		0602	...	0700	...	0737	0806	0837	0857	0905	0937	1007	1037	...	1107	1137	1207	1237	1256	...	1337	1405	1437	1507
Bradford on Avon ... d.		0618	...	0715	...	0748	0821	0848	0912	0920	0948	1022	1048	...	1121	1148	1222	1248	1308	...	1348	1421	1448	1521
Trowbridge ... d.		0624	...	0721	...	0754	0827	0854	0918	0927	0954	1028	1054	...	1127	1154	1228	1254	1315	...	1354	1427	1454	1527
Westbury ... d.		0639r	0703	0728	...	0802	0834	0902	0925	0939r	1002	1034	1102	1107	1134	1202	1235	1302	1327	...	1402	1434	1502	1534
Warminster ... d.		0646	0713	...	...	0809	...	0909	...	0946	1009	...	1109	1116	...	1209	...	1309	1336	...	1409	...	1509	...
Salisbury ... 113 d.		0724c	0737	...	...	0833	...	0933	...	1020c	1032	...	1133	1139	...	1233	...	1333	1359	...	1433	...	1533	...
London Waterloo ... 113 a.		0849	|	...	...	1019	...	1119	...	1149	1219	...	|	1319	...	1419	...	1519	1549	...	1649	...	1719	...
Romsey ... d.		0744	0756	...	...	0851	...	0951	...	...	1050	...	1151	1202	...	1251	...	1351	1419	...	1451	...	1551	...
Southampton Central ... a.		0802	0807	...	...	0902	...	1002	...	...	1102	...	1202	1218	...	1302	...	1402	1432	...	1502	...	1602	...
Fareham ... a.		0826	0859	...	...	0926	...	1026	...	...	1126	...	1226	1259	...	1326	...	1426	1455	...	1526	...	1626	...
Brighton **110** ... a.		|	1018	...	...	1118	...	1218	...	...	1318	...	|	1418	...	1518	...	|	1614	...	1718	...	1818	...
Portsmouth & Southsea ... a.		0845	0940	...	...	0945	...	1045	...	...	1145	...	1245	1340	...	1345	...	1445	1540y	...	1545	...	1645	...
Portsmouth Harbour ... a.		0849	...	...	...	0949	...	1049	...	...	1149	...	1249	...	...	1349	...	1449	...	...	1549	...	1649	...

	⑥ 🍷	⑥	⑥ ◇🍷	⑥ 🍷	⑥ W	⑥ 🍷	⑥ W	⑥ 🍷	⑥	⑥	⑥ 🍷	⑥	⑥ 🍷	⑥ W	⑥ 🍷	⑥	⑥ ◇		⑥			⑦ 🍷		⑦ 🍷
Cardiff Central ... d.	1430	...	...	1530	...	1630	...	1730	...	...	1830	...	1930	...	2030	...	2100	...	2200	...	⑦	0805	...	0909
Newport ... d.	1444	...	...	1544	...	1644	...	1744	...	...	1844	...	1944	...	2044	...	2115	...	2217	...		0819	...	0923
Bristol Temple Meads ... d.	1524r	1543	1552	1624r	1649	1724r	1749	1824r	...	1849	1924r	1949	2024r	2049	2124r	2151	2223	...	2310	...	▲	0910r	...	1010
Bath ... d.	1537	1559	1606	1637	1707	1739	1807	1837	...	1907	1937	2007	2037	2107	2137	2207	2236	...	2327	...		0927	...	1022
Bradford on Avon ... d.	1548	1615	1622	1648	1721	1750	1822	1848	...	1921	1948	2022	2048	2121	2148	2223	2247	...	2342	...		0939	...	1038
Trowbridge ... d.	1554	1621	1628	1654	1727	1756	1828	1854	...	1927	1954	2028	2054	2127	2154	2229	2253	...	2348	...		0945	...	1044
Westbury ... d.	1602	1628	1639	1702	1734	1803	1835	1902	1906	1934	2002	2035	2102	2134	2202	2236	2304	...	2355	...		0955	...	1100c
Warminster ... d.	1609	...	1647	1709	...	1811	...	1909	1915	...	2009	...	2109	...	2209	...	2311	...	...	...		1004	...	1107
Salisbury ... 113 d.	1633	...	1720c	1733	...	1834	...	1933	1939	...	2033	...	2133	...	2232	...	2334	...	...	...		1031	...	1131
London Waterloo ... 113 a.	1819	...	1849	1919	...	2026	...	|	2204	...	2257	...	|	...	|	...	...	...	...	...		1303	...	1404
Romsey ... d.	1651	...	...	1751	...	1853	...	1951	2002	...	2051	...	2151	...	2251	...	...	...	...	...		1050	...	1149
Southampton Central ... a.	1702	...	...	1802	...	1903	...	2002	2018	...	2102	...	2202	...	2302	...	...	...	...	...		1100	...	1204
Fareham ... a.	1726	...	...	1826	...	1926	...	2026	2059	...	2126	...	2225	...	2325	...	...	...	...	...		1137	...	1228
Brighton **110** ... a.	1918	...	...	2020	...	2118	...	|	2222	...	2318a	...	0025a	...	|	...	...	...	...	...		...	...	...
Portsmouth & Southsea ... a.	1745	...	...	1846	...	1945	...	2044	2140	...	2145	...	2245	...	2344	...	...	...	...	...		...	...	...
Portsmouth Harbour ... a.	1749	...	...	1849	...	1949	...	2049	...	...	2149	...	2249	...	2348	...	...	...	...	...		...	...	...

	⑦ 🍷		⑦ 🍷		⑦ 🍷	⑦ W	⑦ 🍷		⑦ 🍷	⑦ ◇🍷	⑦ 🍷		⑦ 🍷	⑦ W	⑦ 🍷	⑦ 🍷	⑦ 🍷	⑦ 🍷	⑦ 🍷	⑦ W	⑦ 🍷	⑦ ◇	⑦	⑦ 🍷
Cardiff Central ... d.	1009	...	1109	...	1209	...	1309	...	1409	...	1509	...	1609	...	1709	...	1809	1835	1909	...	2009	...	...	2205
Newport ... d.	1023	...	1123	...	1223	...	1323	...	1423	...	1523	...	1623	...	1723	1759	1823	1859	1923	...	2023	...	...	2219
Bristol Temple Meads ... d.	1110r	...	1210r	...	1310	1320	1410r	...	1510r	1604	1610	...	1710	1750	1810r	1850b	1910	1950b	2010r	2050	2110r	2135	2215	2310
Bath ... d.	1127	...	1222	...	1327	1337	1423	...	1527	1620	1622	...	1727	1807	1827	1902	1927	2002	2022	2107	2122	2149	2232	2322
Bradford on Avon ... d.	1139	...	1238	...	1339	1354	1439	...	1539	1631	1638	...	1739	1823	1843	1914	1939	|	2038	2124	2136	2200	2249	2334
Trowbridge ... d.	1146	...	1244	...	1346	1400	1445	...	1545	1637	1644	...	1745	1829	1850	1920	1945	2018	2044	2130	2142	2206	2255	2340
Westbury ... d.	1203c	...	1255	...	1403c	1407	1500r	...	1558r	1646	1700c	...	1800r	1836	1901	1929	1955	2027	2055	2137	2155r	2215	2302	2350
Warminster ... d.	1212	...	1302	...	1412	...	1507	...	1607	1653	1707	...	1809	...	1910	1937	2004	2034	2103	...	2202	2222	...	2358
Salisbury ... 113 d.	1236	...	1329	...	1448c	...	1531	...	1631	1726c	1731	...	1833	...	1936	2000	2030	2058	2129	...	2229	2246	...	...
London Waterloo ... 113 a.	1458	...	1604	...	1658	...	1804	...	|	1858	2004	...	2058	...	|	2204	|	2258	|	...	|	...	...	...
Romsey ... d.	1259	...	1347	...	1515	...	1551	...	1649	...	1749	...	1851	...	1959	2019	2048	2116	2148	...	2247	...	...	...
Southampton Central ... a.	1310	...	1358	...	1525	...	1606	...	1704	...	1804	...	1904	...	2010	2029	2059	2127	2158	...	2258	...	...	...
Fareham ... a.	1333	...	1420	...	1550	...	1629	...	1728	...	1828	...	1929	...	2033	...	2121	2149	2221	...	2320	...	...	...
Brighton **110** ... a.	1504	...	...	...	1705	...	...	...	...	...	...	...	...	...	2200	...	...	...	...	...	...	...	...	...
Portsmouth & Southsea ... a.	1428*	...	...	...	1653*	...	...	...	...	...	...	...	...	...	2125‡	...	...	...	...	...	...	...	...	...
Portsmouth Harbour ... a.	1435*	...	...	...	1700*	...	...	...	...	...	...	...	...	...	2132‡	...	...	...	...	...	...	...	...	...

W – To Weymouth.

a – Change at Fratton.
b – Arrives 16 minutes earlier.

c – Arrives 9–11 minutes earlier.
r – Arrives 6–8 minutes earlier.
y – Change at Fareham.
z – Change at Havant.

‡ – By 🚌 (change at Havant).
* – By 🚌 (change at Cosham).
◇ – Also conveys [1].

▲ – Services on ⑦ are subject to alteration due to enginering work. Allow ± 60 minutes for replacement connections (partly by 🚌) Fareham - Portsmouth.

138 (PORTSMOUTH -) RYDE - SHANKLIN

2nd class IL

km		⚒	Ⓐ		⚒		⚒						Ⓑ	⚒	⑦	⚒	⑦	⚒
	Portsmouth Harbour ⛴ d.	0515	0545	0615	0645	0715	0745	0815	0845	and at the same	1815	1845	1915	1945	2015	2045	2115	2145
0	**Ryde** Pier Head ... d.	0549	0608	0649	0708	0749	0808	0849	0908	minutes past each	1849	1908	1949	2008	2049	2108	2149	2208
14	**Shanklin** ... a.	0613	0632	0713	0732	0813	0832	0913	0932	hour until	1913	1932	2013	2032	2113	2132	2213	2232

⛴ – Operated by Wightlink. Through rail fares available.

GW 2nd class — PORTSMOUTH - SALISBURY - BRISTOL - CARDIFF — 137

	Ⓐ	Ⓐ		Ⓐ	Ⓐ	Ⓐ ◇	Ⓐ W	Ⓐ	Ⓐ	Ⓐ W	Ⓐ	Ⓐ		Ⓐ	Ⓐ W	Ⓐ	Ⓐ	Ⓐ	Ⓐ	Ⓐ	Ⓐ		Ⓐ W	Ⓐ
Portsmouth Harbour d.		...	...	...	...	...	...	...	0600	...	...	0651	...	...	...	0822	...	0922	...	0932y	1022	...	...	1122
Portsmouth & Southsea d.		...	...	...	...	...	...	...	0604	...	...	0655	...	...	...	0827	...	0927	...	0936y	1027	...	...	1127
Brighton 110 d.		...	...	...	...	...	...	...	|	...	...	*0530*	...	*0633*	...	*0706*	...	*0803a*	...	0900	*0903a*	...	...	*1003a*
Fareham d.		...	...	...	...	...	...	...	0624	...	...	0718	...	*0747*	...	0847	...	0947	...	1014	1047	...	...	1147
Southampton Central d.		...	...	...	...	...	...	...	0646	...	...	0747	...	0824	...	0910	...	1010	...	1040	1110	...	...	1210
Romsey d.		...	...	...	...	...	...	...	0700	...	...	0800	...	0835	...	0921	...	1021	...	1051	1121	...	...	1221
London Waterloo 113 d.		...	...	...	...	...	...	...	|	...	...	|	...	*0710*	...	*0750*	...	*0850*	*0920*	|	*0950*	...	...	*1050*
Salisbury 113 d.		...	...	0612	...	0640	...	...	0720	...	...	0821	...	0903	...	0941	...	1041	1052	1111	1141	...	...	1241
Warminster d.		...	...	0632	...	0700	...	0723	0742	...	...	0843	...	0923	...	1001	1028	1101	1112	1131	1201	...	...	1301
Westbury d.		0558	...	0642	0657	0707	0718	0738r	0752	0817	0845	0854	...	0933	0938	1008	1038	1108	1119	1138	1208	...	1249	1308
Trowbridge d.		0604	...	0648	0703	0713	0724	0744	0758	0823	0851	0900	...	...	0944	1014	1044	1114	1125	1144	1214	...	1255	1314
Bradford on Avon d.		0610	...	0654	0709	0720	0730	0750	0804	0829	0857	0908	...	...	0950	1020	1050	1120	1131	1150	1220	...	1301	1320
Bath a.		0626	...	0710	0726	0732	0747	0806	0820	0845	0913	0922	...	...	1007	1033	1107	1133	1145	1207	1233	...	1317	1333
Bristol Temple Meads a.		0646	...	0729	0745	0752	0806	0825	0839	0904	0932	0939	...	...	1026	1047	1126	1147	1205	1226	1247	...	1336	1347
Newport a.		0726	...	...	0824	...	*0904q*	...	0923	*0958*	...	1023	...	...	...	1124	...	1224	*1304*	...	1324	...	...	1424
Cardiff Central a.		0745	...	...	0842	...	*0923q*	...	0940	*1017*	...	1040	...	...	...	1141	...	1241	*1327*	...	1341	...	...	1441

	Ⓐ	Ⓐ		Ⓐ	Ⓐ ◇	Ⓐ W	Ⓐ	Ⓐ		Ⓐ	Ⓐ W	Ⓐ	Ⓐ	Ⓐ	Ⓐ W	Ⓐ	Ⓐ	Ⓐ	Ⓐ	Ⓐ	Ⓐ ◇	Ⓐ W	Ⓐ	Ⓐ
Portsmouth Harbour d.	...	...	...	1222	...	...	1322	...	...	1422	...	1522	...	1622	...	1722	1732y	1822	...	1922	...	...	2022	...
Portsmouth & Southsea d.	...	...	...	1227	...	...	1327	...	...	1427	...	1527	...	1627	...	1727	1736y	1827	...	1927	...	...	2027	...
Brighton 110 d.	...	*1033*	...	*1103a*	...	...	*1203a*	...	...	*1303a*	...	*1403a*	...	*1503a*	...	*1603a*	1700	*1703a*	...	*1808a*	...	...	*1903a*	...
Fareham d.	...	*1153*	...	1247	...	...	1347	...	...	1447	...	1547	...	1647	...	1747	1813	1847	...	1947	...	...	2047	...
Southampton Central d.	...	1226	...	1310	...	...	1410	...	...	1510	...	1610	...	1710	...	1810	1840	1910	...	2010	...	...	2110	2120
Romsey d.	...	1239	...	1321	...	...	1421	...	...	1521	...	1621	...	1721	...	1821	1851	1921	...	2021	...	...	2121	2131
London Waterloo 113 d.	...	*1120*	...	*1150*	1220	...	*1250*	...	...	*1350*	...	*1450*	...	*1550*	...	*1650*	*1720*	*1750*	...	*1850*	1920	...	*1950*	*2020*
Salisbury 113 d.	...	1308r	...	1341	1352c	...	1441	...	...	1541	...	1641	...	1740	...	1841	1911	1941	...	2041	2057r	...	2141	2158
Warminster d.	...	1331	...	1401	1412	...	1501	1528	...	1601	...	1701	1728	1800	...	1901	1930	2001	...	2101	2117	...	2201	2218
Westbury d.	1338	1342	...	1408	1419	1445	1508	1538	...	1608	1638	1708	1738	1808	1838	1908	1938	2008	2038	2108	2124	2138	2208	2240d
Trowbridge d.	1344	1351	...	1414	1425	1451	1514	1544	...	1614	1644	1714	1744	1814	1844	1914	1944	2014	2044	2114	2130	2144	2214	2246
Bradford on Avon d.	1350	1357	...	1420	1431	1457	1520	1550	...	1620	1650	1720	1750	1822	1850	1920	1950	2020	2050	2121	2136	2150	2220	2252
Bath a.	1407	1413	...	1433	1445	1513	1533	1607	...	1633	1708	1733	1808	1835	1906	1935	2008	2035	2106	2135	2150	2206	2233	2308
Bristol Temple Meads a.	1426	*1442*	...	1447	1500	1532	1547	1626	...	1647	1727	1747	1827	1850	1925	1949	2027	2050	2127	2150	2206	2227	2247	2328
Newport a.	...	...	...	1524	...	...	1624	...	...	1726	...	1826	...	1925	...	2023	...	2128	...	2235	...	...	2335	...
Cardiff Central a.	...	...	...	1541	...	...	1642	...	...	1745	...	1843	...	1941	...	2041	...	2145	...	2254	...	...	2355	...

	Ⓐ	Ⓐ		⑥	⑥	⑥	⑥ ◇	⑥	⑥		⑥ W	⑥		⑥	⑥ W	⑥		⑥	⑥	⑥	⑥	⑥ W	⑥	⑥
Portsmouth Harbour d.	...	2122	...		...	...	...	...	0600	...	...	0704	...	...	...	0822	...	0922	...	...	1022	...	1122	...
Portsmouth & Southsea d.	...	2127	...		...	...	...	...	0604	...	...	0708	...	...	...	0827	...	0927	...	*0936y*	1027	...	1127	...
Brighton 110 d.	*2030*	|	...		...	...	...	...	|	...	...	*0527*	...	*0631*	...	*0703a*	...	*0803a*	...	0900	*0903a*	...	*1003a*	*1033*
Fareham d.	2153	2148	...		...	...	...	...	0625	...	...	0729	...	*0753*	...	0847	...	0947	...	1015	1047	...	1147	*1153*
Southampton Central d.	2217	2222	...		...	...	...	...	0647	...	...	0752	...	0827	...	0910	...	1010	...	1040	1110	...	1210	1226
Romsey d.	...	2233	...		...	...	...	...	0659	...	...	0809	...	0838	...	0921	...	1021	...	1051	1121	...	1221	1237
London Waterloo 113 d.	...	*2120*	...		...	...	...	...	|	...	...	|	...	*0710*	...	*0750*	...	*0850*	*0920*	|	*0950*	...	*1050*	*1120*
Salisbury 113 d.	...	2300	...		0603	...	0640	...	0723	...	...	0832	...	0904	...	0941	...	1041	1052	1111	1141	...	1241	1305
Warminster d.	...	2320	...		0623	...	0700	0728	0743	...	...	0853	...	0925	...	1001	...	1101	1112	1132	1201	...	1301	1325
Westbury d.	...	2330	...		0638r	0651	0707	0738	0752	...	0838	0908c	...	0933	0938	1008	...	1108	1119	1148c	1208	1241	1308	1338
Trowbridge d.	...	...	...		0644	0657	0713	0744	0758	...	0844	0914	...	...	0944	1014	...	1114	1125	1154	1214	1247	1314	1344
Bradford on Avon d.	...	...	...		0649	0703	0719	0750	0805	...	0850	0920	...	...	0950	1020	...	1120	1131	1200	1220	1253	1320	1350
Bath a.	...	...	...		0706	0720	0732	0806	0816	...	0908	0933	...	...	1006	1034	...	1133	1145	1216	1233	1310	1333	1406
Bristol Temple Meads a.	...	...	...		0725	0739	0752	0825	0829	...	0927	0947	...	...	1025	1048	...	1147	1200	1235	1247	1328	1347	1425
Newport a.	...	...	...		...	0823	*0900*	...	0923	...	...	1023	...	...	...	1122	...	1222	*1258*	...	1322	...	1422	...
Cardiff Central a.	...	...	...		...	0842	*0921*	...	0940	...	...	1040	...	...	...	1140	...	1239	*1318*	...	1340	...	1439	...

	⑥	⑥ ◇	⑥ W	⑥		⑥	⑥ W	⑥		⑥	⑥ W	⑥	⑥		⑥		⑥	⑥ ◇	⑥ W	⑥	⑥		⑦ ▲	⑦
Portsmouth Harbour d.	1222	...	...	1322	...	1422	...	1522	...	1622	...	1722	1732y	...	1822	...	1922	...	...	2022	...	...		...
Portsmouth & Southsea d.	1227	...	...	1327	...	1427	...	1527	...	1627	...	1727	1736y	...	1827	...	1927	...	...	2027	...	...		...
Brighton 110 d.	*1103a*	...	...	*1203a*	...	*1303a*	...	*1403a*	...	*1503a*	...	*1603a*	1700	...	*1703a*	...	*1803a*	...	...	*1903a*	*1927*	...		...
Fareham d.	1247	...	...	1347	...	1447	...	1547	...	1647	...	1747	1815	...	1847	...	1947	...	...	2047	*2053*	...		...
Southampton Central d.	1310	...	...	1410	...	1510	...	1610	...	1710	...	1810	1840	...	1910	...	2010	...	...	2110	2127	...		...
Romsey d.	1321	...	...	1421	...	1521	...	1621	...	1721	...	1821	1851	...	1921	...	2021	...	...	2121	2138	...		...
London Waterloo 113 d.	*1150*	1220	...	*1250*	...	*1350*	...	*1450*	...	*1550*	...	*1650*	*1720*	...	*1750*	...	*1850*	1920	...	*1950*	*2020*	...		...
Salisbury 113 d.	1341	1352c	...	1441	...	1541	...	1641	...	1741	...	1841	1911	...	1941	...	2041	2057d	...	2141	2204	...		...
Warminster d.	1401	1412	...	1501	...	1601	...	1701	...	1801	...	1901	1931	...	2001	...	2101	2117	...	2201	2225	...		...
Westbury d.	1408	1419	1438	1508	...	1608	1638	1708	...	1808	1838	1908	1940	...	2008	...	2108	2124	2138	2208	2238	...		0956
Trowbridge d.	1414	1425	1444	1514	...	1614	1644	1714	...	1814	1844	1914	1946	...	2014	...	2114	2130	2144	2214	2244	...		1002
Bradford on Avon d.	1420	1431	1450	1520	...	1620	1650	1720	...	1820	1850	1920	1952	...	2020	...	2122	2136	2150	2222	2250	...		1007
Bath a.	1433	1445	1506	1533	...	1633	1707	1733	...	1833	1906	1933	2008	...	2033	...	2133	2150	2206	2234	2306	...		1023
Bristol Temple Meads a.	1447	1500	1526	1547	...	1647	1725	1747	...	1847	1926	1947	2027	...	2047	...	2147	2206	2227	2248	2325	...		1043
Newport a.	1522	*1559*	...	1624	...	1725	...	1825	...	1924	...	2022	...	...	2126	...	2233	...	...	2333	...	...		...
Cardiff Central a.	1539	*1615*	...	1641	...	1745	...	1841	...	1940	...	2039	...	...	2142	...	2254	...	...	2354	...	...		...

	⑦		⑦		⑦	⑦ ◇	⑦	⑦ W	⑦		⑦		⑦	⑦	⑦	⑦ W	⑦	⑦ ◇	⑦	⑦	⑦ W	⑦		⑦
Portsmouth Harbour d.	...	...	...	...	*1129‡*	...	...	...	...	...	...	...	...	*1613**	...	...	...	...	...	*1729‡*	...	...	...	...
Portsmouth & Southsea d.	...	...	...	...	*1136‡*	...	...	...	...	...	...	...	...	*1620**	...	...	...	...	...	*1736‡*	...	...	...	...
Brighton 110 d.	...	...	...	...	1110	...	...	...	...	...	...	...	...	1547	...	...	...	...	...	1747	...	...	...	...
Fareham d.	0932	...	1132	...	1232	...	1332	...	1432	...	1532	...	1632	1703	1732	...	1832	...	1901	1932	...	2032	...	2232
Southampton Central d.	0954	...	1154	...	1254	...	1354	...	1454	...	1554	...	1654	1726	1754	...	1854	...	1930r	1954	...	2054	...	2254
Romsey d.	1005	...	1206	...	1306	...	1406	...	1506	...	1606	...	1706	1737	1806	...	1906	...	1944	2006	...	2106	...	2305
London Waterloo 113 d.	*0815*	...	*1015*	...	*1115*	1215	|	...	*1315*	...	*1415*	...	*1515*	*1615*	|	...	*1715*	1815	|	|	...	*1915*	...	*2115*
Salisbury 113 d.	1030r	...	1228	...	1328	1358c	1428	...	1528	...	1628	...	1728	1802	1828	...	1928	1958c	2008	2028	...	2128	...	2330
Warminster d.	1050	...	1248	...	1347	1418	1448	...	1548	...	1648	...	1748	1822	1848	...	1948	2018	2028	2048	...	2148	...	2350
Westbury d.	1059	...	1255	...	1355	1425	1501r	1531	1558	...	1659	...	1801	1834	1901r	1940	2001r	2032r	2039	2101r	2146	2201r	...	2357
Trowbridge d.	1105	...	1301	...	1401	1432	1507	1537	1604	...	1705	...	1807	1840	1907	1947	2007	2038	2045	2107	2152	2207	...	...
Bradford on Avon d.	1111	...	1307	...	1407	1438	1513	1545	1610	...	1711	...	|	1846	1913	1954	2013	2044	2051	2113	2158	2213	...	...
Bath a.	1126	...	1325	...	1423	1452	1527	1602	1628	...	1725	...	1825	1903	1927	2011	2027	2059	2109	2127	2215	2228	...	...
Bristol Temple Meads a.	1144	...	1343	...	1442	1506	1540	1621	1641	...	1743	...	1838	1922	1940	2031	2040	2116	2128	2140	2234	2241	...	...
Newport a.	1231	...	1427	...	1533	...	1627	...	1734	...	1827	...	1933	...	2029	...	2132	...	...	2237	...	2334	...	...
Cardiff Central a.	1246	...	1442	...	1548	...	1642	...	1749	...	1842	...	1948	...	2044	...	2148	...	...	2256	...	2349	...	...

W – From Weymouth.
– Change at Fratton.
– Arrives 9–10 minutes earlier.
d – Arrives 14–15 minutes earlier.
q – Change at Bristol Parkway.
r – Arrives 6–8 minutes earlier.
y – Change at Fareham.
‡ – By 🚌 (change at Havant).
* – By 🚌 (change at Cosham).
◇ – Also conveys 🛏.
▲ – Services on ⑦ are subject to alteration due to engineering work. Allow ± 70 minutes for replacement connections (partly by 🚌) Portsmouth - Fareham.

2nd class — SHANKLIN - RYDE (- PORTSMOUTH) — 138

	⚒	⚒		⚒						Ⓑ		Ⓑ	⚒	⑦	⚒	⑦	⚒
Shanklin d.	0617	0636	0717	0736	0817	0836	and at the same	1817	1836	1917	1936	2017	2036	2117	2136	2217	2236
Ryde Pier Head a.	0641	0700	0741	0800	0841	0900	minutes past each	1841	1900	1941	2000	2041	2100	2141	2200	2241	2300
Portsmouth Harbour ⛴ a.	*0703*	*0733*	*0803*	*0833*	*0903*	*0933*	hour until	*1903*	*1933*	*2003*	*2033*	*2103*	*2133*	*2203*	*2233*	*2303*	*2333*

⛴ – Operated by Wightlink. Through rail fares available.

139 WEYMOUTH - WESTBURY

2nd class GW

km			Ⓐ	Ⓐ	Ⓐ	Ⓐ	Ⓐ	Ⓐ	Ⓐ	Ⓐ			⑥	⑥		⑥	⑥	⑥	⑥	⑥			⑦	⑦	⑦
0	**Weymouth** d.	Ⓐ	0540	0632	0811	1111	1311	1511	1711	2001	...	⑥	0627	0811	...	1111	1311	1511	1711	1958	...	⑦	1400	1800	2009
11	Dorchester West d.		0554	0645	0824	1124	1325	1525	1725	2017	...		0640	0824	...	1124	1324	1523	1724	2011	...		1413	1813	2022
44	Yeovil Pen Mill d.		0626	0730v	0856	1203	1404	1557	1757	2049	...		0725v	0857	...	1200	1400	1558	1757	2044	...		1446	1846	2055
63	Castle Cary **115** d.		0646r	0743	0908	1222r	1416	1610	1810	2102	...		0737	0909	...	1212	1412	1610	1810	2056	...		1459	1859	2115r
86	Frome d.		0704	0802	0926	1239	1435	1629	1827	2120	...		0755	0926	...	1229	1429	1627	1827	2115	...		1518	1918	2134
95	**Westbury** **115** a.		0713	0812	0936	1248	1444	1638	1836	2129	...		0805	0935	...	1241	1438	1637	1836	2125	...		1527	1927	2143
	Bristol Temple Meads **137** a.		0806	0904	1026	1336	1532	1727	1925	2227	...		0927	1025	...	1328	1526	1725	1926	2227	...		1621	2031	2234

		Ⓐ	Ⓐ	Ⓐ	Ⓐ	Ⓐ	Ⓐ	Ⓐ	Ⓐ			⑥	⑥	⑥	⑥	⑥	⑥	⑥	⑦			⑦		⑦	⑦
Bristol Temple Meads **137** d.	Ⓐ	*0545*	0840	0949	1149	1449	1649	1749	2049	...	⑥	*0545*	0840	0949	1149	1449	1649	1749	2049	...	⑦	1320	...	1750	2050
Westbury **115** d.		0639	0928	1036	1237	1536	1738	1836	2136	...		0636	0928	1035	1236	1535	1735	1836	2135	...		1430	...	1838	2138
Frome d.		0648	0938	1046	1247	1546	1747	1846	2146	...		0645	0938	1045	1245	1544	1744	1846	2144	...		1449r	...	1847	2148
Castle Cary **115** d.		0704	0954	1103	1304	1610r	1811r	1903	2202	...		0702	0954	1102	1302	1613v	1814v	1905	2200	...		1506	...	1906	2205
Yeovil Pen Mill d.		0721	1008	1116	1317	1623	1824	1916	2215	...		0716	1008	1116	1316	1626	1829	1919	2213	...		1519	...	1920	2218
Dorchester West a.		0753	1040	1149	1350	1655	1856	1949	2247	...		0749	1038	1151	1351	1654	1903	1953	2246	...		1552	...	1953	2251
Weymouth a.		0805	1055	1206	1409	1707	1913	2006	2302	...		0801	1054	1208	1409	1707	1926	2006	2259	...		1605	...	2005	2303

r – Arrives 8–10 minutes earlier.

v – Arrives 13–14 minutes earlier.

140 LONDON AIRPORT LINKS

Gatwick ✈

GATWICK EXPRESS daily non-stop rail service from / to **London Victoria**. Journey time: 30 minutes (35 minutes on ⑦). ✆ +44 (0) 845 850 1530.

From Victoria:
0001, 0030, 0330 ⚒, 0335 ⑦, 0430 ⚒, 0445 ⑦; then every 15 minutes 0500–2345.

From Gatwick:
0005, 0020, 0035, 0050, 0135, 0435 ⚒, 0440 ⑦, 0520 ⚒. 0535 ⑦;then every 15 minutes 0550–2350.

Other rail services:

Table **103** – London Victoria - Gatwick - Brighton; and Bedford (***A***) - Luton (***A***) - London Blackfriars - Gatwick - Brighton.
Table **105** – Tonbridge and Reading (***B***) - Gatwick.
Table **125** – Birmingham - Reading - Gatwick.
Table **141** – Watford Junction (***C***) - Gatwick.

A – Connections from / to Leicester, Nottingham, Derby and Sheffield (Table **170**).
B – Connections from / to Exeter and the South West (Table **115**), Stratford upon Avon and Birmingham (Table **129**), Worcester (Table **131**), Bristol and South Wales (Table **133**).
C – Connections from / to Birmingham (Table **143**), Liverpool, Manchester and Glasgow (Tables **150 / 2**).

Heathrow ✈

HEATHROW EXPRESS daily non-stop rail service from / to **London Paddington**. Journey time: 15–17 minutes (Terminals 1 / 2 / 3), 22–25 minutes (Terminal 4). ✆ +44 (0) 845 600 1515.

From Paddington: Every 15 minutes 0510–2325. **From Heathrow** Terminal 4 (5–6 minutes later from Terminals 1 / 2 / 3): 4 trains per hour from 0503 ⑦, 0507 ⚒ until 2340.

PICCADILLY LINE (London Underground) service.
Frequent trains (every 4–10 minutes) 0530 – 2300 ①–⑥, 0730 – 2330 ⑦, from **King's Cross St Pancras** and **Heathrow** Terminals. Journey time: 50–58 minutes.

RAILAIR LINK 🚌 service from / to **Reading** rail station.

From Reading: Journey time to Heathrow Terminal 1: 40 minutes ▲
Ⓐ: 0400, 0500, 0530, 0600, 0620 and every 20 minutes until 0840, then 0905, 0925 and every 20 minutes until 1805; then 1835, 1905, 1935, 2005, 2035, 2105, 2205, 2305.
Ⓒ: 0515, 0545 and every 30 minutes until 1945; then 2025, 2055, 2115 ⑦, 2205, 2305.
▲ – 42 minutes to Terminal 2; 45 minutes to Terminal 3.

From Heathrow Central Bus Station: Journey time to Reading: 43 minutes
Ⓐ: 0505, 0605, 0635, 0705, 0732, 0752 and every 20 minutes until 0952, then 1005, 1025 and every 20 minutes until 1905; then 1935, 2005, 2035, 2105, 2135, 2205, 2305, 2359.
Ⓒ: 0505, 0610, 0640 and every 30 minutes until 2040; then 2120, 2200, 2305, 2359.

RAILAIR LINK 🚌 from / to **Woking** rail station.

From Woking: Journey time to Heathrow Central Bus Station: 50–70 minutes △
0530 Ⓐ, 0600 Ⓐ, 0630, 0700 and every 30 minutes until 2100; then 2200.
△ – 30–50 minutes to Terminal 4.

From Heathrow Central Bus Station ▽: Journey time to Woking: 50–70 minutes
0545 Ⓐ, 0615 Ⓐ, 0645, 0715 and every 30 minutes until 2015, then 2100, 2200, 2300.
▽ – 15 minutes later from Terminal 4.

Luton ✈

Frequent *First Capital Connect* trains from / to **London Kings Cross Thameslink**, **London Blackfriars**, **Gatwick** and **Brighton** serve Luton Airport Parkway station ★.
Midland Mainline express trains (Table **170**) from / to **London St Pancras**, **Leicester**, **Nottingham**, **Derby** and **Sheffield** serve Luton main rail station ★.
★ – A frequent shuttle 🚌 service operates between each of the rail stations and the airport terminal.

🚌 service **Milton Keynes - Luton** ✈ (journey time 55 minutes) for train connections from / to **Birmingham** (Table **143**), **Liverpool** and **Manchester** (Table **150**).

From Milton Keynes rail station:
⚒: 0640, 0740, 0840, 0955, 1055 and hourly until 2055, then 2155 Ⓐ.
⑦: 0920, 1120, 1220 and hourly until 2120.

From Luton ✈:
⚒: 0550, 0650, 0750, 0905, 1005 and hourly until 2005; then 2105 Ⓐ.
⑦: 0820, 1020, 1220, 1320 and hourly until 2020.

Stansted ✈

STANSTED EXPRESS rail link service from / to **London Liverpool St**. Journey time: ± 45 minutes. Operating company: *one* ✆ +44 (0) 845 600 7245.

From London Liverpool St:
⚒: 0410, 0440, 0510, 0525 and every 15 minutes until 2255; then 2325.
⑦: 0410, 0440, 0510, 0540, 0610, 0625 and every 15 minutes until 2255; then 2325.

From Stansted ✈:
⚒: 0030, 0100, 0130, 0530, 0600, 0615 and every 15 minutes until 2345; then 2359.
⑦: 0030, 0530, 0600, 0630, 0700, 0715 and every 15 minutes until 2345; then 2359.

Trains call at **Tottenham Hale** for London Underground (Victoria Line) connections to / from Kings Cross, Euston, and Victoria stations.

For *Central Trains* services to / from **Cambridge**, **Peterborough** and **Birmingham**, see Tables **206 / 7**.

City ✈

DOCKLANDS LIGHT RAILWAY from / to **Bank** (interchange with London Underground: Central, Circle, District, Northern, and Waterloo & City Lines).
Trains run every 7–10 minutes 0530–0030 on ⚒, 0700–2330 on ⑦. Journey time: ± 22 minutes.

Inter- Airport 🚌 links

From **Gatwick** to **Heathrow** *Journey 70 minutes*
0050, 0250, 0420, 0520, 0605, 0635, 0705, 0750, 0820 and every 30 minutes until 2350.

From **Gatwick** to **Luton** *Journey 150 minutes*
0250, 0450, 0635, 0850, 1050 and every 2 hours until 1850, then 2150.

From **Gatwick** to **Stansted** *Journey 165 minutes*
0420, 0520, 0605, 0705, 0820, 0920 and hourly until 1920, then 2120, 2220.

From **Heathrow** to **Gatwick** *Journey 70 minutes*
0005, 0205, 0435, 0505 and every 30 minutes until 2205, then 2305.

From **Heathrow** to **Luton** *Journey 70 minutes*
0410, 0520 and at 10 mins past even hours, 20 mins past uneven hours until 2010, 2120, then 2310.

From **Heathrow** to **Stansted** *Journey 85 minutes*
0540, 0640 and hourly until 2040, then 2240, 2340.

From **Luton** to **Gatwick** *Journey 145 minutes*
0050, 0450, 0630 Ⓐ, 0650 Ⓒ, 0850, 1050 and every 2 hours until 2250.

From **Luton** to **Heathrow** *Journey 65 minutes*
0050, 0450, 0535, 0630 Ⓐ, 0650 Ⓒ, 0735, 0850 and at 35 mins past uneven hours, 50 mins past even hours until 2135, 2250.

From **Stansted** to **Heathrow** *(80 mins)* and **Gatwick** *(160 mins)*
0305, 0405, 0605, 0650 Ⓐ, 0705 Ⓒ, 0805, 0905 and hourly until 2005.

SN 2nd class — (BRIGHTON -) GATWICK ✈ - WATFORD — 141

km			Ⓐ	Ⓐ	Ⓐ	Ⓐ	Ⓐ		Ⓐ	Ⓐ	Ⓐ	Ⓐ	Ⓐ			⑥	⑥	⑥		⑥	⑥	⑥	⑥
	Brighton **103** ....d.	Ⓐ	0522	0647	0747	0900r	0955	and	1755	1849r	2004r	2049r	2149r	...	⑥	0521	0556	0655	and	1755	1904r	2004r	2049r
0	**Gatwick** Airport ✈ ....d.		0552	0722	0837	0937	1037		1837	1937	2037	2137	2237	...		0552	0637	0737		1837	1937	2037	2137
26	East Croydon ....d.		0610	0738	0909	0952	1052	hourly	1852	1952	2052	2152	2252	...		0610	0653	0752	hourly	1852	1952	2052	2152
38	Clapham Junction ....d.		0630	0757	0927	1003	1103		1903	2003	2103	2203	2303	...		0623	0703	0803		1903	2003	2103	2203
44	Kensington Olympia .....d.		0639	0805	0935	1012	1112	until	1912	2012	2112	2212	2312	...		0632	0712	0812	until	1912	2012	2112	2212
68	**Watford** Junction ....a.		0709	0833	1005	1045	1145		1945	2045	2145	2245	2345	...		0704	0736	0837		1937	2037	2146	2246

		Ⓐ	Ⓐ	Ⓐ	Ⓐ		Ⓐ	Ⓐ	Ⓐ	Ⓐ	Ⓐ	Ⓐ	Ⓐ	Ⓐ	Ⓐ		⑥		⑥	⑥	⑥	⑥	⑥
Watford Junction ....d.	Ⓐ	0605	0740	0842	0911	and	1511	1629	1729	1812	1911	2011	2111	2212	2318	⑥	0611	and	1911	2013	2113	2211	2313
Kensington Olympia ......d.		0631	0807	0907	0937		1537	1653	1755	1836	1937	2036	2136	2241	2345		0642		1942	2042	2142	2242	2342
Clapham Junction ....d.		0653	0828	0923	0954	hourly	1554	1706	1823	1855	1954	2054	2154	2308	0011		0654	hourly	1954	2054	2154	2308	0011
East Croydon ....a.		0703	0839	0933	1007		1607	1718	1833	1907	2007	2107	2207	2318	0024		0707	until	2007	2107	2207	2318	0024
Gatwick Airport ✈ ....a.		0718	0854	0948	1022	until	1622	1733	1849	1923	2022	2123	2223	2338	0042		0722		2022	2122	2223	2338	0042
Brighton **103** ....a.		0802z	0922	1024z	1107		1707	1802	1925	2002r	2100r	2200r	2300r	0015	0114		0808		2107	2200r	2300r	0015	0114

r – Change at East Croydon.
z – Change at Haywards Heath.

☛ No direct services on ⑦. For connections at Watford Junction, see Tables **143** (Birmingham), **150** (Northwest England and Scotland) and **151** (sleeper trains).

LM — NORTHAMPTON - BIRMINGHAM — 142

km			Ⓐ	Ⓐ	Ⓐ	Ⓐ		Ⓐ		Ⓐ	Ⓐ	Ⓐ	Ⓐ	Ⓐ	Ⓐ			⑥		⑥	⑥		⑥ 🚌	⑥ 🚌
0	**Northampton** ....d.	Ⓐ	0519	0615	0700	0800	and	1700	...	1805	1900	2000	2100	2200	2300	...	⑥	0558	and	2058	...	...	...	2245
30	Rugby ....d.		0543	0636	0720	0820		1720	...	1826	1920	2020	2120	2220	2320	...		0620		2120	2156	...	2305	|
52	**Coventry** ....a.		0554	0648	0732	0832	hourly	1732	...	1841	1932	2032	2132	2232	2336	...		0631	hourly	2132	2207	...	2345	2345
69	Birmingham Internat. ✈ a.		0604	0658	0750	0850		1750	...	1910	1950	2050	2150	2250	...	...		0649		2150	2225	...	...	0006
83	**Birmingham** New St ...a.		0622	0715	0804	0906	until	1806	...	1927	2006	2108	2208	2308	...	...		0708	until	2208	2239	...	...	0018

		⑦ 🚌		⑦ 🚌		⑦ 🚌	⑦ 🚌		⑦ 🚌
Northampton ....d.	⑦	0821	and	2021	...	2121	2221	...	2321
Rugby ....d.		0913		2113	...	2213	2313	...	0013
Coventry ....a.		0953	hourly	2153	...	2253	2353	...	0053
Birmingham Internat. ✈ a.		1013		2208	...	2327	0016	...	0120
Birmingham New St ...a.		1030	until	2223	...	2340	0028	...	0133

		Ⓐ	Ⓐ	Ⓐ		Ⓐ	Ⓐ	Ⓐ		Ⓐ
Birmingham New St.........d.	Ⓐ	...	0530	...	...	0643	0748	0848	and	1548
Birmingham Internat. ✈ ......d.		...	0540	...	...	0659	0759	0857		1557
Coventry ....d.		0515	0550	0618	...	0727	0817	0915	hourly	1615
Rugby ....d.		0526	0620	0632	...	0741	0828	0927		1627
Northampton ....a.		0551	0639	0700	...	0805	0859	0928	until	1657

	Ⓐ	Ⓐ	Ⓐ	Ⓐ	Ⓐ	Ⓐ	Ⓐ	Ⓐ		Ⓐ			⑥	⑥		⑥	⑥			⑦ 🚌	⑦ 🚌		⑦ 🚌	⑦
Birmingham New St ...d.	1645	1715	1745	1818	1848	1948	2036	2136	...	2300	...	⑥	0643	0736	and	2136	2248	...	⑦	...	0915	and	2215	2315
Birmingham Internat. ✈ d.	1656	1727	1756	1830	1857	1957	2053	2153	...	2310	...		0659	0752		2152	2304	...		...	0925		2225	2331
Coventry ....d.	1705	1737	1805	1847	1915	2015	2111	2211	...	2320	...		0717	0810	hourly	2210	2322	...		0845	0945	hourly	2245	2347
Rugby ....d.	1717	1754	1817	1858	1927	2027	2122	2222	...	2334	...		0730	0821		2221	2334	...		0926	1026		2326	...
Northampton ....a.	1746	1823	1853	1929	1956	2057	2147	2254	...	2356	...		0753	0846	until	2249	2358	...		1030	1117	until	0017	...

NORTHAMPTON – LONDON Euston *Operator: LM* *106 km*

Ⓐ: 0415, 0443, 0535, 0558 and 2–3 journeys each hour until 2246; then 2346.
⑥: 0515, 0602, 0632 and 2 journeys each hour until 2147; then 2242.
⑦: 0645 🚌, 0930, 0956, 1026 and every 30 minutes until 2156; then 2256, 2356.

LONDON Euston – NORTHAMPTON Journey time: ± 65 mins (± 85 mins on ⑦)

Ⓐ: 0004 ②–⑤, 0034, 0524, 0555, 0637 and 2–3 journeys each hour until 2254; then 2340.
⑥: 0004, 0034, 0534, 0634, 0704, 0754 and 2 journeys each hour until 2134; then 2234, 2304, 2345.
⑦: 0843, 0913 and every 30 minutes until 2343.

VT — LONDON - BIRMINGHAM - WOLVERHAMPTON — 143

Service are subject to alteration on ⑥⑦

km			Ⓐ	Ⓐ		Ⓐ	Ⓐ	Ⓐ	Ⓐ	Ⓐ	Ⓐ	Ⓐ	Ⓐ	Ⓐ	Ⓐ	Ⓐ	Ⓐ			⑥	⑥	⑥	⑥	⑥
0	**London** Euston .... **150** d.	Ⓐ	0636	0740		1640	1710	1730	1810	1840	1910	1940	2010	2040	2140	2240	2340	...	⑥	0610	0655	0720	0759	0816
28	Watford Junction .... △ **150** d.		0651	|	and at	|	|	|	1825	|	1925	|	2025	|	2154	2257	|	...		0629	0710	|	0814	|
80	Milton Keynes .... **150** d.		0711	0810	the same	1711	|	|	|	1911	|	2012	|	2111	2214	2324	0024	...		0658	0730	0752	|	0848
133	Rugby .... **150** a.		|	|	minutes	|	|	|	|	|	|	|	|	|	|	0023s	0120s	...		|	|	|	|	|
151	**Coventry** ....a.		0744	0844	past	1744	1814	1832	1914	1944	2013	2044	2113	2144	2310	0035s	0133s	...		0740	0814	0841	0915	0940
168	Birmingham International ✈ a.		0757	0857	each	1756	1826	1844	1926	1957	2026	2057	2126	2157	2327	0047s	0146s	...		0755	0827	0855	0927	0955
182	**Birmingham** New St...........a.		0809	0909	hour	1809	1839	1857	1939	2009	2039	2109	2139	2209	2339	0101s	0158s	...		0811	0839	0911	0939	1011
190	Sandwell & Dudley ....a.		0822	0922	until	1822	1853	1922	1959	2022	2052	2122	2159	2222	2351	|	|	...		0821	|	0921	|	1021
202	**Wolverhampton** ....a.		0836	0936		1836	1906	1936	2013	2036	2106	2136	2213	2236	0005	0134	0232	...		0833	0907	0933	1007	1033

	⑥	⑥	⑥	⑥	⑥	❖	⑥	⑥	⑥	⑥	⑥		⑦	⑦	⑦	⑦	⑦	❖	⑦	⑦	⑦	⑦	⑦
London Euston .... **150** d.	0855	0929	0952	1028	1058		1758	1827	1857	1924	2013	⑦	0936	1036	1136	1236	1350		1953	2036	2136	2240	2340
Watford Junction .... △ **150** d.	0910	|	1007	|	1113	and at	1813	|	1911	1938	2029		0952	1052	1152	1252	1407	and at	2011	2053	2152	2257	2357
Milton Keynes .... **150** d.	|	1000	|	1100	|	the same	|	1900	|	2014	2120		1037	1137	1237	1337	|	the same	|	2137	2237	2330	0032
Rugby .... **150** a.	|	|	|	|	|	minutes	|	|	|	|	2155		|	|	|	|	|	minutes	|	2201	|	2351	0056
Coventry ....a.	1015	1042	1115	1140	1215	past	1915	1941	2015	2110	2207		1113	1213	1313	1413	1513	past	2113	2213	2315	0004	0108
Birmingham International ✈ a.	1027	1055	1127	1155	1227	each	1927	1955	2027	2125	2225		1125	1225	1325	1424	1525	each	2125	2226	2327	0016	0120
Birmingham New St ....a.	1039	1111	1139	1211	1239	hour	1939	2011	2039	2139	2239		1139	1239	1339	1439	1539	hour	2139	2239	2340	0028	0133
Sandwell & Dudley ....a.	|	1121	|	1221	|	until	|	2021	2056	2159	2256		1156	1256	1356	1456	1559	until	2156	2251	|	|	|
Wolverhampton ....a.	1107	1133	1207	1233	1307		2007	2033	2108	2214	2311		1208	1308	1408	1508	1611		2208	2303	0005	0053	0155

		Ⓐ	Ⓐ	Ⓐ	Ⓐ	Ⓐ	Ⓐ	Ⓐ	❖	Ⓐ		Ⓐ	Ⓐ		Ⓐ		Ⓐ			⑥	⑥	⑥	⑥	⑥
Wolverhampton ....d.	Ⓐ	0505	0545	0615	0635	0705	0735	0805		1805	...	1905	2005	...	2105	...	2239	...	⑥	0537	0605	0635	0705	0735
Sandwell & Dudley ....d.		0515	0555	0625	0645	0715	0745	0815	and at	1815	...	1915	2015	...	2115	...	|	...		0547	0615	0648	0716	0748
Birmingham New St ....d.		0530	0610	0640	0700	0730	0800	0830	the same	1830	...	1930	2030	...	2130	...	2300	...		0600	0630	0700	0730	0800
Birmingham International ✈ d.		0540	0621	0650	0710	0740	0810	0840	minutes	1840	...	1940	2040	...	2140	...	2310	...		0610	0641	0710	0741	0810
Coventry ....d.		0550	0632	0700	0720	0756	0824	0850	past	1850	...	1950	2050	...	2150	...	2320	...		0621	0655	0722	0754	0821
Rugby .... **150** d.		0604	|	0714	|	|	|	|	each	|	...	|	|	...	|	...	2334	...		0635	|	0736	|	|
Milton Keynes .... **150** a.		0625	0707	|	0756	|	|	0925	hour	1922	...	2022	2122	...	2224	...	0015s	...		0711	0741	|	0836	|
Watford Junction .... ▽ **150** a.		0647	0728	|	|	|	0920	|	until	|	...	2043	2143	...	2247	...	0038	...		0731	|	0827	|	0930
London Euston .... **150** a.		0709	0750	0809	0839	0901	0944	1003		2000	...	2104	2204	...	2326	...	0102	...		0752	0818	0847	0915	0953

	⑥	⑥	⑥	❖	⑥	⑥	⑥		⑥	⑥		⑥			⑦		⑦	⑦	❖	⑦		⑦	⑦
Wolverhampton ....d.	0811	0835	0911		1711	1735	1811	...	1935	2011	...	2111	...	⑦	0935	...	1036	1105		2004	...	2135	2235
Sandwell & Dudley ....d.	|	0848	|	and at	|	1748	|	...	1948	|	...	|	...		0947	...	1047	1117	and at	2017	...	2148	2247
Birmingham New St ....d.	0833	0900	0933	the same	1733	1800	1833	...	2000	2033	...	2133	...		1000	...	1100	1130	the same	2030	...	2200	2300
Birmingham International ✈ d.	0843	0910	0945	minutes	1745	1810	1845	...	2010	2043	...	2143	...		1010	...	1110	1141	minutes	2041	...	2210	2310
Coventry ....d.	0856	0922	0956	past	1757	1821	1857	...	2021	2054	...	2154	...		1021	...	1121	1153	past	2053	...	2221	2321
Rugby .... **150** d.	|	0936	1010	each	1811	1835	1911	...	2035	|	...	|	...		|	...	|	|	each	|	...	2235	2335
Milton Keynes .... **150** a.	0939	|	1041	hour	1842	|	|	...	2111	2139	...	2241	...		1055	...	1157	1227	hour	2128	...	2258	2358
Watford Junction .... ▽ **150** a.	|	1030	|	until	|	1926	1959	...	2202	2222	...	2319	...		1131	...	1236	1306	until	2206	...	2328	0028
London Euston .... **150** a.	1016	1051	1118		1919	1948	2025	...	2226	2246	...	2343	...		1151	...	1258	1329		2227	...	2348	0047

s – Stops to set down only.
△ – Trains stop here to pick up only.
▽ – Trains stop here to set down only.
❖ – Timings may vary by up to 4 minutes on some journeys.
☛ All trains convey 🍸. On Ⓐ trains from London until 0940 and from Wolverhampton until 0905 also convey ✕ in 1st class.

Additional trains **London** Euston - **Birmingham** New St:
Ⓐ: 0708, 0810, 0910, 1010, 1110, 1210, 1310, 1410, 1510, 1610, 1651, 1751, 1857.
⑥: 0704, 0751, 0805, 0851, 0905, 0947, 1005, 1051, 1105, 1151, 1205, 1251, 1305, 1351, 1405, 1451, 1505, 1551, 1605, 1651, 1705.

Additional trains **Birmingham** New St - **London** Euston:
Ⓐ: 0715, 0745, 0900, 1000, 1100, 1200, 1300, 1400, 1500, 1600, 1700, 1800, 1900.
⑥: 0930, 0950, 1030, 1050, 1130, 1151, 1230, 1251, 1330, 1351, 1430, 1451, 1530, 1550, 1630, 1651, 1730, 1751, 1830, 1851, 1900, 1933, 2030, 2053.

145 BIRMINGHAM - SHREWSBURY

AW, LM

km			Ⓐ	✖ A	⑥	Ⓐ C	⑥ C	Ⓐ	✖	✖ 🍷 A	✖	✖ 🍷 C	✖	✖ 🍷 B	✖	✖ 🍷 C	✖	✖ 🍷 B	✖	✖ 🍷 C	✖	✖ 🍷 B	✖	✖ 🍷 C	✖
0	**Birmingham** New St ... d.	✖	*0603*	0633	*0637*	0717	0733	*0718*	0757	0833	0857	0933	0957	1033	1057	1133	1157	1233	1257	1333	1357	1433	1457	1533	1557
21	Wolverhampton ... d.		0627	0648	0715	0733	0748	0747	0815	0848	0915	0948	1015	1048	1115	1148	1215	1248	1315	1348	1415	1448	1515	1548	1615
46	Telford Central ... d.		0656	0704	0743	0759	0804	0807	0843	0904	0943	1004	1043	1104	1143	1204	1243	1304	1343	1404	1443	1504	1543	1604	1643
52	Wellington ... d.		0704	0710	0750	0805	0810	0815	0850	0910	0950	1010	1050	1110	1150	1210	1250	1310	1350	1410	1450	1510	1550	1610	1650
68	**Shrewsbury** ... a.		0720	0722	0809	0822	0825	0837	0909	0922	1009	1025	1109	1122	1209	1225	1309	1322	1409	1425	1509	1522	1609	1625	1709

	✖ 🍷 A	✖	Ⓐ	⑥ 🍷 C	Ⓐ 🍷 C	✖	✖ 🍷 B	✖	✖ C	✖	✖ 🍷 A	✖	⑥ C	✖	✖ D	✖	✖		⑦	⑦	⑦ C	⑦		⑦ 🍷 A	⑦ C
Birmingham New St ... d.	1633	1657	1724	1733	1733	1757	1833	1857	1933	1957	2033	2057	2133	2157	2233	2333	*2343*r	...	⑦	1027	1127	1227	...	1327	1427
Wolverhampton ... d.	1648	1715	1748	1748	1748	1815	1848	1915	1948	2015	2048	2115	2148	2215	2248	2350	0026	...		1043	1144	1244	...	1348	1448
Telford Central ... d.	1704	1743	1809	1804	1813	1843	1904	1943	2004	2043	2104	2147r	2204	2243	2304	0018	0044	...		1111	1211	1311	...	1404	1504
Wellington ... d.	1710	1750	1815	1810	1819	1850	1910	1950	2010	2050	2110	2154r	2210	2250	2310	0024	0050	...		1119	1219	1319	...	1411	1512
Shrewsbury ... a.	1722	1809	1830	1825	1835	1909	1922	2009	2025	2109	2127r	2209	2225	2309	2325	0040	0106	...		1133	1232	1333	...	1429	1525

	⑦	⑦ 🍷 B	⑦ C	⑦	⑦ 🍷 C	⑦ 🍷 A	⑦	⑦	⑦ H	⑦
Birmingham New St ... d.	1507	1607	1657	1757	1857	1957	2057	2157	2254	...
Wolverhampton ... d.	1526	1626	1714	1816	1914	2016	2116	2216	2311	2325
Telford Central ... d.	1553	1642	1730	1843	1941	2032	2143	2243	2327	2353
Wellington ... d.	1601	1650	1738	1851	1949	2039	2151	2251	2334	0001
Shrewsbury ... a.	1615	1703	1751	1905	2002	2052	2205	2305	2347	0018

		✖	Ⓐ	Ⓐ	⑥ C	⑥	Ⓐ	✖ 🍷 A	Ⓐ	⑥
Shrewsbury ... d.	✖	0524	0554	0605	0622	0640	0648	0712	0737	0740
Wellington ... d.		0537	0607	0618	0635	0653	0702	0722	0750	0753
Telford Central ... d.		0543	0613	0626	0641	0702	0709	0729	0756	0802
Wolverhampton ... a.		0600	0630	0655	0658	0731	0727	0758	0819	0831
Birmingham New St ... a.		0618	0648	*0724*	0718	0751	0748	0818	0836	0851

	Ⓐ	✖ 🍷 C	✖	✖ 🍷 A	✖ ✣	✖ 🍷 C	✖ ✣	✖ 🍷 B	✖ ✣	✖ 🍷 C	✖ ✣	✖ 🍷 B	✖ ✣	✖ 🍷 C	✖ ✣	✖ 🍷 B	✖ ✣	✖ 🍷 C	✖ ✣	✖ 🍷 B	✖ ✣	✖ 🍷 C	✖	✖ 🍷 B	⑥ C
Shrewsbury ... d.	0747	0822	0840	0922	0935	1022	1035	1122	1135	1222	1235	1322	1335	1422	1435	1522	1535	1622	1635	1722	1735	1822	1838	1922	2022
Wellington ... d.	0800	0835	0853	0935	0948	1035	1048	1135	1148	1235	1248	1335	1348	1435	1448	1535	1548	1635	1648	1735	1748	1835	1851	1935	2035
Telford Central ... d.	0807	0841	0902	0941	0957	1041	1057	1141	1157	1241	1257	1341	1357	1441	1457	1541	1557	1641	1657	1741	1757	1841	1900	1941	2041
Wolverhampton ... a.	0835	0858	0931	0958	1027	1058	1127	1158	1227	1258	1327	1358	1427	1458	1527	1558	1627	1658	1727	1758	1827	1858	1931	1958	2058
Birmingham New St ... a.	0855	0918	0951	1018	1048	1119	1148	1218	1248	1318	1348	1418	1448	1518	1548	1618	1648	1718	1748	1819	1848	1918	1948d	2018	2118

	Ⓐ	⑥	✖ 🍷 H	✖ C		✖ J			⑦	⑦		⑦		⑦ 🍷 C	⑦	⑦	⑦ 🍷 A	⑦ C	⑦	⑦ 🍷 B	⑦ C	⑦ 🍷 A	⑦ C	⑦ 🍷 H	⑦ C
Shrewsbury ... d.	2031	2040	2126	2222	...	2331	...	⑦	0841	0941	...	1050	...	1208	1253	1342	1424	1525	1628	1726	1827	1925	2025	2120	2229
Wellington ... d.	2044	2053	2139	2235	...	2343	...		0854	0954	...	1104	...	1222	1307	1355	1438	1538	1641	1740	1840	1939	2038	2134	2242
Telford Central ... d.	2052	2102	2145	2241	...	2351	...		0903	1003	...	1113	...	1230	1313	1404	1444	1544	1650	1749	1849	1945	2047	2143	2251
Wolverhampton ... a.	2121	2131	2202	2258	...	0020v	...		0930	1030	...	1130	...	1258	1330	1431	1501	1614	1717	1816	1916	2003	2114	2216	2318
Birmingham New St ... a.	2144	2153	2218	2318	...	...	...		0947	1047	...	1148	...	1315	1349	1449	1518	1633	1734	1835	1934	2019	2132	2236	*2345*

A – To / from Aberystwyth.
B – To / from Aberystwyth and Pwllheli.
C – To / from Chester.
D – To Chester (and Holyhead on Ⓐ).

H – To / from Holyhead.
J – From Holyhead on Ⓐ.

d – 1951 on ⑥.

r – 4–6 minutes earlier on ⑥.
v – 0027 on ⑦.

✣ – Runs 3–6 minutes later on ⑥.

☛ Birmingham - Wolverhampton and v.v., see also Tables **143** and **150**.

146 SHREWSBURY - LLANDRINDOD - SWANSEA

2nd class AW

km			✖ C	✖		✖	✖			⑦	⑦ C
0	**Shrewsbury** .... 162 d.	✖	0519	0905	...	1405	1805	...	⑦	1207	1624
20	Church Stretton .. 162 d.		0536	0922	...	1423	1823	...		1225	1642
32	Craven Arms ...... 162 d.		0550	0935	...	1436	1835	...		1236	1653
52	Knighton ... d.		0612	0957	...	1458	1857	...		1259	1716
84	**Llandrindod** ... a.		0648	1033	...	1534	1933	...		1334	1752
84	**Llandrindod** ... d.		0655	1035	...	1538	1935	...		1338	1757
110	Llanwrtyd ... d.		0724	1109r	...	1607	2013v	...		1410	1826
128	**Llandovery** ... d.		0748	1133	...	1632	2037	...		1434	1851
146	Llandeilo ... d.		0809	1154	...	1652	2058	...		1507p	1911
159	Pantyffynnon ... d.		0825	1210	...	1709	2114	...		1523	1928
178	**Llanelli** .... 136 a.		0843	1230	...	1728b	2142	...		1542	1949
196	**Swansea** .... 136 a.		0907	1301	...	1806	2213	...		1607	2013

		✖	✖ C	✖		✖			⑦	⑦ R
Swansea .... 136 d.	✖	0436	0915	1316	...	1821	...	⑦	1109	1516
Llanelli .... 136 d.		0455	0937r	1337	...	1841	...		1129	1538
Pantyffynnon ... d.		0515	0957	1356	...	1900	...		1149	1558
Llandeilo ... d.		0534	1016	1416	...	1920	...		1209	1617
Llandovery ... d.		0556	1038	1438	...	1942	...		1231	1639
Llanwrtyd ... d.		0621	1107r	1502	...	2008	...		1255	1704
Llandrindod ... a.		0649	1136	1531	...	2037	...		1324	1732
Llandrindod ... d.		0655	1138	1539	...	2039	...		1405	1758
Knighton ... d.		0731	1215	1615	...	2116	...		1441	1834
Craven Arms ...... 162 d.		0753	1236	1637	...	2137	...		1502	1855
Church Stretton ... 162 d.		0806	1250	1650	...	2150	...		1515	1908
Shrewsbury .... 162 a.		0821	1307	1710	...	2212	...		1533	1923

C – To / from Cardiff. R – To Crewe. b – 1734 on ⑥. p – Arrives 1452. r – Arrives 6–7 minutes earlier. v – Arrives 2002.

147 SHREWSBURY - CHESTER

AW

km			✖	✖	✖ 🍷 C	✖	✖ C	✖ 🍷	✖ 🍷 C	✖ 🍷	✖ 🍷 C	✖ 🍷	✖ 🍷 C	✖ 🍷	✖ 🍷 C	⑥ 🍷	Ⓐ 🍷	✖ 🍷 C	✖	Ⓐ C	⑥ CL	✖	✖	✖
	Birmingham New St **145** ... d.	✖	...	...	*0633*	0717p	*0833*	0933	*1033*	1133	*1233*	1333	*1433*	1533	*1633*	1733	1733	*1833*	1933	*2033*	*2033*	*2057*z	2233	...
0	**Shrewsbury** ... d.		0520	0610	0730	0828	0930	1026	1130	1226	1330	1426	1530	1626	1730	1826	1836	1930	2026	2138	2138	2226	2329	2335
29	Gobowen ... d.		0539	0629	0749	0847	0949	1046	1149	1246	1349	1446	1549	1646	1749	1846	1856	1949	2046	2157	2157	2246	|	2354
41	Ruabon ... d.		0550	0640	0800	0858	1000	1057	1200	1257	1400	1457	1600	1657	1800	1857	1907	2000	2057	2208	2208	2257	◧	0005
48	Wrexham General ... d.		0557	0647	0807	0905	1007	1103	1207	1303	1407	1503	1607	1703	1807	1903	1913	2013	2103	2215	2215	2306	|	0012
68	**Chester** ... a.		0616	0709	0828	0927	1028	1121d	1228r	1326	1428	1522v	1628	1722v	1825	1922	1934	2031b	2123v	2232	2232	2326	0026	0035
	Holyhead **165** ... a.		*0821*	*0930*	1020	*1130*	1220	*1330*	1430	*1530*	1630	*1720*	1830	*1920*	2030	*2133*	*2140*	2235	*2330*	0047	*0145*q	...	0215n	...

		⑦	⑦	⑦ 🍷	⑦	⑦	⑦ 🍷	⑦ 🍷	⑦
Birmingham New St **145** ... d.	⑦	...	1127	*1227*	1427	1657	1857	...	2254
Shrewsbury ... d.		1016	1234	1352	1536	1753	2014	2046	2350
Gobowen ... d.		1035	1253	1412	1557	1812	2033	|	|
Ruabon ... d.		1046	1304	1424	1608	1823	2044	|	◧
Wrexham General ... d.		1053	1311	1441	1614	1830	2051	2116	|
Chester ... a.		1111	1329	1459	1633	1848	2109	2134	0048
Holyhead **165** ... a.		*1322*	...	1658	...	...	*2314*	2351	0227

		Ⓐ C	⑥	✖ 🍷 C		✖ 🍷	✖ C	✖ 🍷	✖ C	✖ 🍷
Holyhead **165** ... d.	✖	...	...	0427	...	*0532*v	0615	*0715*	0810p	*0928*
Chester ... d.		0507	0518	0612	...	0728	0820	0928	1020	1128
Wrexham General ... d.		0524	0534	0628	...	0744	0837	0944	1037	1144
Ruabon ... d.		0530	0541	0635	...	0751	0844	0951	1043	1151
Gobowen ... d.		0542	0552	0646	...	0802	0855	1002	1055	1202
Shrewsbury ... a.		0607	0613	0707	...	0822	0916	1022	1115	1222
Birmingham New St **145** a.		*0748*	0718	*0818*	...	0918	*1018*	1118	*1218*	1318

	✖ 🍷 C	✖ 🍷	✖ 🍷 C	✖ 🍷	✖ 🍷 C	✖	✖ 🍷 C		⑥	Ⓐ	✖ 🍷	✖	✖ X			⑦	⑦ 🍷	⑦ 🍷 C	⑦	⑦	⑦ 🍷 C	⑦	⑦ 🍷	⑦ W
Holyhead **165** ... d.	1030	...	1235	*1320*a	1435	...	1635	...	...	*1727*	1835	...	2035	...	⑦	...	...	1035	...	...	1725	...	1840	...
Chester ... d.	1220	1328	1420	1528	1620	1728	1820	...	1928	1956	2028	2128	2229	...		0953	1112	1220	1424	1730	1907	1928	2024	2131
Wrexham General ... d.	1237	1344	1437	1544	1636	1744	1836	...	1944	2012	2044	2144	2246	...		1010	1128	1237	1444	1747	1923	1944	2040	2148
Ruabon ... d.	1243	1351	1443	1551	1643	1751	1843	...	1951	2019	2051	2151	2252	...		1016	1135	1244	1451	1753	1930	1951	2047	2155
Gobowen ... d.	1255	1402	1455	1602	1654	1802	1854	...	2002	2030	2102	2202	2304	...		1028	1146	1255	1502	1805	1941	2002	2058	2207
Shrewsbury ... a.	1315	1422	1515	1622	1715	1822	1915	...	2022	2055	2123	2222	2326	...		1048	1207	1315	1523	1825	1959	2023	2119	2227
Birmingham New St **145** ... a.	*1418*	1518	*1618*	1718	*1819*	1918	*2018*	...	2118	...	2218	2318	...	...		...	1315	*1449*	1633	1934	...	2132	2236	*2345*y

C – From / to Cardiff.
L – To Llandudno Junction.
W – To Wolverhampton.
X – To Wolverhampton on Ⓐ.

a – Ⓐ only.
b – 2026 on ⑥.
d – 1127 on ⑥.
n – Not ⑦.

p – 15–16 minutes later on ⑥.
q – By 🚌. Change at Llandudno Junction.
r – 1225 on ⑥.
v – 3–4 minutes later on ⑥.

y – Change at Wolverhampton.
z – 2133 on ⑥.

◧ – Via Crewe.

AW 2nd class — SHREWSBURY - ABERYSTWYTH — 148

km			⚒	⚒	Ⓐ	⚒	⚒ 🍷	⚒ A 🍷	⚒ 🍷	⚒ 🍷	⚒ 🍷	⚒	❖	⑤			⑦	⑦	⑦	⑦ P 🍷	⑦		⑦ 🍷	⑦
	Birmingham New St **145**	d.	⚒	...	...	...	0633	0833	1033	1233	1433	1633	1833	2033	2033	...	⑦	...	...	0937	1137	...	...	1539	1937
0	**Shrewsbury**	d.		...	...	...	0728	0928	1128	1328	1528	1728	1928	2128	2128	...	▲	...	0833	1101	1245	...	...	1718	2100
32	Welshpool	d.		...	...	...	0751	0951	1151	1351	1551	1751	1951	2151	2151	...		...	0855	1124	1308	...	...	1741	2129r
54	Newtown	d.		...	...	...	0807	1007	1207	1407	1607	1807	2007	2207	2207	...		...	0911	1145r	1324	...	...	1757	2145
63	Caersws	d.		...	...	...	0813	1013	1213	1413	1613	1813	2013	2217	2217	...		...	0918	1152	1331	...	...	1804	2152
98	**Machynlleth 149**	d.		0435	0630	0810	0845	1045	1245	1445	1645	1845	2045	2252r	2305z	...		0800	0950	1222	1402	1408	...	1836	2222
04	Dovey Junction **149**	d.		0441	0636	0816	0851	1051	1251	1451	1651	1851	2051	2259	2312	...		0807	0957	1229	1408	1415	...	1843	2228
18	Borth	d.		0452	0647	0827	0902	1102	1302	1502	1702	1902	2102	2309	2323	...		0817	1007	1239	...	1425	...	1854	2239
31	**Aberystwyth**	a.		0505	0700	0840	0922	1122	1322	1522	1722	1922	2122	2330	2343	...		0831	1021	1253	...	1439	...	1907	2252

			⚒ 🍷		⚒ 🍷	⚒ 🍷	⚒ 🍷	⚒ A 🍷	⚒ 🍷	⚒ 🍷	⚒	⚒	❖	⑤			⑦	⑦		⑦ 🍷	⑦ 🍷		⑦ W		⑦
erystwyth	d.	⚒	0512	...	0727	0927	1127	1327	1527	1727	1927	2136	2340	2353	...	⑦	0837	1035	...	1329	1531	...	2003	...	2304
rth	d.		0525	...	0739	0939	1139	1339	1539	1739	1939	2148	2352	0005	...	▲	0849	1047	...	1341	1543	...	2015	...	2316
ovey Junction **149**	d.		0537	...	0750	0950	1150	1350	1550	1750	1950	2159	0003	0016	...		0900	1058	...	1352	1554	...	2026	...	2327
achynlleth 149	d.		0545	...	0802	1002	1202	1402	1602	1802	2002	2211	0013	0026	...		0909	1108	...	1405	1606	...	2035	...	2335
aersws	d.		0617	...	0833	1033	1233	1433	1633	1833	2033	...	...	...	...		0937	1136	...	1434	1634	...	2103	...	...
ewtown	d.		0624	...	0840	1040	1240	1440	1640	1840	2040	...	...	...	...		0944	1144	...	1441	1641	...	2110	...	...
elshpool	d.		0639	...	0855	1055	1255	1455	1655	1855	2055	...	...	...	...		1000	1200	...	1457	1657	...	2127	...	...
hrewsbury	a.		0705	...	0921	1121	1321	1521	1721	1921	2121	...	...	...	...		1023	1223	...	1520	1722	...	2150	...	...
Birmingham New St **145**	a.		0818	...	1018	1218	1418	1618	1819	2018	*2218*	...	...	...	...		1121	1324	...	1620	1832	...	*2350y*	...	...

– Conveys (2) Birmingham - Machynlleth - Pwllheli and v.v.
P – To Pwllheli.
W – To Wolverhampton.
r – Arrives 6–7 minutes earlier.
y – Change at Wolverhampton.
z – Arrives 2245.
❖ – ①–④ and ⑥.
▲ – Services on ⑦ are subject to alteration from July 8.

AW 2nd class — MACHYNLLETH - PWLLHELI — 149

km				⚒	⚒	⚒	⚒	⚒ 🍷	⚒	⚒	⑤	⚒			⑦		⑦ 🍷		⑦
	Birmingham New St **148**	d.	⚒	...	...	*0633*	*0833*	1033	*1233*	*1433*	*1633*	*1833*	...	⑦	...	...	1137	...	*1539*
0	**Machynlleth 148**	d.		0530	0649	0905	1100	1256	1456	1700	1900	2117	...	▲	0954	...	1402	...	1840
6	Dovey Junction **148**	d.		0544c	0655	0911	1106	1302	1502	1706	1906	2123	...		1001	...	1409	...	1847
16	Aberdovey	d.		0556	0707	0923	1118	1314	1514	1718	1918	2135	...		1012	...	1421	...	1859
22	Tywyn	d.		0602	0715	0930	1126	1322	1522	1726	1926	2141	...		1019	...	1427	...	1906
37	Fairbourne	d.		0619	0733	0948	1144	1340	1540	1744	1944	2159	...		1037	...	1445	...	1924
41	**Barmouth**	d.		0631	0750f	0957	1156	1352	1552	1756	1956	2208	...		1045	...	1501c	...	1933
58	Harlech	d.		0651	0832j	1021	1224	1430r	1620c	1824c	...	2229	...		1107	...	1523	...	1957
67	Penrhyndeudraeth	d.		|	0843	1032	1235	1441	1631	1835	...	2240	...		1119	...	1535	...	2008
69	Minffordd **166**	d.		|	0846	1036	1239	1445	1635	1839	...	2243	...		1121	...	1538	...	2012
72	Porthmadog	d.		0707	0852	1042	1247	1453	1642	1846	...	2248	...		1127	...	1543	...	2016
80	Criccieth	d.		|	0859	1050	1255	1501	1650	1854	...	2255	...		1134	...	1550	...	2024
93	**Pwllheli**	a.		0727	0912	1109	1314	1518	1709	1913	...	2313	...		1148	...	1604	...	2038

			⚒	⚒	⚒		⚒ 🍷	⚒ 🍷	⚒	⚒	⚒		⚒	⑤			⑦	⑦ 🍷		⑦
wllheli	d.	⚒	...	0610	0734	...	0936	1132	1332	1532	1732	...	2000	...	...	⑦	1156	1355	...	1827
riccieth	d.		...	0623	0746	...	0949	1145	1345	1545	1745	...	2013	...	...	▲	1209	1408	...	1840
orthmadog	d.		...	0632	0755	...	0958	1156	1356	1556	1756	...	2023	...	...		1218	1417	...	1850
inffordd **166**	d.		...	0636	0759	...	1002	1200	1400	1600	1800	...	2027	...	...		1223	1422	...	1854
enrhyndeudraeth	d.		...	0639	0803	...	1005	1203	1403	1603	1803	...	2030	...	...		1226	1425	...	1858
arlech	d.		...	0720b	0832z	...	1022c	1225f	1430r	1620	1825f	...	2046	...	...		1238	1437	...	1910
armouth	d.		0646	0749c	0859c	...	1049c	1249	1452	1650f	1849	...	2114c	2212	...		1301	1500	...	1933
airbourne	d.		0653	0756	0906	...	1056	1256	1459	1657	1856	...	2121	2219	...		1308	1507	...	1941
ywyn	d.		0716c	0815	0931c	...	1127d	1323c	1523c	1727d	1926d	...	2146c	2238	...		1327	1526	...	2000
berdovey	d.		0722	0821	0937	...	1133	1329	1529	1733	1932	...	2152	2244	...		1333	1532	...	2006
ovey Junction **148**	d.		0735	0835	0951	...	1147	1341	1541	1746	1946	...	2207	2258	...		1346	1545	...	2019
achynlleth 148	a.		0744	0844	1000	...	1158	1352	1548	1757	1957	...	2216	2307	...		1353	1552	...	2026
Birmingham New St **148**	a.		*1018*	...	...	...	*1418*	1618	*1819*	*2018*	...	...	...	...	...		*1620*	*1832*	...	...

b – Arrives 0650.
c – Arrives 6–8 minutes earlier.
d – Arrives 12–13 minutes earlier.
f – Arrives 9–11 minutes earlier.
j – Arrives 0811.
r – Arrives 16–17 minutes earlier.
z – Arrives 0813.

▲ – Services on ⑦ are subject to alteration from Sept. 16.

VT, LM, XC — LONDON and BIRMINGHAM - MANCHESTER and LIVERPOOL — 150

km				Ⓐ	Ⓐ 🍴 G		Ⓐ 🍷 E	Ⓐ 🍷	Ⓐ 🍷	Ⓐ 🍷	Ⓐ	Ⓐ 🍷 G	Ⓐ 🍴	Ⓐ 🍷	Ⓐ 🍷	Ⓐ 🍴 G	Ⓐ 🍷 S	Ⓐ 🍴	Ⓐ	Ⓐ 🍷 BE	Ⓐ 🍴	Ⓐ 🍴	Ⓐ 🍷 T	Ⓐ 🍷	Ⓐ 🍴 L	Ⓐ 🍷	Ⓐ 🍴
0	**London** Euston	d.	Ⓐ	...	...	...	...	...	...	...	...	...	0620	...	...	0646	...	0657	...	...	0700	0735	...	...	0746	...	0805
28	Watford Junction △	d.		...	...	...	...	...	...	...	...	...	0635	...	...	|	...	0712	...	...	0716	|	...	...	0801	...	|
80	Milton Keynes	d.		...	...	...	...	...	...	...	...	...	0655	...	...	0717	...	|	...	...	0736	|	...	...	|	...	0836
33	Rugby	d.		...	...	...	...	...	...	...	0629	...	|	...	...	0739	...	|	...	...	|	|	...	...	0839	...	|
56	Nuneaton	d.		...	...	...	...	...	...	...	0643	...	|	...	...	|	...	|	...	...	0809	|	...	...	|	...	|
	Birmingham New St	d.		0520	0530	...	0601	0603	0607	0630	|	0703	|	0718	0721	|	0748	|	0751	0800	|	|	0818	0826	|	0848	|
	Wolverhampton	d.		0538	0549	...	*0621*	0621	0639	0705	|	0721	|	0739	0744	|	0806	|	0809	0821	|	|	0839	0844	|	0906	|
15	**Stafford**	d.		0552	0605	...	0639	0634	0700	0718	0725	0734	|	0754	0801	|	0818	|	0826	|	0835	|	0854	0901	|	0918	|
35	Stoke on Trent	a.		|	|	...	0656	|	|	0736	|	|	0804	0812	|	|	0836	0841	|	|	|	0906	0912	|	|	0936	0941
57	Macclesfield	a.		|	|	...	0717	|	|	0756	|	|	0820	0832	|	|	0852	0857	|	|	|	|	0931	|	|	0952	0957
54	**Crewe**	a.		0616	0625	...	|	|	0722	|	0745	0753	|	|	0822	0830	|	|	0851	0854	0858	|	|	0922	0930	|	|
	Holyhead ¶ **165**	a.		0821	*0930*	...	|	|	|	|	|	|	|	|	|	|	|	|	*1130*	|	|	|	|	|	|	|	|
	Stockport	a.		|	*0714*	...	0730	|	|	0809	|	|	0835s	0846	|	|	0905	0912s	|	|	|	0934s	0946	|	|	1005	1012s
96	**Manchester** P'dilly	a.		*0713r*	*0728*	...	0741	0802	|	0827	|	|	0848	0902	|	|	0920	0925	|	|	|	0946	1002	|	|	1020	1024
90	Runcorn	a.		...	*0703*	...	|	...	0747	...	0810	|	...	...	0845	|	...	...	0908	|	0915	...	...	0945	|	...	...
12	**Liverpool** Lime St	a.		...	*0727*	...	|	...	0810	...	0835	|	...	...	0909	|	...	...	0931	|	0938	...	...	1009	|	...	...
	Preston **152**	a.		...	0717	...	0826	...	...	...	...	0841	...	...	...	0914	...	...	...	0938	...	...	...	...	1014	...	...

		Ⓐ 🍷	Ⓐ 🍷 XG	Ⓐ 🍴	Ⓐ 🍴	Ⓐ 🍷 T	Ⓐ 🍷	Ⓐ 🍴 G	Ⓐ 🍴	Ⓐ 🍷	Ⓐ 🍴	Ⓐ 🍷	Ⓐ 🍷 UE	Ⓐ 🍴	Ⓐ 🍴	Ⓐ 🍷 R	Ⓐ 🍷	Ⓐ 🍴 C	Ⓐ 🍷	Ⓐ 🍴	Ⓐ 🍷	Ⓐ 🍷 PG	Ⓐ 🍴 G	Ⓐ 🍴	Ⓐ 🍴	Ⓐ 🍴	Ⓐ 🍷 R
ondon Euston	d.	...	...	0817	0835	...	...	0846	0900	...	0905	...	...	0917	0935	...	...	0946	...	1005	...	...	1029	1035	...	1015	...
atford Junction △	d.	...	...	0832	|	...	...	0901	|	...	0920	...	...	|	|	...	...	|	...	|	...	...	|	|	...	1030	...
lton Keynes	d.	...	...	|	|	...	...	|	|	...	|	...	...	0948	|	...	...	1020	...	1036	...	...	|	|	...	|	...
ugby	d.	...	...	|	|	...	...	|	0950	...	|	...	...	|	|	...	...	1040	...	|	...	...	|	|	1047	|	...
uneaton	d.	...	...	0922	|	...	...	|	|	...	|	...	...	1022	|	...	...	|	...	|	...	...	|	|	1100	1120	...
Birmingham New St	d.	0851	0903	|	|	0918	0921	|	|	0948	|	0951	1003	|	|	1018	1021	|	1048	|	1051	1103	|	|	|	|	1118
Wolverhampton	d.	0910	0921	|	|	0939	0944	|	|	1006	|	1010	1021	|	|	1039	1044	|	1106	|	1110	1121	|	|	|	|	1139
afford	d.	0924	|	0948	|	|	1001	|	|	1018	|	1024	|	1048	|	|	1101	|	1118	|	1124	|	|	|	|	1146	|
Stoke on Trent	a.	|	|	|	1006	1012	|	|	|	1036	1041	|	|	|	1106	1112	|	|	1136	1141	|	|	|	1206	|	|	1212
Macclesfield	a.	|	|	|	|	1032	|	|	|	1052	1057	|	|	|	|	1131	|	|	1152	1157	|	|	|	|	|	|	1232
ewe	a.	0946	0953	1008	|	|	1021	1031	1041	|	|	1046	1053	1108	|	|	1122	1131	|	|	1150	1154	|	|	1200	1208	|
Holyhead ¶ **165**	a.	|	|	|	|	|	|	|	1303	|	|	|	*1330*	|	|	|	|	|	|	|	|	|	|	|	|	|	|
Stockport	a.	*1039*	|	|	1034s	1046	|	|	...	1105	1112s	*1139*	|	|	1134s	1146	|	|	1205	1212s	*1239*	|	|	1234s	1241s	|	1246
Manchester P'dilly	a.	*1054*	|	|	1046	1102	|	|	...	1120	1124	*1154*	|	|	1146	1202	|	|	1220	1224	*1254*	|	|	1246	1255	|	1302
uncorn	a.	1003	|	1026	...	...	1045	|	...	...	...	1103	|	1126	...	...	1145	|	...	...	...	|	|	...	...	1227	...
verpool Lime St	a.	1026	|	1048	...	...	1109	|	...	...	...	1126	|	1148	...	...	1209	|	...	...	...	|	|	...	...	1248	...
Preston **152**	a.	...	1037	...	...	...	...	1115	...	...	...	...	1137	...	...	...	...	1215	...	...	...	1234	1243	...	...	...	...

– From Bristol.
– To Carlisle.
– To Edinburgh.
– To Glasgow.
L – To Lancaster.
P – From Plymouth.
R – From Reading.
S – From Southampton.
T – From Gatwick.
U – From Bournemouth.
X – From Exeter.
r – Change at Crewe.
s – Stops to set down only.
△ – Trains stop here to pick up only.
¶ – For Birmingham to Holyhead via Shrewsbury, see Table **147**.

150 LONDON and BIRMINGHAM - MANCHESTER and LIVERPOOL

VT, LM, XC

		Ⓐ	Ⓐ	Ⓐ	Ⓐ	Ⓐ	Ⓐ	Ⓐ	Ⓐ	Ⓐ	Ⓐ	Ⓐ	Ⓐ	Ⓐ	Ⓐ	Ⓐ	Ⓐ	Ⓐ	Ⓐ	Ⓐ	Ⓐ	Ⓐ	Ⓐ	Ⓐ	Ⓐ	Ⓐ
		🍷	🍷	🍷	🍷	🍷	🍷	🍷	🍷	🍷	🍷	🍷	🍷	🍷	🍷	🍷	🍷	🍷	🍷	🍷	🍷	🍷	🍷	🍷	🍷	🍷
			L	U			E		Q		R		G				G			Z		L	U			E	
London Euston	d.	...	1046	...	1105	...	...	1117	1128	1135	...	...	1146	...	1205	...	...	1217	1235	...	...	1246	...	1305	...	...	131
Watford Junction △	d.	...	1101	...	1120	...	...	|	|	|	...	...	|	...	|	...	...	1232	|	...	...	|	...	1320	...	...	|
Milton Keynes	d.	...	|	...	|	...	...	1148	|	|	...	...	1217	...	1236	...	...	|	|	...	...	1317	...	|	...	...	134
Rugby	d.	...	1139	...	|	...	...	|	|	|	...	...	1239	...	|	...	...	|	|	...	...	1339	...	|	...	...	|
Nuneaton	d.	...	|	...	|	...	...	1222	|	|	...	...	|	...	|	...	...	1321	|	...	...	|	...	|	...	...	142
Birmingham New St	d.	1121	|	1148	|	1151	1203	|	|	|	1218	1221	|	1248	|	1251	1303	|	|	1318	1321	|	1348	|	1351	1403	|
Wolverhampton	d.	1144	|	|	|	1210	1221	|	|	|	1239	1244	|	1306	|	1310	1321	|	|	1339	1344	|	1406	|	1410	1421	|
Stafford	d.	1201	|	1218	|	1224	|	1248	|	|	|	1301	|	1318	|	1324	|	1347	|	|	1401	|	1418	|	1424	|	144
Stoke on Trent	a.	|	|	1236	1241	|	|	|	|	1306	1312	|	|	1336	1341	|	|	|	1406	1412	|	|	1436	1441	|	|	|
Macclesfield	a.	|	|	1252	1257	|	|	|	|	|	1331	|	|	1352	1357	|	|	|	|	1432	|	|	1452	1457	|	|	|
Crewe	a.	1222	1231	|	|	1245	1253	1309	1312	|	|	1322	1331	|	|	1350	1353	1407	|	|	1422	1431	|	|	1445	1453	150
Holyhead ¶ **165**	a.	|	|	|	|	|	|	*1530*	*1530*j	|	|	|	|	|	|	|	|	|	|	|	|	|	|	|	|	*1720*	|
Stockport	a.	|	|	1305	1312s	*1339*	|	|	...	1334s	1346	|	|	1405	1412s	*1439*	|	|	1434s	1446	|	|	1505	1512s	*1539*	|	|
Manchester P'dilly	a.	|	|	1320	1324	*1354*	|	|	...	1346	1402	|	|	1420	1424	*1454*	|	|	1446	1502	|	|	1520	1524	*1554*	|	|
Runcorn	a.	1245	|	...	...	1303	|	1326	...	...	...	1345	|	...	...	...	|	1425	...	...	1445	|	...	...	1503	|	152
Liverpool Lime St	a.	1309	|	...	...	1326	|	1349	...	...	...	1409	|	...	...	...	|	1447	...	...	1509	|	...	...	1526	|	154
Preston **152**	a.	...	1315	...	...	...	1337	...	...	...	...	...	1415	...	...	...	1441	...	...	...	...	1515	...	...	...	1537	...
		Ⓐ	Ⓐ	Ⓐ	Ⓐ	Ⓐ	Ⓐ	Ⓐ	Ⓐ	Ⓐ	Ⓐ	Ⓐ	Ⓐ	Ⓐ	Ⓐ	Ⓐ	Ⓐ	Ⓐ	Ⓐ	Ⓐ	Ⓐ	Ⓐ	Ⓐ	Ⓐ	Ⓐ	Ⓐ	Ⓐ
		🍷	🍷	🍷	🍷	🍷	🍷	🍷	🍷	🍷	🍷	🍷	🍷	🍷	🍷	🍷	🍷	🍷	✕	✕	🍷	🍷	✕	🍷	🍷	🍷	🍷
			R		G				G			Z		G	U			E			R		G				
London Euston	d.	1335	...	...	1346	...	1405	...	...	1417	1435	...	...	1446	...	1505	...	...	1517	1535	...	...	1546	1549	...	1605	...
Watford Junction △	d.	|	...	...	1401	...	|	...	...	1432	|	...	...	|	...	1520	...	...	|	|	...	...	|	|	...	|	...
Milton Keynes	d.	|	...	...	|	...	1436	...	...	|	|	...	...	1517	...	|	...	...	1548	|	...	...	|	|	...	1636u	...
Rugby	d.	|	...	...	1439	...	|	...	...	|	|	...	...	1539	...	|	...	...	|	|	...	...	|	1639	...	|	...
Nuneaton	d.	|	...	...	|	...	|	...	...	1521	|	...	...	|	...	|	...	...	1621	|	...	...	|	|	...	|	...
Birmingham New St	d.	|	1418	1421	|	1448	|	1451	1503	|	|	1518	1521	|	1548	|	1551	1603	|	|	1618	1621	|	|	1648	|	165
Wolverhampton	d.	|	1439	1444	|	1506	|	1510	1521	|	|	1539	1544	|	|	|	1610	1621	|	|	1639	1644	|	|	1706	|	171
Stafford	d.	|	|	1501	|	1518	|	1524	|	1547	|	|	1601	|	1618	|	1624	|	1647	|	|	1701	|	|	1718	|	172
Stoke on Trent	a.	1506	1512	|	|	1536	1541	|	|	|	1606	1612	|	|	1636	1641	|	|	|	1706	1712	|	|	|	1736	1741	|
Macclesfield	a.	|	1531	|	|	1552	1557	|	|	|	|	1632	|	|	1652	1657	|	|	|	1721	1732	|	|	|	1752	1757	|
Crewe	a.	|	|	1522	1531	|	|	1550	1555	1607	|	|	1622	1631	|	|	1645	1653	1707	|	|	1722	1731	1734	|	|	174
Holyhead ¶ **165**	a.	|	|	|	|	|	|	|	|	|	|	|	|	|	|	|	|	*1920*	|	|	|	*1941*	|	1941	|	|	|
Stockport	a.	1534s	1546	|	|	1605	1612s	*1640*	|	|	1634s	1646	|	|	1705	1712s	*1738*	|	|	1735s	1746	|	|	...	1805	1811s	*183*
Manchester P'dilly	a.	1546	1602	|	|	1620	1624	*1654*	|	|	1646	1702	|	|	1720	1724	*1754*	|	|	1749	1802	|	|	...	1820	1825	*185*
Runcorn	a.	...	...	1545	|	...	...	...	|	1625	...	...	1645	|	...	...	1703	|	1725	...	...	1745	|	...	...	...	|
Liverpool Lime St	a.	...	...	1609	|	...	...	...	|	1648	...	...	1709	|	...	...	1726	|	1747	...	...	1809	|	...	...	...	|
Preston **152**	a.	...	...	...	1615	...	...	...	1640	...	...	...	...	1715	...	...	...	1737	...	...	...	...	1815	...	...	...	183
		Ⓐ	Ⓐ	Ⓐ	Ⓐ	Ⓐ	Ⓐ	Ⓐ	Ⓐ	Ⓐ	Ⓐ	Ⓐ	Ⓐ	Ⓐ	Ⓐ	Ⓐ	Ⓐ	Ⓐ	Ⓐ	Ⓐ	Ⓐ	Ⓐ	Ⓐ	Ⓐ	Ⓐ	Ⓐ	Ⓐ
		🍷	🍷	🍷	🍷	🍷	🍷	🍷	🍷	🍷	🍷	✕	🍷	✕	✕	✕	🍷	🍷	✕	✕	✕	🍷	🍷	✕	🍷	✕	✕
		G			P		E	U				G	E				H		L					G	G		
London Euston	d.	...	1617	1635	...	...	1646	...	1649	1705	...	1715	...	1717	1721	1735	...	...	1745	1748	1805	...	...	1808	...	1817	183
Watford Junction △	d.	...	1632	|	...	...	|	...	|	1720	...	|	...	|	|	|	...	...	|	1803	|	...	...	|	...	|	|
Milton Keynes	d.	...	|	|	...	...	|	...	1720u	|	...	|	...	|	|	|	...	...	|	|	|	...	...	|	...	1849u	|
Rugby	d.	...	|	|	...	...	|	...	|	|	...	|	...	|	1810	|	...	...	1834	|	|	...	...	1856	...	|	|
Nuneaton	d.	...	1721	|	...	...	|	...	|	|	...	|	...	|	1824	|	...	...	|	|	1904	...	...	|	...	|	|
Birmingham New St	d.	1703	|	|	1718	1721	|	1748	|	|	1751	|	1803	|	|	|	1818	1821	|	|	|	1843	1851	|	1903	|	|
Wolverhampton	d.	|	|	|	1739	1744	|	1806	|	|	1810	|	1821	|	|	|	1839	1844	|	|	|	1906	1910	|	1921	|	|
Stafford	d.	|	1747	|	|	1801	1811	1818	|	|	1827	|	|	|	1850	|	|	1903	1910	|	|	1927	1924	|	1936	1945	|
Stoke on Trent	a.	|	|	1806	1812	|	|	1836	|	1841	|	|	|	|	|	1906	1912	|	|	|	1939	1945	|	|	|	|	200
Macclesfield	a.	|	|	1821	1832	|	|	1852	|	1857	|	|	|	|	|	1922	1931	|	|	|	1957	2001	|	|	|	|	202
Crewe	a.	1753	1807	|	|	1822	1831	|	1841	|	1848	|	1854	1907	1911	|	|	1929	|	1934	|	|	1949	1952	1958	2007	|
Holyhead ¶ **165**	a.	|	|	|	|	|	|	|	|	|	|	|	|	|	2140	|	|	|	|	|	|	|	|	|	|	|	|
Stockport	a.	|	|	1835s	1846	|	|	1905	1909s	1912s	*1939*	|	|	|	...	1936s	1946	|	|	2002s	2012s	2016	*2039*	|	|	|	2036
Manchester P'dilly	a.	|	|	1849	1902	|	|	1920	1921	1924	*1957*	|	|	|	...	1950	2002	|	|	2014	2020	2035	*2054*	|	|	|	205
Runcorn	a.	|	1825	...	...	1845	|	...	...	...	1905	|	|	1925	...	...	...	1953	|	...	...	...	...	|	|	2025	...
Liverpool Lime St	a.	|	1847	...	...	1909	|	...	...	...	1929	|	|	1945	...	...	...	2018	|	...	...	...	...	|	|	2047	...
Preston **152**	a.	1839	...	...	...	...	1915	...	...	...	...	1937	1942	...	...	...	...	...	2013	...	...	...	...	2032	2042	...	...
		Ⓐ	Ⓐ	Ⓐ	Ⓐ	Ⓐ	Ⓐ	Ⓐ	Ⓐ	Ⓐ	Ⓐ	Ⓐ	Ⓐ	Ⓐ	Ⓐ	Ⓐ	Ⓐ	Ⓐ	Ⓐ	Ⓐ	Ⓐ	Ⓐ	Ⓐ	Ⓐ		Ⓐ	Ⓐ
		🍷	🍷	🍷	🍷	🍷	🍷	🍷	🍷	🍷	🍷	🍷	🍷	🍷	🍷	🍷	🍷	🍷	🍷	🍷	🍷	🍷	🍷	2		🍷	🍷
			P		C		U			D			C		B			P					U	✣			
London Euston	d.	1820	...	...	1845	1905	...	1917	1935	...	...	1938	1946	2005	...	...	2017	...	...	2046	2105	2110	...	...	...	...	220
Watford Junction △	d.	|	...	...	1900	|	...	1932	|	...	...	|	|	|	...	...	|	...	...	2101	2120	|	...	...	...	...	222
Milton Keynes	d.	|	...	...	|	|	...	|	|	...	...	|	2019	2036	...	...	2048	...	...	|	|	|	...	...	...	...	224
Rugby	d.	|	...	...	|	|	...	|	|	...	...	|	2041	|	...	...	|	...	...	2138	|	|	...	...	...	...	232
Nuneaton	d.	|	...	...	|	|	...	2020	|	...	...	|	|	|	...	...	2121	...	...	|	|	2215	...	...	...	...	233
Birmingham New St	d.	|	1918	1921	|	|	2003	|	|	2018	2021	|	|	|	2048	2103	|	2118	2121	|	|	|	2218	2233	...	2307	|
Wolverhampton	d.	|	1939	1944	|	|	2021	|	|	2039	2044	|	|	|	2111	2121	|	2139	2144	|	|	|	2239	2248	...	2334	|
Stafford	d.	1952	|	2001	|	|	2034	|	2057	|	2101	|	|	|	2124	2136	2147	2154	2201	|	|	2241	2254	|	...	2351	0003
Stoke on Trent	a.	|	2012	|	|	2040	|	|	|	2112	|	|	|	2139	2145	|	|	2212	|	|	2244	|	2312	|	...	|	|
Macclesfield	a.	|	2032	|	|	2057	|	|	|	2128	|	|	|	2157	2202	|	|	2232	|	|	2300	|	|	|	...	|	|
Crewe	a.	2014	|	2022	2031	|	2054	2103	|	|	2123	2129	2137	|	|	2158	2207	|	2222	2235	|	2301	|	0001	...	0021	0032
Holyhead ¶ **165**	a.	|	|	|	|	|	|	|	|	|	|	2330	|	|	|	|	|	|	|	|	|	|	|	0215	...	|	|
Stockport	a.	2044	2046	|	|	2112s	2125	|	2142s	2146	|	...	|	2212s	2215	|	|	2246	*2333*	|	2315s	|	|	...	...	|	0058
Manchester P'dilly	a.	2104	2102	|	|	2124	2148	|	2154	2202	|	...	|	2224	2232	|	|	2302	*2349*	|	2329	|	0007	...	...	*0135*	011
Runcorn	a.	...	...	2045	|	...	...	2121	...	...	2145	...	|	...	...	|	2225	...	2245	|	...	2319	...	...	...	...	|
Liverpool Lime St	a.	...	...	2109	|	...	...	2145	...	...	2209	...	|	...	...	|	2247	...	2312	|	...	2347	...	...	...	...	|
Preston **152**	a.	...	...	...	2115	...	...	...	...	...	...	...	2221	...	...	2304	...	...	...	2324	...	...	...	...	...	...	*021*
			⑥	⑥		⑥	⑥		⑥	⑥	⑥	⑥	⑥	⑥	⑥	⑥	⑥	⑥	⑥	⑥	⑥	⑥	⑥	⑥	⑥	⑥	⑥
				🍷					🍷	🍷		🍷	🍷	🍷	🍷	🍷		🍷	🍷	🍷	🍷	🍷	🍷		🍷	🍷	🍷
				G					G			G		E		T					G		X		G		
London Euston	d.		...	...	...	...	...	...	...	...	...	0525	0531	...	0630	...	*0610*	0647	0655	0704	...	0740	...	*0720*	0751	0759	080
Watford Junction △	d.	⑥	...	...	...	...	...	...	...	...	...	0540	|	...	0646	...	*0629*	0703	0710	0719	...	|	...	|	0806	0814	|
Milton Keynes	d.	●	...	...	...	...	...	...	...	...	...	0610	0616	...	|	...	*0658*	0722	0730	|	...	0812	...	*0752*	|	|	083
Rugby	d.		...	...	...	...	...	...	...	...	...	|	0711	...	|	...	|	|	|	0812	...	|	...	|	0857	|	091
Nuneaton	d.		...	...	...	...	...	...	...	...	...	|	|	...	|	...	|	|	|	|	...	|	...	|	|	|	|
Birmingham New St	d.		0520	0530	...	0620	0607	...	0703	0720	0721	|	|	0803	|	0820	0821	|	0848	0850s	0903	|	0920	0921	0940	0948	0950
Wolverhampton	d.		0538	0549	...	0640	0633	...	0721	0740	0744	|	|	0821	|	0840	0844	|	0909	|	0921	|	0940	0944	|	1009	|
Stafford	d.		0552	0605	...	0654	0700	...	0733	0754	0802	0818	|	|	|	0854	0902	0916	0926	|	|	|	0954	1002	1019	1026	|
Stoke on Trent	a.		|	|	...	0712	|	...	|	0812	|	|	|	|	0903	0912	|	|	0943	|	|	1005	1012	|	|	1042	|
Macclesfield	a.		|	|	...	0732	|	...	|	0832	|	|	|	|	0919	0929	|	|	0959	|	|	1021	1032	|	|	1058	|
Crewe	a.		0616	0625	...	|	0722	...	0754	|	0823	0836	0846	0854	|	|	0923	0934	|	0949	0954	|	|	1022	1038	|	104
Holyhead ¶ **165**	a.		0821	*0930*	...	|	|	...	|	|	|	|	*1130*	|	|	|	|	|	|	|	|	|	|	*1253*	|	|	*133*
Stockport	a.		|	*0713*	...	0746	|	...	|	0846	|	|	|	|	0933s	0946	|	|	1014	|	|	1034s	1046	|	|	1113	|
Manchester P'dilly	a.		|	*0740*	...	0802	|	...	|	0902	*0940*	|	|	|	0949	1003	|	|	1025	|	|	1049	1104	|	|	1128	|
Runcorn	a.		|	|	...	...	0746	...	|	...	0846	|	0904	|	...	...	0945	|	...	1009	|	...	...	1045	|	...	110
Liverpool Lime St	a.		*0728*r	|	...	...	0810	...	|	...	0910	|	0931	|	...	...	1009	|	...	1031	|	...	...	1109	|	...	113
Preston **152**	a.		...	0718	...	...	...	...	0839	...	...	0920	...	0938	...	...	...	1026	...	...	1038	...	...	...	1122	...	...

B – From Bristol.
C – To Carlisle.
D – From Guildford.
E – To Edinburgh.
G – To Glasgow.
H – From Brighton.
L – To Lancaster.
P – From Plymouth.
Q – To Llandudno.
R – From Reading.
S – From Southampton.
T – From Gatwick.
U – From Bournemouth.
X – From Exeter.
Z – From Penzance.

NOTES CONTINUE ON FACING PAGE ▶▶

For explanation of standard symbols see page 4

VT, LM, XC — LONDON and BIRMINGHAM - MANCHESTER and LIVERPOOL — 150

	⑥ 🍷 E	⑥ 🍷	⑥ 🍷 U	⑥ 🍷	⑥ 🍷 G	⑥ 🍷	⑥ 🍷	⑥ 🍷 G	⑥ 🍷	⑥ 🍷 P	⑥ 🍷	⑥ 🍷	⑥ 🍷	⑥ 🍷	⑥ 🍷 E	⑥ 🍷	⑥ 🍷 U	⑥ 🍷	⑥ 🍷	⑥ 🍷	⑥ 🍷	⑥ 🍷 G	⑥ 🍷	⑥ 🍷 Z	⑥ 🍷	⑥ 🍷 G
London Euston d.	...	0842	...	*0816*	0851	0855	0905	...	0941	...	*0929*	0947	0952	1005	...	1042	...	*1028*	1051	1058	1105	...	1141	...	*1129*	1151
Watford Junction △ d.	...	0857	...			0910	0921	...		...		1002	1007		...	1057	...			1113	1121	...		...		1206
Milton Keynes d.	...		...	*0848*	0923			...	1013	...	*1000*			1037	...		...	*1100*	1123			...	1213	...	*1201*	
Rugby d.	...		...		0958		1012	...		...		1057		1112	...		...		1158		1212	...		...		1257
Nuneaton d.	...		...					...		...					...		...					...		...		
Birmingham New St d.	1003		1020	1021	1040	1048	1050s	1103		1120	1121	1140	1148	1150s	1203		1220	1221	1240	1248	1250s	1303		1320	1321	1340
Wolverhampton d.	1021		1040	1044		1109		1121		1140	1144		1209		1221		1240	1244		1309		1321		1340	1344	
Stafford d.			1054	1102	1121	1126				1154	1202	1219	1226				1254	1302	1319	1326				1354	1402	1419
Stoke on Trent a.		1105	1112			1143			1205	1212			1243			1305	1312			1343			1405	1412		
Macclesfield a.		1121	1129			1159			1221	1232			1259			1321	1329			1359			1421	1432		
Crewe a.	1054			1123	1140		1149	1154			1223	1238		1248	1254			1323	1338		1350	1354			1423	1438
Holyhead ¶ **165** a.															*1530*											
Stockport a.		1134s	1146			1213			1234s	1246			1313			1334s	1346			1413			1434s	1446		
Manchester P'dilly a.		1149	1202			1228			1248	1304			1332			1349	1404			1428			1449	1504		
Runcorn a.		...	...	1145		...	1209		...	...	1246		...	1308		...	...	1345		...	1408		...	...	1445	
Liverpool Lime St a.		...	...	1209		...	1231		...	...	1309		...	1330		...	...	1409		...	1432		...	...	1509	
Preston **152** a.	1137	...	...	...	1224	...	...	1239	...	...	...	1326	...	...	1336	...	...	...	1423	...	...	1439	...	...	...	1522

	⑥ 🍷	⑥ 🍷	⑥ 🍷 E	⑥ 🍷	⑥ 🍷 U	⑥ 🍷	⑥ 🍷 G	⑥ 🍷	⑥ 🍷	⑥ 🍷 G	⑥ 🍷	⑥ 🍷 Z	⑥ 🍷	⑥ 🍷 G	⑥ 🍷	⑥ 🍷	⑥ 🍷 E	⑥ 🍷	⑥ 🍷 U	⑥	⑥ 🍷 G	⑥ 🍷	⑥ 🍷	⑥ 🍷 G	⑥ 🍷	⑥ 🍷 P
London Euston d.	1158	1205	...	1242	...	*1229*	1251	1258	1305	...	1341	...	*1326*	1351	1358	1405	...	1442	...	*1426*	1451	1458	1505	...	1541	...
Watford Junction △ d.	1213		...	1257	...			1313	1320	...		...		1406	1413		...	1457	...			1513	1520	...		...
Milton Keynes d.		1237	...		...	*1301*	1323			...	1413	...	*1400*			1437	...		...	*1500*	1523			...	1613	...
Rugby d.		1312	...		...		1358		1411	...		...		1457		1512	...		...		1558		1612	...		...
Nuneaton d.			...		...					...		...					...		...					...		...
Birmingham New St d.	1348	1350s	1403		1420	1421	1440	1448	1450s	1503		1520	1521	1540	1548	1550s	1603		1620	1621	1640	1648	1650s	1703		1720
Wolverhampton d.	1409		1421		1440	1444		1509		1521		1540	1544		1609		1621		1640	1644		1709		1721		1740
Stafford d.	1426				1454	1502	1519	1526				1554	1602	1619	1626				1654	1702	1719	1726				1754
Stoke on Trent a.	1443			1505	1512			1543			1605	1612			1643			1705	1712			1743			1805	1812
Macclesfield a.	1459			1521	1529			1559			1621	1633			1659			1721	1729			1759			1821	1832
Crewe a.		1449	1454			1523	1538		1549	1554			1623	1638		1649	1654			1723	1738		1750	1754		
Holyhead ¶ **165** a.		*1720*														*1920*				*1936*				*2046*		
Stockport a.	1513			1534s	1546			1613			1634s	1646			1713			1734s	1746			1813			1834s	1846
Manchester P'dilly a.	1528			1552	1604			1632			1649	1702			1732			1753	1802			1828			1856	1902
Runcorn a.	...	1509		...	...	1545		...	1609		...	...	1646		...	1709		...	...	1745		...	1809		...	...
Liverpool Lime St a.	...	1531		...	...	1609		...	1633		...	...	1709		...	1730		...	...	1809		...	1828		...	...
Preston **152** a.	...	...	1539	...	...	...	1622	...	...	1639	...	...	...	1723	...	...	1739	...	...	...	1822	...	...	1839	...	...

	⑥	⑥ 🍷 C	⑥ 🍷	⑥ 🍷	⑥ 🍷	⑥ 🍷	⑥ 🍷 U	⑥	⑥ 🍷	⑥ 🍷	⑥ 🍷	⑥ 🍷	⑥ 🍷	⑥ 🍷 P	⑥	⑥ 🍷	⑥ 🍷	⑥ 🍷	⑥ 🍷	⑥ 🍷 U	⑥	⑥ 🍷	⑥ 🍷	⑥ 🍷	⑥ 🍷	⑥ 🍷 P
London Euston d.	*1526*	1551	1558	1605	...	1641	...	*1626*	1651	1658	1705	...	1741	...	*1728*	1751	1758	1805	1839	...	...	1846	1857	1905	1920	...
Watford Junction △ d.		1606	1613		...	1657	...			1713	1720	...		...		1807	1813		1854	...	...		1911	1919		...
Milton Keynes d.	*1600*			1637	...		...	*1700*	1723			...	1813	...	*1800*			1837		...	...	1923		1941	1955	...
Rugby d.		1657		1712	...		...		1758		1812	...		...				1912		...	...			2017		...
Nuneaton d.					...		...					...		...						...	...					...
Birmingham New St d.	1721	1740	1748	1750s	1803		1820	1821	1840	1848	1850s	1903		1920	1921		1948			2020	2021		2048			2120
Wolverhampton d.	1744		1809		1820		1840	1844		1909		1921		1940	1944		2009			2040	2044		2110			2140
Stafford d.	1802	1819	1826				1854	1902	1919	1926		1933		1954	2002	2015	2026			2054	2102	2115	2126			2154
Stoke on Trent a.			1843			1905	1912			1943			2005	2012			2043		2105	2112			2144		2201	2212
Macclesfield a.			1859			1921	1929			1959			2021	2032			2059		2121	2129			2200		2217	2232
Crewe a.	1823	1838		1849	1854			1923	1938		1949	1954			2023	2034		2050			2132	2134		2149		
Holyhead ¶ **165** a.					*2133*													*2330*			...					
Stockport a.			1913			1934s	1946			2015			2034s	2046			2116		2134s	2146	...		2212		2232s	2246
Manchester P'dilly a.			1928			1950	1959			2030			2054	2102			2130		2158	2202	...		2225		2245	2302
Runcorn a.	1843		...	1908		...	...	1945		...	2008		...	...	2045		...	2108	...	...	...		...	2208		...
Liverpool Lime St a.	1909		...	1932		...	...	2009		...	2030		...	...	2109		...	2127	...	...	...		...	2227		...
Preston **152** a.	...	1925	...	...	1943	...	...	...	2027	...	...	2051	...	...	...	2124	...	...	...	...	...	2224	...	...	*0006*	...

	⑥	⑥ 🍷	⑥ 🍷	⑥ 🍷 U	⑥ 2 ❖			⑦ 🍷 G	⑦ 🍷	⑦		⑦ 🍷 E	⑦ 🍷	⑦ 🍷	⑦ 🍷 G	⑦ 🍷 B	⑦ 🍷 G	⑦	⑦ 🍷	⑦ 🍷	⑦ 🍷	⑦ 🍷 E	⑦ 🍷 S	⑦ 🍷	⑦ 🍷	⑦ 🍷
London Euston d.	...	1936	2000	...	...	...	⑦	...	...	...	...	...	...	...	...	...	0931	...	0936	0940	1010	...	...	1031	1036	1110
Watford Junction △ d.	...	1950	2014	...	...	...		...	...	...	...	...	...	...	...	...	0946	...	0952	0957	1027	...	...		1052	
Milton Keynes d.	...	2038	2101	...	...	...	●	...	...	...	...	...	...	...	...	...	1031	...	1037	1043	1112	...	...	1131	1137	1212
Rugby d.	...	2116	2139	...	...	...		...	...	...	...	...	...	...	...	...	1057	...		1108		...	...	1157		
Nuneaton d.	...			...	...	...		...	...	...	...	...	...	...	...	...		...				...	...			
Birmingham New St d.	2121			2220	2233	...		0903	0918	0930	...	1003	1018	1048	1103	1118		1130	1148			1203	1218		1248	
Wolverhampton d.	2144			2240	2248	...		0921	0938	0946	...	1021	1038	1110	1121	1138		1148	1210			1221	1238		1310	
Stafford d.	2202	2217	2249	2254		...		0935	0953	1003	...		1053			1153	1201	1206			1240		1253	1301		1340
Stoke on Trent a.			2307	2313s		...			1010		...		1110	1142		1210			1240		1258		1310		1343	1358
Macclesfield a.			2323	2330s		...			1027		...		1127	1158		1227			1256		1314		1327		1359	1414
Crewe a.	2230	2236			0001	...		0955		1025	...	1053			1153		1220	1225		1237		1253		1320		
Holyhead ¶ **165** a.	...				...	...					...	*1322*														
Stockport a.	...	*2333*	2337s	2346s	...	...			1041		...		1141	1215		1241			1310		1330		1341	*1405*	1413	1430s
Manchester P'dilly a.	...	*2350*	2351	0002	...	...			1101		...		1157	1230		1257			1323		1344		1357	*1420*	1430	1456
Runcorn a.	...	2254	...	...	...	...			...	1047	...			...		...		1245		1255	...				...	...
Liverpool Lime St a.	...	2315	...	...	...	...			...	1113	...		*1257*	...		...		1311	*1428*	1318	...		*1457*		...	...
Preston **152** a.	...	...	...	...	...	...		1040	...	...	...	1136	...	...	1239	...	1304	...	...	...	...	1337	...	1408	...	...

	⑦ 🍷 G	⑦ 🍷 X	⑦ 🍷 G	⑦	⑦ 🍷	⑦ 🍷	⑦ 🍷	⑦ 🍷 E	⑦ 🍷 U	⑦ 🍷 G	⑦ 🍷	⑦ 🍷	⑦ 🍷 G	⑦ 🍷	⑦ 🍷 X	⑦ 🍷 G	⑦	⑦ 🍷	⑦ 🍷	⑦ 🍷 E	⑦ 🍷	⑦ 🍷 U	⑦ 🍷 G	⑦ 🍷	⑦ 🍷 G	⑦ 🍷
London Euston d.	...	...	1131	...	1136	1140	1210	...	...	1231	1236	1240	...	1310	...	1340	...	1350	1355	...	1436	...	1450	1453	...	1536
Watford Junction △ d.	...	...	1146	...	1152	1157	1227	...	...	1331	1252		...		...	1358	...	1407	1411	...	1452	...		1510	...	
Milton Keynes d.	...	...		...	1237	1243		...	...		1337	1343	...	1413	...		...		1444	...		...	1535		...	1622
Rugby d.	...	...	1257	...		1308		...	...	1357		1408	...		...	1457	...		1509	...		...	1557		...	
Nuneaton d.	...	...		...				...	...				...		...		...			...		...			...	
Birmingham New St d.	1303	1318		1330	1348			1403	1418		1448		1503		1518		1530	1551		1603		1618		1648	1703	
Wolverhampton d.	1321	1338		1352	1410			1421	1438		1510		1521		1538		1550	1613		1621		1638		1710	1721	
Stafford d.		1353	1401	1409					1453	1501		1520			1553	1601	1605					1653	1701			
Stoke on Trent a.		1410			1442		1456		1510		1543			1558	1610			1644			1659	1710		1743		1758
Macclesfield a.		1427			1458		1512		1527		1559			1614	1627			1700			1715	1727		1759		1814
Crewe a.	1353		1420	1431		1439		1452		1520		1541	1553			1620	1626		1642	1653			1720		1753	
Holyhead ¶ **165** a.												*1802*											*2000*			
Stockport a.		1441			1513		1530s		1541		1614			1630s	1641			1713			1730s	1741	*1811*	1814		1830s
Manchester P'dilly a.		1457			1530		1600		1558		1630			1659	1657			1727			1756	1757	*1826*	1830		1900
Runcorn a.		...		1452	...	1500	...		...		...	1600		...	...		1644		1701		...			...		...
Liverpool Lime St a.		...		1518	...	1526	...		...		...	1624		...	...		1709	*1829*	1727		...	*1857*		...		...
Preston **152** a.	1437	...	1504	...	...	...	...	1538	...	1603	...	...	1637	...	...	1704	...	...	...	1736	...	...	1804	...	1837	...

►► *NOTES CONTINUED FROM FACING PAGE*

j – Change at Llandudno Junction.
r – Change at Chester.
s – Stops to set down only.
u – Stops to pick up only.
y – *0218* on ⑥.
❖ – Via Shrewsbury.
¶ – For Birmingham to Holyhead via Shrewsbury, see Table **147**.
△ – Trains stop here to pick up only.
● – Services on ⑥⑦ are subject to alteration from Feb. 2.

150 LONDON and BIRMINGHAM - LIVERPOOL and MANCHESTER

VT, LM, XC

	⑦ 🍷 X	⑦ 🍷 G	⑦	⑦ 🍷	⑦ 🍷	⑦ 🍷 E	⑦ 🍷	⑦ 🍷 U	⑦ 🍷 L	⑦ 🍷	⑦ 🍷	⑦ 🍷 G	⑦ 🍷	⑦ 🍷 X	⑦ 🍷 G	⑦	⑦ 🍷	⑦ 🍷	⑦ 🍷	⑦ 🍷	⑦ 🍷 U	⑦ 🍷 C	⑦ 🍷	⑦ 🍷	⑦ 🍷	⑦ 🍷 X
London Euston d.	...	1550	...	1553	1558	...	1636	...	1650	1653	1658	...	1736	...	1750	...	1753	1758	...	1836	...	1850	1853	1858	1936	...
Watford Junction △ d.	...	1606	...	1611	1614	...	1652	...	|	1710	|	...	|	...	1806	...	1811	1814	...	1856	...	|	1910	|	|	...
Milton Keynes d.	...	|	...	|	1643	...	|	...	1732	|	1742	...	1822	...	|	...	|	|	...	|	...	1932	|	1943	2022	...
Rugby d.	...	1657	...	|	1709	...	|	...	1757	|	1808	...	|	...	1857	...	|	1909	...	|	...	1957	|	2008	|	...
Nuneaton d.	...	|	...	|	|	...	|	...	|	|	|	...	|	...	|	...	|	|	...	|	...	|	|	|	|	...
Birmingham New St d.	1718	|	1730	1748	|	1803	|	1818	|	1848	|	1903	|	1918	|	1930	1948	|	2003	|	2018	|	2048	|	|	2118
Wolverhampton d.	1738	|	1750	1810	|	1821	|	1838	|	1910	|	1921	|	1938	|	1950	2010	|	2022	|	2038	|	2110	|	|	2138
Stafford d.	1753	1801	1807	|	|	|	|	1853	1903	|	1920	1934	|	1953	2001	2007	|	|	2038	|	2053	2101	|	2122	2143	2153
Stoke on Trent a.	1810	|	|	1843	|	|	1858	1910	|	1943	|	|	1958	2010	|	|	2044	|	|	2059	2110	|	2144	|	2201	2210
Macclesfield a.	1827	|	|	1859	|	|	1914	1927	|	1959	|	|	2014	2027	|	|	2100	|	|	2115	2127	|	2200	|	2217	2227
Crewe a.	|	1820	1828	|	1839	1852	|	|	1923	|	1941	1954	|	|	2020	2027	|	2043	2057	|	|	2120	|	2141	|	|
Holyhead ¶ **165** a.	|	|	|	|	|	|	|	|	*2126*	|	|	|	|	|	*2250*	|	|	|	2314	|	|	|	|	*0026*	|	|
Stockport a.	1841	|	|	1913	|	|	1930s	1941	|	2014	|	|	2030s	2041	|	|	2113	|	...	2130s	2141	|	2214	|	2230s	2241
Manchester P'dilly a.	1857	|	|	1930	|	|	1957	1957	|	2026	|	|	2100	2055	|	|	2128	|	...	2145	2157	|	2227	|	2249	2257
Runcorn a.	...	|	1850	...	1858	|	...	...	|	...	2000	|	...	...	|	2049	...	2102	...	...	...	|	...	2159	...	...
Liverpool Lime St a.	...	|	1913	...	1926	|	...	...	|	...	2024	|	...	...	|	2115	...	2125	...	...	...	|	...	2224	...	...
Preston **152** a.	...	1904	...	...	...	1941	...	...	2011	...	...	2038	...	...	2105	...	...	...	...	...	...	2208	...	...	...	...

	⑦ 🍷	⑦	⑦ 🍷	⑦ 🍷	⑦ 🍷 U	⑦ 🍷	⑦ 🍷	⑦ 🍷	⑦ 🍷	⑦ 2 ❖	⑦ 🍷
London Euston d.	1950	...	1953	1958	...	2010	2031	2040	2110	...	2140
Watford Junction △ d.	2006	...	2011	2014	...	2027	2046	2058	|	...	2157
Milton Keynes d.	2034	...	|	2043	...	|	2131	2143	2212	...	2243
Rugby d.	2057	...	|	2109	...	2141	2157	2207	|	...	2314
Nuneaton d.	|	...	|	|	...	|	|	|	|	...	|
Birmingham New St d.	2135	2140	2148	|	2218	|	|	|	|	2254	|
Wolverhampton d.	2154	2157	2210	|	2238	|	|	|	|	2311	|
Stafford d.	2210	2217	|	|	2253	2258	2304	2318	2350	|	0014
Stoke on Trent a.	|	|	2240	|	2310s	2316	|	|	|	|	|
Macclesfield a.	|	|	2256	|	2327s	2332	|	|	|	|	|
Crewe a.	2235	2242	|	2249	|	|	2330	2342	0015s	0020	0039s
Holyhead ¶ **165** a.	|	...	¶	|	|	|	|	|	*0227*	0227	|
Stockport a.	|	...	2311	|	2341s	2347s	|	|	0043s	...	0104s
Manchester P'dilly a.	|	...	2326	|	2357s	2359	|	|	0056	...	0116
Runcorn a.	|	...	...	2307	...	...	|	0001	|	...	...
Liverpool Lime St a.	|	...	...	2335	...	...	|	0039	|	...	...
Preston **152** a.	2336	...	...	...	...	...	0027	...	*0210*	...	...

Ⓐ	Ⓐ 🍷		Ⓐ 🍴	Ⓐ 🍷 U	Ⓐ 🍷	Ⓐ 🍴	Ⓐ 🍴	Ⓐ 🍴	Ⓐ 🍴 L
Preston **152** d.	...	...	...	...	...	...	...	*0517*	0554
Liverpool Lime St d.	...	...	*0338*	...	...	0544	...	|	|
Runcorn d.	...	...	|	...	...	0600	...	|	|
Manchester P'dilly d.	...	...	0520	...	...	|	0602	0617	|
Stockport d.	...	...	0531u	...	...	|	0611u	0625	|
Holyhead ¶ **165** d.	0215	...	|	...	...	|	|	|	|
Crewe d.	0402	...	0559	0545	0609	0624	|	|	0649
Macclesfield d.	|	...	|	|	|	|	0624	0638	|
Stoke on Trent d.	|	...	|	0604	|	|	0640	0654	|
Stafford d.	0430	...	0618	0624	0630	0643	|	0715	|
Wolverhampton a.	0444	...	|	0641	0647	|	|	0732	|
Birmingham New St a.	0512	...	|	0658	0708	|	|	0755	|
Nuneaton d.	|	...	0651	...	...	0707	...	...	|
Rugby a.	*0602*	...	0704	...	...	|	0727	...	0745
Milton Keynes a.	*0625*	...	|	...	...	|	|	...	|
Watford Junction ▽ a.	*0647*	...	0744	...	...	0757	|	...	|
London Euston a.	*0709*	...	0804	...	...	0819	0827	...	0840

	Ⓐ 🍴	Ⓐ 🍷	Ⓐ 🍴	Ⓐ 🍴	Ⓐ 🍷	Ⓐ 🍴 L	Ⓐ 🍷 R	Ⓐ 🍴	Ⓐ 🍴	Ⓐ 🍴	Ⓐ 🍴	Ⓐ 🍴 C	Ⓐ 🍷	Ⓐ 🍷 U	Ⓐ 🍷	Ⓐ 🍴	Ⓐ 🍷	Ⓐ 🍴 C	Ⓐ 🍴	Ⓐ 🍷	Ⓐ 🍷 H	Ⓐ 🍴	Ⓐ 🍷	Ⓐ 🍷 P	Ⓐ 🍷	Ⓐ 🍴
Preston **152** d.	...	0615	...	...	...	0651	...	...	...	...	...	0718	...	...	0729	...	...	0743	...	...	...	...	...	...	0829	...
Liverpool Lime St d.	0627	|	...	...	0635	|	...	...	0707	...	...	|	0718	...	|	...	0740	|	0815	...	...	...	0819	...	|	...
Runcorn d.	0643	|	...	...	0653	|	...	...	0722u	...	...	|	0735	...	|	...	0758	|	0831	...	...	...	0835	...	|	...
Manchester P'dilly d.	|	|	0635	0645	|	|	0654	0705	|	...	0715	|	|	0724	|	0745	|	|	|	...	0754	0815	|	0824	|	0845
Stockport d.	|	|	0644u	0653u	|	|	|	0714u	|	...	0723u	|	|	0733	|	0755u	|	|	|	...	0803	0824u	|	0834	|	0855u
Holyhead ¶ **165** d.	|	|	|	|	|	|	|	|	|	0532	|	|	|	|	|	|	|	|	|	0645	|	|	|	|	|	|
Crewe d.	0705	0710	0713	|	0723	|	|	|	|	0748	|	|	0756	|	0815	|	0825	0834	|	0850	|	0854	0900	|	0915	|
Macclesfield d.	|	|	|	0709	|	|	|	|	|	|	0737	|	|	0747	|	0807	|	|	|	|	0816	|	|	0847	|	0908
Stoke on Trent d.	|	|	|	0724	|	|	0733	|	|	|	0753	|	|	0808	|	0822	|	|	|	|	0839	|	|	0904	|	0924
Stafford d.	0726	|	|	|	0746	0748	0754	|	|	|	|	0816	0821	0826	|	|	0846	|	|	|	0857	0913	0921	0926	|	|
Wolverhampton a.	|	0748	|	|	0805	|	0812	|	|	|	|	|	0837	0841	0848	|	0906	|	|	|	0912	|	0936	0941	0948	|
Birmingham New St a.	|	0811	|	|	0829	|	0830	|	|	|	|	|	0858	0858	0911	|	0930	|	|	|	0930	|	0958	0958	1011	|
Nuneaton d.	0749	...	|	|	...	|	...	|	|	|	0831	|	...	...	...	|	...	|	0926	|	...	|	...	...	...	|
Rugby a.	|	...	|	|	...	|	...	|	|	|	|	0849	...	...	...	|	...	0923	|	|	...	|	...	...	...	|
Milton Keynes a.	|	...	|	|	...	|	...	|	|	|	0904	|	...	...	...	0931	...	0946	|	|	...	1011	...	...	...	|
Watford Junction ▽ a.	|	...	|	|	...	|	...	|	|	0914	|	0928	...	...	...	|	...	|	|	1021	...	|	...	...	...	1046
London Euston a.	0858	...	0901	0907	...	0914	...	0911	0917	0936	0945	0953	...	...	...	1009	...	1027	1035	1046	...	1050	...	...	...	1109

	Ⓐ 🍷	Ⓐ 🍷 R	Ⓐ 🍴 G	Ⓐ 🍴	Ⓐ 🍴	Ⓐ 🍷	Ⓐ 🍷 U	Ⓐ 🍷 E	Ⓐ 🍴	Ⓐ 🍷	Ⓐ 🍴 G	Ⓐ 🍷 R	Ⓐ 🍴	Ⓐ 🍴	Ⓐ 🍷	Ⓐ 🍷 P	Ⓐ 🍴	Ⓐ 🍷 G	Ⓐ 🍷	Ⓐ 🍴 G	Ⓐ 🍷 R	Ⓐ 🍷	Ⓐ 🍷	Ⓐ 🍷	Ⓐ 🍷	Ⓐ 🍷 U
Preston **152** d.	...	...	0849	...	...	...	...	0929	...	...	0949	...	...	...	...	...	...	1028	...	1049	...	...	...	...	...	...
Liverpool Lime St d.	0840	...	|	...	0915	0919	...	|	...	0940	|	...	...	1015	1019	...	...	|	1040	|	...	...	...	1115	1119	...
Runcorn d.	0858	...	|	...	0931	0935	...	|	...	0958	|	...	...	1031	1035	...	...	|	1058	|	...	...	...	1131	1135	...
Manchester P'dilly d.	|	0854	|	0915	|	|	0924	|	0945	|	|	0954	1015	|	|	1024	1045	|	|	|	1054	1115	...	|	|	1124
Stockport d.	|	0903	|	0923u	|	|	0933	|	0954u	|	|	1003	1024u	|	|	1033	1054u	|	|	|	1103	1123u	...	|	|	1133
Holyhead ¶ **165** d.	|	|	|	|	*0715*	|	|	|	|	|	|	|	|	|	|	|	|	|	|	|	|	|	0950	|	|	|
Crewe d.	0925	|	0934	|	0953	1000	|	1015	|	1025	1034	|	|	1053	1100	|	|	1114	1125	1134	|	|	1149	1153	1200	|
Macclesfield d.	|	0916	|	|	|	|	0947	|	1007	|	|	1016	|	|	|	1047	1107	|	|	|	1116	|	|	|	|	1147
Stoke on Trent d.	|	0939	|	0950	|	|	1004	|	1023	|	|	1039	1050	|	|	1104	1123	|	|	|	1139	1150	|	|	|	1204
Stafford d.	0946	|	|	|	1012	1021	1026	|	|	1046	|	|	|	1112	1121	1126	|	|	1146	|	|	|	|	1212	1221	1226
Wolverhampton a.	1006	1012	|	|	|	1036	1041	1047	|	1107	|	1112	|	|	|	1141	|	1148	1206	|	1212	|	|	|	1236	1241
Birmingham New St a.	1030	1030	|	|	|	1058	1058	1111	|	1130	|	1130	|	|	|	1158	|	1211	1230	|	1230	|	|	|	1258	1258
Nuneaton d.	...	...	|	|	1035	...	...	...	|	...	|	...	|	1135	1202	...	|	...	...	|	...	|	|	1235	...	...
Rugby a.	...	...	1023	|	|	...	...	...	|	...	1123	...	|	|	1216	...	|	...	...	1223	...	|	|	|	...	...
Milton Keynes a.	...	...	|	|	|	...	...	...	1128	...	1145	...	|	1209	|	...	|	...	...	|	...	|	|	|	...	...
Watford Junction ▽ a.	...	...	1102	|	1125	...	...	...	|	...	|	...	|	|	|	...	1246	...	...	1303	...	|	|	1324	...	...
London Euston a.	...	...	1127	1128	1148	...	...	...	1207	...	1226	...	1226	1248	1318	...	1309	...	...	1327	...	1328	1340	1347	...	...

	Ⓐ 🍷 E	Ⓐ 🍷	Ⓐ 🍷 G	Ⓐ 🍷	Ⓐ 🍷 R	Ⓐ 🍷	Ⓐ 🍷 L	Ⓐ 🍷	Ⓐ 🍷	Ⓐ 🍷 Z	Ⓐ 🍷	Ⓐ 🍷	Ⓐ 🍷 D	Ⓐ 🍷 G	Ⓐ 🍷 E	Ⓐ 🍷	Ⓐ 🍷	Ⓐ 🍷	Ⓐ 🍷 U	Ⓐ 🍷 E	Ⓐ 🍷	Ⓐ 🍷	Ⓐ 🍷 R	Ⓐ 🍷 G	Ⓐ 🍷	Ⓐ 🍷
Preston **152** d.	1129	...	1152	...	...	...	1156	...	...	...	...	...	...	1232	1249	...	...	...	...	1329	...	...	...	1349	...	...
Liverpool Lime St d.	|	...	|	1140	...	...	|	1215	...	...	...	1240	...	|	|	...	1315	1319	...	|	...	1340	...	|	...	1415
Runcorn d.	|	...	|	1158	...	...	|	1231	...	...	...	1258	...	|	|	...	1331	1335	...	|	...	1358	...	|	...	1431
Manchester P'dilly d.	|	1145	|	|	1154	1215	|	|	...	1224	1245	|	1254	|	|	1315	|	|	1324	|	1345	|	1354	|	1415	|
Stockport d.	|	1154u	|	|	1203	1224u	|	|	...	1233	1254u	|	1303	|	|	1324u	|	|	1333	|	1354u	|	1403	|	1424u	|
Holyhead ¶ **165** d.	|	|	|	|	|	|	|	|	...	|	|	|	|	|	|	|	|	|	|	*1140*	|	|	|	|	|	|
Crewe d.	1213	|	|	1224	|	*1207*	1244	1253	1300	|	|	1325	|	1333	1334	|	1353	1400	|	1414	|	1425	|	1434	|	1453
Macclesfield d.	|	1207	|	|	1216	|	|	|	|	1247	1307	|	1316	|	|	|	|	|	1347	|	1407	|	1416	|	|	|
Stoke on Trent d.	|	1223	|	|	1239	1250	|	|	|	1304	1323	|	1339	|	|	1349	|	|	1404	|	1423	|	1439	|	1450	|
Stafford d.	|	|	|	1246	|	|	|	1312	1321	1326	|	1346	|	|	|	|	1412	1421	1426	|	|	1446	|	|	|	1512
Wolverhampton a.	1248	|	|	1306	1312	|	|	|	1336	1341	|	1406	1412	1417	|	|	|	1436	1441	1447	|	1506	1512	|	|	|
Birmingham New St a.	1311	|	|	1330	1330	|	|	|	1358	1358	|	1430	1430	1441	|	|	|	1458	1458	1511	|	1530	1530	|	|	|
Nuneaton d.	...	|	|	...	...	|	|	1335	...	...	|	...	...	...	|	|	1435	...	...	...	|	...	...	|	|	1535
Rugby a.	...	|	|	...	...	|	1338	|	...	...	|	...	...	...	1423	|	|	...	...	...	|	...	...	1523	|	|
Milton Keynes a.	...	|	|	...	...	|	1401	1409	...	...	|	...	...	...	|	|	|	...	...	...	1528	...	...	1546	|	1609
Watford Junction ▽ a.	...	|	|	...	...	|	|	|	...	...	1446	...	...	...	1502	|	1525	...	...	...	|	...	...	|	|	|
London Euston a.	...	1404	1404	...	...	1426	1440	1449	...	...	1508	...	...	...	1526	1528	1548	...	...	...	1607	...	...	1627	1628	1648

C – To / from Carlisle.
D – To Guildford.
E – To / from Edinburgh.
G – To / from Glasgow.
H – To Brighton.
L – To / from Lancaster.
P – To Plymouth.
Q – From Llandudno.
R – To Reading.
S – To Southampton.
T – To Gatwick.
U – From / to Bournemouth.
X – From Exeter.
Z – To Penzance.

NOTES CONTINUE ON FACING PAGE ▶▶

LIVERPOOL and MANCHESTER - BIRMINGHAM and LONDON 150

	Ⓐ 🍷	Ⓐ 🍷 Z	Ⓐ 🍷 G	Ⓐ 🍷	Ⓐ 🍷	Ⓐ 🍷 H	Ⓐ 🍷 G	Ⓐ 🍷	Ⓐ 🍷 L	Ⓐ 🍷	Ⓐ 🍷	Ⓐ 🍷 U	Ⓐ 🍷 E	Ⓐ 🍷	Ⓐ 🍷	Ⓐ 🍷	Ⓐ 🍷 R	Ⓐ 🍷 C	Ⓐ 🍷	Ⓐ 🍷 Q	Ⓐ 🍷	Ⓐ	Ⓐ 🍷 P	Ⓐ 🍷	Ⓐ 🍷 G	Ⓐ 🍷
Preston **152** d.	...	...	1430	...	...	...	1502	...	1449	...	...	...	1529	...	...	...	...	1548	...	...	...	...	...	...	1629	...
Liverpool Lime St d.	...	...	|	...	1440	...	|	...	|	1515	1519	...	|	...	1540	...	...	|	...	...	1615	...	...	...	|	1640
Runcorn d.	...	...	|	...	1458	...	|	...	|	1531	1535	...	|	...	1558	...	...	|	...	...	1631	...	...	...	|	1658
Manchester P'dilly d.	...	1424	|	1445	|	1454	|	1515	|	|	|	1524	|	1545	|	...	1554	|	1615	...	|	...	1624	1645	|	|
Stockport d.	...	1433	|	1454u	|	1503	|	1524u	|	|	|	1533	|	1554u	|	...	1603	|	1624u	...	|	...	1633	1654u	|	|
Holyhead ¶ **165** d.	...	|	|	|	|	|	|	|	|	|	|	|	*1335*	|	*1414*	1414	|	|	|	...	|	...	|	|	|	|
Crewe d.	1500	|	1515	|	1525	|	|	*1507*	1538	1553	1600	|	1611	|	1625	1628	|	1634	|	1649	1653	1700	|	|	1715	1724
Macclesfield d.	|	1447	|	1507	|	1516	|	|	|	|	|	1547	|	1607	|	|	1616	|	|	|	|	|	1647	1708	|	|
Stoke on Trent d.	|	1504	|	1523	|	1539	|	1550	|	|	|	1604	|	1623	|	|	1639	|	1650	|	|	|	1704	1724	|	|
Stafford d.	1521	1526	|	|	1546	|	|	|	|	1612	1621	1626	|	|	1646	|	|	|	|	|	1712	1720	1726	|	|	1746
Wolverhampton a.	1536	1541	1548	|	1606	1612	|	|	|	|	1636	1641	1648	|	1705	|	1712	|	|	|	|	|	1741	|	1748	1806
Birmingham New St a.	1558	1558	1611	|	1630	1630	|	|	|	|	1658	1658	1711	|	1730	|	1730	|	|	|	|	|	1758	|	1811	1830
Nuneaton d.	...	...	...	|	...	...	|	|	|	1635	...	...	...	|	...	|	...	|	|	|	1735	1800	...	|	...	...
Rugby a.	...	...	...	|	...	...	|	|	1638	|	...	...	...	|	...	|	...	1723	|	|	1749	1814	...	|	...	...
Milton Keynes a.	...	...	...	|	...	...	|	|	|	|	...	...	...	1728	...	1740	...	1746	|	|	1811	|	...	|	...	...
Watford Junction ▽ a.	...	...	...	1646	...	...	|	|	1717	1725	...	...	...	|	...	|	...	|	|	1817	|	|	...	1849	...	...
London Euston a.	...	...	...	1708	...	...	1717	1727	1740	1747	...	...	...	1807	...	1821	...	1827	1828	1842	1850	1918	...	1911	...	...

	Ⓐ 🍷 T	Ⓐ 🍷 L	Ⓐ 🍷	Ⓐ 🍷	Ⓐ 🍷	Ⓐ 🍷 U	Ⓐ 🍷	Ⓐ 🍷 E	Ⓐ 🍷	Ⓐ 🍷 G	Ⓐ 🍷 T	Ⓐ 🍷	Ⓐ 🍷	Ⓐ 🍷 P	Ⓐ 🍷 G	Ⓐ 🍷	Ⓐ 🍷	Ⓐ 🍷	Ⓐ 🍷	Ⓐ 🍷 G	Ⓐ 🍷	Ⓐ 🍷 S	Ⓐ 🍷 E	Ⓐ 🍷	Ⓐ 🍷	Ⓐ 🍷
Preston **152** d.	...	1649	...	...	...	...	...	1729	...	1749	...	...	...	...	1829	...	...	...	*1808*	1910	...	...	1929	...	...	*1914*
Liverpool Lime St d.	...	|	...	1715	1718	...	...	|	1737	|	...	...	1815	...	|	1840	...	...	|	|	1919	...	|	1940	...	*1852*
Runcorn d.	...	|	...	1731	1736	...	...	|	1756	|	...	...	1831	...	|	1858	...	...	|	|	1935	...	|	1958	...	|
Manchester P'dilly d.	1654	|	1715	|	|	1724	1745	|	|	|	1754	1815	|	1824	|	*1834*	1845	1854	1915	|	|	1924	|	|	1954	2015
Stockport d.	1703	|	1723u	|	|	1733	1755u	|	|	|	1803	1824u	|	1833	|	*1842*	1854u	1903	1924u	|	|	1933	|	|	2003	2024u
Holyhead ¶ **165** d.	|	|	|	|	|	|	|	*1539*	|	|	|	|	|	|	|	|	|	|	|	*1727*	|	|	|	|	|	|
Crewe d.	|	1734	|	1754	1800	|	|	1815	1825	1834	|	|	1853	|	1915	1927	|	|	*1907*j	1954	2000	|	2015	2024	|	|
Macclesfield d.	1716	|	|	|	|	1747	1808	|	|	|	1816	|	|	1847	|	|	1907	1916	1937	|	|	1947	|	|	2016	2037
Stoke on Trent d.	1739	|	1750	|	|	1804	1824	|	|	|	1839	1851	|	1904	|	|	1924	1939	1953	|	|	2004	|	|	2039	2053
Stafford d.	|	|	|	1813	1821	1826	|	|	1846	|	|	|	1912	1926	|	1948	|	1958	|	2014	2021	2026	|	2046	2057	|
Wolverhampton a.	1812	|	|	|	1836	1841	|	1848	1905	|	1912	|	|	1941	1948	2006	|	2012	|	|	2036	2041	2049	2105	2112	|
Birmingham New St a.	1830	|	|	|	1858	1858	|	1911	1930	|	1930	|	|	1958	2011	2030	|	2035	|	|	2058	2058	2111	2130	2135	|
Nuneaton d.	...	|	|	1836	...	...	|	...	...	|	...	|	1935	...	...	...	|	...	|	|	...	...	...	...	...	|
Rugby a.	...	1823	|	|	...	...	|	...	...	1923	...	|	|	...	...	...	|	...	|	2047	...	...	...	...	...	|
Milton Keynes a.	...	|	|	|	...	...	1928	...	...	1946	...	|	2009	...	...	...	2028	...	|	|	...	...	...	...	...	2155
Watford Junction ▽ a.	...	1902	|	1928	...	...	|	...	...	|	...	2010	|	...	...	...	|	...	2113	2126	...	...	...	...	...	|
London Euston a.	...	1925	1928	1950	...	...	2007	...	...	2026	...	2033	2048	...	...	...	2107	...	2136	2151	...	...	...	...	...	2252

	Ⓐ 🍷	Ⓐ 🍷 G	Ⓐ 🍷	Ⓐ 2 ❖	Ⓐ 🍷	Ⓐ 🍷	Ⓐ 🍷 G		Ⓐ 🍷 E	Ⓐ 🍷	Ⓐ 🍷			⑥		⑥ 🍷	⑥ 🍷 U	⑥ 🍷	⑥ 🍷 L	⑥ 🍷	⑥ 🍷	⑥ 🍷	⑥ 🍷	⑥ 🍷	⑥	⑥ 🍷 L
Preston **152** d.	...	2021	...	...	...	...	2049	...	2129	...	...	...	⑥	...	...	...	...	...	0540	...	...	*0517*	...	0615	...	0645
Liverpool Lime St d.	1949	|	...	...	2040	...	|	...	|	2140	...	...		...	...	*0338*	...	...	|	...	0607	|	...	|	0633	|
Runcorn d.	2005	|	...	...	2058	...	|	...	|	2159	...	...	●	...	...	|	...	...	|	...	0624	|	...	|	0653	|
Manchester P'dilly d.	|	|	2024	...	*2034*	2045	|	...	*2103*	|	2154	...		...	...	0505	...	...	|	0603	|	0621	0641	|	|	|
Stockport d.	|	|	2033	...	*2046*	2054u	|	...	*2115*	|	2203	...		...	...	0515u	...	...	|	0612	|	0630	0651	|	|	|
Holyhead ¶ **165** d.	|	|	|	1835	|	|	|	...	*1935*	|	|	...		0215	...	|	...	...	|	|	|	|	|	|	|	|
Crewe d.	2039	2105	|	|	2125	2134	2135	...	2216	2224	|	...		0402	...	0544	0542	0609	0633	|	0645	|	*0652*j	0710	0723	0730
Macclesfield d.	|	|	2047	|	|	|	|	...	|	|	2216	...		|	...	|	|	|	|	0625	|	0643	0705	|	|	|
Stoke on Trent d.	|	|	2104	|	|	2151	|	...	|	|	2239	...		|	...	|	0601	|	|	0641	|	0659	0723	|	|	|
Stafford d.	2104	|	2126	|	2146	|	2155	...	2236	2247	2257	...		0430	...	0610	0620	0630	|	|	0706	0719	|	|	0744	0747
Wolverhampton a.	|	|	2141	2202	2208	|	2216	...	2248	2306	2312	...		0445	...	|	0641	0647	|	|	|	0735	|	0747	0807	|
Birmingham New St a.	|	|	2204	2218	2230	|	2238	...	2311	2330	2347	...		0508	...	|	0658	0708	|	|	|	0756	|	0810	0827	|
Nuneaton d.	2129	|	...	...	...	2234	|	...	...	...	...	...		|	...	|	...	...	|	|	|	|	|	...	...	|
Rugby a.	2142	|	...	...	...	2248	*2332*	...	...	...	...	...		*0633*	...	0724	...	...	|	|	0827	|	|	...	...	|
Milton Keynes a.	2205	2216	...	...	...	2310	*0015*s	...	...	...	...	...		*0711*	...	|	...	...	0830	0841	0900	|	0927	...	...	|
Watford Junction ▽ a.	2225	|	...	...	...	2330	*0038*	...	...	...	...	...		*0731*	...	0814	...	...	0851	0902	|	0930	|	...	...	0952
London Euston a.	2305	2314	...	...	...	0009	*0102*	...	...	...	...	...		*0752*	...	0836	...	...	0912	0924	0939	0953	1005	...	...	1013

	⑥ 🍷	⑥ 🍷	⑥ 🍷 U	⑥ 🍷	⑥	⑥ 🍷	⑥ 🍷 C	⑥ 🍷	⑥ 🍷	⑥ 🍷 P	⑥ 🍷	⑥ 🍷	⑥	⑥ 🍷 G	⑥ 🍷	⑥ 🍷	⑥ 🍷 U	⑥ 🍷 E	⑥ 🍷	⑥	⑥ 🍷 G	⑥ 🍷	⑥ 🍷	⑥ 🍷	⑥ 🍷 G	⑥ 🍷
Preston **152** d.	...	...	...	0720	...	...	0744	...	...	...	...	0829	...	0847	...	...	...	0929	...	...	0947	...	...	...	1029	...
Liverpool Lime St d.	...	0712	...	|	0739	...	|	...	0812	...	...	|	0838	|	...	0915	...	|	...	0937	|	...	1015	...	|	...
Runcorn d.	...	0728	...	|	0757	...	|	...	0828	...	...	|	0855	|	...	0931	...	|	...	0955	|	...	1031	...	|	...
Manchester P'dilly d.	0655	|	0724	|	|	0742	*0728*	0754	|	0824	0840	|	|	*0834*	0854	|	0924	|	0940	|	*0934*	0954	|	1024	|	1040
Stockport d.	0704	|	0733	|	|	0753u	*0737*	0804	|	0833	0850u	|	|	*0844*	0904	|	0933	|	0950u	|	*0942*	1003	|	1033	|	1050u
Holyhead ¶ **165** d.	|	|	|	*0535*	|	|	|	|	|	|	|	*0645*	|	|	|	*0715*	|	|	|	|	|	|	|	|	|	|
Crewe d.	|	0750	|	0811	0822	|	0829	|	0849	|	|	0913	0922	0931	|	0953	|	1015	|	1022	1031	|	1053	|	1115	|
Macclesfield d.	0717	|	0746	|	|	0806	|	0817	|	0846	0906	|	|	|	0920	|	0946	|	1005	|	|	1020	|	1046	|	1105
Stoke on Trent d.	0733	|	0804	|	|	0822	|	0839	|	0907	0922	|	|	|	0939	|	1004	|	1021	|	|	1039	|	1107	|	1121
Stafford d.	|	|	0826	|	0844	|	0848	|	0910	0926	|	|	0944	|	|	1013	1026	|	|	1044	|	|	1113	1126	|	|
Wolverhampton a.	0811	|	0841	0847	0905	|	|	0911	|	0941	|	0947	1005	|	1011	|	1041	1048	|	1105	|	1111	|	1141	1148	|
Birmingham New St a.	0830	|	0858	0910	0927	|	0924	0930	|	0958	|	1011	1027	1024	1030	|	1058	1111	|	1127	1124	1130	|	1158	1211	|
Nuneaton d.	|	|	...	...	...	|	|	|	|	...	|	...	...	|	|	|	...	...	|	...	|	|	|	...	...	|
Rugby a.	|	0925	...	...	...	|	|	1008	|	...	|	...	...	|	1108	|	...	...	|	...	|	1208	|	...	...	|
Milton Keynes a.	0939	|	...	...	...	|	1033	1041	1102	...	|	...	...	1132	|	|	...	...	1213	...	1232	1241	1302	...	...	|
Watford Junction ▽ a.	|	1022	...	...	...	1034	|	|	|	...	1135	...	...	|	1202	1218	...	...	|	...	|	|	|	...	...	1335
London Euston a.	1016	1043	...	...	...	1056	1112	1118	1140	...	1158	...	...	1211	1223	1240	...	...	1258	...	1311	1318	1340	...	...	1358

	⑥	⑥ 🍷 G	⑥ 🍷	⑥ 🍷	⑥ 🍷 U	⑥ 🍷 E	⑥ 🍷	⑥	⑥ 🍷	⑥ 🍷	⑥ 🍷	⑥ 🍷 Z	⑥ 🍷 G	⑥ 🍷	⑥	⑥ 🍷 G	⑥ 🍷	⑥ 🍷	⑥ 🍷	⑥ 🍷 U	⑥ 🍷 E	⑥	⑥ 🍷 G	⑥ 🍷	⑥ 🍷	⑥ 🍷 Z
Preston **152** d.	...	1047	...	...	...	1128	...	...	1147	...	...	...	1229	...	...	1247	...	...	...	...	1329	...	1347	...	...	...
Liverpool Lime St d.	1037	|	...	1115	...	|	...	1137	|	...	1215	...	|	...	1237	|	...	1315	...	...	|	1337	|	...	1415	...
Runcorn d.	1055	|	...	1131	...	|	...	1155	|	...	1231	...	|	...	1255	|	...	1331	...	...	|	1355	|	...	1431	...
Manchester P'dilly d.	|	*1034*	1055	|	1124	|	1140	|	*1134*	1155	|	1224	|	1240	|	|	1258	|	1340	1324	|	|	*1334*	1355	|	1424
Stockport d.	|	*1043*	1107	|	1133	|	1149u	|	*1142*	1207	|	1233	|	1250u	|	|	1307	|	1350u	1333	|	|	*1342*	1407	|	1433
Holyhead ¶ **165** d.	|	|	|	*0928*	|	*0950*	|	|	|	|	|	|	|	|	|	|	|	|	|	|	*1140*	|	|	|	|	|
Crewe d.	1122	1131	|	1153	|	1213	|	1222	1231	|	1253	|	1315	|	1322	1331	|	1354	|	|	1415	1422	1431	|	1453	|
Macclesfield d.	|	|	1120	|	1146	|	1205	|	|	1220	|	1246	|	1305	|	|	1320	|	1405	1346	|	|	|	1420	|	1446
Stoke on Trent d.	|	|	1139	|	1204	|	1221	|	|	1239	|	1307	|	1320	|	|	1339	|	1421	1404	|	|	|	1439	|	1507
Stafford d.	1144	|	|	1213	1226	|	|	1244	|	|	1313	1326	|	|	1344	|	|	1414	|	1426	|	1444	|	|	1513	1526
Wolverhampton a.	1206	|	1211	|	1241	1248	|	1305	|	1311	|	1341	1348	|	1405	|	1411	|	|	1441	1448	1505	|	1511	|	1541
Birmingham New St a.	1227	1224	1230	|	1258	1311	|	1327	1324	1330	|	1358	1411	|	1427	1424	1430	|	|	1458	1511	1527	1524	1530	|	1558
Nuneaton d.	...	|	|	|	...	...	|	...	|	|	|	...	...	|	...	|	|	|	|	...	...	...	|	|	|	...
Rugby a.	...	|	1309	|	...	...	|	...	|	1409	|	...	...	|	...	|	1509	|	|	...	...	...	|	1609	|	...
Milton Keynes a.	...	1332	|	|	...	...	1413	...	1432	1442	1502	...	...	|	...	1534	|	|	1613	...	...	...	1632	1642	1702	...
Watford Junction ▽ a.	...	|	1401	1418	...	...	|	...	|	|	|	...	...	1535	...	|	1559	1618	|	...	...	...	|	|	|	...
London Euston a.	...	1411	1422	1441	...	...	1458	...	1511	1518	1540	...	...	1558	...	1615	1620	1640	1658	...	...	...	1713	1719	1740	...

►► *NOTES CONTINUED FROM FACING PAGE*

j – Change at Stoke.
s – Stops to set down only.
u – Stops to pick up only.

△ – Trains stop here to pick up only.
▽ – Trains stop here to set down only.

❖ – Via Shrewsbury.

¶ – For Birmingham to Holyhead and v.v. via Shrewsbury, see Table **147**.

● – Services on ⑥ are subject to alteration from Feb. 2.

150 LIVERPOOL and MANCHESTER - BIRMINGHAM and LONDON

VT, LM, XC

	⑥ 🍷 G	⑥ 🍷	⑥	⑥ 🍷	⑥ 🍷	⑥ 🍷	⑥ 🍷 U	⑥ 🍷 E	⑥ 🍷	⑥	⑥ 🍷 G	⑥ 🍷	⑥ 🍷	⑥ 🍷 X	⑥ 🍷 G	⑥ 🍷	⑥	⑥ 🍷	⑥ 🍷	56	⑥ 🍷	⑥ 🍷 U	⑥ 🍷 E	⑥ 🍷	⑥	⑥ 🍷 G
Preston **152** d.	1429	...	...	1447	...	...	...	1529	...	...	1547	...	...	...	1629	...	...	1647	...	...	...	...	1724	...	...	1747
Liverpool Lime St d.	|	...	1437	|	...	1510	...	|	...	1537	|	...	1615	...	|	...	1637	|	...	...	1715	...	|	...	...	|
Runcorn d.	|	...	1455	|	...	1526	...	|	...	1555	|	...	1631	...	|	...	1655	|	...	...	1731	...	|	...	...	|
Manchester P'dilly d.	|	1440	|	*1434*	1455	|	1524	|	1540	|	*1534*	1555	|	1624	|	1640	|	*1634*	1656	...	|	1724	|	1740	1737	|
Stockport d.	|	1450u	|	*1442*	1507	|	1533	|	1550u	|	*1542*	1607	|	1633	|	1650u	|	*1643*	1707	...	|	1733	|	1751u	1755	|
Holyhead ¶ **165** d.	|	|	|	|	|	|	|	*1335*	|	*1413*	|	|	|	|	|	|	|	|	|	...	|	|	*1539*	|	|	|
Crewe d.	1513	|	1522	1531	|	1548	|	1613	|	1622	1631	|	1653	|	1715	|	1722	1731	|	...	1753	|	1813	|	1821	1832
Macclesfield d.	|	1505	|	|	1520	|	1546	|	1605	|	|	1620	|	1646	|	1705	|	|	1720	...	|	1746	|	1806	|	|
Stoke on Trent d.	|	1521	|	|	1539	|	1604	|	1621	|	|	1639	|	1707	|	1721	|	|	1739	...	|	1804	|	1822	|	|
Stafford d.	|	|	1544	|	|	1609	1626	|	|	1644	|	|	1713	1726	|	|	1744	|	|	...	1813	1826	|	|	1844	|
Wolverhampton a.	1546	|	1605	|	1611	|	1641	1648	|	1708	|	1711	|	1741	1748	|	1807	|	1811	...	|	1841	1848	|	1907	|
Birmingham New St a.	1611	|	1627	1624	1630	|	1658	1711	|	1727	1724	1730	|	1758	1811	|	1827	1824	1830	...	|	1858	1911	|	1927	|
Nuneaton d.	...	|	...	|	|	|	...	...	|	...	|	|	|	...	...	|	...	|	|	...	|	...	...	|	...	|
Rugby a.	...	|	...	|	1709	|	...	...	|	...	|	1809	1828	...	...	|	...	|	1909	...	|	...	...	|	...	2000
Milton Keynes a.	...	|	...	|	|	|	...	...	1813	...	1833	1842	1902	...	...	|	...	|	|	...	|	...	...	2018	...	2035
Watford Junction ▽ a.	...	1735	...	1751	1759	1818	...	...	|	...	|	|	|	...	...	1932	...	1949	1959	...	2055	...	...	|	...	|
London Euston a.	...	1758	...	1813	1820	1840	...	...	1858	...	1912	1919	1939	...	...	1955	...	2011	2025	...	2123	...	...	2128	...	2137

	⑥ 🍷	⑥ 🍷	⑥ 🍷 X	⑥ 🍷 G	⑥ 🍷	⑥	⑥ 🍷 G	⑥ 🍷	⑥ 🍷 S	⑥ 🍷 E	⑥	⑥ 🍷 G	⑥ 🍷	⑥ 🍷	⑥ 🍷 V	⑥ 2🍷 ✣	⑥ 🍷 G	⑥	⑥	⑥ 🍷		⑦ ▲	⑦ 🍷 X	⑦ 🍷	⑦ 🍷 R	⑦
Preston **152** d.	...	...	...	1830	...	...	1847	...	...	1929	...	1948	...	...	...	...	2043	...	...	2128	...		...	...	...	...
Liverpool Lime St d.	...	1810	...	|	...	1840	|	...	...	|	1937	|	...	2010	...	...	|	...	2116	|	...		...	...	...	...
Runcorn d.	...	1826	...	|	...	1858	|	...	...	|	1955	|	...	2026	...	...	|	...	2134	|	...		...	...	...	...
Manchester P'dilly d.	1757	|	1824	|	1840	|	|	1858	1924	|	|	*1934*	1958	|	2017	...	*2034*	2054	|	|	...		0810	...	...	...
Stockport d.	1807	|	1833	|	1850u	|	|	1907	1933	|	|	*1942*	2007	|	2026	...	*2046*	2104	|	|	...		0824	...	...	...
Holyhead ¶ **165** d.	|	|	|	|	|	|	|	|	|	*1735*	|	|	|	|	|	1835	|	|	|	*1935*	...		|	...	...	...
Crewe d.	|	1848	|	1915	|	1923	1931	|	|	2015	2022	2032	|	2048	|	|	2128	|	2200	2216	...		0846	...	0933	0940
Macclesfield d.	1820	|	1846	|	1905	|	|	1920	1946	|	|	|	2020	|	2040	|	|	2117	|	|	...		|	...	|	|
Stoke on Trent d.	1839	|	1907	|	1921	|	|	1939	2007	|	|	|	2036	|	2058	|	|	2139	|	|	...		0905	...	|	|
Stafford d.	|	1908	1926	|	|	1944	1952	|	2026	|	2044	|	|	|	2118	|	2151	2158	2222	2235	...		0926	0939	0953	1001
Wolverhampton a.	1911	|	1941	1948	|	2007	|	2011	2041	2048	2108	|	2111	|	2135	2202	2209	2213	2243	2249	...		0940	|	1009	1023
Birmingham New St a.	1930	|	1958	2011	|	2030	|	2030	2058	2111	2127	|	2130	|	2156	2218	2230	2237	2304	2311	...		0958	|	1030	1043
Nuneaton d.	|	|	...	...	|	...	|	|	...	...	...	|	|	|	|	...	...	...	...	...	...		...	|	...	...
Rugby a.	|	|	...	...	|	...	2101	|	...	...	...	2200	|	2209	|	...	...	...	...	...	...		...	1041	...	...
Milton Keynes a.	2040	2101	...	...	|	...	|	2139	...	...	...	2235	2241	2247	|	...	...	...	...	...	...		...	1105	...	...
Watford Junction ▽ a.	2118	|	...	...	2208	...	2216	2222	...	...	...	2310	2319	2325	|	...	...	...	...	...	...		...	|	...	...
London Euston a.	2142	2201	...	...	2234	...	2242	2246	...	...	...	2330	2343	2349	*0050**	...	...	...	...	...	...		...	1200	...	...

	⑦ 🍷	⑦ 🍷 U	⑦ 🍷	⑦ 🍷	⑦ 🍷	⑦ 🍷	⑦ 🍷	⑦ 🍷 X	⑦ 🍷	⑦ 🍷	⑦ 🍷	⑦ 🍷	⑦ 🍷 U	⑦ 🍷	⑦ 🍷	⑦	⑦ 🍷	⑦ 🍷	⑦ 🍷 X	⑦ 🍷 L	⑦ 🍷	⑦ 🍷	⑦ 🍷	⑦ 🍷	⑦ 🍷 U	⑦ 🍷 C
Preston **152** d.	...	...	...	...	...	...	1004	...	...	1028	...	...	...	*1030*	1125	...	...	...	...	1203	...	1228	...	...	...	1308
Liverpool Lime St d.	...	*0822*	...	*0830*	0953	...	|	...	...	|	1053	...	...	|	|	1135	1156	...	...	|	...	|	1256	...	...	|
Runcorn d.	...	|	...	|	1009	...	|	...	...	|	1109	...	...	|	|	1153	1214	...	...	|	...	|	1314	...	...	|
Manchester P'dilly d.	0900	0924	...	0944	|	0953	|	1024	1044	|	|	1053	1124	1144	|	|	|	1153	1208	|	1245	|	|	1253	1324	|
Stockport d.	0910	0933	...	0953u	|	1002	|	1033	1053u	|	|	1102	1133	1153u	|	|	|	1202	1222	|	1256u	|	|	1302	1333	|
Holyhead ¶ **165** d.	|	|	...	|	|	|	|	|	|	|	|	|	|	|	|	|	*0956*	|	|	|	|	|	|	|	|	|
Crewe d.	0948	|	1012	|	1035	|	1048	|	|	1113	1135	|	|	|	1212	1219	1235	|	|	1248	|	1313	1338	|	|	1353
Macclesfield d.	|	0946	|	1006	|	1015	|	1045	1105	|	|	1115	1146	1205	|	|	|	1215	1235	|	1309	|	|	1315	1346	|
Stoke on Trent d.	|	1005	|	1022	|	1031	|	1105	1121	|	|	1131	1205	1221	|	|	|	1231	1258	|	1325	|	|	1331	1405	|
Stafford d.	1008	1026	1032	1041	1055	|	1108	1126	|	|	1155	|	1226	|	|	1243	1256	|	1326	|	|	|	1358	|	1426	|
Wolverhampton a.	|	1040	1048	|	|	1105	|	1140	|	1148	|	1205	1240	|	1248	1302	|	1305	1340	|	|	1348	|	1405	1440	|
Birmingham New St a.	|	1058	1111	|	|	1126	|	1158	|	1206	|	1226	1258	|	1311	1321	|	1326	1358	|	|	1411	|	1416	1458	|
Nuneaton d.	|	...	...	|	|	|	|	...	|	...	|	|	...	|	...	...	|	|	...	|	|	...	|	|	...	|
Rugby a.	1126	...	...	1139	1158	|	|	...	|	...	1258	|	...	|	...	...	1358	|	...	1422	|	...	1458	|	...	1523
Milton Keynes a.	1151	...	...	|	1221	1227	1250	...	1300	...	1322	1328	...	|	...	...	|	1426	...	1450	1500	...	1521	1527	...	|
Watford Junction ▽ a.	1231	...	...	1243	1300	1306	1331	...	|	...	|	1403	...	1431	...	...	1446	|	...	1513	|	...	|	|	...	1612
London Euston a.	1251	...	...	1304	1323	1329	1356	...	1400	...	1423	1429	...	1456	...	...	1508	1516	...	1538	1556	...	1607	1616	...	1636

	⑦	⑦ 🍷	⑦ 🍷 E	⑦ 🍷	⑦ 🍷	⑦ 🍷 G	⑦ 🍷 X	⑦ 🍷	⑦ 🍷 G	⑦ 🍷	⑦ 🍷	⑦ 🍷	⑦ 🍷 U	⑦ 🍷	⑦	⑦ 🍷 E	⑦ 🍷	⑦ 🍷	⑦ 🍷 G	⑦ 🍷 X	⑦ 🍷	⑦ 🍷 G	⑦ 🍷	⑦ 🍷 U	⑦ 🍷 G	⑦ 🍷
Preston **152** d.	...	...	1329	...	...	1400	...	...	1427	...	...	1502	...	...	...	1528	...	...	1600	...	...	1623	...	...	1702	...
Liverpool Lime St d.	1326	...	|	1356	...	|	...	...	|	1456	...	|	...	...	1531	|	1556	...	|	...	...	|	...	*1622*	|	*1630*
Runcorn d.	1344	...	|	1414	...	|	...	...	|	1514	...	|	...	...	1549	|	1614	...	|	...	...	|	...	|	|	|
Manchester P'dilly d.	|	1345	|	|	1353	|	1424	1445	|	|	1453	|	1524	1545	|	|	|	1554	|	1624	1645	|	1653	1724	|	1745
Stockport d.	|	1355u	|	|	1403	|	1433	1455u	|	|	1502	|	1533	1555u	|	|	|	1603	|	1633	1655u	|	1702	1733	|	1755u
Holyhead ¶ **165** d.	|	|	|	|	|	|	|	|	|	*1314*	|	|	|	|	|	|	|	|	|	|	|	|	|	|	|	|
Crewe d.	1410	|	1417	1437	|	1445	|	|	1513	1535	|	1546	|	|	1611	1613	1635	|	1646	|	|	1709	|	*1716j*	1747	|
Macclesfield d.	|	1408	|	|	1416	|	1446	1508	|	|	1515	|	1546	1608	|	|	|	1615	|	1646	1708	|	1715	1746	|	1808
Stoke on Trent d.	|	1424	|	|	1432	|	1505	1524	|	|	1531	|	1605	1624	|	|	|	1631	|	1705	1724	|	1731	1805	|	1824
Stafford d.	1431	|	|	1458	|	1507	1526	|	|	1555	|	|	1626	|	1636	|	1655	|	1708	1726	|	|	|	1826	|	|
Wolverhampton a.	1449	|	1454	|	1504	|	1540	|	1548	|	1604	|	1640	|	1654	1648	|	1704	|	1740	|	1748	1804	1840	|	|
Birmingham New St a.	1508	|	1516	|	1526	|	1558	|	1611	|	1626	|	1658	|	1714	1711	|	1726	|	1758	|	1811	1826	1858	|	|
Nuneaton d.	...	|	...	|	|	|	...	|	...	|	|	|	...	|	...	...	|	|	|	...	|	...	|	...	|	|
Rugby a.	...	|	...	1558	|	1626	...	|	...	1658	|	1723	...	|	...	...	1758	|	1826	...	|	...	|	...	1923	|
Milton Keynes a.	...	|	...	|	1625	1651	...	1700	...	1722	1727	|	...	|	...	...	1822	1827	1850	...	1900	...	1925	...	|	|
Watford Junction ▽ a.	...	1632	...	1646	|	|	...	|	...	|	|	1812	...	1830	...	...	1845	|	|	...	|	...	1950	...	2012	2031
London Euston a.	...	1656	...	1708	1711	1739	...	1756	...	1808	1811	1838	...	1851	...	...	1914	1917	1933	...	1953	...	2011	...	2038	2053

	⑦	⑦ 🍷 E	⑦ 🍷	⑦ 🍷	⑦ 🍷 G	⑦ 🍷 X	⑦ 🍷	⑦ 🍷 G	⑦ 🍷	⑦ 🍷	⑦ 🍷 G	⑦ 🍷 S	⑦ 🍷	⑦	⑦ 🍷 E	⑦ 🍷	⑦ 🍷	⑦ 🍷 G	⑦ 🍷	⑦ 🍷 G	⑦	⑦ 2 ✣		⑦ 🍷 E	⑦	⑦
Preston **152** d.	...	1729	...	...	1800	...	...	1830	...	...	1900	...	...	...	1935	...	...	2006	...	2028	...	...	...	2134	...	...
Liverpool Lime St d.	1725	|	1756	...	|	...	...	|	1856	...	|	...	...	1930	|	...	1956	|	...	|	...	...	...	|	*2030*	2147
Runcorn d.	1743	|	1814	...	|	...	...	|	1914	...	|	...	...	1947	|	...	2014	|	...	|	...	...	...	|	|	2205
Manchester P'dilly d.	|	|	|	1753	|	1824	1845	|	|	1853	|	1924	1945	|	|	1956	|	|	2023	|	2055	...	...	*2106*	2155	|
Stockport d.	|	|	|	1802	|	1833	1855u	|	|	1902	|	1933	1955u	|	|	2005	|	|	2032	|	2104	...	...	|	2204	|
Holyhead ¶ **165** d.	*1557*	|	|	|	|	|	|	*1648*	|	|	|	|	|	|	|	|	|	|	|	|	|	1840	...	|	|	|
Crewe d.	1809	1815	1835	|	1847	|	|	1915	1936	|	1945	|	|	2008	2020	|	2035	2051	|	2113	|	|	...	2220	|	2243
Macclesfield d.	|	|	|	1815	|	1846	1908	|	|	1915	|	1946	2008	|	|	2017	|	|	2045	|	2117	|	...	|	2217	|
Stoke on Trent d.	|	|	|	1831	|	1905	1924	|	|	1931	|	2005	2024	|	|	2033	|	|	2101	|	2134	|	...	|	2234	|
Stafford d.	1830	|	1855	|	1908	1926	|	|	1955	|	2008	2026	|	2031	|	2053	2059	2111	2121	2132	2153	|	...	2240	2253	2307
Wolverhampton a.	1848	1851	|	1904	|	1940	|	1948	|	2004	|	2040	|	2047	2052	2108	|	|	2135	2154	2209	2216	...	2254	2309	2325
Birmingham New St a.	1904	1914	|	1926	|	1958	|	2011	|	2026	|	2058	|	2108	2115	2132	|	|	2156	2217	2230	2236	...	2317	2330	2345
Nuneaton d.	...	...	|	|	|	...	|	...	|	|	|	...	|	...	...	...	|	|	|	...	|	...	...	...	...	...
Rugby a.	...	...	1958	|	2026	...	|	...	2058	|	2123	...	2139	...	...	...	2158	|	2233	...	*2333*	...	...	...	...	...
Milton Keynes a.	...	...	2022	2027	2051	...	2101	...	2122	2128	2150	...	2204	...	...	...	2221	2250	2258	...	*2358*	...	...	...	...	...
Watford Junction ▽ a.	...	...	2047	2051	2131	...	|	...	2200	2206	2231	...	2241	...	...	...	2300	2316	2328	...	*0028*	...	...	...	...	...
London Euston a.	...	...	2114	2117	2154	...	2157	...	2223	2227	2251	...	2300	...	...	...	2325	2341	2348	...	*0047*	...	...	...	...	...

C – From Carlisle.
E – From Edinburgh.
G – From Glasgow.
L – From Lancaster.
R – To Reading.
S – To Southampton.
U – To Bournemouth.
V – To Coventry.
X – To Exeter.
Z – To Penzance.
j – Change at Stoke.
u – Stops to pick up only.
¶ – For Holyhead to Birmingham via Shrewsbury, see Table 147.
* – By 🚌. Change at Coventry.
✣ – Via Shrewsbury.
▽ – Trains stop here to set down only.
● – Services on ⑥⑦ are subject to alteration from Feb. 2.

VT, TP (LONDON and BIRMINGHAM -) CREWE and MANCHESTER - GLASGOW and EDINBURGH 152

km		Ⓐ	Ⓐ 🍷		Ⓐ 🍷		Ⓐ 🍷	Ⓐ 🍷	Ⓐ ✕	Ⓐ 🍷	Ⓐ ✕	Ⓐ 🍷	Ⓐ 🍷	Ⓐ ✕	Ⓐ 🍷	Ⓐ ✕	Ⓐ 🍷	Ⓐ ✕	Ⓐ 🍷	Ⓐ ✕	Ⓐ 🍷	Ⓐ 🍷	Ⓐ 🍷	Ⓐ 🍷
	London Euston **150** d.		...	...	...	...	...	...	0646	...	0746	...	...	0846	*0900*r	0946	...	1029	...	1046	...	1146	...	...
	Birmingham New St **150** d.		...	...	0530	...	...	0703	|	0803	|	...	0903	*0921*	1003	*1021*	...	|	1103	*1121*	1203	*1221*	...	1303
0	**Crewe** d.		...	...	0626	...	...	0756	0831	0856	0931	...	0956	1032	1056	1132	...	|	1156	1232	1256	1332	...	1356
39	Warrington Bank Quay d.		...	...	0645	...	...	0813	0850	0913	0950	...	1013	1051	1113	1151	...	|	1214	1251	1313	1351	...	1415
58	Wigan North Western d.		...	...	0704	...	...	0824	0901	0924	1001	...	1024	1102	1124	1202	...	|	1226	1302	1324	1402	...	1427
	Manchester Piccadilly ‡ d.		0458	...	*0605*	...	0745	|	*0811*	*0845*	|	0945	|	*1011*	*1045*	*1111*	1145	|	|	|	*1245*	*1311*	1345	|
	Bolton ‡ d.		|	...	*0626*	...	0804	|	*0832*	*0905*	|	1005	|	*1032*	*1105*	*1132*	1205	|	|	|	*1305*	*1332*	1405	|
82	**Preston** ‡ d.		0604	...	0720	...	0828	0843	0918	0940	1018	1029	1040	1119	1140	1219	1229	1244	1250	1319	1340	1419	1429	1443
	Blackpool North ‡ a.		|	...	*0756*	...	|	*0933*	*0957*	*1021*	*1057*	|	*1121*	*1154*	*1220*	*1254*	|	*1321*	*1321*g	*1354*	*1421*	*1454*	|	*1521*
116	Lancaster ‡ a.		0618	...	0734	...	0844	0900	0931	0955	1035	1044	|	1132	1154	1232	1244	|	1304	1338	1354	1432	1444	1457
146	Oxenholme ‡ a.		0634	...	0747	...	0858	0917	0945	1010	...	1103	1111	1146	|	1246	1259	|	|	...	1408	1446	1459	1512
198	Penrith a.		0700	...	0813	...	0924	0943	1012	1035	...	1129	|	|	1233	1312	|	|	1343	...	|	1512	1524	|
227	**Carlisle** **214** a.		0718	...	0834	...	0947	1001	1029	1052	...	1148	1156	1228	1251	1336	1340	1343	1400	...	1451	1530	1542	1555
371	Motherwell ▽ a.		0835	...	0950	...	|	1104	1127	|	...	1257	|	|	|	...	|	|	|	...	|	1627	|	|
391	**Glasgow** Central **214** a.		0858	...	1018	...	|	1128	1150	|	...	1314	1322	1346	|	...	|	1454	1525	...	|	1655	|	1721
389	**Edinburgh** a.		*0912*c	...	*1056*v	...	1111	...	...	1219	...	...	...	...	1419	...	1511	...	...	...	1616	...	1714	...

	Ⓐ 🍷	Ⓐ 🍷	Ⓐ 🍷	Ⓐ 🍷	Ⓐ 🍷	Ⓐ 🍷	Ⓐ 🍷	Ⓐ 🍷	Ⓐ ✕	Ⓐ 🍷	Ⓐ 🍷	Ⓐ 🍷	Ⓐ ✕	Ⓐ 🍷	Ⓐ 🍷	Ⓐ ✕	Ⓐ ✕	Ⓐ 🍷	Ⓐ 🍷		Ⓐ 🍷	Ⓐ 🍷		Ⓐ 🍷
London Euston **150** d.	1246	...	1346	...	...	1446	...	...	1546	*1549*r	...	1646	1715	...	...	1745	1808	...	1845	...	1946	...	...	2046
Birmingham New St **150** d.	*1321*	1403	*1421*	...	1503	*1521*	1603	...	*1621*	1651	1703	*1721*	|	1803	...	*1821*f	|	1903	*1921*	...	*2021*	2103	...	*2121*
Crewe d.	1432	1456	1532	...	1557	1632	1656	...	1732	1749	1756	1832	|	1856	...	|	1954	1959	2032	...	2138	2159	...	2236
Warrington Bank Quay d.	1451	1513	1551	...	1615	1651	1713	...	1751	1807	|	1852	1909	1913	...	1947	|	2017	2051	...	2157	2217	...	2254
Wigan North Western d.	1502	1524	1602	...	1627	1702	1724	...	1802	1817	|	1903	1920	1924	...	1958	|	2029	2102	...	2208	2234	...	2304
Manchester Piccadilly ‡ d.	|	*1445*	*1511*	1545	|	*1611*	*1644*	1711	|	|	*1732*	*1811*	*1831*	|	1845	|	*1911*	*1944*	*2011*	...	*2116*t	|	...	|
Bolton ‡ d.	|	*1505*	*1532*	1605	|	*1632*	*1705*	1730	|	|	*1753*	*1832*	*1851*	|	1912	|	*1932*	*2004*	*2032*	...	*2132*	|	...	|
Preston ‡ d.	1519	1540	1619	1629	1643	1718	1740	1758	1818	1839	1840	1918	1940	1945	1950	2016	2035	2045	2119	...	2224	2304	...	2324
Blackpool North ‡ a.	*1554*	*1621*	*1654*	|	*1734*	*1758*	*1822*	|	*1900*	...	*1923*	*1957*	|	*2036*	|	*2056*	|	*2136*	*2156*	...	*2328*	*2333*	...	*0038*
Lancaster ‡ a.	1538	1556	1632	1644	1658	1732	1754	1813	1831	...	1858	1933	|	1959	2005	2032	|	2100	2134	...	2238	...	...	...
Oxenholme ‡ a.	...	|	1646	1659	1715	|	1811	1828	1847	...	1913	1946	|	2013	2020	...	2059	2114	2148	...	2251	...	...	...
Penrith a.	...	1633	1712	1725	|	|	1837	1853	1913	...	|	2012	|	2039	2046	...	2125	2141	2214	...	2322	...	...	...
Carlisle **214** a.	...	1651	1729	1743	1757	1826	1855	1911	1931	...	1954	2029	2039	2058	2103	...	2143	2158	2237	...	2345	...	...	...
Motherwell ▽ a.	...	|	|	|	1913	|	|	|	2030	...	|	|	|	|	|	...	2249	2304	...	...	...	...	...	...
Glasgow Central **214** a.	...	|	1846	|	1937	1947	|	2031	2057	...	2111	|	2155	|	2231	...	2304	2333	...	...	...	...	...	...
Edinburgh a.	...	1819	...	1911	...	...	2019	...	...	...	...	2156	...	2225	*0038*	...	...	...	...	...	...	...	...	...

	⑥ ▲	⑥ 🍷		⑥ 🍷		⑥ 🍷	⑥ 🍷	⑥ 🍷	⑥ 🍷	⑥ 🍷	⑥ 🍷	⑥ 🍷	⑥ 🍷	⑥ 🍷	⑥ 🍷	⑥ 🍷	⑥ 🍷	⑥ 🍷	⑥ 🍷	⑥ 🍷	⑥ 🍷	⑥ 🍷	⑥ 🍷	⑥ 🍷
London Euston **150** d.		...	...	...	...	...	...	0525	...	0647	...	*0704*	0751	*0805*	0851	...	*0905*	0947	*1005*	1051	...	*1105*	1151	*1205*
Birmingham New St **150** d.		...	...	0530	...	...	0703	*0721*	0803	*0821*f	...	0903	0940	1003	1040	...	1103	1140	1203	1240	...	1303	1340	1403
Crewe d.		...	...	0628	...	...	0755	0839	0855	0937	...	0955	1041	1055	1143	...	1155	1241	1255	1341	...	1355	1441	1455
Warrington Bank Quay d.		...	...	0645	...	...	0813	0856	0912	0957	...	1013	1058	1113	1200	...	1213	1258	1312	1358	...	1413	1458	1513
Wigan North Western d.		...	...	0704	...	...	0824	0907	0923	1008	...	1024	1109	1124	1211	...	1225	1309	1323	1409	...	1424	1509	1524
Manchester Piccadilly ‡ d.		0510	...	*0605*	...	0745	|	*0816*t	*0831*	|	0945	|	*1016*t	*1045*	*1116*t	1145	|	|	*1245*	*1316*t	1345	|	*1416*t	*1445*
Bolton ‡ d.		|	...	*0626*	...	0804	|	*0832*	*0854*	|	1005	|	*1032*	*1105*	*1132*	1205	|	|	*1305*	*1332*	1405	|	*1432*	*1505*
Preston ‡ d.		0604	...	0720	...	0828	0840	0923	0939	1026	1029	1040	1125	1140	1227	1229	1241	1326	1338	1426	1429	1440	1525	1540
Blackpool North ‡ a.		|	...	*0756*	...	|	*0932*	*1002*	*1021*	...	|	*1123*	*1201*	*1220*	*1301*	|	*1321*	...	*1421*	*1501*	|	*1521*	*1601*	*1621*
Lancaster ‡ a.		0618	...	0733	...	0844	0859	0937	0953	...	1044	|	1140	1154	1241	1244	1255	...	1353	1439	1444	1454	1539	1554
Oxenholme ‡ a.		0633	...	0747	...	0858	0916	0950	1008	...	1103	1108	1153	|	1254	1259	|	...	1407	1453	1459	1509	1552	|
Penrith a.		0659	...	0813	...	0924	0942	1016	1034	...	1129	|	1219	1231	1320	|	1332	...	|	1519	1525	1536	1618	1633
Carlisle **214** a.		0719	...	0831	...	0941	1000	1033	1052	...	1146	1150	1237	1249	1338	1343	1350	...	1448	1537	1543	1554	1636	1649
Motherwell ▽ a.		0830	...	0934	...	|	1103	|	|	...	1300	|	|	|	|	|	|	...	|	1634	|	1653	1734	|
Glasgow Central **214** a.		0900	...	0959	...	|	1127	1157	|	...	1318	1316	1359	|	1458	|	1517	...	|	1658	|	1717	1757	|
Edinburgh a.		*0954*v	...	...	...	1111	...	...	1219	...	...	...	...	1416	...	1511	...	...	1619	...	1714	...	...	1816

	⑥ 🍷	⑥ 🍷	⑥ 🍷	⑥ 🍷	⑥ 🍷	⑥ 🍷	⑥ 🍷	⑥ 🍷	⑥ 🍷	⑥ 🍷	⑥ 🚌	⑥ 🚌	⑥ 🍷	⑥ 🍷	⑥ 🚌	⑥ 🚌	⑥ 🍷	⑥ 🍷		⑦ ▲	⑦ 🍷	⑦ 🍷	⑦ 🍷	⑦ 🍷
London Euston **150** d.	1251	...	*1305*	1351	*1405*	...	1451	*1505*	1551	*1605*	...	...	1651	*1705*	...	...	1751	1846	...		...	...	...	...
Birmingham New St **150** d.	1440	...	1503	1540	1603	...	1640	1703	1740	1803	...	...	1840	1903	...	...	*1921*	*2021*f	...		0903	1003	...	1103
Crewe d.	1541	...	1555	1641	1655	...	1741	1755	1841	1855	...	...	1941	1955	...	...	2037	2137	...		0957	1055	...	1155
Warrington Bank Quay d.	1558	...	1613	1658	1713	...	1758	1813	1858	1913	...	...	1958	2013	...	...	2054	2154	...		1014	1112	...	1212
Wigan North Western d.	1609	...	1624	1709	1724	...	1809	1824	1909	1924	...	...	2009	2024	...	...	2105	2205	...		1025	1123	...	1223
Manchester Piccadilly ‡ d.	*1516*t	1545	|	*1616*t	*1644*	1711	*1715*	*1730*	*1816*t	|	*1845*	...	|	|	*1944*	...	|	|	...		|	*1025*	1142	|
Bolton ‡ d.	*1532*	1605	|	*1632*	*1705*	1730	*1737*	*1753*	*1832*	|	*1912*	...	|	|	*2005*	...	|	|	...		|	*1045*	1200	|
Preston ‡ d.	1625	1629	1640	1726	1740	1758	1825	1840	1925	1943	2000	1955	2027	2051	2100	2055	2124	2224	...		1040	1139	1225	1240
Blackpool North ‡ a.	*1701*	|	*1734*	*1803*	*1830*	|	*1904*	*1921*	*2007*	*2036*	|	|	...	*2136*	|	|	*2236*	*2328*	...		*1134*	*1216*	|	*1334*
Lancaster ‡ a.	1638	1644	1657	1740	1755	1813	1839	1858	1939	...	|	2045	...	*2119*	|	2145	...	...	...		*1115*	1153	1240	1255
Oxenholme ‡ a.	1652	1659	1712	1753	1809	1828	1852	1913	1952	...	|	2130	...	...	|	2230	...	...	...		...	1207	1255	|
Penrith a.	1718	1725	1738	1819	|	|	1919	|	2018	...	|	2225	...	...	|	2325	...	...	...		...	1235	1321	1333
Carlisle **214** a.	1736	1743	1756	1837	1855	1909	1936	1954	2041	...	2200	2300	...	...	2300	2359	...	...	...		...	1253	1338	1350
Motherwell ▽ a.	|	|	1900	|	|	|	2039	|	...	...	...	...	...	...	...	...	...	...	...		...	|	|	|
Glasgow Central **214** a.	1858	|	1927	1958	|	2028	2059	2118	...	...	...	...	...	...	...	...	...	...	...		...	|	|	1509
Edinburgh a.	...	1911	...	...	2022	...	*0038*	...	...	...	...	...	...	...	...	...	...	...	...		...	1420	1508	...

	⑦ 🍷	⑦ 🍷	⑦ 🍷	⑦ 🍷	⑦ 🍷	⑦ 🍷	⑦ 🍷	⑦ 🍷	⑦ 🍷	⑦ 🍷	⑦ 🍷	⑦ 🍷	⑦ 🍷	⑦ 🍷	⑦ 🍷	⑦ 🍷	⑦ 🍷	⑦ 🍷	⑦ 🍷	⑦ 🍷	⑦ 🍷		⑦ 🍷	⑦ 🍷
London Euston **150** d.	0931	*0940*r	1031	...	*1036*	1131	*1140*r	1231	...	*1240*r	1340	*1355*r	1450	...	*1453*	1550	*1558*r	1650	*1658*r	1750	1850	...	1950	2031
Birmingham New St **150** d.	*1118*f	1203	*1218*f	...	1303	*1318*f	1403	*1418*f	...	1503	*1518*f	1603	*1618*f	...	1703	*1718*f	1803	*1818*f	1903	*1918*f	*2018*f	...	2135	*2218*f
Crewe d.	1223	1255	1323	...	1355	1423	1455	1522	...	1555	1623	1655	1723	...	1755	1823	1855	1926	1955	2023	2123	...	2238	2333
Warrington Bank Quay d.	1240	1312	1340	...	1411	1440	1511	1539	...	1611	1640	1711	1740	...	1812	1840	1911	1943	2012	2040	2140	...	2255	2350
Wigan North Western d.	1251	1323	1351	...	1422	1451	1522	1550	...	1623	1651	1722	1751	...	1823	1851	1922	1954	2023	2051	2151	...	2306	0001
Manchester Piccadilly ‡ d.	*1203*	*1225*	|	1342	|	*1403*	*1443*	*1503*	1542	|	*1603*	*1642*	*1703*	1742	|	*1803*	*1842*	|	*1926*	*2003*	*2103*	...	|	|
Bolton ‡ d.	*1222*	*1245*	|	1400	|	*1422*	*1500*	*1522*	1600	|	*1622*	*1700*	*1722*	1800	|	*1822*	*1900*	|	*1945*	*2022*	*2122*	...	|	|
Preston ‡ d.	1307	1340	1408	1425	1439	1507	1539	1606	1625	1639	1707	1739	1807	1825	1839	1907	1942	2014	2040	2108	2211	...	2336	0027
Blackpool North ‡ a.	*1338*	*1416*	*1447*	|	*1516*	*1528*	*1616*	*1647*	|	*1716*	*1738*	*1816*	*1847*	|	*1916*	*1947*	|	*2047*	*2116*	*2147*	*2247*	...	*0016*	...
Lancaster ‡ a.	1320	1354	...	1440	1453	1521	1555	1620	1640	1653	1721	1753	1820	1840	1853	1920	1956	2031	2054	2122	2224	...	...	...
Oxenholme ‡ a.	1334	1409	...	1455	1508	1534	|	1633	1655	1708	1734	|	1834	1844	1908	1934	2010	*2057*	2109	2135	2238	...	...	...
Penrith a.	1400	|	...	1521	1536	1600	1631	1659	1721	|	1800	1829	1900	1921	1935	2000	2036	...	2135	2201	2304	...	...	...
Carlisle **214** a.	1418	1450	...	1538	1552	1618	1648	1717	1738	1749	1818	1848	1918	1938	1952	2018	2052	...	2213	2219	2342	...	...	...
Motherwell ▽ a.	|	|	...	|	|	|	|	|	|	1851	|	|	|	2047	|	|	|	...	2316	|	...	...	...	...
Glasgow Central **214** a.	1537	|	...	|	1711	1737	|	1840	|	1916	1936	|	2048	2107	2114	2137	|	...	2338	2341	...	...	...	...
Edinburgh a.	...	1614	...	1708	...	...	1814	...	1908	...	...	2014	...	...	...	...	2218	...	...	...	...	...	...	...

c – Change at Carstairs.
f – Change at Stafford.
g – Change at Wigan.
r – Change at Crewe.

t – Change at Warrington.
v – Change at Motherwell.

▽ – Trains stop here to set down only.

‡ – For Manchester - Oxenholme, see also Table **157**. For Manchester - Blackpool, see Table **163**.

▲ – Services on ⑥⑦ are subject to alteration from Feb. 2.

GREAT BRITAIN

152 EDINBURGH and GLASGOW - MANCHESTER and CREWE (- BIRMINGHAM and LONDON) VT, TP

Ⓐ	Ⓐ 🍴	Ⓐ 🍷	Ⓐ 🍴	Ⓐ 🍴	Ⓐ 🍷	Ⓐ 🍴		Ⓐ 🍷	Ⓐ 🍴	Ⓐ 🍷	Ⓐ 🍷	Ⓐ 🍴	Ⓐ 🍷	Ⓐ 🍴	Ⓐ 🍷	Ⓐ 🍷	Ⓐ 🍴	Ⓐ 🍷	Ⓐ 🍷	Ⓐ 🍷		Ⓐ 🍷	Ⓐ 🍷
Edinburgh d.	...	...	...	...	...	...	...	...	...	0636	...	...	...	*0725*v	0821	0851	...	...	...	1010	...	1051	...
Glasgow Central 214 d.	...	...	...	...	...	...	...	...	0555	|	0640	0710	0745	0810	|	|	0939	...	1010	|	...	|	1110
Motherwell △ d.	...	...	...	...	...	...	...	...	0610	|	|	|	|	0828	|	|	|	...	|	|	...	|	1126
Carlisle 214 d.	...	...	...	0544	...	0609	...	...	0714	0753	0804	0821	0914	0934	1006	1017	1050	...	1122	1134	...	1213	1234
Penrith d.	...	...	...	0558	...	0623	...	...	0729	0809	0819	|	0929	0949	1022	|	|	...	|	1149	...	1229	1249
Oxenholme ‡ d.	...	...	...	0622	...	0647	...	...	0753	0833	0859	|	0954	1013	1046	1053	|	...	|	1213	...	1253	1313
Lancaster ‡ d.	0536	...	0633	0638	...	0723	...	*0759*	0829	0909	0914	0929	1009	1029	1105	1110	|	1129	1212	1229	...	1309	1329
Blackpool North ‡ d.	*0519*	*0530*	*0609*	*0634*	...	*0703*	...	*0741*	*0809*	*0841*	|	*0911*	*0938*	*1011*	|	*1041*	*1111*	|	*1141*	*1211*	...	*1241*	*1311*
Preston ‡ d.	0554	0615	0651	0718	0729	0743	...	0829	0849	0929	0938	0949	1028	1049	1138	1129	1152	1156	1232	1249	...	1329	1349
Bolton ‡ a.	|	|	|	*0802*	|	*0824*	...	|	*0934*	|	0958	*1034*	*1058*	*1134*	1158	*1158*	*1235*	|	*1312*	*1334*	...	*1358*	*1434*
Manchester Piccadilly ‡ a.	|	|	|	*0825*	|	*0847*	...	|	*0957*	|	1020	*1057*	*1120*	*1157*	1220	*1220*	*1257*	|	*1335*	*1357*	...	*1420*	*1457*
Wigan North Western d.	0606	0627	0703	0730	0741	0755	...	0841	0901	0941	...	1002	1042	1101	...	1141	|	1208	1245	1301	...	1341	1401
Warrington Bank Quay d.	0627	0645	0714	0741	0753	0807	...	0852	0912	0953	...	1013	1053	1112	...	1152	|	1220	1259	1312	...	1353	1412
Crewe a.	0646	0708	|	|	0812	0831	...	0913	0931	1012	...	1032	1113	1131	...	1212	|	1241	1327	1332	...	1412	1432
Birmingham New St 150 a.	|	0811	*0830*f	*0858*f	0911	*0958*	...	1011	*1058*	1111	...	|	1211	*1258*	...	1311	|	*1358*	1441	*1458*	...	1511	*1558*
London Euston 150 a.	0840	...	0914	0953	...	1027	...	...	1127	...	...	1226	...	1327	...	...	1404	1440	...	1526	...	...	1627

	Ⓐ 🍷	Ⓐ 🍷	Ⓐ 🍷	Ⓐ 🍷	Ⓐ 🍷	Ⓐ 🍷	Ⓐ 🍷	Ⓐ 🍷	Ⓐ 🍷		Ⓐ 🍷	Ⓐ 🍷		Ⓐ 🍷	Ⓐ 🍷	Ⓐ 🍷	Ⓐ 🍷		Ⓐ 🍷	Ⓐ 🍷	Ⓐ 🍷	Ⓐ 🍷		Ⓐ 🍷
Edinburgh d.	1152	...	...	...	1251	...	...	...	...	...	1451	...	...	1552	...	...	1651	...	...	1752	...	1851	...	*2015*c
Glasgow Central 214 d.	|	1210	...	1249	|	...	1340	1410	...	...	|	1510	...	|	1610	1646	|	...	1740	|	1810	|	...	2010
Motherwell △ d.	|	|	...	|	|	...	|	|	...	...	|	1529	...	|	|	|	|	...	|	|	1827	|	...	|
Carlisle 214 d.	1311	1321	...	1400	1414	1434	1508	1521	...	...	1614	1634	...	1715	1721	1759	1811	...	1906	1916	1932	2011	...	2147
Penrith d.	1325	|	...	|	1429	1448	1523	|	...	...	1629	1649	...	1729	1736	|	1827	...	1920	1931	|	2027	...	2202
Oxenholme ‡ d.	1349	1359	...	|	1453	1512	1547	|	...	...	1653	1713	...	1753	1800	1834	1851	...	1944	1955	2007	2052	...	2227
Lancaster ‡ d.	1406	|	1429	|	1508	1528	1603	1609	1629	...	1709	1729	...	1816	|	1851	1908	...	2001	2011	2023	2107	...	2244
Blackpool North ‡ d.	|	*1341*	*1411*	*1421*	*1441*	*1511*	|	*1541*	*1610*	...	*1638*	*1710*	...	|	*1738*	*1830*	*1838*	...	*1942*	|	|	*2028*	...	|
Preston ‡ d.	1438	1430	1449	1502	1529	1548	1638	1629	1649	...	1729	1749	...	1838	1829	1910	1929	...	2021	2032	2049	2129	...	2323
Bolton ‡ a.	1458	*1458*	|	|	*1558*	*1634*	1658	*1658*	|	...	*1813*	*1834*	...	1858	*1858*	*1945*y	*2012*	...	|	2053	*2154*	*2253*	...	*2351*
Manchester Piccadilly ‡ a.	1520	*1520*	|	|	*1620*	*1657*	1720	*1720*	|	...	*1838*	*1859*	...	1920	*1920*	*2004*y	*2034*	...	|	2114	*2201*t	*2305*t	...	0016
Wigan North Western d.	...	1442	1501	|	1541	1600	...	1641	1701	...	1741	1800	...	...	1841	1922	1941	...	2033	...	2101	2142	...	2339s
Warrington Bank Quay d.	...	1454	1512	|	1552	1611	...	1653	1712	...	1753	1812	...	...	1853	1933	1953	...	2044	...	2113	2154	...	...
Crewe a.	...	1512	1535	|	1611	1631	...	1713	1732	...	1812	1831	...	...	1912	1952	2013	...	2103	...	2132	2213	...	...
Birmingham New St 150 a.	...	1611	*1658*	|	1711	|	...	1811	*1858*	...	1911	|	...	...	2011	*2058*f	2111	...	*2230*	...	2238	2311	...	...
London Euston 150 a.	...	...	1740	1717	*1821*r	1827	...	...	1925	...	...	2026	...	...	...	2151	*2305*r	...	2314	...	*0102*	...	...	...

⑥ ▲	⑥ 🍷	⑥ 🍷	⑥ 🍷	⑥ 🍷	⑥ 🍷	⑥ 🍷	⑥ 🍷	⑥ 🍷	⑥ 🍷	⑥ 🍷	⑥ 🍷	⑥ 🍷		⑥ 🍷	⑥ 🍷	⑥ 🍷	⑥ 🍷	⑥ 🍷	⑥ 🍷	⑥ 🍷	⑥ 🍷	⑥ 🍷	⑥ 🍷
Edinburgh d.	...	...	...	...	...	...	...	0652	...	...	...	...	...	0851	0841	...	...	...	1051	...	1152	...	...
Glasgow Central 214 d.	...	...	...	...	...	...	0610	|	0658	0710	0740	0806	...	|	|	...	1010	1020	|	1110	|	1210	...
Motherwell △ d.	...	...	...	...	...	...	0625	|	|	0728	|	0826	...	|	|	...	|	|	|	1125	|	|	...
Carlisle 214 d.	...	...	...	...	0630	...	0728	0813	0820	0832	0914	0923	...	1010	1015	...	1122	1132	1213	1232	1311	1321	...
Penrith d.	...	...	...	...	0644	...	0743	0829	0835	0847	0930	0938	...	|	1030	...	|	1147	1229	1247	1325	|	...
Oxenholme ‡ d.	...	...	...	...	0708	...	0807	0853	0859	0911	0954	1006	...	1047	1054	...	|	1211	1253	1311	1350	1358	...
Lancaster ‡ d.	0520	...	0625	...	0724	...	0827	0909	0914	0927	1009	1022	...	1106	1112	...	1211	1227	1309	1327	1417	|	...
Blackpool North ‡ d.	*0443*	*0530*	*0608*	*0634*	*0703*	*0741*	*0809*	*0841*	|	|	*0940*	|	...	*1041*	|	...	*1141*	|	*1241*	|	|	*1341*	...
Preston ‡ d.	0540	0615	0645	0720	0744	0829	0847	0929	0938	0947	1029	1047	...	1128	1138	1147	1229	1247	1329	1347	1438	1429	1447
Bolton ‡ a.	|	|	|	|	*0833*	|	*0934*	|	0958	*1034*	*1058*	*1134*	...	|	1158	|	*1258*	*1334*	*1358*	*1434*	1458	*1458*	|
Manchester Piccadilly ‡ a.	|	|	|	|	*0853*	|	*0957*	|	1020	*1057*	*1120*	*1157*	...	|	1220	|	*1320*	*1357*	*1420*	*1457*	1520	*1520*	|
Wigan North Western d.	0552	0627	0657	0732	0756	0840	0859	0941	...	0959	1041	1059	...	1140	...	1159	1241	1259	1341	1359	...	1441	1459
Warrington Bank Quay d.	0609	0647	0708	0744	0807	0852	0910	0953	...	1010	1053	1110	...	1153	...	1210	1253	1310	1353	1410	...	1452	1510
Crewe a.	0630	0708	0728	0803	0827	0911	0929	1012	...	1029	1113	1129	...	1212	...	1229	1312	1329	1412	1428	...	1510	1528
Birmingham New St 150 a.	|	0810	*0858*f	0910	0924	1011	1024	1111	...	1124	1211	1224	...	1311	...	1324	1411	1424	1511	|	...	1611	1624
London Euston 150 a.	0912	...	1013	...	1112	...	1211	...	...	1311	...	1411	...	...	...	1511	...	1615	...	1713	...	...	1813

	⑥ 🍷	⑥ 🍷	⑥ 🍷	⑥ 🍷	⑥ 🍷	⑥ 🍷	⑥ 🍷	⑥ 🍷	⑥ 🍷	⑥ 🍷	⑥ 🍷	⑥ 🍷	⑥ 🍷	⑦ 🍷	⑥ 🍷	
Edinburgh d.	1251	...	...	...	...	1451	...	1552	...	...	1651	...	1752	...	...	...
Glasgow Central 214 d.	|	1310	1340	1410	...	|	1510	|	1603	1610	|	1707	|	1810	...	...
Motherwell △ d.	|	1324	|	|	...	|	1525	|	|	|	|	|	|	1827	...	...
Carlisle 214 d.	1413	1432	1508	1521	...	1609	1631	1715	1721	1733	1811	1833	1916	1932	...	...
Penrith d.	1428	1447	1523	|	...	1624	1647	1729	1736	1747	1827	1848	1931	|	...	...
Oxenholme ‡ d.	1453	1511	1547	|	...	1648	1711	1753	1800	1811	1851	1912	1955	2008	...	...
Lancaster ‡ d.	1509	1527	1603	1610	...	1704	1727	1816	|	1827	1907	1928	2011	2021	...	...
Blackpool North ‡ d.	*1441*	|	|	*1541*	*1610*	*1638*	*1710*	|	*1738*	|	*1842*	*1910*	|	*1942*	*2030*	...
Preston ‡ d.	1529	1547	1638	1629	1647	1724	1747	1838	1830	1847	1929	1948	2032	2043	2128	...
Bolton ‡ a.	*1558*	*1634*	1658	*1658*	|	*1759*	*1834*	1858	*1912*	*1934*	*2011*	*2040*	2108	*2153*	|	...
Manchester Piccadilly ‡ a.	*1620*	*1657*	1720	*1720*	|	*1820*	*1859*	1920	*1936*	*1959*	*2034*	*2059*t	2127	*2201*t	|	...
Wigan North Western d.	1541	1559	...	1641	1659	1736	1758	...	1842	1859	1941	2000	...	2057	2145	...
Warrington Bank Quay d.	1553	1610	...	1652	1710	1748	1810	...	1853	1910	1953	2011	...	2107	2156	...
Crewe a.	1612	1629	...	1713	1729	1807	1829	...	1913	1929	2013	2029	...	2126	2214	...
Birmingham New St 150 a.	1711	1724	...	1811	1824	1911	|	...	2011	*2058*f	2111	|	...	2230	2311	...
London Euston 150 a.	...	1912	...	...	2011	...	2137	...	...	2242	...	2336	...	...	...	...

⑦ ▲	⑦ 🍷	⑦ 🍷		⑦ 🍷	⑦ 🚌	⑦ 🍷	⑦ 🍷
Edinburgh d.	...	...	...	...	...	...	...
Glasgow Central 214 d.	...	...	...	...	...	...	...
Motherwell △ d.	...	...	...	...	...	...	...
Carlisle 214 d.	...	...	...	...	0915	...	...
Penrith d.	...	...	...	...	0950	...	...
Oxenholme ‡ d.	...	...	...	...	1045	...	...
Lancaster ‡ d.	...	...	...	...	1130	1143	...
Blackpool North ‡ d.	...	*0928*	...	*1028*	...	*1128*	...
Preston ‡ d.	1004	1028	...	1125	...	1203	1228
Bolton ‡ a.	|	|	...	|	...	|	|
Manchester Piccadilly ‡ a.	|	|	...	|	...	|	|
Wigan North Western d.	1015	1040	...	1137	...	1215	1240
Warrington Bank Quay d.	1026	1051	...	1149	...	1226	1252
Crewe a.	1046	1112	...	1208	...	1245	1313
Birmingham New St 150 a.	*1158*f	1206	...	1311	...	|	1411
London Euston 150 a.	1356	*1423*r	...	*1508*r	...	1538	*1607*r

	⑦ 🍷	⑦ 🍷	⑦ 🍷	⑦ 🍷	⑦ 🍷	⑦ 🍷	⑦ 🍷	⑦ 🍷	⑦ 🍷	⑦ 🍷	⑦ 🍷	⑦ 🍷	⑦ 🍷	⑦ 🍷	⑦ 🍷	⑦ 🍷	⑦ 🍷	⑦ 🍷	⑦ 🍷	⑦ 🍷		⑦ 🍷		⑦ 🍷
Edinburgh d.	...	1056	...	1143	...	...	1252	...	...	...	...	1453	...	1543	...	...	1653	...	1739	...	...	1852	...	*1937*v
Glasgow Central 214 d.	...	|	1127	|	1155	...	|	1325	1335	1403	1426	|	1525	|	1603	1626	|	1733	|	1803	...	|	...	2003
Motherwell △ d.	...	|	1149	|	1213	...	|	1345	|	|	1445	|	1545	|	|	1645	|	1750	|	|	...	|	...	2022
Carlisle 214 d.	1151	1214	1245	1307	1315	...	1413	1445	1503	1516	1547	1614	1645	1707	1718	1745	1819	1852	1907	1915	...	2018	...	2130
Penrith d.	1208	1229	1300	1321	1330	...	1428	1500	1517	|	1602	1629	1700	1721	|	1800	1834	1906	1921	|	...	2034	...	2145
Oxenholme ‡ d.	1232	1253	1324	1345	|	...	1453	1524	1541	|	1626	1653	1724	1745	1755	1824	1858	1930	1945	1952	...	2058	...	2209
Lancaster ‡ d.	1321	1309	1340	1401	1407	...	1509	1540	1557	1604	1642	1709	1740	1801	1810	1840	1916	1946	2001	2008	...	2114	...	2226
Blackpool North ‡ d.	*1228*	|	*1312*	|	*1328*	*1428*	|	*1512*	|	*1528*	*1628*	*1645*	*1717*	|	*1745*	*1817*	*1828*	*1928*	|	|	...	*2028*	...	|
Preston ‡ d.	1308	1329	1400	1420	1427	1502	1528	1600	1620	1623	1702	1729	1800	1823	1830	1900	1935	2006	2023	2028	...	2134	...	2301
Bolton ‡ a.	*1352*	*1426*	|	*1452*	*1526*	|	*1626*	|	1642	*1726*	*1741*	*1826*	|	1842	*1926*	*1941*	*2026*	|	2042	*2126*	...	*2226*	...	2337s
Manchester Piccadilly ‡ a.	*1415*	*1441*t	|	*1515*	*1549*	|	*1649*	|	1701	*1749*	*1801*	*1849*	|	1901	*1949*	*2001*	*2049*	|	2101	*2149*	...	*2249*	...	2359
Wigan North Western d.	1321	1340	1413	...	1440	1514	1541	1613	...	1636	1714	1741	1813	...	1842	1912	1947	2018	...	2040	...	2146	...	2323s
Warrington Bank Quay d.	1332	1353	1424	...	1452	1525	1552	1624	...	1647	1725	1753	1834	...	1853	1923	1958	2029	...	2052	...	2158	...	...
Crewe a.	1350	1413	1443	...	1512	1544	1612	1643	...	1707	1744	1812	1844	...	1912	1942	2018	2048	...	2111	...	2217	...	...
Birmingham New St 150 a.	*1508*	1516	*1456*f	...	1611	|	1711	*1758*f	...	1811	*1904*	1914	*1958*f	...	2011	*2058*f	2115	*2156*f	...	2217	...	2317	...	...
London Euston 150 a.	1636	*1708*r	1739	...	*1808*r	1838	*1914*r	1933	...	*2011*	2038	*2114*r	2154	...	*2223*r	2251	*2325*r	2341	...	*0047*	...	...	...	...

c – Change at Carstairs.
f – Change at Stafford.
r – Change at Crewe.
s – Stops to set down only.
t – Change at Warrington.
v – Change at Motherwell.
y – Change at Oxenholme.
△ – Trains stop here to pick up only.
‡ – For Oxenholme - Manchester, see also Table **157**.
For Blackpool - Manchester - Blackpool, see Table **163**.
▲ – Services on ⑥⑦ are subject to alteration from Feb. 2.

AW 2nd class

MANCHESTER - CREWE - HEREFORD - CARDIFF

155

Services on ⑥ are subject to alteration from March 29. Services on ⑦ are subject to alteration from February 3.

km		Ⓐ	⑥	Ⓐ 🍷 M	⑥ 🍷 M	Ⓐ	⑥	⚒ C	⚒	⚒ 🍷 M	⚒ 🍷 C	⚒ 🍷	⚒ 🍷 M	⚒ 🍷 C	⚒ 🍷	⚒ 🍷 M	⚒ 🍷 C	⚒ 🍷	⚒ 🍷 M	⚒ 🍷 C	⚒ 🍷	⚒ 🍷 M	⑥ 🍷 C	Ⓐ 🍷 C	Ⓐ 🍷
0	**Manchester** P'dilly d.	...	...	...	...	...	...	...	...	0638	0728	...	0834	0934	...	1034	1134	...	1234	1334	...	1434	1534	1534	...
10	Stockport d.	...	...	...	...	...	...	...	...	0648	0737	...	0844	0942	...	1042	1142	...	1242	1342	...	1442	1542	1542	...
	Holyhead 165 d.	...	...	*0215*	*0215*	...	...	...	0427	|	*0532*	0615	*0645*	*0715*	0810y	|	*0950*	1030	|	*1140*	1235	|	*1335*	*1335*	1435
	Chester 147 165 d.	...	...	*0340*	*0340*	0507	*0518*	...	0612	*0630*	*0730*	0820	*0830*	*0928*e	1020	*1029*	*1128*	1220	*1229*	*1333*	1420	*1430*	*1530*	*1530*	1620
50	**Crewe** ‡ d.	...	...	0454	0454	|	|	0555	|	0718	0808	...	0917	1017	|	1118	1218	|	1318	1418	|	1518	1615	1618	|
72	Whitchurch ‡ d.	...	...	0512	0512	|	|	0614	|	|	0826	|	|	|	|	|	|	|	|	|	|	|	1633	1636	|
103	**Shrewsbury** ‡ a.	...	...	0532	0532	0607	*0613*	0640	0707	0747	0844	0916	0946	1046	1115	1146	1246	1315	1346	1446	1515	1546	1654	1657	1715
103	**Shrewsbury** 146 d.	...	...	0540	0540	0620	0623	0645	0716	0749	0849	0918	0949	1049	1118	1149	1249	1318	1349	1449	1518	1549	1655	1658	1718
123	Church Stretton 146 d.	...	...	0555	0555	|	|	0700	|	0804	0904	|	1004	1104	|	1204	1304	|	1404	1504	|	1604	1710	1714	|
135	Craven Arms 146 d.	...	...	0603	0603	|	|	0708	|	0812	0912	|	1012	1112	|	1212	1312	|	1412	1512	|	1612	1718	1722	|
146	Ludlow d.	...	...	0611	0611	0647	0649	0716	0743	0820	0920	0944	1020	1120	1145	1220	1320	1345	1420	1520	1545	1620	1726	1730	1745
164	Leominster d.	...	...	0622	0622	0658	0700	0727	0753	0831	0931	|	1031	1131	|	1231	1331	|	1431	1531	|	1631	1736	1741	|
184	**Hereford** a.	...	...	0636	0636	0712	0714	0745	0808	0845	0945	1008	1045	1145	1208	1245	1345	1408	1445	1545	1608	1645	1751	1752	1808
184	**Hereford** d.	0523	0542	0642	0649	0716	0716	0748	0809	0848	0947	1008	1048	1148	1209	1248	1348	1409	1448	1548	1609	1648	1753	1756	1809
223	Abergavenny d.	0548	0607	0705	0712	0739	0739	0811	0832	0911	1010	1032	1111	1211	1232	1311	1411	1432	1511	1611	1632	1711	1816	1819	1833
238	Pontypool & New Inn d.	0559	0618	0715	0722	0749	0749	|	0842	|	1020	|	|	|	1242	|	|	1442	|	|	1642	|	|	|	1842
243	Cwmbrân d.	0604	0623	0720	0727	0754	0754	0824	0847	0923	1024	1046	1123	1223	1247	1323	1423	1447	1523	1623	1647	1723	1829	1831	1847
254	Newport a.	0616	0634	0733	0739	0804	0804	0834	0858	0934	1034	1058	1134	1234	1258	1334	1434	1458	1534	1634	1658	1734	1839	1845	1858
273	**Cardiff** Central a.	0659	0654	0750	0757	0829	0825	0853	0918	0953	1054	1120	1154	1254	1321	1354	1454	1520	1554	1654	1715z	1755	1854	1901	1924

	⑥ 🍷	⚒ 🍷 M	⚒ 🍷 D	⚒ 🍷	⚒ 🍷 C	⑥	Ⓐ	⚒	⚒	⚒		⑦ 🚌	⑦	⑦ 🍷 C	⑦ 🍷	⑦ 🍷 M	⑦ 🍷 P	⑦ 🍷	⑦	⑦ 🍷 M	⑦ 🍷	⑦ 🍷	⑦ 🍷	⑦	⑦
Manchester P'dilly d.	...	1634	1734	...	1834	1934	1934	2034	2134	2234	...	...	...	*0914*	...	1233	1434	1549	...	1637	*1706*	...	1837	2046	2246
Stockport d.	...	1642	1742	...	1842	1942	1943	2046	2145	2242	...	...	...	|	...	1242	1442	1558	...	1645	|	...	1845	2054	2254
Holyhead 165 d.	1435	|	*1539*	1635	|	*1735*	*1727*	*1835*e	*1935*	|	...	...	...	|	1035	|	|	*1314*	...	|	*1557*	1725	|	*1840*e	|
Chester 147 165 d.	1620	*1631*	*1731*	1820	*1830*	*1934*	*1922*	*2030*	*2133*	*2214*j	...	...	...	*1011*	1220	*1225*	*1446*	*1525*	...	*1625*	*1752*	1907	|	*2055*	*2225*
Crewe ‡ d.	|	1718	1818	|	1918	2018	2018	2118	2218	2316	...	0640	...	1050	|	1323	1524	1632	...	1722	1840	|	1920	2135	2325
Whitchurch ‡ d.	|	|	1836	|	|	|	|	2139	2238	2338	...	0720	...	1110	|	1344	|	|	...	1743	|	|	1941	|	2346
Shrewsbury ‡ a.	1715	1746	1857	1915	1947	2046	2046	2204	2304	0007	...	0750	...	1136	1315	1409	1552	1705	...	1808	1913	1959	2006	2209	0014
Shrewsbury 146 d.	1718	1749	1859	1917	1949	2049	2049	2207	2306	...	...	0750	...	1145	1316	1410	1608	1708	...	1809	1918	2013	2013	2213	...
Church Stretton 146 d.	|	1804	1914	|	2004	2104	2104	2222	2322	...	...	0815	...	1201	1332	1426	1624	|	...	1825	|	2029	2029	2228	...
Craven Arms 146 d.	|	1812	1922	|	2012	2112	2112	2230	2330	...	...	0835	...	1209	1341	1435	1632	|	...	1834	|	2037	2037	2236	...
Ludlow d.	1747	1820	1930	1945	2020	2120	2120	2238	2338	...	...	0855	...	1218	1349	1443	1641	1737	...	1842	1947	2046	2046	2244	...
Leominster d.	|	1831	1941	|	2031	2131	2131	2249	2348	...	...	0920	...	1229	1401	1455	1652	|	...	1854	|	2057	2057	2255	...
Hereford a.	1810	1845	1955	2008	2045	2145	2145	2303	0003	...	...	0950	...	1244	1415	1509	1707	1800	...	1908	2010	2112	2112	2309	...
Hereford d.	1811	1848	1957	2009	2048	2148	2149	2305	0004	...	...	...	1011	1246	1417	1511	1709	1802	1850	1910	2012	2113	2113	2314	...
Abergavenny d.	1834	1911	2020	2033	2111	2211	2212	2328	0027	...	...	...	1034	1310	1440	1534	1732	1825	1913	1933	2035	2137	2137	2337	...
Pontypool & New Inn d.	1844	|	|	2042	|	2221	2222	|	0037	...	...	...	1045	1320	1451	1545	1743	|	1924	1944	|	2147	2147	2347	...
Cwmbrân d.	1848	1923	2032	2047	2123	2223	2224	2340	0042	...	...	...	1050	1325	1456	1550	1748	1838	1929	1949	2048	2152	2152	2352	...
Newport a.	1900	1934n	2045	2059	2135	2240	2238	2352	0056b	...	...	...	1100	1337	1509	1600	1758	1851	1946	2000	2100	2203	2203	0001	...
Cardiff Central a.	1922	1954z	2101	2120	2157z	2301	2304	0017	0122q	...	...	...	1117	1354	1531	1617	1816	1913	2005	2017	2121	2228	2228	0029	...

	⑥	②–⑤	⚒	⚒ 🍷	⚒ 🍷	⚒ 🍷 C	⚒	Ⓐ C	⑥ C	⚒ 🍷 M	⚒ 🍷	⚒ 🍷 M	⚒ 🍷 C	⚒ 🍷	Ⓐ 🍷 M	⑥ 🍷 M	⚒ 🍷 C	⚒ 🍷	Ⓐ 🍷 M	⑥ 🍷 M	⚒ 🍷 C	⚒ 🍷	Ⓐ 🍷 M	⑥ 🍷 M	⚒
Cardiff Central d.	0030	0030	0400	0510	0535	0650	0720	0750	0750	0850	0920	0950	1050	1120	1150	1150	1250	1320	1350	1350	1450	1520	1550	1550	1606
Newport d.	0053	0057	0418	0528r	0553	0704	0734	0804	0804	0904	0934	1004	1104	1134	1204	1204	1304	1334	1404	1404	1504	1534	1604	1604	1622
Cwmbrân d.	0104	0108	0428	0538	0603	0715	0744	0816	0815	0915	0944	1015	1115	1144	1215	1215	1315	1343	1415	1415	1515	1544	1615	1615	1632
Pontypool & New Inn d.	0110	0114	0434	0544	0609	|	0749	|	|	0920	|	|	|	1149	|	|	|	1348	|	|	|	1549	|	|	1638
Abergavenny d.	0120	0125	0445	0554	0618z	0728	0800	0829	0828	0928	0957	1028	1128	1200	1228	1228	1328	1400	1428	1428	1528	1600	1628	1628	1655
Hereford a.	0146	0153	0512	0619	0647	0754	0825	0854	0854	0954	1022	1054	1154	1225	1254	1254	1354	1425	1454	1454	1553	1625	1654	1654	...
Hereford d.	0148	...	0523	0625	0648	0756	0828	0856	0856	0956	1023	1056	1156	1228	1256	1256	1356	1428	1456	1456	1554	1628	1656	1656	...
Leominster d.	0201	...	0536	0638	0702	0809	|	0909	0909	1009	|	1109	1209	|	1309	1309	1409	|	1509	1509	1607	|	1709	1709	...
Ludlow d.	0212	...	0547	0649	0713	0820	0849	0920	0920	1020	1045	1120	1220	1249	1320	1320	1420	1449	1520	1520	1618	1649	1720	1720	...
Craven Arms 146 d.	0222	...	0556	0658	0721	0829	|	0929	0929	1029	|	1129	1229	|	1329	1329	1429	|	1529	1529	1627	|	1729	1729	...
Church Stretton 146 d.	0231	...	0608	0707	0730	0838	|	0938	0938	1038	|	1138	1238	|	1338	1338	1438	|	1538	1538	|	|	1738	1738	...
Shrewsbury 146 a.	0249	...	0622	0722	0744	0852	0915	0952	0952	1052	1112	1152	1252	1315	1352	1352	1452	1517	1552	1552	1648	1715	1752	1752	...
Shrewsbury ‡ d.	...	...	0626	0730	0746	0854	0930	0954	0954	1054	1130	1154	1254	1330	1354	1354	1454	1530	1554	1554	1649	1730	1754	1754	...
Whitchurch ‡ d.	...	...	0647	|	0807	|	|	|	|	|	|	|	|	|	|	|	|	|	|	|	1710	|	|	|	...
Crewe ‡ a.	...	...	0705	|	0825z	0925z	|	1025	1028	1125z	|	1225z	1324z	|	1424	1428	1524z	|	1625	1628	1728	|	1824	1828	...
Chester 147 165 a.	...	...	*0759*	0828	*0926*	*1027*	1028	*1117*	*1109*	*1227*	1228r	*1326*e	*1427*	1428	*1522*e	*1526*e	*1627*	1628	*1722*e	*1726*e	|	1825	*1925*	*1922*e	...
Holyhead 165 a.	...	...	|	1020	*1130*	|	1220	*1303*	*1253*	|	1430	*1530*	|	1630	*1720*	*1720*	|	1830	*1920*	*1920*	|	2030	*2140*	*2133*	...
Stockport a.	...	...	0746r	...	0853z	0954z	...	1053	1058	1153z	...	1253z	1353z	...	1453	1458	1553z	...	1653	1658	1754z	...	1853	1858	...
Manchester P'dilly a.	...	...	0810v	...	0913	1013	...	1113	1113	1213	...	1313	1413	...	1513	1513	1613	...	1711	1713	1812	...	1913	1916	...

	⚒ C	⚒ 🍷	Ⓐ 🍷 M	⑥ 🍷 M	⚒ 🍷 C	⚒ T	⚒ 🍷 M	⑥ 🍷 C	Ⓐ 🍷 C	⑥ M	Ⓐ M	⑦	⑦ 🚌	⑦	⑦ 🍷	⑦ 🍷	⑦ 🍷 C	⑦ 🍷 C	⑦ 🍷	⑦ 🍷 M	⑦ 🍷	⑦ 🍷 M	⑦ 🍷	⑦ 🍷 M	⑦ P
Cardiff Central d.	1650	1720	1750	1750	1850	1934	2010	2053	2053	2150	2156	0834	...	...	1135	1135	1235	1435	1535	1635	1705	1835	1835	2035	2246
Newport d.	1704	1734	1803	1804	1905	1949	2025	2109	2110	2208	2215	0854	...	...	1149	1149	1249	1449	1550	1651	1720	1850	1850	2050	2309
Cwmbrân d.	1715	1744	1815	1815	1915	1958	2035	2120	2121	2219	2225	0904	...	...	1200	1200	1300	1501	1600	1702	1730	1900	1900	2100	2319
Pontypool & New Inn d.	|	1749	1820	1821	|	2003	2041	|	|	2225	2231	0910	...	...	|	|	1306	1507	|	1708	1736	|	|	2107	2325
Abergavenny d.	1728	1800	1828	1828	1928	2013	2048	2133	2134	2234	2240	0920	...	...	1214	1214	1316	1517	1614	1716	1746	1914	1914	2117	2335
Hereford a.	1754	1824	1854	1854	1955	2039	2114	2157	2200	2259	2305	0950	...	...	1240	1240	1340	1541	1640	1744	1813	1938	1938	2143	0004
Hereford d.	1756	1826	1856	1856	1956	2040	2116	2159	2201	2300	2306	▬	1000	...	1244	1244	1342	1542	1642	1746	▬	1940	1940	2145	▬
Leominster d.	1809	1839	1909	1909	2009	2054	2129	2212	2215	2313	2320	...	1025	...	1257	1257	1355	1556	1655	1759	⑦	1953	1953	2158	...
Ludlow d.	1820	1849	1920	1920	2020	2101	2140	2223	2226	2324	2331	...	1050	...	1309	1309	1407	1607	1707	1811	Q	2005	2005	2210	...
Craven Arms 146 d.	1829	|	1929	1929	2029	2113	2149	2232	2234	2333	2339	...	1110	...	1318	1318	1416	1617	|	1820	1855	2014	2014	2219	...
Church Stretton 146 d.	1838	|	1938	1938	2038	2122	2202	2241	2243	2342	2348	...	1130	...	1328	1328	1426	1624	|	1830	1908	2024	2024	2229	⑦
Shrewsbury 146 a.	1852	1916	1952	1952	2052	2136	2216	2255	2257	2356	0002	⑦	1200	...	1343	1343	1441	1639	1735	1845	1923	2039	2039	2244	B
Shrewsbury ‡ d.	1854	1930	1954	1954	2054	2138	2217	2256	2259	2357	0012	1058	*1234*	1240	1344	1352	1446	1641	1737	1846	1925	2042	2046	2245	2350
Whitchurch ‡ d.	|	|	|	|	|	|	2242	2322	2324	0021	0037	|	|	1306	|	|	|	1709	|	|	1951	|	|	2311	|
Crewe ‡ a.	1925z	|	2026	2026	2124z	|	2303	2344	2346	0044	0058	1130	|	1334	1421	|	1523	1737	1812	1927	2015	2124	|	2336	0030
Chester 147 165 a.	*2002*	2031r	*2123*e	*2126*e	*2211*	2232	*2326*e	0010	0027v	...	...	*1220*	*1329*	|	|	1459	*1617*	*1820*	*1848*e	*2020*	*2056*	|	2134	...	0048
Holyhead 165 a.	|	2235	*2330*	*2330*	|	0047d	|	...	*0215*	...	...	|	...	|	|	1658	*1802*	|	|	|	*2250*	|	2351	...	0227
Stockport a.	1953n	...	2053	2056	2153z	...	2333	...	...	...	...	1201	...	1405	1455	...	1555	1811	|	1959	|	2156	...	...	...
Manchester P'dilly a.	2018r	...	2113	2113	2213	...	2350	...	...	...	...	1216	...	1420	1511	...	1612	1826	*1921*	2014	*2120*	2207	...	...	...

B – From Birmingham.
C – To / from Carmarthen.
D – To Haverfordwest (and Milford Haven on Ⓐ).
M – To / from Milford Haven.
P – To / from Pembroke Dock.

Q – From Swansea via Llandrindod.
T – Terminates at Llandudno Junction on ⑥.

b – 0053 on ⑥⑦.
d – *0145* by 🚌 from Llandudno Junction on ⑦.
e – Via Wrexham. Change at Shrewsbury.

n – 6–7 minutes later on ⑥.
j – *2233* on ⑥.
q – 0114 on ⑥. 0119 on ⑦.
r – 3–5 minutes earlier on ⑥.
v – 10–11 minutes earlier on ⑥.
y – 0825 on ⑥.

z – 3–5 minutes later on ⑥.

‡ – Additional local services operate between these stations.

157 (MANCHESTER -) PRESTON - WINDERMERE and BARROW

TP, NT

km		Ⓐ	Ⓐ	Ⓐ 2	Ⓐ	Ⓐ	Ⓐ 🍷	Ⓐ 2C	Ⓐ	Ⓐ	Ⓐ 🍷	Ⓐ 🍷	Ⓐ 2C	Ⓐ 2	Ⓐ	Ⓐ 🍷	Ⓐ	Ⓐ	Ⓐ 2C	Ⓐ 🍷	Ⓐ 2S	Ⓐ 🍷	Ⓐ	Ⓐ 🍷	Ⓐ 2M	Ⓐ
	Manchester Airport .. d.		...	0340	...	...	0619	0722	0722	...	0827	0847	...	0927	0927	1027	1047	1127	1127	1227	...	1247	1327	1427	...	1527
	Manchester P'dilly ... d.		...	0355	0458	...	0644	0745	0745	...	0845	0911	...	0945	0945	1045	1111	1145	1145	1245	...	1311	1345	1445	...	1545
0	**Preston** d.		...	0524	0604	0720	0729	0828	0828	0918	0934	1004	1010	1029	1119	1129	1223	1229	1250	1329	1340	1409	1443	1529	1540	1629
34	**Lancaster** d.		0522	0545	0620	0735	0745	0854	0844	0933	0950	1023	1030	1111	1134	1145	1239	1245	1312	1346	1417	1426	1459	1552	1639	1645
64	Oxenholme d.		0553	|	0651	0756	|	|	0906	0953	|	1044	|	|	1155	|	1257	1354	|	|	|	1451	1551	|	|	1704
68	Kendal d.		0557	|	0655	0800	|	|	0910	0957	|	1048	|	|	1159	|	1301	1358	|	|	|	1455	1555	|	|	1708
81	**Windermere** a.		0612	|	0710	0815	|	|	0922	1012	|	1101	|	|	1214	|	1318	1413	|	|	|	1509	1610	|	|	1723
44	Carnforth d.		...	0610	...	...	0754	0903	...	...	0958	...	1040	1120	...	1154	...	...	1321	1355	1427	...	...	1601	1649	...
53	Arnside d.		...	0620	...	...	0804	0913	...	...	1007	...	1050	1130	...	1204	...	...	|	1403	1437	...	...	1611	1659	...
58	Grange over Sands d.		...	0626	...	...	0809	0919	...	...	1012	...	1056	1136	...	1209	...	...	1336	1409	1443	...	...	1616	1705	...
74	Ulverston d.		...	0642	...	...	0825	0935	...	...	1025	...	1112	1152	...	1225	...	...	1349	1421	1459	...	...	1633	1722	...
90	**Barrow in Furness** a.		...	0705	...	...	0849	0957	...	...	1047	...	1133	1216	...	1249	...	...	1407	1443	1521	...	...	1656	1744	...

	Ⓐ	Ⓐ 2L	Ⓐ 🍷	Ⓐ	Ⓐ 🍷	Ⓐ 2	Ⓐ	Ⓐ	Ⓐ	Ⓐ	Ⓐ 2	Ⓐ	Ⓐ	⑥ △	⑥	⑥	⑥	⑥	⑥ 2C	⑥	⑥	⑥ 🍷	⑥ 🍷	⑥ 2C	⑥	⑥ 🍷
Manchester Airport .. d.	...	1527	1627	1647	1732	...	...	1827	1927	...	1947	2127	...		...	...	...	0619	...	0722	...	0827	0847	0927	0927	1027
Manchester P'dilly ... d.	...	1545	1644	1711	1750	...	...	1845	1944	...	2011	2143	...		...	0510	...	0644	...	0745	...	0845	0911	0945	0948	1045
Preston d.	1643	1656	1729	1818	1838	1840	1918	2035	2027	2119	2129	2234	...		...	0604	0720	0729	...	0828	0923	0932	1006	1029	1125	1129
Lancaster d.	1659	1716	1745	1822	1854	1939	1934	2006	2051	2136	2149	2250	2257		0550	0619	0735	0745	0850	0844	0938	0948	1025	1101	1141	1145
Oxenholme d.	1748	|	|	1852	|	|	1959	2105	|	2153	|	|	|		0604	0700	0756	|	|	0905	0955	|	1050	|	1158	|
Kendal d.	1752	|	|	1856	|	|	2003	2109	|	2157	|	|	|		0608	0704	0800	|	|	0909	0959	|	1054	|	1202	|
Windermere a.	1804	|	|	1913	|	|	2018	2124	|	2212	|	|	|		0625	0719	0815	|	|	0921	1014	|	1111	|	1217	|
Carnforth d.	...	1726	1753	...	1903	1949	...	...	2100	...	2159	2258	2325		...	...	...	0754	0859	...	...	0957	...	1110	...	1154
Arnside d.	...	1736	1803	...	1914	1959	...	...	2110	...	2209	2309	2334		...	...	...	0804	0909	...	...	1005	...	1119	...	1204
Grange over Sands d.	...	1744	1809	...	1919	2005	...	...	2116	...	2215	2314	2340		...	...	...	0809	0915	...	...	1011	...	1125	...	1209
Ulverston d.	...	1800	1825	...	1936	2021	...	...	2132	...	2231	2330	2353		...	...	...	0825	0931	...	...	1023	...	1138	...	1226
Barrow in Furness a.	...	1823	1850	...	1959	2042	...	...	2156	...	2254	2354	0014		...	...	...	0849	0954	...	...	1045	...	1156	...	1249

	⑥	⑥	⑥ 🍷	⑥ 2C	⑥ 🍷	⑥	⑥ 🍷	⑥ 2C	⑥	⑥	⑥ 2LM	⑥ 🍷	⑥	⑥ 🍷	⑥	⑥	⑥	⑥	⑥ 2	⑦ ▲	⑦	⑦	⑦	⑦	⑦	⑦
Manchester Airport .. d.	1047	1127	1227	...	1247	1327	1427	...	1527	...	1527	1627	1647	1732	...	1827	1927	...	...		0947	1047	1127	1147	...	1327
Manchester P'dilly ... d.	1111	1145	1245	...	1311	1345	1445	...	1545	...	1545	1644	1711	1750	...	1845	1944	...	...		1003	1103	1142	1203	...	1342
Preston d.	1219	1229	1329	1338	1409	1525	1530	1540	1629	1640	1656	1729	1758	1838	1925	1938	2105	...	2135*		1100	1159	1307	1325	1340	1507
Lancaster d.	1235	1245	1345	1418	1425	1540	1550	1614	1645	1659	1717	1745	1821	1854	1940	1955	2119	2143	2245		1116	1215	1322	1341	1356	1522
Oxenholme d.	1259	1355	|	|	1443	1558	|	|	1704	1748	|	|	1840	|	2000	|	|	|	|		|	1231	1339	|	1439	1539
Kendal d.	1303	1359	|	|	1447	1602	|	|	1708	1752	|	|	1844	|	2004	|	|	|	|		|	1235	1343	|	1443	1543
Windermere a.	1320	1414	|	|	1501	1617	|	|	1723	1804	|	|	1902	|	2019	|	|	|	|		|	1252	1358	|	1455	1558
Carnforth d.	...	...	1354	1428	...	...	1558	1623	...	...	1726	1753	...	1903	...	2004	2128	2154	2254		1124	...	...	1349	...	...
Arnside d.	...	...	1402	1438	...	...	1608	1633	...	...	1737	1803	...	1914	...	2012	2139	2204	2304		1134	...	...	1359	...	...
Grange over Sands d.	...	...	1408	1444	...	...	1613	1639	...	...	1743	1809	...	1919	...	2018	2144	2210	2310		1140	...	...	1405	...	...
Ulverston d.	...	...	1420	1501	...	...	1630	1655	...	...	1759	1825	...	1936	...	2030	2201	2226	2326		1156	...	...	1421	...	...
Barrow in Furness a.	...	...	1442	1523	...	...	1653	1717	...	...	1821	1850	...	1959	...	2051	2224	2250	2350		1218	...	...	1444	...	...

	⑦	⑦	⑦	⑦	⑦	⑦	⑦	⑦	⑦	⑦	⑦ 2
Manchester Airport .. d.	1427	...	...	1527	1627	...	1727	1827	...	2027	...
Manchester P'dilly ... d.	1443	...	...	1542	1642	...	1742	1842	...	2042	...
Preston d.	1525	1606	...	1707	1725	1807	1907	1925	2014	2125	2211
Lancaster d.	1541	1621	1645	1722	1741	1822	1922	1941	2042	2141	2300
Oxenholme d.	|	1639	|	1739	|	1839	1939	|	2058	|	|
Kendal d.	|	1643	|	1743	|	1843	1943	|	2102	|	|
Windermere a.	|	1655	|	1758	|	1858	1958	|	2116	|	|
Carnforth d.	1549	...	1655	...	1749	...	...	1949	...	2149	2309
Arnside d.	1559	...	1707	...	1759	...	...	1959	...	2159	2319
Grange over Sands d.	1605	...	1713	...	1805	...	...	2005	...	2205	2325
Ulverston d.	1621	...	1729	...	1821	...	...	2021	...	2221	2341
Barrow in Furness a.	1644	...	1751	...	1844	...	...	2044	...	2244	0013

	Ⓐ	Ⓐ	Ⓐ 🍷	Ⓐ 🍷	Ⓐ	Ⓐ 🍷	Ⓐ 2L	Ⓐ	Ⓐ 2A	Ⓐ
Barrow in Furness d.		0420	0500	0615	...	0701	0717	...	0758	...
Ulverston d.		0435	0515	0634	...	0718	0736	...	0817	...
Grange over Sands d.		0448	0528	0650	...	0733	0752	...	0833	...
Arnside d.		0455	0534	0656	...	0739	0758	...	0839	...
Carnforth d.		0505	0543	0708	...	0751	0810	...	0851	...
Windermere d.		|	|	|	0620	|	|	0724	|	0820
Kendal d.		|	|	|	0634	|	|	0738	|	0834
Oxenholme a.		|	|	|	0640	|	|	0744	|	0840
Lancaster a.		0514	0553	0715	0722	0757	0819	0827	0859	0914
Preston a.		0551	0627	0735	0740	0817	0842	0846	0925	0933
Manchester Piccadilly a.		...	0715	0825	...	0920	0957	...	1020	1020
Manchester Airport a.		...	0740	0842	...	0940	1019	...	1040	1040

	Ⓐ	Ⓐ 🍷	Ⓐ	Ⓐ 2M	Ⓐ 🍷	Ⓐ	Ⓐ 🍷	Ⓐ 2C	Ⓐ	Ⓐ 2	Ⓐ 🍷	Ⓐ 🍷	Ⓐ	Ⓐ 2C	Ⓐ	Ⓐ 🍷	Ⓐ	Ⓐ	Ⓐ 2S	Ⓐ	Ⓐ	Ⓐ	Ⓐ	Ⓐ	Ⓐ 2	Ⓐ
Barrow in Furness d.	...	0915	...	0957	1118	...	...	1206	...	1256	...	1410	...	1528	...	1621	...	1706	1743	...	...	1910	...	...	2145	...
Ulverston d.	...	0934	...	1016	1134	...	...	1222	...	1314	...	1426	...	1547	...	1637	...	1724	1801	...	...	1929	...	...	2204	...
Grange over Sands d.	...	0950	...	1032	1148	...	...	1235	...	1330	...	1439	...	1603	...	1650	...	1739	1817	...	...	1945	...	...	2220	...
Arnside d.	...	0956	...	1038	1155	...	...	1241	...	1336	...	1445	...	1609	...	1656	...	1745	1823	...	...	1951	...	...	2226	...
Carnforth d.	...	1008	...	1050	1210	...	...	1253	...	1350	...	1455	...	1622	...	1706	...	1755	1834	...	...	2007	...	...	2238	...
Windermere d.	0928	|	1018	|	|	1130	1221	|	1324	|	1418	|	1521	|	1628	|	1727	|	|	1809	1918	|	2027	2128	|	2216
Kendal d.	0942	|	1029	|	|	1144	1232	|	1338	|	1429	|	1535	|	1642	|	1738	|	|	1823	1932	|	2041	2142	|	2230
Oxenholme a.	0948	|	1035	|	|	1150	1238	|	1344	|	1435	|	1541	|	1648	|	1744	|	|	1829	1938	|	2047	2148	|	2236
Lancaster a.	1008	1015	1052	1100	1217	1227	1258	1305	1405	1400	1454	1503	1602	1633	1708	1714	1809	1804	1844	1855	1959	2015	2107	2242	2249	2253
Preston a.	1027	1034	1112	1127	1236	1246	1317	1346	1424	1446	1534	1534	1622	1726	1726	1735	1828	1836	...	1914	2018	2035	2126	2302	2325	2325
Manchester P'dilly ... a.	...	1120	1220	...	1320	...	1420	1520	1520	...	1620	1620	1720	...	...	1820	1920	1920	...	2004	2114	2130	...	0016	0009v	0009v
Manchester Airport .. a.	...	1140	1240	...	1340	...	1440	1540	1540	...	1640	1640	1740	...	...	1842	1940	1940	...	2026	2137	2151	...	...	0045p	...

	⑥ △	⑥	⑥	⑥ 🍷	⑥	⑥ 🍷	⑥	⑥	⑥ 2A	⑥	⑥ 🍷	⑥	⑥ 2M	⑥ 🍷	⑥	⑥ 🍷	⑥	⑥ 2	⑥ 🍷	⑥ 🍷	⑥	⑥ 2C	⑥	⑥ 🍷	⑥	⑥
Barrow in Furness d.		0415	0515	0615	...	0705	...	...	0758	...	0915	...	0958	1116	...	...	...	1256	...	1410	...	1528	...	1621	...	1706
Ulverston d.		0430	0530	0634	...	0722	...	...	0817	...	0934	...	1016	1135	...	...	...	1315	...	1426	...	1547	...	1637	...	1724
Grange over Sands d.		0443	0543	0650	...	0737	...	...	0833	...	0950	...	1032	1150	...	...	...	1331	...	1439	...	1603	...	1650	...	1739
Arnside d.		0450	0549	0656	...	0743	...	...	0839	...	0956	...	1038	1156	...	...	...	1337	...	1445	...	1609	...	1656	...	1745
Carnforth d.		0502	0558	0708	...	0755	...	...	0851	...	1008	...	1050	1208	...	...	...	1349	...	1455	...	1620	...	1706	...	1755
Windermere d.		|	|	|	0635	|	0724	0828	|	0926	|	1018	|	|	1130	1223	1325	|	1418	|	1522	|	1622	|	1727	|
Kendal d.		|	|	|	0649	|	0738	0842	|	0940	|	1029	|	|	1144	1234	1339	|	1429	|	1536	|	1636	|	1738	|
Oxenholme a.		|	|	|	0655	|	0744	0848	|	0946	|	1035	|	|	1150	1240	1345	|	1435	|	1542	|	1642	|	1744	|
Lancaster a.		0511	0608	0715	0723	0802	0825	0908	0902	1009	1015	1052	1101	1215	1225	1302	1407	1359	1454	1503	1602	1632	1703	1714	1809	1805
Preston a.		0537	0627	0735	0741	0821	0844	0926	0935	1027	1034	1113	1132	1235	1244	1322	1426	1435	1534	1534	1622	1721	1721	1735	1829	1836
Manchester P'dilly ... a.		...	0715	0825	...	0920	...	1020	1020	...	1120	1220	1220	1320	...	1420	1520	1520	1620	1620	1720	...	...	1820	1920	1920
Manchester Airport .. a.		...	0740	0843	...	0940	...	1040	1040	...	1140	1240	1240	1340	...	1440	1540	1540	1640	1640	1740	...	...	1842	1940	1940

	⑥	⑥ 2C	⑥	⑥	⑥	⑥ 2		⑦ ▲	⑦		⑦	⑦	⑦	⑦	⑦	⑦	⑦	⑦	⑦	⑦	⑦	⑦	⑦	⑦ 2	⑦	⑦
Barrow in Furness d.	...	1814	...	1915	...	2130	...		0958	...	1200	...	1330	1400	...	...	...	1600	...	...	1800	...	...	1957	2050	...
Ulverston d.	...	1832	...	1933	...	2149	...		1017	...	1219	...	1348	1419	...	...	...	1619	...	...	1819	...	...	2015	2109	...
Grange over Sands d.	...	1848	...	1950	...	2205	...		1033	...	1235	...	1405	1435	...	...	...	1635	...	...	1835	...	...	2031	2125	...
Arnside d.	...	1854	...	1956	...	2211	...		1039	...	1241	...	1411	1441	...	...	...	1641	...	...	1841	...	...	2037	2131	...
Carnforth d.	...	1907	...	2008	...	2223	...		1050	...	1252	...	1423	1453	...	...	...	1653	...	...	1853	...	...	2050	2143	...
Windermere d.	1810	|	1928	|	2024	|	...		|	...	|	1259	|	|	1415	1459	1602	|	1659	1802	|	1902	2002	|	|	2120
Kendal d.	1824	|	1942	|	2038	|	...		|	...	|	1313	|	|	1429	1513	1613	|	1713	1813	|	1916	2013	|	|	2134
Oxenholme a.	1830	|	1948	|	2044	|	...		|	...	|	1319	|	|	1435	1519	1619	|	1719	1819	|	1922	2019	|	|	2140
Lancaster a.	1849	1917	2010	2016	2103	2235	...		1057	...	1259	1338	1434	1500	1507	1538	1640	1700	1738	1838	1900	1945	2038	2100	2151	2156
Preston a.	1909	1943	2029	2035	2145	...	...		1117	...	1319	1357	...	1520	1526	1557	1659	1720	1757	1857	1920	2003	...	2131	2220	2220
Manchester P'dilly ... a.	2004	2104	2127	2140	...	...	...		1215	...	1415	...	...	1601	...	1701	...	1801	1901	...	2001	2101	...	...	2301	2301
Manchester Airport .. a.	2026	2123	...	2216	...	...	...		1233	...	1435	...	...	1618	...	1718	...	1818	1918	...	2018	2118	...	...	2318	2318

A – From Maryport.
C – To / from Carlisle.
L – From / to Liverpool.
M – To / from Millom.
S – To / from Sellafield.
p – Change at Preston.
v – Manchester Victoria.
* – By 🚌.
▲ – Services on ⑦ are subject to alteration from Feb. 2.
△ – Services on ⑥ are subject to alteration from Mar. 29.

NT 2nd class BARROW - WHITEHAVEN - CARLISLE 158

km		⚒	⑥	Ⓐ	⑥	⑥	Ⓐ	Ⓐ	⑥	⚒	⚒	⚒	⑥	Ⓐ P	⑥	Ⓐ	⑥	Ⓐ	⑥	Ⓐ	⑥	Ⓐ	⑥	Ⓐ	Ⓐ	Ⓐ
	Lancaster **157** .... d.		...	...	...	...	...	...	...	...	...	0854r	...	1030	1101	...	...	...	...	1312	...	...	1418	1417	...	...
0	**Barrow in Furness** .. d.		...	...	...	0557	0556	0647	0734	...	0846	0958	1109	1135	1158	...	1258	1300	1355	1409	...	1453	1525	1530	...	1712
26	Millom .... d.		...	...	...	0625	0625	0716	0801	...	0916	1026	1136	1202	1225	...	1325	1330	1422	1433	...	1520	1553	1558	...	1739
47	Ravenglass ‡ .... d.		...	...	...	0643	0643	0734	0818	...	▬	1043	...	1219	1242	...	1341	...	1439	1448	...	1537	1610	1615	...	1756
56	Sellafield .... d.		...	...	...	0656	0658	0748	0830	...	⚒	1055	...	1231	1254	...	1351	...	1451	1456	...	1549	1622	1631	...	1808
74	**Whitehaven** .... d.		0554	0634	0637	0717	0722	0808	0852	0857	0947	1113	...	1249	1312	1403	1411	...	1509	1517	1604	1608	1642	...	1654	1829
85	Workington .... d.		0612	0651	0655	0735	0740	0826	...	0915	1005	1131	...	1307	1330	1421	1429	...	1527	1535	1622	1626	1700	...	1712	1847
92	Maryport .... d.		0620	0659	0703	0743	0748	0834	...	0923	1013	1139	...	1315	1338	1429	1437	...	1535	1543	1630	1634	1708	...	1720	1855
119	Wigton .... d.		0639	0719	0723	0802	0807	0854	...	0942	1032	1159	...	1335	1358	1448	1457	...	1555	1602	1649	1653	1728	...	1739	1914
138	**Carlisle** .... a.		0703	0743	0746	0825	0831	0917	...	1007	1058	1222	...	1357	1421	1512	1519	...	1618	1626	1712	1717	1751	...	1803	1938

	⑥	Ⓐ	⑥ L	⚒	⚒		⑦	⑦	⑦	⑦
Lancaster **157** .... d.	1614	1639	1717	...	...	...		...	...	...
Barrow in Furness ... d.	1719	1758	1824	1910	2119	...		...	...	...
Millom .... d.	1747	1829	1854	1940	2149	...		...	...	...
Ravenglass ‡ .... d.	1804	▬	▬	▬	...	...		...	...	...
Sellafield .... d.	1816	⑥	Ⓐ	⚒	...	...		...	...	...
Whitehaven .... d.	1836	1915	1919	1950	...	...		1250	1610	2015
Workington .... d.	1854	1933	1937	2008	...	...		1307	1627	2032
Maryport .... d.	1902	1941	1945	2016	...	...		1315	1635	2040
Wigton .... d.	1922	2000	2004	2035	...	...		1334	1654	2059
Carlisle .... a.	1946	2024	2028	2059	...	...		1357	1717	2122

	⚒	Ⓐ	⑥	⚒ Q	Ⓐ	⑥	Ⓐ	⑥	Ⓐ	⑥	⑥
Carlisle .... d.		...	...	...	...	0728	0746	0815	0835	0839	...
Wigton .... d.		...	...	...	...	0745	0803	0832	0852	0856	...
Maryport .... d.		...	...	0604	...	0805	0823	0852	0912	0916	...
Workington .... d.		...	...	0615	...	0817	0835	0904	0924	0928	...
Whitehaven .... d.		...	...	0635	0723	0838	0856	0925	0945	0947	...
Sellafield .... d.		...	...	0655	0741	▬	...	▬	...	1005	...
Ravenglass for Eskdale ... d.		...	...	0704	0750	⑥	...	⚒	...	1015	...
Millom .... d.		0608	0615	0723	0810	0810	...	0924	...	1034	1147
Barrow in Furness .... a.		0639	0647	0756	0842	0842	...	0956	...	1106	1219
Lancaster **157** .... a.		...	...	0859v	...	...	...	1101	...	...	...

	Ⓐ	⚒	⑥	Ⓐ	Ⓐ	⑥	⑥	Ⓐ	⑥	Ⓐ	Ⓐ	⑥ P	⚒	Ⓐ	⑥	⑥	Ⓐ	⚒	⚒	⑤	⑥	Ⓐ	⑦	⑦	⑦	⑦
Carlisle .... d.	0927	1014	1111	1144	1241	1241	1346	1418	1428	...	1540	1545	1633	1727	1734	1757	1804	1836	2009	2050	2145	2153		1447	1856	2142
Wigton .... d.	0944	1031	1128	1201	1258	1258	1403	1435	1445	...	1557	1602	1650	1744	1751	1814	1821	1853	2026	2107	2202	2210		1504	1913	2159
Maryport .... d.	1004	1051	1148	1221	1318	1318	1423	1455	1505	...	1620	1622	1710	1804	1811	1835	1841	1913	2046	2127	2222	2230		1524	1933	2219
Workington .... d.	1017	1103	1200	1233	1330	1330	1435	1507	1517	...	1629	1634	1722	1816	1823	1847	1853	1925	2058	2139	2234	2242		1536	1945	2231
Whitehaven .... d.	1036	1124	1219	1254	1349	1349	1456	1526	1536	...	1650	1653	1741	1836	1843	1909	1914	1946	2119	2200	2255	2302		1557	2006	2252
Sellafield .... d.	1054	1145	1238	▬	1411	1415	...	1554j	1556	1640	...	1711	1803	1854	1901	▬	...	...	▬	...	...	...		...	...	...
Ravenglass ‡ .... d.	1104	1154	1247	Ⓐ	1420	1424	...	1604	1606	1649	...	1721	1812	1903	1910	⚒	...	...	⚒	...	...	...		...	...	...
Millom .... d.	1124	1214	1307	1356	1440	1444	...	1624	1625	1709	...	1740	1832	1922	1929	1955	...	...	2155	...	...	...		...	...	...
Barrow in Furness ... a.	1156	1246	1339	1428	1516	1516	...	1657	1657	1741	...	1814	1904	1955	2002	2027	...	...	2227	...	...	...		...	...	...
Lancaster **157** .... a.	1305	...	...	...	1633	1632	...	...	...	1844	...	1917	...	...	...	...	...	...	...	...	...	...		...	...	...

L – From Liverpool.
P – From / to Preston.
Q – To Preston on Ⓐ.
j – Arrives 1544.
v – 0902 on ⑥.
r – 0850 on ⑥.
‡ – Ravenglass for Eskdale.

SR Sleeper trains LONDON - SCOTLAND 159

km		Ⓐ	Ⓐ	...	⑤	①–④	⑦	⑦	...	⑦
0	**London** Euston **150** .... d.		2115	...	2300	2345		2001	...	2330
28	Watford Junction **150** .... d.		2133	...	2319	0004		2025	...	2351
254	Crewe **150 152** .... d.		2345	...	|	|		2314	...	|
336	Preston **152** .... d.		0044	...	|	|		0033	...	|
481	Carlisle **152** .... a.		|	...	0429	0503		|	...	0458
625	Motherwell **152** .... a.		|	...	0611	0658		|	...	0658
646	**Glasgow** Central **152** .... ◧ a.		|	...	0630	0717		|	...	0717
646	**Edinburgh 152** .... ◧ a.		|	...	0640	0716		|	...	0716
	Perth **221** .... a.		0544	...	...	...		0544	...	...
	Dundee **224** .... a.		0610	...	...	...		0610	...	...
	Aberdeen **224** .... ◧ a.		0737	...	...	...		0737	...	...
	Inverness **221** .... a.		0830	...	...	...		0830	...	...
	Fort William **218** .... a.		0954	...	...	...		0954	...	...

	Ⓐ	①–④	⑤	⑤	①–④		⑦	⑦	⑦
Fort William **218** .... d.		...	...	1950	1950	...		...	1900
Inverness **221** .... d.		...	...	2040	2040	...		...	2025
Aberdeen **224** .... d.		...	...	2140	2140	...		...	2140
Dundee **224** .... d.		...	...	2306	2306	...		...	2304
Perth **221** .... d.		...	...	2318	2318	...		...	2259
Edinburgh 152 .... d.		2340	2340	|	|	...		2315	|
Glasgow Central **152** .... d.		2341	2341	|	|	...		2315	|
Motherwell **152** .... d.		2356	2356	|	|	...		2330	|
Carlisle **152** .... d.		0139	0139	|	|	...		0124	|
Preston **152** .... a.		|	|	0405	0429	...		|	0422
Crewe **150 152** .... a.		|	|	0502	0530	...		|	0529
Watford Junction **150** .... a.		0635	0650	|	|	...		0628	|
London Euston **150** .... ◧ a.		0700	0718	0804	0743	...		0654	0743

◧ – Sleeping-car passengers may occupy their cabins until 0800 following arrival at these stations.
☛ All trains in this table convey 🛏 1, 2 cl., (2) (reservation compulsory) and 🍷.

NT 2nd class PRESTON - LIVERPOOL 160

km		⚒	⚒		⚒ A	⚒		⚒		⚒	⚒	⚒	⚒		⚒		⑦ ▲	⑦		⑦		⑦
	Blackpool North **162 190** .... d.		0657	...	*0809*	0925		1625	...	*1710*	1825	1925	*1942*	...	2203	...		0817	and	2017	...	2217
0	**Preston 152 162 190** .... d.		0725	...	0850	0950	and	1650	...	1750	1850	1950	2027	...	2227	...		0842	every	2042	...	2242
24	Wigan North Western **152**....‡ a.		0744	...	0910	1010	hourly	1709	...	1811	1910	2011	2047	...	2247	...		0901	two	2101	...	2311
38	St Helens Central ....‡ a.		0801	...	0926	1026	until	1727	...	1827	1926	2027	2105	...	2305	...		0918	hours	2118	...	2328
57	**Liverpool** Lime St ....‡ a.		0827	...	0953	1052		1753	...	1855	1952	2052	2139	...	2338	...		0949	until	2149	...	2359

	⚒	⚒	Ⓐ	⚒		⚒	⚒ B	Ⓐ	⑥	⚒	⚒	⚒	⚒	⚒	⚒		⑦ ▲	⑦		⑦		⑦
Liverpool Lime St ....‡ d.		0730	0828	0857		1457	1557	1630	1630	1720	1745	1804	1904	2148	2305	...		0800	and	2000	...	2200
St Helens Central ....‡ d.		0748	0853	0917	and	1517	1617	1652	1655	1739	1811	1832	1932	2217	2334	...		0826	every	2026	...	2226
Wigan North Western **152**....‡ d.		0802	0913	0931	hourly	1531	1631	1710	1712	1754	1828	1851	1951	2238	2351	...		0842	two	2042	...	2242
Preston 152 162 190 .... a.		0824	0938	0954	until	1554	1654	1740	1740	1817	1854	1917	2017	2302	0015	...		0905	hours	2105	...	2315
Blackpool North **162 190** .... a.		0851	...	1021		1621	*1734*	*1822*	*1830*	1848	1923	*1957*v	*2056*	2328	...	...		0934	until	2134	...	2343

A – From Barrow on Ⓐ.
B – To Barrow (and Millom on ⑥).
v – *2001* on ⑥.
‡ – Additional services operate Wigan - Liverpool and v.v.
▲ – Services on ⑦ are subject to alteration from Feb. 3.

GC SUNDERLAND - YORK - LONDON 161

The start date for this new service had not been announced as we went to press

km		Ⓐ	Ⓐ ✗		Ⓐ ✗		Ⓐ ✗			⑥	⑥ 🍷		⑥ 🍷		⑥ 🍷			⑦	⑦ 🍷		⑦ 🍷		⑦ 🍷	
0	**Sunderland** .... **211** d.		0646	...	1230	...	1730	...	...		0653	...	1230	...	1730	...	...		0910	...	1342	...	1842	...
29	Hartlepool .... **211** d.		0710	...	1254	...	1756	...	...		0717	...	1254	...	1756	...	...		0934	...	1406	...	1906	...
53	Eaglescliffe .... d.		0729	...	1316	...	1815	...	...		0745	...	1313	...	1828	...	...		0955	...	1432	...	1925	...
76	Northallerton .... **186 187** d.		0746	...	1338	...	1836	...	...		0806	...	1331	...	1845	...	...		1013	...	1457	...	1948	...
89	Thirsk .... **187** d.		0757	...	1347	...	1845	...	...		0815	...	1342	...	1854	...	...		1026	...	1506	...	1957	...
124	**York** .... **186 187** a.		0818	...	1407	...	1904	...	...		0844	...	1403	...	1913	...	...		1045	...	1528	...	2013	...
124	**York** .... **185** d.		0822	...	1410	...	1906	...	...		0847	...	1405	...	1916	...	...		1047	...	1531	...	2015	...
428	**London** Kings Cross ...... **185** a.		1032	...	1605	...	2108	...	...		1045	...	1602	...	2118	...	...		1251	...	1731	...	2220	...

	Ⓐ	Ⓐ ✗		Ⓐ ✗		Ⓐ ✗			⑥	⑥ 🍷		⑥ 🍷		⑥ 🍷			⑦	⑦ 🍷		⑦ 🍷		⑦ 🍷		
London Kings Cross ..... **185** d.		0804	...	1127	...	1650	...	...		0757	...	1127	...	1650	...	...		0855	...	1345	...	1820	...	...
York .... **185** a.		1007	...	1319	...	1844	...	...		0957	...	1325	...	1850	...	...		1051	...	1551	...	2023	...	...
York .... **186 187** d.		1014	...	1322	...	1847	...	...		1000	...	1330	...	1852	...	...		1054	...	1553	...	2025	...	...
Thirsk .... **187** d.		1030	...	1338	...	1905	...	...		1021	...	1351	...	1921	...	...		1110	...	1610	...	2042	...	...
Northallerton .... **186 187** d.		1039	...	1347	...	1916	...	...		1032	...	1409	...	1930	...	...		1121	...	1620	...	2100	...	...
Eaglescliffe .... a.		1057	...	1404	...	1933	...	...		1048	...	1426	...	1949	...	...		1139	...	1639	...	2117	...	...
Hartlepool .... **211** a.		1120	...	1423	...	2000	...	...		1120	...	1445	...	2008	...	...		1206	...	1658	...	2136	...	...
Sunderland .... **211** a.		1150	...	1450	...	2035	...	...		1150	...	1511	...	2035	...	...		1252	...	1736	...	2206	...	...

162 MANCHESTER and LIVERPOOL local services — 2nd class

Manchester – Blackburn – Clitheroe

NT

km		⚒	⚒	⚒	⚒	⚒	⚒	⚒	⚒		⚒	⚒	⚒	⚒	⚒	⚒	⚒	⚒		⚒	⚒	⚒		⚒
0	**Manchester** Victoria ... d.		...	0626	0700	0723	0800	0823	0900	and	1500	1550	1623	1700	1729	1800	1821	1858	...	1958	2058	2158	...	2308
17	Bolton ... d.		...	0645	0719	0744	0819	0844	0919	hourly	1519	1609	1642	1719	1751	1819	1844	1918	...	2018	2118	2218	...	2328
39	Blackburn ... d.		0625	0719	0748	0823	0848	0921	0948		1548	1638	1715	1750	1824	1848	1920	1948	...	2048	2148	2249	...	2359
57	**Clitheroe** ... a.		0650	0744	0813	...	0913	...	1013	until	1613	1703	1740	1815	...	1913	...	2013	...	2113	2213	...	...	...

	⑦	⑦		⑦	⑦	⑦		⑦	⑦	
Manchester Victoria ... d.		0800	...	0900	1000	1100	and	2100	2200	...
Bolton ... d.		0813	...	0918	1018	1118	hourly	2118	2218	...
Blackburn ... d.		0843	...	0955z	1050	1145		2145	2247	...
Clitheroe ... a.		0908	...	1020	1115	1210	until	2210	...	...

	⚒	⚒	⚒	⚒	⚒	⚒	⚒	⚒	⚒
Clitheroe ... d.		...	...	0708	0735	0756	...	0826	...
Blackburn ... d.		0630	0700	0730	0800	0819	0830	0900	0930
Bolton ... d.		0658	0730	0800	0830	...	0901	0930	1001
Manchester Victoria ... a.		0725	0751	0821	0850	...	0925	0950	1022

	⚒		⚒	⚒	⚒	⚒	⚒	⚒	⚒	⚒	⚒	⚒		⚒	
Clitheroe ... d.	0936	and	1436	1526	1636	1712	1808	1836	...	1936	2036	2136	...	2246	...
Blackburn ... d.	1000	hourly	1500	1550	1658	1734	1831	1900	1930	2000	2100	2200	...	2310	...
Bolton ... d.	1030		1530	1620	1730	1803	1902	1930	2000	2030	2130	2233	...	2340	...
Manchester Victoria ... a.	1050	until	1550	1642	1751	1823	1923	1950	2022	2050	2150	2256p	...	0001	...

	⑦	⑦	⑦		⑦	⑦		⑦
Clitheroe ... d.		...	0917	...	1027	1124	and	2224
Blackburn ... d.		0848	0948z	...	1048	1148	hourly	2248
Bolton ... d.		0916	1016	...	1116	1216		2316
Manchester Victoria ... a.		0935	1035	...	1135	1235	until	2335

p – Manchester Piccadilly. z – Arrives 9–10 minutes earlier.

Manchester – Buxton

Journey time: ± 56 minutes *41 km* NT

From Manchester Piccadilly:
Trains call at Stockport ± 11 minutes and at New Mills Newtown ± 31 minutes later.
Ⓐ: 0651, 0737, 0829, 0859, 0937, 1037, 1137, 1237, 1337, 1437, 1506, 1540, 1637, 1707, 1737, 1806, 1838, 1936, 2036, 2149, 2258.
⑥: 0650, 0735, 0830, 0937, 1037 and hourly until 1937; then 2036, 2149, 2257.
⑦: 0853, 0956, 1103, 1156, 1256, 1356, 1456, 1554, 1653 and hourly until 2153; then 2251.

From Buxton:
Trains call at New Mills Newtown ± 21 minutes and at Stockport ± 46 minutes later.
Ⓐ: 0554, 0634, 0704, 0740, 0757, 0836, 0936, 1037, 1134, 1237, 1334, 1437, 1547, 1636, 1706, 1734, 1822, 1855, 1955, 2138, 2255.
⑥: 0554, 0634, 0733, 0757, 0837, 0936, 1037, 1134, 1237, 1334, 1437, 1534, 1636, 1734, 1822, 1855, 1955, 2138, 2255.
⑦: 0825, 0925, 1025, 1120, 1220, 1325, 1425 and hourly until 2225.

Manchester – Northwich – Chester

Journey time: ± 87 minutes *73 km* NT

From Manchester Piccadilly:
Trains call at Stockport ± 9 mins, Altrincham ± 26 mins, and Northwich ± 53 mins later.
Ⓐ: 0635, 0739, 0924, 1024 and hourly until 2224 (***also*** 1651, 1753); then 2309.
⑥: 0635, 0739, 0917, 1017 and hourly until 1917; then 2024, 2124, 2224, 2309.
⑦ ★ From **Altrincham** to Chester: 1010, 1337, 1630, 1840, 2130.

From Chester:
Trains call at Northwich 28 mins, at Altrincham ± 55 mins, and at Stockport ± 73 mins later.
Ⓐ: 0557, 0654, 0730, 0805, 1005, 1105, 1205, 1305, 1405, 1505, 1549, 1600, 1705, 1756, 1856, 1956, 2059, 2245.
⑥: 0555, 0653, 0804, 1005, 1105, 1205, 1305, 1405, 1505, 1600, 1705, 1756, 1858, 1956, 2059, 2245.
⑦ ★ From Chester to **Altrincham**: 0848, 1200, 1520, 1731, 2010.

★ – No trains Manchester - Altrincham and v.v. on ⑦. There is a frequent Metrolink tram service (journey time ± 30 minutes) between Manchester Piccadilly and Altrincham.

Manchester – St Helens – Liverpool

Journey time: ± 63 minutes *51 km* NT

From Manchester Victoria:
Trains call at St Helens Junction ± 29 minutes later.
⚒: 0545, 0607, 0710, 0731, 0801, 0840, 0901, 1001 and hourly until 1801; then 1831, 1901, 2001, 2101, 2201, 2311.
⑦**P**: 0916, 1016 and hourly until 2216.

From Liverpool Lime Street:
Trains call at St Helens Junction ± 28 minutes later.
⚒: 0547, 0639, 0718, 0747, 0848, 0948 and hourly until 1548; then 1618, 1648, 1712, 1735, 1748, 1848, 1918, 2018, 2118, 2218, 2318.
⑦**Q**: 0830, 0930 and hourly until 2230.

P – From Manchester Piccadilly.
Q – To Manchester Piccadilly.

☛ Manchester - Warrington - Liverpool and v.v.: see Tables **189**, **196**.
St Helens Central - Liverpool and v.v.: see Table **158**.

Manchester – Wigan – Southport

Journey time: ± 71 minutes *62 km* NT

From Manchester Piccadilly:
Trains call at Bolton 20 minutes and at Wigan Wallgate ± 39 minutes later.
⚒: 0651 **v**, 0828, 0923, 1023, 1123, 1223, 1323, 1423, 1523, 1623, 1826, 1933, 2032, 2135, 2235.
⑦: 0849 **v**, 0945, 1045, 1146, 1245, 1349, 1449, 1546, 1646, 1746, 1845, 1945, 2046.

From Southport:
Trains call at Wigan Wallgate ± 30 minutes and at Bolton ± 48 minutes later.
⚒: 0635, 0835, 0938, 1038, 1138, 1238, 1338, 1438, 1551, 1643, 1742, 1828, 1934, 2034, 2134 **v**, 2229.
⑦: 0913, 1013 and hourly until 2213.

v – Manchester Victoria.

☛ Additional trains (not calling at Bolton) run Manchester Victoria - Southport and v.v. on ⚒.

Liverpool – Birkenhead – Chester

Journey time: 43 minutes *29 km* ME

From Liverpool Lime Street:
Trains call at Birkenhead Central 9 minutes later.
⚒: 0558, 0628 and every 30 minutes until 2328 (also 1643 Ⓐ, 1713 Ⓐ, 1743 Ⓐ).
⑦: 0758, 0828 and every 30 minutes until 2328.

From Chester:
Trains call at Birkenhead Central 34 minutes later.
⚒: 0615, 0645 and every 30 minutes until 2315 (also 0730 Ⓐ, 0800 Ⓐ).
⑦: 0745, 0815, and every 30 minutes until 2315.

Liverpool – Southport

Journey time: 44 minutes *30 km* ME

From Liverpool Central:
⚒: 0608, 0623 and every 15 minutes until 2308, then 2338 (also 1713 Ⓐ).
⑦: 0808, 0823, 0853 and every 30 minutes until 2323, then 2338.

From Southport:
⚒: 0543, 0558 and every 15 minutes until 2258, then 2316 (also 0748 Ⓐ, 0803 Ⓐ).
⑦: 0758, 0828 and every 30 minutes until 2258, then 2316.

163 MANCHESTER - BLACKPOOL — 2nd class NT

Services on ⑥⑦ are subject to alteration from February 2

km		⚒	Ⓐ	⑥		⚒		⚒		⚒	❖	⚒	
0	Manchester Airport ✈ d.		0106	0106	...	0340	...	0547	...	0647	and	2247	...
16	**Manchester** Piccadilly d.		0125	0125	...	0355	...	0605	...	0711		2311	...
34	Bolton ... d.		0139s	0139s	...	0409s	...	0626	...	0732	hourly	2332	...
66	Preston ... 190 a.		0210s	0218s	...	0441s	...	0659	...	0806		0006	...
94	**Blackpool** North.. 190 a.		0234	0246	...	0507	...	0731	...	0836	until	0038	...

km		⑦	⑦ 🚌		⑦ 🚌		⑦ 🚌		⑦		⑦		⑦
0	Manchester Airport ✈ d.		0110	...	0310	...	0545	...	0736	...	0847	and	2247
16	**Manchester** Piccadilly d.		0130	...	0330	...	0605	...	0751	...	0903		2303
34	Bolton ... d.		0155s	...	0355s	...	0630s	...	0810	...	0922	hourly	2322
66	Preston ... 190 a.		0230s	...	0430s	...	0710s	...	0835	...	0947		2346
94	**Blackpool** North.. 190 a.		0310	...	0510	...	0805	...	0916	...	1016	until	0016

	⚒	Ⓐ	⑥	⑥	Ⓐ	⚒	⚒	⚒	⚒	❖	⚒	⚒	⚒	⚒
Blackpool North.. 190 d.		0143	0143	0350	0353	0519	0634	0741	0841	and	1942	2053	2152	2313
Preston ... 190 d.		0208u	0208u	0416u	0418u	0548	0703	0812	0908		2011	2123	2221	2342
Bolton ... a.		0237u	0243u	0443u	0448u	0629	0733	0833	0934	hourly	2032	2156r	2253	0012
Manchester Piccadilly a.		0253	0258	0501u	0505u	0656	0754	0853	0957		2058	2218	2330	0029
Manchester Airport ✈ a.		0309	0313	0521	0522	0715	0820	0913	1019	until	2119	2239	2358r	0045

	⑦	⑦ 🚌		⑦ 🚌		⑦ 🚌		⑦		⑦	⑦
Blackpool North.. 190 d.		0100	...	0320	...	0520	...	0802	and	2202	2302
Preston ... 190 d.		0140u	...	0400u	...	0600u	...	0830		2230	2330
Bolton ... a.		0215u	...	0435u	...	0635u	...	0851	hourly	2251	0001
Manchester Piccadilly a.		0240u	...	0500u	...	0700u	...	0915		2315	0017
Manchester Airport ✈ a.		0300	...	0520	...	0720	...	0933	until	2333	0033

r – 3 minutes earlier on ⑥. s – Stops to set down only. u – Stops to pick up only. ❖ – Timings may vary by up a few minutes on some journeys.

AW 2nd class HOLYHEAD and LLANDUDNO - CREWE and MANCHESTER 165

Services on ⑥ are subject to alteration from March 29. Services on ⑦ are subject to alteration from February 3.

km		⚒ ◇ B		Ⓐ	⑥	⚒ C	⑥	Ⓐ	Ⓐ ✕ ◇	⑥ 🍷 ◇	⚒ 🍷	⚒ 🍷 C	⑥ 🍷 ◇	Ⓐ 🍷 ◇	⚒ 🍷	⚒	⚒ 🍷	⚒ C	⚒ 🍷	⚒ 🍷	Ⓐ 🍷 ◇	⑥ 🍷 ◇	Ⓐ 🍷	⑥ 🍷
	Dublin ⛴ 2040 d.	2055n	...	...	...	...	...	...	...	...	...	...	...	...	...	...	...	...	...	...	...	...	...	...
0	Holyhead d.	0215	...	...	...	0427	...	...	0532	0535	0600	0615	0645	0645	...	0715	...	0810f	...	0928	0950	0950	...	...
40	Bangor d.	0242	...	...	...	0500	...	...	0601	0604	0628	0659	0712	0712	...	0801	...	0904	...	1007	1018	1018	...	...
	Llandudno d.	|	...	...	...	|	...	...	|	|	0639	0703	|	|	0747	|	0847	|	0947	1014	|	|	1044	1047
64	Llandudno Junction d.	0300	...	0455	0500	0518	0545	0545	0621	0624	0653	0717	0730	0731	0756	0827	0856	0927	0956	1030	1036	1036	1053	1056
69	Llandudno a.	|	...	|	|	|	|	|	0635	0701	|	0743	0816	0816	|	0937	|	1001	|	|	1135	1135	|	|
71	Colwyn Bay d.	|	...	0501	0506	0524	0551	0551	0629	0632	0659	0723	0737	0737	0802	0833	0902	0933	1002	|	1042	1042	1059	1102
81	Abergele & Pensarn d.	|	...	0508	0513	|	0559	0559	|	|	0706	0730	|	|	0809	|	0909	|	1009	|	|	|	1106	1109
88	Rhyl d.	|	...	0514	0519	0535	0606	0606	0642	0645	0712	0736	0748	0748	0815	0843	0915	0943	1015	|	1053	1053	1112	1115
94	Prestatyn d.	|	...	0519	0524	0540	0612	0612	|	|	0717	0742	0753	0754	0821	0849	0921	0949	1021	|	1059	1059	1118	1121
116	Flint d.	|	...	0533	0538	0554	0627	0627	|	|	0731	0755	0806	0807	0834	0902	0934	1002	1034	|	1112	1112	1131	1134
136	Chester a.	0338	...	0550	0555	0608	0645	0645	0712	0715	0749	0812	0820	0821	0851	0917	0951	1016	1051	1109	1126	1126	1148	1151
170	Crewe a.	0359	...	0614	0623	0655	0720	0724	0738	0741	0824	...	0845	0845	0924	0943	1024	1050	1124	1143	1147	1150	1227	1224
	London Euston 150 a.	...	...	|	|	...	|	|	0936	|	|	...	|	1046	|	|	|	...	|	|	1340	|	|	|
165	Warrington Bank Quay a.	...	...	0644	|	...	0715r	0715r	0752r	0752r	0820	...	0911	0912e	0919	1012	1019	...	1119	1213	|	|	1217	1219
201	Manchester Piccadilly a.	...	...	0713	0740	...	0754r	0754r	0840r	0840r	0902	...	0955	0954e	0958	1055	1058	...	1158	...	1254e	1255	1258	1258

	⚒ C	⚒ 🍷	⚒ 🍷	⚒ 🍷	⚒ 🍷 C	⚒ 🍷	Ⓐ 🍷	⚒ 🍷	⚒ 🍷	⑥ 🍷 ◇	Ⓐ 🍷 ◇	⑥ 🍷 ◇	Ⓐ 🍷 ◇	⚒ C	⚒ 🍷	⚒ 🍷	⚒ 🍷	⚒ 🍷 C	⚒ 🍷	Ⓐ 🍷	⑥ 🍷	⚒	⚒ 🍷 B	⚒	⚒ 🍷
Dublin ⛴ 2040 d.	...	...	0845	...	...	...	...	...	...	...	...	...	...	...	...	...	...	...	...	1430	1430	...	...	...	...
Holyhead d.	1030	...	1140	...	1235	...	1320	1335	...	1413	1414	...	...	1435	...	1539	...	1635	...	1727	1735	...	1835	...	1935
Bangor d.	1103	...	1219	...	1304	...	1349	1414	...	1441	1443	...	...	1504	...	1617	...	1704	...	1806	1814	...	1914	...	2014
Llandudno d.	|	1147	|	1247	1314	1347	|	|	1435	|	|	1508	1508	|	1547	1614	1647	|	1747	|	|	1847	|	1947	|
Llandudno Junction d.	1126	1156	1242	1256	1327	1356	1407	1437	1444	1459	1503	1516	1517	1527	1556	1640	1656	1727	1756	1829	1837	1856	1932	1956	2037
Llandudno a.	1235	|	1301	|	1427	|	1427	|	|	1536	1536	|	|	1601	|	1735	|	1835	|	1937	1937	|	2035	|	2108
Colwyn Bay d.	1132	1202	1248	1302	1333	1402	1413	1443	1450	|	|	1523	1523	1533	1602	1646	1702	1733	1802	1835	1843	1902	1938	2002	2043
Abergele & Pensarn d.	|	1209	|	1309	|	1409	|	|	1457	|	|	|	|	|	1609	|	1709	|	1809	|	|	1909	|	2009	|
Rhyl d.	1143	1215	1258	1315	1344	1415	1423	1453	1503	|	|	1534	1534	1543	1615	1656	1715	1743	1815	1845	1853	1915	1948	2015	2053
Prestatyn d.	1148	1221	1304	1321	1349	1421	1429	1459	1509	|	|	1539	1540	1549	1621	1702	1721	1749	1821	1851	1859	1921	1954	2021	2059
Flint d.	1202	1234	1317	1334	1403	1434	|	1512	1522	|	|	1552	1553	1602	1634	1715	1734	1802	1834	1904	1912	1934	2007	2034	2112
Chester a.	1216	1251	1332	1351	1417	1451	1457	1527	1539	1545	1545	1607	1606	1616	1651	1729	1751	1816	1851	1920	1930	1951	2022	2051	2126
Crewe a.	1250	1324	1400	1424	1455	1530z	1528	1555	|	1608	1611	1638	1638	1659	1726	1756	1825	1856	1924	1944	1959	2029	2055	2124	2157
London Euston 150 a.	...	|	|	...	|	|	|	...	|	|	1821	|	1842	...	|	...	|	...	|	|	...	|	|	|	...
Warrington Bank Quay a.	...	1319	...	1420	...	1519	1531	...	1619	1619r	1619r	1712	1711e	...	1719	...	1821	...	1919	2016	...	2018	...	2123	...
Manchester Piccadilly a.	...	1358	...	1458	...	1558	1621	...	1658	1658r	1658r	1754	1754e	...	1759	...	1901	...	1959	2054	...	2100	...	2201	...

	⚒	⚒ H		⑦	⑦ 🍷 C		⑦		⑦ 🍷		⑦ 🍷 ◇	⑦ 🍷		⑦ 🍷	⑦ 🍷 ◇	⑦		⑦	⑦ 🍷 C		⑦ 🍷 B	⑦		⑦
Dublin ⛴ 2040 d.	...	...	...	...	...	...	...	...	...	...	0845	...	...	...	...	...	...	...	1430	...	...	...	...	...
Holyhead d.	...	2035	...	0956	1035	...	...	...	...	...	1314	1331	...	...	1557	...	...	1648	1725	...	1840	...	...	2035
Bangor d.	...	2103	...	1034	1104	...	1156	...	1252	...	1341	1358	...	1542	1624	1632	...	1727	1753	...	1909	1955	...	2115
Llandudno d.	2047	2113	...	1015*	|	...	|	...	|	...	1315*	|	...	|	1615*	|	...	|	|	...	|	|	...	|
Llandudno Junction d.	2056	2126	...	1057	1122	...	1214	...	1315	...	1359	1416	...	1600	1642	1654	...	1746	1811	...	1927	2018	...	2133
Llandudno a.	|	2143	...	|	|	...	1330*	...	|	...	|	|	...	1630*	|	|	...	|	|	...	|	|	...	|
Colwyn Bay d.	2102	2132	...	1103	1128	...	1220	...	1321	...	1406	1422	...	1606	1649	1700	...	1752	1817	...	1933	2024	...	2139
Abergele & Pensarn d.	2109	2139	...	|	|	...	|	...	1328	...	|	|	...	|	|	1707	...	1759	|	...	|	2031	...	2146
Rhyl d.	2115	2145	...	1114	1139	...	1230	...	1334	...	1417	1433	...	1616	1700	1713	...	1805	1828	...	1943	2037	...	2152
Prestatyn d.	2121	2150	...	1119	1145	...	1236	...	1339	...	|	1438	...	1622	|	1719	...	1810	1834	...	1949	2042	...	2158
Flint d.	2134	2204	...	1133	1159	...	1249	...	1353	...	|	1452	...	1635	|	1732	...	1824	1848	...	2002	2056	...	2211
Chester a.	2151	2223	...	1147	1217	...	1306	...	1410	...	1444	1505	...	1649	1727	1746	...	1841	1903	...	2016	2113	...	2228
Crewe a.	2238	2307q	...	1211	1249	...	1331	...	1437	...	1506	1549	...	1724	1757	1816	...	1905	1949	...	2049	2140	...	|
London Euston 150 a.	|	|	...	|	...	...	|	...	|	...	|	|	...	|	...	|	...	|	...	...	|	|	...	|
Warrington Bank Quay a.	2221	2350	...	1222r	...	...	1357r	...	1511	...	...	1528	...	1717	...	1807	...	1941	...	...	2048	2148r	...	2301
Manchester Piccadilly a.	2305	0013	...	1301r	...	...	1441r	...	...	...	...	1610	...	1759	...	1851	...	2014	...	...	2134	2227r	...	2341

	②–⑥ 🍷 B	① B		⚒ B ◇	⚒ 🍷	⚒ 🍷	⚒ 🍷	⚒ 🍷 C	⚒ 🍷	⚒ 🍷		⚒ 🍷	⚒ C	Ⓐ 🍷	⑥ 🍷 ◇	Ⓐ ✕ ◇	⚒ 🍷	⚒ 🍷	⚒ 🍷	⚒ C	⚒ 🍷	⚒ 🍷 ◇	⚒ 🍷	⚒ 🍷
Manchester Piccadilly d.	2320y	2317y	...	0520p	0600	...	0716	...	0816	...	...	0916	...	1003	1003r	...	1016	...	1116	...	1216	...	...	1316
Warrington Bank Quay d.	2352y	2349y	...	|	0633	...	0748	...	0849	...	...	0950	...	1040	1040r	...	1050	...	1150	...	1250	...	...	1350
London Euston 150 d.	|	|	...	|	|	...	|	...	|	...	...	|	...	|	|	0900	|	...	|	...	|	1128a	...	|
Crewe d.	0002	0030	...	0618	0635a	0703	0733	0803	0833	0903	...	0933	1003	1033	1044	1050	|	1103	1133	1203	1233	1312	1319j	1333
Chester d.	0040	0054	...	0645	0705	0732	0824	0835	0924j	0935	...	1024	1035	1107	1118	1119	1124	1135	1224	1235	1322	1333	1343	1425
Flint d.	0053	0107	...	0657	0720	0745	0841	0851	0939	0949	...	1039	1049	1120	|	|	1139	1150	1239	1249	|	1346	1358	1440
Prestatyn d.	|	|	...	0710	0733	0758	0854	0904	0952	1002	...	1052	1102	1133	|	|	1152	1204	1252	1302	1347	1359	1412	1453
Rhyl d.	0109	0123	...	0717	0739	0804	0900	0910	0958	1008	...	1058	1108	1139	1146	1148	1158	1210	1258	1308	1353	1405	1418	1459
Abergele & Pensarn d.	|	|	...	|	0745	|	0906	|	1004	|	...	1104	|	|	|	|	1204	|	1304	|	|	|	1424	1505
Colwyn Bay d.	0120	0134	...	0728	0753	0815	0914	0921	1012	1019	...	1112	1119	1150	1157	1201	1212	1220	1312	1319	1404	1416	1432	1513
Llandudno d.	|	|	...	0703	|	0747	|	0847	|	0947	...	|	1044v	|	1147	1147	|	|	|	1247	|	|	1347	|
Llandudno Junction d.	0126	0140	...	0734	0800	0822	0921	0927	1019	1025	...	1119	1125	1156	1203	1209	1219	1227	1319	1325	1411	1423	1438	1520
Llandudno a.	|	|	...	|	0816	|	0937	1001	1037	|	...	1135	|	|	|	|	1235	1301	1335	|	1427	1444q	|	1536
Bangor d.	0142	0156	...	0751	...	0843	...	0943	...	1047	...	...	1141	1212	1220	1228	...	1248	...	...	1348	...	1454	...
Holyhead a.	0215	0227	...	0821	...	0930	...	1020	...	1130	...	...	1220	1247	1253	1303	...	1330	...	...	1430	...	1530	...
Dublin ⛴ 2040 a.	0555	...	...	...	...	...	...	...	...	1358	...	...	...	...	...	...	...	1725	...	...	...	...	...	...

	⚒ 🍷 C		⚒ 🍷	⚒ 🍷		⚒ 🍷	⚒ 🍷 C		⚒ 🍷	⚒	⑥ 🍷 ◇	Ⓐ 🍷 ◇	⚒	⚒ 🍷 C	⚒ 🍷	⚒	⑥ 🍷 ◇	Ⓐ ✕ ◇	⚒ 🍷 C		⑥	Ⓐ 🍷 ◇	⑥ C	Ⓐ 🍷 C	⑥ 🚌
Manchester Piccadilly d.	...	...	1416	...	...	1516	...	...	1616	...	1634	1634e	1720	...	1741	1816	1834	...	1916	...	2016r	2034e	2116	2116	...
Warrington Bank Quay d.	...	...	1450	...	...	1550	...	...	1648	...	1652	1653e	1756	...	1818	1849	1853	1853e	1948	...	2048r	2048r	2149	2149	...
London Euston 150 d.	...	...	|	...	...	|	...	...	|	...	|	1549	|	...	|	|	|	1721	|	...	|	1938	|	|	...
Crewe d.	1403	...	1433	1503	...	1533	1603	...	1633	1703	1736	1735	|	1803	|	1833	1928	1922	2003	...	2103	2129	2206	2217	...
Chester d.	1435	...	1524	1535	...	1624	1635	...	1724	1735	1800	1800	1824	1835	1850	1924	1948	1951	2035	...	2135	2150	2235	2245	...
Flint d.	1450	...	1539	1549	...	1639	1649	...	1739	1750	1813	1813	1839	1851	1903	1939	|	|	2050	...	2150	2203	2251	2300	...
Prestatyn d.	1503	...	1552	1602	...	1652	1703	...	1752	1803	1826	1826	1852	1904	1916	1952	2014	2018	2103	...	2203	2216	2305	2313	...
Rhyl d.	1509	...	1558	1608	...	1658	1709	...	1758	1809	1833	1833	1858	1910	1922	1958	2020	2025	2109	...	2209	2223	2311	2319	...
Abergele & Pensarn d.	|	...	1604	|	...	1704	|	...	1804	|	|	|	1904	|	|	2004	|	|	2115	...	|	|	2317	2325	...
Colwyn Bay d.	1520	...	1612	1619	...	1712	1719	...	1812	1820	1844	1844	1912	1921	1933	2012	2032	2038	2123	...	2220	2234	2325	2333	...
Llandudno d.	1508	...	|	1547	...	|	1647	...	|	1747	|	|	|	1847	|	|	1947	1947	2113	...	2147	2147	|	|	...
Llandudno Junction d.	1526	...	1619	1625	...	1719	1726	...	1819	1826	1850	1850	1919	1927	1940	2019	2038	2046	2130	...	2226	2240	2333	2340	2343
Llandudno a.	1601	...	1635	|	...	1735	|	...	1835	|	|	|	1937	|	|	2035	2108	2108	2143	...	|	|	|	|	|
Bangor d.	1548	...	...	1647	...	...	1748	...	...	1848	1907	1907	...	1949	2000	...	2057	2105	2152	...	2242	2257	...	0002	0025
Holyhead a.	1630	...	...	1720	...	...	1830	...	...	1920	1936	1941	...	2030	2046	...	2133	2140	2235	...	2330	2330	...	0047	0145
Dublin ⛴ 2040 a.	1924	...	...	...	...	...	...	...	...	...	...	...	...	...	...	...	...	...	...	...	...	...	...	...	0555

B – To / from Birmingham.
C – To / from Cardiff.
H – To Shrewsbury (and Wolverhampton on Ⓐ).

a – Ⓐ only.
e – Change at Crewe.
f – 0825 on ⑥.
j – 3–4 minutes earlier on ⑥.

n – Previous day.
p – 0505 on ⑥.
q – 11 minutes earlier on ⑥.
r – Change at Chester.

v – 1047 on ⑥.
y – Previous day. Change at Chester.
z – ⑥ only.

◇ – Conveys 🛏.
* – By 🚌.

165 MANCHESTER and CREWE - LLANDUDNO and HOLYHEAD — 2nd class AW

Services on ⑦ are subject to alteration from February 3

⑦		⑦	⑦	⑦	⑦	⑦	⑦	⑦	⑦	⑦	⑦	⑦	⑦	⑦	⑦
	🍷		🍷		🍷	🍷 C	🍷	🍷	🍷	🍷	🍷 ◇		🍷 B◇	🍷 C	
Manchester Piccadilly d.	*0900*	...	*0958*r	1134j	*1315*r	...	*1457*r	*1629*r	*1637*	1732	*1837*	*1906*	*2014*r	...	*2114*r
Warrington Bank Quay d.	|	...	*1030*r	1203	*1348*r	...	*1529*r	*1701*r	|	1805	*1904*r	*1958*	*2048*r	...	*2147*r
London Euston **150** d.	|	...	|	|	|	...	|	|	|	|	|	|	|	...	|
Crewe d.	1005	...	1115	*1155*	1355	*1425*	1555	1705	1740	*1755*	1934	2035	2107	...	2220
Chester d.	1032	...	1138	1232	1420	1503	1621	1736	1803	1836	1955	2058	2135	2150	2243
Flint d.	1047	...	1153	1247	1435	1518	1634	1751	1816	1851	|	2113	|	2205	2258
Prestatyn d.	1100	...	1206	1300	1448	1532	1647	1804	1829	1904	2018	2126	|	2220	2311
Rhyl d.	1106	...	1212	1306	1454	1538	1653	1810	1835	1910	2024	2132	2204	2228	2317
Abergele & Pensarn d.	1112	...	1218	1312	|	1545	|	1816	1841	1916	|	2138	|	2235	|
Colwyn Bay d.	1120	...	1226	1320	1505	1553	1704	1824	1849	1924	2035	2146	2217	2243	2328
Llandudno d.	*1015**	...	|	|	|	|	*1615**	|	|	|	|	|	|	|	|
Llandudno Junction d.	1127	1145	1233	1327	1511	1600	1711	1831	1859	1931	2042	2153	2225	2250	2334
Llandudno a.	|	|	*1330**	|	|	*1630**	|	|	*1930**	|	|	|	|	|	|
Bangor d.	1146	1213	1249	1351	1534	1623	1727	1851	1915	1952	2058	2214	2244	2312	2350
Holyhead a.	...	...	1322	...	...	1658	1802	...	2000	2025	2126	2250	2314	2351	0026
Dublin ⛴ **2040** a.	...	...	*1725*	...	...	...	...	...	...	...	...	...	...	...	*0555*

B – From Birmingham. C – From Cardiff. j – Manchester Oxford Rd. r – Change at Chester. * – By 🚌. ◇ – Conveys 🚃(12).

166 LLANDUDNO - BLAENAU FFESTINIOG - PORTHMADOG — 2nd class AW

km		⚒	⚒	⚒	b F	⚒	a F	⚒	⚒	⑦ 🚌	⑦ 🚌	c F	⑦ 🚌
0	**Llandudno** d.	...	*0703*	1014	...	1314	...	1614	*1847*	1015	1315	...	1615
5	Llandudno Junction d.	0535	0739	1033	...	1333	...	1633	1900	1040	1340	...	1640
18	Llanrwst d.	0553	0801	1054	...	1354	...	1654	1921	1101	1401	...	1701
24	Betws y Coed d.	0559	0807	1100	...	1400	...	1700	1927	1110	1410	...	1710
44	**Blaenau Ffestiniog** d.	0627	0837	1130	1145	1430	1510	1730	1957	1145	1445	1510	1745
63	Minffordd **149** a.	...	...	...	1240	...	1605	...	...	...	...	1605	...
66	**Porthmadog** Harbour a.	...	...	...	1300	...	1620	...	...	...	...	1620	...

	⚒	⚒	a F	⚒	b F	⚒	⚒	⚒	c F	⑦ 🚌	c F	⑦ 🚌	⑦ 🚌
Porthmadog Harbour d.	...	...	1015	...	1335	...	...	...	1015	...	1335	...	...
Minffordd **149** d.	...	...	1025	...	1345	...	...	...	1025	...	1345	...	...
Blaenau Ffestiniog d.	0630	0854	1125	1154	1445	1454	1754	2000	1125	1200	1445	1500	1800
Betws y Coed d.	0656	0920	...	1220	...	1520	1820	2026	...	1230	...	1530	1830
Llanrwst d.	0702	0926	...	1226	...	1526	1826	2032	...	1240	...	1540	1840
Llandudno Junction a.	0726	0950	...	1250	...	1550	1851	2056	...	1315	...	1615	1915
Llandudno a.	*0743*	1001	...	1301	...	1601	*1937*	2108	...	1330	...	1630	1930

F – Ffestiniog Railway. Selected journeys from the timetable valid December 5–31 (www.festrail.co.uk ✆ +44 (0) 1766 516 000).

a – Dec. 5, 6, 12, 13, 20 and 26–31.
b – Dec. 5, 6, 12, 13, 19, 20 and 26–31.
c – Dec. 29.

167 CREWE - MANCHESTER AIRPORT ✈ — 2nd class NT

From CREWE — *37 km*

⚒: 0050 ②–⑥, 0743, 0840, 0938, 1038 and hourly until 1538; then 1642, 1738, 1819 Ⓐ, 1842 ⑥.
⑦: 1025, 1227, 1427, 1627, 1827, 2027, 2225.

From MANCHESTER AIRPORT ✈ — Journey: ± 33 minutes

⚒: 0657, 0800, 0900 and hourly until 1800.
⑦: 0933, 1132, 1326, 1525, 1724, 1924, 2125.

168 CREWE - STOKE - DERBY — 2nd class EM

km		Ⓐ	⑥	Ⓐ	⑥	⚒		⚒	⚒	⚒	⚒	⑦▲	⑦	⑦	⑦	⑦	⑦	⑦	⑦
0	**Crewe** d.	0550	0607	0640	0652	0807		1707	1807	1907	2050	1416	1516	1616	1716	1816	1916	2016	2123
24	Stoke on Trent d.	0623	0633	0702	0716	0833	and	1733	1833	1933	2114	1440	1540	1640	1741	1841	1941	2040	2147
51	Uttoxeter d.	0646	0656	0725	0739	0858	hourly	1757	1857	1957	2137	1503	1603	1704	1805	1905	2005	2104	2211
82	**Derby** a.	0712	0726	0751	0810	0928	until	1827	1927	2027	2211r	1533	1634	1732	1827	1937	2035	2132	2234
	Nottingham **124** a.	*0753*	*0832*	*0832*	*0910*	*1005*		*1905*	*2006*v	*2107*v	*2305*	...	*1710*	...	*1911*	*2107*	*2143*	...	2306

	⚒	⚒	Ⓐ	⑥	⚒		⚒	⑥	Ⓐ	⑥	Ⓐ	⚒	Ⓐ	⑥	⑦▲	⑦	⑦	⑦	⑦	⑦	⑦
Nottingham **124** d.	0555r	*0638*r	*0734*	*0734*	*0832*		*1534*	*1634*	*1700*	*1734*	*1800*	*1834*	*1934*	*1940*	*1401*	*1502*	*1514*	...	*1806*	*1908*	*2008*
Derby d.	0639	0730r	0828	0832	0928	and	1628	1728	1744	1828	1844	1928	2028	2033	1443	1543	1638	1745	1844	1944	2044
Uttoxeter d.	0702	0754	0853	0856	0951	hourly	1651	1752	1808	1851	1907	1951	2055	2056	1506	1606	1704	1808	1907	2007	2107
Stoke on Trent a.	0728	0821	0918	0921	1017	until	1717	1821	1832	1917	1932	2017	2121	2122	1531	1631	1730	1833	1932	2032	2132
Crewe a.	0757	0850	0947	0950	1047		1747	1850	1859	1951	2001	2047	2151	2152	1603	1702	1759	1905	2003	2105	2204

r – 3–4 minutes earlier on ⑥. v – 4 minutes later on ⑥. ▲ – Services on ⑦ are subject to alteration from Feb. 3.

169 NOTTINGHAM and DERBY local services — 2nd class EM

Nottingham – Mansfield – Worksop

No service on ⑦. Journey time: ± 65 minutes *51 km*

From Nottingham:
Trains call at Mansfield ± 35 minutes later. Additional trains run Nottingham - Mansfield.
⚒: 0539 ⑥, 0544 Ⓐ, 0610, 0703 Ⓐ, 0714 ⑥, 0823, 0926, 1026, 1126, 1226, 1326, 1426, 1526, 1626, 1726, 1755, 1856, 1956, 2105.

From Worksop:
Trains call at Mansfield ± 32 minutes later. Additional trains run Mansfield - Nottingham.
⚒: 0550 Ⓐ, 0603 ⑥, 0656 Ⓐ, 0701 ⑥, 0737, 0838, 0940, 1040, 1140, 1240, 1340, 1440, 1540, 1642, 1745, 1852, 1921, 2015, 2121.

Derby – Matlock

Journey time: ± 31 minutes *28 km*

From Derby:
Ⓐ: 0542, 0657, 0827, 1026, 1226, 1425, 1620, 1735, 1855, 2030, 2220.
⑥: 0537, 0702, 0821, 0949, 1152, 1330, 1448, 1622, 1748, 1921, 2151.
⑦: 0959, 1132, 1351, 1546, 1756, 1949, 2153.

From Matlock:
Ⓐ: 0620, 0738, 0904, 1112, 1312, 1517, 1658, 1813, 1938, 2110, 2259.
⑥: 0614, 0739, 0858, 1038, 1238, 1410, 1538, 1701, 1838, 2020, 2228.
⑦: 1042, 1241, 1436, 1640, 1838, 2040, 2233.

EM LONDON - LEICESTER - NOTTINGHAM, DERBY and SHEFFIELD 170

Services are subject to alteration from January 28

km		⚒	Ⓐ 🍷	⑥ Y🍷	Ⓐ 🍷		Ⓐ 🍷	⑥ 🍷	Ⓐ ✕	⑥ 🍷	⚒ 🍷	⚒ 🍷§	⚒ 🍷	⚒ 🍷§	⚒ 🍷	⑥ 🍷	Ⓐ ✕	⚒ 🍷	⚒ 🍷§	⚒ 🍷	⚒ ✕	⚒ 🍷	⚒ ✕	Ⓐ 🍷
0	**London** St Pancras ‡ d.		0610	0620	0635	...	0700	0700	0725	0725	0730	0755	0800	0825	0830	0855	0855	0900	0925	0930	0955	1000	1025	1030
47	Luton ✈ Parkway ‡ d.		*0605*	*0605*	0657	...	0722	0725	*0735*	|	*0736*z	|	0822	|	*0835*	|	|	0922	*0925*y	*0940*y	|	1022	|	*1035*
49	Luton ‡ d.		0633	0644	|	...	*0704*	*0656*	0750	0749	0753	|	*0756*	*0808*d	0853	|	|	*0854*	0948	0953	|	*0954*	|	1053
80	Bedford ‡ d.		0648	0701	|	...	0738	0741	|	|	0808	|	0838	0900	0908	|	|	0938	|	1008	|	1038	|	1108
105	Wellingborough d.		0701	0716	0721	...	0751	0753	|	|	0821	|	0851	|	0921	|	|	0951	|	1021	|	1051	|	1121
116	Kettering d.		0708	0724	0728	...	0758	0801	|	|	0828	|	0858	|	0928	|	|	0958	|	1028	|	1058	|	1128
133	Market Harborough d.		0718	0736	0738	...	0808	0811	|	|	0838	|	0908	|	0938	|	|	1008	|	1038	|	1108	|	1138
159	**Leicester** a.		0735	0754	0755	...	0823	0827	0838	0839	0855	0904	0923	0938	0955	1004	1004	1023	1038	1055	1104	1123	1134	1155
159	**Leicester 193** d.		0735	0754	0756	...	0824	0827	0839	0840	0856	0905	0924	0939	0956	1005	1005	1024	1039	1056	1105	1124	1135	1156
180	Loughborough **193** a.		0746	0806	0807	...	0834	0838	0850	0851	0907	0916	0934	|	1007	|	|	1034	|	1107	1116	1134	|	1207
204	**Nottingham 193** a.		|	|	0829	...	|	0856	*0920*	|	0926	0937	*1020*	|	1028	1034	1036	*1120*j	|	1127	1136	*1219*j	|	1226
207	**Derby 127** a.		0812	0832	|	...	0855	...	0909	0914	|	...	0956	1005	|	|	...	1056	1105	|	...	1156	1205	|
246	Chesterfield **127 208** a.		0839	0856	*0918*	...	...	...	0930	0938	*1018*	...	...	1026	*1118*	*1118*	...	...	1126	*1218*	...	...	1226	*1318*
265	**Sheffield 127 208** a.		0905	0913	*0938*	...	...	...	0946	0956	*1038*	...	...	1046	*1138*	*1138*	...	...	1146	*1238*	...	...	1246	*1338*

	⑥ 🍷	⚒ 🍷	⚒ 🍷	⚒ 🍷	⚒ 🍷	⚒ 🍷	⚒ 🍷	⚒ 🍷	⚒ 🍷	⚒ 🍷	⚒ 🍷	⚒ 🍷	⚒ 🍷	⚒ 🍷	⚒ 🍷	⚒ 🍷	⚒ 🍷	⚒ 🍷	⚒ 🍷	⑥ 🍷	Ⓐ 🍷	⚒ 🍷	⑥ 🍷	Ⓐ 🍷
London St Pancras ‡ d.	1030	1055	1100	1125	1130	1155	1200	1225	1230	1255	1300	1325	1330	1355	1400	1425	1430	1455	1500	1525	1525	1530	1555	1555
Luton ✈ Parkway ‡ d.	*1035*	|	1122	|	*1135*	|	1222	|	*1235*	|	1322	|	*1335*	|	1422	|	*1435*	|	1522	|	*1535*	|	*1605*	*1605*
Luton ‡ d.	1053	|	*1054*	|	1153	|	*1154*	|	1253	|	*1254*	|	1353	|	*1354*	*1424*	1453	|	*1454*	1548	1548	1553	1618	1618
Bedford ‡ d.	1108	|	1138	|	1208	|	1238	|	1308	|	1338	|	1408	|	1438	1500	1508	|	1538	|	|	1608	|	|
Wellingborough d.	1121	|	1151	|	1221	|	1251	|	1321	|	1351	|	1421	|	1451	|	1521	|	1551	|	|	1621	|	1644
Kettering d.	1128	|	1158	|	1228	|	1258	|	1328	|	1358	|	1428	|	1458	|	1528	|	1558	|	1618	1628	|	|
Market Harborough d.	1138	|	1208	|	1238	|	1308	|	1338	|	1408	|	1438	|	1508	|	1538	|	1608	|	|	1638	|	|
Leicester a.	1155	1204	1223	1234	1255	1304	1323	1334	1355	1404	1423	1435	1455	1504	1523	1538	1555	1604	1623	1638	1640	1655	1708	1713
Leicester 193 d.	1156	1205	1224	1236	1256	1305	1324	1336	1356	1405	1424	1436	1456	1505	1524	1539	1556	1605	1624	1639	1644	1656	1710	1713
Loughborough **193** a.	1207	|	1234	|	1307	1316	1334	|	1407	|	1434	|	1507	1517	1534	|	1607	1615a	1634	|	|	1707	|	1724
Nottingham 193 a.	1227	1235	*1318*	|	1326	1336	*1421*j	|	1426	1437	*1518*	|	1526	1536	*1618*	|	1626	1636	*1718*	|	|	1728	1734	1750
Derby 127 a.	|	|	1256	1305	|	|	1356	1405	|	...	1456	1505	|	|	1556	1605	|	...	1656	1705	1708	|	|	...
Chesterfield **127 208** a.	1341	*1322*z	...	1328	*1418*	*1418*a	...	1426	*1518*	...	...	1526	*1618*	*1618*z	...	1626	*1718*	...	...	1726	1730	*1818*	*1818*	...
Sheffield 127 208 a.	1400	*1339*z	...	1347	*1438*	*1438*a	...	1446	*1538*	...	...	1546	*1638*	*1638*z	...	1646	*1734*	...	...	1743	1748	*1838*	*1838*	...

	⑥ 🍷	Ⓐ 🍷	Ⓐ 🍷	⑥ L🍷	⚒ 🍷	Ⓐ L🍷	⑥ 🍷	Ⓐ 🍷	⑥ 🍷	Ⓐ 🍷	⑥ 🍷	Ⓐ 🍷	⑥ L🍷	Ⓐ L🍷	⑥ 🍷	Ⓐ 🍷	⑥ 🍷	Ⓐ 🍷	Ⓐ 🍷	⑥ L🍷	Ⓐ L🍷	Ⓐ 🍷	⑥ 🍷	Ⓐ 🍷
London St Pancras ‡ d.	1600	1600	1625	1625	1630	1655	1655	1700	1700	1715	1730	1730	1740	1745	1755	1755	1800	1800	1815	1825	1825	1830	1830	1855
Luton ✈ Parkway ‡ d.	1622	1622	|	|	*1635*	|	|	|	1722	1739	*1735*	|	|	*1756*	*1805*	*1800*	1822	1823	|	|	|	*1840*	*1840*	*1850*
Luton ‡ d.	|	|	|	|	1653	|	|	|	*1654*	|	1753	*1736*	|	1810	1819	1820	|	|	|	|	|	1854	1853	|
Bedford ‡ d.	1638	|	|	|	1708	|	|	|	1738	|	1808	1810	1819	|	|	|	1838	1838	1854	|	|	|	1908	1930
Wellingborough d.	1651	1651	|	|	1721	|	1740	1744	1751	1803	1821	1823	1833	1834	|	1844	1851	1851	|	|	1912	1918	1921	1942
Kettering d.	1658	1658	1714	1715	1728	|	1748	1752	1758	1810	1828	1833	1841	1841	1849	1853	1858	1858	1912	1915	1919	1926	1928	|
Market Harborough d.	1708	1708	|	|	1738	|	1759	1803	1808	1820	1838	|	|	1853	1900	|	1908	1909	1923	1926	1931	1938	1938	|
Leicester a.	1723	1723	1739	1739	1756	1804	1817	1821	1824	1835	1855	1857	1905	1908	1921	1918	1926	1925	1938	1942	1948	1955	1956	2011
Leicester 193 d.	1724	1724	1740	1739	1756	1806	1817	1821	1824	1836	1856	1857	1906	1909	1922	1919	1927	1926	1942	1943	1948	1956	1956	2011
Loughborough **193** a.	1734	1734	1751	1750	1808	|	|	|	1834	1846	1907	|	|	|	1933	1932	1937	1937	|	|	1959	2007	2007	2023
Nottingham 193 a.	*1816*	|	|	|	1826	|	1841	1848	*1916*	*1920*	1926	|	|	1935	1952	1953	*2019*	*2022*	|	|	|	2027	2034	2038
Derby 127 a.	1754	1756	1810	1816	|	1835	...	...	1856	1909	|	1925	1931	|	...	...	1957	1959	2015	2009	2022	...	...	...
Chesterfield **127 208** a.	*1832*	...	1831	1838	*1918*z	1856	...	...	*1932*	...	2012	1946	1952	2018	...	...	2020	*2032*	2037	2030	2043	...	...	...
Sheffield 127 208 a.	*1851*	...	1847	1859	*1939*z	1913	...	...	*1948*	...	2028	2002	2008	2033	...	...	2038	*2048*	2053	2047	2059	...	...	...

	⑥ 🍷	⑥ 🍷	Ⓐ 🍷	⑥ L🍷	Ⓐ L🍷	⚒ 🍷	⚒ 🍷	⚒ 🍷	⚒ 🍷	⚒ 🍷	Ⓐ 🍷	⑥ 🍷	⑥ 🍷	Ⓐ 🍷	⑥ 🍷	⑥ 🍷	Ⓐ 🍷	Ⓐ 🍷	Ⓐ 🍷		Ⓐ 🍷	⑥ 🍷		Ⓐ 🍷
London St Pancras ‡ d.	1855	1900	1900	1925	1925	1930	1955	2000	2025	2030	2055	2055	2100	2100	2125	2135	2125	2130	2200	...	2225	2210	...	2315
Luton ✈ Parkway ‡ d.	*1905*	1922	1922	*1937*	*1928*	*1940*	|	2022	|	*2037*v	|	|	2122	2122	|	|	|	*2137*	*2207*	...	*2225*	*2227*	...	*2331*
Luton ‡ d.	1918	|	*1904*	1949	1951	1953	|	*1957*j	|	2053	|	|	*2054*	*2054*	|	|	|	2153	2222	...	2248	2245	...	2345
Bedford ‡ d.	|	1938	1938	|	|	2008	|	2038	|	2108	|	|	2138	2138	|	|	|	2207	2238	...	2305	2308	...	0009
Wellingborough d.	1942	1951	1951	|	|	2021	2039	2051	|	2121	|	|	2151	2151	|	2220	|	2220	2251	...	2319	2321	...	0022
Kettering d.	|	1958	1958	2019	2019	2028	|	2058	2114	2128	|	|	2158	2158	2215	2227	2217	2235	2304	...	2329	2334	...	0034
Market Harborough d.	|	2008	2008	|	|	2038	|	2108	|	2138	2151	2151	2208	2208	|	2237	|	◐	◐	...	◐	◐	...	◐
Leicester a.	2013	2023	2023	2043	2044	2056	2106	2123	2139j	2155	2206	2207	2223	2223	2239	2252	2319	2346	0002	...	0034	0036	...	0133
Leicester 193 d.	2014	2024	2024	2043	2044	2056	2107	2124	2139	2157	2206	2209	2224	2224	2240	2257	2324	2351	0008	...	0039	0042	...	0139
Loughborough **193** a.	2024	2034	2034	|	|	2107	2118	2134	|	2209	2217	2221	2235	2234	2252	2308	2335	0006	0020	...	0057	|	...	0156
Nottingham 193 a.	2039	*2117*	*2123*	|	|	2128	2139	|	|	2229	2239	2238	|	2252	|	2325	|	0035	0046	...	|	|	...	0212
Derby 127 a.	...	2056	2056	2110	2112	...	|	2156	2208j	...	...	...	2256	2326	2312	...	0002	...	...	...	0131	0149	...	0236
Chesterfield **127 208** a.	...	...	...	2131	2133	...	2220v	...	2230	...	...	...	...	...	...	...	0024	...	...	...	0152	...	...	...
Sheffield 127 208 a.	...	...	...	2147	2149	...	2240	...	2246	...	...	...	...	...	...	...	0041	...	...	...	0208	...	...	...

	⑦	⑦ Y🍷		⑦ 🍷		⑦ 🍷		⑦ 🍷		⑦ 🍷	⑦ 🍷		⑦ 🍷		⑦ 🍷	⑦ 🍷		⑦ 🍷		⑦ 🍷	⑦ 🍷		⑦ 🍷	⑦ 🍷
London St Pancras ‡ d.		...	...	0900	...	0930	...	1000	...	1030	1100	...	1130	...	1200	1230	...	1300	...	1330	1400	...	1430	1500
Luton ✈ Parkway ‡ d.		...	...	*0915*	...	*0945*	...	*1015*	...	*1045*	1128	...	*1135*	...	*1205*	*1248*	...	1327	...	*1348*	*1418*	...	*1435*	1529
Luton ‡ d.		...	...	0930	...	1002	...	1030	...	*1049*	1133	...	*1139*	...	1231	*1252*	...	1333	...	*1352*	1432	...	*1439*	1534
Bedford ‡ d.		...	...	0950	...	1022	...	1050	...	1124	1155	...	1223	...	1255	1324	...	1354	...	1422	1446	...	1516	1551
Wellingborough d.		...	...	1003	...	1035	...	1105	...	1136	1209	...	1237	...	1308	1337	...	1407	...	1435	1500	...	1529	1604
Kettering d.		...	...	1017	...	1048	...	1117	...	1149	1221	...	1250	...	1322	1350	...	1419	...	1443	1513	...	1550	1616
Market Harborough d.		...	...	◐	...	◐	...	◐	...	◐	◐	...	◐	...	◐	◐	...	◐	...	◐	◐	...	◐	◐
Leicester a.		...	...	1119	...	1152	...	1223	...	1259	1323	...	1353	...	1428	1454	...	1523	...	1550	1617	...	1654	1717
Leicester 193 d.		1005	...	1124	...	1200	...	1229	...	1304	1329	...	1400	...	1433	1500	...	1529	...	1557	1623	...	1700	1723
Loughborough **193** a.		1015	...	1138	...	1211	...	1239	...	1315	1340	...	1412	...	1444	1514	...	1540	...	1609	1624	...	1712	1734
Nottingham 193 a.		|	...	1156	...	|	...	1256	...	|	1359	...	|	...	1459	|	...	1557	...	|	1651	...	|	1751
Derby 127 a.		1034	...	...	...	1231	...	...	...	1332	...	...	1434	...	...	1533	...	...	...	1628	...	...	1731	...
Chesterfield **127 208** a.		1055	...	...	...	1251	...	...	...	1352	...	...	1455	...	...	1555	...	...	...	1649	...	...	1752	...
Sheffield 127 208 a.		1109	...	...	...	1305	...	...	...	1407	...	...	1515	...	...	1613	...	...	...	1707	...	...	1808	...

	⑦ 🍷	⑦ 🍷	⑦ 🍷		⑦ 🍷		⑦ L🍷	⑦ 🍷		⑦ L🍷	⑦ 🍷		⑦ 🍷		⑦ 🍷	⑦ L🍷		⑦ 🍷		⑦ 🍷		⑦ 🍷		⑦ 🍷
London St Pancras ‡ d.	1530	1600	1630	...	1700	...	1730	1800	...	1830	1900	...	1930	...	2000	2030	...	2100	...	2130	...	2230	...	2300
Luton ✈ Parkway ‡ d.	*1535*	*1618*	*1635*	...	*1705*	...	*1735*	*1805*	...	1857	1926	...	*1935*	...	*2005*	*2035*	...	*2117*r	...	*2135*	...	*2235*	...	*2315*r
Luton ‡ d.	*1539*	1632	1701	...	1731	...	1753	1822	...	1901	*1909*	...	1956	...	2026	*2039*	...	2125	...	*2139*	...	2255	...	2326
Bedford ‡ d.	1616	1648	1715	...	1747	...	1817	1846	...	1919	1945	...	2017	...	2047	2113	...	2150	...	2219	...	2319	...	2352
Wellingborough d.	1628	1701	1728	...	1801	...	1830	1859	...	1933	1958	...	2031	...	2101	2127	...	2202	...	2232	...	2331	...	0005
Kettering d.	1648	1714	1741	...	1814	...	1843	1911	...	1947	2012	...	2041	...	2115	2140	...	2215	...	2246	...	2344	...	0019
Market Harborough d.	◐	◐	◐	...	◐	...	◐	◐	...	◐	◐	...	◐	...	◐	◐	...	◐	...	◐	...	◐	...	◐
Leicester a.	1750	1818	1845	...	1915	...	1948	2013	...	2050	2116	...	2146	...	2219	2244	...	2319	...	2349	...	0053	...	0124
Leicester 193 d.	1757	1834	1850	...	1920	...	1953	2019	...	2101	2123	...	2155	...	2224	2250	...	2324	...	2355	...	0058	...	0129
Loughborough **193** a.	1809	|	1902	...	1932	...	2004	2030	...	2112	2137	...	|	...	2238	|	...	|	...	0009	...	0114	...	0146
Nottingham 193 a.	|	1849	|	...	1950	...	|	2049	...	|	2154	...	|	...	2256	|	...	0002	...	|	...	0141	...	|
Derby 127 a.	1828	...	1919	...	...	...	2027	|	...	2136	...	...	2223	...	...	2320	...	...	...	0036	...	...	...	0206
Chesterfield **127 208** a.	1850	...	1939	...	...	...	2051	2130	...	2157	...	...	2249	...	...	2345	...	...	...	0131*	...	...	...	...
Sheffield 127 208 a.	1907	...	1956	...	...	...	2110	2146	...	2213	...	...	2308	...	...	2359	...	...	...	0202*	...	...	...	...

L – To Leeds.
Y – To York.

a – Ⓐ only.
d – *0824* on ⑥.

j – 3 minutes earlier on ⑥.
r – Change at Bedford.
v – 4–5 minutes later on ⑥.
y – *0935* on ⑥.
z – ⑥ only.

§ – Also conveys ✕ on Ⓐ.

‡ – Frequent suburban trains operate between these stations.

* – By 🚌.

◐ – Replacement 🚌 services (journey: 25 minutes) operate Kettering - Harborough and Harborough - Leicester during line engineering work.

170 SHEFFIELD, DERBY and NOTTINGHAM - LEICESTER - LONDON

EM

Services are subject to alteration from January 28

	⚒	Ⓐ 🍷		Ⓐ 🍴	⑥ 🍷		⑥ 🍷	Ⓐ 🍴		Ⓐ 🍴	⑥ 🍷	Ⓐ 🍷	⑥ 🍷	⑥ 🍷	Ⓐ 🍴	Ⓐ 🍴	Ⓐ 🍴	⑥ 🍷	Ⓐ 🍴	⑥ 🍷	Ⓐ 🍷	Ⓐ 🍴	⑥ 🍷	Ⓐ 🍷
Sheffield 127 208 d.		...	...	...	...	...	...	...	...	0520	0500	...	...	...	...	...	0600	0616	0625	...	...	0630	*0623*	*0645*
Chesterfield **127 208** d.		...	...	...	...	...	...	...	...	0533	0512	...	...	...	...	...	0614	0629	0638	...	...	0645	*0635*	*0657*
Derby 127 d.		...	...	0500	0500	...	...	...	...	0556	0600	...	...	...	...	0639	|	0653	0701	...	...	|	0734	0725
Nottingham 193 d.		...	...	|	|	...	0529	0530	...	|	|	0607	0607	0625	0625	|	0653	|	|	0707	0707	0729	|	|
Loughborough **193** d.		...	...	|	|	...	0544	0545	...	0615	0620	|	0626	0640	0641	|	|	0710	0718	0723	0722	|	0752	0752
Leicester 193 a.		...	...	0525	0529	...	0557	0558	...	0628	0632	0634	0635	0651	0653	0701	0713	0722	0730	0734	0737	0755	0804	0804
Leicester d.		0500	...	0525	0530	...	0557	0600	...	0630	0632	0635	0635	0655	0655	0704	0715	0723	0730	0735	0737	0757	0805	0805
Market Harborough d.		|	...	0541	|	...	0613	0615	...	0645	|	0650	0653	0710	0710	|	0729	|	0747	0749	0753	|	0819	0819
Kettering d.		0521	...	0552	0554	...	0624	0626	...	0656	0657	0702	0703	0721	0720	0729	0739	0747	0758	0759	0803	0817	0829	0829
Wellingborough d.		0529	...	0600	0602	...	0632	0634	...	0704	0705	0710	0711	0729	0728	0739	0746	0755	0806	0806	0812	|	0836	0840
Bedford ‡ a.		0550	...	0618	0616	...	0650	0651	...	|	|	|	0724	|	|	0753	|	|	|	0820	0825	|	0851	0903
Luton ‡ a.		*0623*	...	0635	0637	...	0708	0708	...	0729	0730	|	*0803*	|	0752	|	0810	|	|	0836	*0853*	|	*0933*	*0933*
Luton ✈ Parkway ‡ a.		0607	...	*0652*	*0651*	...	*0721*	*0722*	...	|	|	0738	0742	|	*0804*	|	*0830*	|	|	*0851*	*0906*	|	0907	0920
London St Pancras a.		0641	...	0706	0705	...	0738	0736	...	0759	0805	0806	0809	0821	0824	0838	0842	0845	0855	0904	0906	0912	0934	0945

	Ⓐ 🍴	Ⓐ L🍴	⑥ 🍴	⚒ 🍷	Ⓐ 🍷	⑥ 🍷	⚒ 🍷	⑥ L🍷	Ⓐ L🍷	⚒ 🍷		⚒ 🍷	⚒ 🍷		Ⓐ L🍷	⑥ L🍷	⚒ 🍷	⚒ 🍷	⚒ 🍷		⚒ 🍷	⚒ 🍷	⚒ 🍷	⚒ 🍷
Sheffield 127 208 d.	0705	0727	0727	...	0714	0732	*0723*a	0827	0827	...	...	...	0836p	...	0927	0927	...	...	*0953*	...	1027	...	...	*1053*
Chesterfield **127 208** d.	0719	0740	0740	...	0727	0745	*0735*a	0839	0840	...	...	...	0848p	...	0940	0940	...	...	|	...	1040	...	...	|
Derby 127 d.	0746	|	0803	...	|	|	0834	0902	0904	...	...	...	0934	...	1004	1004	...	...	1034	...	1104	...	...	1134
Nottingham 193 d.	|	|	|	0807	0828	0835	|	|	*0835*	0907	...	0930	|	...	*0938*	*0938*	1007	1030	|	...	*1038*	1107	1130	|
Loughborough **193** d.	|	|	|	0822	0843	|	0852	|	*0901*	0922	...	0944	0952	...	*1000*	*1001*	1022	|	1052	...	*1100*	1122	1143	1152
Leicester 193 a.	0812	|	0827	0834	0855	0857	0904	0927	0928	0935	...	0957	1004	...	1028	1028	1034	1057j	1104	...	1128	1134	1158	1204
Leicester d.	0814	|	0828	0835	0856	0900	0905	0928	0930	0935	...	1000	1005	...	1030	1030	1035	1100	1105	...	1130	1135	1200	1205
Market Harborough d.	|	|	0843	0849	|	|	0919	|	|	0949	...	1015z	1019	...	|	|	1049	|	1119	...	|	1149	|	1219
Kettering d.	|	|	0854	0859	0918	0923	0929	0951	|	0959	...	|	1029	...	|	1053	1059	|	1129	...	|	1159	|	1229
Wellingborough d.	|	|	|	0906	|	0931	0936	|	|	1006	...	|	1036	...	|	1101	1106	|	1136	...	|	1206	|	1236
Bedford ‡ a.	|	|	|	0921	|	0944	0953	|	|	1021	...	|	1051	...	1110	1115	1120	|	1151	...	|	1220	|	1251
Luton ‡ a.	|	|	|	0938	|	*1018*	*1033*	|	|	1036	...	|	*1133*	...	|	|	1136	|	*1233*	...	1220	1236	|	*1333*
Luton ✈ Parkway ‡ a.	|	|	|	*0951*	|	*1021*	1009	|	|	*1051*	...	|	1107	...	|	|	*1151*	|	1207	...	*1236*	*1251*	|	1307
London St Pancras a.	0929	0933	0949	1004	1019	1029	1036	1046	1048	1104	...	1117	1134	...	1151	1159	1204	1215	1234	...	1251	1304	1315	1334

	⚒ 🍷	⚒ 🍷	⚒ 🍷	⚒ 🍷	⚒ 🍷	⚒ 🍷	⚒ 🍷	⚒ 🍷		⚒ 🍷	⚒ 🍷	⚒ 🍷	⚒ 🍷	⚒ 🍷	⚒ 🍷	⚒ 🍷	⚒ 🍷		⚒ 🍷	⚒ 🍷	⑥ 🍷	Ⓐ 🍷	⚒ 🍷	⚒ 🍷
Sheffield 127 208 d.	1127	...	...	*1153*	1227	...	...	*1253*	...	1327	...	...	*1353*	1427	...	...	*1453*	...	1527	...	...	...	*1553*	1627
Chesterfield **127 208** d.	1140	...	...	|	1240	...	...	|	...	1340	...	...	|	1440	...	...	|	...	1540	...	...	...	|	1640
Derby 127 d.	1204	...	...	1234	1304	...	...	1334	...	1404	...	...	1434	1504	...	...	1534	...	1604	...	...	...	1634	1703
Nottingham 193 d.	*1138*	1207	1230	|	*1238*	1307	1330	|	...	*1338*	1407	1430	|	*1438*	1507	1530	|	...	*1538*	1607	1630	1630	|	*1638*
Loughborough **193** d.	*1200*	1222	|	1252	*1300*	1322	1343	1352	...	*1400*	1422	|	1452	*1500*	1522	1544	1552	...	*1600*	1622	|	1644	1652	*1702*
Leicester 193 a.	1228	1234	1257	1304	1328	1334	1357	1404	...	1428	1434	1457j	1504	1528	1534	1558	1604	...	1628	1634	1655	1658	1704	1730
Leicester d.	1230	1235	1300	1305	1330	1335	1400	1405	...	1430	1435	1500	1505	1530	1535	1600	1605	...	1630	1635	1700	1700	1705	1730
Market Harborough d.	|	1249	|	1319	|	1349	|	1419	...	|	1449	|	1519	|	1549	|	1619	...	|	1649	|	|	1719	|
Kettering d.	|	1259	|	1329	|	1359	|	1429	...	|	1459	|	1529	|	1559	|	1629	...	|	1659	|	1721	1729	|
Wellingborough d.	|	1306	|	1336	|	1406	|	1436	...	|	1506	|	1536	|	1606	|	1636	...	|	1706	|	|	1736	|
Bedford ‡ a.	|	1320	|	1351	|	1420	|	1451	...	|	1520	|	1551	|	1620	|	1651	...	1712	1720	|	|	1751	|
Luton ‡ a.	|	1336	|	*1433*	|	1436	|	*1533*	...	1520	1536	|	*1633*	|	1636	|	*1717*c	...	|	1736	|	|	*1833*	1821
Luton ✈ Parkway ‡ a.	|	*1351*	|	1407	|	*1451*	|	1507	...	*1536*	*1551*	|	1607	|	*1651*	|	1707	...	*1746*a	*1751*	|	|	1807	*1836*
London St Pancras a.	1345	1404	1415	1434	1445	1504	1515	1534	...	1551	1604	1615	1634	1645	1704	1713v	1734	...	1753	1804	1815	1819	1834	1851

	⚒ 🍷	⚒ 🍷	⚒ 🍷		Ⓐ 🍷	⑥ 🍷	Ⓐ 🍷	⑥ 🍷	⚒ 🍷	⚒ 🍷	⚒ 🍷	Ⓐ 🍷	⑥ 🍷	⚒ 🍷	⚒ 🍷	⑥ Y🍷	Ⓐ 🍷	⚒ 🍷		⑥ 🍷	Ⓐ 🍷		Ⓐ 🍷	Ⓐ 🍷
Sheffield 127 208 d.	...	...	*1653*	...	1727	1727	...	...	...	*1753*	1827	...	...	...	*1853*	1907	1927	...	...	...	*1938*	...	2039	...
Chesterfield **127 208** d.	...	...	|	...	1740	1740	...	...	...	|	1840	...	...	...	|	1919	1940	...	...	...	*1956*	...	2051	...
Derby 127 d.	...	...	1734	...	1802	1804	...	...	...	1834	1902	...	...	...	1934	1951	2002	...	...	...	|	...	2116	...
Nottingham 193 d.	1707	1730	|	...	*1738*	*1738*	1807	1807	1830	|	*1838*	1907	1907	1930	|	*1933*	*1938*	2007	...	2030	2047	...	|	2130
Loughborough **193** d.	1722	1744	1752	...	1818	1820	1822	1825	1844	1852	1917	1922	1924	1944	1952	2015	2018	2022a	...	2049	2100	...	2130	2145
Leicester 193 a.	1734	1758	1804	...	1830	1833	1835	1839	1857	1904	1930	1935	1938	1956	2004	2026	2029	2035	...	2102	2112	...	2143	2156
Leicester d.	1735	1800	1805	...	1830	1834	1835	1840	1900	1905	1930	1935	1939	2000	2005	2027	2030	2035	...	2103	2115	...	2145	2200
Market Harborough d.	1749	|	1819	...	|	|	1851	1851	|	1919	|	1951	1953	|	2019	2041	|	2049	...	2118	2128	...	2159	2213
Kettering d.	1759	|	1829	...	|	|	1901	1901	|	1929	|	2001	2003	|	2029	2051	|	2059	...	2128	2138	...	2209	2223
Wellingborough d.	1806	|	1836	...	|	|	1909	1911	|	1936	|	2009	2011	|	2036	2059	|	2107	...	2136	2145	...	2216	2230
Bedford ‡ a.	1821	|	1853	...	|	|	1923	1925	|	1951	|	2023	2024	|	2051	2112	2111	2123	...	2149	2200	...	|	2245
Luton ‡ a.	1839j	|	|	...	1922	|	1939	1941	|	|	|	2039	2040	|	|	2128	|	2139	...	2209	2216	...	|	2301
Luton ✈ Parkway ‡ a.	*1852*	|	1907	...	*1946*	|	*1952*	|	|	2007	|	*2052*	*2052*	|	2108	*2146*	*2146*	*2152*	...	*2222*	*2236*	...	|	*2336*
London St Pancras a.	1904	1917q	1935	...	1952	1945	2004	2009	2011v	2035	2041b	2104	2108	2112	2135	2152	2153	2204	...	2243	2240	...	2304	2332

	⑦	⑦ 🍷		⑦ 🍷	⑦ 🍷		⑦ 🍷		⑦ 🍷	⑦ 🍷		⑦ 🍷		⑦ 🍷		⑦ 🍷		⑦ L🍷	⑦ 🍷		⑦ 🍷	⑦ L🍷		⑦ 🍷
Sheffield 127 208 d.		...	...	...	...	...	...	...	...	...	...	*0746**	...	...	...	0926	...	0940	1031	...	...	1127	...	...
Chesterfield **127 208** d.		...	...	...	...	...	...	...	...	...	...	*0817**	...	...	...	0940	...	0953	1042	...	...	1140	...	...
Derby 127 d.		0531	...	...	0627	...	...	...	0727	...	...	0913	...	...	...	1003	...	1016	1104	...	...	1203	...	...
Nottingham 193 d.		|	...	0651	|	...	0740	...	|	0828	...	|	...	0942	...	|	...	1044	|	...	1143	|	...	1246
Loughborough **193** d.		|	...	|	0727	...	|	...	0828	0849	...	0932	...	0959	...	1026	...	1059	1124	...	1159	1221	...	1300
Leicester 193 a.		0642	...	0713	0741	...	0808	...	0841	0902	...	0943	...	1010	...	1039	...	1113	1135	...	1211	1237	...	1311
Leicester d.		0647	...	0719	0745	...	0814	...	0846	0907	...	0948	...	1016	...	1043	...	1118	1140	...	1215	1241	...	1316
Market Harborough d.		|	...	◐	◐	...	◐	...	◐	◐	...	◐	...	◐	...	◐	...	◐	◐	...	◐	◐	...	◐
Kettering d.		0751	...	0822	0849	...	0919	...	0950	1019	...	1052	...	1121	...	1150	...	1221	1248	...	1321	1348	...	1420
Wellingborough d.		0800	...	0831	0859	...	0929	...	0959	1029	...	1101	...	1131	...	1200	...	1231	1258	...	1331	1358	...	1429
Bedford ‡ a.		0815	...	0846	0915	...	0945	...	1015	1045	...	1116	...	1145	...	1216	...	1245	1313	...	1345	1415	...	1444
Luton ‡ a.		0837	...	0908	*1003*	...	1008	...	*1103*	1107	...	*1203*	...	1210	...	1238	...	1313	*1343*	...	1409	*1449*	...	1500
Luton ✈ Parkway ‡ a.		*0852*	...	*0922*	0942	...	*1022*	...	*1106*	*1122*	...	1141	...	*1222*	...	*1252*	...	*1322*r	*1346*	...	*1420*r	*1452*	...	*1516*
London St Pancras a.		0916	...	0945	1017	...	1046	...	1119	1149	...	1219	...	1250	...	1318	...	1348	1419	...	1445	1511	...	1535

	⑦ 🍷		⑦ 🍷		⑦ 🍷		⑦ 🍷	⑦ 🍷		⑦ 🍷	⑦ 🍷		⑦ 🍷		⑦ 🍷	⑦ 🍷		⑦ 🍷		⑦ Y🍷		⑦ 🍷		⑦ 🍷
Sheffield 127 208 d.	1227	...	...	...	1334	...	...	1425	...	...	1510	...	1526	...	1626	...	...	1709	...	1733	...	1851	...	...
Chesterfield **127 208** d.	1240	...	...	...	1347	...	...	1438	...	...	1523	...	1539	...	1640	...	...	1722	...	1745	...	1904	...	...
Derby 127 d.	1302	...	...	...	1414	...	...	1501	...	...	1553	...	|	...	1702	...	...	1746	...	|	...	1925	...	*1941*
Nottingham 193 d.	|	...	1331	...	|	...	1448	|	...	1540	|	...	1630	...	|	1724	...	|	...	1841	...	|	...	2030
Loughborough **193** d.	1323	...	1348	...	1435	...	1502	1521	...	1558	1607	...	|	...	1722	1743	...	1808	...	|	...	1944	...	2043
Leicester 193 a.	1339	...	1400	...	1444	...	1512	1534	...	1607	1621	...	1658	...	1736	1754	...	1823	...	1908	...	1958	...	2055
Leicester d.	1344	...	1406	...	1449	...	1517	1539	...	1612	1630	...	1707	...	1740	1759	...	1832	...	1913	...	2002	...	2103
Market Harborough d.	◐	...	◐	...	◐	...	◐	◐	...	◐	◐	...	◐	...	◐	◐	...	◐	...	◐	...	◐	...	◐
Kettering d.	1450	...	1511	...	1555	...	1627	1644	...	1717	1744	...	1814	...	1845	1907	...	1938	...	2018	...	2107	...	2206
Wellingborough d.	1500	...	1521	...	1605	...	1639	1654	...	1727	1753	...	1824	...	1855	1917	...	1948	...	2032	...	2116	...	2216
Bedford ‡ a.	1515	...	1534	...	|	...	1654	1710	...	1741	1808	...	1839	...	1910	1932	...	2004	...	2049	...	2131	...	2230
Luton ‡ a.	*1549*	...	1559	...	|	...	1712	*1743*	...	*1813*	1828	...	1901	...	*1943*	1951	...	*2103*	...	2108	...	2150	...	2250
Luton ✈ Parkway ‡ a.	*1552*	...	*1616*	...	1634	...	|	*1746*	...	1759	*1846*	...	*1916*	...	*1946*	*2016*	...	*2106*	...	*2136*	...	*2206*	...	*2306*
London St Pancras a.	1608	...	1630	...	1706	...	1742	1755	...	1828	1857	...	1929	...	1956	2022	...	2049	...	2137	...	2219	...	2322

L – From Leeds.
Y – From York.

a – Ⓐ only.
b – 2048 on ⑥.
c – *1733* on ⑥.

j – 3–4 minutes earlier on ⑥.
p – 20–21 minutes later on ⑥.
q – 1908 on ⑥.
r – Change at Bedford.
v – 4 minutes later on ⑥.
z – ⑥ only.

§ – Also conveys 🍴 on Ⓐ.

‡ – Frequent suburban trains operate between these stations.

* – By 🚌.

◐ – Replacement 🚌 services (journey: 25 minutes) operate Leicester - Harborough and Harborough - Kettering during line engineering work.

NT 2nd class — LEEDS - HARROGATE - YORK — 173

km		⚒	⚒	Ⓐ	⑥	⚒	⚒	⑥	Ⓐ	⚒	⚒		⚒	⚒	⚒	⚒	⚒	⚒	Ⓐ	⚒	⚒	Ⓐ	⚒	⚒	⑥	Ⓐ
0	**Leeds** d.		0606	0629	0637	0713	0743r	0754	0759	0829	0859	and at the	1529	1559	1629	1659	1713	1729	1744	1759	1829	1859	1929	2029	2120	2129
29	**Harrogate** d.		0645	0705	0714	0749	0816	0829	0834	0905	0935	same mins	1605	1635	1708	1735	1749	1805	1816	1835	1905	1935	2005	2105	2156	2205
36	Knaresborough d.		0655	0718	0723	0759	0828	0840	0845	0915	0945	past each	1614	1645	1721	1745	1759	1814	1826	1845	1914	1945	2014	2114	2206	2215
62	**York** a.		0721	0749	0749	0830r	0858	...	...	0945	...	hour until	1645	...	1748	...	...	1846	...	...	1945	...	2044	2147	...	...

	⑦	⑦	⑦	⑦	⑦	⑦	⑦	⑦	⑦	⑦	
Leeds d.		1054	1254	1454	1554	1654	1754	1854	1954	2116	...
Harrogate d.		1130	1330	1530	1630	1730	1830	1930	2030	2153	...
Knaresborough d.		1140	1340	1540	1645	1744	1844	1944	2045	2203	...
York a.		1208	1408	1608	1710	1811	1912	2010	2113	...	...

	⚒	⑥	Ⓐ	⑥	Ⓐ	Ⓐ	⑥	Ⓐ	⚒	⑥	Ⓐ	⚒
York d.		...	...	0652	0652	...	...	...	0757	...	...	0845
Knaresborough d.		0647	0700	0721	0724	0742	0751	0756	0821	0851	0856	0909
Harrogate d.		0656	0711	0731	0740	0751	0800	0806	0830	0900	0905	0918
Leeds a.		0734	0748	0808	0817	0829	0838	0840	0908	0937	0937	0956

	⚒	⚒		⚒	⚒	⚒	⚒	⚒	⚒	⚒	Ⓐ	⚒	⚒	Ⓐ	⑥	Ⓐ	⑦	⑦	⑦	⑦	⑦	⑦	⑦	⑦	⑦	⑦
York d.	0910	...	and at the	...	1611	...	1654	1717	...	1811	...	1911	2011	2111	2157	2211		...	1218	1419	1618	1717	1817	1917	2018	2126
Knaresborough d.	0935	1005	same mins	1605	1635	1705	1718	1741	1805	1835	1905	1935	2035	2135	2221	2236		1142	1242	1443	1642	1742	1842	1942	2042	2150
Harrogate d.	0944	1014	past each	1614	1644	1714	1730	1750	1818	1844	1914	1944	2044	2145	2237	2247		1153	1253	1453	1653	1753	1853	1953	2053	2202
Leeds a.	1022	1052	hour until	1652	1722	1755	1807	1828	1855	1922	1952	2022	2122	2223	2314	2325		1230	1330	1530	1730	1830	1930	2030	2130	2240

r – 4 minutes earlier on ⑥.

☛ Leeds - Harrogate also at: 0954⑦, 2223⑦, 2229⚒, 2321⑥, 2322⑦, 2329Ⓐ.
Harrogate - Leeds also at: 0606⚒, 0630Ⓐ, 0728Ⓐ, 0744⑥, 0953⑦, 1053⑦, 2305⑦.

NT 2nd class — LEEDS - LANCASTER and CARLISLE — 174

km		Ⓐ	Ⓐ	⑥	⑥	⚒	⚒	⑦	⚒	Ⓐ	⑥	⚒		⚒	⑦	⚒	⚒	⑦	⑥	Ⓐ	⑦	⑦	⑥	Ⓐ		⚒
0	**Leeds** 176 d.	...	...	0555	0619	0819	0849	0900	0947	1019	1019	1049	...	1249	1315	1349	1449	1500	1649	1652	1723	1733	1749	1756	...	1919
17	Shipley d.	...	...	0608	0632	0832	0902	0914	1002	1032	1032	1102	...	1302	1329	1403	1502	1513	1702	1705	1736	1746	1802	1809	...	1932
27	Keighley 176 d.	...	...	0621	0642	0842	0912	0928	1012	1040	1040	1112	...	1312	1339	1413	1512	1523	1712	1715	1746	1756	1813	1823	...	1942
42	**Skipton** 176 d.	0543	...	0640	0656	0856	0926	0946	1026	1054	1054	1126	...	1326	1354	1427	1526	1537	1731	1732	1800	1811	1830	1840	...	1959
58	Hellifield d.	0557	...	0654	0708	0910	0940	0957	|	1108	1111	1137	...	1340	1408	1441	1537	1551	1745	1746	1814	1822	1846	1854	...	2014
66	Giggleswick d.	0609	...	0705	|	0920	|	|	|	1118	1121	|	...	|	|	1451	|	1602	1755	1756	1825	|	|	|	...	|
103	Carnforth 157 a.	0643	...	0739	|	0954	|	|	|	1152	1155	|	...	|	|	1525	|	1636	1829	1830	1857	|	|	|	...	|
113	**Lancaster** 157 a.	0653	...	0753	|	1004	|	|	|	1201	1204	|	...	|	|	1538	|	1647	1842	1843	1911	|	|	|	...	|
66	Settle d.	...	...	...	0715	...	0950	1006	1044	...	...	1146	...	1348	1417	...	1545	...	...	...	...	1830	1854	1903	...	2022
76	Horton in Ribblesdale d.	...	...	...	0724	...	0958	1015	|	...	...	1154	...	1357	1426	...	1553	...	...	...	...	1839	1903	1911	...	2031
84	Ribblehead d.	...	...	...	0732	...	1006	1023	|	...	...	1202	...	1405	1434	...	1601	...	...	...	...	1847	1911	1919	...	2041
99	Garsdale d.	...	...	...	0747	...	1021	1039	|	...	...	1217	...	1420	1450	...	1616	...	...	...	...	1902	1926	1934	...	...
115	Kirkby Stephen d.	...	0728	...	0759	...	1034	1052	1122	...	...	1230	...	1432	1503	...	1629	...	...	...	...	1915	1938	1947	...	...
132	Appleby d.	...	0740	...	0812	...	1047	1105	1136	...	...	1243	...	1445	1515	...	1641	...	...	...	...	1928	1951	1959	...	...
166	Armathwaite d.	...	0808	...	0839	...	1115	1133	|	...	...	1311	...	1512	1543	...	1709	...	...	...	...	1956	2018	2027	...	...
182	**Carlisle** a.	...	0824	...	0858	...	1136	1149	1217	...	...	1329	...	1532	1600	...	1728	...	...	...	...	2013	2037	2047	...	...

	⚒	Ⓐ	⑥	⑥	Ⓐ	⑥⑦	⑥	Ⓐ	Ⓐ	⑥	⚒	⑦	Ⓐ	⑥	Ⓐ	⑥	⚒	⑥	Ⓐ	⑦	⑦	Ⓐ	⑥	⚒	⑦	Ⓐ
Carlisle d.	...	0620	...	0752	0853	0924v	...	...	1151	1151	...	1351	1400	1426	1503	1548	...	1614	1618	1637	...	1755	1800	...	...	...
Armathwaite d.	...	0634	...	0806	0907	0938v	...	...	1205	1205	...	1405	1414	1440	|	|	...	1628	1632	1651	...	1809	1814	...	...	...
Appleby d.	...	0703	...	0834	0935	1006v	...	...	1233	1233	...	1433	1443	1509	1540	1625	...	1657	1701	1720	...	1837	1842	...	...	...
Kirkby Stephen d.	...	0717	...	0846	0948	1019v	...	...	1245	1245	...	1446	1455	1521	1553	1638	...	1709	1714	1733	...	1849	1854	...	...	...
Garsdale d.	...	▬	...	0900	1001	1033v	...	...	1259	1302	...	1500	1509	1535	|	|	...	1723	1728	1747	...	1903	1908	...	...	...
Ribblehead d.	0714	...	...	0914	1017	1048	...	...	1313	1316	...	1515	1523	1549	|	|	...	1737	1742	1802	...	1917	1923	...	...	2100
Horton in Ribblesdale d.	0721	...	...	0921	1023	1055	...	...	1320	1323	...	1522	1529	1556	|	|	...	1744	1749	1809	...	1924	1929	...	...	2106
Settle d.	0729	Ⓐ	...	0929	1031	1103	...	...	1328	1331	...	1530	1538	1605	1635	1715	...	1753	1758	1818	...	1932	1937	...	...	2114
Lancaster 157 d.	|	0715	0811	|	|	|	1056	1102	|	|	1315r	|	|	|	|	|	1653	|	|	|	1804	|	|	1924r	2015	|
Carnforth 157 d.	|	0724	0820	|	|	|	1105	1111	|	|	1323	|	|	|	|	|	1702	|	|	|	1812	|	|	1931	2024	|
Giggleswick d.	|	0757	0853	|	|	|	1138	1144	|	|	1356	|	|	|	|	|	1735	|	|	|	1847	|	|	2004	2058	|
Hellifield d.	0737	0808	0904	0936	1039	1112	1154	1155	1336	1339	1410	1538	1546	1612	|	|	1746	1806	1806	1825	1902	1939	1946	2017	2109	2123
Skipton 176 a.	0754	0825	0923	0953	1054	1129	1212	1211	1353	1356	1426	1555	1605	1627	1655	1736	1803	1823	1823	1840	1918	1954	2005	2035	2125	2140
Keighley 176 a.	0808	0837	0937	1007	1108	1139	1222	1222	1408	1408	1438	1606	1621	1638	1707	1750	*1829*	1837	1837	1851	1927	2016	2016	2046	2135	*2200*
Shipley a.	0818	0847	0949	1018	1118	1149	1232	1232	1418	1418	1449	1616	1631	1648	1720	1800	*1842*	1848	1848	1901	1937	2027	2027	2057	2146	*2213*
Leeds 176 a.	0837	0904	1008	1037	1136	1206	1249	1254	1437	1437	1507	1634	1651	1707	1740	1817	*1859*	1907	1907	1919	1956	2044	2044	2115	2203	*2232*

r – 5–6 minutes earlier on ⑥.

v – 3–4 minutes later on ⑥.

NT 2nd class — WEST YORKSHIRE local services — 176

BRADFORD Forster Square – **ILKLEY** *22 km*

Ⓐ: 0615, 0644, 0711, 0746, 0816 and every 30 minutes until 1616; then 1644, 1716, 1746, 1816, 1846, 1941, 2038, 2138, 2238, 2320.

⑥: 0615, 0716, 0816, 0846 and every 30 minutes until 1616; then 1644, 1716, 1746, 1816, 1846, 1941, 2038, 2138, 2238, 2320.

⑦: 1038, 1238, 1438, 1638, 1838, 2038, 2238.

ILKLEY – BRADFORD Forster Square Journey: ± 31 minutes

Ⓐ: 0617, 0650, 0722, 0750, 0824, 0854, 0921, 0951 and every 30 minutes until 1921; then 2005, 2040, 2140, 2240.

⑥: 0619, 0722, 0821, 0851 and every 30 minutes until 1921, then 2005, 2040, 2140, 2240.

⑦: 0953, 1153, 1353, 1553, 1753, 1953, 2153.

BRADFORD Forster Square – **SKIPTON** *30 km*

Ⓐ: 0610, 0640, 0715, 0742, 0811, 0841 and every 30 minutes until 1611; then 1640, 1711, 1738, 1811, 1841, 1908, 1936, 2006, 2105, 2205, 2309.

⑥: 0611, 0711, 0811, 0841 and every 30 minutes until 1841; then 1907, 1936, 2007, 2105, 2205, 2305.

⑦: 1048, 1248, 1448, 1648, 1848, 2048, 2248.

SKIPTON – BRADFORD Forster Square Journey: ± 38 minutes

Ⓐ: 0602, 0627, 0701, 0732, 0801, 0832, 0902 and every 30 minutes until 1602; then 1636, 1702, 1732, 1802, 1832, 1900, 1932, 1954, 2054, 2154.

⑥: 0602, 0701, 0732, 0801, 0832, 0902 and every 30 minutes until 1702; then 1730, 1802, 1832, 1900, 1932, 1954, 2054, 2154.

⑦: 0936, 1137, 1337, 1537, 1737, 1937, 2137.

HUDDERSFIELD – WAKEFIELD Westgate *No service on ⑦ 25 km*

⚒: 0532Ⓐ, 0641, 0732⑥, 0749Ⓐ, 0837, 0935, 1035 and hourly until 1635; then 1733, 1834, 1935, 2035, 2135.

WAKEFIELD Westgate – **HUDDERSFIELD** Journey: ± 33 minutes

⚒: 0629Ⓐ, 0729, 0829 and hourly until 2129; then 2242.

LEEDS – DONCASTER ❖ *48 km*

Ⓐ: 0619, 0727, 0819, 0919 and hourly until 1919; then 2021, 2128, 2239.

⑥: 0619, 0726, 0819, 0919 and hourly until 1819; then 1922, 2021, 2134, 2216.

⑦: 1009, 1209, 1409, 1609, 1809, 2020, 2109.

❖ – Stopping trains. For fast trains Leeds - Doncaster and v.v., see Tables **127** and **185**.

DONCASTER – LEEDS ❖ Journey: ± 48 minutes

Ⓐ: 0625, 0714, 0758, 0826, 0914, 1014, 1126, 1225, 1327, 1427, 1514, 1614, 1727, 1827, 1929, 2038, 2138, 2230.

⑥: 0625, 0714, 0829, 0914, 1014 and hourly until 1514; then 1628, 1727, 1829, 1927, 2045, 2128, 2249.

⑦: 0910, 1110, 1310, 1510, 1710, 1929, 2149.

LEEDS – ILKLEY *26 km*

Ⓐ: 0602, 0627, 0702, 0729, 0735, 0802, 0835, 0902, 0932 and every 30 minutes until 1702; then 1715, 1732, 1802, 1832, 1902, 1932, 2002, 2106, 2202, 2315.

⑥: 0602, 0702, 0802, 0832 and every 30 minutes until 2002; then 2102, 2202, 2315.

⑦: 0912, 1012 and hourly until 2212; then 2314.

ILKLEY – LEEDS Journey: ± 30 minutes

Ⓐ: 0609, 0640, 0710, 0740, 0805, 0817, 0840, 0910 and every 30 minutes until 1640; then 1714, 1740, 1804, 1810, 1840, 1910, 1940, 2021, 2121, 2221, 2321.

⑥: 0609, 0710, 0810, 0840 and every 30 minutes until 1940; then 2021, 2121, 2221, 2321.

⑦: 0930, 1021, 1121 and hourly until 2321.

LEEDS – SKIPTON *See also Table 174* *42 km*

Ⓐ: 0555, 0621, 0656, 0725, 0751, 0825, 0856, 0926 and every 30 mins until 1626; then 1645, 1720, 1751, 1826, 1850, 1925, 1956, 2026, 2055, 2126, 2156, 2226, 2256, 2318.

⑥: 0555, 0619, 0656, 0756, 0825, 0849, 0856, 0926 and every 30 mins (also 0947, 1049, 1749) until 1856; then 1925, 2006, 2026, 2055, 2126, 2156, 2226, 2256, 2318.

⑦: 0900, 1008, 1108 and hourly until 2208; then 2310.

SKIPTON – LEEDS Journey: ± 45 minutes

Ⓐ: 0548, 0618, 0642, 0708, 0724, 0747, 0815, 0843, 0918, 0948 and every 30 mins until 1618; then 1649, 1719, 1749, 1816, 1848, 1918, 1948, 2018, 2048, 2118, 2148, 2218.

⑥: 0548, 0648, 0747, 0756, 0818, 0848 and every 30 mins until 1618; then 1629, 1649, 1719, 1741, 1749, 1816, 1848, 1918, 1948, 2006, 2018, 2048, 2118, 2148, 2218.

⑦: 0835, 0915, 1015 and hourly until 1815; then 1923, 2015, 2115, 2215, 2315.

177 SHEFFIELD - HUDDERSFIELD and LEEDS

2nd class NT

km		⚒	Ⓐ	Ⓐ	⚒	⚒	Ⓐ	Ⓐ	⑥	⚒	⚒	⚒		⚒	⚒	⚒	⑥	Ⓐ	⚒	⚒	⑥	Ⓐ	⚒	⚒
0	**Sheffield** d.		0536	0550	0614	0636	0649	0704	0708	0736	0751	0808	and at	1636	1651	1708	1736	1736	1751	1808	1836	1836	1851	1908
26	Barnsley d.		0601	0611	0641	0701	0710	0731	0735	0801	0812	0835	the same	1703	1712	1735	1803	1803	1818	1835	1903	1909	1918	1935
59	**Huddersfield** a.		0650	|	|	0749	|	|	|	0849	|	|	mins past	1750	|	|	1850	1857	|	|	1951	1957	|	|
44	Wakefield Kirkgate d.		...	0629	0658	...	0729	0747	0751	...	0829	0852	each hour	...	1729	1752	...	...	1836	1852	...	...	1936	1952
70	**Leeds** a.		...	0650	0733	...	0750	0823	0827	...	0851	0927	until	...	1750	1827	...	...	1855	1927	...	...	1957	2027

	⚒	⚒	⚒	⚒	⚒	⚒	⑤⑥	①–④	⑤⑥	⚒	①–④		⑦	⑦	⑦		⑦	⑦	⑦	⑦	⑦	⑦		⑦	⑦
Sheffield d.	1938	1951	2008	2041	2108	2141	2208	2208	...	2241	2324	...		0839	0939	...	1039	1132	1139	1239	1332	1339	...	1439	1532
Barnsley d.	2007	2012	2035	2106	2135	2206	2234	2235	...	2306	2351	...		0909	1006	...	1109	1153	1206	1309	1353	1406	...	1509	1553
Huddersfield a.	2054	|	|	2154	|	2254	...	|	...	2355	|	...		|	1053	...	|	|	1254	|	|	1453	...	|	|
Wakefield Kirkgate d.	...	2029	2052	...	2152	...	...	2252	2252	...	0010	...		0929	...	...	1129	1211	...	1329	1411	...	...	1529	1611
Leeds a.	...	2050	2127	...	2227	...	...	2327	2327	...	...	...		1004	...	...	1207	1231	...	1404	1431	...	...	1604	1631

	⑦		⑦	⑦	⑦	⑦	⑦		⑦	⑦
Sheffield d.	1539	...	1639	1739	1839	1939	2039	...	2143	2239
Barnsley d.	1606	...	1709	1807	1909	2006	2109	...	2209	2309
Huddersfield a.	1655	...	|	1854	|	2053	|	...	...	|
Wakefield Kirkgate d.	...	...	1729	...	1929	...	2129	...	...	2329
Leeds a.	...	...	1804	...	2004	...	2204	...	...	0004

	⚒	⑥	Ⓐ	Ⓐ	⚒	⚒	⚒	⚒	Ⓐ	⑥
Leeds d.		...	...	0605	...	0638	0716	...	0723	0723
Wakefield Kirkgate d.		...	0610	0622	...	0710	0732	...	0755	0755
Huddersfield d.		...	|	|	0610	|	|	0710	|	|
Barnsley d.		0627	0627	0646	0658	0728	0748	0758	0814	0817
Sheffield a.		0657	0657	0712	0729	0759	0815	0828	0845	0847

	⚒	⚒	⚒	⚒	⚒		⚒	⚒	⚒	Ⓐ	⑥	Ⓐ	⚒	⚒	⚒	⚒	⚒	⚒	⚒	⚒	⚒		⚒	Ⓐ
Leeds d.	0816	...	0834	0916	...	and at	...	1734	1816	...	...	...	1834	1916	...	1934	2016	...	2034	...	2134	...	...	2234
Wakefield Kirkgate d.	0832	...	0903	0932	...	the same	...	1803	1832	...	...	...	1903	1932	...	2003	2033	...	2103	...	2203	...	...	2303
Huddersfield d.	|	0810	|	|	0913	mins past	1713	|	|	1756	1813	1822	|	|	1918	|	|	2018	|	2118	|	...	2218	|
Barnsley d.	0848	0858	0926	0948	1001	each hour	1801	1826	1848	1858	1901	1916	1926	1948	2006	2026	2048	2106	2126	2206	2226	...	2306	2326
Sheffield a.	0915	0930	0957	1015	1029	until	1829	1857	1915	1928	1929	1944	1957	2015	2035	2057	2115	2135	2157	2235	2257	...	2335	2357

	⑦	⑦	⑦	⑦	⑦	⑦	⑦		⑦	⑦	⑦		⑦	⑦		⑦		⑦	⑦		⑦	⑦		⑦	⑦
Leeds d.		0830	...	1014	1017	1114	...	...	1217	1314	...	...	1417	...	...	1617	...	...	1817	...	...	2017	...	...	2217
Wakefield Kirkgate d.		0900	...	1030	1046	1130	...	...	1246	1330	...	...	1446	...	...	1646	...	...	1846	...	...	2046	...	...	2246
Huddersfield d.		|	0919	|	|	|	1119	...	|	|	1319	...	|	1519	...	|	...	1719	|	...	1919	|	...	...	|
Barnsley d.		0921	1012	1049	1112	1149	1212	...	1312	1349	1412	...	1512	1612	...	1712	...	1812	1912	...	2012	2112	...	2221	2312
Sheffield a.		0951	1043	1115	1143	1215	1243	...	1343	1415	1443	...	1543	1643	...	1743	...	1847	1943	...	2046	2143	...	2251	2343

☛ For trains Sheffield - Leeds and v.v. via Wakefield Westgate, see Table **127**.

☛ Also: **Sheffield - Barnsley** at 0516 ⚒, 0548 ⑥; **Barnsley - Sheffield** at 0518 ⚒, 0553 ⚒.

178 HULL - DONCASTER - SHEFFIELD

2nd class NT, HT

km		⚒	⚒	Ⓐ	⚒	⑥	Ⓐ	Ⓐ	⑥	⑥	Ⓐ	⚒	⚒	⑥	Ⓐ	⚒	⚒	Ⓐ	⚒	⑥	⚒	⚒	⑥	Ⓐ	⚒	⚒
				L		L	L			L	L			L	L			L		L			L	L		
0	**Hull 181** d.		0520	0625	0640	0650	0700	0804	0808	0802	0812	0856	0956	1005	1012	1057	1155	1245	1257	1305	1357	1457	1506	1518	1557	1654
¶	Selby **181** d.		|	0700	|	0723	0732	|	|	0837	0845	|	|	1041	1047	|	|	1320	|	1340	|	|	1542	1557	|	|
38	Goole d.		0547	|	0715	|	|	0830	0834	|	|	0922	1022	|	|	1123	1222	|	1323	|	1423	1523	|	|	1623	1722
66	Doncaster a.		0616	0716	0745	0740	0753	0856	0857	0900	0903	0947	1046	1101	1104	1146	1246	1337	1346	1403	1446	1547	1601	1615	1646	1747
66	Doncaster **127 194** d.		0625	0735	0746	0752	0817	0857	0859	0924	0924	0948	1048	1124	1127	1148	1248	...	1348	1424	1448	1548	1624	1624	1647	1748
96	**Sheffield 127 194** a.		0703z	0800	0831	0820	0856	0927	0927	1004	1004	1018	1117	1205	1205	1218	1317	...	1417	1504	1518	1617	1704	1704	1717	1818

	Ⓐ	⚒	⑥	⚒	Ⓐ	⚒	⚒	⑥	Ⓐ	⑦	⑦	⑦	⑦	⑦	⑦	⑦	⑦	⑦	⑦	⑦	⑦	⑦	⑦	⑦	⑦	⑦
	L		L		L							L				L			L		L		L			
Hull 181 d.	1706	1755	1812	1853	1918	2003	2056r	2222	2220d		0842	1012	1041	1241	1341	1410	1441	1541	1621	1641	1730	1741	1830	1838	2030	2115
Selby **181** d.	1743	1826	1847	|	1953	|	|	|	|		|	1047	|	|	|	1445	|	|	1656	|	1805	|	1905	|	|	|
Goole d.	|	|	|	1919	|	2036	2122r	2248	2251		0915	|	1109	1309	1409	|	1509	1609	|	1709	|	1809	|	1906	2058	2148
Doncaster a.	1800	1845	1904	1945	2010	2105	2146	2318	2321		0938	1103	1132	1332	1432	1505	1532	1632	1714	1731	1823	1833	1921	1935	2121	2217
Doncaster **127 194** d.	1826	1847	1925	1949	2042	2107	2148	2319	2321		0939	1113	1133	1333	1433	1513	1533	1633	...	1732	...	1834	...	1937	2123	2220
Sheffield 127 194 a.	1905	1919r	2005	2018	2118	2145	2218	2358	0001		1009	1152	1203	1403	1504	1551	1603	1703	...	1802	...	1903	...	2007	2156	2259

	⚒	⚒	⚒	⚒	Ⓐ	⚒	⚒	⚒	⑥	Ⓐ	⚒	⚒	⚒	⚒	Ⓐ	⚒	⑥	⚒	⚒	Ⓐ	Ⓐ	⑥	Ⓐ	⑥	Ⓐ	Ⓐ
					L				L	L			L		L		L			L				L	L	
Sheffield 127 194 d.		0529	0618	0741	0811	0841	0941	1041	1054	1054	1141	1241	1254	1341	1425	1441	1454	1540	1641	1657	1741	1741	1757	1757	1824	1841
Doncaster **127 194** a.		0606	0657	0820	0840	0910	1012	1109	1116	1115	1211	1311	1322r	1414r	1504	1511	1515	1612	1711	1735	1813	1810	1835	1837	1854	1911
Doncaster d.		0614	0728	0822	0905	0916	1016v	1117	1124	1135	1214	1317z	1327	1417	1512	1514	1525	1618r	1714	1742	1816	1824	1841	1848	1905	1914
Goole d.		0639	0753	0842	|	0939	1035v	1137	|	|	1235	1337	|	1436	|	1533z	|	1636	1735	|	1836	1844	1906	|	|	1934
Selby **181** a.		|	|	|	0921	|	|	|	1139	1151	|	|	1344	|	1527	|	1540	|	|	1759	|	|	|	1907	1920	|
Hull 181 a.		0722	0834	0913	1004	1010	1106v	1209	1220	1232	1307	1410	1425r	1507v	1610	1604z	1620	1708	1806z	1840	1909	1915	1947	1947	2000	2007

	⑥	⚒	⚒	⑥	⚒	Ⓐ	⑥	Ⓐ	⑦	⑦	⑦	⑦	⑦	⑦	⑦	⑦	⑦	⑦	⑦	⑦	⑦	⑦	⑦	⑦	⑦	⑦
			L	L		L						L					L				L		L	L		
Sheffield 127 194 d.	1841	1944	1954	2051	2114	...	2226	2221		0845	1026	1154	1228	1324	1428	1528	...	1628	1728	1828	1854	2003	2008	2112	2124	2226
Doncaster **127 194** a.	1910	2011	2020r	2113	2155	...	2304	2304		0922	1051	1216	1254	1401	1456	1554	...	1654	1757	1854	1916	2030	2033	2138	2202	2303
Doncaster d.	1913	2014	2031r	2120	2156	2212	2305	2325		0926	1053	1224	1255	1403	1459	1556	1621	1655	1803	1855	1926	2030	2058	2154	2204	2307
Goole d.	|	2036r	|	|	2222	|	2333	2353		0947	1112	|	1315	1425	1519	1617	|	1715	1822	1921	|	2049	|	|	2223	2328
Selby **181** a.	1934	|	2046r	2135	|	2229	...	...		|	|	1241	|	|	|	|	1641	|	|	|	1940	|	2115	2208	|	|
Hull 181 a.	2011	2106	2128	2215	2258	2313	...	...		1021	1145	1321	1348	1459	1557	1650	1721	1748	1857	1954	2022	2123	2156	2250	2256	0002

L – 🚃12 Hull - London and v.v. (see Table **185**).

d – 2225 on ⑤.

r – 3–5 minutes earlier on ⑥.

v – 5–6 minutes later on ⑥.

z – 3–4 minutes later on ⑥.

¶ – Selby - Doncaster: *30 km.*

179 HULL - BRIDLINGTON - SCARBOROUGH

2nd class NT

km		⚒	⚒	⚒	⚒	⚒	⚒	⚒	⚒	⚒	⚒	⚒	⚒	⚒	⚒	⚒	⚒	⚒	⚒	⚒	⚒	⚒	⑦	⑦	⑦	⑦	⑦
																					A						
0	**Hull** d.		0624	0654	0752	0814	0915	0944	1044	1114	1214	1314	1344	1444	1520	1600	1652	1730	1800	1914	2010	2148		1200	1400	1657	1900
13	Beverley d.		0637	0707	0805	0827	0928	0957	1057	1127	1227	1327	1357	1457	1533	1613	1705	1743	1813	1927	2023	2201		1213	1413	1710	1913
31	Driffield d.		0649	0724	0822r	0841	0942	1011	1111	1139	1239	1339	1411	1511	1545	1630	1720	1800	1828	1941	2040	2215		1227	1427	1724	1927
50	**Bridlington** a.		0704	0739	0839r	0856	1001	1026	1128	1152	1254	1352	1428	1526	1602	1645	1737	1815	1845	1957	2057	2232		1244	1444	1741	1944
50	**Bridlington** d.		...	0749	...	0900	...	1036	...	1204	...	1404	...	1530	...	1654	...	1818	...	1959	...	...		...	...	...	...
71	Filey d.		...	0811	...	0922	...	1058	...	1226	...	1426	...	1552	...	1716	...	1840	...	2021	...	...		...	...	...	...
87	**Scarborough** a.		...	0829	...	0940	...	1118	...	1243	...	1445	...	1610	...	1735	...	1857	...	2039	...	...		...	...	...	...

	⚒	⚒	⚒	⚒	⚒	⚒	⚒	⚒	⚒	⚒	⚒	⚒	⚒	⚒	⚒	⚒	⚒	⚒	⚒	⚒	⚒	⚒	⑦	⑦	⑦	⑦	⑦
Scarborough d.		...	0653	...	...	0903	1000	...	1128	...	...	1328	...	1454	...	1618	...	1738	...	2000	...	...		...	...	...	...
Filey d.		...	0708	...	...	0917	1014	...	1142	...	...	1342	...	1508	...	1632	...	1752	...	2014	...	...		...	...	...	...
Bridlington a.		...	0730	...	...	0939	1036	...	1204	...	...	1404	...	1530	...	1653	...	1814	...	2036	...	...		...	...	...	...
Bridlington d.		0646	0738	0808	0906	0942	1042	1112	1212	1312	1342	1412	1442	1540	1614	1706	1746	1825	1910	2038	2135	2240		1253	1453	1750	2015
Driffield d.		0701	0753	0823	0921	0957	1057	1125	1225	1325	1357	1425	1457	1555	1629	1720	1801	1840	1925	2053	2150	2255		1308	1508	1805	2030
Beverley d.		0715	0809	0837	0937	1011	1111	1137	1237	1337	1411	1437	1511	1609	1643	1734	1817	1854	1939	2107	2204	2309		1322	1522	1819	2044
Hull a.		0731	0825	0853	0953	1026	1126	1153	1254	1353	1426	1453	1529	1624	1658	1749	1833	1912	1954	2123	2219	2325		1337	1537	1834	2059

A – Runs 4 minutes later on ⑥.

r – 3 minutes earlier on ⑥.

☛ Additional trains **Hull - Bridlington** on ⚒ at 0714, 1014, 1144, 1244, 1414.
Additional trains **Bridlington - Hull** on ⚒ at 0714, 1012, 1142, 1242, 1512.

HULL - YORK and LEEDS — 181

TP, NT

km			⚒	⚒	⑥	⚒	Ⓐ	⚒	⑥	⚒	⚒	⚒	⑥	Ⓐ	⚒	Ⓐ	⑥	⚒	⚒	Ⓐ	⚒	⚒	⚒	⑥	Ⓐ	⚒
0	**Hull** 178 d.	⚒	0600	0635	0657	*0700*c	0707	0733	*0802*	0837	0902	0937	1005	1012	1037	1105	1108	1137	1237	*1245*	1312	1337	1437	1451	1506	1537
50	Selby 178 d.		0638	0706	0740	0743	0748	0808	0843	0908	0938	1008	1040	1046	1108	1139	1140	1208	1308	1343	1354	1408	1508	1522	1538	1608
84	**York** a.		*0720*	|	0814	|	0822	|	|	*0948*z	1007p	|	*1116*	*1120*	|	1210	1210	*1315*q	|	|	1427	|	|	1555	1606	|
83	**Leeds** a.		0705	0735	...	0819	...	0837	0919	0935	*1019**	1037	...	...	1133	*1219**	...	1233	1333	1419	...	1434	1533	*1619**	*1619**	1636

	⚒	⚒	⚒	⚒	⚒	⑥	⚒	Ⓐ	⚒	⚒			⑦	⑦	⑦	⑦	⑦	⑦	⑦		⑦	⑦	⑦	⑦	⑦	⑦
Hull 178 d.	1610	1637	1700	1718	1802	1846	1859	1910	1955	2133	...	⑦ ▲	0854	0905	1100	1154	1250	1428	1450	...	1650	1723	1810	1904	2022	2100
Selby 178 d.	1647	1708	1731	1806	1833	1922	1930	1947	2026	2207	...		0925	0936	1131	1225	1321	1504	1521	...	1721	1754	1841	1935	2053	2131
York a.	1713	|	|	1836	|	1950	|	2015	*2100*	*2253*j	...		0954	|	|	1256	|	1530	|	...	|	1823	|	|	2118	|
Leeds a.	...	1735	1759	...	1858	...	1956	...	2059	2235	...		...	1003	1201	...	1349	...	1549	...	1749	...	1912	1959	...	2159

		⚒	⚒	⚒	Ⓐ	⚒	⚒	⚒	⚒	⑥	Ⓐ	⚒	⚒	⑥	Ⓐ	⚒	Ⓐ	⑥	⚒	⚒	⚒	⑥	Ⓐ	⑥	Ⓐ	Ⓐ
Leeds d.	⚒	0723	...	0838	...	0938	...	1038	1138	...	...	1238	1338	...	...	1438	...	...	1538	...	1638	...	...	1738	*1715*	1738
York d.		|	0730	*0834*j	*0843*	|	0952	*1022*r	|	1149	1153	*1218*	|	1338	1345	|	1459	1505	|	1612	|	1718	1727	|	|	|
Selby 178 d.		0743	0749	0859	0922	0959	1012	1059	1159	1209	1218	1259	1359	1404	1409	1459	1519	1524	1559	1639	1659	1737	1746	1800	1800	1807
Hull 178 a.		0821	0845	0931	1004	1034	1056	1134	1236	1254	1302	1334	1434	1445	1448	1534	1558	1603	1634	1727	1736	1821	1829	1837	1840	1845

	Ⓐ	⚒	⚒	⚒	⑥	⚒	Ⓐ	⚒			⑦	⑦		⑦	⑦	⑦		⑦	⑦	⑦	⑦	⑦	⑦		⑦	⑦
Leeds d.	1749	...	1838	1938	...	2105	...	2222	...	⑦ ▲	1025	...	...	1210	...	1410	...	...	1610	1654	1754	...	1956	...	...	2217
York d.	|	1813	|	*1923*	2017	|	2203	*2145*j	...		|	1040	...	|	1323	|	...	1543	|	|	|	1910	|	...	2141	|
Selby 178 d.	1825	1842	1902	2002	2036	2128	2222	2244	...		1048	1059	...	1232	1342	1433	...	1602	1634	1714	1816	1929	2019	...	2200	2239
Hull 178 a.	...	1932r	1937	2037	2122	2204	2308	2321	...		1124	1138	...	1311	1421	1512	...	1641	1711	1753	1853	2008	2058	...	2239	2316

c – *0650* on ⑥.
j – ⑥ only.
p – 1010 on ⑥.
q – 1323 on ⑥.
r – 4–5 minutes earlier on ⑥.
z – *0941* on ⑥.
* – Change at Selby.
▲ – Services on ⑦ are subject to alteration from Feb. 3.

LINCOLN - DONCASTER and SHEFFIELD — 182

NT, EM 2nd class

km			⚒	⚒	⚒	⚒	⑥	Ⓐ S	⚒	⚒	⚒	⚒	⚒	Ⓐ P	⚒	⑥ P	⚒	⑥	⚒	⚒	⚒	⚒	⚒	Ⓐ S	⑥	Ⓐ S	⚒
0	**Lincoln** d.	⚒	...	...	0704	0827	0915	0918	0927	1027	1127	1155	1227	1318	1327	1409	1427	1510	1527	1627	1722	...	1824	1829	1930	1933	1943
26	Gainsborough ‡ d.		...	...	0726	0849	0937	0940	0949	1049	1149	1217	1249	1340	1349	1431	1449	1532	1549	1649	1744	...	1846	1857	1952	1954	2005
60	**Doncaster** a.		...	...	|	|	1006	1009	|	|	|	1247	|	1417	|	1501	|	1601	|	|	|	...	|	1925	2021	2022	|
40	Retford d.		...	0703	0740	0903	...	...	1003	1103	1203	...	1303	...	1403	...	1503	...	1603	1703	1758	1810	1904	...	...	...	2019
52	Worksop d.		0630	0716	0752	0915	...	...	1015	1115	1215	...	1315	...	1415	...	1515	...	1615	1715	1810	1821	1916	...	...	...	2031
78	**Sheffield** a.		0702	0747	0826	0948	...	...	1048	1148	1248	...	1348	...	1448	...	1548	...	1648	1748	1835	1854	1954	...	...	...	2105

	⚒	⚒ ✣	⚒	⚒			⑦	⑦	⑦	⑦	⑦	⑦
Lincoln d.	2027	2127	...	...	...	⑦	...	1515	1735	1935	2115	...
Gainsborough ‡ d.	2049	2149	...	...	...		...	1537	1757	1957	2137	...
Doncaster a.	|	|	...	...	...		...	|	|	|	|	...
Retford d.	2103	2203	2245	...	...		1450	1551	1811	2011	2151	2224
Worksop d.	2115	2215	2258	2328	...		1501	1603	1823	2023	2203	2235
Sheffield a.	2143	2250	2331	0003	...		1533	1635	1855	2056	2234	2307

		⚒	⚒	⚒	⚒	⚒	⚒	⚒	⚒	⚒	⚒
Sheffield d.	⚒	0539	0551	0644	0730	0844	0944	...	1044	1144	...
Worksop d.		0601	0623	0714	0759	0913	1013	...	1113	1213	...
Retford d.		0610	0638	0724	0809	0923	1023	...	1123	1223	...
Doncaster d.		|	...	|	|	|	|	1022r	|	|	1304
Gainsborough ‡ d.		0625	...	0738	0824	0938	1038	1052	1138	1238	1330
Lincoln a.		0653	...	0806	0852	1006	1106	1118	1205	1305	1356

	⚒	⚒	Ⓐ S	⑥ P	Ⓐ	⑥	⚒	⑥ S	⚒	⚒	⚒	⚒	Ⓐ	⚒	⚒	⚒	⚒	⚒			⑦	⑦	⑦		⑦	⑦	⑦
Sheffield d.	1244	1344	...	...	1444	1444	1544	...	1644	1718	1744	1844	...	1948	...	2044	2144	2244	...	⑦	1348	1401	1600	...	1801	1924	2106
Worksop d.	1313	1413	...	...	1513	1513	1613	...	1713	1747	1813	1914	...	2017	...	2121	2215	2318	...		1408	1429	1629	...	1829	1952	2134
Retford d.	1323	1423	...	...	1523	1523	1623	...	1723	1801	1823	1924	...	2027	...	...	2230	...	...		1418	1444	1639	...	1839	2002	2149
Doncaster d.	|	|	1425	1507	|	|	|	1627	|	...	|	|	1934	|	2033	...	...	...	...		|	...	|	...	|	|	...
Gainsborough ‡ d.	1339	1438	1454	1533	1538	1545	1638	1656	1738	...	1838	1939	2000	2042	2100	...	...	...	...		1432	...	1653	...	1853	2016	...
Lincoln a.	1406	1506	1518	1557	1605	1609	1706	1720	1806	...	1907	2006	2025	2110	2126	...	...	...	...		1500	...	1720	...	1921	2044	...

P – From / to Peterborough.
S – From / to Sleaford.
r – 1019 on ⑥.
‡ – Gainsborough Lea Rd.
✣ – Runs 3–4 minutes earlier on ⑥.
Retford - Sheffield: on ⑥ also at 1237, 1621, 1933.
Sheffield - Retford: on ⑥ also at 0802, 1201, 1530.

PETERBOROUGH - LINCOLN — 183

EM 2nd class — No service on ⑦

km		⚒	⚒	⚒	⚒	Ⓐ	⚒	⚒	Ⓐ	⚒	Ⓐ	⑥	Ⓐ	⑥	Ⓐ	⚒	⑥	Ⓐ	⑥	⚒	Ⓐ	⚒	Ⓐ	⑥	⚒
0	**Peterborough** d.	...	0628	...	0730	...	0840	0934	1043	1150	1241	1243	1348	1509	1509	1624	...	...	...	1731	...	1834	...	...	2027
27	Spalding d.	...	0657	...	0758	...	0902	0957	1105	1212	1303	1305	1410	1531	1532	1647	...	...	...	1801r	...	1902v	...	...	2054
57	Sleaford d.	0655	...	0745	...	0846	0931	1026	1133	1244	1332	1337	1440	1607	1610	1716	1733	1755	1811	...	1901	...	2011	2020	...
91	**Lincoln** a.	0726	...	0817	...	0916	1004	1058	1206	1316	1402	1408	1511	1640	1645	1750	1803	1826	1844	...	1931	...	2041	2052	...
	Doncaster **182** a.	...	...	...	...	1009	...	...	...	1417a	...	1501	...	...	...	...	...	1925	...	...	2022	...	...	...	...

	⚒	⚒	⚒	⚒	Ⓐ	⑥	Ⓐ	⚒	Ⓐ	⑥	Ⓐ		⚒	Ⓐ	⑥	Ⓐ	⑥	Ⓐ	⚒	⑥	Ⓐ	⚒	⚒	⚒	Ⓐ
Doncaster **182** d.	...	...	...	...	...	...	...	...	...	...	...	...	...	1425	1507	...	...	...	...	1627	...	...	...	...	...
Lincoln d.	...	0709	...	0804	0911	1015	1017	1112	1214	1328	1331	...	1450	1520	1559	1602	1655	1713	...	1722	1815	...	1930	...	2040
Sleaford d.	...	0740	...	0838	0943	1051	1055	1143	1246	1359	1403	...	1522	1553	1631	1634	1728	1747	...	1755	1848	...	2008r	...	2114
Spalding d.	0701	...	0803	0903	1008	1116	1120	1208	1311	1424	1428	...	1546	...	1656	1658	...	...	1802	...	...	1953	...	2058	...
Peterborough a.	0726	...	0828	0929	1037	1141	1145	1236	1338	1453	1453	...	1613	...	1721	1724	...	...	1829	...	...	2021	...	2126r	...

N – To Nottingham.
a – Ⓐ only.
r – 3–4 minutes earlier on ⑥.
v – 1905 on ⑥.

LONDON - PETERBOROUGH stopping trains — 184

FC

km			Ⓐ	Ⓐ		Ⓐ	Ⓐ	Ⓐ	✣	Ⓐ	Ⓐ	Ⓐ	Ⓐ	Ⓐ	Ⓐ	Ⓐ	Ⓐ	Ⓐ	Ⓐ	Ⓐ	Ⓐ	Ⓐ
0	**London** Kings Cross 185 d.	Ⓐ	0036	0136	...	0521	0622	0636	and at the	1522	1536	1640	1707	1723	1737	1807	1837	1907	1923	2007	2022	2107
44	Stevenage 185 d.		0118	0218	...	0557	0646	0712	same minutes	1546	1612	|	|	1750	1800	|	|	|	1946	|	2046	|
95	Huntingdon a.		0202s	0259s	...	0634	0720	0747	past each	1620	1647	1722	1750	1825	1830	1850	1920	1949	2021	2049	2120	2151
123	**Peterborough** 185 a.		0224	0321	...	0654	0738	0809	hour until	1637	1704	1741	1810	1855	1858	1912	1941	2005	2037	2105	2136	2208

	Ⓐ	Ⓐ	Ⓐ			⑥	⑥	⑥		⑥	⑥	⑥		⑥	⑥	⑥	⑥	⑥	⑥			⑦
London Kings Cross 185 d.	2122	2222	2322	...	⑥	0001	0036	0136	...	0521	0622	0636	and at the	2122	2136	2222	2236	2312	2350	...	⑦	0004
Stevenage 185 d.	2146	2246	2346	...		|	0112	0218	...	0557	0646	0712	same minutes	2146	2212	2246	2312	2346	|	...		0036
Huntingdon a.	2220	2326	0026	...		0100s	0155s	0259s	...	0634	0720	0747	past each	2220	2247	2320	2347	0020	0100s	...		*0150*j
Peterborough 185 a.	2236	2342	0042	...		0120	0220	0321	...	0655	0736	0805	hour until	2236	2305	2343	0014	0042	0119	...		*0212*j

	⑦		⑦		⑦		⑦		⑦
London Kings Cross 185 d.	0036	...	0922	and	2122	...	2222	...	2325
Stevenage 185 d.	|	...	0946	hourly	2146	...	2246	...	2349
Huntingdon a.	*0329**	...	1020	until	2220	...	2327	...	0033
Peterborough 185 a.	*0404**	...	1036		2236	...	2349	...	0055

		Ⓐ		Ⓐ		Ⓐ	Ⓐ	Ⓐ	Ⓐ
Peterborough 185 d.	Ⓐ	0358	...	0512	...	0600	0620	0632	0654
Huntingdon d.		0412	...	0526	...	0615	0635	0647	0713
Stevenage 185 d.		0453	...	0603	...	0652	|	0723	|
London Kings Cross 185 a.		0545	...	0630	...	0723	0727	0750	0800

	Ⓐ	Ⓐ	Ⓐ	Ⓐ	Ⓐ	Ⓐ	Ⓐ	Ⓐ	Ⓐ	✣	Ⓐ	Ⓐ	Ⓐ		Ⓐ		Ⓐ		Ⓐ			⑥
Peterborough 185 d.	0714	0726	0734	0759	0816	0845	0915	0944	1015	and at the	1845	1915	1941	...	2018	...	2128	...	2225	...	⑥	0358
Huntingdon d.	0732	0740	0750	0813	0831	0900	0930	0959	1033	same minutes	1859	1933	1959	...	2033	...	2142	...	2239	...		0412
Stevenage 185 d.	|	|	0827	|	0905	0935	0956	1033	1109	past each	1933	2009	2033	...	2109	...	2217	...	2317	...		0453
London Kings Cross 185 a.	0819	0831	0858	0901	0932	1002	1020	1100	1149	hour until	2003	2049	2100	...	2148	...	2256	...	0001	...		0545

	⑥	⑥	⑥	✣	⑥	⑥	⑥	⑥	⑥			⑦	⑦		⑦		⑦		⑦		⑦
Peterborough 185 d.	0514	0545	0618	and at the	2045	2115	2145	2218	2242	...	⑦	*0815*j	0858	...	0945		2045	...	2145	...	2248
Huntingdon d.	0528	0559	0633	same minutes	2059	2133	2159	2233	2256	...		*0829*j	0912	...	0959	and	2059	...	2159	...	2259
Stevenage 185 d.	0609	0633	0709	past each	2133	2209	2233	2309	2330	...		0916	0947	...	1033	hourly	2133	...	2233	...	2333
London Kings Cross 185 a.	0649	0702	0749	hour until	2202	2249	2316	2353	0007	...		0944	1016	...	1102	until	2202	...	2309	...	0013

j – Change at Hitchin.
s – Stops to set down only.
* – By 🚌. Change at Welwyn Garden City.
✣ – Timings may vary by a few minutes on some journeys.

185 LONDON - HULL, LEEDS and YORK GR

Services on ⑥ are subject to alteration from March 29. Services on ⑦ are subject to alteration from February 3.

km			Ⓐ ✕	Ⓐ ✕	Ⓐ ✕	Ⓐ ✕	Ⓐ ✕	Ⓐ ✕	Ⓐ ✕	Ⓐ ✕	Ⓐ ✕	Ⓐ ✕	Ⓐ ✕	Ⓐ ✕	Ⓐ ✕	Ⓐ ✕	Ⓐ ✕	Ⓐ ✕	Ⓐ ✕	Ⓐ ✕	Ⓐ ✕	Ⓐ ✕ A	Ⓐ 🍷	Ⓐ ✕
0	**London Kings Cross 184** d.	Ⓐ	0600	0615	0635	0700	0710	0720	0730	0735	0800	0810	0830	0835	0900	0910	0930	0935	0948	1000	1010	1030	1035	1100
44	Stevenage 184 d.		0619	0634	|	0719	0729	0744u	0750	0756	|	|	0849	0855	|	|	0949	0954	1009u	|	|	*1012*	|	*1046*
123	Peterborough 184 208 d.		0651	0706	0721	0751	0801	|	0821	|	0846	0859	0921	0927	0946	0956	1021	1027	|	1045	1056	1117	1123	1146
170	Grantham 208 d.		0710	0725	0740	|	|	0831	0845	|	|	|	|	0948	|	|	|	1046	1054	|	1115	|	1142	|
193	Newark North Gate d.		0722	0737	|	|	0828	|	|	|	|	|	0948	|	|	|	1048	|	|	|	1127	|	1155	|
223	Retford d.		0737	0752	|	|	|	0852	|	|	|	|	|	1011	|	|	|	|	1117	|	1142	|	|	|
251	**Doncaster 127 176 178** a.		0751	0807	0812	|	0858	0904	0916	|	|	|	|	1026	1033	|	1112	1117	1132	|	1157	|	1218	|
330	**Hull 178** a.		|	|	*0913*	|	|	1004	*1049*	|	|	|	|	|	*1153*	|	*1209*	|	1232	|	*1306*	|	*1352*	|
283	Wakefield Westgate 127 a.		0810	|	0836	|	0916	...	|	0925	|	1001	|	1051	|	1056	|	1136	...	|	1215	|	1239	|
299	**Leeds 127 176** a.		0832	|	0852	|	0935	...	|	0946	|	1021	|	1109	|	1118	|	1155	...	|	1235	|	1302	|
303	**York 127** a.		...	0831	*0848*d	0855	...	...	0939	...	0951	...	1033	...	1101	...	1137	...	...	1153	...	1226	...	1251
	Newcastle 186 a.		...	0938	*1001*d	1002	...	...	1044	...	1058	...	1141	...	1203	...	1250	...	...	1255	...	1322	...	1350
	Edinburgh 186 a.		...	1114	...	1130	...	...	...	...	1230	...	...	...	1338	...	...	...	...	1424	...	1454	...	1520
	Glasgow Central 186 a.		...	*1221z*	...	1245	...	...	...	...	*1336z*	...	...	...	1445	...	...	...	...	*1536z*	...	*1606z*	...	1625

	Ⓐ 🍷	Ⓐ ✕	Ⓐ ✕	Ⓐ ✕	Ⓐ ✕ N	Ⓐ ✕	Ⓐ ✕	Ⓐ ✕	Ⓐ ✕	Ⓐ ✕	Ⓐ ✕	Ⓐ ✕	Ⓐ ✕	Ⓐ ✕ A	Ⓐ ✕	Ⓐ 🍷	Ⓐ 🍷	Ⓐ ✕	Ⓐ ✕	Ⓐ ✕	Ⓐ 🍷	Ⓐ ✕ A	Ⓐ ✕	Ⓐ 🍷
London Kings Cross 184 d.	1110	1130	1135	1148	1200	1210	1230	1235	1300	1310	1330	1333	1335	1400	1410	1430	1435	1500	1510	1530	1535	1600	1605	1610
Stevenage 184 d.	|	1150	1154	|	|	1229	|	1258	|	|	|	|	*1312*	|	*1346*	*1412*	1454	|	*1446*	*1512*	1554	|	|	|
Peterborough 184 208 d.	1157	1221	1227	|	1247	1301	1317	|	1346	1358	|	|	1425	|	1456	1516	|	|	1557	1617	1626	|	|	1656
Grantham 208 d.	1215	|	1246	1254	|	1320	|	1345	|	1417	|	1435	1444	|	1515	|	|	|	1618	|	1645	|	1707	1715
Newark North Gate d.	1227	1250	1258	|	|	|	|	|	|	1429	|	|	1501	|	1527	|	|	|	1629	|	|	|	|	1727
Retford d.	|	|	|	1316	|	1342	|	|	|	|	1448	1456	|	|	|	|	|	|	1645	|	|	|	1728	|
Doncaster 127 176 178 a.	1259	1314	|	1329	|	1357	1406	1420	1433	1453	1502	1511	1525	1529	1555	|	1609	|	1700	1706	1719	1729	1741	|
Hull 178 a.	*1408*	|	|	1425	|	|	*1507*	|	*1551*	|	*1604*	1610	|	*1649*	|	|	*1708*	|	|	*1806*	|	|	1840	|
Wakefield Westgate 127 a.	1317	|	1337	...	|	1414	|	1439	|	1514	*1542*	...	1551	|	1613	|	1630	|	1718	|	1736	|	...	1804
Leeds 127 176 a.	1341	|	1355	...	|	1435	|	1501	|	1535	*1600*	...	1609	|	1635	|	1648	|	1736	|	1756	|	...	1823
York 127 a.	...	1339	...	...	1400	...	1434	...	1458	...	1526	...	...	1553	...	1621	*1640*d	1645	...	1734	...	1754	...	...
Newcastle 186 a.	...	1447	...	...	1458	...	1547	...	1557	...	1631	...	...	1653	...	1726	*1752*d	1739	...	1845	...	1857	...	...
Edinburgh 186 a.	...	...	...	...	1627	...	...	...	1733	...	1805	...	...	1824	...	*1857*y	...	1912	...	2019	...	2028	...	...
Glasgow Central 186 a.	...	...	...	...	*1737z*	...	...	...	1841	...	*1906z*	...	...	*1936z*	...	...	...	2015	...	*2123z*	...	*2150z*	...	...

	Ⓐ ✕	Ⓐ ✕	Ⓐ ✕	Ⓐ ✕	Ⓐ ✕	Ⓐ ✕	Ⓐ ✕ B	Ⓐ ✕	Ⓐ 🍷	Ⓐ ✕	Ⓐ ✕	⑤ ✕	Ⓐ ✕	Ⓐ ✕ A	Ⓐ ✕	Ⓐ ✕	Ⓐ ✕	Ⓐ ✕	Ⓐ ✕	Ⓐ ✕	Ⓐ ✕	Ⓐ 🍷	Ⓐ 🍷	Ⓐ 🍷
London Kings Cross 184 d.	1630	1635	1700	1703	1720	1730	1733	1800	1750	1803	1820	1830	1833	1850	1900	1903	1930	2000	2003	2027	2030	2100	2130	2200
Stevenage 184 d.	1649	*1612*	|	|	|	|	1752	|	|	|	1841	|	|	|	|	|	*1847*	|	*1947*	|	|	2120	|	*2146*
Peterborough 184 208 d.	|	1725	|	1752	1807	1816	|	|	1839	1853	1913	|	1923	|	1946	1952	2017	2046	2052	|	2120	2153	2217	2247
Grantham 208 d.	1734	|	|	1811	|	|	1839	|	1905	1914	|	1936	|	1956	2005	|	2035	|	2114	2132	2139	|	2238	2308
Newark North Gate d.	1746	|	|	|	1835	|	|	|	1917	|	1940	|	1952	|	|	2021	2047	|	2126	|	2151	2222	2249	2319
Retford d.	|	1803	|	|	|	|	1901	|	|	|	|	1958	|	2016	|	|	2102	|	|	2153	|	|	2305	|
Doncaster 127 176 178 a.	1809	1818	|	1841	1904	|	1917	1927	1941	1946	|	2014	2018	2030	2037	2049	2116	2136	2152	2211	2217	2247	2324	2349
Hull 178 a.	*1909*	*1947*	|	|	2000	|	|	|	*2055*	*2106*	|	|	|	2128	*2145*	|	|	*2257*	|	2313	|	|	|	|
Wakefield Westgate 127 a.	|	1836	|	1901	...	|	1934	|	2001	2006	|	|	2038	*2110*d	|	2114	2135	|	2213	...	2235	|	2342	|
Leeds 127 176 a.	|	1858	|	1921	...	|	1953	|	2021	2025	|	|	2054	*2127*d	|	2134	2153	|	2233	...	2253	|	2359	|
York 127 a.	1834	...	1851	...	...	1923	...	1951	...	...	2022	2040	...	...	2101	...	...	2159	...	...	...	2312	...	0039
Newcastle 186 a.	1949	...	1952	...	...	2026	...	2052	...	...	2132	2149	...	...	2207	...	...	2313	...	...	...	0042	...	*0223*
Edinburgh 186 a.	2120p	...	2123	...	...	2213	...	2222	...	...	*2328*	2329	...	...	2354p	...	...	...	...	...	...	...	...	...
Glasgow Central 186 a.	...	...	*2251z*	...	...	*2324z*	...	2333	...	...	...	...	...	...	...	...	...	...	...	...	...	...	...	...

	Ⓐ 🍷			⑥ 🍷		⑥ 🍷	⑥ 🍷		⑥ 🍷	⑥ 🍷	⑥ 🍷	⑥ 🍷	⑥ 🍷	⑥ 🍷	⑥ ✕	⑥ 🍷	⑥ 🍷	⑥ 🍷 A	⑥ 🍷	⑥ 🍷	⑥ 🍷	⑥ 🍷	⑥ ✕	⑥ 🍷 N
London Kings Cross 184 d.	2330	...	⑥	0615	...	0700	0710	...	0800	0810	0830	0900	0905	0930	0934	1000	1010	1030	1040	1100	1110	1130	1148	1200
Stevenage 184 d.	|	...		0634	...	*0646*	|	...	0820	|	0849	|	0924	0949	|	|	|	*1012*	|	*1046*	|	1150	|	|
Peterborough 184 208 d.	0023s	...		0706	...	0746	0756	...	0851	0857	0921	0946	|	1021	|	1046	1056	1118	1127	1146	1156	1221	|	1247
Grantham 208 d.	0044s	...		0725	...	0805	0815	...	|	0916	0940	|	|	1040	1044	|	1115	|	1148	|	1216	1243	1248	|
Newark North Gate d.	0056s	...		0737	...	0817	0827	...	|	0928	|	|	1018	|	|	|	1127	|	|	|	1228	|	|	|
Retford d.	|	...		0752	...	|	0842	...	|	|	|	1024	|	|	1106	|	|	|	|	|	1243	|	1314	|
Doncaster 127 176 178 a.	0124s	...		0807	...	0841	0857	...	0937	0956	1013	1038	1047	1113	1124	1132	1153	|	1219	1233	1258	1314	1326	|
Hull 178 a.	|	...		*0913*	...	*0955*	*1010*	...	*1050*	|	*1112*	*1153*	*1208*	|	1220	*1250*	*1307*	|	|	*1350*	*1410*	|	1422	|
Wakefield Westgate 127 a.	|	...		*0856*	...	|	0915	...	|	1014	|	|	1111	|	...	|	1213	|	|	|	1316	|	...	|
Leeds 127 176 a.	0235	...		*0914*	...	|	0935	...	|	1035	|	|	1135	|	...	|	1235	|	|	|	1335	|	...	|
York 127 a.	...	...		0831	...	0904	*0948*d	...	1001	...	1039	1102	...	1139	...	1156	...	1227	1246	1256	...	1339	...	1356
Newcastle 186 a.	...	...		0934	...	1005	*1059*d	...	1104	...	1143	1202	...	1244	...	1302	...	1324	1353	1359	...	1446	...	1457
Edinburgh 186 a.	...	...		1112	...	1137	...	...	1245	...	1319	1332	...	1416	...	1431	...	1454	...	1535	...	1619	...	1630
Glasgow Central 186 a.	...	...		*1221z*	...	1249	...	...	*1351z*	...	*1421z*	1447	...	*1521z*	...	*1536z*	...	*1608z*	...	1648	...	*1721z*	...	*1736z*

	⑥ 🍷	⑥ 🍷	⑥ 🍷	⑥ 🍷	⑥ 🍷	⑥ ✕	⑥ 🍷 A	⑥ 🍷	⑥ 🍷	⑥ 🍷	⑥ 🍷	⑥ 🍷	⑥ 🍷	⑥ ✕	⑥ 🍷	⑥ 🍷	⑥ 🍷	⑥ 🍷 B	⑥ 🍷	⑥ 🍷	⑥ 🍷	⑥ 🍷	⑥ ✕	⑥ 🍷
London Kings Cross 184 d.	1210	1230	1300	1310	1330	1338	1400	1430	1500	1530	1600	1630	1700	1705	1730	1740	1800	1830	1835	1840	1900	1930	1941	2000
Stevenage 184 d.	|	*1212*	*1246*	|	1349	|	|	*1412*	*1446*	1549	|	*1612*	*1646*	|	1750	|	|	|	*1827*	|	1919	|	|	*1946*
Peterborough 184 208 d.	1256	1316	1346	1356	1420	|	1447	1516	1546	1621	1646	1716	1746	|	1821	1826	1846	|	1921	1927	1951	2016	|	2046
Grantham 208 d.	1315	1335	|	1415	1439	1443	|	1535	|	1640	|	1735	|	1810	1842	1847	|	1930	|	|	|	2035	2043	2105
Newark North Gate d.	1327	|	|	1427	1451	|	|	1547	|	1652	|	1747	|	|	1854	1859	|	|	|	1956	|	2047	|	2117
Retford d.	|	|	|	1442	|	1510	|	1602	|	|	|	1802	|	1831	|	|	|	|	|	2011	|	|	2105	2132
Doncaster 127 176 178 a.	1352	1407	1433	1457	|	1524	1535	1620	1632	1716	1735	1817	1833	1846	1917	1923	1933	2001	2008	2027	2039	2111	2119	2147
Hull 178 a.	|	*1512*	*1551*	*1607*	|	1620	*1650*	|	*1753*	|	*1857*	*1915*	|	1947	|	|	*2052*	*2104*	|	2127	*2145*	|	2215	*2258*
Wakefield Westgate 127 a.	1413	*1442*	|	1515	|	...	|	1638	|	1733	|	1835	|	|	1935	*1959*	|	2019	|	*2053*d	*2134*	|	*2157*d	2205
Leeds 127 176 a.	1435	*1502*	|	1535	|	...	|	1701	|	1753	|	1853	|	|	1952	*2022*	|	2036	|	*2115*d	*2154*	|	*2218*d	2224
York 127 a.	...	1430	1458	...	1535	...	1559	...	1656	...	1801	...	1856	*1949*d	...	1954	1958	...	2034	...	2103	2138	...	...
Newcastle 186 a.	...	1543	1601	...	1641	...	1659	...	1800	...	1905	...	2000	*2054*d	...	2100	2102	...	2144	...	2214	2245	...	...
Edinburgh 186 a.	...	1715	1739	...	1816	...	1828	...	1933	...	2037	...	2134	*2231*d	...	...	2248	...	...	...	...	...	...	...
Glasgow Central 186 a.	...	*1821z*	1850	...	*1921z*	...	*1936z*	...	2044	...	*2151z*	...	2246	...	...	...	*0003z*	...	...	...	...	...	...	...

	⑥ 🍷			⑦ 🍷	⑦ 🍷	⑦ 🍷	⑦ 🍷	⑦ 🍷	⑦ 🍷	⑦ ✕	⑦ 🍷 A		⑦ 🍷	⑦ 🍷	⑦ 🍷 N	⑦ 🍷	⑦ 🍷	⑦ 🍷	⑦ 🍷 A	⑦ 🍷	⑦ 🍷	⑦ ✕	⑦ 🍷	⑦ 🍷
London Kings Cross 184 d.	2030	...	⑦	0900	0910	0930	1000	1010	1030	1042	1100	...	1200	1210	1230	1300	1310	1330	1400	1410	1430	1444	1500	1510
Stevenage 184 d.	*2012*	...		0920	|	|	*0946*	|	1049	|	|	...	*1146*	1229	|	1319	|	1349	|	|	|	|	1519	|
Peterborough 184 208 d.	2117	...		0949	0955	1014	1046	1059	1119	|	1145	...	1244	1259	1315	1349	1356	1419	1445	1454	1514	|	1549	1555
Grantham 208 d.	2138	...		1011	|	|	|	1121	|	1146	|	...	|	1321	|	|	1419	|	|	1516	|	1545	|	1618
Newark North Gate d.	2149	...		|	1027	|	1116	|	|	|	|	...	1314	|	|	|	1431	|	|	1528	|	|	|	1631
Retford d.	|	...		|	1043	|	|	1143	|	1207	|	...	|	1343	|	|	|	|	|	1543	|	1606	|	|
Doncaster 127 176 178 a.	2214	...		1044	1100	1106	1141	1159	1209	1223	1237	...	1339	1359	1407	1439	1456	1509	1538	1559	1608	1620	|	1657
Hull 178 a.	|	...		*1145*	|	|	|	|	|	1321	*1348*	...	*1459*	|	|	*1557*	|	|	*1650*	|	|	1721	|	|
Wakefield Westgate 127 a.	*2238*	...		|	1119	*1144*	|	1217	*1244*	...	*1338*	...	|	1416	*1444*	|	1514	*1544*	|	1617	*1644*	...	|	1714
Leeds 127 176 a.	*2300*	...		|	1138	*1202*	|	1236	*1301*	...	*1358*	...	|	1436	*1501*	|	1533	*1601*	|	1637	*1701*	...	|	1734
York 127 a.	2238	...		1107	...	1129	1205	...	1238	...	1305	...	1404	...	1433	1505	...	1536	1604	...	1634	...	1702	...
Newcastle 186 a.	2346	...		1210	...	1228	1308	...	1341	...	1409	...	1512	...	1533	1610	...	1642	1704	...	1737	...	1801	...
Edinburgh 186 a.	...	...		1346	...	1400	1436	...	1510	...	1542	...	1646	...	1701	1736	...	1824	1832	...	1908	...	1934	...
Glasgow Central 186 a.	...	...		*1452z*	...	*1517*	*1552z*	...	1614	...	*1651z*	...	*1752z*	...	*1822z*	1844	...	...	*1951z*	...	*2022z*	...	2035	...

A – To Aberdeen.
B – To Bradford.
N – To Inverness.
d – Change at Doncaster.
p – ⑤ only.
s – Stops to set down only.
u – Stops to pick up only.
y – Change at York.
z – Glasgow Queen St.

For explanation of standard symbols see page 4

Services on ⑥ are subject to alteration from March 29. Services on ⑦ are subject to alteration from February 3.

	⑦	⑦	⑦	⑦	⑦	⑦	⑦	⑦	⑦	⑦	⑦	⑦	⑦	⑦	⑦	⑦	⑦	⑦	⑦	⑦	⑦	⑦	⑦	⑦
	🍷	🍷	🍷	🍷	🍷	🍷	🍷	✕	🍷	🍷	🍷	🍷	🍷	🍷	🍷	🍷	🍷	✕	🍷	🍷	🍷	🍷	🍷	🍷
London Kings Cross **184** ...... d.	1530	1600	1610	1630	1700	1710	1730	1740	1800	1810	1830	1840	1900	1910	1930	1935	2000	2005	2010	2030	2100	2130	2200	2210
Stevenage **184** ...... d.	*1519*	*1546*	1629	1649	|	|	1749	|	|	|	1850	|	|	|	1949	1954	|	|	|	|	*2046*	|	*2146*	|
Peterborough 184 208 ...... d.	1615	1645	1659	1719	1744	1754	1819	|	1844	1855	1919	1925	1944	1955	2019	2025	2044	|	|	2114	2145	2215	2245	2259**s**
Grantham **208** ...... d.	1639	|	|	|	|	1816	|	1851	1906	|	|	1947	|	2019	|	|	|	2118	|	2136	|	2239	|	2331**s**
Newark North Gate ...... d.	1650	|	|	|	1814	|	1849	|	|	1926	|	|	|	2030	|	|	|	|	|	2148	|	2250	|	2342**s**
Retford ...... d.	|	|	1739	|	|	|	|	1911	|	1942	|	|	|	|	|	|	|	2139	|	2203	|	2306	|	|
Doncaster 127 176 178 ...... a.	1718	1739	1755	1809	1839	1849	1914	1926	1942	1958	2012	2020	2035	2056	2109	2116	2136	2153	|	2219	2242	2327	2342	0012**s**
Hull 178 ...... a.	|	|	*1857*	|	*1954*	|	|	2022	|	|	|	*2123*	|	2156	|	|	|	2250	|	|	*0002*	|	|	|
Wakefield Westgate **127** ...... a.	|	|	1812	*1844*	|	1906	*1957*	...	|	2016	|	2038	|	...	2127	|	|	...	2156	2240	|	|	|	|
Leeds 127 176 ...... a.	|	|	1832	*1901*	|	1928	*2019*	...	|	2041	|	2059	|	...	2147	|	|	...	2215	2300	|	0022	|	0136**s**
York 127 ...... a.	1745	1805	...	1834	1903	...	1946	...	2007	...	2038	...	2100	...	...	2147	2200	...	...	...	2311	...	0039	...
Newcastle **186** ...... a.	1851	1905	...	1946	2007	...	2058	...	2106	...	2146	...	2202	...	...	2252	2334	...	...	...	0052	...	...	...
Edinburgh **186** ...... a.	...	2035	...	...	2136	...	...	...	2244	...	2329	...	...	...	...	...	...	...	...	...	...	...	...	...
Glasgow Central **186** ...... a.	...	*2155***z**	...	...	2237	...	...	...	*2355***z**	...	...	...	...	...	...	...	...	...	...	...	...	...	...	...

Ⓐ	Ⓐ	Ⓐ	Ⓐ	Ⓐ	Ⓐ	Ⓐ	Ⓐ	Ⓐ	Ⓐ	Ⓐ	Ⓐ	Ⓐ	Ⓐ	Ⓐ	Ⓐ	Ⓐ	Ⓐ	Ⓐ	Ⓐ	Ⓐ	Ⓐ	Ⓐ	Ⓐ
	✕	✕	✕	✕	✕	✕	✕	✕	✕	✕	✕	✕	✕	✕	✕	✕	✕	✕	🍷	✕	✕	✕	🍷
									B														
Glasgow Central **186** ...... d.	...	...	...	...	...	...	...	...	...	...	...	...	...	...	...	...	...	...	...	...	...	*0600***z**	...
Edinburgh **186** ...... d.	...	...	...	...	...	...	...	...	...	...	...	...	...	...	0550	...	0600	...	...	*0605*	...	0700	...
Newcastle **186** ...... d.	...	...	0431**b**	...	0526	...	0600	...	...	...	0630	...	...	0700	0720	...	0740	...	...	0749	...	0830	...
York 127 ...... d.	*0409*	...	0600	...	0630	...	0700	...	...	...	0736	...	...	0800	0810	...	0837	...	...	0849	...	0935	...
Leeds 127 176 ...... d.	0505	0530	|	0605	*0614*	0640	|	...	0700	0720	|	...	0740	|	|	0805	|	...	0840	|	0905	|	0940
Wakefield Westgate **127** ...... d.	0517	0542	|	0618	*0626*	0652	|	...	0712	0732	|	...	0752	|	|	0817	|	...	0852	|	0919	|	0952
Hull 178 ...... d.	|	|	*0520*	|	|	|	|	0625	|	|	|	0700	|	|	|	|	|	0812	|	|	|	*0856*	|
Doncaster 127 176 178 ...... d.	0535	0600	0623	|	0654	|	|	0719	0730	|	|	0755	|	|	|	0836	|	0905	|	0917	0936	1004	1015
Retford ...... d.	0550	|	|	0648	|	|	|	0732	|	|	|	|	0819	|	|	|	|	0919	|	|	0951	|	|
Newark North Gate ...... d.	0605	0624	0646	0704	|	0729	|	|	|	|	|	|	0834	|	|	|	|	|	0940	0945	1006	|	1038
Grantham **208** ...... d.	0618	0637	0659	0717	0725	|	|	0757	|	|	|	0829	|	|	0900	|	0927	0943	|	0957	|	1036	|
Peterborough 184 208 ...... a.	0637	0658	0718	0737	0745	|	0803	|	|	0832	|	0850	|	|	|	0926	0947	|	1008	1017	1033	1056	1106
Stevenage **184** ...... a.	*0757*	|	*0826*	|	|	|	*0905*	|	|	*0935*	0906	*0956*	|	|	|	0957	|	|	1042	|	*1133*	|	|
London Kings Cross **184** ...... a.	0730	0753	0812	0834	0842	0848	0859	0918	0906	0926	0935	0945	0951	0954	1010	1025	1040	1051	1110	1113	1127	1150	1203

	Ⓐ	Ⓐ	Ⓐ	Ⓐ	Ⓐ	Ⓐ	Ⓐ	Ⓐ	Ⓐ	Ⓐ	Ⓐ	Ⓐ	Ⓐ	Ⓐ	Ⓐ	Ⓐ	Ⓐ	Ⓐ	Ⓐ	Ⓐ	Ⓐ	Ⓐ	Ⓐ	Ⓐ
	✕	✕	✕	✕	🍷	🍷	✕	🍷	✕	✕	✕	✕	🍷	✕	✕	✕	✕	🍷	✕	✕	✕	🍷	✕	✕
												A					N				A			
Glasgow Central **186** ...... d.	*0600*	...	0650	...	...	...	0750	...	*0831***z**	...	...	*0915***z**	...	...	...	0950	*1030***z**	...	...	*1100***z**	*1130***z**	...	...	...
Edinburgh **186** ...... d.	*0705*	...	0800	...	...	...	0900	...	0930	...	...	1030	...	...	...	1100	1130	...	...	1200	1230	...	...	...
Newcastle **186** ...... d.	0900	...	0930	*0935***d**	...	...	1034	...	1100	...	1130	1159	...	...	...	1235	1301	...	...	1329	1400	...	...	1405
York 127 ...... d.	1006	...	1029	*1034***d**	...	...	1135	...	1200	...	1231	1253	...	...	...	1336	1354	...	...	1426	1453	...	...	1511
Leeds 127 176 ...... d.	|	1005	|	|	1040	1105	|	1140	|	1205	|	|	1240	...	1305	|	|	1340	1405	|	|	1440	1505	|
Wakefield Westgate **127** ...... d.	|	1018	|	|	1052	1117	|	1154	|	1217	|	|	1252	...	1318	|	|	1353	1418	|	|	1452	1517	|
Hull 178 ...... d.	|	*0925*	*0956*	1012	|	*1022*	*1057*	|	|	*1122*	*1155*	|	|	1245	|	*1257*	|	|	|	*1325*	|	*1357*	|	*1425*
Doncaster 127 176 178 ...... d.	1030	1035	1053	1105	1113	1137	1200	1212	|	1236	1255	|	1314	1337	1338	1403	|	1415	|	1450	|	1515	|	1536
Retford ...... d.	|	|	1108	1120	|	|	|	|	|	1251	|	|	|	|	1355	|	|	|	|	|	|	|	|	1551
Newark North Gate ...... d.	|	1059	|	|	1141	|	|	1237	|	|	|	|	1342	|	1410	|	|	|	|	1513	|	1541	|	1606
Grantham **208** ...... d.	|	1111	|	1140	1154	1209	|	|	|	1314	|	|	|	1409	1423	|	|	|	1503	1526	|	1554	|	1619
Peterborough 184 208 ...... a.	1116	1131	1148	|	1213	1228	1246	1305	1311	|	1342	1403	1409	|	1442	1449	|	1505	1522	1545	1601	|	1617	|
Stevenage **184** ...... a.	1147	*1233*	|	|	1243	|	1316	|	|	|	1416	|	*1508*	|	1512	|	|	|	1552	1617	|	|	1648	|
London Kings Cross **184** ...... a.	1217	1225	1242	1244	1310	1322	1343	1402	1410	1420	1444	1457	1505	1520	1540	1544	1551	1558	1622	1646	1657	1704	1715	1730

	Ⓐ	Ⓐ	Ⓐ	Ⓐ	Ⓐ	Ⓐ	Ⓐ	Ⓐ	Ⓐ	Ⓐ	Ⓐ	Ⓐ	Ⓐ	Ⓐ	Ⓐ	Ⓐ	Ⓐ	Ⓐ	Ⓐ	Ⓐ	Ⓐ	Ⓐ	Ⓐ	Ⓐ
	✕	🍷	✕	✕	✕	🍷	🍷	🍷	✕	✕	✕	✕	✕	✕	✕	🍷	🍷	🍷	✕	✕	🍷	✕	🍷	🍷
																						A		
Glasgow Central **186** ...... d.	1150	...	...	...	...	*1300***z**	...	...	1350	...	...	...	...	...	*1500***z**	...	...	...	1550	...	...	*1615***z**	...	1750
Edinburgh **186** ...... d.	1300	...	*1305*	...	...	1400	...	*1405*	1500	...	...	...	*1505*	...	1600	...	*1605*	...	1700	...	...	1730	...	1900
Newcastle **186** ...... d.	1434	...	1456	...	...	1530	...	1555	1628	...	...	*1627***d**	1655	...	1732	...	1810	...	1835	...	...	1908	*1925***d**	2037
York 127 ...... d.	1535	...	1555	...	...	1632	...	1656	1721	...	...	*1734***d**	1755	...	1830	...	1913	...	1935	...	...	2008	*2031***d**	2138
Leeds 127 176 ...... d.	|	1540	|	...	1605	|	1640	|	|	1705	...	1740	|	1805	|	1840	|	1905	|	...	1942	|	2040	|
Wakefield Westgate **127** ...... d.	|	1552	|	...	1617	|	1652	|	|	1717	...	1752	|	1817	|	1852	|	1917	|	...	1954	|	2055	|
Hull 178 ...... d.	*1457*	|	|	1518	*1521*	*1557*	|	|	|	|	1706	|	|	|	*1756*	|	*1822*	|	*1853*	1918	|	|	*2003*	*2056*
Doncaster 127 176 178 ...... d.	1601	|	|	1615	1636	1657	1710	1720	|	1737	1802	1811	1821	1835	1854	1912	1937	1936	2000	2010	2015	2032	2112	2203
Retford ...... d.	|	|	|	1634	|	|	|	|	|	1757	1816	|	1836	|	|	|	|	|	|	|	|	|	2127	|
Newark North Gate ...... d.	|	|	|	|	|	1720	1733	1744	|	|	|	1834	1851	|	1917	1934	|	2005	|	|	2039	|	2142	2226
Grantham **208** ...... d.	|	|	1644	1655	|	|	|	1757	|	|	1836	1847	|	|	|	1949	|	2017	|	2042	2051	|	2155	2239
Peterborough 184 208 ...... a.	1647	1655	1704	|	1727	1748	|	|	1826	|	|	1906	1919	1925	1945	|	2024	2037	2046	|	2111	2120	2214	2258
Stevenage **184** ...... a.	|	|	1734	1746**s**	*1835*	|	|	1842	*1933*	1900	1924**s**	|	1950	|	2015	2035	|	|	2117	2131**s**	|	2153	2251**s**	2335
London Kings Cross **184** ...... a.	1741	1750	1804	1812	1823	1845	1848	1911	1918	1929	1949	1959	2018	2021	2042	2103	2117	2133	2144	2159	2204	2227	2333	0018

⑥	⑥	⑥	⑥	⑥	⑥	⑥	⑥	⑥	⑥	⑥	⑥	⑥	⑥	⑥	⑥	⑥	⑥	⑥	⑥	⑥	⑥	⑥	⑥
	🍷	🍷	🍷	🍷	🍷	🍷	🍷	🍷	🍷	🍷	🍷	🍷	✕	🍷	🍷	🍷	🍷	🍷	🍷	✕	🍷	🍷	🍷
										B													
Glasgow Central **186** ...... d.	...	...	...	...	...	...	...	...	...	...	...	...	...	...	...	*0600***z**	...	...	0650	...	*0730***z**	...	0750
Edinburgh **186** ...... d.	...	...	...	...	...	...	...	...	...	...	...	...	...	0615	...	0700	0730	...	0800	...	0835	...	0900
Newcastle **186** ...... d.	...	0431	...	0600	...	...	0635	...	0700	...	...	0730	...	0754	...	0833	0900	...	0932	...	1003	...	1032
York 127 ...... d.	*0419*	0600	...	0700	...	...	0736	...	0803	...	...	0830	...	0851	...	0936	1005	...	1031	...	1100	...	1133
Leeds 127 176 ...... d.	0505	|	0610	*0619*	0700	...	|	0740	|	0805	0815	|	...	*0819*	0905	|	*0919*	1005	|	...	*1019*	1105	|
Wakefield Westgate **127** ...... d.	0517	|	0622	*0632*	0712	...	|	0752	|	0818	|	|	...	*0834*	0918	|	*0933*	1018	|	...	*1032*	1117	|
Hull 178 ...... d.	|	*0520*	|	*0607*	|	0650	|	|	|	|	|	*0736*	0802	*0808*	|	*0856*	|	*0925*	*0956*	1005	|	*1025*	*1057*
Doncaster 127 176 178 ...... d.	0535	0623	0640	0723	0730	0740	0800	|	|	|	0845	0855	0901	0915	0935	1003	1029	1036	1055	1101	1124	1139	1157
Retford ...... d.	0550	|	0655	|	|	|	|	0820	|	|	|	0910	0921	|	|	|	|	|	1110	1117	|	|	|
Newark North Gate ...... d.	0605	|	0710	|	0754	|	0824	0834	|	0854	|	|	|	|	0959	|	|	1100	|	|	|	1201	|
Grantham **208** ...... d.	0617	|	0723	|	0806	|	0837	0846	|	0906	|	|	0942	|	1012	|	|	1112	|	1138	1155	1214	1228
Peterborough 184 208 ...... a.	0637	0709	0742	0809	0826	0832	0857	0906	0912	0926	0932	0948	|	1006	1032	1054	1115	1132	1148	|	1214	1233	1249
Stevenage **184** ...... a.	*0733*	*0808*	|	*0908*	|	*0933*	*0945*	|	0945	|	*1033*	|	|	|	1104	|	1147	*1233*	|	|	|	1303	|
London Kings Cross **184** ...... a.	0729	0804	0840	0903	0918	0926	0951	1000	1013	1020	1027	1041	1049	1058	1132	1150	1214	1224	1241	1246	1310	1333	1344

	⑥	⑥	⑥	⑥	⑥	⑥	⑥	⑥	⑥	⑥	⑥	⑥	⑥	⑥	⑥	⑥	⑥		⑥	⑥	⑥	⑥	⑥	⑥
	🍷	🍷	🍷	🍷	🍷	🍷	✕	🍷	🍷	🍷	🍷	🍷	🍷	✕	🍷	🍷	🍷		🍷	🍷	🍷	✕	🍷	🍷
				A				N			A													
Glasgow Central **186** ...... d.	*0830***z**	...	0850	*0915***z**	...	0950	...	*1015***z**	...	*1045***z**	*1115***z**	...	1150	...	*1215***z**	...	*1245***z**	...	1350	...	*1500***z**	...	...	1550
Edinburgh **186** ...... d.	0930	...	1000	1030	...	1100	...	1130	...	1200	1230	...	1300	...	1330	...	1400	...	1500	...	1600	...	...	1700
Newcastle **186** ...... d.	1100	...	1129	1200	...	1233	...	1304	...	1331	1359	...	1429	...	1459	...	1528	...	1629	...	1729	...	...	1834
York 127 ...... d.	1159	...	1231	1302	...	1334	...	1357	...	1440	1501	...	1530	...	1557	...	1634	...	1731	...	1828	...	...	1940
Leeds 127 176 ...... d.	*1119*	1205	|	|	1305	|	...	|	1405	|	|	1505	|	...	*1519*	1605	|	...	*1619*	1740	|	...	1840	|
Wakefield Westgate **127** ...... d.	*1132*	1217	|	|	1317	|	...	|	1417	|	|	1517	|	...	*1532*	1617	|	...	*1632*	1752	|	...	1854	|
Hull 178 ...... d.	|	*1122*	*1157*	|	*1222*	*1257*	1305	|	*1325*	*1357*	|	*1425*	*1457*	1506	|	*1525*	*1557*	...	*1654*	|	*1755*	1812	|	*1853*
Doncaster 127 176 178 ...... d.	1221	1235	1257	|	1338	1358	1404	|	1435	1504	|	1535	1555	1602	1621	1638	1658	...	1755	1810	1852	1905	1914	2004
Retford ...... d.	|	1250	|	|	|	|	1419	|	1450	|	|	|	|	1617	|	1653	|	...	|	1825	|	1920	1929	|
Newark North Gate ...... d.	|	1305	|	|	1401	|	|	|	1505	|	|	1559	|	|	|	1708	|	...	1818	1840	|	|	1944	|
Grantham **208** ...... d.	|	1317	|	|	|	1429	1439	|	1518	|	|	1611	|	1637	1652	|	1729	...	|	1852	|	1940	1956	|
Peterborough 184 208 ...... a.	1307	|	1346	1412	1429	1449	|	1504	1537	1550	|	1631	1642	|	1711	1736	1748	...	1846	1912	1938	|	2016	2051
Stevenage **184** ...... a.	*1408*	|	1417	|	*1533*	|	|	*1608*	|	1619	|	1700	1716	|	|	|	1819	...	|	1943	2007	|	2048	2120
London Kings Cross **184** ...... a.	1359	1427	1444	1510	1521	1541	1549	1558	1630	1647	1657	1728	1743	1745	1810	1828	1846	...	1940	2012	2035	2046	2115	2148

A – From Aberdeen.
B – From Bradford.
N – From Inverness.
b – 0422 on ①.
d – Change at Doncaster.
s – Stops to set down only.
z – Glasgow Queen St.

185 YORK, LEEDS and HULL - LONDON GR

Services on ⑥ are subject to alteration from March 29. Services on ⑦ are subject to alteration from February 3.

	⑥ 🍷 A	⑥ 🍷		⑦	⑦ 🍷	⑦ 🍷		⑦ 🍷	⑦ 🍷	⑦ 🍴	⑦ 🍷	⑦ 🍷	⑦ 🍷	⑦ 🍷	⑦ 🍷	⑦ 🍷	⑦ 🍷	⑦ 🍷	⑦ 🍷	⑦ 🍷	⑦ 🍷	⑦ 🍴	⑦ 🍷 A	⑦ 🍷
Glasgow Central **186** d.	*1615z*	...	...		...	...	...	...	...	...	...	*0750z*	...	*0830z*	...	...	*0930z*	...	...	...	1050	...	...	...
Edinburgh **186** d.	1730	...	...		...	...	...	...	...	...	...	0900	0930	1000	1030	...	1100	...	1130	...	1200	...	1230	...
Newcastle **186** d.	1906	...	...		...	0758	...	0855	0925	...	...	1030	1057	1132	1200	...	1232	...	1303	1320	1332	...	1403	...
York 127 d.	2005	...	...		*0722*	0900	...	1002	1023	...	...	1129	1153	1229	1257	...	1333	...	1405	1419	1436	...	1501	...
Leeds 127 176 d.	*1922*	2015	...		0824	*0835*	...	*0920*	*1000*	*1009*d	1040	|	|	*1200*	*1240*	1240	*1300*	1340	|	|	*1400*	*1409*d	|	1440
Wakefield Westgate **127** d.	*1932*	2031	...		0836	*0847*	...	*0932*	*1012*	*1022*d	1053	|	|	*1212*	*1252*	1252	*1312*	1352	|	|	*1412*	*1422*d	|	1452
Hull 178 d.	|	*1924*	...		|	|	...	*0842*	*0941*	1012	|	*1041*	|	*1141*	|	|	*1241*	|	|	*1341*	|	1410	|	|
Doncaster 127 176 178 d.	2030	2048	...		0854	0926	...	1029	1048	1104	1113	1153	|	1254	1321	1310	1357	1410	1429	1448	1500	1505	|	1510
Retford d.	|	2103	...		|	0941	...	|	|	1119	1128	|	|	|	|	1334	|	|	|	|	|	1520	|	1525
Newark North Gate d.	|	2118	...		0918	|	...	1052	|	|	1142	|	1234	|	|	1348	|	1433	|	|	|	|	|	1539
Grantham **208** d.	|	2131	...		0930	1003	...	1104	|	1139	1154	|	|	1326	|	1400	|	|	1459	|	|	1540	|	1552
Peterborough 184 208 a.	2118	2151	...		0952	1025	...	1126	1137	|	1216	1240	1303	|	1409	1422	1443	|	|	1535	1547	|	|	1613
Stevenage **184** a.	2151	2220	...		|	1100	...	|	1209	|	*1333*	|	1334	1414	|	|	|	1528	|	|	1617	|	|	1649
London Kings Cross **184** a.	2217	2247	...		1047	1128	...	1219	1237	1248	1313	1336	1404	1442	1511	1515	1538	1555	1611	1629	1645	1650	1711	1717

	⑦ 🍷	⑦ 🍷	⑦ 🍷 N	⑦ 🍷	⑦ 🍷	⑦ 🍴	⑦ 🍷	⑦ 🍷 A	⑦ 🍷	⑦ 🍷	⑦ 🍷	⑦ 🍷	⑦ 🍷	⑦ 🍷	⑦ 🍷	⑦ 🍷	⑦ 🍴	⑦ 🍷 A	⑦ 🍷	⑦ 🍷	⑦ 🍷	⑦ 🍷		⑦ 🍷
Glasgow Central **186** d.	*1130z*	...	...	1250	...	...	...	*1300z*	...	*1330z*	...	*1400z*	...	...	1450	...	...	*1500z*	1550	*1600z*	...	*1630z*	...	1750
Edinburgh **186** d.	1300	...	1330	1400	...	...	...	1430	...	1500	...	1530	...	...	1600	...	...	1630	1700	1730	...	1800	...	1900
Newcastle **186** d.	1432	...	1501	1530	...	...	1550	1559	...	1633	...	1706	...	1712	1730	...	...	1810	1829	1857	...	1935	...	2031
York 127 d.	1534	...	1603	1629	...	...	1653	1701	...	1735	...	1807	...	1812	1829	...	...	1905	1930	2002	...	2040	...	2128
Leeds 127 176 d.	*1500*	1540	|	|	1640	...	|	|	1705	|	1740	|	...	|	*1800*	1840	...	|	|	*1900*	2015	|	...	*2020*
Wakefield Westgate **127** d.	*1512*	1552	|	|	1652	...	|	|	1718	|	1752	|	...	|	*1812*	1852	...	|	|	*1912*	2027	|	...	*2033*
Hull 178 d.	*1441*	|	|	*1541*	|	1621	|	|	|	*1641*	|	*1730*	1730	|	*1741*	|	1830	|	*1838*	|	|	|	...	*2030*
Doncaster 127 176 178 d.	1558	1610	1628	1653	1710	1715	1719	1726	1736	1802	|	1831	1823	1837	1853	1910	1922	1930	1954	2026	2047	2105	...	2152
Retford d.	|	|	|	|	|	1730	|	|	1751	|	|	|	1844	|	|	|	1937	|	|	|	|	2120	...	|
Newark North Gate d.	1620	|	|	|	|	|	1746	|	1805	|	|	|	|	1905	|	|	|	|	2016	|	|	2134	...	|
Grantham **208** d.	|	1640	|	|	1740	1749	|	|	|	|	1835	|	1906	|	|	1940	1957	|	|	2056	|	|	...	2222
Peterborough 184 208 a.	1650	1701	1718	1740	1802	|	|	1821	|	1848	1857	1918	1928	1935	1941	2001	|	2025	2046	2117	2135	2204	...	2243
Stevenage **184** a.	1722	|	|	1811	|	|	1842	|	1901	1920	|	|	|	2008	2012	2032	|	2057	2120	2148	2209	2234	...	|
London Kings Cross **184** a.	1749	1755	1815	1840	1855	1906	1912	1916	1933	1947	1951	2012	2023	2036	2042	2059	2112	2125	2147	2216	2237	2314	...	2350

A – From Aberdeen. **N** – From Inverness. **d** – Change at Doncaster. **z** – Glasgow Queen St.

186 YORK - NEWCASTLE - EDINBURGH - GLASGOW GR, XC

For TransPennine Express services York - Newcastle, see Table **187**

km		⚒ △	②–⑥ 🍷		Ⓐ 🍷	⑥ 🍷		Ⓐ 🍷	⑥ 🍷		Ⓐ 🍷 A	⑥ 🍷 A	Ⓐ 🍷	⚒ 🍷	⚒ 🍷‡	⚒ 🍷	Ⓐ 🍴	⑥ 🍷	⚒ 🍷	Ⓐ 🍴	⚒ 🍷	Ⓐ 🍴	⑥ 🍷	Ⓐ 🍷 B	⑥ 🍷 B
	London Kings Cross **185** d.		...	...	...	...	...	...	...	...	...	...	...	...	0615	...	0700	0700	...	0730	...	0800	0800	...	...
	Birmingham New St **127** d.		...	...	...	...	...	...	...	...	...	...	...	0600	|	0630	|	|	0703	|	0730	|	|	0803	0803
	Doncaster **127 185** d.		...	...	...	...	...	0615	0620	...	...	...	0749	|	0808	0825	|	0842	|	0917	0922	|	0937	|	|
	Leeds **127** d.		...	...	...	...	...	|	|	...	0710	0710	|	0757	|	|	|	|	0905	|	|	|	|	1005	1005
0	**York** d.		0050	...	...	...	...	0637	0642	...	0737	0737	0812	0827	0833	0850v	0857	0906	0935	0942	0951	0955	1003	1031	1035
48	Northallerton d.		|	...	...	...	...	|	0701	...	|	|	|	|	|	|	|	|	|	|	|	|	|	|	|
71	Darlington d.		0126s	...	...	...	...	0706	0715	...	0805	0809	0839	0853	0901	0921	0931	0936	1002	1010	1018	1023	1031	1101	1103
106	Durham d.		0144s	...	...	...	...	0723	0733	...	0823	0826	0857	0909	0918	0938	|	|	1018	|	1034	1040	1048	1118	1121
129	**Newcastle** d.		0223	...	0625	0630	...	0741	0752	...	0841	0845	0922	0929	0939c	1001	1004	1007	1039	1044	1055v	1059	1108	1136	1139
185	Alnmouth d.		...	...	0652	0657	...	0807	0820	...	|	|	...	0956	|	...	|	|	|	...	...	|	1134	1203	1206
237	Berwick upon Tweed d.		...	...	0714	0719	...	0829	0842	...	0928	0929	...	|	1022	...	1047	1050	1121	...	...	1142	|	|	|
329	**Edinburgh** a.		...	...	0805	0809	...	0919	0935	...	1020	1020	...	1102	1114	...	1130	1137	1213	...	...	1230	1244	1316	1313
422	**Glasgow** Central a.		...	...	0925	0916	...	1024	1048	...	*1121*r	*1121*r	...	*1206*r	*1221*r	...	1245	1249	*1321*r	...	...	*1337*r	*1351*r	*1421*r	*1421*r

	Ⓐ 🍴	⑥ 🍷	Ⓐ 🍷 B	⑥ 🍷	⑥ 🍷	Ⓐ 🍴	⑥ 🍷 S	Ⓐ 🍷 S	⑥ 🍷	Ⓐ 🍴	⑥ 🍷 B	Ⓐ 🍷 C	Ⓐ 🍴	⑥ 🍷	⚒ 🍷‡ A	⚒ 🍷 P	⚒ 🍷 Q	⑥ 🍷	Ⓐ 🍴	⑥ 🍷	⚒ 🍷 UA	Ⓐ 🍴	⑥ 🍷	⚒ 🍷 R	⑥ 🍷 N
London Kings Cross **185** d.	0830	0830	...	...	0900	0900	...	...	0930	0930	...	...	1000	1000	1030	...	...	1040	1100	1100	...	1130	1130	...	1200
Birmingham New St **127** d.	|	|	0830	0830	|	|	0903	0903	|	|	0930	0930	|	|	|	1003	1030	|	|	|	1103	|	|	1130	|
Doncaster **127 185** d.	|	1014	1017	1020	1039	1035	|	|	1114	1112	1120	1117	|	1132	|	|	1217	1220	|	1234	|	1315	1315	1323	|
Leeds **127** d.	|	|	|	|	|	|	1105	1105	|	|	|	|	|	|	|	1205	|	|	|	|	1305	|	|	|	|
York d.	1035	1042	1043	1046	1103	1103	1135	1132	1141	1141	1147	1146	1154	1157	1229	1234	1246	1249	1252	1258	1332v	1342	1342	1350	1357
Northallerton d.	|	|	|	|	|	|	|	|	|	1200	|	|	|	1220	|	|	|	|	|	|	|	|	|	|	|
Darlington d.	1106	1111	1114	1117	1132	1133	1203	1200	1210	1214	1217	1221	1226	1233	|	1302	1313	1317	1320	1326	1402	1411	1412	1418	|
Durham d.	1123	|	1130	1134	|	|	1219	1223	1227	1232	1234	1245y	|	|	|	1319	1329	1335	|	|	1419	1428	1430	1435	|
Newcastle d.	1141	1145	1154	1157	1203	1204	1239	1240	1246	1250	1257	1307	1257	1304	1324	1337	1350	1353	1351	1401	1439	1447	1448	1456	1458
Alnmouth d.	...	|	...	...	|	1230	|	|	|	...	...	...	|	|	|	1401	...	...	|	|	|	...	|	...	|
Berwick upon Tweed d.	...	1231	...	...	|	1252	1321	1322	1329	...	...	...	|	|	|	|	...	...	1434	1444	1521	...	|	...	|
Edinburgh a.	...	1319	...	...	1332	1338	1413	1416	1416	...	...	...	1424	1431	1451v	1516c	...	...	1520	1535	1616v	...	1619	...	1630
Glasgow Central a.	...	*1421*r	...	...	1447	1445	*1521*r	*1521*r	*1521*r	...	...	...	*1536*r	*1536*r	*1608*r	*1621*r	...	...	1625	1648	*1721*r	...	*1721*r	...	*1736*r

	Ⓐ 🍴 N	Ⓐ 🍷 P	⑥ 🍷 P	⑥ 🍷	Ⓐ 🍴	⑥ 🍷 B	Ⓐ 🍷 B	Ⓐ 🍴	⑥ 🍷	Ⓐ 🍴	⑥ 🍷 U	Ⓐ 🍷 U	⑥ 🍷	⚒ 🍷 G	Ⓐ 🍴 A	⑥ 🍷 A	Ⓐ 🍷	Ⓐ 🍷 ZD	⑥ 🍷 ZD	Ⓐ 🍴	Ⓐ 🍷 B	⑥ 🍷 B	⑥ 🍷	⚒ 🍷 U	Ⓐ 🍴
London Kings Cross **185** d.	1200	...	...	1230	1230	...	...	1300	1300	1330	...	...	1330	...	1400	1400	1430	...	...	1500	...	...	1500	...	1530
Birmingham New St **127** d.	|	1203	1203	|	|	1230	1230	|	|	|	1303	1303	|	1330	|	|	|	1403	1403	|	1430	1430	|	1503	|
Doncaster **127 185** d.	|	|	|	1407	1407	1417	1420	1434	1434	1503	|	|	|	1517	|	1536	|	|	|	|	1617	1617	1632	|	1709
Leeds **127** d.	|	1405	1405	|	|	|	|	|	|	|	1505	1505	|	|	|	|	|	1605	1605	|	|	|	|	1705	|
York d.	1402	1433	1434	1436	1436	1449	1446	1500	1500	1528	1535	1534	1540	1544	1555	1601	1622	1632	1635	1646	1643	1651	1657	1733	1736
Northallerton d.	|	|	|	1456	1458	|	|	|	|	|	|	|	|	|	|	|	|	|	|	|	|	|	|	|	1756
Darlington d.	|	1500	1502	1509	1511	1517	1518	1528	1528	1601	1602	1607	1608	1613	1623	1629	1651	1659	1702	|	1715y	1718	1726	1805c	1810
Durham d.	|	1516	1518	1527	1529	1534	1535	|	1545	|	1618	1625	1625	1630	|	|	1708	|	1718	|	1732	1734	1744	1821c	1827
Newcastle d.	1500	1535	1539	1544	1547	1555	1600	1559	1603	1632	1639	1641	1643	1652	1654	1701	1726	1731	1739	1740	1754	1758	1801	1839	1846
Alnmouth d.	|	1602	1606	|	...	...	...	|	|	1658	|	|	|	...	|	|	...	1755	1803	|	...	...	|	|	1913
Berwick upon Tweed d.	|	|	|	|	...	...	...	1642	1652	|	1721	1725	|	...	1738	|	...	|	|	1826	...	...	1848	1921	|
Edinburgh a.	1626	1716	1714	1715	...	...	...	1734	1739	1804	1816	1816	1816	...	1823	1828	...	1857	1912	1912	...	...	1933	2013	2019
Glasgow Central a.	*1736*r	*1821*r	...	*1821*r	...	...	...	1841	1850	*1906*r	*1921*r	*1921*r	*1921*r	...	*1936*r	*1936*r	...	...	...	2015	...	...	2044	2128	*2122*r

	⚒ 🍷 Q	Ⓐ 🍴 A	⑥ 🍷	⚒ 🍷 P	Ⓐ 🍴	⑥ 🍷 B	Ⓐ 🍷 B	Ⓐ 🍴	⑥ 🍷	Ⓐ 🍴	⑥ 🍷 U	Ⓐ 🍷 U	Ⓐ 🍷 G	Ⓐ 🍴	⑥ 🍷	⑥ 🍷	⑥ 🍷	Ⓐ 🍴	⑥ 🍷 P	Ⓐ 🍷 P	⑥ 🍷	①–④ 🍴	⑤ 🍴	Ⓐ 🍷 B	⑥ 🍷 B
London Kings Cross **185** d.	...	1600	1600	...	1630	...	...	1700	1700	1730	...	...	...	1800	...	1740	1800	1820	...	...	1835	1830	1830	...	...
Birmingham New St **127** d.	1530	|	|	1603	|	1630	1630	|	|	|	1703	1703	1730	|	1730	|	|	|	1803	1803	|	|	|	1830	1830
Doncaster **127 185** d.	1717v	1730	1735	|	1810	1823	1818	|	1833	|	|	|	1919	1928	1921	1925	1934	|	|	|	2008	2015	2015	2022	2018
Leeds **127** d.	|	|	|	1805	|	|	|	|	|	|	1905	1905	|	|	|	|	|	|	2005	2009	|	|	|	|	|
York d.	1746	1756	1803	1832	1839	1849	1844	1853	1858	1925	1935	1938	1947	1953	1952	1955	2001	2023	2036	2037	2041	2044	2044	2051	2046
Northallerton d.	|	|	1822	|	1900	|	|	|	|	|	|	|	|	|	|	|	|	|	|	|	|	2103	|	|	|
Darlington d.	1817	1827	1835	1859v	1913	1916	1919	1923	1927	1953	2004	2005	2014	2023	2019	2024	2030	2051	2104	2109	2109	2116	2116	2122	2125
Durham d.	1833	|	|	1916	1930	1932	1941y	|	1944	2010	2023	2021	2031	|	2035	2041	|	2109	2122	2126	2126	2134	2134	2139	2211
Newcastle d.	1856	1859	1906	1939	1949	1953	2004	1954	2002	2029	2039	2040	2054	2054	2057	2100	2103	2127	2141	2148y	2144	2152	2153	2201	2234
Alnmouth d.	...	|	|	2003	|	...	...	|	|	2100	2103	2108	...	|	|	...	2135	...	...	2215	...	...	|	...	...
Berwick upon Tweed d.	...	1943	1949	2024	|	...	...	|	|	2122	2124	2130	...	2137	2139	...	2157	...	...	2236	...	...	2241	...	...
Edinburgh a.	...	2027	2037	2108v	2120j	...	...	2123	2134	2214	2213	2224	...	2222	2231	...	2248	...	...	2328	...	...	2329	...	...
Glasgow Central a.	...	*2151*r	*2151*r	2243	*2223*r	...	...	*2251*r	2246	*2325*r	*2325*r	...	...	2333	...	...	*0003*r	...	...	...	...	...	...	...	...

FOR NOTES, SEE FACING PAGE ▷▷

YORK - NEWCASTLE - EDINBURGH - GLASGOW

For TransPennine Express services York - Newcastle and v.v., see Table 187

	①–④ ✕	⑤ ✕	⑥ 🍷	Ⓐ 🍷 U	⑥ 🍷	Ⓐ 🍷 G	⑥ 🍷 U	Ⓐ ✕		⑥ 🍷	Ⓐ 🍷		⑦ ▲	⑦ 🍷		⑦ 🍷		⑦ 🍷	⑦ 🍷	⑦ 🍷	⑦ 🍷	⑦ 🍷	⑦ 🍷	⑦ 🍷 A	⑦ 🍷 A
London Kings Cross 185 .. d.	1900	1900	1900	...	1930	...	...	2000	...	2030	2100	...		...	...	...	...	0900	0930	...	1000	...	1030	1100	...
Birmingham New St 127 ... d.	|	|	|	1903	|	1930	1903	|	...	|	|	...		...	...	...	...	|	|	0846	0903	0903	|	1003	1003
Doncaster 127 185 ... d.	2038	2038	2040	|	2112	|	|	2136	...	2214	2247	...		...	...	0942	...	1044	1106	|	1141	1117	1210	1238	1219
Leeds 127 ... d.	|	|	|	2110	|	|	2110	|	...	|	|	...		...	...	0905	...	|	|	1108	|	1208	|	|	1308
York ... d.	2103	2103	2106	2138	2141	2150	2137	2200	...	2239	2314	...		0900	...	1006	...	1109	1130	1136	1206	1236	1240	1307	1336
Northallerton ... d.	|	|	2126	|	|	|	|	2221	...	|	|	...		0920	...	|	...	|	|	|	|	|	|	|	|
Darlington ... d.	2131	2131	2139	2205	2210	2220	|	2234	...	2308	2349	...		0933	...	1036	...	1137	1158	1205	1234	1304	1312	1335	1406
Durham ... d.	2149	2149	2156	2221	2227	2236	2249	2254	...	2325	0007	...		0950	...	1053	...	1154	|	1221	1252	1320	|	1353	1422
Newcastle ... d.	2207	2208	2214	2242	2245	2300	2311	2313	...	2346	0042	...		1010	...	1111	...	1215	1233	1240	1309	1348q	1343	1413	1442
Alnmouth ... d.	...	2238	...	...	...	...	...	...	...	...	...	...		1041	...	|	...	|	|	|	|	1415	|	|	|
Berwick upon Tweed ... d.	...	2300	...	...	...	...	...	...	...	...	...	...		1103	...	1154	...	1258	|	1322	|	|	1426	|	1524
Edinburgh ... a.	...	2354	...	...	...	...	...	...	...	...	...	...		1156	...	1239	...	1346	1400	1412	1436	1521	1510	1542	1624
Glasgow Central ... a.	...	...	...	...	...	...	...	...	...	...	...	...		1305	...	1344	...	1452r	...	1517	1552r	...	1614	1651r	...

	⑦ 🍷	⑦ 🍷 N	⑦ 🍷	⑦ 🍷	⑦ 🍷 B	⑦ 🍷	⑦ 🍷 A	⑦ 🍷 SD	⑦ 🍷	⑦ 🍷	⑦ 🍷 E	⑦ 🍷	⑦ 🍷	⑦ 🍷 U	⑦ 🍷	⑦ 🍷	⑦ 🍷 E	⑦ 🍷	⑦ 🍷	⑦ 🍷 U	⑦ 🍷	⑦ 🍷 E	⑦ 🍷		⑦ 🍷
London Kings Cross 185 .. d.	1200	1230	...	1300	...	1330	1400	...	1430	1500	...	1530	1600	...	1630	1700	...	1730	1800	...	1900	...	2000	...	2100
Birmingham New St 127 ... d.	1103	|	1103	1203	1203	|	1303	1303	|	|	1403	|	1503	1503	|	1603	1603	|	1703	1703	1803	1803	1903	...	|
Doncaster 127 185 ... d.	1340	1409	1317	1441	1417	1510	1539	1517	1609	|	1617	1720	1740	1720	1810	1840	1817	1920	1942	1917	2035	2017	2136	...	2243
Leeds 127 ... d.	|	|	1408	|	1508	|	|	1608	|	|	1708	|	|	1808	|	|	1908	|	|	2008	|	2108	|	...	|
York ... d.	1406	1435	1440	1507	1536	1539	1606	1636	1640	1703	1736	1746	1807	1836	1838	1905	1936	1948	2008	2036	2102	2136	2202	...	2313
Northallerton ... d.	1425	|	|	|	|	|	|	|	|	|	|	|	|	|	1858	|	|	2008	|	|	|	|	|	...	2347
Darlington ... d.	1438	1503	1509	1535	1603	1608	1634	1703	1708	1731	1803	1815	1835	1903	1911	1934	2003	2022	2036	2105	2130	2205	2243	...	0001
Durham ... d.	1456	|	1526	1553	1619	1625	|	1724	|	|	1819	1832	|	1919	1928	1951	2019	2040	|	2121	|	2221	2301	...	0019
Newcastle ... d.	1514	1534	1545	1611	1640	1644	1705	1745y	1739	1805	1839	1851	1906	1943n	1946	2009	2045n	2058	2107	2145n	2202	2242	2334	...	0052
Alnmouth ... d.	|	|	1612	|	|	1715	|	1809	|	|	|	...	|	2008	...	|	2109	...	2134	2209	...	...	...	...	...
Berwick upon Tweed ... d.	1557	|	|	|	1722	1737	|	|	1822	1848	1921	...	|	2028	...	2052	2130	...	2157	2230	...	...	...	...	...
Edinburgh ... a.	1646	1701	1718	1736	1814	1824	1832	1910	1908	1934	2013	...	2035	2113	...	2136	2222	...	2244	2318	...	...	...	...	...
Glasgow Central ... a.	1752r	...	1822r	1844	1922r	...	1951r	...	2022r	2035	2119	...	2155r	2225	...	2237	...	...	2355r	0025r	...	...	...	...	...

	⚒ △	① 🍷	②–⑥ 🍷		Ⓐ ✕	Ⓐ ✕	⑥ 🍷	Ⓐ 🍷 G	Ⓐ ✕	⑥ 🍷	Ⓐ 🍷 U	⑥ 🍷 B	Ⓐ ✕	⑥ 🍷	Ⓐ ✕	Ⓐ 🍷 B	⑥ 🍷	Ⓐ ✕	⑥ 🍷 P	Ⓐ 🍷 P	Ⓐ ✕	⑥ 🍷	⑥ 🍷 B	Ⓐ 🍷 G	Ⓐ ✕
Glasgow Central ... d.		...	...	...	...	...	...	...	...	...	...	...	...	...	...	...	...	...	...	...	...	...	...	...	0600r
Edinburgh ... d.		...	...	...	...	...	...	...	...	...	...	...	...	...	0550	...	...	0600	0605	0605	...	0615	...	...	0700
Berwick upon Tweed ... d.		...	...	...	...	...	...	...	...	...	...	...	...	...	0629	...	...	0643	0647	0649	...	0659	...	...	0740
Alnmouth ... d.		...	...	...	...	...	...	...	...	...	...	...	...	...	|	...	...	0703	0707	0711	...	0719	...	...	|
Newcastle ... d.		0422	0431	...	0526	0600	0600	0619	0630	0635	0644	0650	0700	0700	0720	0723	0730	0740	0740y	0744	0749	0754	0824	0824	0830
Durham ... d.		0437	0445	...	0538	0612	0612	0638	0642	0648	0656	0702	0712	0712	|	0737	0742	|	0754	0756	0801	|	0840	0840	0844
Darlington ... d.		0455	0503	...	0556	0630	0630	0655	0701	0706	0714	0730	0730	0730	|	0754	0800	|	0812	0814	0819	0821	0857	0857	0905
Northallerton ... d.		0522	0530	...	0608	|	|	|	0712	|	|	0741	|	0741	|	|	|	|	|	|	|	|	|	|	|
York ... a.		0557	0557	...	0628	0657	0657	0722	0734	0734	0741	0816	0758	0801	0809	0824	0828	0835	0841	0841	0847	0850	0924	0924	0934
Leeds 127 ... a.		|	|	...	|	|	|	|	|	|	0808	|	|	|	|	|	|	|	0908	0908	|	|	|	|	|
Doncaster 127 185 ... a.		0622	0622	...	0653	|	0722	0749	|	0759	|	|	|	|	|	0850	0854	|	|	|	0916	0915	0949	0954	1003
Birmingham New St 127 ... a.		|	|	...	|	|	|	0936	|	|	0958	1036	|	|	|	1036	|	|	1104	1104	|	|	1136	1136	|
London Kings Cross 185 .. a.		0812	0812b	...	0842	0859	0903	...	0935	0951	...	...	0954	1013	1010	...	1041	1040	...	...	1113	1058	...	...	1150

	⑥ 🍷	⚒ 🍷 U	⑥ 🍷	Ⓐ ✕	⑥ 🍷 B	⚒ 🍷‡	Ⓐ 🍷 B	⑥ 🍷 P	Ⓐ 🍷 DP	⑥ 🍷	⚒ 🍷 P	⚒ 🍷‡	⚒ 🍷 DU	⑥ 🍷	Ⓐ ✕	Ⓐ 🍷 B	⑥ 🍷	Ⓐ ✕	⚒ 🍷 Z	Ⓐ ✕ A	⑥ 🍷 A	⑥ 🍷 B	Ⓐ 🍷 P	⑥ 🍷	Ⓐ ✕
Glasgow Central ... d.	0600r	0600f	...	...	...	0650	...	0700r	0700r	0730r	...	0750	0800r	0830r	0831r	...	0850	...	0900	0915r	0915r	...	...	0950	0950
Edinburgh ... d.	0700	0705	0730	...	...	0800	...	0805	0813	0835	...	0900	0905	0930	0930	...	1000	...	1005	1030	1030	...	...	1100	1100
Berwick upon Tweed ... d.	0740	0749	0811	...	...	|	...	0846	0852	0914	...	0941	0949	1011	1010	...	|	...	|	|	|	...	...	1141	1141
Alnmouth ... d.	|	0808v	|	...	...	0856	...	0906	0912	|	...	|	|	|	|	...	|	...	1104	|	|	...	...	|	1201
Newcastle ... d.	0833	0840	0900	0900	0925	0930	0935	0940	0940	1003	1025	1032	1040	1100	1100	1125	1129	1130	1140	1159	1200	1217	1219	1233	1235
Durham ... d.	0846	0852	0913	0912	0937	|	0947	0952	0952	|	1041	1045	1052	|	|	1137	1142	1143	1152	|	1213	1236	1240	1246	1248
Darlington ... d.	0905	0910	0931	0930	0956	0958v	1004	1011	1010	1031	1058	1106c	1110	1127	1128	1156	1201	1202	1210	|	1231	1253	1300	1304	1306
Northallerton ... d.	|	|	0942	0943	|	|	|	|	|	|	|	|	|	|	|	|	|	|	|	|	|	|	|	|	|
York ... a.	0934	0941	1003	1005	1023	1029	1031	1041	1041	1059	1124	1133	1141	1157	1157	1223	1230	1229	1241	1250	1300	1324	1327	1332	1335
Leeds 127 ... a.	|	1008	|	|	|	|	|	1108	1108	|	|	|	1209	|	|	|	|	|	1308	|	|	|	|	|	|
Doncaster 127 185 ... a.	1002	|	1028	1030	1048	1054	1057	|	|	1124	1151	1200c	|	1220	|	1250	1255	1254	|	|	|	1352	1353	1358	1403
Birmingham New St 127 ... a.	|	1158	|	|	1236	|	1236	1304	1304	|	1336	|	1358	|	|	1436	|	|	1506	|	|	1536	1536	|	|
London Kings Cross 185 .. a.	1150	...	1214	1217	...	1242	...	...	...	1310	...	1344	...	1359	1410	...	1444	1444	...	1457	1510	...	...	1541	1544

	⚒ 🍷 AU	Ⓐ ✕ N	⑥ 🍷 N	Ⓐ ✕	⑥ 🍷 B	Ⓐ 🍷 B	⑥ 🍷	⚒ 🍷 P	Ⓐ ✕ A	⑥ 🍷 A	Ⓐ ✕	⚒ 🍷 C	⑥ 🍷	Ⓐ ✕	⚒ 🍷 U	Ⓐ ✕	⑥ 🍷	⚒ 🍷 B	Ⓐ ✕	⑥ 🍷	⑥ 🍷 E	Ⓐ 🍷 P	Ⓐ ✕	⑥ 🍷	Ⓐ ✕
Glasgow Central ... d.	1000r	1030r	1015r	1100r	...	...	1045r	1100r	1130r	1115r	...	...	1150	1150	1200r	...	1215r	...	1300r	1245r	1300r	...	...	...	1350
Edinburgh ... d.	1105	1130	1130	1200	...	...	1200	1205	1230	1230	...	...	1300	1300	1305	...	1330	...	1400	1400	1405	1405	...	...	1500
Berwick upon Tweed ... d.	1149	|	|	1239	...	...	1239	|	|	|	...	...	|	1341	1349	...	1410	...	1440	1439	|	|	...	...	|
Alnmouth ... d.	|	|	1229	|	...	...	|	1303	|	|	...	...	|	|	|	...	|	...	|	|	1504	1505	...	...	|
Newcastle ... d.	1240	1301	1304	1329	1327	1333	1331	1340	1400	1359	1405	1422	1429	1434	1440	1456	1459	1522	1530	1528	1540	1540	1555	1620	1628
Durham ... d.	1252	|	|	|	1339	1346	1344	1352	|	1412	1417	1438	1442	|	1452	1508	|	1534	|	1541	1552	1552	1608	1636	|
Darlington ... d.	1309	|	|	1356	1358	1403	1403	1409	|	1430	1437	1455	1500	1504	1509	1526	1526	1551	1602	1604	1609	1610	1626	1654	|
Northallerton ... d.	|	|	|	|	|	|	1414	|	|	|	1449	|	|	|	|	|	|	|	|	|	|	|	|	|	|
York ... a.	1342	1352	1355	1424	1424	1429	1437	1441	1451	1459	1509	1526	1528	1533	1541	1553	1555	1623	1630	1632	1641	1641	1654	1722	1720
Leeds 127 ... a.	1408	|	|	|	|	|	|	1508	|	|	|	|	|	|	1608	|	|	|	|	|	1708	1708	|	|	|
Doncaster 127 185 ... a.	|	|	|	1449	1453	1455	1503	|	|	|	1535	1554c	1555	1600	|	|	1620	1650	1656	1657	|	|	1720	1750	|
Birmingham New St 127 ... a.	1558	|	|	|	1636	1636	|	1707c	|	|	|	1736	|	|	1758	|	|	1836	|	|	1904	1908	|	1941	|
London Kings Cross 185 .. a.	...	1551	1558	1646	...	...	1647	...	1657	1657	1730	...	1743	1741	...	1804	1810	...	1845	1846	...	...	1911	...	1918

	⑥ 🍷	Ⓐ 🍷 B	⚒ 🍷 S	Ⓐ ✕	⚒ 🍷	⑥ 🍷	Ⓐ ✕	⚒ 🍷 B	Ⓐ 🍷	Ⓐ 🍷	Ⓐ ✕	⑥ 🍷	Ⓐ 🍷 B	⑥ 🍷	⑥ 🍷 A	Ⓐ ✕ A	Ⓐ 🍷 H	Ⓐ 🍷	⑥ 🍷	Ⓐ 🍷	Ⓐ 🍷	Ⓐ 🍷	⑥ 🍷		Ⓐ 🍷
Glasgow Central ... d.	1350	...	1400r	...	...	1500r	1500r	...	...	...	1550	1550	1600r	...	1615r	1615r	...	1700r	1700r	1715r	...	1750	1750	...	1950
Edinburgh ... d.	1500	...	1505	...	...	1600	1600	1605	...	...	1700	1700	1705	...	1730	1730	...	1805	1805	1835	...	1900	1900	...	2100
Berwick upon Tweed ... d.	|	...	1549	...	...	1639	1643	|	...	...	|	|	1749	...	1814	1816	...	|	1851	1918	...	1946	1946	...	2145
Alnmouth ... d.	|	...	|	...	...	|	|	1708	...	...	1759	1759	|	...	|	|	...	1905	1911	1940	...	|	2008	...	2207
Newcastle ... d.	1629	1627	1640	1655	1717	1729	1732	1740	1810	1820	1835	1834	1840	1840	1906	1908	1925	1940	1945n	2018	2026	2037	2046	...	2246
Durham ... d.	1642	1649	1652	1707	1733	|	|	1754	1822	1836	|	1847	1852	1856	|	|	1944	1952	1957	...	2038	2050	2059	...	2301
Darlington ... d.	1700	1706	1709d	1725	1750	1756	1759	1811	1840	1856	1904	1905	1910	1913	1934	1938	2002	2010	2014	...	2055	2108	2117	...	2319
Northallerton ... d.	|	|	|	|	|	|	|	|	1851	|	|	|	|	|	|	|	|	|	|	...	|	|	2129	...	|
York ... a.	1729	1732	1741	1753	1818v	1826	1828	1842	1911	1925	1933	1934	1941	1941	2003	2006	2028	2041	2041	...	2121	2136	2150	...	0016
Leeds 127 ... a.	|	|	1808	|	|	|	|	1908	|	|	|	|	2008	2008	|	|	|	2108	2108	...	|	|	|	...	...
Doncaster 127 185 ... a.	1754	1756	|	1820	1849	1851	1853	|	1937	1955	1959	2003	|	|	2029	2031	2054	|	|	...	|	2202	2216	...	...
Birmingham New St 127 ... a.	|	1936	1958	|	2043	|	|	2104	|	2144	|	|	2208	2213	|	|	...	2321	2320	...	2359	|	...	...	...
London Kings Cross 185 .. a.	1940	...	...	2018	...	2035	2042	...	2117	...	2144	2148	...	...	2217	2220	...	...	...	...	...	0015	...	...	...

A – To / from Aberdeen.
B – From / to Bristol.
C – From / to Cardiff.
D – To / from Dundee.
E – From / to Exeter.
G – From / to Paignton.
H – To Sheffield.
N – To / from Inverness.

P – From / to Plymouth.
Q – From Bristol (and Plymouth on Ⓐ).
R – From Bristol (and Cardiff on ⑥).
S – From Southampton.
U – From / to Bournemouth.
Z – From / to Penzance.

b – 8 minutes earlier on ⑥.

c – 3 minutes earlier on ⑥.
d – ⑥ only.
f – 0550 on ⑥.
j – ⑤ only.
n – Arrives 8–9 minutes earlier.
q – Arrives 1336.
r – Glasgow Queen St.
v – 3–5 minutes later on ⑥.

y – Arrives 6–7 minutes earlier.

‡ – Also conveys ✕ on Ⓐ.

△ – Services on ⑥ are subject to alteration from Mar. 29.

▲ – Services on ⑦ are subject to alteration from Feb. 3.

186 GLASGOW - EDINBURGH - NEWCASTLE - YORK

GR, XC

For TransPennine Express services Newcastle - York, see Table **187**

		⑦ 🍷		⑦ 🍷	⑦ 🍷	⑦ 🍷 U		⑦ 🍷 E	⑦ 🍷	⑦ 🍷	⑦ 🍷 U	⑦ 🍷	⑦ 🍷	⑦ 🍷 E	⑦ 🍷		⑦ 🍷	⑦ 🍷	⑦ 🍷 U	⑦ 🍷	⑦ 🍷 A	⑦ 🍷 E	⑦ 🍷	⑦ 🍷 N
Glasgow Central d.	⑦	...	...	...	...	...	...	...	*0750*r	...	*0830*r	...	...	*0930*r	...	...	...	...	1030	1050	...	1130	...	...
Edinburgh d.		...	...	...	...	...	...	0850	0900	0930	0950	1000	1030	1050	1100	...	1130	...	1150	1200	1230	1250	1300	1330
Berwick upon Tweed d.	▲	...	...	...	...	...	...	0931	0941	|	|	1041	1111	1135	|	...	|	...	|	1241	|	1335	1342	1411
Alnmouth d.		...	...	...	...	...	...	|	|	|	1048	|	|	|	|	...	|	...	1248	|	1330	|	|	|
Newcastle d.		0758	...	0855	0925	0928	...	1025n	1030	1057	1125n	1132	1200	1225	1232	...	1303	1320	1325n	1332	1403	1425	1432	1501
Durham d.		0810	...	0907	|	0941	...	1037	|	1110	1137	|	|	1237	1245	...	|	|	1337	1345	|	1438	|	1515
Darlington d.		0828	...	0925	0952	0958	...	1054	1059	|	1154	|	1227	1254	1303	...	1330	1346	1354	1404	1431	1455	1500	1533
Northallerton d.		|	...	0939	|	|	...	|	|	|	|	|	|	|	|	...	1342	|	|	|	|	|	1511	|
York a.		0858	...	1000	1020	1027	...	1122	1128	1151	1222	1228	1255	1322	1331	...	1403	1417	1422	1434	1500	1522	1532	1602
Leeds **127** a.		|	...	|	|	1053	...	1151	|	|	1251	|	|	1351	|	...	|	|	1451	|	|	1551	|	|
Doncaster **127 185** a.		0925	...	1025	1047	1147	...	1245	1153	|	1343	1254	1320	1448	1356	...	1428	1443	1546	1459	|	1648	1557	1628
Birmingham New St **127** a.		*1153*	...	*1251*	|	1353	...	1451	*1451*	|	1553	|	*1553*	1651	|	...	|	*1651*	1753	*1753*	|	1851	|	*1851*
London Kings Cross **185** a.		1128	...	1219	1237	...	...	...	1336	1404	...	1442	1511	...	1538	...	1611	1629	...	1645	1711	...	1749	1815

	⑦ 🍷 S	⑦ 🍷	⑦ 🍷 A	⑦ 🍷 AB	⑦ 🍷		⑦ 🍷	⑦ 🍷	⑦ 🍷 B	⑦ 🍷		⑦ 🍷 A	⑦ 🍷	⑦ 🍷	⑦ 🍷	⑦ 🍷	⑦ 🍷		⑦ 🍷	⑦ 🍷		⑦ 🍷		⑦ 🍷
Glasgow Central d.	*1230*r	1250	*1300*r	*1330*r	...	...	*1400*r	...	*1430*r	1450	...	*1500*r	1545	1550	*1600*r	*1630*r	...	...	*1730*r	1750	...	*1830*r	...	1950
Edinburgh d.	1350	1400	1430	1450	1500	...	1530	...	1550	1600	...	1630	1650	1700	1730	1750	1800	...	1850	1900	...	2000	...	2100
Berwick upon Tweed d.	|	|	|	1535	1541	...	1611	...	|	|	...	1711	1733	|	|	|	1841	...	|	|	...	2045	...	2144
Alnmouth d.	1448	|	|	|	|	...	|	...	1648	|	...	1734	|	|	|	1852	1903	...	|	|	...	|	...	2206
Newcastle d.	1525n	1530	1559	1625	1633	...	1706	1712	1725	1730	...	1810	1825y	1829	1857	1925	1935	...	2025q	2031	...	2140	...	2241
Durham d.	1537	|	1612	1637	1646	...	|	1724	1737	|	...	|	1837	1842	1910	1937	1948	...	2037	|	...	2153	...	...
Darlington d.	1554	1559	1630	1654	1704	...	1733	1742	1754	1759	...	|	1854	1900	1928	1954	2006	...	2054	2058	...	2211	...	...
Northallerton d.	|	|	|	|	|	...	1745	|	|	|	...	|	|	|	1939	|	|	...	|	|	...	2241	...	...
York a.	1622	1628	1659	1722	1732	...	1806	1810	1822	1828	...	1904	1922	1928	2000	2022	2038	...	2121	2126	...	2319	...	...
Leeds **127** a.	1651	|	|	1752	|	...	|	|	1851	|	...	|	1951	|	|	2051	|	...	|	|	...	...	...	...
Doncaster **127 185** a.	1747	1653	1725	1845	1802	...	1831	1837	1948	1853	...	1930	|	1953	2025	|	2105	...	2149	2151	...	...	...	...
Birmingham New St **127** a.	1953	|	*1953*	2053	|	...	|	*2053*	2153	|	...	*2153*	2225	|	|	2326	|	...	2352	|	...	...	...	...
London Kings Cross **185** a.	...	1840	1916	...	1947	...	2012	2036	...	2042	...	2125	...	2147	2216	...	2314	...	...	2350	...	...	...	...

A – From Aberdeen.
B – To Bristol.
E – To Exeter.
N – From Inverness.
S – To Southampton.
U – To Bournemouth.
n – Arrives 6–8 minutes earlier.
q – Arrives 2013.
r – Glasgow Queen St.
y – Arrives 1819.
▲ – Services on ⑦ are subject to alteration from Feb. 3.

187 NEWCASTLE and MIDDLESBROUGH - YORK

TP

For GNER and Virgin Trains services Newcastle - York and v.v., see Table **186**

km																								
			⚒ A	⚒ L	⚒ A	Ⓐ A	⑥ A	⚒ A	⚒ A	⚒ A	⚒ A	⚒ A	⚒ A	⚒ A	⚒ A	⚒ A	Ⓐ A	⑥ A	Ⓐ A	⑥ A	⚒	⚒ A	⚒ A
0	**Newcastle** d.	⚒	...	0613	...	0726	0733	...	0912	...	1015	...	1115	...	1215	...	1315	...	...	1412	1415	...	1512r	...
23	Durham d.		...	0629	...	0743	0749	...	0927	...	1027	...	1127	...	1227	...	1327	...	...	1424	1427	...	1525	...
	Middlesbrough 211 d.		0558	|	0721	|	|	0900	|	0959	|	1100	|	1200	|	1251	*1255*	1350	1400	*1355*	|	1450	*1455*	1550
58	Darlington 211 d.		|	0647	|	0801	0806	|	0945	|	1045	|	1145	|	1245	|	1345	|	|	1445	1445	|	1545r	|
81	Northallerton d.		0626	0658	0754c	0812	0818	0928	0956	1027	1056	1128	1156	1228	1256	1321	1356	1418	1428	1456	1456	1518	1554	1618
93	Thirsk d.		0633	0707	0802c	0820	0826	0936	|	1035	|	1136	|	1236	|	1329	|	1426	1436	|	|	1526	|	1626
129	**York** a.		0652	0732	0819	0854	0853	0956	1022	1055	1122	1155	1221	1255	1324r	1349	1422	1448	1454	1525	1522	1541p	1621	1649
	Manchester Piccadilly **188** a.		0828	0905	0950	1022	1022	1122	1150	1222	1250	1322	1350	1422	1450	1522	1550	1622	1622	1650	1652	1726	1751	1822

	⚒ A	Ⓐ	⑥	⚒ A	Ⓐ A	⑥ A	⚒	⑥ A	Ⓐ A	⚒ A	⚒	Ⓐ	⑥	Ⓐ A			⑦ L	⑦ A	⑦ A	⑦ A	⑦ A	⑦ L	⑦ A	⑦ A
Newcastle d.	1606	...	...	1710	...	...	...	1852	1858	...	...	...	...	2147	...	⑦	0933	...	1103	...	1249	...	1410	1457
Durham d.	1622	...	...	1722	...	...	...	1904	1910	...	...	...	...	2200	...		0949	...	1116	...	1305	...	1422	1509
Middlesbrough 211 d.	*1555*	1650	1700	*1657*a	1750	1807	1900	|	|	2010	2050	2140	2150	|	...		*0915*	1015	*1053*	1215	*1225*	1345	|	*1438*
Darlington 211 d.	1639	|	|	1740	|	|	|	1922	1928	|	|	2207	2219	2218	...		1005	|	1134	|	1323	|	1440	1527
Northallerton d.	1651	1718	1728	1751	1818	1835	1928	1936	1939	2038	2121r	2218	2230	2229	...		1017	1042	1145	1242	1335	1412	|	1538
Thirsk d.	1659	1726	1736	1759	1826	1843	1936	|	|	2046	2125z	2226	2238	|	...		|	1050	|	1250	|	1419	|	|
York a.	1725c	1750	1755	1824	1851	1904	1959	2002	2003	2107	2142	2252	2257	2304	...		1044	1109	1212	1312	1411	1440	1514	1612
Manchester Piccadilly **188** a.	1852	1924	1924	1950	2035	2035	...	2135	2135	2235	2305	...	0029	0050	...		1205	1233	1333	1433	1533	1605	1634	1733

	⑦ L	⑦ A	⑦ A	⑦ L	⑦ A	⑦ L	⑦ A	⑦ A	
Newcastle d.	...	1608	1648	...	1757	1920	...	*2106*j	...
Durham d.	...	1620	1704	...	1809	1932	...	*2124*j	...
Middlesbrough 211 d.	1545	*1550*	|	1745	*1749*	*1853*	2015	2207	...
Darlington 211 d.	|	1638	1721	|	1827	1950	|	|	...
Northallerton d.	1614	|	1733	1812	|	2001	2042	2234	...
Thirsk d.	1622	|	|	1820	|	|	2050	2242	...
York a.	1641	1712	1759	1839	1900	2032	2109	2309	...
Manchester Piccadilly **188** a.	1805	1833	1933	2005	2033	2205	2233	0033	...

		⚒	⚒	⚒	Ⓐ A	⑥ A	⑥	Ⓐ L	⑥ A	Ⓐ A
Manchester Piccadilly **188** d.	⚒	0338	0539	*0557*	0653	0653	*0712*	0712	0725	0725
York d.		0540	0706	0732	0822	0822	0842	0842	0857	0903
Thirsk d.		0601	0722	0754	0838	0844	|	|	|	|
Northallerton d.		0617	0730	0802	0849	0855	0903	0903	0918	0924
Darlington 211 d.		0636	0743	|	|	|	0915	0915	0930	0938
Middlesbrough 211 a.		0701	*0812*a	0832	0920	0932	*0952*	*0957*	*1016*	*1023*
Durham a.		...	0759	...	...	...	0931	0931	0946	0954
Newcastle a.		...	0820	...	...	...	0949	0949	1004	1012

	⚒ A	Ⓐ A	⑥ A	⚒ A	⚒ A	⚒ A	⑥ A	Ⓐ A	⚒ A	Ⓐ A	⑥ A	⚒ A	⚒ A	Ⓐ A	⑥ A	⚒ A	⚒ A	⚒ A	Ⓐ A	⑥ A	⚒ L	⚒ A	⚒ A	⑥ A
Manchester Piccadilly **188** d.	0755	0825	0825	0857	0925	0957	1027	1027	1057	1127	1127	1157	1227	1257	1257	1327	1357	1457	1527	1527	1612	1655	1725	1755
York d.	0926	1000	0956	1026	1054	1126	1154	1201	1226	1259	1254	1326	1354	1426	1426	1454	1526	1626	1658	1702	1743	1826	1859r	1926
Thirsk d.	0946	|	|	1046	|	1143	|	|	1246	|	|	1346r	|	1443	1446	|	1546	1646	1714	1720	1800	1844	|	1942
Northallerton d.	0955	1021	1025	1055	1115	1155	1215	1222	1255	1320	1323	1355	1416n	1454	1501	1523	1555	1655	1722	1728	1810	1855	1921	1950
Darlington 211 d.	|	1033	1038	|	1128	|	1228	1234	|	1332	1336	|	1434	|	|	1535	|	|	1738	1741	|	|	1934	|
Middlesbrough 211 a.	1030	*1122*	*1108*	1130	*1200*a	1230	*1258*	*1317*	1330	|	*1418*	1430	*1522*v	1530	1534	*1623*	1630	1730v	*1828*	*1825*	1842	1930	|	2023
Durham a.	...	1050	1054	...	1144	...	1245	1250	...	1348	1352	...	1451	...	...	1551	...	...	1755	1757	...	...	1951	...
Newcastle a.	...	1111	1115	...	1202	...	1301	1309	...	1410	1413	...	1506n	...	...	1614	...	...	1816	1818	...	...	2012	...

	Ⓐ A	⚒	⚒ A		Ⓐ A			⑦	⑦	⑦ A	⑦ L	⑦ A	⑦ A	⑦ A	⑦ A	⑦ A	⑦ A	⑦	⑦ A	⑦ A	⑦ A	⑦ A	⑦ A	⑦ L
Manchester Piccadilly **188** d.	1755	1857	1942	...	2142	...	⑦	0642	0742	0842	0912	0944	1042	1142	1242	1342	1442	1456	1542	1642	1742	1842	1942	2112
York d.	1931	2026	2112	...	2322	...		0810	0910	1010	1032	1110	1210	1310	1411	1512	1610	1623	1710	1810	1910	2010	2110	2240
Thirsk d.	1947	2042	2128	...	2339	...		0827	|	1027	|	|	1227	|	1428	|	|	1639	|	1827	|	2027	2128	2306
Northallerton d.	1959	2050	2136	...	2355	...		0835	0931	1035	|	1133	1236	1333	1436	1533	|	1649	1733	1835	1931	2035	2138	2316
Darlington 211 d.	|	|	2149	...	0008	...		|	0943	|	1104	1145	|	1345	|	1545	1642	|	1745	|	1943	|	2150	2332
Middlesbrough 211 a.	2031	2125	*2310*q	...	|	...		0910	*1018*	1110	|	*1224*	1310	*1432*	1509	*1641*	|	1724	*1853*	1910	*2055*	2110	*2310*	|
Durham a.	...	...	2205	...	0024	...		...	0959	...	1120	1201	...	1407	...	1601	1658	...	1801	...	2005	...	2206	2348
Newcastle a.	...	...	2224	...	0057	...		...	1018	...	1141	1220	...	1423	...	1620	1717	...	1823	...	2021	...	2225	0021

A – To / from Manchester Airport.
L – To / from Liverpool.
a – Ⓐ only.
c – 5–6 minutes earlier on ⑥.
j – Change at Thornaby.
n – 6–7 minutes later on ⑥.
p – 1552 on ⑥.
q – *2257* on ⑥.
r – 3–4 minutes earlier on ⑥.
v – 4–5 minutes later on ⑥.
z – ⑥ only.

TP LIVERPOOL - MANCHESTER - HUDDERSFIELD - LEEDS - YORK 188

km		⚒	①	②–⑥	①	②–⑥ M		⚒ N	⚒ S	⚒ M	⚒ S	⚒ N	⚒ M	⚒ S		⚒ N	⚒ M	⚒ S		⚒ S	⚒ M	⚒ S	⚒ M	⚒ S
0	**Liverpool** Lime St .... d.		...	...	...	...	...	...	...	...	0618	...	...	0715c	...	...	...	0821	and at the same minutes (❖) past each hour until	...	1522	...	...	1622
30	Warrington Central .... d.		...	...	...	...	...	...	...	...	0642	...	...	0739c	...	...	...	0844		...	1544	...	...	1644
‡	Manchester Airport ✈ d.		0122	0122	0322	0317	...	*0434*	0534	0623	*0644*v	0702	0734	*0734*	...	0804	0833	|		1534	|	1604	1634	|
56	**Manchester** Piccadilly d.		0138	0138	0338	0338	...	0539	0557	0653	0712	0725	0755	0812	...	0825	0857	0912		1557	1612	1627	1655	1712
68	Stalybridge .... d.		|	|	|	|	...	0552	|	0706	0725	0738	0808	0825	...	|	|	0925		|	1625	|	1708	1725
97	**Huddersfield** .... d.		0213	0227	0411	0427	...	0611	0627	0725	0745	0757	0827	0845	...	0857	0927	0945		1627	1645	1657	1727	1745
110	Dewsbury .... d.		|	|	|	|	...	|	0637	|	0755	0807	0837	|	...	0907	0937	|		1637	|	1707	1737	|
125	**Leeds** ..... 127 189 190 a.		0250	0250	0450	0450	...	0632	0652	0747	0810	0823	0854	0906	...	0922	0952	1009		1652	1709	1722	1752	1809
166	**York** .... 127 189 190 a.		0320	0335	0518	0532r	...	0703	0722	0820	0835	0855	0925	0936	...	0954	1023	1036		1722	1738	1757	1825	1837

	⚒ N	⚒ M	⚒ S	⚒	⚒ M	⚒ S	⚒ N	⚒	⚒ S	⚒	⚒	⚒	⑥	Ⓐ	⑥	Ⓐ	⑦ ▲	⑦		⑦	⑦ M	⑦ N	⑦ M	⑦ N	⑦ N
Liverpool Lime St .... d.	...	...	1722	...	...	1822	...	1922	...	2022	...	...	2230	2230	...	...		...	...	...	...	...	...	0822	...
Warrington Central .... d.	...	...	1744	...	...	1844	...	1944	...	2044	...	...	2252	2252	...	...		...	...	...	...	...	...	0844	...
Manchester Airport ✈ d.	1704	1734	|	*1752*	1834	|	1922n	*1930*	2022	|	2122	2222	|	*2247*	2322	2322		0122	...	0442	0622	0722	0822	*0847*	0925
Manchester Piccadilly d.	1725	1755	1812	1825	1857	1912	1942	2012	2042	2112	2142	2242	2319	2319	2342	2342		0142	...	0502	0642	0742	0842	0912	0944
Stalybridge .... d.	1738	1808	1825	|	|	1925	|	2025	|	2125	2155	|	2333	2333	|	|		|	...	|	0655	0755	0855	|	|
Huddersfield .... d.	1757	1827	1845	1857	1927	1945	2016	2045	2115	2145	2215	2315	2351	2351	0015	0015		0213	...	0533	0712	0812	0912	0942	1014
Dewsbury .... d.	1807	1837	|	1907	1937	|	2025	|	2125	|	2225	2325	|	|	0024	0024		|	...	|	0722	0822	0922	|	1025
Leeds ..... 127 189 190 a.	1822	1853	1909	1924	1952	2009	2040	2109	2139	2209	2239	2339	0013	0023	0039	0046		0234	...	0554	0739	0839	0938	1003	1041
York .... 127 189 190 a.	1852	1922	1935	1955c	2024	2036	2109	2140	2208r	2238	2312r	0008	0041	0106	0108	0129		0304	...	0624	0809	0907	1006	1029	1109

	⑦ S	⑦ M	⑦ N	⑦ S	⑦ M	⑦ N	⑦ S	⑦ N	⑦ M	⑦	⑦ N	⑦ S	⑦ M	⑦	⑦ N	⑦ S	⑦ M	⑦ S	⑦ N	⑦	⑦	⑦ N	⑦	⑦	⑦
Liverpool Lime St .... d.	0922	...	...	1122	...	...	1322	...	...	1422	...	1522	...	1622	...	1722	...	1822	...	1922	...	2022	...	2152	...
Warrington Central .... d.	0945	...	...	1144	...	...	1344	...	...	1444	...	1544	...	1644	...	1744	...	1844	...	1944	...	2044	...	2215	...
Manchester Airport ✈ d.	*0947*	1022	1122	*1147*	1222	1322	*1347*	1422	*1427*	*1447*	1517	*1547*	1622	*1647*	1722	*1747*	1822	*1847*	1922	*1947*	2022	*2047*	2122	*2147*	2322
Manchester Piccadilly d.	1012	1042	1142	1212	1242	1342	1412	1442	1456	1512	1542	1612	1642	1712	1742	1812	1842	1912	1942	2012	2042	2112	2142	2242	2342
Stalybridge .... d.	1025	|	|	1225	|	|	1425	|	|	1525	|	1625	|	1725	|	1825	|	1925	|	2025	|	2125	|	2255	|
Huddersfield .... d.	1044	1112	1212	1244	1312	1412	1444	1512	1530	1544	1612	1644	1712	1744	1812	1844	1912	1944	2012	2044	2112	2144	2212	2312	0012
Dewsbury .... d.	|	1122	1222	|	1322	1422	|	1522	|	|	1622	|	1722	|	1822	|	1922	|	2022	|	2122	|	2222	2322	|
Leeds ..... 127 189 190 a.	1105	1138	1237	1307	1337	1437	1506	1537	1552	1606	1637	1706	1737	1805	1837	1906	1937	2005	2039	2107	2137	2205	2237	2338	0033
York .... 127 189 190 a.	1136	1205	1307	1337	1405	1507	1540	1605	1619	*1704*	1709	1737	1809	1837	1907	1938	2005	2037	2109	2138	2206	2238	2321	0008	0102

	⚒	②–⑥	①	②–⑥	①	⚒	⚒	⚒	⚒	⚒	⚒ M	⚒ S	⚒ N	⚒ S	⚒ M	⚒ S	⚒ N	⚒		⚒ M	⚒ N	⚒ S	⚒ M	⚒ N
York .... 127 189 190 d.		0200	0213	0300	0313	0409d	0526	0558	0628	...	0658	0724c	0740	0754c	0824	0840	0858	0928	and at the same minutes (❖) past each hour until	1458	1528	1538	1558	1628
Leeds ..... 127 189 190 d.		0235	0240	0335	0340	0445q	0555	0625	0655	0710	0725	0755	0810	0825	0855	0910	0925	0955		1525	1555	1610	1625	1655
Dewsbury .... d.		|	|	|	|	|	0606	0637	0707	|	0737	0807	|	0837	0907	|	0937	1007		1537	1607	|	1637	1707
Huddersfield .... d.		0259	0304	0359	0404	0505	0615	0646	0716	0728	0746	0816	0828	0842c	0916	0928	0946	1016		1546	1616	1628	1646	1716
Stalybridge .... d.		|	|	|	|	|	0633	0705	0735	0746	0808	|	0846	|	|	0946	|	|		|	|	1646	|	|
Manchester Piccadilly a.		0359	0359	0458	0458	0600	0650	0722	0753	0805	0828	0852	0905	0923	0950	1005	1022	1050		1622	1650	1705	1724	1752
Manchester Airport ✈ a.		0415	0415	0519	0519	0629	0712	0749	0822	*0842*	0851	0918	*0940*	0944	1014	*1040*	1044	1114		1651	1714r	*1740*	*1805*	1814
Warrington Central .... a.		...	...	...	...	...	...	...	...	0829	...	...	0929	...	...	1028	...	...		...	...	1728	*1802*	...
Liverpool Lime St .... a.		...	...	...	...	...	...	...	...	0857	...	...	0957	...	...	1057	...	...		...	...	1800	*1832*	...

	⚒ S	⚒ M	⚒ N	⚒ S	⚒ M	⚒ N	⚒ S	⚒ M	⚒ S	⚒ N	⚒ S	⚒ M	⚒ M	⑥ M	Ⓐ N		⑦ ▲	⑦	⑦	⑦	⑦	⑦	⑦	⑦	⑦
York .... 127 189 190 d.	1640	1658	1728	1740	1758	1828	1838	1910	1938	2010r	2040	2110	2145	2307	2307	...		0240	0355	0510	0610	0722	0810	...	0915
Leeds ..... 127 189 190 d.	1710	1725	1755	1810	1825	1852	1910	1940	2010	2040	2110	2140	2210	2335	2335	...		0310	0425	0540	0640	0752	0840	0910	0940
Dewsbury .... d.	|	1737	1807	|	1837	|	|	1951	|	2051	|	2151	|	2346	2346	...		|	|	0551	0651	0803	0851	|	0951
Huddersfield .... d.	1728	1746	1816	1828	1846	1913	1928	2000	2028	2100	2128	2200	2228	2356	2356	...		0328	0443	0601	0701	0813	0901	0928	1001
Stalybridge .... d.	1746	1807	|	1846	1907	|	1946	|	2046	|	2146	|	2246	|	|	...		|	|	|	0719	0831	0919	0946	|
Manchester Piccadilly a.	1805	1822	1852	1905	1924	1950	2005	2035	2105	2135	2205	2235	2305	0029	0050	...		0400	0515	0633	0734	0846	0934	1005	1033
Manchester Airport ✈ a.	*1842*	1846	1914	*1940*	*2005*	2012	|	2058	*2137*	2158	*2239*	2258	...	0057	0110	...		0421	0536	0653	0758	0905	0958	*1033*	1104
Warrington Central .... a.	1828	...	...	1928	...	...	2028	...	2128	...	2229	...	...	...	...	...		...	...	...	...	...	...	1028	...
Liverpool Lime St .... a.	1857	...	...	1957	...	...	2055	...	2155	...	2255	...	...	...	...	...		...	...	...	...	...	...	1058	...

	⑦ S	⑦ N	⑦ M	⑦ S	⑦ N	⑦	⑦ M	⑦ S	⑦ N	⑦ M	⑦ N	⑦ S	⑦ N	⑦ M	⑦ N	⑦ S	⑦ N	⑦ M	⑦ N	⑦ S	⑦ N	⑦ M	⑦ S	⑦ S	⑦ M
York .... 127 189 190 d.	1015	1045	1115	1140	1215	1245	1315	1342	1415	1445	1515	1539	1615	1645	1714	1740	1815	1845	1915	1942	2045	2115	2138	2242	2312
Leeds ..... 127 189 190 d.	1040	1110	1140	1210	1240	1310	1340	1410	1440	1510	1540	1610	1640	1710	1740	1810	1840	1910	1940	2010	2110	2140	2210	2310	2340
Dewsbury .... d.	1051	|	1151	|	1251	|	1351	|	1451	|	1551	|	1651	|	1751	|	1851	|	1951	2021	2121	2151	|	|	2351
Huddersfield .... d.	1101	1128	1201	1228	1301	1328	1401	1428	1501	1528	1601	1628	1701	1728	1801	1828	1901	1928	2001	2030	2130	2201	2228	2328	0001
Stalybridge .... d.	|	1146	|	1246	|	1346	|	1446	|	1546	|	1646	|	1746	|	1846	|	1946	|	2048	2148	|	2246	|	|
Manchester Piccadilly a.	1133	1205	1233	1305	1333	1405	1433	1505	1533	1605	1634	1705	1733	1805	1833	1905	1933	2005	2033	2105	2205	2233	2303	0003	0033
Manchester Airport ✈ a.	1156	*1233*	1258	*1333*	1358	*1433*	1458	*1533*	1558	*1633*	1658	*1733*	1758	*1833*	1858	*1933*	1958	*2033*	2058	*2133*	*2233*	2258	*2333*	*0033*	0054
Warrington Central .... a.	...	1228	...	1328	...	1428	...	1528	...	1628	...	1728	...	1828	...	1929	...	2028	...	2128	2228	...	...	...	...
Liverpool Lime St .... a.	...	1257	...	1357	...	1457	...	1557	...	1657	...	1757	...	1857	...	1957	...	2057	...	2157	2300	...	...	...	...

M – To/from Middlesbrough.
N – To/from Newcastle.
S – To/from Scarborough.
c – 3–4 minutes later on ⑥.
d – 0419 on ⑥.
n – 1915 on ⑥.
q – 0440 on ①.
r – 3–5 minutes earlier on ⑥.
v – *0628* on ⑥.
❖ – Timings on some services may vary by a few minutes.
‡ – Manchester Airport - Manchester Piccadilly: *16 km*.
▲ – Services on ⑦ are subject to alteration from Feb. 3.

TP SCARBOROUGH - YORK 189

km		⚒	Ⓐ A	⑥ A	Ⓐ A	⑥ A	⚒ L	⚒ L	⚒ L	⚒ L		⚒ L	⚒	⚒		⑦	⑦ A	⑦ L	⑦ L	⑦ L	⑦ L	⑦ L	⑦ M	⑦ M
0	**Scarborough** .... d.		0630	0634	0700	0705	0747	0847	0947	1045	and hourly until	1945	2037	2207	...		0920	1045	1245	1445	1645	1845	2045	2145
34	Malton .... d.		0653	0657	0723	0728	0810	0910	1010	1108		2008	2100	2230	...		0943	1108	1308	1508	1708	1908	2108	2208
68	**York** 127 188 190 .... a.		0721	0724	0751	0755	0837	0937	1037	1137		2037	2128	2257	...		1010	1135	1335	1535	1735	1935	2135	2235
	Leeds **127 188 190** .. a.		0752	0752	0823	0823	0904	1004	1104	1205		2104	2200y	*2333*	...		1038	1207	1407	1607	1807	2007	2204	2308

	⚒	⚒	⚒ A	⚒ L		⚒ L	⚒ A	⚒ A	⑥ L	Ⓐ L	⚒ L	⚒ L	⚒ A		⑦	⑦	⑦ L	⑦ L		⑦ L	⑦ L	⑦ L	⑦ L	⑦ A
Leeds **127 188 190** .. d.		...	0655	0812	and hourly until	1612	1657	1724	1812	1812	1912	2012	2142	...		0910	1110	1310	...	1510	1710	1910	2010	2140
York 127 188 190 .... d.		0638	0725	0838		1638	1726	1800	1838	1842	1938	2038	2208	...		0938	1138	1338	...	1544	1738	1938	2038	2208
Malton .... d.		0702	0749	0902		1702	1750	1824	1902	1906	2002	2102	2232	...		1002	1202	1402	...	1608	1802	2002	2102	2232
Scarborough .... a.		0730	0814	0930		1730	1817	1851	1930	1930	2030	2130	2302	...		1027	1230	1429	...	1633	1829	2030	2129	2301

A – To/from Manchester Airport.
L – To/from Liverpool.
M – To/from Manchester Piccadilly.
y – *2208* on ⑥.

190 LEEDS - HALIFAX - BLACKPOOL and MANCHESTER

2nd class NT

Services on ⑦ are subject to alteration from February 3

km	⚒	Ⓐ	⚒	⚒	⚒	⚒	⚒	⚒	⚒	⚒	⚒	⚒	⚒	⚒	⚒		⚒	⚒	⚒	⚒	⚒	⚒	⚒
	York 127 188 189 d.	...	...	...	...	0613	...	...	0706	...	...	0807z	...	...	0909		...	...	1810	...	1904	...	...
0	Leeds 127 188 189 d.	0508	0551	0603	0637	0651	0709	0737	0751	0808	0837	0851	0908	0937	0951		1808	1837	1851	1937	1951	2037	2137
15	Bradford Interchange d.	0531	0614	0625	0700	0714	0732	0800	0814	0831	0900	0911v	0931	1000	1014	and at	1831	1900	1914	2000	2014	2100	2200
28	Halifax d.	0543	0627	0637	0712	0726	0744	0812	0826	0843	0912	0925	0943	1012	1026	the	1843	1912	1926	2012	2026	2112	2212
42	Hebden Bridge d.	0559	0642	0649	0728	0738	0800	0828	0838	0859	0928	0937	0959	1028	1038	same	1859	1928	1938	2028	2038	2128	2228
63	Burnley Manchester Rd d.	│	│	0708	│	0757	│	│	0857	│	│	0957	│	│	1057	minutes	│	│	1957	│	2057	│	│
72	Accrington d.	│	│	0717	│	0806	│	│	0906	│	│	1005	│	│	1106	(❖)	│	│	2005	│	2105	│	│
81	Blackburn d.	│	│	0725	│	0815	│	│	0915	│	│	1014	│	│	1115	past	│	│	2014	│	2114	│	│
100	Preston 152 a.	│	│	0747	│	0833	│	│	0934	│	│	1032	│	│	1134	each	│	│	2031	│	2131	│	│
129	Blackpool North 152 a.	│	│	0812	│	0904	│	│	1002	│	│	1103	│	│	1201	hour	│	│	2056	│	2156	│	│
49	Todmorden d.	0606	0650	...	0735	...	0807	0835	...	0906	0936	...	1006	1035	...	until	1906	1935	...	2035	...	2135	2235
63	Rochdale d.	0624	0706	...	0752	...	0824	0852	...	0922	0953	...	1023	1050	...		1923	1952	...	2052	...	2152	2252
81	Manchester Victoria a.	0646	0729	...	0816	...	0846	0909	...	0940	1010	...	1041	1110	...		1940	2014	...	2114	...	2214	2314

	⚒		⑦	⑦	⑦	⑦	⑦	⑦	⑦	⑦	⑦	⑦	⑦	⑦	⑦	⑦ ⊡	⑦	⑦ ⊡	⑦	⑦	⑦	⑦		⑦
York 127 188 189 d.	...	...	...	...	...	...	...	...	...	...	...	...	...	...	...	1552	...	1655	...	...	...	...	...	2057
Leeds 127 188 189 d.	2237	...	0821	0902	...	1002	1102	...	1204	1302	...	1402	1502	...	1602	1635	1702	1735	1802	1902	...	2002	...	2135
Bradford Interchange d.	2300	...	0845	0926	...	1026	1126	...	1228	1326	...	1426	1526	...	1626	1655	1726	1755	1826	1926	...	2026	...	2158
Halifax d.	2312	...	0901	0939	...	1038	1138	...	1240	1338	...	1438	1538	...	1638	1707	1738	1807	1838	1938	...	2039	...	2211
Hebden Bridge d.	2328	...	0917	0954	1000*	1054	1154	1200*	1256	1354	1400*	1454	1554	1600*	1654	1725*	1754	1825*	1854	1954	2000*	2054	...	2226
Burnley Manchester Rd d.	│	...	│	│	1037	│	│	1237	│	│	1437	│	│	1637	│	1800	│	1900	│	│	2037	│	...	│
Accrington d.	│	...	│	│	1047	│	│	1247	│	│	1447	│	│	1647	│	1810	│	1912	│	│	2047	│	...	│
Blackburn d.	│	...	│	│	1056	│	│	1256	│	│	1456	│	│	1656	│	1819	│	1920	│	│	2056	│	...	│
Preston 152 a.	│	...	│	│	1113	│	│	1313	│	│	1513	│	│	1713	│	1837	│	1938	│	│	2113	│	...	│
Blackpool North 152 a.	│	...	│	│	1138	│	│	1338	│	│	1538	│	│	1738	│	1905	│	2003	│	│	2138	│	...	│
Todmorden d.	2335	...	0924	1002	...	1101	1201	...	1303	1401	...	1501	1601	...	1701	...	1801	...	1901	2001	...	2101	...	2234
Rochdale d.	2352	...	0941	1018	...	1118	1218	...	1319	1418	...	1518	1618	...	1718	...	1818	...	1918	2018	...	2118	...	2250
Manchester Victoria a.	0008	...	1001	1039	...	1138	1238	...	1340	1438	...	1538	1638	...	1738	...	1838	...	1938	2038	...	2138	...	2311

⚒	⚒	⚒	⚒	⚒	⚒	⚒	⚒	⚒	⚒	⚒		⚒	⚒	⚒	⚒	⚒	⚒	Ⓐ	⑥	⚒	⚒	⚒	Ⓐ
Manchester Victoria d.	0554	...	0618z	0649	...	0718	0747	...	0819	0854		...	1718	1749	...	1819	...	1918	1926	2019	...	2119	2219
Rochdale d.	0609	...	0639	0709	...	0739	0807	...	0839	0909		...	1739	1809	...	1839	...	1939	1947	2039	...	2139	2239
Todmorden d.	0626	...	0656	0726	...	0756	0824	...	0856	0926	and at	...	1756	1826	...	1856	...	1956	2004	2056	...	2156	2256
Blackpool North 152 d.	│	0530	│	│	0627	│	│	0730	│	│	the	1630	│	│	1719	│	1830	│	│	│	2028	│	│
Preston 152 d.	│	0555	│	│	0654	│	│	0755	│	│	same	1655	│	│	1744	│	1855	│	│	│	2054	│	│
Blackburn d.	│	0611	│	│	0711	│	│	0811	│	│	minutes	1711	│	│	1811	│	1911	│	│	│	2111	│	│
Accrington d.	│	0619	│	│	0718	│	│	0819	│	│	(❖)	1719	│	│	1819	│	1919	│	│	│	2118	│	│
Burnley Manchester Rd d.	│	0628	│	│	0727	│	│	0828	│	│	past	1728	│	│	1828	│	1928	│	│	│	2127	│	│
Hebden Bridge d.	0633	0650	0703	0733	0750	0803	0833	0850	0903	0933	each	1750	1803	1833	1850	1903	1950	2003	2011	2103	2150	2203	2303
Halifax d.	0649	0702	0719	0749	0802	0819	0850	0902	0919	0949	hour	1802	1819	1849	1902	1919	2002	2019	2027	2119	2202	2219	2319
Bradford Interchange d.	0705	0718	0735	0805	0818	0833	0906	0918	0935	1005	until	1818	1835	1905	1918	1935	2018v	2033	2043	2135	2218	2235	2335
Leeds 127 188 189 a.	0727	0737	0759	0828	0839	0857	0928	0939	0958	1028		1837	1859	1928	1937	1958	2040	2057	2107	2158	2238	2258	2358
York 127 188 189 a.	...	0819	...	...	0923r	...	...	1020	...	...		1920	...	...	2021	...	2130	...	...	...	2333v	...	...

	⑥	Ⓐ		⑦	⑦	⑦	⑦	⑦	⑦	⑦	⑦	⑦	⑦	⑦	⑦	⑦ ⊠	⑦	⑦ ⊠	⑦	⑦	⑦	⑦	⑦	⑦
Manchester Victoria d.	2249	2319	...	0914	1015	1115	...	1215	1315	...	1415	1515	...	1615	1715	...	1815	...	1915	...	2015	2115	...	2215
Rochdale d.	2309	2339	...	0934	1034	1134	...	1234	1334	...	1434	1534	...	1634	1734	...	1834	...	1934	...	2034	2134	...	2234
Todmorden d.	2326	2356	...	0951	1051	1151	...	1251	1351	...	1451	1551	...	1651	1751	...	1851	...	1951	...	2051	2151	...	2251
Blackpool North 152 d.	│	│	...	│	│	│	1112	│	│	1312	│	│	1512	│	│	1645	│	1745	│	1912	│	│	2112	│
Preston 152 d.	│	│	...	│	│	│	1138	│	│	1338	│	│	1538	│	│	1711	│	1811	│	1938	│	│	2138	│
Blackburn d.	│	│	...	│	│	│	1155	│	│	1355	│	│	1555	│	│	1728	│	1828	│	1955	│	│	2155	│
Accrington d.	│	│	...	│	│	│	1202	│	│	1402	│	│	1602	│	│	1738	│	1835	│	2002	│	│	2202	│
Burnley Manchester Rd d.	│	│	...	│	│	│	1220*	│	│	1420*	│	│	1620*	│	│	1757*	│	1856*	│	2020*	│	│	2220*	│
Hebden Bridge d.	2333	0003	...	0958	1058	1158	1250*	1258	1358	1450*	1458	1558	1650*	1658	1758	1832	1858	1932	1958	2050*	2058	2158	2250*	2258
Halifax d.	2349	0019	...	1014	1114	1214	...	1314	1414	...	1514	1614	...	1714	1814	1845	1914	1945	2014	...	2114	2214	...	2314
Bradford Interchange d.	0005	0035	...	1031	1131	1231	...	1331	1431	...	1531	1631	...	1731	1831	1902	1931	2002	2031	...	2131	2231	...	2331
Leeds 127 188 189 a.	0028	0054	...	1052	1154	1252	...	1352	1453	...	1552	1654	...	1752	1854	1921	1953	2022	2054	...	2154	2253	...	2352
York 127 188 189 a.	...	...	...	...	...	...	...	...	...	...	...	...	...	...	...	1959	...	2102	...	...	...	...	...	...

r – 0920 on ⑥.
v – 3 minutes earlier on ⑥.
z – ⑥ only.
z – 0624 on ⑥.
* – By 🚌.
❖ – Timings may vary by up to 5 minutes on some journeys.
⊡ – Change to 🚌 at Hebden Bridge. Change to train at Burnley.
⊠ – Change to 🚌 at Burnley. Change to train at Hebden Bridge.

191 GRIMSBY - LINCOLN - NEWARK

2nd class EM

km		Ⓐ N	Ⓐ	Ⓐ	Ⓐ	Ⓐ	Ⓐ	Ⓐ	Ⓐ	Ⓐ	Ⓐ	Ⓐ	Ⓐ	⑥	⑥	⑥	⑥	⑥	⑥	⑥	⑥	⑥
0	Cleethorpes 194 d.	...	0551	0618	...	0900	1100	...	1328	1528	...	1728	2114	...	0618	...	0900	1113	1300	1500	...	1728
5	Grimsby Town 194 d.	...	0558	0703	...	0928	1128	...	1352	1603	...	1830	2121	...	0659	...	0928	1130	1325	1528	...	1806
52	Market Rasen d.	...	0634	0739	...	1003	1203	...	1427	1636	...	1906	2154	...	0733	...	1001	1203	1359	1601	...	1842
76	Lincoln d.	0523	0654	0759	0910	1023	1223	1404	1447	1656	1817	1926	2215	0655	0754	0910	1023	1223	1419	1622	1809	1910r
102	Newark North Gate a.	0551	0717	0822	0933	1049	1249	1428	1511	1722	1842	1950	...	0723	0815	0933	1045	1245	1444	1652	1832	1934
	London Kings Cross 185 a.	0730	0848	0951	1110	1225	1505	1646	1704	1848	2018	2133	...	0918	0951	1132	1224	1427	1630	1828	2012	2115

	⑥	⑥ N		⑦	⑦	⑦ N	⑦ N	⑦ N
Cleethorpes 194 d.	1900	...	...	...	...	...	...	...
Grimsby Town 194 d.	1928	...	...	...	...	...	...	...
Market Rasen d.	2002	...	...	...	...	...	...	...
Lincoln d.	2020	2041	...	1105	1305	1459	1800	2059
Newark North Gate a.	...	2109	...	1128	1328	1527	1829	2127
London Kings Cross 185 a.	...	2247	...	1313	1515	1717	2036	2314

	Ⓐ	Ⓐ	Ⓐ	Ⓐ	Ⓐ	Ⓐ	Ⓐ	Ⓐ	Ⓐ
London Kings Cross 185 d.	...	0615	0710	0830	1035	1135	1235	1410	...
Newark North Gate d.	...	0746	0835	0957	1207	1305	1433	1537	...
Lincoln d.	0557	0817	0900	1022	1238r	1328	1457	1600	1718
Market Rasen d.	0613	0834	...	1039	1255	...	1514	...	1735
Grimsby Town 194 a.	0657	0915	...	1120	1335	...	1556	...	1814
Cleethorpes 194 a.	0750	0958	...	1154	1354	...	1648	...	1850

	Ⓐ	Ⓐ	Ⓐ	Ⓐ N	Ⓐ N	⑥	⑥	⑥	⑥	⑥	⑥	⑥	⑥	⑥	⑥	⑥	⑥ N	⑦	⑦	⑦ N	⑦ N	⑦ N	⑦ N
London Kings Cross 185 d.	1610	1750	1833	1930	2130	...	...	0700	0810	1010	1210	1330	...	1530	1630	1840	2030	1000	1200	1530	1730	1910	2130
Newark North Gate d.	1734	1924	2000	2111	2258	...	...	0831	0956	1134	1335	1503	...	1751	1851	2015	2127	1134	1334	1717	1917	2115	2318
Lincoln d.	1757	1952	2028	2144	2333	0557	0829	0854	1021	1159	1406r	1526	1650	1816	1919	2040	2236	1156	1356	1751	1950	2149	2352
Market Rasen d.	...	2009	...	...	...	0613	0845	...	1037	1215	1422	...	1707	1833	...	2056	...	...	...	...	...	...	...
Grimsby Town 194 a.	...	2052	...	...	...	0653	0923	...	1117	1255	1501	...	1754	1914	...	...	...	...	...	...	...	...	...
Cleethorpes 194 a.	...	2101	...	...	...	0750	0958	...	1154	1354	1554	...	1850	2009	...	...	...	...	...	...	...	...	...

N – To / from Nottingham.
r – Arrives 8–9 minutes earlier.

KNOW SOMETHING . . . we don't?

We constantly strive to keep the information in this book accurate and up-to-date. So if you have 'inside information' on forthcoming changes or spot an inaccuracy, do drop us a line and tell us. Write to The Editor, Thomas Cook European Rail Timetable, P.O. Box 227, Peterborough PE3 8SB, United Kingdom, or e-mail us at timetables@thomascook.com

EM 2nd class — LINCOLN - NOTTINGHAM - LEICESTER — 192

km		Ⓐ	Ⓐ	Ⓐ	Ⓐ	Ⓐ	Ⓐ	Ⓐ	Ⓐ	Ⓐ	Ⓐ	Ⓐ	Ⓐ	Ⓐ	Ⓐ	Ⓐ	Ⓐ	Ⓐ	Ⓐ	Ⓐ	Ⓐ		⑥	⑥	⑥
0	**Lincoln** d.		0523	...	0710	0729	0834	0931	1036	1143	1231	1335	1438	1532	1640	...	1729	1833	...	2043	2231	...		0550	...
27	Newark Castle d.		0608	...	0733	0757	0905	0958	1103	1205	1258	1403	1501	1558	1705	...	1759	1855	...	2110	2258	...		0617	...
55	**Nottingham** a.		0648	...	0812	0832	0930	1033	1131	1228	1332	1428	1535	1630	1728	...	1840	1930	...	2147	2335	...		0656	...
55	**Nottingham** 170 d.		*0707*	0738	*0826*	0836	0938	1038	1138	1238	1338	1438	1538	1638	1738	1838	*1907*	1938	2038	...	...	...		*0707*	0738
79	Loughborough 170 a.		*0722*	0801	*0843*	0901	1000	1100	1200	1300	1400	1500	1600	1702	1802	1900	*1922*	2001	2100	...	...	...		*0722*	0801
99	**Leicester** 170 a.		*0737*	0825	*0855*	0925	1025	1125	1225	1325	1425	1525	1625	1725	1826	1925	*1935*	2025	2125	...	...	...		*0734*	0825

	⑥	⑥	⑥	⑥	⑥	⑥	⑥	⑥	⑥	⑥	⑥	⑥	⑥	⑥	⑥	⑥		⑦ ▲	⑦		⑦	⑦	⑦	⑦	⑦
Lincoln d.	0655	0730	0834	0923	1036	1141	1231	1335	1432	1535	1640	1735	...	1843	1940	2041	...		1459	...	1800	1910	2012	2058	2212
Newark Castle d.	0735	0757	0905	0954	1104	1207	1258	1404	1458	1601	1706	1802	...	1907	2008	2125	...		1542	...	1844	1939	2039	2140	2240
Nottingham a.	0815	0831	0932	1029	1133	1232	1332	1431	1533	1631	1730	1836	...	1933	2051	2203	...		1622	...	1922	2018	2118	2208	2320
Nottingham 170 d.	*0835*	0838	0938	1038	1138	1238	1338	1438	1538	1638	1738	1838	1933	*2007*	*2130*	...	...		*1630*	...	...	*2030*	...	...	...
Loughborough 170 a.	|	0901	1001	1101	1201	1301	1401	1501	1601	1702	1802	1901	1957	|	*2146*	...	...		|	...	...	|	...	...	...
Leicester 170 a.	*0857*	0925	1025	1125	1225	1325	1425	1525	1625	1725	1825	1925	2022	*2034*	*2200*	...	...		*1658*	...	...	*2055*	...	...	...

	Ⓐ	Ⓐ	Ⓐ		Ⓐ	Ⓐ		Ⓐ	Ⓐ	Ⓐ	Ⓐ	Ⓐ	Ⓐ	Ⓐ	Ⓐ	Ⓐ	Ⓐ	Ⓐ	Ⓐ	Ⓐ	Ⓐ	Ⓐ		⑥	⑥
Leicester 170 d.		...	...	...	*0640*	0724	...	0835	0936	1035	1135	1235	1335	1435	1535	1635	*1656*	1735	1833	1936	2034	*2107*	...		...
Loughborough 170 d.		...	...	...	*0700*	0743	...	0855	0956	1055	1155	1255	1355	1455	1555	1655	*1707*	1755	1855	1957	2054	*2118*	...		...
Nottingham 170 a.		...	...	...	*0730*	0820	...	0920	1020	1120	1219	1318	1421	1518	1618	1718	*1726*	1818	1920	2022	2123	*2137*	...		...
Nottingham d.		0603	0658	...	0809	...	...	0926	1026	1126	1226	1326	1426	1525	1625	1721	1746	1825	...	2024	...	2222	...		0603
Newark Castle d.		0635	0729	...	0841	...	...	0949	1058	1151	1252	1358	1452	1557	1646	1753	1814	1858	...	2056	...	2243	...		0635
Lincoln a.		0711	0803	...	0910	...	...	1018	1132	1219	1326	1428	1527	1634	1713	1825	1848	1932	...	2144	...	2333	...		0711

	⑥	⑥	⑥	⑥	⑥	⑥	⑥	⑥	⑥	⑥	⑥	⑥	⑥	⑥	⑥	⑥		⑦ ▲	⑦	⑦	⑦	⑦	⑦		⑦
Leicester 170 d.	...	*0640*	0728	0832	0930	1030	1130	1230	1330	1430	1530	1630	1730	1830	1929	*2030*	...		*1529*	*1623*	*1723*	*1824*	*1920*	...	*2123*
Loughborough 170 d.	...	*0700*	0753	0852	0952	1052	1152	1252	1352	1452	1552	1652	1752	1852	1952	*2052*	...		*1540*	*1634*	*1734*	|	*1933*	...	*2137*
Nottingham 170 a.	...	*0727*	0816	0916	1018	1117	1216	1316	1418	1518	1616	1716	1816	1916	2019	*2117*	...		*1557*	*1651*	*1751*	*1849*	*1950*	...	*2154*
Nottingham d.	0700	0806	...	0927	1025	1124	1226	1326	1424	1524	1626	1724	1826	1926	2026	2127	...		1630	1730	1830	1930	2030	...	2230
Newark Castle d.	0730	0838	...	0949	1057	1151	1253	1358	1449	1557	1659	1756	1859	1959	2048	2151	...		1702	1803	1902	2002	2102	...	2302
Lincoln a.	0805	0912	...	1018	1127	1221	1327	1427	1525	1631	1730	1830	1930	2034	2125	2236	...		1751	1837	1950	2037	2149	...	2352

▲ – Services on ⑦ are subject to alteration from Mar. 30.

XC 2nd class — LEICESTER - NUNEATON - BIRMINGHAM — 193

km		⚒	⑥	Ⓐ		⑥	Ⓐ	⚒	Ⓐ	⑥	Ⓐ	⚒		⚒	⚒		⚒	⚒	⚒	⚒	⚒	⚒		⚒	⚒
								C		A	A			C			A		A		A			A	
	Peterborough 207 d.		...	...	...	...	...	0608	...	0650	0655	...	...	0746q	...	...	0854	...	0954	...	1054	...	...	1154	...
0	**Leicester** d.		0545	0603	...	0647	0652	0707	0724	0746	0751	0808	...	0852	0909	...	0952	1009	1052	1109	1152	1209	...	1252	1309
22	Hinckley d.		0603	0624	...	0707	0710	0726	|	0804	0809	0828	...	|	0926	...	|	1028	|	1126	|	1228	...	|	1326
30	Nuneaton a.		0610	0631	...	0714	0717	0733	0742	0811	0816	0836	...	0914	0934	...	1014	1035	1113	1135	1214	1235	...	1314	1335
47	Coleshill Parkway a.		0631	0646	...	0730	0732	0753	0757	0830	|	0857	...	0929	0953	...	1029	1054	1129	1156	1229	1254	...	1329	1356
62	**Birmingham** New St a.		0646	0705	...	0746	0750	0809	0815	0848	0848	0909	...	0947	1009	...	1047	1109	1147	1209	1247	1309	...	1347	1409

	⚒	⚒	⚒	⚒	⚒	⚒	⚒	⚒	⑥	Ⓐ	⑥	Ⓐ	⚒	⚒	Ⓐ	⑥	⚒	⚒	⚒	Ⓐ	⑥		⑥	Ⓐ	Ⓐ
	A		A		A		A		A	A			A		A	A		A		A	A				A
Peterborough 207 d.	1254	...	1354	...	1454	...	1554	...	1654	1654	...	...	1754	...	1844	1854	...	1954	...	2041	2045	...	...	...	2154
Leicester d.	1352	1409	1452	1509	1552	1609	1652	1709	1752	1752	1809	1823	1852	1909	1941	1952	2009	2052	2109	2136	2139	...	2226	2227	2249
Hinckley d.	|	1428	|	1529r	|	1628	|	1728	|	1810	1829	1842	|	1928	|	|	2027	|	2128	|	|	...	2244	2246	|
Nuneaton a.	1414	1435	1513	1536r	1613	1635	1714	1736	1813	1817	1836	1849	1914	1937	2000	2013	2035	2113	2135	2157	2200	...	2251	2253	2308
Coleshill Parkway a.	1429	1454	1529	1552	1629	1654	1729	1752	1829	|	1852	|	1929	1954	2015	2029	2057d	2129	2152z	2216	2217	...	2310	2314	2326
Birmingham New St a.	1447	1509	1547	1609	1647	1712	1747	1809	1847	1848	1908	1918	1947	2009	2037	2047	2109d	2147	2204	2236	2235	...	2322	2334	2343

	⑦ ▲	⑦		⑦	⑦	⑦		⑦	⑦	⑦	⑦	⑦	⑦	⑦	⑦	⑦	⑦	⑦		⑦		⑦	⑦		⑦
					C				A		C		A		A		A			A		A			
Peterborough 207 d.		...	...	...	1152	...	...	...	1335	...	1441	...	1533	...	1640	...	1741	...	...	1901	...	2006	...	...	...
Leicester d.		1115	...	1215	1248	1315	...	1415	1440	1515	1544	1615	1634	1715	1743	1813	1838	1914	...	2009	...	2102	2112	...	2308
Hinckley d.		1135	...	1236	|	1336	...	1436	|	1536	|	1635	|	1735	|	1834	|	1934	...	|	...	|	2135	...	2335
Nuneaton a.		1142	...	1243	1311	1344	...	1444	1501	1643	1611	1642	1654	1743	1803	1842	1858	1941	...	2029	...	2122	2143	...	2343
Coleshill Parkway a.		1203	...	1301	1329	1400	...	1501	1518	1559	1629	1658	1715	1800	1820	1859	1917	1959	...	2049	...	2142	2159	...	|
Birmingham New St a.		1217	...	1317	1347	1417	...	1517	1537	1613	1648	1713	1732	1814	1838	1914	1936	2014	...	2106	...	2200	2212	...	0012

	⚒	⚒		Ⓐ	⑥		⑥	Ⓐ	Ⓐ	⑥	Ⓐ	⑥	⚒	⚒	⚒	⚒	⚒	⚒	⚒	⚒	⚒	⚒	⚒	⚒	⚒
		A						A			A	A		A		A		A		A		A		A	
Birmingham New St d.		0520	...	0555	0554	...	0636	0637	0654	0652	0721	0724	0754	0824	0854	0924	0954	1024	1054	1124	1154	1224	1254	1324	1354
Coleshill Parkway d.		|	...	|	0607	...	|	0649	|	0706	|	0737	0807z	0837	0910z	0937	1007	1037	1108	1137	1207	1237	1309	|	1407
Nuneaton d.		0546	...	0621	0624	...	0704	0705	0722	0724	0748	0753	0824	0853	0925	0953	1023	1053	1125	1153	1224	1253	1325	1353	1424
Hinckley d.		|	...	0628	0631	...	|	|	0728	0731	0755	|	0831	|	0932	|	1030	|	1132	|	1231	|	1332	|	1431
Leicester a.		0608	...	0646	0651	...	0725	0728	0748	0750	0813	0813	0850	0913	0951	1013	1050	1113	1150	1213	1250	1313	1350	1413	1450
Peterborough 207 a.		0708	...	...	...	...	0831	0828	...	...	0914	0914	...	1014	...	1114	...	1214	...	1314	...	1414	...	1514	...

	⚒	⚒	⚒	⚒	Ⓐ	⑥	Ⓐ	⚒	Ⓐ	⑥	Ⓐ		Ⓐ	⑥	⚒	⚒	Ⓐ	⑥		⚒	Ⓐ	⑥		⑥	Ⓐ
	A		A		C	C	A			A	C				C		C			C					
Birmingham New St d.	1424	1454	1524	1554	1612	1624	1624	1654	1712	1724	1724	...	1759	1805	1824	1854	1926	1954	...	2027	2054	2115	...	2209	2215
Coleshill Parkway d.	1437	1509	1537z	1607	1626	1637	1640	1708	1728	1737	1739	...	|	|	1837	1907	|	|	...	|	2108	2128	...	|	|
Nuneaton d.	1453	1525	1553	1623	1641	1653	1656	1725	1746	1753	1755	...	1827	1833	1853	1924	1951	2024	...	2054	2124	2144	...	2236	2245
Hinckley d.	|	1532	|	1630	|	|	|	1732	1753	|	|	...	1834	1840	|	1931	|	2031	...	|	2131	2150	...	2243	2252
Leicester a.	1513	1550	1613	1650	1701	1713	1727	1750	1812	1813	1816	...	1853	1859	1913	1951	2015	2050	...	2114	2151	2211	...	2302	2310
Peterborough 207 a.	1614	...	1716	...	1758	1814	1832	...	...	1914	1919	...	...	...	2014q	...	2116	...	...	2215	...	...	...	...	...

	⑦ ▲	⑦		⑦	⑦	⑦		⑦		⑦	⑦	⑦	⑦	⑦	⑦	⑦	⑦	⑦	⑦	⑦		⑦	⑦		⑦
					A					A		A		C		A		A		A			C		
Birmingham New St d.		0953	...	1055	1126	1155	...	1255	...	1336	1353	1434	1455	1532	1555	1634	1655	1734	1755	1834	...	1955	2028	...	2153
Coleshill Parkway d.		1007	...	1109	1139	1209	...	1310	...	1349	1406	1447	1508	1547	1609	1648	1708	1747	1809	1847	...	2008	2042	...	2207
Nuneaton d.		1023	...	1125	1153	1225	...	1326	...	1404	1423	1502	1525	1601	1625	1703	1724	1803	1825	1902	...	2025	2058	...	2223
Hinckley d.		1031	...	1132	|	1232	...	1333	...	|	1430	|	1532	|	1631	|	1731	|	1832	|	...	2032	|	...	2231
Leicester a.		1052	...	1153	1219	1252	...	1353	...	1426	1450	1523	1551	1625	1652	1726	1751	1825	1853	1924	...	2054	2119	...	2251
Peterborough 207 a.		...	...	...	1319	...	...	...	...	1525	...	1626	...	1726	...	1827	...	1928	...	2023	...	...	2223	...	...

A – From / to Stansted Airport.
C – From / to Cambridge.
d – 8–9 minutes earlier on ⑥.
q – 8 minutes later on ⑥.
r – 3 minutes earlier on ⑥.
z – ⑥ only.
▲ – Services on ⑦ are subject to alteration from Feb. 3.

LM — NUNEATON - COVENTRY — 193a

From NUNEATON *16 km*

Ⓐ: 0646, 0742, 0842, 0942, 1040, 1138, 1238, 1342, 1438, 1553, 1650, 1748, 1847, 1948, 2117, 2230.

⑥ (🚌): 0648, 0748 and hourly until 1748; then 1924, 2048, 2248.

⑦ (🚌): 1148, 1348, 1448, 1548, 1648, 1748, 1948, 2148.

From COVENTRY Journey time: ± 18 minutes (🚌 36 minutes)

Ⓐ: 0615, 0714, 0811, 0910, 1010, 1112, 1206, 1306, 1410, 1508, 1617, 1717, 1817, 1917, 2018, 2150.

⑥ (🚌): 0635, 0735 and hourly until 1635; then 1715, 1835, 2005, 2135.

⑦ (🚌): 1135, 1335, 1435, 1535, 1635, 1735, 1935, 2135.

194 CLEETHORPES - SHEFFIELD - MANCHESTER - LIVERPOOL EM, TP

Services on ⑥ are subject to alteration from March 29. Services on ⑦ are subject to alteration from February 3.

km			⚒	⚒	⚒	⚒	⚒ 2 T	⚒ 🍷	⚒ 2 T	⚒ 🍷	⚒ 2 T	⚒ 🍷	⚒ 2 N	⚒ 🍷	⚒ 2 C	⚒ 🍷	⚒ 2 N	⚒ 🍷	⚒ 2 N	⚒ 🍷	⚒ 2	⚒ 🍷	⚒ 2 N	⚒ 🍷	⚒ 2 N	⚒ 🍷
0	**Cleethorpes** d.	⚒	...	...	...	...	...	0518	...	0618	...	0718	...	0828	...	0928	...	1028	...	1128	...	1228	...	1328	...	1428
5	Grimsby Town d.		...	...	...	...	...	0526	...	0626	...	0726	...	0836	...	0936	...	1036	...	1136	...	1236	...	1336	...	1436
47	Scunthorpe d.		...	...	...	...	...	0600	...	0700	...	0800	...	0910	...	1010	...	1110	...	1210	...	1310	...	1410	...	1510
84	Doncaster 127 178 d.		...	...	...	0542	...	0640	...	0735	...	0842	...	0942	...	1042	...	1142	...	1242	...	1342	...	1442	...	1542
113	**Sheffield** 127 178 a.		...	...	...	0608	...	0707	...	0800	...	0907	...	1008	...	1107	...	1207	...	1307	...	1407	...	1507	...	1607
113	**Sheffield** d.		0150	0345	0511	0611	0620	0710	0736	0805	0842	0911	0942	1011	1042	1111	1142	1211	1242	1311	1342	1411	1442	1511	1542	1611
173	Stockport a.		|	|	0553	0653	0723	0755	0826	0851	0925	0953	1024	1053	1124	1153	1224	1253	1324	1353	1424	1453	1524	1553	1624	1653
182	**Manchester** Piccadilly a.		0242	0440	0604	0705	0735	0808	0836	0901	0936	1003	1036	1103	1136	1203	1236	1303	1336	1403	1436	1503	1536	1603	1637	1703
198	Manchester Airport a.		0306	0501	0634	0735	0802	0833	0906	0933	1002	1033	1101	1133	1201	1233	1301	1333	1401	1433	1501	1533	1601	1633	1714r	1739
208	Warrington Central a.		...	...	|	...	0754	...	0857	...	0957	...	1057	...	1157	...	1257	...	1357	...	1457	...	1557	...	1657	...
238	**Liverpool** Lime St a.		...	...	0748p	...	0829	...	0929	...	1029	...	1129	...	1229	...	1329	...	1429	...	1529r	...	1629	...	1729	...

	⚒ 2 N	⚒ 🍷	⚒ 2 N	⚒ 🍷	⑥ 2 N	Ⓐ 2 N	⚒	⑥ 2 N	Ⓐ 2 N	⚒ 🍷	⑥ 2 N	Ⓐ 2 N	⚒ 2	⚒	Ⓐ	⑥	⑥ 2	Ⓐ 2	⑥ 2	⚒ 2		⑦ 🚌	⑦	⑦ 🚌	⑦	⑦
Cleethorpes d.	...	1528	...	1628	...	...	1728	...	...	1828	...	...	...	1928	2028	2028	...	...	...	...	⑦	...	...	...	...	...
Grimsby Town d.	...	1536	...	1636	...	...	1736	...	...	1836	...	...	...	1936	2036	2036	...	...	...	...		...	...	...	...	...
Scunthorpe d.	...	1610	...	1710	...	...	1810	...	...	1910	...	...	...	2010	2110	2110	...	...	2221	2221		...	...	...	...	...
Doncaster 127 178 d.	...	1642	...	1742	...	...	1842	...	...	1942	...	...	...	2042	2142	2142	...	...	2319	2322		...	0803	...	0939	...
Sheffield 127 178 a.	...	1707	...	1808	...	...	1908	...	...	2008	...	...	...	2118	2207	2207	...	...	2358	0001		...	0841	...	1009	...
Sheffield d.	1642	1711	1742	1811	1842	1842	1911	1942	1942	2011	2029	2031	2032	...	2211	...	2224	2247	...	...		0740	...	0920	1020*	...
Stockport a.	1725	1753	1826	1853	1924	1924	1953	2025	2026	2053	2111	2117	|	...	2253	...	2321	2346	...	...		|	...	|	|	...
Manchester Piccadilly a.	1736	1803	1836	1903	1935	1936	2003	2036	2036	2103	2125	2130	2203	...	2303	...	2336	2359	...	...		0900	...	1040	1140*	1207
Manchester Airport a.	1805	1839	1909	1934	2005	2005	2035	2109	2109	2134	2158	2215	2239	...	2328	...	0045	0045	...	...		0925	...	1105	1205*	|
Warrington Central a.	1802	...	1857	...	2028	1957	...	2128	2057	...	2221	2229	...	...	...	...	...	...	...	...		|	...	|	...	1228
Liverpool Lime St a.	1832	...	1929	...	2038	2029	...	2155	2129	...	2241	2241	...	...	...	...	...	...	...	...		1022p	...	1221p	...	1257

	⑦ 🚌 T	⑦	⑦	⑦	⑦ 🚌 T	⑦	⑦ 🚌	⑦	⑦ 🚌	⑦	⑦ 🚌	⑦	⑦ 🚌	⑦	⑦ 🚌	⑦	⑦ 🚌	⑦	⑦ 🚌	⑦	⑦ 🚌	⑦	⑦ 🚌	⑦	⑦	⑦
Cleethorpes d.	...	...	...	0941	...	1028	...	...	...	1228	...	1328	...	1428	...	1528	...	1628	...	1728	...	1828	...	1928	2028	...
Grimsby Town d.	...	...	...	0949	...	1036	...	...	...	1236	...	1336	...	1436	...	1536	...	1636	...	1736	...	1836	...	1936	2036	...
Scunthorpe d.	...	...	...	1023	...	1110	...	...	...	1310	...	1410	...	1510	...	1610	...	1710	...	1810	...	1910	...	2010	2110	...
Doncaster 127 178 d.	...	1042	...	1055	...	1142	...	1242	...	1342	...	1442	...	1542	...	1642	...	1742	...	1842	...	1942	...	2042	2142	2220
Sheffield 127 178 a.	...	1109	...	1125	...	1212	...	1308	...	1412	...	1512	...	1612	...	1712	...	1812	...	1912	...	2012	...	2117	2211	2259
Sheffield d.	1045	1120*	...	...	1145	1220*	1220	1320*	1320	1420*	1420	1520*	1520	1620*	1620	1720*	1720	1820*	1820	1920*	1920	2020*	2020	2130*	...	...
Stockport a.	1210	|	...	...	1310	1340*	|	1440*	|	1540*	|	1640*	|	1740*	|	1840*	|	1940*	|	2040*	|	2140*	|	2250*	...	...
Manchester Piccadilly a.	1226	1240*	1307	...	1336	|	1350	|	1450	|	1550	|	1650	|	1750	|	1850	|	1950	|	2050	|	2150	2315*	...	...
Manchester Airport a.	|	1305*	|	...	|	1400*	|	1500*	|	1600*	|	1700*	|	1800*	|	1900*	|	2000*	|	2100*	|	2200*	|	...	...	...
Warrington Central a.	1256	...	1328	...	1356	...	1428	...	1528	...	1628	...	1728	...	1828	...	1929	...	2028	...	2128	...	2228	...	...	...
Liverpool Lime St a.	1331	...	1357	...	1428	...	1457	...	1557	...	1657	...	1757	...	1857	...	1957	...	2057	...	2157	...	2300	...	...	...

		①	②–⑤		⚒		⚒ 🍷	⚒ 2 N	⚒ 🍷	⚒ 2 N	⚒ 🍷	⚒ 2 N	⚒ 🍷	⚒ 2 N	⚒ 🍷	⚒ 2 N	⚒ 🍷	⚒ 2 N	⚒ 🍷	⚒ 2 N	⚒ 🍷	⚒ 2 T	⚒ 🍷	⚒ 2 N		⚒ 🍷
Liverpool Lime St d.	⚒	...	...	...	...	...	...	0647	...	0747	...	0852	...	0952	...	1052	...	1152	...	1252	...	1352	...	1452	...	...
Warrington Central d.		...	...	...	...	...	...	0715	...	0816	...	0917	...	1017	...	1117	...	1217	...	1317	...	1417	...	1517	...	...
Manchester Airport d.		0318	0321	...	0515	...	0644	0705	0752	0807	0852	0907	0952	1007	1052	1107	1152	1207	1252	1307	1352	1407	1452	1507	...	1552
Manchester Piccadilly d.		0337	0340	...	0548	...	0718	0743	0817	0842	0918	0942	1018	1042	1118	1142	1218	1242	1318	1342	1418	1442	1518	1542	...	1618
Stockport d.		|	|	...	0556	...	0726	0754	0826	0853	0926	0955	1026	1055	1126	1155	1226	1255	1326	1355	1426	1455	1526	1551	...	1626
Sheffield a.		0437	0431	...	0648	...	0810	0835	0909	0935	1008	1035	1108	1135	1208	1235	1308	1335	1408	1435	1508	1535	1608	1635	...	1708
Sheffield 127 178 d.		0440	0440	...	0655	...	0811	...	0911	...	1011	...	1111	...	1211	...	1311	...	1411	...	1511	...	1611	...	...	1711
Doncaster 127 178 d.		0514	0514	...	0724	...	0842	...	0942	...	1042	...	1142	...	1242	...	1342	...	1442	...	1542	...	1642	...	...	1742
Scunthorpe d.		...	...	...	0750	...	0908	...	1008	...	1108	...	1208	...	1308	...	1408	...	1508	...	1608	...	1708	...	...	1808
Grimsby Town a.		...	...	...	0826	...	0942	...	1047	...	1142	...	1244v	...	1342	...	1444v	...	1542	...	1644v	...	1742	...	...	1846v
Cleethorpes a.		...	...	...	0846	...	0958	...	1059r	...	1154	...	1256	...	1354	...	1457	...	1554	...	1656	...	1754	...	...	1900

	⚒ 2 N		⚒ 🍷	⑥ 2 C	Ⓐ 2 T	⚒ 🍷	⑥ 2 N	Ⓐ 2 C	⚒	⚒ 2 T	Ⓐ	⑥ 🍷	⚒ 2 T	⑥	Ⓐ	⚒	⑥ 2 T		Ⓐ	⑥ 2	Ⓐ 2	Ⓐ 2 T		Ⓐ		Ⓐ
Liverpool Lime St d.	1552	...	...	1652	1652	...	1752	1752	...	1852	...	...	1952	...	...	2022	...	...	...	...	...	2135	...	2230	...	...
Warrington Central d.	1617	...	...	1717	1717	...	1817	1817	...	1917	...	...	2017	...	...	2044	...	...	...	...	...	2201	...	2252	...	...
Manchester Airport d.	1607	...	1652	1704	1704	1752		1810	1852	1912	1952	1952	2015	2052	2052	|	...	...	2152	...	...	|	...	|	...	2352
Manchester Piccadilly d.	1642	...	1718	1742	1742	1818	1844	1844	1918	1942	2018	2018	2042	2118	2118	2110	2142	...	2218	...	...	2227	...	2317	...	0015
Stockport d.	1653	...	1726	1755	1753	1826	1855	1855	1926	1955	2026	2026	2055	2126	2126	...	2152	...	2226	...	...	2238	...	...	...	|
Sheffield a.	1737	...	1815r	1835	1841	1908	1935	1936	2008	2039r	2108	2109	2134	2209	2209	...	2231	...	2313	...	...	2335	...	...	...	0113
Sheffield 127 178 d.	...	...	1824	...	...	1911	...	...	2011	...	2111	2111	...	2211	2211	...	...	...	...	2324	2327	...	...	...	...	...
Doncaster 127 178 d.	...	...	1853	...	...	1942	...	...	2042	...	2142	2142	...	2238	2243	...	...	...	...	0003	0007	...	...	...	...	...
Scunthorpe d.	...	...	1923	...	...	2008	...	...	2108	...	2208	2211	...	2313	2318	...	...	...	...	...	...	...	...	...	...	...
Grimsby Town a.	...	...	1958	...	...	2043v	...	...	2146	...	2242	2246	...	2349	2357	...	...	...	...	...	...	...	...	...	...	...
Cleethorpes a.	...	...	2009	...	...	2057	...	...	2200	...	2256	2259	...	0001	0009	...	...	...	...	...	...	...	...	...	...	...

		⑦		⑦	⑦ 🚌	⑦ 🚌	⑦	⑦ 🚌	⑦	⑦ 🚌	⑦	⑦ 🚌	⑦	⑦ 🚌	⑦	⑦ 🚌	⑦	⑦ 🚌	⑦	⑦ 🚌	⑦	⑦ 🚌	⑦ 🚌 T	⑦	⑦ 🚌	⑦
Liverpool Lime St d.	⑦	...	...	...	0930	1122	...	1130	...	1322	...	1422	...	1522	...	1622	...	1722	...	1822	...	1922	1952	...	2022	...
Warrington Central d.		...	...	...	|	1144	...	|	...	1344	...	1444	...	1544	...	1644	...	1744	...	1844	...	1944	2018	...	2044	...
Manchester Airport d.		...	...	...	|	|	1215*	|	1315*	|	1415*	|	1515*	|	1615*	|	1715*	|	1815*	|	1915*	|	|	...	|	...
Manchester Piccadilly d.		0800*	...	1015*	1115	1225	|	1325	|	1425	|	1525	|	1625	|	1725	|	1825	|	1925	|	2025	2043	...	2125	...
Stockport d.		0825*	...	1040*	1140	|	1235*	|	1335*	|	1435*	|	1535*	|	1635*	|	1735*	|	1835*	|	1935*	2050	2100	...	2150	...
Sheffield a.		0945*	...	1200*	1300	1355	1355*	1455	1455*	1555	1555*	1655	1655*	1755	1755*	1855	1855*	1955	1955*	2055	2055*	2210	2225	...	2310	...
Sheffield 127 178 d.		0958	...	1208	...	...	1408	...	1508	...	1608	...	1708	...	1808	...	1908	...	2008	...	2108	...	...	2230	...	2320
Doncaster 127 178 d.		1027	...	1236	...	...	1436	...	1536	...	1636	...	1736	...	1836	...	1936	...	2042	...	2142	...	...	2258	...	2358
Scunthorpe d.		1053	...	1302	...	...	1502	...	1602	...	1702	...	1802	...	1902	...	2002	...	2106	...	2208	...	...	2324	...	...
Grimsby Town a.		1127	...	1338	...	...	1536	...	1638	...	1736	...	1838	...	1936	...	2036	...	2144	...	2244	...	...	2358	...	...
Cleethorpes a.		1139	...	1351	...	...	1548	...	1650	...	1748	...	1850	...	1950	...	2049	...	2156	...	2256	...	...	0010	...	...

C – From / to Cambridge.
N – From / to Norwich.
T – From / to Nottingham.
p – Change at Manchester Piccadilly.
r – 3–5 minutes earlier on ⑥.
v – 3–4 minutes later on ⑥.
* – By 🚌.

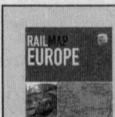

SKEGNESS - NOTTINGHAM — 195

EM 2nd class

km			Ⓐ	⑥	⚒	⚒	⚒	⑥	Ⓐ	Ⓐ	⑥	⚒	⚒	⚒	⚒	⚒	⚒	⚒	⚒	⑥	Ⓐ	⑥	Ⓐ	⑥	Ⓐ
0	**Skegness** d.	⚒	...	...	...	0715	0811	0932	0938	1003	1000	1132	1206	1332	1402v	1532	1610	1732	1821	1918	1918	2020	2025	2059	2110
38	Boston d.		...	...	0615	0750	0845	1006	1014	1040	1040r	1206	1242	1406	1439	1606	1646	1806	1855	1952	1952	2055	2058	2133	2145
66	Sleaford d.		...	...	0637	0815	0907	1029	1037	1102	1102	1229	1304	1429	1503	1629	1708	1829	1920	2014	2017	2117	2120	2154	2206
89	Grantham a.		...	...	0707	0842	0934	|	|	1133	1142	|	1336	|	1533	|	1734	|	1950	2042	2045	|	2146	2220	|
89	Grantham 208 d.		0609	0617	0710	0846	0940	|	|	1140	1146	|	1340	|	1540	|	1740	|	1953	2046	2049	|	2152	2224	|
126	**Nottingham** 208 a.		0648	0656	0752	0922	1022	1120	1129	1222	1229	1320	1422	1520	1622	1721	1822	1920	2037	2122	2125	2208	2237	2308	2256

		⑦		⑦		⑦		⑦	⑦	⑦
Skegness d.	⑦	...	...	1410	...	1612	...	1806	1913	...
Boston d.		1219	...	1443	...	1645	...	1839	1948	...
Sleaford d.		1240	...	1504	...	1707	...	1902	2012	2132
Grantham a.		1309	...	1532	...	1733	...	1929	2039	2200
Grantham 208 d.		...	...	1539	...	1737	...	1936	2042	2204
Nottingham 208 a.		...	...	1622	...	1807	...	2022	2126	2243

		⚒	⚒	⚒		⚒	⑥	Ⓐ	⚒	⚒	⑥
Nottingham 208 d.	⚒	...	0550	0650	...	0759z	0850	0850	0950	1050	1150
Grantham 208 a.		...	0630	0727	...	|	0929	0929	|	1130	|
Grantham d.		...	0637	0730	...	|	0935	0935	|	1135	|
Sleaford d.		...	0703	0758	...	0844	1005	1005	1035	1201	1235
Boston d.		0633	0726	0823	...	0906	1034r	1037r	1058	1223	1258
Skegness a.		0712	0809	0904	...	0948	1114	1117	1138	1306	1340

	Ⓐ	Ⓐ	⑥	⚒	⚒	⚒	⚒	⚒	⑥	Ⓐ		Ⓐ	⑥			⑦	⑦		⑦		⑦		⑦		⑦
Nottingham 208 d.	1150	1250	1250	1350	1450	1550	1650	1750	1842	1850	...	2051	2059	...	⑦	1200	*1232*	...	1444	...	1622	...	1823	...	1941
Grantham 208 a.	|	1331	1331	|	1529	1630	1730	1832	1921	1929	...	2131	2141	...		1234	*1313*	...	1527	...	1703	...	1907	...	2021
Grantham d.	|	1337	1336	|	1535	1634	1736	1835	1924	1932	...	2148	2145	...		1238	1329	...	1534	...	1706	...	1913	...	2027
Sleaford d.	1241r	1409	1409	1439	1603	1708r	1804	1901	1952	2000	...	2216	2213	...		1304	1355	...	1604	...	1735	...	1940	...	2052
Boston d.	1303	1436	1439r	1501	1628	1731	1828	1924	2014	2022	...	2239	2234	...		1326	1417	...	1626	...	1758	...	2005	...	...
Skegness a.	1343	1516	1519	1541	1710	1811	1908	2007	2054	2102	...	...	...	...		1406	1457	...	1705	...	1837	...	...	...	...

r – Arrives 6–9 minutes earlier. v – 1405 on ⑥. z – 0755 on ⑥.

PETERBOROUGH - KINGS LYNN — 197

First *Excel* service **X1**

		⚒	⚒		⚒		⚒		⚒		⚒		⚒			⑦		⑦
Peterborough rail station d.	⚒	0748	0818	and every	1918	...	2018	...	2118	...	2218	...	2318	...	⑦	0818	and every	2318
Wisbech bus station a.		0835	0905	30 minutes	2005	...	2105	...	2205	...	2305	...	0005	...		0905	60 minutes	0005
Kings Lynn bus station a.		0907	0937	until	2037	...	2137	...	2237	...	2337	...	0037	...		0937	until	0037

		⚒	⚒		⚒		⚒		⚒		⚒		⚒			⑦		⑦
Kings Lynn bus station d.	⚒	0629	0659	and every	1759	...	1859	...	1959	...	2059	...	2159	...	⑦	0659	and every	2159
Wisbech bus station d.		0701	0731	30 minutes	1831	...	1931	...	2031	...	2131	...	2231	...		0731	60 minutes	2231
Peterborough rail station a.		0743	0813	until	1913	...	2013	...	2113	...	2213	...	2313	...		0813	until	2313

Rail Link service – through rail tickets are available.

LONDON - ELY - KINGS LYNN — 198

FC

km			Ⓐ	Ⓐ	Ⓐ	Ⓐ	Ⓐ	Ⓐ	Ⓐ		Ⓐ	Ⓐ	Ⓐ	Ⓐ	Ⓐ	Ⓐ	Ⓐ	Ⓐ	Ⓐ	Ⓐ	Ⓐ	Ⓐ	Ⓐ
0	**London** Kings Cross ¶ d.	Ⓐ	...	0545	0645	0715	0745	0845	0945		1545	1558r	1645	1658r	1745	1758r	1845	1858r	1945	2015	2115	2215	2315
93	Cambridge ¶ 205 d.		0623	0656	0735	0804	0838	0933	1033	and	1635	1722	1740	1814	1840	1919	1946	2015	2040	2110	2210	2311	0013
117	**Ely** 205 a.		0638	0711	0751	0820	0853	0950	1048	hourly	1650	1740	1755	1829	1855	1934	2001	2031	2055	2125	2225	2326	0029
142	Downham Market a.		0654	0727	0807	0837	0910	1006	1104	until	1706	...	1811	1848	1912	1951	2017	2047	2111	2141	2241	2342	0045z
160	**Kings Lynn** a.		0710	0743	0822	0852	0925	1026	1120		1721	...	1826	1905	1929	2008	2033	2105	2126	2156	2256	2357	0100z

		⑥	⑥	⑥	⑥		⑥	⑥	⑦	⑦			⑦		⑦		⑦		⑦		⑦	⑦
London Kings Cross ¶ d.	⑥	...	0645	0658r	0745		1945	2052	2152	2308	...	⑦	0752j	...	1015	...	1215	...	1415		2115	2215
Cambridge ¶ 205 d.		0632	0733	0820	0833	and	2033	2156	2256	0016	...		0907	...	1102	...	1302	...	1502	and	2202	2311
Ely 205 a.		0647	0748	0837	0848	hourly	2048	2211	2311	0031	...		0922	...	1117	...	1317	...	1517	hourly	2217	2326
Downham Market a.		0703	0804	...	0904	until	2104	2227	2327	0047	...		0938	...	1133	...	1333	...	1533	until	2233	2342
Kings Lynn a.		0720	0820	...	0921		2121	2243	2343	0104	...		0954	...	1150	...	1350	...	1550		2250	2359

		Ⓐ	Ⓐ	Ⓐ	Ⓐ	Ⓐ	Ⓐ	Ⓐ	Ⓐ	Ⓐ	Ⓐ	Ⓐ		Ⓐ	Ⓐ	Ⓐ		Ⓐ		Ⓐ	Ⓐ	Ⓐ	Ⓐ
Kings Lynn d.	Ⓐ	...	0521	0553	0618	...	0653	0723	0755	0827	0859	0956		1556	1654	1736	...	1836	...	1939	2039	2136	2232
Downham Market d.		...	0535	0606	0632	...	0706	0736	0808	0840	0912	1009	and	1609	1707	1749	...	1849	...	1952	2052	2149	2245
Ely 205 d.		0526	0553	0623	0650	0658	0723	0753	0825	0857	0929	1026	hourly	1626	1724	1806	...	1906	...	2009	2109	2206	2302
Cambridge ¶ 205 a.		0544	0609	0643	0709	0713	0744	0814	0844	0915	0945	1044	until	1644	1743	1822	...	1922	...	2027	2127	2223	2319
London Kings Cross ¶ a.		0635	0733r	0740	0833r	0815	0845	0912	0942	1011	1038	1135		1736	1835	1933	...	2033	...	2130	2230	2335	0042

		⑥		⑥	⑥	⑥	⑥	⑥		⑥			⑦		⑦		⑦		⑦	⑦		⑦
Kings Lynn d.	⑥	0556		1756	1834	1934	2034	2134	...	2315	...	⑦	0826	...	1026	...	1226		2026	2126	...	2226
Downham Market d.		0609	and	1809	1847	1947	2047	2147	...	2331	...		0839	...	1039	...	1239	and	2039	2139	...	2239
Ely 205 d.		0626	hourly	1826	1905	2005	2105	2205	...	2347	...		0856	...	1056	...	1256	hourly	2056	2156	...	2256
Cambridge ¶ 205 a.		0644	until	1844	1921	2021	2121	2221	...	0006	...		0914	...	1114	...	1314	until	2114	2214	...	2313
London Kings Cross ¶ a.		0734		1933	2032	2132	2232	2347	...	...	...		1003	...	1204	...	1405		2203	2315	...	0032

j – From Mar. 30. r – London Liverpool Street. z – ⑥ only. ¶ – **London** - **Cambridge** and v.v., see Table **199**.

LONDON - CAMBRIDGE — 199

London Kings Cross – **Cambridge** ★ Operator: FC *93 km*

Ⓐ: 0007, 0545, 0645, 0715 and every 30 minutes until 2015, then 2052, 2115, 2152, 2215, 2252, 2315.

⑥: 0004, 0545, 0645. 0745, 0815 and every 30 minutes until 1945; then 1952, 2052, 2152, 2308, 2315.

⑦: 0913, 0952, 1015, 1052 and at 15 and 52 minutes past each hour until 2315.

Cambridge – **London** Kings Cross ★ Journey time: ± 55 minutes

Ⓐ: 0545, 0615 and every 30 minutes until 1945; then 2028, 2045, 2128, 2228, 2319.

⑥: 0555, 0628, 0645, 0728, 0745, 0815 and every 30 minutes until 1845; then 1928, 2028, 2128, 2228, 2306.

⑦: 0840, 0915, 0928 and at 15 and 28 minutes past each hour until 2215; then 2241, 2313.

London Liverpool St – **Cambridge** Operator: LE *90 km*

Ⓐ: 0558, 0628 and every 30 minutes until 2358.
Also: 1642, 1712, 1742, 1812, 1842, 1912.

⑥: 0558, 0628 and every 30 minutes until 2358.

⑦: 0743, 0828, 0928 and hourly until 2228.

Cambridge – **London** Liverpool St Journey time: ± 80 minutes

Ⓐ: 0448, 0521, 0542, 0551, 0618, 0648, 0718, 0748, 0818, 0851, 0932, 0951 and at 32 and 51 minutes past each hour until 1451; 1521, 1551 and every 30 minutes until 1951; then 2032, 2051, 2132, 2151, 2232, 2251.

⑥: 0425, 0521, 0551, 0632, 0651 and at 32 and 51 minutes past each hour until 2251.

⑦: 0732, 0832 and hourly until 2232.

★ – Selected trains.

200 LONDON - IPSWICH - NORWICH
LE

km			Ⓐ	Ⓐ	Ⓐ	Ⓐ 🍷	Ⓐ 🍷	Ⓐ ✕	Ⓐ ✕	Ⓐ ✕	Ⓐ ✕	Ⓐ ✕	Ⓐ 🍷	Ⓐ 🍷		Ⓐ 🍷	Ⓐ ✕	Ⓐ 🍷	Ⓐ 🍷	Ⓐ 🍷	Ⓐ 🍷	Ⓐ 🍷	Ⓐ 🍷	Ⓐ ✕
0	**London** Liverpool St. ‡ d.	Ⓐ	0600	0625	0700	0730	0800	0830	0900	0930	1000	1030	1100	1130	and at	1500	1530	1600	1630	1700	1730	1750	1800	1820
48	Chelmsford ‡ d.		*0602*	0657	*0712*	0804	*0812*	0902	*0912*	1002	*1012*	1102	*1112*	1202	the same	*1512*	1602	1630	*1645*	|	*1751*	*1805*	*1814*	*1840*
84	**Colchester** ‡ d.		0650	0722	0750	0825	0850	0925	0950	1025	1050	1123	1150	1223	minutes	1550	1623	1650	1718	*1726*	*1811*	1843	1853	1912
97	Manningtree ‡ d.		0659	0732	0759	0834	0859	0934	0959	1034	1059	1132	1159	1232	past	1559	1632	1659	|	*1735*	1827	1852	1902	1921
111	**Ipswich** 205 ‡ d.		0709	0742	0809	0844	0909	0944	1009	1044	1109	1142	1209	1242	each	1609	1642	1709	1734	1759	1837	1903	1912	1932
130	Stowmarket 205 d.		0720	0753	0820	0855	|	0955	|	1055	|	1153	|	1253	hour	|	1653	1720	1745	|	1848	|	1923	|
153	Diss d.		0732	0805	0832	0907	0930	1007	1030	1107	1130	1205	1230	1305	until	1630	1705	1732	1757	|	1900	|	1935	|
185	**Norwich** a.		0759	0832	0859	0927	0952	1027	1052	1127	1152	1227	1252	1327		1652	1727	1755	1820	1839	1923	1944	1958	2014

	Ⓐ 🍷	Ⓐ 🍷	Ⓐ ✕	Ⓐ 🍷	Ⓐ ✕	Ⓐ 🍷	Ⓐ 🍷	Ⓐ 🍷		⑥	⑥	⑥	⑥	⑥ 🍷	⑥ 🍷		⑥	⑥ 🍷	⑥ 🍷	⑥ 🍷	⑥ 🍷			⑦
London Liverpool St. ‡ d.	1830	1900	1930	2000	2030	2130	2230	2330	⑥	0530	...	0630	0700	0730	0800	and at	2000	2030	2130	2230	2330	...	⑦	0830
Chelmsford ‡ d.	|	*1913*	1959	*2011*	2103	2203	2302	0003		0607	...	0702	*0712*	0802	*0812*	the same	*2012*	2103	2203	2302	0003	...		*0842*
Colchester ‡ d.	1923	1953	2021	2050	2123	2223	2323	0027		0637	...	0723	0750	0823	0850	minutes	2050	2123	2223	2323	0027	...		0924
Manningtree ‡ d.	|	2002	2030	2059	2132	2232	2332	0036		0645	...	0732	0759	0832	0859	past	2059	2132	2232	2332	0036	...		0933
Ipswich 205 ‡ d.	1940	2012	2041	2109	2143	2243	2343	0048		0656	0709	0742	0809	0842	0909	each	2109	2143	2243	2343	0048	...		0944
Stowmarket 205 d.	1951	2023	2051	2120	2154	2254	2354	0059		...	0720	0753	|	0853	|	hour	|	2154	2254	2354	0059	...		0955
Diss d.	2003	2035	2103	2132	2206	2306	0006	0112		...	0732	0805	0830	0905	0930	until	2130	2206	2306	0006	0112	...		1007
Norwich a.	2026	2057	2126	2154	2228	2328	0039	0144		...	0752	0827	0852	0927	0952		2152	2228	2328	0029	0132	...		1029

	⑦ 🍷		⑦ 🍷	⑦ 🍷	⑦ 🍷	⑦ 🍷	⑦ 🍷		⑦ 🍷	⑦
London Liverpool St. ‡ d.	0930		1830	1900	1930	2030	2130	...	2230	2330
Chelmsford ‡ d.	*0942*		*1842*	|	*1942*	*2042*	*2142*	...	*2242*	*2342*
Colchester ‡ d.	1024	and	1924	|	2024	2124	2224	...	2324	0028
Manningtree ‡ d.	1033	hourly	1933	|	2033	2133	2233	...	2333	0037
Ipswich 205 ‡ d.	1044	until	1944	2006	2044	2144	2244	...	2344	0048
Stowmarket 205 d.	1055		1955	2017	2055	2155	2255	...	2355	0059
Diss d.	1107		2007	2029	2107	2207	2307	...	0007	0111
Norwich a.	1129		2029	2051	2129	2229	2329	...	0039	0143

		Ⓐ 🍷	Ⓐ 🍷	Ⓐ ✕	Ⓐ 🍷	Ⓐ ✕	Ⓐ ✕	Ⓐ 🍷	Ⓐ 🍷
Norwich d.	Ⓐ	0510	0540	0605	0620	0635	0650	0705	0730
Diss d.		0528	0558	0624	0639	0654	0709	0724	|
Stowmarket 205 d.		0540	0610	0637	0652	0707	0722	0737	|
Ipswich 205 ‡ d.		0553	0623	0651	0706	0721	0736	0751	0818
Manningtree ‡ a.		0602	0632	0701	0716	0731	0746	0801	|
Colchester ‡ a.		0615	0645	0713	0728	0743	0758	0813	|
Chelmsford ‡ a.		*0641*	*0714*	|	*0756*	*0813*	*0829*	*0844*	|
London Liverpool St ‡ a.		0710	0737	0809	0823	0839	0855	0910	0927

	Ⓐ ✕	Ⓐ ✕	Ⓐ 🍷	Ⓐ 🍷	Ⓐ 🍷		Ⓐ 🍷	Ⓐ 🍷	Ⓐ ✕	Ⓐ 🍷	Ⓐ ✕	Ⓐ 🍷	Ⓐ ✕	Ⓐ 🍷	Ⓐ 🍷		Ⓐ 🍷		Ⓐ 🍷		Ⓐ			⑥ 🍷
Norwich d.	0740	0800	0830	0900	0930	and at	1500	1530	1600	1630	1700	1730	1800	1830	1900	...	2000	...	2100	...	2200	...	⑥	0500
Diss d.	0758	0817	0847	0917	0947	the same	1517	1547	1617	1647	1717	1747	1817	1847	1917	...	2017	...	2117	...	2217	...		0517
Stowmarket 205 d.	0810	0829	|	0929	|	minutes	1529	|	1629	|	1729	1759	1829	|	1929	...	2029	...	2129	...	2229	...		0529
Ipswich 205 ‡ d.	0823	0842	0908	0942	1008	past	1542	1608	1642	1708	1742	1811	1842	1908	1942	...	2042	...	2142	...	2242	...		0542
Manningtree ‡ a.	0832	0851	0917	0951	1017	each	1551	1617	1651	1717	1751	1820	1851	1917	1951	...	2051	...	2151	...	2251	...		0551
Colchester ‡ a.	0843	0901	0927	1001	1027	hour	1601	1627	1701	1727	1801	1830	1901	1927	2001	...	2101	...	2201	...	2301	...		0601
Chelmsford ‡ a.	0902	*0942*	0946	*1039*	1045	until	*1639*	1645	*1739*	1745	*1839*	1848	*1939*	1945	*2039*	...	*2139*	...	*2239*	...	2324	...		*0633*
London Liverpool St. ‡ a.	0938	0956	1024	1054	1124		1654	1724	1754	1824	1854	1927	1954	2024	2054	...	2154	...	2254	...	0003	...		0654

	⑥ 🍷	⑥ 🍷		⑥ 🍷	⑥ 🍷		⑥ 🍷		⑥ 🍷		⑥			⑦ 🍷		⑦ 🍷	⑦ 🍷	⑦ 🍷		⑦ 🍷		⑦
Norwich d.	0530	0600	and at	1830	1900	...	2000	...	2100	...	2200	...	⑦	0700		1600	1620	1700		2100	...	2200
Diss d.	0547	0617	the same	1847	1917	...	2017	...	2117	...	2217	...		0717		1617	1637	1717		2117	...	2217
Stowmarket 205 d.	|	0629	minutes	|	1929	...	2029	...	2129	...	2229	...		0729	and	1629	1649	1729	and	2129	...	2229
Ipswich 205 ‡ d.	0608	0642	past	1908	1942	...	2042	...	2142	...	2242	...		0742	hourly	1642	1703	1742	hourly	2142	...	2242
Manningtree ‡ a.	0617	0651	each	1917	1951	...	2051	...	2151	...	2251	...		0751	until	1651	|	1751	until	2151	...	2251
Colchester ‡ a.	0627	0701	hour	1927	2001	...	2101	...	2201	...	2301	...		0801		1701	1719	1801		2201	...	2301
Chelmsford ‡ a.	0645	*0739*	until	1945	*2039*	...	*2139*	...	*2239*	...	2324	...		*0829*		*1729*	*1757*	*1829*		*2229*	...	2324
London Liverpool St. ‡ a.	0724	0754		2024	2054	...	2154	...	2254	...	0003	...		0903		1801	1828	1901		2301	...	0007

‡ – Additional trains operate between these stations.

202 NORWICH and IPSWICH local services
2nd class LE

NORWICH – GREAT YARMOUTH *30 km (33 km via Reedham)*

Ⓐ: 0515, 0636, 0705, 0736 **r**, 0836, 0936, 1036 **r**, 1136, 1236, 1336, 1436, 1536, 1640, 1705, 1736, 1840, 1936, 2040, 2140, 2300.

⑥: 0536 **r**, 0636, 0705, 0736 **r**, 0836, 0936, 1036 **r**, 1136, 1236, 1336, 1436, 1536, 1640, 1705, 1736, 1840, 1936, 2040, 2140, 2300.

⑦: 0736 **r**, 0845, 0936 **r**, 1045, 1136 **r**, 1245, 1336 **r**, 1445, 1536 **r**, 1645, 1736 **r**, 1845, 1936 **r**, 2045, 2136 **r**, 2236.

GREAT YARMOUTH – NORWICH Journey time: ± 32 mins

Ⓐ: 0600, 0642 ✣, 0717, 0744, 0817, 0917, 1017, 1117, 1217, 1317, 1412 **r**, 1517, 1617, 1717, 1747 **r**, 1817, 1917, 2017, 2117, 2217, 2333 **r**.

⑥: 0617, 0717, 0744, 0817, 0917, 1017, 1117, 1217, 1317, 1412 **r**, 1517, 1617, 1717, 1817, 1917, 2017, 2117, 2217, 2333 **r**.

⑦: 0820 **r**, 0922, 1018 **r**, 1122, 1218 **r**, 1322, 1420 **r**, 1522, 1620 **r**, 1722, 1822 **r**, 1922, 2022 **r**, 2122, 2222 **r**, 2320 **r**.

NORWICH – LOWESTOFT *38 km*

⚒: 0545 Ⓐ **r**, 0549 ⑥ **r**, 0626 Ⓐ **r**, 0655 **r**, 0754 **r**, 0857, 0957 **r**, 1057, 1157 **r**, 1257, 1357 **r**, 1457, 1557 **r**, 1657 **r**, 1757 **r**, 1857 **r**, 1957 **r**, 2057 **r**, 2157 **r**, 2240 **r**.

⑦: 0725, 0857 **r**, 1057 **r**, 1257 **r**, 1457 **r**, 1657 **r**, 1857 **r**, 2057 **r**.

LOWESTOFT – NORWICH Journey time: ± 38 mins

⚒: 0540 Ⓐ **r**, 0640 **r**, 0740 **r**, 0752 Ⓐ **r**, 0842 **r**, 0942 **r**, 1050, 1142 **r**, 1250, 1342 **r**, 1450, 1542 **r**, 1647 **r**, 1747 **r**, 1847 **r**, 1947 **r**, 2050, 2142 **r**, 2245 **r**, 2330 **r**.

⑦: 0950 **r**, 1150 **r**, 1350 **r**, 1550 **r**, 1750 **r**, 1950 **r**, 2150 **r**, 2325 **r**.

NORWICH – CROMER – SHERINGHAM *49 km*

⚒: 0520, 0545 ⑥, 0550 Ⓐ, 0715, 0823, 0945, 1045 and hourly until 1945; then 2115, 2245.

⑦: 0836, 1036, 1236, 1436, 1636, 1836, 2036.

SHERINGHAM – CROMER (△) – NORWICH Journey time: ± 57 mins

⚒: 0622 ⑥, 0632 Ⓐ, 0717, 0825, 0946, 1046 and hourly until 1546; then 1649, 1748, 1849, 1948, 2049, 2216, 2346.

⑦: 0943, 1143, 1343, 1543, 1743, 1943, 2143.

IPSWICH – FELIXSTOWE *25 km*

⚒: 0504 Ⓐ, 0604 Ⓐ, 0627 ⑥, 0713 Ⓐ, 0727 ⑥, 0827, 0927 and hourly until 2027; then 2227.

⑦: 1202, 1302 and hourly until 2002.

FELIXSTOWE – IPSWICH Journey time: ± 25 mins

⚒: 0534 Ⓐ, 0638 Ⓐ, 0656 ⑥, 0750 Ⓐ, 0756 ⑥, 0856, 0956 and hourly until 2056; then 2256

⑦: 1232, 1332 and hourly until 2032.

r – Calls at **Reedham**: *20 km*, 18–21 mins from Norwich; *14 km*, 12–14 mins from Yarmouth; *18 km*, 18–21 mins from Lowestoft.

✣ – (12) to London Liverpool St (a. 0925).

△ – Trains depart Cromer 11 mins after leaving Sheringham. Additional journey Cromer - Norwich at 0603 on Ⓐ.

203 (LONDON -) IPSWICH - LOWESTOFT
2nd class LE

km			Ⓐ	⑥	Ⓐ	⚒	⚒	⚒	⚒	⚒	Ⓐ	Ⓐ	⑥	Ⓐ	⑥	⚒			⑦	⑦	⑦	⑦	⑦	⑦	⑦
	London Liverpool St d.	⚒	...	...	*0600*	0738	0938	1138	1338	1538	*1700*	*1730*	1746	1932	1938	2100	...	⑦	*0830*	*1030*	*1230*	*1430*	*1630*	*1830*	*2030*
	Colchester d.		*0622*	*0538*	*0650*	0838	1038	1238	1438	1641r	*1726*	*1811*	1840	2026	2038	2150	...		*0924*	*1124*	*1324*	*1524*	*1724*	*1924*	*2124*
0	**Ipswich** d.		0648	0650	0735	0902	1102	1302	1502	1702	1813	1855	1902	2052	2102	2215	...		0950	1150	1350	1550	1750	1950	2150
17	Woodbridge d.		0707	0709	0754	0921	1121	1321	1521	1721	1832	1914	1921	2111	2121	2234	...		1009	1209	1409	1609	1809	2009	2209
36	Saxmundham d.		0728	0730	0816	0942	1142	1342	1542	1742	1853	1935	1942	2132	2142	2255	...		1030	1230	1430	1630	1830	2030	2230
65	Beccles d.		0759	0801	...	1013	1213	1413	1613	1813	1931	2006	2013	2203	2213	2326	...		1101	1301	1501	1701	1901	2101	2301
79	**Lowestoft** a.		0818	0820	...	1032	1232	1432	1632	1833	1950	2025	2032	2222	2232	2345	...		1120	1320	1520	1720	1920	2120	2320

		Ⓐ	⑥	Ⓐ	⑥	Ⓐ	⚒	⚒	⚒	⑥	Ⓐ	⚒	Ⓐ	⑥		⚒			⑦	⑦	⑦	⑦	⑦	⑦	⑦
Lowestoft d.	⚒	0531	0558	0644	0658	...	0858	1058	1258	1458	1458	1658	1843	1858	...	2058	...	⑦	0805	1005	1205	1405	1605	1805	2005
Beccles d.		0547	0614	0700	0714	...	0914	1114	1314	1514	1514	1714	1859	1914	...	2114	...		0821	1021	1221	1421	1621	1821	2021
Saxmundham d.		0619	0646	0732	0746	0821	0946	1146	1346	1546	1546	1746	1936	1946	...	2146	...		0853	1053	1253	1453	1653	1853	2053
Woodbridge d.		0640	0707	0753	0807	0842	1007	1207	1407	1607	1607	1807	1957	2007	...	2207	...		0914	1114	1314	1514	1714	1914	2114
Ipswich a.		0659	0726	0812	0826	0901	1026	1226	1426	1626	1626	1826	2016	2026	...	2226	...		0933	1133	1333	1533	1733	1933	2133
Colchester a.		*0728*	0748	*0843*	0848	*0927*	1048	1248	1448	1648	*1648*	1848	2048	2048	...	*2301*	...		*1001*	*1201*	*1401*	*1601*	*1801*	*2001*	*2201*
London Liverpool St a.		*0823*	0845	0925	0938	*1024*	1145r	1345	1545	1745	*1749*	1947	2145	2145	...	*0003*y	...		*1103*	*1301*	*1501*	*1701*	*1901*	*2101*	*2301*

r – 3 minutes earlier on ⑥.

y – *0007* on ⑦.

LE — HARWICH - MANNINGTREE (- LONDON) — 204

For boat trains Harwich International – London and v.v., see Table **15a**

km		Ⓐ	Ⓐ	Ⓐ	Ⓐ	Ⓐ		Ⓐ	Ⓐ	Ⓐ	Ⓐ	Ⓐ	Ⓐ	Ⓐ	Ⓐ	Ⓐ	Ⓐ	Ⓐ	Ⓐ		⑥	⑥		⑥
0	**Harwich Town** d.		0537	0622	0708	0800	and	1500	1605	1700	1753	1825	1853	1928	2000	2033	2100	2154	2305	...		0600	and	2100
3	Harwich International d.		0542	0627	0713	0806	hourly	1506	1611	1706	1758	1830	1858	1933	2006	2038	2106	2159	2310	...		0606	hourly	2106
18	**Manningtree** 200 a.		0558	0643	0729	0822	until	1522	1626	1722	1814	1846	1914	1949	2022	2055	2122	2215	2326	...		0622	until	2122
	Colchester 200 a.		*0613*	0653	*0743*	0832		1532	1640	1732	*1830*	*1901*	*1927*	*2001*	2032	2106	2132	*2228*	*2339*	...		0632		2132
	London Liverpool St. 200 a.		*0710*	*0759*	*0839*	0935		1635	1749	1836	*1924*	*1954*	*2024*	*2054*	2133	*2219*	2236	*2334*	...	...		0733		2238

	⑥		⑥			⑦		⑦	⑦
Harwich Town d.	2154	...	2310	...		0853	and	2153	2253
Harwich International d.	2159	...	2315	...		0858	and	2158	2258
Manningtree 200 a.	2215	...	2331	...		0914	hourly	2214	2314
Colchester 200 a.	*2228*	...	*2345*	...		*0929*	until	*2229*	2324
London Liverpool St. 200 a.	*2338*	...	...	...		*1042*		2342	...

		Ⓐ	Ⓐ	Ⓐ	Ⓐ	Ⓐ	Ⓐ	Ⓐ		Ⓐ
London Liverpool St. 200 d.		...	...	*0625*	0718	*0808*	0918	1018	and	1518
Colchester 200 d.		0543	*0622*	*0722*	0821	0914	1021	1118	and	1618
Manningtree 200 d.		0551	0636	0735	0829	0922	1029	1126	hourly	1626
Harwich International a.		0609	0652	0751	0846	0939	1047	1144	until	1644
Harwich Town a.		0614	0657	0756	0851	0944	1052	1149		1649

	Ⓐ	Ⓐ	Ⓐ	Ⓐ	Ⓐ	Ⓐ	Ⓐ	Ⓐ	Ⓐ	Ⓐ		⑥	⑥	⑥		⑥	⑥	⑥			⑦	⑦		⑦
London Liverpool St. 200 d.	1615	1645	*1720*	*1750*	*1820*	*1900*	1918	2018	*2130*	*2230*		...	...	0618	and	2018	*2130*	*2230*	...		...	*0802*	and	*2102*
Colchester 200 d.	1713	1747	*1811*	*1843*	*1912*	*1953*	2017	2117	*2223*	*2323*		0518	0618	0718	and	2118	*2223*	*2323*	...		0808	*0912*	and	*2212*
Manningtree 200 d.	1721	1755	1825	1857	1927	2007	2025	2125	2238	2338		0526	0626	0726	hourly	2126	2238	2338	...		0826	0926	hourly	2226
Harwich International a.	1738	1812	1841	1913	1943	2023	2042	2142	2254	2354		0543	0643	0743	until	2143	2254	2354	...		0842	0942	until	2242
Harwich Town a.	1745	1819	1846	1918	1948	2028	2047	2147	2259	2359		0549	0649	0749		2149	2259	2359	...		0847	0947		2247

LE 2nd class — IPSWICH - ELY and CAMBRIDGE — 205

km		⚒	⚒	⚒	⚒	Ⓐ	⑥	⚒	⚒	⚒	⚒	⚒	⚒	⚒	⚒	⚒	⚒	⚒	⚒	⚒	⚒	⚒	Ⓐ	⑥	⚒
0	**Ipswich** 200 d.		0510	0600	0613	0652	0716	0803	0816	0916	1003	1016	1116	1203	1216	1316	1403	1416	1516	1603	1616	1716	1749	1803	1816
19	Stowmarket 200 d.		0526	0611	0629	0708	0732	0814	0832	0932	1014	1032	1132	1214	1232	1332	1414	1432	1532	1614	1632	1732	1803	1814	1832
42	Bury St Edmunds d.		0549	0627	0651	0730	0755	0830	0855	0955	1030	1055	1155	1230	1255	1355	1430	1455	1555	1630	1655	1755	1823	1830	1855
82	**Ely** a.		|	0657	|	|	|	0859	|	|	1059	|	|	1259	|	|	1459	|	|	1659	|	|	1852	1859	|
	Peterborough **206** a.		|	0737	|	|	|	0941r	|	|	1138	|	|	1338	|	|	1539	|	|	1738	|	|	1944	1938	|
66	Newmarket d.		0610	...	0713	0751	0817	...	0915	1017	...	1115	1217	...	1315	1417	...	1515	1617	...	1717	1817	...	...	1915
89	**Cambridge** a.		0632v	...	0739	0819	0839	...	0939	1039	...	1139	1239	...	1339	1439	...	1539	1639	...	1739	1839	...	...	1939

	⚒	⑥	Ⓐ	⑥	Ⓐ	⚒			⑦	⑦	⑦		⑦	⑦	⑦	⑦	⑦	⑦		⑦	⑦		⑦		⑦
Ipswich 200 d.	1916	2003	2016	2016	2116	2216	...		0945	0902	0955	...	1102	1155	1302	1355	1502	1555	...	1702	1755	...	1902	...	2102
Stowmarket 200 d.	1932	2014	2030	2032	2132	2232	...		0859	0918	1007	...	1118	1207	1318	1407	1518	1607	...	1718	1807	...	1918	...	2118
Bury St Edmunds d.	1955	2030	2050	2055	2155	2255	...		0917	0940	1023	...	1140	1223	1340	1423	1540	1623	...	1740	1823	...	1940	...	2140
Ely a.	|	2059	2119	|	|	...			...	|	1051	...	|	1251	|	1451	|	1651	...	|	1852	...	|	...	|
Peterborough **206** a.	|	2138	2158	|	|	...			...	|	1141	...	|	1342	|	1542	|	1736	...	|	1936	...	|	...	|
Newmarket d.	2017	...	...	2115	2215	...			...	1000	...	...	1200	...	1400	...	1600	...	...	1800	...	...	2000	...	2200
Cambridge a.	2039	...	...	2139	2239	...			...	1024	...	...	1224	...	1424	...	1627	...	...	1824	...	...	2024	...	2224

		Ⓐ	⚒	⚒		⚒	⚒	⚒	⚒	⚒	⚒	⚒	⚒	⚒	⚒	⚒	⚒	⚒	⚒	⚒	⚒	⚒	⚒	⚒	Ⓐ
Cambridge d.		...	...	0641	...	0743	...	0843	0943	...	1043	1143	...	1243	1343	...	1443	1543	...	1643	1743	...	1843	1943	...
Newmarket d.		...	...	0701	...	0804	...	0903	1004	...	1103	1204	...	1303	1404	...	1503	1604	...	1704	1804	...	1903	2004	...
Peterborough **206** d.		...	...	|	...	|	0752	|	|	0947z	|	|	1148	|	|	1347	|	|	1547	|	|	1747	|	|	1949
Ely d.		...	...	|	...	|	0830	|	|	1030	|	|	1230	|	|	1430	|	|	1630	|	|	1830	|	|	2027
Bury St Edmunds d.		0536	0622	0723	...	0823	0856	0923	1023	1056	1123	1223	1256	1323	1423	1456	1523	1623	1656	1725	1825	1856	1923	2023	2052
Stowmarket 200 d.		0557	0644	0745	...	0845	0912	0945	1045	1112	1145	1245	1312	1345	1445	1512	1545	1645	1712	1746	1846	1912	1945	2045	2108
Ipswich 200 a.		0614	0702	0802	...	0903	0926	1002	1102	1127	1202	1302	1327	1402	1502	1525	1602	1702	1727	1803	1903	1925	2002	2102	2125

	⑥	⚒	⑥	⑥	Ⓐ	Ⓐ		⑦		⑦	⑦	⑦		⑦	⑦	⑦	⑦	⑦	⑦	⑦		⑦		⑦
Cambridge d.	...	2043	2143	...	...	2243		...	...	1112	...	1312	...	...	1512	...	1712	...	1912	...	...	2112	...	2300
Newmarket d.	...	2103	2204	...	...	2304		...	...	1133	...	1333	...	...	1533	...	1733	...	1933	...	...	2133	...	2321
Peterborough **206** d.	1946	|	|	2149	2205	|		...	...	|	1146	|	...	1348	|	1547	|	1747	|	1944	...	|	...	|
Ely d.	2030	|	|	2230	2242	|		...	...	|	1230	|	...	1430	|	1630	|	1830	|	2022	...	|	...	|
Bury St Edmunds d.	2056	2123	2225	2258	2308	2325		0955	...	1155	1256	1355	...	1456	1555	1656	1755	1856	1955	2047	...	2155	...	2342
Stowmarket 200 d.	2112	2145	2246	2317	2324	2346		1017	...	1217	1312	1417	...	1512	1617	1712	1817	1912	2017	2105	...	2217	...	0004
Ipswich 200 a.	2127	2203	2303	2332	2337	0003		1034	...	1234	1325	1434	...	1527	1634	1725	1834	1927	2034	2118	...	2234	...	0021

r – 0938 on ⑥. v – 0636 on ⑥. z – 0955 on ⑥.

LE, EM, XC — NORWICH - (CAMBRIDGE) - PETERBOROUGH — 206

km			Ⓐ 2 B	⑥ 2 B		⑥ 2 B	Ⓐ 2 B	Ⓐ	⑥	⑥ 2 L	Ⓐ 2 L	⚒ J	Ⓐ 2 B	⑥ 2 B	Ⓐ	⑥	⚒ 2 L	Ⓐ 2 B	⑥ 2 B	⚒	Ⓐ 2 L	⑥ 2 L	⑥ J	Ⓐ J	⚒ 2 B
0	**Norwich** d.		...	...	...	...	...	0533	0538	0552	0552	...	...	...	0633	0640	...	...	...	0737v	0757	0757	...	...	...
49	Thetford d.		...	...	...	...	...	0605	0610	0625	0625	...	...	...	0705	0712	...	...	...	0809v	0824	0824	...	...	...
	Stansted Airport ✈ d.		...	...	...	0521	0521	|	|	|	|	...	...	...	|	|	...	0725	0727	|	|	|	...	...	0821v
	Cambridge 198 d.		0507	0511	...	0551	0558	|	|	*0620*	*0623*	0632z	0650	0655	|	|	0725	0759	0804	|	*0812*	*0820*	*0833*	*0838*	0904
86	Ely 198 d.		0524	0528	...	0608	0613	0630	0635	0651	0651	0657	0705	0710	0733	0738	0744	0816	0819	0838	0851	0852	0859	0859	0919
110	**Cambridge** 198 a.		|	|	...	|	|	0650	0652	*0744*	*0713*	|	|	|	0751	0755	|	|	|	0855	*0915*	*0922*	|	|	|
112	March d.		0540	0544	...	0627	0632	...	...	0707	0707	0714	0717	0726	...	...	0801	0833	0835	...	0907	0909	0916	0916	0935
136	**Peterborough** a.		0602	0606	...	0648	0654	...	...	0725	0725	0737	0743	0752	...	...	0824	0850	0854	...	0925	0927	0938	0941	0953

	⚒	⚒ 2 L	⚒ 2 B	⚒	⚒ 2 L	⚒ J	⚒ 2 B	⚒	⚒ 2 L	⚒ 2 B	⚒	⚒ 2 L	⚒ J	⚒ 2 B	⚒	⚒ 2 L	⚒ 2 B	⚒	⚒ 2 L	⚒ J	⚒ 2 B	⚒	Ⓐ 2 L	⑥ 2 M	⚒ 2 B
Norwich d.	0840	0857	...	0940	0957	...	...	1040	1057	...	1140	1157	...	...	1240	1257	...	1340	1357	...	...	1440	1457	1457	...
Thetford d.	0912	0924	...	1012	1024	...	...	1112	1124	...	1212	1224	...	...	1312	1324	...	1412	1424	...	...	1512	1524	1524	...
Stansted Airport ✈ d.	|	|	0925	|	|	...	1020v	|	|	1125	|	|	...	1225	|	|	1325	|	|	...	1425	|	|	|	1525
Cambridge 198 d.	|	*0912*	1004	|	*1012*	*1033*	1104	|	*1112*	1204	|	*1212*	*1233*	1304	|	*1312*	1404	|	*1412*	*1433*	1504	|	*1512*	|	1604
Ely 198 d.	0938	0951	1019	1038	1052	1059	1119	1138	1152	1219	1238	1251	1259	1319	1338	1352	1419	1438	1452	1459	1519	1537	1552	1555	1619
Cambridge 198 a.	0955	*1008*	|	1055	*1108*	|	|	1155	*1208*	|	1255	*1308*	|	|	1355	*1408*	|	1457	*1508*	|	|	1555	*1608*	*1608*	|
March d.	...	|	1035	...	|	1116	1135	...	|	1235	...	|	1316	1335	...	|	1435	...	|	1516	1535	...	|	|	1635
Peterborough a.	...	1025	1053	...	1125	1138	1153	...	1225	1253	...	1325	1338	1353	...	1425	1453	...	1525	1539	1553	...	1625	1627	1654

B – To Birmingham. J – From Ipswich. L – To Liverpool. M – To Manchester. v – 3–5 minutes later on ⑥. z – ⑥ only.

ALL TRAINS **Stansted Airport** – **Cambridge**

Ⓐ: 0533, 0725, 0821, 0925, 1020, 1125, 1225, 1325, 1425, 1525, 1620, 1717, 1820, 1918, 2020.

⑥: 0521, 0727, 0825, 0925, 1025, 1125, 1225, 1325, 1425, 1525, 1625, 1725, 1825, 1918, 2057.

⑦: 1205, 1405, 1518, 1612, 1735, 1835, 2019, 2119, 2219.

ALL TRAINS **Cambridge** – **Stansted Airport**

Ⓐ: 0459, 0632, 0732, 0809, 0923, 1009, 1109, 1209, 1309, 1409, 1509, 1609, 1709, 1818, 1930.

⑥: 0439, 0625, 0724, 0809, 0924, 1009, 1109, 1209, 1309, 1409, 1509, 1609, 1709, 1818, 2013.

⑦: 1123, 1324, 1420, 1509, 1624, 1724, 1924, 2024, 2119.

206 NORWICH - (CAMBRIDGE) - PETERBOROUGH

LE, EM, XC

	⚒	⑥ 2 L	Ⓐ 2 L	⚒ J	⚒ 2 B	⚒	⑥ 2 M	Ⓐ 2 M	Ⓐ 2 B	⑥ 2 B	⚒	⑥ 2 N	Ⓐ 2 N	⚒ J	⚒ 2 B	⚒	⑥ 2 N	Ⓐ 2 N	⚒ 2 B		⑥	Ⓐ	⑥ J	Ⓐ 2 B	Ⓐ J
Norwich d.	1540c	1552	1552	...	...	1638	1657	1657	...	...	1735	1757	1754	...	...	1840	1857	1857	...	...	1940	1945	...	...	...
Thetford d.	1612	1622	1627	...	...	1712	1724	1724	...	...	1812	1824	1824	...	...	1912	1924	1924	...	...	2012	2017	...	...	...
Stansted Airport ✈ d.	|	|	|	...	1620v	|	|	|	1717	1725	|	|	|	...	1820v	|	|	|	1918	...	|	|		2020	...
Cambridge 198 d.	|	*1612*	*1624*	*1633*	1704	|	*1712*	1722	1749	1802	|	*1812*	*1825*	*1833z*	1904	|	*1912*	*1925*	1950	...	|	|	*2033*	2057	...
Ely 198 d.	1638	1651	1652	1659	1719	1738	1751	1750	1806	1817	1840r	1852	1852	1859	1919	1938	1952	1952	2005	...	2038	2044	2059	2114	2119
Cambridge 198 a.	1655	*1708*	*1743*	|	|	1755	*1815*	*1816*	|	|	1857	*1908*	*1922*	|	|	1955	*2008*	*2011*	|	...	2055	2101	|	|	|
March d.	...	|	|	1716	1735	...	|	1807	1824	1835	...	1909	|	1916	1935	...	|	|	2021	...	...	...	2116	2130	2136
Peterborough a.	...	1724	1726	1738	1753	...	1824	1824	1843	1853	...	1926	1931	1944c	1953	...	2025	2025	2039	...	...	...	2138	2152	2158

	⑥	Ⓐ		⚒ 2			⑦		⑦ J	⑦ 2 B		⑦ 2 S		⑦		⑦ 2 B	⑦ J	⑦	⑦ 2		⑦ 2 B	⑦		⑦ 2 S	⑦ 2 B
Norwich d.	2040	2048	...	2210	...	⑦	0915	...	...	...	...	1047	...	1115	...	...	...	1215	...	...	...	1315	...	1349	...
Thetford d.	2112	2120	...	2243	...		0947	...	...	...	...	1114	...	1147	...	...	...	1247	...	...	...	1347	...	1416	...
Stansted Airport ✈ d.	|	|	...	|	...	▲	|	...	...	...	...	|	...	|	...	1205	...	|	...	...	...	|	...	|	1405
Cambridge 198 d.	|	|	...	|	...		|	...	...	1048	...	*1102*	...	|	...	1236	...	|	1309	...	1343	|	...	|	1436
Ely 198 d.	2138	2145	...	2311r	...		1021	...	1057	1109	...	1139	...	1218	...	1254	1257	1317	1327	...	1400	1417	...	1445	1453
Cambridge 198 a.	2155	2202	...	2328r	...		1038	...	|	|	...	|	...	1234	...	|	|	1334	|	...	|	1434	...	*1509*	|
March d.	...	...	...	...	...		...	...	1114	1125	...	|	...	...	...	1310	1315	...	1344	...	1416	...	...	|	1510
Peterborough a.	...	...	...	...	...		...	...	1141	1150	...	1216	...	...	...	1331	1342	...	1406	...	1439	...	...	1524	1531

	⑦ J	⑦		⑦ 2 B	⑦		⑦ 2 S	⑦ J	⑦ 2 B	⑦		⑦ 2 S	⑦	⑦ 2 B	⑦ 2 N	⑦ J	⑦	⑦ 2 B	⑦ 2 N		⑦ 2 N		⑦		⑦ 2 N
Norwich d.	...	1415	...	...	1515	...	1553	...	...	1615	...	1657	1715	...	1754	...	1815	...	1857	...	1944	...	2015	...	2052
Thetford d.	...	1447	...	...	1547	...	1620	...	...	1647	...	1724	1747	...	1821	...	1847	...	1924	...	2011	...	2047	...	2119
Stansted Airport ✈ d.	...	|	...	1518	|	...	|	...	1612	|	...	|	|	1735	|	...	|	1835	|	...	|	...	|	...	|
Cambridge 198 d.	...	|	...	1547	|	...	|	*1602*	1647	|	...	*1702*	|	1809	|	...	|	1908	|	...	*2002*	...	|	...	*2102*
Ely 198 d.	1457	1517	...	1604	1614	...	|	1657	1704	1717	...	1751	1812	1826	1848	1857	1912	1928	1956	...	2035	...	2112	...	2144
Cambridge 198 a.	|	1534	...	|	1631	...	|	|	|	1734	...	*1814*	1829	|	*1914*	|	1930	|	*2014*	...	*2114*	...	2129	...	*2214*
March d.	1515	...	...	1621	...	...	|	1714	1720	...	...	|	...	1842	|	1914	...	1944	|	...	|	...	...	...	|
Peterborough a.	1542	...	...	1638	...	...	1710	1736	1740	...	...	1823	...	1900	1920	1936	...	2002	2029	...	2108	...	...	...	2220

km			Ⓐ 2	⑥ 2	Ⓐ 2 N	⑥	Ⓐ	⚒ 2 B	Ⓐ 2 N	⑥ 2 N	⚒	⚒ J		⚒ 2 B	⑥ 2 N	⚒	Ⓐ 2 N	⚒ 2 B	Ⓐ 2 S	⑥ 2 N	⚒	Ⓐ J	⑥ J	⚒ 2 B	Ⓐ 2 L
0	**Peterborough** d.	⚒	...	...	0627	...	...	0710	0735	0739	...	0752	...	0831	0846	...	0859	0918	0941	0946	...	0947	0955	1018	1043
24	March d.		...	...	0643	...	...	0730	0751	0755	...	0811	...	0847	|	...	|	0934	|	|	...	1006	1014	1034	|
	Cambridge 198 d.		0617	0620	*0623*	0659	0705	|	*0735*	*0733*	0812	|	...	|	*0833*	0912	|	|	*0933*	*0933*	1012	|	|	|	*1033*
49	Ely 198 d.		0634	0637	0705	0714	0720	0751	0816	0818	0827	0830	...	0905	0922	0927	0944	0953	1018	1022	1028	1030	1032	1053	1120
73	**Cambridge** 198 a.		|	|	*0744*	|	|	0807	*0844*	*0844*	|	*0855*	...	0922	*0944*	|	|	1008	*1044*	*1044*	|	*1055*	*1055*	1108	*1144*
113	Stansted Airport ✈ a.		|	|	|	|	|	0843v	|	|	|	...	...	0958	|	|	|	1049	|	|	|	...	...	1149	|
	Thetford d.		0658	0701	0729	0741	0745	...	0837	0839	0852	...	...	...	0944	0948v	1005	...	1039	1044	1052	...	...	...	1141
	Norwich a.		0744	0744	0810	0822	0829	...	0916	0912	0929	...	...	...	1017	1030	1043	...	1114	1117	1129	...	...	...	1215

	⑥ 2 L	Ⓐ	⑥	⚒ 2 B	⚒ 2 L	⚒	⚒ J	⚒ 2 B	⑥ 2 L	Ⓐ 2 L	⚒	⚒ 2 B	⚒ 2 L	⚒	⚒ J	⚒ 2 B	⚒ 2 L	⚒	⚒ 2 B	⚒ 2 L	⚒	⚒ J		⚒ 2 B	Ⓐ 2 L
Peterborough d.	1046	...	...	1118	1136	...	1148	1218	1239	1243	...	1318	1340r	...	1347	1418	1440	...	1518	1535	...	1547	...	1618	1636
March d.	|	...	...	1134	|	...	1207	1234	|	|	...	1334	|	...	1406	1434	|	...	1534	|	...	1606	...	1634	|
Cambridge 198 d.	*1033*	1112	1116	|	*1133*	1212	|	|	*1233*	*1233*	1312	|	*1333*	1412	|	|	*1433*	1512	|	*1533*	1612	|	...	|	*1635*
Ely 198 d.	1123	1127	1131	1153	1216	1227	1230	1253	1315	1320	1327	1353	1416	1427	1430	1453	1516	1527	1553	1612	1627	1630	...	1653	1713
Cambridge 198 a.	*1144*	|	|	1208	*1244*	|	*1255*	1309	*1344*	*1344*	|	1408	*1444*	|	*1457*	1508	*1544*	|	1608	*1644*	|	*1655*	...	1708	*1743*
Stansted Airport ✈ a.	|	|	|	1249	|	|	...	1349	|	|	|	1449	|	|	...	1549	|	|	1649	|	|	...	...	1743v	|
Thetford d.	1144	1151	1155	...	1237	1251	...	...	1336	1341	1352	...	1437	1452	...	...	1537	1552	...	1633	1652	...	...	...	1734
Norwich a.	1217	1229	1230	...	1313	1330	...	...	1413	1414	1429	...	1513	1529	...	...	1613	1629	...	1713	1729	...	...	...	1813

	⑥ 2 L	⚒	⚒ 2 B	Ⓐ	⑥	⚒ J	Ⓐ 2 B	⑥ 2 B	Ⓐ 2 B	⑥ 2 L	Ⓐ 2 L	⑥		⑥ 2 B	Ⓐ 2 B	⚒ 2 L	⑥	⑥ J	Ⓐ J	Ⓐ	⑥ 2 B	Ⓐ 2 B	⑥ 2 L	⚒	Ⓐ 2 B
Peterborough d.	1638	...	1718	...	...	1747	1800	1818	1833	1842	1850	...	...	1918	1919	1935	...	1946	1949	...	2018	2024	2039	...	2118
March d.	|	...	1737	...	...	1806	1816	1834	1851	1858	1907	...	...	1934	1937	|	...	2005	2008	...	2034	2040	2055	...	2134
Cambridge 198 d.	*1633*	1712	|	1805	1812	|	|	|	|	*1833*	*1904*	1912	1925	|	|	*1950*	2012	|	|	2020	|	|	|	2112	|
Ely 198 d.	1717	1727	1758	1820	1827	1830	1834	1853	1910	1919	1928	1927	1940	1953	1956	2015	2027	2030	2026	2035	2053	2058	2115	2127	2152
Cambridge 198 a.	*1744*	|	1816	|	|	*1855z*	1851	1908	1929	*1955*	*1955*	|	|	2008	2011	|	|	*2055*	*2101*	|	2111	2116	2131	|	2208
Stansted Airport ✈ a.	|	|	1847d	|	|	...	...	...	2005	...	|	|	|	2049	...	|	|	...	...	|	...	...	...	|	...
Thetford d.	1738	1751	...	1844	1852	...	...	...	...	1940	1949	1952	2005	...	...	2036	2052	...	...	2059	...	...	...	2152	...
Norwich a.	1813	1829	...	1923	1929	...	...	...	...	2013	2022	2029	2040	...	...	2113	2129	...	...	2135	...	...	...	2230	...

	⑥ 2 B	Ⓐ 2 L	⑥ 2 L	⑥	Ⓐ J	⑥	⚒ 2 B	Ⓐ			⑦		⑦ J		⑦		⑦	⑦ 2 B	⑦ 2 N	⑦ J	⑦ 2	⑦		⑦ 2 N	⑦
Peterborough d.	2121	2137	2139	2149	2205	...	2217	...	...	⑦	...	...	1146	...	...	...	...	1321	1343	1348	1412	...	...	1456	...
March d.	2137	|	2155	2208	2224	...	2237	...	...		...	...	1205	...	...	...	...	1337	|	1407	1428	...	...	|	...
Cambridge 198 d.	|	|	*2156*	|	|	2230	|	2255	...	▲	1044	...	|	...	1246	...	1338	|	*1343*	|	|	1446	...	*1502*	1538
Ely 198 d.	2156	2213	2218	2230	2242	2245	2255	2310	...		1101	...	1228	...	1301	...	1353	1402	1428	1430	1453	1501	...	1538	1553
Cambridge 198 a.	2216	2229	|	...	...	|	2314r	|	...		|	...	*1314*	...	|	...	|	1419	|	...	1509	|	...	*1614*	|
Stansted Airport ✈ a.	...	...	|	...	...	|	...	|	...		|	...	...	...	|	...	|	1458	|	...	1543	|	...	|	|
Thetford d.	...	...	2239	...	...	2309	...	2334	...		1129	...	...	...	1328	...	1418	...	1449	...	...	1526	...	1559	1620
Norwich a.	...	...	2320	...	...	2345	...	0010	...		1209	...	...	...	1409	...	1458	...	1528	...	...	1609	...	1637	1655

	⑦ 2 B	⑦ J	⑦ 2 N	⑦	⑦ 2 B		⑦ 2 N	⑦	⑦ 2 B	⑦ J	⑦ 2 S	⑦	⑦ 2 B	⑦ 2 S	⑦	⑦ 2 B	⑦ J	⑦ 2 S		⑦ 2 B		⑦		⑦ 2 S	⑦ 2 B
Peterborough d.	1528	1547	1605	...	1628	...	1700	...	1728	1747	1753	...	1829	1855	...	1929	1944	1955	...	2030	...	...	...	2155	2224
March d.	1544	1606	|	...	1644	...	|	...	1744	1806	|	...	1845	|	...	1945	2003	|	...	2045	...	...	...	|	2240
Cambridge 198 d.	|	|	*1602*	1638	|	...	*1702*	1744	|	|	*1809*	1838	|	*1902*	1938	|	|	*2002*	...	|	...	2138	...	*2202*	|
Ely 198 d.	1608	1629	1641	1653	1706	...	1739	1759	1802	1827	1835	1853	1903	1932	1953	2005	2021	2031	...	2104	...	2153	...	2231	2300
Cambridge 198 a.	1622	...	*1714*	|	1723	...	*1814*	|	1821	...	*1914*	|	1920	*2014*	|	2021	...	*2114*	...	2119	...	|	...	*2313*	2317
Stansted Airport ✈ a.	1659	...	|	|	1758	...	|	|	...	...	|	|	1958	|	|	2058	...	|	...	2153	...	|	...	|	|
Thetford d.	...	...	1702	1718	...	...	1800	1824	...	...	1856	1918	...	1955	2018	...	...	2052	...	...	...	2218	...	2252	...
Norwich a.	...	...	1735	1753	...	...	1835	1859	...	...	1929	1953	...	2028	2053	...	...	2125	...	...	...	2253	...	2335	...

B – To / from Birmingham.
J – From / to Ipswich.
L – To / from Liverpool.
M – To Manchester.
N – To / from Nottingham.
S – To / from Sheffield.
c – 5–6 minutes earlier on ⑥.
d – 1858 on ⑥.
r – 3–4 minutes earlier on ⑥.
v – 5–6 minutes later on ⑥.
z – ⑥ only.
▲ – Services on ⑦ are subject to alteration from Feb. 3.
☛ For all trains Cambridge - Stansted, see previous page.

XC 2nd class — PETEROROUGH - LEICESTER (- BIRMINGHAM) — 207

Services on ⑥ are subject to alteration from March 29. Services on ⑦ are subject to alteration from February 3.

km		Ⓐ	Ⓐ	Ⓐ	Ⓐ	Ⓐ	Ⓐ	Ⓐ	Ⓐ	Ⓐ	Ⓐ	Ⓐ	Ⓐ	Ⓐ	Ⓐ	Ⓐ	Ⓐ	Ⓐ	Ⓐ	Ⓐ		⑥	⑥	⑥	⑥
																			SN						
	Stansted Airport ✈ **206** d.	Ⓐ	...	0521	...	0725	0821	0925	1020	1125	1225	1325	1425	1525	1620	1717	1820	1918	...	2020		⑥	...	0521	...
	Cambridge **206** d.		0507	0558	0650	0759	0904	1004	1104	1204	1304	1404	1504	1604	1704	1749	1904	1950	...	2057	...		0511	0551	0655
0	**Peterborough** d.		0608	0655	0746	0854	0954	1054	1154	1254	1354	1454	1554	1654	1754	1844	1954	2041	2130	2154	...		0608	0650	0754
19	Stamford d.		0621	0708	0759	0907	1007	1107	1207	1307	1407	1507	1607	1707	1807	1857	2007	2054	2143	2207	...		0621	0703	0807
41	Oakham d.		0639	0724	0815	0923	1023	1123	1223	1323	1423	1523	1623	1723	1823	1913	2023	2109	2158	2223	...		0635	0718	0823
61	Melton Mowbray d.		0650	0735	0826	0934	1034	1134	1234	1334	1434	1534	1634	1734	1834	1924	2034	2120	2210	2234	...		0646	0729	0834
84	**Leicester** a.		0707	0750	0846	0951	1051	1151	1251	1352	1451	1551	1651	1751	1851	1940	2051	2135	...	2248	...		0705	0745	0852
	Birmingham New St **193** a.		0809	0848	0947	1047	1147	1247	1347	1447	1547	1647	1747	1848	1947	2037	2147	2236	...	2343	...		0808	0848	0947

	⑥	⑥	⑥	⑥	⑥	⑥	⑥	⑥	⑥	⑥	⑥	⑥	⑥		⑦	⑦		⑦	⑦	⑦	⑦	⑦	⑦	⑦	⑦
																									RN
Stansted Airport ✈ **206** d.	0727	0825	0925	1025	1125	1225	1325	1425	1525	1625	1725	1825	1918	...	⑦	...	...	1205	...	1405	1518	1612	1735	1835	...
Cambridge **206** d.	0804	0904	1004	1104	1204	1304	1404	1504	1604	1704	1802	1904	1950	...		1048	...	1236	1343	1436	1547	1647	1809	1908	*2002*y
Peterborough d.	0856	0954	1054	1154	1254	1354	1454	1554	1654	1754	1854	1954	2045	...		1152	...	1335	1441	1533	1640	1741	1901	2006	2110
Stamford d.	0907	1007	1107	1207	1307	1407	1507	1607	1707	1807	1907	2007	2058	...		1205	...	1348	1454	1546	1653	1754	1914	2019	2123
Oakham d.	0923	1023	1123	1223	1323	1423	1523	1623	1723	1823	1923	2023	2113	...		1219	...	1409	1508	1600	1707	1808	1928	2033	2137
Melton Mowbray d.	0934	1034	1134	1234	1334	1434	1534	1634	1734	1834	1934	2034	2124	...		1230	...	1421	1519	1611	1718	1819	1939	2044	2147
Leicester a.	0950	1048	1149	1250	1350	1448	1549	1649	1749	1850	1950	2051	2138	...		1247	...	1439	1540	1633	1742	1837	2002	2101	...
Birmingham New St **193** a.	1047	1147	1247	1347	1447	1547	1647	1747	1847	1947	2047	2147	2235	...		1347	...	1537	1648	1732	1838	1936	2106	2200	...

		Ⓐ	Ⓐ	Ⓐ	Ⓐ	Ⓐ	Ⓐ	Ⓐ	Ⓐ	Ⓐ	Ⓐ	Ⓐ	Ⓐ	Ⓐ	Ⓐ	Ⓐ	Ⓐ	Ⓐ	Ⓐ	Ⓐ			⑥	⑥	⑥
		NR		NR																				NR	
Birmingham New St **193** a.	Ⓐ	...	0520	...	0637	0721	0824	0924	1024	1124	1224	1324	1424	1524	1612	1624	1724	1824	1926	2027	...	⑥	0520	...	0636
Leicester d.		...	0612	...	0729	0814	0914	1014	1114	1214	1314	1414	1514	1614	1703	1731	1816	1914	2017	2115	...		0607	...	0729
Melton Mowbray d.		0529	0628	0652	0745	0830	0930	1030	1130	1230	1330	1430	1530	1630	1719	1746	1832	1930	2032	2132	...		0625	0656	0745
Oakham d.		0541	0641	0704	0757	0841	0941	1041	1141	1241	1341	1441	1541	1641	1730	1757	1844	1941	2044	2144	...		0637	0708	0757
Stamford d.		0602	0655	0718	0813	0857	0957	1057	1157	1257	1357	1457	1557	1657	1745	1814	1902	1957	2100	2159	...		0653	0723	0813
Peterborough a.		0617	0708	0733	0828	0914	1014	1114	1214	1314	1414	1514	1614	1716	1758	1832	1919	2022	2116	2215	...		0708	0738	0831
Cambridge **206** a.		*0744*y	0807	*0844*y	0921	1008	1108	1208	1308	1408	1508	1608	1708	1816	1851	1929	2011	2116	2208	2314	...		0806	*0844*y	0922
Stansted Airport ✈ **206** a.		...	0843	...	0958	1049	1149	1249	1349	1449	1549	1649	1743	1847	...	2005	...	...	...	...	...		0849	...	0958

	⑥	⑥	⑥	⑥	⑥	⑥	⑥	⑥	⑥	⑥	⑥	⑥	⑥	⑥			⑦		⑦	⑦	⑦	⑦	⑦	⑦	⑦
Birmingham New St **193** a.	0724	0824	0924	1024	1124	1224	1324	1424	1524	1624	1724	1824	1924	2027	...	⑦	1126	...	1336	1434	1532	1634	1734	1834	2028
Leicester d.	0814	0914	1014	1114	1214	1314	1414	1514	1614	1714	1814	1914	2019	2115	...		1221	...	1428	1524	1627	1728	1828	1926	2121
Melton Mowbray d.	0830	0930	1030	1130	1230	1330	1430	1530	1630	1730	1830	1930	2036	2133	...		1238	...	1445	1543	1644	1746	1846	1941	2141
Oakham d.	0841	0941	1041	1141	1241	1341	1441	1541	1641	1741	1841	1941	2047	2145	...		1250	...	1457	1555	1656	1758	1859	1952	2153
Stamford d.	0857	0957	1057	1157	1257	1357	1457	1557	1657	1757	1857	1957	2104	2159	...		1304	...	1511	1609	1710	1812	1913	2008	2207
Peterborough a.	0914	1014	1114	1214	1314	1414	1514	1614	1714	1814	1914	2014	2120	2215	...		1319	...	1525	1626	1726	1827	1928	2023	2223
Cambridge **206** a.	1008	1108	1208	1308	1408	1508	1608	1708	1815	1908	2008	2111	2216	2311	...		1419	...	1622	1723	1821	1920	2021	2119	2317
Stansted Airport ✈ **206** a.	1049	1149	1249	1349	1449	1549	1649	1749	1858	...	2049	...	...	...	...		1458	...	1659	1758	...	1958	2058	2153	...

N – To / from Nottingham. **R** – From / to Norwich. **S** – From Spalding. **y** – Change at Ely.

EM 2nd class — PETERBOROUGH - NOTTINGHAM - SHEFFIELD — 208

Services on ⑥ are subject to alteration from March 29. Services on ⑦ are subject to alteration from February 3.

km			⚒	⚒	Ⓐ	⑥	⚒	⑥	Ⓐ	⚒	⑥	Ⓐ	Ⓐ	⑥	⚒	⚒	⚒	⚒	⚒	⚒	⚒	Ⓐ	⑥	Ⓐ
					🍷				🍷			🍷	🍷									🍷		
								C	C													L		
	Norwich **206** d.	⚒	...	...	...	...	0552	...	...	0757	0857	0857	0957	0957	1057	1157	1257	1357	1457	1552	1657	...	1757	1754
0	**Peterborough 185** d.		...	...	...	...	0727	0825	0830	0927	1026	1030	1125	1127	1225	1325	1424	1526	1627v	1725	1825	...	1928	1931
46	Grantham **185 195** d.		...	...	*0609*	*0617*	0759	0857	0900	0959	1058	1112	1157	1158	1259	1356	1458	1556	1702	1800r	1856	...	2002	2004
83	**Nottingham 195** a.		...	...	*0648*	*0656*	0839	0927	0939	1028d	1128	1141	1234	1238	1328	1433z	1528	1626	1738	1830	1926	...	2044	2044
83	**Nottingham** d.		0519v	0634v	0742	0742	0842	0942	0940	1042	1142	1142	1242	1247	1345r	1442	1542	1642	1742	1840	1927	1942	...	...
129	Chesterfield **127 170** d.		0554	0714	0818	0818	0918	1018	1018	1118	1218	1218	1318	1322	1418	1518	1618	1718	1818	1918	2008	2018	...	...
148	**Sheffield 127 170** a.		0610	0732	0838	0838	0938	1038	1038	1138	1238	1238	1338	1339	1438	1538	1638	1734	1838	1939	2027	2033	...	...
	Manchester Piccadilly **194** a.		0735	0836	0936	0936	1036	1136	1136	1236	1336	1336	1436	1436	1536	1637	1736	1836	1936	2036	2130r	...	...	...
	Liverpool Lime St **194** a.		0829	0929	1029	1029	1129	1229	1229	1329	1427	1429	1529	1525	1629	1729	1832	1929	2029a	2129a	...	...	...	...

	Ⓐ	Ⓐ	⑥	⑥	⑥	Ⓐ			⑦	⑦	⑦	⑦	⑦	⑦	⑦	⑦	⑦	⑦	⑦	⑦	⑦	⑦	⑦	⑦
	🍷			🍷					🚌	🚌											🍷			
	L			L	S	S			T	T											L			
Norwich **206** d.	...	1857	1857	...	...	...	...	⑦	...	...	...	...	1047	...	...	1349	...	1553	1657	1754	...	1857	1944	2052
Peterborough 185 d.	...	2026	2027	...	2127	2130	...		...	...	...	...	1218	...	...	1526	...	1715	1830	1922	...	2032	2110	2222
Grantham **185 195** d.	*2049*	2056	2100	...	2202	|	...		...	...	...	...	1251	...	...	1559	...	1749	1900	1957	...	2103	|	2251
Nottingham 195 a.	*2125*	2135	2130	...	2233	2256	...		...	...	...	...	1329	...	...	1629	...	1827	1930	2031	...	2132	2231	2329
Nottingham d.	2142	...	...	2147	...	...	...		0905	1005	1146	1239	1333	1436	1535	1642	1731	1833	1939	...	2055	...	...	...
Chesterfield **127 170** d.	2221	...	...	2224	...	...	...		1005	1105	1221	1317	1417	1514	1614	1720	1814	1914	2014	...	2131	...	...	...
Sheffield 127 170 a.	2238	...	...	2240	...	...	...		1040	1140	1237	1334	1433	1531	1632	1744	1831	1932	2031	...	2146	...	...	...
Manchester Piccadilly **194** a.	...	...	...	...	...	...	...		...	...	...	...	...	...	...	...	...	...	...	...	...	...	...	...
Liverpool Lime St **194** a.	...	...	...	...	...	...	...		...	...	...	...	...	...	...	...	...	...	...	...	...	...	...	...

		Ⓐ	⚒	Ⓐ	⑥	Ⓐ	⚒	⑥	Ⓐ	Ⓐ	⑥	Ⓐ	⑥	⚒	⚒	⚒	⚒	⚒	⚒	⚒	⑥	⚒	⑥	Ⓐ	⚒
						🍴	🍷‡			🍷														🍷	
						L	L			L	L										L				
Liverpool Lime St **194** d.	⚒	...	...	...	...	...	...	...	...	...	...	...	...	0647	0747	0852	0952	1052	1152	1252	...	1352	1452	1452	1552
Manchester Piccadilly **194** d.		...	...	...	...	...	...	...	...	...	...	...	...	0743	0842	0942	1042	1142	1242	1342	...	1442	1542	1542	1642
Sheffield 127 170 d.		...	...	...	...	0600	0630v	...	...	0714	0732	0740	...	0838	0938	1038	1138	1238	1338	1438	1502	1538	1638	1638	1741
Chesterfield **127 170** d.		...	...	...	...	0614	0645	...	...	0727	0745	0753	...	0852	0953	1053	1153	1253	1353	1453	1514	1553	1655	1655	1755
Nottingham a.		...	...	...	...	0645	0723	...	...	0809	0826	0829	...	0930	1025	1130	1229	1329	1430	1530	1600	1635	1731	1729	1829
Nottingham 195 d.		0456	0509	0613	0619	...	...	0739	0752	...	...	0831	0833	0935r	1031	1132	1234r	1331	1431	1531	...	*1650*	1736	1739	1831
Grantham **185 195** a.		|	0548	|	|	...	...	0813	0824	...	...	0907	0909	1006v	1105	1206	1308	1406	1505	1605	...	*1730*	1812	1814	1905
Peterborough 185 a.		0617	0627	0733	0738	...	...	0844	0857	...	...	0938	0943	1043	1136	1242r	1338r	1439	1534	1634v	...	...	1840	1849	1936r
Norwich **206** a.		0810	...	0916	0912	...	...	1017	1043	...	...	1114	1117	1217	1313	1414	1513	1613	1713	1813	...	...	2013	2022	2113

	⑥	Ⓐ	⑥	Ⓐ	⚒	⚒	⑥	Ⓐ			⑦	⑦	⑦	⑦	⑦	⑦	⑦	⑦	⑦	⑦	⑦	⑦	⑦	⑦	⑦
		🍷		🍷							🍷					🍷			🍷						🚌
	C			C							L					L			L						T
Liverpool Lime St **194** d.	1652	1652	1752	1752	1852	1952	...	2135	...	⑦	...	...	...	...	...	...	...	...	...	...	...	...	...	...	...
Manchester Piccadilly **194** d.	1742	1742	1844	1844	1942	2042	2142	2227	...		...	...	...	...	...	...	...	...	...	...	...	...	...	...	...
Sheffield 127 170 d.	1838	1845	1938	1938	2040	2137	2236	2338	...		0940	...	1252	1358	1441	1527	1539	1639	1735	1739	1840	1937	2038	2141	2230
Chesterfield **127 170** d.	1853	1901	1953	1956	2055	2153	2250	2359	...		0953	...	1306	1413	1456	1540	1554	1654	1747	1753	1854	1953	2054	2156	2305
Nottingham a.	1929	1937	2029	2031	2138r	2238	2326	0046	...		1036	...	1342	1446	1534	1618	1630	1731	1824	1830	1934	2030	2135	2238	0010
Nottingham 195 d.	1932	...	2032	2036	...	...	...	...	...		...	1232	1344	1454	1548	...	1640	1738	...	1846	*1941*	2035	...	...	...
Grantham **185 195** a.	2009	...	2109	2107	...	...	...	...	...		...	1313	1417	|	1623	...	1715	1813	...	1920	*2021*	2118	...	...	...
Peterborough 185 a.	2038	...	2137	2136	...	...	...	...	...		...	1341	1453	1604	1655	...	1751	1852	...	1951	...	2151	...	...	...
Norwich **206** a.	...	...	2320	...	...	...	...	...	...		...	1528	1637	1735	1835	...	1929	2028	...	2125	...	2335	...	...	...

C – From / to Cambridge.
L – [12] from / to London.
S – From Spalding.
T – To / from Stockport.
a – Ⓐ only.
d – 1037 on ⑥.
r – 3–5 minutes earlier on ⑥.
v – 3–4 minutes later on ⑥.
z – 1426 on ⑥.
‡ – Conveys 🍴 on Ⓐ.

211 WHITBY - MIDDLESBROUGH - NEWCASTLE

2nd class NT

km		⚒	Ⓐ	⚒	⚒	⚒	⚒	⚒	⚒	⑥	Ⓐ	⚒	⚒	⚒	⚒	⚒	⚒	⚒	⚒	⑥	⚒	Ⓐ	⚒	⚒	⚒	⚒
0	**Whitby** d.		...	...	...	...	...	...	...	0845	0852	...	...	...	...	1241	...	...	...	1550	...	1605	...	...	...	1915
10	Grosmont d.		...	...	...	...	...	...	...	0902	0909	...	...	...	...	1258	...	...	...	1607	...	1622	...	...	...	1932
56	**Middlesbrough 187** ‡ d.		0545	0649	0656	0732	0742	0832	0932	1011	1018	1032	1132	1232	1332	1407	1432	1532	1632	1716	1730	1735	1830	1920	2030	2041
81	Darlington **187** ‡ a.		0614	0720	|	|	0815	|	|	*1054*	*1053*	|	|	|	|	*1452*	|	|	|	*1752*	|	*1824*	|	|	|	*2124*
65	Stockton d.		|	|	0708	0743	|	0843	0943	...	...	1043	1143	1243	1343	...	1443	1543	1643	...	1741	...	1841	1931	2041	...
84	Hartlepool d.		|	|	0727	0802	|	0902	1002	...	...	1102	1202	1302	1402	...	1502	1602	1702	...	1802	...	1900	1949	2100	...
113	Sunderland d.		|	|	0755	0830	|	0930	1030	...	...	1130	1230	1330	1430	...	1530	1630	1730	...	1830	...	1927	2027**p**	2127	...
133	**Newcastle** a.		0655	0801	0817	0853	0859**r**	0954	1052	...	...	1152	1252	1352	1451	...	1552	1652	1752	...	1853	...	1948	2048	2148	...

	⑦ ▲	⑦		⑦	⑦		⑦	⑦		⑦
Whitby d.		...	...	...	...	...	...	...	...	...
Grosmont d.		...	...	...	...	...	...	...	...	...
Middlesbrough 187 ‡ d.		0930	...	1130	1330	...	1530	1730	...	1930
Darlington **187** ‡ a.		|	...	|	|	...	|	|	...	|
Stockton d.		0941	...	1141	1341	...	1541	1741	...	1941
Hartlepool d.		1000	...	1200	1400	...	1600	1800	...	2000
Sunderland d.		1028	...	1228	1428	...	1628	1828	...	2028
Newcastle a.		1048	...	1248	1448	...	1648	1848	...	2049

	⚒	⚒	⚒	⚒	⚒	⚒	⚒	⚒	⚒	⚒	⑥
Newcastle d.		...	0700	0730	0830	...	0930	1030	1130	1230	...
Sunderland d.		...	0720	0750	0850	...	0950	1050	1150	1250	...
Hartlepool d.		...	0745	0815	0915	...	1015	1115	1215	1315	...
Stockton d.		...	0804	0833	0933	...	1033	1133	1233	1333	...
Darlington **187** ‡ d.		*0636*	|	|	|	*0951*	|	|	|	|	*1331*
Middlesbrough 187 ‡ d.		0706	0818	0848	0948	1038	1048	1148	1249	1348	1412
Grosmont d.		0820**c**	...	...	...	1144	...	...	...	...	1518
Whitby a.		0841**c**	...	...	...	1205	...	...	...	...	1539

	Ⓐ	⚒	⚒	⚒	⚒	⚒	⚒	⚒	⚒	⚒	⚒	⑥	Ⓐ	
Newcastle d.	...	1330	1430	1530	...	1630	1653	1729	1830	1928	2030	2150	2200	...
Sunderland d.	...	1350	1450	1550	...	1650	1715	1750	1850	1950	2050	|	|	...
Hartlepool d.	...	1415	1515	1615	...	1715	1739	1815	1915	2015	2115	|	|	...
Stockton d.	...	1433	1533	1633	...	1733	1757	1833	1933	2033	2133	|	|	...
Darlington **187** ‡ d.	*1330*	|	|	|	*1659*v	|	|	|	|	|	|	2230	2242	...
Middlesbrough 187 ‡ d.	1416	1448	1548	1647	1738	1749	1812	1848	1948	2050	2148	2257	2310	...
Grosmont a.	1522	...	...	...	1846	...	...	...	...	...	...	...	...	...
Whitby a.	1543	...	...	...	1907	...	...	...	...	...	...	...	...	...

	⑦ ▲	⑦		⑦		⑦	⑦		⑦		⑦	⑦
Newcastle d.		1000	...	1200	...	1400	1600	...	1800	...	2000	2106
Sunderland d.		1021	...	1221	...	1421	1621	...	1821	...	2021	|
Hartlepool d.		1045	...	1245	...	1445	1645	...	1845	...	2045	|
Stockton d.		1104	...	1304	...	1504	1704	...	1904	...	2104	|
Darlington **187** ‡ d.		|	...	|	...	|	|	...	|	...	|	2146
Middlesbrough 187 ‡ d.		1117	...	1320	...	1520	1717	...	1920	...	2120	2207
Grosmont a.		...	...	...	...	...	...	...	...	...	...	...
Whitby a.		...	...	...	...	...	...	...	...	...	...	...

c – 6 minutes earlier on ⑥.
p – Arrives 2020.
r – 0856 on ⑥.
v – *1704* on ⑥.
‡ – Local services run Middlesbrough - Darlington and v.v.: ± 2 trains per hour on ⚒, ± 1 train per hour on ⑦.
▲ – Services on ⑦ are subject to amendment from Mar. 23.

212 NEWCASTLE - CARLISLE

2nd class NT

km		⚒	Ⓐ	⑥ G	Ⓐ G	⚒	⚒	⚒	⚒	⚒	⚒	⚒	⚒ S	⚒	⚒	⚒	⚒	⚒	⚒ W	⚒ S	⚒	⚒	⚒	⚒	⚒	Ⓐ
0	**Newcastle** ‡ d.		0630	0634	0654	0756	0824	0924	1024	1054	1122	1154	1239	1324	1354	1424	1454	1524	1624	1711	1754	1824	1910	2010**v**	2110	2230
36	Hexham ‡ d.		0710	0711	0720	0840	0859	0954	1055	1136	1156	1236	1308	1355	1436	1457	1536	1554	1703	1745	1831	1903	1949	2051**v**	2149	2311
62	Haltwhistle d.		...	0733	0743	...	0921	1012	1114	...	1219	...	1326	1414	...	1516	...	1617	1723	1808	1854	1921	2009	...	2211	...
99	**Carlisle** a.		...	0807	0817	...	0956	1045	1146	...	1254	...	1359	1445	...	1547	...	1654	1755	1843	1928	1956	2042	...	2245	...

	⑦	⑦	⑦	⑦	⑦	⑦	⑦	⑦	⑦	⑦	⑦	⑦
Newcastle d.		0910	1010	1110	1210	1310	1410	1510	1612	1710	1810	2015
Hexham d.		0949	1049	1149	1249	1349	1449	1549	1651	1749	1849	2054
Haltwhistle d.		1011	1111	1208	1311	1408	1508	1611	1710	1808	1911	2116
Carlisle a.		1045	1145	1238	1345	1438	1538	1645	1740	1838	1945	2150

	⚒	⚒	⚒	⚒ D	⚒	⚒	⚒ R	⚒	⚒	⚒
Carlisle d.		...	0625	0713	...	0830	0933	...	1036	1134
Haltwhistle d.		...	0656	0745	...	0901	1001	...	1104	1202
Hexham ‡ d.		0613	0718	0807	0844	0923	1019	1044	1122	1223
Newcastle ‡ a.		0652	0803	0857	0927	0958**v**	1051	1125	1159	1257

	⚒	⚒	⚒ S	⚒	⚒	⚒	⚒	⚒	⚒	⚒ G	⚒	⚒	⚒	Ⓐ
Carlisle d.	...	1230	1336	...	1436	1530	...	1629	1720	1818	1933	...	2120	...
Haltwhistle d.	...	1301	1405	...	1504	1558	...	1700	1752	1846	2001	...	2152	...
Hexham ‡ d.	1244	1323	1424	1444	1522	1616	1644	1722	1814	1904	2019	2114	2214	2314
Newcastle ‡ a.	1326	1357**v**	1456	1528	1600	1650	1726	1800	1855	1945	2101	2156	2259	2357

	⑦	⑦	⑦	⑦	⑦	⑦	⑦	⑦	⑦	⑦	⑦	⑦
Carlisle d.		0905	1005	1112	1205	1312	1412	1505	1612	1712	1805	2015
Haltwhistle d.		0936	1036	1140	1236	1340	1440	1536	1640	1740	1836	2043
Hexham ‡ d.		0959	1059	1159	1259	1359	1459	1559	1659	1759	1859	2059
Newcastle ‡ a.		1040	1140	1240	1340	1440	1540	1640	1740	1840	1940	2143

D – From Dumfries.
G – To / from Glasgow.
R – From Girvan.
S – To / from Stranraer.
W – To Whitehaven.
v – 3–4 minutes later on ⑥.
‡ – Additional local trains run Newcastle - Hexham and v.v. on ⚒.

214 CARLISLE - DUMFRIES - GLASGOW

2nd class SR

km		⚒	⚒	⚒	⑥	⚒	⑥	⚒	⚒	⚒	⑥	⚒	⑥	⚒	⚒	⑥	Ⓐ	⑥	Ⓐ	⑥	⑦	⑦		⑦	⑦
	Newcastle **212** d.	...	...	0654**b**	...	...	...	...	1239	...	...	...	...	...	1711	...	...	...	...	...	...	...	...	...	...
0	**Carlisle** **160** d.	0540	0609	0819	0952	1107	1218	1309	1422	1500	1522	1611	1724	1751	1851	2008	2108	2108	2253	2256	1252	1347	...	1935	2112
28	Annan d.	0600	0631	0838	1012	1126	1238	1332	1442	1523	1543	1631	1744	1812	1910	2028	2128	2128	2313	2316	1311	1407	...	1954	2132
53	**Dumfries** d.	0618	0650	0855	1029	1143	1255	1349	1459	1541	1600	1650	1801	1829	1929	2044	2144	2145	2330	2333	1328	1424	...	2011	2149
124	Auchinleck d.	...	0738	0943	...	1231	...	1437	1548	1629	...	...	...	1917	2017	2132	2232	...	...	...	1416	...	...	2059	...
146	**Kilmarnock 215** d.	...	0758	1004	...	1250	...	1455	1609	1647	...	...	...	1950	2037	2150	2250	...	...	...	1435	...	...	2118	...
	Stranraer **215** a.	...	|	|	...	|	...	|	1755	|	...	...	...	|	2224	|	|	...	...	...	|	...	...	|	...
185	**Glasgow** Central .. **160** a.	...	0837	1041	...	1329	...	1533	*1709*v	1731	...	...	...	2027	*2127*z	2227	2328	...	...	...	1514	...	...	2155	...

	⚒	⚒ □	⚒ G	⚒	⑥	⚒	⑥	Ⓐ	⚒	⑥	⚒	⑥	⚒	⚒	⑥	Ⓐ	⑥	⚒	⑥	⚒	⑦	⑦	⑦	⑦	⑦
Glasgow Central .. **160** d.	...	...	*0642*	0828	...	0953	*1103*z	*1103*z	1203	...	1303	...	...	1548	...	1730	1730	2003	...	2203	...	...	1448	...	2228
Stranraer **215** d.	...	...	|	*0709*	...	|	1000	1000	|	...	*1148*	...	...	|	...	|	|	|	...	|	...	...	|	...	|
Kilmarnock 215 d.	...	...	0741	0913**r**	...	1039	1146	1150	1241	...	1342	...	...	1627	...	1809	1815	2040	...	2243	...	...	1528	...	2305
Auchinleck d.	...	...	0757	0929**r**	...	1056	1203	1209	1257	...	1359	...	...	1644	...	1828	1833	2057	...	2259	...	...	1545	...	2322
Dumfries d.	0628	0731	0849	1015	1039	1147	1253	1257	1348	1426	1447	1615	1701	1731	1820	1918	1924	2147	2210	2353	1300	1437	1635	2214	0012
Annan d.	0643	0746	0906	1030	1054	1202	1308	1312	1403	1443	1504	1630	1716	1747	1835	1933	1939	2202	2225	0008	1315	1452	1650	2229	0027
Carlisle **160** a.	0706	0808	0928	1056**r**	1114	1226	1331	1335	1426	1503	1528	1652	1738	1816**d**	1859	1955	2001	2224	2247	0034	1337	1519	1718	2251	0049
Newcastle **212** a.	0857	...	1051	...	...	...	1456	1455	...	...	...	...	...	1945	...	...	...	...	...	...	...	...	...	...	...

G – From Girvan.
b – 0634 on ⑥.
d – 1810 on ⑥.
v – Change at Troon.
z – Change at Kilmarnock.
□ – Runs 3 minutes earlier on ⑥.

215 GLASGOW and KILMARNOCK - STRANRAER

2nd class SR

km		⚒	⚒	⚒	⚒	⚒		⚒	⚒		⚒ N	⚒	⚒	Ⓐ	⑥	⚒	⚒ N		⚒		⑦	⑦		⑦
0	**Glasgow** Central **216** d.		...	0713	...	0903	...	1142	...	...	...	...	...	...	...	...	...	...	...	...		1142	...	1625
12	Paisley Gilmour St **216** d.		...	0724	...	|	...	1153	...	...	...	...	...	...	...	...	...	...	...	...		1153	...	1639
43	Kilwinning **216** d.		...	0741	...	|	...	1210	...	...	...	...	...	...	...	...	...	...	...	...		1210	...	1656
	Kilmarnock 214 d.		...	|	0910	0955	...	|	1310	...	1609	1631	...	1811	1819	...	2037	...	2244	...		|	...	|
56	Troon **216** d.		...	|	0924	1007	...	|	1322	...	1619	1644	...	1824	1831	...	2050	...	2256	...		|	...	|
61	Prestwick Airport ✈ **216** d.		...	|	0929	1012	...	|	1327	...	|	1649	...	1829	1836	...	|	...	2301	...		|	...	|
67	**Ayr** **216** d.		0600	0800	0943	1022	...	1230	1338	...	1634	1700	1810	1838	1845	1931	2101	...	2311	...		1235	...	1719
101	Girvan d.		0627	0826	1009	1051	...	1301	1405	...	1700	1727	1837	...	...	1957	2127	...	2337	...		1301	...	1745
121	Barrhill d.		...	0845	1035	...	...	1320	...	...	1719	...	...	...	...	2016	2146	...	0001	...		1319	...	1804
163	**Stranraer** a.		...	0921	1111	...	...	1356	...	...	1755	...	...	...	...	2052	2224	...	0037	...		1356	...	1840
	Belfast Port ⛴ **2070** a.		...	*1140*	...	...	...	*1635*	...	...	*2135*	...	...	...	...	...	...	...	...	...		*1635*	...	*2135*

N – From Newcastle.

SR 2nd class — STRANRAER - KILMARNOCK and GLASGOW — 215

km			⚒ N	⚒		⚒ N	⚒	⚒		⚒	⚒	⚒	⚒	⚒	⚒		Ⓐ			⑦		⑦		⑦
	Belfast Port ⛴ **2070**	d.	...	...	...	*0735*	...	...	...	...	*1220*	...	...	*1720*	...	...	...	...	⑦	*0735*	...	*1220*	...	*1720*
0	**Stranraer**	d.	...	0709	...	1000	...	1148	...	...	1437	...	...	1940	2110	...	2325	...		1040	...	1440	...	1940
42	Barrhill	d.	...	0743	...	1034	...	1222	...	...	1511	...	...	2019	2150	...	2359	...		1114	...	1514	...	2015
62	Girvan	d.	0640	0801	...	1052	1140	1240	...	1440	1529	1732	1842	2037	2208	...	0019	...		1132	...	1532	...	2033
95	**Ayr**	216 d.	0710	0836	...	1122	1209	1309	...	1517	1558	1800	1909	2106	2238	...	0047	...		1201	...	1601	...	2102
101	Prestwick Airport ✈	216 d.	|	0843	...	|	1216	1316	...	1524	|	...	1916	|	|	...	...	...		|	...	|	...	|
103	Troon	216 d.	0718	0848	...	1130	1221	1321	...	1529	|	...	1921	|	|	...	...	...		|	...	|	...	|
120	**Kilmarnock 214**	a.	0740	0903	...	1149r	1237	1337	...	1542	|	...	1940	|	|	...	...	...		|	...	|	...	|
	Kilwinning	216 d.	...	|	...	...	...	|	...	|	1613	...	...	2121	2254	...	...	...		1216	...	1617	...	2117
	Paisley Gilmour St	216 a.	...	|	...	...	...	|	...	|	1633	...	...	2144	2314	...	...	...		1236	...	1637	...	2136
	Glasgow Central	216 a.	...	0950	...	...	...	1427	...	1632	1645	...	...	2155	2326	...	...	...		1251	...	1649	...	2148

N – To Newcastle. r – 1145 on ⑥.

SR 2nd class — GLASGOW - AYR — 216

km			②–⑥		⚒	⚒	❖	⚒	⚒		Ⓐ			⑦	⑦		⑦	⑦	⑦		⑦
0	**Glasgow** Central	215 d.	0015	...	0600	0630	and at	2300	2330	...	1730	...	⑦ ▲	0900	0930	and at	1730	1800	1900		2300
12	Paisley Gilmour St	215 d.	0026	...	0611	0641	the same	2311	2341	...	1741u	...		0911	0941	the same	1741	1811	1911	and	2311
43	Kilwinning	215 d.	0042	...	0629	0659	minutes	2329	2359	...	|	...		0929	0959	minutes	1759	1829	1929		2330
48	Irvine	d.	0046	...	0633	0703	past	2333	0003	...	1759	...		0933	1003	past	1803	1833	1933	hourly	2334
56	Troon	215 d.	0054	...	0639	0711	each	2339	0011	...	1807	...		0941	1009	each	1809	1841	1941		2341
61	Prestwick Airport ✈	215 d.	0058	...	0643	0715	hour	2343	0015	...	1811	...		0945	1013	hour	1813	1845	1945	until	2345
67	**Ayr**	215 a.	0110	...	0652	0724	until	2352	0024	...	1820	...		1001	1022	until	1822	1854	1954		2354

			⚒	⚒	⚒	⚒	⚒	⚒	◐	⚒	⚒	⚒		⑦	⑦		⑦	⑦	⑦		⑦	⑦
Ayr	215 d.		0540	0613	0643	0713	0743	0813	and at	2143	2213	2300	⑦ ▲	0913	0943	and at	1713	1743	1843		2143	2300
Prestwick Airport ✈	215 d.		0548	0621	0651	0721	0750	0821	the same	2150	2221	2308		0920	0950	the same	1720	1750	1850	and	2150	2307
Troon	215 d.		0552	0625	0655	0725	0754	0825	minutes	2154	2225	2312		0924	0954	minutes	1724	1754	1854		2154	2311
Irvine	d.		0559	0632	0702	0732	0759	0832	past	2159	2232	2319		0929	1001	past	1729	1801	1901	hourly	2201	2318
Kilwinning	215 d.		0604	0637	0707	0737	0804	0837	each	2204	2237	2324		0934	1006	each	1734	1806	1906		2206	2323
Paisley Gilmour St	215 a.		0631	0655	0725	0757r	0822	0856	hour	2224	2257	2346		0952	1031	hour	1755	1824	1924	until	2224	2341
Glasgow Central	215 a.		0643	0707	0738	0809r	0834	0907	until	2236	2310	2358		1004	1043	until	1807	1836	1936		2236	2353

r – 7 minutes later on ⑥.
u – Stops to pick up only.
❖ – For the 1730 Ⓐ service from Glasgow, see separate column. Some services run up to 8 minutes later Kilwinning - Ayr.
◐ – The 1743 service from Ayr arrives Paisley 1828, Glasgow 1841.
▲ – Services on ⑦ are subject to alteration from Dec. 30.

SR 2nd class — GLASGOW - ARDROSSAN - LARGS — 217

km				⚒	⚒	⚒	Ⓐ	⚒	⚒	⚒		⚒	⚒	⚒	⚒	⚒	⚒	⚒	⚒	⚒		⚒	⚒	Ⓐ
0	**Glasgow** Central **215**	d.		0615	0645	0715	0815	0833	0845	0915	and at	1515	1545	1618	1650	1720	1735	1745	1815	1845	and at	2215	2245	2315
12	Paisley Gilmour St **215**	d.		0626	0656	0726	0826	0844	0856	0926	the same	1526	1556	1629	1701	1732	1746	1756	1826	1856	the same	2226	2256	2326
43	Kilwinning **215**	d.		0654	0720	0752	0854	0910	0918	0954	minutes	1554	1618	1657	1727	1754	1814	1820	1854	1918	minutes	2254	2318	2354
50	**Ardrossan** South Beach	d.		0702	0727r	0802	0902	0918	0926	1002	past	1602	1626	1710	1736	1802	1822	1828	1902	1926	past	2302	2326	0002
54	Fairlie	d.		0713	...	0814	...	...	0937	...	each hour	...	1637	1722	...	1813	...	1839	...	1937	each hour	...	2337	...
69	**Largs**	a.		0720	...	0822	...	...	0944	...	until	...	1644	1728	...	1820	...	1848	...	1944	until	...	2344	...

		⑥	Ⓐ		⑦		⑦	Ⓐ		⑦
Glasgow Central 215	d.	2315	2345	⑦	0945	and	1745	1840	and	2240
Paisley Gilmour St **215**	d.	2326	2356		0956	hourly	1756	1851		2251
Kilwinning **215**	d.	2354	0024		1024		1824	1919	hourly	2318
Ardrossan South Beach	d.	0002	0032		1032	(A)	1832	1927		2326
Fairlie	d.	0014	0043		1044	until	1844	1939	until	2338
Largs	a.	0019	0049		1052		1850	1945		2344

			⚒	⚒	Ⓐ	⚒	Ⓐ	⑥	Ⓐ	Ⓐ
Largs	d.		...	0641	0723	0742	...	...	0828	...
Fairlie	d.		...	0646	0728	0747	...	...	0833	...
Ardrossan South Beach	d.		0634	0657	0739	0758	0817	0834	0844	0907
Kilwinning **215**	d.		0643	0710	0748	0808	0825	0842	0853	0916
Paisley Gilmour St **215**	a.		0710	0734	0812	0834	0853	0910	0917	0939
Glasgow Central **215**	a.		0722	0747	0824	0846	0904	0922	0930	0953

		⑥	⚒	⚒	⚒		⚒	⚒ *	⚒	⚒	⚒	⚒	⚒	⚒		⚒	⚒			⑦		⑦	⑦
Largs	d.	0851	...	0953	...	and at	1553	...	1650	...	1735	...	...	1853	and at	...	2253	...	⑦	0958	and	2158	2258
Fairlie	d.	0856	...	0958	...	the same	1558	...	1655	...	1740	...	...	1858	the same	...	2258	...		1003	hourly	2203	2303
Ardrossan South Beach	d.	0907	0936	1009	1034	minutes	1609	1634	1706	1740	1751	1806	1834	1909	minutes	2234	2309	...		1014		2214	2314
Kilwinning **215**	d.	0916	0945	1018	1043	past	1618	1643	1715	1748	1800	1816	1843	1918	past	2243	2318	...		1023	(B)	2223	2327
Paisley Gilmour St **215**	a.	0939	1010	1040	1110	each hour	1640	1710	1740	1812	1822	1840	1910	1940	each hour	2310	2342	...		1051	until	2251	2354
Glasgow Central **215**	a.	0953	1022	1052	1122	until	1652	1722	1755	1823	1834	1852	1922	1952	until	2322	2354	...		1104		2303	0005

A – Also: 1115, 1405, 1655 Glasgow - Ardrossan.
B – Also: 1240, 1509, 1805 Ardrossan - Glasgow.
r – 0730 on ⑥.
* – By 🚌. Change at Johnstone.
▲ – Services on ⑦ are subject to alteration from Dec. 30.

SR 2nd class — GLASGOW - OBAN, FORT WILLIAM and MALLAIG — 218

km			⚒	⚒ A	⚒ 🍸	⚒ 🍸	⚒ 🍸	⚒ 🍸		🍸	🍸
	Edinburgh **220**	d.	...	0450	*0715*	...	*1115*	...	...	*1715c*	...
0	**Glasgow** Queen St	d.	...	*0530*	0821	0821	1221	1221	...	1820	1820
10	Westerton	d.	...	0556	*0823*	*0823*	*1223*	*1223*	...	*1823r*	*1823r*
16	Dalmuir	d.	...	0604	0839	0839	1242	1242	...	1835	1835
26	Dumbarton Central	d.	...	|	0848	0848	1248	1248	...	1845	1845
40	Helensburgh Upper	d.	...	0628	0906	0906	1306	1306	...	1903	1903
51	Garelochhead	d.	...	0641	0917	0917	1317	1317	...	1914	1914
68	Arrochar & Tarbet	d.	...	0707	0937	0937	1337	1337	...	1934	1934
81	Ardlui	d.	...	0721x	0953	0953	1353	1353	...	1951	1951
95	**Crianlarich**	a.	...	0742	1009	1009	1409	1409	...	2008	2008
95	**Crianlarich**	d.	...	0743	1015	1021	1415	1421	...	2014	2017
123	Dalmally	d.	...	|	1042	|	1442	|	...	2041	|
142	Taynuilt	d.	...	|	1103	|	1503	|	...	2102	|
162	**Oban**	a.	...	|	1127	|	1527	|	...	2126	|
115	Bridge of Orchy	d.	...	0813	...	1046	...	1446	...	...	2042
140	Rannoch	d.	...	0845	...	1108	...	1508	...	...	2107
177	Roy Bridge	d.	...	0929x	...	1146	...	1546	...	...	2145
183	Spean Bridge	d.	...	0937	...	1154	...	1553	...	...	2152
197	**Fort William**	a.	...	0954	...	1207	...	1606	...	...	2205
197	**Fort William**	d.	0830	...	...	1212	...	1619	...	...	2210
223	Glenfinnan	d.	0904	...	...	1245	...	1654	...	...	2243
251	Arisaig	d.	0936	...	...	1318	...	1727	...	...	2316
259	Morar	d.	0945	...	...	1326	...	1735	...	...	2324
264	**Mallaig**	a.	0952	...	...	1334	...	1743	...	...	2331

		Ⓐ	⚒ 🍸	⚒ 🍸	⚒ 🍸	⚒ 🍸	🍸	🍸	⑦ A	⚒	Ⓐ A
Mallaig	d.	...	...	0603	...	1010	1605	...	...	1815	...
Morar	d.	...	...	0609	...	1016	1611	...	...	1821	...
Arisaig	d.	...	...	0619	...	1026	1621	...	...	1831	...
Glenfinnan	d.	...	...	0651	...	1058	1651	...	...	1903	...
Fort William	a.	...	...	0725	...	1132	1727	...	...	1937	...
Fort William	d.	...	...	0742	...	1140	1737	...	1900	...	1950
Spean Bridge	d.	...	...	0755	...	1153	1750	...	1920	...	2010
Roy Bridge	d.	...	...	0802	...	1200	1757	...	1927x	...	2017x
Rannoch	d.	...	...	0843	...	1243	1836	...	2015	...	2106
Bridge of Orchy	d.	...	...	0903	...	1302	1856	...	2047	...	2134
Oban	d.	...	0811	|	1211	|	|	1811	|	...	|
Taynuilt	d.	...	0835	|	1235	|	|	1835	|	...	|
Dalmally	d.	...	0856	|	1256	|	|	1856	|	...	|
Crianlarich	a.	...	0928	0930	1329	1330	1926	1927	2116	...	2204
Crianlarich	d.	...	0935	0935	1336	1336	1933	1933	2118	...	2205
Ardlui	d.	...	0952	0952	1352	1352	1953	1953	2139x	...	2226x
Arrochar & Tarbet	d.	0708	1007	1007	1407	1407	2008	2008	2157	...	2244
Garelochhead	d.	0730	1029	1029	1427	1427	2028	2028	2223	...	2310
Helensburgh Upper	d.	0742	1041	1041	1439	1439	2040	2040	2237	...	2324
Dumbarton Central	d.	0757	1058	1058	1452	1452	2053	2053	|	...	|
Dalmuir	d.	|	1108	1108	1504	1504	2104	2104	2304	...	2351
Westerton	a.	|	*1125*	*1125*	*1525*	*1525*	*2130*	*2130*	2311	...	2356
Glasgow Queen St	a.	0837	1128	1128	1528	1528	2129	2129	|	...	*0019*
Edinburgh **220**	a.	*0948*	...	*1236*	...	*1639*	...	*2251v*	0015	...	0050

A – Ⓡ, 🛏 (limited accommodation), 🛋 1, 2 cl. and 🍸 London - Fort William and v.v. (Table 159).
c – *1700* on ⑦.
r – *1810* on ⑦.
v – *2324* on ⑦.
x – Stops on request.
☛ Services on ⑥⑦ are subject to alteration from Mar. 22

⛴ SCOTTISH ISLAND FERRIES — 219

Caledonian MacBrayne Ltd operates numerous ferry services linking the Western Isles of Scotland to the mainland and to each other. Principal routes – some of which are seasonal – are listed below (see also the map on page **98**). Service frequencies, sailing-times and reservations: ✆ +44 (0)1475 650 100 ; fax +44 (0)1475 637 607 ; www.calmac.co.uk

Ardrossan – Brodick (Arran)
Claonaig – Lochranza (Arran)
Kennacraig – Port Askaig (Islay)
Kennacraig – Port Ellen (Islay)
Kilchoan – Tobermory (Mull)
Leverburgh (Harris) – Otternish (North Uist)
Mallaig – Armadale (Skye)
Mallaig – Eigg, Muck, Rum and Canna
Oban – Castlebay (Barra) and Lochboisdale (South Uist)
Oban – Coll and Tiree
Oban – Colonsay, Port Askaig (Islay) and Kennacraig
Oban – Craignure (Mull)
Uig (Skye) – Lochmaddy (North UIst)
Uig (Skye) – Tarbert (Harris)
Ullapool – Stornaway (Lewis)
Wemyss Bay – Rothesay (Bute)

220 EDINBURGH - GLASGOW SR

From EDINBURGH *76 km*

⚒: 0555, 0630, 0700, 0715 and every 15 minutes until 1900; then 1930, 2000 and every 30 minutes until 2330.

⑦: 0800, 0900, 1000, 1100, 1200, 1230 and every 30 minutes until 2100; then 2200, 2300, 2330.

☛ All services call at Falkirk High (*41 km* ± 27 mins from Edinburgh).

From GLASGOW Queen St Journey time: ± 51 minutes

⚒: 0600, 0630, 0700, 0715 and every 15 minutes until 1900; then 1930, 2000 and every 30 minutes until 2330.

⑦: 0750, 0830, 0930, 1030, 1130, 1230, 1300 and every 30 minutes until 2130; then 2230, 2330.

☛ All services call at Falkirk High (*35 km* ± 21 mins from Glasgow).

221 EDINBURGH and GLASGOW - INVERNESS SR

km		Ⓐ 🍷 A	⚒	⚒ 🍷	⚒ 🍷	⚒	⚒ 🍷	⚒ 🍷	⚒ 🍷	⚒ 🍷	⚒ 🍷‡	⚒ 🍷	Ⓐ 🍷	⑥ 🍷	⚒ 2	
	London Kings Cross **186** d.	2115**d**	...	...	...	...	...	...	...	...	1200	...	...	...	...	...
0	**Edinburgh** 224 d.	|	0640	...	0838**r**	0936	...	1136	1336	*1533*j	1634	1740	1936	1936	2133	...
42	Kirkcaldy 224 d.	|	0715	...	0911**r**	1012	...	1212u	1410u	|	|	1815	2009	2010	|	...
54	Markinch 224 d.	|	0724	...	0920**r**	1022	...	1221	|	|	|	|	2018	2019	|	...
	Glasgow Queen St 224 d.	|	|	0706	*0841*	|	1011	*1141*	*1341*	1611	*1641*j	*1741*	*1942*	*1942*	|	...
	Falkirk Grahamston d.	|	|	|	|	|	|	|	|	|	1704	|	|	|	2207	...
	Stirling 224 d.	0457	|	0731	*0906*	|	1041	*1207*	*1407*	1639	1720	*1814*	*2007*	*2007*	2223	...
91	**Perth** 224 d.	0544	0754	0805	0955	1056	1120	1257	1455	1721	1757	1855	2052	2059	2302**z**	...
116	Dunkeld & Birnam d.	0605	...	0824	|	...	1138	1315	1512	1739	|	1913	2109	2117	...	...
137	Pitlochry d.	0619	...	0841	1024	...	1151	1328	1525	1752	1832	1926	2122	2130	...	...
148	Blair Atholl d.	0630	...	0851	|	...	1200	1337	1535	1802	|	|	2132	2139	...	...
186	Dalwhinnie d.	0701	...	0917	|	...	1228	|	1603	|	|	|	2157	2204	...	...
202	Newtonmore d.	0713	...	0927	|	...	|	1410	|	1834	|	|	2208	2215	...	...
207	Kingussie d.	0718	...	0930	1107	...	1240	1415	1616	1839	1916	2008	2217	2220	...	...
226	Aviemore d.	0740	...	0943	1119	...	1253	1431	1629	1852	1929	2020	2229	2231	...	...
282	**Inverness** a.	0830	...	1026	1159	...	1335	1518	1707	1934	2008	2058	2310	2313	...	...

	⑦ 🍷	⑦ 🍷	⑦ 🍷 E	⑦ 🍷	⑦	⑦ 🍷 E	⑦ 2
London Kings Cross **186** d.	...	...	...	1230	...	...	...
Edinburgh 224 d.	0925	1355	...	1712	1750	...	2234
Kirkcaldy 224 d.	1010	1433	...	|	1823	...	|
Markinch 224 d.	|	|	...	|	|	...	|
Glasgow Queen St 224 d.	*0938*	*1345*	1440	*1615*j	|	1810	|
Falkirk Grahamston d.	|	|	|	1737	|	|	2306
Stirling 224 d.	*1010*	*1412*	1509	1753	|	1839	2324
Perth 224 d.	1051	1513	1546	1830	1902	1916	0006
Dunkeld & Birnam d.	1108	1531	|	|	...	1934	...
Pitlochry d.	1121	1544	1617	1900	...	1947	...
Blair Atholl d.	1133	1554	|	|	...	1956	...
Dalwhinnie d.	1200	1621	|	|	...	2021	...
Newtonmore d.	1211	1632	|	|	...	2032	...
Kingussie d.	1216	1638	1700	1953	...	2037	...
Aviemore d.	1228	1653	1712	2005	...	2050	...
Inverness a.	1309	1738	1750	2044	...	2134	...

	⚒ 2	⚒	⚒ 🍷	⚒ 🍷‡	⚒	⚒ 🍷	⚒ 🍷	⚒ 🍷	⚒ 🍷	⚒ 🍷	⚒	⚒ 🍷	⚒	⚒ 2	Ⓐ 🍷 B
Inverness d.	...	...	0645	0755	...	0919	1053	1240	1441	1656	...	1827	2010	...	2040
Aviemore d.	...	...	0722	0829	...	1004	1138	1325	1518	1733	...	1911	2055	...	2123
Kingussie d.	...	...	0736	0842	...	1016	1150	1337	1531	1746	...	1931	2107	...	2138
Newtonmore d.	...	...	|	|	...	1021	|	|	1535	1750	...	1935	2112	...	2144
Dalwhinnie d.	...	...	|	|	...	1032	|	|	|	1802	...	1947	2123	...	2159
Blair Atholl d.	...	...	|	|	...	1054	|	|	1605	1823	...	2009	2145	...	2225
Pitlochry d.	...	...	0816	0924	...	1103	1231	1417	1615	1833	...	2018	2155	...	2237
Dunkeld & Birnam d.	...	...	0828	|	...	1116	1244	1429	1627	1845	...	2031	2207	...	2252
Perth 224 d.	0640	0703	0848	0956	1108	1139	1304	1449	1648	1908	1913	2051	2228	...	2318
Stirling 224 a.	0715	|	*0940*	1030	|	1211	*1341*	*1541*	*1741*	1940	|	*2146*	2302	2312	0007
Falkirk Grahamston a.	0734	|	|	1045	|	|	|	|	|	|	|	|	|	2330	0024
Glasgow Queen St 224 a.	|	|	*1015*	*1115*j	|	1244	*1414*	*1614*	*1818*	2017	|	*2217*	2339	|	|
Markinch 224 d.	|	0734	|	|	1142	|	|	1518	1722	...	1945	|	...	|	|
Kirkcaldy 224 d.	|	0744	0925	|	1152	|	1344	1528	1731	...	1954	2133	...	|	|
Edinburgh 224 a.	0815	0823	1001	1120	1228	*1332*j	1421	1604	1811	...	2032	2209	...	0007	|
London Kings Cross **186** a.	...	...	...	1551**p**	...	...	...	...	...	...	...	...	...	...	0743**c**

	⑦ 2	⑦ 🍷	⑦ 🍷	⑦ 🍷	⑦ 🍷	⑦ 2	⑦ 🍷	⑦ 🍷 B
Inverness d.	...	0938	1230	1325	1615	...	1830	2025
Aviemore d.	...	1017	1317	1402	1655	...	1909	2108
Kingussie d.	...	1030	1330	1415	1714	...	1922	2122
Newtonmore d.	...	1035	1335	|	|	...	1926	2129
Dalwhinnie d.	...	|	1346	|	|	...	1939	2143
Blair Atholl d.	...	1107	1408	|	1747	...	2002	2209
Pitlochry d.	...	1121	1417	1454	1756	...	2012	2221
Dunkeld & Birnam d.	...	1134	1430	|	1809	...	2024	2236
Perth 224 d.	0927	1155	1450	1525	1827	...	2046	2259
Stirling 224 a.	1002	1232	1522	|	1901	1907	*2140*	2344
Falkirk Grahamston a.	1019	1247	|	|	|	1924	|	2358
Glasgow Queen St 224 a.	|	*1405*j	1556	|	1936	|	*2215*	|
Markinch 224 d.	|	|	...	|	...	|	|	|
Kirkcaldy 224 d.	|	|	...	1602	...	|	2125	|
Edinburgh 224 a.	1058	1318	...	1643	...	2005	2206	|
London Kings Cross **186** a.	...	1815	...	...	...	...	...	0740**q**

A – R. 🛏 1,2 class and [2]. Train stops to set down only.
B – R. 🛏 1,2 class and [2]. Train stops to pick up only.
E – To Elgin.
c – London Euston. 0804 on ⑥.
d – London Euston. Previous day. 2000 on ⑦.
j – Change at Stirling.
p – 1558 on ⑥.
q – London Euston. 0928 Feb. 4 - Mar. 24.
r – 3 minutes earlier on ⑥.
u – Stops to pick up only.
z – 2305 on ⑥.
‡ – Also conveys ✕ on Ⓐ.

222 EDINBURGH - STIRLING SR

From EDINBURGH *75 km*

Ⓐ: 0518, 0632, 0703, 0733, 0759, 0833, 0903, 0933 and every 30 minutes until 2033 (also 1636, 1726); then 2133, 2233, 2333.

⑥: 0518, 0633, 0703, 0733 and every 30 minutes until 2033 (also 1636); then 2133, 2233, 2333.

⑦: 0933, 1033, 1134, 1234, 1338, 1434, 1534, 1634, 1712, 1734, 1834, 1934, 2034, 2134, 2234.

From STIRLING Journey time: ± 50 minutes

Ⓐ: 0530, 0636, 0716, 0731, 0748, 0806, 0836 and every 30 minutes until 2106 (also 1030); then 2206, 2312.

⑥: 0530, 0636, 0716, 0806, 0836 and every 30 minutes until 2106 (also 1030); then 2206, 2312.

⑦: 0905, 1002, 1106, 1207, 1232, 1307, 1407, 1507, 1607, 1707, 1807, 1907, 2007, 2107, 2207.

☛ All trains (except the 1726 Ⓐ from Edinburgh and the 0731 Ⓐ from Stirling) call at **Falkirk Grahamston**: *41 km* (± 31 minutes) from Edinburgh; *34 km* (± 16 minutes) from Stirling.

223 GLASGOW - STIRLING SR

From GLASGOW Queen St *47 km*

Ⓐ: 0555, 0613, 0648, 0706, 0718, 0741, 0748 and at 18, 41 and 48 minutes past each hour until 2218 (also 1011, 1611, 1811; not 1641); then 2248, 2318, 2348.

⑥: 0555, 0613, 0648, 0706, 0718, 0741, 0748 and at 18, 41 and 48 minutes past each hour until 2218 (also 1011, 1611, 1703, 1811); then 2248, 2318, 2348.

⑦: 0938, 1015, 1115, 1145, 1215, 1315, 1345, 1415, 1440, 1515, 1545, 1615, 1715, 1745, 1810, 1815, 1915, 1945, 2015, 2115, 2145, 2215, 2335.

From STIRLING Journey time: ± 35 minutes

Ⓐ: 0553, 0622, 0649, 0722, 0738, 0752, 0810, 0823, 0844, 0853, 0923, 0941, 0953 and at 23, 41 and 53 minutes past each hour until 2123 (also 1212, 1958; not 1810); then 2147, 2153, 2223, 2247, 2253, 2303.

⑥: 0553, 0622, 0653, 0722, 0730, 0752, 0810, 0823, 0844, 0853, 0910, 0941, 0953 and at 23, 41 and 53 minutes past each hour until 2123 (also 1212, 1958; not 1810); then 2147, 2153, 2223, 2247, 2253, 2303.

⑦: 0925, 0938, 1025, 1125, 1138, 1225, 1325, 1338, 1425, 1522, 1525, 1538, 1625, 1725, 1738, 1825, 1902, 1925, 1954, 2025, 2125, 2140.

224 EDINBURGH and GLASGOW - ABERDEEN SR

km		Ⓐ 2 D	⚒ 🍷 Z▽	⚒ 🍷	⚒	⚒ 🍷	⚒ 🍷 D	⚒	⚒ 🍷 D	⚒ 🍷	⚒ 🍷	⚒ 🍷	⚒ 🍷	⚒ 🍷	⚒ 🍷	⚒ 🍷 L	⚒ 🍷	⚒ 🍷	⚒ 🍷	⚒ 🍷 D	⚒ 🍷	⚒ 🍷	⚒ 🍷
	London Kings Cross **186** d.	...	2115**q**	...	...	...	...	...	...	...	...	...	...	...	...	...	...	...	...	...	...	...	...
0	**Edinburgh** 221 d.	...	|	...	...	0533	...	0640	0708	...	0810	...	0910	...	1010	1026	...	1110	...	1210	...	1310	...
42	Kirkcaldy 221 d.	...	0517	...	...	|	...	0715	0743	...	0842	...	0944	...	1042	1105	...	1143	...	1242	...	1343	...
54	Markinch 221 d.	...	|	...	...	0637	...	0724	0752	...	0851	...	|	...	1051	|	...	1152	...	1251	...	1352	...
82	Leuchars d.	...	0546	...	...	0656	...	|	0813	...	0913	...	1009	...	1112	1131	...	1211	...	1312	...	1411	...
	Glasgow Queen St 221 d.	...	|	...	...	|	0555	|	|	0741	|	0841	|	0941	|	|	1041	|	1141	|	1241	|	1341
	Stirling 221 d.	...	|	...	...	|	0625	|	|	0807	|	0906	|	1007	|	|	1107	|	1207	|	1307	|	1407
	Perth 221 d.	...	|	...	0632	|	0701	0755	|	0837	|	0937	|	1037	|	|	1137	|	1237	|	1337	|	1437
95	**Dundee** d.	...	0610	0635	0656	0718	0724	0821	0828	0900	0926	1000	1022	1100	1125	1145	1200	1224	1300	1325	1400	1424	1500
123	Arbroath d.	...	0631	0651	0715	...	0743	...	0844	0918	0945	1018	1038	1118	1142	1203	1218	1241	1318	1342	1418	1441	1518
145	Montrose d.	0630	0650	0705	0729	...	0757	...	0859	0932	|	1032	1053	1132	|	1219	1232	1255	1332	|	1432	1455	1543
184	Stonehaven d.	0652	0716	0726	0751	...	0819	...	0920	|	1019	1052	1114	|	1215	1242	|	1317	|	1417	1452	1517	|
210	**Aberdeen** a.	0715	0737	0750	0813	...	0840	...	0940	1018	1038	1117	1134	1219	1235	1304	1313	1336	1413	1436	1513	1536	1621

D – To Dyce.
L – From Leeds.
Z – R. 🛏 1,2 class and [2]. Train stops to set down only.
q – London Euston. Previous day. 2001 on ⑦.

SR

EDINBURGH and GLASGOW - ABERDEEN

224

	⚒ 🍷 D	⚒ 🍷	⚒ 🍷‡	⚒ 🍷	⚒ 🍷 D	⚒ 🍷 U	⑥ 🍷	Ⓐ 🍷	⚒ 🍷 D	Ⓐ 2	⚒ 2	⑥ 🍷	Ⓐ 🍷	⚒ 🍷 J	⚒ 🍷‡	⚒ 🍷	Ⓐ 🍷 E	⚒ 🍷	⑥ 🍷 E	⚒ 🍷	⚒ 2	Ⓐ ✕	⚒ 2	⑥ 🍷
London Kings Cross **186** ....d.	...	...	1030	...	...	...	...	...	...	...	...	...	...	...	1400	...	...	...	...	...	...	1600	...	...
Edinburgh .... **221** d.	1410	...	1500	...	1605	1630	...	...	1704	...	1714	...	...	1810	1832	...	1901	1910	1912	...	2011	2030	...	2110
Kirkcaldy .... **221** d.	1442	...	1538	...	1641	1703	...	...	1737	...	1801	...	...	1844	1911	...	1935	1943	1950	...	2057	2107	...	2143
Markinch .... **221** d.	1451	...	|	...	1650	1712	...	...	1746	...	1810	...	...	1853	|	...	1944	1952	2000	...	2106	|	...	2152
Leuchars .... d.	1512	...	1602	...	1711	1732	...	...	1805	...	1834	...	...	1915	1936	...	2005	2013	2030	...	2128	2139	...	2213
Glasgow Queen St ..... **221** d.	|	1441	|	1541	|	|	1641	1642	|	1712	|	1741	1741	|	|	1841	|	|	|	1942	|	|	2041	|
Stirling .... **221** d.	|	1507	|	1607	|	|	1707	|	|	1745	|	1807	1814	|	|	1907	|	|	|	2007	|	|	2108	|
Perth .... **221** d.	|	1537	|	1637	|	|	1737	1738	|	1823	|	1844	1850	|	|	1944	|	|	|	2037	|	|	2144	|
Dundee .... d.	1525	1600	1619	1700	1727	1748	1800	1801	1824	...	1848	1908	1915	1929	1951	2009	2025	2027	2050	2100	2141	2153	2209	2228
Arbroath .... d.	1544	1616	1636	1718	1749	1804	1818	1821	1840	...	...	1931	1934	1945	2009	2025	...	2043	...	2118	...	2211	2225	2244
Montrose .... d.	|	1631	1651	1732	1803	1818	1832	|	1855	...	...	1945	1948	|	2024	2038	...	2058	...	2133	...	2227	2240	2259
Stonehaven .... d.	1617	|	1714	1752	1825	1838	1852	1855	1916	...	...	2007	2010	2019	2048	|	...	2119	...	2153	...	2250	2301	2320
Aberdeen .... a.	1637	1709	1738	1815	1846	1902	1916	1915	1938	...	...	2027	2031	2044r	2110	2120	...	2139	...	2215	...	2313	2321	2340

	⚒ 2	⚒ 🍷	⚒ 2	⚒ 2	⚒ 2	⚒ 2		⑦	⑦ 🍷	⑦ 🍷	⑦ 2	⑦ 🍷	⑦ 🍷	⑦ 2	⑦ 🍷	⑦ 🍷	⑦ 2	⑦ 🍷	⑦ 2	⑦ 🍷	⑦ 🍷	⑦ 🍷 B	⑦ 🍷	⑦ 2
London Kings Cross **186** ....d.	...	...	...	...	...	...	...		...	...	...	...	...	...	...	...	...	...	...	...	1100	...	...	...
Edinburgh .... **221** d.	2124	...	2235	...	2310	...	...		0805	0910	0915	...	1055	1115	...	1240	1315	...	1515	...	1600	1635	1705	1715
Kirkcaldy .... **221** d.	2210	...	2320	...	2351	...	...		0839	0949	1003	...	1131	1203	...	1316	1403	...	1603	...	1641	1709	1738	1800
Markinch .... **221** d.	2219	...	2329	...	0001	...	...		0849	|	1012	...	|	1212	...	|	1412	...	1612	...	|	1718	|	1809
Leuchars .... d.	2241	...	2353	...	0022	...	...		0909	1013	1034	...	1155	1233	...	1340	1433	...	1633	...	1710	1737	1802	1830
Glasgow Queen St ..... **221** d.	|	2141	|	2248	|	2348	...		|	|	|	0938	|	|	1145	|	|	1345	|	1545	|	|	|	|
Stirling .... **221** d.	|	2207	|	2331	|	0031	...		|	|	|	1010	|	|	1212	|	|	1412	|	1612	|	|	|	|
Perth .... **221** d.	|	2237	|	0015	|	0119d	...		|	|	|	1048	|	|	1248	|	|	1448	|	1648	|	|	|	|
Dundee .... d.	2255	2300	0007	...	0036	...	...		0923	1028	1049	1111	1208	1248	1311	1353	1448	1511	1648	1711	1724	1751	1815	1846
Arbroath .... d.	...	2319	...	...	...	...	...		0940	1045	...	1130	1225	...	1327	1410	...	1527	...	1727	1742	1807	1832	...
Montrose .... d.	...	2333	...	...	...	...	...		0954	1101	...	1144	1237	...	1342	1424	...	1542	...	1742	1800	1821	1846	...
Stonehaven .... d.	...	2355	...	...	...	...	...		1015	1124	...	1206	1259	...	1403	1446	...	1603	...	1803	1823	1841	1908	...
Aberdeen .... a.	...	0017	...	...	...	...	...		1039	1147	...	1227	1323	...	1423	1505	...	1623	...	1823	1844	1905	1930	...

	⑦ 🍷	⑦ 🍷	⑦ 2	⑦ 🍷 P	⑦ 🍷	⑦ 🍷	⑦ 🍷	⑦ 2	⑦
London Kings Cross **186** ....d.	...	1400	...	...	...	...	...	...	...
Edinburgh 221 .... d.	...	1843	1915	1925	...	2100	...	2225	...
Kirkcaldy **221** .... d.	...	1922	2000	2006	...	2133	...	2310	...
Markinch **221** .... d.	...	|	2009	2015	...	2144	...	2319	...
Leuchars (for St Andrews) ..... d.	...	1947	2030	2046	...	2205	...	2340	...
Glasgow Queen St **221** ..... d.	1745	|	|	|	1945	|	2145	|	2335
Stirling **221** .... d.	1812	|	|	|	2012	|	2212	|	0014
Perth 221 .... d.	1845	|	|	|	2048	|	2248	|	0056
Dundee .... d.	1909	2001	2046	2105	2111	2218	2310	2356	...
Arbroath .... d.	1927	2019	...	...	2127	2235	2327	...	...
Montrose .... d.	1942	2035	...	...	2142	2249	2342	...	...
Stonehaven .... d.	2003	2058	...	...	2203	2311	0003	...	...
Aberdeen .... a.	2026	2121	...	...	2224	2333	0025	...	...

km		⚒	⚒ 2	Ⓐ 2	⚒ 2	Ⓐ 🍷 P	⚒	⚒ 🍷	⚒ 2	⚒ 🍷 U
0	**Aberdeen** .... d.		...	...	...	...	0527	0600	...	...
26	Stonehaven .... d.		...	...	...	...	0544	0616	...	...
65	Montrose .... d.		...	...	...	...	0605	0638	...	...
87	Arbroath .... d.		...	...	...	...	0619	0652	...	...
115	**Dundee** .... d.		...	...	0616	0638	0648	0711	0717	0733
149	**Perth** .... **221** d.		0515	0609	|	|	0714	|	|	|
202	Stirling .... **221** d.		0553	0649	|	|	0752	|	|	|
249	**Glasgow** Queen St .... **221** a.		0633	0735	|	|	0834	|	|	|
	Leuchars .... d.		...	...	0628	0651	...	0723	0730	0746
	Markinch .... **221** d.		...	...	0652	0713	...	|	0754	0809
	Kirkcaldy .... **221** d.		...	...	0702	0725	...	0750	0805	0818
	Edinburgh .... **221** a.		...	...	0751	0806	...	0826	0852	0903
	London Kings Cross **186** ... a.		...	...	...	...	...	...	...	...

	⚒ 🍷	⚒ 2	⚒ 🍷 D	⚒ 🍷 N	⚒	⚒ 🍷‡	⚒ 🍷 U	⚒ 🍷	⚒ 🍷	⚒ 🍷 D	⚒ 🍷‡	⚒ 🍷 D	⚒ 🍷	⚒ 🍷	⚒ 🍷	⚒ 🍷	⚒ 🍷	⚒ 🍷	⚒ 🍷	⚒ 🍷	⚒ 🍷	⚒ 🍷‡	⚒ 🍷 D	⚒ 🍷
Aberdeen .... d.	0634	...	0707	0720	...	0753	0820	0839	0850	0936	0952	1022	1041	1122	1142	1224	1242	1321	1342	1425	1440	1450	1520	1533
Stonehaven .... d.	0653	...	0723	0736	...	0810	0837	|	0906	0953	1009	1038	|	1138	|	1243	1256	1337	|	1441	|	1507	1536	|
Montrose .... d.	0715	...	0745	0758	...	0833	0858	0914	|	1014	1032	1100	1115	1200	1215	|	1315	1359	1415	|	1515	1530	1600	1613
Arbroath .... d.	0729	...	0759	0812	...	0848	0915	0928	0942	1028	1047	1114	1128	1214	1228	1317	1330	1413	1428	1515	1528	1545	1614	1627
Dundee .... d.	0752	0759	0821	0831	0847	0906	0932	0950	0959	1050	1105	1130	1150	1230	1250	1333	1350	1430	1450	1532	1550	1603	1631	1647
Perth .... **221** d.	0813	|	0843	|	0908	|	|	1012	|	1112	|	|	1212	|	1312	|	1412	|	1512	|	1612	|	|	1710
Stirling .... **221** d.	0844	|	0910q	|	0941	|	|	1041	|	1141	|	|	1241	|	1341	|	1441	|	1541	|	1641	|	|	1741
Glasgow Queen St ..... **221** a.	0915	|	0944	|	1015	|	|	1115	|	1215	|	|	1314	|	1414	|	1514	|	1614	|	1718	|	|	1818
Leuchars .... d.	...	0811	...	0843	...	0920	0945	...	1011	...	1119	1142	...	1242	...	1345	...	1442	...	1544	...	1617	1643	...
Markinch .... **221** d.	...	0834	...	0906	...	|	1004	...	1034	...	|	1202	...	1304	...	1405	...	1504	...	1604	...	|	1707	...
Kirkcaldy .... **221** d.	...	0843	...	0915	...	0944	1012	...	1043	...	1143	1212	...	1314	...	1415	...	1514	...	1614	...	1641	1717	...
Edinburgh .... **221** a.	...	0920	...	0950	...	1025	1051v	...	1120	...	1222	1250	...	1350	...	1450	...	1550	...	1650	...	1723	1753	...
London Kings Cross **186** ....a.	...	...	...	...	...	1457c	...	...	...	...	1657	...	...	...	...	...	...	...	...	...	...	2220r	...	...

	⚒ 🍷	⚒ 🍷	⚒ 🍷 D	⚒ 🍷	Ⓐ 🍷	⑥ 🍷	⚒ 🍷	⚒ 🍷 D	⑥ 2	⚒ 🍷	Ⓐ 2	⑥ 2 D	⚒ 🍷	⚒	⚒	Ⓐ 🍷 Z	①–④	⑤		⑦	⑦ 2		⑦	⑦ 2
Aberdeen .... d.	1621	1641	1721	1754	1820	1825	1841	1925	...	1941	...	2020	2026	2045	2122	2140	2230	2329	...		...	...	...	...
Stonehaven .... d.	1637	1656	1741	1812	1837	1842	|	1941	...	2000	...	2036	2043	2101	2138	2158	2249	2349	...		...	...	...	...
Montrose .... d.	|	1715	1805	1833	1900	1904	1915	|	...	2024	...	2058	2104	2123	2200	2227	2311	0010	...		...	...	...	...
Arbroath .... d.	1711	1728	1819	1847	1915	1919	1928	2015	...	2038	...	2112	2121	2137	2216	2245	2325	0024	...		...	...	...	...
Dundee .... d.	1731	1750	1835	1911	1933	1935	1950	2032	2054	2057	2128	2128	2138v	2156	2234	2306	2347	0047	...		0725	...	0845	0925
Perth .... **221** d.	|	1812	|	1933	|	|	2012	|	|	2118	|	|	|	2218	|	|	0011	0111	...		|	...	0905	|
Stirling .... **221** d.	|	1841	|	1958	|	|	2041	|	|	2147	|	|	|	2247	|	|	...	...	...		|	...	0938	|
Glasgow Queen St ..... **221** a.	|	1914	|	2038	|	|	2115	|	|	2217	|	|	|	2318	|	|	...	...	...		|	...	1015	|
Leuchars .... d.	1743	...	1847	...	1947	1947	...	2044	2106	...	2140	2140	2152	...	2246	2324	...	...	...		0737	...	...	0937
Markinch .... **221** d.	1805	...	1907	...	|	|	...	2106	2130	...	2203	2203	2212v	...	2309	|	...	...	...		0759	...	...	0959
Kirkcaldy .... **221** d.	1815	...	1917	...	2011	2013	...	2116	2140	...	2213	2213	|	...	2318	2353	...	...	...		0809	...	...	1009
Edinburgh .... **221** a.	1850	...	1957	...	2050	2050	...	2156r	2232	...	2305	2305	2325	...	0009	|	...	...	...		0900	...	...	1104
London Kings Cross **186** ....a.	...	...	...	...	...	...	...	...	...	...	...	...	...	...	...	0743j	...	...	...		...	...	...	...

	⑦ 🍷	⑦ 🍷	⑦ 2		⑦ 🍷	⑦ 🍷	⑦ 🍷 S	⑦ 2		⑦ 🍷	⑦ 🍷	⑦ 2	⑦ 🍷	⑦ 🍷	⑦ 2	⑦ 🍷	⑦ 🍷	⑦ 2	⑦ 🍷	⑦ 🍷	⑦ 🍷	⑦ 🍷	⑦ 🍷 Z	⑦
Aberdeen .... d.	0930	0950	...	...	1128	1142	1158	...	...	1330	1350	...	1510	1530	...	1710	1750	...	1910	1935	2010	2051	2140	2229
Stonehaven .... d.	0946	1007	...	...	1144	1159	1216	...	...	1346	1407	...	1529	1546	...	1726	1806	...	1926	1951	2029	2108	2158	2248
Montrose .... d.	1008	1030	...	...	1206	1222	1239	...	...	1408	1430	...	1551	1608	...	1748	1828	...	1948	2013	2050	2129	2225	2311
Arbroath .... d.	1022	1045	...	...	1220	1237	1256	...	...	1422	1445	...	1605	1622	...	1802	1842	...	2002	2027	2104	2146	2243	2325
Dundee .... d.	1043	1103	1125	...	1243	1258	1314	1325	...	1443	1503	1525	1625	1643	1725	1819	1902	1925	2020	2046	2121	2203	2304	2347
Perth .... **221** d.	1105	|	|	...	1305	|	|	|	...	1505	|	|	|	1705	|	|	1924	|	|	2108	|	|	|	0009
Stirling .... **221** d.	1138	|	|	...	1338	|	|	|	...	1538	|	|	|	1738	|	|	1954	|	|	2140	|	|	|	...
Glasgow Queen St ..... **221** a.	1212	|	|	...	1412	|	|	|	...	1612	|	|	|	1812	|	|	2032	|	|	2215	|	|	|	...
Leuchars .... d.	...	1117	1137	...	...	1312	|	1339	...	...	1517	1537	1637	...	1737	1831	...	1937	2032	...	2133	2216	2322	...
Markinch .... **221** d.	...	|	1159	...	...	|	1349	1401	...	...	|	1601	|	...	1759	|	...	1959	|	...	2156	2238	|	...
Kirkcaldy .... **221** d.	...	1141	1209	...	...	1336	1358	1411	...	...	1541	1611	1703	...	1809	1856	...	2009	2059	...	2205	2246	2351	...
Edinburgh .... **221** a.	...	1224	1304	...	...	1424	1433	1504	...	...	1626	1659	1741	...	1900	1935	...	2059	2138	...	2244	2326	|	...
London Kings Cross **186** ....a.	...	1711	...	...	...	1916	...	...	...	...	2125	...	...	...	...	...	...	...	...	...	...	...	0743	...

B – From Birmingham.
D – To / from Dyce.
E – From Penzance.
J – To Inverurie on Ⓐ.
N – From Inverness.

P – From / to Plymouth.
S – To Southampton.
U – From / to Bournemouth.
Z – Ⓡ. 🛏 1, 2 class and 2 (couchette). Train stops to pick up only.

c – 1510 on ⑥.
d – 0116 on ⑦.
j – London Euston. 0804 on ⑥.
q – ⑥ only.

r – 3–4 minutes earlier on ⑥.
v – 3–4 minutes later on ⑥.

‡ – Also conveys ✕ on Ⓐ.

La explicación de los signos convencionales se da en la página 4

225 INVERNESS - ELGIN - ABERDEEN SR

km		⚒ E	⚒ 🍷	⑥	Ⓐ	⚒ 🍷	⚒	⚒ 🍷	⚒	⚒ 🍷	⚒	⚒ 🍷	⚒ 🍷	⚒ 🍷	⚒	⚒	⚒
0	**Inverness** d.	0500	0557	...	...	0842	...	1044	...	1219	...	1357	1525	1712	1808	1953	2120
24	Nairn d.	0517	0614	...	...	0859	...	1101	...	1236	...	1414	1542	1728	1825	2014	2139
40	Forres d.	0528	0625	...	...	0910	...	1112	...	1247	...	1425	1553	1739	1836	2025	2150
59	**Elgin** d.	0544	0641	...	...	0927	...	1132	...	1304	...	1442	1608	1755	1854	2041	2208
89	Keith d.	0605	0702	...	0932	0946	...	1153	...	1326	...	1503	1630	1817	1916	—	2229
109	Huntly d.	0619	0721	...	0946	1002	...	1208	...	1340	...	1517	1644	1836	1936	...	2246
130	Insch d.	0635	0738	...	1002	1018	...	1224	...	1356	...	1533	1700	1855	1953	⚒	2302
147	**Inverurie** d.	0651	0751	0840	1014	1030	1135	1236	1308	1408	1442	1548	1712	1907	2005	2128	2314
164	Dyce ✈ d.	0703	0803	0856	1026	1042	1150	1248	1323	1420	1454	1600	1726	1919	2018	2140	2327
174	**Aberdeen** a.	0714	0815	0907	1037	1053	1201	1259	1334	1431	1505	1611	1737	1930	2029	2151	2338

⑦	⑦ 🍷	⑦ 🍷	⑦ 🍷	⑦ 🍷	⑦ H 🍷	⑦ 🍷	⑦ H 🍷
Inverness d.	0955	1219	1525	1710	1800	2052	2142
Nairn d.	1012	1236	1542	1728	1817	2110	2159
Forres d.	1023	1247	1553	1739	1828	2121	2210
Elgin d.	1038	1304	1608	1755	1844	2137	2226
Keith d.	1059	1326	1630	1817	...	2158	...
Huntly d.	1118	1340	1644	1836	...	2217	...
Insch d.	1134	1356	1700	1853	...	2234	...
Inverurie d.	1147	1408	1712	1905	...	2247	...
Dyce ✈ d.	1159	1420	1726	1917	...	2259	...
Aberdeen a.	1210	1431	1737	1928	...	2310	...

	⚒	⚒	⚒	⑥	Ⓐ	⚒ 🍷	⚒	⚒ 🍷	⚒	⚒ 🍷	⚒	⚒ 🍷	⚒ 🍷	⚒ 🍷	⚒ 🍷	⚒ A	⚒	⚒	
Aberdeen d.	...	0625	0728	0752	0822	0927	1100	1140	1238	1312	1411	1523	1715	1821	2007	2054	2155	2250	...
Dyce ✈ d.	...	0637	0739	0804	0831	0936	1110	1149	1249	1321	1423	1532	1727	1830	2019	2103	2204	2259	...
Inverurie d.	...	0650	0751	0818	0843	0948	1121	1201	1303	1333	1437	1546	1739	1842	2031	2116	2216	2313	...
Insch d.	...	0703	0803	...	0855	1003	...	1213	...	1345	...	1558	1751	1854	2043	...	2228	...	...
Huntly d.	...	0720	0819	...	0911	1024	...	1229	...	1402	...	1614	1808	1909	2100	...	2246	...	...
Keith d.	...	0734	0833	...	0927	1037	...	1243	...	1416	...	1635	1823	1924	2114	...	2300	...	...
Elgin d.	0700	0756	0855	...	...	1058	...	1304	...	1439	...	1657	1847	1945	2136	...	2320	...	...
Forres d.	0714	0810	0915	...	...	1117	...	1319	...	1454	...	1711	1901	2000	2156	...	2335	...	...
Nairn d.	0725	0821	0926	...	...	1128	...	1330	...	1505	...	1729	1912	2013	2207	...	2346	...	...
Inverness a.	0743	0841	0944	...	...	1146	...	1348	...	1523	...	1747	1934	2031	2225	...	0005	...	...

⑦	⑦ 🍷	⑦ 🍷	⑦ 🍷	⑦ 🍷	⑦ 🍷
Aberdeen d.	1000	1312	1523	1715	2100
Dyce ✈ d.	1009	1321	1532	1727	2109
Inverurie d.	1022	1333	1547	1740	2121
Insch d.	1034	1345	1559	1752	2133
Huntly d.	1050	1402	1615	1808	2149
Keith d.	1105	1416	1634	1822	2203
Elgin d.	1127	1438	1657	1844	2229
Forres d.	1141	1453	1711	1858	2243
Nairn d.	1153	1504	1729	1911	2255
Inverness a.	1212	1523	1747	1934	2314

Other trains on ⚒:
Dyce – **Aberdeen** at 0650 **G**, 0745 Ⓐ, 0908 **G**, 1008 **E**, 1508 **E**, 1700 **E**, 1756, 1905 **E**, 1955 **B**.
Aberdeen – **Dyce** at 0718 Ⓐ **M**, 0752 ⑥, 0846 **H**, 0947 **F**, 1442 **F**, 1641 **F**, 1742, 1846 **F**, 1939 **F**.

A – From Edinburgh on Ⓐ.
B – To Edinburgh on ⑥.
E – To Edinburgh.
F – From Edinburgh.
G – To Glasgow.
H – From Glasgow.
M – From Montrose.

226 INVERNESS - KYLE, THURSO and WICK 2nd class SR

km		⚒	⚒	⚒	⚒	⑦	⚒	⚒	⚒	⑦	⚒	⚒
0	**Inverness** ‡ d.	0714	0853	1039	1052	1118	1217	1241	1752	1800	1815	2039
16	Beauly ‡ d.	0728	0908	1056	1109	1132	1232	1258	1807	1817	1830	2053
21	Muir of Ord ‡ d.	0734	0914	1103	1116	1138	1238	1304	1813	1823	1837	2101
30	Dingwall ‡ d.	0745	0924	1113	1126	1148	1248	1314	1823	1833	1850	2111
49	Garve d.	|	0945	|	1147	1209	|	1336	|	|	1911	|
75	Achnasheen d.	|	1010	|	1213	1234	|	1401	|	|	1936	|
104	Strathcarron d.	|	1038	|	1243	1304	|	1430	|	|	2005	|
116	Stromeferry d.	|	1056	|	1301	1322	|	1448	|	|	2023	|
124	Plockton d.	|	1107	|	1313	1333	|	1459	|	|	2034	|
133	**Kyle of Lochalsh** a.	|	1120	|	1325	1346	|	1512	|	|	2047	|
51	Invergordon ‡ d.	0802	...	1130	...	...	1304	...	1840	1850	...	2128
71	Tain d.	0820	...	1147	...	...	...	...	1857	1909	...	2145
93	Ardgay d.	0836	...	1203	...	...	...	...	1913	1924	...	...
108	Lairg d.	0858	...	1222	...	...	...	...	1933	1944	...	...
136	Golspie d.	0923	...	1247	...	...	...	...	0958	2008	...	...
146	Brora d.	0934	...	1258	...	...	...	...	2009	2019	...	...
163	Helmsdale d.	0949	...	1313	...	...	...	...	2024	2034	...	...
237	Georgemas Jcn a.	1050	...	1415	...	...	...	...	2125	2134	...	...
248	**Thurso** a.	1102	...	1427	...	...	...	...	2137	2146	...	...
248	**Thurso** d.	1104	...	1430	...	...	...	...	2139	2148	...	...
237	Georgemas Jcn d.	1114	...	1440	...	...	...	...	2149	2158	...	...
260	**Wick** a.	1134	...	1457	...	...	...	...	2206	2215	...	...

	⚒	⚒	⚒	⚒	⚒	⑦	⚒	⑦	⚒	⚒	⚒
Wick d.	...	...	0622	0813	...	1156	1237	...	...	1552	...
Georgemas Jcn a.	...	...	0638	0829	...	1212	1253	...	...	1608	...
Thurso a.	...	...	0648	0839	...	1222	1303	...	...	1618	...
Thurso d.	...	...	0651	0842	...	1225	1306	...	...	1621	...
Georgemas Jcn d.	...	...	0703	0854	...	1237	1318	...	...	1633	...
Helmsdale d.	...	...	0803	0949	...	1339	1421	...	...	1733	...
Brora d.	...	...	0818	1005	...	1354	1436	...	...	1748	...
Golspie d.	...	...	0828	1015	...	1403	1446	...	...	1758	...
Lairg d.	0633	...	0857	1041	...	1429	1512	...	...	1824	...
Ardgay d.	0650	...	0914	1055	...	1446	1529	...	...	1841	...
Tain d.	0705	...	0930	1111	...	1501	1544	...	...	1900	2149
Invergordon § d.	0723	...	0947	1130	...	1519	1602	...	...	1918	2206
Kyle of Lochalsh d.	|	0725	|	|	1159	|	|	1517	1648	|	|
Plockton d.	|	0738	|	|	1212	|	|	1530	1701	|	|
Stromeferry d.	|	0751	|	|	1224	|	|	1542	1713	|	|
Strathcarron d.	|	0808	|	|	1242	|	|	1559	1730	|	|
Achnasheen d.	|	0835	|	|	1309	|	|	1626	1757	|	|
Garve d.	|	0900	|	|	1337	|	|	1651	1823	|	|
Dingwall § d.	0744	0925	1007	1146	1400	1539	1621	1715	1849	1936	2226
Muir of Ord § d.	0754	0936	1017	1156	1408	1548	1630	1724	1857	1945	2235
Beauly § d.	0800	0943	1023	|	1415	1554	1637	1730	1904	1951	2241
Inverness § a.	0814	0957	1037	1213	1429	1608	1651	1745	1919	2005	2255

‡ – Inverness - Invergordon also at 0915 ⚒, 1433 ⚒, 1703 ⚒.

§ – Invergordon - Inverness also at 1033 ⚒, 1312 ⚒, 1531 ⚒, 1946 ⚒.

227 🚌 / ⛴ INVERNESS - ULLAPOOL - STORNOWAY

	B	A	B	A	B
Inverness 🚌 d.	0705	0805	1330	1435	1950
Ullapool a.	0825	0925	1450	1555	2110

	B	A	B	A	B
Ullapool ⛴ d.	0930	1030	1550	1715	2200
Stornoway a.	1215	1315	1835	2000	0045

	B	A	B	A	B
Stornoway ⛴ d.	0615	0715	1240	1345	1900
Ullapool a.	0900	1000	1525	1630	2145

	B	A	B	A	B
Ullapool 🚌 d.	0905	1005	1530	1635	2150
Inverness a.	1025	1125	1650	1755	2310

A – ①–⑥ until June 21 and from Sept. 1; ①②④⑥ June 23 - Aug. 30;
B – ③⑤ June 25 - Aug. 29.

🚌 Operated by Scottish Citylink (service **961**). Runs in conjunction with Ullapool - Stornaway ferry.

⛴ Operated by Caledonian MacBrayne Ltd.

228 🚌 INVERNESS - FORT WILLIAM - OBAN

Service number	919 ⚒	918 ⚒	919 ⚒		919		919 ⚒	918 ③–⑥	919		19 ⚒
Inverness d.	0930	...	1130	...	1315	...	1530	...	1735	...	2015
Fort Augustus d.	1028	...	1228	...	1413	...	1628	...	1833	...	2113
Fort William d.	1120	1130	1320	...	1505	...	1720	1835	1925	...	2205
Ballachulish d.	...	1158	...	...	...	...	...	1903	...	...	...
Oban a.	...	1257	...	...	...	...	...	2002	...	...	...

Service number	19 ⚒	919 ⚒	918 ⚒	919 ⚒		919		919 ⚒		918 ③–⑥	919
Oban d.	...	...	0840	...	...	...	...	...	...	1600	...
Ballachulish d.	...	...	0939	...	...	...	...	...	...	1659	...
Fort William d.	0730	0845	1007	1030	...	1230	...	1430	...	1727	1815
Fort Augustus d.	0822	0937	...	1122	...	1322	...	1522	...	...	1907
Inverness a.	0920	1035	...	1220	...	1420	...	1620	...	...	2005

☛ Operated by Highland Country Buses / Scottish Citylink: www.citylink.co.uk, ✆ +44 (0) 8705 50 50 50. No services on Dec. 25, 26, Jan. 1, 2.

229 ISLE OF MAN RAILWAYS ✆ +44 (0)1624 663366

km	Manx Electric Railway	Feb. 3 - Apr. 1, 2007 ⑥⑦		⑥⑦		Service Apr. 2 - Nov. 4, 2007	A		B				A			B	A	
0	**Douglas** Derby Castle ‡ ⊙ d.	0940	...	1340	...	0940	1010	1040	1110	1140	1240	...	1340	1410	1510	1540	1610	1640
4	Groudle ⊙ d.	0952	...	1352	...	0952	1022	1052	1122	1152	1252	...	1352	1422	1522	1552	1622	1652
11	Laxey ▲ d.	1010	...	1410	...	1010	1040	1110	1140	1210	1310	...	1410	1440	1540	1610	1640	1710
28	**Ramsey** a.	1055	...	1455	...	1055	1125	1155	1225	1255	1355	...	1455	1525	1625	1655	...	1755

	Feb. 3 - Apr. 1, 2007 ⑥⑦		⑥⑦		Service Apr. 2 - Nov. 4, 2007		A		B				A		A		B
Ramsey d.	1140	...	1510	...	1010	1110	1140	1210	1240	...	1340	1440	1510	1540	...	1640	1710
Laxey ▲ d.	1225	...	1555	...	1055	1155	1225	1255	1325	...	1425	1525	1555	1625	1655	1725	1755
Groudle ⊙ d.	1243	...	1613	...	1113	1213	1243	1313	1343	...	1443	1543	1613	1643	1713	1743	1813
Douglas Derby Castle ‡ ⊙ a.	1255	...	1625	...	1125	1225	1255.	1325	1355	...	1455	1555	1625	1655	1725	1755	1825

A – Daily May 28 - Sept. 9, 2007.
B – ①–⑤ July 2 - Aug. 31, 2007.

‡ – 🚌 services **23**, **24**, **25**, **26** connect Derby Castle and the Steam Railway Station.

⊙ – A service of illuminated trams operates Douglas - Groudle and v.v. in connection with **Groudle Glen Railway** evening services on ② July 31 - Aug. 21 and ③ July 4 - Aug. 22, 2007. Departures from Douglas at 1845, 1915, 1945, 2015, 2045, 2115 and from Groudle at 1900, 1930, 2000, 2030, 2100, 2130.

▲ – **Snaefell Mountain Railway** operates daily Apr. 30 - Sept. 30, 2007, subject to weather conditions. First departure from Laxey 1015, last departure 1545. Journey time to summit: 30 mins.

km	Isle of Man Steam Railway	Service Apr. 2 - Nov. 4, 2007							
0	**Douglas** Railway Station ‡ d.	1015	...	1215	...	1415	...	1615	...
9	Santon *(request stop)* d.	1036	...	1236	...	1436	...	1636	...
16	**Castletown** d.	1052	...	1252	...	1452	...	1652	...
25	Port Erin a.	1112	...	1312	...	1512	...	1712	...

	Service Apr. 2 - Nov. 4, 2007							
Port Erin d.	1015	...	1215	...	1415	...	1615	...
Castletown d.	1037	...	1237	...	1437	...	1637	...
Santon *(request stop)* d.	1053	...	1253	...	1453	...	1653	...
Douglas Railway Station ‡ a.	1112	...	1312	...	1512	...	1712	...

IRELAND

SEE MAP PAGE 98

Operators: Iarnród Éireann (**IÉ**) and Northern Ireland Railways (**NIR**), Bus Éireann, Ulsterbus and Dublin Area Rapid Transit (**DART**). Most cross-border services are jointly operated.

Timings: **Rail:** **NIR** services are valid from **October 1, 2007** until further notice. **IÉ** and **DART** services are valid from **December 9, 2007** until further notice..

Bus: **Ulsterbus** services are valid from **February 5, 2006**, incorporating amendments from **November 20, 2006** and **February 19, 2007**, until further notice. **Bus Éireann** services are valid until **May 10, 2008.**

Rail services: Except for *Enterprise* cross-border expresses (for details, see Table **230** below), **all trains** convey *Standard* (2nd) class seating. Most express trains in the Republic of Ireland, as noted in the tables, also have first class accommodation.
On public holiday dates in the **Republic of Ireland**, DART trains run as on Sundays; outer-suburban services to or from Drogheda and Dundalk do not run. Other services may be amended, though most main-line trains run normally. All services are subject to alteration during the Christmas, New Year and Easter holiday periods.

Bus services: **Bus Éireann** and **Ulsterbus**: services are shown in detail where there is no comparable rail service; only basic information is given for other routes. Buses do not always call at the rail station, but usually stop nearby. Where possible the stop details are given in the station bank or as a footnote. On longer routes, a change of bus may be required – please check with the driver. At holiday times bus travellers should consult detailed leaflets or seek further information from the operator. **Bus Éireann**: ✆ +353 1 836 6111 (Dublin) or + 353 21 450 8188 (Cork); **Ulsterbus**: ✆ + 028 9033 3000 (Translink, Belfast). **Dublin Busaras** (bus station) is a 5 minute walk from Dublin Connolly station.

The Dublin Tram service (Luas) connects Dublin Connolly and Heuston stations at frequent intervals. Journey time is 10–20 minutes, depending on traffic conditions. See Dublin City Plan on page 30.

NIR, IÉ — BELFAST - DUNDALK - DUBLIN — 230

Enterprise express trains (*E*) convey Standard (2nd) class and Premium (1st) class seating, 🍸 (Café Bar and trolley service) and ✗ (at-seat meal service in Premium)

km		Ⓐ	Ⓐ	⑥	Ⓐ	⚒	⚒ E	⑥	⚒	⚒ E	⚒	⚒	⚒	⚒ E	⚒	⚒	⚒ E	⚒	⚒ E	⚒	⑤	⚒	⚒ E	⚒	⚒	⑥	Ⓐ
0	**Belfast Central** § d.	...	...	...	...	...	0650	...	0700z	0800	...	...	1000	1030	...	1200	1230	1330	1410	...	...	1530	1610	...	...	1700	1710
13	Lisburn § d.	...	...	...	...	...	│	...	0801z	│	...	...	1032	│	...	1231	│	1401	│	...	...	1602	│	...	...	1732	1731
42	Portadown § d.	...	...	...	...	...	0717	...	0826z	0827	...	...	1057	1058	...	1257	1258	1428	1441	...	...	1630	1638	...	...	1800	1800
71	Newry d.	...	...	...	...	...	0739	...	▬	│	...	...	▬	1121	...	▬	1321	▬	1502	...	...	▬	1700	...	...	1825	1825
95	**Dundalk** d.	0540	0635	0703	0703	...	0757	0810	Ⓐ	│	0955	1045	⚒	1138	...	⚒	1338	⚒	1520	...	1620	⚒	1717	...	...	...	...
131	Drogheda d.	0604	0659	0729	0727	0758	0818	0835	0832	│	1020	1109	1135	1200	1208	1303	1359	1415	1541	1555	1645	1655	1738	1748	1805	...	...
148	Balbriggan d.	0617	0713	0745	0742	0811	│	0850	0847	│	1033	1123	1150	│	1223	1318	│	1430	│	1610	│	1711	│	│	1819	...	...
154	Skerries d.	0623	0720	0751	0749	0817	│	0856	0853	│	1039	1130	1156	│	1229	1324	│	1436	│	1616	│	1717	│	│	1825	...	...
168	Malahide d.	│	│	0806	│	0832	│	0913	0909	│	│	1145	1211	│	1244	1339	│	1451	│	1631	│	1735	│	│	1840	...	...
183	**Dublin Connolly** a.	0654	0755	0824	0828	0859	0905	0929	0929	0955	1112	1202	1229	1240	1304	1357	1440	1510	1620	1657	1734	1756	1820	1830	1858	...	...

	Ⓐ	⚒ E	⚒	⚒ E	⚒	⑦	⑦ E	⑦ E	⑦ E	⑦ E	⑦ E
Belfast Central § d.	1750	1810	1900	2010	...	...	1000	1300	1500	1600	1900
Lisburn § d.	1811	│	1932	│	...	...	1013	*1301*	*1501*	*1601*	*1901*
Portadown § d.	1836	1841	2005	2041	...	...	1040	1332	1532	1632	1932
Newry d.	▬	1902	▬	2102	...	...	1102	1354	1554	1654	1954
Dundalk d.	⚒	1920	⚒	2120	...	0920	1119	1413	1613	1713	2013
Drogheda d.	1855	1941	2000	2141	2205	0945	1140	1434	1634	1734	2034
Balbriggan d.	1910	│	2014	│	2219	1000	│	│	│	│	│
Skerries d.	1916	│	2020	│	2226	1006	│	│	│	│	│
Malahide d.	1931	│	2035	│	2242	1021	│	│	│	│	│
Dublin Connolly a.	1952	2020	2054	2220	2300	1040	1213	1513	1715	1815	2105

	Ⓐ	⚒	Ⓐ	⚒ E	⚒	⚒ E	⚒	⚒	⚒ E	⚒	⚒	⚒ E
Dublin Connolly d.	...	...	0711	0735	0853	0935	1003e	1035	1100	1106	1237	1320
Malahide d.	...	...	0725	│	0912	│	1025	1053	│	1127	1255	│
Skerries d.	...	...	0739	│	0926	│	1039	1107	│	1141	1310	│
Balbriggan d.	...	...	0745	│	0932	│	1045	1113	│	1147	1315	│
Drogheda d.	...	...	0800	0805	0946	1006	1100	1127	1133	1204	1335	1350
Dundalk d.	...	...	...	0830	1010	1030	▬	▬	1155	▬	▬	1415
Newry d.	0650	0735	...	0848	...	1048	Ⓐ	⑥	1213	Ⓐ	⑥	1433
Portadown § d.	0720	0800	...	0909	...	1109	1115	1130	1234	1245	1300	1454
Lisburn § a.	0745	0825	...	*0940*p	...	│	1140	1155	│	1310	1325	│
Belfast Central § a.	0804	0845g	...	0945g	...	1145g	1209	1224	1315	1339	1354	1535h

	⚒	⚒ E	⚒	⚒	⚒ E	⚒ g	⑥	Ⓐ	Ⓐ	⑥	Ⓐ	⑥	⚒	⚒ E	⚒	Ⓐ	⚒ E	⚒	⚒	Ⓐ	⚒	⑦ E	⑦ E	⑦ E	⑦ E	⑦ E	⑦
Dublin Connolly d.	1322	1520	1549	1623	1650	1651	...	...	1721	1721	1758	1759	1840	1900	1921	2017	2045	...	2125	2229	2320	1000	1300	1600	1800	1900	2122
Malahide d.	1340	│	1609	1643	│	1710	...	...	│	1739	1820	1820	│	│	1942	2035	│	...	2143	2248	2335	│	│	│	│	│	2140
Skerries d.	1355	│	1623	1658	│	1725	...	...	1745	1754	1835	1834	1901	│	1956	2049	│	...	2157	2302	2350	│	│	│	│	│	2154
Balbriggan d.	1400	│	1629	1703	│	1731	...	...	1751	1759	1840	1840	1907	│	2002	2055	│	...	2203	2308	2355	│	│	│	│	│	2200
Drogheda d.	1418	1553f	1645	1720	│	1746	...	...	1807	1816	1857	1857	1922	1931	2018	2111	2115	...	2219	2324	0016	1030	1330	1630	1830	1930	2219
Dundalk d.	...	1615	▬	...	1743	▬	...	...	1832	1840	1922	...	1946	1955	▬	▬	2140	...	2243v	2348	0040	1052	1352	1652	1852	1952	2243
Newry d.	...	1633	⚒h	...	1801	⚒g	1835	1850	...	...	...	...	...	2013	Ⓐ	⑥	2158	...	...	...	...	1110	1410	1710	1910	2010	...
Portadown § d.	...	1654	1705	...	1822	1830	1900	1915	...	...	...	...	...	2034	2045	2100	2219	2225	...	...	...	1132	1432	1732	1932	2032	...
Lisburn § a.	...	│	1730	...	│	1855	1925	1940	...	...	...	...	...	│	2110	2125	│	2250	...	...	...	1201	*1525*	*1825*	*2025*	*2125*	...
Belfast Central § a.	...	1735h	1759	...	1857	1924	1954	2009	...	...	...	...	...	2110	2139	2154	2255	2319	...	...	...	1216	1507	1807	2010	2107	...

e – 1006 on ⑥.
f – Not ⑤.
g – 3–9 mins. later on ⑥.
h – 5 mins. earlier on ⑥.
p – *0955* on ⑥.
v – ⑤ only.
z – On ⑥ depart Belfast 0730, Lisburn 0801, arrive Portadown 0827.
§ – Other local trains run Belfast - Lisburn - Portadown and v.v.

NIR — BELFAST - LONDONDERRY and PORTRUSH — 231

km		⚒	⑥	Ⓐ	Ⓐ	⚒	Ⓐ	⑥	⚒	Ⓐ	⑥	Ⓐ	Ⓐ	Ⓐ	⑥	Ⓐ	Ⓐ	⑥	Ⓐ	⑥	⑦	⑦	⑦	⑦	⑦	⑦
	Belfast GVSt. ★ d.	...	0840	0841	0909	1040	1218	1220	1415e	1520	1557	1600	1647	1715	1755	1755	1935	1950	2115	2120	0950	1250	1550	1840	...	2120
0	**Belfast Central** d.	0657	0850	0850	0925	1050	1228	1229	1425e	1530	1607	1609	1658	1725	1805	1805	1945	2000	2125	2130	1000	1300	1600	1850	...	2130
33	Antrim d.	0720	0913	0913	0952	1113	1251	1252	1451	1554	1630	1633	1722	1754	1827	1829	2007	2023	2149	2153	1024	1324	1624	1917	...	2154
52	Ballymena d.	0735	0930	0930	1005	1126	1310	1312	1505	1606	1650	1653	1736	1807	1841	1841	2028	2036	2201	2207	1035	1335	1635	1933	...	2205
97	**Coleraine** ▲ d.	0820	1015	1015	...	1210	1355	1400x	1550	...	1735	1735	1825	1857	1925	1930x	2112	2120	2245	2250	1120	1420	1720	2025x	2022	2250
107	Portrush ▲ a.	│	│	│	...	│	│	│	│	...	│	│	1835	1907	│	│	│	│	│	│	│	│	│	2038	│	│
151	**Londonderry** a.	0910	1105	1105	...	1300	1445	1447	1640	...	1825	1825	...	...	2015	2015	2200	2210	2335	2340	1210	1510	1810	...	2110	2340

	Ⓐ	⑥	Ⓐ	Ⓐ	⚒	Ⓐ	Ⓐ	⑥	⚒	Ⓐ	⚒	⑥	Ⓐ	⑥	Ⓐ	Ⓐ	⑥		⑦	⑦	⑦	⑦		⑦	⑦	
Londonderry d.	...	0540	...	...	0733	...	1125	1125	1309	...	1505	1650	1705	1840	1838	2028	2035	...	1035	1335	...	1635	...	1935	2120	...
Portrush ▲ d.	...	│	0638	...	│	...	│	│	│	...	│	│	│	│	│	│	│	...	│	│	1533	│	...	│	│	...
Coleraine ▲ d.	...	0625	0648	0718	0820	...	1212	1212	1355	...	1550	1736	1756	1925	1930	2115	2120	...	1120	1420	1547	1720	...	2020	2206	...
Ballymena d.	0635	0710	0735	0805	0905	1012	1257	1257	1439	1616	1635	1821	1841	2010	2015	2204	2207	...	1205	1505	1638	1805	...	2105	...	...
Antrim d.	0648	0723	0753	0820	0918	1025	1311	1310	1453	1630	1648	1842	1854	2023	2029	2218	2220	...	1218	1518	1652	1818	...	2118	...	...
Belfast Central a.	0711	0750	0821	0843	0943	1050	1333	1334	1521	1654	1713	1906	1918	2047	2051	2240	2244	...	1242	1542	1720	1842	...	2142	...	...
Belfast GVSt. ★ a.	0722	0759	0830	0855	0953	1102	1343	1344	1531	1702	1723	1916	1930	2057	2100	2250	2254	...	1253	1553	1730	1853	...	2153	...	...

km		Ⓐ	⑥	⚒	⚒e	⚒	⚒	⚒	⚒	⚒e	⚒	⚒e	⚒	⚒	⚒e	Ⓐy	⑥	Ⓐy	Ⓐ	⑥	Ⓐ	⑥	Ⓐ	⑥	Ⓐ	⑥	Ⓐ	⑥	
0	Coleraine d.	0623	0632	0740	0825	0930	1025	1130	1220	1315	1405	1510	1600	1700	1740	1825	1850	1857	1931	1935	2040	2045	2120	2130	2215	2220	2250	2255	...
10	Portrush a.	0633	0642	0752	0837	0942	1037	1142	1232	1327	1417	1522	1612	1712	1752	1835	1900	1907	1941	1945	2050	2055	2130	2140	2225	2230	2300	2305	...

	⚒e	Ⓐy	⑥	⚒	⚒e	⚒	⚒v	⚒	⚒v	⚒	⚒v	⚒	⑥	Ⓐ	⑥	Ⓐ	⚒	Ⓐ	⚒c	⚒	Ⓐ	⑥	Ⓐ	⑥	Ⓐ	⑥			
Portrush d.	0605	0638	1650	0758	0840	0953	1040	1150	1235	1333	1420	1530	1615	1620	1715	1718	1800	1843	1905	1950	2055	2100	2140	2145	2230	2235	...	...	...
Coleraine a.	0615	0648	0700	0810	0852	1005	1052	1202	1245	1345	1430	1542	1625	1632	1725	1730	1812	1853	1915	2000	2105	2110	2150	2155	2240	2245	...	...	...

	⑦	⑦	⑦	⑦	⑦	⑦	⑦	⑦y	⑦	⑦				
Coleraine d.	1040	1130	1340	1430	1640	1730	1940	2025	2210	2255	...	...	...	...
Portrush a.	1052	1142	1352	1442	1650	1740	1950	2038	2220	2305	...	...	...	...

	⑦	⑦	⑦	⑦y	⑦	⑦	⑦	⑦	⑦				
Portrush d.	1100	1200	1400	1533	1700	1800	2000	2100	2235	...	...	...	...
Coleraine a.	1112	1212	1412	1545	1710	1810	2010	2112	2245	...	...	...	...

c – 10 mins. later on Ⓐ.
e – 5 mins. later on ⑥.
v – 5 mins. later on Ⓐ.
x – Arrive 3–8 mins. earlier.
y – Through train to / from Belfast Great Victoria St.
▲ – **COLERAINE - PORTRUSH** (for all trains see panel).
★ – Belfast GVSt. (Belfast Great Victoria St.) is the nearest station to Belfast City Centre and the Europa Buscentre is adjacent.

Ulsterbus 212 express 🚌 service, Belfast - Londonderry. Journey time: 1 hour 40 minutes.
Ⓐ: 0645, 0800, 0830, 0900, 0930, 1000, 1030, 1100, 1130, 1200, 1230, 1300, 1330, 1400, 1430, 1500, 1530, 1545, 1600, 1615, 1630, 1645, 1700, 1715, 1730, 1745, 1800, 1830, 1900, 1930, 2030, 2215.
⑥: 0645, 0930, 1030, 1130, 1230, 1330, 1400 and every 30 minutes to 1800, 1830 then 1930, 2030, 2215.
⑦: 0830, 1000, 1130, 1330, 1430, 1600, 1730, 1930, 2030, 2130, 2215.

Ulsterbus 212 express 🚌 service, Londonderry - Belfast. Journey time: 1 hour 40 minutes.
Ⓐ: 0530, 0600, 0615, 0630, 0645, 0700, 0730 0800, 0830, 0900, 0930, 1000, 1030, 1100, 1130, 1200, 1230, 1300, 1400, 1430, 1500, 1530, 1600, 1630, 1700, 1800, 1900, 2000.
⑥: 0700, 0800, 0830, 0900, 0930, 1000, 1030, 1100, 1130, 1200, 1230, 1300, 1400, 1500, 1600, 1700, 1800, 1900, 2000.
⑦: 0800, 0900, 1030, 1200, 1330, 1500, 1600, 1700, 1800, 1900.

232 BELFAST - ENNISKILLEN and ARMAGH

Ulsterbus 251, 261

From Belfast ★ to Enniskillen (Bus Stn) (journey time 2 hours 20 mins)

Ⓐ: 0805, 0935, 1005, 1135, 1205, 1335, 1405, 1535, 1605, 1735, 1805, 1905, 2005.
⑥: 0905, 1005, 1105, 1205, 1305, 1505, 1605, 1805, 2005.
⑦: 1605, 2005.

From Enniskillen (Bus Stn) to Belfast ★

Ⓐ: 0655, 0725, 0855, 0925, 1055, 1125, 1255, 1325, 1455, 1525, 1625, 1725, 1825 ◧.
⑥: 0725, 0925, 1025, 1225, 1325, 1525, 1725.
⑦: 1225, 1525, 1725, 1825.

From Belfast ★ to Armagh (Bus Stn) (journey time 1 hour 25 mins)

Ⓐ: 0800, 1000, 1100, 1200, 1300, 1400, 1500, 1600, 1645, 1745, 1845, 2000, 2115.
⑥: 1030, 1130, 1300, 1645, 1745, 1845, 2015.
⑦: 1735, 2015, 2130.

From Armagh (Bus Stn) to Belfast ★

Ⓐ: 0630, 0715, 0800, 0900, 1000, 1100, 1200, 1300, 1500, 1600, 1710, 1800.
⑥: 0725, 0900, 1000, 1100, 1515, 1600, 1710.
⑦: 1400, 1610, 1830, 2015.

Buses call at **Portadown (Market Street)** 40–75 minutes from Belfast and **Portadown (Northern Bank)** 20–30 minutes from Armagh (Bus Stn).

◧ – Change at Dungannon. ★ – Europa Buscentre / Great Victoria St. Rail Station.

233 BELFAST - LARNE

NIR

From Belfast Central – Ⓐ: 0555 **H**, 0647, 0745 **H**, 0842 **H**, and hourly until 1442 **H**, 1512 **H**, 1612, 1635, 1715 **H**, 1735, 1810, 1850, 1930 **H**, 2030 **H**, 2130 **H**, 2230 **H**, 2330 **H**.
⑥: 0612 **H**, 0712 **H**, and hourly until 2012 **H**, 2113 **H**, 2212, 2312 **H**. ⑦: 0833 **H**, 1003 **H**, 1133 **H**, 1303 **H**, 1433 **H**, 1603 **H**, 1733 **H**, 1903 **H**, 2033 **H**, 2203 **H**.

From Larne Town – Ⓐ: 0600, 0630 **S**, 0700 **S**, 0730 **S**, 0757, 0809 **S**, 0900 **S**, 1000 **S** and hourly until 1500 **S**, 1553 **S**, 1630 **S**, 1715, 1743, 1820, 1845, 1912, 1950, 2033 **S**, 2133 **S**, 2233 **S**.
⑥: 0550 **S**, 0630 **S**, 0730 **S**, 0830 **S** and hourly until 2030 **S**, 2130 **S**, 2230 **S**. ⑦: 0826 **S**, 0956 **S**, 1126 **S**, 1256 **S**, 1426 **S**, 1556 **S**, 1726 **S**, 1856 **S**, 2026 **S**, 2156 **S**.

Trains call at: **Carrickfergus** 27–29 minutes from Belfast and 28–31 minutes from Larne and **Whitehead** 38–40 minutes from Belfast, 18–21 minutes from Larne.

Trains marked **H** arrive Larne **Harbour** 4 minutes after Larne **Town**. Trains marked **S** depart Larne **Harbour** 3 minutes before Larne **Town**. Journey time Belfast Central - Larne Harbour 57–65 mins.

234 DUBLIN - LONDONDERRY

Bus Éireann 33 / Ulsterbus 274

Dublin ● d.	...	0715	0915	1145	1345	1545	1745	1945	2145	2300	...
Dublin Airport ✈, △ d.	...	0735	0935	1205	1405	1605	1805	2005	2205	2320	...
Monaghan a.	...	0910	1110	|	|	1740	|	2140	|	|	...
Monaghan d.	...	0925	1125	1355u	1555u	1755	1955u	2155	2340u	0055u	...
Omagh ▽ a.	...	1010	1210	1440	1640	1840	2040	2240	0025	0140	...
Strabane ▽ a.	...	1045	1245	1515	1715	1915	2115	2315	0100	0215	...
Londonderry a.	...	1115	1315	1545	1745	1945	2145	2345	0130	0245	...

Londonderry d.	...	0045	0615	0815	1015	1215	1415	1615	1815	2045	...
Strabane △ d.	...	0105	0645	0845	1045	1245	1445	1645	1845	2115	...
Omagh △ d.	...	0130	0720	0920	1120	1320	1520	1720	1920	2150	...
Monaghan a.	...	0210	0805	1005	1205	1405	1605	1805	2005	2235	...
Monaghan d.	...	0210	0820	1020	1220	1420	1620	1820	2020	2235	...
Dublin Airport ✈, ▽ a.	...	0350	0955	1155	1355	1555	1755	1955	2155	0025	...
Dublin ● a.	...	0410	1015	1215	1415	1615	1815	2015	2215	0045	...

u – Stops to pick up only. △ – Busses stop here to pick up only. ☛ The calling point in each town is the bus station unless otherwise indicated.
● – Dublin **Busaras**. ▽ – Busses stop here to set down only.

234a DUBLIN - DONEGAL

Bus Éireann 30

	⚒	⑦	⚒	⚒	⑦	⚒	⑦	⚒	⑤	⚒	⑦	⑦
Dublin ● d.	0800	0900	1000	1145	1145	1330	1330	1600	1715	1800	1800	2030
Navan ◧ d.	0845u	0947u	1045u	1230u	1232u	|	|	|	|	1845u	1850u	|
Cavan a.	0940	1040	|	1325	1325	1510	1510	|	1855	1940	1940	|
Cavan d.	0950	1055	|	1335	1340	1520	1520	|	1900	1950	1955	2220u
Enniskillen d.	1100	1205	1220	1445	1450	1625	1610	1820	1950	2040	2045	2305
Ballyshannon d.	1145	1250	1305	1530	1535	1725	1655	1905	2035	2125	2130	2345
Donegal ⊡ a.	1210	1315	1330	1555	1600	1735	1720	1930	2105	2155	2155	0010

	⚒	⑦	⚒	⚒	⑦	⚒	⑦	⚒	⑦	⚒	⑦
Donegal ⊡ d.	0730	0730	0845	1100	1100	1315	1500	1515	1600	1730	1730
Ballyshannon d.	0750	0750	0910	1125	1125	1340	1525	1540	|	1755	1755
Enniskillen d.	0835	0835	0950	1210	1210	1425	1610	1625	|	1840	1840
Cavan a.	|	0915	|	1320	1320	|	1720	1735	|	1950	1950
Cavan d.	|	0915	|	1330	1335	|	1735	1745	|	2000	2005
Navan ◐ d.	|	|	|	1420s	1427s	|	1827s	1840s	|	2050s	2057s
Dublin ● a.	1100	1100	1230	1510	1515	1700	1915	1925	1930	2140	2145

s – Stops to set down only. u – Stops to pick up only. ● – Dublin **Busaras**. ◧ – Navan **Mercy Convent**. ⊡ – Donegal **Abbey Hotel**. ◐ – Navan **Bypass**.

235 LONDONDERRY - GALWAY - CORK

Bus Éireann 51, 64

	⚒	⚒	⚒	⚒	⚒	⚒	⑦	⑦	⑦	⑦
Londonderry d.	...	...	0720	0830	1200	1600	...	1130	1440	1715
Letterkenny d.	...	...	0755	0905	1235	1635	...	1205	1515	1750
Donegal (Abbey Hotel) d.	...	...	0845	0955	1330	1730	...	1255	1605	1840
Ballyshannon d.	...	...	0905	1015	1350	1750	...	1315	1625	1900
Sligo d.	...	0815	1000	1115	1500	1900	1115	1415	1720	2000
Knock d.	...	0925	1110	1225	1610	2010	1220	1525	1830	2110
Claremorris (Dalton St.) d.	...	|	1122	|	1622	|	1232	|	|	2122
Galway (Bus Station) a.	...	1045	1230	1345	1730	2130	1345	1645	1950	2230
❖ change buses ❖		❖	❖	❖	❖		❖	❖		
Galway (Bus Station) d.	0705	1205	1405	1505	1905	...	1505	1805	...	...
Ennis d.	0820	1320	1520	1620	2020	...	1620	1920	...	...
Shannon Airport ✈ d.	0850	1350	1550	1650	2050	...	1650	1950	...	...
Limerick (Rail Station) a.	0920	1420	1620	1720	2120	...	1720	2020	...	...
Limerick (Rail Station) d.	0935	1435	1635	1735	...	...	1735	2035	...	...
Charleville d.	1010	1510	1710	1810	...	...	1810	2110	...	...
Mallow (Town Park) d.	1040	1540	1740	1840	...	...	1840	2140	...	...
Cork a.	1125	1625	1825	1925	...	...	1925	2225	...	...

	⚒	⚒	⚒	⚒	⚒	⚒	⑦	⑦	⑦	⑦
Cork d.	...	...	0825	1025	1225	1825	...	0825	1025	1525
Mallow (Town Park) d.	...	...	0900	1100	1300	1900	...	0900	1100	1600
Charleville d.		...	0930	1130	1330	1930	...	0930	1130	1630
Limerick (Rail Station) a.	...	...	1010	1210	1410	2010	...	1010	1210	1710
Limerick (Rail Station) d.	...	0825	1025	1225	1425	2025	...	1025	1225	1725
Shannon Airport ✈ d.	...	0855	1055	1255	1455	2055	...	1055	1255	1755
Ennis d.	...	0925	1125	1325	1525	2125	...	1125	1325	1825
Galway (Bus Station) a.	...	1045	1245	1445	1645	2245	...	1245	1445	1945
❖ change buses ❖		❖	❖	❖	❖	▬		❖	❖	❖
Galway (Bus Station) d.	0900	1200	1400	1600	1815	...	1000	1400	1600	2100
Claremorris (Dalton St.) d.	|	1308	|	|	1923	...	|	|	|	2208
Knock d.	1020	1320	1520	1720	1935	⑤	1120	1520	1720	2220
Sligo d.	1145	1445	1645	1845	2045	2050	1245	1645	1900	2330
Ballyshannon d.	1225	1525	1725	1925	...	2130	1325	1725	1940	...
Donegal (Abbey Hotel) d.	1250	1550	1750	1950	...	2155	1350	1750	2005	...
Letterkenny d.	1340	1640	1840	2040	...	2245	1440	1840	2055	...
Londonderry a.	1415	1715	1915	2115	...	2325	1515	1915	2130	...

❖ – Change buses. Minimum conection time 45 minutes. ☛ The calling point in each town is the bus station unless otherwise indicated.

236 DUBLIN - SLIGO

IÉ

Service to January 20. *For service from January 21 see page 541*

km	*Valid until January 20*	⚒ 🍷	⚒ 🍷	Ⓐ	⚒ 🍷	⑤	⚒ 🍷	⚒ 🍷	Ⓐ	⑥	⚒ 🍷		⑦ 🍷	⑦ 🍷	⑦	⑦ 🍷	⑦ 🍷	
0	**Dublin Connolly** d.	0800	1105	1158	1405	1600	1705	1715	1818	1818	1905	...	0805	1405	1616	1705	1905	...
26	Maynooth d.	0822	1130	1222	1430	1625	|	1755	1859	1900	1928	...	0828	1430	1652	|	1928	...
83	Mullingar d.	0911	1210	1306	1510	1712	1811	1838	1943	1942	2017	...	0911	1510	1743	1810	2014	...
125	**Longford** d.	0943	1241	1344	1541	1743	1843	1910	2026	...	2049	...	0943	1542	1821	1843	2045	...
143	Dromod d.	1000	1300	...	1600	1757	1900	...	...	...	2104	...	1001	1600	...	1900	2101	...
159	Carrick on Shannon d.	1017	1317	...	1617	1813	1917	...	...	...	2120	...	1018	1616	...	1916	2116	...
173	Boyle d.	1029	1329	...	1629	1828	1929	...	...	...	2132	...	1030	1628	...	1928	2131	...
219	**Sligo** a.	1110	1410	...	1710	1914	2010	...	...	...	2214	...	1110	1710	...	2010	2210	...

Valid until January 20	Ⓐ	Ⓐ	⚒ 🍷	⚒ 🍷	⚒ 🍷	Ⓐ	⚒ 🍷	⑥ 🍷	Ⓐ 🍷	Ⓐ		⑦ 🍷	⑦ 🍷	⑦ 🍷	⑦ 🍷	⑦	⑦ 🍷	
Sligo d.	...	...	0655	0855	1155	...	1455	1755	1755	...	...	0855	1155	1455	1550	...	1755	...
Boyle d.	...	...	0730	0930	1230	...	1530	1830	1830	...	...	0931	1230	1530	1629	...	1830	...
Carrick on Shannon d.	...	...	0741	0941	1241	...	1541	1841	1841	...	...	0944	1241	1541	1642	...	1841	...
Dromod d.	...	...	0800	1000	1300	...	1600	1900	1900	...	...	1002	1300	1559	1658	...	1859	...
Longford d.	0618	0700	0816	1016	1316	1413	1616	1916	1916	2050	...	1018	1316	1616	1712	1840	1917	...
Mullingar d.	0651	0733	0849	1049	1349	1445	1649	1949	1954	2122	...	1050	1349	1649	1746	1912	1950	...
Maynooth d.	0734	0815	0928	1125	1426	1532	1725	2028	2035	2201	...	1130	1425	1725	1823	1956	2027	...
Dublin Connolly a.	0820	0904	1000	1200	1500	1557	1800	2100	2109	2250	...	1201	1500	1800	1855	2025	2100	...

236a BALLYBROPHY - ROSCREA - LIMERICK

IÉ

km	*Valid until August 30*	⚒	⚒	⑦	
0	Dublin Heuston d.	0900	1725	1825	...
107	Ballybrophy a.	1005	1845	1943	...
	change trains				
	Ballybrophy d.	1010	1855	1950	...
123	Roscrea d.	1027	1912	2007	...
154	Nenagh d.	1102	1947	2042	...
199	**Limerick** a.	1155	2039	2135	...

Valid until August 30	⚒	⚒		⑦	
Limerick d.	0644	1645	...	1745	...
Nenagh d.	0735	1739	...	1838	...
Roscrea d.	0810	1814	...	1913	...
Ballybrophy a.	0829	1831	...	1930	...
change trains					
Ballybrophy d.	0835	1844	...	1939	...
Dublin Heuston a.	0955	2008	...	2105	...

IÉ — DUBLIN - ROSSLARE — 237

km		Ⓐ	⚒	⚒	⚒🍷	WⒶ	Ⓐ	Ⓐ	⚒🍷§	⑦	⑦🍷	⑦🍷§
0	**Dublin Connolly** ▲ d.	...	0726	1135	1305	1640	1725	...	1837	0949	1320	1830
11	Dún Laoghaire ▲ d.	...	0752	1157	1320	|	1749	...	1853	1009	1336	1845
21	Bray ▲ d.	...	0815	1216	1337	1723	1806	...	1910	1029	1353	1900
47	Wicklow d.	...	0838	1244	1400	1749	1835	...	1938	1053	1417	1925
80	Arklow d.	0544	0906	1313	1429	1818	1906	...	2011	1125	1446	1954
97	Gorey d.	0557	0920	1327	1443	1833	1920	...	2025	1139	1500	2008
126	Enniscorthy d.	0625	0940	...	1503	...	1939	1950	2049	1159	1525	2028
150	**Wexford** d.	0648	1004	...	1527	...	...	2013	2112	1223	1550	2052
160	Rosslare Strand d.	0712	1022	...	1544	...	...	2030	2129	1240	1608	2109
166	**Rosslare** Europort a.	0718	1028	...	1553	...	...	2037	2135	1248	1616	2117

	Ⓐ	Ⓐ	⑥	⚒🍷§	⚒🍷	⚒	⚒	WⒶ	Ⓐ	Ⓐ	⑦🍷	⑦🍷	⑦
Rosslare Europort d.	...	0535	...	0740	1300	...	1740	...	1855	...	0855	1435	1750
Rosslare Strand d.	...	0541	...	0745	1306	...	1745	...	1901	...	0900	1440	1755
Wexford d.	...	0600	...	0804	1325	...	1805	...	1920	...	0920	1500	1815
Enniscorthy d.	...	0623	...	0827	1348	...	1828	...	1942	2005	0943	1523	1838
Gorey d.	0600	0645	0645	0850	1410	1448	1850	1923	...	2027	1005	1547	1900
Arklow d.	0613	0659	0659	0905	1431	1500	1904	1935	...	2040	1018	1600	1913
Wicklow d.	0644	0733	0733	0939	1501	1530	1938	2010	...	2109	1053	1630	1953
Bray ▲ d.	0713	0805	0805	1001	1523	1601	2001	2037	...	2133	1117	1653	2016
Dún Laoghaire ▲ d.	0731	0823	0823	1018	1537	1622	2017	2057	...	2150	1134	1713	2037
Dublin Connolly ▲ a.	0757	0851	0851	1036	1603	1641	2032	2118	...	2212	1152	1730	2054

▲ – Additional surburban trains (*DART*) run Howth - Dublin Connolly - Dún Laoghaire - Bray. Trains run every 10–15 minutes on ⚒, every 20–30 minutes on ⑦.

W – From May 6, 2008.

§ – Does not connect with Ferry: Rosslare - Fishguard and v.v.

Bus Éireann 12, 13 — 🚌 DUBLIN - LIMERICK - TRALEE — 238

									⑦			
Dublin Busaras d.	...	...	0730	0930	1130	1330	1530	1630	...	1730	1830	2000
Kildare (Boyle's) d.	...	...	0830	1030	1230	1430	1630	1730	...	1830	1930	2100
Portlaoise (JFL Ave.) d.	...	...	0900	1100	1300	1500	1700	1800	...	1900	2000	2130
Roscrea d.	...	...	0950	1150	1350	1550	1750	1850	...	1950	2050	2220
Nenagh d.	...	...	1025	1225	1425	1625	1825	1925	...	2025	2125	2255
Limerick (Bus Stn) ✥ a.	...	...	1110	1310	1510	1710	1910	2010	...	2110	2210	2340
Limerick (Bus Stn) ✥ d.	0835	0935	1135	1335	1535	1735	1935	2035	2035	2135	...	...
Adare d.	0855	0955	1155	1355	1555	1755	1955	2055	2055	2155	...	...
Newcastlewest d.	0920	1020	1220	1420	1620	1820	2020	2120	2120	2220	...	...
Abbeyfeale d.	0940	1040	1240	1440	1640	1840	2040	2140	2140	2240	...	...
Listowel (Square) d.	1000	1100	1300	1500	1700	1900	2100	...	2200	2300	...	...
Tralee (Station) a.	1040	1140	1340	1540	1740	1940	2140	...	2240	2340	...	...

		⚒										
Tralee (Station) d.	...	0615	...	0800	0900	1100	1300	1500	...	1700	1800	1900
Listowel (Square) d.	...	0645	...	0830	0930	1130	1330	1530	...	1730	1830	1930
Abbeyfeale d.	...	0710	...	0855	0955	1155	1355	1555	1655	1755	1855	1955
Newcastlewest d.	...	0730	...	0915	1015	1215	1415	1615	1715	1815	1915	2015
Adare d.	...	0755	...	0940	1040	1240	1440	1640	1740	1840	1940	2040
Limerick (Bus Stn) ✥ a.	...	0820	...	1005	1105	1305	1505	1705	1805	1905	2005	2105
Limerick (Bus Stn) ✥ d.	0730	...	0830	1030	1130	1330	1530	1730	1830	1930	...	...
Nenagh d.	0810	...	0910	1110	1210	1410	1610	1810	1910	2010	...	...
Roscrea d.	0840	...	0940	1140	1240	1440	1640	1840	1940	2040	...	...
Portlaoise (JFL Ave.) d.	0930	...	1030	1230	1330	1530	1730	1930	2030	2130	...	...
Kildare (Boyle's) d.	1000	...	1100	1300	1400	1600	1800	2000	2100	2200	...	...
Dublin Busaras a.	1110	...	1210	1410	1510	1710	1910	2110	2210	2310	...	...

Dublin - Limerick (service **12**) also: 0830, 1030, 1230, 1430.
Limerick - Dublin (service **12**) also: 0930, 1230, 1430, 1630.

✥ – A change of 🚌 is required at Limerick (Bus Station). Adjacent to Limerick railway station.

IÉ; Bus Éireann 40, 55, 372 — LIMERICK - WATERFORD - ROSSLARE — 239

km		⚒	⚒	⚒	⚒		🚌	🚌 ⚒	🚌	🚌 ⚒	🚌
0	**Limerick** d.	*0755*	*1055*	*1455*	*1755*	...	0825	1230	1615	1740	2040
35	**Limerick Jct.** d.	0850	1145	1546	1845	...	0855	1300	1645	1810	2110
40	Tipperary d.	0902	1156	1556	1856	...	0900	1305	1650	1815	2115
62	Cahir d.	0926	1220	1620	1920	...	0930	1335	1720	1845	2145
79	Clonmel d.	0944	1238	1638	1938	...	0950	1355	1740	1905	2205
101	Carrick on Suir d.	1008	1302	1707	2002	...	1010	1415	1800	1925	2225
124	**Waterford** a.	1032	1326	1732	2026	...	1050	1455	1840	2005	2305
	Waterford d.	...	...	1734	...	...	*1130c*	*1630c*	*1930*	...	...
	Wexford d.	...	...	|	...	...	*1230c*	1730c	*2030*	...	...
186	**Rosslare** Europort a.	...	...	1850	...	...	*1255c*	...	*2050*	...	...

	⚒	⚒	⚒	⚒	⚒	🚌 ⚒	🚌 ⑦	🚌 ⚒	🚌	🚌
Rosslare Europort d.	...	0705	...	...	...	*0700*	*0715*	...	*1300c*	*1900*
Wexford d.	...	|	...	...	...	*0725*	*0740*	...	*1325c*	*1925*
Waterford a.	...	0823	...	...	...	*0845*	*0840*	...	*1425c*	*2020*
Waterford d.	0635	...	0935	1230	1638	0850	0850	1250	1450	2030
Carrick on Suir d.	0700	...	1009	1303	1704	0920	0920	1320	1520	2100
Clonmel d.	0723	...	1033	1326	1727	0945	0945	1345	1545	2125
Cahir d.	0742	...	1052	1345	1746	1010	1010	1410	1610	2150
Tipperary d.	0805	...	1115	1409	1809	1035	1035	1435	1635	2215
Limerick Jct. a.	0817	...	1125	1419	1819	1040	1040	1440	1640	2220
Limerick a.	*0915*	...	*1212*	*1508*	*1903*	1115	1115	1515	1715	2300

Additional journeys: Limerick - Waterford 🚌 1130⑦, 1840⑦. Waterford - Limerick 🚌 0950 ⚒; 1630⑤, 1830⑦. Waterford - Wexford 🚌 0700⚒, 0900⚒. Wexford - Waterford 🚌: 1745⚒; 1840Ⓐ.

c – ⚒ only.

Buses call at rail stations **except**: Limerick (Bus Station), Limerick Junction (Bit and Bridle Pub), Tipperary (Abbey St), Cahir (Castle St), Carrick (Greenside), Waterford (Bus Station).

IÉ — ✥ DUBLIN - GALWAY, BALLINA and WESTPORT ✥ — 240

km		⚒	⚒h ◇🍴	⚒ 🍷	⚒ 🍷	⚒ ◇🍷	⚒ 🍷	⚒ ◇🍷	⑤ 🍷	⚒h ◇🍴	⚒	⚒ 🍷	⚒	⚒ 🍷	⚒ ◇🍷
0	**Dublin Heuston 245** d.	...	0710	0820	0910	1110	1240	1435	1615	1650	1710	1745	...	1750	1915
48	Kildare **245** d.	...	|	|	0948	1144	1314	|	1653	|	1747	|	...	|	1954
67	Portarlington **245** d.	...	0754	|	1002	|	1329	1519	1708	|	1805	|	...	1839	2007
93	Tullamore d.	...	0812	0924	1021	1212	1347	1539	1727	|	1823	|	...	1858	2025
129	**Athlone** d.	0705	0845	0954	1048	1245	1414	1605	1753	1813	1853	1909	...	1932	2051
152	Ballinasloe d.	0721	0903	|	1105	1303	|	1623	|	1831	...	|	...	1950	2109
187	Athenry d.	0800	0931	|	1137	1329	|	1650	|	1856	...	|	...	2012	2134
208	**Galway** a.	0821	0955	|	1159	1351	|	1715	|	1916	...	|	...	2031	2155
160	Roscommon d.	...	...	1020	—	...	1442	—	1821	...	...	1937	...	...	...
186	Castlerea d.	...	...	1040	...	...	1503	...	1841	...	...	1957	...	...	...
204	Ballyhaunis d.	...	...	1055	...	...	1518	...	1856	...	...	2012	...	...	...
222	Claremorris d.	...	...	1110	⚒	...	1532	⚒	1913	...	...	2027	...	...	...
240	Manulla Junction § d.	...	...	1125	1128	...	1548	1551	|	...	...	2042	2045	...	...
273	**Ballina** a.	...	...	|	1157	...	|	1619	2002	...	...	|	2113	...	...
246	Castlebar d.	...	...	1136	...	...	1558	...	...	...	...	2051	...	...	...
264	**Westport** a.	...	...	1158	...	...	1621	...	...	...	...	2114	...	...	...

	⑦ 🍷	⑦	⑦ 🍷	⑦ 🍷	⑦	⑦ ◇🍷	⑦ 🍷	⑦ 🍷	⑦	⑦ ◇🍷	⑦ ◇
Dublin Heuston 245 d.	0840	...	1210	1305	...	1345	1605	1805	...	1850	2040
Kildare **245** d.	0918	...	|	1342	...	|	|	1842	...	1924	|
Portarlington **245** d.	0932	...	|	1355	...	|	1650	1856	...	1938	2128
Tullamore d.	0951	...	|	1413	...	|	1708	1914	...	1959	2146
Athlone d.	1026	1035	|	1445	...	1506	1739	1956	...	2031	2215
Ballinasloe d.	1045	|	|	|	...	1529	1757	|	...	2049	2233
Athenry d.	1116	|	|	|	...	1556	1831	|	...	2115	2256
Galway a.	1140	|	1438	|	...	1618	1847	|	...	2134	2315
Roscommon d.	...	1058	—	1520	...	...	...	2020	...	...	...
Castlerea d.	...	1119	...	1551	...	...	...	2040	...	...	...
Ballyhaunis d.	...	1134	...	1556	...	...	...	2055	...	...	...
Claremorris d.	...	1148	⑦	1610	...	...	...	2110	...	...	...
Manulla Junction § d.	...	1203	1207	1625	1629	...	...	2125	2128	...	...
Ballina a.	...	|	1236	|	1657	...	...	|	2156	...	...
Castlebar d.	...	1213	...	1635	...	...	...	2135	...	...	...
Westport a.	...	1231	...	1650	...	...	...	2151	...	...	...

	Ⓐ	Ⓐ ◇🍷	⚒h ◇🍴	⚒	⚒ 🍷	⚒ 🍷	⚒h ◇🍴	⚒ 🍷	⚒	⚒ 🍷	⚒ ◇🍷	⚒	⚒ 🍷	Ⓐ
Westport d.	...	...	...	...	0700	...	...	...	...	1310	...	...	1805	...
Castlebar d.	...	...	...	...	0713	...	...	...	...	1323	...	...	1818	...
Ballina d.	...	...	...	0650	|	...	...	...	1300	|	...	1755	|	...
Manulla Junction § d.	...	...	...	0718	0722	...	...	...	1328	1332	...	1823	1828	...
Claremorris d.	...	...	...	...	0737	...	...	...	...	1347	...	—	1843	...
Ballyhaunis d.	...	...	...	...	0753	...	...	...	...	1403	...	...	1859	...
Castlerea d.	...	...	...	...	0808	...	...	...	...	1417	...	⚒	1913	...
Roscommon d.	...	...	...	...	0829	...	...	...	...	1438	...	◇🍷	1935	...
Galway d.	...	0520	0715	...	|	0915	1050	1310	...	|	1505	1805	|	2145
Athenry d.	...	0533	0728	...	|	0928	1103	1328	...	|	1518	1818	|	2208
Ballinasloe d.	...	0559	0751	...	|	0956	1130	1354	...	|	1545	1853	|	2237
Athlone d.	0505	0617	0808	...	0855	1013	1147	1413	...	1508	1606	1910	2003	2255
Tullamore d.	0531	0646	0837	...	0925	1043	1216	1443	...	1536	1635	1939	2046	...
Portarlington **245** d.	0550	0706	|	...	0944	|	1238	1503	...	1601	1654	1958	2105	...
Kildare **245** d.	0604	0718	|	...	|	|	|	|	...	1614	|	|	|	...
Dublin Heuston 245 a.	0700	0810	0945	...	1036	1158	1338	1603	...	1651	1748	2054	2157	...

	⑦ ◇🍷	⑦	⑦ 🍷	⑦ 🍷	⑦ 🍷	⑦	⑦ 🍷	⑦ 🍷	⑦ A🍷	⑦ ◇🍷	⑦	⑦ 🍷
Westport d.	...	...	0745	...	...	...	1330	...	1530	...	...	1755
Castlebar d.	...	...	0758	...	...	...	1343	...	1543	...	...	1808
Ballina d.	...	0735	|	...	...	1320	|	...	|	...	1745	|
Manulla Junction § d.	...	0803	0807	...	...	1348	1352	...	|	...	1813	1817
Claremorris d.	...	...	0822	...	...	—	1407	...	1612	...	...	1836
Ballyhaunis d.	...	...	0838	...	...	...	1423	...	1629	...	...	1852
Castlerea d.	...	...	0853	...	...	⑦	1438	...	1645	...	...	1907
Roscommon d.	...	...	0914	...	...	◇🍷	1459	...	1707	...	...	1928
Galway d.	0825	...	|	1130	1320	1455	|	1615	|	1815	...	|
Athenry d.	0838	...	|	|	1335	1508	|	1631	|	1828	...	|
Ballinasloe d.	0904	...	|	|	1405	1531	|	1657	|	1857	...	|
Athlone d.	0921	...	0941	|	1423	1548	1526	1718	1742	1914	...	1955
Tullamore d.	0950	...	1015	|	1506	1617	1555	1748	1814	1940	...	2023
Portarlington **245** d.	1012	...	1038	|	1531	1637	|	1811	1836	2004	...	2043
Kildare **245** d.	1024	...	|	|	|	1649	|	1826	1851	2016	...	|
Dublin Heuston 245 a.	1110	...	1131	1354	1628	1731	1715	1910	1934	2057	...	2137

A – Dec. 9 - May 28.

h – 🍴 on Ⓐ, 🍷 on ⑥.

◇ – Also conveys [1].

§ – Passenger transfer point only.

✥ – Services affected by engineering works on ⑥⑦.

IÉ — ✥ DUBLIN - KILKENNY - WATERFORD ✥ — 241

km		⚒ 🍷	⚒ 🍷	⚒h ◇🍴	⚒ 🍷	⚒ 🍷	⚒	⚒ ◇🍷	Ⓐ	⑦ 🍷	⑦ 🍷	⑦ ◇🍷	⑦ 🍷
0	**Dublin Heuston** △ d.	0730	0930	1130	1505	1625	1735	1825	2005	0930	1430	1735	1840
48	Kildare △ d.	0811	1011	1204	1545	1712	|	|	2043	1010	1512	1813	1914
72	Athy d.	0831	1031	1223	1604	1730	1829	1918	2106	1030	1533	1831	1926
90	Carlow d.	0854	1046	1238	1621	1745	1845	1933	2119	1048	1555	1845	1953
106	Muine Bheag d.	0906	1100	1253	1636	1759	...	1947	...	1102	1609	1859	2007
130	**Kilkenny** a.	0925	1119	1312	1654	1818	...	2006	...	1121	1628	1923	2026
	Kilkenny d.	0929	1123	1322	1701	1828	...	2015	...	1131	1632	1932	2035
147	Thomastown d.	0941	|	1333	1713	1840	...	2027	...	1142	1644	1944	2047
179	**Waterford** a.	1009	1202	1353	1740	1905	...	2050	...	1211	1713	2010	2109

	Ⓐ	⚒ 🍷	⚒h ◇🍴	⚒ 🍷	⚒ 🍷	⚒ ◇🍷	⚒ 🍷	Ⓐ	⑦ ◇🍷	⑦ 🍷	⑦ 🍷	⑦ 🍷
Waterford d.	...	0610	0735	1045	1315	1500	1825	...	0925	1300	1430	1800
Thomastown d.	...	0630	0755	1107	|	1521	1855	...	0949	1321	1450	1824
Kilkenny a.	...	0647	0812	1123	1358	1538	1912	...	1007	1337	1509	1842
Kilkenny d.	...	0656	0821	1127	1403	1548	1919	...	1016	1347	1518	1848
Muine Bheag d.	...	0711	0837	1143	1419	1603	1947	...	1032	1404	1535	1905
Carlow d.	0630	0724	0850	1201	1432	1621	2002	2125	1046	1417	1551	1919
Athy d.	0641	0737	0905	1222	1448	1633	2018	2137	1059	1430	1605	1934
Kildare △ d.	0659	0759	0925	1241	1508	1653	2040	2154	1118	1451	1625	1954
Dublin Heuston △ a.	0752	0845	1005	1326	1553	1734	2126	2240	1208	1534	1708	2042

h – 🍴 on Ⓐ, 🍷 on ⑥.

◇ – Also conveys [1].

△ – For additional trains Dublin - Kildare and v.v, see Tables **240**, **245**.

✥ – Services affected by engineering works on ⑥⑦.

245 ✣ DUBLIN - LIMERICK, TRALEE and CORK ✣ IÉ

km		⚒h ◇✕	⚒	⚒h ◇✕	⚒	⚒ ◇🍷	⚒ ◇🍷	⚒ ◇🍷	⚒	⚒ ◇🍷	⚒ ◇🍷	⚒h ◇✕	⚒	⚒h ◇✕	⚒ 🍷	⚒ ◇🍷	⚒	⚒h ◇✕	⚒ ◇🍷	⚒h ◇✕	⚒	⚒h ◇✕	Hh ◇✕	⑤ ◇✕	⚒ ◇🍷
0	**Dublin Heuston 240** d.	0700	...	0800	...	0900	0925	1000	...	1100	1125	1200	...	1300	1325	1400	...	1500	1525	1600	...	1700	1705	1705	1725
48	Kildare **240** d.	│	...	│	...	│	1000	│	...	│	1158	│	...	│	1358	│	...	│	1558	│	...	│	│	│	1807
67	Portarlington **240** d.	│	...	│	...	│	1013	│	...	│	1213	│	...	│	1412	│	...	│	1612	│	...	│	│	│	1819
82	Portlaoise d.	0753	...	│	...	│	1024	│	...	│	1224	│	...	│	1424	│	...	│	1624	│	...	│	│	│	1831
107	Ballybrophy d.	│	...	│	...	1005	│	│	...	│	│	│	...	│	1439	│	...	│	1639	│	...	│	│	│	1845
127	Templemore d.	│	...	│	...	│	1048	│	...	│	1248	│	...	│	1451	│	...	│	1651	│	...	│	1819	1819	1857
139	Thurles d.	0822	...	0919	...	│	1057	1119	...	1219	1257	1319	...	│	1500	1519	...	│	1700	1719	...	│	1828	1835	1907
172	**Limerick Junction** § d.	0844	0846	0941	0943	│	│	1141	1143	│	│	1341	1343	│	│	1541	1543	│	│	1741	1832	1838	│	│	│
208	**Limerick** § a.	│	0915	│	1012	│	1148	│	1212	│	1348	│	1412	│	1554	│	1612	│	1751	│	1903	│	1917	1917	1955
**	Ennis a.	│	*1000*	│	*1145*	│	*1325*	│	*1325*	│	*1500*	│	*1500*	│	*1700*	│	*1700*	│	*1840*	│	*2010*	│	*2010*	2010	...
208	Charleville d.	│	...	│	...	1058	...	│	...	1258	...	│	...	1455	...	│	...	1655	...	│	...	│	...	...	...
232	**Mallow** d.	0918	...	1015	...	1115	...	1215	...	1315	...	1415	...	1512	...	1615	...	1712	...	1815	...	1912	...	...	...
	Tralee **246** a.	│	...	│	...	│	...	│	...	│	...	│	...	│	...	│	...	│	...	│	...	│	...	...	...
266	**Cork** a.	0953	...	1050	...	1150	...	1250	...	1350	...	1450	...	1545	...	1650	...	1745	...	1850	...	1945	...	...	...

	⚒h ◇✕	⚒	⚒h ◇✕	⚒	⚒	⚒ ◇🍷	⚒ ◇🍷	⚒	⚒ ◇	⚒		⑦ 🍷	⑦	⑦	⑦ ◇🍷	⑦	⑦ ◇🍷	⑦ ◇🍷	⑦ ◇🍷	⑦ ◇🍷	⑦ ◇🍷	⑦ ◇🍷	⑦ ◇🍷	⑦ ◇🍷	⑦ ◇🍷
Dublin Heuston 240 d.	1800	...	1830	...	1835	1900	2000	...	2100	...	...	0810	...	...	1000	...	1100	1125	1200	1300	1325	1400	1500	1525	1600
Kildare **240** d.	│	...	│	...	1912	│	2034	...	│	...	...	│	...	...	│	...	│	1200	│	│	1400	│	│	1600	│
Portarlington **240** d.	│	...	│	...	1925	│	│	...	2145	...	...	│	...	...	│	...	│	1213	│	│	1413	│	│	1613	│
Portlaoise d.	│	...	│	...	1936	1953	│	...	2156	...	...	0909	...	...	│	...	│	1224	│	│	1424	│	│	1624	│
Ballybrophy d.	│	...	│	...	1953	│	│	...	│	...	...	│	...	...	│	...	│	1239	│	│	1439	│	│	1639	│
Templemore d.	│	...	│	...	2006	│	│	...	│	...	...	│	...	...	│	...	│	1251	│	│	1451	│	│	1651	│
Thurles d.	1926	...	1954	...	2016	2024	2122	...	2225	...	...	0945	...	...	1119	...	1219	1300	1319	1419	1500	1519	1619	1700	1719
Limerick Junction § d.	1948	1952	│	...	...	│	2144	2148	2249	2248	...	1008	1012	...	1141	1143	1241	│	1341	│	│	1541	│	│	1741
Limerick § a.	│	2029	│	...	...	│	│	2216	│	2316	...	│	1040	...	│	1211	│	1351	*1409*	│	1551	*1611*	│	1751	*1811*
Ennis a.	│	...	│	...	...	│	│	...	│	...	...	│	*1130*	...	│	*1310*	│	*1520*	*1520*	│	*1720*	*1720*	│	*1905*	*1905*
Charleville d.	│	...	2034	...	...	2103	│	...	│	...	...	1034	...	...	│	...	│	...	│	1458	...	│	│	...	│
Mallow d.	2020	...	2055	2100	...	2118	2220	...	2321	...	...	1052	...	1100	1215	...	1315	...	1415	1515	...	1615	1712	...	1815
Tralee **236** a.	│	...	2235	│	...	│	│	...	│	...	...	1228	...	│	│	...	│	...	│	│	...	│	│	...	│
Cork a.	2052	...	...	2126	...	2155	2255	...	2355	...	...	...	...	1128	1250	...	1350	...	1450	1550	...	1650	1745	...	1850

	⑦ ◇🍷	⑦ ◇🍷	⑦ ◇🍷	⑦ ◇🍷	⑦ ◇🍷	⑦	⑦ ◇	⑦ ◇
Dublin Heuston 240 d.	1700	1800	1825	1900	1910	...	...	2100
Kildare **240** d.	│	│	1905	│	│	...	...	│
Portarlington **240** d.	│	│	1917	│	1955	...	...	2145
Portlaoise d.	│	│	1929	│	│	...	...	│
Ballybrophy d.	│	│	1943	│	│	...	...	│
Templemore d.	│	│	1955	│	│	...	...	│
Thurles d.	1819	1919	2005	2019	2032	...	...	2222
Limerick Junction § d.	│	1941	│	│	2054	2028	...	2244
Limerick § a.	│	│	2052	│	│	2126	...	│
Ennis a.	│	│	*2135*	│	│	...	...	│
Charleville d.	│	│	...	│	2114	...	...	│
Mallow d.	1912	│	...	2112	2129	...	2135	2318
Tralee **246** a.	│	│	...	│	2315	...	│	│
Cork a.	1945	2045	...	2145	...	...	2203	2355

	⚒ ◇🍷	⚒ ◇🍷	⚒ ◇🍷	⚒	⚒h ◇✕	⚒h ◇✕	⚒	⚒h ◇✕	⚒	⚒	⚒	⚒h ◇✕
Cork d.	...	0515	...	...	0630	...	...	0730	0830	...	...	...
Tralee **246** d.	...	│	...	...	│	...	...	│	│	...	...	0715
Mallow d.	...	0537	...	...	0652	...	...	0752	0855	...	...	0857
Charleville d.	...	0552	...	...	│	...	...	│	...	...	...	0910
Ennis d.	...	│	...	...	│	*0645*	...	│	...	0800	...	│
Limerick § d.	0535	│	0635	0655	│	0735	0755	│	...	0840	0855	│
Limerick Junction § d.	│	0614	│	0722	0726	│	0825	0829	...	...	0927	0932
Thurles d.	0618	0635	0718	...	│	0818	...	0849	...	...	...	0952
Templemore d.	0627	0644	0728	...	│	│	...	│	...	...	...	│
Ballybrophy d.	│	0658	│	...	│	0835	...	│	...	...	...	│
Portlaoise d.	0651	0711	0750	...	│	0850	...	│	...	...	...	│
Portarlington **240** d.	│	0724	0804	...	│	│	...	│	...	...	...	│
Kildare **240** d.	0713	│	0814	...	│	│	...	│	...	...	...	│
Dublin Heuston 240 a.	0757	0825	0905	...	0915	0955	...	1020	...	...	...	1115

	⚒	⚒ ◇🍷	⚒ ◇🍷	⚒	⚒ ◇🍷	⚒ ◇🍷	⚒h ◇✕	⚒	⚒h ◇✕	⚒ ◇🍷	⚒ ◇🍷	⚒	⚒	⚒ ◇🍷	⚒h ◇✕	⚒ 🍷	⚒	⚒h ◇✕	⚒ ◇🍷	⚒	⚒	⚒ ◇🍷	⚒	⚒ ◇🍷	
Cork d.	...	0930	1030	...	1130	...	1230	...	1330	...	1430	...	...	1530	1630	...	...	1730	1830	...	...	1930	...	2030	...
Tralee **246** d.	...	│	│	...	│	...	│	...	│	...	│	...	...	│	│	...	...	│	│	...	...	│	...	│	...
Mallow d.	...	0952	1052	...	1152	...	1252	...	1352	...	1452	...	...	1552	1652	...	...	1752	1852	...	...	1952	...	2052	...
Charleville d.	...	│	1107	...	│	...	│	...	│	...	1507	...	...	│	1707	...	...	│	1907	...	...	│	...	│	...
Ennis d.	...	│	│	*1005*	│	*1150*	│	...	│	*1330*	│	1505	...	│	│	...	*1705*	│	│	1845	...	│	...	│	...
Limerick § d.	0955	│	│	1155	│	1235	│	1355	│	1415	│	1545	1555	│	│	1735	1755	│	│	1925	1950	│	...	│	...
Limerick Junction § d.	1023	1026	│	1223	1226	│	│	1423	1426	│	│	...	1623	1626	│	│	1823	1826	│	...	2020	2026	...	│	...
Thurles d.	...	1046	│	...	1246	1317	│	...	1446	1459	1546	...	...	1646	│	1822	...	1846	│	...	...	2046	2100	2143	...
Templemore d.	...	│	1151	...	│	1327	│	...	│	1507	│	...	...	│	1751	1830	...	│	│	...	...	│	2109	│	...
Ballybrophy d.	...	│	│	...	│	1337	│	...	│	│	│	...	...	│	│	1844	...	│	│	...	...	│	2122	│	...
Portlaoise d.	...	1115	│	...	│	1352	1409	...	│	1531	│	...	...	│	│	1857	...	│	│	...	...	│	2139	2214	...
Portarlington **240** d.	...	│	│	...	│	1403	│	...	│	1542	│	...	...	│	│	1909	...	│	│	...	...	│	2149	│	...
Kildare **240** d.	...	│	│	...	│	1415	│	...	│	1554	│	...	...	│	│	1921	...	│	│	...	...	│	2202	│	...
Dublin Heuston 240 a.	...	1225	1320	...	1420	1500	1515	...	1620	1635	1715	...	...	1820	1920	2008	...	2020	2115	...	...	2220	2247	2315	...

	⑦ ◇🍷	⑦ ◇🍷	⑦	⑦ ◇🍷	⑦ ◇🍷	⑦ ◇🍷	⑦ ◇🍷	⑦ ◇🍷	⑦	⑦ ◇🍷	⑦ ◇🍷	⑦ ◇🍷	⑦	⑦🍷 ◇	⑦	⑦ ◇🍷	⑦ ◇🍷	⑦ ◇🍷	⑦	⑦ ◇🍷	⑦ ◇🍷	⑦ ◇🍷	⑦	⑦ 🍷	⑦ 🍷
Cork d.	0730	...	...	0930	...	1130	...	1230	...	1330	...	1430	1450	...	...	1530	...	1630	...	1730	...	1830	...	...	1930
Tralee **246** d.	│	...	...	│	...	│	...	│	...	│	...	│	│	1345	...	│	...	│	...	│	...	│	...	1745	│
Mallow d.	0752	...	...	0952	...	1152	...	1252	...	1352	...	1452	1515	1522	...	1552	...	1652	...	1752	...	1852	...	1927	1952
Charleville d.	0807	...	...	1007	...	1207	...	│	...	│	...	1507	...	1537	...	│	...	1707	...	│	...	1907	...	│	│
Ennis d.	│	*0750*	...	│	*0945*	│	*1145*	│	...	│	*1350*	│	...	│	...	│	*1545*	│	...	│	*1740*	│	...	│	*1910*
Limerick § d.	│	0835	0930	│	1035	│	1235	│	1355	│	1435	│	...	│	1555	│	1635	│	1755	│	1835	│	1855	│	*1955*
Limerick Junction § d.	0829	│	1000	1029	│	│	│	│	1423	1426	│	│	...	│	1623	1626	│	│	1823	1826	│	│	1923	2006	2026
Thurles d.	│	0918	...	│	1118	1246	1318	1343	...	1446	1518	1546	...	1617	...	1646	1718	1746	...	1846	1918	1946	...	2029	2046
Templemore d.	│	0926	...	│	1126	│	1326	│	...	│	1526	│	...	│	...	│	1726	│	...	│	1928	│	...	│	│
Ballybrophy d.	│	0938	...	│	│	│	1338	│	...	│	1538	│	...	│	...	│	1738	│	...	│	1939	│	...	│	│
Portlaoise d.	│	0953	...	│	1150	│	1353	│	...	│	1553	│	...	│	...	│	1753	│	...	│	1958	│	...	│	│
Portarlington **240** d.	│	│	...	│	1202	│	1405	│	...	│	1605	│	...	│	...	│	1805	│	...	│	2012	│	...	│	│
Kildare **240** d.	│	1013	...	│	1214	│	1417	│	...	│	1617	│	...	│	...	│	1817	│	...	│	2024	│	...	│	│
Dublin Heuston 240 a.	1020	1055	...	1220	1257	1420	1500	1515	...	1620	1700	1720	...	1745	...	1820	1905	1920	...	2020	2105	2120	...	2206	2220

H – ①②③④⑥. h – ✕ on Ⓐ, 🍷 on ⑥. ◇ – Also conveys [1]. § – See also Table **247**. ** – Limerick - Ennis: *40 km*. ✣ – Services affected by engineering works on ⑥⑦.

246 (DUBLIN -) CORK - MALLOW - TRALEE IÉ

km		⚒	⚒	⚒	⚒	⚒	⚒	⚒	⚒	⚒	⚒h ◇✕	⚒		⑦	⑦ 🍷	⑦	⑦	⑦	⑦	⑦ ◇🍷	
	Dublin Heuston **245** d.	...	...	*0700*	*0900*	*1100*	*1300*	*1500*	*1600*	*1700*	1830	*2000*	...	...	0810	*1000*	*1100*	*1300*	*1500*	1910	...
0	**Cork** d.	0545	0615	0850	*1030*	*1230*	*1430*	*1655*	1755	*1855*	*2030*	2155	...	0900	*1020*	1210	*1230*	1450	*1630*	*2055*	...
34	**Mallow** d.	0615	0656	0925	1125	1325	1525	1725	1843	1925	2055	2225	...	0938	1052	1245	1325	1528	1725	2129	...
66	Millstreet d.	0647	0719	0948	1148	1348	1548	1748	1906	1948	2123	2248	...	1001	1117	1308	1348	1551	1748	2159	...
100	Killarney d.	...	0750	1029	1229	1429	1629	1829	...	2029	2156	2319	...	1032	1151	1339	1423	1629	1829	2232	...
134	**Tralee** a.	...	0825	1103	1303	1503	1703	1903	...	2103	2235	2353	...	1106	1228	1420	1459	1705	1905	2315	...

		⚒	⚒h ◇✕	⚒	⚒	⚒	⚒	⚒	⚒	⚒			⑦	⑦	⑦ ◇🍷	⑦	⑦	⑦ 🍷	⑦		
Tralee d.	...	0525	0715	0915	1115	1315	1515	1715	1915	2115	...	...	0810	1115	1345	1515	1715	1745	1915	...	...
Killarney d.	...	0600	0752	0950	1150	1350	1550	1750	1950	2157	...	...	0844	1150	1422	1550	1750	1829	1950	...	...
Millstreet d.	...	0624	0822	1017	1217	1417	1617	1817	2017	2224	...	...	0911	1217	1452	1617	1817	1859	2017	...	...
Mallow d.	...	0700	0857	1044	1244	1444	1644	1844	2100	2258	...	...	0945	1256	1522	1641	1856	1927	2051	...	...
Cork a.	...	0724	*0925*	*1111*	*1311*	*1511*	*1745*	*1945*	2126	2324	...	...	1010	1320	│	*1711*	1925	│	2115	...	...
Dublin Heuston **245** a.	...	*0915*	1115	*1320*	*1515*	*1715*	*1920*	*2115*	*2315*	...	...	...	*1220*	*1515*	1745	*1920*	*2120*	2206	...	...	...

NOTES

h – ✕ on Ⓐ, 🍷 on ⑥.
◇ – Also conveys [1].

Will the times be the same in the next edition?

They may be, but many of the services in this timetable are likely to change frequently, and without advance notice.

For details of subscription rates, see the order form at the back of this book.

247 LIMERICK JUNCTION - LIMERICK IÉ

Shuttle service connecting with main-line trains. *35 km*. Journey time: 25–40 minutes. For through services to or from Dublin Heuston see Table **245** above. For notes see Table **246**.

From Limerick Junction ⚒: 0800, 0846, 0943, 1032, 1143, 1232, 1343, 1440, 1543, 1632, 1832, 1952, 2032, 2148, 2248. ⑦: 1012, 1143, 1343, 1432, 1543, 1632, 1743, 1832, 1955, 2058.

From Limerick ⚒: 0655, 0755, 0855, 0955, 1055, 1155, 1255, 1355, 1455, 1555, 1755, 1900, 1950, 2105, 2200. ⑦: 0930, 1055, 1255, 1355, 1455, 1555, 1655, 1755, 1855, 1955.

FRANCE

SEE MAP PAGES 172/3

Operator: Société Nationale des Chemins de Fer Français (SNCF), unless otherwise shown.

Services: Trains convey first and second classes of accommodation unless otherwise shown. **Sleeping** cars (🛏) and couchette cars (▬) are of the normal European types, see page 10 for more details. **Restaurant** cars (✕) offer full dining services at meal times either in a restaurant car or at first class seats, in addition to refreshment services at other times, and may be limited to first class only. **Refreshment** services (🍷) consist of self-service buffet cars, bar cars or trolleys wheeled through the train. Catering services shown in the tables may not be available for the full length of the journey and may be suspended at weekends and holidays. It is important in France to state whether meals may be required when booking first class travel, as some meals are served at your reserved seat. Night trains often have coin-operated vending machines offering light refreshments. Where two **TGV** units are coupled together, they will often carry different train numbers for reservation purposes.

Timings: **Valid December 9, 2007 - June 14, 2008**. Engineering work can often affect schedules; variations are shown where possible but other changes may occur. Amended services operate on and around **public holidays** and, whilst we try to show holiday variations, passengers are advised to confirm their train times locally before travelling during these periods. Public holidays are Jan. 1, Easter Monday (Mar. 24), May 1, 8, Whit Monday (May 12), July 14, Aug. 15, Nov. 1, 11, Dec. 25.

Tickets: **Seat reservations** are available (for a small fee) on most long distance trains and are compulsory for travel by all *TGV* trains and trains marked Ⓡ. Advance reservations are strongly recommended for travel to ski resorts during the season. **Supplements** (which include the cost of seat reservation) are payable for travel in sleeping cars and couchettes and for travel on all *TGV* trains and other trains marked ⁄. Rail tickets must be date-stamped by the holder before boarding the train using the self-service validating machines (composteurs) at the platform entrances – this applies to all tickets except passes and hand-written tickets.

Note: The *TGV* services **Lille Europe - Charles de Gaulle ✈ - Marne-la-Vallée - Lyon / Bordeaux / Rennes / Nantes** are shown in the International section (Table **11**).

PARIS - LILLE - TOURCOING — 250

TGV Nord high-speed trains

For slower trains via Douai see Table **256**. For **Charles de Gaulle ✈ - Lille** see Table **11**. Certain trains continue to Dunkerque, Calais or Boulogne - see Table **265**.

km		*TGV* 7001 ① g	*TGV* 7005 Ⓐ	*TGV* 7207 Ⓐ	*TGV* 7211	*TGV* 7015 ①–⑥ n	*TGV* 7021	*TGV* 7229	*TGV* 7029 ⑦ e	*TGV* 7033	*TGV* 7235	*TGV* 7043	*TGV* 7045 Ⓐ	*TGV* 7049	*TGV* 7053 Ⓐ	*TGV* 7059	*TGV* 7061 Ⓐ	*TGV* 7065	*TGV* 7275 Ⓐ	*TGV* 7277	*TGV* 7281 Ⓐ	*TGV* 7079 ⑤ f	*TGV* 7285 ‡	
0	**Paris Nord** d.	0628	0658	0728	0758	0828	0858	0958	0958	1058	1158	1258	1428	1458	1528	1558	1628	1658	1728	1758	1828	1849	1858	...
227	**Lille Europe** a.	|	|	0827	|	|	|	1057	1057	|	|	|	|	|	|	|	|	|	1827	|	1926	|	1956	...
227	**Lille Flandres** a.	0730	0800	...	0900	0930	1000	...	...	1200	1303	1400	1530	1600	1630	1700	1730	1800	...	1900	...	1951	...	...
227	**Lille Flandres 405** d.	...	...	...	0912	...	...	...	...	...	1313	...	...	...	...	...	...	...	...	1910	...	...	...	...
237	Roubaix **405** a.	...	...	...	0926	...	...	...	...	...	1327	...	...	...	...	...	...	...	...	1924	...	...	...	...
240	**Tourcoing 405** a.	...	...	...	0932	...	...	...	...	...	1333	...	...	...	...	...	...	...	...	1930	...	...	...	...

	TGV 7087 Ⓐ	*TGV* 7291 ①–⑥ n	*TGV* 7091 ⑦ e	*TGV* 7093 ⑥ t	*TGV* 7089 Ⓐ ⊡	*TGV* 7293 ⑦ e	*TGV* 7097 ⑤⑦ q	*TGV* 7099 ⊡			*TGV* 7000 Ⓐ	*TGV* 7002 Ⓐ	*TGV* 7206 ①–⑥ n	*TGV* 7214 Ⓐ	*TGV* 7218 ⑥ t	*TGV* 7220 Ⓐ	*TGV* 7222 ⑦ e	*TGV* 7022 ①–⑥ n	*TGV* 7028 Ⓐ	
Paris Nord d.	1928	1958	1958	2058	2058	2058	2158	2258	...	**Tourcoing 405** d.	...	...	0630	...	...	...	0747	...	...	...
Lille Europe a.	|	|	|	|	|	|	|	|	...	Roubaix **405** d.	...	...	0636	...	...	...	0753	...	...	...
Lille Flandres a.	2030	2100	2100	2200	2219	2200	2300	0018	...	**Lille Flandres 405** a.	...	...	0650	...	...	...	0807	...	...	...
Lille Flandres 405 d.	...	2112	...	...	...	2212	...	...	...	**Lille Flandres** d.	0600	0630	0700	...	...	...	0817	0817	0830	...
Roubaix **405** a.	...	2126	...	...	...	2225	...	...	...	**Lille Europe** d.	|	|	|	0732	0732	0802	|	|	|	...
Tourcoing 405 a.	...	2132	...	...	...	2232	...	...	...	**Paris Nord** a.	0702	0732	0802	0832	0832	0902	0920	0920	0932	...

	TGV 7030	*TGV* 7036	*TGV* 7040	*TGV* 7246	*TGV* 7050	*TGV* 7254 ①–⑥ n	*TGV* 7256	*TGV* 7058 Ⓐ	*TGV* 7062	*TGV* 7066 Ⓐ	*TGV* 7070	*TGV* 7072 Ⓐ	*TGV* 7074	*TGV* 7082 Ⓐ	*TGV* 7288 Ⓑ h	*TGV* 7088 ⑥ t	*TGV* 7092 ⑥⑦ b	*TGV* 7292 Ⓐ	*TGV* 7294 ⑤⑦ q	*TGV* 7098 ⑥ t	*TGV* 7298 ⑦ e	*TGV* 7096 Ⓐ ⊡		
Tourcoing 405 d.	...	...	...	1130	...	...	1430	...	...	...	...	...	...	...	...	...	...	...	2030	...	...	...	...	...
Roubaix **405** d.	...	...	...	1136	...	...	1436	...	...	...	...	...	...	...	...	...	...	...	2036	...	...	...	...	...
Lille Flandres 405 a.	...	...	...	1150	...	...	1450	...	...	...	...	...	...	...	...	...	...	...	2050	...	...	...	...	...
Lille Flandres d.	...	1000	1100	1200	1300	...	1500	1530	1600	1630	1700	1730	1800	1830	...	1900	...	...	2100	...	...	...	...	...
Lille Europe d.	0902	|	|	|	|	1329	|	|	|	|	|	|	|	|	1902	|	2002	2011	|	2202	2202	2209	...	...
Paris Nord a.	1002	1102	1202	1302	1402	1429	1602	1632	1702	1732	1802	1832	1902	1932	2002	2002	2102	2111	2202	2302	2302	2323	...	...

b – Also Dec. 25, Jan. 1, Mar. 24, May 1, 8, 12.
e – Also Dec. 25, Jan. 1, Mar. 24, May 12.
f – Also Apr. 30, May 7; not May 2.
g – Also Dec. 26, Jan. 2, Mar. 25, May 13; not Dec. 24, 31, Mar. 24, May 12.
h – Not May 1, 8.
n – Not Dec. 25, Jan. 1, Mar. 24, May 12.
q – Also Dec. 25, Jan. 1, Mar. 24, Apr. 30, May 7, 12; not May 2.
t – Also May 1, 8.

TGV –Ⓡ, supplement payable.
⊡ – Via Arras (Table **256**).
‡ – Also runs as **7289** on ⑦.

PARIS - LAON — 251

km		⚒	⚒	†	⑥	Ⓐ	Ⓐ		Ⓐ	†	⑥	Ⓐ		Ⓐ	⑥	Ⓐ	Ⓐ	Ⓐ	Ⓒ	Ⓐ			Ⓐ		
0	**Paris Nord** d.	0558	0707	0806	0806	0831	0957	...	1202	1246	1326	1326	...	1448	1448	1530	1631	1745	1752	1847	...	2005	2118	...	...
61	Crépy-en-Valois d.	0651	0744	0844	0856	0908	1038	...	1244	1323	1402	1403	...	1536	1537	1612	1706	1831	1834	1927	...	2043	2153	...	...
105	Soissons d.	0730	0814	0921	0928	0938	1110	...	1316	1357	1431	1434	...	1614	1615	1645	1735	1904	1904	1958	...	2113	2223	...	...
140	**Laon** a.	0758	0838	0951	0954	1004	1136	...	1340	1429	1456	1501	...	1652	1653	1712	1804	1933	1930	2023	...	2139	2248	...	...

	Ⓐ	Ⓐ	Ⓐ	⑥	†	⚒	†	⚒		Ⓐ	⚒	†	Ⓐ	⑥	†	Ⓐ	†	Ⓐ	⑥		Ⓑ	Ⓐ	⚒	†	Ⓐ	†
Laon d.	0506	0532	0635	0640	0710	0753	0848	0933	...	1119	1222	1231	1405	1554	1555	1621	1711	1718	1739	...	1800	1907	2011	2022	2114	2106
Soissons d.	0533	0600	0707	0708	0737	0822	0916	1001	...	1149	1254	1258	1432	1625	1623	1649	1738	1750	1806	...	1829	1935	2039	2051	2143	2133
Crépy-en-Valois d.	0601	0630	0741	0740	0806	0852	0947	1031	...	1220	1329	1330	1502	1657	1702	1724	1816	1821	1841	...	1900	2006	2110	2122	2215	2208
Paris Nord a.	0637	0706	0826	0818	0853	0927	1022	1110	...	1253	1417	1420	1539	1749	1753	1802	1855	1902	1918	...	1937	2039	2158	2201	2305	2305

AMIENS - LAON - REIMS — 252

Some trains 2nd class only

km		⑥	Ⓐ	Ⓐ	†	⚒b	⚒	†	⑥	Ⓐ	Ⓑ	⑥	Ⓐ	Ⓐ	Ⓐ	Ⓒ	Ⓒ	Ⓐ	†	Ⓒ	Ⓐ	⚒	Ⓐ	Ⓐ	†
0	**Amiens** d.	0602	0612	0724	0800	0830	...	...	...	...	1226	1237	1453	...	1612	1612	...	...	...	1759	1806	1847	...	1927	2125
	Cambrai 257 d.	|	|	|	|	|	0858	...	...	...	|	|	|	...	|	|	...	...	...	|	|	|	...	|	|
	St Quentin **255/7** d.	|	|	|	|	|	0941	...	...	...	|	|	|	1637	|	|	1715	1730	...	|	|	|	1940	|	|
80	Tergnier **255/7** a.	0712	0720	0832	0907	0932	0958	...	...	...	1334	1344	1549	1654	1714	1720	1737	1750	...	1908	1911	1957	1959	2027	2228
80	Tergnier d.	0723	0733	0833	0912	...	1000	...	...	1233	1346	1354	1550	1656	1722	...	1751	1806	...	1920	1924	...	2002	*2036*c	2230
108	Laon a.	0753	0803	0901	0935	...	1023	...	...	1301	1411	1421	1613	1720	1745	...	1818	1831	...	1946	1950	...	2028	*2101*c	2252
108	Laon d.	...	0805	...	...	...	1027	1214	1256	1302	...	...	*1659*	*1726*	...	...	*1837*r	1836	1925	1947	...	...	2030	...	...
160	**Reims** a.	...	0843	...	...	...	1107	1259	1343	1354	...	...	*1742*	*1807*	...	...	*1925*r	1925	2013	2026	...	...	2105	...	...

	Ⓐ	⚒	Ⓐ	⚒	†	⚒	Ⓐ	†	Ⓐ	Ⓒ	Ⓐ	Ⓐ	⑥	Ⓐ	⑥	Ⓐ	Ⓒ	Ⓐ	Ⓐ	†	Ⓐ	Ⓐ	†	⚒	
Reims d.	...	...	...	0627	...	...	0735	1058	1118	...	1217	...	1219	1509	1509	...	...	...	1653	1705	1726	...	1822	1845	...
Laon a.	...	...	...	0709	...	...	0811	1143	1152	...	1311	...	1312	1543	1545	...	...	...	1737	1741	1820	...	1910	1940	...
Laon d.	0553	0628	0654	0711	0720	0742	0814	...	1156	1202	...	1313	1313	1544	...	1625	1706	*1722*	1739	1743	1825	...	...	...	2008
Tergnier a.	0619	0653	0720	0733	0745	0809	0837	...	1222	1225	...	1339	1337	1608	...	1651	1732	*1748*	1758	1805	1852	...	...	...	2035
Tergnier **255/7** d.	0624	0655	0722	0735	0747	0812	...	...	1233	1232	...	1341	...	1614	...	1652	1742	1807	1759	...	1854	1856	...	...	2036
St Quentin **255/7** a.	0641	|	|	0755	|	|	...	...	|	|	...	|	...	1630	...	|	|	|	1818	...	|	1917	...	...	|
Cambrai 257 a.	...	|	|	0845	|	|	...	...	|	|	...	|	...	...	...	|	|	|	...	...	|	...	...	...	|
Amiens a.	...	0801	0825	...	0843	0911	...	...	1337	1338	...	1449	...	...	...	1753	1848	1913	...	...	2001	...	...	...	2144

b – Not Mar. 10 - 15.
c – Daily.
r – ⑥ only.

Additional journey on ⚒: Laon d. 0630 - Reims a. 0724.

🚐 AMIENS - TGV HAUTE-PICARDIE — 253

SNCF 🚐 service

🚐 runs to connect with *TGV* services at TGV Haute-Picardie station (Table **11**). Journey time 40 minutes. Available only to passengers with appropriate *TGV* tickets and reservations.

Amiens depart: 0610, 0902, 1018, 1203, 1215, 1534, 1631, 1718, 2135, 2214

TGV Haute-Picardie depart: 0715, 0956, 1131, 1255, 1310, 1626, 1724, 1821, 1846 Ⓐ, 2147, 2228, 2307.

Subject to confirmation

LONDON
BELGIUM
GERMANY
SWITZ.

Brussels
Gent
Namur
Charleroi
Mons
Tournai
Givet
Luxembourg
Saarbrücken
Wissembourg
Haguenau
STRASBOURG
Kehl 912
Basel
Bern
Lausanne
Le Locle
Neuchâtel
Martigny 572
Chamonix
Aosta

Dunkerque
De Panne
Calais
Fréthun
Boulogne
Étaples
Hazebrouck
Tourcoing
LILLE
Béthune
St Pol
Arras
Douai
Valenciennes
Jeumont
Maubeuge
Aulnoye
Cambrai
Hirson
Charleville-Mézières
Sedan
Longwy
Longuyon
Thionville
METZ
Forbach
Sarrebourg
Lunéville
NANCY
Lorraine TGV
Toul
St Dié
Colmar
Mulhouse
Épinal
Remiremont
Belfort
Verdun
Meuse TGV
Bar le Duc
Vitry
St Dizier
Châlons en Champagne
REIMS
Champagne Ardenne TGV
Épernay
Laon
St Quentin
Tergnier
Haute Picardie
Compiègne
Amiens
Longueau
Abbeville
Le Tréport
Creil
Beauvais
CDG
Marne la Vallée (Disneyland)
PARIS
Versailles
Dreux
Chartres
Fontainebleau
Troyes
Chaumont
Langres
Culmont
Laroche
Auxerre
Avallon
Autun
Étang
Le Creusot
Montchanin
DIJON
Besançon
Dole
Frasne
Pontarlier
Vallorbe
Morez
St Claude
Chalon sur Saône
Mâcon
Paray
TGV
GENÈVE
Évian
La Roche sur Foron
St Gervais
Culoz
Annecy
Aix les Bains
Saint Exupéry
LYON
see inset
Roanne
Vichy
St Germain des Fossés
Moulins
Nevers
Saincaize
CLERMONT FERRAND
Gannat
Montluçon
Bourges
Vierzon
ORLÉANS
Les Aubrais
Châteaudun
Blois
St Pierre des Corps
TOURS
Chinon
Châteauroux
Limoges
Poitiers
Saumur
Angers
Cholet
Niort
La Rochelle
Rochefort
Saintes
La Roche sur Yon
Les Sables d'Olonne
NANTES
Savenay
St Nazaire
Le Croisic
Redon
Vannes
Auray
Quiberon
Lorient
Rosporden
Quimper
BREST
Landerneau
Morlaix
Roscoff
Plouaret
Lannion
Guingamp
St Brieuc
Lamballe
Dinan
Dinard
St Malo
Dol
Mont St Michel
RENNES
Laval
LE MANS
Alençon
Surdon
Argentan
Villedieu
Folligny
Granville
Coutances
Lison
Cherbourg
Bayeux
CAEN
Mézidon
Lisieux
Trouville-Deauville
Dives
Serquigny
ROUEN
Dieppe
Fécamp
Le Havre

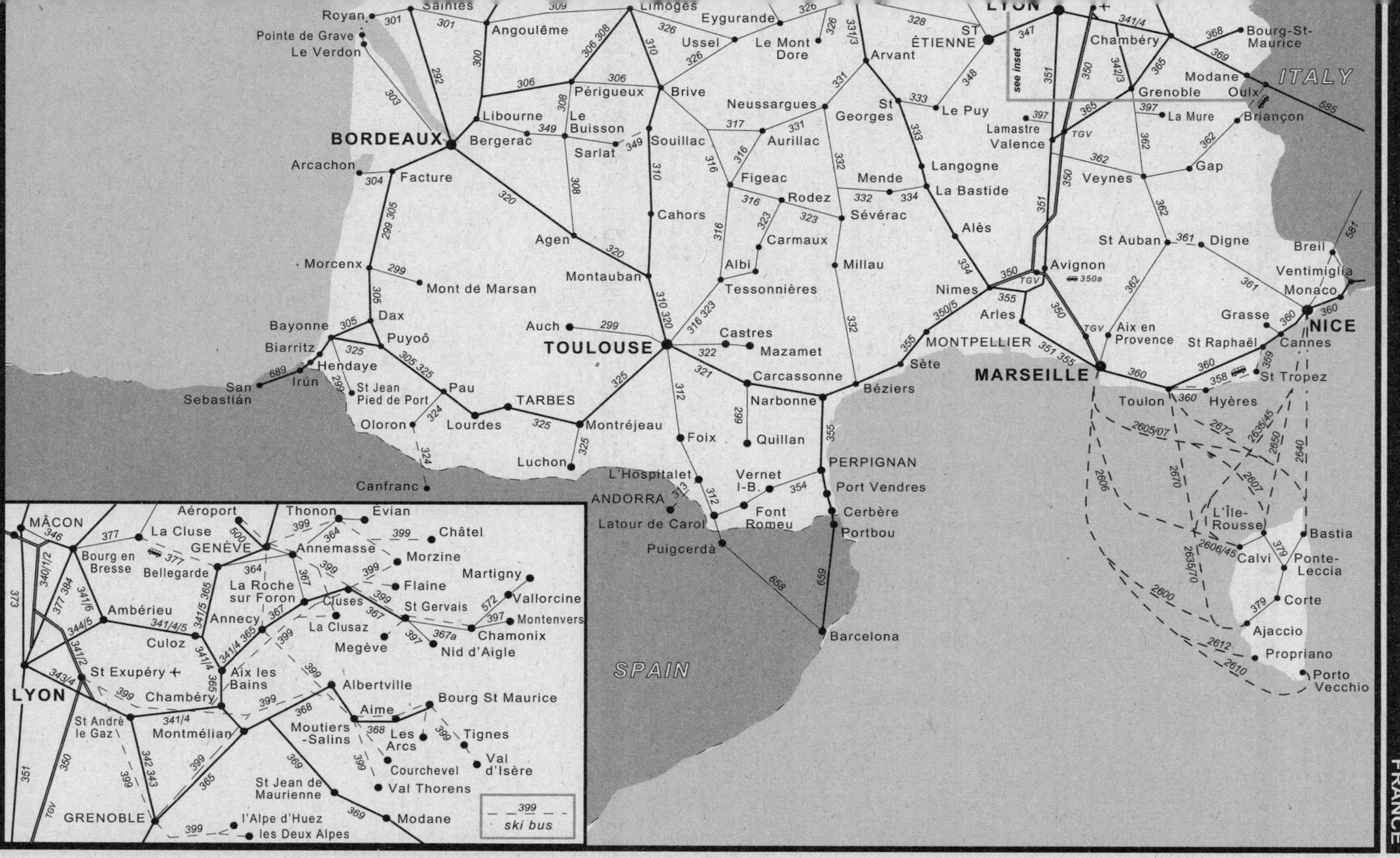
ITALY
SPAIN
Royan
Saintes
Pointe de Grave
Le Verdon
Angoulême
Limoges
Eygurande
Ussel
Le Mont Dore
Arvant
ST ÉTIENNE
LYON
see inset
Chambéry
Bourg-St-Maurice
Modane
Oulx
Grenoble
La Mure
Briançon
Périgueux
Brive
Neussargues
St Georges
Le Puy
Lamastre
Valence
Libourne
Bergerac
Le Buisson
Sarlat
Souillac
Aurillac
BORDEAUX
Arcachon
Facture
Figeac
Rodez
Mende
Langogne
La Bastide
Sévérac
Veynes
Gap
Cahors
Carmaux
Agen
Alès
St Auban
Digne
Breil
Ventimiglia
Monaco
Morcenx
Mont de Marsan
Montauban
Albi
Tessonnières
Millau
Nimes
Avignon
Arles
Aix en Provence
Grasse
NICE
Cannes
St Raphaël
Dax
Bayonne
Biarritz
Puyoô
Auch
TOULOUSE
Castres
Mazamet
MONTPELLIER
Sète
MARSEILLE
Hendaye
Irún
San Sebastián
St Jean Pied de Port
Pau
Carcassonne
Narbonne
Béziers
Toulon
Hyères
St Tropez
TARBES
Oloron
Lourdes
Montréjeau
Luchon
Foix
Quillan
PERPIGNAN
Canfranc
L'Hospitalet
ANDORRA
Latour de Carol
Puigcerdà
Vernet I-B.
Font Romeu
Port Vendres
Cerbère
Portbou
Barcelona
L'Île-Rousse
Calvi
Bastia
Ponte-Leccia
Corte
Ajaccio
Propriano
Porto Vecchio
MÂCON
Aéroport
La Cluse
GENÈVE
Thonon
Évian
Annemasse
Châtel
Morzine
Bourg en Bresse
Bellegarde
La Roche sur Foron
Flaine
Martigny
Vallorcine
Montenvers
Cluses
St Gervais
Chamonix
Nid d'Aigle
Ambérieu
Annecy
La Clusaz
Megève
Culoz
Aix les Bains
St Exupéry
LYON
Chambéry
Albertville
Aime
Bourg St Maurice
Les Arcs
Tignes
Val d'Isère
Moutiers -Salins
Courchevel
Val Thorens
St André le Gaz
Montmélian
St Jean de Maurienne
Modane
GRENOBLE
l'Alpe d'Huez
les Deux Alpes
399
ski bus

254 AMIENS - COMPIÈGNE

km		Ⓐ	⑥	⚒	†	Ⓐ		Ⓐ		⚒	†	⚒	†
0	**Amiens** d.	0553	0608	0805	0920	1049	1224	1439	1617	1733	1837	1857	2224
5	Longueau d.	0604	0614	0817	0927	1056	1229	1446	1624	1741	1845	1903	2231
76	**Compiègne** a.	0734	0738	0930	1034	1203	1351	1556	1758r	1856	2001	2021	2341

	⚒	⚒	†	①g	Ⓐ		Ⓐ		Ⓐ	†	⚒	†
Compiègne d.	0602	0655	0754	0811	1045	1229	1435	1623	1724	1840	1904	2020
Longueau a.	0720	0811	0903	0927	1158	1349	1548	1739	1855	1958	2013	2124
Amiens a.	0727	0822	0910	0934	1205	1356	1555	1746	1902	2005	2020	2131

g – Also Dec. 26, Jan. 2, Mar. 25, May 2, 9, 13; not Mar. 24, May 12.

r – 1751 on Ⓒ.

255 PARIS - COMPIÈGNE - ST QUENTIN - MAUBEUGE

km		12301	12305		12309	12313	12319	12321		12327	12325			12331	2335		12337	12339		12341	12343			12349		
		Ⓐ	①-⑥	Ⓐ	Ⓑ		①-⑥	⚒	†	Ⓒ	Ⓐ	Ⓒ	Ⓐ			Ⓐ	Ⓐ	Ⓑ	†	①-⑥		Ⓒ	Ⓐ	Ⓑ	⑥	Ⓑ
			n	⊡	s	u	k			f								h		n				h		
0	**Paris Nord** ▶ d.	0640	0734	0749	0837	1037	1207	1237	1243	1437	1437	1616	1616	1637	1737	1740	1804	1837	1840	1907	1937	1943	2010	2104	2134	2234
51	Creil ▶ d.	0707	|	0823	|	|	1233	|	1316	|	|	1643	1643	|	|	1807	|	|	1917	1934	|	2019	2042	|	2208	2305
84	**Compiègne** ▶ d.	0726	0816	0847	0917	1118	1259	1319	1339	1518	1532	1706	1722	1719	1819	1829	1853	1925	1941	1959	2018	2054	2105	2145	2247	2327
108	Noyon d.	0741	|	0900	|	|	1314	|	1353	|	|	1719	1744	|	|	1843	1908	|	1955	2013	|	2117	2127	2200	2302	2343
124	Chauny d.	0754	|	0911	|	|	1326	|	1405	|	|	1731	1756	|	|	1855	1920	|	2006	2026	|	2131	2139	2212	2313	2355
131	Tergnier 257 d.	0802	|	0918	|	|	1334	|	1412	|	|	1743	1804	|	|	1901	1928	|	2017	2034	|	2138	2145	2220	2320	0001
154	**St Quentin 257** a.	0816	0848	...	0951	1153	1348	1352	1427	1551	1605	1802	1822	1752	1852	▬	1942	1957	2034	2049	2053	...	...	2234	2334	0019
154	**St Quentin 257** d.	...	0850	...	...	1155	...	1354	...	1553	1607	...	...	1754	1854	2	...	1959	...	...	2055	...	...	2236x	...	...
181	Busigny 257 d.	...	|	...	...	|	...	|	...	|	|	...	...	|	1912	1920	...	|	...	...	|	...	...	|	...	...
207	*Cambrai Ville 257* a.	...	|	...	...	|	...	|	...	|	|	...	...	|	1934	|	...	|	...	...	|	...	...	|	...	...
217	Aulnoye Aymeries 262 d.	...	0924	...	...	1228	...	1427	...	1626	1638	...	...	1827	...	1946	...	2034	...	...	2127	...	...	2315x	...	...
229	**Maubeuge 262** d.	...	0934	...	...	1238	...	1438	...	1636	1649	...	...	1837	...	2000c	...	2045	...	...	2137	...	...	...	...	...

	12300		12302	12304	2306			12308	12312	2312	12316	12318	12320		12326		12330	12330	12334	12336	12338	12340		12342		12346
	①-⑤	⑥	①-⑥	Ⓐ	Ⓐ	Ⓒ	Ⓐ		Ⓐ	Ⓒ	Ⓐ			†		Ⓐ	Ⓐ	Ⓑ		Ⓑ	Ⓒ	Ⓐ	Ⓑ	⑦	†	⑦
	q		n	m				b		z			w		⊕			y	△	y				g		e
Maubeuge 262 d.	...	...	...	0547	...	...	...	0647	...	...	...	1050	...	...	1450	...	1549	...	1628v	1750	1849	1913	...	1945	...	2042
Aulnoye Aymeries 262 d.	...	...	...	0559	...	...	...	0659	...	...	...	1102	...	...	1502	...	1601	...	1640v	1802	1901	1925	...	1957	...	2055
Cambrai Ville 257 d.	...	...	...	|	0612	...	...	|	...	0728	...	|	...	...	|	...	|	...	|	|	|	|	...	|	...	|
Busigny 257 d.	...	...	...	|	0642	0645r	0651	|	...	0757	...	|	...	...	|	...	|	...	|	|	|	|	...	|	...	|
St Quentin 257 a.	...	...	...	0629	0656	0703r	0709	0730	...	0811	...	1130	...	...	1531	...	1630	...	1709v	1832	1934	1954	...	2030	...	2125
St Quentin 257 d.	0507	0508	0600	0631	0658	0703	0711	0732	0812	0813	1008	1132	1213	1429	1533	...	1632	1632	1711	1834	1936	1956	2000a	2032	2053	2127
Tergnier 257 d.	0523	0523	0617	|	|	0719	0726	|	0828	0828	1024	|	1230	1448	|	1608	|	|	1728	|	|	|	2012	|	2108	|
Chauny d.	0531	0530	0625	|	|	0726	0732	|	0837	0837	1032	|	1238	1454	|	1615	|	|	1736	|	|	|	2020	|	2114	|
Noyon d.	0543	0541	0637	|	0724	0736	0744	|	0849	0849	1043	|	1249	1506	|	1626	|	|	1748	|	|	|	2032	|	2124	|
Compiègne ▶ d.	0558	0555	0652	0708	0739	0750	0759	0808	0905	0904	1059	1208	1304	1527	1609	1641	1709	1709	1804	1909	2012	2032	2047	2108	2139	2202
Creil ▶ d.	0624	0624	|	|	|	0814	0821	|	0924	0924	1124	|	1324	1605	|	1703	|	|	1823	|	|	|	2110	|	2207	|
Paris Nord ▶ a.	0650	0659	0741	0750	0820	0847	0847	0853	0953	0953	1150	1250	1350	1638	1650	1738	1750	1750	1850	1950	2056	2114	2144	2150	2241	2244

▶	⑥	†d	Ⓐ	Ⓒ	⑦t	⑥	Ⓐ◧	⑥	Ⓐ	Ⓒ	Ⓐ	
Paris Nord d.	0634	0640	*0707*	0904	*1137*	*1243*	1422	*1619*	1707	1749	1819	2134
Creil d.	0708	0714	0739	0944	1214	1343	1459	1707	1741	1825	1853	2208
Compiègne a.	0751	0752	0805	1024	1251	1420	1540	1746	1811	1908	1920	2246

▶	Ⓐ	⚒	†◐	⑥	Ⓐ	Ⓒ	Ⓒ	Ⓐ▷	Ⓑ	⑥	Ⓑ	⑥
Compiègne d.	0504	0620	0650	0657	0657	1045	1226	1242	1719	1741	1822	2023
Creil d.	0543	0704	0714	0735	0747	1115	1307	1307	1803	1806	1905	2107
Paris Nord a.	0617	0738	0741	0805	0817	1150	1341	1341	1838	1838	1941	2141

a – Ⓐ only.
b – Not Dec. 25, Jan. 1.
c – Ⓒ (not Mar. 15, 16).
d – To Tergnier (a. 0833), St Quentin (a. 0901).
e – Also Dec. 25, Jan. 1, Mar. 24, May 12; not Mar. 23, May 11.
f – Not Mar. 23, May 11.
g – Also Dec. 25, Jan. 1, Mar. 24, May 12; not Dec. 23, 30, Mar. 23, May 11.
h – Not May 1, 8.
k – Not Dec. 25, Jan. 1, Mar. 24, May 2, 9, 12.
m – Not May 2, 9.
n – Not Dec. 25, Jan. 1, Mar. 24, May 12.
q – Not Dec. 25, May 1, 8.
r – † only.
s – Not Mar. 10-14, 17-21, May 1, 2, 8, 9.
t – To Tergnier (a. 1333), St Quentin (a. 1353).
u – Not on ①-⑤ Mar. 10-28; not May 2, 9.
v – ⑦ (also Dec. 25, Jan. 1, Mar. 24, May 12).
w – Not Mar. 10-14, 17-21, 23, 25-28, May 11.
x – ⑦ (also Dec. 25, Jan. 1, Mar. 24, May 12; not Mar. 23).
y – Not Mar. 23, May 1, 8, 11.
z – On Apr. 12, 13 by 🚌 Tergnier - Compiègne.
▶ – For additional local trains see panel below main table. Additional suburban trains run Paris - Creil and v.v.
◐ – From Tergnier (depart 0611).
◧ – To Tergnier (arrive 1613).
⊕ – Not Mar. 17-21, 24-28, May 2, 9.
△ – Not May 2, 9.
▷ – By 🚌 Compiègne - Creil Mar. 17-28.
⊡ – By 🚌 Compiègne - Tergnier Mar. 10-21.

256 PARIS and AMIENS - ARRAS - DOUAI - VALENCIENNES and LILLE

Most trains (except *TGV*) are 2nd class only. For fast trains Paris - Lille see Table 250

km ★					◇				*TGV* 7101	*TGV* 7105				*TGV* 7111	*TGV* 7113		*TGV* 5163			*TGV* 7121					*TGV* 5422
		Ⓐ	⚒	Ⓐ	Ⓐ	⑥	Ⓐ	⑥	①	①-⑥	Ⓐ	⑥	†	Ⓒ	Ⓐ			Ⓒ	Ⓐ	⑤⑥	Ⓐ	†	⑥	Ⓐ	
									g	n	R	R					W		R	v	d				S
0	**Paris Nord 265** d.	...	...	...	...	...	...	...	0722	0752	...	...	...	0952	1022	...	...	...	...	1222	...	...	...	...	...
131	**Amiens** d.	...	...	0601	...	0635	0655	0705	|	|	0816	0921	0930	|	|	1050	...	1155	1208	|	1337	...	1359	1408	...
162	Albert d.	...	...	0625	...	0657	0721	0725	|	|	0839	0943	0952	|	|	1119	...	1219	1228	|	1359	...	1421	1428	...
199	Arras 265 a.	...	...	0650	...	0742	0742	0746	0812	0842	0859	1003	1015	1042	1112	1142	...	1246	1248	1312	1418	...	1444	1452	...
199	Arras d.	0525	0609	0652	0747	...	0744	0748	0815	0845	0900	1005	1017	1045	1115	1147	1154	1248	1250	1315	1419	1417	1446	1454	1523
224	Douai a.	0550	0637	0706	|	...	0802	0804	0830	0900	0913	1019	1032	1059	1129	1202	1207	1303	1304	1330	1437	1437	1500	1508	1538
224	Douai 257 ▶ d.	0557	0639	0708	|	...	...	0806	0838	0910	0915	1021	1034	1109	1137	1204	1210	1305	1306	1338	1439	1439	1502	1510	1541
260	Valenciennes ▶ a.	|	|	|	|	...	...	|	0904	0937	|	|	|	1135	1202	|	|	|	|	1404	|	|	|	|	|
257	**Lille Europe** a.	|	|	|	0807	...	...	|	...	...	|	|	|	...	...	|	|	|	|	...	|	|	|	|	1559
257	**Lille Flandres 257** a.	0636	0716	0730	...	...	...	0830	...	...	0936	1042	1056	...	...	1230	1235	1327	1327	...	1508	1508	1523	1529	...

		TGV 7131			*TGV* 7137	*TGV* 7139		*TGV* 7141	*TGV* 7343			*TGV* 7145	*TGV* 5279		*TGV* 7347		*TGV* 7149		*TGV* 7151	*TGV* 5192	*TGV* 7155	*TGV* 5181	*TGV* 5288	*TGV* 7159	*TGV* 7099
			Ⓐ	⑥	⑤	①-④		Ⓑ	Ⓐ	†	Ⓐ			Ⓐ	Ⓑ	Ⓐ	①-④		⑤-⑦	Ⓐ	Ⓐ	Ⓒ		⑦	
					f	m		h					W		h		m⊕	R	b⊕	W	⊕	W	W	e⊗	
Paris Nord 265 d.	...	1452	...	...	1622	1652	...	1722	1752	...	...	1822	...	...	1852	...	1922	...	1952	...	2058	...	...	2152	2258
Amiens d.	...	|	1600z	...	|	|	1658x	|	|	1751	1803	|	...	1852	|	...	|	1939	|	...	|	...	...	|	|
Albert d.	...	|	1623	...	|	|	1722	|	|	1814	1824	|	...	1914	|	...	|	2001	|	...	|	...	...	|	|
Arras 265 a.	...	1542	1648	...	1712	1741	1745	1812	1842	1839	1845	1912	...	1939	1942	...	2012	2020	2042	...	2149	...	...	2242	2348
Arras d.	1539	1548	1650	1650	1715	1744	1747	1815	...	1841	1847	1915	1927	...	...	1951	2015	2022	2048	2052	2156	2202	2240	2245	2354
Douai a.	1556	1604	1704	1704	1729	1758	1804	1829	...	1854	1910	1929	1940	...	...	2007	2029	2035	2103	2107	2211	2214	2254	2300	|
Douai 257 ▶ d.	1558	1612	1706	1706	1737	1806	1806	1837	...	1856	1912	1937	1943	...	...	2009	2037	2037	2111	2110	2219	2217	2257	2310	|
Valenciennes ▶ a.	|	1639	|	|	1802	1840	|	1903	...	|	|	2003	|	...	...	|	2104	|	2137	|	2246	|	|	2337	|
Lille Europe a.	|	...	|	|	...	...	|	...	...	|	|	...	|	...	...	|	...	|	...	2128	...	2238	2318	...	|
Lille Flandres 257 a.	1621	...	1730	1727	...	...	1831	...	...	1914	1941	...	2003	...	...	2031	...	2058	...	...	...	...	...	...	0018

	TGV 7100	*TGV* 5200	*TGV* 7102			*TGV* 5110	*TGV* 7104			*TGV* 7108				*TGV* 7110	*TGV* 5214			*TGV* 7118		*TGV* 5402				*TGV* 7124	
	Ⓐ		Ⓐ	⑥	Ⓐ		Ⓐ	⑥	Ⓐ	①-⑥	⑥	†	Ⓐ	⑦		⚒			Ⓐ		⑥	Ⓐ	†	①-⑥	Ⓐ
		W			R	W				n	R		△	e	W			L	R	S				n	
Lille Flandres 257 d.	...	...	...	0620	0620	...	...	0704	0705	...	0805	0805	0805	...	...	0910	1010	...	1103	...	1203	1202	1202	...	1257
Lille Europe d.	...	0558	...	|	|	0643	...	|	|	...	|	|	|	...	0846	|	|	...	|	1121	|	|	|	...	|
Valenciennes ▶ d.	0533	|	0600	|	|	|	0638	|	|	0733	|	|	|	0813	|	|	|	1006	|	|	|	|	|	1156	|
Douai 257 ▶ a.	0558	0625	0625	0640	0642	0706	0704	0727	0726	0759	0825	0824	0831	0841	0906	0934	1035	1032	1122	1139	1224	1224	1224	1222	1320
Douai d.	0606	0628	0633	0642	0644	0709	0712	0728	0727	0810	0827	0826	0833	0849	0908	0936	1037	1042	1124	1142	1226	1226	1226	1232	1322
Arras a.	0620	0644	0649	0655	0659	0724	0728	0744	0741	0825	0841	0839	0847	0903	0925	0954	1054	1059	1141	1155	1240	1242	1242	1246	1338
Arras 265 d.	0623	...	0656	0657	0701	...	0735	0746	0743	0835	0843	0841	0849	0906	...	...	1056c	1106	1143	...	1242	1244	...	1249	1340
Albert d.	|	...	|	0716	0720	...	|	0811	0808	|	0904	0904	0915	|	...	...	1122c	|	1202	...	1310	1311	...	|	1407
Amiens a.	|	...	|	0737	0741	...	|	0842	0828	|	0923	0923	0936	|	...	...	1145c	|	1225	...	...	1341	...	|	1428
Paris Nord 265 a.	0714	...	0747	...	...	...	0826	...	...	0926	...	...	...	0956	...	...	...	1156	...	...	...	...	...	1338	...

LILLE and VALENCIENNES - DOUAI - ARRAS - AMIENS and PARIS 256

Most trains (except *TGV*) are 2nd class only. For fast trains Lille - Paris see Table **250**.

	Ⓒ	⑥	*TGV* **7136** ⑤–⑦ b		Ⓐ	*TGV* **7342**	Ⓐ	⑥	*TGV* **7144** Ⓑ h	Ⓐ R	*TGV* **7148** Ⓑ h	Ⓒ R	Ⓐ	◇ Ⓐ ⊡	*TGV* **7152** ⑤⑥ v	Ⓐ	*TGV* **5136** ①–⑥ Wn	*TGV* **7156** ⑦ e	*TGV* **7154** ①–④ m	Ⓐ	*TGV* **7158** ⑤ f⊕	*TGV* **5138** ⑦ We	*TGV* **7160** ⑦ e		*TGV* **7096** Ⓐ
ille Flandres 257 d.	1301	1410	...	1540	1605	...	1634	1638	...	1705	...	1805	1804	...	...	1909	...	...	...	2013	...	2021	...	2110	2209
ille Europe d.	|	|	...	|	|	...	|	|	...	|	...	|	|	1839	...	|	1915	...	...	|	...	|	...	|	|
Valenciennes ▶ d.	|	|	1438	|	|	...	|	|	1641	|	1739	|	|	|	1845	|	|	1938	1942	|	2008	|	2038	|	|
ouai 257 ▶ a.	1322	1437	1504	1607	1630	...	1656	1701	1707	1725	1805	1826	1829	|	1910	1928	1933	2004	2008	2037	2034	2040	2106	2136	|
ouai d.	1324	1439	1512	1609	1632	...	1658	1703	1717	1730	1813	1828	1831	|	1918	1930	1936	2012	2018	2039	2042	2043	2116	2138	|
rras a.	1340	1459	1528	1629	1650	...	1713	1719	1733	1745	1829	1846	1851	1900	1933	1943	1949	2028	2032	2054	2058	2056	2132	2156	2229
rras 265 d.	1342	...	1535	1632	...	1706	*1725*	...	1736	1747	1836	1848	1852	...	1940	1945	...	2035	2035	2055	2105	...	2135	...	2235
Albert d.	1407	...	|	1656	...	|	*1755*	...	|	1809	|	1910	1921	...	|	2007	...	|	|	2119	|	...	|	...	|
Amiens a.	1427	...	|	1719	...	|	*1817*	...	|	1829	|	1932	1944	...	|	2028	...	|	|	2141	|	...	|	...	|
aris Nord 265 a.	...	...	1626	...	...	1756	...	...	1826	...	1926	...	...	...	2032	...	...	2126	2126	...	2156	...	2226	...	2323

2nd class

LOCAL TRAINS DOUAI - VALENCIENNES

	⚒	⚒	Ⓐ	⚒	Ⓐ		⚒	†	Ⓐ		Ⓐ	⚒		⚒		Ⓐ	⊙	Ⓐ	Ⓐ	†	Ⓐ	⚒	Ⓐ	⑥	Ⓐ	†
ouai d.	0600	0659	0725	0755	0814	0855	0953	1048	1155	1216	1248	1309	1351	1623	1650	1721	1755	1822	1855	1914	1921	1958	2056	2116	2144	2214
alenciennes a.	0629	0728	0758	0833	0847	0933	1022	1116	1226	1250	1321	1345	1422	1659	1718	1753	1833	1852	1927	1948	1951	2032	2130	2147	2215	2246

	Ⓐ	⚒	⚒	⚒	⚒	Ⓑ	Ⓐ	Ⓐ	Ⓒ		†	⑥	Ⓐ	⚒		⚒	⚒		⚒	Ⓑ	⚒	Ⓑ	Ⓐ	⑥	Ⓑ	Ⓐ
alenciennes d.	0508	0543	0624	0654	0753	0803	0839	0934	0945	...	1120	1148	1201	1223	1301	1402	1455	1602	1650	1720	1751	1820	1858	1858	1928	2142
ouai a.	0537	0616	0701	0727	0826	0837	0910	1004	1015	...	1151	1218	1230	1257	1335	1434	1526	1638	1725	1754	1825	1855	1932	1935	1959	2212

– ①⑥⑦ (also Dec. 25, 26, Jan. 1, 2, Mar. 25, May 13; not Dec. 24, 31).
– To/from Rouen (Table **268**).
– To/from Strasbourg (Table **391**).
– For origin/destination see Table **11**.
– Also Dec. 25, Jan. 1, Mar. 24, Apr. 30, May 1, 7, 8, 12; not May 2.
– Ⓒ only.
– Not Feb. 4 - Mar. 14.
– Also Dec. 25, Jan. 1, Mar. 24, May 12.
– Also Apr. 30, May 7; not May 2.

g – Also Dec. 26, Jan. 2, Mar. 25, May 13; not Dec. 24, 31, Mar. 24, May 12.
h – Not May 1, 8.
m – Also May 2; not Dec. 25, Jan. 1, Mar. 24, Apr. 30, May 1, 7, 8, 12.
n – Not Dec. 25, Jan. 1, Mar. 24, May 12.
v – Also Apr. 30, May 1, 7, 8; not May 2.
x – 1700 on Ⓒ.
z – 1556 on ⑤.
TGV – Ⓡ, supplement payable.

◇ – TER à Grande Vitesse (via high-speed line). Supplement *Côte d'Opale* is payable (€3 per day).
★ – Paris - Arras via high-speed line is *179 km*.
▶ – For local trains see panel below main table.
⊙ – On ⑥ depart 1754, arrive 1826.
△ – Runs 10 - 18 minutes later Arras - Amiens on Ⓐ Feb. 25 - Mar. 14.
⊕ – By 🚌 Douai - Valenciennes and v.v. on Ⓐ Feb. 15 - Mar. 21.
⊗ – By 🚌 Douai - Valenciennes Dec. 9, 16, Jan. 6, 13, 20.

LILLE - CAMBRAI - ST QUENTIN 257

Most trains 2nd class. For other journeys Paris - Cambrai change at Douai (see Table **256** for Paris - Douai).

km		Ⓐ	Ⓐ	Ⓐ	Ⓒ	⚒	Ⓐ	Ⓐ	⚒	⚒		†	Ⓐ	⚒b	†	⚒c	⚒	⚒d	⚒	†	⑥	⑥	Ⓑ	⑥	Ⓐ
0	**Lille Flandres 256** d.	...	...	0534	...	*0620*	...	*0647*	0733	...	0852	...	*0910*	...	1108	...	1130	*1202*	...	*1301*	...	1505	*1540*	*1540*	...
34	Douai **256** a.	...	...	0614	...	*0642*	...	*0723*	0800	...	0917	...	*0934*	...	1131	...	1200	*1224*	...	*1322*	...	1529	*1607*	*1607*	...
34	Douai d.	...	...	0616	...	0649	...	0728	0802	...	0919	...	0944	...	1133	...	1202	1238	1342	1342	...	1531	1627	1627	...
66	**Cambrai Ville** a.	...	...	0657	...	0724	...	0757	0830	...	0947	...	1014	...	1201	...	1235	1315	1413	1414	...	1559	1658	1658	...
66	**Cambrai Ville** d.	0520	0612	...	0728	...	0742	...	...	0858	...	1000	...	1040	...	1216	...	1317	...	1416	1431	...	...	1700	1715
82	Caudry d.	0535	0629	...	0743	...	0756	...	...	0912	...	1013	...	1053	...	1234	...	1333	...	1429	1444	...	...	1714	1733
92	Busigny **255** d.	0546	0642	...	0757	...	0807	...	...	0921	...	1022	...	1103	...	1248	...	1344	...	1438	1453	...	...	1724	1747
119	**St Quentin 255** d.	0607	0658	...	0813	...	0827	...	...	0941	...	1044	...	1126	...	1312	...	...	...	...	1517	...	...	1747	1808
142	Tergnier **255** a.	...	|	...	0826	...	...	...	...	0958	...	...	...	...	...	...	...	...	...	...	...	...	...	...	...
273	*Paris Nord* **255** a.	...	0820	...	0953	...	...	...	...	R	...	...	...	...	...	...	...	...	...	...	...	...	...	...	...

	Ⓐ	Ⓒ	Ⓐ	Ⓐ	†	⚒	Ⓐ	⑥	Ⓐ	Ⓐ
Lille Flandres 256 d.	*1634*	1705	*1705*	1738	1818	...	1838	1920	*1909*	*2013*
Douai **256** a.	*1656*	1729	*1725*	1802	1842	...	1903	1942	*1928*	*2037*
Douai d.	1705	1731	1734	1810	1844	1844	1909	1944	1950	2044
Cambrai Ville a.	1737	1801	1810	1840	1913	1914	1943	2014	2018	2110
Cambrai Ville d.	...	1805	1812	1842	1916	...	1945	2016	...	...
Caudry d.	...	1818	1828	1858	1928	...	1958	2029	...	...
Busigny **255** d.	...	1827	1840	1910	1939	...	2007	2037	...	...
St Quentin 255 d.	...	1846	1858	1932	2001	...	2028	...	...	...
Tergnier **255** a.	...	1906	1916	...	...	...	...	...	...	...
Paris Nord **255** a.	...	...	...	...	...	...	...	...	...	...

	Ⓐ	Ⓐ	Ⓐ	⚒	Ⓐ	⚒	Ⓐ	⚒ R	⚒
Paris Nord **255** d.	...	...	...	...	...	...	...	...	...
Tergnier **255** d.	...	...	0524	...	...	...	...	0735	...
St Quentin 255 d.	...	0508	0540	0617	...	0650	...	0758	...
Busigny **255** d.	...	0535	0601	0635	...	0712	...	0822	...
Caudry d.	...	0543	0609	0643	...	0722	...	0833	...
Cambrai Ville a.	...	0555	0621	0655	...	0736	...	0845	...
Cambrai Ville d.	0513	0557	0623	0657	0719	0804	0834	...	0855
Douai a.	0543	0628	0652	0730	0755	0833	0902	...	0918
Douai **256** d.	*0557*	0630	*0708*	0732	0807	0835	*0915*	...	0920
Lille Flandres 256 a.	*0636*	0658	*0730*	0758	0830	0902	*0936*	...	0943

	†	⚒b	⚒	†	⚒	⚒	Ⓑ	Ⓐ	⑥	†	Ⓐ	⑥	Ⓐd	Ⓒ	Ⓐ	⑥	†	Ⓐ	Ⓐ	⑥	†			
Paris Nord **255** d.	...	...	...	...	...	...	...			...	...	...	...	...	...	...	...	...	...	...	...	1737	...	...
Tergnier **255** d.	...	...	...	...	...	...	...	...	...	...	...	...	...	...	...	...	...	...	...	...	1811	|	...	...
St Quentin 255 d.	...	0858	...	1120	...	1159	...	1402	1402	...	...	1602	...	...	...	...	1724	1720	1828	1829	1829	1854	...	2103
Busigny **255** d.	...	0925	...	1141	...	1225	...	1423	1423	1423	...	1624	1638	...	...	...	1743	1745	1852	1853	1854	1912	...	2126
Caudry d.	...	0936	...	1151	...	1235	...	1432	1433	1433	...	1634	1648	...	...	...	1753	1756	1901	1902	1903	1922	...	2137
Cambrai Ville a.	...	0949	...	1203	...	1247	...	1444	1444	1444	...	1646	1701	...	...	...	1804	1808	1914	1914	1914	1934	...	2148
Cambrai Ville d.	0852	...	1129	1205	1210	1249	1319	...	1446	1446	1632	...	1703	1703	1741	1809	1809	1814	1917	1917	1917	...	...	...
Douai a.	0919	...	1157	1234	1236	1320	1345	...	1515	1515	1704	...	1731	1731	1816	1833	1833	1849	1947	1947	1947	...	...	...
Douai **256** d.	0921	...	*1204*	*1244*	1237	...	1347	...	*1558*	*1558*	...	...	1733	1733	*1829*	1835	1835	*1912*	1949	1949	1949	...	...	...
Lille Flandres 256 a.	0947	...	*1230*	*1322*	1301	...	1410	...	*1621*	*1621*	...	...	1758	1758	*1854*	1858	1858	*1941*	2013	2014	2014	...	...	...

– To/from Reims (Table **252**).
– Subject to alteration Mar. 2 - 22.
c – Subject to alteration Mar. 17 - 28.
d – Subject to alteration Cambrai - Busigny and v.v. Mar. 2 - 21.

AMIENS - ST QUENTIN 258

2nd class only

km		Ⓐ	⑥	Ⓐ	⚒§	†	⚒b	Ⓐ	Ⓐ	⚒	†	Ⓐ
0	Amiens d.	0639	0648	0749	0830	1025	1212	1442	1718	1826	1851	2035
76	St Quentin a.	0735	0747	0843	1001	1121	1312	1539	1814	1926	1949	2135

	⑥	Ⓐ	Ⓐ	†		⚒d	Ⓐf	Ⓐ	Ⓐ	⑥	†
St Quentin d.	0629	0637	0745	0755	...	1221	1325	1716	1838	1851	2017
Amiens a.	0729	0736	0843	0857	...	1319	1425	1813	1937	1951	2115

– Arrive St Quentin 1333 on Ⓐ Mar. 10 - 21, arrive 1320 on Ⓐ Mar. 25 - Apr. 18.
– Not Mar. 17 - 21, 25 - 28.
f – By 🚌 Mar. 17 - 28.
§ – Via Tergnier (depart 0941). Subject to alteration on Ⓐ Mar. 10 - 21.

CALAIS - DUNKERQUE - DE PANNE 259

km			Ⓐ		⚒		⚒		Ⓐ	
0	**Calais Ville** d.	...	0534	...	0638	...	1222	...	1719	...
23	Gravelines d.	...	0553	...	0701	...	1249	...	1742	...
46	**Dunkerque** a.	...	0616	...	0731	...	1316	...	1810	...

	⚒	🚌 Ⓐ		⚒	⑥	Ⓐ		Ⓐ	Ⓐ
Dunkerque d.	0629	0734	...	1217	1328	1542	...	1711	1827
Gravelines d.	0701	0825	...	1247	1352	1609	...	1743	1854
Calais Ville a.	0724	0855	...	1309	1412	1627	...	1808	1918

🚌 **BOULOGNE - CALAIS - DUNKERQUE** (serving the railway stations) is operated by Autocars BCD ✆ 03 21 83 51 51, approx. 5 journeys on Ⓐ, 2 journeys on ⑥ (no service on ⑦).

🚌 **DUNKERQUE GARE - ADINKERKE (DE PANNE STATION)** Operator DK'BUS Marine. Journey 40 - 50 minutes. Connects at De Panne station with coastal tram service (Table **404**).
rom Dunkerque Gare: ⚒ (service 2): 0702 and approx hourly to 1806, 1908, 2012. † (service 3): 0755 and hourly to 1955.
rom Adinkerke: ⚒ (service 2): 0700, 0807 and approx hourly to 1809, 1906, 2006, 2106. † (service 3): 0910 and hourly to 1910, 2014, 2105.

260 PARIS - AMIENS - BOULOGNE - CALAIS

For *TGV* service Paris - Boulogne / Calais (and connections via Hazebrouck) see Table **265**. Other services available by changing at Lille (Tables **250** and **265**).

km		2 Ⓐ	2 Ⓐ	2 ⚒	⚒	2 Ⓐ	12001 Ⓐ z	2003 ①–⑥ n	⑥	2007	2007 ⑦ q	2 †	⚒	2 ⑥	12011 ①–⑥ n	†	2015	2 †	12019 Ⓐ		2 †		12023 x	2 ⑥	2 Ⓐ
0	**Paris Nord** △ d.	...	...	...	...	...	0634	0707	0710	0804	0804	...	0819	...	0910	0919	1007	...	1104	...	...	1137	1231	...	...
51	Creil △ d.	...	...	...	...	...	0701	0734	0744	0831	0831	...	0853	...	0940	0955	|	...	|	...	...	1211	1257	...	...
66	Clermont-de-l'Oise △ d.	...	...	...	...	...	|	|	0802	|	|	...	0903	...	0951	1011	|	...	|	...	...	1228	|	...	...
126	Longueau d.	...	...	...	...	...	0738	0812	0846	0909	0909	...	0950	...	1027	1054	1107	...	1204	...	...	1318	1338	...	...
131	**Amiens** a.	...	...	...	...	...	0744	0817	0852	0914	0914	...	0956	...	1033	1059	1112	...	1210	...	...	1323	1344	...	...
131	**Amiens** d.	...	...	...	...	0638	▬	0828	▬	▬	0925	...	▬	...	▬	▬	1123	...	▬	1224	...	▬	▬	...	1428
176	Abbeville d.	...	...	...	...	0715	...	0853	...	...	0950	...	...	...	...	...	1148	...	...	1312	...	Ⓐ ▷	...	...	1514
216	Rang du Fliers ⊙ d.	...	0611	...	0657	0745	...	0917	...	...	1014	...	...	...	...	...	1221	...	...	▬	L	1303	...	L	1544
227	Étaples-Le Touquet **263** d.	...	0618	...	0705	0755	...	0927	⚒	①–④	1024	...	⑤	...	Ⓐ	⚒	1231	...	Ⓐ	⑥	1314	1311	©	1458	1552
254	**Boulogne Ville 263** a.	...	0642	...	0724	0823	2	0944	2	m ⊖	1041	...	2	...	2 ⊡	2	1248	...	2 ▷	2	1330	1333	2	1516	1608
254	**Boulogne Ville** d.	0602	0644	0702	0726	...	0829	...	0957	1036	...	1051	1138	1148	1157	1224	...	1258	1303	1303	1331	1335	1444	1517	*1613*
261	Wimille-Wimereux d.	0609	0651	0711	0734	...	0837	...	1006	1043	...	1058	1146	1156	1205	1232	...	1307	1311	1311	|	1343	1451	1524	*1621*
271	Marquise-Rinxent d.	0617	0659	0719	0743	...	0845	...	1015	1051	...	1106	1153	1205	1213	1240	...	1315	1320	1320	1342	1351	1459	1532	*1628*
288	Calais Fréthun ▶ d.	0629	0711	0734	0759	...	0856	...	|	|	...	|	|	1217	1224	1251	...	|	1334	1334	1353	1405	|	1544	*1639*
296	**Calais Ville** ▶ a.	0637	0718	0742	0807	...	0903	...	1031	1108	...	1122	1210	1224	1231	1258	...	1333	1343	1343	1400	1414	1517	1551	*1649*
	Lille Flandres **265** a.	0801	...	0902	...	...	1033	...	...	1242	...	1249	...	1403	1403	...	...	1508	...	1511	...	...	1643	...	...

	2 ©	2025	2 Ⓐ	2 Ⓐ	2 ©	2 Ⓐ	2 ©	12031 ①–⑥ n	2 Ⓐ	⑥	2033 ⊕	©	12035 Ⓐ	Ⓐ	12037	12039 Ⓐ	2041	†	Ⓐ	⑥	2045 Ⓐ	2045 ⑤ f	2049 b	2049 ⑦ q	
Paris Nord △ d.	...	1419	...	...	...	...	...	1610	...	...	1704	1719	1734	1749	1807	1834	1904	1910	1910	1940	2004	2004	2107	2107	2149
Creil △ d.	...	|	...	...	...	...	...	|	...	...	|	1753	|	1823	|	|	|	1940	1943	2012	2031	2031	|	|	2217
Clermont-de-l'Oise △ d.	...	|	...	...	...	...	...	|	...	...	|	1810	|	1834	|	1908	|	1956	2000	2026	|	|	|	|	2234
Longueau d.	...	1519	...	...	...	...	...	1710	...	...	1804	1859	1834	1928	1911	1945	2004	2039	2050	2108	2109	2109	2207	2207	2317
Amiens a.	...	1524	...	...	...	...	...	1716	...	...	1809	1905	1840	1933	1917	1951	2008	2044	2056	2113	2114	2114	2212	2212	2323
Amiens d.	...	1535	...	...	...	...	...	▬	1724	1726	1820	▬	*1855*	...	...	...	2019	...	...	...	...	2125	...	2223	...
Abbeville d.	...	1601	...	...	...	...	...	...	1757	1814	1846	...	*1946*	...	...	...	2046	...	...	...	...	2150	...	2248	...
Rang du Fliers ⊙ d.	...	1631	...	...	...	...	1817	Ⓐ	1828	...	1916	...	▬	...	...	...	2119	...	...	...	...	2223	...	2321	...
Étaples-Le Touquet **263** d.	...	1641	...	...	...	*1729*	1826	1826	1837	...	1925	Ⓐ	©	...	...	...	2129	...	...	...	...	2233	...	2331	...
Boulogne Ville 263 a.	...	1659	...	...	...	*1752*	1843	1841	1853	...	1942	2	2	...	...	...	2146	...	...	...	...	2250	...	2348	...
Boulogne Ville d.	1644	...	1703	1731	1739	1818	1845	1842	1913	...	...	1952	1949	...	...	...	...	...	...	...	...	...	...	...	...
Wimille-Wimereux d.	1652	...	1712	1740	1747	1826	1854	1849	1921	...	...	1958	1957	...	...	...	...	...	...	...	...	...	...	...	...
Marquise-Rinxent d.	1700	...	1721	1751	1755	1834	1903	1857	1929	...	...	2005	2005	...	...	...	...	...	...	...	...	...	...	...	...
Calais Fréthun ▶ d.	|	...	1732	1807	|	1852	|	1908	1941	...	...	2016	2016	...	...	...	...	...	...	...	...	...	...	...	...
Calais Ville ▶ a.	1716	...	1739	1816	1816	1900	1921	1915	1949	...	...	2023	2023	...	...	...	...	...	...	...	...	...	...	...	...
Lille Flandres **265** a.	1840	...	...	2002	1947	...	2058	...	...	...	...	2158r	...	...	...	...	...	...	...	...	...	...	...	...	...

	⚒	2004 ①–⑥ v	†	⑥	12006 Ⓐ	2008 ①–⑥ u	12010 Ⓑ y	2 Ⓐ	12012 Ⓐ z	2 ⑥	2 ⚒ ◧	2014 s	2 Ⓐ	2 ⚒	Ⓐ	2 ⑥	2 Ⓐ ▷	†	2 Ⓐ ▷	2022	2 ©	⚒ ⊗	†	2 ©	⑥
Lille Flandres **265** d.	...	...	...	...	...	...	...	...	...	...	...	...	...	0627a	0700	0727	0800	...	0815	...	0922	...	...	1124	...
Calais Ville ▶ d.	...	...	...	...	...	...	...	0548	...	0601	0642	...	0739	0804	0822	0904	0917	0951	0953	...	1046	1227	...	1305	1327
Calais Fréthun ▶ d.	...	...	...	...	...	...	...	|	...	|	0653	...	|	0812	0829	0911	0925	1000	1000	...	|	1237	...	|	1334
Marquise-Rinxent d.	...	...	...	...	...	...	...	0607	...	0619	0713	...	0755	0824	0840	0922	0940	1012	1012	...	1104	1254	...	1322	1346
Wimille-Wimereux d.	...	...	...	...	...	...	...	0616	...	0627	0721	...	0803	0831	0847	0929	0947	1020	1020	...	1112	1303	...	1331	1354
Boulogne Ville a.	...	...	...	...	...	...	...	0625	...	0635	0730	...	0809	0838	0854	0936	0954	1027	1027	...	1119	1310	...	1338	1401
Boulogne Ville 263 d.	...	0429c	...	...	...	0538	...	0627	...	0637	...	0746	▬	▬	...	...	▬	▬	▬	1046	▬	1319	1324	▬	1402
Étaples-Le Touquet **263** d.	...	0447c	...	...	...	0556	...	0646	...	0654	...	0804	...	...	...	...	...	...	...	1104	...	1337	1342	...	1418
Rang du Fliers ⊙ d.	...	0457c	...	...	...	0606	...	0655	...	0703	...	0815	...	...	...	...	**12018**	**12020**	...	1115	**12026**	1347	1352	...	1426
Abbeville d.	...	0530c	...	...	...	0638	...	0730	...	0733	...	0838	...	...	...	...	①–⑥	Ⓐ	...	1138	①–⑥	1419	1424	**12030**	...
Amiens a.	...	0554c	...	...	...	0701	...	0804	...	0812	...	0902	Ⓐ	©	...	...	d	z	...	1202	n	1456	1501	k	...
Amiens d.	0520	0605	0612	0625	0646	0715	0747	...	0812	...	...	0913	0928	0930	...	...	1012	1112	1218	1213	1311	...	...	1508	...
Longueau d.	0526	0613	0618	0631	0654	0723	0755	...	0821	...	...	0921	0934	0935	...	...	1020	1120	1225	1221	1319	...	...	1516	...
Clermont-de-l'Oise △ d.	0616	0649	0706	0723	|	|	|	...	|	...	...	|	1021	1019	...	...	|	|	1317	|	|	...	...	|	...
Creil △ a.	0632	|	0721	0738	|	|	|	...	|	...	...	|	1036	1034	...	...	|	|	1334	|	1355	...	...	1552	...
Paris Nord △ a.	0708	0723	0759	0817	0753	0823	0856	...	0923	...	...	1020	1111	1111	...	...	1120	1220	1411	1320	1423	...	...	1620	...

	Ⓐ	2 Ⓐ	2032	2 Ⓐ ▷	2 ⑥	2 ⑥	2 Ⓐ	2 Ⓐ	2 ©	2038 ⑦ e	2 Ⓐ	©	2042	Ⓐ	Ⓐ	2 ©	2044 ⑦ q	Ⓐ	2 Ⓐ	2 Ⓐ	2 Ⓐ	2 ©	2048 ⑦ q	2 Ⓐ	2 ©
Lille Flandres **265** d.	...	...	...	...	...	1338	1403	...	1421	...	...	...	...	1557	...	1621	...	...	1700	...	1806	1821	...	1914	2020
Calais Ville ▶ d.	1328	1349	...	1427	1430	1503	1529	...	1552	...	1644	1652	...	1727	...	1745	...	1755	1820	1910	1931	1950	...	2041	2154
Calais Fréthun ▶ d.	|	1356	...	1437	1437	1511	|	...	|	...	1653	1659	...	1736	...	|	...	1804	1828	1918	1939	|	...	2048	|
Marquise-Rinxent d.	1349	1407	...	1449	1449	1523	1547	...	1609	...	1706	1711	...	1754	...	1802	...	1818	1840	1933	1950	2007	...	2100	2211
Wimille-Wimereux d.	1357	1415	...	1457	1457	1532	1557	...	1618	...	1714	1719	...	1803	...	1810	...	1829	1849	1942	1957	2015	...	2107	2220
Boulogne Ville a.	1405	1423	...	1504	1504	1540	1604	...	1626	...	1721	1726	...	1811	...	1818	...	1836	1858	1948	2004	2022	...	2114	2228
Boulogne Ville 263 d.	▬	▬	1437	...	...	▬	▬	1619	▬	1630	1723	1728	1742	▬	1824	▬	1832	1844	▬	...	*2015*	▬	2048	...	...
Étaples-Le Touquet **263** d.	...	...	1455	...	...	...	...	1640	...	1649	1748	1745	1800	...	1852	...	1850	1908	...	...	*2031*	...	2106	...	...
Rang du Fliers ⊙ d.	...	...	1505	...	...	...	**12036**	1648	...	1659	L	▬	1811	...	1902	**2044**	1901	...	...	...	*2039*	**12046**	2117	...	...
Abbeville d.	...	...	1539	...	...	Ⓐ	Ⓑ	1720	**2038**	1733	...	...	1834	...	1933	Ⓑ	1935	...	...	...	...	Ⓑ	2140	...	...
Amiens a.	©	Ⓐ	1602	...	...		h	1756		1758	...	©	1858	†	1959	h	2000	...	†	...	...	w	2205	...	...
Amiens d.	1524	1534	1613	...	...	1625	1708	...	1809	1809	...	1822	1909	1925	...	2011	2011	...	2025	...	...	2112	2216	...	...
Longueau d.	1529	1540	1621	...	...	1631	1716	...	1817	1817	...	1828	1916	1932	...	2018	2018	...	2032	...	...	2120	2224	...	...
Clermont-de-l'Oise △ d.	1616	1619	|	...	...	1719	|	...	|	|	...	1919	|	2019	...	|	|	...	2114	...	...	2156	|	...	...
Creil △ a.	1632	1632	|	...	...	1732	1752	...	1852	1852	...	1937	1953	2035	...	2053	2053	...	2131	...	...	|	|	...	...
Paris Nord △ a.	1708	1708	1720	...	...	1808	1820	...	1920	1920	...	2011	2020	2111	...	2123	2123	...	2208	...	...	2229	2323	...	...

SNCF 🚌 service — 🚌 **CALAIS VILLE - CALAIS FRÉTHUN** — *Subject to confirmation*

	⑥	Ⓐ	†	Ⓐ	⑥	⚒	†	⑥	†	
Calais Ville d.	0627	0658	1046	1125	1143	1607	1820	1913	2055	...
Calais Fréthun a.	0642	0713	1101	1140	1158	1622	1835	1928	2110	...

				†	⑥			†		
Calais Fréthun d.	...	0952	...	1737	1810	...	2038	2251	...	...
Calais Ville a.	...	1007	...	1752	1825	...	2053	2306	...	...

- K – June 29 - Aug. 31.
- L – To/from Lille Flandres (Table **263**).
- a – Ⓐ only.
- b – Not Dec. 24, 31, Mar. 23, May 11.
- c – ① (also Dec. 26, Jan. 2, Mar. 25; not Dec. 24, 31, Mar. 24, May 12).
- d – Not Dec. 25, Jan. 1, Mar. 24, May 2, 9, 12.
- e – Also Dec. 25, Jan. 1, Mar. 24, May 12.
- f – Also Apr. 30, May 7; not May 2, 9.
- h – Not May 1, 8.
- k – Not Mar. 23, May 11.
- m – Not Dec. 25, Jan. 1, Mar. 24, May 1, 7, 8, 12.
- n – Not Dec. 25, Jan. 1, Mar. 24; May 12.
- q – Also Dec. 25, Jan. 1, Mar. 24, May 12; not Mar. 23, May 11.
- r – Subject to alteration Jan. 7 - Feb. 1.
- s – Not Dec. 25, Jan. 1.
- u – Not Dec. 25, Jan. 1, Mar. 24, May 3, 10, 12.
- v – Not Dec. 24, 25, 31, Jan. 1, Mar. 24, May 12.
- w – Not Dec. 24, 31, May 1, 8.
- x – Not Mar. 23, May 2, 9, 11.
- y – Not May 1, 2, 8, 9.
- z – Not May 2, 9.
- ⊕ – Not May 8.
- ⊗ – Subject to alteration on Ⓐ Mar. 31 - Apr. 11.
- ⊖ – Subject to alteration Apr. 7 - 17.
- ⊡ – Subject to alteration Mar. 25 - Apr. 18.
- ⊙ – Rang du Fliers-Verton-Berck.
- △ – Frequent local trains run Paris - Creil. Infrequent local trains run Paris or Creil - Clermont-de-l'Oise.
- ▷ – Subject to alteration Feb. 11 - 22, Mar. 25 - May 23.
- ◧ – Runs 2–5 minutes later on ⑥.
- ▶ – For additional 🚌 service see below main table.
- § – Connections are by train.

261 AMIENS - ABBEVILLE - LE TRÉPORT

37 km	🚌 ①–⑥ u	† K	🚌 ①–⑥ n	🚌 ⑦ q	🚌	🚌	🚌 ①–⑥ n	©	Ⓐ	Ⓐ	⑥	🚌 ⑤⑥
Amiens **260** § d.	...	0833	*0828*	*0925*	*1123*	*1224*	*1535*	*1557*	*1650*	*1820*	*1837*	*2019*
Abbeville d.	0645	0904	0907	1000	1151	1322	1606	1644	1743	1854	1921	2054
Le Tréport a.	0750	0938	1015	1106	1259	1430	1713	1734	1829	1940	2007	2202

	⚒	⚒	🚌 Ⓐ	🚌 ©	🚌 ⚒	🚌 †	🚌 ⑥	🚌 Ⓑ	🚌 Ⓑ	🚌	† K
Le Tréport d.	0632	0734	0755	1020	1202	1301	1413	1437	1600	1720	1912
Abbeville a.	0718	0816	0902	1128	1310	1409	1523	1523	1708	1823	1946
Amiens **260** § a.	*0804*	*0902*	*1005*	*1202*	*1409*	*1501*	*1602*	*1602*	*1758*	*1858*	2018

FOR NOTES SEE TABLE 260 ABOVE

LILLE - VALENCIENNES - MAUBEUGE and CHARLEVILLE MÉZIÈRES — 262

Most trains 2nd class

km		Ⓐ	⚒	⚒	Ⓐ	⚒	⑥	Ⓐ	Ⓐ	⚒	⚒	Ⓐ		⚒	†	Ⓐ	Ⓒ	†		⚒	Ⓐ	⑥	⚒	†	⚒	
0	**Lille Flandres** d.	0554	0554	...	0655	0655	...	0754	...	0817	...	0855	0917	...	...	0943	1011	1117	...	1200	1219	1219	...	1224	1237	1318
48	Valenciennes d.	0634	0634	...	0736	0736	...	0832	...	0856	...	0932	0955	...	...	1029	1059	1157	...	1233	1257	1257	...	1308	1325	1357
82	Aulnoye Aymeries a.	0704	0704	...	0802	0802	...	0900	...	0925	...	0957	1022	...	...	...	...	1227	...	1259	1324	1324	...	...	...	1423
82	Aulnoye Aymeries d.	0706	...	0716	0810	0812	0835	0908	0909	0928	0938	1005	1027	1039	1039	...	...	1235	1235	1301	1333	1333	1332	...	...	1430
94	**Maubeuge** a.	0718	...	|	0824	|	0848	|	0923	0940	|	|	1037	|	|	...	...	|	1249	1315	|	|	1346	...	...	1442
104	Jeumont a.	0727	...	|	0833	|	0857	|	0932	0951	|	|	1046	|	|	...	...	|	1257	1324	|	|	1359	...	...	1451
94	Avesnes d.	...	...	0732	...	0826	...	0920	...	...	0950	1016	...	1050	1056	...	...	1246	...	...	1344	1344	...	...	...	...
123	Hirson a.	...	...	0759	...	0856	...	0946	...	...	1013	1039	...	1121	1122*	...	...	1310*	...	...	1407	1407	...	...	...	...
184	**Charleville-Mézières** a.	...	...	...	...	0935	...	...	...	...	...	1120	...	...	1200*	...	...	...	...	...	...	1450	...	...	...	...

	*	⚒	⚒	⚒	Ⓐ	Ⓐ	Ⓐ	Ⓐ			†	Ⓐ	Ⓐ	Ⓐ	Ⓒ	Ⓐ	Ⓐ	Ⓐ	Ⓐ	Ⓐ	Ⓒ	Ⓐ	Ⓒ	Ⓐ	Ⓐ	Ⓐ
ille Flandres d.	...	1337	1415	...	1515	...	1551	1551	1616	...	...	1654	1717	1717	1721	1727	...	1752	1808	...	1813	1820	...	1848	1855	...
alenciennes d.	...	1425	1453	...	1555	...	1628	1628	1657	...	...	1730	1752	1756	1807	1810	...	1827	1837	1842	1856	1859	...	1921	1932	...
ulnoye Aymeries a.	...	...	1521	...	1621	...	1654	1654	1728	...	...	1756	1813	|	...	1840	...	...	1900	|	1926	1928	...	|	1958	...
ulnoye Aymeries d.	1437	...	1523	1540	1623	1645	1703	1707	1730	1740	1740	1802	1815	|	...	1842	1847	...	1902	|	1933	1933	1946	|	2005	2007
Maubeuge a.	|	...	1534	|	1634	|	1717	|	1742	|	|	1815	1823	|	...	1854	|	...	1910	|	|	1945	2000	|	|	2018
Jeumont a.	|	...	1543	|	1641	|	1729	|	1751	|	|	1826	1832	|	...	1903	|	...	1919	|	|	1955	2012	|	|	2028
vesnes d.	1449	...	...	1552	...	1659	...	1718	...	1756	1756	...	...	1822	...	...	1902	...	...	1913	1946	...	...	1948	2016	...
irson a.	1512	...	...	1621	...	1727	...	1741	...	1821	1821	...	...	1842	...	...	1927	...	...	1938	2011	...	...	2009	2040	...
harleville-Mézières a.	...	...	...	...	...	...	...	...	...	...	1900	...	...	1919	...	...	...	...	...	...	2052	...	...	2050	...	...

	†	⑥	Ⓐ	Ⓐ		⊕	Ⓐ	Ⓐ	Ⓐ	Ⓒ	
ille Flandres d.	1911	1921	1928	...	2016	...	2037	2116	...	2120	2144
alenciennes d.	1958	2007	2007	...	2056	...	2121	2153	...	2206	2231
ulnoye Aymeries a.	...	...	2036	...	2124	...	...	2220	...	...	...
ulnoye Aymeries d.	...	...	2038	2047	2131	2136	...	2222	2235	...	...
Maubeuge a.	...	...	2049	|	2143	|	...	2233	|	...	...
Jeumont a.	...	...	2058	|	2154	|	...	2242	|	...	...
vesnes d.	...	...	...	2057	...	2148	...	...	2247	...	...
irson a.	...	...	...	2124	...	2217	...	...	2310	...	...
harleville-Mézières a.	...	...	...	...	...	...	...	...	...	...	...

	⚒	Ⓐ	Ⓐ	Ⓐ	⚒	⚒	⚒	Ⓐ	Ⓐ	⚒
Charleville-Mézières d.	...	...	...	...	...	...	...	...	0557	...
Hirson d.	...	...	...	0518	...	0541	...	...	0634	0614
Avesnes d.	...	...	...	0541	...	0612	...	...	0656	0640
Jeumont d.	...	0501	0527	|	...	|	0611	0635	|	|
Maubeuge d.	...	0508	0535	|	...	|	0619	0644	|	|
Aulnoye Aymeries a.	...	0519	0547	0551	...	0624	0631	0653	|	0651
Aulnoye Aymeries d.	...	0521	...	0601	...	...	0633	0656	|	0708
Valenciennes d.	0439	0552	...	0628	0632	...	0704	0718	0724	0739
Lille Flandres a.	0525	0630	...	0706	0723	...	0742	0746	0751	0817

	⚒		Ⓐ	Ⓐ	⚒	⚒	⚒ ⊡	Ⓐ	Ⓒ		Ⓐ	Ⓐ	Ⓐ	Ⓒ		Ⓐ	⚒ ◧	⚒	⚒	Ⓐ	⑥	Ⓒ	† *	†	Ⓐ	Ⓐ
harleville-Mézières d.	...	...	...	...	...	...	...	...	...	...	...	...	0956	1013*	...	...	...	...	...	1150	1150	...	1309	...	...	...
irson d.	0644	...	...	0720	...	0748	...	0825	0832*	...	0936	...	1031	1055*	...	1115	1153	...	...	1232	1232	...	1347	...	1421	...
vesnes d.	0707	...	...	0744	...	0813	...	0847	0856	...	1000	...	1053	1120	...	1143	1219	...	...	1254	1256	...	1410	...	1444	...
Jeumont d.	|	0708	0738	|	...	|	0815	|	|	0912	|	1003	|	|	1114	|	|	1215	1232	|	|	...	|	1404	|	1500
Maubeuge d.	|	0716	0746	|	...	|	0823	|	|	0920	|	1011	|	|	1123	|	|	1223	1244	|	|	...	|	1413	|	1508
ulnoye Aymeries a.	0721	0729	0757	0753	...	0828	0835	0857	0911	0932	1011	1022	|	1129	1134	1154	1234	1235	1302	1305	1305	...	1420	1425	1454	1520
ulnoye Aymeries d.	...	0731	0759	0804	...	...	0837	...	...	0934	...	1024	|	...	1136	1204	...	1237	...	1316	1318	...	...	1427	...	1523
alenciennes d.	...	0759	0820	0831	0835	...	0908	...	...	1003	...	1053	1121	...	1206	1232	...	1307	...	1348	1348	1352	...	1500	...	1550
ille Flandres a.	...	0837	0848	0907	0924	...	0944	...	...	1042	...	1132	1149	...	1245	1306	...	1344	...	1428	1428	1440	...	1542	...	1627

	Ⓒ	† *	†	⑥	⚒	Ⓐ ⊖	Ⓐ	Ⓐ	Ⓐ	Ⓒ	Ⓐ	Ⓐ	† *	† △	⚒	⚒ △	Ⓐ	Ⓐ	† △	†	⑥	Ⓐ	† △	†	⚒ △	⚒
harleville-Mézières d.	...	...	...	...	...	...	...	...	...	...	...	...	...	...	...	...	...	...	...	...	...	...	...	1921	...	2045
irson d.	...	1534	...	1540	...	...	1616	1645	...	...	...	1719	1737	...	1748	...	1814	...	...	1855*	...	...	...	2000	...	2124
vesnes d.	...	1601	...	1606	...	...	1639	1711	...	...	...	1741	1801	...	1815	...	1841	...	...	1921	...	...	...	2025	...	2148
Jeumont d.	...	|	1555	|	1606	1626	|	|	1711	...	1727	|	|	1803	|	1812	|	1858	1901	|	...	...	2020	|	2124	|
Maubeuge d.	...	|	1604	|	1614	1638	|	|	1719	...	1737	|	|	1812	|	1820	|	1907	1912	|	...	...	2028	|	2131	|
ulnoye Aymeries a.	...	1615	1616	1615	1626	1652	1649	1724	1730	...	1749	1750	1814	1824	1828	1831	1854	1919	1926	1929	...	...	2038	2034	2141	2200
ulnoye Aymeries d.	...	...	1624	...	1628	...	1703	...	1736	...	...	1759	...	1826	...	1833	...	1921	...	1937	...	...	...	2046	...	2208
alenciennes d.	1553	...	1655	...	1659	...	1731	...	1805	1815	...	1824	...	1859	...	1902	...	1954	...	2006	2017	2035	...	2112	...	2235
ille Flandres a.	1641	...	1737	...	1739	...	1805	...	1844	1903	...	1903	...	1942	...	1943	...	2035	...	2043	2104	2121	...	2149	...	2312

– Not Feb. 4 - 22.
– Subject to alteration on Ⓒ Mar. 29 - Apr. 13.
– On Mar. 15, 16 subject to alteration Jeumont - Aulnoye.
– On Ⓐ Feb. 4 - 22 depart Jeumont 0754, Maubeuge 0803.

◧ – Subject to alteration on Ⓐ Mar. 10 - 21.
* – Subject to alteration on Apr. 20, 27, May 25.

Engineering Work Ⓐ Jan. 14 - Apr. 11: Certain journeys are subject to 🚌 substitution between Aulnoye and Jeumont

BOULOGNE - ST POL - ARRAS and LILLE — 263

2nd class

Engineering work between Béthune and Don Sainghin will affect timings between Béthune and Lille Feb. 9 - 24 and Apr. 5 - 20

km		⚒	⚒	⚒	Ⓐ	Ⓐ	⚒	⚒	Ⓐy	†	†	Ⓐ	⚒	⚒	†	Ⓐ	†	Ⓐ	Ⓐ	Ⓒ	Ⓒ	Ⓐ	Ⓐ	Ⓒ	Ⓒ	Ⓐ
	Calais Ville **260** d.	...	...	...	...	...	...	...	...	...	...	...	...	...	...	...	...	...	...	...	...	...	1644	1652	...	1755
0	**Boulogne Ville** § d.	...	...	0519	...	...	0652	...	0845	0915	...	...	...	1229	1346	1527x	1537	...	...	1646	...	...	1723	1728	...	1844
27	Étaples Le Touquet § d.	...	...	0553	...	...	0711	...	0937	0933	...	...	...	1300	1404	1546	1556	...	...	1705	...	...	1803	1807	...	1909
39	Montreuil sur Mer d.	...	...	0603	...	...	0721	...	0949	0944	...	...	...	1310	1415	1556	1606	...	...	1716	...	...	1813	1817	...	1919
88	St Pol sur Ternoise d.	0534	0612	0647	0656	0727	0811v	0814	1027	1030v	1029	1046	1210	1404	1455	1648	1647	*1720*r	1737	1801	1810	1826	1906	1857	1913	2004
127	**Arras** a.	|	|	0725	|	0759	0845	|	...	|	1101	|	|	1438	1522	1724	1718	|	1816	|	1841	1906	|	1924	|	...
120	Béthune a.	0605	0643	...	0729	...	...	0844	...	1100	...	1116	1242	...	...	...	...	*1813*r	...	1831	...	...	1939	...	1939	...
120	Béthune ▶ d.	0615	0655	...	0731	...	...	0846z	...	1102	...	1118	*1255*	...	...	...	...	1822	...	1833	...	...	1941	...	1941	...
162	**Lille Flandres** ▶ a.	0658	0742	...	0821	...	...	0919z	...	1142	...	1159	*1351*	...	...	...	...	1906	...	1920	...	...	2026	...	2026	...

	⚒	⚒	Ⓐ	⚒	Ⓐ	⑥	Ⓐ	Ⓒ	Ⓒ	†	†	⑥	⚒	Ⓐ	⑥	Ⓐ	Ⓐ	Ⓐ	Ⓒ	Ⓐ	Ⓐ	Ⓐ	Ⓒ	Ⓒ		⚒
lle Flandres ▶ d.	...	...	...	0631	*0752*	0807	...	...	0909	...	1102	...	...	1237	1236	1550	...	1630	...	...	1730	...	1748	...	...	1855
éthune ▶ a.	...	...	...	0723	*0836*	0853	...	...	0949	...	1156	...	...	1325	1325	1637	...	1713	...	...	1818	...	1829	...	...	1937
éthune d.	...	...	...	0732	0857	0857	...	...	0950	...	1157	...	...	1327	1327	1644	...	1715	...	...	1820	...	1832	...	...	1942
Arras d.	...	...	0640	|	|	|	0906	0942	|	1143	|	1223	1319	|	|	|	1645	|	1736	1736	|	1842	|	1849	1935	|
Pol sur Ternoise d.	0554	0712	0723	0805	0929	0929	0942	1017	1025	1215	1227	1301	1355	1406	1406	1712	1729	1748	1808	1815	1853	1914	1904	1926	2006	2016
ontreuil sur Mer d.	0647	0803	...	...	...	...	1028	...	1104	...	1304	1353	...	1448	1449	...	1816	...	1856	1857	...	2002	...	2004	...	2101
aples Le Touquet § d.	0716	0813	...	...	...	...	1037	...	1113	...	1314	1402	...	1456	1458	...	1826	...	1906	1907	...	2012	...	2015	...	2111
oulogne Ville § a.	0742	0837	...	...	...	...	1057x	...	1133	...	1330	1419	...	...	1516	...	1841	...	1921	1924	...	2028	...	2031	...	2128
Calais Ville **260** a.	...	...	...	...	...	...	...	...	...	...	1400	...	...	...	1551	...	1915	...	...	...	...	...	...	...	...	...

– By 🚌.
– Arrives 9 minutes earlier.
– Not Mar. 31 - Apr. 11.

y – Subject to alteration Feb. 18 - 22.
z – On ⑥ depart 0859, arrive 0948.
§ – See also Table **260**.

▶ – **Additional trains** Béthune - Lille and v.v.
From Béthune: 0522 Ⓐ, 0550 Ⓐ, 0749 ⚒, 0843 †, 0859 ⚒, 0956 Ⓒ, 1214 ⚒, 1355 †, 1425 ⑥, 1609, 1719, 2028 Ⓑ.
From Lille Flandres: 0830 Ⓐ, 1010 Ⓒ, 1154 ⚒, 1237 †, 1332 ⚒, 1509 Ⓒ, 1608 Ⓐ, 1658 Ⓐ, 1800 Ⓐ, 1815 Ⓐ, 1855, 1918 Ⓐ, 1945 ⑥, 2027 ⚒, 2056 ⚒, 2114 †.

🚌 RENNES / ST MALO - LE MONT ST MICHEL — 264

By 🚌 *Courriers Bretons*

68 km	❖	⚒	†			❖	①–⑥	†		Ⓑ	⑥
ennes (Gare SNCF) d.	**Sept. 17 -**	0930	1040	1130	1730	**June 15 -**	0940	1040	1130	1830	1840
e Mont St Michel a.	**June 14**	1100	1200	1300	1900	**Sept. 14**	1100	1200	1300	2000	2010
	❖		⚒	†		❖					
Mont St Michel d.	**Sept. 17 -**	0930	1515	1530	1645	**June 15 -**	0945	...	1515	...	1715
nnes (Gare SNCF) a.	**June 14**	1050	1645	1650	1815	**Sept. 14**	1105	...	1645*	...	1845

To July 4, 2008	C	B	⚒S	E	F
St Malo (Gare SNCF) d.	0840	0940	1030	1630	1745
Le Mont St Michel a.	1018*	1128*	1213*	1811*	1930*
			C	B	⚒S
Le Mont St Michel d.	0927	...	1550	1615	1720
St Malo (Gare SNCF) a.	1108*	...	1738*	1808*	1858*

– To Sept. 2, 2007.
– Sept. 3, 2007 - July 4, 2008.
– From Sept. 3 (not on ⑤ during school term).

F – ⑤ during school term (daily to Sept. 2).
S – July 5 - Sept. 2, 2007.
* – Change buses at Pontorson.

❖ – Subject to alteration from Dec. 9, 2007.

Connections (not guaranteed) are available at Rennes with *TGV* services to/from Paris. Special fares are available in conjunction with rail tickets.

265 PARIS and LILLE - DUNKERQUE and CALAIS

Local trains are 2nd class

km		Ⓐ	⚒	Ⓐ	Ⓐ	⚒	Ⓐ	⚒	◇ Ⓐ	Ⓐ	Ⓐ	⑥	◇ Ⓐ	Ⓐ	Ⓐ	TGV 7207 Ⓐ	©	Ⓐ	†	TGV 7301 Ⓐ	Ⓐ ▷	⑥	Ⓐ	Ⓐ	◇	Ⓐ
0	**Paris Nord 256** ▶ d.	...	...	...	...	...	...	...	...	...	...	...	...	...	...	0728	...	...	...	0722	...	...	...	...	...	...
199	Arras **256** d.	...	...	...	0610	...	...	0634	...	...	...	...	...	0721	...	|	...	...	...	0818	...	0805	0805	...	...	0845
219	Lens d.	...	...	...	0626	...	...	0650	...	...	...	...	...	0739	...	|	...	...	...	0832	...	0822	0822	...	...	0901
238	Béthune d.	...	0605a	...	0643	...	...	0709	...	...	...	...	...	0758	...	|	...	...	...	0845	...	0850	0853	...	...	0918
	Lille Europe d.	...	|	...	|	...	...	|	0722	...	...	...	0822	|	...	0832	...	...	...	|	...	|	|	...	0914	|
• 46	**Lille Flandres** ▶ d.	...	|	0627	|	0640	0700	|	|	0715	0731	0727	|	|	0800	|	0813	0815	...	|	0841	|	|	0902	|	|
• 25	Armentières d.	...	|	0643	|	0654	0716	|	|	0730	|	0746	|	|	|	|	0828	0830	...	|	0855	|	|	0917	|	|
272	Hazebrouck a.	...	0635a	0701	0706	0717	0731	0735	|	0754	0801	0803	|	0825	0830	|	0847	0854	...	0905	0913	0917	0920	0938	|	0943
272	Hazebrouck d.	0545	0637	0703	0708	0719	0733	0736	|	0756	0803	0805	|	...	0832	|	0849	0856	0900	0908	0915	0919	...	0940	|	...
Δ 312	**Dunkerque** a.	|	|	|	0736	0753	|	0802	0757	|	0829	|	|	...	|	0905	0923	|	|	0929	0943	0945	...	|	|	...
293	St Omer d.	0600	0653	0720	...	...	0747	...	...	0811	...	0821	|	...	0847	...	...	0910	0914	...	...	...	...	0953	|	...
	Calais Fréthun **260** a.	|	|	|	...	...	|	...	...	|	...	|	0850	...	|	...	...	|	|	...	...	...	...	|	0942	...
336	**Calais Ville 260** a.	0627	0728	0748	...	...	0812	...	...	0842	...	0848	|	...	0909	...	...	0943	0940	...	...	...	...	1018	|	...
	Boulogne Ville **260** a.	...	...	0838	...	...	0854	...	...	...	...	0936	0925	...	0954z	...	...	1027z	...	...	...	...	...	...	1011	...

	†	©	†	Ⓐ ▷	TGV 7303 ⑥ t	⚒ ▷	Ⓐ ⊗	©	TGV 7229 ①–⑥ n	◇ †	TGV 7311 ©	©	©	◇ Ⓐ ⊕	⚒	⚒ ▷	⑥	◇ ⚒	Ⓐ ⊙	Ⓐ	⑥	Ⓐ ⊙	⚒	†	TGV 7321 ①–⑥ n	⑥
Paris Nord 256 ▶ d.	...	...	...	...	0822	...	...	...	0958	...	0952	...	...	...	...	...	...	...	...	...	...	...	...	...	1222	...
Arras **256** d.	0852	...	...	...	0915	0920	...	...	|	...	1048	1052	...	...	...	...	...	...	1213	...	...	...	1220	...	1318	...
Lens d.	0908	...	...	...	0928	0937	...	...	|	...	1102	1110	...	...	...	...	...	...	1229	...	...	...	1243	...	1332	...
Béthune d.	0926	...	...	...	0941	0955	...	...	|	...	1115	1128	...	...	...	...	...	...	1246	...	...	...	1306	...	1345	...
Lille Europe d.	|	...	...	...	|	|	...	...	1101	1119	|	|	...	...	1247	...	...	1303	|	...	...	...	|	...	|	...
Lille Flandres ▶ d.	|	0922	...	0931	|	|	0957	1017	|	|	|	|	1124	1203	|	1233	...	|	|	1243	1241	1257	|	1316	|	1338
Armentières d.	|	0937	...	0946	|	|	1011	1035	|	|	|	|	1139	1223	|	|	...	|	|	1259	1302	|	|	1334	|	1354
Hazebrouck a.	0952	0955	←	1004	1004	1019	1028	1053	|	|	1135	1156	1159	1242	|	1305	...	|	1310	1318	1321	1330	1336	1356	1405	1412
Hazebrouck d.	→	0957	1009	1006	1006	1021	1030	1055	|	|	1137	1209	1201	1244	|	1307	1316	|	1312	1320	1323	1332	1338	1357	1407	1414
Dunkerque a.	...	|	1041	1031	1028	1047	|	1123	|	1151	1158	1245	*1245*	|	|	1332	|	1336	|	1356	1356	|	1406	1421	1429	|
St Omer d.	...	1009	...	...	...	...	1043	...	|	...	...	...	1215	1257	|	...	1335	...	1328	...	...	1346	...	...	...	1428
Calais Fréthun **260** a.	...	|	...	...	...	...	|	...	1131	...	...	...	|	|	1315	...	|	...	|	...	...	|	...	...	...	|
Calais Ville 260 a.	...	1037	...	...	...	...	1112	...	1140	...	...	...	1247	1319	|	...	1407	...	1358	...	...	1410	...	...	...	1453
Boulogne Ville **260** a.	...	1119	...	...	...	...	...	...	...	...	...	...	1338	...	1343	...	1504	...	...	...	...	...	...	...	...	1540

	Ⓐ	⑥	Ⓐ	Ⓐ	©	†	Ⓐ	©	Ⓐ	◇ †	Ⓐ	TGV 7331	Ⓐ	◇ †	©	©	Ⓐ	Ⓐ	Ⓐ	Ⓐ	◇ Ⓐ	Ⓐ	©	◇ Ⓐ	◇ ⑥	Ⓐ
Paris Nord 256 ▶ d.	...	...	...	...	...	...	...	...	...	...	...	1452	...	...	...	...	...	...	...	...	...	...	...	...	...	...
Arras **256** d.	...	1324	1324	...	...	1405	1442	...	...	...	...	1545	1537	...	...	1548	...	...	...	...	...	1643	...	...	...	...
Lens d.	...	1341	1341	...	...	1422	1500	...	...	...	...	1600	1603	...	...	1606	...	...	...	...	...	1700	...	...	...	...
Béthune d.	...	1357	1359	...	...	1439	1520	...	...	...	...	1613	1621	...	...	1624	...	1649	...	...	...	1720	...	...	...	...
Lille Europe d.	...	|	|	...	...	|	|	...	...	1554	...	|	|	1648	...	|	...	|	...	...	1715	|	...	1721	1731	...
Lille Flandres ▶ d.	1339	|	|	1403	1421	|	|	1535	1538	|	1557	|	|	|	1621	|	1634	|	1646	1700	|	|	1718	|	|	1729
Armentières d.	1354	|	|	1418	1439	|	|	1552	1554	|	|	|	|	|	1637	|	|	|	1703	|	|	|	1736	|	|	|
Hazebrouck a.	1413	1420	1425	1436	1457	1503	1547	1612	1612	|	1628	1633	1645	|	1655	1650	1703	1718	1725	1730	|	1749	1752	|	|	1759
Hazebrouck d.	1415	1422	1446	1438	1459	1505	...	1614	1614	|	1630	1636	1647	|	1657	1705	1704	1719	1727	1732	|	1751	1754	|	|	1801
Dunkerque a.	1440	1447	1523	*1523*	|	1534	...	1638	1647	|	|	1657	1713	|	|	1733	1728	|	1805	|	1747	1823	1826	|	|	|
St Omer d.	...	...	...	1451	1512	...	...	...	...	|	1645	...	...	|	1709	...	...	1734	...	1745	...	...	...	|	|	1819
Calais Fréthun **260** a.	...	...	...	|	|	...	...	...	...	1622	|	...	...	1716	|	...	...	|	...	|	...	...	...	1749	1759	|
Calais Ville 260 a.	...	...	...	1520	1542	...	...	...	...	|	1711	...	...	|	1735	...	...	1802	...	1811	...	...	...	|	|	1848
Boulogne Ville **260** a.	...	...	...	1604	1626	...	...	...	...	1650	1811	...	...	1744	1818	...	...	...	...	1858	...	...	...	1817	1829	...

	TGV 7337 ⑤–⑦ w		Ⓐ	Ⓐ	Ⓐ	TGV 7339 ①–④ m	◇ †	©	Ⓐ	TGV 7275 Ⓐ	Ⓐ	◇ ⑥	Ⓐ	TGV 7343 Ⓐ	TGV 7281 Ⓐ	Ⓐ	Ⓐ	©	Ⓐ	◇ †	TGV 7285	TGV 7289 ⑦ e	†	⑥	TGV 7347 Ⓑ h	Ⓐ
Paris Nord 256 ▶ d.	1622	...	...	...	...	1652	...	...	...	1728	...	...	...	1752	1828	...	...	...	...	...	1858	1858	...	...	1852	...
Arras **256** d.	1718	1722	...	...	1728	1747	...	...	...	|	1806	...	...	1845	|	...	1851	...	...	...	|	|	1926	1936	1945	...
Lens d.	1733	1738	...	...	1749	1801	...	...	...	|	1822	...	...	1858	|	...	1906	...	...	...	|	|	1942	1953	1959	...
Béthune d.	1746	1756	...	...	1828	1815	...	...	...	|	1842	...	...	1911	|	...	1924	...	...	...	|	|	2000	2012	2012	...
Lille Europe d.	|	|	...	...	|	|	1825	...	...	1830	|	1905	...	|	1930	...	|	...	...	1943	2000	2003	|	|	|	...
Lille Flandres ▶ d.	|	|	1745	1806	|	|	|	1821	1832	|	|	|	1840	|	|	1914	|	1920	1930	|	|	|	|	|	|	2013
Armentières d.	|	|	1803	|	|	|	|	1837	|	|	|	|	1856	|	|	|	|	1937	1944	|	|	|	|	|	|	2028
Hazebrouck a.	1807	1820	1821	1841	1856	1835	|	1857	1901	|	1907	|	1913	1931	|	1946	1950	1956	2001	|	|	|	2023	2036	2032	2047
Hazebrouck d.	1809	1822a	1824	1843	1858	1838	|	1859	1903	|	1909	|	1915	1933	|	1948	...	1958	2003	|	|	|	...	2038	2035	2049
Dunkerque a.	1830	1848a	1858	|	1922	1902	|	|	1928	|	|	1937	1949	|	2001	|	...	2032	2037	|	|	2035	...	2102	2056	*2121*
St Omer d.	...	...	...	1856	...	...	|	1911	...	|	1927	...	...	1946	...	2000	...	...	...	|	|	...	...	...	...	2102
Calais Fréthun **260** a.	...	...	...	|	...	...	1854	|	...	1858	|	...	...	...	...	|	...	...	...	2011	2031	...	...	...	...	|
Calais Ville 260 a.	...	...	...	1921	...	...	|	1940	...	|	1957	...	...	...	...	2028	...	...	...	|	|	...	...	...	...	2132
Boulogne Ville **260** a.	...	...	...	2004	...	...	1922	2022	...	1927	...	...	...	...	...	2114	...	...	...	2039	2101	...	...	...	...	...

	©		TGV 7351 ⑤–⑦ w	Ⓐ ◧	©	◇ †	Ⓐ ◧	g	† u	TGV 7357 ⑤ d
Paris Nord 256 ▶ d.	...	...	1952	...	...	...	...	...	...	2131
Arras **256** d.	...	2020	2045	...	...	...	...	2151	...	2224
Lens d.	...	2039	2059	...	...	...	...	2206	...	2238
Béthune d.	...	2100	2112	...	...	...	...	2225	...	2251
Lille Europe d.	...	|	|	...	...	2213	...	|	...	|
Lille Flandres ▶ d.	2020	|	|	2108	2118	|	2210	|	2223	|
Armentières d.	2036	|	|	2127	2133	|	2228	|	2238	|
Hazebrouck a.	2056	2128	2132	2147	2153	|	2245	2250	2257	2311
Hazebrouck d.	2058	2128c	2135	2151	2155	|	2247	...	2259	2313
Dunkerque a.	|	2152c	2156	2223	2223	|	2311	...	|	2335
St Omer d.	2112	...	...	...	...	|	...	...	2312	...
Calais Fréthun **260** a.	|	...	...	...	...	2241	...	...	|	...
Calais Ville 260 a.	2144	...	...	...	...	|	...	...	2342	...
Boulogne Ville **260** a.	2228	...	...	...	...	2309	...	...	...	...

	Ⓐ	TGV 7302 Ⓐ	⚒	Ⓐ	TGV 7304 Ⓐ	⚒	Ⓐ	Ⓐ	⚒	◇ Ⓐ	TGV 7214 Ⓐ
Boulogne Ville **260** d.	...	...	...	...	...	...	...	...	...	...	...
Calais Ville 260 d.	0503	...	...	0542	...	...	0558	...	...	...	...
Calais Fréthun **260** d.	|	...	...	|	...	...	|	...	...	...	...
St Omer d.	0530	...	...	0611	0623	...	0629	...	...	...	...
Dunkerque d.	*0507*	0535	0541a	|	|	0559	|	0620	0636	0642	0646
Hazebrouck a.	0542	0556	0607a	0624	0636	0633	0642	0654	0704	|	|
Hazebrouck d.	0544	0559	0609	0626	0638	0639	0644	0656	0706	|	|
Armentières d.	0601	|	|	|	|	0703	|	0716	|	|	|
Lille Flandres ▶ a.	0617	|	|	0658	|	0721	|	0735	|	|	|
Lille Europe a.	...	|	|	...	|	...	|	...	|	0712	0719
Béthune d.	...	0621	0638	...	0700	...	0714	...	0743	...	|
Lens d.	...	0634	0657	...	0712	...	0734	...	0800	...	|
Arras **256** a.	...	0646	0712	...	0725	...	0746	...	0818	...	|
Paris Nord 256 ▶ a.	...	0747	...	...	0826	...	...	...	...	...	0832

	TGV 7218 ⑥ t	†	Ⓐ	⑥	⑥	Ⓐ	TGV 7220 Ⓐ	TGV 7308 ①⑥ v	Ⓐ	⑥	Ⓐ	⚒	⚒	◇ ⚒	◇ Ⓐ	Ⓐ	⚒	©	Ⓐ	Ⓐ			TGV 7318 ▷	◇ Ⓐ	Ⓐ ▷	◇ †
Boulogne Ville **260** d.	0623	...	0602	...	...	...	0657	...	...	...	...	...	0702	0748	...	...	...	...	...	...	...	0829	...	0940	...	...
Calais Ville 260 d.	|	...	0647	0643	...	...	|	...	0705	0705	...	...	0750	|	...	...	...	...	0838	...	...	0913	...	|	...	...
Calais Fréthun **260** d.	0654	...	|	|	...	...	0729	...	|	|	...	...	|	0817	...	...	...	...	|	...	...	|	...	1011	...	...
St Omer d.	|	...	0712	0715	...	...	|	...	0739	0743	...	...	0816	|	...	...	...	...	0908	...	...	0946	...	|	...	...
Dunkerque d.	|	...	|	|	0655	0701	|	0717	|	|	0737	0743	|	|	0817	0821	...	0842	|	0910	0909c	|	0944	|	1023	1035
Hazebrouck a.	|	...	0725	0733	0730	0736	|	0738	0754	0756	0802	0817	0830	|	|	0845	...	0910	0921	0935	0943c	0959	1005	|	1047	|
Hazebrouck d.	|	0724	0727	0735	0737	0739	|	0740	0756	0758	0804	...	0832	|	|	0847	0854	0912	0923	0937	0945	1001	1008	|	1049	|
Armentières d.	|	|	|	|	0804	0805	|	|	|	0822	|	...	|	|	|	0903	|	0932	0946	1001	|	1017	|	|	1110	|
Lille Flandres ▶ a.	|	|	0801	0802	0819	0821	|	|	|	0842	0831	...	0902	|	|	0916	|	0947	1003	1019	|	1033	|	|	1125	|
Lille Europe a.	0724	|	...	...	...	...	0758	|	|	...	...	...	...	0847	0850	...	|	...	...	...	|	...	|	1043	...	1107
Béthune d.	|	0750	...	...	...	...	|	0802	0824	...	...	...	...	...	...	...	0924	...	...	...	1012	...	1030	...	...	...
Lens d.	|	0807	...	...	...	...	|	0815	0841	...	...	...	...	...	...	...	0942	...	...	...	1031	...	1043	...	...	...
Arras **256** a.	|	0820	...	...	...	...	|	0828	0855	...	...	...	...	...	...	...	0959	...	...	...	1047	...	1056	...	...	...
Paris Nord 256 ▶ a.	0832	...	...	...	...	...	0902	0926	...	...	...	...	...	...	...	...	...	...	...	...	...	...	1156	...	...	...

Local trains are 2nd class

CALAIS and DUNKERQUE - LILLE and PARIS 265

	Ⓐ ▷	Ⓐ	Ⓐ q	Ⓒ	Ⓐ ▷	⑥	◇ †	Ⓐ ◐	⑥ b	†	◇ Ⓐ	◇ ⑥	⚒ △	⚒	Ⓐ △	⑥	◇ ⑥	Ⓐ k	⑥	*TGV* **7254** ①–⑥ n	Ⓐ ⊖	Ⓒ	Ⓒ	†	*TGV* **7336** ▽	⑥
Boulogne Ville **260** . d.	...	...	...	...	...	...	1042	1036r	...	1051	1133	1139	...	...	...	...	...	...	1148	...	1157	...	...	1258	...	1303
Calais Ville 260 .... d.	...	...	1038	...	...	...	|	1118	1120	1132	|	|	...	...	...	...	...	1231	1234	1239	1246	...	...	1343	...	1353
Calais Fréthun **260** . d.	...	...	|	...	...	...	1111	|	|	|	1202	1208	...	...	...	...	...	|	|	1248	|	...	...	|	...	|
St Omer..................... d.	...	...	1107	...	...	...	|	1148	1150	1200	|	|	...	...	...	...	...	1257	1308	|	1313	...	...	1415	...	1425
Dunkerque .... d.	1044	...	|	1057	1108	1118	|	|	|	|	|	|	1157	...	1213	1212	1227	|	|	|	|	1307	1340	|	1413	|
Hazebrouck .... a.	1112	...	1120	1121	1143	1146	|	1205	1202	1212	|	|	1225	...	1245	1244	|	1314	1321	|	1327	1335	1417	1429	1434	1438
Hazebrouck .... d.	1114	...	1122	1123	1145	1148	|	1207	1204	1214	|	|	1227	1229	1247	1246	|	1316	1328	|	1329	1337	1419	1431	1437	1440
Armentières............ d.	|	...	1141	1140	1204	|	|	1226	1225	1235	|	|	|	|	1310	1309	|	|	1349	|	1348	1358	|	1452	|	1457
Lille Flandres .... ▶ a.	|	...	1157	1157	1220	|	|	1242	1240	1249	|	|	1302	|	1326	1330	|	1348	1403	|	1403	1414	|	1508	|	1511
Lille Europe .... a.	|	...	...	...	...	|	1142	...	...	...	1232	1238	...	|	...	...	1300	...	...	1319	...	...	|	...	|	...
Béthune.................... d.	1139	1220	...	...	...	1216	...	...	...	...	...	...	...	1302	...	...	...	...	...	|	...	...	1447	...	1459	...
Lens .... d.	...	1239	...	...	...	1235	...	...	...	...	...	...	...	1320	...	...	...	...	...	|	...	...	1506	...	1512	...
Arras **256**.................. a.	...	1259	...	...	...	1253	...	...	...	...	...	...	...	1335	...	...	...	...	...	|	...	...	1522	...	1525	...
Paris Nord 256 ..... ▶ a.	...	...	...	...	...	...	...	...	...	...	...	...	...	...	...	...	...	...	...	1429	...	...	...	...	1626	...

	Ⓐ	⑥	Ⓐ k	Ⓐ	Ⓐ	Ⓐ	Ⓐ	Ⓒ	*TGV* **7342**	Ⓒ	◇ Ⓐ	◇ ⚒	Ⓐ	Ⓐ	Ⓒ	Ⓐ		*TGV* **7348**	Ⓐ	Ⓐ	Ⓐ	Ⓐ	Ⓒ	Ⓐ	Ⓒ	◇ †
Boulogne Ville **260** . d.	...	...	...	...	...	...	...	1444	...	...	...	1600	...	...	...	...	...	...	...	...	...	...	1644	...	...	1714
Calais Ville 260 .... d.	...	...	1437	...	...	...	1525	1527	...	...	...	|	...	...	...	1615	...	...	...	...	1715	...	1726	...	...	|
Calais Fréthun **260** . d.	...	...	|	...	...	...	|	|	...	...	...	1632	...	...	...	|	...	...	...	...	|	...	|	...	...	1744
St Omer..................... d.	...	...	1506	...	...	...	1556	1556	...	...	...	|	...	...	...	1647	...	...	...	...	1744	...	1754	...	...	|
Dunkerque .... d.	...	1438	| •	...	1511	1535	|	*1528*	1552	1528	1623	|	1614	...	1633	|	1639a	1711	1715	1724	|	...	*1725*	...	...	|
Hazebrouck .... a.	...	1506	1519	...	1545	1602	1608	1608	1613	1600	|	|	1644	...	1657	1700	1715a	1734	1740	1758	1801	...	1806	...	...	|
Hazebrouck .... d.	1454	1508	1521	1541	1547	1604	1610	1610	1616	1623	|	|	1646	1649	1659	1702	1717	1737	1742	1800	1803	1806	1806	1815	1824	|
Armentières............ d.	|	1527	1541	|	1605	|	1629	1627	|	|	|	|	1706	|	1720	1725	|	|	1806	|	|	1830	1825	|	|	|
Lille Flandres .... ▶ a.	|	1542	1556	|	1620	|	1645	1643	|	|	|	|	1721	|	1739	1743	|	|	1821	1830	|	1846	1840	|	|	|
Lille Europe .... a.	|	...	...	|	...	|	...	...	|	|	1658	1703	...	|	...	...	|	|	...	...	|	...	...	|	|	1815
Béthune.................... d.	1522	...	...	1606	...	1642	...	...	1638	1650	...	...	...	1723	...	...	1746	1800	...	...	1831	...	...	1845	1853	...
Lens .... d.	1540	...	...	1627	...	1701	...	...	1651	1708	...	...	...	1742	...	...	1806	1813	...	...	1851	...	...	1903	1912	...
Arras **256**.................. a.	1555	...	...	1643	...	1717	...	...	1703	1722	...	...	...	1759	...	...	1822	1826	...	...	1902	...	...	1918	1928	...
Paris Nord 256 ..... ▶ a.	...	...	...	...	...	...	...	...	1756	...	...	...	...	...	...	...	...	1926	...	...	...	...	...	...	...	...

	◇ Ⓐ	Ⓐ	Ⓒ	Ⓐ	◇ ⑥	*TGV* **7288** Ⓑ h	*TGV* **7352** ⑦ e	Ⓐ	Ⓒ	Ⓐ		Ⓐ	◇ †	*TGV* **7292** Ⓐ	◇ ⑥	*TGV* **7356** ⑦ e	Ⓒ	Ⓐ	Ⓐ	*TGV* **7358** ⑤ f	Ⓒ	Ⓐ	Ⓒ	Ⓐ ⊡	◇ †	*TGV* **7298** ⑦ e
Boulogne Ville **260** . d.	...	...	...	...	...	...	...	...	1739	1731	...	...	1815	1904	1906	...	...	...	...	...	1845	...	...	1952	2045	...
Calais Ville 260 .... d.	...	1746	...	...	...	...	...	...	1826	1827	...	...	|	|	|	...	...	1914	...	...	1932	...	...	2036	|	...
Calais Fréthun **260** . d.	...	|	...	...	...	...	...	...	|	|	...	...	1845	1934	1936	...	...	|	...	...	|	...	...	|	2114	...
St Omer..................... d.	...	1815	...	...	...	...	1832	...	1900	1856	...	...	|	|	|	...	...	1942	...	...	2005	...	...	2108	|	...
Dunkerque .... d.	1801	|	1807	1810	1816	1823	|	1836	|	|	1845	...	|	|	|	1912	1917	|	1930	1943	|	...	2050	|	|	2115
Hazebrouck .... a.	|	1828	1836	1843	|	|	1845	1858	1913	1911	1917	←	|	|	|	1934	1944	1956	1959	2004	2018	...	2115	2120	|	|
Hazebrouck .... d.	|	1830	1838	1845	|	|	1847	1900	1915	→	1919	1922	|	|	|	1937	1946	...	2001	2007	2020	2037	2117	2122	|	|
Armentières............ d.	|	|	1858	1909	|	|	|	|	1932	...	|	1946	|	|	|	|	2004	...	2022	|	2042	|	2135	2142	|	|
Lille Flandres .... ▶ a.	|	1858	1916	1923	|	|	|	1930	1947	...	|	2002	|	|	|	|	2020	...	2038	|	2058	|	2150	2158	|	|
Lille Europe .... a.	1834	...	...	...	1847	1859	|	...	...	...	|	...	1915	2003	2006	|	...	...	...	|	...	|	...	...	2143	2147
Béthune.................... d.	...	...	...	...	...	|	1909	...	...	...	1946	...	...	|	...	2000	...	...	...	2029	...	2105	...	...	...	|
Lens .... d.	...	...	...	...	...	|	1921	...	...	...	2004	...	...	|	...	2013	...	...	...	2042	...	2123	...	...	...	|
Arras **256**.................. a.	...	...	...	...	...	|	1933	...	...	...	2019	...	...	|	...	2025	...	...	...	2055	...	2138	...	...	...	|
Paris Nord 256 ..... ▶ a.	...	...	...	...	...	2002	2026	...	...	...	...	...	...	2111	...	2126	...	...	...	2156	...	...	...	...	...	2302

a – Ⓐ only.
b – Not May 24.
c – Ⓒ only.
d – Also Apr. 30, May 7; not May 2.
e – Also Dec. 25, Jan. 1, Mar. 24, May 12.
f – Also Apr. 30, May 7; not May 2.
g – Not Jan. 13, 20, 27, Feb. 2. Runs 6 - 12 minutes later on Ⓐ.
h – Not May 1, 8.
k – Subject to alteration Mar. 31 - Apr. 4, Apr. 14 - 18.
m – Not Dec. 25, Jan. 1, Mar. 24, Apr. 30, May 1, 7, 8, 12.
n – Not Dec. 25, Jan. 1, Mar. 24, May 12.
q – Not Apr. 7 - 11.

r – ①–④ (not Dec. 25, Jan. 1, Mar. 24, May 1, 8, 12.).
t – Also May 1, 8.
u – Not Jan. 13, 20, 27, Mar. 2.
v – Also Dec. 26, Jan. 2, Mar. 25, May 1, 8, 13; not Dec. 24, 31, Mar. 24, May 12.
w – Also Dec. 25, Jan. 1, Mar. 24, Apr. 30, May 1, 7, 8, 12; not May 2.
z – Subject to alteration on Ⓐ Feb. 11 - 22, Mar. 25 - May 23.

TGV – Ⓡ, supplement payable.

⊖ – Subject to alteration Mar. 25 - Apr. 18.
⊗ – Runs 6 - 8 mins later Dec. 10 - 14, Apr. 21 - 25.
⊕ – Runs 3 - 6 mins earlier Dec. 10 - 14, Apr. 21 - 25.

⊙ – Subject to alteration Hazebrouck - Calais on Ⓐ Mar. 25 - Apr. 11.
⊡ – Subject to alteration Hazebrouck - Lille Jan. 7 - Feb. 2.
Δ – *303 km* by *TGV* via Lille Europe.
▷ – Subject to alteration Hazebrouck - Dunkerque and v.v. Ⓐ Mar. 10 - Apr. 4.
△ – Subject to alteration Hazebrouck - Dunkerque and v.v. on Ⓐ Mar. 3 - Apr. 4.
▽ – Subject to alteration Hazebrouck - Dunkerque and v.v. Mar. 3 - 7.
• – Distance from Hazebrouck.
◧ – Subject to alteration Jan. 7 - Feb. 1.
◐ – Subject to alteration Boulogne - Hazebrouck Apr. 7 - 18.
▶ – For *TGV* connections Paris - Lille and v.v. see Table **250**.
◇ – TER à Grande Vitesse (TER GV) via high-speed line, *TGV* train, 1, 2 class. Supplement *Côte d'Opale* payable (€3, valid all day). Reservation not necessary.

PARIS - BEAUVAIS 266

km		Ⓐ	⑥	Ⓐ	Ⓐ	⑥	†	Ⓐ	⑥	Ⓐ			⚒	Ⓐ	Ⓒ	Ⓐ	⑥	Ⓐ	Ⓐ	Ⓒ	Ⓐ	⑥	Ⓐ	Ⓐ	Ⓒ	Ⓐ
0	**Paris Nord** ....d.	0615	0632	0657	0743	0748	0859	0928	0933	1018	1118	1218	1318	1418	1433	1619	1630	1649	1719	1733	1749	1801	1819	1836*	1901	1919
80	**Beauvais** ....a.	0729	0739	0806	0853	0901	1007	1040	1049	1131	1233	1336	1438	1537	1549	1728	1739	1758	1833	1844	1905	1913	1926	1959	2011	2029

	Ⓐ	⑥	Ⓑ	Ⓒ	
Paris Nord ....d.	1949	1948	2048	2148	...
Beauvais...........a.	2100	2105	2201	2300	...

	Ⓐ	⑥	Ⓐ	⑥	†r	Ⓐ	Ⓐ	⑥	†r	Ⓐ	⑥	Ⓐ	†s		⚒	⚒	†
Beauvais .... d.	0508	0511	0614	0621	0633	0642	0717	0719	0742	0759	0844	0847	0922	1031	1144	1239	1253
Paris Nord.............. a.	0628	0624	0725	0729	0744	0757	0829	0831	0854	0912	0959	0956	1029	1144	1259	1400	1401

	⚒		Ⓐ	⑥	Ⓒ	Ⓐ	Ⓐ	†	⑥	Ⓐ	⑥	†	⑥	†	Ⓐ	†
Beauvais...........d.	1349	1428	1558	1613	1717	1740	1814	1824	1826	1908	1918	1924	2004	2005	2010	2111
Paris Nord........a.	1500	1544	1714	1729	1831	1847	1933	1931	1931	2017	2032	2031	2108	2129	2115	2217

Most trains call at Persan-Beaumont (30 minutes from Paris). Trains also run Creil - Beavais and v.v. (11 trains each way on Ⓐ, 7 on ⑥, 4 on †).

r – Not May 12
s – On May 12 depart 0937, arrive 1044.
* – Suburban station.

BEAUVAIS - LE TRÉPORT 267

km		Ⓐ	R	†S	⚒	⑤	Ⓐ	⑥	†	†	⑥	⑤
	Paris Nord **266** .. d.	...	...	0803	...	...	...	...	...	...	...	...
0	**Beauvais**.............. d.	0734	0907	0918	1243	1450	1844	1856	1856	2027	2027	2037
49	Abancourt .... d.	0827	0952	0957	1335	1539	1936	1945	1956	2115	2116	2126
103	Eu .... d.	0913	1039	|	1420	1629	2021	2031	2041	2159	2201	2211
106	**Le Tréport** .... a.	0917	1044	1039	1425	1633	2025	2036	2046	2203	2205	2215

	Ⓐ	⑥	†	①g	⚒	†	⑤	†	⚒	†
Le Tréport........... d.	0613	0643	0740	0951	1205	1247	1545	1648	1720	1830
Eu .... d.	0618	0648	0745	0956	1210	1252	1550	1653	1724	1835
Abancourt .... d.	0706	0741	0832	1050	1259	1339	1647	1738	1815	1922
Beauvais............. a.	0749	0826	0916	1134	1344	1424	1731	1822	1903	2003
Paris Nord **266** . a.	...	...	...	...	...	...	...	1931	...	2129

R – ①⑥ (also Dec. 26, Jan. 2, Mar. 25, May 2, 9, 13; not Mar. 24, May 12).
S – June 29 - Aug. 31.
g – Also Dec. 26, Jan. 2, Mar. 25, May 2, 9, 13; not Mar. 24, May 12.

Most trains 2nd class

AMIENS - ROUEN 268

km		Ⓐ	⑥	†	Ⓐ	⑥	†	⑤		Ⓐ	Ⓒ
	Lille Flandres **256**.........d.	0620	0805	...	1103	...	...	...	...	1705	1805
0	**Amiens**...........................d.	0752	0931	0950	1227	1228	1442	1605	1736	1831	1940
31	Poix de Picardie ....d.	0811	0950	1010	1247	1254	1504	1628	1757	1848	1959
52	Abancourt..........................d.	0827	1003	1025	1301	1310	1520	1644	1813	1900	2012
73	Serqueux............................d.	0840	1016	1042	1313	1327	1539	1701	1830	1913	2025
121	**Rouen Rive-Droite** ....a.	0909	1045	1115	1344	1408	1613	1739	1903	1944	2056

	Ⓐ	⑥	†	Ⓐ	⚒	Ⓐ		⑤	†
Rouen Rive-Droite.......d.	0703	0805	0916	1043	1215	1628	1811r	1920	1927
Serqueux.......................d.	0732	0834	0947	1112	1257	1705	1844	1959	2004
Abancourt.....................d.	0745	0848	1001	1126	1314	1721	1857	2016	2020
Poix de Picardie............d.	0757	0901	1014	1139	1330	1733	1909	2030	2032
Amiens ....a.	0814	0919	1032	1156	1353	1752	1926	2050	2050
Lille Flandres **256**......a.	0936	1042	...	1327	...	...	2058	...	...

r – 1814 on Ⓒ.

270 PARIS - ROUEN - LE HAVRE

km					3131		3133	3133		13141	13101	13103	13103	3135		3193	3193	3103					13105	3139
		⚒	Ⓐ	⑥	Ⓐ	⚒	Ⓐ	⑥	†	Ⓐ	⑦	Ⓐ	⑥		†	⑦	⑥	Ⓐ	†	Ⓐ	⑥	⑥	①–⑥	①–⑥
		2	2	2	🍷			t	2		d		t	🍷	2	De	Dt	x	2	2	2	2	n	🍷n
0	**Paris St Lazare** § d.	...	...	...	0639	0645	0731	0731	...	0807	0807	0815	0839	0915	0932	1044	1051	1051	...	...	...	...	1204	1240
57	Mantes la Jolie § d.	...	0627	0630	|	0718	|	|	...	|	0838	0848	0913	|	1027	|	|	|	...	...	...	...	1236	|
79	Vernon (Eure) d.	...	0648	0650	0719	0739	|	|	...	|	0851	0904	0927	|	1048	1123	|	|	...	...	...	...	1251	|
111	Val de Reuil d.	...	0708	0711	|	0803	|	|	...	|	0912	0921	0948	|	...	1140	|	|	...	...	...	...	1314	|
126	Oissel d.	...	0719	0722	|	0816	|	|	...	|	0922	0932	0958	|	...	|	|	|	...	...	...	...	1324	|
140	**Rouen** Rive-Droite a.	...	0735	0740	0750	0837	0840	0840	...	0917	0936	0945	1012	1022	...	1157	1157	1158	...	...	...	...	1336	1349
140	**Rouen** Rive-Droite d.	0639	...	...	0752	...	0842	0842	0849	...	...	...	...	1024	...	...	...	1200	1207	1220	1230	1253	...	1351
178	Yvetot d.	0704	...	...	0812	...	0902	0902	0911	...	...	...	...	1045	...	...	...	1221	1230	1251	1257	1324	...	1411
203	Bréauté-Beuzeville ▲ d.	0719	...	...	0825	...	|	0916	0925	...	...	...	...	1059	...	...	...	1235	1243	1313	1310	1343	...	1425
228	**Le Havre** a.	0735	...	...	0839	...	0926	0930	0938	...	...	...	...	1113	...	...	...	1250	1257	1335	1325	1407	...	1439

		3141	13143	3137	3143	13107	3145	13145	3147			13109	3149	3151			3157	13109	13117	3159			13111	
	Ⓐ	⑥	⑤		⑦	①–⑥	①–⑥	⑦	Ⓐ	Ⓐ	⑥	Ⓐ	⑤	Ⓐ	†	Ⓐ	⑥	⑦	①–④	⑤	①–④	⑥	Ⓐ	Ⓐ
	2	u		Z	e	n	n	q		2	2		s		2		t	e	m	f	2m			2
Paris St Lazare § d.	...	1345	1356	1356	1425	1423	1512	1544	1551	...	...	1623	1645	1650	...	1653	1709	1709	1725	1725	...	1723	1730	1745
Mantes la Jolie § d.	...	|	|	|	|	1455	|	|	|	...	...	|	|	|	...	1726	|	|	|	|	...	1756	1803	1818
Vernon (Eure) d.	...	1425	|	|	1506	1509	|	|	|	...	...	1705	|	|	...	1747	1750	1751	|	|	...	1816	1818	1837
Val de Reuil d.	...	|	|	|	1523	1526	|	|	|	...	...	1722	|	|	...	1805	1807	1812	|	|	...	1836	1840	...
Oissel d.	...	|	|	|	1533	1536	|	|	|	...	...	1733	|	|	...	1817	1817	1821	|	|	...	1846	1850	...
Rouen Rive-Droite a.	...	1455	1505	1505	1544	1548	1618	1653	1701	...	...	1747	1752	1759	...	...	1829	1833	1834	1833	...	1856	1902	...
Rouen Rive-Droite d.	1416	1457	...	1508	1546	...	1621	...	1703	1715	1736	...	1754	1802	1805	...	1831	...	...	1836	1839	...	...	...
Yvetot d.	1439	1517	...	1531	1606	...	1642	...	1724	1748	1759	...	1815	1823	1838	...	1852	...	...	1857	1902	...	...	...
Bréauté-Beuzeville ▲ d.	1452	1531	...	1547	1622	...	1655	...	|	1807	1812	...	1829	1837	1851	...	1907	...	...	1911	1915	...	...	...
Le Havre a.	1505	1545	...	1603	1636	...	1708	...	1748	1822	1826	...	1844	1852	1904	...	1921	...	...	1926	1929	...	...	...

	3161	3161	13113	3105	13115		3163	13119	3169	13147		3165	3167	5376	13149		3175	3171	13121	3179	3173	13151	13123	3177
	Ⓒ	Ⓐ	Ⓐ	Ⓐ		†	①–④	⑤	⑥	⑦	⑥	⑤	⑦	*TGV*	Ⓐ	Ⓐ	⑥	①–④	⑤	⑦	⑤	⑦		⑤⑦
						2	m	f	t	y	2	f	e	♥		2	t	w	f	y	f	q	N	z
Paris St Lazare § d.	1758	1805	1810	1845	1850	...	1931	1931	1935	1935	...	1953	2005	...	2022	2025	2036	2120	2120	2136	2153	2237	2314	2350
Mantes la Jolie § d.	|	|	1842	|	|	...	|	|	|	|	...	|	|	2047	|	2122	|	2151	2153	2208	|	|	2346	|
Vernon (Eure) d.	|	|	1857	|	1932	...	2012	2012	|	|	...	|	2046	|	|	2141	2117	2205	2208	2221	|	|	2359	0031
Val de Reuil d.	|	|	1918	|	1954	...	2030	2029	|	|	...	|	|	|	|	...	|	2222	2226	2239	|	|	0017	0049
Oissel d.	|	|	1928	|	2004	...	|	|	|	|	...	|	|	|	|	...	|	2232	2237	2248	|	|	0026	0058
Rouen Rive-Droite a.	1908	1914	1939	1953	2017	...	2047	2048	2042	2043	...	2100	2117	2126	2133	...	2148	2243	2248	2259	2301	2346	0038	0106
Rouen Rive-Droite d.	1911	1917	...	1955	...	2025	2049	...	2044	...	2052	2102	2119	2129	...	...	2150	2245	...	2301	2303	...	...	0108
Yvetot d.	1933	1939	...	2016	...	2050	2110	...	2105	...	2119	2123	2140	|	...	...	2211	2305	...	2322	2323	...	...	0129
Bréauté-Beuzeville ▲ d.	1948	1954	...	|	...	2105	2124	...	|	...	2133	2138	2155	|	...	...	2226	2320	...	2337	2338	...	...	0142
Le Havre a.	2003	2009	...	2040	...	2120	2139	...	2130	...	2148	2152	2210	2215	...	...	2241	2335	...	2352	2353	...	...	0157

	13100			13102	3130		13104	3132	13106	3134	3100		13108				3136	3136	5316		13140		13142	13110
	Ⓐ	Ⓐ	⑥	Ⓐ	Ⓐ	Ⓐ	⑦	⑥	Ⓐ	Ⓐ	Ⓐ	⑥	①–⑥		⚒	Ⓐ	†	⚒	*TGV*	⑥	⑥	Ⓐ	Ⓐ	
							e	t				2	n		2	2		🍷	♥	2	t	2		
Le Havre d.	...	...	...	...	0543	...	...	0613	...	0631	0702	...	...	...	0708	0726	0751	0754	0806	0837	...	0856	...	...
Bréauté-Beuzeville ▲ d.	...	...	...	...	0601	...	...	0629	...	0648	|	0700	...	...	0724	0744	0807	|	|	0852	...	0911	...	...
Yvetot d.	...	...	...	...	0617	...	...	0643	...	0703	0728	0715	...	...	0743	0800	0821	0820	|	0906	...	0926	...	...
Rouen Rive-Droite a.	...	...	...	...	0637	...	...	0704	...	0724	0748	0743	...	...	0817	0823	0842	0841	0847	0928	...	0948	...	...
Rouen Rive-Droite d.	0536	...	...	0615	0640	0650	0658	0706	0710	0727	0750	...	0755	...	...	...	0846	0846	0852	...	0944	...	0954	1007
Oissel d.	0547	0605	0619	0625	|	0700	0709	0717	|	|	|	...	0807	...	...	...	|	|	|	...	|	...	|	1017
Val de Reuil d.	0559	0619	0634	0637	|	0712	0719	0730	0732	|	|	...	0820	...	...	...	|	|	|	...	|	...	|	1028
Vernon (Eure) d.	0621	0646	0657	0700	|	0737	0740	0748	0751	0803	|	...	0842	...	...	...	|	|	|	...	|	...	|	1051
Mantes la Jolie § a.	|	0709	0720	0715	|	0756	0755	|	0803	|	|	...	0857	...	...	...	|	|	0936	...	|	...	|	1106
Paris St Lazare § a.	0705	0745	0757	0754	0757	0835	0829	0831	0838	0849	0903	...	0932	...	...	...	0958	0958	...	...	1054	...	1104	1140

	13144	3138		13146	3140	13112	3142			3166	13114	3144	3146		13148	13150			3102	3162	3194	13116	3148	
	⑦	①–⑥		Ⓐ	⑦	①–⑥	①–⑥	⑥	Ⓐ	Ⓐ	①–⑥	⑦	①–⑥		⑦	⑤	†	⚒	Ⓐ		Ⓒ	Ⓐ	⑦	⑥
	q	🍷c			🍷e	n	n	2	2		n	e	n		e	b				Y	D🍷		q	2
Le Havre d.	...	1010	...	...	1106	...	1202	1231	1236	1304	...	1326	1359	...	...	...	...	...	1604	1607	...	...	1639	1636
Bréauté-Beuzeville ▲ d.	...	1025	...	...	1121	...	1217	1256	1255	|	...	1343	1416	...	...	...	...	...	|	1623	...	...	1655	1700
Yvetot d.	...	1039	...	...	1135	...	1231	1314	1313	1330	...	1358	1430	...	...	...	...	...	1631	1636	...	...	1709	1719
Rouen Rive-Droite a.	...	1059	...	...	1156	...	1250	1344	1344	1350	...	1418	1451	...	...	...	...	...	1652	1656	...	...	1730	1750
Rouen Rive-Droite d.	1101	1101	...	1146	1159	1210	1252	...	...	1352	1416	1422	1453	...	1602	1613	1640	1649	1654	1659	1719	1718	1733	...
Oissel d.	|	|	...	|	1209	1220	|	...	...	|	1427	|	|	...	|	|	1653	1708	|	1710	1728	1728	|	...
Val de Reuil d.	|	|	...	|	1222	1233	|	...	...	|	1438	|	|	...	|	|	1707	1720	|	1721	1740	1740	|	...
Vernon (Eure) d.	|	|	...	|	1240	1255	|	...	...	|	1457	|	|	...	|	|	1730	1749	|	1744	1800	1804	|	...
Mantes la Jolie § a.	|	|	...	|	1255	1308	|	...	...	|	1511	|	|	...	|	|	1751	1807	|	|	|	|	|	...
Paris St Lazare § a.	1211	1211	....	1259	1331	1341	1401	...	...	1503	1544	1532	1603	...	1712	1727	1825	...	1810	1829	1841	1850	1844	...

		3104	13118				3152	3150		3150		3196		13122	3156	3154	13124	3158		13126			13128	3160
	Ⓐ		⑦	Ⓐ	⚒	⑥		Ⓐ	⑥	⑦		⑦	Ⓐ	Ⓐ	⑦	⑥	⑦	Ⓐ	†	⑦	Ⓐ	⑥	⑦	⑦
	2		q		2	2	Y	🍷	2	y		De	2		🍷y	🍷t	e	🍷	2	e	2	2	q	🍷e
Le Havre d.	1644	1704	...	...	1710	...	1804	1816	1815	1826	...	...	1829	...	1921	1927	...	1949	2010	...	2051	2051	...	2126
Bréauté-Beuzeville ▲ d.	1709	1720	...	...	1731	...	1821	1831	1830	1842	...	...	1856	...	1937	1943	...	2005	2025	...	2106	2106	...	2142
Yvetot d.	1728	1734	...	...	...	...	1836	1846	1843	1856	...	...	1916	...	1951	1958	...	2019	2038	...	2119	2120	...	2156
Rouen Rive-Droite a.	1812	1755	...	...	...	...	1856	1906	1905	1915	...	...	1950	...	2011	2018	...	2039	2100	...	2142	2143	...	2217
Rouen Rive-Droite d.	...	1758	1821	1817	...	1844	1858	1908	...	1918	...	1953	...	2003	2014	2020	2034	2041	...	2125	...	...	2158	2219
Oissel d.	...	|	1831	1836	...	1857	|	|	...	|	...	|	...	2014	|	2031	2045	|	...	2135	...	...	|	|
Val de Reuil d.	...	|	1845	1850	...	1908	|	|	...	|	...	|	...	2026	|	2042	2056	|	...	2146	...	...	|	|
Vernon (Eure) d.	...	|	1902	1914	...	1930	|	|	...	|	...	|	...	2043	|	2101	2113	|	...	2208	...	...	|	|
Mantes la Jolie § a.	...	|	1915	1935	...	1948	|	|	...	|	...	|	...	|	|	2115	2127	|	...	2223	...	...	|	|
Paris St Lazare § a.	...	1907	1950	2011	...	...	2008	2017	...	2027	...	2103	...	2126	2125	2147	2200	2151	...	2255	...	...	2309	2330

D – (12) Paris - Rouen - Dieppe and v.v. (Table **270a**).
E – ①②④⑤ (not holidays).
K – June 15 - Sept. 14.
N – ①②③④⑥ (also Dec. 23, 30, Mar. 23, May 2, 9, 11; not Dec. 25, Jan. 1, Mar. 24, May 12).
Y – Dec. 25, Jan. 1, 6, Mar. 24, May 4, 12 only.
Z – Dec. 21, 28, Mar. 21, Apr. 18, 30, May 7 only.
b – Also Apr. 30, May 7.
c – Not Dec. 25, Jan. 1, Mar. 18, 24, May 12.
d – Also Dec. 25, Jan. 1, Mar. 24, May 8, 12.
e – Also Dec. 25, Jan. 1, Mar. 24, May 12.
f – Also Apr. 30, May 7; not May 2, 9.
m – Not Dec. 25, Jan. 1, Mar. 24, Apr. 30, May 1, 7, 8, 12.
n – Not Dec. 25, Jan. 1, Mar. 24, May 12.
q – Also Dec. 25, Jan. 1, Mar. 24, May 12; not Dec. 23, 30, Mar. 23, May 11.
s – Also Dec. 25, Jan. 1, 6, Mar. 24, Apr. 30, May 4, 7, 12; not May 2, 9.
t – Also May 1, 8.
u – Also Dec. 25, Jan. 1, 6, Mar. 24, May 1, 8, 12.
w – Also May 2, 9; not Dec. 25, Jan. 1, Mar. 24, Apr. 30, May 1, 7, 8, 12.
x – Also May 12.
y – Also Dec. 25, Jan. 1, Mar. 24, May 12; not Mar. 23, May 11
z – Also Dec. 25, Jan. 1, Mar. 24, May 12; not Dec. 23, 30, Mar 23, May 2, 9, 11.

TGV – [R], supplement payable, 🍷.

♥ – To/from Lyon and Marseille (Table **335**).
▲ – Connecting trains run Bréauté-Beuzeville - Fécamp and v.v
§ – Frequent suburban trains run Paris - Mantes-la-Jolie and v.v

Note: certain departures towards Paris are 2 - 3 mins later to May 9

270a ROUEN - DIEPPE

63 km. Most trains 2nd class

	Ⓐ	⑥	Ⓐ	Ⓐ	⑥	Ⓐ	†		Ⓐ	⑦e	⑥t	⑥	†K	⑥	Ⓐ	⑥	Ⓐ	Ⓐ	⚒	Ⓐ	⑥K	Ⓐ	†	Ⓐ
Paris **270** d.	...	...	...	...	...	...	...	...	...	1044	1051	...	...	...	...	...	...	...	...	...	...	...	...	...
Rouen Rive-Droite d.	0607	0624	0745	0812	0853	0925	0944	1032	1210	1214	1214	1222	1325	1357	1404	1504	1610	1643	1708	1807	1816	1844	1920	1922
Dieppe a.	0706	0724	0831	0910	0935	1012	1031	1131	1250	1254	1254	1328	1418	1444	1451	1548	1708	1724	1809	1851	1905	1939	2009	2005

	⑥	Ⓐ	⑤b	†	Ⓐ	⑥	
Paris **270** d.	...	...	...	...	...	...	...
Rouen Rive-Droite d.	1943	2012	2109	2141	2154	2157	...
Dieppe a.	2022	2058	2148	2222	2230	2242	...

	Ⓐ	Ⓐ	⑥	Ⓐ	⑥	†	Ⓐ	⑥	Ⓐ	Ⓐ	Ⓐ
Dieppe d.	0554	0636	0638	0714	0749	0753	0754	0822	0840	1049	1155
Rouen Rive-Droite a.	0654	0730	0737	0801	0830	0836	0834	0922	0939	1138	1231
Paris **270** a.	...	...	...	...	...	...	...	...	...	...	...

	⑥	E	⑥	③	†	Ⓐ	Ⓐ	Ⓒ	⑦K	Ⓐ	†	Ⓐ	⑥	Ⓐ	⑦e	⑥	Ⓐ	†	⑥K	†K
Dieppe d.	1158	1223	1300	1308	1303	1507	1603	1619	1648	1726	1805	1810	1838	1854	1853	1923	1942	2021	2054	2125
Rouen Rive-Droite a.	1239	1320	1353	1402	1403	1555	1643	1704	1741	1820	1846	1903	1937	1939	1937	2010	2027	2114	2138	2205
Paris **270** a.	...	...	...	...	...	...	...	1841	...	...	...	...	...	...	2103	...	...	...	...	...

FOR NOTES SEE TABLE 270 ABOVE

 French public holidays are on Dec. 25, Jan. 1, Mar. 24, May 1, 8, 12

CAEN - LE MANS - TOURS 271

km		⚒	① g	Ⓐ	Ⓐ	Ⓐ		⑥	Ⓑ	⑥	⚒	⑤⑦ u	N	①–④ m		†	①–④ 2m	⑤ 2d	⚒	⑥ 🚌	Ⓐ	Ⓐ	⑦ q	⑤ f	N	⑦ y
0	**Caen** 275 d.	...	0505	...	...	0739	0838	...	...	...	...	1305	1304	...	...	1621	1625	1625	...	...	...	1726	1755	1824	1824	2140
23	Mézidon 275 d.	...	0520	...	...	0754	0854	...	...	...	...	1322	1322	...	...	|	1641	1641	...	...	...	1742	1813	1839	1838	2154
67	Argentan 273 d.	...	0542	...	0653	0819	0922	...	...	...	...	1351	1351	...	...	1703	1708	1708	...	...	...	1817	1841	1906	1908	2216
82	Surdon 273 d.	...	0552	...	0703	|	|	...	...	...	...	1402	1402	...	...	|	|	|	...	...	...	1827	1852	1917	|	|
91	Sées d.	...	0559	...	0711	0834	|	...	...	...	...	1410	1409	...	...	1718	1723	1723	...	...	...	1835	1859	1924	1924	2231
11	Alençon d.	...	0613	*0639*z	0725	0846	0949	...	*1144*a	...	1251	1423	1423	...	...	1733	1737	1737	...	...	*1830*	1847	1913	1938	1936	2243
66	**Le Mans** a.	...	0654	*0731*z	0809	0914	1020	...	*1214*a	...	1336	1451	1452	...	...	1807	1809	1809	...	...	*1912*	...	1941	2008	2006	2312
66	**Le Mans** d.	0615	...	0736	...	...	1036	1212	1242	1309	...	1453	...	1502	1640	1810	*1820*	1824	1840	...	2019	...	2026	...	...	...
15	Château du Loir d.	0649	...	0803	...	...	1105	1255	1312	1344	...	1523	...	1531	1718	1839	*1846*	1854	1929	1950	2054	...	2055	...	...	...
62	St Pierre des Corps a.	|	...	|	...	...	1135	|	|	|	...	|	...	1602	|	|	|	1923	...	|	|	...	|	...	...	...
65	**Tours** a.	0735	...	0832	...	...	*1143*	1332	1340	1416	...	1553	...	1615	1747	1909	*1915*	1934	...	2035	2127	...	2125	...	...	...

	Ⓐ 2	Ⓐ	⑥ 2	① g	Ⓐ	⚒	†	†	①–④ m	⑤⑥ k	⚒		⑥	①–④ m	①–④ m	⑤ d	⑦ q	①–⑥ n	Ⓐ 2	Ⓑ	⑥	⑤ d	†	①–④ m	⑦ q	⑤⑦ y
Tours d.	...	...	...	0551	0645	0756	...	0900	*0941*	0947	...	1205	1225	1359	...	1523	1653	1700	...	1831	...	...	...	...	2008	2319
St Pierre des Corps d.	...	...	...	|	|	|	...	0911	*0951*	0957	...	|	|	|	...	|	|	|	...	|	...	...	...	...	2017	|
Château du Loir d.	...	...	...	0625	0721	0826	...	0940	*1021*	1027	...	1235	1312	1428	...	1556	1724	1732	...	1902	...	...	...	...	2048	2357
Le Mans a.	...	...	...	0716	0804	0856	...	1010	*1053*	1059	...	1308	1400	1459	...	1624	1752	1800	...	1934	...	...	...	...	2117	0032
Le Mans d.	0631g	0705	...	...	*0849*	...	1005	...	1105	1105	1238	...	...	...	...	1634	1800	1805	1823	...	1955	1958	2004	2021	2119	...
Alençon d.	0701	0745	0745	...	*0925*	...	1034	...	1136	1136	1326	...	...	...	1725	1723	1838	1838	1914	...	2031	2030	2038	2105	2150	...
Sées d.	0714	0758	0758	...	...	...	1047	...	1150	1150	1338	...	...	...	1737	1737	1853	1853	1928	...	...	2044	2052	2121	2204	...
Surdon 273 d.	0722	0805	0805	...	...	...	1054	...	1157	1157	1344	...	...	...	1744	1745	1901	1901	1935	...	...	2052	2100	2129	|	...
Argentan 273 d.	0733	0814	0814	...	...	...	1104	...	1209	1209	1353	...	...	...	1753	1757	1912	1912	...	...	...	2103	2112	2140	2219	...
Mézidon 275 d.	0800	0840	0840	...	...	...	1129	...	1231	1235	1419	...	...	...	1822	1834	1936	1937	...	...	...	2130	2141	...	|	...
Caen 275 a.	0814	0853	0856	...	...	...	1142	...	1244	1251	1432	...	...	...	1835	1850	1952	1953	...	...	...	2145	2156	...	2257	...

– ①②③④⑥ (also May 2; not Dec. 25, Jan. 1, Mar. 24, Apr. 30, May 7, 12).
– Ⓐ only.
– Also Apr. 30, May 7.
– Also Apr. 30, May 7; not May 2, 9.

g – ① (also Dec. 26. Jan. 2, Mar. 25, May 13; not Dec. 24, 31, Mar. 24, May 12).
k – Also Apr. 30, May 1, 7, 8; not May 2.
m – Not Dec. 25, Jan. 1, Mar. 24, Apr. 30, May 1, 7, 8, 12.
n – Not Dec. 25, Jan. 1, Mar. 24, May 12.

q – Also Dec. 25, Jan. 1, Mar. 24, May 12; not Mar. 23, May 11.
u – Also Dec. 25, Jan. 1, Mar. 24, Apr. 30, May 7, 12; not Mar. 23, May 2, 11.
y – Also Dec. 25, Jan. 1, Mar. 24, May 12; not Dec. 23, 30, Mar. 23, May 11.
z – ⚒ only.

CAEN - COUTANCES - RENNES 272

km		① g	⚒	⑥ 2	Ⓐ	⑥	Ⓐ 2	Ⓐ 2	Ⓒ 2	Ⓐ	🚌 Ⓐ		⑥	E	Ⓐ	⑥		⚒	Ⓐ	⚒	†	①–④ 2m	⑤ d	⑤ d	⑤ d
0	**Caen** 275 d.	0555	0640	0728	0731	0843	0905	1057	1108	1232	...	1321	1419	1429	1520	1620	1655	1718	1812	1812	1855	1907	1914	*2003*	2047
30	Bayeux 275 d.	0611	0657	0746	0747	0900	0924	1115	1125	1248	...	1344	1437	1446	1536	1636	1712	1741	1833	1833	1912	1924	1932	|	2105
57	Lison 275 d.	0626	0713	0802	0802	0916	0940	1131	1141	1300	1306	1402	1453	1501	1551	1650	1728	1759	1851	1851	1928	1940	1948	2036	2121
75	St Lô d.	0640	0728	0815	0815	0929	0952	1144	1154	...	1326	1418	1506	1514	1602	1702	1741	1814	1907	1907	1941	1956	2001	2049	2134
105	**Coutances** d.	0703	0749	0835	0836	0950	1012	1204	1214	...	1356	1440	1527	1535	...	*1740**	1805	...	*1945**	...	2003	2018	2023	2112	2154
	Granville ▲ a.	|	*0825*a	*0911*	|	|	...	...	...	...	1426	*1515*	*1613*n	*1620*n	...	...	*1839*	...	...	...	*2037*	...	*2057*	...	...
132	Folligny d.	0726	...	...	0858	1013	...	...	...	...	...	...	1549	1556	...	...	1828	...	...	...	2023	...	2044	...	...
151	Avranches d.	0741	...	...	0913	1027	...	...	...	...	...	...	1603	1611	...	...	1842	...	...	...	2039	...	2100	...	...
173	Pontorson ⊡ d.	0801	...	...	0931	1044	...	...	...	...	...	...	1619	1628	...	...	1859	...	...	...	2058	...	2118	...	...
194	Dol 281 d.	0819	...	...	0949	1101	...	...	...	...	...	...	1635	1645	...	...	1917	...	...	...	2116	...	2136	...	...
252	**Rennes** 281 a.	0850	...	...	1020	1137	...	...	...	...	...	...	1705	1725	...	...	1950	...	...	...	2145	...	2206	...	...

	Ⓐ 2	🚌 Ⓐ	⚒ 2	① g	🚌 P		Ⓐ	Ⓒ 2	⑥	Ⓐ	⚒ 2	🚌 Ⓒ	Ⓒ	Ⓐ	†	⚒	⑤ d	†	2	①–④ m	⑤–⑦ w	①–④ m	†	⑤ d	⑦ y
Rennes 281 d.	...	...	...	0550	...	...	...	...	0848	0906	...	...	...	...	1306	...	1421	...	...	...	1616	1650	1807	1821	2045
Dol 281 d.	...	...	...	0627	...	...	...	...	0919	0939	...	...	...	...	1336	...	1456	...	...	...	1649	1732	1846	1902	2121
Pontorson ⊡ d.	...	...	...	0644	...	...	...	...	0935	0955	...	...	...	...	1353	...	1514	...	...	...	1705	1748	1902	1919	2137
Avranches d.	...	...	...	0707	...	...	...	...	0956	1016	...	...	...	...	1414	...	1537	...	...	...	1727	1810	1924	1943	2158
Folligny d.	...	...	...	0725	...	...	...	...	1011	1031	...	...	...	...	1429	...	1555	...	...	...	1742	1827	1939	1959	2213
Granville ▲ d.	...	0604	*0625*c	*0655*n	0708	...	...	*0825*	*0952*c	*1012*	*1205*	...	...	*1313*x	*1359*n	...	*1525*n	...	*1637*s	*1712**	*1724*	*1758*n	*1922*	*1942*	*2143*n
Coutances d.	0615	0635	0705	0752	0739	...	0900	0905	1032	1052	1245	1347	...	1354	1450	...	1615	...	1717	*1743**	1804	1851	2002	2022	2234
St Lô d.	0641	0707	0729	0816	0813	...	0921	0930	1054	1114	1306	1417	...	1418	1515	1613	1637	1700	1742	1825	1826	1914	2023	2050	2255
Lison 275 d.	0656	0727	0744	0829	0833	0850	0934	0942	1107	1127	1320	1437	1447	1431	1529	1625	1649	1712	1756	1839	1838	1932	2036	2103	2308
Bayeux 275 d.	0714	...	0802	0844	...	0904	0950	1001	1121	1143	1335	...	1501	1447	1543	1639	1704	1725	1811	1856	1854	1947	2051	2117	2323
Caen 275 a.	0737	...	0824	0901	...	0920	1007	1018	1137	1201	1352	...	1517	1504	1559	1700	1720	1740	1828	1917	1911	2003	2106	2133	2339

– ①⑤⑦ (also Dec. 25, 26, Jan. 1, 2, Mar. 24, 25, Apr. 30, May 1, 7, 8, 13; not Dec. 24, 31).
– ②–⑤ only.
– Ⓐ only.
– ⑥ only.
– Also Apr. 30, May 7.

g – Also Dec. 26. Jan. 2, Mar. 25, May 13; not Dec. 24, 31, Mar. 24, May 12.
m – Not Dec. 25, Jan. 1, Mar. 24, Apr. 30, May 1, 7, 8, 12.
n – 🚌 Folligny - Granville and v.v.
s – Ⓑ only.
w – Also Dec. 25, Jan. 1, Mar. 24, Apr. 30, May 1, 7, 8, 12.

x – ⑤ (also Apr. 30, May 7).
y – Also Dec. 25, Jan. 1, Mar. 24, May 12; not Dec. 23, 30, Mar. 23, May 11.

▲ – Connection by 🚌 (timings subject to confirmation).
⊡ – Pontorson-Mont St Michel (10 km from Mont St Michel).
* – By 🚌.

PARIS - DREUX - GRANVILLE 273

km			3411	3413	16511			3421	3423	3431	3433	3435			3441	3443			3445			3453	3451	
		Ⓐ	Ⓐ	Ⓒ	⑦ q	Ⓐ	⑥	①–⑥ n	⑦ e	①–⑥ n	⑦ e	⑤ f	Ⓐ 2v	⑥	①–⑥ n	⑦ y	⑤ d	①–④ m	⑤ f	Ⓐ	⚒ 2	Ⓒ	Ⓐ	Ⓐ 2v
0	**Paris Montparnasse** ⊖ 274 d.	...	0706	0820	0914	0926	0927	1030	1040	1330	1340	1451	1455	1519	1635	1635	*1718*	*1733*	1735	1820	1833	1935	1938	1948
17	Versailles Chantiers ▲ 274 d.	...	|	0833	0929	0939	0940	|	|	|	|	|	1508	1533	|	|	*1732*	*1747*	|	1833	1847	1948	|	2002
82	**Dreux** d.	0515	0756	0908	1016	1016	1035	1118	1128	↓	|	|	1604	1622	1722	1725	1832	1848	|	1917	1944	2026	2026	2101
118	Verneuil sur Avre d.	0546	|	0927	1046	1039	...	|	|	1432	1442	|	...	1653	1741	1745	1857	1912	|	1942	...	2045	2045	...
142	L'Aigle d.	0604	0825	0941	1104	1053	...	1147	1156	1446	1456	1606	...	1711	1755	1758	1913	1928	1852	1958	...	2059	2059	...
183	Surdon 271 d.	0635	0845	1001	1139	1122	...	|	|	1506	1516	|	...	1736	1815	1819	1940	1955	1913	2026	...	2119	2119	...
198	Argentan 271 d.	0646	0856	1012	1150	1132	...	1217	1226	1517	1527	1635	...	1745	1826	1829	1950	2005	1923	2038	...	2130	2130	...
226	Briouze d.	0708	0912	1028	1206	...	...	|	|	1533	1543	|	...	...	|	|	...	...	1939	...	...	2146	2145	...
243	Flers d.	0720	0923	1038	1217	...	...	1239	1249	1543	1553	1658	...	...	1849	1853	...	...	1951	...	...	2156	2156	...
272	Vire d.	0737	0939	1055	1233	...	...	1256	1305	1559	1609	1714	...	...	1906	1910	...	...	2007	...	...	2212	2213	...
298	Villedieu d.	0757	0956	1109	1248	...	...	1310	1319	1614	1624	1728	...	...	1920	1926	...	...	2022	...	...	2227	2227	...
313	Folligny 272 d.	0808	1007	1121	1300	...	...	|	|	|	|	|	...	...	|	|	...	...	2033	...	...	|	|	...
328	**Granville** 272 a.	0818	1016	1130	1310	...	...	1329	1338	1632	1642	1748	...	...	1939	1944	...	...	2043	...	...	2245	2245	...

			16510				3410		3412		3420		3430		3432	3440	3442		3444		13272	3450		3454
	Ⓐ	Ⓐ 2v	① g	Ⓐ	⑥	†	①–⑥ n	⚒ 2	⑦ e	† 2		⑥	①–⑥ n	Ⓐ	⑦ e	①–⑥ n	⑦ e	Ⓐ	⑦ q	Ⓐ	⑦ q		⑦ q	⑦ q
Granville 272 d.	...	...	0444	...	...	...	0604	...	0657	...	0937	...	1224	...	1354	1521	1537	1635	1700	...	...	1830	...	1945
Folligny 272 d.	...	...	|	...	...	...	|	...	|	...	|	...	|	...	|	|	|	1647	|	...	...	1840	...	1956
Villedieu d.	...	...	0502	...	...	...	0621	...	0714	...	0955	...	1241	...	1411	1539	1554	1657	1717	...	...	1851	...	2006
Vire d.	...	...	0517	...	...	...	0637	...	0731	...	1012	...	1257	...	1426	1555	1610	1715	1733	...	...	1907	...	2022
Flers d.	...	...	0535	...	...	...	0654	...	0747	...	1030	...	1314	...	1443	1611	1627	1736	1749	...	...	1925	...	2038
Briouze d.	...	...	0547	...	...	...	0705	...	0759	...	|	...	1325	...	1454	|	|	1748	1800	...	...	1937	...	2050
Argentan 271 d.	0513	...	0610	0610	0620	0620	0723	...	0816	...	1057	1117	1343	1430	1511	1636	1652	1809	1818	1857	1920	1953	2010	2107
Surdon 271 d.	0524	...	0621	0621	0631	0630	0733	...	0826	...	1108	1127	1355	1440	1521	|	|	...	|	1908	1931	2005	2020	|
L'Aigle d.	0551	...	0649	0649	0656	0702	0753	...	0847	...	1130	1152	1417	1509	1542	1703	1719	...	1849	1946	2000	2025	2048	2136
Verneuil sur Avre d.	0607	...	0703	0703	0711	0715	0807	...	0900	...	1143	1210	|	1523	1556	|	|	...	|	2001	2013	2039	2105	|
Dreux d.	0630	0638	0728	0728	0735	0739	0827	0916	0921	1033	|	1241	|	1547	|	1733	1750	...	|	2023	2037	2100	2134	|
Versailles Chantiers ▲ 274 a.	...	0729	0814	0814	0830	0840	|	1012	|	1129	|	1330	|	1629	|	|	|	...	|	...	2114	|	2230	|
Paris Montparnasse ⊖ 274 a.	...	0742	0828	0828	0843	0852	0916	1026	1008	1143	1248	1343	1541	1642	1657	1828	1837	...	2004	...	2125	2146	2242	2249

– Also Dec. 25, Jan. 1, Mar. 24, May 12.
- Also Apr. 30, May 7; not May 2, 9.
– Also Dec. 26. Jan. 2, Mar. 25, May 13; not Dec. 24, 31, Mar. 24, May 12.
– Not Dec. 24 - Jan. 1, Mar. 24, Apr. 30, May 1, 7, 8, 12.

n – Not Dec. 25, Jan. 1, Mar. 24, May 12.
q – Also Dec. 25, Jan. 1, Mar. 24, May 12; not Mar. 23, May 11.
v – Not Dec. 22 - Jan. 1.
y – Also Dec. 25, Jan. 1, Mar. 24, May 12; not Dec. 23, 30, Mar. 23, May 11.

⊖ – Most trains use **Vaugirard** platforms (5 - 10 mins walk).
▲ – Local travel to / from Paris not permitted on certain trains (see Table **274** for local services).

274 PARIS - VERSAILLES

RER (express Métro) Line C: **Paris Austerlitz** - St Michel Notre Dame - **Versailles Rive Gauche** (for Château). Every 15 - 30 minutes. Journey 40 minutes.
Alternative service: RER Line C: Paris Austerlitz - St Michel Notre Dame - Versailles Chantiers. Journey 39 minutes.
SNCF suburban services: Paris St Lazare - Versailles Rive Droite (journey 28 - 35 minutes); Paris Montparnasse - Versailles Chantiers (journey 12 - 28 minutes). See also Table **278**.

275 PARIS - CAEN - CHERBOURG

For other trains Paris - Lisieux (- Trouville-Deauville) see Table **276**. For other trains (Rouen) - Serquigny - Lisieux - Caen see Table **277**. Many express trains convey 🍷 in July / August.

km	🍷 on most fast trains	3301							3331	3303					3333	3337	3313		3305	3339		3307	13337			3341
		①	Ⓐ	⑥	Ⓐ	Ⓐ	⑥	Ⓐ	Ⓐ	Ⓐ	⑥	⑥	†	Ⓐ	⑥	Ⓐ		Ⓐ	Ⓒ	Ⓒ	⑥	Ⓐ	Ⓑ	Ⓐ	⑥	Ⓒ
		g									2				t		Z	2								
0	**Paris St Lazare** .... ▷ d.	0025	...	...	...	...	...	...	0642	0712	*0616*	...	...	...	0810	0840	0904	...	0908	1010	...	1043	1100	...	...	1200
57	Mantes la Jolie ...... ▷ d.	|	...	...	...	...	...	...	|	|	0724	...	...	...	|	|	|	...	|	|	...	|	1134	...	...	|
108	Evreux .... d.	0133	...	...	...	0609	...	...	0737	|	0758	...	...	...	0905	0934	|	...	|	1106	...	|	1208	...	...	1257
150	Serquigny .... d.	|	...	...	...	0637	...	...	|	|	▬	...	...	...	|	|	|	...	|	|	...	|	1245	...	...	|
160	Bernay .... d.	0212	...	...	...	0644	...	...	0802	|	...	...	...	...	0930	1000	|	...	|	1131	...	|	▬	...	...	1322
191	Lisieux .... d.	0239	...	...	0636	0659	*0705*	...	0820	|	...	...	0900	0950	0947	1016	|	...	1037	1149	...	1208	...	1235	1241	1340
216	Mézidon **271** .... d.	|	...	...	0650	0713	*0720*	...	|	|	Ⓐ	...	0914	1004	1003	|	|	...	|	|	...	|	...	1249	1256	|
239	**Caen 271** .... a.	0317	...	...	0707	0731	*0738*	...	0846	0858	2	...	0931	1016	1018	1044	1051	...	1058	1218	...	1230	†	1306	1308	1405
239	**Caen 272** .... d.	0320	0604	0630	0709	...	0800	0825	...	0900	0905	0920	0932	1017	...	...	1053	1057	1100	...	1228	1232	1315	*1321*	*1321*	...
269	Bayeux **272** .... d.	0342	0620	0646	0724	...	0815	0846	...	|	0924	0939	0948	1032	...	...	1108	1115	1115	...	1246	1248	1331	*1344*	*1344*	...
296	Lison **272** .... d.	0403	0634	0700	0738	...	0829	0901	...	|	0939	0957	1003	1045	...	...	1122	1130	1129	...	1302	1301	1346	*1401*	*1401*	...
314	Carentan .... d.	0418	0644	0710	0748	...	0839	...	...	0932	...	1007	1013	1055	...	...	1132	...	1139	...	1312	1312	1356	...	...	...
343	Valognes .... d.	0439	0702	0725	0806	...	0857	...	...	0946	...	1022	1026	1110	...	...	1145	...	1153	...	1327	1326	1413	...	...	...
371	**Cherbourg** .... a.	0500	0716	0740	0820	...	0911	...	...	1002	...	1037	1040	1126	...	...	1202	...	1210	...	1342	1342	1427	...	...	...

	3341	3309	13339	3309	3343				3345	3311		3315		3347			3349	3349		3317			3351	3319	3355	3321
		Ⓐ	Ⓐ	⑥	⑤	Ⓐ	⑥	Ⓐ		Ⓐ	Ⓐ	⑦	⑥	⑥	†	Ⓐ	①–④	⑤	Ⓐ	Ⓐ	⑥			⑤	①–④	⑤
	Z			t	f							e		t			w	d						f	m	d
Paris St Lazare .... ▷ d.	1200	1225	1231	1305	1308	...	...	...	1430	1457	...	1600	...	1613	...	...	1633	1633	...	1705	...	1710	1733	1813	1830	1830
Mantes la Jolie ..... ▷ d.	|	|	1303	|	|	...	...	...	|	|	...	|	...	|	...	...	|	|	...	|	...	1741	|	|	|	|
Evreux .... d.	1257	|	1337	|	1403	...	...	...	1525	|	...	|	...	|	...	...	|	|	...	|	...	1831	1828	|	|	|
Serquigny .... d.	|	|	▬	|	|	...	...	...	|	|	...	|	...	|	...	...	|	|	...	|	...	1909	|	|	|	|
Bernay .... d.	1322	|	...	|	|	...	...	...	1551	|	...	|	...	|	...	...	|	1747	...	|	...	...	1855	|	1948	1955
Lisieux .... d.	1340	|	...	|	1442	...	...	1459	1609	|	1716	|	1719	|	...	1745	1801	1804	...	|	...	...	1915	|	2005	2013
Mézidon **271** .... d.	|	|	...	|	|	...	...	1515	|	|	1730	|	1734	|	...	1759	|	|	...	|	...	...	|	|	|	|
Caen 271 .... a.	1405	1409	Ⓐ	1449	1510	...	...	1529	1637	1642	1742	1745	1751	1757	...	1812	1825	1829	...	1855	...	...	1941	2001	2032	2036
Caen 272 .... d.	1407	1411	1448	1451	...	1520	1527	...	...	1646	1744	1747	...	1759	1812	...	...	...	1840	1857	1907	...	...	2003	2034	2038
Bayeux **272** .... d.	1424	1428	1504	1508	...	1536	1543	...	...	1702	1759	1802	...	1814	1831	...	...	...	1859	1913	1928	...	...	|	2050	2055
Lison **272** .... d.	1438	1442	1518	1522	...	1550	1557	...	...	1716	1815	1816	...	1827	1847	...	...	...	1912	1926	1945	...	...	2029	2105	2112
Carentan .... d.	1450	1454	1528	1534	...	...	1607	...	...	1727	1825	1827	...	1837	1857	...	...	...	1922	1937	1955	...	...	2041	2116	2124
Valognes .... d.	1505	1507	1543	1548	...	...	1622	...	...	1741	1839	1841	...	1851	1912	...	...	...	1940	1951	2012	...	...	2057	2131	2140
Cherbourg .... a.	1520	1523	1557	1602	...	...	1636	...	...	1757	1855	1858	...	1908	1926	...	...	...	1954	2009	2026	...	...	2111	2149	2156

	3323	3357	3323	3325	3361	3327	3327	3329	3369	3367
	⑦	Ⓐ	⑥	⑤	Ⓒ	①–④	⑥	⑤⑦	①–④	⑤
	e		t	f		m	t	z	m	f
Paris St Lazare ..... ▷ d.	1843	1907	1919	1940	1940	2039	2039	2052	2155	2159
Mantes la Jolie ...... ▷ d.	|	|	|	|	|	2110	2110	2123	|	|
Evreux .... d.	|	2002	|	|	2035	2138	2138	2151	2250	2254
Serquigny .... d.	|	|	|	|	|	|	|	|	|	|
Bernay .... d.	|	2029	|	|	2100	2204	2204	2217	|	2319
Lisieux .... d.	|	2047	|	2105	2118	2221	2221	2236	2330	2336
Mézidon **271** .... d.	|	|	|	|	|	|	|	|	|	|
Caen 271 .... a.	2028	2115	2107	2129	2146	2246	2246	2304	2355	0003
Caen 272 .... d.	2030	...	2109	2131	...	2248	...	2306	...	...
Bayeux **272** .... d.	2046	...	2126	2147	...	2305	...	2322	...	...
Lison **272** .... d.	2100	...	2140	2200	...	2321	...	2337	...	...
Carentan .... d.	2110	...	2151	2211	...	2333	...	2348	...	...
Valognes .... d.	2124	...	2206	2224	...	2349	...	0004	...	...
Cherbourg .... a.	2140	...	2220	2241	...	0005	...	0023	...	...

	3330	3332	3300	3334			3340				3302
	①–⑥	①–⑥	Ⓐ	①	Ⓐ	⑥		Ⓐ	Ⓐ	Ⓐ	
	n	n		g	2						
Cherbourg .... d.	...	...	0551	...	...	0623	...	0648	0730	...	0811
Valognes .... d.	...	...	0607	...	...	0638	...	0703	0745	...	0825
Carentan .... d.	...	...	0621	...	...	0656	...	0718	0802	...	0839
Lison **272** .... d.	...	...	0632	...	0656	0707	...	0728	0813	...	0850
Bayeux **272** .... d.	...	...	0646	...	0714	0722	...	0742	0826	...	0904
Caen 272 .... a.	...	...	0703	...	0737	0740	...	0757	0841	...	0920
Caen 271 .... d.	0517	0614	0705	0733	...	...	0752	0759	...	0855	0924
Mézidon **271** .... d.	|	|	|	|	...	...	|	0812	...	0915	|
Lisieux .... d.	0543	0639	|	|	...	...	0818	0825	...	0929	|
Bernay .... d.	0601	0658	|	|	...	...	0838	...	...	...	|
Serquigny .... d.	|	|	|	|	...	...	|	...	...	...	|
Evreux .... d.	0628	0728	|	0838	...	...	0905	...	...	...	|
Mantes la Jolie .... ▷ a.	|	|	|	|	...	...	0931	...	...	...	|
Paris St Lazare .... ▷ a.	0726	0826	0900	0935	...	...	1004	...	...	...	1111

	3360			3342		3346				3306					3306	3348					3354	3316	3310	3312	3350	
	Ⓒ	⑥	Ⓐ	Ⓐ	⑥	⑥	Ⓐ	Ⓐ	⑥	①–④	Ⓐ	Ⓐ	†	Ⓐ	⑤	Ⓒ	⑥	①–④	Ⓐ	⑤	Ⓐ		Ⓐ	Ⓒ	⑥	Ⓐ
						t				m					d			m	2	d		Y			t	
Cherbourg .... d.	...	0939	0941	...	...	...	...	...	1051	1110	...	...	1137	...	1205	...	1215	1215	...	1300	...	1355	1404	1406	...	...
Valognes .... d.	...	0954	0956	...	...	...	...	...	1107	1126	...	...	1152	...	1221	...	1230	1230	...	1315	...	1410	1420	1422	...	...
Carentan .... d.	...	1009	1011	...	...	...	...	...	1122	1142	...	...	1206	...	1237	...	1244	1244	...	1329	...	1424	1433	1436	...	...
Lison **272** .... d.	...	1019	1021	...	...	*1107*	...	1127	1133	|	...	...	1217	1219	|	...	1254	1254	...	1340	...	1436	1444	1447	...	1532
Bayeux **272** .... d.	...	1033	1035	...	...	*1121*	...	1143	1147	|	...	...	1230	1235	|	...	1311	1311	...	1354	...	1450	1458	1501	...	1545
Caen 272 .... a.	...	1048	1050	...	...	*1137*	...	1201	1203	1216	...	...	1245	1255	1311	...	1328	1331	...	1409	...	1506	1514	1517	...	1600
Caen 271 .... d.	0937	...	...	1103	1130	1157	1158	...	*1206*	1218	1226	...	1246	...	1313	1320	...	...	1350	...	1424	1507	1516	1519	1526	1603
Mézidon **271** .... d.	|	...	...	|	1146	|	1211	...	*1221*	|	1245	...	1303	...	|	|	...	...	1404	...	|	|	|	|	|	1617
Lisieux .... d.	1005	...	...	1132	1158	|	1224	...	*1235*	|	1257	...	1315	...	|	1348	...	...	1418	...	1451	|	|	|	1553	1630
Bernay .... d.	1023	...	...	1150	...	|	...	...	...	|	...	...	...	...	|	1406	...	...	...	...	1510	|	|	|	1611	...
Serquigny .... d.	|	...	...	|	...	|	...	...	...	|	...	1300	...	...	|	|	...	...	...	...	|	|	|	|	|	...
Evreux .... d.	1051	...	...	1217	...	|	...	...	...	|	...	1328	...	...	|	1434	...	...	...	...	1538	1605	|	|	1638	...
Mantes la Jolie ...... ▷ a.	|	...	...	|	...	|	...	...	...	|	...	|	...	...	|	|	...	...	...	...	|	|	|	|	|	...
Paris St Lazare ..... ▷ a.	1146	...	...	1312	...	1345	...	...	...	1409	...	1426	...	...	1506	1529	...	...	...	...	1632	1700	1702	1706	1733	...

	3352	3336	3356		3356	3358					3314			3362	3344	3364		3318		3322	3324	3320	3366			3328
		⑦	⑤	Ⓒ	①–④	Ⓒ	Ⓐ	⚒	Ⓐ	†	Ⓐ	Ⓐ	⑥	⑦		Ⓐ	⑥	⑦	Ⓐ	⑦	⑥	Ⓐ	⑦	①–④	⑤	⑦
	Y	y	d		m									e	X			e		s	t			m	d	e
Cherbourg .... d.	1454	...	...	1527	...	...	...	...	1626	...	1652	...	1650	...	1707	1723	...	1730	...	1819	1831	1844	...	1924	1944	2013
Valognes .... d.	1511	...	...	1542	...	...	...	...	1641	...	|	...	1705	...	1722	1739	...	1746	...	1837	1846	1858	...	1939	1959	2029
Carentan .... d.	1528	...	...	1557	...	...	...	...	1659	...	|	...	1722	...	1739	1754	...	1802	...	1853	1902	1912	...	1954	2014	2045
Lison **272** .... d.	1541	...	...	1607	...	...	...	1625	1709	1712	|	...	1733	...	1751	1806	...	1815	...	1906	1913	1922	...	2004	2024	2057
Bayeux **272** .... d.	1556	...	...	1621	...	...	...	1639	1723	1725	|	...	1746	...	1807	1821	...	1830	...	1922	1928	1936	...	2018	2038	2113
Caen 272 .... a.	1612	...	...	1636	...	...	...	1700	1738	1740	1748	...	1801	...	1823	1838	...	1848	...	1939	1946	1953	...	2033	2053	2130
Caen 271 .... d.	1614	1631	1631	...	1641	1649	1659	...	▬	1741	1750	1757	...	1813	1826	1840	1840	1850	1928	1941	1948	1955	2025	...	...	2132
Mézidon **271** .... d.	|	|	|	...	|	|	1718	...	...	1800	|	1815	...	1829	|	|	1859	|	1946	|	|	|	|	...	...	|
Lisieux .... d.	|	1658	1659	...	1709	1717	1730	...	⑦	1812	|	1828	...	|	1853	1907	1911	1917	1959	|	2014	2016	2053	...	...	|
Bernay .... d.	|	|	1718	...	1728	1736	...	...	e	...	|	1843	...	1858	|	1925	...	|	...	|	2032	|	2111	...	...	|
Serquigny .... d.	|	|	1727	...	|	|	...	...	1815	...	|	1850	...	|	|	|	...	|	...	|	|	|	|	...	...	|
Evreux .... d.	|	1740	1756	...	1756	1803	...	...	1846	...	|	1918	...	1926	1935	1953	...	|	...	|	2057	|	2137	...	...	|
Mantes la Jolie ...... ▷ a.	|	|	|	...	|	|	...	...	1920	...	|	...	...	|	|	|	...	|	...	|	|	|	|	...	...	|
Paris St Lazare ..... ▷ a.	1811	1835	1853	...	1853	1859	...	...	1958	...	1936	...	...	2024	2030	2051	...	2049	...	2136	2152	2145	2234	...	...	232

X – Dec. 25, Jan. 1, 6, Mar. 24, May 4, 12 only.
Y – Dec. 25, Jan. 1, 6, Mar. 24, Apr. 27, May 4, 12 only.
Z – Dec. 22, 29, Mar. 22, Apr. 19, 26, May 1, 8 only.

d – Also Apr. 30, May 7.
e – Also Dec. 25, Jan. 1, Mar. 24, May 12.
f – Also Apr. 30, May 7; not May 2, 9.
g – Also Dec. 26, Jan. 2, Mar. 25, May 13; not Dec. 24, 31, Mar. 24, May 12.
m – Not Dec. 25, Jan. 1, Mar. 24, Apr. 30, May 1, 7, 8, 12.

n – Not Dec. 25, Jan. 1, Mar. 24, May 12.
s – Also Dec. 25, Jan. 1, Mar. 24, May 12; not Dec. 23, 30, Mar. 23, May 11.
t – Also May 1, 8.
w – Not Dec. 25, Jan. 1, Mar. 24, May 1, 7, 8, 12.
y – Also Dec. 25, Jan. 1, Mar. 24, May 12; not Mar. 23, May 11.
z – Also Dec. 25, Jan. 1, Mar. 24, Apr. 30, May 7, 12.
▷ – Frequent suburban trains run Paris St Lazare - Mantes-la-Jolie and v.v. Some trains this table do not carry passengers locally Paris - Mantes-la-Jolie and v.v.

PARIS - LISIEUX - TROUVILLE DEAUVILLE 276

km		13371 Ⓐ	3373 Ⓒ	3375 U	3379 W	3381 Ⓐ	3383 ⑥ S	3389 W	3391 ①–④ m	3393 ⑤ d	3395 ⑤ d
0	**Paris St Lazare** ..... ▷ d.	0800	0849	1004	1155	1200	1336	1336	1813	1825	1923
57	Mantes la Jolie ...... ▷ d.	0832	|	|	|	|	|	|	|	|	|
108	Evreux .... ▷ d.	0905	0944	|	1250	1258	|	1429	1909	1919	|
150	Serquigny .... ▷ d.	0931	|	|	|	|	|	|	|	|	|
160	Bernay .... ▷ d.	|	1010	|	1316	1324	1452	1457	|	|	|
191	Lisieux .... ▷ d.	|	1028	1133	1335	1344	1510	1517	1948	2000	|
221	**Trouville-Deauville** ... a.	1007	1051	1151	1357	1400	1529	1534	2011	2020	2105

	3370 Ⓐ	13374 Ⓐ	3398 Z	3376 Y	3386 ⑦ P	3384 Ⓒ	3388 Ⓐ ⊡	3390 ⑦ T	3396 X	3394 ⑦ T
Trouville-Deauville .. d.	0710	1049	1340	1622	1707	1809	1854	1928	2044	2104
Lisieux .... ▷ d.	0733	1109	1401	1643	1730	1831	1917	|	2107	|
Bernay .... ▷ d.	0751	1125	|	|	|	|	|	|	2125	|
Serquigny .... ▷ d.	|	1133	|	|	|	|	|	|	|	|
Evreux .... ▷ d.	0817	1158	1442	|	|	|	|	|	2153	|
Mantes la Jolie ...... ▷ a.	|	1232	|	|	|	|	|	|	|	|
Paris St Lazare .... ▷ a.	0914	1306	1539	1816	1903	2001	2059	2122	2249	2250

		⚒	†	Ⓐ		⑥t	Ⓐ		†	Ⓐ		⑥t	Ⓐ		⑦e	Y	⑥	Ⓐ		Ⓐ					
aris St Lazare 275 ....d.	...	...	...	...	...	...	...	...	...	...	...	...	...	...	...	...	...	...	...	...	...	...	...	...	...
isieux .... d.	...	0748	0827	0845	...	0958	1026	...	1206	1240	...	1349	1458	...	1614	1614	1617	1621	...	1812	...	1923	...	...	...
rouville-Deauville .....a.	...	0810	0846	0904	...	1017	1045	...	1225	1302	...	1410	1516	...	1634	1640	1636	1644	...	1833	...	1942	...	...	...

	Ⓐb	⚒	†	Ⓐ		Ⓐ	†	⑥		Ⓐ	Ⓒ	Ⓐ		⑥S	W	V	Ⓐ	Ⓒ	Ⓐ		Ⓐ	†	⑥t	⑦u	
rouville-Deauville .....d.	0549	0721	0748	0815	...	0915	0932	0933	...	1155	1311	1419	...	1506	1511	1520	1623	1646	1708	...	1839	1843	1947	2022	...
sieux .... a.	0631	0743	0808	0837	...	0935	0952	0953	...	1217	1332	1441	...	1534	1539	1540	1647	1706	1732	...	1859	1902	2007	2042	...
aris St Lazare 275 ....a.	...	...	...	...	...	...	...	...	...	...	...	...	...	...	...	...	...	...	...	...	...	...	...	...	...

– May 1, 8 only.
– ⑦ to June 1 (also Dec. 25, Jan. 1, Mar. 24, May 12).
– ⑥ from June 7.
– ⑦ from June 8.
– ⑥ Apr. 19 - June 28 (also Dec. 22, 29, Mar. 22, May 1, 8).
– ⑥ Jan. 5 - May 31 (also Dec. 15; not Mar. 22, Apr. 19, 26).
/ – Dec. 22, 29, Mar. 22, Apr. 19, 26, May 1, 8 only.
– Mar. 24, May 4, 12 only.
– Dec. 25, Jan. 1, 6, Mar. 24, Apr. 27, May 4, 12 only.
– Dec. 25, Jan. 1, 6, Mar. 24, May 4, 12 only.

b – By 🚌.
d – Also Apr. 30, May 7.
e – Also Dec. 25, Jan. 1, Mar. 24, May 12.
g – Also Dec. 26, Jan. 2, Mar. 25, May 13; not Dec. 24, 31, Mar. 24, May 12.
m – Not Dec. 25, Jan. 1, Mar. 24, Apr. 30, May 1, 7, 8, 12.
t – Also May 1, 8.
u – Also Dec. 25, Jan. 1; not May 4.
v – Not May 1, 8.

⊡ – Also runs Mar. 24, May 4, 12 (depart 1844).
▷ – For other trains see Table **275**.

TROUVILLE DEAUVILLE - DIVES CABOURG 276a

		Ⓒ	⑥U	⑥t	E	⑦e	⑦T	⑦T	④v	⑤d	
0	Trouville Deauville .... d.	1101	1203	1416	1540	1650	1803	1933	2027	2115	...
24	Dives Cabourg .... a.	1128	1231	1446	1610	1720	1833	2003	2057	2145	...

	①g		Ⓒ	E	Y		Ⓒ	⑦T	⑦T	
Dives Cabourg .... d.	0629	...	1238	1454	1542	...	1727	1847	2023	...
Trouville Deauville .... a.	0700	...	1306	1525	1612	...	1757	1918	2054	...

OR NOTES SEE TABLE 276

ROUEN - LISIEUX - CAEN 277

km		Ⓐ	Ⓐ 2◇	⑥	⑥	†	Ⓐ	†		Ⓐ	⑥	⑤ d	⑤ d	⑦ e	Ⓐ	⑥ t	①–④ m	†	⑥	⑤ d	①–④ m	⑤ d	†	
0	**Rouen Rive Droite** .... d.	0604	0655	0656	0900	0904	1038	1049	...	1220	1324	1437	1623	1630	1711	1726	1805	1809	1819	1848	1915	1925	1934	...
23	Elbeuf-St Aubin .... d.	0619	0714	0713	0915	0919	1053	1104	...	1235	1340	1452	1640	1645	1726	1741	1825	1835	1837	1905	1930	1941	1949	...
73	Serquigny .... ▷ d.	0647	|	|	0943	|	|	1132	...	1303	1417	1521	1708	|	1751	|	1901	1914	1910	1941	|	2006	|	...
83	Bernay .... ▷ d.	0655	0745	0743	0950	0950	1126	1140	...	1311	1424	1528	1716	1718	1759	1813	1909	1922	1919	1948	2002	2013	2020	...
114	Lisieux .... ▷ d.	0712	0800	0758	1007	1007	1141	1156	...	1328	1441	1544	1734	1734	1814	1829	1927	1938	1938	2004	2018	2029	2037	...
139	Mézidon **271** .... ▷ d.	0726	0814	0813	1022	1022	1156	1211	...	|	1455	1558	1748	1748	1829	1843	1943	1953	1955	2018	2032	2043	|	...
162	**Caen 271** .... ▷ a.	0740	0828	0826	1037	1037	1209	1224	...	1352	1508	1612	1801	1801	1843	1856	1958	2006	2010	2031	2045	2057	2102	...

	Ⓐ	⑥	Ⓐ		†		Ⓒ	Ⓐ	⑥	Ⓐ		Ⓒ	Ⓐ	Ⓐ	⑥	†	Ⓐ		⑥ S	†	⑤ d			
aen 271 .... ▷ d.	0557	0712	0721	...	0951	...	1101	1114	1237	1246	...	1710	1713	1831	1832	1831	1857	...	2004	2010	2018	...	...	...
ézidon **271** .... ▷ d.	0611	0726	0734	...	1005	...	|	|	1251	1300	...	1724	1727	1845	|	1845	1912	...	2019	2024	2037	...	...	...
isieux .... ▷ d.	0625	0740	0748	...	1019	...	1126	1139	1305	1314	...	1738	1741	1859	1856	1859	1925	...	2033	2039	2056	...	...	...
ernay .... ▷ d.	0641	0756	0804	...	1036	...	1143	1156	1321	1330	...	1754	1758	1915	1913	1915	1941	...	2050	2056	2117	...	...	...
erquigny .... ▷ d.	0649	0804	0812	...	1043	...	|	|	1329	1338	...	|	|	1923	1921	1923	|	...	|	2104	|	...	...	...
lbeuf-St Aubin .... d.	0721	0831	0837	...	1113	...	1215	1226	1357	1406	...	1826	1829	1951	1949	1951	2012	...	2122	2137	2153	...	...	...
ouen Rive Droite .... a.	0740	0850	0855	...	1126	...	1230	1242	1414	1423	...	1843	1846	2010	2005	2006	2027	...	2137	2154	2209	...	...	...

– ⑥ from Apr. 12 (also Mar. 22).
– Also Apr. 30, May 7.
– Also Dec. 25, Jan. 1, Mar. 24, May 12.

m – Not Dec. 25, Jan. 1, Mar. 24, Apr. 30, May 1, 7, 8, 12.
t – Also May 1, 8.

◇ – From Dieppe (Table **270a**).
▷ – See also Table **275**.

PARIS - CHARTRES - LE MANS 278

For TGV trains Paris - Le Mans see Table 280

km		Ⓐ	Ⓐ	⚒		⚒			Ⓒ	Ⓐ	§		Ⓐ§	Ⓐ§	Ⓒ	⚒	⚒	†	⚒	⚒	⊕	⚒	†	Ⓐ	Ⓐ
0	**Paris Montparnasse 274** d.	...	0538	0620	0700	0720	...	0815	0910	0915	0930	...	1025	1115	1115	1215	1230	1300	1315	1400	1425	1500	1500	...	1600
17	Versailles Chantiers **274** ..d.	...	0551	0634	0714	0733	...	0829	0926	0928	0944	...	1040	1128	1128	1228	1243	1313	1329	1413	1438	1514	1514	...	1613
48	Rambouillet .... d.	...	|	0652	|	0753	...	0849	0948	0948	|	...	1059	1148	1148	1248	|	1332	|	1433	|	1533	1534	...	1631
88	**Chartres** .... d.	0611	0649	0730	0758	0830	...	0927	1024	1024	1031	...	1132	1226	1226	1326	1332	1410	1420	1510	1523	1610	1618	1630	1710
149	Nogent le Rotrou .... d.	0656	0740	...	0833	...	...	...	...	...	1109	...	1219	1316	1317	...	1408	...	...	...	1559	...	1717	1725	...
211	**Le Mans** .... a.	0745	...	...	0913	...	...	...	...	...	1148	...	1311	...	1407	...	1447	...	...	...	1650	...	1810	1816	...

	Ⓒ	Ⓐ	Ⓐ		Ⓐ		†	Ⓐ	Ⓐ		Ⓐ	Ⓐ	Ⓒ	Ⓐ	Ⓒ	Ⓐ	Ⓒ	Ⓐ	⑤f		Ⓐ	⑦v		⑦v	
aris Montparnasse 274 .d.	1600	1625	1630	1700	1715	1725	1730	1730	1745	1800	1815	1830	1830	1846	1855	1900	1930	1944	2018	2030	2125	2130	2230	2330	0030
ersailles Chantiers **274** ...d.	1613	1639	1644	1713	1729	1740	1744	1744	1759	1813	1829	1843	1843	1900	1908	1914	1943	1958	2030	2044	2138	2143	2244	2343	0043
ambouillet .... d.	|	|	1704	1735	1750	|	|	1805	1820	1835	1850	1905	1905	|	1924	1935	2002	2020	|	2102	|	2201	2304	0001	0102
hartres .... d.	1708	1717	1733	1813	1823	1820	1838	1843	1850	1913	1918	1948	1958	1938	1955	2014	2040	2057	2109	2140	2224	2230	2345	0029	0140
ogent le Rotrou .... d.	1759	1754	1826	...	...	1900	...	...	...	...	...	2036	2050	2018	2037	...	...	...	2146	...	2302	2311	...	...	...
e Mans .... a.	...	1839	1915	...	...	1945	...	...	...	...	...	...	...	2105	2129	...	...	...	2233	...	2343	2350	...	...	...

	⚒	Ⓐ	Ⓐ	⑥	⚒	Ⓐ		Ⓐ	Ⓐ	⚒		Ⓐ		Ⓐ	Ⓐ	⑥				Ⓐ		Ⓐ§	Ⓐ	Ⓒ	
e Mans .... d.	...	0400	...	...	...	...	...	...	0535	...	...	...	...	...	...	...	...	0656	...	0748	...	0905	...	0940	...
ogent le Rotrou .... d.	...	0437	...	...	...	...	...	...	0614	...	...	...	0636	0658	...	...	...	0745	0820	0836	...	0943	...	1019	...
hartres .... d.	0445	0519	0524	0536	0604	0627	0633	0652	0658	0703	...	0725	0730	0741	0745	0752	...	0830	0913	0918	0939	1024	1053	1100	...
ambouillet .... d.	|	|	0601	0616	0643	0658	0713	0728	|	0743	...	|	0759	0814	0829	|	...	0901	|	...	1018	|	1131	1131	...
ersailles Chantiers **274** ...d.	0541	0604	0623	0634	0704	0718	0733	0749	0736	0803	...	0806	0820	0834	0849	0849	...	0920	1006	...	1037	1107	1150	1149	...
aris Montparnasse 274 .a.	0554	0616	0636	0647	0716	0731	0746	0801	0750	0816	...	0820	0833	0846	0901	0901	...	0932	1019	...	1050	1120	1204	1201	...

	Ⓐ▷					Ⓐ			Ⓐ		Ⓐ	Ⓒ				Ⓐ		⚒	⑦v			Ⓐ	†	⑦v	
e Mans .... d.	1044	...	...	1239	...	...	...	1550	...	...	1643	...	...	...	1736	1800	...	1845	1846	1935	...	...	...	2059	...
ogent le Rotrou .... d.	1125	...	...	1334	...	...	...	1630	...	...	1730	1728	...	...	1833	1853	...	1942	1941	2013	...	...	...	2139	...
hartres .... d.	1206	1223	1341	1431	1526	1550	1648	1712	1720	1750	1823	1824	...	1845	1922	1945	1955	2020	2039	2055	...	2120	2146	2227	...
ambouillet .... d.	|	1301	|	1501	|	1628	1726	|	1800	|	1852	|	...	1922	|	...	2035	...	2109	|	...	2159	2225	2259	...
ersailles Chantiers **274** ...d.	1250	1320	1435	1520	1619	1649	1745	1749	1819	1849	1911	1911	...	1938	2006	...	2054	...	2129	2138	...	2219	2244	2317	...
aris Montparnasse 274 .a.	1304	1334	1447	1533	1631	1701	1757	1800	1831	1901	1924	1924	...	1950	2018	...	2107	...	2141	2150	...	2231	2257	2329	...

– Also Apr. 30, May 7; not May 2, 9.
– Also Dec. 25, Jan. 1, Mar. 24, May 12; not Dec. 23, 30, Mar. 23, May 11.
– Subject to alteration Chartres - Le Mans and v.v. on Ⓐ Feb. 18 - Mar. 14.

▷ – Subject to alteration Le Mans - Chartres on Ⓐ Feb. 18 - Mar. 28.
⊕ – Subject to alteration on ①–④ Feb. 4 - Mar. 6.

On May 11 subject to alteration or cancellation Le Mans - Nantes and v.v.

280 PARIS - LE MANS - RENNES and NANTES

TGV Atlantique

TGV trains convey 🍷. Many trains continue to destinations in Tables **281**, **284**, **285** and **288**. For other trains Massy - Nantes via St Pierre des Corps see Table **335**.

km		Ⓐ	⑥	Ⓐ	TGV 8801 Ⓐ k	TGV 8001 Ⓐ k	TGV 8903 Ⓐ	TGV 8603* ①–⑥ n	TGV 8805 ①–⑥ n	Ⓐ	TGV 8081 Ⓐ	TGV 8807 ①–⑥ n	TGV 8009*	TGV 8909	TGV 8611	TGV 5486 ☆	TGV 8813	TGV 8715	†		TGV 8921* ①–⑥ n	TGV 8619 ©	TGV 8617 Ⓐ	TGV 5214
	Lille Europe **11** d.	...	...	...	...	...	...	...	...	...	...	...	...	...	...	...	...	...	...	...	...	...	...	0846
	Charles de Gaulle ✈ d.	...	...	...	...	...	...	...	...	...	...	...	...	...	...	...	...	...	...	...	...	...	...	1027
	Marne la Vallée - Chessy § d.	...	...	...	...	...	...	...	...	...	...	...	...	...	...	0900	...	...	...	...	...	...	...	1042
0	**Paris Montparnasse** d.	...	...	...	0630	0635	0700	0705	0730	...	0735	0800	0805	0900	0905	|	1000	1005	...	...	1100	1105	1105	|
14	Massy TGV d.	...	...	...	|	|	|	|	0741	...	0747	|	|	|	|	0933	|	|	...	...	|	|	|	1117
202	**Le Mans** d.	0625	0637	0650	0727	0733	|	|	0832	0838	|	|	0902	|	|	1025	1057	|	1104	1104	|	1202	1202	1210
292	Laval d.	0728	0730	|	|	0815	|	|	|	|	|	|	0943	|	|	|	|	|	1150	|	|	1244	1244	|
327	Vitré d.	0755	0754	|	|	|	|	|	|	|	|	|	|	|	|	|	|	|	1214	|	|	|	1304	|
365	**Rennes** a.	0815	0815	|	|	0852	|	0908	|	|	0949	|	1020	|	1108	|	|	1208	1245	|	|	1321	1323	1327
251	Sablé d.	...	...	0713	|	...	|	...	0852	0859	...	|	...	|	...	|	|	...	...	1124	|	...	...	...
299	Angers St Laud **289** d.	...	...	0738	0805	...	|	...	0916	0922	...	0933	...	1033	...	1102	1137	...	...	1145	|	...	...	...
387	**Nantes 289** a.	...	...	0818	0841	...	0901	...	0952	1001	...	1008	...	1108	...	1140	1212	...	...	1226	1304	...	...	...

	TGV 5213	TGV 5350* ♠	TGV 5365 ⑥ ♣t	TGV 8823	TGV 5470 ☆	TGV 8717	TGV 8929 ⑤ f	TGV 8621 ⑤ f	TGV 5224	TGV 5227	TGV 8933*	TGV 8623* Ⓐ	TGV 8625 ©	TGV 8835 ⑤ f	⑤ d	TGV 8837* c	TGV 8729*	TGV 5375 ⑦ ♠e	TGV 5371 ⑦ ♠e	TGV 8843 Ⓑ h	TGV 8033* Ⓑ h	TGV 8031 ⑥ t	⚒ c	TGV 5232 ①–⑥ n	TGV 5216 ⑦ e
Lille Europe **11** d.	0846	...	...	...	...	...	...	...	1210	1210	...	...	...	...	...	...	...	...	...	...	...	...	...	1447	1447
Charles de Gaulle ✈ d.	1027	...	...	...	...	...	...	...	1316	1316	...	...	...	...	...	...	...	...	...	...	...	...	...	1542	1542
Marne la Vallée - Chessy § d.	1042	...	...	...	1122	...	...	...	1329	1329	...	...	...	...	...	...	...	...	...	...	...	...	...	1557	1557
Paris Montparnasse d.	|	...	...	1200	|	1205	1300	1305	|	|	1400	1405	1405	1430	...	1500	1505	...	...	1600	1605	1605	...	|	|
Massy TGV d.	1117	1131	1131	|	1201	|	|	|	1401	1401	|	|	|	|	...	|	|	1532	1532	|	|	|	...	1631	1631
Le Mans d.	1213	1222	1225	|	1253	1302	|	1402	1453	1502	1457	|	|	1524	1535	|	|	1622	1626	|	|	1702	1706	1723	|
Laval d.	|	|	|	|	1335	|	|	|	|	|	|	1539	1539	...	|	|	|	|	1707	|	|	1743	|	|	|
Vitré d.	|	|	|	|	|	|	|	|	|	|	|	|	1558	...	|	|	|	|	|	|	|	|	|	|	◐
Rennes a.	|	1340	|	|	1410	1413	|	1515	1607	|	|	1615	1619	...	|	|	1708	|	1743	|	1808	1820	|	1836	|
Sablé d.	|	...	|	|	...	...	|	...	...	|	|	...	...	...	1555	|	...	|	...	|	...	...	1726	...	|
Angers St Laud **289** d.	1254	...	1305	1339	...	...	1431	...	...	1542	1538	...	...	...	1618	1632	...	1702	...	1733	...	...	1749	...	1816
Nantes 289 a.	1333	...	1342	1414	...	...	1505	...	...	1617	1612	...	...	...	1657	1707	...	1736	...	1808	...	...	1830	...	1856

	TGV 8737* Ⓐ	Ⓐ	†	TGV 8845 Ⓐ	TGV 8847 Ⓐ	TGV 8849 ⑥ t	TGV 8747* ①–⑥ n	Ⓐ	TGV 8743 ⑦ e	TGV 8953* a	TGV 8645 ①–④ m	TGV 8649* ⑤ f	TGV 8857 ⑦ e	TGV 8855 Ⓐ	TGV 8861 Ⓐ	TGV 8655* Ⓐ	TGV 8659 ⑦ e	TGV 8653 ⑥ t	TGV 8093 Ⓐ	TGV 8965 ①–⑥ n	TGV 8873 © a	TGV 8867 ①–④ m	TGV 8869 ⑤ f	TGV 8871 ①–⑤ p	TGV 5373 ①–⑥ ♠n
Lille Europe **11** d.	...	...	...	...	...	...	...	...	...	...	...	...	...	...	...	...	...	...	...	...	...	...	...	...	...
Charles de Gaulle ✈ d.	...	...	...	...	...	...	...	...	...	...	...	...	...	...	...	...	...	...	...	...	...	...	...	...	...
Marne la Vallée - Chessy § d.	...	...	...	...	...	...	...	...	...	...	...	...	...	...	...	...	...	...	...	...	...	...	...	...	...
Paris Montparnasse d.	1635	...	...	1650	1700	1700	1705	...	1705	1730	1735	1735	1750	1750	1800	1805	1805	1805	1835	1830	1845	1845	1845	1900	...
Massy TGV d.	|	...	...	|	|	|	|	...	|	|	|	|	|	|	|	|	|	|	|	|	|	|	|	|	1901
Le Mans d.	1732	1738	1745	1747	|	1757	|	1800	1801	|	|	1832	1847	1847	|	|	1902	1902	|	|	1942	1942	1942	|	1952
Laval d.	1813	1824	|	|	|	|	|	|	1843	|	1909	1913	|	|	|	|	|	1943	2012	|	|	|	|	|	2034
Vitré d.	|	1842	|	|	|	|	|	|	|	|	|	|	|	|	|	|	|	2003	2031	|	|	|	|	|	|
Rennes a.	1850	1904	|	|	|	|	1908	|	1920	|	1945	1950	|	|	|	2008	2015	2024	2049	|	|	|	|	|	2110
Sablé d.	...	...	1805	|	|	|	...	1820	...	|	...	...	|	|	|	...	...	...	...	|	2002	2002	2002	|	...
Angers St Laud **289** d.	...	...	1828	1827	1832	1836	...	1843	...	|	...	...	1926	1930	|	...	...	...	...	|	2025	2031	2031	|	...
Nantes 289 a.	...	...	1908	1907	1910	1912	...	1923	...	1930	...	...	2003	2008	2002	...	...	...	...	2033	2102	2108	2112	2102	...

	TGV 5363 ①–⑥ ♠n	TGV 8665 ①–⑥ n	TGV 8669 ⑦ e	TGV 5236* Ⓑ h	Ⓑ	TGV 5231 Ⓑ h	TGV 8761* ①–⑥ n	TGV 8879* Ⓑ h	TGV 8071*	TGV 5387 ①–④ ♣m	TGV 8777 ⑤ f	TGV 8887* a	TGV 5488 ☆ Ba	TGV 8077 ①–④ w	TGV 8679 ⑤ f	TGV 8069 ⑦ e	TGV 5234 ①–④ m⊙	TGV 5248 ⑥ t	TGV 5245 ⑥ c	TGV 5390 ⑤⑦ ♣⊡	TGV 5210 ⑤⑦ ⊡	TGV 5247 ⑦ e	TGV 8893 Ⓑ j	TGV 8073 ⑤ f	TGV 8075 ⑦ e
Lille Europe **11** d.	...	...	...	1729	...	1729	...	...	...	...	...	...	...	...	...	...	1939	1939	1939	...	2014	2014	...	...	...
Charles de Gaulle ✈ d.	...	...	...	1824	...	1824	...	...	...	...	...	...	...	...	...	...	2034	2034	2034	...	2109	2109	...	...	...
Marne la Vallée - Chessy § d.	...	...	...	1840	...	1840	...	...	...	...	...	...	2024	...	...	...	2050	2050	2050	...	2125	2125	...	...	...
Paris Montparnasse d.	...	1905	1905	|	...	|	1935	2000	2005	...	2035	2100	|	2105	2105	2105	|	|	|	...	|	|	2200	2205	2205
Massy TGV d.	1901	|	|	1916	...	1921	|	|	|	2032	|	|	2101	|	|	|	2131	2134	2134	2137	2201	2201	|	|	|
Le Mans d.	1956	2002	|	2008	2020	|	|	|	2102	2122	2132	|	2157	|	2202	2202	2223	2227	2230	2227	2253	2258	2257	|	2302
Laval d.	|	|	2039	2048	|	|	|	|	2143	|	|	|	|	|	|	2243	|	2309	|	|	|	|	|	2339	2344
Vitré d.	|	|	2058	|	|	◐	|	|	|	|	|	|	|	|	|	|	|	|	|	|	|	|	|	2358	0004
Rennes a.	|	2115	2119	2125	|	|	2138	|	2220	2234	2243	|	|	2308	2315	2320	|	2344	|	2340	|	0010	|	0019	0024
Sablé d.	|	...	...	...	2040	|	...	|	...	...	...	|	|	...	...	...	|	...	|	...	|	...	|	...	...
Angers St Laud **289** d.	2038	...	...	...	2103	2108	...	2133	...	...	...	2231	2239	...	...	...	2304	...	2307	...	2331	...	2337	...	...
Nantes 289 a.	2116	...	...	...	2143	2147	...	2208	...	...	...	2308	2314	...	...	...	2338	...	2343	...	0007	...	0016	...	...

	TGV 8800 ① g	TGV 8802 Ⓐ	TGV 8002 Ⓐ q	TGV 8804 Ⓐ	TGV 8602 ①–⑤ u	TGV 5252 ①–⑥ n	TGV 5254 ①–⑥ n	TGV 8904* Ⓐ	TGV 8706* ①–⑤ u	TGV 8808 Ⓐ	TGV 8806 ⑥ t	Ⓐ	TGV 8810 ①–⑤ v	TGV 8608 ⑥ t	TGV 8610 Ⓐ	Ⓐ	TGV 8820 Ⓐ	TGV 8812 ©	TGV 8712 Ⓐ	TGV 5312 ♠	Ⓐ	TGV 8814 Ⓐ	TGV 8012 Ⓐ	TGV 8014 ©	TGV 8816 Ⓐ
Nantes 289 d.	0500	0530	...	0600	...	0604	...	0630	...	...	0634	0634	0700	...	...	...	0730	0730	...	0735	0739	0800	...	...	0830
Angers St Laud **289** d.	0542	0608	...	0639	...	0643	...	|	...	0715	0715	0719	|	...	...	...	0809	0809	...	0813	0820	|	...	...	0907
Sablé d.	|	0630	...	|	...	|	...	|	...	|	|	0744	|	...	...	...	|	|	...	|	0841	|	...	...	|
Rennes d.	|	|	0535	|	0605	|	0610	|	0635	|	|	|	|	0705	0705	0710	|	|	0735	|	|	|	0805	0805	|
Vitré d.	|	|	0556	|	|	|	|	|	|	|	|	|	|	|	|	0728	|	|	|	|	|	|	|	|	|
Laval d.	|	|	0616	|	0639	|	|	|	|	|	|	|	|	|	|	0748	|	|	|	|	|	|	0841	0841	|
Le Mans d.	0623	0652	0703	|	|	0730	0730	|	|	0759	0759	0805	|	|	0819	0835	|	0849	0849	0854	0903	|	0925	0929	|
Massy TGV a.	|	|	|	|	|	0818	0818	|	|	|	|	...	|	|	|	...	|	|	|	0943	...	|	|	|	|
Paris Montparnasse a.	0720	0750	0800	0810	0820	|	|	0835	0840	0855	0855	...	0905	0910	0915	...	0940	0945	0945	...	...	1005	1020	1025	1040
Marne la Vallée - Chessy § a.	...	...	...	...	...	0900	0900	...	...	...	...	...	...	...	...	...	...	...	...	...	...	...	...	...	...
Charles de Gaulle ✈ a.	...	...	...	...	...	0914	0914	...	...	...	...	...	...	...	...	...	...	...	...	...	...	...	...	...	...
Lille Europe **11** a.	...	...	...	...	...	1009	1009	...	...	...	...	...	...	...	...	...	...	...	...	...	...	...	...	...	...

	TGV 5478 ☆ B	TGV 8618* ①–⑥ n	TGV 8016 ⑦ e	TGV 8818	TGV 5318 ♠	TGV 5272	TGV 5270	TGV 8922	TGV 8620*	TGV 8028 ① g		TGV 8828 Ⓐ	TGV 8022 Ⓐ	TGV 8826 ⑥ t	⚒	TGV 5324 F ♣	TGV 5322 ♠	TGV 8932 ⑦ e	TGV 8834 Ⓐ	TGV 8084	TGV 8730*	TGV 8836	TGV 5326 G ♠	TGV 5278 a	TGV 5280
Nantes 289 d.	0834	...	...	0900	...	...	0910	1100	...	...	1144	1200	...	1200	...	...	1252	1300	1300	...	...	1400	...	1435	...
Angers St Laud **289** d.	0913	...	...	0937	...	...	0948	1138	...	...	1227	1237	...	1237	...	...	1338	|	|	...	...	1438	...	1513	...
Sablé d.	|	...	...	|	...	...	|	|	...	...	1248	|	...	|	...	...	|	|	|	...	...	|	...	|	...
Rennes d.	|	0905	0905	|	0910	0915	|	|	1105	1125	|	|	1205	|	...	1230	|	|	|	1305	1405	|	1414	|	1435
Vitré d.	|	|	|	|	|	|	|	|	|	|	|	|	|	|	...	|	◐	|	|	|	|	|	|	|	|
Laval d.	|	|	|	|	0946	|	|	|	1142	|	|	|	|	|	1240	|	|	|	|	1340	|	|	|	|	|
Le Mans d.	0956	|	|	1019	1029	1041	1041	|	1228	|	1309	|	1319	1319	1341	1350	|	|	1413	|	|	1519	1529	1557	1557
Massy TGV a.	1047	|	|	|	1118	1133	1133	|	|	|	...	|	|	|	...	1438	1518	|	|	|	|	|	1618	1647	1647
Paris Montparnasse a.	|	1110	1110	1115	...	|	|	1310	1325	1330	...	1410	1415	1415	...	...	...	1505	1510	1515	1610	1615	...	|	|
Marne la Vallée - Chessy § a.	1123	...	...	...	...	1223	1223	...	...	...	...	...	...	...	...	...	...	...	...	...	...	...	...	1728	172
Charles de Gaulle ✈ a.	...	...	...	...	...	1237	1237	...	...	...	...	...	...	...	...	...	...	...	...	...	...	...	...	1741	174
Lille Europe **11** a.	...	...	...	...	...	1341	1341	...	...	...	...	...	...	...	...	...	...	...	...	...	...	...	...	1838z	1838

B – From Mar. 31.
F – ①②③④⑦ (not Apr. 30, May 1, 7, 8).
G – ⑤⑥ (also Apr. 30, May 1, 7, 8).
a – Not May 10, 11.
b – Not Dec. 25, Jan. 1, Mar. 24, May 1, 8, 12.
c – Not May 10.
d – Also Apr. 30, May 7.
e – Also Dec. 25, Jan. 1, Mar. 24, May 12.
f – Also Apr. 30, May 7; not May 2.
g – Also Dec. 26, Jan. 2, Mar. 25, May 13; not Dec. 24, 31, Mar. 24, May 12.
h – Not May 1, 8.
j – Not Dec. 24, 25, 31, May 1, 8, 11.
k – Not Dec. 24 - Jan. 4.
m – Not Dec. 25, Jan. 1, Mar. 24, Apr. 30, May 1, 7, 8, 12.
n – Not Dec. 25, Jan. 1, Mar. 24, May 12.
p – Not Dec. 24 - 26, 31, Jan. 1, 2, Mar. 24, Apr. 30, May 1, 7, 8, 1
q – Not Dec. 31.
r – Not Dec. 24, 25, 31, Jan. 1, Mar. 24, Apr. 30, May 1, 7, 8, 12.
s – Also Dec. 25, Jan. 1, Mar. 24, May 12; not Dec. 23, 30.
t – Also May 1, 8.
u – Not Dec. 24, 25, 28, 31, Jan. 1, Mar. 24, May 1, 8, 12.
v – Not Dec. 24, 25, 31, Jan. 1, Mar. 24, May 1, 8, 12.

NOTES CONTINUED ON NEXT PAGE →

NANTES and RENNES - LE MANS - PARIS — 280

	TGV 8844	TGV 8942	TGV 8040	TGV 8042	TGV 5346	TGV 5480			TGV 8848	TGV 8646	TGV 8752	TGV 8952*	TGV 5334	TGV 5460		TGV 8956*	TGV 8090		TGV 8088	TGV 8660	TGV 8862	TGV 8862	TGV 8860	TGV 8864*	TGV 8762
	⑤		⑤⑦	①–④	①–④		Ⓑ	⑥	Ⓑ				⑦		†	Ⓐ	⑥	Ⓐ	Ⓑ	Ⓑ	①–④	⑤	Ⓒ	Ⓐ	
	f	a	y	m	♠m	☆	b	c	h				♣e	☆			t		h	h	m	d	a		
antes 289 ... d.	...	1500	...	...	...	1520	1527	1527	1600	...	...	1700	1708	...	1724	1730	...	1734	...	...	1800	1800	1800	1830	...
ngers St Laud 289 ... d.	...	1537	...	...	...	1600	1609	1610	1637	...	...	1737	1744	...	1806	|	...	1816	...	...	1838	1838	1838	|	...
ablé ... d.	...	|	...	...	...	|	1631	1633	|	...	...	|	|	...	1827	|	...	1838	...	...	1901	1901	1858	|	...
Rennes ... d.	...	|	1505	1505	1514	|	|	|	|	1605	1705	|	|	1710	|	|	1735	|	1735	1805	|	|	|	|	1835
Vitré ... d.	...	|	|	|	|	|	|	|	|	|	|	|	|	|	|	|	|	|	1757	|	|	|	|	|	|
Laval ... d.	...	|	|	|	|	|	|	|	|	1641	|	|	|	1746	|	|	1812	|	1819	|	|	|	|	|	|
e Mans ... d.	1609	|	|	1619	1630	1640	1652	1703	|	1725	|	1819	1824	1835	1848	|	1859	1859	1904	|	|	|	|	|	|
lassy TGV ... a.	|	|	|	|	1718	1727	...	...	|	|	|	|	1912	1922	...	|	|	...	|	|	|	|	|	|	|
aris Montparnasse ... a.	1705	1710	1715	1715	...	|	...	...	1810	1820	1910	1915	...	|	...	1935	1955	...	2000	2010	2015	2020	2020	2035	2040
Marne la Vallée - Chessy § a.	...	...	...	...	...	1803	...	...	...	...	...	...	...	2003	...	...	...	...	...	...	...	...	...	...	...
Charles de Gaulle ✈ ... a.	...	...	...	...	...	...	...	...	...	...	...	...	...	...	...	...	...	...	...	...	...	...	...	...	...
Lille Europe 11 ... a.	...	...	...	...	...	...	...	...	...	...	...	...	...	...	...	...	...	...	...	...	...	...	...	...	...

	TGV 8864	TGV 5338	TGV 5290	TGV 5288		TGV 8668*	TGV 8866*	TGV 5344	TGV 5342	TGV 8886	TGV 8774*	TGV 8980*	TGV 8780	TGV 8782	TGV 8096		TGV 5294	TGV 8688	TGV 8894	TGV 8682*	TGV 8892	TGV 8896	TGV 8996	TGV 8686	
	⑦	⑦			⑤			⑤	⑤	⑦	⑦		①–④	⑤	Ⓒ	†	⑦	⑦	①–④	Ⓑ	⑤	⑦	⑦	⑦	
	e	♣e		a	d		a	♣f	♣f	e	e		m	f			e	e	r	△	f	e	e	s	
antes 289 ... d.	1830	...	...	1835	1839	...	1900	...	1904	1930	...	2000	...	...	...	1934	...	...	2045	...	2100	2100	2200	...	...
ngers St Laud 289 ... d.	|	...	...	1912	1922	...	1939	...	1944	|	...	2039	...	...	...	2048	...	...	2122	...	2139	2143	|	...	...
ablé ... d.	|	...	...	|	1947	...	|	...	|	|	...	|	...	...	...	2112	...	...	|	...	|	|	|	...	...
Rennes ... d.	|	1827	1840	|	|	1905	|	1909	|	|	1935	|	2005	2005	2005	|	2020	2035	|	2105	|	|	|	2205	...
Vitré ... d.	|	|	|	|	|	|	|	|	|	|	|	|	|	|	2026	|	|	|	|	|	|	|	|	|	...
Laval ... d.	|	|	|	|	|	|	|	|	|	|	|	|	2041	2044	2047	|	|	|	|	|	|	|	|	|	...
e Mans ... d.	1948	1952	2000	2000	2011	|	2019	2029	2029	|	|	|	|	2129	2132	2135	2138	|	|	|	2219	2225	|	|	...
lassy TGV ... a.	|	2043	2048	2048	...	|	|	2118	2118	|	|	|	|	|	|	...	2228	|	|	|	|	|	|	|	...
aris Montparnasse ... a.	2045	...	|	|	...	2110	2115	...	...	2135	2140	2210	2215x	2225	2230	...	|	2240	2255	2310	2315	2325	0005	0010	...
Marne la Vallée - Chessy § a.	...	...	2129	2129	...	...	...	...	...	...	...	...	...	...	...	...	2301	...	...	...	...	...	...	...	...
Charles de Gaulle ✈ ... a.	...	...	2146	2146	...	...	...	...	...	...	...	...	...	...	...	...	2316	...	...	...	...	...	...	...	...
Lille Europe 11 ... a.	...	...	2318	2318	...	...	...	...	...	...	...	...	...	...	...	...	0010	...	...	...	...	...	...	...	...

OTES - CONTINUED FROM PREVIOUS PAGE

- – Not Dec. 24, 25, 31, Jan. 1, Mar. 24, Apr. 30, May 1, 7, 8, 12.
- – Arrive 2304 May 26 - July 10.
- – Also Dec. 25, Jan. 1, Mar. 24, Apr. 30, May 7, 12.
- – Lille **Flandres**.

GV – 🅁, supplement payable, 🍷.

- ♣ – From/to Lyon (Table **335**).
- ♠ – From/to Lyon and Marseille (Table **335**).
- – Via St Pierre des Corps (Table **335**).
- – Also Dec. 25, Jan. 1, Mar. 24, Apr. 30, May 7, 12; not May 2.
- – Arrives up to 30 mins later night of ①–④ Jan. 21 - Feb. 28.
- ☆ – From/to Strasbourg (Table **391**).
- – Arrive 2355 on ①–④ Jan. 21 - Feb. 28, May 26 - July 10.
- – Station for Disneyland Paris.

* – **The train number shown is altered as below**:

5236 runs as 5238 on ⑤**f**.
5350 runs as 5360 on ⑥ (also May 1, 8), from Lyon.
8009 runs as 8711 on Ⓒ.
8033 runs as 8633 on ⑤⑦.
8071 runs as 8773 on ⑦**e**.
8603 also runs as 8705 on Ⓐ.
8618 also runs as 8718.
8620 runs as 8622 on Ⓒ. Also runs as 8722 ①-⑥, 8724 ⑦.
8623 runs as 8023 on ⑤.
8649 also runs as 8691.
8655 runs as 8657 on ⑤**f** (also as 8759 on ①–④**m**).
8668 runs as 8670 on Ⓒ.
8682 runs as 8696/8794 on ⑦**e** (also as 8790 on ⑤**f**).
8706 runs as 8704 on ①.
8729 runs as 8027 on ⑤.
8730 runs as 8734 on ⑦**e**, also as 8634 Ⓐ, 8636 ⑦**e**.
8737 runs as 8739 on ⑤**f**.
8747 runs as 8741 on ⑥**t**; also runs as 8643 on ①–④**m**.
8761 runs as 8763 on ⑤**f**.
8774 also runs as 8676.
8837 runs as 8937 on ⑥ (also Nov. 1).
8864 runs as 8964 on ⑤**f**.
8866 runs as 8966 on ⑦**e**.
8879 runs as 8979 on ⑤**f**.
8887 runs as 8987 on ⑤**f**.
8904 runs as 8902 on ①**g**.
8921 runs as 8819 on ⑤**f**, 8919 on ⑥**t**.
8933 runs as 8833 on ⑤⑥.
8952 runs as 8852 on ⑤-⑦.
8953 runs as 8951 on ⑤**f**.
8956 runs as 8856 on ⑤**f**.
8980 runs as 8880 on ⑤**f**.

RENNES - ST MALO — 281

km		2	2			TGV 8081	TGV 8091		TGV 8083	2	2			2		2	2	2	2	2	2		2	
		⚒	⚒	Ⓐ	Ⓒ	Ⓐ	Ⓒ	Ⓒ		Ⓐ	③⑥	⚒	†	⚒	⑤	Ⓒ	Ⓐ	Ⓐ	⑦	Ⓐ	Ⓑ	⑥	Ⓐ	⑥
					b										d				e		h			
	Paris Montparnasse 280 ... d.	...	...	...	...	0735	0805	...	1005	...	...	...	...	...	...	...	...	...	...	...	...	...	...	...
0	**Rennes 272** ... d.	0630	0730	0920	0930	0952	1027	1130	1215	1230	1300	1340	1350	1430	1530	1645	1645	1730	1730	1800	1830	1830	1900	1930
58	Dol **272** ... d.	0709	0809	0956	1006	1025	1058	1209	|	1310	1342	1414	1426	1506	1606	1720	1725	1806	1808	1844	1907	1910	1938	2006
81	**St Malo** ... a.	0730	0825	1010	1020	1038	1113	1222	1258	1328	1400	1430	1440	1520	1620	1734	1742	1820	1822	1903	1920	1933	1952	2020

			2	2	TGV 8093	TGV 8099	2		
	†	①–④	⑤	†	Ⓐ	⑦	①–⑥	⑤	
		m	d	v		e	n⊕	d	
Paris Montparnasse 280 ... d.	...	...	...	...	1835	1905	...	...	...
ennes 272 ... d.	1930	2000	2020	2030	2058	2126	2150	2253	...
ol 272 ... d.	2009	2038	2059	2106	|	|	2228	2327	...
t Malo ... a.	2022	2051	2112	2119	2144	2210	2241	2341	...

	2	TGV 8080	2		2	2		2	2
	⚒	Ⓐ	Ⓐ	⑥	Ⓐ	Ⓐ	Ⓒ	Ⓐ	⚒
							b		
St Malo ... d.	0550	0605	0620	0650	0650	0720	0750	0750	0950
Dol **272** ... d.	0604	0621	0638	0703	0706	0734	0805	0805	1004
Rennes 272 ... a.	0641	0655	0718	0740	0744	0816	0840	0845	1039
Paris Montparnasse 280 ... a.	...	0915	...	...	...	...	...	...	...

	2		TGV 8084	2	2	2	2	2		TGV 8088	TGV 8090	2		2	2	2		2		2	TGV 8096			
	†	⑥		③	†	⚒	⚒	Ⓐ	†	Ⓑ	⑥	⑤	⑥	†	Ⓐ	Ⓐ	†	⑥	⑦	Ⓐ	Ⓒ		⑦	
	w			k						h	t	d							z			s	z	
t Malo ... d.	0950	1050	1214	1220	1250	1250r	1450	1550	1550	1640	1640	1650	1720	1720	1720	1750	1750	1820	1830	1840	1915	1950	2050	...
ol 272 ... d.	1005	1109	|	1239	1304	1309	1505	1604	1604	1657	1657	1704	1734	1734	1739	1810	1809	1839	1844	1857	|	2004	2104	...
ennes 272 ... a.	1043	1148	1300	1320	1341	1350	1541	1636	1642	1730	1730	1736	1807	1808	1817	1848	1850	1918	1916	1936	2000	2038	2136	...
Paris Montparnasse 280 ... a.	...	...	1515	...	...	...	...	...	...	2000	1955	...	...	...	...	...	...	...	...	...	2230	...	...	...

- – Subject to alteration Apr. 13, 20.
- – Also Apr. 30, May 7.
- – Also Dec. 25, Jan. 1, Mar. 24, May 12.
- – Not May 1, 8.
- – Not Mar. 26, Apr. 9.
- – Not Dec. 25, Jan. 1, Mar. 24, Apr. 30, May 1, 7, 8, 12.
- **n** – Not Dec. 25, Jan. 1, Mar. 24, May 12.
- **r** – 1235 on Mar. 25 - 27, Apr. 7 - 10.
- **s** – 20 minutes earlier on Apr. 19.
- **t** – Also May 1, 8.
- **v** – Not Mar. 23, May 11.
- **w** – On Apr. 20 runs 37 minutes later.
- **z** – Also Dec. 25, Jan. 1, Mar. 24, May 12; not Mar. 23, May 11.
- ⊙ – To/from St Brieuc (Table **299**).
- ⊕ – Subject to alteration on Apr. 19.
- △ – Subject to alteration Apr. 14 - 18, 21 - 25.
- ▷ – 20 minutes later on ⑤ (also Apr. 30, May 7).
- § – Runs 7 minutes later on ①–④**m**.

DOL - DINAN — 282

2nd class

28 km	Ⓐ	⑥	Ⓐ	Ⓒ	⑥	Ⓐ	†	⑥		Ⓐ	†	Ⓐ	†
			⊙△	⊙		△			§			▷	
ol ... d.	0702	0818	1032	1105	1350	1419	1431	1511	1730	1814	1911	2045	2109
inan ... a.	0725	0841	1054	1128	1413	1442	1454	1541	1801	1842	1934	2108	2132

	Ⓐ	⚒	⑥		⑥		⑤	①–④	†	⚒	†
				△		△§	d	m	⊙		
Dinan ... d.	0629	0732	0929	1230	1432	1617	1657	1705	1816	1849	2036
Dol ... a.	0657	0800	0959	1300	1455	1640	1720	1728	1839	1912	2059

OR NOTES SEE TABLE 281 ABOVE

Additional journeys Dol - Dinan: 2141 Ⓐ 🚌, 2235 ⑤⑥.

Additional journey Dinan - Dol: 0543 Ⓐ 🚌.

MORLAIX - ROSCOFF — 283

2nd class

km		🚌	🚌					🚌	🚌	🚌	🚌	🚌	🚌	🚌	🚌	🚌
		Ⓐ	⚒	①–⑥	⑦	⚒	†	⑥	①–④	⑤	①–④	Ⓒ	⑤	†	①–④	⑤
				n	e				w		w		f		w	f
0	**Morlaix** ... d.	0803	0929	1053	1151	1305	1515	1515	1640	1705	1756	1806	1950	2010	2057	2122
28	**Roscoff** ... a.	0833	1004	1122	1220	1334	1544	1545	1710	1735	1826	1836	2025	2040	2132	2157

	🚌	🚌	🚌		🚌		🚌				🚌		🚌	🚌	🚌	🚌
	Ⓐ	⑥	Ⓐ	⚒	†		⚒	†	⑥	Ⓐ	⑥	†	①–④	Ⓐ	†	⑤
													w			f
oscoff ... d.	0643	0830	0835	1133	1135	...	1330	1341	1442	1531	1630	1640	1712	1835	1925	2030
orlaix ... a.	0713	0905	0910	1201	1210	...	1405	1409	1510	1559	1705	1708	1742	1910	2000	2105

- **e** – Also Dec. 25, Jan. 1, Mar. 24, May 12.
- **f** – Also Apr. 30, May 7; not May 2, 9.
- **n** – Not Dec. 25, Jan. 1, Mar. 24, May 12.
- **w** – Not Dec. 25, Jan. 1, Mar. 24, May 1, 8, 12.

All services call at St Pol de Léon (*21 km* / 15 mins from Morlaix). 🚌 call at Roscoff port on days of sailings.

284 RENNES - ST BRIEUC - MORLAIX - BREST

km	*TGV* trains convey 🍷	2	2	2	2	2	2	2	55803	2		*TGV* 8603	2	2				*TGV* 8611	2	2	2		*TGV* 8619	2	*TGV* 8617
		Ⓐ	Ⓐ	Ⓐ	⑥	Ⓐ	Ⓐ	⑥	Ⓐ	Ⓐ	⑥	①–⑥	⚒	Ⓐ	⑦	⑥	Ⓐ		⚒	Ⓑ	⑥	⑥	Ⓒ	Ⓒ	Ⓐ
						u						n			e	t									
	Paris ⊡ **280** d.	...	...	...	...	...	...	...	...	...	...	0705	...	...	...	...	...	0905	...	...	...	...	1105	...	1105
0	**Rennes** d.	...	...	0605	...	...	0620	0640	0700	0720	0830	0911	...	...	1006	1035	1032	1111	...	...	...	1236	1324	...	1326
80	Lamballe **299** d.	...	...	0647	...	0704	0724	0745	|	0809	0909	|	...	...	|	1111	1122	1152	...	...	...	1311	|	...	|
101	**St Brieuc 299** d.	...	...	0701	0701	0724	0737	0759	0748	0823	0922	1000	...	...	1053	1123	1136	1205	...	...	1215	1323	1413	...	1417
132	Guingamp d.	...	...	0719	0720	0747	...	...	|	...	0940	1017	1026	...	1111	1141	...	1223	...	1230	1235	1340	1432	...	1434
158	Plouaret-Trégor d.	...	...	0735	0735	0808	...	...	|	...	0954	|	1046	...	1126	1156	...	|	...	1251	1253	1354	1446	1450	1449
175	Lannion a.	...	...	|	|	0826	...	...	|	...	|	|	1103	...	*1151*	*1230*	...	|	...	1308	1309	|	|	1507	*1509*
189	Morlaix d.	0616	0637	0759	0757	...	...	...	0831	...	1012	1046	...	1055	1144	1213	...	1252	1301	...	...	1412	1505	...	1507
215	Landivisiau d.	0632	0700	0815	0814	...	...	...	|	...	1027	|	...	1112	1159	1228	...	|	1325	...	...	1427	|	...	|
230	Landerneau **286** d.	0643	0715	0830	0828	...	...	...	|	...	1037	|	...	1122	1208	1238	...	|	1337	...	...	1438	1530	...	1533
248	**Brest 286** a.	0657	0732	0842	0840	...	...	...	0902	...	1048	1119	...	1134	1220	1249	...	1325	1354	...	...	1450	1542	...	1545

	2	*TGV* 8627			2	2	*TGV* 8621	2	2	2		*TGV* 8623	2	*TGV* 8625	2	2	2		2		2		2	*TGV* 8633	55845
		①–④	⑤	Ⓒ	Ⓐ	①–④	⑤	⑤	①–④	⑦	⑤	①–④	Ⓐ	Ⓒ	Ⓒ	⑥	①–④	⑤	Ⓐ	⑦	⑦	Ⓐ	Ⓐ	⑤⑦	①–④
		w	f			m	f	d	m	e	d	m				t	m	d		e	e			q	w
Paris ⊡ **280** d.	...	1205	...	...	...	...	1305	...	...	...	...	1405	...	1405	...	...	...	...	...	...	...	...	...	1605	...
Rennes d.	1333	1420	1426	1426	...	...	1518	...	...	...	1603	1618	...	1622	...	...	...	1650	1700	1723	...	1746	...	1812	1821
Lamballe **299** d.	1440	|	1501	1501	...	...	1559	...	...	...	1639	|	...	1703	...	...	1713	1729	1804	1759	...	1821	...	|	1858
St Brieuc 299 d.	1457	1511	1514	1514	...	...	1612	...	...	...	1651	1707	...	1716	...	1727	1737	1742	1818	1811	...	1834	...	1900	1911
Guingamp d.	...	1530	1532	1532	...	...	1629	...	...	...	1710	1724	...	1734	...	1756	1807	1801	...	1830	...	1852	...	1918	|
Plouaret-Trégor d.	...	|	1547	1546	...	1637	|	...	...	1707	1724	|	...	|	...	1819	1827	1817	...	1844	1900	1907	1931	|	|
Lannion a.	...	|	|	|	...	1654	|	...	...	1724	*1746*	|	...	|	...	1836	1844	*1842*	...	|	1917	|	1948	|	|
Morlaix d.	...	1600	1604	1604	1630	...	1658	1705	1722	...	1742	1753	1759	1803	1809	...	...	1836	...	1902	...	1925	...	1946	|
Landivisiau d.	...	|	|	1619	1646	...	|	1730	1746	...	1757	|	1818	|	1828	...	...	1855	...	1917	...	1940	...	|	|
Landerneau **286** d.	...	|	1627	1629	1656	...	|	1742	1758	...	1807	|	1828	|	1838	...	...	1906	...	1927	...	1949	...	2011	|
Brest 286 a.	...	1630	1638	1640	1708	...	1732	1800	1815	...	1818	1827	1843	1838	1853	...	...	1918	...	1938	...	2000	...	2023	2023

	2		2		*TGV* 8647		2	*TGV* 8643	2	2			*TGV* 8645	*TGV* 8691	*TGV* 8649	*TGV* 8655	*TGV* 8657	*TGV* 8659	2	*TGV* 8653	*TGV* 8665	*TGV* 8669	*TGV* 5238	*TGV* 8679	*TGV* 8689
	⑦	⑥	⑥	Ⓑ	⑤	⑤	⑤	①–④	①–④	Ⓐ	⑦	⑦	①–④	⑤	⑤	①–④	⑤	⑦	⑦	⑥	①–⑥	⑦	⑤	⑤	⑦
	y	t	t	h	f	f	d	m	m		y	y	m	f	f	m	f	e	e	t	n⊕	e	♥f	f	b
Paris ⊡ **280** d.	...	...	...	...	1710	...	...	1705	...	...	...	...	1735	1735	1735	1805	1805	1805	...	1805	1905	1905	...	2105	2355
Rennes d.	...	1846	...	1840	|	1920	...	1914	...	1925	1935	...	1948	2001	1953	2011	2011	2018	...	2027	2120	2122	2130	2318	|
Lamballe **299** d.	...	1921	...	1938	|	2001	...	|	...	2017	2011	...	2029	2041	|	|	|	|	...	|	2202	2204	2212	|	|
St Brieuc 299 d.	...	1934	...	1949	1959	2014	...	2003	...	2028	2023	...	2040	2054	|	2059	2103	2108	...	2118	2215	2217	2226	0007	0423
Guingamp d.	...	1951	...	...	|	2033	...	2020	2028	▬	2041	...	...	2111	|	|	2123	2126	2134	2134	2232	2234	2245	0024	0440
Plouaret-Trégor d.	2005	2005	2011	...	|	2049	2052	|	2048	🚌	2055	2102	...	|	|	|	|	|	2154	|	2247	2249	|	|	|
Lannion a.	2022	|	2028	...	|	|	2109	|	2105	①–④	|	2119	...	2141	|	|	|	|	2211	|	*2309*	*2311*	|	|	|
Morlaix d.	...	2023	...	...	|	2107	...	2049	...	2055	2112	...	...	...	2119	|	2152	2154	...	2202	2305	2307	2317	0053	0512
Landivisiau d.	...	2038	...	...	|	|	...	|	...	2113	2127	...	...	...	|	|	|	|	...	|	|	|	|	|	|
Landerneau **286** d.	...	2048	...	...	|	2131	...	|	...	2133	2137	...	...	...	|	|	|	|	...	|	2330	|	|	|	0537
Brest 286 a.	...	2059	...	...	2109	2142	...	2122	...	...	2148	...	...	...	2153	2208	2222	2229	...	2237	2343	2341	2348	0126	0552

	TGV 8690	*TGV* 8608	*TGV* 8610	2	2	2	2	55802	2	2	2	*TGV* 8618	2	2	2	2	2	*TGV* 8622	*TGV* 8620	2			2	2	
	Ⓐ	⑥	Ⓐ	Ⓐ	⑥	Ⓐ	Ⓐ	Ⓐ	Ⓐ	†	⚒	①–⑥	Ⓐ	Ⓐ	⑥	Ⓐ	Ⓒ	Ⓒ	Ⓐ	⑦	⑥	†	Ⓐ	⑥	⑥
	k	t			⊖		u			⊗		n								e				t	t
Brest 286 d.	...	0448	0452	...	...	0528	...	0545	...	...	...	0648	0702	0749	0818	...	...	0844	0848	...	1022	1037	1132	...	1142
Landerneau **286** d.	...	|	|	...	...	0541	...	|	...	...	...	0701	0720	0802	0833	...	...	|	|	...	1034	1049	1144	...	1154
Landivisiau d.	...	|	|	...	...	0551	...	|	...	...	...	|	0732	0812	0845	...	...	|	|	...	|	1058	1154	...	1203
Morlaix d.	...	0519	0523	...	...	0606	...	0615	...	...	...	0723	0755	0827	0908	...	...	0916	0921	...	1055	1113	1210	...	1219
Lannion d.	...	|	|	...	...	...	...	*0606*	...	...	0654	|	...	▬	▬	0904	0910	|	|	1055	|	|	▬	1150	|
Plouaret-Trégor d.	...	|	|	...	...	...	...	0631	...	...	0711	|	...	...	...	0922	0927	0935	|	1112	|	1130	2	1207	1236
Guingamp d.	...	0548	0551	...	...	...	0623	0645	0707	0720	0732	0752	...	†c	⚒	0940	...	0951	0951	...	1124	1144	⚒	...	1250
St Brieuc 299 d.	0510	0607	0609	0617	0639	...	0648	0703	0728	0738	0756	0811	...	0930	0934	...	...	1011	1011	...	1141	1201	1221	...	1306
Lamballe **299** d.	0522	0619	|	0628	0650	...	0706	0717	0744	0751	...	|	...	0942	0946	...	...	|	|	...	1152	1212	1235	...	1318
Rennes a.	0600	0700	0700	0725	0750	...	...	0755	0840	0850	...	0900	...	1040	1045	...	...	1056	1056	...	1230	1250	1345	...	1355
Paris ⊡ **280** a.	0820	0910	0915	...	...	...	...	...	...	...	...	1110	...	...	...	...	...	1325	1325	...	...	...	...	...	...

	TGV 8634	*TGV* 8636		2	2	2	*TGV* 8646			2		2	2	*TGV* 8660	2			*TGV* 5290	2		2	2	*TGV* 8670	*TGV* 8668	2
	Ⓐ	⑦	⑤	⚒		†		①–④	⑤	⑥	Ⓒ	①–④	Ⓑ	Ⓑ	⑦	⑦	①–④	⑦	⑤	⑤	①–④	⑥	Ⓒ	Ⓐ	⑥
		e	d					m	d			m	h	h	y	y	m	♥e	d	d	m	t			t
Brest 286 d.	1148	1151	1207	1229	...	1308	1345	1433	1437	...	1437	1529	...	1544	...	1601	...	1621	...	1621	...	...	1644	1700	...
Landerneau **286** d.	|	|	1219	1246	...	1326	|	1445	1449	...	1449	1543	...	|	...	1613	...	|	...	1634	...	...	|	|	...
Landivisiau d.	|	|	1228	1259	...	1338	|	1455	1459	...	1459	1553	...	|	...	1623	...	|	...	1644	...	...	|	|	...
Morlaix d.	1220	1223	1244	1321	...	1401	1418	1512	1515	...	1515	1608	...	1615	...	1639	...	1654	...	1659	...	...	1716	|	...
Lannion d.	*1211*	|	|	...	1355	...	|	|	|	1512	|	...	1605	|	1633	|	...	|	1650	|	1701	1701	|	|	...
Plouaret-Trégor d.	1238	|	1301	...	1412	...	|	1529	1532	1529	1533	...	1622	1633	1650	1656	...	|	1707	1719	1717	1718	|	|	...
Guingamp d.	1253	1253	1315	...	1432	...	1448	1544	1547	...	1547	...	...	1648	...	1710	...	1725	...	1737	1736	1736	1746	|	...
St Brieuc 299 d.	1312	1312	1331	...	1455	...	1509	1601	1603	...	1603	...	...	1710	...	1727	1731	1743	...	1756	1800	...	1807	1812	1827
Lamballe **299** d.	|	|	1343	...	...	...	1521	1614	1614	...	1614	...	...	1722	...	1739	1744	1756	...	1809	...	...	1820	|	1841
Rennes a.	1400	1400	1420	...	...	...	1600	1653	1655	...	1655	...	...	1800	...	1817	1825	1834	...	1855	...	...	1900	1900	1944
Paris ⊡ **280** a.	1610	1610	...	...	...	...	1820	...	...	...	...	...	...	2010	...	...	...	...	...	...	...	...	2110	2110	...

	2	2	2	*TGV* 8676	2	2			2	*TGV* 8688	2	2	2	2		2	*TGV* 8696	*TGV* 8682		2	2	2	2		
	①–④	⑤	⚒	⑦	Ⓐ	⑦	⑦	Ⓐ	⑦	⑦	⑦	Ⓐ	⑤	⑥	⑤⑥	①–④	⑦	Ⓐ	⑦	①–④	⑤	⑤	†	⑦	⑦
	m	d		e		e	e		e	e	e		d	⊕	d⊕	m	e	v	y	m	d	d		y	y
Brest 286 d.	...	...	1705	1718	...	...	1725	1745	...	1811	...	1805	...	...	1834	...	...	1851	1902	1920	1935	...	...	...	2058
Landerneau **286** d.	...	...	1721	|	...	...	1738	1757	...	|	...	1823	...	...	1847	...	...	|	1914	1938	1952	...	...	...	2110
Landivisiau d.	...	...	1732	|	...	...	1748	|	...	|	...	1835	...	...	1857	...	...	|	1923	1950	2005	...	...	...	|
Morlaix d.	...	...	1749	1751	...	...	1806	1819	...	1842	...	1858	...	...	1912	...	...	1924	1939	2005	2020	...	...	...	2132
Lannion d.	1734	1753	|	|	...	1757	|	|	1819	|	...	...	1851	1900	|	1910	1921	|	|	...	...	2020	2029	2128	|
Plouaret-Trégor d.	1751	1810	1815	|	...	1814	1825	|	1836	|	...	...	1908	1917	1927	1927	|	|	1956	...	...	2037	2046	2145	2149
Guingamp d.	1809	1828	...	1821	...	...	1841	1848	1858	1917	...	...	...	...	1944	1945	1950	1954	2010	...	...	...	...	...	2203
St Brieuc 299 d.	1833	...	...	1839	1841	...	1900	1905	1922	1940	1947	...	...	...	2000	...	2009	2013	2027	...	...	...	...	...	2220
Lamballe **299** d.	...	...	...	|	1855	...	1913	1917	...	|	2001	...	...	...	2012	...	2022	|	2038	...	...	...	...	...	2232
Rennes a.	...	...	...	1926	1945	...	1955	1955	...	2030	2055	...	...	...	2050	...	2100	2100	2115	...	...	...	...	...	2310
Paris ⊡ **280** a.	...	...	...	2140	...	...	...	...	...	2240	...	...	...	...	...	...	2310	2310x	...	...	...	...	...	...	...

- **b** – Also Dec. 25, Jan. 1, Mar. 24, May 12; not Dec. 23, 30.
- **c** – Not Feb. 17, 24, Mar. 30, Apr. 6, 20, June 8, 15.
- **d** – Also Apr. 30, May 7.
- **e** – Also Dec. 25, Jan. 1, Mar. 24, May 12.
- **f** – Also Apr. 30, May 7; not May 2.
- **h** – Not May 1, 8.
- **k** – Not Dec. 24, 28, 31.
- **m** – Not Dec. 25, Jan. 1, Mar. 24, Apr. 30, May 1, 7, 8, 12.
- **n** – Not Dec. 25, Jan. 1, Mar. 24, May 12.
- **q** – Also Dec. 25, Jan. 1, Mar. 24, Apr. 30, May 7, 12; not May 2.
- **t** – Also May 1, 8.
- **u** – From/to Dinan, Table **299**.
- **v** – Not Dec. 31.
- **w** – Also May 2; not Dec. 25, Jan. 1, Mar. 24, Apr. 30, May 1, 7, 8, 12.
- **x** – Arrive 2355 on ①–④ Jan. 21 - Feb. 28, May 26 - July 10.
- **y** – Also Dec. 25, Jan. 1, Mar. 24, May 12; not Mar. 23, May 11.

TGV –Ⓡ, supplement payable, 🍷.

- ⊡ – Paris Montparnasse.
- ⊕ – Subject to alteration on Apr. 19.
- ⊗ – Not Jan. 27, Feb. 3, 17, 24, Mar. 2, 30, Apr. 6, 13, 20, June 8, 15.
- ⊖ – 10 minutes earlier on Feb. 16, 23.
- ♥ – To/from Lille (Table **11**).

TGV trains convey 🍷

RENNES and NANTES - QUIMPER 285

km								4549	4546 4547					*TGV* 8705							*TGV* 8711				*TGV* 8715	
		2 Ⓐ	2 ⑥	2 Ⓐ	2 Ⓐ	Ⓐ	2 ⑥	[R] X	[R] X	2 Ⓐ	Ⓐ	Ⓐ	Ⓒ	Ⓐ	⑥	⑥	†	Ⓐ	†	⑥	Ⓒ	Ⓐ	Ⓐ	⑥		⑥
0	*Paris* ⊡ **280** d.	...	...	...	...	...	...	...	...	...	...	...	...	0705	...	...	...	...	...	...	0805	...	...	...	1005	...
365	**Rennes 287** d.	...	...	...	0626	...	0625	...	...	0645	...	0723	0830	0914	0925	...	0930	...	...	...	1023	1030	...	1118	1211	...
	Nantes ◧ d.	...	...	...	|	0612	|	0641	0641	|	0651	|	|	|	|	0910	|	0920	1003	1008	|	|	1019	|	|	1226
	Savenay ◧ d.	...	...	...	|	0636	|	|	|	|	0715	|	|	|	|	|	|	0942	1026	1030	|	|	1041	|	|	1247
437	Redon **287** ◧ d.	...	...	...	0712	0712	0711	0726	0726	0737	0742	0759	0908	|	1007	1007	1005	1010	1053	1056	1101	1117	1117	1153	1249	1313
492	Vannes d.	0637	0640	0705	0742	0742	...	0754	0754	0808	...	0825	...	1014	1033	1033	1031	...	...	...	1128	1147	1147	1223	1316	1343
511	Auray d.	0652	0655	0718	0754	0754	...	0811	0811	0819	...	|	...	1027	1044	1044	1044	...	...	...	1141	1200	1200	1236	1329	1356
545	Lorient d.	0725	0724	0748	0815	0815	...	0831	0831	0843	...	0852	...	1047	1103	1103	1103	...	...	...	1200	1221	1221	1258	1350	1418
565	Quimperlé d.	0743	...	...	0827	0827	...	0845	0845	...	...	|	...	|	1115	1115	1115	...	...	...	|	1233	1233	1310	1403	1429
612	**Quimper** a.	0813	...	...	0853	0853	...	0915	0915	...	...	0926	...	1123	1142	1142	1142	...	...	...	1235	1259	1259	1336	1431	1457

			TGV 8717			13895	*TGV* 8723										*TGV* 8729									
	⑥	Ⓐ		2	◇		⑤ f	2 ①–④ w	⑤ f	①–④ m	①–④ m	⑥	⑥	†	⑤ d	⑤ f	A	2	①–④	†	⑤ d	Ⓑ	2 Ⓐ	⑤ d	2 †	⑥
Paris ⊡ **280** d.	...	...	1205	...	...	...	1345	...	...	...	...	...	...	...	...	...	1505	...	...	...	...	...	...	...	...	...
Rennes 287 d.	...	1341	1416	...	1426	...	|	...	1610	1639	...	1637	...	...	...	1654	1711	...	...	...	...	1745	1750	...	1803	1815
Nantes ◧ d.	1312	|	|	...	|	1440u	|	...	|	|	1622	|	1622	1622	1622	|	|	...	1705	1723	1725	|	|	1809	|	|
Savenay ◧ d.	1336	|	|	...	|	|	|	...	|	|	1644	|	1644	1649	1645	|	|	...	1749	1748	1748	|	|	|	|	|
Redon **287** ◧ d.	1403	1416	|	...	1503	1526	|	...	1649	1723	1723	1718	1723	1720	1716	1733	|	1753	1821	1813	1817	1828	1846	1853	1857	1855
Vannes d.	...	1443	1517	...	...	1556	1647	1708	1717	1748	1748	...	1753	...	...	1800	1812	1830	...	...	...	1857	...	1922	...	...
Auray d.	...	1457	1530	...	...	1609	1700	1721	1729	1801	1801	...	1805	...	...	1813	1826	1846	...	...	...	1910	...	1935	...	...
Lorient d.	...	1514	1551	1558	...	1630	1720	1754	1750	1820	1820	...	1826	...	...	1834	1847	1916	...	...	...	1931	...	1957	...	...
Quimperlé d.	...	...	|	1610	...	1642	|	1811	1802	|	|	...	1838	...	...	1846	|	...	...	...	...	1943	...	2008	...	...
Quimper a.	...	...	1626	1643	...	1709	1754	1843	1829	1854	1854	...	1904	...	...	1913	1924	...	...	...	...	2009	...	2035	...	...

	3854 3855	*TGV* 5232		*TGV* 8737	*TGV* 8739	*TGV* 8747	*TGV* 8741	*TGV* 8743	*TGV* 8759	*TGV* 8757							*TGV* 5236	*TGV* 5236	3856	*TGV* 8763		*TGV* 8761	*TGV* 8773	*TGV* 8777		*TGV* 8799
	♠ 🍷	⑤ ♥d	2 ⑦ e	①–④ m	⑤ f	Ⓐ	⑥ t	⑦ e	①–④ w	⑤ f	Ⓐ	①–④ m	⑦ y	2 ⑥	⑤ d	⑦ y	①–④ ♥w	⑦ ♥e	⑤⑦ z	⑤ f	Mu	L	⑦ e	⑤ f		⑦ q
Paris ⊡ **280** d.	...	...	...	1635	1635	1705	1705	1705	1805	1810	...	...	...	...	...	...	...	...	...	1935	...	1935	2005	2035	...	2355
Rennes 287 d.	...	1844	...	1853	1855	1911	1911	1923	2014	|	...	2020	2030	2034	...	...	2129	2129	...	2141	...	2141	2223	2246	...	|
Nantes ◧ d.	1826	|	...	|	|	|	|	|	|	|	1944	|	|	|	2022	2041	|	|	2116	|	2126	|	|	|	...	|
Savenay ◧ d.	1848	|	...	|	|	|	|	|	|	|	2016	|	|	|	2045	2104	|	|	2141	|	2147	|	|	|	...	|
Redon **287** ◧ d.	1915	1928	1924	1931	1937	|	1949	|	|	|	2044	2108	2106	2111	2114	2135	2206	2206	2207	2219	2212	2219	2300	2323	...	|
Vannes d.	1945	1955	1954	1959	2004	2016	2015	2025	2114	2115	...	2137	2132	...	...	...	2233	2233	...	2246	...	2246	2327	2350	...	0449
Auray d.	1958	2009	2009	...	2017	2029	2028	2039	|	2128	...	...	2145	...	...	...	2246	2246	...	2258	...	2258	2340	0003	...	0505
Lorient d.	2018	2028	2030	...	2036	2049	2048	2059	2142	2148	...	...	2204	...	...	...	2303	2305	...	2318	...	2318	2359	0023	...	0525
Quimperlé d.	|	2040	2041	...	|	2102	2102	|	|	|	...	...	2215	...	...	...	...	2319	...	|	...	2332	0012	0036	...	|
Quimper a.	2055	2107	2107	...	2116	2128	2130	2132	2216	2222	...	...	2242	...	...	...	...	2346	...	2354	...	2359	0041	0104	...	0600

	TGV 8704	*TGV* 8706	*TGV* 8712						*TGV* 8718	*TGV* 5272					3832 3833		*TGV* 8724	*TGV* 8722			13894	*TGV* 8730	*TGV* 8734			
	① g	②–⑤ j	Ⓐ	2 Ⓐ	Ⓐ	2 Ⓒ	Ⓐ	2 ⚒	①–⑥ n	①⑥ ♣v	2 ②–⑤ s	2 ① g	2 ⑥	Ⓐ	♠ 🍷	Ⓐ	⑦ e	①–⑥ n		Ⓒ		①–⑥ n	⑦ e	①–④ m	⑤ d	2 ⚒
Quimper d.	0418	...	0525	...	0532	...	0613	...	0635	0646	0644	0653	0700	0727	0740	...	0840	0842	...	1007	1112	1144	1147	1234	1240	...
Quimperlé d.	|	...	|	...	0600	...	|	...	0704	0716	0717	0727	0733	0754	|	...	0908	0910	...	1035	1139	|	|	1301	1308	...
Lorient d.	0453	0457	0601	...	0611	...	0647	...	0717	0729	0734	0744	0749	0806	0817	...	0922	0925	...	1049	1153	1219	1222	1314	1321	1331
Auray d.	0511	|	|	...	0632	...	0704	...	0737	0749	0806	0815	...	0827	0837	...	0941	0944	...	1107	1218	1239	1242	1333	1340	1401
Vannes d.	0524	0524	0630	...	0644	...	0717	...	0750	0802	0819	0828	...	0839	0851	...	0955	0958	...	1120	1233	1254	1255	1346	1354	1416
Redon **287** d.	0553	0553	|	0646	0716	0734	0747	0750	0820	0829	...	...	...	0910	0917	1015	1024	|	...	1147	1303	1321	|	1420	1420	...
Savenay ◧ d.	|	|	|	0734	|	|	|	0817	|	|	...	...	...	|	|	|	|	|	...	|	1327*	|	|	|	|	...
Nantes ◧ a.	|	|	|	0810	|	|	|	0840	|	|	...	...	...	|	1001	|	|	|	...	|	1350*	|	|	|	|	...
Rennes 287 ◧ a.	0630	0630	0730	...	0755	0814	0826	...	0856	0904	...	...	...	0945	...	1052	1100	1100	...	1220	...	1357	1357	1455	1455	...
Paris ⊡ **280** a.	0840	0840	0945	...	...	...	...	...	1110	...	...	...	...	...	...	...	1325	1325	...	...	...	1610	1610	...	...	...

						TGV 8752										*TGV* 8762							*TGV* 8774			
	⑤ d	⑥	†	Ⓒ u	2 Ⓐ		Ⓐ	⑦ x	2 ①–④ m	2 ①–④ m	①–④ m	†	⑤ d	2 ⑤ c	†		2 ⚒	⑦ y	2 Ⓐ	2 ⑥	①–④ m	⑦ x	⑦ e	⑥	2 ⑤ d	2 ①–④ m
Quimper d.	1325	1333	1335	...	...	1437	1512	...	...	...	...	1547	1553	...	...	1617	...	1633	...	...	1715	...	1717	...	...	...
Quimperlé d.	1353	1400	1404	...	...	1505	1539	...	...	...	...	1614	1620	...	...	|	...	1700	...	...	|	...	|	...	...	...
Lorient d.	1406	1412	1417	...	...	1523	1552	...	...	1623	...	1627	1632	...	...	1654	...	1712	1713	1732	1750	...	1753	...	1745	1755
Auray d.	1423	1434	1439	...	...	1542	1614	...	...	1647	...	1649	1654	...	...	1715	...	1734	1738	1802	|	...	1811	...	1811	1820
Vannes d.	1436	1446	1451	...	...	1556	1627	...	...	1701	...	1702	1706	...	...	1730	...	1746	1755	1815	1820	...	1824	...	1825	1834
Redon **287** d.	1508	1520	1522	1526	1532	1626	1658	1700	1719	1736	1741	1736	1737	1745	1749	|	1809	1818	...	1850	1847	1851	1854	1901	1858	1904
Savenay ◧ d.	1530	|	|	1549	|	|	1722	1735	|	...	1813	|	|	1816	1815	|	|	|	...	...	|	1919	|	1928	...	...
Nantes ◧ a.	1550	|	|	1610	|	|	1745	1758	|	...	1835	|	|	1840	1836	|	|	|	...	...	|	1941	|	1950	...	...
Rennes 287 ◧ a.	...	1555	1555	...	1609	1700	...	...	1804	...	...	1811	1811	...	...	1829	1906	1855	...	...	1920	...	1930	...	...	...
Paris ⊡ **280** a.	...	...	...	...	...	1910	...	...	...	...	...	...	...	...	...	2040	...	...	...	...	...	...	2140	...	...	...

	4446 4447					*TGV* 8776	*TGV* 8780	*TGV* 8782					4448	*TGV* 8794				*TGV* 8790			*TGV* 8798					3856
	[R] X	2 ①–④ m	⑤ d	Ⓐ	⑥	⑦ e	①–④ b	⑤ f	⑦ e	2 ①–④ m	2 ⑤ d	†	[R] X	⑦ e	①–④ m	①–④ m	⑤ d	⑤ f	⑦ x	⑦ k	⑦ q	①–④ m	⑤ d	⑦ y	M	⑤⑦ z
Quimper d.	1715	1728	1735	...	1740	1746	1748	1750	1757	...	1757	...	1820	1836	1838	1838	...	1846	1918	...	1950	2000	2003	2030	...	...
Quimperlé d.	1747	1800	1803	...	1808	|	|	|	1825	←	1831	...	1853	1905	1905	1905	...	|	1945	...	|	2027	2030	2058	...	...
Lorient d.	1803	1816	1815	...	1820	1822	1827	1827	1838	1835	1847	...	1907	1919	1918	1918	...	1922	1958	...	2026	2039	2042	2112	...	...
Auray d.	1858	→	1833	...	1839	1842	1847	1847	1857	1905	1917	...	1928	1939	1936	1936	...	1941	2021	...	2045	2100	2102	2131	...	...
Vannes d.	1912	...	1845	...	1851	1857	1901	1901	1910	1918	1930	...	1942	1953	1948	1948	...	1955	2034	...	2058	2111	2114	2145	...	...
Redon **287** d.	1941	...	1918	1921	1922	|	|	|	1937	...	...	1951	2010	2020	2021	2026	2026	|	2105	2130	|	2141	2144	2212	2227	2228
Savenay ◧ d.	|	...	|	1949	|	|	|	|	|	...	...	2019	|	|	|	2052	2054	|	|	2156	|	...	2211	|	|	|
Nantes ◧ a.	2025	...	|	2012	|	|	|	|	|	...	...	2039	2053	|	|	2115	2116	|	|	2216	|	...	2233	|	|	|
Rennes 287 ◧ a.	...	...	1950	...	1955	|	2000	2000	2010	...	...	...	...	2056	|	...	...	2056	2139	...	2200	...	...	2245	2305	2307
Paris ⊡ **280** a.	...	...	...	...	...	2200	2215	2225	...	...	...	...	...	2310	2055	...	...	2310	...	...	0010	...	...	...	...	...

A – Daily except ⑤ (also runs May 2; will not run Apr. 30, May 7).
L – ①②③④⑥ (not Dec. 25, Jan. 1, Mar. 24, Apr. 30, May 7, 12).
M – ①②③④⑥ (not Dec. 25, Jan. 1, Mar. 24, Apr. 30, May 1, 7, 8, 12.).
X – For days of running and composition see Table **290** Night Trains panel.

b – Not Dec. 25, 31, Jan. 1, Mar. 24, Apr. 30, May 1, 7, 8, 12.
c – Also Apr. 30, May 7; not May 2, 9.
d – Also Apr. 30, May 7.
e – Also Dec. 25, Jan. 1, Mar. 24, May 12.
f – Also Apr. 30, May 7; not May 2.
g – Also Dec. 26, Jan. 2, Mar. 25, May 13; not Dec. 24, 31, Mar. 24, May 12.
j – Not Dec. 25, 26, 28, Jan. 1, 2, Mar. 25, May 1, 8, 13.
k – Also Dec. 25, Jan. 1, Mar. 24, May 1, 8, 12; not Dec. 23, 30, Mar. 23, May 11.
m – Not Dec. 25, Jan. 1, Mar. 24, Apr. 30, May 1, 7, 8, 12.
n – Not Dec. 25, Jan. 1, Mar. 24, May 12.
q – Also Dec. 25, Jan. 1, Mar. 24, May 12; not Dec. 23, 30.
s – Not Dec. 25, 26, Jan. 1, 2, Mar. 25, May 1, 8, 13.
t – Also May 1, 8.
u – Subject to alteration on May 24.
v – Also Dec. 26, Jan. 2, Mar. 25, May 1, 8, 13; not Dec. 24, 31, Mar. 24, May 12.
w – Also May 2; not Dec. 25, Jan. 1, Mar. 24, Apr. 30, May 1, 7, 8, 12.
x – Also Dec. 25, Jan. 1, Mar. 24, May 1, 8, 12; not Mar. 23, May 11.
y – Also Dec. 25, Jan. 1, Mar. 24, May 12; not Mar. 23, May 11.
z – Also Dec. 25, Jan. 1, Mar. 24, Apr. 30, May 7, 12; not Mar. 23, May 2, 9, 11.

TGV – [R], supplement payable, 🍷.

⊡ – Paris Montparnasse.
◇ – On Ⓒ depart 1430, arrive 1510.
◧ – See also **287** Nantes - Redon, **287/8** Nantes - Savenay.
♥ – From Lille Europe (**5232** departs 1447, **5236** departs 1729, Table **11**).
♣ – To Lille Europe (arrive 1341, Table **11**).
♠ – [12] Bordeaux - Nantes - Quimper and v.v.
* – Subject to alteration on May 25.

AURAY - QUIBERON

Rail service runs June 28 - Aug. 31 only.

🚌 operates 4 - 5 times daily all year.

286 BREST - QUIMPER

2nd class

km		Ⓐ	Ⓐ	⑥	⚒	†	⊕	⑤ d	Ⓒ	Ⓐ	†	①-④ m	⑤ d	⑥	⑤ d	⑦ q
	Brest 284 d.	0553	0716	0719	0920	1019	1201	1535	1659	1713	1834	1841	1844	1920	2001	2006
	Landerneau **284** d.	0606	0728	0732	0931	1032	1215	1548	1712	1725	1847	1855	|	1935	2017	2021
	Châteaulin d.	0644	0804	0812	1009	1109	1250	1624	1749	1803	1922	1927	1927	2013	2052	2059
	Quimper a.	0705	0825	0832	1029	1130	1311	1646	1810	1823	1942	1948	1949	2033	2113	2119

km		Ⓐ	Ⓐ	⑥	†	⚒	⊕	⑤ d	Ⓒ	Ⓐ	†	①-④ m	⑤ d	⑤ d	⑦ q
0	**Quimper** d.	0621	0741	0749	0925	0944	1443	1601	1727	1740	1859	1905	1905	2029	2035
30	Châteaulin d.	0646	0806	0814	0946	1011	1504	1626	1751	1805	1924	1929	1929	2054	2101
84	Landerneau **284** d.	0725	0841	0852	1021	1047	1539	1704	1830	1843	1959	|	2003	2135	2141
102	**Brest 284** a.	0737	0854	0904	1034	1100	1552	1720	1843	1856	2012	2013	2016	2147	2153

CAT 🚌, journey approx 90 minutes, rail tickets valid:
From Brest: 0700 Ⓐ, 0930 †, 1000 ⚒, 1415 †, 1440 ⚒, 1612 ⑤, 1800 Ⓐ.
From Quimper: 0713 Ⓐ, 1135 ⑤, 1247 †, 1255 ⚒, 1639 ⚒, 1720 ①-④ m, 1730 ⑤, 1740 †.

d – Also Apr. 30, May 7.
m – Not Dec. 25, Jan. 1, Mar. 24, Apr. 30, May 1, 7, 8, 12.
q – Also Dec. 25, Jan. 1, Mar. 24, May 12; not Mar. 23, May 11.
⊕ – By 🚌 on ①-④ Apr. 7 - 24 in revised timings.

287 RENNES - REDON - NANTES

Some trains 2nd class

km		⑥	⚒	Ⓐ	Ⓒ	3832	Ⓐ	Ⓒ	Ⓐ	8715 ☆		⑥	Ⓐ	Ⓒ	⑤ d	⑤ f	Ⓐ	⑤ f	①-④ m	⑤ f	†	Ⓐ	Ⓑ	Ⓐ	⑦ y	†	⑥
0	**Rennes** § d.	0625	...	0710	0830	...	0855	1130	1223	1211	...	1245	*1426*	*1430*	1537	1610	...	1647	*1644*	*1654*	1729	1736	1745	...	...	1803	1815
72	Redon § a.	0711	...	|	0908	...	|	1225	|	1249	...	|	*1503*	*1510*	|	1649	...	|	*1736*	*1731*	|	|	1826	...	...	1857	1855
72	Redon ◇ d.	...	0750	|	...	0917	|	...	|	...	1303	|	1508	1526	|	...	1658	|	1741	1745	|	|	...	1832	1851	...	1901
106	Savenay ◇ d.	...	0817	|	...	|	|	...	|	...	1327	|	1530	1549	|	...	1722	|	1813	1816	|	|	...	1904	1919	...	1928
145	**Nantes** ◇ a.	...	0840	0826	...	1001	1013	...	1337	...	1350	1359	1550	1610	1652	...	1745	1808	1835	1840	1845	1852	...	1929	1941	...	1950

	①-④ m	⑤ d	†	①-④ m	⑤⑥ d	⑤ d	①-④ m	①-④ m	⑤ d	⑥	⑦ z
Rennes § d.	1831	1835	1858	1920	1921	...	*1925*	2020	*2020*	2034	2041
Redon § a.	1916	1917	1939	|	2018	...	*2024*	2107	*2106*	2111	2119
Redon ◇ d.	1921	1922	1951	⌉	...	2021	2026	...	2144	...	2130
Savenay ◇ d.	1950	1949	2019	|	...	2054	2052	...	2211	...	2156
Nantes ◇ a.	2012	2012	2039	2034	...	2116	2116	...	2233	...	2216

	Ⓐ	Ⓒ	Ⓐ	Ⓐ a	Ⓐ	†	⑥		⑥	8730 n☆	Ⓐ	⑥	⑦ e
Nantes ◇ d.	0612	...	0651	0725	0920	1003	1008	...	1226	...	1231	1312	...
Savenay ◇ d.	0636	...	0715	|	0942	1026	1030	...	1247	...	|	1336	...
Redon ◇ a.	0701	..	0744	|	1010	1053	1056	...	1311	...	|	1403	...
Redon § d.	*0716*	0734	0754	|	1015	1102	1102	1238	...	1321	|	...	1408
Rennes § a.	*0755*	0814	0834	0843	1052	1151	1151	1340	...	1357	1347	...	1455

	Ⓐ	⊗	⑥ ⊗	Ⓐ	⑥	†	⑤ d	①-④ m	†	①-④ m	⑤ d	⑥ ⊗	†	⑦ y	⑤ d	⚒	3854	⑤ d	⑥	①-④ m	⑤⑦ w	⑥	⑤ d		⑤⑦ b	①-④ m	⑥ ⊗
Nantes ◇ d.	1434	1440	1445	...	...	...	1520	1602	...	1622	1622	1622	1622	1723	1725	1758	1826	...	...	1903	1918	...	2022	...	2116	2126	2126
Savenay ◇ d.	|	|	|	...	...	...	|	|	...	1644	1645	1644	1649	1748	1748	|	1848	...	...	|	|	...	2045	...	2141	2147	2147
Redon ◇ a.	|	1523	|	...	...	...	|	|	...	1712	1716	1712	1720	1813	1817	|	1913	...	...	|	|	...	2114	...	2207	2212	2212
Redon § d.	|	...	|	1532	1536	1540	|	|	1646	*1719*	*1737*	...	*1736*	*1818*	...	|	...	1918	1922	|	|	2025	2119	...	2228	2227	2227
Rennes § a.	1548	...	1603	1609	1616	1617	1635	1718	1742	*1804*	*1811*	...	*1811*	*1855*	...	1912	...	1950	1955	2024	2035	2110	2155	...	2307	2305	2305

a – From Angers (depart 0618).
b – Also Dec. 25, Jan. 1, Mar. 24, Apr. 30, May 7, 12; not Mar. 23, May 2, 9, 11. From Bordeaux (train **3856**).
d – Also Apr. 30, May 7.
e – Also Dec. 25, Jan. 1, Mar. 24, May 12.
f – Also Apr. 30, May 7; not May 2, 9.
m – Not Dec. 25, Jan. 1, Mar. 24, Apr. 30, May 1, 7, 8, 12.
n – ①-⑥ (not Dec. 25, Jan. 1, Mar. 24, May 12).
w – Also Dec. 25, Jan. 1, Mar. 24, Apr. 30, May 1, 7, 8, 12.
y – Also Dec. 25, Jan. 1, Mar. 24, May 12; not Mar. 23, May 11.
z – Also Dec. 25, Jan. 1, Mar. 24, May 12; not Dec. 23, 30, Mar. 23, May 11.
§ – For other trains Rennes - Redon see Table **285**.
◇ – For other trains Redon - Nantes see Table **285**, for Savenay - Nantes see Tables **285** and **288**.
☆ – *TGV* train, 🅁. Supplement payable.
⊗ – Subject to alteration on May 24.

288 NANTES - ST NAZAIRE - LE CROISIC

Subject to alteration May 10, 11, 24, 25

km	*TGV* trains convey 🍷	B	Ⓐ	⑥	Ⓐ	*TGV* 8903 Ⓐ	Ⓐ △	⑥ O	† O	*TGV* 8909 ◇	Ⓐ	◧	*TGV* 8919 ⑥ t	*TGV* 8921 ①-④ w◇	Ⓐ k	Ⓐ O	⑥	*TGV* 8929 ⑤ f	⑤ d	*TGV* 8933 N	2 Ⓐ	*TGV* 8937 ⑥ t	2 ①-④ m	2 ⑤ d	⑥
	Paris ⊡ **280** d.	...	...	...	...	0700	...	...	...	0900	...	...	1100	1100	...	...	...	1300	...	1400	...	1500	...	...	...
0	**Nantes 285/7** d.	0656	0753	0800	0800	0905	1005	1003	1007	1112	1200	1222	1307	1303	1312	1355	1454	1509	1605	1616	1643	1710	1721	1730	1735
39	Savenay **285/7** d.	0720	0821	0832	0834	|	1026	1026	1040	|	1233	1243	|	|	1334	1429	1530	|	1640	|	1704	|	1745	1753	1801
64	**St Nazaire** d.	0739	0835	0851	0858	0939	1041	1042	1054	1148	1248	1258	1344	1344	1348	1445	1547	1546	1659	1652	1728	1747	1803	1810	1818
79	Pornichet d.	0752	...	0901	0910	...	1052	1054	1105	1201r	...	1309	1356	|	...	...	1558	|	1711	|	1739	|	1814	1822	1828
83	La Baule Escoublac d.	0800	...	0908	0918	...	1059	1102	1113	1204	...	1319	1403	1403	...	...	1606	1604	1719	1709	1747	1802	1821	1831	1838
90	**Le Croisic** a.	0815	...	0920	0930	...	1111	1116	1126	1217	...	1332	1416	1412	...	...	1618	1613	1730	1717	1800	1811	1835	1844	1851

	2 Ⓐ	† T	Ⓐ	⚒	*TGV* 5216 ⑦ ♥e	⑤⑥ Od	⑦ y	①-④ m	①-④ m	*TGV* 8953 A	*TGV* 8951 ⑤ f	①-④ m	⑥	⑤ d	⑦ y	*TGV* 8965 ①-⑥ n	①-④ m	*TGV* 5231 ⑤ ♥f	⑤ d	*TGV* 8979 ⑤ f	L ⊙	*TGV* 8987 ⑤ f	⑦ y	⑤⑥ d	▷ ①-④ m
Paris ⊡ **280** d.	...	...	...	...	...	...	...	...	...	1730	1730	...	...	...	...	1830	...	...	...	2000	...	2100	...	...	...
Nantes 285/7 d.	1740	1807	1809x	1834	1858	1858	1906	1907	1927	1935	1935	...	...	1927	2018	2037	2130	2150	2157	2212	2220	2310	2322	2323	2325
Savenay **285/7** d.	1815	1832	|	1910	|	|	1928	1945	2001	|	|	←	...	2005	2044	|	2152	|	2218	|	2249	|	2345	2353	2353
St Nazaire d.	1837	1847	1847	1923	1934	1933	1943	2006	2016	2009	2012	2021	2021	2025	2113	2112	2207	2225	2233	2248	2303	2347	0001	0008	0006
Pornichet d.	...	1857	1858	...	1946	1944	1955	→	...	...	2024	2032	2032	2036	2124	|	2217	2237	2245	2300	...	|	0013	0019	...
La Baule Escoublac d.	...	1907	1907	...	1952	1951	2002	...	...	...	2031	2040	2040	2044	2131	2128	2222	2244	2252	2307	...	0003	0021	0026	...
Le Croisic a.	...	1922	1922	...	2004	2003	2015	...	...	...	2043	2053	2053	2056	2144	2137	2233	2257	2306	2319	...	0012	0035	0036	...

	① g	*TGV* 8902 ① g	*TGV* 8904 ②-⑤ a	2 Ⓐ	⑥ O	Ⓐ	⚒	2 Ⓐ	Ⓐ	⚒	† O	*TGV* 5270 ①⑥ ♥v	Ⓒ	Ⓐ ⊖	Ⓐ ⊖	*TGV* 8922 ⊖		Ⓐ ⊖	*TGV* 8932 ⑦ e	Ⓐ	Ⓒ	Ⓐ ⊖	*TGV* 8942 ⊕	Ⓐ	
Le Croisic d.	0456	...	...	...	0600	0610	...	0634	...	0730	0734	0800	0851	0903	0939	0954	...	1141	1146	...	1220	...	1351	...	...
La Baule Escoublac d.	0509	...	...	...	0610	0624	...	0647	...	0743	0748	0814	0906	0916	0952	1005	...	1152	1202	...	1232	...	1402	...	...
Pornichet d.	0516	...	...	...	0616	0632	...	0654	...	0751	0755	0821	0911	0921	0959	|	...	1200	1210	...	1239	...	|	...	...
St Nazaire d.	0526	0547	0551	0608	0626	0644	0644	0705	0746	0803	0807	0833	0922	0933	1010	1021	...	1210	1222	1237	1251	1402	1418	1453	...
Savenay **285/7** d.	0541	0602	|	0629	0641	0659	0706	0730	|	0821	0822	|	0936	0948	1024	|	...	|	|	1258	1308	1418	|	1509	...
Nantes 285/7 a.	0605	0625	0625	0706	0703	0720	0743	0750	0820	0848	0846	0906	0957	1009	1045	1055	...	1242	1255	1333	1335	1450	1455	1541	...
Paris ⊡ **280** a.	...	0835	0835	...	...	...	...	...	...	...	...	...	...	...	...	1310	...	...	1505	...	...	...	1710	...	...

	Ⓑ ◧z	*TGV* 8952 ①-④ w⊕	Ⓐ	*TGV* 8956 ①-④ m	⑥	Ⓐ O	†	Ⓐ	*TGV* 8964 ⑤ f	*TGV* 8966 ⑦ e	Ⓐ	Ⓐ	⑥ O		*TGV* 8980 A	† O	Ⓐ	⑤ d	①-④ m	†		*TGV* 8996 ⑦ e	Ⓐ	⑤ d	
Le Croisic d.	1513	1551	...	...	1637	...	1652	...	1717	1748	...	1816	1823	...	1855	1902	...	1937	1943	2019	...	2040	...	...	...
La Baule Escoublac d.	1522	1603	...	...	1650	...	1707	...	1731	1802	...	1830	1836	...	1906	1917	...	1949	1955	2031	...	2054	...	...	...
Pornichet d.	1530	|	...	...	1657	...	1714	...	1738	1808	...	1836	1843	...	|	1923	...	1955	2001	2038	...	2100	...	...	...
St Nazaire d.	1540	1621	1635	1650	1708	1704	1727	1736	1750	1821	1823	1847	1856	...	1921	1935	1939	2006	2011	2050	...	2115	2120	2214	...
Savenay **285/7** d.	1558	|	1653	|	1722	1727	1744	1754	|	|	1838	1909	1912	...	|	|	1954	2022	2027	2110	...	|	2136	2230	...
Nantes 285/7 a.	1625	1655	1717	1725	1750	1800	1816	1820	1825	1855	1910	1943	1939	...	1955	2009	2020	2045	2049	2137	...	2150	2205	2252	...
Paris ⊡ **280** a.	...	1915	...	1935	...	...	...	...	2035	2115	...	...	...	...	2210	...	...	...	...	...	...	0005	...	...	...

A – Daily except ⑤ (will not run Apr. 30, May 7, 10, 11).
B – ⚒ to St Nazaire, Ⓐ to Le Croisic.
L – ①②③④⑦ (not Apr. 30, May 7).
N – ①②③④⑦ (also May 2; not Apr. 30, May 1, 7, 8, 11).
O – To/from Orléans (Table **289**).
T – 🚌12 Le Croisic - Nantes - Tours and v.v.
a – Also Dec. 24, 31; not Dec. 25, 26, Jan. 1, 2, Mar. 25, May 1, 8, 13.
d – Also Apr. 30, May 7.
e – Also Dec. 25, Jan. 1, Mar. 24, May 12.
f – Also Apr. 30, May 7; not May 2.
g – Also Dec. 26, Jan. 2, Mar. 25, May 13; not Dec. 24, 31, Mar. 24, May 12.
k – Not Jan. 7 - Feb. 29.
m – Not Dec. 25, Jan. 1, Mar. 24, Apr. 30, May 1, 7, 8, 12.
n – Not Dec. 25, Jan. 1, Mar. 24, May 12.
r – Calls on Ⓐ.
t – Also May 1, 8.
v – Also Dec. 26, Jan. 2, Mar. 25, May 1, 8, 13; not Dec. 24, 31, Mar. 24, May 12.
w – Also May 2; not Dec. 25, Jan. 1, Mar. 24, Apr. 30, May 1, 7, 8, 12.
x – 1802 on ⑤ (also Apr. 30, May 7).
y – Also Dec. 25, Jan. 1, Mar. 24, May 1, 8, 12; not Mar. 23, May 11.
z – Not Dec. 23, 30, Mar. 23. To Nevers (Table **290**).

TGV – 🅁, supplement payable, 🍷.
♥ – To/from Lille Europe (Table **11**).
◧ – On Jan. 21 - 24, 28 - 31 by 🚌 St Nazaire (1312) - Le Croisic (a. 1412 / d. 1427) - St Nazaire (1530).
⊙ – Subject to alteration Mar. 3 - 8, 10 - 15, 17 - 22.
⊡ – Paris Montparnasse.
△ – From Le Mans (Table **280**).
▷ – Subject to alteration Mar. 3 - 20, May 13 - 19.
◇ – On ①-④ Jan. 21 - 31 terminates at St Nazaire.
⊕ – On ①-④ Jan. 21 - 31 starts from St Nazaire.
⊖ – Subject to alteration on Ⓐ Jan. 7 - Feb. 29.

NANTES - ANGERS - TOURS 289

For other *TGV* trains Nantes - Lyon (via Massy) see Table **335**. For night trains see panel below Table **290**. *Subject to alteration on May 11.*

km		TGV 5302 ①–④ m	Ⓐ	TGV 5304 ⑥ t	TGV 8310 ①–⑥ P n	⚒	Ⓐ ⊕	†	Ⓐ	Ⓐ	▽	TGV 5322 ♠	4406 4407 †	TGV 5328 Ⓐ b	⑤ d	⑥	Ⓑ ☆f	①–④ m	⑤ d	†	⑥ △	Ⓐ	† w	⑥ ⊗	†	⑦ ⊖q
	Le Croisic **288** d.	...	...	...	...	0600y	...	0734	...	...	...	...	...	...	...	...	1513	...	...	...	...	...	...	1823	1902	...
0	**Nantes 280** d.	0455	...	0630	...	0706	0837	0849	...	1123	...	1252	1505	1555	...	...	1628	1636	1636	...	...	1818	1854	1945	2012	2218
88	Angers St Laud **280** d.	0533	0655	0708	...	0743	0921	0931	1100	1201	1231	1338	1548	1633	1640	...	1708	1750	1750	1749	1810	1859	1934	2030	2051	2301
132	Saumur d.	0556	0719	0730	0733	0805	0944	0954	1121	1222	1302	|	1610	1656	1706	1701	1732	1815	1815	1822	1842	1920	1958	2056	2112	2322
196	St Pierre des Corps a.	0629	|	0804	|	0837	1022	1033	|	1255	|	1427	|	1724	|	1746	|	|	1852	1858	1920	1952	|	2134	2141	2352
199	**Tours** a.	0638	0759	0816	|	0847	1033	1045	1158	1305	1355	1437	1642	1737	1744	1757	1804	1854	1902	1907	1931	2009	2035	2144	2151	0002
202	St Pierre des Corps a.	|	...	|	0813	|	...	|	...	|	...	|	1710	|	...	...	1822	...	...	...	...	|	...	|	|	...
	Orléans **296** a.	|	...	|	...	0935	...	1132	...	1352	...	|	|	|	...	...	...	...	...	...	...	2043	...	2227	2236	...
	Lyon Part Dieu **290** a.	0935	...	1103	...	...	...	...	...	...	...	1731	2149	2031	...	...	...	...	...	...	...	...	...	...	...	...

	Ⓐ	Ⓐ	⑥	†	Ⓐ ▷	TGV 5352 Ⓐ	Ⓐ	†	⚒	①–④ jm	⊗	①–⑥ n⊗	⑦ e	TGV 5368 ①–⑥ ♠n	⑤⑥ d⊗	Ⓐ	①–④ m	⚒	†	TGV 8367 ①–④ Pm	TGV 5378 ⑦ ♠e	TGV 5231 Ⓑ ♥h	4506 4507 ⑤–⑦ x		TGV 5380 k	TGV 8383 ⑤⑦ Pa
Lyon Part Dieu **290** d.	...	...	...	...	...	0656	...	...	...	...	...	...	...	1326	...	...	...	...	...	...	1656	...	1526	...	1826	...
Orléans **296** d.	...	0641	0727	0727	...	|	1105	...	...	...	...	...	...	|	1626	...	1726	...	1759	...	|	...	|	...	|	...
St Pierre des Corps d.	...	|	|	|	...	|	|	...	...	...	...	...	...	|	|	...	|	...	|	1945	|	...	2004	...	|	2134
Tours d.	0639	0727	0809	0809	0914	0944	1151	1202	1228	1325	1432	1611	1619	1612	1709	1732	1804	1837	1844	1958	1939	2004	2020	2042	2112	2146
St Pierre des Corps d.	|	0737	0820	0820	|	0954	1200	|	|	1336	|	|	|	1626	1723	|	1819	|	1855	|	1955	2014	|	2054	2125	|
Saumur d.	0717	0809	0856	0856	0955	|	1233	1248	1317	1412	1505	1648	1657	|	1754	1822	1851	1930	1927	2029	|	|	2053	2130	2205	2220
Angers St Laud **280** d.	0743	0833	0921	0921	1023	1049	1257	...	1349	...	1528	1713	1720	1722	1817	1845	1914	1954v	1950	...	2049	2108	2117	2206u	2226	...
Nantes 280 a.	0822	0910	1001	1001	...	1125	1337	...	...	...	1608	1759	1804	1803	1855	...	1956	...	2029	...	2127	2147	2158	...	2304	...
Le Croisic **288** a.	...	...	1116	1126	...	...	...	...	...	...	...	...	1922	...	2003	...	...	...	...	...	...	2257v	...	...	...	...

FOR NOTES SEE BELOW

Additional trains: Saumur - Tours 0612 Ⓐ, 0635 ⚒, 0812 Ⓐ, 0836 Ⓒ, 1623 ⑤ **d**, 1629 ⑦ **q**, 1704 ①–④ **m**, 1854 †.
Tours - Saumur 0719 Ⓐ, 1450 ⑤ **d**, 1450 ⑥, 1935 †, 2315 ⑦ **q**.

TOURS - BOURGES - LYON 290

For faster TGV trains Nantes / Tours - Massy - Lyon and v.v. see Table **335**. For night trains see panel below table.

km		⚒	16831		4402 B	⑥	⚒ D	†	16834 D•	⑥	◐	Ⓐ 2	4406 ⚒	†	⚒ 2	⑤ d	Ⓒ	4406 †	⚒	Ⓐ	Ⓑ f		Ⓑ	Ⓐ	†
	Nantes **289** d.	...	...	...	...	...	...	...	...	...	...	...	...	...	...	...	...	1505	...	...	1628	...	...	...	...
0	**Tours** d.	0617	...	...	0845	...	0900	1022	1213	1225	1405	1419	1505	1505	...	1609	1633	1705	1705	1727	1817	1928	1928	2053	2057
3	St Pierre des Corps d.	0624	...	...	0851	...	0906	1029	1219	1231	1411	1425	1512	1512	...	1615	1639	1712	1712	1733	1824	1935	1935	2100	2104
	Orléans **315** d.	|	0705	...	|	...	|	|	|	|	|	|	|	|	...	|	|	|	|	|	|	|	|	|	|
113	Vierzon **290 315** d.	0739	0748	...	0950	...	1023	1148	1326	1356	1516	1554	1616	1626	...	1724	1758	1814	1813	1905	1930	2049	2049	2234	2232
145	**Bourges 290 315** d.	0757	0805	...	1010	...	1046	1206	1348	▬	1537	1620	1636	1646	1724	1802	...	1835	1833	...	1951	2107	2112	2256	2253
	Nevers d.	...	0820	...	1032	...	...	|	1400	...	|	|	1653	...	|	...	...	1852	|	...	|	...	|	...	|
203	Saincaize d.	...	0836	0848	1043	1054	...	|	1418	1432	|	|	1709	...	|	...	...	1907	|	...	|	...	|	...	|
214	**Nevers 330** a.	...	|	0856	|	1102	...	1251	|	1440	1615	1713	1720	...	1814	...	...	1928	1910	...	2030	...	2153	...	2334
252	Moulins-sur-Allier **330** d.	...	0901	...	1111	...	...	...	1443	...	...	...	1735	...	...	...	...	1936	...	...	...	...	...	...	...
293	St Germain des Fossés **328** d.	...	|	...	1134	...	...	...	|	...	...	...	1758	...	...	...	...	2000	...	...	...	...	...	...	...
360	Roanne **328** d.	...	⊙	...	1217	...	...	...	⊙	...	...	...	1839	...	...	...	...	2042	...	...	...	...	...	...	...
457	**Lyon Part Dieu 328** a.	...	1139	...	1324	...	...	...	|	...	...	...	1947	...	...	...	...	2149	...	...	...	...	...	...	...
461	**Lyon Perrache 328** a.	...	1151	...	1336	...	...	...	1727	...	...	...	2003	...	...	...	...	2205	...	...	...	...	...	...	...

	Ⓐ	⑥	Ⓐ	⚒	⚒ 2		D	Ⓐ E		4504 ⚒ F		16842		⚒	†	2	†		4506	Ⓐ	†	⑤† c		16846	† 2
Lyon Perrache 328 d.	...	...	...	...	...	...	...	...	...	0904	...	1226	...	...	...	...	...	...	1511	...	...	...	...	1751	...
Lyon Part Dieu 328 d.	...	...	...	...	...	...	...	...	...	0918	...	1239	...	...	...	...	...	...	1526	...	...	...	...	1804	...
Roanne **328** d.	...	...	...	...	...	...	...	...	...	1032	...	⊙	...	...	...	...	...	...	1637	...	...	...	...	⊙	...
St Germain des Fossés **328** d.	...	...	...	...	...	...	...	...	...	1114	...	|	...	...	...	...	...	...	1719	...	...	...	...	|	...
Moulins-sur-Allier **330** d.	...	...	...	...	...	...	...	...	...	1137	...	1522	...	...	...	...	...	...	1742	...	...	...	...	2055	...
Nevers 330 d.	...	...	0547	0710r	0741	...	0919	...	1149	|	1528	|	...	1627	...	1632	...	1751	|	1936	1941	...	2104	|	2120
Saincaize d.	...	...	|	|	|	...	|	...	1158	1206	1536	1549	1600	|	...	|	...	1800	1808	|	|	...	2112	2120	|
Nevers a.	...	...	|	|	|	...	|	...	...	1220	...	|	1609	|	...	|	...	...	1820	|	|	...	...	2138	|
Bourges 290 315 d.	...	...	0635	0750	0831	0849	0959	1203	...	1238	...	1620	...	1709	1709	1721	1745	...	1840	2017	2028	2135	...	2151	2209
Vierzon **290 315** d.	0556	0625	0656	0809	...	0914	1020	1224	...	1300	...	1640	...	1728	1728	...	1808	...	1901	2038	2047	2154	...	2211	...
Orléans **315** a.	|	|	|	|	...	|	|	|	...	|	...	|	...	|	|	...	|	...	|	|	|	|	...	2249	...
St Pierre des Corps a.	0726	0800	0809	0914	...	1030	1129	1339	...	1401	...	1747	...	1843	1843	...	1918	...	2002	2156	2200	2258	...	...	...
Tours a.	0732	0806	0816	0921	...	1037	1136	1344	...	1407	...	1754	...	1850	1850	...	1924	...	2009	2203	2206	2304	...	...	...
Nantes **289** a.	...	...	...	...	...	...	...	...	...	...	...	...	...	...	...	...	...	...	2158x	...	...	...	...	...	...

Night Trains	4548 4549 🅁 T ◇	4550 4551 🅁 U ◇
Bourg St Maurice d.	...	1746
Chambéry d.	...	1943
Aix les Bains d.	...	1956
Lyon Perrache d.	2207	|
Lyon Part Dieu d.	2221	2134
Lyon Perrache d.	|	2223
St Pierre des Corps a.	0456	0456
Saumur a.	0528	0528
Angers a.	0551	0551
Nantes a.	0637	0637
Quimper **285** a.	0915	0915

Night Trains	4448 4449 🅁 X ◇	4450 4451 🅁 Y ◇
Quimper **285** d.	1820	1820
Nantes d.	2105	2105
Angers d.	2151	2151
Saumur d.	2214	2214
St Pierre des Corps d.	2247	2247
Lyon Perrache a.	|	0656
Lyon Part Dieu a.	0647	0729
Lyon Perrache a.	0701	|
Aix les Bains a.	...	0839
Chambéry a.	...	0852
Bourg St Maurice a.	...	1053

NOTES FOR TABLES 289 AND 290

- **B** – ⑥ (also Dec. 21, 24, 26 - 28, 31, Jan. 2 - 4); ⚒ from Mar. 31.
- **D** – By 🚌 Tours - Vierzon and v.v. on Ⓐ Dec. 10 - 21, Ⓐ Jan. 3 - Feb. 1, Ⓐ Mar. 25 - Apr. 4 (🚌 departs Tours approx 0845 and 1130, arrives Tours approx 1245).
- **E** – By 🚌 Vierzon - Tours (a. 1450) on Ⓐ Dec. 10 - 21, Ⓐ Jan. 2 - Feb. 8.
- **F** – By 🚌 St Germain des Fossés - Tours on Ⓐ Dec. 10 - 21, Ⓐ Jan. 2 - Feb. 1.
- **P** – (12) Saumur - Tours - Paris (Table **295**) and v.v.
- **T** – ⑤ to Mar. 21 (also Dec. 9, 16, 26, 27, Jan. 2, 3, ①–④ Feb. 11 - Mar. 6); also Mar. 30, daily Apr. 4 - May 4, May 7 - 12; ⑤⑦ from May 16.
- **U** – ⑥⑦ Dec. 22 - Mar. 23 (also Dec. 25, Jan. 1, Mar. 24).
- **X** – Dec. 9, 14, 16, 25 - 27, Jan. 1 - 3, ⑦ Jan. 6 - Mar. 16 (also ①–④ Feb. 11 - Mar. 6), Mar. 24, 28, 30, May 4, 7 - 12, ⑤⑦ from May 16.
- **Y** – ⑤⑥ Dec. 21 - Mar. 22 (also Dec. 23, 30, Mar. 23; not Feb. 22, 29, Mar. 7.
- **a** – Also Dec. 25, Jan. 1, Apr. 30, Mar. 24, May 7, 12; not May 2.
- **b** – Not May 2. To Grenoble on ⑤ (train **5332**).
- **c** – Also Apr. 30, May 7; not Mar. 23, May 11.
- **d** – Also Apr. 30, May 7.
- **e** – Also Dec. 25, Jan. 1, Mar. 24, May 12.
- **f** – Not Dec. 25, Jan. 1, Mar. 24, May 1, 2, 8, 9.
- **h** – Also May 1, 8.
- **j** – Subject to alteration Feb. 25 - Mar. 20.
- **k** – From Montpellier (Table **350**).
- **m** – Not Dec. 25, Jan. 1, Mar. 24, Apr. 30, May 1, 7, 8, 12.
- **n** – Not Dec. 25, Jan. 1, Mar. 24, May 12.
- **q** – Also Dec. 25, Jan. 1, Mar. 24, May 12; not Dec. 23, 30, Mar. 23, May 11.
- **r** – ① (also Dec. 26, Jan. 2, Mar. 25, May 2, 9, 13; not Mar. 24, May 12).
- **t** – Also May 1, 8.
- **u** – ⑤† (also Apr. 30, May 7; not Mar. 23, May 11).
- **v** – ⑤ (also Apr. 30, May 7).
- **w** – Not Mar. 23, May 11.
- **x** – ⑤⑥⑦ (also Dec. 25, Jan. 1, Mar. 24, May 1, 8, 12; not Nov. 10, 11).
- **y** – ⑥ only.

TGV – 🅁, supplement payable, 🍷.

- ⊙ – Via Paray le Monial (Table **372**).
- ⊖ – From Rennes (Table **287**).
- ☆ – To Nevers (Table **290**).
- ◇ – 🛏 1, 2 cl. and (2) (reclining).
- ⊕ – Not via St Pierre des Corps Feb. 25 - Mar. 7.
- ⊗ – Not May 10, 11.
- ◐ – Subject to alteration Apr. 2 - 7 Tours - Vierzon.
- ♥ – From Lille (Table **11**).
- ♠ – To / from Marseille (Table **335**).
- △ – Not Angers - Saumur on May 10.
- ▽ – Subject to alteration Ⓐ Mar. 25 - Apr. 18.
- ▷ – Subject to alteration Ⓐ Mar. 25 - Apr. 11, Apr. 21 - 25.
- • – On Apr. 2, 3, 4, 7 Tours 1206, St Pierre des Corps 1212, Vierzon 1319.

ROANNE - ST ÉTIENNE 291

km		Ⓐ	Ⓐ	⚒	Ⓐ			Ⓐ		Ⓐ				Ⓐ	Ⓐ		Ⓑ			Ⓐ				†
0	**Roanne** d.	0527	0547	0612	0641	0716	...	0819	0841	0941	1041	...	1237	1341	1441	...	1541	1641	...	1719	1818	1925	...	2047
80	**St Étienne** Châteaucreux a.	0647	0707	0732	0803	0839	...	0939	1003	1103	1204	...	1403	1503	1603	...	1703	1803	...	1843	1939	2044	...	2203

		Ⓐ	Ⓐ	⚒			Ⓐ			Ⓐ				Ⓐ			⚒	Ⓐ			Ⓐ			
St Étienne Châteaucreux d.	...	0550	0621	0714	...	0815	0850	0950	...	1150	1247	...	1450	1550	1650	...	1734	1750	1822	...	1850	1950	2050	...
Roanne a.	...	0704	0743	0829	...	0929	1004	1104	...	1304	1400	...	1604	1704	1804	...	1849	1905	1936	...	2005	2104	2204	...

292 NANTES - LA ROCHELLE - BORDEAUX

km									3832 3833		3835								3837		3839			4624 4625	
		Ⓐ	①–⑥ n	Ⓐ ◇	†	① g		⚒	🍷			A	⑤ f	①–④ m◇	⑤ f	⑤ f	†	L			⑤⑦ w	①–④ u		Ⓡ F	
	Quimper **285** d.	...	...	...	...	...	...	...	0740	...	...	...	...	...	...	...	...	...	...	...	...	...	...	...	...
0	**Nantes 293** d.	...	...	...	...	...	...	...	1019	...	1409	...	...	...	...	...	...	...	1727	...	1903	1933	...	2046	...
77	La Roche sur Yon **293** d.	...	...	...	...	...	...	...	1103	...	1454	...	...	...	...	...	...	...	1812	...	1950	2031	...	2130	...
180	**La Rochelle** d.	...	0606	0642	0750	0751	...	1122	1207	...	1558	...	1638	1649	...	1753	1758	1814	1919	...	2054	2132	...	2233	...
209	Rochefort d.	...	0631	0705	0815	0816	...	1144	1227	...	1619	...	1702	1712	...	1817	1825	1840	1939	...	2114	...	...	2254	...
253	Saintes d.	0608	0703	0741	0845	0846	...	1218	1258	...	1648	1741	1737	1747	1755	1858	1901	1916	2009	...	2144	...	...	2324	...
376	**Bordeaux St Jean** a.	0750	0835	...	1016	1016	...	1351	1419	...	1814	1922	...	...	1926	2043	...	...	2134	...	2304	...	...	0043	...
	Toulouse **320** a.	...	...	...	...	...	...	...	...	...	2056	...	...	...	...	...	...	...	...	...	...	...	...	|	...
	Marseille **355** a.	...	...	...	...	...	...	...	...	...	...	...	...	...	...	...	...	...	...	...	...	...	...	0708	...
	Nice **360** a.	...	...	...	...	...	...	...	...	...	...	...	...	...	...	...	...	...	...	...	...	...	...	1015	...

		🚌			4724 4725			🚌		3852			3854 3855				3856				3888	3858			
	⚒	① g	Ⓐ 2	②–⑤ v	Ⓡ F⊕	Ⓐ	Ⓐ ◇	Ⓐ	Ⓒ		Ⓐ	L		⚒	⚒ 2◇	† ◇	▽	†	⑥	⑦ e	①–④ z	⑤⑦ w	⑦ e	⑤ f	⑤ f
Nice **360** d.	...	...	...	...	1835	...	...	...	...	...	...	...	...	...	...	...	...	...	...	...	...	...	...	...	...
Marseille **355** d.	...	...	...	...	2214	...	...	...	...	...	...	...	...	...	...	...	...	...	...	...	...	...	...	...	...
Toulouse **320** d.	...	...	...	...	|	...	...	...	...	0748r	...	...	...	...	...	...	...	...	...	...	...	...	...	...	...
Bordeaux St Jean d.	...	...	...	...	0457	...	...	...	0819	1022	...	1215	1403	...	...	...	1703	1756	1818	...	1851	1851	1957	2027	2153
Saintes d.	...	...	...	...	0618	0636	0736	...	0946	1141	...	1352	1525	...	1742	1742	1827	1943	2009	...	2017	2014	2133	2205	2332
Rochefort d.	...	...	...	...	0647	0718	0814	1010	1018	1210	1312	1423	1554	1718	1820	1821	1859	...	...	...	2047	2044	2204	2234	0001
La Rochelle d.	...	0543	...	0640	0715	0748	0836	1046	1040	1231	1338	1445	1615	1746	1842	1845	1922	...	...	...	2107	2105	2229	2258	0024
La Roche sur Yon **293** d.	0620	0711	0724	0749	0822	...	...	...	...	1338	...	...	1722	...	...	...	2025	...	...	2117	...	2208	...	...	...
Nantes 293 a.	0720	...	0820	0846	0905	...	...	...	...	1424	...	...	1810	...	...	...	2113	...	...	2204	...	2252	...	...	...
Quimper **285** a.	...	...	...	...	...	...	...	...	...	...	...	...	2055	...	...	...	...	...	...	...	...	...	...	...	...

A – Daily except ⑤ (also runs May 2, 9; not Apr. 30, May 7).
F – ⑤⑦ (not Mar. 23), also Dec. 21 - Jan. 6 (not Dec. 24, 31), Feb. 8 - Mar. 9, Mar. 24, Apr. 4 - May 4, May 7 - 12. 🛏 1,2 cl. and (2) (reclining) Nantes - Nice and v.v.
L – ①②③④⑥ (also May 2, 9; not Dec. 25, Jan. 1, Mar. 24, Apr. 30, May 1, 7, 8, 12).
e – Also Dec. 25, Jan. 1, Mar. 24, May 12; not Mar. 23, May 11.
f – Also Apr. 30, May 7; not May 2, 9.
g – Also Dec. 26, Jan. 2, Mar. 25, May 13; not Dec. 24, 31, Mar. 24, May 12.
m – Also May 2, 9; not Dec. 25, Jan. 1, Mar. 24, Apr. 30, May 1, 7, 8, 12.
n – Not Dec. 25, Jan. 1, Mar. 24, May 1, 8.
r – 0653 on Ⓐ Feb. 18 - Mar. 14.
u – Not Dec. 25, Jan. 1, Mar. 24, Apr. 30, May 1, 7, 8, 12.
v – Not Dec. 25, 26, Jan. 1, 2, Mar. 25, May 1, 2, 8, 9, 13.
w – Also Dec. 25, Jan. 1, Mar. 24, Apr. 30, May 7, 12; not Mar. 23, May 2, 9, 11.
z – Also May 2; not Dec. 25, Jan. 1, Mar. 24, Apr. 30, May 7, 12.
◇ – To/from Angoulême (Table **301**).
▽ – To Rennes on dates in Table **287**.
⊕ – Subject to delay morning of Apr. 6, 13, 20, 27 (arrive Nantes 1036).

293 NANTES - LES SABLES D'OLONNE

km		Ⓐ 🚌	Ⓐ b	⚒ b	Ⓐ k	†	Ⓐ d	Ⓒ	Ⓒ	⑤ f	H 🚌	Ⓐ d	⑤f 🚌	Ⓐ d	Ⓐ d	Ⓒ	Ⓐ d	Ⓐ d	⑥	Ⓐ d	†	⑤ h	Ⓒ u	⑤ h
0	**Nantes 292** d.	...	*0615*	0708	0858	0926	1223	1224	1232	...	...	1424	...	1625	1645	1730	1735	1815	1926	2015	2014	2022	2126	2131
77	La Roche sur Yon **292** d.	0650	0729	0827	0948	1030	1320	1308	1342	1350	1350	1521	1615	1718	1803	1844	1844	1913	2014	2102	2111	2121	2210	2221
114	**Les Sables d'Olonne** a.	0730	0808	0901	1015	1100	1349	1335	1411	1428	1435	1555	1700	1752	1843	1920	1920	1943	2045	2129	2141	2152	2237	2250

	Ⓐ b	Ⓐ b	Ⓐ b	Ⓒ	Ⓐ b	Ⓐ	⚒ b	Ⓐ k	⑥	Ⓐ k	Ⓒ	⑤ h	A	Ⓐ d	Ⓐ d	Ⓒ	† v	Ⓐ d	† v	⑥	Ⓐ d	Ⓐ 🚌	† v	Ⓐ d	
Les Sables d'Olonne d.	0531	0632	0654	0710	0728	*0755*r	0917	1126	1157	1221	1232	1356	1420	1521	1628	1631	1712	1717	1746	1802	1810	1830	1932	1948	...
La Roche sur Yon **292** d.	0559	0700	0724	0739	0808	0846	0947	1155	1231	1251	1259	1429	1449	1558	1658	1658	1743	1755	1814	1830	1845	1915	1959	2016	2025
Nantes 292 a.	0645	0748	0820	0850	...	0953	1038	1242	1330	1345	1345	...	...	1650	1806	1745	1842	1850	1917	1934	1943	...	2050	...	2113

A – Daily except ⑤ (will not run Apr. 30, May 7).
H – ①–④ (not Dec. 24, 25, 31, Jan. 1, Mar. 24, May 1, 8, 12).
b – By 🚌 La Roche sur Yon - Les Sables and v.v. on ②–⑤ Jan. 8 - May 23 (not Mar. 25, May 13).
d – By 🚌 La Roche sur Yon - Les Sables and v.v. on ①–④ Jan. 7 - May 22 (not Apr. 30, May 7).
f – Also Apr. 30, May 7; not May 2, 9.
h – Also Apr. 30, May 7.
k – By 🚌 La Roche sur Yon - Les Sables and v.v. on Ⓐ Jan. 7 - May 23.
r – By 🚌.
u – Not Jan. 19.
v – Not Mar. 23, May 11.

Timings of replacement buses were not available at press date.

294 PARIS - LES AUBRAIS - ORLÉANS

Selected trains

Timings may vary due to engineering work

km		⚒	Ⓐ	⚒	⑥		⚒			⚒r		◇	⚒	⚒		⑤d			Ⓐ				Ⓑ	⚒	⑦q
0	**Paris Austerlitz** § d.	0557	0624	0648	0706	0722	0806	0921	...	1047	1141	1217	1208	1241	1335	1456	...	1547	1632	1703	1721	...	1736	1803	1803
56	Étampes § d.	0626	|	0718	|	|	|	|	...	|	|	|	1239	|	|	|	...	|	|	|	1752	...	|	|	|
119	Les Aubrais-Orléans a.	0719	0722	0817	0759	0820	0903	1017	...	1145	1240	1311	1332	1340	1433	1553	...	1647	1733	1802	1845	...	1832	1902	1902
121	**Orléans** a.	0724	0728	0822	*0807*	*0828*	0910	*1029*	...	1151	1246	*1319*	1338	*1348*	1439	*1602*	...	*1656*	1739	1808	1850	...	*1841*	1908	*1918*

	Ⓑ	⑤d					⑤⑦v	c		
Paris Austerlitz § d.	1833	1848	1901	1907	...	1952	2153	2253	2344	...
Étampes § d.	|	|	|	1937	...	|	|	|	|	...
Les Aubrais-Orléans a.	1932	1949	1956	2037	...	2049	2251	2354	0048	...
Orléans a.	1938	1955	*2007*	2046	...	2055	2257	*0003*	0054	...

	⚒u	Ⓐ	⚒u	⚒	Ⓐu		⚒	⚒	†	⚒	
Orléans d.	0506	0608z	*0621*	0617	*0652*	...	0708	*0724*	0738	0750	0839
Les Aubrais-Orléans d.	0512	0615	0629	0623	0702	...	0714	0736	0744	0755	0845
Étampes § a.	|	|	|	0723	|	...	|	|	|	0840	|
Paris Austerlitz § a.	0614	0716	0730	0800	0803	...	0818	0833	0842	0912	0947

	†	⚒	u	u	⚒		⚒	x	⚒	Ⓐ	Ⓒ		⚒				⚒	⑦q		Ⓑ		†	Ⓐ		
Orléans d.	0900	0941	1036	*1125*	1143	...	1226	1235	*1319*	*1402*	1432	1629	1717	*1752*	...	1814	*1822*	*1822*	1856	1924	*1944*	2043	2100	2216	...
Les Aubrais-Orléans d.	0906	0947	1042	1134	1149	...	1231	1243	1328	1411	1438	1635	1722	1801	...	1819	1832	1834	1900	1930	2006	2049	2107	2221	...
Étampes § a.	|	|	|	|	|	...	1329	|	|	|	|	1701	|	|	...	1921	|	1906	|	|	|	2120	|	|	...
Paris Austerlitz § a.	1026	1050	1141	1228	1250	...	1359	1341	1423	1511	1538	1734	1838	1859	...	1953	1926	1935	1959	2052	2104	2152	2205	2321	...

c – Not Dec. 24, 31.
d – Also Apr. 30, May 7.
q – Also Dec. 25, Jan. 1, Mar. 24, May 12; not Dec. 23, 30, Mar. 23, May 11.
r – Change at Les Aubrais Apr. 14 - 18.
u – Subject to alteration Apr. 24 - May 17.
v – Also Dec. 25, Jan. 1, Mar. 24, Apr. 30, May 7, 12.
x – Subject to alteration Apr. 14 - May 15.
z – *0606* on ① (also Dec. 26, Jan. 2, Mar. 25; not Mar. 24, May 5, 12.
◇ – Timings may vary up to 20 minutes earlier due to engineering work.
§ – Suburban trains run Paris Austerlitz - Étampes and v.v. approximately every 30 minutes (journey 55 minutes).

PARIS - TOURS — 295

TGV trains — *SUBJECT TO ALTERATION MAY 8 – 11*

km	*TGV* trains convey 🍸	TGV 8405	TGV 8315	TGV 5200	TGV 8317	TGV 5212 9802	TGV 8417	TGV 8417	TGV 8323	TGV 8333	TGV 5218	TGV 8441	TGV 8343	TGV 8345	TGV 8349	TGV 5216	TGV 5205	TGV 8347	TGV 8353	TGV 8451	TGV 5222	TGV 8363	TGV 8357	TGV 8365	TGV 8367
			①–⑥							‡			⑤	⑤	①–④	⑦	①–④	⑤	⑤		⑤⑥	①–④	⑤	D	Ⓐe
			p			b	A	¶					d	d	m	v	k	d	d		a	m	d		s
	Lille Europe **11** d.	...	...	0558	...	0759	...	...	...	...	1238f	...	...	...	...	1447	1447	...	...	...	1541	...	...	...	...
	Charles de Gaulle ✈ d.	...	...	0739	...	0856	...	...	...	...	1337	...	...	...	...	1542	1542	...	...	...	1638	...	...	...	...
	Marne la Vallée - Chessy d.	...	...	0756	...	0910	...	...	...	...	1351	...	...	...	...	1557	1557	...	...	...	1653	...	...	...	...
0	**Paris Montparnasse** d.	0650	0750	|	0910	|	1040	1050	1225	1350	|	1515	1535	1610	1615	|	|	1645	1655	1715	|	1740	1755	1810	1840
14	Massy-TGV d.	0702	|	0831	|	0946	|	|	|	|	1431	|	|	|	|	1631	1636	|	|	|	1730	|	|	|	|
162	Vendôme-Villiers d.	|	0835	|	|	|	|	|	1310	|	|	|	|	1654	|	|	|	|	|	|	|	|	1839	1855	1923
221	St Pierre des Corps a.	0752	0853	0921	1006	1035	1140	1146	1327	1447	1521	1611	1631	1712	1712	1721	1727	1739	1751	1811	1821	1836	1858	1914	1942
221	St Pierre des Corps d.	0757	0855	0927	1011	1040	1145	1158	1330	1454	1527	1616	1633	1714	1714	1726	1732	1742	1756	1816	1830	1838	1900	1916	1945
224	**Tours** a.	0802	0900	0932	1016	1045	1150	1203	1335	1459	1532	1621	1639	1719	1719	1731	1737	1747	1801	1821	1835	1842	1905	1921	1950

TGV trains convey 🍸	TGV 8469	TGV 5231	TGV 8375	TGV 8377	TGV 5242	TGV 8483	TGV 8383	TGV 8489	TGV 8391	TGV 8587
		Ⓑ	①–⑥	⑦	⑤–⑦	①–④	⑤⑦	⑦	⑤	⑤⑦
		c	p	v	r	m	u◐	v	d	g
Lille Europe **11** d.	...	1729	...	...	1829	...	...	...	...	...
Charles de Gaulle ✈ d.	...	1824	...	...	1925	...	...	...	...	...
Marne la Vallée - Chessy d.	...	1840	...	...	1942	...	...	...	...	...
Paris Montparnasse d.	1850	|	1930	1930	|	2020	2030	2110	2120	2245
Massy-TGV d.	|	1921	|	|	2018	|	|	|	|	2258
Vendôme-Villiers d.	|	|	2015	|	|	2105	2114	|	|	|
St Pierre des Corps a.	1946	2011	2033	2026	2109	2125	2132	2206	2216	0000
St Pierre des Corps d.	1952	2018	2036	2033	2114	2134	2134	2211	2220	0005
Tours a.	1957	2023	2041	2038	2119	2139	2139	2216	2225	0010

	TGV 8300	TGV 8320	TGV 8302	TGV 8332	TGV 8304	TGV 5260	TGV 8310	TGV 8312	TGV 5260	TGV 5260
	①–④	⑤	Ⓐ	⑥	Ⓐ	①–⑥	①–⑥	⑦	⑦G	E
	m	d		z		H	p◐	v		
Tours d.	0610	0624	0652	0727	0740	0753	0757	0809	0831	0852
St Pierre des Corps a.	0615	0629	0657	0732	0745	0758	0802	0814	0836	0857
St Pierre des Corps d.	0618	0632	0700	0735	0747	0803	0816	0823	0841	0902
Vendôme-Villiers d.	0640	0653	0722	0757	|	|	0837	|	|	|
Massy-TGV a.	|	0731	|	|	|	|	|	|	|	0952
Paris Montparnasse a.	0725	0740	0805	0840	0845	|	0920	0920	|	|
Marne la Vallée - Chessy a.	...	...	...	...	...	0926	...	...	1006	1036
Charles de Gaulle ✈ a.	...	...	...	...	...	0942	...	...	1021	1050
Lille Europe **11** a.	...	...	...	...	...	1044	...	...	1128	1151

	TGV 8414	TGV 5264	TGV 8318	TGV 8420	TGV 8322	TGV 8324	TGV 5276	TGV 8328	TGV 8436	TGV 8540	TGV 5279 9816	TGV 8346	TGV 8548	TGV 8350	TGV 8358	TGV 8364	TGV 8362	TGV 5284	TGV 8466	TGV 8472	TGV 8474	TGV 8378	TGV 5292	TGV 8584	TGV 8390
		Ⓑ	①–④	◇				⑤				Ⓑ		⑤	⑤	⑤–⑦	①–④	Ⓑ	⑦	①–⑥	⑦	⑦	①–⑥		⑦
	x		m					d		y	b	c		d	d	t	n	w	v	j	v	v	h▲	▲	v
Tours d.	0928	1013	1020	1024	1208	1252	1322	1412	1442	1612	1645	1712	1742	1755	1829	1857	1912	1920	1957	2022	2035	2054	2112	2208	2308
St Pierre des Corps a.	0933	1018	1025	1029	1213	1257	1327	1417	1447	1617	1650	1717	1747	1800	1834	1902	1917	1925	2002	2027	2040	2059	2117	2213	2313
St Pierre des Corps d.	0938	1023	1036	1036	1216	1303	1333	1422	1452	1622	1655	1720	1753	1805	1836	1908	1922	1928	2007	2032	2047	2101	2122	2221	2318
Vendôme-Villiers d.	|	|	|	|	1237	|	|	|	|	|	|	1748	|	|	1857	|	|	|	|	|	|	2122	|	|	|
Massy-TGV a.	|	1113	|	|	|	|	1423	|	|	|	1747	|	|	|	|	|	|	2018	|	|	2140	|	2213	|	|
Paris Montparnasse a.	1035	|	1135	1135	1320	1400	|	1520	1550	1720	|	1830	1850	1905	1940	2005	2020	|	2105	2130	2150	2205	|	2320	0015
Marne la Vallée - Chessy a.	...	1152	...	...	...	...	1506	...	...	...	1827	...	...	...	...	...	...	2058	...	...	...	...	2251	...	...
Charles de Gaulle ✈ a.	...	1207	...	...	...	...	1521	...	...	...	1841	...	...	...	...	...	...	2112	...	...	...	...	2306	...	...
Lille Europe **11** a.	...	1304	...	...	...	...	1615	...	...	...	2003f	...	...	...	...	...	...	2219	...	...	...	...	0007	...	...

A – ①–⑤ Jan. 7 - Feb. 20 and ①–⑤ Mar. 10 – 21.
D – ①②③④⑥⑦ (not Apr. 30, May 7).
E – Until Mar. 30.
G – ⑦ from Apr. 6 (also May 12; not May 11).
H – ①–⑥ from Mar. 31 (not May 10, 12).

a – Also Apr. 30, May 1, 7, 8; not May 2, 9, 10.
b – To / from Lille Europe and Brussels (Table **11**).
c – Not May 1, 8.
d – Also Apr. 30, May 7; not May 2.
e – Not May 2.
f – Lille **Flandres**.
g – Also Dec. 25, Jan. 1, Mar. 24, Apr. 30, May 7, 12; not May 2, 30, June 6, 13.
h – Not Dec. 25, Jan. 1, Mar. 24, May 9, 10, 12.
j – Not Dec. 25, Jan. 1, Mar. 24, May 2, 8, 9, 10, 12. Runs 5 minutes later on ⑤ **d**.
k – Also May 2; not Dec. 25, Jan. 1, Mar. 24, Apr. 30, May 1, 7, 8, 12.
m – Not Dec. 25, Jan. 1, Mar. 24, Apr. 30, May 1, 7, 8, 12.
n – Also May 2, 9; not Dec. 25, Jan. 1, Mar. 24, Apr. 30, May 1, 7, 8, 12.
p – Not Dec. 25, Jan. 1, Mar. 24, May 12.
r – Also Dec. 25, Jan. 1, Mar. 24, Apr. 30, May 1, 7, 8, 12; not May 2.
s – Train number **8371** on ⑤ **d**. To Saumur on ①–④ **m** (Table **289**).
t – Also Dec. 25, Jan. 1, Mar. 24, Apr. 30, May 1, 7, 8, 12; not May 2, 9.
u – Also Dec. 25, Jan. 1, Mar. 24, Apr. 30, May 7, 12; not May 2.
v – Also Dec. 25, Jan. 1, Mar. 24, May 12.
w – Not May 1, 8, 9.
x – Not Feb. 24.
y – Not Mar. 29, 30.
z – Also May 1, 8.

TGV – Ⓡ, supplement payable, 🍸.
¶ – Daily except when train **A** runs.
▲ – Subject to alteration on ①–④ from May 26.
‡ – Train number **8331** on ⑦ **v**.
◇ – Train number **8422** on ⑦ **v**.
◐ – To / from Saumur (Table **289**).

ORLÉANS - BLOIS - TOURS — 296

For fast *TGV* services Paris - Tours and v.v. see Table **295**

km																								
		⚒	Ⓐ	Ⓐ	⚒	Ⓒ	Ⓐ	Ⓐ	⚒	⚒		†		Ⓐ	Ⓐ	⊡	⚒q	⚒		⚒q	⊡		⑤	⑤
						n								⊕				❖	⊖				f	f
	Paris Austerlitz **294** d.	...	...	...	...	...	...	0624	...	...	0722	...	0921	...	...	1047	1047	...	1141	1241	1241	1335	...	1456
0	**Orléans** d.	...	0641	0624	0702	0727	0727	0738	0738	0746	0813	0852	1010	1023	1105	1125	1201	1216	1256	1332	1332	1449r	1540	1546
2	Les Aubrais-Orléans d.	...	|	|	|	|	|	0724x	|	|	0822	|	1019	1031	|	1147	1147x	|	1242x	1342	1358	1435x	|	1555
30	Beaugency d.	...	|	0643	0723	|	|	0801	0801	0815	0839	0919	1038	1055	|	1207	1222	1241	1317	|	|	1510	1558	|
61	Blois d.	0637	0709	0712	0743	0754	0754	0822	0822	0839	0900	0944	1102	1113	1132	1229	1244	1306	1339	1412	1428	1531	1616	1625
93	Amboise d.	0703	|	0731	0801	|	|	0844	0844	...	0920	1008	1124	...	|	1250	1305	1331	1400	|	|	1552	1635	|
115	St Pierre des Corps a.	0720	0735	0744	0814	0818	0818	0859	0859	...	0937	1025	1136	...	1159	1302	1318	1348	1412	1443	1451	1605	1647	1652
118	**Tours** a.	0727	0745	0751	0820	0830	0825	0906	0906	...	0944	1031	1143	...	1209	1308	1325	1355	1419	1450	1500	1612	1653	1659
	Nantes **289** a.	...	0910	...	...	1001	...	...	...	...	...	...	...	...	1337	...	...	...	...	...	...	...	...	...

	①–④	⑤	⑤⑥	①–④	Ⓐ		①–④	†	⚒	†	Ⓐ	⚒		⑥	Ⓑ	Ⓐ	⑦	⚒	Ⓑ	Ⓐ		Ⓑ		
	m	f	y	m		◐	m			n			t				k							s
Paris Austerlitz **294** d.	...	...	...	...	...	1547	...	...	...	...	1632	...	1703	1703	1736	...	1803	1803	1833	...	1952	...	...	2253
Orléans d.	1558	1605	1626	1610	...	1640	1726	1713	1733	1759	1749	...	1818	1818	1822	1847	1856	1918	1948	1953	2105	2141	...	2348
Les Aubrais-Orléans d.	|	|	|	|	...	1649	|	|	|	|	1735x	...	1804x	1804x	1834	|	1905	1904x	1934x	|	2051x	2153	...	2356
Beaugency d.	1616	1631	|	1637	...	1707	|	1738	1801	|	1810	...	1838	1838	|	1913	1925	1940	|	2020	2126	2212	...	|
Blois d.	1635	1649	1655	1658	1658	1730	1753	1804	1825	1825	1832	1837	1858	1900	1905	1938	1945	2002	2023	2038	2148	2232	...	0028
Amboise d.	1653	...	|	1722	1722	1751	|	1830	...	1840	1853	1903	...	1921	|	2003	2006	2024	...	...	2209	2252	...	|
St Pierre des Corps a.	1705	...	1721	1743	1743	1803	1817	1846	...	1853	1905	1922	...	1935	1930	2020	2020	2038	...	...	2222	2303	...	0054
Tours a.	1712	...	1731	1750	1750	1810	1828	1853	...	1903	1912	1929	...	1941	1937	2027	2027	2045	...	...	2228	2309	...	0100
Nantes **289** a.	...	...	1855	...	...	...	1956	...	...	2029	...	...	...	...	...	...	...	...	...	...	...	...	...	...

	⚒		⚒	Ⓐ	⚒	⚒	Ⓐ	⚒		⚒	Ⓐ	⚒	⚒		†	†	⚒		⚒	⑥	Ⓐ	Ⓐ	Ⓒ	
														◇		n	◇	◇‡	⊕					
Nantes **289** d.	...	...	...	...	...	...	...	...	...	...	...	...	0706	...	...	0849	...	...	...	...	...	1123	...	...
Tours d.	...	...	0534	...	...	0630	...	0647	0708	...	0802	0813	0829	0903	0940	1022	1027*	1100	...	1230	1230	1241	1300	...
St Pierre des Corps d.	...	...	0541	...	...	0638	...	0653	0714	...	0809	0820	0839	0910	0946	1035	1034*	1106	...	1236	1237	1257	1306	...
Amboise d.	...	...	0553	...	...	0650	...	0710	0727	...	|	0832	|	0922	1001	1047	|	1119	...	1252	1254	|	1318	...
Blois d.	0546	...	0615	0629	0632	0707	0713	0736	0749	0753	0834	0852	0906	0943	1026	1104	1101*	1142	1225	1317	1325	1322	1340	...
Beaugency d.	0607	...	0635	|	0651	|	0732	...	0810	0818	|	0912	|	1003	1050	|	|	1204	1251	...	1347	|	1400	...
Les Aubrais-Orléans a.	0627	...	0712v	0700	|	0733	|	...	0843v	|	|	0945v	|	1040v	|	|	1147v	1239v	1319	...	1409e	|	1436v	...
Orléans a.	0639	...	0657	0712	0719	0745	0759	...	0830	0845	0904	0931	0935	1026	1118	1132	1133	1225	1328	...	|	1352e	1422	...
Paris Austerlitz **294** a.	0733	...	0818	0806	...	0836	...	...	0948	...	...	1052	...	1141	...	...	1250	1341	...	...	1511e	...	1539	...

		Ⓐ	Ⓐ		Ⓐ				Ⓐ		Ⓐ	†	Ⓐ	Ⓐ	⑥				⑥	†		†	Ⓐ	
												z					s		p	n				
Nantes **289** d.	...	...	...	...	...	...	...	...	...	...	...	...	...	1818	...	...	...	...	1945	2012	...	...	...	...
Tours d.	1500	1550	1630	1655	...	1723	1735	...	1811	1841	1852	1910	1912	1944	1947	...	2046b	...	2126	2133	...	2219	2223	...
St Pierre des Corps d.	1506	1557	1636	1702	...	1730	1741	...	1818	1848	1858	1917	1919	1954	1954	...	2053b	...	2136	2143	...	2225	2229	...
Amboise d.	1519	1611	1652	|	...	1742	1756	...	|	1901	1914	1929	1931	|	2005	...	2105b	...	|	|	...	2236	2241	...
Blois d.	1539	1631	1718	1728	1735	1805	1820	...	1846	1923	1939	1952	1951	2018	2025	...	2126	...	2200	2208	...	2255	2300	...
Beaugency d.	1558	1656	...	|	1800	1826	1839	...	|	1944	...	2013	2011	|	2042	...	2146	...	|	|	...	2312	2320	...
Les Aubrais-Orléans a.	1633v	|	...	1758	|	|	|	...	|	2004	...	2047v	|	|	|	...	2219v	...	|	|	...	|	|	...
Orléans a.	1619	1724	...	1808	1827	1846	1905	...	1915	|	...	2033	2028	2043	2100	...	2206	...	2227	2236	...	2330	2339	...
Paris Austerlitz **294** a.	1736	...	...	1902	...	2001	...	...	...	2107	...	2155	...	...	...	...	2324	...	...	...	...	...	...	...

b – 7 minutes earlier on ①–④ from May 26.
e – 3 – 5 minutes later Apr. 14 - May 15.
f – Also Apr. 30, May 7.
k – Also Dec. 25, Jan. 1, Mar. 24, May 12; not Dec. 23, 30, Mar. 23, May 11.
m – Not Dec. 25, Jan. 1, Mar. 24, Apr. 30, May 1, 7, 8, 12.
n – Not May 11.
p – Not May 10.
q – Not Apr. 14 – 18.
r – Not May 18.
s – Not Dec. 24, 31.
t – Not Mar. 23, May 11.
v – Calls after Orléans.
x – Calls before Orléans.
y – Also Apr. 30, May 7; not May 10.
z – Not Dec. 23, 30, Mar. 23, May 11.

⊡ – Apr. 14 – 18 only.
⊕ – Not Ⓐ Apr. 14 - May 15.
❖ – 22 – 28 minutes later on May 20.
⊖ – On May 18, 20 runs up to 11 minutes later Beaugency - Tours.
◐ – On May 18 Paris d. 1538, Orléans d. 1629, Les Aubrais d. 1639.
◇ – On Ⓐ Apr. 14 - May 15 does not call at Orléans.
‡ – On May 20 runs 10 – 14 minutes later Tours - Beaugency and does not call at Orléans.
* – 10 minutes later on Ⓐ Apr. 21 - May 15.

299 OTHER LOCAL SERVICES

ANGERS - CHOLET: *60 km* Journey 50 - 65 minutes

Angers depart: 0646 Ⓐ, 0722 Ⓐ, 0756 ⚒, 0938 ⚒, 1148, 1304 Ⓐ, 1309 ⑥, 1559, 1638 ⑥, 1725 Ⓐ, 1741 Ⓐ, 1846 ⚒, 1934 Ⓑ, 2041 †, 2043 ⚒, 2138 ⑤, 2244 Ⓐ, 2245 † **v**.

Cholet depart: 0611 Ⓐ, 0635 ⚒, 0658 Ⓐ, 0711 ⑥, 0742 Ⓐ, 0842 ⚒, 0844 †, 1046 ⚒, 1237 ⚒, 1349 †, 1357 ⚒, 1649 Ⓑ, 1737, 1840 ⑦ **v**, 1842 Ⓐ, 1941 Ⓑ, 1944 ⑥, 2204 ⑦ **v**.

BAYONNE - ST JEAN PIED DE PORT *50 km*

	①g	M		△			⚒		⑤d	†
Bayonne .... d.	0745	0824	...	1200	1437	...	1813	...	2106	2106
St Jean Pied de Port.... a.	0858	0937	...	1313	1550	...	1935	...	2218	2218

	Ⓐ	⑥			▽				†	
St Jean Pied de Port.... d.	0619	0658	0945	...	1320	...	1556	...	1838	...
Bayonne .... a.	0737	0816	1058	...	1433	...	1709	...	1951	...

BORDEAUX - MONT DE MARSAN *147 km*

	Ⓐ	Ⓐ	⑥		⚒	†	Ⓐz	⚒	†	⚒
Bordeaux 305 .... d.	...	0631	...	...	...	...	1030	1230	1322	1440
Morcenx **305** .... d.	0652	0730	0744	...	0917	0935	1128	1334	1418	1537
Mont de Marsan .... a.	0721	0757	0810	...	0940	1003	1150	1357	1438	1559

	Ⓐ		Ⓑy
Bordeaux 305 .... d.	1721	...	2110
Morcenx **305** .... d.	1819	1939	2206
Mont de Marsan .... a.	1844	2008	2228

	Ⓐ	⚒	Ⓐ
Mont de Marsan .... d.	0552	0616	0726
Morcenx **305** .... d.	0617	0643	0754
Bordeaux 305 .... a.	0717	...	...

	⚒		⚒u	Ⓐ	†	⚒	†	⑥	†	Ⓐ
Mont de Marsan .... d.	0848	1011	1206	1436	1552	1613	1758	1851	1858	1901
Morcenx **305** .... d.	0914	1032	1234	1457	1615	1634	1828	1920	1928	1931
Bordeaux 305 .... a.	1005	...	1332	1554	1711	1730	...	...	2024	2027

CARCASSONNE - LIMOUX - QUILLAN

km		🚌	⚒	🚌†	⚒k	⚒k	🚌†	⚒	⚒	⚒	🚌†
0	Carcassonne .... d.	0610	0717	0915	1050	1241	1326	1612	1727	1843	1839
26	Limoux .... a.	0643	0747	0948	1120	1311	1359	1642	1757	1913	1912
54	Quillan .... a.	0723	...	1028	*1210*r	1347	1439	*1735*r	...	1949	1952

	⚒	⚒	🚌†	⚒k	🚌†	⚒k	⚒	🚌†	⚒	🚌⚒	🚌†
Quillan .... d.	0602	...	0736	*1035*r	1040	1354	*1555*r	1606	...	1750	2007
Limoux .... d.	0637	0754	0816	1127	1122	1429	1649	1650	1802	1833	2047
Carcassonne ..... a.	0708	0824	0849	1157	1200	1500	1719	1727	1832	1910	2120

CHARLEVILLE MÉZIÈRES - GIVET: *64 km* Journey 65 - 75 minutes

Charleville Mézières depart: 0605 ⚒, 0650 ⚒, 0743 Ⓐ, 0839 Ⓐ, 1010 ⚒, 1115, 1220 ⚒, 1258 ⑥, 1330, 1440, 1615, 1635 Ⓐ, 1730 ⚒, 1806 Ⓐ, 1833 Ⓐ, 1915 ⑥, 1932 Ⓑ, 2015.

Givet depart: 0450 Ⓐ, 0511 ⑥, 0520 Ⓐ, 0555 Ⓐ, 0609 ⑥, 0645 Ⓐ, 0650 †, 0653 ⑥, 0738 ⑥, 0743 Ⓐ, 1015, 1114 Ⓐ, 1210 ⑥, 1233 ⚒, 1351 Ⓐ, 1359 ⑥, 1501 Ⓐ, 1519 †, 1610 Ⓑ, 1651 ⚒, 1744 Ⓐ, 1753 ⑥, 1822 Ⓐ, 1905 Ⓑ, 2013 †.

DINARD - ST MALO

🚌 : 7 - 10 times per day (3 - 5 on †), journey 24 minutes. Operator: TIV. *11 km*

⛴ : *Le Bus de Mer* passenger ferry operates 10 - 15 times daily from April to October. Journey time 10 minutes.

LILLE - LENS: *39 km* Journey 31 - 48 minutes

Lille Flandres depart: 0548 Ⓐ, 0700 ⚒, 0726 Ⓐ, 0756 ⑥, 0759 Ⓐ, 0825 Ⓐ, 0901 ⚒, 1003 †, 1142 ⑥, 1156 Ⓑ, 1242 ⚒, 1329, 1558, 1626 Ⓐ, 1658, 1726 Ⓐ, 1758, 1807 Ⓐ, 1830 Ⓐ, 1857 Ⓐ, 1934 ⑥, 1942 Ⓑ, 2026.

Lens depart: 0455 Ⓐ, 0525 ⚒, 0626 ⚒, 0652 ⚒, 0724 ⚒, 0756 ⚒, 0830 Ⓐ, 0851, 0958 ⑥, 1054 Ⓒ, 1119 Ⓐ, 1230 ⚒, 1255 Ⓑ, 1345 ⑥, 1431 Ⓒ, 1556 ⚒, 1630 Ⓑ, 1658 ⚒, 1731 Ⓑ, 1758 ⚒, 1846 ⚒, 1900 †, 2002.

MONTLUÇON - USSEL

km				⚒t		†		⑤f §	
0	Montluçon .... d.	...	...	1546	...	1634	...	2041	...
94	Eygurande-Merlines **326** .... d.	...	...	1742	...	1834	...	2246	...
112	Ussel **326** .... a.	...	...	1759	...	1851	...	2305	...

					⑦x§				
Ussel **326** .... d.	...	...	1323	...	1638	...	...	...	...
Eygurande-Merlines **326** .... d.	...	...	1341	...	1657	...	...	...	...
Montluçon .... a.	...	...	1541	...	1856	...	...	...	...

NANTES - CHOLET: *65 km* Journey 51 - 65 minutes

Nantes depart: 0634 ⚒, 0805 Ⓐ 🚌, 0915 ⑥ 🚌, 0915 ① 🚌, 1236, 1635 ⚒ 🚌, 1709 Ⓐ, 1735 🚌, 1845, 1920 ⑤ 🚌.

Cholet depart: 0605 ⚒, 0635 Ⓐ 🚌, 0739 Ⓐ, 0805 ⑥ 🚌, 1019, 1216 †, 1240 ⚒ 🚌, 1505 ⑤ 🚌, 1654 Ⓐ, 1745 ⑤ 🚌, 1825 Ⓐ, 2042 ⑦.

PARIS - CHÂTEAUDUN

km			⚒		⑤d	Ⓐ	⚒	†v	⑤d	†v
0	Paris Austerlitz .... d.	0824	1150	1350	1614	1748	1851	1912	2211	2238
134	Châteaudun .... a.	0958	1319	1520	1749	1926	2026	2043	2339	0006

		⚒	⚒		⚒		†v	⑤d	†v	
Châteaudun .... d.	...	0617	0721	1023	1527	1656	1823	2033	2047	...
Paris Austerlitz .... a.	...	0757	0857	1153	1704	1832	1956	2202	2217	...

PARIS - DISNEYLAND (Marne la Vallée - Chessy): *32 km* Journey 39 minutes

Trains run approximately every 15 minutes 0500 - 2400 on RER Line A:
Paris Châtelet les Halles - Paris Gare de Lyon - Marne la Vallée Chessy (for Disneyland).
Operator: RATP. For *TGV* services serving Marne la Vallée see Tables **11**, **391**.

ST BRIEUC - DINAN

km		Ⓐ	⑥		†	⚒ ⊕		⑥	Ⓐ	† ◇	
0	St Brieuc **284**.... d.	0648	0717	...	1220	1320	...	1713	1718	1718	...
21	Lamballe **284**.... d.	0707	0735	...	1237	1337	...	1730	1736	1734	...
62	Dinan .... a.	0746	0810	...	1312	1412	...	1805	1810	1813	...

	Ⓐ	⑥		Ⓐ ◇⊕	Ⓒ ◇		⑥	Ⓐ	†	
Dinan .... d.	0622	0655	...	1057	1131	...	1820	1831	1920	...
Lamballe **284** .... a.	0702	0729	...	1128	1203	...	1853	1905	1954	...
St Brieuc **284** .... a.	0722	0747	...	1147	1221	...	1912	1923	2012	...

TOULOUSE - AUCH: *88 km* Journey 90 - 100 minutes

Toulouse Matabiau depart: 0627 Ⓐ, 0727 **b**, 1040 **a**, 1227 **c**, 1427 Ⓐ **q**, 1615 ⚒ 🚌, 1627 Ⓐ **b**, 1727, 1827, 2027, 2120 🚌.

Auch depart: 0607 Ⓐ, 0707, 0747 ⚒ 🚌, 0807 Ⓐ **b**, 0907 **q**, 1107 **c**, 1407 Ⓐ **a**, 1407 Ⓒ, 1500 🚌, 1707, 1807, 1907.

🚌 services depart from Toulouse gare routière.

TOURS - CHINON: *49 km* Journey 45 - 50 minutes (70 minutes by 🚌)

Tours depart: 0534 Ⓐ, 0640 ⚒ 🚌, 0735 Ⓐ, 0800 † 🚌, 0909 ⑥, 0915 Ⓐ 🚌, 1145 † 🚌, 1220 ⚒ **s**, 1408, 1633 ⚒, 1719 Ⓐ, 1750 Ⓐ 🚌, 1832, 1929 Ⓐ, 2058 ⑤ **d**, 2058 † **v**.

Chinon depart: 0635 Ⓐ, 0640 ⑥, 0716 Ⓐ, 0745 ⚒, 0837 Ⓐ, 0919 🚌, 1100 Ⓐ 🚌, 1116 ⑥, 1317 ⚒ **s**, 1335 † 🚌, 1516 ⑥, 1615 Ⓑ, 1728 ⚒, 1816 Ⓐ, 1915 ①–④ **m** 🚌, 1934 ⑤ **d**, 1934 ⑥, 1949 †, 2010 ⑤ **d** 🚌.

VALENCIENNES - CAMBRAI: *40 km* Journey 36 - 44 minutes

Valenciennes depart: 0631 ⚒, 0732 ⚒, 0805 ⚒ **n**, 1013 Ⓐ, 1220 ⚒, 1309 ⚒ **w**, 1717, 1745 Ⓐ, 1837 Ⓐ, 1928 Ⓐ, 2007 †.

Cambrai depart: 0605 Ⓐ, 0644 ⚒, 0744 ⚒, 0759 Ⓐ, 0957 ⑥, 1102 Ⓐ **h**, 1211 ⚒, 1314 Ⓐ, 1352 ⑥, 1713 Ⓐ, 1812 Ⓒ, 1836 Ⓐ, 1921 †, 1942 Ⓐ.

M – ②–⑦ (not Dec. 26, Jan. 2, May 13). By 🚌 on ②–⑤ Dec. 11 - 21, Mar. 4 - 28.

a – Depart / arrive Toulouse Arènes (⊖).
b – Depart / arrive Toulouse Arènes (⊖) on Jan. 2, 3, Ⓐ Jan. 28 - Feb. 15.
c – Depart / arrive Toulouse Arènes (⊖) on Jan. 2, 3, Jan. 26 - Feb. 15, Mar. 10 - 14, 17 - 21.
d – Also Apr. 30, May 7.
f – Also Apr. 30, May 7; not May 2, 9.
g – Also Dec. 26, Jan. 2, Mar. 25, May 13; not Dec. 24, 31.
h – Subject to alteration Jan. 21 - Feb. 1, Mar. 31 - Apr. 4.
k – By 🚌 on Ⓐ Feb. 25 - Mar. 28.
m – Not Dec. 25, Jan. 1, Mar. 24, Apr. 30, May 1, 7, 8, 12.
n – Subject to alteration on Ⓐ Jan. 21 - Feb. 1.
q – Depart / arrive Toulouse Arènes (⊖) on ①–⑤ Mar. 10 - 21.
r – By 🚌.
s – Subject to alteration on Ⓐ Feb. 25 - Mar. 7.
t – Not May 2, 9.
u – Subject to alteration Mar. 17 - Apr. 4.
v – Not Mar. 23, May 11.
w – Subject to alteration Mar. 31 - Apr. 4.
x – Also Dec. 25, Jan. 1, Mar. 24, May 12; not Dec. 23, 30, Mar. 23, May 11.
y – Subject to alteration Mar. 10 - 13.
z – Subject to alteration Apr. 7 - 25.
◇ – To / from Dol (Table **282**).
△ – By 🚌 on ①–⑤ Dec. 10 - 21, Mar. 3 - 28.
▽ – By 🚌 on ①–⑤ Dec. 10 - 21.
⊖ – Connection by métro with main station.
⊕ – Subject to alteration on ①–⑤ Apr. 14 - 25.
§ – To/from Paris (Table **315**).

NOTES FOR TABLE 300 (for page 193 opposite) →

A – Daily except ⑤ (will not run Apr. 30, May 7).
G – ⑤⑦ (also Dec. 25, Jan. 1, Mar. 24, Apr. 30, May 7, 12; not May 2). On ⑤ from May 30 Paris d. 2145, Massy d. 2204 (train **8595**).
L – ①②③④⑥ (also May 2, 9; not Dec. 25, Jan. 1, Mar. 24, Apr. 30, May 1, 7, 8, 12).
M – ①②③④⑦ (also May 2; not Apr. 30, May 1, 7, 8).
N – ①②③④⑥ (not Dec. 25, Jan. 1, Mar. 24, Apr. 30, May 7, 12).
P – ⑤⑥⑦ from Apr. 4 (also Apr. 30, May 1, 7, 8, 12; not May 2).
Q – ①–④ from Mar. 31 (also May 2; not Apr. 30, May 1, 7, 8, 12).
R – Daily from Mar. 31.

a – Also Dec. 25, Jan. 1, Mar. 24, Apr. 30, May 1, 7, 8, 12; not May 2.
b – Not Mar. 29, 30.
c – Lille **Flandres**.
d – Also Apr. 30, May 7; not May 2.
e – Also Dec. 25, Jan. 1, Mar. 24, May 12.
f – Also Apr. 30, May 7; not May 2, 9.
g – Also Dec. 26, Jan. 2, Mar. 25, May 13; not Mar. 24, May 12.
h – Not May 1, 8.
j – Not Dec. 25, 26, Jan. 1, 2, Mar. 25, May 1, 8, 13.
k – Not Mar. 29.
m – Not Dec. 25, Jan. 1, Mar. 24, Apr. 30, May 1, 7, 8, 12.
n – Not Dec. 25, Jan. 1, Mar. 24, May 12.
o – 0022 night of ①–④ Jan. 14 - Feb. 21.
q – Also Apr. 30, May 1, 7, 8; not May 2, 9, 10.
r – 0955 on Ⓐ Jan. 7 - Feb. 20, Mar. 13 - 21.
s – Not Dec. 25, Jan. 1, Mar. 24, 29, May 12.
t – Also May 1, 8.
u – 1650 certain dates (1717 Feb. 18 - 20, 27 - 29, Mar. 3 - 7, 10 - 14).
v – Depart 1150 Jan. 7 - Feb. 20, also Mar. 18 - 21.
w – Also May 2; not Dec. 25, Jan. 1, Mar. 24, Apr. 30, May 1, 7, 8, 12.
x – 1732 on ⑤ (also Apr. 30, May 7; not May 2).
y – Not Dec. 25, Jan. 1, Mar. 24, May 8, 12.
z – ⑥ (also May 1, 8).

TGV – [R], supplement payable, 🍷.
♥ – From Lyon (Table **335**).
♣ – [12] Brussels (d. 0732) - Bordeaux (Table **11**); [12] Lille Europe (train **5212**) - Charles de Gaulle ✈ - Bordeaux.
★ – For alternative daily overnight train Paris - Irún/ Tarbes see Table **305**.
☆ – From Strasbourg (Table **391**).
△ – Paris Austerlitz - St Pierre des Corps = 232 km.
⊖ – Not for journeys to/from Poitiers or Châtellerault.
⊕ – Extends to Hendaye (a. 1744) on ⑤ Jan. 11 - Feb. 1.
⊗ – Will not run Bordeaux - Irún on Ⓐ Apr. 7 - 25.
⊙ – Runs 9 minutes later on ①②③④⑥.
⊡ – Departs 10 minutes earlier on certain dates.
▽ – Also calls at Vendôme-Villiers (2105).
§ – Depart 0617 on ① (also Dec. 26, Jan. 2, Mar. 25, May 13). Runs up to 19 mins earlier Dec. 10 - 21.

PARIS - POITIERS - LA ROCHELLE and BORDEAUX 300

km	TGV trains convey 🍷							TGV 8501		TGV 8405	TGV 8405	TGV 8305		TGV 8505	TGV 8507		TGV 8411	TGV 8511	TGV 8513	TGV 5200	TGV 5356	TGV 8317	TGV 8415
		Ⓐ	Ⓐ §	Ⓐ	⑥	⚒	① g	②-⑤ j	Ⓐ	②-⑤ j	Ⓐ	Ⓒ	①-⑥ n	†	⊗	①-⑥ s	⑥	⑦ e	Ⓐ	Ⓒ		⑥ ♥t		①-⑥ y
	Lille Europe 11 d.	...	...	...	...	...	...	...	...	...	...	...	...	...	...	...	...	...	...	...	0558	...	...	...
	Charles de Gaulle ✈ d.	...	...	...	...	...	...	...	...	...	...	...	...	...	...	...	...	...	...	...	0739	...	...	...
	Marne la Vallee - Chessy d.	...	...	...	...	...	...	...	...	...	...	...	...	...	...	...	...	...	...	...	0756	...	...	...
0	**Paris Montparnasse 295** d.	...	...	...	...	...	...	...	0610	...	0650	0650	0720	...	0715	0745	...	0755	0810	0810	|	...	0910	0915
△	*Paris Austerlitz 296* d.	...	...	...	...	...	...	...	|	...	|	|	|	...	|	|	...	|	|	|	|	...	|	|
14	Massy TGV 295 d.	...	...	...	...	...	...	...	|	...	0702	0702	|	...	|	|	...	|	|	|	0831	0901	|	|
	Tours d.	...	...	...	...	0601	0644	0644	|	...	*0745*	*0745*	|	...	|	|	0824	|	|	|	*0915*	*0944*	*0959*	|
221	St Pierre des Corps 295 d.	...	...	...	...	|	|	|	|	...	0755	0755	|	...	|	|	0834	|	|	|	0925	0954	1009	|
289	Châtellerault d.	...	...	...	...	0652	0716	0717	|	...	0823	0823	|	...	|	|	0907	|	|	|	|	|	|	|
311	Futuroscope ⊖ d.	...	...	...	...	|	|	|	|	...	|	|	|	...	|	|	|	|	0936	0936	1003	1037	|	|
321	**Poitiers** a.	...	...	...	...	0726	0731	0734	0739	←	0838	0838	0848	...	|	0914	0920	0922	|	|	1011	1044	1047	|
321	**Poitiers** d.	0620	0624	0713	0723	...	0733	→	0742	0755	0845	0845	0851	0901	|	0917	0923	0925	|	|	1014	...	1050	|
401	Niort d.	0723	|	0802	0814	...	0826	...	|	0840	|	|	0937	0946	|	|	1006	|	|	|	|	...	1136	|
468	**La Rochelle** a.	0803	|	0840	0851	...	0907	...	|	0920	|	|	1016	1028	|	|	1045	|	|	|	|	...	1217	|
434	Angoulême d.	...	0729	...	...	...	...	...	|	...	0931	0934	...	...	|	1003	...	1013	|	|	1101	...	...	|
517	Coutras 306 d.	...	0816	...	...	...	...	...	|	...	...	|	...	...	|	|	...	|	|	|	|	...	...	|
533	Libourne 306 349 d.	...	0827	...	...	...	...	...	|	...	...	|	...	...	|	1048	...	1053	|	|	|	...	...	|
570	**Bordeaux St Jean 306 349** a.	...	0851	...	...	...	...	...	0920	...	...	1034	...	...	1020	1113	...	1117	1120	1120	1200	...	...	1222
	Hendaye 305 a.	...	...	...	...	...	...	...	|	...	...	...	...	...	1242	|	...	...	|	|	1417z	...	...	...
	Irún 305 a.	...	...	...	...	...	...	...	|	...	...	...	...	...	1251	|	...	...	|	|	1426z	...	...	...
	Tarbes 305 a.	...	...	...	...	...	...	...	|	...	...	...	...	...	...	1400	...	...	|	|	...	...	...	...
	Toulouse 320 a.	...	...	...	...	...	...	...	1136	...	...	...	...	...	...	...	...	...	1330	1336	...	...	...	...

	TGV 9802	TGV 8515	TGV 8516		TGV 8319	TGV 8417	TGV 5450		TGV 8519	TGV 8425	TGV 8525	TGV 8525	TGV 8529	TGV 8329	TGV 8333	TGV 8331	TGV 8535	TGV 8335		TGV 8539	TGV 5218	TGV 5221	TGV 8339	
	♣		b			⊡	☆	⚒		⑤ ⊕f	①-④ m	⑥	f	⑤ f	①-⑥ n	⑦ e		⑤ d	⑤ f	k		⑦ e	N	⑦ e
Lille Europe 11 d.	0759	...	...	...	...	...	...	...	...	...	...	...	...	...	...	...	...	...	...	...	1238c	1238c	...	...
Charles de Gaulle ✈ d.	0856	...	...	...	...	...	...	...	...	...	...	...	...	...	...	...	...	...	...	...	1337	1337	...	...
Marne la Vallee - Chessy d.	0910	...	...	...	...	...	1023	...	...	...	...	...	...	...	...	...	...	...	...	...	1351	1351	...	...
aris Montparnasse 295 d.	|	1010r	1010r	...	1045	1050	|	...	1130	1210v	1210v	1210	1310	1310	1350	1350	1410	1420	...	1440	|	|	1445	...
Paris Austerlitz 296 d.	|	|	|	...	|	|	|	...	|	|	|	|	|	|	|	|	|	|	...	|	|	|	|	...
assy TGV 295 d.	0946	|	|	...	|	|	1101	...	|	|	|	|	|	|	|	|	|	|	...	|	1431	1431	|	...
Tours d.	*1024*	|	|	...	|	*1139*	*1139*	...	|	|	|	|	|	|	*1442*	*1442*	|	|	...	|	*1514*	*1514*	|	...
Pierre des Corps 295 d.	1038	|	|	...	|	1149	1155	...	|	|	|	|	|	|	1459	1459	|	|	...	|	1525	1525	|	...
hâtellerault d.	|	|	|	...	|	|	|	...	|	|	|	|	|	|	1532	1531	|	|	...	|	|	|	|	...
uturoscope ⊖ d.	|	|	|	...	|	|	1232	...	|	|	|	|	|	|	|	|	|	|	...	|	1603	1603	|	...
oitiers a.	1117	|	|	...	1212	|	1239	...	|	1339	1339	1340	1436	1436	1547	1546	|	|	...	|	1611	1611	1615	...
oitiers d.	1120	|	|	...	1215	|	1242	1257	|	1341	1341	1342	1439	1445	...	1549	|	|	1600	|	1613	1613	1618	1619
Niort d.	|	|	|	...	1259	|	|	1359	|	|	|	|	|	1526	...	1636	|	1633	1647	|	|	|	1702	1706
La Rochelle a.	|	|	|	...	1333	|	|	1448	|	|	|	|	|	1605	...	1716	|	1715	1730	|	|	|	1742	1746
ngoulême d.	1206	|	|	1227	...	1313	1329	...	|	1427	1427	1429	1523	...	...	...	1618	...	...	|	1659	1659	...	...
outras 306 d.	|	|	|	1315	...	|	|	...	|	|	|	|	|	...	...	...	|	...	...	|	|	|	...	...
bourne 306 349 d.	|	|	|	1327	...	1358	|	...	|	|	|	|	|	...	...	...	|	...	...	|	1739	1739	...	...
ordeaux St Jean 306 349 a.	1305	1310	1310	1355	...	1423	1428	...	1432	1524	1524	1528	1624	...	...	...	1714	...	...	1739	1803	1803	...	...
Hendaye 305 a.	...	1532	|	...	...	...	...	...	|	...	1744	1745	1838	...	...	...	|	...	...	|	|	2025	...	...
Irún 305 a.	...	1540	|	...	...	...	...	...	|	...	...	...	...	...	...	...	|	...	...	|	|	2034	...	...
Tarbes 305 a.	...	...	1611	...	...	...	...	...	|	...	...	...	...	...	...	...	|	...	...	2039	|	...	...	...
Toulouse 320 a.	...	...	...	...	...	...	...	...	1642u	...	...	...	...	...	...	...	1926	...	...	...	2017	...	...	...

		TGV 5452	TGV 8441			TGV 8543	TGV 8445	TGV 8545		TGV 5229	TGV 5205				TGV 8353		TGV 5222	TGV 5452	TGV 8451	TGV 8355	TGV 8549	TGV 8557	TGV 8361	
	⑤ f	P ☆		Ⓒ	Ⓐ		①-④ m	⑤ f	①-④ m	⑦ e	①-④ w	⑤† f	⑤ d	①-④ w	⑤ d	A	⑤⑥ q	Q ☆		⑦ e			M	⚒ ⊙
Lille Europe 11 d.	...	...	...	...	...	...	...	...	...	1447	1447	...	...	...	...	...	1541	...	...	...	...	...	...	...
Charles de Gaulle ✈ d.	...	...	...	...	...	...	...	...	...	1542	1542	...	...	...	...	...	1638	...	...	...	...	...	...	...
Marne la Vallee - Chessy d.	...	1421	...	...	...	...	...	...	...	1557	1557	...	...	...	...	...	1653	1657	...	...	...	...	...	...
aris Montparnasse 295 d.	...	|	1515	...	...	1550	1610	1620	...	|	|	...	...	...	1655	...	|	|	1715	1715	1720	1745	1755	...
Paris Austerlitz 296 d.	...	|	|	...	...	|	|	|	...	|	|	...	...	...	|	...	|	|	|	|	|	|	|	...
assy TGV 295 d.	...	1501	|	...	...	|	|	|	...	1631	1636	...	...	...	|	...	1730	1731	|	|	|	|	|	...
Tours d.	...	*1545*	*1603*	...	...	|	|	|	1643	*1715*	*1717*	...	1712	...	*1742*	1736	*1814*	*1814*	*1804*	*1804*	|	|	|	1840
Pierre des Corps 295 d.	...	1555	1614	...	...	|	|	|	|	1730	1730	...	|	...	1754	|	1824	1824	1814	1814	|	|	|	|
hâtellerault d.	...	|	|	...	...	|	|	|	1738	|	|	...	1758	...	|	1824	|	|	1843	1843	|	|	|	1925
uturoscope ⊖ d.	...	|	|	...	...	|	|	|	|	|	|	...	|	...	|	|	|	|	1901	1901	|	|	|	|
oitiers a.	...	1632	1652	...	...	|	1738	|	1805	1807	1809	...	1813	...	1833	1840	1903	1902	1908	1908	|	|	1922	1940
oitiers d.	1646	1635	1655	1706	1727x	|	1741	|	...	...	1812	...	*1821*	1831	1836	...	1906	1905	1915	1920	|	|	1927	...
Niort d.	1738	|	|	1756	1823	|	|	|	...	...	|	...	|	1922	1922	...	|	|	|	2002	|	|	2014	...
La Rochelle a.	1816	|	|	1835	1910	|	|	|	...	...	|	...	|	2005	2001	...	|	|	|	2041	|	|	2053	...
ngoulême d.	...	1721	1744	...	...	|	|	|	...	...	1901	1902	*1941*	...	...	...	1951	1950	2008	...	|	1958	...	...
outras 306 d.	...	|	|	...	...	|	|	|	...	...	|	2000	...	...	...	...	|	|	|	...	|	|	...	...
bourne 306 349 d.	...	|	1825	...	...	|	|	|	...	...	|	2009	...	...	...	...	|	|	2048	...	|	|	...	...
ordeaux St Jean 306 349 a.	...	1823	1848	...	...	1852	1917	1918	...	...	2000	2036	...	...	...	...	2051	2052	2111	...	2023	2056	...	...
Hendaye 305 a.	...	...	...	...	...	2114	...	|	...	...	...	...	...	...	...	...	2308	...	...	...	|	|	...	...
Irún 305 a.	...	...	...	...	...	2125	...	|	...	...	...	...	...	...	...	...	...	...	...	...	|	|	...	...
Tarbes 305 a.	...	...	...	...	...	...	...	2210	...	...	...	...	...	...	...	...	...	...	...	...	|	2352o	...	...
Toulouse 320 a.	...	...	...	...	...	...	...	...	...	...	...	...	...	...	...	...	...	...	...	...	2241	...	...	...

	TGV 8359	TGV 8565	TGV 8469	TGV 8369		TGV 8477	TGV 8577	TGV 8579	TGV 8377	TGV 8479	TGV 5240	TGV 5454			TGV 8379	TGV 5242	TGV 8483	TGV 8495	TGV 8489	TGV 8491	TGV 8391	TGV 8497	TGV 8587	TGV 8588
	⑤ d	Ⓑ h		N	⑤ f	①-④ m	⑤ f	⑤ f	⑦ e		Ⓑ h	R ☆	L	†	⑤ d	⑤-⑦ a	①-④ m▽	⑤ f	⑦ e	⑤ f	⑤ d	⑤ f	G ★	G ★
Lille Europe 11 d.	...	...	...	...	...	...	...	...	...	...	1809	...	...	...	...	1829	...	...	...	...	...	...	...	...
Charles de Gaulle ✈ d.	...	...	...	...	...	...	...	...	...	...	1911	...	...	...	...	1925	...	...	...	...	...	...	...	...
Marne la Vallee - Chessy d.	...	...	...	...	...	...	...	...	...	...	1927	1912	...	...	...	1942	...	...	...	...	...	...	...	...
aris Montparnasse 295 d.	1820	1825	1850	1850	...	1925	1925	1925	1930	1950	|	|	...	...	2020	|	2020	2110	2110	2115	2120	2135	2245	2245
Paris Austerlitz 296 d.	|	|	|	|	...	|	|	|	|	|	|	|	...	...	|	|	|	|	|	|	|	|	|	|
assy TGV 295 d.	|	|	|	|	...	|	|	|	|	|	2000	1951	...	...	|	2018	|	|	|	|	|	|	2258	2258
Tours d.	|	|	*1939*	*1939*	...	|	|	|	*2019*	|	|	*2035*	...	...	|	*2101*	|	|	*2159*	|	*2208*	*2223*	*2353*	*2353*
Pierre des Corps 295 d.	|	|	1949	1949	...	|	|	|	2029	|	|	2046	...	...	|	2112	2128	|	2209	|	2219	2233	0003	0003
hâtellerault d.	|	|	2018	2018	...	|	|	|	|	|	|	|	...	...	2138	|	2200	|	2238	2233	|	|	|	|
uturoscope ⊖ d.	|	|	|	|	...	|	|	|	|	|	|	|	...	...	|	|	|	|	|	|	|	|	|	|
oitiers a.	1947	|	2033	2033	...	|	|	|	2108	2118	2123	2127	...	...	2153	2158	2215	|	2253	2248	|	2312	0048	0048
oitiers d.	1958	|	2036	2040	2041	|	|	|	2110	2120	2126	2130	2146	2150	2156	2201	2218	|	2256	2251	|	2315	0103	0103
Niort d.	2048	|	|	2121	2127	|	|	|	2156	|	|	|	2233	2244	2242	|	|	|	|	|	2342	|	|	|
La Rochelle a.	2125	|	|	2156	2206	|	|	|	2236	|	|	|	2311	2323	2321	|	|	|	|	|	0021	|	|	|
ngoulême d.	...	|	2122	...	...	|	|	|	...	2208	2212	2219	...	...	...	2249	2304	|	2343	2343	...	0001	|	|
outras 306 d.	...	|	|	...	...	|	|	|	...	|	|	|	...	...	...	|	|	|	|	|	...	|	|	|
bourne 306 349 d.	...	|	2202	...	...	|	|	|	...	|	|	|	...	...	...	|	|	|	0025	0024	...	|	|	|
ordeaux St Jean 306 349 a.	...	2126	2225	...	...	2229	2229	2229	...	2308	2312	2319	...	...	...	2352	0004	0011	0048	0048	...	0103	|	|
Hendaye 305 a.	...	2343	...	...	...	...	0045	|	...	...	...	...	...	...	...	...	...	...	...	...	...	...	0616	|
Irún 305 a.	...	...	...	...	...	...	...	|	...	...	...	...	...	...	...	...	...	...	...	...	...	...	0626	|
Tarbes 305 a.	...	...	...	...	...	...	...	|	...	...	...	...	...	...	...	...	...	...	...	...	...	...	...	0703
Toulouse 320 a.	...	...	...	...	...	...	...	0042	...	...	...	...	...	...	...	...	...	...	...	...	...	...	...	...

— **FOR NOTES SEE FOOT OF PREVIOUS PAGE**

Timings at Toulouse may vary by a few minutes due to engineering work

300 BORDEAUX and LA ROCHELLE - POITIERS - PARIS

TGV trains convey 🍷	*TGV* 8308	*TGV* 8406			*TGV* 8408	*TGV* 8306	*TGV* 5260	*TGV* 8312		*TGV* 8410	*TGV* 8412	*TGV* 5260		*TGV* 5440	*TGV* 5260			*TGV* 8414	*TGV* 8314	*TGV* 8416		*TGV* 5264	*TGV* 5268	
	①	Ⓐ	⑥	Ⓐ	Ⓐ	①–⑥		⑦	Ⓐ	①–⑥	Ⓐ		⑥	☆		Ⓐ	†		①	Ⓐ	⚒		①⑥	
	g					n	Q	e		n		R		S	P			⊕	g				q	
Toulouse 320 d.	...	...	...	...	...	...	...	...	...	...	...	...	...	...	...	...	...	...	...	...	...	0527	...	...
Tarbes 305 d.	...	...	...	...	...	...	...	...	...	...	...	...	...	...	...	...	...	...	...	...	...	|	...	...
Hendaye 305 d.	...	...	...	...	...	...	...	...	...	...	...	...	...	...	...	...	...	...	...	...	...	|	0529	...
Bordeaux St Jean 306 349 d.	...	0440	...	...	0513	...	0535	...	...	0552	0627	0614	...	0633	0634	...	...	0659	...	0728	...	0750	0750	...
Libourne 306 349 d.	...	0506	...	...	|	...	|	...	...	0619	|	|	...	|	|	...	...	0724	...	|	...	|	|	...
Coutras 306 d.	...	|	...	...	|	...	|	...	...	|	|	|	...	|	|	...	...	|	...	|	...	|	|	...
Angoulême d.	...	0547	...	...	0611	...	0638	...	...	0700	|	0714	...	0733	0734	...	...	0804	...	|	...	0850	0850	...
La Rochelle d.	...	|	...	...	|	0547	|	...	...	|	|	|	0640	|	|	0650	0715	|	0727	|	0746	|	|	...
Niort d.	...	|	...	...	|	0628	|	...	...	|	|	|	0721	|	|	0735	0754	|	0804	|	0828	|	|	...
Poitiers a.	...	0633	...	...	|	0714	0722	...	...	0746	|	0758	0805	0817	0818	0823	0838	0851	0843	|	0915	0933	0933	...
Poitiers d.	0506	0636	0635	0641	|	0716	0724	0733	0736	0749	|	0801	...	0819	0821	...	...	0856	0856	|	...	0935	0935	...
Futuroscope ⊖ d.	|	|	|	|	|	|	|	|	|	|	|	|	...	|	|	...	...	|	|	|	...	0946	0946	...
Châtellerault d.	|	0654	0700	0658	|	|	|	0751	0753	0806	|	|	...	|	|	...	...	|	|	|	...	|	|	...
St Pierre-des-Corps 295 a.	0546	|	|	|	|	|	0800	0818	|	|	|	0838	...	0859	0859	...	...	0935	0935	|	...	1020	1020	...
Tours a.	*0556*	|	0744	0752	|	|	*0810*	*0830*	0830	|	|	*0849*	...	*0910*	*0910*	...	...	*0944*	*0944*	|	...	*1030*	*1030*	...
Massy TGV 295 a.	0638	|	...	...	|	|	|	|	...	|	|	|	...	0952	0952	...	...	|	|	|	...	1113	1113	...
Paris Austerlitz 296 a.	|	|	...	...	|	|	|	|	...	|	|	|	...	|	|	...	...	|	|	|	...	|	|	...
Paris Montparnasse 295 a.	0650	0815	...	...	0830	0850	|	0920	...	0925	0930	|	...	|	|	...	...	1035	1035	1030	...	|	|	...
Marne la Vallee - Chessy a.	...	...	...	...	...	...	0926	...	...	...	...	1006	...	1034	1036	...	...	...	...	...	...	1152	1152	...
Charles de Gaulle ✈ a.	...	...	...	...	...	...	0942	...	...	...	...	1021	...	...	1050	...	...	...	...	...	...	1207	1207	...
Lille Europe 11 a.	...	...	...	...	...	...	1044	...	...	...	...	1128	...	...	1151	...	...	...	...	...	...	1304	1304	...

	TGV 8518	*TGV* 8420	*TGV* 8422	*TGV* 5442	*TGV* 8524	*TGV* 8527	*TGV* 8324	*TGV* 5442	*TGV* 5276	*TGV* 8528	*TGV* 8330		*TGV* 8436	*TGV* 8334	*TGV* 8534		*TGV* 8541	*TGV* 8542	*TGV* 8438	*TGV* 8338	*TGV* 9816		*TGV* 8444	*TG* 854
	①–⑥	①–⑥	⑦	☆	⊖	⊖		☆			⑤	Ⓐ						Ⓐ	Ⓐ		♣	Ⓐ		
	n	n	e	©U		y		ⒶT			d	▷					y	u	§△					
Toulouse 320 d.	0608	...	...	...	...	...	...	...	...	0922	...	...	...	...	...	...	...	...	...	...	...	...	...	131
Tarbes 305 d.	|	...	...	...	...	0722	...	...	...	|	...	...	...	...	...	...	1054	...	...	...	...	...	...	|
Hendaye 305 d.	|	...	...	...	0758	|	...	...	0839x	|	...	...	...	...	1026	...	|	1122	...	...	...	...	...	|
Bordeaux St Jean 306 349 d.	0825	...	0755	1019	1026	1026	...	1030	1100	1124	...	...	1201	...	1251	...	1355	1355	1416	...	1422	...	1458	152
Libourne 306 349 d.	|	...	|	|	|	|	...	|	|	|	...	...	1228	...	|	...	|	|	|	...	1446	...	|	|
Coutras 306 d.	|	...	|	|	|	|	...	|	|	|	...	...	|	...	|	...	|	|	|	...	|	...	|	|
Angoulême d.	|	0854	0857	1122	1128	1128	...	1135	1202	|	...	...	1311	...	|	...	1457	1457	|	...	1526	...	|	162
La Rochelle d.	|	|	|	|	|	|	1056	|	|	|	...	1200	|	1228	|	...	|	|	|	1447	|	...	|	|
Niort d.	|	|	|	|	|	|	1137	|	|	|	...	1246	|	1309	|	...	|	|	|	1524	|	...	|	|
Poitiers a.	|	0945	0947	1207	1211	1211	1217	1221	1248	|	...	1346	1357	1353	|	...	|	|	1555	1604	1611	...	|	170
Poitiers d.	|	0948	0950	1210	1214	1214	1220	1224	1250	|	1331	...	1402	1402	|	...	|	|	1556	1607	1614	1619	|	171
Futuroscope ⊖ d.	|	|	|	|	|	|	|	|	|	|	|	...	|	|	|	...	|	|	|	|	|	|	|	|
Châtellerault d.	|	1004	1008	|	|	|	|	|	|	|	|	...	1420	1420	|	...	|	|	|	|	|	1635	|	|
St Pierre-des-Corps 295 a.	|	1030	1035	1248	|	|	1300	1304	1329	|	1412	...	1449	1449	|	...	1619	1619	|	|	1652	...	|	175
Tours a.	|	*1045*	*1045*	*1305*	|	|	*1314*	*1314*	*1341*	|	*1437*	...	*1459*	*1459*	|	...	*1632*	*1632*	|	|	*1702*	...	|	*180*
Massy TGV 295 a.	|	|	|	1342	|	|	|	1358	1423	|	|	...	|	|	|	...	|	|	|	|	1747	...	|	|
Paris Austerlitz 296 a.	|	|	|	|	|	|	|	|	|	|	|	...	|	|	|	...	|	|	|	|	|	...	|	|
Paris Montparnasse 295 a.	1130	1135	1135	|	1345	1345	1400	|	|	1435	1520	...	1550	1550	1555	...	1720	1720	1730	1740	|	...	1800	185
Marne la Vallee - Chessy a.	...	...	...	1421	...	...	...	1437	1506	...	...	...	...	...	...	...	...	...	...	...	1827	...	...	...
Charles de Gaulle ✈ a.	...	...	...	...	...	...	...	...	1521	...	...	...	...	...	...	...	...	...	...	...	1841	...	...	...
Lille Europe 11 a.	...	...	...	...	...	...	...	...	1615	...	...	...	...	...	...	...	...	...	...	...	2003c	...	...	...

	TGV 8348				*TGV* 5444	*TGV* 8558	*TGV* 8354	*TGV* 8364	*TGV* 5284		*TGV* 8362	*TGV* 8456	*TGV* 5444	*TGV* 8562	*TGV* 8466		*TGV* 5336		*TGV* 8370	*TGV* 8472			*TGV* 8474	
	⑤	⚒	†	Ⓐ	⑦		①–④	⑤–⑦	Ⓑ		①–④	⑤–⑦	①–⑥		⑦	⑦	⑦	Ⓐ	⑤⑦	①–⑥	⑦	⑤	⑦	Ⓐ
	d				☆e		m▽	w	h		v	w	☆n		e	e	♥e	k	b	n	e	f	e	
Toulouse 320 d.	...	...	...	...	...	...	...	...	...	...	...	...	...	...	...	...	...	...	...	...	...	...	...	...
Tarbes 305 d.	...	...	...	...	...	...	...	...	...	...	...	...	...	1433z	...	...	...	...	...	...	...	...	...	...
Hendaye 305 d.	...	...	...	...	...	1411	...	...	...	...	...	...	...	|	...	...	...	...	...	...	...	...	...	...
Bordeaux St Jean 306 349 d.	...	...	...	...	1613	1632	...	...	1643	...	...	1647	1708	1725	1733	...	...	...	...	1751	...	...	1805	175
Libourne 306 349 d.	...	...	...	...	|	|	...	...	|	...	...	|	|	|	|	...	...	...	...	1821	...	...	1829	182
Coutras 306 d.	...	...	...	...	|	|	...	...	|	...	...	|	|	|	|	...	...	...	...	|	...	...	|	185
Angoulême d.	...	...	...	...	1716	1733	...	...	1745	...	...	1750	1812	|	1835	...	...	...	...	1904	...	...	1910	194
La Rochelle d.	1549	...	...	1625	|	|	...	1647	|	...	1708	|	|	|	|	1747	...	1750	...	|	1802	1805	|	...
Niort d.	1630	...	...	1706	|	|	...	1728	|	...	1749	|	|	|	|	1832	...	1836	...	|	1848	1851	|	...
Poitiers a.	1714	...	...	1804*	1802	|	...	1813	1831	...	1837	1838	1856	|	1920	1926	...	1934	...	1948	1948	1949	1956	...
Poitiers d.	1717	1735	1737	...	1805	|	1821	1821	1834	...	1840	1841	1902	|	1923	1928	1932	1936	1941	1951	...	...	2004	...
Futuroscope ⊖ d.	|	|	|	...	1815	|	|	|	1850	...	|	|	1912	|	|	|	1943	|	1952	|	...	...	|	...
Châtellerault d.	|	1809	1802	...	|	|	1840	1839	|	...	|	|	|	|	|	1945	|	1953	|	|	...	...	|	...
St Pierre-des-Corps 295 a.	1756	|	|	...	1851	|	|	1905	1925	...	1919	|	1946	|	2004	|	2018	|	|	2029	...	...	2044	...
Tours a.	*1810*	1858	1848	...	*1903*	|	|	*1915*	*1940*	...	*1929*	|	*1957*	|	*2015*	2016	*2034*	2025	|	*2045*	...	...	*2054*	...
Massy TGV 295 a.	|	...	...	...	1943	|	|	|	2018	...	|	|	2043	|	|	...	2118	...	|	|	...	...	2137	...
Paris Austerlitz 296 a.	|	...	...	...	|	|	|	|	|	...	|	|	|	|	|	...	...	...	|	|	...	...	|	...
Paris Montparnasse 295 a.	1905	...	...	...	|	1945	2005	2005	|	...	2020	2015	|	2030	2105	...	...	...	2120	2135	...	...	2150	...
Marne la Vallee - Chessy a.	...	...	...	...	2025	...	...	...	2058	...	...	...	2120	...	...	...	...	...	...	...	...	...	...	...
Charles de Gaulle ✈ a.	...	...	...	...	...	...	...	...	2112	...	...	...	...	...	...	...	...	...	...	...	...	...	...	...
Lille Europe 11 a.	...	...	...	...	...	...	...	...	2219	...	...	...	...	...	...	...	...	...	...	...	...	...	...	...

		TGV 8568	*TGV* 8374	*TGV* 8570	*TGV* 8382			*TGV* 5292	*TGV* 5292	*TGV* 8384		*TGV* 8580	*TGV* 8482		*TGV* 8584	*TGV* 8583		*TGV* 8494	*TGV* 8586	*TGV* 8590		*TGV* 8390	*TGV* 8592	*TG* 859
	⑥	Ⓑ		⑥	⑤	†	†	Ⓐ	⑥	⑦	⑤	Ⓑ	⑦	⚒				⑦	⑦	⑦		⑦	G	G
		h	L	t	d		⊗	⊙	t	e	f	h⊡	e			s		e	e	e		e	★	★
Toulouse 320 d.	...	1608	...	1631	...	...	...	...	...	...	...	1736	...	...	...	...	...	...	1826	...	...	...	...	...
Tarbes 305 d.	...	|	...	|	...	...	...	...	...	...	...	|	...	...	...	1646	...	...	|	...	...	...	...	224
Hendaye 305 d.	...	|	...	|	...	...	...	...	1625	...	...	|	...	...	1726	|	...	...	|	1817	...	...	2314	|
Bordeaux St Jean 306 349 d.	1759	1824	...	1846	...	...	1831	1841	1841	...	1901	1947	1947	...	1951	1951	...	2017	2041	2041	...	...	|	|
Libourne 306 349 d.	1833	|	...	|	...	...	1909	|	|	...	1940	|	|	...	|	|	...	2042	|	|	...	...	|	|
Coutras 306 d.	1846	|	...	|	...	...	1918	|	|	...	1949	|	|	...	|	|	...	|	|	|	...	...	|	|
Angoulême d.	1934	|	...	|	...	...	2004	1951	1946	...	2037	|	|	...	2053	2053	...	2123	|	|	...	...	|	|
La Rochelle d.	...	|	1828	|	1855	1906	...	|	|	1929	...	|	|	1945	|	|	...	|	|	|	...	2112	|	|
Niort d.	...	|	1909	|	1932	1947	...	|	|	2006	...	|	|	2030	|	|	...	|	|	|	...	2153	|	|
Poitiers a.	...	|	1954	|	2012	2038	...	2035	2033	2046	...	|	|	2130	2137	2137	...	2214	|	|	...	2236	|	|
Poitiers d.	...	|	2002	|	2017	...	...	2039	2040	2048	...	|	|	...	2140	2140	...	2222	|	|	...	2238	|	|
Futuroscope ⊖ d.	...	|	2014	|	|	...	...	|	2050	|	...	|	|	...	|	|	...	|	|	|	...	|	|	|
Châtellerault d.	...	|	|	|	|	...	...	|	|	|	...	|	|	...	|	|	...	2241	|	|	...	|	|	|
St Pierre-des-Corps 295 a.	...	|	|	|	|	...	...	2119	2124	|	...	|	|	...	2218	2218	...	|	|	|	...	2316	0456	045
Tours a.	...	|	|	|	|	...	...	*2139*	*2144*	|	...	|	|	...	*2225*	*2225*	...	|	|	|	...	*2326*	*0508*	*050*
Massy TGV 295 a.	...	|	|	|	|	...	...	2213	2217	|	...	|	|	...	|	|	...	|	|	|	...	|	|	|
Paris Austerlitz 296 a.	...	|	|	|	|	...	...	|	|	|	...	|	|	...	|	|	...	|	|	|	...	|	|	|
Paris Montparnasse 295 a.	...	2130	2140	2150	2150	...	...	|	|	2220	...	2250	2250	...	2320r	2320r	...	0000	2345	2345	...	0015	0600	060
Marne la Vallee - Chessy a.	...	...	...	...	...	...	...	2251	2251	...	...	...	...	...	...	...	...	...	...	...	...	...	...	...
Charles de Gaulle ✈ a.	...	...	...	...	...	...	...	2306	2306	...	...	...	...	...	...	...	...	...	...	...	...	...	...	...
Lille Europe 11 a.	...	...	...	...	...	...	...	0007	0007	...	...	...	...	...	...	...	...	...	...	...	...	...	...	...

G – ⑤⑦ (also Dec. 25, Jan. 1, Mar. 24, Apr. 30, May 7, 12; not May 2).
L – ①②③④⑥ (not Dec. 25, Jan. 1, Mar. 24, Apr. 30, May 12).
P – Dec. 9 - Mar. 30.
Q – ①–⑥ from Mar. 31 (not May 9, 10, 12).
R – ⑦ from Apr. 6 (also May 12; not May 11).
S – From Mar. 31.
T – Ⓐ from Mar. 31 (not May 2, 9).
U – © from Apr. 5 (also May 2; not May 10, 11).

NOTES CONTINUED AT FOOT OF NEXT PAGE →

ANGOULÊME - SAINTES - ROYAN — 301

Some trains 2nd class

km		Ⓐ ◇	Ⓐ	Ⓐ △	Ⓐ ▽	Ⓒ	Ⓐ ⊖		⚒	◇	⑤⑦ y	①–④ w	N	⑤ f	⚒	†	①–④ w	⑤ f	Ⓐ	⑥	N	⑤⑦ y	†	⑤ f	⑤ f	Ⓑ
0	**Angoulême** ◐ d.	0613	...	0720	0936	1018	1235	...	1437	1639	...	...	...	...	1750	...	...	...	1905	1905	2016	2016	...	...	2125	2221
49	Cognac d.	0702	...	0804	1015	1101	1315	...	1520	1720	...	...	...	...	1833	...	...	...	1946	1946	2100	2102	...	...	2206	2304
	Niort ◐ d.	|	0654	|	|	|	|	1322	|	|	1652	...	1718	1742	|	1825	1836	1838	|	|	|	|	2029	2051	|	|
75	**Saintes** a.	0722	0757	0825	1037	1120	1334	1416	1538	1739	1747	...	1821	1849	1851	1940	1950	1952	2004	2004	2120	2123	2126	2150	2226	2323
75	**Saintes** d.	*0731*	0759	...	1044r	1125	...	1418z	1544*	...	1749	1752	1840	...	1903c	...	...	...	2020	...	2127	...	2137	2153	2234	2332
111	**Royan** a.	*0800*	0831	...	1113r	1154	...	1447z	1616*	...	1817	1820	1909	...	1930c	...	...	...	2048	...	2155	...	2205	2221	2302	0000

	Ⓐ	Ⓐ b	Ⓐ	① g §	②–⑤ n	Ⓐ ◇	⑥	⚒	⊕			Ⓐ	①–④ w	⑥	⑤⑦ h	⑤⑦ y	☆	⑤ f	†	N	⑤ f	①–④ w	⑤ f	⑤⑦ y	†	†
Royan d.	...	...	0608	0628	0656	...	0708	0812	...	0955s	1224x	1339x	...	1555	1555	...	1707	1820	1820	...	...	1850	...	1935	2056	...
Saintes a.	...	...	0635	0657	0723	...	0736	0840	...	1024s	1251x	1408x	...	1625	1623	...	1734	1849	1849	...	...	1920	...	2003	2124	...
Saintes d.	0540	0615	0640	0711	...	0743	0742	...	0955	1036	1321	1418	1609	1634	1625	1634	1749	...	1853	1900	1906	1925	1925	2015	2155	2154
Niort ◐ a.	|	0729	|	0811	...	|	|	...	|	1131	|	1515	|	|	1722	|	|	...	1957	2004	2010	|	|	|	|	2256
Cognac d.	0559	...	0701	...	...	0803	0802	...	1016	...	1343	...	1630	1655	...	1654	1809	...	...	...	...	1945	1945	2035	2216	...
Angoulême ◐ a.	0642	...	0745	...	...	0843	0841	...	1058	...	1420	...	1714	1736	...	1736	1852	...	...	...	...	2024	2024	2115	2300	...

N – ①②③④⑥ (also May 2, 9; not holidays or Apr. 30, May 7).
b – Not Dec. 24, 31.
c – ⑤⑥ (also Apr. 30, May 7; not May 2, 9).
f – Also Apr. 30, May 7; not May 2, 9.
g – Also Dec. 26, Jan. 2, May 13; not Dec. 24, 31, Mar. 24, May 12.
h – Also holidays; not May 2, 9.
n – Also Dec. 24, 31; not Dec. 25, 26, Jan. 1, 2, Mar. 25, May 1, 8, 13.
r – By 🚌 ①–④ Feb. 25 - Apr. 3 (arrive 1135 / 1635).
s – By 🚌 on ⑤ Feb. 29 - Apr. 4.

w – Also May 2, 9; not Dec. 25, Jan. 1, Mar. 24, Apr. 30, May 1, 7, 8, 12.
x – By 🚌 ①–④ Feb. 25 - Apr. 3 (not Mar. 24), Royan d. 1150 / 1315.
y – Also holidays and Apr. 30, May 7; not May 2, 9.
z – By 🚌 on ①–④ Feb. 25 - Apr. 3 (not Mar. 24).
◐ – See Table **300** for *TGV* connections to / from Paris.
◇ – To / from La Rochelle (Table **292**).
△ – By 🚌 (d. 0735, a. 0845) on Dec. 24, 31, Feb. 11, 18, Apr. 7, 14.
▽ – By 🚌 ②③④ Mar. 4 - 27 (arrivals up to 30 mins later).

⊕ – By 🚌 on ②③④ Feb. 26 - Mar. 20 (d. 0950, a. 1107).
⊖ – By 🚌 on ②③④ Feb. 26 - Mar. 20.
☆ – Change at Saintes on ①–④ **m**.
§ – To Poitiers (arrive 0859).
* – 20 - 25 minutes later on ①–④ Feb. 25 - Apr. 3 (not Mar. 24).

BORDEAUX - LE VERDON - POINTE DE GRAVE — 303

Some trains 2nd class

km		Ⓐ	⑥	🚌 ⑥ ⊖	Ⓐ	Ⓒ		⚒ △	Ⓐ	🚌 Ⓐ ◇	†	⑥	🚌 ⑥ ◇		Ⓐ	Ⓑ	🚌 Ⓐ ◇	Ⓐ	🚌 ⑥ ⊖	Ⓐ	†	Ⓐ	①–④ w	⑤ f	†
0	**Bordeaux** St Jean d.	0636	0724	...	0724	0905	...	1057	1234	...	1332	1332	...	...	1542	1627	...	1716	1800	1803	1803	1850	1928	1954	2003
23	Blanquefort d.	0712	0800	...	0800	0947	...	1118	1311	...	1403	1403	...	...	1613	1658	...	1747	1842	1836	1836	1924	1959	2026	2026
39	Margaux d.	0730	0820	...	0820	1008	...	1133	1326	...	1418	1418	...	...	1627	1717	...	1805	1907*	1857	1856	1945	2014	2040	2040
61	Pauillac d.	0751	0842	...	0842	1030	...	1154	1345	...	1436	1436	...	...	1647	1738	...	1825	1940	1918	1918	2006	2034	2059	2100
80	Lesparre d.	0806	0856	0906	0857	1046	...	1207	1400	1405	1450	1450	1500	...	1703	1755	1805	1842	2006	1932	1933	2020	...	...	2114
106	Soulac sur Mer d.	...	...	0937	0916	1105	...	...	1420	1443	1509	...	1538	...	...	...	1836	1902	2038	...	1953	2039	...	...	...
113	**Le Verdon** a.	...	...	0949	0924	1113	...	...	1427	1455*	1517	...	1550*	...	...	...	1846*	1910	2049	...	2000	2047	...	...	...
116	Pointe de Grave § a.	...	...	0953	...	1118	...	...	...	1500	...	...	1555	...	...	...	1850	...	...	...	...	...	...	...	...

	Ⓐ	Ⓐ	Ⓐ		Ⓐ ▽	🚌 ⑥ ⊖	Ⓐ ▽		🚌 ⚒ ◇	Ⓐ ⊕	⑥		Ⓐ ⊗		🚌 ⑥ ⊖	Ⓑ		Ⓐ	🚌 † ◇		🚌 Ⓐ ⊖	Ⓑ		
Pointe de Grave § d.	...	...	...	...	...	...	...	...	1100	...	...	...	...	...	...	...	...	...	1700	...	1705	...	...	...
Le Verdon d.	...	...	0615	...	0706	0732	...	...	1105*	1152	...	...	...	...	1454	1604	...	...	1706*	...	1709	...	...	...
Soulac sur Mer d.	...	...	0622	...	0713	0744	...	...	1113	1159	...	...	...	...	1506	1611	...	...	1717	...	1721	...	...	...
Lesparre d.	...	0601	0642	...	0733	0814	0824	...	1155	1219	1219	...	1449	...	1541	1631	...	1719	1800	...	1752	1807	...	...
Pauillac d.	0523	0615	0657	...	0750	...	0841	...	...	1233	1233	...	1503	...	1608	1646	...	1737	...	...	...	1824	...	...
Margaux d.	0542	0636	0717	...	0807	...	0857	...	...	1253	1253	...	1523	...	1641*	1704	...	1754	...	...	...	1844	...	...
Blanquefort d.	0558	0655	0738	...	0823	...	0909	...	...	1312	1312	...	1536	...	1703	1720	...	1810	...	...	...	1900	...	...
Bordeaux St Jean a.	0617	0729	0812	...	0858	...	0946	...	...	1345	1345	...	1607	...	1733	1754	...	1840	...	...	...	1930	...	...

f – Also Apr. 30, May 7; not May 2, 9.
w – Also May 2, 9; not Dec. 25, Jan. 1, Mar. 24, Apr. 30, May 1, 7, 8, 12.
⊖ – Subject to confirmation.
⊕ – Subject to alteration Feb. 11 - Mar. 14, Apr. 7 - 18.

⊗ – Subject to alteration Feb. 11 - 22.
◇ – Non SNCF service, rail tickets valid for through journeys.
△ – Subject to alteration on Ⓐ Feb. 11 - Mar. 14, Mar. 25 - Apr. 4.
▽ – Subject to alteration on Ⓐ Apr. 7 - 18.
* – Serves town centre, not railway station.

§ – ⛴ operates Pointe de Grave - Royan every 30 - 45 minutes in high summer (June 30 - Aug. 28), 0630 - 2030 from Pointe de Grave, 0715 - 2115 from Royan). Reduces to 6 - 9 per day in winter. ✆ 05 56 73 37 73.

BORDEAUX - ARCACHON — 304

km		⚒	Ⓐ △	⑥	Ⓐ △b	△	⊗	*TGV* **8411** ⑦ q	*TGV* **8415** ①–⑥ v		Ⓐ ⊕	⊙	⚒	Ⓐ		Ⓐ	Ⓐ		Ⓐ	Ⓐ		Ⓑ	*TGV* **8467** ⑤ f	Ⓑ
	Paris Montparnasse **300** d.	...	...	...	...	...	...	0755	0915	...	...	...	...	...	...	...	...	...	...	...	...	...	1826	...
0	**Bordeaux St Jean** d.	0645	0717	0750	0744	0831	1037	1121	1226	1238	1326	1444	1604	1646	1710	1725	1749	1821	1837	1904	1940	2032	2135	2148
40	Facture Biganos d.	0720	0746	0818	0817	0900	1104	1144	1250	1312	1352	1514	1638	1713	1733	1758	1818	1900	1905	1931	2009	2056	2158	2213
56	La Teste a.	0739	0803	0836	0834	0917	1121	|	|	1331	1408	1534	1657	1730	1751	1818	1836	1920	1924	1949	2026	2109	2210	2230
59	**Arcachon** a.	0747	0807	0840	0839	0921	1125	1158	1305	1336	1412	1539	1702	1734	1755	1823	1840	1925	1929	1953	2030	2114	2215	2234

	⚒	Ⓐ	⚒	Ⓐ	⚒	Ⓐ		⊖	⊡	◇	*TGV* **8438** ①–④ m▽	⊕	*TGV* **8456** ⑤–⑦ w		Ⓐ	†	⚒	①–④ m	⑤ f	⑦ e	①–⑥ n	*TGV* **8482** ⑦ e	Ⓑ	⚒
Arcachon d.	0618	0638	0711	0730	0755	0847	0903	1048	1239	1314	1333	1519	1600	1602	1657	1657	1725	1744	1803	1817	1823	1852	1918	2016
La Teste d.	0622	0642	0715	0735	0800	0851	0908	1052	1243	1318	|	1523	|	1607	1702	1701	1729	1749	1808	1821	1827	1859	1922	2020
Facture-Biganos d.	0638	0700	0731	0752	0819	0907	0927	1109	1259	1334	1349	1541	1617	1626	1717	1718	1746	1808	1827	1837	1843	1913	1940	2037
Bordeaux St Jean a.	0711	0723	0756	0825	0853	0936	1001	1135	1327	1402	1411	1611	1642	1657	1744	1750	1817	1833	1850	1906	1912	1935	2007	2104
Paris Montparnasse **300** a.	...	...	...	...	...	...	...	...	...	...	1730	...	2015	...	...	...	...	...	...	...	...	2250	...	...

b – Not Dec. 24, 31, May 15, 26.
e – Also Dec. 25, Jan. 1, Mar. 24, May 12.
f – Also Apr. 30, May 7; not May 2, 9.
g – Also Dec. 26, Jan. 2, Mar. 25, May 13; not Dec. 24, 31, Mar. 24, May 12.
m – Also May 2, 9; not Dec. 25, Jan. 1, Mar. 24, Apr. 30, May 1, 7, 8, 12.
n – Not Dec. 25, Jan. 1, Mar. 24, May 12.
q – Also Dec. 25, Jan. 1, Mar. 24, May 12; not May 11.

v – Not Dec. 25, Jan. 1, Mar. 24, May 8, 9, 10, 12.
w – Also Dec. 25, Jan. 1, Mar. 24, Apr. 30, May 1, 7, 12; not May 2, 9, 10.
TGV – 🅁, supplement payable, 🍷.
△ – Subject to alteration on Ⓐ Apr. 7 - 25.
▽ – Not Mar. 17 - Apr. 3.
⊖ – Subject to alteration on Ⓐ Jan. 14 - Feb. 8.
⊕ – Subject to alteration on ①–④ Jan. 14 - Feb. 7.

⊗ – Subject to alteration Ⓐ Feb. 11 - Mar. 7, Apr. 7 - 25, May 26 - June 13.
⊡ – Subject to alteration Ⓐ Feb. 11 - Mar. 7, May 26 - June 13.
⊙ – Subject to alteration on ①–④ Feb. 11 - Mar. 6, May 26 - June 12.
◇ – Subject to alteration on Ⓐ Mar. 17 - Apr. 4.

Additional journeys:
From Bordeaux: 0557 ① **g**, 2250 ⑤ **f**, 2250 †.
From Arcachon: 0528 Ⓐ, 0559 Ⓐ, 0645 Ⓐ, 2104 †, 2151 †.

← NOTES FOR TABLE 300 (continued from page 194)

b – Also Dec. 25, Jan. 1, Mar. 24, Apr. 30, May 7, 12; not May 2.
c – Lille **Flandres**.
d – Also Apr. 30, May 7; not May 2.
e – Also Dec. 25, Jan. 1, Mar. 24, May 12.
f – Also Apr. 30, May 7; not May 2, 9.
g – Also Dec. 26, Jan. 2, Mar. 25, May 13; not Dec. 24, 31, Mar. 24, May 12.
h – Not May 1, 8.
k – On ⑤ depart Poitiers 1931.
m – Not Dec. 25, Jan. 1, Mar. 24, Apr. 30, May 1, 7, 8, 12.
n – Not Dec. 25, Jan. 1, Mar. 24, May 12.
q – Also Dec. 26, Jan. 2, Mar. 25, May 1, 8, 13; not Dec. 24, 31, Mar. 24, May 10, 12.
r – 0002 on night of ①–④ May 26 - July 10.
s – Not Mar. 29.

t – Also May 1, 8.
u – Not Mar. 17 - Apr. 4.
v – Also May 2, 9; not Dec. 25, Jan. 1, Mar. 24, Apr. 30, May 1, 7, 8, 12.
w – Also Dec. 25, Jan. 1, Mar. 24, Apr. 30, May 1, 7, 12; not May 2, 9.
x – ⑦ (also Dec. 25, Jan. 1, Mar. 24, May 12).
y – Not Mar. 29, 30.
z – 1418 on ①–④ Feb. 25 - Mar. 6.
TGV – 🅁, supplement payable, 🍷.
♥ – To Lyon (Table **335**).
♣ – (12) Bordeaux - Brussels (arrive 2003, Table **11**); (12) Bordeaux - Charles de Gaulle ✈ (**5279**) - Lille Flandres.
★ – For alternative overnight train see Table **305**.
☆ – To Strasbourg (Table **391**).

⊖ – Not for journeys to/from Poitiers or Châtellerault.
⊝ – Arrive Paris 1355 on Ⓐ Dec. 10 - 21, 1350 on Feb. 21, 22, 25, 26.
△ – Subject to alteration on ①–④ Mar. 17 - Apr. 3.
▽ – Also calls at Vendôme-Villiers (1921).
▷ – Runs earlier on ①–④ Mar. 3 - 20 (d. 1127, a. 1312).
⊡ – On ①–④ May 26 - July 10 arrive Paris **Austerlitz** 2354 (also calls at St Pierre des Corps, arrive 2200).
⊙ – On ①–④ May 26 - July 10 departs 10 - 15 minutes earlier, arrive Lille 0010.
⊕ – On Feb. 24 runs 2½ - 3 hours later.
⊗ – On May 1, 8 depart 1825 and runs up to 10 mins later.
§ – Train **8442** on ⑤ (also Apr. 30, May 7; not May 2, 9).
* – 1837 on ⑤ (also Apr. 30, May 7; not May 2, 9).

305 BORDEAUX - TARBES and IRÚN

km	All *TGV* trains convey 🍸	Ⓐ	Ⓐ	Ⓐ ‡	▷ ⑤ f‡	⑥ ‡	67751 ⑥	67733 Ⓐ	⚒ ◧	4720 Ⓡ Uy	⚒ ⊕	4720 Ⓡ Uz	4778 4779 Ⓡ ♥	†	† a		*TGV* 8505 ⊗	*TGV* 8507 ①–⑥ s	Ⓐ	Ⓐ △	*TGV* 5200 ⑥ t	⑤⑥ f	①–④ m	Ⓐ
	Lille Europe **11** d.	...	...	...	...	...	...	...	...	...	...	...	...	...	...	...	...	...	...	...	0558	...	...	...
	Charles de Gaulle ✈ **300** d.	...	...	...	...	...	...	...	...	...	...	...	...	...	...	...	...	...	...	...	0739	...	...	...
	Paris Montparnasse **300** d.	...	...	...	...	...	...	...	...	...	...	...	...	...	...	...	0715	0745	...	...	|	...	...	...
0	**Bordeaux St Jean** d.	...	...	0641	0641	0645	0645	0641	0820	0820	...	0825	...	0825	...	...	1025	1118	...	...	1205	...	1221	1221
109	Morcenx d.	...	...	0735	0735	0743	0743	0735	0908	|	...	|	...	0926	...	...	|	|	...	...	|	...	|	|
148	Dax a.	...	...	0755	0755	0802	0802	0755	0927	0926	...	0941	...	0945	...	...	1133	|	...	...	1310	...	1327	1327
148	Dax d.	0618	0711	0800	0800	0806	0811	0805	0933	0929	0936	0944	0954	0959	1019	...	1136	|	1238	1248	1313	1323	1332	1341
179	Puyoô **325** d.	|	|	0818	0818	0823	|	|	|	|	|	|	|	|	1037	...	|	|	|	1307	|	|	|	|
193	Orthez **325** d.	|	|	0828	0828	0834	|	|	|	|	1003	|	|	|	1049	...	|	|	|	1318	|	|	|	1407
233	Pau **325** d.	|	|	0855	0857	0900	|	|	|	|	1028	|	|	|	1118	...	|	1316	|	1345	|	|	|	1432
272	Lourdes **325** d.	|	|	...	0927	0930	|	|	|	|	...	|	|	|	1150	...	|	1345	|	...	|	|	|	...
293	**Tarbes 325** a.	|	|	...	0942	0947	|	|	|	|	...	|	|	|	1205	...	|	1400	|	...	|	|	|	...
199	**Bayonne 325** d.	0703	0751	...	...	...	0841	0838	1003	1000	...	1015	1024	1030	...	...	1206	...	1320	...	1343	1403	1405	...
209	Biarritz **325** d.	0713	0801	...	...	...	0852	0848	...	1011	...	1027	1036	1041	...	...	1219	...	...	...	1355	1414	1415	...
222	St Jean de Luz **325** d.	0724	0814	...	...	...	0902	0858	...	1024	...	1039	1049	1055	...	...	1233	...	...	...	1407	1426	1425	...
235	Hendaye **325** a.	0739	0826	...	...	...	0912	0907	...	1034	...	1048	1058	1104	...	...	1242	...	...	...	1417	1438	1435	...
237	**Irún 325** a.	...	...	...	...	...	0919	...	...	1044	...	1057	1107	1114	...	...	1251	...	...	...	1426	1444	...	...

	TGV 8515	*TGV* 8516 b	14013 ⑤ f	Ⓐ	*TGV* 8525 ①–④ m	*TGV* 8525 ⑥	Ⓐ	Ⓐ	*TGV* 8529 ⑤ f	◇	①–④ m	①–④ m	⑤ f	⑤ f‡	⚒	†	*TGV* 8539 k	*TGV* 5221 ⑦ e	14171 14170 k	4678 4679 Ⓡ ♣	*TGV* 8543	14172 Ⓒ D	*TGV* 8545 ⑤ f	*TGV* 5222 ⑤⑥ q
Lille Europe **11** d.	...	...	...	...	...	...	...	...	...	...	...	...	...	...	...	...	...	1238c	...	...	...	...	...	1541
Charles de Gaulle ✈ **300** d.	...	...	...	...	...	...	...	...	...	...	...	...	...	...	...	...	...	1337	...	...	...	...	...	1638
Paris Montparnasse **300** d.	1010r	1010r	...	...	1210v	1210	...	...	1310	...	...	...	...	...	...	...	1440	|	...	...	1550	...	1620	|
Bordeaux St Jean d.	1314	1314	1429	1500	1528	1532	...	...	1630	...	1642	1642	1637	1637	1703	...	1743	1811	1817	...	1855	...	1921	2055
Morcenx d.	|	|	|	|	|	|	...	...	|	...	|	|	|	|	1808	...	|	|	1913	...	|	...	|	|
Dax a.	1423	1423	1537	1607	1636	1637	...	...	1733	...	1748	1748	1746	1746	1827	...	1853	1917	1934	...	2004	...	2029	2200
Dax d.	1426	1430	1539	1609	1639	1640	...	1710	1735	...	1753	1758	1751	1756	1830	1834	1856	1920	1935	1958	2007	2022	2032	2203
Puyoô **325** d.	|	|	|	|	|	|	...	|	|	...	|	|	|	1815	|	|	|	|	1956	2017	|	2041	|	|
Orthez **325** d.	|	1459	|	1637	|	|	...	|	|	...	|	1825	|	1826	|	|	|	|	2007	2029	|	2053	|	|
Pau **325** d.	|	1526	|	1700	|	|	...	|	|	...	|	1847	|	1848	|	|	1954	|	2039	2058	|	2122	2124	|
Lourdes **325** d.	|	1556	|	...	|	|	...	|	|	...	|	|	|	...	|	|	2024	|	2112	2131	|	2153	2154	|
Tarbes 325 a.	|	1611	|	...	|	|	...	|	|	...	|	|	|	...	|	|	2039	|	2129	2145	|	2211	2210	|
Bayonne 325 d.	1457	...	1614	...	1710	1711	1726	1756	1804	1802	1825	...	1824	...	1922	1916	...	1950	...	...	2039	...	...	2233
Biarritz **325** d.	1509	...	1625	...	1722	1723	1736	...	1815	1814	1835	...	1834	...	1932	1926	...	2002	...	...	2052	...	...	2245
St Jean de Luz **325** d.	1523	...	1637	...	1735	1736	1747	...	1829	1830	1848	...	1847	...	1945	1938	...	2015	...	...	2105	...	...	2258
Hendaye **325** a.	1532	...	1648	...	1744	1745	1759	...	1838	1839	1900	...	1858	...	1957	1949	...	2025	...	...	2114	...	...	2308
Irún 325 a.	1540	...	...	...	...	...	1805	...	...	1846	...	...	...	...	2004	1956	...	2034	...	...	2125	...	...	...

	TGV 8557	Ⓑ	*TGV* 8565 Ⓑ h	14003 ⑥⑦ E	*TGV* 8577 ⑤ f	⑤ f p	*TGV* 8587 G	*TGV* 8588 G	4053 Ⓡ Z⊖	4055 Ⓡ Z⊖
Lille Europe **11** d.	...	...	...	...	...	...	...	...	...	...
Charles de Gaulle ✈ **300** d.	...	...	...	...	...	...	...	...	...	...
Paris Montparnasse **300** d.	1745	...	1825	...	1925	...	2245	2245	...	...
Paris Austerlitz **300** d.	|	...	|	...	|	...	|	|	2311	2311
Bordeaux St Jean d.	2100	...	2130	2231	2233	...	|	|	|	|
Morcenx d.	|	...	|	|	|	...	|	|	0535	0535
Dax a.	2208	...	|	2339	2338	...	0500	0500	0558	0558
Dax d.	2211	2215	|	2341	2341	2349	0503	0508	0608	0626
Puyoô **325** d.	|	|	|	|	|	0007	|	|	|	|
Orthez **325** d.	2241	|	|	|	|	0018	|	0544	|	0655
Pau **325** d.	2307	|	|	|	|	0048	|	0617	|	0725
Lourdes **325** d.	2337	|	|	|	|	0118	|	0649	|	0756
Tarbes 325 a.	2352o	|	|	|	|	0133	|	0703	|	0811
Bayonne 325 d.	...	2249	2309	0010	0011	...	0538	...	0640	...
Biarritz **325** d.	...	2259	2321	0022	0022	...	0550	...	0654	...
St Jean de Luz **325** d.	...	2310	2333	0033	0036	...	0607	...	0710	...
Hendaye **325** a.	...	2320	2343	0043	0045	...	0616	...	0722	...
Irún 325 a.	...	...	...	...	...	...	0626	...	0732	...

	① g	*TGV* 5268 ①⑥ w	①⑥ F	②–⑤ n	②–⑤ n	Ⓐ ‡	Ⓐ	
Hendaye 325 d.	...	0529	...	0524	...	...	0645	...
St Jean de Luz **325** d.	...	0542	...	0538	...	...	0657	...
Biarritz **325** d.	...	0554	...	0551	...	...	0711	...
Bayonne 325 d.	0547	0606	...	0602	...	...	0722	...
Tarbes 325 d.	|	|	0438	|	...	...	|	...
Lourdes **325** d.	|	|	0454	|	...	...	|	...
Pau **325** d.	|	|	0525	|	0547	0657	|	...
Orthez **325** d.	|	|	0557	|	0618	0722	|	...
Puyoô **325** d.	|	|	0609	|	0628	|	|	...
Dax a.	0623	0634	0628	0640	0646	0748	0752	...
Dax d.	...	0637	0644	...	0648	0757	0757	...
Morcenx d.	...	|	0704	...	0708	0817	0817	...
Bordeaux St Jean a.	...	0743	0805	...	0808	0905	0905	...
Paris Austerlitz **300** a.	...	|	...	...	...	...	...	...
Paris Montparnasse **300** a.	...	|	...	...	...	...	...	...
Charles de Gaulle ✈ **300** a.	...	1207	...	...	...	...	...	...
Lille Europe **11** a.	...	1304	...	...	...	...	...	...

	⚒ H	*TGV* 8527 b	*TGV* 8524	4778 4779 Ⓡ ♥	*TGV* 5276 ⑦ e		14167 ▽ b	*TGV* 8534	Ⓐ J	Ⓐ L‡	*TGV* 8542 Ⓐ u	*TGV* 8541 v		⚒	*TGV* 8558	Ⓐ △	⑤ ⊖f	†	*TGV* 8563 ⊙	Ⓐ	*TGV* 5292 ⑥ t	①–④ m	①–④ m	⑤ f
Hendaye 325 d.	0745	...	0758	...	0839	...	...	1026	...	...	1122	...	...	1327	1411	...	...	...	...	1530	1625	1628	...	...
St Jean de Luz **325** d.	0758	...	0812	...	0853	...	...	1040	...	...	1136	...	...	1340	1426	...	...	...	...	1542	1638	1639	...	...
Biarritz **325** d.	0812	...	0826	...	0906	...	...	1054	...	...	1149	...	...	1352	1440	...	...	...	...	1554	1651	1651	...	...
Bayonne 325 d.	0822	...	0838	...	0918	...	...	1105	1120	...	1201	...	...	1402	1453	...	1528	1528	...	1603	1702	1703	...	...
Tarbes 325 d.	|	0722	|	0746	|	...	0830	|	|	...	|	1054	...	...	|	...	...	...	1433	...	|	|	...	...
Lourdes **325** d.	|	0742	|	0804	|	...	0848	|	|	...	|	1114	...	...	|	...	...	...	1451	...	|	|	...	...
Pau **325** d.	|	0811	|	0834	|	...	0921	|	|	1056	|	1142	...	...	|	1434	...	...	1520	...	|	|	1638	1638
Orthez **325** d.	|	0840	|	0900	|	...	0951	|	|	1123	|	|	...	...	|	1502	...	...	|	...	|	|	1707	1707
Puyoô **325** d.	|	|	|	|	|	...	1002	|	|	|	|	|	...	...	|	|	...	...	|	...	|	|	1717	1717
Dax a.	0854	0905	0909	0930	0945	...	1020	1134	1154	1150	1229	1234	...	...	|	1528	1600	1600	1609	...	1729	1738	1734	1734
Dax d.	...	0914	0914	...	0948	...	1022	1137	1159	1159	1239	1239	...	...	|	1530	...	...	1612	...	1732	1743	1743	1739
Morcenx d.	...	|	|	...	|	...	1044	|	|	|	|	|	...	...	|	|	...	...	|	...	|	|	|	|
Bordeaux St Jean a.	...	1021	1021	...	1055	...	1140	1246	1305	1305	1350	1350	...	...	1627	1645	...	...	1720	...	1837	1849	1849	1854
Paris Montparnasse **300** a.	...	1345x	1345x	...	|	...	...	1555	...	...	1720	1720	...	...	1945	...	...	...	2030	...	|	...	...	...
Charles de Gaulle ✈ **300** a.	...	...	...	...	1521	...	...	...	...	...	...	...	...	...	...	...	...	...	...	...	2306	...	...	...
Lille Europe **11** a.	...	...	...	...	1615	...	...	...	...	...	...	...	...	...	...	...	...	...	...	...	0007	...	...	...

	14169 ⑦ ad	14006 ⑦ d	①–④ m	†	14008 ⑤ f	*TGV* 8584	*TGV* 8583 k	Ⓐ	*TGV* 8590 ⑦ e	4678 4679 Ⓡ ♣	①–④ m	①–④ m	⑥	⑥	⑤ f	⑤ f	4620 Ⓡ T	†	†		4052 Ⓡ Z⊡	4051 Ⓡ Z⊡	*TGV* 8591 G	*TGV* 8592 G
Hendaye 325 d.	...	1647	1650	1701	1708	1726	...	...	1817	1831	1838	...	1838	...	1836	...	1853	...	1922	...	2219	...	...	2314
St Jean de Luz **325** d.	...	1658	1703	1715	1719	1740	...	...	1831	1843	1852	...	1852	...	1851	...	1906	...	1934	...	2236	...	...	2328
Biarritz **325** d.	...	1710	1713	1728	1730	1752	...	...	1844	1855	1904	...	1904	...	1904	...	1919	...	1946	...	2253	...	...	2341
Bayonne 325 d.	...	1721	1725	1740	1742	1803	...	1811	1857	1907	1916	...	1916	...	1916	...	1930	...	1957	...	2306	...	...	2353
Tarbes 325 d.	1604	|	|	|	|	|	1646	|	|	|	|	...	|	1810	|	1810	|	1830	|	...	|	2157	2240	|
Lourdes **325** d.	1622	|	|	|	|	|	1705	|	|	|	|	...	|	|	|	|	|	1846	|	...	|	2215	2259	|
Pau **325** d.	1653	|	|	|	|	|	1733	|	|	|	|	1853	|	1853	|	1853	|	1918	|	...	|	2248	2328	|
Orthez **325** d.	1723	|	|	|	|	|	1803	|	|	|	|	1922	|	1922	|	1922	|	1948	|	...	|	2317	2357	|
Puyoô **325** d.	1733	|	|	|	|	|	|	|	|	|	|	1933	|	1933	|	1933	|	2000	|	...	|	|	|	|
Dax a.	1751	1755	1759	1813	1816	1833	1828	1851	|	1938	1948	1953	1948	1953	1949	1953	2001	2018	2031	...	2340	2344	0022	0027
Dax d.	...	1757	...	1815	1820	1838	1838	...	|	...	1958	1958	1958	1958	2014	2014	2003	2051	2051	...	0007	0007	0032	0032
Morcenx d.	...	1817	...	1835	1841	|	|	...	|	...	2016	2016	2016	2016	2034	2034	|	2111	2111	...	0032	0032	|	|
Bordeaux St Jean a.	...	1910	...	1942	1936	1947	1947	...	2036	...	2114	2114	2114	2114	2135	2135	2128	2210	2210	...	|	|	|	|
Paris Austerlitz **300** a.	...	...	...	...	...	|	|	...	|	...	...	...	...	...	...	...	...	...	...	...	0710	0710	|	|
Paris Montparnasse **300** a.	...	...	...	...	...	2320j	2320j	...	2345	...	...	...	...	...	...	...	...	...	...	...	...	...	0600	0600
Charles de Gaulle ✈ **300** a.	...	...	...	...	...	...	...	...	...	...	...	...	...	...	...	...	...	...	...	...	...	...	...	...
Lille Europe **11** a.	...	...	...	...	...	...	...	...	...	...	...	...	...	...	...	...	...	...	...	...	...	...	...	...

IRÚN and TARBES - BORDEAUX 305

– Not Mar. 23, 29, May 11.
– Also Dec. 25, Jan. 1, Mar. 24, May 12; not Dec. 23, 30, Mar. 23, May 11. On Mar. 24, May 12 runs 4 minutes earlier.
– Also Dec. 26, Jan. 2, Mar. 25, May 1, 8, 10, 13; not Dec. 24, 31, Mar. 24, 29, May 10, 12.
– ⑤⑦ (also Dec. 25, Jan. 1, Mar. 24, Apr. 30, May 7, 12; not May 2). On ⑤ from May 30 Paris d. 2145 (train **8595**).
– On Dec. 26 runs 15 minutes earlier.
– To Mar. 14 / from Apr. 7.
– Not on ②–⑤ Jan. 8 - Feb. 22.
– ⑤⑦ (not Mar. 23), also daily Dec. 21 - Jan. 6 (not Dec. 24, 31), Feb. 8 - Mar. 9, Mar. 24, Apr. 4 - May 4, May 7 - 12. 🛏 2 cl., [2] (reclining) Hendaye - Bordeaux - Nice.
– 🛏 2 cl. and [2] (reclining) Nice - Bordeaux - Irún.
– *CORAIL LUNÉA* – 🛏 1, 2 cl. and [2] (reclining). Not Dec. 24, 31 (not Mar. 28, 29 Paris - Tarbes or Mar. 29 Tarbes - Paris).

– Not Mar. 30.
– Not Mar. 29, 30.
– Lille **Flandres**.
– Also Dec. 25, Jan. 1, Mar. 24, May 12; not Mar. 23, May 11.
– Also Dec. 25, Jan. 1, Mar. 24, May 12.
– Also Apr. 30, May 7; not May 2, 9.
– Also Dec. 26, Jan. 2, Mar. 25, May 13; not Dec. 24, 31, Mar. 24, May 12.
– Not May 1, 8.
– 0002 on night of ①–④ May 26 - July 10.
– Not Mar. 29.
– Not Dec. 25, Jan. 1, Mar. 24, Apr. 30, May 1, 7, 8, 12.
– Not Dec. 25, 26, Jan. 1, 2, Mar. 25, May 1, 8, 13.
– 0022 night of ①–④ Jan. 14 - Feb. 21.
– Not Mar. 28.
– Also Apr. 30, May 1, 7, 8; not May 2, 9, 10.

r – 0955 on Ⓐ Jan. 7 - Feb. 20, Mar. 13 - 21.
s – Not Dec. 25, Jan. 1, Mar. 24, 29, May 12.
t – Also May 1, 8.
u – Not Mar. 17 - Apr. 4.
v – Not Mar. 17 - 21, Mar. 25 - Apr. 4.
w – Also Dec. 26, Jan. 2, Mar. 25, May 1, 8, 13; not Dec. 24, 31, Mar. 24, May 10, 12.
x – 1355 on Ⓐ Dec. 10 - 21, 1350 on Feb. 21, 22, 25, 26.
y – From Bordeaux ⑦ Dec. 23 - Jan. 6, ⑦ Feb. 10 - Mar. 9, ⑦ Apr. 6 - May 11 (also May 1, 8, 12).
z – From Bordeaux on ①⑥ (also Dec. 26 - 28, Jan. 2 - 4, ②–⑤ Feb. 12 - Mar. 7, Mar. 25, Apr. 29, 30, May 2, 9, 13; not Mar. 24, Apr. 7, 14, 21).
TGV – Ⓡ, supplement payable, 🍷.
♥ – *CORAIL LUNÉA* – for days of running see Table **325**. 🛏 1, 2 cl. and [2] (reclining) Genève / Nice - Bayonne - Irún. Nice portion is **4730**.
♣ – *CORAIL LUNÉA* – for days of running see Table **325**. 🛏 1, 2 cl. and [2] (reclining) Hendaye - Genève and Nice. Nice portion is **4630**.
◧ – Subject to alteration on Ⓐ Apr. 7 - 25.
⊕ – Subject to alteration on ②–⑤ Jan. 8 - Feb. 22 (also Mar. 29).
⊗ – Not on Ⓐ Apr. 7 - 25.
△ – Subject to alteration on Ⓐ Jan. 7 - Feb. 22.
▽ – On Mar. 10 - 13 runs approx one hour later.
▷ – On Mar. 28 runs later (Dax 0810, Tarbes 1022).
⊡ – Subject to alteration on Apr. 5, 12, 19, 26, May 24, 31, June 6.
⊙ – On ①–④ Feb. 25 - Mar. 6 Tarbes 1418, Lourdes 1436.
⊖ – Depart Paris 2105 on Apr. 5, 12, 19, 26, May 17, 24, 31, June 6 (train **4059**), arriving up to 2 hours later.
⊖ – On Dec. 21 runs 12 minutes earlier.
◇ – From Toulouse (Table **325**). Runs 3 - 4 minutes later on ①–④, 6 - 7 minutes later on ⑤.
‡ – A change of trains at Dax may be necessary.

BORDEAUX - PÉRIGUEUX - BRIVE and LIMOGES 306

km							4490				4492	4480		2											
		Ⓐ	Ⓐ	Ⓐ		⚒	V 🍷	R	Ⓐ	⑥ y	⑥ ⊖z	△	⚒ U	Ⓐ	⑥				⑤ f	①–④ w	⑤ f	†	Ⓐ ⊡	⑥	⑥
0	**Bordeaux St Jean 300/7** d.	...	0606	...	...	0641	0734	0732	0814	...	0908	1047	...	1223	1228	...	1359	...	...	1558	1600	1621	1659	1659	...
37	Libourne **300/7** d.	...	0633	...	...	0715	0800	0759	|	...	|	1115	...	1252	1253	...	1426	...	...	|	1624	1647	1728	1728	...
53	Coutras **300** d.	...	0645	...	...	0726	0812	0814	|	...	|	1125	...	1302	1304	...	1436	...	...	|	1633	|	1737	1737	...
93	Mussidan d.	...	0713	...	...	0753	0840	0842	|	...	|	1145	...	1332	1333	...	1504	...	...	|	1700	1714	1806	1806	...
129	Périgueux a.	...	0732	...	...	0822	0902	0907	0920	...	1022	1202	...	1352	1358	...	1525	...	...	1707	1720	1735	1826	1826	...
129	Périgueux **308** ▷ d.	0610	...	0735	0740	...	0904	0909	0925	0925	1024	1208	1221	...	...	1429	...	1602	1652	1715	...	...	1836	...	1840
203	**Brive la Gaillarde** ▷ a.	|	...	0828	|	...	0958	1006	|	|	1109	|	1311	...	...	|	...	|	|	|	...	...	|	...	|
228	**Limoges 308** a.	0724	...	...	0838	...	...	...	1024	1024	...	1306	...	...	...	1535	...	1709	1801	1820	...	...	1955	...	1953
639	*Lyon Part Dieu* **327** a.	...	...	...	...	...	...	...	...	...	...	1816	...	...	...	...	...	...	...	...	...	...	...	...	...
643	*Lyon Perrache* **327** a.	...	...	...	...	...	...	...	...	...	...	1829	...	...	...	...	...	...	...	...	...	...	...	...	...

	⑤⑥ f	Ⓑ	N	⑤ f	Ⓑ	⚒	Ⓑ	⑤ f	†	†
Bordeaux St Jean 300/7 d.	...	1739	1807	1806	...	1856	2009	2009	2009	2156
Libourne **300/7** d.	...	1809	1835	1833	...	1928	2036	2036	2036	2220
Coutras **300** d.	...	1821	|	|	...	1943	2046	2046	2046	2230
Mussidan d.	...	1850	1906	1907	...	2016	2112	2112	2112	2252
Périgueux a.	...	1911	1925	1933	...	2042	2133	2133	2133	2313
Périgueux **308** ▷ d.	1846	...	1932	1946	1939	...	...	2138	2138	...
Brive la Gaillarde ▷ a.	1948	...	|	|	2035	...	...	|	|	...
Limoges 308 a.	...	...	2032	2049	...	...	...	2248	2248	...
Lyon Part Dieu **327** a.	...	...	...	...	...	...	...	...	...	...
Lyon Perrache **327** a.	...	...	...	...	...	...	...	...	...	...

	⚒	Ⓐ	Ⓐ	Ⓐ	⑥	Ⓐ			⚒	⚒
Lyon Perrache **327** d.	...	...	...	...	...	...	...	...	...	...
Lyon Part Dieu **327** d.	...	...	...	...	...	...	...	...	...	...
Limoges 308 d.	...	...	...	0611	...	...	0720	...	1021	...
Brive la Gaillarde ▷ d.	...	...	0620	|	...	...	|	0731	|	1110
Périgueux **308** ▷ a.	...	...	0724	0722	...	...	0825	0822	1119	1200
Périgueux d.	0559	0652	...	0734	0734	0800	0827	0827	1125	...
Mussidan d.	0625	0714	...	0755	0755	|	0848	0848	1145	...
Coutras **300** d.	0701	0742	...	0822	0822	|	0915	0915	1210	...
Libourne **300/7** d.	0713	0754	...	0832	0832	|	0925	0925	1221	...
Bordeaux St Jean 300/7 a.	0744	0820	...	0859	0859	0913	0949	0949	1249	...

			2											2	4590	4595		4580							
	Ⓐ	⑥	Ⓑ		⑤ f		†	Ⓑ ⊕	⑤ f	①–④ w		⑤ f		Ⓐ	V 🍷	⑦ ⊖q	⑥	▽	†	Ⓐ	Ⓑ	⑤–⑦ b		Ⓑ	
Lyon Perrache **327** d.	...	...	...	...	...	...	...	...	...	...	...	...	...	...	...	...	...	1251	...	...	...	...	...	...	...
Lyon Part Dieu **327** d.	...	...	...	...	...	...	...	...	...	...	...	...	...	...	...	...	...	1305	...	...	...	...	...	...	...
Limoges 308 d.	1110	...	...	1248	...	1455r	...	...	...	1705	1705	...	...	1735	...	...	...	1809	...	1929	2035	2125	2155	2259	...
Brive la Gaillarde ▷ d.	|	...	...	|	...	|	1557	...	1714	|	|	...	...	|	1801	1801	1803	|	...	|	|	|	|	|	...
Périgueux **308** ▷ a.	1206	...	...	1355	...	1559	1647	...	1813	1815	1815	...	...	1852	1856	1856	1900	1906	...	2055	2136	2226	2256	2356	...
Périgueux d.	...	1215	1218	...	1439	1606	...	1658	...	1820	...	1820	1836	...	1859	1859	...	1912	2031	...	...	...	...	...	...
Mussidan d.	...	1240	1240	...	1501	1627	...	1723	...	|	...	1841	1905	...	|	|	...	1931	2052	...	...	...	...	...	...
Coutras **300** d.	...	1310	1310	...	1525	1654	...	1757	...	|	...	1905	1936	...	|	|	...	1956	2117	...	...	...	...	...	...
Libourne **300/7** d.	...	1320	1320	...	1536	1705	...	1808	...	|	...	1915	1946	...	1952	1951	...	2009	2128	...	...	...	...	...	...
Bordeaux St Jean 300/7 a.	...	1346	1347	...	1559	1731	...	1837	...	1926	...	1940	2012	...	2018	2018	...	2037	2152	...	...	...	...	...	...

ADDITIONAL TRAINS PÉRIGUEUX - BRIVE AND V.V.

	Ⓐ	†	⑤ f	†	①–④ w	
Périgueux d.	0629	1454	1704	1704	1802	...
Brive la Gaillarde a.	0726	1545	1758	1758	1907	...

	⚒ 2	①–④ m	①–④ w	⑤ f	†	
Brive la Gaillarde d.	1349	1612	1822	2037	2115	...
Périgueux a.	1450	1715	1922	2127	2205	...

N – ①②③④⑦ (also May 2, 9; not Apr. 30, May 7).
R – ①②③④⑥ (also May 2, 9; not Dec. 25 - 27, Jan. 1 - 3, Mar. 24, Apr. 30, May 1, 7, 8, 12).
U – [12] Périgueux - Ussel.
V – ⑤ (also Dec. 26, 27, Jan. 2, 3, Apr. 30, May 7; not May 2, 9). To / from Ussel (Table **326**).

b – Also Dec. 25, Jan. 1, Mar. 24, May 1, 8, 12.
f – Also Apr. 30, May 7; not May 2, 9.
m – Not Dec. 25, Jan. 1, Mar. 24, May 1, 8, 12.
q – Also Dec. 25, Jan. 1, Mar. 24, May 12; not Dec. 23, 30, Mar. 23, May 11.
r – 1450 on Ⓐ Feb. 25 - Mar. 7.

w – Also May 2, 9; not Dec. 25, Jan. 1, Mar. 24, Apr. 30, May 1, 7, 8, 12.
y – Also Dec. 25, Jan. 1, Mar. 24, May 1, 8, 12.
z – Also May 8; not May 10.

⊖ – To / from Clermont Ferrand (Table **326**).
△ – Not Dec. 15, Mar. 3 - 6, 10 - 13, 17 - 20, 25 - 27, 29.
▽ – Not Dec. 15, Mar. 3 - 6, 10 - 13, 17 - 21, 25 - 27, 29.
⊕ – On May 8 subject to alteration Libourne - Bordeaux.
⊡ – Change at Périgueux on ⑤.
▷ – For additional trains see panel below main table.

308 LIMOGES - PÉRIGUEUX - AGEN *2nd class*

km		①g	Ⓐ	Ⓐb	⑥	†		Ⓐn	⚒	Ⓐ	†
0	**Limoges 306** d.	...	...	1110	...	*1248*	1450	...	...	1735	...
99	Périgueux **306** a.	...	...	1206	...	*1355*	1559	...	...	1852	...
99	Périgueux d.	0512	0720	1210	1210	1407	...	1603	1722	1902	1904
139	Les Eyzies d.	0542	0750	1243	1243	1438	...	1634	1758	1935	1937
156	Le Buisson a.	0557	0805	1259	1259	1453	...	1649	1813	1951	1952
156	Le Buisson d.	0558	0806	1301	1301	1454	...	1650	1817	2000f	2000
251	**Agen** a.	0727	0926	1419	1419	1616	...	1813	1943	2123f	2120

	Ⓐ	Ⓐ	①–⑥	b		Ⓐn	†		⑤f	
Agen d.	...	0642	...	1107	...	1502	1535	1828	2043	...
Le Buisson a.	...	0759	...	1224	...	1617	1656	1953	2201	...
Le Buisson d.	0618	0815	...	1225	...	1618	1657	1955	2202	...
Les Eyzies d.	0633	0830	...	1244	...	1635	1713	2010	2217	...
Périgueux a.	0713	0904	...	1314	...	1704	1743	2041	2248	...
Périgueux **306** d.	*0740*	...	0925	1319	1429	...	...	...	...	...
Limoges 306 a.	*0838*	...	1024	1429	1535	...	...	...	...	...

b – Subject to alteration Ⓐ Feb. 18 - Mar. 21.
f – ⑤ (also Apr. 30, May 7; not May 2, 9).
g – Also Dec. 26, Jan. 2, Mar. 25, May 13; not Dec. 24, 31, Mar. 24, May 12.
n – Subject to alteration ①–④ Feb. 4 - Mar. 20, June 9 - 12

309 LIMOGES - ANGOULÊME and POITIERS

km		①g	⑥	R	⑥	b			⑤f	†v	⑤f
0	**Limoges** d.	0530	0530	0636	0821	1224	...	1707	1836	1836	2042
122	**Angoulême** a.	0722	0722	0842	1006	1418	...	1856	2028	2028	2235

	⚒	Ⓐ		⚒b	†	⑤f	H	G	⑤f
Angoulême d.	0550	0754	...	1223	1512	1632	1835	1900	2011
Limoges a.	0756	0941	...	1416	1655	1825	2039	2100	2201

km		①g			⚒d	†v	⑤f		⑤f	†	
0	**Limoges** d.	0509	0630	...	1319	1459	1606	1720	1838	1838	...
139	**Poitiers** a.	0710	0832	...	1524	1659	1810	1932	2052	2050	...

	Ⓐ	c	d	⑤z	⑥	†	⚒	⑤f	†
Poitiers d.	0538	1056	1236	1817	1817	1817	1942	2150	2156
Limoges a.	0750	1258	1442	2027	2027	2027	2147	2349	2355

G – ⑤–⑦ (also Dec. 25, Jan. 1, Mar. 24, May 1, 8, 12).
H – ①–④ (not Dec. 25, Jan. 1, Mar. 24, Apr. 30, May 1, 7, 8, 12).
R – ②–⑤ (not Dec. 25, 26, Jan. 1, 2, Mar. 25, May 1, 8, 13).
b – Subject to alteration Ⓐ Jan. 28 - Feb. 22, Mar. 31 - Apr. 4.
c – Subject to alteration Ⓐ Jan. 14 - Mar. 14.
d – Subject to alteration ①–④ Mar. 17 - Apr. 10 (not Mar. 24).
f – Also Apr. 30, May 7; not May 2, 9.
g – Also Dec. 26, Jan. 2, Mar. 25, May 2, 9, 13; not Mar. 24, May 12.
v – Not Mar. 23, May 11.
z – Also Dec. 24, 31, Apr. 30, May 7.

310 PARIS - LIMOGES - TOULOUSE

For faster TGV services Paris - Agen - Toulouse and v.v. see Table 320. Additional relief trains run on peak dates

km									★ 3601			★ 3611	★ 3621		★ 3623			★ 3631				3635	★ 3637	★ 3641
		⚒	Ⓐ	⊡	⚒	⚒	Ⓐ	⑥	Ⓐ	Ⓐ △	Ⓐ ⊖	▽		⚒	V⊖	Ⓐ ⊕	© ⊖	Y	⑥	Ⓐ ⊖b	⑤ f	⑤⑦ q	⊗	
	Lille Europe d.	...	...	...	...	...	...	...	...	...	...	...	...	...	...	...	...	...	...	...	...	...	...	...
0	**Paris Austerlitz 294 315** d.	...	...	...	...	...	...	...	0641	...	...	0754	0909r	...	0924	...	...	1017	...	...	...	1247	1250	1356
	Orléans 315 d.	...	...	...	...	...	0627	0627	|	...	0759	*0839*	|	...	|	1020	1020	|	1214	1309	...	|	|	|
119	Les Aubrais-Orléans **294 315** d.	...	...	...	...	...	|	|	|	...	0808	0848	|	...	|	1030	1030	|	|	1320	...	|	|	|
200	Vierzon **315** d.	...	...	...	...	0636	0728	0728	|	...	0858	|	1037	...	|	1119	1119	1143	1314	1411	...	|	1422	|
236	Issoudun d.	...	...	...	...	0659	0749	0749	0817	...	0915	|	|	...	|	1136	1136	|	1335	1433	...	|	1441	|
263	Châteauroux d.	...	...	...	...	0716	0803	0802	0832	...	0929	0948	1109	...	1128	1150	1149	|	1350	1446	...	1452	1457	1553
294	Argenton sur Creuse d.	...	...	...	...	0735	0819	▬	|	...	0944	|	|	...	|	1206	...	|	1406	...	...	|	1515	|
341	La Souterraine d.	...	...	...	...	0802	0844	...	|	...	▬	1025	1145	...	1204	1232	...	|	1435	...	...	|	1540	|
400	**Limoges** a.	...	...	...	...	0835	▬	...	0932	...	...	1054	1215	...	1234	1306	...	1310	1509	...	...	1558	1610	1655
400	**Limoges** d.	...	...	0621	0733	▬	...	...	0934	...	...	1056	1217	1223	...	...	...	1313	▬	...	...	1600	...	1659
459	Uzerche d.	...	...	0657	0814	...	...	...	|	...	...	1132	|	1311	...	...	...	|	...	...	...	1636	...	|
499	**Brive la Gaillarde** a.	...	...	0727	0843	...	...	...	1034	...	†	1157	1320	1341	...	...	...	1412	...	...	...	1702	...	1759
499	**Brive la Gaillarde** d.	...	0603	0733	...	...	...	...	...	1112	1203	1159	...	...	...	...	...	1415	...	...	1720	▬	...	1802
536	Souillac d.	...	0628	0757	...	...	⚒	...	...	1135	1226	|	...	...	...	...	...	1440	...	...	1745	...	...	|
559	Gourdon d.	...	0643	0812	...	...	k	†	...	1149	1240	|	...	...	...	...	...	1456	Ⓐ	...	1800	†	...	|
600	Cahors d.	0626	0710	0838	...	...	1035	1035	...	1215	1306	1301	...	...	...	...	...	1524	1827	...	1827	1827	...	1903
639	Caussade d.	0652	0735	0904	...	Ⓐ	1100	1100	...	1240	1330	|	...	...	...	...	...	1550	1853	...	1853	1853	...	|
662	Montauban **320** d.	0710	0752	0919	...	1045	1115	1114	...	1254	1345	1340	...	...	...	...	...	1607	1910	...	1910	1913	...	|
713	**Toulouse Matabiau 320** a.	0737	0828	0946	...	1121	1143	...	...	1321	1412	1405	...	...	...	...	...	1633	1947	...	1947	1950	...	2005
	Portbou **355** a.	...	...	...	...	...	...	...	...	...	...	...	...	...	...	...	...	...	...	...	...	...	...	...

					★ 3651				★ 3657	★ 3661		★ 3665	★ 3667			*TGV* 5298	★ 3673	★ 3681	*TGV* 5298		3731	3971	3733	3751
	Ⓐ	Ⓐ	Ⓐ	Ⓐ	Ⓐ	†	⑥	Ⓐ	⑤ f	Ⓑ h	Ⓐ	⑤–⑦ w		Ⓐ	©	⑦ ♠e	⑤ f		①–⑥ ♣n		♦ 🅁	♦ 🅁	M 🅁 ◇	♦ 🅁
Lille Europe d.	...	...	...	...	...	...	...	...	...	...	...	...	...	...	...	1740	...	...	1815	...	...	...	...	...
Paris Austerlitz 294 315 d.	...	...	...	...	1608	...	...	...	1700	1733	...	1818	1830	...	...	|	1919	1949	|	...	2156	2156	2202	2256
Orléans 315 d.	...	...	...	...	|	1647	1647	1709	|	|	...	|	|	1929	1929	*1944*	|	|	*2033*	...	*2246*	*2246*	*2246*	*2348*
Les Aubrais-Orléans **294 315** d.	...	...	...	...	|	1656	1656	|	|	|	...	|	|	|	|	2014	|	|	2055	...	2257	2257	2303	2359
Vierzon **315** d.	...	...	1636	...	1736	1751	1751	1757	|	|	1901	1942	1959	2025	2023	2053	|	2114	2130	...	2337	2337	2346	|
Issoudun d.	...	...	1656	...	|	1811	1811	1818	|	|	1922	|	2019	2044	...	|	|	|	|	...	|	|	|	|
Châteauroux d.	...	1639	1713	...	1807	1827	1829	1836	1857	1926	1939	2013	2035	2058	...	2123	|	2144	2201	...	|	|	0017	|
Argenton sur Creuse d.	...	1657	▬	...	|	...	1845	1851	|	|	1958	|	2053	...	...	|	|	|	|	...	|	|	|	|
La Souterraine d.	...	1727	⑦	...	1845	...	1915	1921	1934	|	2026	|	2118	...	...	2201	|	|	2239	...	|	|	|	|
Limoges a.	...	1804	u	...	1916	...	1948	1955	2004	2028	2056	2115	2147	...	...	2231	2212	2246	2309	...	0115	0115	0120	|
Limoges d.	1730	...	1826	1826	1918	...	...	...	...	2030	...	2117	...	...	...	2234	...	2248	2312	...	0117	0117	0122	|
Uzerche d.	1815	...	1915	1914	|	...	...	...	...	2107	...	|	...	...	...	|	...	|	|	...	|	|	|	|
Brive la Gaillarde a.	1845	...	1945	1943	2016	...	...	...	...	2131	...	2215	...	...	...	2333	...	2348	0012	...	|	|	0223	|
Brive la Gaillarde d.	...	...	1949	...	...	...	...	...	...	2133	...	2217	...	...	...	...	...	...	...	...	|	|	0227	|
Souillac d.	...	...	2012	...	...	...	...	...	...	2158	...	2242	...	...	...	...	...	...	...	...	|	|	|	0445
Gourdon d.	...	...	2028	...	...	...	...	...	...	2214	...	2258	...	...	...	...	...	...	...	...	|	|	|	0501
Cahors d.	...	...	2055	...	...	...	...	...	...	2240	...	2325	...	...	...	...	...	...	...	...	|	|	|	0530
Caussade d.	...	...	2120	...	...	...	...	...	...	...	...	|	...	...	...	...	...	...	...	...	|	|	|	0556
Montauban **320** d.	...	...	2136	...	...	...	...	...	...	...	...	|	...	...	...	...	...	...	...	...	|	|	|	0614
Toulouse Matabiau 320 a.	...	...	2202	...	...	...	...	...	...	...	...	0027	...	...	...	...	...	...	...	...	|	0432s	0439	0641
Portbou **355** a.	...	...	...	...	...	...	...	...	...	...	...	...	...	...	...	...	...	...	...	...	0821	...	0854	...

		★ 3600	★ 3604			*TGV* 5296			★ 3610	★ 3612				★ 3620				★ 3624		★ 3626	★ 3630		★ 3640	
	⚒	Ⓐ	§	⚒	⚒	♥	Ⓐ	Ⓐ	①–⑥ ⊙	⑦	① g	⚒	Ⓐ ❖	①–⑥ n	⚒ ❖	†	⚒		Ⓐ L	⑦ p	▽	⚒		⑥
Cerbère **355** d.	...	...	...	...	...	...	...	...	...	...	...	...	...	...	...	...	...	...	...	...	0748	...	...	...
Toulouse Matabiau 320 d.	...	...	...	...	...	...	...	...	...	...	0630	0657	...	0720	...	0728	0734	...	0941	...	1124	...	...	1225
Montauban **320** d.	...	...	...	...	...	...	...	...	...	...	0700	0732	...	0750	...	0756	0811	...	1017	...	1151	...	...	1305
Caussade d.	...	...	...	...	...	...	...	...	...	...	0716	0749	...	|	...	0814	▬	...	▬	...	1207	...	...	1323
Cahors d.	...	...	...	...	...	...	...	...	0635	...	0741	0819	...	0829	...	0841	...	...	...	...	1234	...	...	1349
Gourdon d.	...	...	...	...	...	...	...	...	0702	...	0806	0843	...	|	...	0906	...	...	...	...	1300	...	...	▬
Souillac d.	...	...	...	...	...	...	...	...	0719	...	0822	0858	...	|	...	0922	...	...	...	...	1317	...	...	...
Brive la Gaillarde a.	...	...	...	...	...	...	...	...	0743	...	0845	0921	...	0929	...	0944	...	...	...	...	1341	...	...	...
Brive la Gaillarde d.	...	0448	...	...	0616	0633	0728	...	0746	0746	▬	...	...	0931	...	▬	...	...	1238	1308	1345	...	1444	...
Uzerche d.	...	0513	...	...	0644	|	0755	...	|	|	...	...	...	|	...	...	⚒	...	1307	1335	|	...	1509	...
Limoges a.	...	0550	...	...	0730	0735	0833	...	0845	0845	...	...	...	1029	...	...	❖	...	1355	1412	1444	...	1546	...
Limoges d.	0527	0552	0604	0614	0741a	0738	▬	...	0849	0849	...	...	1016	1032	...	...	1250	1350	...	1415	1448	...	1549	...
La Souterraine d.	0558	|	0635	0648	0815a	0813	...	0903	|	|	Ⓐj	...	1051	1103	...	⚒	1334	1421	...	|	|	...	|	⚒
Argenton sur Creuse d.	0626	|	|	0716	...	|	...	0930	|	|	←	...	1119	|	←	◐▽	1401	1445	...	|	|	1630	|	←
Châteauroux d.	0643	0654	0714	0733	...	0851	0858	0945	0953	0953	0957	...	1134	1141	1146	1228	1421	1504	...	1520	|	1646	1654	1703
Issoudun d.	0657	|	0730	0751	...	|	0912	→	|	|	1011	...	→	|	1200	1245	...	1520	...	|	|	→	|	1720
Vierzon **315** d.	0725	|	0751	0813	...	0922	0934	...	|	|	1030	...	...	|	1222	1306	...	1541	...	|	|	...	|	1759
Les Aubrais-Orléans **294 315** a.	|	|	|	|	...	0953	|	...	|	|	|	...	...	|	1316	1352	...	|	...	|	|	...	|	1851
Orléans 315 a.	0820	|	|	0901	...	|	1021*	...	|	|	1118	...	...	|	1325	1400	...	|	...	|	|	...	|	1900
Paris Austerlitz 294 315 a.	...	0845	0918	...	...	|	...	...	1144	1144	...	...	...	1335z	...	...	...	1707	...	1710	1740	...	1850	...
Lille Europe a.	...	...	...	...	...	1226	...	...	...	...	...	...	...	...	...	...	...	...	...	...	...	...	...	...

TOULOUSE - LIMOGES - PARIS 310

		★ 3652	★ 3654			★ 3664	3660		★ 3672		★ 3680				★ 3690								3750	3730	3732
	⚒	⑦	⑤	⚒	⚒	⑦	①–⑥	Ⓐ	⑦	†	Ⓑ	Ⓐ	Ⓐ	⑦		⑥	⑤	①–④	⑤	Ⓐ	Ⓒ	Ⓐ	◆	◆	N
		p	f		△	e	n	△	e		h			u				m	f				🄡	🄡	🄡 ◇
Cerbère **355** ... d.	...	...	...	...	...	...	...	...	...	...	...	...	...	...	...	...	...	...	...	...	...	...	...	2121	2134
Toulouse Matabiau 320 ... d.	...	1355	...	...	1349	...	...	1353	1508	...	...	...	...	...	1656	*1700*	1713	1750	1806	1853	1936	2005	2235	0049	0127
Montauban **320** ... d.	...	|	...	...	1417	...	...	1427	|	...	...	...	...	...	|	1731	1753	1824	1833	1940	2003	2039	2309	|	|
Caussade ... d.	...	|	...	...	1431	...	...	▬	|	...	...	...	...	...	|	1747	1811	1839	1847	1957	2018	...	2321c	|	|
Cahors ... d.	...	1501	...	...	1456	...	...	...	1613	1645	...	...	1730	...	1802	1815	1839	1905	1914	2023	2045	...	2353	|	|
Gourdon ... d.	...	|	...	...	1522	...	...	...	1640	1711	...	...	1759	...	|	1841	1903	1930	1940	...	2112	...	0022c	|	|
Souillac ... d.	...	|	...	...	1537	...	...	...	1656	1727	...	...	1814	...	|	1857	1919	1946	1956	...	2129	...	0040c	|	|
Brive la Gaillarde ... a.	...	1600	...	...	1600	...	...	...	1720	1750	...	...	1840	...	1903	1920	1942	2011	2019	...	2153	...	|	|	0329
Brive la Gaillarde ... d.	...	1603	...	...	▬	...	1622	...	1723	▬	1757	1829	...	1845	1905	...	...	*2041*	2021	...	2155	...	|	|	0331
Uzerche ... d.	...	|	...	...	...	...	|	...	|	⑤	1822	1901	...	1914	|	...	...	*2106*	2047	...	2221	...	|	|	|
Limoges ... a.	...	1702	...	...	...	...	1720	Ⓐ	1823	d	1859	1942	...	1956	2007	...	...	*2144*	2125	...	2259	...	|	|	0436
Limoges ... d.	1632	1705	1705	...	...	1716	1723	1731	1826	1826	1902	...	...	...	2009	...	...	...	...	...	...	...	|	|	0438
La Souterraine ... d.	1712	|	|	...	†	1747	1752	1815	|	1916	1934	...	...	...	|	...	...	...	...	...	...	...	|	|	|
Argenton sur Creuse ... d.	1740	|	|	←	1744	1811	1815	1843	|	1947	|	...	...	...	|	...	...	...	...	...	...	...	|	|	|
Châteauroux ... d.	1800	1809	1809	1813	1813	1830	1833	1900	1930	2020	2013	...	...	...	2112	...	...	...	...	...	...	...	|	|	0547
Issoudun ... d.	→	|	|	1830	1830	1846	1848	...	|	2037	|	...	...	...	|	...	...	...	...	...	...	...	|	|	|
Vierzon **315** ... d.	...	1840	1840	1909	1910	1905	1906	...	|	2058	2043	...	...	...	2140	...	...	...	...	...	...	...	|	0538	0620
Les Aubrais-Orléans **294 315** a.	...	|	|	1955	1955	|	|	...	|	...	|	...	...	...	2214	...	...	...	...	...	...	...	0546	0622	0704
Orléans 315 ... a.	...	|	|	2004	2004	|	|	...	|	...	|	...	...	...	*2224*	...	...	...	...	...	...	...	*0601*	*0639*	|
Paris Austerlitz 294 315 ... a.	...	2008	2008	...	...	2034	2034	...	2122	...	2208	...	...	...	2309	...	...	...	...	...	...	...	0655	0727	0812
Lille Europe ... a.	...	...	...	...	...	...	...	...	...	...	...	...	...	...	...	...	...	...	...	...	...	...	...	...	...

◆ – **NOTES** (LISTED BY TRAIN NUMBER):

3730 – *CORAIL LUNÉA* – 🛏 1,2 cl. and (2) (reclining) Cerbère - Paris and Latour de Carol (**3970**) - Toulouse - Paris. Not Dec. 24, 31.

3731 – *CORAIL LUNÉA* – 🛏 1,2 cl., (2) (reclining) Paris - Portbou. Not Dec. 24, 31.

3750 – *CORAIL LUNÉA* – 🛏 1,2 cl. and (2) (reclining) Toulouse - Paris. Not Dec. 24, 31. Train **3752** on dates in note **c**. Conveys (from Brive) portions from Rodez and Carmaux on dates in Table **316**.

3751 – *CORAIL LUNÉA* – 🛏 1,2 cl. and (2) (reclining) Paris - Toulouse. Not Dec. 24, 31. Train **3753** on dates in note **x**. Conveys (to Brive) portions for Rodez and Carmaux on dates in Table **316**.

3971 – CORAIL LUNÉA – 🛏 1,2 cl., (2) (reclining) Paris - Latour de Carol. Not Dec. 24, 31. Train **3985** Mar. 24 - Apr. 24.

L – Subject to alteration Jan. 7 - 25.
M – Dec. 21, 28, Apr. 30, May 7 only.
N – Dec. 25, Jan. 1, May 3, 12 only.
V – Dec. 21, 22, 24, 28, 29, 31, Feb. 22, 23, 29, Mar. 1, 21, 22, Apr. 18, 19, 25, 26, 30, May 1, 7, 8 only.
Y – To Cerbère (Table **355**). Depart Paris 1006 on Mar. 10 - 14, 20, 21; depart Paris 0956 on Mar. 19, 26, 27.

a – Ⓐ only.
b – Runs earlier Mar. 7, 17 - 19 (Paris d. 1232). Subject to alteration Mar. 3 - 6.
c – Calls on night of ⑤⑥⑦ (also Dec. 25, Jan. 1, Mar. 24, Apr. 30, May 1, 7, 8, 12).
d – Also Apr. 30, May 7.
e – Also Dec. 25, Jan. 1, Mar. 24, May 12.
f – Also Apr. 30, May 7; not May 2, 9.
g – Not Mar. 24, May 12.
h – Not May 1, 8.
j – Subject to alteration Châteauroux - Orléans Ⓐ Feb. 11 - 29. Runs 12 mins later Vierzon - Orléans Mar. 10 - 14, 20, 21.
k – Runs up to 20 mins earlier Jan. 21 - 25, Feb. 18 - 22, Mar. 10 - 14, 17 - 21; up to 30 mins later Jan. 8 - 11, 14 - 18, May 6, 7.

m – Not Dec. 25, Jan. 1, Mar. 24, Apr. 30, May 1, 8, 12.
n – Not Dec. 25, Jan. 1, Mar. 24, May 12.
p – Also Dec. 25, Jan. 1, Mar. 24, May 12; not Mar. 23.
q – Also Dec. 25, Jan. 1, Mar. 24, Apr. 30, May 7, 12; not Mar. 23.
r – 0821 on Apr. 7 - 10, 21 - 25.
s – Service stop - does not set down passengers.
u – Also Dec. 25, Jan. 1, Mar. 24, May 1, 8, 12; not Mar. 23, May 11.
w – Also Dec. 25, Jan. 1, Mar. 24, Apr. 30, May 1, 7, 8, 12.
x – Calls on morning of ①⑥⑦ (also Dec. 26, Jan. 2, Mar. 25, May 1, 2, 8, 9, 13).
y – Depart 1311 Feb. 25 - 29, Mar. 10 - 14, 20, 21, 25, 26, 31, Apr. 1; depart 1340 Apr. 7 - 10, 21 - 25.
z – 1350 Dec. 10 - 14, 1353 Feb. 11 - 29.

TGV – 🄡, supplement payable, 🍸.

⊕ – Subject to alteration Mar. 19, 26, 27, 31, Apr. 1 - 4, 7 - 10, 21 - 25, May 5 - 7.
⊗ – Subject to delay of up to 25 minutes Feb. 25 - 29, Mar. 10 - 14, 20, 21, 25 - 28, 31, Apr. 1 - 4.
⊙ – Runs up to 22 mins earlier on Ⓐ Feb. 11 - 29.
⊡ – Subject to alteration Montauban - Toulouse Ⓐ Jan. 14 - 25.
⊖ – Timings may vary by up to 10 minutes earlier or later.
△ – Timings may vary by up to 15 minutes earlier or later.
▽ – May arrive up to 30 minutes later on certain dates.
◇ – 🛏 1, 2 cl. and (2) (reclining).
★ – CORAIL TÉOZ. 🄡. 🍸.
♥ – Not Apr. 12, 13. Also calls at Marne la Vallée (a. 1117), Charles de Gaulle ✈ (a. 1131).
♠ – Also calls at Charles de Gaulle ✈ (d. 1835), Marne la Vallée (d. 1853).
♣ – Also calls at Charles de Gaulle ✈ (d. 1917), Marne la Vallée (d. 1933).
◐ – Subject to alteration Mar. 3 - 22.
✣ – Subject to alteration due to engineering work.
• – Arrive 1740.
§ – Runs up to 3 mins earlier Apr. 24 - May 17.
* – Subject to alteration Mar. 25 - 28, 31, Apr. 1 - 4, 8 - 10, 22 - 25.

TOULOUSE - LATOUR DE CAROL 312

Subject to alteration Mar. 25 - Apr. 25

km		3971 ◇ 🄡		B	△	△	d				
	Paris Austerlitz **310** d.	2156	...	...	...	...	...	...	...	...	...
0	**Toulouse Matabiau** .. d.	|	0650	0750	0850	1050	1450	1650	1750	1850	1950
65	Pamiers ... d.	0545	0750	0850	0950	1150	1550	1750	1850	1950	2050
83	Foix ... a.	0555	0800	0905	1000	1200	1600	1800	1905	2000	2105
83	Foix ... d.	0558	0801	0906	1001	1201	1601	1801	1906	2001	2106
123	Ax les Thermes ... d.	0647	0849	0945	1049	1249	1649	1849	1945	2049	2145
144	L'Hospitalet ⊖ ... a.	0720	0920	...	1120	1320	1720	1920	...	2120	...
163	**Latour de Carol** ... a.	0751	0952	...	1152	1352	1752	1952	...	2152	...

	Ⓐ		Ⓒ	Ⓐ	△	Ⓐ				3970 ◇ 🄡
Latour de Carol ... d.	0521	0721	0921	*0903**	1321	*1530**	...	1721	1921	2021
L'Hospitalet ⊖ ... d.	0552	0752	0952	*0930**	1352	*1600**	...	1752	1952	2049
Ax les Thermes ... d.	0620	0820	1020	1020	1420	*1625**	1748	1820	2020	2120
Foix ... a.	0704	0904	1104	1104	1504	*1720**	1829	1904	2104	2210
Foix ... d.	0705	0907	1107	1107	1507	1734	1831	1907	2107	2220
Pamiers ... d.	0721	0921	1121	1121	1521	1751	1851	1921	2121	2237
Toulouse Matabiau ... a.	0816	1016	1216	1216	1616	1846	1946	2016	2216	2317
Paris Austerlitz **310** a.	...	...	...	...	...	...	...	...	...	0727

B – ①–⑤ (daily from Mar. 17).
d – Runs 25 mins earlier on ⑥⑦ Mar. 29 - Apr. 20.
⊖ – For 🚌 connections to / from Andorra see Table **313**.

△ – On Apr. 28 - 30, May 5 - 7, Ⓐ May 13 - June 6 subject to alteration Ax les Thermes - Latour de Carol and v.v.
* – By 🚌.

◇ – 🛏 1,2 cl. and (2) (reclining). Not Dec. 24, 31. Southbound train arrives up to 15 mins later night of Mar. 24 - Apr. 24.

ANDORRA 🚌 313

Subject to cancellation when mountain passes are closed by snow. The service to / from Latour de Carol has been withdrawn.

L'Hospitalet Gare ... d.	0735	...	...	...	...	...	1945	...	...
Pas de la Casa ... d.	0815	1030	1230	1400	1630	1830	2000	2130	...
Soldeu ... ⊙ d.	0840	1055	1255	1425	1655	1855	2025	2155	...
Andorra la Vella ... a.	0905	1205	1405	1505	1805	1935	2105	2215	...

Andorra la Vella ... d.	0545	0730	0900	1030	1200	1430	1700	1830	2000
Soldeu ... ⊙ d.	0610	0805	0945	1105	1245	1505	1735	1905	2030
Pas de la Casa ... d.	0640	0825	1000	1125	1300	1530	1815	1925	2100
Hospitalet Gare ... a.	0710	...	...	...	...	...	1930	...	...

⊙ – Also calls at Canillo, Encamp and Escaldes.

Operator: La Hispano Andorrana, Av. Santa Coloma, entre 85 - 87, Andorra la Vella, ✆ + 376 821 372. www.andorrabus.com
Additional service: approx hourly (5 per day on ⑦) Escaldes - Andorra la Vella - Sant Julià de Lòria - Seu d'Urgell (Spain).

315 PARIS - VIERZON - BOURGES - MONTLUÇON

Some trains 2nd class

km					3903	3905					3909					3913	3913				3917	3921	3923	
		⚒	Ⓐ		Ⓐ	⑥	⚒	Ⓒ					Ⓐ	Ⓐ	Ⓐ	Ⓑ	⑤	†	①–④	†		⑤	⑦	†
				♥		t			⊕	◐	⊗	◇		s		h	f△		m			d	e	v
0	**Paris Austerlitz** 310 d.	...	...	...	0706	0706	...	...	...	...	1217	...	...	...	...	1715	1715	...	...	...	1901	2050	2047	...
	Orléans 310 d.	...	...	0705	*0750*	*0750*	...	...	0900	...	*1300*	1459	...	1632	1756	|	|	...	...	...	*1944*	*2135*	*2135*	...
119	Les Aubrais-Orléans 310 d.	...	...	|	0802	0801	...	...	0909	...	1313	|	...	|	|	|	|	...	...	...	1958	2147	2147	...
200	Vierzon 310 a.	...	...	0746	0835	0837	...	...	0957	...	1345	1547	...	1723	1839	1843	1843	...	...	...	2037	2224	2223	...
200	Vierzon ▷ d.	...	0625	0748	0845	0839	0842	0907	1002	1046	1347	1549	*1654*	1725	1840	1847	1847	1851	1851	...	2039	2231	2229	2235
	Bourges ▷ a.	...	0650	0803	0903	0857	|	0930	1026	|	1403	1608	*1718*	1751	1857	1904	1904	|	|	...	2058	2251	2245	|
	Bourges d.	0530	*0659*	...	...	...	|	*1025*z	...	|	1413	...	1745	*1822*c	...	...	1914	|	|	2001	2113	2303	...	|
291	St Amand-Montrond-Orval d.	0653	*0750*	...	...	...	0937	*1111*z	...	1144	1456	...	1840	*1920*c	...	...	2001	1942	1948	2046	2159	2345	...	2329
341	**Montluçon** a.	0734	...	...	...	...	1010	...	...	1218	1527	...	1916	...	...	...	2033	2015	2022	2129	2236	0020	...	0002

		3904				3908		3914						3918	3920							3924	
	⚒	⚒	①–⑥	⚒	Ⓐ	⚒		⚒	①–⑥	†	Ⓐ	Ⓑ	Ⓑ		⚒	†	Ⓐ	†	Ⓑ	Ⓐ	Ⓐ	Ⓐ	⑦	♥
			n				⊖		n⊡						▽	▽							q△	
Montluçon d.	...	0508	...	0615	...	...	0856	1108	...	...	...	...	...	...	1558	1635	1726	1755	...	...	1843	...	1902	...
St Amand-Montrond-Orval d.	...	0543	...	0650	...	...	0936	1146	...	1148	...	...	...	...	1632	1710	1810	1838	...	...	1921	...	1943	...
Bourges a.	...	0630	...	|	...	...	1020	|	...	1231	...	...	...	...	1723	1755	1907	1925	...	...	|	...	2025	...
Bourges ▷ d.	0608	...	0645	|	0736	*0750*	1035	|	1232	...	1513r	1604r	...	1633	1735	1807	...	...	1934	...	|	2017	2038	2151
Vierzon ▷ a.	0627	...	0703	0740	0755	*0807*	1058	1242	1248	...	1533	1623	...	1656	1751	1823	...	...	1953	...	2022	2036	2054	2209
Vierzon 310 d.	0632	...	0705	...	0757	0813	1100	...	1253	...	1544	...	1632	1659	1753	1825	...	...	...	2010	...	...	2056	2211
Les Aubrais-Orléans 310 a.	0721	...	0743	...	|	|	1132	...	1326	...	1630	...	1711	1749	1830	1905	...	...	...	2056	...	...	2130	|
Orléans 310 a.	0731	...	*0755*	...	0830	0901	*1141*	...	*1338*	...	1638	...	*1720*	1758	*1841*	*1918*	...	...	...	2104	...	...	*2157*	2249
Paris Austerlitz 310 a.	...	...	0842	...	...	...	1228	...	1423	...	...	...	1810	...	1926	2005	...	...	...	...	...	...	2225	...

ADDITIONAL TRAINS VIERZON - BOURGES (see also Table **290**)

	⚒	Ⓐ				Ⓐ	Ⓐ			
Vierzon d.	0659	0802	1043	1431*	1516	1654	1740	1828	2049	...
Bourges a.	0725	0828	1102	1450	1532	1718	1802	1854	2107	...

	⚒	†			Ⓐ	⚒		⚒	†	†	
Bourges d.	0704	0720	0849	0902	1015	1247r	1620	1741	1745	2028	...
Vierzon a.	0730	0740	0908	0928	1035	1313	1638	1807	1806	2045	...

c – ⚒ only.
d – Also Apr. 30, May 7.
e – Also Dec. 25, Jan. 1, Mar. 24, May 12.
f – Also Apr. 30, May 7; not May 2, 9.
h – Not May 1, 8.
m – Also May 2, 9; not Dec. 25, Jan. 1, Mar. 24, Apr. 30, May 1, 7, 8, 12.
n – Not Dec. 25, Jan. 1, Mar. 24, May 12.
q – Also Dec. 25, Jan. 1, Mar. 24, May 12; not Dec. 23, 30, Mar. 23, May 11.
r – 5 minutes earlier Apr. 8 - 11.
s – Subject to alteration Mar. 11.
t – Also May 1, 8.
v – Not Mar. 23, May 11.
z – † only.
♥ – To / from Lyon (Table **290**).
◐ – Runs up to 5 minutes earlier Jan. 28, 29, Feb. 4, 7.
◇ – Timings may vary up to 10 minutes earlier.
⊖ – Subject to delay Jan. 31, Feb. 1, 5, 6, 8 (Paris a. 1253), Mar. 26, 27 (a. 1305).
⊕ – Runs 16 mins earlier to Vierzon on Ⓐ Mar. 25 - Apr. 4.
⊗ – Runs up to 20 minutes earlier to Bourges Jan. 28, 29, Feb. 4 - 7, 25 - 29, Mar. 10 - 14, 20, 21, 25 - 28, 31, Apr. 1 - 4, 7 - 10, 21 - 25.
⊡ – Depart Bourges up to 5 minutes earlier Jan. 31, Feb. 1, 5, 6, 8, Apr. 8 - 11.
▷ – See also panel below table (also Table **290**).
△ – To / from Ussel (Table **299**).
▽ – Subject to alteration Apr. 24 - May 17.
* – 1425 on Jan. 28, 29, Feb. 4 - 7; 1449 (a. 1514) Apr. 2 - 4, 7.

316 BRIVE and AURILLAC - FIGEAC - TOULOUSE

km		3751/3 3755	3751/3 3755/7	2	2	2	2	2	2			2		2	2	🚌	2	2	2	2	2	🚌		2
			⑤f	Ⓐ		⚒		Ⓐ	Ⓐ	⚒		Ⓐ	Ⓐ				Ⓐ		⑦			⑤	⑤	
		DⓇ	CⓇ		⊡			⊕	⊗			⊖	△	⊙	▽		▷		W			d	d	
	Paris Austerlitz 310 d.	2256	2256	...	...	...	...	...	...	...	...	...	...	...	...	...	...	...	...	...	...	...	...	...
0	**Brive la Gaillarde** 317 d.	|	|	...	0600	...	...	...	0830	...	...	...	1109	...	1333	...	1614	...	...	...	1827r	...	...	2133
27	St Denis-près-Martel 317 d.	0449	0449	...	0626	...	...	...	0856	...	...	...	1130	...	1356	...	1636	...	...	...	1858	...	...	2202
45	Rocamadour-Padirac d.	0509	0509	...	0641	...	...	...	0913	...	...	...	1144	...	1411	...	1652	...	...	...	1917	...	...	2217
	Clermont Ferrand 331 d.	|	|	...	|	...	...	...	|	0636	...	...	|	...	|	...	|	...	...	...	|	...	...	|
	Aurillac d.	|	|	...	|	0651	...	...	|	0907	...	...	|	1304	|	...	|	1652	1750	1830	|	1907	2122	|
88	Figeac d.	0549	0549	0612	0715	0815	0815	0908	0954	1016	1016	1211	1218	1415	1443	1448	1728	1812	1902	1955	1951	2020	2237	2252
94	Capdenac a.	0556	0556	0619	0721	0821	0821	0914	1001	1022	1022	1217	1224	1421	1450	|	1734	1819	1909	...	1957	2030	2244	2258
94	Capdenac d.	0602	0620	0621	0727	0823	0823	0915	...	1024	1024	1223	1225	1423	1453	|	1736	1821	...	...	1958	...	...	2259
161	**Rodez** a.	0741	|	|	0826	|	|	1019	...	|	|	|	1329	|	1557	|	1839	|	...	...	2055	...	...	0002
123	Villefranche de Rouergue d.	...	0647	0650	...	0851	0851	...	...	1052	1052	1251	...	1451	...	1527	...	1851	...	...	...	...	...	...
140	Najac d.	...	0703	0705	...	0906	0906	...	...	1107	1107	1305	...	1505	...	...	...	1905	...	...	...	...	...	...
189	Tessonnières 323 a.	...	0755	|	...	|	|	...	...	|	|	|	...	|	...	...	...	|	...	...	...	...	...	...
	Carmaux 323 a.	...	0923	|	...	|	|	...	...	|	|	|	...	|	...	...	...	|	...	...	...	...	...	...
193	Gaillac 323 a.	...	...	0751	...	0950	0950	...	...	1150	1150	1352	...	1552	...	...	...	1950	...	...	...	...	...	...
247	**Toulouse Matabiau** 323 a.	...	...	0834	...	1033	1033	...	...	1233	1233	1434	...	1633	...	...	...	2034	...	...	...	...	...	...

		2	2			2	2		🚌	2		2	2	2	2	🚌	2		2	2	🚌		3754 3750/2	3759/8 3750/2
	⚒		Ⓐ	Ⓐ	Ⓐ		⚒	Ⓐ						E	⑤	Ⓐ	Ⓐ			Ⓐ	⑤			⑦v
					⊕			▽		⊖	♥	u	u		f						d		DⓇ	CⓇ
Toulouse Matabiau 323 d.	...	...	...	0639	...	0839	0839	...	...	...	1240	...	...	1637	1637	...	...	1838	...	1947	...	...	...	...
Gaillac 323 d.	...	...	...	0717	...	0915	0915	...	...	...	1318	...	...	1717	1717	...	...	1915	...	2030	...	...	...	...
Carmaux 323 d.	...	...	...	|	...	|	|	...	...	...	|	...	...	|	|	...	...	|	...	|	...	...	...	2103
Tessonnières 323 d.	...	...	...	|	...	|	|	...	...	...	|	...	...	|	|	...	...	|	...	|	...	...	...	2159
Najac d.	...	...	...	0804	...	1004	1004	...	...	...	1404	...	...	1803	1803	...	...	2004	...	2115	...	...	...	2247
Villefranche de Rouergue d.	...	...	...	0819	...	1019	1019	...	1210	...	1419	...	...	1819	1819	...	...	2019	...	2130	...	...	...	2304
Rodez d.	...	0650	...	|	0840	|	|	...	|	1150	|	1422	1631	|	|	1726	...	|	2000	|	...	...	2220	|
Capdenac a.	...	0756	...	0848	0945	1049	1049	...	|	1255	1448	1527	1735	1849	1849	1845	...	2046	2104	2156	...	...	2330	2329
Capdenac d.	0546	0757	...	0849	0946	1050	1050	1110	|	1256	1451	1529	1737	1850	1854	1845	1909z	2049	2106	2157	...	...	2355	2355
Figeac d.	0554	0804	0834	0856	0953	1057	1107	1117	1250	1303	1458	1538	1744	1856	1901	1900	1917	2057	2113	2204	2216	...	0007	0007
Aurillac a.	0718	|	0959	...	...	...	1219	|	...	|	1605	|	|	...	2018	...	|	2212	|	...	2329	...	|	|
Clermont Ferrand 331 a.	...	|	...	...	...	...	...	|	...	|	1854	|	|	...	...	...	|	...	|	...	...	...	|	|
Rocamadour-Padirac d.	...	0838	...	...	...	...	...	1200	...	1340	...	1618	1819	...	...	...	1953	...	|	...	...	...	0050	0050
St Denis-près-Martel 317 d.	...	0853	...	...	...	...	...	1215	...	1355	...	1636	1834	...	...	...	2008	...	2206	...	...	...	0107	0107
Brive la Gaillarde 317 a.	...	0914c	...	...	...	...	...	1237	...	1421	...	1657	1854	...	...	...	2032	...	2226	...	...	...	|	|
Paris Austerlitz 310 a.	...	...	...	...	...	...	...	...	...	...	...	...	...	...	...	...	...	...	...	...	...	...	0655	0655

C – 🛏 1,2 cl. and (2) (reclining) Paris - Carmaux and v.v.
D – 🛏 1,2 cl. and (2) (reclining) Paris - Rodez and v.v. Not Dec. 24, 31.
E – Daily except ⑤ (also runs May 2, 9; not Apr. 30, May 7).
W – ⑦ Dec. 9 - Mar. 9.
c – On Ⓐ Dec. 10 - 21 by 🚌 (arrive 0941).
d – Also Apr. 30, May 7.
f – Also Apr. 30, May 7; not May 2, 9.
r – 1816 Dec. 9 - 21.
u – Runs up to 20 minutes earlier Dec. 9 - 21.
v – Also Dec. 25, Jan. 1, Mar. 24, May 12; not Dec. 23, 30, Mar. 23, May 11.
z – ⑤ (also May 7; not May 9).
♥ – Subject to alteration Toulouse - Capdenac on Ⓐ Jan. 21 - Feb. 8.
△ – Subject to alteration Dec. 10 - 21, May 13 - 23.
▽ – Subject to alteration Dec. 9 - 21, May 12 - 16.
▷ – Subject to alteration Dec. 10 - 21.
⊕ – Subject to alteration May 19 - 23.
⊗ – Runs up to 10 minutes earlier Dec. 10 - 21. Subject to alteration Rocamadour - Capdenac Dec. 10 - 14, May 13 - 16.
⊡ – Runs up to 6 minutes earlier Dec. 9 - 21.
⊙ – Subject to alteration on Ⓐ Jan. 21 - Feb. 8.
⊖ – Subject to alteration Jan. 22 - Feb. 8.
⊝ – Subject to alteration Dec. 9 - 21, May 12 - 16, 19 - 23.

317 BRIVE - AURILLAC

km	To June 7	W	Ⓐ		⑥				Ⓑ	⑥
0	**Brive la Gaillarde** 316 d.	0758	1044r	...	1211	1431	...	1807	2143	2233
27	St Denis-près-Martel 316 d.	0822	1107	...	1234	1456	...	1832	2205	2257
102	**Aurillac** a.	0940	1231	...	1351	1622	...	1957	2322	0014

To June 7	⚒	⚒			† v	⑤		◇	
Aurillac d.	0538	0732	...	1144	1410	1545	...	1712	...
St Denis-près-Martel 316 d.	0700	0858	...	1306	1532	1718	...	1832	...
Brive la Gaillarde 316 a.	0724	0921r	...	1329r	1553	1739	...	1858	...

W – Dec. 9 - Mar. 9. To Le Lioran (arrive 1014).
r – By 🚌 on Ⓐ Dec. 10 - 21.
v – Not Mar. 23, May 11.
◇ – From Neussargues on dates in Table 331.

BORDEAUX - TOULOUSE 320

km		TGV 5171 ♦ ⊗	4652 4653 ★ ⊕	⚒ △	4654 4655 ★	TGV 8501 Ⓐ	†	4656 4657 ★ ⊖	TGV 8511 Ⓐ	TGV 8513 Ⓒ	4660 4661 ★ u	TGV 8519 ▽	4662 4663 ★	⊖	4664 4665 ★ ⊗	TGV 8535	R	TGV 5218 ♦	3835 🍷	14109 Ⓐ ⊡	14111 ⑦ q	⑥	TGV 8549	4621 [R] ♦	TGV 8579 ⑤ f	4624 4625 [R] ♦
	Paris M'parnasse **300** d.	...	...	...	...	0610	...	...	0810	0810	...	1130	...	...	...	1410	...	...	...	...	...	...	1720	...	1925	...
	Nantes **292** d.	...	...	...	...	|	...	...	|	|	...	|	...	...	...	|	...	...	1409	...	...	...	|	...	|	2046
0	**Bordeaux St Jean** d.	0539	0552	0727	0816	0923	1008	1057	1124	1124	1209	1436	1431	1446	1627	1718	1721	1807	1837	1930	1930	1939	2027	2148	2236	0101
79	Marmande d.	|	|	0808	0852	|	1049	|	|	|	|	|	|	1536	|	|	1806	|	1921	2008	2018	2027	|	2227	|	|
136	Agen d.	0638	|	0846	0922	1024	1127	|	|	1226	1310	1539	|	1613	1730	1818	1850	1906	1949	2036	2057	2100	2129	2257	2336	|
206	Montauban d.	|	|	0938	1008	1104	1215	|	|	1304	|	1616	|	...	1818	1903	1937	1951	2032	2119	2147	...	2210	2340	0017	|
257	**Toulouse Matabiau** a.	0744	0759	1007	1033	1136	1245	1302	1330	1336	1420	1650	1644	...	1843	1926	2002	2017	2100	2150	2218	...	2241	0006	0045	|
	Narbonne **321** a.	0901	|	...	1201	...	...	|	...	...	1539	...	|	...	2004	...	...	...	...	...	...	...	...	|	...	|
	Marseille **355** a.	...	1142	...	1453	...	...	1639	...	...	1825	...	2018	...	2243	...	...	...	...	...	...	...	...	0532	...	0708
	Nice **360** a.	...	1430	...	...	...	...	1923	...	...	...	...	...	...	...	...	...	...	...	...	...	...	...	0837	...	1015

	⑥	Ⓐ	TGV 5264 ♦	4720 [R] ♦	TGV 8518 ①–⑥ n	14100 Ⓐ y	†	3852 ▷ 🍷	TGV 8528	❖	4752 4753 ★	4754 4755 ★ ⊙	4756 4757 ★ ⊙	TGV 8548	⊖	TGV 8568 Ⓑ h	4758 4759 ★ c	TGV 8570 ⑥ t		TGV 8580 Ⓑ h	TGV 8586 ⑦ e	4762 4763 ★	4764 4765 ★	TGV 5116 ♦	4766 ★ ⑤⑦ ♦w	4724 4725 [R] ♦
Nice **360** d.	...	...	...	2058	...	...	...	...	...	...	...	...	...	...	...	...	1008	...	...	...	...	...	1330	...	...	1835
Marseille **355** d.	...	...	...	0010	...	...	...	...	...	...	0554	0714	0920	...	...	...	1254	...	...	...	...	1500	1619	...	1912	2214
Narbonne **321** d.	...	...	...	|	...	...	...	...	...	...	0840	0955	|	...	...	...	|	...	...	...	...	1745	|	1958	2148	|
oulouse Matabiau d.	...	...	0527	0536	0608	0653	...	0748	0922	...	1003	1121	1310	1312	...	1608	1628	1631	1700	1736	1826	1908	1956	2117	2311	|
ontauban d.	...	...	0553	0603	0636	0721	...	0816	|	...	|	1148	|	1341	...	1636	|	1701	1726	1803	1855	1935	|	|	2339	|
gen d.	0525	0615	0630	0641	0714	0756	0833	0853	|	1027	1107	1226	|	1418	1439	1714	|	1739	1812	1839	1931	2013	|	2219	|	|
'armande d.	0603	0647	|	0717	|	0825	0907	0923	|	1103	|	1256	|	|	1514	|	|	|	1851	|	|	2044	|	|	|	|
ordeaux St Jean a.	0654	0731	0739	0810	0820	0903	0955	1002	1119	1153	1209	1331	1512	1520	1559	1822	1829	1841	1937x	1942	2032	2122	2157	2320	0117	0437
Nantes **292** a.	...	...	...	...	|	...	...	1424	|	...	...	...	...	|	...	|	...	|	...	|	|	...	...	...	...	0905
Paris M'parnasse **300** a.	...	...	...	...	1130	...	...	...	1435	...	...	...	...	1850	...	2130	...	2150	...	2250z	2345	...	...	...	...	...

OR NOTES SEE TABLE 321 BELOW *Services in this table are subject to alteration on May 10, 11*

TOULOUSE - NARBONNE 321

For night train Hendaye / Bordeaux - Marseille - Nice see Table **355**; for night train Nantes - Marseille - Nice see Table **320** or **355**

km		3731 [R] ♦	3733 [R] ♦	2 b	TGV 5301 ⊗	2 ⊗	TGV 5171 ♦ ⊗	4652 4653 ★ ⊕	E	4654 4655 ★	a ⊗	4656 4657 ★ ⊖	4660 4661 ★ u	TGV 5315 Ⓑ h⊗	4659 ★ F	⚒ 2	TGV 5186 L⊗	4662 4663 ★	3631 ★	2 Ⓐ	Ⓑ ⊗	Ⓐ 2⊗	4664 4665 ★ ⊗	4666 4667 ★ ⑤⑦ v	4678 4679 [R] ♦Z
	Paris Austerlitz **310** d.	2156	2202	...	...	...	...	...	...	...	...	...	...	...	...	...	...	...	1017s	...	...	...	...	...	...
	Nantes **292** d.	|	|	...	...	...	...	...	...	...	...	...	...	...	...	...	...	...	|	...	...	...	...	...	...
	Bordeaux **320** d.	|	|	...	...	...	0539	0552	...	0816	...	1057	1209	...	...	...	...	1431	|	...	...	...	1627	...	...
	Hendaye **325** d.	|	|	...	...	...	|	|	...	|	...	|	|	...	...	...	...	|	|	...	...	...	|	...	1831
0	**Toulouse Matabiau** d.	|	0509	...	0655	0705	0749	0803	0809	1042	1154	1306	1419	1434	1517	...	1608	1649	1638	...	1732	1832	1848	2045	0017
55	Castelnaudary d.	0519	0544	...	|	0743	|	|	0849	1112	1227	|	|	|	1546	1601	|	|	1719	...	1804	1902	|	|	|
91	Carcassonne d.	0541	0604	0714	0742	0806	0834	|	0903	1133	1252	|	1511	1520	1607	1627	1654	|	1737	1804	1825	1924	1935	2131	|
128	Lézignan d.	0602	0625	0735	|	0825	|	|	|	|	1312	|	|	|	|	1649	|	|	|	1826	...	|	|	|	|
150	**Narbonne** a.	0616	0637	0748	0809	0838	0901	|	0931	1201	1325	|	1539	1547	1636	1703	1725	|	1805	1840	...	1954	2004	2202	|
	Marseille **355** a.	|	|	...	1040	...	|	1142	|	1453	...	1639	1825	|	1926	...	|	2018	|	...	...	|	2243	0043	|
	Nice **360** a.	|	|	...	...	...	|	1430	|	...	...	1923	...	|	2217	...	|	...	|	...	...	|	...	...	|
	Lyon Part Dieu **350/1** a.	|	|	...	...	...	1154	...	|	...	...	...	...	1846	...	...	2020	...	|	...	...	|	...	...	0644
	Genève **345** a.	|	|	...	...	...	...	...	|	...	...	...	...	...	...	...	...	...	|	...	...	|	...	...	0845
	Perpignan **355** a.	0718	0742	...	...	...	...	...	1030	...	...	...	...	...	...	...	...	...	1902	...	...	2100	...	...	...
	Cerbère **355** a.	0813	0839	...	...	...	...	...	1113	...	...	...	...	...	...	...	...	...	1951	...	...	...	...	...	...
	Portbou **355** a.	0821	0854	...	...	...	...	...	...	...	...	...	...	...	...	...	...	...	...	...	...	...	...	...	...

	4778 4779 [R] ♦Z	Ⓐ 2p	⚒ 2	4752 4753 ★	3630 ★	4754 4755 ★ ⊙	TGV 5355 Ⓑ h	4756 4757 ★ ⊙	2	TGV 5104 L	Ⓐ 2	4768 ★ G	4758 4759 ★ c	Yb	Ⓐ	Ⓐ 2	4762 4763 ★	4764 4765 ★	Ⓒ 2	Ⓐ 2	E	TGV 5116 ♦	4766 ★ ⑤⑦ ♦w	TGV 5398	3730 [R] ♦
Cerbère **355** d.	...	...	...	...	0748	...	...	...	1039	...	...	...	...	...	...	...	...	...	...	...	1730	...	...	...	2121
Perpignan **355** d.	...	...	...	...	0842	...	...	...	1119	...	...	...	...	...	...	...	...	...	...	...	1812	...	...	...	2214
Genève **345** d.	2044	...	...	...	|	...	...	...	|	...	...	...	...	...	...	...	...	...	...	...	|	...	...	...	|
Lyon Part Dieu **350/1** d.	2250	...	...	...	|	...	0710	...	|	0937	...	...	...	...	...	...	...	...	...	...	|	1707	...	...	|
Nice **360** d.	|	...	...	...	|	...	|	...	|	|	...	0856	1008	...	...	...	...	1335	...	...	|	|	...	...	|
Marseille **355** d.	|	...	...	0554	|	0714	|	0920	|	|	...	1153	1254	...	...	...	1500	1619	...	...	|	|	1912	1936	|
arbonne d.	|	0649	0744	0840	0938	0955	1002	|	1210	1238	1310	1449	|	1533	...	1710	1745	|	1845	1847	1912	1958	2148	2204	2305
ézignan d.	|	0703	0759	|	|	|	|	|	1224	|	1323	|	|	1546	...	1723	|	|	1859	1901	|	|	|	|	2319
:arcassonne d.	|	0725	0819	0911	1010	1027	1034	|	1245	1312	1342	1521	|	1608	1723	1742	1817	|	1919	1922	1944	2028	2220	2236	2340
:astelnaudary d.	|	0746	0840	|	1031	1047	|	|	1307	|	1405*	1543	|	1630	1746	...	|	|	...	1943	2006	|	|	|	2359
oulouse Matabiau a.	0511	0831	0917	0958	1101	1117	1121	1305	1345	1356	...	1612	1623	1703	1822	...	1903	1951	...	...	2037	2112	2306	2321	0029
Irún **325** a.	1107	...	...	|	|	|	...	|	...	...	...	...	|	...	...	...	|	|	...	...	...	|	|	...	|
Bordeaux **320** a.	...	...	...	1208	|	1331	...	1512	...	...	...	...	1829	...	...	...	2121	2157	...	...	...	2320	0117	...	|
Nantes **292** a.	...	...	...	...	|	...	...	...	...	...	...	...	...	...	...	...	...	...	...	...	...	...	...	...	|
Paris Austerlitz **310** a.	...	...	...	...	1740r	...	...	...	...	...	...	...	...	...	...	...	...	...	...	...	...	...	...	...	0727

– **NOTES FOR TABLES 320/1** (LISTED BY TRAIN NUMBER):

730 – *CORAIL LUNÉA* – 🛏 1,2 cl. and [2] (reclining) Cerbère - Paris. Not Dec. 24, 31. Additional relief train **3732** runs on certain peak dates – see Table **355**.
731 – *CORAIL LUNÉA* – 🛏 1,2 cl. and [2] (reclining) Paris - Portbou. Not Dec. 24, 31. Additional relief train **3733** runs on certain peak dates – see Table **355**.
733 – Dec. 21, 28, Apr. 30, May 7 only. 🛏 1,2 cl. and [2] (reclining) Paris - Portbou.
621 – *CORAIL LUNÉA* – 🛏 1,2 cl. and [2] (reclining) Bordeaux - Nice. Not Dec. 24, 31. Starts from Hendaye on dates in Table **305**.
624/5 – ⑤⑦ (not Mar. 23), also Dec. 21 - Jan. 6 (not Dec. 24, 31), Feb. 8 - Mar. 9, Mar. 24, Apr. 4 - May 4, May 7 - 12. 🛏 1,2 cl. and [2] (reclining) Nantes - Nice and v.v.
678/9 – *CORAIL LUNÉA* – 🛏 1,2 cl. and [2] (reclining) Hendaye - Lyon - Genève.
720 – *CORAIL LUNÉA* – 🛏 1,2 cl. and [2] (reclining) Nice - Bordeaux. Not Dec. 24, 31. Continues to Irún on dates in Table **305**.
724/5 – ⑤⑦ (not Mar. 23), also Dec. 21 - Jan. 6 (not Dec. 24, 31), Feb. 8 - Mar. 9, Mar. 24, Apr. 4 - May 4, May 7 - 12. 🛏 1,2 cl. and [2] (reclining) Nice - Nantes. Subject to delay morning of Apr. 6, 13, 20, 27 (arrive Nantes 1036).
766 – [12] Toulon - Marseille - Bordeaux.
778/9 – *CORAIL LUNÉA* – 🛏 1,2 cl. and [2] (reclining) Genève - Lyon - Irún.
116 – [12] and 🍷 Dijon - Lyon - Bordeaux.
171 – [12] and 🍷 Bordeaux - Toulouse - Lyon - Dijon.
218 – [12] and 🍷 Lille Flandres - Charles de Gaulle ✈ - Bordeaux - Toulouse (Table **11**).
264 – [12] and 🍷 Toulouse - Bordeaux - Charles de Gaulle ✈ - Lille Europe (Table **11**).

– ⑥⑦ from June 21.
– ⑤⑥⑦ Dec. 21 - Jan. 6, Feb. 15 - Mar. 9, Apr. 11 - 27 (also Dec. 25, Jan. 1, Mar. 21, 22, 24, Apr. 30, May 1, 4, 7, 8, 12).
– ⑤⑥⑦ Dec. 23 - Jan. 6, Feb. 15 - Mar. 9, Apr. 12 - 27 (also Dec. 25, Jan. 1, Mar. 22, 24, Apr. 30, May 1, 4, 7, 8, 12). On Jan. 4, Feb. 15 Castelnaudary 1612, Toulouse 1700.
– [12] Toulouse - Lyon - Charles de Gaulle ✈ - Lille Europe and v.v. (Table **11**).
– Daily to Agen, Ⓑ to Toulouse.
– Daily to Carcassonne, Ⓑ to Toulouse. Subject to alteration Mar. 17 - Apr. 12.
– ⑤⑦, also daily Dec. 21 - Jan. 6 (not Dec. 24, 31), Feb. 8 - Mar. 9, Mar. 24 (not Mar. 23), Apr. 4 - May 12 (not May 5, 6).

a – To Avignon Centre on Ⓐ.
b – To / from Avignon Centre.
c – On ⑥ Jan. 5 - Feb. 9 arrive Bordeaux 1848. On ①–④ Mar. 17 - Apr. 10 (not Mar. 24) Toulouse 1728, Bordeaux 1933. On ⑤ Mar. 21 - Apr. 11 arrive Bordeaux 1842.
e – Also Dec. 25, Jan. 1, Mar. 24, May 12.
f – Also Apr. 30, May 7; not May 2, 9.
h – Not May 1, 8.
n – Not Dec. 25, Jan. 1, Mar. 24, May 12.
p – Arrive Toulouse 0845 Dec. 10 - 21, Jan. 2 - Feb. 22.
q – Also Dec. 25, Jan. 1, Mar. 24, May 12; not Mar. 23, May 11.
r – Arrival times vary between 1740 and 1810.
s – 1006 on Mar. 10 - 14, 20, 21; 0956 on Mar. 19, 26, 27.
t – Also May 1, 8.
u – Timings vary (depart Bordeaux 1149 Feb. 18 - 22, 25 - 29, Mar. 3 - 7, 13, 14; 1204 Jan. 7 - 27, 29 - 31, Feb. 1 - 4, 8; 1215 Dec. 9 - 16 and from Apr. 12).
v – Also Dec. 24, Jan. 1, Mar. 24, Apr. 30, May 7, 12; not Mar. 23, May 2, 11.
w – Also Dec. 24, Jan. 1, Mar. 24, Apr. 30, May 7, 12; not Mar. 23, May 2, 9.
x – 1957 on ①–④ Mar. 17 - Apr. 10 (not Mar. 24).
y – On Ⓐ Feb. 18 - Mar. 14 runs as train **3852**.
z – On ①–④ May 26 - July 10 arrive Paris **Austerlitz** 2354.

TGV – [R], supplement payable, 🍷.
★ – *CORAIL TÉOZ*, [R], 🍷.
❖ – Timings vary - please check before travelling.
⊙ – Arrives up to 20 minutes later on certain dates.
⊡ – Not Dec. 24, 31. Subject to alteration Feb. 18 - Mar. 14.
⊖ – Departs up to 10 minutes earlier on certain dates.
⊕ – Depart 5 minutes earlier Jan. 7 - Feb. 8, Feb. 18 - 22.
⊗ – Depart 5 minutes earlier Jan. 7 - Feb. 8.
△ – Runs approx 45 minutes later Jan. 14 - 18.
▽ – On Feb. 18 - 20, 27 - 29, Mar. 3 - 7, 10 - 14 runs later (Bordeaux 1454, Toulouse 1717).
▷ – On Ⓐ Feb. 18 - Mar. 14 runs 55 minutes earlier Toulouse - Bordeaux.
* – Not Mar. 17 - Apr. 11.

322 TOULOUSE - CASTRES - MAZAMET

Most trains 2nd class

km		Ⓐ		❖	❖	Ⓐ	Ⓐ	Ⓐ			
0	**Toulouse Matabiau** ... d.	0646	0746	1146	1346	1546	1644	1726	1746	1846	2046
86	Castres ... a.	0753	0852	1255	1453	1653	1753	1834	1854	1953	2153
105	**Mazamet** ... a.	0820	0923	1320	1520	1720	1818	1903	1927	2020	2220

	Ⓐ	Ⓐ	Ⓐ		Ⓐ❖	❖	❖	Ⓐ		
Mazamet ... d.	0531	0556	0631	0731	0931	1126	1431	1731	1821	1931
Castres ... d.	0555	0627	0657	0756	0956	1157	1456	1756	1857	1957
Toulouse Matabiau d.	0704	0736	0804	0904	1104	1304	1603	1903	2004	2102

❖ – Subject to alteration Feb. 11 – 15, 18 – 22.

323 TOULOUSE - ALBI - RODEZ - MILLAU

Most trains 2nd class

km		Ⓐ			🅁P		Ⓐ		Ⓐd				Ⓑ🚌		Ⓐ		⚒🚌	Ⓐ			Ⓐ		Ⓐ	▲
0	**Toulouse Matabiau 316** ... d.	0620	...	0721	...	0900	1018	1120	...	1158	1300	1420	...	1600	1700	1712	...	1731	1800	...	1815	1900	1928	2120
54	Gaillac **316** ... d.	0701	...	0806	...	0953	1104	1205	...	1244	1353	1501	...	1652	1742	1756	...	1820	1854	...	1905	1939	2021	2214
58	Tessonnières **316** ... d.	|	...	|	0828	1001	|	|	...	1249	1358	|	...	1657	1747	|	...	1824	|	...	1911	|	2027	2222
75	**Albi Ville** ... d.	0715	...	0826	0906	1017	1117	1224	...	1305	1412	1515	...	1711	1803	1815	...	1841	1909	...	1925	2001	2044	2237
92	Carmaux ... d.	0732	...	0845	0923	1032	1132	1241	...	1320	1429	1532	...	1728	...	1831	...	1903	1925	...	...	2018	2101	2252
158	**Rodez** ... d.	0830	0852	0947c	...	...	1230r	1345	1427	...	...	1628	1636	...	...	1937	1942	...	2025k	2106	...	2119k	...	...
202	Sévérac-le-Château **332** ... d.	...	0936	...	...	...	...	...	1511	...	...	...	1717	...	...	...	2023	...	...	2147	...	...	...	...
232	**Millau 332** ... a.	...	1003	...	...	...	...	...	1538	...	...	...	1751	...	...	...	2053	...	...	2214	...	...	...	...

	Ⓐ	Ⓐ			Ⓐ				Ⓐ🚌			Ⓐ	Ⓐ	Ⓐ				Ⓐe	Ⓐ	†🚌		🅁P	Ⓒ	★
Millau 332 ... d.	...	...	...	...	...	0618	...	...	0900	...	...	1026	...	...	...	...	...	1605	...	1650	...	...	1917	...
Sévérac-le-Château **332** ... d.	...	...	...	...	...	0648	...	...	0930	...	...	1057	...	...	...	...	...	1636	...	1725	...	...	1949	...
Rodez ... d.	...	...	...	...	0633n	0729	0744f	0833c	1014	1024c	...	1138	1233	...	1433	...	1634	1716	1731	1808	1824	...	2033	2058
Carmaux ... d.	0514	0554	0624	0654	0733	...	0846	0933	...	1133	1205	...	1330	1455	1533	1654	1731	...	1832	...	1926	2103	...	2153
Albi Ville ... d.	0531	0612	0642	0716	0750	...	0904	0949	...	1150	1223	...	1346	1516	1550	1720	1748	...	1849	...	1943	2122	...	2209
Tessonnières **316** ... d.	0543	0629	0657	0731	|	...	|	|	...	|	1237	...	|	1532	|	1736	|	...	|	...	|	2137	...	|
Gaillac **316** ... d.	0547	0633	0700	0735	0805	...	0924	1004	...	1204	1242	...	1404	1536	1603	1741	1805	...	1914	...	2002	...	...	2225
Toulouse Matabiau 316 ... a.	0635	0725	0749	0830	0843	...	1007	1043	...	1244	1329	...	1449	1625	1641	1832	1841	...	1950	...	2043	...	...	2304

P – 🛏 1, 2 cl. and [2] (reclining) Paris - Carmaux and v.v. For days of running see Table **316**.
c – Subject to alteration Feb. 26, 27, 28, Ⓐ Mar. 3 – 28.
d – Not Feb. 11 - Mar. 7, May 27, 28, 29, June 3, 4, 5.
e – Not ①–④ Feb. 11 - Mar. 6, May 27, 28, 29, June 3, 4, 5.
f – Not Feb. 26 – 28.
k – Not Mar. 20.
n – Not Mar. 21.
r – 1318 Mar. 3 – 28.
▲ – Subject to alteration Albi - Carmaux on ①–④ Jan. 14 - Feb. 14 and ①–④ June 2 – 12. Subject to alteration Toulouse - Albi on ①–④ Mar. 31 - Apr. 29 (also May 5, 6).
★ – Subject to alteration Rodez - Carmaux on Mar. 19, 20, 25. Subject to alteration Albi - Toulouse on ①–④ Mar. 31 - Apr. 29 (also May 5, 6).

324 PAU - CANFRANC

Subject to alteration Mar. 29, 30

km		Ⓐb	d	b		Ⓑ	⚒	†	⚒	⑤f	
0	**Pau** ... d.	0730	0905	1210	1345	1532	1705	1749	1831	1957	2131
36	Oloron-Ste-Marie ... a.	0808	0943	1248	1423	1610	1743	1827	1909	2035	2209
36	Oloron-Ste-Marie 🚌 d.	*0816*	*0950*	...	*1440*	...	...	...	...	...	...
90	**Canfranc** ... 🚌 a.	*0937*	*1111*	...	*1601*	...	...	...	...	...	...

	Ⓐy	Ⓒ	Ⓐc	d	Ⓐb	Ⓒ		⚒◇	†	⚒
Canfranc ... 🚌 d.	...	...	...	...	*1114*	...	*1257*	...	*1654*	*173*
Oloron-Ste-Marie 🚌 a.	...	...	...	...	*1235*	...	*1418*	...	*1815*	*185*
Oloron-Ste-Marie ... d.	0647	0719	0813	1052	1255	1255	1428	1748	1832	1914
Pau ... a.	0725	0757	0851	1130	1333	1333	1506	1826	1910	1952

b – Subject to alteration on Ⓐ Mar. 31 - Apr. 11, May 26 - June 20.
c – Subject to alteration on Ⓐ Jan. 7 - 25, Mar. 31 - Apr. 11, May 26 - June 20.
d – Subject to alteration on Ⓐ Jan. 7 - 25, Mar. 31 - Apr. 25, May 26 - June 20.
f – Also Apr. 30, May 7; not May 2, 9.
y – On ① (also Dec. 26, Jan. 2, Mar. 25, May 2, 9, 13; not Dec. 24, 31) d. 0630, a. 0708.
◇ – Additional journeys: 1615 Ⓐ, 1640 †, 2201 †
🚌 – By 🚌 Oloron - Canfranc and v.v. (rail tickets valid).

325 HENDAYE - BAYONNE - TARBES - TOULOUSE

km		Ⓐ ‡		⚒ r	Ⓐ	14140 ⊕		14142 △		14150 h	k	Ⓑ	⑤ f	A	†	Ⓐ	14132 ⚒	14132 †	①–④ m	Ⓐ	†	Ⓐ	4678 4679 🅁 G	3990 🅁 Y	†
0	**Hendaye 305** ... d.	...	...	...	...	0604	...	0835	...	...	...	...	...	...	...	1530	...	...	1628	...	*1701*	...	1831	...	*1922*
13	St Jean de Luz **305** ... d.	...	...	...	...	0615	...	0847	...	...	...	...	...	...	...	1542	...	...	1639	...	*1715*	...	1843	...	*1934*
26	Biarritz **305** ... § d.	...	...	...	...	0628	...	0859	...	...	...	...	...	...	...	1554	...	...	1651	...	*1728*	...	1855	...	*194*
36	**Bayonne 305** ... § a.	...	...	...	...	0638	...	0912	...	...	...	...	...	...	...	1603	...	...	1700	...	*1738*	...	1905	...	*195*
36	**Bayonne 305** ... § d.	...	...	0544g	0610	0659	...	0936	...	1215	...	...	...	...	...	▬	1622	1622	...	1717	1808	1820	1907	...	2008
	Dax **305** ... d.	...	...	|	|	|	...	|	...	|	...	...	...	...	...	...	|	|	...	|	|	|	1958	...	|
87	Puyoô **305** ... d.	...	...	0618g	0700	0735	...	|	...	1254	...	...	...	...	...	...	1657	1657	...	1757	1843	1858	2017	...	2057
101	Orthez **305** ... d.	...	...	0630g	0711	0747	...	|	...	1305	...	...	...	...	...	†	1709	1709	...	1807	1854	1908	2029	...	2111
141	**Pau 305** ... d.	...	0558a	0701	0739	0814	...	1046	...	1335	...	...	1545	1601d	...		1734	1736	...	1834	1921	1934	2058	...	2142
180	Lourdes **305** ... d.	0553	0630b	0735	...	0846	...	1114	...	1406	...	...	1619	1634	...	1754	1807	1807	...	1910	1956	...	2131	...	2214
201	**Tarbes 305** ... d.	0609	0648	0753	...	0903	1048j	1130	...	1423	1444	...	1636	1650	...	1810	1825	1825	...	1926	2012	...	2148	...	2229
238	Lannemezan ... d.	0631	0715	0831	...	0928	1113	|	...	|	1508	...	1712	1714	...	1839	1854	1859	...	...	...	...	2213	...	...
◧	Luchon ... ▶ d.	|	|	|	...	|	|	|	1112e	|	|	...	|	|	1723	|	|	|	...	...	...	...	|	2136	...
255	Montréjeau ... d.	0642	0727	0843	...	0940	1124	|	1211	|	1520	1611	1723	1726	1829	1852	1906	1912	...	...	...	...	|	2254	...
268	St Gaudens ... d.	0652	0737	0853	...	0950	1134	|	1223	|	1530	1621	1733	1735	1839	1903	1918	1924	...	...	...	...	2234	2305	...
293	Boussens ... d.	0706	0751	0908	...	1004	1149	|	1237	|	1544	1637	1747	1749	1859	1920	1935	1941	...	...	...	...	|	2321	...
359	**Toulouse Matabiau** ... a.	0755	0849	0959	...	1038	1222	1252	1325	1553k	1621	1725	1837	1837	1950	1958	2019	2020	...	...	...	...	2321	0004	...

	Ⓐ	⚒	3991 🅁 W	4778 4779 🅁 G	Ⓐ	⚒		⊗	14131 14137 ▽	⚒ ▷	14143 14145 ⊖	⚒	Ⓐ	⑤	14147 14149	Ⓐ		Ⓑ	⑤†	Ⓐ	Ⓐ			⑤⑦ v	
Toulouse Matabiau ... d.	...	...	0541	0609	0614	0715	0731	0908	1008	1209	1357	1437	...	1557	1631y	1640	1715	1715	1715	1731	1811	1936	2115	2341	...
Boussens ... d.	...	...	0623	|	0710	|	0824	0943	1048	1301	1437	1528	...	1637	|	1737	1756	1756	1756	1827	1902	2026	2202	0019	...
St Gaudens ... d.	...	...	0638	0656	0733	0817	0837	0958	1104	1322	1449	1544	...	1652	|	1755	1811	1811	1811	1847	1915	2042	2216	0033	...
Montréjeau ... d.	...	...	0706	|	0744	0827	0855	1008	1115	1333	1500	1552	...	1701	|	1804	1821	1821	1821	1856	1925	2053	2226	0047	...
Luchon ... ▶ a.	...	...	0805	|	|	|	0948	|	|	|	|	...	...	|	|	...	|	|	|	...	|	|	|	|	...
Lannemezan ... d.	...	...	...	0716	0755	0838	...	1019	1127	1344	1512	...	...	1713	|	...	1833	1833	1833	...	1936	2107	2237	|	...
Tarbes 305 ... d.	...	0622	...	0742	0823	0906	...	1042	1153	1411	1537	...	...	1737	1750	...	1855	1857	1857	...	1959	2137	2305	0126	...
Lourdes **305** ... d.	...	0639	...	0800	...	0920p	...	...	1210	1425	1553	...	...	...	1807	...	...	1912	1912	...	...	2154	2318	0143	...
Pau 305 ... d.	0630	0713	...	0833	...	...	...	...	1244	1451z	1625	...	1755	...	1838	...	...	1942	1944	...	...	2228	2348z	0212	...
Orthez **305** ... d.	0658	0739	...	0900	...	...	...	...	1310	...	1653	...	1822	...	|	...	...	...	2010	...	...	2259	...	...	...
Puyoô **305** ... d.	0708	0750	...	|	...	...	...	...	1322	...	1705	...	1832	...	|	...	...	...	2021	...	...	2310	...	...	...
Dax ... d.	|	|	...	0950	...	...	...	...	|	...	|	...	|	...	|	...	...	...	|	...	...	|	...	...	...
Bayonne 305 ... § a.	0748	0825	...	1021	...	...	...	...	1355	...	1745	...	1910	...	1944	...	...	...	2056	...	...	2343	...	...	...
Bayonne 305 ... § d.	...	...	...	1021	...	...	...	...	...	...	1802	...	...	...	2004	...	...	...	2116	...	...	...	...	...	...
Biarritz **305** ... § d.	...	...	...	1034	...	...	...	...	...	...	1814	...	...	...	2015	...	...	...	2127	...					
St Jean de Luz **305** ... d.	...	...	...	1047	...	...	...	...	...	...	1830	...	...	...	2029	...	...	...	2137	...					
Hendaye **305** ... a.	...	...	...	1058	...	...	...	...	...	...	1843	...	...	...	2038	...	...	...	2148	...					
Irún 305 ... a.	...	...	...	1107	...	...	...	...	...	...	1850	...	...	...	2046	...	...	...	...	...	...	...	...	...	...

Subject to alteration Mar. 29, 30. Timings may vary from June 1.

A – ①②③④⑥ (not Dec. 25, Jan. 1, Mar. 24, Apr. 30, May 1, 7, 8, 12).
G – *CORAIL LUNÉA* – ⑤† (②–⑦ Dec. 21 - Jan. 6; daily Feb. 8 - Mar. 9 and Apr. 4 - May 4; also May 7, 10; not Mar. 23). 🛏 1, 2 cl. and [2] (reclining) Hendaye - Lyon - Genève and Genève - Lyon - Irún.
W – From Paris on ⑤⑥ Dec. 14 - Mar. 28, ⑤ from Apr. 4 (also Apr. 30, May 7; not May 2, 9). 🛏 1, 2 cl. Paris Austerlitz (d. 2156) - Luchon.
Y – Ⓒ Dec. 9 - Mar. 24 (not Dec. 23, 30, Mar. 23); ⑦ from Mar. 30. 🛏 1, 2 cl. Luchon - Paris Austerlitz (arrive 0727).

a – Ⓐ only.
b – Ⓑ only.
d – ⑥ only.
e – ⚒ only.
f – Also Apr. 30, May 7; not May 2, 9.
g – ① (not Dec. 24, 31, Mar. 24, May 12).
h – Not Dec. 25, Jan. 1, Mar. 24, May 12.
j – 1023 Mar. 31 - Apr. 3.
k – 25 – 29 minutes later Mar. 31 - Apr. 3.
m – Not Dec. 25, Jan. 1, Mar. 24, Apr. 30, May 1, 7, 8, 12.
p – ①⑥ (not Mar. 24, May 12).
r – Not Dec. 26, Jan. 2, Mar. 25, 29, May 13.
v – Not Mar. 28, Apr. 25, May 2, 9.
y – 1624 on ⑤**f**.
z – ⑤⑥ (not Mar. 29).
◧ – Montréjeau - Luchon is 35 km.
⊕ – On ①–④ Mar. 10 – 20 runs 39 – 40 mins later Lourdes - Toulouse. On Mar. 26, 27, 28 runs 31 – 32 mins later Tarbes - Toulouse. May 26 – 30 Toulouse d. 1050.
⊗ – Runs 10 min earlier Jan. 2, 3, Ⓐ Jan. 28 - Feb. 15. On Ⓐ from May 26 runs up to one hour earlier.
⊖ – Timings vary up to 5 minutes later.
‡ – 12 minutes later Jan. 28 - Feb. 15 (also Jan. 2, 3).
△ – On Mar. 26, 27, 28 runs 25 - 31 minutes earlier Tarbes - Lourdes. Mar. 31 - Apr. 3 departs Pau 1043, Lourdes 1112, Tarbes 1131, arrives Toulouse 1336.
▽ – Runs up to 20 mins earlier Feb. 25 - 29, Mar. 3 - 7, up to 34 mins earlier from May 26. Depart Toulouse 1004 certain dates Jan. 2 - Feb. 15.
▷ – Subject to alteration Jan. 26, Feb. 2 and from May 26
§ – 🚌 services are available from Bayonne and Biarritz stations to Biarritz town.
▶ – 🚌 connections Luchon - Montréjeau and v.v.: From Luchon 0620 ⚒, 0830, 0940 ⚒, 1353, 1616 ⚒, 1755 ⚒, 1945 †. From Montréjeau 0720 ⚒, 0800 ⚒, 1130, 1405 ⚒, 1527 †, 1557 ⚒, 1830, 2103. Journey 50 - 53 mins.

BRIVE and LE MONT DORE - CLERMONT FERRAND — 326

Some 2nd class only

km		⚒	⚒	⑦G	🚌 ①g	⑦G	🚌	4490/1 ⑤h	🚌 ⑤h	4492/3 ⑥e	Ⓐ	🚌 ⑥	⚒P	🚌	🚌 Ⓒ	🚌 ⑥	†w	🚌 H	🚌 ⑤d	⑤A	⑤B	⑤z	⚒	🚌 ⑤d	Ⓐ	†w
0	*Bordeaux* **306** d.	...	...	...	...	...	...	0734	❖	0908	...	...	...	...	...	...	...	...	...	...	...	...	...	...	...	...
203	**Brive la Gaillarde** d.	...	0622	0648	...	...	...	1001	...	1111	...	...	1314	...	...	...	...	...	...	1540	1540	1615	1734	...	...	1816
229	Tulle d.	...	0652	0713	...	...	...	1037	...	1146	...	...	1348	...	...	...	...	...	...	1606	1606	1645	1808	...	...	1843
◇	**Limoges** ▶ d.	...	|	|	...	0645	...	|	...	|	...	...	|	...	...	...	...	...	...	|	|	|	|	...	1714v	|
282	Meymac ▶ d.	...	0746	0805	...	0822	...	1135	...	1246	...	...	1437	...	...	...	...	...	...	1705	1705	1743	1857	...	1913	1943
295	**Ussel** ▶ a.	...	0758	0817	...	0835	...	1149	...	1300	...	...	1450	...	...	...	...	...	...	1718	1718	1756	1910	...	1925	1955
295	**Ussel** d.	...	▬	...	0820	0839	1004	▬	1200	1302	...	...	...	1526	1620	...	...	...	...	1721	*1726*	1800	▬	...	1930	1958
313	Eygurande-Merlines d.	...	⚒	...	0842	0856	1024	...	1222	1322	...	...	...	1548	1636	...	...	...	...	1739	*1748*	1818	...	...	1948	2020
*13	**Le Mont Dore** d.	0539	*0810*c	...	|	|	|	1102	*1218*c	|	1424	1419	...	*1546*c	|	1655	1653	1730	1735	|	|	|	🚌	1943	|	*2013*c
*8	La Bourboule d.	0546	*0818*c	...	|	|	|	1110	*1226*c	|	1431	1427	...	*1552*c	|	1703	1700	1738	1743	|	|	|	⑤d	1951	|	*2021*c
335	Laqueuille d.	0557	0853	...	0904	0920	1044	1121	1244	1348	1442	1440	...	1610	1705	1715	1718	1750	1755	1804	*1810*	1842	1850	2003	2013	2046
395	Royat-Chamalières d.	0708	1002	...	|	...	...	1225	|	1453	1548	1547	...	|	...	|	1829	|	...	1923	|	...	|	...	2119	2154
400	**Clermont Ferrand** a.	0717	1010	...	1005	...	...	1235	1335	1500	1557	1602	...	1701	...	1815	1837	1855	...	1932	*1901*	...	1951	...	2125	2202

	🚌 ①g	①–⑥	🚌 ⚒L	⑦G	🚌	🚌	🚌 ⑥m	⑧n	🚌	4595/4 ⑦r	🚌 ⑤h	4591/0 ⑤h	🚌	⑦G	🚌 ⑥	🚌 ⑥	⑤d	🚌 †w	†w	⑧w	†w	🚌 H	⑤d	🚌 ⑤d	†w	🚌 ⑤d
Clermont Ferrand d.	0630	0650	...	0807	1036	...	1240	1243	...	1407	1415	...	...	...	1737	...	*1737*c	1747	...	1758	1842	1940	2000	...	2035	*2136*
Royat-Chamalières d.	|	0659	...	0814	|	...	|	1252	...	1415	|	...	...	...	|	...	|	|	...	1807	1850	|	2007	...	2044	|
Laqueuille d.	0731	0803	0816	0926	1137	1146	1353	1401	1420	1525	1515	...	1615	1717	1837	1842	1847	1837	...	1921	1955	2040	2124	2129	2154	2235
La Bourboule a.	|	▬	0829	0938	|	1158	1406	1412	|	*1548*c	*1538*c	...	1628	|	1849	|	|	|	...	1932	|	2052	2136	|	*2211*c	2248
Le Mont Dore a.	|	...	0837	0944	|	1204	1414	1418	|	*1556*c	*1544*c	...	1636	|	1857	|	|	|	...	1938	|	2100	2142	|	*2219*c	2256
Eygurande-Merlines d.	0753	...	▬	▬	1159	▬	...	...	1440	1551	1540	...	▬	1742	...	1900	1911	1857	...	...	2020	...	...	2147	2218	...
Ussel a.	0815	⚒	⑦w	...	1221	...	...	...	1500	1609	1604	...	...	1758	...	1920	1927	1917	...	...	2037	...	...	2207	2234	...
Ussel ▶ d.	...	0830	0847	⚒q	...	1231	...	...	...	1612	...	1612	1612	...	...	...	1928	...	1928	...	2039	...	...	...	2235	...
Meymac ▶ d.	...	0843	0900	0900	...	1245	...	...	...	1627	...	1627	1627	...	...	...	1942	...	1942	...	2052	...	...	...	2248	...
Limoges ▶ a.	...	1012x	|	|	...	|	...	...	...	|	...	|	|	...	...	...	|	...	|	...	|	...	...	...	|	...
Tulle d.	...	...	0954	0954	...	1343	...	...	...	1734	...	1734	1734	...	...	...	2035	...	2035	...	2148	...	...	...	2343	...
Brive la Gaillarde a.	...	...	1017	1021	...	1409	...	...	...	1757	...	1757	1757	...	...	...	2057	...	2057	...	2211	...	...	...	0004	...
Bordeaux **306** a.	...	...	...	...	...	...	...	...	...	2018	...	2018	...	...	...	...	...	...	...	...	...	...	...	...	...	...

LIMOGES - USSEL

	Ⓐ	⑦G	Ⓐ	⑥	‡	⑤z	⑥	H	†	⑤d	
Limoges d.	0555j	0645	1023	1132	1325	1700	1700	1714	1731	1834	2034
Meymac d.	0731	0822	1157	1304	1457	1913	1913	1913	1905	2009	2206
Ussel a.	0743	0835	1210	1316	1510	1925	1925	1925	1918	2021	2219

	①g	⚒	⚒		⑥m	⑧n‡	†w	⑤⑥z	†	⑧
Ussel d.	*0534*	0624	0830	...	*1231*	1249	1521	*1612*	1629	1801
Meymac d.	0552	0637	0843	...	1302	1302	1534	1634	1643	1814
Limoges a.	0727	0813x	1012x	...	1437	1437y	1705	1811	1815	1948

A – ⑤ to June 6 (also Apr. 30, May 7; not May 2, 9).
B – ⑤ from June 13. By 🚌 Ussel - Clermont.
G – Until Mar. 9.
H – ①–④ (not Dec. 25, Jan. 1, Mar. 24, Apr. 30, May 1, 7, 8, 12).
L – Runs 17 minutes later on ⑥.
P – From Périgueux (Table **306**).
c – Connection by 🚌.
d – Also Apr. 30, May 7.
e – Also May 8; not May 10.
g – Also Dec. 26, Jan. 2, Mar. 25, May 13; not Mar. 24, May 12.
h – Also Dec. 26, 27, Jan. 2, 3, Apr. 30, May 7; not May 2, 9.
j – 0546 on Apr. 28, May 2, 5, 9, 13.
m – Also May 8.
n – Not May 8.
q – Also Mar. 23, May 8, 11.
r – Also Dec. 25, Jan. 1, Mar. 24, May 12; not Dec. 23, 30, Mar. 23, May 11.
v – 1700 on ⑤z
w – Not Mar. 23, May 11.
x – Subject to alteration on Apr. 12.
y – Subject to alteration on Apr. 6.
z – Also Apr. 30, May 7; not May 2, 9.
❖ – Subject to confirmation.
‡ – Runs 2–3 minutes **earlier** Mar. 17–21, 25–28.
◇ – Limoges - Meymac: 98 km.
* – Distance from Laqueuille.
▶ – See below main table.

LIMOGES - MONTLUÇON - LYON — 327

Most trains 2nd class

km		🚌 ⚒	🚌 ⚒	①g	⑥▲	4403 ⚒	4480/1 △	🚌 Ⓐ		⑤	
	Bordeaux **306** d.	...	...	...	...	...	1047	...	...	...	...
0	**Limoges** d.	...	...	0559e	0805	...	1313	...	1553	1840	...
78	Guéret d.	...	...	0704	0908	...	1416	...	1705	1944	...
156	**Montluçon 329** d.	0520	0755	0757	1007	...	1515	1748	1804	2045	...
224	Gannat **329** d.	|	|	...	1108	...	1619	1906	...	...	...
247	**St Germain des Fossés** d.	|	|	...	1121	1139	|	|	...	...	...
	Vichy **330** a.	0645	0927	...	...	|	|	1927	...	...	...
314	Roanne **328** d.	...	...	...	...	1220	1713	...	...	...	...
411	**Lyon Part Dieu 328** a.	...	...	...	...	1328	1816	...	...	...	...
411	**Lyon Perrache 328** a.	...	...	...	...	1340	1829	...	...	...	...

	①g	⚒		4580/1 ▽		⑤†r	🚌 ⑧	🚌	⑤†r
Lyon Perrache 328 d.	...	...	...	1251	...	...	...	...	...
Lyon Part Dieu 328 d.	...	...	...	1305	...	...	...	...	...
Roanne **328** d.	...	...	...	1414	...	...	...	...	...
Vichy **330** d.	...	...	...	|	...	...	1839	1932	...
St Germain des Fossés d.	...	...	...	|	...	...	|	|	...
Gannat **329** d.	...	...	...	1508	...	...	|	1953	...
Montluçon 329 d.	0617	0800	...	1605	...	1912	2006	2111	2146
Guéret d.	0738	0910	...	1704	...	2012	...	...	2243
Limoges a.	0842	1014*	...	1804	...	2110	...	...	2343
Bordeaux **306** a.	...	...	...	2037	...	...	...	...	...

e – 0555 Apr. 28 - May 13.
f – Also Apr. 30, May 7.
g – Also Dec. 26, Jan. 2, Mar. 25, May 2, 9, 13; not Mar. 24, May 12.
r – Also Apr. 30, May 7; not Mar. 23, May 2, 9, 11.
▲ – On Dec. 15, Mar. 29 Gannat d. 1125, St Germain a. 1200 (by 🚌 from Montluçon). Departs Limoges 0757 on Apr. 5. Subject to alteration Limoges - Guéret on Apr. 12.
△ – Not Dec. 15, Mar. 3-6, 10-13, 17-20, 25-27, 29.
▽ – Not Dec. 15, Mar. 3-6, 10-13, 17-21, 25-27, 29.
* – Subject to alteration on Apr. 12.

CLERMONT FERRAND - ST ÉTIENNE and LYON — 328

km		m	2 Ⓐ		⚒	⚒	2 ⚒			2	4403 ⚒			§		2		†	⚒		Ⓐ	†	
0	**Clermont Ferrand 327/30** d.	...	...	...	0623	...	0747	...	0858	0903	*1040*	1116	1213	1406	1505	1611	...	1744	1756	1817	1906	1958	...
14	Riom-Châtel-Guyon **327/30** d.	...	...	...	0633	...	|	...	0907	|	*1053*	|	1223	1415	1514	|	...	1754	1805	|	1915	2007	...
55	Vichy **330** d.	...	...	...	0656	...	|	...	0929	|	|	|	1245	1436	1536	|	...	1818	1826	|	1937	2028	...
65	St Germain des Fossés **290 330** d.	...	...	...	|	...	|	...	|	|	1139	|	|	|	|	|	...	|	|	|	|	|	...
132	Roanne **290** d.	0559	...	0729	0745	0829	|	0929	1014	|	1220	|	1332	1520	1620	|	1752	1907	1914	|	2021	2114	...
•112	Montbrison d.	|	0713	|	|	|	0936	|	|	1048	|	1301	|	|	|	1805	|	|	|	2015	|	|	...
•145	**St Étienne** Châteaucreux a.	|	0755	|	|	|	1008	|	|	1124	|	1335	|	|	|	1837	|	|	|	2048	|	|	...
229	**Lyon Part Dieu 290** a.	0731	...	0847	0856	0946	...	1047	1117	...	1328	...	1443	1625	1724	...	|	2017	2017	...	2125	2217	...
229	**Lyon Perrache 290** a.	0743	...	0859	0908	...	...	1129	1129	...	1340	...	1455	1638	1736	...	1925	2029	2029	...	2137	2229	...

	⚒	⚒		2 Ⓐ		*			2		4506 n	Ⓐk		2				2					
Lyon Perrache 290 d.	...	0620	0705	...	...	1120	1156	...	...	1420	1511	...	1620	...	1720	1820	...	...	...	1956	2020	2056	...
Lyon Part Dieu 290 d.	...	0634	|	...	0808	1134	1208	...	...	1434	1526	...	1634	...	1734	1834	1908	...	...	2008	2034	2108	...
St Étienne Châteaucreux d.	0608	|	|	0807	|	|	|	1228	1405	|	|	...	|	1729	|	|	|	1915	2007	|	|	|	...
Montbrison d.	0653	|	|	0847	|	|	|	1259	1434	|	|	...	|	1803	|	|	|	1943	2048	|	|	|	...
Roanne **290** d.	|	0739	0833	...	0933	1239	1325	|	|	1539	1637	...	1744	|	1839	1949	2023	|	...	2126	2139	2223	...
St Germain des Fossés **290 330** d.	|	|	...	...	...	|	...	|	|	|	1717	1739	|	|	|	|	...	|	...	...	|	...	...
Vichy **330** d.	|	0823	...	...	...	1321	...	|	|	1624	...	1747	1829	|	1922	2036	...	|	...	...	2222	...	...
Riom-Châtel-Guyon **327/30** d.	|	0847	...	...	...	1344	...	|	|	1648	...	1812	1853	|	1944	2101	...	|	...	...	2244	...	...
Clermont Ferrand 327/30 a.	0849	0856	...	...	...	1353	...	1437	1610	1656	...	1822	1902	1944	1952	2111	...	2124	...	...	2252	...	...

k – Not Dec. 24 - Jan. 4.
m – Not May 17, 18.
n – Not May 10, 11.
• – Distance from Clermont Ferrand.
§ – Train **5528** or **5530** on ⑤⑦.
* – Train **5526** on ⑤⑦.

MONTLUÇON - CLERMONT FERRAND — 329

2nd class

km		⚒	Ⓐ	†	Ⓐ	⚒	⊖		Ⓑ	⊖	†
0	**Montluçon 327** d.	0600	0715	0840	0929	*1001*r	1228	*1507*v	1710	1818	1925
68	Gannat **327** d.	0705	0818	0936	1032	1134	1335	1644	1814	1929	2022
96	Riom-Châtel-Guyon d.	0730	0836	0952	1053	1200	1356	1711	1831	1948	2039
110	**Clermont Ferrand** a.	0742	0845	1002	1103	1212	1405	1722	1841	1956	2048

	Ⓐ	⚒	Ⓐ	†	⚒⊖	♥	⑤†f	Ⓐ	Ⓑ	⑥⊖	Ⓑ	⑤†z
Clermont Ferrand d.	0556	0655	0744	1037	1300	1418	1449	1612	1734	1808	1820	2003
Riom-Châtel-Guyon d.	0608	0705	0756	1047	1311	1431	1502	1625	1747	1821	1830	2013
Gannat **327** d.	0625	0724	0818	1107	1336	1456	1526	1643	1813	1849	1849	2039
Montluçon 327 a.	0726	0828	0920	1208	1438	*1603*q	*1631*	1740	1911	1957	1954	2137

f – Also Apr. 30, May 7.
q – Not Dec. 15, Mar. 29.
r – ⑥ only. By 🚌 on Dec. 15, Mar. 29.
v – Not Dec. 15, Mar. 29. Departs 1520 on Mar. 11.
z – Also Apr. 30, May 7; not Mar. 23, May 11.
⊖ – By 🚌 on Dec. 15, Mar. 29 (journey time extended by up to 30 minutes).
♥ – ①②③④⑥ (not Dec. 25, Jan. 1, Mar. 24, Apr. 30, May 1, 7, 8, 12).
Subject to alteration Mar. 4-30

330 PARIS - NEVERS - CLERMONT FERRAND

km					5951 Ⓡ★	5903	5953 Ⓡ★	5955 Ⓡ★	5905	5957 Ⓡ★	5959 Ⓡ★	5911	5963 Ⓡ★	5967 Ⓡ★	5971 Ⓡ★	5907	5975 Ⓡ★	5979 Ⓡ★	5909	5983 Ⓡ★	5915	5917	5985 Ⓡ★	5919
		①	⚒	⚒	①-⑥									⑤		Ⓐ	Ⓐ	Ⓑ			Ⓐ	Ⓒ		Ⓑ
		g			n		R	⊕	⊕	S				f				h					T	s
0	**Paris Gare de Lyon** d.	...	...	...	0701	0713	0807	0901	1113	1138	1301	1334	1404	1501	1601	1642	1701	1801	1804	1935	1911	2013	2041	2131
119	Montargis d.	...	...	...	|	0832	|	|	1219	|	|	1432	|	|	|	1759	|	|	1914	|	2035	2119	|	2228
155	Gien d.	...	...	...	|	0856	|	|	1244	|	|	1456	|	|	|	1825	|	|	1939	|	2100	2139	|	2250
196	Cosne d.	...	...	0724	|	0921	|	|	1308	|	|	1521	|	|	|	1852	|	|	2004	|	2126	2201	|	2312
228	La Charité d.	...	...	0753	|	0946	|	|	1326	|	|	1538	|	|	|	1909	|	|	2021	|	2144	2219	|	2330
254	**Nevers** d.	0601	0640	0823	0857	1008	1028	1100	1345	1356	1458	1553	1601	1657	1757	1923	|	2001	2035	2132	2158	2233	2238	2344
314	Moulins sur Allier ▷ d.	0632	0727	...	0927	...	1118	1131	...	1436	1527	...	1630	1727	1828	...	|	2030	...	2202	...	...	2308	...
355	St Germain des Fossés ▷ d.	0655	0804	...	|	...	|	|	...	|	|	...	|	|	|	...	|	|	...	|	...	...	|	...
365	Vichy ▷ d.	0703	0813	...	0955	...	1151	1159	...	1506	1555	...	1658	1755	1856	...	|	2058	...	2229	...	...	2335	...
406	Riom-Châtel-Guyon ▷ d.	0724	0840	...	1020	...	1216	1223	...	1531	1620	...	|	1819	1920	...	|	2123	...	2254	...	...	0000	...
420	**Clermont Ferrand** ▷ a.	0732	0852	...	1028	...	1224	1232	...	1540	1628	...	1727	1828	1928	...	2008	2131	...	2302	...	...	0008	...

	5904	5906	5950 Ⓡ★	5954 Ⓡ★	5908	5910	5950 Ⓡ★	2	5962 Ⓡ★	5912	5914	5966 Ⓡ★	5968 Ⓡ★	5916	5970 Ⓡ★	5974 Ⓡ★	5918	5978 Ⓡ★	5924	5920	5982 Ⓡ★	5986 Ⓡ★	5922	5990 Ⓡ★
		①-⑥										①-⑥												
	Ⓐ	n	Ⓐ	Ⓐ	Ⓐ	⑦	⑥	⚒		Ⓐ	⑥	⊗n	V	⊗		⑦	Ⓑ		†	⚒	Ⓑ	⑦	⑦	
				c		e	t				t					e	h				h	e	e	
Clermont Ferrand ▷ d.	...	...	0526	0552	...	...	0629	0740	0824	...	...	1020	1150	...	1320	1426	...	1618	...	...	1725	1826	...	1925
Riom-Châtel-Guyon ▷ d.	...	...	0537	|	...	...	0640	0749	0834	...	...	1031	1201	...	1332	1437	...	1628	...	...	|	1837	...	1936
Vichy ▷ d.	...	...	0559	|	...	...	0703	0810	0858	...	...	1054	1226	...	1355	1500	...	1651	...	...	1758	1900	...	1958
St Germain des Fossés ▷ d.	...	...	|	|	...	...	|	0817	|	...	...	|	|	...	|	|	...	|	...	...	|	|	...	|
Moulins sur Allier ▷ d.	...	...	0627	|	...	...	0731	0841	0926	...	...	1123	1254	...	1423	1528	...	1718	...	...	1826	1927	...	2026
Nevers d.	0522	0558	0657	|	0736	0758	0801	0910	0958	1035	1041	1155	1326	1339	1455	1558	1639	1749	1806	1829	1857	1957	2001	2056
La Charité d.	0536	0618	|	|	0752	0820	|	...	|	1055	1101	|	|	1402	|	|	1653	|	1825	1849	|	|	2022	|
Cosne d.	0553	0635	|	|	0810	0837	|	...	|	1111	1118	|	|	1423	|	|	1712	|	1847	1906	|	|	2042	|
Gien d.	0619	0700	|	|	0835	0857	|	...	|	1135	1138	|	|	1449	|	|	1734	|	1912	1930	|	|	2106	|
Montargis d.	0643	0725	|	|	0854	0917	|	...	|	1158	1157	|	|	1513	|	|	1756	|	1935	1959	|	|	2128	|
Paris Gare de Lyon a.	0756	0831	0852	0900	0953	1019	0955	...	1155	1302	1302	1352	1528	1623	1652	1752	1905	1946	2046	2110	2053	2155	2235	2252

ADDITIONAL TRAINS MOULINS SUR ALLIER - CLERMONT FERRAND — Some trains 2nd class

	⚒	Ⓐ	⑦ q	Ⓐ	⚒	Ⓐ		Ⓐ	†	D
Moulins sur Allier d.	0632	0713	0804	...	1230	1430	1651	1809	1834	1956
St Germain des Fossés d.	0654	0740	0831	0911	1257	1453	1721	1835	1900	2021
Vichy d.	0702	0749	0839	0919	1305	1501	1730	1844	1908	2030
Riom-Châtel-Guyon d.	0724	0813	0903	0943	1329	1523	1753	1907	1929	2052
Clermont Ferrand a.	0732	0822	0912	0952	1342	1532	1802	1917	1937	2100

	Ⓐ D	Ⓐ	Ⓒ D	⚒	⑥	Ⓐ		⚒	Ⓐ	
Clermont Ferrand d.	0616	0650	0829	1040	1130	1530	1659	1800	1830	2030
Riom-Châtel-Guyon d.	0626	0700	0839	1053	1139	1540	1709	1809	1840	2040
Vichy d.	0649	0722	0903	|	1203	1602	1730	1833	1902	2104
St Germain des Fossés a.	0657	0730	0910	1130	1210	1610	1737	1841	1910	2112
Moulins sur Allier a.	0728	0802	0934	1200	1237	1637	1801	1904	1937	2140

D – (12) Clermont Ferrand - Dijon and v.v.
R – Dec. 22, 26, 29, Jan. 2, Mar. 22, May 1, 8 only.
S – Dec. 21, 22, 28, 29, Mar. 21, 22, Apr. 30, May 1, 7, 8 only.
T – Dec. 21, 28, Mar. 21 only.
V – Dec. 21, 22, 24, 26, 28, 29, 31, Jan. 2, Apr. 30, May 1, 7, 8 only.

c – Not Dec. 24, 31.
e – Also Dec. 25, Jan. 1, Mar. 24, May 12.
f – Also May 7; not May 2, 9.
g – Also Dec. 26, Jan. 2, Mar. 25, May 2, 9, 13; not Mar. 24, May 12.

h – Not May 1, 8.
n – Not Dec. 25, Jan. 1, Mar. 24, May 12.
q – Also Dec. 25, Jan. 1, Mar. 24, May 1, 8, 12; not Mar. 23, May 11.
s – Not Dec. 24, 31, May 1, 8.
t – Also May 1, 8.

★ – *CORAIL TÉOZ* service, Ⓡ, 🍷.
⊕ – Not Mar. 31 - Apr. 4, Apr. 7 - 11.
⊗ – Not Apr. 14 - 18, 21 - 25.
▷ – See also panel below main table (also Table **328** for Vichy - Clermont Ferrand).

331 CLERMONT FERRAND - NEUSSARGUES - AURILLAC

km		⚒	⑦ W		2	E	⑦ W		Ⓑ	⚒ 2	Ⓑ 2	⑤⑦ 2v
0	**Clermont Ferrand** ▷ d.	0636	0710	1038	*1240*	...	...	1637	1738	1841	1942	2142
36	Issoire ▷ d.	0702	0738	1104	*1309*	...	...	1705	1806	1908	2008	2208
61	Arvant ▷ d.	0728	0759	1124	*1330*	...	...	1723	1823	1927	2025	2228
85	Massiac-Blesle d.	0749	0820	1148	*1352*	...	...	1745	1846	1948	2045	2249
111	**Neussargues** a.	0809	|	1208	*1415*	...	...	1805	1907	2010	2107	2308
111	**Neussargues** d.	0810	|	1209	1443	1550	1650	1806	1908	2012	2113	2309
120	Murat (Cantal) d.	0819	0848	1218	1452	1601	1704	1817	1918	2022	2122	2318
131	Le Lioran d.	0831	0859	1229	1504	1613	1718	1828	|	2036	2136	2330
168	**Aurillac** a.	0902	...	1259	1534	1645	1748	1858	1958	2105	2204	2359
476	*Toulouse* **316** a.	1233	...	...	...	...	...	...	...	...	...	...

	⚒	Ⓐ	2	2		Ⓐ	Ⓑ 2	† 2z	⑤ 2f
Toulouse **316** d.	...	...	...	...	1240r	...	...	...	...
Aurillac ◇ d.	0553	0737	1034	1331	1617	1731	1828	2017	2036
Le Lioran ◇ d.	0625	|	1106	1403	1649	1803	1904	2049	2110
Murat (Cantal) d.	0636	0820	1118	1415	1702	1816	1917	2101	2124
Neussargues a.	0644	0829	1126	1423	1711	1824	1925	2108	2133
Neussargues d.	0645	0830	1127	*1433*	1715	1825	1926	2111	2134
Massiac-Blesle d.	0706	0850	1153	*1456*	1747	1848	1949	2132	2155
Arvant ▷ d.	0726	|	|	*1518*	1811	1909	2009	2152	2215
Issoire ▷ a.	0744	0926	1230	*1537*	1829	1926	2027	2210	2233
Clermont Ferrand ▷ a.	0814	0957	1300	*1603*	1854	1952	2053	2236	2259

E – Daily to Mar. 9; ⑤ from Mar. 14 (also Apr. 30, May 7; not Dec. 25, Jan. 1, May 2, 9). To Brive (Table **317**).
W – ⑦ Dec. 9 - Mar. 9.
f – Also Apr. 30, May 7; not May 2, 9.

r – Not on ①-⑤ Jan. 21 - Feb. 8.
v – Also Dec. 25, Jan. 1, Mar. 24, Apr. 30, May 1, 7, 8, 12; not Mar. 23, May 2, 9, 11.
z – Not Mar. 23, May 11.

▷ – See also Table **333**.
◇ – Additional journeys: Aurillac d. 0754 - Le Lioran a. 0826 on ⑥ Dec. 15 - Mar. 8 (daily Feb. 17 - Mar. 2).
Aurillac d. 0943 - Le Lioran a. 1014 daily Dec. 9 - Mar. 9 (from Brive d. 0805).

332 CLERMONT FERRAND - MILLAU - BÉZIERS

km		2 ⚒	2 ① g	2 ⚒	2	15941	2 ⑤ f◇	2 †	🚌 ⑤ d	🚌 ⑦ e	2 ⑤ f
0	**Clermont Ferrand** ▷ d.	...	...	...	...	1240	...	...	...	...	...
85	Massiac-Blesle ▷ d.	...	...	...	...	1352	...	...	1750	...	...
111	**Neussargues** ▷ d.	...	...	...	...	1435	...	1724	|	2114	2140
130	St Flour d.	...	...	...	...	1503	...	1747	1815	2145	2203
168	St Chély d'Apcher d.	...	...	1147	...	1548	1642	1826	1842	2215	2241
201	Marvejols d.	...	...	1226	1242	1629	1717	1901	1920	...	2328*
236	**Mende** a.	...	...	|	1329	|	|	|	|	...	|
243	Sévérac le Château d.	...	...	1310	▬	1716	1813	1947	2012	...	0009
273	Millau ⊙ d.	0552	0848	1356	2	1746	1843	2023	2047	...	0037
352	Bédarieux ▶ d.	0708	1008	1512	1730	1902	2002	2139	...	...	...
394	**Béziers** ▶ a.	0740	1040	1545	1805	1936	2036	2212	...	...	...

	2 ⚒	2	15940	2 †	2 ⑤ f	2 ①-④ m	2 Ⓐ	2	🚌 Ⓑ	2 ⑦ q
Béziers ▶ d.	...	0807	0910	...	1238	1300	...	1826	...	1907
Bédarieux ▶ d.	...	0840	0943	...	1312	1333	...	1901	...	1944
Millau ⊙ d.	0853	▬	1103	1400	1430	1447	1842	2021	2033	2116*
Sévérac le Château d.	0920	⚒2	1132	1428	1457	...	1910	...	2102	2151
Mende d.	|	1125	|	|	|	...	|	...	|	|
Marvejols d.	1010	1211	1222	1510	1541	...	1954	...	2212	2239
St Chély d'Apcher d.	1044	...	1301	1545	1618	...	2029	...	2242	2313
St Flour d.	...	...	1340	1623	...	...	2108c	...	...	...
Neussargues ▷ a.	...	...	1402	1645	...	...	2129c	...	...	...
Massiac-Blesle ▷ a.	...	...	1456	...	...	...	...	...	...	...
Clermont Ferrand ▷ a.	...	...	1603	...	...	...	...	...	...	...

SNCF 🚌 service	🚌 ⚒	🚌	🚌	🚌	🚌 Ⓑ	🚌 Ⓐ	🚌 ⑤f	🚌 ⑤d	🚌 Ⓑ
Clermont Ferrand ▷ d.	...	...	1640	...	...	...	1940	...	2145
Massiac-Blesle ▷ d.	0805	1155	|	1750	1849	1952	|	2051	|
St Flour d.	0830	1219	|	1815	1914	2017	|	2116	2303
St Chély d'Apcher d.	...	...	1815	...	...	...	2115	...	2324
Marvejols d.	...	...	1853	...	...	...	2151	...	2358
Mende a.	...	...	1930	...	...	...	2230	...	0037

SNCF 🚌 service	🚌 ⚒	🚌 ⚒	🚌 Ⓐ	🚌	🚌	🚌 ⑦e	🚌 ⑦e	🚌 ⑤f	🚌 Ⓐ	🚌 ⑦e
Mende d.	...	...	0700	...	1010	...	1532	1552	...	...
Marvejols d.	...	...	0740	...	1052	...	1614	1634	...	1815
St Chély d'Apcher d.	...	...	0816	...	1128	...	1650	1710	...	1854
St Flour d.	0631	0730	0843	1116	|	1550	1718	1738	1810	1918
Massiac-Blesle ▷ a.	0656	|	|	1140	|	1617	|	|	1835	|
Clermont Ferrand ▷ a.	...	0800	1000	...	1300	1716	1836	1856	...	2040

b – Also Apr. 30, May 7; not May 2, 9. To Millau, a. 2245.
c – St Chély d'Apcher - Neussargues runs on ⑤**f** only.
d – Also Apr. 30, May 7.
e – Also Dec. 25, Jan. 1, Mar. 24, May 1, 8, 12; not Mar. 23, May 11.
f – ⑤ (also Apr. 30, May 7; not May 2, 9).
g – Also Mar. 25, May 13; not Dec. 24, 31, Feb. 18, 25, Mar. 24, Apr. 14, 21, 28, May 12.
m – Also May 2, 9; not Dec. 25, Jan. 1, Mar. 24, Apr. 30, May 1, 7, 8, 12.

q – Also Mar. 24, May 12; not Dec. 23, 30, Feb. 17, 24, Mar. 23, Apr. 13, 20, May 11. From Montpellier (d. 1800).

◇ – To Montpellier (a. 2137) except on Dec. 28, Jan. 4, Feb. 22, 29, Apr. 18, 25.
▷ – For connections see Table **331**.
* – Arrives 13 - 15 minutes earlier.

▶ – Additional trains Bédarieux - Béziers and v.v.:
From Bédarieux: 0626 ⚒, 0708, 0800 ⚒, 1202, 1508 †.
From Béziers: 0712 ⚒, 1300 Ⓒ, 1642, 1737 Ⓐ, 2055 ⑤ **b**.

⊙ – Additional 🚌 service Millau - Montpellier and v.v.:
From Millau 0710, 1716. From Montpellier 0710, 1715 ⚒, 2115 ⑤ **f**, 2200. Journey 95 minutes.

CLERMONT FERRAND - LE PUY EN VELAY — 333

km		2 Ⓐ	①–⑥ ▽	🚌 ⚒ ◐		2 Ⓐ		🚌 Ⓒ		⑥	△	🚌		▽	🚌 Ⓑ ◐	Ⓑ	🚌 ⑤ d		2 Ⓐ	2 Ⓑ	🚌 ⑤ d		2 ⑦ q	
0	**Clermont Ferrand** 331 d.	0602	0645	...	...	0929	1038	...	...	1153	1252	...	...	1641	...	1738	...	...	1900	1942	...	...	2058	...
36	Issoire 331 d.	0628	0712	...	...	0955	1104	...	...	1220	1320	...	...	1714	...	1806	...	...	1930	2008	...	...	2123	...
61	Arvant 331 d.	0647	0734	...	...	1014	1123	1130	...	1240	1340	...	...	1734	...	1822	1831	...	1951	2024	2029	...	2142	...
71	Brioude d.	0656	0745	...	...	1022	...	1141	...	1249	1350	1400	...	1755	...	...	1844	...	2001	...	2040	...	2154	...
95	St Georges d'Aurac d.	0722	|	...	...	1044	...	|	...	1313	|	|	...	1819	1824	...	|	...	2022	...	|	...	2217	...
103	Langeac d.	|	0814	0819	...	|	...	1209	...	|	1416	|	...	1827	|	...	1921	...	|	...	2107	...	|	...
147	**Le Puy en Velay** a.	0810	...	0906	...	1133	...	1254	...	1401	...	1507	...	...	1914	...	2004	...	2108	...	2150	...	2305	...

	2 ① g	2 ②–⑤ w		2 ⑥		▽		Ⓐ	⑥		🚌	△		①–⑤ u	2 ⑦ v		🚌 Ⓐ	2 Ⓑ		2 Ⓑ ▽		2 ⑦ q		
Le Puy en Velay d.	0545	0631	...	0800	...	...	...	1200	1221	...	1620	...	...	1726	1726	...	1841	...	...	...	...	2042	...	...
Langeac d.	|	|	...	|	...	1131	...	|	|	...	1712	1722	...	|	|	...	|	...	...	2104	...	|	...	...
St Georges d'Aurac d.	0633	0720	...	0845	...	|	...	1249	1312	...	...	1731	...	1820	1820	...	|	...	...	|	...	2133	...	...
Brioude d.	0701	0746	...	0907	...	1158	...	1308	1331	...	...	1752	...	1838	1838	...	1944	...	...	2131	...	2153	...	...
Arvant 331 d.	0710	0754	...	0917	...	|	...	1316	1341	...	...	1802	...	|	|	...	1954	2009	...	2140	...	2202	...	...
Issoire 331 d.	0733	0813	...	0937	...	1224	...	1339	1404	...	...	1822	...	1901	1901	...	...	2028	...	2159	...	2222	...	...
Clermont Ferrand 331 a.	0802	0842	...	1005	...	1253	...	1411	1435	...	...	1847	...	1929	1932	...	...	2053	...	2224	...	2247	...	...

d – Also Apr. 30, May 7.
g – Also Dec. 26, Jan. 2, Mar. 25, May 2, 9, 13; not Mar. 24, May 12.
q – Also Dec. 25, Jan. 1, Mar. 24, May 1, 8, 12; not Mar. 23, May 11.
u – Not Mar. 24, May 12.
v – Also Mar. 24, May 12; not Dec. 23, 30, Feb. 17, 24, Mar. 23, Apr. 13, 20, May 11.
w – Not Dec. 25, 26, Jan. 1, 2, Mar. 25, May 1, 2, 8, 9, 13.
◐ – Subject to confirmation.
△ – (12) Clermont Ferrand - Nimes - Marseille and v.v. (Table **334**).
▽ – (12) Clermont Ferrand - Nimes and v.v. (Table **334**).

CLERMONT FERRAND and MENDE - NIMES - MONTPELLIER — 334

km		2 ⚒	2 ②–⑥ n	①–⑥	2 ⑦	🚌 ⑤⑥	2 ⚒	🚌	15945		
0	*Clermont Ferrand* 333 d.	...	...	0645	...	...	...	...	1252	...	1641
103	**Langeac** d.	...	...	0816	...	...	...	...	1417	...	1828
170	Langogne d.	...	...	0936	...	...	1233	...	1531	...	1944
*47	**Mende** d.	0512	0838	|	0835	1130	|	1420	|	1650	|
188	La Bastide-St Laurent d.	0629	0951	0957	0957	1240	1254	1530	1550	1807	2004
241	Grand Combe la Pise d.	0721	...	1051	1051	...	1347	...	1645	1908	2058
254	Alès ▶ d.	0740	...	1111	1113	...	1408	...	1702	1931	2118
303	**Nimes 355** ▶ a.	0818	...	1150	1150	...	1444	...	1740	2007	2155
	Marseille 355 a.	|	...	...	|	...	...	...	1915	|	...
353	**Montpellier 355** a.	0844	...	...	1221	...	...	...	...	2036	...

	2 ⚒		2 ⚒ b	2	15942	🚌	2 Ⓑ	2	🚌
Montpellier 355 d.	0643	...	...	1212r	...	...	1624	1740	...
Marseille 355 d.	|	...	...	|	1212	...	|	|	...
Nimes 355 ▶ d.	0721	0800	...	1250	1354	...	1714	1808	2145
Alès ▶ d.	0807	0842	...	1333	1434	...	1801	1851	2225
Grand Combe la Pise d.	0822	0858	...	1348	1451	...	1817	1910	2245
La Bastide-St Laurent d.	0916	0956	1010	1450	1552	1600	1925	2006	...
Mende a.	|	|	1123	1606	|	1710	|	2118	...
Langogne d.	0934	1015	...	...	1611	...	1949	...	...
Langeac a.	...	1130	...	...	1721	...	2103	...	...
Clermont Ferrand 333 a.	...	1253	...	...	1847	...	2224	...	...

b – Subject to alteration on Ⓐ from June 2.
n – Not Dec. 25, 26, Jan. 1, 2, Mar. 25, May 2, 9, 13. Subject to alteration from June 3.
r – ⑦ (also Mar. 24, May 12; not Dec. 23, 30, Feb. 17, 24, Mar. 23, Apr. 13, 20, May 11).
* – Distance from La Bastide.

▶ – Additional services Alès - Nimes and v.v.:
From Alès 0606 ⚒, 0640 Ⓐ, 0704, 0810 Ⓐ, 0841 Ⓑ, 0920 Ⓐ, 1208 Ⓐ, 1256, 1509, 1615 🚌, 1805 Ⓑ, 1845 🚌.
From Nimes 0627 Ⓐ, 0655 Ⓐ, 0904 Ⓐ, 1000 Ⓐ, 1047, 1215 Ⓐ, 1520 🚌, 1635, 1714 ⑥, 1900 Ⓐ, 1945 🚌, 2045.

TGV services

LYON - MASSY - TOURS, RENNES and NANTES — 335

For slower services via Bourges see Table **290**. For Lille - Massy - Rennes / Nantes see Table **11**. For Strasbourg - Massy - Rennes / Nantes see Table **391**.

	TGV 5352 ① g	*TGV* 5352 Ⓐ	*TGV* 5356 ⑥ t		*TGV* 5350 Ⓑ h	*TGV* 5360 ⑥ t	*TGV* 5364 ⑥ t	*TGV* 5365 ⑥ t		*TGV* 5374 ⑦ e	*TGV* 5371 ⑦ e	*TGV* 5368 ①–⑥ n	*TGV* 5233 ①–⑥ ♥n		*TGV* 5372 ①–⑥ n	*TGV* 5363 ①–⑥ n	*TGV* 5378 ⑦ ez	*TGV* 5236 ⑦ ♥e		*TGV* 5380 ◇	*TGV* 5387 ①–④ ◇m	*TGV* 5394 ⑥ F	*TGV* 5394 ⑥ F	*TGV* 5390 ⑤⑦ w
Bourg St Maurice d.	...	...	...	...	...	...	...	...	...	...	...	...	...	...	...	...	...	...	...	...	...	1644	1644	...
Chambéry d.	...	...	...	...	...	...	...	...	...	...	...	...	...	...	...	...	...	...	...	...	...	1832	1832	...
Grenoble 343 d.	0532	...	...	...	...	...	0811	...	...	...	...	...	...	...	...	...	...	...	...	...	...	|	|	...
Marseille 350 d.	|	...	...	...	0739	...	|	...	...	1133	1133	1133	...	...	1509	1509	1509	...	...	...	...	|	|	...
Avignon TGV 350 d.	|	...	...	...	|	...	|	...	...	1209	1209	1209	...	...	1546	1546	1546	...	...	...	...	|	|	...
Lyon Perrache d.	|	...	...	...	|	...	|	...	...	|	|	|	...	...	|	|	|	...	...	...	...	|	|	1908
Lyon Part Dieu d.	0656	0656	0656	...	0926	0926	0926	0926	...	1326	1326	1326	...	...	1656	1656	1656	...	...	1826	1826	|	|	1926
Massy TGV d.	0901	0901	0901	...	1131	1131	1131	1131	...	1532	1532	1533	1631	...	1901	1901	1901	1916	...	2036	2032	2128	2128	2137
St Pierre des Corps a.	0951	0951	0951	...	|	|	|	|	...	|	|	1622	|	...	|	|	1953	|	...	2129	|	|	|	|
Futuroscope 300 a.	|	|	1028	...	|	|	|	|	...	|	|	|	|	...	|	|	|	|	...	|	|	|	|	|
Poitiers 300 a.	|	|	1044	...	|	|	|	|	...	|	|	|	|	...	|	|	|	|	...	|	|	|	|	|
Le Mans 280 a.	|	|	...	...	1219	1219	1219	1219	...	1619	1619	|	1720	...	1949	1949	|	2005	...	|	2119	2215	2215	2224
Rennes 280 a.	|	|	...	...	1340	1340	1340	|	...	|	1743	|	1836	...	2110	|	|	2125	...	|	2234	|	2334	2340
Angers St Laud 280 a.	1046	1046	...	...	...	...	...	1302	...	1659	...	1719	...	...	...	2035	2046	...	...	2223	...	2252	...	...
Nantes 280 a.	1125	1125	...	...	...	...	...	1342	...	1736	...	1803	...	...	...	2116	2127	...	...	2304	...	2328	...	...

	TGV 5302 ①–④ m	*TGV* 5308 ⑥ F	*TGV* 5310 ⑥ F	*TGV* 5304 ⑥ t	*TGV* 8712 Ⓐ	*TGV* 5312	*TGV* 5311 △	*TGV* 8818	*TGV* 5318		*TGV* 5324 G	*TGV* 5322 z	*TGV* 8836	*TGV* 5326 ⑤⑥ y	*TGV* 5346 ①–④ m	*TGV* 5332 ⑤ f	*TGV* 5328 ①–④ m		*TGV* 5334 ⑦ e	*TGV* 5338 ⑦ e	*TGV* 5344 ⑤ f	*TGV* 5342 ⑤ f	*TGV* 5336 ⑦ e	*TGV* 5340 ⑦ ez
Nantes 280 d.	0455	0623	...	0630	...	0735	0735	0900	...	...	...	1252	1400	...	...	1555	1555	...	1708	...	...	1904	...	1849
Angers St Laud 280 d.	0533	0701	...	0708	...	0813	0813	0937	...	...	...	1338	1438	...	...	1633	1633	...	1744	...	...	1944	...	1927
Rennes 280 d.	|	|	0629	|	0735	|	|	|	0910	...	1230	|	|	1414	1514	|	|	...	|	1827	1909	|	...	|
Le Mans 280 d.	|	0748	0748	|	0846	0854	0854	1016	1029	...	1350	|	1516	1529	1630	|	|	...	1824	1952	2029	2029	...	|
Poitiers 300 d.	|	|	|	|	...	|	|	...	|	...	|	|	...	|	|	|	|	...	|	|	|	|	1932	|
Futuroscope 300 a.	|	|	|	|	...	|	|	...	|	...	|	|	...	|	|	|	|	...	|	|	|	|	1943	|
St Pierre des Corps d.	0632	|	|	0807	...	|	|	...	|	...	|	1430	...	|	|	1727	1727	...	|	|	|	|	2028	2028
Massy TGV d.	0723	0843	0843	0901	...	0948	0948	...	1121	...	1451	1521	...	1621	1721	1821	1821	...	1915	2046	2121	2121	2126	2126
Lyon Part Dieu a.	0935	|	|	1103	...	1201	1201	...	1331	...	1655	1731	...	1831	1931	2031	2031	...	2131	2255	2331	2331	2331	2331
Lyon Perrache a.	0950	|	|	1115	...	|	...	...	|	...	...	|	...	|	|	|	...	...	|	|	2346	2346	2347	2347
Avignon TGV 350 a.	...	|	|	...	...	1309	...	...	1446	...	...	1846	...	1945	2046	|	...	...	|	0016	...	...	...	...
Marseille 350 a.	...	|	|	...	...	1349	...	...	1523	...	...	1918	...	2024	2117	|	...	...	|	0055	...	...	...	...
Grenoble 343 a.	...	|	|	...	...	...	...	...	...	...	...	...	...	...	...	2153	...	...	2253	...	...	...	...	...
Chambéry a.	...	1204	1204	...	...	...	...	...	...	...	...	...	...	...	...	...	...	...	...	...	...	...	...	...
Bourg St Maurice a.	...	1410	1410	...	...	...	...	...	...	...	...	...	...	...	...	...	...	...	...	...	...	...	...	...

LYON - ROUEN	*TGV* 5366 ⑥t	*TGV* 5376
Marseille 350 d.	...	1539
Avignon TGV 350 d.	...	1610
Lyon Perrache d.	1212	|
Lyon Part Dieu d.	1226	1726
Massy-Palaiseau d.	1500	1940
Versailles Chantiers d.	1518	2010
Mantes la Jolie a.	|	2045
Rouen Rive Droite a.	1624	2126
Le Havre 270 a.	...	2215

ROUEN - LYON	*TGV* 5316	*TGV* 5320 ⑦e
Le Havre 270 d.	0806	...
Rouen Rive Droite d.	0852	1251
Mantes la Jolie d.	0938	|
Versailles Chantiers d.	1005	1401
Massy-Palaiseau d.	1021	1418
Lyon Part Dieu a.	1231	1631
Lyon Perrache a.	|	...
Avignon TGV 350 a.	1347	...
Marseille 350 a.	1418	...

F – ⑥ Dec. 15 - Mar. 29.
G – ①②③④⑦ (not Apr. 30, May 1, 7, 8).
e – Also Dec. 25, Jan. 1, Mar. 24, May 12.
f – Also Apr. 30, May 7; not May 2.
g – Also Dec. 26, Jan. 2, Mar. 25, May 13; not Dec. 24, 31, Mar. 24, May 12.
h – Not May 1, 8.
m – Not Dec. 25, Jan. 1, Mar. 24, Apr. 30, May 1, 7, 8, 12.
n – Not Dec. 25, Jan. 1, Mar. 24, May 12.
t – Also May 1, 8.
w – Also Dec. 25, Jan. 1, Mar. 24, Apr. 30, May 12; not May 2.
y – Also Apr. 30, May 1, 7, 8; not May 2.
z – Not May 11.

TGV – Ⓡ, supplement payable, 🍷.

♥ – To / from Lille (Table **11**).
◇ – From Montpellier (depart 1630, Table **350**).
△ – To Montpellier (arrive 1402, Table **350**).

Nantes and Angers times are subject to alteration on May 10, 11.

340 PARIS - LYON *TGV Sud-Est*

For Charles de Gaulle ✈ - Marne la Vallée - Lyon see Table **11**. For Paris - Lyon St Exupéry ✈ see Table **342**. Trains not serving Lyon Perrache continue to/from other destinations.

km	*TGV* trains convey 🍸	*TGV* 6601	*TGV* 6641	*TGV* 6681	*TGV* 6603		*TGV* 6643		*TGV* 6605	*TGV* 6645	*TGV* 6607		*TGV* 6609	*TGV* 6611		*TGV* 6613	*TGV* 6685	*TGV* 6615	*TGV* 6657		*TGV* 6617		*TGV* 6619	*TGV* 6621
		Ⓐ	①–⑤	①–⑥	①–⑥					①–④	①–⑥								⑤					
		z	w	n	u		⊗			m	n							⊕	f					
0	**Paris Gare de Lyon** ▷ d.	0554	0624	0654	0654	...	0724	...	0754	0824	0854	...	0954	1054	...	1154	1254	1254	1324	...	1354	...	1454	1554
303	Le Creusot TGV d.	0718	|	|	|	...	|	...	0917	|	|	...	1118	|	...	|	|	|	|	...	1517	...	|	1718
363	Mâcon Loché TGV ▷ a.	|	|	|	|	...	0859	...	|	|	|	...	|	|	...	|	|	|	|	...	|	...	|	|
427	**Lyon Part-Dieu** a.	0757	0821	0851	0851	...	0924	...	0957	1021	1051	...	1157	1251	...	1351	1451	1451	1521	...	1557	...	1651	1757
431	**Lyon Perrache** a.	0809	0833	...	0903	...	0936	...	1009	1033	1103	...	1209	1303	...	1403	...	1503	1533	...	1609	...	1703	1809

	TGV 6659	*TGV* 6687	*TGV* 6623	*TGV* 6663		*TGV* 6627	*TGV* 6665		*TGV* 6689	*TGV* 6629		*TGV* 6669		*TGV* 6631		*TGV* 6671	*TGV* 6633		*TGV* 6673	*TGV* 6635		*TGV* 5139		
	Ⓐ			Ⓐ			Ⓑ					⑤				⑦	Ⓑ		⑤	Ⓑ		⑦		
			q				c			s		f				e	h		d	h		⊡ e		
Paris Gare de Lyon ▷ d.	1624	1654	1654	1724	...	1754	1824	...	1854	1854	...	1924	...	1954	...	2024	2054	...	2124	2154	...	...	...	...
Le Creusot TGV d.	|	|	|	|	...	1918	|	...	|	|	...	|	...	2118	...	|	|	...	|	|	...	2322	...	...
Mâcon Loché TGV ▷ a.	|	|	|	|	...	|	|	...	|	|	...	|	...	|	...	|	|	...	|	|	...	|	...	...
Lyon Part-Dieu a.	1819	1853	1853	1921	...	1957	2021	...	2051	2051	...	2121	...	2157	...	2221	2251	...	2321	2351	...	2358	...	...
Lyon Perrache a.	1833	...	1905	1933	...	2009	2033	...	...	2103	...	2133	...	2209	...	2233	2303	...	2333	0003	...	0013	...	...

	TGV 6640	*TGV* 6602	*TGV* 5154		*TGV* 6642	*TGV* 6604	*TGV* 6690		*TGV* 6644	*TGV* 6648	*TGV* 6608	*TGV* 6608		*TGV* 6610		*TGV* 6612		*TGV* 6692	*TGV* 6614	*TGV* 6908		*TGV* 6616	*TGV* 6618	*TGV* 6694
	①	Ⓐ	①–⑥		①–⑤	①–⑥	①–⑥		①		Ⓐ	Ⓒ												
	g		⊙ n		w	v	n		g	⊖									y	▽				
Lyon Perrache d.	0516	0546	...	...	0616	0641	...	...	0731	0716	0746	0746	...	0846	...	0946	...	...	1040	...	...	1146	1240	...
Lyon Part-Dieu d.	0530	0600	0613	...	0630	0700	0700	...	0745	0730	0800	0800	...	0900	...	1000	...	1100	1100	...	...	1200	1300	1300
Mâcon Loché TGV ▷ d.	|	0625	|	...	|	|	|	...	|	|	|	0827	...	|	...	|	...	|	|	...	...	|	|	|
Le Creusot TGV d.	|	0645	0651	...	|	|	|	...	|	|	0840	0848	...	|	...	|	...	|	|	1150	...	|	1343	1343
Paris Gare de Lyon ▷ a.	0727	0807	...	...	0827	0857	0857	...	0943	0927	1003	1009	...	1057	...	1159	...	1257	1257	1313	...	1359	1505	1505

	TGV 6620	*TGV* 6620		*TGV* 6622	*TGV* 6624	*TGV* 6664		*TGV* 6626	*TGV* 6668		*TGV* 6628	*TGV* 6638	*TGV* 6696	*TGV* 6630		*TGV* 6632		*TGV* 6674	*TGV* 6634		*TGV* 6588	*TGV* 6676	*TGV* 6676	
		⑤				⑤			Ⓐ			Ⓑ						⑦			⑦	⑤	⑦	
	A	f				f			⊖			k		b				a	N		x △	f	a	
Lyon Perrache d.	1346	1346	...	1446	1546	1616	...	1646	1716	...	1746	1816	...	1841	...	1946	...	2016	2046	...	...	2146	2146	...
Lyon Part-Dieu d.	1400	1400	...	1500	1600	1630	...	1700	1730	...	1800	1830	1900	1900	...	2000	...	2030	2100	...	...	2200	2200	...
Mâcon Loché TGV ▷ d.	|	|	...	|	|	|	...	|	|	...	|	|	|	|	...	|	...	|	|	...	...	|	2226	...
Le Creusot TGV d.	|	1440	...	|	1641	|	...	|	|	...	1841	|	|	|	...	2040	...	|	|	...	2236	2241	|	...
Paris Gare de Lyon ▷ a.	1559	1603	...	1659	1803	1827	...	1857	1927	...	2003	2027	2057	2057	...	2203	...	2227	2257	...	2359	0003	0003	...

A – Daily except ⑤ (will not run Apr. 30, May 7).
N – ①②③④⑥ (not Apr. 30, May 1, 7, 8).

a – Also Dec. 25, Jan. 1, Mar. 24, May 12; not Mar. 23.
b – Not Dec. 24, 28, 31, Jan. 3.
c – Not Mar. 23, May 1, 8, 9.
d – Also Apr. 30, May 7; not May 2, 9.
e – Also Dec. 25, Jan. 1, Mar. 24, May 12.
f – Also Apr. 30, May 7; not May 2.
g – Also Dec. 26, Jan. 2, Mar. 25, May 13; not Dec. 24, 31, Mar. 24, May 12.
h – Not May 1, 8.
k – Not Mar. 23, May 1, 8.
m – Not Dec. 25, Jan. 1, Mar. 24, Apr. 30, May 1, 7, 8, 12.
n – Not Dec. 25, Jan. 1, Mar. 24, May 12.
q – Not Dec. 31, Feb. 11, 18, 19, 25, Mar. 3, 10, 23.
r – Not Dec. 31, May 1, 8.
s – Not Dec. 31, Feb. 23, Mar. 1, 8, 23, May 2.
u – Not Dec. 24 - Jan. 6, Mar. 24, May 2, 9, 12.
v – Not Dec. 24, 25, 27, 28, 31, Jan. 1, Mar. 24, May 2, 9, 12.
w – Not Dec. 25, Jan. 1, Mar. 24, May 1, 2, 8, 9, 12.
x – Also Dec. 25, Jan. 1, Mar. 24, May 12; not Dec. 23, 30, Mar. 23.
y – Not Mar. 23.
z – Not Dec. 24, 31.

TGV –Ⓡ, supplement payable, 🍸.

▷ – For other trains Paris - Mâcon Loché TGV and v.v. see Table **341**.
△ – From Genève (Table **341**).
▽ – From Grenoble (Table **342**).
⊙ – Grenoble - Lyon - Lille Europe (Table **11**).
⊡ – Lille - Lyon (Table **11**).
⊕ – Not May 2.
⊗ – Not May 9.
⊖ – Not May 2, 9.

341 PARIS - GENÈVE, CHAMBÉRY and ANNECY *TGV trains*

For the night trains Paris Austerlitz - Aix les Bains - Chambéry - Bourg St Maurice / Modane see Tables **368** and **369** (Paris - Annecy see Table **367**).

km	All trains convey 🍸	*TGV* 6931	*TGV* 6561	*TGV* 9241	*TGV* 6565	*TGV* 6937	*TGV* 6939	*TGV* 6569		*TGV* 6573	*TGV* 9247	*TGV* 6941	*TGV* 6577	*TGV* 9249	*TGV* 6947	*TGV* 6949	*TGV* 6581		*TGV* 6951	*TGV* 6585	*TGV* 6453	*TGV* 6953	*TGV* 6449	*TGV* 6589
				M	Ⓐ					Ⓑ	M			M		Ⓑ					⑤	⑤	④	⑤
				△						h	△			△		h			u		D	E	G	f
0	**Paris Gare de Lyon** 340 d.	0650	0710	0742	0910	0950	1050	1110	...	1310	1350	1350	1504	1524	1650	1750	1810	...	1850	1907	1950	1950	2010	2010
365	Mâcon Loché TGV 340 d.	|	|	|	|	1128	|	|	...	|	1528	1528	1642	|	|	1928	|	...	|	2046	2128	2128	|	|
406	Bourg-en-Bresse d.	|	0903	|	|	|	|	1303	...	1503	|	|	1703	|	|	1950	|	...	|	2109	|	|	|	|
	Lyon St Exupéry TGV ✈ d.	0846	|	|	|	|	1246	|	...	|	|	|	|	1720	1846	|	|	...	2046	|	|	|	|	|
489	Culoz 345 d.	|	|	|	|	|	|	|	...	|	|	|	|	|	|	|	|	...	|	2156	|	|	|	|
522	Bellegarde ▲ 345 a.	|	1007	|	1203	|	|	1407	...	1607	|	|	1808	|	|	|	2103	...	|	2218	|	|	|	2303
555	**Genève** 345 a.	|	1035	|	1232	|	|	1435	...	1635	|	|	1835	|	|	|	2132	...	|	2245	|	|	|	2335
*532	Chambéry a.	0942	...	1041	...	|	1343	...	...	...	1708	|	...	1826	1943	|	...	...	2143	...	2259	2300	2309	...
*532	Chambéry 344 365 d.	0951	...	...	...	|	1352	...	...	...	|	|	...	...	1952	|	...	...	2152	...	|	|	...	...
*546	Aix les Bains 344 365 a.	1001	...	...	...	1250	1401	...	...	...	1652z	1652	...	...	2001	2052	...	...	2201	...	2245z	2245z	...	...
*560	**Annecy** 344 365 a.	1032	...	...	...	1330	1432	...	...	...	...	1731	...	...	2032	2129	...	...	2232	...	...	...	...	...

All trains convey 🍸	*TGV* 6560	*TGV* 6960	*TGV* 6962	*TGV* 6564		*TGV* 6964	*TGV* 6568	*TGV* 6968	*TGV* 9240	*TGV* 9242	*TGV* 6972	*TGV* 6572	*TGV* 6424	*TGV* 6976	*TGV* 6576	*TGV* 6576	*TGV* 6580		*TGV* 6980	*TGV* 6984	*TGV* 6584	*TGV* 9248	*TGV* 6494	*TGV* 6588
	Ⓐ	①–⑥	Ⓐ			Ⓒ			M	M			⑥				Ⓐ			Ⓑ		M		⑦
		n							△	△			H		B	C			F	k	q	△	L	e ⊖
Annecy 344 365 d.	...	0532	0632	...	...	0830	...	0935	...	...	1232	...	...	1535	...	...	...	...	1735	1832	...	...	1946	...
Aix les Bains 344 365 d.	...	0601	0709	...	...	0907	...	1004	...	...	1309	...	1508	1604	...	...	...	...	1804	1909	...	...	2047	...
Chambéry 344 365 a.	...	0612	|	...	...	|	...	1014	...	...	|	...	|	1614	...	...	...	...	1815	|	...	...	|	...
Chambéry 348 d.	...	0622	|	...	...	|	...	1024	1058	1225	|	...	|	1624	...	...	...	...	1825	|	...	2027	|	...
Genève 345 d.	0535	|	|	0717	...	|	0917	|	|	|	|	1317	|	|	1614	1614	1717	...	|	|	1917	|	|	201
Bellegarde ▲ 345 d.	0603	|	|	0749	...	|	0948	|	|	|	|	1348	|	|	1641	1641	1748	...	|	|	1948	|	|	204
Culoz 345 d.	|	|	|	|	...	|	|	|	|	|	|	|	|	|	|	|	|	...	|	|	|	|	|	|
Lyon St Exupéry TGV ✈ a.	|	|	|	|	...	|	|	|	|	|	|	|	|	|	|	|	|	...	|	|	|	2124	|	|
Bourg-en-Bresse d.	0710	|	|	0856	...	|	1056	|	|	|	|	1454	|	|	|	1748	1856	...	|	|	2056	|	|	215
Mâcon Loché TGV 340 d.	|	|	0829	|	...	1030	|	1146	|	|	1430	|	|	|	1805	1816	|	...	|	2029	|	|	|	|
Paris Gare de Lyon 340 a.	0903	0915	1007	1049	...	1207	1249	1323	1355	1515	1607	1649	1807	1915	1943	1955	2049	...	2115	2207	2249	2319	2347	235

B – Daily except dates in note **C**.
C – Ⓒ May 1 - July 6.
D – ⑤ Dec. 21 - Apr. 25.
E – ⑤ from May 9 (also Apr. 30, May 7; not May 2).
F – Daily to Apr. 4; Ⓑ from Apr. 6 (not May 1, 8).
G – ④ Dec. 20 - Mar. 27.
H – ⑥ Dec. 15 - Apr. 26.
L – ⑥ Dec. 29 - Apr. 19. From St Gervais.
M – 🚆 Paris - Modane - Torino - Milano and v.v. (Table **44**).

e – Also Dec. 25, Jan. 1, Mar. 24, May 12; not Dec. 23, 30, Mar. 23, May 11.
f – Also Apr. 30, May 7; not May 2, 9.
h – Not May 1, 8.
k – Not Dec. 31, May 1, 8.
n – Not Dec. 25, Jan. 1, Mar. 24, May 12.
q – Not Dec. 24, 31.
u – Not Dec. 31.
z – Calls before Chambéry.

TGV –Ⓡ, supplement payable, 🍸.

* – Via Lyon St Exupéry TGV (Paris - Aix les Bains via Bourg en Bresse = *511* km).
△ – Special 'global' fares payable.
▲ – Additional trains operate Paris - Bellegarde - (Évian les Bains) and v.v. at weekends – see Table **364**.
⊖ – Also call at Le Creusot TGV (d. 2236).

PARIS - LYON ST EXUPÉRY ✈ - GRENOBLE 342

Shows complete service Paris - Lyon St Exupéry ✈ and v.v. Journeys not serving Grenoble continue to destinations in other tables

km	All trains convey 🍷	TGV 6901	TGV 6905	TGV 6191	TGV 6905	TGV 6193	TGV 6911	TGV 6943		TGV 6915	TGV 6919	TGV 9249	TGV 6921	TGV 6947	TGV 6195	TGV 6923		TGV 6925	TGV 6951	TGV 6927	TGV 6197	TGV 6927	TGV 6929	
		Ⓐ		①–⑥	⑦					⑥						Ⓑ		Ⓐ		⑤			⑤⑦	
			F	n	E					t					⊙	d			z	f		B	w	
0	**Paris Gare de Lyon** d.	0638	0738	0746	0746	0946	0946	1050	...	1238	1346	1524	1638	1650	1746	1746	...	1838	1850	1938	1946	1946	2038	...
441	Lyon St Exupéry ✈ a.	|	|	0938	0939	1139	1139	1243	...	|	1539	1717	|	1843	1939	1939	...	|	2043	|	2139	2139	|	...
441	Lyon St Exupéry ✈ d.	|	|	...	0946	...	1146	...	...	|	1546	...	|	...	...	1946	...	|	...	|	...	2146	|	...
553	**Grenoble** a.	0933	1033	...	1050	...	1249	...	...	1535	1650	...	1933	...	...	2050	...	2133	...	2236	...	2248	2333	...

	TGV 6900	TGV 6192	TGV 6902		TGV 6904	TGV 6194		TGV 6908	TGV 6912		TGV 6196	TGV 6916		TGV 6920	TGV 6198		TGV 6922	TGV 6924		TGV 6926	TGV 9248		TGV 6928	
	①–④	Ⓐ	Ⓐ		①–⑥				⑥								Ⓐ			⑤			⑦	
	m				n			⊡	u									A		f			e	
renoble d.	0521	...	0601	...	0725	...	...	1005	1205	...	...	1322	...	1605	...	...	1805	1921	...	2005	...	...	2122	...
yon St Exupéry ✈ a.	|	...	0710	...	0830	...	...	1110	|	...	...	|	...	1710	...	...	1910	|	...	2110	...	...	|	...
yon St Exupéry ✈ d.	|	0647	0713	...	0833	0933	...	1112	|	...	1417	|	...	1713	1816	...	1913	|	...	2113	2127	...	|	...
aris Gare de Lyon a.	0819	0841	0907	...	1027	1127	...	1313	1507	...	1611	1619	...	1907	2011	...	2107	2219	...	2307	2319	...	0019	...

– Daily except ⑤ (will not run Dec. 24, 31, Apr. 30, May 7).
– Daily except ⑤ (also runs May 2; not Apr. 30, May 7).
– ⑦ Dec. 9 - Mar. 30 (also Dec. 25, Jan. 1; not Feb. 24, Mar. 2, 9).
– ⑥⑦ Feb. 23 - Mar. 9.
– Not May 1, 2, 8.
– Also Dec. 25, Jan. 1, Mar. 24, May 12; not Dec. 23, 30.

f – Also Apr. 30, May 7; not May 2.
m – Not Dec. 25, Jan. 1, Mar. 24, Apr. 30, May 1, 7, 8, 12.
n – Not Dec. 25, Jan. 1, Mar. 24, May 12.
t – Also May 1, 8.
u – Also Mar. 2, 9, May 1, 8.
w – Also Dec. 25, Jan. 1, Mar. 24, Apr. 30, May 7, 12.

z – Not Dec. 31.
TGV – Ⓡ, supplement payable, 🍷.
⊡ – Also calls at Le Creusot TGV (depart 1150).
⊙ – Not May 2. Train **6923** on ⑤⑦.

LYON - GRENOBLE 343

km																										
						Ⓐ					Ⓐ		Ⓐ		Ⓐ		Ⓐ		Ⓐ							Ⓐ
							◇			◇		◇		◇		◇		◇		◇	◇		◇		◇	
0	**Lyon Part-Dieu** . 344 d.	0557	0645	0703	0745	0815	0845	0945	...	1045	1115	1145	1215	1245	1315	1345	1415	1445	1515	1545	1603	...	1645	1715	1745	1811
41	Bourgoin-Jallieu . 344 d.	0627	0715	0732	0813	|	0913	1013	...	1115	|	1213	|	1314	|	1413	|	1515	|	1613	1632	...	1714	1745	1815	1836
56	La Tour du Pin ... 344 d.	0637	0726	0743	0824	|	0924	1024	...	1126	|	1224	|	1325	|	1424	|	1525	|	1624	1643	...	1725	1755	1825	|
104	Voiron d.	0713	0755	|	0854	|	0954	1054	...	1155	|	1254	|	1354	|	1454	|	1554	|	1654	1714	...	1755	1825	1854	|
129	**Grenoble** a.	0730	0811	0831	0911	0929	1011	1111	...	1211	1229	1311	1329	1411	1429	1511	1529	1611	1629	1711	1731	...	1811	1846	1911	1929

				TGV 5333		TGV 5123	TGV 5335		TGV 5132	
		Ⓐ		⑤		①–⑥	⑦		⑦	⑤–⑦
	◇			Nf		Ln	Ne		Le	w
yon Part-Dieu .... 344 d.	1845	1915	1945	2037	2045	2111	2137	2145	2207	2245
ourgoin-Jallieu .... 344 d.	1912	1944	2014	|	2116	|	|	2215	|	2314
a Tour du Pin ...... 344 d.	1924	1955	2024	|	2126	|	|	2226	|	2325
oiron d.	1954	2028	2054	|	2154	|	|	2256	|	2355
renoble a.	2011	2046	2111	2153	2211	2225	2253	2312	2317	0011

	TGV 5154		TGV 5352	TGV 5160						TGV 5364
	①–⑥	⚒	①	⑦		Ⓐ		Ⓐ		⑥
	Ln		Ng	Le	◇		◇		◇	Nt
Grenoble d.	0451	0458	0532	0540	0544	0615	0644	0714	0744	0811
Voiron d.	|	0515	|	|	0601	0634	0701	|	0801	|
La Tour du Pin ... 344 d.	|	0545	|	|	0631	0706	0731	0759	0831	|
Bourgoin-Jallieu ... 344 d.	|	0557	|	|	0642	0717	0743	0810	0843	|
Lyon Part-Dieu ... 344 a.	0604	0629	0650	0653	0712	0746	0812	0842	0912	0920

	Ⓐ		Ⓐ		Ⓐ		Ⓐ		Ⓐ		Ⓐ				Ⓐ					Ⓐ		Ⓐ				
		◇		◇		◇		◇		◇		◇							◇		◇		◇			
renoble d.	0826	0844	0926	0944	1026	1044	1126	1144	1226	1244	1326	1344	1444	1544	1625	1644	...	1725	1744	1825	1844	1926	1944	2043	2144	...
oiron d.	|	0900	|	1001	|	1101	|	1201	|	1301	|	1401	1501	1601	1642	1701	...	1742	1801	|	1901	|	2001	2101	2202	...
a Tour du Pin ..... 344 d.	|	0930	|	1031	|	1132	|	1231	|	1331	|	1431	1531	1631	1713	1730	...	1816	1831	1911	1931	|	2031	2131	2232	...
ourgoin-Jallieu ... 344 d.	|	0942	|	1043	|	1143	|	1243	|	1343	|	1443	1543	1643	1725	1741	...	1828	1843	1921	1943	|	2043	2143	2245	...
yon Part-Dieu ... 344 a.	0942	1012	1042	1112	1142	1212	1242	1312	1342	1412	1442	1512	1612	1712	1759	1812	...	1859	1912	1946	2012	2042	2112	2212	2312	...

– 🚃12 Grenoble - Charles de Gaulle ✈ - Lille Europe and v.v. (Table **11**).
– 🚃12 Grenoble - Massy - Nantes and v.v. (Table **335**).
– Also Dec. 25, Jan. 1, Mar. 24, May 12.

f – Also Apr. 30, May 7; not May 2.
g – Also Dec. 26, Jan. 2, Mar. 25, May 13; not Dec. 24, 31, Mar. 24, May 12.
n – Not Dec. 25, Jan. 1, Mar. 24, May 12.
t – Also May 1, 8.

w – Also Dec. 25, Jan. 1, Mar. 24, May 1, 8, 12.
TGV – Ⓡ, supplement payable, 🍷.
◇ – To / from Dijon (Table **502**).

LYON - CHAMBÉRY - ANNECY 344

km		D			⚒		⚒						V		E		⑥B						Z		
		△							◇				§				△	§		△			△		⊖
	Lyon Perrache d.	...	...	...	...	...	...	...	...	...	...	...	...	...	1316	...	...	...	...	...	...	...	...	...
0	**Lyon Part Dieu** 343 d.	0633	...	0738	0741	...	0841	...	0941	1038	...	1138	1230	1241	1338	...	1425	1441	1445	1541	1638	1641	...	1738
41	Bourgoin-Jallieu 343 d.	0658	...	|	0807	...	0906	...	|	|	...	|	|	1307	|	...	|	1506	|	1605	|	1706	...	|
56	La Tour du Pin 343 d.	0709	...	|	|	...	|	...	|	|	...	|	|	|	|	...	|	|	|	|	|	|	...	|
50	Ambérieu ▷ d.	|	...	0809	|	...	|	...	|	1109	...	1212	|	|	|	...	|	|	1510	|	1709	|	...	1808
*106	**Chambéry** a.	0756	...	|	0901	...	0955	...	1059	|	...	1311	1402	1356	1449	...	1602	1600	|	1657	|	1755	...	|
*106	**Chambéry** 341 365 d.	...	0814	|	...	...	...	1014	...	|	...	|	...	1405	1455	...	|	...	|	...	|	...	...	|
*120	Aix les Bains 341 365 a.	...	0825	0855	...	...	...	1025	...	1159	...	1256x	...	1416	1506	...	1549x	...	1557	...	1756	...	...	1854
*159	**Annecy** 341 365 a.	...	0908	0933	...	...	...	1107	...	1245	...	...	...	1456	1556	...	...	...	1642	...	1852	...	...	1929

	§			◇§					
yon Perrache d.	...	...	...	...	...	...	...	...	...
yon Part Dieu 343 d.	1741	1841	...	1941	...	2041	...	2141	...
ourgoin-Jallieu 343 d.	|	|	...	|	...	|	...	2209	...
a Tour du Pin 343 d.	|	1913	...	|	...	|	...	|	...
Ambérieu ▷ d.	|	|	...	|	...	|	...	|	...
hambéry a.	1859r	1956	...	2100	...	2156	...	2258	...
hambéry 341 365 d.	...	2004	...	...	2114	2205	...	...	...
ix les Bains 341 365 a.	...	2015	...	...	2125	2216	...	...	...
nnecy 341 365 a.	...	2055	...	...	2204	2249	...	...	...

		⚒		⚒	V			Y	Z
				△		△		§	§
Annecy 341 365 d.	...	0523	0609	...	...	...	0730	...	...
Aix les Bains 341 365 d.	...	0601	0644	0704z	...	...	0814	...	...
Chambéry 341 365 a.	...	|	0655	|	...	...	|	...	...
Chambéry d.	0601	|	0701	0651	0735	0801	|	0858	0901
Ambérieu ▷ d.	|	0651	|	0806	|	|	0901	0959	0959
La Tour du Pin 343 d.	|	|	|	|	|	|	|	|	|
Bourgoin-Jallieu 343 d.	0652	|	0753	|	0828	0851	|	|	|
Lyon Part Dieu 343 a.	0716	0726	0816	0843	0854	0916	0926	1026	1026v
Lyon Perrache a.	...	...	...	0855	...	...	...	...	...

		⚒	F		Z	⚒	Y	Z		W		Y					Z	Y		Ⓑ		d		Ⓑ
	d	▽		△			§			△		§	◇		◇		§	§				△		
nnecy 341 365 d.	0853	...	1039	...	...	...	...	...	1333	...	1435	...	...	...	...	1629	...	...	1815	...	1900	...	1931	...
ix les Bains 341 365 d.	0941	...	1116	...	1216z	...	...	...	1408	...	1516	1555z	...	...	...	1712	...	...	1850	...	1935	...	2013	...
hambéry 341 365 a.	0952	...	|	...	|	...	...	...	|	...	|	|	...	...	...	|	...	...	|	∴	1946	...	|	...
hambéry d.	...	1001	|	1201	1204	1301	1400	1401	|	1450	|	1540	1601	...	1701	|	1801	1801	|	1901	...	2001	|	2101
Ambérieu ▷ d.	...	|	1200	|	1300	|	|	|	1453	|	1601	|	|	...	|	1800	|	|	1940	|	...	|	2100	|
a Tour du Pin 343 d.	...	|	|	|	|	|	|	|	|	|	|	|	|	...	|	|	|	|	|	|	...	2044	|	|
ourgoin-Jallieu 343 d.	...	1053	|	1251	|	|	1451	1452	|	|	|	|	1652	...	|	|	1852	1854	|	|	...	|	|	|
yon Part Dieu 343 a.	...	1116	1226	1316	1323	1416	1516	1516	1517	1614	1626c	1719	1716	...	1816	1826	1916	1920	2006	2016	...	2116	2126	2221
yon Perrache a.	...	...	1247	...	...	...	...	...	...	1628	...	...	...	...	...	...	...	...	...	...	...	...	...	...

B – ⑥ Dec. 15 - Apr. 26.
D – Daily to May 3; ⚒ from May 5.
E – Ⓐ to Mar. 28 (also Dec. 9, 16, 25); Ⓑ Mar. 31 - Apr. 25; daily from Apr. 27.
F – Not Dec. 14 - 17, 22, 23, 29, 30, Jan. 5, 6, Feb. 9, 10, 16, 17, 23, 24, Mar. 1, 2, 8, 9, 15, 22, 29, May 13 - 16, 19 - 23.
V – For days of running see Table **368**.
W – For days of running see Table **369**.
Y – ⑥⑦ to Apr. 27 (also Dec. 25, Jan. 1, Mar. 24, May 1).

Z – Ⓐ to Apr. 30; daily from May 2.
c – 1649 on Jan. 7 - 11, 14, 15.
d – Not Feb. 23, Mar. 1, 8.
r – Arrive 1920 on ⑥ Dec. 15 - Mar. 29.
v – Subject to alteration Mar. 31 - Apr. 18.
x – Calls at Aix les Bains before Chambéry.
z – Calls at Aix les Baims after Chambéry.

◇ – To / from Dijon (Table **373**).
△ – To / from Modane (Table **369**).
▽ – From Modane on dates in Table **369**.
⊖ – To Annemasse and Évian les Bains (Tables **367** / **364**).
▷ – Lyon - Ambérieu: see also Table **345**.
§ – To / from Bourg St Maurice (Table **368**).
* – Distances via Ambérieu: Chambéry *138 km*, Aix les Bains *124 km*, Annecy *163 km*.

FRANCE

345 LYON - BELLEGARDE - GENÈVE

Certain trains convey through portions Lyon - Bellegarde - Annemasse - St Gervais (see Table **367**)

km		⚒r	Ⓐr	4678 4679 ®Z		Ⓐr	⚒			b	Ⓐr	△		D		TGV 6866 M	⊖ Ⓐ	⊖ Ⓒ		TGV 6886 N	Ⓐr			TGV 6874 L
0	**Lyon Part Dieu** 344 d.	...	...	0651	0704	...	0804	0904	1104	...	...	1304	...	1350	1504	1556	1704	1704	...	1804	...	1904	2004	2056
50	Ambérieu 344 d.	...	...	|	0730	...	0830	0930	1130	...	...	1330	...	|	1530	|	1731	1730	...	|	...	1930	2032	|
102	Culoz d.	...	...	|	0805	...	0902	1002	1202	...	...	1402	...	|	1602	|	1802	1803	...	|	...	2003	2106	|
135	Bellegarde 341 365 d.	0619	0645	|	0828	0845	0929	1028	1228	1307	1345	1428	1507	1520	1628	1710	1828	1826	1903	1917	1945	2028	2132	2210
168	**Genève** 341 365 a.	0654	0726	0845	0857	0926	0957	1057	1257	1332	1426	1457	1532	...	1657	1735	1857	...	1932	1942	2026	2057	2157	2233

	⚒		Ⓐr	TGV 6806 L	Ⓐ	Ⓒ			Ⓐr	Ⓐr	TGV 6816 M		TGV 6818 N	c				Ⓐr	Ⓐr		Ⓐr			4778 4779 ®Y
Genève 341 365 d.	0558	0658	0735	0817	0858	0858	1016	1058	1142	1205	1244	1258	1344	1358	1417	1617	1658z	1735	1755	1817	1835	1858	1958	2044
Bellegarde 341 365 d.	0627	0729	0813	0848	0928	0923	1045	1126	1222	1245	1311	1328	1411	1425	1446	1650	1729z	1811	1827	1845	1911	1928	2028	|
Culoz d.	0648	0752	...	|	0955	...	...	1146	...	...	|	1351	|	1451	...	...	1751	...	...	...	...	1951	2051	|
Ambérieu 344 d.	0724	0823	...	|	1036	...	...	1223	...	...	|	1423	|	1523	...	...	1823	...	...	...	...	2023	2123	|
Lyon Part Dieu 344 a.	0751	0847	...	1001	1101	...	...	1247	...	...	1426	1447	1531	1550	...	...	1847	...	...	...	...	2047	2147	2245

B – Ⓑ to Apr. 25; daily from Apr. 27.
D – ⑥ Dec. 15 - Apr. 26 (also ⑦ Dec. 23 - Jan. 6, Feb. 10 - Mar. 9). To Évian les Bains (Table **364**).
L – [12] Genève - Lyon - Marseille and v.v. (Table **350**).
M – [12] Genève - Lyon - Montpellier and v.v. (Table **350**).
N – [12] Genève - Lyon - Marseille - Nice and v.v. (Table **350**).
Y – 🛏 1, 2 cl. and [2] (reclining) Genève - Lyon - Toulouse - Irún. For days of running see Table **355**.
Z – 🛏 1, 2 cl. and [2] (reclining) Hendaye - Toulouse - Lyon - Genève. For days of running see Table **355**.
b – Not on ⑥ Dec. 22 - Apr. 12.
c – Not Feb. 23, Mar. 1, 8.
r – Also May 8; not Dec. 26, Jan. 2, Mar. 21.
z – On ⑥ Dec. 15 - Apr. 26 Genève d. 1644, Bellegarde 1724.

TGV – ®, supplement payable, 🍷.
△ – Runs 9 - 20 minutes later on ⑥⑦ Dec. 22 - Jan. 6, ⑥⑦ Feb. 9 - Mar. 2 (also Mar. 9).
⊖ – From Lyon Perrache, depart 1650.

346 MÂCON - BOURG EN BRESSE - AMBÉRIEU - (LYON)

Mostly 2nd class

km		⚒		Ⓐ	Ⓐ	🚌	🚌 Ⓐ	Ⓐ	🚌 ⑥	Ⓐ	🚌 ⚒	🚌	🚌	⑥	Ⓐ	🚌	⚒c	🚌	🚌	⚒	🚌 Ⓐ	Ⓐ	🚌	🚌	🚌	🚌
0	**Mâcon Ville** d.	...	...	0655	...	0710	0725	...	...	0810	...	0925	...	1156	1156	...	1310	1455	...	1650	...	1755	...	1855	...	2055
37	Bourg en Bresse d.	0653	0712	0726	0734	0815	0805	0827	0827	0841	0927	1025	1027	1223	1224	1312	1340	1555	1627	1723	1825	1826	1827	1955	2027	2150
68	Ambérieu ▷ a.	0712	0750	...	0750	...	...	0850	0905	...	1005	...	1105	...	1248	1350	...	...	1705	1749	1855	...	1905	...	2105	...
118	**Lyon Part-Dieu** ▷ a.	0747	...	...	0826	...	...	...	...	...	...	...	...	...	...	...	...	...	...	...	...	...	...	...	...	...

	🚌 Ⓐ	h	🚌 ⑥	Ⓐd	🚌	🚌 Ⓐ	h	⚒k	⚒r	🚌	🚌	Ⓐ	🚌	⚒s	b	Ⓐ	🚌	🚌	Ⓐ	⚒	L	🚌	🚌	🚌	Ⓐ	†b
Lyon Part-Dieu ▷ d.	...	...	...	...	...	...	...	...	...	...	...	...	...	...	1550	...	...	...	...	...	1838	...	...	...	2112	2122
Ambérieu ▷ d.	...	...	0700	0707	0800	0807	...	0917	...	1217	...	1317	1417	...	1617	...	...	1717	...	1817	1909	...	1917	2117	2154	2158
Bourg en Bresse d.	0640	0732	0740	0734	0842	0840	0932	0940	1231	1257	1332	1341	1457	1612	1635	1715	1732	1757	1832	1840	1930	1932	1957	2157	2212	2216
Mâcon Ville a.	0715	0803	...	...	...	...	1003	...	1300	...	1435	...	...	1643	...	1746	1835	...	1903	...	...	2030	...	...	...	...

L – ①②③④⑥.
b – To Besançon (Table **384**).
c – Not Feb. 9, 11.
d – To Dijon (see panel to right).
h – By 🚌 on Ⓒ (arrive Mâcon Ville 30 minutes later).
k – By 🚌 on ⑥ (arrive Bourg en Bresse 0957).
r – 10 minutes earlier on ⑥ Dec. 22 - Apr. 19.

km		⚒		⚒	Ⓐ		
0	Dijon d.	0645	0941	1249	1738	1756	1924
86	Louhans d.	0758	1053	1401	1843	1856	2039
140	Bourg en Bresse a.	0830	1124	1433	1917	1930	2112

	Ⓐ		⚒		Ⓑ
Bourg en Bresse d.	0534	0736	1136	1720	1839
Louhans d.	0608	0810	1215	1754	1911
Dijon a.	0717	0912	1335	1855	2008

s – 30 minutes later on ⑥ Dec. 22 - Apr. 19.
▷ – See also Tables **344**/**345**.

347 LYON - ST ÉTIENNE

Engineering work may affect journeys from Mar. 3

km	*TGV* trains convey 🍷		⚒	⚒	⚒	⚒		⚒		Ⓐ		Ⓐ	TGV 6681 P		Ⓐ		Ⓐ		Ⓐ			Ⓐ		⚒		Ⓐ
	Paris ▽ **340** d.	...	...	...	...	...	...	...	...	...	...	...	0654	...	...	...	...	...	...	...	...	...	...	...	...	...
0	**Lyon Part-Dieu** d.	0019	0619	...	0649	...	0719	...	0749	...	0819	0849	0858	0919	0949	1019	1049	1119	1149	1219	...	1249	1319	1349	1419	1449
	Lyon Perrache d.	|	|	0636	|	0706	|	0733	|	0806	|	|	|	|	|	|	|	|	|	|	1236	|	|	|	|	|
22	Givors Ville d.	0038	0638	0654	0708	0724	0738	0754	0808	0824	0838	0908	|	0938	1008	1038	1108	1138	1208	1238	1254	1308	1338	1409	1438	1508
47	St Chamond d.	0058	0658	0715	0728	0745	0758	0815	0828	0845	0858	0928	|	0958	1028	1058	1128	1158	1228	1258	1315	1328	1358	1428	1458	1528
59	**St Étienne** ⊙ a.	0108	0708	0724	0738	0754	0808	0824	0838	0854	0908	0938	0941	1008	1038	1108	1138	1208	1238	1310	1329	1338	1408	1438	1508	1538

	TGV 6685		Ⓐ	Ⓐ		⚒	Ⓑ	Ⓑ			Ⓐ	Ⓐ			Ⓐ	TGV 6687	Ⓐ			Ⓐ		Ⓑ	TGV 6689		Ⓑ	
Paris ▽ **340** d.	1254	...	...	...	...	...	...	...	...	...	...	...	...	...	...	1654	...	...	...	...	...	...	1854	...	...	...
Lyon Part-Dieu d.	1458	1519	1549	...	1619	...	1649	...	1719	...	1749	...	1819	...	1849	1900	...	1919	...	1949	2019	2049	2058	2119	2219	2319
Lyon Perrache d.	|	|	|	1606	|	1636	|	1706	|	1736	|	1806	|	1836	|	|	1906	|	1936	|	|	|	|	|	|	|
Givors Ville d.	|	1538	1608	1624	1638	1655	1708	1724	1738	1754	1808	1824	1838	1854	1908	|	1924	1938	1954	2008	2038	2108	|	2138	2238	2338
St Chamond d.	|	1558	1628	1645	1658	1718	1728	1745	1758	1815	1828	1845	1858	1915	1928	|	1945	1958	2015	2028	2058	2128	|	2158	2258	2358
St Étienne ⊙ a.	1541	1608	1638	1700	1708	1730	1738	1754	1808	1824	1838	1854	1908	1924	1938	1941	1954	2008	2024	2038	2108	2138	2141	2208	2308	0008

	⚒		TGV 6691 P	⚒	Ⓐ		⚒	⚒	Ⓐ	⚒		⚒	Ⓐ	⚒		⚒ b	Ⓐ		TGV 6693	Ⓐ				TGV 6695	⚒	
St Étienne ⊙ d.	0518	0548	0615	0618	0631	0648	0701	0718	0731	0737	0748	0801	0818	0831	0848	0901	0918	0948	1014	1018	1048	1118	1148	1214	1218	1248
St Chamond d.	0529	0558	|	0629	0640	0659	0710	0729	0740	0747	0759	0810	0830	0840	0859	0911	0929	0959	|	1029	1059	1129	1159	|	1229	1259
Givors Ville d.	0550	0618	|	0650	0703	0719	0732	0750	0802	0808	0820	0832	0850	0902	0920	0931	0950	1020	|	1050	1120	1150	1220	|	1250	1320
Lyon Perrache a.	|	|	|	|	0723	|	0750	|	0820	|	|	0850	|	0920	|	0950	|	|	|	|	|	|	|	|	|	|
Lyon Part-Dieu a.	0608	0638	0654	0708	...	0738	...	0808	...	0826	0838	...	0908	...	0938	...	1008	1038	1054	1108	1138	1208	1238	1254	1308	1338
Paris ▽ **340** a.	...	...	0857	...	...	...	...	...	...	...	...	...	...	...	...	...	...	...	1257	...	...	...	...	1505	...	...

		Ⓐ	◇	Ⓐ		Ⓐ	Ⓐ	Ⓐ	Ⓐ				Ⓐ			TGV 6697	Ⓐ		Ⓑ		Ⓑ		Ⓑ			
St Étienne ⊙ d.	1301	1318	1348	1418	1448	1518	1548	1618	1631	1648	1701	1718	1731	1748	1801	1814	1818	1831	1848	1901	1918	1948	2018	2048	2118	2218
St Chamond d.	1310	1329	1359	1429	1459	1529	1559	1629	1640	1659	1710	1729	1740	1759	1810	|	1829	1840	1859	1910	1929	1959	2028	2059	2129	2229
Givors Ville d.	1332	1350	1420	1450	1520	1550	1620	1650	1702	1720	1732	1750	1802	1820	1832	|	1850	1902	1920	1932	1950	2020	2048	2120	2150	2250
Lyon Perrache a.	1350	|	|	|	|	|	|	|	1720	|	1750	|	1820	|	1850	|	|	1920	|	1950	|	|	|	|	|	|
Lyon Part-Dieu a.	...	1408	1438	1508	1538	1608	1638	1708	...	1738	...	1808	...	1838	...	1854	1908	...	1938	...	2008	2038	2108	2138	2208	2308
Paris ▽ **340** a.	...	...	...	...	...	...	...	...	...	...	...	...	...	...	...	2057	...	...	...	...	...	...	...	...	...	...

P – ①-⑥ (not Dec. 25, Jan. 1, Mar. 24, May 12).
b – Not Apr. 21 - 25, 28 - 30, May 5 - 10, 13 - 16, 19 - 23.
TGV – ®, supplement payable, 🍷.
◇ – From Le Puy en Velay (Table **348**).
▽ – Paris Gare de Lyon.
⊙ – St Étienne Châteaucreux.

Additional journeys:
Lyon Perrache - St Étienne 0536 Ⓐ.
St Étienne - Lyon Perrache 0531 ⚒, 0601 ⚒.

348 ST ÉTIENNE - LE PUY

km		⚒		⚒					Ⓐ		
	Lyon Part Dieu **347** d.	...	...	...	...	...	...	...	...	...	...
0	**St Étienne** ⊙ d.	0612	0813	0953	1222	1553	1713	1818	1913	2019	2152
15	Firminy d.	0629	0831	1011	1240	1611	1735	1836	1935	2037	2214
88	**Le Puy en Velay** a.	0741	0938	1116	1354	1720	1837	1949	2039	2138	2315

	⚒	Ⓐ	†	⚒						†
Le Puy en Velay d.	0603	0746	0806	0837	1039	1209	1617	1735	1841	1911
Firminy d.	0713	0852	0913	0943	1143	1321	1725	1856	1953	2016
St Étienne ⊙ a.	0738	0909	0931	1000	1201	1343	1743	1912	2010	2034
Lyon Part Dieu **347** a.	...	...	...	...	...	1438	...	...	...	2138

⊙ – St Étienne Châteaucreux.

Additional journeys: Le Puy - St Étienne 0445 Ⓐ, 0535 Ⓐ.

BORDEAUX - BERGERAC - SARLAT - SOUILLAC 349

Some trains 2nd class

km																									
		①	Ⓐ	⚒		⚒	†			Ⓐ	Ⓒ	Ⓐ	Ⓐ				Ⓐ	Ⓐ			⚒	⑤	Ⓑ		
		g		⊗					△	d			b	⊕								f			
0	**Bordeaux St Jean 300/6** d.	...	0556	0707	...	0801	0834	...	1047	...	1043	1223	...	1334	...	1604	1651	1729	...	1811	1920	2032	2144	...	...
37	Libourne **300/6** d.	...	0624	0746	...	0829	0911	...	1114	1113	1113	1251	1257	1403	...	1631	1722	1813	...	1845	1949	2108	2215	...	...
99	Bergerac d.	0550	0727	0849	...	0915	1005	...	...	1203	1203	...	1355	1449	...	1724	1817	1919	...	1932	2040	2201	2300	...	...
135	Le Buisson a.	0630	0806	0923	...	...	1039	...	...	1238	1238	...	...	1521	...	1803	...	...	...	2007	...	2236	...	...	...
135	Le Buisson d.	0631	0817	0924	...	...	1047	...	...	1239	1239	...	...	1522	...	1804x	...	...	...	2013	...	2237	...	...	...
168	**Sarlat** a.	0712	0900	1005	...	...	1129	...	...	1321	1321	...	...	1603	...	1847x	...	...	...	2055	...	2318	...	...	...

	①	⚒		Ⓐ	Ⓐ	⑥				†	Ⓐb			Ⓐb	⑥				Ⓑ				⑤⑦		
	g				c								k			m							w		
Sarlat d.	...	...	...	...	0602z	...	...	0728	...	...	...	...	1012	...	...	1205	...	1608	...	...	1736	...	1942	...	...
Le Buisson a.	...	...	...	...	0644z	...	...	0809	...	...	...	...	1051	...	...	1247	...	1647	...	...	1818	...	2022	...	...
Le Buisson d.	...	...	...	...	0645	...	...	0810	...	...	...	...	1052	...	...	1252	...	1648	...	...	1819	...	2023	...	...
Bergerac d.	0520	0601	...	0642	0726	0725	...	0853	...	1013	1013	...	1129	1215	1236	1330	...	1721	1819	...	1857	...	2059	...	...
Libourne **300/6** a.	0606	0653	...	0741	0816	0816	...	0939	...	1102	1102	...	1214	1312	1333	1420	...	1811	1917	...	1948	...	2141	...	...
Bordeaux St Jean 300/6 a.	0632	0725	...	0810	0847	0845	...	1009	...	1129	...	...	1245	1343	1404	1451	...	1840	1953	...	2032	...	2209	...	...

km	By 🚌 §										
							†				
0	**Sarlat** d.	...	1219	...	...	...	1824	...	...	...	...
30	**Souillac** a.	...	1300	...	...	...	1905	...	...	...	...

By 🚌 §										
		⑥				⑤		Ⓐ		
Souillac d.	...	0910	...	1501	...	1843	...	2210	...	...
Sarlat a.	...	0951	...	1539	...	1921	...	2250	...	...

b – Subject to alteration Mar. 3 - Apr. 4.
c – Not Dec. 24, 31.
d – Subject to alteration Mar. 3 - Apr. 4 (also Bergerac - Sarlat on ①–④ Jan. 7 - 31, Apr. 7 - 29).
f – Also Apr. 30, May 7; not May 2, 9.
g – Also Dec. 26, Jan. 2, Mar. 25, May 13; not Dec. 24, 31, Mar. 24, May 12.
k – Subject to alteration Mar. 3 - Apr. 4 (also Sarlat - Bergerac on ①–④ Jan. 7 - 31).
m – Subject to alteration ①–④ Mar. 3 - Apr. 3 (also Sarlat - Bergerac Ⓐ Jan. 7 - Feb. 1, ①–④ Apr. 7 - 29).
w – Also Dec. 25, Jan. 1, Mar. 24, Apr. 30, May 1, 7, 8, 12; not May 2, 9.
x – On ⑤ (also Apr. 30, May 7; not May 2, 9) depart Le Buisson 1828, arrive Sarlat 1910.
z – On ① (also Dec. 26, Jan. 2, Mar. 25, May 13; not Mar. 24, May 12) depart Sarlat d. 0531, Le Buisson a. 0617.

⊕ – Subject to alteration Libourne - Bergerac on ①–④ Mar. 3 - Apr. 3.
⊗ – Subject to alteration Bergerac - Sarlat on Ⓐ Jan. 7 - Feb. 1, Ⓐ Mar. 3 - Apr. 4.
△ – Not Dec. 15, Mar. 3 - 6, 10 - 13, 17 - 20, 25 - 27, 29.
§ – Rail tickets not valid. Most journeys continue beyond the SNCF stations to and from the town centres of Sarlat and Souillac. Timings subject to alteration.

Subject to alteration Bergerac - Sarlat and v.v. Dec. 9 - 21 (also Apr. 12, 13) with 🚌 substitution

PARIS and LYON - MONTPELLIER, MARSEILLE and NICE via high-speed line 350

TGV Méditerranée

km	All *TGV* trains are 🅁	*TGV* 6831	*TGV* 6815	*TGV* 5355	*TGV* 6803	*TGV* 6133	*TGV* 6801	*TGV* 6805	*TGV* 6101	*TGV* 6201	*TGV* 6809	*TGV* 6811	*TGV* 6103	*TGV* 5301	*TGV* 6203	*TGV* 5102	*TGV* 6171	*TGV* 9804	*TGV* 5104	*TGV* 6105	*TGV* 6205	*TGV* 6807	*TGV* 6813	*TGV* 5110
		①	Ⓐ	Ⓑ	⑥	Ⓐ	Ⓐ	Ⓒ	Ⓐ	Ⓐ	Ⓐ	Ⓒ						Ⓐ	Ⓒ					
		g		h	t						⊡			A			⊕							
	Brussels Midi **11** d.	...	...	...	...	...	...	...	...	...	...	...	...	...	...	...	...	0540	...	...	...	...	...	...
	Lille Europe **11** d.	...	...	...	...	...	...	...	...	...	...	...	...	...	...	0559	...	0625	0625	...	...	...	...	0643r
	Charles de Gaulle ✈ d.	...	...	...	...	...	...	...	...	...	...	...	...	...	...	0654	...	0725	0725	...	...	...	...	0821
	Marne la Vallée-Chessy § d.	...	...	...	...	...	...	...	...	...	...	...	...	...	...	0710	...	0740	0740	...	...	...	...	0835
0	**Paris Gare de Lyon** d.	...	...	...	...	0606	...	...	0616	0620	...	...	0716	...	0720	|	0804	|	|	0816	0820	...	...	|
	Genève **345** d.	...	...	...	...	|	...	...	|	|	...	...	|	...	|	|	|	|	|	|	|	0817	...	|
	Dijon **373** d.	...	...	...	...	|	0549	...	|	|	...	0645	|	...	|	|	|	|	|	|	|	|	0816x	|
	Lyon Part Dieu d.	0050p	0637	0710	0710	|	0736	0737	|	|	0837	0837	|	...	|	0907	|	0937	0937	|	|	1007	1011	1037
527	Valence TGV d.	|	|	|	|	|	0816	0816	|	0834	0915	0915	|	...	|	|	|	1016	1016	|	1034	|	|	1115
657	**Avignon TGV** d.	|	0743	|	|	|	0853	0853	0901	|	0951	0951	0959	1004	|	1012	1046	|	|	|	|	1113	|	1149
686	Nîmes **355** d.	|	|	0830	0830	|	|	|	|	0919	|	|	|	|	1013	|	|	1102	1102	|	1120	|	1128	|
736	**Montpellier 355** a.	|	|	0855	0855	|	|	|	|	0944	|	|	|	|	1038	|	|	1129	1129	|	1147	|	1155	|
	Sète **355** a.	|	|	|	|	|	|	|	|	...	|	|	|	|	|	|	|	|	|	|	...	|	...	|
	Agde **355** a.	|	|	|	|	|	|	|	|	...	|	|	|	|	|	|	|	|	|	|	...	|	...	|
	Béziers **355** a.	|	|	0941	0941	|	|	|	|	...	|	|	|	|	1125	|	|	1213	1213	|	...	|	...	|
	Narbonne **355** a.	|	|	0959	0959	|	|	|	|	...	|	|	|	|	1145	|	|	1235	1235	|	...	|	...	|
	Toulouse **321** a.	|	|	1121	|	|	|	|	|	...	|	|	|	|	|	|	|	1356	1356	|	...	|	...	|
	Perpignan 355 a.	|	|	...	1035	|	|	|	|	...	|	|	|	|	1221	|	|	...	...	|	...	|	...	|
731	Aix en Provence TGV d.	|	0807	...	...	0902	|	|	|	...	|	|	1022	1029	...	1035	|	...	...	|	...	1136	...	1213
750	**Marseille St Charles** a.	|	0819	...	...	|	0923	0923	0929	...	1025	1025	1035	1040	...	1047	|	...	...	1119	...	1147	...	1225
750	**Marseille St Charles 360** d.	|	0832	...	...	|	...	0935	...	...	...	...	...	...	...	1100	|	...	...	1131	...	...	...	...
817	**Toulon 360** a.	0550	0912	...	...	0948	...	1015	...	...	...	...	...	...	...	1138	|	...	...	1215	...	...	...	...
885	Les Arcs-Draguignan **360** a.	0629	|	...	...	...	...	|	...	...	...	...	...	...	...	1213	1220	...	...	...	...	...	...	...
911	St Raphaël-Valescure **360** a.	0648	1005	...	...	...	...	1108	...	...	...	...	...	...	...	1231	1238	...	...	...	...	...	...	...
944	Cannes **360** a.	0715	1031	...	...	...	...	1136	...	...	...	...	...	...	...	1255	1303	...	...	...	...	...	...	...
955	Antibes **360** a.	0727	1043	...	...	...	...	1148	...	...	...	...	...	...	...	1307	1315	...	...	...	...	...	...	...
975	**Nice 360** a.	0745	1101	...	...	...	...	1206	...	...	...	...	...	...	...	1325	1336	...	...	...	...	...	...	...

	TGV 6107	*TGV* 6207	*TGV* 5148	*TGV* 6173	*TGV* 9928	*TGV* 5112	*TGV* 6109		*TGV* 5312	*TGV* 5311	*TGV* 5316	*TGV* 6111	*TGV* 6209	*TGV* 6175	*TGV* 5405	*TGV* 9826	*TGV* 5164	*TGV* 5318		*TGV* 6816	*TGV* 6113	*TGV* 6211	*TGV* 9833	*TGV* 5115
	①–⑥																							
	n		M		T		◇		N	N	H			w	S			R						
Brussels Midi **11** d.	...	...	...	...	0825	...	...	...	...	...	...	...	...	...	...	1021	...	...	...	...	...	...	1110	...
Lille Europe **11** d.	...	...	...	...	|	0828	...	...	...	...	...	...	...	...	...	|	1030	...	...	...	...	...	1156	1156
Charles de Gaulle ✈ d.	...	...	...	...	|	0925	...	...	...	...	...	...	...	...	...	1142	1142	...	...	...	...	...	1258	1258
Marne la Vallée-Chessy § d.	...	...	...	...	|	0940	...	...	...	...	...	...	...	...	...	1156	1156	...	...	...	...	...	1311	1311
Paris Gare de Lyon d.	0916	0920	...	0942	|	|	1016	...	...	...	...	1116	1120	1146	...	|	|	...	...	...	1316	1320	|	|
Genève **345** d.	|	|	...	|	|	|	|	...	...	...	...	|	|	|	...	|	|	...	...	1244	|	|	|	|
Dijon **373** d.	|	|	0916	|	|	|	|	...	...	...	...	|	|	|	...	|	|	...	...	|	|	|	|	|
Lyon Part Dieu d.	|	|	1107	|	|	1137	|	...	1207	1211	1237	|	|	|	1323	|	|	1337	...	1437	|	|	1507	1511
Valence TGV d.	|	|	|	|	1155	1215	|	...	|	|	1315	|	1334	|	|	1406	1406	1414	...	1516	|	1534	1546	|
Avignon TGV d.	1159	|	1214	|	1230	|	|	...	1312	|	1350	1359	|	|	1432	1440	1440	1449	...	|	1559	|	|	|
Nîmes **355** d.	|	1213	|	|	|	1301	|	...	|	1330	|	|	1418	|	|	|	|	|	...	1602	|	1619	1632	|
Montpellier 355 a.	|	1250	|	|	|	1342v	|	...	|	1402	|	|	1446	|	|	|	|	|	...	1626	|	1645	1657	|
Sète **355** a.	|	...	|	|	|	...	|	...	|	...	|	|	1506	|	|	|	|	|	...	...	|	...	1721	|
Agde **355** a.	|	...	|	|	|	...	|	...	|	...	|	|	1521	|	|	|	|	|	...	...	|	...	1737	|
Béziers **355** a.	|	...	|	|	|	...	|	...	|	...	|	|	1536	|	|	|	|	|	...	...	|	...	1751	|
Narbonne **355** a.	|	...	|	|	|	...	|	...	|	...	|	|	1554	|	|	|	|	|	...	...	|	...	1807	|
Toulouse **321** a.	|	...	|	|	|	...	|	...	|	...	|	|	|	|	|	|	|	|	...	...	|	...	|	|
Perpignan 355 a.	|	...	|	|	|	...	|	...	|	...	|	|	1640	|	|	|	|	|	...	...	|	...	1844	|
Aix en Provence TGV d.	1222	...	1238	1246	1254	...	|	...	1334	...	|	1422	...	1445	1501	|	|	1512	...	...	1622	...	...	1637
Marseille St Charles a.	1235	...	1249	|	1308	...	1321	...	1349	...	1418	1435	...	|	1513	1509	1509	1523	...	...	1634	...	...	1649
Marseille St Charles 360 d.	...	...	1301	|	...	...	1333	...	...	...	...	...	...	|	...	1521	1521	...	...	...	...	...	...	...
Toulon 360 a.	...	...	1342	|	...	...	1412	...	...	...	...	...	...	1532	...	1559	1559	...	...	...	...	...	...	...
Les Arcs-Draguignan **360** a.	...	...	|	1409	...	...	...	...	...	...	...	...	...	|	...	1634	1634	...						
St Raphaël-Valescure **360** a.	...	...	1437	1428	...	...	...	...	...	...	...	...	...	1621	...	1651	1651	...						
Cannes **360** a.	...	...	1502	1453	...	...	...	...	...	...	...	...	...	1646	...	1714	1714	...						
Antibes **360** a.	...	...	1514	1505	...	...	...	...	...	...	...	...	...	1701	...	1727	1727	...						
Nice 360 a.	...	...	1532	1523	...	...	...	...	...	...	...	...	...	1725	...	1750	1750	...						

Arrival times at stations between Marseille and Nice may be a few minutes later Jan. 3 - Feb. 22.

A – 🚃12 Toulouse - Montpellier - Marseille (Table **355**).
H – 🚃12 Le Havre - Rouen - Lyon - Marseille (Table **335**).
M – From Metz (Table **392**).
N – From Nantes via Massy TGV (Table **335**).
R – From Rennes via Massy TGV (Table **335**).
S – From Strasbourg (Table **384**).
T – ⑥ June 21 - Aug. 30. *Thalys* train. Calls at Valence / Avignon to set down only.

g – Also Dec. 26, Jan. 2, Mar. 25, May 13; not Dec. 24, 31, Mar. 24, May 12.
h – Not May 1, 8.
n – Not Dec. 25, Jan. 1, Mar. 24, May 12.
p – Lyon **Perrache**.
r – 0647 on ⑥.
t – Also May 1, 8.
v – 1328 on ⑤–⑦ and holidays.
w – To Ventimiglia (Table **360**).

x – ①⑥ (also Dec. 26, Jan. 2, Mar. 25, May 1, 8, 13; not Dec. 24, 31, Mar. 24, May 12).

TGV – 🅁, supplement payable, 🍷.

◇ – To Hyères (Table **360**).
⊡ – From Melun (Table **370**).
⊕ – Arrivals Les Arcs - Nice are up to 30 minutes later Jan. 3 - Feb. 22, Feb. 25 - 29, Mar. 31 - Apr. 18.
§ – Station for Disneyland Paris.

350 PARIS and LYON - MONTPELLIER, MARSEILLE and NICE via high-speed line *TGV Méditerranée*

All *TGV* trains are R	*TGV* 6177	*TGV* 6115	*TGV* 6818	*TGV* 9828	*TGV* 6821	*TGV* 6117	*TGV* 6213	*TGV* 5117	*TGV* 6179	*TGV* 5322	*TGV* 6119	*TGV* 6231	*TGV* 6829	*TGV* 5118		*TGV* 6121	*TGV* 5326	*TGV* 6123	*TGV* 6215	*TGV* 5398	*TGV* 9834	*TGV* 6181	*TGV* 5346	
												Ⓐ					⑤⑥						①–④	
								B	L	N	△						Rs			A			Rm	
Brussels Midi **11** d.	...	...	...	1210	...	...	...	...	...	...	...	...	...	...	...	...	...	...	...	...	1509	...	...	...
Lille Europe **11** d.	...	...	...	1258	...	...	...	...	...	...	...	...	...	1454o	...	...	...	...	...	...	1557	...	...	...
Charles de Gaulle ✈ d.	...	...	...	1354	...	...	...	...	...	...	...	...	...	1553	...	...	...	...	...	...	1652	...	...	...
Marne la Vallée-Chessy § d.	...	...	...	1409	...	...	...	...	...	...	...	...	...	1610	...	...	...	...	...	...	1710	...	...	...
Paris Gare de Lyon d.	1342	1416	...	|	...	1516	1520	...	1546	...	1616	1620	...	|	...	1646	...	1716	1720	...	|	1742	...	...
Genève **345** d.	|	|	1344	|	...	|	|	...	|	...	|	|	...	|	...	|	...	|	|	...	|	|	...	...
Dijon **373** d.	|	|	|	|	...	|	|	1516	|	...	|	|	1616	|	...	|	...	|	|	...	|	|	...	...
Lyon Part Dieu d.	|	|	1537	1607	1637	|	|	1707	|	1737	|	|	1807	1811	...	|	1837	|	|	...	1907	|	1937	...
Valence TGV d.	|	|	|	|	1715	|	1735	1745	|	1814	|	1834	1848	|	...	|	1914	|	1935	...	|	|	2014	...
Avignon TGV d.	1626	|	1646	1712	|	1759	|	|	|	1849	|	|	|	|	...	1929	1948	1959	|	2014	2014	|	2049	...
Nîmes **355** d.	|	|	|	|	|	|	|	1832	|	|	|	1920	|	1930	...	|	|	|	2023	2034	|	|	|	...
Montpellier 355 a.	|	|	|	|	|	|	1842	1856	|	|	|	1944	|	1955	...	|	|	|	2049	2059	|	|	|	...
Sète **355** a.	|	|	|	|	|	|	1905	|	|	|	|	...	|	2014	...	|	|	|	2109	2117	|	|	|	...
Agde **355** a.	|	|	|	|	|	|	1920	|	|	|	|	...	|	2030	...	|	|	|	2124	|	|	|	|	...
Béziers **355** a.	|	|	|	|	|	|	1933	1940	|	|	|	...	|	2044	...	|	|	|	2137	2144	|	|	|	...
Narbonne **355** a.	|	|	|	|	|	|	1949	1955	|	|	|	...	|	2101	...	|	|	|	2153	2201	|	|	|	...
Toulouse **321** a.	|	|	|	|	|	|	|	2112	|	|	|	...	|	|	...	|	|	|	|	2321	|	|	|	...
Perpignan 355 a.	|	|	|	|	|	|	2024	...	|	|	|	...	|	2135	...	|	|	|	2229	...	|	|	|	...
Aix en Provence TGV d.	|	|	|	1736	1807	1822	...	...	1845	|	|	...	|	...	...	|	2011	2022	...	...	2037	2045	|	...
Marseille St Charles a.	|	1721	1717	1747	1819	1834	...	...	|	1918	1922	...	1946	...	...	1958	2024	2034	...	...	2049	|	2117	...
Marseille St Charles 360 d.	|	...	1729	...	...	...	...	...	|	...	1934	...	1957	...	...	...	...	...	...	...	2101r	|	...	...
Toulon 360 a.	1731	...	1809	...	...	...	...	...	|	...	2012	...	2044	...	...	...	...	...	...	...	2141r	2134	...	...
Les Arcs-Draguignan **360** a.	|	...	|	...	...	...	...	...	2005	...	...	...	|	...	...	...	...	...	...	...	...	|	...	...
St Raphaël-Valescure **360** a.	1819	...	1906	...	...	...	...	...	2021	...	...	...	2137	...	...	...	...	...	...	...	...	2224	...	...
Cannes **360** a.	1845	...	1932	...	...	...	...	...	2047	...	...	...	2201	...	...	...	...	...	...	...	...	2248	...	...
Antibes **360** a.	1856	...	1944	...	...	...	...	...	2059	...	...	...	2213	...	...	...	...	...	...	...	...	2259	...	...
Nice 360 a.	1914	...	2006	...	...	...	...	...	2117	...	...	...	2232	...	...	...	...	...	...	...	...	2317	...	...

	TGV 6127	*TGV* 6187	*TGV* 6217	*TGV* 9836	*TGV* 9836	*TGV* 6183	*TGV* 6125	*TGV* 6135	*TGV* 6135		*TGV* 5126	*TGV* 6129	*TGV* 5124	*TGV* 6219	*TGV* 6219	*TGV* 6219	*TGV* 6131	*TGV* 6221	*TGV* 5142	*TGV* 5135	*TGV* 6137	*TGV* 5136	*TGV* 5136	*TGV* 5338
		⑤			⑤⑦				⑤		⑦		①–⑥		①–④	⑤			⑦	⑦	⑤	①–⑥	⑤⑥	⑦
	Y	Q			r	E	Z	W	X		e		n		m	f			e	e	f	n⊖	s	Re
Brussels Midi **11** d.	...	...	...	1609	1609	...	...	...	...	...	...	...	...	...	...	...	...	...	...	...	...	...	...	...
Lille Europe **11** d.	...	...	...	1654	1654	...,	...	...	...	...	1752	...	1752	...	...	...	...	...	1931	1931	...	1915	1915	...
Charles de Gaulle ✈ d.	...	...	...	1751	1751	...	...	...	...	...	1854	...	1854	...	...	...	...	...	2026	2006	...	2048	2048	...
Marne la Vallée-Chessy § d.	...	...	...	1810	1810	...	...	...	...	...	1908	...	1908	...	...	...	...	...	2040	2040	...	2103	2103	...
Paris Gare de Lyon d.	1816	1816	1820	|	|	1842	1842	1846	1846	...	|	1916	|	1920	1920	1920	2016	2020	|	|	2116	|	|	...
Genève **345** d.	|	|	|	|	|	|	|	|	|	...	|	|	|	|	|	|	|	|	|	|	|	|	|	...
Dijon **373** d.	|	|	|	|	|	|	|	|	|	...	|	|	|	|	|	|	|	|	|	|	|	|	|	...
Lyon Part Dieu d.	|	|	|	2007	2007	|	|	|	|	...	|	|	2107	|	|	|	|	|	2237	2241	|	2259	2305	2305
Valence TGV d.	|	|	2034	2045	2045	|	|	|	|	...	2117	|	|	|	|	|	|	2234	|	2318	|	...	2344	2342
Avignon TGV d.	|	|	|	|	|	|	|	2129	2129	...	2151	2159	2211	|	|	|	2258	|	2346	|	0000	...	0021	0019
Nîmes **355** d.	|	|	2120	2130	2130	|	|	|	|	...	|	|	|	2214	2214	2214	|	2320	|	0005	|	...	|	|
Montpellier 355 a.	|	|	2148	2155	2155	|	|	|	|	...	|	|	|	2238	2238	2238	|	2344	|	0030	|	...	|	|
Sète **355** a.	|	|	2206	...	2214	|	|	|	|	...	|	|	|	...	|	2258	|	...	|	...	|	...	|	|
Agde **355** a.	|	|	2222	...	2229	|	|	|	|	...	|	|	|	...	|	2314	|	...	|	...	|	...	|	|
Béziers **355** a.	|	|	2236	...	2244	|	|	|	|	...	|	|	|	...	2323	2328	|	...	|	...	|	...	|	|
Narbonne **355** a.	|	|	...	...	2300	|	|	|	|	...	|	|	|	...	...	2344	|	...	|	...	|	...	|	|
Toulouse **321** a.	|	|	...	...	|	|	|	|	|	...	|	|	|	...	...	|	|	...	|	...	|	...	|	|
Perpignan 355 a.	|	|	...	...	2335	|	|	|	|	...	|	|	|	...	...	0021g	|	...	|	...	|	...	|	|
Aix en Provence TGV d.	|	|	...	...	...	2143	2143	|	2156	...	|	2222	2234	...	...	...	|	...	0009	...	0023	...	0044	0044
Marseille St Charles a.	2121	2121	...	...	...	|	|	2158	2210	...	2221	2235	2245	...	...	...	2326	...	0020	...	0035	...	0055y	0055
Marseille St Charles 360 d.	...	2133	...	...	...	|	|	...	2222	...	...	...	...	...	...	...	2338	...	...	...	...	...	...	...
Toulon 360 a.	...	2213	...	...	...	2231	2231	...	2308	...	...	...	...	...	...	...	0018	...	...	...	...	...	...	...
Les Arcs-Draguignan **360** a.	...	|	...	...	...	|	...	...	...	...	...	...	...	...	...	...	...	...	...	...	...	...	...	...
St Raphaël-Valescure **360** a.	...	2301	...	...	...	2320	...	...	...	...	...	...	...	...	...	...	...	...	...	...	...	...	...	...
Cannes **360** a.	...	2326	...	...	...	2344	...	...	...	...	...	...	...	...	...	...	...	...	...	...	...	...	...	...
Antibes **360** a.	...	2339	...	...	...	2355	...	...	...	...	...	...	...	...	...	...	...	...	...	...	...	...	...	...
Nice 360 a.	...	2357	...	...	...	0012	...	...	...	...	...	...	...	...	...	...	...	...	...	...	...	...	...	...

	TGV 6102	*TGV* 9854	*TGV* 5158		*TGV* 6202	*TGV* 6104	*TGV* 9856	*TGV* 9856	*TGV* 6852	*TGV* 6136	*TGV* 6230		*TGV* 5162	*TGV* 5162	*TGV* 5144		*TGV* 6204	*TGV* 6106	*TGV* 5350	*TGV* 6850		*TGV* 6108		
	Ⓐ	Ⓐ	⑥		Ⓐ	Ⓐ	⑥	⑦	Ⓐ		Ⓐ			①⑥					Ⓑ	Ⓒ		①–⑥		
			t				t	e						b					Rh			n		
Nice 360 d.	...	...	...	...	...	...	...	...	...	...	...	...	...	...	...	...	...	...	...	...	...	...	...	...
Antibes **360** d.	...	...	...	...	...	...	...	...	...	...	...	...	...	...	...	...	...	...	...	...	...	...	...	...
Cannes **360** d.	...	...	...	...	...	...	...	...	...	...	...	...	...	...	...	...	...	...	...	...	...	...	...	...
St Raphaël-Valescure **360** d.	...	...	...	...	...	...	...	...	...	...	...	...	...	...	...	...	...	...	...	...	...	...	...	...
Les Arcs-Draguignan **360** d.	...	...	...	...	...	...	...	...	...	...	...	...	...	...	...	...	...	...	...	...	...	...	...	...
Toulon 360 d.	...	...	...	...	...	0525	0517	...	...	0537c	...	...	...	...	...	...	...	...	...	...	...	0727	...	...
Marseille St Charles 360 a.	...	...	...	...	...	|	0557	...	...	0616c	...	...	...	...	...	...	...	...	...	...	...	0817	...	...
Marseille St Charles d.	0528	0539	0539	...	...	|	0609	0609	0613	0628	...	...	...	...	0710	...	...	0728	0739	0806	...	0828	...	...
Aix en Provence TGV d.	0542	|	0554	...	...	0617	0624	0624	0628	|	...	...	...	...	0725	...	...	0743	0753	0820	...	|	...	...
Perpignan 355 d.	|	|	|	...	...	|	|	|	|	|	...	...	...	0505	|	...	...	|	|	|	...	|	...	...
Toulouse **321** d.	|	|	|	...	...	|	|	|	|	|	...	...	...	|	|	...	...	|	|	|	...	|	...	...
Narbonne **355** d.	|	|	|	...	...	|	|	|	|	|	...	...	...	0544	|	...	...	|	|	|	...	|	...	...
Béziers **355** d.	|	|	|	...	0447	|	|	|	|	|	0534	...	...	0601	|	...	...	|	|	|	...	|	...	...
Agde **355** d.	|	|	|	...	0501	|	|	|	|	|	0549	...	...	0615	|	...	...	|	|	|	...	|	...	...
Sète **355** d.	|	|	|	...	0517	|	|	|	|	|	0604	...	...	0630	|	...	...	|	|	|	...	|	...	...
Montpellier 355 d.	|	|	|	...	0539	|	|	|	|	|	0623	...	0652	0652	|	...	0720	|	|	|	...	|	...	...
Nîmes **355** d.	|	|	|	...	0605	|	|	|	|	|	0650	...	0718	0718	|	...	0750	|	|	|	...	|	...	...
Avignon TGV d.	0604	0611	0616	...	|	0640	0647	0647	|	|	|	...	|	|	0747	...	|	0805	|	|	...	|	...	...
Valence TGV d.	|	0645	0650	...	0656	|	|	|	|	|	0736	...	0810	0810	|	...	|	|	0845	0913	...	|	...	...
Lyon Part Dieu a.	|	0720	|	...	|	|	0750	0750	0750	|	|	...	0846	0846	0850	...	|	|	0920	0950	...	|	...	...
Dijon **373** a.	|	|	|	...	|	|	|	|	0943	|	|	...	|	|	|	...	|	|	...	1143	...	|	...	...
Genève **345** a.	|	|	|	...	|	|	|	|	...	|	|	...	|	|	|	...	|	|	...	...	...	|	...	...
Paris Gare de Lyon a.	0845	|	|	...	0911	0919	|	|	...	0931	0949	...	|	|	|	...	1041	1045	...	...	...	1131	...	...
Marne la Vallée-Chessy § a.	...	0915	0857	...	...	...	0945	0945	...	...	...	...	1045	1045	1045	...	...	...	...	...	...	...	...	...
Charles de Gaulle ✈ a.	...	0930	0918	...	...	...	0959	0959	...	...	...	...	1059	1059	1059	...	...	...	...	...	...	...	...	...
Lille Europe **11** a.	...	1028	...	...	...	...	1100	1100	...	...	...	...	1235v	1235v	1235v	...	...	...	...	...	...	...	...	...
Brussels Midi **11** a.	...	1115	...	...	...	...	1150	1150	...	...	...	...	...	...	...	...	...	...	...	...	...	...	...	...

NOTES FOR PAGES 210/211

A – (12) Toulouse - Montpellier - Marseille and v.v. (Table **355**).
B – (12) Dijon - Lyon - Toulouse - Bordeaux and v.v.
D – ⑥ Dec. 15 - Mar. 29.
E – ⑤ from Apr. 4 (also Apr. 30, May 7; not May 2).
G – Apr. 1 - Sept. 21.
H – (12) Marseille - Lyon - Rouen - Le Havre.
L – Mar. 31 - Sept. 20.
M – To/from Metz (Table **378**).
N – To/from Nantes via Massy TGV (Table **335**).
Q – ⑤ from Apr. 4 (also Apr. 30, May 7; not May 2).
R – To/from Rennes via Massy TGV (Table **335**).
S – To Strasbourg (Table **384**).
T – ⑥ June 21 - Aug. 30. *Thalys* train. Calls at Avignon and Valence to pick up only.
U – ⑦ Apr. 6 - June 29 (also May 12).
V – ⑦ from Apr. 6 (also May 12).
W – ①②③④⑦ to Apr. 3; ⑧ from Apr. 4 (not May 1, 8).
X – ⑤ to Mar. 28.
Y – Daily to Apr. 3; ①②③④⑥⑦ from Apr. 5 (not Apr. 30, May 7).
Z – Daily except ⑤ (will not run Apr. 30, May 7).

b – Also Dec. 26, Jan. 2, Mar. 25, May 1, 8, 13; not Dec. 24, 31, Mar. 24, May 12.
c – Ⓒ only.

NOTES CONTINUED ON NEXT PAGE →

TGV Méditerranée NICE, MARSEILLE and MONTPELLIER - LYON and PARIS via high-speed line 350

All *TGV* trains are 🅁	*TGV* 5166	*TGV* 9860	*TGV* 9860	*TGV* 6172	*TGV* 6206	*TGV* 6112	*TGV* 5301	*TGV* 6854	*TGV* 6114	*TGV* 5170	*TGV* 6208		*TGV* 5368	*TGV* 5374	*TGV* 9862	*TGV* 5198	*TGV* 6174	*TGV* 6116	*TGV* 5430	*TGV* 9864	*TGV* 6176	*TGV* 6210	*TGV* 6118	*TGV* 6866
		⑥											①–⑥	⑦e										
		t					A			B			Nn	NR		M	w	△	S					
Nice 360 d.	...	...	...	0632	...	...	...	0656	...	...	...	...	...	...	...	0929	0937	...	...	1032	1042	...	...	...
Antibes **360** d.	...	...	...	0650	...	...	...	0717	...	...	...	...	...	...	...	0947	0955	...	...	1049	1100	...	...	...
Cannes **360** d.	...	...	...	0702	...	...	...	0728	...	...	...	...	...	...	...	0958	1007	...	...	1101	1111	...	...	...
St Raphaël-Valescure **360** d.	...	...	...	0729	...	...	...	0754	...	...	...	...	...	...	...	1023	1034	...	...	1125	1135	...	...	...
Les Arcs-Draguignan **360** d.	...	...	...	|	...	...	...	|	...	...	...	...	...	...	...	|	1052	...	...	1142	1152	...	...	...
Toulon 360 d.	...	0745	...	0824	...	...	...	0846	...	...	...	...	...	...	...	1117	|	1132	...	1218	|	...	...	...
Marseille St Charles 360 a.	...	0827	...	|	...	...	...	0927	...	...	...	...	...	...	...	1158	|	1216	...	1258	|	...	...	...
Marseille St Charles d.	...	0839	0839	|	...	0928	...	0939	1028	...	...	...	1133	1133	...	1208	|	1228	1246	1309	|	...	1328	...
Aix en Provence TGV d.	...	0853	0853	|	...	0943	...	0953	1042	...	...	...	1147	1147	...	|	1213	|	1300	|	|	...	1343	...
Perpignan 355 d.	0642	|	|	|	0732	|	...	|	|	...	...	...	|	|	...	|	|	|	|	|	|	...	|	...
Toulouse **321** d.	|	|	|	|	|	|	0655q	|	|	0749	...	...	|	|	...	|	|	|	|	|	|	...	|	...
Narbonne **355** d.	0720	|	|	|	0815	|	0812	|	|	0903	...	...	|	|	...	|	|	|	|	|	|	...	|	...
Béziers **355** d.	0737	|	|	|	0833	|	0827	|	|	0918	...	...	|	|	...	|	|	|	|	|	|	...	|	...
Agde **355** d.	0751	|	|	|	0846	|	|	|	|	|	...	...	|	|	...	|	|	|	|	|	|	...	|	...
Sète **355** d.	0807	|	|	|	0901	|	0855	|	|	|	...	...	|	|	...	|	|	|	|	|	|	...	|	...
Montpellier 355 d.	0826	|	|	|	0921	|	0915	|	|	1002	1013	...	|	|	1156	|	|	|	|	|	|	1315	|	1356
Nîmes **355** d.	0853	|	|	|	0948	|	0943	|	|	1029	1050	...	|	|	1227	|	|	|	|	|	|	1350	|	1424
Avignon TGV d.	|	0916	0916	0932	|	1005	1001	1017	|	|	|	...	1209	1209	|	1245	1238	|	1324	1339	1332	|	1405	|
Valence TGV d.	0938	|	|	|	|	|	...	|	|	1117	1136	...	1243	1243	|	|	|	|	|	1414	|	|	|	1513
Lyon Part Dieu a.	1016	1020	1020	|	|	|	...	1123	|	1154	|	...	1320	1320	1346	1350	|	|	1430	|	|	|	|	1550
Dijon **373** a.	|	|	|	|	|	|	...	...	|	1343	|	...	...	...	|	1539	|	|	...	|	|	|	|	|
Genève **345** a.	|	|	|	|	|	|	...	...	|	...	|	...	...	...	|	...	|	|	...	|	|	|	|	1735
Paris Gare de Lyon a.	|	|	|	1211*	1241	1245	...	...	1337	...	1349	...	...	...	|	...	1519	1531	...	|	1615	1641	1645	...
Marne la Vallée-Chessy § a.	1216	1216	1216	...	...	...	...	...	...	...	...	...	...	...	1545	...	...	...	...	1619	...	...	...	...
Charles de Gaulle ✈ a.	1230	1230	1230	...	...	...	...	...	...	...	...	...	...	...	1559	...	...	...	...	1633	...	...	...	...
Lille Europe **11** a.	1326	1326	1326	...	...	...	...	...	...	...	...	...	...	...	1707	...	...	...	...	1738	...	...	...	...
Brussels Midi **11** a.	1412	1412	1412	...	...	...	...	...	...	...	...	...	...	...	1754	...	...	...	...	1822	...	...	...	...

	TGV 9866	*TGV* 9954	*TGV* 6120	*TGV* 6212	*TGV* 9868		*TGV* 5372	*TGV* 5378	*TGV* 6122	*TGV* 6214	*TGV* 5376	*TGV* 6124		*TGV* 6886	*TGV* 6178	*TGV* 6126	*TGV* 6216	*TGV* 5380	*TGV* 6168		*TGV* 5314	*TGV* 6868	*TGV* 5180	*TGV* 5180
							①–⑥	⑦											⑦		Ⓑ	⑥	Ⓐ	Ⓒ
		T					Rn	Nd			H				G	◇		N	U		h	t		
Nice 360 d.	...	...	...	...	...	...	...	...	...	...	...	...	...	1326	1343	...	...	...	1430	...	...	...	...	...
Antibes **360** d.	...	...	...	...	...	...	...	...	...	...	...	...	...	1344	1359	...	...	...	1447	...	...	...	...	...
Cannes **360** d.	...	...	...	...	...	...	...	...	...	...	...	...	...	1355	1410	...	...	...	1500	...	...	...	...	...
St Raphaël-Valescure **360** d.	...	...	...	...	...	...	...	...	...	...	...	...	...	1421	1435	...	...	...	1524	...	...	...	...	...
Les Arcs-Draguignan **360** d.	...	...	...	...	...	...	...	...	...	...	...	...	...	|	1452	...	...	...	1541	...	...	...	...	...
Toulon 360 d.	...	...	1325	...	...	...	...	...	...	...	...	...	...	1517	|	1538	...	...	1616	...	...	...	...	...
Marseille St Charles 360 a.	...	...	1409	...	...	...	...	...	...	...	...	...	...	1559	|	1616	...	...	|	...	...	...	...	...
Marseille St Charles d.	1340	1409	1421	...	...	...	1509	1509	1528	...	1539	1558	...	1610	|	1628	...	...	|	...	...	...	1709	1709
Aix en Provence TGV d.	1356	1424	1436	...	...	...	1523	1523	|	...	|	|	...	|	1618	1644	...	...	|	...	...	...	1723	1723
Perpignan 355 d.	|	|	|	...	1240	...	|	|	|	1336	|	|	...	|	|	|	...	...	|	...	...	1511	|	|
Toulouse **321** d.	|	|	|	...	|	...	|	|	|	|	|	|	...	|	|	|	...	...	|	...	1434q	|	|	|
Narbonne **355** d.	|	|	|	...	1320	...	|	|	|	1420	|	|	...	|	|	|	...	...	|	...	1550	1550	|	|
Béziers **355** d.	|	|	|	...	1337	...	|	|	|	1437	|	|	...	|	|	|	...	...	|	...	1605	1605	|	|
Agde **355** d.	|	|	|	...	1351	...	|	|	|	1451	|	|	...	|	|	|	...	...	|	...	|	|	|	|
Sète **355** d.	|	|	|	...	1407	...	|	|	|	1506	|	|	...	|	|	|	...	...	|	...	|	|	|	|
Montpellier 355 d.	|	|	|	1423	1430	...	|	|	|	1525	|	|	...	|	|	|	1620	1630	|	...	1652	1652	|	|
Nîmes **355** d.	|	|	|	1450	1457	...	|	|	|	1553	|	|	...	|	|	|	1650	1700	|	...	1720	1720	|	|
Avignon TGV d.	1418	1446	1458	|	|	...	1546	1546	1600	|	1610	1630	...	1644	|	|	|	|	1732	...	|	|	|	|
Valence TGV d.	|	1520	|	1537	1544	...	|	|	|	|	1645	|	...	|	|	|	1736	1745	|	...	|	|	1815	1815
Lyon Part Dieu a.	1520	|	|	|	1620	...	1650	1650	|	|	1720	|	...	1750	|	|	|	1820	|	...	1846	1846	1850	1850
Dijon **373** a.	|	|	|	|	|	...	...	...	|	|	...	|	...	|	|	|	|	...	|	...	...	...	|	|
Genève **345** a.	|	|	|	|	|	...	...	...	|	|	...	|	...	1942	|	|	|	...	|	...	...	...	|	|
Paris Gare de Lyon a.	|	|	1737	1749	|	...	...	...	1841	1845	...	1911	...	...	1920	1931	1949	...	2015	...	...	...	|	|
Marne la Vallée-Chessy § a.	|	|	...	...	1816	...	...	...	...	...	...	...	...	...	...	...	...	...	...	...	...	...	2045	2045
Charles de Gaulle ✈ a.	1724	|	...	...	1830	...	...	...	...	...	...	...	...	...	...	...	...	...	...	...	...	...	2103	2103
Lille Europe **11** a.	1820	|	...	...	1936	...	...	...	...	...	...	...	...	...	...	...	...	...	...	...	...	...	2206	2238
Brussels Midi **11** a.	1910	1847	...	...	2022	...	...	...	...	...	...	...	...	...	...	...	...	...	...	...	...	...	...	...

	TGV 6218	*TGV* 6128	*TGV* 6870	*TGV* 6130	*TGV* 5184		*TGV* 5186	*TGV* 6138	*TGV* 6220	*TGV* 6184	*TGV* 6874	*TGV* 6222	*TGV* 6132	*TGV* 5398		*TGV* 6880	*TGV* 6876	*TGV* 6180	*TGV* 6134	*TGV* 6224		*TGV* 6140	*TGV* 6186	
		Ⓑ																		⑦		⑦	⑦	
		h	⊡											A					u	e		e	V	
Nice 360 d.	...	...	...	...	1534	...	...	...	...	1636	...	...	...	...	...	...	1725	1735	...	...	...	...	1842	...
Antibes **360** d.	...	...	...	...	1551	...	...	...	...	1654	...	...	...	...	...	...	1745	1754	...	...	...	...	1900	...
Cannes **360** d.	...	...	...	...	1603	...	...	...	...	1706	...	...	...	...	...	...	1758	1806	...	...	...	...	1911	...
St Raphaël-Valescure **360** d.	...	...	...	...	1628	...	...	...	...	1732	...	...	...	...	...	...	1823	1831	...	...	...	...	1935	...
Les Arcs-Draguignan **360** d.	...	...	...	...	1645	...	...	...	...	|	...	...	...	...	...	...	|	|	...	...	...	...	|	...
Toulon 360 d.	...	...	...	...	1720	...	...	...	...	1824	...	...	...	...	...	...	1917	1923	...	...	...	...	2026	...
Marseille St Charles 360 a.	...	...	...	...	1759	...	...	...	...	|	...	...	...	...	...	...	1958	|	...	...	...	...	|	...
Marseille St Charles d.	...	1728	1739	1758	1810	...	...	1828	...	|	1908	...	1928	1936	...	...	2009	|	2028	...	...	2058	|	...
Aix en Provence TGV d.	...	1743	|	1812	1824	...	...	|	...	1916	1924	...	1943	1951	...	...	|	2013	|	...	...	|	2117	...
Perpignan 355 d.	1531	|	|	|	|	...	...	|	...	|	|	1737	|	|	...	...	|	|	|	1835	...	|	|	...
Toulouse **321** d.	|	|	|	|	|	...	1608x	|	...	|	|	|	|	|	...	...	|	|	|	|	...	|	|	...
Narbonne **355** d.	1610	|	|	|	|	...	1728	|	...	|	|	1817	|	|	...	...	|	|	|	1914	...	|	|	...
Béziers **355** d.	1627	|	|	|	|	...	1745	|	...	|	|	1834	|	|	...	...	|	|	|	1930	...	|	|	...
Agde **355** d.	|	|	|	|	|	...	|	|	...	|	|	1848	|	|	...	...	|	|	|	1945	...	|	|	...
Sète **355** d.	|	|	|	|	|	...	|	|	...	|	|	1904	|	|	...	...	|	|	|	2000	...	|	|	...
Montpellier 355 d.	1717	|	|	|	|	...	1830	|	1823	|	|	1923	|	|	...	1928	|	|	|	2023	...	|	|	...
Nîmes **355** d.	1744	|	|	|	|	...	1857	|	1850	|	|	1950	|	|	...	1955	|	|	|	2050	...	|	|	...
Avignon TGV d.	|	1805	1812	|	1846	...	|	|	|	|	1946	|	2005	2011	...	|	|	|	2059	|	...	2129	|	...
Valence TGV d.	1828	|	1848	|	|	...	1945	|	1936	|	|	|	|	...	...	2044	2111	|	|	2136	...	|	|	...
Lyon Part Dieu a.	|	|	1925	|	1950	...	2020	|	|	|	2050	|	|	...	...	2120	2150	|	|	|	...	|	|	...
Dijon **373** a.	|	|	...	|	|	...	|	|	|	|	|	|	|	...	...	2305z	2340	|	|	|	...	|	|	...
Genève **345** a.	|	|	...	|	|	...	|	|	|	|	2233	|	|	...	...	...	...	|	|	|	...	|	|	...
Paris Gare de Lyon a.	2041	2045	...	2111	|	...	|	2131	2149	2215	...	2241	2245	...	...	...	...	2311	2337	2345	...	0011	0015	...
Marne la Vallée-Chessy § a.	...	...	...	...	2145	...	2215	...	...	...	...	...	...	...	...	...	...	...	...	...	...	...	...	...
Charles de Gaulle ✈ a.	...	...	...	...	2159	...	2229	...	...	...	...	...	...	...	...	...	...	...	...	...	...	...	...	...
Lille Europe **11** a.	...	...	...	...	2301	...	2332	...	...	...	...	...	...	...	...	...	...	...	...	...	...	...	...	...
Brussels Midi **11** a.	...	...	...	...	...	...	...	...	...	...	...	...	...	...	...	...	...	...	...	...	...	...	...	...

NOTES FOR PAGES 210/211 – CONTINUED

- **d** – Also Dec. 25, Jan. 1, Mar. 24, May 12; not May 11.
- **e** – Also Dec. 25, Jan. 1, Mar. 24, May 12.
- **f** – Also Apr. 30, May 7; not May 2.
- **g** – Night of ⑤ (also Apr. 30, May 7; not Dec. 14, Jan. 18, Feb. 8, Mar. 14, May 2).
- **h** – Not May 1, 8.
- **m** – Not Dec. 25, Jan. 1, Mar. 24, Apr. 30, May 1, 7, 8, 12.
- **n** – Not Dec. 25, Jan. 1, Mar. 24, May 12.
- **o** – 1458 on Ⓐ.
- **q** – 5 minutes earlier Jan. 7 - Feb. 8.
- **r** – ⑤⑦ (also Dec. 25, Jan. 1, Mar. 24, Apr. 30, May 7, 12; not May 2).
- **s** – Also Apr. 30, May 1, 7, 8; not May 2.
- **t** – Also May 1, 8.
- **u** – Not Dec. 31 or Ⓐ Mar. 10 - Apr. 11.
- **v** – Lille **Flandres**.
- **w** – From Ventimiglia (Table **360**).
- **x** – 1603 on Jan. 12, 13, 19, 20, 27, Feb. 3.
- **y** – Runs Aix - Marseille morning of ⑦ (also May 2, 9).
- **z** – ⑤⑦ (also Dec. 25, Jan. 1, Mar. 24, Apr. 30, May 7, 12).

TGV – 🅁, supplement payable, 🍸.

- ⊡ – To Melun (Table **370**) on ①–④ **m**. On other dates train number is **6872**.
- ◇ – To/from Hyères (Table **360**).
- △ – To/from Hyères on dates in Table **360**.
- ⊖ – Also calls at Le Creusot TGV (a. 2220).
- § – Station for Disneyland Paris.
- * – Up to 10 minutes later on certain dates.

← *FOR OTHER NOTES SEE PREVIOUS PAGE*

Departure times from Nice and stations to Marseille may be a few minutes earlier Jan. 3 - Feb. 22.

350a 🚌 AVIGNON CENTRE - AVIGNON TGV

City 🚌 service *Navette TGV* operated by TCRA ✆ 04 32 74 18 32. Journey time 13 minutes (10 minutes Gare TGV - Avignon Centre). Rail tickets not valid. *Subject to confirmation*

Avignon Centre (Poste) ▲ depart: 0538, 0612, 0638, 0659, 0732 ©, 0752 Ⓐ, 0831, 0850, 0904, 0930, 0941, 1002, 1018, 1031, 1047, 1114, 1141, 1150, 1213, 1234, 1255, 1307, 1323, 1332, 1359, 1422, 1442, 1511, 1536, 1554, 1618, 1636, 1649, 1707, 1732, 1813, 1832, 1849, 1903, 1933, 1945, 2001, 2032, 2109, 2132, 2152, 2206, 2235, 2316 ⑦ **b**.

Avignon TGV depart: 0614, 0646, 0714, 0745, 0802 ©, 0827 Ⓐ, 0847, 0908, 0920, 0944, 1007, 1017, 1032, 1047, 1116, 1130, 1158, 1213, 1228, 1256, 1310, 1320, 1339, 1349, 1414, 1441, 1502, 1525, 1551, 1614, 1633, 1653, 1711, 1725, 1748, 1828, 1846, 1909, 1927, 1948, 2009, 2039, 2108, 2140, 2150, 2212, 2225, 2306, 2327 ⑦ **b**.

b – Not July 1 - Aug. 26.

▲ – Cross road in front of station, through city 'gate', turn first left, first bus stop. On ⑦ (until approx 1300) departs from Cité Administrative (cross road, through ramparts, first stop on the right).

351 LYON - VALENCE - AVIGNON - MARSEILLE

Via 'classic' line. For TGV trains via high-speed line see Table 350. Night trains Paris - Nice are shown in Table 360.

km	All *TGV* trains are Ⓡ						17443	17701				17705		TGV 6191	17709	17433		TGV 6193	17713		TGV 6199	17717	4240 4241	4251 4240
		Ⓐ		Ⓐ	Ⓐ	Ⓑ	⑥ w	⚒	⚒			△		①–⑥ n	△	U	⚒		△	b △	⑥ E	⚒ ▷	S 🍷	S 🍷
	Paris Gare de Lyon ▲ d.													0746				0946			1058			
	Lille Flandres **13** d.																							
	Metz **392** d.																						0820r	
	Strasbourg **384** d.																							0815
	Dijon **373** d.																						1216	1216
	Genève **345** d.																							
	Lyon St Exupéry TGV ✈ d.													0942				1142						
0	**Lyon Perrache** ▶ d.																							
0	**Lyon Part-Dieu** d.											0725			0925		1025		1111	1123		1327	1405	1405
32	Vienne ▶ d.											0745			0945		1044		1131			1347		
87	Tain-Hermitage-Tournon ▶ d.											0818			1019		1124		1206			1422		
105	**Valence Ville** ▶ a.											0828		1012	1029		1135	1212	1217	1221	1322	1433	1505	1505
105	**Valence Ville** d.							0604	0650		0717	0832	0923	1015	1032		1141	1215	1220			1436	1508	1508
150	Montélimar d.							0627	0718		0744	0855	0950	1037	1055		1208	1237	1243			1459		
202	Orange d.							0702	0753		0822	0931	1026		1130		1242	1303	1317			1533		
230	**Avignon Centre** a.							0717	0817		0840	0946	1049	1112	1145		1307	1317	1332			1548	1607	1607
230	**Avignon Centre** d.	0545	0554	0632	0634	0655	0657	0720		0823		0949			1148	1305		1320	1335			1551	1610	1610
	Montpellier **355** a.																						1713	1713
	Béziers **355** a.																						1807	1807
	Perpignan **355** a.																						1916	1916
	Portbou **355** a.																						2011	2011
265	Arles § d.	0604			0653	0715	0716	0740		0843		1008			1208	1324		1338	1355			1610		
299	Miramas § d.	0626	0647	0723	0711	0734	0735	0802		0906		1025			1226			1353	1413			1627		
351	**Marseille St Charles** § a.	0703	0734	0804	0745	0808	0806	0840		0940		1054			1302	1408			1447			1702		
	Toulon **360** a.						0919									1510								
	Nice **360** a.						1109									1704								

		17721						17725				TGV 6295			TGV 6195	17729	4264 4265	TGV 6197		4778 4779	4238 4239	4296 4297	5799
		Ⓐ				⚒					k	⑤ ◇	⑤⑦ q			N		⑤ d			♦ Ⓡ	♦ Ⓡ	♦ Ⓡ	♦ Ⓡ
Paris Gare de Lyon ▲ d.													1710			1746			1946					2205a
Lille Flandres **13** d.																								
Metz **392** d.																		1545				2044		
Strasbourg **384** d.																							2056	
Dijon **373** d.																		1907						
Genève **345** d.																					2044			
Lyon St Exupéry TGV ✈ d.																1942			2142					
Lyon Perrache ▶ d.							1638				1738				1838									
Lyon Part-Dieu d.			1525			1625			1725					1825			1925	2102		2125	2250			
Vienne ▶ d.			1545			1644	1700		1746		1800			1845	1900		1944	2124		2144				
Tain-Hermitage-Tournon ▶ d.			1618			1724	1740		1819		1840			1925	1941		2018			2225				
Valence Ville ▶ a.			1629			1735	1750		1829		1850		1928	1935	1951	2012	2029	2201	2212	2235	2351			0354
Valence Ville d.			1632		1710	1740		1810	1832			1907	1931	1940		2015	2032	2205	2215		2354			
Montélimar d.			1656		1739	1810		1839	1856			1933	1956	2008		2037	2056	2229	2237					
Orange d.			1731		1814	1848		1915	1931			2006	2031	2043		2103	2131	2309						
Avignon Centre a.			1745		1836	1913		1938	1945			2025	2050	2105		2117	2145	2324	2312			0412	0444	
Avignon Centre d.	1624	1640	1748	1829					1948	2025			2053			2120	2148	2329				0415	0447	
Montpellier **355** a.																		0034						
Béziers **355** a.																					c			
Perpignan **355** a.																								
Portbou **355** a.																								
Arles § d.		1701	1808	1848					2008	2045			2112			2138	2208						0509	
Miramas § d.	1726	1723	1828	1909					2026	2104			2128			2153	2226							
Marseille St Charles § a.	1813	1802	1904	1954					2102	2132							2254					0515	0556	
Toulon **360** a.																						0616	0707	
Nice **360** a.																						0820	0912	

		TGV 6192		17702					17706	TGV 6194			17704	4340 4341	4340 4351		17352	17714	TGV 6196			TGV 6190		17716
	Ⓐ	Ⓐ	⊖	⚒	⚒	⊖	⚒		⊙		Ⓐ ▽		⊙	T 🍷	T 🍷	⊡	b				Ⓐ	⑥ E	⚒	
Nice **360** d.													0600											
Toulon **360** d.													0751											
Marseille St Charles § d.				0505				0558	0702		0748		0904					1113			1305			1405
Miramas § d.				0533				0636	0731	0715	0823		0933					1150			1341			1433
Arles § d.				0552				0657	0753	0735	0844		0952					1207			1403			1452
Cerbère **355** d.														0607	0607									
Perpignan **355** d.														0701	0701									
Béziers **355** d.														0819	0819									
Montpellier **355** d.														0924	0924									
Avignon Centre a.				0610				0714	0811	0752		0902	1010	1025	1025			1224			1421			1510
Avignon Centre d.		0511	0532	0613	0617	0641	0654		0814	0755			1013	1029	1029			1227	1239	1311				1513
Orange d.			0548	0629	0634	0659	0717		0829	0810			1029					1243		1335				1529
Montélimar d.	0538	0550	0625	0705	0711	0737	0752		0904	0836			1103	1111	1111			1313	1320	1411				1605
Valence Ville a.	0600	0612	0653	0725	0738	0805	0819		0925	0858			1125	1133	1133			1335	1341	1437				1625
Valence Ville ▶ d.	0607	0615	0707	0728	0740	0807	0822		0928	0900	1022		1128	1137	1137	1222	1334	1338	1344			1550	1607	1628
Tain-Hermitage-Tournon ▶ d.	0618		0718	0740	0743	0818	0833		0939		1033		1140			1233		1351					1618	1639
Vienne ▶ d.	0658		0758	0813	0829	0901	0914		1012		1113		1213			1313		1426					1658	1714
Lyon Part-Dieu a.				0834					1034		1134		1234	1246	1246	1334	1434	1446						1734
Lyon Perrache ▶ a.	0719		0819		0850	0920	0934																1719	
Lyon St Exupéry TGV ✈ a.		0644								0930									1414					
Genève **345** a.																								
Dijon **373** a.														1439	1439									
Strasbourg **384** a.															1828									
Metz **392** a.														1808										
Lille Flandres **13** a.																								
Paris Gare de Lyon ▲ a.		0841								1127									1611			1811		

Jan. 3 - Feb. 22: timings may vary by 10 minutes earlier or later in the Nice / Marseille area

MARSEILLE - AVIGNON - VALENCE - LYON — 351

		17718	*TGV* 6198							17724					17726	4322 4323	17726		17434	4394 4395	4330 4331	5790	4678 4679	
	Ⓑ					Ⓑ		† s	Ⓑ			Ⓐ			Ⓑ	⑦ e	Ⓑ	M	⑤⑦ y	◆ R	◆ R	◆ R	◆ R	
Nice **360** d.	...	...	...	...	...	...	...	...	...	...	...	...	...	...	...	...	...	...	1750	1946	2017	...	...	...
Toulon **360** d.	...	...	...	...	...	...	...	...	...	...	...	...	...	...	...	...	...	...	1950	2154	2214	...	...	...
Marseille St Charles § d.	...	1505	...	...	...	...	1554	...	1632	1705	...	1745	...	1844	1923	...	...	2042	2042	2251	2310	...	...	...
Miramas § d.	...	1533	1554	...	...	...	1641	...	1702	1742	...	1826	...	1922	2001	...	...	2119	2120	|	|	...	...	...
Arles § d.	...	1552	1615	...	...	...	|	...	|	1800	...	|	...	1945	2019	...	...	2136	2137	2342	|	...	...	...
Cerbère **355** d.	...	|	|	...	...	...	|	...	|	|	...	|	...	|	|	1650	...	|	|	|	|	...	...	...
Perpignan **355** d.	...	|	|	...	...	...	|	...	|	|	...	|	...	|	|	1742	...	|	|	|	|	...	...	...
Béziers **355** d.	...	|	|	...	...	...	|	...	|	|	...	|	...	|	|	1849	...	|	|	|	|	...	c	...
Montpellier **355** d.	...	|	|	...	...	...	|	...	|	|	...	|	...	|	|	1942	...	|	|	|	|	...	|	...
Avignon Centre a.	...	1609	1634	...	...	...	1729	...	1802	1817	...	1908	...	2004	2036	2047	...	2154	2153	0001	0022	...	|	...
Avignon Centre d.	...	1612	1637	1641	1705	...	...	1756	...	1820	1830	...	1949	...	2039	2050	...	...	2155	0014	0025	...	|	...
Orange d.	...	1628	1652	1705	1730	...	...	1815	...	1835	1856	...	2014	...	2055	|	...	...	2211	|	|	...	|	...
Montélimar d.	...	1704	1719	1741	1807	...	...	1847	...	1911	1935	...	2057	...	2127	2131	...	...	|	|	|	...	|	...
Valence Ville a.	...	1725	1741	1805	1832	...	...	1911	...	1932	2003	...	2124	...	2148	2153	←	...	2256	|	|	...	0538	...
Valence Ville ▶ d.	1707	1728	1744	1807	1835	1907	...	...	...	1935	2006	...	...	...	→	2157	2201	...	2259	|	|	0049	0541	...
Tain-Hermitage-Tournon ▶ d.	1718	1740	|	1819	1847	1918	...	...	...	1949	2017	...	...	...	...	|	2212	...	2312	|	|	|	|	...
Vienne ▶ d.	1758	1814	|	1858	|	1958	...	...	...	2023	2058	...	...	...	...	|	2245	...	|	|	|	|	|	...
Lyon Part-Dieu a.	|	1834	|	|	1954	|	...	...	...	2046	|	...	...	...	...	2251	2304	...	|	|	|	|	0644	...
Lyon Perrache ▶ a.	1818	...	|	1919	...	2019	...	...	...	...	2119	...	...	...	...	|	...	...	0010	|	|	|	|	...
Lyon St Exupéry TGV ✈ a.	...	...	1813	...	...	...	...	...	...	...	...	...	...	...	...	|	...	...	...	|	|	|	|	...
Genève **345** a.	...	...	|	...	...	...	...	...	...	...	...	...	...	...	...	|	...	...	...	|	|	|	0845	...
Dijon **373** a.	...	...	|	...	...	...	...	...	...	...	...	...	...	...	...	|	...	...	...	|	|	|	...	...
Strasbourg **384** a.	...	...	|	...	...	...	...	...	...	...	...	...	...	...	...	0519	...	...	...	0758	|	|	...	...
Metz **392** a.	...	...	|	...	...	...	...	...	...	...	...	...	...	...	...	...	...	...	...	...	0745	|	...	...
Lille Flandres **13** a.	...	...	|	...	...	...	...	...	...	...	...	...	...	...	...	...	...	...	...	...	...	|	...	...
Paris Gare de Lyon ▲ a.	...	...	2011	...	...	...	...	...	...	...	...	...	...	...	...	...	...	...	...	...	...	0646a	...	...

ADDITIONAL TRAINS LYON - VALENCE VILLE AND V.V.

Some 2nd class only

	Ⓐ	⚒	⚒	⚒	Ⓐ	Ⓐ	⚒	Ⓐ	Ⓐ	Ⓐ	⊕	Ⓐ	†	⚒⊗	Ⓐ	Ⓐ		Ⓐ	⚒	Ⓐ	Ⓐ	Ⓑ		⚒
Lyon Perrache d.	0538	...	0638	0722	0738	...	0822	0922	1022	1122	...	1322	...	1438	1538	1622	1654	1708	1722	1810	1852	1939	...	2022
Lyon Part Dieu d.	|	0622	|	|	|	0825	|	|	|	|	1225	|	1425	|	|	|	|	|	|	|	|	|	2025	|
Vienne d.	0602	0642	0704	0754	0800	0845	0854	0954	1054	1154	1244	1356	1444	1500	1600	1654	1726	1731	1754	1831	1924	2000	2044	2054
Tain-Hermitage-Tournon d.	0644	0724	0748	...	0840	0925	...	...	...	...	1325	...	1525	1540	1640	...	...	1811	...	1911	...	2041	2124	...
Valence Ville a.	0654	0735	0759	...	0851	0936	...	...	...	...	1335	...	1535	1551	1651	...	...	1821	...	1921	...	2051	2135	...

	Ⓐ	Ⓐ	⚒	⚒	⚒		⚒	Ⓐ	⚒	Ⓐ	Ⓐg	Ⓐ	⚒		Ⓐ	Ⓐ	Ⓐ	Ⓐ		⚒	⚒	⚒		
Valence Ville d.	0537	...	...	0622	0637	...	...	...	...	...	...	...	...	...	...	...	...	...	...	...	...	...	...	...
Tain-Hermitage-Tournon d.	0548	...	...	0635	0649	...	...	...	...	...	...	...	...	...	...	...	...	...	...	...	...	...	...	...
Vienne d.	0628	0634	0704	0712	0728	...	0804	0834	0904	1004	1104	1204	1304	...	1504	1634	1704	1734	...	1804	1904	2004	...	...
Lyon Part Dieu a.	|	|	|	0734	|	...	|	|	|	|	|	|	|	...	|	|	|	|	...	|	|	|	...	...
Lyon Perrache a.	0649	0707	0737	...	0749	...	0837	0907	0937	1037	1137	1237	1337	...	1537	1707	1737	1805	...	1837	1937	2036	...	...

◆ – **NOTES** (LISTED BY TRAIN NUMBER)

4238/9 – *CORAIL LUNÉA* – ⑤⑦, also daily Dec. 19 - Jan. 6 (not Dec. 24, 31), Feb. 6 - Mar. 9, Mar. 24, 25 (not Mar. 23), Apr. 2 - May 13 (not May 3), June 6 - Sept. 2. 🛏 1,2 cl. and (2) (reclining) Luxembourg - Metz - Nice. Conveys on dates in Table **382**, 🛏 2 cl., (2) (reclining) Reims - Nice.

4296/7 – *CORAIL LUNÉA* – daily except Dec. 15, 24, 31, Jan. 12, 19, 26, Feb. 2, Mar. 15, 22, 23, 29, May 3, 17, 24, 31. 🛏 1,2 cl. and (2) (reclining) Strasbourg - Nice. Train **4294/5** on certain dates.

4330/1 – *CORAIL LUNÉA* – ⑤⑦, also daily Dec. 19 - Jan. 6 (not Dec. 24, 31), Feb. 6 - Mar. 9, Mar. 24, 25 (not Mar. 23), Apr. 2 - May 13 (not May 3), June 6 - Sept. 2. 🛏 1,2 cl. and (2) (reclining) Nice - Metz - Luxembourg. Conveys on dates in Table **382**, 🛏 2 cl., (2) (reclining) Nice - Reims.

4394/5 – *CORAIL LUNÉA* – daily except Dec. 15, 24, 31, Jan. 12, 19, 26, Feb. 2, Mar. 15, 22, 23, 29, May 3, 17, 24, 31. 🛏 1,2 cl. and (2) (reclining) Nice - Strasbourg. Train **4388/9** on certain dates.

4678/9 – *CORAIL LUNÉA* – for days of running and composition see Table **355**.

4778/9 – *CORAIL LUNÉA* – for days of running and composition see Table **355**.

5790 – *CORAIL LUNÉA* – 🛏 1,2 cl. and (2) (reclining) Briançon - Paris. Not Dec. 24, 31. Train **15790** on certain dates.

5799 – *CORAIL LUNÉA* – 🛏 1,2 cl. and (2) (reclining) Paris - Briançon. Not Dec. 24, 31. Train **15799** on certain dates.

E – ⑥ Dec. 15 - Mar. 29.
M – ①②③④⑥ (not Dec. 25, Jan. 1, Mar. 24, May 1, 8, 12).
N – ①②③④⑥ (not Dec. 25, Jan. 1, Mar. 24, Apr. 30, May 7, 12).
S – June 13 - Sept. 19.
T – June 14 - Sept. 21.
U – June 15 - Sept. 13.

a – Paris **Austerlitz**.
b – To/from Briançon (Table **362**).
c – To Irún/from Hendaye (Table **355**).
d – Also Dec. 24, 31, Apr. 30, May 7; not May 2, 9.
e – Also Dec. 25, Jan. 1, Mar. 24, May 12; not Mar. 23, May 11.
g – Not Dec. 10 - 14.
k – Not Feb. 16, 23.
n – Not Dec. 25, Jan. 1, Mar. 24, May 12.
q – Also Dec. 25, Jan. 1, Mar. 23, Apr. 30, May 7, 12; not May 2.
r – 0833 on ©.
s – To Chambéry (Table **365**).
w – To Ventimiglia.
y – Also Dec. 25, Jan. 1, Mar. 24, May 1, 8.

TGV – R, supplement payable, 🍸.

▲ – For *TGV* services via high-speed line see Table **340** Paris - Lyon, Table **350** Paris - Marseille/Montpellier.
▶ – For additional trains Lyon Perrache - Valence Ville and v.v. see panel below main table.
⊕ – Subject to alteration on Ⓐ Jan. 8 - 25.
⊗ – Subject to alteration on Ⓐ Jan. 14 - 25.
⊡ – Subject to alteration Jan. 6 - 11.
◇ – From Annecy and Grenoble (Table **365**).
▽ – Depart 15 mins earlier Dec. 10 - 14. Subject to alteration on Ⓐ Jan. 7 - 25.
△ – On Jan. 13 diverted via St Peray and will not call at Tain or Valence.
▷ – On Jan. 14 - 18 diverted via St Peray and will not call at Tain or Valence.
⊖ – On Jan. 6, 13 diverted via St Peray and will not call at Tain or Valence.
⊙ – On Jan. 6 - 11, 13 diverted via St Peray and will not call at Tain or Valence.
§ – See also Table **355**.

Subject to alteration on Dec. 9.

PERPIGNAN - VILLEFRANCHE - LATOUR DE CAROL — 354

Subject to alteration on ①–⑤ Apr. 7 - 25

km		⚒			Ⓐv	©	Ⓐ		Ⓑ	
0	**Perpignan** d.	0636	0741	0848	1210	1211	1505	1700	1832	1950
40	Prades-Molitg les Bains d.	0727	0832	0936	1311	1302	1553	1751	1923	2041
46	**Villefranche-Vernet les Bains** a.	0734	0839	0943	1318	1309	1600	1758	1930	2048

	⚒		x		Ⓐ			Ⓑ
Villefranche-Vernet les Bains d.	0639	0746	1105	1215	1351	1702	1835	1953
Prades-Molitg les Bains d.	0647	0754	1113	1223	1359	1710	1843	2001
Perpignan a.	0734	0841	1200	1310	1446	1757	1930	2048

Villefranche - Latour de Carol is narrow gauge, 2nd class only ('Petit Train Jaune'). In summer most trains include open sightseeing carriages.

km		J	K	S	S	b	F	S	d	
0	**Villefranche-Vernet les Bains** d.	0905	0905	0905	1005	1330	1610	1725	1825	...
28	Mont Louis la Cabanasse d.	1021	1040	1040	1134	1444	1746	1842	1935	...
35	Font Romeu-Odeillo-Via d.	1042	1058	1102	1154	1503	1804	1900	1952	...
56	Bourg Madame d.	1139	1145	1159	1245	...	1851	1946	2037	...
63	**Latour de Carol** a.	1152	1200	1212	1300	...	1905	2001	2052	...

	①g	b	K	S	b	b	S	
Latour de Carol d.	0526	0810	0905	0905	...	1527	1620	...
Bourg Madame d.	0540	0827	0922	0922	...	1542	1635	...
Font Romeu-Odeillo-Via d.	0624	0917	1021	1021	1520	1638	1732	...
Mont Louis la Cabanasse d.	0638	0935	1040	1040	1540	1659	1754	...
Villefranche-Vernet les Bains a.	0735	1051	1155	1155	1650	1809	1908	...

F – ⑦ Dec. 9 - June 1 (also Dec. 25, Jan. 1; not Mar. 16, 23), also ⑤⑥ Feb. 8 - Mar. 8, ⑤⑥ Mar. 29 - May 3 (also May 1, 12).
J – Daily Dec. 9 - Feb. 8; ①–⑤ Feb. 11 - Mar. 7; ①–⑤ Mar. 31 - May 9 (not May 1); daily May 10 - June 1.
K – © Feb. 9 - Mar. 9; © Mar. 29 - May 4.
S – June 2 - 29.

b – Not Mar. 10 - 28.
d – Not Mar. 10 - 27.
g – ① to May 5 (also Dec. 26, Jan. 2, May 2, 13; not Dec. 24, 31, Mar. 17, 24).
v – By 🚌 Perpignan - Ille sur Tet (a. 1246, train d. 1253).
x – On Ⓐ by 🚌 Ille sur Tet (d. 1140) - Perpignan (a. 1205).

355 AVIGNON and MARSEILLE - NARBONNE - PORTBOU

km			3731			3733	3741		4248 4249	4293 4248		463		4752 4753						TGV 6803	TGV 5355	4754 4755		
		Ⓐ	♦	Ⓐ	Ⓐ	♦	♦	Ⓐ	S	S	Ⓐ	[R]✕	Ⓐ	★	⚒	⚒		E	⚒	⑥	Ⓑ	★	Ⓐ	⑥
		2	[R]	2	2	[R]	[R]	2	[R]	[R]	2	♦⁄	2		2	2	2		2	t	h		2	2
	Paris Gare de Lyon **350** d.	...	...	...	...	...	...	...	...	...	...	...	...	...	...	...	...	...	...	...	...	...	...	...
	Paris Austerlitz **310** d.	...	2156	...	...	2202	2217	...	...	...	...	...	...	...	...	...	...	...	...	...	...	...	...	...
	Brussels Midi **11** d.	...	|	...	...	|	|	...	...	...	...	...	...	...	...	...	...	...	...	...	...	...	...	...
	Lille Europe **11** d.	...	|	...	...	|	|	...	...	...	...	...	...	...	...	...	...	...	...	...	...	...	...	...
	Charles de Gaulle ✈ **350** d.	...	|	...	...	|	|	...	...	...	...	...	...	...	...	...	...	...	...	...	...	...	...	...
	Metz **392** d.	...	|	...	...	|	|	...	2112	...	...	...	...	...	...	...	...	...	...	...	...	...	...	...
	Strasbourg **384** d.	...	|	...	...	|	|	...	|	2019	...	...	...	...	...	...	...	...	...	...	...	...	...	...
	Dijon **373** d.	...	|	...	...	|	|	...	0116	0116	...	...	...	...	...	...	...	...	...	...	...	...	...	...
	Genève **345** d.	...	|	...	...	|	|	...	|	|	...	...	...	...	...	...	...	...	...	...	...	...	...	...
	Lyon Part Dieu **350** d.	...	|	...	...	|	|	...	|	|	...	...	...	...	...	...	...	...	...	0710	0710	...	...	...
	Nice **360** d.	...	|	...	...	|	|	...	|	|	...	...	...	...	...	...	...	...	...	|	|	...	...	...
▵	**Marseille St Charles** d.	...	|	...	...	|	|	...	|	|	...	...	...	0554	...	...	...	...	...	|	|	0714	...	...
	Arles d.	...	|	...	...	|	|	...	|	|	...	...	...	0638	...	...	...	...	...	|	|	0758	...	...
0	**Avignon Centre** d.	...	|	...	...	|	|	...	|	|	0558	...	...	|	...	0638	0726	...	...	|	|	|	...	...
21	Tarascon-sur-Rhône d.	...	|	...	...	|	|	...	|	|	0610	...	...	|	...	0652	0739	...	...	|	|	|	...	...
49	Nimes a.	...	|	...	...	|	|	...	0552	0552	0629	...	...	0702	...	0718	0756	...	...	0827	0827	0822	...	...
49	Nimes d.	...	|	...	0515	|	|	...	0555	0555	0631	...	0654	0705	...	0720	0758	...	0821	0830	0830	0825	0843	...
99	**Montpellier** a.	...	|	...	0545	|	|	...	0627	0627	0659	...	0727	0733	...	0752	0829	...	0844	0855	0855	0850	0911	...
99	**Montpellier** d.	...	|	...	0547	|	|	0620	0630	0630	0702	0726	0730	0737	...	0755	0832	...	...	0859	0859	0854	0914	0914
126	Sète d.	...	|	...	0604	|	|	0644	0651	0651	0721	|	0747	|	...	0815	0853	...	...	|	|	0911	0934	0934
149	Agde d.	...	|	...	0618	|	|	0700	0707	0707	0737	|	0802	|	...	0829	0907	...	...	|	|	|	0949	0949
170	Béziers d.	...	|	...	0632	|	|	0716	0723	0723	0751	0806	0816	0822	...	0840	0925	...	...	0943	0943	0936	1004	1002
196	**Narbonne** a.	...	0616	...	0647	0637	0658	0734	0739	0739	0805	0820	0830	0836	←	...	0941	...	...	0959	0959	0952	1020	...
196	**Narbonne** d.	...	0636	0642	0649	0658	0718	0737	0752	0752	...	0822	→	0840	0846	...	0943	0949	...	1002	1002	0955	...	...
	Carcassonne **321** a.	...	|	|	0723	|	|	|	|	|	...	|	...	0909	|	...	|	|	...	|	1032	1024	...	...
	Toulouse **321** a.	...	|	|	0831c	|	|	|	|	|	...	|	...	0958	|	...	|	|	...	|	1121	1117	...	...
	Irún **325** a.	...	|	|	...	|	|	|	|	|	...	|	...	|	|	...	|	|	...	|	▬	|	...	...
	Bordeaux **320** a.	...	|	|	...	|	|	|	|	|	...	|	...	1208	|	...	|	|	...	|	...	1331s	...	...
	Nantes **292** a.	...	|	|	...	|	|	|	|	|	...	|	...	...	|	...	|	|	...	|	2	...	...	...
259	**Perpignan** a.	...	0718	0728	...	0742	0803	0821	0826	0826	...	0854	...	...	0933	...	1026	1030	...	1035	←	...	...	...
259	**Perpignan** d.	0620	0722	...	...	0746	0807	...	0829	0829	...	0856	...	...	0936	...	→	1032	...	...	1045	...	...	...
281	Argelès sur Mer d.	0639	0745	...	...	0809	0826	...	0849	0849	...	|	...	...	0953	...	...	1051	...	...	1104	...	...	...
286	Collioure d.	0645	0753	...	...	0818	0833	...	0856	0856	...	|	...	...	0959	...	...	1057	...	...	1110	...	...	...
289	Port Vendres d.	0649	0759	...	...	0823	0838	...	0902	0902	...	|	...	...	1003	...	...	1100	...	...	1114	...	...	...
294	Banyuls sur Mer d.	0654	0805	...	...	0831	0846	...	0909	0909	...	|	...	...	1009	...	...	1106	...	...	1119	...	...	...
301	Cerbère a.	0700	0813	...	...	0839	0853	...	0916	0916	...	0921	...	...	1015	...	...	1113	...	...	1126	...	...	...
303	**Portbou** a.	...	0821	...	...	0854	...	...	0927	0927	...	0948	...	...	...	...	...	...	...	...	...	...	...	...

	17390	TGV 6201		TGV 6203	4756 4757			TGV 5104	TGV 9804		TGV 6205	TGV 6813	TGV 6207		4768 4769	TGV 5112	TGV 5311	15942 15943		4758 4759		TGV 6209		
		Ⓐ	2		★	2	2	Ⓒ	Ⓐ	2				⚒	★				Q	★				
														2	F		△	C	2	⊡	2		2	
Paris Gare de Lyon **350** d.	...	0620	...	0720	...	...	...	...	...	...	0820	...	0920	...	...	...	...	...	...	...	...	1120	...	...
Paris Austerlitz **310** d.	...	|	...	|	...	...	...	...	...	...	|	...	|	...	...	...	...	...	...	...	...	|	...	...
Brussels Midi **11** d.	...	|	...	|	...	...	...	...	0540	...	|	...	|	...	...	...	...	...	...	...	...	|	...	...
Lille Europe **11** d.	...	|	...	|	...	...	...	0625	0625	...	|	...	|	...	...	0828	...	...	...	...	...	|	...	...
Charles de Gaulle ✈ **350** d.	...	|	...	|	...	...	...	0725	0725	...	|	...	|	...	...	0925	...	...	...	...	...	|	...	...
Metz **392** d.	...	|	...	|	...	...	...	|	|	...	|	...	|	...	...	|	...	...	...	...	...	|	...	...
Strasbourg **384** d.	...	|	...	|	...	...	...	|	|	...	|	...	|	...	...	|	...	...	...	...	...	|	...	...
Dijon **373** d.	...	|	...	|	...	...	...	|	|	...	|	0816x	|	...	...	|	...	...	...	...	...	|	...	...
Genève **345** d.	...	|	...	|	...	...	...	|	|	...	|	|	|	...	...	|	...	...	...	...	...	|	...	...
Lyon Part Dieu **350** d.	...	|	...	|	...	...	...	0937	0937	...	|	1011	|	...	...	1137	1211	...	...	...	...	|	...	...
Nice **360** d.	...	|	...	|	...	...	...	|	|	...	|	|	|	...	0856	|	|	...	...	1008	...	|	...	...
Marseille St Charles d.	0743	|	...	|	0920	...	...	|	|	...	|	|	|	...	1153	|	|	1212	...	1254	...	|	...	...
Arles d.	0836	|	...	|	|	...	...	|	|	...	|	|	|	...	1244	|	|	1304	...	|	...	|	...	...
Avignon Centre d.	|	|	0903	|	|	1012	...	|	|	1039	|	|	|	1151	|	|	|	|	...	|	1322	|	...	...
Tarascon-sur-Rhône d.	0847	|	0916	|	|	1024	...	|	|	1053	|	|	|	1203	|	|	|	1315	...	|	1335	|	...	...
Nimes a.	0906	0916	0932	1010	|	1045	...	1059	1059	1107	1117	1125	1210	1226	1308	1258	1327	1332	...	|	1351	1415	...	...
Nimes d.	0909	0919	0934	1013	|	1048	...	1102	1102	1110	1120	1128	1213	1228	1311	1301	1330	...	1341	|	1359	1418	...	...
Montpellier a.	0939	0944	1005	1038	1056	1117	...	1129	1129	1141	1147	1155	1250	1259	1336	1342z	1402	...	1409	1420	1425	1446	...	...
Montpellier d.	...	...	1007	1042	1100	...	...	1133	1133	1145	...	...	...	1308	1341	...	...	...	1412	1424	1430	1450	...	...
Sète d.	...	...	1030	|	|	...	...	|	|	1207	...	...	...	1330	1359	...	...	...	1430	|	1450	1508	...	...
Agde d.	...	...	1045	|	|	...	...	|	|	1224	...	...	...	1343	1416	...	...	...	1444	|	1504	1524	...	...
Béziers d.	...	...	1059	1127	|	...	...	1216	1216	1240	...	...	...	1357	1432	...	...	...	1455	|	1517	1538	...	...
Narbonne a.	...	...	1114	1145	|	...	...	1235	1235	1256	...	...	...	1410	1446	...	...	...	...	|	1530	1554	...	...
Narbonne d.	...	...	1116	1148	|	...	1220	1238	1238	1258	...	...	...	1412	1449	...	...	...	...	|	1533	1602	1616	...
Carcassonne **321** a.	...	...	|	|	|	...	|	1309	1309	|	...	...	...	|	1518	...	...	...	...	|	1604	|	|	...
Toulouse **321** a.	...	...	|	|	1306	...	|	1356	1356	|	...	...	...	|	1613j	...	...	...	...	1623	1707r	|	|	...
Irún **325** a.	...	...	|	|	|	...	|	...	...	|	...	...	...	|	...	...	...	...	...	|	...	|	|	...
Bordeaux **320** a.	...	...	|	|	1512y	...	|	...	...	|	...	...	...	|	...	...	...	...	...	1829	...	|	|	...
Nantes **292** a.	...	...	|	|	...	...	|	...	...	|	...	...	...	|	...	...	...	...	...	...	...	|	|	...
Perpignan a.	...	...	1156	1221	...	...	1308	...	...	1336	...	...	...	1444	...	...	...	...	...	...	...	1640	1700	...
Perpignan d.	...	...	1206	...	...	...	...	...	...	1340	...	...	...	...	...	...	...	...	...	...	...	...	1703	...
Argelès sur Mer d.	...	...	1224	...	...	...	...	...	...	1358	...	...	...	...	...	...	...	...	...	...	...	...	1719	...
Collioure d.	...	...	1230	...	...	...	...	...	...	1404	...	...	...	...	...	...	...	...	...	...	...	...	1724	...
Port Vendres d.	...	...	1234	...	...	...	...	...	...	1408	...	...	...	...	...	...	...	...	...	...	...	...	1727	...
Banyuls sur Mer d.	...	...	1240	...	...	...	...	...	...	1413	...	...	...	...	...	...	...	...	...	...	...	...	1732	...
Cerbère a.	...	...	1246	...	...	...	...	...	...	1420	...	...	...	...	...	...	...	...	...	...	...	...	1738	...
Portbou a.	...	...	...	...	...	...	...	...	...	1428	...	...	...	...	...	...	...	...	...	...	...	...	...	...

♦ – **NOTES** (LISTED BY TRAIN NUMBER)

463 – MARE NOSTRUM – [12] and ✕ Montpellier - Barcelona - Alacant - Cartagena. In France calls to pick up only.

3731 – *CORAIL LUNÉA* – not Dec. 24, 31. ▬ 1, 2 cl. and [2] (reclining) Paris - Portbou.

3733 – Dec. 21, 28, Apr. 30, May 7 and ⑤⑥ from June 27. ▬ 1, 2 cl. and [2] (reclining) Paris - Portbou.

3741 – ①②③④⑦ June 29 - Aug. 28. ▬ 1, 2 cl. and [2] (reclining) Paris - Toulouse - Cerbère.

C – [12] Marseille - Clermont Ferrand (Table **334**).

E – ⑥⑦ June 21 - Aug. 24. [12] Toulouse - Cerbère.

F – ⑤⑥⑦ Dec. 23 - Jan. 6, Feb. 15 - Mar. 9, Apr. 12 - 27 (also Dec. 25, Jan. 1, Mar. 22, 24, Apr. 30, May 1, 4, 7, 8, 12).

Q – Daily to Montpellier, ⚒ to Béziers. Starts from Alès (Table **334**).

S – Runs (from Metz and Strasbourg) on ⑤⑦ (not Mar. 23), also Dec. 20 - Jan. 6 (not Dec. 24, 31), Feb. 9, 16, 23, Mar. 1, 8, 24, 27, 29, Apr. 4 - 27, 30, May 7, 10, 12, June 6 - 26. ▬ 1, 2 cl. and [2] (reclining) Metz and Strasbourg - Portbou.

c – 0845 on Ⓐ Dec. 9 - 21, Jan. 2 - Feb. 22.

h – Not May 1, 8.

j – 1700 on Jan. 4, Feb. 15.

r – Ⓑ to Mar. 16; ⑤⑦ Mar. 21 - Apr. 13; Ⓑ from Apr. 14.

s – 1339 on Ⓒ Jan. 5 - Feb. 10; 1343 on Jan. 2 - 4 and Ⓐ Jan. 14 - Feb. 15; 1348 Jan. 7 - 11; 1349 Ⓐ Feb. 18 - Mar. 14 and daily Mar. 17 - Apr. 4, Apr. 11 - 25.

t – Also May 1, 8.

x – ①⑥ (also Dec. 26, Jan. 2, Mar. 25, May 1, 8, 13; not Dec. 24, 31, Mar. 24, May 12).

y – Arrive 1530 Jan. 4 - 6, Jan. 12 - Feb. 15, Feb. 18 - 22. Arrive 1550 Ⓐ Jan. 7 - 11.

z – 1328 on ⑤-⑦ and holidays.

TGV – [R], supplement payable, 🍷.

⁄ – Special 'global' fares payable.

⊡ – On Ⓑ Jan. 2 - Feb. 11 arrive Toulouse 1628, Bordeaux 1833. On ⑥ Jan. 5 - Feb. 9 arrive Toulouse 1628, Bordeaux 1848. On ①-④ Mar. 17 - Apr. 10 (not Mar. 24) Montpellier a. 1433 / d. 1440, arrive Toulouse 1723, Bordeaux 1933. On ⑤ Mar. 21 - Apr. 11 arrive Toulouse 1637, Bordeaux 1842.

△ – From Nantes (Table **335**).

★ – *CORAIL TÉOZ*, [R], 🍷.

▵ – *135 km* from Nîmes via Avignon TGV, *128 km* via Arles.

AVIGNON and MARSEILLE - NARBONNE - PORTBOU 355

				TGV 6816	4762 4763	TGV 6211		70 71	TGV 9833	3631	4240 4241	76437		4764 4765				TGV 6213	TGV 5117					TGV 6231
	⚒ 2	⑥ 2	Ⓐ 2		★		Ⓐ 2	♦ ⁄ 🅁 ✕		★	S 🍷	V 2	Ⓐ 2	★	Ⓐ 2	2	Ⓑ 2			2y	Ⓐ 2	⑥ 2	⚒ 2	Ⓐ
Paris Gare de Lyon **350** d.	...	...	...	...	...	1320	...	...	...	...	...	...	...	...	...	...	...	1520	...	...	...	...	...	1620
Paris Austerlitz **310** d.	...	...	...	...	...	|	...	...	...	1017x	...	...	...	...	...	...	...	|	...	...	...	...	...	|
Brussels Midi **11** d.	...	...	...	...	...	|	...	...	1110	|	...	...	...	...	...	...	...	|	...	...	...	...	...	|
Lille Europe **11** d.	...	...	...	...	...	|	...	...	1156	|	...	...	...	...	...	...	...	|	...	...	...	...	...	|
Charles de Gaulle ✈ **350** d.	...	...	...	...	...	|	...	...	1258	|	...	...	...	...	...	...	...	|	...	...	...	...	...	|
Metz **392** d.	...	...	...	...	...	|	...	...	|	|	0820z	...	...	...	...	...	...	|	...	...	...	...	...	|
Strasbourg **384** d.	...	...	...	...	...	|	...	...	|	|	0813	...	...	...	...	...	...	|	...	...	...	...	...	|
Dijon **373** d.	...	...	...	...	...	|	...	...	|	|	1216	...	...	...	...	...	...	|	1516	...	...	...	...	|
Genève **345** d.	...	...	...	1244	...	|	...	...	|	|	|	...	...	...	...	...	...	|	|	...	...	...	...	|
Lyon Part Dieu **350** d.	...	...	...	1437	...	|	...	...	1507	|	1405	...	...	...	...	...	...	|	1707	...	...	...	...	|
Nice **360** d.	...	...	...	|	...	|	...	...	|	|	|	...	...	1330	...	...	...	|	|	...	...	...	...	|
Marseille St Charles d.	...	...	...	|	1500	|	...	...	|	|	|	...	...	1619	...	...	1643	|	|	...	...	...	...	|
Arles d.	...	...	...	|	1546	|	...	...	|	|	|	...	...	|	...	...	1742	|	|	...	...	...	...	|
Avignon Centre d.	...	...	1525r	|	|	|	...	...	|	|	1610	1610	...	|	...	1706	|	|	|	...	1800	...	1845	|
Tarascon-sur-Rhône d.	...	...	1537	|	|	|	...	...	|	|	|	1624	...	|	...	1719	1752	|	|	...	1816	...	1857	|
Nimes a.	...	...	1552	1559	1610	1616	...	...	1629	|	1639	1639	...	|	...	1734	1805	|	1829	...	1833	...	1912	1917
Nimes d.	1454	...	1554	1602	1612	1619	1623	...	1632	|	1642	1642	1700	|	...	1736	1808	|	1832	...	1835	...	...	1920
Montpellier a.	1525	...	1623	1626	1638	1645	1653	...	1657	|	1713	1713	1742	1745	←	1812	1838	1842	1856	...	1915	...	...	1944
Montpellier d.	1528	1626	1626	...	1642	...	1656	1702	1707	|	1716	1716	→	1749	1754	1815	1841	1847	1900	...	1918	1918	...	...
Sète d.	1549	1646	1646	...	1700	...	1719	|	1723	|	1738	1738	...	|	1816	1840	1901	1907	|	...	1937	1937	...	...
Agde d.	1605	1701	1701	...	|	...	1734	|	1740	|	1754	1754	...	|	1833	1856	1916	1922	|	...	1950	1950	...	...
Béziers d.	1620	1712	1714	...	1727	...	1747	1742	1754	|	1809	1809	...	|	1850	1914	1929	1936	1943	...	2001	2001	...	...
Narbonne a.	1638	▬	1734	...	1742	...	1801	1756	1807	1805	1823	1823	...	|	1906	1930	1941	1949	1955	...	...	...	...	...
Narbonne d.	...	...	1737	...	1745	...	...	1758	1810	1825	1829	1829	...	|	...	...	...	1952	1958	2010	...	...	...	...
Carcassonne **321** a.	...	...	|	...	1814	...	...	|	|	|	|	|	...	|	...	...	...	|	2026	|	...	...	...	...
Toulouse **321** a.	...	...	|	...	1903	...	...	|	|	|	|	|	...	1951	...	...	...	|	2112	|	...	...	...	...
Irún **325** a.	...	...	|	...	|	...	...	|	|	|	|	|	...	|	...	...	...	|	|	|	...	...	...	...
Bordeaux **320** a.	...	...	|	...	2121	...	...	|	|	|	|	|	...	2157	...	...	...	|	2320	|	...	...	...	...
Nantes **292** a.	...	...	|	...	...	...	...	|	|	|	|	|	...	...	...	...	...	|	...	|	...	...	...	...
Perpignan a.	...	2	1822	...	...	...	...	1835	1844	1902	1916	1915	...	...	...	...	...	2024	...	2100	...	...	...	...
Perpignan d.	...	1726	1824	...	...	...	...	1837	...	1906	1919	1918	...	...	...	...	...	...	...	...	...	...	...	...
Argelès sur Mer d.	...	1744	1840	...	...	...	...	|	...	1925	1939	1937	...	...	...	...	...	...	...	...	...	...	...	...
Collioure d.	...	1749	1845	...	...	...	...	|	...	1932	1944	1943	...	...	...	...	...	...	...	...	...	...	...	...
Port Vendres d.	...	1753	1849	...	...	...	...	|	...	1938	1950	1948	...	...	...	...	...	...	...	...	...	...	...	...
Banyuls sur Mer d.	...	1758	1854	...	...	...	...	|	...	1944	1957	1955	...	...	...	...	...	...	...	...	...	...	...	...
Cerbère a.	...	1804	1900	...	...	...	...	1904	...	1951	2003	2003	...	...	...	...	...	...	...	...	...	...	...	...
Portbou a.	...	1812	...	...	...	...	...	1931	...	...	2011	2011	...	...	...	...	...	...	...	...	...	...	...	...

	TGV 5118	17394				4766 4767	TGV 6215		TGV 5398	17396		TGV 6217	TGV 9836	TGV 9836		TGV 6219	TGV 6219	TGV 6219	TGV 6221	4724 4725	TGV 5135	4264 4265	4778 4779	4720
			2	2	2	⑤⑦ ♦u		2			⑤⑦ 2			⑤⑦ w	⑦ 2		①–④ m	⑤ f		♦ 🅁	⑦ e	⑤ d	♦ 🅁	♦ 🅁
Paris Gare de Lyon **350** d.	...	...	...	...	...	...	1720	...	...	...	...	1820	...	...	...	1920	1920	1920	2020	...	...	...	...	...
Paris Austerlitz **310** d.	...	...	...	...	...	...	|	...	...	...	...	|	...	...	...	|	|	|	|	...	...	...	...	...
Brussels Midi **11** d.	...	...	...	...	...	...	|	...	...	...	...	|	1609	1609	...	|	|	|	|	...	...	...	...	...
Lille Europe **11** d.	1454c	...	...	...	...	...	|	...	...	...	...	|	1654	1654	...	|	|	|	|	...	1931	...	...	...
Charles de Gaulle ✈ **350** d.	1553	...	...	...	...	...	|	...	...	...	...	|	1751	1751	...	|	|	|	|	...	2026	...	...	...
Metz **392** d.	|	...	...	...	...	...	|	...	...	...	...	|	|	|	...	|	|	|	|	...	|	1545	...	...
Strasbourg **384** d.	|	...	...	...	...	...	|	...	...	...	...	|	|	|	...	|	|	|	|	...	|	|	...	...
Dijon **373** d.	|	...	...	...	...	...	|	...	...	...	...	|	|	|	...	|	|	|	|	...	|	1907	...	...
Genève **345** d.	|	...	...	...	...	...	|	...	...	...	...	|	|	|	...	|	|	|	|	...	|	|	2044	...
Lyon Part Dieu **350** d.	1811	...	...	...	...	...	|	...	...	...	...	|	2007	2007	...	|	|	|	|	...	2241	2102	2250	...
Nice **360** d.	|	...	...	...	...	...	|	...	...	...	...	|	|	|	...	|	|	|	|	1835	|	|	|	2058
Marseille St Charles d.	|	1805	...	...	...	1912	|	...	1936	1916	...	|	|	|	...	|	|	|	|	2214	|	|	|	0010
Arles d.	|	1853	...	...	...	|	|	...	|	2012	...	|	|	|	...	|	|	|	|	|	|	|	|	|
Avignon Centre d.	|	|	...	1928	...	|	|	1958	2014v	|	...	|	|	|	...	|	|	|	|	|	|	2329	|	|
Tarascon-sur-Rhône d.	|	1911	...	1943	...	|	|	|	|	2022	...	|	|	|	...	|	|	|	|	|	|	2343	|	|
Nimes a.	1927	1931	...	2000	...	2015	2020	2025	2031	2038	...	2117	2127	2127	...	2211	2211	2211	2317	2330	0002	0001	|	|
Nimes d.	1930	1934	...	...	2009	2018	2023	...	2034	2041	...	2120	2130	2130	...	2214	2214	2214	2320	2335	0005	0003	|	|
Montpellier a.	1955	2003	...	...	2036	2044	2049	...	2059	2108	...	2148	2155	2155	...	2238	2238	2238	2344	0006	0030	0034	|	|
Montpellier d.	1959	2006	...	...	2039	2048	2054	...	2103	2111	...	2152	...	2159	2226	...	2244	2244	...	0011	...	...	|	|
Sète d.	2016	2024	...	...	2058	2106	2111	...	2120	2130	...	2209	...	2216	2244	...	|	2301	...	|	...	...	|	|
Agde d.	2032	2038	...	...	2111	|	2126	...	|	2144	...	2224	...	2232	2257	...	|	2316	...	|	...	...	|	|
Béziers d.	2047	2051	...	...	2123	2131	2140	...	2147	2156	...	2236	...	2246	2309	...	2323	2330	...	|	...	...	|	|
Narbonne a.	2101	2104	...	...	...	2146	2153	...	2201	2209	...	...	...	2300	2325	...	...	2344	...	|	...	...	|	|
Narbonne d.	2104	...	2120	...	...	2148	2156	...	2204	...	2219	...	...	2303	...	...	...	2347n	...	|	...	...	|	|
Carcassonne **321** a.	|	...	|	...	...	2217	|	...	2233	...	|	...	...	|	...	...	...	|	...	|	...	...	|	|
Toulouse **321** a.	|	...	|	...	...	2306	|	...	2321	...	|	...	...	|	...	...	...	|	...	|	...	...	0511	0514
Irún **325** a.	|	...	|	...	...	|	|	...	...	...	|	...	...	|	...	...	...	|	...	|	...	...	1107	|
Bordeaux **320** a.	|	...	|	...	...	0117	|	...	...	...	|	...	...	|	...	...	...	|	...	0437	...	...	...	0810
Nantes **292** a.	|	...	|	...	...	...	|	...	...	...	|	...	...	|	...	...	...	|	...	0905j	...	...	...	...
Perpignan a.	2135	...	2157	...	...	...	2229	...	...	...	2257	...	...	2335	...	...	...	0021n	...	...	...	...	...	...
Perpignan d.	...	...	2159	...	...	...	...	...	...	...	...	...	...	...	...	...	...	...	...	...	...	...	...	...
Argelès sur Mer d.	...	...	2216	...	...	...	...	...	...	...	...	...	...	...	...	...	...	...	...	...	...	...	...	...
Collioure d.	...	...	2221	...	...	...	...	...	...	...	...	...	...	...	...	...	...	...	...	...	...	...	...	...
Port Vendres d.	...	...	2225	...	...	...	...	...	...	...	...	...	...	...	...	...	...	...	...	...	...	...	...	...
Banyuls sur Mer d.	...	...	2231	...	...	...	...	...	...	...	...	...	...	...	...	...	...	...	...	...	...	...	...	...
Cerbère a.	...	...	2237	...	...	...	...	...	...	...	...	...	...	...	...	...	...	...	...	...	...	...	...	...
Portbou a.	...	...	...	...	...	...	...	...	...	...	...	...	...	...	...	...	...	...	...	...	...	...	...	...

♦ – **NOTES** (LISTED BY TRAIN NUMBER)

70/1 – CATALAN TALGO – [12] and ✕ Montpellier - Barcelona. In France calls to pick up only.

4720 – *CORAIL LUNÉA* – not Dec. 24, 31. ▬ 1,2 cl. and [2] (reclining) Nice - Bordeaux. To Irún on dates in Table **305**.

4724/5 – ⑤⑦ (not Mar. 23), also Dec. 21 - Jan. 6 (not Dec. 24, 31), Feb. 8 - Mar. 9, Mar. 24, Apr. 4 - May 4, May 7 - 12. ▬ 1,2 cl. and [2] (reclining) Nice - Nantes.

4766/7 – [12] Toulon - Marseille - Bordeaux.

4778/9 – *CORAIL LUNÉA* – ⑤⑦, also daily Dec. 21 - Jan. 6 (not Dec. 24, 31), Feb. 8 - Mar. 9, Mar. 24 (not Mar. 23), Apr. 4 - May 12 (not May 5, 6). ▬ 1,2 cl. and [2] (reclining) Genève - Lyon - Irún.

S – June 13 - Sept. 20: [12] Metz - Dijon - Portbou; [12] and 🍷 Strasbourg (**4251/0**) - Dijon - Portbou.

V – Dec. 9 - June 12.

c – 1458 on Ⓐ.

d – Also Dec. 24, 31, Apr. 30, May 7; not May 2, 9.

e – Also Dec. 25, Jan. 1, Mar. 24, May 12.

f – Also Apr. 30, May 7; not May 2.

j – 1036 on Apr. 6, 13, 20, 27.

m – Not Dec. 25, Jan. 1, Mar. 24, Apr. 30, May 1, 7, 8, 12.

n – Night of ⑤ (also Apr. 30, May 7; not Dec. 14, Jan. 18, Feb. 8, Mar. 14, May 2).

r – 1509 on Ⓐ Feb. 25 - Mar. 7, Apr. 14 - 25.

u – Also Dec. 24, Jan. 1, Mar. 24, Apr. 30, May 7, 12; not Mar. 23, May 2, 9.

v – Avignon **TGV** station.

w – Also Dec. 25, Jan. 1, Mar. 24, Apr. 30, May 7, 12; not May 2.

x – Depart 0956 Mar. 19, 26, 27. Depart 1006 Mar. 10 - 14, 20, 21.

y – From Toulouse on Ⓐ.

z – 0833 on ©.

TGV – 🅁, supplement payable, 🍷.

⁄ – Special 'global' fares payable.

★ – *CORAIL TÉOZ*, 🅁, 🍷.

355 CERBÈRE - NARBONNE - AVIGNON and MARSEILLE

		4624 4625	TGV 6202				TGV 6230			TGV 5162	TGV 5162	TGV 6204						TGV 5166			4340 4341		TGV 5301	TGV 6206
	Ⓐ 2	♦ R	Ⓐ	Ⓐ	Ⓐ 2	⑥ 2	Ⓐ	Ⓐ 2	⑥ 2		①⑥ y		2	Ⓐ 2	⚒ 2	⚒ 2	† 2			2	♦	⚒ 2		
Cerbère d.	...	...	...	...	...	...	...	...	...	...	...	...	...	...	...	0545	0545	...	...	...	0607	0640	...	...
Banyuls sur Mer d.	...	...	...	...	...	...	...	...	...	...	...	...	...	...	...	0552	0552	...	...	...	0616	0647	...	...
Port Vendres d.	...	...	...	...	...	...	...	...	...	...	...	...	...	...	...	0558	0558	...	...	...	0623	0653	...	...
Collioure d.	...	...	...	...	...	...	...	...	...	...	...	...	...	...	...	0602	0602	...	...	...	0628	0657	...	...
Argelès sur Mer d.	...	...	...	...	...	...	...	...	...	...	...	...	...	...	...	0607	0607	...	...	...	0635	0702	...	...
Perpignan a.	...	...	...	...	...	...	...	...	...	...	...	...	...	...	...	0625	0625	...	...	...	0658	0719	...	...
Perpignan d.	...	...	...	...	...	...	...	...	...	...	0505	...	...	0552	...	0628	0628	0642	...	...	0701	0721	...	0732
Nantes **292** d.	...	2046	...	...	...	...	...	...	...	...	|	...	...	|	...	|	|	|	...	...	|	|	...	|
Bordeaux **320** d.	...	0101	...	...	...	...	...	...	...	...	|	...	...	|	...	|	|	|	...	...	|	|	...	|
Hendaye **325** d.	...	|	...	...	...	...	...	...	...	...	|	...	...	|	...	|	|	|	...	...	|	|	...	|
Toulouse **321** d.	...	|	...	...	...	...	...	...	...	...	|	...	...	|	...	|	|	|	...	...	|	|	0655*	|
Carcassonne **321** d.	...	|	...	...	...	...	...	...	...	...	|	...	...	|	...	|	|	|	...	0714	|	|	0742	|
Narbonne a.	...	|	...	...	...	...	...	...	...	...	0541	...	...	0643	...	0715	0715	0717	...	0748	0744	0806	0809	0813
Narbonne d.	...	|	...	0440	...	...	...	...	...	...	0544	...	0610	0647	0655	0724	0724	0720	...	0750	0803	...	0812	0815
Béziers d.	...	|	0447	0455	0513	...	0534	0555	...	...	0601	...	0625	0704	0710	0745	0745	0737	...	0805	0819	...	0827	0833
Agde d.	...	|	0501	0508	0525	...	0549	0608	...	...	0615	...	0639	0717	0724	0758	0758	0751	...	0818	0833	...	|	0846
Sète d.	...	|	0517	0523	0539	...	0604	0622	...	...	0630	...	0657	0731	0741	0812	0812	0807	...	0832	0848	...	0855	0901
Montpellier a.	...	0523	0534	0541	0556	...	0619	0640	...	...	0645	...	0721	0748	0803	0830	0830	0822	...	0849	0903	...	0910	0916
Montpellier d.	...	0526	0539	0544	0559	0559	0623	0643	0643	0652	0652	0720	0724	0751	0806	0836	...	0826	...	0852	0924	...	0915	0921
Nimes a.	...	0555	0602	0610	0642	0642	0647	0711	0711	0715	0715	0747	0753	0824	0838	0904	...	0850	...	0923	0954	...	0941	0945
Nimes d.	0530	0557	0605	0612	0710	0710	0650	...	...	0718	0718	0750	0756	0826	...	0906	...	0853	...	0925	0957	...	0943	0948
Tarascon-sur-Rhône d.	0549	|	|	0628	0733	0733	|	...	...	|	|	|	0812	0843	...	0925	...	|	...	0944	|	...	|	|
Avignon Centre a.	0600	|	|	|	0745	0745	|	...	...	|	|	|	|	0856	...	0938	...	|	...	0955	1025	...	1004v	|
Arles d.	...	|	|	0638	...	...	|	...	...	|	|	|	0823	...	...	...	...	|	...	...	|	...	|	|
Marseille St Charles a.	...	0708	|	0738	...	...	|	...	...	|	|	|	0918	...	...	...	...	|	...	...	|	...	1040	|
Nice **360** a.	...	1015	|	...	...	...	|	...	...	|	|	|	...	...	...	...	...	|	...	...	|	...	...	|
Lyon Part Dieu **350** a.	...	...	|	...	...	...	|	...	...	0846	0846	|	...	...	...	...	...	1016	...	...	1246	...	...	|
Genève **345** a.	...	...	|	...	...	...	|	...	...	|	|	|	...	...	...	...	...	|	...	...	|	...	...	|
Dijon **373** a.	...	...	|	...	...	...	|	...	...	|	|	|	...	...	...	...	...	|	...	...	1439	...	...	|
Strasbourg **384** a.	...	...	|	...	...	...	|	...	...	|	|	|	...	...	...	...	...	|	...	...	1829	...	...	|
Metz **392** a.	...	...	|	...	...	...	|	...	...	|	|	|	...	...	...	...	...	|	...	...	1808	...	...	|
Charles de Gaulle + **350** a.	...	...	|	...	...	...	|	...	...	1059	1059	|	...	...	...	...	...	1230	...	...	...	...	...	|
Lille Europe **11** a.	...	...	|	...	...	...	|	...	...	1235	1235	|	...	...	...	...	...	1326	...	...	...	...	...	|
Brussels Midi **11** a.	...	...	|	...	...	...	|	...	...	...	...	|	...	...	...	...	...	1412	...	...	...	...	...	|
Paris Austerlitz **310** a.	...	...	|	...	...	...	|	...	...	...	...	|	...	...	...	...	...	...	...	...	...	...	...	|
Paris Gare de Lyon **350** a.	...	...	0911	...	...	...	0949	...	...	...	...	1041	...	...	...	...	...	...	...	...	...	...	...	1241

			17342		TGV 5170	4652 4653	TGV 6208	3630	TGV 9862				4654 4655		TGV 6210	73		TGV 6866			TGV 6212	TGV 9868		
	Ⓐ W	⚒		2	·	★		★		⑥⑦ 2b	2		★ ▽	⊡ 2		♦ R ✕	2		⚒D 2	E 2			Ⓐ 2	Ⓒ 2
Cerbère d.	...	0713	...	...	...	...	...	0748	...	...	...	...	...	1039	...	1114	...	...	...	1122	...	...	...	...
Banyuls sur Mer d.	...	0721	...	...	...	...	...	0757	...	...	...	...	...	1045	...	|	...	...	...	1129	...	...	...	...
Port Vendres d.	...	0726	...	...	...	...	...	0803	...	...	...	...	...	1050	...	|	...	...	...	1134	...	...	...	...
Collioure d.	...	0730	...	...	...	...	...	0808	...	...	...	...	...	1054	...	|	...	...	...	1138	...	...	...	...
Argelès sur Mer d.	...	0735	...	...	...	...	...	0815	...	...	...	...	...	1059	...	|	...	...	...	1144	...	...	...	...
Perpignan a.	...	0754	...	...	...	...	...	0838	...	...	...	...	...	1117	...	1143	...	...	...	1203	...	...	...	...
Perpignan d.	...	...	0757	...	...	...	...	0842	...	...	1024	...	...	1119	...	1145	...	...	1205	1205	...	1240	...	...
Nantes **292** d.	...	...	|	...	...	...	...	|	...	...	|	...	...	|	...	|	...	...	|	|	...	|	...	...
Bordeaux **320** d.	...	...	|	...	0543*	0552*	...	|	...	...	|	...	0816r	|	...	|	...	...	|	|	...	|	...	...
Hendaye **325** d.	...	...	|	...	|	|	...	|	...	...	|	...	|	|	...	|	...	...	|	|	...	|	...	...
Toulouse **321** d.	...	...	|	...	0749*	0803*	...	|	...	...	|	...	1042*	|	...	|	...	...	|	|	...	|	1154*	1154*
Carcassonne **321** d.	...	...	|	...	0834	|	...	|	...	...	|	...	1133	|	...	|	1210	...	|	|	...	|	1252	1252
Narbonne a.	...	...	0838	...	0901	|	...	0916	...	...	1108	...	1201	1200	...	1219	1244	...	1250	1250	...	1317	1325	1325
Narbonne d.	0822	...	0841	...	0903	|	...	0938	...	...	1110	...	1204	...	...	1221	1247	...	...	...	...	1320	1327	1327
Béziers d.	0838	...	0856	...	0918	|	...	|	...	1123	1127	...	1221	...	...	1239	1304	...	...	...	...	1337	1343	1343
Agde d.	0852	...	0909	...	|	|	...	|	...	1135	1140	...	|	...	...	|	1315	...	...	...	...	1351	1356	1356
Sète d.	0907	...	0923	...	|	|	...	|	...	1151	1156	...	1244	...	...	|	1329	...	...	...	...	1407	1412	1412
Montpellier a.	0921	...	0941	...	0955	1002	...	|	...	1209	1214	...	1259	...	...	1322	1346	...	...	...	...	1425	1431	1431
Montpellier d.	0925	...	0944	...	1002	1006	1013	|	1156	1212	1226	...	1303	...	1315	...	1349	1356	...	...	1423	1430	1434	...
Nimes a.	0954	...	1010	...	1026	|	1037	|	1222	1240	1304	...	1330	...	1343	...	1418	1421	...	...	1447	1454	1503	...
Nimes d.	...	...	1012	1022	1029	|	1050	|	1227	...	1318	...	1340	...	1350	...	...	1424	...	...	1450	1457	1507	...
Tarascon-sur-Rhône d.	...	...	1029	|	|	|	|	|	|	...	1336	...	|	...	|	...	...	|	...	...	|	|	1523	...
Avignon Centre a.	...	...	|	1054	|	|	|	|	|	...	1349	...	|	...	|	...	...	|	...	...	|	|	1536	...
Arles d.	...	...	1041	...	|	|	|	|	|	...	...	...	1406	...	|	...	...	|	...	...	|	|	...	...
Marseille St Charles a.	...	...	1136	...	|	1142	|	|	|	...	...	...	1453	...	|	...	...	|	...	...	|	|	...	...
Nice **360** a.	...	...	...	...	|	1430	|	|	|	...	...	...	...	...	|	...	...	|	...	...	|	|	...	...
Lyon Part Dieu **350** a.	...	...	...	...	1154	...	|	|	1346	...	...	...	...	...	|	...	...	1550	...	...	|	1620	...	...
Genève **345** a.	...	...	...	...	|	...	|	|	|	...	...	...	...	...	|	...	...	1735	...	...	|	|	...	...
Dijon **373** a.	...	...	...	...	1343	...	|	|	|	...	...	...	...	...	|	...	...	...	...	...	|	|	...	...
Strasbourg **384** a.	...	...	...	...	...	...	|	|	|	...	...	...	...	...	|	...	...	...	...	...	|	|	...	...
Metz **392** a.	...	...	...	...	...	...	|	|	|	...	...	...	...	...	|	...	...	...	...	...	|	|	...	...
Charles de Gaulle + **350** a.	...	...	...	...	...	...	|	|	1559	...	...	...	...	...	|	...	...	...	...	...	|	1830	...	...
Lille Europe **11** a.	...	...	...	...	...	...	|	|	1707	...	...	...	...	...	|	...	...	...	...	...	|	1936	...	...
Brussels Midi **11** a.	...	...	...	...	...	...	|	|	1754	...	...	...	...	...	|	...	...	...	...	...	|	2022	...	...
Paris Austerlitz **310** a.	...	...	...	...	...	...	|	1740x	...	...	...	...	...	...	|	...	...	...	...	...	|	...	...	...
Paris Gare de Lyon **350** a.	...	...	...	...	...	...	1349	...	...	...	...	...	...	...	1641	...	...	...	...	...	1749	...	...	...

♦ – **NOTES FOR PAGES 216/217** (LISTED BY TRAIN NUMBER)

73 – CATALAN TALGO – 12 and ✕ Barcelona - Montpellier.

460 – MARE NOSTRUM – 12 and ✕ Cartagena - Alacant - Barcelona - Montpellier. After Cerbère calls to set down only.

3730 – *CORAIL LUNÉA* – not Dec. 24, 31. 1, 2 cl. and 2 (reclining) Cerbère - Paris.

3732 – Dec. 25, Jan. 1, May 3, 12 and ⑥ from June 28. 1, 2 cl. and 2 (reclining) Cerbère - Paris.

3740 – ①-⑤ June 30 - Aug. 29. 1, 2 cl. and 2 (reclining) Cerbère - Paris.

4340/1 – June 14 - Sept. 21 : 12 Cerbère - Dijon - Metz; 12 Cerbère - Dijon (**4351**) - Strasbourg.

4348/9 – ⑤⑦ (not Mar. 23), also Dec. 20 - Jan. 6 (not Dec. 24, 31), Feb. 9, 16, 23, Mar. 1, 8, 24, 27, 29, Apr. 4 - 27, 30, May 7 - 12, 17, June 6 - 26. 1, 2 cl. and 2 (reclining) Cerbère - Metz.

4620/1 – *CORAIL LUNÉA* – not Dec. 24, 31. 1, 2 cl. and 2 (reclining) Bordeaux - Nice. From Hendaye on dates in Table **305**.

4624/5 – ⑤⑦ (not Mar. 23), also Dec. 21 - Jan. 6 (not Dec. 24, 31), Feb. 8 - Mar. 9, Mar. 24, Apr. 4 - May 4, May 7 - 12. 1, 2 cl. and 2 (reclining) Nantes - Nice and v.v.

4678/9 – *CORAIL LUNÉA* – ⑤⑦, also daily Dec. 21 - Jan. 6 (not Dec. 24, 31), Feb. 8 - Mar. 9, Mar. 24 (not Mar. 23), Apr. 4 - May 12 (not May 5, 6). 1, 2 cl. and 2 (reclining) Hendaye - Lyon - Genève.

C – 12 Clermont Ferrand - Marseille (Table **334**).

D – ⚒ to May 31.

E – ①-⑥ June 2 - 28.

F – ⑤⑥⑦ Dec. 21 - Jan. 6, Feb. 15 - Mar. 9, Apr. 11 - 27 (also Dec. 25, Jan. 1, Mar. 21, 22, 24, Apr. 30, May 1, 4, 7, 8, 12).

W – Dec. 9 - June 13.

Y – ⑤⑦ (not Mar. 23), also Dec. 20 - Jan. 6 (not Dec. 24, 31), Feb. 9, 16, 23, Mar. 1, 8, 24, 27, 29, Apr. 4 - 27, 30, May 7 - 12, 17, June 6 - 26. 1, 2 cl. and 2 (reclining) Cerbère - Strasbourg.

b – Also Mar. 24, May 12; not Mar. 23, May 11.

c – Runs up to 10 minutes earlier certain dates (depart 1133 Mar. 10 - 12, 1157 Apr. 7 - 10).

d – Also Dec. 25, Jan. 1, Mar. 24, May 12; not Mar. 23, May 11.

e – Also Dec. 25, Jan. 1, Mar. 24, May 12.

h – Not May 1, 8.

j – 1442 Dec. 9 - 16 and from Apr. 12.

m – ⑤ to Apr. 11, ⑤ May 16 - June 27 (also Apr. 30, May 7; not Dec. 28, Jan. 4, Feb. 22, 29).

r – Departure times vary (0759 Jan. 14 - 18, 0804 Jan. 21 - 25, otherwise 0816, 0820 or 0825).

s – On Mar. 22 runs Montpellier (1826) - Avignon (1928) only.

t – Also May 1, 8.

u – Not Dec. 31.

v – Avignon **TGV** station.

w – Also Dec. 24, Jan. 1, Mar. 24, Apr. 30, May 7, 12; not Mar. 23, May 2, 11.

x – Arrival times varies between 1740 and 1810.

y – Also Dec. 26, Jan. 2, Mar. 25, May 1, 8, 13; not Dec. 24, 31, Mar. 24, May 12.

z – ⑤⑦ (also Dec. 25, Jan. 1, Mar. 24, Apr. 30, May 7, 12; not May 2).

NOTES CONTINUED ON NEXT PAGE →

CERBÈRE - NARBONNE - AVIGNON and MARSEILLE 355

	4656 4657 ★	2	*TGV* 6214	17384 ⚒	2	*TGV* 6216	2	*TGV* 5380 △	4660 4661 ★	*TGV* 5314 Ⓑ h	*TGV* 6868 ⑥ t	2	*TGV* 6218	Ⓐ 2	15944 15945 C	2	4658 ★ F	Ⓐ 2	Ⓐ 2	2s	*TGV* 6220 u	*TGV* 5186	17386 ⚒	4662 4663 ★
Cerbère d.	...	1226	...	...	...	...	...	...	...	...	...	...	...	...	...	...	...	...	...	1542	...	...	...	...
Banyuls sur Mer d.	...	1233	...	...	...	...	...	...	...	...	...	...	...	...	...	...	...	...	...	1550	...	...	...	...
Port Vendres d.	...	1239	...	...	...	...	...	...	...	...	...	...	...	...	...	...	...	...	...	1556	...	...	...	...
Collioure d.	...	1242	...	...	...	...	...	...	...	...	...	...	...	...	...	...	...	...	...	1601	...	...	...	...
Argelès sur Mer d.	...	1248	...	...	...	...	...	...	...	...	...	...	...	...	...	...	...	...	...	1608	...	...	...	...
Perpignan a.	...	1307	...	...	...	...	...	...	...	...	...	...	...	...	...	...	...	...	...	1626	...	...	...	...
Perpignan d.	...	1310	1336	...	...	...	...	...	...	...	1511	...	1531	...	...	...	...	...	1553	1628	...	...	...	...
Nantes **292** d.	...	|	|	...	...	...	...	...	...	...	|	...	|	...	...	...	...	...	|	|	...	...	...	...
Bordeaux **320** d.	1102*	|	|	...	...	...	...	...	1209c	...	|	...	|	...	...	...	...	...	|	|	...	...	...	1431j
Hendaye **325** d.	|	|	|	...	...	...	...	...	|	...	|	...	|	...	...	...	...	...	|	|	...	...	...	|
Toulouse **321** d.	1307	|	|	...	...	...	...	...	1424*	1434*	|	...	|	...	...	...	1517	...	|	|	...	1608*	...	1649*
Carcassonne **321** d.	|	|	|	...	...	...	...	...	1511	1520	|	...	|	...	...	...	1607	...	|	|	...	1654	...	|
Narbonne a.	|	1357	1413	...	...	...	...	...	1539	1547	1547	...	1607	...	...	...	1636	...	1640	1708	...	1725	...	|
Narbonne d.	|	1359	1420	1425	...	...	...	...	1542	1550	1550	1555	1610	1617	...	...	1638	...	1642	1713	...	1728	...	|
Béziers d.	|	1415	1437	1443	1509	...	...	...	1558	1605	1605	1610	1627	1632	...	1646	1655	...	1704	1729	...	1745	...	|
Agde d.	|	1429	1451	1457	1522	...	...	...	|	|	|	1622	|	1645	...	1659	1709	...	1717	1742	...	|	...	|
Sète d.	|	1445	1506	1512	1537	...	...	...	1622	|	|	1637	|	1700	...	1716	1725	...	1730	1758	...	|	...	|
Montpellier a.	1507	1503	1520	1527	1555	...	...	...	1638	1645	1645	1656	1712	1718	...	1736	1741	...	1749	1812	...	1825	...	1847
Montpellier d.	1511	1515	1525	1530	1558	1620	1625	1630	1644	1652	1652	1659	1717	1721	...	1740	1745	...	1752	1814	1823	1830	1834	1851
Nimes a.	|	1543	1550	1555	1629	1647	1653	1657	1708	1717	1717	1735	1741	1749	...	1805	1810	...	1840	1843	1847	1854	1902	|
Nimes d.	|	1545	1553	1557	1631	1650	...	1700	1711	1720	1720	1737	1744	...	1800	...	1813	1820	...	1846	1850	1857	1905	|
Tarascon-sur-Rhône d.	|	1602	|	|	1651	|	...	|	|	|	|	1801	|	...	1818	...	|	1838	...	1903	|	|	1922	|
Avignon Centre a.	|	1614	|	|	1703	|	...	|	|	|	|	1813	|	...	|	...	|	1850	...	1915	|	|	|	|
Arles d.	|	...	|	1622	...	|	...	|	1736	|	|	...	|	...	1829	...	1840	...	...	...	|	|	1939	|
Marseille St Charles a.	1639	...	|	1712	...	|	...	|	1825	|	|	...	|	...	1918	...	1926	...	...	...	|	|	2030	2018
Nice **360** a.	1923	...	|	...	...	|	...	|	...	|	|	...	|	...	...	...	2217	...	...	...	|	|	...	...
Lyon Part Dieu **350** a.	...	...	|	...	...	|	...	1820	...	1846	1846	...	|	...	...	...	...	...	...	...	|	2020	...	...
Genève **345** a.	...	...	|	...	...	|	...	...	...	...	...	...	|	...	...	...	...	...	...	...	|	|	...	...
Dijon **373** a.	...	...	|	...	...	|	...	...	...	...	...	...	|	...	...	...	...	...	...	...	|	|	...	...
Strasbourg **384** a.	...	...	|	...	...	|	...	...	...	...	...	...	|	...	...	...	...	...	...	...	|	|	...	...
Metz **392** a.	...	...	|	...	...	|	...	...	...	...	...	...	|	...	...	...	...	...	...	...	|	|	...	...
Charles de Gaulle ✈ **350** a.	...	...	|	...	...	|	...	...	...	...	...	...	|	...	...	...	...	...	...	...	|	2229	...	...
Lille Europe **11** a.	...	...	|	...	...	|	...	...	...	...	...	...	|	...	...	...	...	...	...	...	|	2332	...	...
Brussels Midi **11** a.	...	...	|	...	...	|	...	...	...	...	...	...	|	...	...	...	...	...	...	...	|	...	...	...
Paris Austerlitz **310** a.	...	...	|	...	...	|	...	...	...	...	...	...	|	...	...	...	...	...	...	...	|	...	...	...
Paris Gare de Lyon **350** a.	...	...	1845	...	...	1949	...	...	...	...	...	...	2041	...	...	...	...	...	...	...	2149	...	...	...

	TGV 6222	*TGV* 6880	Ⓐ 2	⑥ 2	4322 4323 ⑦ d	Ⓑ 2		*TGV* 6224 ⑦ e	Ⓐ 2	2	4664 4665 ★	460 Ⓡ✗ ♦⚡	⑦ 2	⑤ m	4666 4667 ⑤⑦ ★w		3740 ♦ Ⓡ	4348 4349 ♦ Ⓡ	4348 4392 Y Ⓡ		3730 ♦ Ⓡ	3732 ♦ Ⓡ	4620 4621 ♦ Ⓡ	4678 4679 ♦ Ⓡ
Cerbère d.	...	...	...	...	1650	1725	...	...	...	1823	...	1906	...	...	...	...	2025	2042	2042	...	2121	2134	...	...
Banyuls sur Mer d.	...	...	...	...	1659	1732	...	...	...	1830	...	|	...	...	...	...	2033	2051	2051	...	2129	2143	...	...
Port Vendres d.	...	...	...	...	1705	1737	...	...	...	1835	...	|	...	...	...	...	2041	2058	2058	...	2135	2149	...	...
Collioure d.	...	...	...	...	1711	1741	...	...	...	1839	...	|	...	...	...	...	2046	2103	2103	...	2140	2154	...	...
Argelès sur Mer d.	...	...	...	...	1718	1747	...	...	...	1844	...	|	...	...	...	...	2053	2110	2110	...	2147	2201	...	...
Perpignan a.	...	...	...	...	1739	1806	...	...	...	1901	...	1936	...	...	...	...	2116	2130	2130	...	2210	2224	...	...
Perpignan d.	1737	...	1725	...	1742	1808	...	1835	...	1903	...	1939	1957	...	...	...	2119	2133	2133	...	2214	2227	...	...
Nantes **292** d.	|	...	|	...	|	|	...	|	...	|	...	|	|	...	...	...	|	|	|	...	|	|	...	...
Bordeaux **320** d.	|	...	|	...	|	|	...	|	...	|	1627*	|	|	...	...	...	|	|	|	...	|	|	2148	...
Hendaye **325** d.	|	...	|	...	|	|	...	|	...	|	|	|	|	...	...	...	|	|	|	...	|	|	|	1831
Toulouse **321** d.	|	...	|	...	|	|	...	|	...	|	1848*	|	|	...	2045*	...	|	|	|	...	|	|	0011	0017
Carcassonne **321** d.	|	...	|	...	|	|	...	|	...	|	1935	|	|	...	2131	...	|	|	|	...	|	|	|	|
Narbonne a.	1814	...	1818	...	1828	1853	...	1911	...	1948	2004	2013	2032	...	2200	...	2204	2208	2208	...	2247	2310	|	|
Narbonne d.	1817	...	1820	...	1831	1856	...	1914	1925	...	2007	2015	2034	...	2202	...	2226	2213	2213	...	2305	2330	|	|
Béziers d.	1834	...	1839	...	1849	1911	...	1930	1944	...	2024	2030	2050	2051	2219	...	|	2230	2230	...	|	|	|	|
Agde d.	1848	...	1852	...	1902	1924	...	1945	1956	...	|	|	|	2104	|	...	|	2244	2244	...	|	|	|	|
Sète d.	1904	...	1908	...	1918	1939	...	2000	2012	...	|	|	2114	2119	2246	...	|	2301	2301	...	|	|	|	|
Montpellier a.	1918	...	1928	...	1938	1957	...	2016	2030	...	2102	2109	2135	2137	2302	...	|	2316	2316	...	|	|	|	|
Montpellier d.	1923	1928	1931	1931	1942	2000	...	2023	2033	...	2106	...	2138	...	2306	...	|	2319	2319	...	|	|	|	|
Nimes a.	1947	1952	2001	2001	2012	2030	...	2047	2104	...	2131	...	2209	...	2334	...	|	2347	2347	...	|	|	|	|
Nimes d.	1950	1955	...	...	2015	2033	...	2050	...	...	2134	...	...	...	2337	...	|	2349	2349	...	|	|	|	|
Tarascon-sur-Rhône d.	|	|	...	...	2033	2049	...	|	...	...	|	...	...	...	|	...	|	|	|	...	|	|	|	|
Avignon Centre a.	|	|	...	...	2047	2102	...	|	...	...	|	...	...	...	|	...	|	|	|	...	|	|	|	|
Arles d.	|	|	...	...	|	...	...	|	...	...	2200	...	...	...	|	...	|	|	|	...	|	|	|	|
Marseille St Charles a.	|	|	...	...	|	...	...	|	...	...	2243	...	...	...	0043	...	|	|	|	...	|	|	0532	|
Nice **360** a.	|	|	...	...	|	...	...	|	...	...	...	...	...	...	...	...	|	|	|	...	|	|	0837	|
Lyon Part Dieu **350** a.	|	2120	...	...	2251	...	...	|	...	...	...	...	...	...	...	...	|	|	|	...	|	|	...	0644
Genève **345** a.	|	|	...	...	|	...	...	|	...	...	...	...	...	...	...	...	|	|	|	...	|	|	...	0845
Dijon **373** a.	|	2305z	...	...	|	...	...	|	...	...	...	...	...	...	...	...	|	|	|	...	|	|	...	...
Strasbourg **384** a.	|	...	...	...	0519	...	...	|	...	...	...	...	...	...	...	...	|	|	0834	...	|	|	...	...
Metz **392** a.	|	...	...	...	...	...	...	|	...	...	...	...	...	...	...	...	|	0818	...	...	|	|	...	...
Charles de Gaulle ✈ **350** a.	|	...	...	...	...	...	...	|	...	...	...	...	...	...	...	...	|	...	...	...	|	|	...	...
Lille Europe **11** a.	|	...	...	...	...	...	...	|	...	...	...	...	...	...	...	...	|	...	...	...	|	|	...	...
Brussels Midi **11** a.	|	...	...	...	...	...	...	|	...	...	...	...	...	...	...	...	|	...	...	...	|	|	...	...
Paris Austerlitz **310** a.	|	...	...	...	...	...	...	|	...	...	...	...	...	...	...	...	0652	...	...	...	0727	0812	...	...
Paris Gare de Lyon **350** a.	2241	...	...	...	...	...	...	2345	...	...	...	...	...	...	...	...	...	...	...	...	...	...	...	...

NOTES (CONTINUED FROM PREVIOUS PAGE)

TGV – Ⓡ, supplement payable.
⚡ – Special 'global' fares payable.
⊡ – To Toulouse (Table **321**).
★ – *CORAIL TÉOZ* Ⓡ, 🍷.
△ – To Nantes (Table **335**).
▽ – To Toulon on ⑤⑦ (Table **360**).
* – Timings may vary up to 10 minutes earlier on certain dates.

SODETRAV 🚌 route 103 — 🚌 TOULON - ST TROPEZ 358

September 24, 2007 - June 8, 2008. *Additional journeys operate Toulon - Hyères - Le Lavandou*

km		⚒	⚒	⚒	⚒c	⚒	⚒	⚒	⚒
0	**Toulon** Gare SNCF d.	0625	0800	0920	1120	1300	1440	1600	1830
23	Hyères, Centre d.	0653	0837	0955	1155	1338	1515	1650	1858
46	Le Lavandou d.	0724	0909	1026	1226	1410	1546	1727	1923
67	Cavalaire-sur-Mer d.	0756	0942	1059	1258	1450	1620	1801	1955
78	Gassin - La Foux a.	0824	1005	1121	1320	1512	1643	1824	2017
84	**St Tropez** Gare Routière a.	0832	1015	1130	1330	1524	1655	1835	2025

	⚒	⚒	⚒	⚒	⚒	⚒	⚒	⚒		
St Tropez Gare Routière d.	0535	0845	1035	1200	1350	1555	1730	1920	...	For service on † see below
Gassin - La Foux d.	0542	0855	1045	1208	1358	1603	1740	1928	...	
Cavalaire-sur-Mer d.	0601	0919	1106	1229	1419	1625	1803	1948	...	
Le Lavandou d.	0631	0953	1138	1300	1452	1658	1837	2020	...	
Hyères, Centre d.	0703	1026	1210	1339	1523	1735	1908	2049	...	
Toulon Gare SNCF a.	0738	1107	1245	1418	1605	1820	1947	2114	...	

c – Runs 10 minutes later on ③⑥.

Service on † Sept. 30 - Mar. 30 (also May 1): from Toulon: 0915, 1330, 1615; from St Tropez 0813, 1350, 1845.

Service on † Apr. 6 - June 8 (not May 1): from Toulon 0750, 0900, 1130, 1345, 1600, 1945; from St Tropez: 0830, 1020, 1350, 1505, 1605, 1905.

Operator: SODETRAV, 'Le Palatin' Centre Europe, 6 rue Georges Simenon, 83401 Hyères les Palmiers. ✆ 04 94 12 55 12, fax 04 94 12 55 19.

359 🚐 ST RAPHAËL - ST TROPEZ

SODETRAV 🚐 routes 100/104

September 24, 2007 - June 8, 2008 (subject to confirmation)

km			⚒	⚒	⚒	⚒	⚒	⚒	⚒	⚒	⚒	⚒			†	†	†	†	†	†	†	†	
0	**St Raphaël** (Gare SNCF) d.	⚒	0630	0830	1005	...	1215	1330	1545	1740	...	1935	...	†	0800	...	1020	1245	1345	1715	1900	...	...
4	Fréjus (Av. Provence) d.		0635	0835	1010	...	1220	1335	1550	1745	...	1940	...		0808	...	1025	1250	1350	1720	1905	...	...
9	St Aygulf d.		0640	0840	1015	...	1225	1340	1555	1755	...	1945	...		0815	...	1032	1257	1357	1727	1912	...	...
	Les Arcs (Gare SNCF) d.		|	|	|	1020	|	|	|	|	1925	|	...		|	1020	|	|	|	|	|	2015	...
23	Ste Maxime (Office du Tourisme) d.		0700	0902	1035	1052	1250	1402	1619	1820	1952	2005	...		0830	1052	1050	1315	1415	1745	1930	2047	...
28	Port Grimaud d.		|	|	|	1104	|	|	|	|	...	2019	...		|	1104	|	|	|	|	|	2100	...
29	Gassin - La Foux a.		0733	0943	1117	1111	1325	1435	1657	1855	...	2025	...		0905	1111	1127	1352	1455	1822	2007	2105	...
35	**St Tropez** (Gare Routière) a.		0740	0955	1130	1125	1340	1450	1707	1905	...	2035	...		0915	1125	1140	1405	1505	1835	2020	2115	...

		⚒	⚒	⚒	⚒	⚒	⚒	⚒	⚒	⚒	⚒			†	†	†	†	†	†	†	†	
St Tropez (Gare Routière) d.	⚒	0625	0830	0900	1020	1145	1410	1520	1725	1805	1920	...	†	0835	0900	1020	1220	1445	1520	1635	1900	...
Gassin - La Foux d.		0632	0838	0910	1028	1155	1418	1528	1735	1815	1927	...		0843	0910	1028	1228	1453	1528	1643	1910	...
Port Grimaud d.		|	|	0915	|	|	|	|	|	1820	|	...		|	0915	|	|	|	|	|	1919	...
Ste Maxime (Office du Tourisme) d.		0710	0917	0926	1103	1234	1455	1603	1811	1835	1957	...		0910	0926	1103	1300	1528	1603	1718	1938	...
Les Arcs (Gare SNCF) a.		|	|	1005	|	|	|	|	|	1910	|	...		|	1005	|	|	|	|	|	2005	...
St Aygulf d.		0730	0940	...	1123	1255	1515	1623	1831	...	2017	...		0930	...	1123	1320	1548	1623	1738	...	...
Fréjus (Av. Provence) d.		0738	0948	...	1132	1305	1525	1634	1840	...	2026	...		0940	...	1132	1329	1557	1632	1749	...	...
St Raphaël (Gare SNCF) a.		0750	0955	...	1145	1315	1535	1645	1850	...	2035	...		0950	...	1140	1337	1605	1640	1800	...	...

Service by 🚐, operated by SODETRAV, 175 chemin du Palyvestre, B.P. 007, 83401 Hyères Les Palmiers. ✆ 04 94 12 55 12 www.sodetrav.fr

A much reduced service operates on Dec. 25, Jan. 1, May 1.

360 MARSEILLE - NICE - VENTIMIGLIA

Jan. 3 - Feb. 22
Trains are liable to run up to 10 minutes earlier or later Marseille - Nice - Ventimiglia

km										*TGV*				4238			4620				4296				
									17471	6831		5771		4239			4621				4297				17441
		①–⑤		①–⑤		①–⑤		①–⑥	⚒	①		♦		♦	⑦		♦	⚒	⑥	①–⑤	♦			⚒	Ⓐ
								n		g		🅁		🅁	e		🅁				🅁				
	Paris Gare de Lyon **350/1** d.	...	...	...	...	...	...	...	...	...	...	2117a	...	...	...	...	...	...	...	...	...	...	...	...	...
	Lille Europe **11** d.	...						...	...	...	...	|	...	...	...	...	...	...	...	...	...	...	...	...	...
	Metz **392** d.	...						...	...	...	...	|	...	2044	...	...	...	...	...	...	...	...	...	...	...
	Strasbourg **384** d.	...						...	...	...	...	|	...	|	...	...	...	...	...	...	2056	...	...	...	...
	Dijon **373** d.	...						...	...	...	...	|	...	|	...	...	...	...	...	...	|	...	...	...	...
	Genève **345** d.	...						...	...	...	...	|	...	|	...	...	...	...	...	...	|	...	...	...	...
	Lyon Part-Dieu **350/1** d.	...						...	...	...	...	|	...	|	...	...	...	...	...	...	|	...	...	...	...
	Lyon Perrache **350/1** d.	...						...	...	0050	...	|	...	|	...	...	...	...	...	...	|	...	...	...	...
	Nantes **292** d.	...	...	...	...	...	...	...	...	|	...	|	...	|	...	...	...	...	...	...	|	...	...	...	...
	Bordeaux **320** d.	...	...	...	...	...	...	...	...	|	...	|	...	|	...	...	2148	...	...	...	|	...	...	...	...
	Toulouse **321** d.	...	...	...	...	...	...	...	...	|	...	|	...	|	...	...	0011	...	...	...	|	...	...	...	...
	Cerbère **355** d.	...	...	...	...	...	...	...	...	|	...	|	...	|	...	...	|	...	...	...	|	...	...	...	...
	Narbonne **355** d.	...	...	...	...	...	...	...	...	|	...	|	...	|	...	...	|	...	...	...	|	...	...	...	...
	Montpellier **355** d.	...	...	...	...	...	...	...	...	|	...	|	...	|	...	...	|	...	...	...	|	...	...	...	...
0	**Marseille St Charles 350** d.	...	...	...	...	...	...	...	...	|	...	|	...	0535	...	...	0557	0602	...	...	0623	...	0635	0700	0721
37	La Ciotat d.	...	...	...	...	...	...	...	...	|	...	|	...	|	...	...	|	0632	...	...	|	...	0704	0731	|
51	Bandol d.	...	...	...	...	...	...	...	...	|	...	|	...	|	...	...	|	0644	...	...	|	...	0717	0743	|
67	**Toulon 350** a.	...	...	...	...	...	...	...	...	0550	...	0557	...	0616	...	...	0642	0659	...	...	0707	...	0731	0759	0803
67	**Toulon** d.	...	...	...	...	...	...	0535	0543	0553	...	0600	...	0620	0629	...	0645	▬	...	...	0710	0727	...	▬	0806
87	Hyères a.	...	...	...	...	...	...	0557	|	|	...	|	...	|	0652	...	|	...	...	...	|	0748	...	...	|
135	Les Arcs-Draguignan d.	...	...	...	...	...	...	▬	0623	0632	...	0639	...	0658	...	0649	0721	...	...	0732	0749	...	...	...	0845
161	St Raphael-Valescure d.	...	...	...	...	...	0605	...	0642	0651	...	0704	...	0718	...	0710	0739	①–⑤	...	0752	0810	...	...	...	0906
**	Grasse d.	...	...	...	...	0555	|	...	|	|	0701	|	...	|	...	|	|	0741	...	|	|	...	...	0825	|
194	**Cannes** a.	...	...	...	...	0619	0634	①–⑥	0706	0715	0727	0733	...	0744	...	0739	0801	0807	...	0831	0837	...	...	0853	0927
194	**Cannes** d.	...	0522	...	0559	0621	0636	0653	0709	0720	0729	0736	...	0747	...	0751	0805	0811	0831	0833	0840	...	...	0901	0930
203	Juan les Pins d.	...	0533	...	0608	0631	0646	0704	|	|	0739	|	...	|	...	0802	|	0822	0842	0843	|	...	...	0911	|
205	Antibes d.	...	0536	...	0612	0634	0649	0707	0720	0730	0743	0752	...	0759	...	0805	0818	0825	0845	0847	0853	...	...	0914	0939
216	Cagnes sur Mer d.	...	0548	...	0625	0640	0701	0719	0729	|	0754	|	...	|	...	0817	|	0836	0853	0854	|	...	...	0926	|
225	**Nice Ville** a.	...	0605	...	0641	0653	0716	0734	0741	0745	0810	0815	...	0820	...	0832	0837	0851	0907	0907	0913	...	...	0941	0952
225	**Nice Ville** d.	0525	0608	0635	0644	0703	0719	0737	0751	...	0812	0820	...	...	...	0834	...	0854	0910	0910	...	...	...	0944	...
230	Villefranche sur Mer d.	0532	0616	|	0652	|	0728	0746	|	...	|	|	...	...	...	0842	...	0901	|	|	...	...	...	0951	...
232	Beaulieu sur Mer d.	0536	0619	0643	0655	0711	0731	0749	0803	...	0820	|	...	...	...	0846	...	0904	0919	0919	...	...	...	0955	...
241	**Monaco-Monte Carlo** d.	0547	0633	0652	0709	0721	0746	0804	0815	...	0830	0838	...	...	...	0902	...	0918	0929	0929	...	...	...	1008	...
245	Cap Martin-Roquebrune d.	|	0638	|	0714	|	0752	0810	|	...	|	|	...	...	...	0907	...	0923	|	|	...	...	...	1014	...
248	Menton d.	0557	0645	0701	0721	0731	0759	0818	0826	...	0839	0848	...	...	...	0914	...	0930	0940	0940	...	...	...	1021	...
258	**Ventimiglia** a.	0608	0657	...	0733	0741	0813	0832	0840	...	...	0859	...	...	...	0929	...	0943	0951	0951	...	...	...	1035	...

	EC	4624					4208		*TGV*			*TGV*					*TGV*		*TGV*	*EC*					4652
	139	4625					4209		6815	17443		6805					5102		6171	145					4653
	♦§	♦	①–⑥	Ⓐ			♦		Ⓐ			Ⓒ						①–⑥		♦§				Ⓐ	★
	🅁	🅁				b	🅁			⊡			k						⊕	🅁					
Paris Gare de Lyon **350/1** d.	...	...	...	...	...	...	...	...	...	...	...	...	...	...	...	...	...	...	0804	...	...	...	...	...	...
Lille Europe **11** d.	...	...	...	...	...	...	2125f	...	...	...	...	...	...	...	...	...	0559	...	|	...	...	...	...	...	...
Metz **392** d.	...	...	...	...	...	...	|	...	...	...	...	...	...	...	...	...	|	...	|	...	...	...	...	...	...
Strasbourg **384** d.	...	...	...	...	...	...	|	...	...	...	...	...	...	...	...	...	|	...	|	...	...	...	...	...	...
Dijon **373** d.	...	...	...	...	...	...	|	...	...	...	...	...	...	...	...	...	|	...	|	...	...	...	...	...	...
Genève **345** d.	...	...	...	...	...	...	|	...	...	...	...	...	...	...	...	...	|	...	|	...	...	...	...	...	...
Lyon Part-Dieu **350/1** d.	...	...	...	...	...	...	|	...	0637	...	...	0737	...	...	...	...	0907	...	|	...	...	...	...	...	...
Lyon Perrache **350/1** d.	...	...	...	...	...	...	|	...	|	...	...	|	...	...	...	...	|	...	|	...	...	...	...	...	...
Nantes **292** d.	...	2046	...	...	...	...	|	...	|	...	...	|	...	...	...	...	|	...	|	...	...	...	...	...	...
Bordeaux **320** d.	...	0055	...	...	...	...	|	...	|	...	...	|	...	...	...	...	|	...	|	...	...	...	...	...	0552z
Toulouse **321** d.	...	|	...	...	...	...	|	...	|	...	...	|	...	...	...	...	|	...	|	...	...	...	...	...	0803z
Cerbère **355** d.	...	|	...	...	...	...	|	...	|	...	...	|	...	...	...	...	|	...	|	...	...	...	...	...	|
Narbonne **355** d.	...	|	...	...	...	...	|	...	|	...	...	|	...	...	...	...	|	...	|	...	...	...	...	...	|
Montpellier **355** d.	...	0526	...	...	...	...	|	...	|	...	...	|	...	...	...	...	|	...	|	...	...	...	...	...	1006
Marseille St Charles 350 d.	...	0726	...	0744	0744	...	0801	...	0832	0837	0843	0935	...	...	...	...	1100	...	|	...	...	1113	...	1135	1159
La Ciotat d.	...	|	...	0814	0814	...	|	...	|	|	0912	|	...	...	...	...	|	...	|	...	...	1143	...	1211	|
Bandol d.	...	|	...	0826	0826	...	|	...	|	|	0924	|	...	...	...	...	|	...	|	...	...	1155	...	1223	|
Toulon 350 a.	...	0814	...	0842	0842	...	0850	...	0912	0919	0939	1015	...	...	...	...	1138	...	|	...	...	1210	...	1238	1243
Toulon d.	...	0817	...	0844	...	...	0853	...	0915	0922	▬	1018	...	...	...	...	1141	...	|	...	...	1214	1225	▬	1246
Hyères a.	...	|	...	0908	...	...	|	...	|	|	...	|	...	...	...	...	|	...	|	...	...	1236	|	...	|
Les Arcs-Draguignan d.	...	0856	...	...	...	0905	0932	...	|	0959	...	|	...	...	...	...	1216	...	1223	...	1230	...	1322	...	|
St Raphael-Valescure d.	...	0921	...	...	...	0925	0949	...	1009	1018	...	1112	...	...	...	1208	1234	...	1241	...	1249	...	▬	...	1341
Grasse d.	...	|	0907	...	...	|	|	0952	|	|	...	|	1106	...	1214	|	|	...	|	...	|	...	...	1313	|
Cannes a.	...	0944	0934	...	...	1005	1012	1016	1031	1038	...	1136	1132	...	1238	1243	1255	...	1303	...	1321	...	...	1342	1403
Cannes d.	...	0948	0953	...	...	1007	1017	...	1035	1040	...	1139	1147	1225	...	1245	1258	...	1306	...	1323	...	...	1344	1405
Juan les Pins d.	...	|	1003	...	...	1018	|	...	|	|	...	|	1156	1236	...	1256	|	...	|	...	1334	...	...	1353	|
Antibes d.	...	0959	1006	...	...	1021	1033	...	1046	1050	...	1151	1159	1240	...	1259	1310	...	1318	...	1337	...	...	1356	1415
Cagnes sur Mer d.	...	|	1013	...	...	1033	|	...	|	1059	①–⑥	|	1210	1252	...	1307	|	...	|	...	1349	...	...	1403	|
Nice Ville a.	...	1015	1026	...	...	1049	1055	...	1101	1109		1206	1224	1308	...	1320	1324	...	1336	...	1405	...	...	1416	1430
Nice Ville d.	1004	...	1031	...	...	1051	...	...	...	1113	1209	...	1236	1310	...	...	...	1335	...	1405	1409	...	...	...	...
Villefranche sur Mer d.	|	...	|	...	...	1059	...	...	...	|	|	...	1244	1317	...	...	...	|	...	|	1417	...	...	...	...
Beaulieu sur Mer d.	|	...	1040	...	...	1102	...	...	...	1122	1218	...	1248	1321	...	...	...	1344	...	|	1420	...	...	...	...
Monaco-Monte Carlo d.	1021	...	1049	...	...	1116	...	...	...	1134	1228	...	1300	1334	...	...	...	1354	...	1420	1434	...	...	...	...
Cap Martin-Roquebrune d.	|	...	|	...	...	1121	...	...	...	|	|	...	1305	1340	...	...	...	|	...	|	1439	...	...	...	...
Menton d.	1030	...	1059	...	...	1128	...	...	...	1146	1239	...	1311	1347	...	...	...	1403	...	1431	1446	...	...	...	...
Ventimiglia a.	1042	...	1110	...	...	1140	...	...	...	1156	1250	...	1323	1359	...	...	...	1414	...	1442	1459	...	...	...	...

FOR NOTES SEE NEXT PAGE →

MARSEILLE - NICE - VENTIMIGLIA 360

	17483			*TGV* 6173	*TGV* 5148			*TGV* 6109			17433			*TGV* 6175		4655 4654	*TGV* 5164						17487		
												①-⑤			①-⑤	⑤⑦		Ⓐ	Ⓒ		①-⑤	Ⓐ	Ⓐ		Ⓐ
			U													★	B							Y	
Paris Gare de Lyon **350/1** d.	...	...	...	0942	...	...	...	1016	...	...	...	...	...	1142	...	...	...	...	...	...	...	...	...	...	...
Lille Europe **11** d.	...	...	...	|	...	...	...	|	...	...	...	...	...	|	...	...	1030	...	...	...	...	...	...	...	...
Metz **392** d.	...	...	...	|	0611	...	...	|	...	...	...	...	...	|	...	...	|	...	...	...	...	...	...	...	...
Strasbourg **384** d.	...	...	...	|	|	...	...	|	...	...	...	...	...	|	...	...	|	...	...	...	...	...	...	...	...
Dijon **373** d.	...	...	...	|	0916	...	...	|	...	...	...	...	...	|	...	...	|	...	...	...	...	...	...	...	...
Genève **345** d.	...	...	...	|	|	...	...	|	...	...	...	...	...	|	...	...	|	...	...	...	...	...	...	...	...
Lyon Part-Dieu **350/1** d.	...	...	...	|	1107	...	...	|	...	...	...	...	...	|	...	...	|	...	...	...	...	...	...	...	...
Lyon Perrache **350/1** d.	...	...	...	|	|	...	...	|	...	...	...	...	...	|	...	...	|	...	...	...	...	...	...	...	...
Nantes **292** d.	...	...	...	|	|	...	...	|	...	...	...	...	...	|	...	...	|	...	...	...	...	...	...	...	...
Bordeaux **320** d.	...	...	...	|	|	...	...	|	...	...	...	...	...	|	...	0825	|	...	...	...	...	...	...	...	...
Toulouse **321** d.	...	...	...	|	|	...	...	|	...	...	...	...	...	|	...	1042	|	...	...	...	...	...	...	...	...
Cerbère **355** d.	...	...	...	|	|	...	...	|	...	...	...	...	...	|	...	|	|	...	...	...	...	...	...	...	...
Narbonne **355** d.	...	...	...	|	|	...	...	|	...	...	...	...	...	|	...	1204	|	...	...	...	...	...	...	...	...
Montpellier **355** d.	...	...	...	|	|	...	...	|	...	...	...	...	...	|	...	1303	|	...	...	...	...	...	...	...	...
Marseille St Charles 350 d.	1210	1219	...	|	1301	...	1305	1333	...	1408	1425	...	...	|	...	1509	1521	1525	1525	...	...	1545	1607	1612	1620
La Ciotat d.	|	1249	...	|	|	...	1342	|	...	1437	|	...	...	|	...	|	|	1554	1554	...	...	1616	|	1642	1651
Bandol d.	|	1302	...	|	|	...	1353	|	...	1449	|	...	...	|	...	|	|	1606	1606	...	...	1628	|	1655	1703
Toulon 350 a.	1250	1318	...	|	1342	...	1408	1412	...	1504	1510	...	...	1532	...	1553	1559	1621	1621	...	...	1643	1651	1709	1715
Toulon d.	1253	▬	...	|	1345	...	▬	1416	...	▬	1512	...	...	1535	...	...	1602	1624	▬	...	...	▬	1655	1711	▬
Hyères a.	|	...	...	|	|	...	...	1431	...	...	|	...	...	|	...	...	|	|	...	...	...	...	|	1732	...
Les Arcs-Draguignan d.	1332	...	...	1411	|	1426	...	...	...	...	1547	...	...	|	...	...	1636	1723	...	...	...	...	1732	...	...
St Raphael-Valescure d.	1352	...	1356	1431	1441	1445	...	...	...	...	1608	...	...	1624	...	...	1654	▬	①-⑤	...	...	1715	1753	...	...
Grasse d.	|	1400	|	|	|	|	...	...	1526c	①-⑤	|	...	...	|	...	...	|	...	1654	1716	...	|	|	...	1804
Cannes a.	1413	1425	1434	1453	1502	1514	...	...	1550c	...	1632	...	...	1646	...	...	1714	...	1720	1740	...	1754	1813	...	1827
Cannes d.	1416	▬	1437	1456	1506	1516	...	...	1552	1609	1635	...	1639	1649	1709	...	1718	*EC*	1722	1743	...	1756	1816	...	1829
Juan les Pins d.	|	...	1448	|	|	1526	...	...	1602	1620	|	...	1649	|	1719	...	|	**147**	1731	1752	...	1807	|	...	1839
Antibes d.	1426	...	1451	1508	1517	1529	...	...	1605	1624	1646	...	1652	1704	1722	...	1730	♦§	1735	1755	...	1811	1827	...	1842
Cagnes sur Mer d.	|	...	1458	|	|	1542	...	...	1617	1637	|	...	1704	|	1730	...	|	🅁	1747	1803	1813	1823	|	...	1853
Nice Ville a.	1441	⑥⑦	1511	1523	1532	1558	①-⑤	...	1632	1653	1704	...	1718	1725	1743	...	1749	...	1802	1815	1828	1839	1844	...	1908
Nice Ville d.	...	1447	1524	...	...	1602	1614	...	1634	1656	...	1710	1721	1739	1746	...	...	1805	...	1818	1831	1841	1854	...	1911
Villefranche sur Mer d.	...	1454	|	...	...	1609	|	...	1642	1703	...	1717	1729	|	1753	...	...	|	...	1825	1839	1849	|	...	1918
Beaulieu sur Mer d.	...	1457	1533	...	...	1613	1623	...	1645	1707	...	1720	1732	|	1757	...	...	|	...	1828	1843	1852	1905	...	1921
Monaco-Monte Carlo d.	...	1510	1543	...	...	1627	1634	...	1658	1721	...	1735	1746	1755	1810	...	...	1820	...	1842	1855	1908	1916	...	1934
Cap Martin-Roquebrune d.	...	1516	|	...	...	1632	|	...	1703	1726	...	1740	1751	|	1816	...	...	|	...	1847	...	1913	|	...	1939
Menton d.	...	1523	1556	...	...	1639	1644	...	1709	1732	...	1746	1758	1805	1824	...	...	1830	...	1853	...	1920	1928	...	1945
Ventimiglia a.	...	1535	1606	...	...	1653	...	...	1722	1745	...	...	1810	1815	1836	...	...	1842	...	1905	...	1935	1940	...	1957

	TGV 6177	4656 4657				*TGV* 6818		17439		*TGV* 6179				*TGV* 6119	4658 4659		*TGV* 6829			*TGV* 6181	*TGV* 6187	17495	*TGV* 6183		
					Ⓑ		①-⑤				⚒		Ⓐ								⑤	Ⓑ	⑤		
		★			M					L		D			★ F						E	△	E		
Paris Gare de Lyon **350/1** d.	1342	...	...	...	...	...	...	...	...	1546	...	...	...	1616	...	...	...	...	...	1742	1816	...	1842	...	...
Lille Europe **11** d.	|	...	...	...	...	...	...	...	...	|	...	...	...	|	...	...	...	...	...	|	|	...	|	...	...
Metz **392** d.	|	...	...	...	...	...	...	...	...	|	...	...	...	|	...	...	...	...	...	|	|	...	|	...	...
Strasbourg **384** d.	|	...	...	...	...	...	...	...	...	|	...	...	...	|	...	...	...	...	...	|	|	...	|	...	...
Dijon **373** d.	|	...	...	...	...	...	...	...	...	|	...	...	...	|	...	...	1616	...	...	|	|	...	|	...	...
Genève **345** d.	|	...	...	...	...	1344	...	...	...	|	...	...	...	|	...	...	|	...	...	|	|	...	|	...	...
Lyon Part-Dieu **350/1** d.	|	...	...	...	...	1537	...	...	...	|	...	...	...	|	...	...	1807	...	...	|	|	...	|	...	...
Lyon Perrache **350/1** d.	|	...	...	...	...	|	...	...	...	|	...	...	...	|	...	...	|	...	...	|	|	...	|	...	...
Nantes **292** d.	|	...	...	...	...	|	...	...	...	|	...	...	...	|	...	...	|	...	...	|	|	...	|	...	...
Bordeaux **320** d.	|	1057z	...	...	...	|	...	...	...	|	...	...	...	|	...	...	|	...	...	|	|	...	|	...	...
Toulouse **321** d.	|	1307	...	...	...	|	...	...	...	|	...	...	...	|	1517	...	|	...	...	|	|	...	|	...	...
Cerbère **355** d.	|	|	...	...	...	|	...	...	...	|	...	...	...	|	|	...	|	...	...	|	|	...	|	...	...
Narbonne **355** d.	|	|	...	...	...	|	...	...	...	|	...	...	...	|	1638	...	|	...	...	|	|	...	|	...	...
Montpellier **355** d.	|	1511	...	...	...	|	...	...	...	|	...	...	...	|	1745	...	|	...	...	|	|	...	|	...	...
Marseille St Charles 350 d.	|	1654	...	1659	1703	1729	...	1734	1745	|	1807	1833	1906	1934	1938	1942	1957	2014	2027	|	2133	2138	|	2156	2306
La Ciotat d.	|	|	...	1730	1739	|	...	1759	1827	|	1836	1902	1941	|	|	2013	|	2044	2100	|	|	|	|	2225	2336
Bandol d.	|	|	...	1743	1751	|	...	|	1839	|	1848	1915	1953	|	|	2024	|	2057	2113	|	|	|	|	2237	2347
Toulon 350 a.	1731	1737	...	1758	1805	1809	...	1817	1854	|	1904	1929	2008	2012	2025	2039	2044	2112	2129	2134	2213	2219	2231	2252	0002
Toulon d.	1734	1740	1745	▬	1816	1812	...	1819	1856x	|	1908s	1940	▬	2024v	2029	...	2047	▬	...	2137	2216	2222	2234	...	▬
Hyères a.	|	|	|	...	1837	|	...	|	|	|	1930s	|	...	2041v	|	...	|	...	...	|	|	|	|	...	...
Les Arcs-Draguignan d.	|	|	1845	1820	...	|	...	1904	1953x	2007	...	2037	...	...	2109	...	|	...	...	|	|	2257	|	...	...
St Raphael-Valescure d.	1823	1833	▬	1840	...	1909	...	1925	▬	2025	...	▬	...	...	2128	...	2140	...	...	2227	2305	2315	2323	...	...
Grasse d.	|	|	...	|	...	|	1904	|	*1940*	|	...	...	2049	...	|	...	|	2157	...	|	|	|	|	...	...
Cannes a.	1845	1855	...	1919	...	1932	1928	1946	*2004*	2047	...	...	2114	...	2151	...	2201	2222	...	2248	2326	2337	2344	...	...
Cannes d.	1848	1858	...	1921	...	1935	1940	1948	2026	2051	...	...	2117	...	2153	...	2205	2224	...	2251	2330	2340	2348	...	0004
Juan les Pins d.	|	|	...	1932	...	|	1952	|	2036	|	...	...	2130	...	|	...	|	2234	...	|	|	|	|	...	0013
Antibes d.	1859	1909	...	1935	...	1947	1956	2002	2039	2102	...	**369**	2134	...	2203	...	2216	2237	...	2302	2342	2350	2358	...	0017
Cagnes sur Mer d.	|	|	...	1946	...	|	2004	|	2052	|	...	♦	2146	...	|	...	|	2248	...	|	|	|	|	...	0024
Nice Ville a.	1914	1923	①-⑤	2002	...	2006	2017	2020	2109	2117	...	🅁	2203	...	2217	...	2232	2301	...	2317	2357	0002	0012	...	0037
Nice Ville d.	...	...	1934	2005	...	...	2020	...	2113	...	...	2150	2206	...	...	...	...	2303	...	...	...	...	...	...	0039
Villefranche sur Mer d.	...	...	|	2013	...	...	|	...	2121	...	...	|	|	...	...	...	...	2310	...	...	...	...	...	...	0046
Beaulieu sur Mer d.	...	...	1942	2016	...	...	2030	...	2124	...	...	|	2215	...	...	...	...	2313	...	...	...	...	...	...	0049
Monaco-Monte Carlo d.	...	...	1952	2031	...	...	2040	...	2137	...	...	2205	2225	...	...	...	...	2326	...	...	...	...	...	...	0102
Cap Martin-Roquebrune d.	...	...	|	2036	...	...	|	...	2142	...	...	|	|	...	...	...	...	2331	...	...	...	...	...	...	|
Menton d.	...	...	2001	2043	...	...	2050	...	2148	...	...	|	2235	...	...	...	...	2338	...	...	...	...	...	...	0111
Ventimiglia a.	...	...	2012	2055	...	...	...	...	2201	...	...	2223	2246	...	...	...	...	2351	...	...	...	...	...	...	...

♦ – **NOTES (LISTED BY TRAIN NUMBER)**

139 – RIVIERA DEI FIORI – 🚃12 and 🍷 Nice - Ventimiglia - Genova - Milano.

145 – SAN REMO – 🚃12 and 🍷 Nice - Ventimiglia - Genova - Milano.

147 – LIGURE – 🚃12 and 🍷 Nice - Ventimiglia - Genova - Milano.

369 – MONTECARLO – 🛏 1,2 cl. and ▬ 2 cl. (4/6 berth) Nice - Firenze - Roma; 🛏 1,2 cl. and ▬ 2 cl. (4 berth) Nice - Venezia (Table **90**).

4208/9 – *CORAIL LUNÉA* – for days of running see Table **13**: ▬ 1,2 cl. and 🚃2 (reclining) Lille Flandres - Nice.

4238/9 – *CORAIL LUNÉA* – ⑤⑦ (not Mar. 23), also Dec. 19 - Jan. 6 (not Dec. 24, 31), Feb. 6 - Mar. 9, Mar. 24, 25, Apr. 2 - May 13 (not May 3), daily June 6 - Sept. 2. ▬ 1,2 cl. and 🚃2 (reclining) Luxembourg - Metz - Nice. Also runs in train **4296/7** (arrive Nice 0912) on dates in Table **392**. Conveys on dates in Table **382**, ▬ 2 cl. and 🚃2 (reclining) Reims - Nice.

4296/7 – *CORAIL LUNÉA* – daily except Dec. 15, 24, 31, Jan. 12, 19, 26, Feb. 2, Mar. 15, 22, 23, 29, May 3, 17, 24, 31. ▬ 1,2 cl., 🚃2 (reclining) Strasbourg - Nice. Train **4294/5** on certain dates.

4620/1 – *CORAIL LUNÉA* – not Dec. 24, 31. ▬ 1,2 cl. and 🚃2 (reclining) Bordeaux - Nice. From Hendaye on dates in Table **305**.

4624/5 – ⑤⑦ (not Mar. 23), also Dec. 21 - Jan. 6 (not Dec. 24, 31), Feb. 8 - Mar. 9, Mar. 24, Apr. 4 - May 4, May 7 - 12. ▬ 1,2 cl. and 🚃2 (reclining) Nantes - Nice and v.v.

5771 – *CORAIL LUNÉA* – not Dec 24, 31. ▬ 1,2 cl. and 🚃2 (reclining) Paris Austerlitz - Nice - Ventimiglia. Relief train **5773** also operates Dec. 21, 28, Jan. 5, Apr. 18, 25, 30, May 7, 13 (Paris Austerlitz d. 2132, Nice a. 0844).

B – 🚃12 Lille Europe - Charles de Gaulle (**9826**) - Nice; 🚃12 Brussels (**9826**) - Nice (Table **11**).

D – Daily to Toulon, Ⓑ to Les Arcs.
E – ⑤ from Apr. 4 (also Apr. 30, May 7; not May 2).
F – ⑤⑥⑦ Dec. 21 - Jan. 6, Feb. 15 - Mar. 9, Apr. 11 - 27 (also Dec. 25, Jan. 1, Mar. 21, 22, 24, Apr. 30, May 1, 4, 7, 8, 12).
L – Mar. 31 - Sept. 20.
M – Ⓑ to Toulon, daily Toulon - Hyères.
U – Daily St Raphael - Nice; ⑥⑦ Nice - Ventimiglia.
Y – Ⓐ to Toulon, daily Toulon - Hyères.

a – Paris **Austerlitz**.
b – Runs 6 minutes later Nice - Ventimiglia on Ⓐ (not Dec. 24 - Jan. 4, Apr. 14 - 18).
c – ⑥⑦ only.
e – Also Dec. 25, Jan. 1, Mar. 24, May 12.
f – Lille **Flandres**.
g – Also Dec. 26, Jan. 2, Mar. 25, May 13; not Dec. 24, 31, Mar. 24, May 12.
k – Runs 3 - 9 minutes later Antibes - Nice on Ⓒ (daily from May 13).
n – Not Dec. 25, Jan. 1, Mar. 24, May 12.
s – Ⓑ only.
v – ⑤⑦ (also Dec. 25, Jan. 1, Mar. 24, Apr. 30, May 7, 12; not May 2).
x – Ⓐ only.
z – Timings vary up to 7 minutes earlier or later.

TGV – 🅁, supplement payable, 🍷.

⊡ – From Avignon Centre on ⑥ (Table **351**).
△ – Runs 30 - 40 minutes later Jan. 2 - Feb. 22.
⊕ – Arrivals Les Arcs - Nice are up to 30 min later Jan. 3 - Feb. 22, Feb. 25 - 29, Mar. 31 - Apr. 18.
★ – *CORAIL TÉOZ*, 🅁, 🍷.
** – Grasse - Cannes = *17 km*.

FRANCE

360 VENTIMIGLIA - NICE - MARSEILLE

								17704		TGV 6172			TGV 6854		17476				17484			368		4768 4769	
	①–⑥		Ⓐ		Ⓐ		Ⓐ					Ⓐ		①–⑤	Ⓐ			①–⑤				♦		★	
		s					p															🅁	N	F	
Ventimiglia d.	...	...	...	...	...	0455	...	...	0516	...	0545	...	...	0622	...	0640	0710	...	...	...	0745	0751	0803	...	...
Menton d.	...	...	...	...	...	0508	...	...	0528	...	0557	...	...	0634	...	0654	0721	0741	...	...	0757	|	0815	...	...
Cap Martin-Roquebrune d.	...	...	...	...	...	0514	...	...	0535	...	0604	...	...	0641	...	0700	|	|	...	...	0804	|	|	...	...
Monaco-Monte Carlo d.	...	...	...	...	...	0521	...	...	0542	...	0610	...	...	0648	...	0707	0732	0752	...	...	0811	0820	0827	...	...
Beaulieu sur Mer d.	...	...	...	...	...	0529	...	...	0556	...	0623	...	...	0700	...	0720	0741	0800	...	...	0824	|	0837	...	...
Villefranche sur Mer d.	...	...	...	...	...	|	...	...	0559	...	0626	...	...	0703	...	0723	|	|	...	...	0827	|	|	...	...
Nice Ville a.	...	...	...	...	...	0537	...	...	0606	...	0633	...	...	0710	...	0729	0749	0808	...	...	0834	0840	0845	...	←
Nice Ville d.	0513	...	...	...	...	0539	...	0600	0608	0632	0636	...	0656	▬	0720	0732	0752	0813	0833	...	0837	...	→	0856	0900
Cagnes sur Mer d.	0528	...	...	...	...	0554	...	|	0623	|	0650	...	|	...	0731	0749	0807	0827	|	...	0853	...	...	|	0915
Antibes d.	0541	...	...	...	...	0607	...	0615	0636	0650	0658	...	0717	...	0740	0800	0815	0840	0851	...	0904	...	...	0913	0927
Juan les Pins d.	0544	...	...	...	...	0610	...	|	0639	|	0701	...	|	...	|	0804	0818	0843	|	...	0908	...	...	|	0930
Cannes a.	0553	...	...	...	...	0620	...	0625	0649	0658	0711	...	0725	...	0749	0813	0829	0853	0901	...	0917	...	...	0923	0940
Cannes d.	▬	...	...	...	...	0623	...	0628	0651	0702	0713	...	0728	...	0752	0815	0831	0855	0904	...	0931	...	...	0926	0942
Grasse a.	...	...	...	...	...	0648	...	|	0716	|	|	...	|	...	|	0840	|	0921	|	...	|	...	...	|	1008
St Raphael-Valescure d.	...	...	...	...	...	▬	...	0652	▬	0729	0744	...	0754	...	0815	▬	0913	▬	0927	...	1010	...	...	0951	...
Les Arcs-Draguignan d.	...	...	...	...	0600	...	...	0713	...	|	0803	...	|	...	0835	...	0930	...	0946	...	...	...	...	1010	...
Hyères d.	...	...	0615	0615x	|	...	0703	|	...	|	...	0818	|	...	|	...	...	0955	|	...	...	...	...	|	...
Toulon a.	Ⓐ	...	0636	0636x	0659	...	0725	0748	...	0821	...	0839	0843	Ⓐ	0909	...	...	1016	1020	←	...	...	...	1046	...
Toulon 350 d.	0532	0553	0638	0642	0701	0709	0731	0751	0755	0824	...	...	0846	0852	0912	0920	...	→	1022	1030	...	...	...	1050	...
Bandol d.	0548	0608	0650	0657	0716	0724	0746	|	0810	|	...	...	|	0908	|	0935	...	...	|	1045	...	...	...	|	...
La Ciotat d.	0601	0620	0700	0709	0728	0736	0757	0810	0821	|	...	...	|	0920	|	0947	...	...	|	1058	...	...	...	|	...
Marseille St Charles 350 a.	0632	0656	0731	0748	0756	0813	0824	0836	0856	|	...	...	0927	0950	0954	1021	...	...	1102	1128	...	...	...	1133	...
Montpellier **355** a.	...	...	...	...	...	...	...	|	...	|	...	...	|	...	...	...	...	...	...	...	...	...	...	1336	...
Narbonne **355** a.	...	...	...	...	...	...	...	|	...	|	...	...	|	...	...	...	...	...	...	...	...	...	...	1446	...
Portbou **355** a.	...	...	...	...	...	...	...	|	...	|	...	...	|	...	...	...	...	...	...	...	...	...	...	|	...
Toulouse **321** a.	...	...	...	...	...	...	...	|	...	|	...	...	|	...	...	...	...	...	...	...	...	...	...	1611*	...
Bordeaux **320** a.	...	...	...	...	...	...	...	|	...	|	...	...	|	...	...	...	...	...	...	...	...	...	...	...	...
Nantes **292** a.	...	...	...	...	...	...	...	|	...	|	...	...	|	...	...	...	...	...	...	...	...	...	...	...	...
Lyon Perrache **350/1** a.	...	...	...	...	...	...	...	|	...	|	...	...	|	...	...	...	...	...	...	...	...	...	...	...	...
Lyon Part-Dieu **350/1** a.	...	...	...	...	...	...	...	1234	...	|	...	...	1123	...	...	...	...	...	...	...	...	...	...	...	...
Genève **345** a.	...	...	...	...	...	...	...	...	...	|	...	...	...	...	...	...									...
Dijon **373** a.	...	...	...	...	...	...	...	...	...	|	...	...	...	...	...	...									...
Strasbourg **384** a.	...	...	...	...	...	...	...	...	...	|	...	...	...	...	...	...									...
Metz **392** a.	...	...	...	...	...	...	...	...	...	|	...	...	...	...	...	...	...	...	...	...	...	...	...	...	...
Lille Europe **11** a.	...	...	...	...	...	...	...	...	...	|	...	...	...	...	...	...	...	...	...	...	...	...	...	...	...
Paris Gare de Lyon **350/1** a.	...	...	...	...	...	...	...	...	...	1211y	...	...	...	...	...	...	...	...	...	...	...	...	...	...	...

For *TGV* trains from Toulon and Marseille to Paris and Lille see Table **350**

		TGV 5198	TGV 6174		TGV 6116		4758 4759		TGV 9864	TGV 6176		17488							EC 142			TGV 6886	4764 4765	TGV 6178	
							★	△				Ⓐ			⑥⑦	①–⑥	①–⑥	⑦	♦§		①–⑥		★		
									B							▷			🅁		b			G	
Ventimiglia d.	0827	...	0851	...	...	...	...	0923z	...	...	0955	1019	...	...	...	1050	1115	...	1125	1151	1212	...	...	...	1246
Menton d.	0841	...	0903	0910	...	...	...	0936	...	...	1007	1031	...	...	...	1103	1126	...	1137	1203	1225	...	...	...	1300
Cap Martin-Roquebrune d.	0848	...	|	|	...	...	...	0943	...	...	1014	|	...	...	...	1110	|	...	|	1210	1232	...	...	...	1306
Monaco-Monte Carlo d.	0855	...	0913	0921	...	...	...	0949	...	...	1021	1040	...	...	...	1116	1137	...	1147	1217	1238	...	...	...	1313
Beaulieu sur Mer d.	0909	...	|	0930	...	...	...	1003	...	...	1034	1050	...	...	...	1129	1146	...	|	1230	1252	...	...	...	1326
Villefranche sur Mer d.	0913	...	|	|	...	...	...	1007	...	...	1037	|	...	...	...	1133	|	...	|	1233	1255	...	...	...	1330
Nice Ville a.	0920	...	0927	0938	...	...	...	1014	...	...	1044	1101	...	...	...	1140	1155	...	1201	1240	1302	...	...	...	1338
Nice Ville d.	▬	0929	0937	0941	...	...	1008	▬	1032	1042	1047	1112	...	...	1125	▬	1158	1158	▬	1243	1305	1326	1330	1343	1347
Cagnes sur Mer d.	...	|	|	0955	...	...	|	...	|	|	1103	|	...	...	1138	...	1212	1212	...	1259	1321	|	|	|	1403
Antibes d.	...	0947	0955	1009	...	...	1023	...	1049	1100	1116	1128	...	...	1146	...	1222	1222	...	1312	1333	1344	1350	1359	1416
Juan les Pins d.	...	|	|	1012	...	...	|	...	|	|	1119	|	...	...	1149	...	1226	1226	...	1315	1336	|	|	|	1419
Cannes a.	...	0955	1003	1022	...	...	1033	...	1057	1107	1129	1137	...	...	1158	...	1235	1235	①–⑥	1325	1346	1352	1359	1407	1427
Cannes d.	...	0958	1007	1024	...	...	1037	1053	1101	1111	▬	1140	...	...	1204	1204	1236	1236	1305	1328	1348	1355	1402	1410	1433v
Grasse a.	...	|	|	|	...	...	|	1121	|	|	...	|	...	...	1229	1229	|	|	1328	|	1415	|	|	|	1458v
St Raphael-Valescure d.	...	1023	1034	1052	...	...	1103	...	1125	1135	...	1204	...	...	...	...	1316	1316	...	1400	...	1421	1427	1435	▬
Les Arcs-Draguignan d.	...	|	1052	...	...	...	|	...	1142	1152	...	1224	...	1229	...	...	...	...	...	...	...	|	1444	1452	...
Hyères d.	...	|	|	...	1102c	...	|	...	|	|	...	|	1246	|	...	...	...	...	...	...	...	|	|	|	...
Toulon a.	...	1114	|	...	1120c	...	1152	...	1215	|	...	1258	1307	1325	...	...	...	...	...	...	...	1514	1519	|	...
Toulon 350 d.	1053	1117	|	...	1132	1136	1156	...	1218	|	1229	1301	1308	...	...	...	...	...	...	...	...	1517	1522	|	1541
Bandol d.	1109	|	|	...	|	1153	|	...	|	|	1246	|	1323	...	...	...	...	...	...	...	...	|	|	|	1556
La Ciotat d.	1122	|	|	...	|	1205	|	...	|	|	1258	|	1336	...	...	...	...	...	...	...	...	|	|	|	1609
Marseille St Charles 350 a.	1151	1158	|	...	1216	1234	1238	...	1258	|	1335	1342	1405	...	...	...	...	...	...	...	...	1559	1604	|	1647
Montpellier **355** a.	...	|	|	...	|	...	1420	...	|	|	...	...	...	...	...	...	...	...	...	...	...	|	1745	|	...
Narbonne **355** a.	...	|	|	...	|	...	|	...	|	|	...	...	...	...	...	...	...	...	...	...	...	|	|	|	...
Portbou **355** a.	...	|	|	...	|	...	|	...	|	|	...	...	...	...	...	...	...	...	...	...	...	|	|	|	...
Toulouse **321** a.	...	|	|	...	|	...	1623	...	|	|	...	...	...	...	...	...	...	...	...	...	...	|	1951	|	...
Bordeaux **320** a.	...	|	|	...	|	...	1829	...	|	|	...	...	...	...	...	...	...	...	...	...	...	|	2157	|	...
Nantes **292** a.	...	|	|	...	|	...	...	...	|	|	...	...	...	...	...	...	...	...	...	...	...	|	...	|	...
Lyon Perrache **350/1** a.	...	|	|	...	|	...	...	...	|	|	...	...	...	...	...	...	...	...	...	...	...	|	...	|	...
Lyon Part-Dieu **350/1** a.	...	1350	|	...	|	...	...	...	|	|	...	...	...	...	...	...	...	...	...	...	...	1750	...	|	...
Genève **345** a.	...	|	|	...	|	...	...	...	|	|	...	...	...	...	...	...	...	...	...	...	...	1942	...	|	...
Dijon **373** a.	...	1539	|	...	|	...	...	...	|	|	...	...	...	...	...	...	...	...	...	...	...	...	...	|	...
Strasbourg **384** a.	...	|	|	...	|	...	...	...	|	|	...	...	...	...	...	...	...	...	...	...	...	...	...	|	...
Metz **392** a.	...	1848	|	...	|	...	...	...	|	|	...	...	...	...	...	...	...	...	...	...	...	...	...	|	...
Lille Europe **11** a.	...	...	|	...	|	...	...	...	1738	|	...	...	...	...	...	...	...	...	...	...	...	...	...	|	...
Paris Gare de Lyon **350/1** a.	...	...	1519	...	1531	...	...	...	...	1615	...	...	...	...	...	...	...	...	...	...	...	...	...	1920	...

♦ – **NOTES (LISTED BY TRAIN NUMBER)**

142 – LIGURE – (12) and 🍷 Milano - Genova - Ventimiglia - Nice.

144 – SAN REMO – (12) and 🍷 Milano - Genova - Ventimiglia - Nice.

160 – RIVIERA DEI FIORI – (12) and 🍷 Milano - Genova - Ventimiglia - Nice.

368 – MONTE CARLO – 🛏 1,2 cl. and ▬ 2 cl. (4/6 berth) Roma - Firenze - Nice; 🛏 1,2 cl. and ▬ 2 cl. (4 berth) Venezia - Nice (Table **90**).

4308/9 – *CORAIL LUNÉA* – for days of running see Table **13**: ▬ 1,2 cl. and (2) (reclining) Nice - Lille Flandres.

4328/9 – *CORAIL LUNÉA* – ①–④ Dec. 10 - 18, Jan. 7 - Feb. 5, Mar. 10 - Apr. 1 (not Mar. 24, 25), May 14 - June 5. ▬ 1,2 cl., (2) (reclining) Nice - Metz - Luxembourg.

4330/1 – *CORAIL LUNÉA* – ⑤⑦ (not Mar. 23), also Dec. 19 - Jan. 6 (not Dec. 24, 31), Feb. 6 - Mar. 9, Mar. 24, 25, Apr. 2 - May 13 (not May 3), daily June 6 - Sept. 2. ▬ 1,2 cl., (2) (reclining) Nice - Metz - Luxembourg. Conveys on dates in Table **382**, ▬ 2 cl., (2) (reclining) Nice - Reims.

4394/5 – *CORAIL LUNÉA* – daily except Dec. 15, 24, 31, Jan. 12, 19, 26, Feb. 2, Mar. 15, 22, 23, 29, May 3, 17, 24, 31. ▬ 1,2 cl. and (2) (reclining) Nice - Strasbourg. Train **4388/9** on certain dates.

4720 – *CORAIL LUNÉA* – not Dec. 24, 31. ▬ 1,2 cl. and (2) (reclining) Nice - Bordeaux. To Irún on dates in Table **305**.

4724/5 – ⑤⑦ (not Mar. 23), also Dec. 21 - Jan. 6 (not Dec. 24, 31), Feb. 8 - Mar. 9, Mar. 24, Apr. 4 - May 4, May 7 - 12. ▬ 1,2 cl. and (2) (reclining) Nice - Nantes.

5770 – *CORAIL LUNÉA* – not Dec. 24, 31. ▬ 1,2 cl. and (2) (reclining) Ventimiglia - Nice - Paris Austerlitz. Additional relief train **5772** runs on Dec. 20, 25, Jan. 1, Apr. 17, 24, 26, May 3, 12 (Nice d. 2103, Paris Austerlitz a. 0815).

B – To Brussels (Table **11**).
F – ⑤⑥⑦ Dec. 23 - Jan. 6, Feb. 15 - Mar. 9, Apr. 12 - 27 (also Dec. 25, Jan. 1, Mar. 22, 24, Apr. 30, May 1, 4, 7, 8, 12).
G – Apr. 1 - Sept. 21.
N – ①–⑤ (daily Nice - Grasse).
R – ⑥⑦ (daily Nice - Grasse).
U – ⑦ from Apr. 6 (also May 12).

a – Paris **Austerlitz**.
b – Runs daily Cannes - Grasse.
c – © only.
d – Menton - Nice runs ①–⑥ Mar. 29 - June 14.
f – Lille **Flandres**.
p – Daily Hyères - Toulon.
q – Also Dec. 25, Jan. 1, Mar. 24, May 1, 8.
s – 8 minutes later on ⑥.
u – ⑤⑦ (also Dec. 25, Jan. 1, Mar. 24, May 1, 8).
v – ⑥⑦ only.
w – Also Dec. 24, Jan. 1, Mar. 24, Apr. 30, May 7, 12; not Mar. 23, May 2, 9.
x – ⑥ only.
y – Up to 10 minutes later on certain dates.
z – ①–⑥ only.

TGV – 🅁, supplement payable, 🍷.
△ – 9 - 12 minutes later on Ⓐ to Dec. 21 and from Jan. 7 (not Apr. 14 - 18).
▷ – 9 - 11 minutes earlier on Mar. 5, May 22, 23, 28.
★ – CORAIL TÉOZ, 🅁, 🍷.
§ – Calls to set down only.
* – 1700 on Jan. 4, Feb. 15.

Jan. 3 - Feb. 22
Trains are liable to run up to 7 minutes earlier Ventimiglia - Nice - Marseille

VENTIMIGLIA - NICE - MARSEILLE 360

	TGV 6126	①-⑥	17490 ⑦ q	TGV 6168 ⑦ U		⑥⑦	R	TGV 5184 ⊕	①-⑥	17446	①-⑥	4766 4767 ⑤⑦ ★w	EC 144 ◆§ [R]		TGV 6186			①-⑤ b	TGV 6876	①-⑤	TGV 6180	①-⑥	17434	①-⑥
Ventimiglia d.	...	1314	...	...	...	1354	1434	...	1500	...	...	...	1525	1531	...	...	1557	1629	...	...	...	1649	1700	...
Menton d.	...	1327	...	...	...	1406	1446	...	1512	...	...	...	1537	1542	...	...	1609	1640	...	1657	...	1702	1713	...
Cap Martin-Roquebrune d.	...	1334	...	...	...	1413	1453	...	1519	...	...	...	|	|	...	...	1616	|	...	|	...	1708	|	...
Monaco-Monte Carlo d.	...	1340	...	...	...	1420	1459	...	1525	...	...	...	1548	1554	...	...	1623	1650	...	1708	...	1715	1727	...
Beaulieu sur Mer d.	...	1353	...	...	...	1433	1511	...	1537	...	...	...	|	1603	...	...	1636	1658	...	1718	...	1727	1737	...
Villefranche sur Mer d.	...	1357	...	...	...	1437	1515	...	1540	...	...	...	|	|	...	...	1639	|	...	|	...	1730	|	...
Nice Ville a.	...	1404	...	...	...	1444	1521	...	1546	...	←	...	1601	1611	...	...	1646	1707	...	1726	...	1736	1746	...
Nice Ville d.	...	...	1404	1430	...	1447	1539	1531	→	1554	1558	...	▬	1613	1636	...	1649	1710	1725	1729	1735	1739	1750	...
Cagnes sur Mer d.	...	...	|	|	...	1504	1552	|	▬	|	1611	...	...	1630	|	...	1705	1723	|	1742	|	1756	|	...
Antibes d.	...	...	1425	1447	...	1517	1558	1551	...	1610	1619	...	...	1643	1654	...	1718	1738	1745	...	1754	1806	1811	...
Juan les Pins d.	...	...	|	|	...	1520	1601	|	...	|	1623	...	...	1646	|	...	1721	1741	|	...	|	1809	|	...
Cannes a.	...	...	1437	1456	...	1529	1610	1559	...	1619	1633	...	...	1655	1703	←	1731	1749	1754	...	1802	1817	1820	←
Cannes d.	...	...	1443	1500	...	1531	1612	1603	...	1622	1644	...	...	→	1706	1716	1733	1751	1758	...	1806	→	1822	1829
Grasse a.	...	...	|	|	...	|	1637	|	...	|	1709	...	...	...	|	|	|	1819	|	...	|	▬	|	1854
St Raphael-Valescure d.	...	...	1506	1524	...	1610	▬	1628	...	1646	...	...	...	...	1732	1745	1815	▬	1823	...	1831	...	1849	...
Les Arcs-Draguignan d.	...	...	1528	1541	...	▬	...	1645	...	1705	...	...	...	...	|	1805	1833	...	|	...	|	...	1909	...
Hyères d.	1514	...	|	|	...	...	...	|	...	|	...	...	1743	...	|	...	...	...	|	...	|	...	|	...
Toulon a.	1532	...	1600	1613	...	Ⓐ	...	1717	Ⓐ	1743	...	...	1804	...	1821	...	...	Ⓐ	1914	...	1920	...	1947	...
Toulon 350 d.	1538	...	1602	1616	1619	1635	1657	1720	1724	1746	...	1802	1806	...	1824	...	...	1850	1917	...	1923	1930	1950	...
Bandol d.	|	...	|	|	1634	1651	1712	|	1740	|	...	|	1821	...	|	...	...	1907	|	...	|	1945	|	...
La Ciotat d.	|	...	|	|	1647	1704	1724	|	1752	|	...	|	1833	...	|	...	...	1919	|	...	|	1956	|	...
Marseille St Charles 350 a.	1616	...	1644	|	1716	1740	1754	1759	1822	1826	...	1845	1903	...	|	...	...	1952	1958	...	|	2026	2030	...
Montpellier **355** a.	|	...	...	|	...	...	...	|	...	...	...	2044	...	...	|	...	...	...	|	...	|	...	|	...
Narbonne **355** a.	|	...	...	|	...	...	...	|	...	...	...	2146	...	...	|	...	...	...	|	...	|	...	|	...
Portbou **355** a.	|	...	...	|	...	...	...	|	...	...	...	|	...	...	|	...	...	...	|	...	|	...	|	...
Toulouse **321** a.	|	...	...	|	...	...	...	|	...	...	...	2306	...	...	|	...	...	...	|	...	|	...	|	...
Bordeaux **320** a.	|	...	...	|	...	...	...	|	...	...	...	0117	...	...	|	...	...	...	|	...	|	...	|	...
Nantes **292** a.	|	...	...	|	...	...	...	|	...	...	...	...	...	...	|	...	...	...	|	...	|	...	|	...
Lyon Perrache **350/1** a.	|	...	...	|	...	...	...	|	...	...	...	...	...	...	|	...	...	...	|	...	|	...	0010u	...
Lyon Part-Dieu **350/1** a.	|	...	...	|	...	...	...	1950	...	...	...	...	...	...	|	...	...	...	2150	...	|	...	...	...
Genève **345** a.	|	...	...	|	...	...	...	|	...	...	...	...	...	...	|	...	...	...	|	...	|	...	...	...
Dijon **373** a.	|	...	...	|	...	...	...	|	...	...	...	...	...	...	|	...	...	...	2340	...	|	...	...	...
Strasbourg **384** a.	|	...	...	|	...	...	...	|	...	...	...	...	...	...	|	...	...	...	...	...	|	...	...	...
Metz **392** a.	|	...	...	|	...	...	...	|	...	...	...	...	...	...	|	...	...	...	...	...	|	...	...	...
Lille Europe **11** a.	|	...	...	|	...	...	...	2301	...	...	...	...	...	...	|	...	...	...	...	...	|	...	...	...
Paris Gare de Lyon **350/1** a.	1931	...	...	2015	...	...	...	...	...	...	...	...	...	...	2215	...	...	...	...	...	2311	...	...	...

			①-⑤	4724 4725 ◆ [R]	TGV 6186 ⑦ U	17494 Ⓐ		①-⑤	4308 4309 ◆ [R]		①-⑤	4394 4395 ◆ [R]	4328 4329 ◆ [R]		EC 160 ◆§ [R]	4330 4331 ◆ [R]		5770 ◆ [R]	4720 ◆ [R]		Ⓐ		①-⑥ d	
Ventimiglia d.	1712	...	1739	...	...	...	1758	...	...	1836	...	...	...	1900	1922	...	1930	2001	...	2016	2030	...	...	2332
Menton d.	1724	...	1750	...	...	...	1811	1832	...	1847	...	...	...	1912	1934	...	1944	2014	...	2028	2042	2140	2206	2344
Cap Martin-Roquebrune d.	1731	...	|	...	...	...	1817	|	...	|	...	...	...	1919	|	...	1951	|	...	2034	2049	|	2213	2351
Monaco-Monte Carlo d.	1738	...	1801	...	...	...	1824	1843	...	1858	1915	...	...	1926	1945	...	1958	2025	...	2040	2056	2151	2219	2357
Beaulieu sur Mer d.	1751	...	1810	...	...	...	1837	1851	...	1907	1929	...	...	1939	|	...	2011	|	...	2054	2107	2201	2232	0009
Villefranche sur Mer d.	1754	...	|	...	...	...	1841	|	...	|	1933	...	...	1942	|	...	2014	|	...	2057	|	|	2235	0013
Nice Ville a.	1801	...	1818	...	...	...	1848	1900	...	1916	1939	...	...	1949	1958	...	2021	2040	...	2104	2117	2208	2242	0021
Nice Ville d.	1804	...	1821	1835	1842	1846	1850	...	1911	1920	...	1946	1946	1951	▬	2017	2029	2049	2058	2107	...	2210	2244	0024
Cagnes sur Mer d.	1820	...	1836	|	|	|	1904	...	|	1936	...	|	|	2008	...	|	2045	|	|	2123	...	2225	2300	0040
Antibes d.	1832	...	1843	1854	1900	1904	1917	...	1933	1947	...	2007	2007	2020	...	2034	2058	2108	2116	2135	...	2232	2312	0053
Juan les Pins d.	1835	...	1846	|	|	|	1920	...	|	1951	...	|	|	2024	...	|	2102	|	|	2138	...	2235	2315	0056
Cannes a.	1844	...	1855	1904	1907	1914	1928	...	1945	2000	...	2016	2016	2033	...	2044	2112	2119	2127	2148	...	2244	2325	0106
Cannes d.	1846	...	▬	1907	1911	1917	1930	...	1948	▬	...	2019	2019	2034	2039	2047	2115	2122	2130	...	...	2246	...	...
Grasse a.	|	...	...	|	|	|	1955	...	|	...	...	|	|	|	2105	|	2139	|	|	...	...	2311	...	...
St Raphael-Valescure d.	1929	...	...	1934	1935	1942	...	...	2015	...	...	2045	2045	2105	...	2112	...	2149	2208	...	...	...	...	...
Les Arcs-Draguignan d.	1947	...	Ⓑ	2010	|	2000	...	...	2034	...	...	2107	2107	...	...	2132	...	2214	2228	...	...	...	...	...
Hyères d.	...	2010	2010	|	|	|	...	...	|	...	...	|	|	...	...	|	...	|	|	...	...	...	...	...
Toulon a.	...	2031	2031	2049	2023	2041	...	...	2109	...	...	2150	2150	...	...	2210	...	2249	2305	...	...	...	...	...
Toulon 350 d.	...	...	2034	2054	2026	...	...	...	2113	2135	...	2154	2154	...	...	2214	...	2253	2308	...	...	...	...	...
Bandol d.	...	...	2049	|	|	...	...	...	|	2151	...	|	|	...	...	|	...	|	|	...	...	...	...	...
La Ciotat d.	...	...	2101	|	|	...	...	...	|	2203	...	|	|	...	...	|	...	|	|	...	...	...	...	...
Marseille St Charles 350 a.	...	...	2131	2139	|	...	...	...	2152	2233	...	2237	2237	...	...	2256	...	|	2350	...	...	...	...	...
Montpellier **355** a.	...	...	...	0006	|	...	...	...	|	...	...	|	|	...	...	|	...	|	|	...	...	...	...	...
Narbonne **355** a.	...	...	...	|	|	...	...	...	|	...	...	|	|	...	...	|	...	|	|	...	...	...	...	...
Portbou **355** a.	...	...	...	|	|	...	...	...	|	...	...	|	|	...	...	|	...	|	|	...	...	...	...	...
Toulouse **321** a.	...	...	...	|	|	...	...	...	|	...	...	|	|	...	...	|	...	|	0514	...	...	...	...	...
Bordeaux **320** a.	...	...	...	0437	|	...	...	...	|	...	...	|	|	...	...	|	...	|	0810	...	...	...	...	...
Nantes **292** a.	...	...	...	0905	|	...	...	...	|	...	...	|	|	...	...	|	...	|	...	...	...	...	...	...
Lyon Perrache **350/1** a.	...	...	...	...	|	...	...	...	|	...	...	|	|	...	...	|	...	|	...	...	...	...	...	...
Lyon Part-Dieu **350/1** a.	...	...	...	...	|	...	...	...	|	...	...	|	|	...	...	|	...	|	...	...	...	...	...	...
Genève **345** a.	...	...	...	...	|	...	...	...	|	...	...	|	|	...	...	|	...	|	...	...	...	...	...	...
Dijon **373** a.	...	...	...	...	|	...	...	...	|	...	...	|	|	...	...	|	...	|	...	...	...	...	...	...
Strasbourg **384** a.	...	...	...	...	|	...	...	...	|	...	...	0758	|	...	...	|	...	|	...	...	...	...	...	...
Metz **392** a.	...	...	...	...	|	...	...	...	|	...	...	...	0745	...	...	0745	...	|	...	...	...	...	...	...
Lille Europe **11** a.	...	...	...	...	|	...	...	...	0827f	...	...	...	...	...	...	...	...	|	...	...	...	...	...	...
Paris Gare de Lyon **350/1** a.	...	...	...	...	0015	...	...	...	...	...	...	...	...	...	...	...	...	0745a	...	...	...	...	...	...

← FOR NOTES SEE PREVIOUS PAGE

NICE - ANNOT - DIGNE - ST AUBAN and VEYNES 361

2nd class only

km	CP ▲	①								
0	**Nice** (Gare CP) d.	...	0625	...	0850	1255	...	1715	1813	...
65	Puget Théniers d.	...	0748	...	1015	1420	...	1839	1937	...
72	Entrevaux d.	...	0756	...	1023	1428	...	1848	1945	...
87	Annot d.	0541	0816	...	1042	1446	...	1908	2001	...
106	Thorame Haute d.	0605	0841	...	1106	1510	...	1932	...	...
118	St André les Alpes d.	0619	0854	...	1119	1524	...	1945	...	...
166	**Digne** a.	0715	0950	...	1216	1620	...	2041	...	...

CP ▲		⚒	†						
Digne d.	...	...	...	0729	1055	...	1425	1730	...
St. André les Alpes d.	...	...	...	0826	1153	...	1523	1828	...
Thorame Haute d.	...	...	...	0840	1206	...	1536	1841	...
Annot d.	...	0540	0639	0906	1231	...	1602	1910	...
Entrevaux d.	...	0558	0657	0923	1248	...	1620	1927	...
Puget Théniers d.	...	0606	0705	0931	1256	...	1628	1936	...
Nice (Gare CP) a.	...	0731	0830	1054	1421	...	1752	2057	...

🚌 services to/from Digne. Subject to confirmation

SNCF 🚌	🚌 ①g	🚌	🚌 ⑤⑦	🚌 Ⓑ	🚌 ⑥
Digne (Gare) d.	0600	1220	1720	2015	2015
Château Arnoux § **362** d.	0634	1243	1743	2055	2049
Sisteron **362** d.	...	1258	1758	...	2104
Veynes-Dévoluy 362 a.	...	1400	1900	...	2200

SNCF 🚌	🚌 n	🚌 Ⓐ	🚌 Ⓒ	🚌 ⑤⑦
Veynes-Dévoluy 362 d.	0645	1600	1615	1925
Sisteron **362** d.	0746	1701	1716	2026
Château Arnoux § **362** d.	|	|	|	|
Digne (Gare) a.	0825	1740	1755	2105

g – Also Mar. 25, May 13; not Mar. 24, May 12.
n – Not May 1.
§ – Château Arnoux - St Auban.
▲ – Narrow gauge railway, operated by Chemins de Fer de Provence (CP).

362 BRIANÇON - GRENOBLE, VALENCE and MARSEILLE

km																								
										🚌													5790
			⚒	Ⓐ				F	⑥		⚒	⑥		⑥	Ⓑ	⑦		Ⓐ	⑥⑦	Ⓒ	Ⓒ	Ⓒ	Ⓐ	Ⓡ
		▷					⊕	⊕▷	L§	⊕▷				y		q	▽		G		v		▽	D
0	**Briançon** d.	...	...	0446r	0606	0736	0908	...	1110	...	1140	1218	1247	1445	1502	...	...	1634	1635	...	1718	...	1729	2009
13	L'Argentière les Écrins d.	...	...	0458r	0621	0752	0925	...	1126	...	1200	1234	1301	1501	1515	...	...	1649	1649	...	1733	...	1740	2025
28	Montdauphin-Guillestre d.	...	...	0509r	0633	0804	0937	...	1139	...	1215	1246	1313	1516	1527	...	...	1701	1701	...	1745	...	1752	2038
45	Embrun d.	...	...	0526r	0652	0824	0957	...	1158	...	1245	1304	1333	1547	1547	...	...	1719	1719	...	1804	...	1810	2101
82	**Gap** a.	...	...	0601r	0732	0904	1039	...	1237	...	1330	1340	1413	1626	1626	...	...	1757	1757	...	1844	...	1846	2146
82	**Gap** d.	0501	0531	0603	0734	0908	1042	1125	1239	1325	...	1343	1415	1631	1631	1652	1724	1759	1800	1833	1847	...	1849	2153
109	Veynes-Dévoluy a.	0528	0553	0624	0758	0931	1109	1147	1305	1347	...	1409	1439	1654	1654	1721	1748	1829	1829	1856	1913	←	1911	2223
109	Veynes-Dévoluy d.	0531	0555	0627	0759	0933	1113	1150	1307	1351	...	1412	1442	1659	1659	1724	1755	1831	1832	→	1916	1923	1915	2227
199	St Georges de Commiers d.	0700	|	|	|	|	|	1322	|	1520	...	|	|	|	|	|	|	|	|	▬	|	2053	2053	|
218	**Grenoble** a.	0723	|	|	0959*	|	|	1341	|	1542	...	1612	|	|	|	|	1956	|	|	...	|	2113	2113	|
172	Die d.	...	|	0720	...	|	1213	...	1408	...	...	...	|	1752	1752	|	▬	|	|	...	|	▬	...	2325
244	**Valence Ville** a.	...	|	0824	...	|	1326	...	1510	...	...	...	|	1855	1855	|	...	|	|	...	|	...	...	0029
254	Valence TGV **350** a.	...	|	0838	...	|	|	...	|	...	...	...	|	1906	1906	|	...	|	|	...	|	...	...	|
	Lyon Part-Dieu 351 a.	...	|	▬	...	|	1434	...	1633	...	...	...	|	...	...	|	...	|	|	...	|	...	...	|
	Paris Austerlitz **351** a.	...	|	...	...	|	...	...	...	...	...	...	|	...	...	|	...	|	|	...	|	...	...	0646
159	Sisteron d.	...	0635	...	...	1022	...	...	...	...	...	...	1523	...	...	1809	🚌	1913	1913	🚌	2013	🚌	...	...
176	Château Arnoux - St Auban d.	...	0648	🚌	...	1037	...	...	...	...	...	...	1537	...	...	1825	⑦	1928	|	Ⓐ	2028	Ⓒ	...	...
209	Manosque-Gréoux d.	...	0714	⚒	...	1101	...	...	...	...	...	...	1602	...	...	1858	q	1953	1949	...	2104	...	...	...
252	Meyrargues d.	...	0738	0745	...	1125	...	...	...	...	...	...	1625	...	...	1922	1925	2017	2015	2024	2129	2135	...	...
278	Aix en Provence ▲ d.	...	0758	|	...	1154	...	...	...	...	...	...	1650	...	...	1941	|	2037	2033	|	2150	|	...	...
315	**Marseille St Charles** ▲ a.	...	...	0845	...	1245	...	...	...	...	...	...	1741	...	...	...	2015	...	...	2110	...	2220	...	...

		5799					🚌								🚌				🚌					🚌
	Ⓐ	Ⓡ	⑥⑦	⚒				⑥					⑥				Ⓐ	b	Ⓑ	Ⓑ	⑤	Ⓐ	Ⓑ	†
		D	G	▷	⊕	⊕▷	s	d	▷	u	▷		L	▽				▽						
Marseille St Charles ▲ d.	...	...	...	...	0648	...	...	...	...	...	...	1315	...	...	1700	...	...	...	1903	...	...	...	...	...
Aix en Provence ▲ d.	...	...	0610	...	0800	...	...	...	...	...	...	1429	...	...	|	1749	...	...	|	1955	...	...	...	...
Meyrargues d.	...	...	|	...	0821	...	...	...	...	...	...	1448	...	...	1755	1809	...	...	2003	2016	...	...	...	...
Manosque-Gréoux d.	...	...	0649	...	0844	...	...	...	...	...	...	1511	...	...	...	1831	...	...	...	2039	...	...	...	...
Château Arnoux - St Auban d.	...	...	|	...	0911	...	...	...	...	...	...	1538	...	...	...	1857	...	...	...	2103	...	...	...	...
Sisteron d.	...	...	0727	...	0925	...	...	...	...	...	...	1552	...	...	...	1912	...	...	...	2116	...	...	...	...
Paris Austerlitz **351** d.	...	2205	|	...	|	...	...	...	...	...	...	|	...	...	...	|	...	...	...	|	...	...	...	...
Lyon Part-Dieu 351 d.	...	|	|	...	|	...	...	...	...	1123	...	|	...	...	...	|	...	...	...	|	...	...	...	...
Valence TGV **365** d.	...	|	|	...	|	...	...	1053	...	|	...	|	1432	...	...	|	1747	...	...	|	...	2013	2013	...
Valence Ville 365 d.	...	0414	|	...	|	...	...	1107	...	1224	...	|	1458	...	...	|	1758	...	...	|	...	2026	2026	...
Die d.	...	0521	|	...	|	...	...	1215	...	1329	...	|	1608	...	...	|	1910	...	...	|	...	2128	2128	...
Grenoble d.	...	|	|	0757	|	1013	...	|	1213	|	1413	|	|	1613	...	|	|	1813	...	|	2013	|	|	...
St Georges de Commiers d.	...	|	|	0818	|	1034	...	|	1235	|	1433	|	|	1634	...	|	|	1838	...	|	2039	|	|	...
Veynes-Dévoluy a.	...	0626	0803	0950	1009	1205	...	1315	1406	1428	1605	1635	1706	1802	...	1953	2005	2020	...	2156	2216	2223	2223	...
Veynes-Dévoluy d.	...	0628	0806	0953	1014	1212	...	1317	1411	1440	1607	1657	1716	1804	...	1955	2009	2023	...	2158	...	2226	2226	...
Gap a.	...	0656	0827	1015	1036	1235	...	1339	1437	1502	1629	1719	1747	1826	...	2015	2030	2045	...	2222	...	2248	2248	...
Gap d.	0613	0658	0830	...	1040	...	1245	1341	...	1504	...	1723	1805	1848z	...	2017	...	2105	...	...	...	2253	...	2301
Embrun d.	0651	0743	0915	...	1121	...	1325	1424	...	1545	...	1809	1849	1925z	...	2058	...	2151	...	...	...	2328	...	2341
Montdauphin-Guillestre d.	0709	0805	0940	...	1141	...	1355	1444	...	1604	...	1828	1908	1943z	...	2117	...	2210	...	...	...	2346	...	2356
L'Argentière les Écrins d.	0720	0819	0952	...	1153	...	1410	1459	...	1616	...	1840	1920	|	...	2130	...	2223	...	...	...	2356	...	0006
Briançon a.	0733	0838	1005	...	1206	...	1430	1516	...	1631	...	1854	1933	2005z	...	2143	...	2239	...	...	...	0009	...	0021

▲ RAIL REPLACEMENT 🚌 SERVICE MARSEILLE - AIX EN PROVENCE Journey time: 50–70 minutes. *By 🚌 to Dec. 2008 during track reconstruction*

From Marseille St Charles: 0520Ⓐ, 0610Ⓐ, 0640⚒, 0700Ⓐ, 0730Ⓐ, 0745Ⓐ, 0800, 0830, 0910Ⓐ, 1000, 1030, 1130, 1215, 1300, 1330, 1415, 1500, 1530Ⓐ, 1600, 1635, 1640Ⓐ, 1650Ⓐ, 1710, 1720Ⓐ, 1735Ⓐ, 1750, 1800Ⓒ, 1815Ⓐ, 1830Ⓑ, 1845Ⓐ, 1900, 1925, 2000, 2030, 2145, 2315. *Timings subject to confirmation.*

From Aix en Provence: 0500, 0540Ⓐ, 0600, 0630, 0645Ⓐ, 0650Ⓐ, 0705⚒, 0710Ⓒ, 0720⚒, 0730, 0745⚒, 0755⚒, 0800, 0815, 0845Ⓐ, 0930Ⓑ, 1000, 1015, 1120Ⓒ, 1130Ⓐ, 1205, 1240⚒, 1300, 1400, 1430Ⓐ, 1500, 1545, 1615, 1635, 1710⚒, 1715†, 1730⚒, 1745Ⓐ, 1830Ⓐ, 1910, 1940Ⓑ, 2015, 2130. *Timings subject to confirmation.*

D – *CORAIL LUNÉA* – 🛏 1,2 cl., (2) (reclining). Not Dec. 24, 31. Train **15790/9** on certain dates. A relief train (**5792/3**) operates on peak dates.
F – ⚒ to Apr. 26; daily from Apr. 28.
G – ⑥⑦ Jan. 12 - Feb. 3, ⑥⑦ Mar. 15 - 23.
L – ⑥ Dec. 15 - Mar. 29.
S – July 1 - Aug. 31.

b – Not Mar. 1, 2, 7 - 9 Gap - Briançon.
d – On Feb. 23, Mar. 1, 8 runs earlier (Valence Ville 0928, Briançon 1437). On Feb. 23, Mar. 1 an additional train runs Valence Ville 1107, Gap 1417, Briançon 1600).

q – Also Mar. 24, May 1, 8; not Dec. 23, 30, Feb. 10, 17, Apr. 13, 20.
r – ① (also Mar. 25; not Mar. 24). By 🚌 on ②–⑤ (not holidays), Briançon d. 0430.
s – Not May 1.
u – Not Mar. 1, 8. On Jan. 13 Lyon 1123, Gap 1605, Briançon 1833, not calling at Valence.
v – Not May 12.
y – On Feb. 23, Mar. 1, 8 runs earlier (Briançon 1334, Gap 1506, Valence Ville 1751).
z – Ⓑ to Mar. 6; daily from Mar. 10 (not Dec. 23, Mar. 2, 7 - 9).

▲ – For 🚌 Aix - Marseille see below table.
⊕ – On Ⓐ Apr. 7 - 25 by 🚌 Veynes - Gap / Briançon and v.v.
▽ – Subject to alteration on ①–④ May 19 - June 5.
▷ – Subject to alteration on Ⓐ May 19 - June 6.
§ – Runs up to 30 mins later on Feb. 23, Mar. 1, 8.
* – Subject to alteration ②–⑤ May 20 - June 6.

🚌 Briançon station - Oulx station (connects with *TGV* to / from Paris, Table **44**)
Subject to confirmation

			S						S	
Briançon d.	0740	1005	1420	1655	Oulx d.	0845	1310	1520	1925
Oulx a.	0845	1110	1520	1800	Briançon a.	0950	1415	1625	2030

364 BELLEGARDE - ANNEMASSE - ÉVIAN LES BAINS

km																								
		5675				🚌		*TGV*		*TGV*	*TGV*													
		Ⓡ						**6501**		**6503**	**6509**													
		A	Ⓐ	①–⑥				⑥	⚒	⑥	⑦					①–⑥	①–⑥			①–⑤	Ⓐ			
		◇		v				D	d	F	R	⊕	Y	⊗		2v	v			v		Lz		u
	Paris Gare de Lyon **341** d.	2226a	...	...	...	...	...	0810	...	0910	0910	...	...	...	...	...	...	...	...	...	...	...	...	...
	Lyon Part-Dieu **345** d.	|	...	...	...	...	...	|	...	|	|	...	1350	...	...	...	...	...	1704	...	...	...	...	...
0	**Bellegarde** ▷ d.	0642	0653	...	...	0915	1032x	1120	...	1210	1210	1232x	1535	...	1632n	...	...	...	1833	...	1932	...	2032	2232
	Genève Eaux Vives **367** d.	|	|	0732	...	|	|	|	1232	|	|	|	|	1632r	|	1732	1802	1832	|	1932	|	...	|	|
38	Annemasse ▷ a.	0722	0732	0743	...	1010	1108x	1151	1243	1243	1243	1311x	1605	1643r	1712n	1743	1813	1843	1912	1943	2012	...	2112	2315
38	Annemasse d.	0736	...	0753	0753	1010	1112	1156	1246	1252	1252	1318	1610	1646	1718	1746	1818	1846	1918	1946	2016	2034	2118	2317
68	Thonon les Bains d.	0810	...	0828	0828	1055	1141	1231	1316	1323	1323	1347	1641	1715	1744	1816	1845	1915	1946	2015	2041	2059	2144	2341
77	**Évian les Bains** a.	0818	...	0837	0837	1110	1148	1239	1324	1331	1331	1355	1648	1722	1752	1824	1852	1924	1957	2024	2049	2107	2151	2350

															TGV		*TGV*	*TGV*					5676	
															6502		**6504**	**6506**					Ⓡ	
	Ⓐ	Ⓐ		①–⑥	Ⓐ	⑥	⚒		⚒	Ⓑ			⑥	①–⑤	⑥		⑥	⑦		①–⑥		①–⑥	F	
		d		v										⊗v	E	△	G	S		v		w	◇	
Évian-les-Bains d.	0450	0532	0558	0632	0658	...	0732	0758	0858	...	...	1158	1334	1334	1431	1558	1625	1628	1732	1832	1903	1932	2030	...
Thonon-les-Bains d.	0459	0542	0608	0642	0708	...	0741	0807	0908	...	...	1209	1345	1345	1444	1608	1637	1640	1744	1844	1914	1946	2041	...
Annemasse a.	0522	0610	0638	0710	0736	...	0812	0836	0937	...	...	1236	1413	1413	1509	1636	1703	1703	1811	1911	1943	2014	2109	...
Annemasse ▷ d.	0524	0617	0644	0717	0738	0738	0817	0844	...	1040	...	1244x	...	1417	1514	1644x	1713	1721	1817	1917	1945	2017	2120	...
Genève Eaux Vives **367** a.	|	0628	|	0728	|	|	0828	|	...	|	...	|	...	1428	|	|	|	|	1828	1928	|	2028	|	...
Bellegarde ▷ a.	0555	...	0719	...	0817	0817	...	0919	...	1118	...	1318x	...	...	1543	1719x	1747	|	...	...	2019	...	2151	...
Lyon Part-Dieu **345** a.	...	...	...	...	...	...	...	1107c	...	...	...	...	...	...	|	...	|	|	...	...	...	...	|	...
Paris Gare de Lyon **341** a.	...	...	...	...	...	...	...	...	...	...	...	...	...	...	1849	...	2046	2049	...	...	...	...	0636a	...

A – ⑤ Dec. 21 - Mar. 28.
D – ⑥ Dec. 22 - Apr. 26.
E – ⑥ Dec. 15 - Apr. 26.
F – ⑥ Dec. 22 - Mar. 29.
G – ⑥ Dec. 22 - Apr. 19.
L – (2) Lyon - Annecy - Annemasse - Évian les Bains.
R – ⑦ Dec. 23 - Apr. 13 (also Dec. 25, Jan. 1, Mar. 24).
S – ⑦ Dec. 23 - Apr. 20 (also Dec. 25, Jan. 1, Mar. 24).
Y – ⑥ Dec. 15 - Apr. 26 (also ⑦ Dec. 23 - Jan. 6, Feb. 10 - Mar. 9).

a – Paris **Austerlitz**.
c – Ⓒ only.
d – Not Jan. 2, Mar. 21 Genève Eaux-Vives - Annemasse or v.v.
n – ⚒ to Jan. 19; ⑤⑥ Jan. 25 - June 21.
r – ①–⑥ (not Dec. 25, Jan. 1, 2, Mar. 21, 24, May 1, 12).
u – Not Feb. 23, Mar. 1, 8.
v – Not Dec. 25, Jan. 1, 2, Mar. 21, 24, May 1, 12.
w – Not Dec. 25, Jan. 1, 2, Feb. 23, Mar. 1, 8, 21, 24, May 1, 12.
x – Daily to Jan. 20; Ⓒ Jan. 26 - June 22.
z – Runs 12 - 20 minutes later on ⑥ Dec. 22 - Mar. 29.

TGV – Ⓡ, supplement payable, 🍷.
◇ – 🛏 1, 2 cl. and (2) (reclining).
▷ – See also Table **367**.
△ – Subject to alteration Évian - Annemasse on Ⓐ Apr. 21 - May 9.
⊖ – Subject to alteration Annemasse - Bellegarde on Apr. 7 - 11, 14 - 18.
⊕ – Subject to alteration on Ⓐ Apr. 7 - May 9.
⊗ – Subject to alteration Apr. 21 - 25, 28 - 30, May 1, 2, 5 - 7, 9.

GENÈVE and ANNECY - CHAMBÉRY - GRENOBLE - VALENCE 365

For *TGV* trains Genève - Lyon - Valence TGV - Montpellier / Nice and v.v. see Table **350**

km																									
		Ⓐ			⚒		Ⓐ	⚒	Ⓐ		Ⓐ	Ⓐ		⚒n	🚌 ①d		x	Ⓐ		⚒	Lb		Ⓐ	🚌	
0	**Genève** .... **341 345** d.	...	...	...	...	...	...	...	*0558*	...	...	...	...	...	...	...	...	...	1016	...	...	...	...	...	...
33	Bellegarde .... **341 345** d.	...	...	...	...	...	...	...	*0627*	...	...	...	...	...	...	...	...	...	1048	...	...	...	...	...	...
66	Culoz .... d.	...	...	...	...	...	...	...	0658	...	...	...	...	...	...	...	...	0947	|	...	...	...	...	...	...
	Annecy .... **341 344** d.	...	...	...	...	0600	...	...	|	0700	...	0716	0800	0836	...	...	0910	|	|	...	...	...	...	...	1300
88	Aix les Bains .... **341 344** d.	...	...	...	...	0635	...	0701	0722	0735	...	0754	0835	0916	...	...	0952	1010	1132	1200	...	...	*1300*	...	1335
102	**Chambéry** .... **341 344** a.	...	...	...	...	0646	...	0712	0732	0746	...	0805	0846	0926	...	...	1003	1021	1145	1211	...	...	*1311*	...	1346
102	**Chambéry** .... d.	...	0506	...	0615	0649	0654	0715	...	0749	0754	0815	0849	▬	...	0915	▬	▬	1148	1215	...	1249	1315	...	1349
116	Montmélian .... d.	...	0519	...	0625	|	0708	0726	...	|	0806	0826	|	...	...	0926	🚌	...	|	1227	...	|	1325	...	|
165	**Grenoble** .... a.	...	0553	...	0712	0734	0752	0812	...	0834	0853	0912	0934	⑥	...	1012	Ⓐ	🚌	1232	1312	...	1332	1412	...	1432
165	**Grenoble** .... d.	0548	0556	0638	...	0738	0755	...	...	0838	...	...	...	u	0955	1020	1055	1155	1238	...	...	1338	...	1415	...
242	Romans-Bourg de Péage .... d.	0651	0713	0754	...	0853	0913	...	...	0938	...	...	...	1043	|	1114	|	|	1345	...	1424	1445	...	|	...
249	Valence TGV .... ⊙ d.	0701	0723	0803	...	0903	0922	...	...	0948	...	...	...	1053	1055	1124	1155	1255	1354	...	1432	1454	...	1515	...
259	**Valence Ville** .... ⊙ a.	0709	0731	0810	...	0911	0929	...	...	0956	...	...	...	1101	...	1131	...	...	1407	...	1440	1502	...	...	...

	⚒		🚌		🚌			⊡		⚒			Ⓑg	Ⓐ	🚌 ⑤⑦r	y		Ⓐ		Ⓐ		Ⓐ	s	△
Genève .... **341 345** d.	...	...	...	1417	...	...	...	...	...	...	1624	...	...	...	...	...	...	...	...	1817	...	...	1944	...
Bellegarde .... **341 345** d.	...	...	...	1448	...	...	...	...	...	...	1651	...	...	...	...	...	...	...	...	1847	...	...	2012	...
Culoz .... d.	...	...	...	1514	...	...	...	...	...	...	|	...	...	...	...	...	...	...	1833	1914	...	...	2040	...
Annecy .... **341 344** d.	...	1355	...	|	1500	...	...	1600	...	...	|	1700	...	...	...	*1715*	1800	...	|	|	1900	...	|	2010
Aix les Bains .... **341 344** d.	...	1435	...	1528	1535	...	...	1635	...	...	1730	1735	...	...	...	*1758*	1835	...	1852	1931	1935	2025	2059	2055
Chambéry .... **341 344** a.	...	1446	...	▬	1546	...	...	1645	...	...	...	1746	...	...	...	*1809*	1846	...	1901	1942	1946	2036	2110	2106
Chambéry .... d.	1415	1449	...	...	1549	...	1615	1648	1654	1715	...	1749	...	1754	...	1815	1849	1854	*1915*	...	1949	2039	...	2114
Montmélian .... d.	1426	|	...	...	|	...	1626	|	1707	1727	...	|	...	1808	...	1826	|	1907	*1926*	...	2001	|	...	2124
Grenoble .... a.	1512	1532	...	Ⓐ	1632	...	1712	1731	1751	1811	...	1834	...	1853	...	1913	1934	1951	*2012*	...	2034	2125	...	2157
Grenoble .... d.	...	1538	1610	g	1638	1710	1715	1734	1753	...	...	1838	...	...	1915	...	1938	1954	...	...	2038	...	...	...
Romans-Bourg de Péage .... d.	...	1644	|	1737	1743	|	1828	1843	1900	...	...	1943	2005	...	|	...	2039	2101	...	...	2139	...	...	...
Valence TGV .... ⊙ d.	...	1654	1715	1747	1753	1815	1838	1853	1910	...	...	1953	2013	...	2015	...	2049	2111	...	...	2149	...	...	...
Valence Ville .... ⊙ a.	...	1702	...	1755	1802	...	1846	1902	1918	...	...	2002	2021	...	...	...	2058	2119	...	...	2157	...	...	...

	⚒	2 ▽	Ⓐ	⚒	Ⓐ				Ⓐ			Ⓐg	Ⓐ	E	🚌	F	Ⓐ	Ⓑ		Ⓐ			N	Ⓐ
Valence Ville .... ⊙ d.	...	...	...	...	...	...	0552	0603	0650	0703	0752	0830	...	...	...	...	...	...	1100	1124	1200	1200	1300	...
Valence TGV .... ⊙ d.	...	...	...	...	...	...	0603	0615	0701	0715	0804	0841	...	...	0955	...	...	...	1111	1136	1211	1211	1311	...
Romans-Bourg de Péage .... d.	...	...	...	...	...	...	0612	0626	0711	0726	0814	0848	...	...	|	...	...	...	1121	1145	1219	1219	1321	...
Grenoble .... a.	...	...	...	...	...	...	0718	0742	0822	0842	0916	▬	...	...	1055	...	...	...	1220	1303	1320	1320	1415	...
Grenoble .... d.	...	0545	0622	...	0645	0705	0725	0745	▬	...	0925	...	1005	1050	...	1105	...	1205	1225	1305	1325	1325	1425	1505
Montmélian .... d.	...	0633	0659	...	0732	0751	|	0832	...	...	|	...	1050	1139	...	1155	...	1252	|	1352	|	|	|	1552
Chambéry .... a.	...	0642	0708	...	0742	0800	0810	0842	B	...	1010	Ⓐ	1100	1148	...	1204	...	1302	1310	1402	1410	1410	1509	1602
Chambéry .... **341 344** d.	0610	0645	0713	0727	...	...	0814	0845	0901	...	1014	1101	...	1151	...	1209	1213	...	1313	...	1414	1414	1520	...
Aix les Bains .... **341 344** d.	0623	0701	0725	0740	...	...	0832	0856	0912	...	1035	1112	...	1204	...	1224	1226	...	1334	...	1434	1430	1534	...
Annecy .... **341 344** a.	|	0751	|	0820	...	...	0908	...	...	...	1107	...	...	|	...	|	1313	...	1418	...	1514	|	1621	...
Culoz .... a.	0638	...	0740	...	...	...	...	...	...	...	...	...	...	1220	...	1240	...	...	...	...	...	|	...	...
Bellegarde .... **341 345** a.	0705	...	0805	...	...	...	...	...	...	...	...	...	...	1252	...	1305	...	...	...	...	...	1505	...	...
Genève 347 348 ...... **341 345** a.	0732	...	0835	...	...	...	...	...	...	...	...	...	...	1332	...	1332	...	...	...	...	...	1532	...	...

		🚌	Ⓐ	Ⓐ		Ⓐ	z	⚒		Ⓐ	⚒					🚌 Ⓐ		b⊖	☆	🚌		🚌 ⑦q	⑦	🚌 P
Valence Ville .... ⊙ d.	1400	...	...	...	1500	...	...	...	1600	...	...	1638	1656	1738	...	...	1838	1858	1939	...	2038	...	2213	...
Valence TGV .... ⊙ d.	1412	1430	...	...	1512	...	...	...	1611	...	...	1650	1708	1750	...	1905	1849	1908	1950	2000	2049	2150	2224	2258
Romans-Bourg de Péage .... d.	1421	|	...	...	1521	...	...	...	1619	...	...	1659	1716	1759	...	|	1859	1915	2002	|	2100	|	2235	2313
Grenoble .... a.	1520	1530	...	...	1620	...	...	...	1718	...	...	1820	1842	1920	...	2005	2020	...	2056	2100	2150	2250	2328	0020
Grenoble .... d.	1525	▬	1535	1605	1625	1635	...	1705	1725	1735	1803	1825	1845	1925	1945	...	2025	...	2101	▬	2155	...	...	...
Montmélian .... d.	|	...	1623	1652	|	1722	...	1751	|	1822	1851	1901	1934	|	2032	...	|	...	|	...	|	...	...	...
Chambéry .... a.	1610	Ⓐ	1632	1701	1710	1732	...	1802	1810	1832	1903	1910	1943	2010	2042	...	2110	...	2146	...	2238	...	...	...
Chambéry .... **341 344** d.	1614	1631	...	...	1714	*1737*	...	...	1814	...	...	1914	1949	2014	...	...	2114	...	...	2205	...	...	...	...
Aix les Bains .... **341 344** d.	1634	1645	...	...	1731	*1751*	1828	...	1834	...	...	1933	1958c	2027	...	...	2134	...	...	2216	...	...	...	...
Annecy .... **341 344** a.	1714	|	...	...	1814	|	|	...	1920	...	...	2009	...	2104	...	...	2204	...	...	2248	...	...	...	...
Culoz .... a.	...	1706	...	...	...	*1812*	|	...	...	...	...	...	...	...	...	...	...	...	...	...	...	...	...	...
Bellegarde .... **341 345** a.	...	...	...	...	...	...	1901	...	...	...	...	...	...	...	...	...	...	...	...	...	...	...	...	...
Genève 347 348 ...... **341 345** a.	...	...	...	...	...	...	1932	...	...	...	...	...	...	...	...	...	...	...	...	...	...	...	...	...

B – Ⓐ to Apr. 30; daily from May 2.
E – ⑥ Dec. 15 - Apr. 12.
F – Daily except dates in note **E** (not Dec. 9, 17 - 21).
L – ⑥ Dec. 15 - Mar. 29.
N – Dec. 9 - Mar. 7 (not Dec. 22, 25, 29, Feb. 10, 16, 17, 23, 24, Mar. 1, 2)
P – ①-⑥ (also Dec. 23, 30, Mar. 23, May 11; not Dec. 25, Jan. 1, Mar. 24, May 1, 8, 12).

b – To / from Briançon (Table **362**).
c – Daily except ⑥.
d – Also Mar. 25, May 13; not Dec. 24, 31, Mar. 24, May 12.
g – To / from Gap or Briançon (Table **362**).
n – Not Feb. 9, 16, 23, Mar. 1, 8. From St Gervais (Table **367**).
q – Also Dec. 25, Jan. 1, Mar. 24, May 1, 8, 12; not Dec. 23, 30, Mar. 23, May 11.
r – Also Dec. 25, Jan. 1, Mar. 24, Apr. 30, May 1, 7, 8, 12; not Dec. 23, 30, Mar. 23, May 2, 9, 11.
s – Not Feb. 22, Mar. 8, Apr. 5.
u – Not Feb. 23, Mar. 1, 8. To Briançon (Table **362**).
x – Not Feb. 23, Mar. 1, 8.
y – Not Dec. 29, Jan. 1, Feb. 23, Mar. 1, 8 Annecy - Chambéry.
z – Not Feb. 16, 23.

△ – On © to Apr. 27 (also May 1) arrive Grenoble 2202.
▽ – Runs 10 - 20 minutes earlier Dec. 22, 29, Jan. 5, Feb. 16, 23, Mar. 1.
⊡ – To Avignon Centre (arrive 2025) on ⑤.
⊙ – Additional 🚌 Valence Ville - Valence TGV runs 2 - 4 times per hour.
☆ – From Avignon Centre on † (Table **351**).
⊖ – On Feb. 23, Mar. 1, 8 runs 11 - 14 minutes earlier.

Via Mont Blanc road tunnel — 🚌 CHAMONIX - COURMAYEUR - AOSTA 366

July 2007 - June 2008																	
	→	R§	R‡	R§	R‡	R§	R‡	→	R§ ⚒	R‡ ⚒	→	R§	R§ B	R‡	→	R§ ⚒	R‡ ⚒
Chamonix (rail station) .... d.	**July 1 - Sept 9**	0900	1000	1330	1500	1600	1745	**Sept. 10 - Dec. 16**	0830	1615	**Dec. 17 - Apr. 20** (not Dec. 25)	0830	1430	1615	**Apr. 21 - June 30**	0830	1615
Courmayeur .... a.		0945	1045	1415	1545	1645	1830		0915	1700		0915	1515	1700		0915	1700
Aosta .... a.		*1100*	*1200*	*1630*	*1730*	*1830*	1905		*1045*	*1830*		*1045*	*1630*	*1830*		*1045*	*1830*
	→	R‡	R§	R‡	R§	R‡	R§	→	R§ ⚒	R‡ ⚒	→	R§	R‡	R§ B	→	R§ ⚒	R‡ ⚒
Aosta .... d.	**July 1 - Sept 9**	0815	*0945*	*1045*	*1220*	*1545*	*1645*	**Sept. 10 - Dec. 16**	*0750*	*1335*	**Dec. 17 - Apr. 20** (not Dec. 25)	*0750*	*1220*	*1545*	**Apr. 21 - June 30**	*0750*	*1220*
Courmayeur .... d.		0900	1045	1300	1430	1645	1745		0925	1510		0925	1340	1715		0925	1340
Chamonix (rail station) .... a.		0945	1130	1345	1515	1730	1830		1005	1555		1005	1425	1800		1005	1425

B – Dec. 26 - Jan. 6, Feb. 4 - Apr. 20. § – Operated by SAT, Le Fayet. ‡ – Operated by SAVDA, Aosta.

Reservations by day before departure: Courmayeur (AG Mont Blanc ✆ 0165 841 305), Chamonix station (SAT ✆ 04 50 530 115), Aosta bus station (SAVDA ✆ 0165 262 027).

Connecting 🚌 service **Courmayeur - Pré St Didier - Aosta** (journey 60 minutes): Pré St Didier is 10 mins from Courmayeur. See also Table **586**. Operator: SAVDA, Aosta.

From Courmayeur: 0645, 0800, 0900, 0945, 1100, 1225, 1325, 1430 (⚒, schooldays only), 1530, 1630, 1730, 1830, 1945, 2145, 2245.
From Aosta: 0645, 0750, 0945, 1045, 1220, 1305 (⚒, schooldays only), 1335, 1445, 1545, 1645, 1745, 1845, 1945, 2045, 2145.

Service to June 30, 2008 (no service Dec. 25)

ST GERVAIS - CHAMONIX 367a

Subject to alteration Mar. 24 - Apr. 13. Many journeys continue to / from Le Châtelard or Martigny (Table **572**).

km											
0	**St Gervais** .... d.	0651	0732	0832	0932	1032	1232	1332	1532	and	2032
9	Les Houches .... d.	0718	0756	0856	0955	1056	1256	1356	1556	hourly	2056
20	**Chamonix** .... a.	0733	0811	0911	1011	1111	1311	1411	1611	until	2111

	M	N							
Chamonix .... d.	0639	0655	0739	0839	0939	1039	1239	and	1939
Les Houches .... d.	0657	0717	0757	0857	0957	1057	1257	hourly	1957
St Gervais .... a.	0720	0742	0820	0920	1020	1120	1320	until	2020

M – © (also Dec. 24 - 28, 31, Jan. 1 - 4, Feb. 18 - 22, 25 - 29, Apr. 14 - 18, 21 - 25, May 1, 8, 12). **N** – Daily except when train in previous column runs.

367 (PARIS / LYON) - ANNECY / GENÈVE - ST GERVAIS

km	TGV trains convey 🍷	5583				5595						TGV 6561		TGV 6463		TGV 5108	TGV 6467	TGV 6473			TGV 6569				
		D ◇	Ⓐ	Ⓐ	Ⓐ	B		⚒	①-⑤	⚒	Ⓐ			⑦	①-⑥	⑥	⑥	⑥	①-⑤				F	K	Ⓐ
		[R]				[R]			v				⊕	W	v ⊖	L	N	N	v	⊗		⊗			
	Paris Gare de Lyon **341** d.	2208n	...	...	...	2226g	...	...	...	...	...	0710	...	0810	...	...	0910	1006	...	...	1110	...	...	...	...
	Lyon Part-Dieu **345** d.	|	...	...	...	|	...	...	...	0704	...	|	0904	|	...	...	|	|	...	...	|	1304	...	...	...
	Chambéry **341/4 365** d.	|	...	...	...	0532	...	...	...	|	...	|	|	|	...	...	|	|	...	...	|	|	...	...	...
	Aix les Bains **365** d.	0422	...	...	...	0600	...	...	...	|	...	|	|	|	...	...	|	|	...	...	|	|	...	...	...
0	**Annecy** d.	0504	...	0703	...	0712	...	0903	...	|	1103	|	|	|	...	...	|	|	...	...	|	|	1622	1703	...
	Bellegarde d.	|	...	|	...	|	...	|	...	0832	|	1007	1032	|	...	...	1210	|	...	1332	1407	1432	|	|	...
*23	**Genève Eaux-Vives** ▷ d.	|	0602x	|	0702x	|	0802	|	0902	|	|	...	|	|	1202	...	|	|	1402	|	...	|	|	|	1702x
*17	Annemasse ▷ d.	|	0618	|	0718	|	0818	|	0913	0918	|	...	1118	|	1218	1216	1301	|	1413	1418	...	1518	|	|	1718
39	La Roche sur Foron a.	0537	0636	0735	0736	0813	0836	0935	...	0936	1135	...	1136	|	1236	|	1316	|	...	1436	...	1536	1703	1735	1736
39	La Roche sur Foron d.	0551	0640	...	0740	0831	0840	...	...	0940	...	...	1140	|	1240	|	1320	|	...	1440	...	1540	1711	...	1740
61	Cluses (Haute-Savoie) d.	0620	0706	...	0806	0851	0906	...	...	1005	...	...	1206	1237	1306	1306	1350	1438	...	1506	...	1606	1736	...	1806
80	Sallanches Megève d.	0641	0720	...	0820	0905	0920	...	...	1019	...	...	1220	1253	1320	1323	1406	1455	...	1520	...	1620	1754	...	1820
116	**St Gervais** a.	0647	0726	...	0825	0911	0925	...	...	1025	...	...	1225	1259	1325	1328	1412	1501	...	1525	...	1625	1800	...	1825

				TGV 6577						TGV 6477
	G	Ⓑ	①-⑤			①-⑤	Ⓐ	①-⑥		⑤
			v			v		v		T
Paris Gare de Lyon **341** d.	...	...	...	1504	...	...	...	...	...	1732
Lyon Part-Dieu **345** d.	...	...	...	|	1704	...	...	...	1904	|
Chambéry **341/4 365** d.	...	...	...	|	|	...	...	...	|	|
Aix les Bains **365** d.	...	...	...	|	|	...	...	...	|	|
Annecy d.	1722	1822	...	|	|	...	...	...	|	|
Bellegarde d.	|	|	...	1808	1832	...	...	...	2032	|
Genève Eaux-Vives ▷ d.	|	|	1902	...	|	1932	...	2032	|	|
Annemasse ▷ d.	|	|	1913	...	1918	1943	1958	2043	2118	|
La Roche sur Foron a.	1812	1902	...	...	1937	...	2014	...	2137	|
La Roche sur Foron d.	1825	1918	...	...	1940	...	2019	...	2140	|
Cluses (Haute-Savoie) d.	1848	1940	...	...	2006	...	2042	...	2206	2226
Sallanches Megève d.	1904	1955	...	...	2020	...	2059	...	2220	2242
St Gervais a.	1909	2001	...	...	2025	...	2105	...	2225	2248

		TGV 6564						TGV 6964		TGV 6568
			①-⑤	Ⓐ	⚒	⚒	⚒	Ⓒ		
			v			u	d			
St Gervais d.	0530	...	...	...	0555	0630	0645	...	0730	...
Sallanches Megève d.	0536	...	...	...	0602	0636	0651	...	0736	...
Cluses (Haute-Savoie) d.	0551	...	...	...	0617	0651	0707	...	0750	...
La Roche sur Foron a.	0615	...	...	...	0639	0716	0731	...	0816	...
La Roche sur Foron d.	0619	...	...	0621	0653	0719	0743	...	0819	...
Annemasse ▷ a.	0639	...	0647	|	|	0739	|	...	0839	...
Genève Eaux-Vives ▷ a.	|	...	0658	|	|	0758	|	...	|	...
Bellegarde a.	0719	0749	...	|	|	...	|	...	0919a	0948
Annecy a.	|	|	...	0652	0735	...	0824	0830	|	|
Aix les Bains **365** a.	|	|	...	...	...	...	0914	0857	|	|
Chambéry **341/4 365** a.	|	|	...	...	...	...	0926	|	|	|
Lyon Part-Dieu **345** a.	0847	|	...	...	...	...	...	|	1101a	|
Paris Gare de Lyon **341** a.	...	1049	...	...	...	...	...	1227	...	1249

			TGV 6968		17582	TGV 6480							TGV 6580	TGV 5178	TGV 6482		TGV 6486	TGV 6484	TGV 6984			TGV 6584	TGV 6494		5596
	H			①-⑤		⑥	①-⑥	Ⓐ	⚒		①-⑤	⚒	Ⓐ	⑥	⑦		⑥	⑦	Ⓑ		①-⑤		⑥	Ⓐ	B
				q	C	P	v ⊖		⊕ ⊗		v	k		L	X		Q	Y	w		v	b	R		[R] §
St Gervais d.	...	0745	...	0830	0853	0930	1130	...	1330	1530	...	...	...	1542	1610	1645	1651	1654	...	1730	...	...	1810	1827	2050
Sallanches Megève d.	...	0751	...	0836	0904	0941	1136	...	1336	1536	...	...	...	1552	1621	1651	1701	1704	...	1736	...	...	1821	1833	2100
Cluses (Haute-Savoie) d.	...	0807	...	0850	0923	1001	1150	...	1351	1550	...	...	...	1608	1636	1707	1717	1720	...	1751	...	...	1836	1849	2122
La Roche sur Foron a.	...	0830	...	0916	0939	|	1216	...	1416	1616	...	...	...	|	|	1730	|	|	...	1816	...	...	|	1913	2139
La Roche sur Foron d.	0821	0843	...	0918	0953	|	1219	1221	1419	1618	...	1621	...	|	|	1743	|	|	...	1819	...	...	|	1922	2158
Annemasse ▷ a.	|	|	...	0939	|	|	1239	|	1439	1633	1647	|	...	1645	1711	|	|	1755	...	1839	1847	...	|	1938	|
Genève Eaux-Vives ▷ a.	|	|	...	0958	|	|	1258x	|	|	|	1658	|	...	...	|	|	|	|	...	|	1858	...	|	...	|
Bellegarde a.	|	|	...	...	|	|	...	|	1515	1719	...	|	1748	...	|	|	|	|	...	1919	...	1948	|	...	|
Annecy a.	0852	0925	0935	...	1030	|	...	1252	...	|	...	1652	|	...	|	1821	|	|	1832	|	...	|	1932	...	2232
Aix les Bains **365** a.	...	...	1004	...	1107	|	...	...	...	|	...	...	|	...	|	...	|	|	1859	|	...	|	2037	...	2322
Chambéry **341/4 365** a.	...	...	|	...	|	|	...	...	...	|	...	...	|	...	|	...	|	|	|	|	...	|	|	...	2337
Lyon Part-Dieu **345** a.	...	...	|	...	1226	|	...	...	...	*1847*r	...	...	|	...	|	...	|	|	|	2047	...	|	|	...	|
Paris Gare de Lyon **341** a.	...	...	1323	...	...	1433	...	...	...	...	...	...	2049	...	2049	...	2143	2143	2207	...	...	2249	2347	...	0636p

GENÈVE EAUX-VIVES - ANNEMASSE - ANNECY showing through trains Annemasse - Annecy

See also above	①-⑤	Ⓐ	①-⑤	①-⑤	①-⑤	①-⑥	H		①-⑥	①-⑤	①-⑤	Ⓐ	Ⓐ	①-⑥	①-⑥	①-⑤	①-⑤	Ⓐ	⚒	①-⑥	①-⑤	①-⑥	①-⑥		Ⓐ
	v		v	v	v	△ v			u	v	v			v	△ v	v	v		k	△ v	v	△ v	△ v	△	
Genève Eaux-Vives d.	0532	...	0602	0632	0702	0732	...	0802	0832	0902	0932	...	...	1202	1232	1302	1332	1432	...	1632	1702	1732	1802	1832	...
Annemasse d.	0550	0602	0613	0643	0713	0743	0802	0813	0843	0913	0943	1002	1202	1213	1243	1313	1343	1443	1602	1643	1713	1743	1813	1843	1855
La Roche sur Foron a.	...	0618	...	...	...	...	0818	...	...	...	...	1018	1218	...	...	...	...	...	1617	...	...	...	...	...	1912
Annecy a.	...	0652	...	...	...	...	0852	...	...	...	...	1052	1252	...	...	...	...	...	1652	...	...	...	...	...	1959

See also above	①-⑤	①-⑤	①-⑥		Ⓐ	⚒	①-⑤	①-⑤	①-⑤	⚒	Ⓐ	①-⑥	①-⑤	①-⑤	①-⑤	Ⓐ	①-⑤	①-⑥	①-⑥	①-⑥	K		①-⑥	①-⑥	
	v	△ v	△ v	u		△	v	v	q			v	v	v	v		△ v	v	v	v		△	△ v	△ w	E
Annecy d.	...	...	...	...	0659	...	...	...	...	0903	1103	...	...	...	...	1303	...	...	...	...	1703	...	...	...	1935
La Roche sur Foron d.	...	...	...	...	0741	...	...	...	...	0941	1141	...	...	...	...	1341	...	...	...	...	1741	...	...	...	2016
Annemasse d.	0547	0617	0717	0747	0755	0817	0847	0917	0947	0955	1155	1217	1247	1317	1347	1355	1417	1617	1717	1747	1755	1817	1917	2017	2031
Genève Eaux-Vives d.	0558	0628	0728	0758	...	0828	0858	0928	0958	...	...	1228	1258	1328	1358	...	1428	1628	1728	1758	...	1828	1928	2028	...

B – *CORAIL LUNÉA* – Dec. 9, 14-16, 20-23, 25-30; daily Jan. 1 - Mar. 30; ⑤⑥⑦ from Apr. 4 (also Apr. 30, May 1, 7, 8, 12; not May 2). 🛏 1, 2 cl., [2] (reclining).
C – ⑥⑦ Dec. 22 - Jan. 6, ⑥⑦ Feb. 9 - Mar. 9, ⑥ Mar. 15-29.
D – ⑤⑥ Feb. 8 - Mar. 7 (not Mar. 1).
E – [2] Lyon - Annecy - Évian les Bains.
F – Ⓑ to Dec. 24; Ⓐ Dec. 26 - Apr. 18; Ⓑ from Apr. 21.
G – Daily Dec. 9-21; Ⓑ Dec. 23 - Apr. 18 (not Feb. 24, Mar. 2, 9); daily from Apr. 20.
H – ⚒ to Dec. 21; Ⓐ Dec. 24 - Feb. 29; ⚒ from Mar. 3.
K – ⚒ to Dec. 28; Ⓐ Dec. 31 - Apr. 25; ⚒ from Apr. 28.
L – ⑥ Dec. 15 - Apr. 26. To / from Lille Europe (Table 9).
N – ⑥ Dec. 15 - Apr. 12.
P – ⑥ Dec. 22 - Apr. 19.
Q – ⑥ Dec. 29 - Apr. 26.
R – ⑥ Dec. 29 - Apr. 19.
T – ⑤ Dec. 21 - Apr. 25.

W – ⑦ Dec. 23 - Apr. 13 (also Dec. 25, Jan. 1, Mar. 24).
X – ⑦ Dec. 23 - Apr. 20 (also Dec. 25, Jan. 1, Mar. 24).
Y – ⑦ Dec. 30 - Apr. 20 (also Dec. 25, Jan. 1, Mar. 24).
a – Ⓐ only.
b – Not Dec. 24, 31.
d – Not Feb. 9, 16, 23, Mar. 1, 8.
g – Paris **Austerlitz**. Depart 2246 on ④⑤⑥ Dec. 20 - Mar. 29 (also Dec. 23, 25, 26, 30, Jan. 1, 2, Mar. 23, Apr. 18-20, 25-27, 30, May 1, 3, 4, 7-11).
k – Not Dec. 22, Feb. 16, 23, Mar. 1, 8.
n – Paris **Austerlitz**.
p – Paris **Austerlitz**. Arrive 0620 certain dates.
q – Not Dec. 25, Jan. 1, Mar. 24, May 1, 12.
r – Ⓑ (daily from Apr. 27).
u – Not Feb. 9, 16, 23, Mar. 1.
v – Not Dec. 25, Jan. 1, 2, Mar. 21, 24, May 1, 12.

w – Not Dec. 25, Jan. 1, 2, Feb. 23, Mar. 1, 8, 21, 24, May 1, 12.
x – ①-⑤ (not Dec. 25, Jan. 1, 2, Mar. 21, 24, May 1, 12).
z – Not Dec. 31, May 1, 8.
TGV – [R], supplement payable, 🍷.
◇ – 🛏 1, 2 cl. only.
△ – To / from Évian les Bains (Table **364**).
▷ – For additional trains Genève Eaux-Vives - Annemasse see panel below main table.
⊕ – Not Apr. 14-18, 21-25.
⊗ – Not Apr. 7-11, 14-18 Bellegarde - Annemasse.
⊖ – Not Apr. 14-18, 21-25 Annemasse - St Gervais or v.v.
§ – Relief train **5598** also runs Feb. 16, Mar. 7, 8 (d. 2026).
* – Distance from La Roche sur Foron.

FOR TABLE 367a SEE PAGE 223

368 CHAMBÉRY - ALBERTVILLE - BOURG ST MAURICE

km	TGV trains convey 🍷						TGV 6417					TGV 6419	TGV 6421	TGV 5106	TGV 6429	TGV 6433	TGV 6427				TGV 5308	TGV 6435		
		⑥⑦	Ⓐ	①		⑥⑦	⑥			⑥⑦		⑦	⑥	⑥	⑥	①⑤	⑦	⑥⑦			⑥ v	⑥⑦		
		Y		g	Z	Y	B	d	b	Y		M	C	C ▽	D	U	M	Y	Z		E ▷	R	d §	b
	Paris Gare de Lyon **341** d.	...	...	...	...	...	0638	...	...	...	...	0742	0838	...	0850	0850	0854	...	...	...	...	0950	...	...
	Lyon Part Dieu **344** d.	...	...	...	...	...	|	...	...	...	...	|	|	...	|	|	|	...	...	...	...	|	...	...
	Aix les Bains **341/4** d.	...	...	...	...	...	|	...	...	...	...	|	|	...	|	|	|	...	...	...	...	|	...	...
0	**Chambéry** **369** d.	0611	0618	0618	0818	0834	|	1011	1011	1010	...	|	|	1153	|	|	|	1204	1205	...	1220	|	1405	1405
14	Montmélian **369** d.	|	0629	0629	0829	|	|	|	|	|	...	|	|	|	|	|	|	|	1216	...	|	|	|	|
26	St Pierre d'Albigny **369** d.	|	0638	0638	0837	|	|	|	|	|	...	|	|	|	|	|	|	|	1226	...	|	|	|	|
62	Albertville a.	0653	0702	0702	0900	0911	1002	1045	1045	1045	...	1122	1206	1223	1230	1230	1230	1238	1249	...	1255	1339	1438	1438
62	Albertville d.	0712	...	0708	0913	0927	1013	1058	...	1110	...	1134	1216	1233	1240	1240	1240	1251	1302	...	1305	1351	1451	...
104	Moûtiers-Salins d.	0742	...	0734	0939	1000	1037	1126	...	1134	...	1154	1241	1255	1303	1310	1302	1315	1327	...	1336	1411	1517	...
126	Aime la Plagne d.	0800	...	0748	0953	1016	1056	1140	...	1149	...	1209	1256	1312	1319	1326	1317	1333	1340	...	1352	1426	1531	...
137	Landry d.	0814	...	0756	1001	1026	1106	1149	...	1159	...	1218	1305	1321	1330	1336	1328	1342	1348	...	1403	1436	1539	...
146	**Bourg St Maurice** a.	0822	...	0804	1008	1034	1113	1156	...	1207	...	1224	1312	1328	1337	1343	1335	1350	1355	...	1410	1443	1546	...

CHAMBÉRY - ALBERTVILLE - BOURG ST MAURICE 368

TGV trains convey 🍷	DD	*TGV* 6437 ⑥ D	*TGV* 6439 ⑥⑦ S		*TGV* 6443 ⑥ A	Z§	⑥⑦ Y	Ⓐ	🚌 Ⓐ	Z	⑥⑦ Y	*TGV* 6447 ⑤ F	Z		Z	⑥⑦ Y	*TGV* 6451 ⑤ F		*TGV* 6453 ⑤ G	*TGV* 6449 ④ V	5707 [R]◇ AA	*TGV* 6455 ⑤ H	5709 [R] W
*Paris Gare de Lyon **341** d.*	...	1158	1210	...	1250	...	...	...	...	...	...	1610	...	...	...	...	1858	...	1950	2010	2223a	2307	2226a
*Lyon Part Dieu **344** d.*	1230	|	|	...	|	1441	1441	...	...	...	...	|	1741	...	1941	1941	|	...	|	|	|	|	|
*Aix les Bains **341/4** d.*	|	|	|	...	|	|	|	...	...	...	...	|	|	...	|	|	|	...	2248	|	|	|	|
Chambéry **369** d.	1406	|	|	...	|	1605	1625	1720	...	1820	1825	|	1910	...	2105	2117	|	...	2307	2313	|	|	0537
Montmélian **369** d.	|	|	|	...	|	|	|	1731	...	1831	|	|	1922	...	2116	|	|	...	|	|	|	|	|
St Pierre d'Albigny **369** d.	|	|	|	...	|	|	|	1740	...	1839	|	|	1932	...	2126	|	|	...	|	|	|	|	|
Albertville a.	1443	1536	1543	...	1614	1638	1715	1803	...	1902	1910	1949	1956	...	2149	2152	2237	...	2338	2346	0513	0540	0617
Albertville d.	1456	1546	1555	...	1628	1651	1731	...	1807	1915	1923	1959	2009	...	2203	2205	2247	...	2347	2356	0526	0550	0640
Moûtiers-Salins d.	1519	1608	1617	...	1656	1716	1804	...	1847	1941	1946	2021	2029	...	2233	2241	2310	...	0010	0017	0600	0632	0708
Aime la Plagne d.	1539	1624	1641	...	1711	1731	1824	...	...	1955	2002	2037	2043	...	2246	2302	2326	...	0026	0032	0622	0649	0733
Landry d.	1551	1634	1651	...	1726	1739	1833	...	...	2003	2011	2047	2051	...	2254	2313	2336	...	0036	0042	0631	0703	0743
Bourg St Maurice a.	1559	1641	1658	...	1733	1746	1841	...	...	2010	2019	2054	2058	...	2300	2320	2343	...	0043	0049	0639	0710	0751

	⑥⑦ Y	CC	🚌 Ⓐ	Ⓐ	⑥⑦ Y	Z		⑥⑦ Y	Z	*TGV* 6420 ⑥⑦ P		Ze	⑥⑦ Y	d	b	*TGV* 6422 ⑥⑦ Q	*TGV* 6424 ⑥ C		⑥⑦ Y		d	b	
Bourg St Maurice d.	0517	0535	...	...	0646	0702	...	0807	0810	0851	...	1014	1114	1210	...	1225	1254	...	1351	...	1409	...	...
Landry d.	0525	0543	...	...	0658	0710	...	0816	0818	0901	...	1023	1124	1218	...	1233	1304	...	1401	...	1417	...	...
Aime la Plagne d.	0534	0552	...	...	0715	0718	...	0826	0826	0911	...	1031	1134	1225	...	1243	1317	...	1411	...	1426	...	...
Moûtiers-Salins d.	0551	0607	0647	...	0736	0735	...	0844	0841	0933	...	1046	1207	1240	...	1320	1339	...	1431	...	1442	...	...
Albertville a.	0614	0633	0730	...	0757	0800	...	0905	0905	0953	...	1112	1232	1301	...	1341	1409	...	1452	...	1508	...	...
Albertville d.	0627	0646	...	0742	0810	0808	...	0918	0918	1008	...	1125	1256	1314	1314	1351	1419	...	1502	...	1517	1517	...
St Pierre d'Albigny **369** d.	|	0710	...	0806	|	0836	...	|	|	|	...	|	|	1333	1333	|	|	...	|	...	1536	1536	...
Montmélian **369** d.	|	0719	...	0814	|	0845	...	|	|	|	...	|	|	1341	1341	|	|	...	|	...	1544	1544	...
Chambéry **369** a.	0703	0729	...	0824	0846	0853	...	0950	0950	|	...	1156	1332	1350	1350	|	|	...	1534	...	1553	1553	...
*Aix les Bains **341/4** a.*	...	|	...	...	0910	0910	...	...	...	|	...	...	|	...	...	|	1505	...	1552	...	...	...	...
*Lyon Part Dieu **344** a.*	...	0854c	...	...	1026	1026x	...	...	...	|	...	...	1516	...	...	|	|	...	1719	...	...	...	...
*Paris Gare de Lyon **341** a.*	...	...	...	...	...	...	...	...	...	1403	...	...	...	...	...	1715	1807	...	...	...	...	...	...

	TGV 6432 ⑥ D	*TGV* 6430 ⑦ N	*TGV* 5182 ⑥ C▽	*TGV* 6434 ①⑤ T		⑥⑦ Y	Z	*TGV* 6444 ⑦ L	*TGV* 6436 ⑥ A	*TGV* 5394 ⑥ E▷		*TGV* 6438 ⑥ A	Ⓐ	⑥⑦ Y	Z		*TGV* 6446 ⑦ K	*TGV* 6442 ⑥⑦ T		5710 [R]◇ BB	5708 [R] X	*TGV* 6456 ⑤ J	
Bourg St Maurice d.	1445	1453	1504	1508	...	1602	1606	1619	1623	1644	...	1708	...	1755	1802	...	1823	1905	...	2108	2130	2323	...
Landry d.	1455	1503	1515	1519	...	1611	1614	1628	1632	1654	...	1719	...	1813	1810	...	1833	1915	...	2119	2139	2333	...
Aime la Plagne d.	1506	1513	1527	1530	...	1621	1621	1637	1642	1709	...	1730	...	1822	1819	...	1843	1925	...	2131	2150	2343	...
Moûtiers-Salins d.	1527	1536	1543	1547	...	1642	1635	1655	1700	1731	...	1748	...	1838	1834	...	1900	1948	...	2151	2212	2358	...
Albertville a.	1546	1553	1610	1605	...	1706	1707	1722	1730	1748	...	1806	...	1902	1857	...	1920	2006	...	2222	2242	0022	...
Albertville d.	1559	1603	1619	1615	...	1720	1715	1732	1742	1758	...	1816	1815	1915	1911	...	1930	2017	...	2237	2259	0032	...
St Pierre d'Albigny **369** d.	|	|	|	|	...	|	1737	|	|	|	...	|	1833	|	1933	...	|	|	...	|	|	|	...
Montmélian **369** d.	|	|	|	|	...	|	1745	|	|	|	...	|	1843	|	1941	...	|	|	...	|	|	|	...
Chambéry **369** a.	|	|	1647	|	...	1752	1753	|	|	1827	...	|	1853	1951	1951	...	2004	|	...	2315	2335	|	...
*Aix les Bains **341/4** a.*	|	|	...	|	...	|	|	|	|	...	...	|	...	...	...	...	|	|	...	2329	|	|	...
*Lyon Part Dieu **344** a.*	|	|	...	|	...	1920	1916	|	|	...	...	|	...	...	...	...	|	|	...	|	|	|	...
*Paris Gare de Lyon **341** a.*	2015	1957	...	2015	...	...	...	2107	2115	...	...	2207	...	...	...	...	2307	0007	...	0559a	0620a	0711	...

A – ⑥ Dec. 22 - Mar. 29.
B – ⑥ Dec. 22 - Mar. 29 (not Jan. 5).
C – ⑥ Dec. 15 - Apr. 26.
D – ⑥ Dec. 22 - Apr. 26.
E – ⑥ Dec. 15 - Mar. 29.
F – ⑤ Dec. 14 - Mar. 28.
G – ⑤ Dec. 21 - Apr. 25.
H – ⑤ Dec. 21 - Mar. 28 (not Jan. 4, Feb. 8, 15).
J – ⑤ Jan. 4 - Mar. 28 (not Feb. 8, 15, 22).
K – ⑦ Dec. 16 - Mar. 30 (also Dec. 25, Jan. 1, Mar. 24; not Dec. 23).
L – ⑦ Dec. 30 - Mar. 30 (also Dec. 25, Jan. 1, Mar. 24).
M – ⑦ Dec. 23 - Mar. 30 (also Dec. 25, Jan. 1, Mar. 24; not Mar. 23).
N – ⑦ Dec. 9 - Apr. 27 (also Dec. 25, Jan. 1, Mar. 24).
P – ⑥⑦ Dec. 22 - Apr. 27 (also Jan. 1, Mar. 24).
Q – ⑥⑦ Dec. 22 - Mar. 30 (also Jan. 1, Mar. 24).
R – ⑥⑦ Dec. 15 - Apr. 13 (also Dec. 25, Jan. 1, Mar. 24; not Apr. 5, 12).
S – ⑥⑦ Dec. 15 - Apr. 20 (also Dec. 25, Jan. 1, Mar. 24; not Mar. 23).
T – ⑥⑦ Dec. 29 - Apr. 20 (also Jan. 1, Mar. 24; not Dec. 30).

U – ①⑤ Dec. 21 - Mar. 21 (also Dec. 26, 27, Jan. 2, 3, Feb. 26 - 28, Mar. 4 - 6, 25, 28).
V – ④ Dec. 20 - Mar. 27.
W – *CORAIL LUNÉA* – Dec. 9, 14 - 16; daily Dec. 20 - Mar. 30 (not Dec. 24, 31); ⑤⑥⑦ from Apr. 4 (also Apr. 30, May 1, 7, 8, 12; not May 2). 🛏 1,2 cl., (2) (reclining).
X – *CORAIL LUNÉA* – Dec. 14 - 16; daily Dec. 20 - Mar. 30 (not Dec. 24, 31); ⑤⑥⑦ from Apr. 4 (also Apr. 30, May 1, 7, 8, 12; not May 2). 🛏 1,2 cl., (2) (reclining).
Y – ⑥⑦ Dec. 9 - Apr. 27 (also Dec. 25, Jan. 1, Mar. 24, May 1).
Z – Ⓐ to Apr. 30; daily from May 2.
AA – ⑤ Dec. 21 - Mar. 28 (also ⑥ Dec. 22 - Jan. 5, ⑥ Feb. 9 - Mar. 8).
BB – Dec. 25, Jan. 1, 5, ⑦ Jan. 6 - Feb. 3; ⑥⑦ Feb. 9 - Mar. 9, also Mar. 16, 24, 30.
CC – Ⓐ to Apr. 30; ⚒ May 2 - June 21.
DD – © to May 1 (not Dec. 22, 29, Feb. 16, 23, 24, Mar. 1, 2, 8, 9).
a – Paris **Austerlitz**.

b – May 2 - June 27.
c – Daily to May 3 (not Jan. 1, 6, Feb. 23, Mar. 1, 8); ⚒ May 5 - June 21.
d – Ⓐ to Apr. 30.
e – Not Dec. 10 - 14.
g – Also Mar. 25, May 2, 9, 13; not Dec. 24, 31, Feb. 18, 25, Mar. 24, Apr. 14, 21, May 12.
n – Not Feb. 23, Mar. 1.
v – Not Feb. 16.
x – Subject to alteration Mar. 31 - Apr. 18.

TGV – [R], supplement payable, 🍷.
◇ – 🛏 1,2 cl. only.
▽ – To/from Lille Europe (Table **9**).
▷ – To/from Nantes/Rennes (Table **335**).
§ – Subject to alteration Mar. 10 - 28.

CHAMBÉRY - MODANE 369

km		🚌 ⚒	5559 [R] N ◇	Ⓐ	🚌 †	⑥	①–⑤ y	⑦ E	🚌 ⚒		*TGV* 9241 M	*TGV* 6401 ⑥ A	⊖	*TGV* 6407 © R	🚌 ⚒	Ⓐ			*TGV* 9247 M	Ⓐ	Z	*TGV* 9249 M	Ⓐ	†
	*Paris Gare de Lyon **341** d.*	...	2308a	...	...	...	...	...	...	...	0742	0742	...	1038	...	...	...	...	1350	...	...	1524	...	...
	*Lyon Part Dieu **344** d.*	...	|	...	...	0633	0633	0633	...	...	|	|	...	|	...	...	1425c	1541	|	...	1641	1720z	...	...
	*Aix les Bains **341/4** d.*	...	0526	...	...	|	|	|	...	...	|	|	...	|	...	...	1552c	|	1658	...	|	|	1953	...
0	**Chambéry** **368** d.	0550	0550	0609	0629	0800	0807	0814	...	1014	1045	1049	1210	|	1230	1410	1610	1703	1711	1727	1800	1839	2008	2008
14	Montmélian **368** d.	0610	|	0619	0649	|	0818	0825	...	1024	|	|	1221	|	1250	1422	1620	|	|	1737	1811	|	2018	2018
26	St Pierre d'Albigny **368** d.	0628	|	0628	0704	|	0828	0834	...	1033	|	|	1230	|	1316	1431	1629	|	|	1747	1821	|	2027	2027
71	St Jean de Maurienne d.	0745	0643	0707	0759	0848	0905	0914	1030	1112	1129	1140	1311	1433	1417	1511	1711	1757	|	1826	1900	|	2111	2111
83	St Michel-Valloire d.	...	0657	0717	0815	0858	0916	0927	1048	1122	|	1151	1322	1445	1432	1522	1722	1808	|	1836	1910	|	2122	2122
99	**Modane** a.	...	0714	0730	0835	0912	0930	0944	1107	1136	1150	1205	1336	1459	1449	1536	1736	1822	1813	1850	1924	1940	2136	2136

	⚒			Z	Y	*TGV* 9240 M		*TGV* 9242 M	🚌	D	*TGV* 6406 ⑥ B	Z ⊕	Y §	Ⓐ	*TGV* 6414 © S			Ⓐ	†	🚌 ⚒		*TGV* 9248 M		5558 [R] P ◇
Modane d.	0525	0630	0722	0835	0845	0950	1029	1116	1131	1325	1354	1423	1440	1545	1604	1624	...	1715	1715	1701	1835	1920	...	2130
St Michel-Valloire d.	0541	0645	0741	0850	0859	|	1044	|	1150	1342	1409	1438	1457	1600	1620	1639	...	1731	1731	1718	1849	|	...	2148
St Jean de Maurienne d.	0552	0655	0754	0900	0910	|	1055	1141	1208	1354	1421	1448	1509	1611	1632	1650	...	1742	1742	1745	1859	|	...	2202
St Pierre d'Albigny **368** d.	0631	0734	0832	0939	|	|	1134	|	1309	|	|	1527	|	|	|	1728	...	1820	1820	1859	1940	|	...	|
Montmélian **368** d.	0639	0744	0841	0947	|	|	1142	|	1325	|	|	1537	|	|	|	1738	...	1829	1829	1919	1948	|	...	|
Chambéry **368** a.	0648	0752	0850	0956	0953	1052	1151	1220	1345	1445	|	1545	1555	1653	|	1746	...	1838	1838	1939	1958	2022	...	2250
*Aix les Bains **341/4** a.*	0701	|	...	...	|	|	|	|	...	|	|	...	|	...	|	...	...	1851	...	...	|	|	...	2334
*Lyon Part Dieu **344** a.*	0843	0916	...	...	1116	|	1316	|	...	1614	|	...	1716	...	|	...	...	...	...	...	2116x	2124z	...	|
*Paris Gare de Lyon **341** a.*	...	...	...	...	...	1355	...	1515	...	...	1819	...	...	...	2019	...	...	...	...	...	...	2319	...	0556a

A – ⑥ Dec. 15 - Apr. 12.
B – ⑥ Dec. 22 - Apr. 19.
D – ⑥ Feb. 9 - Mar. 8 (also Dec. 29, Jan. 5).
E – ⑦ Dec. 9 - Apr. 27.
M – (12) and 🍷 Paris - Milano and v.v. (Table **44**). [R], special 'global' fares payable.
N – ⑤⑥ Dec. 21 - Mar. 28 (not Mar. 8, 15, 22).
P – ⑤⑥⑦ Dec. 22 - Mar. 8 (also Dec. 25, Jan. 1, Mar. 15, 22, 29; not Dec. 23, 30).

R – ⑥⑦ Dec. 22 - Mar. 30 (also Dec. 25, Jan. 1).
S – ⑥⑦ Dec. 23 - Mar. 30 (also Jan. 1, Mar. 24).
Y – ⑥⑦ Dec. 9 - Apr. 27 (also Dec. 25, Jan. 1, Mar. 24, May 1).
Z – Ⓐ to Apr. 30; daily from May 2.
a – Paris **Austerlitz**.
c – ⑥ Dec. 15 - Apr. 26.
x – Not Feb. 23, Mar. 1, 8.
y – Not May 1, 8, 12.
z – Lyon St Exupéry ✈ (not Lyon Part Dieu).

TGV – [R], supplement payable, 🍷.
◇ – 🛏 1,2 cl. and (2) (reclining).
⊕ – Runs 12 minutes earlier Mar. 10 - 28.
⊖ – On Dec. 22, 29, Feb. 2, 9 runs 8 - 13 minutes later.
§ – To Dijon (Table **373**).

370 PARIS - DIJON

Many *TGV* trains continue to Besançon or Belfort (Table **374**), Lausanne or Bern (Table **375**)

km	*TGV* trains convey 🍸	TGV 6751	TGV 9265	TGV 9281	TGV 6755	TGV 6757		TGV 6759	TGV 6711	TGV 9269	TGV 6713	TGV 9271	TGV 6765	TGV 6715	TGV 6719	TGV 9285		TGV 6789	TGV 6769	TGV 9277	TGV 6731	TGV 6773		TGV 6735	TGV 6775	TGV 6777
		Ⓐ			Ⓐ	Ⓒ			①-⑥		⑤	⑦	Ⓐ	⑥	⑤						①-④			①-④	⑤	⑤⑦
			X	◇					n		f	v		t	f						k			w	f	u
0	**Paris Gare de Lyon** . d.	0658	0658	0758	0828	0828	...	1028	1128	1258	1410	1410	1428	1428	1528	1558	...	1658	1728	1758	1858	1928	...	2028	2028	2128
212	Montbard d.	0806	|	|	|	0936	...	|	1236	|	|	|	|	|	1636	|	...	1806	|	|	2006	|	...	|	|	|
284	**Dijon** a.	0840	0839	0935	1005	1010	...	1205	1310	1437	1547	1547	1605	1605	1710	1735	...	1840	1905	1935	2040	2107	...	2205	2207	2305

	TGV 6700	TGV 6704	TGV 6784	TGV 6756		TGV 9260	TGV 6710	TGV 9262	TGV 6714	TGV 9284	TGV 6762		TGV 6766	TGV 9266	TGV 6718	TGV 9268	TGV 6722	TGV 6726		TGV 6774	TGV 6776	TGV 6734	TGV 9270	TGV 9288	TGV 6770	TGV 9274
	Ⓐ	⑥	Ⓐ				⑥						Ⓐ		Ⓒ		Ⓐ				Ⓑ	⑦		Ⓑ	⑦	⑤-⑦
	d	t					t	Y						Z							s	q	V	h	e	w
Dijon d.	0620	0650	0652	0758	...	0924	0957	1026	1052	1125	1152	...	1359	1404	1457	1515	1621	1652	...	1758	1858	1918	1955	2020	2121	2144
Montbard d.	|	0730	0730	|	...	|	|	|	1130	|	|	...	|	|	|	|	|	1730	...	|	|	1954	|	|	|	|
Paris Gare de Lyon .. a.	0800	0837	0837	0938	...	1103	1137	1211	1237	1303	1331	...	1537	1544	1637	1655	1751	1837	...	1940	2037	2103	2156	2159	2303	2324

STOPPING TRAINS

km																									
			†	⚒											Ⓐ	Ⓐ						†	⚒		
				B			A	⊙				⊙		A				B					⊖		
0	**Paris Gare de Lyon** ... d.	...	0631	0704b	...	0813	0836b	...	1131	1231	1338	...	1613	1639b	1704	1737	1807	1837b	1831	1904	1942	2020	2025	2218b	2246
45	Melun d.	...	0700	|	...	0839	|	...	1156	|	1403	...	|	|	1729	|	1832	|	1858	|	2012	|	|	|	2314
60	Fontainebleau-Avon .... d.	...	0712	|	...	0851	|	...	1209	|	1416	...	|	|	1740	|	1842	|	1912	|	2025	|	2102	|	2328
79	Montereau d.	...	0729	|	...	0909	|	...	1225	|	1435	...	|	|	1756	|	1859	|	1931	|	2041	|	2121	|	2343
113	Sens d.	0551	0756	0804	...	0934	0932	...	1250	1326	1502	...	1720	1736	1822	1840	1926	1939	1958	2009	2108	2123	2140	2315	0009
147	Joigny d.	0617	0820	0820	...	1001	0949	...	1313	|	1527	...	1739	1753	1844	1856	...	1956	2028	2028	...	2141	2158	2333	0029
156	**Laroche Migennes** ▷ d.	0625	0827	0827	0844	1008	0955	1054	1319	1349	1534	1626	1746	1759	1851	1905	...	2003	2035	2038	...	2148	2204	2339	0036
197	Tonnerre ▷ d.	0649	...	...	0911	...	...	1119	...	1412	...	1651	1814	...	...	1931	...	...	...	2103	...	...	...	...	...
243	Montbard ▷ d.	0715	...	...	0940	...	...	1144	...	1436	...	1715	1843	...	...	2001	...	...	...	2127	...	...	...	...	...
315	**Dijon** ▷ a.	0758	...	...	1017	...	...	1224	...	1515	...	1756	1923	...	...	2045	...	...	...	2202	...	...	...	...	...

	⚒	▽	Ⓐ	Ⓐ		Ⓒ			†	⚒	Ⓐ										†			†	†	
	A				B								B	⊙		△		A			B	⊙				
Dijon ▷ d.	...	...	0439	...	...	...	0556	...	...	*0706*	...	...	...	1046	...	...	...	...	1639	...	...	1726	1824	...	...	2035
Montbard ▷ d.	...	...	0520	...	...	...	0639	...	...	*0746*	...	...	...	1124	...	...	...	...	1717	...	...	1807	1906	...	...	2112
Tonnerre ▷ d.	...	...	0545	...	...	...	0705	...	...	*0810*	...	...	...	1151	...	...	...	...	1740	...	...	1833	1932	...	...	2137
Laroche Migennes ▷ d.	0509	0519	0612	0626	0637	0655	0731	0738a	0837	0841	...	1109	1158	1216	1231	1346	1547	1644	1803	1821	1851	1859	1958	2016	2132	2201
Joigny d.	0517	0526	0621	0633	0645	0702	0739	0746a	0846	0850	...	1116	1207	...	1239	1354	1556	1652	1811	1829	1859	...	2006	2026	2138	|
Sens d.	0535	0555	0641	0701	0702	0726	0800	0804	0912	0917	1030	1138	1225	...	1300	1417	1620	1710	1830	1858	1918	...	2028	2044	2201	2221
Montereau d.	|	0622	|	0732	|	0749	|	0832	0940	0945	1051	1203	|	...	1322	1442	1649	|	|	1925	|	...	2052	|	2227	|
Fontainebleau-Avon ... d.	|	0640	|	0748	|	0810	|	0853	0956	1001	1111	1219	|	...	1340	1459	1707	|	|	1943	|	...	|	|	2243	|
Melun d.	|	0651	|	0758	|	0825	|	0906	1010	1014	1133	1230	|	...	1353	1513	1720	|	|	2003	|	...	|	|	2256	|
Paris Gare de Lyon .. a.	0638b	0720	0741	0824	0759b	0851	0855	0935	1039	1043	1202	1257	1319b	...	1419	1541	1747	1811b	1935	2034	2025b	...	2142	2146	2323	2329

A – (2) Paris - Auxerre and v.v. (Table **376**).
B – (2) Paris - Auxerre - Avallon and v.v. (Table **376**).
V – Dec. 22, 29, Mar. 1, 8 only.
X – Dec. 22, 23, 29, Feb. 23, 24, Mar. 1, 2, Apr. 19, 26, May 1, 8 only.
Y – Dec. 22, 27, Mar. 21, May 1, 8 only.
Z – Dec. 26, 29, 30, Jan. 1, 2, Mar. 15, 22, 29 only.

a – Ⓐ only.
b – Paris **Bercy**.
d – Not Dec. 24, 28, 31, Jan. 4
e – Also Dec. 25, Jan. 1, Mar. 24, May 12.
f – Also Apr. 30, May 7; not May 2.
h – Not May 1, 8.
k – Not Dec. 24, 31, Apr. 30, May 7.
m – Not Dec. 25, Jan. 1, Mar. 24, Apr. 30, May 1, 7, 8, 12.
n – Not Dec. 25, Jan. 1, Mar. 24, May 12.
q – Also Dec. 25, Jan. 1, Mar. 24, May 12; not Dec. 23.

s – Not Dec. 24, 31, May 1, 8.
t – Also May 1, 8.
u – Also Dec. 25, Jan. 1, Mar. 24, Apr. 30, May 7, 12; not Mar. 23, May 2.
v – Also Dec. 25, Jan. 1, Feb. 23, Mar. 1, 24, May 12.
w – Also Dec. 25, Jan. 1, Mar. 24, Apr. 30, May 1, 7, 8, 12; not May 2.

TGV – Ⓡ, supplement payable, 🍸.

◇ – Train **9261** on ⑥ (also May 1, 8).
△ – Runs 8 - 10 minutes later on ⑥.
▽ – Runs 8 - 12 minutes later on Ⓒ.
⊙ – To/from Auxerre (Table **376**).
⊖ – On ⑥ depart Paris 2023, calling at Melun 2049.

▷ – Additional trains Laroche Migennes - Dijon:
From Laroche 0733 Ⓐ, 0808, 1434 ⚒, 1635 †, 1808 Ⓐ, 1841 ⑥, 2057 ⑤⑦.
From Dijon 0803 ⚒, 1001, 1226 ⑥, 1430, 1544, 1737.

Melun - Marseille	TGV 6809 Ⓐ	
Melun d.	0603	...
Sens d.	0639	...
Laroche Migennes d.	0702	...
Le Creusot TGV d.	0751	...
Lyon Part Dieu a.	0831	...
Marseille **350** a.	1025	...

Marseille - Melun	TGV 6870 ①-④ m	TGV 6824 ⑤ f
Marseille **350** d.	1739	1908
Lyon Part Dieu d.	1939	2056
Le Creusot TGV d.	2020	|
Laroche Migennes a.	2107	2221
Sens a.	2131	2242
Melun a.	2204	2316

371 DIJON - CHAGNY - ÉTANG - AUTUN and NEVERS

km																									
		⚒		Ⓐ	Ⓐ					⚒		Ⓐ			Ⓐ	Ⓐ	Ⓐ	Ⓐ				①-④		⑤⑦	
										2		2		🚌		2		🚌	C			m		q	
0	**Dijon 373** d.	...	0603	...	0702	...	0903	...	1103	1340	...	1603	...	...	...	1703	...	...	1716	...	1803	1903	...	2003	...
37	Beaune **373** d.	...	0628	...	0726	...	0928	...	1128	1405	...	1628	...	...	...	1728	...	...	1738	...	1831	1929	...	2028	...
	Chalon sur Saône **373** d.	0609	|	0708	|	0909	|	...	|	|	1609	|	...	1614	1709	|	...	...	|	1806	|	|	2009	|	...
52	Chagny **373** d.	0622	|	0721	|	0921	|	←	|	|	1621	|	←	1643	1722	|	←	...	1756	1819	|	|	2021	|	...
81	Montchanin § d.	0647	0700	0747	0758	0947	1000	1012	1200	1437	1647	1659	1712	|	1747	1800	1813	...	1813	1847	1903	2001	2048	2100	...
	Paray le Monial **372** a.	...	|	...	|	→	|	|	|	|	→	|	|	|	→	|	|	...	1858	...	|	|	2135	|	...
89	Le Creusot § d.	...	0707	...	0807	...	1007	1023	1207	1445	...	1707	1724	|	...	1807	1824	1825	...	...	1911	2008	...	2107	...
111	Étang d.	...	0723	...	0823	...	1022	1045	1222	1500	...	1722	1745	|	...	1822	1847	|	...	...	1926	2024	...	2123	...
	Autun (see below) a.	...	|	...	|	...	|	...	|	|	...	|	...	1804	...	|	...	1905	...	...	|	|	...	|	...
179	Decize d.	...	0810	...	|	...	1110	...	1309	|	...	|	...	...	...	1909	...	...	...	...	2015	|	...	|	...
216	**Nevers** a.	...	0837	...	0929	...	1137	...	1337	1606	...	1826	...	...	...	1937	...	...	...	...	2044	2127	...	2226	...

	Ⓐ	Ⓐ	⚒	Ⓐ	Ⓐ	Ⓐ		Ⓐ	Ⓐ	Ⓒ				†	⚒		⑤⑦	Ⓐ	Ⓐ	Ⓑ				⑦e	Ⓑ
					🚌			🚌	C	C		🚌					e	🚌						🚌	
Nevers d.	...	0517	...	0614	...	...	0716	...	...	...	1123	...	1215	1519	1525	...	...	...	...	1716	...	1817	...	...	2050
Decize d.	...	0544	...	0641	...	...	0745	...	...	...	1151	...	1243	1547	1553	...	...	...	...	1744	...	1845	...	...	|
Autun (see below) d.	...	|	...	|	0715	...	|	0832	...	...	|	...	|	|	|	...	1640	1740	...	|	...	|	...	1933	|
Étang d.	...	0633	0650	0731	|	0750	0834	|	...	...	1240	...	1332	1635	1637	...	1704	|	1813	1834	...	1935	...	|	2159
Le Creusot § d.	...	0650	0714	0748	0755	0814	0851	|	...	...	1257	...	1348	1652	1652	...	1720	|	1830	1851	...	1952	...	|	2216
Paray le Monial **372** d.	0535	|	|	|	...	|	|	|	0825	1032	|	...	|	|	|	1602	|	|	|	|	...	|	...	|	|
Montchanin § d.	0622	0700	0724	0800	...	0823	0900	|	0910	1117	1305	1309	1400	1700	1700	1710	1728	|	1839	1900	1910	2000	2010	|	2225
Chagny **373** d.	0710t	|	0809*	|	...	0848	|	|	0932	1139	|	1351	|	|	|	1731	1754	1854	...	|	1936	|	2035	2046	|
Chalon sur Saône **373** a.	0726	|	0825	|	...	0905	|	0943	|	|	|	1413	|	|	|	1748	1806	...	...	|	1948	|	2048	2105	|
Beaune **373** a.	...	0729	...	0828	...	...	0929	...	0943	1150	1334	...	1428	1733	1729	...	...	...	...	1929	...	2029	...	...	2253
Dijon 373 a.	...	0754	...	0854	...	...	0954	...	1010	1217	1359	...	1454	1759	1754	...	...	...	...	1953	...	2054	...	...	2316

km													
		Ⓐ 🚌	⚒	⚒	🚌	⑥	Ⓐ	†	⑤-⑦ q	①-④ m	Ⓐ	⑤-⑦ 🚌 r	Ⓐ
0	Étang d.	0611	0727	0810	1051	1251	1254	1421	1620	1643	1750	1939	1950
15	Autun a.	0632	0745	0827	1112	1309	1312	1439	1638	1701	1807	1957	2007

	⚒	⚒	⚒ 🚌	⚒	🚌	⑤⑦ e	⚒	Ⓐ	🚌	†
Autun d.	0609	0749	1150	1230	1602	1640	1727	1811	1906	2100
Étang a.	0627	0806	1211	1248	1623	1657	1745	1829	1924	2117

C – (12) Dijon - Clermont Ferrand and v.v.

e – Also Dec. 25, Jan. 1, Mar. 24, May 1, 8, 12; not Mar. 23, May 11.
m – Not Dec. 24, 25, 31, Jan. 1, Mar. 24, Apr. 30, May 1, 7, 8, 12.
q – Also Dec. 24, 25, 31, Jan. 1, Mar. 24, Apr. 30, May 1, 7, 8, 12; not Mar. 23, May 11.
r – Also Dec. 24, 25, 31, Jan. 1, Mar. 24, Apr. 30, May 1, 7, 8, 12.

t – Arrive 0647.
* – Arrive 0748.
§ – 🚌 services also run between these points and Le Creusot TGV station connecting with *TGV* trains to and from Paris (Table **340**). Rail tickets not valid.

MOULINS SUR ALLIER - PARAY LE MONIAL - MONTCHANIN and LYON — 372

km																								
		Ⓐ		⚒		Ⓐ	Ⓐ		ⒶC		O	ⒸC				T						†		
0	**Moulins sur Allier** d.	...	...	...	...	0555	...	...	0733	...	0901	0939	...	1157	...	1443	...	...	1648	...	1755	...	...	...
56	Digoin d.	...	...	...	...	0649	...	...	0815	...	0943	1022	...	1249	...	1526	...	...	1740	...	1848	...	...	...
67	Paray le Monial d.	0535	0602	0608	...	0700	0708	...	0825	...	0954	1032	...	1300	...	1537	1602	...	1800	...	1900	2024	...	...
102	Montceau les Mines d.	0607	0636	|	...	0736	|	...	0857	...	|	1104	...	1336	...	|	1635	...	1836	...	1937	|	...	...
117	Montchanin a.	0621	0650	|	...	0750	|	...	0910	...	|	1117	...	1350	...	|	1650	...	1850	...	1950	|	...	...
	Chalon sur Saône **371** a.	0726	...	|	...	...	|	...	|	...	|	|	...	...	...	|	1748	...	...	...	...	|	...	...
	Dijon **371** a.	...	...	|	...	...	|	...	1010	...	|	1217	...	...	...	|	...	...	...	...	...	|	...	...
131	Lamure sur Azergues d.	...	...	0706	...	...	0805	...	...	...	1049	...	...	...	...	1631	...	...	...	...	...	2118	...	...
191	**Lyon Part Dieu** a.	...	...	|	...	...	|	...	...	...	1139	...	...	...	...	|	...	...	...	...	...	2205	...	...
195	**Lyon Perrache** a.	...	...	0810	...	...	0910	...	...	...	1151	...	...	...	...	1727	...	...	...	...	...	2217	...	...

	Ⓐ			†				⚒		T					Ⓐ		Ⓐ	C			O		Ⓐ	
Lyon Perrache d.	...	...	...	0740	...	...	...	...	...	1226	...	...	...	...	...	...	1654	...	...	...	1751	...	1849	...
Lyon Part Dieu d.	...	...	...	0752	...	...	...	...	...	1239	...	...	...	...	...	...	|	...	...	...	1804	...	|	...
Lamure sur Azergues d.	...	...	...	0852	...	...	...	...	...	1329	...	...	...	...	...	...	1759	...	...	...	1903	...	2000	...
Dijon **371** d.	...	...	...	|	...	...	...	...	...	|	...	...	...	...	...	...	|	1716	...	...	|	...	|	...
Chalon sur Saône **371** d.	0538	...	...	|	...	...	...	...	...	|	...	...	...	...	...	...	|	|	...	...	|	...	|	2009
Montchanin d.	0616	0706	...	|	...	1006	...	1206	...	|	...	1444	...	...	1705	...	|	1815	...	1906	|	...	|	2048
Montceau les Mines d.	0630	0720	...	|	...	1020	...	1221	...	|	...	1459	...	...	1722	...	|	1828	...	1921	|	...	|	2102
Paray le Monial d.	0702	0754	...	0947	...	1054	...	1256	...	1425	...	1533	...	...	1801	...	1854	1900	...	1952	2002	...	2056	2135
Digoin d.	...	0803	...	...	...	1103	...	1306	...	1434	...	1543	...	...	1811	...	...	1909	...	...	2011	...	...	...
Moulins sur Allier a.	...	0856	...	...	...	1156	...	1356	...	1520	...	1634	...	...	1902	...	...	1951	...	...	2053	...	...	...

C – From / to Clermont Ferrand (Table **330**). **O** – From / to Orléans (Table **290**). **T** – From / to Tours (Table **290**).

DIJON - CHALON SUR SAÔNE - LYON — 373

For *TGV* trains Paris - Mâcon Loché TGV and v.v. see Table **340**. For overnight trains not stopping between Dijon and Lyon see Table **350**.

km																								
					TGV **6801**					*TGV* **6811**				*TGV* **6813**		*TGV* **6781**	*TGV* **5148/9**						**4240 4241**	
		Ⓐ	⚒ ◇	Ⓐ	Ⓐ ♠	Ⓐ	⑥	Ⓐ	Ⓒ	Ⓒ ♠	Ⓐ	2	Ⓐ C	①⑥ z♥		Ⓐ	M	Ⓐ				Ⓐ	E	
0	*Paris Gare de Lyon* **370** d.	...	...	...	...	...	...	...	...	...	...	...	...	...	...	0658	...	...	...	...	...	...	...	...
315	**Dijon 371** d.	...	...	0535	0549	...	...	0635	0635	0645	...	0720	0735	0816	0835	0846	0916	0935	1020	1035	...	1135	1216	1220
352	Beaune **371** d.	...	...	0554	|	...	...	0654	0654	|	...	0748	0754	|	0854	0907	|	0954	1048	1054	...	1154	|	1248
367	Chagny **371** d.	...	...	0604	|	...	...	0704	0704	|	...	0800	0804	|	0904	|	|	1005	1100	1105	...	1205	|	1300
382	**Chalon sur Saône** d.	...	...	0616	0623	...	...	0715	0715	0721	...	0809	0815	0851	0915	0924	0954	1016	1109	1116	...	1216	1251	1309
440	Mâcon Ville d.	0553	0632	0646	0653	0712	0725	0745	0745	0752	0816	...	0845	0922	0948	...	1024	1046	...	1146	1232	1246	1320	...
478	Villefranche sur Saône ▲ d.	0626	0706	0709	|	0739	0759	0809	0814	|	0841	...	0909	|	1011	...	|	1109	...	1209	1304	1309	|	...
512	**Lyon Part Dieu** a.	0651	|	0735	0727	0804	|	0835	0837	0831	0905	...	0935	0957	1035	...	1057	1135	...	1235	|	1335	1358	...
	Grenoble **343** a.	...	|	0911	...	|	|	1011	1011	...	|	...	...	...	1211	...	...	1311	...	1411	|	1511	...	...
512	**Lyon Perrache** a.	...	0733	...	...	0817	0837	...	...	...	0917	...	...	...	...	...	...	...	...	...	1333	...	...	...

					4262 4263	*TGV* **5117/6**		*TGV* **6829**							*TGV* **6789**		**4264 4265**			**4266 4267**				
	Ⓑ q	⑥ r	Ⓐ	⊕	A	B		N	Ⓐ ◇			Ⓐ C				Ⓐ	⑤f T	Ⓐ		A	⚒	† e	2	⑤⑦
Paris Gare de Lyon **370** d.	...	...	...	...	...	...	...	...	...	...	...	...	...	...	1658	...	...	...	...	...	...	...	...	...
Dijon 371 d.	1235	1235	1335	1435	1455	1516	1535	1616	...	1620	1635	...	1735	1835	1843	1850	1907	1935	2035	2048	2120	2135	2220	2320
Beaune **371** d.	1254	1254	1354	1454	|	|	1554	|	...	1648	1654	...	1754	1855	1905	1915	|	1954	2054	|	2148	2154	2248	2348
Chagny **371** d.	1305	1305	1405	1505	|	|	1604	|	...	1700	1705	...	1804	1905	|	1924	|	2004	2104	|	2200	2204	2300	2359
Chalon sur Saône d.	1316	1316	1416	1516	|	1552	1616	1652	...	1709	1716	...	1815	1916	1921	1934	1945	2015	2115	2123	2209	2215	2309	0009
Mâcon Ville d.	1346	1346	1447	1546	|	1623	1646	1722	1734	...	1746	1834	1846	1946	...	...	2015	2045	2146	2153	...	2245	...	...
Villefranche sur Saône ▲ d.	1409	1416	1514	1608	|	|	1709	|	1804	...	1809	1904	1909	2010	...	...	|	2109	2214	|	...	2309	...	...
Lyon Part Dieu a.	1435	1439	1546	1635	1631	1701	1735	1757	|	...	1835	|	1935	2035	...	...	2055	2135	2237	2229	...	2335	...	...
Grenoble **343** a.	1611	1611	1731	1811	...	...	1911	...	|	...	2011	|	...	2211	...	...	...	|	|	|	...	|	...	...
Lyon Perrache a.	...	...	...	...	...	...	...	...	1833	...	...	1934	...	...	...	...	...	2147	2251	2242	...	2351	...	...

		TGV **6784**			*TGV* **6786**		**4336 4337**				*TGV* **6852**				*TGV* **6850**			*TGV* **5170**	*TGV* **6792**		**4340 4341**			*TGV* **5198/9**
	Ⓐ	Ⓐ	① m	⚒	⑥ k	Ⓐ	A			Ⓐ ◐	Ⓐ ♠	Ⓐ		2	Ⓒ ♠	Ⓐ		B	Ⓐ	Ⓐ	D		Ⓐ	M
Lyon Perrache d.	...	...	0508	...	...	0608	0635	...	...	0724	...	...	...	...	...	...	...	...	...	...	...	...	1323	...
Grenoble **343** d.	...	...	|	...	...	|	|	...	0544	|	...	0644	0744	...	...	0844	0944	...	...	1044	...	1144	|	...
Lyon Part Dieu d.	...	...	0522	...	...	0622	0648	...	0722	|	0800	0822	0922	...	1000	1022	1122	1200	...	1222	1253	1322	|	1400
Villefranche sur Saône ▲ d.	...	...	0549	...	...	0649	|	...	0749	0754	|	0849	0949	...	|	1049	1149	|	...	1249	|	1349	1355	|
Mâcon Ville d.	...	...	0613	...	...	0713	0725	...	0813	0822	0837	0913	1013	...	1040	1113	1213	1238	...	1313	1337	1413	1426	1436
Chalon sur Saône d.	0534	0604	0645	0648	0708	0745	0754	0759	0846	...	0906	0945	1045	1049	1110	1145	1245	1307	1311	1345	1405	1444	...	1506
Chagny **371** d.	0545	|	0655	0659	|	0755	|	0809	0856	...	|	0955	1056	1059	|	1155	1255	|	|	1355	|	1454	...	|
Beaune **371** d.	0555	0622	0705	0710	0726	0805	|	0821	0906	...	|	1005	1106	1111	|	1205	1305	|	1329	1405	|	1504	...	|
Dijon 371 a.	0620	0641	0723	0739	0747	0823	0827	0849	0924	...	0943	1023	1125	1139	1143	1223	1323	1343	1348	1423	1439	1523	...	1539
Paris Gare de Lyon **370** a.	...	0837	...	...	0938	...	...	...	...	...	...	...	...	...	...	...	...	...	1537	...	...	...	...	...

				TGV **6794**											**4342 4343**						*TGV* **6880**		*TGV* **6876**	
	Ⓐ			⑦ w		Ⓑ		Ⓐ	Ⓐ	C			⚒ ◇	Ⓐ	A	C	Ⓑ ◇		◧	Ⓐ	⑤⑦ b♥		N	Ⓐ
Lyon Perrache d.	...	...	...	...	...	1608	...	1623	1639	...	...	...	1723	1739	1759	...	1823	...	1923	...	...	...	...	2203
Grenoble **343** d.	1244	...	1344	...	...	|	...	|	|	...	...	...	|	|	|	...	|	1744	|	1844	...	1944	...	|
Lyon Part Dieu d.	1422	...	1522	...	...	1622	...	|	1652	1722	...	...	|	1752	1812	1822	|	1922	|	2022	2126	2122	2156	2217
Villefranche sur Saône ▲ d.	1449	...	1549	...	...	1649	...	1654	1719	1749	...	...	1754	1820	|	1849	1856	1949	1954	2048	|	2152	|	2247
Mâcon Ville d.	1513	...	1613	...	...	1713	...	1724	1744	1813	...	...	1824	1845	1855	1913	1926	2013	2022	2113	2203	2217	2236	2308
Chalon sur Saône d.	1545	1625	1645	1712	1725	1745	1749	...	...	1844	1849	...	...	...	1923	1944	...	2045	...	2145	2232	2248	2304	...
Chagny **371** d.	1555	1639	1655	|	1740	1754	1803	...	...	1854	1859	...	...	...	|	1954	...	2055	...	2155	|	2259	|	...
Beaune **371** d.	1605	1649	1705	1730	1749	1805	1815	...	...	1904	1911	...	...	...	|	2004	...	2105	...	2205	|	2309	|	...
Dijon 371 a.	1623	1714	1723	1749	1814	1823	1844	...	...	1923	1939	...	...	...	1957	2023	...	2123	...	2223	2305	2328	2340	...
Paris Gare de Lyon **370** a.	...	...	...	1938	...	...	...	...	...	...	...	...	...	...	...	...	...	...	...	...	...	...	...	...

A – (12) Metz - Dijon - Lyon and v.v.
B – (12) and 🍷 Dijon - Montpellier - Toulouse - Bordeaux and v.v.
C – To / from Chambéry (Table **344**).
D – June 14 - Sept. 21. (12) Cerbère - Nancy - Metz; (12) Cerbère - Dijon (**4351**) - Strasbourg (Table **351**).
E – June 13 - Sept. 20. (12) Metz - Nancy - Portbou; (12) Strasbourg (**4251**) - Dijon - Portbou (Table **351**).
M – (12) and 🍷 Metz - Lyon - Marseille - Nice and v.v.
N – (12) and 🍷 Dijon - Lyon - Marseille - Nice and v.v.
T – (12) Metz - Lyon - Avignon - Montpellier (Table **351**).

b – Also Dec. 25, Jan. 1, Mar. 24, Apr. 30, May 7, 12; not May 2.
e – Not Mar. 23, May 11.
f – Also Dec. 24, 31, Apr. 30, May 7; not May 2, 9.
k – Also May 1, 8.
m – Also Dec. 26, Jan. 2, Mar. 25, May 2, 9, 13; not Mar. 24, May 12.
q – Also May 3, 10; not May 1, 8.
r – Also May 1, 8; not May 3, 10.
w – Also Dec. 25, Jan. 1, Mar. 24, May 12.
z – Also Dec. 26, Jan. 2, Mar. 25, May 1, 8, 13; not Dec. 24, 31, Mar. 24, May 12.

TGV – [R], supplement payable, 🍷.

♠ – To / from Marseille (Table **350**).
♥ – To / from Montpellier (Table **350**).
◇ – To / from Valence Ville (Table **351**).
⊕ – Subject to alteration on Ⓐ Mar. 3 - 28.
◐ – From Montélimar (Table **351**).
◧ – From Avignon (Table **351**).
▲ – Villefranche is also served by 🚌 service to Mâcon Loché TGV station, connecting with *TGV* trains to and from Paris (Table **340**).

374 DIJON - BESANÇON - BELFORT

Timings at Montbéliard and Belfort are subject to alteration from Feb. 25. See notes ▲ and ★.

km													TGV 6751			TGV 6755	TGV 6757				TGV 6759				
		Ⓐ	⑥	Ⓐ	Ⓐ	⚒	⚒	⚒	⚒	Ⓐ	Ⓒ	Ⓐ	Ⓐ	Ⓒ	Ⓐ	Ⓐ	Ⓒ		t	⚒			⚒	Ⓒ	⚒
		2	2	2	2	2	2	2	2	2	2	2		2	2			2	2	2		2	t 2	2	t 2
	Paris Gare de Lyon **370** d.	...	...	...	...	...	...	...	...	...	...	...	0658	...	...	0828	0828	...	...	...	1028	...	...	...	...
0	**Dijon 375** d.	...	...	0512	...	...	0602	0641	0705	0731	0734	0820	0843	0945	0948	1008	1013	1039	...	1136	1208	1215	...	1320	...
46	Dole **375** d.	...	...	0544	...	...	0644	0714	0742	0804	0808	0853	0909	1016	1021	1034	1039	1110	...	1216	|	1253	...	1352	...
91	**Besançon Viotte** a.	...	...	0617	...	...	0726	0743	0818	0832	0835	0921	0934	1047	1053	1101	1104	1138	...	1253	1257	1328	...	1421	...
91	**Besançon Viotte** 384 d.	0541	0620	0619	0647	0703	...	0745	...	0834	...	...	...	1049	...	...	...	...	1210	...	1300	...	1338	...	1520
170	Montbéliard 384 d.	0642	0721	0725	0745	0812	...	0846	...	0934	...	...	...	1147	...	...	...	...	1310	...	1351	...	1438	...	1621
188	**Belfort** ▲ 384 a.	0656	0735	0741	0800	0827	...	0901	...	0949	...	...	...	1202	...	...	...	...	1325	...	1405	...	1455	...	1636

	4351 4350				TGV 6765								TGV 6769	TGV 6769				TGV 6773	TGV 6773		TGV 5130/1	TGV 6775		TGV 6777	
	A	Ⓐ		⑤f	Ⓐ		Ⓑ			Ⓐ	Ⓐ	†		①–④	⑥	Ⓑ			⑤⑦*	n		⑤	①–④	⑤⑦	⑤–⑦
		2	2	2		2	2	2	2	2	2	2		h	2	2	2		k	2	L	d	e 2	w	v 2
Paris Gare de Lyon **370** d.	...	...	...	...	1428	...	...	...	...	...	...	...	1728	1728	...	...	...	1928	1928	...	...	2028	...	2128	...
Dijon 375 d.	1450	1453	...	1557	1608	1615	1642	1716	1750	1814	1831	1836	1908	1908	1851	1915	2004	2111	2111	2115	2142	2210	2219	2308	2315
Dole **375** d.	1516	1526	...	1629	1634	1647	1727	1750	1829	1846	1908	1910	1934	1934	1923	1950	2036	2137	2137	2146	2208	2238	2251	2334	2344
Besançon Viotte a.	1539	1558	...	1656	1703	1724	1803	1818	1906	1915	1944	1943	1959	1959	1951	2018	2107	2205	2205	2214	2232	2301	2319	0001	0009
Besançon Viotte 384 d.	1541	...	1631	...	...	1728	...	1820	1909	...	...	...	...	2006	...	2020p	...	...	2208	2223q	...	...	...	...	...
Montbéliard 384 d.	1634	...	1732	...	...	1827	...	1922	2019	...	...	...	...	2055	...	2118p	...	...	2259	2321q	...	...	...	...	...
Belfort ▲ 384 a.	1652	...	1745	...	...	1841	...	1937	2035	...	...	...	...	2110	...	2134p	...	...	2313	2336q	...	...	...	...	...

		TGV 6700	TGV 5152/3		TGV 6754					TGV 5156/7	TGV 6756	TGV 6756										TGV 6762	TGV 6762	4251 4250	
	Ⓐ	①	Ⓐ	Ⓐ	Ⓐ	①⑦	T		②–⑥	Ⓒ	Ⓒ	Ⓐ	⚒	⚒	Ⓐ		Ⓒ	Ⓐ				⑥j		B	⚒
	2	g	L	2	z	R 2	2	2	R 2	L	m		2	2	2	2	2	2	2	2	2				2
Belfort ★ 384 d.	...	...	...	...	...	0453	0501	...	0519	...	...	0552	...	0556	0625	0638	...	0729	0812	0917	...	0945	...	0951	...
Montbéliard ★ 384 d.	...	...	...	...	...	0509	0517	...	0534	...	...	0606	...	0611	0640	0653	...	0745	0827	0933	...	0959	...	1004	...
Besançon Viotte 384 a.	...	...	...	...	...	0620	0620	...	0642	...	...	0655	...	0723	0740	0815	...	0844	0930	1032	...	1048	...	1103	...
Besançon Viotte d.	0508	0524	0540	0545	0556	...	...	0626	...	0652	0702	0705	0710	0728	0742	0817	0909	...	...	...	...	1055	1055	1105	1227
Dole **375** d.	0535	0549	0605	0613	0621	...	...	0657	...	0717	0727	0731	0753	0757	0817	0900	0938	...	...	...	1110	|	|	1129	1306
Dijon 375 a.	0605	0613	0629	0641	0645	...	...	0734	...	0741	0751	0755	0821	0831	0849	0932	1011	...	...	...	1141	1145	1145	1152	1343
Paris Gare de Lyon **370** a.	...	0800	...	...	0837	...	...	...	...	...	0938	0938	...	...	...	...	...	...	...	...	...	1331	1331	...	...

		TGV 6766							TGV 6774				TGV 6776									TGV 6770			
	t	Ⓐ	†	⚒			Ⓐ					Ⓐ	Ⓑ	Ⓐ	Ⓒ	⚒	⚒	†	Ⓐ	Ⓑ	†	⑦r	Ⓐ	N	
	2		2	2	2	2	2	2		2	2	2	y	2	2	2	2	2	2	2	2		2	2	2
Belfort ★ 384 d.	1138	...	...	1217t	1326t	...	...	1535	1546	...	...	1623	...	1710	...	1735	...	1805	1815	...	1910	...	1934	2014	...
Montbéliard ★ 384 d.	1153	...	...	1233t	1341t	...	...	1550	1600	...	...	1639	...	1726	...	1751	...	1820	1830	...	1925	...	1949	2030	...
Besançon Viotte 384 a.	1255	...	...	1343t	1445t	...	...	1652	1657	...	...	1750	...	1825	...	1907	...	1924	1934	...	2025	...	2049	2129	...
Besançon Viotte d.	...	1301	1308	1346	1448	1530	1638	...	1703	1710	1727	1752	1800	1827	1835	...	1914	...	...	2001	...	2030	...	2132	2132
Dole **375** d.	...	1327	1339	1417	1525	1605	1714	...	1728	1746	1807	1830	1826	1905	1911	...	1959	...	...	2031	...	|	...	2202	2202
Dijon 375 a.	...	1352	1409	1450	1559	1638	1748	...	1754	1819	1843	1906	1851	1936	1940	...	2031	...	...	2102	...	2118	...	2236	2236
Paris Gare de Lyon **370** a.	...	1537	...	...	...	...	...	...	1940	...	...	...	2037	...	...	...	...	...	...	...	...	2303	...	...	...

A – June 14 - Sept. 21. (12) Cerbère (**4340**) - Dijon - Strasbourg.
B – June 13 - Sept. 20. (12) Strasbourg - Dijon (**4241**) - Portbou.
L – (12) Lille - Charles de Gaulle ✈ - Besançon and v.v.
N – Until Feb. 24 only.
R – From Feb. 19 only.
T – Until Feb. 18 only.

d – Also Apr. 30, May 7; not May 2.
e – Not Dec. 25, Jan. 1, Mar. 24, Apr. 30, May 1, 7, 8, 12.
f – Also Apr. 30, May 7.
g – Also Dec. 26, Jan. 2, Mar. 25, May 13; not Dec. 24, 31, Mar. 24, May 12.
h – Also May 2; not Dec. 25, Jan. 1, Mar. 24, Apr. 30, May 1, 7, 8, 12.

j – Also May 1, 8.
k – Also Dec. 25, Jan. 1, Mar. 24, Apr. 30, May 7, 12; not May 2.
m – Not Mar. 23.
n – Not Apr. 30, May 7.
p – Ⓑ to Mar. 2; ⑦ from Mar. 9 (also Mar. 24, May 12).
q – ⑤⑥† to Feb. 17; ⑥⑦ from Feb. 23 (also Mar. 24, May 12).
r – Also Dec. 25, Jan. 1, Mar. 24, May 12.
t – Not Mar. 17–21, 25–28.
v – Also Dec. 25, Jan. 1, Mar. 24, Apr. 30, May 1, 7, 8, 12.
w – Also Dec. 25, Jan. 1, Mar. 24, Apr. 30, May 7, 12; not Mar. 23, May 2.

y – Not Dec. 24, 31, May 1, 8.
z – Not Dec. 24, 31.

TGV– Ⓡ, supplement payable, 🍸.

▲ – Arrivals at Belfort may be up to 7 minutes later from Feb. 25.
★ – Departures from Belfort and Montbéliard may be up to 8 minutes **earlier** from Feb. 25.

375 DIJON - LAUSANNE and BERN

km	*Special global fares payable for international journeys*				TGV 6751		TGV 9281	TGV 9261				TGV 9269			TGV 9271			TGV 9273	TGV 9285	TGV 9287			TGV 9277		
		Ⓐ	⚒	Ⓐ	Ⓐ	Ⓑ	Ⓑh		Ⓒ	⑥	⑥		⚒	†	⑦	Ⓒ	Ⓐ		⑤			⑤		⑤†	⑤†
		2	2	2		2		B	2	2	2		2	2	k	2	2	B	f	L	2	2d		2d	2d
0	*Paris Gare de Lyon* **370** d.	...	...	...	0658	...	0758	0758	...	...	...	1258	...	...	1410	...	...	1558	1558	1658	...	...	1758	...	...
315	**Dijon 374** d.	0512	...	...	0843	...	0938	0938	0956	*1136*	*1215*	1440	...	...	1550	1700	1700	1738	1738	1846	...	...	1938	...	...
361	Dole **374** a.	0543	...	...	0907	...	|	|	1020	*1211*	*1252*	1504	...	...	|	1734	1729	1802	1802	|	...	...	|	...	...
361	Dole d.	...	0626	...	...	0931	|	|	1021	1220	1258	1506	...	1555	|	1739	1735	1805	1805	|	1810	...	|	2032	2141
393	Mouchard d.	...	0644	...	...	0955	1022	1022	1100c	1244	1327	|	...	1616	|	1759	1758	|	|	1935	1844	...	2022	2103c	2200
417	Andelot d.	...	0708	0712	...	1020	|	|	1122	1313	1351	|	...	|	|	1821	1822	|	|	|	1905	1910	|	2128	2218
466	Morez a.	...	|	0821	...	1117	|	|	1218	|	1444	|	...	|	|	1915	1926	|	|	|	|	2009	|	2221	|
466	Morez d.	...	|	0849	...	1121	|	|	1234	|	1517	|	...	|	|	1924	1930	|	|	|	|	2013	|	2225	|
489	**St Claude** a.	...	|	0914	...	1145	|	|	1258	|	1542	|	...	|	|	1949	1954	|	|	|	|	2037	|	2250	|
438	Frasne d.	...	0722	...	...	...	1059	1102	...	1327	...	1601	1608	1646	1707	...	...	1900	1900	2010	1926	...	2059	...	2233
454	Pontarlier 🏛 a.	...	0739	...	...	...	1110	|	...	1342	...	|	1619	1700	|	...	...	|	1911	2021	1942	...	|	...	2243
462	Vallorbe 🏛 a.	...	...	...	...	...	|	1117	...	...	...	1616	...	...	1723	...	...	1917	|	|	...	...	2114	...	...
508	**Lausanne** a.	...	...	...	...	...	|	1152	...	...	...	1652	...	...	1758	...	...	1952	|	|	...	...	2152	...	...
518	Neuchâtel **511** a.	...	...	...	...	...	1156	...	...	...	...	...	...	...	...	...	...	...	1957	2107	...	...	...	...	...
561	**Bern 511** a.	...	...	...	...	...	1243	...	...	...	...	...	...	...	...	...	...	...	2034	2141	...	...	...	...	...

Special global fares payable for international journeys						TGV 9260		TGV 9284	TGV 9264				🚌		TGV 9268		TGV 6774					TGV 9288	TGV 9272		TGV 9274
	⚒	Ⓐ	①	Ⓐ	⚒				①–⑥	Ⓒ	⚒	Ⓒ	†	⚒		⚒		Ⓒ	†	Ⓐ		Ⓑh	Ⓑh	†	⑤–⑦
	2	2	g2	2	2		2		n	2	2	2			B	2		2	2	2	2			2	mB
Bern 511 d.	...	...	...	...	...	...	...	0817	...	...	...	...	...	...	...	...	...	...	...	...	...	1717	...	...	...
Neuchâtel **511** d.	...	...	...	...	...	...	...	0902	...	...	...	...	...	...	...	...	...	...	...	...	...	1802	...	...	...
Lausanne d.	...	...	...	...	...	0703	...	|	0903	...	...	...	...	...	1303	...	...	...	...	...	...	|	1803	...	1922
Vallorbe 🏛 d.	...	...	...	...	...	0745	...	|	0940	...	...	...	...	...	1342	...	...	...	...	...	...	|	1840	...	2005
Pontarlier 🏛 d.	0502	...	...	0557	...	|	...	0945	|	1220	...	...	1340	1346	|	...	...	1627	1718	1730	...	1845	|	...	|
Frasne d.	0514	...	...	0611	...	0805	...	1007	1007	1236	...	...	1400	1357	1402	...	...	1641	1736	1748	...	1906	1906	...	2025
St Claude d.	|	...	0443	|	0616	|	0821	|	|	|	...	1207	...	...	|	1448	...	|	|	|	1637	|	|	1852	|
Morez a.	|	...	0507	|	0642	|	0847	|	|	|	...	1232	...	...	|	1514	...	|	|	|	1702	|	|	1917	|
Morez d.	|	...	0511	|	0650	|	0852	|	|	|	...	1246	...	...	|	1524	...	|	|	|	1706	|	|	1922	|
Andelot d.	0528	...	0610	0626	0759c	|	0950	|	|	1250	...	1345	...	...	|	1624	...	1702	1751	1802	1811c	|	|	2018	|
Mouchard d.	0546	...	0642c	0646	0819	0840	1014r	|	|	1319c	...	1409	...	...	|	1656	...	1719	1816	...	1844	1936	1936	2045	2058
Dole a.	0604	...	0701	0711	0845	|	1041	1056	1056	1343	...	1432	...	...	|	1718	...	1738	1836	...	1901	|	|	2106	2115
Dole **374** d.	...	0613	...	0713	*0900*	|	...	1058	1058	...	1417	1435	...	...	|	...	1728	*1746*	1837	...	1902e	|	|	...	2117
Dijon 374 a.	...	0641	...	0747	*0932*	0921	...	1122	1122	...	1450	1509	...	...	1512	...	1754	*1819*	1907	...	1927e	2017	2017	...	2141
Paris Gare de Lyon **370** a.	...	...	...	...	...	1103	...	1303	1303	...	...	...	...	...	1655	...	1938	...	...	...	...	2159	2159	...	2324

B – To / from Brig on dates in Table **42**.
L – ①②③④⑥⑦ (also May 2; not Apr. 30, May 7).
c – Arrives 9–13 minutes earlier.
d – Also Apr. 30, May 7.
e – ⑤⑥† (also Apr. 30, May 7).

f – Also Apr. 30, May 7.
g – Also Dec. 26, Jan. 2, Mar. 25, May 2, 9, 13; not Mar. 24, May 12.
h – Not May 1, 8.
k – Also Dec. 25, Jan. 1, Feb. 23, Mar. 1, 24, May 12.
m – Also Dec. 25, Jan. 1, Mar. 24, Apr. 30, May 1, 7, 8, 12; not May 2.

n – Not Dec. 25, Jan. 1, Mar. 24, May 12.
r – 1019 on Ⓐ.

TGV – Ⓡ, supplement payable, 🍸.

LAROCHE MIGENNES - AUXERRE - AUTUN — 376

2nd class only

km		Ⓐ	⚒		⚒		†	⊙		⚒	⚒	⚒	Ⓐ	†w			⑥	⊙			F	G	A	D	H	⑤d
	Paris Lyon 370 d.	...	...	...	...	...	...	...	*1231*	*1231*	*1338*	...	...	...	...	...	...	*1704*a	...	...	...	...	*1904*	*1904*	*2025*k	*2025*
	Paris Bercy 370 d.	...	...	...	0704	0836	...	...	|	|	|	...	...	...	1639	...	...	|	1837	...	...	...	|	|	|	|
0	**Laroche Migennes** d.	0604	0642	0745	0833	0957	...	1221	1356	1356	1611	1721	1721	1721	1801	1812	1812	1907	2007	2026	2026	2026	2057	2117	2220	2229
19	**Auxerre** a.	0620	0702	0800	0845	1010	...	1243	1413	1413	1627	1736	1736	1737	1816	1831	1831	1920	2019	2043	2043	2043	2112	2132	2236	2245
19	**Auxerre** d.	0623	...	...	0846	▬	1038	...	...	1414	...	...	1738	1738	...	1834	1834	...	2023	▬	2045	2045	...	2133	...	...
36	Cravant Bazarnes a.	0639	...	...	0902	...	1055	...	...	1429	...	...	1750	1754	...	1851	1851	...	2040	...	2102	2102	...	2147	...	...
36	Cravant Bazarnes d.	0646	...	...	0909	...	1102	...	...	1436	...	...	1802	1801	...	...	1857	...	2047	...	...	2136	...	2156	...	...
60	Sermizelles-Vézelay d.	0717	...	...	0941	⚒	1132	...	...	1506	...	...	1832	1831	...	...	1928	...	2117	⑤f	...	2206	...	2224	...	...
74	Avallon d.	0733	...	...	0957	1033	1148	...	...	1524	...	...	1848	1848	...	...	1944	...	2133	2138	...	2222	...	2240	...	...
161	**Autun** a.	...	...	...	...	1229	...	...	...	1721	...	...	...	2046	...	...	...	...	...	2335	...	...	...	...	...	...
	Étang **371** a.	...	...	...	...	1248	...	...	...	1745	...	...	...	...	...	...	...	...	...	...	...	...	...	...	...	...

	⚒	⚒		⚒		Ⓐ		⊙	†	⚒	⚒				Ⓐ		⑥		†	Ⓐ	†w	†w	Ⓐ	Ⓐ		⑤⑥f
Étang **371** d.	...	...	...	...	...	...	...	...	...	0810	...	...	...	...	1254	...	...	...	...	...	1620	...	...	...	...	1620
Autun d.	...	...	...	...	...	...	...	...	...	0836	...	...	...	...	1324	...	...	...	...	...	1638	...	...	...	...	1725
Avallon d.	...	...	0506	0558	...	0658	...	...	1011	1029	1032	...	...	...	1520	...	1627	...	1709	...	1834	1851	...	1900	...	1918
Sermizelles-Vézelay d.	...	...	0524	0614	...	0715	...	...	1027	...	1050	...	...	...	▬	...	1645	...	1726	...	▬	1907	...	1917	...	...
Cravant Bazarnes a.	...	...	0555	0644	...	0744	...	...	1057	...	1120	...	...	...	...	...	1715	...	1756	...	...	1935	...	1946	...	...
Cravant Bazarnes d.	...	0528	0603	0652	...	0751	...	...	1112	...	1127	1127	...	1504a	...	...	1722	1722	1806	...	...	1943	1940	2000	...	...
Auxerre a.	...	0545	0621	0708	...	0807	...	...	1129	...	1143	1143	...	1519a	⊙	...	1737	1737	1822	...	⑥	1955	1957	2014	...	...
Auxerre d.	0454	0546	0623	0709	0709	0808	0808	1028	...	...	1144	1144	1323	1520	1600	1629	1739	1739	1836	1847	1931	1956	1958	...	2137	...
Laroche Migennes a.	0507	0603	0636	0725	0725	0823	0823	1043	...	...	1156	1156	1340	1537	1615	1642	1758	1758	1849	1909	1949	2012	2014	...	2153	...
Paris Bercy **370** a.	0638	|	0759	|	|	|	|	|	...	...	1319	1319	|	|	...	1811	|	|	2025	|	|	|	...	...	|	...
Paris Lyon **370** a.	...	*0741*a	...	*0855*	*0855*	*1043*	*1043*q	*1257*	...	...	...	...	*1541*h	*1747*	...	...	*1935*	*1935*	...	*2142*	*2142*	*2323*	...	...	*2329*	...

A – ①②③④⑥ (not Dec. 24, 25, 31, Jan. 1, Mar. 24, Apr. 30, May 1, 7, 8, 12).
D – ①–④ (not Dec. 24, 25, 31, Jan. 1, Mar. 24, Apr. 30, May 1, 7, 8, 12).
F – ⑤⑥† (also Dec. 24, 31, Apr. 30, May 7).
G – ⑤† (also Dec. 24, 31, Apr. 30, May 7).
H – ①②③④⑥⑦ (also May 2; not Apr. 30, May 7).

a – Ⓐ only.
d – Also Apr. 30, May 7; not May 2.
f – Also Dec. 24, 31, Apr. 30, May 7.
h – *1549* on ⑥.
k – *2020* on †. *2023* on ⑥.

q – *1039* on †.
w – Not Mar. 23, May 11.

⊙ – From / to Dijon (Table **370**).

LYON - ST CLAUDE - MOREZ — 377

Most 2nd class

All services Bourg en Bresse - Oyonnax and v.v. are currently operated by 🚌.

km			⚒	⚒🚌	🚌	🚌					G
	Lyon Perrache 384 d.	...	0804	...	...	...	1604	...	...	1704	1824
0	**Lyon Part Dieu 384** d.	...	0816	1116	1316	1516	1616	...	...	1716	1838
65	Bourg en Bresse **384** a.	...	0926	1229	1429	1629	1726	...	...	1826	1930
		Ⓐ	⚒	⚒			Ⓐ				¶
65	Bourg en Bresse 🚌 d.	0624	0928	1310	1515	1646	1745	...	...	1844	1947
101	Brion-M-La Cluse ⊠ 🚌 d.	0709	1013	1350	|	1731	1825	...	...	1958	2034
114	Oyonnax 🚌 a.	0729	1033	1406	1614	1757	1840	...	...	2030	2055
		⚒	¶	⚒⊡				†	⚒		¶
114	Oyonnax d.	0747	1047	1410	1650	...	...	1925	1951	...	2105
147	**St Claude 375** a.	0821	1120	1443	1723	...	...	1959	2025	...	2138
170	**Morez 375** a.	0847	...	1514	...	...	...	2025	2050r	...	...

		D								◇
Morez 375 d.	...	...	...	0644	...	1121b	...	...	...	...
St Claude 375 d.	...	0523	...	0709	...	1146	...	1527	1727	2002
Oyonnax a.	...	0557	...	0743	...	1220	...	1600	1800	2036
	Ⓐ	⚒	Ⓐ							▬
Oyonnax 🚌 d.	0507	0609	0637	0752	1015	1230	1404	1652	1810	...
Brion-M-La Cluse ⊠ 🚌 d.	0527	0629	0702	0813	1040	1248	1424	1715	1827	...
Bourg en Bresse 🚌 a.	0612	0714	0753	0910	1125	1330	1509	1800	1945	...
	⚒	¶	⚒	⚒🚌	🚌		🚌		†	⚒🚌
Bourg en Bresse **384** d.	0630	0730	0830	0930	1130	1445	1530	1830	2030	2030
Lyon Part Dieu 384 a.	0739	0839	0939	1048	1248	1529	1648	1939	2139	2148
Lyon Perrache 384 a.	0751	0851	0954	...	...	...	...	1951	2151	...

km				⚒🚌			🚌				
0	Oyonnax d.	...	...	*1330*a	...	...	*1810*	...	...	...	...
13	Brion-M-La Cluse ⊠ d.	...	...	1405	...	...	1840	...	...	...	...
41	Bellegarde a.	...	...	1450	...	...	1925	...	...	...	...

						⚒🚌			🚌	
Bellegarde d.	...	...	...	...	...	1255	...	...	1730	...
Brion-M-La Cluse ⊠ a.	...	...	...	...	...	1340	...	...	1815	...
Oyonnax a.	...	...	...	...	...	*1406*	...	...	*1857*	...

D – ②–⑥ (not Dec. 25, 26, Jan. 1, 2, Mar. 25, May 1, 2, 8, 9, 13).
G – ①②③④⑥.

a – Ⓐ only.
b – Ⓑ only.
– Also Dec. 24, 26, 27, 31.
– 2105 on ⑤ (also Apr. 30, May 7).

| – Daily.
⊠ – Brion-Montréal-La Cluse.

⊡ – Also runs Oyonnax - St Claude on † (depart 1415, arrive 1449).
◇ – On ⚒ departs St Claude 2027, arrives Oyonnax 2101.

Additional stopping trains Lyon Part Dieu - Bourg en Bresse and v.v. (see also Table **384** for other fast trains).
From Lyon Part Dieu: 0716⚒, 0916†, 0916Ⓐ🚌, 1016⚒🚌, 1116†, 1216⑤⑥†**f**, 1416⑤⑥†**f**, 1640Ⓐ, 1740Ⓐ, 1816Ⓐ, 1842Ⓐ, 1916, 2016 and 2116🚌.
From Bourg en Bresse: 0530⚒, 0600Ⓐ, 0700Ⓐ, 1030⚒🚌, 1030†, 1230⑤⑥†**f**, 1330⑤⑥**f**, 1430⑤, 1630Ⓐ, 1730 and 1930.

BESANÇON - LE LOCLE - LA CHAUX DE FONDS — 378

2nd class

km		A		Ⓐ		⑥	⑦v	A	Ⓐ		†
0	**Besançon Viotte** d.	...	...	0715	1003	1225	1346	1356	1722	1824	1950
67	Morteau d.	0624	0726	0840	1124	1350	1502	1520	1856	1952	2112
80	Le Locle **512** a.	0640	0741	...	1140	...	...	1540	...	2008	...
88	**La Chaux de F 512** a.	0650*	0751*	...	1150*	...	...	1550*	...	2017*	...

	A	⚒		Ⓐ	⑥		Ⓐ	⑥	†	
La Chaux de F 512 d.	0554*	...	0810*	...	...	1610*	1710*	...	...	2041*
Le Locle **512** d.	0601	...	0820	...	...	1620	1720	...	...	2051
Morteau d.	0617	0650	0842	1137	1227	1639	1738	1825	1955	2108
Besançon Viotte a.	...	0811	1001	1301	1348	1755	1858	1947	2111	...

A – ①–⑤ (not Dec. 25, 26, Jan. 1, 2, Mar. 21, 24, May 1, 12).
v – Also Dec. 25, 26, Jan. 1, 2, Mar. 21, 24, May 1, 12.

* – Subject to alteration from Mar. 1.

CORSICAN RAILWAYS — 379

Narrow gauge. 2nd class only

Service November 19 - April 13

During track renewal service is by 🚌 between Corte and Ajaccio (to mid-April) and between Ponte Leccia and Calvi (to mid-June)

km	⚒		⚒		⚒		⚒		⚒		⚒	⚒		Ⓐ	
0	**Bastia** d.	...	0638	...	0903	...	1011	...	1520	...	1655	...	...	1823	...
21	Casamozza a.	...	0704	...	0932	...	1045	...	1546	...	1721	...	...	1857	...
21	Casamozza d.	...	0706	...	0934	...	1050*	...	1548	...	1723	...	...	1859	...
47	Ponte Leccia a.	...	0739	...	1005	...	1122*	...	1619	...	1757	...	...	1933	...
47	Ponte Leccia d.	...	0741	...	1007	...	1132*	...	1621	...	1759	1802*	...	1935	...
99	Ile Rousse a.	...	|	...	|	...	1215*	...	|	...	|	1845*	...	|	...
99	Ile Rousse d.	...	|	...	|	...	1215*	...	|	...	|	1845*	...	|	...
120	**Calvi** a.	...	|	...	|	...	1244*	...	|	...	|	1914*	...	|	...
74	Corté d.	...	0825	...	1051	...	...	...	1704	...	1841	...	...	2009	...
152	**Ajaccio Gare** a.	...	1015*	...	1241*	...	...	...	1854*	...	2031*	...	...	...	...

†	†		†		†	†	†	
Bastia d.	0935	...	1040	...	1712	1825	...	...
Casamozza a.	1001	...	1114	...	1738	1858	...	...
Casamozza d.	1003	...	1117*	...	1740	1900	...	...
Ponte Leccia a.	1034	...	1149*	...	1816	1931	...	...
Ponte Leccia d.	1036	...	1158*	...	1818	1935	1940*	...
Ile Rousse a.	|	...	1239*	...	|	|	2021*	...
Ile Rousse d.	|	...	1239*	...	|	|	2021*	...
Calvi a.	|	...	1308*	...	|	|	2050*	...
Corté d.	1119	...	...	...	1901	2009	...	...
Ajaccio Gare a.	1309*	...	...	...	2051*	...	...	...

⚒		⚒		⚒		⚒		⚒			⚒	⚒		⚒	
Ajaccio Gare d.	...	...	...	0630*	...	...	...	0851*	...	...	...	1503*	...	1640*	...
Corté d.	...	0644	...	0824	...	...	...	1053	...	...	...	1702	...	1838	...
Calvi d.	...	|	...	|	...	0849*	...	|	...	...	1621*	|	...	|	...
Ile Rousse a.	...	|	...	|	...	0921*	...	|	...	...	1653*	|	...	|	...
Ile Rousse d.	...	|	...	|	...	0921*	...	|	...	...	1653*	|	...	|	...
Ponte Leccia a.	...	0717	...	0858	...	1001*	...	1127	...	...	1733*	1736	...	1912	...
Ponte Leccia d.	...	0719	...	0900	...	1010*	...	1129	...	...	...	1738	...	1914	...
Casamozza a.	...	0751	...	0932	...	1045*	...	1200	...	...	...	1811	...	1947	...
Casamozza d.	...	0753	...	0934	...	1049	...	1202	...	...	...	1813	...	1949	...
Bastia a.	...	0825	...	1000	...	1121	...	1230	...	...	...	1842	...	2015	...

†	†		†		†		†	
Ajaccio Gare d.	...	...	0919*	...	...	...	1701*	...
Corté d.	...	...	1119	...	...	...	1900	...
Calvi d.	0920*	...	|	...	1658*	...	|	...
Ile Rousse a.	0950*	...	|	...	1728*	...	|	...
Ile Rousse d.	0950*	...	|	...	1728*	...	|	...
Ponte Leccia a.	1030*	...	1153	...	1808*	...	1935	...
Ponte Leccia d.	1039*	...	1155	...	1823	...	1937*	...
Casamozza a.	1110*	...	1226	...	1856	...	2008	...
Casamozza d.	1116	...	1228	...	1858	...	2010	...
Bastia a.	1148	...	1254	...	1924	...	2036	...

* – By 🚌.

Additional "Tramway de la Balagne" services operate between Ile Rousse and Calvi from April to October.
Additional "Tramway Suburbain" local services operate between Bastia and Casamozza.

380 PARIS - TROYES - BELFORT - MULHOUSE

km	*For TGV see Table **390**																							
			1541	1039		1041	1841	1545	1545		1043	1043	1043	1547	1045	1045	11641	1047	1641	1741	1049	1643	1549	1645
		Ⓐ	①–⑥	①–⑥	Ⓐ	⑦	⚒	Ⓐ	Ⓒ		⑦	⑥	Ⓐ		①–⑤	⑦	Ⓐ		Ⓐ			Ⓐ		Ⓑ
		2	n	🍷n	2	e				2y	e	t			🍷h	🍷		🍷			🍷w		⊗	z◇
0	**Paris Est** d.	...	0642	0711	...	0812	0942	1209	1213	...	1243	1313	1313	1409r	1509	1516	1611	1641	1711	1811	1841	1911	2013	2213
110	Nogent sur Seine d.	0650	0739	|	...	0910	1040	1308	1308	...	|	|	|	1512	|	|	1717	|	1813	1911	|	2011	2108	2310
129	Romilly sur Seine d.	0702	0751	|	...	0924	1053	1320	1320	...	|	|	|	1523	|	|	1730	|	1827	1924	|	2024	2121	2324
166	**Troyes** d.	0722	0810	0836	...	0946	1115	1340	1340	...	1408	1438	1438	1544	1638	1638	1751	1805	1850	1946	2007	2046	2141	2346
221	Bar sur Aube d.	0753	0841	|	...	1020	|	1412	1412	...	|	|	|	1615	|	|	...	1841	...	2020	|	...	2212	▬
262	Chaumont **382** d.	0813	0903	0926	...	1045	1205	1433	1433	...	1500	1528	1528	1637	1728	1728	...	1906	...	2045	2057	...	2235	...
296	Langres **382** d.	▬	0923	|	...	1107	|	1453	1453	...	|	|	|	1657	|	|	...	1927	...	2107	|	...	2254	...
307	Culmont Chalindrey **382** d.	...	0931	|	...	1117	|	1501	1501	...	|	|	|	1706	|	|	...	1937	...	2117	|	...	2303	...
380	Vesoul d.	...	▬	1029	...	1156	1307	▬	...	...	1605	1631	1631	...	1829	1829	...	2015	...	...	2159	...	...	2
410	Lure d.	Ⓐ	2s	1049	...	1217	...	2	...	...	|	|	|	...	1849	1849	...	2035	...	...	2219	...	...	⚒
442	**Belfort** ▷ **384** d.	0805	1010	1110	1155	1238	...	1355	...	1635	1640	1706	1708	...	1912	1912	...	2059	...	...	2242	...	...	0659
491	**Mulhouse** ▷ **384** a.	0836	1044	...	1234	...	...	1434	...	1709	...	...	1739	...	1943	1943	...	2130	...	...	2309	...	...	0736

	1640	11640	1740	1940	1940	1742	1540	1040	1542			1642	1042	1644	1840	1544		1044	1548		1048	1046	1046	
	①–⑥	Ⓐ	Ⓐ	⑥	Ⓐ	⑦	①–⑥			Ⓐ	Ⓒ	⚒		Ⓐ	Ⓑ		Ⓐ			Ⓒ	⑦	Ⓐ	①–⑥	
	n⊕			🍷t	🍷b	e	n	🍷		2	2v		🍷		h		2	🍷	⊗	2	🍷e	🍷w	nw	2u
Mulhouse ▷ **384** d.	...	...	...	0349	0422	...	...	0745	...	0855	0936	...	1246	...	...	...	1555	...	...	1659	...	1817	...	1955
Belfort ▷ **384** d.	...	...	...	0419	0452	...	...	0820	...	0930	1022	...	1321	...	...	...	1629	1649	...	1754	1824	1847	1847	2035
Lure d.	...	...	...	0439	0514	...	...	0844	...	...	...	...	1344	...	...	...	...	1711	...	...	1846	1909	1909	...
Vesoul d.	...	...	...	0500	0534	...	...	0903	...	...	...	...	1404	...	1601	...	...	1731	...	...	1906	1929	1929	...
Culmont Chalindrey **382** d.	...	...	0529	0540	0614	0713	0852	|	1049	...	...	...	|	...	|	1649	...	|	1823	...	1945	2008	2008	...
Langres **382** d.	...	...	0540	0550	0625	0724	0902	|	1059	...	...	...	|	...	|	1700	...	|	1833	...	1956	|	|	...
Chaumont **382** d.	...	...	0602	0611	0646	0746	0922	1005	1119	...	...	...	1506	...	1706	1720	...	1834	1854	...	2017	2035	2035	...
Bar sur Aube d.	...	...	0624	0634	0709	0808	0943	|	1140	...	...	...	|	...	|	1741	...	|	1915	...	2038	|	|	...
Troyes d.	0509	0602	0658	0707	0742	0841	1015	1051	1211	...	...	1443	1552	1643	1751	1812	...	1921	1946	...	2112	2121	2121	...
Romilly sur Seine d.	0530	0625	0720	0729	0804	0903	1035	|	1231	...	...	1504	|	1705	|	1832	...	|	2006	...	2134	|	|	...
Nogent sur Seine d.	0543	0639	0734	0742	0817	0916	1048	|	1243	...	...	1517	|	1717	|	1844	...	|	2018	...	2147	|	|	...
Paris Est a.	0645	0745	0830	0841	0915	1015	1146	1218	1341	...	...	1615	1714	1814	1914	1944	...	2044	2115	...	2244	2244	2244	...

b – Not May 9.
e – Also Dec. 25, Jan. 1, Mar. 24, May 12.
h – Not May 1, 8.
n – Not Dec. 25, Jan. 1, Mar. 24, May 12.
r – 1416 on Ⓒ.
s – On Ⓒ d. 1052, a. 1130.
t – Also May 1, 8.
u – Arrive 2049 on ⑥.
v – On ⑥ d. 0955, a. 1034.
w – Not Dec. 24, 31.
y – On Ⓒ depart 1640, arrive 1718.
z – Not Dec. 24, 31, Mar. 23, May 1, 8, 11.
◇ – On Ⓐ Jan. 7 - Mar. 4 Paris d. 2017, Troyes a. 2150.
▷ – Other local trains run.
⊕ – Subject to alteration on Apr. 14.
⊗ – Subject to alteration on Apr. 13.

381 PARIS - CHÂLONS EN CHAMPAGNE - BAR LE DUC

km											2777						2785							
		Ⓐ	Ⓐ	Ⓐ	Ⓒ	Ⓒ	⑥	Ⓐ	†				Ⓐ		①–⑤		Ⓑ		①–⑤	⑤	Ⓒ	Ⓐ	⑤	†
					2	2					♥	2					♥h	2		u			d	
0	**Paris Est** d.	0635	0735	0835	0835	...	1035	1035	1035	1235	1357	...	1435	1635	1735	1835	1927	...	1935	1935	2035	2135	2135	2235
95	Château Thierry d.	0730	0830	0930	0930	...	1123	1123	1123	1324	|	...	1523	1722	1830	1930	|	...	2030	2030	2122	2222	2222	2323
142	Épernay d.	0758	0858	0954	0957	...	1147	1147	1147	1351	|	...	1547	1750	1854	1958	|	...	2057	2057	2150	2246	2246	2348
	Champagne-Ardenne TGV d.	|	|	|	|	...	|	|	|	|	1440	...	|	|	|	|	2010	...	|	|	|	|	|	|
172	**Châlons en Champagne** ▷ d.	0814	0915	1010	1014	...	1203	1203	1203	1408	1503	...	1604	1807	1910	2015	2033	...	2114	2115	2206	2303	2304	0004
205	Vitry le François ▷ d.	0832	0933	...	1032	1047	1221	1221	...	1426	1521	1530	1622	1825	...	2033	2052	2057	...	2133	...	...	2322	...
234	**St Dizier** ▷ a.	0850	*1000*	...	|	1107	1241	*1255*	...	1444	|	1550	1641	|	...	2051	|	2115	...	2151	...	...	|	...
255	**Bar le Duc** ▷ a.	...	0957	...	1056	...	...	1247	...	...	1545	...	...	1851	...	...	2114	...	...	...	...	...	2347	...

				2778															2784					
	Ⓐ	①–⑥	⚒	①–⑥	Ⓐ	①	Ⓒ		†			Ⓐ	⑥		Ⓐ		Ⓑ			Ⓐ	⑥	†	①–④	
				♥n		g			2									2	♥				H	
Bar le Duc ▷ d.	...	...	...	0614	...	...	...	...	...	0925	...	...	0936	1132	1341	...	...	...	1713	...	...	...	...	1937
St Dizier ▷ d.	...	...	0611	|	0637	0738	0738	...	0918	|	...	0940	*0935*	*1122*	|	1539	...	1703	|	1738	1825	1828	1930	|
Vitry le François ▷ d.	...	...	0630	0639	0658	0758	0758	...	0938	0949	...	1001	1001	1156	1406	1600	...	1722	1738	1759	1845	1849	1950	2002
Châlons en Champagne ▷ d.	0519	0614	0649	0657	0715	0815	0815	0815	0955	1006	1019	1019	1019	1214	1424	1617	1716	1741	1757	1816	...	1906	...	2021
Champagne-Ardenne TGV d.	|	|	...	0720	|	|	|	|	...	...	|	|	|	|	|	|	|	...	1819	|	...	|	...	|
Épernay d.	0537	0632	...	|	0731	0832	0832	0832	...	...	1036	1036	1036	1231	1440	1633	1733	...	|	1832	...	1922	...	2037
Château Thierry d.	0600	0700	...	|	0800	0900	0900	0900	...	...	1100	1100	1100	1259	1503	1700	1800	...	|	1900	...	1950	...	2100
Paris Est a.	0650	0752	...	0800	0853	0953	0953	0953	...	...	1153	1153	1153	1350	1558	1751	1850	...	1900	1951	...	2038	...	2151

CHÂLONS EN CHAMPAGNE - VERDUN

2nd class

km		Ⓐv	Ⓒ	Ⓐz	Ⓐx	⑥	H◇	†	⑤k	
0	**Châlons en Champagne** d.	0821	1022	1223	1828	2026	2039	2040	2053	...
62	Ste Menehould d.	0907	1108	1311	1928	2113	2129	2127	2142	...
107	**Verdun** a.	0946	1147	1350	2006	2153	2210	2206	2222	...

	①	⚒v	†		Ⓐz	Ⓐ◇		x	
Verdun d.	0503	0613	0641	...	1043	1539	...	1845	...
Ste Menehould d.	0542	0651	0720	...	1120	1617	...	1923	...
Châlons en Champagne a.	0631	0740	0807	...	1208	1706	...	2009	...

H – ①–④ (not Dec. 24, 25, 31, Jan. 1, Mar. 24, Apr. 30, May 1, 7, 8, 12).
d – Also Apr. 30, May 7.
g – Also Dec. 26, Jan. 2, Mar. 25, May 13.
h – Not May 1, 8.
k – Also Dec. 24, 31, Apr. 30, May 7. To Metz (**393a**).
n – Not Dec. 25, Jan. 1, Mar. 24, May 12.
u – Also Dec. 24, 25, 31, Jan. 1, Mar. 24, Apr. 30, May 7, 12.
v – Subject to alteration Apr. 29, 30, May 6, 7.
x – Subject to alteration Apr. 28, 29, May 5, 6.
z – Subject to alteration ①–④ Apr. 28 - May 22.
♥ – *TGV* train, R, supplement payable, 🍷.
◇ – Subject to alteration Apr. 28 - May 7.
▷ – For other trains see Table **382**.

382 REIMS - CHÂLONS EN CHAMPAGNE - METZ / NANCY / DIJON

Some 2nd class

km		⑥t		Ⓐ	Ⓒ		①⑤y	⚒		⑤	†
0	**Reims** d.	...	...	0619	0751	...	...	...	1647	...	...
31	Épernay d.	0612	...	0646	0817	...	...	1620	1717	...	1822
61	**Châlons en Champ.** ◇ d.	0631	...	0704	0835	1140	...	1637	1736	...	1839
94	Vitry le François ◇ d.	0648	...	0722	0852	1157	...	1655	1753	...	1856
143	Bar le Duc ◇ d.	0717	0721	0748	0918	1225	1229	1720	1822	1922	1922
250	**Metz** a.	|	0814	|	|	|	1323	1814	|	2016	2014
183	Commercy d.	0739	...	0809	0939	1247	...	...	1843	...	...
209	Toul d.	0755	...	0825	0955	1303	...	...	1859	...	...
242	**Nancy** a.	0818	...	0846	1013	1322	...	...	1917	...	...

				①⑤y					†	⑤
Nancy d.	0701	...	1002	...	1330	1602	1801	...	2034	2041
Toul d.	0719	...	1023	...	1350	1621	1824	...	2055	2100
Commercy d.	0733	...	1044	...	1410	1636	1839	...	2110	2115
Metz d.	|	0829	|	1333	|	|	|	1830	|	|
Bar le Duc ◇ d.	0755	0925	1108	1425	1434	1659	1902	1928	2132	2137
Vitry le François ◇ d.	0823	0949	...	...	1501	...	1930	...	2159	2201
Châlons en Champ. ◇ d.	0841	1006	...	...	1519	...	1949	...	2217	2219
Épernay d.	0904	...	...	...	1535	...	2013	...	...	2236
Reims a.	0924	...	...	...	...	...	2036	...	...	...

km			14255						4287	
		Ⓑ	⑥		Ⓑ	Ⓒ	Ⓐ	L	P	⑤⑦
		b	t		2		2	2	R	d
0	**Reims** d.	0610	0853	1236	1640	1730	1748	1942	2019	2042
58	**Châlons en Champ.** ◇ d.	0655	0934	1317	1721	1815	1825	2038	2057	2124
91	Vitry le François ◇ d.	0715	0955	1338	1742	1835	1844	2057	2116	2144
120	St Dizier ◇ d.	0736	1015	1359	1806	1853	1901	2117	2138	2203
193	Chaumont § d.	0824	1102	1444	1853	▬	...	2201	2221	2246
227	Langres § d.	0846	1123	1506	1916	...	...	2222	|	2306
238	Culmont Chalindrey § a.	0855	1131	1514	1927	...	...	2230	2247	2314
238	Culmont Chalindrey d.	0857	1133	1516	...	1951	...	...	...	2317
315	**Dijon** a.	0949	1225	1606	...	2036	...	...	...	0012
	Lyon Part Dieu **373** a.	...	...	...	...	2229	...	...	...	...
	Lyon Perrache **373** a.	...	...	...	...	2242	...	...	...	...

		4332									14355
	⚒	P	Ⓐ	①	⑥⑦	⚒			⑤⑦	Ⓑ	⑥
	2	R	2	g	z	2	2		w	b	t
Lyon Perrache **373** d.	...	...	...	...	*0635*	...	...	...	...	...	...
Lyon Part Dieu **373** d.	...	...	...	...	*0648*	...	...	...	...	...	...
Dijon d.	...	...	...	...	*0839*	...	...	1553	1703	1852	1941
Culmont Chalindrey a.	...	...	...	...	*0924*	...	...	1659	1748	1950	2028
Culmont Chalindrey § d.	0534	0557	0655	0912	0945	1222v	...	1700	1755	1952	2030
Langres § d.	0545	|	0705	0921	0954	1232v	...	1711	1806	2002	2039
Chaumont § d.	0607	0628	0725	0942	1015	1252	...	1734	1826	2023	2100
St Dizier ◇ d.	0654	0713	0822	1026	1058	1340	1703	1824	1915	2106	2146
Vitry le François ◇ d.	0716	0735	0841	1047	1119	1400	1722	1848	1937	2128	2208
Châlons en Champ. ◇ d.	0741	0756	0902	1116	1140	...	1744	1912	1959	2148	2227
Reims a.	0825	0833	0943	1153	1222	...	1820	1951	2040	2226	2304

L – ①②③④⑥ (not Dec. 24, 25, 31, Jan. 1, Mar. 24, Apr. 30, May 1, 7, 8, 12)
P – From Reims and Nice on ⑤⑦ (not Mar. 23), also Dec. 19 - Jan. 6 (not Dec. 24, 31), Feb. 8 - 24, Mar. 24, Apr. 4 - 20, May 7 - 13. ▬ 2 cl. and [2] (reclining) Reims - Nice and v.v. (see Table 392).
b – Also May 3, 10; not May 1, 8.
d – Also Dec. 24, 25, 31, Jan. 1, Mar. 24, Apr. 30, May 1, 7, 8, 12.
g – Also Dec. 25, 26, Jan. 1, 2, Mar. 25, May 1, 2, 8, 9, 13; not Mar. 24, May 12.
t – Also May 1, 8; not May 3, 10.
v – ⑥ only.
w – Also Dec. 24, 25, 31, Jan. 1, Mar. 24, Apr. 30, May 1, 7, 8, 12.
y – Also Dec. 26, Jan. 2, Mar. 25, May 13; not Mar. 24, May 12.
z – 2nd class on ⑥.
◇ – For other trains see Table **381**.
§ – For other trains see Table **380**.

Additional trains: Bar le Duc - Nancy: 0603 Ⓐ, 0710 †, 0716 ⚒, 1010 Ⓐ, 1611 Ⓐ, 1911. Nancy - Bar le Duc: 1702 Ⓐ, 1704 Ⓒ, 1907 Ⓐ, 1939 ①–④ (not hols), 2032 ⑥.

METZ and NANCY - STRASBOURG 383

Some trains 2nd class

km														91									97			
		Ⓐ z	⑥	Ⓐ z	①–⑥	⚒ z	Ⓐ z	Ⓐ z			⚒ z	⑥	† u	V	Ⓐ z	⚒ z	⑥	Ⓐ z	† u	Ⓑ	Ⓐ z	† u	R	⚒ z	Ⓐ z	⚒ z
	Luxembourg **388** d.	...	...	...	0543	...	...	...	...	...	...	...	...	1046	...	...	...	...	...	...	...	...	1603	...	...	...
0	**Metz** d.	...	...	...	0631	...	0748	...	0857	...	...	...	...	1132	...	1225	...	1334	1334	...	...	...	1653	...	1711	1742
• 80	**Nancy** d.	...	...	0615	|	0715	|	0815	|	0915	0915	1115	1115	|	1215	|	1315	|	|	1415	1615	1615	|	1715	|	|
• 47	Lunéville d.	...	...	0633	|	0733	|	0833	|	0935	0935	1134	1132	|	1234	|	1332	|	|	1433	1634	1633	|	1732	|	|
88	Sarrebourg d.	0622	0623	0656	|	0759	0845	0858	0955	1000	1000	1202	1201	|	1259	1328	1402	|	1431	1454	1658	1656	|	1758	1811	|
91	Réding d.	0628	0629	0700	0729	|	|	|	|	|	|	|	|	|	|	1332	|	1422	|	|	|	|	|	1802	1816	1829
114	Saverne d.	0645	0648	0717	0747	0815	0902	0915	1011	1015	1015	1218	1217	|	1315	1350	1417	1438	1448	1512	1714	1712	|	1815	1830	1845
159	**Strasbourg** a.	0719	0719	0739	0817	0839	0931	0938	1040	1039	1039	1239	1239	1250	1343	1415	1439	1505	1514	1539	1739	1735	1813	1840	1856	1909
	Mulhouse **385** a.	0816	...	0845	...	0945	...	...	...	...	1146	...	...	1353	1454	...	...	...	...	...	1846	...	1922	...	...	...
	Basel **385** a.	0840	...	0910	...	1009	...	...	...	...	1210	...	...	1420	1519	...	...	...	...	...	1910	...	1948	...	...	...

										2583		295
	Ⓑ	⚒ z	⑥	Ⓐ z	†	Ⓐ z	† u	⑥	⑥	Ⓑ ♥h	† u	Ⓑ M
Luxembourg **388** d.	...	...	...	...	...	...	...	...	...	...	...	2026
etz d.	...	1820	...	...	...	1928	1931	1934	...	...	2051	2115
Nancy d.	1815	|	1915	1918	1920	|	|	|	2006	2045	|	|
Lunéville d.	1833	|	1934	1937	1937	|	|	|	2024	|	|	|
arrebourg d.	1858	1926	1959	2001	2000	|	|	|	2047	2124	|	|
éding d.	|	...	2003	|	|	2026	2020	2022	|	|	|	|
averne d.	1916	...	2016	2016	2015	2041	2037	2036	2104	2142	2147	2212
trasbourg a.	1941	...	2039	2041	2039	2110	2059	2059	2130	2204	2210	2238
Mulhouse **385** a.	2045	...	...	2146	...	...	...	...	...	...	...	2346
Basel **385** a.	2109	...	...	2211	...	...	...	...	...	...	...	0013

	2584							
	①–⑥ ♥n	Ⓐ z	⚒ z	Ⓐ z	⑥	† u	Ⓐ z	⑥
Basel **385** d.	...	...	...	0537	0534	...	...	...
Mulhouse **385** d.	...	...	...	0559	0559	...	0617	...
Strasbourg d.	0550	0558	0628	0707	0717	0706	0740	0740
Saverne d.	0613	0623	0651	0729	0742	0728	0802	0802
Réding d.	|	0639	|	0752	0759	|	0817	0817
Sarrebourg d.	0631	0650	0708	|	|	0753	0821	0821
Lunéville d.	|	|	0731	|	|	|	0845	0844
Nancy a.	0710	|	0752	|	|	|	0904	0902
Metz a.	...	0741	...	0845	0846	0846	...	...
Luxembourg **388** a.	...	...	...	...	...	...	...	...

	296										90							96								
	Ⓑ M	Ⓐ z	†		Ⓑ	⑥	Ⓐ z	Ⓐ z	⑥	⑥	V		Ⓐ z	Ⓐ	† u	Ⓒ u	Ⓐ z	R	⑥	Ⓐ z	Ⓐ	† u		Ⓑ	⑥	Ⓑ
Basel **385** d.	0648	0718	...	...	...	...	...	...	...	...	1307	...	...	1518	...	...	...	1607	...	...	1718	...	...	1818	...	...
Mulhouse **385** d.	0712	0742	...	...	...	...	...	...	...	...	1334	...	...	1541	...	...	...	1634	...	...	1741	...	...	1841	...	...
trasbourg d.	0806	0841	0841	1002	1026	1026	1143	1219	1220	1237	1436	1437	1535	1636	1636	1649	1652	1738	1741	1741	1837	1837	1904	1937	1937	2000
averne d.	|	0903	0906	1027	1048	1049	1204	1246	1252	1302	|	1503	1559	1702	1659	1714	1716	|	1805	1805	1903	1900	1929	2003	2003	2024
éding d.	|	|	|	|	|	|	1221	|	|	1318	|	|	1615	|	|	1730	1739	|	|	|	1917	1914	|	|	|	2039
arrebourg d.	|	0920	0922	1051	1104	1105	1229	1302	1309	1328	|	1519	1631	1718	1717	1742	|	|	1820	1821	1921	1919	1956	2018	2018	|
Lunéville d.	|	0941	0946	|	1132	1133	|	1332	1335	|	|	1541	|	|	|	|	|	|	1847	1846	1944	1944	|	2048	2048	|
Nancy a.	|	1000	1004	|	1155	1152	|	1352	1354	|	|	1602	|	1757	1757	|	|	|	1906	1907	2002	2003	|	2107	2107	|
etz a.	0926	...	...	1141	...	...	1331	...	...	1426	1554	...	1730	...	...	1830	1829	1853	...	...	...	...	2043	...	...	2127
Luxembourg **388** a.	1014	...	...	...	...	...	...	...	...	...	1645	...	...	...	...	...	...	1936	...	...	...	...	...	...	...	2214

– JEAN MONNET – [12] Brussels - Basel and v.v. (Table **40**).
– IRIS – [12] Brussels - Zürich - Chur and v.v. (Table **40**).
– VAUBAN – [12] Brussels - Basel - Zürich and v.v. (Table **40**).

h – Not May 1, 8.
n – Not Dec. 25, Jan. 1, Mar. 24, May 12.
u – Also Dec. 26, Mar. 21.

z – Not Dec. 26, Mar. 21.
♥ – *TGV* train, 🅁, 🍷. To/from Paris (Table **390**).
• – Distance from Sarrebourg.

STRASBOURG - BELFORT - BESANÇON - LYON 384

km						4211	4251	*TGV*		4213		4215						4217		4219	4221	4299	4293	4297
		2	2	2	2	4210	4250	5405/4	2	4212	2	4214	2	2	2	2	2	4216	2	4218	4220	4298	4248	4296
		①⑥		⚒	⑦	①–⑥	S						⑤	Ⓑ	⑥	Ⓑ	①–④	⑤⑦		P	⑤⑦	D	F	M
		y				n		🍷				🍷					m	d	⊙		d	🅁	🅁	🅁
0	**Strasbourg** 385 d.	...	...	...	...	0612r	0813	0834	...	1014	...	1149	...	...	...	...	...	1530	...	1713	1816	2019	2019	2056
43	Sélestat 385 d.	...	...	...	...	|	|	|	...	1034	...	|	...	...	...	...	...	|	...	|	|	2041	2041	2118
65	Colmar 385 d.	...	...	...	...	0648	0844	0858	...	1046	...	|	...	...	...	...	...	1556	...	1739	|	2056	2054	2132
106	Mulhouse 385 d.	...	...	...	...	0720	0916	0926	...	1117	...	1242	...	...	...	...	...	1628	...	1811	1909	2131	2134	2206
155	**Belfort** a.	...	...	...	...	0745	0941	|	...	1147	...	|	...	...	...	...	...	|	...	1839	1936	2156	2159	2229
155	**Belfort** 374 d.	...	...	...	...	0755	0951	|	...	1150	...	|	...	...	...	...	...	|	...	1845	1943	2208	2212	2241
173	Montbéliard 374 d.	...	...	...	...	|	1004	0959	...	1204	...	1324	...	...	...	...	...	1704	...	1859	1956	2221	2225	2253
252	**Besançon Viotte** 374 a.	...	...	...	...	0857	1103	1056	...	1303	...	1418	...	...	...	...	...	1803	...	1956	2054	2319	2319	2351
252	**Besançon Viotte** d.	0453	0639	0722	0850	0859	...	1058	1235	1305	1340	1420	1451	1659	1716	1734	1803	1806	1830	1958	2057	2322	2322	2355
292	Mouchard d.	0520	0712	0751	0920	|	...	|	1315	|	1422	|	1519	1744	1807	1808	1831	|	1911	|	|	|	|	|
341	Lons-le-Saunier d.	0606	0754	0836	0958	1000	...	1156	1355	1408	1502	1520	1557	1829	1852	1852	1911	1912	1957	2058	2156	|	|	|
405	Bourg-en-Bresse 377 d.	0653	0837	...	1039	1039	...	1236	...	1445	...	|	...	1908	...	...	...	|	...	2135	2233	|	|	|
465	**Lyon Part-Dieu** 377 a.	0750	0923	...	1126	1128	...	1316	...	1529	...	1639	...	...	...	...	...	2033	...	2221	2320	|	|	|
470	**Lyon Perrache** 377 a.	0759	0932	...	1135	1137	...	|	...	...	...	...	...	...	...	...	...	2042	...	2230	2329	|	|	|
	Marseille **350** a.	...	...	...	...	...	...	1513	...	...	...	...	...	...	...	...	...	...	...	...	...	|	|	0556
	Nice **360** a.	...	...	...	...	...	...	...	...	...	...	...	...	...	...	...	...	...	...	...	...	|	|	0913
	Montpellier **355** a.	...	...	...	...	...	...	...	...	...	...	...	...	...	...	...	...	...	...	...	...	0534	0627	...
	Portbou **355** a.	...	...	...	...	...	...	...	...	...	...	...	...	...	...	...	...	...	...	...	...	0836	0927	...

					4310		4312		4314		4351	*TGV*			4316	4318	4318	4320			4322	4394	4398	4348
	2	2	2	2	4311	2	4313	2	4315	2	4350	5430/1	2	2	4317	4319	4319	4321	2	2	4323	4395	4399	4392
	⚒	⚒	⑦	⚒	①–⑥					⑥	T				⑤⑦	①–④	⑥	⑤⑦	⑥	⑤⑦	⑦	N	E	G
					🍷 n		🍷	k	🍷			🍷			d	w		d		u	e	🅁	🅁	🅁
Cerbère **355** d.	...	...	...	...	...	...	...	...	...	...	...	...	...	...	...	...	...	...	...	...	1650	...	2020	2042
Montpellier **355** d.	...	...	...	...	...	...	...	...	...	...	...	...	...	...	...	...	...	...	...	...	1942	...	2313	2319
Nice **360** d.	...	...	...	...	...	...	...	...	...	...	...	...	...	...	...	...	...	...	...	...	|	1946	|	|
Marseille **350** d.	...	...	...	...	...	...	...	...	...	...	...	1246	...	...	...	...	...	...	...	...	|	2251	|	|
yon Perrache 377 d.	...	...	...	...	0707	...	0917	...	1235	...	...	|	...	1538	1654	1654	1732	1824	1919	2108	|	|	|	|
yon Part-Dieu 377 d.	...	...	...	...	0721	...	0931	...	1249	...	...	1437	...	1550	1708	1708	1746	1838	1933	2122	2254	|	|	|
ourg-en-Bresse 377 d.	0541	...	...	0655a	0803	...	|	...	|	...	...	1525	...	1637	1753	1753	1833	|	2017	2218	2347	|	|	|
ons-le-Saunier d.	0630	0728	0805	0812	0841	1020	1048	1334	|	1416	...	1600	1610	1719	1830	1830	1912	1954	2059	2259	0027	|	|	|
ouchard d.	0713	0811	0845	0856	|	1057	|	1423	|	1503	...	|	1650	1803	|	|	|	|	2133	2337	0115	|	|	|
esançon Viotte a.	0739	0840	0915	0925	0939	1125	1145	1450	1506	1531	...	1659	1717	1836	1932	1932	2009	2051	2200	0006	0142	0449	0530	0530
esançon Viotte 374 d.	...	...	...	...	0941	...	1147	...	1507	...	1541	1701	...	...	1935	1934	2011	2054	...	...	0145	0452	0533	0533
ontbéliard 374 d.	...	...	...	...	1033	...	|	...	1600	...	1635	1749	...	...	2028	2026	2103	2147	...	...	0242	0544	0627	0627
elfort 374 a.	...	...	...	...	|	...	1254	...	|	...	1651	|	...	...	|	2039	2122	2205	...	...	0300	0604	0645	0645
elfort d.	...	...	...	...	|	...	1258	...	|	...	1701	|	...	...	|	2049	2127	2210	...	...	0315	0615	0655	0655
ulhouse 385 d.	...	...	...	...	1118	...	1325	...	1645	...	1727	1825	...	...	2113	2115	2152	2237	...	...	0357	0646	0726	0726
olmar 385 d.	...	...	...	...	1138	...	1352	...	|	...	1756	1852	...	...	2134	2143	2220	2304	...	...	0436	0717	0755	0755
élestat 385 d.	...	...	...	...	|	...	|	...	|	...	|	|	...	...	2146	2156	2233	|	...	...	0454	0733	0808	0808
trasbourg 385 a.	...	...	...	...	1216	...	1423	...	1735	...	1829	1919	...	...	2213	2219	2300	2337	...	...	0519	0758	0834	0834

– *CORAIL LUNÉA* – June 27 - Sept. 20. 🛏 1, 2 cl. and [2] (reclining) Strasbourg - Portbou.
– *CORAIL LUNÉA* – June 28 - Sept. 21. 🛏 1, 2 cl. and [2] (reclining) Cerbère - Strasbourg.
– *CORAIL LUNÉA* – ⑤⑦ (not Mar. 23), also Dec. 20 - Jan. 6 (not Dec. 24, 31), Feb. 9, 16, 23, Mar. 1, 8, 24, 27, 29, Apr. 4 - 27, 30, May 7, 10, 12, June 6 - 26. 🛏 1, 2 cl. and [2] (reclining) Strasbourg - Portbou.
– CORAIL LUNÉA – ⑤⑦ (not Mar. 23), also Dec. 20 - Jan. 6 (not Dec. 24, 31), Feb. 9, 16, 23, Mar. 1, 8, 24, 27, 29, Apr. 4 - 27, 30, May 7 - 12, 17, June 6 - 26. 🛏 1, 2 cl. and [2] (reclining) Cerbère - Strasbourg.
– *CORAIL LUNÉA* – daily except Dec. 15, 24, 31, Jan. 12, 19, 26, Feb. 2, Mar. 15, 22, 23, 29, May 3, 17, 24, 31. 🛏 1,2 cl. and [2] (reclining) Strasbourg - Nice. Train **4294/5** on certain dates.
– *CORAIL LUNÉA* – daily except Dec. 15, 24, 31, Jan. 12, 19, 26, Feb. 2, Mar. 15, 22, 23, 29, May 3, 17, 24, 31. 🛏 1,2 cl. and [2] (reclining) Nice - Strasbourg. Train **4388/9** on certain dates.
– ①②③④⑥ (also May 2; not Dec. 25, Jan. 1, Mar. 24, Apr. 30, May 7, 12).
– June 13 - Sept. 20. [12] Strasbourg - Dijon (**4241**) - Portbou.
– June 14 - Sept. 21. [12] Cerbère (**4340**) - Dijon - Strasbourg.

a – Ⓐ only.
d – Also Dec. 25, Jan. 1, Mar. 24, Apr. 30, May 7, 12; not May 2.
e – Also Dec. 25, Jan. 1, Mar. 24, May 12; not Mar. 23, May 11.
k – On ⑥ depart Lons-le-Saunier 1220, Mouchard 1323, arrive Besançon 1401.
m – Not Dec. 25, Jan. 1, Mar. 24, Apr. 30, May 7, 12.
n – Not Dec. 25, Jan. 1, Mar. 24, May 12.
r – 0620 to Feb. 23.
u – Also Dec. 25, Jan. 1, Mar. 24, May 1, 8, 12; not Apr. 4, 11.
w – Also May 2; not Dec. 25, Jan. 1, Mar. 24, Apr. 30, May 7, 12.
y – Also Dec. 26, Jan. 2, Mar. 25, May 2, 9, 13; not Mar. 24, May 12.

TGV – 🅁, supplement payable, 🍷.

⊙ – 17 mins later on ⑤†.

385 STRASBOURG - MULHOUSE - BASEL

See also Tables 390 and 384

For faster *TGV* trains Paris - Strasbourg - Mulhouse - Basel see Table **390**. For trains Strasbourg - Mulhouse - Belfort - Lyon see Table **384**.

km		Ⓐ	Ⓐ	Ⓐ	Ⓐ	⑥	Ⓐ	⑥	Ⓐ	⚒ ◇	†	Ⓐ	◇	⚒	†		⚒	†			91 V	Ⓒ	Ⓐ	Ⓑ	⑥
	Luxembourg 388 d.	...	...	...	...	...	...	...	...	...	...	...	...	...	...	...	...	...	...	...	1046	...	...	...	...
	Metz 383 d.	...	...	...	...	...	...	...	...	...	...	...	...	...	...	...	...	...	...	...	1132	...	...	...	...
0	**Strasbourg** d.	...	...	0520	0623	...	0653	0653	0723	0753	0753	0823	0853	0953	0953	...	1053	1053	1153	...	1253	1353	1353	1453	1453
43	Sélestat d.	...	...	0539	0642	...	0712	0720	0743	0812	0819	0842	0912	1012	1012	...	1112	1119	1212	...	1316	1412	1416	1512	1519
65	Colmar d.	...	...	0551	0655	...	0724	0732	0754	0824	0832	0854	0924	1024	1024	...	1124	1134	1224	...	1329	1424	1430	1524	1531
106	**Mulhouse** a.	...	...	0616	0714	...	0744	0803	0816	0845	0854	0915	0945	1045	1048	...	1146	1203	1245	...	1353	1445	1454	1545	1552
106	**Mulhouse** d.	0442	0530	0618	0716	0730	0746	0805	0818	0847	0856	0917	0947	1047	1050	...	1148	1205	1247	...	1356	1447	1456	1547	1553
140	**Basel** a.	0516	0555	0639	0739	0755	0808	0833	0840	0910	0918	0939	1009	1109	1111	...	1210	1227	1309	...	1420	1509	1519	1609	1614

	⚒	†	Ⓐ		Ⓒ	Ⓐ	⚒ ◇	†		97 R	Ⓐ	⑥	†	Ⓑ 2	◇	Ⓐ		†	①–⑤ z	⑥	Ⓑ △	Ⓒ y	295 Ⓑ M	⑥	
Luxembourg 388 d.	...	...	...	...	...	...	...	...	...	1603	...	...	...	...	...	...	...	...	...	...	...	...	2026	...	...
Metz 383 d.	...	...	...	...	...	...	...	...	...	1653	...	...	...	...	...	...	...	...	...	...	...	...	2115	...	...
Strasbourg d.	1553	1553	1623	1653	...	1723	1753	1753	...	1823	1853	1853	1853	1923	1953	2053	...	2123	...	2153	2153	...	2253	2253	...
Sélestat d.	1612	1611	1642	1712	...	1742	1812	1812	...	1844	1912	1913	1920	1944	2012	2112	...	2152	...	2218	2216	...	2312	2316	...
Colmar d.	1624	1623	1654	1724	...	1754	1825	1824	...	1857	1924	1925	1936	1957	2024	2125	...	2206	...	2231	2230	...	2325	2329	...
Mulhouse a.	1645	1652	1715	1745	...	1815	1846	1848	...	1922	1945	1953	2009	2021	2045	2146	...	2228	...	2252	2254	...	2346	2354	...
Mulhouse d.	1647	1654	1717	1747	1803	1817	1848	1850	...	1924	1947	1955	...	...	2047	2148	...	...	2252	2254	...	2303	2351	...	...
Basel a.	1709	1716	1739	1809	1838	1839	1910	1912	...	1948	2009	2017	...	...	2109	2211	...	...	2326	2315	...	2338	0013	...	...

	⚒	Ⓐ	⑥	Ⓐ	†	Ⓐ ◇	Ⓐ	⑥	296 Ⓑ M	⚒ ◇	Ⓐ		⚒	†	†	⚒	Ⓐ		⚒	†			90 V	Ⓑ	⑥
Basel d.	...	0518	0534	0537	0537	...	0618	0618	0648	0718	0746	...	0818	0918	0918	1004	1018	1048	1118	1218	...	...	1307	1418	1418
Mulhouse a.	...	0540	0556	0558	0558	...	0641	0640	0710	0740	0810	...	0841	0940	0939	1025	1041	1109	1139	1239	...	...	1332	1439	1439
Mulhouse d.	0502	0542	0559	0559	0559	0617	0643	0642	0712	0742	0812	...	0843	0942	0941	1027	1043	1111	1141	1241	1238	...	1334	1441	1441
Colmar d.	0525	0601	0625	0625	0625	0646	0705	0708	0732	0801	0832	...	0902	1001	1005	1054	1102	1130	1201	1301	1306	...	1356	1501	1501
Sélestat d.	0539	0612	0636	0636	0636	0659	0717	0719	0743	0812	0843	...	0913	1012	1016	1105	1113	1141	1212	1313	1322	...	1409	1512	1512
Strasbourg a.	0603	0634	0704	0704	0704	0733	0740	0748	0803	0838	0904	...	0935	1034	1038	1134	1135	1203	1234	1335	1354	...	1433	1534	1541
Metz 383 a.	...	...	0846	0845	...	...	...	...	0926	...	...	...	...	...	...	...	...	...	...	...	...	...	1554	...	...
Luxembourg 388 a.	...	...	...	...	...	...	...	...	1014	...	...	...	...	...	...	...	...	...	...	...	...	...	1645	...	...

	⚒ ◇	†	Ⓐ	96 R		Ⓐ	Ⓐ ◇	Ⓒ	†	Ⓐ		◇	†	Ⓐ	†	⑥		†	Ⓐ	Ⓑ	Ⓑ	Ⓐ	⑥	
Basel d.	1518	1518	1548	1607	...	1648	1718	1718	1730	1748	...	1818	...	1917	1918	1914	2018	...	2125	2226	2243	...	2334	2343	...
Mulhouse a.	1539	1540	1609	1631	...	1709	1739	1739	1800	1809	...	1839	...	1939	1939	1942	2039	...	2147	2252	2317	...	0009	0018	...
Mulhouse d.	1541	1542	1611	1634	...	1711	1741	1741	1812	1811	...	1841	1905	1941	1941	1944	2041	...	2149	...	...	2323	...	...	...
Colmar d.	1600	1602	1631	1656	...	1730	1800	1809	1833	1830	...	1900	1928	2001	2008	2012	2101	...	2215	...	...	2347	...	...	...
Sélestat d.	1612	1613	1643	1709	...	1741	1812	1820	1844	1842	...	1912	1941	2013	2023	2027	2112	...	2228	...	...	0000	...	...	...
Strasbourg a.	1633	1641	1704	1732	...	1804	1833	1842	1905	1904	...	1933	2004	2036	2052	2058	2134	...	2249	...	...	0026	...	...	...
Metz 383 a.	...	...	...	1853	...	...	...	...	...	...	...	...	...	...	...	...	...	...	...	...	...	...	...	...	...
Luxembourg 388 a.	...	...	...	1936	...	...	...	...	...	...	...	...	...	...	...	...	...	...	...	...	...	...	...	...	...

M – JEAN MONNET – 🚃 Brussels - Basel and v.v.
R – IRIS – 🚃 Brussels - Zürich - Chur and v.v. (Table **40**).
V – VAUBAN – 🚃 Brussels - Basel - Zürich and v.v. (Table **40**).

y – Not May 8.
z – Not Dec. 25, 26, Jan. 1, Mar. 21, 24, May 1, 12, 19, 20.
◇ – To/from Nancy on days in Table **383**.
△ – Runs 12 mins later on Ⓐ Mar. 3 - Apr. 1 (not Mar. 21, 28).

On Dec. 26 and Mar. 21 service is as on ⑦.

386 NANCY - ÉPINAL - REMIREMONT

Most trains 2nd class

km		⚒	Ⓐ	⚒	△	Ⓐ		†	⚒		⚒	2571 ♥		Ⓐ		Ⓐ		Ⓐ	⚒	Ⓐ		2573 Ⓒ ♥	2573 Ⓐ ♥	Ⓐ		k
	Paris Est 390 d.	...	...	...	...	...	...	...	...	...	...	1212	...	...	...	...	...	...	...	...	...	1812	1812	...	...	...
0	**Nancy** d.	0605	...	0617	0705	0820	0905	1006	1119	1205	1303	1346	1405	1506	1605	1704	1720	1752	1805	1820	1904	1945	1950	2008	2105	2204
74	Épinal a.	0705	...	0723	0759	0914	1000	1100	1215	1302	1402	1427	1500	1600	1700	1802	1827	1845	1901	1923	2000	2026	2030	2105	2200	2300
	Épinal d.	...	0720	...	0801	0916	1002	1102	1227	1304	...	1430	1502	*1616*	1702	1804	...	...	1903	...	2002	2029	2033	...	2202	...
100	**Remiremont** a.	...	0750	...	0828	0942	1028	1128	1252	1332	...	1451	1528	*1645*	1726	1832	...	...	1929	...	2028	2052	2054	...	2228	...

	⚒	2574 Ⓐ ♥	⚒		⚒	⚒		2576 Ⓒ ♥	Ⓐ	Ⓐ	Ⓒ	⚒	Ⓒ	Ⓐ		Ⓐ	2578 ①–⑥ ♥n	⚒	†	Ⓒ		2580 ⑦ ♥e	Ⓐ		⚒	Ⓑ u
Remiremont d.	0534	0600	...	0629	0701	...	0832	0906	...	...	1038	...	1215	1418	...	1536	1604	...	1625	...	1730	1808	...	1835	1935	...
Épinal a.	0558	0620	...	0658	0729	...	0856	0928	...	...	1103	...	1244	1443	...	1559	1624	...	1654	...	1758	1828	...	1902	2000	...
Épinal d.	0600	0623	0624	0700	0731	0800	0858	0931	1000	1104	1104	1200	1246	...	1500	1601	1627	1656	1656	1726	1800	1831	1830	1904	2002	2110
Nancy a.	0659	0705	0732	0758	0835	0856	0954	1012	1057	1159	1159	1257	1342	...	1557	1658	1710	1752	1752	1834	1857	1912	1933	1957	2057	2203
Paris Est 390 a.	...	0845	...	...	...	...	...	1145	...	...	...	...	...	...	...	...	1845	...	...	...	...	2045	...	...	...	...

km		⚒c	Ⓐ	⑥	⚒	
0	**Nancy** d.	0605	*0905*	...	...	1752a
74	Épinal a.	0705	*1000*	...	...	1845a
74	Épinal d.	0710	1022	1308	1440	1850
132	Luxeuil les Bains d.	0758	1106	1351	1526	1935
150	Lure 380 d.	0814	1120	1405	1540	1948
182	**Belfort** 380 a.	0835	1140	1423	1601	2009
200	Montbéliard a.	...	...	...	1622	...

	⚒	⚒	†	Ⓐ	⑥	⑤⑦r	
Montbéliard d.	0536*	...	...	1642	1647	...	...
Belfort 380 d.	0559	1120	1631	1700	1705	1940	...
Lure 380 d.	0622	1141	1654	1724	1729	2001	...
Luxeuil les Bains d.	0635	1154	1707	1738	1743	2014	...
Épinal a.	0721	1240	1754	1826	1829	2059	...
Épinal d.	*0731*	...	...	...	...	2100	...
Nancy a.	*0835*	...	...	...	...	2159	...

Additional trains: Nancy - Épinal 0720⚒, 1222⚒, 1620Ⓐ. Épinal - Nancy 0500Ⓐ, 1235⚒, 1246Ⓐ, 1640Ⓐ.

a – Ⓐ only.
c – Change at Épinal on ②–⑤.
e – Also Dec. 25, Jan. 1, Mar. 24, May 12.
k – On ⑤⑦ and holidays depart 2255, arrive 2354.
n – Not Dec. 25, Jan. 1, Mar. 24, May 12.
r – ⑤⑦ and holidays to Nancy, also Apr. 30, May 7 to Épinal.
u – On ⑤⑦ and holidays depart 2100.
♥ – *TGV* train, 🅁, 🍸, supplement payable.
△ – From Luxembourg on † (Table **388**).
* – Not Apr. 15 - 26.

387 NANCY - ST DIÉ and STRASBOURG - ÉPINAL

Most trains 2nd class

km	*Also see below*	⚒	Ⓐ			Ⓐ		2511 ⑦ ♥e			2593 Ⓐ ♥	2595 ⑦ ♥e
	Paris Est 390 d.	...	...	...	...	...	...	1412	...	...	1812	2012
0	**Nancy** d.	0627	0758	0901	1230	1259	1400	1546	1600	1756	1946	2145
33	Lunéville d.	0655	0825	0923	1249	1325	1422	1606	1620	1822	2007	2205
84	**St Dié** a.	0804	0915	1006	1345	1408	1509	1636	1714	1914	2036	2235

Also see below	2596 ①–⑥ ♥n	Ⓒ	Ⓐ	Ⓒ	Ⓐ	Ⓐ	⚒			2598 ⑦e ♥	
St Dié d.	0719	0853	0855	1059	1202	1450	1558	1641	1755	1923	1944
Lunéville d.	0751	0941	0945	1142	1242	1545	1640	1742	1842	1954	2039
Nancy a.	0810	1000	1006	1203	1303	1610	1702	1803	1902	2012	2102
Paris Est 390 a.	0945	...	...	...	...	...	...	...	...	2145	...

km		⚒	Ⓐ	Ⓐ u	†	⑥	⑥	Ⓑ	Ⓐ	Ⓐ	†	⑥	Ⓑ	Ⓐ	Ⓐ	⑥	†	⚒	Ⓐ	†	†
0	**Strasbourg** d.	...	...	0645	0816	0855	...	0955	...	1210	...	1250	...	1555	...	...	1743	1755	...	1820	...
87	St Dié d.	0602	0733	0838*	0945	1018	1037	1129*	1235	1348*	1352	1426	1650	1734*	1825	1900	1906	1926*	1944	1950	2001
147	**Épinal** a.	0712	0840	...	...	...	1144	...	1345	...	1500	...	1805	...	1932	2007	...	...	2049	...	2110

	Ⓐ	Ⓐ u	†	⚒	⚒	†	Ⓐ	⑥	⚒	⚒	†	†	Ⓐ	Ⓐ	†	⑥	⑥	Ⓐ	†	†	⚒
Épinal d.	0604	...	...	0732	...	1030	...	...	1239	...	1515	...	1652	...	...	1710	...	1825	1836	...	2042
St Dié d.	0708	0730*	0819	0840	0850*	1135	1210*	1220	1344	1540*	1619	1629	1759	1804*	1816	1815	1835	1931	1943	2000	2151
Strasbourg a.	...	0855	0945	...	1014	...	1349	1355	...	1715	...	1800	...	1930	2001	...	2016	...	...	2125	...

e – Also Dec. 25, Jan. 1, Mar. 24, May 12.
n – Not Dec. 25, Jan. 1, Mar. 24, May 12.
u – Not Dec. 26, Mar. 21.
♥ – *TGV* train, 🅁, 🍸, supplement payable.
* – Subject to alteration on Ⓐ from June 2.

Additional trains:
Nancy - St Dié: 0550⚒, 1201Ⓐ, 1657Ⓐ, 1725, 1853†, 1857⚒, 1958, 2101Ⓐ.
St Dié - Nancy: 0540Ⓐ, 0612⚒, 0637, 0729⚒, 1214, 1545†, 1853Ⓐ.
Additional local trains run Nancy - Lunéville

LUXEMBOURG - METZ - NANCY — 388

Many trains 2nd class only

For *TGV* trains Luxembourg - Metz - Paris see Table **390**. For long distance trains to the south of France see Table **392**. *Subject to alteration on May 8.*

km																										
																					91					
		Ⓐ	⚒	⚒	†r	⚒s	†	⚒	⚒	⚒z	Ⓐ	⚒	†	Ⓐz		Ⓐ	Ⓒ	Ⓐ	Ⓐ	Ⓒ	⑥⑦c	V	⚒	Ⓐ		Ⓐ
0	**Luxembourg** d.		...	0502	0529	0543	...	0615	...	0655	...	0730	...	0755	0835	0855	0935	...	1034	...	...	1046	...	...	1135	...
34	Thionville d.	...	...	0531	0558	0605	...	0642	...	0724	0738	0800	0806	0823	0900	0923	1000	1010	1101	...	1104	1111	...	...	1200	*1210*
46	Hagondange d.	...	...	0542	0611	|	...	0653	...	0733	0747	0809	0818	0832	0909	0934	1008	1019	1109	...	1113	|	...	...	1208	*1222*
64	**Metz** a.	...	...	0600	0625	0623	...	0707	...	0745	0758	0821	0836	0844	0921	0953	1021	1031	1120	...	1125	1129	...	...	1222	*1237*
64	**Metz** d.	0556	0558	...	0628	*0636*	0657	0709	0729	...	0800	0824	0838	*0900*	0924	...	1024	1035	1124	1124	...	...	1156	1200	1224	1259
93	Pont-à-Mousson d.	0616	0635	...	0648	*0657*	0727	0727	0749	...	0821	0845	0907	*0919*	0944	...	1045	1056	1144	1144	...	...	1228	1221	1244	1320
121	**Nancy** a.	0632	0705	...	0704	*0720*	0759	0743	0806	...	0837	0902	0936	*0938*	1000	...	1101	1112	1200	1201	...	...	1252	1237	1300	1337

							97											295								
		Ⓐ	Y			Ⓐb	R	Ⓐ	Ⓐz		Ⓐz		Ⓐ	Ⓐ			Ⓐ	ⒷM	Ⓒ	⑥⑦c	⚒	†	Ⓐ	⚒	†	△
Luxembourg d.	1235	1255	1330	1430	1535	...	1603	...	1615	1640	1655	1730	...	1755	1830	1935	2016	2026	...	...	...	2115	2145	2215	2235	...
Thionville d.	1300	1322	1353	1453	1559	...	1632	...	1642	1707	1724	1800	...	1824	1900	2000	2040	2051	...	2104	2142	2142	2215	2243	2300	...
Hagondange d.	1309	1331	1406	1502	1608	...	|	...	1653	1718	1734	1809	...	1835	1909	2009	2050	|	...	2113	2153	2153	2227	2251	2309	...
Metz a.	1321	1343	1421	1518	1621	...	1650	...	1711	1731	1746	1822	...	1850	1921	2021	2108	2112	...	2125	2211	2211	2243	2303	2321	...
Metz d.	1324	...	1426	1524	1624	1634	...	1701	...	1733	*1800*	1826	1838	1900	1924	2024	2116	...	2116	...	2214	*2224*	...	...	...	2324
Pont-à-Mousson d.	1344	...	1449	1543	1644	|	...	1719	...	1754	*1819*	1849	1856	1920	1944	2044	2146	...	2145	...	2235	*2245*	...	...	...	2353
Nancy a.	1400	...	1505	1601	1702	1709	...	1738	...	1810	*1835*	1905	1913	1938	2000	2100	2216	...	2215	...	2251	*2301*	...	...	...	0023

														296											
	Ⓐz	Ⓐz	⚒	Ⓐ	⚒	⚒	⚒	Ⓐr	⚒	†	Ⓐ	Ⓐz		ⒷM	Ⓐ	Ⓒ		Ⓐ	Ⓒ	Ⓐ			Ⓐ		Ⓐ	
Nancy d.	...	...	...	0540	0620	0639	0657	0705	0719	0723	0749	...	0819	...	0852	0916	...	0953	1020	...	1122	...	1151	1220	1253	1319
Pont-à-Mousson d.	...	...	...	0602	0638	0701	0714	|	0739	0754	0808	...	0836	...	0915	0933	...	1010	1037	...	1139	...	1208	1237	1310	1336
Metz a.	...	...	...	0632	0657	0729	0733	0739	0758	0828	0828	...	0857	...	0935	0953	...	1032	1057	...	1158	...	1225	1257	1327	1355
Metz d.	0534	0558	0619	0635	0700	0739	...	0747	0800	...	...	0840	0900	0930	...	...	1019	...	1100	1100	1200	1219	...	1300	...	1400
Hagondange d.	0546	0610	0638	0649	0713	0753	...	0803	0812	...	...	0853	0912	|	...	...	1040	...	1113	1119	1213	1234	...	1314	...	1413
Thionville d.	0557	0621	0651	0702	0724	0803	...	0814	0826	...	...	0902	0923	0952	...	...	1051	...	1124	1129	1224	1247	...	1324	...	1424
Luxembourg a.	0623	0646	0719	0730	0750	0830	...	...	0849	...	...	...	0945	1014	...	...	...	...	1150	1156	1247	1315	...	1345	...	1445

			90											96											
	Ⓐ	Ⓒ	V		Ⓐz	Ⓐ		Ⓐz	Ⓐz		Ⓑ	Ⓐ	Ⓐ	R	⚒	†	Ⓐz	Ⓒ	Ⓐ			Ⓑs	Ⓐ	Ⓐ		
Nancy d.	1418	1418	...	1520	...	*1552*	1620	...	*1651*	1719	1752	...	1757	...	1820	1820	*1853*	1920	1920	...	2020	...	2053	2155	...	2250
Pont-à-Mousson d.	1436	1436	...	1537	...	*1609*	1638	...	*1709*	1736	1810	...	1819	...	1837	1837	*1913*	1937	1938	...	2037	...	2123	2212	...	2320
Metz a.	1457	1457	...	1557	...	*1626*	1657	...	*1728*	1757	1826	...	1844	...	1857	1857	*1931*	1957	1957	...	2057	...	2152	2230	...	2350
Metz d.	1500	1500	1556	1600	1619	1639	1700	1718	1740	1800	...	1839	...	1855	1900	1900	1939	2000	2000	2020	2100	2130	...	...	2321	...
Hagondange d.	1513	1513	|	1613	1634	1652	1715	1734	1752	1813	...	1852	...	|	1913	1914	1951	2013	2014	2038	2113	|	...	...	2338	...
Thionville d.	1522	1524	1620	1624	1647	1703	1727	1746	1803	1824	...	1905	...	1914	1924	1929	2003	2024	2029	2049	2126	2153	...	...	2350	...
Luxembourg a.	...	1550	1645	1650	1715	1730	1752	...	1830	1850	...	1930	...	1936	1945	1951	2032	2045	2050	...	2154	2214	...	...	0017	...

M – JEAN MONNET – (12) Brussels - Basel and v.v. (Table **40**).
R – IRIS – (12) Brussels - Zürich - Chur and v.v. (Table **40**).
V – VAUBAN – (12) Brussels - Basel - Zürich and v.v. (Table **40**).
Y – Daily to Metz, ⑤–⑦ (also holidays) Metz - Nancy.

b – To / from St Dié (Table **387**).
c – Also Dec. 25, 26, Jan. 1, Mar. 21, 24, May 12.
r – To / from Remiremont (Table **386**).
s – To / from Strasbourg (Table **383**).

z – Not Dec. 26 Luxembourg - Metz and v.v.
△ – Not on ①–④ Apr. 28 - May 15. On ⑤ runs 7 - 11 mins later.

PARIS - REIMS - CHARLEVILLE MÉZIÈRES - SEDAN — 389

km																									
					TGV		*TGV*			*TGV*		*TGV*		*TGV*			*TGV*				*TGV*			*TGV*	*TGV*
		2	2	2	**2709**	2	**2713**	2	2	**2723**	2	**2733**	2	**2777**	2	2	**2743**	2	2	2	**2747**			**2751**	**2753**
		Ⓐ	⚒	Ⓐ	①–⑥	⚒		†	⚒						Ⓐ	⚒			⚒	†	Ⓑ	Ⓑ		N	⑤⑦
					n									△				d			h				w
0	**Paris Est** d.	...	...	...	0757	...	0857	...	...	1127	...	1257	...	1357	...	...	1557	...	...	...	1727	...	...	1827	1827
136	Champagne-Ardenne TGV ▷ d.	...	...	...	|	...	|	0951	0959	|	...	|	...	1437	1453	...	|	...	...	...	|	...	1853	|	|
147	**Reims** ▷ a.	...	...	...	0842	...	0942	0959	1007	1212	...	1342	...	...	1501	...	1642	...	...	...	1812	...	1901	1913	1913
147	**Reims** d.	0631	0705	0739	...	0857	...	1002	1010	...	1231	1345	1407	...	1504	1622	...	1646	1718	1724	...	1825	1904	1917	1917
186	Rethel d.	0655	0729	0805	...	0923	...	1028	1036	...	1257	|	1430	...	1531	1643	...	1713	1745	1748	...	1853	1927	1940	|
235	**Charleville-Mézières** a.	0726	0758	0838	...	0950	...	1055	1103	...	1324	1431	1458	...	1601	1714	...	1743	1820	1819	...	1922	1954	2006	2003
255	**Sedan** a.	0754	0820	0856	...	1011	...	1116	1124	...	1359v	...	1519	...	1620	1737	...	1814	1849	1838	...	1945	2013	2029	...

			TGV		*TGV*				*TGV*		*TGV*
			2785	2	**2757**		2	2	**2759**		**2765**
	⑤⑦	P	Ⓑ	Ⓑ	⑤⑦	⑤⑦	P	⑤⑦	N	P	⑤⑦
	q		h△		w	q		q			w
Paris Est d.	...	...	1927	...	2004	...	...	...	2057	...	2127
Champagne-Ardenne TGV ▷ d.	...	...	2007	2021	|	...	2106	2107	|	...	|
Reims ▷ a.	...	...	...	2033	2049	...	2114	2115	2142	...	2213
Reims d.	1937	2016	...	...	...	2058	2118	2119	...	2154	2216
Rethel d.	2003	2042	...	...	...	2123	2141	2142	...	2221	2239
Charleville-Mézières a.	2033	2109	...	...	...	2152	2207	2209	...	2253	2305
Sedan a.	2056	...	...	...	...	...	...	...	...	2317	2327

		TGV		*TGV*			*TGV*	*TGV*
	2	**2706**	2	**2778**	2	2	**2712**	**2714**
	Ⓐ	Ⓐ	⚒	①–⑥	⑥	Ⓐ	①–⑥	Ⓐ
				n△			n	
Sedan d.	...	...	0527	...	0606	0607	...	0700
Charleville-Mézières d.	0547	...	0555	...	0631	0631	...	0721
Rethel d.	0617	...	0629	...	0702	0705	...	0750
Reims a.	0638	...	0653	...	0727	0733	...	0812
Reims ▷ d.	...	0645	0657	...	...	...	0745	0815
Champagne-Ardenne TGV ▷ d.	...	|	0705	0720	...	...	|	|
Paris Est a.	...	0730	...	0800	...	...	0830	0900

		TGV			*TGV*		*TGV*			*TGV*	*TGV*		*TGV*		*TGV*				*TGV*			*TGV*			*TGV*
		2720	2	2	**2722**		**2732**	2	2	**2738**	**2746**	2	**2752**		**2784**	2		2	**2756**	2		**2762**		2	**2766**
	Ⓐ	Ⓒ		⚒	①–⑥			⚒		Ⓑ	⑥	Ⓑ	Ⓑ			⚒	†	Ⓑ	⑤⑦					†	⑦
					n					h	t		h		△	c			w						e
Sedan d.	0705	0757	0733	0849	...	1116	...	1215	1451v	...	...	1544	...	...	...	1629	1642	1704	...	1746	1849	...	2012	2100	...
Charleville-Mézières d.	0738	0818	0804	0910	...	1138	...	1241	1512	...	1527	1609	1622	...	...	1659	1711	1727	...	1815	1908	...	2035	2116	2127
Rethel d.	0814	0847	0832	0938	...	1206	...	1314	1545	...	|	1638	|	...	...	1732	1739	1800	...	1844	1937	...	2103	...	|
Reims a.	0838	0910	0904	0959	...	1228	...	1335	1604	...	1612	1702	1710	...	...	1758	1801	1825	...	1908	2000	...	2125	...	2212
Reims ▷ d.	...	0915	0919	...	1015	...	1245	...	...	1615	1615	...	1715	1750	...	1808r	1805x	...	1845	1922z	...	2015	...	...	2215
Champagne-Ardenne TGV ▷ d.	...	|	0927	...	|	...	|	...	...	|	|	...	|	1758	1819	1815r	1814x	...	|	1933z	...	|	...	...	|
Paris Est a.	...	1000	...	...	1100	...	1330	...	...	1700	1700	...	1800	...	1900	...	...	...	1930	...	...	2100	...	...	2300

N – ①②③④⑥ (not Dec. 25, Jan. 1, Apr. 30, Mar. 24, May 7, 12).
P – ①②③④⑥ (not Dec. 25, Jan. 1, Mar. 24, May 1, 8, 12).
c – Not May 9, 10.
d – Depart Reims 1650 on ⑥.
e – Also Dec. 25, Jan. 1, Mar. 24, May 12.
h – Not May 1, 8.
n – Not Dec. 25, Jan. 1, Mar. 24, May 12.

q – Also Dec. 25, Jan. 1, Mar. 24, May 1, 8, 12.
r – From Mar. 31.
s – To / from Longwy (d. 0620 / a. 1826). See also Table **393**.
t – Also May 1, 8.
v – Ⓒ (daily Feb. 9 - 24, Apr. 5 - 20).
w – Also Dec. 25, Jan. 1, Apr. 30, Mar. 24, May 7, 12; not May 2.
x – † from Apr. 6 (not May 8).

z – From Mar. 31 (not May 10, 11).
TGV – Ⓡ, supplement payable, 🍷.
△ – To / from Bar le Duc (Table **381**).
▷ – For full service see Table **391**.

CHARLEVILLE MÉZIÈRES - LONGWY and METZ — 389a

2nd class

km										
		⚒	Ⓐ	⚒		⚒	†	P	⑤⑦	
		s							q	
	Reims **389** d.	...	0631	0705	1407	1622	1724	...	1937	...
0	**Charleville-Mézières** **389** d.	...	0735	0807	1503	1719	1824	2024	2039	...
20	Sedan **389** a.	...	0754	0820	1519	1737	1838	2042	2056	...
20	Sedan d.	...	0756	0821	1520	1738	1839	2043	2057	...
69	Montmédy d.	...	0828	0853	1555	1809	1910	2116	2129	...
91	Longuyon **393** d.	0634	0847	0906	1615	1824	1923	2135	2148	...
107	**Longwy** **393** a.	|	0859	|	1627	|	|	2148	2200	...
	Hayange d.	0705	...	0936	...	1853	1951	...	...	...
170	**Metz** a.	0732	...	0958	...	1915	2016	...	...	...

	Ⓐ	Ⓒ		⚒	Ⓑ			⚒	
								s	
Metz d.	...	...	...	0704	...	...	...	1714	1835
Hayange d.	...	...	...	0731	...	...	...	1740	1859
Longwy **393** d.	0548	0645	...	|	1013	...	1748	|	|
Longuyon **393** d.	0607	0702	...	0759	1031	...	1805	1811	1927
Montmédy d.	0620	0717	...	0814	1044	...	1818	...	1941
Sedan a.	0651	0748	...	0848	1114	...	1848	...	2011
Sedan **389** d.	0705	0804	...	0849	1116	...	1849	...	2012
Charleville-Mézières **389** a.	0733	0817	...	0904	1133	...	1903	...	2027
Reims **389** a.	0838	...	...	0959	1228	...	2000	...	2125

FOR NOTES SEE TABLE 389 ABOVE

390 TGV EST EUROPÉEN

PARIS - STRASBOURG - BASEL

km		TGV 9201 ①–⑤ h	TGV 2405 Ⓐ	TGV 9203 ⑥ t	TGV 9571	TGV 9211 ①–⑥ n△	TGV 9211 ⑦ e		TGV 2419 Ⓑ h	TGV 2421 ⑥ t	TGV 9573	TGV 9213	TGV 2431 ⑤ f		TGV 2365 Ⓐ	TGV 2367 Ⓒ	TGV 9575 ⊙	TGV 2443 N	TGV 2373 ⑤⑦ d	TGV 2445 ⑤ f	TGV 2447 ⑦ e		TGV 9577 Ⓑ k	TGV 244 ⑥ u
0	**Paris Est** d.	0624	0654	0654	0724	0824	0824	...	1024	1024	1124	1224	1324	...	1424	1424	1524	1624	1624	1654	1654	...	1724	172
405	Saverne a.	|	|	|	|	|	|	...	|	1222	|	|	|	...	1624	|	|	|	|	|	1852	...	|	|
450	**Strasbourg** a.	0843	0913	0913	0942	1043	1043	...	1244	1246	1342	1443	1543	...	1645	1645	1742	1843	1843	1913	1916	...	1942	194
450	**Strasbourg** 385 d.	0847	...	0917	0947	1047	1047	...	...	...	1347	1447	...	...	1649	1649	1747	...	1847	...	...	...	1947	...
	Stuttgart Hbf **930** a.	|	...	|	1103	|	|	...	...	...	1503	|	...	...	|	|	1903	...	|	...	...	...	2103	...
515	Colmar 385 d.	0913	...	0942	...	|	1114	...	...	...	...	|	...	...	1714	1714	...	...	|	...	...	...	...	...
556	Mulhouse 385 d.	0937	...	1006	...	1132	1138	...	...	...	...	1533	...	...	1735	1735	...	...	1928	...	...	...	...	...
590	**Basel** 385 a.	0956	...	1025	...	1150	1156	...	...	...	...	1551	...	...	...	...	...	...	...	...	...	...	...	...
	Zürich HB **510** a.	...	...	...	...	1300	1300	...	...	...	...	1700c	...	...	...	...	...	...	...	...	...	...	...	...

	TGV 9217 Ⓑ	TGV 2457	TGV 2583 Ⓑ h◇		TGV 2375 Ⓑ h	TGV 9219 ⑥	TGV 2467 Ⓑ h	TGV 2469 ⑤⑦ d	
Paris Est d.	1754	1824	1912	...	1924	1924	2024	2124	...
Saverne a.	|	|	2140	...	|	|	|	|	...
Strasbourg a.	2011	2043	2204	...	2143	2143	2243	2345	...
Strasbourg 385 d.	2015	...	...	...	2147	2147	...	...	...
Stuttgart Hbf **930** a.	|	...	...	...	|	|	...	...	...
Colmar 385 d.	|	...	...	...	2213	2213	...	...	...
Mulhouse 385 d.	2058	...	...	...	2234	2237	...	...	...
Basel 385 a.	2115	...	...	...	...	2255	...	...	...
Zürich HB **510** a.	2214	...	...	...	...	2356	...	...	...

	TGV 2584 ①–⑥ n◇	TGV 2404 Ⓐ	TGV 2350 Ⓐ	TGV 2406 ⑥ t	TGV 2410 Ⓑ h	TGV 2352 ⑥ t	TGV 9578 ①–⑥ n	TGV 2412 ⑦ e	
Zürich HB **510** d.	...	...	...	...	...	...	...	...	...
Basel 385 d.	...	...	...	...	...	...	...	...	...
Mulhouse 385 d.	...	...	0553	...	...	0622	...	...	...
Colmar 385 d.	...	...	0613	...	...	0643	...	...	...
Stuttgart Hbf **930** d.	...	...	|	...	...	|	0654	...	...
Strasbourg 385 a.	...	...	0640	...	...	0710	0811	...	...
Strasbourg d.	0550	0615	0645	0645	0715	0715	0816	0816	...
Saverne d.	0613	|	|	|	|	|	|	|	...
Paris Est a.	0845	0834	0904	0904	0934	0934	1034	1034	...

	TGV 9212 ①–⑥ n	TGV 9212 ⑦ e	TGV 9576 ⊙	TGV 2424 ①–⑥ n	TGV 2426 ⑦ e	TGV 9204 B	TGV 9204 ①–⑥	TGV 2354 ⑦	TGV 9574	TGV 2356 ⑤–⑦ w	TGV 2440	TGV 9216	TGV 2448 ⑦ e	TGV 2446 ⑤ f	TGV 2450 Ⓑ h	TGV 2452 Ⓐ	TGV 9572 ⑥⑦ b	TGV 2360 Ⓑ h	TGV 2460 ⑥ t	TGV 9570 ①–⑤ n	TGV 9218 Ⓐ	TGV 9218 ⑥ t▽	TGV 9218 ⑦ e	TGV 2472 ⑦ e
Zürich HB **510** d.	0702	0702	...	...	...	...	...	...	...	...	...	1402	...	...	...	...	...	...	...	...	1802	1802	1802	...
Basel 385 d.	0804	0804	...	...	...	1101	...	...	...	...	...	1504	...	...	...	...	...	...	...	...	1904	1903	1904	...
Mulhouse 385 d.	0828	0826	...	...	...	1123	...	1123	...	1325	...	1527	...	...	...	...	...	1823	...	...	1925	1924	1928	...
Colmar 385 d.	|	0846	...	...	...	1143	...	1143	...	|	...	|	...	...	...	...	...	1843	...	...	|	1944	|	...
Stuttgart Hbf **930** d.	|	|	0854	...	...	|	...	|	1254	|	...	|	...	...	...	...	1654	|	...	1854	|	|	|	...
Strasbourg 385 a.	0910	0912	1012	...	...	1210	...	1210	1411	1407	...	1610	...	...	...	...	1811	1910	...	2011	2007	2011	2011	...
Strasbourg d.	0915	0915	1017	1111	1115	1215	1215	1215	1416	1416	1515	1615	1641	1645	1715	1816	1816	1915	1915	2017	2017	2017	2017	2115
Saverne d.	|	|	|	1135	|	|	|	|	|	|	|	|	1705	|	|	|	|	|	|	|	|	|	|	|
Paris Est a.	1134	1134	1234	1334	1334	1434	1434	1434	1634	1634	1734	1834	1904	1904	1934	2034	2034	2134	2134	2234	2234	2234	2234	2334

PARIS - NANCY

Certain trains continue beyond Nancy to Épinal and Remiremont (Table **386**) or to Lunéville and St Dié (Table **387**). Train **2583/4** continues to / from Strasbourg.

km		TGV 2501 ①–⑥ n		TGV 2503 Ⓑ h⊡	TGV 2505 ①–⑥ n		TGV 2507 Ⓒ	TGV 2571		TGV 2509 Ⓐ	TGV 2591 ⑦ e		TGV 2513 ⑥ t	TGV 2515 Ⓑ h	TGV 2517 Ⓐ		TGV 2573	TGV 2583 Ⓑ h		TGV 2519 ①–⑥ n	TGV 2595 ⑦ e		TGV 2521 ⑦ e	
0	**Paris Est** d.	0712	...	0812	0905	...	1042	1212	...	1412	1412	...	1512	1612	1712	...	1812	1912	...	2012	2012	...	2112	...
330	**Nancy** a.	0842	...	0948	1035	...	1212	1342	...	1543	1543	...	1642	1742	1842	...	1942	2042	...	2142	2142	...	2242	...

	TGV 2531 Ⓐ	TGV 2584 ①–⑥ n	TGV 2596 ①–⑥ n	TGV 2533 ⑦ e		TGV 2576 Ⓒ	TGV 2535 Ⓐ		TGV 2537	TGV 2539 ①–④ m		TGV 2541 ⑤–⑦ w	TGV 2543 Ⓑ h		TGV 2578 ①–⑥ n	TGV 2545 Ⓑ h⊡		TGV 2547 ⑤⑥ v	TGV 2580 ⑦ e		TGV 2549 Ⓐ	TGV 2598 ⑦ e	TGV 2551 ⑦ e	
Nancy d.	0615	0715	0815	0815	...	1015	1028	...	1215	1345	...	1515	1615	...	1715	1811	...	1915	1915	...	2015	2015	2115	...
Paris Est a.	0745	0845	0945	0945	...	1145	1200	...	1345	1515	...	1645	1745	...	1845	1946	...	2045	2045	...	2145	2145	2245	...

PARIS - METZ - LUXEMBOURG

km		TGV 2601 ① g	TGV 2803 ①–⑥ n	TGV 2503 Ⓑ ☆h		TGV 2809 Ⓐ	TGV 2809 Ⓒ		TGV 2615	TGV 2621	TGV 2827		TGV 2831	TGV 2833 ⑦ e	TGV 2633 Ⓐ		TGV 2835 Ⓐ	TGV 2837 Ⓒ		TGV 2639 Ⓑ h	TGV 2643 Ⓐ	TGV 2843 ⑦ e	TGV 2647 ⑤⑦ q	
0	**Paris Est** d.	0639	0709	0812	...	0839	0839	...	1039	1239	1409	...	1609	1739	1739	...	1839	1839	...	1939	2039	2039	2139	...
236	Meuse TGV a.	|	|	0912	...	|	0938	...	|	|	|	...	|	|	1838	...	|	1938	...	|	|	|	|	...
315	**Metz** a.	0802	0832	...	...	1002	1009	...	1202	1402	1533	...	1732	1902	1908	...	2002	2008	...	2102	2202	2202	2302	...
315	**Metz** 388 d.	...	0835	...	...	1005	1012	...	...	...	1537	...	1736	1905	...	...	2005	2011	...	...	...	2205	...	...
345	Thionville 388 a.	...	0852	...	...	1022	1029	...	...	...	1554	...	1753	1922	...	...	2022	2028	...	...	...	2222	...	...
379	**Luxembourg** 388 a.	...	0915	...	...	1045	1052	...	...	...	1617	...	1815	1945	...	...	2045	2051	...	...	...	2245	...	...

	TGV 2650 Ⓐ	TGV 2652 Ⓐ	TGV 2857 ⑥ t	TGV 2855 Ⓐ		TGV 2660 ②–⑤ z	TGV 2861 ① g	TGV 2863 ⑦ e	TGV 2662 ⑥ t		TGV 2865 ①–⑥ n	TGV 2664 ⑦ e		TGV 2869	TGV 2672 ⑥ t	TGV 2672 Ⓑ h	TGV 2676 Ⓑ h	TGV 2881	TGV 2545 Ⓑ ☆h	TGV 2684 ⑤⑦ q		TGV 2889 x	TGV 2893 ⑦ e	
Luxembourg 388 d.	...	...	0640	0643	...	...	0810	0807	...	...	1000	...	...	1308	...	...	...	1712	...	...	...	1912	2013	...
Thionville 388 d.	...	...	0701	0704	...	...	0832	0828	...	...	1021	...	...	1329	...	...	...	1735	...	...	...	1935	2034	...
Metz 388 a.	...	...	0720	0722	...	...	0850	0846	...	...	1039	...	...	1348	...	...	...	1752	...	...	...	1952	2052	...
Metz d.	0625	0649	0725	0725	...	0855	0855	0849	0919	...	1042	1042	...	1353	1549	1555	1655	1755	...	1855	...	1955	2055	...
Meuse TGV d.	|	0719	|	|	...	|	|	0919	0950	...	|	|	...	|	|	|	|	|	1847	|	...	|	|	...
Paris Est a.	0749	0819	0849	0849	...	1019	1019	1019	1049	...	1205	1205	...	1519	1720	1720	1820	1920	1946	2019	...	2119	2219	...

PARIS - SAARBRÜCKEN

km		ICE 9551 ①–⑥ n	ICE 9553 ⑦ e	ICE 9553 ①–⑥ n		ICE 9555		ICE 9557 Ⓑ k	ICE 9559 s	
0	**Paris Est** d.	0658	0901	0909	...	1309	...	1709	1905	...
304	Lorraine TGV d.	0815	1017	|	...	|	...	|	|	...
372	Forbach d.	0849	1049	|	...	|	...	|	2050	...
383	**Saarbrücken** a.	0858	1058	1058	...	1458	...	1858	2058	...
	Frankfurt (Main) Hbf **919** a.	1058	1258	1258	...	1658	...	2058	2258	...

	ICE 9558 ①–⑥ n	ICE 9556 ①–⑥ n	ICE 9556 ⑦ e		ICE 9554		ICE 9552 Ⓑ k	ICE 9552 ⑥ u	ICE 9550 Ⓑ k
Frankfurt (Main) Hbf **919** d.	0600	0901	0901	...	1301	...	1701	1701	1901
Saarbrücken d.	0800	1101	1101	...	1501	...	1901	1901	2101
Forbach d.	0810	|	1111	...	|	...	1911	1911	|
Lorraine TGV d.	|	|	|	...	|	...	|	1944	2140
Paris Est a.	0950	1249	1253	...	1650	...	2051	2057	2253

B – ①–⑥ to Feb. 23; ⑥ Mar. 1 - Apr. 5 (also Mar. 24); ①–⑥ from Apr. 7.
N – ①②③④⑥ (not Dec. 25, Jan. 1, Mar 24, Apr. 30, May 7, 12).
b – Also Dec. 25, Jan. 1, Mar. 24, May 1, 12.
c – 1707 on ⑥.
d – Also Dec. 25, Jan. 1, Mar. 24, Apr. 30, May 7, 12; not May 2.
e – Also Dec. 25, Jan. 1, Mar. 24, May 12.
f – Also Apr. 30, May 7; not May 2.
g – Also Dec. 26, Jan. 2, Mar. 25, May 13; not Dec. 24, 31, Mar. 24, May 12.

h – Not May 1, 8.
k – Not Dec. 24, 31, Mar. 23, May 11.
m – Not Dec. 25, Jan. 1, Mar. 24, May 1, 7, 8, 12.
n – Not Dec. 25, Jan. 1, Mar. 24, May 12.
q – Also Dec. 25, Jan. 1, Mar. 24, Apr. 30, May 7, 12; not May 2.
s – Not Mar. 23, May 11.
t – Also May 1, 8.
u – Also Dec. 24, 31, Mar. 23, May 11.
v – Also Apr. 30, May 1, 7, 8; not May 2.
w – Also Dec. 25, Jan. 1, Mar. 24, Apr. 30, May 1, 7, 8, 12; not May 2.

x – On ⑤**f** Luxembourg 1910, Thionville 1931 (train **2891**).
z – Also Dec. 24, 31; not Dec. 25, 26, Jan. 1, 2, Mar. 25, May 1, 8, 13.
ICE – 🅁 (Paris - Saarbrücken and v.v.); supplement payable, 🍷.
TGV – 🅁, supplement payable, 🍷.
⊙ – To / from München (Table **32**).
◇ – Via Nancy, calling also at Sarrebourg (Table **383**).
△ – To Chur (Table **40**) on ⑥ Dec. 15 - Mar. 29, train **9221**.
▽ – From Chur (Table **40**) on ⑥ Dec. 15 - Mar. 29, train **9222**.
⊡ – Via Meuse TGV (see Paris - Metz section).
☆ – To / from Nancy.

STRASBOURG - NORTHERN and WESTERN FRANCE 391

	TGV	TGV	TGV	TGV	TGV	TGV	TGV	TGV	TGV	TGV	TGV	
	5420	**5486**	**5450**	**5450**	**5470**	**5452**	**5422**	**5452**	**5454**	**5488**	**5426**	
			⑦	①–⑥		⑤–⑦		①–④	**B**	**B**		
	△	⊗	**e**	**n**		**Bd**		**Bk**	⊖	⊙		
trasbourg d.	0611	0625	0741	0745	0856	1153	1206**r**	1420	1636*	1756	1900	...
orraine TGV d.	0725	0740	0852	0859	1008	1307	1326	1539	1748*	1909	2012	...
leuse TGV d.	|	|	0912	0923	|	|	|	|	|	|	|	...
hampagne-Ardenne TGV d.	0812	0828	0944	0949	1049	1347	1407	1624	1832	1948	2057	...
larne la Vallée - Chessy a.	|	0856	1018	1018	1122	1416	|	1652	1908	2020	|	...
lassy TGV a.	|	0930	1058	1058	1158	1458	|	1728	1946	2058	|	...
aris Charles de Gaulle ✈ a.	0843	|	|	|	|	|	1437	|	|	|	2128	...
GV Haute Picardie a.	0914	|	|	|	|	|	|	|	|	|	|	...
rras a.	|	|	|	|	|	|	1520	|	|	|	|	...
ouai a.	|	|	|	|	|	|	1538	|	|	|	|	...
ille Europe a.	0946	|	|	|	|	|	1559	|	|	|	2223**z**	...
Le Mans a.	...	1022	|	|	1250	|	...	|	|	2151	...	...
Angers a.	...	1059	|	|	|	|	...	|	|	2236	...	...
Nantes a.	...	1140	|	|	|	|	...	|	|	2314	...	...
Laval a.	...	...	|	|	1333	|	...	|	|	...	...	...
Rennes a.	...	...	|	|	1410	|	...	|	|	...	...	...
t Pierre des Corps a.	...	...	1152	1152	...	1552	...	1821	2041	...	...	...
uturoscope a.	...	...	1229	1229	...	|	...	|	|	...	...	...
oitiers a.	...	...	1239	1239	...	1632	...	1902	2127	...	...	...
ngoulême a.	...	...	1326	1326	...	1719	...	1948	2216	...	...	...
ordeaux St Jean a.	...	...	1428	1428	...	1823**v**	...	2052	2319	...	...	...

	TGV	TGV	TGV	TGV	TGV	TGV	TGV	TGV	TGV	TGV	TGV	
	5400	**5440**	**5478**	**5402**	**5442**	**5442**	**5480**	**5416**	**5460**	**5444**	**5444**	
		B	**B**		⑥⑦	①–⑤				⑦	①–⑥	
		⊡	⊗		**Bs**	**Bq**	⊕			**e**	**n**	
ordeaux St Jean d.	...	0633	...	...	1019	1030	...	...	...	1613	1708**x**	...
ngoulême d.	...	0733	...	...	1122	1135	...	...	...	1716	1812	...
oitiers d.	...	0819	...	...	1210	1224	...	...	...	1805	1902	...
uturoscope d.	...	|	...	...	|	|	...	...	...	1815	1912	...
t Pierre des Corps d.	...	0902	...	...	1251	1307	...	...	...	1854	1949	...
Rennes d.	...	|	...	...	|	|	...	...	1710	|	|	...
Laval d.	...	|	...	...	|	|	...	...	1746	|	|	...
Nantes d.	...	|	0834	...	|	|	1520	...	|	|	|	...
Angers d.	...	|	0913	...	|	|	1600	...	|	|	|	...
Le Mans d.	...	|	0956	...	|	|	1640	...	1835	|	|	...
ille Europe d.	0652	|	|	1121	|	|	|	1858	|	|	|	...
ouai d.	|	|	|	1142	|	|	|	|	|	|	|	...
rras d.	|	|	|	1201	|	|	|	|	|	|	|	...
GV Haute Picardie d.	|	|	|	1223	|	|	|	|	|	|	|	...
aris Charles de Gaulle ✈ d.	0746	|	|	1254	|	|	|	1953	|	|	|	...
lassy TGV d.	|	0958	1050	|	1349	1402	1730	|	1926	1947	2046	...
larne la Vallée - Chessy d.	|	1039	1128	|	1429	1445	1808	|	2009	2029	2125	...
hampagne-Ardenne TGV a.	0816	1107	1157	1324	1458	1515	1838	2023	2036	2057	2152	...
leuse TGV a.	|	|	|	|	|	|	|	|	|	2127	2219	...
orraine TGV a.	0857	1148	1246	1405	1542	1555	1919	2104	2115	2148	2239	...
trasbourg a.	1010	1304	1359	1517	1657	1717	2032	2217	2227	2302	2352	...

B – From Mar. 31.
a – Not May 2, 9.
c – Not May 11.
d – Also Apr. 30, May 7; not May 2, 9, 10.
e – Also Dec. 25, Jan. 1, Mar. 24, May 12.
k – Also May 2; not Apr. 30, May 1, 7, 8, 12.
m – Also May 2; not Dec. 25, Jan. 1, Mar. 24, Apr. 30, May 1, 7, 8, 12.
n – Not Dec. 25, Jan. 1, Mar. 24, May 12.
q – Not Dec. 25, Jan. 1, Mar. 24, May 1, 2, 8, 9, 12.
r – 1210 on Ⓒ.
s – Also Dec. 25, Jan. 1, Mar. 24, May 1, 2, 8, 12.
u – Not Apr. 28, May 5, 26.
v – Subject to alteration on May 8.
w – Also Apr. 30, May 1, 7, 8, 12; not May 2, 9, 10.
x – Subject to alteration May 8 - 10.
z – 2227 on †.
△ – On ⑦**e** depart Strasbourg 0620, Lorraine TGV 0732.
⊕ – Subject to alteration May 10, 11 Nantes - Le Mans.
⊗ – Subject to alteration May 11 Le Mans - Nantes and v.v.
⊡ – Not May 9 - 11.
⊙ – Not May 10, 11.
⊖ – Not May 8 - 10.
TGV – 🅁, supplement payable, 🍷.
* – 3 minutes earlier on ⑤⑦ (also Apr. 30, May 1, 7, 12).

CONNECTING 🚌 SERVICES

Bus services connect with the trains in Table **391** on the following routes:

Nancy - Lorraine TGV (journey 35 minutes)

Metz - Lorraine TGV (journey 25 minutes)

Verdun - Meuse TGV (journey 25 mins)

For further details ✆ 03 87 78 67 09.

Subject to alteration May 10, 11 — RAIL CONNECTIONS CHAMPAGNE ARDENNES TGV - REIMS — 2nd class

	⚒	†		†	⚒ **u**		Ⓐ	Ⓒ	**B**		⑤–⑦ **Bw**			Ⓒ **B**	Ⓐ **Ba**	①–④ **Bk**			**B**	Ⓑ			†	⚒
hampagne-Ardenne TGV d.	0818	0824	0838	0951	0956	1101	1114	1122	1211	1339	1400	1419	1453	1510	1524	1629	1848	1853	1959	2018	2047	2106	2118	2202
eims a.	0827	0832	0847	0959	1003	1111	1122	1131	1219	1346	1408	1427	1501	1518	1532	1637	1856	1901	2007	2025	2056	2115	2125	2210

	⚒	Ⓒ	Ⓐ					**Bc**		⑤–⑦ **Bw**		Ⓒ **B**	Ⓐ **Ba**	①–④ **Bk**		†	⚒ **B**	⚒	Ⓑ **B**	⑥ **B**			⚒	
eims d.	0657	0741	0749	0757	0919	1024	1049	1150	1308	1319	1340	1441	1500	1601	1750	1805	1808	1817	1922	1924	2006	2025	2135	...
hampagne-Ardenne TGV a.	0705	0749	0757	0805	0927	1034	1057	1158	1316	1327	1350	1449	1508	1609	1758	1814	1815	1825	1933	1933	2013	2036	2143	...

METZ - NANCY - DIJON 392

km		TGV 5148	4240 4241	4262 4263	4264 4265	4266 4267	4239 4238	4235 4234	4248 4249	4246 4247
			F		⑤		**R**	**P**	**A**	**B**
					f		🅁◐	🅁◧	🅁◇	🅁◇
0	**Luxembourg** 388 d.	...	...	...	...	...	1946	1946	...	...
34	Thionville 388 d.	...	...	...	...	...	2014	2014	...	...
64	**Metz** 388 d.	0611	0820*	1140**r**	1545	1721	2044	2044	2112	2151
121	**Nancy** 388 d.	0651	0912*	1229	1631	1807	2133	2133	2200	2237
154	Toul d.	|	0933*	1251	1651	1828	2156	2156	2221	2258
198	Neufchâteau d.	|	1002*	1316	1715	1854	2221	2221	2249	2323
272	Culmont Chalindrey a.	|	|	|	|	1939	2308	2308	2334	0010
272	Culmont Chalindrey d.	|	|	|	|	1951	2323	2323	2357	0030
349	**Dijon** a.	0906	1148	1443	1847	2036	|	|	0045	|
	Lyon Part-Dieu **373** a.	1057	1358	1631	2055	2229	|	|	|	|
	Lyon Perrache **373** a.	|	|	...	|	2242	|	|	|	|
	Avignon Centre **351** a.	|	1607	...	2324	...	0412	0438	|	|
	Avignon TGV **350** a.	1211	|	...	|	...	|	|	|	|
	Montpellier **355** a.	|	1713	...	0034	...	|	|	0627	0627
	Perpignan **355** d.	|	1916	...	...	...	|	|	0826	0826
	Portbou **355** a.	|	2011	...	...	...	|	|	0927	0927
	Marseille **350** a.	1249	...	...	...	...	0515	0556	...	...
	Nice **360** a.	1532	...	...	...	...	0820	0912	...	...

	4328 4329	4330 4331	4346 4347	4348 4349		4336 4337	4340 4341	TGV 5198	4342 4343
	P	**R**	**C**	**D**			**G**		
	🅁◧	🅁◐	🅁◇	🅁◇					
Nice **360** d.	1946	2017	...	...	...	...	...	0929**c**	...
Marseille **350** d.	2251	2310	...	...	...	...	...	1208	...
Cerbère **355** d.	|	|	2038	2042	...	...	0607	|	...
Perpignan **355** d.	|	|	2132	2133	...	...	0701	|	...
Montpellier **355** d.	|	|	2319	2319	...	...	0924	|	...
Avignon TGV **350** d.	|	|	|	|	...	...	|	1245	...
Avignon Centre **351** d.	0014	0025	|	|	...	...	1029	|	...
Lyon Perrache **373** d.	|	|	|	|	...	0635	|	|	1759
Lyon Part-Dieu **373** d.	|	|	|	|	...	0648	1253	1400	1812
Dijon d.	|	|	|	0445	...	0839	1505	1546	2007
Culmont Chalindrey a.	0509	0504	0530	0530	...	0924	|	|	|
Culmont Chalindrey d.	0523	0523	0547	0547	...	0935	|	|	|
Neufchâteau d.	0610	0610	0637	0637	...	1023	1635	|	2137
Toul d.	0635	0635	0709	0709	...	1049	1703	|	2202
Nancy 388 a.	0655	0655	0730	0730	...	1107	1722	1759	2221
Metz 388 a.	0745	0745	0818	0818	...	1152	1808	1848	2306
Thionville 388 a.	0815	0815	...	...	...	...	...	...	...
Luxembourg 388 a.	0845	0845	...	...	...	...	...	...	...

A – ⑤⑦ (not Mar. 23), also Dec. 20 - Jan. 6 (not Dec. 24, 31), Feb. 9, 16, 23, Mar. 1, 8, 24, 27, 29, Apr. 4 - 27, 30, May 7, 10, 12, June 6 - 26.
B – June 27 - Sept. 20.
C – June 28 - Sept. 21.
D – ⑤⑦ (not Mar. 23), also Dec. 20 - Jan. 6 (not Dec. 24, 31), Feb. 9, 16, 23, Mar. 1, 8, 24, 27, 29, Apr. 4 - 27, 30, May 7 - 12, 17, June 6 - 26.
– June 13 - Sept. 20.
G – June 14 - Sept. 21.
P – ①–④ Dec. 10 - 18, Jan. 7 - Feb. 5, Mar. 10 - Apr. 1 (not Mar. 24, 25), May 14 - June 5.
R – ⑤⑦ (not Mar. 23), also Dec. 19 - Jan. 6 (not Dec. 24, 31), Feb. 6 - Mar. 9, Mar. 24, 25, Apr. 2 - May 13 (not May 3), daily June 6 - Sept. 2.
c – 0923 Jan. 3 - Feb. 22.
f – Also Dec. 24, 31, Apr. 30, May 7; not May 2, 9.
r – 1136 on Ⓒ.
* – On Ⓒ depart 13 - 17 minutes later.
◇ – 🛏 1, 2 cl. and 🪑2 (reclining).
◐ – *CORAIL LUNÉA* – 🛏 1, 2 cl. and 🪑2 (reclining) Luxembourg - Nice and v.v. Conveys on dates in Table **382** 🛏 2 cl. and 🪑2 (reclining) Reims - Culmont Chalindrey - Nice and v.v.
◧ – CORAIL LUNÉA – 🛏 1, 2 cl. and 🪑2 (reclining) Luxembourg - Nice and v.v.
TGV – 🅁, supplement payable, 🍷.

VERDUN - METZ 392a

km		Ⓐ	⚒		🚌 Ⓐ	Ⓐ		Ⓐ	🚌 Ⓐ	Ⓐ	†	⑤**f**
0	**Verdun** d.	0639	...	1050	1205	1238	...	...	1700	1815	1927	2225
40	Conflans-Jarny d.	0718	0731	1130	1256	1318	...	1642	1752	1854	2007	2307
66	Hagondange 388 d.	|	0812	1204	|	1356	1406	1713	|	1927	|	|
84	**Metz** 388 a.	0752	0827	1218	1335	...	1421	1727	1840	1943	2039	2340

	🚌 ①	🚌 ②–⑤	⚒	⚒	†	🚌 Ⓐ	Ⓐ	†	Ⓐ	⑥	🚌 Ⓐ
Metz 388 d.	0620	0715	0728	1230	1230	1420	1628	1706	1821	1828	1850
Hagondange 388 d.	|	|	0742	1244	1244	|	|	1721	|	1844	|
Conflans-Jarny d.	0704	0759	0814	1325	1324	1504	1709	1800	1855	1929	1934
Verdun a.	0750	0845	...	1400	...	1550	1744	1836	1929	2003	2020

– Also Dec. 24, 31, Apr. 30, May 7.

393 LONGWY - NANCY / LUXEMBOURG

Most trains 2nd class only

km		Ⓐ	⚒	Ⓐ	⑥	Ⓐ	†	⑥	†	Ⓐ	†
0	**Longwy** ▷ d.	0540	0640	0839	1051	1219	1240	1658	1741	1827	1940
16	Longuyon ▷ d.	0554	0654	0853	1104	1233	1254	1711	1755	1840	1954
57	Conflans-Jarny d.	0624	0724	0924	1135	1305	1324	1741	1825	1909	2024
100	Pont-à-Mousson d.	0652	0755	0952	1205	1335	1353	1810	1854	1938	2053
128	**Nancy** a.	0710	0814	1012	1222	1354	1412	1826	1912	1956	2110

	Ⓐ	Ⓐ	⑥	†	⑥	Ⓐ	†	Ⓐ	Ⓐ	⑥	†	†
Nancy d.	0606	0849	0906	1006	1254	1402	1708	1735	1836	1856	1937	2246
Pont-à-Mousson d.	0625	0907	0923	1025	1311	1424	1725	1752	1854	1914	1954	2303
Conflans-Jarny d.	0655	0937	0953	1056	1340	1457	1755	1821	1924	1944	2024	2333
Longuyon ▷ d.	|	1007	1024	1124	1410	1525	1824	1852	1953	2014	2054	0003
Longwy ▷ a.	0735	1020	1037	1137	1422	1537	1836	1905	2005	2027	2108	0016

km	★	①–⑤	①–⑥	①–⑥		①–⑤	①–⑤	⑥	①–⑤	
0	**Longwy** d.	0621	0641	0741	...	1314	1850	1855	1912	...
6	Pétange d.	0640	0656	0755	...	1328	1909	1909	1926	...
27	**Luxembourg** a.	0702	0722	0820	...	1350	1934	1934	2010	...

★	⑥	①–⑤		①–⑤	①–⑤	①–⑤	①–⑤	①–⑤	①–⑥	①–⑤	①–⑤
Luxembourg d.	0547	1211	...	1611	1626	1711	1726	1745	1811	1826	1911
Pétange d.	0609	1235	...	1635	1652	1735	1752	1810	1835	1852	1935
Longwy a.	0623	1248	...	1648	1705*	1749	1806	1823	1848	1906	1948

▷ – See also Table **389a**.
* – To Longuyon (arrive 1720).

★ – No service Dec. 25, 26, Jan. 1, Mar. 24, May 1, 12.

LONGWY - METZ Journey 72 mins (55 mins by 🚌).
From Longwy: 0620 ⚒ (also 🚌 at 0515 Ⓐ, 0735, 0930 ⚒, 1240 ⚒, 1645 Ⓐ, 1845 †, 1920 ⚒).
From Metz: 1714 ⚒ (also 🚌 at 0620 Ⓐ, 0842 ⚒, 0850 †, 1220 ⚒, 1615 Ⓐ, 1805 ⚒, 2020 Ⓒ, 2115 Ⓐ).

394 METZ - FORBACH - SAARBRÜCKEN

km		⚒ △	⚒	Ⓐ	⚒	†	Ⓐ ◇	⑥	†	Ⓐ	⑥	⚒			Ⓐ		Ⓐ	Ⓐ	†	⑥	Ⓐ		⚒	①–④ m	⑤	†
0	**Metz** d.	0642	0741	0814	0842	0842	0930	1042	1042	1216	1216	1242	1342	1549	1642	1747	1816	1834	1842	1919	1924	2019	...	2216	2334	2334
50	St Avold d.	0721	0813	0856	0917	0917	1005	1117	1120	1257	1256	1319	1416	1625	1718	1822	1855	1916	1929	2008	2003	2055	...	2253	0008	0009
70	Forbach a.	0738	0839	0913	0931	0931	1019	1135	1138	1316	1313	1335	1431	1640	1735	1840	1913	1933	1948	2026	2020	2112	...	2309	0024	0024
70	Forbach d.	0743	0844	0916	0936	0936	1024	1140	1143	1321	1316	1340a	1436	1645	1740	1845	1918	1938	1953	2031	2025	...	2117	2314	0029	0029
81	**Saarbrücken** a.	0752	0853	0925	0945	0945	1033	1149	1152	1330	1325	1349a	1445	1654	1749	1854	1927	1947	2002	2040	2034	...	2126	2323	0038	0038

	⚒ △	Ⓐ	⚒	⚒	Ⓐ	Ⓐ	Ⓒ	Ⓐ	†	⚒	Ⓐ	⑥	⚒			Ⓐ	Ⓒ	Ⓐ	†	Ⓐ	Ⓐ	⑥	Ⓑ	▽	Ⓐ
Saarbrücken d.	0503	0553	...	0631	0651	0731	0731	0831	0917	0925	1131	1153	...	1233	1431	1631	1631	...	...	1731	...	1753	1831	1931	2240
Forbach a.	0512	0602	...	0640	0700	0740	0740	0840	0926	0934	1140	1202	...	1241	1440	1640	1642	...	...	1740	...	1802	1840	1940	2249
Forbach d.	0517	...	0607	0645	0707	0745	0745	0845	0931	0939	1145	...	1207	1244	1445	1645	1645	1707	1707	1745	1807	1807	1846	1945	...
St Avold d.	0534	...	0624	0701	0725	0802	0800	0859	0948	0953	1159	...	1224	1303	1459	1700	1700	1724	1723	1801	1824	1825	1900	1959	...
Metz a.	0613	...	0705	0735	0806	0837	0830	0935	1029	1029	1236	...	1306	1335	1535	1735	1731	1804	1810	1838	1906	1913	1937	2034	...

a – Ⓐ only.
m – Not Dec. 25, 26, Jan. 1, Mar. 24, May 1, 8, 12.

◇ – Change at Forbach on ①.
△ – Change at Forbach on Ⓐ.
▽ – Change at Forbach on ⑤.

Note: on Dec. 26 and Mar. 21 a Sunday service will operate.

METZ - SARREGUEMINES Journey 63 - 70 mins:
From Metz: 1212 ⚒, 1707 Ⓐ, 1816 ⑥, 1919 Ⓑ.
From Sarreguemines: 0621 ⚒. 0728 Ⓐ, 1210 ⚒, 1714 †.

395 STRASBOURG - SAARBRÜCKEN

2nd class

km		Ⓐ	⑥ 🚌	Ⓐ	⑥	Ⓐ	Ⓒ			Ⓐ	⑥	†	Ⓐ	Ⓐ	⑥	Ⓐ	Ⓐ	⑥	Ⓐ	†	⑥	Ⓐ	†	
0	**Strasbourg** d.	0555	0551	0637	0752	0757	0845	...	1100	1222	1300	1430	1431	1530	1600	1626	1729	1729	1830	1910	1930	1951	2010	...
71	Diemeringen d.	0646	0719	0732	0848	0850	0941	...	1154	1323	1354	1523	1523	1622	1656	1729	1832	1833	1929	2004	2023	2045	2112	...
97	Sarreguemines a.	0711	|	0752	0911	0911	1006	...	1217	1349	1418	1544	1544	1644	1720	1753	1856	1856	1953	2023	2044	2105	2136	...
97	Sarreguemines 🏛 ▲ d.	0712	|	...	0912	0912	1023	...	1223	1355	1424	1555	...	1655	...	...	...	...	...	2026	2055	2126	...	...
115	**Saarbrücken** ▲ a.	0728	0820	...	0927	0927	1042	...	1244	1415	1441	1615	...	1715	...	...	...	...	...	2043	2114	2143	...	...

	Ⓐ	Ⓐ	⑥	Ⓐ	⚒			Ⓒ	Ⓐ	⑥	⚒	†	Ⓐ	⑤	①–④ m	†	Ⓒ	Ⓐ	†	Ⓐ
Saarbrücken ▲ d.	0443	...	...	...	...	0745	...	1024	1124	1124	...	1224	1324	1511	1524	...	1714	...	...	1814
Sarreguemines 🏛 ▲ a.	0459	...	...	...	...	0802	...	1044	1144	1144	...	1244	1344	1529	1544	...	1732	...	...	1832
Sarreguemines d.	0501	0535	0605	0605	0705	0805	...	1045	1145	1145	1245	1245	1345	1536	1553	1641	1742	1743	1824	1835
Diemeringen d.	0519	0554	0629	0630	0729	0829	...	1106	1205	1207	1308	1308	1406	1557	1615	1704	1806	1807	1850	1858
Strasbourg a.	0625	0700	0735	0735	0830	0927	...	1200	1304	1300	1404	1404	1505	1654	1711	1800	1900	1901	1952	2001

m – Not Dec. 25, 26, Jan. 1, Mar. 24, May 1, 8, 12.

Note: on Dec. 26 and Mar. 21 a Sunday service will operate.

▲ – Additional light rail service operates **Sarreguemines Bahnhof - Saarbrücken Hbf** (continuing to / from Ludwigstrasse and Riegelsberg Süd).

From Sarreguemines:
Ⓐ: hourly 0516 - 0016 (every 30 mins 0516 - 0916, 1216 - 2116);
⑥: hourly 0516 - 0016 (every 30 mins 0816 - 1816);
⑦: hourly 0716 - 0016 (every 30 mins 1216 - 1816).

From Saarbrücken:
Ⓐ: hourly 0440 - 2340 (every 30 mins 0440 - 0840, 1140 - 2040);
⑥: hourly 0440 - 2340 (every 30 mins 0740 - 1740);
⑦: hourly 0740 - 2340 (every 30 mins 1140 - 1740).

Journey time: 30 minutes.

On holidays service is as on ⑦.

396 STRASBOURG - HAGUENAU - WISSEMBOURG

2nd class only

km		⚒	Ⓐ	Ⓐ	Ⓒ	Ⓒ	Ⓑ		⑥	Ⓑ	⑥	Ⓐ			Ⓒ	Ⓐ		Ⓐ	Ⓒ	Ⓒ	Ⓐ	Ⓑ			
0	**Strasbourg** ▲ d.	0615	0729	0810	0810	0910	0955	1055	1200	1201	1210	1224	1354	1455	1555	1640	1719	1750	1750	1824	1825	1853	1926	2027	...
34	Haguenau ▲ d.	0646	0803	0843	0841	0942	1026	1126	1223	1234	1242	1252	1429	1528	1649	1706	1743	1822	1820	1859	1857	1930	1953	2059	...
66	**Wissembourg** a.	0722	0831	0917	...	1017	...	1157	...	...	1318	1325	1457	...	1724	1738	1824	1849	...	1939	1939	...	2026	...	...

	Ⓐ	⚒	Ⓐ	†	⑥	⑥	†	Ⓐ	Ⓒ	Ⓐ	Ⓒ	Ⓐ	†	⑥		⑥	†				⚒	Ⓐ	Ⓐ	Ⓐ b	†
Wissembourg d.	0609	0640	0727	...	0744	0830	...	0846	...	0930	1036	1218	...	1238	1336	...	...	1541	...	1745	1859	...	1956	...	2036
Haguenau ▶ d.	0647	0723	0757	0805	0812	0901	0902	0916	1002	1003	1110	1303	1305	1318	1402	1453	1502	1609	1756	1821	1940	2016	2029	2034	2103
Strasbourg ▶ a.	0724	0750	0825	0839	0845	0935	0936	0950	1036	1035	1142	1330	1338	1350	1427	1525	1535	1635	1820	1855	2017	2050	...	2114	2137

b – By 🚌.

Note: on Dec. 26, Mar. 21 a Sunday service will operate.

▲ – Additional journeys Strasbourg - Haguenau: 0655 ⚒, 0718 Ⓐ, 0829 Ⓐ, 0850 Ⓐ, 1020 Ⓐ, 1120 Ⓐ, 1241 Ⓐ, 1254 ⚒, 1324 Ⓐ, 1427 Ⓐ, 1525 Ⓐ, 1540 Ⓐ, 1555 Ⓐ, 1610 Ⓐ, 1625 Ⓐ, 1700 Ⓐ, 1725 Ⓐ, 1810 Ⓐ, 1842 Ⓐ, 1955 Ⓐ, 2055 Ⓐ **b**, 2155 ⚒ **b**, 2255 Ⓐ **b**.

▶ – Additional journeys Haguenau - Strasbourg: 0539 ⚒, 0603 Ⓐ, 0633 ⚒, 0647 †, 0704 ⚒, 0738 ⚒, 0818 Ⓐ, 0837 Ⓐ, 0848 Ⓐ, 0948 Ⓐ, 1018 Ⓐ, 1117 Ⓐ, 1148 Ⓐ, 1218 Ⓐ, 1248 Ⓐ, 1320 Ⓐ, 1347 Ⓐ, 1418 Ⓐ, 1448 Ⓐ, 1518 Ⓐ, 1548 Ⓐ, 1618 Ⓐ, 1644 Ⓐ, 1702 Ⓐ, 1730 Ⓐ, 1811 Ⓐ, 1845 Ⓐ, 1940 †, 2100 ⑥ **b**, 2145 Ⓐ **b**.

397 PRIVATE TOURIST RAILWAYS

CHEMIN DE FER DE LA MURE. Scenic electric railway. 2008 service

Days of running: daily April 1 - October 31.

30 km	D	B	C	B
St Georges de C ‡ d.	0945	1200	1430	1700
La Mure Gare a.	1135	1345	1620	1835

	B	B	D	C
La Mure Gare d.	0945	1200	1430	1700
St Georges de C ‡ a.	1115	1330	1605	1835

B – July 1 - Aug. 31. C – May 1 - Sept. 30. D – Apr. 1 - Oct. 31.
‡ – St Georges de Commiers. For SNCF connections see Table **362**.

Operator: Chemin de fer de la Mure, 38450 St Georges de Commiers, ✆ 04 76 735 734. Fax 04 76 735 736. www.trainlamure.com E-mail trainmure@aol.com

VIVARAIS RAILWAY. Scenic steam (🚂) and diesel line. 2007 service

Days of running: ⑥⑦ in Apr. and Oct.; ②③④⑥⑦ in May, June, Sept; daily in July and August. Journey time is 2 hours by steam train, 1 hour by railcar. *33* km. 2008 season starts Mar. 23.

Apr / Oct: Tournon d. 1000 ⑦ 🚂, 1130 ⑥⑦, 1800 ⑥⑦.
Lamastre d. 0800 ⑥⑦, 1500 ⑦ 🚂, 1600 ⑥⑦.

May / June / Sept: Tournon d. 1000 ②③④⑥⑦ 🚂, 1130 ⑥⑦, 1800 ②③④⑥⑦.
Lamastre d. 0800 ②③④⑥⑦, 1500 ②③④⑥⑦ 🚂, 1600 ⑥⑦.

July / Aug: Tournon d. 1000 🚂, 1800. Additional journey departs 1400 to Boucieu-le-Roi.
Lamastre d. 0800, 1500 🚂.

Note: on Apr. 9, 30, May 1, 7, 8, 17, 18, 28 service is as on ⑦.

Operator: Chemin de Fer du Vivarais, La Gare, 07300 Tournon sur Rhône, ✆ 04 75 08 20 30

TRAMWAY DU MONT BLANC *Tramway du Mont Blanc* ✆ 04.50.47.51.83, fax 04.50.78.32.75. The highest rack railway in France. www.compagniedumontblanc.fr

Winter Season Dec. 22, 2007 - Apr. 13, 2008: runs from St Gervais Le Fayet (opposite SNCF station) to Bellevue (altitude 1800 metres), journey 60 minutes.
Depart St Gervais 0900, 1000 Ⓒ, 1100, 1300, 1430, returning from Bellevue 1000, 1100 Ⓒ, 1200, 1430, 1630 (1650 Feb. 9 - Apr. 13).

Summer Season June 14 - Sept. 28, 2008 (timings subject to confirmation): runs from St Gervais Le Fayet (opposite SNCF station) to Nid d'Aigle (altitude 2380 metres), journey 75 minutes.
June 14 - July 4, Aug. 25 - Sept. 28: from St Gervais Le Fayet 0745, 0910, 1015, 1140, 1340, 1440, returning from Nid d'Aigle at 0900, 1025, 1150, 1325, 1535, 1635.
July 5 - Aug. 24: from St Gervais Le Fayet 0745, 0910, 1015, 1045, 1140, 1310, 1340, 1410, 1540, 1640, 1710, returning at 0900, 1025, 1150, 1225, 1250, 1430, 1525, 1550, 1650, 1750, 1840

CHAMONIX - MONTENVERS *Train du Montenvers* ✆ 04.50.53.12.54, fax 04.50.53.83.93. www.compagniedumontblanc.fr Journey 20 mins each way.
From Chamonix (200 metres from SNCF station) to Montenvers 'Mer de Glace' (altitude 1913 metres). A cable car takes visitors to the ice grotto inside the glacier (not all year).
Dec. 1 - 21, 2007 depart Chamonix 1000, 1200, 1400, 1500, 1600; depart Montenvers 1130, 1330, 1430, 1530, 1630.
Dec. 22, 2007 - Apr. 26, 2008 depart Chamonix 0900, 1000 and every 30 minutes to 1600; depart Montenvers 1000 and every 30 minutes to 1630. In summer runs every 20 - 30 minutes.

VLISSINGEN - ROTTERDAM - DEN HAAG - AMSTERDAM 450

For INTERNATIONAL TRAINS **Paris – Brussels – Amsterdam**, see Table **18**
For OTHER TRAINS **Breda – Rotterdam – Den Haag**, see Table **470**
For NIGHT NETWORK **Rotterdam – Amsterdam – Utrecht**, see Table **454**
For OTHER TRAINS **Haarlem – Amsterdam**, see Table **470**

km																								
										Ⓐ		Ⓐ	Ⓐ				Ⓐ	⚒	⚒		Ⓐ			⚒
	Vlissingen d.	...	...	...	...	...	...	...	...	...	...	...	...	...	...	...	...	...	...	...	...	...	...	...
	Middelburg d.	...	...	...	...	...	...	...	...	...	...	...	...	...	...	...	...	...	...	...	...	...	...	...
	Goes d.	...	...	...	...	...	...	...	...	...	...	...	...	...	...	...	...	...	...	...	...	...	...	...
	Bergen op Zoom d.	...	...	...	...	...	...	...	...	...	...	...	...	...	...	...	...	...	...	...	0535	...	...	...
	Roosendaal 410 a.	...	...	...	...	...	...	...	...	...	...	...	...	...	...	...	...	...	...	...	0545	...	...	...
	Roosendaal d.	...	...	...	...	...	...	...	...	...	...	...	...	...	...	...	...	...	...	...	0549	...	...	...
0	**Breda** d.	...	...	0020	...	...	...	...	...	...	...	...	...	...	...	...	...	...	...	...	|	...	...	...
29	Dordrecht d.	...	...	0048	...	...	...	...	...	0436	...	...	...	...	...	...	...	0533	...	...	0612	...	...	...
42	Rotterdam Lombardijen d.	...	...	0102	...	...	...	...	...	0449	...	...	...	...	...	...	...	0550	...	...	|	...	...	...
49	**Rotterdam** Centraal d.	0100	...	0114	...	0200	...	...	0500	0459	...	0528	...	...	0559	...	...	0600	0611	...	0628	0628	...	...
64	Delft d.	0114	...	...	...	0215	...	...	0514	...	...	|	...	...	|	...	...	0617	0624	...	|	|	...	...
72	**Den Haag** HS d.	|	...	...	...	|	...	...	|	...	...	0552	...	...	0616	...	...	0630	0632	...	0647	0647	...	...
	Den Haag Centraal d.	0127	...	...	...	0229	...	...	0528	...	...	|	0558	...	|	...	0628	0633	|	...	|	|	...	0658
92	Leiden Centraal **457** d.	0142	...	...	...	0245	...	...	0550	...	...	0607	0613	...	0630	...	0643	...	0645	...	0700	0700	...	0713
121	Haarlem d.	|	...	...	...	|	...	...	|	...	...	|	|	...	|	...	|	...	0706	...	|	|	...	|
	Schiphol ✈ 457 d.	0200	...	...	...	0303	...	...	0608	...	...	0624	0630	...	0648	...	0700	...	|	...	0718	0718	...	0730
	Amsterdam Sloterdijk **457** d.	|	...	...	...	|	...	...	|	...	...	|	0642	...	|	...	0712	...	0716	...	|	|	...	0742
	Amsterdam Centraal **457** a.	0215	...	...	...	0316	...	...	0625	...	...	0638	0649	...	0703	...	0719	...	0722	...	0733	0733	...	0749

	Ⓐ	⚒		Ⓐ			⚒	⚒			Ⓐ	⑥		Ⓐ			⚒						⚒	
Vlissingen d.	...	...	...	...	...	...	...	...	...	...	0545	...	...	...	...	...	0612	...	...	...	...	...	0643	...
Middelburg d.	...	...	...	...	...	...	...	...	...	...	0552	...	...	...	...	...	0620	...	...	...	...	...	0651	...
Goes d.	...	...	...	...	...	...	...	...	...	...	0606	...	...	...	...	...	0634	...	...	...	...	...	0705	...
Bergen op Zoom d.	...	...	...	0605	...	...	...	...	...	...	0634	...	...	...	...	...	0707	...	...	...	...	...	0737	...
Roosendaal 410 a.	...	...	...	0615	...	...	...	...	...	...	0644	...	...	...	...	...	0716	...	...	...	...	...	0747	...
Roosendaal d.	...	...	...	0619	...	...	...	...	...	...	0648	...	...	...	...	...	0717	...	...	...	...	...	0748	...
Breda d.	0550	...	...	|	...	...	...	0620a	...	...	|	...	...	0650	...	...	|	...	...	...	0720v	...	|	...
Dordrecht d.	0622	...	...	0643	0643	...	...	0648	...	...	0712	0712	...	0718	...	...	0743	...	...	...	0752	...	0812	0812
Rotterdam Lombardijen d.	0631	...	...	|	|	...	...	0657	...	...	|	|	...	0727	...	...	|	...	...	...	0801	...	|	|
Rotterdam Centraal d.	0641	0641	...	0658	0658	...	...	0711	0711	...	0728	0728	...	0741	0741	...	0758	0758	...	...	0811	...	0828	0828
Delft d.	0654	0654	...	|	|	...	...	0724	0724	...	|	|	...	0754	0754	...	|	|	...	...	0824	...	|	|
Den Haag HS d.	0702	0702	...	0717	0717	...	...	0732	0732	...	0747	0747	...	0802	0802	...	0817	0817	...	...	0832	...	0847	0847
Den Haag Centraal d.	|	|	...	|	|	...	0728	|	|	...	|	|	0758	|	|	...	|	|	...	0828	|	...	|	|
Leiden Centraal **457** d.	0715	0715	...	0730	0730	...	0743	0745	0745	...	0800	0800	0813	0815	0815	...	0830	0830	...	0843	0845	...	0900	0900
Haarlem d.	0736	0736	...	|	|	...	|	0806	0806	...	|	|	|	0836	0836	...	|	|	...	|	0906	...	|	|
Schiphol ✈ 457 d.	|	|	...	0748	0748	...	0800	|	|	...	0818	0818	0830	|	|	...	0848	0848	...	0900	|	...	0918	0918
Amsterdam Sloterdijk **457** d.	0746	0746	...	|	|	...	0812	0816	0816	...	|	|	0842	0846	0846	...	|	|	...	0912	0916	...	|	|
Amsterdam Centraal **457** a.	0752	0752	...	0803	0803	...	0819	0822	0822	...	0833	0833	0849	0852	0852	...	0903	0903	...	0929	0922	...	0933	0933

		▽																⑥d			★		
Vlissingen d.	...	...	0716	...	...	...	0752	and at the same minutes past each hour until	...	...	2116	...	...	...	2152	...	2216	...	...	...	...	2316	...
Middelburg d.	...	...	0723	...	...	...	0759		...	...	2123	...	...	...	2159	...	2223	...	...	...	...	2323	...
Goes d.	...	...	0737	...	...	...	0811		...	...	2137	...	...	...	2211	...	2237	...	...	...	...	2337	...
Bergen op Zoom d.	...	...	0805	...	...	...	0835		...	...	2205	...	...	...	2235	...	2305	...	...	...	...	0005	...
Roosendaal 410 a.	...	...	0815	...	...	...	0845		...	...	2215	...	...	...	2245	...	2315	...	...	...	...	0015	...
Roosendaal d.	...	...	...	0830	...	...	0849		...	...	...	2230	...	...	2249	...	...	2330	...	...	...	...	...
Breda d.	...	0750a	...	|	...	0820	|		...	...	...	|	...	2220	|	...	...	|	...	...	2322	...	...
Dordrecht d.	...	0822	...	0854	...	0852	0912		...	2222	...	2254	...	2252	2312	2322	...	2354	...	...	2348	...	...
Rotterdam Lombardijen d.	...	0831	...	|	...	0901	|		...	2231	...	|	...	2301	|	2331	...	|	...	...	2357	...	...
Rotterdam Centraal d.	...	0841	...	0908	...	0911	0928		...	2241	...	2308	...	2311	2328	2341	...	0008	...	...	0011	...	...
Delft d.	...	0854	...	|	...	0924	|		...	2254	...	|	...	2324	|	2354	...	|	...	...	0024	...	...
Den Haag HS d.	...	0902	...	0926	...	0932	0947		...	2302	...	2326	...	2332	2347	0002	...	0026	...	...	0032	...	...
Den Haag Centraal d.	0858	|	...	|	0928	|	|		2258	|	...	|	2328	|	|	|	...	|	0025	...	|	...	...
Leiden Centraal **457** d.	0913	0915	...	|	0943	0945	1000		2313	2315	...	|	2343	2345	0000	0015	...	|	0042	...	0053	...	...
Haarlem d.	|	0936	...	|	|	1006	|		|	2336	...	|	|	0006	|	0043	...	|	|	...	0117	...	...
Schiphol ✈ 457 d.	0931	|	...	0949s	1001	|	1018		2331	|	...	2349s	0001	|	0018	|	...	0049s	0100	...	|	...	...
Amsterdam Sloterdijk **457** d.	0944	0946	...	|	1014	1016	|		2344	2346	...	|	0014	0016	|	0057	...	|	|	...	0129	...	...
Amsterdam Centraal **457** a.	0950	0952	...	1006	1020	1022	1033		2350	2352	...	0006	0020	0022	0033	0102	...	0106	0115	...	0135	...	...

a – Ⓐ only.
d – Also Apr. 30, May 1.
s – Stops to set down only.
v – ⚒ only.
▽ – From Breda at 0850 Ⓐ, 1550 Ⓐ, 1650 Ⓐ and 1750 Ⓐ. Other services in this pattern start from Dordrecht.
★ – On certain dates runs 4–25 minutes later between Dordrecht and Amsterdam.

UTRECHT - SCHIPHOL ✈ 452

From Utrecht Centraal *45 km*

0643 Ⓐ, 0713 Ⓐ, 0743 ⚒, 0813 ⚒, 0843, 0913 and every 30 minutes until 2343.

These trains also call at Amsterdam Zuid 24 minutes later.

From Schiphol ✈ Journey time: ± 33 minutes

0614 Ⓐ, 0644 ⚒, 0714, 0744 and every 30 minutes until 2344.

These trains also call at Amsterdam Zuid 9 minutes later.

UTRECHT - AMSTERDAM - DEN HAAG - ROTTERDAM Night Network 454

km									
							Ⓒ		Ⓐ
0	**Utrecht** Centraal d.	0026	...	0106	0206	0306	0406	0406	...
40	Amsterdam Centraal a.	|	...	0140	0240	0340	0442	0442	...
40	Amsterdam Centraal d.	|	0042	0142	0242	0342	0442	0442	...
57	Schiphol ✈ d.	|	0100	0200	0300	0400	0500	0500	...
84	Leiden Centraal d.	0111	0117	0217	0317	0417	0517	0517	...
99	Den Haag Centraal a.	...	0129	0229	0329	0429	0529	0529	...
99	Den Haag Centraal d.	...	0134	0234	0334	0434	0534	...	0551
109	Delft d.	...	0143	0243	0343	0443	0543	...	0603
124	**Rotterdam** Centraal a.	...	0157	0256	0355	0454	0554	...	0615

							Ⓒ	Ⓐ	Ⓐ
Rotterdam Centraal d.	2346	...	0100	0200	0300	0400	0500	0500	...
Delft d.	2358	...	0111	0211	0311	0411	0511	0511	...
Den Haag Centraal a.	0010	...	0122	0224	0323	0423	0520	0523	...
Den Haag Centraal d.	...	0025	0127	0225	0325	0425	0525	0525	...
Leiden Centraal d.	...	0042	0141	0239	0339	0439	0539	0539	...
Schiphol ✈ d.	...	0100	0200	0300	0400	0500	0600	0605	...
Amsterdam Centraal a.	...	0114	0215	0315	0415	0515	0615	0619	...
Amsterdam Centraal d.	...	0117	0217	0317	0417	0517	0617	...	0622
Utrecht Centraal a.	...	0152	0253	0355	0449	0555	0646	...	0649

HOEK VAN HOLLAND - ROTTERDAM 455

For connections to shipping services, see Table **15a**

From Hoek van Holland Haven *27 km*

0007 **N**, 0013 **P**, 0037, 0107 **N**, 0134 **P**, 0537 Ⓐ, 0607 Ⓐ, 0637 Ⓐ, 0652 Ⓐ, 0707 ⚒, 0722 Ⓐ, 0737 ⚒, 0752 Ⓐ, 0807, 0822 Ⓐ, 0837, 0907, 0937 and at 07 and 37 minutes past each hour until 2337.

From Rotterdam Centraal Journey time: ± 30 minutes

0013 **N**, 0043 **D**, 0100 **P**, 0450 **T**, 0513 **E**, 0543 Ⓐ, 0613 Ⓐ, 0628, 0643 ⚒, 0658 Ⓐ, 0713 ⚒, 0728 Ⓐ, 0743, 0758 Ⓐ, 0813, 0843 and at 13 and 43 minutes past each hour until 2343.

D – ⑥⑦ (also May 1, 2).
E – ① (not Mar. 24, May 12).
N – ①⑥⑦ (also Dec. 26, 27, Jan. 2, Mar. 25, May 1, 2, 13).
P – ②–⑤ (not Dec. 26, 27, Jan. 2, Mar. 25, May 1, 2, 13).
T – ②–⑤ (not Dec. 25, 26, Jan. 1, Apr. 30, May 1).

457 LEIDEN and AMSTERDAM - UTRECHT and AMERSFOORT

km		△			Ⓐ	Ⓐ	Ⓐ	⚒	Ⓐ	⚒	⚒		⚒										
0	**Leiden** Centraal 450 d.	...	...	...	...	...	...	...	...	0618	...	0648	...	0718	...	0748	...	and at the same minutes past each hour until	...	2318	...	2348	...
27	Schiphol ✈ 450 d.	...	...	...	0540	...	0610	...	...	0640	...	0710	...	0740	...	0810	...		...	2340	...	0010	...
36	Amsterdam Zuid d.	...	...	...	0548	...	0618	...	...	0648	...	0718	...	0748	...	0818	...		...	2348	...	0018	...
41	Duivendrecht d.	...	...	...	0556	...	0626	...	...	0656	...	0726	...	0756	...	0826	...		...	2356	...	0026	...
	Amsterdam Centraal 450 d.	0036	...	...	|	0606	|	...	0636	|	0706	|	0736	|	0806	|	0836		2336	|	0006	|	...
49	Weesp d.	0053	...	...	0613	0623	0643	...	0653	0713	0723	0743	0753	0813	0823	0843	0853		2353	0013	0023	0043	...
58	Naarden-Bussum d.	0100	...	...	0620	0630	0650	0650	0700	0720	0730	0750	0800	0820	0830	0850	0900		0000	0020	0030	0050	...
64	Hilversum d.	0109	...	...	0631	0639	0701	0701	0709	0731	0739	0801	0809	0831	0839	0901	0909		0009	0031	0039	0101	...
81	**Utrecht** Centraal a.	|	...	...	0651	|	0721	0721	|	0751	|	0821	|	0851	|	0921	|		|	0051	|	0121	...
71	Baarn d.	0115	...	...	...	0645	...	...	0715	...	0745	...	0815	...	0845	...	0915		0015	...	0045	...	...
80	**Amersfoort** a.	0125	...	...	...	0652	...	...	0722	...	0752	...	0822	...	0852	...	0922		0022	...	0052	...	...

km						Ⓐ		Ⓐ		Ⓐ												N	
0	**Amersfoort** d.	0006	...	...	0436	0456	...	0536	...	0606	...	0636	...	0706	and at the same minutes past each hour until	2206	...	2236	...	2306	...	2336	...
9	Baarn d.	0013	...	...	0443	0504	...	0543	...	0613	...	0643	...	0713		2213	...	2243	...	2313	...	2343	...
	Utrecht Centraal d.	|	0028	...	|	|	0513	|	0543	|	0608	|	0638	|		|	2208	|	2238	|	2308	|	2338
16	Hilversum d.	|	0046	...	0450	|	0534	0550	0604	0620	0629	0650	0659	0720		2220	2229	2250	2259	|	2329	2350	2359
22	Naarden-Bussum d.	0028	0053	...	0458	0519	0540	0558	0610	0628	0639	0658	0709	0728		2228	2239	2258	2309	2328	2339	2358	0009
31	Weesp d.	0037	...	...	0507	0529	0553	0607	0623	0637	0653	0707	0723	0737		2237	2253	2307	2323	2337	2353	0007	0023
45	**Amsterdam** Centraal 450 a.	0055	...	...	0525	0549	|	0622	|	0652	|	0722	|	0752		2252	|	2322	|	2352	|	0022	...
39	Duivendrecht d.	...	...	...	...	...	0604	...	0634	...	0704	...	0734	...		...	2304	...	2334	...	0004	...	0034
43	Amsterdam Zuid d.	...	...	...	...	...	0611	...	0641	...	0711	...	0741	...		...	2311	...	2341	...	0011	...	0041
53	Schiphol ✈ 450 a.	...	...	...	...	...	0619	...	0649	...	0719	...	0749	...		...	2319	...	2349	...	0019	...	0049
80	**Leiden** Centraal 450 a.	...	...	...	...	...	0642	...	0712	...	0742	...	0812	...		...	2342	...	0012	...	...	...	...

N – ⑤⑥ (also Apr. 30, May 1).

△ – Runs 6–10 minutes later on certain dates.

458 SCHIPHOL ✈ and AMSTERDAM - LELYSTAD

km		△			Ⓐ	Ⓐ	Ⓐ	Ⓐ	⚒	Ⓐ K	⚒		Ⓐ K	⚒		Ⓐ K			Ⓐ K			Ⓐ K			Ⓐ K
0	**Schiphol** ✈ 450 d.	...	0026	...	...	0555	...	0626	...	0641	0655	...	0711	0726	...	0741	0755	...	0811	0826	...	0841	0855	...	0911
9	Amsterdam Zuid d.	...	0034	...	...	0604	...	0634	...	|	0704	...	|	0734	...	|	0804	...	|	0834	...	|	0904	...	|
14	Duivendrecht d.	...	0042	...	...	0612	...	0642	...	|	0712	...	|	0742	...	|	0812	...	|	0842	...	|	0912	...	|
	Amsterdam Sloterdijk 450 d.	...	|	...	...	|	...	|	...	0653	|	...	0723	|	...	0753	|	...	0823	|	...	0853	|	...	0923
	Amsterdam Centraal 450 a.	...	|	...	...	|	...	|	...	0700	|	...	0730	|	...	0800	|	...	0830	|	...	0900	|	...	0930
	Amsterdam Centraal d.	0020	|	...	0550	|	0620	|	0650	0703	|	0720	0733	|	0750	0803	|	0820	0833	|	0850	0903	|	0920	0933
22	Weesp d.	0038	0101	...	0608	0624	0638	0654	0708	|	0724	0738	|	0754	0808	|	0824	0838	|	0854	0908	|	0924	0938	|
37	Almere Centrum d.	0051	0110	...	0621	0637	0651	0707	0721	0726	0737	0751	0756	0807	0821	0826	0837	0851	0856	0907	0921	0926	0937	0951	0956
42	Almere Buiten d.	0058	0121	...	0628	0644	0658	0714	0728	0732	0744	0758	0802	0814	0828	0832	0844	0858	0902	0914	0928	0932	0944	0958	1002
62	**Lelystad** Centrum a.	0113	0136	...	...	0658	...	0728	...	0744	0758	0812y	0814	0828	0842y	0844	0858	0912y	0914	0928	0942y	0944	0958	1012y	1014

			⚒ K			⚒ K				⚒ K			⚒ K										
Schiphol ✈ 450 d.	0926	...	0941	0955	...	1011	and at the same minutes past each hour until	1855	...	1911	1926	...	1941	then	1955	...	2026	...	and at the same minutes past each hour until	...	2326	...	2355
Amsterdam Zuid d.	0934	...	|	1004	...	|		1904	...	|	1934	...	|		2004	...	2034	...		...	2334	...	0004
Duivendrecht d.	0942	...	|	1012	...	|		1912	...	|	1942	...	|		2012	...	2042	...		...	2342	...	0012
Amsterdam Sloterdijk 450 d.	|	...	0953	|	...	1023		|	...	1923	|	...	1953		|	...	|	...		...	|	...	|
Amsterdam Centraal 450 a.	|	...	1000	|	...	1030		|	...	1930	|	...	2000		|	...	|	...		...	|	...	|
Amsterdam Centraal d.	|	0950	1003	|	1020	1033		|	1920	1933	|	1950	2003		|	2020	|	2050		2320	|	2350	|
Weesp d.	0954	1008	|	1024	1038	|		1924	1938	|	1954	2008	|		2024	2038	2054	2108		2338	2354	0008	0024
Almere Centrum d.	1007	1021	1026	1037	1051	1056		1937	1951	1956	2007	2021	2026		2037	2051	2107	2121		2351	0007	0021	0037
Almere Buiten d.	1014	1028	1032	1044	1058	1102		1944	1958	2002	2014	2028	2032		2044	2058	2114	2128		2358	0014	0028	0044
Lelystad Centrum a.	1028	1042y	1044	1058	1112y	1114		1958	2012y	2014	2028	2042y	2044		2058	2112	2128	2142		0012	0028	0043	0058

km					Ⓐ			Ⓐ	Ⓐ K		Ⓐ	Ⓐ K			Ⓐ K			Ⓐ K			Ⓐ K				⚒ K
0	**Lelystad** Centrum d.	0000	...	0430	0450	...	0516	0530	0545	0546c	0600	0615	0616c	0630	0645	0646c	0700	0715	0716c	0730	0745	0746y	...	0800	0815
20	Almere Buiten d.	0015	...	0445	0505	...	0530	0545	0557	0600	0615	0627	0630	0645	0657	0700	0715	0727	0730	0745	0757	0700	...	0815	0827
25	Almere Centrum d.	0023	...	0453	0516	...	0538	0553	0603	0608	0623	0633	0638	0653	0703	0708	0723	0733	0738	0753	0803	0708	...	0823	0833
40	Weesp d.	0037	...	0507	0527	...	0553	0607	|	0623	0637	|	0653	0707	|	0723	0737	|	0753	0807	|	0723	...	0837	|
53	**Amsterdam** Centraal a.	|	...	|	|	...	0608	|	0627	0640	|	0655	0710	|	0725	0740	|	0755	0810	|	0825	0740	...	|	0855
53	**Amsterdam** Centraal 450 d.	|	...	|	|	...	...	|	0632	...	|	0702	...	|	0732	...	|	0802	...	|	0832	...	...	|	0902
58	Amsterdam Sloterdijk 450 a.	|	...	|	|	...	...	|	0639	...	|	0709	...	|	0739	...	|	0809	...	|	0839	...	...	|	0909
	Duivendrecht d.	0047	...	0517	0537	...	...	0617	|	...	0647	|	...	0717	|	...	0747	|	...	0817	|	...	...	0847	|
	Amsterdam Zuid a.	0054	...	0523	0545	...	...	0625	|	...	0653	|	...	0723	|	...	0753	|	...	0823	|	...	...	0853	|
	Schiphol ✈ 450 a.	0104	...	0533	0601	...	...	0632	0649	...	0702	0719	...	0732	0749	...	0802	0819	...	0832	0849	...	...	0902	0919

			⚒ K				⚒ K			⚒ K												N	
Lelystad Centrum d.	0816y	0830	0844	0846y	and at the same minutes past each hour until	1900	1915	1916y	1930	1945	1946y	then	2000	2016	2030	2046	and at the same minutes past each hour until	2230	2246	2300	2316	2330	2346
Almere Buiten d.	0830	0845	0856	0900		1915	1927	1930	1945	1957	2000		2015	2030	2045	2100		2345	2300	2315	2330	2345	0000
Almere Centrum d.	0838	0853	0902	0908		1923	1933	1938	1953	2003	2008		2023	2038	2053	2108		2353	2308	2323	2338	2353	0008
Weesp d.	0853	0907	|	0923		1937	|	1953	2007	|	2023		2037	2053	2107	2123		2307	2323	2337	2353	0007	0023
Amsterdam Centraal a.	0910	|	0922	0940		|	1955	2010	|	2025	2010		|	2110	|	2140		|	2340	|	0010	|	0040
Amsterdam Centraal 450 d.	...	|	0932	...		|	2002	...	|	2032	...		|	...	|	...		|	...	|	...	|	...
Amsterdam Sloterdijk 450 a.	...	|	0939	...		|	2009	...	|	2039	...		|	...	|	...		|	...	|	...	|	...
Duivendrecht d.	...	0917	|	...		1947	|	...	2017	|	...		2047	...	2117	...		2317	...	2347	...	0017	...
Amsterdam Zuid a.	...	0923	|	...		1953	|	...	2023	|	...		2053	...	2123	...		2323	...	2353	...	0023	...
Schiphol ✈ 450 a.	...	0932	0949	...		2002	2019	...	2032	2049	...		2102	...	2132	...		2332	...	0002	...	0032	...

K – Runs daily Schiphol - Amsterdam Centraal and v.v.
N – ⑤⑥ (also Apr. 30, May 1).

c – Ⓒ only.
y – † only.

△ – Runs 6–6 minutes later on certain dates.

459 ENKHUIZEN - SCHIPHOL ✈ and AMSTERDAM

km		⑥k	Ⓐ	Ⓐ	Ⓐ	⚒	⚒	Ⓐ	⚒		⚒											
0	**Enkhuizen** d.	...	0442	0530	...	0553	0623a	...	0653	0723	...	0753	0823	...	and at the same minutes past each hour until	2123	...	2153	2223	2253	2323	2353
18	Hoorn d.	0504	0505	0551	0611	0617	0647	0711	0717	0747	0811	0817	0847	0911		2147	2211	2217	2247	2317	2347	0017
50	Zaandam 466 d.	0531	0534	0618	0639	0645	0715	0739	0745	0815	0839	0845	0915	0939		2215	2239	2245	2315	2345	0015	0045
58	Amsterdam Sloterdijk 466 a.	|	|	0623	|	0650	0720	|	0750	0820	|	0850	0920	|		2220	|	2250	2320	2350	0021	0058
	Schiphol ✈ a.	0550	0552	*0649*	0654	*0719*	*0749*	0754	*0819*	*0849*	0854	*0919*	*0949*	0954		*2249*	2254	*2319*	|	*0019*	*0049*p	|
62	**Amsterdam** Centraal 466 a.	*0545*r	*0548*r	0629	...	0657	0727	...	0757	0827	...	0857	0927	...		2227	...	2257	2327	2357	0028	0105

		Ⓐ		Ⓐ	⚒			⚒	Ⓐ				⚒								
Amsterdam Centraal 466 d.	0033	...	0603	...	0633	...	0703	...	0733	...	0803	...	0833	...	...	0903	0933	...	and at the same minutes past each hour until	2303	2333	...
Schiphol ✈ d.	*0011*	...	|	...	*0611*	0636	*0641*	...	*0711*	0735	*0741*	...	*0811*	0835	...	*0841*	*0911*	0935		*2241*	*2311*	2335
Amsterdam Sloterdijk 466 d.	0039	...	0609	...	0639	|	0709	...	0739	|	0809	...	0839	|	...	0909	0909	|		2309	2339	|
Zaandam 466 d.	0046	...	0616	...	0646	0653	0716	...	0746	0753	0816	...	0846	0853	...	0916	0946	0953		2316	2346	2353
Hoorn d.	0116	...	0646	...	0716	0721	0746	...	0816	0821	0846	...	0916	0921	...	0946	1016	1021		2346	0016	0021
Enkhuizen a.	0139	...	0708	...	0738	...	0808	...	0838	...	0908	...	0938	...	...	1008	1038	...		0008	0038	...

a – Ⓐ only.

k – Also Apr. 30, May 1.

p – ②–⑤ (not Dec. 26, 27, Jan. 2, Mar. 25, May 1, 2, 13).

r – Change at Zaandam.

For traffic arrangements on Dutch holiday dates, see page 248

HAARLEM - ALKMAAR - HOORN 461

km		Ⓐ	Ⓐ	Ⓐ	⚒	Ⓐ	⚒	⚒		⚒													
0	**Haarlem** d.	...	...	0643	...	0713	...	0743	...	0813	0843	0913	and every 30 minutes until	1913	1943	2013	2043	...	2143	...	2243	...	2343
11	Beverwijk d.	...	...	0653	...	0723	...	0753	...	0823	0853	0923		1923	1953	2023	2053	...	2153	...	2253	...	2353
22	Castricum 466 d.	...	...	0704	...	0734	...	0804	...	0834	0904	0934		1934	2004	2034	2104	...	2204	...	2304	...	0004
34	**Alkmaar** 466 d.	0616	0646	0716	0716	0746	0746	0816	0816	0846	0916	0946		1946	2016	2045	2116	...	2216	...	2316	...	0016
40	Heerhugowaard 466 a.	0624	0654	0724	0742	0754	0754	0824	0824	0854	0924	0954		1954	2024	*2058*	2124	...	2224	...	2324	...	0024
57	**Hoorn** a.	0640	0710	0740	0740	0810	0810	0840	0840	0910	0940	1010		2010	2040	...	2140	...	2240	...	2340	...	0040

	Ⓐ	Ⓐ	⚒	⚒		⚒			⚒														
Hoorn d.	0557	0621	0651	0721	0751	0821	...	0851	0921	...	0951	1021	and every 30 minutes until	1921	1951	...	2051	...	2151	...	2251	...	2351
Heerhugowaard 466 d.	0612	0636	0706	0736	0806	0836	...	0906	0936	...	1006	1036		1936	2006	...	2106	...	2206	...	2306	...	0006
Alkmaar 466 d.	0621	0645	0715	0745	0815	0845	0845	0915	0945	0945	1015	1045		1945	2015	...	2115	...	2215	...	2315	...	0014
Castricum 466 d.	0632	0656	0726	0756	0826	0856	0856	0926	0956	0956	1026	1056		1956	2026	...	2126	...	2226	...	2326	...	...
Beverwijk a.	0642	0708	0738	0808	0838	0908	0908	0938	1008	1008	1038	1108		2008	2038	...	2136	...	2236	...	2336	...	...
Haarlem a.	0652	0718	0748	0818	0848	0918	0918	0948	1018	1018	1048	1118		2018	2048	...	2148	...	2248	...	2348	...	...

LEIDEN - ALPHEN - UTRECHT 463

km			Ⓐ	⚒	⚒				
0	**Leiden** Centraal ‡d.	0022	0552	0622	0652	0722	0752	and every 30 minutes until	2352
15	Alphen aan den Rijn △‡d.	0038	0608	0638	0708	0738	0808		0008
34	Woerden d.	0057	0625	0655	0725	0755	0825		0025
50	**Utrecht** Centraal a.	0110	0636	0708	0736	0808	0836		0036

		Ⓐ	⚒	⚒				
Utrecht Centraal d.	0020	0556	0626	0656	0726	0756	and every 30 minutes until	2356
Woerden d.	0040	0608	0638	0708	0738	0808		0008
Alphen aan den Rijn △‡d.	0057	0624	0654	0724	0754	0824		0024
Leiden Centraal ‡a.	0111	0637	0707	0737	0807	0837		0037

‡ – Additional peak-hour services run Leiden - Alphen and v.v. on Ⓐ.

△ – Connecting lightrail services run at least hourly Alphen - Gouda and v.v. *17 km.* Journey: ± 20 mins.

AMSTERDAM - GOUDA - ROTTERDAM 465

For fast trains **Amsterdam** – **Rotterdam** and v.v. via **Den Haag**, see Table **450**

km		Ⓐ		Ⓐ		⚒		⚒								Q	R		Q	R		
0	**Amsterdam** Centraal 468 470 d.	0555	...	0625	...	0655	...	0725	...	0755	...	0825	and every 30 minutes until	2255	...	2325	2325	...	2355	2355	...	...
9	Duivendrecht 468 470 d.	0607	...	0637	...	0707	...	0737	...	0807	...	0837		2307	...	2337	2337	...	0007	0007	...	...
27	Breukelen d.	0623	...	0653	...	0723	...	0753	...	0823	...	0853		2323	...	2353	2353	...	0023	0023	...	...
40	Woerden d.	0633	...	0703	...	0733	...	0803	...	0833	...	0903		2333	...	0003	0003	...	0039	0039	...	...
56	**Gouda** 483 d.	0646	...	0716	...	0746	...	0816	...	0846	...	0916		2346	...	0016	0021	...	0052	0111	...	...
70	Rotterdam Alexander 483 d.	0658	...	0728	...	0758	...	0828	...	0858	...	0928		2358	...	0028	0033	...	0104	0123	...	...
80	**Rotterdam** Centraal 483 a.	0708	...	0738	...	0808	...	0838	...	0908	...	0938		0008	...	0038	0043	...	0114	0133	...	...

	Ⓐ		Ⓐ		⚒		⚒									
Rotterdam Centraal 483 d.	0520	...	0550	...	0620	...	0650	...	0720	...	0750	and every 30 minutes until	2250	...	2320	...
Rotterdam Alexander 483 d.	0531	...	0601	...	0631	...	0701	...	0731	...	0801		2301	...	2331	...
Gouda 483 d.	0545	...	0615	...	0645	...	0715	...	0745	...	0815		2315	...	2345	...
Woerden d.	0558	...	0628	...	0658	...	0728	...	0758	...	0828		2328	...	2358	...
Breukelen d.	0608	...	0638	...	0708	...	0738	...	0808	...	0838		2338	...	0008	...
Duivendrecht 468 470 d.	0623	...	0653	...	0723	...	0753	...	0823	...	0853		2353	...	0022	...
Amsterdam Centraal 468 470 a.	0637	...	0707	...	0737	...	0807	...	0837	...	0907		0007	...	0036	...

Q – ⑤⑥⑦ (also Dec. 25, 26, Jan. 1, Mar. 24, Apr. 30, May 1, 24).

R – ①–④ (not Dec. 25, 26, Jan. 1, Mar. 24, Apr. 30, May 1, 24).

AMSTERDAM - DEN HELDER 466

km							Ⓐ	Ⓐ	⚒	⑥j	Ⓐ	Ⓐ										Q		
	Utrecht Centraal 468 d.	2340	...	0017p	...	...	...	...	...	...	...	...	0640v	...	0710	0740	and every 30 minutes until	2210	2240	...	...	...	...
0	**Amsterdam** Centraal 459 d.	0013	...	0108	...	...	0518	0547	...	0616	0625	0643	0713	...	0743	0813		2243	2313	...	2346	...	...
5	Amsterdam Sloterdijk 459 d.	0019	...	0116	...	...	0524	0553	...	0622	0631	0649	0719	...	0749	0819		2249	2319	...	2351	...	...
12	Zaandam 459 d.	0026	...	0123	...	...	0532	0603	...	0629	0638	0656	0726	...	0756	0826		2256	2326	...	0003	...	...
29	Castricum 461 d.	0040	...	0145	...	...	0600	0626	...	0650	0652	0708	0738	...	0808	0838		2308	2338	...	0025	...	...
41	**Alkmaar** 461 d.	0051	...	0157	...	...	0611	0637	0650	0702	0706	0720	0750	...	0820	0850		2320	2350	...	0036	...	...
48	Heerhugowaard 461 a.	0059	...	0204	...	...	*0624*	...	0658	...	...	0728	0758	...	0828	0858		2328	2358	...	...	...	...
83	**Den Helder** ▲ a.	0126	...	...	...	...	*0655*	...	0725	...	...	0756	0826	...	0856	0926		2356	0026	...	...	...	...

	A			⚒	Ⓐ	Ⓐ	Ⓐ	Ⓐ		⚒	Ⓐ	⚒	⚒										
Den Helder ▲ d.	0034	...	...	...	...	...	0534	0604	...	0634	0645	0704	0715a	...	0734	0804	and every 30 minutes until	2204	2234	...	...	...	2334
Heerhugowaard 461 d.	0100	...	...	...	...	...	0600	0630	...	0700	0712	0730	0742a	...	0800	0830		2230	2300	...	...	...	0000
Alkmaar 461 d.	0109	...	...	0455	0528	0542	0612	0642	...	0712	0724	0742	0754	...	0812	0842		2242	2312	...	2328	...	0016
Castricum 461 d.	...	...	...	0507	0540	0551	0621	0651	...	0721	0736	0751	0806	...	0821	0851		2251	2321	...	2340	...	0029
Zaandam 459 d.	...	...	...	0532	0603	0606	0636	0706	...	0736	0752	0806	0822	...	0836	0906		2306	2336	...	0003	...	0054*
Amsterdam Sloterdijk 459 d.	...	...	...	0539	0609	0613	0643	0713	...	0743	0758	0813	0828	...	0843	0913		2313	2343	...	0009	...	0101*
Amsterdam Centraal 459 a.	...	...	...	0548	0615	0619	0649	0719	...	0749	0804	0819	0834	...	0849	0919		2319	2349	...	0115	...	0108*
Utrecht Centraal 468 a.	...	...	...	...	...	0649	0719	0749	...	0819	0834	0849	0904	...	0919	0949		2349	0019	...	...	...	...

A – ⑥⑦ (also May 1, 2).

Q – ⑤⑥⑦ (also Dec. 25, 26, Jan. 1, Mar. 24, Apr. 30, May 1, 24).

a – Ⓐ only.

j – Also Apr. 30, May 1.

p – 0024 on certain dates.

v – ⚒ only.

* – 9–11 minutes later on certain dates.

▲ – For 🚌 / ⛴ Den Helder - Texel and v.v., see Table **499**.

AMSTERDAM - ARNHEM - NIJMEGEN 468

For INTERNATIONAL TRAINS **Amsterdam** – **Arnhem** – **Köln** and v.v., see Table **28**   For NIGHT NETWORK **Rotterdam** – **Amsterdam** – **Utrecht** and v.v., see Table **454**

km		⑦		Ⓐ	⚒	Ⓐ	⚒	Ⓐ	⚒	⚒		⚒											L
	Alkmaar 466 d.	...	...	...	...	...	...	0542	...	0612a	...	0642a	...	0712v	0742v	...	0812	0842	and every 30 minutes until	2212	2242	...	*2328*
0	**Amsterdam** Centraal 470 d.	*0117*	...	...	...	*0531*	...	0622	...	0652	...	0722	...	0752	0822	...	0852	0922		2252	2322	...	0022
5	Amsterdam Amstel 470 d.	|	...	...	...	*0541*	...	0630	...	0700	...	0730	...	0800	0830	...	0900	0930		2300	2330	...	0030
39	**Utrecht** Centraal 470 a.	*0146*	...	...	...	*0614*	...	0649	...	0719	...	0749	...	0819	0849	...	0919	0949		2319	2350	...	0050
39	**Utrecht** Centraal d.	0153	...	0553	...	0623	...	0653	0653	0723	...	0753	0753	0823	0853	...	0923	0953		2323	2353	...	0053
79	Ede-Wageningen d.	0222	...	0621	...	0651	...	0721	0721	0751	...	0821	0821	0851	0921	...	0951	1021		2351	0021	...	0121
96	**Arnhem** a.	0232	...	0632	...	0702	...	0732	0732	0802	...	0832	0832	0902	0932	...	1002	1032		0002	0032	...	0132
96	**Arnhem** 475 d.	0239	...	0637	0637	0707	0707	0737	0737	0807	0807	0837	0837	0907	0937	...	1007	1037		0007	0037	...	0137
114	**Nijmegen** 475 a.	0254	...	0651	0651	0721	0721	0751	0751	0821	0821	0851	0851	0921	0951	...	1021	1051		0021	0053	...	0152

	Ⓐ	⚒		⚒		⚒																	F
Nijmegen 475 d.	0535	...	...	0609	...	0639	...	...	0709v	...	0739d	...	0809	0839	and every 30 minutes until	2109	2139	...	2209	2239	...	2309	...
Arnhem 475 a.	0552	...	...	0621	...	0651	...	...	0721v	...	0751e	...	0821	0851		2121	2151	...	2221	2251	...	2321	...
Arnhem d.	0558	...	...	0628	...	0658	...	...	0728	...	0758	...	0828	0858		2128	2158	...	2228	2258	...	2328	...
Ede-Wageningen d.	0610	...	...	0640	...	0710	...	...	0740	...	0810	...	0840	0910		2141	2211	...	2240	2310	...	2340	...
Utrecht Centraal a.	0637	...	...	0707	...	0737	...	...	0808	...	0838	...	0908	0938		2208	2238	...	2308	2338	...	0008	...
Utrecht Centraal 470 d.	0640	0640	...	0710	0710	0740	0740	...	0810	...	0840	...	0910	0940		2210	2240	...	2310	2340	...	...	0017
Amsterdam Amstel 470 a.	0701	0701	...	0731	0731	0801	0801	...	0831	...	0901	...	0931	1001		2231	2301	...	2331	0001	...	...	0049
Amsterdam Centraal 470 a.	0710	0710	...	0740	0740	0810	0810	...	0840	...	0910	...	0940	1010		2240	2310	...	2340	0010	...	...	0058
Alkmaar 466 a.	0748	0748	...	0818	0818	0848	0848	...	0918	...	0948	...	1018	1048		2318	2348	...	...	0049	...	...	0156

F – ①⑥⑦ (also Dec. 26, 27, Jan. 2, Mar. 25, May 1, 2, 13).

L – Runs 4–19 minutes later on certain dates.

a – Ⓐ only.

d – 0734 on †.

e – 0755 on †.

v – ⚒ only.

470 MAASTRICHT, HEERLEN and VENLO - DEN HAAG and AMSTERDAM

km		Ⓐ	Ⓐ	Ⓐ	Ⓐ	Ⓐ	Ⓐ ◄	Ⓐ	⚒	⚒ ◄	⚒		◄	⚒		◄		◄		◄	and at the same minutes past each hour until		◄
0	**Maastricht** d.	...	...	...	...	0523	...	0553	...	...	0623	...	...	0653	...	...	0723	...	0753	...		2053	...
	Heerlen d.	...	...	...	...	0521	...	0551	...	...	0621	...	...	0651**d**	...	...	0721**r**	...	0751	...		2051	...
22	Sittard d.	...	...	...	...	0542	...	0612	...	...	0642	...	...	0712	...	...	0742	...	0812	...		2112	...
46	Roermond d.	...	...	...	...	0558	...	0628	...	...	0658	...	...	0728	...	...	0758	...	0828	...		2128	...
70	Weert d.	...	...	...	...	0612	...	0642	...	...	0712	...	...	0742	...	...	0812	...	0842	...		2142	...
	Venlo d.	...	...	...	...	|	0549	|	...	0619**a**	|	...	0649**v**	|	...	0719	|	0749	|	0819		|	2119
	Helmond d.	...	...	...	...	|	0620	|	...	0650**a**	|	...	0720**v**	|	...	0750	|	0820	|	0850		|	2150
99	**Eindhoven** a.	...	...	...	...	0632	0630	0700	...	0700**a**	0730	...	0730**v**	0800	...	0800	0830	0830	0900	0900		2200	2200
99	**Eindhoven** d.	0532	0532	0602	0602	0632	0632	0702	0702	0702	0732	0732	0732	0802	0802	0802	0832	0832	0902	0902		2202	2202
136	Tilburg **475** d.	|	0555	|	0625	|	0655	|	|	0725	|	|	0755	|	|	0825	|	0855	|	0925		|	2225
157	Breda **450 475** d.	|	0609	|	0639	|	0709	|	|	0739	|	|	0809	|	|	0839	|	0909	|	0939		|	2239
187	Dordrecht **450** d.	|	0628	|	0658	|	0728	|	|	0758	|	|	0828	|	|	0858	|	0928	|	0958		|	2258
207	**Rotterdam** Centraal **450** a.	|	0641	|	0711	|	0741	|	|	0811	|	|	0841	|	|	0911	|	0941	|	1011		|	2311
207	**Rotterdam** Centraal **450** d.	|	0644	|	0714	|	0744	|	|	0814	|	|	0844	|	|	0914	|	0944	|	1014		|	2314
230	Den Haag HS **450** a.	|	0705	|	0735	|	0805	|	|	0835	|	|	0905	|	|	0935	|	1005	|	1035		|	2335
231	**Den Haag** Centraal a.	|	0710	|	0740	|	0810	|	|	0840	|	|	0910	|	|	0940	|	1010	|	1040		|	2340
131	's-Hertogenbosch d.	0553	...	0623	...	0653	...	0723	0723	...	0753	0753	...	0823	0823	...	0853	...	0923	...		2223	...
179	**Utrecht** Centraal a.	0622	...	0652	...	0722	...	0752	0752	...	0822	0822	...	0852	0852	...	0922	...	0952	...		2252	...
179	**Utrecht** Centraal **468** d.	0625	...	0655	...	0725	...	0755	0755	...	0825	0825	...	0855	0855	...	0925	...	0955	...		2255	...
213	Amsterdam Amstel **468** a.	0644	...	0714	...	0744	...	0814	0814	...	0844	0844	...	0914	0914	...	0944	...	1014	...		2314	...
219	**Amsterdam** Centraal **468** a.	0652	...	0722	...	0752	...	0822	0822	...	0852	0852	...	0922	0922	...	0952	...	1022	...		2322	...

		◄		◄		◄			
Maastricht d.	2123	...	2153	...	2223	...	2253	...	2353
Heerlen d.	2121	...	2151	...	2221	...	2251	...	2351
Sittard d.	2142	...	2212	...	2242	...	2312	...	0012
Roermond d.	2158	...	2228	...	2258	...	2328	...	0028
Weert d.	2212	...	2242	...	2312	...	2342	...	0042
Venlo d.	|	2149	|	2219	|	2249	|	2319	|
Helmond d.	|	2220	|	2250	|	2320	|	2350	|
Eindhoven a.	2230	2230	2300	2300	2330	2330	2400	2400	0113
Eindhoven d.	2232	2232	2302	2302	2332	2332	▬	*0005*	...
Tilburg **475** d.	|	2255	|	2325	|	2355	...	|	...
Breda **450 475** d.	|	2309	|	2339	|	0009	...	|	...
Dordrecht **450** d.	|	2328	|	2358	|	0028	...	|	...
Rotterdam Centraal **450** a.	|	2341	|	0011	|	0043	...	|	...
Rotterdam Centraal **450** d.	|	2344	|	0014**f**	|	...	0100	|	...
Den Haag HS **450** a.	|	0005	|	0035**f**	|	...	|	|	...
Den Haag Centraal a.	|	0010	|	0040**f**	|	...	0122	|	...
's-Hertogenbosch d.	2253	...	2323	...	2353	...	...	*0034*	...
Utrecht Centraal a.	2322	...	2352	...	0022	...	...	...	...
Utrecht Centraal **468** d.	2325	...	2355	...	0025	...	...	...	...
Amsterdam Amstel **468** a.	2344	...	0014	...	0050	...	...	...	...
Amsterdam Centraal **468** a.	2352	...	0022	...	0059	...	...	...	...

km		Ⓐ	Ⓐ	Ⓐ	Ⓐ ◄	Ⓐ	⚒	⚒ ◄	Ⓐ	
0	**Amsterdam** Centraal **468** d.	...	...	...	...	0607	...	...	0637	...
6	Amsterdam Amstel **468** d.	...	...	...	...	0615	...	...	0645	...
40	**Utrecht** Centraal **468** a.	...	...	...	...	0634	...	...	0704	...
40	**Utrecht** Centraal d.	...	...	...	...	0638	...	...	0708	...
87	's-Hertogenbosch d.	*0556*	...	...	...	|	...	...	|	...
	Den Haag Centraal d.	|	...	...	...	|	...	0551**a**	|	...
	Den Haag HS **450** d.	|	...	...	...	|	...	0556**a**	|	...
	Rotterdam Centraal **450** a.	|	...	...	...	|	...	0615**a**	|	...
	Rotterdam Centraal **450** d.	|	...	...	0547	|	...	0617	|	...
	Dordrecht **450** d.	|	...	...	0601	|	...	0631	|	...
	Breda **450 475** d.	|	...	...	0621	|	...	0651	|	...
	Tilburg **475** d.	|	...	...	0636	|	...	0706	|	...
120	**Eindhoven** a.	*0624*	...	...	0700	0727	...	0730	0757	...
120	**Eindhoven** d.	0632	0632	0702	0702	0732	0732	0732	0802	0802
133	Helmond d.	|	0641	|	0711	|	|	0741	|	|
171	**Venlo** a.	|	0713	|	0743	|	|	0815	|	|
149	Weert d.	0649	...	0719	...	0749	0749	...	0819	0819
173	Roermond d.	0704	...	0734	...	0804	0804	...	0834	0834
197	Sittard a.	0719	...	0749	...	0819	0819	...	0849	0849
216	**Heerlen** a.	0739	...	0809	...	0839	0839	...	0909	0909
219	**Maastricht** a.	0735	...	0805	...	0835	0835	...	0905	0905

	⚒ ◄	⚒		⚒ ◄			◄		◄		◄	and at the same minutes past each hour until		◄		◄		◄		◄			
Amsterdam Centraal **468** d.	...	0707	...	...	...	0737**v**	...	0807	...	0837	...		2107	...	2137	...	2207	...	2237	...	2307	...	2337
Amsterdam Amstel **468** d.	...	0715	...	...	...	0745**v**	...	0815	...	0845	...		2115	...	2145	...	2215	...	2245	...	2315	...	2345
Utrecht Centraal **468** a.	...	0734	...	...	...	0804**v**	...	0834	...	0904	...		2134	...	2204	...	2234	...	2304	...	2334	...	0004
Utrecht Centraal d.	...	0738	...	...	...	0808	...	0838	...	0908	...		2138	...	2208	...	2238	...	2308	...	2338	...	*0014*
's-Hertogenbosch d.	...	0808	...	...	...	0838	...	0908	...	0938	...		2208	...	2238	...	2308	...	2338	...	0008	...	*0056*
Den Haag Centraal d.	0621	|	...	0651	...	|	0721	|	0751	|	0821		|	2051	|	2121	|	2151	|	2221	|	2251	▬
Den Haag HS **450** d.	0626	|	...	0656	...	|	0726	|	0756	|	0826		|	2056	|	2126	|	2156	|	2226	|	2256	...
Rotterdam Centraal **450** a.	0645	|	...	0715	...	|	0745	|	0815	|	0845		|	2115	|	2145	|	2215	|	2245	|	2315	...
Rotterdam Centraal **450** d.	0647	|	...	0717	...	|	0747	|	0817	|	0847		|	2117	|	2147	|	2217	|	2247	|	2317	...
Dordrecht **450** d.	0701	|	...	0731	...	|	0801	|	0831	|	0901		|	2131	|	2201	|	2231	|	2301	|	2331	...
Breda **450 475** d.	0721	|	...	0751	...	|	0821	|	0851	|	0921		|	2151	|	2221	|	2251	|	2321	|	2351	...
Tilburg **475** d.	0736	|	...	0806	...	|	0836	|	0906	|	0936		|	2206	|	2236	|	2306	|	2336	|	0006	...
Eindhoven a.	0800	0827	...	0830	...	0857	0900	0927	0930	0957	1000		2227	2230	2257	2300	2327	2330	2357	2400	0027	0031	...
Eindhoven d.	0802	0832	0832	0832	0832	0902	0902	0932	0932	1002	1002		2232	2232	2302	2302	2332	2332	0002	*0016*	...	0032	0034**f**
Helmond d.	0811	|	|	0841	0841	|	0911	|	0941	|	1011		|	2241	|	2311	|	2341	|	*0029*	...	0041	|
Venlo a.	0843	|	|	0913	0913	|	0943	|	1013	|	1043		|	2313	|	2343	|	0015	|	...	...	0113	|
Weert d.	...	0849	0849	...	...	0919	...	0949	...	1019	...		2249	...	2319	...	2349	...	0019	...	...	...	0056**f**
Roermond d.	...	0904	0904	...	...	0934	...	1004	...	1034	...		2304	...	2334	...	0004	...	0034	...	...	...	...
Sittard a.	...	0919	0919	...	...	0949	...	1019	...	1049	...		2319	...	2349	...	0021	...	0113*	...	...	...	...
Heerlen a.	...	0939	0939	...	...	1009	...	1039	...	1109	...		2339	...	0009	...	0054*	...	0132*	...	...	...	...
Maastricht a.	...	0935	0935	...	...	1005	...	1035	...	1105	...		2335	...	0005	...	0050*	...	0131*	...	...	...	...

a – Ⓐ only.
d – 0638 on ⑥.
f – ①⑥⑦ (also Dec. 26, 27, Jan. 2, Mar. 25, May 1, 2, 13).
r – 0711 on ✝. Later services depart at xx21 daily.
v – ⚒ only.
◄ – Connects at Eindhoven with train in preceding column.
* – Arrival is earlier on certain dates.

For traffic arrangements on Dutch holiday dates, see page 248

MAASTRICHT - HEERLEN - KERKRADE 472

Operated by **Veolia** ★ 2nd class

km							Ⓐ		⚒		⚒													
0	**Maastricht** d.	0009	...	0039	...	...	0515	...	0545a	...	0615	...	0645v	...	0715	...	0745	and	2315	...	2345	...	...	...
11	Valkenburg d.	0028	...	0058	...	...	0528	...	0558a	...	0628	...	0658v	...	0728	...	0758	every 30	2328	...	2358	...	...	...
24	**Heerlen** d.	0047	...	0118	...	...	0545	...	0615	...	0645	...	0715	...	0745	...	0815	minutes	2345	...	0015	...	...	...
33	**Kerkrade** Centrum a.	...	...	...	...	...	0600	...	0628	...	0658	...	0728	...	0758	...	0828	until	2358	...	0028	...	...	...

						Ⓐ		Ⓐ		⚒		⚒											
Kerkrade Centrum d.	0001	...	0031	...	...	...	...	...	...	0601	...	0631a	...	0701v	...	0731	...	0801	and	2301	...	2331	...	...
Heerlen d.	0015	...	0045	...	...	0515	...	0545	...	0615	...	0645	...	0715	...	0745	...	0815	every 30	2315	...	2345	...	...
Valkenburg d.	0032	...	0102	...	...	0532	...	0602	...	0632	...	0702	...	0732	...	0802	...	0832	minutes	2332	...	0002	...	...
Maastricht a.	0045	...	0115	...	...	0545	...	0615	...	0645	...	0715	...	0745	...	0815	...	0845	until	2345	...	0015	...	...

a – Ⓐ only. v – ⚒ only. ★ – NS tickets valid.

WINTERSWIJK - ARNHEM 474

Operated by **Syntus** ★ 2nd class

km		Ⓐ	⚒	⚒						
0	**Winterswijk** d.	0549	...	0649	...	...	0749	and	2249	...
34	Doetinchem d.	0622	0622	0722	0722	...	0822	hourly	2322	...
50	Zevenaar d.	0641	0641	0741	0741	...	0841	until	2341	...
64	**Arnhem** a.	0656	0656	0756	0756	...	0856		2356	...

	Ⓐ	⚒							
Arnhem d.	0634	0734	...	...	0834	and	2234	...	2334
Zevenaar d.	0648	0748	...	...	0848	hourly	2248	...	2348
Doetinchem a.	0706	0806	0807	...	0906	until	2306	...	0006
Winterswijk a.	0740	0840	0840	...	0940		2340	...	0040r

r – ①⑦ (also Dec. 26, 27, Jan. 2, Mar. 25, May 2, 13. ★ – NS tickets valid. ☛ Additional services operate.

ROOSENDAAL - 's-HERTOGENBOSCH - NIJMEGEN - ZWOLLE 475

For faster connections **Roosendaal** - **Zwolle** and v.v., changing at **Rotterdam**, see Tables **450** and **481**

km		Ⓐ	Ⓐ	⚒	⚒	Ⓐ	⚒	Ⓐ	⚒	⚒														
0	**Roosendaal** d.	...	...	...	...	0521	...	0551	...	0621	...	0651r	...	0721	...	and at	2121	...	2151	...	2221	...	2251	2321
23	Breda 470 d.	...	...	...	...	0540	...	0610	...	0640	...	0710r	...	0740	...	the	2140	...	2210	...	2240	...	2310	2340
44	Tilburg 470 d.	...	...	...	...	0555	...	0625	...	0655	...	0725	...	0755	...	same	2155	...	2225	...	2255	...	2325	2355
67	**'s-Hertogenbosch** d.	...	...	...	...	0614	...	0644	...	0714	...	0744	...	0814	...	minutes	2214	...	2244	...	2314	...	2344	0012
86	Oss d.	...	...	...	...	0626	...	0656	...	0726	...	0756	...	0826	...	past	2226	...	2256	...	2326	...	2356	...
110	**Nijmegen** 468 d.	...	*0535*	0628a	0644	0644	0658a	0714	0728	0744	0758	0814	0828	0844	0858	each	2244	2258	2314	2328	2344	...	0014	...
129	Arnhem 468 d.	...	0600	0642a	0704	0704	0712	0734	0742	0804	0812	0834	0842	0904	0912	hour	2304	2312	2334	2342	0004	0022	0035	...
145	Dieren d.	...	0619	0654a	...	...	0724	...	0754	...	0824	...	0854	...	0924	until	...	2324	...	2354	...	0041	...	...
159	Zutphen d.	0604	0634	0704	...	...	0734	...	0804	...	0834	...	0904	...	0934		...	2334	...	0004	...	0054	...	...
174	Deventer d.	0620	0650	0720	...	...	0750	...	0820	...	0850	...	0920	...	0950		...	2350	...	0020	...	...	...	...
204	**Zwolle** a.	0643	0713	0743	...	...	0813	...	0843	...	0913	...	0943	...	1013		...	0013	...	0043	...	...	...	...

	Ⓐ	Ⓐ	Ⓐ			⚒		⚒																
Zwolle d.	...	...	...	...	...	0620a	...	0650a	...	0720v	...	0750	...	0820	...	and at	...	2150	...	2220	...	2250	...	2350
Deventer d.	...	...	...	...	...	0644a	...	0714a	...	0744v	...	0814	...	0844	...	the	...	2214	...	2244	...	2314	...	0014
Zutphen d.	...	...	...	...	...	0657	...	0727	...	0757	...	0827	...	0857	...	same	...	2227	...	2257	...	2327	...	0027
Dieren d.	...	...	...	...	...	0707	...	0737	...	0807	...	0837	...	0907	...	minutes	...	2237	...	2307	...	2337	...	0037
Arnhem 468 d.	...	...	0558	0628a	0658v	0721	0728v	0751	0758	0821	0828	0851	0858	0921	0928	past	2228	2251	2258	2321	2328	2351	*0007*	0050
Nijmegen 468 d.	...	...	0619	0649a	0719v	0735	0749v	0805	0819	0835	0849	0905	0919	0935	0949	each	2249	2305	2319	2335	2349	0005	0024	...
Oss d.	...	...	0634	0704a	0734v	...	0804v	...	0834	...	0904	...	0934	...	1004	hour	2304	...	2334	...	0004	...	0044	...
's-Hertogenbosch d.	...	0620	0650	0720v	0750	...	0820	...	0850	...	0920	...	0950	...	1020	until	2320	...	2350	...	0020	...	0120	...
Tilburg 470 d.	*0555*	0637	0707	0737v	0807	...	0837	...	0907	...	0937	...	1007	...	1037		2337	...	0007	...	0043	...	...	...
Breda 470 d.	0622	0652	0722	0752	0822	...	0852	...	0922	...	0952	...	1022	...	1052		2352	...	0022	...	0104	...	...	...
Roosendaal a.	0641	0711	0741	0811	0841	...	0911	...	0941	...	1011	...	1041	...	1111		0011	...	0041	...	0133	...	...	...

a – Ⓐ only. r – 6 minutes earlier on ✝. Later services in this pattern depart Roosendaal at xx51 and Breda at xx10 daily. v – ⚒ only.

NIJMEGEN - VENLO - ROERMOND 477

Operated by **Veolia** ★ 2nd class

km					Ⓐ	Ⓐ	Ⓐ	⚒		Ⓐ	⚒	⚒		⚒											
0	**Nijmegen** d.	0009	...	...	...	...	0539	...	...	0609	...	0639	...	0709	...	...	0739	...	0809	and	2239	...	2309	...	2339
24	Boxmeer d.	0030	...	...	...	...	0600	...	...	0630	...	0700	...	0730	...	...	0800	...	0830	every 30	2300	...	2330	...	0000
39	Venray d.	0046	...	...	...	...	0616	...	...	0646	...	0716	...	0746	...	...	0816	...	0846	minutes	2316	...	2346	...	0016
61	**Venlo** d.	0102	...	...	0534	0604	0634	0634	...	0704	0704	0734	0734	0804	0804	...	0834	...	0904	until	2334	...	0004	...	0032
84	**Roermond** a.	...	...	...	0556	0627	0657	0657	...	0727	0727	0757	0757	0827	0827	...	0857	...	0927		2357	...	0027	...	...

					Ⓐ	Ⓐ	⚒	Ⓐ	⚒	Ⓐ		⚒		⚒										
Roermond d.	0004	0034	...	...	...	...	...	0604	...	0634	...	0704	...	0734	...	...	0804	...	0834	and	2234	...	2304	...	2334
Venlo d.	0027	0057	...	...	0500	0530	0600	0630	0630	0700	0700	0730	0730	0800	0800	...	0830	...	0900	every 30	2300	...	2330	...	2357
Venray d.	...	...	...	...	0517	0547	0617	0647	0647	0717	0717	0747	0747	0817	0817	...	0847	...	0917	minutes	2317	...	2347	...	...
Boxmeer d.	...	...	...	...	0529	0559	0629	0659	0659	0729	0729	0759	0759	0829	0829	...	0859	...	0929	until	2329	...	2359	...	...
Nijmegen a.	...	...	...	...	0549	0619	0649	0719	0719	0749	0749	0819	0819	0849	0849	...	0919	...	0949		2349	...	0019	...	...

★ – NS tickets valid.

TIEL - UTRECHT 478

km					Ⓐ	Ⓐ	⚒	⚒																
0	**Tiel** d.	0005	...	...	0551	0621	0651	0721	...	0751	...	0821	and	2021	...	2051	...	2105	2135	2205	...	2235	2305	2335
12	Geldermalsen 479 d.	0025	...	...	0608	0638	0708	0738	...	0808	...	0838	every 30	2038	...	2108	...	2125	2155	2225	...	2255	2325	2355
20	Culemborg d.	0032	...	...	0614	0644	0714	0744	...	0814	...	0844	minutes	2044	...	2114	...	2132	2202	2232	...	2302	2332	0002
38	**Utrecht** Centraal a.	0049	...	...	0628	0658	0728	0758	...	0828	...	0858	until	2058	...	2128	...	2149	2219	2249	...	2319	2349	0019

	Ⓐ		Ⓐ	Ⓐ	⚒																			
Utrecht Centraal d.	0531	...	0601	0631	0701	...	0731	...	0801	and	1931	...	2001	...	2014	2044	2114	...	2143	2214	2243	...	2314	2343
Culemborg d.	0545	...	0615	0645	0715	...	0745	...	0815	every 30	1945	...	2015	...	2030	2100	2130	...	2200	2230	2300	...	2330	0000
Geldermalsen 479 d.	0553	...	0623	0653	0723	...	0753	...	0823	minutes	1953	...	2023	...	2038	2108	2138	...	2208	2238	2308	...	2338	0008
Tiel a.	0605	...	0635	0705	0735	...	0805	...	0835	until	2005	...	2035	...	2051	2120	2149	...	2220	2249	2320	...	2349	0020

ARNHEM - TIEL Operated by *Syntus* (NS tickets valid)

Ⓐ: 0633, 0703, 0733, 0803, 0833, 0933 and hourly until 2333 (also 1603, 1703, 1803).

Ⓒ: 0033⑦, 0833⑥, 0933, 1033 and hourly until 2333.

TIEL - ARNHEM Journey time ± 40 minutes *44 km*

Ⓐ: 0618, 0648, 0718, 0748, 0818, 0848, 0948 and hourly until 1948 (also 1618, 1718, 1818); then 2051, 2151, 2251.

Ⓒ: 0748⑥, 0848, 0948 and hourly until 1948; then 2051, 2151, 2251, 2351⑥.

DORDRECHT - GELDERMALSEN 479

km							Ⓐ	⚒	⚒									
0	**Dordrecht** d.	0007	0037	0107	...	...	0437	0507	0537	...	0607	...	0637	and	2307	...	2337	Operated by Arriva
10	Sliedrecht d.	0017	0047	0117	...	...	0447	0517	0547	...	0617	...	0647	every 30	2317	...	2347	(NS tickets valid)
24	Gorinchem d.	0032	0058	0128	...	...	0502	0532	0602	...	0632	...	0702	minutes	2332	...	0002	
49	**Geldermalsen** 478 a.	0103	...	...	...	...	0533	0603	0633	...	0703	...	0733	until	0003	...	0033	

						Ⓐ	Ⓐ	⚒	⚒	⚒														
Geldermalsen 478 d.	0009	0039	0109	...	...	...	0539	...	0609	0639	...	...	0709	...	0739	and	2309	...	2339	...	...	...	...	...
Gorinchem d.	0032	0102	0132	...	...	0534	0604	0604	0634	0704	0704	...	0734	...	0804	every 30	2334	...	0004	...	...	...	...	...
Sliedrecht d.	0046	0116	0146	...	...	0546	0616	0616	0646	0716	0716	...	0746	...	0816	minutes	2346	...	0016	...	...	...	...	...
Dordrecht a.	0055	0125	0155	...	...	0555	0625	0625	0655	0725	0725	...	0755	...	0825	until	2355	...	0025	...	...	...	...	...

481 UTRECHT and AMSTERDAM - AMERSFOORT - ZWOLLE

For other (stopping) trains **Schiphol ✈** and **Amsterdam Centraal** – **Amersfoort**, see Table **457**

km		Ⓐ	Ⓐ	Ⓐ	⚒	⚒	Ⓐ	⚒	⚒	⚒	⚒			Ⓐ		⚒		Ⓐ	Ⓒ				Ⓐ	
	Rotterdam Centraal **483** d.	...	...	...	...	0602**a**	...	...	...	0632	...	...	...	0702	0702**z**	...	...	0732	0732	...	...	...	0802	0802**z**
	Den Haag Centraal **483** d.	...	...	...	...	0606**a**	...	...	...	|	0636	...	...	|	0706**v**	...	...	|	|	0736	...	...	|	0806
0	**Utrecht** Centraal ‡ d.	...	0620	...	...	0650	...	...	...	0720	0720	...	...	0747	0750	...	...	0817	0820	0820	...	...	0847	0850
	Schiphol ✈ d.	...	|	0551	...	|	0621	...	...	|	|	0651	...	|	|	0718	...	|	|	|	0751	...	|	|
	Amsterdam Zuid d.	...	|	0558	...	|	0628	...	...	|	|	0658	...	|	|	0728	...	|	|	|	0758	...	|	|
	Duivendrecht d.	...	|	0604	...	|	0634	...	...	|	|	0704	...	|	|	0734	...	|	|	|	0804	...	|	|
	Amsterdam Centraal d.	0556	|	|	0627	|	|	...	0657	|	|	|	0727	|	|	|	0757	|	|	|	|	0827	|	|
21	**Amersfoort** ⊙ ‡ a.	0632	0634	0637	0702	0704	0705	...	0732	0734	0734	0735	0802	0801	0804	0805	0832	0831	0834	0834	0837	0902	0901	0904
21	**Amersfoort** ⊙ ‡ d.	...	0638	0641	...	0710	0710	0710	...	0738	0738	0741	...	0804	0810	0808	...	0834	0838	0838	0841	...	0904	0910
	Deventer **484** a.	...	|	0718	...	0748	|	|	...	|	|	0818	...	|	0848	|	...	|	|	|	0918	...	|	0948
	Enschede **484** a.	...	|	0805	...	0835	|	|	...	|	|	...	...	|	0935	|	...	|	|	|	1005	...	|	1035
88	**Zwolle** ‡ a.	...	0716	...	...	...	0746	0746	...	0814	0814	...	...	0843	...	0846	...	0911	0914	0914	...	...	0943	...
	Leeuwarden **486** a.	...	|	...	...	...	|	|	...	0914	|	...	...	0954	...	0954**z**	...	1014	1014	|	...	...	1054	...
	Groningen **486** a.	...	0816	...	...	...	0852	0852	...	...	0914	...	...	...	...	0953	...	...	...	1014	...	...	...	...

			Ⓐ	Ⓒ				Ⓐ				Ⓐ	Ⓒ											
Rotterdam Centraal **483** d.	...	...	0832	0832	...	...	...	0902	...	...	...	0932	0932	...	...	...	1002**b**	...	...	1032	...	...	...	1102
Den Haag Centraal **483** d.	...	...	|	|	0836	...	...	|	0906	...	...	|	|	0936	...	...	1006	...	...	|	1036	...	...	1106
Utrecht Centraal ‡ d.	...	...	0917	0920	0920	...	...	0947	0950	...	...	1017	1020	1020	...	...	1050	...	...	1120	1120	...	...	1150
Schiphol ✈ d.	0818	...	|	|	|	0851	...	|	|	0918	...	|	|	|	0951	...	|	1018	...	|	|	1050	...	|
Amsterdam Zuid d.	0828	...	|	|	|	0858	...	|	|	0928	...	|	|	|	0958	...	|	1028	...	|	|	1057	...	|
Duivendrecht d.	0834	...	|	|	|	0904	...	|	|	0934	...	|	|	|	1004	...	|	1034	...	|	|	1101	...	|
Amsterdam Centraal d.	|	0857	|	|	|	|	0927	|	|	|	0957	|	|	|	|	1027	|	|	1057	|	|	|	1127	|
Amersfoort ⊙ ‡ a.	0905	0932	0931	0934	0934	0937	1002	1001	1004	1005	1032	1031	1034	1034	1037	1102	1104	1105	1132	1134	1134	1132	1202	1204
Amersfoort ⊙ ‡ d.	0908	...	0934	0938	0938	0941	...	1004	1010	1008	...	1034	1038	1038	1041	...	1110	1108	...	1138	1138	...	...	1210
Deventer **484** a.	|	...	|	|	|	1018	...	|	1048	|	...	|	|	|	1118	...	1148	|	...	|	|	...	...	1248
Enschede **484** a.	|	...	|	|	|	1105	...	|	1135	|	...	|	|	|	1205	...	1235	|	...	|	|	...	...	1335
Zwolle ‡ a.	0944	...	1011	1014	1014	...	...	1043	...	1044	...	1111	1114	1114	...	...	...	1144	...	1214	1214	...	...	...
Leeuwarden **486** a.	1054**c**	...	1114	1114	|	...	...	1154	...	1154**c**	...	1214	1214	|	...	...	...	1254	...	1314	|	...	...	...
Groningen **486** a.	1053	...	...	...	1114	...	...	...	...	1153	...	...	...	1214	...	...	...	1253	...	...	1314	...	...	...

																					Ⓐ			
Rotterdam Centraal **483** d.	...	...	1132	...	...	...	1202**v**	...	...	1232	...	...	...	1302**v**	...	...	1332	...	...	...	1402	1402**c**	...	...
Den Haag Centraal **483** d.	...	...	|	1136	...	...	1206	...	...	|	1236	...	...	1306	...	...	|	1336	...	...	|	1406	...	...
Utrecht Centraal ‡ d.	...	...	1220	1220	...	...	1250	...	...	1320	1320	...	...	1350	...	...	1420	1420	...	...	1447	1450	...	...
Schiphol ✈ d.	1118	...	|	|	1151	...	|	1218	...	|	|	1251	...	|	1318	...	|	|	1351	...	|	|	1418	...
Amsterdam Zuid d.	1128	...	|	|	1158	...	|	1228	...	|	|	1258	...	|	1328	...	|	|	1358	...	|	|	1428	...
Duivendrecht d.	1134	...	|	|	1204	...	|	1234	...	|	|	1304	...	|	1334	...	|	|	1404	...	|	|	1434	...
Amsterdam Centraal d.	|	1157	|	|	|	1227	|	|	1257	|	|	|	1327	|	|	1357	|	|	|	1427	|	|	|	1457
Amersfoort ⊙ ‡ a.	1205	1232	1234	1234	1237	1302	1304	1305	1332	1334	1334	1337	1402	1404	1405	1432	1434	1434	1437	1502	1501	1504	1505	1532
Amersfoort ⊙ ‡ d.	1208	...	1238	1238	1241	...	1310	1308	...	1338	1338	1341	...	1410	1408	...	1438	1438	1441	...	1504	1510	1508	...
Deventer **484** a.	|	...	|	|	1318	...	1348	|	...	|	|	1418	...	1448	|	...	|	|	1518	...	|	1548	|	...
Enschede **484** a.	|	...	|	|	1405	...	1435	|	...	|	|	1505	...	1535	|	...	|	|	1605	...	|	1635	|	...
Zwolle ‡ a.	1244	...	1314	1314	...	...	...	1344	...	1414	1414	...	...	...	1444	...	1514	1514	...	...	1543	...	1544	...
Leeuwarden **486** a.	1354	...	1414	|	...	...	...	1454	...	1514	|	...	...	...	1554	...	1614	|	...	...	1654	...	1654**c**	...
Groningen **486** a.	1353	...	...	1414	...	...	...	1453	...	...	1514	...	...	...	1553	...	...	1614	...	...	...	...	1653	...

	Ⓐ	Ⓒ				Ⓐ				Ⓐ	Ⓒ				Ⓐ				Ⓐ	Ⓒ				Ⓐ
Rotterdam Centraal **483** d.	1432	1432	1432**c**	...	...	1502	1502**c**	...	...	1532	1532	...	...	...	1602	1602**c**	...	...	1632	1632	...	...	...	1702
Den Haag Centraal **483** d.	|	|	1436	...	...	|	1506	...	...	|	|	1536	...	...	|	1606	...	...	|	|	1636	...	...	|
Utrecht Centraal ‡ d.	1517	1520	1520	...	...	1547	1550	...	...	1617	1620	1620	...	...	1647	1650	...	...	1717	1720	1720	...	...	1747
Schiphol ✈ d.	|	|	|	1451	...	|	|	1518	...	|	|	|	1551	...	|	|	1618	...	|	|	|	1651	...	|
Amsterdam Zuid d.	|	|	|	1458	...	|	|	1528	...	|	|	|	1558	...	|	|	1628	...	|	|	|	1658	...	|
Duivendrecht d.	|	|	|	1504	...	|	|	1534	...	|	|	|	1604	...	|	|	1634	...	|	|	|	1704	...	|
Amsterdam Centraal d.	|	|	|	|	1527	|	|	|	1557	|	|	|	|	1627	|	|	|	1657	|	|	|	|	1727	|
Amersfoort ⊙ ‡ a.	1531	1534	1534	1537	1602	1601	1604	1605	1632	1631	1634	1634	1637	1702	1701	1704	1705	1732	1731	1734	1734	1737	1802	1801
Amersfoort ⊙ ‡ d.	1534	1538	1538	1541	...	1604	1610	1608	...	1634	1638	1638	1641	...	1704	1710	1708	...	1734	1738	1738	1741	...	1804
Deventer **484** a.	|	|	|	1618	...	|	1648	|	...	|	|	|	1718	...	|	1748	|	...	|	|	|	1818	...	|
Enschede **484** a.	|	|	|	...	...	|	1735	|	...	|	|	|	1805	...	|	1835	|	...	|	|	|	...	...	|
Zwolle ‡ a.	1614	1614	1614	...	...	1641	...	1644	...	1714	1714	1714	...	...	1743	...	1744	...	1814	1814	1814	...	...	1841
Leeuwarden **486** a.	1714	1714	|	...	...	1754	...	1754**c**	...	1814	1814	|	...	...	1854	...	1854**c**	...	1914	1914	|	...	...	1954
Groningen **486** a.	...	...	1714	...	...	...	...	1753	...	...	...	1814	...	...	...	...	1853	...	...	...	1914	...	...	...

				Ⓐ	Ⓒ				Ⓐ				Ⓐ	Ⓒ										
Rotterdam Centraal **483** d.	1702**c**	...	...	1732	1732	...	...	...	1802	1802**n**	...	...	1832	1832	1832**c**	...	...	...	...	...	1932	1932**a**	...	...
Den Haag Centraal **483** d.	1706	...	...	|	|	1736	...	...	|	1806	...	...	|	|	1836	...	...	1906	...	...	|	1936	...	...
Utrecht Centraal ‡ d.	1750	...	...	1817	1820	1820	...	...	1847	1850	...	...	1917	1920	1920	...	...	1950	...	...	2020	2020	...	...
Schiphol ✈ d.	|	1718	...	|	|	|	1751	...	|	|	1818	...	|	|	|	1851	...	|	1918	...	|	|	1951	...
Amsterdam Zuid d.	|	1728	...	|	|	|	1758	...	|	|	1828	...	|	|	|	1858	...	|	1928	...	|	|	1958	...
Duivendrecht d.	|	1734	...	|	|	|	1804	...	|	|	1834	...	|	|	|	1904	...	|	1934	...	|	|	2004	...
Amsterdam Centraal d.	|	|	1757	|	|	|	|	1827	|	|	|	1857	|	|	|	|	1927	|	|	1957	|	|	|	2027
Amersfoort ⊙ ‡ a.	1804	1805	1832	1831	1834	1834	1837	1902	1901	1904	1905	1932	1931	1934	1934	1937	2002	2004	2005	2032	2034	2034	2037	2102
Amersfoort ⊙ ‡ d.	1810	1808	...	1834	1838	1838	1841	...	1904	1910	1908	...	1934	1938	1938	1941	...	2010	2008	...	2038	2038	2041	...
Deventer **484** a.	1848	|	...	|	|	|	1918	...	|	1948	|	...	|	|	|	2018	...	2048	|	...	|	|	2118	...
Enschede **484** a.	1935	|	...	|	|	|	2005	...	|	2035	|	...	|	|	|	2105	...	2135	|	...	|	|	2205	...
Zwolle ‡ a.	...	1844	...	1914	1914	1914	...	...	1941	...	1944	...	2014	2014	2014	...	...	...	2044	...	2114	2114	...	...
Leeuwarden **486** a.	...	1954**c**	...	2014	2014	|	...	...	2054	...	2054**c**	...	2114	2114	|	...	...	...	2154	...	2214	|	...	...
Groningen **486** a.	...	1953	...	...	...	2014	...	...	...	...	2053	...	...	...	2114	...	...	...	2153	...	...	2214	...	...

																							y	
Rotterdam Centraal **483** d.	2002**v**	...	...	2032	...	...	...	2102	...	...	2132	...	...	...	2202	2202**d**	...	...	2232	...	...	2302	...	...
Den Haag Centraal **483** d.	2006	...	...	|	2036	...	...	2106	...	...	2136**n**	2136	...	...	|	2206	...	...	2236	...	...	|	2306	...
Utrecht Centraal ‡ d.	2050	...	...	2120	2120	...	...	2150	...	...	2220	2220	...	...	2250	2250	...	...	2320	...	...	2350	2350	...
Schiphol ✈ d.	|	2018	...	|	|	2051	...	|	2118	...	|	|	2151	...	|	|	2221	...	|	2251	...	|	|	2318
Amsterdam Zuid d.	|	2028	...	|	|	2058	...	|	2128	...	|	|	2158	...	|	|	2228	...	|	2258	...	|	|	2328
Duivendrecht d.	|	2034	...	|	|	2104	...	|	2134	...	|	|	2204	...	|	|	2234	...	|	2304	...	|	|	2334
Amsterdam Centraal d.	|	|	2057	|	|	|	2127	|	|	2157	|	|	|	2227	|	|	|	2257	|	|	2327	|	|	|
Amersfoort ⊙ ‡ a.	2104	2105	2132	2134	2134	2137	2202	2204	2205	2232	2234	2234	2237	2302	2304	2304	2305	2332	2334	2337	0002	0004	0004	0005
Amersfoort ⊙ ‡ d.	2110	2108	...	2138	2138	2141	...	2210	2208	...	2238	2238	2241	...	...	2310	2310	...	2339	2341	...	0010**r**	0010	0008
Deventer **484** a.	2148	|	...	|	|	2218	...	2248	|	...	|	|	2318	...	...	2348	|	...	|	0018	...	0048**r**	0048	|
Enschede **484** a.	2235	|	...	|	|	2305	...	2335	|	...	|	|	0005	...	...	0036	|	...	|	0105	...	0135**r**	0135	|
Zwolle ‡ a.	...	2144	...	2214	2214	...	...	...	2244	...	2314	2314	...	...	...	...	2346	...	0016	...	...	...	...	0049
Leeuwarden **486** a.	...	2254	...	2314	|	...	...	...	2354	...	0015	|	...	...	...	...	0056	...	...	...	...	...	...	0157**p**
Groningen **486** a.	...	2253	...	...	2314	...	...	...	2353	...	...	0014	...	...	...	...	0056	...	...	...	...	...	...	0157**q**

b – ①–④ and ⑦ (not Dec. 25, 26, Jan. 1, Mar. 24, May 12).
c – Ⓒ only.
d – Not ⑤.
n – † only.
p – ⑥⑦ (also May 1, 2).
q – Morning after ⚒ only.

r – ①⑦ (also Dec. 26, 27, Jan. 2, Apr. 10, May 1, 18, 29).
v – ⚒ only.
y – ⑤⑥⑦ (also Dec. 25, 26, Jan. 1, Mar. 24, Apr. 30, May 1, 12).
z – ⑥ (also Apr. 30, May 1).

⊙ – Trains are in connection at Amersfoort where the interval between their arrival and departure times is at least 2 minutes.

‡ – Trains with the same timings Utrecht - Amersfoort - Zwolle run coupled together over these sections. Passengers should take care to join the appropriate portion of the train for their destination.

For traffic arrangements on Dutch holiday dates, see page 248

ZWOLLE - AMERSFOORT - AMSTERDAM and UTRECHT 481

For other (stopping) trains **Amersfoort – Schiphol ✈** and **Amsterdam Centraal**, see Table **457**

km		Ⓐ	Ⓐ	Ⓐ	⚒	Ⓐ	Ⓐ	Ⓐ	Ⓐ	Ⓐ	Ⓐ	⚒	⚒	⚒	Ⓐ	⚒	⚒	⚒	Ⓐ	Ⓒ				Ⓐ
	Groningen **486** d.	...	...	...	...	...	...	0504	...	...	...	0545**a**	...	...	...	0604**a**	...	...	...	...	0644**y**	...	...	...
	Leeuwarden **486** d.	...	...	...	...	...	...	0500	...	...	0540	|	...	...	0604	|	...	...	0643	0635**z**	|	...	...	0704
0	**Zwolle** ‡ d.	0517	...	0546	...	...	...	0618	...	...	0641	0646	...	...	0711	0716	...	...	0741	0746	0746	...	...	0811
	Enschede **484** d.	|	...	|	0454**a**	...	...	|	0527	...	|	|	0557**a**	...	|	|	0627	...	|	|	|	0657**v**	...	|
	Deventer **484** d.	|	...	|	0546**a**	...	...	|	0615	...	|	|	0645	...	|	|	0715	...	|	|	|	0745	...	|
67	**Amersfoort** ⊙ ‡ a.	0614	...	0623	0623**a**	...	...	0653	0653	...	0720	0723	0723	...	0750	0753	0753	...	0820	0823	0823	0823	...	0850
67	**Amersfoort** ⊙ ‡ d.	0615	0622	0625	0625	0628	0652	0655	0655	0658	0722	0725	0725	0728	0752	0755	0755	0758	0822	0825	0825	0825	0828	0852
111	**Amsterdam** Centraal a.	|	|	|	|	0701	|	|	|	0731	|	|	|	0801	|	|	|	0831	|	|	|	|	0901	|
106	Duivendrecht a.	|	|	|	0654	...	|	0726	|	...	|	|	0754	...	|	0826	|	...	|	|	|	0854	...	|
111	Amsterdam Zuid a.	|	|	|	0701	...	|	0731	|	...	|	|	0801	...	|	0831	|	...	|	|	|	0901	...	|
120	**Schiphol** ✈ a.	|	|	|	0708	...	|	0738	|	...	|	|	0808	...	|	0838	|	...	|	|	|	0908	...	|
88	**Utrecht** Centraal ‡ a.	0636	0637	0640	...	...	0707	...	0710	...	0737	0740	...	...	0807	...	0810	...	0837	0840	0840	...	...	0907
	Den Haag Centraal **483** a.	...	|	0725	...	...	|	...	0755	...	|	0825	...	...	|	...	0855	...	|	|	0925	...	...	|
	Rotterdam Centraal **483** a.	...	0727	...	...	...	0757	...	...	...	0827	...	...	...	0857	...	...	...	0927	0927	...	...	...	0957

				Ⓐ	Ⓒ				⚒				⑥**d**	Ⓑ**e**				⚒						
Groningen **486** d.	0704	...	...	...	...	0744	...	...	...	0804	...	...	...	...	0844	...	...	...	0904	...	...	...	0944	...
Leeuwarden **486** d.	0704**z**	...	...	0745	0745**r**	|	...	...	0804	0804**n**	...	...	0845	0845	|	...	...	0904	0904**n**	...	...	0945	|	...
Zwolle ‡ d.	0816	...	...	0841	0846	0846	...	...	0911	0916	...	...	0941	0946	0946	...	...	1011	1016	...	...	1046	1046	...
Enschede **484** d.	|	0727	...	|	|	|	0757	...	|	|	0827	...	|	|	|	...	...	|	|	0927	...	|	|	0957
Deventer **484** d.	|	0815	...	|	|	|	0845	...	|	|	0915	...	|	|	|	0945	...	|	|	1015	...	|	|	1045
Amersfoort ⊙ ‡ a.	0853	0853	...	0920	0923	0923	0923	...	0950	0953	0953	...	1020	1023	1023	1023	...	1050	1053	1053	...	1123	1123	1123
Amersfoort ⊙ ‡ d.	0855	0855	0858	0922	0925	0925	0925	0928	0952	0955	0955	0958	1022	1025	1025	1025	1028	1052	1055	1055	1058	1125	1125	1125
Amsterdam Centraal a.	|	|	0931	|	|	|	|	1001	|	|	|	1031	|	|	|	|	1101	|	|	|	1131	|	|	|
Duivendrecht a.	0926	|	...	|	|	|	0954	...	|	1026	|	...	|	|	|	1054	...	|	1126	|	...	|	|	1154
Amsterdam Zuid a.	0931	|	...	|	|	|	1001	...	|	1031	|	...	|	|	|	1101	...	|	1131	|	...	|	|	1201
Schiphol ✈ a.	0938	|	...	|	|	|	1008	...	|	1038	|	...	|	|	|	1108	...	|	1138	|	...	|	|	1208
Utrecht Centraal ‡ a.	...	0910	...	0937	0940	0940	...	...	1007	...	1010	...	1037	1040	1040	...	...	1107	...	1110	...	1140	1140	...
Den Haag Centraal **483** a.	...	0955	...	|	|	1025	...	...	|	...	1055	...	|	|	1125	...	...	|	...	1155	...	|	1225	...
Rotterdam Centraal **483** a.	...	0957**c**	...	1027	1027	...	...	...	1057	...	1057**n**	...	1127	1127	...	...	...	1157	...	1157**n**	...	1227	...	...

Groningen **486** d.	...	1004	...	...	...	1044	...	...	1104	...	...	1144**n**	1144	...	...	1204	...	...	...	1244	...	...	1304	...
Leeuwarden **486** d.	...	1004	...	...	1045	|	...	...	1104	...	...	1145	1145**p**	...	...	1204	...	...	1245	|	...	...	1304	...
Zwolle ‡ d.	...	1116	...	...	1146	1146	...	...	1216	...	...	1246	1244	...	...	1316	...	...	1346	1346	...	...	1416	...
Enschede **484** d.	...	|	1027	...	|	|	1057	...	|	1127	...	|	|	1157	...	|	1227	...	|	|	...	...	|	1327
Deventer **484** d.	...	|	1115	...	|	|	1145	...	|	1215	...	|	|	1245	...	|	1315	...	|	|	1345	...	|	1415
Amersfoort ⊙ ‡ a.	...	1153	1153	...	1223	1223	1223	...	1253	1253	...	1323	1323	1323	...	1353	1353	...	1423	1423	1423	...	1453	1453
Amersfoort ⊙ ‡ d.	1128	1155	1155	1158	1225	1225	1225	1228	1255	1255	1258	1325	1325	1325	1328	1355	1355	1358	1425	1425	1425	1428	1455	1455
Amsterdam Centraal a.	1201	|	|	1231	|	|	|	1301	|	|	1331	|	|	|	1401	|	|	1431	|	|	|	1501	|	|
Duivendrecht a.	...	1226	|	...	|	|	1254	...	1326	|	...	|	|	1354	...	1426	|	...	|	|	1454	...	1526	|
Amsterdam Zuid WTC a.	...	1231	|	...	|	|	1301	...	1331	|	...	|	|	1401	...	1431	|	...	|	|	1501	...	1531	|
Schiphol ✈ a.	...	1238	|	...	|	|	1308	...	1338	|	...	|	|	1408	...	1438	|	...	|	|	1508	...	1538	|
Utrecht Centraal ‡ a.	...	...	1210	...	1240	1240	...	...	...	1310	...	1340	1340	...	...	...	1410	...	1440	1440	...	...	...	1510
Den Haag Centraal **483** a.	...	...	1255	...	|	1325	...	...	...	1355	...	|	1425	...	...	...	1455	...	|	1525	...	...	...	1555
Rotterdam Centraal **483** a.	...	...	1257	...	1327	...	...	...	...	1357**a**	...	1427	...	...	...	...	1457	...	1527	...	...	...	...	1557**v**

						Ⓐ				Ⓐ	Ⓒ				Ⓐ				Ⓐ	Ⓒ				Ⓐ
Groningen **486** d.	...	1344**p**	1344	...	...	...	1404	...	...	...	1444**n**	1444	...	...	...	1504	...	...	...	1544**n**	1544	...	...	...
Leeuwarden **486** d.	...	1345	|	...	...	1404	1404**c**	...	...	1445	1445	|	...	...	1504	1504**c**	...	...	1545	1545	|	...	...	1604
Zwolle ‡ d.	...	1446	1446	...	...	1511	1516	...	...	1541	1546	1546	...	...	1611	1616	...	...	1641	1646	1646	...	...	1711
Enschede **484** d.	...	|	|	1357	...	|	|	1427	...	|	|	|	1457	...	|	|	1527	...	|	|	|	1557	...	|
Deventer **484** d.	...	|	|	1445	...	|	|	1515	...	|	|	|	1545	...	|	|	1615	...	|	|	|	1645	...	|
Amersfoort ⊙ ‡ a.	...	1523	1523	1523	...	1550	1553	1553	...	1620	1623	1623	1623	...	1650	1653	1653	...	1720	1723	1723	1723	...	1750
Amersfoort ⊙ ‡ d.	1458	1525	1525	1525	1528	1552	1555	1555	1558	1622	1625	1625	1625	1628	1652	1655	1655	1658	1722	1725	1725	1725	1728	1752
Amsterdam Centraal a.	1531	|	|	|	1601	|	|	|	1631	|	|	|	|	1701	|	|	|	1701	|	|	|	|	1801	|
Duivendrecht a.	...	|	|	1554	...	|	1626	|	...	|	|	|	1654	...	|	1726	|	...	|	|	|	1754	...	|
Amsterdam Zuid WTC a.	...	|	|	1601	...	|	1631	|	...	|	|	|	1701	...	|	1731	|	...	|	|	|	1801	...	|
Schiphol ✈ a.	...	|	|	1608	...	|	1638	|	...	|	|	|	1708	...	|	1738	|	...	|	|	|	1808	...	|
Utrecht Centraal ‡ a.	...	1540	1540	...	...	1607	...	1610	...	1637	1640	1640	...	...	1707	...	1710	...	1737	1740	1740	...	...	1807
Den Haag Centraal **483** a.	...	|	1625	...	...	|	...	1655	...	|	|	1725	...	...	|	...	1755	...	|	|	1825	...	...	|
Rotterdam Centraal **483** a.	...	1627	...	...	...	1657	...	1657**c**	...	1727	1727	...	...	...	1757	...	1757**j**	...	1827	1827	...	...	...	1857

								Ⓐ											†	⚒				
Groningen **486** d.	1604	...	...	1644**p**	1644	...	...	...	1702	...	...	1744**q**	1744	...	...	1804	...	...	...	1844	1844	...	...	1904
Leeuwarden **486** d.	1604**c**	...	...	1645	|	...	...	1704	1704**c**	...	...	1745	|	...	...	1804	...	...	1845	1845	|	...	...	1904**v**
Zwolle ‡ d.	1716	...	...	1746	1746	...	...	1811	1816	...	...	1846	1846	...	...	1916	...	...	1941	1946	1946	...	...	2016
Enschede **484** d.	|	1627	...	|	|	...	...	|	|	1727	...	|	|	1757	...	|	1827	...	|	|	|	1857	...	|
Deventer **484** d.	|	1715	...	|	|	1738	...	|	|	1815	...	|	|	1845	...	|	1915	...	|	|	|	1945	...	|
Amersfoort ⊙ ‡ a.	1753	1753	...	1823	1823	1819	...	1850	1853	1853	...	1923	1923	1923	...	1953	1953	...	2020	2023	2023	2023	...	2053
Amersfoort ⊙ ‡ d.	1755	1755	1758	1825	1825	1825	1828	1852	1855	1855	1858	1925	1925	1925	1928	1955	1955	1958	2022	2025	2025	2025	2028	2055
Amsterdam Centraal a.	|	|	1831	|	|	|	1901	|	|	|	1931	|	|	|	2001	|	|	2031	|	|	|	|	2101	|
Duivendrecht a.	1826	|	...	|	|	1854	...	|	1926	|	...	|	|	1954	...	2026	|	...	|	|	|	2054	...	2126
Amsterdam Zuid WTC a.	1831	|	...	|	|	1901	...	|	1931	|	...	|	|	2001	...	2031	|	...	|	|	|	2101	...	2131
Schiphol ✈ a.	1838	|	...	|	|	1908	...	|	1938	|	...	|	|	2008	...	2038	|	...	|	|	|	2108	...	2138
Utrecht Centraal ‡ a.	...	1810	...	1840	1840	...	...	1907	...	1910	...	1940	1940	...	...	...	2010	...	2037	2040	2040	...	...	...
Den Haag Centraal **483** a.	...	1855	...	|	1925	...	...	|	...	1955	...	|	2025	...	...	...	2055	...	|	|	2125	...	...	...
Rotterdam Centraal **483** a.	...	1857**c**	...	1927	...	...	...	1957	...	1957**c**	...	2027	...	...	...	...	2057	...	2127	2127	...	...	...	...

Groningen **486** d.	...	...	1944**b**	1944	...	...	2004	...	...	2044**a**	2044	...	...	2104	...	...	...	2144	...	...	2204	...	...	...
Leeuwarden **486** d.	...	...	1945	|	...	...	2004	...	...	2044	|	...	...	2104	...	...	2145	2145**p**	...	...	2204	...	...	...
Zwolle ‡ d.	...	...	2046	2046	...	...	2116	...	...	2146	2146	...	...	2216	...	...	2246	2246	...	...	2316	...	...	2347
Enschede **484** d.	1927	...	|	|	1957	...	|	2027	...	|	|	...	...	|	2127	...	|	|	2157	...	|	2227	...	|
Deventer **484** d.	2015	...	|	|	2045	...	|	2115	...	|	|	2145	...	|	2215	...	|	|	2245	...	|	2315	...	|
Amersfoort ⊙ ‡ a.	2053	...	2123	2123	2123	...	2153	2153	...	2223	2223	2223	...	2253	2253	...	2323	2323	2323	...	2353	2353	...	0043
Amersfoort ⊙ ‡ d.	2055	2058	2125	2125	2125	2128	2155	2155	2158	2225	2225	2225	2228	2255	2255	2258	2325	2325	2325	2328	2355	2355	2358	0044
Amsterdam Centraal a.	|	2131	|	|	|	2201	|	|	2231	|	|	|	2301	|	|	2301	|	|	|	0001	|	|	0031	|
Duivendrecht a.	|	...	|	|	2154	...	2226	|	...	|	|	2254	...	2324	|	...	|	|	2354	...	0026	|	...	|
Amsterdam Zuid WTC a.	|	...	|	|	2201	...	2231	|	...	|	|	2301	...	2331	|	...	|	|	0001	...	0031	|	...	|
Schiphol ✈ a.	|	...	|	|	2208	...	2238	|	...	|	|	2308	...	2338	|	...	|	|	0008	...	0040	|	...	|
Utrecht Centraal ‡ a.	2110	...	2140	2140	...	...	...	2210	...	2240	2240	...	...	...	2310	...	2340	2340	...	...	...	0010	...	0110
Den Haag Centraal **483** a.	2155	...	|	2225	...	...	...	2255	...	|	2325	...	...	...	2355	...	|	0024	...	...	...	...	...	...
Rotterdam Centraal **483** a.	2157**v**	...	2227	...	...	...	...	...	...	2327	...	...	...	...	2357	...	0027**f**	...	...	...	...	...	...	...

a – Ⓐ only.
b – ①–④ (not Dec. 25, 26, Jan. 1, Mar. 24, Apr. 30, May 1, 12).
c – Ⓒ only.
d – Also Apr. 30, May 1.
e – Not Apr. 30, May 1.
f – ①⑥⑦ (also Dec. 26, 27, Jan. 2, Mar. 25, May 1, 2, 13).

j – Ⓒ only. Starts from Deventer on ⑥, Apr. 30, May 1.
n – † only.
p – ⑤ only.
q – ⑤⑥ (also Apr. 30, May 1).
r – 0734 on †.
v – ⚒ only.
y – ⚒ only (0638 on ⑥, Apr. 30, May 1).
z – ⑥ (also Apr. 30, May 1).

⊙ – Trains are in connection at Amersfoort where the interval between their arrival and departure times is at least 2 minutes.

‡ – Trains with the same timings Zwolle - Amersfoort - Utrecht run coupled together over these sections. Passengers should take care to join the appropriate portion of the train for their destination.

483 DEN HAAG and ROTTERDAM - GOUDA - UTRECHT

Most of these journeys are through services to / from **Deventer**, **Enschede**, **Leeuwarden** and / or **Groningen**. For details, see Table **481**

km					Ⓐ	Ⓐ	Ⓐ	Ⓐ	Ⓐ	⚒	⚒	⚒	⚒	⚒	⚒		⚒	⚒			⚒	⚒		
0	**Den Haag** Centraal d.	...	0006	...	0525	...	0606	...	0621	...	0636	...	0651	...	0706	...	...	0721	...	0736	...	0751	...	0806
	Rotterdam Centraal **465** d.	0002	|	...	|	0602	|	0617	|	0632	|	0647	|	0702	|	...	0717	|	0732	|	0747	|	0802	|
	Rotterdam Alexander **465** d.	0011	|	...	|	0611	|	0626	|	0641	|	0656	|	0711	|	...	0726	|	0741	|	0756	|	0811	|
28	Gouda **465** d.	0022	0025	...	0551	0622	0625	0638	0641	0652	0655	0708	0711	0722	0725	...	0738	0741	0752	0755	0808	0811	0822	0825
60	**Utrecht** Centraal **463** a.	0043	0046	...	0625	0641	0644	0656	0701	0711	0714	0726	0731	0741	0745	...	0756	0801	0811	0814	0826	0831	0842	0844

			⚒	⚒			⚒	⚒											
Den Haag Centraal d.	and at the	...	1006	...	1021	...	1036	...	1051	...	...	...	1106	...	1121	...	1136	...	1151	and at the
Rotterdam Centraal **465** d.	same minutes	1002	|	1017	|	1032	|	1047	|	...	...	1102	|	1117	|	1132	|	1147	|	same minutes
Rotterdam Alexander **465** d.	past	1011	|	1026	|	1041	|	1056	|	...	...	1111	|	1126	|	1141	|	1156	|	past
Gouda **465** d.	each hour	1023	1025	1038	1041	1052	1055	1108	1111	...	...	1122	1125	1138	1141	1152	1155	1208	1211	each hour
Utrecht Centraal **463** a.	until	1042	1045	1056	1101	1111	1114	1126	1131	...	...	1141	1144	1156	1201	1211	1214	1226	1231	until

Den Haag Centraal d.	...	1921	...	1936	...	1951	...	2006	...	...	2036	...	2106	...	2136	...	2206	...	2236	...	2306	...	2336	...
Rotterdam Centraal **465** d.	1917	|	1932	|	1947	|	2002	|	...	2032	|	2102	|	2132	|	2202	|	2232	|	2302	|	2332	|	...
Rotterdam Alexander **465** d.	1926	|	1941	|	1956	|	2011	|	...	2041	|	2111	|	2141	|	2211	|	2241	|	2311	|	2351	|	...
Gouda **465** d.	1938	1941	1952	1955	2008	2011	2022	2025	...	2052	2055	2123	2125	2152	2155	2222	2225	2252	2255	2322	2325	2352	2355	...
Utrecht Centraal **463** a.	1956	2001	2011	2014	2026	2031	2041	2044	...	2111	2114	2142	2145	2211	2214	2241	2244	2311	2314	2341	2344	0011	0014	...

km		A	A			Ⓐ	Ⓐ	Ⓐ	Ⓐ	Ⓐ	Ⓐ	⚒	⚒	⚒	Ⓐ	⚒	⚒	⚒	⚒	⚒	⚒			⚒
0	**Utrecht** Centraal **463** d.	0015	...	....	...	0559	0603	0629	0633	0645	0648	0659	0703	0715	0718	0729	0733	0745	0747	0759	0803	0815	0818	0829
32	Gouda **465** d.	0047	0052	...	...	0620	0623	0650	0653	0705	0709	0720	0723	0735	0739	0750	0753	0805	0809	0820	0823	0835	0839	0850
46	Rotterdam Alexander **465** d.	|	0104	...	...	|	0633	|	0703	|	0718	|	0733	|	0748	|	0803	|	0818	|	0833	|	0848	|
56	**Rotterdam** Centraal **465** a.	|	0114	...	...	|	0642	|	0712	|	0727	|	0742	|	0757	|	0812	|	0827	|	0842	|	0857	|
	Den Haag Centraal a.	0113	...	...	...	0638	...	0708	...	0725	...	0738	...	0755	...	0808	...	0825	...	0838	...	0855	...	0908

	⚒				⚒			⚒	⚒			⚒										
Utrecht Centraal **463** d.	0833	0845	0848	and at the	1033	1045	1048	1059	1103	1115	1118	1129	...	...	1133	1145	1148	1159	1203	1215	1218	1229
Gouda **465** d.	0853	0905	0909	same minutes	1053	1105	1109	1120	1123	1135	1139	1150	...	...	1153	1205	1209	1221	1223	1235	1239	1250
Rotterdam Alexander **465** d.	0903	|	0918	past	1103	|	1118	|	1133	|	1148	|	...	...	1203	|	1218	|	1233	|	1248	|
Rotterdam Centraal **465** a.	0912	|	0927	each hour	1112	|	1127	|	1142	|	1157	|	...	...	1212	|	1227	|	1242	|	1257	|
Den Haag Centraal a.	...	0925	...	until	...	1125	...	1138	...	1155	...	1208	...	...	...	1225	...	1239	...	1255	...	1308

																					B
Utrecht Centraal **463** d.	and at the	1959	2003	2015	2018	2029	2033	2045	2048	...	2115	2118	2145	2148	2215	2218	2245	2248	2315	2318	2345	2348
Gouda **465** d.	same minutes	2020	2023	2035	2039	2050	2053	2105	2109	...	2135	2139	2205	2209	2235	2239	2305	2309	2335	2339	0005	0009
Rotterdam Alexander **465** d.	past	|	2033	|	2048	|	2103	|	2118	...	|	2148	|	2218	|	2248	|	2318	|	2348	|	0018
Rotterdam Centraal **465** a.	each hour	|	2042	|	2057	|	2112	|	2127	...	|	2157	|	2227	|	2257	|	2327	|	2357	|	0027
Den Haag Centraal a.	until	2038	...	2055	...	2108	...	2125	...	...	2155	...	2225	...	2255	...	2325	...	2355	...	0024	...

A – ①⑥⑦ (also Dec. 26, 27, Jan. 2, Mar. 25, May 1, 2, 13).

B – ⑤⑥⑦ (also Dec. 25, 26, Jan. 1, Mar. 24, Apr. 30, May 1, 12).

484 AMERSFOORT - DEVENTER - ENSCHEDE

For through journeys from / to **Rotterdam**, **Den Haag**, **Schiphol** ✈ and **Amsterdam**, see table **481**

km		A	N			Ⓐ		Ⓐ	Ⓐ	⚒												B	P
0	**Amersfoort** d.	0010	0022	...	...	...	...	...	0641	0710	...	0741	0810	...	0841	and at	2241	...	2310	...	2341	2341
43	Apeldoorn d.	0037	0100	...	...	0614	...	0644	0707	0737	...	0807	0837	...	0907	the same	2307	...	2337	...	0007	0005
58	**Deventer** d.	0050	0116	...	...	0629	...	0659	0720	0750	...	0820	0850	...	0920	minutes past	2320	...	2350	...	0020	0017
96	Almelo **492** d.	0115	0153	...	...	0701	...	0731	0745	0815	...	0845	0915	...	0945	each	2345	...	0015	...	0045	0049
111	Hengelo **492** a.	0127	0204	...	...	0718	...	0748	0757	0827	...	0857	0927	...	0957	hour	2357	...	0027	...	0057	0101
119	**Enschede 492** a.	0135	0212	...	...	0727	...	0757	0805	0835	...	*0907*	0935	...	1005	until	0005	...	0036	...	0105	0109

	Ⓐ		Ⓐ	⚒	Ⓐ	⚒		⚒													Z	
Enschede 492 d.	0454	...	0527	...	0557	0627	...	0657	...	0727	...	0757	and at	2157	...	2227	...	*2247*	...	2347	...	...
Hengelo **492** d.	0505	...	0536	...	0606	0636	...	0706	...	0736	...	0806	the same	2206	...	2236	...	*2258*	...	2358	...	...
Almelo **492** d.	0517	...	0549	...	0619	0649	...	0719	...	0749	...	0819	minutes past	2219	...	2249	...	2331	...	0012	0031	...
Deventer d.	0546	...	0615	0645	0645	0715	0745	0745	...	0815	...	0845	each	2245	...	2315	...	0003	...	...	0102	...
Apeldoorn d.	0557	...	0627	0657	0657	0727	0757	0757	...	0827	...	0857	hour	2257	...	2327	...	0016	...	...	...	...
Amersfoort a.	0623	...	0653	0723	0723	0753	0823	0823	...	0853	...	0923	until	2323	...	2353	...	...	...	...	...	...

A – ①⑥⑦ (also Dec. 26, 27, Jan. 2, Mar. 25, May 1, 2, 13).

B – ⑤⑥⑦ (also Dec. 25, 26, Jan. 1, Mar. 24, Apr. 30, May 1, 12).

N – ②–⑤ (not Dec. 26, 27, Jan. 2, Mar. 25, May 1, 2, 13).

P – ①–④ (not Dec. 25, 26, Jan. 1, Mar. 24, Apr. 30, May 1, 12).

Z – ⑥⑦ (also May 1, 2).

486 ZWOLLE - LEEUWARDEN and GRONINGEN

For through journeys from / to **Rotterdam**, **Den Haag**, **Schiphol** ✈ and **Amsterdam**, see table **481**

km		Ⓐ	Ⓐ		Ⓐ	Ⓐ	⚒	⚒		Ⓐ	⚒			⚒	⚒	⚒						
0	**Zwolle** d.	0547	0552	...	0622	0623	0647	0652	0719	0722	0725	0737	0752	0817	0822	0823	...	0847	0852	0917	0922	and at
27	Meppel d.	0603	0609	...	0638	0640	0703	0709	|	|	0741	0805	0809	|	|	0840	...	0903	0909	|	|	the
41	Steenwijk d.	|	0618	...	0647	|	|	0718	|	0746	|	|	0818	|	0844	|	...	|	0918	|	0944	same
65	Heerenveen d.	|	0633	...	0703	|	|	0733	|	0802	|	|	0833	|	0857	|	...	|	0933	|	0957	minutes
94	**Leeuwarden** a.	|	0654	...	0725	|	|	0754	|	0818	|	|	0854	|	0913	|	...	|	0954	|	1013	past
47	Hoogeveen d.	0614	...	...	...	0653	0714	...	|	...	0754	0846	...	|	...	0853	...	0914	...	|	...	each
77	Assen d.	0634	...	...	...	0711	0734	...	0759	...	0813	0834	...	0857	...	0911	...	0934	...	0957	...	hour
104	**Groningen** a.	0653	...	...	...	0731	0753	...	0816	...	0832	0853	...	0914	...	0931	...	0953	...	1014	...	until

							B	P	
Zwolle d.	2222	2247	2252	2317	2322	...	2347	2347	2352
Meppel d.	|	2303	2309	|	2338	...	0003	0003	0009
Steenwijk d.	2244	|	2318	|	2347	...	|	|	0018
Heerenveen d.	2257	|	2333	|	0001	...	|	|	0033
Leeuwarden a.	2313	|	2354	|	0017	...	|	|	0056
Hoogeveen d.	...	2314	...	|	...	...	0014	0015	...
Assen d.	...	2334	...	2357	...	...	0034	0050	...
Groningen a.	...	2353	...	0014	...	...	0053	0112	...

	Ⓐ	Ⓐ		Ⓐ	Ⓐ	Ⓐ	Ⓐ	Ⓐ	⑥ d	Ⓐ
Groningen d.	...	0504	...	...	0545	...	0604	0625	...	...
Assen d.	...	0526	...	...	0601	...	0622	0644	...	...
Hoogeveen d.	...	0546	...	...	|	...	0642	0703	...	...
Leeuwarden d.	0500	|	...	0540	|	0604	|	|	0636	0643
Heerenveen d.	0523	|	...	0601	|	0626	|	|	0657	0659
Steenwijk d.	0542	|	...	0615	|	0642	|	|	0713	0713
Meppel d.	0553	0559	...	0624	|	0653	0657	0716	0723	0723
Zwolle a.	0609	0615	...	0639	0644	0709	0713	0732	0739	0739

	⑥ d	Ⓐ	⚒		⚒	†	⚒															
Groningen d.	0638	0644	...	0704	0725	...	...	0744	...	0804	...	and at	...	2144	...	2204	...	...	2234	...	2325	...
Assen d.	0657	0702	...	0722	0744	...	...	0800	...	0822	...	the	...	2200	...	2222	...	...	2253	...	2344	...
Hoogeveen d.	0715	|	...	0742	0803	...	...	|	...	0842	...	same	...	|	...	2242	...	...	2313	...	0003	...
Leeuwarden d.	|	|	0704	|	|	0734	0745	|	0804	|	0845	minutes	2145	|	2204	|	...	2234	|	...	|	2332
Heerenveen d.	|	|	0725	|	|	0755	0801	|	0826	|	0901	past	2201	|	2226	|	...	2255	|	...	|	2356
Steenwijk d.	|	|	0742	|	|	0812	0815	|	0842	|	0915	each	2215	|	2242	|	...	2312	|	...	|	0012
Meppel d.	0728	|	0753	0757	0816	0823	|	|	0853	0857	|	hour	|	|	2253	2257	...	2323	2326	...	0016	0023
Zwolle a.	0744	0744	0809	0813	0832	0839	0839	0844	0909	0913	0939	until	2239	2243	2309	2313	...	2339	2342	...	0037	0043

☛ Additional services **Zwolle** – **Groningen** (same timings as the 0823 ⚒ service shown above): 0923 ⚒ and hourly until 1523 ⚒, then 1623, 1723, 1823, 1923, 2023, 2123 **B**, 2223 †.

Additional services **Groningen** – **Zwolle** (same timings as the 0725 ⚒ service shown above): 0825 ⚒ and hourly until 1425 ⚒, then 1525, 1625, 1725, 1825, 1925, 2025, 2125 **B**.

B – ⑤⑥⑦ (also Dec. 25, 26, Jan. 1, Mar. 24, Apr. 30, May 1, 12).

P – ①–④ (not Dec. 25, 26, Jan. 1, Mar. 24, Apr. 30, May 1, 12).

d – Also Apr. 30, May 1.

For traffic arrangements on Dutch holiday dates, see page 248

OLDENZAAL - HENGELO - ZUTPHEN — 488

Operated by Syntus ★

km					Ⓐ	Ⓐ	⚒																	Ⓐ	
0	**Oldenzaal** d.	0029	...	...	0559	0629	0659	0729v	...	0759	0829	and at the same minutes past each hour until	2029	2059	...	2129	...	2159	2229	...	2259	2329	2329	2359
11	Hengelo d.	0044	...	...	0614	0644	0714	0744v	...	0814	0844v		2044v	2114	...	2144a	...	2214	2244a	...	2314	2340	2344	0014
26	Goor d.	0056	...	...	0629	0659	0729	0759	...	0829	0859v		2059v	2129	...	2159a	...	2229	2259a	...	2329	...	2359	0029
39	Lochem d.	...	...	...	0638	0708	0738	0808	...	0838	0908v		2108v	2138	...	2208a	...	2238	2308a	...	2338	...	0008	0038
56	**Zutphen** a.	...	...	...	0653	0723	0753	0823	...	0853	0923v		2123v	2153	...	2223a	...	2253	2323a	...	2353	...	0023	0053

				Ⓐ	Ⓐ	⚒	⚒																	
Zutphen d.	0007	...	...	...	...	0607a	0637a	0707v	...	0737	0807v	and at the same minutes past each hour until	2007v	2037	...	2107a	...	2137	2207a	...	2237	2307a	...	2337
Lochem d.	0019	...	...	...	...	0619a	0649a	0719v	...	0749	0819v		2019v	2049	...	2119a	...	2149	2219a	...	2249	2319a	...	2349
Goor d.	0028	...	...	0529	0559	0629	0659	0729	...	0759	0829v		2029v	2059	...	2129a	...	2159	2229a	...	2259	2329a	...	2359
Hengelo d.	...	...	...	0545	0615	0645	0715	0745	...	0815	0845		2045	2115	...	2145	...	2215	2245	...	2315	2345	...	0015
Oldenzaal a.	...	...	...	0554	0624	0654	0724	0754	...	0824	0854		2054	2124	...	2154	...	2224	2254	...	2324	2354	...	0024

a – Ⓐ only. v – ⚒ only. ★ – NS tickets valid.

ZUTPHEN - WINTERSWIJK — 490

Operated by Syntus ★

km		Q		Ⓐ	Ⓐ	Ⓐ	⑥r	Ⓐ	Ⓐ	⑥	Ⓐ						Ⓐ	Ⓐ	⚒	⚒	⚒	⚒	⚒	⚒	Ⓐ
0	**Zutphen** d.	0007	...	0701	0731	0801	0807	0831	0901	0907	0931	1007	and hourly until	2307	...	ALSO	1036	1136	1236	1336	1436	1536	1636	1736	1837
22	Ruurlo d.	0023	...	0717	0747	0817	0823	0847	0917	0923	0947	1023		2323	...		1052	1152	1252	1352	1452	1552	1652	1752	1853
43	**Winterswijk** a.	0042	...	0736	0806	0836	0842	0906	0936	0942	1006	1042		2342	...		1111	1211	1311	1411	1511	1611	1711	1811	1912

	Ⓐ	⚒z	Ⓐ	Ⓐ	©	Ⓐ	Ⓐ	©	Ⓐ	Ⓐ	©	Ⓐ				Y		Ⓐ	⚒	⚒	⚒	⚒	⚒	⚒	Ⓐ
Winterswijk d.	0615	0645	0715	0745	0751	0815	0845	0851	0915	0945	0951	1021	1051	and hourly until	2151	2251	ALSO	1121	1221	1321	1421	1521	1621	1721	1821
Ruurlo d.	0633	0703	0733	0803	0809	0833	0903	0909	0933	1003	1009	1039	1109		2209	2309		1139	1239	1339	1439	1539	1639	1739	1839
Zutphen a.	0649	0719	0745	0819	0824	0849	0919	0924	0949	1024	1024	1054	1124		2224	2324		1154	1254	1354	1454	1554	1654	1754	1854

– ⑥⑦ (also May 1, 2). Y – ⑤⑥ (also Apr. 30, May 1). z – Runs 6 minutes later on ⑥ (also Apr. 30, May 1). ★ – NS tickets valid.

ZWOLLE - EMMEN and ENSCHEDE — 492

km		N		Ⓐ		Ⓐ	Ⓐ	⚒	⚒			⚒			P			P					
0	**Zwolle** d.	0026	...	0556	...	0626	0656	0728	0756	0826	and at the same mins past each hour until	1456	1526	then	1556	1626	and at the same mins past each hour until	2056	2126	...	2226	...	2326
23	Ommen d.	0044	...	0615	...	0644	0715	0745	0815	0844		1515	1544		1615	1644		2115	2144	...	2244	...	2344
34	Mariënberg **497** d.	0051	...	|	...	0651	|	0752	|	0851		|	1551		|	1651		|	2151	...	2251	...	2351
55	Coevorden d.	0107	...	0636	...	0707	0736	0808	0836	0907		1536	1607		1636	1707		2136	2207	...	2307	...	0007
75	**Emmen** a.	0128	...	0651	...	0728	0751	0829	0851	0929		1551	1628		1651	1728		2151	2228	...	2328	...	0028

	Ⓐ	Ⓐ	Ⓐ	Ⓐ	⚒	⚒	⚒			⚒			P			P							
Emmen d.	0503	0533	0608	0633	0708	0733	0808	0833	and at the same mins past each hour until	1508	1533	then	1608	1633	and at the same mins past each hour until	1908	1933	...	2033	2133	...	2233	2333
Coevorden d.	0522	0552	0624	0652	0724	0752	0824	0852		1524	1552		1624	1652		1924	1952	...	2052	2152	...	2252	2352
Mariënberg **497** d.	0538	0608	|	0708	|	0808	|	0908		|	1608		|	1708		|	2008	...	2108	2208	...	2308	0008
Ommen d.	0546	0616	0645	0716	0745	0816	0845	0916		1545	1616		1645	1716		1945	2016	...	2116	2216	...	2316	0016
Zwolle a.	0605	0635	0704	0735	0804	0835	0904	0935		1604	1635		1704	1735		2004	2035	...	2135	2235	...	2335	0035

km				Ⓐ	⚒		Ⓐ	Ⓐ	⚒		⚒	⚒			⚒		⚒							
0	**Zwolle** d.	...	...	...	...	...	0606	0636	0706	...	0736	0806	0836	...	0906	0936	1006	...	1036	1106	and every 30 minutes until	2306	2336	...
18	Raalte d.	...	...	...	...	...	0622	0652	0722	...	0752	0822	0852	...	0922	0952	1022	...	1052	1122		2322	2352	...
44	Almelo **484 497** d.	0049	...	...	0619a	...	0649	0719	0749	...	0819	0849	0919	...	0949	1019	1049	...	1119	1149		2349	0019	...
59	Hengelo **484** d.	0105	...	0612	0635	...	0705	0735	0805	...	0835	0905	0935	...	1005	1035	1105	...	1135	1205		0005	0035	...
67	**Enschede 484** a.	0117	...	0622	0645	...	0715	0745	0815	...	0845	0915	0945	...	1015	1045	1115	...	1145	1215		0015	0045	...

		Q	Ⓐ	Ⓐ		Ⓐ	Ⓐ	⚒	⚒		⚒		⚒		⚒								
Enschede 484 d.	0017	0047	...	0517	...	0547	0617	0647	0717	0747	0817	0847	0917	0947	1017	...	1047	1117	and every 30 minutes until	2247	2317	...	2347
Hengelo **484** d.	0028	0057	0500	0528	...	0558	0628	0658	0728	0758	0828	0858	0928	0958	1028	...	1058	1128		2258	2328	...	2358
Almelo **484 497** d.	0042	...	0514	0542	...	0612	0642	0712	0742	0812	0842	0912	0942	1012	1042	...	1112	1142		2312	2342	...	0012
Raalte d.	...	...	0540	0610	...	0640	0710	0740	0810	0840	0910	0940	1010	1040	1110	...	1140	1210		2340	0010	...	...
Zwolle a.	...	...	0557	0627	...	0657	0727	0757	0827	0857	0927	0957	1027	1057	1127	...	1157	1227		2357	0027	...	...

a – Ⓐ only. N – ②–⑦ (not Dec. 26, 27, Jan. 2, Apr. 10, May 29). P – Not Dec. 25, 30, Jan. 1, Mar. 23, May 4, 11. Q – ⑥⑦ (also May 1, 2).

LEEUWARDEN - GRONINGEN — 494

Operated by Arriva ★

km		2		Ⓐ 2		Ⓐ 2		⚒ 2	Ⓐ	⚒ 2		Ⓐ 2	Ⓐ	2	⚒ 2		⚒ 2	Ⓐ	2	E 2	Ⓐ	2	⑦ 2
0	**Leeuwarden** d.	0003	...	0533	...	0603	...	0633	0658	0703	...	0733	0758	0803	0833	and at the same minutes past each hour until	1733	1758	1803	1833	1858	1903	1933
25	Buitenpost d.	0027	...	0557	...	0627	...	0657	0714	0727	...	0757	0814	0827	0857		1757	1814	1827	1857	1914	1927	1957
54	**Groningen** a.	0052	...	0622	...	0652	...	0722	0732	0752	...	0822	0832	0852	0922		1822	1832	1852	1922	1932	1952	2022

	2		⑦ 2		2		⑦ 2	2		2
Leeuwarden d.	2003	...	2033	...	2103	...	2133	2203	...	2303
Buitenpost d.	2027	...	2057	...	2127	...	2157	2227	...	2327
Groningen a.	2052	...	2122	...	2152	...	2222	2252	...	2352

	2		Ⓐ 2	Ⓐ	⚒ 2	Ⓐ	⚒ 2		⚒ 2	Ⓐ	2
Groningen d.	0001	...	0531	0601	0631	0652	0701	...	0733	0752	0801
Buitenpost d.	0027	...	0557	0628	0657	0711	0727	...	0758	0811	0827
Leeuwarden a.	0053	...	0623	0653	0723	0728	0755	...	0823	0828	0853

		⚒ 2	Ⓐ	2		E 2	Ⓐ	2		E 2	Ⓐ	2		⑦ 2	2		⑦ 2	2		⑦ 2	2		2
Groningen d.	and at the same minutes past each hour until	1633	1652	1701	...	1733	1752	1801	...	1833	1852	1901	...	1933	2001	...	2033	2101	...	2133	2201	...	2301
Buitenpost d.		1658	1711	1727	...	1758	1811	1827	...	1858	1911	1927	...	1958	2027	...	2058	2127	...	2158	2227	...	2327
Leeuwarden a.		1723	1728	1753	...	1823	1828	1853	...	1923	1928	1953	...	2023	2053	...	2123	2153	...	2223	2253	...	2353

E – Not Dec. 25, 26, Jan. 1, Mar. 24, May 1, 12. ★ – NS tickets valid.

GRONINGEN - NIEUWESCHANS - LEER — 495

Operated by Arriva

km				Ⓐ	⚒	⚒	⑦	⚒	⚒		⚒		⚒			⚒		⚒						
0	**Groningen** d.	0019	...	0520	0546	0620	0641	0646	0720	...	0746	0820	0846	0920	and in the same pattern **every two hours** until	1746	1820	1846	1920	2020	2120	...	2220	2320
34	Winschoten d.	0054	...	0555	0620	0655	0715	0721	0755	...	0821	0856	0920	0955		1821	1856	1920	1955	2055	2155	...	2255	2355
46	Nieuweschans a.	0104	...	0603	...	0703	...	0731	0805	...	0831	0909	...	1005		1831	1905	...	2005	2105	2205	...	2305	0005
46	Nieuweschans d.	...	...	0603	...	0703	...	...	0810n	...	...	0910	...	...		...	1910	...	...	...	...	...	...	...
57	Weener d.	...	...	0612	...	0712	...	...	0819n	...	...	0919	...	...		...	1919	...	...	...	...	...	...	...
72	**Leer** a.	...	...	0625	...	0725	...	...	0832n	...	...	0932	...	...		...	1932	...	...	...	...	...	...	...

				Ⓐ	⚒	Ⓐ	Ⓐ	©	⚒		⚒		⚒			⚒		⚒					
Leer d.	...	...	...	...	...	...	0639	...	...	...	0824	0846n	...	and in the same pattern **every two hours** until	1846n	...	...	2024	...	2046n	...	...	...	...
Weener d.	...	...	...	...	...	...	0652	...	...	...	0837	0859n	...		1859n	...	...	2037	...	2059n	...	...	...	...
Nieuweschans a.	...	...	...	...	...	...	0703	...	...	...	0846	0908n	...		1908n	...	...	2046	...	2108n	...	...	...	...
Nieuweschans d.	0010	0108	...	...	...	0645	0710	0710	0745	0810	0846	0910	...		1910	...	2010	2046	...	2110	...	2210	...	2310
Winschoten d.	0020	0118	...	0520	0620	0656	0720	0720	0756	0820	0856	0920	0956		1920	1956	2020	2056	...	2120	...	2220	...	2320
Groningen a.	0056	0154	...	0556	0656	0734	0756	0756	0834	0856	0934	0956	1034		1956	2034	2056	2134	...	2156	...	2256	...	2356

n – ⑦ only. ☛ NS tickets are valid Groningen - Nieuweschans and v.v.

497 OTHER BRANCH LINES

ALMELO – MARIËNBERG Operated by **Connexxion** (NS tickets valid)

From Almelo:

0621 Ⓐ, 0644 Ⓐ, 0721 ⚒, 0744 ⚒, 0821 ⚒, 0844 ⚒, 0921 ⚒, 0944 ⚒, 1021 ⚒, 1044 ⚒, 1121 ⚒, 1144 and at 21 ⚒ and 44 minutes past each hour until 1844; then 1844, 1944, 2044, 2144.

19 km Journey time: 23 minutes 2nd clas

From Mariënberg:

0649 Ⓐ, 0714 Ⓐ, 0749 ⚒, 0814 ⚒, 0849 ⚒, 0914 ⚒, 0949 ⚒, 1014 ⚒, 1049 ⚒, 1114 ⚒, 1149 ⚒, 1214, 1249 ⚒ and at 14 and 49 ⚒ minutes past each hour until 1849 ⚒; then 191 2014. 2114, 2214.

AMERSFOORT – EDE-WAGENINGEN Operated by **Connexxion** (NS tickets valid)

From Amersfoort:

0016, 0046, 0516, 0546 and every 30 minutes until until 2346.

34 km Journey time: 37 minutes

From Ede-Wageningen:

0002, 0032, 0102, 0532 Ⓐ, 0602, 0632 Ⓐ, 0702, 0732 and every 30 minutes until 2332.

APELDOORN – ZUTPHEN

From Apeldoorn:

0010 **Q**, 0703 Ⓐ, 0733 Ⓐ, 0803 ⚒, 0833, 0903, 0933, 1003, 1033, 1103, 1133, 1203, 1240, 1310 and every 30 minutes until 2310.

18 km Journey time: ± 21 minutes

From Zutphen:

0632 Ⓐ, 0702 Ⓐ, 0732 ⚒, 0802, 0832, 0902, 0932, 1002, 1032, 1102, 1132, 1202, 1236, 13 and every 30 minutes until 2236; then 2336 **R**.

GRONINGEN – DELFZIJL Operated by **Arriva** (NS tickets valid)

From Groningen:

0024, 0533 Ⓐ, 0603 ⚒, 0633, 0703 **D**, 0733, 0803 ⚒, 0833 and at 03 ⚒ and 33 minutes past each hour until 1833; then 1903 Ⓐ, 1933, 2033, 2103 **F**, 2133, 2233, 2333.

38 km Journey time: ± 40 minutes

From Delfzijl:

0015, 0105, 0515 **E**, 0615 Ⓐ, 0645 ⚒, 0715, 0745 **D**, 0815, 0845 ⚒ and at 15 and 45 ⚒ minute past each hour until 1915; then 1945 Ⓐ, 2015, 2115, 2215, 2315.

GRONINGEN – ROODESCHOOL Operated by **Arriva** (NS tickets valid)

From Groningen:

0020, 0529 ⚒, 0559 Ⓐ, 0629 **J**, 0659 Ⓐ, 0729, 0829 and hourly until 2329.
Also: 1459 Ⓐ, 1559 Ⓐ, 1659 Ⓐ, 1759 Ⓐ, 2059 **F**.

38 km Journey time: 43 minutes

From Roodeschool:

0015, 0107, 0615 ⚒, 0645 Ⓐ, 0715 ⚒, 0745 Ⓐ, 0815, 0915 and hourly until 2315.
Also: 1545 Ⓐ, 1645 Ⓐ, 1745 Ⓐ, 1845 Ⓐ.

HAARLEM – ZANDVOORT AAN ZEE

From Haarlem:

0001, 0042, 0558 Ⓐ, 0631 ⚒, 0701 ⚒, 0731, 0801 and every 30 minutes until 2331.
Also (May 31 - Aug. 31): 0946, 1016 and every 30 minutes until 1846.

8 km Journey time: ± 11 minutes

From Zandvoort:

0018, 0058, 0614 Ⓐ, 0648 ⚒, 0718 ⚒, 0748, 0818 and every 30 minutes until 2348.
Also (May 31 - Aug. 31): 1001, 1031 and every 30 minutes until 1901.

HEERLEN – AACHEN

From Heerlen: *Trains call at Herzogenrath 11 minutes later*

0532 **P**, 0632 **N**, 0732, 0832 and hourly until 2232.

24 km Journey time: ± 30 minutes

From Aachen Hbf: *Trains call at Herzogenrath 18 minutes later*

0632 **P**, 0732 **N**, 0832, 0932 and hourly until 2332.

LEEUWARDEN – HARLINGEN ¶ Operated by **Arriva** (NS tickets valid)

From Leeuwarden:

0459 Ⓐ, 0559 ⚒, 0633 Ⓐ, 0659 ⚒, 0733 ⚒, 0759, 0833, 0859 and at 33 (▲) and 59 minutes past each hour until 1959; then 2059, 2159, 2323.

26 km Journey time: ± 26 minutes 2nd clas

From Harlingen Haven:

0528 Ⓐ, 0628 ⚒, 0703 Ⓐ, 0728 ⚒, 0803 ⚒, 0828, 0903, 0928 and at 03 (▼) and 28 minut past each hour until 2028; then 2128, 2228, 2352.

LEEUWARDEN – SNEEK – STAVOREN Operated by **Arriva** (NS tickets valid)

Leeuwarden – **Sneek** (*22 km*, ± 22 minutes):

0530 Ⓐ, 0601 ⚒, 0632 ⚒, 0703, 0735 ⚒ and at 03 and 35 ⚒ minutes past each hour until 1903; then 1935 ⑤, 2003, 2103, 2203, 2320.

Leeuwarden – **Sneek** – **Stavoren**:

0530 Ⓐ, 0601 ⚒, 0632 Ⓐ, 0703 ⚒, 0803, 0903 and hourly until 2103; then 2203 ⑤⑥.

50 km Journey time: ± 54 minutes 2nd cla

Sneek – **Leeuwarden**:

0629 Ⓐ, 0701 ⚒, 0729 and at 01 ⚒ and 29 minutes past each hour until 1929; then 2001 ⑤ 2029, 2129, 2229, 2346.

Stavoren – **Sneek** (*29 km*, 28 minutes) – **Leeuwarden**:

0624 Ⓐ, 0655 ⚒, 0726 ⚒, 0758 ⚒, 0858, 0958 and hourly until 2158; then 2317 ⑤⑥.

ZWOLLE – KAMPEN

From Zwolle:

0103 **K**, 0549 Ⓐ, 0619 Ⓐ, 0649 ⚒, 0719 ⚒, 0749 and at 19 ⚒ and 49 minutes past each hour until 1349; then 1419, 1449 and every 30 minutes until 2349.

13 km Journey time: 10 minutes 2nd cla

From Kampen:

0003, 0117 **K**, 0603 Ⓐ, 0633 Ⓐ, 0703 ⚒, 0733 ⚒, 0803, 0833 ⚒ and at 03 and 33 ⚒ minute past each hour until 1333 ⚒; then 1403, 1433 and every 30 minutes until 2333.

D – Not Mar. 24, May 12.
E – ① (not Mar. 24, May 12).
F – ④ (not May 1).
J – ⑥ (also Apr. 30, May 1).
K – ⑥⑦ (also May 1, 2).
N – ①–⑥ (not German public holidays).
P – ①–⑤ (not German public holidays).
Q – ①⑥⑦ (also Dec. 26, 27, Jan. 2, Mar. 25, May 1, 2, 13).
R – ⑤⑥⑦ (also Dec. 25, 26, Jan. 1, Mar. 24, Apr. 30, May 1, 12).
▲ – The services at 0933, 1033, 1133, 1533 and 163 run on ⚒ only.
▼ – The services at 1003, 1103, 1203, 1603 and 170 run on ⚒ only.
¶ – For ⛴ to/from Terschelling and Vlieland.

499 OTHER 🚌 and ⛴ LINES

ALKMAAR – HARLINGEN Haven ¶ 🚌 *Connexxion Snelbus/Qliner* route **350/132**

From Alkmaar rail station:

★ 0527 Ⓐ, 0627 ⚒, 0727 ⚒, 0827, 0927 and hourly until 2127; also 2227 ⑦.

Journey time: ± 1 hour 35 minutes

From Harlingen Haven ¶:

★ 0628 Ⓐ, 0728 ⚒, 0828, 0928 and hourly until 2228.

ALKMAAR – LEEUWARDEN 🚌 *Connexxion Snelbus/Qliner* route **350**

From Alkmaar rail station:

0527 Ⓐ, 0627 ⚒, 0727 ⚒, 0827, 0927 and hourly until 2127; also 2227 ⑦.

Journey time: ± 2 hours

From Leeuwarden rail station:

0601 Ⓐ, 0701 ⚒, 0801, 0901 and hourly until 2201.

DEN HELDER – TEXEL ⛴ *TESO*: ✆ +31 (0) 222 36 96 00

🚌 route **33**: Den Helder rail station (d. 18 minutes before ships sail) to Havenhoofd.

From Den Helder Havenhoofd: 0630 ⚒, 0730 ⚒, 0830, 0930 and hourly until 2130.

Journey time: 20 minutes

From Texel ('t Horntje ferryport): 0600 ⚒, 0700 ⚒, 0800, 0900 and hourly until 2100.

🚌 route **33**: Den Helder Havenhoofd (d. 3 minutes after ships arrive) to rail station.

ENKHUIZEN – STAVOREN ⛴ *Rederij V & O*: ✆ +31 (0) 228 32 60 06 (reservations)

From Enkuizen Spoorhaven: 0830 **A**, 1230 **B**, 1630 **A**. Journey time: 1 hour 20 minutes

From Stavoren: 1005 **A**, 1415 **B**, 1805 **A**. Journey time: ± 1 hour 30 minut

LELYSTAD – ENKHUIZEN 🚌 *Connexxion* route **150**

From Lelystad rail station:

Ⓐ: 0814, 1406, 1606, 1736.

Journey time: 35 minutes NO SERVICE ON ⑥

From Enkhuizen rail station:

Ⓐ: 0725, 1313, 1643, 1813.

LELYSTAD – ZWOLLE 🚌 *Interliner* (✆ 0900 89 98 998) route **330**

From Lelystad rail station:

Ⓐ: 0607, 0637 and every 30 minutes until 1937; then 2037, 2137.
⑥: 0807, 0837 and every 30 minutes until 1937; then 2037, 2137.
⑦: 1237, 1337 and hourly until 2137.

Journey time: 65 minutes

From Zwolle rail station:

Ⓐ: 0600, 0630 and every 30 minutes until 2000; then 2100.
⑥: 0730, 0800 and every 30 minutes until 1900; then 2000, 2100.
⑦: 1200, 1300 and hourly until 2100.

VLISSINGEN – BRESKENS ⛴ *BBA fast ferry* ▲ Journey time: 20 minutes

0750, 0850 and hourly until 2050; ***also*** 0620 Ⓐ, 0650 Ⓐ, 0720 Ⓐ, 0820 Ⓐ, 1620 Ⓐ, 1720 Ⓐ. (Additional sailings operate May 1 - Sept. 30).

BRESKENS ferryport – **BRUGGE** 🚌 *Veolia* route **2** Journey time: 87 minutes

0619 Ⓐ, 0718 ⚒, 0819 ⚒, 0919, 1019 and hourly until 2019.

BRUGGE – BRESKENS ferryport 🚌 *Veolia* route **2** Journey time: 79 minut

0654 ⚒, 0754 ⚒, 0854, 0954 and hourly until 1954; then 2054 ⚒.

BRESKENS – VLISSINGEN ⛴ *BBA fast ferry* ▲ Journey time: 20 minut

0820, 0920 and hourly until 2120; ***also*** 0650 Ⓐ, 0720 Ⓐ, 0750 Ⓐ, 0850 Ⓐ, 1650 Ⓐ, 1750 (Additional sailings operate May 1 - Sept. 30).

A – ②–⑦ Apr. 5–29.
Daily May 1 - Sept. 30, Oct. 18–26.
⑥⑦ Oct. 4–12.
B – Daily May 1 - Sept. 30.
★ – Change at Kop Afsluitdijk on all services. Additional, direct services run June 1 - Aug. 31: at 1257, 1757 ⑦ from Alkmaar; and at 1459, 2000 ⑦ from Harlingen Haven.
▲ – Conveys foot passengers, cycles and mopeds only
¶ – For ⛴ to/from Terschelling and Vlieland.

For traffic arrangements on Dutch holiday dates, see page 248

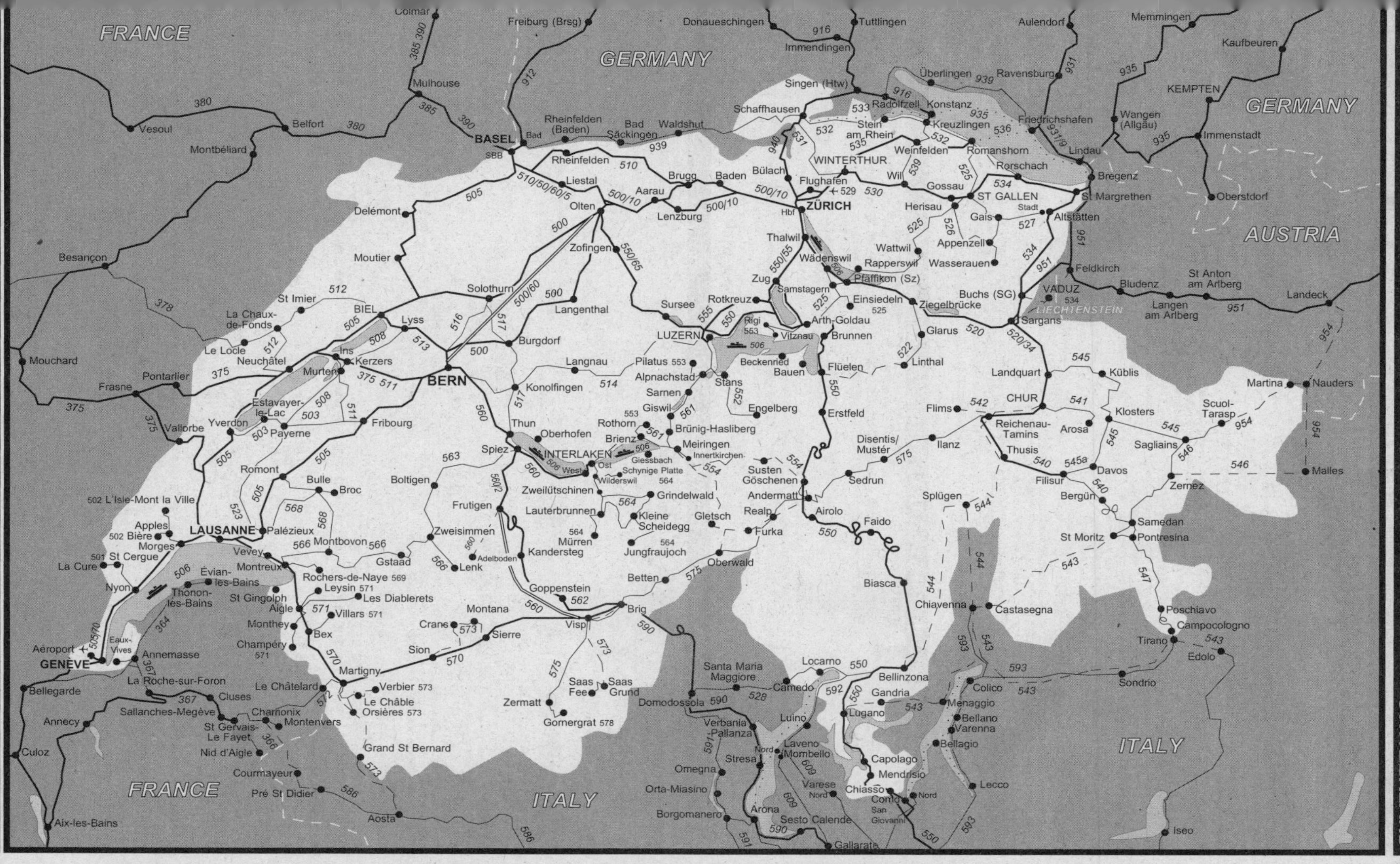
FRANCE
GERMANY
AUSTRIA
ITALY
LIECHTENSTEIN
BASEL
ZÜRICH
BERN
LUZERN
LAUSANNE
GENÈVE
CHUR
ST GALLEN
WINTERTHUR
INTERLAKEN
BIEL
VADUZ
Colmar
Freiburg (Brsg)
Donaueschingen
Tuttlingen
Immendingen
Aulendorf
Memmingen
Kaufbeuren
KEMPTEN
Immenstadt
Oberstdorf
Wangen (Allgäu)
Überlingen
Ravensburg
Friedrichshafen
Lindau
Bregenz
Mulhouse
Belfort
Vesoul
Montbéliard
Besançon
Mouchard
Frasne
Pontarlier
Vallorbe
Yverdon
Neuchâtel
La Chaux-de-Fonds
Le Locle
St Imier
Delémont
Moutier
Solothurn
Olten
Liestal
Rheinfelden
Rheinfelden (Baden)
Bad Säckingen
Waldshut
Aarau
Brugg
Baden
Lenzburg
Zofingen
Langenthal
Burgdorf
Sursee
Schaffhausen
Singen (Htw)
Radolfzell
Konstanz
Kreuzlingen
Stein am Rhein
Weinfelden
Romanshorn
Rorschach
St Margrethen
Altstätten
Feldkirch
Bludenz
St Anton am Arlberg
Langen am Arlberg
Landeck
Buchs (SG)
Sargans
Landquart
Küblis
Klosters
Davos
Filisur
Bergün
Thusis
Reichenau-Tamins
Arosa
Flims
Ilanz
Disentis/Mustér
Sedrun
Andermatt
Göschenen
Airolo
Faido
Biasca
Bellinzona
Locarno
Lugano
Chiasso
Como
Brig
Visp
Zermatt
Gornergrat
Saas Fee
Saas Grund
Sierre
Sion
Martigny
Montreux
Vevey
Aigle
Bex
Chamonix
St Moritz
Pontresina
Samedan
Poschiavo
Tirano
Scuol-Tarasp
Zernez
Martina
Nauders
Malles
Domodossola
Spiez
Thun
Meiringen
Grindelwald
Lauterbrunnen
Mürren
Kandersteg
Zweisimmen
Gstaad
Montbovon
Fribourg
Romont
Payerne
Murten
Kerzers
Lyss
Zug
Arth-Goldau
Brunnen
Flüelen
Erstfeld
Engelberg
Stans
Sarnen
Glarus
Rapperswil
Einsiedeln
Wädenswil
Thalwil
Bülach
Gossau
Wil
Appenzell
Herisau
Évian-les-Bains
Thonon-les-Bains
Annemasse
Nyon
Morges

SWITZERLAND

Operators: There are numerous operators of which Schweizerische Bundesbahnen (SBB)/Chemins de fer Fédéraux (CFF)/Ferrovie Federali Svizzere (FFS) is the principal. Bus services are provided by PostAuto/Autopostale (PA). Table headings show the operators' initials; abbreviations used in the European Timetable are:

AB	Appenzeller Bahnen	MGB	Matterhorn Gotthard Bahn	SGV	Schifffahrtsgesellschaft des Vierwaldstättersees
BAM	Bière - Apples - Morges	MOB	Montreux - Oberland Bernois	SMC	Sierre - Montana - Crans
BLM	Bergbahn Lauterbrunnen - Mürren	MThB	Mittelthurgau Bahn	SNCF	Société Nationale des Chemins de Fer Français
BLS	BLS Lötschbergbahn	NStCM	Nyon-St Cergue-Morez	SOB	Schweizerische Südostbahn
BOB	Berner Oberland Bahnen	PA	PostAuto / Autopostale / AutoDaPosta	SPB	Schynige Platte Bahn
BRB	Brienz - Rothorn Bahn	PB	Pilatus Bahn	THURBO	an alliance of MThB and SBB
CGN	Compagnie Générale de Navigation	RA	RegionAlps	TMR	Transports de Martigny et Régions
CP	CarPostal Suisse	RB	Rigi Bahnen	TPC	Transports Publics du Chablais
FART	Ferrovie Autolinee Regionali Ticinesi	RBS	Regionalverkehr Bern - Solothurn	TPF	Transports Publics Fribourgeois
FS	Ferrovie dello Stato	RhB	Rhätische Bahn	URh	Untersee und Rhein
GGB	Gornergrat Bahn	RM	Regionalverkehr Mittelland	WAB	Wengernalpbahn
JB	Jungfraubahn	SBB	Schweizerische Bundesbahnen	ZB	Zentralbahn
MIB	Meiringen - Innertkirchen Bahn	SBS	Schweizerische Bodensee-Schifffahrtsgesellschaft	ZSG	Zürich Schifffahrtsgesellschaft

Services: All trains convey first and second class seating, **except** where shown otherwise in footnotes or by a '1' or '2' in the train column, or where the footnote shows sleeping and/or couchette cars only. For most local services you **must** be in possession of a valid ticket before boarding your train. Some international trains convey sleeping cars (🛏) and/or couchette cars (🛏), descriptions of which appear on page **10**.

Train Categories:

CIS	Italian high-speed **Cisalpino** tilting (*Pendolino*) train.	*CNL*	**City Night Line** quality international overnight hotel train.
TGV	French high-speed **Train à Grande Vitesse**.	*IC*	**InterCity** quality internal express train.
ICE	German high-speed **InterCity Express** train.	*ICN*	**InterCity Neigezug** high-speed tilting train.
EC	**EuroCity** quality international express train.	*IR*	**InterRegio** fast inter-regional trains.
EN	**EuroNight** quality international overnight express train.	*RE*	**RegioExpress** semi-fast regional trains.

Catering: ✕ – Restaurant; (✕) – Bistro; (🍸) – Bar coach; 🍸 – Minibar.
Details of catering is shown in the tables where known, but as a general guide *CIS*, *ICE*, *EC* and *ICN* trains convey ✕ or (✕), *IC* services convey ✕ or (🍸), and *TGV* and *IR* trains convey (🍸) or 🍸. Catering facilities may not be open for the whole journey.

Timings: Valid from **December 9, 2007** unless otherwise stated in the table concerned. Local services are subject to alteration on **public holidays**.

Supplements: *TGV*, *CIS* and *ICE* high-speed trains may be used for internal Swiss journeys without supplement. For international journeys however, *TGV* services are priced as 'global' fares and *CIS* services are subject to the payment of a supplement; both types require compulsory reservation for international travel.

Reservations: Seat reservations may be made on all *ICE*, *CIS*, *TGV*, *EC*, *IC*, *ICN* and *EN* (where seats are conveyed) trains. Reservation is recommended for travel in first class observation cars. Fares in Switzerland are calculated according to distance and many Swiss railways use artificially inflated tariff-kilometres. Distances shown in tables below, however, are actual kilometres.

CAR-CARRYING TRAINS through the ALPINE TUNNELS

BLS, MGB, RhB, SBB

TUNNEL	CAR TERMINALS	FIRST TRAIN*	LAST TRAIN*	NORMAL FREQUENCY	INFORMATION ✆
ALBULA:	Thusis - Samedan	0810 (0750 from Samedan)	2010 (1750 from Samedan)	7–10 services per day	081 288 47 16, 081 288 55 11
FURKA:	Oberwald - Realp	0600 (0630 from Realp)	2100 (2130 from Realp)	every 60 minutes more frequent on ①⑤⑥⑦.	027 927 76 66, 027 927 76 76
LÖTSCHBERG:	Kandersteg - Goppenstein	0600	2300	every 30 minutes, more frequent 0730–1900 on ⑤⑥⑦ and mid-June – mid-Oct.	0900 55 33 33
OBERALP:	Andermatt - Sedrun	unspecified	unspecified	every 60 minutes	027 927 77 07, 027 927 77 40
SIMPLON:	Brig - Iselle (Italy)	0531 (0620 from Iselle)	2201 (2250 from Iselle)	11–12 services per day	0900 300 300
VEREINA:	Selfranga (Klosters) - Sagliains	0520 (0550 from Sagliains)	2050 (2120 from Sagliains) Dec. 9 - Apr. 30 and Dec. 1-13, services continue for a further 2 hours	every 30 minutes 0850–1920	081 288 37 37

* – Not necessarily daily.

500 BERN and BIEL - ZÜRICH

SBB

km		*IR* 1903	*IR* 2005	*ICN* 2107	*IR* 1909	*ICN* 509	*IR* 2009	*IC* 809	*IR* 3209	*IC* 709	*ICN* 2109	*IR* 1911	*ICN* 1511	*IR* 2011	*IC* 811	*IR* 3211	*IC* 711	*ICN* 2111	*IR* 1915	*ICN* 515	*IR* 2015	*IC* 815	*IR* 3215	
		⑥⑦					Ⓐ	**S**		**F**														
	Genève Aéroport ✈ **505** d.	...	...	...	...	...	...	...	...	...	...	...	...	...	...	...	...	...	...	...	...	...	...	...
	Genève **505** d.	...	...	...	...	...	...	...	...	...	...	...	...	...	...	...	0536	...	...	0614	...	...	...	...
	Lausanne **505** d.	...	...	...	...	...	...	...	...	...	...	...	0539	...	...	...	0620	...	...	|	...	...	...	...
	Brig **560** d.	...	...	...	...	...	...	...	...	...	...	...	|	...	0545	...	|	...	...	|	...	0649	...	...
	Interlaken Ost **560** d.	...	...	...	...	...	...	...	...	...	...	...	|	...	|	...	|	...	...	|	...	|	...	...
0	**Bern** d.	0422	0451	...	...	...	0539	0602	0607	0632	...	0636	|	0639	0702	0707	0732	...	0736	|	0739	0802	0807	...
23	Burgdorf d.	|	0505	...	...	...	0552	|	0620	|	...	|	|	0652	|	0720	|	...	|	|	0752	|	0820	...
47	Langenthal d.	|	0523	...	...	...	0611	|	0641	|	...	|	|	0711	|	0741	|	...	|	|	0811	|	0841	...
	Biel/Bienne d.	|	|	0515	...	0543	|	|	|	|	0615	|	0644	|	|	|	|	0715	|	0745	|	|	|	...
	Solothurn d.	|	|	0533	...	0601	|	|	|	|	0633	|	0702	|	|	|	|	0733	|	0801	|	|	|	...
67	**Olten** a.	0448	0536	0556	...	0618	0624	0628	0654	|	0656	0702	0718	0724	|	0754	|	0756	0802	0818	0824	|	0854	...
67	**Olten** d.	0450	0539	0559	0604	0620	...	0631	...	|	0659	0704	0720	0729	|	...	|	0759	0804	0820	0829	|	...	...
80	Aarau d.	0501	0550	|	0615	0630	...	|	...	|	|	0715	0730	|	|	...	|	|	0815	0830	|	|	...	...
90	Lenzburg d.	|	0558	|	|	|	...	|	...	|	|	|	|	|	|	...	|	|	|	|	|	|	...	...
	Brugg d.	|	|	|	0630	|	...	|	...	|	|	0730	|	|	|	...	|	|	0830	|	|	|	...	...
	Baden a.	|	|	|	0638	|	...	|	...	|	|	0738	|	|	|	...	|	|	0838	|	|	|	...	...
122	**Zürich HB** a.	|	|	0630	0654	0656	...	0702	...	0728	0730	0754	0756	0802	0758	...	0828	0830	0854	0856	0902	0858	...	...
	Zürich Flughafen ✈ **530/5** a.	0530	0625	0646	...	0720	...	0716	...	0750	0746	...	0820	...	0816	...	0850	0846	...	0920	...	0916	...	...
	St Gallen **530** a.	...	...	|	...	0815	...	|	...	0853	|	...	0915	...	|	...	0953	|	...	1015	...	|	...	...
	Konstanz **535** a.	...	...	0754	...	...	...	|	...	...	0854	...	...	...	|	...	...	0954	...	...	...	|	...	...
	Romanshorn **535** a.	...	...	...	...	...	...	0818	...	...	...	...	...	...	0918	...	...	...	...	...	...	1018	...	...

km		*IC* 715	*ICN* 2115	*IR* 1917	*ICN* 1517	*IR* 2017	*IC* 817	*IR* 3217	*IC* 717	*ICN* 2117	*IR* 1919	*ICN* 519	*IR* 2019		*IC* 819	*IR* 3219	*IC* 719	*ICN* 2119	*IR* 1921	*ICN* 1521	*IR* 2021	*IC* 821	*IR* 3221	*IC* 721
	Genève Aéroport ✈ **505** d.	0636	...	...	...	...	...	...	0736	...	...	0805	...	...	...	...	0836	...	...	...	...	...	...	0936
	Genève **505** d.	0645	...	...	...	...	...	...	0745	...	...	0814	...	...	...	...	0845	...	...	...	...	...	...	0945
	Lausanne **505** d.	0720	...	...	0745	...	...	...	0820	...	...	|	...	...	...	...	0920	...	...	0945	...	...	...	1020
	Brig **560** d.	|	...	...	|	...	0749	...	|	...	...	|	...	...	0849	...	|	...	...	|	...	0949	...	|
	Interlaken Ost **560** d.	|	...	...	|	...	|	...	|	...	...	|	...	...	|	...	|	...	...	|	...	|	...	|
	Bern d.	0832	...	0836	|	0839	0902	0907	0932	...	0936	|	0939	...	1002	1007	1032	...	1036	|	1039	1102	1107	1132
	Burgdorf d.	|	...	|	|	0852	|	0920	|	...	|	|	0952	...	|	1020	|	...	|	|	1052	|	1120	|
	Langenthal d.	|	...	|	|	0911	|	0941	|	...	|	|	1011	...	|	1041	|	...	|	|	1111	|	1141	|
0	**Biel/Bienne** d.	|	0815	|	0845	|	|	|	|	0915	|	0945	|	...	|	|	|	1015	|	1045	|	|	|	|
25	Solothurn d.	|	0833	|	0901	|	|	|	|	0933	|	1001	|	...	|	|	|	1033	|	1101	|	|	|	|
60	**Olten** a.	|	0856	0902	0918	0924	|	0954	|	0956	1002	1018	1024	...	|	1054	|	1056	1102	1118	1124	|	1154	|
60	**Olten** d.	|	0859	0904	0920	0929	|	...	|	0959	1004	1020	1029	...	|	...	|	1059	1104	1120	1129	|	...	|
73	Aarau d.	|	|	0915	0930	|	|	...	|	|	1015	1030	|	...	|	...	|	|	1115	1130	|	|	...	|
	Lenzburg d.	|	|	|	|	|	|	...	|	|	|	|	|	...	|	...	|	|	|	|	|	|	...	|
91	Brugg d.	|	|	0930	|	|	|	...	|	|	1030	|	|	...	|	...	|	|	1130	|	|	|	...	|
100	Baden a.	|	|	0938	|	|	|	...	|	|	1038	|	|	...	|	...	|	|	1138	|	|	|	...	|
122	**Zürich HB** a.	0928	0930	0954	0956	1002	0958	...	1028	1030	1054	1056	1102	...	1058	...	1128	1130	1154	1156	1202	1158	...	1228
	Zürich Flughafen ✈ **530/5** a.	0950	0946	...	1020	...	1016	...	1050	1046	...	1120	...	...	1116	...	1150	1146	...	1220	...	1216	...	1250
	St Gallen **530** a.	1053	|	...	1115	...	|	...	1153	|	...	1215	...	...	|	...	1253	|	...	1315	...	|	...	1353
	Konstanz **535** a.	...	1054	...	...	...	|	...	...	1154	...	...	...	...	|	...	...	1254	...	...	...	|	...	...
	Romanshorn **535** a.	...	...	...	...	...	1118	...	...	...	...	...	...	...	1218	...	...	...	...	...	...	1318	...	...

F – From Fribourg. **S** – From Spiez.

SBB BERN and BIEL - ZÜRICH 500

	ICN 2121	IR 1923	ICN 523	IR 2023		IC 823	IR 3223	IC 723	ICN 2123	IR 1925	ICN 1525	IR 2025		IC 825	IR 3225	IC 725	ICN 2125	IR 1927	ICN 527	IR 2027		IC 827	IR 3227	IC 727
Genève Aéroport ✈ **505** d.	...	...	1005	...	...	...	...	1036	...	...	...	...	...	...	...	1136	...	...	1205	...	...	...	...	1236
Genève **505** d.	...	...	1014	...	...	...	...	1045	...	...	...	...	...	...	...	1145	...	...	1214	...	...	...	...	1245
Lausanne **505** d.	...	...	|	...	...	...	...	1120	...	...	1145	...	...	...	...	1220	...	...	|	...	...	...	...	1320
Brig **560** d.	...	...	|	...	...	1049	...	|	...	...	|	...	...	1149	...	|	...	...	|	...	...	1249	...	|
Interlaken Ost **560** d.	...	...	|	...	...	|	...	|	...	...	|	...	...	|	...	|	...	...	|	...	...	|	...	|
Bern d.	...	1136	|	1139	...	1202	1207	1232	...	1236	|	1239	...	1302	1307	1332	...	1336	|	1339	...	1402	1407	1432
Burgdorf d.	...	|	|	1152	...	|	1220	|	...	|	|	1252	...	|	1320	|	...	|	|	1352	...	|	1420	|
Langenthal d.	...	|	|	1211	...	|	1241	|	...	|	|	1311	...	|	1341	|	...	|	|	1411	...	|	1441	|
Biel/Bienne d.	1115	|	1145	|	...	|	|	|	1215	|	1245	|	...	|	|	|	1315	|	1345	|	...	|	|	|
Solothurn d.	1133	|	1201	|	...	|	|	|	1233	|	1301	|	...	|	|	|	1333	|	1401	|	...	|	|	|
Olten a.	1156	1202	1218	1224	...	|	1254	|	1256	1302	1318	1324	...	|	1354	|	1356	1402	1418	1424	...	|	1454	|
Olten d.	1159	1204	1220	1229	...	|	...	|	1259	1304	1320	1329	...	|	...	|	1359	1404	1420	1429	...	|	...	|
Aarau d.	|	1215	1230	|	...	|	...	|	|	1315	1330	|	...	|	...	|	|	1415	1430	|	...	|	...	|
Lenzburg d.	|	|	|	|	...	|	...	|	|	|	|	|	...	|	...	|	|	|	|	|	...	|	...	|
Brugg d.	|	1230	|	|	...	|	...	|	|	1330	|	|	...	|	...	|	|	1430	|	|	...	|	...	|
Baden a.	|	1238	|	|	...	|	...	|	|	1338	|	|	...	|	...	|	|	1438	|	|	...	|	...	|
Zürich HB a.	1230	1254	1256	1302	...	1258	...	1328	1330	1354	1356	1402	...	1358	...	1428	1430	1454	1456	1502	...	1458	...	1528
Zürich Flughafen ✈ **530/5** a.	1246	...	1320	...	...	1316	...	1350	1346	...	1420	...	...	1416	...	1450	1446	...	1520	...	...	1516	...	1550
St Gallen **530** a.	|	...	1415	...	...	|	...	1453	|	...	1515	...	...	|	...	1553	|	...	1615	...	...	|	...	1653
Konstanz **535** a.	1354	...	...	...	...	|	...	...	1454	...	...	...	...	|	...	...	1554	...	...	...	...	|	...	...
Romanshorn **535** a.	...	...	...	...	...	1418	...	...	...	...	...	...	...	1518	...	...	...	...	...	...	...	1618	...	...

	ICN 2127	IR 1929	ICN 1529	IR 2029	IC 829	IR 3229	IC 729	ICN 2129	IR 1931	ICN 531	IR 2031		IC 831	IR 3231	IC 731	ICN 2131	IR 1935	ICN 1535	IR 2035		IC 835	IR 3235	IC 735	ICN 2135
Genève Aéroport ✈ **505** d.	...	...	...	...	...	...	1336	...	...	1405	...	...	...	...	1436	...	...	...	...	...	...	...	1536	...
Genève **505** d.	...	...	...	...	...	...	1345	...	...	1414	...	...	...	...	1445	...	...	...	...	...	...	...	1545	...
Lausanne **505** d.	...	...	1345	...	...	...	1420	...	...	|	...	...	...	...	1520	...	...	1545	...	...	...	...	1620	...
Brig **560** d.	...	...	|	...	1349	...	|	...	...	|	...	...	1449	...	|	...	...	|	...	...	1549	...	|	...
Interlaken Ost **560** d.	...	...	|	...	|	...	|	...	...	|	...	...	|	...	|	...	...	|	...	...	|	...	|	...
Bern d.	...	1436	|	1439	1502	1507	1532	...	1536	|	1539	...	1602	1607	1632	...	1636	|	1639	...	1702	1707	1732	...
Burgdorf d.	...	|	|	1452	|	1520	|	...	|	|	1552	...	|	1620	|	...	|	|	1652	...	|	1720	|	...
Langenthal d.	...	|	|	1511	|	1541	|	...	|	|	1611	...	|	1641	|	...	|	|	1711	...	|	1741	|	...
Biel/Bienne d.	1415	|	1445	|	|	|	|	1515	|	1545	|	...	|	|	|	1615	|	1645	|	...	|	|	|	1715
Solothurn d.	1433	|	1501	|	|	|	|	1533	|	1601	|	...	|	|	|	1633	|	1701	|	...	|	|	|	1733
Olten a.	1456	1502	1518	1524	|	1554	|	1556	1602	1618	1624	...	|	1654	|	1656	1702	1718	1724	...	|	1754	|	1756
Olten d.	1459	1504	1520	1529	|	...	|	1559	1604	1620	1629	...	|	...	|	1659	1704	1720	1729	...	|	...	|	1759
Aarau d.	|	1515	1530	|	|	...	|	|	1615	1630	|	...	|	...	|	|	1715	1730	|	...	|	...	|	|
Lenzburg d.	|	|	|	|	|	...	|	|	|	|	|	...	|	...	|	|	|	|	|	...	|	...	|	|
Brugg d.	|	1530	|	|	|	...	|	|	1630	|	|	...	|	...	|	|	1730	|	|	...	|	...	|	|
Baden a.	|	1538	|	|	|	...	|	|	1638	|	|	...	|	...	|	|	1738	|	|	...	|	...	|	|
Zürich HB a.	1530	1554	1556	1602	1558	...	1628	1630	1654	1656	1702	...	1658	...	1728	1730	1754	1756	1802	...	1758	...	1828	1830
Zürich Flughafen ✈ **530/5** a.	1546	...	1620	...	1616	...	1650	1646	...	1720	...	...	1716	...	1750	1746	...	1820	...	...	1816	...	1850	1846
St Gallen **530** a.	|	...	1715	...	|	...	1753	|	...	1815	...	...	|	...	1853	|	...	1915	...	...	|	...	1953	|
Konstanz **535** a.	1654	...	...	...	|	...	...	1754	...	...	...	...	|	...	...	1855	...	...	...	...	|	...	...	1954
Romanshorn **535** a.	...	...	...	...	1718	...	...	...	...	...	...	...	1818	...	...	...	...	...	...	...	1918	...	...	...

	IR 1937	ICN 537	IR 2037	IC 837	IR 3237		IC 737	ICN 2137	IR 1939	ICN 1539	IR 2039	IC 839	IR 3239	IC 739	ICN 2139	IR 1941	ICN 541		IR 2041	IC 841	IR 3241	IC 741	ICN 2141	IR 1943
Genève Aéroport ✈ **505** d.	...	1605	...	...	...	...	1636	...	...	...	...	...	...	1736	...	...	1805	...	...	...	...	1836	...	...
Genève **505** d.	...	1614	...	...	...	...	1645	...	...	...	...	...	...	1745	...	...	1814	...	...	...	...	1845	...	...
Lausanne **505** d.	...	|	...	...	...	...	1720	...	...	1745	...	...	...	1820	...	...	|	...	...	...	...	1920	...	...
Brig **560** d.	...	|	...	1649	...	...	|	...	...	|	...	1749	...	|	...	...	|	...	...	1849	...	|	...	...
Interlaken Ost **560** d.	...	|	...	|	...	...	|	...	...	|	...	|	...	|	...	...	|	...	...	|	...	|	...	...
Bern d.	1736	|	1739	1802	1807	...	1832	...	1836	|	1839	1902	1907	1932	...	1936	|	...	1939	2002	2007	2032	...	2036
Burgdorf d.	|	|	1752	|	1820	...	|	...	|	|	1852	|	1920	|	...	|	|	...	1952	|	2020	|	...	|
Langenthal d.	|	|	1811	|	1841	...	|	...	|	|	1911	|	1941	|	...	|	|	...	2011	|	2041	|	...	|
Biel/Bienne d.	|	1745	|	|	|	...	|	1815	|	1845	|	|	|	|	1915	|	1945	...	|	|	|	|	2015	|
Solothurn d.	|	1801	|	|	|	...	|	1833	|	1901	|	|	|	|	1933	|	2001	...	|	|	|	|	2033	|
Olten a.	1802	1818	1824	|	1854	...	|	1856	1902	1918	1924	|	1954	|	1956	2002	2018	...	2024	|	2054	|	2056	2102
Olten d.	1804	1820	1829	|	...	...	|	1859	1904	1920	1929	|	...	|	1959	2004	2020	...	2029	|	...	|	2059	2104
Aarau d.	1815	1830	|	|	...	...	|	|	1915	1930	|	|	...	|	|	2015	2030	...	|	|	...	|	|	2115
Lenzburg d.	|	|	|	|	...	...	|	|	|	|	|	|	...	|	|	|	|	...	|	|	...	|	|	|
Brugg d.	1830	|	|	|	...	...	|	|	1930	|	|	|	...	|	|	2030	|	...	|	|	...	|	|	2130
Baden a.	1838	|	|	|	...	...	|	|	1938	|	|	|	...	|	|	2038	|	...	|	|	...	|	|	2138
Zürich HB a.	1854	1856	1902	1858	...	...	1928	1930	1954	1956	2002	1958	...	2028	2030	2054	2056	...	2102	2058	...	2128	2130	2154
Zürich Flughafen ✈ **530/5** a.	...	1920	...	1916	...	...	1950	1946	...	2020	...	2016	...	2050	...	...	2120	...	...	2116	...	2150	...	...
St Gallen **530** a.	...	2015	...	|	...	...	2053	|	...	2115	...	|	...	2153	...	...	2215	...	...	|	...	2253	...	...
Konstanz **535** a.	...	...	...	|	...	...	...	2054	...	...	...	|	...	...	...	...	...	...	...	|	...	...	...	...
Romanshorn **535** a.	...	...	...	2018	...	...	...	...	...	...	...	2118	...	...	...	...	...	...	...	2218	...	...	...	...

	ICN 1543	IR 2043	IC 843		IR 3243	ICN 2143	IC 743		IR 1945	ICN 545	IR 2045		IC 845	IR 1947	IR 3245	IC 745	IR 2047	IC 847	ICN 1547	RE 3649	IR 3247	IC 747		IC 849
Genève Aéroport ✈ **505** d.	...	...	...	...	...	...	1936	...	...	2005	...	...	...	...	...	2036	...	...	...	...	...	2136	...	...
Genève **505** d.	...	...	...	...	...	...	1945	...	...	2014	...	...	...	...	...	2045	...	...	...	...	...	2145	...	...
Lausanne **505** d.	1945	...	...	...	...	...	2020	...	...	|	...	...	...	...	...	2120	...	...	2145	...	...	2220	...	...
Brig **560** d.	|	...	1949	...	...	...	|	...	...	|	...	...	...	...	...	|	...	...	|	...	...	|	...	...
Interlaken Ost **560** d.	|	...	|	...	...	...	|	...	...	|	...	...	...	...	...	|	...	...	|	...	...	|	...	...
Bern d.	|	2039	2102	...	2107	...	2132	...	...	|	2139	...	2202	...	2207	2232	2239	2302	|	...	2307	2332	...	0004
Burgdorf d.	|	2052	|	...	2120	...	|	...	...	|	2152	...	|	...	2220	|	2252	|	|	...	2320	|	...	0018
Langenthal d.	|	2111	|	...	2141	...	|	...	...	|	2211	...	|	...	2241	|	2311	|	|	...	2341	|	...	0036
Biel/Bienne d.	2045	|	|	...	|	2115	|	...	...	2145	|	...	|	...	|	|	|	|	2245	...	|	|	...	|
Solothurn d.	2101	|	|	...	|	2133	|	...	...	2203	|	...	|	...	|	|	|	|	2305	...	|	|	...	|
Olten a.	2118	2124	|	...	2154	2155	2158	...	...	2219	2224	...	|	...	2254	2258	2324	|	2330	...	2354	2358	...	0048
Olten d.	2120	...	|	...	...	...	2200	...	2204	2220	...	...	|	2235	...	2300	...	|	2334	2340	...	0000	...	0050
Aarau d.	2130	...	|	...	...	...	|	...	2215	2230	...	...	|	2245	...	|	...	|	2343	2349	...	0010	...	0059
Lenzburg d.	|	...	|	...	...	...	|	...	|	|	...	...	|	|	...	|	...	|	|	|	...	0018	...	0107
Brugg d.	|	...	|	...	...	...	|	...	2230	|	...	...	|	2301	...	|	...	|	|	0002	...	|	...	|
Baden a.	|	...	|	...	...	...	|	...	2238	|	...	...	|	2312	...	|	...	|	|	0012	...	|	...	|
Zürich HB a.	2156	...	2158	...	...	...	2231	...	2254	2256	...	...	2258	2328	...	2331	...	2358	0007	0042	...	0038	...	0127
Zürich Flughafen ✈ **530/5** a.	2220	...	2216	...	...	...	...	...	...	2320	...	...	2316	...	...	...	...	...	0027	...	...	...	...	...
St Gallen **530** a.	2317	...	|	...	...	...	...	...	...	0018	...	...	|	...	...	...	...	...	0125	...	...	...	...	...
Konstanz **535** a.	...	...	|	...	...	...	...	...	...	...	...	...	|	...	...	...	...	...	...	...	...	...	...	...
Romanshorn **535** a.	...	...	2318	...	...	...	...	...	...	...	...	...	0018	...	...	...	...	...	...	...	...	...	...	...

500 ZÜRICH - BIEL and BERN

SBB

	IR 2006	IC 706	ICN 2106	IR 3208	RE 3606	IC 808	IR 2008	ICN 508	IR 1908	ICN 2108	IC 708	IR 3210		IR 2010	IC 810	ICN 1510	IR 1910	IC 1010	ICN 2110	ICN 2104	IC 710	IR 3212	IR 2012	IC 812
																		Ⓐ						
Romanshorn **535** d.	...	...	...	...	...	...	...	...	...	...	...	...	...	...	0538	...	...	...	0559a	...	...	...	...	0638
Konstanz **535** d.	...	...	...	...	...	...	...	...	...	...	...	...	...	...	|	...	...	...	|	0603j	...	...	...	|
St Gallen **530** d.	...	...	...	...	...	...	...	...	...	...	0511	...	...	...	|	0544	...	...	|	|	0611	...	...	|
Zürich Flughafen + **530/5** d.	...	...	...	...	...	...	...	...	...	...	0613	...	...	0633	0639	0643	...	...	0709	0709	0713	...	...	0743
Zürich HB d.	...	0522	...	...	...	0600	0602	0604	0606a	0630	0632	...	...	0658	0700	0704	0706	0718	0730	0730	0732	...	0758	0800
Baden d.	...	|	...	...	0547	|	|	|	0622	|	|	...	...	|	|	|	0722	|	|	|	|	...	|	|
Brugg d.	...	|	...	...	0559	|	|	|	0632	|	|	...	...	|	|	|	0732	|	|	|	|	...	|	|
Lenzburg d.	...	0544	...	...	|	|	|	|	|	|	|	...	...	|	|	|	|	|	|	|	|	...	|	|
Aarau d.	...	0552	...	...	0614	|	|	0630	0646	|	|	...	...	|	|	0730	0746	|	|	|	|	...	|	|
Olten a.	...	0601	...	...	0623	|	0634	0639	0656	0701	|	...	...	0729	|	0739	0756	|	0801	0801	|	...	0829	|
Olten d.	0536	0603	0603	0606	...	|	0636	0641	0658	0703	|	0706	...	0736	|	0741	0758	|	0803	0803	|	0806	0836	|
Solothurn d.	|	|	0628	|	...	|	|	0659	|	0728	|	|	...	|	|	0759	|	|	0828	0828	|	|	|	|
Biel/Bienne a.	|	|	0645	|	...	|	|	0713	|	0745	|	|	...	|	|	0813	|	|	0845	0845	|	|	|	|
Langenthal d.	0548	|	...	0618	...	|	0648	|	|	...	|	0718	...	0748	|	|	|	|	...	...	|	0818	0848	|
Burgdorf d.	0607	|	...	0639	...	|	0707	|	|	...	|	0739	...	0807	|	|	|	|	...	...	|	0839	0907	|
Bern a.	0621	0629	...	0653	...	0657	0721	|	0725	...	0729	0753	...	0821	0757	|	0825	0815	...	...	0829	0853	0921	0857
Interlaken Ost **560** a.	...	|	...	...	...	|	...	|	...	...	|	...	...	...	|	|	...	...	...	...	|	...	...	|
Brig **560** a.	...	|	...	...	...	0811	...	|	...	...	|	...	...	...	0911	|	...	...	...	...	|	...	...	1011
Lausanne **505** a.	...	0740	...	...	...	...	...	|	...	...	0840	...	...	...	...	0915	...	...	...	...	0940	...	...	...
Genève **505** a.	...	0815	...	...	...	...	...	0846	...	...	0915	...	...	...	...	...	...	...	...	...	1015	...	...	...
Genève Aéroport + **505** a.	...	0824	...	...	...	...	...	0855	...	...	0924	...	...	...	...	...	...	...	...	...	1024	...	...	...

	ICN 512	IR 1912	ICN 2112	IC 712	IR 3216	IR 2016		IC 816	ICN 1516	IR 1916	ICN 2116	IC 716	IR 3218	IR 2018	IC 818	ICN 518	IR 1918	ICN 2118	IC 718	IR 3220	IR 2020		IC 820	ICN 1520
Romanshorn **535** d.	...	...	...	...	...	...	...	0741	...	...	...	...	...	...	0841	...	...	...	...	...	...	...	0941	...
Konstanz **535** d.	...	...	0703	...	...	...	...	|	...	...	0803	...	...	...	|	...	...	0903	...	...	...	...	|	...
St Gallen **530** d.	0642	...	|	0711	...	...	...	|	0748	...	|	0811	...	...	|	0848	...	|	0911	...	...	...	|	0948
Zürich Flughafen + **530/5** d.	0739	...	0809	0813	...	...	...	0839	0843	...	0909	0913	...	...	0939	0943	...	1009	1013	...	...	...	1039	1043
Zürich HB d.	0804	0806	0830	0832	...	0858	...	0900	0904	0906	0930	0932	...	0958	1000	1004	1006	1030	1032	...	1058	...	1100	1104
Baden d.	|	0822	|	|	...	|	...	|	|	0922	|	|	...	|	|	|	1022	|	|	...	|	...	|	|
Brugg d.	|	0832	|	|	...	|	...	|	|	0932	|	|	...	|	|	|	1032	|	|	...	|	...	|	|
Lenzburg d.	|	|	|	|	...	|	...	|	|	|	|	|	...	|	|	|	|	|	|	...	|	...	|	|
Aarau d.	0830	0846	|	|	...	|	...	|	0930	0946	|	|	...	|	|	1030	1046	|	|	...	|	...	|	1130
Olten a.	0839	0856	0901	|	...	0929	...	|	0939	0956	1001	|	...	1029	|	1039	1056	1101	|	...	1129	...	|	1139
Olten d.	0841	0858	0903	|	0906	0936	...	|	0941	0958	1003	|	1006	1036	|	1041	1058	1103	|	1106	1136	...	|	1141
Solothurn d.	0859	|	0928	|	|	|	...	|	0959	|	1028	|	|	|	|	1059	|	1128	|	|	|	...	|	1159
Biel/Bienne a.	0913	|	0945	|	|	|	...	|	1013	|	1045	|	|	|	|	1113	|	1145	|	|	|	...	|	1213
Langenthal d.	|	|	...	|	0918	0948	...	|	|	|	...	|	1018	1048	|	|	|	...	|	1118	1148	...	|	|
Burgdorf d.	|	|	...	|	0939	1007	...	|	|	|	...	|	1039	1107	|	|	|	...	|	1139	1207	...	|	|
Bern a.	|	0925	...	0929	0953	1021	...	0957	|	1025	...	1029	1053	1121	1057	|	1125	...	1129	1153	1221	...	1157	|
Interlaken Ost **560** a.	|	...	...	|	...	...	...	|	|	...	...	|	...	...	|	|	...	...	|	...	...	...	|	|
Brig **560** a.	|	...	...	|	...	...	...	1111	|	...	...	|	...	...	1211	|	...	...	|	...	...	...	1311	|
Lausanne **505** a.	|	...	...	1040	...	...	...	...	1115	...	...	1140	...	...	...	|	...	...	1240	...	...	...	...	1315
Genève **505** a.	1046	...	...	1115	...	...	...	...	...	...	...	1215	...	...	...	1246	...	...	1315	...	...	...	...	...
Genève Aéroport + **505** a.	1055	...	...	1124	...	...	...	...	...	...	...	1224	...	...	...	1255	...	...	1324	...	...	...	...	...

	IR 1920	ICN 2120	IC 720	IR 3222	IR 2022	IC 822	ICN 522	IR 1922	ICN 2122	IC 722	IR 3224	IR 2024		IC 824	ICN 1524	IR 1924	ICN 2124	IC 724	IR 3226	IR 2026		IC 826	ICN 526	IR 1926
Romanshorn **535** d.	...	...	...	...	...	1041	...	...	...	...	...	...	...	1141	...	...	...	...	...	...	...	1241	...	...
Konstanz **535** d.	...	1003	...	...	...	|	...	...	1103	...	...	...	...	|	...	...	1203	...	...	...	...	|	...	...
St Gallen **530** d.	...	|	1011	...	...	|	1048	...	|	1111	...	...	...	|	1148	...	|	1211	...	...	...	|	1248	...
Zürich Flughafen + **530/5** d.	...	1109	1113	...	...	1139	1143	...	1209	1213	...	...	...	1239	1243	...	1309	1313	...	...	...	1339	1343	...
Zürich HB d.	1106	1130	1132	...	1158	1200	1204	1206	1230	1232	...	1258	...	1300	1304	1306	1330	1332	...	1358	...	1400	1404	1406
Baden d.	1122	|	|	...	|	|	|	1222	|	|	...	|	...	|	|	1322	|	|	...	|	...	|	|	1422
Brugg d.	1132	|	|	...	|	|	|	1232	|	|	...	|	...	|	|	1332	|	|	...	|	...	|	|	1432
Lenzburg d.	|	|	|	...	|	|	|	|	|	|	...	|	...	|	|	|	|	|	...	|	...	|	|	|
Aarau d.	1146	|	|	...	|	|	1230	1246	|	|	...	|	...	|	1330	1346	|	|	...	|	...	|	1430	1446
Olten a.	1156	1201	|	...	1229	|	1239	1256	1301	|	...	1329	...	|	1339	1356	1401	|	...	1429	...	|	1439	1456
Olten d.	1158	1203	|	1206	1236	|	1241	1258	1303	|	1306	1336	...	|	1341	1358	1403	|	1406	1436	...	|	1441	1458
Solothurn d.	|	1228	|	|	|	|	1259	|	1328	|	|	|	...	|	1359	|	1428	|	|	|	...	|	1459	|
Biel/Bienne a.	|	1245	|	|	|	|	1313	|	1345	|	|	|	...	|	1413	|	1445	|	|	|	...	|	1513	|
Langenthal d.	|	...	|	1218	1248	|	|	|	...	|	1318	1348	...	|	|	|	...	|	1418	1448	...	|	|	|
Burgdorf d.	|	...	|	1239	1307	|	|	|	...	|	1339	1407	...	|	|	|	...	|	1439	1507	...	|	|	|
Bern a.	1225	...	1229	1253	1321	1257	|	1325	...	1329	1353	1421	...	1357	|	1425	...	1429	1453	1521	...	1457	|	1525
Interlaken Ost **560** a.	...	...	|	...	...	|	|	...	...	|	...	...	...	|	|	...	...	|	...	...	...	|	|	...
Brig **560** a.	...	...	|	...	...	1411	|	...	...	|	...	...	...	1511	|	...	...	|	...	...	...	1611	|	...
Lausanne **505** a.	...	...	1340	...	...	...	|	...	...	1440	...	...	...	...	1515	...	...	1540	...	...	...	...	|	...
Genève **505** a.	...	...	1415	...	...	...	1446	...	...	1515	...	...	...	...	...	...	...	1615	...	...	...	...	1646	...
Genève Aéroport + **505** a.	...	...	1424	...	...	...	1455	...	...	1524	...	...	...	...	...	...	...	1624	...	...	...	...	1655	...

	ICN 2126	IC 726	IR 3228	IR 2028		IC 828	ICN 1528	IR 1928	ICN 2128	IC 728	IR 3230		IR 2030	IC 830	ICN 530	IR 1930	ICN 2130	IC 730	IR 3232	IR 2032	IC 832	ICN 1532	IR 1932	
Romanshorn **535** d.	...	...	...	...	...	1341	...	...	...	...	...	...	...	1441	...	...	...	...	...	...	1541	...	...	...
Konstanz **535** d.	1303	...	...	...	...	|	...	...	1403	...	...	...	...	|	...	...	1503	...	...	...	|	...	...	...
St Gallen **530** d.	|	1311	...	...	...	|	1348	...	|	1411	...	...	...	|	1448	...	|	1511	...	...	|	1548	...	...
Zürich Flughafen + **530/5** d.	1409	1413	...	...	...	1439	1443	...	1509	1513	...	...	...	1539	1543	...	1609	1613	...	...	1639	1643	...	...
Zürich HB d.	1430	1432	...	1458	...	1500	1504	1506	1530	1532	...	...	1558	1600	1604	1606	1630	1632	...	1658	1700	1704	1706	...
Baden d.	|	|	...	|	...	|	|	1522	|	|	...	...	|	|	|	1622	|	|	...	|	|	|	1722	...
Brugg d.	|	|	...	|	...	|	|	1532	|	|	...	...	|	|	|	1632	|	|	...	|	|	|	1732	...
Lenzburg d.	|	|	...	|	...	|	|	|	|	|	...	...	|	|	|	|	|	|	...	|	|	|	|	...
Aarau d.	|	|	...	|	...	|	1530	1546	|	|	...	...	|	|	1630	1646	|	|	...	|	|	1730	1746	...
Olten a.	1501	|	...	1529	...	|	1539	1556	1601	|	...	...	1629	|	1639	1656	1701	|	...	1729	|	1739	1756	...
Olten d.	1503	|	1506	1536	...	|	1541	1558	1603	|	1606	...	1636	|	1641	1658	1703	|	1706	1736	|	1741	1758	...
Solothurn d.	1528	|	|	|	...	|	1559	|	1628	|	|	...	|	|	1659	|	1728	|	|	|	|	1759	|	...
Biel/Bienne a.	1545	|	|	|	...	|	1613	|	1645	|	|	...	|	|	1713	|	1745	|	|	|	|	1813	|	...
Langenthal d.	...	|	1518	1548	...	|	|	|	...	|	1618	...	1648	|	|	|	...	|	1718	1748	|	|	|	...
Burgdorf d.	...	|	1539	1607	...	|	|	|	...	|	1639	...	1707	|	|	|	...	|	1739	1807	|	|	|	...
Bern a.	...	1529	1553	1621	...	1557	|	1625	...	1629	1653	...	1721	1657	|	1725	...	1729	1753	1821	1757	|	1825	...
Interlaken Ost **560** a.	...	|	...	...	...	|	|	...	...	|	...	...	...	|	|	...	...	|	...	...	|	|	...	...
Brig **560** a.	...	|	...	...	...	1711	|	...	...	|	...	...	...	1811	|	...	...	|	...	...	1911	|	...	...
Lausanne **505** a.	...	1640	...	...	...	...	1715	...	...	1740	...	...	...	...	|	...	...	1840	...	...	...	1915	...	...
Genève **505** a.	...	1715	...	...	...	...	...	...	...	1815	...	...	...	...	1846	...	...	1915	...	...	...	...	...	...
Genève Aéroport + **505** a.	...	1724	...	...	...	...	...	...	...	1824	...	...	...	...	1855	...	...	1924	...	...	...	...	...	...

a – Ⓐ only.

j – 0557 on Ⓐ.

SBB ZÜRICH - BIEL and BERN 500

km		ICN 2132	IC 732	IR 3236	RE 3732	IR 2036	IC 836	ICN 536	IR 1936	ICN 2136	IC 736	IR 3238	IR 2038		IC 838	ICN 1538	IR 1938	ICN 2138	IC 738	IR 3240	IR 2040	IC 840	ICN 1540	IR 1940
(via hsl)					Ⓐ																			
	Romanshorn **535** d.	...	...	...	...	...	1641	...	...	...	...	...	...	...	1741	...	...	...	...	...	...	1841	...	...
	Konstanz **535** d.	1603	...	...	...	...	|	...	...	1703	...	...	...	...	|	...	...	1803	...	...	...	|	...	...
	St Gallen **530** d.	|	1611	...	...	...	|	1648	...	|	1711	...	...	...	|	1748	...	|	1811	...	...	|	1848	...
	Zürich Flughafen ✈ **530/5** d.	1709	1713	...	...	...	1739	1743	...	1809	1813	...	...	...	1839	1843	...	1909	1913	...	...	1939	1943	...
	Zürich HB d.	1730	1732	...	1715	1758	1800	1804	1806	1830	1832	...	1858	...	1900	1904	1906	1930	1932	...	1958	2000	2004	2006
	Baden d.	|	|	...	|	|	|	|	1822	|	|	...	|	...	|	|	1922	|	|	...	|	|	|	2022
	Brugg d.	|	|	...	|	|	|	|	1832	|	|	...	|	...	|	|	1932	|	|	...	|	|	|	2032
	Lenzburg d.	|	|	...	1741	|	|	|	|	|	|	...	|	...	|	|	|	|	|	...	|	|	|	|
	Aarau d.	|	|	...	1758	|	|	1830	1846	|	|	...	|	...	|	1930	1946	|	|	...	|	|	2030	2046
	Olten a.	1801	|	...	1807	1829	|	1839	1856	1901	|	...	1929	...	|	1939	1956	2001	|	...	2029	|	2039	2056
0	**Olten** d.	1803	|	1806	...	1836	|	1841	1858	1903	|	1906	1936	...	|	1941	1958	2003	|	2006	2036	|	2041	2058
	Solothurn d.	1828	|	|	...	|	|	1859	|	1928	|	|	|	...	|	1959	|	2028	|	|	|	|	2059	|
	Biel/Bienne a.	1845	|	|	...	|	|	1913	|	1945	|	|	|	...	|	2013	|	2045	|	|	|	|	2113	|
	Langenthal d.	...	|	1818	...	1848	|	|	|	...	|	1918	1948	...	|	|	|	...	|	2018	2048	|	|	|
	Burgdorf d.	...	|	1839	...	1907	|	|	|	...	|	1939	2007	...	|	|	|	...	|	2039	2107	|	|	|
62	**Bern** a.	...	1829	1853	...	1921	1857	|	1925	...	1929	1953	2021	...	1957	|	2025	...	2029	2053	2121	2057	|	2125
	Interlaken Ost **560** a.	...	|	...	...	...	|	|	...	...	|	...	...	...	|	|	...	...	|	...	...	...	|	...
	Brig **560** a.	...	|	...	...	...	2011	|	...	...	|	...	...	...	2111	|	...	...	|	...	...	...	|	...
	Lausanne **505** a.	...	1940	...	...	...	...	|	...	...	2040	...	...	...	...	2115	...	...	2140	...	...	...	2215	...
	Genève **505** a.	...	2015	...	...	...	...	2046	...	...	2115	...	...	...	...	...	...	...	2215	...	...	...	...	...
	Genève Aéroport ✈ **505** a.	...	2024	...	...	...	...	2055	...	...	2124	...	...	...	...	...	...	...	2224	...	...	...	...	...

km		ICN 2140	IC 740	IR 3242	IR 2042	IC 842	ICN 1542	IR 1942	ICN 2142	IC 742	IR 3244	IR 1944	IC 844	IR 2044	ICN 1544	IC 744	IR 1946	IC 846	IR 2046	ICN 1546		IC 800	IR 2048	IR 700
(via hsl)										F												⑥⑦q		⑥⑦q
	Romanshorn **535** d.	...	...	...	...	1941	...	...	...	...	...	...	2041	...	...	...	...	2141	...	...	...	...	...	...
	Konstanz **535** d.	1903	...	...	...	|	...	...	...	...	...	...	|	...	...	...	...	|	...	...	...	...	...	...
	St Gallen **530** d.	|	1911	...	...	|	1948	...	...	2011	...	...	|	...	2048	2111	...	|	...	2144	...	...	...	...
	Zürich Flughafen ✈ **530/5** d.	2009	2013	...	...	2039	2043	...	...	2113	...	...	2139	...	2143	2213	...	2239	...	2243	...	...	...	...
	Zürich HB d.	2030	2032	...	2058	2100	2104	2106	2130	2132	...	2136	2200	...	2204	2232	2236	2300	...	2304	...	0008	0010	0111
	Baden d.	|	|	...	|	|	|	2122	|	|	...	2152	|	...	|	|	2252	|	...	|	...	|	|	|
	Brugg d.	|	|	...	|	|	|	2132	|	|	...	2200	|	...	|	|	2300	|	...	|	...	|	|	|
	Lenzburg d.	|	|	...	|	|	|	|	|	|	...	|	|	...	|	|	|	|	...	|	...	|	0032	0133
	Aarau d.	|	|	...	|	|	2130	2146	|	|	...	2213	|	...	2230	|	2313	|	...	2330	...	|	0040	0140
	Olten a.	2101	|	...	2129	|	2139	2156	2201	|	...	2222	2231	...	2239	2303	2322	2331	...	2339	...	0040	0048	0149
0	**Olten** d.	2103	|	2106	2136	|	2141	...	2203	|	2206	...	2233	2236	2241	2305	...	2335	2336	2341	...	0042	0051	0151
	Solothurn d.	2128	|	|	|	|	2159	...	2228	|	|	...	|	|	2258	|	...	|	|	0004	...	|	|	|
58	**Biel/Bienne** a.	2145	|	|	|	|	2213	...	2245	|	|	...	|	|	2314	|	...	|	|	0022	...	|	|	|
	Langenthal d.	...	|	2118	2148	|	|	...	...	|	2218	...	|	2248	|	|	...	|	2348	...	...	|	0104	|
	Burgdorf d.	...	|	2139	2207	|	|	...	...	|	2239	...	|	2307	|	|	...	|	0007	...	...	|	0122	|
	Bern a.	...	2129	2153	2221	2157	|	...	...	2229	2253	...	2300	2321	|	2332	...	0002	0021	...	...	0109	0136	0218
	Interlaken Ost **560** a.	...	|	...	...	...	|	...	...	...	...	...	...	...	|	...	...	...	...	...	...	...	...	...
	Brig **560** a.	...	|	...	...	...	|	...	...	...	...	...	...	...	|	...	...	...	...	...	...	...	...	...
	Lausanne **505** a.	...	2240	...	...	...	2315	...	...	...	...	...	...	...	0015	...	...	...	...	...	...	...	...	...
	Genève **505** a.	...	2318	...	...	...	...	...	...	...	...	...	...	...	...	...	...	...	...	...	...	...	...	...
	Genève Aéroport ✈ **505** a.	...	2327	...	...	...	...	...	...	...	...	...	...	...	...	...	...	...	...	...	...	...	...	...

F – To Fribourg.
q – Also Jan. 1. June 8-30 runs to special FIFA *EURO 2008* schedule.

NStCM. Narrow gauge. 2nd class only NYON - ST CERGUE - LA CURE 501

km		j	k	j	j		j	j					j			j		j		j		j		j		j					m
0	**Nyon** d.	0528	0553	...	0628	0653	0728	0753	0817	0917	1017	1117	1153	1217	1317	1353	1417	1453	1517	1553	1617	1653	1717	1753	1817	1853	1917	1953	2130	2253	0017
19	St Cergue a.	0606	0625	0638	0701	0725	0758	0825	0848	0948	1048	1148	1225	1248	1348	1425	1448	1525	1548	1625	1648	1725	1748	1825	1848	1925	1948	2025	2159	2324	0048
27	La Cure a.	0620	0650	0650	...	0741	0813	...	0911	1003	1103	1203	...	1303	1403	...	1503	...	1603	...	1703	...	1803	...	1903j	...	2003	...	...	...	...

	j		j	⚒	j	j		j						j			j			j			j			j				
La Cure d.	...	...	0623	0653	...	0750	0817	...	0917	1017	1117	1213	...	...	1317	1417	...	1517	1617	...	...	1717	...	1817	...	1917	2017	...	...	...
St Cergue d.	0540	0609	0645	0708	0732	0809	0832	0909	0932	1032	1132	1232	...	1309	1332	1432	1509	1532	1632	1709	...	1732	1809	1832	1909	1932	2032	2209	2332	...
Nyon a.	0610	0643	0718	0743	0805	0843	0905	0943	1005	1105	1205	1305	...	1343	1405	1505	1543	1605	1705	1743	...	1805	1843	1905	1943	2005	2105	2243	0005	...

– Ⓐ (not Sept. 22).
k – ⑥ (also Sept. 22).
m – ⑥⑦ (not Mar. 22, Aug. 2).

BAM. Narrow gauge. 2nd class only MORGES - BIÈRE and L'ISLE MONT LA VILLE 502

km		⚒		⚒		⚒		⚒			⚒		⚒		⚒			⚒		⚒				F	
0	**Morges** d.	0621	0702	0746	0846	0946	1046	1136	...	1216	1316	1403	1503	1603	1646	1736	...	1816	1846	1946	2036	2207	2336	0103	...
12	Apples a.	0633	0717	0801	0901	1001	1101	1151	...	1231	1331	1418	1518	1618	1701	1751	...	1831	1901	2001	2051	2222	2351	0118	...
19	**Bière** a.	0646	0730	0814	0914	1014	1114	1204	...	1244	1344	1431	1531	1631	1714	1804	...	1844	1914	2014	2104	2235	0004	0131	...

	⚒		⚒	Ⓐ		⚒		⚒			⚒		⚒		⚒		⚒			⚒				F	
Bière d.	0545	0625	0653	0709	0753	0853	0953	1053	1126	...	1222	1306	1353	1453	1553	1653	1726	...	1811	1853	1953	2126	2253	0026	...
Apples d.	0555	0635	0704	0719	0803	0903	1003	1103	1136	...	1232	1316	1403	1503	1603	1703	1736	...	1821	1903	2003	2136	2303	0036	...
Morges a.	0615	0655	0724	0736	0823	0923	1023	1123	1156	...	1251	1336	1423	1523	1623	1723	1756	...	1841	1923	2023	2156	2323	0056	...

km			⚒		Ⓐ🚌	Ⓒ	Ⓐ🚌	Ⓒ		Ⓐ🚌	Ⓒ		Ⓐ		⚒	A🚌	B	A🚌	C	A🚌	B	C	C	F✗	
0	Apples d.	0602	0635	0719	0903	0903	1103	1103	1233	1420	1420	1620	1703	1753	1833	1903	1903	2003	2003	2053	2053	2224	2353	0120	...
11	L'Isle Mont la Ville d.	0614	0647	0731	0917	0917	1117	1117	1247	1434	1434	1634	1717	1805	1846	1917	1917	2017	2017	2107	2107	2238	0007	0134	...

		⚒			Ⓐ🚌	Ⓒ	Ⓐ🚌	Ⓒ		Ⓐ🚌	Ⓒ			Ⓐ		⚒	A🚌	B	A🚌	C	A🚌	B	C	F	
L'Isle Mont la Ville d.	0618	0648	0746	...	0946	0946	1119	1119	1259	1446	1446	1646	...	1719	1805	1846	1946	1946	2036	2036	2119	2119	2246	0019	...
Apples a.	0632	0702	0801	...	1001	1001	1134	1134	1314	1501	1501	1701	...	1734	1819	1901	2001	2001	2051	2051	2134	2134	2301	0034	...

A – ①②③④ (not Dec. 25, 26, Jan. 1, 2, Mar. 24, May 1, 12).
B – ⑤⑥⑦ (also Dec. 25, 26, Jan. 1, 2, Mar. 24, May 1, 12).
C – ⑤⑥ (not Mar. 21, Aug. 1).
F – ⑥⑦ (not Mar. 22, Aug. 2).
✗ – Supplement payable.

SBB YVERDON - FRIBOURG 503

km		Ⓐ		Ⓐ						
0	**Yverdon** d.	0520	0601	0620	...	0701	and	2101	2201	...
18	Estavayer-le-Lac d.	0538	0619	0638	...	0719	hourly	2119	2219	...
28	Payerne d.	0554	0630	0654	...	0730	until	2130	2230	...
50	**Fribourg** a.	0622	0658	0722	...	0758		2158	2259	...

		Ⓐ	Ⓒ				G	⑤⑥	
Fribourg d.	0601a	0701	0703	0803	and	2203	2303	2342	...
Payerne d.	0630	0730	0730	0830	hourly	2230	2330	0009	...
Estavayer-le-Lac d.	0640	0740	0740	0840	until	2240	2340	0019	...
Yverdon a.	0657	0757	0757	0857		2257	2357	0036	...

G – ①②③④⑦ only.
a – Ⓐ only.

505 GENÈVE - LAUSANNE - BIEL, BASEL and BERN

SBB

km		ICN 509	ICN 1609	ICN 1511	IC 2511	ICN 611	IR 1711	IC 711	IC 2515	ICN 515	ICN 1615	RE 2615	IC 715	RE 2917	IC 2517	ICN 617	ICN 1517	RE 2617	IC 717	IC 2519	ICN 519	ICN 1619	RE 2619	IC 719	IC 2521	ICN 621
							B							Ⓐ												
0	Genève A ✈ 570 d.	...	...	...	...	...	...	...	...	...	...	0612	0636	...	...	0705	...	0712	0736	0801	0805	...	...	0836	0901	0905
6	**Genève 570** d.	...	...	...	0456	...	0521	0536	0556	0614	...	0621	0645	0648	0710	0714	...	0721	0745	0810	0814	...	0821	0845	0910	0914
27	Nyon **570** d.	...	...	...	0510	...	0537	0550	0610	0627	...	0637	|	0705	|	0727	...	0737	|	|	0827	...	0837	|	|	0927
53	Morges **570** d.	...	...	...	0528	...	0600	0604	0628	0641	...	0700	|	0724	|	0741	...	0800	|	|	0841	...	0900	|	|	0941
66	**Lausanne 570** a.	...	...	...	0540	...	0612	0615	0640	|	...	0712	0718	0736	0743	|	...	0812	0818	0843	|	...	0912	0918	0943	|
	Lausanne 508 d.	...	...	0539	0545	...	...	0620	0645	|	0645	...	0720	...	0745	|	0745	...	0820	0845	|	0845	...	0920	0945	|
	Yverdon d.	...	...	0603	|	...	...	|	|	0703	0706	...	|	...	|	0803	0806	...	|	|	0903	0906	...	|	|	1003
	Neuchâtel d.	...	...	0624	|	...	...	|	|	0724	0727	...	|	...	|	0824	0827	...	|	|	0924	0927	...	|	|	1024
	Biel/Bienne a.	...	...	0640	|	...	...	|	|	0740	0742**k**	...	|	...	|	0840	0842**k**	...	|	|	0940	0942**k**	...	|	|	1040
	Biel/Bienne d.	0543	0550	0644	|	0650	...	|	|	0745	0750	...	|	...	|	0850	0845	...	|	|	0945	0950	...	|	|	1050
	Moutier d.	|	0608	|	|	0708	...	|	|	|	0808	...	|	...	|	0908	|	...	|	|	|	1008	...	|	|	1108
	Delémont d.	|	0623	|	|	0723	...	|	|	|	0823	...	|	...	|	0923	|	...	|	|	|	1023	...	|	|	1123
	Basel a.	|	0653	|	|	0753	...	|	|	|	0853	...	|	...	|	0953	|	...	|	|	|	1053	...	|	|	1153
87	Palézieux **508** d.	|	...	|	0601	...	...	|	0701	|	...	...	|	...	0801	...	|	...	|	0901	|	...	...	|	1001	...
106	Romont d.	|	...	|	0616	...	...	|	0716	|	...	...	|	...	0816	...	|	...	|	0916	|	...	...	|	1016	...
132	Fribourg d.	|	...	|	0634	...	...	0704	0734	|	...	...	0804	...	0834	...	|	...	0904	0934	|	...	...	1004	1034	...
163	**Bern** a.	|	...	|	0656	...	...	0726	0756	|	...	...	0826	...	0856	...	|	...	0926	0956	|	...	...	1026	1056	...
	Olten **500** a.	0618	...	0718	|	...	...	|	|	0818	...	...	|	...	|	...	0918	...	|	|	1018	...	...	|	|	...
	Luzern **565** a.	|	...	|	0800	...	...	|	0900	|	...	...	|	...	1000	...	|	...	|	1100	|	...	...	|	1200	...
	Zürich HB **500** a.	0656	...	0756	...	...	...	0828	...	0856	...	...	0928	...	...	...	0956	...	1028	...	1056	...	...	1128	...	...
	Zürich Flug ✈ **530** a.	0720	...	0820	...	...	...	0850	...	0920	...	...	0950	...	...	...	1020	...	1050	...	1120	...	...	1150	...	...
	St Gallen **530** a.	0815	...	0915	...	...	...	0953	...	1015	...	...	1053	...	...	...	1115	...	1153	...	1215	...	...	1253	...	...

km		ICN 1521	RE 2621	IC 721	IC 2523	ICN 523	ICN 1623	RE 2623	IC 723	IC 2525	ICN 625	ICN 1525	RE 2625	IC 725	IC 2527	ICN 527	ICN 1627	RE 2627	IC 727	IC 2529	ICN 629	ICN 1529	RE 2629	IC 729	IC 2531	ICN 531
	Genève A ✈ 570 d.	...	...	0936	1001	1005	...	...	1036	1101	1105	...	...	1136	1201	1205	...	...	1236	1301	1305	...	...	1336	1401	1405
	Genève 570 d.	...	0921	0945	1010	1014	...	1021	1045	1110	1114	...	1121	1145	1210	1214	...	1221	1245	1310	1314	...	1321	1345	1410	1414
	Nyon **570** d.	...	0937	|	|	1027	...	1037	|	|	1127	...	1137	|	|	1227	...	1237	|	|	1327	...	1337	|	|	1427
	Morges **570** d.	...	1000	|	|	1041	...	1100	|	|	1141	...	1200	|	|	1241	...	1300	|	|	1341	...	1400	|	|	1441
	Lausanne 570 a.	...	1012	1018	1043	|	...	1112	1118	1143	|	...	1212	1218	1243	|	...	1312	1318	1343	|	...	1412	1418	1443	|
0	**Lausanne 508** d.	0945	...	1020	1045	|	1045	...	1120	1145	|	1145	...	1220	1245	|	1245	...	1320	1345	|	1345	...	1420	1445	|
39	Yverdon d.	1006	...	|	|	1103	1106	...	|	|	1203	1206	...	|	|	1303	1306	...	|	|	1403	1406	...	|	|	1503
75	Neuchâtel d.	1027	...	|	|	1124	1127	...	|	|	1224	1227	...	|	|	1324	1327	...	|	|	1424	1427	...	|	|	1524
105	**Biel/Bienne** a.	1042**k**	...	|	|	1140	1142**k**	...	|	|	1240	1242**k**	...	|	|	1340	1342**k**	...	|	|	1440	1442**k**	...	|	|	1540
105	**Biel/Bienne** d.	1045	...	|	|	1145	1150	...	|	|	1250	1245	...	|	|	1345	1350	...	|	|	1450	1445	...	|	|	1545
129	Moutier d.	|	...	|	|	|	1208	...	|	|	1308	|	...	|	|	|	1408	...	|	|	1508	|	...	|	|	|
140	Delémont d.	|	...	|	|	|	1223	...	|	|	1323	|	...	|	|	|	1423	...	|	|	1523	|	...	|	|	|
179	**Basel** a.	|	...	|	|	|	1253	...	|	|	1353	|	...	|	|	|	1453	...	|	|	1553	|	...	|	|	|
	Palézieux **508** d.	|	...	|	1101	|	...	...	|	1201	...	|	...	|	1301	|	...	...	|	1401	...	|	...	|	1501	|
	Romont d.	|	...	|	1116	|	...	...	|	1216	...	|	...	|	1316	|	...	...	|	1416	...	|	...	|	1516	|
	Fribourg d.	|	...	1104	1134	|	...	...	1204	1234	...	|	...	1304	1334	|	...	...	1404	1434	...	|	...	1504	1534	|
	Bern a.	|	...	1126	1156	|	...	...	1226	1256	...	|	...	1326	1356	|	...	...	1426	1456	...	|	...	1526	1556	|
	Olten **500** a.	1118	...	|	|	1218	...	...	|	|	...	1318	...	|	|	1418	...	...	|	|	...	1518	...	|	|	1618
	Luzern **565** a.	|	...	|	1300	|	...	...	|	1400	...	|	...	|	1500	|	...	...	|	1600	...	|	...	|	1700	|
	Zürich HB **500** a.	1156	...	1228	...	1256	...	...	1328	...	...	1356	...	1428	...	1456	...	...	1528	...	...	1556	...	1628	...	1656
	Zürich Flug ✈ **530** a.	1220	...	1250	...	1320	...	...	1350	...	...	1420	...	1450	...	1520	...	...	1550	...	...	1620	...	1650	...	1720
	St Gallen **530** a.	1315	...	1353	...	1415	...	...	1453	...	...	1515	...	1553	...	1615	...	...	1653	...	...	1715	...	1753	...	1815

km		ICN 1631	RE 2631	IC 731	IC 2535	ICN 635	ICN 1535	RE 2635	IC 735	IC 2537	ICN 537	ICN 1637	RE 2637	IC 737	IC 2539	ICN 639	ICN 1539	RE 2639	IC 739		RE 2941	IC 2541	ICN 541	ICN 1641	RE 2641	IC 741
																					Ⓐ					
	Genève A ✈ 570 d.	...	1412	1436	...	1505	...	...	1536	1601	1605	...	...	1636	1701	1705	...	...	1736	...	...	1801	1805	...	...	1836
	Genève 570 d.	...	1421	1445	...	1514	...	1521	1545	1610	1614	...	1621	1645	1710	1714	...	1721	1745	...	1748	1810	1814	...	1821	1845
	Nyon **570** d.	...	1437	|	...	1527	...	1537	|	|	1627	...	1637	|	|	1727	...	1737	|	...	1805	|	1827	...	1837	|
0	Morges **570** d.	...	1500	|	...	1541	...	1600	|	|	1641	...	1700	|	|	1741	...	1800	|	...	1824	|	1841	...	1900	|
	Lausanne 570 a.	...	1512	1518	...	|	...	1612	1618	1643	|	...	1712	1718	1743	|	...	1812	1818	...	1836	1843	|	...	1912	1918
	Lausanne 508 d.	1445	...	1520	1545	|	1545	...	1620	1645	|	1645	...	1720	1745	|	1745	...	1820	...	...	1845	|	1845	...	1920
39	Yverdon d.	1506	...	|	|	1603	1606	...	|	|	1703	1706	...	|	|	1803	1806	...	|	...	...	|	1903	1906	...	|
	Neuchâtel d.	1527	...	|	|	1624	1627	...	|	|	1724	1727	...	|	|	1824	1827	...	|	...	...	|	1924	1927	...	|
	Biel/Bienne a.	1542**k**	...	|	|	1640	1642**k**	...	|	|	1740	1742**k**	...	|	|	1840	1842**k**	...	|	...	...	|	1940	1942**k**	...	|
	Biel/Bienne d.	1550	...	|	|	1650	1645	...	|	|	1745	1750	...	|	|	1850	1845	...	|	...	...	|	1945	1950	...	|
	Moutier d.	1608	...	|	|	1708	|	...	|	|	|	1808	...	|	|	1908	|	...	|	...	...	|	|	2008	...	|
	Delémont d.	1623	...	|	|	1723	|	...	|	|	|	1823	...	|	|	1923	|	...	|	...	...	|	|	2023	...	|
	Basel a.	1653	...	|	|	1753	|	...	|	|	|	1853	...	|	|	1953	|	...	|	...	...	|	|	2053	...	|
	Palézieux **508** d.	...	...	|	1601	...	|	...	|	1701	|	...	...	|	1801	...	|	...	|	...	...	1901	|	...	...	|
	Romont d.	...	...	|	1616	...	|	...	|	1716	|	...	...	|	1816	...	|	...	|	...	...	1916	|	...	...	|
	Fribourg d.	...	...	1604	1634	...	|	...	1704	1734	|	...	...	1804	1834	...	|	...	1904	...	...	1934	|	...	...	2004
	Bern a.	...	...	1626	1656	...	|	...	1726	1756	|	...	...	1826	1856	...	|	...	1926	...	...	1956	|	...	...	2026
	Olten **500** a.	...	...	|	|	...	1718	...	|	|	1818	...	...	|	|	...	1918	...	|	...	...	|	2018	...	...	|
	Luzern **565** a.	...	...	|	1800	...	|	...	|	1900	|	...	...	|	2000	...	|	...	|	...	...	2100	|	...	...	|
	Zürich HB **500** a.	...	...	1728	...	...	1756	...	1828	...	1856	...	...	1928	...	...	1956	...	2028	...	...	...	2056	...	...	2128
	Zürich Flug ✈ **530** a.	...	...	1750	...	...	1820	...	1850	...	1920	...	...	1950	...	...	2020	...	2050	...	...	...	2120	...	...	2150
	St Gallen **530** a.	...	...	1853	...	...	1915	...	1953	...	2015	...	...	2053	...	...	2115	...	2153	...	...	...	2215	...	...	2253

	IC 2543	ICN 643	ICN 1543	RE 2643	IC 743	IC 2545	ICN 545	ICN 1645	RE 2645	IC 745	IR 2687	ICN 647	ICN 1547	RE 2647	IC 747		IR 2689	ICN 1647	RE 2649	IR 2691	ICN 1649	IR 2699	RE 2601	RE 2603	
																								⑥⑦ **p**	
Genève Aéroport ✈ 570 d.	1901	1905	...	...	1936	2001	2005	...	...	2036	2047	2105	...	...	2136	...	2147	...	...	2247	...	...	0012	...	...
Genève 570 d.	1910	1914	...	1921	1945	2010	2014	...	2021	2045	2056	2114	...	2121	2145	...	2156	...	2221	2256	...	2356	0021	0118	...
Nyon **570** d.	|	1927	...	1937	|	|	2027	...	2037	|	2110	2127	...	2137	|	...	2210	...	2237	2310	...	0010	0037	0137	...
Morges **570** d.	|	1941	...	2000	|	|	2041	...	2100	|	2128	2141	...	2200	|	...	2228	...	2300	2328	...	0028	0100	0200	...
Lausanne 570 a.	1943	|	...	2012	2018	2043	|	...	2112	2118	2140	|	...	2212	2218	...	2240	...	2312	2340	...	0040	0112	0212	...
Lausanne 508 d.	1945	|	1945	...	2020	2045	|	2045	...	2120	2145	|	2145	...	2220	...	2245	2245	...	2345	2345	...	...	...	...
Yverdon d.	|	2003	2006	...	|	|	2103	2106	...	|	|	2203	2206	...	|	...	|	2306	...	|	0006	...	...	...	...
Neuchâtel d.	|	2024	2027	...	|	|	2124	2127	...	|	|	2224	2227	...	|	...	|	2327	...	|	0027	...	...	...	...
Biel/Bienne a.	|	2040	2042**k**	...	|	|	2140	2142**k**	...	|	|	2240	2242**k**	...	|	...	|	2342	...	|	0042	...	...	...	...
Biel/Bienne d.	|	2050	2045	...	|	|	2145	2150	...	|	|	2250	2245	...	|	...	|	2350	...	|	...	...	...	...	...
Moutier d.	|	2108	|	...	|	|	|	2208	...	|	|	2308	|	...	|	...	|	0008	...	|	...	...	...	...	...
Delémont d.	|	2123	|	...	|	|	|	2223	...	|	|	2323	|	...	|	...	|	0018	...	|	...	...	...	...	...
Basel a.	|	2153	|	...	|	|	|	2253	...	|	|	2353	|	...	|	...	|	...	...	|	...	...	...	...	...
Palézieux **508** d.	2001	...	|	...	|	2101	|	...	...	|	2201	...	|	...	|	...	2301	...	...	0001	...	...	...	...	...
Romont d.	2016	...	|	...	|	2116	|	...	...	|	2216	...	|	...	|	...	2316	...	...	0016	...	...	...	...	...
Fribourg d.	2034	...	|	...	2104	2134	|	...	...	2204	2234	...	|	...	2304	...	2334	...	...	0034	...	...	...	...	...
Bern a.	2056	...	|	...	2126	2156	|	...	...	2226	2256	...	|	...	2326	...	2356	...	...	0056	...	...	...	...	...
Olten **500** a.	|	...	2118	...	2158	...	2219	...	...	2258	...	...	2330	...	2358	...	...	...	...	...	...	...	...	...	...
Luzern **565** a.	2200	...	|	...	|	...	|	...	...	|	...	...	|	...	|	...	...	...	...	...	...	...	...	...	...
Zürich HB **500** a.	...	...	2156	...	2231	...	2256	...	...	2331	...	...	0007	...	0038	...	...	...	...	...	...	...	...	...	...
Zürich Flughafen ✈ **530** a.	...	...	2220	...	...	...	2320	...	...	...	...	...	0027	...	...	...	...	...	...	...	...	...	...	...	...
St Gallen **530** a.	...	...	2317	...	...	...	0018	...	...	...	...	...	0125	...	...	...	...	...	...	...	...	...	...	...	...

B – To Brig. **k** – Connects with train in previous column. **p** – Also Jan. 1, Aug. 1.

SBB — BERN, BASEL and BIEL - LAUSANNE - GENÈVE — 505

	RE 2900	IR 1402	RE 2602	ICN 1604	ICN 504	IC 2504	IC 704	RE 2606	ICN 1506	ICN 606	IC 2506	RE 2906	IC 706	RE 2608	ICN 1608	ICN 508	IC 2508	IC 708	RE 2610	ICN 1510	ICN 610	IC 2510	IC 710	RE 2612	ICN 1612
					Ⓐ							Ⓐ													
St Gallen 530 d.	...	...	...	...	...	...	...	...	...	...	...	...	...	...	...	...	...	0511	...	0544	...	...	0611	...	...
Zürich Flughafen + 530 d.	...	...	...	...	...	...	...	...	...	...	...	...	...	...	...	...	...	0613	...	0643	...	...	0713	...	...
Zürich HB 500 d.	...	...	...	...	...	...	...	...	...	...	...	...	0522	...	...	0604	...	0632	...	0704	...	...	0732	...	...
Luzern 565 d.	...	...	...	...	...	...	...	...	...	...	...	...	|	...	...	|	0600	|	...	|	...	0700	|	...	...
Olten 500 d.	...	...	...	...	...	...	...	...	...	...	...	...	|	...	...	0641	|	|	...	0741	...	|	|	...	...
ern d.	...	...	...	...	...	0504	0534	...	...	...	0604	...	0634	...	...	|	0704	0734	...	|	...	0804	0834	...	...
ribourg d.	...	...	...	...	...	0526	0555	...	...	...	0626	...	0655	...	...	|	0726	0755	...	|	...	0826	0855	...	...
omont d.	...	...	...	...	...	0544	|	...	...	...	0644	...	|	...	...	|	0744	|	...	|	...	0844	|	...	...
alézieux 508 d.	...	...	...	...	...	0559	|	...	...	...	0659	...	|	...	...	|	0759	|	...	|	...	0859	|	...	...
Basel d.	...	...	...	...	...	|	|	...	...	...	|	...	|	...	0603	|	|	|	...	|	0703	|	|	...	0803
Delémont d.	...	...	...	...	...	|	|	...	...	0542	|	...	|	...	0642	|	|	|	...	|	0742	|	|	...	0842
Moutier d.	...	...	...	...	...	|	|	...	...	0552	|	...	|	...	0652	|	|	|	...	|	0752	|	|	...	0852
Biel/Bienne a.	...	...	...	...	...	|	|	...	...	0610k	|	...	|	...	0710	0713k	|	|	...	0813	0810k	|	|	...	0910
Biel/Bienne d.	...	...	...	0513	0519	|	|	...	0613	0619	|	...	|	...	0716	0719	|	|	...	0816	0819	|	|	...	0916
Neuchâtel d.	...	...	...	0531	0537	|	|	...	0631	0637	|	...	|	...	0734	0737	|	|	...	0834	0837	|	|	...	0934
Yverdon d.	...	...	...	0550	0556	|	|	...	0650	0656	|	...	|	...	0753	0756	|	|	...	0853	0856	|	|	...	0953
ausanne 508 a.	...	...	...	0612z	|	0615	0640	...	0715	|	0715	...	0740	...	0815	|	0815	0840	...	0915	|	0915	0940	...	1015
ausanne 570 d.	0430	0520	0548	...	|	0617	0642	0648	...	|	0717	0725	0742	0748	...	|	0817	0842	0848	...	|	0917	0942	0948	...
orges 570 d.	0442	0532	0600	...	0619	|	|	0700	...	0719	|	0736	|	0800	...	0819	|	|	0900	...	0919	|	|	1000	...
yon 570 d.	0505	0550	0623	...	0633	|	|	0723	...	0733	|	0756	|	0823	...	0833	|	|	0923	...	0933	|	|	1023	...
enève 570 a.	0524	0604	0639	...	0646	0650	0715	0739	...	0746	0750	0812	0815	0839	...	0846	0850	0915	0939	...	0946	0950	1015	1039	...
Genève Aéroport + 570 d.	0533	0613	...	...	0655	0659	0724	...	...	0755	0759	...	0824	...	...	0855	0859	0924	...	...	0955	0959	1024	...	...

	ICN 512	IC 2512	IC 712	RE 2614	ICN 1516	ICN 616	IC 2516	IC 716	RE 2618	ICN 1618	ICN 518	IC 2518	IC 718	RE 2620	ICN 1520	ICN 620		IC 2520	IC 720	RE 2622	ICN 1622	ICN 522	IC 2522	IC 722	RE 2624
St Gallen 530 d.	0642	...	0711	...	0748	...	...	0811	...	...	0848	...	0911	...	0948	...	...	...	1011	...	...	1048	...	1111	...
Zürich Flughafen + 530 d.	0739	...	0813	...	0843	...	...	0913	...	...	0943	...	1013	...	1043	...	...	...	1113	...	...	1143	...	1213	...
Zürich HB 500 d.	0804	...	0832	...	0904	...	...	0932	...	...	1004	...	1032	...	1104	...	...	...	1132	...	...	1204	...	1232	...
Luzern 565 d.	|	0800	|	...	|	...	0900	|	...	...	|	1000	|	...	|	...	...	1100	|	...	...	|	1200	|	...
Olten 500 d.	0841	|	|	...	0941	...	|	|	...	...	1041	|	|	...	1141	...	...	|	|	...	...	1241	|	|	...
ern d.	|	0904	0934	...	|	...	1004	1034	...	...	|	1104	1134	...	|	...	...	1204	1234	...	...	|	1304	1334	...
ribourg d.	|	0926	0955	...	|	...	1026	1055	...	...	|	1126	1155	...	|	...	...	1226	1255	...	...	|	1326	1355	...
omont d.	|	0944	|	...	|	...	1044	|	...	...	|	1144	|	...	|	...	...	1244	|	...	...	|	1344	|	...
alézieux 508 d.	|	0959	|	...	|	...	1059	|	...	...	|	1159	|	...	|	...	...	1259	|	...	...	|	1359	|	...
Basel d.	|	|	|	...	|	0903	|	|	...	1003	|	|	|	...	|	1103	...	|	|	...	1203	|	|	|	...
Delémont d.	|	|	|	...	|	0942	|	|	...	1042	|	|	|	...	|	1142	...	|	|	...	1242	|	|	|	...
Moutier d.	|	|	|	...	|	0952	|	|	...	1052	|	|	|	...	|	1152	...	|	|	...	1252	|	|	|	...
Biel/Bienne a.	0913k	|	|	...	1013	1010k	|	|	...	1110	1113k	|	|	...	1213	1210k	...	|	|	...	1310	1313k	|	|	...
Biel/Bienne d.	0919	|	|	...	1016	1019	|	|	...	1116	1119	|	|	...	1216	1219	...	|	|	...	1316	1319	|	|	...
Neuchâtel d.	0937	|	|	...	1034	1037	|	|	...	1134	1137	|	|	...	1234	1237	...	|	|	...	1334	1337	|	|	...
Yverdon d.	0956	|	|	...	1053	1056	|	|	...	1153	1156	|	|	...	1253	1256	...	|	|	...	1353	1356	|	|	...
ausanne 508 a.	|	1015	1040	...	1115	|	1115	1140	...	1215	|	1215	1240	...	1315	|	...	1315	1340	...	1415	|	1415	1440	...
ausanne 570 d.	|	1017	1042	1048	...	|	1117	1142	1148	...	|	...	1242	1248	...	|	...	1317	1342	1348	...	|	1417	1442	1448
orges 570 d.	1019	|	|	1100	...	1119	|	|	1200	...	1219	...	|	1300	...	1319	...	|	|	1400	...	1419	|	|	1500
yon 570 d.	1033	|	|	1123	...	1133	|	|	1223	...	1233	...	|	1323	...	1333	...	|	|	1423	...	1433	|	|	1523
enève 570 a.	1046	1050	1115	1139	...	1146	1150	1215	1239	...	1246	...	1315	1339	...	1346	...	1350	1415	1439	...	1446	1450	1515	1539
Genève Aéroport + 570 d.	1055	1059	1124	...	...	1155	1159	1224	...	...	1255	...	1324	1348	...	1355	...	1359	1424	...	...	1455	1459	1524	...

	ICN 1524	ICN 624	IC 2524	IC 724	RE 2626	ICN 1626	ICN 526	IC 2526	IC 726	RE 2628	ICN 1528	ICN 628	IC 2528	IR 2928	IC 728	RE 2630	ICN 1630	ICN 530	IC 2530	IC 730	RE 2632	ICN 1532	ICN 632	IC 2532	IC 732
														Ⓐ											
St Gallen 530 d.	1148	...	...	1211	...	...	1248	...	1311	...	1348	...	...	...	1411	...	...	1448	...	1511	...	1548	...	...	1611
Zürich Flughafen + 530 d.	1243	...	...	1313	...	...	1343	...	1413	...	1443	...	...	...	1513	...	...	1543	...	1613	...	1643	...	...	1713
Zürich HB 500 d.	1304	...	...	1332	...	...	1404	...	1432	...	1504	...	...	...	1532	...	...	1604	...	1632	...	1704	...	...	1732
Luzern 565 d.	|	...	1300	|	...	...	|	1400	|	...	|	...	1500	...	|	...	...	|	1600	|	...	|	...	1700	|
Olten 500 d.	1341	...	|	|	...	...	1441	|	|	...	1541	...	|	...	|	...	...	1641	|	|	...	1741	...	|	|
ern d.	|	...	1404	1434	...	...	|	1504	1534	...	|	...	1604	...	1634	...	...	|	1704	1734	...	|	...	1804	1834
ribourg d.	|	...	1426	1455	...	...	|	1526	1555	...	|	...	1626	...	1655	...	...	|	1726	1755	...	|	...	1826	1855
omont d.	|	...	1444	|	...	...	|	1544	|	...	|	...	1644	...	|	...	...	|	1744	|	...	|	...	1844	|
alézieux 508 d.	|	...	1459	|	...	...	|	1559	|	...	|	...	1659	...	|	...	...	|	1759	|	...	|	...	1859	|
Basel d.	|	1303	|	|	...	1403	|	|	|	...	|	1503	|	...	|	...	1603	|	|	|	...	|	1703	|	|
Delémont d.	|	1342	|	|	...	1442	|	|	|	...	|	1542	|	...	|	...	1642	|	|	|	...	|	1742	|	|
Moutier d.	|	1352	|	|	...	1452	|	|	|	...	|	1552	|	...	|	...	1652	|	|	|	...	|	1752	|	|
Biel/Bienne a.	1413	1410k	|	|	...	1510	1513k	|	|	...	1613	1610k	|	...	|	...	1710	1713k	|	|	...	1813	1810k	|	|
Biel/Bienne d.	1416	1419	|	|	...	1516	1519	|	|	...	1616	1619	|	...	|	...	1716	1719	|	|	...	1816	1819	|	|
Neuchâtel d.	1434	1437	|	|	...	1534	1537	|	|	...	1634	1637	|	...	|	...	1734	1737	|	|	...	1834	1837	|	|
Yverdon d.	1453	1456	|	|	...	1553	1556	|	|	...	1653	1656	|	...	|	...	1753	1756	|	|	...	1853	1856	|	|
ausanne 508 a.	1515	|	1515	1540	...	1615	|	1615	1640	...	1715	|	1715	...	1740	...	1815	|	1815	1840	...	1915	|	1915	1940
ausanne 570 d.	...	|	1517	1542	1548	...	|	1617	1642	1648	...	|	1717	1723	1742	1748	...	|	1817	1842	1848	...	|	1917	1942
orges 570 d.	...	1519	|	|	1600	...	1619	|	|	1700	...	1719	|	1736	|	1800	...	1819	|	|	1900	...	1919	|	|
yon 570 d.	...	1533	|	|	1623	...	1633	|	|	1723	...	1733	|	1756	|	1823	...	1833	|	|	1923	...	1933	|	|
enève 570 a.	...	1546	1550	1615	1639	...	1646	1650	1715	1739	...	1746	1750	1812	1815	1839	...	1846	1850	1915	1939	...	1946	1950	2015
Genève Aéroport + 570 d.	...	1555	1559	1624	...	...	1655	1659	1724	...	...	1755	1759	...	1824	...	...	1855	1859	1924	...	...	1955	1959	2024

	RE 2636	ICN 1636	ICN 536	IC 2536	IC 736	RE 2638	ICN 1538	ICN 638	IC 2538	IC 738	RE 2640	ICN 1640	ICN 1540	IC 2540	IC 740	RE 2642	ICN 642	ICN 1542	IC 2542	RE 2644	ICN 1644	ICN 1544	IR 2694	ICN 646	RE 2646
						†																			⑥⑦ p
St Gallen 530 d.	...	...	1648	...	1711	...	1748	...	...	1811	...	...	1848	...	1911	...	...	1948	...	...	...	2048	...	...	...
Zürich Flughafen + 530 d.	...	...	1743	...	1813	...	1843	...	...	1913	...	...	1943	...	2013	...	...	2043	...	...	...	2143	...	...	...
Zürich HB 500 d.	...	...	1804	...	1832	...	1904	...	...	1932	...	...	2004	...	2032	...	...	2104	...	...	...	2204	...	...	...
Luzern 565 d.	...	...	|	1800	|	...	|	...	1900	|	...	...	|	2000	|	...	...	|	2100	...	...	|	...	...	...
Olten 500 d.	...	...	1841	|	|	...	1941	...	|	|	...	...	2041	|	|	...	...	2141	|	...	...	2241	...	...	...
ern d.	...	...	|	1904	1934	...	|	...	2004	2034	...	...	|	2104	2134	...	...	|	2204	...	...	|	2307	...	...
ribourg d.	...	...	|	1926	1955	...	|	...	2026	2055	...	...	|	2126	2155	...	...	|	2226	...	...	|	2329	...	...
omont d.	...	...	|	1944	|	...	|	...	2044	|	...	...	|	2144	|	...	...	|	2244	...	...	|	2347	...	...
alézieux 508 d.	...	...	|	1959	|	...	|	...	2059	|	...	...	|	2159	|	...	...	|	2259	...	...	|	0002	...	...
Basel d.	...	1803	|	|	|	...	|	1903	|	|	...	2003	|	|	|	...	2103	|	|	...	2203	|	|	2303	...
Delémont d.	...	1842	|	|	|	...	|	1942	|	|	...	2042	|	|	|	...	2142	|	|	...	2242	|	|	2337	...
Moutier d.	...	1852	|	|	|	...	|	1952	|	|	...	2052	|	|	|	...	2152	|	|	...	2252	|	|	...	...
Biel/Bienne a.	...	1910	1913k	|	|	...	2013	2010k	|	|	...	2110	2113	|	|	...	2210	2213	|	...	2310	2314	|	...	...
Biel/Bienne d.	...	1916	1919	|	|	...	2016	2019	|	|	...	...	2116	|	|	...	...	2216	|	...	...	2316	|	...	...
Neuchâtel d.	...	1934	1937	|	|	...	2034	2037	|	|	...	...	2134	|	|	...	...	2234	|	...	...	2334	|	...	...
Yverdon d.	...	1953	1956	|	|	...	2053	2056	|	|	...	...	2153	|	|	...	...	2253	|	...	...	2353	|	...	...
ausanne 508 a.	...	2015	|	2015	2040	...	2115	|	2115	2140	...	...	2215	2215	2240	...	...	2315	2315	...	...	0015	0018	...	...
ausanne 570 d.	1948	...	|	2020	2042	2048	...	|	2120	2142	2148	...	...	2220	2245	2248	...	...	2320	2348	...	...	0020	...	0048
orges 570 d.	2000	...	2019	2032	|	2100	...	2119	2132	|	2200	...	...	2232	|	2300	...	...	2332	0000	...	...	0032	...	0100
yon 570 d.	2023	...	2033	2050	|	2123	...	2133	2150	|	2223	...	...	2250	|	2323	...	...	2350	0023	...	...	0050	...	0123
enève 570 a.	2039	...	2046	2104	2115	2139	...	2146	2204	2215	2239	...	...	2304	2318	2339	...	...	0004	0039	...	...	0104	...	0142
Genève Aéroport + 570 d.	...	...	2055	2113	2124	...	...	2155	2213	2224	2248	...	...	2313	2327	...	...	...	...	...	...	...	...	...	...

- – Connects with train in previous column. p – Also Jan. 1, Aug. 1. z – Arrive 0615 on Ⓐ.

506 SWISS LAKES

BRIENZERSEE — Operator: BLS

Services from Interlaken Ost, Bönigen, Iseltwald, Oberried am Brienzersee, Giessbach See and Brienz.

April 6 - May 31 and September 8 - October 19, 2008

Interlaken Ost - Brienz:- from Interlaken: 0915**v**, 1115**t**, 1215**v**, 1415**t**, 1615**q**;
from Brienz: 1045**v**, 1250**t**, 1350**v**, 1550**t**, 1800**q**.

June 1 - September 7, 2008

Interlaken Ost - Brienz:- from Interlaken: 0915, 1115**Q**, 1215, 1415**Q**, 1615;
from Brienz: 1045, 1250**Q**, 1350, 1550**Q**, 1800.

No Winter service

LAC LÉMAN — Operator: CGN

Services from Genève (Mont-Blanc / Jardin-Anglais / Pâquis / Eaux-Vives), Hermance, Coppet, Nyon, Yvoire, Thonon-les-Bains, Evian-les-Bains, Rolle, Morges, Lausanne-Ouchy, Vevey-Marché, Vevey-La Tour, Montreux, Territet, Château-de-Chillon, Villeneuve, Bouveret, St Gingolph.

December 9, 2007 - March 20, 2008

Genève - Lausanne:- no direct sailings.
Genève - Nyon:- from Genève: 0900⚒**e**, 1220†**f**, 1710⚒**e**, 1805⚒**e**; from Nyon: 0730⚒**e**, 1410†**f**, 1715⚒**e**, 1820⚒**e**.
Lausanne - Evian-les-Bains:- from Lausanne: 0455⚒**e**, 0622⚒**e**, 0740⚒**e**, 0925, 1100, 1230, 1400, 1530, 1715, 1840, 2000⚒**e**, 2130⚒**e**; from Evian-les-Bains: 0540⚒**e**, 0700⚒**e**, 0820⚒**e**, 1005, 1145, 1320, 1445, 1615, 1800, 1920, 2045⚒**e**, 2215⚒**e**.
Vevey-Marché - St Gingolph / Bouveret:- from Vevey-Marché: 1205Ⓒ**f**, 1405Ⓒ**f**, 1605Ⓒ**f**; from St Gingolph / Bouveret: 1125Ⓒ**f**, 1325Ⓒ**f**, 1525Ⓒ**f**.

March 21 - May 31 and September 23 - November 2, 2008

Genève - Evian-les-Bains:- from Genève: 1000; from Evian-les-Bains: 1350.
Genève - Lausanne:- no direct sailings.
Genève - Nyon - Yvoire:- from Genève: 0900⚒, 1000, 1430**V**; from Yvoire: 1516, 1640**V**.
Genève - Nyon only:- from Genève: 1710⚒; from Nyon: 1715⚒, 1892⚒.
Genève - Thonon-les-Bains:- from Genève: 1805⚒; from Thonon-les-Bains: 0700⚒.
Lausanne - Evian-les-Bains:- from Lausanne: 0455⚒, 0622⚒, 0740⚒, 0930, 1100, 1230, 1400, 1530, 1715, 1840, 2000⚒, 2130⚒; from Evian-les-Bains: 0540⚒, 0700⚒, 0820⚒, 1015, 1145, 1320, 1445, 1615, 1800, 1920, 2045⚒, 2215⚒.
Vevey-Marché - St Gingolph / Bouveret:- from Vevey-Marché: 0950**d**, 1205, 1405; from St Gingolph / Bouveret: 0850**d**, 1125, 1325, 1525.

June 1 - September 22, 2008

Genève - Lausanne:- from Genève: 1000**S**, 1430, 1805; from Lausanne: 1035, 1430**S**.
Genève - Nyon - Yvoire:- from Genève: 0900⚒, 1115, 1840**S**; from Yvoire: 2020**S**.
Genève - Nyon only:- from Genève: no sailings; from Nyon: 0950, 1715.
Genève - Thonon-les-Bains:- from Genève: no sailings; from Thonon-les-Bains: 0700⚒.
Lausanne - Evian-les-Bains:- from Lausanne: 0455⚒, 0622⚒, 0740⚒, 0930, 1100, 1230, 1400, 1530, 1715, 1840, 2035, 2115, 2215, 2305; from Evian-les-Bains: 0540⚒, 0700⚒, 0820⚒, 1015, 1145, 1320, 1445, 1615, 1800, 1920, 2100, 2150, 2240, 2330.
Lausanne - St Gingolph / Bouveret:- from Lausanne: 0925**S**, 1230**S**, 1415**W**, 1700; from St Gingolph / Bouveret: 1020**S**, 1320**S**, 1505**W**, 1750.
Vevey-Marché - St Gingolph / Bouveret:- from Vevey-Marché: 0950, 1205, 1405, 1605, 1805, 1950, 2230; from St Gingolph / Bouveret: 0850, 1020**S**, 1125, 1320**S**, 1325, 1525, 1725, 1925, 2200.

Other local sailings operate throughout the year.

THUNERSEE — Operator: BLS

Services from Thun, Hünibach, Hilterfingen, Oberhofen am Thunersee, Gunten, Spie[z] Schiffstation, Faulensee, Merligen, Beatenbucht and Interlaken West.

December 9, 2007 - April 5 and October 20 - December 7, 2008

Thun - Interlaken:- from Thun: 1133**n**; from Interlaken: 1409**n**.

April 6 - May 31 and September 8 - October 19, 2008

Thun - Interlaken:- from Thun: 0933, 1033**m**, 1133, 1233**m**, 1504, 1633**v**;
from Interlaken: 0909**v**, 1209, 1309**m**, 1409, 1512**m**, 1725.

June 1 - September 7, 2008

Thun - Interlaken:- from Thun: 0833, 0933, 1033, 1133, 1233**S**, 1404, 1504, 1633;
from Interlaken: 0909, 1109, 1209, 1309, 1409, 1512**S**, 1640, 1725.

VIERWALDSTÄTTERSEE — Operator: SG[V]

Services from Luzern (Bahnhofquai), Verkehrshaus Lido, Kehrsiten Bürgenstock, Hertenstei[n], Küssnacht am Rigi, Weggis, Vitznau, Beckenried, Gersau, Treib, Brunnen, Rütli, Sisiko[n], Tellsplatte, Bauen, Isleten-Isenthal and Flüelen; and Luzern - Verkehrshaus Lido, Kehrsite[n] Bürgenstock, Kehrsiten Dorf, Hergiswil, Stansstad, Alpnachstad.

December 9, 2007 - March 20, 2008

Luzern - Vitznau - Brunnen:- from Luzern: 0921, 1032, 1621; from Brunnen: 0946, 1246, 164[6]
Luzern - Vitznau - Flüelen:- from Luzern: 0921†, 1321†; from Flüelen: 1241†, 1555†.

March 21 - May 24 and September 22 - October 19, 2008

Luzern - Alpnachstad:- 0922**p**, 1015**p**, 1121**p**, 1300**p**, 1400**p**; from Alpnachstad: 1050**p**, 1210**p**, 1310**p**, 1435**p**, 1555**p**.
Luzern - Küssnacht am Rigi:- from Luzern: 1021†, 1335†, 1545†;
from Küssnacht am Rigi: 1119†, 1434†, 1655†.
Luzern - Stansstad only:- from Luzern: 1015†**y**, 1121**y**, 1300†**y**, 1400**y**, 1521**y**;
from Stansstad: 1122†**y**, 1230**y**, 1403†**y**, 1516**y**, 1702**y**.
Luzern - Vitznau - Flüelen:- from Luzern: 0832**r**, 0921**Z**, 1032, 1125**P**, 1321**h**, 1421;
from Flüelen: 0927, 1220**Z**, 1350, 1425**r**, 1503**P**, 1613**h**.
Luzern - Vitznau only:- 0555Ⓐ, 0744**p**, 1200, 1525†, 1725, 1821Ⓐ; from Vitznau: 0647Ⓐ, 0835**p**, 1010, 1256, 1640†, 1922⚒.

May 25 - September 21, 2008

Luzern - Alpnachstad:- from Luzern: 0815**w**, 0922, 1015**T**, 1121, 1300, 1400**T**, 1515;
from Alpnachstad: 0935**w**, 1050, 1210**T**, 1310, 1435, 1555**T**, 1650.
Luzern - Küssnacht am Rigi:- from Luzern: 1021, 1335, 1545; from Küssnacht am Rigi: 111[9], 1435, 1655.
Luzern - Vitznau - Flüelen:- from Luzern: 0832, 0921**S**, 1000**S x**, 1032, 1125**S**, 1232, 1321**S**, 1421, 1625; from Flüelen: 0927, 1134**x**, 1220**S**, 1300**S x**, 1350, 1503**S**, 1530, 1613**S**, 1741.
Luzern - Vitznau only:- from Luzern: 0555Ⓐ, 0744, 1200, 1525**S**, 1725, 1821Ⓐ, 1921;
from Vitznau: 0647Ⓐ, 0835, 1010, 1256, 1640**S**, 2025.

Other local sailings operate throughout the year.

ZÜRICHSEE — Operator: ZS[G]

Services from Zürich (Bürkliplatz), Erlenbach, Thalwil, Oberrieden, Wädenswil an[d] Rapperswil.

December 9, 2007 - March 20, 2008

Zürich - Thalwil - Rapperswil:- from Zürich: 1330; from Rapperswil: 1525.
Zürich - Thalwil only:- from Zürich: 1300, 1430, 1548; from Thalwil: 1220, 1340, 1520.

March 21 - October 19, 2008

Zürich - Thalwil - Rapperswil:- from Zürich: 0930**k**, 0955**k**, 1030, 1130, 1230**k**, 1330, 143[0], 1530**k**, 1730**j**; from Rapperswil: 1125**k**, 1230, 1325, 1430**g**, 1455**k**, 1525, 163[0], 1725**k**, 1730†, 1945**j**.
Zürich - Thalwil only:- from Zürich: 0900, 1000, 1100, 1130 and every 30 minutes until 183[0] then 1900**j**, 1930**j** from Thalwil: 0704Ⓐ, 0740Ⓐ, 1020, 1120, 1140 and every 3[0] minutes until 1840, then 1920, 1940**j**, 2020**j**.

P – Daily. Normally operated by historic Steamship on † (daily from May 1).
Q – Daily. Normally operated by historic Steamship on ②–⑦.
S – Normally operated by historic Steamship.
T – Daily. Normally operated by historic Steamship on † (daily July 1 - Aug. 24).
V – Daily. Normally operated by historic Steamship from Apr. 27.
W – Daily. Normally operated by historic Steamship June 29 - Sept. 7.
Z – Daily. Normally operated by historic Steamship on † from May 1.

d – From May 1.
e – Also Dec. 26.
f – Not Dec. 26.
g – ⚒ June 2 - Sept. 30.
h – † Mar. 21 - Apr. 27; daily May 1-24, Sept. 22 - Oct. 19.
j – May 1 - Sept. 30.
k – † Mar. 21 - May 25; daily June 1 - Sept. 30; † Oct. 5 - 19.
m – ⑦ Apr. 6 - 27; daily May 1 - 31, Sept. 8 - Oct. 19.
n – † Dec. 9 - Mar. 30; ⑦ Oct. 26 - Dec. 7.
p – May 1-24, Sept. 22 - Oct. 19.
q – † May 1-25; ⑦ Sept. 14 - Oct. 19.
r – † Mar. 21 - May 18; daily Sept. 22 - Oct. 19.
t – ⑤⑥⑦ Apr. 6 - 27; daily May 1 - 31, Sept. 8 - 19.
v – May 1 - 31, Sept. 8 - Oct. 19.
w – July 1 - Aug. 24.
x – † (daily July 1 - Aug. 24).
y – Mar. 21 - Apr. 30.

Operators:

BLS – Schifffahrt Berner Oberland: ✆ +41 (0)33 334 52 11; fax +41 (0)33 334 52 1[…] (www.bls.ch)
CGN – Compagnie Générale de Navigation: ✆ +41 (0)848 811 848; fax +41 (0)21 614 62 0[…] (www.cgn.ch)
SGV – Schifffahrtsgesellschaft Vierwaldstättersee: ✆ +41 (0)41 367 67 67; fax +41 (0)41 36[…] 68 68. (www.lakelucerne.ch)
ZSG – Zürich Schifffahrtsgesellschaft: ✆ +41 (0)44 487 13 33; fax +41 (0)44 487 13 2[…] (www.zsg.ch)

508 PAYERNE - MURTEN - KERZERS (- LYSS) — BL[S]

km			⚒			⚒															⚒		⚒					
0	Payerne 523 ...... d.	...	0556	0635	...	0701	0735	0835	0935	...	1035	1135	1235	...	1335	1435	1535	...	1635	1735	1801	1835	1901	1935	...	2035	2235	...	234
11	Avenches .... d.	...	0609	0648	...	0710	0748	0848	0948	...	1048	1148	1248	...	1348	1448	1548	...	1648	1748	1810	1848	1910	1948	...	2048	2248	...	235
18	Murten .... a.	...	0616	0656	...	0716	0756	0856	0956	...	1056	1156	1256	...	1356	1456	1556	...	1656	1756	1816	1856	1916	1956	...	2056	2256	...	000

km		Ⓐ	Ⓒ	Ⓐ	Ⓐ	Ⓒ	Ⓐ	Ⓐ										Ⓐ		Ⓐ	Ⓒ	Ⓐ	Ⓐ	Ⓒ	Ⓐ				
0	Murten .... d.	0547	0617	0618	0647	0717	0718	0747	0817	0917	1017	1117	1217	1317	1417	1517	1617	1647	1717	1747	1817	1818	1847	1917	1918	2017	2147	2247	000
8	Kerzers .... ▲ a.	0556	0626	0626	0656	0726	0726	0756	0826	0926	1026	1126	1226	1326	1426	1526	1626	1656	1726	1756	1826	1826	1856	1926	1926	2026	2156	2256	001

	Ⓐ	Ⓐ	Ⓐ	Ⓐ	Ⓒ	Ⓐ		Ⓐ										Ⓐ	⚒	†	Ⓐ	⚒	†	Ⓐ					①–⑤	⑥⑦
Kerzers .... ▲ d.	0504	0534	0604	0634	0634	0704	0734	0804	0834	0934	1034	1134	1234	1334	1434	1534	1634	1704	1734	1734	1804	1834	1834	1904	1934	2034	2204	2304	0015	005
Murten .... a.	0513	0543	0613	0642	0643	0713	0743	0813	0843	0943	1043	1143	1243	1343	1443	1543	1643	1713	1742	1743	1813	1842	1843	1913	1943	2043	2213	2313	0024	005

	Ⓐ	⚒	†		⚒																	⚒		⚒							
Murten .... d.	0514	0602	0603	...	0643	0703	...	0803	0903	1003	1103	1203	...	1303	1403	1503	...	1603	1703	...	1743	1803	1843	1903	...	2003	2103	...	2315	...
Avenches .... d.	0522	0611	0611	...	0649	0711	...	0811	0911	1011	1111	1211	...	1311	1411	1511	...	1611	1711	...	1749	1811	1849	1911	...	2011	2111	...	2323	...
Payerne 523 ...... a.	0534	0623	0623	...	0657	0723	...	0823	0923	1023	1123	1223	...	1323	1423	1523	...	1623	1723	...	1757	1823	1857	1923	...	2023	2123	...	2335	...

▲ – **Rail service KERZERS - LYSS and v.v.**: *17 km*, journey 20 minutes.
From **Kerzers**: 0606 and hourly until 2106, then 2306.
From **Lyss**: 0534, 0632 and hourly until 2032, then 2232, 0011.

SBB BASEL - ZÜRICH 510

km		IR	IR	IR	IR	IC	IR	IR	ICE	IR	IC	CNL	IR	IR	IR	ICE	CNL	EC	IR	IR	IC	IR	IR	IR	ICE	IR	IR
		2057	**1953**	**557**	**2059**	**759**	**1955**	**559**	**1009**	**2061**	**761**	**409**	**1961**	**561**	**2065**	**275**	**458**	**163**	**565**	**2067**	**767**	**1967**	**567**	**2069**	**271**	**1969**	**569**
												♦				✕ ♦	♦	♦							✕ ♦		
0	**Basel SBB** d.	0440	0514	0522	0540	0607	0614	0622	0637	0640	0707	0710**s**	0714	0722	0740	0807	0810**s**	0814	0822	0842	0907	0914	0922	0942	1007	1014	1022
17	Rheinfelden d.	0452	0526	|	|	|	0626	|	|	|	|	|	0726	|	|	|	|	0826	|	|	|	0926	|	|	|	1026	|
	Liestal d.	|	|	0531	|	|	|	0631	|	|	|	|	|	0731	|	|	|	|	0831	|	|	|	0931	|	|	|	1031
	Aarau d.	|	|	0557	|	|	|	0657	|	|	|	|	|	0757	|	|	|	|	0857	|	|	|	0957	|	|	|	1057
	Lenzburg d.	|	|	0604	|	|	|	0704	|	|	|	|	|	0804	|	|	|	|	0904	|	|	|	1004	|	|	|	1104
57	Brugg d.	0520	0600	|	0620	|	0700	|	|	0720	|	|	0800	|	0820	|	|	0900	|	0920	|	1000	|	1020	|	1100	|
66	Baden d.	0530	0608	|	0630	|	0708	|	|	0730	|	0759**s**	0808	|	0830	|	0859**s**	0908	|	0930	|	1008	|	1030	|	1108	|
88	**Zürich HB** a.	|	0624	0626	|	0700	0724	0726	0732	|	0800	0822	0824	0826	|	0900	0918	0924	0926	|	1000	1024	1026	|	1100	1124	1126
	Zürich Flug ✈ **530/5** a.	0556	...	...	0656	|	...	|	...	0756	|	...	...	|	0856	...	...	...	|	0956	|	...	|	1056	...	...	|
	Chur **520** a.	...	...	...	...	0843	...	0852	...	...	0943	...	...	0952	...	...	...	...	1052	...	1143	...	1152	...	...	...	1252

	IR	IC	IR	IR	IR	TGV	IR	IR	IR	IC	IR	IR	IR	EC	IR	IR	IC	IR	ICE	IR	IR	IR	TGV	TGV	EC	IR	EC
	2071	**771**	**1971**	**571**	**2073**	**9211**	**1973**	**573**	**2075**	**777**	**1975**	**575**	**2077**	**7**	**1977**	**577**	**91**	**2079**	**73**	**1979**	**579**	**2081**	**9213**	**9213**	**103**	**1981**	**101**
						(✕) ♦								♦			♦		✕ Z				(✕) ♦⑥	(✕) ♦⑧	♦		♦
Basel SBB d.	1042	1107	1114	1122	1142	1207	1214	1222	1242	1307	1314	1322	1342	1407	1414	1422	1440	1442	1507	1514	1522	1542	1558	1607	1607	1614	1622
Rheinfelden d.	|	|	1126	|	|	|	1226	|	|	|	1326	|	|	|	1426	|	|	|	|	1526	|	|	|	|	|	1626	|
Liestal d.	|	|	|	1131	|	|	|	1231	|	|	|	1331	|	|	|	1431	|	|	|	|	1531	|	|	|	|	|	1631
Aarau d.	|	|	|	1157	|	|	|	1257	|	|	|	1357	|	|	|	1457	|	|	|	|	1557	|	|	|	|	|	1657
Lenzburg d.	|	|	|	1204	|	|	|	1304	|	|	|	1404	|	|	|	1504	|	|	|	|	1604	|	|	|	|	|	1704
Brugg d.	1120	|	1200	|	1220	|	1300	|	1320	|	1400	|	1420	|	1500	|	|	1520	|	1600	|	1620	|	|	|	1700	|
Baden d.	1130	|	1208	|	1230	|	1308	|	1330	|	1408	|	1430	|	1508	|	|	1530	|	1608	|	1630	|	|	|	1708	|
Zürich HB a.	|	1200	1224	1226	|	1300	1324	1326	|	1400	1424	1426	|	1500	1524	1526	1540	|	1600	1624	1626	|	1707	1700	1700	1724	1726
Zürich Flug ✈ **530/5** a.	1156	...	...	|	1256	|	...	|	1356	|	...	|	1456	|	...	|	...	1556	...	...	|	1656	...	...	|	...	|
Chur **520** a.	...	...	...	1352	...	1425**r**	...	1452	...	1543	...	1552	...	1643	...	1652	...	...	...	...	1752	...	...	...	1843	...	1852

	IR	IR	ICE	IR	IR	IR	IC	IR	IR	IR	ICE	IR	IR	IR	IC	IR	IR	ICE	IR	TGV	IR	IR	IR	IR	TGV	IR	IR
	581	**2085**	**75**	**1985**	**585**	**2087**	**787**	**1987**	**587**	**2089**	**77**	**1989**	**589**	**2091**	**97**	**1991**	**591**	**79**	**1993**	**9217**	**593**	**1995**	**595**	**1997**	**9219**	**597**	**1999**
	⑥		✕ H								✕ H				♦			✕ H		(✕) ♦					(✕) ♦		
Basel SBB d.	1622	1642	1707	1714	1722	1742	1807	1814	1822	1842	1907	1914	1922	1942	2007	2014	2022	2107	2114	2120	2122	2152	2222	2252	2301	2322	0008
Rheinfelden d.	|	|	|	1726	|	|	|	1826	|	|	|	1926	|	|	|	2026	|	|	2126	|	|	2204	|	2304	|	|	0020
Liestal d.	1631	|	|	|	1731	|	|	|	1831	|	|	|	1931	|	|	|	2031	|	|	|	2131	|	2231	|	|	2331	|
Aarau d.	1657	|	|	|	1757	|	|	|	1857	|	|	|	1957	|	|	|	2057	|	|	|	2157	|	2257	|	|	2357	|
Lenzburg d.	1704	|	|	|	1804	|	|	|	1904	|	|	|	2004	|	|	|	2104	|	|	|	2204	|	2304	|	|	0004	|
Brugg d.	|	1720	|	1800	|	1820	|	1900	|	1920	|	2000	|	2020	|	2100	|	|	2200	|	|	2235	|	2335	|	|	0053
Baden d.	|	1730	|	1808	|	1830	|	1908	|	1930	|	2008	|	2030	|	2108	|	|	2208	|	|	2244	|	2344	|	|	0101
Zürich HB a.	1726	|	1800	1824	1826	|	1900	1924	1926	|	2000	2024	2026	|	2100	2124	2126	2200	2224	2214	2226	2300	2326	2400	2356	0026	0117
Zürich Flug ✈ **530/5** a.	|	1756	...	...	|	1856	|	...	|	1956	...	...	...	2056	|	...	...	...	...	...	...	...	...	...	...	...	...
Chur **520** a.	1852	...	...	...	1952	...	2045	...	2052	...	...	...	...	...	2245	...	...	...	...	...	...	...	...	...	...	...	...

km		IR	ICE	IR	IR	IR	TGV	IR	IR	IR	ICE	IR	IR	IR	IC	IR		IR	IR	ICE	IR	IR	IR	EC	EC	IR	IR
		556	**78**	**2058**	**558**	**1958**	**9212**	**2060**	**560**	**1960**	**76**	**2062**	**562**	**1962**	**764**	**2066**		**566**	**1966**	**74**	**2068**	**568**	**1968**	**102**	**100**	**2070**	**570**
			✕ H				(✕) ♦				✕ Z									✕ Z				♦	♦		
	Chur **520** d.	...	...	...	...	...	...	...	0606**d**	...	...	...	0709	...	...	...	...	0809	...	...	...	0909	...	0916	0916	...	1009
	Zürich Flug ✈ **530/5** d.	...	...	0604	...	...	...	0704	|	...	...	0804	|	...	...	0904	...	|	...	...	1004	|	...	|	|	1104	|
0	**Zürich HB** d.	0534	0554	|	0634	0636	0702	|	0734	0736	0802	|	0834	0836	0902	|	...	0934	0936	1002	|	1034	1036	1102	1102	|	1134
	Baden d.	|	0610	0630	|	0652	|	0730	|	0752	|	0830	|	0852	|	0930	...	|	0952	|	1030	|	1052	|	|	1130	|
	Brugg d.	|	0619	0640	|	0702	|	0740	|	0802	|	0840	|	0902	|	0940	...	|	1002	|	1040	|	1102	|	|	1140	|
32	Lenzburg d.	0555	|	|	0655	|	|	|	0755	|	|	|	0855	|	|	|	...	0955	|	|	|	1055	|	|	|	|	1155
41	Aarau d.	0603	|	|	0703	|	|	|	0803	|	|	|	0903	|	|	|	...	1003	|	|	|	1103	|	|	|	|	1203
77	Liestal d.	0628	|	|	0728	|	|	|	0828	|	|	|	0928	|	|	|	...	1028	|	|	|	1128	|	|	|	|	1228
	Rheinfelden d.	|	|	0716	|	0735	|	|	|	0835	|	|	|	0935	|	|	...	|	1035	|	|	|	1135	|	|	|	|
91	**Basel SBB** a.	0638	0658	0733	0738	0748	0756	0820	0838	0848	0856	0920	0938	0948	0956	1020	...	1038	1048	1056	1120	1138	1148	1156	1156	1220	1238

	IR	ICE	IR	IR	IR		EC	IR	IR	IR	TGV	IR	IR		IR	IC	IR	IR	IR	IC	IR	ICE		IR	IR	IC	IR
	90	**72**	**2072**	**572**	**1972**		**6**	**2074**	**574**	**1974**	**9216**	**2076**	**96**		**1976**	**776**	**2078**	**578**	**1978**	**780**	**2080**	**1030**		**580**	**1980**	**782**	**2082**
	♦	✕ H					♦				(✕) ♦		♦									✕					
Chur **520** d.	...	...	...	1109	...	...	1116	...	1209	...	...	...	1309	...	...	...	...	1409	...	...	...	...	...	1509	...	1516	...
Zürich Flug ✈ **530/5** d.	...	...	1204	|	...	...	|	1304	|	...	...	1404	|	...	...	...	1504	|	...	...	1604	...	...	|	...	|	1704
Zürich HB d.	1136	1202	|	1234	1236	...	1302	|	1334	1336	1402	|	1434	...	1436	1502	|	1534	1536	1602	|	1628	...	1634	1636	1702	|
Baden d.	1152	|	1230	|	1252	...	|	1330	|	1352	|	1430	|	...	1452	|	1530	|	1552	|	1630	|	...	|	1652	|	1730
Brugg d.	1202	|	1240	|	1302	...	|	1340	|	1402	|	1440	|	...	1502	|	1540	|	1602	|	1640	|	...	|	1702	|	1740
Lenzburg d.	|	|	|	1255	|	...	|	|	1355	|	|	|	1455	...	|	|	|	1555	|	|	|	|	...	1655	|	|	|
Aarau d.	|	|	|	1303	|	...	|	|	1403	|	|	|	1503	...	|	|	|	1603	|	|	|	|	...	1703	|	|	|
Liestal d.	|	|	|	1328	|	...	|	|	1428	|	|	|	1528	...	|	|	|	1628	|	|	|	|	...	1728	|	|	|
Rheinfelden d.	1235	|	|	|	1335	...	|	|	|	1435	|	|	|	...	1535	|	|	|	1635	|	|	|	...	|	1735	|	|
Basel SBB a.	1248	1256	1320	1338	1348	...	1356	1420	1438	1448	1456	1520	1538	...	1548	1556	1620	1638	1648	1656	1722	1722	...	1738	1748	1756	1822

	IR	IR	TGV	IR	IR	EC	ICE	IR	IR	IR		CNL	IC	IR	IR	IR	CNL	IC	IR	IR	IR	IR	ICE	IR	IR	IR	
	582	**1982**	**9218**	**2086**	**586**	**162**	**270**	**2088**	**588**	**1988**		**459**	**790**	**2090**	**590**	**1990**	**408**	**792**	**2092**	**592**	**794**	**594**	**1996**	**596**	**798**	**1950**	
			(✕) ♦			♦	✕ ♦					♦					♦									⑥⑦**q**	
Chur **520** d.	1609	...	1633	...	1709	...	...	...	1809	...	...	...	1816	...	...	...	...	1916	...	...	2013	...	...	...	2213	...	...
Zürich Flug ✈ **530/5** d.	|	...	|	1804	|	...	...	1904	|	...	...	...	|	2004	...	...	...	|	2104	...	|	...	...	...	|	...	...
Zürich HB d.	1734	1736	1802	|	1834	1836	1902	|	1934	1936	...	1944	2002	|	2034	2036	2042	2102	|	2134	2206	2234	2306	2334	0006	0106	...
Baden d.	|	1752	|	1830	|	1852	|	1930	|	1952	...	1958**u**	|	2030	|	2052	2058**u**	|	2130	|	2222	|	2322	|	0022	0122	...
Brugg d.	|	1802	|	1840	|	1902	|	1940	|	2002	...	|	|	2040	|	2102	|	|	2140	|	2232	|	2332	|	0032	0132	...
Lenzburg d.	1755	|	|	|	1855	|	|	|	1955	|	...	|	|	|	2055	|	|	|	|	2155	|	2255	|	2355	|	|	...
Aarau d.	1803	|	|	|	1903	|	|	|	2003	|	...	|	|	|	2103	|	|	|	|	2203	|	2303	|	0003	|	|	...
Liestal d.	1828	|	|	|	1928	|	|	|	2028	|	...	|	|	|	2128	|	|	|	|	2228	|	2328	|	0028	|	|	...
Rheinfelden d.	|	1835	|	|	|	1935	|	|	|	2035	...	|	|	|	|	2135	|	|	|	|	2304	|	0003	|	0104	0204	...
Basel SBB a.	1838	1848	1856	1922	1938	1948	1956	2020	2038	2048	...	2051**u**	2056	2120	2138	2148	2151**u**	2156	2220	2238	2316	2338	0015	0038	0116	0216	...

♦ – **NOTES** (LISTED BY TRAIN NUMBER)

– [12] and ✕ Chur - Basel - Köln - Dortmund (- Hamburg ⑧, not Dec. 24, 25, 31, Mar. 21, 23, May 11, Oct. 3).

– [12] and ✕ (①–⑥, not Dec. 25, 26, Jan. 1, Mar. 22, 24, May 12, Oct. 4, Hamburg -) Dortmund - Basel - Chur.

0/1 – VAUBAN – Brussels - Luxembourg - Basel - Zürich and v.v.

6/7 – IRIS – [12] Chur - Zürich - Basel - Luxembourg - Brussels and v.v.

00 – ①–⑥ (also Dec. 23, 30, Mar. 23, May 11; not Dec. 26, Jan. 1, Mar. 24, May 12): [12] Chur - Zürich - Basel - Hamburg.

01 – ⑧: [12] Hamburg - Basel - Zürich - Chur.

02 – ⑦ (also Dec. 26, Jan. 1, Mar. 24, May 12; not Dec. 23, 30, Mar. 23, May 11): [12] Chur - Zürich - Basel - Hamburg - Kiel.

03 – ⑥: [12] Hamburg - Basel - Zürich - Chur.

62/3 – TRANSALPIN – [12] Wien - Innsbruck - Basel and v.v.

70/1 – [12] and ✕ Zürich - Frankfurt (Main) and v.v.

75 – [12] and ✕ Karlsruhe - Zürich.

08 – *City Night Line* KOMET – 🛏 1, 2 cl., ▬ 2 cl., [2] [reclining] and ✕ (⑥ Dec. 22 - Mar. 29, Brig -) Zürich - Hamburg / Amsterdam. Special fares payable.

09 – *City Night Line* KOMET – 🛏 1, 2 cl., ▬ 2 cl., [2] [reclining] and ✕ Hamburg / Amsterdam - Zürich (- Brig ⑥ Dec. 22 - Mar. 29). Special fares payable.

458/9 – *City Night Line* SEMPER – 🛏 1, 2 cl., ▬ 2 cl., [2] [reclining] and ✕ Berlin / Dresden - Basel - Zürich and v.v. Special fares payable.

9211 – [12] and (✕) Paris Est - Basel - Zürich (- Chur, ⑥ Dec. 15 - Mar. 29). On ⑥ Dec. 15 - Mar. 29 runs Basel - Zürich - Chur only as train **9221**.

9212 – [12] and (✕) Zürich - Basel - Paris Est.

9213 – [12] and (✕) Paris Est - Basel - Zürich.

9216 – [12] and (✕) Zürich - Basel - Paris Est.

9217 – ⑧: [12] and (✕) Paris Est - Basel - Zürich.

9218 – [12] and (✕) (Chur, ⑥ Dec. 15 - Mar. 29 -) Zürich - Basel - Paris Est. On ⑥ Dec. 15 - Mar. 29 runs Chur - Zürich - Basel only as train **9222**.

9219 – ⑥: [12] and (✕) Paris Est - Basel - Zürich.

H – [12] and ✕ Zürich - Basel - Hamburg and v.v.

Z – [12] and ✕ Zürich - Basel - Hamburg - Kiel and v.v.

d – ⚒ only.

q – Also Jan. 1. June 8 - 30 runs to special FIFA *EURO 2008* schedule.

r – ⑥ Dec. 15 - Mar. 29.

s – Stops to set down only.

u – Stops to pick up only.

511 BERN and FRIBOURG - NEUCHÂTEL

BLS, TPF*

km		⚒	⚒p	⚒q		p	q		▲		p	q				p	q			⑤⑥	Gr	G	⑤⑥t		①-⑤	⑥⑦
0	**Bern** d.	0537	...	...	0637	...	...	0706	and at	1937	...	...	2006	...	2038	...	...	2138	...	2238	...	2238	...	...	2342	0019
22	Kerzers d.	0559	...	...	0700	...	...	0729	the same	2000	...	...	2029	...	2100	...	...	2200	...	2300	...	2300	...	...	0008	0045
	Fribourg d.	|	0533	0533	|	0633	0633	|	minutes	|	1933	1933	|	...	|	2033	2033	|	2132	|	2232	|	2332	...	|	|
	Murten d.	|	0600	0600	|	0700	0700	|	past each	|	2000	2000	|	...	|	2100	2100	|	2200	|	2300	|	0000	...	|	|
30	Ins d.	0605	0611	0618	0705	0711	0718	0735	hour	2005	2011	2018	2035	...	2106	2111	2118	2207	2211	2306	2310	2313	0010	...	0015	0051
43	**Neuchâtel** a.	0618	0626	0632	0717	0726	0731	0753	until	2017	2026	2031	2053	...	2121	2129	2131	2220	2228	2322	...	2328	...	...	0032	0107

km		Ⓐ	⚒	Ⓒ	Ⓐ		†	⚒		Ⓐ				▲												
	Neuchâtel d.	0510	...	0537	0543	0603	...	0636	0643	0654	0703	0736	0743	and at	1903	1936	1943	...	2003	2035	2043	2133	2142	2233	2242	2357
0	Ins d.	0525	0550	0552	0554	0622	0650	0650	0654	0707	0722	0750	0754	the same	1922	1950	1954	...	2022	2050	2053	2150	2152	2250	2252	0010
10	Murten d.	|	0601	|	|	|	0701	0701	|	|	|	0801	|	minutes	|	2001	|	...	|	2101	|	2201	|	2301	|	|
32	**Fribourg** a.	|	0627	|	|	|	0727	0728	|	|	|	0827	|	past each	|	2027	|	...	|	2127	|	2227	|	2326	|	|
	Kerzers d.	0533	...	0601	0601	0632	...	...	0701	0717	0732	...	0801	hour	1932	...	2001	...	2032	...	2102	...	2202	...	2302	0021
	Bern a.	0554	...	0622	0623	0654	...	...	0723	0736	0754	...	0823	until	1954	...	2023	...	2054	...	2122	...	2222	...	2322	0046

G – ①②③④⑦ only.

p – Not Apr. 14 - June 22.

q – Apr. 14 - June 22.

r – Also Mar. 21, Aug. 1.

t – Not Mar. 21, Aug. 1.

▲ – Variations: 1033, 1133 from Fribourg; 0936, 1036 from Neuchâtel: run only Murten - Ins - Neuchâtel and v.v. on Oct. 5.

* – Operators: BLS, Bern - Ins - Neuchâtel TPF, Fribourg - Ins.

512 BIEL and NEUCHÂTEL - LA CHAUX DE FONDS - LE LOCLE

SBB

km				Ⓒ	Ⓐ																		G		⑤⑥
0	**Biel/Bienne** d.	...	0614	...	...	0649	0717	...	...	0749	and at	1917	...	...	1949	...	2017	...	2117	...	2217	...	2319	...	2349
28	St Imier d.	...	0641	...	...	0731	0744	...	...	0831	the same	1944	...	...	2031	...	2052	...	2152	...	2252	...	2352	...	0029
	Neuchâtel d.	0537	|	0631	0631	|	|	0731	0737	|	minutes	|	1931	1937	|	2031	|	2037	|	2137	|	2237	|	2337	|
44	La Chaux de Fonds d.	0615	0655	0702	0705	0747	0758	0802	0818	0847	past each	1958	2002	2018	2047	2059	2110	2115	2210	2215	2310	2315	0010	0015	0045
52	**Le Locle** a.	0623	...	0710	0713	...	...	0810	0827	...	hour until	...	2010	2026	...	...	...	2123	...	2223	...	2323	...	0023	...

km																									
0	**Le Locle** d.	0546	...	0630	0650	...	0724r	0750	...	...	0832	and at	1850	...	...	1932	1950	...	2032	...	2132	...	2232	2332	...
8	La Chaux de Fonds d.	0557	0559	0642	0701	0702	0742	0801	0802	0813	0842	the same	1901	1902	1913	1942	2001	2002	2042	2051	2142	2151	2242	2342	2351
37	**Neuchâtel** a.	0626	|	0719	0730	|	0819	0830	|	|	0919	minutes	1930	|	|	2019	2030	|	2119	|	2219	|	2319	0019	|
	St Imier d.	...	0613	...	...	0716	...	...	0816	0830	...	past each	...	1916	1930	...	...	2016	...	2109	...	2209	...	...	0009
	Biel/Bienne a.	...	0640	...	...	0741	...	...	0841	0910	...	hour until	...	1941	2010	...	...	2041	...	2141	...	2241	...	...	0041

G – ①②③④⑦ only.

r – 0732 on Ⓒ.

513 BERN - BIEL

SBB

Valid December 9 - June 7

km																								⑥⑦j
0	**Bern** d.	0530	0600	0612	0630	0642	and at the	2000	2012	2030	2042	...	2100	2112	2130	2200	2212	2230	2300	2312	2330	0000	0012	0115
23	Lyss d.	0552	0622	0630	0652	0700	same minutes past each	2022	2030	2052	2100	...	2122	2130	2152	2222	2230	2252	2322	2330	2352	0022	0030	0137
34	**Biel/Bienne** a.	0606	0636	0639	0706	0709	hour until	2036	2039	2106	2109	...	2135	2139	2205	2235	2239	2305	2335	2339	0005	0035	0039	0145

	Ⓐ	Ⓒ																						⑥⑦j
Biel/Bienne d.	0518	0519	0551	0554	0621	0624	and at the	1951	1954	2021	2024	...	2051	2055	2121	2125	2155	2221	2225	2255	2321	2325	2355	0026
Lyss d.	0531	0532	0600	0607	0630	0637	same minutes past each	2000	2007	2030	2037	...	2100	2107	2130	2137	2207	2230	2237	2307	2330	2337	0007	0035
Bern a.	0554	0554	0618	0630	0648	0700	hour until	2018	2030	2048	2100	...	2118	2130	2148	2200	2230	2248	2300	2330	2348	2400	0030	0053

j – Also Jan. 1.

514 BERN - LUZERN via Langnau

BLS

For faster services Bern - (Olten -) Luzern see Tables 505/565

km									
0	**Bern** d.	...	0637	0712	and at	2137	2212	2237	2342
21	Konolfingen d.	...	0653	0733	the same	2153	2233	2253	2356
38	Langnau d.	0606	0706	0751	minutes	2206	2251	2306	0008
75	Wolhusen d.	0645	0745	...	past each	2245	...	2345	...
96	**Luzern** a.	0702	0802	...	hour until	2302	...	0007	...

										n
Luzern d.	0554	...	0657	...	and at	2057	...	...	...	2315
Wolhusen d.	0615	...	0715	...	the same	2115	...	...	...	2344
Langnau d.	0654	0738	0754	0808	minutes	2154	2208	2254	0008	0023
Konolfingen d.	0708	0756	0808	0826	past each	2208	2226	2308	0026	...
Bern a.	0726	0817	0826	0847	hour until	2226	2247	2326	0047	...

n – Daily Dec. 9 - Apr. 26; ⑤⑥ May 2 - Aug. 9; daily Aug. 14 - Dec. 13 (also May 1, 11).

516 BERN - SOLOTHURN

Narrow gauge. RBS

km																			
0	**Bern RBS** d.	0606	0636	and at the same minutes past	1906	1936	...	2006	...	2041	2111	and at the same minutes past	2241	2311	...	2341	...	0011	...	...
34	Solothurn a.	0643	0713	each hour until	1943	2013	...	2043	...	2124	2154	each hour until	2324	2354	...	0024	...	0054	...	...

Solothurn d.	0548	...	0618	0648	and at the same minutes past	1918	1948	...	2005	...	2035	2107	and at the same minutes past	2135	2207	...	2235	2307	2335	...
Bern RBS a.	0625	...	0655	0725	each hour until	1955	2025	...	2050	...	2120	2150	each hour until	2220	2250	...	2320	2350	0020	...

517 SOLOTHURN - BURGDORF - THUN

BLS

Valid December 9 - September 30

km																											
0	**Solothurn** d.	0601	0701	...	0801	0901	...	1001	1101	...	1201	1301	...	1401	1501	...	1601	1701	...	1801	...	1901	...	...	...	...	...
5	Biberist d.	0606	0706	...	0806	0906	...	1006	1106	...	1206	1306	...	1406	1506	...	1606	1706	...	1806	...	1906	...	...	...	...	...
21	**Burgdorf** a.	0627	0727	...	0827	0927	...	1027	1127	...	1227	1327	...	1427	1527	...	1627	1727	...	1827	...	1927	...	...	...	...	...
21	**Burgdorf** d.	0631	0731	*0747*	0831	0931	*0947*	1031	1131	*1147*	1231	1331	*1347*	1431	1531	*1547*	1631	1731	*1747*	1831	*1847*	1931	*1947*	*2047*	*2147*	*2247*	*2347*
28	Hasle-Rüegsau d.	0640	0740	0801	0840	0940	1001	1040	1140	1201	1240	1340	1401	1440	1540	1601	1640	1740	1801	1840	1901	1940	2001	2101	2201	2301	0001
46	Konolfingen a.	0700	0800	0822	0900	1000	1022	1100	1200	1222	1300	1400	1422	1500	1600	1622	1700	1800	1822	1900	1922	2000	2022	2122	2222	2322	0022
46	Konolfingen d.	0701	0801	0835	0901	1001	1035	1101	1201	1235	1301	1401	1435	1501	1601	1635	1701	1801	1835	1901	1935	2001	2035	2135	2235	2335	0035
61	**Thun** a.	0718	0818	0856	0918	1018	1056	1118	1218	1256	1318	1418	1456	1518	1618	1656	1718	1818	1856	1918	1956	2018	2056	2156	2255	2355	0055

	Ⓐ																									
Thun d.	0532	0639	0739	0839	0903	0939	1039	1103	1139	1239	1303	1339	1439	1503	1539	1639	1703	1739	1803	1839	1903	1939	2009	2109	2209	2309	0009
Konolfingen a.	0553	0658	0758	0858	0924	0958	1058	1124	1158	1258	1324	1358	1458	1524	1558	1658	1724	1758	1824	1858	1924	1958	2030	2129	2229	2329	0029
Konolfingen d.	0600	0700	0800	0900	0935	1000	1100	1135	1200	1300	1335	1400	1500	1535	1600	1700	1735	1800	1835	1900	1935	2000	2035	2135	2235	2335	0035
Hasle-Rüegsau d.	0620	0720	0820	0920	0957	1020	1120	1157	1220	1320	1357	1420	1520	1557	1620	1720	1757	1820	1857	1920	1957	2020	2057	2157	2257	2357	0058
Burgdorf a.	0629	0729	0829	0929	*1012*	1029	1129	*1212*	1229	1329	*1412*	1429	1529	*1612*	1629	1729	*1812*	1829	*1912*	1929	*2012*	2029	*2112*	*2212*	*2312*	*0008*	0107
Burgdorf d.	0632	0732	0832	0932	...	1032	1132	...	1232	1332	...	1432	1532	...	1632	1732	...	1832	...	1932	...	...	...	...	...	...	...
Biberist a.	0650	0750	0850	0950	...	1050	1150	...	1250	1350	...	1450	1550	...	1650	1750	...	1850	...	1950	...	...	...	...	...	...	...
Solothurn a.	0657	0757	0857	0957	...	1057	1157	...	1257	1357	...	1457	1557	...	1657	1757	...	1857	...	1957	...	...	...	...	...	...	...

X – ⑦ (also Dec. 25, 26, Jan. 1, 2, Mar. 21, 24, May 1, 12, Aug. 1).

h – Change at Hasle-Rüegsau.

Additional services operate:
Solothurn - Burgdorf: 0448Ⓐ, 0518⚒, 0636⚒, 0736⚒, 1236⚒, 1336⚒, 1636, 1736, 1836, 2015, 2115, 2215, 2315, 0015 **X**.
Burgdorf - Thun: 0451⚒, 0517Ⓐ, 0547Ⓐ **h**, 0551†, 0647 **h**, 0847 **h**, 1047 **h**, 1247 **h**, 1447 **h**, 1647 **h**.

Thun - Burgdorf: 0503⚒ **h**, 0603 **h**, 0703 **h**, 0803 **h**, 1003 **h**, 1203 **h**, 1403 **h**, 1603 **h**.
Burgdorf - Solothurn: 0500Ⓐ, 0532Ⓐ, 0555⚒, 0632Ⓒ, 0655⚒, 1155⚒, 1255⚒, 1555, 1655, 1755, 1855Ⓒ, 2015, 2115, 2215, 2315

SBB ZÜRICH - SARGANS - CHUR 520

km		IR 757	IC 553		IR 759	IC 559	IC 169	IR 761	IC 561		IR 765	IC 565	EC 163	IR 767	IC 567		IR 769	IC 569		IR 773	IC 571		TGV 9221 (✕)	IR 775	IC 573	EC 161	IR 777
							F						♦				B						♦			♦	
	Basel SBB **510** d.	...	0514	...	0607	0622	...	0707	0722	...	...	0822	0814	0907	0922	...	...	1022	...	...	1122	...	1207	...	1222	...	1307
0	**Zürich HB** d.	0612	0637	...	0712	0737	0740	0812	0837	...	0912	0937	0940	1012	1037	...	1112	1137	...	1212	1237	...	1307	1312	1337	1340	1412
12	Thalwil d.	0622	|	...	0722	|	|	0822	|	...	0922	|	|	1022	|	...	1122	|	...	1222	|	...	|	1322	|	|	1422
24	Wädenswil d.	0632	|	...	0732	|	|	0832	|	...	0932	|	|	1032	|	...	1132	|	...	1232	|	...	|	1332	|	|	1432
33	Pfäffikon d.	0641	|	...	0741	|	|	0841	|	...	0941	|	|	1041	|	...	1141	|	...	1241	|	...	|	1341	|	|	1441
57	Ziegelbrücke d.	0659	|	...	0759	|	|	0859	|	...	0959	|	|	1059	|	...	1159	|	...	1259	|	...	|	1359	|	|	1459
90	**Sargans 534** d.	0721	0733	0748	0821	0833	0837	0921	0933	0948	1021	1033	1037	1121	1133	1148	1221	1233	1248	1321	1333	1348	1405	1421	1433	1437	1521
106	Buchs **534** a.	|	|	0759	|	|	0850	|	|	0959	|	|	1050	|	|	1159	|	|	1259	|	|	1359	|	|	|	1450	|
103	Landquart d.	0736	0743	...	0834	0843	...	0934	0943	...	1034	1043	...	1134	1143	...	1234	1243	...	1334	1343	...	1415	1434	1443	...	1534
116	**Chur** a.	0745	0752	...	0843	0852	...	0943	0952	...	1043	1052	...	1143	1152	...	1243	1252	...	1343	1352	...	1425	1443	1452	...	1543
	St Moritz **540** a.	...	*0958*	...	...	*1058*	...	...	*1158*	...	...	*1258*	...	...	*1358*	...	...	*1458*	...	...	*1558*	...	...	...	*1658*	...	...

	IC 575		EC 7	IC 577		IR 779	IC 579		IR 781	EC 103	EC 101	IC 581	EC 165	IR 785	IC 585		IR 787	IC 587		IR 789	IC 599		IR 97	EN 465	IR 793	EN 467	IR 795
			♦						Ⓑ	♦	♦	⑥	♦										♦	♦		♦	
Basel SBB **510** d.	1322	...	1407	1422	...	...	1522	...	...	1607	1622	1622	...	...	1722	...	1807	1822	...	...	...	...	2007	*2022*	...	*2122*	...
Zürich HB d.	1437	...	1512	1537	...	1612	1637	...	1712	1712	1737	1737	1740	1812	1837	...	1912	1937	...	2012	2037	...	2112	2140	2212	2240	2312
Thalwil d.	|	...	1522	|	...	1622	|	...	1722	1722	|	|	|	1822	|	...	1922	|	...	2022	|	...	2122	|	2222	|	2322
Wädenswil d.	|	...	1532	|	...	1632	|	...	1732	1732	|	|	|	1832	|	...	1932	|	...	2032	|	...	2132	|	2232	|	2332
Pfäffikon d.	|	...	1541	|	...	1641	|	...	1741	1741	|	|	|	1841	|	...	1941	|	...	2041	|	...	2141	|	2241	|	2341
Ziegelbrücke d.	|	...	1559	|	...	1659	|	...	1759	1759	|	|	|	1859	|	...	1959	|	...	2059	|	...	2159	|	2259	|	2359
Sargans 534 d.	1533	1548	1621	1633	1648	1721	1733	1748	1821	1821	1833	1833	1837	1921	1933	1948	2021	2033	2048	2121	2133	2144	2221	2237	2321	2337	0025
Buchs **534** a.	|	1559	|	|	1659	|	|	1759	|	|	|	|	1850	|	|	1959	|	|	2059	|	|	2154	|	2250	|	2350	|
Landquart d.	1543	...	1634	1643	...	1734	1743	...	1834	1834	1843	1843	...	1934	1943	...	2036	2043	...	2136	2143	...	2236	...	2336	...	0040
Chur a.	1552	...	1643	1652	...	1743	1752	...	1843	1843	1852	1852	...	1943	1952	...	2045	2052	...	2145	2152	...	2245	...	2345	...	0049
St Moritz **540** a.	*1758*	...	...	*1858*	...	...	*1958*	...	...	...	*2058*	*2058*	...	...	*2159*	...	...	*2259*	...	...	...	...	...	...	...	...	...

	EN 466	IR 758		IC 560	IR 760	EN 464	IC 562	IR 762		IC 566	IR 766		IC 568	EC 100	EC 102		IC 570	IR 770	EC 164	IC 572	EC 6		IC 574	IR 772		IC 96	IR 774
	♦			⚒		♦								♦	♦				♦		♦					♦	B
St Moritz **540** d.	...	...	...	...	...	...	...	...	...	...	...	...	*0704*	...	...	...	*0804*	...	...	*0904*	...	...	*1004*	...	...	*1104*	...
Chur d.	...	0513	...	0606	0613	...	0709	0713	...	0809	0816	...	0909	0916	0916	...	1009	1016	...	1109	1116	...	1209	1216	...	1309	1316
Landquart d.	...	0523	...	0615	0623	...	0719	0723	...	0819	0826	...	0919	0926	0926	...	1019	1026	...	1119	1126	...	1219	1226	...	1319	1326
Buchs **534** d.	0510	|	0607	|	|	0710	|	|	0801	|	|	0901	|	|	|	1001	|	|	1110	|	|	1201	|	|	1301	|	|
Sargans 534 d.	0524	0539	0622	0625	0639	0724	0728	0739	0812	0828	0839	0912	0928	0939	0939	1012	1028	1039	1124	1128	1139	1212	1228	1239	1312	1328	1339
Ziegelbrücke d.	|	0601	...	0647	0701	|	|	0801	...	|	0901	...	|	1001	1001	...	|	1101	|	|	1201	...	|	1301	...	|	1401
Pfäffikon d.	|	0619	...	|	0719	|	|	0819	...	|	0919	...	|	1019	1019	...	|	1119	|	|	1219	...	|	1319	...	|	1419
Wädenswil d.	|	0628	...	|	0728	|	|	0828	...	|	0928	...	|	1028	1028	...	|	1128	|	|	1228	...	|	1328	...	|	1428
Thalwil d.	|	0638	...	|	0738	|	|	0838	...	|	0938	...	|	1038	1038	...	|	1138	|	|	1238	...	|	1338	...	|	1438
Zürich HB a.	0620	0647	...	0723	0747	0820	0823	0847	...	0923	0947	...	1023	1047	1047	...	1123	1147	1220	1223	1247	...	1323	1347	...	1423	1447
Basel SBB **510** a.	*0738*	...	...	0838	...	*0938*	0938	...	...	1038	...	...	1138	1156	1156	...	1238	...	*1338*	1338	1356	...	1438	...	...	1538	...

		IC 578	IR 778	EC 160	IC 580	IR 782		IC 582	IR 784		TGV 9222 (✕)	EC 162	IC 586	IR 788		IC 588	IR 790	IC 168	IC 598	IR 792		IR 794		IR 796		IR 798	
				♦							♦	♦															
St Moritz **540** d.	...	*1204*	...	...	*1304*	...	...	*1404*	...	...	...	...	*1504*	...	...	*1604*	...	...	*1704*	*1704*	...	*1804*	...	*1904*	...	*2004*	...
Chur d.	...	1409	1416	...	1509	1516	...	1609	1616	...	1633	...	1709	1716	...	1809	1816	...	1909	1916	...	2013	...	2113	...	2213	...
Landquart d.	...	1419	1426	...	1519	1526	...	1619	1626	...	1645	...	1719	1726	...	1819	1826	...	1919	1926	...	2023	...	2123	...	2223	...
Buchs **534** d.	1401	|	|	1510	|	|	1601	|	|	...	|	1710	|	|	1801	|	|	1910	|	|	2010	|	2120	|	2201	|	...
Sargans 534 d.	1412	1428	1439	1524	1528	1539	1612	1628	1639	...	1655	1724	1728	1739	1812	1828	1839	1924	1928	1939	2025	2039	2135	2139	2212	2239	...
Ziegelbrücke d.	...	|	1501	|	|	1601	...	|	1701	...	|	|	|	1801	...	|	1901	|	|	2001	...	2101	...	2201	...	2301	...
Pfäffikon d.	...	|	1519	|	|	1619	...	|	1719	...	|	|	|	1819	...	|	1919	|	|	2019	...	2119	...	2219	...	2319	...
Wädenswil d.	...	|	1528	|	|	1628	...	|	1728	...	|	|	|	1828	...	|	1928	|	|	2028	...	2128	...	2228	...	2328	...
Thalwil d.	...	|	1538	|	|	1638	...	|	1738	...	|	|	|	1838	...	|	1938	|	|	2038	...	2138	...	2238	...	2338	...
Zürich HB a.	...	1523	1547	1620	1623	1647	...	1723	1747	...	1753	1820	1823	1847	...	1923	1947	2020	2023	2047	...	2147	...	2247	...	2347	...
Basel SBB **510** a.	...	1638	...	...	1738	1756	...	1838	...	...	1856	1948	1938	...	...	2038	2056	...	...	2156	...	2316	...	...	...	0116	...

♦ – **NOTES** (LISTED BY TRAIN NUMBER)

- **6** – [12] and ✕ Chur - Basel - Köln - Dortmund (- Hamburg Ⓑ, not Dec. 24, 25, 31, Mar. 21, 23, May 11, Oct. 3).
- **7** – [12] and ✕ (①–⑥, not Dec. 25, 26, Jan. 1, Mar. 22, 24, May 12, Oct. 4, Hamburg -) Dortmund - Basel - Chur.
- **96/7** – IRIS – [12] Chur - Zürich - Basel - Luxembourg - Brussels and v.v.
- **100** – ①–⑥ (also Dec. 23, 30, Mar. 23, May 11; not Dec. 26, Jan. 1, Mar. 24, May 12): [12] Chur - Zürich - Basel - Hamburg.
- **101** – Ⓑ: [12] Hamburg - Basel - Zürich - Chur.
- **102** – ⑦ (also Dec. 26, Jan. 1, Mar. 24, May 12; not Dec. 23, 30, Mar. 23, May 11): [12] Chur - Zürich - Basel - Hamburg - Kiel.
- **103** – ⑥: [12] Hamburg - Basel - Zürich - Chur.
- **160/1** – VORARLBERG – [12] Zürich - Innsbruck - Wien and v.v.
- **162/3** – TRANSALPIN – [12] and ✕ Wien - Innsbruck - Basel and v.v.
- **164/5** – KAISERIN ELISABETH – [12] and ✕ Salzburg - Innsbruck - Zürich and v.v.
- **464/5** – ZÜRICHSEE – 🛏 1, 2 cl., ▬ 2 cl. and [2] Graz - Innsbruck - Feldkirch - Zürich and v.v.; 🛏 1, 2 cl. and ▬ 2 cl. Zagreb (**414/5**) - Villach - Zürich and v.v.; [2] Beograd (**414/5**) - Zagreb - Zürich and v.v.; [12] Buchs - Zürich and v.v.
- **466/7** – WIENER WALZER – 🛏 1, 2 cl., ▬ 2 cl. and [2] [reclining] Wien - Zürich and v.v.; ▬ 2 cl. and [2] Budapest - Wien - Zürich and v.v.; 🛏 1, 2 cl. and ▬ 2 cl. Praha (**206/7**) - Linz - Zürich and v.v.; [12] Buchs - Zürich and v.v.
- **9221/2** – ⑥ Dec. 15 - Mar. 29: [12] and (✕) Paris Est - Basel - Zürich - Chur and v.v.

- **B** – [12] Chur - Zürich - Bern and v.v.
- **F** – [12] From / to Feldkirch.

SBB ZIEGELBRÜCKE - LINTHAL 522

km										Ⓒ	Ⓒ
0	Ziegelbrücke d.	0605	and	1905	2005	2105	2205	2305	EXTRA	0921	1121
11	Glarus d.	0620	hourly	1920	2020	2120	2220	2320	SERVICES	0939	1139
16	Schwanden d.	0628	until	1928	2027	2127	2227	2327	▶▶▶	0946	1146
27	Linthal ▲ a.	0646		1946	*2052*y	*2152*y	*2252*y	*2352*j		0959	1159

									Ⓒ	Ⓒ
Linthal ▲ d.	0515d	0612	and	2012	*2106*y	*2206*y	*2306*y	EXTRA	1601	1801
Schwanden d.	0534	0631	hourly	2031	2131	2231	2331	SERVICES	1614	1814
Glarus d.	0543	0641	until	2041	2141	2241	2341	▶▶▶	1623	1823
Ziegelbrücke a.	0557	0655		2055	2155	2255	2355		1637	1837

- d – ⚒ only.
- j – ⑤⑥⑦ (also Dec. 25, 26, Jan. 1, 2, Mar. 24, May 1, 12). Connection by 🚌.
- q – Also Aug. 15.
- y – Connection by 🚌.

▲ – 🚌 service **Linthal - Flüelen** Bahnhof (Table **550**) and v.v. operates **June 28 - September 28, 2008** over the Klausenpass. Ⓡ. Journey time: 2 hours 25 minutes. **NO WINTER SERVICE**.
From **Linthal**: 0805Ⓒ **q**, 0905, 1005, 1505, 1700Ⓒ **q**. From **Flüelen**: 0550Ⓒ **q**, 0730, 0930, 1450Ⓒ **q**, 1530.
Reservations: ✆ (Flüelen) 041 870 21 36.
Operator: PostAuto Zentralschweiz, Luzern. ✆ (Luzern) 041 368 10 10, fax: 041 368 10 11.

SBB LAUSANNE - PALÉZIEUX - PAYERNE 523

km																	Ⓐ										⚡Z		
0	**Lausanne 505** d.	0524	0624	0724	...	0824	0924	1024	1124	1224	...	1324	1424	1524	1624	...	1700	1724	1824	1924	2024	2124	...	2302	0002	...	0116	...	...
21	Palézieux **505** d.	0541	0641	0741	...	0841	0941	1041	1141	1241	...	1341	1441	1541	1641	...	1718	1741	1841	1941	2041	2141	...	2325	0025	...	0139	...	...
38	Moudon d.	0600	0700	0800	...	0900	1000	1100	1200	1300	...	1400	1500	1600	1700	...	1733	1800	1900	2000	2100	2200	...	2345	...	...	...	...	...
58	Payerne **508** a.	0619	0722	0821	...	0919	1019	1119	1219	1321	...	1419	1519	1619	1721	...	1752	1819	1921	2019	2119	2219	...	0004	...	...	...	...	...

			Ⓐ																											
Payerne **508** d.	0539	0639	0708	...	0738	...	0839	...	0939	1039	...	1139	1238	...	1339	1439	1539	...	1639	1736	...	1839	1939	...	2039	2139	...	2239	...	...
Moudon d.	0559	0659	0726	...	0759	...	0859	...	0959	1059	...	1159	1259	...	1359	1459	1559	...	1659	1759	...	1859	1959	...	2059	2159	...	2259	...	...
Palézieux **505** d.	0618	0718	0742	...	0818	...	0918	...	1018	1118	...	1218	1318	...	1418	1518	1618	...	1718	1818	...	1918	2018	...	2118	2218	...	2318	...	...
Lausanne 505 a.	0636	0736	0800	...	0836	...	0936	...	1036	1136	...	1236	1336	...	1436	1536	1636	...	1736	1836	...	1936	2036	...	2136	2236	...	2336	...	...

- Z – ⑥⑦ (also Jan. 1).
- ⚡ – Supplement payable.

525 ARTH GOLDAU - ST GALLEN - ROMANSHORN

SBB, SOB*

km			⚒	IR 2401	Ⓐ		IR 2405			IR 2407	IR 2409 V	IR 2411 V	IR 2415 V	IR 2417 V	IR 2419 V	IR 2421 V		IR 2423 V	IR 2425 V	IR 2427 V	IR 2429 V	IR 2431 V	IR 2435 V	IR 2437 V		
	Luzern **550** d.	...	...	...	...	...	...	...	...	...	0740	0840	0940	1040	1140	1240	...	1340	1440	1540	1640	1740	1840	1940	...	...
0	**Arth Goldau** d.	...	...	...	0523	...	...	*0618*	*0657*	...	0813	0913	1013	1113	1213	1313	...	1413	1513	1613	1713	1813	1913	2013	2114	2214
20	Biberbrugg ◐ d.	...	...	...	0547	0550	...	0650	0750	...	0835	0935	1035	1135	1235	1335	...	1435	1535	1635	1735	1835	1935	2035	2136	2236
26	Samstagern ◐ d.	...	...	...	...	0557	...	0657	0757	...	|	|	|	|	|	|	...	|	|	|	|	|	|	|	2144	2244
34	Pfäffikon d.	...	...	...	...	0615	...	0715	0815	...	0854	0954	1054	1154	1254	1354	...	1454	1554	1654	1754	1854	1954	2054	2158	2258
38	Rapperswil a.	...	...	...	...	0622	...	0722	0822	...	0859	0959	1059	1159	1259	1359	...	1459	1559	1659	1759	1859	1959	2059	2202	2302
38	Rapperswil d.	...	...	0602d	...	...	0703	...	...	0803	0903	1003	1103	1203	1303	1403	...	1503	1603	1703	1803	1903	2003	2103	2203	2303
66	Wattwil d.	...	...	0630d	...	...	0730	...	...	0830	0930	1030	1130	1230	1330	1430	...	1530	1630	1730	1830	1930	2030	2130	2230	2330
89	Herisau d.	0546	*0608*	0651	...	...	0751	...	...	0851	0951	1051	1151	1251	1351	1451	...	1551	1651	1751	1851	1951	2051	2151	2253	2353
97	**St Gallen** a.	0554	*0617*	0658	...	...	0758	...	...	0858	0958	1058	1158	1258	1358	1458	...	1558	1658	1758	1858	1958	2058	2158	2302	0002
97	**St Gallen 532** d.	0601	0631	0701	...	...	0801	...	...	0901	1001	1101	1201	1301	1401	1501	...	1601	1701	1801	1901	2001	2101	2201	2302	0002
119	**Romanshorn 532** a.	0627	0657	0727	...	...	0827	...	...	0927	1027	1127	1227	1327	1427	1527	...	1627	1727	1827	1927	2027	2127	2227	2329	0029

					IR 2408 V	IR 2410 V	IR 2412 V	IR 2416 V	IR 2418 V	IR 2420 V	IR 2422 V	IR 2424 V	IR 2426 V	IR 2428 V	IR 2430 V	IR 2432 V	IR 2436 V	IR 2438		IR 2442						
Romanshorn 532 d.	...	...	0532d	...	0634	0734	0834	0934	1034	1134	1234	1334	1434	1534	1634	1734	1834	1934	...	*2034*	...	*2134*	...	*2234*	...	2334
St Gallen 532 a.	...	...	0556d	...	0659	0759	0859	0959	1059	1159	1259	1359	1459	1559	1659	1759	1859	1959	...	*2059*	...	*2159*	...	*2259*	...	2359
St Gallen d.	...	...	0557	...	0702	0802	0902	1002	1102	1202	1302	1402	1502	1602	1702	1802	1902	2002	...	2102	...	2202	...	2302	...	0002
Herisau d.	...	...	0606	...	0710	0810	0910	1010	1110	1210	1310	1410	1510	1610	1710	1810	1910	2010	...	2110	...	2211	...	2311	...	0011
Wattwil d.	...	...	0630	...	0732	0832	0932	1032	1132	1232	1332	1432	1532	1632	1732	1832	1932	2032	...	2132	...	2232	...	2332	...	0032
Rapperswil a.	...	...	0657	...	0757	0857	0957	1057	1157	1257	1357	1457	1557	1657	1757	1857	1957	2057	...	2157	...	2257	...	2357	...	...
Rapperswil d.	0559	0636	0700	...	0800	0900	1000	1100	1200	1300	1400	1500	1600	1700	1800	1900	2000	...	2103	...	2203	...	2303	...	0003	...
Pfäffikon d.	0606	0647	0706	...	0806	0906	1006	1106	1206	1306	1406	1506	1606	1706	1806	1906	2006	...	2107	...	2207	...	2307	...	0007	...
Samstagern ◐ d.	0615	0658	0715	...	|	|	|	|	|	|	|	|	|	|	|	|	|	...	2118	...	2218	...	2320	...	0020	...
Biberbrugg ◐ d.	*0625*	*0706*	0724	...	0824	0924	1024	1124	1224	1324	1424	1524	1624	1724	1824	1924	2024	...	2125	...	2225	...	...	...	...	...
Arth Goldau a.	*0650*	*0730*	0746	...	0846	0946	1046	1146	1246	1346	1446	1546	1646	1746	1846	1946	2046	...	2150	...	2250	...	...	...	...	...
Luzern **550** a.	...	...	*0837*	...	0919	1019	1119	1219	1319	1419	1519	1619	1719	1819	1919	2019	2119	...	...	...	...	...	...	...	...	...

d – ⚒ only.

V – VORALPEN EXPRESS – (12) Luzern - Rapperswil - St Gallen - Romanshorn and v.v. Also conveys (🍷) or 🍷 on most services.

◐ – For service to Einsiedeln see panel below.

* – Operated by SOB, except Rapperswil - Wattwil (SBB).

km				Ⓐ								
0	**Wädenswil** d.	0559	0629	0659	0734	0804	and every 30 minutes until	2204	2234	2304	2334	0004
6	Samstagern d.	0607	0637	0707	0741	0811		2211	2241	2321	2341	0021
11	Biberbrugg ● d.	0620	0650	0720	0750	0820		2220	2250	2328	2350	0028
17	**Einsiedeln** ● a.	0627	0657	0727	0757	0827		2227	2257	2334	2357	0034

			Ⓐ								
Einsiedeln ● d.	0518	0600	0630	0659	0730	0800	and every 30 minutes until	2230	2300	2327	...
Biberbrugg ● d.	0524	0607	0637	0707	0737	0807		2237	2307	2337	...
Samstagern d.	0534	0615	0645	0715	0745	0815		2245	2315	2345	...
Wädenswil a.	0543	0624	0654	0724	0754	0824		2254	2324	2354	...

● – Additional services run Biberbrugg - Einsiedeln and v.v.

526 GOSSAU - APPENZELL - WASSERAUEN

Narrow gauge. AB

km		⚒																									
0	**Gossau** d.	0548	0647	0717	0747	0817	0847	0917	0947	1017	1047	1117	1147	1247	1347	1447	1517	1547	1617	1647	1717	1747	1847	1947	2047	2147	2312
5	Herisau a.	0553	0653	0723	0753	0823	0853	0923	0953	1023	1053	1123	1153	1253	1353	1453	1523	1553	1623	1653	1723	1753	1853	1953	2053	2153	2318
5	Herisau d.	0554a	0654	0724	0754p	0824	0854	0924p	0954	1024p	1054	1124	1154	1254	1354	1454	1524	1554	1624	1654	1724	1754	1854	1954	2054	2154	2319
15	Urnäsch d.	0608a	0708	0738	0808p	0838	0908	0938p	1008	1038p	1108	1138	1208	1308	1408	1508	1538	1608	1638	1708	1738	1808	1908	2008	2108	2208	2333
26	**Appenzell** d.	0630a	0730	0800	0830p	0900	0930	1000p	1030	1100p	1130	1200	1230	1330	1430	1530	1600	1630	1657	1730	1800	1833	1927	2027	2127	2227	2350
32	**Wasserauen** a.	0641a	0741	0811	0841p	0911	0941	1011p	1041	1111p	1141	1211a	1241	1341	1441	1541	1611p	1641	...	1741	1811a	1844	*1941*y	*2041*y	*2141*y	...	...

																									🚌p	
Wasserauen d.	...	...	0646a	0749	0819	0849p	0919	0949p	1019	1119	1149a	1219	1310	1419	1519	1549p	1619	1649p	1719	1749a	1819	1849	...	*1942*y	*2042*y	2142	...
Appenzell d.	0603a	0633	0703a	0803	0833	0903p	0933	1003p	1033	1133	1203	1233	1333	1433	1533	1603	1633	1703	1733	1803	1833	1903	1933a	2003	2103	2153	2203
Urnäsch d.	0620a	0650	0720a	0820	0850	0920p	0950	1020p	1050	1150	1220	1250	1350	1450	1550	1620	1650	1720	1750	1820	1850	1920	1950a	2020	2120	...	2220
Herisau a.	0636a	0706	0736a	0836	0906	0936p	1006	1036p	1106	1206	1236	1306	1406	1506	1606	1636	1706	1736	1806	1836	1906	1936	2006a	2036	2136	...	2236
Herisau d.	0637	0707	0737	0837	0907	0937	1007	1037	1107	1207	1237	1307	1407	1507	1607	1637	1707	1737	1807	1837	1907	1937	2007	2037	2137	...	2237
Gossau a.	0643	0713	0743	0843	0913	0943	1013	1043	1113	1213	1243	1313	1413	1513	1613	1643	1713	1743	1813	1843	1913	1943	2013	2043	2143	...	2243

a – Ⓐ only. **p** – May 18 - Oct. 26. **y** – Connection by 🚌.

527 ST GALLEN - APPENZELL

Narrow gauge rack railway. AB

km		⚒	⚒	Ⓐ	🚌Ⓒ			⚒							q							Ⓐ		🚌	🚌	🚌z
0	**St Gallen** d.	0605	0642a	0705	0723	0742d	0811	0837	0907	0937	and every 30 minutes until	1637	1707	1737	1752	1807	1837	1907	1937	2007	2037	2107	2137	2230	2330	0030
7	Teufen d.	0622	0659a	0722	0735	0759d	0828	0854	0924	0954		1654	1724	1754	1808	1824	1854	1924	1954	2024	2054	2124	2154	2242	2342	0042
14	Gais ▲ d.	0637	0713	0737	0746	0813	0848	0910	0940	1010		1710	1740	1810	1820	1840	1910	1940	2010	2039	2109	2139	2210	2252	2352	0052
20	**Appenzell** a.	0649	0724	0749	0757	0824	0859	0921	0951	1021		1721	1751	1821p	1831	1851	1921	1951	2021	*2057*y	*2121*y	...	2221	*2307*	0002	0102

	⚒	Ⓐ	Ⓐ	⚒		⚒									Ⓒ	Ⓐ							🚌	🚌	🚌
Appenzell d.	0508	0611	0635	0650	0711	0750	0811a	0834	0908d	0938	1008	and every 30 minutes until	1638	1708	1738	1738	1808	1838	1908	1938	2008	2038	2108	2155	*2246*
Gais ▲ d.	0520	0623	0646	0700	0723	0800	0823	0850	0920	0950	1020		1650	1720	1750	1755	1820	1850	1920	1950	2020	2050	2117	2204	2258
Teufen d.	0534	0637	0701	0712	0737	0812	0837	0903	0933	1003	1033		1703	1733	1803	1808	1833	1903	1933	2003	2033a	2103	2127	2213	2308
St Gallen a.	0555	0656	0720	0732	0756	0832	0856	0920	0950	1020	1050		1720	1750	1820	1825	1850	1920	1950	2020	2050a	2120	2140	*2228*	2321

a – Ⓐ only.
d – ⚒ only.
p – Ⓒ (daily Dec. 22 - Jan. 2, July 7 - Aug. 8; also Apr. 30, May 2).
q – Ⓐ Dec. 10 - 21, Jan. 3 - July 4, Aug. 11 - Dec. 12 (not Apr. 30, May 2).
y – Connection by 🚌.
z – ⑥⑦ (not Mar. 22).

▲ – Rail service **Gais - Altstätten Stadt** and v.v. *8 km*. Journey time: 22 minutes. **Operator**: AB.
From **Gais**: 0552Ⓐ🚌, 0652Ⓐ, 0700⑥🚌, 0700†, 0800, 0851 and hourly until 1751, 1911🚌, 2011🚌.
From **Altstätten Stadt**: 0617Ⓐ🚌, 0717Ⓐ, 0725⑥🚌, 0725†, 0828 and hourly until 1828, 1928🚌, 2028🚌.
A bus connects Altstätten Stadt with Altstätten SBB station (Table **534**). Journey time: 7 minutes.

528 LOCARNO - DOMODOSSOLA

FART

km				h 🍷	🍷	🍷	C 🍷	h	P 🍷	Cj 🍷	S	
0	**Locarno** d.	0650	0812	0950	1050	1212	1412	1455	1612	1630	1750	1912
20	Camedo 🏛 d.	0729	0847	1032	1132	1252	1447	1532	1650	1709	1832	1949
26	Re ⊗ d.	0744	0903	1047	1145	1307	1503	1547	1705	1724	1847	2004
34	S M Maggiore § ⊗ d.	0755	0915	1057	1155	1317	1515	1605	1716	1736	1857	2015
53	**Domodossola** a.	0835	0956	1140	1235	1356	1556	1645	1756	1817	1936	2056

		j 🍷	C 🍷	j 🍷	P 🍷	🍷	P 🍷	🍷	⊡	
Domodossola d.	0525r	0925	1005	1025	1128	1205	1405	1525	1805	2025
S. M. Maggiore § ⊗ d.	0606r	1004	1045	1104	1209	1245	1444	1605	1845	2105
Re ⊗ d.	0614	1016	1057	1115	1220	1259	1455	1616	1857	2117
Camedo 🏛 d.	0630	1032	1113	1131	1236	1318	1514	1632	1913	2133
Locarno a.	0710	1110	1155	1210	1312	1355	1555	1710	1955	2210

C – Conveys observation cars (supplement payable).
P – Conveys observation cars Mar. 16 - Oct. 26 (supplement payable).
S – Conveys observation cars Mar. 16 - June 7, Sept. 8 - Oct. 26 (supplement payable).
h – Mar. 16 - Oct. 26.
j – † Mar. 16 - June 8; daily June 9 - Sept. 6; ⑦ Sept. 7 - Oct. 26.
r – ①–⑤ only.
⊡ – Conveys 🍷 Apr. 6 - Oct. 26.
⊗ – Request stop.
§ – Full name is Santa Maria Maggiore.

529 ZÜRICH - ZÜRICH FLUGHAFEN ✈

Journey time: 9 - 13 minutes

Additional services are available at peak times

From **Zürich Hbf:**
0502, 0527, 0539, 0545, 0601, 0607, 0610, 0617, 0627, 0637, 0639, 0647, 0707, 0710, 0717, 0727, 0737, 0739, 0747, 0801, 0807, 0810, 0817, 0827, 0837, 0839, 0847, and xx01, xx07, xx10, xx17, xx27, xx37, xx39, xx47 minutes past each hour until 2001, 2007, 2010, 2017, 2027, 2039, 2047, then 2107, 2110, 2117, 2127, 2139, 2147, 2207, 2210, 2217, 2227, 2239, 2247, 2307, 2310, 2327, 0017.

From **Zürich Flughafen:**
0503, 0546, 0602, 0613, 0620, 0632, 0633, 0639, 0643, 0702, 0709, 0713, 0720, 0732, 0739, 0743, 0802, 0809, 0813, 0820, 0832, 0839, 0843, 0847, 0902, 0909, 0913, 0920, 0932, 0939, 0943, 0947, and xx02, xx09, xx13, xx20, xx32, xx39, xx43, xx47 minutes past each hour until 2002, 2009, 2013, 2020, 2032, 2039, 2043, 2047, then 2102, 2113, 2120, 2132, 2139, 2143, 2202, 2213, 2220, 2232, 2234, 2239, 2243, 2302, 2320, 2339, 2343, 0010, 0043⑥⑦.

SBB — ZÜRICH - ST GALLEN — 530

km		*IC* 705	*ICN* 507	*IC* 707		*ICN* 509	*EC* 191	*IC* 709	*ICN* 1511	*IC* 711		*ICN* 515	*EC* 193	*IC* 715	*ICN* 1517	*IC* 717	*ICN* 519	*IC* 719		*ICN* 1521	*IC* 721	*ICN* 523	*EC* 195	*IC* 723
							M	**F**					**M**										**M**	
	Genève Aéroport ✈ **505** ....d.	...	...	...	...	...	...	...	...	...	...	...	...	0636	...	0736	0805	0836	...	...	0936	1005	...	1036
	Genève **505** ....d.	...	...	...	...	...	...	...	...	0536	...	0614	...	0645	...	0745	0814	0845	...	...	0945	1014	...	1045
	Lausanne **505** ....d.	...	...	...	...	...	...	...	0539	0620	...	|	...	0720	0745	0820	|	0920	...	0945	1020	|	...	1120
	Biel **500** ....d.	...	...	...	...	0543	...	...	0644	|	...	0745	...	|	0845	|	0945	|	...	1045	|	1145	...	|
	Bern **500** ....d.	...	...	...	...	|	...	0632	|	0732	...	|	...	0832	|	0932	|	1032	...	|	1132	|	...	1232
0	**Zürich HB 535** ....d.	0539	0610	0639	...	0710	0716	0739	0810	0839	...	0910	0916	0939	1010	1039	1110	1139	...	1210	1239	1310	1316	1339
10	**Zürich Flughafen** ✈ **535** ....d.	0552	0622	0652	...	0722	0728	0752	0822	0852	...	0922	0928	0952	1022	1052	1122	1152	...	1222	1252	1322	1328	1352
30	Winterthur **535** ....d.	0607	0637	0707	...	0737	0742	0807	0837	0907	...	0937	0942	1007	1037	1107	1137	1207	...	1237	1307	1337	1342	1407
57	Wil **539** ....d.	0625	0654	0725	...	0754	|	0825	0854	0925	...	0954	|	1025	1054	1125	1154	1225	...	1254	1325	1354	|	1425
78	Gossau ....d.	0645	0710	0745	...	0807	|	0845	0907	0945	...	1007	|	1045	1107	1145	1207	1245	...	1307	1345	1407	|	1445
87	**St Gallen** ....a.	0653	0717	0753	...	0815	0818	0853	0915	0953	...	1015	1018	1053	1115	1153	1215	1253	...	1315	1353	1415	1418	1453

	ICN 1525	*IC* 725	*ICN* 527	*IC* 727	*ICN* 1529	*IC* 729	*ICN* 531	*IR* 3831	*IC* 731	*ICN* 1535	*EC* 197	*IC* 735	*ICN* 537	*IC* 737	*ICN* 1539	*IC* 739		*ICN* 541	*IC* 741	*ICN* 1543	*IR* 3841	*ICN* 545	*ICN* 1547	
								Ⓐ			**M**													
Genève Aéroport ✈ **505** ....d.	...	1136	1205	1236	...	1336	1405	...	1436	...	...	1536	1605	1636	...	1736	...	1805	1836	...	...	2005	...	...
Genève **505** ....d.	...	1145	1214	1245	...	1345	1414	...	1445	...	...	1545	1614	1645	...	1745	...	1814	1845	...	...	2014	...	...
Lausanne **505** ....d.	1145	1220	|	1320	1345	1420	|	...	1520	1545	...	1620	|	1720	1745	1820	...	|	1920	1945	...	|	2145	...
Biel **500** ....d.	1245	|	1345	|	1445	|	1545	...	|	1645	...	|	1745	|	1845	|	...	1945	|	2045	...	2145	2245	...
Bern **500** ....d.	|	1332	|	1432	|	1532	|	...	1632	|	...	1732	|	1832	|	1932	...	|	2032	|	...	|	|	...
Zürich HB 535 ....d.	1410	1439	1510	1539	1610	1639	1710	1733	1739	1810	1816	1839	1910	1939	2010	2039	...	2110	2139	2210	2239	2310	0017	...
Zürich Flughafen ✈ **535** ....d.	1422	1452	1522	1552	1622	1652	1722	1745	1752	1822	1828**u**	1852	1922	1952	2022	2052	...	2122	2152	2222	2252	2322	0029	...
Winterthur **535** ....d.	1437	1507	1537	1607	1637	1707	1737	1800	1807	1837	1842**u**	1907	1937	2007	2037	2107	...	2137	2207	2237	2307	2337	0044	...
Wil **539** ....d.	1454	1525	1554	1625	1654	1725	1754	|	1825	1854	|	1925	1954	2025	2054	2125	...	2154	2225	2254	2325	2354	0100	...
Gossau ....d.	1507	1545	1607	1645	1707	1745	1807	|	1845	1907	|	1945	2007	2045	2107	2145	...	2207	2245	2310	2345	0011	0118	...
St Gallen ....a.	1515	1553	1615	1653	1715	1753	1815	1839	1853	1915	1919**u**	1953	2015	2053	2115	2153	...	2215	2253	2317	2353	0018	0125	...

		IC 708	*ICN* 1510	*IC* 710	*ICN* 512	*IR* 3810	*IC* 712	*ICN* 1516	*IC* 716	*ICN* 518		*IC* 718	*ICN* 1520	*IC* 720	*EC* 196	*ICN* 522	*IC* 722	*ICN* 1524		*IC* 724	*ICN* 526	*IC* 726	*ICN* 1528	*IC* 728
						R									**M**									
St Gallen ....d.	0432	0511	0544	0611	0642	0644	0711	0748	0811	0848	...	0911	0948	1011	1042	1048	1111	1148	...	1211	1248	1311	1348	1411
Gossau ....d.	0439	0519	0551	0619	0650	0652	0719	0756	0819	0856	...	0919	0956	1019	|	1056	1119	1156	...	1219	1256	1319	1356	1419
Wil **539** ....d.	0456	0539	0610	0639	0706	0711	0739	0810	0839	0910	...	0939	1010	1039	|	1110	1139	1210	...	1239	1310	1339	1410	1439
Winterthur **535** ....d.	0515	0558	0628	0658	0725	0733	0758	0828	0858	0928	...	0958	1028	1058	1119	1128	1158	1228	...	1258	1328	1358	1428	1458
Zürich Flughafen ✈ **535** ....a.	0529	0611	0641	0711	0737	|	0811	0841	0911	0941	...	1011	1041	1111	1132	1141	1211	1241	...	1311	1341	1411	1441	1511
Zürich HB 535 ....a.	...	0623	0653	0723	0749	0759	0823	0853	0923	0953	...	1023	1053	1123	1144	1153	1223	1253	...	1323	1353	1423	1453	1523
Bern **500** ....a.	...	0729	|	0829	|	...	0929	|	1029	|	...	1129	|	1229	...	|	1329	|	...	1429	|	1529	|	1629
Biel **500** ....a.	...	|	0813	|	0913	...	|	1013	|	1113	...	|	1213	|	...	1313	|	1413	...	|	1513	|	1613	|
Lausanne **505** ....a.	...	0840	0915	0940	|	...	1040	1115	1140	|	...	1240	1315	1340	...	|	1440	1515	...	1540	|	1640	1715	1740
Genève **505** ....a.	...	0915	...	1015	1046	...	1115	...	1215	1246	...	1315	...	1415	...	1446	1515	...	...	1615	1646	1715	...	1815
Genève Aéroport ✈ **505** ....a.	...	0924	...	1024	1055	...	1124	...	1224	1255	...	1324	...	1424	...	1455	1524	...	...	1624	1655	1724	...	1824

	ICN 530	*IC* 730	*EC* 194	*ICN* 1532	*IC* 732	*ICN* 536		*IC* 736	*ICN* 1538	*IC* 738	*ICN* 1540	*IC* 740		*EC* 192	*ICN* 1542	*IC* 742	*ICN* 1544	*IC* 744		*EC* 190	*ICN* 1546	*ICN* 548	*ICN* 500	
			M											**M**		**F**				**M**			⑤⑥	
St Gallen ....d.	1448	1511	1542	1548	1611	1648	...	1711	1748	1811	1848	1911	...	1942	1948	2011	2048	2111	...	2142	2144	2244	2344	...
Gossau ....d.	1456	1519	|	1556	1619	1656	...	1719	1756	1819	1856	1919	...	|	1956	2019	2056	2119	...	|	2151	2251	2351	...
Wil **539** ....d.	1510	1539	|	1610	1639	1710	...	1739	1810	1839	1910	1939	...	|	2010	2039	2110	2139	...	|	2210	2310	0010	...
Winterthur **535** ....d.	1528	1558	1619	1628	1658	1728	...	1758	1828	1858	1928	1958	...	2019	2028	2058	2128	2158	...	2219	2228	2328	0028	...
Zürich Flughafen ✈ **535** ....a.	1541	1611	1632	1641	1711	1741	...	1811	1841	1911	1941	2011	...	2032	2041	2111	2141	2211	...	2232	2241	2341	0041	...
Zürich HB 535 ....a.	1553	1623	1644	1653	1723	1753	...	1823	1853	1923	1953	2023	...	2044	2053	2123	2153	2223	...	2244	2253	2353	0055	...
Bern **500** ....a.	|	1729	...	|	1829	|	...	1929	|	2029	|	2129	...	...	|	2229	|	2332	...	...	|	...	...	...
Biel **500** ....a.	1713	|	...	1813	|	1913	...	|	2013	|	2113	|	...	...	2213	...	2314	...	...	...	0022	...	...	...
Lausanne **505** ....a.	|	1840	...	1915	1940	|	...	2040	2115	2140	2215	2240	...	...	2315	...	0015	...	...	...	...	...	...	...
Genève **505** ....a.	1846	1915	...	...	2015	2046	...	2115	...	2215	...	2318	...	...	...	...	...	...	...	...	...	...	...	...
Genève Aéroport ✈ **505** ....a.	1855	1924	...	...	2024	2055	...	2124	...	2224	...	2327	...	...	...	...	...	...	...	...	...	...	...	...

F – From/to Fribourg.
M – 🚃12 Zürich - München and v.v.
R – Ⓐ: 🚃12 Rorschach - Zürich.
u – Stops to pick up only.

SBB — WINTERTHUR - SCHAFFHAUSEN — 531

			Ⓐ				Ⓐ			Ⓐ	Ⓐ			Ⓐ	Ⓐ			Ⓐ			Ⓐ			
Winterthur ....d.	0542	0606	0619	0642	and at the same	1606	1619	1642	1706	1719	1730	1742	1806	1819	1830	1842	1906	1919	1942	2006	2019	2042	2142	2242	2342
Schaffhausen ....a.	0614	0638	0644	0714	minutes past each hour until	1638	1644	1714	1738	1744	1759	1814	1838	1844	1859	1914	1938	1944	2014	2038	2044	2114	2214	2314	0014

km																								
				Ⓐ		Ⓐ			Ⓐ	Ⓐ				Ⓐ				Ⓐ						
0	Schaffhausen .. d.	0521	0544	0614	0621	0631	0643	...	0701	0714	0721	0744	...	0814	0821	0846	and at the same	2014	2021	2046	...	2146	2246	2346	...
30	Winterthur ..... a.	0554	0619	0642	0654	0659	0719	...	0729	0742	0754	0819	...	0842	0854	0919	minutes past each hour until	2042	2054	2119	...	2219	2319	0019	...

SBB, THURBO* — SCHAFFHAUSEN - ROMANSHORN - RORSCHACH — 532

km																									
0	**Schaffhausen 939/40** ... d.	...	0531	0601	0631	0701	0731	0801	0901	1001	1101	1131	1201		1731	1801	1831	1901	1931	...	2031	...	*2131*	*2201*	2301
20	Stein am Rhein .... d.	0527	0557	0627	0657	0727	0757	0825	0925	1025	1125	1157	1227		1757	1827	1857	1927	1957	...	2057	...	*2157*	2301	2327
46	**Kreuzlingen** .... a.	0556	0626	0656	0726	0756	0826	▬	▬	▬	▬	1226	1256	and at	1826	1856	1926	1956	2026	...	2126	...	*2226*	2327	2356
46	**Kreuzlingen** .... d.	0600	0630	0700	0730	0800	0830	0900	1000	1100	1200	1230	1300	the same	1830	1900	1930	2000	2030	2100	2130	2200	2300	2330	...
47	Kreuzlingen Hafen .... d.	0602	0632	0702	0732	0802	0832	0902	1002	1102	1202	1232	1302	minutes	1832	1902	1932	2002	2032	2102	2132	2202	2302	2332	...
65	**Romanshorn** .... a.	0625	0655	0725	0755	0825	0855	0925	1025	1125	1225	1255	1325	past each	1855	1925	1955	2025	2055	2125	2155	2225	2325	2355	...
65	**Romanshorn** .... d.	0628	0704**d**	0732	0804	0832	0904	0932	1032	1132	1232	1304	1332	hour	1904	1932	...	2032	...	2132	...	2232	2332	...	...
	St Gallen **525** .... a.	|	0729**d**	|	0829	|	0929	|	|	|	|	1329	|	until	1929	|	...	|	...	|	...	|	|	...	...
73	Arbon .... a.	0636	...	0741	...	0841	...	0941	1041	1141	1241	...	1341		...	1941	...	2041	...	2141	...	2241	2341	...	...
79	Rorschach Hafen .... a.	0643	...	0748	...	0848	...	0948	1048	1148	1248	...	1348		...	1948	...	2048	...	2148	...	2248	2348	...	...
80	**Rorschach** .... a.	0647	...	0752	...	0852	...	0952	1052	1152	1252	...	1352		...	1952	...	2052	...	2152	...	2252	2352	...	...

Rorschach .... d.	...	0607	...	0707	...	0807	...	0907	...	1007	...	1107	...		1807	...	1907	...	2007	...	2107	...	2207	2307	...
Rorschach Hafen .... d.	...	0608	...	0708	...	0808	...	0908	...	1008	...	1108	...		1808	...	1908	...	2008	...	2108	...	2208	2308	...
Arbon .... d.	...	0617	...	0717	...	0817	...	0917	...	1017	...	1117	...	and at	1817	...	1917	...	2017	...	2117	...	2217	2317	...
St Gallen **525** .... d.	...	|	0631**d**	|	0731**d**	|	0831	|	0931	|	1031	|	1131	the same	|	1831	|	1931	|	...	|	...	|	|	...
Romanshorn .... a.	...	0627	0657**d**	0727	0757**d**	0827	0857	0927	0957	1027	1057	1127	1157	minutes	1827	1857	1927	1957	2027	...	2127	...	2227	2327	...
Romanshorn .... d.	0602	0632	0702	0732	0802	0832	0902	0932	1002	1032	1102	1132	1202	past each	1832	1902	1932	2002	2032	2102	2132	2202	2232	2332	0032
Kreuzlingen Hafen .... d.	0624	0654	0724	0754	0824	0854	0924	0954	1024	1054	1124	1154	1224	hour	1854	1924	1954	2024	2054	2124	2154	2224	2254	2354	0054
Kreuzlingen .... a.	0626	0656	0726	0756	0826	0856	0926	0956	1026	1056	1126	1156	1226	until	1856	1926	1956	2026	2056	2126	2156	2226	2256	2356	0056
Kreuzlingen .... d.	0631	0701	0731	▬	0831	▬	0931	▬	1031	▬	1131	1201	1231		1901	1931	▬	2031	▬	2131	▬	2231	*2331*	...	...
Stein am Rhein .... d.	0700	0730	0800	0830	0900	0930	1000	1030	1100	1130	1200	1230	1300		1930	2000	2030	2100	2130	2200	2230	2257	*2357*	...	...
Schaffhausen 939/40 ... a.	0726	0756	0826	0856	0926	0956	1026	1056	1126	1156	1226	1256	1326		1956	2026	2056	2126	2156	2226	2256	...	...	...	...

d – ⚒ only.
* – SBB operate Romanshorn - Rorschach; THURBO operate Schaffhausen - Romanshorn.

533 SCHAFFHAUSEN - KREUZLINGEN
Valid March 21 - October 19 (no winter service) URh

		✕A		✕B		✕A		✕A	
Schaffhausen d.	...	0910	...	1110	...	1310	...	1510	...
Stein am Rhein d.	...	1115	...	1315	...	1515	...	1715	...
Kreuzlingen Hafen a.	...	1350	...	1550	...	1750	...	1950y	...

		✕A		✕A		✕A		✕B	
Kreuzlingen Hafen d.	...	0900	...	1100	...	1400	...	1600	...
Stein am Rhein d.	...	1130	...	1330	...	1630	...	1830	...
Schaffhausen a.	...	1245	...	1445	...	1745	...	1945y	...

A – Ⓒ Mar. 21 - Apr. 20; daily Apr. 26 - Oct. 19. B – † Apr. 27 - June 29; daily July 5 - Sept. 7; † Sept. 14 - Oct. 3 (also May 22, Oct. 3). y – Not Aug. 9.

534 ST GALLEN - BUCHS - CHUR
SBB

Subject to alteration on Ⓒ Aug. 9 - 17

km		*RE* 3803	*RE* 3805	*RE* 3807	*EC* 191 M	*RE* 3809	*RE* 3811	*EC* 193 M	*RE* 3815	*RE* 3817	*RE* 3819	*RE* 3821	*EC* 195 M	*RE* 3823	*RE* 3825	*RE* 3827	*RE* 3829	*RE* 3833	*IR* 787	*EC* 197 M	*RE* 3835	*RE* 3837	*IR* 97		
0	**St Gallen** d.	0600	0704	0804	0819	0904	1004	1019	1104	1204	1304	1404	1419	1504	1604	1704	1804	1904	...	1919	2004	2104	...	2221	2321
16	Rorschach d.	0621	0721	0821	|	0921	1021	|	1121	1221	1321	1421	|	1521	1621	1721	1821	1921	...	|	2021	2121	...	2240	2340
27	**St Margrethen** d.	0631	0731	0831	0840	0931	1031	1040	1131	1231	1331	1431	1440	1531	1631	1731	1831	1931	...	1940	2031	2131	...	2251	2351
39	Altstätten **527** d.	0642	0742	0842	...	0942	1042	...	1142	1242	1342	1442	...	1542	1642	1742	1842	1942	...	...	2042	2142	...	2303	0003
65	**Buchs 520** ⊖ d.	0701	0801	0901	...	1001	1101	...	1201	1301	1401	1501	...	1601	1701	1801	1901	2001	...	...	2101	2201	...	2325	0025
81	Sargans **520** ⊖ d.	0713	0813	0913	...	1013	1113	...	1213	1313	1413	1513	...	1613	1713	1813	1913	2012	2021	...	2113	2212	2221	2338	0038
93	Landquart **520** d.	0728	0828	0928	...	1028	1128	...	1228	1328	1428	1528	...	1628	1728	1828	1928	...	2036	...	2128	...	2236	...	...
107	**Chur 520** a.	0738	0838	0938	...	1038	1138	...	1238	1338	1438	1538	...	1638	1738	1838	1938	...	2045	...	2138	...	2245	...	...
	St Moritz **540** a.	*0958*	*1058*	*1158*	...	*1258*	*1358*	...	*1458*	*1358*	*1658*	*1758*	...	*1858*	*1958*	*2058*	*2159*	...	*2259*	...	...	...	...	...	...

			IR 758	*RE* 3812	*RE* 3816	*RE* 3818	*RE* 3820	*EC* 196 M	*RE* 3822	*RE* 3824	*RE* 3826	*RE* 3828	*IC* 96	*RE* 3830	*EC* 194 M	*RE* 3832	*RE* 3834	*RE* 3836	*RE* 3838	*EC* 192 M	*RE* 3840	*RE* 3842	*EC* 190 M	*IR* 794	*RE* 3844
St Moritz **540** d.	...	...	...	...	...	...	...	...	*0704*	*0804*	*0904*	*1004*	*1104*	*1104*	...	*1204*	*1304*	*1404*	*1504*	...	*1604*	*1704*	...	*1804*	...
Chur 520 d.	...	...	0513	...	0622	0722	0822	...	0922	1022	1122	1222	1309	1322	...	1422	1522	1622	1722	...	1822	1922	...	2013	...
Landquart **520** d.	...	...	0523	...	0633	0733	0833	...	0933	1033	1133	1233	1319	1333	...	1433	1533	1633	1733	...	1833	1933	...	2023	...
Sargans **520** ⊖ d.	...	...	0537	0541	0648	0748	0848	...	0948	1048	1148	1248	1327	1348	...	1448	1548	1648	1748	...	1848	1948	...	2037	2048
Buchs 520 ⊖ d.	...	...	...	0600	0701	0801	0901	...	1001	1101	1201	1301	...	1401	...	1501	1601	1701	1801	...	1901	2001	...	...	2101
Altstätten **527** d.	...	0551	...	0615	0717	0817	0917	...	1017	1117	1217	1317	...	1417	...	1517	1617	1717	1817	...	1917	2017	...	...	2117
St Margrethen d.	0508	0605	...	0626	0729	0829	0929	1020	1029	1129	1229	1329	...	1429	1520	1529	1629	1729	1829	1920	1929	2029	2120	...	2129
Rorschach d.	0519	0619	...	0637	0740	0840	0940	|	1040	1140	1240	1340	...	1440	|	1540	1640	1740	1840	|	1940	2040	|	...	2140
St Gallen a.	0538	0638	...	0655	0756	0856	0956	1041	1056	1156	1256	1356	...	1456	1541	1556	1656	1756	1856	1941	1956	2056	2141	...	2156

⊖ – 🚌 services to **VADUZ (LIECHTENSTEIN)**

[line 12]	⚒	⚒							and at the				⑥										
Buchs (Bahnhof) d.	0533	0603	0633	0703	0733	...	0803	0833	same minutes	1603	1633	1703	1733	1803	1833	1903	1933	2003	2033	2103	2133	2203	2233
Vaduz Post d.	0550	0620	0650	0720	0750	...	0820	0850	past each	1620	1650	1720	1750	1820	1850	1920	1950	2020	2050	2120	2150	2220	2250
Sargans (Bahnhof) a.	0621	0651	0721	0751	0821	...	0851	0921	hour until	1651	1721	1751	1821	1851	1921	1951	2021	2051	2121	...	2221	...	2321j

[line 12]	⚒									and at the											Ⓑ	k	
Sargans (Bahnhof) d.	0606	0636	0706	0736	0806	0836	...	0906	0936	same minutes	1806	1836	...	1906	1936	2006	2036	2106	2136	...	2226	2346	...
Vaduz Post d.	0638	0708	0738	0808	0838	0908	...	0938	1008	past each	1838	1908	...	1938	2008	2038	2108	2138	2208	...	2256	0016	...
Buchs (Bahnhof) a.	0655	0725	0755	0825	0855	0925	...	0955	1025	hour until	1855	1925	...	1955	2025	2055	2125	2155	2225	...	...	...	...

🚌 [line 14] **Feldkirch** (Bahnhof) - **Vaduz** (Post) and v.v. Journey time: 36 minutes. Service shown operates on Ⓐ; a reduced service operates on Ⓒ.
Operator: Liechtenstein Bus Anstalt LBA, Städtle 38, 9490 Vaduz. ✆ +423 236 63 10, fax +423 236 63 11.

From **Feldkirch**: 0620, 0650, 0720, 0750 and hourly until 1550, then 1620, 1650, 1720, 1750, 1820, 1850, 1950.

From **Vaduz**: 0632, 0702, 0732 and hourly until 1532, then 1602, 1632, 1702, 1732, 1802, 1832, 1902.

M – 🚆12 Zürich HB - München and v.v. j – ⑤⑥ (not Mar. 21, Aug. 1, 15). k – ⑤⑥ (also Dec. 8; not Feb. 2, Nov. 1).

535 ZÜRICH - KONSTANZ and ROMANSHORN
SBB

km		*IC* 807	*ICN* 2107	*IC* 809 S	*ICN* 2109	*IC* 811	*ICN* 2111	*IC* 815	*ICN* 2115	*IC* 817	*ICN* 2117	*IC* 819	*ICN* 2119	*IC* 821	*ICN* 2121	*IC* 823	*ICN* 2123	*IC* 825	*ICN* 2125	*IC* 827	*ICN* 2127	*IC* 829	*ICN* 2129	*IC* 831	*ICN* 2131	*ICN* 933 Ⓐ
	Brig **560** d.	...	...	...	...	0545	...	0649	...	0749	...	0849	...	0949	...	1049	...	1149	...	1249	...	1349	...	1449	...	...
	Interlaken Ost **560** d.	...	...	...	...	|	...	|	...	|	...	|	...	|	...	|	...	|	...	|	...	|	...	|	...	...
	Bern **500** d.	...	...	0602	...	0702	...	0802	...	0902	...	1002	...	1102	...	1202	...	1302	...	1402	...	1502	...	1602	...	...
	Biel **500** d.	...	0515	|	0615	|	0715	|	0815	|	0915	|	1015	|	1115	|	1215	|	1315	|	1415	|	1515	|	1615	1615
0	**Zürich HB 530** d.	0607	0637	0707	0737	0807	0837	0907	0937	1007	1037	1107	1137	1207	1237	1307	1337	1407	1437	1507	1537	1607	1637	1707	1737	1737
10	**Zürich Flug ✈ 530** d.	0618	0648	0718	0748	0818	0848	0918	0948	1018	1048	1118	1148	1218	1248	1318	1348	1418	1448	1518	1548	1618	1648	1718	1748	1748
30	Winterthur **530** d.	0635	0705	0735	0805	0835	0905	0935	1005	1035	1105	1135	1205	1235	1305	1335	1405	1435	1505	1535	1605	1635	1705	1735	1805	1805
46	Frauenfeld d.	0647	0717	0747	0817	0847	0917	0947	1017	1047	1117	1147	1217	1247	1317	1347	1417	1447	1517	1547	1617	1647	1717	1747	1817	1817
64	Weinfelden **539** ▲ d.	0700	0730	0800	0830	0900	0930	1000	1030	1100	1130	1200	1230	1300	1330	1400	1430	1500	1530	1600	1630	1700	1730	1800	1830	1845
	Kreuzlingen ▲ a.	|	0750	|	0850	|	0950	|	1050	|	1150	|	1250	|	1350	|	1450	|	1550	|	1650	|	1750	|	1851	|
	Konstanz ▲ a.	|	0754	|	0854	|	0954	|	1054	|	1154	|	1254	|	1354	|	1454	|	1554	|	1654	|	1754	|	1855	|
86	**Romanshorn** a.	0718	...	0818	...	0918	...	1018	...	1118	...	1218	...	1318	...	1418	...	1518	...	1618	...	1718	...	1818	...	1903

	IC 835	*ICN* 2135	*IC* 837	*ICN* 2137	*IC* 839	*IC* 841	*IC* 843	*IC* 845
Brig **560** d.	1549	...	1649	...	1749	1849	1949	...
Interlaken Ost **560** d.	|	...	|	...	|	|	|	...
Bern **500** d.	1702	...	1802	...	1902	2002	2102	2202
Biel **500** d.	|	1715	|	1815	|	|	|	|
Zürich HB 530 d.	1807	1837	1907	1937	2007	2107	2207	2307
Zürich Flughafen ✈ 530 d.	1818	1848	1918	1948	2018	2118	2218	2318
Winterthur **530** d.	1835	1905	1935	2005	2035	2135	2235	2335
Frauenfeld d.	1847	1917	1947	2017	2047	2147	2247	2347
Weinfelden **539** ▲ d.	1900	1930	2000	2030	2100	2200	2300	0000
Kreuzlingen ▲ a.	|	1950	|	2050	|	|	|	|
Konstanz ▲ a.	|	1954	|	2054	|	|	|	|
Romanshorn a.	1918	...	2018	...	2118	2218	2318	0018

	IC 810	*ICN* 2110 Ⓐ	*ICN* 2104 Ⓐ	*ICN* 2110 Ⓒ	*ICN* 2104 Ⓒ	*IC* 812	*ICN* 2112	*IC* 816	*ICN* 2116	*IC* 818	*ICN* 2118
Romanshorn d.	0538	0559z	...	...	...	0638	...	0741	...	0841	...
Konstanz ▲ d.	|	|	0557	...	0603	|	0703	|	0803	|	0903
Kreuzlingen ▲ d.	|	|	0602	...	0607	|	0707	|	0807	|	0907
Weinfelden **539** ▲ d.	0559	0629	0629	0629	0629	0659	0729	0759	0829	0859	0929
Frauenfeld d.	0612	0642	0642	0642	0642	0713	0742	0812	0842	0912	0942
Winterthur **530** d.	0625	0655	0655	0655	0655	0728	0755	0825	0855	0925	0955
Zürich Flughafen ✈ 530 a.	0637	0707	0707	0707	0707	0741	0807	0837	0907	0937	1007
Zürich HB 530 a.	0649	0720	0720	0720	0720	0753	0820	0849	0920	0949	1020
Biel **500** d.	|	0845	0845	0845	0845	|	0945	|	1045	|	1145
Bern **500** a.	0757	...	...	...	...	0857	...	0957	...	1057	...
Interlaken Ost **560** a.	|	...	...	...	...	|	...	|	...	|	...
Brig **560** a.	0911	...	...	...	...	1011	...	1111	...	1211	...

km		*IC* 820	*ICN* 2120	*IC* 822	*ICN* 2122	*IC* 824	*ICN* 2124	*IC* 826	*ICN* 2126	*IC* 828	*ICN* 2128	*IC* 830	*ICN* 2130	*IC* 832	*ICN* 2132	*IC* 836	*ICN* 2136	*IC* 838	*ICN* 2138	*IC* 840	*ICN* 2140	*IC* 842	*IC* 844	*IC* 846	*IC* 848	
	Romanshorn d.	0941	...	1041	...	1141	...	1241	...	1341	...	1441	...	1541	...	1641	...	1741	...	1841	...	1941	2041	2141	2238	...
0	**Konstanz** ▲ d.	|	1003	|	1103	|	1203	|	1303	|	1403	|	1503	|	1603	|	1703	|	1803	|	1903	|	|	|	|	...
1	Kreuzlingen ▲ d.	|	1007	|	1107	|	1207	|	1307	|	1407	|	1507	|	1607	|	1707	|	1807	|	1907	|	|	|	|	...
24	Weinfelden **539** ▲ d.	0959	1029	1059	1129	1159	1229	1259	1329	1359	1429	1459	1529	1559	1629	1659	1729	1759	1829	1859	1929	1959	2059	2159	2259	...
	Frauenfeld d.	1012	1042	1112	1142	1212	1242	1312	1342	1412	1442	1512	1542	1612	1642	1712	1742	1812	1842	1912	1942	2012	2112	2212	2312	...
	Winterthur **530** d.	1025	1055	1125	1155	1225	1255	1325	1355	1425	1455	1525	1555	1625	1655	1725	1755	1825	1855	1925	1955	2025	2125	2225	2325	...
	Zürich Flug ✈ 530 a.	1037	1107	1137	1207	1237	1307	1337	1407	1437	1507	1537	1607	1637	1707	1737	1807	1837	1907	1937	2007	2037	2137	2237	2337	...
	Zürich HB 530 a.	1049	1120	1149	1220	1249	1320	1349	1420	1449	1520	1549	1620	1649	1720	1749	1820	1849	1920	1949	2020	2049	2149	2249	2349	...
	Biel **500** d.	|	1245	|	1345	|	1445	|	1545	|	1645	|	1745	|	1845	|	1945	|	2045	|	2145	|	|	|	...	...
	Bern **500** a.	1157	...	1257	...	1357	...	1457	...	1557	...	1657	...	1757	...	1857	...	1957	...	2057	...	2157	2300	0002	...	...
	Interlaken Ost **560** a.	|	...	|	...	|	...	|	...	|	...	|	...	|	...	|	...	|	...	...	...	...	...	...	...	...
	Brig **560** a.	1311	...	1411	...	1511	...	1611	...	1711	...	1811	...	1911	...	2011	...	2111	...	...	...	...	...	...	...	...

S – From Spiez.

z – Train *ICN* **910** to Weinfelden.

▲ – Additional services operate **Weinfelden - Kreuzlingen - Konstanz and v.v.** journey time: 30 – 36 minutes.
From **Weinfelden**: 0602, and hourly until 1802, then 2002, 2102, 2202, 2307, 0002.
From **Konstanz**: 0524, 0621, 0721, 0821, 0918, 1321, 1418, 1521, 1621, 1721, 1821, 1918, 2021, 2121, 2221, 2321.

SBS ⛴ ROMANSHORN - FRIEDRICHSHAFEN car ferry service 536

Journey time: 41 minutes. ✕ available 0836 - 1936 from Romanshorn; 0841 - 1941 from Friedrichshafen. 🍸 on other sailings. Operator: SBS ✆ 071 466 78 88

From **Romanshorn**: 0936 and hourly until 1636.
From **Friedrichshafen**: 0941 and hourly until 1641.

Services shown operate daily. Additional hourly service available on certain dates from 0536 - 0836 and 1736 - 2136 from Romanshorn; 0541 - 0841 and 1741 - 2041, 2241 from Friedrichshafen.

THURBO WEINFELDEN - WIL 539

km		Ⓐ		Ⓐ		Ⓐ					y
0	Weinfelden **535**.......... d.	0457	0532	0557	0632	0657	0732	and	hourly	2232	2332
19	Wil **530**...................... a.	0520	0555	0622	0655	0722	0755	hourly	until	2255	2355

	Ⓐ		Ⓐ		Ⓐ					z
Wil **530**................... d.	0525	0601	0625	0701	0732	0801	and	hourly	2301	0011
Weinfelden **535**........ a.	0550	0624	0650	0724	0757	0824	hourly	until	2324	0034

y – ⑤⑥ (daily June 8 - 29; also Dec. 31, Mar. 20, 23, Apr. 30, July 31).

z – ⑥⑦ (daily June 9 - 30; also Jan. 1, Mar. 21, 24, May 1, Aug. 1).

RhB. Narrow gauge CHUR - ST MORITZ 540

km		⊗ 2⚒		⊡◐	961 ♦🅁⚡	1325 ♦	951 ♦🅁⚡	953 ♦🅁⚡	🍸‡	◐🍸	⊡‡	‡	⊡‡	◐🍸	904 ♣	🍸‡	902 ♣	906 ♣	908 ♣	910 ♣	⊡		⊡‡	‡	‡		S
0	**Chur 575**.................d.	0458	0648	0758	...	...	0828	0857	0858	0958	1058	1158	1258	1358	1457	1458	1503	1530	1531	1557	1558	1658	1758	1858	1956	2056	...
10	Reichenau-Tamins **575** d.	0509	0701	0808	...	...	0838u	0908u	0908	1008	1108	1208	1308	1408	|	1508	|	|	|	1607s	1608	1708	1808	1908	2007	2107	...
27	Thusis.........................d.	0536	0730	0830	...	...	|	0930u	0930	1030	1130	1230	1330	1430	1527s	1530	1533s	1601s	1602s	1627s	1630	1730	1830	1930	2033	2133	...
41	Tiefencastel.................d.	0552	0747	0847	...	...	0917u	0947u	0947	1047	1147	1247	1347	1447	1546s	1547	1553s	1626s	1627s	1646s	1647	1747	1847	1947	2050	2150	...
51	**Filisur 545a**..............d.	0612	0802	0902	0917	...	|	1002u	1002	1102	1202	1302	1402	1502	1600s	1602	1611	1641s	1642s	1700s	1702	1802	1902	2002	2105	2205	...
59	Bergün/Bravuogn.......d.	0630	0814	0914	0929u	...	|	1014u	1014	1114	1214	1314	1414	1514	1612s	1614	...	1655s	1656s	1713s	1714	1814	1914	2014	2117	2217	...
72	Preda..........................d.	0646	0830	0930	|	...	|	1030u	1030	1130	1230	1330	1430	1530	|	1630	...	|	|	|	1730	1830	1930	2030	2134	2234	...
84	**Samedan**..................a.	0702	0847	0946	|	...	|	1046	1046k	1146	1246	1346	1446	1546	1645s	1646	...	1731s	1732s	1745s	1746	1847	1947	2047	2149	2249	...
84	**Samedan 546**...........d.	...	0850	0950	1008u	1011	|	1050	1050	1150	1250	1350	1450	1550	|	1650	...	|	|	|	1750	1850	1950	2050	2151	2251	2339
89	Pontresina **546/7**...a.	...	|	|	1014	|	1027	1057	|	|	|	|	|	|	|	|	...	|	|	|	|	|	|	|	|	|	|
87	Celerina **546/7**..........d.	...	0853	0953	...	|	...	...	1053	1153	1253	1353	1453	1553	1652s	1653	...	1738s	1739s	1752s	1753	1853	1953	2053	2154	2254	2342
89	**St Moritz 546/7**........a.	...	0858	0958	...	1018	...	...	1058	1158	1258	1358	1458	1558	1657	1658	...	1742	1743	1757	1758	1858	1958	2058	2159	2259	2346

	S⚒	⚒	†		‡	903 ♣		905 ♣	907 ♣	909 ♣	911 ♣	⊡◐	◐🍸	🍸‡	⊡		⊡‡	952 ♦🅁⚡	🍸‡	950 ♦🅁⚡	1360 ♦	960 ♦🅁⚡	954 ♦🅁⚡	🍸‡	◐⊡‡		⊡‡
St Moritz 546/7.........d.	0500	0540	0557	0704	0804	0901	0904	0918	0919	...	1001	1004	1104	1204	1304	1404	1504	...	1604	...	1635	...	...	1704	1804	1904	2004
Celerina **546/7**..........d.	0503	0543	0600	0707	0807	0904u	0907	0923u	0924u	...	1005u	1007	1107	1207	1307	1407	1507	...	1607	...	|	...	...	1707	1807	1907	2007
Pontresina **546/7**...d.	|	|	|	|	|	|	|	|	|	...	|	|	|	|	|	|	|	1556	|	1625	|	1638	1701	|	|	|	|
Samedan 546..........a.	0507	0548	0605	0711	0811	|	0917	|	|	...	|	1011	1111	1211	1311	1411	1511	1602	1611	|	1642	1644	1708	1711	1811	1911	2011
Samedan.................d.	...	0550	0605	0717	0817	0916u	0917	0929u	0930u	...	1017u	1017	1117	1217	1317	1417	1517	1617	1617	|	...	1648	1717	1717	1817	1917	2017
Preda.........................d.	...	0604	0620	0730	0830	|	0930	|	|	...	|	1030	1130	1230	1330	1430	1530	1629s	1630	|	...	|	1730s	1730	1830	1930	2030
Bergün/Bravuogn .....d.	...	0621	0637	0747	0847	|	0947	|	|	...	|	1047	1147	1247	1347	1447	1547	1647s	1647	|	...	1732s	1747s	1747	1847	1948	2048
Filisur 545a.............d.	...	0634	0650	0801	0901	1000u	1001	1017u	1018u	1044	1101u	1101	1201	1301	1401	1501	1601	1700s	1701	|	...	1744	1808s	1801	1901	2001	2101
Tiefencastel................d.	...	0651	0704	0815	0915	1014u	1015	1032u	1033u	1100u	1115u	1115	1215	1315	1415	1515	1615	1714s	1715	1732s	...	...	1814s	1815	1915	2015	2115
Thusis........................d.	...	0711	0721	0833	0933	1032u	1033	1051u	1052u	1116u	1133u	1133	1233	1333	1433	1533	1633	1731s	1733	1751s	...	...	1831s	1833	1933	2033	2133
Reichenau-Tamins **575** d.	...	|	0747	0853	0953	|	1053	|	|	|	|	1153	1253	1353	1453	1553	1653	1752s	1753	1818s	...	...	1852s	1853	1953	2055	2155
Chur 575.................a.	...	0741	0759	0903	1003	1103	1103	1127	1127	1153	1202	1203	1303	1403	1503	1603	1703	1804	1803	1829	...	...	1904	1903	2003	2109	2209

♦ – **NOTES** (LISTED BY TRAIN NUMBER)

950/1 – BERNINA EXPRESS – May 10 - Oct. 19: [12] [observation cars] and 🍸 Tirano - Pontresina - Chur and v.v.
952 – BERNINA EXPRESS – Dec. 9 - Feb. 29, Oct. 20 - Dec. 13: [12] [observation cars] Tirano - Pontresina - Chur.
953 – BERNINA EXPRESS – Dec. 9 - May 9, Oct. 20 - Dec. 13: [12] [observation cars] Chur - Pontresina - Tirano.
954 – BERNINA EXPRESS – Mar. 1 - May 9: [12] [observation cars] Tirano - Pontresina - Chur.
960/1 – BERNINA EXPRESS – May 10 - Oct. 19: [12] [observation cars] and 🍸 Tirano - Pontresina - Davos and v.v.
1325/60 – ENGADIN STAR – May 10 - Oct. 19: [12] Landquart - Klosters - St Moritz and v.v.

S – [12] St Moritz - Klosters and v.v.

k – Connects with train in previous column.
s – Stops to set down only.
u – Stops to pick up only.
♣ – GLACIER EXPRESS – For composition and days of running see Table **579**.
⊗ – Mixed train. Times subject to variation.
‡ – Conveys ✕ on some dates.
⊡ – Conveys 🍸 on some dates.
◐ – Conveys [12] [observation cars] Dec. 22 - Mar. 30, 🅁, ⚡.
⚡ – Supplement payable.

RhB. Narrow gauge CHUR - AROSA 541

km		⚒	⚒	†								
0	**Chur**.................d.	0526	0622	0626	...	0808	and	1908	...	2004	2104	2255
18	Langwies............d.	0607	0709	0707	...	0849	hourly	1949	...	2045	2145	2336x
26	Arosa.................a.	0625	0727	0727	...	0909	until	2009	...	2103	2205	2353

	⚒	Ⓐ	Ⓒ								
Arosa.............d.	0551	0637	0651	...	0748	and	1948	...	2108	0000	...
Langwies ....d.	0607	0653	0708	...	0804	hourly	2004	...	2124	0016x	...
Chur..............a.	0653	0738	0752	...	0852	until	2052	...	2209	0059	...

x – Stops on request only.

Additional services run Ⓒ Jan. 2 - Mar. 2: Chur depart 0852, 0952; Arosa depart. 1533, 1633.

PA 🚌 CHUR - FLIMS 542

🚌 **Chur** (Bahnhof) - **Flims Dorf** (Post), ± 35 minutes, and **Flims Waldhaus** (Post), ± 40 minutes.

From **Chur**:
Ⓐ: 0603, 0658, 0758, 0858, 0958, 1058, 1120, 1158, 1245, 1258, 1358, 1458, 1558, 1620, 1658, 1720, 1740, 1758, 1820, 1858, 2000, 2100, 2200, 2300.
Ⓒ: 0603⑥, 0658, 0758 and hourly until 1658, 1720⑥, 1758, 1858, 2000, 2100, 2200, 2300.

From **Flims Waldhaus** (± 5 minutes from Flims Dorf):
Ⓐ: 0516, 0614, 0659, 0714 and hourly until 1214, 1259, 1314 and hourly until 1814, 1843, 1918, 2018, 2113, 2213, 2313.
Ⓒ: 0516⑥, 0614, 0714 and hourly until 1814, 1918, 2018, 2113, 2213, 2313.

PA 🚌 ST MORITZ and TIRANO - LUGANO 543

		A⚒	A⚒		H🅁		M🅁▪	A⚒		A⚒	
St Moritz Bahnhof ◧......d.	...	...	...	...	1220	...	...	...	...	...	...
Tirano Stazione..........d.	...	1030	1205	...	|	...	1425	1430	...	1650	...
Aprica.........................a.	...	1115	1250	...	|	...	|	1510	...	1735	...
Edolo..........................a.	...	...	...	...	|	...	|	*1600*	...	*1910*	...
Chiavenna Stazione ....d.	...	...	...	...	1410	...	|	...	...	...	...
Menaggio ◐....................d.	...	...	...	...	1505x	...	◐	...	...	...	...
Lugano Stazione ....a.	...	...	...	...	1610s	...	1730	...	...	...	...
Lugano Via S. Balestra .a.	...	...	...	...	1620	...	1740	...	...	...	...

	A⚒		A⚒		M🅁▪		G🅁	A⚒	A⚒	
Lugano Via S. Balestra. d.	...	...	...	...	0945	...	1120	...	...	...
Lugano Stazione ◐.......d.	...	...	...	...	1000	...	1140u	...	...	...
Menaggio ....d.	...	...	...	...	◐	...	1230x	...	...	...
Chiavenna Stazione ......d.	...	...	...	...	|	...	1400	...	...	...
Edolo ....d.	*0600*	...	...	...	|	...	|	...	...	...
Aprica ....d.	0645	...	1120	...	|	...	|	1515	1740	...
Tirano Stazione.........a.	0730	...	1200	...	1245	...	|	1555	1820	...
St Moritz Bahnhof ◧.....a.	...	...	...	...	...	...	1525	...	...	...

A – Aprica Pass service. **Tirano - Aprica** operator: Automobilistica Perego; **Aprica - Edolo** operator: FNM. Contact FNM: ✆ (0364) 361 015, (030) 980 061. *Aprica - Edolo is subject to confirmation.*
G – Palm Express service. Runs ①⑥⑦ Dec. 9 - 17; daily Dec. 22 - Jan. 7; ①⑥⑦ Jan. 12 - June 16; daily June 21 - Oct. 20; ①⑥⑦ Oct. 25 - Dec. 13. Reservation: ✆ St Moritz (081) 833 94 40; fax (081) 833 94 45.
H – Palm Express service. Runs ⑤⑥⑦ Dec. 9 - 16; daily Dec. 21 - Jan. 6; ⑤⑥⑦ Jan. 11 - June 15; daily June 20 - Oct. 19; ⑤⑥⑦ Oct. 24 - Dec. 13. Reservation: ✆ St Moritz (081) 833 94 40; fax (081) 833 94 45.
M – Bernina Express service. Runs Mar. 1 - 30, May 10 - Oct. 19. Reservation: ✆ Poschiavo (081) 288 54 54; fax (081) 288 54 47.

s – Stops to set down only.
u – Stops to pick up only.
x – Calls only if advance reservation is made.
▪ – **Operator**: RhB.
◧ – 🛃 is at Castasegna.
◐ – 🛃 is at Gandria.

544 🚌 CHUR - BELLINZONA and CHIAVENNA PA

km		Ⓐ	Ⓐm	Ⓒ	V[R]n		V[R]		Yh	V[R]			V[R]		V[R]		V[R]	Yh		V[R]			[R]⚡g	[R]⚡g
0	**Chur** Bahnhof **540** d.	...	...	...	0810	...	0810	...	...	1010	...	...	1210	...	1410	...	1610	...	...	1810	...	...	...	...
40	Thusis Bahnhof **540** d.	0615	...	0637	|	0737	0837u	0937	...	1037u	1107	1137	1237u	1337	1437u	1537	1637u	...	1737	1837u	1937	...	2235	2355
64	Splügen Post d.	0647	0649	0709	|	0815	0906	1015	1020	1106	1143	1215	1306	1415	1506	1615	1706	1715	1815	1906	2009s	...	2315	0035
	Chiavenna Stazione ◐ a.	...	|	...	|	|	|	|	1215	|	...	|	|	|	|	|	|	1910	|	|	|	...	...	...
179	**Bellinzona** Stazione a.	...	*0835z*	...	0950	*1005z*	1025	*1205z*	...	1225	...	*1405z*	1425	*1605z*	1625	*1805z*	1825	...	*2005z*	2025	*2205z*	...	...	...

	Ⓐ	Ⓐ	Ⓒq	p	Yh	V[R]	p		V[R]		V[R]			V[R]	Yh		V[R]k	V[R]j		V[R]	V[R]n	[R]⚡g	[R]⚡f	
Bellinzona Stazione d.	...	...	*0655z*	...	...	0835	*0855z*	...	1030	*1055z*	1235	...	*1255z*	1430	...	*1455z*	1630	1630	*1655z*	1830	1930	...	...	...
Chiavenna Stazione ◐ d.	...	...	|	...	0750	|	|	...	|	|	|	...	|	|	1430	|	|	|	|	|	|	...	...	...
Splügen Post d.	0632	0737	0835	0837	0940	0944	1037	...	1144	1237	1344	...	1437	1544	1625	1637	1741	1744	1842	1944	2044	2327	0047	...
Thusis Bahnhof **540** d.	0708	0817	...	0917	...	1017s	1117	...	1217s	1317	1417s	...	1517	1617s	...	1717	1806s	1817s	1918	2017s	2117s	2354	0114	...
Chur Bahnhof **540** a.	...	...	...	...	...	1044	...	...	1244	...	1444	...	...	1644	...	...	1835	1844	...	2044	2144	...	...	...

V – San Bernardino Route Express.
Y – Splügen Pass service.
f – ⑥⑦ (not Mar. 22).
g – ⑤⑥ (not Mar. 21, Aug. 1).
h – June 8 - Oct. 12.
j – Dec. 9 - June 6, Oct. 13 - Dec. 13.
k – June 7 - Oct. 12.
m – Also Jan. 2; not Mar. 19, May 22, Aug. 15, Dec. 8.
n – May 10 - Oct. 19.
p – Mar. 15 - Oct. 19.
q – Also Mar. 19, May 22, Aug. 15, Dec. 8; not Jan. 2.
s – Stops to set down only.
u – Stops to pick up only.
z – Change at San Bernardino Posta.
◐ – 🏨 is at Splügen Pass.
⚡ – Supplement payable.
Reservations: ✆ Chur (081) 256 32 83.

545 LANDQUART - KLOSTERS - DAVOS / SCUOL TARASP Narrow gauge. RhB

km		⊗Ⓐ	⚒	Ⓐ					2p		E			2p									
	Chur d.	...	...	*0550*	...	...	0720	...	...	0752	...	...	0820	...	...	0920	...	...	1020		...	1820	...
0	**Landquart** d.	0451	0525	0615	0647	0747	0749k	...	0752	0809	0820	0847	0849k	0852	0947	0949k	...	1047	1049k	and at	1847	1849k	...
21	Küblis d.	0511x	0555	0644	0713	0811	0815	...	0822	...	0847	0911	0915	0922	1011	1015	...	1111	1115	the same	1911	1915	...
30	Klosters Dorf d.	0524x	0609	0658	0726	|	0828	...	0844	...	|	|	0928	0944	|	1028	...	|	1128	minutes	|	1928	...
32	**Klosters** 🚗 d.	0529	0617	0702	0734	0828	0834	...	0851	...	0903	0928	0934	0952	1028	1034	...	1128	1134	past each	1928	1934	...
	Sagliains **546** 🚗 § a.	|	|	|	0754	|	0853	...	|	...	...	|	0953	|	|	1053	...	|	1153	hour	|	1953	...
	Scuol-Tarasp 546 a.	|	|	|	0819	|	0917	...	|	...	...	|	1017	|	|	1117	...	|	1217	until	|	2017	...
47	Davos Dorf d.	0550	0640	0725	...	0850	...	...	0914	...	...	0950	...	1014	1050	...	...	1150	...		1950	...	...
50	**Davos Platz 545a** a.	0556	0647	0730	...	0855	...	...	0925	...	...	0955	...	1025	1055	...	...	1155	...		1955	...	...

Chur d.	*1920*	...	*1952*	...	*2052*	...	*2152*	...	...
Landquart d.	1947	...	2047	...	2147	...	2247	...	...
Küblis d.	2013	...	2113	...	2213	...	2313	...	...
Klosters Dorf d.	2026	...	2126	...	2225	...	2326	...	...
Klosters 🚗 d.	2030	2034	2130	2134	2230	...	2330	...	...
Sagliains **546** 🚗 § a.	|	2054	|	2154	|	...	|	...	...
Scuol-Tarasp 546 a.	|	2119r	|	2219r	|	...	|	...	...
Davos Dorf d.	2052	...	2152	...	2252	...	2352	...	...
Davos Platz 545a a.	2057	...	2157	...	2257	...	2357	...	...

	⚒		Ⓐ						
Davos Platz 545a d.	0454	0550	0627	0702	...	0802	...	0902	...
Davos Dorf d.	0457	0553	0630	0705	...	0805	...	0905	...
Scuol-Tarasp 546 d.	|	|	|	|	0738	|	0842	|	0942
Sagliains **546** 🚗 § d.	|	|	|	|	0803	|	0903	|	1003
Klosters 🚗 d.	0520	0617	0654	0729	0825	0832	0925	0932	1025
Klosters Dorf d.	0523	0620	0657	0732	0828	|	0928	|	1028
Küblis d.	0538	0634	0712	0746	0843	0848	0943	0948	1043
Landquart a.	0607	0706	0738	0813	0910	0913k	1010	1013k	1110
Chur a.	0629a	0730a	...	...	0938	...	1038	...	1138j

km										E					🚌			🚌			🚌		🚌
	Davos Platz 545a d.	1002	...	...	1102		...	1702	...	...	...	1802	...	1902	...	...	2002	...	...	2102	...	...	...
	Davos Dorf d.	1005	...	...	1105	and at	...	1705	...	...	...	1805	...	1905	...	...	2005	...	...	2105	...	...	...
0	**Scuol-Tarasp 546** d.	|	...	1042	|	the same	1642	|	...	...	1742	|	1842	|	...	1942	|	...	2038	|	...	2138r	...
17	Sagliains **546** 🚗 § d.	|	...	1103	|	minutes	1703	|	...	...	1803	|	1903	|	...	2003	|	...	2103	|	...	2203	...
39	**Klosters** 🚗 d.	1032	...	1125	1132	past each	1725	1732	...	1754	1825	1832	1925	1932	...	2024	2029	...	2124	2129	...	2229	...
	Klosters Dorf d.	|	...	1128	|	hour	1728	|	...	|	1828	|	1928	|	...	...	2032	...	...	2132	...	2232	...
	Küblis d.	1048	...	1143	1148	until	1743	1748	...	1813	1843	1848	1943	1948	...	...	2046	...	...	2146	...	2246	...
	Landquart a.	1113k	...	1210	1213k		1810	1813k	...	1836	1910	1913k	2010	2013k	2045	...	2113	2142	...	2213	2242	2313	2342
	Chur a.	...	...	1238	...		1838	...	...	...	1938	...	2038	...	2109	...	...	2206	...	...	2306	...	0014

E – ENGADIN STAR – May 10 - Oct. 19: [12] St Moritz - Klosters - Landquart and v.v.
a – Ⓐ only.
j – By connecting train on Ⓐ.
k – Connects with train in previous column.
p – Dec. 22 - Mar. 8.
r – By 🚌 Ardez (between Sagliains and Scuol-Tarasp) - Scuol-Tarasp and v.v. on Ⓐ Mar. 31 - Nov. 14 (not May 2). Arrive 6 minutes later; depart 8 minutes earlier.
x – Stops on request only.
§ – Sagliains station can only be used for changing trains.
⊗ – Mixed train. Times subject to variation.
🚗 – Car-carrying shuttle available (see page 260).

545a DAVOS - FILISUR Narrow gauge. RhB

km		⚒				961 ♦[R]⚡				909 ♦[R]⚡						p							
0	**Davos Platz 545** d.	0605	0732	0832	...	0850u	...	0932	...	1010u	...	1032	and hourly	1932	...	2032	...	...	...	...	...	...	...
16	**Filisur 540** a.	0630	0757	0857	...	0917u	...	0957	...	1044u	...	1057	until	1957	...	2057	...	...	...	...	...	...	...

	⚒					902 ♦[R]⚡				960 ♦[R]⚡						p						
Filisur 540 d.	0635	0803	and hourly	1603	...	1611s	...	1703	...	1744s	...	1803	1903	2003	...	2107	...	...	...	...	...	...
Davos Platz 545 a.	0700	0828	until	1628	...	1647s	...	1728	...	1809s	...	1828	1928	2028	...	2132	...	...	...	...	...	...

♦ – **NOTES** (LISTED BY TRAIN NUMBER)
960/1 – BERNINA EXPRESS – May 10 - Oct. 19: [12] [observation cars] and 🍷 Tirano - Pontresina - Davos and v.v.
902/9 – GLACIER EXPRESS – June 14 - Sept. 28: [1] [observation car] and [12] Zermatt - Davos and v.v.
p – May 10 - Oct. 19.
s – Stops to set down only.
u – Stops to pick up only.
⚡ – Supplement payable.

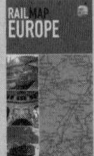

PONTRESINA / ST MORITZ - SCUOL TARASP — 546

Narrow gauge. RhB

km		⚒S	⚒	†P									Y	E							2		
0	**Pontresina 540/7** ....d.	...	...	0557	0702	0802	0902	...	1002	1102		1602	1638	...	1702	1802	1902	2002	...	2102	...	2202	...
	St Moritz **540/7** ....d.	0500	0540	0557	0704	0804	0904	...	1004	1104	and at	1604	|	1635	1704	1804	1904	2004	2102	|	2202	|	...
5	**Samedan 540** ....a.	0507	0548	0603	0708	0808	0908	...	1008	1108	the same	1608	1644	1642	1708	1808	1908	2008	2110	2108	2210	2208	...
5	**Samedan** ....d.	0507	0555	0617	0712	0814	...	0914	1014	1114	minutes	1614	...	1646	1714	1814	1914	2014	▬	2112	▬	2212	...
15	Zuoz ....d.	0521	0608	0630	0725	0827	...	0927	1027	1127	past each	1627	...	1659	1727	1827	1927	2027	...	2125	...	2225	...
32	Zernez ....⊖ d.	0540	0638	0649	0746	0849	...	0949	1049	1149	hour	1649	...	1720	1749	1849	1949	2047	...	2146	...	2246	...
38	Susch ....d.	0547	0645	0656	0752	0855	...	0955	1055	1155	until	1655	...	...	1755	1855	1955	2053	...	2152	...	2252	...
40	Sagliains **545** ....§ a.	0550	0647	0700	0757	0900"	...	1000	1100	1200		1700	...	...	1800	1900	2000	2057	2059	2157	2159	2255	...
57	**Scuol-Tarasp 545** ....a.	0624t	0709	...	0819	0925	...	1025	1125	1225		1725	...	...	1825	1925	2025	...	2119r	...	2219r	2315r	...

	⚒				E	Y							Z										K
Scuol-Tarasp 545 ....d.	0607t	0642v	0738	0834	...	...	0934	1034	1134	1234	1334	1434	...	1534		1834	1934	...	2038	...	2138r	...	...
Sagliains **545** ....§ d.	|	0702	0803	0856	...	...	0956	1056	1156	1256	1356	1456	...	1556	and at	1856	1956	...	2058	2103	2158	2203	2255
Susch ....d.	0631	0705	0805	0858	...	...	0958	1058	1158	1258	1358	1458	...	1558	the same	1858	1958	...	...	2105	...	2205	2257
Zernez ....⊖ d.	0638	0713	0813	0908	0933	...	1008	1108	1208	1308	1408	1508	1533	1608	minutes	1908	2008	...	...	2113	...	2213	2305
Zuoz ....d.	0657	0734	0834	0927	0956	...	1027	1127	1227	1327	1427	1527	1556	1627	past each	1927	2027	...	...	2134	...	2234	2324
Samedan ....a.	0711	0749	0849	0942	1006	...	1042	1142	1242	1342	1442	1542	1606	1642	hour	1942	2042	...	...	2149	...	2249	2338
Samedan 540 ....d.	0712	0751	0851	0949	1011	1008	1043j	1149	1249	1349	1449	1549	1611	1649	until	1949	2051	2050	...	2151	...	2251	2339
St Moritz **540/7** ....a.	0719	0758	0858	0958	1018	|	1058	1158	1258	1358	1458	1558	1618	1658		1958	|	2058	...	2159	...	2259	2346
Pontresina 540/7 ....a.	...	0757	0857	0956	...	1014	1049j	1156	1256	1356	1456	1556	...	1656		1956	2057	...	...	2157	...	2257	...

E – ENGADIN STAR – May 10 - Oct. 19: 🚃12 St Moritz - Landquart and v.v.
K – 🚃12 Klosters (d. 2230) - St Moritz.
P – 🚃12 Pontresina - Klosters (a. 0725).
S – 🚃12 St Moritz - Klosters (a. 0615).
Y – May 10 - Oct. 19.
Z – ⑥ Dec. 15 - Mar. 29.

j – 6 minutes later May 10 - Oct. 19.
r – By 🚌 Ardez (between Sagliains and Scuol-Tarasp) - Scuol-Tarasp and v.v. on Ⓐ Mar. 31 - Nov. 14 (not May 2). Arrive 6 minutes later; depart 8 minutes earlier.
t – By 🚌 Ardez (between Sagliains and Scuol-Tarasp) - Scuol-Tarasp and v.v. on ②–⑥ Apr. 1 - Nov. 15 (not May 1-3, 13, Aug. 1, 2). Arrive 6 minutes later; depart 8 minutes earlier.
v – By 🚌 Scuol-Tarasp - Ardez (between Scuol-Tarasp and Sagliains) on ②–⑥ Apr. 1 - Nov. 15 (not May 2, 3, 13, Aug. 2). Depart 8 minutes earlier.

§ – Sagliains station can only be used for changing trains.
⊖ – 🚌 service **Zernez - Malles and v.v.** (journey 1 h 35 minutes):
From **Zernez posta**: 0715, 0815**Y**, 0915, 1015**Y**, 1115, 1215**Y**, 1315, 1415**Y**, 1515, 1615**Y**, 1715, 1815**Y**.
From **Malles / Mals bahnhof**: 0703**Y**, 0803**Y**, 0903, 1003**Y**, 1103, 1203**Y**, 1303, 1403**Y**, 1503, 1603**Y**, 1703, 1803**Y**, 1903.
Operator: AutoDaPosta (PA), Agentura Scuol, CH-7550 Scuol. ✆ +41 (0)81 864 16 83, fax +41 (0)81 864 91 48.

ST MORITZ - TIRANO — 547

Narrow gauge. RhB

Valid December 9 - May 9

km		⊗	⊗	©			Y	953 ♦🅁✗	◐	r			ⒶW	ⒶV	T					⊗ Ⓐ		⊗		🚌 ⑤h	🚌
0	**St Moritz** ....d.	...	...	...	0745	0845	0941	...	1045	1145	1245	1345	1345	1345	1444	1445	1540	1645	1845	...	1945	...	2020	...	...
2	Celerina Staz ....⊡ d.	...	...	...	0748	0848	0944	...	1048	1148	1248	1348	1348	1348	1448	1448	1543	1648	1848	...	1948	...	2023	...	...
6	**Pontresina** ....a.	...	...	...	0755	0855	0951	...	1055	1155	1255	1355	1355	1355	1455	1455	1550	1655	1855	...	1955	...	2030	m	...
6	**Pontresina 540** ....d.	...	...	0704	0809	0904	1004	1103	1104	1209	1304	...	1409	1409	1504	1504	1609	1704	...	1904	...	2009	...	2057	...
12	Morteratsch ....⊡ d.	...	...	0713	0818	0913	1013	1113u	1113	1218	1313	...	1418	1418	1513	1513	1618	1713	...	1913	...	2018	...	|	...
17	Bernina Diavolezza ⊡ d.	...	...	0723	0828	0923	1023	1123s	1123	1228	1323	...	1428	1428	1523	1523	1628	1723	...	1921	...	2026	...	|	...
18	Bernina Lagalb ....⊡ d.	...	...	0725	0830	0925	1026	1126s	1125	1230	1325	...	1430	1430	1525	1525	1630	1725	...	1924	...	2029	...	|	...
22	Ospizio Bernina ....d.	...	...	0734	0839	0934	...	1135s	1134	1239	1334	...	1439	1439	1534	1534	1639	1734	...	1933x	...	2038x	...	|	...
27	Alp Grüm ....d.	...	...	0746	0853	0946	...	1145s	1146	1252	1346	...	1453	1453	1546	1546	1653	1746	...	1942x	...	2047x	...	|	...
44	**Poschiavo** ....a.	...	...	0827	0935	1027	...	1227s	1227	...	1427	...	1536	1542	1627	1627	1735	1827	...	2029	...	2134	...	2135	...
44	**Poschiavo** ....d.	0626	0736	0829	0938	1029	...	|	1229	...	1429	...	1540	1550	1628	1629	1738	1829	...	...	...	...	...	...	2137
48	Le Prese ....d.	0634x	0744x	0837	0946	1037	...	1238s	1237	...	1437	...	1548	1558	1637	1637	1746	1837	...	...	...	...	...	...	2143s
51	Miralago ....⊡ d.	0639	0749	0843	0952	1043	...	1243s	1243	...	1443	...	1554	1604	1643	1643	1752	1843	...	...	...	...	...	...	2147s
54	Brusio ....⊡ d.	0647	0757	0851	1000	1051	...	1251s	1251	...	1451	...	1602	1612	1651	1651	1800	1851	...	...	...	...	...	...	2151s
58	Campocologno ▦ ....d.	0657	0807	0903	1012	1103	...	1301s	1303	...	1503	...	1612	1622	1703	1703	1812	1903	...	...	...	...	...	...	2155
61	**Tirano** ....a.	0712	0823	0912	1021	1112	...	1311	1312	...	1512	...	1623	1636	1711	1712	1821	1912	...	...	...	...	...	...	2205

		⊗ ⚒	🚌			T		©		r		952 ♦🅁✗		W	954 ♦🅁✗	q	j		⊗ Ⓐ		⊗		🚌 ⑤h✗	⊗	⊗
Tirano ....d.	...	...	0650	...	0740	0849	0850	0940	1050	...	1250	1337	...	1338	1432	1433	...	1540	1650	...	1740	...	...	1850	1940
Campocologno ▦ ....d.	...	...	0657	...	0752	0901u	0901	0952	1101	...	1301	1348u	...	1348	1441u	1441	...	1552	1701	...	1752	...	...	1901	1952
Brusio ....⊡ d.	...	...	0702	...	0800	0909u	0909	1000	1109	...	1309	1356u	...	1356	1449u	1449	...	1600	1709	...	1800	...	...	1909	2000
Miralago ....⊡ d.	...	...	0707	...	0807	0916u	0916	1007	1116	...	1316	1403u	...	1403	1456u	1456	...	1607	1716	...	1807	...	...	1916	2007
Le Prese ....d.	...	...	0711	...	0813	0922u	0922	1013	1122	...	1322	1409u	...	1409	1502u	1502	...	1613	1722	...	1812x	...	...	1922	2012x
Poschiavo ....a.	...	...	0728	...	0823	|	0931	1023	1131	...	1331	|	...	1419	|	1513	...	1623	1732	...	1823	...	...	1932	2023
Poschiavo ....d.	...	0628	▬	0733	0825	0932u	0933	1025	1133	...	1333	1424u	...	1425	1514u	1515	...	1625	1734	...	1825	...	1915	...	...
Alp Grüm ....d.	...	0705x	...	0815	0907	1014s	1015	1107	1215	1307	1415	1507u	...	1507	1600u	1600	...	1707	1811x	...	1902x	...	|	...	...
Ospizio Bernina ....d.	...	0714x	...	0824	0916	1024s	1024	1116	1224	1316	1424	1516u	...	1516	1609u	1609	...	1716	1820x	...	1911x	...	|	...	...
Bernina Lagalb ....⊡ d.	...	0722	...	0832	0924	1033s	1032	1124	1232	1324	1432	1524u	...	1524	1617u	1617	1620	1724	1828	...	1919	...	|	...	...
Bernina Diavolezza ⊡ d.	...	0724	...	0834	0926	1035s	1034	1126	1234	1326	1434	1527u	...	1526	1620u	1619	1622	1726	1830	...	1921	...	|	...	...
Morteratsch ....⊡ d.	...	0734	...	0844	0936	1046s	1044	1136	1244	1336	1444	1536u	...	1536	1629u	1629	1631	1736	1840	...	1931	...	|	...	...
Pontresina 540 ....a.	...	0750	...	0858	0950	1057s	1058	1150	1258	1350	1458	1549	...	1550	1643	1644	1644	1750	1857	...	1950	...	2000	...	...
Pontresina ....d.	0720	...	0756	0901	0952	|	1101	1156	1301	1356	1501	...	1551	1551	...	1656	1656	1756	...	1901	...	1956	n	...	...
Celerina Staz ....⊡ d.	0725	...	0801	0906	0957	1107s	1106	1201	1306	1401	1506	...	1556	1556	...	1701	1701	1801	...	1906	...	2001	...	...	...
St Moritz ....a.	0731	...	0807	0912	1003	1111	1112	1207	1312	1407	1512	...	1602	1602	...	1707	1707	1807	...	1912	...	2007	...	...	...

♦ – **NOTES** (LISTED BY TRAIN NUMBER)
952 – BERNINA EXPRESS – Dec. 9 - Feb. 29: 🚃12 [observation cars] Tirano - Pontresina - Chur.
953 – BERNINA EXPRESS – 🚃12 [observation cars] Chur - Pontresina - Tirano.
954 – BERNINA EXPRESS – Mar. 1 - May 9: 🚃12 [observation cars] Tirano - Pontresina - Chur.

T – BERNINA EXPRESS – ②③④⑤⑥⑦ (also Mar. 24; not Dec. 27, Jan. 3, Mar. 25): 🚃12 [observation cars] St Moritz - Tirano and v.v. 🅁 and ✗.
V – Mar. 3 - May 9.
W – Dec. 9 - Feb. 29.
Y – Dec. 22 - Mar. 30.

h – Also Mar. 20, Apr. 30; not Mar. 21.
j – Dec. 22 - Feb. 29.
m – From Samedan (d. 2050).
n – To Samedan (a. 2008).
q – Mar. 1 - May 9.
r – Dec. 9 - Mar. 30.
s – Stops to set down only.
u – Stops to pick up only.
x – Stops on request only.

550 LUZERN and ZÜRICH - LOCARNO, CHIASSO and MILANO

SBB, FS

	RE 14023	*EC* 105	*RE* 14025	*EC* 107			*IR* 2257		*CIS* 151		*IR* 2159	*EC* 171	*IR* 2409	*IR* 2255	*CIS* 153		*EC* 109	*IR* 2261	*IR* 2259	*IR* 2411	*EC* 173	*IR* 2165	*IR* 2415	*EC* 111	*IR* 2267
		⊡		⊡			△		✕⊙		△	⊡	(🍷)		✕⊙		⊡	△		(🍷)	⊡	△	(🍷)	⊡	△
	⚒	♦	g	♦					M			♦	R	⑥	F		♦			R	♦		R	♦	
Basel SBB **565** d.	...	...	...	...	...	...	...	...	...	...	0604	...	...	...	...	...	0704	...	...	...	...	0804	...	0904	...
Olten **565** d.	...	...	...	...	...	...	...	...	...	...	0633	...	...	...	...	...	0733	...	...	...	...	0833	...	0933	...
Luzern 565 ⊗ d.	...	...	...	...	...	...	...	...	...	...	0721	...	0740	...	...	...	0821	...	...	0840	...	0921	0940	1021	...
Küssnacht am Rigi ⊗ d.	...	...	...	...	...	...	...	...	...	...	|	...	0758	...	...	...	|	...	...	0858	...	|	0958	|	...
Schaffhausen **939/40** d.	...	...	...	...	...	...	...	...	...	...	|	...	|	...	...	...	|	...	...	|	0809	|	|	|	...
Zürich HB d.	...	...	...	...	...	...	0609	...	0709	...	|	0715	|	0731	0742	...	|	0809	0831	|	0909	|	|	|	1009
Zug d.	...	...	...	...	...	...	0632	...	0732	...	|	|	|	0757	|	...	|	0832	0857	|	0932	|	|	|	1032
Arth-Goldau ⊗ a.	...	...	...	...	...	...	0648	...	0748	...	0746k	0808	0811	0813	0832	...	0846	0848k	0913	0911	0948	0946k	1011	1046	1048k
Arth-Goldau d.	...	...	...	...	...	...	0654	...	0750	...	0754	0809	...	0815	0834	...	0852	0854	0915	▬	0952	0954	▬	1052	1054
Schwyz d.	...	...	...	...	...	...	0703	...	|	...	0803	|	...	|	|	...	|	0903	|	...	|	1003	...	|	1103
Brunnen d.	...	...	...	...	...	...	0707	...	|	...	0807	|	...	|	|	...	|	0907	|	...	|	1007	...	|	1107
Flüelen d.	...	...	...	...	...	...	0717	...	|	...	0817	|	...	|	|	...	|	0917	|	...	|	1017	...	|	1117
Erstfeld d.	...	...	...	...	...	...	0726	...	|	...	0826	|	...	|	|	...	|	0926	|	...	|	1026	...	|	1126
Göschenen d.	...	...	...	...	...	...	0752	...	|	...	0851	0855	...	0902	|	...	|	0952	1001	...	|	1052	...	|	1152
Airolo d.	...	...	...	...	0642	...	0803	...	|	...	0907	|	...	0913	|	...	|	1003	|	...	|	1103	...	|	1203
Faido d.	...	...	...	...	0700	...	0822	...	|	...	0925	|	...	|	|	...	|	1022	|	...	|	1122	...	|	1222
Biasca d.	...	0624g	0701	...	0723	0802	0844	0902	|	...	0947	|	...	|	|	1004	|	1044	|	1102	|	1144	1202	|	1244
Bellinzona a.	...	0636g	0715	...	0736k	0814	0858	0914	0924	...	0959	0952k	...	1003	1012	1016	1036	1058	1102	1114	1136	1158	1214	1236	1258
Bellinzona ▲ d.	...	0643	0715	0743	0750	0815	0900	0915	0925	0945	1000	0954	...	1005	1013	1017	1038	1100	1104	1115	1138	1200	1215	1238	1300
Locarno ▲ a.	...	|	|	|	|	|	0919	|	|	|	1019	|	...	|	|	|	|	1119	|	|	|	1219	|	|	1319
Lugano a.	...	0710	0743	0810	0820	0845	...	0945	0947	1015	...	1019	...	1030	1036	1048	1103	...	1129	1145	1203	...	1245	1303	...
Lugano d.	0651	0711	0745	0811	0824	0854	...	0954	0948	1024	...	1021	...	1032	1037	1054	1105	...	1131	1154	1205	...	1254	1305	...
Capolago-Riva San Vitale d.	|	|	|	|	0838	0908	...	1008	|	1038	...	|	...	1051s	|	1108	|	...	1143	1208	|	...	1308	|	...
Mendrisio d.	0707	0727	0801	0827	0844	0914	...	1014	|	1044	...	|	...	1058	|	1114	|	...	1151	1214	|	...	1314	|	...
Chiasso a.	0714	0735	0809	0835	0853	0923	...	1023	|	1053	...	1044	...	1106	|	1123	1128	...	1158	1223	1228	...	1323	1328	...
Chiasso 🏛 d.	...	0749	...	0848	...	...	...	...	|	...	...	1105	...	...	|	...	1142	...	...	...	1248	...	...	1348	...
Como San Giovanni a.	...	0753	...	0852	...	...	...	...	1012	...	...	1110	...	...	1103	...	1147	...	...	...	1252	...	...	1352	...
Milano Centrale a.	...	0835	...	0935	...	...	...	...	1047	...	...	1150	...	...	1138	...	1235	...	...	...	1335	...	...	1435	...

	IR 2417	*EC* 175	*IR* 2169	*IR* 2419	*EC* 115	*IR* 2271	*IR* 2421	*CIS* 155		*IR* 2173	*IR* 2423	*EC* 117	*IR* 2275	*IR* 2425	*EC* 177	*IR* 2177	*IR* 2427	*EC* 119	*IR* 2279	*IR* 2429	*EC* 179	*IR* 2181	*IR* 2431	*IC* 685	*IR* 2285
	(✕)	⊡		(🍷)	⊡	△	(🍷)	✕⊙		△	(🍷)	⊡		(🍷)	⊡	△	(🍷)	⊡	△	(🍷)	⊡	△	(🍷)		△
	R	♦	W	R	♦		R	T			R	♦	W	R	♦		R	♦		R	♦		R		
Basel SBB **565** d.	...	...	1004	...	1104	...	...	...	...	1204	...	1304	...	...	...	1404	...	1504	...	...	...	1604	...	1704	...
Olten **565** d.	...	...	1033	...	1133	...	...	...	...	1233	...	1333	...	...	...	1433	...	1533	...	...	...	1633	...	1733	...
Luzern 565 ⊗ d.	1040	...	1121	1140	1221	...	1240	...	...	1321	1340	1421	...	1440	...	1521	1540	1621	...	1640	...	1721	1740	1821	...
Küssnacht am Rigi ⊗ d.	1058	...	|	1158	|	...	1258	...	...	|	1358	|	...	1458	...	|	1558	|	...	1658	...	|	1758	|	...
Schaffhausen **939/40** d.	|	1016	|	|	|	...	|	...	...	|	|	|	...	|	...	|	|	|	...	|	...	|	|	|	...
Zürich HB d.	|	1109	|	|	|	1209	|	1309	...	|	|	|	1409	|	1509	|	|	|	1609	|	1709	|	|	|	1809
Zug d.	|	1132	|	|	|	1232	|	1332	...	|	|	|	1432	|	1532	|	|	|	1632	|	1732	|	|	|	1832
Arth-Goldau ⊗ a.	1111	1148	1146k	1211	1246	1248k	1311	1348	...	1346k	1411	1446	1448k	1511	1548	1546k	1611	1646	1648k	1711	1748	1746k	1811	1846	1848k
Arth-Goldau d.	▬	1152	1154	▬	1252	1254	▬	1350	...	1354	▬	1452	1454	▬	1552	1554	▬	1652	1654	▬	1752	1754	▬	1852	1854
Schwyz d.	...	|	1203	...	|	1303	...	|	...	1403	...	|	1503	...	|	1603	...	|	1703	...	|	1803	...	|	1903
Brunnen d.	...	|	1207	...	|	1307	...	|	...	1407	...	|	1507	...	|	1607	...	|	1707	...	|	1807	...	|	1907
Flüelen d.	...	|	1217	...	|	1317	...	|	...	1417	...	|	1517	...	|	1617	...	|	1717	...	|	1817	...	|	1917
Erstfeld d.	...	|	1226	...	|	1326	...	|	...	1426	...	|	1526	...	|	1626	...	|	1726	...	|	1826	...	|	1926
Göschenen d.	...	|	1252	...	|	1352	...	|	...	1452	...	|	1552	...	|	1652	...	|	1752	...	|	1852	...	|	1952
Airolo d.	...	|	1303	...	|	1403	...	|	...	1503	...	|	1603	...	|	1703	...	|	1803	...	|	1903	...	|	2003
Faido d.	...	|	1322	...	|	1422	...	|	...	1522	...	|	1622	...	|	1722	...	|	1822	...	|	1922	...	|	2022
Biasca d.	1302	|	1344	1402	|	1444	1502	|	...	1544	1602	|	1644	1702	|	1744	1802	|	1844	1902	|	1944	2002	|	2044
Bellinzona a.	1314	1336	1358	1414	1436	1458	1514	1524	...	1558	1614	1636	1658	1714	1736	1758	1814	1836	1858	1914	1936	1958	2014	2036	2057
Bellinzona ▲ d.	1315	1338	1400	1415	1438	1500	1515	1525	1545	1600	1615	1638	1700	1715	1738	1800	1815	1838	1900	1915	1938	2000	2015	2038	2059
Locarno ▲ a.	|	|	1419	|	|	1519	|	|	|	1619	|	|	1719	|	|	1819	|	|	1919	|	|	2019	|	|	|
Lugano a.	1345	1403	...	1445	1503	...	1545	1547	1615	...	1645	1703	...	1745	1803	...	1845	1903	...	1945	2003	...	2045	2103	2126
Lugano d.	1354	1405	...	1454	1505	...	1554	1548	1624	...	1654	1705	...	1754	1805	...	1854	1905	...	1954	2005	...	2054	2105	2127
Capolago-Riva San Vitale d.	1408	|	...	1508	|	...	1608	|	1638	...	1708	|	...	1808	|	...	1908	|	...	2008	|	...	2108	|	2142
Mendrisio d.	1414	|	...	1514	|	...	1614	|	1644	...	1714	|	...	1814	|	...	1914	|	...	2014	|	...	2114	|	2149
Chiasso a.	1423	1428	...	1523	1528	...	1623	|	1653	...	1723	1728	...	1823	1828	...	1923	1928	...	2023	2028	...	2123	2128	2158
Chiasso 🏛 d.	...	1448	...	...	1548	...	...	|	...	...	...	1748	...	...	1848	...	...	1948	...	...	2048	...	...	...	...
Como San Giovanni a.	...	1452	...	...	1552	...	...	|	...	...	...	1752	...	...	1852	...	...	1952	...	...	2052	...	...	...	...
Milano Centrale a.	...	1535	...	...	1635	...	...	1642	...	...	...	1835	...	...	1935	...	...	2035	...	...	2135	...	...	...	...

	IR 2435	*CIS* 157	*IR* 2187	*IR* 2437	*IC* 2287	*IR* 2289	*IR* 2189	*IR* 2191	*IR* 2193	*IR* 2293
	(🍷)	✕⊙	△	(🍷)				△		
	R	S		R	j					
Basel SBB **565** d.	...	...	1804	...	...	...	1904	2004	...	...
Olten **565** d.	...	...	1833	...	...	...	1933	2032	...	...
Luzern 565 ⊗ d.	1840	...	1921	1940	...	...	2021	2121	2221	...
Küssnacht am Rigi ⊗ d.	1858	...	|	1958	...	...	|	|	|	...
Schaffhausen **939/40** d.	|	1816	|	|	...	...	|	|	|	...
Zürich HB d.	|	1909	|	|	1931	2009	|	|	|	2209
Zug d.	|	1932	|	|	1957	2032	|	|	|	2232
Arth-Goldau ⊗ a.	1911	1948	1946k	2011	2013	2048	2046	2146	2246	2248
Arth-Goldau d.	▬	1950	1954	▬	2015	...	2054	2154	▬	2254
Schwyz d.	...	|	2003	...	|	...	2103	2203	...	|
Brunnen d.	...	|	2007	...	|	...	2107	2207	...	|
Flüelen d.	...	|	2017	...	|	...	2117	2217	...	|
Erstfeld d.	...	|	2026	...	|	...	2126	2226	...	2316
Göschenen d.	...	|	2052	...	|	...	2152	▬	...	2340
Airolo d.	...	|	2103	...	|	...	2203	...	...	2351
Faido d.	...	|	2122	...	|	...	2222	...	...	0009
Biasca d.	...	|	2144	...	|	...	2244	...	...	0030
Bellinzona a.	...	2124	2157	...	2205	...	2257	...	...	0042
Bellinzona ▲ d.	2115	2125	2159	2215	2207	...	2259	2315	0015	0043
Locarno ▲ a.	|	|	|	|	|	...	|	|	|	|
Lugano a.	2145	2147	2226	2245	2233	...	2326	2345	0045	0112
Lugano d.	2154	2148	2227	2254	...	...	2327	2354	0054	0115
Capolago-Riva San Vitale d.	2208	|	2242	2308	...	...	2342	0008	0108	0130
Mendrisio d.	2214	|	2249	2314	...	...	2349	0014	0114	0137
Chiasso a.	2223	|	2258	2323	...	...	2358	0023	0123	0146
Chiasso 🏛 d.	...	|	...	...	...	...	...	...	...	...
Como San Giovanni a.	...	2212	...	...	...	...	...	...	...	...
Milano Centrale a.	...	2247	...	...	...	...	...	...	...	...

	RE 2920	*IR* 2166	*IC* 2266		*IR* 2268		*IC* 668		*IR* 2170	*RE* 14026
		△	△						△	
										Ⓐ
Milano Centrale d.	...	...	...	...	...	...	...	...	...	...
Como San Giovanni d.	...	...	...	...	...	...	...	...	...	...
Chiasso 🏛 a.	...	...	...	...	...	...	...	...	...	...
Chiasso d.	...	...	0531	0535	0559	...	0628	0635	0658	0720
Mendrisio d.	...	...	|	0544	0608	...	0636	0644	0707	0728
Capolago-Riva San Vitale d.	...	...	|	0547	|	...	|	0647	|	0731
Lugano a.	...	...	0553	0604	0625	...	0653	0704	0723	0748
Lugano d.	...	...	0555	0612	0628	...	0655	0712	0725	0755
Locarno ▲ d.	...	...	|	|	|	...	|	|	|	|
Bellinzona ▲ a.	...	...	0621	0642	0658	...	0721	0742	0750	0823
Bellinzona d.	...	0600	0623	0643	0700	...	0723	0743	0800	...
Biasca d.	...	0613	|	0655	0713	...	0735	0755	0813	...
Faido d.	...	0636	|	▬	0736	...	|	▬	0836	...
Airolo d.	...	0654	|	...	0754	...	|	...	0854	...
Göschenen d.	...	0705	|	...	0805	...	|	...	0905	...
Erstfeld d.	0615	0731	|	...	0831	...	|	...	0931	...
Flüelen d.	0625	0739	|	*IR*	0839	...	|	*IR*	0939	...
Brunnen d.	0638	0750	|	**2408**	0850	...	|	**2410**	0950	...
Schwyz d.	0643	0754	|	(🍷)	0854	...	|	(🍷)	0954	...
Arth-Goldau a.	0653	0804	0808k	R	0904	...	0908k	R	1004	...
Arth-Goldau ⊗ d.	0655	0812	0812	0848	0912	...	0912	0948	1012	...
Zug d.	0720	|	0829	|	0929	...	|	|	|	...
Zürich HB a.	0753	|	0851	|	0951	...	|	|	|	...
Schaffhausen **939/40** a.	...	|	...	|	...	...	|	|	|	...
Küssnacht am Rigi ⊗ d.	...	|	...	0859	...	...	|	0959	|	...
Luzern 565 ⊗ a.	...	0837	...	0919	...	...	0937	1019	1037	...
Olten **565** a.	...	0924	...	...	...	...	1024	...	1124	...
Basel SBB **565** a.	...	0951	...	...	...	...	1051	...	1151	...

FOR NOTES SEE OPPOSITE PAGE

FS, SBB — MILANO, CHIASSO and LOCARNO - ZÜRICH and LUZERN — 550

km		CIS 156 ✕⊙ M		IR 2272 △	IC 672		IR 2174 W	EC 170 ⊡ ♦			IR 2276 △	EC 106 ⊡ ♦		IR 2178 △	CIS 154 ✕⊙ V		IR 2280 W	EC 108 ⊡ ♦			IR 2182 △	EC 172 ⊡ ♦		IR 2286 △	EC 110 ⊡ ♦
0	**Milano Centrale** d.	0710	...	...	...	...	...	0825	...	...	...	0925	...	...	1118	...	...	1125	...	...	...	1225	...	...	1325
47	Como San Giovanni d.	0743	...	...	...	...	...	0907	...	...	...	1007	...	...	│	...	...	1207	...	...	...	1307	...	...	1407
51	**Chiasso** 🛃 a.	│	...	...	...	...	...	0912	...	...	...	1012	...	...	│	...	...	1212	...	...	...	1312	...	...	1412
51	**Chiasso** d.	│	0735	...	0831	0835	...	0931	0935	...	...	1031	1035	...	│	1135	...	1231	1235	...	...	1331	1335	...	1431
58	Mendrisio d.	│	0744	...	│	0844	...	│	0944	...	...	│	1044	...	│	1144	...	│	1244	...	...	│	1344	...	│
63	Capolago-Riva San Vitale d.	│	0747	...	│	0847	...	│	0947	...	...	│	1047	...	│	1147	...	│	1247	...	...	│	1347	...	│
77	**Lugano** a.	0808	0804k	...	0853	0904	...	0953	1004	...	...	1053	1104	...	1208	1204k	...	1253	1304	...	...	1353	1404	...	1453
77	**Lugano** d.	0809	0812	...	0855	0912	...	0955	1012	...	...	1055	1112	...	1209	1212	...	1255	1312	...	...	1355	1412	...	1455
	Locarno ▲ d.	│	│	0837z	│	│	0939	│	│	...	1039	│	│	1139	│	│	1239	│	│	...	1339	│	│	1439	│
106	Bellinzona ▲ a.	0833	0842	0858z	0921	0942	0958	1021	1042	...	1058	1121	1142	1158	1233	1242	1258	1321	1342	...	1358	1421	1442	1458	1521
106	Bellinzona d.	0834	0843	0900	0923	0943	1000	1023	1043	...	1100	1123	1143	1200	1234	1243	1300	1323	1343	...	1400	1423	1443	1500	1523
125	Biasca d.	│	0855	0913	│	0955	1013	│	1055	...	1113	│	1155	1213	│	1255	1313	│	1355	...	1413	│	1455	1513	│
151	Faido d.	│	▬	0936	│	▬	1036	│	▬	...	1136	│	▬	1236	│	▬	1336	│	▬	...	1436	│	▬	1536	│
171	Airolo d.	│	...	0954	│	...	1054	│	...	...	1154	│	...	1254	│	...	1354	│	...	...	1454	│	...	1554	│
187	Göschenen d.	│	...	1005	│	...	1105	│	...	...	1205	│	...	1305	│	...	1405	│	...	...	1505	│	...	1605	│
216	Erstfeld d.	│	...	1031	│	...	1131	│	...	...	1231	│	...	1331	│	...	1431	│	...	...	1531	│	...	1631	│
225	Flüelen d.	│	*IR*	1039	│	*IR*	1139	│	*IR*	...	1239	│	*IR*	1339	│	*IR*	1439	│	*IR*	...	1539	│	*IR*	1639	│
237	Brunnen d.	│	**2412**	1050	│	**2416**	1150	│	**2418**	...	1250	│	**2420**	1350	│	**2422**	1450	│	**2424**	...	1550	│	**2426**	1650	│
240	Schwyz d.	│	(🍸)	1054	│	(🍸)	1154	│	(🍸)	...	1254	│	(🍸)	1354	│	(🍸)	1454	│	(🍸)	...	1554	│	(🍸)	1654	│
248	**Arth-Goldau** a.	1008k	R	1104	1108k	R	1204	1208k	R	...	1304	1308k	R	1404	1408k	R	1504	1508k	R	...	1604	1608k	R	1704	1708k
248	**Arth-Goldau** ⊗ d.	1012	1048	1112	1112	1148	1212	1212	1248	...	1312	1312	1348	1412	1412	1448	1512	1512	1548	...	1612	1612	1648	1712	1712
264	Zug d.	1029	│	1129	│	│	│	1229	│	...	1329	│	│	│	1429	│	1529	│	│	...	│	1629	│	1729	│
293	**Zürich HB** a.	1051	│	1151	│	│	│	1251	│	...	1351	│	│	│	1451	│	1551	│	│	...	│	1651	│	1751	│
—	*Schaffhausen* **939/40** a.	...	│	...	│	│	│	...	│	...	...	│	│	│	1547	│	...	│	│	...	│	...	│	...	│
12*	Küssnacht am Rigi ⊗ d.	...	1059	...	│	1159	│	...	1259	...	...	│	1359	│	...	1459	...	│	1559	...	│	...	1659	...	│
28*	**Luzern 565** ⊗ a.	...	1119	...	1137	1219	1237	...	1319	...	...	1337	1419	1437	...	1519	...	1537	1619	...	1637	...	1719	...	1737
	Olten **565** a.	...	...	...	1224	...	1324	...	...	...	...	1424	...	1524	...	...	...	1624	...	...	1724	...	...	...	1824
	Basel SBB **565** a.	...	...	...	1251	...	1351	...	...	...	...	1451	...	1551	...	...	...	1651	...	...	1751	...	...	...	1851

		IR 2188 △	EC 174 ✕⊡ ♦			IR 2290 △	EC 114 ⊡ ♦		IR 2192 △	EC 176 ✕⊡ ♦		CIS 152 ✕⊙ M		IR 2294 △	IC 694		CIS 150 ✕⊙ F	EC 116 ⊡ ♦		EC 178 ⊡ ♦		EC 198 ⊡ ♦			
Milano Centrale d.	...	...	1425	...	...	...	1525	...	...	1625	...	1738	...	...	...	...	1843	1825	...	1920	...	2020	...	...	...
Como San Giovanni d.	...	...	1507	...	...	...	1607	...	...	1707	...	1813	...	...	...	...	1917	1905	...	1957	...	2103	...	...	...
Chiasso 🛃 a.	...	...	1512	...	...	...	1612	...	...	1712	...	│	...	...	...	...	│	1910	...	2002	...	2109	...	...	...
Chiasso d.	1435	...	1531	1535	...	...	1631	1635	...	1731	1735	│	...	...	1831	1835	│	1920	1935	2014	2035	2121	2135	2241	2344
Mendrisio d.	1444	...	│	1544	...	...	│	1644	...	│	1744	│	...	...	│	1844	│	│	1944	│	2044	2129	2144	2250	2352
Capolago-Riva San Vitale d.	1447	...	│	1547	...	...	│	1647	...	│	1747	│	...	...	│	1847	│	│	1947	│	2047	│	2147	2253	2355
Lugano a.	1504	...	1553	1604	...	...	1653	1704	...	1753	1804	1838	...	...	1853	1904	1945	1942	2004	2035	2104	2145	2204	2311	0012
Lugano d.	1512	...	1555	1612	...	...	1655	1712	...	1755	1812	1839	...	...	1855	1912	1946	1948	2012	2037	2112	2146	2212	2312	0012
Locarno ▲ d.	│	1539	│	│	...	1639	│	│	1739	│	│	│	...	1839	│	│	│	│	│	│	│	│	│	│	│
Bellinzona ▲ a.	1542	1558	1621	1642	...	1658	1721	1742	1758	1821	1842	1902	...	1857k	1921	1942	2008	2014	2042	2102	2142	2215	2242	2342	0042
Bellinzona d.	1543	1600	1623	1643	...	1700	1723	1743	1800	1823	1843	1904	...	1859	1923	1943	2010	2015	▬	2104	...	...	2252	...	...
Biasca d.	1555	1613	│	1655	...	1713	│	1755	1813	│	1855	│	...	1913	│	1955	│	2028	...	│	...	...	2304	...	...
Faido d.	▬	1636	│	▬	...	1736	│	▬	1836	│	▬	│	...	1936	│	...	│	2049	...	│	...	...	2325	...	...
Airolo d.	...	1654	│	...	...	1754	│	...	1854	│	...	│	...	1954	│	...	│	2108	...	│	...	...	2343	...	...
Göschenen d.	...	1705	│	...	...	1805	│	...	1905	│	...	│	...	2005	│	...	│	2119	...	│	...	...	...	...	...
Erstfeld d.	...	1731	│	...	...	1831	│	...	1931	│	...	│	...	2031	│	...	│	│	...	│	...	...	...	...	...
Flüelen d.	*IR*	1739	│	*IR*	...	1839	│	*IR*	1939	│	*IR*	│	...	2039	│	...	│	2149	...	2229	...	...	...	...	...
Brunnen d.	**2428**	1750	│	**2430**	...	1850	│	**2432**	1950	│	**2436**	│	...	2050	│	...	│	│	*IR*	│	...	...	...	...	...
Schwyz d.	(🍸)	1754	│	(🍸)	...	1854	│	(🍸)	1954	│	(🍸)	│	...	2054	│	...	│	│	**2296**	│	...	...	...	...	...
Arth-Goldau a.	R	1804	1808k	R	...	1904	1908k	R	2004	2008k	R	2043k	...	2104	2108k	...	2146	2208		2248	...	...	...	...	...
Arth-Goldau ⊗ d.	1748	1812	1812	1848	...	1912	1912	1948	2012	2012	2048	2046	...	2112	2112	...	2147	2212	2212	2250	...	...	...	...	...
Zug d.	│	│	1829	│	...	1929	│	│	│	2029	│	2103	...	2129	│	...	2205	│	2229	2308	...	...	...	...	...
Zürich HB a.	│	│	1851	│	...	1951	│	│	│	2051	│	2125	...	2151	│	...	2229	│	2251	2331	...	...	...	...	...
Schaffhausen **939/40** a.	│	│	1950	│	...	...	│	│	│	...	│	...	...	...	│	...	...	│	...	...	...	...	...	...	...
Küssnacht am Rigi ⊗ d.	1759	│	...	1859	...	...	│	1959	│	...	2059	...	...	...	│	...	...	│	...	...	...	...	...	...	...
Luzern 565 ⊗ a.	1819	1837	...	1919	...	...	1937	2019	2037	...	2119	...	...	...	2137	...	...	2237	...	...	...	...	...	...	...
Olten **565** a.	...	1924	...	...	...	...	2024	...	2124	...	...	...	...	...	2224	...	...	2324	...	...	...	...	...	...	...
Basel SBB **565** a.	...	1951	...	...	...	...	2051	...	2151	...	...	...	...	...	2251	...	...	2351	...	...	...	...	...	...	...

♦ – **NOTES** (LISTED BY TRAIN NUMBER)

105 – CISALPINO LARIO – [12] Biasca / Bellinzona - Milano.
106/119 – CISALPINO TIZIANO – [12] Milano - Basel and v.v.; 🍸 Bellinzona - Luzern and v.v.
107/198 – CISALPINO BRIANZA – [12] Bellinzona - Milano and v.v.
108/117 – CISALPINO VERDI – [12] and 🍸 Milano - Basel and v.v.
109/110 – CISALPINO TICINO – [12] and 🍸 Basel - Milano and v.v.
111/114 – CISALPINO SAN MARCO – [12] and 🍸 Basel - Milano - Venezia Santa Lucia and v.v.
115/116 – CISALPINO MEDIOLANUM – [12] and 🍸 Basel - Milano and v.v.
170/177 – CISALPINO MONTE CENERI – [12] and 🍸 Milano - Zürich and v.v.
171/178 – CISALPINO TEODOLINDA – [12] and 🍸 Zürich - Milano and v.v.
172/179 – CISALPINO INSUBRIA – [12] and 🍸 Milano - Zürich and v.v.
173/4 – CISALPINO CANALETTO – [12] and ✕ Schaffhausen - Zürich - Milano - Venezia Santa Lucia and v.v.
175 – CISALPINO CINQUE TERRE – [12] and ✕ Schaffhausen - Zürich - Milano - Livorno.
176 – CISALPINO CINQUE TERRE – [12] and ✕ Livorno - Milano - Zürich.

F – [12] and ✕ Firenze - Milano - Zürich and v.v.
M – [12] and ✕ Zürich - Milano and v.v.
R – VORALPEN EXPRESS – [12] Luzern - St Gallen - Romanshorn and v.v.
S – [12] and ✕ Schaffhausen - Zürich - Milano.
T – [12] and ✕ Zürich - Milano - Trieste.

V – [12] and ✕ Trieste - Milano - Schaffhausen.
W – [12] Basel / Zürich - Locarno and v.v. May 1 - Oct. 21 also conveys [1] [observation car] and runs as WILHELM TELL EXPRESS Flüelen - Locarno and v.v. 🅁

g – Ⓐ (also Jan. 2, Mar. 21).
j – ⑤ (also Mar. 20, July 31; not Mar. 21, Aug. 1).
k – Connects with train in previous column(s).
s – Stops to set down only.
u – Stops to pick up only.
z – Ⓒ (not Jan. 2, Mar. 21).

⊙ – *CISALPINO Pendolino* train. 🅁 inclusive of supplement for international journeys; may be used for Swiss internal journeys without reservation.
⊡ – Operated by *CISALPINO*. 🅁 for international journeys; may be used for Swiss internal journeys without reservation.
⁄ – Supplement payable.
§ – Supplement payable in Italy (except for passengers with international tickets).
△ – Also conveys [1] [observation car].
▲ – For additional services Locarno - Bellinzona and v.v. see panel below.
* – Distance from Arth-Goldau.

▲ – Additional services **BELLINZONA - LOCARNO and v.v.**:

km														and at the same minutes past each hour until									
0	**Bellinzona** d.	0528	0540	0558	0610	0640	0658	0710	0740	0800	...	0810	0840		2010	2040	2110	2140	2210	2240	2310	2340	0046
21	**Locarno** a.	0546	0606	0619	0636	0706	0719	0736	0806	0820	...	0836	0906		2036	2106	2136	2206	2236	2306	2336	0006	0110

													and at the same minutes past each hour until															
Locarno d.	0523	0553	0623	0636	0653	0723	0736	0753	0823	0836	0853	0923		1853	1923	1939	1953	2023	2039	2053	2123	2153	2223	2253	2323	2353	0023	0114
Bellinzona a.	0548	0618	0648	0655	0718	0748	0755	0818	0848	0858	0918	0948		1918	1948	1958	2018	2048	2056	2118	2148	2218	2248	2318	2348	0018	0048	0138

552 LUZERN - STANS - ENGELBERG

Narrow gauge rack railway. ZB

km																											
		†	⚒					T			T								🚌			🚌			🚌		🚌
0	**Luzern 561** ..... d.	*0605*	0609	0641	0711	0741	0811	0834	0841	0911	0934	0941	1011		1941	2011	...	2041	...	2111	2141	...	2211	2241	...	2341	...
9	Hergiswil **561** .. d.	0625	0625	0655	0725	0755	0825	│	0855	0925	│	0955	1025	and	1955	2025	...	2055	...	2125	2155	...	2225	2255	...	2355	...
11	Stansstad........ d.	0629	0629	0659	0730	0759	0830	│	0859	0930	│	0959	1030	hourly	1959	2030	...	2059	...	2130	2159	...	2230	2259	...	2359	...
15	Stans .... d.	0633	0633	0703	0735	0803	0835	0852	0903	0935	0952	1003	1035	until	2003	2035	...	2103	...	2133	2203	...	2233	2303	...	0003	...
19	Dallenwil .... d.	0640	0640	0708**a**	0740	...	0840	│	...	0940	│	...	1040		...	2040	...	2109	2111	...	2209	2211	...	2309	2311	0009	0011
34	**Engelberg** ...... a.	0712	0712	...	0812	...	0912	0923	...	1012	1023	...	1112		...	2112	...	...	2132	...	...	2232	...	...	2332	...	0032

			Ⓐ									T			T							🚌		🚌		🚌	
Engelberg ....d.	...	...	...	0645	...	0745	...		1545	...	...	1627	1645	...	1727	1745	...		2045	...	...	2145	...	2245	...	2345	...
Dallenwil..........d.	0550	0607	0709	0718	0749**a**	0818	...	and	1618	...	...	│	1718	1749**a**	│	1818	...	and	2118	...	...	2206	2212	2306	2312	0006	0012
Stans.................d.	0556	0613	0716	0725	0755	0825	0855	hourly	1625	1655	...	1707	1725	1755	1807	1825	1855	hourly	2125	2155	...	...	2225	...	2318	...	0018
Stansstad ....d.	0600	0617	0720	0730	0800	0830	0900	until	1630	1700	...	│	1730	1800	│	1830	1900	until	2130	2200	...	...	2230	...	2322	...	0022
Hergiswil **561** ...d.	0604	0624	0725	0734	0805	0834	0905		1634	1705	...	│	1734	1805	│	1834	1905		2134	2205	...	...	2234	...	2325	...	0025
Luzern 561 ......a.	0616	0636	0734	0749	0819	0849	0919		1649	1719	...	1726	1749	1819	1826	1849	1919		2149	2219	...	...	2249	...	...	...	...

T – TITLIS EXPRESS – © Dec. 9 - Mar. 30, July 5 - Oct. 12.

a – Ⓐ only.

553 MOUNTAIN RAILWAYS IN CENTRAL SWITZERLAND

2nd class only

km																											
			p							S														p	q		
0	Arth-Goldau .... d.	0800	0910	...	...	1010	...	...	...	1015	1110	1210	...	1310	...	...	...	1410	...	1510	...	1610	...	1710	1810	...	...
9	Rigi Kulm .... a.	0845	0947	...	...	1047	...	...	...	1205	1147	1247	...	1347	...	...	...	1447	...	1547	...	1647	...	1747	1847	...	...
	change trains	**y**	**z**	**n**	**r**	**z**	**n**	**y**	**z**		**r**	**z**	**y**	**z**	**n**	**K**	**r**	**z**	**y**	**z**	**y**	**z**	**y**	**m**		**m**	**m**
0	Rigi Kulm .... d.	0925	1000	1010	1040	1050	1100	1140	1145	...	1240	1250	1325	1355	1425	1410	1440	1455	1540	1555	1640	1655	1740	1840	...	2010	2240
7	Vitznau .... a.	1005	1040	1050	1120	1130	1140	1220	1225	...	1320	1330	1405	1440	1505	1509	1520	1540	1620	1640	1720	1735	1820	1920	...	2050	2320

		y	**z**	**n**	**r**	**z**	**n**	**r**	**n**	**K**	**T**	**z**		**y**	**z**		**y**	**z**	**y**	**z**	**y**	**z**	**y**	**m**	**m**	**m**	
Vitznau ....d.	...	0840	0905	0930	0940	1015	1025	1040	1100	1041	1101	1105	1145	1240	1305	...	1340	1415	1440	1515	1540	1615	1640	1740	1930	2205	...
Rigi Kulm ....a.	...	0910	0940	1000	1010	1045	1055	1110	1130	1220	1235	1140	1215	1310	1340	...	1410	1445	1510	1545	1610	1645	1710	1810	2000	2235	...
change trains				p												S							p	q			
Rigi Kulm ....d.	0900	...	...	1005	...	...	1105	...	1205	...	...	...	1305	...	1405	1406	...	1505	...	1605	...	1705	1805	1905	...	...	...
Arth-Goldau......a.	0950	...	...	1050	...	...	1150	...	1250	...	...	...	1350	...	1450	1535	...	1550	...	1650	...	1750	1850	1950	...	...	...

ALPNACHSTAD - PILATUS KULM. Narrow gauge rack railway. *5 km*. Journey time: 30 minutes uphill, 40 minutes downhill. **Operator**: PB, ✆ 041 329 11 11.
Services run daily ***early May - Nov. 23*** (weather permitting). **NO WINTER SERVICE** (December - April).

From **Alpnachstad**: 0810 **j**, 0850, 0930, 1010, 1050, 1130, 1210, 1310, 1350, 1430, 1510, 1600, 1650 **j**, 1735 **k**, 1815 **x**.

From **Pilatus Kulm**: 0845 **j**, 0925, 1005, 1045, 1125, 1205, 1305, 1345, 1425, 1505, 1555, 1645, 1730 **j**, 1810 **k**, 1900 **x**.

BRIENZ - BRIENZER ROTHORN. Narrow gauge rack railway. *8 km*. Most services operated by steam train. Journey time: 55–60 minutes uphill, 60–70 minutes downhill.
Operator: BRB, ✆ 033 952 22 22. Service operates ***May 24 - Oct. 26 (also May 17, 18) only***, and is subject to demand and weather conditions on the mountain. A reduced service operates until June 6. Extra trains may run at busy times. **NO WINTER SERVICE** (November - April).

From **Brienz**: 0737 **w**, 0837, 0937, 1005, 1040, 1145, 1245, 1345, 1445, 1545, 1620 **v**.

From **Brienzer Rothorn**: 0834 **w**, 0936, 1038, 1110, 1215, 1315, 1415, 1515, 1615, 1650, 1725 **v**.

K – 🚂 Steam train. Runs ⑥ July 5 - Sept. 27 (also Sept. 28) from Rigi Kulm; Sept. 27, 28 from Vitznau. Supplement payable (from Vitznau only, CHF 10).
S – 🚂 Steam train. Runs ⑥ July 5 - Sept. 27 from Arth-Goldau; ⑦ July 6 - Sept. 21 from Rigi Kulm. Supplement payable (from Arth-Goldau only, CHF 10).
T – 🚂 Steam train. Runs ⑦ July 6 - Sept. 21 from Vitznau. Supplement payable (CHF 10).
j – Until Oct. 25.
k – May 25 - Aug. 30.
m – May 1 - Oct. 19.
n – May 25 - Sept. 21.
p – ⑥⑦ Dec. 9 - 16; daily Dec. 17 - Mar. 24; ⑥⑦ Mar. 29 - Apr. 27; daily May 1 - Oct. 31; ⑥⑦ Nov. 1 - Dec. 13 (also Dec. 8).
q – Daily Dec. 22 - Jan. 2; ⑤⑥⑦ May 2 - June 27; daily June 28 - Aug. 31; ⑤⑥⑦ Sept. 5 - Oct. 26 (also May 1, 12, 22).
r – Mar. 21 - May 24, Sept. 22 - Oct. 19.
v – June 28 - Aug. 31.
w – ⑦ Aug. 3 - Sept. 21.
x – June 29 - Aug. 30.
y – Mar. 21 - Oct. 19.
z – Dec. 9 - Mar. 20, Oct. 20 - Dec. 13.

554 🚌 MEIRINGEN - ANDERMATT Service June 21 - October 5, 2008 (no winter service)

PA

	R	R	R	R	R	R	R	R	R	
Meiringen Bahnhof............d.	...	...	0920	...	1100	1300	1330	1520	...	...
Susten Passhöhe............d.	...	...	│	...	│	│	1440	│	...	...
Göschenen Bahnhof.......d.	...	...	│	...	│	│	1524	│	...	...
Grimsel Passhöhe..............d.	0842	...	1045	...	1220	1404	│	1630	...	...
Oberwald Bahnhof ....a.	0907	...	1111	...	1251	...	│	1654	...	...
Oberwald Bahnhof ....d.	...	1030	1120	1230	...	...	│	...	1715	...
Furka Passhöhe..................d.	...	1109	│	1415	...	...	│	...	1751	...
Realp Post ....d.	...	...	│	1441	...	...	│	...	1817	...
Andermatt Bahnhof...........a.	...	...	1520	1500	...	...	1539	...	1835	...

	R	R	R	R	R	R	R	R	R	R
Andermatt Bahnhof.........d.	...	0830	...	0910	...	1140	...	1535	...	1545
Realp Post.......................d.	...	0842	...	│	...	│	...	│	...	1557
Furka Passhöhe..............d.	...	0906	1110	│	...	│	...	│	...	1621
Oberwald Bahnhof ....a.	...	1020	1156	1210	...	1510	...	│	...	1706
Oberwald Bahnhof ....d.	0815	1030	...	...	1335	...	...	│	1700	...
Grimsel Passhöhe...........d.	0841	1130	...	...	1407	...	1530	│	1732	...
Göschenen Bahnhof....d.	...	│	...	...	│	...	│	1552	│	...
Susten Passhöhe ....d.	...	│	...	...	│	...	│	1632	│	...
Meiringen Bahnhof.........a.	...	1230	...	...	1511	...	1634	1736	1836	...

555 ZÜRICH FLUGHAFEN ✈ - ZÜRICH - LUZERN

SBB

km																							
																Ⓐ			Ⓐ				
0	**Zürich Flughafen ✈ 530/5** ..d.	...	...	...	...	...	...	...	0847	...	and at	1547	...	...	...	...	1647	...	...	1747	...	1847	...	1947
10	**Zürich HB 530/5** ....d.	0535	0604	0635	0704	0735	0804	0835	0904	0935	the same	1604	1635	...	1641	1704	1735	1741	1804	1835	1904	1935	2004
22	Thalwil..................................d.	0545	0614	0645	0714	0745	0814	0845	0914	0945	minutes	1614	1645	...	1654	1714	1745	1754	1814	1845	1914	1945	2014
39	Zug.......................................d.	0602	0629	0702	0729	0802	0829	0902	0929	1002	past each	1629	1702	...	1712	1729	1802	1812	1829	1902	1929	2002	2029
49	Rotkreuz...............................d.	0610	│	0710	│	0810	│	0910	│	1010	hour	│	1710	...	1720	│	1810	1820	│	1910	│	2010	│
67	**Luzern** ....a.	0625	0650	0725	0750	0825	0850	0925	0950	1025	until	1650	1725	...	1735	1750	1825	1835	1850	1925	1950	2025	2050

Zürich Flughafen ✈ 530/5 ..d.	...	2047	...	...	...	...	...	...	...
Zürich HB 530/5.....................d.	2035	2104	2135	...	2204	2235	2307	2335	0007
Thalwil....................................d.	2045	2114	2145	...	2214	2245	2317	2345	0017
Zug ....d.	2102	2129	2202	...	2229	2302	2332	0002	0035
Rotkreuz..................................d.	2110	│	2210	...	│	2310	│	0010	0046
Luzern ....a.	2125	2150	2225	...	2250	2325	2351	0025	0107

				Ⓐ				Ⓐ	
Luzern..d.	0455	0528	0608	0621	0635	...	0710	0723	0735
Rotkreuz ....d.	0514	0548	│	0636	0648	...	│	0737	0748
Zug..d.	0526	0558	0629	0648	0658	...	0731	0748	0758
Thalwil ....d.	0542	0616	0646	0705	0716	...	0746	0805	0816
Zürich HB 530/5..........................a.	0555	0625	0656	0719	0725	...	0756	0819	0825
Zürich Flughafen ✈ 530/5.........a.	0613	...	...	...	...	...	0813	...	...

Luzern ....d.	0810	0835	and at	1510	1535	...	1610	1635	1710	1735	1810	1835	1910	1935	...	2010	2035	2110	2135	2210	2235	2310	2335
Rotkreuz....................................d.	│	0848	the same	│	1548	...	│	1648	│	1748	│	1848	│	1948	...	│	2048	│	2148	│	2248	│	2348
Zug ....d.	0831	0858	minutes	1531	1558	...	1631	1658	1731	1758	1831	1858	1931	1958	...	2031	2058	2131	2158	2231	2258	2331	2358
Thalwil.......................................d.	0846	0916	past each	1546	1616	...	1646	1716	1746	1816	1846	1916	1946	2016	...	2046	2113	2146	2216	2246	2316	2346	0016
Zürich HB 530/5.....................a.	0856	0925	hour	1556	1625	...	1656	1725	1756	1825	1856	1925	1956	2025	...	2056	2123	2156	2225	2256	2325	2356	0025
Zürich Flughafen ✈ 530/5 ..a.	0913	...	until	1613	...	...	1713	...	1813	...	1913	...	2013	...	...	...	...	...	...	...	...	...	...

SBB BASEL - BERN - INTERLAKEN and BRIG 560

km		IC	IC	ICE	IC	IC	CIS	IC	IC	ICE	IC	IC	CIS	ICE	IC	IC	IC	IC	IC	IC	IC	IC	ICE	IC	CIS	IC	IC	IC	ICE
		3353	3153	1055	955	808	41	959	810	1061	961	812	43	5	816	1067	967	818	1069	969	820	1071	375	822	47	973	824	1075	277
				✕			✕ ⊙			✕			✕ ⊙	✕ ♦									✕ F		✕ ⊙				✕ B
	Romanshorn **535** ... d.	...	...	...	...	...	...	...	0538	...	...	0638	...	...	0741	...	...	0841	...	...	0941	...	...	1041	...	...	1141	...	...
	Zürich Flug ✈ **535** . d.	...	...	...	...	...	...	...	0639	...	...	0743	...	...	0839	...	...	0939	...	...	1039	...	...	1139	...	...	1239	...	...
	Zürich HB **500** .... d.	...	...	...	...	0600	...	...	0700	...	...	0800	...	...	0900	...	...	1000	...	...	1100	...	...	1200	...	...	1300	...	...
0	**Basel SBB** .... d.	...	...	0527	0601	|	0630	0701	|	0730	0801	|	0830	0901	|	0930	1001	|	1030	1101	|	1130	1201	|	1230	1301	|	1330	1401
14	Liestal .... d.	...	...	0537	|	|	0640	|	|	0740	|	|	0840	|	|	0940	|	|	1040	|	|	1140	|	|	1240	|	|	1340	|
39	Olten .... d.	...	...	0600	0629	|	0700	0729	|	0800	0829	|	0900	0929	|	1000	1029	|	1100	1129	|	1200	1229	|	1300	1329	|	1400	1429
101	**Bern** .... a.	...	...	0627	0656	0657k	0727	0756	0757k	0827	0856	0857k	0927	0956	0957k	1027	1056	1057k	1127	1156	1157k	1227	1256	1257k	1327	1356	1357k	1427	1456
101	**Bern** .... d.	0604	0607	0635	0704	0707	0735	0804	0807	0835	0904	0907	0935	1004	1007	1035	1104	1107	1135	1204	1207	1235	1304	1307	1335	1404	1407	1435	1504
132	Thun .... d.	0622	0625	0654	0722	0725	0754	0822	0825	0854	0922	0925	0954	1022	1025	1054	1122	1125	1154	1222	1225	1254	1322	1325	1354	1422	1425	1454	1522
142	**Spiez** .... a.	0631	0634	0702	0731	0734	0802	0831	0834	0902	0931	0934	1002	1031	1034	1102	1131	1134	1202	1231	1234	1302	1331	1334	1402	1431	1434	1502	1531
142	**Spiez** .... ⊗ d.	0632	0636	0703	0732	0736	0805	0832	0836	0903	0932	0936	1005	1032	1036	1103	1132	1136	1205	1232	1236	1303	1332	1336	1405	1432	1436	1503	1532
	Interlaken West.. ⊗ d.	0652	|	0723	0752	|	|	0852	|	0923	0952	|	|	1052	|	1123	1152	|	|	1252	|	1323	1352	|	|	1452	|	1523	1552
	Interlaken Ost .. ⊗ a.	0657	|	0728	0757	|	|	0857	|	0928	0957	|	|	1057	|	1128	1157	|	|	1257	|	1328	1357	|	|	1457	|	1528	1557
197	Visp .... d.	...	0703	...	...	0803	0832	...	0903	...	...	1003	1032	...	1103	...	...	1203	1232	...	1303	...	...	1403	1432	...	1503	...	...
206	**Brig** .... a.	...	0711	...	...	0811	0840	...	0911	...	...	1011	1040	...	1111	...	...	1211	1240	...	1311	...	...	1411	1440	...	1511	...	...
	Milano C **590** .... a.	...	...	...	...	...	1035	...	...	...	...	...	1245	...	...	...	...	...	...	...	...	...	...	...	1640	...	...	...	...

	IC	IC	IC	IC	IC	IC	IC	IC	IC	IC	CIS	ICE	IC	IC	ICE	IC	IC	ICE	IC	IC	IC	IC	IC	IC	EN	IC	IC	ICE	IC
	826	1077	977	828	1079	979	830	1081	981	832	51	373	836	1087	987	838	1089	279	1091	1091	991	3391	1093	3191	313	993	995	3395	3351
											✕ ⊙	✕ B			✕			✕ B	①–⑥	⑦					🅁 ⚡ ♦				M
Romanshorn **535** ....d.	1241	...	...	1341	...	...	1441	...	...	1541	...	...	1641	...	...	1741	...	...	...	...	...	...	...	...	...	...	...	...	...
Zürich Flug ✈ **535**..d.	1339	...	...	1439	...	...	1539	...	...	1639	...	...	1739	...	...	1839	...	...	...	...	...	...	...	...	...	...	...	...	...
Zürich HB **500** ....d.	1400	...	...	1500	...	...	1600	...	...	1700	...	...	1800	...	...	1900	...	...	...	...	...	...	...	...	2127u	...	...	...	...
Basel SBB..........d.	|	1430	1501	|	1530	1601	|	1630	1701	|	1730	1801	|	1830	1901	|	1930	2001	2030	2030	2101	...	2130	...	|	2201	2305	...	...
Liestal ....d.	|	1440	|	|	1540	|	|	1640	|	|	1740	|	|	1840	|	|	1940	|	2040	2040	|	...	2140	...	|	|	|	...	...
Olten ....d.	|	1500	1529	|	1600	1629	|	1700	1729	|	1800	1829	|	1900	1929	|	2000	2029	2100	2100	2129	...	2200	...	2209u	2229	2332	...	...
Bern..........a.	1457k	1527	1556	1557k	1627	1656	1657k	1727	1756	1757k	1827	1856	1857k	1927	1956	1957k	2027	2056	2127	2127	2156	...	2227	...	|	2256	2359	...	...
Bern..........d.	1507	1535	1604	1607	1635	1704	1707	1735	1804	1807	1835	1904	1907	1935	2004	2007	2035	2104	2135	2135	...	2204	...	2239	2304u	2307	...	0009	0115
Thun..........d.	1525	1554	1622	1625	1654	1722	1725	1754	1822	1825	1854	1922	1925	1954	2022	2025	2054	2122	2154	2154	...	2222	...	2258	2322u	2325	...	0029	0136
Spiez..........a.	1534	1602	1631	1634	1702	1731	1734	1802	1831	1834	1902	1931	1934	2002	2031	2034	2102	2131	2202	2202	...	2231	...	2306	|	2334	...	0039	0146
Spiez .... ⊗ d.	1536	1605	1632	1636	1703	1732	1736	1805	1832	1836	1905	1932	1936	2003	2032	2036	2104	2132	2204	2204	...	2232	...	2308	2334u	2335	...	0039	0146
Interlaken West.. ⊗ d.	|	|	1652	|	1723	1752	|	|	1852	|	|	1952	|	2023	2050	|	|	2150	|	|	...	2250	...	|	|	2352	...	0053	0204
Interlaken Ost... ⊗ a.	|	|	1657	|	1728	1757	|	|	1857	|	|	1957	|	2028	2055	|	|	2155	|	|	...	2255	...	|	|	2357	...	0100	0213
Visp..........d.	1603	1632	...	1703	...	...	1803	1832	...	1903	1932	...	2003	...	...	2103	f	...	2231	|	...	...	...	f	|	...	...	...	...
Brig..........a.	1611	1640	...	1711	...	...	1811	1840	...	1911	1940	...	2011	...	...	2111	2209	...	2239	2301	...	...	...	0012	0058u	...	...	...	...
Milano C **590** ....a.	...	...	...	...	...	...	...	...	...	...	2135	...	...	...	...	...	...	...	...	...	...	...	...	...	...	...	...	...	...

km		IC	IC	EN	IC	ICE	IC	IC	IC	IC	IC	ICE	IC	IC	IC	IC	CIS		ICE	IC	IC	IC	IC	IC	ICE	IC	IC	IC	IC
		809	952	314	1058	278	811	1060	956	815	1064	372	817	1066	962	819	40		272	821	1070	968	823	1072	276	825	1074	974	827
				🅁 ⚡ ♦		✕ B						✕ B					✕ ⊙		✕ B						✕ B				
	Milano C **590** .... d.	...	...	...	...	...	...	...	...	...	...	...	...	...	...	...	0725	...	...	...	...	...	...	...	...	...	...	...	...
	Brig.......... d.	...	...	0439s	...	...	0545	...	...	0649	0720	...	0749	...	...	0849	0920	...	...	0949	...	...	1049	1120	...	1149	...	...	1249
	Visp.......... d.	...	...	|	...	...	0553	...	...	0657	0728	...	0757	...	...	0857	0928	...	...	0957	...	...	1057	1128	...	1157	...	...	1257
0	**Interlaken Ost** .. ⊗ d.	...	...	|	0522	0601	f	0627	0701	|	|	0801	|	0831	0901	|	|	...	1001	|	1031	1101	|	|	1201	|	1231	1301	|
2	Interlaken West.. ⊗ d.	...	...	|	0526	0605	|	0630	0705	|	|	0805	|	0835	0905	|	|	...	1005	|	1035	1105	|	|	1205	|	1235	1305	|
18	**Spiez**.......... ⊗ a.	...	...	0543s	0548	0622	0624	0652	0722	0724	0753	0822	0824	0852	0922	0924	0953	...	1022	1024	1052	1122	1124	1153	1222	1224	1252	1322	1324
	Spiez.......... d.	0520	...	|	0550	0623	0625	0654	0723	0725	0754	0823	0825	0854	0923	0925	0954	...	1023	1025	1054	1123	1125	1154	1223	1225	1254	1323	1325
	Thun.......... d.	0530	...	|	0601	0634	0637	0705	0734	0737	0805	0834	0837	0905	0934	0937	1005	...	1034	1037	1105	1134	1137	1205	1234	1237	1305	1334	1337
	Bern.......... a.	0553	...	0620s	0623	0652	0654k	0723	0752	0754k	0823	0852	0854k	0923	0952	0954k	1023	...	1052	1054k	1123	1152	1154k	1223	1252	1254k	1323	1352	1354k
	Bern.......... d.	0602	0604	|	0634	0704	0702	0734	0804	0802	0834	0904	0902	0934	1004	1002	1034	...	1104	1102	1134	1204	1202	1234	1304	1302	1334	1404	1402
	Olten.......... d.	0631	0631	0740s	0702	0731	|	0802	0831	|	0902	0931	|	1002	1031	|	1102	...	1131	|	1202	1231	|	1302	1331	|	1402	1431	|
	Liestal.......... d.	|	|	|	0720	|	|	0819	|	|	0919	|	|	1019	|	|	1119	...	|	|	1219	|	|	1319	|	|	1419	|	|
	Basel SBB .... a.	|	0654	|	0729	0754	|	0829	0854	|	0929	0954	|	1029	1054	|	1129	...	1154	|	1229	1254	|	1329	1354	|	1429	1454	|
	Zürich HB **500** .... a.	0702	...	0834	...	...	0758	...	...	0858	...	...	0958	...	...	1058	...	...	...	1158	...	...	1258	...	...	1358	...	...	1458
	Zürich Flug ✈ **535**. a.	0716	...	...	...	...	0816	...	...	0916	...	...	1016	...	...	1116	...	...	...	1216	...	...	1316	...	...	1416	...	...	1516
	Romanshorn **535** ..... a.	0818	...	...	...	...	0918	...	...	1018	...	...	1118	...	...	1218	...	...	...	1318	...	...	1418	...	...	1518	...	...	1618

	CIS	IC	IC	IC	ICE	IC	IC	IC	IC	ICE	IC	IC	IC	IC	IC	IC	IC	IC	IC	IC	IC	CIS	ICE	IC	ICE	CIS	CIS	ICE	IR
	44	978	829	1078	374	831	1080	982	835	1082	986	837	1086	988	839	1088	990	841	1090	992	843	48	994	845	996	50	50	998	3398
	✕ ⊙				✕ F					✕												✕ ⊙	✕		✕	✕ ⊙ p	✕ ⊙ q	✕	⑤⑥
Milano C **590** ....d.	1120	...	...	...	...	...	...	...	...	...	...	...	...	...	...	...	...	...	...	...	...	1825	...	...	...	2025	2025	...	...
Brig..........d.	1320	...	1349	...	...	1449	1520	...	1549	...	...	1649	1720	...	1749	...	...	1849	1850	...	1949	2020	...	...	...	2220	2226	...	...
Visp..........d.	1328	...	1357	...	...	1457	1528	...	1557	...	...	1657	1728	...	1757	...	...	1857	f	...	1957	2028	...	...	...	2228	|	...	...
Interlaken Ost... ⊗ d.	|	1401	|	1431	1501	|	|	1601	|	1631	1701	|	|	1801	|	1831	1901	|	|	2001	|	|	2101	...	2201	|	|	2301	2331
Interlaken West.. ⊗ d.	|	1405	|	1435	1505	|	|	1605	|	1635	1705	|	|	1805	|	1835	1905	|	|	2005	|	|	2105	...	2205	|	|	2305	2335
Spiez .... ⊗ a.	1353	1422	1424	1452	1522	1524	1553	1622	1624	1652	1722	1724	1753	1822	1824	1852	1922	1924	1953	2022	2024	2053	2122	...	2222	2253	2322	2322	2352
Spiez..........d.	1354	1423	1425	1454	1523	1525	1554	1623	1625	1654	1723	1725	1754	1823	1825	1854	1923	1925	1954	2023	2025	2054	2123	...	2223	2254	2325	2323	2354
Thun..........d.	1405	1434	1437	1505	1534	1537	1605	1634	1637	1705	1734	1737	1805	1834	1837	1905	1934	1937	2005	2034	2037	2105	2134	...	2234	2305	2337	2334	0005
Bern..........a.	1423	1452	1454k	1523	1552	1554k	1623	1652	1654k	1723	1752	1754k	1823	1852	1854k	1923	1952	1954k	2023	2052	2054k	2123	2152	...	2252	2323	2354	2352	0023
Bern..........d.	1434	1504	1502	1534	1604	1602	1634	1704	1702	1734	1804	1802	1834	1904	1902	1934	2004	2002	2034	2104	2102	2134	2204	2202	2304	2334	0006	...	...
Olten ....a.	1502	1531	|	1602	1631	|	1702	1731	|	1802	1831	|	1902	1931	|	2002	2031	|	2102	2131	|	2202	2232	|	2332	0002	0034	...	...
Liestal ....a.	1519	|	|	1619	|	|	1719	|	|	1819	|	|	1919	|	|	2019	|	|	2119	|	|	2219	2254	|	2354	0019	0051	...	...
Basel SBB..........a.	1529	1554	|	1629	1654	|	1729	1754	|	1829	1854	|	1929	1954	|	2029	2054	|	2129	2154	|	2229	2304	|	0004	0029	0100	...	...
Zürich HB **500** ....a.	...	...	1558	...	...	1658	...	...	1758	...	...	1858	...	...	1958	...	...	2058	...	...	2158	...	...	2258	...	...	...	...	...
Zürich Flug ✈ **535**...a.	...	...	1616	...	...	1716	...	...	1816	...	...	1916	...	...	2016	...	...	2116	...	...	2216	...	...	2316	...	...	...	...	...
Romanshorn **535** ....a.	...	...	1718	...	...	1818	...	...	1918	...	...	2018	...	...	2118	...	...	2218	...	...	2318	...	...	0018	...	...	...	...	...

♦ – **NOTES** (LISTED BY TRAIN NUMBER)

5 – (12) and ✕ (①, also Dec. 27, Jan. 2, Mar. 25, May 13, not Dec. 24, 31, Mar. 24, May 12, Hamburg -) Frankfurt - Basel - Interlaken.

313 – LUNA – 🛏 1, 2 cl. and 🛏 2 cl. Zürich - Brig - Roma Termini. Also conveys (12) Zürich - Brig (without supplement).

314 – LUNA – 🛏 1, 2 cl. and 🛏 2 cl. Roma Termini - Brig - Zürich. Also conveys (12) Brig - Zürich (without supplement).

B – (12) and ✕ Interlaken - Basel - Berlin Ost and v.v.
F – (12) and ✕ Interlaken - Basel - Frankfurt and v.v.
M – MOONLINER – ⑥⑦ (also Jan. 1). June 8-30 runs to special FIFA *EURO 2008* schedule.

f – Via Frutigen.
k – Connects with train in previous column.
p – ①–⑥ only.
q – ⑦ only.
s – Stops to set down only.
u – Stops to pick up only.

⚡ – Supplement payable.
⊙ – *CISALPINO Pendolino* train: (12) and ✕ Basel - Milano and v.v. 🅁 inclusive of supplement for international journeys; may be used for Swiss internal journeys without reservation.
🚗 – Car-carrying shuttle available (see page 260).

● – 🚌 **SERVICE FRUTIGEN - ADELBODEN and v.v.:** 20 km, journey 30 minutes.

Operator: AFA, 3715 Adelboden. ✆ +41 (0)33 673 74 74, fax +41 (0)33 673 74 70.

From **Frutigen:** 0615Ⓐ, 0633, 0708Ⓐ, 0733 and hourly until 1633, then 1700Ⓐ, 1733, 1800Ⓐ, 1833, 1900Ⓐ, 1933, 2033, 2130, 2230, 2330.

From **Adelboden:** 0535Ⓐ, 0552, 0622Ⓐ, 0652 and hourly until 1552, then 1630Ⓐ, 1652, 1730Ⓐ, 1752, 1830Ⓐ, 1852, 1952, 2052, 2152, 2228.

561 LUZERN - INTERLAKEN

ZB. Narrow gauge rack railway

km																										
		Ⓐ	P				⚒			⚒	P			P		P				⚒				P		
0	**Luzern 552** d.	...	...	...	0537	0605	0637	0655	0707	0737	0755	0807	0837	0855	0907	0955	1007	1055	1107	1137	1155	1207	1237	1255	1307	1337
9	Hergiswil **552** d.	...	...	...	0553	0623	0653	0706	0723	0753	0806	0823	0853	0906	0923	1006	1023	1106	1123	1153	1206	1223	1253	1306	1323	1353
13	Alpnachstad d.	...	...	...	0558	0628	0658	|	0728	0758	|	0828	0858	|	0928	|	1028	|	1128	1158	|	1228	1258	|	1328	1358
15	Alpnach Dorf d.	...	...	...	0601	0631	0701	0711	0731	0801	0811	0831	0901	0911	0931	1011	1031	1111	1131	1201	1211	1231	1301	1311	1331	1401
21	Sarnen d.	...	...	...	0609	0639	0709	0720	0739	0809	0820	0839	0909	0920	0939	1020	1039	1120	1139	1209	1220	1239	1309	1320	1339	1409
23	Sachseln d.	...	...	...	0614	0644	0714	|	0744	0814	|	0844	0914	|	0944	|	1044	|	1144	1214	|	1244	1314	|	1344	1414
29	Giswil d.	...	...	...	0626	0651	0721	0730	0751	0821	0830	0851	0921	0930	0951	1030	1051	1130	1151	1221	1230	1251	1321	1330	1351	1421
36	Lungern § d.	...	...	...	0639	...	▬	0744	...	▬	0844	...	...	0944	▬	1044	▬	1144	...	▬	1244	...	▬	1344	...	▬
40	Brünig Hasliberg d.	...	...	...	0653	...	...	0756	...	...	0856	...	...	0956	...	1056	...	1156	...	...	1256	...	...	1356	...	...
45	**Meiringen ●** a.	...	...	...	0708	...	...	0812	...	...	0912	...	...	1012	...	1112	⚒	1212	...	...	1312	...	⚒	1412	...	...
45	**Meiringen ●** d.	0547	0614	0647	0720	...	0746	0821	...	0846	0921	...	...	1021	1046	1121	1146	1221	...	1246	1321	...	1346	1421	...	1446
58	**Brienz** d.	0559	0626	0701	0734	...	0800	0838	...	0900	0938	...	...	1038	1100	1138	1200	1238	...	1300	1338	...	1400	1438	...	1500
65	Oberried d.	0609	0638	0713	0744	...	0812	|	...	0912	|	...	...	|	1112	|	1212	|	...	1312	|	...	1412	|	...	1512
74	**Interlaken Ost** a.	0622	0651	0724	0755	...	0824	0855	...	0924	0955	...	...	1055	1124	1155	1224	1255	...	1324	1355	...	1424	1455	...	1524

		P										P						P							
Luzern 552 d.	1355	1407	1455	1507	1537	1555	1607	1637	1655	1707	1737	1755	1807	1837	1855	1907	1937	1955	2007	2037	2107	2137	2207	2311	0030
Hergiswil **552** d.	1406	1423	1506	1523	1553	1606	1623	1653	1706	1723	1753	1806	1823	1853	1906	1923	1953	2006	2023	2053	2123	2153	2223	2326	0043
Alpnachstad d.	|	1428	|	1528	1558	|	1628	1658	|	1728	1758	|	1828	1858	|	1928	1958	|	2028	2058	2128	2158	2228	2330	0048
Alpnach Dorf d.	1411	1431	1511	1531	1601	1611	1631	1701	1711	1731	1801	1811	1831	1901	1911	1931	2001	2011	2031	2101	2131	2201	2231	2332	0050
Sarnen d.	1420	1439	1520	1539	1609	1620	1639	1709	1720	1739	1809	1820	1839	1909	1920	1939	2009	2020	2039	2109	2139	2209	2239	2340	0057
Sachseln d.	|	1444	|	1544	1614	|	1644	1714	|	1744	1814	|	1844	1914	|	1944	2014	|	2044	2114	2144	2214	2244	2344	0100
Giswil d.	1430	1451	1530	1551	1621	1630	1651	1721	1730	1751	1821	1830	1851	1921	1930	1951	2021	2030	2051	2121	2152	2221	2251	2351	0108
Lungern § d.	1444	▬	1544	...	▬	1644	...	▬	1744	...	▬	1844	...	...	1944	...	▬	2043	▬	...	2206	▬	...	...	...
Brünig Hasliberg d.	1456	...	1556	...	...	1656	...	...	1756	...	...	1856	...	...	1956	...	...	2101	...	...	2217	...	...	...	...
Meiringen ● a.	1512	...	1612	...	...	1712	...	...	1812	...	...	1912	...	...	2012	...	...	2116	...	...	2232	...	...	...	...
Meiringen ● d.	1521	1546	1621	...	1646	1721	...	1746	1821	...	1846	1921	...	...	...	...	2018	...	2118	...	...	2237	...	...	...
Brienz d.	1538	1600	1638	...	1700	1738	...	1800	1838	...	1900	1935	...	...	...	...	2032	...	2132	...	...	2249	...	...	...
Oberried d.	|	1612	|	...	1712	|	...	1812	|	...	1912	1944	...	...	...	...	2042	...	2142	...	...	2259	...	...	...
Interlaken Ost a.	1555	1624	1655	...	1724	1755	...	1824	1855	...	1924	1956	...	...	...	...	2055	...	2155	...	...	2311	...	...	...

		⚒		P				Ⓐ		P							P						P	⚒	
Interlaken Ost d.	...	...	...	...	...	...	...	0627	...	0704	0733	...	0804	0833	0904	0933	1004	...	...	1104	1133	...	1204	1233	...
Oberried d.	...	...	...	...	...	...	...	0639	...	0714	0746	...	|	0846	|	0946	|	...	...	|	1146	...	|	1246	...
Brienz d.	...	...	...	...	...	...	...	0650	...	0724	0758	...	0825	0858	0925	0958	1025	...	...	1125	1158	...	1225	1258	...
Meiringen ● a.	...	...	...	...	...	...	...	0703	...	0734	0810	...	0835	0910	0935	1010	1035	...	...	1135	1210	...	1235	1310	...
Meiringen ● d.	...	...	...	0544	...	...	0644	▬	...	0743	▬	...	0844	▬	0944	▬	1044	...	...	1144	▬	...	1244	▬	...
Brünig Hasliberg d.	...	...	...	0555	...	...	0655	...	...	0756	...	...	0855	...	0955	...	1055	...	...	1155	...	...	1255	...	...
Lungern § d.	...	...	...	0610	...	...	0710	...	...	0810	...	...	0910	...	1010	...	1110	...	...	1210	...	...	1310	...	...
Giswil d.	0506	0536	0606	0629	0636	0706	0729	0736	0806	0829	0836	0906	0929	1006	1029	1106	1129	1136	1206	1229	1236	1306	1329	1336	1406
Sachseln d.	0515	0545	0615	|	0645	0715	|	0745	0815	|	0845	0915	|	1015	|	1115	|	1145	1215	|	1245	1315	|	1345	1415
Sarnen d.	0520	0550	0620	0640	0650	0720	0740	0750	0820	0840	0850	0920	0940	1020	1040	1120	1140	1150	1220	1240	1250	1320	1340	1350	1420
Alpnach Dorf d.	0525	0555	0625	0645	0655	0725	0745	0755	0825	0845	0855	0925	0945	1025	1045	1125	1145	1155	1225	1245	1255	1325	1345	1355	1425
Alpnachstad d.	0530	0600	0630	|	0700	0730	|	0800	0830	|	0900	0930	|	1030	|	1130	|	1200	1230	|	1300	1330	|	1400	1430
Hergiswil **552** d.	0539	0609	0639	0654	0709	0739	0754	0809	0839	0854	0909	0939	0954	1039	1054	1139	1154	1209	1239	1254	1309	1339	1354	1409	1439
Luzern 552 a.	0553	0623	0653	0704	0723	0753	0804	0823	0853	0904	0923	0953	1004	1053	1104	1153	1204	1223	1253	1304	1323	1353	1404	1423	1453

				⚒		P						P								P					
Interlaken Ost d.	1304	1333	1404	1433	...	1504	1533	...	1604	1633	...	1704	1733	...	1804	1833	...	1904	1933	2008	...	2105	2200	2315	...
Oberried d.	|	1346	|	1446	...	|	1546	...	|	1646	...	|	1746	...	|	1846	...	|	1946	2020	...	2117	2211	2326	...
Brienz d.	1325	1358	1425	1458	...	1525	1558	...	1625	1658	...	1725	1758	...	1825	1858	...	1925	1958	2031	...	2129	2221	2336	...
Meiringen ● a.	1335	1410	1435	1510	...	1535	1610	...	1635	1710	...	1735	1810	...	1835	1910	...	1935	2010	2043	...	2141	2233	2348	...
Meiringen ● d.	1344	▬	1444	▬	...	1544	▬	...	1644	▬	...	1744	▬	...	1844	▬	...	1944	▬	...	2051	▬	▬	...	...
Brünig Hasliberg d.	1355	...	1455	...	...	1555	...	...	1655	...	...	1755	...	...	1855	...	...	1955	...	...	2102	...	...	...	...
Lungern § d.	1410	...	1510	...	...	1610	...	...	1710	...	...	1810	...	...	1910	...	...	2010	...	...	2115	...	...	...	...
Giswil d.	1429	1506	1529	1536	1606	1629	1636	1706	1729	1736	1806	1829	1836	1906	1929	1936	2006	2029	2106	...	2136	2206	2306	...	...
Sachseln d.	|	1515	|	1545	1615	|	1645	1715	|	1745	1815	|	1845	1915	|	1945	2015	|	2115	...	2145	2215	2315	...	...
Sarnen d.	1440	1520	1540	1550	1620	1640	1650	1720	1740	1750	1820	1840	1850	1920	1940	1950	2020	2040	2120	...	2150	2220	2320	...	...
Alpnach Dorf d.	1445	1525	1545	1555	1625	1645	1655	1725	1745	1755	1825	1845	1855	1925	1945	1955	2025	2045	2125	...	2155	2225	2325	...	...
Alpnachstad d.	|	1530	|	1600	1630	|	1700	1730	|	1800	1830	|	1900	1930	|	2000	2030	|	2130	...	2200	2230	2330	...	...
Hergiswil **552** d.	1454	1539	1554	1609	1639	1654	1709	1739	1754	1809	1839	1854	1909	1939	1954	2009	2039	2054	2139	...	2208	2239	2339	...	...
Luzern 552 a.	1504	1553	1604	1623	1653	1704	1723	1753	1804	1823	1853	1904	1923	1953	2004	2023	2053	2104	2153	...	2222	2253	2353	...	...

P – GOLDENPASS PANORAMIC – Conveys [1] [observation car] and [1/2]. Also conveys ✕ on most services (Reservation recommended for observation car).

p – ⚒ Dec. 10 - May 9; daily May 10 - Aug. 24; ①–⑥ Aug. 25 - Dec. 13.
q – Ⓒ May 10 - Aug. 24.

§ – Buses depart from Lungern **Dorfkapelle**.

● – Rail service **Meiringen - Innertkirchen** and v.v. Narrow gauge. 2nd class only. *5 km*. Journey time: 11 minutes. **Operator**: MIB. Trains run from **Meiringen MIB** (300 metres from SBB station).

From **Meiringen MIB**: 0617Ⓐ, 0642Ⓐ, 0717Ⓐ, 0742, 0817⚒, 0842, 0942, 1042, 1117Ⓐ, 1142, 1217⚒, 1242, 1317 **p**, 1342, 1417 **q**, 1442, 1517 **q**, 1542, 1617 **p**, 1642, 1717Ⓐ, 1742, 1817Ⓐ, 1842, 1917.

From **Innertkirchen**: 0557Ⓐ, 0628Ⓐ, 0700Ⓐ, 0728, 0800, 0828⚒, 0900, 1000, 1100, 1128Ⓐ, 1200, 1228⚒, 1300, 1328 **p**, 1400, 1428 **q**, 1500, 1528 **q**, 1600, 1628 **p**, 1700, 1728Ⓐ, 1800, 1828Ⓐ, 1900.

562 SPIEZ - BRIG (via Lötschberg pass)

BLS

km		RE 3253	RE 3255 T	RE 3257	RE 3259	RE 3261		CNL 409 ♦🅁		RE 3263	RE 3265	RE 3267	RE 3269	RE 3271	RE 3273	RE 3275		RE 3277	RE 3279	RE 3281	IC 1089 B	RE 3285		IC 3191	RE 3251
	Bern d.	...	...	0739	0839	0939	...	...	...	1039c	1139e	1239e	1339e	1439e	1539e	1639	...	1739	1839	1939	2035	...	...	2239	...
0	**Spiez** ⊗ d.	0612	0712	0812	0912	1012	...	1047s	...	1112	1212	1312	1412	1512	1612	1712	...	1812	1912	2012	2104	2212	...	2308	0012
14	Frutigen ● d.	0627	0727	0827	0927	1027	...	1100s	...	1127	1227	1327	1427	1527	1627	1727	...	1827	1927	2027	2117	2227	...	2320	0027
31	Kandersteg 🚗 d.	0643	0743	0843	0943	1043	...	1118s	...	1143	1243	1343	1443	1543	1643	1743	...	1843	1943	2043	2133	2243	...	2337	0043
48	Goppenstein 🚗 d.	0655	0755	0855	0955	1055	...	1132s	...	1155	1255	1355	1455	1555	1655	1755	...	1855	1955	2055	2146	2255	...	2349	0055
74	**Brig** a.	0724	0824	0924	1024	1124	...	1200	...	1224	1324	1424	1524	1624	1724	1824	...	1924	2024	2124	2209	2324	...	0012	0124

	RE 3256	IC 811 R	RE 3256	RE 3258	RE 3260	RE 3262	RE 3264	RE 3266	RE 3268		RE 3270	RE 3272	RE 3274	RE 3276	RE 3278		CNL 408 ♦🅁		RE 3280	RE 3282	IC 1090 B	RE 3284	IC 3194	RE 3288
Brig d.	0535	0545	...	0635	0735	0835	0935	1035	1135	...	1235	1335	1435	1535	1635	...	1652	...	1735	1835	1850	1935	2050	2207
Goppenstein 🚗 d.	0602	|	←	0702	0802	0902	1002	1102	1202	...	1302	1402	1502	1602	1702	...	1717u	...	1802	1902	1913	2002	2113	2234
Kandersteg 🚗 d.	0614	|	0614	0714	0814	0914	1014	1114	1214	...	1314	1414	1514	1614	1714	...	1736u	...	1814	1914	1925	2014	2125	2246
Frutigen ● d.	→	0612	0631	0731	0831	0931	1031	1131	1231	...	1331	1431	1531	1631	1731	...	1756u	...	1831	1931	1942	2031	2142	2303
Spiez ⊗ a.	...	0624	0646	0746	0846	0946	1046	1146	1246	...	1346	1446	1546	1646	1746	...	1813u	...	1846	1946	1953	2046	2153	2319
Bern a.	...	0654	0720	0820	0920	1020c	1120e	1220e	1320e	...	1420e	1520e	1620	1720	1820	...	...	...	1920	...	2023	...	2223	...

♦ – **NOTES** (LISTED BY TRAIN NUMBER)

408 – *City Night Line* KOMET – ⑥ Dec. 22 - Mar. 29: 🛏 1, 2 cl., ▬ 2 cl., [2] [reclining] and ✕ Brig - Hamburg / Amsterdam. Special fares payable.

409 – *City Night Line* KOMET – ⑤ Dec. 21 - Mar. 28 (from Hamburg / Amsterdam): 🛏 1, 2 cl., ▬ 2 cl., [2] [reclining] and ✕ Hamburg / Amsterdam - Brig. Special fares payable.

B – Basel - Brig and v.v.
T – From Thun.
R – Brig - Romanshorn.

c – Ⓒ only.
e – † only.
s – Stops to set down only.
u – Stops to pick up only.

BLS — SPIEZ - ZWEISIMMEN — 563

km				RE 3111		RE 3113 ©		RE 3115 G			RE 3119			RE 3123 G			RE 3127		RE 3129 Ⓐ		RE 3131						
	Interlaken Ost 560	d.	...	...	...	...	...	0908	...	...	...	...	...	1308	...	...	...	...	...	...	...	...	...	...	...	...	...
0	**Spiez 560**	d.	0609	0709	0736	0809	0845	0910	0936	1009	1110	1136	1209	1310	1336	1409	1510	1536	1609	1636	1710	1736	1809	1906	2006	2106	2206	2311
11	Erlenbach im Simmental	d.	0626	0726	0748	0826	|	0926	0948	1026	1126	1148	1226	1326	1348	1426	1526	1548	1626	1648	1726	1748	1826	1920	2020	2120	2220	2326
26	Boltigen	d.	0644	0744	0809	0844	0909	0944	1009	1044	1144	1209	1244	1344	1409	1444	1544	1609	1644	1709	1744	1809	1844	1938	2038	2138	2238	2344
35	**Zweisimmen**	a.	0656	0756	0819	0856	0919	0956	1019	1056	1156	1219	1256	1356	1419	1456	1556	1619	1656	1719	1756	1819	1856	1950	2050	2150	2250	2356

		RE 3106 Ⓐ		RE 3108 Ⓐ		RE 3110 Ⓐ			RE 3114			RE 3118 G			RE 3122			RE 3126 G		RE 3126 ©		RE 3130						
Zweisimmen	d.	0542	0600	0638	0700	0738	0800	0900	0938	1000	1100	1138	1200	1300	1338	1400	1500	1538	1600	1636	1700	1738	1800	1905	2005	2105	2205	2300
Boltigen	d.	0549	0609	0647	0709	0747	0809	0909	0947	1009	1109	1147	1209	1309	1347	1409	1509	1547	1609	1644	1709	1747	1809	1914	2014	2114	2214	2309
Erlenbach im Simmental	d.	0603	0627	0702	0728	0802	0827	0928	1002	1027	1128	1202	1227	1328	1402	1427	1528	1602	1627	|	1728	1802	1827	1933	2033	2133	2233	2327
Spiez 560	a.	0621	0645	0721	0747	0821	0845	0947	1021	1045	1147	1221	1245	1347	1421	1445	1547	1621	1647	1711	1747	1821	1845	1950	2050	2150	2250	2345
Interlaken Ost 560	a.	...	...	...	...	...	...	...	...	...	...	1250	...	...	...	...	...	1650	...	...	...	...	...	...	...	...	...	...

G – GOLDEN PASS PANORAMIC – Ⓡ for groups.

Narrow gauge rack railway. BOB, WAB, JB — INTERLAKEN - KLEINE SCHEIDEGG - JUNGFRAUJOCH — 564

km							j	d			j	j			j	j			j	j			j	j			j
0	**Interlaken Ost**	d.	0600	0604	0705	0705	0735	0735	0805	0805	0835	0835	0905	0905	0935	0935	1005	1005	1035	1035	1105	1105	1135	1135	1205	1205	1235
3	Wilderswil ▲	d.	0605	0609	0710	0710	0740	0740	0810	0810	0840	0840	0910	0910	0940	0940	1010	1010	1040	1040	1110	1110	1140	1140	1210	1210	1240
8	Zweilütschinen	d.	0611	0615	0716	0717	0746	0747	0816	0817	0846	0847	0916	0917	0946	0947	1016	1017	1046	1047	1116	1117	1146	1147	1216	1217	1246
12	**Lauterbrunnen** ●	a.	0620	|	0725	|	0755	|	0825	|	0855	|	0925	|	0955	|	1025	|	1055	|	1125	|	1155	|	1225	|	1255
	change trains			|		|		|		|	j	|		|		|		|	j	|		|		|		|	j
12	**Lauterbrunnen**	d.	0639	|	0739	|	0804	|	0830	|	0914	|	0939	|	1004	|	1030	|	1114	|	1139	|	1204	|	1230	|	1314
16	Wengen	a.	0653	|	0753	|	0818	|	0844	|	0927	|	0953	|	1018	|	1044	|	1127	|	1153	|	1218	|	1244	|	1327
16	Wengen	d.	0659	|	0759	|	0824j	|	0849	|	0934	|	0959	|	1024j	|	1049	|	1134	|	1159	|	1224j	|	1249	|	1334
19	Grindelwald	a.	|	0638	|	0739	|	0809	|	0839	|	0909	|	0939	|	1009	|	1039	|	1109	|	1139	|	1209	|	1239	|
	change trains		|		|		|	j	|		|	j	|		|	j	|		|	j	|		|	j	|		|
19	Grindelwald	d.	|	0655	|	0747	|	0817	|	0847	|	0917	|	0947	|	1017	|	1047	|	1117	|	1147	|	1217	|	1247	|
20	Grindelwald Grund	d.	|	0703	|	0755	|	0825	|	0855	|	0925	|	0955	|	1025	|	1055	|	1125	|	1155	|	1225	|	1255	|
23	**Kleine Scheidegg**	a.	0723	0726	0824	0820	0849j	0850	0914	0920	1002	0950	1024	1020	1049j	1050	1114	1120	1202	1150	1224	1220	1249j	1250	1314	1320	1402

						j			j	j			j	j													
Interlaken Ost	d.	1305	1305	1405	1405	1435	1505	1505	1535	1535	1605	1605	1635	1635	1705	1705	1805	1805	1905	1905	2001	2005	2101	2105	2201	2205	...
Wilderswil ▲	d.	1310	1310	1410	1410	1440	1510	1510	1540	1540	1610	1610	1640	1640	1710	1710	1810	1810	1910	1910	2006	2010	2106	2110	2206	2210	...
Zweilütschinen	d.	1316	1317	1416	1417	1447	1516	1517	1546	1547	1616	1617	1646	1647	1716	1717	1816	1817	1916	1917	2012	2016	2112	2116	2212	2216	...
Lauterbrunnen ●	a.	1325	|	1425	|	|	1525	|	1555	|	1625	|	1655	|	1725	|	1825	|	1925	|	2021	|	2121	|	2221	|	...
change trains			|		|	|		|		|		|		|		|		|		|		|		|		|	
Lauterbrunnen	d.	1339	|	1430	|	|	1539	|	1604	|	1630	|	1713	|	1739	|	1830	|	1930	|	2030	|	2130	|	2230	|	...
Wengen	a.	1353	|	1444	|	|	1553	|	1618	|	1644	|	1727	|	1753	|	1844	|	1944	|	2044	|	2144	|	2244	|	...
Wengen	d.	1359	|	1449	|	|	1559	|	1624k	|	1649	|	...	|	1759j	|	...	|	...	|	...	|	...	|	...	|	...
Grindelwald	a.	|	1339	|	1439	1509	|	1539	|	1609	|	1639	...	1709	|	1739	...	1839	...	1939	...	2035	...	2135	...	2235	...
change trains		|		|		j	|		|	j	|				|											
Grindelwald	d.	|	1347	|	1447	1517	|	1547	|	1617	|	1647	...	...	|	1747	...	1847	...	...	...	...	...	...	...	...	...
Grindelwald Grund	d.	|	1355	|	1455	1525	|	1555	|	1625	|	1655	...	...	|	1755j	...	1852	...	...	...	...	...	...	...	...	...
Kleine Scheidegg	a.	1424	1420	1514	1520	1550	1624	1620	1649k	1650k	1714	1720	...	...	1824j	1820j	...	...	...	...	...	...	...	...	...	...	...

																	j				j						
Kleine Scheidegg	d.	...	...	...	...	...	...	...	...	0729t	0803	...	0831	0833	...	0856j	0903	0925	0933	0944j	1003	1031	1033	...	1056j	1125	1133
Grindelwald Grund	d.	...	...	...	...	...	...	0647	...	|	0838	...	|	0908	...	|	0938	|	1008	|	1038	|	1108	...	|	|	1208
Grindelwald	a.	...	...	...	...	...	...	0651	...	|	0842	...	|	0912	...	|	0942	|	1012	|	1042	|	1112	...	|	|	1212
change trains										|	j		|			|	j	|		|	j	|			|	|	
Grindelwald	d.	0520	...	...	0620	...	...	0720	...	|	0850	...	|	0920	...	|	0950	|	1020	|	1050	|	1120	...	|	|	1220
Wengen	a.	|	...	...	|	...	...	|	...	0758t	|	...	0904	|	...	0929j	|	0953	|	1015j	|	1104	|	...	1129j	1153	|
Wengen	d.	|	0512	0612	|	...	0712	|	0737	0802	|	0828	0911	|	...	0937	|	1002	|	1028	|	1111	|	...	1137	1202	|
Lauterbrunnen	a.	|	0529	0628	|	...	0728	|	0754	0819	|	0845	0928	|	...	0954	|	1019	|	1045	|	1128	|	...	1154	1219	|
change trains		|			|			|	j		|	j		|		j	|		|	j	|		|		j		|
Lauterbrunnen ●	d.	|	0534	0633	|	...	0733	|	0803	0833	|	0903	0933	|	...	1003	|	1033	|	1103	|	1133	|	...	1203	1233	|
Zweilütschinen	d.	0540	0544	0643	0643	...	0743	0743	0813	0843	0913	0913	0943	0943	...	1013	1013	1043	1043	1113	1113	1143	1143	...	1213	1243	1243
Wilderswil ▲	d.	0546	0549	0649	0649	...	0749	0749	0819	0849	0919	0919	0949	0949	...	1019	1019	1049	1049	1119	1119	1149	1149	...	1219	1249	1249
Interlaken Ost	a.	0550	0554	0654	0654	...	0754	0754	0824	0854	0924	0924	0954	0954	...	1024	1024	1054	1054	1124	1124	1154	1154	...	1224	1254	1254

						j					j				j							j					
Kleine Scheidegg	d.	1231	1233	1325	1333	1403	1431	1433	...	1456j	1503	1525	1533	1548j	1603	1631	1633	1656j	1725	1733	...	1833	1830j	...	...	...	...
Grindelwald Grund	d.	|	1308	|	1408	1438	|	1508	...	|	1538	|	1608	|	1638	|	1708	|	|	1808	...	1908	|	...	...	...	...
Grindelwald	a.	|	1312	|	1412	1442	|	1512	...	|	1542	|	1612	|	1642	|	1712	|	|	1812	...	1912	|	...	...	...	...
change trains		|		|		j	|			|	j	|		|	j	|		|	|				|				
Grindelwald	d.	|	1320	|	1420	1450	|	1520	...	|	1550	|	1620	|	1650	|	1720	|	|	1820	|	1920	|	2020	|	2120	|
Wengen	a.	1304	|	1353	|	|	1504	|	...	1529j	|	1553	|	1617j	|	1704	|	1729j	1753	|	...	|	1858j	|	...	|	...
Wengen	d.	1311	|	1402	|	|	1511	|	...	1537	|	1602	|	1628	|	1711	|	1737	1802	|	...	|	1902	|	2002	|	2108
Lauterbrunnen	a.	1328	|	1419	|	|	1528	|	...	1554	|	1619	|	1645	|	1728	|	1754	1819	|	...	|	1919	|	2019	|	2125
change trains			|		|	|		|		j	|		|		|		|	j		|		|		|		|	
Lauterbrunnen ●	d.	1333	|	1433	|	|	1533	|	...	1603	|	1633	|	1703	|	1733	|	1803	1833	|	...	|	1934	|	2034	|	2134
Zweilütschinen	d.	1343	1343	1543	1443	1513	1543	1543	...	1613	1613	1643	1643	1713	1713	1743	1743	1813	1843	1843	...	1940	1944	2040	2044	2140	2144
Wilderswil ▲	d.	1349	1349	1449	1449	1519	1549	1549	...	1619	1619	1649	1649	1719	1719	1749	1749	1819	1849	1849	...	1946	1950	2046	2050	2146	2150
Interlaken Ost	a.	1354	1354	1454	1454	1524	1554	1554	...	1624	1624	1654	1654	1724	1724	1754	1754	1824	1854	1854	...	1950	1954	2050	2054	2150	2154

At times of heavy snowfall (November 1 - April 30) the Eigergletscher - Jungfraujoch service is subject to cancellation

km					t			t		t			t		t		t		t					t	
0	**Kleine Scheidegg**	d.	0735	0830	0900	0930	...	1000	1030	1100	1130	...	1200	1230	1300	1330	1400	1430	1500	1530	...	1630	1730	1840	...
2	Eigergletscher	d.	0745	0840	0910	0940	...	1010	1040	1110	1140	...	1210	1240	1310	1340	1410	1440	1510	1540	...	1640	1740	1850	...
9	**Jungfraujoch**	a.	0827	0922	0952	1022	...	1052	1122	1152	1222	...	1252	1322	1352	1422	1452	1522	1552	1622	...	1722t	...	...	...

				t			t			t		t			t			t					t	
Jungfraujoch	d.	0837	0930	1000	...	1030	1100	1130	...	1200	1230	1300	1330	...	1400	1430	...	1500	1530	1600	1640	...	1750	...
Eigergletscher	d.	|	1008	1038	...	1108	1138	1208	...	1238	1308	1338	1408	...	1438	1510	...	1540	1604	1640	1708	...	1817	...
Kleine Scheidegg	a.	0920	1020	1050	...	1120	1150	1220	...	1250	1320	1350	1420	...	1450	1520	...	1550	1612	1650	1716	...	1825	...

d – ⚒ only.
h – June 30 - Sept. 30.
j – Dec. 15 - Apr. 6, May 3 - Oct. 26.
k – Jan. 26 - Apr. 6, May 3 - Oct. 26.
t – May 3 - Oct. 26.

Additional trains run between Lauterbrunnen, Wengen and Jungfraujoch and between Grindelwald and Jungfraujoch.

● – Cableway operates **Lauterbrunnen - Grütschalp**, and narrow gauge railway **Grütschalp - Mürren**, *total: 5 km.* **Operator**: BLM. Journey time: 20 minutes allowing for the connection.
From **Lauterbrunnen**: 0609, 0629, 0647, 0710, 0731, 0801 and every 30 minutes◆ until 1831, then 1931, 2031**j**.
From **Mürren**: 0604, 0636, 0706 and every 30 minutes◆ until 1906, then 2006**j**.
◆ – Additional services available Dec. 15 - Apr. 6, May 3 - Oct. 26.

▲ – Narrow gauge rack railway operates **May 24 - Oct. 26 Wilderswil - Schynige Platte**. *7 km.* Journey time: 52 minutes. **Operator**: SPB, ✆ 033 828 73 51. Service may be reduced in bad weather.
From **Wilderswil**: 0725, 0805**h**, 0845, 0925, 1005, 1045, 1125, 1205**h**, 1245, 1325, 1405, 1445, 1525, 1605**h**, 1645.
From **Schynige Platte**: 0821, 0901**h**, 0941, 1021, 1101, 1141, 1221**h**, 1301, 1341, 1421, 1501, 1541, 1621, 1701**h**, 1753.

565 BASEL, OLTEN and BERN - LUZERN SBB

km		RE 3555	RE 3557	IR 2455	IC 2509	IR 2159	RE 3559	IR 2457	IC 2511	EC 109	RE 3561	IR 2461	IC 2515	IR 2165	RE 3565	IR 2465	IC 2517	EC 111	RE 3567	IR 2467	IC 2519	IR 2169	RE 3569	IR 2469
					F	△ L				♦				△ L				♦				△ L		
	Genève Aéroport + 505 d.	...	...	...	...	...	...	...	...	...	...	...	...	...	...	...	...	...	...	...	0801	...	...	...
	Genève 505 d.	...	...	...	...	...	...	...	0456	...	...	...	0556	...	...	...	0710	...	...	...	0810	...	...	...
	Lausanne 505 d.	...	...	...	...	...	...	...	0545	...	...	...	0645	...	...	...	0745	...	...	...	0845	...	...	...
0	**Basel SBB** d.	...	...	0544	...	0604	...	0644	|	0704	...	0744	|	0804	...	0844	|	0904	...	0944	|	1004	...	1044
14	Liestal d.	...	...	0553	...	|	...	0653	|	|	...	0753	|	|	...	0853	|	|	...	0953	|	|	...	1053
21	Sissach d.	...	...	0600	...	|	...	0700	|	|	...	0800	|	|	...	0900	|	|	...	1000	|	|	...	1100
39	**Olten** a.	...	...	0614	...	0628	...	0714	|	0728	...	0814	|	0828	...	0914	|	0928	...	1014	|	1028	...	1114
39	**Olten** d.	0525	0602	0616	...	0633	0706	0716	|	0733	0806	0816	|	0833	0906	0916	|	0933	1006	1016	|	1033	1106	1116
	Bern d.	|	|	|	0600	|	|	|	0700	|	|	|	0800	|	|	|	0900	|	|	|	1000	|	|	|
47	Zofingen d.	0531	0609	0623	0627	0641	0712	0723	0727	0741	0812	0823	0827	0841	0912	0923	0927	0941	1012	1023	1027	1041	1112	1123
69	Sursee d.	0551	0629	...	0640	0655	0731	...	0740	0755	0831	...	0840	0855	0931	...	0940	0955	1031	...	1040	1055	1131	...
95	**Luzern** a.	0613	0652	...	0700	0714	0752	...	0800	0814	0852	...	0900	0914	0952	...	1000	1014	1052	...	1100	1114	1152	...

	IC 2521	EC 115	RE 3571	IR 2471	IC 2523	IR 2173	RE 3573	IR 2473	IC 2525	EC 117	RE 3575	IR 2475	IC 2527	IR 2177	RE 3577	IR 2477	IC 2529	EC 119	RE 3579	IR 2479	IC 2531	IR 2181	RE 3581	IR 2483
		♦				△ L				♦				L				♦				△ L		
Genève Aéroport + 505 d.	0901	...	...	...	1001	...	...	...	1101	...	...	...	1201	...	...	...	1301	...	...	...	1401	...	...	...
Genève 505 d.	0910	...	...	...	1010	...	...	...	1110	...	...	...	1210	...	...	...	1310	...	...	...	1410	...	...	...
Lausanne 505 d.	0945	...	...	...	1045	...	...	...	1145	...	...	...	1245	...	...	...	1345	...	...	...	1445	...	...	...
Basel SBB d.	|	1104	...	1144	|	1204	...	1244	|	1304	...	1344	|	1404	...	1444	|	1504	...	1544	|	1604	...	1644
Liestal d.	|	|	...	1153	|	|	...	1253	|	|	...	1353	|	|	...	1453	|	|	...	1553	|	|	...	1653
Sissach d.	|	|	...	1200	|	|	...	1300	|	|	...	1400	|	|	...	1500	|	|	...	1600	|	|	...	1700
Olten a.	|	1128	...	1214	|	1228	...	1314	|	1328	...	1414	|	1428	...	1514	|	1528	...	1614	|	1628	...	1714
Olten d.	|	1133	1206	1216	|	1233	1306	1316	|	1333	1406	1416	|	1433	1506	1516	|	1533	1606	1616	|	1633	1706	1716
Bern d.	1100	|	|	|	1200	|	|	|	1300	|	|	|	1400	|	|	|	1500	|	|	|	1600	|	|	|
Zofingen d.	1127	1141	1212	1223	1227	1241	1312	1323	1327	1341	1412	1423	1427	1441	1512	1523	1527	1541	1612	1623	1627	1641	1712	1723
Sursee d.	1140	1155	1231	...	1240	1255	1331	...	1340	1355	1431	...	1440	1455	1531	...	1540	1555	1631	...	1640	1655	1731	...
Luzern a.	1200	1214	1252	...	1300	1314	1352	...	1400	1414	1452	...	1500	1514	1552	...	1600	1614	1652	...	1700	1714	1752	...

	IC 2535	IC 685	RE 3585	IR 2487	IC 2537	IR 2187	RE 3587	IR 2491	IC 2539	IR 2189	RE 3589	IR 2493	IC 2541	IR 2191	RE 3591	IR 2495	IC 2543	IR 2193	RE 3593	IR 2197	RE 3595	IR 2199	IR 2153	IR 2451
		C				△ C				C				E				A						⑥⑦q
Genève Aéroport + 505 d.	...	...	...	...	1601	...	...	...	1701	...	...	...	1801	...	...	...	1901	...	...	...	...	...	...	...
Genève 505 d.	...	...	...	...	1610	...	...	...	1710	...	...	...	1810	...	...	...	1910	...	...	...	...	...	...	...
Lausanne 505 d.	1545	...	...	...	1645	...	...	...	1745	...	...	...	1845	...	...	...	1945	...	...	...	...	...	...	...
Basel SBB d.	|	1704	...	1744	|	1804	...	1844	|	1904	...	1944	|	2004	...	2044	|	2104	...	2204	...	2308	0015	0116
Liestal d.	|	|	...	1753	|	|	...	1853	|	|	...	1953	|	|	...	2053	|	|	...	2213	...	2317	0025	0128
Sissach d.	|	|	...	1800	|	|	...	1900	|	|	...	2000	|	|	...	2100	|	|	...	2220	...	2323	0031	0134
Olten a.	|	1728	...	1814	|	1828	...	1914	|	1928	...	2014	|	2028	...	2114	|	2128	...	2234	...	2336	0044	0146
Olten d.	|	1733	1806	1816	|	1833	1906	1916	|	1933	2006	2016	|	2033	2106	2116	|	2133	2206	2236	2306	2337	0053	
Bern d.	1700	|	|	|	1800	|	|	|	1900	|	|	|	2000	|	|	|	2100	|	|	|	|	|	|	
Zofingen d.	1727	1741	1812	1823	1827	1841	1912	1923	1927	1941	2012	2023	2027	2041	2112	2123	2127	2141	2212	2243	2312	2344	0100	...
Sursee d.	1740	1755	1831	...	1840	1855	1931	...	1940	1955	2031	...	2040	2055	2131	...	2140	2155	2231	2257	2331	2358	0113	...
Luzern a.	1800	1814	1852	...	1900	1914	1952	...	2000	2014	2052	...	2100	2114	2152	...	2200	2214	2252	2315	2352	0016	0137	...

km (via hsl)		RE 3554	IR 2454	IR 2160	IC 2508	IR 2456	RE 3558	IR 2162	IC 2510	IR 2460	RE 3560	IC 664	IC 2512	IR 2464	RE 3562	IR 2166	IC 2516	IR 2466	RE 3566	IC 668	IC 2518	IR 2468	RE 3568	IR 2170
			⚒													△ B				C				△ C
	Luzern d.	0441	...	0540	0600	...	0605	0645	0700	...	0707	0745	0800	...	0807	0845	0900	...	0907	0945	1000	...	1007	1045
	Sursee d.	0504	...	0559	0619	...	0625	0704	0719	...	0727	0804	0819	...	0827	0904	0919	...	0927	1004	1019	...	1027	1104
0	Zofingen d.	0522	...	0613	0633	0635	0644	0718	0733	0735	0746	0818	0833	0835	0846	0918	0933	0935	0946	1018	1033	1035	1046	1118
63	**Bern** a.	|	...	|	0700	|	|	|	0800	|	|	|	0900	|	|	|	1000	|	|	|	1100	|	|	|
	Olten a.	0530	...	0620	|	0642	0652	0724	|	0742	0752	0824	|	0842	0852	0924	|	0942	0952	1024	|	1042	1052	1124
	Olten d.	...	0558	0623	|	0644	...	0727	|	0744	...	0827	|	0844	...	0927	|	0944	...	1027	|	1044	...	1127
	Sissach d.	...	0613	0636	|	0659	...	|	|	0759	...	|	|	0859	...	|	|	0959	...	|	|	1059	...	|
	Liestal d.	...	0620	0646	|	0705	...	|	|	0805	...	|	|	0905	...	|	|	1005	...	|	|	1105	...	|
	Basel SBB a.	...	0630	0657	|	0716	...	0751	|	0816	...	0851	|	0916	...	0951	|	1016	...	1051	|	1116	...	1151
	Lausanne 505 a.	...	...	...	0815	...	...	...	0915	...	...	...	1015	...	...	...	1115	...	...	...	1215	...	...	...
	Genève 505 a.	...	...	...	0850	...	...	...	0950	...	...	...	1050	...	...	...	1150	...	...	...	...	...	...	...
	Genève Aéroport + 505 a.	...	...	...	0859	...	...	...	0959	...	...	...	1059	...	...	...	1159	...	...	...	...	...	...	...

	IC 2520	IR 2470	RE 3570	IC 672	IC 2522	IR 2472	RE 3572	IR 2174	IC 2524	IR 2474	RE 3574	EC 106	IC 2526	IR 2476	RE 3576	IR 2178	IC 2528	IR 2478	RE 3578	EC 108	IC 2530	IR 2482	RE 3580	IR 2182
				C				△ L				♦				△ L				♦				△ L
Luzern d.	1100	...	1107	1145	1200	...	1207	1245	1300	...	1307	1345	1400	...	1407	1445	1500	...	1507	1545	1600	...	1607	1645
Sursee d.	1119	...	1127	1204	1219	...	1227	1304	1319	...	1327	1404	1419	...	1427	1504	1519	...	1527	1604	1619	...	1627	1704
Zofingen d.	1133	1135	1146	1218	1233	1235	1246	1318	1333	1335	1346	1418	1433	1435	1446	1518	1533	1535	1546	1618	1633	1635	1646	1718
Bern a.	1200	|	|	|	1300	|	|	|	1400	|	|	|	1500	|	|	|	1600	|	|	|	1700	|	|	|
Olten a.	|	1142	1152	1224	|	1242	1252	1324	|	1342	1352	1424	|	1442	1452	1524	|	1542	1552	1624	|	1642	1652	1724
Olten d.	|	1144	...	1227	|	1244	...	1327	|	1344	...	1427	|	1444	...	1527	|	1544	...	1627	|	1644	...	1727
Sissach d.	|	1159	...	|	|	1259	...	|	|	1359	...	|	|	1459	...	|	|	1559	...	|	|	1659	...	|
Liestal d.	|	1205	...	|	|	1305	...	|	|	1405	...	|	|	1505	...	|	|	1605	...	|	|	1705	...	|
Basel SBB a.	|	1216	...	1251	|	1316	...	1351	|	1416	...	1451	|	1516	...	1551	|	1616	...	1651	|	1716	...	1751
Lausanne 505 a.	1315	...	...	...	1415	...	...	...	1515	...	...	...	1615	...	...	...	1715	...	...	...	1815	...	...	...
Genève 505 a.	1350	...	...	...	1450	...	...	...	1550	...	...	...	1650	...	...	...	1750	...	...	...	1850	...	...	...
Genève Aéroport + 505 a.	1359	...	...	...	1459	...	...	...	1559	...	...	...	1659	...	...	...	1759	...	...	...	1859	...	...	...

	IC 2532	IR 2486	RE 3582	EC 110	IC 2536	IR 2490	RE 3586	IR 2188	IC 2538	IR 2492	RE 3588	EC 114	IC 2540	IR 2494	RE 3590	IR 2192	IC 2542	IR 2496	RE 3592	IC 694	RE 3594	EC 116	RE 3596	IR 2198
				♦				△ L				♦				△ L				C		♦		
Luzern d.	1700	...	1707	1745	1800	...	1807	1845	1900	...	1907	1945	2000	...	2007	2045	2100	...	2107	2145	2207	2245	2307	0005
Sursee d.	1719	...	1727	1804	1819	...	1827	1904	1919	...	1927	2004	2019	...	2027	2104	2119	...	2127	2204	2227	2304	2327	0024
Zofingen d.	1733	1735	1746	1818	1833	1835	1846	1918	1933	1935	1946	2018	2033	2035	2046	2118	2133	2135	2146	2218	2246	2318	2346	0038
Bern a.	1800	|	|	|	1900	|	|	|	2000	|	|	|	2100	|	|	|	2200	|	|	|	|	|	|	|
Olten a.	|	1742	1752	1824	|	1842	1852	1924	|	1942	1952	2024	|	2042	2052	2124	|	2142	2152	2224	2252	2324	2352	0045
Olten d.	|	1744	...	1827	|	1844	...	1927	|	1944	...	2027	|	2044	...	2127	|	2144	...	2227	...	2327	...	0053
Sissach d.	|	1759	...	|	|	1859	...	|	|	1959	...	|	|	2059	...	|	|	2159	...	|	...	|	...	0107
Liestal d.	|	1805	...	|	|	1905	...	|	|	2005	...	|	|	2105	...	|	|	2205	...	|	...	|	...	0114
Basel SBB a.	|	1816	...	1851	|	1916	...	1951	|	2016	...	2051	|	2116	...	2151	|	2216	...	2251	...	2351	...	0124
Lausanne 505 a.	1915	...	...	...	2015	...	...	...	2115	...	...	...	2215	...	...	...	2315	...	...	...	...	...	...	...
Genève 505 a.	1950	...	...	...	2104	...	...	...	2204	...	...	...	2304	...	...	...	0004	...	...	...	...	...	...	...
Genève Aéroport + 505 a.	1959	...	...	...	2113	...	...	...	2213	...	...	...	2313	...	...	...	...	...	...	...	...	...	...	...

♦ – NOTES (LISTED BY TRAIN NUMBER)

106/119 – CISALPINO TIZIANO – (12) Milano - Basel and v.v.
108/117 – CISALPINO VERDI – (12) Milano - Basel and v.v.
109/110 – CISALPINO TICINO – (12) Basel - Milano and v.v.
111/114 – CISALPINO SAN MARCO – (12) Basel - Milano - Venezia Santa Lucia and v.v.
115/116 – CISALPINO MEDIOLANUM – (12) Basel - Milano and v.v.

A – To Arth-Goldau.
B – From Bellinzona.
C – From/to Chiasso.
E – To Erstfeld.
F – From Fribourg.
L – From/to Locarno.

q – June 8 - 30 runs to special FIFA *EURO 2008* schedule.
△ – Also conveys (1) [observation car].

Narrow gauge MOB — LENK - ZWEISIMMEN - MONTREUX — 566

km		Ⓐ		Ⓐ										Ⓐ													⑤⑥
0	**Lenk** d.	0537	0638	0703	0738	0838	0938	1003	1038	1103	1138	1203	1238	1308	1338	1438	1538	1603	1638	1738	1803	1838	1932	2032	2132	2232	2326
13	**Zweisimmen** a.	0555	0656	0721	0756	0856	0956	1021	1056	1121	1156	1221	1256	1321	1356	1456	1556	1621	1656	1756	1821	1856	1950	2050	2150	2250	2344

km						2119			3121			2127	2227	3129				2129	2131				2133				
									🍸			(🍸)	🍸	🍸				(🍸)	🍸								
		Ⓐ				G			G☆			C	G	G★				®T	G☆			Ⓐ	C				
0	**Zweisimmen** d.	0430	0518	0605	0705	0826	0905	0934	1026	1105	...	1226	1305	1426	...	1505	1515	...	1626	...	1705	1724	1826	1905	2005	2105	2155
9	Saanenmöser d.	0445	0532	0619	0719	0841	0919	0947	1041	1119	...	1241	1319	1441	...	1519	1530	...	1641	...	1719	1738	1841	1919	2019	2119	2208
11	Schönried d.	0450	0537	0624	0724	0846	0924	0952	1046	1124	...	1246	1324	1446	...	1524	1535	...	1646	...	1724	1743	1846	1924	2024	2124	2212
16	**Gstaad** d.	0500	0548	0635	0737	0855	0937	1000	1055	1137	...	1255	1337	1455	...	1537	1544	...	1655	...	1737	1752	1855	1937	2037	2137	2222
19	Saanen d.	0504	0552	0641	0742	0900	0942	...	1100	1142	...	1300	1342	1500	...	1542	1548	...	1700	...	1742	1756	1900	1942	2042	2142	2226
23	Rougemont d.	0510	0557	0646	0748	0906	0948	...	1106	1148	...	1306	1348	1506	...	1548	...	...	1706	...	1748	...	1906	1948	2048	2148	2231s
29	Château d'Oex d.	0523	0609	0706	0806	0916	1006	...	1116	1206	...	1316	1406	1516	...	1606	...	...	1716	...	1806	...	1916	2006	2106	2206	2240
40	**Montbovon** d.	0540	0626	0723	0826	0931	1026	...	1131	1226	...	1331	1426	1531	...	1626	...	1647	1731	...	1826	...	1931	2026	2130	2233	...
51	Les Avants § d.	0602	0648	0743	0847	0952	1047	...	1152	1247	...	1352	1447	1552	...	1647	...	|	1752	...	1847	...	1952	2047	2150	2253	...
55	Chamby ⊙ § d.	0609	0658	0750	0854	1000	1054	...	1200	1254	...	1400	1454	1600	...	1654	...	|	1800	...	1854	...	2000	2054	2157	2300	...
58	Chernex § d.	0615	0703	0756	0900	1005	1100	...	1205	1300	...	1405	1500	1605	...	1700	...	|	1805	...	1900	...	2005	2100	2202	2305	...
62	**Montreux** § a.	0625	0713	0805	0910	1013	1110	...	1213	1310	...	1413	1510	1613	...	1710	...	1733	1813	...	1910	...	2013	2110	2212	2315	...

							2216		2118	3116	2222				3124		2228	2128				2134				
									(🍸)	🍸	🍸				🍸		(🍸)					🍸				
	Ⓐ	Ⓐ	©				C		®T	G★	G				G☆		C	G		Ⓐ		G☆				
Montreux § d.	...	...	...	0540	0635	0745	...	0845	...	0936	0945	1045	1145	...	1245	1345	...	1445	1545	1645	...	...	1745	1845	1945	2045	2145
Chernex § d.	...	...	...	0550	0645	0755	...	0859	...	|	0955	1059	1155	...	1259	1355	...	1459	1555	1659	...	...	1755	1859	1955	2059	2201
Chamby ⊙ § d.	...	...	...	0556	0650	0800	...	0904	...	|	1000	1104	1200	...	1304	1400	...	1504	1600	1704	...	...	1800	1904	2000	2104	2206
Les Avants § d.	...	...	...	0604	0658	0807	...	0912	...	|	1007	1112	1207	...	1312	1407	...	1512	1607	1712	...	...	1807	1912	2008	2112	2214
Montbovon d.	...	...	...	0625	0722	0828	...	0932	...	1017	1028	1132	1228	...	1332	1428	...	1532	1628	1732	...	...	1828	1932	2032	2132	2234
Château d'Oex d.	...	0541	0550	0641	0737	0843	...	0949	...	...	1043	1149	1243	...	1349	1443	...	1549	1643	1749	...	...	1843	1949	2049	2149	2249
Rougemont d.	...	0556	0603	0654	0750	0853	...	1003	...	...	1053	1203	1253	...	1403	1453	...	1603	1653	1803	...	...	1853	2003	2103	2203	2303
Saanen d.	0522	0602	0620	0700	0756	0859	...	1009	...	...	1059	1209	1259	...	1409	1459	1552	1609	1659	1809	1821	...	1859	2009	2109	2209	2309
Gstaad d.	0527	0607	0625	0706	0803	0904	1005	1014	...	...	1104	1214	1304	...	1414	1504	1557	1614	1704	1814	1827	...	1904	2014	2114	2214	2314
Schönried d.	0537	0615	0634	0715	0812	0913	1014	1023	...	...	1113	1223	1313	...	1423	1513	1606	1623	1713	1823	1836	...	1913	2023	2123	2223	2323
Saanenmöser d.	0542	0619	0639	0720	0817	0918	1019	1028	...	...	1118	1228	1318	...	1428	1518	1611	1628	1718	1828	1841	...	1918	2028	2128	2228	2328
Zweisimmen a.	0556	0633	0653	0734	0834	0932	1034	1043	...	...	1132	1243	1332	...	1443	1532	1625	1643	1732	1843	1854	...	1932	2043	2143	2243	2343

	Ⓐ		Ⓐ											Ⓐ												⑤⑥
Zweisimmen d.	0513	0603	0637	0703	0803	0903	0937	1003	1037	1103	1137	...	1203	1237	1303	1403	1503	1537	1603	1703	1737	1803	1903	1958	2058	2158	2258
Lenk a.	0531	0621	0656	0721	0821	0921	0956	1021	1056	1121	1156	...	1221	1256	1321	1421	1521	1556	1621	1721	1756	1821	1921	2016	2116	2216	2316

§ – ADDITIONAL SERVICES LES AVANTS - MONTREUX and v.v. (2nd class only):

		Ⓐ		q		q		Ⓐ			
Les Avants d.	...	0710	...	1323	...	1720	...	1800	...	2320	...
Chamby ⊙ d.	...	0717	...	1330	...	1728	...	1807	...	2327	...
Chernex d.	...	0723	...	1335	...	1734	...	1812	...	2332	...
Montreux a.	...	0736	...	1345	...	1744	...	1824	...	2342	...

	Ⓐ		q		q		Ⓐ				
Montreux d.	0616	...	1216	...	1606	...	1714	...	2251	...	2345
Chernex d.	0627	...	1226	...	1617	...	1724	...	2304	...	2355
Chamby ⊙ d.	0632	...	1231	...	1622	...	1729	...	2309	...	0000s
Les Avants a.	0639	...	1238	...	1629	...	1736	...	2316	...	0007

C – GOLDEN PASS CLASSIC – [12] and (🍸).
G – GOLDEN PASS PANORAMIC – conveys [12] [observation cars].
T – TRAIN DU CHOCOLAT – ①③④ June 2 - 26; ①-⑤ June 30 - Aug. 29; ①③④ Sept. 1 - Oct. 30: conveys [1] only.

q – Ⓐ Dec. 10 - 21, Jan. 7 - Feb. 8, Feb. 18 - Mar. 14, Mar. 31 - July 4, Aug. 25 - Oct. 10, Oct. 27 - Dec. 12 (not May 2, Sept. 22).
s – Stops to set down only.

★ – Also conveys VIP accommodation. ®
☆ – Also conveys VIP accommodation May 1 - Nov. 30 only. ®
⊙ – Chamby is a request stop.

Narrow gauge. 2nd class only. TPF — MONTBOVON - BULLE - PALÉZIEUX — 568

km																							611		
		Ⓐ		⚒				Ⓐ															®Fw		🚌
0	**Montbovon** d.	...	0540a	0640	0723	0840	...	0940	1040c	1140	...	1240d	1340	1440	...	1540	1640	1740	...	1840	1940	2040	...	2130	...	2154
13	Gruyères d.	...	0558a	0658	0745	0858	...	0958	1058c	1158	...	1258d	1358	1458	...	1558	1658	1758	...	1858	1958	2058	...	|	...	2212
17	**Bulle** ▲ a.	...	0608a	0708	0753	0908	...	1008	1108c	1208	...	1308d	1408	1508	...	1608	1708	1808	...	1908	2008	2108	...	2204	...	2222
17	**Bulle** d.	0513	0613	0713	0813	0913	...	1013	1113	1213	...	1313	1413h	1513	...	1613	1713	1813	...	1913	2013	2113	...	...	...	...
37	Châtel-St Denis a.	0541	0641	0741	0841	0941	...	1041	1141	1241	...	1341	1441h	1541	...	1641	1741	1841	...	1941	2041	2141	...	...	...	...
37	Châtel-St Denis d.	0544	0644	0744	0844	0944	...	1044	1144	1244	...	1344	1444h	1544	...	1644	1744	1844	...	1944	2044	2144	...	...	...	...
44	**Palézieux** a.	0555	0655	0755	0855	0955	...	1055	1155	1255	...	1355	1455h	1555	...	1655	1755	1855	...	1955	2055	2155	...	...	...	...

																	610							
	Ⓐ	⚒			⚒				⚒									®Fw				🚌		
Palézieux d.	...	...	0605a	0705	0805	0905	1005	...	1105a	1205	1305	1405	...	1505h	1605	1705	...	...	1805	1905	...	2005	...	2105	2205
Châtel-St Denis a.	...	...	0616a	0716	0816	0916	1016	...	1116a	1216	1316	1416	...	1516h	1616	1716	...	...	1816	1916	...	2016	...	2116	2216
Châtel-St Denis d.	...	...	0619a	0719	0819	0919	1019	...	1119a	1219	1319	1419	...	1519h	1619	1719	...	...	1819	1919	...	2019	...	2119	2219
Bulle a.	...	...	0647a	0747	0847	0947	1047	...	1147a	1247	1347	1447	...	1547h	1647	1747	...	...	1847	1947	...	2047	...	2147	2247
Bulle ▲ d.	0509	0552	0652	0756	0852a	0952c	1052	...	1152	1252	1352	1452	...	1552	1652	1752	...	1830	1852	1952	...	...	2052	...	...
Gruyères d.	0516	0559	0659	0803	0859a	0959c	1059	...	1159	1259	1359	1459	...	1559	1659	1759	...	|	1859	1959	...	...	2059	...	...
Montbovon a.	0536	0620	0720	0820	0920a	1020c	1120	...	1220	1320	1420	1520	...	1620	1720	1820	...	1904	1920	2020	...	...	2120	...	...

F – TRAIN FONDUE – [1] [observation car], [12] and ✕ Montbovon - Bulle and v.v. ®.
a – Ⓐ only.
c – © only.
d – ⚒ only.
h – † only.
q – Not May 22, Aug. 15, Dec. 8.
w – ⑥ Jan. 5 - Apr. 26, Nov. 8 - Dec. 13 (also Dec. 15; not Jan. 19, Feb. 16, Mar. 8, 22, Apr. 12, Nov. 29, Dec. 6).

▲ – Local TPF rail services **Bulle - Broc** (*5 km*, journey time 11 minutes), **Bulle - Romont** (*18 km*, journey time 22 minutes); TPF 🚌 service **Bulle - Fribourg** (*28 km*, journey time 32 minutes, line **346**). Other services available (some via Sorens) journey time 45 – 60 minutes, line **336**.

From **Bulle**: 0619Ⓐ, 0713⚒, 0813†, 0913⚒, 1013, 1113Ⓐ, 1154Ⓐ, 1213©, 1313, 1413Ⓐ, 1513, 1554Ⓐ, 1613⑥, 1713, 1813, 1913.
From **Broc**: 0632Ⓐ, 0732⚒, 0832†, 0932⚒, 1032, 1132Ⓐ, 1232©, 1249Ⓐ, 1332, 1432Ⓐ, 1532, 1632⚒, 1732, 1832, 1932.
From **Bulle**: 0546Ⓐ, 0646, 0746⚒, 0846, 1046, 1204, 1318Ⓐ, 1418, 1618, 1718, 1818, 1918.
From **Romont**: 0619Ⓐ, 0719, 0819⚒, 0919, 1119, 1247, 1347Ⓐ, 1447, 1647, 1747, 1847, 1947.
From **Bulle** (Gare) 🚌 service: 0556Ⓐ **q**, 0626, 0656Ⓐ **q**, 0726, 0756Ⓐ **q**, 0826 and hourly until 1226, 1256Ⓐ **q**, 1326 and hourly until 1626, 1656Ⓐ **q**, 1726, 1756Ⓐ **q**, 1826, 1926, 2026, 2056, 2145, 2245, 2345⑤⑥.
From **Fribourg** (Gare) 🚌 service: 0602Ⓐ **q**, 0632Ⓐ **q**, 0702, 0732Ⓐ **q**, 0802 and hourly until 1202, 1232Ⓐ **q**, 1302 and hourly until 1602, 1632Ⓐ **q**, 1702, 1732Ⓐ **q**, 1802, 1832Ⓐ **q**, 1902, 2002, 2102, 2202, 2302, 0040⑥⑦.

Narrow gauge rack railway. 2nd class only. MOB — MONTREUX - CAUX - ROCHERS DE NAYE — 569

No service between Caux and Rochers de Naye during bad weather

km																									
0	**Montreux** d.	0545	0645	0745	...	0846	0946	1046	...	1146	1246	...	1346	1446	1546	...	1646	1746	...	1846	1946	2046	2146	2246	...
3	Glion ▲ d.	0558	0658	0758	...	0900	1000	1100	...	1200	1300	...	1400	1500	1600	...	1700	1800	...	1900	2000	2100	2200	2300	...
5	Caux a.	0609	0709	0809	...	0911	1011	1111	...	1211	1311	...	1411	1511	1611	...	1711	1811	...	1911	2011	2111	2211	2311	...
10	**Rochers de Naye** a.	...	...	...	...	0941p	1041p	1141p	...	1241p	1341p	...	1441p	1541p	1641p	...	1741r	1841t	...	...	...	...	...	...	...

Rochers de Naye d.	...	...	...	...	...	0946p	1046p	...	1146p	1246p	...	1346p	1446p	...	1546p	1646p	...	1746r	...	1846t	...	...	...	...
Caux d.	0612	0712	0812	0916	...	1016	1116	...	1216	1316	...	1416	1516	...	1616	1716	...	1816	...	1916	...	2016	2116	2216
Glion ▲ d.	0625	0725	0825	0929	...	1029	1129	...	1229	1329	...	1429	1529	...	1629	1729	...	1829	...	1929	...	2029	2129	2229
Montreux a.	0637	0737	0837	0941	...	1041	1141	...	1241	1341	...	1441	1541	...	1641	1741	...	1841	...	1941	...	2041	2141	2241

p – Daily Dec. 9 - Oct. 26; © Nov. 1 - Dec. 13.
r – May 24 - Sept. 28.
t – June 28 - Aug. 31.

▲ – Funicular railway operates daily (not June 30 - Sept. 5) **Glion - Territet** and v.v. **Operator**: MVR, ✆ 0900 245 245. Depart 0525, 0545, 0600, 0615, 0630, 0645, and every 15 minutes until 2115, then 2145, 2215, 2245, 2315, 2350, 0020, 0045, 0130⑥⑦.

570 GENÈVE - LAUSANNE - SION - BRIG SBB

For Franco - Italian overnight services through Switzerland see Table **44**

km		IR 1709	IR 1411	IR 1711	IR 1415	IR 1715	CIS 121 ⊡ ◆	IR 1417	IR 1717	IR 1419	IR 1719		CIS 123 ⊡ ◆	IR 1421	IR 1721	IR 1423	IR 1723	CIS 125 ⊡ ◆	IR 1425	TGV 9261 (✕) ◆	IR 1725	IR 1427	IR 1727	IR 1429	IR 1729	IR 1431
0	Genève A ✈ 505 d.	...	...	...	...	0627	0658	0647	0727	0747	0827	...	...	0847	0927	0947	1027	...	1047	...	1127	1147	1227	1247	1327	1347
6	**Genève 505** d.	...	...	0521	...	0636	0707	0656	0736	0756	0836	...	0907	0856	0936	0956	1036	1107	1056	...	1136	1156	1236	1256	1336	1356
27	Nyon **505** d.	...	...	0537	...	0650	|	0710	0750	0810	0850	...	|	0910	0950	1010	1050	|	1110	...	1150	1210	1250	1310	1350	1410
53	Morges **505** d.	...	...	0600	...	0705	|	0728	0805	0828	0905	...	|	0928	1005	1028	1105	|	1128	...	1205	1228	1305	1328	1405	1428
66	**Lausanne 505** a.	...	...	0612	...	0715	|	0740k	0815	0840	0915	...	|	0940k	1015	1040	1115	1140	1140k	...	1215	1240	1315	1340	1415	1440
66	**Lausanne** ▲ d.	...	0545	0620	0645	0720	0746u	0750	0820	0845	0920	...	0946u	0950	1020	1045	1120	1146	1150	1157	1220	1245	1320	1345	1420	1445
84	Vevey ▲ d.	...	0559	0634	0659	0734	|	0804	0834	0859	0934	...	|	1004	1034	1059	1134	|	1204	|	1234	1259	1334	1359	1434	1459
92	**Montreux** ▲ d.	...	0605	0640	0705	0740	0806	0810	0840	0905	0940	...	1006	1010	1040	1105	1140	1206	1210	1216	1240	1305	1340	1405	1440	1505
105	Aigle ▲ d.	...	0616	0651	0716	0751	|	0821	0851	0916	0951	...	|	1021	1051	1116	1151	|	1221	1229	1251	1316	1351	1416	1451	1516
114	Bex d.	...	0623	|	0723	|	|	0827	|	0923	|	...	|	1027	|	1123	|	|	1227	|	|	1323	|	1423	|	1523
118	St Maurice d.	...	0628	|	0728	|	|	0832	|	0928	|	...	|	1032	|	1128	|	|	1232	|	|	1328	|	1428	|	1528
133	Martigny d.	...	0638	0708	0738	0808	|	0842	0908	0938	1008	...	|	1042	1108	1138	1208	|	1242	1249	1308	1338	1408	1438	1508	1538
158	**Sion** d.	0624	0654	0724	0754	0824	0843	0858	0924	0954	1024	...	1043	1058	1124	1154	1224	1243	1258	1305	1324	1354	1424	1454	1524	1554
174	Sierre d.	0635	0705	0735	0805	0835	|	0909	0935	1005	1035	...	|	1109	1135	1205	1235	1253	1309	1317	1335	1405	1435	1505	1535	1605
184	Leuk d.	0642	0712	0742	0812	0842	|	|	0942	1012	1042	...	|	|	1142	1212	1242	|	|	1326	1342	1412	1442	1512	1542	1612
203	Visp d.	0655	0723	0755	0823	0855	0907	0924	0955	1023	1055	...	1107	1124	1155	1223	1255	|	1324	1338	1355	1423	1455	1523	1555	1623
212	**Brig** a.	0702	0730	0802	0830	0902	0914	0931	1002	1030	1102	...	1114	1131	1202	1230	1302	1314	1331	1345	1402	1430	1502	1530	1602	1630
368	*Milano C 590* a.	...	...	...	...	...	1135	...	...	...	...	...	1335	...	...	...	...	1535	...	...	...	...	...	...	...	...

	IR 1731	CIS 127 ⊡ ◆	IR 1435	IR 1735	IR 1437	TGV 9267 (✕) ◆	RE 2737 Ⓐ	IR 1737	IR 1439	RE 2739 Ⓐ	IR 1739	CIS 129 ⊡ ◆	IR 1441		IR 1741	IR 1443	TGV 9273 (✕) ◆	IR 1743	IR 1445	IR 1745		IR 311	EN 311 Ⓡ✗ ◆		IR 1749	IR 1449
Genève A ✈ 505 d.	1427	1501	1447	1527	1547	...	...	1627	1647	...	1727	1758	1747	...	1827	1847	...	1927	1947	2027	2124	...	...	...	2227	2312
Genève 505 d.	1436	1510	1456	1536	1556	...	...	1636	1656	...	1736	1807	1756	...	1836	1856	...	1936	1956	2036	2130	2136	2136	...	2236	2321
Nyon **505** d.	1450	|	1510	1550	1610	...	...	1650	1710	...	1750	|	1810	...	1850	1910	...	1950	2010	2050	...	2150	2150u	...	2250	2337
Morges **505** d.	1505	|	1528	1605	1628	...	...	1705	1728	...	1805	|	1828	...	1905	1928	...	2005	2028	2105	...	2205	2205u	...	2305	0000
Lausanne 505 a.	1515	1543	1540k	1615	1640	...	...	1715	1740	...	1815	|	1840k	...	1915	1940	...	2015	2040	2115	...	2215	|	...	2315	0012
Lausanne ▲ d.	1520	1546	1550	1620	1645	1657	1656	1720	1745	1756	1820	1846u	1850	...	1920	1945	1957	2020	2045	2120	...	2220	2220u	...	2320	0024
Vevey ▲ d.	1534	|	1604	1634	1659	|	1711	1734	1759	1811	1834	|	1904	...	1934	1959	|	2034	2059	2134	...	2234	2234u	...	2334	0038
Montreux ▲ d.	1540	1606	1610	1640	1705	1717	1718	1740	1805	1818	1840	1906	1910	...	1940	2005	2016	2040	2105	2140	...	2240	2240u	...	2340	0044
Aigle ▲ d.	1551	|	1621	1651	1716	1727	1732	1751	1816	1832	1851	|	1921	...	1951	2016	2027	2051	2116	2151	...	2251	2251u	...	2351	0055
Bex d.	|	|	1627	|	1723	...	1739	|	1823	1839	|	|	1927	...	|	2023	|	2058	2123	2158	...	2258	2258u	...	2358	0102
St Maurice d.	|	|	1632	|	1728	...	1744	|	1828	1844	|	|	1932	...	|	2028	|	2103	2128	2203	...	2303	2303u	...	0003	0107
Martigny d.	1608	|	1642	1708	1738	...	...	1808	1838	...	1908	|	1942	...	2008	2038	2047	2113	2138	2213	...	2313	2313u	...	0013	0117
Sion d.	1624	1643	1658	1724	1754	...	...	1824	1854	...	1924	1943	1958	...	2024	2054	2104	2127	2154	2229	...	2329	2329u	...	0029	0131
Sierre d.	1635	1653	1709	1735	1805	...	...	1835	1905	...	1935	1953	2009	...	2035	2105	2116	...	2205	2240	...	2340	2340u	...	0040	...
Leuk d.	1642	|	|	1742	1812	...	...	1842	1912	...	1942	|	|	...	2042	2112	2126	...	2212	2247	...	2347	2347u	...	0047	...
Visp d.	1655	|	1724	1755	1823	...	...	1855	1923	...	1955	|	2024	...	2055	2123	2141	...	2223	2258	...	2358	2358u	...	0058	...
Brig a.	1702	1714	1731	1802	1830	...	...	1902	1930	...	2002	2014	2031	...	2102	2130	2147	...	2230	2305	...	0005	0005u	...	0105	...
Milano C 590 a.	...	1935	...	...	...	...	...	...	...	...	...	2235	...	...	...	...	...	...	...	...	...	...	...	...	...	...

	IR 1702	IR 1404	IR 1706	IR 1406	RE 2706 Ⓐ	IR 1708	RE 2708 Ⓐ	IR 1408	EN 316 Ⓡ✗ ◆	IR 316	IR 1410	IR 1712	IR 1412	IR 1714	IR 1414	IR 1718	IR 1418	CIS 120 ⊡ ◆	TGV 9268 (✕) ◆	IR 1720	IR 1420	IR 1722	IR 1422	IR 1724	IR 1424	IR 1726
Milano C 590 d.	...	...	...	...	...	...	...	...	...	...	...	...	...	...	...	...	...	0825	...	...	...	...	...	...	...	...
Brig d.	...	0428	...	0528	...	0600	...	0628	0657s	0657	0728	0757	0828	0857	0928	0957	1028	1046	1032	1057	1128	1157	1228	1257	1328	1357
Visp d.	...	0435	...	0535	...	0607	...	0635	0703s	0707	0735	0807	0835	0907	0935	1007	1035	|	1040	1107	1135	1207	1235	1307	1335	1407
Leuk d.	...	0446	...	0546	...	0618	...	0646	0718s	0718	0746	0818	0846	0918	0946	1018	|	|	1053	1118	1146	1218	1246	1318	1346	1418
Sierre d.	...	0454	...	0554	...	0626	...	0654	0725s	0726	0754	0826	0854	0926	0954	1026	1051	1106	1110	1126	1154	1226	1254	1326	1354	1426
Sion d.	0427	0505	0532	0605	...	0637	...	0705	0735s	0737	0805	0837	0905	0937	1005	1037	1102	1117	1129	1137	1205	1237	1305	1337	1405	1437
Martigny d.	0441	0519	0546	0619	...	0651	...	0719	0750s	0751	0819	0851	0919	0951	1019	1051	1116	|	1145	1151	1219	1251	1319	1351	1419	1451
St Maurice d.	0451	0531	0556	0631	0646	|	0702	0731	|	|	0831	|	0931	|	1031	|	1126	|	|	|	1231	|	1331	|	1431	|
Bex d.	0456	0536	0601	0636	0651	|	0707	0736	|	|	0836	|	0936	|	1036	|	1131	|	|	|	1236	|	1336	|	1436	|
Aigle ▲ d.	0503	0543	0608	0643	0658	0708	0714	0743	0807s	0808	0843	0908	0943	1008	1043	1108	1138	|	1214	1208	1243	1308	1343	1408	1443	1508
Montreux ▲ d.	0514	0554	0619	0654	0712	0719	0726	0754	0818s	0819	0854	0919	0954	1019	1054	1119	1149	1155	1226	1219	1254	1319	1354	1419	1454	1519
Vevey ▲ d.	0521	0601	0626	0701	0720	0726	0735	0801	0825s	0826	0901	0926	1001	1026	1101	1126	1156	|	|	1226	1301	1326	1401	1426	1501	1526
Lausanne ▲ a.	0535	0615	0640	0715	0734	0740	0750	0815	0840s	0840	0915	0940	1015	1040	1115	1140	1210	1214	1245	1240	1315	1340	1415	1440	1515	1540
Lausanne 505 d.	0540	0620	0645	0720	...	0745	...	0820	|	0845	0920	0945	1020	1045	1120	1145	1220	1217	...	1245	1320	1345	1420	1445	1520	1545
Morges **505** d.	0550	0632	0655	0732	...	0755	...	0832	0854s	0855	0932	0955	1032	1055	1132	1155	1232	|	...	1255	1332	1355	1432	1455	1532	1555
Nyon **505** d.	0605	0650	0710	0750	...	0810	...	0850	0909s	0910	0950	1010	1050	1110	1150	1210	1250	|	...	1310	1350	1410	1450	1510	1550	1610
Genève 505 a.	0619	0704	0724	0804	...	0824	...	0904	0924s	0924	1004	1024	1104	1124	1204	1224	1304	1250	...	1324	1404	1424	1504	1524	1604	1624
Genève A ✈ 505 a.	0628	0713	0733	0813	...	0833	...	0913	0933	0933	1013	1033	1113	1133	1213	1233	1313	1259	...	1333	1413	1433	1513	1533	1613	1633

	CIS 122 ⊡ ◆	IR 1426	IR 1728	IR 1428	IR 1730	CIS 124 ⊡ ◆	IR 1430	IR 1732	TGV 9274 (✕) ◆	TGV 9274 (✕) A	IR 1432	IR 1736	IR 1436	CIS 126 ⊡ ◆	IR 1738 †	IR 1738 ⚒	IR 1438	IR 1740	RE 2640	IR 1440	RE 2642	IR 1442	CIS 128 ⊡ ◆	RE 2644	IR 1444	RE 2646
Milano C 590 d.	1225	...	...	...	...	1425	...	...	...	...	...	...	...	1625	...	...	...	...	...	...	...	...	1920	...	...	...
Brig d.	1446	1428	1457	1528	1557	1646	1628	1657	1716	...	1728	1757	1828	1846	1857	1857	1928	1957	...	2028	...	2125	2146	...	2228	...
Visp d.	|	1435	1507	1535	1607	|	1635	1707	1724	...	1735	1807	1835	1854	1907	1907	1935	2007	...	2035	...	2133	2154	...	2235	...
Leuk d.	|	|	1518	1546	1618	|	|	1718	1736	...	1746	1818	|	|	1918	1918	1946	2018	...	2046	...	2144	|	...	2246	...
Sierre d.	1506	1451	1526	1554	1626	1706	1651	1726	1745	...	1754	1826	1851	|	1926	1926	1954	2026	...	2054	...	2151	|	...	2254	...
Sion d.	1517	1502	1537	1605	1637	1717	1702	1737	1759	...	1805	1837	1902	1917	1937	1937	2005	2035	...	2105	...	2202	2217	...	2305	...
Martigny d.	|	1516	1551	1619	1651	|	1716	1751	1814	...	1819	1851	1916	|	1951	1951	2019	...	...	2119	...	2216	|	...	2319	...
St Maurice d.	|	1526	|	1631	|	|	1726	|	|	...	1831	|	1926	|	|	|	2031	...	...	2131	...	2226	|	...	2331	...
Bex d.	|	1531	|	1636	|	|	1731	|	|	...	1836	|	1931	|	|	|	2036	...	...	2136	...	2231	|	...	2336	...
Aigle ▲ d.	|	1538	1608	1643	1708	|	1738	1808	1836	1836	1843	1908	1938	|	2008	2008	2043	...	...	2143	...	2238	|	...	2343	...
Montreux ▲ d.	1555	1549	1619	1654	1719	1755	1749	1819	1849	1849	1854	1919	1949	1955	2019	2019	2054	...	...	2154	...	2249	2255	...	2354	...
Vevey ▲ d.	|	1556	1626	1701	1726	|	1756	1826	|	|	1901	1926	1956	|	2026	2026	2101	...	...	2201	...	2256	|	...	0001	...
Lausanne ▲ a.	1614s	1610	1640	1715	1740	1814s	1810	1840	1908	1908	1915	1940	2010	2014	2040	2040	2115	...	...	2215	...	2310	2314	...	0015	...
Lausanne 505 d.	|	1620	1645	1720	1745	|	1820	1845	...	...	1920	1945	...	2017	2045	2048	...	...	2148	...	2248	...	2317	2348	...	0048
Morges **505** d.	|	1632	1655	1732	1755	|	1832	1855	...	...	1932	1955	...	|	2055	2100	...	...	2200	...	2300	...	|	0000	...	0100
Nyon **505** d.	|	1650	1710	1750	1810	|	1850	1910	...	...	1950	2010	...	|	2110	2123	...	...	2223	...	2323	...	|	0023	...	0123
Genève 505 a.	1653	1704	1724	1804	1824	1853	1904	1924	...	...	2004	2024	...	2050	2124	2139	...	...	2239	...	2339	...	2350	0039	...	0142
Genève A ✈ 505 a.	1702	1713	1733	1813	1833	...	1913	1933	...	...	2013	2033	...	2059	2133	2148	...	...	2248	...	...	...	2359	...	...	...

◆ – **NOTES** (LISTED BY TRAIN NUMBER)

120/127 – CISALPINO VALLESE – [12] Genève Aéroport - Milano and v.v.
121/128 – CISALPINO MONTERVERDI – [12] Genève Aéroport - Milano - Venezia and v.v.
122/129 – CISALPINO MONTE ROSE – [12] Genève Aéroport - Milano and v.v.
123/124 – CISALPINO BORROMEO – [12] Genève - Milano and v.v.
125 – CISALPINO LEMANO – [12] Genève - Milano.
126 – CISALPINO LEMANO – [12] Milano - Genève Aéroport.
311 – LUNA – 1,2 cl. and 2 cl. Genève - Brig (**313**) - Roma.
316 – LUNA – 1,2 cl. and 2 cl. Roma (**314**) - Brig - Genève.
9261 – ⑥ Dec. 15 - Mar. 29; ⑦ July 6 - Aug. 24: [12] and (✕) Paris - Brig.
9267 – ⑦ Dec. 16 - Mar. 30; ⑥ July 12 - Aug. 23 (also Dec. 25, Jan. 1, Mar. 24): [12] and (✕) Paris - Aigle.
9268 – ⑥ Dec. 15 - Mar. 29, July 12 - Aug. 23 (also Aug. 15; not Aug. 16): [12] and (✕) Brig - Paris.
9273 – ⑤ Dec. 14 - Mar. 28, July 11 - Aug. 22 (also Aug. 14; not Aug. 15): [12] and (✕) Paris - Brig.
9274 – ⑥ Dec. 15 - Mar. 29: [12] and (✕) Brig - Paris.

A – ⑦ Dec. 16 - Mar. 30; ⑥ July 12 - Aug. 23 (also Dec. 25, Jan. 1, Mar. 24): [12] and (✕) Aigle - Paris.

k – Connects with train in previous column.
s – Stops to set down only.
u – Stops to pick up only.

✗ – Supplement payable.
⊡ – Operated by *CISALPINO*. Ⓡ for international journeys; may be used for Swiss internal journeys without reservation. Conveys ✕.

▲ – Additional local services operate hourly **Lausanne - Montreux - Villeneuve** and v.v. calling at all stations including Territet and Veytaux-Chillon; **Lausanne** depart xx00, **Villeneuve** depart xx24. Bus connections are available between Villeneuve and Aigle.

Local services from VEVEY, AIGLE and BEX — 571

2nd class only

VEVEY - BLONAY. Narrow gauge. *6 km.* Journey time: 14–16 minutes. **Operator**: MOB.

From **Vevey**: 0639, 0709, 0739, 0809, 0839, 0909, 0939, 1009⚒, 1039, 1109⚒, 1139, 1209⚒, 1239, 1309⚒, 1339, 1409⚒, 1439, 1509⚒, 1546, 1609⚒, 1639, 1709Ⓐ, 1739, 1809Ⓐ, 1839, 1909Ⓐ, 1939, 2009, 2039, 2139, 2239, 2339, 0041⑥⑦.

From **Blonay**: 0602, 0632, 0702, 0732, 0802, 0832, 0902, 0932⚒, 1002, 1032⚒, 1102, 1132⚒, 1202, 1232⚒, 1302, 1332⚒, 1402, 1432⚒, 1502, 1532⚒, 1602, 1632Ⓐ, 1702, 1732Ⓐ, 1802, 1832Ⓐ, 1902, 1932, 2002, 2114, 2214, 2314, 0002⑥⑦.

AIGLE - LEYSIN. Narrow gauge rack railway. *6 km.* Journey time: 29–39 minutes. **Operator**: TPC.

From **Aigle**: 0550⚒, 0620Ⓒ, 0720Ⓐ, 0756 and hourly until 2056, then 2256.

From **Leysin** Grand Hotel: 0525, 0624Ⓐ, 0653Ⓒ, 0753 and hourly until 2153, then 2327.

AIGLE - LES DIABLERETS. Narrow gauge. *23 km.* Journey time: 45–55 minutes. **Operator**: TPC. *Subject to 🚌 substitution March 31 - May 30 owing to engineering work.*

From **Aigle**: 0619, 0720, 0828, 0955, 1057, 1140Ⓐ, 1155Ⓒ, 1240Ⓐ, 1255Ⓒ, 1355, 1457, 1555, 1657, 1755, 1855, 2055, 2159.

From **Les Diablerets**: 0513Ⓐ, 0612Ⓒ, 0622Ⓐ, 0713, 0813, 0948, 1045, 1148, 1248, 1332Ⓐ, 1348Ⓒ, 1445, 1548, 1645, 1748, 1900, 2048, 2145.

AIGLE - CHAMPÉRY. Narrow gauge rack railway. 2nd class only. **Operator**: TPC. *Monthey - Champéry and v.v. subject to 🚌 substitution April 28 - July 18 owing to engineering work.*

km																											
		⚒			⚒				⚒		⚒		⚒					⚒								⑥	
0	**Aigle** d.	0518	0618	0720	0810	0825	0922	1025	1105	1120	1154	1225	1254	1320	1422	1520	1624	1705	1720	1823	1902	1954	2054	2153	2254	...	2354
11	Monthey Ville d.	0547	0647	0747	0829	0849	0947	1047	1124	1147	1213	1247	1313	1347	1447	1547	1647	1724	1749	1845	1926	2020	2113	2213	2313	2330	0013
23	**Champéry** a.	0620	0722	0820	...	0922	1020	1130	...	1220	...	1320	...	1420	1520	1628	1720	...	1822	1918	1959	2053	...	2245	...	0003	...

		⚒		⚒					⚒		⚒		⚒						⚒								⑦
Champéry d.	...	0533	0600c	0633a	0702d	0733	0835	0933	...	1033	...	1133	...	1300	1333	1433	1533	1631	...	1733	1831	1939	2033	2133	2247	...	0004
Monthey Ville d.	0540	0617	0641	0712	0742	0817	0914	1017	1032	1112	1127	1217	1232	1342	1414	1512	1616	1712	1727	1815	1909	2017	2117	2214	2322	2318	0039
Aigle a.	0601	0637	0701	0732	0802	0837	0934	1037	1052	1132	1147	1237	1252	1402	1434	1532	1636	1732	1747	1835	1929	2037	2137	2234	...	2338	...

BEX - VILLARS. *12 km.* Journey time: 40–46 minutes. All trains call at Bex (Place du Marché), and Bévieux (*3 km* and 10 minutes from Bex). **Operator**: TPC.

From **Bex**: 0631, 0739, 0839, 0939, 1039, 1149, 1239, 1339, 1457, 1549, 1639, 1743, 1843, 1934, 2105.

From **Villars**: 0542, 0644, 0733, 0833, 0933, 1033, 1143, 1233, 1333, 1433, 1543, 1633, 1738, 1838, 1947, 2042.

a – Ⓐ only. c – Ⓒ only. d – ⚒ only.

MARTIGNY - CHAMONIX — 572

2nd class only. SNCF, TMR

Narrow gauge rack railway. Through journeys operate as MONT BLANC EXPRESS. Passengers may be required to change trains at Le Châtelard Frontière.

December 9 - June 13

km																								
		Ⓐ								j			k		j			j					⑤⑥	
0	**Martigny** d.	...	...	0540	...	0648	0801	0901	...	1001	...	1101	1201	1301	1401	1501	...	1601	...	1643	1801	1901	2012	...
7	Salvan d.	0515	...	0558	...	0706	0818	0918	...	1018	...	1118	1218	1318	1418	1518	...	1618	...	1700	1818	1918	2029	...
9	Les Marécottes d.	0519	...	0602	...	0710	0822	0922	...	1022	...	1122	1222	1322	1422	1522	...	1622	...	1704	1822	1922	2033	...
14	Finhaut d.	0531	...	0614	...	0722	0834	0934	...	1034	...	1134	1234	1334	1434	1534	...	1634	...	1717	1834	1934	2045*	...
18	Le Châtelard Frontière 🏛 a.	0542	...	0625	...	0733	0845	0945	...	1045	...	1145	1245	1345	1445	1545	...	1645	...	1728	1845	1945	2055*	...
			n						b				b					b	d					
18	Le Châtelard Frontière d.	...	...	...	...	...	0847	0947	...	...	1047	1147	1247	1347	...	...	1547v	1647	...	1747	1847	1947	...	...
21	Vallorcine d.	...	0618	...	0658	...	0858	0958	1030	...	1058	1158	1258	1358	...	...	1558	1656	1721	1758	1858	1958	...	...
28	Argentière Haute Savoie d.	...	0635	...	0714	...	0914	1014	1049	...	1114	1214	1314	1414	...	...	1614	1714	1738	1814	1914	2014	...	...
32	Les Tines d.	...	0645	...	0726	...	0926	1026	1058	...	1126	1226	1326	1426	...	...	1626	1726	1747	1826	1926	2026	...	...
36	**Chamonix** a.	...	0653	...	0733	...	0933	1033	1107	...	1133	1233	1333	1433	...	...	1633	1733	1756	1833	1933	2033	...	...
	St Gervais **367a** ❖ a.	...	0742	...	0820	...	1020	1120	...	...	...	1320	1420	1520	...	...	1720	1820	...	1920	2020	...	...	...

							b		b		b						d	b					
St Gervais **367a** ❖ d.	...	...	...	0651	0732	0832	...	...	0932	1032	...	...	1232	1332	...	...	1532	...	1632	...	1732	1832	1932	...
Chamonix d.	...	...	...	0736	0817	0917	0943	...	1017	1117	1217	...	1317	1417	...	...	1617	1643	1717	...	1817	1917	2017	...
Les Tines d.	...	...	...	0746	0827	0927	0952	...	1027	1127	1227	...	1327	1427	...	...	1627	1652	1727	...	1827	1927	2027	...
Argentière Haute Savoie d.	...	...	...	0755	0836	0936	1002	...	1036	1136	1236	...	1336	1436	...	...	1636	1702	1736	...	1836	1936	2036	...
Vallorcine d.	...	...	...	...	0859	0959	1020	...	1059	1159	1259	...	1359	1459	...	...	1659	1718	1759	...	1859	1959	2052	...
Le Châtelard Frontière a.	...	...	...	...	0905	1005	...	...	1105	1205	1305	...	1405	1505	...	...	1705	...	1805	...	1905	2005	...	...
	Ⓐ								h		k			j			j							
Le Châtelard Frontière 🏛 d.	0547	0638	0807	...	0907	1007	...	...	1107	1207	1307	...	1407	1507	1549	...	1707	...	...	1807	1907	2007	...	...
Finhaut d.	0558	0649	0818	...	0918	1018	...	...	1118	1218	1318	...	1418	1518	1600	...	1718	...	...	1818	1918	2018	...	...
Les Marécottes d.	0611	0701	0830	...	0930	1030	...	...	1130	1230	1330	...	1430	1530	1612	...	1730	...	...	1830	1930	2030	...	...
Salvan d.	0615	0705	0834	...	0934	1034	...	...	1134	1234	1334	...	1434	1534	1616	...	1734	...	...	1834	1934	2034	...	...
Martigny a.	0635	0726	0854	...	0954	1054	...	...	1154	1254	1354	...	1454	1554	1637	...	1754	...	...	1854	1954	2054	...	...

b – Dec. 9 - Mar. 30.
d – Daily Dec. 9 - Mar. 30; Ⓐ Mar. 31 - June 13.
h – Dec. 15 - Mar. 15.
j – Dec. 15 - Mar. 15, June 2 - Sept. 14.
k – Daily Dec. 15 - Mar. 15; ③ Apr. 2 - May 28; daily June 2 - Sept. 14.
n – Ⓐ Dec. 10-21, Jan. 7 - Feb. 15, Mar. 3 - Apr. 11, Apr. 28 - July 2.
v – Dec. 9-14, Mar. 16 - June 14.
* – Runs only if passengers are present at Les Marécottes.
❖ – Timings Chamonix - St Gervais and v.v. are subject to alteration Mar. 24 - Apr. 13.

SION VALLEY RESORTS — 573

MARTIGNY - ORSIÈRES▲ and LE CHÂBLE. *19 km*, 26 minutes to both resorts. A change of train may be necessary at Sembrancher. **Operator**: RA.

From **Martigny**: 0813, 0913, 1027, 1130, 1213, 1334, 1413, 1523, 1613Ⓒ, 1647, 1723, 1823, 1913, 2013, 2124⑤⑥.

From **Orsières and Le Châble**: 0550Ⓐ, 0648, 0809, 0909, 1009, 1057, 1209, 1301, 1409, 1519, 1609, 1643Ⓒ, 1719, 1819, 1909, 2049⑤⑥.

LE CHÂBLE - VERBIER. 🚌 service. Journey time: 25 minutes. **Operator**: PA.

From **Le Châble Gare**: 0655⚒, 0730Ⓐ, 0750⑥ **q**, 0845, 0945, 1100Ⓒ, 1100Ⓐ **r**, 1245, 1405, 1500 **m**, 1610, 1718, 1800 **j**, 1812 **p**, 1905 **w**, 1955, 2050 **w**, 2155 **n**.
From **Verbier Post**: 0618⚒, 0720, 0840⚒, 0915, 1020, 1215, 1335, 1435 **m**, 1525, 1645, 1747, 1840, 1925 **w**, 2020 **w**.

MARTIGNY - AOSTA. 🚌 service via Grand St Bernard tunnel. Service runs daily throughout the year. Journey time: 2 hours. **Operator**: TMR/SAVDA.

From **Martigny Gare**: 0825, 1655. From **Aosta Stazione**: 0810, 1620 (🚌 to Orsières arrive 1805, then train forward depart 1819, Martigny arrive 1845).

SION - CRANS-SUR-SIERRE. 🚌 service. Journey time: 45 minutes. **Operator**: PA.

From **Sion Gare**: 0645⚒, 0750, 0850⚒, 0945, 1045⚒, 1150, 1230⚒ 1345, 1545, 1650, 1800, 1905.

From **Crans-sur-Sierre Post**: 0643, 0745⚒, 0845, 0940⚒, 1045, 1140⚒, 1245, 1345⚒, 1545, 1645, 1803, 1900.

SIERRE - CRANS-sur-SIERRE and MONTANA. 🚌 service. Journey time to Crans is 30–45 minutes, to Montana, 45–60 minutes. **Operator**: SMC.

Principal stop in **Crans-sur-Sierre** is Hotel Scandia; and in **Montana** are Montana Maison Général Guisan, Gare and Barzettes. Approximately hourly on ⚒ (times vary, check locally) between 0700 and 2100 (less frequent on † and Mar. 19, May 22, Aug. 15, Nov. 1, Dec. 8).

BRIG - SAAS FEE. 🚌 service. Journey time: 50–70 minutes. All services call at **Visp** (Post) 15–20 minutes from Brig, and **Saas Grund** (Post) 5–10 minutes from Saas Fee.

From **Brig (Bahnhof)**: 0615, 0645, 0715 and every 30 minutes until 1115, then 1140, 1215, 1251, 1315, 1345 and every 30 minutes until 1845, then 1945, 2045, 2215⑤⑥ **y**.

From **Saas Grund (Post)**: 0611, 0644, 0711, 0735 and hourly until 1835, then 1911, 2011, 2111, 2339⑤⑥ **y**.

j – Daily Dec. 9 - June 27, Sept. 22 - Dec. 13.
m – Daily Dec. 10 - Apr. 13; ⚒ Apr. 15 - Dec. 13.
n – ⑤⑥ Dec. 14 - Mar. 29.
p – June 28 - Sept. 21.
q – Not Nov. 1.
r – 35 minutes later on ③ schooldays.
w – Dec. 14 - Apr. 13.
y – Not Mar. 21, Aug. 1.

575 ZERMATT - BRIG - DISENTIS - CHUR

Narrow gauge rack railway. MGB, RhB*

km			Ⓐ	Ⓒ				⁄Av	★Bm				★Cm	★Yk	★Dm													
0	**Zermatt** d.	0539	0613	0639	0739	0839	...	0900	0913	...	0939	...	1000	1000	1013	...	1039	1139	1239	1339	1439	1539	1639	1739	1839	1913	2013	2113
8	Täsch d.	0551	0626	0651	0751	0851	...	|	|	...	0951	...	|	|	|	...	1051	1151	1251	1351	1451	1551	1651	1751	1851	1928	2028	2128
21	St Niklaus d.	0617	0653	0717	0817	0917	...	0937	|	...	1017	...	|	1037	|	...	1117	1217	1317	1417	1517	1617	1717	1817	1917	1953	2053	2153
29	Stalden-Saas d.	0638	0713	0738	0838	0938	...	|	|	...	1038	...	|	|	|	...	1138	1238	1338	1438	1538	1638	1738	1838	1938	2012	2112	2212
36	Visp d.	0652	0726	0752	0852	0952	...	|	|	...	1052	...	|	|	|	...	1152	1252	1352	1452	1552	1652	1752	1852	1952	2025	2125	2225
45	**Brig** a.	0703	0736	0803	0903	1003	...	1005	1022	...	1103	...	1105	1105	1122	...	1203	1303	1403	1503	1603	1703	1803	1903	2003	2035	2135	2235

km							⁄Av		★Bm	★Cm	★Yk	m	w	p	★Dm											🚌	①–⑥	⑦
	Visp d.	...	...	0708	0808	0908	1006	1008	1025	1106	1106	...	...	1108	1125	1208	1308	1408	1508	1608	1708	1808	1908	2008	2108	...	2236	2255
0	**Brig** d.	...	0623	0723	0823	0923	1016	1023	1041	1116	1116	...	...	1123	1141	1223	1323	1423	1523	1623	1723	1823	1923	2023	2123	...	2250	2310
7	Mörel d.	...	0633	0733	0833	0933	|	1033	|	|	|	...	...	1133	|	1233	1333	1433	1533	1633	1733	1833	1933	2033	2133	...	2259	2319
10	Betten d.	...	0639	0739	0839	0939	|	1039	|	|	|	...	...	1139	|	1239	1339	1439	1539	1639	1739	1839	1939	2039	2139	...	2305	2325
17	Fiesch d.	...	0658	0758	0858	0958	1042	1058	|	|	1142	...	...	1158	|	1258	1358	1458	1558	1658	1758	1858	1958	2058	2157	2158	2323	2343
41	Oberwald 🚗 d.	...	0744	0844	0944	1044	1111	1144	|	|	1211	...	...	1244	|	1344	1444	1544	1644	1744	1844	1944	2044	2144t	...	2239	...	...
59	Realp ▲ 🚗 § d.	...	0805	0905	1005	1105	|	1205	|	|	|	...	...	1305	|	1405	1505	1605	1705	1805	1905	2005	2105	2205t	...	...	...	...
68	**Andermatt** a.	...	0820	0920	1020	1120	1136	1220	1206	1239	1239	...	...	1320	1306	1420	1520	1620	1720	1820	1920	2020	2120	2220t	...	...	...	...
68	**Andermatt** 🚗 d.	0730	*0830*	*0930*	*1030*	*1130*	1159	*1230*j	1223	1247	1247	1328	*1328*	1328	1308	*1430*	*1530*	*1630*	*1730*	*1830*	...	...	...	...	...	...	...	...
78	Oberalppass d.	0757	*0857*	*0957*	*1057*	*1157*	|	*1257*j	|	|	|	1349	1357	*1357*	|	*1457*	*1557*	*1657*	*1757*	*1857*	...	...	...	...	...	...	...	...
87	Sedrun 🚗 d.	0823	*0923*	*1023*	*1123*	*1223*	1246	*1323*j	|	|	|	1423	1423	*1423*	|	*1523*	*1623*	*1723*	*1823*	*1923*	...	...	...	...	...	...	...	...
97	**Disentis/Mustér** a.	0842	*0942*	*1042*	*1142*	*1242*	1305	*1342*j	1321	1349	1352	1442	1442	*1442*	1405	*1542*	*1642*	*1742*	*1842*	*1942*	...	...	...	...	...	...	...	...

km			⚒									⁄Av	★Bm			★Cm	★Dm		★Yk									
0	**Disentis/Mustér** d.	0545	0615	0645	0745	...	0845	0945	1045	1145	1245	1327	1328	...	1345	1414	1415	...	1428	...	1445	...	1545	1645	1745	1845	1945	2045
12	Trun d.	0601	0630	0701	0801	...	0901	1001	1101	1201	1301	|	|	...	1401	|	|	...	|	...	1501	...	1601	1701	1801	1901	2001	2101
30	Ilanz d.	0624	0653	0724	0824	...	0924	1024	1124	1224	1324	|	|	...	1424	|	|	...	1500s	...	1524	...	1624	1724	1824	1924	2024	2124
49	Reichenau-Tamins d.	0650	0720	0750	0850	...	0950	1050	1150	1250	1350	|	|	...	1450	|	|	...	|	...	1550	...	1650	1750	1850	1950	2050	2150
59	**Chur** a.	0704	0734	0804	0902	...	1002	1102	1202	1302	1402	1439	1440	...	1502	1520	1521	...	1540	...	1602	...	1702	1802	1902	2002	2104	2204

	⚒						★Xk		★Gm	★Fm		Ⓐ	Ⓒ		★Hm	⁄Jv												
Chur d.	0611	0656	0756	0856	0956	1056	1115	...	1138	1139	...	1155	1156	...	1214	1215	...	1256	1356	1456	1556	1656	1756	1856	1959	2059	...	2259
Reichenau-Tamins d.	0625	0705	0805	0905	1005	1105	1125u	...	|	|	...	1205	1205	...	|	|	...	1305	1405	1505	1605	1705	1805	1905	2013	2113	...	2310
Ilanz d.	0653	0733	0833	0933	1033	1133	1150u	...	|	|	...	1233	1233	...	|	|	...	1333	1433	1533	1633	1733	1833	1933	2042	2142	...	2336
Trun d.	0714	0753	0853	0953	1053	1153	|	...	|	|	...	1253	1253	...	|	|	...	1353	1453	1553	1653	1753	1853	1953	2101	2201	...	2355
Disentis/Mustér a.	0731	0811	0911	1011	1111	1211	1228	...	1245	1245	...	1311	1311	...	1327	1328	...	1411	1511	1611	1711	1811	1911	2011	2119	2219	...	0012

	🚌											m	★Xk	★Gm		★Fm		★Hm	⁄Jv						t			🚌
Disentis/Mustér d.	...	...	...	...	*0719*	*0819*	*0919*	*1019*	*1119*	1219	...	...	1244	1252	...	1307	*1319*j	1335	1351	...	*1419*	*1519*	*1619*	*1719*	...	*1819*	...	...
Sedrun 🚗 d.	...	...	...	...	*0737*	*0837*	*0937*	*1037*	*1137*	1237	...	...	|	|	...	|	*1337*j	|	1407	...	*1437*	*1537*	*1637*	*1737*	...	*1837*	...	...
Oberalppass d.	...	...	...	...	*0800*	*0900*	*1000*	*1100*	*1200*	1300	...	1400	|	|	...	|	*1400*j	|	|	...	*1500*	*1600*	*1700*	*1800*	...	*1900*	...	...
Andermatt 🚗 a.	...	...	...	...	*0825*	*0925*	*1025*	*1125*	*1225*	1325r	...	1425	1351	1351	...	1413	*1425*j	1434	1457	...	*1525*	*1625*	*1725*	*1825*	...	*1925*	...	...
Andermatt d.	...	...	...	0737	0837	0937	1037	1137	1237	...	1337	...	1354	1354	...	1419	1437	1454	1508	...	1537	1637	1737	1837	1910	1937	2037	...
Realp ▲ 🚗 § d.	...	...	...	0750	0850	0950	1050	1150	1250	...	1350	...	|	|	...	|	1450	|	|	...	1550	1650	1750	1850	1922	1950	2050	...
Oberwald 🚗 d.	0612	...	0712	0812	0912	1012	1112	1212	1312	...	1412	...	1426	|	...	|	1512	|	1543	...	1612	1712	1812	1912	1942	2012	2112	2239
Fiesch d.	0656	0657	0757	0857	0957	1057	1157	1257	1357	...	1457	...	|	|	...	|	1557	|	1614	...	1657	1757	1857	1957	2027	2057	2157	2324
Betten d.	...	0717	0817	0917	1017	1117	1217	1317	1417	...	1517	...	|	|	...	|	1617	|	|	...	1717	1817	1917	2017	2048	2117	2217	...
Mörel d.	...	0724	0824	0924	1024	1124	1224	1324	1424	...	1524	...	|	|	...	|	1624	|	|	...	1724	1824	1924	2024	2055	2124	2224	...
Brig a.	...	0733	0833	0933	1033	1133	1233	1333	1433	...	1533	...	1515	1525	...	1542	1633	1625	1642	...	1733	1833	1933	2033	2103	2133	2233	...
Visp a.	...	0748	0850	0950	1050	1150	1250	1350	1450	...	1550	...	1532	1536	...	1557	1650	1636	1656	...	1750	1850	1950	2050	...	2150	...	...

													★Xk		★Gm		★Fm			★Hm		⁄Jv						
Brig d.	0510	0553	0653	0753	0853	0953	1053	1153	1253	1353	1453	...	1523	...	1528	...	1548	1608	...	1628	...	1648	...	1653	1753	1853	1953	2053
Visp d.	0529	0610	0710	0810	0910	1010	1110	1210	1310	1410	1510	...	1543	...	1543	...	1600	1625	...	1643	...	1700	...	1710	1810	1910	2010	2110
Stalden-Saas d.	0539	0620	0720	0820	0920	1020	1120	1220	1320	1420	1520	...	|	...	|	...	|	1637	...	|	...	|	...	1720	1820	1920	2020	2120
St Niklaus d.	0556	0638	0738	0838	0938	1038	1138	1238	1338	1438	1538	...	1614	...	|	...	|	1655	...	|	...	1728	...	1738	1838	1938	2038	2138
Täsch d.	0622	0703	0803	0903	1003	1103	1203	1303	1403	1503	1603	...	|	...	|	...	|	1722	...	|	...	|	...	1803	1903	2003	2103	2203
Zermatt a.	0633	0714	0814	0914	1014	1114	1214	1314	1414	1514	1614	...	1650	...	1650	...	1710	1733	...	1752	...	1810	...	1814	1914	2014	2114	2214

577 GÖSCHENEN - ANDERMATT

Narrow gauge rack railway. MGB

km																												
0	**Göschenen** d.	0758	0810	0858	0910	0958	1010	1058	1110	1158	1210	1258	1310	1358	1410	1458	1510	1558	1610	1658	1710	1758	1810	1858	1910	2010	2110	2158
4	**Andermatt** a.	0808	0820	0908	0920	1008	1020	1108	1120	1208	1220	1308	1320	1408	1420	1508	1520	1608	1620	1708	1720	1808	1820	1908	1920	2020	2120	2208

Andermatt d.	0725	0744	0828	0844	0928	0944	1028	1044	1128	1144	1228	1244	1328	1344	1428	1444	1528	1544	1628	1644	1728	1744	1828	1844	1944	2044	2128
Göschenen a.	0739	0758	0842	0858	0942	0958	1042	1058	1142	1158	1242	1258	1342	1358	1442	1458	1542	1558	1642	1658	1742	1758	1842	1858	1958	2058	2142

578 ZERMATT - GORNERGRAT

Services liable to be suspended in bad weather — **Valid Dec. 9 - May 28** — Narrow gauge rack railway. GGB

km				y	y	n	y	y	n	y	y	y	n	y	y		y	y		y		y	y		y		y			z
0	**Zermatt** d.	0710	0800	0824	0848	0912	0912	0936	1000	1000	1024	1048	1112	1112	1136	1200	1224	1248	1312	1336	1400	1424	1448	1512	1536	1600	1624	1712	1800	1912
9	**Gornergrat** a.	0743	0833	0857	0921	0945	0954	1018	1033	1042	1106	1130	1145	1154	1209	1233	1257	1321	1345	1409	1433	1457	1521	1545	1609	1633	1657	1745	1833	1945

		y		y			y	y		y			y	y		y		y	y		y	y			y				z	
Gornergrat d.	0755	0843	0907	0931	0955	...	1019	1043	1107	1131	1155	...	1219	1243	1307	1331	1355	1419	1443	1507	1531	1555	...	1619	1643	1707	1755	1843	1957	...
Zermatt a.	0839	0927	0951	1015	1039	...	1103	1127	1151	1215	1239	...	1303	1327	1351	1415	1439	1503	1527	1551	1615	1639	...	1703	1727	1751	1837	1925	2039	...

579 GLACIER EXPRESS summary table

Narrow gauge rack railway. MGB, RhB*

km			910			902	904	906	908
		WINTER	★Y		SUMMER	⁄A	★B	★C	★D
0	**Zermatt** d.	SERVICE	1000	...	SERVICE	0900	0913	1000	1013
45	**Brig** d.	▶▶▶▶	1116	...	▶▶▶▶	1016	1041	1116	1141
113	Andermatt a.		1239	...		1136	1206	1239	1306
113	Andermatt d.		1247	...		1139	1223	1247	1308
142	**Disentis/Mustér** a.	Dec. 9	1352s	...	May 10	1305s	1321s	1349s	1405s
142	**Disentis/Mustér** d.	to	|	...	to	|	|	|	|
191	Reichenau-Tamins d.	May 9	1529s	...	Oct. 19	|	|	|	|
201	**Chur** a.		1540s	...		1439	1440s	1520s	1521s
290	**St Moritz** a.		1758	...		...	1658	1742	1743

		903			905	907	909	911
	WINTER	★X		SUMMER	★G	★F	★H	⁄J
St Moritz d.	SERVICE	0904	...	SERVICE	0918	0919	1004	...
Chur d.	▶▶▶▶	1115u	...	▶▶▶▶	1138u	1139u	1214u	1215
Reichenau-Tamins d.		1125u	...		|	|	|	|
Disentis/Mustér a.		|	...		|	|	|	|
Disentis/Mustér d.	Dec. 9	1244u	...	May 10	1252u	1307u	1335u	1351u
Andermatt a.	to	1351	...	to	1351	1413	1434	1457
Andermatt d.	May 9	1354	...	Oct. 19	1354	1419	1454	1508
Brig a.		1515	...		1525	1542	1625	1642
Zermatt a.		1650	...		1650	1710	1752	1810

NOTES FOR TABLES 575/7/8/9:

- **A** – June 14 - Sept. 28: [12] [observation cars] Zermatt - Chur - Davos Platz; 🍷 Brig - Chur.
- **B** – [12] [observation cars], 🍴 and 🍷 [at seat] Zermatt - Chur - St Moritz.
- **C** – [12] [observation cars] Zermatt - Chur - St Moritz; 🍴 and 🍷 Zermatt - Chur.
- **D** – [12] [observation cars], 🍴 and 🍷 [at seat] Zermatt - Chur - St Moritz.
- **F** – [12] [observation cars] St Moritz - Chur - Zermatt; 🍴 and 🍷 St Moritz - Zermatt.
- **G** – [12] [observation cars], 🍴 and 🍷 [at seat] St Moritz - Chur - Zermatt.
- **H** – [12] [observation cars], 🍴 and 🍷 [at seat] St Moritz - Chur - Zermatt.
- **J** – June 14 - Sept. 28: [12] [observation cars] Davos Platz - Chur - Zermatt; 🍴 Chur - Disentis; 🍷 Chur - Brig.
- **X** – [12] [observation cars], 🍴 and 🍷 [at seat] St Moritz - Chur - Zermatt.
- **Y** – [12] [observation cars], 🍴 and 🍷 [at seat] Zermatt - Chur - St Moritz.
- **⁄** – GLACIER EXPRESS (standard) – [R] with supplement (CHF 10 winter, CHF 15 summer). 🍴 reservations are obligatory in advance – ✆ Chur (081) 252 14 25.
- **★** – GLACIER EXPRESS (premium) – [R] with supplement (CHF 10 winter, CHF 30 summer). 🍴 reservations are obligatory in advance – ✆ Chur (081) 252 14 25.

- § – Realp is a request stop.
- ⊗ – Mixed train. Times subject to variation.
- ▲ – 🚂 service (summer only, not daily) **Realp - Furka - Gletsch.** Operator: Dampfbahn Furka-Bergstrecke ✆ 0848 000 144.
- 🚗 – Car-carrying shuttle available (see page 260).

- j – Not May 10 - Oct. 19.
- k – Dec. 9 - May 9.
- m – May 10 - Oct. 19.
- n – Apr. 21 - May 28.
- p – Mar. 25 - May 9, Oct. 20 - Dec. 13.
- r – ①–⑤ Dec. 10 - 21; daily Mar. 25 - May 9, Oct. 20 - Dec. 13.
- s – Stops to set down only.
- t – ⑤ Dec. 21 - Mar. 14, May 16 - Oct. 17 (also Mar. 20; not Aug. 1).
- u – Stops to pick up only.
- v – June 14 - Sept. 28.
- w – Dec. 9 - Mar. 24.
- y – Dec. 9 - Apr. 20.
- z – Dec. 9 - Apr. 13.

* – Operators: MGB, Zermatt - Andermatt / Göschenen - Disentis; RhB, Disentis - Chur.

SCENIC RAIL ROUTES OF EUROPE

The following is a list of some of the most scenic rail routes of Europe, detailed timings for most of which can be found within the timetable. Routes marked * are the Editor's personal choice. This list does not include specialised mountain and tourist railways.

Many more scenic lines are clearly marked on the Thomas Cook New Rail Map of Europe - see the back of this book for details.

Types of scenery : C-Coastline, F-Forest, G-Gorge, L-Lake, M-Mountain, R-River.

ALBANIA

Route	Scenery
Elbasan - Pogradec	ML G R

AUSTRIA

Route	Scenery
Bruck an der Mur - Villach	R
Gmunden - Stainach Irdning*	ML
Innsbruck - Brennero	M
Innsbruck - Garmisch Partenkirchen*	M
Innsbruck - Schwarzach-St Veit	M G
Klagenfurt - Unzmarkt	M
Landeck - Bludenz*	M
Linz - Krems	R
St Pölten - Mariazell*	M
Salzburg - Villach*	M G
Selzthal - Hieflau - Steyr	M G R
Wiener Neustadt - Semmering - Graz	M

BELGIUM and LUXEMBOURG

Route	Scenery
Liège - Luxembourg*	R
Liège - Marloie	R
Namur - Dinant	R

BULGARIA

Route	Scenery
Septemvri - Dobriniste	M
Sofija - Burgas	M
Tulova - Gorna Orjahovitza	M

CROATIA and BOSNIA

Route	Scenery
Rijeka - Ogulin	M
Ogulin - Split	M
Sarajevo - Ploče	M G R

CZECH REPUBLIC

Route	Scenery
Karlovy Vary - Mariánské Lázně	R F
Karlovy Vary - Chomutov	R
Praha - Děčín	R

DENMARK

Route	Scenery
Struer - Thisted	C

FINLAND

Route	Scenery
Kouvola - Joensuu	L F

Many other lines run through scenic areas.

FRANCE

Route	Scenery
Aurillac - Neussargues	M G
Bastia - Ajaccio	M
Chambéry - Bourg St Maurice	M
Chambéry - Modane	ML
Chamonix - Martigny*	M G
Clermont Ferrand - Béziers	M G
Clermont Ferrand - Nîmes*	M G R
Gap - Briançon	ML
Genève - Aix les Bains	M R
Grenoble - Veynes - Marseille	M
Marseille - Ventimiglia	C
Mouchard - Besançon - Montbéliard	R
Nice - Digne	M
Nice / Ventimiglia - Cuneo*	M G
Perpignan - Latour de Carol*	M G
Portbou - Perpignan	C
Sarlat - Bergerac	R
Toulouse - Latour de Carol	M
Valence - Veynes	M

GERMANY

Route	Scenery
Arnstadt - Meiningen	M
Bonn - Siegen	R
Dresden - Děčín	G R
Freiburg - Donaueschingen	G F
Garmisch Partenkirchen - Kempten	M
Heidelberg - Neckarelz	R
Koblenz - Mainz*	G R
München - Lindau	M
Murnau - Oberammergau	ML
Naumburg - Saalfeld	R

GERMANY - continued

Route	Scenery
Niebüll - Westerland	C
Nürnberg - Pegnitz	G R
Offenburg - Konstanz	M F
Pforzheim - Nagold / Wildbad	F
Plattling - Bayerisch Eisenstein	F
Rosenheim - Freilassing - Berchtesgaden	ML
Rosenheim - Wörgl	M
Stuttgart - Singen	F
Titisee - Seebrugg	L F
Trier - Koblenz - Giessen	R
Ulm - Göppingen	M
Ulm - Tuttlingen	R

GREAT BRITAIN and IRELAND

Route	Scenery
Alnmouth - Dunbar	C
Barrow in Furness - Maryport	C
Coleraine - Londonderry	C
Dun Laoghaire - Wicklow	C
Edinburgh - Aberdeen	C
Exeter - Newton Abbot	C
Glasgow - Oban / Mallaig*	ML
Inverness - Kyle of Lochalsh*	M C
Liskeard - Looe	R
Llanelli - Craven Arms	M
Machynlleth - Pwllheli	M C
Perth - Inverness	M
Plymouth - Gunnislake	R
Rosslare - Waterford	C
St Erth - St Ives	C
Sheffield - New Mills	M
Shrewsbury - Aberystwyth	M R
Skipton - Carlisle	M R

GREECE

Route	Scenery
Korinthos - Patras	C
Diakoptó - Kalávrita	M G

HUNGARY

Route	Scenery
Budapest - Szob	R
Eger - Szilvásvárad	M
Székesfehérvár - Balatonszentgyörgy	L
Székesfehérvár - Tapolca	L

ITALY

Route	Scenery
Bologna - Pistoia	M
Bolzano - Merano	M
Brennero - Verona*	M
Brig - Arona	ML
Domodossola - Locarno*	M G
Firenze - Viareggio	M
Fortezza - San Candido	M
Genova - Pisa	C
Genova - Ventimiglia	C
Lecco - Tirano	ML
Messina - Palermo	C
Napoli - Sorrento	C
Roma - Pescara	M
Salerno - Reggio Calabria	C
Taranto - Reggio Calabria	C
Torino - Aosta	M

NORWAY

Route	Scenery
Bergen - Oslo*	ML
Bodø - Trondheim	ML
Dombås - Åndalsnes	M
Drammen - Larvik	C
Lillestrom - Kongsvinger	R
Myrdal - Flåm*	M C
Oslo / Røros - Trondheim	ML
Stavanger - Kristiansand	M

POLAND

Route	Scenery
Jelenia Góra - Walbrzych	M
Kraków - Zakopane	M
Olsztyn - Elk	L
Olsztyn - Morag	L
Tarnów - Krynica	M

PORTUGAL

Route	Scenery
Guarda - Entroncamento	M R
Pampilhosa - Guarda	M
Porto - Coimbra	C R
Porto - Pocinho*	R
Porto - Valença	M C
Regua - Vila Real	M G
Tua - Mirandela*	M G R

ROMANIA

Route	Scenery
Braşov - Ploeşti	M
Caransebeş - Craiova	M G R
Feteşti - Constanţa	R
Oradea - Cluj Napoca	R

SERBIA and MONTENEGRO

Route	Scenery
Priboj - Bar	ML

SLOVAKIA

Route	Scenery
Banská Bystrica - Brezno - Košice	M
Žilina - Poprad Tatry	M

SLOVENIA

Route	Scenery
Jesenice - Sežana	M R
Maribor - Zidani Most	M
Trieste - Ljubljana - Zagreb	G R

SPAIN

Route	Scenery
Algeciras - Ronda	M R
Barcelona - Latour de Carol	M
Bilbao - San Sebastián	M
Bilbao - Santander	M
Ferrol - Gijón*	C
Granada - Almería	M
Huesca - Canfranc	M G R
León - Monforte de Lemos	M
León - Oviedo	M
Lleida - La Pobla de Segur	ML
Madrid - Aranda - Burgos	ML
Málaga - Bobadilla	G
Santander - Oviedo	M C
Zaragoza - València	M R

SWEDEN

Route	Scenery
Bollnäs - Ånge - Sundsvall	ML
Borlänge - Mora	ML F
Borlänge - Ludvika - Frövi	ML F
Narvik - Kiruna	M F
Östersund - Storlien	L F

Many other lines run through scenic areas.

SWITZERLAND

Route	Scenery
Andermatt - Göschenen	G
Basel - Delémont - Moutier	M R
Chur - Arosa	M G
Chur - Brig - Zermatt*	M
Chur - St Moritz*	M G
Davos - Filisur	M G
Davos - Landquart	M
Interlaken Ost - Jungfraujoch*	M
Interlaken Ost - Luzern	ML
Interlaken West - Spiez	L
Lausanne - Brig	ML R
Lausanne - Neuchâtel - Biel	ML
Montreux - Zweisimmen - Lenk	ML G
Rorschach - Kreuzlingen	L
St Moritz - Scuol Tarasp	M
St Moritz - Tirano*	M
Spiez - Zweisimmen	G
Thun - Brig*	ML
Zürich / Luzern - Chiasso	ML
Zürich - Chur	ML

Many other lines run through scenic areas.

If you are aware of other routes shown in this book that are scenic please write to us. We would like to know about them.

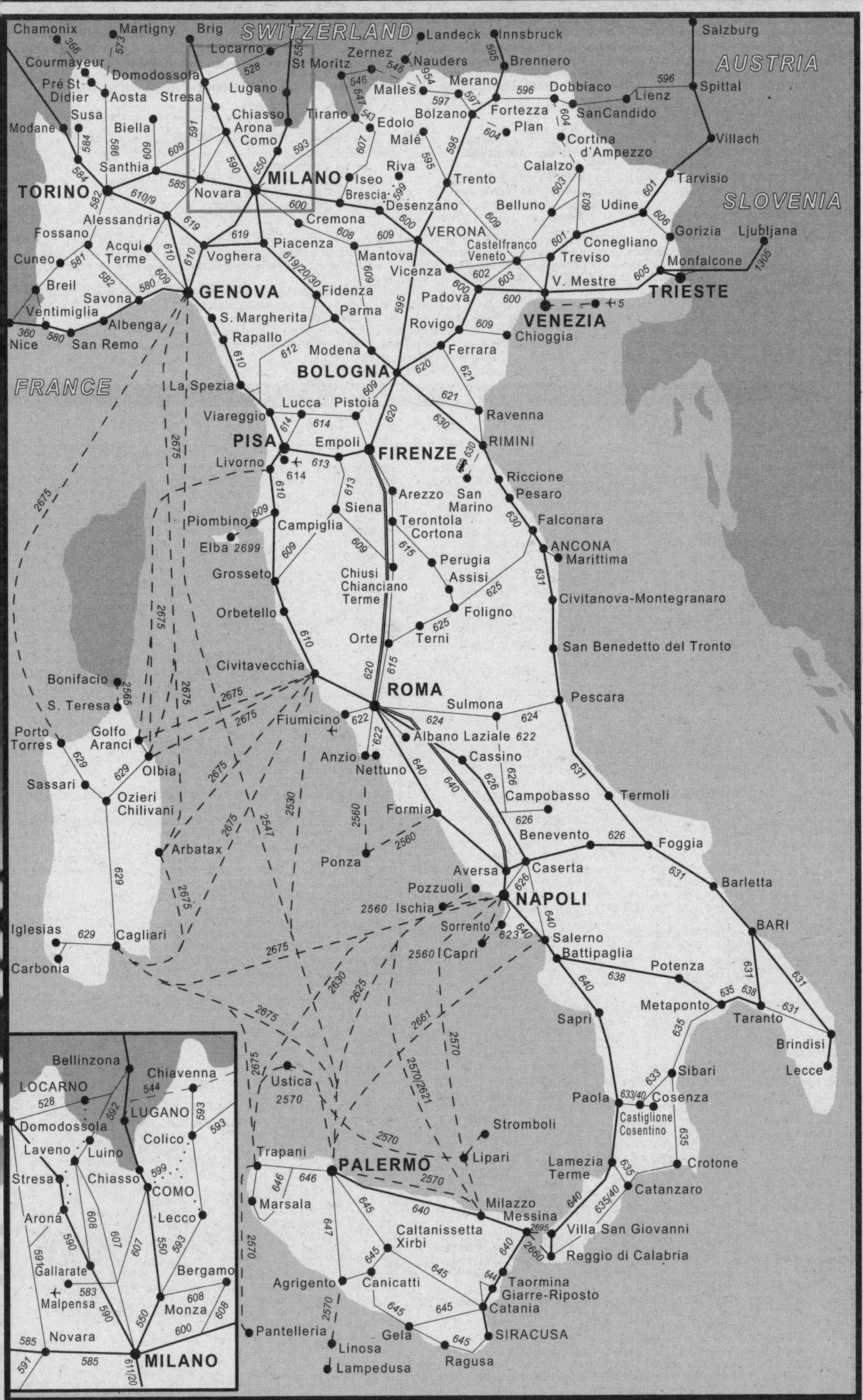
SWITZERLAND
AUSTRIA
SLOVENIA
FRANCE
Chamonix
Martigny
Brig
Locarno
Landeck
Innsbruck
Salzburg
Courmayeur
Domodossola
Zernez
St Moritz
Nauders
Brennero
Pré St-Didier
Aosta
Stresa
Lugano
Malles
Merano
Dobbiaco
Lienz
Spittal
Susa
Chiasso
Arona
Como
Tirano
Edolo
Bolzano
Fortezza
SanCandido
Modane
Biella
Malé
Plan
Cortina d'Ampezzo
Villach
Santhia
Riva
Calalzo
Tarvisio
TORINO
Novara
MILANO
Iseo
Brescia
Trento
Desenzano
Belluno
Udine
Alessandria
Cremona
VERONA
Gorizia
Ljubljana
Fossano
Acqui Terme
Voghera
Piacenza
Mantova
Castelfranco Veneto
Conegliano
Treviso
Cuneo
Vicenza
Monfalcone
Breil
Savona
GENOVA
Fidenza
Padova
V. Mestre
TRIESTE
Ventimiglia
Albenga
S. Margherita
Parma
VENEZIA
Nice
San Remo
Rapallo
Rovigo
Chioggia
Modena
Ferrara
BOLOGNA
La Spezia
Lucca
Pistoia
Viareggio
Ravenna
PISA
Empoli
FIRENZE
RIMINI
Livorno
San Marino
Riccione
Pesaro
Arezzo
Siena
Piombino
Campiglia
Terontola Cortona
Falconara
Elba
ANCONA
Marittima
Perugia
Grosseto
Chiusi Chianciano Terme
Assisi
Civitanova-Montegranaro
Orbetello
Foligno
Orte
Terni
San Benedetto del Tronto
Civitavecchia
Bonifacio
ROMA
S. Teresa
Sulmona
Pescara
Fiumicino
Porto Torres
Golfo Aranci
Albano Laziale
Cassino
Olbia
Anzio
Nettuno
Sassari
Ozieri Chilivani
Campobasso
Termoli
Formia
Benevento
Foggia
Arbatax
Ponza
Aversa
Caserta
Pozzuoli
Barletta
Ischia
NAPOLI
Sorrento
BARI
Iglesias
Cagliari
Salerno
Carbonia
Capri
Battipaglia
Potenza
Metaponto
Taranto
Sapri
Brindisi
Lecce
Ustica
Sibari
Paola
Cosenza
Castiglione Cosentino
Stromboli
Trapani
Lipari
PALERMO
Lamezia Terme
Crotone
Marsala
Milazzo
Messina
Catanzaro
Caltanissetta
Xirbi
Villa San Giovanni
Reggio di Calabria
Agrigento
Canicatti
Taormina
Giarre-Riposto
Catania
Pantelleria
Gela
SIRACUSA
Linosa
Ragusa
Lampedusa
Bellinzona
Chiavenna
LOCARNO
LUGANO
Domodossola
Colico
Laveno
Luino
Stresa
Chiasso
COMO
Arona
Lecco
Gallarate
Bergamo
Malpensa
Monza
Novara
MILANO

ITALY

Operator: Trenitalia, a division of Ferrovie dello Stato SpA (FS), unless otherwise noted.

Services: All trains convey First and Second classes of travel unless otherwise shown by a figure "2" at the top of the column, or in a note in the Table heading. Overnight sleeping ca (🛏) or couchette (▬) trains do not necessarily convey seating accommodation or may convey only second class seats - refer to individual footnotes. Excelsior sleeping cars offer en-suite facilities. Descriptions of sleeping and couchette cars appear on page **10**. Refreshment services (✕ or 🍷) where known, may only be available for part of the journey, and may be added to or taken away from trains during the currency of the timetable.

Train Categories: There are 11 categories of express train:

AV	**Alta Velocità**	premium fare ETR 500 services using high-speed lines.
CIS	**Cisalpino**	Pendolino; for services to / from Switzerland.
EC	**EuroCity**	international express; supplement payable.
EN	**EuroNight**	higher standard of overnight express.
ES	**Eurostar Italia**	high speed (ETR 450 / 460 / 500) services at premium fare.
ESc	**Eurostar City**	high speed services at special premium fare.
IC	**InterCity**	internal day express.
ICN	**InterCityNight**	internal night express.
ICp	**InterCity** Plus	internal express with new coaches; supplement payable.
T-Biz	**TrenBiz**	high speed business class services.
Tok	**TrenOK**	high speed (ETR 450) low-cost services.

Other services are classified:

E	**Espresso**	semi-fast or international services.
*ES*L*	**ES* LINK**	🚌 link.
R	**Regionale**	Local train.

Timings: Valid **December 9, 2007 - May 31, 2008** unless stated otherwise. Readers should note, however, that only partial information was available at press date and that furthe alterations are likely. In particular, details of accommodation conveyed and local services may change. Dates quoted after May 31 refer to last years schedules. Trains may be cancelled or altered at holiday times – for public holiday dates see page 2. Some international trains which are not available for local travel are not shown in this section; these include *City Night Line* services running between Germany and Italy – see International pages.

Tickets: Seat reservations are strongly recommended for travel on **all express trains**. Reservations are compulsory on **Cisalpino** trains and other services indicated by [R] under the train number. Rail tickets must be date-stamped by the holder before boarding the train using the self-service validating machines – this applies to all tickets except passes Tickets for travel on the low cost *Tok* services are sold via the internet, call-centre and self-service ticket machines only.

Supplements: Supplements are calculated according to class of travel and total distance travelled (minimum 10km, maximum 3000km), and are payable on all *EC* and *IC* trains, regardless o the number of changes of train. A higher fare (including supplement) is payable for travel by **Alta Velocità**, **Eurostar Italia** and **Cisalpino** trains. Some trains are only available to passengers holding long distance tickets and the restrictions applying to these are noted in the tables.

580 VENTIMIGLIA - GENOVA

km		2	*ICp* **503** [R] ♦	*ICp* **651** [R]	2	⚒ 2	2	*IC* **515**	2	2	*ICp* **657** [R]	⚒ 2	C2	2	*EC* **139** [R]🍷 ♦	© 2	Ⓐ 2	2	† C2	*ICp* **627** [R]	2	2	† 2	*EC* **145** [R]🍷 ♦	© 2	Ⓐ 2	⚒ 2
0	**Ventimiglia 🚌 581** d.	...	...	0442	0507	0517	...	0633	0646	0750	0858	...	0906	0948	1058	...	...	1150	1206	1258	...	1354	1420	1458	...	...	1526
5	Bordighera d.	...	...	0450	0514	0524	...	0640	0655	0757	0905	...	0915	0956	1105	...	...	1157	1216	1305	...	1401	1427	1505	...	...	1533
16	**San Remo 581** d.	...	...	0501	0522	0533	...	0650	0704	0806	0915	...	0926	1006	1115	...	...	1205	1226	1315	...	1409	1435	1515	...	...	1542
24	Taggia-Arma d.	...	...	0509	0528	0539	...	|	0710	0812	|	...	0935	1015	|	...	...	1212	1233	|	...	1415	1441	|	...	...	1548
39	Imperia Porto Maurizio d.	...	...	0521	0541	0551	...	0707	0722	0824	0932	...	...	1032	1132	...	...	1229	...	1332	...	1432	1453	1532	...	...	1600
41	Imperia Oneglia d.	...	...	|	0545	0555	...	|	0732	0828	|	...	...	1036	|	...	...	1236	...	|	...	1437	1458	|	...	...	1605
46	Diano Marina d.	...	...	|	0551	0601	...	0715	0738	0835	0940	...	...	1042	1140	...	...	1242	...	1340	...	1443	1504	1540	...	...	1612
61	Alassio d.	...	...	0541	0604	0626	...	0730	0804	0849	0956	...	...	1057	1156	...	...	1302	...	1356	...	1502	1523	1556	1610	1610	1639
67	**Albenga** d.	...	...	0548	0611	0636	0657	0738	0811	0855	1004	1015	...	1104	1204	1214	1214	1312	...	1404	1414	1512	1531	1604	1617	1617	1649
76	Loano d.	...	...	|	0622	0651	0711	|	0825	0905	|	1024	...	1122	|	1223	1223	1321	...	|	1422	1521	1553	|	1624	1624	1704
79	Pietra Ligure d.	...	...	|	0626	0655	0716	|	0829	0915	|	1028	...	1130	|	1228	1228	1330	...	|	1426	1531	1557	|	1628	1628	1708
85	Finale Ligure Marina d.	...	...	0603	0634	0659	0725	0752	0838	0923	1018	1035	...	1138	1218	1235	1235	1338	...	1418	1433	1538	1602	1618	1635	1635	1716
108	**Savona** d.	0436	0552	0619	0655	0726	0748	0807	0908	0958	1034	1110	...	1158	1234	1253	1255	1402	...	1434	1452	1601	1618	1634	1655	1655	1732
120	Varazze d.	0451	|	|	0704	0735	0759	|	0921	1013	|	1124	...	1216	|	1301	1304	1416	...	|	1501	1615	...	|	1704	1704	...
151	**Genova Piazza Principe** a.	0537	0631	0702	0744	0815	0844	0849	1002	1101	1106	1209	...	1301	1306	1332	1344	1501	...	1506	1532	1701	...	1706	1732	1747	...
	Milano Centrale **610** a.	...	|	0850	0945	...	...	|	...	...	1250	...	...	...	1450	1535	...	...	...	1650	1737	...	...	1850	1938	...	...
	Pisa Centrale **610** a.	...	0852	...	...	...	...	1057	...	...	...	...	...	...	...	...	...	...	...	...	...	...	...	...	...	...	...
	Roma Termini **610** a.	...	1214	...	...	...	...	1414	...	...	...	...	...	...	...	...	...	...	...	...	...	...	...	...	...	...	...

	V2	† 2	*ICp* **1537** [R] ©	*ICp* **669** [R] Ⓐy	† 2	⚒ 2	⚒ 2	*EC* **147** [R]🍷 ♦	2	2	2	*EN* **369** ♦
Ventimiglia 🚌 581 d.	1554	...	1645	1658	1723	1723	1754	1858	...	1951	...	2245
Bordighera d.	1601	...	1652	1705	1730	1730	1801	1905	...	1958	...	2253
San Remo 581 d.	1610	...	1702	1715	1739	1739	1809	1915	...	2006	...	2304
Taggia-Arma d.	1616	...	1708	1721	1744	1744	1815	|	...	2012	...	2311
Imperia Porto Maurizio d.	1632	...	1722	1734	1756	1756	1832	1932	...	2029	...	2324
Imperia Oneglia d.	1637	...	|	|	1800	1800	1837	|	...	2034	...	|
Diano Marina d.	1643	...	|	|	1806	1806	1843	1940	...	2040	...	2332
Alassio d.	1702	...	1741	1756	1835	1838	1902	1956	...	2102	2225	2346
Albenga d.	1710	1725	1749	1804	1843	1846	1910	2004	2010	2113	2233	2353
Loano d.	1721	1736	1757	|	1856	1859	1918	|	2020	2121	2240	|
Pietra Ligure d.	1730	1747	1807	|	1900	1909	1922	|	2024	2130	2244	|
Finale Ligure Marina d.	1738	1755	1815	1818	1909	1919	1929	2018	2031	2138	2251	0012
Savona d.	1802	1820	1830	1834	1928	1935	1955	2034	2049	2201	2312	0028
Varazze d.	1816	1832	1838	|	...	...	2010	|	2058	2215	2325	|
Genova P P a.	1901	1918	1906	1906	...	...	2056	2106	2136	2301	0009	0107
Milano Centrale **610** a.	...	2130	2050	2050	...	...	...	2250	2335	...	...	|
Pisa Centrale **610** a.	...	...	...	...	...	...	...	...	...	...	...	0525
Roma Termini **610** a.	...	...	...	...	...	...	...	...	...	...	...	0945

	EN **368** ♦	⚒ 2	2	2	⚒ 2	2	⚒ 2	† 2	*EC* **142** [R]🍷 ♦	2
Roma Termini **610** d.	2116	...	...	...	...	...	...	...	...	...
Pisa Centrale **610** d.	0038	...	...	...	...	...	...	...	...	...
Milano Centrale **610** d.	|	...	...	...	...	...	...	0625	0710	...
Genova P P d.	0445	0523	0608	0644	0723	...	0753	0842	0855	0859
Varazze d.	|	0606	0653	0729	0808	...	0839	0926	|	0946
Savona d.	0530	0621	0710	0745	0823	0849	0907	0938	0928	1012
Finale Ligure Marina d.	0544	0637	0729	0801	...	0906	0926	0957	0941	1038
Pietra Ligure d.	|	0643	0737	0807	...	0914	0932	1003	|	1045
Loano d.	|	0648	0742	0812	...	0919	0937	1009	|	1050
Albenga d.	0611	0655	0756	0821	...	0929	0948	1024	1003	1103
Alassio d.	0625	0702	0805	0829	...	0936	...	...	1011	1110
Diano Marina d.	0642	0725	0834	0851	...	0959	...	...	1024	1141
Imperia Oneglia d.	|	0731	0841	0857	...	1007	...	...	|	1148
Imperia Porto Maurizio d.	0652	0735	0845	0904	...	1011	...	...	1033	1153
Taggia-Arma d.	0705	0746	0858	0916	...	1023	...	...	|	1204
San Remo 581 d.	0713	0752	0905	0929	...	1030	...	...	1050	1211
Bordighera d.	0723	0801	0917	0939	...	1042	...	...	1100	1221
Ventimiglia 🚌 581 a.	0731	0808	0926	0948	...	1050	...	...	1107	1231

	2	*ICp* **650** [R] Ⓐ	*ICp* **1536** [R] ©	2	2	*EC* **144** [R]🍷 ♦	A2	T2	2	*ICp* **610** [R]	A2	2	2	2	*EC* **160** [R]🍷 ♦	2	⚒ 2	Ⓐ 2	© 2	*ICp* **660** [R]	2	Ⓐ 2	© 2	*IC* **538**	2	*ICp* **668** [R]	*ICp* **542** [R] ♦
Roma Termini **610** d.	...	...	...	...	...	...	...	...	...	...	...	...	...	...	...	...	...	...	...	...	...	...	...	1546	...	...	1746
Pisa Centrale **610** d.	...	...	...	...	...	...	...	...	...	...	...	...	...	...	...	...	...	...	...	...	...	...	...	1900	...	...	2102
Milano Centrale **610** d.	0820	0910	0910	...	...	1110	...	...	...	1310	...	...	...	1420	1510	...	...	...	1620	1700	...	...	1825	|	2020	2110	|
Genova Piazza Principe d.	1026	1055	1055	1059	1217	1255	1259	...	1417	1455	1459	1523	...	1625	1655	1717	1746	1817	1830	1855	1859	2017	2038	2112	2227	2255	2323
Varazze d.	1057	|	1121	1144	1258	|	1345	...	1458	|	1544	1609	...	1655	|	1758	1828	1858	1904	|	1944	2058	2112	|	2306	|	|
Savona d.	1110	1128	1131	1213	1308	1328	1411	...	1508	1528	1613	1623	1629	1705	1728	1813	1841	1912	1914	1928	2008	2108	2122	2145	2320	2340	0003
Finale Ligure Marina d.	1123	1141	1144	1235	1324	1341	1433	...	1524	1541	1635	...	1645	1723	1741	1835	1900	1932	1932	1941	2031	2124	2142	2157	2340	2353	...
Pietra Ligure d.	1131	|	1150	1241	1331	|	1439	...	1530	|	1641	...	1651	1731	|	1841	1908	1938	1938	|	2038	2131	2148	|	2346	|	...
Loano d.	1136	|	1156	1246	1336	|	1444	...	1535	|	1646	...	1656	1736	|	1845	1913	1943	1943	|	2044	2136	2153	|	2351	|	...
Albenga d.	1144	1203	1207	1254	1347	1403	1453	...	1543	1603	1653	...	1709	1744	1803	1853	1925	1951	1951	2003	2052	2146	2200	2212	2359	0008	...
Alassio d.	...	1211	1215	1301	...	1411	1501	...	1555	1611	1703	...	1723	...	1811	1901	1934	...	...	2011	2101	2155	2209	2220	0006	0016	...
Diano Marina d.	...	|	|	1316	...	1424	1516	...	...	1624	1719	...	1750	...	1824	1917	2000	...	...	|	2116	...	...	2233	0021	0030	...
Imperia Oneglia d.	...	|	|	1322	...	|	1522	1604	...	|	1725	...	1801	...	|	1923	2006	...	...	|	2122	...	...	|	0027	|	...
Imperia Porto Maurizio d.	...	1230	1241	1331	...	1433	1531	1609	...	1633	1733	...	1806	...	1833	1931	2010	...	...	2030	2127	...	...	2242	|	0040	...
Taggia-Arma d.	...	1242	1253	1343	...	|	1543	1621	...	|	1745	...	1818	...	|	1943	2021	...	...	2042	2138	...	...	|	0041	|	...
San Remo 581 d.	...	1250	1302	1350	...	1450	1550	1628	...	1650	1751	...	1824	...	1850	1950	2027	...	...	2050	2144	...	...	2258	0047	0056	...
Bordighera d.	...	1300	1312	1400	...	1500	1600	1638	...	1700	1800	...	1833	...	1900	2000	2037	...	...	2100	2154	...	...	2308	0057	0106	...
Ventimiglia 🚌 581 a.	...	1307	1320	1409	...	1507	1607	1646	...	1707	1811	...	1840	...	1907	2007	2047	...	...	2107	2204	...	...	2315	0104	0113	...

♦ – **NOTES** (LISTED BY TRAIN NUMBER)

139/160 – RIVIERA DEI FIORI – [12] and 🍷 Nice - Genova (**140/159**) - Milano and v.v.
142/147 – LIGURE – [12] and 🍷 Milano (**141/8**) - Genova - Nice and v.v.
144/145 – SANREMO – [12] and 🍷 Milano (**143/6**) - Genova - Nice and v.v.
368 – MONTECARLO – 🛏 1,2 cl. and ▬ 2 cl. (4 berth) Roma (**366**) - Firenze (**367**) Pisa - Genova - Nice; 🛏 1,2 cl. and ▬ 2 cl. (4 berth) Venezia (**358**) - Milano (**359**) - Genova - Nice.
369 – MONTECARLO – 🛏 1,2 cl. and ▬ 2 cl. (4 berth) Nice - Genova - Pisa (**374**) - Firenze (**375**) - Roma; 🛏 1,2 cl. and ▬ 2 cl. (4 berth) Nice - Genova (**362**) - Milano (**363**) - Venezia.
503/542 – BOCCANEGRA – [12] Savona - Napoli and v.v.

A – on © runs up to 14 minutes later between Alassio and Ventimiglia.
C – From / to Cuneo.
T – [12] Torino - Cuneo - Ventimiglia - Imperia Oneglia and v.v.
V – [2] Ventimiglia - Parma.
y – Also Jun. 14.

CUNEO - NICE, VENTIMIGLIA and SAN REMO 581

2nd class only

km		f	z		T	d			L		d				c		d	c	c								
	Torino P.N. **582** d.	...	...	...	...	...	...	...	0730	0835	...	...	...	...	...	...	...	...	...	...	...	...	...	...	...	...	...
0	**Cuneo** d.	...	...	0604	0700	0740	...	0833	0904	1012	1034	...	...	...	1204	1305	1402	1415	1504	1604	1704	1807	1905	2010	2205	...	...
29	Limone d.	...	...	0641	0743	0810	...	0911	0939	1049	1111	...	...	...	1242	1347	1437	1448	1550	1644	1747	1850	1943	2047	2249	...	...
47	Tende d.	...	0610	0700	0801	...	...	0929	0957	1107	...	1210	...	...	1306	1405	...	...	1608	1722	1809	1916	2006	...	...	...	...
75	Breil sur Roya a.	...	0647	0734	0831	...	...	0957	1025	1137	...	1249	...	...	1345	1441	...	...	1643	1802	1844	1945	2034	...	...	...	...
75	Breil sur Roya d.	0610	0647f	0736	0838	...	0914	1008	1026	1139	...	1249	...	...	1348	1443	...	...	1645	1812	1846	1947	2036	...	...	...	...
*	**Nice Ville** a.	0710	0750f	|	|	...	1018	1106	|	|	...	1351	...	...	|	|	...	...	|	1912	|	|	|	...	...	...	...
96	**Ventimiglia** a.	...	...	0801	0902	...	...	...	1045	1203	...	...	...	...	1419	1508	...	...	1718	...	1910	2020	2101	...	...	...	...
96	**Ventimiglia 580** d.	...	...	...	0906	...	...	...	1048	1206	...	...	...	...	...	...	...	...	...	...	...	...	...	...	...	...	...
112	**San Remo 580** a.	...	...	...	0925	...	...	...	1103	1225	...	...	...	...	...	...	...	...	...	...	...	...	...	...	...	...	...

	d	d	d	c						c		T			d	c		d	L							
San Remo 580 d.	...	...	...	...	...	...	...	...	...	...	...	1143	...	...	...	...	...	...	1628	...	...	...	...	...	...	...
Ventimiglia 580 a.	...	...	...	...	...	...	...	...	...	...	...	1200	...	...	...	...	...	...	1646	...	...	...	...	...	...	...
Ventimiglia d.	...	0540	...	0645	...	0812	0908	...	...	1050	...	1204	...	1348	...	...	1556	...	1649	...	1756	...	1947	...	...	...
Nice Ville d.	...	|	...	|	0720	|	|	...	0901	|	...	|	1235	|	...	...	|	...	|	1700	|	1755	|	1920	...	...
Breil sur Roya a.	...	0602	...	0711	0821	0837	0935	...	1002	1115	...	1229	1338	1417	...	...	1620	...	1713	1806	1822	1902	2017	2024	...	...
Breil sur Roya d.	...	0604	...	0713	...	0839	0937	...	1005	1117	...	1231	1346	1419	...	...	1622	...	1715	...	1824	1923	2035	...	...	...
Tende d.	...	0638	...	0802	...	0909	1020	...	1047	1156	...	1305	1428	1455	...	...	1700	...	1750	...	1859	2007	2108	...	...	...
Limone d.	0642	0705	0817	0825	...	0938	1048	1120	...	1217	...	1325	1452	1515	1600	1616	1724	1749	1812	...	1918	2028	2127	...	...	...
Cuneo a.	0723	0739	0854	0903	...	1011	1126	1154	...	1257	...	1357	1526	1550	1640	1656	1754	1827	1846	...	1957	2100	2200	...	...	...
Torino P.N. **582** a.	0835	...	...	...	...	...	...	...	...	...	...	...	...	...	...	...	1925	...	2030	...	...	...	...	...	...	...

L – (12) Torino - Imperia Oneglia and v.v.
T – From/to Taggia-Arma.

c – ⑦ (also Italian public holidays).
d – ①–⑥ (not Italian public holidays).
f – ①–⑥ (not French public holidays).
z – ①–⑥ (not July 14).

⊡ – Conveys (12).
* – Nice - Breil sur Roya: *44 km*.

TORINO - CUNEO and SAVONA 582

Most trains 2nd class only

km			⚒	⚒	⚒	⚒	⚒	L⚒	⚒	⚒	⚒	⚒	⚒	⚒		⚒	⚒	⚒	⚒	⚒	⚒	⚒	⚒	⚒	⚒	⚒	⚒
0	**Torino P N** d.		...	0600	0620	0700	...	0730	0800	0835	0900	1030	1100	1135	...	1200	1235	1300	1335	1400	1435	1500	1535	1600	1635	1700	1735
52	Savigliano d.		...	0646	0717	0752	...	0825	0853	0923	0953	1123	1150	1223	...	1253	1323	1353	1423	1453	1522	1552	1623	1650	1723	1747	1823
64	Fossano d.	⚒	0602	0655	0727	0803	0808	0835	0903	0935	1003	1133	1200	1232	...	1303	1332	1403	1432	1503	1531	1602	1632	1659	1732	1756	1833
90	**Cuneo** a.		|	0723	|	0828	|	0902	|	1000	|	1157	|	1255	...	|	1355	|	1455	|	1555	|	1654	|	1755	|	1855
83	Mondovi d.		0622	...	0741	...	0826	...	0919	...	1019	...	1216	...	...	1325	...	1419	...	1518	...	1619	...	1715	...	1815	...
103	Ceva d.		0641	...	0756	...	0846	...	0933	...	1033	...	1232	...	...	1339	...	1434	...	1533	...	1633	...	1731	...	1832	...
153	**Savona** a.		0744	...	0845	...	0940	...	1026	...	1120	...	1320	...	...	1425	...	1522	...	1625	...	1734	...	1823	...	1920	...

	⚒	⚒	⚒	⚒	⚒	⚒	⚒	⚒	⚒z		†	†	†	†y	L†	†	†	†	†	†	†	†	†	†	†	†	†
Torino P N d.	1800	1835	1900	1935	2000	2100	2135	2235	2304		...	0620	0700	0725	0730	0800	0900	0935	...	1035	1135	...	1235	1325	...	1400	1535
Savigliano d.	1846	1922	1953	2023	2049	2150	2223	2328	0028		...	0717	0752	0810	0825	0849	0953	1023	...	1121	1223	...	1323	1415	...	1453	1623
Fossano d.	1855	1932	2003	2032	2058	2159	2232	2338	0038	†	0636	0727	0803	0822	0835	0857	1003	1031	1040	1130	1232	1240	1332	1425	1430	1503	1632
Cuneo a.	|	1955	|	2055	|	|	2255	2400	0100		|	|	0828	|	0902	|	|	1055	|	|	1255	|	|	1449	|	|	1654
Mondovi d.	1909	...	2019	...	2116	2217	...	...	...		0654	0741	...	0840	...	0911	1019	...	1059	1144	...	1259	1345	...	1449	1518	...
Ceva d.	1932	...	2033	...	2136	2235	...	...	...		0712	0756	...	0857	...	0926	1033	...	1118	1200	...	1318	1400	...	1508	1532	...
Savona a.	2022	...	2122	...	2230	...	...	...	...		0809	0845	...	0946	...	1019	1120	...	1215	1248	...	1415	1447	...	1606	1628	...

	†	†	†	†	†	†	†	†	†	†
Torino P N d.	...	1635	1735	...	1835	1935	...	2000	2135	2235
Savigliano d.	...	1723	1823	...	1922	2023	...	2045	2223	2328
Fossano d.	1640	1732	1832	1845	1931	2032	2037	2054	2232	2338
Cuneo a.	|	1755	1855	|	|	2055	|	|	2255	2400
Mondovi d.	1658	...	...	1906	1943	...	2055	2112	...	...
Ceva d.	1718	...	...	1928	1958	...	2114	2132	...	...
Savona a.	1821	...	...	2023	2046	...	2207	2226	...	...

		⚒	⚒	⚒	⚒	⚒	⚒	⚒	⚒	⚒	⚒	⚒	⚒
Savona d.		...	...	...	...	0516	...	0551	...	0626	...	0724	...
Ceva d.		...	...	0533	...	0613	...	0652	...	0729	...	0831	...
Mondovi d.	⚒	...	...	0550	...	0626	...	0705	...	0746	...	0845	...
Cuneo d.		0435	0500	|	0600	|	0648	|	0725	|	0805	|	0836
Fossano d.		0458	0524	0607	0635	0640	0710	0718	0749	0802	0828	0857	0902
Savigliano d.		0508	0534	0617	0643	0649	0719	0727	0758	0811	0837	...	0911
Torino P N a.		0600	0625	0710	0730	0735	0755	0815	0835	0900	0925	...	1000

	⚒	⚒	⚒	⚒	⚒	⚒	⚒	⚒	⚒	⚒	⚒	⚒	⚒	⚒	⚒	⚒	L⚒	⚒	⚒	⚒	⚒	⚒	⚒	⚒		†	†
Savona d.	....	0942	...	...	...	1240	...	1340	...	1442	...	1538	...	1640	...	1735	...	1840	...	1940	...	2035	...	2116		...	...
Ceva d.	...	1030	...	1227	...	1327	...	1432	...	1530	...	1627	...	1727	...	1830	...	1928	...	2033	...	2129	...	2213		...	...
Mondovi d.	...	1044	...	1242	...	1346	...	1446	...	1547	...	1642	...	1742	...	1844	...	1943	...	2047	...	2146	...	2226	†	...	...
Cuneo d.	0905	|	1203	|	1303	|	1403	|	1503	|	1603	|	1703	|	1756	|	1902	|	2003	|	2105	|	2205	|		0500	0705
Fossano d.	0928	1059	1227	1258	1331	1403	1427	1501	1527	1602	1627	1658	1727	1758	1826	1859	1927	1958	2027	2102	2128	2201	2228	2238		0524	0728
Savigliano d.	0938	1108	1237	1307	1340	1412	1437	1510	1537	1611	1636	1708	1737	1807	1836	1908	1937	2008	2037	2110	2137	2210	2237	2248		0534	0737
Torino P N a.	1035	1205t	1325	1400	1425	1500	1525	1600	1625	1700	1725	1800	1825	1900	1925	2000	2030	2100	2125	2200	2239t	2300	2335	2345		0625	0825

	†	†	†	†	†	†	†	†y	†	†	†	†	†	†	†	†	†	†	†y	†	L†	†	†y	†	†	†	†
Savona d.	0628	...	0725	...	0911	0942	...	1111	1140	...	1311	1341	...	1500	1540	...	1621	1703	1713	1745	...	1838	1854	...	1938	...	2117
Ceva d.	0729	...	0831	...	0958	1036	...	1158	1237	...	1358	1437	...	1549	1634	...	1709	1754	1810	1838	...	1928	1947	...	2034	...	2206
Mondovi d.	0746	...	0849	...	1012	1055	...	1211	1257	...	1412	1456	...	1605	1653	...	1723	1809	1825	1857	...	1943	2001	...	2047	...	2220
Cuneo d.	|	0805	|	0908	|	|	1104	|	|	1303	|	|	1503	|	|	1703	|	|	|	|	1902	|	|	2003	|	2105	|
Fossano d.	0802	0828	0905	0930	1027	1112	1127	1227	1315	1331	1429	1514	1527	1627	1710	1727	1738	1826	1838	1914	1927	1959	2015	2027	2102	2128	2236
Savigliano d.	0811	0837	...	0939	1037	...	1137	1237	...	1340	1438	...	1537	1636	...	1737	1746	...	1848	...	1937	2008	2024	2037	2110	2137	2245
Torino P N a.	0900	0925	...	1025	1125	...	1225	1325	...	1425	1525	...	1625	1725	...	1825	1835	...	1930	...	2030	2100	2110	2125	2200	2230	2335

ADDITIONAL SERVICES FOSSANO - CUNEO and v.v. (2nd class only):

	⚒	⚒		†		⚒	†		⚒	†	⚒	⚒	†	⚒	⚒	†	⚒	⚒	⚒	⚒	†	⚒	⚒	†	
Fossano d.	0627	0734	...	0735	...	0907	0911	...	1107	1134	1207	1307	1336	1407	1507	1535	1607	1707	1800	1900	1936	2007	2107	2136	...
Cuneo a.	0648	0804	...	0758	...	0930	0942	...	1130	1159	1230	1330	1359	1430	1530	1559	1630	1730	1830	1931	1959	2030	2130	2200	...

	⚒		†		⚒	†	⚒	⚒	†	⚒		⚒	†	⚒	†		⚒	⚒		⚒		⚒			
Cuneo d.	0701	...	0959	...	1131	1200	1231	1331	1401	1431	...	1531	1600	1631	1657	...	1731	1809	...	1914	...	2031	...	2204	...
Fossano a.	0727	...	1022	...	1155	1222	1253	1353	1424	1453	...	1553	1622	1653	1718	...	1753	1831	...	1944	...	2053	...	2226	...

L – (12) Torino - Ventimiglia - Imperia Oneglia and v.v.

t – Torino **Porta Susa**.

y – Apr. 1 - Sept. 30.
z – Not days after holidays.

MILANO MALPENSA AEROPORTO ✈ 583

FNM *Malpensa Express*

45 km, journey 40 minutes (50 minutes by 🚌). All rail services call at Milano Nord Bovisa (7 minutes from Cadorna, 33 minutes from Malpensa). Special fare payable.

From **Milano Nord Cadorna**: 0420🚌, 0500🚌, 0557, 0627, 0657 and every 30 minutes until 2057, then 2127†, 2127⚒ 🚌, 2227🚌, 2327🚌.

Operator: Ferrovie Nord Milano, Piazzale Cadorna 14, 20123 Milano. ✆ + 39 02 85 111, fax: + 39 02 85 11 708.

From **Malpensa Aeroporto**: 0553🚌, 0653, 0723, 0753 and every 30 minutes until 2153, then 2223†, 2223⚒ 🚌, 2253🚌, 2323🚌, 0023🚌, 0130🚌.

584 MODANE - OULX - TORINO

Local trains are 2nd class only

km	*For local trains on † see panel below*	⚒	⚒	⚒	⚒	⚒	⚒	⚒	⚒	⚒	*EC* **9241** R P	⚒	⚒	Ⓐ	⚒	Ⓐ	Ⓐ	Ⓐ	⚒	*EC* **9247** R P	Ⓐ	©	⚒	*EC* **9249** R P	Ⓐ
0	**Modane** 🏛 ▶ d.	...	...	...	...	...	...	...	...	...	1155	...	...	...	...	...	...	...	...	1820	...	...	...	1945	...
20	Bardonecchia ▶ d.	0555	...	...	0650	...	0810	...	...	*1152*	1220	*1305*	...	*1502*	*1553*a	1632	...	1740	...	1847	*1856*	1913	*1955*a	2016	*2102*
31	Oulx ▲ d.	0606	...	...	0701	...	0823	...	...	*1204*	1230	*1318*	...	*1513*	*1605*a	1644	...	1750	...	1857	*1907*	1927	*2007*a	2026	*2114*
*	Susa d.	|	0623	0653	|	0739	|	0939	1155	1233	|	1342	1441	1543	1643	|	1738	|	1843	|	1943	|	2043	|	2143
61	Bussoleno d.	0637	0641	0703	0733	0749	0854	0949	1205	1243	|	1352	1451	1553	1653	1717	1748	1818	1853	|	1953	1957	2053	|	2153
106	**Torino Porta Nuova** a.	0715	0740	0755	0810	0840	0945	1040	1255	1340	|	1445	1545	1645	1745	1805	1840	1915	1945	|	2045	2045	2145	|	2245
	Torino Porta Susa a.	...	...	...	...	...	...	...	...	...	1317	...	...	...	...	...	...	...	...	1945	...	...	...	2116	...
	Milano Centrale **585** a.	...	...	...	...	...	...	...	...	...	1450	...	...	...	...	...	...	...	...	2120	...	...	...	2250	...

Italic timings - change at Bussoleno	⚒	⚒	⚒	*EC* **9240** R P	⚒	⚒	*EC* **9242** R P	Ⓐ	⚒	⚒	⚒	⚒	Ⓐ	⚒	Ⓐ	Ⓐ	*EC* **9248** R P	Ⓐ	Ⓐ	Ⓐ	Ⓐ	Ⓐ	⚒	⑥	Ⓐ
Milano Centrale **585** d.	...	...	...	0640	...	...	0810	...	...	...	...	...	...	...	...	...	1610	...	...	...	...	...	...	...	...
Torino Porta Susa d.	...	...	...	0811	...	...	0940	...	...	...	...	...	...	...	...	...	1735	...	...	...	...	...	...	...	...
Torino Porta Nuova d.	0610	0655	0720	|	0815	0900	|	1055	1130	1215	1315	1420	1520	1615	1700	1715	|	1755	1815	1845	1915	1940	2020	2130	2130
Bussoleno d.	0701	0749	0808	|	0911	0945	|	1149	1221	1310	1416	1519	1616	1711	1738	1821	|	1834	1911	1935	2006	2030	2111	2226	2226
Susa a.	|	0757	|	|	0920	|	|	1158	|	1320	1425	1528	1625	1720	|	1830	|	|	1920	|	2015	|	2120	|	2235
Oulx ▲ d.	0732	...	0837	0900	...	1014	1030	...	1247	*1346*	*1450*	...	*1659*	...	1807	...	1825	1907	...	2005	...	2059	...	2254	...
Bardonecchia ▶ d.	0742	...	0850	0912	...	1025	1040	...	1300	*1358*	*1500*	...	*1710*	...	1817	...	1840	1916	...	2015	...	2110	...	2305	...
Modane 🏛 ▶ a.	...	...	...	0938	...	...	1105	...	...	...	...	...	...	...	...	...	1905	...	...	...	...	...	...	...	...

Local trains on †

	†	♣	†
Bardonecchia d.	0513	and	2113
Oulx ▲ d.	0526	every	2127
Susa ⊖ d.	|	two	|
Bussoleno d.	0555	hours	2157
Torino P.N. a.	0645	until	2245

	†	†	♣	†	†	†
Torino P.N. d.	0720	0915	and	1715	1915	2130
Bussoleno d.	0808	1004	every	1821	2004	2226
Susa ⊖ a.	|	|	two	|	|	|
Oulx ▲ d.	0837	1034	hours	1851	2035	2254
Bardonecchia a.	0850	1045	until	1902	2047	2305

♣ – Some services may depart up to ±7 minutes. Service at 11xx from Torino departs 1130.

P – 🚃 and 🍸 Paris - Milano and v.v. (Table **44**). Special 'global' fares payable.
a – Ⓐ only.
⊖ – Service on † is by 🚌 Susa - Bussoleno and v.v.
▲ – Station for the resorts of Cesana, Claviere and Sestriere.
▶ – A connecting 🚌 service operates 4 times daily.
* – Bussoleno - Susa: *8 km*.

585 TORINO - MILANO

km		2	2	*ICp* **607** R	2	*IC* **611** T	*ES* **9491** R ✕ R	2 Ⓐy	2	*AV* **9661** R 🍸 Ⓐx	2	*IC* **613**		2 z	*AV* **9663** R 🍸 x	2	2	*EC* **9241** R 🍸 P	2	*AV* **9665** R 🍸 Ⓐx	*IC* **625**	2	2	2	*AV* **9667** R 🍸 x
0	**Torino Porta Nuova 586** d.	0450	0550	0605	0650	0708	0715	...	0750	0755	0850	0905	...	1050	1118	1150	1250	...	1350	1355	1405	1450	1550	1650	1655
6	**Torino Porta Susa 586** d.	0459	0559	0615	0659	0718	0726	0739	0759	0807u	0859	0915	...	1103	1130u	1159	1259	1320	1359	1407u	1415	1459	1559	1659	1707u
29	Chivasso **586** d.	0515	0615	|	0714	|	|	0754	0815	|	0915	|	...	1119	|	1215	1315	|	1415	|	|	1515	1615	1715	|
60	Santhià d.	0533	0633	|	0733	|	|	0814	0833	|	0933	|	...	1138	|	1233	1333	|	1433	|	|	1533	1633	1733	|
79	Vercelli d.	0545	0645	0656	0745	0801	|	0827	0845	|	0945	0956	...	1152	|	1245	1345	|	1445	|	1456	1545	1645	1745	|
101	Novara d.	0603	0703	0714	0802	0816	|	0845	0903	|	1003	1014	...	1213	|	1303	1403	|	1503	|	1514	1603	1703	1803	|
153	**Milano Centrale** a.	0645	0745	0750	0840	0850	0840p	0925	0945	0917	1045	1050	...	1250	1240	1345	1445	1450	1545	1517	1550	1645	1745	1845	1817
	Verona Porta Nuova **600** a.	...	...	0940	...	1040	...	...	...	...	...	1240	...	...	...	...	...	...	...	...	1740	...	...	...	...
	Venezia Santa Lucia **600** a.	...	...	1109	...	1209	...	...	...	...	...	1410	...	...	...	...	...	...	...	...	1909	...	...	...	...

	IC **635**	2	2	*AV* **9669** R 🍸 x	*EC* **9247** R 🍸 P	2	2	*EC* **9249** R 🍸 P	2	2
Torino Porta Nuova 586 d.	1705	1750	1850	1927	...	1950	2050	...	2150	2250
Torino Porta Susa 586 d.	1715	1759	1859	1939u	1947	1959	2059	2118	2159	2259
Chivasso **586** d.	|	1815	1915	|	|	2015	2115	|	2215	2315
Santhià d.	|	1833	1933	|	|	2033	2133	|	2233	2333
Vercelli d.	1756	1845	1945	|	2028	2045	2145	2158	2245	2345
Novara d.	1814	1903	2003	|	2045	2103	2203	2214	2303	0003
Milano Centrale a.	1850	1945	2044	2049	2120	2145	2245	2250	2345	0045
Verona Porta Nuova **600** a.	2040	...	...	...	...	...	...	...	...	...
Venezia Santa Lucia **600** a.	2209	...	...	...	...	...	...	...	...	...

	2	2	2	*EC* **9240** R 🍸 P	2	*AV* **9660** R 🍸 Ⓐx	*EC* **9242** R 🍸 P	2		2 v
Venezia Santa Lucia **600** d.	...	...	...	...	...	...	...	...	...	...
Verona Porta Nuova **600** d.	...	...	...	...	...	...	...	...	...	...
Milano Centrale d.	0030	0515	0600	0640	0715	0743	0810	0815	...	0915
Novara d.	0116	0559	0645	0714	0759	|	0844	0859	...	0959
Vercelli d.	0132	0613	0700	0728	0813	|	0857	0913	...	1013
Santhià d.	0144	0625	0713	|	0825	|	|	0925	...	1025
Chivasso **586** d.	0204	0643	0730	|	0843	|	|	0943	...	1043
Torino Porta Susa 586 a.	0223	0700	0748	0809	0900	0853s	0937	1000	...	1100
Torino Porta Nuova 586 a.	...	0710	0800	...	0910	0905	...	1010	...	1115

	IC **606**	2		2	2	2	*AV* **9664** R 🍸 Ⓐx	2	*EC* **9248** R 🍸 P	2	*ICp* **618** R	2	*AV* **9666** R 🍸 x	*IC* **622**	2	*AV* **9668** R 🍸 x	Ⓐv	*IC* **624**	2	*ES* **9494** R ✕ R	2	*IC* **626** T	2	2	
Venezia Santa Lucia **600** d.	0752	...	...	...	...	...	...	...	...	...	1352	...	...	1451	...	...	...	1551	...	...	...	1751	...	...	...
Verona Porta Nuova **600** d.	0918	...	...	...	...	...	...	...	...	...	1518	...	...	1618	...	...	...	1718	...	...	...	1918	...	...	...
Milano Centrale d.	1110	1115	...	1215	1315	1415	1443	1515	1610	1615	1710	1715	1743	1810	1815	1843	1848	1910	1915	1944p	2015	2110	2115	2215	...
Novara d.	1148	1159	...	1259	1359	1459	|	1559	|	1659	1746	1759	|	1849	1859	|	1929	1946	1959	|	2059	2146	2159	2259	...
Vercelli d.	1207	1213	...	1313	1413	1513	|	1613	|	1713	1800	1813	|	1903	1913	|	1943	2000	2013	|	2113	2200	2213	2313	...
Santhià d.	|	1225	...	1325	1425	1525	|	1625	|	1725	|	1825	|	|	1925	|	1955	|	2025	|	2125	|	2225	2325	...
Chivasso **586** d.	|	1243	...	1343	1443	1543	|	1643	|	1743	|	1843	|	|	1943	|	2013	|	2043	|	2143	|	2243	2343	...
Torino Porta Susa 586 a.	1246	1300	...	1400	1500	1600	1553s	1700	1733	1800	1840	1900	1853s	1943	2000	1953s	2031	2040	2100	2100	2200	2240	2300	2400	...
Torino Porta Nuova 586 a.	1300	1310	...	1410	1510	1610	1605	1710	...	1810	1855	1910	1905	1955	2010	2005	...	2055	2110	2113	2210	2255	2310	0010	...

P – 🚃 and 🍸 Paris Gare de Lyon - Milano and v.v. Special 'global' fares payable.
R – 🚃 and ✕ Torino - Milano - Bologna - Roma and v.v.
T – 🚃 Trieste - Torino and v.v.
p – Milano **Porta Garibaldi**
s – Stops to set down only.
u – Stops to pick up only.
v – Not July 28 - Aug. 26.
x – Not Aug. 4 - 19.
y – Not July 28 - Aug. 26.
z – Not July 30 - Aug. 26.

586 TORINO - AOSTA - PRÉ ST DIDIER

Most trains 2nd class only

km				⚒	⚒			†				⚒	⚒				Ⓐ	⚒		⚒	†	⚒			⚒	†	
0	**Torino Porta Nuova 585** d.	...	...	...	0625	0735	0825	0925	...	1125	*1150*	1225	...	1325	1425	...	*1450*	...	1625	...	1725	1725	1825	...	1920	2025	2225
6	Torino Porta Susa **585** d.	...	...	...	0634	0744	0835	0933	...	1136	*1159*	1236	...	1334	1433	...	*1459*	...	1636	...	1734	1734	1834	...	1928	2034	2234
29	Chivasso **585** d.	...	...	...	0706	0806	0900	1002	...	1200	1219	1303	...	1400	1500	...	1520	...	1703	1720	1803	1758	1902	...	2000	2101	2300
62	Ivrea d.	...	0627	0650	0747	0836	0925	1028	...	1225	1304	1333	1338	1425	1529	...	1610	1646	1728	1804	1834	1834	1928	1943	2025	2126	2326
79	Pont Saint Martin d.	...	0643	0712	0801	0853	0944	1042	...	1239	1323	...	1354	1439	1544	...	▬	1702	1742	1833	1848	1850	1942	2004	2046	2147	2340
91	Verrès d.	...	0701	0728	0812	0910	0955	1053	...	1249	1333	...	1409	1450	1556	...	...	1720	1753	1850	1859	1901	1953	2023	2057	2158	2351
104	Chatillon-Saint Vincent d.	...	0714	0742	0826	0923	1008	1112	...	1301	1344	...	1421	1509	1615	...	...	1733	1811	1902	1912	1914	2013	2034	2115	2211	0004
129	**Aosta** § a.	...	0735	0811	0852	0942	1032	1134	...	1325	1409	...	1452	1532	1635	...	...	1757	1832	1925	1933	1935	2034	2100	2136	2232	0025
	change trains							†	⚒						©	Ⓐ	©										
129	**Aosta** d.	0641	0745	...	0903	...	1039	1142	1235	1334	1437	...	...	1540	1642	1707	1742	...	1844	...	...	1946	...	...	...	...	...
161	**Pré St Didier** ▲ a.	0734	0838	...	0956	...	1132	1235	1324	1427	1530	...	...	1633	1735	1756	1835	...	1937	...	...	2039	...	...	...	...	...

		⚒																©		Ⓐ	©					
Pré St Didier ▲ d.	...	0638	...	0742	0900	1036	1139	...	...	...	...	1331	1434	1537	...	...	...	1640	...	1658	1740	...	1842	...	1944	2046
Aosta a.	...	0727	...	0831	0949	1125	1228	...	...	...	...	1420	1523	1626	...	...	...	1728	...	1751	1828	...	1930	...	2032	2134
change trains						⚒								†	⚒					⚒	†	⚒				⚒
Aosta § d.	0626	...	0737	0837	1034	1150	1237	...	1337	...	1415	1429	1536	1636	1637	...	1712	...	1735	1759	1833	1846	1937	...	2037	2141
Chatillon-Saint Vincent d.	0647	...	0759	0858	1055	1211	1301	...	1358	...	1435	1451	1557	1656	1657	...	1733	...	1756	1823	1853	1914	1957	...	2059	2200
Verrès d.	0701	...	0812	0910	1108	1223	1313	...	1409	...	1450	1505	1611	1709	1707	...	1753	...	1809	1834	1912	1927	2010	...	2112	2210
Pont Saint Martin d.	0712	...	0822	0921	1118	1239	1323	...	1425	...	1503	1515	1621	1720	1721	...	1807	...	1820	1850	1922	1942	2020	...	2123	2223
Ivrea d.	0724	...	0835	0936	1131	1257	1337	...	1447	...	1518	1528	1636	1740	1741	...	1822	...	1833	1909	1941	2004	2036	...	2137	2236
Chivasso **585** d.	0808	...	0906	1007	1206	1334	1407	...	1533	1543	...	1602	1710	1811	1833	1843	...	...	1905	1953	2014	2048	2106	...	2208	2318
Torino Porta Susa **585** a.	0825	...	0923	1025	1233	...	1425	...	...	1600	...	1621	1727	1830	...	1900	...	...	1922	...	2031	...	2124	...	2225	2339
Torino Porta Nuova 585 a.	0835	...	0935	1035	1245	...	1435	...	...	1610	...	1635	1740	1840	...	1910	...	...	1935	...	2040	...	2135	...	2235	2350

▲ – A connecting 🚌 service is available Pré St Didier - Courmayeur and v.v. (see Table **353**).

BRIG - STRESA - MILANO 590

For night trains from Genève/Basel to Roma and Venezia see Table **82**

km								*CIS* 41		*EC* 121	*CIS* 43	*EC* 123			*EC* 125	*CIS* 47				*EC* 127				*CIS* 51	*EC* 129	
								🅁✕		🅁🍷	🅁✕	🅁🍷			🅁🍷	🅁✕				🅁🍷				🅁✕	🅁🍷	
					⚒	†				V								⚒								
	Genève Aéroport **570** d.	...	...	...	...	...	...	...	...	0658	...	...	...	...	...	...	...	...	...	1501	...	...	...	...	1758	...
	Genève **570** d.	...	...	...	...	...	...	...	...	0707	...	0907	...	...	1107	...	...	...	...	1510	...	...	...	...	1807	...
	Lausanne **570** d.	...	...	...	...	...	...	...	...	0746	...	0946	...	...	1146	...	...	...	...	1546	...	...	...	...	1846	...
	Basel **560** d.	...	...	...	...	...	...	0630	...	|	0830	|	...	...	|	1230	...	...	...	|	...	...	...	1730	|	...
	Bern **560** d.	...	...	...	...	...	...	0735	...	|	0935	|	...	...	|	1335	...	...	...	|	...	...	...	1835	|	...
0	**Brig** 🏛 d.	...	...	...	...	...	...	0844	...	0920	1044	1120	...	...	1320	1444	...	...	...	1720	...	...	...	1944	2020	...
42	**Domodossola** 🏛 § a.	...	...	...	...	...	...	0912	...	0950	1112	1150	...	...	1350	1512	...	...	...	1750	...	...	...	2012	2050	...
42	**Domodossola** d.	0455	0605	0655	0728	0758	0825	0917	0942	1005	1117	1205	1255	1357	1405	1517	1525	1605	1655	1805	1810	1855	1952	2017	2105	2155
72	Verbania-Pallanza d.	0516	0627	0716	0747	0825	0846	|	1008	1023	|	1223	1316	1433	1423	|	1546	1638	1716	1823	1836	1915	2020	|	2123	2223
77	Baveno d.	|	0632	|	|	0830	|	|	1013	|	|	|	|	1438	|	|	|	1642	|	|	1841	|	2025	|	|	2228
81	Stresa d.	0523	0638	0723	0755	0834	0853	|	1018	1031	1139	1231	1323	1443	1431	|	1553	1642	1723	1831	1845	1923	2039	|	2131	2232
98	Arona d.	0536	0704	0736	0808	0853	0906	|	1048	1045	|	1245	1336	1502	1445	|	1606	1700	1736	1845	1903	1936	2059	|	2145	2251
124	Gallarate d.	0558	0731	0758	0832	0922	0928	1003	1128	1103	|	1303	1358	1532	1503	1603	1628	1730	1758	1903	1932	1958	2127	2103	2203	2321
150	Rho d.	|	0800	|	0900	0944	|	|	1149	|	|	|	|	1559	|	|	|	1800	|	|	1959	|	2150	|	|	2345
165	**Milano Porta Garibaldi** a.	|	0813	0835	0913	0957	|	|	1207	|	|	|	|	1613	|	|	|	1813	|	|	2013	|	2202	|	|	2357
167	**Milano Centrale** a.	0635	...	...	...	...	1005	1035	...	1135	1245	1335	1435	...	1535	1640	1705	...	1835	1935	...	2035	...	2135	2235	...

				CIS 40		*EC* 120		*CIS* 44	*EC* 122			*EC* 124				*EC* 126				*CIS* 48		*EC* 128		*CIS* 50		
				🅁✕		🅁🍷		🅁✕	🅁🍷			🅁🍷				🅁🍷				🅁✕		🅁🍷		🅁✕		
							p															V				
Milano Centrale d.	...	...	...	0725	0755	0825	...	1120	1225	...	1325	1425	...	1525	...	1625	...	1725	...	1825	...	1920	1925	2025	...	2125
Milano Porta Garibaldi d.	...	0505	0630	|	|	|	0900	|	|	1247	|	|	1447	|	1600	|	1647	|	1755	|	1835	|	|	|	2047	|
Rho d.	...	0522	0643	|	|	|	0913	|	|	1301	|	|	1500	|	|	|	1701	|	|	|	|	|	|	|	2100	|
Gallarate d.	...	0551	0703	0758	0832	0858	0931	1158	1258	1327	1400	1458	1527	1600	1640	1658	1727	1802	1831	|	1913	1954	2000	2058	2128	2200
Arona d.	...	0618	0734	|	0853	0916	0959	|	1316	1348	1421	1516	1555	1621	1719	1716	1753	1824	1859	|	1934	2012	2021	|	2157	2221
Stresa d.	...	0637	0753	|	0906	0929	1018	|	1329	1407	1434	1529	1613	1634	1741	1729	1812	1837	1924	1921	1953	2025	2034	|	2216	2234
Baveno d.	...	0642	0759	|	|	|	1023	|	|	1412	|	|	1617	|	1746	|	1816	|	1931	|	1958	|	|	|	2220	|
Verbania-Pallanza d.	...	0647	0804	|	|	0936	1028	|	1336	1417	1442	1536	1622	1642	1751	1736	1821	1845	1936	|	2003	2033	2042	|	2225	2242
Domodossola a.	...	0718	0830	0843	0935	0955	1105	1243	1355	1437	1505	1555	1643	1705	1820	1755	1850	1905	1955	1943	2023	2055	2105	2143	2253	2305
Domodossola 🏛 § d.	...	...	...	0848	...	1010	...	1248	1410	...	...	1610	...	...	...	1810	...	...	...	1948	...	2110	...	2148	...	...
Brig 🏛 a.	...	...	...	0916	...	1040	...	1316	1440	...	...	1640	...	...	...	1840	...	...	...	2016	...	2140	...	2216	...	...
Bern **560** a.	...	...	...	1023	...	|	...	1423	|	...	...	|	...	...	...	|	...	...	...	2123	...	|	...	2323	...	...
Basel **560** a.	...	...	...	1129	...	|	...	1529	|	...	...	|	...	...	...	|	...	...	...	2229	...	|	...	0029	...	...
Lausanne **570** a.	...	...	...	...	...	1214	...	...	1614	...	...	1814	...	...	...	2014	...	...	...	...	...	2314	...	...	...	...
Genève **570** a.	...	...	...	...	...	1250	...	...	1653	...	...	1853	...	...	...	2050	...	...	...	...	...	2350	...	...	...	...
Genève Aéroport **570** a.	...	...	...	...	...	1259	...	...	1702	...	...	...	...	...	...	2059	...	...	...	...	...	2359	...	...	...	...

Local service BRIG - DOMODOSSOLA and v.v. (2nd class only):

km		⚒		🚌		🚌 Ⓐ		Ⓒ	🚌		🚌		🚌		🚌	Ⓐ		🚌	Ⓑ		🚌		🚌		🚌	
0	**Brig** d.	0615	0705	...	0825	...	1000	1023	...	1155	...	1335	...	1505	...	1553	1655	...	1753	1855	...	2025	...	2145	...	0023
23	Iselle di Trasquera § d.	0634	0725	0730	0845	0902	1020	1042	1107	1217	1227	1357	1402	1527	1532	1612	1717	1722	1812	1917	1922	2045	2050	2205	2210	0042
42	**Domodossola** a.	0654	...	0800	...	0932	...	1102	1137	...	1258	...	1432	...	1602	1632	...	1752	1832	...	1952	...	2120	...	2240	0102

		Ⓐ		⚒		🚌 Ⓐ		🚌		⑥	🚌			🚌		🚌		🚌		🚌		🚌		🚌		
Domodossola d.	0331	0526	0601	0701	...	0829	...	1034	...	1141	1154	...	...	1327	...	1457	...	1647	...	1847	...	2017	...	2137	...	...
Iselle di Trasquera § d.	0355	0550	0625	0725	...	0900	0905	1105	1110	1205	1225	1235	...	1358	1415	1528	1600	1718	1735	1918	1935	2048	2105	2208	2225	...
Brig a.	0410	0604	0640	0740	...	...	0927	...	1130	1220	...	1257	...	...	1435	...	1620	...	1755	...	1955	...	2125	...	2247	...

V – (12) and ✕ Genève - Milano - Venezia Santa Lucia and v.v. p – Runs up to 7 minutes later Arona - Verbania-Pallanza on †. § – Ticket point is **Iselle**.

DOMODOSSOLA and ARONA - NOVARA 591

2nd class only except where shown

km					1779																				
		⚒		y	z	⚒			⚒	Ⓒ	Ⓒ	⚒				⚒			Ⓐ				Ⓐ	Ⓒ	
0	**Domodossola** d.	0523	...	0618	0618	0615	...	...	0757	...	...	...	...	1237	...	1342	...	1557	...	...	1747	...	1903	1904	...
38	Omegna d.	0618	...	|	|	0655	...	...	0849	...	...	...	...	1338	...	1432	...	1645	...	...	1844	...	1945	1943	...
44	Pettenasco d.	0624	...	|	|	0702	...	...	0855	...	...	...	...	1345	...	|	...	1651	...	...	1851	...	1951	1950	...
47	Orta-Miasino d.	0629	...	|	|	0706	...	...	0900	...	...	...	...	1354	...	1442	...	1655	...	...	1856	...	1959	1959	...
60	Borgomanero d.	0641	...	|	|	0721	...	...	0913	...	...	1253	...	1408	...	1458	...	1715	1812	...	1908	...	2016	2016	...
	Arona d.	|	0637	0704	0704	|	...	0757	|	1005	1207	|	1400	|	...	|	1635	|	|	1845	|	...	|	|	...
	Oleggio d.	|	0658	0720	0720	|	...	0817	|	1024	1228	|	1423	|	...	|	1657	|	|	1911	|	...	|	|	...
90	**Novara** a.	0713	0721	0734	0733	0751	...	0834	0951	1041	1246	1328	1441	1450	...	1533	1717	1751	1841	1931	1942	...	2045	2045	...
	Alessandria a.	...	...	...	0822	...	...	...	...	...	...	...	...	...	...	...	...	...	...	...	...	...	...	...	...

km																									1782
		⚒	⚒		⚒		Ⓒ	⚒	Ⓒ				⚒		Ⓐ		Ⓐ			Ⓐ	y				z
	Alessandria d.	...	...	...	...	...	...	...	...	...	...	...	...	...	...	...	...	...	...	...	...	...	...	...	2118
0	**Novara** d.	0538	0553	0634	0658	0805	0912	0918	1004	1223	1255	...	1348	1413	1421	1516	1632	...	1732	1739	1822	1832	1920	1926	2205
17	Oleggio d.	|	0610	|	0721	|	0930	|	1025	|	1312	...	|	1441	|	|	|	...	|	1800	|	1846	|	1945	2218
37	**Arona** a.	|	0634	|	0742	|	0950	|	1047	|	1334	...	|	1503	|	|	|	...	|	1823	|	1904	|	2005	2230
	Borgomanero d.	0608	...	0720	...	0838	...	0950	...	1252	...	...	1425	...	1456	1557	1700	...	1811	...	1912	|	2003	...	|
	Orta-Miasino d.	0630	...	0736	...	...	...	...	...	1306	...	...	1443	...	...	1613	1713	...	1829	...	1932	|	2017	...	|
	Pettenasco d.	0634	...	0740	...	...	...	...	...	1311	...	...	1447	...	...	1617	1717	...	1834	...	1936	|	2021	...	|
	Omegna d.	0656	...	0801	...	...	...	...	...	1323	...	...	1458	...	...	1624	1724	...	1843	...	1944	|	2027	...	|
	Domodossola a.	0741	...	0851	...	...	...	...	...	1413	...	...	1542	...	...	1713	1804	...	1935	...	2016	1954	2109	...	2314

y – Ⓐ (not July 28 - Aug. 26). z – Ⓒ June 10 - Sept. 30 (daily July 30 - Aug. 26).

592 BELLINZONA - LUINO

2nd class only

km											
0	**Bellinzona 550** .... d.	0554	0803	...	0956	1203	...	1354	*1540*	*1740*	...
9	Cadenazzo .... d.	0602	0811	...	1002	1211	...	1402	1602	1802	...
27	Pino-Tronzano 🏛 .... d.	0623	0831	...	1023	1231	...	1423	1623	1823	...
40	**Luino 608** .... a.	0638	0847	...	1038	1247	...	1438	1638	1838	...

							m			
Luino 608 .... d.	0651	...	1122	1322	1522	...	1624	1722	1922	...
Pino-Tronzano 🏛 .... d.	0709	...	1137	1337	1537	...	1635	1737	1937	...
Cadenazzo .... d.	0730	...	1159	1359	1559	...	1700	1758	1959	...
Bellinzona 550 .... a.	0740	...	1209	1409	1609	...	1709	*1818*	2009	...

Operator: FS – Ferrovie dello Stato / FFS – Ferrovie Federali Svizzere.

m – ③ Apr. 2 - Aug. 27.

593 MILANO - COLICO - TIRANO

km				1858			1854				2590	2592		1860		2594	2596			2598	2600	2602	2604	2606	2608	
		2⚒	⚒	2†	2⚒	2⚒	2†C	2	2†	2			2	†	2			2	2		⚒					
0	**Milano Centrale** .... d.	...	0502	0610	...	...	0620	0635	0710p	...	0815	0915	...	1010	...	1215	1415	...	...	1615	1700	1800	1905	2008	2105	...
12	Monza .... d.	...	0519	0622	...	...	0634	0654	0724	...	0827	0927	...	1021	...	1228	1427	...	...	1627	1718	1812	1922	2024	2123	...
50	Lecco .... d.	...	0605	0651	0645	...	0708	0745	0755	0805	0857	0957	...	1051	...	1257	1457	1507	...	1657	1757	1850	1953	2058	2159	...
72	Varenna .... d.	...	0634	0711	0726	...	|	...	0816	0840	0918	1018	...	1111	...	1319	1520	1541	...	1720	1825	1914	2021	2122	2230	...
75	Bellano .... d.	...	0640	0720	0731	...	|	...	0821	0845	0923	1023	...	1115	...	1324	1525	1546	...	1725	1830	1919	2028	2128	2235	...
89	**Colico ▲** .... d.	...	0705	0734	0748	...	0801	...	0836	0905	0937	1038	...	1136	...	1340	1540	1610	...	1741	1844	1933	2045	2144	2250	...
130	Sondrio .... d.	0659	0750	0813	0830	0854	...	...	0918	1000	1016	1110	1115	1215	1255	1413	1613	1651	1658	1816	1924	2005	2118	2216	...	...
156	**Tirano** .... a.	0741	0826	0840	...	0932	...	...	0950	...	1045	...	1150	1242	1337	1442	1642	...	1739	1846	1958	...	2146	...	...	...

		2585		2589	2591		2593			2595			2597			2599	1855	2603	1853			2605	2607	1861		2609
	2⚒		⚒			2⚒		2	2y		2	2		2	2		†		2†C	2†	2⚒		2⚒y	2†	2⚒	2
Tirano .... d.	...	...	...	0550	0650	...	0850	0959	...	...	1155	...	1245	1355	...	1455	...	1655	...	1743	1759	1855	...	1955	2028	...
Sondrio .... d.	...	0520	0535	0629	0730	0843	0917	1035	1040	1127	1227	1240	1324	1433	1440	1523	1618	1723	...	1817	1837	1923	2014	2022	2101	2125
Colico ▲ .... d.	0501	0557	0618	0704	0804	0924	0952	...	1125	1201	...	1329	1403	...	1528	1602	1657	1802	1823	1850	...	2000	2059	2059	...	2207
Bellano .... d.	0520	0612	0641	0719	0818	0950	1008	...	1145	1216	...	1352	1417	...	1559	1617	1711	1817	|	1905	...	2015	2114	2114	...	2223
Varenna .... d.	0525	0617	0646	0725	0823	0957	1019	...	1150	1221	...	1357	1422	...	1604	1622	1721	1824	1840	1915	...	2020	2123	2123	...	2229
Lecco .... d.	0553	0642	0716	0746	0846	1033	1046	...	1224	1246	...	1428	1446	...	1633	1646	1745	1846	1915	1944	...	2046	2146	2146	...	2254
Monza .... d.	0641	0713	0756	0818	0916	...	1116	...	...	1316	...	...	1516	...	...	1717	1815	1917	1957	2016	...	2115	2218	2218	...	...
Milano Centrale .... a.	0657p	0731	0812	0830	0930	...	1130	...	...	1330	...	...	1530	...	...	1730	1830	1930	2013	2028p	...	2130	2230	2230	...	...

C – 🚌2 Milano - Chiavenna and v.v.

p – Milano **Porta Garibaldi**.

y – Not July 29 - Aug. 26.

z – † (daily July 30 - Aug. 25).

▲ – **Local service COLICO - CHIAVENNA and v.v.:** 27 km, journey 28–35 minutes, 2nd class only.

From **Colico**: 0627⚒y, 0709⚒, 0802†C, 0840, 1043, 1128⚒y, 1230, 1330⚒y, 1432, 1548⚒y, 1631, 1755⚒, 1830†, 1943⚒y, 2049z.

From **Chiavenna**: 0619⚒, 0706⚒y, 0725†, 0753⚒, 0917, 1125, 1228⚒y, 1323, 1425⚒y, 1507, 1628⚒y, 1715, 1758†C, 1848⚒y, 1920y.

595 INNSBRUCK - BOLZANO / BOZEN - VERONA - BOLOGNA

km		*ICp* 577										1871	*ES* 9311		*IC* 717				*EC* 81					*EC* 85	
		Ⓡ m		2 ⚒	2	2	2 ⚒	2	2 ⚒	2	2	2 L	Ⓡ✕		♦		2 †		Ⓡ✕	2 †	2 ⚒		2 ⚒	Ⓡ✕	2 ⚒
	München Hbf **951** .... d.	...	...	...	...	...	...	...	...	...	...	...	...	...	...	...	...	...	0730	...	...	...	...	0932	...
0	**Innsbruck Hbf** .... ▶ d.	...	...	...	...	...	...	0542	...	0636	...	0700	...	...	...	...	...	...	0926	...	...	...	...	1126	1206
18	Matrei .... ▶ d.	...	...	...	...	...	...	0600	...	0656	...	0717	...	...	...	...	...	...	|	...	...	...	...	|	1225
23	Steinach in Tirol .... ▶ d.	...	...	...	...	...	...	0612	...	0701	...	0722	...	...	...	...	...	...	|	...	...	...	...	|	1230
37	**Brennero** 🏛 .... ▶ a.	...	...	...	...	...	...	0624	...	0717	...	0737	...	...	...	...	...	...	1002	...	...	...	...	1202	1246
37	**Brennero** 🏛 .... d.	...	...	...	0540	...	...	▬	0632	▬	0730	0739	...	...	...	...	...	...	1014	...	...	...	1118	1214	...
60	Vipiteno/Sterzing .... d.	...	...	...	0600	...	...	...	0652	...	0749	0757	...	...	...	...	...	...	|	...	...	...	1138	|	...
78	Fortezza/Franzensfeste .... d.	...	...	...	0618	...	0653	...	0710	...	0807	0814	...	...	...	...	...	...	1050	...	1056	...	1156	1250	...
89	Bressanone/Brixen .... d.	...	...	...	0627	...	0703	...	0719	...	0816	...	...	...	...	...	...	...	1059	...	1106	...	1205	1259	...
99	Chiusa/Klausen .... d.	...	...	...	0637	...	0713	...	0729	2	0826	...	...	...	...	...	...	...	|	...	1115	...	1214	|	...
127	**Bolzano/Bozen 597** .... d.	...	0509	0613	0703	...	0739	...	0754	0809	0850	...	0900	...	0931	...	1031	...	1131	...	1140	1231	1240	1331	...
143	Ora/Auer .... d.	...	0521	0626	0717	...	0754	...	...	0825	...	...	0913	...	0943	...	1046	...	|	...	1155	1243	1257	|	...
165	Mezzocorona .... d.	...	0535	0642	0732	...	0813	...	...	0846	...	...	|	...	0957	...	1106	...	|	...	1210	1257	1318	|	...
182	**Trento ▲** .... d.	...	0549	0656	0746	...	0828	...	...	0902	...	...	0940	...	1011	...	1120	...	1207	...	1225	1311	1331	1407	...
206	Rovereto .... d.	...	0603	0710	0801	...	0842	...	...	0916	...	...	0955	...	1027	...	1134	...	1222	...	1239	1326	1345	1422	...
274	**Verona Porta Nuova** .... a.	...	0655	0809	0855	...	0930	©	...	1014	...	...	1035	...	1111	...	1234	...	1301	...	1344	1415	1448	1501	...
274	**Verona Porta Nuova** .... d.	0529	0711	...	...	0902	...	0933	...	...	...	...	1048	...	1131	1137	...	1238	...	1334	...	1437	...	1516	...
388	**Bologna Centrale** .... a.	0716	0853	...	...	1110	...	1123	...	...	...	...	1200	...	1310	1323	...	1423	...	1523	...	1623	...	1630	...
	Milano Centrale **600** .... a.	|	...	...	...	...	...	...	...	...	...	...	|	...	...	...	...	...	...	...	...	...	...	|	...
	Venezia Santa Lucia **600** . a.	|	...	...	...	...	...	...	...	...	...	...	|	...	...	...	...	...	...	...	...	...	...	|	...
	Firenze SMN **620** .... a.	0829c	...	...	...	...	...	...	...	...	...	...	1310	...	...	...	...	...	...	...	...	...	...	1738	...
	Roma Termini **620** .... a.	1103	...	...	...	...	...	...	...	...	...	...	1455	...	...	...	...	...	...	...	...	...	...	2018	...
	Napoli Centrale **620** .... a.	...	...	...	...	...	...	...	...	...	...	...	...	...	...	...	...	...	...	...	...	...	...	...	...

			EC 87		*ES* 9313			1875	*EC* 89 *EC* 92	*E* 1595				*EC* 83		1873		*E* 925	*E* 925 *E* 837	*EC* 189	*E* 1601		*EN* 389	*EN* 389 *EN* 363	
			Ⓡ✕	2 ⚒	Ⓡ✕	2 Ⓐ		2 L⑤j	Ⓡ✕	♦	2 Ⓐ		2 Ⓐ	Ⓡ✕	2 ⚒	2 L		♦	Q	Ⓡ✕	♦	2	Ⓡ ♦	Ⓡ B	
München Hbf **951** .... d.	...	...	1130	...	...	...	...	...	1331	...	...	...	...	1530	...	...	...	...	...	1731	...	...	2103	2103	...
Innsbruck Hbf .... ▶ d.	...	...	1326	...	...	1406	...	1436	1526	...	1606	...	1706	1726	...	1759	...	...	...	1926	...	2043	2304	2304	...
Matrei .... ▶ d.	...	...	|	...	...	1425	...	1453	|	...	1626	...	1726	|	...	1817	...	...	...	|	...	2102	|	|	...
Steinach in Tirol .... ▶ d.	...	...	|	...	...	1430	...	1458	|	...	1631	...	1731	|	...	1822	...	...	...	|	...	2107	|	|	...
Brennero 🏛 .... ▶ a.	...	...	1402	...	...	1446	...	1512	1602	...	1647	...	1747	1802	...	1838	...	...	...	2002	...	2123	2340	2340	...
Brennero 🏛 .... d.	...	1310	1414	1434	...	...	1510	1514	1614	...	...	1710	...	1814	...	1839	1910	...	...	2014	...	...	2355	2355	...
Vipiteno/Sterzing .... d.	...	1330	|	1454	...	...	1530	1535	|	...	...	1730	...	|	...	1857	1930	...	...	|	...	...	|	|	...
Fortezza/Franzensfeste .... d.	...	1350	1450	1514	...	...	1550	1553	1650	...	...	1750	...	1850	1825	1914	1950	...	...	2050	2142	...	0027	0027	...
Bressanone/Brixen .... d.	...	1359	1459	...	...	...	1559	...	1659	...	...	1759	...	1859	1836	...	1959	...	...	2059	2153	...	0036	0036	...
Chiusa/Klausen .... d.	...	1408	|	...	...	...	1608	...	|	...	...	1808	...	|	1846	...	2008	...	...	|	|	...	|	|	...
Bolzano/Bozen 597 .... d.	...	1431	1531	...	1618	...	1631	...	1731	1800	...	1831	...	1931	1909	...	2031	2045	2045	2131	2249	...	0107	0107	...
Ora/Auer .... d.	...	1443	|	...	|	...	1643	...	|	1813	...	1843	...	|	1925	...	2043	2059	2059	|	2302	...	|	|	...
Mezzocorona .... d.	...	1457	|	...	|	...	1657	...	|	1830	...	1857	...	|	1945	...	2101	2115	2115	|	2318	...	|	|	...
Trento ▲ .... d.	...	1511	1607	...	1654	...	1711	...	1807	1846	...	1911	...	2007	2016	...	2115	2131	2131	2207	2333	...	0140	0140	...
Rovereto .... d.	...	1526	1622	...	1708	...	1726	...	1822	1903	...	1926	...	2022	2031	...	2130	2147	2147	2222	2351	...	|	|	...
Verona Porta Nuova .... a.	...	1615	1701	...	1748	...	1815	...	1901	2000	...	2015	...	2101	2125	...	2221	2234	2234	2301	|	...	0235	0235	...
Verona Porta Nuova .... d.	...	1637	1710	...	1800	...	1837	...	1913	2003	...	2037	...	...	...	...	...	2237	2237	...	|	...	0305	0552	...
Bologna Centrale .... a.	...	1823	|	...	1937	...	2023	...	|	2221	...	2223	...	...	...	...	...	0058	0058	...	|	...	0435	|	...
Milano Centrale **600** .... a.	...	...	|	...	|	...	...	...	2045	|	...	...	...	...	...	...	...	...	|	...	|	...	|	|	...
Venezia S.L. **600** .... a.	...	...	1832	...	|	...	...	...	...	|	...	...	...	...	...	...	...	...	|	...	|	...	|	0737	...
Firenze SMN **620** .... a.	...	...	...	...	2033	...	...	...	...	2344c	...	...	...	...	...	...	...	...	|	...	|	...	0618	...	...
Roma Termini **620** .... a.	...	...	...	...	2220	...	...	...	...	|	...	...	...	...	...	...	...	...	0609t	...	0837t	...	0905	...	...
Napoli Centrale **620** .... a.	...	...	...	...	...	...	...	...	...	0432	...	...	...	...	...	...	...	...	0926	...	...	...	...	...	...

ADDITIONAL TRAINS INNSBRUCK - BRENNERO and v.v. (2nd class only):

							⚒	Ⓐ		
Innsbruck Hbf .... d.	0736	0843	1106	1306	1506	1643	1743	1843	1934	2330
Matrei .... d.	0755	0902	1125	1325	1525	1702	1803	1902	1954	2347
Steinach in Tirol .... d.	0800	0907	1130	1330	1530	1707	1808	1907	1959	2351
Brennero 🏛 .... a.	0816	0923	1146	1346	1546	1723	1824	1923	2015	0007

	⚒					⚒				
Brennero 🏛 .... d.	0610	0642	0751	1039	1220	1259	1639	1839	2312	...
Steinach in Tirol .... d.	0627	0659	0808	1056	1237	1316	1656	1856	2328	...
Matrei .... d.	0631	0703	0812	1100	1241	1320	1700	1901	2332	...
Innsbruck Hbf .... a.	0649	0722	0831	1118	1259	1339	1718	1919	2350	...

FOR NOTES SEE NEXT PAGE

BOLOGNA - VERONA - BOLZANO / BOZEN - INNSBRUCK 595

		1870			*E* 1602			*E*824 *E*924	*E* 924	*EC* 188			*E* 1594		*EC*93 *EC*88			*EC* 82				*EC* 84	*ES* 9310		
	2 ⚒	2 L	2 ⚒	2	♦	2 ⚒	2 ⚒	R	♦	[R] ✕	2 ⚒		♦		[R] ✕	y	2 †	[R] ✕	2		2 ⚒	[R] ✕	[R] ✕		2
Napoli Centrale **620** d.	...	...	...	...	...	...	...	1845	...	...	...	...	2302	...	...	...	...	...	...	...	...	...	...	...	...
Roma Termini **620** d.	...	...	...	...	2157t	...	...	2207t	...	...	...	...	|	...	...	...	...	...	...	...	...	0742	0900	...	...
Firenze SMN **620** d.	...	...	...	...	|	...	...	|	...	...	...	...	|	...	...	...	...	...	...	...	...	0957	1047	...	...
Venezia Santa Lucia **600** d.	...	...	...	...	|	...	...	|	...	...	...	...	|	...	...	...	...	...	...	...	...	|	|	...	...
Milano Centrale **600** d.	...	...	...	...	|	...	...	|	...	...	...	...	|	...	0705	...	...	...	...	...	...	|	|	...	...
ologna Centrale d.	...	...	...	...	|	...	...	0400	0400	...	...	...	0535	0613	|	0737	...	...	...	0937h	...	1122	1201	1137	...
erona Porta Nuova a.	...	...	...	...	|	...	...	0615	0615	...	...	...	0758	0803	0844	0925	...	...	...	1127h	...	1245	1330	1324	...
erona Porta Nuova d.	...	...	...	...	|	0525	0605	0620	0620	0659	0632	0748	0801	...	0859	...	0944	1059	...	1148	1217	1259	1342	1347	...
overeto d.	...	...	...	...	0543s	0613	0705	0721	0721	0740	0735	0837	0856	...	0940	...	1036	1140	...	1237	1317	1340	1420	1437	...
rento ▲ d.	...	...	0602	...	0601s	0629	0721	0739	0739	0757	0752	0853	0912	...	0957	...	1052	1157	...	1253	1331	1357	1435	1453	...
ezzocorona d.	...	...	0614	...	0615s	0642	0734	0752	0752	|	0815	0904	0925	...	|	...	1103	|	...	1304	1344	|	|	1504	...
ra/Auer d.	...	...	0635	...	0632s	0708	0754	0826	0826	|	0838	0918	0941	...	|	...	1119	|	...	1318	1403	|	|	1518	...
olzano/Bozen 597 d.	0600	...	0704	...	0650s	0725	0820	0843	0843	0831	0857	0931	0955	...	1031	...	1131	1231	...	1331	1420	1431	1508	1531	...
hiusa/Klausen d.	0623	...	0729	...	|	*0752*	0843	...	...	|	...	0951	...	...	|	...	...	|	...	1351	▬	|	...	1551	...
ressanone/Brixen d.	0631	...	0737	...	0750s	*0800*	0851	...	...	0857	...	1000	...	...	1057	...	...	1257	...	1400	...	1457	...	1600	...
ortezza/Franzensfeste d.	0642	0658	0748	...	0806s	*0812*	0904	...	...	0912	...	1011	...	...	1112	...	...	1312	...	1411	...	1512	...	1611	...
piteno/Sterzing d.	0700	0715	0805	...	...	...	...	...	...	|	...	1028	...	...	|	...	...	|	...	1428	2	|	...	1628	...
rennero 🏛 a.	0719	0736	0824	...	...	...	...	...	...	0948	...	1050	...	...	1148	...	...	1348	...	1450	Ⓐ	1548	...	1650	...
rennero 🏛 ▶ d.	...	0737	...	0839	...	...	...	...	...	1000	...	...	...	...	1200	...	...	1400	1439	...	1537	1600	...	...	1726
teinach in Tirol ▶ d.	...	0755	...	0856	...	...	...	...	...	|	...	...	...	...	|	...	...	|	1456	...	1554	|	...	...	1743
latrei ▶ d.	...	0759	...	0900	...	...	...	...	...	1018	...	...	...	...	|	...	...	|	1500	...	1558	|	...	...	1748
nsbruck Hbf ▶ a.	...	0816	...	0918	...	...	...	...	...	1035	...	...	...	...	1233	...	...	1433	1518	...	1615	1633	...	...	1807
München Hbf **951** a.	...	...	...	...	...	...	...	...	...	1226	...	...	...	...	1427	...	...	1626	...	...	...	1826	...	...	...

	EC 86					1874	*EC* 80			1872				*ES* 9312			*IC* 718		*ICp* 596	*EN*358 *EN*388	*EN* 388				
	[R] ✕	2 Ⓐ		2 ⚒	2 ⚒	2 L⑦	[R]	2		2 L	2 Ⓐ	2		[R] ✕	2 †		♦		[R] n	[R] B	[R] ♦		2		
Napoli Centrale **620** d.	...	...	...	...	...	...	...	...	...	...	...	...	...	...	...	...	...	...	...	...	...	...	...	...	...
Roma Termini **620** d.	...	...	...	...	...	...	...	...	...	...	...	...	...	1605	...	...	...	...	1857	...	1910	...	...	...	...
Firenze SMN **620** d.	...	...	...	...	...	...	...	...	...	...	...	...	...	1756	...	...	...	...	2127c	...	2153	...	...	...	...
Venezia Santa Lucia **600** d.	1328	...	...	...	...	...	...	...	...	...	...	...	...	|	...	...	...	...	|	2251	|	...	...	...	...
Milano Centrale **600** d.	|	...	...	...	...	...	...	...	...	...	...	...	...	|	...	...	...	...	|	|	|	...	...	...	...
ologna Centrale d.	|	...	1337	...	...	...	...	...	1537	...	...	...	1737	1901	...	1937	1958	2107	2244	|	2305	...	...	...	...
erona Porta Nuova a.	1445	...	1527	...	...	...	...	...	1729	...	...	...	1927	2026	...	2124	2140	2249	0022	0025	0031	...	...	...	...
erona Porta Nuova d.	1459	...	1548	...	1615	...	1659	1721	1748	...	1836	1928	2000	2039	2057	2148	2200	...	...	0101	0101	...	...	...	...
overeto d.	1540	...	1637	...	1710	...	1740	1815	1837	...	1934	2026	2049	2122	2145	2237	2245	...	...	|	|	...	...	...	...
rento ▲ d.	1557	1628	1653	...	1727	...	1757	1832	1853	...	1951	2043	2105	2137	2202	2253	2259	...	...	0155	0155	...	...	...	...
ezzocorona d.	|	1642	1704	...	1740	...	|	1845	1904	...	2002	2054	2116	|	2213	2304	2311	...	...	|	|	...	...	...	...
ra/Auer d.	|	1702	1718	...	1801	...	|	1904	1918	...	2022	2114	2130	2158	2227	2318	2325	...	...	|	|	...	...	...	...
olzano/Bozen 597 d.	1631	1720	1731	...	1818	...	1831	1920	1931	...	2039	2130	2143	2211	2240	2329	2339	...	...	0230	0230	...	...	...	...
hiusa/Klausen d.	|	1743	1751	...	1839	...	|	1943	1951	...	...	...	2203	...	2303	...	...	...	...	|	|	...	...	...	...
ressanone/Brixen d.	1657	1751	1800	...	1848	...	1857	1951	2000	...	...	...	2212	...	2311	...	...	...	...	|	|	...	...	...	...
ortezza/Franzensfeste d.	1712	1804	1811	...	1859	1908	1912	2004	2011	2054	...	...	2223	...	2322	...	...	...	...	|	|	...	...	...	...
ipiteno/Sterzing d.	|	...	1828	...	1917a	1924	|	...	2028	2109	...	...	2240	...	2339	...	...	...	...	|	|	...	...	...	...
rennero 🏛 a.	1748	...	1850	...	1937a	1942	1948	...	2050	2125	...	...	2301	...	2359	...	...	...	...	0341	0341	...	...	...	...
rennero 🏛 ▶ d.	1800	...	...	1942	...	1944	2000	...	...	2127	...	...	...	...	...	...	...	...	...	0356	0356	...	0541	...	...
teinach in Tirol ▶ d.	|	...	...	1959	...	1959	|	...	...	2142	...	...	...	...	...	...	...	...	...	|	|	...	0558	...	...
latrei ▶ d.	|	...	...	2003	...	2003	|	...	...	2146	...	...	...	...	...	...	...	...	...	|	|	...	0602	...	...
nsbruck Hbf ▶ a.	1833	...	...	2020	...	2020	2033	...	...	2204	...	...	...	...	...	...	...	...	...	0432	0430	...	0621	...	...
München Hbf **951** a.	2026	...	...	...	...	...	2226	...	...	...	...	...	...	...	...	...	...	...	...	0630	0630	...	...	...	...

♦ – **NOTES** (LISTED BY TRAIN NUMBER)

88/9 – *City Night Line* CAPRI – 🛏 1,2 cl., ▬ 2 cl. and (2) Roma - München and v.v. Supplement payable.

17 – ADIGE – (12) Bolzano - Verona - Mantova (d. 1203) - Modena (d. 1245) - Bologna - Ancona - Bari - Lecce.

18 – ADIGE – (12) Lecce - Bari - Ancona - Bologna - Modena (d. 2022) - Mantova (d. 2112) - Verona - Bolzano.

24 – ①③④⑤⑥⑦; also Jan. 1, Apr. 29, not Dec. 24, 31, Apr. 28 (from Lecce): 🛏 1,2 cl. (T2), ▬ 2 cl. (4 berth) and (2) Lecce - Bologna - Bolzano.

25 – ①②③⑤⑥⑦ (also Dec. 27, Jan. 3, May 1; not Dec. 25, 26, Jan. 1, Apr. 30): 🛏 1,2 cl. (T2), ▬ 2 cl. (4 berth) and (2) Bolzano - Bologna - Lecce.

594 – ⑤ Dec. 14 - Mar. 28; also Dec. 19, 23, 30 (from Reggio): 🛏 1,2 cl. (T2), ▬ 2 cl. and (2) Reggio di Calabria - Bolzano.

595 – ⑥ Dec. 15 - Mar. 29 (also Dec. 20, 26, Jan. 1): 🛏 1,2 cl. (T2), ▬ 2 cl. and (2) Bolzano - Reggio di Calabria.

601 – Daily Dec. 20 - 23, 26 - 30, Jan. 2 - 6; ⑥ Jan. 12 - Feb. 2; ⑥⑦ Feb. 9 - Mar. 16; also Mar. 22, 24. 🛏 1,2 cl. (Excelsior), 🛏 1,2 cl. (T2), 🛏 1,2 cl., ▬ 2 cl. (4 berth) San Candido (**1600**) - Fortezza - Bolzano - Roma Tiburtina.

602 – Daily Dec. 19 - 22, 25 - 29, Jan. 1 - 5; ⑤ Jan. 11 - Feb. 1; ⑤⑥ Feb. 8 - Mar. 22 (from Roma): 🛏 1,2 cl. (Excelsior), 🛏 1,2 cl. (T2), 🛏 1,2 cl. and ▬ 2 cl. (4 berth) Roma Tiburtina - Bolzano - Fortezza (**1603**) - San Candido.

3 – 🛏 1,2 cl., ▬ 2 cl. and (2) Venezia - Verona (**358/363**) - München Hbf and v.v.

. – (2) Innsbruck - San Candido - Lienz and v.v. (Table **596**).

Q – ①②③⑤⑥⑦ (also Dec. 27, Jan. 3, May 1; not Dec. 25, 26, Jan. 1, Apr. 30): 🛏 1,2 cl., ▬ 2 cl. (4 berth) and (2) Bolzano - Bologna (**837**) - Napoli.

R – ①③④⑤⑥⑦; also Jan. 1, Apr. 29, not Dec. 24, 31, Apr. 28 (from Napoli): 🛏 1,2 cl., ▬ 2 cl. (4 berth) and (2) Napoli - Bologna (**924**) - Bolzano.

a – Ⓐ only.
c – Firenze **Campo di Marte**.
h – Ⓒ only.
j – Also Oct. 25, 31; not Oct. 26, Nov. 2.
m – Via Mantova (d. 0600), Modena (d. 0648).
n – Via Modena (d. 2305), Mantova (d. 2352).
s – Stops to set down only.
t – Roma **Tiburtina**.
u – Stops to pick up only.
y – Train number **2256** on Ⓒ (Verona a. 0920).

⊖ – Special fares payable. Service not shown in the German section – see International Tables **65** and **70**.

▶ – For additional trains Innsbruck - Brennero and v.v. see foot of page 294.

▲ – **TRENTO - MALÉ - MARILLEVA and v.v.**
56 *km*, journey 75 – 90 minutes.
Trento - Malé and v.v.: up to 15 departures on ⚒, 10 on †.
5 departures on ⚒, 3 on † extended Malé - Marilleva and v.v. (9 *km*, journey ± 15 minutes).
Operator: Trentino transporti S.p.A, Via Innsbruck 65, 38014 Gardolo. ✆ +39 0 461 821000, fax +39 0 461 031407.

2nd class except where shown — FORTEZZA / FRANZENSFESTE - SAN CANDIDO / INNICHEN - LIENZ 596

km				1871	*E* 1603							*ÖEC* 530							1875						1873	
		⚒	⚒		A					⚒	Ⓐw	⑥L	y	v	⚒	x		x	⑤z	⚒	x		Ⓐ			
	Innsbruck Hbf **595** d.	...	...	0700	...	...	...	...	...	...	...	...	...	...	...	...	...	...	1436	...	...	...	...	...	1759	...
	Brennero 🏛 **595** d.	...	...	0739	...	...	...	...	...	...	...	...	...	...	...	...	...	...	1514	...	...	...	...	...	1839	...
0	**Fortezza / Franzensfeste** d.	...	0658	0815	0759s	0915	1015	1115	...	1215	...	...	1255	1315	1415	...	1515	...	1554	1615	...	1715	1755	1815	1915	2017
33	Brunico / Bruneck d.	...	0729	0851	0905s	0952	1052	1152	...	1252	...	...	1332	1352	1452	...	1552	...	1632	1652	...	1752	1831	1852	1952	2054
61	Dobbiaco / Toblach d.	...	0759	0922	1005s	1021	1121	1221	...	1321	...	...	1405	1421	1521	...	1621	...	1706	1721	...	1821	1905	1921	2023	2123
65	**San Candido / Innichen** a.	...	0803	0928	1011	1025	1125	1225	...	1325	...	...	1409	1425	1525	...	1625	...	1713	1725	...	1825	1910	1925	2029	2127
65	**San Candido / Innichen** 🏛 d.	0646	...	0930	▬	...	...	...	1228	...	1412	...	...	...	...	1532	...	1628	1715j	...	1823	...	...	...	2031	...
78	Sillian 🏛 d.	0659	...	0943	...	...	...	...	1240	...	1425	1427	...	...	...	1545	...	1640	1728j	...	1836	...	...	...	2044	...
108	**Lienz** a.	0730	...	1013	1017	...	...	...	1312	...	1456	1453	...	...	...	1613	...	1711	1801j	...	1909	...	...	...	2114	...
	Spittal-Millstättersee **970** a.	...	...	...	1118	...	...	...	*1419*	...	*1549*	1549	...	...	...	...	...	*1819*	*1919*	...	*2017*	...	...	...	...	...

A – ⑤⑥ June 15 - July 21; daily July 27 - Sept. 1 (from Roma): 🛏 1,2 cl. (Excelsior), 🛏 1,2 cl. (T2), 🛏 1,2 cl. and ▬ 2 cl. (4 berth) Roma Tiburtina (**1602**) - Bolzano - Fortezza - San Candido.

L – (12) and ✕ Sillian - Lienz - Villach - Wien.

j – Not Aug. 3 - 24.
s – Stops to set down only.
v – † (daily June 11 - Sept. 8).
w – Not July 28 - Aug. 22.
x – Not July 26 - Aug. 24.
y – ⚒ Sept. 10 - Dec. 8.
z – Also Oct. 25, 31; not Oct. 26, Nov. 2.

596 LIENZ - SAN CANDIDO / INNICHEN - FORTEZZA / FRANZENSFESTE

2nd class except where shown

											ÖEC													E	
		1870									531									1874			1872	1600	
	⚒		⚒			⚒			⚒		⑥L	m	⚒	x	⚒	x			⚒	⑦	x	Ⓐ		A	Ⓐ
Spittal-Millstättersee **970** ... d.	...	...	...	...	...	...	*0926*	...	...	...	1211	*1211*	...	*1242*	1342	...	...	...	1542	...	...	1742	...	...	...
Lienz ... d.	...	0500	...	...	...	...	1035	...	...	...	1313	1330	...	1408	1445	1527	...	...	1646	1652k	1715	1848	1851	...	...
Sillian ... d.	...	0530	...	...	...	...	1108	...	...	...	1339	1358	...	1445	▬	1601	...	...	...	1728k	1749	▬	1920	...	...
San Candido / Innichen 🏛 .. a.	...	0543	...	...	...	...	1122	...	...	...	...	1410	...	1459	...	1615	...	...	...	1742k	1803	...	1933	...	...
San Candido / Innichen 🏛 .. d.	0530	0545	0650	0836	0936	1036	...	1136	1252	1336	...	...	1436	...	1536	...	1636	1736	...	1745	...	1836	1935	1950	2036
Dobbiaco / Toblach ... d.	0535	0551	0655	0841	0941	1041	...	1141	1256	1341	...	...	1441	...	1541	...	1641	1741	...	1753	...	1841	1942	1955	2041
Brunico / Bruneck ... d.	0604	0622	0729	0914	1014	1114	...	1214	1331	1414	...	...	1514	...	1614	...	1714	1814	...	1831	...	1914	2016	2056	2116
Fortezza / Franzensfeste ..... a.	0641	0657	0759	0945	1045	1145	...	1245	1402	1445	...	...	1545	...	1645	...	1745	1845	...	1907	...	1945	2053	2130	2147
Brennero 🏛 **595** ... a.	...	0736	...	...	...	...	...	...	...	...	...	...	...	...	...	...	...	...	...	1942	...	...	2125	...	...
Innsbruck Hbf **595** ... a.	...	0816	...	...	...	...	...	...	...	...	...	...	...	...	...	...	...	...	...	2020	...	...	2204	...	...

A – ⑥⑦ June 16 - July 22; daily July 28 - Sept. 2: 🛏 1,2 cl. (Excelsior), 🛏 1,2 cl. (T2), 🛏 1,2 cl., ▬ 2 cl. (4 berth) San Candido - Fortezza (**1601**) - Bolzano - Roma Tiburtina.
L – 🚃12 and ✕ Wien - Villach - Lienz - Sillian.

k – Not July 29 - Aug. 26.
m – July 26 - Aug. 26.

u – Stops to pick up only.
x – Not July 26 - Aug. 24.

597 BOLZANO / BOZEN - MERANO / MERAN - MALLES / MALS

2nd class only FS, SAD*

km		⚒	⚒	⚒			and			🚌
0	**Bolzano / Bozen 595** ... d.	0542	0655	0757	0852	0935	hourly	2035	2147	2345
32	Merano / Meran ... a.	0628	0739	0837	0931	1013	until	2113	2225	0030

	⚒	⚒		⚒			and			🚌
Merano / Meran ... d.	0606	0649	0715	0752	0846	0946	hourly	1946	2046	2250
Bolzano / Bozen 595 ... a.	0646	0730	0756	0835	0925	1025	until	2025	2125	2340

km								§		
0	Merano / Meran ... d.	0545	0633	0718	0814	0914	1016	and	2116	...
43	Silandro / Schlanders ... d.	0636	0731	0810	0910	1010	1110	hourly	2210	...
60	Malles / Mals **546 / 954** ... a.	0700	0754	0838	0938	1038	1138	until	2238	...

							§			
Malles / Mals **546 / 954** ... d.	...	0551	0611	0720	...	0820	and	1920	2020	2120
Silandro / Schlanders ... d.	...	0614	0640	0748	...	0848	hourly	1948	2048	2148
Merano / Meran ... a.	...	0704	0732	0843	...	0943	until	2043	2143	2243

§ – Additional services run on ⚒ every 2 hours (journey 70 minutes): Merano / Meran d. 0746 – 1746, Malles / Mals d. 0705 – 1905.

* – Operators: FS Bolzano - Merano; SAD Merano - Malles (*Ferrovia della Val Venosta*).
Servizi Autobus Dolomiti (SAD), Via Conciapelli 60, I-39100 Bolzano. ✆ +39 0471 97 12 59, fax +39 0471 97 00 42

599 ITALIAN LAKES (LAGO MAGGIORE, GARDA, COMO)

Lago Maggiore: ⛴ services link Arona, Stresa, Baveno, Laveno, Luino and Locarno throughout the year on an irregular schedule. For details contact the operator below:
Operator: Navigazione sul Lago Maggiore, Viale F. Baracca 1, 28041 Arona, Italy. ✆ + 39 0322 233 200. Fax: + 39 0322 249 530.

Lago di Garda: ⛴ services link Desenzano, Peschiera, Garda, Salo, Gardone and Riva, (April to September only), on an irregular schedule. For details contact the operator below:
Operator: Navigazione sul Lago di Garda, Piazza Matteotti, 25015 Desenzano del Garda, Italy. ✆ + 39 30 91 41 321, 2, 3. Fax: + 39 30 91 44 640.

Lago Di Como: ⛴ services link Como, Bellagio, Menaggio, Varenna, Bellano and Colico (April to September only) on an irregular schedule. For details contact the operator below:
Hydrofoil service: **October 29, 2007 - March 22, 2008**.

	⚒	†	⚒	⚒	†z	⚒y	⚒	Ⓐy	w	Ⓐv	⑥t
Como ... d.	0733	1110	1215	1330	1400	1420	1615	1710	1805	1910	1910
Tremezzo ... d.	0819r	1153	1252	1419	1443	1507	1651	1757	1853	1947	1957
Bellagio ... d.	0813r	1200	1259	1439r	1450	1514	1658	1804	1900	1953	2004
Menaggio ... d.	0808	1208	1306	1430	1457	1521	1704	1812	1908	1959	2012
Bellano ... d.	...	1218	1318	1455	...	...	1713	1821	1924	2011	2028
Colico ... a.	...	1251	1345	1528	...	...	1740	...	1954	2034	2058

	⚒	⚒q	†p	⚒		†z	⚒y		⚒	Ⓐy	⑥n
Colico ... d.	0604	0622	0722	...	1345	...	...	1610	1741	...	1954
Bellano ... d.	0628	0653	0753	...	1413	...	...	1644	1806	1822	|
Menaggio ... d.	0641	0703	0803	0808	1424	1518	1522	1655	1814	1843	2025
Bellagio ... d.	0647	0712	0812	0814	1431	1527	1531	1704	1820	1852	2034
Tremezzo ... d.	0653	0718	0818	0820	1438	1533	1537	1710	1826	1858	|
Como ... a.	0730	0805	0905	0857	1518	1617	1624	1752	1857	1940	2112

n – Not Dec. 22, 29, Jan. 5.
p – Not Dec. 26.
q – Not Dec. 24, 27, 31, Jan. 2.
r – Via Menaggio.
t – Not holidays.
v – Not Dec. 23, 24, 26, 30, 31.
w – Not Dec. 22, 29, Jan. 5.
y – Not Dec. 22 - Jan. 5.
z – Not Dec. 23, 26, 30.

Operator: Navigazione Lago di Como, Via Per Cernobbio 18, 22100 Como Italy. ✆ +39 (0) 31 579 211, fax: +39 (0) 31 570 080.

600 MILANO - VERONA - VENEZIA

km			*EN*		*IC*		*ESc*	*EC*		*ES*	*ICp*		*ESc*	*IC*		*IC*	*IC*		*EC*	*IC*		*ESc*	*ICp*		
			363		**603**		**9701**	**93**		**9401**	**607**		**9705**	**611**		**1505**	**613**		**121**	**615**		**9707**	**619**		
		2	R	2		2	R 🍷	R ✕	2	R 🍷	R	2	R 🍷		2			2			2	R 🍷	R	2	2
			◆					◆			T			V	†	©	T		◆	Ⓐ			◆		†
0	**Milano Centrale** ... d.	0025	...	...	0600	0615	0655	0705	0715	0755	0805	0815	0855	0905	0910p	1005	1105	...	1155	1205	1215	1255	1305	1315	1314
4	Milano Lambrate ... d.	0031	...	...	|	0623	|	|	0723	|	|	0823	|	|	0921	|	|	1115	|	|	1223	|	|	1323	1325
34	Treviglio ... d.	0100	...	...	|	0645	|	|	0745	|	|	0845	|	|	0941	|	|	1145	|	|	1245	|	|	1345	1352
83	Brescia ... d.	0146	...	...	0652	0723	0742	0800	0823	|	0857	0923	0942	0957	1017	1057	1157	1223	1242	1257	1323	1342	1357	1423	1429
111	Desenzano-Sirmione ... d.	0202	...	...	0708	0746	|	0816	0839	|	0913	0939	|	1013	1034	1113	1213	1239	|	1313	1339	|	1413	1439	1453
125	Peschiera del Garda § ... d.	0212	...	...	0718	0802	|	0827	0850	|	0923	0950	|	1023	1045	1123	1223	1250	|	1323	1350	|	1423	1450	1503
148	**Verona Porta Nuova** ... a.	0232	...	...	0736	0824	0814	0844	0913	|	0940	1007	1014	1040	1101	1140	1240	1304	1314	1340	1407	1414	1440	1513	1522
148	**Verona Porta Nuova** ... d.	...	0552	0604	0739	...	0816	...	0915	|	0943	...	1016	1043	1104	1143	1243	1307	1316	1343	...	1416	1443	...	1525
200	Vicenza ... d.	...	0632	0655	0820	...	0844	...	0950	|	1020	...	1044	1120	1147	1220	1320	1352	1344	1420	...	1444	1518	...	1559
230	Padova **620** ... d.	...	0655	0721	0838	...	0902	...	1009	0948	1038	...	1102	1138	1211	1238	1338	1414	1402	1438	...	1502	...	...	1618
258	**Venezia Mestre 620** ... a.	...	0722	0746	0857	...	0918s	...	1029	1004s	1057	...	1118s	1157	1236	1256	1358	1436	1418	1457	...	1518s	...	...	1639
258	**Venezia Mestre 620** ... d.	...	0727	0750	0859	...	|	...	1031	|	1059	...	|	1159	1238	1258	1400	1438	1420	1459	...	|	...	...	1641
267	**Venezia Santa Lucia 620** a.	...	0737	0802	0909	...	0930	...	1041	1015	1109	...	1130	1209	1249	1308	1410	1449	1430	1509	...	1530	...	...	1651
	Trieste Centrale **605** ... a.	...	...	...	...	...	...	...	...	...	...	...	...	1430	...	...	...	...	...	...	...	...	...	...	...

	ES	*EC*		*ESc*	*EC*		*EC*	*IC*		*CIS*	*IC*		*ES*	*ICp*			*ESc*	*IC*	*ICp*		*IC*		*ICp*		
	9403	**173**		**9713**	**111**		**87**	**625**		**155**	**629**		**9405**	**633**			**9717**	**635**	**637**		**639**		**641**		
	R 🍷	R ✕	2	R 🍷	R 🍷	2	R ✕		2	R ✕		2	R 🍷	R	2	2	R 🍷		R	2		2	R	2	2
		◆			◆		◆	T		◆					Ⓐ	©		T	Ⓑ◆		Ⓑ		◆		
Milano Centrale ... d.	1355	1405	1415	1455	1505	1515	...	1605	1615	1655	1705	1715	1755	1805	1810	1815	1855	1905	1910	1915	2005	2015	2105	2115	2215
Milano Lambrate ... d.	|	|	1423	|	|	1523	...	|	1623	|	|	1723	|	|	1818	1822	|	|	|	1923	|	2023	|	2123	2223
Treviglio ... d.	|	|	1445	|	|	1545	...	|	1645	|	|	1745	|	|	1840	1843	|	|	|	1945	|	2045	|	2145	2245
Brescia ... d.	|	1457	1523	1542	1557	1623	...	1657	1723	1742	1757	1823	|	1907	1914	1921	1942	1957	2004	2023	2057	2123	2157	2223	2323
Desenzano-Sirmione ... d.	|	1513	1539	|	1613	1639	...	1713	1739	|	1813	1839	|	1923	1931	1940	|	2013	2020	2039	2113	2139	2213	2239	2339
Peschiera del Garda § ... d.	|	1523	1550	|	1623	1650	...	1723	1750	|	1823	1850	|	1933	1943	1950	|	2023	2030	2050	2123	2150	2223	2250	2350
Verona Porta Nuova ... a.	|	1540	1607	1614	1640	1707	...	1740	1807	1814	1840	1913	|	1950	2000	2006	2014	2040	2049	2107	2140	2207	2240	2307	0007
Verona Porta Nuova ... d.	|	1543	...	1616	1643	...	1710	1743	...	1816	1843	1915	|	1953	...	...	2016	2043	2052	...	2143	2210	2243	▬	...
Vicenza ... d.	|	1620	...	1644	1720	...	1742	1820	...	1844	1920	1952	|	2030	...	...	2044	2120	2125	...	2220	2248	2320	...	...
Padova **620** ... d.	1548	1638	...	1702	1738	...	1800	1838	...	1902	1938	2011	1948	2048	...	...	2102	2138	...	...	2238	2307	2338	2	...
Venezia Mestre 620 ... a.	1604s	1656	...	1718s	1757	...	1820	1857	...	1918	1956	2031	2004s	2111	...	...	2118s	2157	...	...	2257	2328	2356	...	...
Venezia Mestre 620 ... d.	|	1658	...	|	1759	...	1822	1859	...	1943	1958	2033	|	2113	...	...	|	2159	...	...	2259	2330	...	0006	...
Venezia Santa Lucia 620 a.	1615	1708	...	1730	1809	...	1832	1909	...	|	2008	2043	2015	2123	...	...	2130	2209	...	...	2309	2340	...	0016	...
Trieste Centrale **605** ... a.	...	...	...	...	...	...	...	...	...	2130	...	...	...	...	...	...	...	...	...	...	...	...	...	...	...

◆ – **NOTES** (LISTED BY TRAIN NUMBER)

87 – TIEPOLO – 🚃12 and ✕ München - Innsbruck - Verona - Venezia.
93 – LEONARDO DA VINCI – 🚃12 and ✕ Milano - Verona (**88**) - München.
111 – CISALPINO SAN MARCO – 🚃12 Basel - Chiasso - Milano - Venezia.
121 – CISALPINO MONTEVERDI – 🚃12 and ✕ Genève - Milano - Venezia.
155 – 🚃12 and ✕ Zürich - Milano - Trieste. *CISALPINO Pendolino* train; supplement payable.
173 – CISALPINO CANALETTO – 🚃12 and ✕ Schaffhausen - Zürich - Chiasso - Milano - Venezia.
363 – MONTECARLO – 🛏 1,2 cl. and ▬ 2 cl. (4 berth) Nice (**369**) - Ventimiglia - Genova Piazza Principe (**362**) - Milano - Venezia; 🛏 1, 2 cl., ▬ 2 cl. and 🚃2 München (**389**) - Verona - Venezia.
619 – GIORGIONE – 🚃12 Milano - Treviso (**620**) - Udine.
637 – FOGAZZARO – 🚃12 Milano - Treviso (**638**) - Udine.
641 – VIVALDI – 🚃12 Milano - Venezia Mestre; 🛏 1,2 cl. and ▬ 2 cl. (4 berth) Milano - Venezia Mestre (**234**) - Wien Südbahnhof.

T – 🚃12 Torino Porta Nuova - Milano - Venezia.
V – 🚃12 Torino Porta Nuova - Milano - Venezia - Trieste.

p – Milano **Porta Garibaldi**.
s – Stops to set down only.

§ – Station for Gardaland Park. Free shuttle bus available.

VENEZIA - VERONA - MILANO 600

				ICp	*ESc*		*ICp*	*IC*		*ES*	*IC*	*CIS*	*IC*	*IC*	*ESc*		*EC*		*EC*		*ICp*		*EC*	*ES*	*ICp*
				600	**9700**		**602**	**604**		**9400**	**606**	**154**	**608**	**1506**	**9704**		**174**		**114**		**614**		**86**	**9402**	**618**
	2	2	2	R	R 🍷	2	R		2	R 🍷		R ✕			R 🍷	2	R ✕	2	R 🍷	2	R	2	R ✕	R 🍷	R
				♦			⚒ ♦	⚒			T	♦	Ⓐ	Ⓒ			♦		♦				♦		T
Trieste Centrale **605** d.	...	...	...	...	...	...	...	...	...	...	...	0630	...	...	...	...	...	...	...	...	...	...	...	...	...
enezia Santa Lucia 620 d.	...	...	0519	...	0630	...	...	0651	...	0745	0752	|	0900	0951	1030	...	1051	1118	1151	...	1252	...	1328	1345	1352
enezia Mestre 620 a.	...	...	0529	...	|	...	...	0701	...	|	0802	0820	0912	1001	|	...	1101	1128	1201	...	1302	...	1338	|	1402
enezia Mestre 620 d.	...	...	0531	0603	0642u	...	...	0703	...	0756u	0804	0842	0914	1003	1042u	...	1103	1130	1203	...	1304	...	1340	1356u	1404
adova **620** d.	...	...	0551	0624	0700	...	...	0724	...	0814	0824	0900	0933	1025	1100	...	1124	1151	1224	...	1324	...	1358	1414	1424
icenza d.	...	...	0610	0642	0716	...	0735	0742	...	|	0842	0917	0956	1046	1116	...	1142	1210	1242	...	1342	...	1417	|	1442
erona Porta Nuova a.	...	...	0647	0715	0741	...	0808	0815	...	|	0915	0943	1042	1119	1141	...	1215	1247	1315	...	1415	...	1445	|	1515
erona Porta Nuova d.	0610	0640	0650	0718	0743	0753	0811	0818	0845	|	0918	0945	1050	1122	1143	1153	1218	1250	1318	1343	1418	1445	...	|	1518
eschiera del Garda § d.	0624	0656	0705	0733	|	0807	0826	0833	0901	|	0933	|	1111	1136	|	1207	1233	1306	1333	1401	1433	1501	...	|	1533
esenzano-Sirmione d.	0633	0707	0716	0744	|	0817	0837	0844	0913	|	0944	|	1123	1145	|	1217	1244	1317	1344	1411	1444	1513	...	|	1544
rescia d.	0652	0728	0737	0805	0818	0837	0857	0905	0937	|	1005	1020	1158	1205	1218	1237	1305	1337	1405	1437	1505	1537	...	|	1605
reviglio d.	0729	|	0820	|	|	0915	|	|	1010	|	|	|	|	|	|	1315	|	1415	|	1515	|	1615	...	|	|
ilano Lambrate d.	0748	0823	0842	|	|	0938	|	|	1040	|	|	|	|	|	|	1338	|	1438	|	1538	|	1638	...	|	|
ilano Centrale a.	0755	0830	0850	0855	0905	0945	0950	0955	...	1005	1055	1105	1255	1255	1305	1345	1355	1445	1455	1545	1555	1645	...	1605	1655

	ESc		*IC*		*IC*	*EC*		*ESc*		*EC*	*IC*	*ES*			*IC*	*ESc*			*ICp*	*IC*					*EN*
	9708		**622**		**624**	**128**		**9710**		**92**	**626**	**9404**			**630**	**9716**			**632**	**634**					**358**
	R 🍷	2		2			2	R 🍷	2	R ✕		R ✕	2	2		R 🍷	2	2	R		2	2	2	2	R
			T		T	♦				♦	V			†					♦			†	⚒	†	♦
Trieste Centrale **605** d.	...	...	...	...	...	...	...	...	...	...	1528	...	...	...	...	...	...	...	...	...	...	...	...	...	...
enezia Santa Lucia 620 d.	1430	...	1451	1518	1551	1630	...	1730	1708	...	1751	1845	...	1824	1852	1930	...	1907	...	1951	...	2025	2042	2104	2251
enezia Mestre 620 a.	|	...	1501	1528	1601	1640	...	|	1719	...	1801	|	...	1834	1902	|	...	1918	...	2001	...	2036	2053	2114	2301
enezia Mestre 620 d.	1442u	...	1503	1530	1603	1642	...	1742u	1721	...	1803	1856u	...	1836	1904	1942u	...	1920	...	2003	...	2038	2055	2116	2304
adova **620** d.	1500	...	1524	1550	1624	1700	...	1800	1751	...	1823	1914	...	1858	1924	2000	...	1951	...	2024	...	2112	2129	2139	2328
icenza d.	1516	...	1542	1610	1642	1717	...	1816	1810	...	1842	|	...	1919	1942	2016	...	2022	2034	2042	...	2142	2155	2202	2347
erona Porta Nuova a.	1541	...	1615	1647	1715	1743	...	1841	1849	...	1915	|	...	2006	2015	2041	...	2101	2108	2115	...	2231	2244	2241	0025
erona Porta Nuova d.	1543	1553	1618	1650	1718	1745	1753	1843	1852	1913	1918	|	1945	2009	2018	2043	2053	...	2111	2118	2150	...	...	2244	...
eschiera del Garda § d.	|	1607	1633	1705	1733	|	1807	|	1906	1927	1933	|	2001	2025	2033	|	2107	...	2126	2133	2205	...	...	2259	...
esenzano-Sirmione d.	|	1617	|	1716	1744	|	1817	|	1916	1937	1944	|	2013	2036	2044	|	2117	...	2137	2144	2216	...	...	2311	...
rescia d.	1618	1637	1705	1737	1805	1820	1837	1918	1937	1956	2005	|	2037	2059	2105	2118	2137	...	2157	2205	2237	...	...	2332	...
reviglio d.	|	1715	|	1815	|	|	1915	|	2011	|	|	|	2115	2148	|	|	2212	...	|	|	2315	...	...	0001	...
ilano Lambrate d.	|	1738	|	1838	|	|	1938	|	2033	|	|	|	2138	2209	|	|	2233	...	|	|	2338	...	...	0023	...
ilano Centrale a.	1705	1745	1755	1845	1855	1905	1945	2005	2040	2045	2055	2105	2145	2220p	2155	2205	2240	...	2245	2255	2345	...	...	0030	...

♦ – **NOTES** (LISTED BY TRAIN NUMBER)

6 – TIEPOLO – (12) and ✕ Venezia - Verona - Innsbruck - München.
2 – LEONARDO DA VINCI – (12) and ✕ München (**89**) - Verona - Milano.
14 – CISALPINO SAN MARCO – (12) Venezia - Milano - Chiasso - Basel.
28 – CISALPINO MONTEVERDI – (12) and ✕ Venezia - Milano - Genève.
54 – (12) and ✕ Trieste - Milano - Zürich - Schaffhausen. *CISALPINO Pendolino* train; supplement payable.
74 – CISALPINO CANALETTO – (12) and ✕ Venezia - Milano - Chiasso - Zürich - Schaffhausen.
58 – MONTECARLO – 🛏 1,2 cl. and ▬ 2 cl. (4 berth) Venezia - Milano (**359**) - Genova Piazza Principe (**368**) - Ventimiglia - Nice; 🛏 1, 2 cl., ▬ 2 cl. and (2) Venezia - Verona (**388**) - München.
00 – VIVALDI – (12) Venezia Mestre - Milano; 🛏 1,2 cl. and ▬ 2 cl. (4 berth) Wien Südbahnhof (**235**) - Venezia Mestre - Milano.

602 – FOGAZZARO – (12) Udine (**601**) - Treviso - Milano.
632 – GIORGIONE – (12) Udine (**631**) - Treviso - Milano.

T – (12) Venezia - Milano - Torino Porta Nuova.
V – (12) Trieste - Venezia - Milano - Torino Porta Nuova.

p – Milano **Porta Garibaldi**.
u – Stops to pick up only.

§ – Station for Gardaland Park. Free shuttle bus available.

VENEZIA - UDINE - VILLACH 601

km		*E*	*E*	*ICp* **641**	*EN*			*ICN*				*EC*				*IC*			*EC*		*ICp*				
		1236	**1234**	*EN* **234**	**234**			**774**				**32**				**700**			**30**		**620**				
		R	R	R	R	2	2		2	2	2	R	2	2	2		2	2	R ✕	2	R	2	2	2	2
		♦	♦	J	♦	⚒ p	q	♦		⚒	⚒ C	♦	⚒				B		♦	⚒	♦		⚒	C	
	Roma Termini **620** d.	1700	...	...	1910	...	...	2250t	...	...	...	...	...	...	...	0657	...	...	...	...	...	...	...	...	...
	Firenze SMN **620** d.	2056c	2100	...	2153	...	...	0147c	...	...	...	...	...	...	...	0927c	...	...	...	...	...	...	...	...	...
	Bologna Centrale **620** d.	2223	2223	...	2320	...	...	0318	...	...	...	...	...	...	...	1044	...	...	...	...	...	...	...	...	...
	Milano Centrale **600** d.	|	|	2105	|	...	...	|	...	...	...	...	...	...	...	|	...	...	...	...	1305	...	...	...	...
0	**Venezia Santa Lucia** d.	|	|	|	|	0526	0526	0601	0656	0717	0756	0846	0856	0956	1156	|	1336	1356	1444	1456	|	1556	1656	1733	1756
9	**Venezia Mestre** a.	0011	0011	2356	0102	0536	0536	0611	0706	0728	0806	0856	0906	1006	1206	1226	1347	1406	1454	1506	|	1606	1706	1744	1806
9	**Venezia Mestre** d.	0036	0036	0126	0126	0538	0538	0613	0708	0730	0808	0858	0908	1008	1208	1248	1349	1408	1456	1508	|	1608	1708	1746	1808
30	Treviso Centrale d.	|	|	|	|	0558	0559	0632	0727	0752	0832	0920	0927	1027	1227	1308	1414	1427	|	1530	1612	1627	1729	1808	1827
57	Conegliano **603** d.	|	|	|	|	0618	0617	0653	0746	0818	0854	0938	0946	1046	1246	1325	1434	1446	|	1549	1629	1646	1749	1836	1846
74	Sacile d.	|	|	|	|	0642	0630	0709	0759	0836	...	|	0959	1059	1259	|	...	1459	|	1602	1644	1659	1802	...	1859
87	Pordenone d.	|	|	|	|	0653	0641	0722	0809	0848	...	0956	1009	1109	1309	1344	...	1509	1542	1612	1656	1709	1812	...	1909
136	**Udine** d.	0157	0157	|	|	0734	0735k	0804	0848	0933	...	1028	1045	1148	1348	1415	...	1548	1614	1651	1734	1748	1851	...	1948
	Trieste Centrale **606** a.	|	|	|	|	0843	0908	...	0956	1049	...	|	...	1256j	1456	...	...	1656	|	1759	...	1856	1959	...	2056
230	Tarvisio Boscoverde 🏛 a.	0304	0304	0339	0339	...	...	...	...	...	...	1120	...	...	...	...	...	...	1706	...	...	...	...	...	...
258	**Villach Hbf** a.	0341	0341	0415	0415	...	...	...	...	...	...	1202	...	...	...	...	...	...	1740	...	...	...	...	...	...

		ES				*EN* **239**	*ICp*			*E*	
		9476				*EN* **236**	**637/8**			**1134**	
	2	R ✕	2	2	2	R	R	2	2	R	2
				B		H	z			♦	
Roma Termini **620** d.	...	1452	...	...	...	...	...	...	...	...	...
Firenze SMN **620** d.	...	1637	...	...	...	...	...	...	...	...	...
Bologna Centrale **620** d.	...	1740	...	...	...	...	...	...	...	...	...
Milano Centrale **600** d.	...	|	...	...	...	...	1910	...	...	...	...
enezia Santa Lucia d.	1856	|	1956	2002	2056	2028	|	2156	2256	...	2356
enezia Mestre a.	1906	1910	2006	2013	2106	2038	|	2206	2307	...	0006
enezia Mestre d.	1908	1931	2008	2015	2108	2040	|	2208	2309	0002	0008
reviso Centrale d.	1930	1948	2027	2040	2129	|	2219	2228	2330	|	0027
onegliano **603** d.	1948	2007	2046	2101	2150	|	2237	2247	2352	|	0046
acile d.	2001	|	2059	...	2203	|	2250	2301	0005	|	0059
ordenone d.	2011	2027	2109	...	2215	|	2300	2311	0015	|	0109
dine d.	2047	2056	2148	...	2257	2304r	2331	2354	0051	|	0145
Trieste Centrale **606** a.	...	...	2256	...	...	|	...	0121	...	|	...
arvisio Boscoverde 🏛 a.	...	...	...	...	...	0005	...	...	...	0231	...
illach Hbf a.	...	...	...	...	...	0042	...	...	...	0308	...

	EN	*EN* **235**	*E*	*E*	*E*	*ICp*			*EN* **237**
	235	*ICp* **600**	**1235**	**1237**	**1135**	**601/2**			*EN* **238**
	R	R	R	R	R	R	2	2	R
	♦	K	♦	♦	♦	y	†	⚒	H
Villach Hbf d.	0003	0003	0045	0045	0154	...	...	...	0423
Tarvisio Boscoverde 🏛 d.	0041	0041	0123	0123	0232	...	...	...	0501
Trieste Centrale **606** d.	|	|	|	|	|	...	...	...	|
Udine d.	|	|	0218	0218	|	0516	0523	0525	0619n
Pordenone d.	|	|	|	|	|	0548	0600	0602	|
Sacile d.	|	|	|	|	|	0601	0610	0612	|
Conegliano **603** d.	|	|	|	|	|	0617	0626	0628	|
Treviso Centrale d.	|	|	|	|	|	0642	0652	0653	|
Venezia Mestre a.	0252	0252	0332	0332	0446	|	0713	0713	0833
Venezia Mestre d.	0311	0603	0357	0357	...	|	0715	0715	0835
Venezia Santa Lucia a.	|	|	|	|	...	|	0726	0726	0845
Milano Centrale **600** a.	|	0855	|	|	...	0950	...	...	...
Bologna Centrale **620** a.	0448	...	0541	0541	...	...	...	...	...
Firenze SMN **620** a.	0618	...	0659	0705c	...	...	...	...	...
Roma Termini **620** a.	0905	...	...	1005	...	...	...	...	...

FOR NOTES SEE NEXT PAGE

601 VILLACH - UDINE - VENEZIA

		ES								*EC*				*IC*					*ICp*	EC				*ICN*	
		9465								**31**				**709**					**631/2**	**33**				**771**	
	2	R 🍷	2	2	2	2	2	2	2	R	2	2	2		2	2	2	2	R	R	2	2	2		2
	⚒					⚒C	†C	†	⚒	◆		⚒				⚒	B			◆	Ⓐ		C	◆	
Villach Hbf d.	...	...	...	...	...	...	...	...	...	1037	...	...	...	...	...	...	...	...	...	1749	...	...	...	...	...
Tarvisio Boscoverde 🏛 d.	...	...	...	...	...	...	...	...	...	1111	...	...	...	...	...	...	...	...	...	1823	...	...	...	...	...
Trieste Centrale **606** d.	0502	...	0558	0704	0904	...	...	...	...	|	1104	1134	1304	...	1504	...	...	1704	...	|	1804	1904	...	...	2116
Udine d.	0628	0700	0735	0815	1015	...	...	1050	1110	1205	1215	1306	1415	1530	1615	1713	...	1815	1830	1919	1931	2015	...	2150	2227
Pordenone d.	0705	0728	0813	0852	1052	...	...	1131	1147	1232	1252	1343	1452	1601	1652	1749	...	1852	1901	1950	2009	2052	...	2228	2304
Sacile d.	0715	|	0823	0902	1102	...	...	1144	1157	|	1302	1353	1502	|	1702	1759	...	1902	1911	|	2019	2102	...	2239	2314
Conegliano **603** d.	0727	0749	0842	0914	1114	1129	1147	1202	1208	|	1314	1411	1514	1622	1714	1811	1832	1914	1925	2011	2030	2114	2232	2252	2326
Treviso Centrale d.	0746	0809	0908	0933	1133	1149	1207	1230	1230	|	1333	1430	1533	1643	1733	1830	1851	1933	1944	2031	2048	2133	2252	2311	2345
Venezia Mestre a.	0805	0825	0930	0952	1152	1210	1230	1252	1252	1318	1352	1452	1552	1701	1752	1852	1910	1952	|	2048	2109	2152	2310	2331	0004
Venezia Mestre d.	0807	0850	0932	0954	1154	1212	1232	1254	1254	1320	1354	1454	1554	1732	1754	1854	1912	1954	|	2050	2111	2154	2312	2333	0006
Venezia Santa Lucia a.	0817	|	0942	1004	1204	1223	1243	1304	1304	1330	1404	1504	1604	|	1804	1904	1923	2004	|	2100	2121	2204	2323	2343	0016
Milano Centrale **600** a.	...	|	...	...	...	...	...	...	...	...	...	...	...	|	...	...	...	...	2245	...	...	...	...	|	...
Bologna Centrale **620** a.	...	1020	...	...	...	...	...	...	...	...	...	...	...	1916	...	...	...	...	...	...	...	...	...	0217	...
Firenze SMN **620** a.	...	1123	...	...	...	...	...	...	...	...	...	...	...	2029c	...	...	...	...	...	...	...	...	...	|	...
Roma Termini **620** a.	...	1308	...	...	...	...	...	...	...	...	...	...	...	2303	...	...	...	...	...	...	...	...	...	0656t	...

◆ – **NOTES** (LISTED BY TRAIN NUMBER)

30/1 – ALLEGRO JOHANN STRAUSS – [12] Venezia - Wien Süd and v.v.

32/3 – ALLEGRO STRADIVARI – [12] Venezia - Wien Süd and v.v.

234 – ALLEGRO TOSCA – 🛏 1,2 cl., ▬ 2 cl. (4 berth) and [2] Roma - Venezia Mestre - Villach - Wien Süd. Supplement payable.

235 – ALLEGRO TOSCA – 🛏 1,2 cl., ▬ 2 cl. (4 berth) and [2] Wien Süd - Villach - Venezia Mestre - Roma. Supplement payable.

620 – GIORGIONE – [12] Milano (**619**) - Treviso - Udine.

771 – MARCO POLO – 🛏 1,2 cl. (Excelsior), 🛏 1,2 cl., ▬ 2 cl. (4 berth) and [2] Udine - Venezia Santa Lucia - Napoli.

774 – MARCO POLO – 🛏 1,2 cl. (Excelsior), 🛏 1,2 cl., ▬ 2 cl. (4 berth) and [2] Napoli - Venezia Santa Lucia - Udine.

1134 – ALLEGRO AIDA – ⑥ June 16 - Sept. 8 (from Ancona): 🛏 1,2 cl., ▬ 2 cl. and [2] Ancona - Venezia Mestre - Wien Süd. Supplement payable.

1135 – ALLEGRO AIDA – ⑤ June 15 - Sept. 7 (from Wien): 🛏 1,2 cl., ▬ 2 cl. and [2] Wien Süd - Venezia Mestre - Ancona. Supplement payable.

1234 – ALLEGRO RIGOLETTO – ⑤⑦ June 15 - Sept. 30 (from Livorno): 🛏 1,2 cl. (Excelsior), ▬ 2 cl. and [2] Livorno - Firenze - Wien Süd. Supplement payable.

1235 – ALLEGRO RIGOLETTO – ④⑥ June 14 - Sept. 29 (from Wien): 🛏 1,2 cl. (Excelsior), ▬ 2 cl. and [2] Wien Süd - Firenze - Livorno. Supplement payable.

1236 – ALLEGRO ROSSINI – ⑥ June 16 - Sept. 29 (from Roma): 🛏 1,2 cl. (Excelsior), ▬ 2 cl. and [2] Roma - Wien Süd. Supplement payable.

1237 – ALLEGRO ROSSINI – ⑤ June 15 - Sept. 28 (from Wien): 🛏 1,2 cl. (Excelsior), ▬ 2 cl. and [2] Wien Süd - Roma. Supplement payable.

B – [2] Venezia - Ponte nelle Alpi - Belluno and v.v.

C – [2] Venezia - Ponte nelli Alpi - Calalzo and v.v.

H – ALLEGRO DON GIOVANNI – 🛏 1,2 cl. (Excelsior), ▬ 2 cl. and [2] Venezia - Cervignano - Gorizia Centrale - Udine - Villach - Salzburg - Wien Westbf and v.v.; ▬ 2 cl. Venezia - Salzburg (**206/7**) - Praha and v.v. Supplement payable.

J – ALLEGRO TOSCA – 🛏 1,2 cl. and ▬ 2 cl. (4 berth) Milano (**641**) - Venezia Mestre - Wien Süd. Supplement payable.

K – ALLEGRO TOSCA – 🛏 1,2 cl. and ▬ 2 cl. (4 berth) Wien Süd - Venezia Mestre (**600**) - Milano. Supplement payable.

c – Firenze **Campo di Marte**.
j – ①⑥† (also Aug. 16, Nov. 2).
k – Arrive 0722.
n – Arrive 0557.
p – Ⓐ Sept. 10 - Dec. 7.
q – ⚒ June 11 - Sept. 8; ⑥ Sept. 15 - Dec. 1.
r – Arrive 2242.
t – Roma **Tiburtina**.
y – ⚒ Dec. 10 - June 14.
z – ⑧ Dec. 9 - June 8; daily June 9 - 14.

602 VICENZA - TREVISO

2nd class only except where shown

km													*ICp*												*ICp*
													619												**637**
		⚒	⚒	⚒	⚒	⚒z	†	⚒	†	⚒	⚒		R P	⚒	†	⚒	⚒		†	⚒	⚒	†	⚒	⚒y	R P ⚒
0	**Vicenza** d.	0546	0614	0658	0837	0918	0918	1123	1323	1355	1457	...	1520	1554	1626	1626	1655	...	1736	1750	1853	1926	1926	1954	2127
24	Cittadella d.	0611	0639	0722	0902	0943	0943	1146	1349	1419	1521	...	1541	1620	1650	1650	1716	...	1801	1815	1917	1951	1952	2017	2146
36	Castelfranco Veneto d.	0634	0702	0747	0920	1004	1004	1208	1403	1437	1536	...	1553	1635	1709	1711	1727	...	1816	1830	1932	2012	2012	2033	2200
60	**Treviso Centrale** a.	0656	0727	0812	0947	1028	1028	1232	1426	1501	1600	...	1610	1702	1730	1737	1747	...	1840	1855	1954	2035	2035	2057	2217

					ICp																	*ICp*			
					602																	**632**			
	⚒	⚒	⚒		R P ⚒	⚒			†	⚒	†		†	⚒	⚒	⚒		⚒	⚒	⚒	⚒y	R P	Ⓐw	†	
Treviso Centrale d.	0540	0553	0614	...	0642	0654	0731	...	0938	1003	1125	...	1315	1328	1431	1538	...	1635	1709	1753	1835	1944	2012	2048	...
Castelfranco Veneto d.	0559	0619	0638	...	0701	0721	0756	...	1004	1036	1148	...	1343	1351	1455	1601	...	1657	1737	1815	1905	2002	2040	2110	...
Cittadella d.	0611	0635	0653	...	0712	0736	0810	...	1019	1051	1203	...	1357	1405	1508	1616	...	1710	1753	1831	1920	2013	2055	2124	...
Vicenza a.	0638	0704	0720	...	0733	0805	0836	...	1045	1119	1231	...	1421	1431	1536	1645	...	1735	1821	1859	1945	2032	2125	2151	...

P – [12] Milano Centrale - Udine and v.v.
w – June 11 - Sept. 7 (not July 30 - Aug. 24).
y – Not Aug. 6 - 18.
z – Not Aug. 6 - 25.

603 CONEGLIANO and PADOVA - BELLUNO and CALALZO

2nd class only except where shown

km		*E*																								
		1606																								
		H		⚒	†z	⚒	†	⚒z				†	⚒													
	Venezia S. L. **601** d.	...	...	...	0702	...	...	0756	...	...	...	1202	1202	...	1336	...	...	1502	...	...	...	1733	...	2002	...	...
0	**Conegliano 601** d.	...	0627	...	0802	...	...	0855	...	...	...	1303	1303	...	1435	...	...	1605	...	1803	...	1837	...	2103	...	...
14	Vittorio Veneto d.	...	0642	...	0820	...	...	0909	...	...	...	1320	1330	...	1452	...	...	1625	...	1818	...	1853	...	2118	...	...
	Padova d.	...	|	0600	|	0648	0648	|	0933	...	1134	|	|	...	|	1250	1345	|	1534	|	1705	|	1813	|	1912	2118
	Castelfranco Veneto d.	...	|	0629	|	0724	0724	|	1002	...	1203	|	|	...	|	1322	1425	|	1613	|	1733	|	1847	|	1948	2152
	Montebelluna d.	...	|	0643	|	0746	0746	|	1021	...	1217	|	|	...	|	1336	1443	|	1629	|	1751	|	1908	|	2005	2205
	Feltre d.	...	|	0733	|	0833	0833	|	1054	...	1250	|	|	...	|	1425	1526	|	1709	|	1827	|	1947	|	2046	2240
	Belluno d.	0606s	|	0816	|	0908	0908	|	1125	1156	1325	|	|	...	|	1510	1558	|	1752f	|	1908	|	2023	|	2137f	2312
41	Ponte nelle Alpi d.	|	0726j	0827	0902j	0916	0918	0950j	...	1205	1334	1353	1403	1410	1523	1527j	...	1704j	1804	1853	*1923*	1931j	...	2150	2153j	...
	Belluno a.	|	|	|	|	...	|	|	...	|	|	*1425*	*1425*	|	1530	|	...	|	|	1901	...	|	...	2158	|	...
78	**Calalzo ▲** a.	0732	0805	0915	0942	...	1001	1039	...	1254	1422	...	...	1451	...	1610	...	1747	1850	...	...	2016	...	...	2235	...

km																									*E*	
																									1607	
		†	⚒				⚒	⚒	⚒	⚒	†														**L**	
0	**Calalzo ▲** d.	...	...	...	...	0641	...	0813	...	0954	1015	...	...	1229	1313	...	1503	...	1619	...	1719	1824	...	1929	2043	2105
	Belluno d.	...	...	...	0604	|	0737	|	...	|	|	1126	...	|	|	...	|	...	|	1734	|	|	1945	|	|	|
37	Ponte nelle Alpi d.	...	...	...	0613	0727	0748	0854	*0951*	1046j	1104j	1135	...	1315	1401	1418	1554	1554	1701	1744	1804	1905	1955	2019	|	2150
44	**Belluno** d.	0528	0528	0608	|	0736	|	0909	1018	|	|	|	...	1326	...	1426	|	1602	1711	|	1814	1913	|	2026	2132	|
75	Feltre d.	0601	0601	0643	|	0809	|	0945	1055	|	|	|	...	1400	...	1500	|	1635	1749	|	1847	1946	|	...	...	|
110	Montebelluna d.	0637	0644	0728	|	0847	|	1020	1129	|	|	|	...	1444	...	1546	|	1711	1828	|	1927	2026	|	...	...	|
127	Castelfranco Veneto d.	0650	0701	0746	|	0902	|	1034	1142	|	|	|	...	1504	...	1603	|	1727	1846	|	1944	2044	|	...	...	|
158	**Padova** a.	0723	0741	0820	|	0935	|	1110	1215	|	|	|	...	1538	...	1643	|	1800	1917	|	2017	2118	|	...	...	|
	Vittorio Veneto d.	...	...	...	0643	...	0819	...	...	1114	1132	1204	...	...	...	...	1626	...	...	1818	...	...	2022	...	...	2217
	Conegliano 601 a.	...	...	...	0657	...	0832	...	...	1128	1146	1219	...	...	...	...	1641	...	...	1831	...	...	2037	...	...	2231
	Venezia S. L. **601** a.	...	...	...	0754	...	0934	...	...	1223	1243	1317	...	...	...	...	...	...	...	1923	...	...	2135	...	...	2323

H – ⑤ June 29 - July 20; daily July 27 - Sept. 1 (from Roma): 🛏 1,2 cl. (Excelsior), 🛏 1,2 cl. (T2), 🛏 1,2 cl. and ▬ 2 cl. (4 berth) Roma Tiburtina - Belluno - Calalzo-Cortina.

L – ⑥ June 30 - July 21; daily July 28 - Sept. 2: 🛏 1,2 cl. (Excelsior), 🛏 1,2 cl. (T2), 🛏 1,2 cl. and ▬ 2 cl. (4 berth) Calalzo-Cortina - Belluno - Roma Tiburtina.

f – Arrive 14 – 16 minutes earlier.
j – Arrives 8 – 11 minutes earlier.
s – Stops to set down only.
u – Stops to pick up only.
z – July 1 - Aug. 31.
▲ – Full name of station is Calalzo-Pieve di Cadore-Cortina.

VAL GARDENA / GRÖDNERTAL and CORTINA 🚌 services — 604

ervice **445**	⚒		v				v		
an Candido / Innichen ....d.	...	0750	0850	1111	...	1411	1550	...	1811
obbiaco / Toblach ♣............d.	0659	0759	0859	1120	...	1420	1559	...	1820
ortina...............................a.	0749	0849	0949	1210	...	1510	1649	...	1910

Service **445**	⚒		v						v	
Cortina............................d.	0755	0855	0955	...	1320	...	1555	...	1655	1915
Dobbiaco / Toblach ♣.........d.	0840	0940	1040	...	1405	...	1640	...	1740	2000
San Candido / Innichen ....a.	0849	0949	1049	...	1414	...	1649	...	1749	...

♣ – Dobbiaco town. Services also call at Dobbiaco railway station en route between Dobbiaco town and Cortina (5 minutes from town stop). v – Dec. 26 - Mar. 28.

ervice **350**	⚒		⚒		⚒		⚒	⚒	⚒		
olzano / Bozen ♦ ......d.	0635	0740	0940	1040	1140	1220	1440	1555	1715	1745	1920
onte Gardena/Waidbruck .d.	0706	0811	1011	1111	1211	1251	1511	1626	1746	1816	1951
rtisei / St Ulrich ▲.......d.	0736	0841	1041	1141	1243	1321	1541	1656	1816	1846	2021
anta/St Cristina ▲ ......d.	0746	0851	1051	1151	1253	1331	1551	1706	1826	1856	2031
elva / Wolkenstein ▲ .d.	0755	0900	1100	1200	1302	1340	1600	1715	1835	1905	2040
lan ▲.........................a.	0758	0903	1103	1203	1305	1343	1603	1718	1838	1908	2043

Service **350**	⚒		⚒	⚒		⚒	⚒		⚒		
Plan ▲ ....d.	0608	0712	0747	0842	1002	1117	1217	1322	1432	1612	1750
Selva / Wolkenstein ▲......d.	0611	0715	0750	0845	1005	1120	1220	1325	1435	1615	1753
Santa/St Cristina ▲ ....d.	0620	0724	0759	0854	1014	1129	1229	1334	1444	1624	1802
Ortisei / St Ulrich ▲............d.	0632	0736	0811	0906	1026	1141	1241	1346	1456	1636	1814
Ponte Gardena/Waidbruck .....d.	0700	0804	0839	0934	1054	1209	1309	1414	1524	1704	1842
Bolzano / Bozen ♦ ....a.	0731	0835	0910	1005	1125	1240	1340	1445	1555	1735	1913

♦ – Bolzano/Bozen town. Services also call at Bolzano/Bozen railway station (2 minutes from town stop). ▲ – Extra buses run Ortisei/St Ulrich - Plan and v.v. in summer.

imings shown above are valid **September 10, 2007 - June 20, 2008**.
perator: Servizi Autobus Dolomiti, Via Conciapelli 60, 39100, Bolzano / Bozen. ✆: + 39 0471 450111 Fax: + 39 0471 970042.

🚌 service **30 Cortina - Calalzo**. 35 km. Journey time: 55 minutes. Timings are valid **September 10, 2007 - June 8, 2008**.

rom **Cortina Autostazione** (Bus Station): 0535⚒, 0625⚒, 0650⚒, 0700†, 0832⚒, 0900†, 0930⚒, 1115, 1220⚒, 1240⚒, 1315⚒, 1315†**z**, 1345†**z**, 1402, 1505, 1605⚒, 1705, 1755⚒, 1920, 1940⚒, 2010⚒**y**, 2010†**x**.

From **Calalzo Stazione** (FS rail station): 0625⚒, 0658⚒, 0658**z**, 0740⚒, 0740**w**, 0830, 0935⚒, 1015†, 1055⚒, 1215⚒, 1305, 1400⚒, 1455, 1620, 1755⚒, 1810†, 1900⚒, 2025.

– Dec. 23 - Feb. 24. **x** – Dec. 23 - Jan. 6. **y** – Dec. 22 - Mar. 31. **z** – Dec. 23 - Mar. 24.

perator: Dolomitibus, via Col Da Ren 14, 32100, Belluno, Italy. ✆ +39 00 437 217 111, fax +39 00 437 940 522.

VENEZIA - TRIESTE — 605

km			*ICN* **773**	*ICN* **777**						*IC* **611**					*EC* **61**					*CIS* **155**	*ICp* **707**	*EN* **239** *EN* **236**	*ES* **9479**	*EN* **241**	
			♦	♦	2 ⚒					T	†	⚒			Ⓡ🍷 ♦⊖					Ⓡ✕ ♦	Ⓡ R	Ⓡ M	Ⓡ✕ ♦	Ⓡ ♦⊖	2
	Roma Termini **620** ....d.	...	2250t	...	...	...	...	...	...	...	...	...	...	...	...	...	...	...	...	...	1457	...	1652	...	...
0	**Venezia Santa Lucia**.........d.	0010	0541	...	0737	...	0910	0946	1210	1224	1310	1310	1410	1510	1546	1610	1710	1810	1910	...	|	2028	|	2127	2247
9	**Venezia Mestre**..................a.	0020	0551	...	0748	...	0920	0956	1220	1234	1320	1320	1420	1520	1556	1620	1720	1820	1920	...	2026	2038	2110	2138	2258
9	**Venezia Mestre**..................d.	0022	0553	0705	0750	...	0922	0958	1222	1236	1322	1322	1422	1522	1558	1622	1722	1822	1922	1943	2040	2040	2125	2140	2302
42	Santa Dona di Piave-Jesolo d.	0046	0620	0727	0814	...	0946	1022	1246	1259	1346	1346	1446	1546	|	1646	1746	1846	1946	2005	2103	2100	|	2201	2335
69	Portogruaro-Caorle..............d.	0105	0640	0743	0833	...	1005	1041	1305	1315	1405	1406	1505	1605	1632	1705	1805	1905	2005	2022	2120	2118	2159	2218	2359
83	Latisana-Lignano.................d.	0116	0653	0754	0844	...	1016	1052	1316	1327	1416	1417	1516	1616	|	1716	1816	1916	2016	2034	2132	2130	|	2229	0010
101	San Giorgio di Nogaro.........d.	0128	0709	0806	0856	...	1028	1104	1328	|	1428	1436	1528	1628	|	1728	1828	1928	2028	|	|	|	|	|	0024
112	Cervignano-Aquileia-Grado..d.	0137	0720	0817	0906	...	1037	1112	1337	1346	1437	1447	1537	1637	|	1737	1837	1937	2037	2052	2150	2147	|	2246	0032
	Udine **606**.........................a.	|	|	|	|	...	|	|	|	|	|	|	|	|	|	|	|	|	|	|	|	2242	|	|	|
129	Monfalcone **606** ....d.	0150	0737	0832	0920	...	1050	1125	1350	1404	1450	1500	1550	1650	1705	1750	1850	1950	2050	2107	2206	...	2240	2259	0045
157	**Trieste Centrale 606**.........a.	0219	0802	0856	0943	...	1113	1148	1415	1430	1513	1523	1613	1716	...	1813	1913	2013	2113	2130	2230	...	2304	...	0108

		EN **240**		*CIS* **154**	*EN* **237** *EN* **238**		*ICp* **702**		*ES* **9466**			*EC* **60**				*IC* **626**						*ICN* **778**		*ICN* **772**
	2		Ⓡ ♦⊖		Ⓡ✕ ♦	Ⓡ M		Ⓡ R		Ⓡ✕ ♦			Ⓡ🍷 ♦⊖				T				Ⓑw		♦	2 Ⓐ	♦
rieste Centrale 606..........d.	...	0430	...	0535	0630	...	0647	0713	0835	0856	1047	1147	...	1247	1347	1447	1528	1547	1647	1747	1847	...	1947	2021	2125
onfalcone **606**...................d.	...	0453	0544	0558	0654	...	0710	0738	0858	0920	1110	1210	1257	1310	1410	1510	1554	1610	1710	1810	1910	...	2012	2046	2150
Udine **606** ....d.	...	|	|	|	|	0619	|	|	|	|	|	|	|	|	|	|	|	|	|	|	|	...	|	|	|
ervignano-Aquileia-Grado .. d.	...	0505	0556	0610	0708	0716	0723	0751	0911	|	1123	1223	|	1323	1423	1523	1606	1623	1723	1823	1923	...	2026	2100	2203
an Giorgio di Nogaro ....d.	...	0514	|	0619	|	|	0731	|	0920	|	1132	1232	|	1332	1432	1532	|	1632	1732	1832	1932	...	2035	2109	2212
atisana-Lignano ....d.	...	0526	0614	0631	0727	0737	0748	0810	0932	|	1144	1244	|	1344	1444	1544	1624	1644	1744	1844	1944	...	2049	2129	2226
ortogruaro-Caorle ....d.	0424	0536	0625	0641	0739	0750	0758	0821	0942	0959	1154	1254	1329	1354	1454	1554	1635	1654	1754	1854	1954	...	2102	2140	2238
anta Dona di Piave-Jesolo . d.	0447	0557	0642	0703	0755	0807	0821	0839	1001	|	1213	1313	|	1413	1513	1613	1653	1713	1813	1913	2013	...	2120	...	2255
enezia Mestre..................a.	0521	0622	0704	0728	0820	0833	0856	0906	1026	1035	1238	1338	1409	1438	1538	1638	1720	1738	1838	1938	2038	...	2147	...	2318
enezia Mestre..................d.	0523	0624	0706	0730	...	0835	0858	0921	1028	1050	1240	1340	1411	1440	1540	1640	1722	1740	1840	1940	2040	...	...	...	|
enezia Santa Lucia ....a.	0534	0635	0716	0740	...	0845	0909	|	1038	|	1250	1350	1421	1450	1550	1650	1732	1750	1850	1950	2050	...	...	...	2331
Roma Termini **620**............a.	...	...	...	...	...	...	...	1503	...	1508	...	...	...	...	...	...	...	...	...	...	...	...	...	...	0656t

♦ – NOTES (LISTED BY TRAIN NUMBER)

0/61 – CASANOVA – [12] and 🍷 Venezia - Villa Opicina - Ljubljana and v.v.
54 – [12] and ✕ Trieste - Milano - Zürich - Schaffhausen.
55 – [12] and ✕ Zürich - Milano - Trieste.
40 – VENEZIA – 🛏 1,2 cl., ▬ 2 cl. and [2] Budapest - Zagreb - Ljubljana - Venezia; 🛏 1,2 cl. (also [2] on ①②④⑤⑦) Bucureşti (**625**) - Vinţu de Jos (**354**) - Lökösháza (**735**) - Budapest - Venezia; ▬ 2 cl. Beograd (**412**) - Zagreb - Venezia. Conveys on dates in Table **97**: 🛏 1,2 cl. Moskva - Budapest - Venezia.
41 – VENEZIA – 🛏 1,2 cl., ▬ 2 cl. and [2] Venezia - Ljubljana - Zagreb - Budapest; 🛏 1,2 cl. (also [2] on ②③④⑥⑦) Venezia - Budapest (**734**) - Lökösháza (**355**) - Vinţu de Jos (**626**) - Bucureşti; ▬ 2 cl. Venezia - Zagreb (**413**) - Beograd. Conveys on dates in Table **97**: 🛏 1,2 cl. Venezia - Budapest - Moskva.
72 – MARCO POLO – 🛏 1,2 cl., ▬ 2 cl. (4 berth) and [12] Trieste - Venezia (**771**) - Napoli.
73 – MARCO POLO – 🛏 1,2 cl., ▬ 2 cl. (4 berth) and [12] Napoli (**774**) - Venezia - Trieste.
77 – TERGESTE – ▬ 2 cl. (4 berth) and [12] Lecce (**776**) - Venezia Mestre - Trieste.
78 – TERGESTE – ▬ 2 cl. (4 berth) and [12] Trieste - Venezia Mestre (**779**) - Lecce.

9466 – [12] and ✕ Trieste - Venezia Santa Lucia (**9467**) - Roma.
9479 – [12] and ✕ Roma (**9478**) - Venezia Santa Lucia - Trieste.
M – ALLEGRO DON GIOVANNI – 🛏 1,2 cl. (Excelsior), ▬ 2 cl. and [2] Venezia - Cervignano - Gorizia Centrale - Udine - Villach (**296/7**) - Salzburg (**262/3**) - Wien Westbf and v.v.; ▬ 2 cl. Venezia - Salzburg (**206/7**) - Praha and v.v. Supplement payable.
R – MIRAMARE – [12] Trieste - Venezia Mestre (**703/6**) - Napoli and v.v.
T – [12] Torino - Milano - Venezia Santa Lucia - Trieste and v.v.
t – Roma **Tiburtina**.
w – Not Aug. 14, Oct. 31, Dec. 7.
⊖ – Ⓡ and special fares payable for journeys to / from Slovenia.

UDINE - TRIESTE — 606

ost services 2nd class only

km		⚒	⚒	*EN* **237** ⓇA	z		⚒		V z	V	V ⚒	†	V q		r	†	⚒	V		†p	V	Ⓐ	†		V ⚒	⚒	Ⓐ
0	**Udine**........................d.	0517	0551	0619	0630	0657	0730	...	0735	0847	0932	1000	1147	...	1207	1240	1243	1347	...	1420	1547	1602	1633	...	1650	1705	1731
33	Gorizia Centrale ....d.	0548	0631	0641	0655	0735	|	...	0812	0912	1001	1037	1212	...	1234	1316	1316	1412	...	1456	1612	1634	1709	...	1715	1740	|
55	Monfalcone **605**........d.	0612	0656	...	0716	0800	0813	...	0838	0933	1024	1103	1233	...	1305	1340	1340	1433	...	1520	1633	1656	1734	...	1736	1804	1822
83	**Trieste Centrale 605** a.	0639	0722	...	0739	0829	0836	...	0908	0956	1049	1133	1256	...	1329	1406	1406	1456	...	1548	1656	1724	1802	...	1759	1835	1845

	V	⚒	†	V Ⓐ	Ⓐ	†	V	Ⓒpj		V	V	
dine.......................d.	1747	1810	1818	1850	1915	1915	1947	2021	...	2147	2353	...
orizia Centrale.........d.	1812	1848	1843	1915	1952	1954	2012	2054	...	2212	0028	...
onfalcone **605**.........d.	1833	1912	1904	1936	2017	2019	2033	2116	...	2233	0053	...
rieste Centrale 605 a.	1856	1940	1928	1959	2045	2047	2056	2142	...	2256	0121	...

	V ⚒	⚒	⚒		V	⚒		Ⓐ	V	†
Trieste Centrale 605.....d.	0502	0607	0636	...	0704	0735	...	0757	0904	0935
Monfalcone **605**..............d.	0527	0631	0704	...	0727	0804	...	0820	0927	1004
Gorizia Centrale ....d.	0550	|	0729	...	0747	0826	...	|	0947	1028
Udine ....a.	0624	0727	0803	...	0813	0857	...	0858	1013	1102

	V	V ⚒	†		⚒	V	⚒	⚒		V		Ⓒp	Ⓐ	V	Ⓐ	Ⓐ		V Ⓐ		V		⚒		V		*EN* **236** ⓇA	
rieste Centrale 605 d.	1104	1135	1204	...	1235	1304	1330	1411	1419	1504	...	1600	1635	1704	1730	1735	...	1804	1817	1904	...	1935	2035	2116	...	...	...
onfalcone **605**.........d.	1127	1203	1234	...	1304	1327	1401	1434	1447	1527	...	1629	1703	1727	1753	1804	...	1827	1848	1927	...	2004	2104	2139	...	...	...
orizia Centrale.........d.	1147	1227	1258	...	1329	1347	1426	|	1511	1547	...	1651	1725	1747	|	1828	...	1847	1911	1947	...	2026	2127	2159	...	2218	...
dine.......................a.	1213	1302	1337	...	1403	1413	1506	1516	1543	1613	...	1722	1757	1813	1834	1902	...	1913	1946	2013	...	2057	2200	2225	...	2242	...

– ALLEGRO DON GIOVANNI – For days of running and composition – see Table **605**.
– From / to Venezia (Table **601**).
j – Not Oct. 28.
p – Daily June 10 - Sept. 9.
q – ①⑥† (also Aug. 16, Nov. 2).
r – ②③④⑤ (not Aug. 16, Nov. 2, and holidays).
z – ⑥ (⚒ June 11- Sept. 8).

607 FERROVIE NORD MILANO services

BRESCIA - EDOLO : *103 km* Journey: approximately 120 – 150 minutes 2nd class only

From **Brescia** : ⚒ (not July 30 - Aug. 25): 0537, 0708, 0930, 1159, 1331, 1700, 1800 **b**, 1900 **b**.
† (daily July 30 - Aug. 25): 0609, 0809, 1009, 1409, 1709, 1909 **b**.

From **Edolo** : ⚒ (not July 30 - Aug. 25): 0524 **b**, 0610, 0641 **b**, 0949, 1220, 1324, 1632, 1842.
† (daily July 30 - Aug. 25): 0530 **b**, 0735, 0935, 1535, 1635, 1835.

MILANO - COMO NORD LAGO : *46 km* Journey: 52 – 65 minutes 2nd class only

From **Milano Nord Cadorna** : 0612⚒, 0642, 0712⚒, 0742, 0800Ⓐ, 0842, 0900, 0942, 1042, 1142, 1212⚒, 1242, 1312⚒, 1342, 1400†, 1412Ⓐ, 1442, 1512Ⓐ, 1542, 1612Ⓐ, 1642, 1700Ⓐ, 1712⚒, 1742, 1800Ⓐ, 1812, 1842, 1900Ⓐ, 1912⚒, 1942, 2012⚒, 2042, 2112.

From **Como Nord Lago** : 0546⚒, 0616, 0636Ⓐ, 0646⚒, 0716, 0736Ⓐ, 0746⚒, 0816, 0836⚒, 0916, 0936Ⓐ, 1016, 1116, 1216, 1246⚒, 1316, 1346⚒, 1416, 1446Ⓐ, 1516, 1546Ⓐ, 1616, 1646Ⓐ, 1716, 1746 **k**, 1816, 1836†, 1846⚒, 1916, 1946 **k**, 2016, 2116.

July 30 - Aug. 25 only services shown as daily will operate

MILANO - LAVENO : *72 km* Journey: 87 – 107 mins 2nd class only

From **Milano Nord Cadorna** : 0606⚒, 0636, 0706Ⓐ, 0750, 0850, 0936, 1036, 1136, 1206⚒, 1250, 1350, 1450Ⓐ, 1536, 1606Ⓐ, 1650, 1720Ⓐ, 1750, 1820Ⓐ, 1850, 1920Ⓐ, 2020Ⓐ.

From **Laveno Mombello** : 0537Ⓐ, 0607⚒, 0637, 0707⚒, 0737, 0807Ⓐ, 0837, 0937, 1037, 1137, 1237, 1307⚒, 1337, 1437, 1537, 1637, 1737, 1807Ⓐ, 1837, 1937, 2037.

Other services available by changing at Varese Nord, 1 hour from Milano, 30 mins from Laveno

July 30 - Aug. 25 only services shown as daily will operate

b – By 🚌 Breno - Edolo and v.v. For 🚌 Edolo - Tirano see Table **543**.
k – Not July 30 - Aug. 25.

Operator: Ferrovie Nord Milano, Piazzale Cadorna 14, 20123 Milano.
✆ + 39 02 20 222, fax: + 39 02 85 11 708.

608 MILANO local services

MILANO - BERGAMO : *43 km (56 km* via Treviglio Ovest) Some services 2nd class only

	n	⚒n	⚒	Ⓐ			⚒	†				⚒	†	Ⓐ			Ⓐ	⚒		Ⓐ		Ⓑ					
Milano Centrale .... d.	...	...	...	...	0720	...	0840	...	1115	1155	1220	1320	1325	...	1520	1620	...	...	1720	...	1820	...	1920	...	2125	2225	2337
Milano Porta Garibaldi ... d.	0450	0523	0620	0708	|	0814	|	...	|	|	|	|	|	1415	|	|	1618	...	|	1717	|	1815	|	...	|	|	|
Milano Lambrate .... d.	0459	|	|	|	0727	0824	0847	1016	1122	|	1227	1327	1332	|	1527	1627	|	1658	1727	|	1826	|	1927	2031	2132	|	2344
Bergamo .... a.	0548	0628	0735	0819	0821	0920	0933	1101	1215	1242	1320	1420	1423	1520	1610	1720	1720	1742	1806	1823	1907	1920	2011	2123	2222	2316	0033

		⚒	Ⓐk		⚒	⚒	⚒		⚒	⚒		⚒				Ⓐk											
Bergamo .... d.	0556	0603	0613	0627	0652	0658	0719	0725	0749	0811	0835	0926	0944	1053	...	1226	1232	1332	1438	1538	1635	1747	1835	1935	2034	2133	2311
Milano Lambrate .... a.	|	0653	|	0720	|	0741	|	0806	0834	0853	0926	|	1031	|	...	|	1327	1426	1528	1628	1728	1832	1924	2023	2127	2218	2359
Milano Porta Garibaldi ... a.	|	|	0715	0729	0754	|	0818	|	|	|	...	1025	|	|	...	1323	|	|	|	|	|	|	...	|	|	|	|
Milano Centrale .... a.	0650	0700	...	...	...	0750	...	0815	0845	0900	...	...	1040	1145	...	...	1335	1435	1535	1635	1735	1840	...	2032	2135	2225	0007

MILANO - LUINO : *91 km* 2nd class only

	⚒	⚒	⑥	⚒	⚒	⚒	⚒	⚒	⚒	⚒	⚒
Milano P G .... d.	0510	0656	*0830*	*1230*	*1430*	*1530*	*1630*	*1730*	1858	*1930*	*2204*v
Gallarate **590** ...... § d.	0600	0735	0913	1313	1513	1613	1713	1813	1937	2013	2256
Laveno Mombello § d.	0650	0820	0952	1349	1549	1649	1749	1849	2015	2053	2328
Luino 592 .... § a.	0706	0835	1013	1408	1608	1708	1808	1908	2033	2108	2347

	⚒	⚒	⚒	⑥	⚒	⚒	⚒	⚒	⚒	⚒	⚒
Luino 592 .... § d.	0632	0723	0852	1252	1352	1452	1552	1652	1752	1952	2052
Laveno Mombello § d.	0649	0738	0912	1312	1412	1512	1612	1712	1812	2016	2112
Gallarate **590** ...... § d.	0728	0805	0947	1347	1447	1547	1647	1747	1847	2047	2147
Milano P G .... a.	0805	0843	*1030*	*1430*	*1530*	*1630*	*1730*	*1830*	*1930*	*2130*	*2253*v

§ – Service on † Gallarate - Luino: From **Gallarate** 0655, 0913, 1113, 1313, 1513, 1713, 1813, 2013, 2256. From **Luino** 0552, 0752, 1000, 1152, 1352, 1552, 1652, 1752, 2052, 2152.

MILANO - MANTOVA :

km				n			⚒				Ⓑ	
0	**Milano C** .... d.	0615	0815	1013**p**	1215	1415	1615	1720	1845	2015	2018**p**	...
60	Codogno ...... d.	0703	0904	1104	1304	1504	1704	1804	1926	2100	2146	...
88	Cremona ..... d.	0735	0926	1126	1326	1524	1726	1823	1949	2120	2218	...
151	**Mantova** ..... a.	0830	1017	1217	1413	1617	1814	1917	2044	2208	...	...

			⚒			⚒		n			2†
Mantova .... d.	0525	0612	0647	0943	1143	1330	1437	1543	1737	1943	1953
Cremona .... d.	0620	0658	0734	1030	1230	1500	1525	1630	1835	2030	2058
Codogno .... a.	0641	0719	0754	1053	1254	1536	1546	1653	1855	2054	2132
Milano Centrale .... a.	0745	0810	0840	1145	1345	*1640*	1640	1748**p**	1945	2145	*2245*

NOTES – SEE FOOT OF PAGE

609 Local services in NORTHERN and CENTRAL ITALY

2nd class only

ALESSANDRIA - ACQUI TERME : *34 km* Journey 28 – 38 minutes

From **Alessandria** : 0624⚒, 0649†, 0700⚒, 0911, 1136, 1243, 1337⚒, 1609†, 1643Ⓐ, 1741, 1937.

From **Acqui Terme** : 0621⚒, 0703, 0738⚒, 0946, 1319, 1510, 1543⚒, 1727†, 1818⚒, 1950†.

BOLOGNA - PORRETTA TERME : *59 km* Journey 60 – 72 minutes

From **Bologna Centrale** : 0551⚒, 0701, 0801⚒, 0901, 1001⚒, 1101, 1201, 1301, 1401, 1501, 1601, 1701, 1735⚒, 1801, 1835Ⓐ, 1901, 2001, 2101.

From **Porretta Terme** : 0500⚒, 0552, 0607⚒, 0640, 0717, 0820, 0920⚒, 1020, 1120⚒, 1220, 1320, 1420, 1520, 1620, 1720, 1820, 1920, 2020, 2043Ⓐ.

CAMPIGLIA - PIOMBINO : *16 km* Journey 22 – 30 minutes

From **Campiglia Marittima** : 0603⚒, 0710⚒, 1016⑥, 1330Ⓐ, 1339⑥**z**, 1533, 1647, 1737⑥**z**, 1804.

From **Piombino Marittima** : 0638⚒, 0746⚒, 0925, 1053⑥, 1520⚒, 1609, 1725, 1841.

GENOVA - ACQUI TERME : *58 km* Journey 65 – 81 minutes

From **Genova Piazza Principe** :
⚒: 0612, 0714, 0902, 1021Ⓐ, 1222, 1322, 1422, 1545, 1712Ⓐ, 1741, 1812Ⓐ, 1922, 2044.
†: 0612, 0737, 0907, 1037, 1206, 1342, 1437, 1607, 1741, 1922, 2044.

From **Acqui Terme** :
⚒: 0520, 0612, 0703, 0741, 0853Ⓐ, 1027, 1217, 1316, 1415, 1537, 1717, 1819, 2047.
†: 0602, 0738, 0900, 1036, 1201, 1334, 1601, 1750, 1917, 2047.

PORRETTA TERME - PISTOIA : *40 km* Journey 48 – 55 minutes

From **Porretta Terme** : 0540⚒, 0648⚒, 0720, 0815, 0921⚒, 1021, 1321, 1521, 1728, 1916.

From **Pistoia** : 0515⚒, 0614, 0705†, 0712⚒, 0821⚒, 0921, 1221, 1317, 1421, 1621, 1721, 1926.

ROVIGO - CHIOGGIA : *57 km*

	⚒	†		⚒	†	⚒	†	⚒	†	⚒			⚒
Rovigo ...... d.	0630	0635	...	0815	0917	1017	1217	1250	1455	1617	1817	...	1943
Adria .... d.	0701	0703	...	0846	0944	1044	1245	1323	1522	1648	1843	...	2015
Chioggia ... a.	0740	0737	...	0922	1021	1120	1321	1356	1554	1724	1920	...	2050

	⚒	⚒	†	⚒	⚒	†	⚒	†	⚒	†	⚒		⚒
Chioggia ... d.	0600	0650	0744	0808	0938	1030	1245	1337	1437	1615	1737	1937	2057
Adria .... d.	0635	0725	0819	0845	1013	1107	1322	1413	1514	1652	1813	2013	2126
Rovigo ...... a.	0701	0751	0846	0910	1045	1133	1347	1439	1540	1718	1845	2043	2145

SANTHIÀ - ARONA : *65 km* Journey 60 – 73 minutes

From **Santhià** : 0640⚒, 0840, 0908†, 1240⚒, 1352, 1443Ⓐ, 1744, 1840.

From **Arona** : 0655, 1120†, 1155⚒, 1347⚒, 1511, 1730, 1810Ⓐ, 1845†, 1908†, 2010.

Trains call at Borgomanero approximately 45 mins from Santhia and 15 mins from Arona.

SANTHIÀ - BIELLA SAN PAOLO : *27 km* Journey 20 – 35 minutes

From **Santhià** : 0637⚒, 0737⚒, 0755†, 0837⚒, 0900†, 0937†, 0951⚒, 1152⚒, 1237, 1355⚒, 1437, 1552⚒, 1637⚒, 1657†, 1737⚒, 1837†, 1846⚒, 1925Ⓐ, 1958, 2050, 2141 **z**.

From **Biella** : 0548, 0624⚒, 0711Ⓐ, 0723⚒, 0750†, 0802⚒, 0852†, 0901⚒, 0944⚒, 1145, 1301⚒, 1350⚒, 1353†, 1500⚒, 1545⚒, 1653†, 1702⚒, 1748†, 1800⚒, 1832⚒, 1951, 2036.

SIENA - CHIUSI-CHIANCIANO TERME : *89 km* Journey 71 – 94 minutes

From **Siena** : 0557⚒, 0602†, 0804†, 0806⚒, 1004†, 1217⚒, 1329⚒, 1357⚒, 1404†, 1448, 1558⚒, 1604†, 1659⚒, 1743⚒, 1804†, 1815⚒, 1927⚒, 2004†, 2019⚒.

From **Chiusi** : 0431⚒, 0607⚒, 0626†, 0709⚒, 0834†, 0914⚒, 1034†, 1040⚒, 1234†, 1352⚒, 1512⚒, 1634†, 1709⚒, 1834†, 1845⚒, 1930⚒, 2034†, 2040⚒, 2134†, 2140⚒.

SIENA - GROSSETO : *102 km* Journey 77 – 107 minutes

From **Siena** : 0602⚒, 0753, 1218, 1330, 1543, 1744, 1839, 1943.

From **Grosseto** : 0500, 0620⚒, 0722, 0940, 1336†, 1340⚒, 1547⚒, 1645, 1758, 1953.

TRENTO - VENEZIA :

km											⚒
0	**Trento** .... d.	0705	0805	*1005*d	*1105*	*1205*d	*1305*	*1505*	1705	1905	...
31	Levico Terme .... d.	0754	0854	*1054*d	*1154*	*1254*d	*1354*	*1554*	1754	1954	...
44	Borgo Valsugana Centro .. d.	0807	0907	*1107*d	*1207*	*1307*d	*1407*	*1607*	1807	2007	...
97	Bassano del Grappa .... d.	0903	1010	1237	1317	1422	1545	1742	1908	2106	2115
116	Castelfranco Veneto .... d.	0923	1037	1303	1342	1443	1607	1809	1945	...	2137
148	Venezia Mestre .... a.	1004	1120	1343	1420	1522	1701	1844	2043	...	2222
157	**Venezia Santa Lucia** ...... a.	1015	1133	1356	1433	1533	1714	1856	2056	...	2233

			†	⚒		⚒	†			
Venezia Santa Lucia ...... d.	0601	0741	0844	*0844*n	*1144*	*1345*	*1413*	1544	1652	1945
Venezia Mestre .... d.	0614	0754	0857	*0857*n	*1157*	*1357*	*1426*	1557	1705	1958
Castelfranco Veneto .... d.	0656	0835	0946	*0946*n	*1245*	*1444*	*1514*	1650	1752	2043
Bassano del Grappa .... d.	0718	0915	1015	1115	1315	1515	1615	1715	1815	2108
Borgo Valsugana Centro .. d.	0827	1027	1127	1225	1425	1627	1725	1825	1926	2209
Levico Terme .... d.	0843	1043	1143	1243	1443	1643	1744	1844	1943	2223
Trento .... a.	0927	1127	1227	1327	1527	1727	1827	1927	2027	2303

VERONA PORTA NUOVA - MANTOVA - MODENA :

km		S	⚒		⚒	A	⚒n		⚒				
0	**Verona P N** d.	0529	0637	0902	0936	1131	1227	1355	1548	1700	1745	1854	2003
37	Mantova .... d.	0600	0722	0937	1017	1203	1330	1446	1632	1746	1838	1943	2049
56	Suzzara ..... d.	|	0748	0954	1035	|	1358	1505	1652	1810	1856	2003	2118
98	**Modena** .... a.	0646	0830	1025	1112	1243	1445	1546	1741	1857	1939	2048	2156

	⚒		⚒n	⚒			⚒				A		S
Modena ..... d.	0558	0702	0814	0911	1329	1422	1520	1631	1725	1835d	2022	2031	2305
Suzzara ..... d.	0656	0747	0901	0955	1423	1506	1600	1715	1811	1916d	|	2117	|
Mantova .... d.	0728	0827	0923	1010	1446	1529	1631	1734	1841	1938	2112	2138	2352
Verona P N . a.	0821	0914	1012	...	1533	1601	1712	*1841*	1932	2024	2140	*2313*	0022

NOTES FOR TABLES 608 / 9

A – ADIGE – 🚃 Bolzano - Verona - Bologna - Lecce and v.v.
S – SCALIGERO – 🚃 Verona - Roma and v.v. Ⓡ.

d – ⚒ only.
k – Not July 28 - Aug. 26.
n – Not July 29 - Aug. 26.
p – Milano **Porta Garibaldi**.

v – Milano Porta Garibaldi **Passante**.
z – Not Dec. 8.

TORINO and MILANO - GENOVA - PISA - ROMA 610

km		2	ICp 501	2	ES 9305	2	ICp 503	2		ICp 645	2	2	2	EC 141	IC 515	2	2	1763	2201	ICp 517	2	2	2	ICp 1533	ICp 647	2
			[R]		[R] 🍷		[R]			[R]				[R] 🍷						[R]				[R]	[R]	
			⚒				♦					†A	⚒	♦	♦			♦	♦	Ⓐ	⚒	†		©	Ⓐ	A
0	**Torino Porta Nuova 619** .. d.	...	...	...	...	...	...	...	...	...	0520	...	...	...	...	...	...	...	...	0635	...	...	0720	...	...	...
56	Asti **619** d.	...	...	...	...	...	...	...	...	...	0606	...	...	...	...	...	...	...	...	0713	...	...	0806	...	...	...
91	Alessandria **619** d.	...	...	...	...	...	...	...	...	...	0628	...	...	...	...	...	...	...	...	0732	...	...	0833	...	...	...
12	Novi Ligure d.	...	...	...	...	...	...	...	...	...	0650	...	...	...	...	...	...	...	...	0745	...	...	0850	...	...	...
	Milano Centrale d.	...	...	...	...	...	...	...	...	0610	|	0625	0625	0710	...	...	...	...	...	|	0715	0715	|	0810	0810	0820
	Pavia d.	...	...	...	...	...	...	...	...	0635	|	0700	0700	0735	...	...	...	...	...	|	0751	0751	|	0835	0835	0855
	Voghera **619** d.	...	...	...	...	...	...	...	...	|	|	0716	0716	0751	...	...	...	...	...	|	0811	0811	|	0851	0851	0911
	Tortona **619** d.	...	...	...	...	...	...	...	...	0700	|	0729	0729	|	...	...	...	...	...	|	0824	0824	|	|	|	0923
66	**Genova Piazza Principe 619** a.	...	...	...	...	...	...	...	...	0744	0749	0822	0836	0842	...	...	...	...	...	0830	0908	0910	0943	0942	0942	1014
66	**Genova Piazza Principe** d.	...	...	...	0548	0605	0637	0711	...	0747	0752	...	|	...	0852	...	...	...	...	...	0911	0913	...	0947	0947	...
69	Genova Brignole d.	...	...	...	0557	0614	0645	0720	...	0758	0803	...	0847	...	0900	...	...	...	...	...	0920	0922	...	0958	0958	...
94	Santa Margherita-Portofino d.	...	...	...	|	0647	|	0757	...	0822	0834	...	...	...	|	...	...	...	...	...	0957	1000	...	1022	1030	...
96	Rapallo d.	...	...	...	0619	0652	0711	0801	...	0827	0838	...	...	...	0923	...	...	...	...	...	1002	1005	...	1027	1036	...
05	Chiavari d.	...	...	...	0627	0701	0721	0809	...	0836	0846	...	...	...	0932	...	...	...	...	...	1011	1014	...	1036	1045	...
12	Sestri-Levante d.	...	0515	...	|	0710	0729	0816	...	0844	0856	...	...	...	|	...	...	...	...	...	1025	1027	...	1044	1053	...
35	Levanto d.	...	|	...	|	0730	|	0837	...	0858	0924	...	...	...	|	...	...	...	...	...	1054	1053	...	1058	1111	...
49	Riomaggiore d.	...	|	...	|	|	|	0856	...	|	0949	...	...	...	|	...	...	...	...	...	1121	1123	...	|	|	...
56	**La Spezia Centrale** d.	...	0546	...	0702	0749	0759	0908	...	0919	1002	...	...	...	1006	...	...	...	...	...	1132	1132	...	1119	1138	...
72	Sarzana d.	...	0559	...	|	▬	|	0921	...	|	1016	...	...	...	|	←	...	1057	1057	...	...	...	...	|	|	...
82	Carrara-Avenza d.	...	0608	...	|	...	|	0929	...	|	1023	...	...	...	|	1024	...	1104	1105	...	...	...	...	1137	|	...
89	Massa Centro d.	...	0616	...	0724	...	0822	0936	...	0947	→	...	...	...	|	1030	...	1111	1112	...	...	...	...	1145	1205	...
10	Viareggio d.	...	0630	...	0737	...	0836	0956	...	1002	...	...	...	...	1038	1050	...	1130	1136	...	...	...	...	1206	1223	...
31	**Pisa Centrale** d.	0545	0649	0740	0754	...	0855	1015	...	1021	...	...	...	...	1100	1121j	1145	1147	1201	...	...	...	...	1224	1248	...
	Firenze SMN **614** a.	|	|	|	|	...	|	...	...	|	...	...	...	...	|	|	|	...	...	...	...	...	...	|	|	...
51	**Livorno Centrale** d.	0604	0706	0759	0810	...	0911	...	...	1038	...	...	...	...	1116	1137j	1204	...	...	...	...	...	...	1242	1305	...
74	Rosignano d.	0621	|	0816	|	...	|	...	...	...	...	...	...	...	|	...	1221	...	...	...	...	...	...	|	|	...
85	Cecina d.	0630	0729	0825	|	...	0934	...	...	...	...	...	...	...	1138	...	1230	...	...	...	...	...	...	1306	1339	...
20	Campiglia Marittima d.	0653	0748	0849	|	←	0953	...	...	...	...	...	...	...	|	...	1253	...	...	...	...	...	...	1325	1400	...
37	Follonica d.	0704	0759	0859	|	0900	|	...	...	...	...	...	...	...	|	...	1304	...	...	...	...	...	...	1336	1411	...
79	Grosseto d.	0732	0824	→	0909	0932	1028	...	...	...	...	...	...	...	1228	...	1332	...	...	...	...	...	...	1400	1433	...
17	Orbetello d.	0754	0842	...	|	0954	|	...	...	...	...	...	...	...	|	...	1354	...	...	...	...	...	...	...	...	...
56	Tarquinia d.	0827	|	...	|	1027	|	...	...	...	...	...	...	...	|	...	1427	...	...	...	...	...	...	...	...	...
86	**Civitavecchia ▲** d.	0841	0922	...	1006	1041	1122	...	...	...	...	...	...	...	1322	...	1441	...	...	...	...	...	...	...	...	...
95	Santa Marinella d.	0848	|	...	|	1048	|	...	...	...	...	...	...	...	|	...	1448	...	...	...	...	...	...	...	...	...
17	Ladispoli-Cerveteri d.	0904	|	...	|	1104	|	...	...	...	...	...	...	...	|	...	1504	...	...	...	...	...	...	...	...	...
60	**Roma Ostiense** a.	0937	1000	...	1043	1137	1200	...	...	...	...	...	...	...	1400	...	1537	...	...	...	...	...	...	...	...	...
67	**Roma Termini** a.	0950	1014	...	1057	1150	1214	...	...	...	...	...	...	...	1414	...	1550	...	...	...	...	...	...	...	...	...
	Napoli Centrale **640** a.	...	1236	...	...	...	1436	...	...	...	...	...	...	...	...	...	...	...	...	...	...	...	...	...	...	...

km		2	2	IC 519	ICp 649	EC 143	ICp 523	2	ICp 653	ICp 525	2	2	2	ICp 527	ICp 609	ICp 655	2	ICp 529	EC 159	IC 533	2	EC 175	ICp 537	2	2	2
				🍴	[R]	[R] 🍷	[R] 🍴		[R]	[R]				[R] 🍴	[R]	[R]		[R]	[R] 🍷			[R] 🍴	[R]			
				♦	♦	♦						†	⚒	♦	♦				♦			♦			©A	Ⓐ
	Torino Porta Nuova 619 .. d.	0820	...	0905	...	...	1105	1120	...	1205	...	...	...	1305	...	...	1320	1405	...	1505	1520	...	1605	...	...	...
	Asti **619** d.	0906	...	0943	...	...	1143	1206	...	1243	...	...	...	1343	...	...	1406	1443	...	1543	1606	...	1643	...	...	...
	Alessandria **619** d.	0930	...	1002	...	...	1202	1233	...	1303	...	...	...	1403	...	...	1433	1503	...	1602	1633	...	1703	...	...	...
	Novi Ligure d.	0943	...	|	...	...	|	1250	...	1315	...	...	...	|	...	...	1450	1515	...	|	1650	...	1715	...	...	...
0	**Milano Centrale** d.	|	0845	|	0910	1110	|	|	1210	|	...	1225	1225	|	1310	1410	|	|	1510	|	|	1600	|	...	1620	1625
39	Pavia d.	|	0910	|	0935	1135	|	|	1235	|	...	1300	1300	|	1335	1435	|	|	1535	|	|	1635	|	...	1655	1700
65	Voghera **619** d.	|	0931	|	|	1151	|	|	|	|	...	1316	1316	|	1351	1451	|	|	1551	|	|	1651	|	...	1711	1716
82	Tortona **619** d.	|	...	|	1000	|	|	|	1300	|	...	1328	1328	|	|	|	|	|	|	|	|	|	|	...	1725	1729
54	**Genova Piazza Principe 619** a.	1032	...	1049	1042	1242	1249	1334	1342	1353	...	1418	1434	1449	1442	1542	1536	1553	1642	1649	1734	1742	1753	...	1816	1818
	Genova Piazza Principe d.	|	...	1052	▬	...	1252	|	1347	1357	1411	|	|	1452	...	1547	1539	1557	...	1652	|	1748	|	1811	...	|
	Genova Brignole d.	1041	...	1100	...	...	1300	1342	1358	1403	1420	1427	1442	1500	...	1558	1548	1603	...	1700	1742	1758	1808	1820	...	1829
	Santa Margherita-Portofino d.	...	...	|	...	...	|	...	1422	▬	1456	...	...	|	...	|	1626	...	...	|	▬	1822	...	1849	...	...
	Rapallo d.	...	...	1123	...	...	|	...	1427	...	1500	...	...	1523	...	1627	1630	...	...	|	...	1827	...	1853	...	...
	Chiavari d.	...	...	|	...	...	|	...	1436	...	1508	...	...	1532	...	1636	1638	...	...	1729	...	1836	...	1901	...	...
	Sestri-Levante d.	...	...	|	...	...	1334	...	1444	...	1518	...	...	|	...	1644	1655	...	...	|	...	1844	...	1911	...	...
	Levanto d.	...	...	|	...	...	|	...	1458	...	1538	...	...	|	...	1658	1724	...	...	|	...	1858	...	1931	...	...
	Riomaggiore d.	...	...	|	...	...	|	...	|	...	1552	...	...	|	...	|	1751	...	...	|	...	|	...	1953	...	...
	La Spezia Centrale d.	...	...	1206	...	...	1406	...	1518	...	1602	...	...	1606	...	1718	1802	...	...	1806	...	1919	...	2002	...	...
	Sarzana d.	...	...	|	...	...	|	...	...	...	1616	...	...	|	...	▬	1816	...	...	|	...	|	...	2017	...	...
	Carrara-Avenza d.	...	...	|	...	...	1423	...	...	...	1624	...	...	|	...	...	1824	...	...	|	...	1938	...	2025	...	...
	Massa Centro d.	...	...	1226	...	...	|	...	...	...	1630	...	...	1626	...	...	1830	...	...	1826	...	|	...	2033	...	...
	Viareggio d.	...	...	1240	...	...	1440	...	...	...	1652	...	...	|	...	...	1852	...	...	1840	...	1956	...	2057	...	...
	Pisa Centrale d.	...	...	1300	1345	...	1500	...	...	1545	1722	...	...	1700	...	1745	1919	...	...	1900	1956	2015	...	2122	...	...
	Firenze SMN **614** a.	...	...	|	|	...	|	...	...	|	|	...	...	|	...	|	...	...	...	|	|	|	...	|	...	...
	Livorno Centrale d.	...	...	1316	1404	...	1516	...	...	1604	1738	...	...	1716	...	1804	...	...	...	1916	2014	2030	...	2140	...	...
	Rosignano d.	...	...	|	1421	...	|	...	...	1621	...	...	...	|	...	1821	...	...	...	|	2031	...	...	...	...	...
	Cecina d.	...	...	|	1430	...	|	...	...	1630	...	...	...	|	...	1830	...	...	...	1939	2040	...	...	...	...	...
	Campiglia Marittima d.	...	...	|	1453	...	1553	...	...	1653	...	...	...	|	...	1853	...	...	...	1956	2103	...	...	...	...	...
	Follonica d.	...	...	1403	1504	...	|	...	...	1704	...	...	...	1803	...	1904	...	...	...	2007	2114	...	...	...	...	...
	Grosseto d.	...	...	1428	1532	...	1628	...	...	1732	...	...	...	1828	...	1932	...	...	...	2034	2142	...	...	...	...	...
	Orbetello d.	...	...	|	1554	...	|	...	...	1754	...	...	...	|	...	1954	...	...	...	2052	2204	...	...	...	...	...
	Tarquinia d.	...	...	|	1627	...	|	...	...	1827	...	...	...	|	...	2027	...	...	...	|	2236	...	...	...	...	...
	Civitavecchia ▲ d.	...	...	1522	1641	...	1722	...	...	1841	...	...	...	1922	...	2041	...	...	...	2131	2250	...	...	...	...	...
	Santa Marinella d.	...	...	|	1648	...	|	...	...	1848	...	...	...	|	...	2048	...	...	...	|	2257	...	...	...	...	...
	Ladispoli-Cerveteri d.	...	...	|	1704	...	|	...	...	1904	...	...	...	|	...	2104	...	...	...	|	2312	...	...	...	...	...
	Roma Ostiense a.	...	...	1600	1737	...	1800	...	...	1937	...	...	...	2001	...	2137	...	...	...	2214	2339	...	...	...	...	...
	Roma Termini a.	...	...	1614	1750	...	1814	...	...	1950	...	...	...	2014	...	2150	...	...	...	2228	2358t	...	...	...	...	...
	Napoli Centrale **640** a.	...	...	...	...	...	2036	...	...	...	...	...	...	2236	...	...	...	...	...	...	...	...	...	...	...	...

– **NOTES** (LISTED BY TRAIN NUMBER)

41 – LIGURE – 🚃12 and 🍷 Milano - Genova (**142**) - Nice.
43 – SANREMO – 🚃12 and 🍷 Milano - Genova (**144**) - Nice.
59 – RIVIERA DEI FIORI – 🚃12 and 🍷 Milano - Genova (**160**) - Nice.
75 – CISALPINO CINQUE TERRE – 🚃12 and 🍴 Schaffhausen - Zürich - Chiasso - Milano - Livorno.
3 – BOCCANEGRA – 🚃12 Savona - Napoli.
15 – TIRRENO – 🚃12 Ventimiglia - Genova - Roma.
19 – CARIGNANO – 🚃12 and 🍴 Torino - Roma. On ⑤ July 13 - Aug. 10 runs as train **1519**.
27 – CAPODIMONTE – 🚃12 Torino - Salerno.
09 – ANDREA DORIA – 🚃12 Milano - Genova (**610**) - Ventimiglia.
49 – MAMELI – 🚃12 Milano - Genova (**650**) - Ventimiglia. Train numbers **1535/6** on ©.
763 – FRECCIA DELLA VERSILIA – †: 🚃12 Bergamo - Fidenza - Aulla - Pisa.
201 – FRECCIA DELLA VERSILIA – ⚒: 🚃12 Bergamo - Fidenza - Aulla - Pisa.

A – To Albenga.
j – 8–10 minutes later on ⚒.
t – Roma **Tiburtina**.
▲ – 🚌 service available from / to Civitavecchia Marittima – see panel on page 302.

610 TORINO and MILANO - GENOVA - PISA - ROMA

	E	ICp	IC				ICp	ICp					ICp	IC		ICp	ICp		ICN	ICp		E			ICN
	1941	**659**	**539**				**661**	**541**					**663**	**543**		**665**	**545**		**761**	**667**		**809**			**767**
		R		2	2	2	R	R		2	2	2	R		2	R	R	2		R	2		2	2	
	Z	♦	♦							©A	Ⓐ	⑤		Ⓑ				V	Z	V		Z			♦
Torino Porta Nuova 619 d.	1655	...	1705	...	...	1720	...	1805	...	...	...	...	...	1905	1920	...	2005	...	2050	...	2120	2155	...	2225	230
Asti **619** d.	1730	...	1743	...	...	1806	...	1843	...	...	...	...	...	1943	2006	...	2043	...	2126	...	2206	2237	...	2317	234
Alessandria **619** d.	1750	...	1802	...	...	1831	...	1903	...	...	...	...	...	2002	2033	...	2103	...	2147	...	2230	2300	...	2339	000
Novi Ligure d.	|	...	|	...	...	1847	...	1915	...	...	...	...	...	|	2049	...	2115	...	2200	...	2247	|	...	2356	|
Milano Centrale d.	|	1700	|	...	1705	|	1810	|	...	1825	1825	1853g	1905	|	|	2010	|	2020	|	2110	|	|	2225	|	|
Pavia d.	|	1736	|	...	|	|	1835	|	...	1902	1904	|	1935	|	|	2035	|	2055	|	2135	|	|	2300	|	|
Voghera **619** d.	|	1751	|	...	|	|	1851	|	...	1918	1923	|	1951	|	|	2055	|	2111	|	2151	|	|	2316	|	|
Tortona **619** d.	|	|	|	...	|	|	1903	|	...	1930	1944	|	|	|	|	|	|	2123	|	|	|	|	2329	|	|
Genova Piazza Principe 619 a.	1837	1842	1849	...	|	1934	1945	1953	...	2025	2036	|	2042	2049	2135	2146	2154	2213	2237	2242	2333	2350	0020	0046	005
Genova Piazza Principe d.	1840	...	1852	1903	|	1937	1948	1957	...	...	|	|	2045	2052	|	2149	2157	...	2240	...	|	0001	|	|	022
Genova Brignole d.	1849	...	1900	1920	|	1948	1958	2003	...	...	2045	|	2051	2100	2143	2158	2203	...	2249	...	2341	0011	0028	0054	|
Santa Margherita-Portofino d.	|	...	|	1956	|	2031	2022	...	...	...	...	|	...	|	...	2218	...	...	|	...	...	|	...	...	|
Rapallo d.	|	...	1923	2000	w	2035	2027	...	...	...	...	w	...	2123	...	2223	...	...	|	...	...	0037	...	...	|
Chiavari d.	|	...	1932	2008	|	2045	2036	...	...	...	...	|	...	2133	...	2232	...	...	|	...	...	0047	...	...	|
Sestri-Levante d.	|	...	|	2018	|	2054	2044	...	...	...	...	|	...	2141	...	2243	...	...	|	...	...	|	...	...	|
Levanto d.	|	...	|	2038	|	2126	2058	...	...	...	...	|	...	|	...	2257	...	...	|	...	...	|	...	...	|
Riomaggiore d.	|	...	|	2052	|	2156	|	...	...	...	...	|	...	|	...	|	...	...	|	...	...	|	...	...	|
La Spezia Centrale d.	1955	...	2006	2100	|	2204	2119	...	...	...	...	|	...	2212	...	2318	...	...	2358	...	...	0127	...	...	|
Sarzana d.	|	...	|	...	2044	...	|	...	...	...	...	2241	...	2225	...	...	...	...	|	...	...	|	...	...	|
Carrara-Avenza d.	|	...	|	...	2052	...	|	...	...	...	...	2249	...	2234	...	...	...	...	|	...	...	|	...	...	|
Massa Centro d.	|	...	|	...	2059	...	2141	...	...	...	...	2257	...	2241	...	...	...	...	|	...	...	|	...	...	|
Viareggio d.	|	...	2038	...	2119	...	2156	...	...	...	...	2318	...	2253	...	...	...	...	0030	...	...	|	...	...	|
Pisa Centrale d.	2047	...	2056	...	2138	...	2215	...	...	...	...	2337	...	2313	...	...	...	...	0050	...	...	0219	...	...	053
Firenze SMN **614** a.	|	...	2200	...	|	...	|	...	...	...	...	|	...	|	...	...	...	...	|	...	...	|	...	...	0653
Livorno Centrale d.	2104	...	...	...	2153	...	2230	...	...	...	...	2353	...	2329	...	...	...	...	0107	...	...	0240	...	...	|
Rosignano d.	|	...	...	...	...	...	...	...	...	...	...	...	...	...	...	...	...	...	|	...	...	|	...	...	|
Cecina d.	|	...	...	...	...	...	...	...	...	...	...	...	...	...	...	...	...	...	|	...	...	|	...	...	|
Campiglia Marittima d.	|	...	...	...	...	...	...	...	...	...	...	...	...	...	...	...	...	...	|	...	...	|	...	...	|
Follonica d.	|	...	...	...	...	...	...	...	...	...	...	...	...	...	...	...	...	...	|	...	...	|	...	...	|
Grosseto d.	2209	...	...	...	...	...	...	...	...	...	...	...	...	...	...	...	...	...	0217	...	...	0358	...	...	|
Orbetello d.	...	...	...	...	...	...	...	...	...	...	...	...	...	...	...	...	...	...	|	...	...	|	...	...	|
Tarquinia d.	...	...	...	...	...	...	...	...	...	...	...	...	...	...	...	...	...	...	|	...	...	|	...	...	|
Civitavecchia ▲ d.	...	...	...	...	...	...	...	...	...	...	...	...	...	...	...	...	...	...	|	...	...	0454	...	...	|
Santa Marinella d.	...	...	...	...	...	...	...	...	...	...	...	...	...	...	...	...	...	...	|	...	...	|	...	...	|
Ladispoli-Cerveteri d.	...	...	...	...	...	...	...	...	...	...	...	...	...	...	...	...	...	...	|	...	...	|	...	...	|
Roma Ostiense a.	...	...	...	...	...	...	...	...	...	...	...	...	...	...	...	...	...	...	|	...	...	0558	...	...	|
Roma Termini a.	...	...	...	...	...	...	...	...	...	...	...	...	...	...	...	...	...	...	|	...	...	|	...	...	094
Napoli Centrale **640** a.	...	...	...	...	...	...	...	...	...	...	...	...	...	...	...	...	...	...	0601f	...	...	0911	...	...	...

			E		ICp	ICp		ICp		ICp		ICp	ICN	E		IC	ICp	IC					ICp		ICp
			806		**648**	**500**		**652**		**502**		**654**	**768**	**1940**		**504**	**656**	**506**					**510**		**662**
	2	2		2	R	R		R	2	R	2	R			2		R		2	2	2	2	R	2	R
			Z					♦	V		⚒		Z	Z		⚒		♦		P		†			
Napoli Centrale **640** d.	...	...	2138	...	...	...	...	...	...	...	...	...	...	...	...	...	...	...	...	...	...	...	...	...	...
Roma Termini d.	...	...	|	...	...	...	...	...	...	...	...	...	...	...	...	...	...	...	...	...	...	...	...	0609	...
Roma Ostiense d.	...	...	0005	...	...	...	...	...	...	...	...	...	...	...	...	...	...	...	...	...	...	...	...	0619	...
Ladispoli-Cerveteri d.	...	...	|	...	...	...	...	...	...	...	...	...	...	...	...	...	...	...	...	...	...	...	...	0649	...
Santa Marinella d.	...	...	|	...	...	...	...	...	...	...	...	...	...	...	...	...	...	...	...	...	...	...	...	0705	...
Civitavecchia ▲ d.	...	...	0047	...	...	...	...	...	...	...	...	...	...	...	...	...	...	...	...	...	...	...	...	0715	...
Tarquinia d.	...	...	|	...	...	...	...	...	...	...	...	...	...	...	...	...	...	...	...	...	...	...	...	0729	...
Orbetello d.	...	...	|	...	...	...	...	...	...	...	...	...	...	...	...	...	...	...	0558a	...	...	...	...	0802	...
Grosseto d.	...	...	0148	...	...	...	...	...	...	...	...	...	...	...	...	...	...	...	0628	...	0755	...	...	0828	...
Follonica d.	...	...	|	...	...	...	...	...	...	...	...	...	...	...	...	...	...	...	0654	...	0826	...	...	0854	...
Campiglia Marittima d.	...	...	|	...	...	...	...	...	...	...	...	...	...	...	...	...	...	...	0707	...	0840	...	...	0905	...
Cecina d.	...	...	|	...	...	...	...	...	...	...	...	...	...	...	...	...	...	...	0732	...	0908	...	...	0928	...
Rosignano d.	...	...	|	...	...	...	...	...	...	...	...	...	...	...	...	...	...	...	0744	...	0916	...	...	0936	...
Livorno Centrale d.	...	...	0311	...	...	...	...	...	...	...	...	0526	0542	0531s	0550	0632	...	...	0811	...	0937	...	...	1000	...
Firenze SMN **614** d.	...	...	|	...	...	...	...	...	...	...	...	|	|	|	|	|	...	0751	|	...	|	...	...	|	...
Pisa Centrale d.	...	...	0328	...	...	...	...	...	...	...	...	0544	0600	0548s	0608	0649	...	0902	0826	...	0957	...	...	1015	...
Viareggio d.	...	...	|	...	...	...	...	...	...	...	...	0601	0618	|	0626	0706	...	0919	▬	...	▬	...	...	...	...
Massa Centro d.	...	...	|	...	...	...	...	...	...	...	...	0616	|	|	0650	0719	...	|	...	...	...	...	...	...	...
Carrara-Avenza d.	...	...	|	...	...	...	...	...	...	...	...	|	|	|	0656	0726	...	|	...	...	...	...	...	...	...
Sarzana d.	...	...	|	...	...	...	...	...	...	...	...	|	0642	|	0705	0735	...	|	...	...	...	...	...	...	...
La Spezia Centrale d.	...	...	0416	...	0502	...	...	...	...	...	0627	0640	0701	0706s	|	0750	...	0953	...	1000	...	...	...	...	104
Riomaggiore d.	...	...	|	...	|	...	...	...	...	...	|	|	|	|	|	|	...	|	...	1009	...	...	...	...	|
Levanto d.	...	...	|	...	0525	...	...	...	...	...	0644	0701	|	|	|	|	...	|	...	1023	...	...	...	...	110
Sestri-Levante d.	...	0434	|	...	0542	...	...	...	...	...	0701	0716	|	|	|	0818	...	|	...	1043	...	...	...	...	111
Chiavari d.	...	0445	0510	...	0553	...	...	...	...	...	0711	0724	|	|	|	0826	...	1027	...	1053	...	...	...	...	112
Rapallo d.	...	0453	0520	...	0603	...	...	...	...	...	0721	0733	|	|	w	0835	...	1036	*ICp*	1101	...	...	...	...	113
Santa Margherita-Portofino d.	...	0457	|	...	0608	...	...	...	...	...	0726	0739	|	|	|	|	...	|	**658**	1105	...	...	...	...	|
Genova Brignole d.	0535	0536	0555	0617	0635	0657	...	...	...	0757	0804	0810	0835	0848s	|	0902	0910	1102	R	1142	...	...	1157	...	121
Genova Piazza Principe a.	0541	0542	0601	0623	0641	0703	...	...	...	0803	0810a	0816	0841	0859s	|	0908	0916	1108	V	...	⚒	...	1203	...	121
Genova Piazza Principe 619 d.	0543	0545	0604	0625	0644	0708	...	0719	0758	0808	...	0819	0844	|	|	0912	0919	1112	1119	...	1125	1145	1208	...	121
Tortona **619** d.	|	0634	|	|	|	|	...	|	0844	|	...	0859	|	|	|	|	|	|	|	...	1233	1233	|	...	|
Voghera **619** d.	|	0646	|	|	0734	|	...	0808	0856	|	...	0912	|	|	|	|	1008	|	1208	...	1246	1246	|	...	130
Pavia d.	|	0707	|	|	0751	|	...	0825	0912	|	...	0928	|	|	|	|	1025	|	1225	...	1302	1302	|	...	132
Milano Centrale a.	|	0740	|	|	0820	|	...	0850	0945	|	...	0955	|	|	1025	|	1050	|	1250	...	1335	1335	|	...	135
Novi Ligure d.	0635	...	|	0707	...	0741	...	...	...	0841	...	...	0925	|	...	|	...	|	...	...	...	...	1241	...	...
Alessandria **619** d.	0657	...	0705	0726	...	0757	...	...	...	0856	...	...	0941	0946s	...	0957	...	1157	...	...	...	...	1256	...	...
Asti **619** d.	0720	...	0731	0751	...	0816	...	...	...	0916	...	...	1002	1021s	...	1016	...	1216	...	...	...	...	1316	...	...
Torino Porta Nuova 619 a.	0810	...	0820	0840	...	0855	...	...	...	0955	...	...	1045	1110	...	1055	...	1255	...	...	...	...	1355	...	...

♦ – **NOTES** (LISTED BY TRAIN NUMBER)

506 – DONATELLO – [12] Firenze (**505**) - Pisa - Torino.
539 – DONATELLO – [12] Torino - Pisa (**540**) - Firenze.
652 – MAZZINI – [12] Ventimiglia (**651**) - Genova - Milano.
659 – MAZZINI – [12] Milano - Genova (**660**) - Ventimiglia.
767 – MONTECARLO – 🛏 1, 2 cl. and ▬ 2 cl. (4 berth) Nice (**369**) - Pisa (**374**) - Firenze (**375**) - Roma; 🛏 1, 2 cl. (Excelsior), 🛏 1, 2 cl. and ▬ 2 cl. (4/6 berth) Torino - Genova (**369**) - Pisa (**374**) - Firenze (**375**) - Roma.

A – To Albenga.
P – [2] Parma - Aulla - La Spezia - Genova.
V – From/to Ventimiglia.
Z – For days of running and composition see Table **640**.

a – Ⓐ only.
c – Firenze **Campo di Marte**.
f – Napoli **Campi Flegrei**.
g – Milano **Porta Garibaldi**.
s – Stops to set down only.
w – Via Fidenza and Aulla.

▲ – 🚌 **from/to CIVITAVECCHIA MARITTIMA** Journey 5 minutes
Civitavecchia Marittima depart: 0655, 0750.
Civitavecchia depart: 2105, 2200, 2215.

ROMA - PISA - GENOVA - MILANO and TORINO — 610

		IC 514	EC 140					EC 176			ICp 516	ICp 628			ICp 518	ICp 664			ICp 520	EC 146		ICp 524		ICp 666		ICp 670
	2	✕	[R]	2	2	2	2	[R]✕	2	2	[R]✕	[R]	2	2	[R]	[R]	2	2	[R]✕	[R]🍷	2	[R]	2	[R]	2	[R]
			♦			⚒	†	♦		†	♦	♦	A							♦		⚒				♦
Napoli Centrale 640 ....d.	...	...	...	...	...	...	...	...	...	...	0730	...	...	...	...	...	...	...	0924	...	...	...	...	...	...	...
ma Termini ....d.	...	0735	...	...	...	...	...	...	...	...	0946	...	...	...	...	...	1009	...	1146	...	...	...	...	...	1209	...
ma Ostiense ....d.	...	0745	...	...	...	...	...	...	...	...	0957	...	...	...	...	...	1019	...	1157	...	...	...	...	...	1219	...
dispoli-Cerveteri ....d.	...	|	...	...	...	...	...	...	...	...	|	...	...	...	...	...	1048	...	|	...	...	...	...	...	1249	...
nta Marinella ....d.	...	|	...	...	...	...	...	...	...	...	|	...	...	...	...	...	1105	...	|	...	...	...	...	...	1305	...
vitavecchia ▲ ....d.	...	0825	...	...	...	...	...	...	...	...	1034	...	...	...	...	...	1115	...	1234	...	...	...	...	...	1315	...
rquinia ....d.	...	|	...	...	...	...	...	...	...	...	|	...	...	...	...	...	1129	...	|	...	...	...	...	...	1329	...
betello ....d.	...	0901	...	...	...	...	...	...	...	...	|	...	...	...	...	...	1202	...	|	...	...	...	...	...	1402	...
osseto ....d.	...	0922	...	...	...	...	...	...	...	...	1130	...	...	...	...	...	1228	...	1329	...	...	...	...	...	1428	...
llonica ....d.	...	0944	...	...	...	...	...	...	...	...	1151	...	...	...	...	...	1254	...	|	...	...	...	...	...	1454	...
mpiglia Marittima ....d.	...	0955	...	...	...	...	...	...	...	...	|	...	...	...	...	...	1305	...	1358	...	...	...	...	...	1505	...
cina ....d.	...	1016	...	...	...	...	...	...	...	...	|	...	...	...	...	...	1328	...	|	...	...	...	...	...	1528	...
signano ....d.	...	|	...	...	...	...	...	...	...	...	|	...	...	...	...	...	1336	...	|	...	...	...	...	...	1536	...
vorno Centrale ....d.	...	1042	...	...	...	...	...	1126	1223	...	1242	...	...	...	...	1326	1400	1423	1442	...	...	...	...	...	1600	...
Firenze SMN 614 ....d.	...	|	...	...	...	...	...	|	|	...	|	...	...	...	...	|	|	|	|	...	...	...	...	...	|	...
sa Centrale ....d.	...	1100	...	...	...	1033	1110	1144	1241	...	1300	...	...	...	...	1344	1415	1441	1500	...	...	...	...	...	1615	...
areggio ....d.	...	1117	...	...	...	1053	1131	1201	1301	...	|	...	...	...	...	1401	...	1501	1517	...	...	...	...	...	▬	...
ssa Centro ....d.	...	1131	...	...	...	1111	1149	|	1319	...	1327	...	...	←	...	1416	...	1519	|	...	...	...	...	...	...	...
rrara-Avenza ....d.	...	|	...	...	...	1121	1155	1219	1326	...	|	...	...	1327	...	|	...	1527	1533	...	...	...	←	...	...	...
rzana ....d.	...	|	...	...	...	1144	1204	|	→	...	|	...	...	1336	...	|	...	1536	|	...	...	...	1537	...	...	...
Spezia Centrale ....d.	...	1153	...	...	...	1223	1223	1240	▬	...	1354	...	...	1401	...	1440	...	→	1553	...	...	...	1601	1640	...	...
maggiore ....d.	...	|	...	...	...	1231	1231	|	...	...	|	...	...	1409	...	|	...	▬	|	...	...	...	1609	|	...	...
vanto ....d.	...	|	...	...	...	1245	1245	1301	...	...	|	...	...	1423	...	1501	...	...	|	...	...	...	1633	1701	...	...
stri-Levante ....d.	...	|	...	...	...	1305	1305	1316	...	...	|	...	...	1444	...	1516	...	...	1622	...	...	...	1704	1716	...	...
iavari ....d.	...	1227	...	...	...	1315	1315	1324	...	...	1427	...	...	1454	...	1524	...	...	|	...	...	...	1714	1724	...	...
pallo ....d.	...	|	...	...	...	1323	1323	1333	←	←	1436	...	...	1502	...	1533	...	...	|	...	...	...	1722	1733	...	...
nta Margherita-Portofino .d.	...	|	...	...	...	1327	1327	1339	⚒	†	|	...	...	1506	...	1539	...	...	|	...	...	...	1727	1739	←	...
nova Brignole ....d.	1217	1302	...	1325	...	1413	1413	1410	1416	1416	1502	...	...	1545	1557	1610	...	1617	1702	...	...	1757	1812	1810	1816	...
nova Piazza Principe ....a.	1223	1308	...	1331	...	→	→	1416	1422	1422	1508	...	...	1551	1603	1616	...	1623	1708	...	...	1803	→	1816	1822	...
nova Piazza Principe 619 .d.	1225	1312	1319	1333	1345	...	...	1419	1425	1425	1512	1519	1546	...	1608	1619	...	1625	1712	1719	1745	1808	...	1819	1825	1919
Tortona 619 ....d.	|	|	|	|	1433	...	...	|	|	|	|	|	1634	...	|	1700	...	|	|	|	1833	|	...	1859	|	2000
Voghera 619 ....d.	|	|	1408	|	1446	...	...	1508	|	|	|	1608	1647	...	|	|	...	|	|	1808	1846	|	...	|	|	|
Pavia ....d.	|	|	1425	|	1502	...	...	1525	|	|	|	1625	1703	...	|	1725	...	|	|	1825	1902	|	...	1925	|	2025
Milano Centrale ....a.	|	|	1450	|	1535	...	...	1550	|	|	|	1650	1737	...	|	1750	...	|	|	1850	1938	|	...	1950	|	2050
vi Ligure ....d.	1309	|	...	1414	...	...	...	...	1509	1509	|	...	...	...	1641	...	...	1709	|	...	...	1841	...	...	1909	...
essandria 619 ....d.	1329	1357	...	1429	...	...	...	...	1529	1529	1556	...	...	...	1656	...	...	1729	1757	...	...	1856	...	...	1929	...
ti 619 ....d.	1351	1416	...	1451	...	...	...	...	1551	1551	1616	...	...	...	1716	...	...	1751	1816	...	...	1916	...	...	1951	...
rino Porta Nuova 619 ....a.	1440	1455	...	1540	...	...	...	...	1640	1640	1655	...	...	...	1755	...	...	1840	1855	...	...	1955	...	...	2040	...

		IC 526		ICp 528		ICp 1534	ICp 672				IC 538	EC 148					ES 9308			ICp 542		ICp 546			EN 366	
	2	✕	2	[R]	2	[R]	[R]	2	2	2		[R]🍷	2	2	2	2	[R]🍷	2		[R]✕	2	[R]	2	2		2
					⑦p	©	Ⓐ		F		♦	♦	A				♦			♦		Ⓑ			♦	
Napoli Centrale 640 ....d.	...	...	...	...	...	...	...	...	...	...	...	...	...	...	...	...	...	...	...	1524	...	1724	...	...	...	...
ma Termini ....d.	...	1346	...	...	...	...	...	1409	...	...	1546	...	...	1609	...	...	1700	...	...	1746	1809	1946	2009	2109	2116	2209
ma Ostiense ....d.	...	1357	...	...	...	...	...	1419	...	...	1557	...	...	1619	...	...	1709	...	...	1757	1820	1957	2019	2120	|	2220
dispoli-Cerveteri ....d.	...	|	...	...	...	...	...	1449	...	...	|	...	...	1649	...	...	|	...	...	|	1849	|	2049	2151	|	2256
nta Marinella ....d.	...	|	...	...	...	...	...	1505	...	...	|	...	...	1705	...	...	|	...	...	|	1905	|	2105	2207	|	2311
vitavecchia ▲ ....d.	...	1434	...	...	...	...	...	1515	...	...	1634	...	...	1715	...	...	1747	...	...	1834	1915	2034	2115	2216	|	2319
rquinia ....d.	...	|	...	...	...	...	...	1529	...	...	|	...	...	1729	...	...	|	...	...	|	1929	|	2129	2229	|	...
betello ....d.	...	|	...	...	...	...	...	1602	...	...	|	...	...	1802	...	...	|	...	...	|	2002	2110	2202	2302	|	...
osseto ....d.	...	1529	...	...	...	1604	1610	1628	...	1650	1729	...	...	1828	...	...	1847	...	...	1929	2028	2131	2228	2329	|	...
llonica ....d.	...	1551	...	...	...	1625	1632	1654	...	1714	|	...	...	1854	...	...	|	...	...	|	2054	2153	2254	...	|	...
mpiglia Marittima ....d.	...	|	...	...	...	1636	1643	1705	...	1725	|	...	...	1905	...	←	|	...	...	1958	2105	2205	2305	...	|	...
cina ....d.	...	|	...	...	...	1655	1702	1728	...	1751	1816	...	...	1924	...	1925	|	...	...	2018	2128	2222	2328	...	|	...
signano ....d.	...	|	...	...	...	|	|	1736	...	1800	|	...	...	→	...	1936	|	...	...	|	2136	|	2336	...	|	...
vorno Centrale ....d.	1623	1642	...	...	1705	1718	1726	1800	...	1828	1842	...	...	▬	1850	2000	1950	...	...	2044	2200	2247	0001	...	|	...
Firenze SMN 614 ....d.	|	|	...	...	|	|	|	|	...	|	|	...	...	...	|	|	|	...	...	|	|	|	|	...	2325c	...
sa Centrale ....d.	1641	1700	...	...	1722	1736	1744	1815	1820	1846	1900	...	...	...	1909	2015	2007	...	...	2102	2220	2304	0015	...	0038	...
areggio ....d.	1701	1717	...	...	1740	1753	1801	...	1837	1906	1917	...	...	...	1928	▬	2023	...	...	2119	▬	2321	...	...	|	...
ssa Centro ....d.	1719	1731	...	...	1757	1813	1816	...	1856	1925	|	...	...	←	1945	...	2036	...	...	2134	...	2334	...	...	|	...
rrara-Avenza ....d.	1727	|	←	...	1803	1820	|	...	1902	1931	|	...	...	1932	1952	...	|	...	...	|	...	2340	...	...	|	...
rzana ....d.	1736	|	1737	...	1812	|	|	...	1909	→	|	...	...	1940	2002	...	|	...	...	|	2	2349	...	...	|	...
Spezia Centrale ....d.	→	1753	1801	...	|	1840	1840	...	▬	...	1953	...	...	2001	|	...	2057	2116	...	2200	2222	0006	...	...	|	...
maggiore ....d.	▬	|	1809	...	|	|	|	...	...	...	|	...	...	2009	|	...	|	2124	...	|	2231	|	...	...	|	...
vanto ....d.	...	|	1823	...	|	1901	1901	...	...	...	|	...	...	2022	|	...	|	2138	...	|	2248	|	...	...	|	...
stri-Levante ....d.	...	|	1844	...	|	1916	1916	...	...	...	|	...	...	2042	|	...	|	2159	...	2228	2308	0040	...	...	|	...
iavari ....d.	...	|	1854	...	|	1924	1924	...	...	...	2027	...	...	2052	|	...	2128	2209	...	2236	2315	...	...	...	|	...
pallo ....d.	...	1833	1902	...	w	1933	1933	...	...	...	2036	...	...	2103	w	...	2138	2216	...	2245	2323	...	...	...	|	...
nta Margherita-Portofino .d.	...	|	1906	...	|	1939	1939	...	...	...	|	...	...	2107	|	...	|	2220	...	|	2327	...	...	...	|	...
nova Brignole ....d.	†	1902	1945	1957	|	2010	2010	...	2024	...	2102	...	...	2154	|	2217	2205	2257	...	2313	0016	...	...	...	|	...
nova Piazza Principe ....a.	A	1908	1951	2003	|	2016	2016	...	2030	...	2108	...	...	2200	|	2223	2211	...	...	2319	...	...	...	...	0338	...
nova Piazza Principe 619 .d.	1935	1912	...	2008	|	2019	2019	...	2032	...	...	2119	2149	...	|	2225	...	...	...	...	...	...	...	...	0530	...
Tortona 619 ....d.	2026	|	...	|	|	|	|	...	|	...	...	|	2236	...	|	|	...	...	...	...	...	...	...	...	|	...
Voghera 619 ....d.	2038	|	...	|	|	2108	2108	...	|	...	...	2208	2247	...	|	|	...	...	...	...	...	...	...	...	|	...
Pavia ....d.	2055	|	...	|	|	2125	2125	...	|	...	...	2225	2303	...	|	|	...	...	...	...	...	...	...	...	|	...
Milano Centrale ....a.	2130	|	...	|	2145g	2150	2150	...	|	...	...	2250	2335	...	2315	|	...	...	...	...	...	...	...	...	|	...
vi Ligure ....d.	...	|	...	2041	...	...	...	...	2114	...	...	...	...	...	...	2309	...	...	...	...	...	...	...	...	|	...
essandria 619 ....d.	...	1957	...	2056	...	...	...	...	2134	...	...	...	...	...	...	2329	...	...	...	...	...	...	...	...	0617s	...
ti 619 ....d.	...	2016	...	2116	...	...	...	...	2155	...	...	...	...	...	...	2351	...	...	...	...	...	...	...	...	0638s	...
rino Porta Nuova 619 ....a.	...	2055	...	2155	...	...	...	...	2240	...	...	...	...	...	...	0040	...	...	...	...	...	...	...	...	0720	...

– **NOTES** (LISTED BY TRAIN NUMBER)

0 – RIVIERA DEI FIORI – [12] Nice (**139**) - Genova - Milano.
6 – SANREMO – [12] and 🍷 Nice (**145**) - Genova - Milano.
8 – LIGURE – [12] and 🍷 Nice (**147**) - Genova - Milano.
6 – CISALPINO CINQUE TERRE – [12] and ✕ Livorno - Milano - Chiasso - Zürich.
6 – MONTECARLO – 🛏 1,2 cl. and 🛏 2 cl. (4 berth) Roma - Firenze (**367**) - Pisa (**368**) - Nice; 🛏 1,2 cl. (Excelsior), 🛏 1,2 cl. and 🛏 2 cl. (4/6 berth) Roma - Firenze (**367**) - Pisa (**368**) - Genova (**764**) - Torino.
6 – CAPODIMONTE – [12] and ✕ Salerno - Torino.
8 – TIRRENO – [12] Roma - Ventimiglia.
2 – BOCCANEGRA – [12] Napoli - Genova - Savona.
8 – ANDREA DORIA – [12] Ventimiglia (**627**) - Genova - Milano.
0 – MAMELI – [12] Ventimiglia (**669**) - Genova - Milano. Train number **1537/8** on ©.
08 – [2] and 🍷 Roma - Genova - Savona.

A – From Albenga.
F – FRECCIA DELLA VERSILIA – [12] Pisa - Aulla - Fidenza - Bergamo.
c – Firenze **Campo di Marte**.
g – Milano **Porta Garibaldi**.
p – Also Aug. 15; not Aug. 12.
s – Stops to set down only.
w – Via Aulla, Fidenza.
▲ – 🚌 service available from / to Civitavecchia Marittima – see panel on page 302.

612 PARMA and FIDENZA - SARZANA and LA SPEZIA

Most services 2nd class onl

km							2295	2037	2201												2039	2301		1757		
		⚒				⚒q	H	Y	BX	p		⚒q		⚒q	⚒q	⚒m			⚒	⚒		F	Ⓐ	⑤j	x	⑥
	Milano Centrale ..... d.	...	...	...	...	...	...	0700	...	...	...	...	...	...	...	...	...	...	...	...	1705	...	...	1853g	...	...
0	**Parma** ..... d.	...	...	0512	0617	...	0752	|	...	1116	...	...	1306	...	1345	...	1455	...	1638	1840	|	1855	1950	|	2050	225
*	**Fidenza** ..... d.	...	...	|	|	0734	|	0834	0913	|	...	1242	|	1343	|	...	|	...	|	|	1846	|	|	2037	|	|
23	Fornovo ..... d.	...	...	0531	0638	0751	0819	0900	0930	1136	...	1307	1328	1408	1411	...	1521	...	1709	1904	1905	1916	2014	2103	2113	231
61	Borgo Val di Taro ..... d.	...	0547	0605	0725	...	0851	0934	0959	1210	1310	...	1409	...	1453	...	1603	...	1743	...	1942	2004	...	2136	2157	234
79	Pontremoli ..... d.	0545	0602	0628	0745	...	0907	0950	1017	...	1326	...	1426	...	1509	1548	1622	1643	1802	...	1959	2023	...	2157	2216	235
100	Aulla Lunigiana ..... d.	0606	0623	0653	0811r	...	0926	1011	1039	...	1352	...	1452	...	...	1613	...	1707	1827	...	2022	2052	...	2219	2235	002
108	San Stefano di Magra . d.	0613	0632	0659	0818r	...	0933	1019	1047	...	1359	...	1500	...	...	1620	...	1714	1834	...	2032	2059	...	2227	2242	003
116	**Sarzana** ..... a.	|	0640	|	|	...	|	1032	1056	...	|	...	|	...	...	|	...	|	|	...	2043	|	...	2240	|	|
	Pisa C **610** ..... a.	|	0734	|	|	...	|	1137	1201	...	|	...	|	...	...	|	...	|	|		2135	|	...	2334	|	|
	Livorno **610** ..... a.	|	...	|	|	...	|	1157	...	...	|	...	|	...	...	|	...	|	|	...	2153	|	...	2353	|	|
120	**La Spezia Centrale** .. a.	0632	...	0720	0838	...	0946	...	...	...	1418	...	1518	...	...	1638	...	1735	1851	...	...	2113	...	...	2259	004

						2036	2292											1756		3174		2202	2038	2298	1830	
	⚒	⚒	⚒q	m			S	p	⚒q		⚒q		⚒q	⚒q		⚒	⚒	⑦v	x	V		B		G	J	
La Spezia Centrale ... d.	...	...	...	0540	0627	...	0752	1016	...	1220	...	1320	1445	...	1525	1707	...	...	1817	1835	1902	...	...	2102	2108	...
Livorno **610** ..... d.	...	...	...	|	|	0550	|	|	...	|	...	|	|	...	|	|	...	1705	|	|	|	...	1850	|	|	...
Pisa C **610** ..... a.	...	...	...	|	|	0608	|	|	...	|	...	|	|	...	|	|	...	1722	|	|	|	1820	1909	|	|	...
Sarzana ..... d.	...	...	...	|	|	0705	|	|	...	|	...	|	|	...	|	|	...	1812	|	|	|	1910	2002	|	|	...
San Stefano di Magra .. d.	...	...	...	0552	0645	0715	0810	1032	...	1236	...	1341	1502	...	1543	1729	...	1823	1834	1852	1919	1924	2013	2113	2119	...
Aulla Lunigiana ..... d.	...	...	...	0600	0653	0723	0818	1041	...	1245	...	1352	1510	...	1550	1736	...	1830	1842	1859	...	1934	2022	2122	2126	...
Pontremoli ..... d.	0500	0605	...	0627	0718	0743	0837	1108	...	1313	...	1416	1535	1541	1614	1758	...	1852	1906	1925	...	1957	2043	2144	2145	...
Borgo Val di Taro ..... d.	0517	0621	...	0643	0736	0759	0853	1125	...	1329	...	1434	...	1604	1630	1817	1907	1907	1922	1945	...	2014	2059	2201	2201	...
Fornovo ..... d.	0559	0658	0703	0723	0818	0839	0926	1205	1210	1412k	1414	1520	...	1639	1710	...	1948	1951	2015	2020	...	2045	2135	2231	2231	...
Fidenza ..... a.	|	|	0728	|	|	0904	|	|	1235	|	1439	|	...	|	|	...	|	2013	|	|	...	2103	2154	|	|	...
Parma ..... a.	0630	0722	...	0745	0840	|	0940	1225	...	1434	...	1542	...	1702	1730	...	2015	|	2037	2037	...	...	|	2250	2252	...
Milano Centrale ..... a.	...	...	...	...	...	1025	...	...	...	...	...	...	...	...	...	...	...	2145g	...	...	...	...	2315	...	...	...

B – FRECCIA DELLA VERSILIA – [12] Bergamo - Pisa and v.v.
F – [12] Bologna (**2300**) - Parma - La Spezia (**2302**) - Genova.
G – Dec. 9 - Mar. 22: [12] Ventimiglia (**2297**) - La Spezia - Parma.
H – ①②④⑤⑥⑦: [12] Parma - La Spezia (**2296**) - Genova.
J – June 10 - Sept. 16: [12] (Ventimiglia Ⓐ, train **1829** -) Savona - La Spezia - Parma. Runs as trains **1799/1800** on ©.
S – [12] Genova (**2291**) - La Spezia - Parma (**2293**) - Bologna.
V – † June 10 - Sept. 16: [12] Sestri Levante - La Spezia - Parma.

X – Runs as train **1763** on † (Pisa a. 1147).
Y – Runs as train **1761** on † (Pisa a. 1124, Livorno a. 1143).

g – Milano **Porta Garibaldi**.
j – Also Apr. 24, 30; not Apr. 25, May 2.
k – Arrive 1407.
m – Not July 30 - Aug. 26.
p – © June 10 - Nov. 30; daily Dec. 1 - 8.

q – Not July 30 - Aug. 25.
r – 6–7 minutes later on †.
v – Also Dec. 26, Jan. 1, Mar. 24, June 2; not Dec. 23, 30, Mar. 23, June 1.
x – ⚒ June 10 - Sept. 16; daily Sept. 17 - Dec.
y – ① (also days after holidays).
* – Fidenza - Fornovo is *25 km*.

613 FIRENZE - SIENA, PISA, PISA AEROPORTO ✈ and LIVORNO

Most services 2nd class onl

km		⚒	E	⚒	⚒		R🅁	y		⚒	D				⚒	†	⚒	⚒		⚒		⚒		L			⚒	
0	**Firenze SMN 614** ..... d.	0430	0532	...	0628	0637	0713	0727	...	0732	0751	0757	0810	0805	0827	0850	0857	0910	0927	1010	1027	1037	1057	1100	1110	1127	1157	121
34	Empoli ..... d.	0506	0602	0627	0655	0714	|	0759	0806	0808	0820	0830	0840	0845	0859	0927	0930	0940	0959	1040	1059	1114	1130	|	1140	1159	1230	124
	Poggibonsi ..... d.	|	|	0705	0729	|	|	|	0848	|	|	|	0915	|	|	|	|	1015	|	1115	|	|	|	|	1215	|	|	131
	Siena ..... a.	|	|	0731	0752	|	|	|	0916	|	|	|	0938	|	|	|	|	1038	|	1138	|	|	|	1210	1238	|	|	133
81	**Pisa Centrale 614** ... ¶ d.	0555	0643	...	...	0802	0828	0834	...	0901	0859	0906	...	0925	0934	1013	1020	...	1034	...	1134	1202	1206	...	...	1234	1306	...
	Pisa Aeroporto ✈ ... ¶ a.	|	|	...	...	0807	|	|	...	0906	...	...	...	0930	|	...	1025	...	|	...	|	1207	...	...	...	|	...	...
101	**Livorno** ..... a.	0610	0656	...	...	...	0844	0849	...	...	...	...	...	...	0949	...	...	...	1049	...	1149	...	...	...	...	1249	...	...

km					⚒	⚒				L			⚒	y			⚒	⚒z	Ⓐ									
	Firenze SMN 614 ..... d.	1227	...	1257	1310	1327	1337	1357	1410	1415	1427	1457	1510	1527	1537	1557	1610	1627	1637	1657	1710	1727	1737	1757	1810	1827	1837	185
0	Empoli ..... d.	1259	1308	1330	1340	1359	1414	1430	1440	|	1459	1530	1540	1559	1614	1630	1640	1659	1714	1730	1740	1759	1814	1830	1840	1859	1914	193
38	Poggibonsi ..... d.	|	1349	|	1415	|	|	|	1515	|	|	|	1615	|	|	|	1715	|	|	|	1815	|	|	|	1915	|	|	|
63	**Siena** ..... a.	|	1414	|	1438	|	|	|	1538	1525	|	|	1638	|	|	|	1738	|	|	|	1838	|	|	|	1938	|	|	|
	Pisa Centrale 614 ... ¶ d.	1334	...	1406	...	1434	1504	1506	...	...	1534	1606	...	1634	1659	1706	...	1734	1802	1806	...	1834	1904	1906	...	1934	1959	200
	Pisa Aeroporto ✈ ... ¶ a.	|	...	...	...	|	|	...	...	...	|	...	...	|	...	...	...	|	1807	...	...	|	|	...	...	|	...	...
	Livorno ..... a.	1349	...	...	...	1449	1520	...	...	...	1549	...	...	1649	...	...	...	1749	...	...	...	1849	1922	...	...	1949	...	...

		☆q			L		⚒						
Firenze SMN 614 ..... d.	1910	1923r	1927	1957	2000	2010	2027	2037	2127	...	2157	2307	0037
Empoli ..... d.	1940	|	1959	2030	|	2040	2059	2114	2159	2208	2233	2343	0114
Poggibonsi ..... d.	2015	|	|	|	|	2115	|	|	|	2249	|	|	|
Siena ..... a.	2038	|	|	|	2110	2138	|	|	|	2314	|	|	|
Pisa Centrale 614 .... ¶ d.	...	2007	2034	2109	...	...	2131	2202	2234	...	2322	0032	0159
Pisa Aeroporto ✈ .... ¶ a.	...	...	|	|	...	...	...	2207	|	...	|	|	...
Livorno ..... a.	...	...	2049	2124	...	...	...	...	2249	...	2337	0047	...

			⚒					⚒	⚒	⚒	⚒
Livorno ..... d.	...	0521	...	0620	...	...	...	0711	...	0743	...
Pisa Aeroporto ✈ ¶ d.	...	|	...	|	...	0641	...	|	...	|	...
Pisa Centrale 614 ¶ d.	0412	0539	...	0638	...	0654	...	0729	...	0801	...
Siena ..... d.	|	|	0550	|	0627	|	0639	|	0702	|	073
Poggibonsi ..... d.	|	|	0615	|	0649	|	0703	|	0728	|	080
Empoli ..... d.	0451	0618	0653	0709	0723	0731	0752	0802	0820	0847	085
Firenze SMN 614 ... a.	0526	0652	0728	0737	0750	0803	0828	0833	0855	0923	...

km				⚒L	⚒	†	☆⚒	⚒	†L	⚒		⚒		⚒	⚒				⚒	⚒	⚒z					⚒		⚒
	Livorno ..... d.	0811	...	...	0911	0911	...	...	...	1011	...	...	1111	...	...	...	1211	...	...	...	1311	...	...	1343	1411	...	1435e	151
0	Pisa Aeroporto ✈ ... ¶ d.	|	...	...	|	|	...	...	...	|	1042	...	|	...	1143	...	|	...	1243	...	|	...	...	|	|	...	|	|
2	**Pisa Centrale 614** ... ¶ d.	0829	...	...	0929	0929	0939	...	...	1029	1101	...	1129	...	1154	...	1229	...	1254	1301	1329	...	1354	1401	1429	...	1454	152
	Siena ..... d.	|	0818	0840	|	|	|	0918	0945	|	|	1041	|	1118	|	1141	|	1218	|	|	|	1318	|	|	|	1418	|	|
	Poggibonsi ..... d.	|	0846	|	|	|	|	0946	|	|	|	1112	|	1146	|	1212	|	1246	|	|	|	1346	|	|	|	1446	|	|
	Empoli ..... d.	0902	0921	|	1002	1017	|	1021	|	1102	1147	1152	1202	1221	1231	1252	1302	1321	1331	1347	1402	1421	1431	1447	1502	1521	1531	160
	Firenze SMN 614 ..... a.	0933	0950	0950	1033	1046	1024r	1050	1055	1133	1223	...	1233	1250	1303	...	1333	1350	1403	1423	1433	1450	1503	1523	1533	1550	1603	163

		L			⚒		⚒		L					⚒	†	x	R🅁	⚒	Ⓐ	E		†	D	⚒	y		
Livorno ..... d.	...	...	1543	1611	...	...	1711	...	...	...	1811	...	...	...	...	1911	1927	...	...	2011	...	...	...	...	2111	...	...
Pisa Aeroporto ✈ ..... ¶ d.	...	...	|	|	...	...	|	...	...	1753	|	...	...	...	...	|	|	...	1953	|	...	...	...	...	|	...	222
Pisa Centrale 614 ..... ¶ d.	...	...	1601	1629	...	1654	1729	...	...	1801	1829	...	1854	1901	1913	1929	1947	...	2001	2029	...	2042	2056	2101	2129	...	223
Siena ..... d.	1518	1550	|	|	1618	|	|	1718	1730	|	|	1818	|	|	|	|	|	1918	|	|	2018	|	|	|	|	2118	|
Poggibonsi ..... d.	1546	|	|	|	1646	|	|	1746	|	|	|	1846	|	|	|	|	|	1946	|	|	2046	|	|	|	|	2146	|
Empoli ..... d.	1621	|	1647	1702	1721	1731	1802	1821	|	1847	1902	1921	1931	1947	1953	2002	|	2021	2047	2102	2121	2116	2132	2147	2202	2221	231
Firenze SMN 614 ..... a.	1650	1700	1723	1733	1750	1803	1833	1850	1850	1923	1933	1950	2003	2023	2024	2033	2046	2050	2123	2133	2150	2155	2200	2223	2233	2250	235

D – DONATELLO – [12] Firenze (**505/540**) - Pisa (**506/539**) - Torino and v.v.
E – [12] Firenze - Piombino Marittima and v.v.
L – *ES*Link*: 🚌 link.
R – ALLEGRO RIGOLETTO – ④⑥ June 14 - Sept. 29 (from Wien, one day later from Livorno): 🛏 1, 2 cl. (Excelsior), ▬ 2 cl. and [2] Wien Süd (**1234/5**) - Firenze (**1232/9**) - Livorno and v.v. Supplement payable.

e – † only.
q – Ⓑ (not Aug. 14, Oct. 31, Dec. 7).
r – Firenze **Rifredi**.
x – ⚒ (daily Aug. 27 - Dec. 8).
y – Ⓐ (daily Aug. 27 - Dec. 8).
z – Also † June 2 - Aug. 26.

☆ – *ES* train: [12] and ✕ Torino - Pisa - Firenze - Roma and v.v. 🅁

¶ – For complete service Pisa - Pisa Aeropor see Table **614**.

614 FIRENZE - LUCCA - VIAREGGIO and PISA

Most services 2nd class onl

km		⚒	⚒									†	⚒										
0	**Firenze SMN 613** ..... d.	0510	...	...	...	0708	...	0808	...	0908	...	1008	...	...	1208	...	and at	1908	...	2008	...	2119	220
17	Prato Centrale ..... d.	0533	...	...	...	0731	...	0831	...	0931	...	1031	...	...	1231	...	the same	1931	...	2031	...	2138	223
34	Pistoia ..... d.	0551	...	...	...	0747	...	0847	...	0947	...	1047	...	...	1247	...	minutes	1947	...	2047	...	2153	224
47	Montecatini Centro ..... d.	0604	...	...	...	0805	...	0905	...	1005	...	1105	...	...	1305	...	past each	2005	...	2105	...	2205	230
78	Lucca ..... ⊡ d.	0651	0653	0740	0755	0831	0842	0931	0940	1031	1040	1131	1240	1310	1331	1340	hour	2031	2040	2131	2140	2231	233
101	**Viareggio** ..... a.	0711	|	|	|	0849	|	0949	|	1049	|	1149	|	|	1349	|	until	2049	|	2149	|	2249	234
	Pisa Centrale 613 ..... ⊡ a.	...	0716	0810	0825	...	0910	...	1010	...	1105	...	1310	1340	...	1410		...	2110	...	2210	...	...

⊡ – Additional services operate Lucca - Pisa Centrale on ⚒.

PISA and VIAREGGIO - LUCCA - FIRENZE — 614

Most services 2nd class only

km				q														▲			p			
		⚒									⚒											⚒		
0	**Pisa Centrale 613** . ⊡ d.	0620	...	0750	...	0850	...	0950	...	...	1220	1250	...	1343	...	1450	...	and at	1950	...	2050	...	2150	...
	Viareggio .... d.	|	0630	|	0811	|	0911	|	1011	1211	|	|	1311	|	1411	|	1511	the same	|	2011	|	2111	|	2211
24	Lucca .... ⊡ d.	0645	0650	0820	0832	0915	0932	1015	1032	1232	1245	1315	1332	1408	1432	1515	1532	minutes	2015	2032	2115	2132	2215	2232
	Montecatini Centro ..... d.	...	0718	...	0857	...	0957	...	1057	1257	...	...	1357	...	1457	...	1557	past each	...	2057	...	2158	...	2257
	Pistoia .... d.	...	0732	...	0912	...	1012	...	1112	1312	...	...	1412	...	1512	...	1612	hour	...	2112	...	2214	...	2312
	Prato Centrale .... d.	...	0747	...	0928	...	1028	...	1130	1328	...	...	1428	...	1528	...	1628	until	...	2128	...	2230	...	2328
	Firenze SMN 613 ...... a.	...	0803	...	0952	...	1100	...	1159	1352	...	...	1452	...	1552	...	1652		...	2152	...	2252	...	2350

– Not July 30 - Aug. 25.
– † July 30 - Aug. 25; daily Aug. 26 - Dec. 8.

▲ – 1650 departure from Pisa runs Ⓑ only.
⊡ – Additional services operate Pisa Centrale - Lucca on ⚒.

¶ – **Full service PISA Centrale - PISA Aeroporto ✈ and v.v.**: *2 km*, journey 5 minutes. Most services 2nd class only.

From **Pisa Centrale**: 0620, 0720, 0750, 0802, 0850, 0901⚒, 0925, 0950, 1020⚒, 1050, 1120, 1202⚒, 1220, 1250, 1320, 1350, 1420, 1450, 1520, 1550, 1620, 1650, 1720, 1742, 1802Ⓐ, 1820, 1850, 1920, 2020, 2050, 2120, 2202.

From **Pisa Aeroporto**: 0641, 0735, 0818, 0835, 0915, 0942⚒, 1005, 1042, 1105, 1135, 1143⚒, 1235, 1243⚒, 1305, 1335, 1405, 1435, 1505, 1535, 1605, 1635, 1705, 1735, 1753, 1835, 1905, 1935, 1953Ⓐ, 2035, 2105, 2135, 2220.

FIRENZE - PERUGIA - FOLIGNO and ROMA — 615

Faster express trains Firenze - Arezzo - Chiusi - Roma are shown in Table 620

km		⚒	*ES* **9321** [R] 🍷 ♦	2 ⚒	*IC* **579** ⚒	*EN* **389** [R] ♦	*EN* **235** [R] ♦	†	2 ⚒	2 ⚒	†	2 ⚒	*ICp* **577** [R] ♦		2		*ICp* **585** [R] ♦	⚒	2	Ⓐ		*ICp* **703** [R] ♦	2		*ICp* **591** [R] ♦	2
0	**Firenze SMN** .... d.	...	...	...	0550	0618s	0630	...	...	0645	0709	...	0832c	0809	0909	...	1029r	1100	1109	...	1209	1232c	1309	1409	1427r	1509
88	Arezzo .... d.	...	...	...	0630	|	|	...	...	0746	0810	...	0905	0911	1012	...	1106	1149	1212	...	1311	1305	1412	1511	1506	1612
106	Castiglion Fiorentino ... d.	...	...	...	|	|	|	...	...	0758	0822	...	|	0923	1024	...	|	1206	1224	...	1323	|	1424	1523	|	1624
122	Terontola-Cortona ...... d.	...	...	0607	0650	|	|	...	0712	0811	0836	0840	|	0939	1038	...	|	1224	1238	...	1339	|	1438	1539	|	1638
134	Passignano ▲ .... d.	...	...	0620	|	|	|	...	0722	|	|	0856	|	0951	|	...	|	1236	|	...	1351	|	|	1551	|	|
165	**Perugia** .... a.	...	...	0657	|	|	|	...	0749	|	|	0929	|	1019	|	...	|	1301	|	...	1419	|	|	1619	|	|
165	**Perugia 625** .... d.	0603	0645	0658	|	|	|	0718	0751	|	|	0934	|	1021	|	1118	|	1303	|	1342	1421	|	|	1621	|	|
176	Ponte San Giovanni d.	0612	0654	0709	|	|	|	0727	0805	|	|	0946	|	1030	|	1131	|	1312	|	1351	1430	|	|	1630	|	|
189	Assisi **625** .... d.	0624	0704	0721	|	|	|	0737	0822	|	|	0958	|	1042	|	1142	|	1329	|	1405	1442	|	|	1642	|	|
200	Spello .... d.	0633	|	0729	|	|	|	0746	0831	|	|	1006	|	1051	|	1151	|	1339	|	1417	1451	|	|	1651	|	|
205	**Foligno 625** .... a.	0641	0715	0734	|	|	|	0751	0836	|	|	1012	|	1056	|	1158	|	1344	|	1425	1456	|	|	1656	|	|
133	Castiglion del Lago..... d.	|	|	|	|	|	|	|	...	0819	0844	...	|	...	1046	|	|	...	1246	|	...	|	1446	...	|	1646
151	Chiusi ▼ .... d.	|	|	|	0710	0730s	0732	|	...	0833	0859	...	0935	...	1101	|	1135	...	1301	|	...	1335	1501	...	1535	1701
191	Orvieto .... d.	|	|	|	0730	0755s	0757	|	...	0900	0926	...	0958	...	1128	|	1158	...	1328	|	...	1358	1528	...	1558	1728
233	Orte **625** .... d.	0800	0815	0920	|	|	|	0923	...	0933	1009	...	1022	...	1202	1302	1219	...	1402	1537	...	1422	1602	...	1620	1802
311	Roma Tiburtina **625**.... a.	0837	0849	...	|	|	|	1000	...	1008	1046	...	|	...	1236	1336	|	...	1436	1614	...	|	1636	...	|	1836
316	**Roma Termini 625** .... a.	...	0859	...	0824	0905	0905	1010	...	1019	1055	...	1103	...	1248	1348	1303	...	1448	1622	...	1503	1648	...	1703	1848

		ES **9333** [R] 🍷		*IC* **705** ♦	2		*IC* **595** ♦	2		*IC* **709** ♦	2	*ICp* **597** [R] ♦
Firenze SMN .... d.	...	...	1609	1632c	1709	1809	1829r	1909	2009	2032c	2109	2143
Arezzo .... d.	...	...	1711	1705	1812	1911	1906	2012	2111	2105	2212	2234
Castiglion Fiorentino .. d.	...	...	1723	|	1824	1923	|	2024	2123	|	2224	|
Terontola-Cortona ...... d.	...	...	1739	|	1838	1939	|	2038	2139	|	2238	2258
Passignano ▲ .... d.	...	...	1751	|	|	1951	|	|	2151	|	|	|
Perugia .... a.	...	...	1819	|	|	2019	|	|	2219	|	|	2325
Perugia 625 .... d.	1719	1803	1821	|	|	2021	|	|	2221	|	|	2327
Ponte San Giovanni d.	1732	1812	1830	|	|	2030	|	|	2230	|	|	2337
Assisi **625** .... d.	1746	1822	1842	|	|	2042	|	|	2242	|	|	2346
Spello .... d.	1755	|	1851	|	|	2051	|	|	2251	|	|	|
Foligno 625 .... a.	1802	1835	1856	|	|	2056	|	|	2256	|	|	2359
Castiglion del Lago .... d.	|	|	...	|	1846	...	|	2046	...	|	2246	...
Chiusi ▼ .... d.	|	|	...	1735	1901	...	1935	2101	...	2145	2301	...
Orvieto .... d.	|	|	...	1758	1928	...	1958	2128	...	2206	2328	...
Orte **625** .... d.	1918	1944	...	1825	2002	...	2026	2202	...	2227	0001	...
Roma Tiburtina **625** ... a.	1952	2015	...	|	2036	...	|	2236	...	|	0036	...
Roma Termini 625 .... a.	2008	2025	...	1903	2048	...	2106	2248	...	2303	0048	...

	⚒	*ICp* **580** [R] ♦	2 ⚒		*IC* **700** ♦	2 ⚒		Ⓐ		*IC* **582** ♦
Roma Termini 625 d.	...	...	...	0607	0657	...	0712	...	0814	0855
Roma Tiburtina **625** d.	...	...	...	0615	|	...	0720	...	0821	|
Orte **625** .... d.	...	...	...	0655	0734	...	0758	...	0901	0933
Orvieto .... d.	...	...	...	0729	0758	...	0831	...	|	0957
Chiusi ▼ .... d.	...	...	...	0801	0823	...	0901	...	|	1021
Castiglion del Lago d.	...	...	...	0812	|	...	0915	...	|	|
Foligno 625 .... d.	0530	0600	0640	|	|	0736	|	0919	1013	|
Spello .... d.	0535	|	0645	|	|	0741	|	0924	1019	|
Assisi **625** .... d.	0543	0612	0654	|	|	0750	|	0933	1028	|
Ponte S. Giovanni d.	0554	0628	0710	|	|	0804	|	0945	1046	|
Perugia 625 .... a.	0602	0637	0719	|	|	0815	|	0953	1055	|
Perugia .... d.	0607	0639	0721	|	|	0823	|	0954	...	|
Passignano ▲ ..... d.	0641	|	0754	|	|	0855	|	1025	...	|
Terontola-Cortona .. d.	0656	0710	0806	0821	|	0908	0923	1037	...	|
Castiglion Fiorentino d.	0709	|	...	0834	|	...	0940	|	...	|
Arezzo .... d.	0727	0735	...	0846	0855	...	1001	1101	...	1055
Firenze SMN .... a.	0838	0817	...	0951	0924c	...	1051	1151	...	1124c

		IC **704** ♦	Ⓐ				*ICp* **586** [R] ♦		Ⓐ	*ES* **9328** [R] 🍷	*ICp* **706** [R] ♦		2 ⚒	*IC* **592** ♦			*IC* **594** Ⓑp	2 ⚒	Ⓐ	⚒	Ⓑp	*ICp* **596** [R] ♦		*ES* **9336** [R] 🍷 ♦	*EN* **234** [R] ♦	*EN* **388** [R] ♦
Roma Termini 625 .... d.	0912	1055	...	1112	...	1214	1257	1314	...	1346	1457	1512	...	1657	...	1712	1755	...	...	...	1814	1857	1912	1944	1910	1910
Roma Tiburtina **625** ... d.	0920	|	...	1120	...	1221	|	1321	...	1353	|	1520	...	|	...	1720	|	...	...	...	1821	|	1920	1951	|	|
Orte **625** .... d.	0958	1132	...	1158	...	1301	1334	1359	...	1424	1534	1558	...	1734	...	1758	|	...	...	...	1900	1934	1958	2022	|	|
Orvieto .... d.	1031	1156	...	1231	...	|	1358	1433	...	|	1558	1631	...	1758	...	1831	1845	...	...	...	|	1958	2031	|	2014	2014u
Chiusi ▼ .... d.	1101	1221	...	1301	...	|	1423	1503	...	|	1623	1701	...	1820	...	1901	1911	...	...	...	|	2023	2101	|	2045	2045u
Castiglion del Lago .... d.	1112	|	...	1312	...	|	|	1514	...	|	|	1712	...	|	...	1912	|	...	...	...	|	|	2112	|	|	|
Foligno 625 .... d.	|	|	1104	|	1304	1408	|	|	1504	1521	|	|	1622	|	1704	|	|	1821	1904	1956	2010	|	|	2122	|	|
Spello .... d.	|	|	1109	|	1309	1418	|	|	1509	|	|	|	1629	|	1709	|	|	1830	1909	2002	2017	|	|	|	|	|
Assisi **625** .... d.	|	|	1118	|	1318	1428	|	|	1518	1533	|	|	1643	|	1718	|	|	1842	1918	2012	2028	|	|	2135	|	|
Ponte San Giovanni d.	|	|	1130	|	1331	1446	|	|	1530	1549	|	|	1656	|	1731	|	|	1854	1931	2031	2046	|	|	2146	|	|
Perugia 625 .... a.	|	|	1139	|	1339	1455	|	|	1539	1557	|	|	1705	|	1739	|	|	1902	1940	2039	2055	|	|	2155	|	|
Perugia .... d.	|	|	1141	|	1341	...	|	|	1541	...	|	|	1707	|	1741	|	|	1908	1942	2040	...	|	|	...	|	|
Passignano ▲ .... d.	|	|	1209	|	1409	...	|	|	1609	...	|	|	1752	|	1809	|	|	1952	2009	2106	...	|	|	...	|	|
Terontola-Cortona ...... d.	1121	|	1221	1321	1421	...	|	1523	1621	...	|	1721	1804	|	1821	1921	1932	2004	2021	2118	...	|	2121	...	|	|
Castiglion Fiorentino .. d.	1134	|	1234	1334	1434	...	|	1536	1634	...	|	1734	...	|	1834	1934	|	...	2034	...	...	|	2134	...	|	|
Arezzo .... d.	1146	1255	1246	1346	1446	...	1455	1548	1646	...	1655	1746	...	1855	1846	1946	2002	...	2046	...	...	2055	2146	...	|	|
Firenze SMN .... a.	1251	1324c	1351	1451	1551	...	1524c	1651	1751	...	1724c	1851	...	1924c	1951	2051	2041	...	2150	...	...	2124c	2251	...	2141	2153u

♦ – NOTES (LISTED BY TRAIN NUMBER)

234/5 – ALLEGRO TOSCA – 🛏 1,2 cl., ▬ 2 cl. (4 berth) and (2) Roma - Wien Süd and v.v. Supplement payable.
388/9 – *City Night Line* CAPRI – 🛏 1,2 cl., ▬ 2 cl. and (2) Roma - München and v.v. Supplement payable.
580/97 – TACITO – (12) Terni - Milano and v.v.
582/95 – VESUVIO – (12) Napoli - Milano and v.v.
577/96 – SCALIGERO – (12) Verona - Roma and v.v.
585/92 – BRERA – (12) Milano - Roma and v.v.
586/91 – PARTENOPE – (12) Napoli - Milano and v.v.
700/9 – CANOVA – (12) Roma - Venezia Mestre - Udine and v.v.
703/6 – MIRAMARE – (12) Trieste (**702/7**) - Venezia Mestre - Napoli and v.v.
704/5 – MATILDE SERAO – (12) Napoli - Venezia and v.v.
9321 – ⚒: (12) and 🍷 Perugia - Roma.
9336 – Ⓑ (not days before holidays): (12) and 🍷 Roma - Perugia.

c – Firenze **Campo di Marte**.
p – Not days before holidays.
r – Firenze **Rifredi**.
s – Stops to set down only.
u – Stops to pick up only.

▲ – Passignano sul Trasimeno.
▼ – Chiusi - Chianciano Terme.

Additional local services are available on ⚒ Firenze - Chiusi and v.v. serving Arezzo, Castiglion Fiorentino, Terontola-Cortona and Castiglion del Lago.

619 MILANO and TORINO - BOLOGNA

Trains with intermediate stops only. Express services shown on Tables 620, 630

km		E 907	ICp 577	AV 9425	ICp 551	ESc 9751	ES 9459	ICp 585			IC 1591	IC 1589		IC 587		ES 9307	ICp 507	ES 9413	ICp 553	ICp 591	CIS 153	ICp 557			IC 559	IC 1557
			R	R 🍷	R	R ✕	R 🍷	R								R 🍷	R	R 🍷	R	R	R ✕	R				
		◆	◆		A	◆	◆		R	L	Z	Z	P	F	A	◆	Z	◆	◆			A			◆	◆
0	**Milano Centrale** d.	...	...	0530	0605	0705	...	0710	...	0700	0730	0730	0730	0810	...	...	...	...	0910	1110	1150	1200	...	...	...	1430
	Torino P N 610 d.	2250	...	│	│	│	...	│	...	│	│	│	│	│	0605	0630	0705	0745	│	│	│	│	...	...	1155	│
	Asti **610** d.	2332	...	│	│	│	...	│	...	│	│	│	│	│	0651	0700	0744	0819	│	│	│	│	...	...	1228	│
	Alessandria **610** d.	2356	...	│	│	│	...	│	...	│	│	│	│	│	0716	0724	0810	0840	│	│	│	│	...	...	1251	│
	Tortona **610** d.	0014	...	│	│	│	...	│	0649	│	│	│	│	│	0750	│	│	│	│	│	│	│	...	1250	│	│
	Voghera **610** d.	0027	...	│	│	│	...	│	0703	│	│	│	│	│	0803	0752	0840	0904	│	│	│	│	...	1303	1316	│
72	Piacenza d.	0105	...	0612	0653	0744	...	0752	0757	0805	0822	0822	0843	0853	0857	0830	0917	0942	0953	1152	│	1253	...	1343	1353	1516
107	Fidenza d.	│	...	0633	│	│	0807	│	0819	0827	0854	0854	0906	0910	0919	│	│	│	│	│	│	│	...	...	│	1537
129	Parma d.	│	...	0646	0720	│	0820	0825	0833	...	0908	0908	0918	0922	0933	│	0949	│	1021	1219	1250	1320	...	...	1421	1551
157	Reggio Emilia d.	│	...	0702	0735	│	│	0842	0850	...	0926	0926	0933	0937	0951	│	1006	│	1036	1234	│	1337	...	...	1436	1625
182	Modena d.	│	0648	0717	0752	│	0847	0858	0904	...	0941	0941	0947	0953	1005	│	1021	│	1052	1250	1314	1352	...	...	1452	1655
219	**Bologna Centrale** a.	0234	0716	0742	0821	0852	0908	0922	0930	...	1007	1007	1010	1016	1030	0936	1101	1052	1116	1311	1336	1416	...	...	1516	1720
	Roma Termini **620** a.	...	1103	1030	...	...	1155	1303	...	...	1400t	1400t	...	...	...	1220	1406t	...	...	1703	...	...	...	...	...	1945t
	Napoli C **640** a.	...	...	1212	...	...	...	...	...	...	1658	1658	...	...	...	...	1636	...	...	1936	...	...	...	...	...	2226p

km		IC 593	E 823	IC 595		ICp 561	E 1921	ICp 563		ICp 597			ICp 565			E 1991	ICp 599		E 923	ICp 569	ICN 781	E 833	E 901	ICN 785	E 1911	
						R		R		R			R				R			R						
		F	Z			◆	Z	◆	L	◆	A		A	R	⑤	Z	F		◆	v	◆	◆	◆	◆	◆	
	Milano Centrale d.	1405	1430	1510	...	1605	1635	1710	1705	1750	...	1820	1910	...	1853g	1940	2005	...	2040	2105	2120	2200	...	2300	2320	...
0	**Torino P N 610** d.	│	│	│	1420	│	│	│	│	│	1620	│	│	...	│	│	│	1820	│	│	│	│	2105	│	│	...
56	Asti **610** d.	│	│	│	1506	│	│	│	│	│	1706	│	│	...	│	│	│	1906	│	│	│	│	2139	│	│	...
91	Alessandria **610** d.	│	│	│	1533	│	│	│	│	│	1733	│	│	...	│	│	│	1933	│	│	│	│	2206	│	│	...
113	Tortona **610** d.	│	│	│	1550	│	│	│	│	│	1750	│	│	1850	│	│	│	1950	│	│	│	│	2222	│	│	...
130	Voghera **610** d.	│	│	│	1603	│	│	│	│	│	1803	│	│	1903	│	│	│	2003	│	│	│	│	2235	│	│	...
188	Piacenza d.	1453	1516	1552	1643	1653	1740	1753	1812	1848	1857	1910	1953	1957	2004	│	2049	2057	2139	2153	2204	2252	2314	2346	0011	...
	Fidenza d.	│	│	1609	...	│	│	│	1835	│	1919	1935	│	2020	2028	│	2112	2119	2158	│	│	2317	│	│	│	...
	Parma d.	1521	│	1621	...	1720	1810	1820	...	1917	1933	1949	2020	2033	...	│	2124	2133	2212	2221	2243	2332	2351	0018	0101	...
	Reggio Emilia d.	1537	│	1636	...	1737	1826	1837	...	1936	1951	2006	2037	2051	...	│	2139	2151	2229	2237	2303	2352	0010	0038	│	...
	Modena d.	1553	│	1651	...	1752	1840	1852	...	1954	2005	2020	2052	2105	...	2201	2154	2205	2244	2253	2318	0009	0027	0055	│	...
	Bologna Centrale a.	1616	1636	1711	...	1816	1903	1916	...	2016	2033	2048	2120	2133	...	2225	2216	2233	2310	2316	2352	0039	0054	0124	...	...
	Roma Termini **620** a.	...	2042t	2106	...	...	2319t	...	...	...	...	...	...	...	...	...	...	...	...	...	...	0452t	...	...	0715	...
	Napoli C **640** a.	...	...	2336	...	...	...	...	...	...	...	...	...	...	...	...	...	...	...	...	...	0810	...	...	1007	...

	E 900	ICN 780	E 1910			ICN 784	E 830	E 906		ICp 552	E 926	ICp 578		ICN 752	ICp 556	E 1920		ICp 580		ICp 558	IC 582	IC 584	IC 560	ICp 562	
				2	2					R		R	2		R			R		R			R	R	
	◆	◆	◆			◆	◆	◆		ⒶR	◆	F	L	Z	A	Z	A	◆	A	◆		F	◆	A	
Napoli C **640** d.	...	...	2036	...	...	...	2150	...	...	...	...	...	...	...	...	...	...	...	...	...	0624	...	...	...	...
Roma Termini **620** d.	...	...	2300	...	...	...	0047t	...	...	...	...	...	...	0427t	...	0505t	...	...	...	...	0855	...	...	...	...
Bologna Centrale d.	0325	0412	│	0453	0530	0548	0602	0618	0627	0644	0657	0744	...	0755	0837	0859s	0928	0944	...	1044	1244	1342	1444	1544	...
Modena d.	│	0437	│	0521	0556	0612	0629	0640	0653	0704	0725	0805	...	│	0859	0923s	0953	1008	...	1104	1305	1405	1506	1604	...
Reggio Emilia d.	│	0455	│	0536	0611	0629	0646	0656	0708	0719	0744	0819	...	│	0920	0939s	1008	1023	...	1119	1319	1419	1521	1619	...
Parma d.	│	0514	│	0553	0628	0648	0706	0715	0724	0736	│	0836	...	│	0938	1000s	1025	1039	...	1136	1336	1436	1538	1636	...
Fidenza d.	│	│	│	0607	0642	│	│	│	0739	│	│	0849	0907	│	│	│	1038	│	←	│	1349	│	│	│	...
Piacenza d.	0446	0554	0602	0638	0708	0730	0814	0754	0817	0808	0832	0909	0932	0955	1008	1038s	1102	1108	1117	1209	1409	1509	1609	1708	1717
Voghera **610** d.	0524	│	│	0721	│	│	│	0833	0859	│	│	│	│	│	│	│	→	│	1159	│	│	│	1644	│	1759
Tortona **610** d.	0537	│	│	0736	│	│	│	0847	0910	│	│	│	│	│	│	│	...	│	1212	│	│	│	│	│	1812
Alessandria **610** d.	0554	│	│	0800	│	│	│	0905	...	│	│	│	│	│	│	│	...	│	1229	│	│	│	1709	│	1829
Asti **610** d.	0616	│	│	0822	│	│	│	0927	...	│	│	│	│	│	│	│	...	│	1251	│	│	│	1730	│	1851
Torino P N 610 a.	0705	│	│	0910	│	│	│	1010	...	│	│	│	│	│	│	│	...	│	1340	│	│	│	1805	│	1940
Milano Centrale a.	...	0705	0715	...	0800	0820	0920	...	...	0855	0925	1000	1025	1050	1055	1125	...	1150	...	1255	1450	1555	...	1750	...

	E 1550	CIS 150	ICp 586		ICp 564			ICp 568	ES 9416			ES 9460	IC 588	ICp 530	ES 9300	IC 1554	ICp 592			ES 9450	IC 1590	IC 1588	ICp 570	ICp 596	
		R ✕	R		R			R	R 🍷			R ✕		R	R ✕		R	2		R ✕			R	R	
	◆	◆		A	◆	A	R	◆	◆	R	Lj	◆	Z	Z	◆	◆		L	P		Z	Z	A	◆	
Napoli C **640** d.	...	...	1024	...	...	...	...	...	...	...	...	...	...	1424	...	1300p	...	...	...	...	1442	1442	...	...	...
Roma Termini **620** d.	...	...	1257	...	...	...	...	...	...	...	...	1635	...	1643t	1735	1553t	1657	...	...	1830	1706t	1706t	...	1857	...
Bologna Centrale d.	1557	1633	1644	1727	1744	...	1827	1844	1908	...	...	1923	1944	1951	2022	2004	2050	...	2056	2116	2134	2134	2144	2244	...
Modena d.	1619	1658	1706	1753	1804	...	1853	1904	│	...	...	1947	2005	2013	│	2028	2110	...	2119	2137	2159	2159	2204	2303	...
Reggio Emilia d.	1634	│	1720	1808	1819	...	1908	1919	│	...	...	│	2019	2028	│	2053	2125	...	2135	2151	2214	2214	2219	...	...
Parma d.	1651	1728	1736	1825	1836	...	1925	1936	│	...	...	2015	2036	2045	│	2114	2143	...	2158	2208	2230	2230	2236	...	...
Fidenza d.	│	│	│	1838	│	←	1938	│	│	←	2016	2031	2049	│	│	2128	│	2200	2212	2221	2242	2242	│	...	...
Piacenza d.	1727	│	1809	1902	1909	1917	2003	2009	2016	2027	2040	...	2109	2117	2128	2154	2213	2224	2246	2243	2301	2301	2312	...	...
Voghera **610** d.	│	│	│	→	│	1959	→	│	2049	2116	│	...	│	2201	2210	│	│	│	│	│	│	│	│	...	...
Tortona **610** d.	│	│	│	...	│	2011	...	│	│	2129	│	...	│	│	│	│	│	│	│	│	│	│	│	...	...
Alessandria **610** d.	│	│	│	...	│	2029	...	│	2117	...	│	...	│	2227	2237	│	│	│	│	│	│	│	│	...	...
Asti **610** d.	│	│	│	...	│	2051	...	│	2139	...	│	...	│	2247	2254	│	│	│	│	│	│	│	│	...	...
Torino P N 610 a.	│	│	│	...	│	2140	...	│	2215	...	│	...	│	2325	2330	│	│	│	│	│	│	│	│	...	...
Milano Centrale a.	1810	1830	1850	...	1950	...	...	2050	...	...	2145g	...	2150	...	...	2235	2255	2315	2340	2325	2345	2345	2359	...	...

◆ – **NOTES** (LISTED BY TRAIN NUMBER)

150/3 – (12) and ✕ Firenze - Zürich and v.v.
553/68 – MURGE – (12) Milano - Bari - Taranto (**554/67**) - Metaponto (**555/66**) - Crotone and v.v.
558/63 – D'ANNUNZIO – (12) Pescara Centrale - Milano and v.v.
559/60 – ROSSINI – (12) Torino - Bari and v.v.
561/4 – LEOPARDI – (12) Milano - Pescara and v.v.
580/97 – TACITO – (12) Terni - Milano and v.v.
577/96 – SCALIGERO – (12) Verona - Roma and v.v.
780/1 – FRECCIA SALENTINA – 🛏 1,2 cl. (T2), 🛏 1,2 cl., ▬ 2 cl. (4 berth) and (12) Lecce - Milano and v.v.
784/5 – FRECCIA DEL LEVANTE – Not Dec. 24, 25, 31: ▬ 2 cl. and (12) Crotone (**782/7**) - Metaponto (**783/6**) - Taranto - Milano and v.v.; 🛏 1,2 cl. (T2), 🛏 1,2 cl. and (12) Taranto - Milano and v.v.
830 – ⑦ (also Aug. 15, Nov. 1): (12) Salerno - Milano.
833 – ⑤ (also Aug 14, Oct. 31): (2) Milano - Salerno.
900 – ⑦; also Dec. 26, Jan. 1, Mar. 24, May 1, June 2, not Dec. 23, 30, Mar. 23, June 1 (from Bari): ▬ 2 cl. and (2) (also 🛏 1,2 cl. (T2) June 4 - Sept. 8) Bari - Torino.
901/6 – FRECCIA ADRIATICA – 🛏 1,2 cl. (T2), ▬ 2 cl. and (2) Torino - Lecce and v.v.; ▬ 2 cl. and (2) Torino - Bari (**903/10**) - Taranto (**904/9**) - Metaponto (**905/8**) - Catanzaro Lido and v.v.
907 – ⑤; also Apr. 24, 30, not Apr. 25 (from Torino): ▬ 2 cl. and (2) (also 🛏 1,2 cl. (T2) June 3 - Sept. 7) Torino - Bari.
923/6 – Not Dec. 24, 25, 31: 🛏 1,2 cl. (T2), ▬ 2 cl. (4/6 berth) and (2) Milano - Lecce and v.v.
1550 – APULIA – ⑦ (also Nov. 1): (2) Bari - Milano.
1554 – ⑦ (also Nov. 1): (12) Salerno - Milano.
1557 – ⑤ (also Oct. 31): (12) Milano - Salerno.
1910 – 🛏 1,2 cl. (Excelsior), 🛏 1,2 cl. (T2), 🛏 1,2 cl., ▬ 2 cl. (4 berth) and (2) Napoli - Milano.
1911 – 🛏 1,2 cl. (Excelsior), 🛏 1,2 cl. (T2), 🛏 1,2 cl., ▬ 2 cl. (4 berth) and (2) Milano - Napoli.

9300 – ⑧ (not days before holidays): (12) and ✕ Roma - Torino.
9307 – ⚒: (12) and 🍷 Torino - Roma.
9413/6 – (12) and 🍷 Torino - Lecce and v.v.
9459 – (12) and 🍷 Bergamo (**9458**) - Treviglio - Roma.
9460 – (12) and 🍷 Roma - Bergamo.
9751 – (12) and ✕ Milano - Lecce.

A – From/to Ancona.
F – From/to Firenze.
L – (12) Milano - Aulla - Livorno and v.v.
P – ⑥⑦: (2) Milano - Pescara and v.v.
R – From/to Rimini.
Z – For days of running and composition see Table **640**.

g – Milano **Porta Garibaldi**.
j – ⑦ (also Aug. 15; not Aug. 12).
p – Napoli **Piazza Garibaldi**.
s – Stops to set down only.
t – Roma **Tiburtina**.
v – ①②③④⑦ (not days before holidays).

VENEZIA and MILANO - BOLOGNA - FIRENZE - ROMA 620

km		*E*	*E*	*ICN*	*E*		*IC*	*EN*	*EN*	*ES*	*EN*	*EN*	*E*	*E*	*E*	*ES*	*ES*	*ICp*		*AV*			*T-Biz*	*ES*	*ICp*	*ES*
		833	**837**	**771**	**1911**		**579**	**235**	**389**	**9421**	**313**	**375**	**1235**	**1237**	**1135**	**9423**	**9461**	**577**		**9425**			**9301**	**9463**	**577**	**9427**
								R □	R	R 🍷	R	□	R □	R □	R □	R 🍷	R 🍷	R		R 🍷			R 🍷	R 🍷	R	R 🍷
		♦	♦	Z	Z		⚒	♦	♦		♦	♦	♦	♦	♦			♦				2	x		♦	
0	**Venezia Santa Lucia 600** d.	...	...	0004	...	...	...	...	...	...	...	...	...	...	...	...	...	...	...	...	...	0557	...	0643	...	...
9	**Venezia Mestre 600** d.	...	...	0017	...	...	...	0311	...	...	...	...	0357	0357	0446s	...	0519	...	...	...	...	0610	...	0654u	...	...
37	Padova **600** d.	...	...	0041	...	...	...	|	...	...	...	...	0421	0421	0524s	...	0539	...	0550	...	...	0633	...	0711	...	...
81	Rovigo d.	...	...	0117	...	...	...	|	...	...	...	...	0448	0448	0554s	...	0612	...	0622	...	...	0707	...	|	...	...
113	Ferrara d.	...	...	0141	...	...	...	0419	...	...	...	...	0509	0509	0619	...	0638	...	0643	...	...	0731	...	|	...	...
	Milano C 619/30 d.	2200	...	|	2320	...	...	|	...	...	...	...	|	|	...	...	|	...	|	0530	...	|	0635	|	...	0700
160	**Bologna C 619/30** a.	0039	...	0217	|	...	...	0448	0435s	...	...	...	0541	0541	...	...	0708	...	0720	0742	...	0804	0815	0820	...	0842
160	**Bologna C** d.	0044	0115	0222	|	...	...	0515	|	...	0524s	...	0546	0546	...	0638	0712	0720	...	0746	...	...	0817	0824	...	0846
241	Prato d.	|	|	|	|	...	...	|	|	...	|	...	|	|	...	0728	|	0808	...	|	...	...	|	|	...	|
255	Firenze Campo di Marte d.	|	|	|	|	...	...	|	|	...	0656s	0701	|	0725	...	|	|	0832	...	|	...	...	|	|	...	|
257	**Firenze SMN** a.	|	|	|	|	...	...	0618	0618s	...	|	|	0659	|	...	0744	0811	|	...	0844	...	...	|	0922	...	0944
257	**Firenze SMN** d.	|	|	|	|	...	0550	0630	|	0640	|	|	...	|	...	0752	0819	|	...	0852	...	...	|	0930	←	0952
345	Arezzo d.	|	|	0458	|	...	0630	|	|	0714	|	|	...	|	...	|	|	0903	...	|	...	...	|	|	0905	|
408	Chiusi-Chianciano Terme d.	|	|	0543	|	...	0710	0732	0730s	|	|	|	...	|	...	|	|	→	...	|	...	...	|	|	0935	|
568	Roma Tiburtina a.	0452	0609	0656	|	...	|	|	|	|	|	|	...	|	...	|	|	...	...	|	...	...	|	|	|	|
573	**Roma Termini** a.	|	|	|	0715	...	0824	0905	0905	0830	0912	0945	...	1005	...	0930	0955	...	...	1030	...	...	1040	1108	1103	1130
	Napoli Centrale **640** a.	0810	0926	1000	1007	...	...	...	...	...	...	...	...	...	...	...	...	...	...	1212	...	...	...	...	...	...

	ES	*ES*		*IC*	*ICp*	*AV*			*IC*		*ES*	*IC*	*IC*	*ES*		*ICp*	*ICp*	*AV*	*ES*	*ES*		*ICp*	*ES*		*ICp*	*CIS*
	9459	**9307**		**713**	**585**	**9429**			**1589**		**9467**	**587**	**1589**	**9491**		**507**	**703**	**9433**	**9311**	**9469**		**703**	**9435**		**591**	**153**
	R 🍷	R 🍷			R	R ✕					R ✕			R 🍷		R	R	R ✕	R ✕	R ✕		R	R ✕		R	R ✕
	♦	♦	2 ⚒	♦			2		Z	2			Z	♦		Z	♦		B			♦		2		♦
Venezia Santa Lucia 600 d.	...	...	0657	0723	...	...	0727	...	...	0757	0843	...	...	...	...	...	...	...	...	1043	...	...	...	1057	...	...
Venezia Mestre 600 d.	...	...	0710	0735	...	...	0740	...	...	0810	0854u	...	...	...	...	...	0921	...	...	1054u	...	...	...	1110	...	...
Padova **600** d.	...	...	0733	0756	...	...	0807	...	...	0833	0911	...	...	...	...	...	0941	...	...	1111	...	...	...	1133	...	...
Rovigo d.	...	...	0807	0825	...	...	0843	...	...	0907	|	...	...	...	...	...	1011	...	...	|	...	...	...	1207	...	...
Ferrara d.	...	...	0831	0845	...	...	0900	...	...	0931	|	...	...	...	...	...	1034	...	...	|	...	...	...	1231	...	...
Milano C 619/30 d.	...	...	|	|	0710	0800	|	...	0730	|	|	0810	...	0845g	...	...	|	1000	...	|	...	...	1100	|	1110	1150
Bologna C 619/30 a.	...	...	0904	0916	0922	0942	0938	...	1007	1004	1020	1016	...	1036	...	...	1116	1142	...	1220	...	...	1242	1304	1311	1336
Bologna C d.	0922	0939	...	...	0928	0946	...	...	1012	...	1024	1030	←	1040	...	1105	1120	1146	1204	1224	...	...	1246	...	1315	1340
Prato d.	|	1022	...	...	1016	|	...	...	1123	...	|	1118	1133	|	...	1158	1208	|	|	|	...	...	|	...	1402	|
Firenze Campo di Marte d.	1020r	1036r	...	...	1029r	|	...	...	→	...	|	|	1201	|	...	1220	1232	|	|	|	...	...	|	...	1427r	|
Firenze SMN a.	|	|	...	...	|	1044	...	...	...	...	1122	1138	|	1136	...	|	|	1244	1310	1322	...	...	1344	...	|	1432
Firenze SMN d.	|	|	...	...	|	1052	...	...	...	...	1130	...	|	1144	...	|	|	1252	1320	1330	...	←	1352	...	|	...
Arezzo d.	|	|	...	...	1106	|	...	...	...	...	|	...	|	|	...	|	1303	|	|	|	...	1305	|	...	1506	...
Chiusi-Chianciano Terme d.	|	|	...	...	1135	|	...	...	...	...	|	...	1254	|	...	|	→	|	|	|	...	1335	|	...	1535	...
Roma Tiburtina a.	|	|	...	...	|	|	...	...	...	...	|	...	1400	|	...	1406	...	|	|	|	...	|	|	...	→	...
Roma Termini a.	1203	1220	...	...	1303	1230	...	...	...	...	1308	...	|	1322	...	|	...	1430	1455	1508	...	1503	1530	...	...	...
Napoli Centrale **640** a.	...	...	...	...	...	1412	...	...	...	...	...	...	1658	...	...	1636	...	1612	...	...	...	1736	...	...	...	...

	AV		*ES*	*ICp*		*ES*		*ES*	*IC*	*AV*	*IC*	*ES*	*IC*	*EC*		*E*	*ES*		*IC*	*IC*	*IC*		*AV*	*IC*		*ES*
	9437		**9473**	**591**		**9439**		**9493**	**705**	**9441**	**705**	**9477**	**593**	**85**		**823**	**9443**		**715**	**595**	**1557**		**9445**	**595**		**9481**
	R ✕		R ✕	R		R ✕		R 🍷		R ✕		R 🍷		R ✕			R 🍷						R ✕			R ✕
		2					2			Z				♦		Z		2	♦		⑤				- 2	
Venezia Santa Lucia 600 d.	...	1157	1243	...	...	...	1257	...	1323	...	...	1443	...	...	...	...	...	1457	1523	...	...	...	...	...	1557	1643
Venezia Mestre 600 d.	...	1210	1254u	...	...	...	1310	...	1335	...	...	1454u	...	...	...	...	...	1510	1535	...	...	...	...	...	1610	1654u
Padova **600** d.	...	1233	1311	...	...	...	1333	...	1357	...	...	1511	...	...	...	...	...	1533	1555	...	...	...	...	...	1633	1711
Rovigo d.	...	1307	|	...	...	...	1407	...	1427	...	...	|	...	...	...	...	...	1607	1621	...	...	...	...	...	1707	|
Ferrara d.	...	1331	|	...	...	...	1431	...	1447	...	...	|	...	...	...	...	...	1631	1643	...	...	...	...	...	1731	|
Milano C 619/30 d.	1200	|	|	...	...	1300	|	1330	|	1400	...	|	1405	...	...	1430	1500	|	|	1510	1430	...	1600	...	|	|
Bologna C 619/30 a.	1342	1404	1420	...	...	1442	1504	1512	1516	1542	...	1620	1616	...	...	1636	1642	1704	1712	1711	1720	...	1742	...	1804	1820
Bologna C d.	1346	...	1424	...	...	1446	...	1516	1520	1546	...	1624	1630	1634	...	1640	1646	...	...	1715	1730	...	1746	...	...	1824
Prato d.	|	...	|	...	...	|	...	|	1608	|	...	|	1718	1723	...	1746	|	...	...	1816	1839	...	|	...	...	|
Firenze Campo di Marte d.	|	...	|	...	...	|	...	|	1632	|	...	|	|	|	...	1819	|	...	...	1829r	1903	...	|	...	...	|
Firenze SMN a.	1444	...	1522	...	...	1544	...	1617	|	1644	...	1722	1738	1738	...	|	1744	...	...	|	|	...	1844	...	...	1922
Firenze SMN d.	1452	...	1530	...	...	1552	...	1625	|	1652	←	1730	...	1752	...	|	1752	...	...	|	|	...	1852	←	...	1930
Arezzo d.	|	...	|	←	...	|	...	|	1703	|	1705	|	...	1842	...	|	|	...	...	1904	|	...	|	1906	...	|
Chiusi-Chianciano Terme d.	|	...	|	1535	...	|	...	|	→	|	1735	|	...	|	...	1922	|	...	...	→	|	...	|	1935	...	|
Roma Tiburtina a.	|	...	|	|	...	|	...	|	...	|	|	|	...	|	...	2042	|	...	...	...	2043	...	|	|	...	|
Roma Termini a.	1630	...	1708	1703	...	1730	...	1803	...	1830	1903	1908	...	2018	...	...	1930	...	...	...	|	...	2030	2106	...	2112
Napoli Centrale **640** a.	1812	...	...	1936	...	...	...	...	...	...	2136	...	...	...	...	...	...	...	...	...	2253p	...	2212	2336	...	...

	T-Biz	*AV*	*E*			*IC*	*ES*	*ES*	*IC*		*ES*	*ICp*		*ES*		*E*		*ES*	*E*		*ICN*		*ICp*	*ICN*	*E*	
	9303	**9447**	**1921**			**709**	**9313**	**9449**	**709**		**9485**	**597**		**9451**		**1931**		**9453**	**1991**		**751**		**599**	**779**	**1595**	
	R ✕	R ✕					R ✕	R ✕			R ✕	R		R ✕				R ✕					R			
	w		Z	2		♦	B		♦	2		♦				Z			Z		Z	2		♦	Z	
Venezia Santa Lucia 600 d.	...	...	...	1657	...	...	...	...	...	1757	1836	...	...	...	...	1903	...	...	...	...	...	1957	...	2122	...	...
Venezia Mestre 600 d.	...	...	...	1710	...	1732	...	...	...	1810	1847u	...	...	...	...	1920	...	...	...	...	...	2010	...	2206	...	...
Padova **600** d.	...	...	...	1733	...	1753	...	...	...	1833	1903	...	...	...	...	1942	...	...	...	...	...	2033	...	2230	...	...
Rovigo d.	...	...	...	1807	...	1827	...	...	...	1907	1930	...	...	...	...	2015	...	...	...	...	...	2107	...	2310	...	...
Ferrara d.	...	...	...	1831	...	1847	...	...	...	1931	1950	...	...	...	...	2040	...	...	...	...	...	2131	...	2332	...	...
Milano C 619/30 d.	1655	1700	1635	|	...	|	...	1800	...	|	|	1750	...	1900	...	|	...	2000	1940	...	1945	|	2005	...	...	...
Bologna C 619/30 a.	1829	1842	1903	1904	...	1916	...	1942	...	2004	2020	2016	...	2042	...	2113	...	2142	2225	...	2204	2204	2216	...	...	...
Bologna C d.	1831	1846	1910	...	...	1920	1940	1946	...	...	2024	2030	...	2046	...	2135	...	2146	2233	...	2208	...	2220	...	2226	...
Prato d.	|	|	|	...	...	2008	|	|	...	...	|	2118	...	|	...	|	...	|	|	...	|	...	2320	...	|	...
Firenze Campo di Marte d.	|	|	2100	...	...	2032	|	|	...	...	|	|	...	|	...	2238	...	|	2355	...	2325	...	|	...	2347	...
Firenze SMN a.	|	1944	|	...	...	|	2033	2044	...	...	2122	2131	...	2144	...	...	...	2244	...	...	...	...	2340	...	|	...
Firenze SMN d.	|	1952	|	...	...	|	2043	2052	←	...	2130	2143	...	2152	...	...	...	...	...	...	...	...	...	...	|	...
Arezzo d.	|	|	|	...	...	2103	|	|	2105	...	|	2232	...	|	...	...	...	...	...	...	...	...	...	...	|	...
Chiusi-Chianciano Terme d.	|	|	|	...	...	→	|	|	2145	...	|	...	...	|	...	...	...	...	...	...	...	...	...	...	|	...
Roma Tiburtina a.	|	|	2319	...	...	...	|	|	|	...	|	...	...	|	...	...	...	...	...	...	...	...	...	...	|	...
Roma Termini a.	2100	2130	...	...	...	...	2220	2230	2303	...	2308	...	...	2330	...	...	...	...	...	...	...	...	...	...	|	...
Napoli Centrale **640** a.	...	2312	...	...	...	...	...	...	...	...	...	...	...	...	...	...	...	...	...	...	...	...	...	...	0432	...

♦ – **NOTES** (LISTED BY TRAIN NUMBER)

85 – MICHELANGELO – [12] and ✕ München - Innsbruck - Verona - Roma.
153 – [12] and ✕ Zürich - Firenze.
235 – ALLEGRO TOSCA – 🛏 1,2 cl., ▬ 2 cl. (4 berth) and [2] Wien Süd - Villach - Venezia Mestre - Roma.
313 – LUNA – 🛏 1,2 cl. and ▬ 2 cl. Zürich - Brig - Roma; 🛏 1,2 cl. and ▬ 2 cl. Genève Aéroport (**311**) - Brig - Roma.
375 – MONTECARLO – 🛏 1,2 cl. and ▬ 2 cl. (4 berth) Nice (**369**) - Ventimiglia - Pisa (**374**) - Firenze - Roma; 🛏 1,2 cl. (Excelsior), 🛏 1,2 cl., ▬ 2 cl. (4/6 berth) and [2] Torino (**767**) - Genova (**369**) - Pisa (**374**) - Firenze - Roma.
389 – *City Night Line* CAPRI – 🛏 1,2 cl., ▬ 2 cl. and [2] Roma - München and v.v. Supplement payable.
577 – SCALIGERO – [12] Verona - Roma.
597 – TACITO – [12] Milano - Terni.
703 – MIRAMARE – [12] Trieste (**702**) - Venezia Mestre - Napoli.
709 – CANOVA – [12] Udine - Roma.
713 – ADRIATICO – [12] Venezia - Lecce.
715 – MANIN – [12] Venezia - Pescara.
779 – TERGESTE – ▬ 2 cl. (4 berth) and [12] Trieste (**778**) - Venezia Mestre - Lecce; 🛏 1,2 cl. (T2), 🛏 1,2 cl. and [12] Venezia Santa Lucia (**1599**) - Mestre - Lecce.
833 – ⑤ (also Aug 14, Oct. 31): [2] Milano - Salerno.
837 – ①②③⑤⑥⑦; also Dec. 27, Jan. 3, May 1; not Dec. 25, 26, Jan. 1, Apr. 30 (from Bolzano): 🛏 1,2 cl., ▬ 2 cl. (4 berth) and [2] Bolzano (**925**) - Bologna - Napoli.
1135 – ALLEGRO AIDA – ⑤ June 1 - Sept. 7 (from Wien): 🛏 1,2 cl., ▬ 2 cl. and [2] Wien Süd - Venezia Mestre - Ancona.
1235 – ALLEGRO RIGOLETTO – ④⑥ June 14 - Sept. 29 (from Wien): 🛏 1,2 cl. (Excelsior), ▬ 2 cl. and [2] Wien Süd - Firenze (**1239**) - Livorno.
1237 – ALLEGRO ROSSINI – ⑤ June 15 - Sept. 28 (from Wien): 🛏 1,2 cl. (Excelsior), ▬ 2 cl. and [2] Wien Süd - Roma.
9307 – ⚒: [12] and 🍷 Torino - Roma.
9459 – [12] and 🍷 Bergamo (**9458**) - Treviglio - Roma.
9491 – [12] and ✕ Torino - Roma.

B – [12] and ✕ Bolzano - Bologna - Roma.
Z – For days of running and composition see Table **640**.

g – Milano **Porta Garibaldi**.
p – Napoli **Piazza Garibaldi**.
r – Firenze **Rifredi**.
s – Stops to set down only.
u – Stops to pick up only.
w – ⑧ (not Dec. 22-31, and days before holidays).
x – Not Dec. 24 - Jan. 1.
□ – Supplement payable.

620 ROMA - FIRENZE - BOLOGNA - MILANO and VENEZIA

km			E	ICp		ICN	E	ES		T-Biz	E	ES		ICp	ES		IC	ES	EC	ES	E	ES	ES	IC	
			1992	578		752	1930	9424		9302	1920	9426		580	9462		700	9428	84	9492	834	9430	9466	582	
				[R]				[R] 🍷		[R] 🍷		[R] 🍷		[R]	[R] 🍷			[R] 🍷	[R] ✕	[R] 🍷		[R] 🍷	[R] ✕		
		⚒	Z			Z	Z			x	Z			♦			♦		♦		Z			Z	
	Napoli Centrale **640** d.	...	...	...	...	...	...	...	...	...	...	...	...	...	...	...	...	...	...	...	...	...	...	0624	...
0	**Roma Termini** d.	...	...	...	...	...	...	...	...	0625	...	0630	...	...	0650	...	0657	0730	0742	0755	...	0830	0850	0855	...
5	Roma Tiburtina d.	...	...	...	...	0427	...	...	...	|	0505s	|	...	...	|	...	|	|	|	|	0616	|	|	|	...
165	Chiusi-Chianciano Terme d.	...	...	...	...	|	...	...	...	|	|	|	...	...	|	...	0823	|	|	|	|	|	|	1021	...
229	Arezzo d.	...	...	...	...	|	...	0628	...	|	|	|	...	0735	|	...	0855	|	0905	|	|	|	|	1055	...
316	**Firenze SMN** a.	...	...	...	...	|	...	0700	...	|	|	0806	...	0817	0830	...	|	0906	0945	0931	|	1006	1030	→	...
316	**Firenze SMN** d.	...	...	0628	...	|	...	0708	...	|	|	0814	...	0829	0838	...	|	0914	0957	0939	|	1014	1038	...	...
319	Firenze Campo di Marte d.	...	0559	|	...	0638	0640s	|	...	|	0722s	|	...	|	|	...	0927	|	|	|	0855	|	|	...	...
333	Prato d.	...	|	0649	...	|	|	0724	...	|	|	|	...	0844	|	...	0951	|	1014	|	0915	|	|	...	...
413	**Bologna C** a.	...	0703	0740	...	0746	0755s	0812	...	0850	0859s	0912	...	0930	0936	...	1040	1012	1118	1036	1018	1112	1136	...	...
413	**Bologna C 619/30** d.	0602	0712	0744	0756	0755	|	0816	0856	0852	|	0916	...	0944	0940	0956	1044	1016	...	1040	1023	1116	1140	...	1156
632	**Milano C 619/30** a.	|	1010	1000	|	1050	|	1000	|	1030	1125	1100	...	1150	|	|	|	1200	...	1225	1245	1300	|	...	|
	Ferrara d.	0637	...	...	0830	...	0901s	...	0930	...	...	...	...	...	|	1030	1113	...	...	...	...	...	|	...	1230
	Rovigo d.	0659	...	...	0854	...	0948s	...	0954	...	...	...	...	...	|	1054	1135	...	...	...	...	...	|	...	1254
	Padova **600** d.	0738	...	...	0929	...	1109s	...	1029	...	...	...	...	...	1051	1129	1206	...	...	...	...	...	1251	...	1329
	Venezia Mestre 600 a.	0758	...	...	0950	...	1133s	...	1050	...	...	...	...	...	1106s	1150	1226	...	...	...	...	...	1306s	...	1350
	Venezia Santa Lucia 600 a.	0812	...	...	1003	...	1146	...	1103	...	...	...	...	...	1117	1203	...	...	...	...	...	...	1317	...	1403

km (via hsl)		ES	AV	ES	IC	IC		AV	ES	IC	IC		AV	IC		ES	ICp	ES		AV	CIS	ICp		ES	ES
		9310	9432	9468	714	582		9434	9470	704	584		9436	704		9438	586	9474		9440	150	586		9442	9478
		[R] ✕	[R] ✕	[R] ✕				[R] ✕	[R] ✕				[R] ✕			[R] ✕	[R]	[R] ✕		[R] ✕	[R] ✕	[R]		[R] 🍷	[R] ✕
		B			♦	Z							Z								♦				
	Napoli Centrale **640** d.	...	0748	...	...	...	...	0848	...	0824	...	...	0948	...	...	...	1024	...	...	1148	...	...	...	...	...
0	**Roma Termini** d.	0900	0930	0945	...	...	...	1030	1050	1055	...	...	1130	...	...	1230	1257	1250	...	1330	...	...	...	1430	1450
	Roma Tiburtina d.	|	|	|	...	...	...	|	|	|	...	...	|	...	...	|	|	|	...	|	...	...	...	|	|
	Chiusi-Chianciano Terme d.	|	|	|	...	←	...	|	|	1221	...	...	|	←	...	|	1423	|	...	|	...	←	...	|	|
	Arezzo d.	|	|	|	...	1055	...	|	|	1255	...	...	|	1255	...	|	1453	|	...	|	...	1455	...	|	|
261	**Firenze SMN** a.	1037	1106	1119	...	|	...	1206	1230	→	...	...	1306	|	...	1406	→	1430	...	1506	...	|	...	1606	1630
	Firenze SMN d.	1047	1114	1127	...	|	...	1214	1238	...	1219	...	1314	|	...	1414	...	1438	...	1514	1524	|	...	1614	1638
	Firenze Campo di Marte d.	|	|	|	...	1127	...	|	|	...	|	...	|	1327	...	|	...	|	...	|	|	1527	...	|	|
	Prato d.	|	|	|	...	1151	...	|	|	...	1241	...	|	1351	...	|	...	|	...	|	|	1551	...	|	|
	Bologna C a.	1157	1212	1229	...	1240	...	1312	1336	...	1330	...	1412	1440	...	1512	...	1536	...	1612	1629	1640	...	1712	1736
	Bologna C 619/30 d.	...	1216	1233	1248	1244	1256	1316	1340	...	1342	1356	1416	1444	1456	1516	...	1540	1556	1616	1633	1644	1656	1716	1740
	Milano C 619/30 a.	...	1400	|	|	1450	|	1500	|	...	1555	|	1600	|	|	1700	...	|	|	1800	1830	1850	|	1900	|
	Ferrara d.	...	...	|	1313	...	1330	...	|	...	...	1430	...	1513	1530	...	...	|	1630	...	...	...	1730	...	|
	Rovigo d.	...	...	|	1339	...	1354	...	|	...	...	1454	...	1535	1553	...	...	|	1654	...	...	...	1757	...	|
	Padova **600** d.	...	...	1348	1410	...	1429	...	1451	...	...	1529	...	1607	1629	...	...	1651	1729	...	...	...	1829	...	1851
	Venezia Mestre 600 a.	...	...	1406s	1430	...	1450	...	1506s	...	...	1550	...	1634	1649	...	...	1706s	1750	...	...	...	1850	...	1906s
	Venezia Santa Lucia 600 a.	...	...	1418	1442	...	1503	...	1517	...	...	1603	...	1647	1703	...	...	1717	1803	...	...	...	1903	...	1917

	ICp	ES		AV	ICp		IC	ES	ES	ES	IC	ICp	ES		IC	ICp	IC	IC	AV	ES	T-Biz	IC	ICp		IC
	706	9494		9444	706		1554	9312	9446	9460	588	530	9482		1554	592	1588	1590	9448	9300	9304	716	592		1588
	[R]	[R] ✕		[R] ✕	[R]			[R] ✕	[R] ✕	[R] ✕		[R]	[R] ✕			[R]			[R] ✕	[R] ✕	[R] ✕		[R]		
	♦	♦			♦		⑦j	B		♦		Z			⑦j		Z	Z		♦	w	♦			Z
Napoli Centrale **640** d.	1224	...	...	1348	...	...	1300p	...	...	...	...	1424	...	...	...	...	1442	1442	1548	...	...	...	...	...	...
Roma Termini d.	1457	1505	...	1530	...	...	|	1605	1630	1635	...	|	1650	...	...	1655	|	|	1730	1735	1802	...	...	...	...
Roma Tiburtina d.	|	|	...	|	...	...	1553	|	|	|	...	1643	|	...	...	|	1706	1706	|	|	|	...	...	...	...
Chiusi-Chianciano Terme d.	1623	|	...	|	←	...	1708	|	|	|	...	|	|	...	←	1814	1832	1832	|	|	|	...	←	...	←
Arezzo d.	1653	|	...	|	1655	...	1736	|	|	|	...	|	|	...	1738	1853	1915	1915	|	|	|	...	1853	...	1917
Firenze SMN a.	→	1638	...	1706	|	...	→	1745	1806	|	...	|	1830	...	|	→	→	→	1906	|	|	...	|	...	|
Firenze SMN d.	...	1646	...	1714	|	...	...	1756	1814	|	1819	|	1838	...	|	...	...	...	1914	|	|	...	|	...	|
Firenze Campo di Marte d.	...	|	...	|	1727	...	...	|	|	1821r	|	1823	|	...	1836	...	...	...	|	1922r	|	...	1931r	...	1953
Prato d.	...	|	...	|	1751	...	...	|	|	|	1842	1855	|	...	1902	...	...	...	|	|	|	...	1957	...	2017
Bologna C a.	...	1743	...	1812	1840	...	...	1857	1912	1919	1930	1947	1936	...	1954	...	...	...	2012	2018	2026	...	2046	...	2119
Bologna C 619/30 d.	...	1747	1756	1816	1844	1856	...	...	1916	...	1944	...	1940	1956	2004	...	...	...	2016	...	2029	2048	2050	2056	2134
Milano C 619/30 a.	...	1937g	|	2000	|	|	...	...	2100	...	2150	...	|	|	2235	...	...	...	2200	...	2207	|	2255	|	2345
Ferrara d.	...	...	1830	...	1913	1930	...	...	...	...	...	...	|	2030	...	...	...	...	...	...	...	2117	...	2130	...
Rovigo d.	...	...	1854	...	1936	1954	...	...	...	...	...	...	|	2054	...	...	...	...	...	...	...	2139	...	2154	...
Padova **600** d.	...	...	1929	...	2006	2029	...	...	...	...	...	...	2051	2129	...	...	...	...	...	...	...	2210	...	2229	...
Venezia Mestre 600 a.	...	...	1950	...	2026	2050	...	...	...	...	...	...	2106s	2150	...	...	...	...	...	...	...	2228	...	2250	...
Venezia Santa Lucia 600 a.	...	...	2003	...	...	2103	...	...	...	...	...	...	2117	2203	...	...	...	...	...	...	...	2240	...	2303	...

	IC	E	IC	ES	ES	E	E	ICp	AV		ICp	EN	EN	ES	EN	EN	ES		E	ICN	ICN	E	E	E	
	1590	1134	594	9450	9486	1236	1234	596	9452		596	388	234	9454	314	366	9456		824	774	776	1910	830	1594	
		[R] ⊡		[R] ✕	[R] ✕	[R] ⊡	[R] ⊡	[R]	[R] ✕	2	[R]	[R]	[R] ⊡	[R] ✕	[R] ⊡	⊡	[R] 🍷								
	Z	♦	⑧y			♦	♦	♦			♦	♦	♦		♦	♦			♦	Z	♦	Z	♦	Z	
Napoli Centrale **640** d.	...	...	...	...	...	...	...	...	1748	...	...	...	...	...	...	...	...	...	1845	1957	...	2036	2150	2302	...
Roma Termini d.	...	...	1755	1830	1850	1700	...	1857	1930	...	...	1910	1910	2030	1955	2116	2145	...	|	|	...	2300	|	|	...
Roma Tiburtina d.	...	...	|	|	|	|	...	|	|	...	...	|	|	|	|	|	|	...	2207	2250	...	|	0047	|	...
Chiusi-Chianciano Terme d.	←	...	1911	|	|	|	...	2023	|	...	←	2045u	2045	2127	|	|	|	...	2350	0007	...	|	|	|	...
Arezzo d.	1917	...	2002	|	|	|	...	2053	|	...	2055	|	|	2157	|	|	2302	...	0032	0049	...	|	|	|	...
Firenze SMN a.	|	...	2041	2006	2030	|	...	→	2106	...	|	|	2141	2229	|	|	2332	...	|	|	...	|	|	|	...
Firenze SMN d.	|	...	...	2014	2038	|	2100	...	2114	...	|	2153u	2153	2237	|	|	...	...	|	|	...	|	|	|	...
Firenze Campo di Marte d.	1953	...	...	|	|	2056	|	...	|	...	2127	|	|	|	2200u	2325u	...	...	|	0147	...	|	|	|	...
Prato d.	2017	...	...	|	|	|	|	...	|	...	2153	|	|	2253	|	...	...	...	|	|	...	|	|	|	...
Bologna C a.	2119	...	...	2112	2136	2218	2218	...	2212	...	2240	|	2255	2343	|	...	...	...	0300	0313	...	|	0557	0528	...
Bologna C 619/30 d.	2134	...	...	2116	2140	2223	2223	...	2216	2235	...	2305u	2320	...	2318u	...	...	...	...	0318	...	|	0602	...	...
Milano C 619/30 a.	2345	...	...	2325	|	|	|	...	0005	|	...	...	|	...	...	...	...	...	...	|	...	0715	0920	...	...
Ferrara d.	...	2200	...	...	|	2256	2256	...	...	2307	...	...	2350	...	...	...	...	...	...	0348	0516	...	...	...	...
Rovigo d.	...	2226u	...	...	|	2319	2319	...	...	2328	...	...	|	...	...	...	...	...	...	0411	0540	...	...	...	...
Padova **600** d.	...	2306u	...	...	2251	2349	2349	...	...	2400	...	...	0041	...	...	...	...	...	...	0452	0628	...	...	...	...
Venezia Mestre 600 a.	...	2327u	...	...	2306s	0011	0011	...	...	...	...	...	0102	...	...	...	...	...	...	0512	0648	...	...	...	...
Venezia Santa Lucia 600 a.	...	...	...	...	2317	...	...	...	...	...	...	...	...	...	...	...	...	...	...	0524	0708	...	...	...	...

♦ – **NOTES** (LISTED BY TRAIN NUMBER)

84 – MICHELANGELO – [12] and ✕ Roma - Verona - Innsbruck - München.

150 – [12] and ✕ Firenze - Zürich.

234 – ALLEGRO TOSCA – 🛏 1,2 cl., ▬ 2 cl. (4 berth) and [2] Roma - Venezia Mestre - Villach - Wien Süd.

314 – LUNA – 🛏 1,2 cl. and ▬ 2 cl. Roma - Brig - Zürich; 🛏 1,2 cl. and ▬ 2 cl. Roma - Brig (**316**) - Genève.

366 – MONTECARLO – 🛏 1,2 cl. and ▬ 2 cl. (4 berth) Roma - Firenze (**367**) - Pisa (**368**) - Nice; 🛏 1,2 cl. (Excelsior), 🛏 1,2 cl., ▬ 2 cl. (4/6 berth) and [2] Roma - Firenze - Pisa - Genova (**764**) - Torino.

388 – *City Night Line* CAPRI – 🛏 1,2 cl., ▬ 2 cl. and [2] Roma - München and v.v. Supplement payable.

580 – TACITO – [12] Terni - Milano.

596 – SCALIGERO – [12] Roma - Verona.

700 – CANOVA – [12] Roma - Venezia Mestre - Udine.

706 – MIRAMARE – [12] Napoli - Venezia Mestre (**707**) - Trieste.

714 – ADRIATICO – [12] Bari - Venezia.

716 – MANIN – [12] Pescara - Venezia.

776 – TERGESTE – ▬ 2 cl. (4 berth) and [12] Lecce - Venezia Mestre (**777**) - Trieste; 🛏 1,2 cl. (T2), ▬ 1,2 cl. and [12] Lecce - Venezia Mestre (**1598**) - Venezia Santa Lucia.

824 – ①③④⑤⑥⑦ (also Jan. 1, Apr. 29; not Dec. 24, 31, Apr. 28): 🛏 1,2 cl., ▬ 2 cl. (4 berth) and [2] Napoli - Bologna (**924**) - Bolzano.

830 – ⑦ (also Aug. 15, Nov. 1): [2] Salerno - Milano.

1134 – ALLEGRO AIDA – ⑥ June 16 - Sept. 8: 🛏 1,2 cl., ▬ 2 cl. and [2] Ancona - Venezia Mestre - Wien Süd.

1234 – ALLEGRO RIGOLETTO – ⑤⑦ June 15 - Sept. 30: 🛏 1,2 cl. (Excelsior), ▬ 2 cl. and [2] Livorno - Firenze - Wien Süd.

1236 – ALLEGRO ROSSINI – ⑥ June 16 - Sept. 29: 🛏 1,2 cl. (Excelsior), ▬ 2 cl. and [2] Roma - Wien Süd.

9300 – ⑧ (not days before holidays): [12] and ✕ Roma - Torino.

9460 – [12] and ✕ Roma - Bergamo.

9494 – [12] and ✕ Roma - Torino.

B – [12] and ✕ Roma - Bologna - Bolzano.
Z – For days of running and composition see Table **640**.

g – Milano **Porta Garibaldi**.
j – Also Nov. 1.
p – Napoli **Piazza Garibaldi**.
r – Firenze **Rifredi**.
s – Stops to set down only.
u – Stops to pick up only.
w – ⑧ (not Dec. 22-31, and days before holidays).
x – Not Dec. 24 - Jan. 1.
y – Not days before holidays.
⊡ – Supplement payable.

FERRARA and BOLOGNA - RAVENNA - RIMINI — 621

2nd class only except where shown

For express services Bologna - Faenza - Rimini see Table 630

km																									
		j		n		⚒	⚒		⚒		⚒		p			z		L ①–⑤	x	⚒	r		⚒	n	
0	**Ferrara 620** d.	...	0611	...	...	...	0720	...	0812	...	0913	...	1010	...	...	...	...	...	1211	...	...	...	1309	...	...
	Bologna C 630 d.	...	|	...	...	0650	|	0758	|	...	|	0908	|	...	1108	...	...	1200	|	...	...	1308	|	...	...
	Imola d.	...	|	...	...	0712	|	0823	|	...	|	0935	|	...	1135	...	...	|	|	...	...	1335	|	...	...
	Castelbolognese d.	...	|	...	...	0719	|	0832	|	...	|	0942	|	...	1142	...	...	|	|	...	...	1342	|	...	...
	Lugo d.	...	|	...	...	0734	|	0846	|	...	|	1000	|	...	1200	...	...	|	|	...	...	1400	|	...	...
74	**Ravenna** a.	...	0724	...	...	0803	0826	0912	0925	...	1021	1025	1114	...	1225	...	...	1315	1324	...	...	1425	1429	...	...
74	**Ravenna** d.	0635	...	0733	...	...	0832	0924	0933	...	...	...	1121	...	...	1235	...	...	...	1336	1336	...	...	1435	...
95	Cervia d.	0656	...	0755	...	...	0900	0943	1002	...	...	...	1139	...	...	1304	...	...	...	1400	1400	...	...	1502	...
103	Cesenatico d.	0703	...	0801	...	...	0906	0956	1009	...	...	...	1146	...	...	1310	...	...	...	1407	1406	...	...	1508	...
124	**Rimini 630** a.	0732	...	0836	...	...	0936	1017	1036	...	...	...	1210	...	...	1335	...	...	...	1437	1437	...	...	1535	...
					⚒	L ①–⑤			†	⚒		⚒	†	⚒	Ⓐ	k	x							*ICN* 779 ♦	
	Ferrara 620 d.	...	1412	...	...	...	...	1615	...	...	...	1715	...	...	...	1814	1814	...	...	2014	...	...	...	2334	...
	Bologna C 630 d.	1408	|	...	1508	1600	1608	|	...	...	1708	|	...	...	1755	|	|	1808	1908	|	2008	...	2208	|	...
	Imola d.	1435	|	...	1535	|	1635	|	...	...	1735	|	...	...	|	|	|	1835	1935	|	2034	...	2235	|	...
	Castelbolognese d.	1442	|	...	1542	|	1642	|	...	...	1742	|	...	...	1821	|	|	1842	1942	|	2042	...	2242	|	...
	Lugo d.	1500	|	...	1600	|	1700	|	...	...	1800	|	...	...	1834	|	|	1900	2000	|	2100	...	2256	|	...
	Ravenna a.	1524	1529	...	1625	1715	1725	1725	...	...	1825	1826	...	...	1855	1925	1931	1925	2025	2126	2125	...	2320	0028	...
	Ravenna d.	1535	...	...	...	...	...	...	1730	1735	...	...	1835	1835	...	...	...	1935	...	...	...	2135	...	0030	...
	Cervia d.	1557	...	...	...	...	...	...	1758	1758	...	...	1856	1900	...	...	...	1959	...	...	...	2157	...	|	...
	Cesenatico d.	1602	...	...	...	...	...	...	1805	1805	...	...	1908	1907	...	...	...	2005	...	...	...	2204	...	|	...
	Rimini 630 a.	1631	...	...	...	...	...	...	1836	1836	...	...	1933	1933	...	...	...	2035	...	...	...	2233	...	0111	...

km																									
		ICN 776 ♦		n	⚒	n	⚒	†	†		⚒	r	j		j	⚒	L ①–⑤	q	r		⚒				m
	Rimini 630 d.	0333	...	0518	...	...	0620	0620	...	0652	0736	...	0820	...	0921	...	...	1020	...	...	...	...	...	1230	...
	Cesenatico d.	|	...	0550	...	...	0646	0646	...	0722	0802	...	0852	...	0955	...	...	1054	...	...	...	...	...	1257	...
	Cervia d.	|	...	0557	...	...	0657	0657	...	0728	0809	...	0859	...	1001	...	...	1100	...	...	...	...	...	1303	...
	Ravenna a.	0411	...	0615	...	...	0719	0719	...	0747	0829	...	0920	...	1020	...	...	1118	...	...	...	...	...	1324	...
0	**Ravenna** d.	0413	0505	...	0620	0630	0726	...	0735	0749	0831	0931	0935	...	...	1031	1035	...	1132	1135	1231	1235	...	...	1335
28	Lugo d.	|	0530	...	|	0659	|	...	|	0808	|	|	1000	...	...	|	|	...	|	1200	|	1300	...	...	|
42	Castelbolognese d.	|	0546	...	|	0716	|	...	|	|	|	|	1017	...	...	|	|	...	|	1217	|	1317	...	...	|
50	Imola d.	|	0553	...	|	0724	|	...	|	|	|	|	1024	...	...	|	|	...	|	1224	|	1324	...	...	|
84	**Bologna C 630** a.	|	0620	...	|	0748	|	...	|	0847	|	|	1052	...	...	|	1150	...	|	1252	|	1352	...	...	|
	Ferrara 620 a.	0514	...	...	0737	...	0836	...	0848	...	0946	1047	...	...	...	1140	...	...	1246	...	1345	...	...	...	1451
			n	L ①–⑤	⚒			v	Ⓐ					⚒	m		⚒	†		⚒	r				
	Rimini 630 d.	...	1320	...	...	1420	...	1520	...	...	1615	...	...	1720	...	...	1820	1838	...	1920	1920	...	...	2020	...
	Cesenatico d.	...	1352	...	...	1454	...	1549	...	...	1655	...	...	1751	...	...	1852	1907	...	1952	1952	...	...	2052	...
	Cervia d.	...	1359	...	...	1501	...	1559	...	...	1702	...	...	1757	...	...	1859	1914	...	1958	1958	...	...	2059	...
	Ravenna a.	...	1421	...	...	1521	...	1622	...	...	1725	...	...	1820	...	...	1920	1932	...	2020	2019	...	...	2120	...
	Ravenna d.	1335	...	1435	1438	1531	...	...	1635	...	1732	1735	...	...	1836	1835	...	1935	1950	...	...	2035	...	2133	...
	Lugo d.	1400	...	|	|	1600	...	...	1700	...	|	1800	...	...	|	1900	...	2000	|	...	...	2100	...	|	...
	Castelbolognese d.	1417	...	|	|	1617	...	...	1717	...	|	1817	...	...	|	1917	...	2017	|	...	...	2117	...	|	...
	Imola d.	1424	...	|	|	1624	...	...	1723	...	|	1824	...	...	|	1924	...	2024	|	...	...	2124	...	|	...
	Bologna C 630 a.	1452	...	1550	|	1652	...	...	1745	...	|	1852	...	...	|	1952	...	2052	|	...	...	2152	...	|	...
	Ferrara 620 a.	...	...	...	1551	...	...	...	...	...	1851	...	...	...	1946	...	...	...	2104	...	...	...	...	2238	...

♦ – **NOTES** (LISTED BY TRAIN NUMBER)

776 – TERGESTE – 🛏 2 cl. (4 berth) and 🛋 Lecce - Venezia Mestre (**777**) - Trieste; 🛏 1, 2 cl. (T2), 🛏 1, 2 cl. and 🛋 Lecce - Mestre (**1598**) - Venezia Santa Lucia.

779 – TERGESTE – 🛏 2 cl. (4 berth) and 🛋 Trieste (**778**) - Venezia Mestre - Lecce; 🛏 1, 2 cl. (T2), 🛏 1, 2 cl. and 🛋 Venezia Santa Lucia (**1599**) - Mestre - Lecce.

L – *ES*Link*: 🚌 link.

j – ⚒ (daily until Aug. 26).
k – Sept. 17 - Dec. 8.
m – ⚒ (daily June 10 - Sept. 15).
n – ⚒ (daily June 10 - Sept. 22).
p – † Sept. 23 - Dec. 8.
q – † (daily July 29 - Aug. 26).
r – † June 10 - Sept. 16.
v – ⚒ Sept. 3 - Dec. 8.
x – June 10 - Sept. 16.
z – ⚒ (daily June 17 - Sept. 22).

ROMA AIRPORTS ✈ and other local services — 622

ROMA FIUMICINO AIRPORT ✈

Leonardo Express rail service Roma Termini - Roma Fiumicino ✈. *26 km* Journey time: 31 minutes. Special fare payable.

From **Roma Termini**: 0552, 0622, 0652, and every 30 minutes until 2252.

From **Roma Fiumicino**: 0635, 0705, 0735, and every 30 minutes until 2335.

Additional rail service (2nd class only) operates from Roma Tiburtina **and** Roma Ostiense - Roma Fiumicino ✈. *26 km* Journey times: Tiburtina - ✈ 41–42 minutes; Ostiense - ✈ 27 minutes.

From **Roma Tiburtina** (Ostiense 15 minutes later):
0503, 0533, 0548⚒**x**, 0603, 0618⚒**x**, 0633, 0648⚒**x**, and every 15 minutes (30 †) until 2033, then 2103, 2133, 2203, 2233.

From **Roma Fiumicino** ✈:
0557, 0627, 0642⚒**x**, 0657, 0712⚒**x**, 0727, 0742⚒**x**, 0757, and every 15 minutes (30 †) until 2127, then 2157, 2227, 2257, 2327.

x – Not July 22 - Aug. 26.

ROMA CIAMPINO AIRPORT ✈

Frequent services operate Roma Termini - Ciampino and v.v., journey approximately 15 minutes. There is a 🚌 service between Ciampino station and airport.

ROMA - ANZIO and v.v. *57 km* Journey time: 56–68 minutes. 2nd class only. All services continue to Nettuno (*3 km* and 4–6 minutes from Anzio).

From **Roma Termini**:
⚒: 0505, 0610, 0710, 0810, 0907 and hourly until 1407, then 1428, 1507 and hourly until 2107, then 2150.
†: 0710, 0810, 0907, 1107, 1307, 1407, 1607, 1807, 2007, 2150.

From **Anzio**:
⚒: 0456, 0557, 0634, 0657, 0727, 0755, 0838, 0935 and hourly until 2035, then 2153.
†: 0634, 0727, 0838, 0935, 1235, 1435, 1635, 1835, 1935, 2153.

ROMA - CIAMPINO - ALBANO LAZIALE and v.v. *29 km* Journey time: 40–58 minutes. 2nd class only.

From **Roma Termini**: 0551⚒, 0720, 0837, 1000⚒, 1210, 1306⚒, 1406, 1506⚒, 1606, 1706⚒, 1806, 1906⚒, 2006, 2106⚒.

From **Albano Laziale**: 0635⚒, 0708⚒, 0739⚒, 0823, 1022, 1122⚒, 1338, 1422⚒, 1522, 1622⚒, 1722, 1822⚒, 1922, 2022⚒, 2122.

All trains call at Ciampino, Marino Laziale and Castel Gandolfo approximately 15, 30 and 35 minutes from Roma, 6, 11 and 30 minutes from Albano Laziale respectively.

623 NAPOLI - SORRENTO, BAIANO and SARNO

2nd class only — Circumvesuviana Ferrovia

Services depart from Napoli Porta Nolana station and call at Napoli Piazza Garibaldi ▲ 2 minutes later.

NAPOLI (Porta Nolana) - SORRENTO and v.v. Journey: 55 - 68 minutes. *45 km.* All services call at Ercolano, Pompei Villa di Misteri, Castellammare di Stabia, Vico Equense and Meta.

From **Napoli:** 0509⚒, 0539, 0609⚒, 0640, 0644⚒, 0709, 0739⚒, 0811, 0822, 0839, 0909, 0939 and every 30 minutes until 1309, 1341, 1409, 1439, 1511, 1522⚒, 1539, 1609, 1639, 1709, 1741, 1809, 1839, 1911, 1939, 2009, 2039, 2109, 2139, 2209, 2242.

From **Sorrento:** 0501, 0537, 0607⚒, 0625, 0655, 0722, 0738⚒, 0755, 0826, 0852⚒, 0907, 0937 and every 30 minutes until 1307, 1325, 1356, 1422, 1455, 1526, 1552⚒, 1607, 1637, 1707, 1725, 1756, 1822, 1855, 1926, 2007, 2037, 2107, 2137, 2225.

NAPOLI (Porta Nolana) - BAIANO and v.v. Journey 60 minutes.

From **Napoli:** 0517⚒, 0548, 0618⚒, 0648, 0718, 0748, 0818, 0848⚒, 0918, 0948⚒, 1018, 1048⚒, 1118, 1148⚒, 1218, 1248, 1318, 1348⚒, 1418†, 1430⚒, 1448⚒, 1518, 1548Ⓐ, 1618, 1648Ⓐ, 1718†, 1730⚒, 1748Ⓐ, 1818, 1848Ⓐ, 1918, 1948, 2018, 2048.

From **Baiano:** 0502, 0532⚒, 0602, 0632⚒, 0700, 0730, 0802, 0832, 0902, 0932, 1002, 1032⚒, 1102, 1132⚒, 1202, 1232⚒, 1302, 1332⚒, 1402, 1430, 1502, 1532⚒, 1602, 1632⚒, 1702, 1730Ⓐ, 1802, 1832Ⓐ, 1902, 1932Ⓐ, 2002, 2032Ⓐ, 2102.

NAPOLI (Porta Nolana) - SARNO and v.v. Journey 65 minutes. All services call at Poggiomarino (49 minutes from Napoli, 12 minutes from Sarno).

From **Napoli:** 0502⚒, 0532, 0602⚒, 0632, 0722, 0802, 0832⚒, 0902, 0932⚒, 1002, 1032⚒, 1102, 1132⚒, 1202, 1232, 1302, 1332⚒, 1402, 1432⚒, 1502, 1532Ⓐ, 1602, 1632Ⓐ, 1702, 1732Ⓐ, 1802, 1832Ⓐ, 1902, 1932, 2002, 2042, 2102**p**.

From **Sarno:** 0453, 0519⚒, 0549, 0619⚒, 0649, 0719, 0741, 0759, 0819, 0849, 0919, 0949, 1019⚒, 1049, 1119⚒, 1149, 1219⚒, 1249, 1349, 1419, 1449, 1519⚒, 1549, 1619⚒, 1649, 1719Ⓐ, 1749, 1819Ⓐ, 1849, 1919Ⓐ, 1949, 2019Ⓐ, 2049.

p – To Poggiomarino only.

▲ – Adjacent to **Napoli Centrale** main line station - connection is by moving walkway. Operator: Circumvesuviana Ferrovia ✆ +39 081 777 22 111, fax +39 081 779 24 50.

Frequent 🚌 services operate along the Amalfi Coast between Sorrento and Salerno. Up to 20 services on ⚒, less frequent on †. Change of buses at Amalfi is necessary. Operator: SITA, Via Campegna 23, 80124 Napoli. ✆ +39 081 610 67 11, fax +39 08 239 50 10.

624 ROMA - PESCARA

2nd class only

km				Ⓐ		Ⓐ				⚒	†	
0	**Roma Tiburtina** ▲	d.	...	0746t	1030	1252	1404	1610t	1710	1835t	2026	2115	2302
40	Tivoli ▲	d.	...	0832	1134	|	1445	|	1805	1911	2110	|	2351
108	Avezzano	d.	0612	0937	1242	1426	1547	1744	1922	2014	2218	2252	0054
172	Sulmona **626**	d.	0744	1039	1400	1522	1657	1841	...	2114	...	...	...
226	Chieti	a.	0836	1120	1456	1611	1741	1927	...	2159	...	...	...
240	**Pescara C**	a.	0853	1139	1511	1631	1802	1947	...	2218	...	...	...

			Ⓐ			⚒				†	Ⓐ y	⚒
Pescara C	d.	0616	0623	...	0936	1238	1410	1558	...	1844	1915	1941	2150
Chieti	d.	0628	0637	...	0951	1255	1425	1615	...	1859	1931	2001	2213
Sulmona **626**	d.	0713	0756	...	1040	1358	1521	1713	...	1949	2016	2100	2301
Avezzano	d.	0807	0851	...	1138	*1533*	1620	1823	...	2053	...	...	...
Tivoli ▲	d.	|	|	...	1237	...	1728	1943	...	2155	...	...	...
Roma Tiburtina ▲	a.	0950t	1037	...	1326	...	1809t	2032	...	2240	...	...	...

t – Roma **Termini**.

y – Not days before holidays.

▲ – Additional services operate Roma Tiburtina - Tivoli and v.v., journey 55–60 minutes.

625 ROMA - FOLIGNO - ANCONA

km					*ICp*			*ES*			*ES*					*ES*		*ES*				*ES*				*ES*		
					580			**9320**			**9324**					**9328**		**9330**				**9332**			**12134**	**9336**		
			2	2	🅁	2		🅁 🍷			🅁 🍷	2				🅁 🍷		🅁 🍷	2		2	🅁 🍷			🅁	🅁 🍷		
			⚒	⚒	T	⚒		S				⚒		⚒					Ⓐ		⚒	R	Ⓑh		F	Ⓑh		
0	**Roma Termini 615**	d.	...	...	...	...	0600	0736	...	0814	0938	...	...	1135	1212	1346	1412	1545	...	1612	...	1740	1812	1830	1930	1944	2030	2236
5	**Roma Tiburtina 615**	d.	...	...	...	...	0608	0743	...	0822	0945	...	...	1143	1220	1353	1420	1552	...	1620	...	1747	1820	1838	1938	1951	2038	2244
83	Orte **615**	d.	...	...	...	...	0645	|	...	0900	|	...	...	1219	1300	1424	1459	|	...	1700	...	|	|	1918	|	2022	2114	2321
112	Terni	d.	...	...	0515	...	0707	0828	...	0930	1033	...	...	1239	1326	1441	1521	1639	...	1727	...	1833	1923	1946	2032	2042	2147	2342
141	Spoleto	d.	...	...	0540	...	0734	0853	...	0952	1056	...	...	1307	1349	1504	1545	1703	...	1752	...	1856	1946	2017	|	2105	2209	0010
167	**Foligno**	a.	...	...	0556	...	0753	0906	...	1012	1109	...	...	1326	1406	1519	1603	1716	...	1813	...	1909	2007	2034	2107	2119	2226	0030
167	**Foligno 615**	d.	...	0550	0600	0647	0755	0908	0919	1014	1111	...	1304	1328	1408	1521	1609	1718	...	1815	1821	1911	2010	2038	2109	2122	2228	...
	Assisi **615**	d.	...	|	0612	|	|	|	0933	1028	|	...	1319	|	1428	1533	|	|	...	|	1842	|	2028	|	|	2135	|	...
	Perugia **615**	a.	...	|	0637	|	|	|	0953	1055	|	...	1339	|	1455	1557	|	|	...	|	1902	|	2055	|	|	2155	|	...
224	**Fabriano**	d.	0600	0645	...	0746	0857	0948	...	...	1152	1210	...	1425	...	...	1708	1801	1818	1926	...	2001	...	2137	2153	...	2326	...
268	Jesi	d.	0643	0732	...	0831	0934	1017	...	...	1221	1250	...	1510	...	...	1744	1829	1902	2006	...	2030	...	2209	2225	...	0003	...
286	Falconara Marittima **630**	d.	0706	0748	...	0851	0948	1032	...	...	1236	1306	...	1528	...	...	1800	1843	1921	2019	...	2041	...	2223	2238	...	0019	...
295	**Ancona 630**	a.	0718	0800	...	0906	1000	1040	...	...	1248	1319	...	1538	...	...	1812	1851	1932	2030	...	...	...	2233	2250	...	0030	...
	Ancona Marittima	a.	0729**a**	0809	...	0915	...	...	...	...	...	1328**a**	...	...	...	...	...	...	1941	...	...	...	...	...	...	...	...	...

				ES	*ES*			*ES*											*ES*			*ES*			*ES*					*ICp*
				9321	**9323**			**9325**			**12133**								**9331**			**9333**			**9337**					**597**
				🅁 🍷	🅁 🍷		2	🅁 🍷			🅁		2		2	2		2			🅁 🍷	2		🅁 🍷	2		2	2	🅁
			⚒	⚒		†	⚒	R			F	Ⓐ	⚒		Ⓐz	⚒		⚒				Ⓐ		S			⚒		T
Ancona Marittima	d.	...	...	...	...	...	...	...	...	...	...	...	1216**a**	...	1400	...	...	1535	...	...	1619	...	...	1815**a**	...	1943	...	...
Ancona 630	d.	0336	...	...	0609	...	...	...	0755	...	1110	...	1225	1352	1410	...	1508	1544	...	...	1628	...	1805	1824	1905	1952	2126	...
Falconara Marittima **630**	d.	0347	...	...	0618	...	...	0721	0806	...	1119	...	1236	1403	1420	...	1519	1555	...	...	1641	...	1816	1836	1917	2004	2135	...
Jesi	d.	0359	...	...	0631	...	...	0735	0820	...	1131	...	1255	1417	1440	...	1531	1612	...	...	1702	...	1827	1855	1931	2021	2150	...
Fabriano	d.	0436	...	...	0703	...	...	0807	0858	...	1206	...	1346	1458	1530	...	1603	1709	...	...	1752	...	1902	1947	2012	2100	2239	...
Perugia **615**	d.	|	0603	0645	|	0718	0750	|	|	1118	|	1342	|	|	...	1540	|	|	1719	1803	...	1821	|	...	|	...	|	2327
Assisi **615**	d.	|	0624	0704	|	0737	0823	|	|	1142	|	1405	|	|	...	1603	|	|	1746	1822	...	1841	|	...	|	...	|	2346
Foligno 615	a.	0523	0639	0715	0746	0751	0837	0851	0953	1156	1248	1422	1455	1548	...	1618	1644	1807	1800	1835	...	1856	1944	...	2101	...	2337	2359
Foligno	d.	0529	0641	0718	0748	0757	...	0853	0955	1158	1250	1425	1505	1552	...	...	1646	...	1802	1838	...	...	1946	...	2103	...	...	0005
Spoleto	d.	0555	0700	0734	0804	0821	...	0909	1012	1215	|	1446	1529	1609	...	...	1704	...	1822	1856	...	...	2002	...	2122	...	...	0021
Terni	d.	0625	0729	0758	0826	0854	...	0931	1034	1239	1328	1516	1605	1634	...	...	1727	...	1855	1920	...	...	2025	...	2148	...	...	0045
Orte **615**	d.	0654	0800	0815	0845	0923	...	|	1102	1302	|	1537	1632	1702	...	...	|	...	1918	1944	...	...	|	...	2212	...	...	...
Roma Tiburtina 615	a.	0728	0837	0849	0915	1000	...	1015	1136	1336	1415	1612	...	1736	...	...	1813	...	1952	2015	...	...	2111	...	2246	...	...	...
Roma Termini 615	a.	0738	...	0859	0924	1010	...	1024	1148	1348	1426	1622	...	1748	...	...	1822	...	2008	2025	...	...	2120	...	2258	...	...	...

F – GENTILE DA FABRIANO – 🚃 Ancona - Roma and v.v.

R – 🚃 and 🍷 Roma - Rimini and v.v.

S – 🚃 and 🍷 Roma - Ancona (**9322/35**) - Rimini and v.v.

T – TACITO – 🚃 Terni - Perugia - Milano and v.v.

a – Ⓐ only.

h – Not days before holidays.

z – Not July 28 - Aug. 26.

626 ROMA, SULMONA and CAMPOBASSO - CASERTA - NAPOLI and FOGGIA

km						*E*			*E*		*ES*					*ICp*				*ES*						
						833			**837**		**9351**					**677**				**9353**						
								2			🅁 🍷					🅁				🅁 ✕	2					
			⚒	†	C	B		⚒	Z	C			⚒N		C	q	†N	C	⚒y			⚒	⚒	z	C	
0	**Roma Termini**	d.	...	...	...	0501t	...	...	0617t	0615	0738	...	...	0725	...	0852	...	0915	...	1338	...	...	...	1315	...	...
138	Cassino	d.	...	...	...	|	...	...	0759	0738	|	...	...	0927	...	1017	...	1036	...	|	...	...	...	1449	...	...
	Sulmona 624	d.	...	...	...	|	...	...	|	|	|	...	0632	|	...	|	0804	|	...	|	1100	...	...	|	...	...
	Castel di Sangro	d.	...	...	...	|	...	...	|	|	|	...	0751	|	...	|	0935	|	...	|	1223	1238	...	|	...	...
	Pescolanciano-Chiauci	d.	...	...	...	|	...	...	|	|	|	...	|	|	...	|	1005	|	...	|	...	1313	...	|	...	...
	Campobasso	d.	0518	0518	0550	|	...	0624	|	|	|	...	|	|	0828	|	|	|	1224	|	...	|	1311	|	1415	...
	Carpinone	d.	0559	0559	0632	|	...	0718	|	|	|	...	0839	|	0922	|	1018	|	1309	|	...	1328	1400	|	1500	...
	Isernia	d.	0609	0612	0641	|	...	0736	|	0822	|	...	0849	|	0932	|	1029	1118	1320	|	...	1339	1412	|	1510	...
170	Vairano-Caianello	d.	0648	0653	...	|	...	0814	|	...	|	...	0931	0956	...	1034	1110	...	1444	|	...	...	1457	1511	...	...
216	Caserta	d.	0715	0724	...	0731	...	0843	0853	...	0920	...	1006	1042	...	1103	1141	...	...	1520	...	...	1531	1540	...	...
	Napoli Centrale	a.	0748	0803	...	0810	...	0916	0926	...	|	...	1047	...	...	|	1218	...	...	|	...	...	1602	1612	...	...
279	Benevento	d.	...	...	...	...	...	...	...	...	1002	...	...	...	...	1149	...	...	...	1601	...	...	...	...	...	...
380	**Foggia 631**	a.	...	...	...	...	...	...	...	...	1111	...	...	...	...	1320	...	...	...	1705	...	...	...	...	...	...
	Bari Centrale **630**	a.	...	...	...	...	...	...	...	...	1223	...	...	...	...	1446	...	...	...	1815	...	...	...	...	...	...
	Lecce **630**	a.	...	...	...	...	...	...	...	...	1408	...	...	...	...	...	...	...	...	1940	...	...	...	...	...	...

FOR NOTES SEE OPPOSITE PAGE

ROMA, SULMONA and CAMPOBASSO - CASERTA - NAPOLI and FOGGIA 626

km		⚒C	†C	ES 9355 [R]✕		2 †	ES 9385 [R]🍷 T	†C	⚒C	2	2 †		⚒	ES 9357 [R]🍷		⚒C	†C	2	C	⚒C	†C	E 891 Z		E 951 F	ICN 789 A
	Roma Termini d.	1415	1420	1538	...	...	1638	...	...	...	1647	...	1715	1716	...	...	1728	1815	...	1940	1942	2225	...	2330	2358
	Cassino d.	1543	1545	|	...	...	|	...	...	...	1844	...	1847	|	...	1849	1855	1950	...	|	|	|	...	0108	0140
0	**Sulmona 624** d.	|	|	|	...	1430	|	...	...	1544	|	...	|	|	...	|	|	|	...	|	|	|	...	|	|
77	Castel di Sangro d.	|	|	|	...	1551	|	...	...	1700	|	...	|	|	...	|	|	|	...	|	|	|	...	|	|
106	Pescolanciano-Chiauci d.	|	|	|	...	|	|	...	...	1731	|	...	|	|	...	|	|	|	...	|	|	|	...	|	|
	Campobasso d.	|	|	|	...	|	|	1628	1630	|	|	...	|	|	1803	|	|	|	1943	|	|	|	...	|	|
119	Carpinone d.	|	|	|	...	1641	|	1715	1714	1744	|	...	|	|	1853	|	|	|	2030	|	|	|	...	|	|
130	Isernia d.	1627	1627	|	...	1653	|	1725	1723	1757	|	...	|	|	1904	1942	1942	|	2040	2145	2147	|	...	|	|
176	Vairano-Caianello d.	...	...	|	...	1744	|	...	...	1838	1913	...	1910	|	1958	...	...	2013	...	...	...	|	...	|	|
222	Caserta d.	...	...	1720	...	1820	1836	...	...	1912	1958	...	1942	1918	2029	...	...	2045	...	...	...	0036	...	0155	0236
256	**Napoli Centrale** a.	...	...	|	...	1900	|	...	...	1954	...	...	...	|	2100	...	...	2124	...	...	...	...	...	|	|
	Benevento d.	...	...	1801	...	...	1923	...	...	...	...	...	...	2003	...	...	...	...	...	...	...	...	...	|	0330
	Foggia 631 a.	...	...	1905	...	...	2049	...	...	...	...	...	...	2122	...	...	...	...	...	...	...	...	...	n	0453
	Bari Centrale **630** a.	...	...	2015	...	...	2202	...	...	...	...	...	...	2248	...	...	...	...	...	...	...	...	...	|	0638
	Lecce **630** a.	...	...	2150	...	...	...	...	...	...	...	...	...	...	...	...	...	...	...	...	...	...	...	0922	0825

km		2 †	2 ⚒		C	⚒		2	⚒	C	2 †r	ES 9350 [R]🍷	C	2 †	⚒	ES 9352 [R]🍷 ⚒	ES 9380 [R]🍷 †	C	2 †	⚒	⚒		2	C	2 ⚒
	Lecce **630** d.	...	...	...	...	...	...	...	...	...	...	...	...	...	...	0600	0600	...	...	...	...	...	...	...	...
	Bari Centrale **630** d.	...	...	...	...	...	...	...	...	...	...	0515	...	...	...	0742	0742	...	...	...	...	...	...	...	...
	Foggia 631 d.	...	...	...	...	...	...	...	...	...	...	0639	...	...	...	0853	0853	...	...	...	...	...	...	...	...
	Benevento d.	...	...	...	...	...	...	...	0502	...	...	0750	...	...	...	0957	0958	...	...	...	...	...	...	...	...
	Napoli Centrale d.	...	...	...	...	...	...	0551	|	...	0750	|	...	0830	...	|	|	...	...	...	1214	...	...	...	...
	Caserta d.	0510	0510	0612	...	...	...	0622	0714	...	0827	0836	...	0908	...	1037	1037	...	...	...	1244	1340	1313	...	...
	Vairano-Caianello d.	0555	0555	0647	...	...	...	0655	0748	...	0911	|	...	0943	...	|	|	...	...	...	1317	1411	1359	...	...
	Isernia d.	|	|	|	0642	0645	...	0735	|	0823	|	|	0933	1030	1050	|	|	1119	...	1346	1413	|	|	1511	...
0	Carpinone d.	|	|	|	|	0658	...	0750	|	0834	|	|	|	1042	1101	|	|	1130	...	1404	1424	|	|	|	...
48	**Campobasso** d.	|	|	|	|	0749	...	|	|	0918	|	|	|	|	1153	|	|	1215	...	|	1522	|	|	|	...
	Pescolanciano-Chiauci d.	|	|	|	|	...	...	0803	|	...	|	|	|	|	...	|	|	...	...	1418	...	|	|	|	...
	Castel di Sangro d.	|	|	|	|	...	...	0844	|	...	|	|	|	1124	...	|	|	...	1417	1452	...	|	|	|	1712
	Sulmona 624 d.	|	|	|	|	...	...	1014	|	...	|	|	|	1244	...	|	|	...	1533	...	...	|	|	|	1830
	Cassino a.	0624	0630	0710	0729	...	...	...	0812	...	0940	|	1013	...	...	|	|	...	...	...	...	1436	1431	1553	...
	Roma Termini a.	0835	0835	0848	0853	...	...	...	0945	...	...	1022	1140	...	...	1222	1238	...	...	...	...	1625	1645	1716	...

		⚒C	†C	C	ⒶN	ES 9354 [R]✕	⚒	⚒C	†C		E 824 Z	C	⚒	†	ICp 678 [R] q	ES 9386 [R]🍷 R	⚒C	†C	ES 9356 [R]✕	E 830 D	ICN 752 Z	E 892 Z	E 956 F	ICN 788 H
Lecce **630** d.	...	...	...	...	...	1217	...	...	...	...	...	...	...	...	...	...	...	...	1700	...	...	...	2046	2220
Bari Centrale **630** d.	...	...	...	...	...	1342	...	...	...	...	...	...	...	...	1614	1707	...	...	1842	...	...	...	|	0012
Foggia 631 d.	...	...	...	...	...	1453	...	...	...	...	...	...	...	...	1755	1822	...	...	1953	...	...	...	n	0159
Benevento d.	...	...	...	...	...	1557	...	...	...	...	...	...	...	...	1924	1950	...	...	2103	...	...	...	|	0327
Napoli Centrale d.	1415	...	...	...	1527	|	1730	...	...	...	1845	...	1943	1943	|	|	...	...	|	2150	...	...	|	|
Caserta d.	1445	...	...	...	1603	1637	1801	...	...	...	1916	...	2014	2014	2023	2035	...	...	2142	2224	0157	0347	0426	0418
Vairano-Caianello d.	1521	...	...	...	1648	|	1841	...	...	...	|	...	2042	2043	2052	|	...	...	|	|	|	|	|	|
Isernia d.	1603	1628	1628	1724	1801	|	1922	1943	1943	...	|	2041	2124	2125	|	|	2146	2148	|	|	|	|	|	|
Carpinone d.	1615	1640	1640	|	1815	|	1933	1954	1954	...	|	|	2135	2136	|	|	|	|	|	|	|	|	|	|
Campobasso d.	1709	1730	1730	|	|	|	2028	2046	2046	...	|	|	2220	2225	|	|	2240	2245	|	|	|	|	|	|
Pescolanciano-Chiauci d.	...	...	...	|	1828	|	...	...	...	...	|	|	...	...	|	|	...	...	|	|	|	|	|	|
Castel di Sangro d.	...	...	...	|	1905	|	...	...	...	...	|	|	...	...	|	|	...	...	|	|	|	|	|	|
Sulmona 624 d.	...	...	...	|	2018	|	...	...	...	...	|	|	...	...	|	|	...	...	|	|	|	|	|	|
Cassino a.	...	...	...	1805	...	|	...	...	...	...	2015	2126	...	...	2112	|	...	...	|	|	|	|	|	|
Roma Termini a.	...	...	...	1928	...	1822	...	...	...	...	2158t	2250	...	...	2240	2222	...	...	2326	0042t	0417t	0617	0635	0629

A – TAVOLIERE – ▱ 1, 2 cl., ▬ 2 cl. (4 berth) and [12] Roma - Lecce.
B – ⑤ (also Aug 14, Oct. 31): ▬ 2 cl. and [2] Milano - Napoli - Salerno.
C – [12] Roma - Isernia - Campobasso and v.v.
D – ⑦ (also Aug. 15, Nov. 1): ▬ 2 cl. and [2] Salerno - Napoli - Milano.
F – ▬ 2 cl. and [2] Lecce - Taranto - Roma and v.v.
H – TAVOLIERE – ▱ 1, 2 cl., ▬ 2 cl. (4 berth) and [12] Lecce - Roma.
N – [2] Pescara - Sulmona - Napoli and v.v.
R – ⑦ (also Nov. 1): [12] and 🍷 Taranto - Roma.

T – ⑤ (also Apr. 24, 30; not Apr. 25): [12] and 🍷 Roma - Taranto.
Z – For days of running and composition – see Table **640**.

n – Via Taranto.
q – June 16 - Sept. 2.
r – Also Aug. 11 - 25.
t – Roma **Tiburtina**.
y – Not June 18 - Sept. 2.
z – Not † June 25 - Sept. 3.

SARDINIA 629

Some trains 2nd class only

km		A	⚒y	A		G	⚒		⚒		†	⚒	†	⚒		A	⚒	⚒		A	†	⚒	⚒			C		⚒
0	**Golfo Aranci** d.	...	...	...	...	0728d	...	...	...	...	...	...	...	...	1340	...	...	1525	...	...	...	...	...	*1747*	...	...	...	...
22	**Olbia** d.	...	...	...	0631	0752	0838	...	...	0917	...	...	...	...	1403	1408	...	1548	1649	...	...	...	...	1824	2017	...	...	...
	Cagliari d.	...	...	...	|	|	|	0639t	0700	|	0907	1004	1018	1203	▬	|	1325	▬	|	1443r	1624	1638	...	|	|	1830	1930	2020a
	Decimomannu d.	...	...	...	|	|	|	0651t	0713	|	0920	1015	1036	1217	...	|	1339	...	|	1456r	|	|	...	|	|	1843	1949	|
	Oristano d.	...	...	...	|	|	|	0752	0837	|	1046	1122	1149	1314	1320	|	1519	...	|	1607	1727	1737	...	|	|	1946	2101	2127
	Macomer d.	...	...	...	|	|	|	0853	...	|	1151	*1254*	▬	▬	1417	|	...	...	|	1705	1814	1819	1830	|	|	2034	2207e	2219
92	Ozieri-Chilivani a.	...	...	...	0736	0857	0939	0940	...	1025	...	...	...	...	1507	1510	...	...	1751	1753	1858	|	1912	1936	2119	2122	...	...
92	Ozieri-Chilivani d.	...	0649	...	0743	*0901*	...	0946	...	1034	...	...	A⚒y	A⚒y	...	1521	...	A⚒	...	1758	1903	|	...	...	2126	...	...	...
139	**Sassari** a.	0700	0743	0800	0834	*0942*	...	1034	...	1115	...	...	1315	1418	...	1607	...	1745	...	1844	1945	1937	...	...	2207	...	...	...
158	**Porto Torres** a.	0718	...	0818	...	...	...	...	...	...	...	...	1335	1438	...	1625d	...	1803	...	1902	...	...	...	...	...	...	...	...

km		⚒	†	⚒	⚒		A		G⚒	C†	A⚒§	A†§		⚒y		⚒	†	A⚒y			A⚒y		A		A⚒	†	A	C
	Porto Torres d.	...	...	...	...	...	0734	...	...	...	0928	0928	...	...	...	...	...	1353	...	...	1534	...	1651d	...	1823	...	1919	...
0	**Sassari** d.	...	...	0600j	...	0654	0751	0806	...	...	0946	0946	...	...	...	1330	...	1410	1430	...	1549	...	1708	...	1847	1852	1934	*2033*
47	Ozieri-Chilivani a.	...	...	0640j	...	0734	...	0848	...	...	1027	1027	...	...	...	1412	...	▬	1512	...	...	...	1749	...	1934	1939	...	*2117*
47	Ozieri-Chilivani d.	...	...	0642	*0651*	0741	...	0858d	0859	0859	1032	1033	...	...	...	1414	...	...	1517	1519	...	...	1800	1913	1944	1944	...	2124
107	Macomer d.	0655	0655	|	0753	0827	...	|	0957	0957	1121	1125	...	1311	...	|	1423	...	1607	|	...	1724	|	|	2035	2035	...	|
166	Oristano d.	0753	0753	|	0841	0915	...	|	1045	1045	1210	1214	...	1412	1430t	|	1518	...	1658	|	...	1827	|	|	2126	2124	...	|
244	Decimomannu d.	0850	0854	|	|	|	...	|	1145	1145	1305	1318	...	1521	1549r	|	1634	...	1754	|	...	1945	|	|	2218	2236	...	|
261	**Cagliari** a.	0905	0910	|	0935	1019	...	|	1159	1159	1319	1333	...	1535	1609	|	1655	...	1809	|	...	1959	|	|	2232	2251	...	|
	Olbia d.	...	...	0744	...	...	...	1003d	...	...	...	...	1310	...	...	1520	...	1623	...	1618	...	...	1908	2009	...	...	...	2227
	Golfo Aranci a.	...	...	...	...	...	...	...	...	...	...	...	1334	...	...	...	...	1647	...	*1647*	...	...	...	2036	...	...	...	...

A – From / to Porto Torres **Marittima**; journey 4 – 8 mins.
C – [12] Olbia - Cagliari and v.v.
G – [12] Golfo Aranci - Olbia - Cagliari.

a – Ⓐ only.
d – ⚒ only.
e – † only.
j – Ⓐ from Sept. 15.
n – Not Aug. 1 - 31.
r – 4 – 7 minutes later on ⚒.
t – 6 – 8 minutes later on †.
y – From Sept. 17.
§ – Service may be delayed awaiting arrival of Tirrenia ship.

ADDITIONAL SERVICES:
Cagliari (0km) - Decimomannu (17km) - Villamassargia-Domusnovas (46km) - Iglesias (55km). Journey 55 - 65 minutes. Connections are available Villamassargia-Domusnovas (0km) - Carbonia Stato (22km) and v.v. from / to most services on ⚒. Journey 20 - 25 mins.

From **Cagliari**:
⚒: 0550, 0643, 0753, 1029, 1130, 1213, 1343, 1614 **n**, 1723, 1819, 1926, 2043.
†: 0728, 1130, 1433, 1638, 1723, 1838, 1950, 2047.

From **Iglesias**:
⚒: 0555 **n**, 0627, 0700, 0730, 0802, 0906, 1131, 1255, 1355, 1455, 1758 **n**, 1855, 2002, 2057.
†: 0620, 0830, 1340, 1545, 1740, 1845, 1940, 2054.

Narrow gauge services on Sardinia are operated by Ferrovie della Sardegna (FdS), Via Cugia 1, 09129 Cagliari. ✆ +39 070 342341. Cagliari - Sorgono (166km), Macomer - Bosa Marina (45km), Mandas - Arbatax (160km), Macomer - Nuoro (63km), Sassari - Alghero San Agostino (35km), Sássari - Palau Marina (150km), Sassari - Sorso (11km). Services operate to differing frequencies; some lines have an occasional tourist service only. Fuller details are shown in our *Tourist Railways* feature annually each July.

630 MILANO - BOLOGNA - RIMINI - ANCONA

km		E 901 ♦	ICN 785 ♦	E 925 ♦	E 907 ♦		ES 9325 [R]♀ R	2 ⚒	2 †	2 ⚒	2 Ⓐ		2 ⚒x	E 1135 ♦	ICp 551 [R] m		ESc 9751 [R]✕	2 †y	IC 713	2 ⑥⑦	ES 9413 [R]♀	Ⓒ	Ⓐ	ICp 553 [R] ♦	t	ES 9415 [R]✕
	Torino Porta Nuova **619** d.	2105	...	...	2250	...	...	...	...	...	...	...	...	...	...	...	...	...	...	...	0745	0605	0605	...	...	...
	Venezia Santa Lucia **620** d.	|	...	...	|	...	...	...	...	...	...	...	...	0442v	...	...	...	...	0723	...	|	|	|	...	...	...
0	**Milano Centrale 619/20** d.	...	2300	...	|	...	...	...	...	...	...	...	...	|	0605	...	0705	...	...	0730	|	|	|	0910	...	1105
219	**Bologna Centrale 619/20** a.	0054	0124	...	0234	...	...	...	...	...	...	...	...	r	0821	...	0852	...	0916	1010	1052	1030	1030	1116	...	1252
219	**Bologna Centrale** d.	0059	0129	0139	0239	...	...	...	...	...	...	0638	...	|	0829	0840	0856	0916	0929	1016	1056	1038	1038	1129	1238	1256
254	Imola d.	|	|	|	|	...	...	...	...	...	...	0701	...	|	|	0902	|	0942	|	1042	|	1101	1104	|	1301	|
261	Castelbolognese d.	|	|	|	|	...	...	...	...	...	...	0708	...	|	|	0909	|	0952	|	|	|	1108	1121	|	1308	|
269	Faenza d.	|	|	|	|	...	...	...	...	...	...	0717	...	|	0856	0917	|	1001	0956	1052	|	1117	1136	1156	1317	|
284	Forlì d.	|	|	|	|	...	...	...	...	...	...	0728	...	|	0906	0932	|	1013	1006	1103	|	1132	1157	1206	1332	|
302	Cesena d.	|	|	|	|	...	...	...	...	...	...	0741	...	|	0918	0945	|	1027	1018	1114	|	1145	1214	1218	1345	|
331	**Rimini** ● d.	0202	0237	0245	|	...	0608	0550	0605	0622	...	0807	...	0850s	0940	1007	0953	1052	1040	1134	1153	1207	1247	1240	1407	1353
340	Riccione d.	|	|	|	|	...	0618	0559	0613	0633	...	0817	...	0900s	0950	1017	|	1103	1050	1144	|	1218	1256	|	1417	|
349	Cattolica d.	|	|	|	|	...	|	0609	0620	0642	...	0827	...	0907s	0956j	1026	|	1114	1058	1152	|	1228	1306	|	1427	|
364	Pesaro d.	|	|	|	|	...	0635	0621	0632	0653	0726	0839	0855	0919s	1007	1038	1015	1127	1110	1204	|	1240	1319	1302	1439	|
376	Fano d.	|	|	|	|	...	0644	0629	0640	0702	0735	0847	0903	0928s	|	1046	|	1135	|	|	|	1249	1327	|	1447	|
398	Senigallia d.	|	|	|	|	...	|	0643	0655	0717	0751	0900	0918	0941s	1025	1100	|	1149	1127	1224	|	1304	1341	|	1502	|
415	Falconara Marittima **625** d.	|	|	|	|	...	0707	0658	0709	0733	0809	0911	0932	0954s	|	1110	|	1201	|	|	|	1315	1357	|	1512	|
423	**Ancona 625** a.	0257	0333	0341	0443	...	...	0711	0719	0746	0820	0924	0947	1005	1046	1124	1050	1210	1147	1243	1255	1325	1410	1334	1524	1441
	Ancona Marittima **625** a.	|	|	|	|	...	...	0720	...	0755	0829	...	0956	...	...	...	|	...	|	|	|	...	...	|	...	|
	Pescara Centrale **631** a.	0422	0459	0522	0622	...	...	...	...	...	...	...	...	...	...	...	1204	...	1325	1436	1415	...	...	1509	...	1605
	Bari Centrale **631** a.	0749	0831	0915	1100	...	...	...	...	...	...	...	...	...	...	...	1452	...	1641	...	1715	...	...	1847	...	1853
	Lecce **631** a.	1000	...	1125	...	...	...	...	...	...	...	...	...	...	...	...	1625	...	1828	...	1852	...	...	...	...	2030

	IC 717 ♦	2 ⚒		ICp 557 [R] w	t	ES 9417 [R]✕ ♦	E 1549 2 ⑤z	IC 559	ES 9335 [R]♀ ♦	2 Ⓐ	t	ES 9419 [R]✕	IC 715	p	ICp 561 [R]		ICp 563 [R]		2 q	ICp 565 [R]		E 923 ♦	ICp 569 [R] n	ICN 781 ♦	ICN 779 ♦
Torino Porta Nuova **619** d.	...	...	...	...	...	...	...	1155	...	...	...	...	...	...	...	...	...	...	1620	...	...	...	...	...	...
Venezia Santa Lucia **620** d.	...	...	...	...	...	...	...	|	...	...	...	...	1523	...	...	...	...	...	|	...	...	...	...	...	2122
Milano Centrale 619/20 d.	...	...	...	1200	...	1305	1240	|	...	...	...	1505	|	...	1605	...	1710	...	|	1910	...	2040	2105	2120	|
Bologna Centrale 619/20 a.	...	...	...	1416	...	1452	1508	1516	...	...	...	1652	1712	...	1816	...	1916	...	2033	2120	...	2310	2316	2352	r
Bologna Centrale d.	1329	...	1338	1429	1438	1456	1517	1529	...	...	1638	1656	1729	1738	1829	1840	1929	1938	2038	2129	2138	2315	2323	2357	|
Imola d.	|	...	1401	|	1501	|	|	|	...	...	1701	|	|	1805	|	1903	|	2002	2101	|	2202	|	|	|	|
Castelbolognese d.	|	...	1408	|	1508	|	|	|	...	...	1708	|	|	1812	|	1910	|	2009	2108	|	2209	|	|	|	|
Faenza d.	1356	...	1417	1455	1517	|	|	1556	...	...	1717	|	1755	1820	1855	1917	1955	2017	2117	2155	2217	|	2352	|	|
Forlì d.	1406	...	1428	1506	1532	|	|	1606	...	...	1732	|	1806	1831	1906	1928	2006	2028	2128	2206	2229	|	0002	0034	|
Cesena d.	1418	...	1441	1518	1545	|	|	1618	...	...	1745	|	1818	1845	1918	1941	2018	2044	2141	2218	2246	|	0014	|	|
Rimini ● d.	1440	1445	1507	1540	1607	1553	1618	1640	1652	1700	1807	1753	1840	1911	1940	2007	2040	2113	2207	2240	2319	0030	0040	0104	0113
Riccione d.	1450	1456	1515	1549	1617	|	|	1650	1702	1713	1816	|	|	1920	1949	2017	2050	...	2217	|	...	0041	...	|	|
Cattolica d.	1458	1505	1523	1556j	1626	|	|	|	|	1722	1825	|	1852	1930	|	2026	|	...	2226	2252	...	|	...	|	|
Pesaro d.	1510	1516	1534	1606	1638	|	|	1707	1719	1733	1836	|	1905	1942	2006	2038	2107	...	2238	2305	...	0059	...	|	|
Fano d.	|	1524	1542	1615	1646	|	|	1716	1728	1741	1844	|	1914	1950	2015	2046	|	...	2246	2315	...	|	...	|	|
Senigallia d.	1527	1539	1557	1628	1701	|	|	1729	|	1757	1858	|	|	2005	2028	2101	|	...	2301	2328	...	|	...	|	|
Falconara Marittima **625** d.	|	1551	1607	1640	1712	|	|	|	|	1812	1912	|	1934	2022	|	2111	2131	...	2311	|	...	|	...	|	|
Ancona 625 a.	1547	1603	1619	1700	1724	1641	1712	1747	1755	1828	1924	1842	1947	2036	2047	2124	2141	...	2324	2346	...	0135	...	0201	0209
Ancona Marittima **625** a.	|	1612a	...	...	...	|	|	|	...	|	...	|	|	...	|	...	|	...	...	...	...	|	...	|	|
Pescara Centrale **631** a.	1725	...	...	...	...	1805	1833	1925	...	2055	...	1957	2125	...	2225	...	2315	...	...	...	...	0257	...	0329	0338
Bari Centrale **631** a.	2048	...	...	...	...	2055	2230	2235	...	...	...	2304	...	...	...	...	...	...	...	...	...	0623	...	0647	0706
Lecce **631** a.	2235	...	...	...	...	...	...	...	...	...	...	...	...	...	...	...	...	...	...	...	...	0814	...	0837	0905

	E 900 ♦	E 924 ♦	ICN 780 ♦	ICN 776 ♦	ICN 784 ♦	E 906 ♦	ICp 552 [R] Ⓐ		E 926 ♦	ICp 556 [R]	q		p	Ⓐ	ICp 558 [R]	Ⓒ	IC 714		ES 9322 [R]♀ ♦	ES 9410 [R]✕ ♦	q	IC 560	q	ESc 9752 [R]✕	ICp 562 [R]
Lecce **631** d.	...	1805	1903	1923	...	2125	...	...	2200	...	...	...	...	...	...	...	...	...	...	...	...	...	...	0700	...
Bari Centrale **631** d.	1950	2024	2101	2124	2259	2338	...	...	2357	...	...	...	...	...	...	...	0508	...	...	0653	...	0712	...	0836	...
Pescara Centrale **631** d.	2347	0000	0028	0059	0204	0240	...	...	0322	...	...	...	...	...	0635	...	0817	...	...	0953	...	1030	...	1119	...
Ancona Marittima **625** d.	|	|	|	|	|	|	...	...	|	...	...	...	...	...	|	...	|	...	...	|	...	|	...	|	...
Ancona 625 d.	0126	0132	0159	0234	0330	0406	...	0435	0446	0620	0635	...	0740	0800	0815	0840	1020	1040	1050	1116	1135	1210	1247	1241	1310
Falconara Marittima **625** d.	|	|	|	|	|	|	...	0444	|	|	0646	...	0752	0810	0826	0849	|	1048	1032f	|	1145	|	1257	|	1319
Senigallia d.	|	|	|	|	|	|	...	0457	|	0637	0700	...	0806	0820	|	0900	|	1059	|	|	1159	1229	1307	|	1330
Fano d.	|	|	|	|	|	|	...	0512	|	0649	0714	...	0820	0834	|	0915	1044	1113	1115	|	1213	1242	1321	|	1342
Pesaro d.	|	|	|	|	|	|	...	0520	|	0700	0724	...	0830	0842	0852	0925	1054	1123	1124	|	1223	1252	1330	1316	1352
Cattolica d.	|	|	|	|	|	|	...	0531	|	|	0735	...	0841	0853	|	0936	1106	1134	|	|	1234	|	1341	|	|
Riccione d.	|	|	|	|	|	|	...	0541	|	|	0745	...	0847	0903	0910	0947	|	1143	1142	|	1245	1310	1351	|	1410
Rimini ● d.	|	0230	0256	0333	0427	0502	0530	0600	0542	0722	0800	...	0900	0930	0922	1000	1122	1155	1150	1209	1300	1322	1403	1339	1422
Cesena d.	|	|	|	|	0448	|	0551	0618	|	0742	0818	...	0918	0953	0942	1018	1143	1212	...	|	1318	1342	1421	|	1441
Forlì d.	|	|	|	|	0501	|	0603	0631	|	0754	0831	...	0931	1007	0954	1031	1155	1226	...	|	1331	1354	1434	|	1453
Faenza d.	|	|	|	|	|	|	0614	0642	|	0805	0842	...	0942	1018	1005	1042	1205	1238	...	|	1342	1405	1444	|	1503
Castelbolognese d.	|	|	|	|	|	|	|	0649	|	|	0850	...	0950	1026	|	1050	|	1250	...	|	1349	|	1450	|	|
Imola d.	|	|	|	|	|	|	|	0656	|	|	0857	...	0957	1033	|	1057	|	1257	...	|	1356	|	1456	|	|
Bologna Centrale a.	0320	0330	0408	r	0543	0612	0640	0722	0652	0833	0922	...	1022	1122	1031	1122	1230	1322	...	1304	1422	1431	1520	1504	1528
Bologna Centrale 619/20 d.	0325	...	0412	|	0548	0618	0644	...	0657	0837	0928	...	...	...	1044	...	1248	...	...	1308	...	1444	...	1508	1544
Milano Centrale 619/20 a.	|	...	0705	|	0820	|	0855	...	0925	1055	|	...	...	...	1255	...	|	...	...	1455	...	|	...	1655	1750
Venezia Santa Lucia **620** a.	|	...	...	0705	...	|	...	...	...	...	|	...	...	...	...	...	1442	...	...	...	...	|	...	...	...
Torino Porta Nuova **619** a.	0705	...	...	...	...	1010	...	...	...	...	1340	...	...	...	...	...	...	...	...	...	...	1805	...	...	...

	2 ⚒x	2 ⚒	E 1550 2 ⑦h	2 Ⓐ		ICp 564 [R]	ES 9414 [R]✕	†y	2 ⚒	ICp 568 [R] ♦		IC 718 ♦	ES 9416 [R]♀	2 ⚒	2 Ⓐ	2 ⑥⑦	IC 716		E 1134 [R] ♦	ICp 570 [R]	ES 9418 [R]✕	2 Ⓐx	2 ⚒	q	ES 9334 [R]♀ R
Lecce **631** d.	...	...	...	...	...	...	...	...	...	...	...	1020	1125	...	...	...	...	...	...	...	1335	...	...	...	...
Bari Centrale **631** d.	...	...	0912	...	...	...	1105	...	...	1112	...	1203	1258	...	...	...	...	...	...	...	1508	...	...	...	...
Pescara Centrale **631** d.	...	...	1230	...	...	1320	1348	...	...	1435	...	1530	1550	...	...	1600	1630	...	...	...	1748	...	...	...	...
Ancona Marittima **625** d.	1310	1334	|	1412	...	|	|	...	1543a	|	...	|	|	1716a	1735	|	|	...	...	...	|	1916	2000	...	...
Ancona 625 d.	1323	1343	1400	1421	1435	1503	1518	1524	1552	1620	1635	1710	1715	1725	1744	1748	1810	1835	1845u	1900	1913	1926	2009	2040	2107
Falconara Marittima **625** d.	1335	1354	|	1432	1445	1514	|	|	1604	|	1644	|	|	1736	1755	1758	1822	1844	1855u	1911	|	1938	2019	2054	|
Senigallia d.	1350	1411	|	1447	1457	|	|	|	1619	|	1657	1729	|	1751	1810	1812	1833	1858	1907u	1923	|	1955	2033	2106	2125
Fano d.	1405	1426	|	1502	1512	1535	|	|	1634	|	1712	|	|	1807	1826	1826	|	1913	1920u	1937	|	2010	2047	2120	2136
Pesaro d.	1413	1435	|	1511	1522	1545	|	1600	1642	1652	1721	1752	|	1815	1835	1835	1852	1923	1931u	1947	1946	2018	2056	2129	2145
Cattolica d.	...	1446	|	1522	1533	1555j	|	1611	1652	|	1733	1804	|	...	1846	1847	|	1934	1943u	1957j	|	...	2107	2140	|
Riccione d.	...	1456	|	1532	1543	1601	|	1620	1702	|	1743	1812	|	...	1857	1857	1910	1943	1950u	2004	|	...	2118	2149	2202
Rimini ● d.	...	1510	1451	1546	1555	1620	1609	1631	1716	1722	1755	1828	1809	...	1909	1911	1922	1955	2001u	2022	2009	...	2128	2200	2210
Cesena d.	...	...	|	...	1613	1642	|	1651	...	1742	1813	1847	|	...	...	1930	1940	2013	|	2041	|	...	...	2218	...
Forlì d.	...	...	|	...	1626	1654	|	1704	...	1754	1826	1859	|	...	...	1944	1953	2026	|	2053	|	...	...	2231	...
Faenza d.	...	...	|	...	1638	1705	|	1715	...	1805	1838	1909	|	...	...	1955	2003	2038	|	2103	|	...	...	2242	...
Castelbolognese d.	...	...	|	...	1650	|	|	1722	...	|	1850	|	|	...	...	|	|	2050	|	|	|	...	...	2250	...
Imola d.	...	...	|	...	1657	|	|	1730	...	|	1856	|	|	...	...	2009	|	2057	|	|	|	...	...	2257	...
Bologna Centrale a.	...	...	1553	...	1721	1729	1704	1757	...	1831	1922	1944	1904	...	...	2043	2030	2120	r	2129	2104	...	...	2322	...
Bologna Centrale 619/20 d.	...	...	1557	...	1727	1744	1708	1804	...	1844	...	...	1908	...	...	2056	2048	...	|	2144	2108	...	...	...	...
Milano Centrale 619/20 a.	...	...	1810	...	|	1950	1855	2109g	...	2050	...	...	|	...	...	2340	|	...	|	2359	2300	...	...	...	...
Venezia Santa Lucia **620** a.	...	...	...	...	|	...	...	...	...	...	...	...	|	...	...	...	2240	...	0002v	...	...	...	...	...	...
Torino Porta Nuova **619** a.	...	...	...	...	2140	...	...	...	...	...	...	...	2215	...	...	...	...	...	...	...	...	...	...	...	...

FOR NOTES SEE OPPOSITE PAGE

ANCONA - BARI - LECCE 631

	2 ⚒	2	E 923 ♦	ICN 789 ♦	ICN 781 ♦	ICN 779 ♦	E 951 ♦	2 ⚒	E 903 A	E 901 ♦	ICN 785 ♦	E 925 ♦	L	2		2 ⚒	E 907 ♦	2 ⚒x	ES 9351 [R] 🍷	2	2 ⚒	2	2	ICp 677 [R]	ESc 9751 [R] ✕	2
Torino Porta Nuova **619** d.	...	...	...	...	...	...	...	...	2105	2105	...	...	...	...	...	...	2250	...	...	...	...	...	...	...	...	...
Venezia Santa Lucia **620** d.	...	...	...	...	...	2122	...	...	|	|	...	...	...	...	...	...	|	...	...	...	...	...	...	...	...	...
Milano C **619/20/30** d.	...	...	2040	...	2120	|	...	...	|	|	2300	...	...	...	...	...	|	...	...	...	...	...	...	...	0705	...
Bologna C **619/20/30** d.	...	...	2315	...	2357	r	...	...	0059	0059	0129	0139	...	...	...	...	0239	...	...	...	...	...	...	...	0856	...
Ancona 625/30 d.	...	...	0137	...	0204	0212	...	...	0259	0259	0336	0343	...	...	...	...	0447	...	...	...	0624	0728	...	...	1053	...
Civitanova-Montegranaro d.	...	...	|	...	|	|	...	...	|	|	|	|	...	...	...	...	0514	...	...	...	0704	0805	...	...	|	...
San Benedetto del Tronto d.	...	...	|	...	|	|	...	...	|	|	|	0437	...	...	...	...	0540	...	...	...	0737	0839	...	...	|	...
Pescara Centrale a.	...	...	0257	...	0329	0338	...	...	0422	0422	0459	0522	...	...	...	...	0622	...	...	...	0834	0931	...	...	1204	...
Pescara Centrale d.	...	...	0301	...	0332	0341	...	...	0425	0425	0502	0525	...	...	...	...	0625	...	...	...	▬	▬	...	...	1207	...
Termoli d.	...	...	0403	...	|	0445	...	...	0530	0530	0608	0636	...	...	...	...	0744	...	...	...	...	...	...	...	|	...
Roma Termini **626** d.	...	...	|	2358	|	|	...	...	|	|	|	|	...	...	...	...	|	...	0738	...	...	...	...	0852	|	...
Foggia 626 a.	...	...	0450	0453	0526	0541	...	...	0625	0625	0700	0743	...	...	...	...	0838	...	1111	...	...	...	...	1320	1347	...
Foggia d.	...	...	0453	0509	0530	0545	...	...	0633	0633	0704	0747	...	...	...	...	0908	...	1120	...	...	...	...	1334	1350	...
Barletta d.	...	...	0535	0547	0609	0622	...	...	0710	0710	0746	0822	...	...	...	...	0959	...	1152	...	2	...	...	1406	|	...
Bari Centrale a.	...	...	0623	0638	0647	0706	...	...	0749	0749	0831	0915	...	...	...	...	1100	...	1223	...	⚒	2	...	1446	1452	...
Bari Centrale ▲ d.	0501	0539	0627	0642	0651	0710	...	0712	0804	0805	0850	0929	0930	0936	...	1015	...	1152	1227	1249	1315	1414	1415	...	1456	1608
Gioia del Colle d.	|	|	|	|	|	|	...	0804	0836	|	0934	|	|	|	...	1056	...	|	|	|	1400	1457	|	...	|	1648
Taranto 638 ▲ a.	|	|	|	|	|	|	0713	0857	0914	|	1010	|	1040	|	...	1141	...	|	|	|	1450	1540	|	...	|	1733
Crotone **635** a.	|	|	|	|	|	|	|	...	1244	|	1400	|	...	|	...	...	...	|	|	|	...	...	|	...	|	...
Monopoli d.	0533	0611	0654	0704	0718	0739	|	...	...	0838	...	1000	...	1012	...	...	...	1230	1252	1323	...	...	1450	...	|	...
Fasano d.	0541	0620	0704	0718	0730	0751	|	...	...	0849	...	1011	...	1023	...	...	...	1239	1303	1333	...	...	1459	...	|	...
Ostuni d.	0555	0634	0717	0732	0745	0806	|	...	...	0903	...	1025	...	1038	...	...	...	1254	1316	1346	...	...	1515	...	1532	...
Brindisi ▲ d.	0624	0704	0745	0758	0811	0833	0843	...	...	0931	...	1052	...	1124	...	...	...	1320	1341	1415	...	...	1547	...	1600	...
Lecce a.	0702	0739	0814	0825	0837	0905	0922	...	...	1000	...	1125	...	1206	...	...	...	1354	1408	1447	...	...	1618	...	1625	...

	2 ⚒	IC 713	2 ⑥⑦	ES 9413 [R] 🍷	L	2	ES 9353 [R] ✕	2	ICp 553 [R] ♦	ES 9415 [R] ✕	2	2	ES 9355 [R] ✕	IC 717 ♦	ES 9417 [R] ✕	2 ⚒	ES 9385 [R] 🍷 ⑤z	E 1549 ⑤z	IC 559 🍷	E 981 ♦	ES 9357 [R] 🍷	ES 9419 [R] ✕	2	IC 715	ICp 561 [R]	ICp 563 [R]
Torino Porta Nuova **619** d.	...	...	...	0745	...	...	...	...	...	...	...	...	...	...	...	...	...	...	1155	...	...	...	...	...	...	...
Venezia Santa Lucia **620** d.	...	0723	...	|	...	...	...	...	...	...	...	...	...	...	...	...	...	...	|	...	...	...	...	1523	...	...
Milano C **619/20/30** d.	...	|	0730	|	...	...	...	...	0910	1105	...	...	...	...	1305	...	...	1240	|	...	...	1505	...	|	1605	1710
Bologna C **619/20/30** d.	...	0929	1016	1056	...	...	...	...	1129	1256	...	...	...	1329	1456	...	...	1517	1529	...	...	1656	...	1729	1829	1929
Ancona 625/30 d.	...	1150	1246	1258	...	...	...	...	1337	1444	...	...	...	1550	1644	...	...	1715	1750	...	...	1845	...	1950	2052	2144
Civitanova-Montegranaro d.	...	1217	1320	|	...	...	...	...	1409	|	...	...	...	1617	|	...	...	|	1817	...	...	|	...	2022	2117	2210
San Benedetto del Tronto d.	...	1247	1348	|	...	...	...	...	1432	1530	...	...	...	1647	1730	...	...	|	1847	...	...	|	...	2047	2147	2238
Pescara Centrale a.	...	1325	1436	1415	...	...	...	...	1509	1605	...	...	...	1725	1805	...	...	1833	1925	...	...	1957	...	2125	2225	2315
Pescara Centrale d.	...	1328	...	1418	...	...	...	...	1512	1608	...	...	...	1728	1808	...	...	1836	1928	...	...	2000	...	▬	...	...
Termoli d.	...	1428	...	1516	...	...	...	...	1620	|	...	...	...	1828	|	...	...	1941	2028	...	...	2103	...	...	...	...
Roma Termini **626** d.	...	|	...	|	...	...	1338	...	|	|	...	...	1538	|	|	...	1638	|	|	...	1716	|	...	...	...	...
Foggia 626 a.	...	1528	...	1606	...	...	1705	...	1724	1747	...	...	1905	1921	1946	...	2049	2058	2120	...	2122	2154	...	...	...	...
Foggia d.	...	1531	...	1609	...	...	1714	...	1728	1750	...	...	1914	1924	1949	...	2058	2104	2123	...	2131	2157	...	...	...	...
Barletta d.	...	1603	...	1640	...	...	1745	...	1803	|	...	...	1945	1958	|	...	2128	2137	2155	...	2202	2229	...	...	...	...
Bari Centrale a.	...	1641	...	1715	...	...	1815	...	1847	1853	...	...	2015	2048	2055	...	2203	2230	2235	...	2248	2304	...	2	...	...
Bari Centrale ▲ d.	1610	1645	...	1719	1730	1744	1819	1822	1908	1857	1935	1944	2019	2052	2105	2100	2212	...	...	2248	...	...	2311	2320	...	...
Gioia del Colle d.	|	|	...	|	|	|	|	1904	1940	|	|	2024	|	|	2139	|	2243	...	...	2326	...	...	|	0004	...	...
Taranto 638 ▲ a.	|	|	...	|	1840	|	|	1956	2014	|	|	2115	|	|	2217	|	2320	...	...	0012	...	...	|	0049	...	...
Crotone **635** a.	|	|	...	|	...	|	|	...	2359	|	|	...	|	|	...	|	...	...	...	...	...	...	|	...	...	...
Monopoli d.	1646	1708	...	|	...	1820	|	...	...	1924	2010	...	2040	2116	...	2132	...	...	...	...	...	...	2343	...	...	...
Fasano d.	1655	1720	...	1749	...	1830	|	...	...	|	2020	...	2049	2127	...	2142	...	...	...	...	...	...	2351	...	...	...
Ostuni d.	1711	1734	...	|	...	1845	|	...	...	|	2036	...	2101	2142	...	2156	...	...	...	...	...	...	0004	...	...	...
Brindisi ▲ d.	1740	1800	...	1825	...	1931k	1917	...	...	2004	2107	...	2125	2208	...	2226	...	...	...	...	...	...	0030	...	...	...
Lecce a.	1814	1828	...	1852	...	2004	1940	...	...	2030	...	...	2150	2235	...	2300	...	...	...	...	...	...	0102	...	...	...

♦ – **NOTES FOR TABLES 630/1** (LISTED BY TRAIN NUMBER)

553 – MURGE – [12] Milano - Taranto (**554**) - Metaponto (**555**) - Crotone.
568 – MURGE – [12] Crotone (**566**) - Metaponto (**567**) - Taranto - Milano.
717/8 – ADIGE – [12] Bolzano - Verona - Bologna - Lecce and v.v.
776 – TERGESTE – 🛌 2 cl. (4 berth) and [12] Lecce - Venezia Mestre (**777**) - Trieste; 🛏 1, 2 cl. (T2), 🛏 1, 2 cl. and [12] Lecce - Venezia Mestre (**1598**) - Venezia Santa Lucia.
779 – TERGESTE – 🛌 2 cl. (4 berth) and [12] Trieste (**778**) - Venezia Mestre - Lecce; 🛏 1, 2 cl. (T2), 🛏 1, 2 cl. and [12] Venezia Santa Lucia (**1599**) - Venezia Mestre - Lecce.
780/1 – FRECCIA SALENTINA – 🛏 1, 2 cl. (T2), 🛏 1,2 cl., 🛌 2 cl. (4 berth) and [12] Lecce - Milano and v.v.
784 – FRECCIA DEL LEVANTE – Not Dec. 24, 25, 31: 🛌 2 cl. and [12] Crotone (**782**) - Metaponto (**783**) - Taranto - Milano; 🛏 1, 2 cl. (T2), 🛏 1, 2 cl. and [12] Taranto - Milano.
785 – FRECCIA DEL LEVANTE – Not Dec. 24, 25, 31: 🛌 2 cl. and [12] Milano - Taranto (**786**) - Metaponto (**787**) - Crotone; 🛏 1,2 cl. (T2), 🛏 1, 2 cl. and [12] Milano - Taranto.
789 – TAVOLIERE – 🛏 1, 2 cl., 🛌 2 cl. (4 berth) and [12] Roma - Lecce.
900 – ⑦; also Dec. 26, Jan. 1, Mar. 24, May 1, June 2, not Dec. 23, 30, Mar. 23, June 1 (from Bari): 🛌 2 cl. and [2] (also 🛏 1, 2 cl. (T2) June 4 - Sept. 8) Bari - Torino.
901 – FRECCIA ADRIATICA – 🛏 1,2 cl. (T2), 🛌 2 cl. and [2] Torino - Lecce; 🛌 2 cl. and [2] Torino (**901**) - Bari (**903**) - Taranto (**904**) - Metaponto (**905**) - Catanzaro Lido.
906 – FRECCIA ADRIATICA – 🛏 1,2 cl. (T2), 🛌 2 cl. and [2] Lecce - Torino; 🛌 2 cl. and [2] Catanzaro Lido (**908**) - Metaponto (**909**) - Taranto (**910**) - Bari (**906**) - Torino.
907 – ⑤; also Apr. 24, 30, not Apr. 25 (from Torino): 🛌 2 cl. and [2] (also 🛏 1, 2 cl. (T2) June 3 - Sept. 7, from Torino) Torino - Bari.
923 – Not Dec. 24, 25, 31: 🛏 1, 2 cl. (T2), 🛌 2 cl. (4/6 berth) and [2] Milano - Lecce.
924 – ①③④⑤⑥⑦ (also Jan. 1, Apr. 29; not Dec. 24, 31, Apr. 28): 🛏 1, 2 cl. (T2), 🛌 2 cl. (4 berth) and [2] Lecce - Bologna - Bolzano.
925 – ①②③⑤⑥⑦; also Dec. 27, Jan. 3, May 1; not Dec. 25, 26, Jan. 1, Apr. 30 (from Bolzano): 🛏 1, 2 cl. (T2), 🛌 2 cl. (4 berth) and [2] Bolzano - Bologna - Lecce.
926 – Not Dec. 24, 25, 31: 🛏 1, 2 cl. (T2), 🛌 2 cl. (4/6 berth) and [2] Lecce - Milano.
951 – 🛌 2 cl. and [2] Roma - Taranto - Lecce.
981 – Ⓐ: [2] Bari - Taranto (**982**) - Metaponto (**983**) - Villa S G - Reggio di Calabria.
1134 – ALLEGRO AIDA – ⑥ June 16 - Sept. 8 (from Ancona): 🛏 1, 2 cl., 🛌 2 cl. and [2] Ancona - Venezia Mestre - Wien Süd. Supplement payable.
1135 – ALLEGRO AIDA – ⑤ June 15 - Sept. 7 (from Wien): 🛏 1, 2 cl., 🛌 2 cl. and [2] Wien Süd - Venezia Mestre - Ancona. Supplement payable.
9322 – [12] and 🍷 Roma (**9320**) - Ancona - Rimini (- Ravenna, June 10 - Sept. 8).
9335 – [12] and 🍷 (Ravenna, June 10 - Sept. 8 -) Rimini - Ancona (**9337**) - Roma.
9410/7 – [12] and ✕ Taranto - Bari - Milano and v.v.

A – FRECCIA ADRIATICA – 🛌 2 cl. and [2] Torino (**901**) - Bari - Taranto (**904**) - Metaponto (**905**) - Catanzaro Lido.
L – *ES*Link*: 🚌 link.
R – [12] and 🍷 Roma - Rimini and v.v.

a – Ⓐ only.
f – Via Ancona.
g – Milano **Porta Garibaldi**.
h – Also Nov. 1.
j – June 16 - Sept. 16.
k – Arrive 1912.
m – Not Jan. 26-30, Feb. 23, 24, Mar. 13-16, 29, 30, May 15-18.
n – ①②③④⑦ (not Dec. 8, and days before holidays).
p – Not Jan. 26-30, Feb. 23-26, Mar. 13-16, May 15-18, 29-31, June 8-10, 14.
q – Dec. 9 - May 30.
r – Via Ravenna.
s – Stops to set down only.
t – Dec. 9 - May 28 (not Jan. 26-30, Feb. 23-26, Mar. 13-16, May 15-18).
u – Stops to pick up only.
v – Venezia **Mestre**.
w – Dec. 9 - May 31.
x – Not July 29 - Aug. 26.
y – June 2 - Aug. 26.
z – Also Oct. 31.

▲ – For additional services Taranto - Brindisi/Bari and v.v. – see below.

▲ – LOCAL SERVICES TARANTO - BRINDISI/BARI and v.v. 2nd class only

TARANTO - BRINDISI and v.v.: 70 km, journey 61–84 minutes.

From **Taranto**: 0516⚒, 0536⚒, 0625, 0842⚒x, 1150, 1247⚒x, 1354⚒, 1439⚒, 1628⚒x, 1820, 1906, 2135.

From **Brindisi**: 0507, 0551⚒, 0707⚒x, 0855, 1152⚒, 1305, 1409⚒x, 1432⚒, 1603⚒, 1703, 1842⚒x, 2025.

TARANTO - BARI and v.v. (additional services): 115 km, journey 83–110 minutes.

From **Taranto**: 0442⚒, 0504†, 0627, 0708⚒, 1021†, 1230⚒x, 1424⚒x.

From **Bari**: 0344, 0546⚒, 0649⚒x, 0811†, 1727⚒x.

● – For 🚌 service Rimini - San Marino and v.v. – see below.

● – 🚌 service available **Rimini - San Marino and v.v.**, 27 km, journey 40–50 minutes.
Departures from Rimini (FS railway station).
Operator: F.lli Benedettini s.a. ✆ +378 90 67 48.

631 LECCE - BARI - ANCONA

	ICp 558	*IC* 714	*ES* 9350	*ES* 9410			*IC* 560		*ES* 9352	*ES* 9380	*E* 990		*ESc* 9752	*E* 1550		*ICp* 564	*ES* 9414	*IC* 568		*IC* 718		*ES* 9416		*ES* 9354	*IC* 716	
	[R]		[R] ♀	[R] ✕	2	2		2	[R] ♀	[R] ♀		2	[R] ✕	2	2	[R]	[R] ✕		2			[R] ♀	2	[R] ✕		2
						⚒		⚒	⚒	†	♦	⚒		⑦p	⚒			♦	⚒x	♦	L					⚒
Lecce d.	...	...	...	...	0505	...	...	0530	0600	0600	...	0607	0700	...	...	...	...	...	0946	1020	...	1125	1050	1217	...	1230
Brindisi ▲ d.	...	...	...	...	0536	...	...	0602	0625	0625	...	0638	0725	...	...	...	...	...	1019	1045	...	1149	1127	1242	...	1302
Ostuni d.	...	...	...	...	0559	...	...	0626	0645	0645	...	0700	|	...	...	...	...	...	1043	1107	...	|	1154	|	...	1328
Fasano d.	...	...	...	...	0614	...	...	0639	0658	0658	...	0714	|	...	...	...	...	...	1057	1120	...	1218	1226	|	...	1343
Monopoli d.	...	...	...	...	0622	...	...	0648	0710	0710	...	0722	0801	...	...	...	...	...	1107	1132	...	|	1235	|	...	1352
Crotone **635** d.	...	...	...	...	|	...	...	|	|	|	...	|	|	...	...	...	...	0605	|	|	...	|	|	|	...	|
Taranto 638 ▲ d.	...	...	...	0534	|	0545	...	|	|	|	0610	|	|	...	0808	...	...	0941	|	|	1130	|	|	|	...	|
Gioia del Colle d.	...	...	...	0608	|	0625	...	|	|	|	0659	|	|	...	0859	...	...	1015	|	|	|	|	|	|	...	|
Bari Centrale ▲ a.	...	...	...	0644	0703	0708	...	0728	0738	0738	0748	0802	0832	...	0945	...	...	1048	1149	1159	1240	1254	1314	1338	...	1437
Bari Centrale d.	...	0508	0515	0653	...	...	0712	...	0742	0742	...	...	0836	0912	...	...	1105	1113	...	1203	...	1258	━━	1342	...	...
Barletta d.	...	0546	0558	0728	...	...	0756	...	0813	0813	...	...	|	1000	...	...	|	1148	...	1254	...	1329	...	1413	...	...
Foggia a.	...	0624	0630	0801	...	...	0833	...	0844	0844	...	...	0937	1034	...	...	1207	1224	...	1329	...	1404	...	1444	...	...
Foggia 626 d.	...	0628	0639	0804	...	...	0836	...	0853	0853	...	...	0940	1037	...	...	1210	1227	...	1332	...	1407	*IR*	1453	...	...
Roma Termini **626** a.	...	|	1022	|	...	...	|	...	1222	1238	...	...	|	|	...	...	|	|	...	|	...	|	**1764**	1822	...	...
Termoli d.	...	0719	...	0858	...	...	0928	...	...	...	...	...	1026	1128	...	...	|	1334	...	1426	...	1456	2	...	...	...
Pescara Centrale a.	...	0814	...	0950	...	...	1027	...	...	...	...	...	1116	1227	...	...	1345	1432	...	1527	...	1547	⑥⑦	...	...	...
Pescara Centrale d.	0635	0817	...	0953	...	...	1030	...	...	...	...	...	1119	1230	...	1320	1348	1435	...	1530	...	1550	1600	...	1630	...
San Benedetto del Tronto d.	0714	0900	...	|	...	...	1111	...	...	...	...	...	1152	|	...	1400	1424	1521	...	1611	...	|	1641	...	1711	...
Civitanova-Montegranaro d.	0741	0931	...	|	...	...	1138	...	...	...	...	...	|	|	...	1427	|	1545	...	1638	...	|	1708	...	1738	...
Ancona 625/30 a.	0812	1016	...	1113	...	...	1207	...	...	...	...	...	1238	1356	...	1500	1515	1617	...	1707	...	1712	1745	...	1806	...
Bologna C **619/20/30** a.	1031	1230	...	1304	...	...	1431	...	...	...	...	...	1504	1553	...	1729	1704	1831	...	1944	...	1904	2043	...	2030	...
Milano C **619/20/30** a.	1255	|	...	1455	...	...	|	...	...	...	...	...	1655	1810	...	1950	1855	2050	...	...	...	|	2340	...	|	...
Venezia Santa Lucia **620** a.	...	1442	...	...	...	...	|	...	...	...	...	...	...	...	...	...	...	...	...	...	...	|	...	...	2240	...
Torino Porta Nuova **619** a.	...	...	...	...	...	...	1805	...	...	...	...	...	...	...	...	...	...	...	...	...	...	2215	...	...	...	...

	ES 9418			*ICp* 678			*ES* 9386			*ES* 9356			*E* 900	*E* 924	*ICN* 780		*ICN* 776				*ICN* 784	*E* 956	*E* 906	*E* 908	*E* 926	*ICN* 788
	[R] ✕	2	2	[R]	2	2	[R] ♀	2	2	[R] ✕	2	2							2	2						
		⚒			⚒x		⑦p						♦	♦	♦	L	♦		Ⓑ	⑥	♦	♦	♦	A	♦	♦
Lecce d.	1335	...	1345	...	1425	...	...	1525	...	1700	1720	...	...	1805	1903	...	1923	...	1950	2002	...	2046	2125	...	2200	2220
Brindisi ▲ d.	1400	...	1419	...	1501	...	...	1600	...	1725	1752	...	...	1835	1930	...	1954	...	2035	2035	...	2126	2154	...	2231	2246
Ostuni d.	1420	...	1442	...	1527	...	...	1627	...	1745	1819	...	...	1857	1953	...	2017	...	2102	2102	...	|	2214	...	2253	2308
Fasano d.	|	...	1456	...	1542	...	...	1642	...	1758	1834	...	...	1911	2007	...	2031	...	2117	2117	...	|	2227	...	2307	2323
Monopoli d.	|	...	1505	...	1553	...	...	1651	...	1810	1843	...	...	1922	2018	...	2043	...	2128	2128	...	|	2239	...	2318	2336
Crotone **635** d.	|	...	|	...	|	...	...	|	...	|	|	...	...	|	|	...	|	...	|	|	1730	|	|	1802	|	|
Taranto 638 ▲ d.	|	1340	|	...	|	1515	1550	|	1640	|	|	1806	...	|	|	2000	|	...	|	|	2120	2240	|	2156	|	|
Gioia del Colle d.	|	1431	|	...	|	1607	1624	|	1724	|	|	1846	...	|	|	|	|	...	|	|	2204	...	|	2237	|	|
Bari Centrale ▲ a.	1504	1514	1546	...	1635	1649	1658	1730	1807	1838	1925	1937	...	2000	2056	2110	2119	...	2204	2204	2241	...	2315	2315	2350	0008
Bari Centrale d.	1508	...	...	1614	...	...	1707	...	...	1842	...	...	1950	2024	2101	...	2124	...	...	...	2259	...	2338	2338	2357	0012
Barletta d.	|	...	...	1700	...	...	1738	...	...	1913	...	...	2036	2116	2142	...	2211	...	...	...	2332	...	0011	0011	0045	0102
Foggia a.	1609	...	...	1738	...	...	1813	...	...	1944	...	...	2117	2155	2223	...	2256	...	...	...	0010	...	0046	0046	0125	0143
Foggia 626 d.	1612	...	...	1755	...	...	1822	...	...	1953	...	...	2137	2159	2227	...	2300	...	...	...	0013	...	0050	0050	0130	0159
Roma Termini **626** a.	|	...	...	2240	...	...	2222	...	...	2326	...	...	|	|	|	...	|	...	...	...	|	...	|	|	|	0629
Termoli d.	|	...	...	...	...	...	...	...	...	...	...	...	2238	2256	2320	...	2357	...	...	...	|	...	|	|	0220	...
Pescara Centrale a.	1745	...	...	...	...	...	...	...	...	...	...	...	2344	2358	0025	...	0056	...	...	...	0201	...	0237	0237	0319	...
Pescara Centrale d.	1748	...	...	...	...	...	...	...	...	...	...	...	2347	0000	0028	...	0059	...	...	...	0204	...	0240	0240	0322	...
San Benedetto del Tronto d.	|	...	...	...	...	...	...	...	...	...	...	...	0025	0039	|	...	|	...	...	...	|	...	|	|	|	...
Civitanova-Montegranaro d.	|	...	...	...	...	...	...	...	...	...	...	...	0051	|	|	...	|	...	...	...	|	...	|	|	|	...
Ancona a.	1910	...	...	...	...	...	...	...	...	...	...	...	0123	0130	0156	...	0231	...	...	...	0327	...	0401	0401	0444	...
Bologna C **619/20/30** a.	2104	...	...	...	...	...	...	...	...	...	...	...	0320	0330	0408	...	r	...	...	...	0543	...	0612	0612	0652	...
Milano C **619/20/30** a.	2300	...	...	...	...	...	...	...	...	...	...	...	|	...	0705	...	|	...	...	...	0820	...	|	|	0925	...
Venezia Santa Lucia **620** a.	...	...	...	...	...	...	...	...	...	...	...	...	|	...	...	...	0705	...	...	...	...	...	|	|	...	...
Torino Porta Nuova **619** a.	...	...	...	...	...	...	...	...	...	...	...	...	0705	...	...	...	...	...	...	...	...	...	1010	1010	...	...

♦ – **NOTES** (LISTED BY TRAIN NUMBER)

568 – MURGE – [12] Crotone (**566**) - Metaponto (**567**) - Taranto - Milano.
718 – ADIGE – [12] Lecce - Bologna - Verona - Bolzano.
776 – TERGESTE – ▬ 2 cl. (4 berth) and [12] Lecce - Venezia Mestre (**777**) - Trieste; 🛏 1, 2 cl. (T2), 🛏 1, 2 cl. and [12] Lecce - Venezia Mestre (**1598**) - Venezia Santa Lucia.
780 – FRECCIA SALENTINA – 🛏 1, 2 cl. (T2), 🛏 1, 2 cl., ▬ 2 cl. (4 berth) and [12] Lecce - Milano.
784 – FRECCIA DEL LEVANTE – Not Dec. 24, 25, 31: ▬ 2 cl. and [12] Crotone (**782**) - Metaponto (**783**) - Taranto - Milano; 🛏 1, 2 cl. (T2), 🛏 1, 2 cl. and [12] Taranto - Milano.
788 – TAVOLIERE – 🛏 1, 2 cl., ▬ 2 cl. (4 berth) and [12] Lecce - Roma.
900 – ⑦; also Dec. 26, Jan. 1, Mar. 24, May 1, June 2, not Dec. 23, 30, Mar. 23, June 1 (from Bari): ▬ 2 cl. and [2] (also 🛏 1, 2 cl. (T2) June 4 - Sept. 8) Bari - Torino.
906 – FRECCIA ADRIATICA – 🛏 1,2 cl. (T2), ▬ 2 cl. and [2] Lecce - Torino.
924 – ①③④⑤⑥⑦ (also Jan. 1, Apr. 29; not Dec. 24, 31, Apr. 28): 🛏 1, 2 cl. (T2), ▬ 2 cl. (4 berth) and [2] Lecce - Bologna - Bolzano.
926 – Not Dec. 24, 25, 31: 🛏 1, 2 cl. (T2), ▬ 2 cl. (4/6 berth) and [2] Lecce - Milano.
956 – ▬ 2 cl. and [2] Lecce - Taranto - Roma.
990 – Ⓐ (from Reggio): [2] Reggio di Calabria (**986**) - Villa S G - Metaponto (**989**) - Taranto - Bari.

A – FRECCIA ADRIATICA – ▬ 2 cl. and [2] Catanzaro Lido - Metaponto (**909**) - Taranto (**910**) - Bari (**906**) - Torino.
L – *ES*Link*: 🚌 link.
p – Also Nov. 1.
r – Via Ravenna.
u – Stops to pick up only.
x – Not July 29 - Aug. 26.
▲ – For additional services Taranto - Brindisi / Bari and v.v. – see page 313.

633 ROMA and LAMEZIA - PAOLA - COSENZA - SIBARI

km								*ICp* 511/2			
		2	2	2	2	2	2	[R]	2	2	2
		Ⓒ	⚒		⚒		⚒	S			
	Roma Tiburtina **640** d.	...	...	...	...	...	...	1420	...	...	...
	Napoli Centrale **640** d.	0648	...	0850	...	1250	...	1648	1640	1854	1950
	Lamezia Terme **640** d.	|	...	|	...	|	...	|	|	|	|
0	**Paola 640** ▲ d.	1100	...	1300	...	1700	...	2025	2100	2300	0000
21	Castiglione-Cosentino ▲ a.	1118	...	1318	...	1716	...	2048	2118	2318	0018
26	**Cosenza** ▲ a.	1125	...	1325	...	1725	...	2055	2125	2325	0025
—	**Cosenza** d.	...	1143	...	1417	...	1817	2110	...	...	...
0	Castiglione-Cosentino d.	...	1149	...	1423	...	1823	|	...	...	...
60	**Sibari** a.	...	1242	...	1522	...	1912	2158	...	...	...

			ICp 535/6							
	2	2	[R]	2	2	2	2	2	2	2
			S	Ⓒ	⚒		Ⓐ		⚒	
Sibari d.	...	...	0855	...	1310	...	1505	...	1710	...
Castiglione-Cosentino a.	...	...	|	...	1401	...	1601	...	1801	...
Cosenza a.	...	...	0953	...	1407	...	1607	...	1807	...
Cosenza ▲ d.	0435	0525	1008	1225	...	1425	...	1625	...	1825
Castiglione-Cosentino ▲ d.	0442	0532	1015	1232	...	1434	...	1634	...	1832
Paola 640 ▲ a.	0457	0550	1035	1250	...	1450	...	1650	...	1850
Lamezia Terme **640** a.	|	|	|	|	...	|	...	|	...	|
Napoli Centrale **640** a.	0853	1010	1412	1710	...	1910	...	2112	...	2317
Roma Tiburtina **640** a.	...	...	1640	...	...	...	...	...	...	...

S – SILA – [2] Torino (**507/30**) - Sibari (**513/34**) - Crotone and v.v.

▲ – **Additional services Paola - Cosenza and v.v.** 2nd class only.
From **Paola**: 0530⚒, 0630⚒, 0700⚒, 0730, 0752⚒, 0830⚒, 0900⚒, 0938⚒, 0945†, 1130†, 1200⚒, 1230⚒, 1330⚒, 1400⚒, 1430, 1530⚒, 1600⚒, 1730⚒, 1830, 1900⚒, 2000⚒, 2050†, 2200⚒, 2230⚒.
From **Cosenza**: 0550⚒, 0625⚒, 0650, 0725⚒, 0750⚒, 0825⚒, 0850⚒, 0855†, 0950⚒, 1030†, 1150⚒, 1250, 1325⚒, 1350⚒, 1450⚒, 1510†, 1525⚒, 1650⚒, 1750, 1850⚒, 1950, 2023, 2125, 2225⚒.

REGGIO DI CALABRIA - SIBARI - TARANTO 635

2nd class only except where shown

km		E 986 ♦	ICp 566/7 [R] M	⚒	ICp 534 [R] ♦	⚒		Ⓐ	⚒	†	⚒	⚒	⚒	⚒	†	⚒	⚒	†	†	⚒	⚒	⚒	⚒	⚒	†
0	**Reggio di Calabria** d.	2340	...	...	...	...	...	0637	...	0630	...	0828j	...	...	0830	...	...	1030	...	...	1037	1237	...	...	...
30	Melito di Porto Salvo d.	|	...	...	...	...	...	0702	...	0702	...	0902	...	...	0902	...	...	1102	...	...	1102	1302	...	...	...
96	Locri d.	|	...	...	...	...	...	0810	...	0810	...	1010	...	...	1010	...	...	1210	...	...	1210	1410	...	...	...
101	Siderno d.	|	...	...	...	...	...	0818	...	0818	...	1018	...	...	1018	...	...	1218	...	...	1218	1418	...	...	...
112	Roccella Jonica d.	|	...	...	...	...	...	0833	...	0831	...	1033	...	...	1031	...	...	1233	...	...	1233	1433	...	...	...
160	Soverato d.	|	...	...	...	...	...	0910	...	0917	...	1110	...	...	1115	...	...	1315	...	...	1310	1510	...	...	...
178	Catanzaro Lido a.	|	...	...	...	...	...	0925	...	0933	...	1125	...	...	1132	...	...	1333	...	...	1325	1525	...	...	...
	Catanzaro Lido ▲ d.	|	...	0540	...	...	...	0930	...	0943	...	1136	...	1135	1143	1235	1335	1336	1335	...	1336	...	1535	...	...
	Catanzaro ▲ d.	|	...	|	...	...	...	|	...	0956	...	1156	...	|	1156	|	|	1356	|	...	1356	...	|	...	...
	Lamezia Terme ▲ a.	0114	...	|	...	...	...	|	...	1037	...	1237	...	|	1237	|	|	1433	|	...	1437	...	|	...	...
238	**Crotone** d.	|	0605	0625	0652	...	...	1022	...	...	...	...	...	1220	...	1320	1420	...	1425	...	...	...	1620	...	1650
325	Rossano d.	|	0710	0730	0813	...	...	1117	...	...	...	...	...	1337	...	1440	1529	...	1541	...	...	...	1733	...	1806
336	Corigliano Calabro d.	|	0721	0739	0825	...	...	1127	...	...	...	...	...	1346	...	1449	1539	...	1550	...	...	...	1742	...	1815
351	**Sibari** a.	0318	0731	0757	0839	...	...	1140	...	...	...	...	...	1356	...	1458	1550	...	1601	...	...	...	1754	...	1825
351	**Sibari** d.	0323	0734	...	...	1003	...	...	1155	...	1245	...	1401	...	...	...	...	...	...	1647	...	...	1757	1825	...
366	Trebisacce d.	|	0749	...	...	1018	...	...	1216	...	1258	...	1415	...	...	...	...	...	...	1702	...	...	1810	1840	...
430	Metaponto **638** d.	0455	0848	...	...	1129	...	...	1320	...	1359	...	1514	...	...	...	...	...	...	1801	...	...	1918	1944	...
473	**Taranto 631/8** a.	0550	0926	...	...	*1225*	...	...	1409	...	1454	...	1606	...	...	...	...	...	...	1850	...	...	2006	2027	...
	Bari Centrale **631** a.	0748	1048	...	...	...	...	...	...	...	...	...	...	...	...	...	...	...	...	...	...	...	...	...	...

	ICN 782/783 L	E 908/909 A	⚒	ICN 766 ♦		⚒	ICN 750 ♦	⚒	E 890 ♦
Reggio di Calabria d.	...	...	1437	1610	...	...	1710	1837	1910
Melito di Porto Salvo d.	...	...	1502	1633	...	...	1736	1902	1936
Locri d.	...	...	1610	1740	...	...	1840	2010	2105
Siderno d.	...	...	1618	1747	...	...	1847	2018	2114
Roccella Jonica d.	...	...	1633	1803	...	...	1903	2033	2133
Soverato d.	...	...	1710	1846	...	...	1945	2115	2220
Catanzaro Lido a.	...	...	1725	1903	...	...	2003	2130	2237
Catanzaro Lido ▲ d.	...	1710	...	1906	...	1935	2006	...	2240
Catanzaro ▲ d.	...	|	...	1920	...	|	2020	...	2253
Lamezia Terme ▲ a.	...	|	...	2003	...	|	2100	...	2335
Crotone d.	1730	1802	...	...	...	2028	...	...	...
Rossano d.	1849	1916	...	...	...	2140	...	...	...
Corigliano Calabro d.	1901	1928	...	...	...	2149	...	...	...
Sibari a.	1915	1939	...	...	...	2200	...	...	...
Sibari d.	1918	1942	...	...	...	...	...	...	...
Trebisacce d.	1931	2000	...	...	...	...	...	...	...
Metaponto **638** d.	2023	2054	...	...	...	...	...	...	...
Taranto 631/8 a.	2100	2138	...	...	...	...	...	...	...
Bari Centrale **631** a.	2241	2315	...	...	...	...	...	...	...

	⚒	E 893 ♦	⚒	†	⚒	⚒		ICN 753 ♦	⚒	ICN 763 ♦
Bari Centrale **631** d.	...	...	...	...	...	...	...	...	...	...
Taranto 631/8 d.	...	...	...	...	...	0508	...	...	0654	...
Metaponto **638** d.	...	...	...	...	...	0555	...	...	0740	...
Trebisacce d.	...	...	...	...	...	0654	...	...	0838	...
Sibari a.	...	...	...	...	...	0707	...	...	0850	...
Sibari d.	...	...	...	...	0605	0717	...	...	...	...
Corigliano Calabro d.	...	...	...	...	0615	0740	...	...	...	...
Rossano d.	...	...	...	...	0622	0748	...	...	...	...
Crotone d.	...	...	...	...	0735	0905	...	...	...	...
Lamezia Terme ▲ d.	...	0545	...	...	|	|	...	0940	...	1040
Catanzaro ▲ d.	...	0628	...	...	|	|	...	1026	...	1121
Catanzaro Lido ▲ a.	...	0637	...	...	0825	0958	...	1035	...	1130
Catanzaro Lido d.	0610	0645	0810	0808	...	...	...	1038	...	1133
Soverato d.	0624	0710	0824	0825	...	...	...	1053	...	1150
Roccella Jonica d.	0705	0810	0905	0908	...	...	...	1138	...	1235
Siderno d.	0717	0832	0917	0918	...	...	...	1150	...	1247
Locri d.	0723	0839	0923	0923	...	...	...	1156	...	1254
Melito di Porto Salvo d.	0828	1008	1028	1028	...	...	...	1252	...	1350
Reggio di Calabria a.	0853	1040	1053	1100	...	...	...	1315	...	1415

km		⚒		E 904/905 A	ICN 786/787 L	†	⚒		⚒	†	⚒	⚒	⚒	⚒	†	⚒		†	⚒	⚒	⚒	⚒	ICp 513 [R] ♦	ICp 554/5 [R] M	E 982 ♦
	Bari Centrale **631** d.	...	...	0804	0850	...	...	...	...	...	...	...	...	...	...	...	...	...	...	...	...	...	...	1908	2248
	Taranto 631/8 d.	...	...	0931	1030	...	...	...	...	...	1152	...	...	...	...	1427	...	...	1705	...	1816	1930	...	2032	0030
	Metaponto **638** d.	...	...	1011	1111	...	...	...	...	...	1242	...	...	...	...	1515	...	...	1804	...	1911	2024	...	2119	0115
	Trebisacce d.	...	...	1057	1215	...	...	...	...	...	1338	...	...	...	...	1614	...	...	1910	...	2021	2133	...	2209	|
	Sibari a.	...	...	1110	1227	...	...	...	...	...	1352	...	...	...	...	1629	...	...	1930	...	2038	2147	...	2224	0218
	Sibari d.	...	...	1113	1230	...	...	...	...	...	...	1358	1537	...	...	...	1710	...	...	1957	...	...	2213	2227	0223
	Corigliano Calabro d.	...	...	1128	1245	...	...	...	...	...	...	1409	1555	...	...	...	1721	...	...	2008	...	...	2224	2244	|
	Rossano d.	...	...	1139	1257	...	...	...	...	...	...	1417	1603	...	...	...	1734	...	...	2016	...	...	2234	2256	|
	Crotone d.	...	...	1247	1400	...	...	...	...	...	...	1535	1716	...	...	...	1840	...	...	2140	...	...	2335	2359	|
0	Lamezia Terme ▲ d.	...	...	|	...	1313	1313	...	1513	1513	...	|	|	1713	1713	...	|	...	...	|	...	...	...	...	0422
38	Catanzaro ▲ d.	...	...	|	...	1353	1353	...	1553	1553	...	|	|	1753	1753	...	|	...	...	|	...	...	...	...	|
47	Catanzaro Lido ▲ a.	...	...	1353	...	1405	1405	...	1605	1605	...	1625	1803	1805	1805	...	1925	...	...	2225	...	...	...	...	|
	Catanzaro Lido d.	1210	...	...	...	1408	1410	...	1610	1608	...	...	...	1810	1808	...	...	2008	...	...	...	...	...	...	|
	Soverato d.	1224	...	...	...	1425	1424	...	1624	1625	...	...	...	1824	1825	...	...	2025	...	...	...	...	...	...	|
	Roccella Jonica d.	1305	...	...	...	1508	1505	...	1705	1708	...	...	...	1905	1908	...	...	2109	...	...	...	...	...	...	|
	Siderno d.	1317	...	...	...	1518	1517	...	1717	1718	...	...	...	1917	1918	...	...	2128	...	...	...	...	...	...	|
	Locri d.	1324	...	...	...	1523	1523	...	1723	1723	...	...	...	1923	1923	...	...	2133	...	...	...	...	...	...	|
	Melito di Porto Salvo d.	1428	...	...	...	1628	1628	...	1828	1828	...	...	...	2028	2028	...	...	2237	...	...	...	...	...	...	|
	Reggio di Calabria a.	1453	...	...	...	1700	1653	...	1853	1900	...	...	...	2053	2100	...	...	2300	...	...	...	...	...	...	0610

♦ – **NOTES** (LISTED BY TRAIN NUMBER)

513/34 – SILA – [2] Torino (**507/30**) - Paola (**511/536**) - Cosenza (**512/35**) - Sibari - Crotone and v.v.

750 – PIEPOLI – June 8 - Sept. 16: 🛏 2 cl. (4 berth) and [2] Reggio di Calabria - Lamezia (**752**) - Milano.

753 – PIEPOLI – June 7 - Sept. 17 (from Milano, following day from Lamezia): 🛏 2 cl. (4 berth) and [2] Milano (**751**) - Lamezia - Reggio di Calabria.

763 – SCILLA – June 7 - Sept. 17 (from Torino, following day from Lamezia): 🛏 2 cl. (4 berth) and [2] Torino (**761**) - Lamezia - Reggio di Calabria.

766 – SCILLA – June 8 - Sept. 16: 🛏 2 cl. (4 berth) and [2] Reggio di Calabria - Lamezia (**768**) - Torino.

890/3 – 🛌 1, 2 cl. (T2), 🛏 2 cl. and [2] Reggio di Calabria - Lamezia (**894/5**) - Roma and v.v. Runs as train **898** Lamezia - Roma on ⑥ June 16 - Sept. 8.

982 – Ⓐ: [2] Bari (**981**) - Taranto - Metaponto (**983**) - Reggio di Calabria.

986 – Ⓐ (from Reggio): [2] Reggio di Calabria - Villa S G - Metaponto (**989**) - Taranto (**990**) - Bari.

A – FRECCIA ADRIATICA – 🛏 2 cl. and [2] Torino (**901/6**) - Bari (**903/10**) - Taranto - Catanzaro Lido and v.v.

L – FRECCIA DEL LEVANTE – Not Dec. 24, 25, 31: 🛏 2 cl. and [12] Crotone - Taranto (**784/5**) - Milano and v.v.

M – MURGE – [12] Milano (**553/68**) - Taranto - Crotone and v.v.

j – 0837 on Ⓐ.

▲ – **Local services LAMEZIA TERME - CATANZARO LIDO and v.v.**:
Journey 50 – 75 minutes. All trains call at Catanzaro; 33 – 56 minutes from Lamezia Terme, 10 – 15 minutes from Catanzaro Lido. Some trains 2nd class only.

From **Lamezia Terme**: 0613, 0713⚒, 0813⚒, 0913⚒, 1113⚒, 1213, 1313, 1413⚒, 1513, 1613⚒, 1713, 1813⚒, 1913, 2035⚒, 2113⚒.

From **Catanzaro Lido**: 0536⚒, 0636⚒, 0736⚒, 0743†, 0836, 0936⚒, 0943†, 1136⚒, 1143†, 1236⚒, 1336, 1436⚒, 1536⚒, 1636, 1736⚒, 1836⚒, 1936.

NAPOLI - POTENZA - TARANTO 638

km		E 951 ♦	2	ICp 675 [R]	2 ⚒	2 ⚒	2	2 Ⓑw	2	ES 9363 [R]🍷	2
	Roma Termini **640** d.	2330	...	0719	...	...	...	...	...	1545	...
0	**Napoli Centrale 640** d.	|	0831	0936	...	...	1437p	1528	1634	1742p	1825
26	Pompei d.	|	|	|	...	...	|	1602	1657	|	1852
54	Salerno d.	0246	0928	1012	...	1351	1519	1640	1717	1819	1922
74	Battipaglia d.	0306	0948	1029	...	1415	1539	1659	1735	1838	1944
166	**Potenza** Centrale d.	0440	1119y	1145	1416	1607	1710	1844	1922	1952	2131
273	Metaponto **635** d.	0609	...	1305	1556	...	...	...	2042	2120	...
317	**Taranto 635** a.	0651	...	1340	1641	...	...	...	2124	2154	...

	2 ⚒	2	ES 9360 [R]🍷 ⚒	ES 9382 [R]✕ †	2	2	ICp 676 [R]	2 ⚒	2	E 956 ♦
Taranto 635 d.	...	...	0616	0739	1005	...	1515	...	...	2255
Metaponto **635** d.	...	...	0651	0815	1043	...	1555	...	...	0006
Potenza Centrale d.	0523	0622	0811	0934	1219	1420	1716	1847	2032	0133
Battipaglia d.	0650	0805	0925	1101	1344	1612	1833	2035	2212	0304
Salerno d.	0712	0827	0942	1121	1403	1632	1850	2054	2236	0325
Pompei a.	0732	0844	|	1137	1420	|	|	...	...	|
Napoli Centrale 640 a.	0805	0910	1018p	1200p	1442	1719	1924	...	...	|
Roma Termini **640** a.	...	...	1216	1400	...	...	2139	...	...	0635

♦ – **NOTES** (LISTED BY TRAIN NUMBER)

951 – 🛏 2 cl. and [2] Roma - Taranto - Lecce.

956 – 🛏 2 cl. and [2] Lecce - Taranto - Roma.

p – Napoli **Piazza Garibaldi**.

w – Not days before holidays.

y – Arrive 1126 on †.

640 ROMA - NAPOLI - SICILY

km		*E*	*E*		*E*	*ICN*		*ICN*		*E*		*ES*	*ES*		*E*		*E*	*ICp*	*AV*	*ICp*	*ICp*		*ICN*	*E*	*EN*
		1993	**1991**	2	**1595**	**751**	2	**761**	2	**833**	2	**9371**	**9381**	2	**809**		**837**	**675**	**9601**	**719**	**721**	2	**771**	**1911**	**287**
												R 🍷	R 🍷					R 🍷	R 🍷	R	R				R
		M	◆	⚒	◆	◆		◆		◆		j	⚒ k		◆	⚒	◆	◆	Ⓐ	◆	U	†	◆	◆	◆
	Torino PN **610** d.	...	...	...	...	...	...	2050	...	...	...	...	...	...	2155	...	...	...	...	...	...	...	...	...	...
	Milano C **619/20** d.	1940	1940	...	...	1945	...	│	...	2200	...	...	...	...	│	...	...	...	...	...	...	...	...	2320	...
	Venezia SL **620** d.	│	│	...	...	│	...	│	...	│	...	...	...	...	│	...	...	...	...	...	...	...	0004	│	...
	Bologna C **620** d.	2233	2233	...	2226	2208	...	│	...	0044	...	...	...	...	│	...	0115	...	...	...	...	...	0222	│	0425
0	**Roma Termini 620** d.	│	│	...	│	│	...	│	...	0501t	0550	0645	0645	...	0613o	...	0617t	0719	0725	0745	0745	...	0715t	0732	0816t
62	Latina d.	│	│	...	│	│	...	│	...	0543	0628	│	│	...	0659	...	│	0753	│	│	│	...	│	│	│
129	Formia d.	│	│	...	│	│	...	│	...	0622	0718	│	│	...	0757	...	│	0831	│	│	│	...	0855	│	│
195	Aversa d.	│	│	...	│	│	...	│	...	│	0805	│	│	...	0846	...	│	0906	│	│	│	...	│	│	│
214	**Napoli Centrale 620** a.	│	│	...	0432	│	...	0601f	...	0810	0836	0838p	0838p	...	0911	...	0926	0924	0852	0938p	0938p	...	1000	1007	1023
214	**Napoli Centrale** d.	│	│	...	0444	│	0550	0605f	0648	0822	▬	0842p	0842p	0850	...	...	...	0936	...	0942p	0942p	...	...	...	...
240	Pompei d.	│	│	...	│	│	0619	│	0717	0844	...	0900e	0900g	0919	...	...	...	│	...	│	│	...	...	...	...
268	Salerno d.	│	│	...	0530	0538	0643	0657	0742	0910	...	0919	0919	0942	...	...	...	1012	...	1019	1019	...	...	...	...
288	Battipaglia d.	│	│	...	│	0558	0701	0715	0801	▬	...	│	│	1001	...	...	...	1027	...	│	│	...	...	...	...
318	Agropoli d.	│	│	...	0604	0617	0725	0733	0824	...	...	│	0948	1025	...	...	...	...	...	│	│	...	...	...	...
349	Ascea d.	│	│	...	0627	0645	0751	0756	0848	...	...	│	│	1053	...	...	...	...	...	│	│	...	...	...	...
395	Sapri d.	│	│	...	0654	0717	0845	0829	0930	...	...	1025	1032	1132	...	...	...	...	...	│	│	...	...	...	...
407	Maratea d.	│	│	...	│	0728	0859	0840	0940	...	...	│	1040g	1145	...	...	...	...	...	│	│	...	...	...	...
455	Belvedere Marittimo d.	│	│	...	│	│	0942	│	1014	...	...	│	│	1220	...	...	...	...	...	│	│	...	...	...	...
489	Paola d.	0722	0722	...	0750	0820	1015	0936	1100	...	...	1112	1128	1300	...	...	...	...	...	1218	1218	...	...	...	...
	Cosenza a.	│	│	...	│	│	...	│	1125c	...	...	│	│	1325	...	...	...	...	...	│	│	...	...	...	...
546	**Lamezia Terme C** a.	0757	0757	...	0825	0900	...	1017	▬	...	...	1137	1200	...	...	...	...	...	...	1250	1250	...	...	...	...
546	**Lamezia Terme C** d.	0800	0800	...	0855	0908	...	1025	...	...	...	1140	1203	...	...	...	...	...	...	1253	1253	...	...	...	...
638	Gioia Tauro d.	│	│	...	0943	0955	...	1107	...	...	...	1220	1242	...	...	...	...	...	...	│	│	...	...	...	...
675	Villa San Giovanni a.	0913	0913	...	1018	1027	...	1147	...	...	...	1247	1312	...	...	...	...	...	...	1355	1355	...	...	...	...
675	Villa San Giovanni d.	0928	0928	...	1040	1030	...	1150	...	...	...	1250	1315	...	...	...	...	...	...	1407	1407	...	...	...	...
	Reggio di Calabria a.	│	│	...	1100	1050	...	1205	...	2	2	1308	1328	...	...	...	...	...	...	│	│	...	...	...	...
684	**Messina Centrale** a.	1105	1105	...	...	...	...	...	⚒	†	⚒	...	...	...	...	...	...	...	...	1523	1523	...	...	...	...
684	**Messina Centrale** d.	1130	1138	1200	...	...	...	...	1310	1350	1410	...	...	...	...	1420	...	...	...	1526	1538	1540	...	...	...
	Taormina-Giardini d.	│	1219	1318	...	...	...	...	1403	1453	1456	...	...	...	...	│	...	...	...	│	1620	│	...	...	...
	Giarre-Riposto **644** d.	│	1236	1337	...	...	...	...	1421	1516	1522	...	...	...	...	│	...	...	...	│	1635	│	...	...	...
	Catania Centrale a.	│	1305	1402	...	...	...	...	1450	1545	1550	...	...	...	...	│	...	...	...	│	1700	│	...	...	...
	Catania Centrale d.	│	1310	1420	...	...	...	...	...	...	...	...	...	...	...	│	...	...	...	│	1703	│	...	...	...
	Augusta d.	│	1413	1514	...	...	...	...	...	...	...	...	...	...	...	│	...	...	...	│	1806	│	...	...	...
	Siracusa a.	│	1445	1545	...	...	...	...	...	...	...	...	...	...	...	│	...	...	...	│	1825	│	...	...	...
720	Milazzo d.	1156	...	...	...	...	...	...	...	...	...	...	...	...	...	1444	...	...	...	1552	...	1616	...	...	...
849	Cefalù d.	1344	...	...	...	...	...	...	...	...	...	...	...	...	...	1644	...	...	...	1745	...	1840	...	...	...
879	Termini Imerese **645/7** d.	1410	...	...	...	...	...	...	...	...	...	...	...	...	...	1705	...	...	...	1806	...	1916	...	...	...
916	**Palermo C 645/7** a.	1440	...	...	...	...	...	...	...	...	...	...	...	...	...	1735	...	...	...	1835	...	1955	...	...	...

km				*ICp*	*ICp*	*AV*	*AV*	*ES*	*ICp*	*AV*			*AV*	*IC*	*ICp*	*ICp*	*ICp*	*AV*				*ES*	*ICp*	*IC*	*IC*
		2	2	**581**	**1571**	**9605**	**9603**	**9373**	**501**	**9425**	2	2	**9607**	**583**	**729**	**725**	**503**	**9429**		2	2	**9375**	**589**	**1589**	**1591**
(via hsl)				R	R	R 🍷	R 🍷	R ✕	R	R 🍷			R 🍷	🍷	R	R	R	R ✕				R ✕	R		
		⚒	⚒		†	Ⓐ	Ⓒ q	⚒	◆				Ⓐ		V	◆	◆		2 ⚒		⚒			◆	◆
	Torino PN **610** d.	...	...	...	...	...	...	...	...	...	...	...	...	...	...	...	...	...	...	...	...	...	...	...	...
	Milano C **619/20** d.	...	...	...	...	...	...	...	...	0530	...	...	...	...	...	...	...	0800	...	...	...	...	...	0730	0730
	Venezia SL **620** d.	...	...	...	...	...	...	...	...	│	...	...	...	...	...	...	...	│	...	...	...	...	...	│	│
	Bologna C **620** d.	...	...	...	...	...	...	...	...	0746	...	...	...	...	...	...	...	0946	...	...	...	...	...	1012	1012
0	**Roma Termini 620** d.	...	...	0827	0900	0925	0925	0945	1027	1045	...	1049	1125	1128	1145	1145	1227	1245	...	1249	...	1345	1327	1409t	1409t
	Latina d.	...	...	0858	0932	│	│	│	1058	│	...	1127	│	1158	│	│	1258	│	...	1327	...	│	1358	1450	1450
	Formia d.	...	...	0935	1009	│	│	│	1135	│	...	1213	│	1235	│	│	1335	│	...	1413	...	│	1433	1545	1545
	Aversa d.	...	...	1013	1044	│	│	│	1209	│	...	1301	│	1313	│	│	1409	│	...	1459	...	│	1513	1636	1636
216	**Napoli Centrale 620** a.	...	...	1036	1108	1052	1052	1138p	1236	1212	...	1328	1252	1336	1338p	1338p	1436	1412	...	1530	...	1538p	1536	1658	1658
—	**Napoli Centrale** d.	...	...	▬	...	...	...	1142p	...	...	1250	▬	...	▬	1342p	1342p	...	...	1450	...	...	1542p	1548	1710	1710
km	Pompei d.	...	...	...	...	...	...	│	...	...	1319	...	...	...	│	│	...	...	1519	...	...	│	│	│	│
	Salerno d.	...	...	...	...	...	...	1219	...	...	1342	...	...	...	1419	1419	...	...	1542	...	...	1619	1626	1755	1755
	Battipaglia d.	...	...	...	...	...	...	│	...	...	1401	...	...	...	│	│	...	...	1601	...	...	│	1644	│	│
	Agropoli d.	...	...	...	...	...	...	│	...	...	1425	...	...	...	│	│	...	...	1625	...	...	│	│	│	│
	Ascea d.	...	...	...	...	...	...	│	...	...	1453	...	...	...	│	│	...	...	1653	...	...	│	│	1841	1841
	Sapri d.	...	...	...	...	...	...	1325	...	...	1532	...	...	...	1527	1527	...	...	1734	...	...	1725	1745	1916	1916
	Maratea d.	...	...	...	...	...	...	│	...	...	1545	...	...	...	│	│	...	...	1747	...	...	│	1755	│	│
	Belvedere Marittimo d.	...	...	...	...	...	...	│	...	...	1620	...	...	...	│	│	...	...	1835	...	...	│	│	│	│
0	Paola d.	...	...	...	...	...	...	1412	...	...	1700	...	...	...	1618	1618	...	...	1930	...	...	1812	1845	2013	2013
26	Cosenza a.	...	...	...	...	...	...	│	...	...	1725	...	...	...	│	│	...	...	│	...	...	│	│	│	│
—	**Lamezia Terme C** a.	...	...	...	...	...	...	1437	...	...	...	...	...	...	1650	1650	...	...	2008	...	...	1837	1922	2050	2050
	Lamezia Terme C d.	...	...	...	...	...	...	1440	...	...	...	...	...	...	1653	1653	...	...	2010	...	...	1840	1925	2053	2053
	Gioia Tauro d.	...	...	...	...	...	...	1520	...	...	...	...	...	...	│	│	...	...	2055	...	...	1920	2010	2138	2246
	Villa San Giovanni a.	...	...	...	...	...	...	1547	...	...	...	...	...	...	1755	1755	...	...	2130	...	...	1947	2042	2207	2317
0	Villa San Giovanni d.	...	...	...	...	...	...	1550	...	...	...	...	...	...	1807	1807	...	...	2132	...	...	1950	2045	2210	2320
15	**Reggio di Calabria** a.	...	...	...	...	...	...	1605	...	...	...	2	...	...	│	│	...	...	2150	...	...	2005	2100	2230	2335
—	**Messina Centrale** a.	...	...	†	...	...	...	...	...	...	...	...	...	⚒	1923	1923	...	...	...	...	...	...	...	...	...
0	**Messina Centrale** d.	1600	1715	1720	...	...	...	...	...	...	...	1830	...	1835	1926	1940	...	...	...	...	2145	...	...	...	...
47	Taormina-Giardini d.	1646	│	1816	...	...	...	...	...	...	...	│	...	1926	│	2025	...	...	...	...	2226	...	...	...	...
65	Giarre-Riposto **644** d.	1704	│	1834	...	...	...	...	...	...	...	│	...	1945	│	2042	...	...	...	...	2242	...	...	...	...
95	**Catania Centrale** a.	1730	│	1900	...	...	...	...	...	...	...	│	...	2013	│	2107	...	...	...	...	2305	...	...	...	...
95	**Catania Centrale** d.	1733	│	1903	...	...	...	...	...	...	...	│	...	2015	│	2110	...	...	...	...	...	...	...	...	...
151	Augusta d.	1837	│	1950	...	...	...	...	...	...	...	│	...	2118	│	2208	...	...	...	...	...	...	...	...	...
182	**Siracusa** a.	1900	│	2015	...	...	...	...	...	...	...	│	...	2140	│	2230	...	...	...	...	...	...	...	...	...
	Milazzo d.	...	1741	...	...	...	...	...	...	...	...	1855	...	...	1951	...	...	...	...	...	...	...	...	...	...
	Cefalù d.	...	1929	...	...	...	...	...	...	...	...	2103	...	...	2128	...	...	...	...	...	...	...	...	...	...
	Termini Imerese **645/7** d.	...	1953	...	...	...	...	...	...	...	...	2125	...	...	2150	...	...	...	...	...	...	...	...	...	...
	Palermo C 645/7 a.	...	2020	...	...	...	...	...	...	...	...	2155	...	...	2220	...	...	...	...	...	...	...	...	...	...

◆ – **NOTES** (LISTED BY TRAIN NUMBER)

287 – CAPRI – 🛏 1,2 cl., ▬ 2 cl. (4/6 berth) and [2] München - Napoli.
501 – CARDUCCI – ⚒: [12] Sestri Levante - Napoli.
503 – BOCCANEGRA – [12] Savona - Genova - Napoli.
675 – [12] Roma - Taranto.
719 – PELORITANO – [12] Roma - Palermo.
725 – ARCHIMEDE – [12] Roma - Siracusa.
751 – PIEPOLI – 🛏 1,2 cl. (T2), ▬ 2 cl. and [12] Milano - Reggio. Conveys until Sept. 17 (from Milano): ▬ 2 cl. (4 berth) and [2] Milano - Lamezia (**753**) - Reggio.
761 – SCILLA – 🛏 1,2 cl. (T2), ▬ 2 cl. and [12] Torino - Reggio. Conveys until Sept. 17 (from Torino): ▬ 2 cl. (4 berth) and [2] Torino - Lamezia (**763**) - Reggio.
771 – MARCO POLO – 🛏 1,2 cl. (Excelsior), 🛏 1,2 cl., ▬ 2 cl. (4 berth) and [2] Udine - Napoli; 🛏 1,2 cl., ▬ 2 cl. (4 berth) and [12] Trieste (**772**) - Venezia - Napoli.
809 – 🛏 1,2 cl.(T2), ▬ 2 cl. (4 berth) and [2] Torino - Napoli.
833 – ⑤ (also Aug 14, Oct. 31): [2] Milano - Salerno.
837 – ①②③⑤⑥⑦; also Dec. 27, Jan. 3, May 1, not Dec. 25, 26, Jan. 1, Apr. 30 (from Bolzano): 🛏 1,2 cl., ▬ 2 cl. (4 berth) and [2] Bolzano (**925**) - Bologna - Napoli.
1589 – ASPROMONTE – ⑤ Sept. 7 - Dec. 7 (also Oct. 31): [12] Milano - Reggio.
1591 – ASPROMONTE – ⑤ June 15 - Aug. 31: [12] Milano - Reggio.
1595 – ⑥ Dec. 15 - Mar. 29; also Dec. 20, 26, Jan. 1 (from Bolzano): 🛏 1,2 cl. (T2), ▬ 2 cl. and [2] Bolzano - Reggio.
1911 – 🛏 1,2 cl. (Excelsior), 🛏 1,2 cl. (T2), 🛏 1,2 cl., ▬ 2 cl. (4 berth) and [2] Milano - Napoli.
1991 – MONGIBELLO – ⑤ (also Dec. 18, Mar. 18, Apr. 24, 30; not Apr. 25, May 2): 🛏 1,2 cl. (T2), ▬ 2 cl. and [2] Milano - Siracusa.

M – MONGIBELLO – ▬ 2 cl. and [2] Milano (**1991**) - Messina - Palermo. See train **1991** for running dates.
U – PELORITANO – [12] Roma (**719**) - Messina - Siracusa.
V – ARCHIMEDE – [12] Roma (**725**) - Messina - Palermo.

c – Ⓒ only.
e – ⑦ only.
f – Napoli **Campi Flegrei**.
g – ⑥ only.
j – Sept. 9 - Dec. 8.
k – June 10 - Sept. 8.
o – Roma **Ostiense**.
p – Napoli **Piazza Garibaldi** (situated under Centrale).
q – Daily Aug. 6 - 17.
s – Stops to set down only.
t – Roma **Tiburtina**.

ROMA - NAPOLI - SICILY 640

	AV 9611	*ICp* 507		*AV* 9433			*AV* 9615	*ICp* 703	*ES* 9363	*AV* 9437	*ICp* 521			*ICp* 591		*ES* 9377			*AV* 9621	*AV* 9441		*ICp* 523	*AV* 9623	*IC* 705	*ES* 9379
	R 🍸 Ⓐ	R ♦		R ✕	2	2	R 🍸 Ⓐ	R ♦	R 🍸 ♦	R ✕	R	2	2	R ✕		R ✕		2	R 🍸	R ✕	⚒	R ✕	R 🍸 Ⓐ	🍸	R ✕
Torino PN 610 d.	...	0705	...	...	...	...	...	...	...	...	...	...	...	...	...	...	...	...	...	...	...	1105	...	...	...
Milano C 619/20 d.	...	|	...	1000	...	...	...	...	...	1200	...	...	...	1110	...	...	...	...	...	1400	...	|	...	...	...
Venezia SL 620 d.	...	|	...	|	...	...	...	0921z	...	|	...	...	...	|	...	...	...	...	...	|	...	|	...	1323	...
Bologna C 620 d.	...	|	...	1146	...	...	...	1120	...	1346	...	...	...	1320	...	...	...	...	...	1546	...	|	...	1520	...
Roma Termini 620 d.	1425	1420t	...	1445	...	1449	1525	1527	1545	1645	1627	...	1649	1727	...	1745	...	...	1825	1845	...	1827	1925	1927	1945
Latina d.	|	1457	...	|	...	1527	|	1558	|	|	1658	...	1727	1758	...	|	...	...	|	|	...	1858	|	1957	|
Formia d.	|	1535	...	|	...	1613	|	1633	|	|	1733	...	1813	1835	...	|	...	...	|	|	...	1935	|	2035	|
Aversa d.	|	1609	...	|	...	1701	|	1713	|	|	1809	...	1901	1913	...	|	...	...	|	|	...	2009	|	2113	|
Napoli Centrale 620 a.	1552	1636	...	1612	...	1728	1652	1736	1738p	1812	1836	...	1928	1936	...	1938p	...	...	1952	2012	...	2036	2052	2136	2138p
Napoli Centrale d.	...	1648	...	...	1640	...	...	...	1742p	...	1848	1854	...	...	...	1942p	...	1950	...	2024	...	...	...	...	2142p
Pompei d.	...	|	...	...	1716	...	...	...	|	...	|	1919	...	...	...	|	...	2019	...	|	...	...	...	...	2201
Salerno d.	...	1731	...	...	1743	...	...	...	1819	...	1931	1942	...	...	...	2019	...	2042	...	2102	...	...	...	...	2226
Battipaglia d.	...	1747	...	...	1801	...	...	...	1836	...	1947	2001	...	...	...	|	...	2101	...	...	...	...	...	...	...
Agropoli d.	...	1803	...	...	1825	...	...	...	...	...	|	2025	...	...	...	|	...	2125	...	...	...	...	...	...	...
Ascea d.	...	1828	...	...	1853	...	...	...	...	...	|	2053	...	...	...	|	...	2153	...	...	...	...	...	...	...
Sapri d.	...	1901	...	...	1932	...	...	...	...	...	2048	2132	...	...	...	2125	...	2232	...	...	...	...	...	...	...
Maratea d.	...	|	...	...	1945	...	...	...	...	...	2059	2145	...	...	...	|	...	2245	...	...	...	...	...	...	...
Belvedere Marittimo d.	...	|	...	...	2020	...	...	...	...	...	|	2220	...	...	...	|	...	2320	...	...	...	...	...	...	...
Paola d.	...	2006	...	...	2100	...	...	...	...	...	2148	2300	...	...	...	2212	...	0000	...	...	...	...	...	...	...
Cosenza a.	...	|	...	...	2125	...	...	...	...	...	|	2325	...	...	...	|	...	0025	...	...	...	...	...	...	...
Lamezia Terme C a.	...	2040	...	...	...	...	...	...	...	...	2227	...	...	...	...	2237	...	...	...	...	...	...	...	...	...
Lamezia Terme C d.	...	2043	...	...	...	...	...	...	...	...	2230	...	...	...	...	2240	...	...	...	...	...	...	...	...	...
Gioia Tauro d.	...	2127	...	...	...	...	...	...	...	...	2314	...	...	...	...	2320	...	...	...	...	...	...	...	...	...
Villa San Giovanni a.	...	2200	...	...	...	...	...	...	...	...	2339	...	...	...	...	2347	...	...	...	...	...	...	...	...	...
Villa San Giovanni d.	...	2203	...	...	...	...	...	...	...	...	2342	...	...	...	...	2350	...	...	...	...	...	...	...	...	...
Reggio di Calabria a.	...	2220	...	...	...	...	...	...	...	...	2355	...	...	...	...	0005	...	...	...	...	...	...	...	...	...
Messina Centrale a.	...	...	...	...	...	...	...	...	...	...	...	...	...	...	...	...	...	...	...	...	...	...	...	...	...
Messina Centrale d.	...	...	...	...	...	...	...	...	...	...	...	...	...	...	...	...	...	...	...	...	0430	...	...	...	...
Taormina-Giardini d.	...	...	...	...	...	...	...	...	...	...	...	...	...	...	...	...	...	...	...	...	|	...	...	...	...
Giarre-Riposto 644 d.	...	...	...	...	...	...	...	...	...	...	...	...	...	...	...	...	...	...	...	...	|	...	...	...	...
Catania Centrale a.	...	...	...	...	...	...	...	...	...	...	...	...	...	...	...	...	...	...	...	...	|	...	...	...	...
Catania Centrale d.	...	...	...	...	...	...	...	...	...	...	...	...	...	...	...	...	...	...	...	...	|	...	...	...	...
Augusta d.	...	...	...	...	...	...	...	...	...	...	...	...	...	...	...	...	...	...	...	...	|	...	...	...	...
Siracusa a.	...	...	...	...	...	...	...	...	...	...	...	...	...	...	...	...	...	...	...	...	|	...	...	...	...
Milazzo d.	...	...	...	...	...	...	...	...	...	...	...	...	...	...	...	...	...	...	...	...	0501	...	...	...	...
Cefalù d.	...	...	...	...	...	...	...	...	...	...	...	...	...	...	...	...	...	...	...	...	0704	...	...	...	...
Termini Imerese 645/7 d.	...	...	...	...	...	...	...	...	...	...	...	...	...	...	...	...	...	...	...	...	0730	...	...	...	...
Palermo C 645/7 a.	...	...	...	...	...	...	...	...	...	...	...	...	...	...	...	...	...	...	...	...	0755	...	...	...	...

	E 1925		*AV* 9445		*ICp* 527	*IC* 1557	*E* 823		*IC* 595	*AV* 9447	*E* 1939	*E* 985	*E* 891		*E* 1921	*E* 1923		*E* 895	*E* 1941	*E* 1945		*E* 1935	*E* 1931	*E* 1933	
	♦	2 ⚒	R ✕		R ✕	⑤v	♦		🍸	R ✕	♦	♦	♦		♦	Z		♦	♦	R		B	♦	T	
Torino PN 610 d.	...	...	...	...	1305	...	...	...	...	...	...	...	...	...	...	...	...	...	1655	1655	...	...	...	...	...
Milano C 619/20 d.	...	...	1600	...	|	1350	1430	...	1510	1700	...	...	...	...	1635	1635	...	...	|	|	...	...	...	...	...
Venezia SL 620 d.	...	...	|	...	|	|	|	...	|	|	...	...	...	...	|	|	...	...	|	|	...	1903	1903	1903	...
Bologna C 620 d.	...	...	1746	...	|	1614	1640	...	1720	1846	...	...	...	...	1910	1910	...	...	|	|	...	2135	2135	2135	...
Roma Termini 620 d.	1958	...	2045	...	2027	2047t	2047t	...	2127	2145	2118	...	2225	...	2326t	2326t	...	2310	|	|	...	|	|	|	...
Latina d.	2029	...	|	...	2057	2119	|	...	2157	|	2150	...	2301	...	|	|	...	|	|	|	...	|	|	|	...
Formia d.	2105	...	|	...	2135	2156	|	...	2235	|	2227	...	2346	...	|	|	...	|	|	|	...	|	|	|	...
Aversa d.	|	...	|	...	2209	|	|	...	2309	|	|	...	|	...	|	|	...	|	|	|	...	|	|	|	...
Napoli Centrale 620 a.	2158	...	2212	...	2236	2253p	|	...	2336	2312	2318	...	|	...	|	|	...	|	|	|	...	|	|	|	...
Napoli Centrale d.	2210	...	...	...	2248	2230p	|	...	...	...	2330	...	|	...	|	|	...	|	|	|	...	|	|	|	...
Pompei d.	|	...	...	...	2317	2252	|	...	...	...	|	...	|	...	|	|	...	|	|	|	...	|	|	|	...
Salerno d.	2249	...	...	...	2339	2316	|	...	...	...	|	...	|	...	|	|	...	0219	|	|	...	0437s	0437s	0437s	...
Battipaglia d.	|	...	...	...	...	...	|	...	...	...	|	...	|	...	|	|	...	|	|	|	...	|	|	|	...
Agropoli d.	|	...	...	...	...	...	|	...	...	...	|	...	|	...	|	|	...	|	|	|	...	|	|	|	...
Ascea d.	|	...	...	...	...	...	|	...	...	...	|	...	|	...	|	|	...	|	|	|	...	|	|	|	...
Sapri d.	|	...	...	...	...	...	|	...	...	...	|	...	0247	...	|	|	...	0347	|	|	...	0555s	0555s	0555s	...
Maratea d.	|	...	...	...	...	...	|	...	...	...	|	...	|	...	|	|	...	|	|	|	...	|	|	|	...
Belvedere Marittimo d.	|	...	...	...	...	...	|	...	...	...	|	...	|	...	|	|	...	|	|	|	...	|	|	|	...
Paola d.	|	...	...	...	...	...	0144	...	...	...	|	...	0348	...	|	|	...	0449	|	|	...	0649s	0649s	0649s	...
Cosenza a.	|	...	...	...	...	...	|	...	...	...	|	...	|	...	|	|	...	|	|	|	...	|	|	|	...
Lamezia Terme C a.	|	...	...	...	...	...	0224	...	...	...	|	...	0427	...	|	|	...	0527	0531s	0531s	...	0725s	0725s	0725s	...
Lamezia Terme C d.	|	...	...	...	...	...	0227	...	...	...	|	0422	0430	...	|	|	...	0539	|	|	...	|	|	|	...
Gioia Tauro d.	|	...	...	...	...	...	|	...	...	...	|	0510	0521	...	|	|	...	0722	0618s	0618s	...	0813s	0813s	0813s	...
Villa San Giovanni a.	0255	...	...	...	...	...	0335	...	...	...	0415	0550	0607	...	0615	0615	...	0800	0655s	0655s	...	0845s	0845s	0845s	...
Villa San Giovanni d.	0310	...	...	...	...	...	0350	...	...	...	0430	0553	0610	...	0630	0630	...	0815	|	|	...	0900	|	|	...
Reggio di Calabria a.	|	...	...	...	...	...	|	...	...	...	|	0610	0630	...	|	|	...	0832	|	|	...	0920	|	|	...
Messina Centrale a.	0435	...	...	...	...	...	0520	...	...	...	0555	...	...	...	0800	0800	...	...	0835s	0835s	...	...	1035s	1035	...
Messina Centrale d.	0459	0520	...	0530	...	...	0540	...	...	...	0618	...	...	0655	0829	0838	...	...	|	0855	...	...	|	1105	...
Taormina-Giardini d.	|	0602	...	|	...	...	0630	...	...	...	0712	...	...	|	|	0911s	...	...	|	0933s	...	...	1135s	|	...
Giarre-Riposto 644 d.	|	0621	...	|	...	...	0647	...	...	...	0735	...	...	|	|	0927s	...	...	|	0955s	...	...	1151s	|	...
Catania Centrale a.	|	0650	...	|	...	...	0715	...	...	...	0800	...	...	|	|	0957s	...	...	|	1020s	...	...	1216s	|	...
Catania Centrale d.	|	0653	...	|	...	...	0755	...	...	...	0813	...	...	|	|	|	...	...	|	|	...	...	|	|	...
Augusta d.	|	0750	...	|	...	...	0851	...	...	...	0913	...	...	|	|	1059s	...	...	|	1118s	...	...	1319s	|	...
Siracusa a.	|	0815	...	|	...	...	0925	...	...	...	0940	...	...	|	|	1130	...	...	|	1145	...	...	1355	|	...
Milazzo d.	0524	...	...	0555	...	...	...	...	...	...	...	...	...	0724	0855	...	...	...	0924s	...	...	...	...	1130	...
Cefalù d.	0718	...	...	0812	...	...	...	...	...	...	...	...	...	0913	1104	...	...	...	1120s	...	...	...	...	1320	...
Termini Imerese 645/7 d.	0741	...	...	0834	...	...	...	...	...	...	...	...	...	0935	1127	...	...	...	1141s	...	...	...	...	1342	...
Palermo C 645/7 a.	0810	...	...	0900	...	...	...	...	...	...	...	...	...	1000	1155	...	...	...	1215	...	...	...	...	1415	...

♦ – **NOTES** (LISTED BY TRAIN NUMBER)

507 – SILA – 1,2 Torino - Firenze - Reggio; 2 Torino - Paola (**511**) - Cosenza (**512**) - Sibari (**513**) - Crotone.

703 – MIRAMARE – 1,2 Trieste (**702**) - Venezia Mestre - Napoli.

823 – FRECCIA DEL SUD – ①③⑤⑦ (also Aug. 14; not Aug. 15): 2 cl. and 2 Milano - Catania - Agrigento; 2 Milano - Catania (**827**) - Siracusa.

891 – ⑤ (also Aug. 14, Oct. 31): 2 cl. and 2 Roma - Reggio.

895 – 1,2 cl. (T2), 2 cl. and 2 Roma - Reggio; 1,2 cl. (T2), 2 cl. and 2 Roma - Lamezia (**893**) - Reggio.

985 – Ⓐ (from Bari): 2 Bari (**981**) - Taranto (**982**) - Metaponto (**983**) - Reggio.

1921 – TRINACRIA – 1,2 cl. (T2), 1,2 cl. and 2 cl. (4/6 berth) Milano - Palermo; 2 Messina - Palermo.

1925 – IL GATTOPARDO – 1,2 cl., 2 cl. (4 berth) and 2 Roma - Palermo.

1931 – FRECCIA DELLA LAGUNA – 1,2 cl. and 2 cl. (4 berth) Venezia - Siracusa.

1939 – BELLINI – 1,2 cl., 2 cl. (4 berth) and 2 Roma - Siracusa.

1941 – TRENO DEL SOLE – 1,2 cl., and 2 cl. (4 berth) Torino - Palermo; 2 Messina - Palermo.

9363 – 1,2 and 🍸 Roma - Taranto.

B – FRECCIA DELLA LAGUNA – 1,2 cl. and 2 cl. (also 1,2 cl. (T2) on ①⑤⑥⑦) Venezia (**1931**) - Villa SG - Reggio.

R – TRENO DEL SOLE – 1,2 cl. and 2 cl. (4 berth) Torino (**1941**) - Messina - Siracusa.

T – FRECCIA DELLA LAGUNA – 1,2 cl. and 2 cl. (4 berth) Venezia (**1931**) - Messina - Palermo.

Z – TRINACRIA – 1,2 cl. (T2), 1,2 cl. and 2 cl. (4/6 berth) Milano (**1921**) - Messina - Siracusa.

p – Napoli **Piazza Garibaldi** (situated under Centrale).

s – Stops to set down only.

t – Roma **Tiburtina**.

v – Also Oct. 31.

z – Venezia **Mestre**.

640 SICILY - NAPOLI - ROMA

	E	*E*	*E*	*E*	*E*			*E*		*E*			*E*		*IC*	*ES*		*AV*	*AV*		*ICp*	*AV*	*AV*	*IC*		*AV*
	894	**1922**	**1920**	**892**	**834**			**1924**		**986**			**1938**		**582**	**9370**		**9602**	**9432**		**516**	**9604**	**9434**	**704**		**9436**
											2	2			🍷	R 🍷	2	R 🍷	R 🍷		R ✕	R 🍷	R ✕	🍷	2	R ✕
	♦	Z	♦	♦	X			♦		♦			♦			⚒		Ⓐ				Ⓐ				
Palermo C 645/7 d.	...	...	1700	...	...	...	1805	1840	...	...	2030	...	...	...	...	...	...	...	...	...	...	...	...	...	...	...
Termini Imerese **645/7** d.	...	...	1725	...	...	...	1833	1908	...	...	2056	...	...	...	...	...	...	...	...	...	...	...	...	...	...	...
Cefalù d.	...	...	1747	...	...	...	1858	1930	...	...	2128	...	...	...	...	...	...	...	...	...	...	...	...	...	...	...
Milazzo d.	...	...	1942	...	...	...	2055	2112	...	...	2303	...	...	...	...	...	...	...	...	...	...	...	...	...	...	...
Siracusa d.	...	1715	│	...	1740	...	│	│	...	...	│	...	2025	...	...	...	...	...	...	...	...	...	...	...	...	...
Augusta d.	...	1741	│	...	1805	...	│	│	...	...	│	...	2048	...	...	...	...	...	...	...	...	...	...	...	...	...
Catania Centrale a.	...	1840	│	...	1900	...	│	│	...	...	│	...	2145	...	...	...	...	...	...	...	...	...	...	...	...	...
Catania Centrale d.	...	1844	│	...	1920	...	│	│	...	...	│	...	2205	...	...	...	...	...	...	...	...	...	...	...	...	...
Giarre-Riposto **644** d.	...	1909	│	...	1945	...	│	│	...	...	│	...	2232	...	...	...	...	...	...	...	...	...	...	...	...	...
Taormina-Giardini d.	...	•1928	│	...	2007	...	│	│	...	...	│	...	2250	...	...	...	...	...	...	...	...	...	...	...	...	...
Messina Centrale a.	...	2010	2010	...	2100	...	2130	2140	...	...	2330	...	2335	...	...	...	...	...	...	...	...	...	...	...	...	...
Messina Centrale d.	...	2030	2030	...	2120	...	...	2200	...	...	...	...	2355	...	...	...	...	...	...	...	...	...	...	...	...	...
Reggio di Calabria d.	2035	│	│	2140	│	...	...	│	...	2340	...	...	│	...	...	...	...	...	...	...	...	...	...	...	...	...
Villa San Giovanni a.	2051	2155	2155	2154	2245	...	...	2325	...	2355	...	...	0120	...	...	...	...	...	...	...	...	...	...	...	...	...
Villa San Giovanni d.	2120	2220	2220	2157	2310	...	...	2340	...	2358	...	...	0145	...	...	...	...	...	...	...	...	...	...	...	...	...
Gioia Tauro d.	2205	│	│	2242	│	...	...	│	...	0030	...	...	│	...	...	...	...	...	...	...	...	...	...	...	...	...
Lamezia Terme C a.	2330	│	│	2340	0014	...	...	│	...	0114	...	...	│	...	...	...	...	...	...	...	...	...	...	...	...	...
Lamezia Terme C d.	0022	│	│	2343	0017	...	...	│	...	...	...	...	│	...	...	...	...	...	...	...	...	...	...	...	...	...
Cosenza d.	│	│	│	│	│	...	...	│	...	...	...	...	│	...	...	...	...	...	...	...	...	...	...	...	0435	...
Paola d.	0111	│	│	0033	0059	...	...	│	...	...	...	...	│	...	...	...	...	...	...	...	...	...	...	...	0500	...
Belvedere Marittimo d.	│	│	│	│	│	...	...	│	...	...	...	...	│	...	...	...	...	...	...	...	...	...	...	...	0527	...
Maratea d.	│	│	│	│	│	...	...	│	...	...	...	...	│	...	...	...	...	...	...	...	...	...	...	...	0602	...
Sapri d.	0211	│	│	0132	│	...	...	│	...	...	...	...	│	...	...	...	...	...	...	...	...	...	...	...	0615	...
Ascea d.	│	│	│	│	│	...	...	│	...	...	...	...	│	...	...	...	...	...	...	...	...	...	...	...	0649	...
Agropoli d.	│	│	│	│	│	...	...	│	...	...	...	...	│	...	...	...	...	...	...	...	...	...	...	...	0717	...
Battipaglia d.	│	│	│	│	│	...	...	│	...	...	...	...	│	...	...	...	...	...	...	...	...	...	...	...	0742	...
Salerno d.	0341	│	│	0258	│	...	...	│	...	...	...	...	│	...	...	0540	...	...	...	...	0630	...	...	...	0801	0856
Pompei d.	│	│	│	│	│	...	...	│	...	...	...	...	│	...	...	0601	...	...	...	...	0652	...	...	...	0820	│
Napoli Centrale a.	0421	│	│	│	│	...	...	0430	...	...	...	...	0618	...	...	0624p	...	...	...	...	0718	...	...	...	0853	0936
Napoli Centrale 620 d.	0433	│	│	│	│	...	...	0442	...	...	...	0530	0630	...	0624	0628p	0636	0710	0748	...	0730	0810	0848	0824	...	0948
Aversa d.	0452	│	│	│	│	...	...	│	...	...	...	0547	│	...	0646	│	0657	│	│	...	0746	│	│	0846	...	│
Formia d.	0535	│	│	0440	│	...	...	0548	...	...	...	0633	0734	...	0725	│	0746	│	│	...	0825	│	│	0925	...	│
Latina d.	0620	│	│	0530	│	...	...	0634	...	...	...	0709	0817	...	0801	│	0834	│	│	...	0859	│	│	0959	...	│
Roma Termini 620 a.	0705	0505t	0505t	0617	0611t	...	...	0723	...	...	...	0753	0856	...	0833	0816	0918	0837	0915	...	0933	0937	1015	1033	...	1115
Bologna C **620** a.	...	0859	0859	...	1018	...	...	...	...	...	...	...	...	...	1240	...	...	...	1212	...	│	...	1312	1440	...	1412
Venezia SL **620** a.	...	│	│	...	│	...	...	...	...	...	...	...	...	...	│	...	...	...	│	...	│	...	│	1647	...	│
Milano C **619/20** a.	...	1125	1125	...	1245	...	...	...	...	...	...	...	...	...	1450	...	...	...	1400	...	│	...	1500	...	...	1600
Torino PN **610** a.	...	...	...	...	...	...	...	...	...	...	...	...	...	...	...	...	...	...	...	...	1655	...	...	...	...	...

	ICp		*ES*	*ICp*	*AV*		*ICp*	*AV*	*ES*		*ES*	*ICp*			*IC*	*AV*	*ICp*	*AV*		*ICp*	*IC*	*IC*		*ES*		
	520		**9360**	**586**	**9608**		**522**	**9440**	**9382**		**9372**	**706**			**1554**	**9612**	**590**	**9444**		**530**	**1590**	**1588**		**9374**		
	R ✕	2	R 🍷	R ✕	R 🍷		R	R ✕	R 🍷		R ✕	R ✕				R 🍷	R	R ✕		R ✕				R ✕	2	2
			♦						♦	⚒		♦	⚒	⚒	⑦v	Ⓐ				♦	♦	♦			⚒	†
Palermo C 645/7 d.	...	...	...	...	...	...	...	...	...	...	...	...	...	0405	...	...	...	...	...	...	...	...	...	...	...	...
Termini Imerese **645/7** d.	...	...	...	...	...	...	...	...	...	...	...	...	...	0430	...	...	...	...	...	...	...	...	...	...	...	...
Cefalù d.	...	...	...	...	...	...	...	...	...	...	...	...	...	0450	...	...	...	...	...	...	...	...	...	...	...	...
Milazzo d.	...	...	...	...	...	...	...	...	...	...	...	...	...	0713	...	...	...	...	...	...	...	...	...	...	...	...
Siracusa d.	...	...	...	...	...	...	...	...	...	...	...	...	0500	│	...	...	...	...	...	...	...	...	...	...	...	...
Augusta d.	...	...	...	...	...	...	...	...	...	...	...	...	0521	│	...	...	...	...	...	...	...	...	...	...	...	...
Catania Centrale a.	...	...	...	...	...	...	...	...	...	...	...	...	0609	│	...	...	...	...	...	...	...	...	...	...	...	...
Catania Centrale d.	...	...	...	...	...	...	...	...	...	...	...	...	0615	│	...	...	...	...	...	...	...	...	...	...	...	...
Giarre-Riposto **644** d.	...	...	...	...	...	...	...	...	...	...	...	...	0639	│	...	...	...	...	...	...	...	...	...	...	...	...
Taormina-Giardini d.	...	...	...	...	...	...	...	...	...	...	...	...	0700	│	...	...	...	...	...	...	...	...	...	...	...	...
Messina Centrale a.	...	...	...	...	...	...	...	...	...	...	...	...	0748	0753	...	...	...	...	...	...	...	...	...	...	...	...
Messina Centrale d.	...	...	...	...	...	...	...	...	...	...	...	...	...	...	...	...	...	...	...	...	...	...	...	...	...	...
Reggio di Calabria d.	...	...	...	...	...	...	0550	...	...	0605	0755	...	...	...	...	...	0745	...	...	0830	0840	0915	...	0955	...	...
Villa San Giovanni a.	...	...	...	...	...	...	0600	...	...	0620	0808	...	...	...	...	...	0757	...	...	0845	0855	0930	...	1008	...	...
Villa San Giovanni d.	...	...	...	...	...	...	0603	...	...	0622	0811	...	...	...	...	...	0800	...	...	0848	0858	0933	...	1011	...	...
Gioia Tauro d.	...	...	...	...	...	...	0632	...	...	0700	0837	...	...	...	...	...	0829	...	...	0921	0929	1004	...	1037	...	...
Lamezia Terme C a.	...	...	...	...	...	...	0715	...	...	0742	0914	...	...	...	...	...	0922	...	...	1005	1051	1053	...	1114	...	...
Lamezia Terme C d.	...	...	...	...	...	...	0718	...	...	0744	0917	...	...	...	...	...	0925	...	...	1008	1054	1056	...	1117	...	...
Cosenza d.	...	0525	...	...	...	...	│	...	...	│	│	...	...	...	...	...	│	...	...	│	│	│	...	│	...	...
Paola d.	...	0553	...	...	...	...	0757	...	...	0823	0948	...	...	...	...	...	1005	...	...	1107	1140	1135	...	1148	...	...
Belvedere Marittimo d.	...	0622	...	...	...	...	│	...	...	0857	│	...	...	...	...	...	│	...	...	│	│	│	...	│	...	...
Maratea d.	...	0706	...	...	...	...	0848	...	...	0938	│	...	...	...	...	...	1053	...	...	│	│	│	...	│	...	...
Sapri d.	...	0720	...	...	...	...	0902	...	...	0949	1034	...	...	...	...	...	1107	...	...	1207	1234	1228	...	1234	...	...
Ascea d.	...	0810	...	...	...	...	│	...	...	│	│	...	...	...	...	...	│	...	...	1236	1304	1257	...	│	...	...
Agropoli d.	...	0840	...	...	...	...	│	...	...	1037	│	...	...	...	...	...	│	...	...	1258	│	│	...	│	...	...
Battipaglia d.	...	0902	0925	...	...	...	1006	...	1101	1100	│	...	...	...	...	...	1216	...	...	1320	│	│	...	│	...	...
Salerno d.	...	0922	0942	...	...	...	1022	...	1121	1121	1142	...	...	...	1207	...	1233	...	...	1336	1356	1356	...	1344	...	...
Pompei d.	...	0940	│	...	...	...	│	...	1138	1142	...	...	...	...	1230	...	│	...	...	│	│	│	...	│	...	...
Napoli Centrale a.	...	1010	1018p	...	...	...	1112	...	1200p	1214	1218p	...	2	...	1256p	...	1312	...	...	1412	1430	1430	...	1418p	...	...
Napoli Centrale 620 d.	0924	...	1022p	1024	1110	...	1124	1148	1204p	...	1222p	1224	1230	...	1300p	1310	1324	1348	...	1424	1442	1442	...	1422p	1430	1430
Aversa d.	0946	...	│	1046	│	...	1146	│	│	...	│	1246	1252	...	│	│	1346	│	...	1446	1459	1459	...	│	1452	1502
Formia d.	1023	...	│	1126	│	...	1223	│	│	...	│	1323	1344	...	1401	│	1423	│	...	1523	1542	1542	...	│	1544	1551
Latina d.	1059	...	│	1200	│	...	1259	│	│	...	│	1359	1430	...	1451	│	1459	│	...	1559	1618	1618	...	│	1630	1637
Roma Termini 620 a.	1133	...	1216	1233	1237	...	1333	1315	1400	...	1416	1433	1513	...	1546t	1437	1533	1515	...	1640t	1653t	1653t	...	1616	1713	1721
Bologna C **620** a.	│	...	...	1640	...	...	...	1612	...	...	...	1840	...	...	1954	...	...	1812	...	│	2119	2119	...	...	...	...
Venezia SL **620** a.	│	...	...	│	...	...	...	│	...	...	...	2026z	...	...	│	...	...	│	...	│	│	│	...	...	...	...
Milano C **619/20** a.	│	...	...	1850	...	...	...	1800	...	...	...	...	...	...	2235	...	...	2000	...	│	2345	2345	...	...	...	...
Torino PN **610** a.	1855	...	...	...	...	...	...	...	...	...	...	...	...	...	...	...	...	...	...	2325	...	...	...	...	...	...

♦ – **NOTES** (LISTED BY TRAIN NUMBER)

530 – SILA – [12] Reggio - Firenze - Torino; [2] Crotone (**534**) - Sibari (**535**) - Cosenza (**536**) - Paola - Torino.

706 – MIRAMARE – [12] Napoli - Venezia Mestre (**707**) - Trieste.

892 – ⑦ (also Aug. 15, Nov. 1): ▬ 2 cl. and [2] Reggio - Roma.

894 – 🛏 1, 2 cl. (T2), ▬ 2 cl. and [2] Reggio - Roma; 🛏 1, 2 cl. (T2), ▬ 2 cl. and [2] Reggio (**890**) - Catanzaro Lido - Lamezia - Roma. Runs as train **898** on ⑥ June 16 - Sept. 8.

986 – Ⓐ: [2] Reggio - Metaponto (**989**) - Taranto (**990**) - Bari.

1588 – ASPROMONTE – ⑦ Sept. 9 - Dec. 2 (also Nov. 1): [12] Reggio - Milano.

1590 – ASPROMONTE – ⑦ June 17 - Sept. 2: [12] Reggio - Milano.

1920 – TRINACRIA – 🛏 1, 2 cl. (T2), 🛏 1,2 cl. and ▬ 2 cl. (4/6 berth) Palermo - Milano; [2] Palermo - Messina.

1924 – IL GATTOPARDO – Dec. 9 - May 31: 🛏 1,2 cl., ▬ 2 cl. (4 berth) and [2] Palermo - Roma.

1938 – BELLINI – 🛏 1,2 cl., ▬ 2 cl. (4 berth) and [2] Siracusa - Roma.

9360 – ⚒: [12] and 🍷 Taranto - Roma.

9382 – †: [12] and ✕ Taranto - Roma.

X – FRECCIA DEL SUD – ③⑤⑥⑦: ▬ 2 cl. and [2] Agrigento - Catania - Milano; [2] Siracusa (**836**) - Catania - Milano.

Z – TRINACRIA – 🛏 1, 2 cl. (T2), 🛏 1, 2 cl. and ▬ 2 cl. (4/6 berth) Siracusa - Messina (**1920**) - Milano.

p – Napoli **Piazza Garibaldi** (situated under Centrale).

s – Stops to set down only.

t – Roma **Tiburtina**.

v – Also Nov. 1.

z – Venezia **Mestre**.

SICILY - NAPOLI - ROMA 640

	2 ⚒	AV 9616 R 🍷 Ⓐ	ICp 542 R ✕ ♦	2 ⚒	AV 9448 R ✕	ICp 720 R ♦	ICp 722 R U	2	AV 9620 R 🍷 Ⓐ	ICp 546 R ✕ ♦	ICp 1572 R ♦	2	AV 9452 R ✕	AV 9624 R 🍷	y	2 x	ES 9376 R ✕	2 †	ICp 598 R 🍷	2	E 824 ♦	ICp 730 R V	ICp 726 R ♦	ICp 676 R 🍷 ♦	EN 286 R ♦	ICN 774 ♦
Palermo C 645/7 d.	...	...	...	0605	...	0730	...	...	...	...	...	...	...	...	0825	...	...	0840	...	...	...	1020	...	...	...	...
Termini Imerese 645/7 d.	...	...	...	0632	...	0754	...	...	...	...	...	...	...	...	0850	...	...	0916	...	...	...	1045	...	...	...	...
Cefalù d.	...	...	...	0700	...	0813	...	...	...	...	...	...	...	...	0914	...	...	0940	...	...	...	1105	...	...	...	...
Milazzo d.	...	...	...	0855	...	0952	...	...	...	...	...	...	...	...	1057	...	...	1152	...	...	...	1248	...	...	...	...
Siracusa d.	0630	...	...	|	...	|	0800	...	...	...	...	...	...	...	|	0850	...	|	...	...	...	|	1045	...	...	...
Augusta d.	0653	...	...	|	...	|	0820	...	...	...	...	...	...	...	|	0912	...	|	...	...	...	|	1105	...	...	...
Catania Centrale a.	0737	...	...	|	...	|	0907	...	...	...	...	...	...	...	|	1001	...	|	...	...	...	|	1155	...	...	...
Catania Centrale d.	0744	...	...	|	...	|	0910	...	...	...	...	...	...	...	|	1005	...	|	...	...	...	|	1200	...	...	...
Giarre-Riposto 644 d.	0808	...	...	|	...	|	0934	...	...	...	...	...	...	...	|	1026	...	|	...	...	...	|	1224	...	...	...
Taormina-Giardini d.	0826	...	...	|	...	|	0950	...	...	...	...	...	...	...	|	1045	...	|	...	...	...	|	1242	...	...	...
Messina Centrale a.	0920	...	...	0925	...	1025	1030	...	...	...	...	...	...	...	1125	1140	...	1235	...	...	...	1320	1325	...	...	...
Messina Centrale d.	...	...	...	...	...	1040	1040	...	...	...	...	...	...	...	...	...	...	...	...	...	...	1335	1335	...	...	...
Reggio di Calabria d.	...	...	...	...	...	|	|	...	...	...	...	...	...	...	...	...	1355	...	...	...	...	|	|	...	...	...
Villa San Giovanni a.	...	...	...	...	...	1145	1145	...	...	...	...	...	...	...	...	...	1408	...	...	...	...	1440	1440	...	...	...
Villa San Giovanni d.	...	...	...	...	...	1205	1205	...	...	...	...	...	...	...	...	...	1411	...	...	...	...	1505	1505	...	...	...
Gioia Tauro d.	...	...	...	...	...	|	|	...	...	...	...	...	...	...	...	...	1437	...	...	...	...	|	|	...	...	...
Lamezia Terme C a.	...	...	...	...	...	1302	1302	...	...	...	...	...	...	...	...	...	1514	...	...	...	...	1602	1602	...	...	...
Lamezia Terme C d.	...	...	...	...	...	1305	1305	...	...	...	...	...	...	...	2	...	1517	...	...	...	...	1605	1605	...	...	...
Cosenza d.	...	...	...	...	...	|	|	...	...	...	...	1225c	...	...	1425	...	|	...	...	...	...	|	|	...	...	...
Paola d.	...	...	...	...	...	1340	1340	...	...	...	...	1253	...	...	1453	...	1548	...	...	...	...	1640	1640	...	...	...
Belvedere Marittimo d.	...	...	...	...	...	|	|	...	...	...	...	1322	...	...	1522	...	|	...	...	...	...	|	|	...	...	...
Maratea d.	...	...	...	...	...	|	|	...	...	...	...	1406	...	...	1606	...	|	...	...	...	...	|	|	...	...	...
Sapri d.	...	...	...	...	...	1428	1428	...	...	...	...	1420	...	...	1620	...	1634	...	...	...	...	|	|	...	...	...
Ascea d.	...	...	...	...	...	|	|	...	...	...	...	1502	...	...	1702	...	|	...	...	...	...	|	|	...	...	...
Agropoli d.	...	...	...	...	...	|	|	...	...	...	...	1535	...	...	1732	...	|	...	...	...	...	|	|	...	...	...
Battipaglia d.	...	...	...	...	...	|	|	...	...	...	...	1602	...	...	1757	...	|	...	...	...	...	|	|	1833	...	...
Salerno d.	...	...	...	...	...	1542	1542	...	...	...	...	1622	...	...	1820	...	1742	...	...	...	...	1842	1842	1850	...	...
Pompei d.	...	...	...	...	...	|	|	...	...	...	...	1640	...	...	1839	...	|	...	...	...	...	|	|	|	...	...
Napoli Centrale a.	...	...	...	...	...	1618p	1618p	...	...	...	...	1710	...	...	1910	...	1818p	...	...	...	...	1918p	1918p	1924	...	...
Napoli Centrale 620 d.	...	1510	1524	...	1548	1622p	1622p	1630	1710	1724	1724	...	1748	1810	...	...	1822p	...	1824	1830	1845	1922p	1922p	1936	1930	1957
Aversa d.	...	|	1546	...	|	|	|	1652	|	1746	1746	...	|	|	...	...	|	...	1846	1852	|	|	|	1953	|	|
Formia d.	...	|	1623	...	|	|	|	1744	|	1823	1823	...	|	|	...	...	|	...	1926	1944	|	|	|	2029	|	2121
Latina d.	...	|	1659	...	|	|	|	1830	|	1859	1859	...	|	|	...	...	|	...	1959	2030	|	|	|	2101	|	2159
Roma Termini 620 a.	...	1637	1733	...	1715	1816	1816	1913	1837	1933	1933	...	1915	1937	...	...	2016	...	2033	2111	2158t	2116	2116	2139	2150t	2245t
Bologna C 620 a.	...	...	...	...	2012	...	...	...	...	...	...	...	2212	...	...	...	...	...	...	...	0300	...	...	...	0118	0313
Venezia S L 620 a.	...	...	...	...	|	...	...	...	...	...	...	...	|	...	...	...	...	...	...	...	...	...	...	...	...	0524
Milano C 619/20 a.	...	...	...	...	2200	...	...	...	...	...	...	...	0005	...	...	...	...	...	...	...	...	...	...	...	...	...
Torino P N 610 a.	...	...	...	...	...	...	...	...	...	...	...	...	...	...	...	...	...	...	...	...	...	...	...	...	...	...

	E 1910 ♦	⚒	2 ⚒	2 †	ES 9388 R ✕ ⚒k	ES 9378 R ✕ j	E 806 ♦	E 830 ♦	2	E 1594 ♦		⚒	2 ⚒	2 †	ICN 768 ♦	E 1942 R	E 1940 ♦	ICN 752 ♦	E 1992 ♦	E 1990 M	2 Ⓐ		E 1934 B	E 1930 ♦	E 1932 T	2 ⚒
Palermo C 645/7 d.	...	1135	...	...	...	...	...	...	...	...	...	...	1305	1320	...	...	1430	...	...	1500	1527	...	...	...	1600	...
Termini Imerese 645/7 d.	...	1201	...	...	...	...	...	...	...	...	...	...	1334	1357	...	...	1454	...	...	1525	1551	...	...	...	1623	...
Cefalù d.	...	1222	...	...	...	...	...	...	...	...	...	...	1400	1424	...	...	1518	...	...	1547	1609	...	...	...	1646	...
Milazzo d.	...	1439	...	...	...	...	...	...	...	...	...	...	1603	1625	...	...	1702	...	...	1740	1803	...	...	...	1832	...
Siracusa d.	...	|	...	...	...	...	...	...	...	...	...	...	|	|	...	1450	|	...	1530	|	|	...	...	1555	|	1700
Augusta d.	...	|	...	...	...	...	...	...	...	...	...	...	|	|	...	1515	|	...	1552	|	|	...	...	1620	|	1727
Catania Centrale a.	...	|	...	...	...	...	...	...	...	...	...	...	|	|	...	1602	|	...	1642	|	|	...	...	1715	|	1820
Catania Centrale d.	...	|	1345	1345	...	...	...	...	...	...	...	1422	|	|	...	1605	|	...	1648	|	|	...	...	1733	|	1824
Giarre-Riposto 644 d.	...	|	1407	1412	...	...	...	...	...	...	...	1448	|	|	...	1630	|	...	1715	|	|	...	...	1758	|	1848
Taormina-Giardini d.	...	|	1430	1439	...	...	...	...	...	...	...	1512	|	|	...	1647	|	...	1735	|	|	...	...	1818	|	1909
Messina Centrale a.	...	1520	1528	1545	...	...	...	...	...	...	...	1605	1632	1705	...	1725	1730	...	1825	1815	1835	...	...	1905	1910	2000
Messina Centrale d.	...	...	...	...	...	...	...	...	...	...	...	...	...	...	...	1750	1750	...	1845	1845	...	...	...	1925	1925	...
Reggio di Calabria d.	...	...	...	...	1630	1655	...	...	...	1617	...	...	...	...	1820	|	|	1935	|	|	...	...	2025	|	|	...
Villa San Giovanni a.	...	...	...	...	1642	1708	...	...	...	1632	...	...	...	...	1837	1910	1910	1948	2010	2010	...	...	2040	2050	2050	...
Villa San Giovanni d.	...	...	...	...	1645	1711	...	...	...	1655	...	...	...	...	1840	1935	1935	1951	2040	2040	...	...	2115	2115	2115	...
Gioia Tauro d.	...	...	...	...	1713	1737	...	...	...	1732	...	...	...	...	1913	|	|	2021	|	|	...	...	2146	2146	2146	...
Lamezia Terme C a.	...	...	...	...	1752	1814	...	...	...	1825	...	...	...	...	2000	2039	2039	2107	2145	2145	...	...	2232	2230	2230	...
Lamezia Terme C d.	...	...	...	2	1755	1817	...	...	...	1855	...	...	...	...	2025	2042	2042	2130	2148	2148	...	...	2235	2233	2233	...
Cosenza d.	...	...	...	1625	|	|	...	...	1825	|	...	...	...	...	|	|	|	|	|	|	...	...	|	|	|	...
Paola d.	...	...	...	1653	1832	1848	...	...	1853	1933	...	...	...	...	2102	2117	2117	2215	2223	2223	...	...	2313	2313	2313	...
Belvedere Marittimo d.	...	...	...	1722	|	|	...	...	1923	|	...	...	...	...	|	|	|	|	|	|	...	...	|	|	|	...
Maratea d.	...	...	...	1806	1914g	|	...	...	2006	|	...	...	...	...	2150	|	|	2306	|	|	...	...	|	|	|	...
Sapri d.	...	...	...	1820	1926	1934	...	...	2020	2034	...	...	...	...	2202	2209	2209	2326	|	|	...	...	0006	0006	0006	...
Ascea d.	...	...	...	1902	|	|	...	...	2102	2102	...	...	...	...	2233	|	|	2358	|	|	...	...	|	|	|	...
Agropoli d.	...	...	...	1935	2009	|	...	...	2135	2128	...	...	...	...	2301	|	|	0025	|	|	...	...	|	|	|	...
Battipaglia d.	...	...	...	2002	|	|	...	...	2202	|	...	...	...	...	2328	|	|	0047	|	|	...	...	|	|	|	...
Salerno d.	...	...	...	2022	2042	2042	...	2048	2222	2208	...	...	...	...	2347	2327	2327	0105	0031	0031	...	...	0130	0130	0130	...
Pompei d.	...	...	...	2040	2057g	2057e	...	2110	2243	|	...	...	...	...	|	|	|	|	|	|	...	...	|	|	|	...
Napoli Centrale a.	...	2	...	2112	2118p	2118p	...	2138	2317	2250	...	...	...	...	|	|	|	|	|	|	...	...	|	|	|	...
Napoli Centrale 620 d.	2036	2042	...	...	2122p	2122p	2138	2150	...	2302	...	...	...	...	|	|	|	|	|	|	...	...	|	|	|	...
Aversa d.	|	2100	...	...	|	|	2156	|	...	|	...	...	...	...	|	|	|	|	|	|	...	...	|	|	|	...
Formia d.	|	2147	...	...	|	|	2239	2318	...	|	...	...	...	...	|	|	|	|	|	|	...	...	|	|	|	...
Latina d.	|	2232	...	...	|	|	2317	2356	...	|	...	...	...	...	|	|	|	|	|	|	...	...	|	|	|	...
Roma Termini 620 a.	2245	2321	...	...	2315	2315	2357o	0042t	...	...	...	...	...	...	|	|	|	0417t	|	|	...	...	|	|	|	...
Bologna C 620 a.	|	...	...	...	...	...	|	0557	...	0528	...	...	...	...	|	|	|	0746	0703	0703	...	...	0755	0755	0755	...
Venezia S L 620 a.	|	...	...	...	...	...	|	|	...	...	...	...	...	...	|	|	|	|	|	|	...	...	1146	1143	1143	...
Milano C 619/20 a.	0715	...	...	...	...	...	|	0920	...	...	...	...	...	...	|	|	|	1050	1010	1010	...	...	...	...	...	...
Torino P N 610 a.	...	...	...	...	...	...	0820	...	...	...	...	...	...	...	1045	1110	1110	...	...	...	...	...	...	...	...	...

♦ – **NOTES** (LISTED BY TRAIN NUMBER)

286 – CAPRI – 🛏 1,2 cl., ▬ 2 cl. (4/6 berth) and (2) Napoli - München.
542 – BOCCANEGRA – (12) Napoli - Genova - Savona.
546 – CARDUCCI – ⑧ (not days before holidays): (12) and ✕ Napoli - Sestri Levante.
676 – (12) Taranto - Roma.
720 – PELORITANO – (12) Palermo - Roma.
726 – ARCHIMEDE – (12) Siracusa - Roma.
752 – PIEPOLI – 🛏 1,2 cl. (T2), ▬ 2 cl. and (12) Reggio - Milano. Conveys until Sept. 16: ▬ 2 cl. (4 berth) and (2) Reggio (**750**) - Lamezia - Milano.
768 – SCILLA – 🛏 1,2 cl. (T2), ▬ 2 cl. and (12) Reggio - Torino. Conveys until Sept. 16: ▬ 2 cl. (4 berth) and (2) Reggio (**766**) - Lamezia - Torino.
774 – MARCO POLO – 🛏 1,2 cl. (Excelsior), 🛏 1,2 cl., ▬ 2 cl. (4 berth) and (2) Napoli - Udine; 🛏 1,2 cl., ▬ 2 cl. (4 berth) and (12) Napoli - Venezia (**773**) - Trieste.
806 – Not Dec. 24, 25, 31: 🛏 1,2 cl. (T2), ▬ 2 cl. (4 berth) and (2) Napoli - Torino.
824 – ①③④⑤⑥⑦ (also Jan. 1, Apr. 29; not Dec. 24, 31, Apr. 28): 🛏 1,2 cl., ▬ 2 cl. (4 berth) and (2) Napoli - Bologna (**924**) - Bolzano.
830 – ⑦ (also Aug. 15, Nov. 1): (2) Salerno - Milano.
1572 – CARDUCCI – ⑥ (also Aug. 14, Oct. 31, Dec. 7): (12) Napoli - Roma.
1594 – ⑤ Dec. 14 - Mar. 28 (also Dec. 19, 23, 30): 🛏 1,2 cl. (T2), ▬ 2 cl. and (2) Reggio - Bolzano.
1910 – 🛏 1,2 cl. (Excelsior), 🛏 1,2 cl. (T2), 🛏 1,2 cl., ▬ 2 cl. (4 berth) and (2) Napoli - Milano.
1930 – FRECCIA DELLA LAGUNA – 🛏 1,2 cl. and ▬ 2 cl. (4 berth) Siracusa - Venezia.
1940 – TRENO DEL SOLE – 🛏 1,2 cl. and ▬ 2 cl. (4 berth) Palermo - Torino; (2) Palermo - Messina.
1992 – MONGIBELLO – ⑦ June 10 - Sept. 9 (also Oct. 28, Nov. 4): 🛏 1,2 cl. (T2), ▬ 2 cl. and (2) Siracusa - Milano.

B – FRECCIA DELLA LAGUNA – 🛏 1,2 cl. and ▬ 2 cl. (also 🛏 1,2 cl. (T2) on ④⑤⑥⑦) Reggio - Villa S G (**1930**) - Venezia.
M – MONGIBELLO – ▬ 2 cl. and (2) Palermo - Messina (**1992**) - Milano. See train **1992** for running dates.
R – TRENO DEL SOLE – 🛏 1,2 cl. and ▬ 2 cl. (4 berth) Siracusa - Messina (**1940**) - Torino.
T – FRECCIA DELLA LAGUNA – 🛏 1,2 cl. and ▬ 2 cl. (4 berth) Palermo - Messina (**1930**) - Venezia.
U – PELORITANO – (12) Siracusa - Messina (**720**) - Roma.
V – ARCHIMEDE – (12) Palermo - Messina (**726**) - Roma.

c – © only.
e – ⑦ only.
g – ⑥ only.
j – Sept. 9 - Dec. 8.
k – June 10 - Sept. 8.
o – Roma **Ostiense**.
p – Napoli **Piazza Garibaldi** (situated under Centrale).
t – Roma **Tiburtina**.
x – Not Dec. 25, Mar. 23.
y – Not Dec. 25, Jan. 1, Mar. 23.

644 CATANIA - RANDAZZO - RIPOSTO

Ferrovia Circumetnea

Winter service valid from September 17, 2007. No service on †

km		⚒	⚒	⚒	⚒	⚒	⚒	⚒	⚒	⚒	⚒	⚒	⚒	⚒	⚒	⚒
0	**Catania ▲** ..d.	...	...	0550	0648	0748	...	0930	...	1113	1209	1315	1436	1642	1822	1915
20	Paternò ....d.	...	...	0625	0720	0821	...	1006	...	1147	1244	1349	1510	1716	1855	1949
36	Adrano ....d.	...	...	0654	0753	0856	...	1037	...	1218	1317	1425	1544	1747	1924	2019
52	Bronte ....d.	...	...	0725	0822	0926	...	1108	...	1247	1352	1457	1613	1816	1953	2047
71	Randazzo ....d.	0637	0746	0755	0854	0957	1000	1138	1155	1325	1422	1527	1645	1847	2023	2117
109	Giarre **640** ...a.	0747	0853	...	...	...	1106	...	1302	1430	...	...	1750	...	...	...
111	**Riposto** ......a.	0751	0857	...	...	...	1109	...	1305	1433	...	...	1753	...	...	...

	⚒	⚒	⚒	⚒	⚒	⚒	⚒	⚒	⚒	⚒	⚒	⚒	⚒
Riposto ... d.	...	...	...	0653	0830	1014	...	...	1236	1339	1436	...	1805
Giarre **640** d.	...	...	...	0658	0834	1018	...	...	1241	1343	1440	...	1809
Randazzo . d.	0520	0616	0654	0820	1001	1130	1216	1320	1426	1457	1552	1711	1921
Bronte ...... d.	0551	0648	0724	0851	1032	...	1248	1352	1456	...	...	1741	1952
Adrano ..... d.	0619	0716	0752	0919	1101	...	1316	1423	1522	...	...	1810	2018
Paternò .... d.	0650	0745	0822	0949	1131	...	1348	1455	1551	...	...	1840	2049
Catania ▲ a.	0724	0816	0854	1020	1202	...	1420	1527	1623	...	...	1912	2119

▲ – Catania Borgo station. The Metropolitana di Catania operates a metro service Borgo - Porto and v.v. (3.8 km) via Catania Centrale station. Weekdays only, every 15 minutes 0700 – 2045.

645 PALERMO and AGRIGENTO - CATANIA

2nd class only except where shown

km*	km*		3874 ⚒	⚒	⚒	3884 ⚒G	⚒	3860 †G	⚒	3832		⚒	3866 ⚒	†	†	3836 †	⚒	⚒	⚒	*E* 834 Bx	†z	3858 ⚒	†	G	3872		
0		**Palermo C 647**........d.	...	...	0555	...	0635	...	...	0815	...	...	1205	...	...	1445	...	...	...	...	...	1605	...	1722	...	...	...
37		Termini Imerese **647** . d.	...	...	0620	...	0705	...	...	0841	...	...	1231	...	...	1511	...	...	...	...	...	1631	...	1752	...	...	...
70		Roccapalumba Alia **647** d.	...	...	0649	...	0744	...	...	0913	...	...	1258	...	...	1537	...	...	...	...	...	1703	...	1821	...	...	...
		Agrigento C 647.. d.	...	...	|	...	|	...	...	|	1220	...	|	...	...	|	...	...	...	1500	...	|	...	|	1850	...	...
		Aragona-Caldare **647** d.	...	...	|	...	|	...	...	|	1240	...	|	...	...	|	...	...	...	1518	...	|	...	|	1905	...	...
	0	**Siracusa**..........d.	...	...	|	...	|	...	0515	|	|	...	|	1035	...	|	...	...	...	|	1255	|	1450	|	|	*1740*d	2032
	62	Pozzallo...........d.	...	...	|	...	|	...	0638	|	|	...	|	1136	...	|	...	...	...	|	1357	|	1551	|	|	*1843*d	2132
	92	Modica.............d.	...	...	|	...	|	...	0718	|	|	...	|	1217	...	|	...	...	1335	|	1435	|	1626	|	|	1955	2205
	112	**Ragusa**.............d.	...	...	|	...	|	...	0742	|	|	...	|	1240	...	|	...	...	1408	|	1458	|	1650	|	|	2020	...
	153	Vittoria ....d.	...	...	|	...	|	...	0826	|	|	...	|	1320	...	|	...	...	1449	|	1537	|	1730	|	|	2100	...
	183	Gela.................d.	...	...	|	0620	|	0715	0855	|	|	1215	|	1350	1420	|	1420	...	1517	|	1603	|	1755	|	|	2130	...
	218	Licata...............d.	...	...	|	0649	|	0744	...	|	|	1250	|	...	1451	|	1451	...	1547	|	1633	|	...	|	|	...	...
	264	Canicattì...............d.	...	...	|	0729	|	0826	...	|	1315	1332	|	...	1534	|	1538	...	...	1608	1713	|	...	|	1937	...	...
		Caltanisetta Xirbi .. a.	...	...	0740	|	0839	|	...	0958	|	|	1350	...	|	1621	|	...	...	|	|	1752	...	1913	|	...	...
	293	Caltanisetta Centrale d.	0540	0700	0750	0755	0850	0852	...	|	1345	1400	1402	...	1610	|	1615	1620	...	1641	1740	1805	...	1923	2003	...	...
127		Caltanisetta Xirbi......d.	0548	0708	...	0802	...	0859	...	1000	1355	...	...	...	1618	1623	...	1633	...	1652	...	...	...	...	2011	...	...
154		Enna.......................d.	0612	0731	...	...	...	...	...	1023	1418	...	...	...	...	1646	...	1655	...	1725	...	...	...	...	2037	...	...
243		**Catania Centrale**.....a.	0733	0845	...	...	...	...	...	1145	1530	...	...	...	...	1800	...	1815	...	1850	...	...	...	...	2148	...	...

	⚒	3899 ⚒	⚒	⚒	3885 ⚒G	3843 †	†	3861 †G	*.E* 823 By	3897 †z	⚒	3845 ⚒		⚒	⚒	⚒	†	⚒		3831 †	3833 ⚒	3837 ⚒	⚒	3895 †z	†z	G	3839
Catania Centrale ..... d.	...	...	0545	...	...	0640	...	...	0738	...	...	...	...	1045	...	...	1305	1335	...	...	1415	1605	...	...	1605	...	1915
Enna........................ d.	...	...	0705	...	...	0755	...	...	0905	...	...	...	...	1205	...	...	1420	1500	...	...	1538	1721	...	...	1726	...	2036
Caltanisetta Xirbi....... a.	...	...	0731	...	...	0818	...	...	0937	...	...	...	...	1231	...	...	1444	1523	...	...	1600	1745	...	...	1748	1916	2058
Caltanisetta Centrale. d.	...	0603	0740	0800	0755	0831	0810	0852	0950	1025	...	1125	1135	1240	1245	1428	1454	1534	...	1550	|	|	1735	1745	1800	1924	|
Caltanisetta Xirbi ... d.	...	0613	▬	|	0805	|	|	0903	|	1035	...	1135	|	▬	1255	|	|	|	...	1600	1604	1753	|	1756	...	|	2059
Canicattì................ d.	...	|	...	0835	|	0909	0846	|	1035	|	...	|	1205	...	|	1501	1533	1610	...	|	|	|	1810	|	...	1958	|
Licata................. d.	...	|	†	|	|	|	0926	|	|	|	...	|	1251	...	|	1551	|	|	...	|	|	|	|	|	...	2041	|
Gela .... d.	0618	|	0715	|	|	|	0957	|	|	|	1255	|	1325	1415	|	1625	|	|	1718	|	|	|	|	|	...	2115	|
Vittoria .... d.	0653	|	0743	|	|	|	1023	|	|	|	1324	|	...	1450	|	...	|	|	1748	|	|	|	|	|	...	...	|
Ragusa .... d.	0741	|	0826	|	|	|	1105	|	|	|	1410	|	...	1534	|	...	|	|	1830	|	|	|	|	|	...	...	|
Modica................ d.	0803	|	0848	|	|	|	1127	|	|	|	1436	|	...	1600	|	...	|	|	1850	|	|	|	|	|	...	...	|
Pozzallo.............. d.	0842	|	0922	|	|	|	1201	|	|	|	1523	|	...	1632	|	...	|	|	1927	|	|	|	|	|	...	...	|
Siracusa .... a.	0950	|	1030	|	|	|	1315	|	|	|	1625	|	...	1735	|	...	|	|	2030	|	|	|	|	|	...	...	|
Aragona-Caldare **647** d.	...	|	...	0913	|	0939	...	|	1115	|	...	|	...	...	|	...	1601	1646	...	|	|	|	1842	|	...	...	|
Agrigento C 647... a.	...	|	...	0930	|	0955	...	|	1130	|	...	|	...	...	|	...	1615	1700	...	|	|	|	1900	|	...	...	|
Roccapalumba Alia **647** d.	...	0710	...	...	0856	...	...	0958	...	1129	...	1223	...	...	1345	...	...	...	...	1700	1703	1845	...	1846	...	...	2146
Termini Imerese **647** . d.	...	0736	...	...	0927	...	...	1025	...	1200	...	1300	...	...	1415	...	...	...	...	1730	1730	1912	...	1912	...	...	2215
Palermo C 647......... a.	...	0800	...	...	0955	...	...	1055	...	1230	...	1330	...	...	1455	...	...	...	...	1755	1800	1940	...	1940	...	...	2245

B – FRECCIA DEL SUD – 🛏 2 cl. and (2) Agrigento - Milano and v.v.
G – (2) Palermo - Gela and v.v.
d – ⚒ only.
x – ③⑤⑥⑦ only.
y – ①②④⑥ only.

z – Sept. 16 - Dec. 8.
* – Other distances: Palermo *0*, Caltanisetta Xirbi *126*, Caltanisetta C *132*, Canicatti *161*, Aragona-Caldare *190*, Agrigento C *203*.

CATANIA - GELA and v.v. 2nd class only, *137 km*, journey 2½ hours (approximately).
From **Catania**: 0550⚒, 0920⚒, 1210⚒z, 1320⚒, 1434⚒, 1740⚒.
From **Gela**: 0530⚒, 0645⚒, 0910⚒z, 1215⚒z, 1305⚒, 1420⚒, 1735⚒.

646 PALERMO - TRAPANI

2nd class only

km		⚒	⚒	⚒	⚒	†	⚒	†	†	⚒	⚒	†	†	⚒	⚒	⚒			⚒					⚒
0	**Palermo Centrale** ....d.	...	...	...	...	...	0630	0730	...	...	0940	0940	...	...	1140	...	1350	...	...	1540	1740	...	1840	1940
73	Castellammare del Golfo.......d.	...	0647	...	...	...	0822	0859	...	1034	1103	1115	...	...	1302	...	1516	...	...	1716	1902	...	2009	2113
79	Alcamo Diramazione............d.	...	0657	0703	...	...	0830	0907	0915	1042	1110	1125	1130	...	1313	1325	1525	1530	...	1724	1910	1920	2017	2122
121	Castelvetrano ....d.	0625	0739	|	0820	0825	0908	|	0955	1120	|	|	1210	1315	|	1403	|	1608	1730	1805	1952	|	|	2200
144	Mazara del Vallo ....d.	0644	0805	|	0843	0845	0928	|	1020	1143	|	|	1230	1339	|	1422	|	1627	1749	1829	2014	|	|	...
165	Marsala............................d.	0706	0826	|	0902	0905	0945	|	1038	1209	|	|	1250	1358	|	1450	|	1648	1806	1856	2031	|	|	...
196	**Trapani** ....a.	0740	0855	0747	0930	0935	1015	0945	1105	1235	1150	1205	1320	1435	1352	1520	1605	1715	1840	1920	2100	2010	2055	...

km		⚒	⚒	⚒	⚒	†	⚒	⚒	⚒	⚒	†	†	†	⚒		⚒	⚒				⚒			
0	**Trapani** ....d.	0502	0540	0650	0605	0730	0757	0810	0940	0830	0910	1030	1120	1140	1250	1325	1423	1425	1725	1620	1735	1815	1940	2030
	Marsala............................d.	|	|	|	0640	|	0825	|	|	0902	0936	|	1146	1208	1320	1358	1449	|	|	1649	1807	1838	|	2101
	Mazara del Vallo ....d.	|	|	|	0710	|	0842	|	|	0928	0955	|	1204	1225	1339	1423	1508	|	|	1706	1828	1857	|	2118
	Castelvetrano ....d.	|	|	|	0738	|	0900	|	|	0947	1015	|	1230	1245	1410	1445	1528	|	|	1726	1850	1920	|	2140
47	Alcamo Diramazione............d.	0538	0615	0725	0815	0807	...	0851	1020	1025	1057	1107	...	1327	1450	...	...	1503	1805	1810	...	2000	2018	...
53	Castellammare del Golfo.......d.	0546	...	0733	0822	0815	...	0858	...	1033	...	1114	...	1336	...	...	...	1517	...	1818	...	...	2025	...
126	**Palermo Centrale** ....a.	0725	...	0905	0955	0955	...	...	...	1205	...	1255	...	1525	...	...	...	1635	...	1955	...	...	2155	...

647 PALERMO - AGRIGENTO

2nd class only

km		⚒				⚒	†	⚒	⚒	y		⚒	
0	**Palermo C 645**.......... d.	0735	0835	1035	1235	1335	1435	1435	1535	1635	1735	1835	2015
37	Termini-Imerese **645**.. d.	0803	0901	1101	1301	1403	1501	1501	1601	1701	1801	1902	2043
70	Roccapalumba-Alia **645**. d.	0834	0930	1128	1329	1433	1527	1533	1632	1734	1831	1935	2112
125	Aragona-Caldare **645**. d.	0924	1019	1220	1430	1521	1616	1635	1723	1826	1928	2024	2200
139	**Agrigento C 645** .... a.	0940	1035	1235	1445	1540	1635	1650	1740	1840	1945	2040	2215

	⚒	⚒	⚒				⚒	y			
Agrigento C 645 .... d.	0450	0543	0655	0815	1100	1325	1415	1530	1620	1810	2005
Aragona-Caldare **645**. d.	0505	0558	0710	0830	1115	1340	1434	1545	1635	1826	2024
Roccapalumba-Alia **645** d.	0558	0647	0800	0931	1206	1433	1533	1632	1734	1918	2112
Termini-Imerese **645**. d.	0630	0720	0835	1000	1230	1500	1600	1700	1800	1942	2140
Palermo C 645 .... a.	0700	0750	0900	1030	1300	1530	1630	1730	1830	2010	2210

y – ⚒ (daily Sept. 15 - Dec. 8).

MALTA

Bus services are operated by ATP (www.atp.com.mt) on behalf of the Government's Transport Department ADT (www.maltatransport.com) and operate frequently throughout Malta.

649 PRINCIPAL BUS SERVICES

Approx frequency (in minutes) shown in *italics*

Routes from Valletta: 1/2/4/6 Vittoriosa (*10-15*), 3 Senglea (*20*), 8 Airport (*30*), 11-13 Birzebugia (*10-15*), 17-21 Zabbar / Marsascala (*10*), 27-30 Marsaxlokk (*10-15*), 32/34 Zurrieq (*20-30*), 45 Cirkewwa for Gozo ferry (*20*), 49/57-59 Mosta / Bugibba (*7-10*), 54-56 Naxxar (*15*), 62/64/66/67/68 Sliema / St Julians (*5*), 80/81/84 Rabat / Dingli (*10-15*), 88 Zebbug (*15*), 89 Siggiewi (*20*).
Routes from Sliema: 65 Mosta / Rabat (*30*), 645 Bugibba / Cirkewwa for Gozo ferry (*30*), 652 Bugibba / Golden Bay (*30*). **Gozo**: service 25 Victoria - Mgarr connects with ferries.

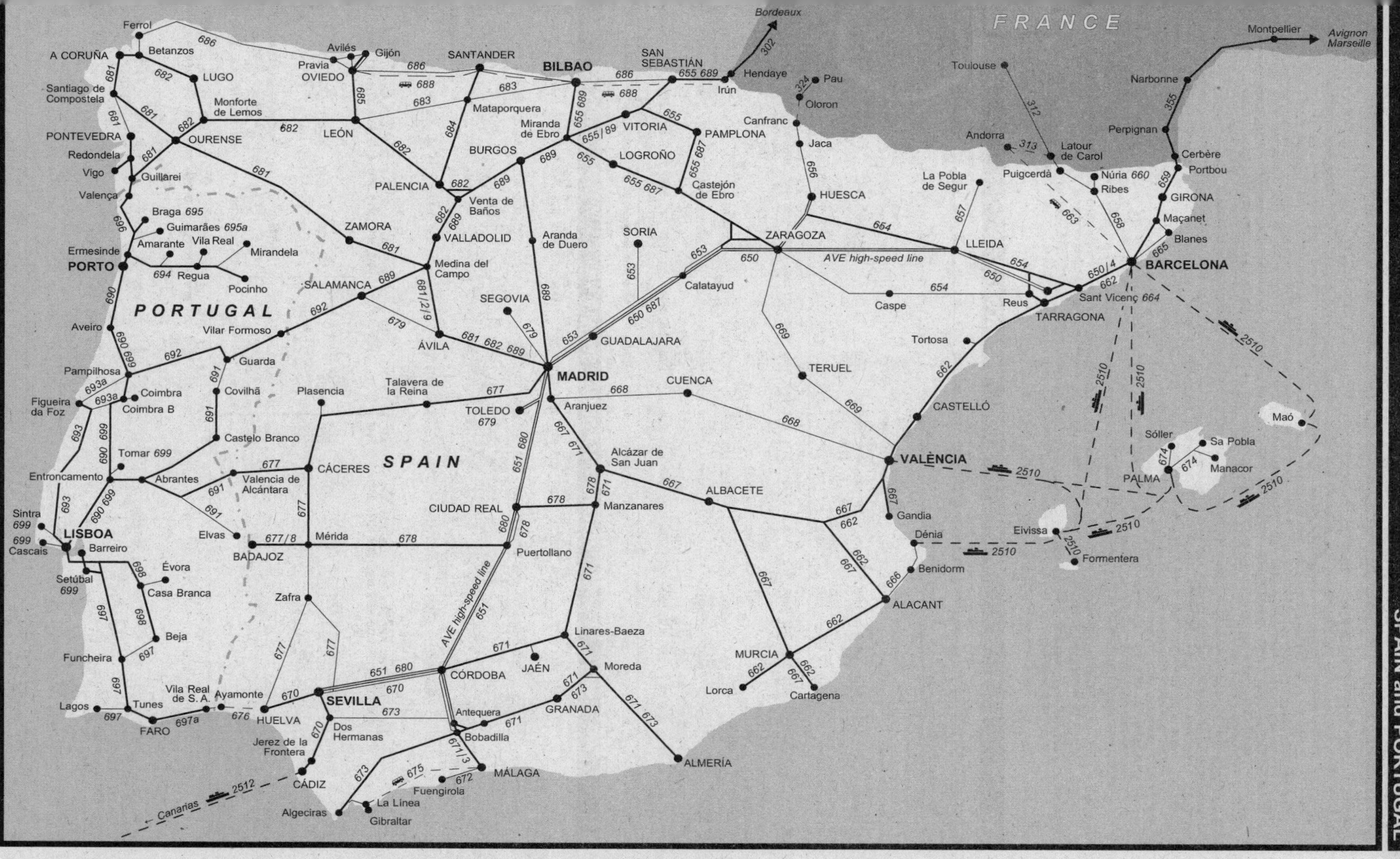
FRANCE
SPAIN
PORTUGAL
Avignon Marseille
Montpellier
Narbonne
Perpignan
Cerbère
Portbou
GIRONA
Maçanet
Blanes
BARCELONA
Núria 660
Ribes
Latour de Carol
Puigcerdà
Toulouse
Andorra
La Pobla de Segur
LLEIDA
Sant Vicenç 664
TARRAGONA
Reus
Tortosa
Caspe
CASTELLÓ
VALÈNCIA
Gandia
Dénia
Benidorm
ALACANT
Eivissa
Formentera
PALMA
Sóller
Sa Pobla
Manacor
Maó
Bordeaux
Hendaye
Irún
Pau
Oloron
Canfranc
Jaca
HUESCA
ZARAGOZA
AVE high-speed line
PAMPLONA
Castejón de Ebro
SAN SEBASTIÁN
VITORIA
LOGROÑO
SORIA
Calatayud
GUADALAJARA
TERUEL
CUENCA
ALBACETE
MURCIA
Cartagena
Lorca
ALMERÍA
BILBAO
Miranda de Ebro
BURGOS
Aranda de Duero
MADRID
Aranjuez
Alcázar de San Juan
Manzanares
SANTANDER
Mataporquera
Venta de Baños
VALLADOLID
SEGOVIA
TOLEDO 679
CIUDAD REAL
Puertollano
Linares-Baeza
Moreda
GRANADA
JAÉN
CÓRDOBA
Antequera
Bobadilla
MÁLAGA
Fuengirola
La Línea
Gibraltar
Algeciras
Gijón
Avilés
Pravia
OVIEDO
LEÓN
PALENCIA
Medina del Campo
ÁVILA
Talavera de la Reina
CÁCERES
Mérida
BADAJOZ
Zafra
SEVILLA
Dos Hermanas
HUELVA
Jerez de la Frontera
CÁDIZ
Ayamonte
ZAMORA
SALAMANCA
Plasencia
Valencia de Alcántara
Elvas
A CORUÑA
Ferrol
Betanzos
LUGO
Monforte de Lemos
OURENSE
Santiago de Compostela
PONTEVEDRA
Redondela
Vigo
Valença
Guillarei
Braga 695
Guimarães 695a
Amarante
Vila Real
Mirandela
Regua
Pocinho
Ermesinde
PORTO
Aveiro
Vilar Formoso
Guarda
Covilhã
Castelo Branco
Abrantes
Tomar 699
Coimbra
Coimbra B
Pampilhosa
Figueira da Foz
Entroncamento
LISBOA
Sintra 699
Cascais 699
Barreiro
Setúbal 699
Évora
Casa Branca
Beja
Funcheira
Tunes
Lagos
FARO
Vila Real de S. A.
Canarias
AVE high-speed line

 For new high-speed services from Dec. 23/24, see page 54

SPAIN

Operator: **Renfe Operadora** (www.renfe.es) – unless otherwise indicated.

Services: On long-distance trains first class is known as *Preferente* and second class as *Turista*; a 'super-first class' – *Club* – is additionally available on *AVE* trains. Unless otherwise indicated (by '2' in the train column or [2] in the notes), all trains convey both first- and second-class seating accommodation.

🍸 indicates a buffet car (*cafeteria*) or a mobile trolley service. 🍴 indicates a full restaurant car service or the availability of hot meals served from the buffet car. Meals a served free of extra charge to holders of *Club* and *Preferente* tickets on all *AVE* trains and to holders of *Preferente* tickets on *Alaris*, *Altaria*, *Alvia*, *Euromed*, *Talgo 200*, a *Trenhotel* services. Note that catering services may not be available throughout a train's journey, particularly in the case of trains with multiple origins / destinations.

🛏 indicates coaches equipped with couchettes: for occupancy of these a standard supplement is payable in addition to the normal *Turista* fare. 🛌 indicates sleeping-ca with single, double, and 3- or 4-berth compartments. The *Turista* fare is payable plus a sleeping-car supplement corresponding to the type and standard of accommodatic **Trenhotel** services additionally convey *Gran Clase* accommodation: *de luxe* single- and double-occupancy compartments with *en suite* shower and toilet. *Preferente* fare payable for travel in *Gran Clase* plus a sleeping-car supplement corresponding to the type and standard of accommodation.

Train categories:

- ☐ ***Alaris***: Fast tilting trains on the Madrid - Albacete - València line.
- ☐ ***Altaria*** (*Alta*) and ***Talgo 200*** (*T200*): Talgo trains which can change gauge and run on the high-speed lines as well as the broad-gauge system.
- ☐ ***Alta Velocidad Española*** (*AVE*): High-speed trains running on the Madrid - Sevilla and Madrid - Huesca / Camp de Tarragona standard-gauge lines.
- ☐ ***Alvia***: The newest high-speed trains running between Madrid and Barcelona.
- ☐ ***Arco*** and ***Intercity*** (*IC*): Quality day express trains.
- ☐ ***Avant*** (*AV*): Medium-distance high-speed trains on the standard-gauge line
- ☐ ***Diurno*** (*D*): Ordinary long-distance day trains.
- ☐ ***Estrella*** (*Estr*): Night trains, conveying 🛌, 🛏, [1] and [2] as indicate
- ☐ ***Euromed*** (*Em*): Trains similar of similar construction to *AVE* but running o the broad-gauge Barcelona - València - Alacant route.
- ☐ ***Talgo***: Quality express trains using light, articulated stock.
- ☐ ***Trenhotel*** (*Hotel*): Quality night express trains (see Services, above)

Local ('Regional') trains are shown without an indication of category except for fast ***Tren Regional Diesel*** (*TRD*) and ***R-598*** services.

Reservations: Reservations are available on services for which a train number is shown. They are **compulsory** for all journeys by services for which a **train category** (e.g. *D*, *IC*, *TRD*) shown in the timing column. A reservation fee paid to the conductor on board the train costs more than one bought in advance.

Supplements: Higher fares, incorporating a supplement, are payable for travel by *Alaris*, *Altaria*, *Alvia*, *Arco*, *Euromed*, *InterCity*, *Talgo*, and *Talgo 200* trains. 'Global' fares – i.e. inclusive accommodation – are payable for travel by the international hotel trains from Barcelona to Milano / Paris / Zürich and v.v., and Madrid - Paris and v.v.

Timings: Timings have been compiled from the latest information supplied by operators.

650 MADRID - ZARAGOZA - BARCELONA — High-speed services

km		Alvia 1069 ①–⑥	AVE 9815 ①–⑤	Alta 601 ①–⑤	Alvia 1079	AVE 9819	Alvia 1109	AVE 9823 ①–⑤	Alvia 1119	AVE 9827 Ⓑ	Alta 1138	Alta 609	AVE 9831 Ⓑ	Alvia 1159 Ⓑ	AVE 9881 ①–④	AVE 9881 ⑤⑦	AVE 9835	Alvia 1169	Alvia 1189	Alta 701 Ⓑ	AVE 9887	AVE 9839	Alvia 1199 ⑤⑦	AVE 9841 Ⓑ	AV 989 Ⓑ
	Cádiz **670** d.	...	...	...	...	...	...	...	...	...	0740	...	...	...	...	...	...	...	...	...	...	...	...	...	...
0	**Madrid** Pta de Atocha d.	0625	0705	0715	0815	0905	1025	1115	1145	1250	1305	1405	1500	1545	1615	1615	1700	1715	1755	1810	1855	1905	1940	2010	213
64	Guadalajara - Yebes d.	|	0728	0743	0843	0928	|	|	1213	|	|	1433	|	|	|	|	|	1743	|	1838	|	1928	|	|	215
221	Calatayud d.	|	0809	0838	0936	1009	|	|	1306	|	|	1528	|	|	|	|	|	1836	|	1933	|	2009	|	|	223
307	**Zaragoza** Delicias d.	0810	0837	...	1010	1037	1210	1237	1340	1412	1450	...	1622	|	1736	1737	1822	1910	1940	...	2017	2037	|	2132	230
	Huesca **656** a.	|	|	...	|	|	|	|	|	|	|	...	|	|	...	1821	|	|	|	...	|	2122	|	|	...
447	Lleida d.	0905	0925	...	1105	1125	1305	1325	1435	|	1549	...	1710	|	...	...	1910	2005	2035	...	|	...	|	2220	...
526	Camp de Tarragona a.	|	0955	...	|	1155	|	1353	|	1518	1620	...	1738	|	...	...	1938	|	|	...	2123	...	|	2248	...
610	**Barcelona** Sants a.	1043	...	...	1243	...	1443	...	1613	...	1742	...	...	1942	...	...	...	2143	2213	...	...	...	2335	...	...
	Barcelona França a.	1107	...	...	1305	...	1505	...	1635	...	...	...	...	2005	...	...	...	2207	2235	...	...	...	2356	...	...

	AVE 9814 ①–⑥	AVE 9816 ①–⑥	AVE 9898	Alta 802 ①–⑥	AVE 9868	Alta 702 ①–⑥	Alvia 1578		Alvia 1598	AVE 9876 ①–⑤	Alta 1619	AVE 9830 Ⓑ	Alvia 1638	AVE 9884	Alvia 1658 Ⓑ	Alta 606 Ⓑ	AVE 9886 Ⓑ	Alvia 1668	AVE 9888 Ⓑ	Alvia 1678 Ⓑ	AVE 9890 ①–④	AVE 9890 ⑤⑦	Alvia 1688	AVE 9892 Ⓑ	Alvi 169 ⑤⑦
Barcelona França d.	...	...	...	...	...	...	0700	...	0900	...	...	...	1300	...	1500	...	...	1600	...	1700	...	...	1800	...	190
Barcelona Sants d.	...	...	...	...	...	...	0730	...	0930	...	1130	...	1330	...	1530	...	...	1630	...	1730	...	...	1830	...	193
Camp de Tarragona d.	...	0645	...	...	0815	...	|	...	|	1155	1243	1345	|	1615	|	...	1725	|	1820	|	...	...	|	2005	|
Lleida d.	...	0712	...	...	0842	...	0902	...	1103	1222	1315	|	1502	1642	|	...	|	1800	1847	|	...	...	2001	2033	205
Huesca **656** d.	...	|	0745	...	|	...	|	...	|	|	|	|	|	|	|	...	|	|	|	|	...	1935	|	|	|
Zaragoza Delicias d.	0700	0800	0830	...	0930	...	1005	...	1200	1310	1410	1450	1600	1730	|	...	1826	1900	1935	|	2020	2020	2100	2125	215
Calatayud d.	0727	|	0857	0913	|	1016	1038	...	|	|	|	|	1632	|	|	1832	|	1932	|	|	|	|	|	2152	|
Guadalajara - Yebes d.	0808	|	0938	1007	|	1110	1131	...	|	|	|	|	1725	|	|	1925	|	2025	|	|	|	|	|	2233	|
Madrid Pta de Atocha a.	0835	0925	1005	1037	1055	1140	1200	...	1350	1435	1600	1615	1755	1855	1930	1955	2000	2055	2100	2130	2145	2145	2250	2300	234
Cádiz **670** a.	...	...	...	...	...	...	...	...	...	...	2129	...	...	...	...	...	...	...	...	...	...	...	...	...	...

☛ All trains convey 🍸. *AVE* trains also convey 🍴. For other high-speed trains Madrid – Calatayud, see Table **687**. **Trains showed shaded do not run in August.**

651 MADRID - CÓRDOBA - SEVILLA — High-speed services

km		AVE 9662 ①–⑤	AVE 9614 ①–⑤	T200 9114	AVE 9664	Alta 9214 ①–⑥	AVE 9616 ①–⑥	AVE 9666 ①–⑥	Alta 9366	AVE 9618	T200 9118	AVE 9620 ①–⑥	Alta 9320	AVE 9622	Alta 9222 ⑦	AVE 9624	T200 9124	AVE 9626	AVE 9628	T200 9128	AVE 9630 Ⓑ	AVE 9632	AVE 9682 ⑤⑦	Alta 1619	AVE 9634	Alt 938
	Barcelona Sants **650** d.	...	...	...	...	...	...	...	...	...	...	...	...	...	...	...	...	...	...	...	...	...	...	1130	...	...
0	**Madrid** Pta de Atocha d.	0630	0700	0705	0730	0735	0800	0830	0835	0900	0930	1000	1005	1100	1135	1200	1210	1300	1400	1435	1500	1600	1630	1610	1700	170
171	Ciudad Real d.	0721	|	|	0821	0837	|	|	0936	0951	1031	|	1106	|	|	|	|	1351	|	|	|	|	|	1716	1751	|
210	Puertollano d.	0737	|	|	0837	0855	|	|	0952	1007	1047	|	1122	|	|	|	|	1407	|	|	|	|	|	1738	1807	|
345	**Córdoba** d.	0822	0844	0907	0922	0946	|	1014	1038	1052	1136	1144	1210	1244	|	1344	1412	1452	1544	1637	1644	1744	1814	1825	1852	190
	Málaga **671** a.	|	|	1053	|	|	|	|	|	|	1330	|	|	|	|	|	1606	|	|	1828	|	|	|	|	|	|
	Algeciras **673** a.	|	|	...	|	|	|	|	1400	|	...	|	|	|	|	|	...	|	|	...	|	|	|	|	|	222
	Granada **671 / 3** a.	|	|	...	|	1215	|	|	...	|	...	|	|	|	1608	|	...	|	|	...	|	|	|	|	|	...
471	**Sevilla** a.	0905	0930	...	1005	...	1020	1100	...	1135	...	1230	1318	1330	...	1430	...	1535	1630	...	1730	1830	1900	1934	1935	...
	Huelva **670** a.	...	...	...	...	...	...	...	...	...	...	...	|	...	...	...	...	...	...	...	...	...	...	|	...	...
	Cádiz **670** a.	...	...	...	...	...	...	...	...	...	...	...	1500	...	...	...	...	...	...	...	...	...	...	2129	...	...

	AVE 9636	Alta 9386	T200 9136	AVE 9638 Ⓑ	Alta 9238	AVE 9688	AVE 9640 Ⓑ	T200 9140	AVE 9642		AVE 9644
Barcelona Sants **650** d.	...	...	...	...	...	...	...	...	...	...	...
Madrid Pta de Atocha d.	1800	1805	1825	1900	1905	1930	2000	2010	2100	...	2200
Ciudad Real d.	|	|	1926	|	|	2021	|	|	|	...	2251
Puertollano d.	|	|	1942	|	|	2037	|	|	|	...	2307
Córdoba d.	1944	2013	2031	2044	2106	2122	2144	2212	2244	...	2352
Málaga **671** a.	|	|	2225	|	|	|	|	2357	|	...	|
Algeciras **673** a.	|	|	...	|	|	|	|	...	|	...	|
Granada **671 / 3** a.	|	|	...	|	2333	|	|	...	|	...	|
Sevilla a.	2030	|	...	2130	...	2205	2230	...	2330	...	0035
Huelva **670** a.	...	2223	...	...	...	...	...	...	...	...	...
Cádiz **670** a.	...	...	...	...	...	...	...	...	...	...	...

	AVE 9663 ①–⑤	AVE 9615 ①–⑤	AVE 9665	AVE 9617 ①–⑥	T200 9115	AVE 9667 ①–⑥	Alta 9213 ①–⑥	AVE 9619	Alta 9365	Alta 113
Cádiz **670** d.	...	...	...	...	...	...	...	...	...	074
Huelva **670** d.	...	...	...	...	...	...	...	...	0740	|
Sevilla d.	0630	0700	0730	0800	...	0830	...	0900	|	092
Granada **671 / 3** d.	|	|	|	|	...	|	0650	|	|	|
Algeciras **673** d.	|	|	|	|	...	|	|	|	|	|
Málaga **671** d.	|	|	|	|	0700	|	|	|	|	|
Córdoba d.	0713	0744	0813	|	0847	0914	0918	0943	0953	103
Puertollano d.	0755	|	0855	|	|	|	|	1025	|	112
Ciudad Real d.	0811	|	0911	|	|	|	|	1041	|	114
Madrid Pta de Atocha a.	0905	0930	1005	1020	1051	1100	1125	1135	1204	124
Barcelona Sants **650** a.	...	...	...	...	...	...	...	...	...	174

	AVE 9621 ①–⑥	T200 9119	AVE 9623	Alta 9367	AVE 9625	Alta 9221 ⑦	AVE 9627	AVE 9629	T200 9127	AVE 9631 Ⓑ		AVE 9633	T200 9131	AVE 9683 ⑤⑦	AVE 9635	AVE 9637	Alta 9333	AVE 9639 Ⓑ	T200 9137	Alta 9383	AVE 9689	AVE 9641 Ⓑ	Alta 9237	AVE 9643	T200 9141	AV 964
Cádiz **670** d.	...	...	...	...	...	...	...	...	...	...	...	...	...	...	...	...	1615	...	...	...	...	...	...	...	...	...
Huelva **670** d.	...	...	...	...	...	...	...	...	...	...	...	...	...	...	...	...	|	...	...	...	...	...	...	...	...	...
Sevilla d.	1000	...	1100	...	1200	...	1300	1400	...	1500	...	1600	...	1630	1700	1800	1800	1900	...	...	1930	2000	...	2100	...	220
Granada **671 / 3** d.	|	...	|	...	|	1025	|	|	...	|	...	|	...	|	|	|	|	|	...	...	|	|	1850	|	...	|
Algeciras **673** d.	|	...	|	0840	|	|	|	|	...	|	...	|	...	|	|	|	|	|	...	1640	|	|	|	|	...	|
Málaga **671** d.	|	0915	|	|	|	|	|	|	1305	|	...	|	1500	|	|	|	|	|	1800	|	|	|	|	|	2005	|
Córdoba d.	1044	1107	1144	1155	1244	|	1343	1444	1450	1544	...	1644	1647	1714	1743	1844	1908	1944	1946	1958	2013	2044	2116	2144	2151	224
Puertollano d.	|	1157	|	|	|	|	1425	|	|	|	...	|	1735	|	1825	|	1955	|	|	2046	2055	|	2204	|	|	232
Ciudad Real d.	|	1214	|	|	|	|	1441	|	|	|	...	|	1755	|	1841	|	2011	|	|	2103	2111	|	2221	|	|	234
Madrid Pta de Atocha a.	1230	1318	1330	1402	1430	1458	1535	1630	1654	1730	...	1830	1900	1900	1935	2030	2122	2130	2148	2214	2205	2230	2325	2330	2353	003
Barcelona Sants **650** a.	...	...	...	...	...	...	...	...	...	...	...	...	...	...	...	...	...	...	...	...	...	...	...	...	...	...

☛ All trains convey 🍸. *AVE* trains also convey 🍴. For other high-speed trains Madrid – Puertollano and Córdoba – Sevilla, see Table **680**.

MADRID - SORIA and ZARAGOZA — 653

km	For high-speed trains see Table 650		TRD 8801			7308	TRD 8803		7012			TRD 8805						TRD 8807				7304			Estr 370
		2	2	2	2	2	2	2	2	2		2	2		2	2	2	2	2	2		2	2		B
		①–⑤	①–⑤	⑥⑦	①–⑤		①–⑤	⑥⑦		①–⑥		①–⑤	⑦				⑤	①–⑤	b	⑤					
0	**Madrid** Chamartín d.	...	...	...	0700	0815	...	0915	1030	...	...	...	...	...	...	*1422*	1548	...	*1637*	1715	...	1915	2010	...	2200
55	Guadalajara d.	...	...	...	0739	0853u	...	0952	1105	...	...	...	...	...	...	1528	1626u	...	1751	1751	...	1955u	2048	...	2242
138	Sigüenza d.	...	...	...	0842	0945	...	1055	1158	...	...	...	...	...	...	1631	1720	...	1854	1854	...	2052	2150	...	2335
248	**Soria** a.	...	...	...	|	1112	...	|	|	...	...	...	...	...	...	...	1850	...	|	...	...	2215	|	...	|
178	Arcos de Jalón d.	0645	...	0855	0910	...	...	1124	1223	1255	...	...	...	...	1735j	...	...	...	1922d	...	...	...	2219	...	0004
241	Calatayud d.	0731	0815	0939	...	...	1140	...	1259	1341	...	1515	1630	...	1825	...	...	2020	...	...	...	...	...	...	0042
339	**Zaragoza** Delicias a.	0853	0925	1102	...	...	1237	...	1400	1452	...	1612	1750	...	1945	...	...	2117	...	...	...	...	...	...	...

For high-speed trains see Table 650	Estr 373			7305		7303	TRD 8800				TRD 8802					TRD 8804			7309	7011	TRD 8806				
	C	2		2	2	2	2	2		2	2	2		2	2	2	2	2	2	2	2	2	2		2
		①–⑤		①–⑤	⑥⑦	⑥⑦	①–⑤	①–⑤		⑥⑦	①–⑤			b	⑤	①–⑤		⑦	①–⑥		①–⑤	⑦			
Zaragoza Delicias d.	...	...	...	...	...	...	0645	0745	...	0915	0935	...	...	...	...	1410	1510	...	...	1725	1840	...	...	...	2020
Calatayud d.	0417	...	...	...	...	...	0751	0909	...	1035	1038	...	...	...	...	1507	1626	...	...	1823	1937	...	...	...	2139
Arcos de Jalón d.	0455	0621	...	...	0840	...	...	0957	...	1125	...	1230	...	...	...	...	1715f	...	...	1900	...	...	1935d	...	2228
Soria d.	|	|	...	0740	|	0845	...	...	...	...	...	|	...	...	...	...	...	1645	1740	|	...	1825	|	...	...
Sigüenza d.	0523	0652	...	0900	0911	1006	...	...	...	...	...	1301	...	1645	1700	...	...	1813	1903	1925	...	1947	2005	...	...
Guadalajara a.	0612	0753	...	0949s	1012	1054s	...	...	...	...	...	1402	...	1746	1801	...	...	1903s	1954s	2015	...	2039s	2103	...	...
Madrid Chamartín a.	0721	0833	...	1028	1052	1135	...	...	...	...	...	*1515*q	...	*1900*	1840	...	...	1945	2035	2055	...	2123	2143	...	...

☛ **FOR NOTES**, SEE TABLE **655** BELOW.

ZARAGOZA - BARCELONA — 654

km	For high-speed trains see Table 650	Estr 370			Estr 930			Estr 920	5650		5550				Talgo 530							Talgo 620		5508
		B		2	P🍷 ¶	2	2	G🍷	2	2	2	2	2	2	M🍷	2	2	2	2	2	2	D🍷	2	2
									①–⑤		⑥⑦						①–⑤	①–⑥	⑦					
	Madrid Chamartín **653** d.	2200	...	...	...	...	...	...	...	...	...	...	...	...	...	...	...	...	...	...	...	...	...	...
0	**Zaragoza** Delicias d.	|	...	...	0359	...	...	0600	0630	...	0905	...	1220	...	1445	...	1510	...	...	1650	...	1908	2030	2045
114	Caspe d.	|	...	...	|	...	0720	|	|	...	|	...	1345	...	|	...	|	...	...	1813	...	|	2200	|
★	Lleida d.	|	...	...	0614	0710	|	0803	0835	...	1115	1310	|	1545	1651	...	1715	1750	1750	|	...	2109	...	2310
239	Reus d.	0536	...	0643	0719	|	0911	0926	...	1110	...	1437	1540	1714	1803	1841	...	|	|	2003	2118	|	...	...
257	Tarragona **662** d.	0610	...	0700	0736	|	0925	0943	...	1125	...	1454	1557	1728	1816	1857	...	|	|	2020	2134	|	...	...
282	Sant Vicenç de Calders **662** d.	0638	...	0719	0800	0845	0945	|	...	1145	...	1515	1618	1747	|	1917	...	1910	1927	2040	2200	2227	...	...
342	**Barcelona** Sants **662** a.	0735	...	0819	0900	0942	1038	1108	...	1238	...	1608	1708	1836	1921	2011	...	2008	2015	2138	2302	2324	...	...
345	Barcelona Pass. de Gràcia a.	|	...	0823	...	0947	1046	...	...	1243	...	1613	1713	1841	...	2016	...	2013	2021	2143	2307	...	...	...
	Cerbère **659** a.	1035	...	...	...	|	|	...	...	|	...	...	|	|	...	...	...	|	|	...	...	...	...	...
350	**Barcelona** França a.	...	...	...	...	0955	1056	...	...	1251	...	...	1721	1849	...	...	...	2021	2029	...	...	...	...	...

For high-speed trains see Table 650		5507			Talgo 623	5517						Talgo 533	5657							Estr 923			Estr 933	Estr 373
	2	2	2	2	E🍷	2	2	2	2		2	N🍷	2	2		2	2	2	2	G🍷	2	2	Q🍷 ¶	C
	①–⑥	①–⑤	⑦			⑥																		
Barcelona França d.	...	...	...	...	...	...	...	...	...	...	...	...	...	1347	...	...	1648	1717	1847	...	2018	2118	...	...
Portbou **659** d.	...	...	...	...	...	...	...	...	...	...	...	...	...	|	...	...	|	|	|	...	|	|	...	1940
Barcelona Pass. de Gràcia d.	...	...	...	0624	...	...	0701	0728	0855	...	1158	...	...	1355	...	1555	1656	1725	1855	...	2026	2126	...	|
Barcelona Sants **662** d.	...	...	...	0633	0703	...	0706	0733	0903	...	1203	1230	...	1403	...	1603	1703	1733	1903	2000	2033	2133	2200	2220
Sant Vicenç de Calders **662** d.	...	...	...	0718	0744	...	0814	0818	0948	...	1248	|	...	1447	...	1648	1747	1818	1948	|	2118	2222	2242	2317
Tarragona **662** d.	...	...	...	0739	|	...	|	0839	1009	...	1308	1327	...	1509	...	1708	1809	1837	|	2056	2139	2243	2300	2341
Reus d.	...	...	...	0754	|	...	|	0855	1028	...	1326	1341	...	1529	...	1724	1827	1852	|	2110	2154	2258	2314	2356
Lleida d.	...	0620	...	...	0855	0925	1005	...	|	...	1455	1441	1500	1650	...	|	1958	|	2124	2216	...	...	0015	|
Caspe d.	0655	|	0828	...	|	|	...	...	1240	...	...	|	|	...	...	1920	...	2047	...	|	...	...	|	0135
Zaragoza Delicias a.	0820	0845	0954	...	1045	1148	...	...	1411	...	...	1643	1720	...	...	2100	...	...	...	0010	...	...	0214	|
Madrid Chamartín **653** a.	...	...	...	...	...	...	...	...	...	...	...	...	...	...	...	...	...	...	...	...	...	...	...	0721

☛ **FOR NOTES**, SEE TABLE **655** BELOW.

ZARAGOZA - IRÚN and BILBAO — 655

km		Estr 923	Estr 933	Estr 933	8069	8071	6023 6013*	Alta 601	Talgo 623	Alta 605	8021	8073	6025 6015*	Alta 609	8023	Talgo 533	Talgo 533	6071	6017	8075	6781	8077	Alta 701	Alta 801	
		G🍷	Q🍷 ¶	Q🍷	2V	2	2	🍷	E🍷	🍷	2	2	2	🍷	2	N🍷	N🍷	2	2	2	2	2	🍷	🍷	2
						①–⑥	①–⑥	①–⑤							⑤			①–⑤			⑦		Ⓑ	Ⓑ	Ⓑ
	Barcelona Sants **654** d.	2000	2200	2200	...	...	...	...	0703	...	...	...	...	...	...	1230	1230	...	...	...	...	...	...	...	...
	Madrid Pta de Atocha **650** d.	|	|	|	...	...	...	0715	|	0950	...	...	...	1405	...	|	|	...	...	...	...	...	1810	1930	...
0	**Zaragoza** Delicias d.	0015	0215	0215	...	0630	...	|	1050	|	1130	1433	...	|	1620	1648	1648	...	...	1745	...	1930	|	|	2117
94	Castejón de Ebro ★ d.	0106	0324	0440	...	0727	0730	1001	1141	|	1239	1541	1545	|	1715	1745	1755	...	...	1846	1900	2037	|	|	2224
182	**Pamplona / Iruña** d.	|	|	0536	...	|	0845	1055	1236	1320	1345	|	1639	1746	1822	1842	|	...	1940	|	2005	|	|	2259	...
234	Altsasu **689** d.	|	|	0610	...	|	0916p	...	|	...	...	|	1719p	|	...	1916	|	...	2015p	|	...	|	|	|	...
275	Vitoria / Gasteiz **689** d.	|	|	|	...	|	0947	...	1325	...	...	|	1753	|	...	|	|	...	2045	|	...	|	|	2348	...
321	San Sebastián / Donostia d.	|	|	0745	...	|	...	...	|	...	...	|	...	1924	...	2043	|	...	...	|	...	|	|	...	...
337	**Irún** **689** a.	|	|	0808	...	|	...	...	|	...	...	|	...	1941	...	2105	|	...	...	|	...	|	|	...	...
339	Hendaye **689** a.	|	|	0815	...	|	...	...	|	...	...	|	...	1946	...	2116	|	...	...	|	...	|	|	...	...
171	**Logroño** d.	0156	0420	...	0736	0830a	...	...	|	...	...	1637	...	...	...	...	1848	1900	...	1947	...	2140y	2150	...	...
242	Miranda de Ebro **689** d.	...	0610	...	0832	...	...	...	1344	...	...	...	...	...	...	...	1951	1957	...	...	...	...	...	...	...
347	**Bilbao** Abando **689** a.	...	0753	...	...	...	...	...	...	...	...	...	...	...	...	...	2142	...	...	...	...	...	...	...	...

	Estr 920		Alta 802	8072	Alta 702		6007	6070	Alta 602	Talgo 530	Talgo 530	6022	8076	Alta 606	6021	6078	8020	Talgo 620	Alta 610	8022	6011 6024*	8078	8017	Estr 930	Estr 930
	G🍷		🍷	2	🍷	2	2	2	🍷	M🍷	M🍷	2	2	🍷	2A	2	2	D🍷	🍷	2	2	2	2V	P🍷	P🍷 ¶
		①–⑤	①–⑥		①–⑥		①–⑥	①–⑤	Ⓑ			①–⑥		Ⓑ		y				⑦					
Bilbao Abando **689** d.	...	...	...	...	...	...	...	...	...	...	1005	...	...	...	...	...	...	...	...	...	...	...	...	...	2225
Miranda de Ebro **689** d.	...	...	...	...	...	...	...	0836	...	...	1151	...	...	...	1501	...	...	1601	...	...	...	...	2130	...	0043
Logroño d.	0404	...	...	0730a	0800	...	...	0935	...	...	1246	...	1337	...	|	1645	...	|	...	...	...	2010	2230	...	0141
Irún **689** d.	|	...	...	|	|	...	...	...	...	1030	|	...	|	...	|	|	...	|	1705	...	...	|	...	2240	|
San Sebastián / Donostia d.	|	...	...	|	|	...	...	...	...	1045	|	...	|	...	|	|	...	|	1721	...	...	|	...	2259	|
Vitoria / Gasteiz **689** d.	|	...	0610	|	|	...	0740	...	...	|	|	...	|	...	1530	|	...	1623	|	...	1905	|	...	|	|
Altsasu **689** d.	|	...	|	|	|	...	0810p	...	...	1159	|	...	|	...	1601p	|	...	|	|	...	1936p	|	...	0021	|
Pamplona / Iruña d.	|	...	0700	|	|	...	0842	...	1220	1232	|	1325	|	1617	1635	|	1645	1717	1900	1905	2010	|	...	0057	|
Castejón de Ebro d.	0457	0625	0750	0830	|	1030	...	...	|	1345	1345	1422	1433	|	...	1739	1747	1816	|	2006	2105	2116	...	0253	0253
Zaragoza Delicias a.	0555	0733	|	0940	|	1138	...	...	|	1440	1440	...	1535	|	...	...	1850	1905	|	2100	...	2224	...	0358	0358
Madrid Pta de Atocha **650** a.	|	...	1037	...	1140	...	...	...	1543	|	|	...	...	1955	...	...	...	|	2234	...	...	...	...	|	|
Barcelona Sants **654** a.	1108	...	...	...	...	...	...	...	...	1921	1921	...	...	...	...	...	...	2324	...	...	...	...	...	0900	0900

A – From Burgos on ①–⑥. Train **6009** from Vitoria.
B – COSTA BRAVA – 🛏, ▬ and (12) Madrid - Cerbère.
C – COSTA BRAVA – 🛏, ▬ and (12) Portbou - Madrid.
D – LAGOS DE COVADONGA – (12) Gijón - Barcelona. FINISTERRE – ①③⑤⑦: (12) A Coruña - Barcelona; ②④⑥: (12) Vigo - Barcelona.
E – LAGOS DE COVADONGA – (12) Barcelona - Gijón. FINISTERRE – ①③⑤: (12) Barcelona - Vigo; ②④⑥⑦: (12) Barcelona - A Coruña.
G – GALICIA – 🛏, ▬ and (1) A Coruña and Vigo - Barcelona and v.v.
M – MIGUEL DE UNAMUNO – (12) Bilbao, Irún and Salamanca - Barcelona.
N – MIGUEL DE UNAMUNO – (12) Barcelona - Bilbao, Hendaye and Salamanca.
P – PÍO BAROJA – Ⓑ. 🛏, ▬ and (1) Bilbao and Irún - Barcelona; 🛏, ▬ and (12) Gijón - Barcelona.
Q – PÍO BAROJA – Ⓑ. 🛏, ▬ and (1) Barcelona - Bilbao and Hendaye; 🛏, ▬ and (12) Barcelona - Gijón.
V – To / from Valladolid.

a – ①–⑤.
b – Not ⑤.
d – ⑦ only.
f – ⑤ only.
j – ⑤⑦ only.
p – Altsasu Pueblo (*230 km*).
q – *1530* on ⑥⑦.
s – Stops to set down only.
u – Stops to pick up only.
y – ⑤⑥⑦.

¶ – On ⑤⑦ conveys through cars from / to Salamanca (Table **689**).
* – Number from Pamplona.
★ – Calatayud - Castejón: *140 km*. Lleida - Reus: *90 km*. Lleida - Sant Vicenç: *106 km*. Zaragoza - Lleida: *189 km*.

656 ZARAGOZA - HUESCA - CANFRANC

2nd class (except *AVE* trains)

km		*TRD* 8821 ①–⑤		*TRD* 8823 ①–⑤	5646	*TRD* 8825 ①–⑤	*TRD* 8827 ①–⑥		*AVE* 9881 ⑤⑦	*TRD* 8829 Ⓑ	*AVE* 9839	*TRD* 8504 V
	Madrid ◇ **650** ... d.	...	...	...	...	...	...	...	1615	...	1905	...
0	**Zaragoza** Delicias d.	0645	0745	0905	1020	1205	1420	1520	1737	1840	2037	2041
58	Tardienta d.	0720	0835	0940	1115	1240	1455	1604	|	1915	2109	2134
80	**Huesca** d.	0735	0856	0955	1134	1255	1510	1624	1821	1930	2122	2146
115	Ayerbe d.	...	0948	...	1206	...	...	1708	...	...	...	...
174	Sabiñánigo d.	...	1052	...	1308	...	...	1819	...	...	...	...
190	Jaca ‡ d.	...	1110	...	1325	...	...	1837	...	...	...	...
215	**Canfranc 324** ‡ a.	...	1142	...	...	...	...	1913	...	...	...	...

	TRD 8511 V	*AVE* 9898	*TRD* 8861 ①–⑤		*TRD* 8863 ①–⑤	*TRD* 8865 ①–⑤	*TRD* 8867 ①–⑥	5647	*AVE* 9890 ⑤⑦	*TRD* 8869 Ⓑ	
Canfranc 324 ‡ d.	...	...	...	0715	...	...	...	...	...	...	1810
Jaca ‡ d.	...	...	...	0745	...	...	...	1545	...	...	1840
Sabiñánigo d.	...	...	...	0802	...	...	...	1602	...	...	1857
Ayerbe d.	...	...	...	0904	...	...	...	1704	...	...	2000
Huesca d.	0704	0745	0805	1000	1100	1305	1520	1743	1935	1947	2045
Tardienta d.	0718	0757	0819	1017	1114	1319	1534	1759	|	2001	2100
Zaragoza Delicias a.	0808	0825	0855	1105	1150	1355	1610	1840	2015	2037	2148
Madrid ◇ **650** ... a.	...	1005	...	...	...	...	...	...	2145	...	...

V – From / to Valencia.　　◇ – Madrid Puerta de Atocha.　　‡ – 🚌 Jaca bus station (± *2 km* from rail station) - Canfranc and v.v.: daily at 1455 from Jaca, 1330 from Canfranc; journey 30 minutes; operated by *Mancobús*.

657 LLEIDA - LA POBLA DE SEGUR

2nd class FGC

km											
0	**Lleida** d.	0600	0715	0905	...	1145	1345	1515	1750	...	2030
27	Balaguer d.	0623	0744	0934	...	1214	1419	1544	1819	...	2059
77	Tremp d.	...	...	1039	...	...	1524	...	...	...	2204
90	**La Pobla de Segur** a.	...	...	1055	...	...	1540	...	...	...	2220

La Pobla de Segur d.	...	0640	...	...	...	1256	...	...	...	1805
Tremp d.	...	0655	...	...	...	1311	...	...	...	1820
Balaguer d.	0630	0800	0945	...	1225	1416	...	1600	1830	1925
Lleida a.	0659	0830	1014	...	1254	1446	...	1629	1859	1955

658 BARCELONA - PUIGCERDÀ - LATOUR DE CAROL

2nd class

km											
0	**Barcelona** Sants d.	0700	0757	0917	1106	1206	1406	1516	1706	1857	2015
33	Granollers-Canovelles d.	0742	0836	0953	1148	1242	1447	1553	1747	1934	2051
74	Vic d.	0819	0922	1034	1234	1319	1522	1626	1820	2010	2129
90	Torelló d.	0834	0939	1051	1249	1335	1535	1644	1838	2029	2144
110	Ripoll d.	0855	1005	1112	1311	1357	1555	1706	1902	2053	2205
124	Ribes de Freser **660** d.	0914	1023	1134	...	1416	...	1727	1923	2114	...
145	La Molina d.	0951	...	1211	...	1454	...	1804	2004	2148	...
159	Puigcerdà d.	1011	...	1232	...	1516	...	1825	2024	2209	...
163	**Latour de Carol** 🏛 **312** a.	1017	...	1238	...	1522	...	1831	...	...	...

	Ⓐ									
Latour de Carol 🏛 **312** d.	...	...	0815	1031	...	1315	...	1628	...	1842
Puigcerdà d.	...	0631	0822	1042	...	1326	...	1636	...	1853
La Molina d.	...	0653	0844	1105	...	1348	...	1658	...	1916
Ribes de Freser **660** d.	...	0724	0916	1138	...	1421	1620c	1729	...	1948
Ripoll d.	0634	0745	0938	1157	1329	1440	1639	1751	1832	2007
Torelló d.	0654	0806	0958	1217	1356	1505	1706	1819	1858	2031
Vic d.	0708	0821	1013	1233	1413	1520	1724	1838	1912	2046
Granollers-Canovelles d.	0742	0857	1051	1308	1506	1600	1808	1912	1953	2118
Barcelona Sants a.	0819	0937	1128	1346	1548	1637	1858	1949	2036	2158

☛ **Barcelona - Ripoll**: also at 1306**a**, 1616. **Ripoll - Barcelona**: also at 0901 ⚒, 1112 ⚒**b**.　　a – Continues to Ribes (a. 1529) on †.　　b – Starts from Ribes (d. 1055).　　c – † only.

659 BARCELONA - GIRONA - PORTBOU

For hotel trains Barcelona - Paris and v.v., see Table **45**; Barcelona - Zürich and v.v., see Table **49**; Barcelona - Milano and v.v., see Table **90**

km		2 ①–⑤	2 ①–⑤	2 ①–⑤	2 ⑥	2 ①–⑤	2 ①–⑤	*Estr* 370 🍷 C	*Talgo* 73 🍷 L	2	2	2	2	2	2 ⑥⑦	2 ①–⑤	2 ①–⑤	2 ①–⑥	2 ⑦	2	2 ⑦	2 ①–⑤	2	*Talgo* 460 🍷 A
0	**Barcelona** Sants **665** d.	...	0555	0625	0655	0655	0746	0752	0845a	0825	0925	1025	1125	1225	1325	1325	1355	1425	1425	1525	1555	1555	1625	1642
3	Barcelona Passeig de Gràcia d.	...	0600	0630	0700	0700	0751	|	|	0830	0930	1030	1129	1230	1330	1330	1359	1430	1430	1530	1600	1600	1630	|
31	Granollers Centre d.	...	0622	|	0724	0724	|	0827	|	0855	|	1049	1153	|	1351	1351	|	|	|	1557	|	|	|	|
72	Maçanet-Massanes **665** d.	...	0659	|	0803	0803	|	|	|	0934	|	|	1231	|	1432	1432	|	|	|	1632	|	|	|	|
86	Caldes de Malavella d.	...	0710	0729	0814	0814	0851	0906	|	0951	1031	1131	1242	1329	1443	1443	1502	1534	1534	1643	1703	1703	1731	|
102	**Girona** d.	...	0724	0740	0830	0830	0902	0925	0955	1007	1042	1142	1257	1340	1458	1459	1513	1545	1545	1659	1713	1714	1742	1748
118	Flaçà d.	...	0739	0752	0842	0845	0914	0938	|	1022	1054	1154	1312	1352	1511	1514	1525	1557	1557	1714	...	1726	1754	|
143	Figueres d.	0609	0802	0808	0859	0908	0930	0958	1025	1045	1110	1210	1335	1408	1531	1537	1541	1612	1613	1737	...	1742	1810	1815
162	Llançà d.	0625	0817	...	0912	0922	...	1016	|	1059	...	1223	1350	...	1544	1551	...	...	1627	1751	...	...	...	|
169	**Portbou** 🏛 a.	0634	0827	...	0922	0931	...	1025s	1049	1108	...	1230	1400	...	1554	1600	...	...	1634	1800	...	...	...	1837
171	**Cerbère** 🏛 **355** a.	0640	...	...	0926	0936	...	1035	1115	1113	...	...	1406	...	1600	1605	...	...	...	1805	...	...	...	1902

	2	2 ①–⑤	2	2 ①–⑤	2	2 ①–⑤	2	2 ⑦	2
Barcelona Sants **665** d.	1725	1755	1825	1855	1925	1955	2025	2055	2125
Barcelona Passeig de Gràcia d.	1730	1800	1829	1900	1930	2000	2030	2100	2130
Granollers Centre d.	1756	|	|	|	1954	|	|	|	|
Maçanet-Massanes **665** d.	1832	|	|	|	2029	|	|	|	|
Caldes de Malavella d.	1843	1906	1935	2005	2040	2105	2132	2200	2231
Girona d.	1858	1917	1946	2016	2055	2116	2144	2211	2242
Flaçà d.	1913	1929	1958	2028	2110	2128	2156	2223	...
Figueres d.	1936	1945	2014	2044	2134	2144	2212	2240	...
Llançà d.	1951	...	...	...	2150	...	...	...	...
Portbou 🏛 a.	2001	...	...	...	2201	...	...	...	...
Cerbère 🏛 **355** a.	2007	...	...	...	2207	...	...	...	...

	2	2 ①–⑤	2 ①–⑥	2 ⑦	2 ①–⑥	2		2	*Talgo* 463 🍷 A
Portbou 🏛 **355** d.	...	...	0710	...	...	0810	...	...	0952
Llançà d.	...	...	0719	...	...	0822	...	...	|
Figueres d.	0657z	0728	0734	0800	0832	0838	...	1000	1013
Flaçà d.	0713z	0745	0756	0815	0850	0901	...	1017	|
Girona d.	0727	0759	0812	0828	0903	0919	...	1030	1042
Caldes de Malavella d.	0738	0810	0826	0838	0915	0933	...	1042	|
Maçanet-Massanes **665** d.	|	|	0837	|	|	0944	...	|	|
Granollers Centre d.	|	|	0909	|	|	1019	...	|	|
Barcelona Passeig de Gràcia a.	0841	0911	0937	0937	1011	1041	...	1137	|
Barcelona Sants **665** a.	0846	0916	0942	0942	1016	1046	...	1142	1146

	2 Ⓑ	2 ⑥		2	2		2	2 ①–⑤	2 ①–⑤	2 ⑥⑦	2	2 ①–⑤	2 ①–⑤	2 ⑥⑦	2 ⑦	2 ①–⑥	2 ⑦	2 Ⓑ	2	2	*Talgo* 70 🍷 L	*Estr* 373 🍷 D	2 ①–⑤	2 ⑥⑦
Portbou 🏛 **355** d.	1014	1020	...	...	1215	...	1340	...	1412	1422	...	...	1612	1618	...	...	1740	...	1817y	1910	1935	1940	...	2030
Llançà d.	1023	1029	...	...	1224	...	1348	...	1421	1431	...	...	1621	1627	...	...	1747	...	1826y	1919	|	1950	...	2038
Figueres d.	1038	1045	...	1203	1239	...	1402	1431	1437	1447	1600	1630	1636	1643	...	1801	1801	1832	1840	1934	1954	2005	2033	2052
Flaçà d.	1100	1104	...	1220	1301	...	1417	1446	1459	1509	1616	1646	1658	1702	...	1815	1815	1847	1903	1956	|	2023	2050	2109
Girona d.	1115	1118	...	1233	1316	...	1430	1459	1515	1525	1629	1659	1713	1715	1756	1828	1828	1900	1918	2011	2020	2042	2103	2123
Caldes de Malavella d.	1131	1131	...	1244	1332	...	1441	1510	1529	1539	1640	1710	1729	1729	1807	1839	1839	1911	1934	2027	|	2055	2114	2134
Maçanet-Massanes **665** d.	1142	1142	...	|	1343	...	|	|	1540	1550	|	|	1740	1740	|	|	|	|	1945	2038	|	|	|	2145
Granollers Centre d.	1216	1216	...	|	1418	...	1516	|	1615	1624	|	|	1815	1815	|	|	|	|	2022	2119	|	2131	|	2218
Barcelona Passeig de Gràcia a.	1241	1241	...	1341	1441	...	1541	1611	1641	1648	1741	1811	1841	1841	1911	1941	1945	2011d	2046	2143	|	|	2211	2241
Barcelona Sants **665** a.	1246	1246	...	1346	1446	...	1546	1616	1646	1653	1746	1816	1846	1846	1916	1946	1950	2016d	2051	2148	2145a	2202	2216	2246

A – MARE NOSTRUM – (12) Cartagena - Montpellier and v.v.
C – COSTA BRAVA – 🛏, 🛏 and (12) Madrid - Cerbère.
D – COSTA BRAVA – 🛏, 🛏 and (12) Portbou - Madrid.
L – CATALÁN TALGO – (12) Barcelona - Montpellier and v.v.
V – From / to València.
a – Barcelona França.
d – 3 minutes later on ⑦.
s – Stops to set down only.
y – Not ⑥.
z – Not ⑦.

660 VALL DE NÚRIA

2nd class

Ribes Enllaç - **Queralbs** - **Núria** rack railway

From Ribes:
Ⓐ: 0925, 1105, 1245, 1510, 1650, 1740, 1840⑤, 2040⑤.
Ⓒ: 0830, 0920, 1010, 1100, 1150, 1240, 1330, 1420, 1510, 1600, 1650, 1740.

From Núria:
Ⓐ: 0830, 1015, 1155, 1400, 1600, 1740, 1830, 1930⑤, 2130⑤.
Ⓒ: 0830, 0920, 1010, 1100, 1150, 1240, 1330, 1420, 1510, 1650, 1740, 1830.

Journey times **Ribes** – **Queralbs** (*6 km*) 24 minutes, **Ribes** – **Núria** (*12 km*) 40 minutes.
Operator: Ferrocarrils de la Generalitat de Catalunya (FGC) ✆ +34 972 73 20 20.

661 AEROPORT ✈ BARCELONA

2nd class

Local rail service **Aeroport** ✈ - **Barcelona**　　Journey time ± 20 minutes

From Aeroport:
0600, 0630, 0700, 0731, 0801, 0830, 0901, 0930, 0959, 1029 and every 30 minutes until 1959; then 2028, 2059, 2129, 2159, 2229, 2259, 2344.

From Barcelona Sants:
0525, 0555 and every 30 minutes until 2255.
(Also 13 minutes earlier from **Barcelona** França.)

BARCELONA - VALÈNCIA - ALACANT - CARTAGENA 662

km			Alaris			Em		Arco		Em		Em		Arco			Talgo		Alaris		Em	Talgo		Em	
			1075			1071		697		1091	8093	1101	8093	1111			463		1155		1441	165		1161	
		2	🍷	2	2	🍷	2	🍷	2	🍷	2	🍷	2	🍷	2	2	🍷	2	🍷	2	🍷	🍷	2	🍷	2
				①–⑤	①–⑥	①–⑥	⑥	F								⑤⑦	M				⑧				
	Portbou **659** d.	...	...	...	...	...	...	...	...	...	...	...	...	...	...	...	0952	...	...	...	...	...	...	...	...
0	**Barcelona** França d.	...	...	...	...	...	...	...	...	...	0919	...	...	1030	1047	...	|	...	...	1318	...	...	...	...	...
5	Barcelona Pass. de Gràcia d.	...	...	...	0558	...	...	...	0755	...	0927	...	...	|	1055	...	|	...	...	1326	...	...	1455	...	1628
8	**Barcelona** Sants **654** d.	...	...	...	0603	0700	...	0800	0803	0900	0933	1000	...	1100u	1103	...	1200	...	...	1333	1430	1500	1503	1600	1633
68	Sant Vicenç de Calders **654** d.	...	...	...	0648	|	...	|	0848	|	1012	|	...	|	1147	...	|	...	...	1416	|	|	1547	|	1716
82	Altafulla-Tamarit d.	...	...	...	0658	|	...	|	|	|	1023	|	...	|	1158	...	|	...	...	1426	|	|	1558	|	1727
93	**Tarragona 654** d.	...	...	...	0707	0754	...	0856	0909	0955	1034	1055	...	1155	1207	...	1254	...	...	1435	1524	1555	1608	1657	1738
103	Port Aventura d.	...	...	...	0720	|	...	|	0917	|	1042	|	...	|	1216	...	|	...	...	1443	|	|	1616	|	1747
105	Salou d.	...	...	...	0724	|	...	0907	0922	|	1046	|	...	1204	1219	...	1307	...	...	1447	|	1606	1620	|	1751
163	L'Aldea-Amposta d.	...	...	...	0807	|	...	0940	1006	|	1129	|	←	1235	1302	...	1335	...	...	1532	|	1633	1707	|	1836
176	Tortosa d.	...	...	0645	0817	|	0751	|	1015	|	1142	|	1142	|	1312	...	|	1316	...	1542	|	|	1717	|	1847
202	Vinaròs d.	...	...	0720	...	|	0828	0956	...	|	→	|	1219	1250	▬	...	1350	1356	...	▬	|	1648	▬	|	▬
208	Benicarló-Peñíscola d.	...	...	0726	...	|	0833	1002	...	|	...	|	1226	1256	...	...	1355	1402	...	...	|	1654	...	|	...
280	Castelló de la Plana d.	...	0650	0815	...	0915	0922	1036	...	1117	...	1215	1319	1334	2	...	1427	1449	1455	...	1643	1727	...	1812	2
353	**València** Nord a.	...	0740	0905	...	0959	1017	1121	...	1159	...	1300	1418	1425	①–④	...	1515	1548	1540	2	1730	1821	...	1859	⑤
353	**València** Nord **667** d.	0704	0750	...	...	1005	...	1128	...	...	...	1306	...	1440	1435	1515	1520	...	1550	1620	...	1827	...	1905	1935
409	Xátiva **667** d.	0736	|	...	...	|	...	1224	...	...	...	|	...	|	1514	1552	1604	...	|	1655	...	1906	...	|	2015
	Madrid Pta de Atocha **667** a.	|	1114	...	...	|	...	|	...	...	...	|	...	|	|	|	|	...	1914	|	...	|	...	|	|
	Badajoz **678** a.	|	▬	...	...	|	...	2205	...	...	...	|	...	|	|	|	|	...	...	|	...	|	...	|	|
	Granada **671** a.	|	...	...	...	|	...	1939	...	...	...	|	...	|	|	|	|	...	...	|	...	|	...	|	|
	Almería **671** a.	|	...	...	...	|	...	2025	...	...	...	|	...	|	|	|	|	...	...	|	...	|	...	|	|
	Málaga **671** a.	|	...	...	...	|	...	2110	...	...	...	|	...	|	|	|	|	...	...	|	...	|	...	|	|
	Sevilla Santa Justa **670** a.	|	...	...	...	|	...	1955	...	...	...	|	...	|	|	|	|	...	...	|	...	|	...	|	|
495	Elda-Petrer d.	0836	...	...	...	|	...	...	...	...	...	|	...	|	1614	1649	1701	...	...	1751	...	1946	...	|	2105
536	**Alacant** Terminal a.	0902	...	...	...	1140	...	...	...	...	...	1500	...	1645	1651	1716	1724	...	...	1817	...	2014	...	2040	2130
536	**Alacant** Terminal § d.	0905	...	...	...	...	...	...	...	...	...	...	...	...	...	...	1734	...	...	1820	...	2024	...	...	...
614	Murcia § a.	1023	2	...	...	...	...	...	...	...	...	...	...	...	...	...	1849	...	...	1933	...	2136	2	...	...
614	Murcia **667** § d.	...	1205z	...	...	...	...	...	...	...	...	...	...	...	...	...	1905	...	...	*1945*	...	2144	2145	...	...
677	**Lorca** Sutullena § a.	...	|	...	...	...	...	...	...	...	...	...	...	...	...	...	|	...	...	|	...	2250	|	...	...
679	**Cartagena 667** § a.	...	1257z	...	...	...	...	...	...	...	...	...	...	...	...	...	1952	...	...	*2037*	...	...	2241	...	...

	Arco		Em		Arco		Em		Hotel	Hotel
	1171		1181		1191		1501		997	947
	🍷	2	🍷	2	🍷	2	🍷	2	🍴	🍴
		⑦					⑧		T	Q
Barcelona França d.	1630	...	...	1749	1830	1917	...	...	...	...
Barcelona Pass. de Gràcia d.	|	...	...	1757	|	1925	...	2055	...	...
Barcelona Sants **654** d.	1700u	...	1800	1803	1900u	1933	2030	2100	2130	2230
Sant Vicenç de Calders **654** d.	|	...	|	1848	|	2012	|	2147	|	|
Altafulla-Tamarit d.	|	...	|	1900	|	2024	|	2159	|	|
Tarragona 650 d.	1755	...	1854	1909	1956	2035	2123	2208	2224	2325
Sevilla Santa Justa **670** a.	|	...	|	|	|	|	|	|	|	0840
Port Aventura d.	|	...	|	1923	|	2048	|	2219	|	...
Salou d.	1807	...	|	1926	2008	2051	|	2223	2238	...
L'Aldea-Amposta d.	1841	...	|	2017	2040	2133	|	2306	2311	...
Tortosa d.	|	...	|	2028	|	2143	|	2316	|	...
Vinaròs d.	1858	1903	|	...	2057	2223	|	...	|	...
Benicarló-Peñíscola d.	1904	1908	|	...	2103	...	|	...	|	...
Castelló de la Plana d.	1941	1957	2013	...	2143	...	1241	...	2359	...
València Nord a.	2025	2050	2059	...	2232	...	2325	...	0049	...
València Nord **667** d.	2031	...	2105	...	...	...	...	...	0051	...
Xátiva **667** d.	2121	...	|	...	...	...	...	...	|	...
Granada **671** a.	|	...	|	...	...	...	...	...	0840	...
Málaga **671** a.	|	...	|	...	...	...	...	...	0949	...
Elda-Petrer d.	2158	...	|	...	...	...	...	...	...	...
Alacant Terminal a.	2219	...	2240	...	...	...	...	...	...	...
Alacant Terminal § d.	2234	...	...	...	...	...	...	...	...	...
Murcia § a.	2340	...	...	...	...	...	...	...	...	...
Murcia **667** § d.	...	...	...	...	...	...	...	...	...	...
Lorca Sutullena § a.	...	...	...	...	...	...	...	...	...	...
Cartagena 667 § a.	...	...	...	...	...	...	...	...	...	...

	Hotel		Hotel	Em			Em		
	944		994	1362			1382		
	🍴	2	🍴	🍷	2	2	🍷	2	2
	Q	①–⑥	T	①–⑥				①–⑥	
Cartagena 667 § d.	...	...	...	...	...	...	...	...	...
Lorca Sutullena § d.	...	...	...	...	...	...	...	...	...
Murcia **667** § a.	...	...	...	...	...	...	...	...	...
Murcia § d.	...	...	...	...	...	...	...	0555	...
Alacant Terminal § a.	...	...	...	...	...	...	...	0718	...
Alacant Terminal d.	...	...	...	...	...	...	0655	0721	...
Elda-Petrer d.	...	...	...	...	...	...	|	0753	...
Málaga **671** d.	...	...	2035	...	...	...	|	|	...
Granada **671** d.	...	...	2125	...	...	...	|	|	...
Xátiva **667** d.	...	...	|	...	...	...	|	0846	...
València Nord **667** a.	...	...	0505	...	...	...	0827	0929	...
València Nord d.	...	...	0511	0640	...	...	0835	...	...
Castelló de la Plana d.	...	...	0606	0717	...	...	0918	...	...
Benicarló-Peñíscola d.	...	...	|	|	...	...	|	...	...
Vinaròs d.	...	...	|	|	0710	...	|	...	...
Tortosa d.	...	0615	|	|	0750	0918	|	...	1045
L'Aldea-Amposta d.	...	0626	|	|	0801	0930	|	...	1055
Salou d.	...	0707	0740	|	0837	1013	|	...	1142
Port Aventura d.	...	0710	|	|	0839	1015	|	...	1145
Sevilla Santa Justa **670** d.	2122	|	|	|	|	|	|	...	1156
Tarragona 650 d.	0640s	0721	0755	0836	0852	1025	1040	...	1216
Altafulla-Tamarit d.	|	|	|	|	0900	1032	|	...	1308
Sant Vicenç de Calders **654** d.	|	0743	|	|	0913	1045	|	...	1313
Barcelona Sants **654** a.	0806	0836	0927	0947	1000	1137	1142	...	...
Barcelona Passeig de Gràcia a.	...	0841	...	...	1005	1142	...	...	...
Barcelona França a.	...	...	...	...	1013	1151	...	...	...

	Arco		Em	Alaris		Talgo	Em		Arco	Em		Arco		Talgo		Em			Em	Arco		Arco		Alaris	
	1102		1112	1084		460	1142		1152	1162		694	8096	264		1182	8096		1492	1202		1212		1184	
	🍷	2	🍷	🍷	2	🍷	🍷	2	🍷	🍷	2	🍷	2	🍷	2	🍷	2	2	🍷	🍷	2	🍷	2	🍷	2
	L					M	⑧					G			①–⑤			⑧		①–⑥	⑧	⑦			⑦
Cartagena 667 § d.	...	...	...	...	...	0835	...	...	...	...	1055	...	...	...	1415	...	...	...	...	...	...	...	*1643*	...	...
Lorca Sutullena § d.	...	...	...	...	...	|	...	...	...	...	|	...	...	1300	|	...	...	...	...	...	...	...	|	...	...
Murcia **667** § a.	...	...	...	...	...	0920	...	...	...	...	1147	...	...	1358	1514	...	...	...	...	...	...	...	*1736*	...	...
Murcia § d.	0635	...	...	...	...	0945	...	...	...	...	▬	...	...	1400	▬	...	...	...	...	...	...	1630	1740v	...	...
Alacant Terminal § a.	0746	...	...	...	...	1059	...	...	...	...	...	...	...	1503	...	...	...	...	...	...	...	1739	1859	...	...
Alacant Terminal d.	0806	...	0925	...	...	1109	...	...	...	1420	...	...	...	1523	...	1616	...	1728	...	1820	...	1809	1900	...	2045
Elda-Petrer d.	0831	...	|	...	...	1135	...	...	...	|	...	...	...	1547	...	|	...	1800	...	|	...	1846	1930	...	2114
Sevilla Santa Justa **670** d.	|	...	|	...	...	|	...	...	...	|	...	0820	...	|	...	|	...	|	...	|	...	|	|	...	|
Málaga **671** d.	|	...	|	...	...	|	...	...	...	|	...	0715	...	|	...	|	...	|	...	|	...	|	|	...	|
Almería **671** d.	|	...	|	...	...	|	...	...	...	|	...	0740	...	|	...	|	...	|	...	|	...	|	|	...	|
Granada **671** d.	|	...	|	...	...	|	...	...	...	|	...	0845	...	|	...	|	...	|	...	|	...	|	|	...	|
Badajoz **678** d.	|	...	|	...	...	|	...	...	...	|	...	0640	...	|	...	|	...	|	...	|	...	|	|	...	|
Madrid Pta de Atocha **667** d.	|	...	|	0800	...	|	...	...	...	|	...	|	...	|	...	|	...	|	...	|	...	|	|	1800	|
Xátiva **667** d.	0913	...	|	1050	...	1213	...	...	...	|	...	1552	...	1626	...	|	...	1849	...	|	...	1933	2025	|	2207
València Nord a.	0952	...	1055	1123	...	1257	...	...	...	1555	...	1650	...	1707	...	1800	...	1929	...	1959	...	2019	2104	2120	2238
València Nord d.	1000	1035	1105	1128	...	1308	1405	...	1505	1605	...	1655	1700	1715	...	1805	...	...	1935	2005	2010	2035	...	2130	...
Castelló de la Plana d.	1043	1132	1144	1215	...	1352	1446	...	1551	1647	...	1744	1757	1801	...	1845	←	...	2016	2048	2102	2120	...	2215	...
Benicarló-Peñíscola d.	1119	1224	|	...	...	1426	|	...	1632	|	...	1815	1846	1831	...	|	1846	...	|	2123	2147	2157	...	...	...
Vinaròs d.	1125	1230	|	...	...	1431	|	...	1638	|	2	1820	→	1836	2	|	1853	...	|	2129	2154	2202	...	...	...
Tortosa d.	|	1304	|	...	1324	|	|	1554	|	|	1725	|	...	|	1850	|	1936	...	|	|	2230	|	...	...	...
L'Aldea-Amposta d.	1140	...	|	...	1336	1447	|	1605	1654	|	1735	1836	...	1851	1903	|	1950	...	|	2144	...	2219	...	...	...
Salou d.	1215	...	|	...	1413	1520	|	1645	1726	|	1818	1914	...	1927	1943	|	2039	...	|	2213	...	|	...	...	...
Port Aventura d.	|	...	|	...	1416	|	|	1647	|	|	1821	|	...	|	1947n	|	2041	...	|	|	...	|	...	...	...
Tarragona 650 d.	1234	...	1309	...	1428	1539	1610	1657	1738	1811	1830	1928	...	1940	1957	2010	2100	...	2137	2242	...	2306	...	...	...
Altafulla-Tamarit d.	|	...	|	...	1435	|	|	1707	|	|	1838	|	...	|	2005	|	2108	...	|	|	...	|	...	...	...
Sant Vicenç de Calders **654** d.	|	...	|	...	1447	|	|	1719	|	|	1849	1947	...	|	2017	|	2118	...	|	|	...	|	...	...	...
Barcelona Sants **654** a.	1341s	...	1411	...	1537	1637	1713	1808	1839	1910	1938	2051	...	2041	2108	2113	2213	...	2237	2346	...	2358	...	...	...
Barcelona Pass. de Gràcia a.	|	...	...	...	1542	|	...	1813	|	...	1944	...	...	...	2113	...	2218	...	...	...	...	...	...	...	...
Barcelona França a.	1405	...	...	...	1550	|	...	1821	1855	...	1953	...	...	...	2122	...	2227	...	...	...	...	...	...	...	...
Cerbère **659** a.	...	...	...	...	...	1902	...	...	...	...	...	...	...	...	...	...	...	...	...	...	...	...	...	...	...

F – GARCÍA LORCA – Daily: [12] Barcelona - Málaga and Sevilla, [2] Barcelona - Badajoz. ①④⑥: [2] Barcelona - Almería. ③⑤⑦: [2] Barcelona - Granada.

G – GARCÍA LORCA – Daily: [12] Málaga and Sevilla - Barcelona; [2] Badajoz - Barcelona. ③⑤⑦: [2] Almería - Barcelona. ①④⑥: [2] Granada - Barcelona.

L – Murcia - Valencia ①–⑥. Valencia - Barcelona daily.

M – MARE NOSTRUM – [12] Montpellier - Cartagena and v.v.

Q – 🛏 and [1] Barcelona - Cádiz and v.v.

T – 🛏 and [2] Barcelona - Granada and Málaga and v.v.

n – Not ⑦.

s – Stops to set down only.

u – Stops to pick up only.

v – 1755 on ⑥⑦.

z – 20 minutes earlier on ⑦.

§ – Additional local trains operate between these stations.

663 BARCELONA - ANDORRA

From Barcelona Nord bus station:
0615▲**N**, 0630**S**, 0730**P**, 1030∇**N**,
1500∇**N**, 1500**S**, 1700**P**, 1800∇**B**.

From Andorra la Vella bus station:
0600▲**B**, 0600**S**, 0645**P**, 1030▲**N**,
1500∇**N**, 1500**S**, 1700**P**, 1900∇**N**.

B – Via Berga. Journey: 3 hrs 45 mins.
N – Non-stop. Journey: 3 hrs 30 mins.
P – Via Ponts. Journey: 4 hrs.
S – Via Solsona. Journey: 4 hrs.
▲ – Not Dec. 25, Jan. 1.
∇ – Not Dec. 25.

Operator: Alsina Graells (AG), Barcelona ✆ +34 93 265 65 92, Andorra ✆ +376 82 65 67.

664 SITGES — 2nd class

Local rail service **Barcelona** - **Sitges** - **Sant Vicenç de Calders**.
From Barcelona Sants: 0606, 0636 and every 30 minutes until 2206; then 2306.
From Sant Vicenç: 0559, 0615 ⚒, 0629 Ⓐ, 0646, 0708 Ⓐ, 0729, 0753, 0813 Ⓐ, 0831, 0900, 0930 and every 30 minutes until 2100; then 2200.

Additional trains operate **Barcelona** - **Sitges** and v.v.
Journey times: **Barcelona** – **Sitges** (*34 km*) 30 minutes,
Barcelona – **Sant Vicenç** (*60 km*) 56 minutes.

665 BARCELONA - MATARÓ, BLANES and MAÇANET — 2nd class

Cercanías (suburban) line **C1**. For faster services Barcelona - Maçanet via Granollers, see Table **659**.

Barcelona Sants – **Mataró** and v.v. *35 km*
Ⓐ: 4–6 trains per hour.
From Barcelona 0554–2311; from Mataró 0530–2235.
Ⓒ: 2–4 trains per hour.
From Barcelona 0610–2300; from Mataró 0603–2218.

Barcelona Sants – **Blanes** *67 km*
0610, 0642 and every 30 mins until 2042, then 2124, 2158, 2233.
Blanes - **Barcelona** Sants
0611, 0640, 0657, 0709 and every 30 mins until 2139.

Barcelona Sants - **Maçanet-Massanes** *82 km*
0610, 0712, 0812 Ⓐ, 0842 Ⓒ, 0942, 1042 and hourly until 1842, then 1912, 2042, 2158.
Maçanet-Massanes - **Barcelona** Sants
0626, 0655, 0724, 0824 and hourly until 1827, then 1954, 2124.

Approximate journey times (in mins) to/from **Barcelona** Sants: Mataró (43), Arenys de Mar (55), Calella (71), Pineda de Mar (74), Malgrat de Mar (80), Blanes (85), Maçanet-Massanes (98).

666 ALACANT - BENIDORM - DÉNIA — 2nd class

By tram																										
Alacant ⊙ ‡ d.	...	...	0602	0702	...	0802	0902	...	1002	1102	1202	...	1302	1402	...	1502	1602	...	1702	1802	...	1902	2002	...	2102
El Campello ‡ d.	...	...	0625	0725	...	0825	0925	...	1025	1125	1225	...	1325	1425	...	1525	1625	...	1725	1825	...	1925	2025	...	2125
La Creueta a.	...	...	0647	0747	...	0847	0947	...	1047	1147	1247	...	1347	1447	...	1547	1647	...	1747	1847	...	1947	2047	...	2147
By train																										
La Creueta d.	...	...	0651	0751	...	0851	0951	...	1051	1151	1251	...	1351	1451	...	1551	1651	...	1751	1851	...	1951	2051	...	2151
Benidorm d.	0607	...	0708	0807	...	0908	1007	...	1108	1207	1306	...	1408	1507	...	1608	1707	...	1808	1907	...	2008	2107	...	2207
Altea d.	0620	...	0721	0820	...	0921	1020	...	1121	1220	...	...	1421	1520	...	1620	1720	...	1820	1920	...	2021	2120	...	2220
Calpe d.	...	...	0738	...	...	0938	...	...	1138	...	...	...	1438	...	...	1638	...	...	1838	...	...	2038	...	...	...
Teulada d.	...	...	0755	...	...	0955	...	...	1155	...	...	...	1455	...	...	1655	...	...	1855	...	...	2055	...	...	...
Gata d.	...	...	0804	...	...	1004	...	...	1204	...	...	...	1504	...	...	1704	...	...	1904	...	...	2104	...	...	...
Dénia a.	...	...	0817	...	...	1017	...	...	1217	...	...	...	1517	...	...	1717	...	...	1917	...	...	2117	...	...	...

By train																									
Dénia d.	...	0625	...	...	0825	...	...	1025	...	...	...	...	1325	...	...	1525	...	...	1725	...	...	1925	...	...	...
Gata d.	...	0639	...	...	0839	...	...	1039	...	...	...	...	1339	...	...	1539	...	...	1739	...	...	1939	...	...	...
Teulada d.	...	0648	...	...	0848	...	...	1048	...	...	...	...	1348	...	...	1548	...	...	1748	...	...	1948	...	...	...
Calpe d.	...	0705	...	...	0905	...	...	1105	...	...	...	...	1405	...	...	1605	...	...	1805	...	...	2005	...	...	...
Altea d.	0624	0722	...	0824	0922	...	1024	1122	...	1224	...	...	1422	...	1524	1622	...	1724	1822	...	1924	2022	...	2124	2224
Benidorm d.	0636	0736	...	0836	0936	...	1036	1136	...	1236	1336	...	1436	...	1536	1636	...	1736	1836	...	1936	2036	...	2136	2235
La Creueta a.	0652	0752	...	0852	0952	...	1052	1152	...	1252	1352	...	1452	...	1552	1652	...	1752	1852	...	1952	2052	...	2152	...
By tram																									
La Creueta d.	0655	0755	...	0855	0955	...	1055	1155	...	1255	1355	...	1455	...	1555	1655	...	1755	1855	...	1955	2055	...	2155	...
El Campello § d.	0717	0817	...	0917	1017	...	1117	1217	...	1317	1417	...	1517	...	1617	1717	...	1817	1917	...	2017	2117	...	2217	...
Alacant ⊙ § a.	0740	0840	...	0940	1040	...	1140	1240	...	1340	1440	...	1540	...	1640	1740	...	1840	1940	...	2040	2140	...	2240	...

‡ – 3–4 trams per hour 0602–2252.
§ – 3–4 trams per gour 0603–2217.
⊙ – Alacant Mercat: ± 1000m from Alacant Renfe station.

Operator: Tram Metropolitano / FGV ✆ 900 72 04 72.

667 MADRID - CARTAGENA, ALACANT and VALÈNCIA

km		*Hotel*			*Alaris*		*Alta*	*Alta*	*Alaris*	*Alaris*	*Alta*		*Alta*	*Alaris*	*Alta*	*Arco*	*Alta*	*Alaris*	*Alta*		*Alaris*		*Alta*	*Alta*	*Alaris*
		994		**8024**	**1074**	**8018**	**1076**	**220**	**1084**	**1094**	**1096**	**8081**	**222**	**1414**	**1126**	**694**	**228**	**1144**	**76**	**8040**	**1454**		**78**	**224**	**1174**
		✕		2	✕	2	🍷	🍷	✕	✕	🍷	2	🍷	✕	🍷	🍷	🍷	✕	🍷	2	✕	2	🍷	🍷	✕
		J		①–⑤	①–⑤	⑥⑦	①–⑥	①–⑤	**K**							**F**	Ⓑ	Ⓑ	**A**			⑤⑦	**N**		
0	**Madrid** Chamartín ‡ d.	...	...	...	...	...	0700	0710	...	...	0905	...	0935	...	1205	...	1240	...	1405	1422	...	...	1605	1630	...
8	**Madrid** Atocha Cercanías ‡ d.	...	...	...	...	...	0715	0725	...	...	0920	...	0950	...	1220	...	1255	...	1420	1437	...	...	1620	1645	...
	Madrid Pta de Atocha ‡ d.	...	...	...	0700	...	|	|	0800	0900	|	...	|	1120	|	...	|	1400	|	|	1520	...	|	|	1700
57	Aranjuez **668** ‡ d.	...	...	...	|	...	|	|	|	|	|	...	|	|	|	...	|	|	1448	1508	|	...	|	|	|
	Badajoz **678** d.	...	...	...	|	...	|	|	|	|	|	...	|	|	|	0640	|	|	|	|	|	...	|	|	|
	Ciudad Real **678** d.	...	...	0555**y**	|	...	|	|	|	|	|	0920	|	|	|	1138	|	|	|	|	|	...	|	|	|
157	Alcázar de San Juan ‡ a.	...	...	0658**y**	|	...	0824	0837	|	|	|	1029	|	|	1328	1302	|	|	|	1606	1626	...	|	|	|
157	Alcázar de San Juan d.	0230	...	0701	|	0800	0825	0838	|	|	|	1032	|	|	1329	1350	|	|	|	1607	1627	...	|	|	|
288	**Albacete** d.	0327	...	0820	0900	0917	0924	0935	0958	1059	1121	1145	1154	1318	1422	1450	1500	1558	1623	1724	1720	1735	1825	1854	1858
354	Hellín d.	|	...	|	|	|	|	1010	|	|	|	|	|	|	|	|	|	|	|	...	|	|	|	|	|
458	Alcantarilla d.	|	...	|	|	|	|	1120	|	|	|	|	|	|	|	|	|	|	|	...	|	|	|	|	|
466	Murcia **662** d.	|	...	|	|	|	|	1132	|	|	|	|	1338	|	|	|	1638	|	|	...	|	|	|	2048	|
531	**Cartagena 662** a.	|	...	|	|	|	|	...	|	|	|	|	1425	|	|	|	1730	|	|	...	|	|	|	2130	|
424	Elda-Petrer d.	|	...	|	|	|	1025	...	|	|	1213	1259	...	|	1522	|	...	|	1726	...	|	|	1930	...	|
464	**Alacant** Terminal a.	|	...	|	|	|	1055	...	|	|	1245	1325	...	|	1550	|	...	|	1755	...	|	|	1957	...	|
435	Xátiva **662** d.	|	...	0935	|	1040	...	...	1050	|	...	...	...	1411	...	1552	...	|	...	...	1814	1917	...	...	|
491	**València** Nord **662** △ a.	0505	...	1014	1022	1120	...	...	1123	1220	...	...	...	1442	...	1650	...	1720	...	...	1844	2001	...	...	2020
	Barcelona Sants **662** a.	0927	...	...	...	...	...	...	...	|	...	...	...	...	...	2051	...	...	...	...	...	...	...	...	|
553	Gandia △ a.	...	...	...	...	...	...	...	...	1321	...	...	...	...	...	...	...	...	...	...	...	...	...	...	2119

		Alaris	*Alta*	*Alta*	*Alaris*		*Alta*	*Alta*	*Alaris*	
	8044	**1184**	**1186**	**74**	**1194**	**8032**	**226**	**1196**	**1504**	**7000**
	2	✕	🍷	🍷	✕	2	🍷	🍷	✕	2
	⑤	**K**	Ⓑ	**C**			Ⓑ	Ⓑ	Ⓑ	
Madrid Chamartín ‡ d.	1640	...	1805	1813	...	1825	1905	1945	...	2045
Madrid Atocha Cercanías ‡ d.	1655	...	1820	1828	...	1840	1920	2000	...	2100
Madrid Pta de Atocha ‡ d.	|	1800	|	|	1900	|	|	|	2020	|
Aranjuez **668** ‡ d.	1724	|	|	|	|	1911	|	|	|	2131
Alcázar de San Juan ‡ a.	1824	|	|	1937	|	2000	2029	2107	|	2230
Alcázar de San Juan d.	1825	|	|	1938	|	2010**b**	2030	2108	|	...
Albacete d.	1940	2000	2019	2036	2058	2121**b**	2130	2200	2218	...
Hellín d.	...	|	|	|	|	...	2205	|	|	...
Alcantarilla d.	...	|	|	|	|	...	|	|	|	...
Murcia **662** d.	...	|	|	|	|	...	2321	|	|	...
Cartagena 662 a.	...	|	|	|	|	...	0010	|	|	...
Elda-Petrer d.	...	|	2115	2144	|	...	...	2258	|	...
Alacant Terminal a.	...	|	2145	2212	|	...	...	2328	|	...
Xátiva **662** d.	...	|	...	...	2151	...	...	...	|	...
València Nord **662** △ a.	...	2120	...	...	2222	...	...	...	2340	...
Barcelona Sants **662** a.	...	...	...	...	...	...	...	...	...	...
Gandia △ a.	...	...	...	...	...	...	...	...	...	...

	Hotel			*Alta*	✣	*Alaris*	*Alta*	*Alaris*	*Alaris*
	997		**8041**	**221**	**8031**	**1065**	**1077**	**1075**	**1085**
	✕	2	2	🍷	2	✕	🍷	✕	✕
	J	①–⑤	①–⑤	①–⑤		①–⑤	①–⑥	**K**	①–⑥
Gandia △ d.	...	...	...	...	...	...	...	...	...
Barcelona Sants **662** d.	2130	...	...	...	...	...	...	...	...
València Nord **662** △ d.	0051	...	...	...	...	0650	...	0750	0850
Xátiva **662** d.	|	...	...	...	...	0719	...	|	|
Alacant Terminal d.	|	...	...	...	...	|	0705	|	|
Elda-Petrer d.	|	...	...	...	...	|	0727	|	|
Cartagena 662 d.	|	...	...	0530	...	|	|	|	|
Murcia **662** d.	|	...	...	0611	...	|	|	|	|
Alcantarilla d.	|	...	...	|	...	|	|	|	|
Hellín d.	|	...	...	|	...	|	|	|	|
Albacete d.	0244	0425**y**	0635	0749	0730**z**	0810	0822	0908	1008
Alcázar de San Juan a.	0348	0547**y**	0742	|	0845**z**	|	|	|	|
Alcázar de San Juan ‡ d.	...	0548	0743	|	0846	|	|	|	|
Aranjuez **668** ‡ d.	...	0640	0839	|	0941	|	|	|	|
Madrid Pta de Atocha ‡ a.	...	0714	|	|	|	1017	|	1114	1215
Madrid Atocha Cercanías ‡ a.	...	...	0915	0957	1015	...	1029	...	...
Madrid Chamartín ‡ a.	...	...	0929	1012	1029	...	1043	...	...

FOR OTHER NOTES SEE FACING PAGE ▶▶

VALÈNCIA, ALACANT and CARTAGENA - MADRID 667

	Alta	*Alta*	*Alta*	*Alaris*	*Alta*	*Arco*	*Alta*	*Alta*	*Alaris*		*Alaris*	*Alta*		*Alaris*	*Alta*		*Alaris*		*Alta*		*Alaris*	*Alta*	*Alta*	*Alaris*	*Alaris*
	129	**223**	**79**	**1415**	**77**	**697**	**229**	**1147**	**1445**		**1155**	**1167**	**8043**	**1165**	**225**	**8083**	**1175**	**8045**	**1187**	**8027**	**1185**	**227**	**1207**	**1505**	**11505**
	🍷	🍷	🍷	🍴	🍷	🍷	🍷	🍷	🍴	2	🍴	🍷	2	🍴	🍷	2	🍴	2	🍷	2	🍴	🍷	🍷	🍴	🍴
	D		**N**		**A**	**G**	**Q**		Ⓑ	⑤⑦	**K**	Ⓑ						⑦				Ⓑ	Ⓑ	Ⓑ	⑦
Gandia △ d.	...	...	...	...	...	...	...	...	...	...	...	...	...	1538	...	...	...	...	...	...	...	...	...	...	...
Barcelona Sants **662** d.	...	...	...	...	...	0800	...	...	...	...	...	...	...	│	...	...	...	...	...	...	...	...	...	...	...
València Nord **662** △ d.	...	...	...	1125	...	1128	...	...	1420	1435	1550	...	...	1650	...	...	1750	...	...	1805	1850	...	...	2020	2120
Xátiva **662** d.	...	...	...	1154	...	1224	...	...	│	1515	│	...	...	│	...	...	1819	...	...	1840	│	...	...	2049	│
Alacant Terminal d.	0940	...	1035	│	1200	│	...	1405	│	│	│	1605	...	│	...	1700	│	...	1805	│	│	...	2000	│	│
Elda-Petrer d.	1002	...	1056	│	1223	│	...	1427	│	│	│	1626	...	│	...	1728	│	...	1827	│	│	...	2023	│	│
Cartagena 662 d.	│	0855	│	│	│	│	1220a	│	│	│	│	│	...	│	1600	│	│	...	│	│	│	1820	│	│	│
Murcia **662** d.	│	0943	│	│	│	│	1306	│	│	│	│	│	...	│	1648	│	│	...	│	│	│	1908	│	│	│
Alcantarilla d.	│	0953	│	│	│	│	│	│	│	│	│	│	...	│	│	│	│	...	│	│	│	│	│	│	│
Hellín d.	│	1100	│	│	│	│	│	│	│	│	│	│	...	│	│	│	│	...	│	│	│	2026	│	│	│
Albacete d.	1112	1135	1158	1246	1321	1330	1453	1521	1538	1702	1708	1717	1740	1808	1837	1845	1910	1915	1923	1958	2008	2105	2120	2139	2238
Alcázar de San Juan a.	1207	1236	│	│	1417	1430	│	│	│	...	│	│	1852	│	│	1958	2002	2026	│	2125	│	2201	2214	│	│
Alcázar de San Juan ‡ d.	1208	1237	│	│	1418	1505	│	│	│	...	│	│	1853	│	│	2008	2003	2027	│	2128d	│	2202	2215	│	│
Ciudad Real **678** a.	│	│	│	│	│	1612	│	│	│	...	│	│	│	│	│	2114	│	│	│	2240d	│	│	│	│	│
Badajoz **678** a.	│	│	│	│	│	2205	│	│	│	...	│	│	│	│	│	...	│	│	│	...	│	│	│	│	│
Aranjuez **668** ‡ d.	│	│	│	│	1506	...	│	│	│	...	│	│	1957	│	│	...	│	2122	│	...	│	│	│	│	│
Madrid Pta de Atocha ‡ a.	│	│	│	1455	│	...	│	│	1746	...	1914	│	│	2014	│	...	2128	│	│	...	2214	│	│	2348	0044
Madrid Atocha Cercanías ‡ a.	1322	1357	1414	...	1548	...	1704	1732	...	...	...	1926	2035	...	2043	...	...	2152	2129	...	...	2316	2334	...	...
Madrid Chamartín ‡ a.	1338	1415	1428	...	1602	...	1719	1746	...	...	...	1940	2048	...	2058	...	...	2206	2143	...	...	2330	2348	...	...

A – [12] Santander - Alacant and v.v.
C – ⑥. [12] A Coruña and Pontevedra - Alacant.
D – ⑦. [12] Alacant - A Coruña and Pontevedra.
F – GARCÍA LORCA – [2] Badajoz - Barcelona, [12] Málaga and Sevilla - Alcázar - Barcelona. ③⑤⑦: [2] Almería - Alcázar - Barcelona. ①④⑥: [2] Granada - Alcázar - Barcelona.
G – GARCÍA LORCA – [2] Barcelona - Badajoz, [12] Barcelona - Alcázar - Málaga and Sevilla. ①④⑥: [2] Barcelona - Alcázar - Almería. ③⑤⑦: [2] Barcelona - Alcázar - Granada.
J – 🛏 and [2] Granada and Málaga - Alcázar - Barcelona and v.v.
K – [12] Madrid - Castelló and v.v.
N – [12] Gijón - Alacant and v.v.
Q – Ⓑ (daily July 22 - Sept. 7).
a – ⑦ (daily July 27 - Sept. 2).
b – Not ⑥.
d – ⑦ only.
y – ① only.
v – ⑤ only.
z – ⑥ only.
❖ – Train **8049** on ⑥⑦.
‡ – See also Table **671**.

△ – *Cercanías* (suburban) line **C1**: **Valencia** - **Gandia** and v.v. 2nd class. Journey time: 54–60 minutes.

From **València** Nord
Ⓐ: 0611, 0641 and every 30 minutes until 1941; then 1956, 2033, 2041, 2111, 2141, 2211, 2241.
Ⓒ: 0030⑦, 0641, 0741 and hourly until 2241.

From **Gandia**
Ⓐ: 0608, 0638, 0653, 0708, 0723, 0738, 0753, 0823, 0838, 0853, 0913, 0923, 0953 and every 30 minutes until 2223.
Ⓒ: 0653, 0753 and hourly until 2053; then 2223.

MADRID - CUENCA - VALÈNCIA 668

2nd class

km			①–⑤							
0	**Madrid** Puerta de Atocha d.	...	...	0850	...	1223	...	1600	...	1940
49	Aranjuez **667 671** d.	...	0610	0923	...	1255	...	1633	...	2014
201	**Cuenca** d.	0735	0837	1139r	...	1449	...	1850	...	2223
327	Requena d.	0922	...	1322	...	1631	...	2034	...	...
404	**València** Nord a.	1049	...	1450	...	1755	...	2154	...	...

				①–⑤					
València Nord d.	...	...	0808	...	1230	...	1508	...	1808
Requena d.	...	...	0944	...	1344	...	1651	...	1935
Cuenca d.	0705	...	1137	1320	1552	1620	1841	1855v	2132
Aranjuez **667 671** d.	0908	...	1326	1536	...	1817	...	2051	...
Madrid Puerta de Atocha a.	0945	...	1400	1617	...	1856	...	2126	...

r – Arrives 1116.
v – 1845 on ⑦.

VALÈNCIA - TERUEL - ZARAGOZA 669

2nd class

km					*TRD* **8502**			*TRD* **8504** H		
0	**València** Nord d.	...	...	...	0933	...	...	1547	...	1847
34	Sagunt d.	...	...	...	0959	...	...	1613	...	1915
65	Segorbe d.	...	...	...	1032	...	...	1639	...	1945
171	**Teruel** ‡ d.	0708	...	...	1206	...	...	1814	...	2135
242	Calamocha ‡ d.	0808	...	...	1251	...	...	1908	...	...
305	Cariñena ‡ d.	0912	...	...	1334	...	...	1958	...	...
359	**Zaragoza** Delicias ‡ a.	1003	...	...	1413	...	...	2037	...	...

			TRD **8511** H			*TRD* **8513**			
Zaragoza Delicias ‡ d.	...	...	0837	...	...	1600	...	...	1915
Cariñena ‡ d.	...	...	0914	...	...	1636	...	...	1957
Calamocha ‡ d.	...	...	1002	...	...	1727	...	...	2112
Teruel ‡ d.	0800	...	1049	...	...	1812	...	...	2206
Segorbe d.	0938	...	1228	...	...	1948	...	...	...
Sagunt d.	1017	...	1301	...	...	2019	...	...	...
València Nord a.	1046	...	1328	...	...	2045	...	...	...

H – To / from Huesca.

CÓRDOBA - SEVILLA - HUELVA and CÁDIZ 670

km					*Hotel*						*Alta*								*Alta*		*Arco*			*Alta*	
		3000	**3002**	**3030**	**947**	**3004**	**3037**	**3006**	**3021**	**3008**	**9320**	**3010**	**3032**	**3012**	**3039**	**3014**	**3016**		**1619**	**3035**	**697**	**3018**	**3095**	**9386**	**3073**
		2	2	2	🍴	2	2	2	2	2	🍴	2	2	2	2	2	2		🍷	2	🍷	2	2	🍷	2
		①–⑤	①–⑥	①–⑤	**A**			①–⑤	**J**	①–⑤				①–⑤					**T**	**J**	**G**				**J**
	Madrid Pta de Atocha **651** d.	...	...	...	...	...	...	...	...	...	1005	...	...	...	...	...	...	...	1610	...	...	...	...	1805	...
0	**Córdoba 651** ◇ d.	...	...	0715	0720	...	...	...	0936	...	1210	...	1335	...	...	...	...	...	1825	1832	1840	...	...	2013	2013
51	Palma del Río d.	...	...	0744	│	...	...	...	1007	...	│	...	1404	...	...	...	...	...	│	1901	│	...	...	│	2042
129	**Sevilla** Santa Justa **651** ◇ a.	...	...	0831	0840	...	...	...	1056	...	1318	...	1456	...	...	...	...	...	1934	1949	1955	...	...	│	2134
129	**Sevilla** Santa Justa **673** § d.	0635	0755	...	0845	0900	0910	1005	1100	1210	1323	1405	...	1535	1640	1700	1800	...	1938	...	...	2005	2030	│	2135
204	La Palma del Condado d.	│	│	...	│	│	1010	│	│	│	│	│	...	│	1739	│	│	...	│	...	...	│	2127	2155s	│
244	**Huelva** Término a.	│	│	...	│	│	1045	│	│	│	│	│	...	│	1815	│	│	...	│	...	...	│	2200	2223	│
145	Dos Hermanas **673** § d.	0650	0808	...	│	0913	...	1018	1113	1223	│	1420	...	1550	...	1713	1813	...	│	...	...	2018	...	...	2148
162	Utrera § d.	0700	│	...	│	0924	...	│	│	1235	│	│	...	1601	...	│	1824	...	│	...	...	│	...	...	2159
236	Jerez de la Frontera d.	0745	0857	...	0946	1011	...	1109	1208	1320	1416	1515	...	1646	...	1808	1908	...	2041	...	...	2113	...	...	2241
250	Puerto de Santa María d.	0755	0907	...	0956	1021	...	1119	1218	1330	1429	1525	...	1656	...	1818	1918	...	2052	...	...	2123	...	...	2251
271	San Fernando - Bahía Sur d.	0818	0933	...	1014	1041	...	1143	1238	1353	1448	1547	...	1714	...	1839	1940	...	2112	...	...	2150	...	...	2311
284	**Cádiz** a.	0834	0949	...	1030	1056	...	1156	1251	1406	1503	1603	...	1729	...	1852	1953	...	2129	...	...	2203	...	...	2325

			Arco			*Alta*		*Alta*										*Alta*						*Hotel*	
	3001	**3023**	**694**	**3041**	**3003**	**9365**	**3025**	**1138**	**3005**	**3007**	**3009**	**3047**	**3011**	**3071**	**3013**	**3043**	**3015**	**9333**	**3027**	**3017**	**3031**	**3049**	**3019**	**944**	**3033**
	2	2	🍷	2	2	🍷	2	🍷	2	2	2	2	2	2	2	2	2	🍷	2	2	2	2	2	🍴	2
	①–⑤	①–⑤	**G**		①–⑥			**T**		①–⑤			①–⑤	**J**	①–⑤				**J**					**A**	
Cádiz d.	0545	...	...	...	0647	...	...	0740	0850	1000	1105	...	1300	...	1355	...	1500	1615	1700	1800	...	...	1900	1935	2005
San Fernando - Bahía Sur d.	0559	...	...	...	0702	...	...	0751	0901	1012	1116	...	1311	...	1410	...	1515	1631	1713	1812	...	...	1911	1947	2019
Puerto de Santa María d.	0619	...	...	...	0725	...	...	0809	0922	1034	1135	...	1331	...	1433	...	1540	1649	1733	1832	...	...	1931	2007	2038
Jerez de la Frontera d.	0630	...	...	...	0736	...	...	0822	0932	1044	1145	...	1341	...	1444	...	1550	1702	1743	1842	...	...	1941	2018	2048
Utrera § d.	0715	...	...	...	0818	...	...	│	│	│	│	...	1421	...	│	...	1632	│	│	│	...	...	2024	│	2129
Dos Hermanas **673** § d.	0727	...	...	...	0830	...	...	│	1024	1134	1235	...	1433	...	1535	...	1644	│	1831	1935	...	...	2036	│	2141
Huelva Término d.	│	...	...	0710	│	0740	...	│	│	│	│	...	│	...	│	1440	│	│	│	│	...	1850	│	│	│
La Palma del Condado d.	│	...	...	0739	│	0806	...	│	│	│	│	...	│	...	│	1513	│	│	│	│	...	1922	│	│	│
Sevilla Santa Justa **673** § a.	0741	...	...	0844	0844	│	...	0922	1040	1147	1248	...	1447	...	1548	1612	1657	1755	1845	1948	...	2020	2049	2114	2156
Sevilla Santa Justa **651** ◇ d.	...	0750	0820	...	...	│	0900	0925	...	...	...	1325	...	1500	...	...	...	1800	1848	...	2015	...	...	2122	...
Palma del Río d.	...	0840	│	...	...	│	0949	│	...	...	...	1414	...	1548	...	...	...	│	1939	...	2104	...	...	│	...
Córdoba 651 ◇ a.	...	0911	0937	...	...	0952	1026	1032	...	...	...	1445	...	1621	...	...	...	1907	2010	...	2135	...	...	2233	...
Madrid Pta de Atocha **651** a.	...	...	...	...	...	1204	...	1247	...	...	...	...	...	...	...	...	...	2122	...	...	...	...	...	...	...

A – ANTONIO MACHADO – 🛏 and [1] Barcelona - Córdoba - Cádiz and v.v.
G – GARCÍA LORCA – [12] Barcelona - València - Sevilla and v.v.
J – From / to Jaén.
T – [12] Barcelona - Madrid - Cádiz and v.v.
s – Stops to set down only.
◇ – For *Avant* high-speed services Córdoba - Sevilla and v.v., see Table **680**
§ – Frequent suburban services operate Sevilla - Utrera and v.v.

For new high-speed services from Dec. 23/24, see page 540

671 MADRID - ALMERÍA, GRANADA and MÁLAGA

For other trains Madrid – Córdoba – Granada and v.v. via the AVE high-speed line, see Table **651**

km		*Hotel*	*Hotel*	*Estr*	*T200*			*Alta*	*Alta*	*T200*		*Talgo*			*T200*			*T200*		*Arco*	*Arco*	*Arco*		
		997	**997**	**940**	**9114**	**7008**	**3021**	**9214**	**9366**	**9118**	**3097**	**276**	**3068**	**8030**	**9124**	**8776**		**9128**	**3058**	**697**	**697**	**697**	**3035**	**3090**
		A✕	A✕	P🍷	✕	2	2C	🍷	🍷	✕	2	🍷	2	2	✕	2B		✕	2	J🍷	2G🍷	2H🍷	2	2
						①–⑤		①–⑥											①–⑤					
0	**Madrid** Chamartín § d.	...	...	...	...	...	...	...	...	...	...	0810	...	...	...	...	...	...	...	...	...	...	...	...
8	**Madrid** Atocha Cercanías § d.	...	...	...	...	...	...	...	...	...	...	0825	...	0900	...	...	...	...	...	...	...	...	...	...
	Madrid Pta de Atocha § d.	...	...	...	0705	0730	...	0735	0835	0930	...	|	...	|	1210	1315	...	1435	...	...	...	...	...	...
57	Aranjuez § d.	...	...	...	|	0805	...	|	|	|	...	|	...	0931	|	1347	...	|	...	...	...	...	...	...
	Barcelona Sants **662** d.	2130	2130	...	|	|	...	|	|	|	...	|	...	|	|	|	...	|	...	0800	0800	0800	...	...
	València Nord **667** d.	0051	0051	...	|	|	...	|	|	|	...	|	...	|	|	|	...	|	...	1128	1128	1128	...	...
157	Alcázar de San Juan **678** § d.	0403	0403	...	|	0856	...	|	|	|	...	0947	...	1027	|	1439	...	|	...	1448	1448	1448	...	...
	Bilbao Abando **689** d.	|	|	2035	|	...	...	|	|	|	...	|	...	|	|	|	...	|	...	|	|	|	...	...
206	Manzanares **678** d.	|	|	0518	|	...	...	|	|	|	...	|	...	1054	|	1505	...	|	...	1511	1511	1511	...	...
323	Linares-Baeza a.	0541	0541	0639	|	...	...	|	|	|	...	1118	...	1220	|	...	...	|	...	1634	1634	1634	...	...
323	Linares-Baeza d.	0548	0610	0640	|	...	...	|	|	|	...	1133	...	1221	|	...	...	|	...	1644	1655	1655	...	1724
382	**Jaén** a.	|	|	|	|	...	...	|	|	|	...	|	...	1305	|	...	...	|	...	|	|	|	...	|
441	Moreda **673** d.	|	|	|	|	...	...	|	|	|	...	|	...	...	|	...	...	|	...	|	1839	1839	...	1910
466	Guadix **673** d.	|	|	|	|	...	...	|	|	|	...	1330	...	...	|	...	...	|	...	|	1901	|	...	|
565	**Almería 673** a.	|	|	|	|	...	...	|	|	|	...	1455	...	...	|	...	...	|	...	|	2025	|	...	|
	Jaén d.	|	|	|	|	...	0805	|	|	|	1000	...	...	...	|	...	...	|	...	|	...	|	1650	|
371	Andújar d.	0622	|	|	|	...	0846	|	|	|	1040	...	...	...	|	...	...	|	...	1721	...	|	1738	|
450	**Córdoba** a.	0710	|	0759	0905	...	0934	0945	1037	1134	1136	...	...	...	1410	...	...	1635	...	1810	...	|	1830	|
450	**Córdoba** d.	0712	|	0802	0907	...	...	0946	1038	1136	...	...	1215	...	1412	...	...	1637	1750	1820	...	|	...	|
501	Montilla d.	0747	|	|	|	...	...	|	|	|	...	...	1252	...	|	...	...	|	1833	1855	...	|	...	|
527	Puente Genil d.	0806	|	0927	|	...	...	|	|	1205r	...	...	1317	...	|	...	...	|	1855	1914	...	|	...	|
574	Bobadilla **673** d.	0852	|	1008	|	...	...	1026z	1118z	1219z	...	...	1405	...	|	...	...	1717z	1935	1946	...	|	...	|
	Algeciras **673** a.	|	|	|	|	...	...	|	1400	|	...	...	...	...	|	...	...	|	...	|	...	|	...	|
	Granada a.	|	0840	|	|	...	...	1215	...	|	...	...	...	...	|	...	...	|	...	|	...	1939	...	2000
643	**Málaga 673** a.	0949	...	1115	1053	...	...	...	...	1330	...	...	...	...	1606	...	...	1828	...	2110	...	...	...	...

	Alta		*Talgo*	*R-598*		*T200*		*T200*	
	9384	**8034**	**278**	**8914**	**3073**	**9136**	**8032**	**9140**	
	🍷	2	🍷	2	2S	✕	2	✕	
		①–⑤		⑧					
Madrid Chamartín § d.	...	1540	1647	...	...	...	1825	...	...
Madrid Atocha Cercanías § d.	...	1555	1702	...	...	...	1840	...	...
Madrid Pta de Atocha § d.	1705	|	|	1740	...	1825	|	2010	...
Aranjuez § d.	|	1628	|	|	...	|	1911	|	...
Alcázar de San Juan **678** § d.	|	1720	1812	1841	...	|	2005	|	...
Manzanares **678** d.	|	1747	1837	1912	...	|	2031	|	...
Linares-Baeza a.	|	1906	1952	2031	...	|	2156	|	...
Linares-Baeza d.	|	1907	2008	2031	...	|	2157	|	...
Jaén a.	|	1952	|	2118	...	|	2242	|	...
Moreda d.	|	...	|	...	...	|	...	|	...
Guadix **673** d.	|	...	2211	...	...	|	...	|	...
Almería 673 a.	|	...	2330	...	...	|	...	|	...
Jaén d.	|	...	...	...	1840	|	...	|	...
Andújar d.	|	...	...	...	1922	|	...	|	...
Córdoba a.	1905	...	...	...	2011	2029	...	2210	...
Córdoba d.	1906	...	...	...	...	2031	...	2212	...
Montilla d.	|	...	...	...	...	|	...	|	...
Puente Genil d.	|	...	...	...	...	2102r	...	|	...
Bobadilla **673** d.	|	...	...	...	...	2116z	...	|	...
Algeciras **673** a.	2225	...	...	...	...	|	...	|	...
Granada a.	...	...	...	...	...	|	...	|	...
Málaga 673 a.	...	...	...	...	...	2225	...	2357	...

km					*R-598*	*T200*	*R-598*		*Talgo*
		3069	**3093**	**8031**	**8915**	**9115**	**8917**	**8033**	**277**
		2	2	2	2	✕	2	2	🍷
		①–⑤		①–⑤	①–⑤		⑦	①–⑥	
	Málaga 673 d.	...	...	...	...	0700	...	...	...
0	**Granada** d.	...	...	...	...	|	...	...	...
	Algeciras **673** d.	...	...	...	...	|	...	...	...
	Bobadilla **673** d.	0610	...	...	...	0804z	...	...	...
	Puente Genil d.	0649	...	...	...	0818r	...	...	...
	Montilla d.	0710	...	...	...	|	...	...	...
	Córdoba a.	0754	...	...	...	0845	...	...	...
	Córdoba d.	...	0800	...	...	0847	...	...	...
¶	Andújar d.	...	0858	...	...	|	...	...	...
¶	**Jaén** a.	...	0945	...	...	|	...	...	...
	Almería 673 d.	...	...	...	...	|	...	...	0715
	Guadix **673** d.	...	...	...	...	|	...	...	0841
58	Moreda d.	...	...	...	...	|	...	...	|
	Jaén d.	...	...	0600	0645	|	0838	0838	|
176	Linares - Baeza a.	...	...	0639	0725	|	0918	0920	1037
176	Linares - Baeza d.	...	...	0639	0725	|	0919	0921	1047
293	Manzanares **678** d.	...	...	0757	0843	|	1040	1038	|
342	Alcázar de San Juan **678** § d.	...	...	0827	0906	|	1104	1105	1228
	Aranjuez § d.	...	...	0921	|	|	|	1157	|
	Madrid Pta de Atocha § a.	...	...	|	1025	1051	1219	|	|
	Madrid Atocha Cercanías § a.	...	...	1001	...	...	...	1232	1352
	Madrid Chamartín § a.	...	...	1017	...	...	...	1246	1406

	Arco	*Arco*	*Arco*	*T200*	*Alta*			*T200*				*T200*				*T200*	*Alta*		*Talgo*	*Alta*	*T200*	*Hotel*	*Hotel*	*Estr*
	694	**694**	**694**	**9119**	**9367**	**7041**	**3047**	**9127**	**3091**	**8035**	**3071**	**9131**	**3067**	**7801**	**8037**	**9137**	**9383**	**3027**	**279**	**9237**	**9141**	**994**	**994**	**941**
	2H🍷	2G🍷	J🍷	✕	🍷	2D	2	✕	2	2	2S	✕		2B	2	✕	🍷	2C	🍷	🍷	✕	A✕	A✕	Q🍷
															⑦									
Málaga 673 d.	...	...	0715	0915	...	...	...	1305	...	...	...	1500	...	...	...	1800	...	...	...	...	2005	...	2035	2048
Granada d.	...	0845	|	|	...	...	...	|	1335	...	...	|	...	...	...	|	...	...	...	1850	|	2125	|	|
Algeciras **673** d.	...	|	|	|	0840	...	...	|	|	...	...	|	...	...	...	|	1640	...	...	|	|	|	|	|
Bobadilla **673** d.	...	|	0805	1023z	|	...	...	|	|	...	...	|	1558	...	...	|	1915z	...	...	2037z	2109z	|	2125	2145
Puente Genil d.	...	|	0833	1037r	|	...	...	|	|	...	...	1617r	1633	...	...	|	|	...	...	|	|	|	2152	2219
Montilla d.	...	|	0854	|	|	...	...	|	|	...	...	|	1655	...	...	|	|	...	...	|	|	|	2211	|
Córdoba a.	...	|	0935	1105	1154	...	...	1448	|	...	...	1645	1738	...	...	1944	1956	...	...	2115	2149	|	2250	2322
Córdoba d.	...	|	1000	1107	1155	...	1447	1450	|	...	1623	1647	...	...	...	1946	1958	2012	...	2116	2151	|	2252	2324
Andújar d.	...	|	1051	|	|	...	1543	|	|	...	1718	|	...	...	...	|	|	2103	...	|	|	|	2343	|
Jaén a.	...	|	|	|	|	...	1634	|	|	...	1812	|	...	...	...	|	|	2149	...	|	|	|	|	|
Almería 673 d.	0740	|	|	|	|	...	...	|	|	...	...	|	...	...	...	|	|	...	1615	|	|	|	|	|
Guadix **673** d.	0907	|	|	|	|	...	...	|	|	...	...	|	...	...	...	|	|	...	1746	|	|	|	|	|
Moreda d.	0931	0937	|	|	|	...	...	|	1425	...	...	|	...	...	...	|	|	...	|	|	|	|	|	|
Jaén d.	|	|	|	|	|	...	...	|	|	1538	...	|	...	...	1715	|	|	...	|	|	|	|	|	|
Linares - Baeza a.	1105	1110	1123	|	|	...	...	|	1558	1617	...	|	...	...	1756	|	|	...	1944	|	|	2350	0018	0040
Linares - Baeza d.	1147	1147	1147	|	|	...	...	|	...	1618	...	|	...	...	1757	|	|	...	1956	|	|	0040	0040	0041
Manzanares **678** d.	1307	1307	1307	|	|	1524	...	|	...	1743	...	|	...	1826	1922	|	|	...	2114	|	|	|	|	0201
Bilbao Abando **689** a.	|	|	|	|	|	|	...	|	...	|	...	|	...	|	|	|	|	...	|	|	|	|	|	1118
Alcázar de San Juan **678** § d.	1350	1350	1350	|	|	1555	...	|	...	1812	...	|	...	1903	1950	|	|	...	2140	|	|	0230	0230	...
València Nord **667** a.	1650	1650	1650	|	|	|	...	|	...	|	...	|	...	|	|	|	|	...	|	|	|	0505	0505	...
Barcelona Sants **662** a.	2051	2051	2051	|	|	|	...	|	...	|	...	|	...	|	|	|	|	...	|	|	|	0927	0927	...
Aranjuez § d.	...	...	...	|	|	1654	...	|	...	1905	...	|	...	1958	2041	|	|	...	|	|	|	...	...	...
Madrid Pta de Atocha § a.	...	...	...	1318	1402	|	...	1654	...	|	...	1900	...	2039	|	2148	2214	...	|	2325	2353	...	...	...
Madrid Atocha Cercanías § a.	...	...	...	...	...	1726	...	...	...	1943	...	...	...	...	2115	...	...	...	2301	...	...	...	...	...
Madrid Chamartín § a.	...	...	...	...	...	1740	...	...	...	1957	...	...	...	...	2129	...	...	...	2316	...	...	...	...	...

A – 🛏 and [2] Barcelona - Granada and Málaga and v.v.
B – To / from Badajoz.
C – To / from Cádiz.
D – From Ciudad Real.
G – GARCÍA LORCA – ①④⑥.
H – GARCÍA LORCA – ③⑤⑦.
J – GARCÍA LORCA – [12] Barcelona - Málaga and v.v.; [12] Barcelona - Córdoba - Sevilla and v.v.
P – PICASSO – ⑤. 🛏, couchette and [12] Bilbao - Málaga.
Q – PICASSO – ⑦. 🛏, couchette and [12] Málaga - Bilbao.
S – To / from Sevilla.
r – Puente Genil - Herrera (± *8 km* from Puente Genil).
z – Antequera - Santa Ana (± *17 km* from Antequera).
¶ – Andújar - Jaen: *54 km*.
§ – See also Table **667**.

672 MÁLAGA - TORREMOLINOS - FUENGIROLA

2nd class

km				⚒		⚒			
0	Málaga Centro - Alameda d.	0530	0600	0630	0700	0730	0800	and every 30 minutes until	2230
1	**Málaga 671** d.	0532	0602	0632	0702	0732	0802		2232
9	Aeropuerto ✈ d.	0544	0614	0644	0714	0744	0814		2244
17	**Torremolinos** d.	0555	0625	0655	0725	0755	0825		2255
21	Benalmádena d.	0602	0632	0703	0733	0803	0833		2303
32	**Fuengirola** a.	0617	0649	0719	0749	0819	0849		2319

		⚒		⚒						
Fuengirola d.	0627	0657	0727	0757	0827	and every 30 minutes until	2157	2227	2257	2327
Benalmádena d.	0641	0711	0741	0811	0841		2211	2241	2311	2341
Torremolinos d.	0648	0718	0748	0818	0848		2218	2248	2318	2348
Aeropuerto ✈ d.	0659	0729	0759	0829	0859		2229	2259	2329	2359
Málaga 671 a.	0713	0743	0813	0843	0913		2243	2311	2341	0011
Málaga Centro - Alameda a.	0716	0746	0816	0846	0916		2246	2314	2344	0014

SEVILLA and ALGECIRAS - MÁLAGA, GRANADA and ALMERÍA 673

2nd class

km		R-598 3920	3061 ①–⑥	R-598 3900	3063		Alta 9367 M	R-598 3902		R-598 3926		R-598 3904	3077		R-598 3910 ⑤⑦		R-598 3922		3065	R-598 3906	Alta 9383 M	R-598 3924	3079 ①–⑤	R-598 3908
0	**Sevilla** ¶ d.	0700	...	0740	...	...	...	1105	...	1150	...	1315	...	...	1510	...	1553	...	...	1705	...	1740	...	2010
15	Dos Hermanas **670** ¶ d.	0713u	...	0753u	...	...	...	1118u	...	1203u	...	1328u	...	...	1523u	...	1606u	...	...	1718u	...	1753u	...	2023u
	Algeciras d.	|	...	|	0715	...	0840	|	...	|	...	|	1210	...	|	...	|	...	1535	|	1640	|	1835	|
	San Roque - La Línea d.	|	...	|	0729	...	|	|	...	|	...	|	1224	...	|	...	|	...	1548	|	|	|	1848	|
	Ronda d.	|	0752	|	0903	...	1009	|	...	|	...	|	1406	...	|	...	|	...	1720	|	1811	|	2026	|
167	Bobadilla **671** d.	|	0845	0917	0955	...	...	1239	...	|	...	1456	1503	...	1645	...	|	...	1812	1844	|	|	...	2144
236	**Málaga 671** a.	|	0942	1007	|	...	...	1336	...	|	...	1552	|	...	1740	...	|	...	|	1938	|	|	...	2236
183	Antequera d.	0842	...	...	1010	...	...	...	...	1337	...	...	1519	...	...	...	1731	...	1827	...	1914z	1932	...	...
290	**Granada** a.	0959	...	...	1131	...	...	...	...	1459	...	...	1648	...	...	...	1844	...	2000	...	...	2102	...	...
290	**Granada 671** d.	1003	...	...	...	...	...	...	...	1503	...	...	...	...	...	...	1848	...	...	...	...	2106	...	...
372	Guadix **671** d.	1107	...	...	...	...	...	...	...	1600	...	...	...	...	...	...	1953	...	...	...	...	2203	...	...
471	**Almería 671** a.	1221	...	...	...	...	...	...	...	1715	...	...	...	...	...	...	2100	...	...	...	...	2314	...	...

km		3074 ①–⑤	R-598 3901	3064		R-598 3941		R-598 3903	Alta 9366 M		R-598 3943		R-598 3905	3076		R-598 3907	R-598 3945	3062	Alta 9384 M	R-598 3909 ⑤⑦	3057 ①–⑥		R-598 3911	R-598 3947
0	**Almería 671** d.	...	...	...	...	0600	...	...	...	...	0925	...	...	...	...	...	1415	...	...	...	...	...	...	1800
99	Guadix **671** d.	...	...	...	...	0717	...	...	...	...	1037	...	...	...	...	...	1529	...	...	...	...	...	...	1921
181	**Granada 671** a.	...	...	...	...	0814	...	...	...	...	1129	...	...	...	...	...	1626	...	...	...	...	...	...	2020
181	**Granada** d.	...	...	0715	...	0818	...	...	...	...	1133	...	...	1355	...	...	1632	1735	...	...	...	...	...	2024
288	Antequera d.	...	...	0841	...	0943	...	...	1118z	...	1245	...	...	1520	...	...	1800	1905	...	...	...	...	...	2130
	Málaga 671 d.	...	0745	|	...	|	...	1030	|	...	|	...	1400	|	...	1635	|	|	...	1900	1915	...	2010	|
304	Bobadilla **671** d.	...	0835	0857	...	|	...	1122	|	...	|	...	1452	1534	...	1723	|	1919	...	1952	2025	...	2101	|
376	Ronda d.	0715	|	1003	...	|	...	|	1223	...	|	...	|	1630	...	|	|	2018	2054	|	2122	...	|	|
468	San Roque - La Línea d.	0850	|	1138	...	|	...	|	|	...	|	...	|	1807	...	|	|	2144	|	|	...	...	|	|
480	**Algeciras** a.	0908	|	1152	...	|	...	|	1400	...	|	...	|	1822	...	|	|	2157	2225	|	...	...	|	|
456	Dos Hermanas **670** ¶ a.	...	1004s	...	...	1109s	...	1243s	...	...	1413s	...	1621s	...	...	1849s	1930s	...	...	2118s	...	...	2228s	2257s
471	**Sevilla** ¶ a.	...	1018	...	...	1127	...	1258	...	...	1430	...	1639	...	...	1905	1945	...	...	2134	...	...	2242	2310

M – (12) and 🍷 Algeciras - Madrid and v.v. See Table **651**.

s – Stops to set down only.
u – Stops to pick up only.

z – Antequera - Santa Ana (*17 km* from Antequera).

¶ – Frequent suburban services run Sevilla - Dos Hermanas and v.v.

MALLORCA 674

ALMA DE MALLORCA - INCA - **SA POBLA**
: 0550, 0650 and hourly until 1950; then 2050 (to Inca), 2125.
: 0600, 0725, 0840, 0955, 1110, 1225, 1340, 1455, 1610, 1725, 1840, 1955, 2110.

ALMA DE MALLORCA - INCA - **MANACOR**
: 0621, 0720, 0825, 0925 and hourly until 2025; then 2200.
: 0645, 0800, 0915, 1030, 1145, 1300, 1415, 1530, 1645, 1800, 1915, 2030, 2200.

ourney times from Palma: Inca 35–40 mins, Sa Pobla 57 mins, Manacor 66 mins.

SA POBLA - INCA - **PALMA DE MALLORCA**
Ⓐ: 0710, 0823, 0923 and hourly until 2123; then 2230.
Ⓒ: 0730, 0845, 1000, 1115, 1230, 1345, 1500, 1615, 1730, 1845, 2000, 2115, 2230.

MANACOR - INCA - **PALMA DE MALLORCA**
Ⓐ: 0623, 0734, 0839, 0939 and hourly until 2039; then 2143.
Ⓒ: 0645, 0800, 0915, 1030, 1145, 1300, 1415, 1530, 1645, 1800, 1915, 2030, 2145.

Operator: Serveis Ferroviaris de Mallorca (SFM) ✆ +34 971 752 245.

ALMA DE MALLORCA - SÓLLER
800, 1050, 1215, 1330, 1510, 1930.

3 km Journey time: 55 minutes.

SÓLLER - PALMA DE MALLORCA
0700, 0910, 1050, 1215, 1400, 1830, 1900 Ⓒ.

Operator: Ferrocarril de Sóller (FS) ✆ +34 971 752 051.

connecting tram service operates **Sóller** - **Port de Sóller** at 0700, 0800 and every 30 mins until 1930 (also 2025), returning approximately 25 mins later. *5 km*. Journey time: 15–20 mins.

MÁLAGA and ALGECIRAS - LA LÍNEA (for Gibraltar) 675

MÁLAGA - LA LÍNEA bus station (for **Gibraltar** ▲) and v.v.

rom Málaga: 700, 1015, 1400, 1715.
From La Línea: 0715, 1030, 1415, 1700.

ourney time: 3 hours. *Timings subject to confirmation.*
perator: Automóviles Portillo, Málaga ✆ +34 952 360 191.

ALGECIRAS - LA LÍNEA bus station (for **Gibraltar** ▲) and v.v.

From Algeciras: Ⓐ: every 30 mins 0700–2130*. ⑥: every 45 mins 0700–2115*. †: every 45 mins 0800–2130*.
From La Línea: Ⓐ: every 30 mins 0745–2215§. ⑥: every 45 mins 0745–2200§. †: every 45 mins 0845–2215§.

Journey time: 45 mins.
Operator: Transportes Generales Comes SA, Algeciras ✆ +34 956 653 456.

* – Also 2230. § – Also 2315.

▲ – There are no cross-border bus services: passengers to/from **Gibraltar** must cross the frontier on foot (walking-time about 5 minutes) and transfer to/from Gibraltar local bus services.

SEVILLA - HUELVA - FARO 676

DAMAS / EVA joint service ★

	Ⓐ			⚒			Ⓐ	Ⓐ					Ⓐ	Ⓐ		Ⓐ	⚒
evilla Plaza de Armas d.	0730	*0730*	...	0930	...	1100	...	1230	...	*1330*	...	1530	1630	*1630*	1800	*1830*	1930
uelva d.	0845u	0900	...	1100	...	1230	1300	1400	...	1515	...	1700	1745u	1830	1930	2000	2100
yamonte △ ES d.	0930u	1000	...	1200	...	1330	1400	1500	...	1615	...	1800	1830u	1930	2030	2100	2200
ila Real de Santo António △ PT a.	0855s	...	...	...	...	...	...	...	...	...	...	...	1755s	...	...	...	...
aro a.	1010	...	...	...	...	...	...	...	...	...	...	...	1910	...	...	...	...

		Ⓐ	⚒			Ⓐ					⚒	†	Ⓐ	Ⓐ	Ⓐ		
aro d.	...	...	...	...	...	0820	...	...	...	...	...	...	...	...	1535	...	...
ila Real de Santo António △ PT d.	...	...	...	...	...	0935u	...	...	...	...	...	...	...	...	1650u	...	...
yamonte △ ES d.	0645	0730	0845	0945	...	1100s	1145	...	1345	...	1515	1615	1645	1715	1815s	...	1930
uelva a.	0745	0830	0945	1045	...	1150s	1245	...	1445	...	1615	1715	1745	1815	1905s	...	2030
evilla Plaza de Armas a.	0910	*1010*	*1110*y	1210	...	1300	*1410*	...	*1610*	...	1740	1840	1910	*2010*	2015	...	2210

Sevilla Plaza de Armas bus station is ± 2 km from Santa Justa rail station.

Huelva bus station is ± 1 km from the rail station.

Ayamonte bus station is ± 1.5 km from the ferry terminal.

△ – **Ayamonte - Vila Real de Santo António Guadiana** and v.v. Journey time: 10 minutes. Operator: Empresa de Transportes do Rio Guadiana, Vila Real ✆ +351 281 543 152.
From Ayamonte ES – ⚒: 0940, 1020 and every 40 minutes until 1900; then 2000. †: 1030, 1130 and hourly until 1830.
From Vila Real PT – ⚒: 0900, 0940 and every 40 minutes until 1900. †: 1000, 1100 and hourly until 1600; then 1730.

u – Stops to pick up only.
s – Stops to set down only.

y – Ⓐ only.

ES – Spain (Central European Time).
PT – Portugal (West European Time).

★ – DAMAS, Huelva ✆ +34 959 256 900; EVA, Faro ✆ +351 289 899 700/1.

677 MADRID - CÁCERES - BADAJOZ

km			R-598			R-598			TRD	R-598						TRD			Talgo		TRD			Hotel
			7904	8772		7902	8774		7014	7900			7804			7016	7824	7824	194		7018			332
		2	2	2	2	2	2	2	2	2	2	2	2	2	2	2	2	2	🍷	2	2	2	2	✕
		①–⑥	①–⑤	①–⑤	①–⑤	⑥⑦	⑥⑦	⑥⑦			P		△			●	⑤⑦	⑤		①–⑤	⑧	①–⑥	⑦	L
0	**Madrid** Puerta de Atocha d.	...	...	...	...	...	...	...	0740	0955	...	...	1328	...	1430	1525	1525	1525	1640	1755	1905	2007	2050	2245
138	Talavera de la Reina d.	...	...	...	...	...	...	...	0902	1121	...	...	|	...	1605	1653	1706	1706	1803	1925	2034	2135	2222	0039
270	Plasencia a.	...	...	...	...	...	...	...	1022	1242	...	...	|	...	▬	1820	1838	|	|	...	2148	...	...	|
	Plasencia d.	...	0538	...	...	0720	...	...	1025	1245	...	...	|	...	...	...	...	|	|	...	2151	...	...	|
335	**Cáceres** d.	...	0644	...	...	0830	...	...	1141	1350	...	1900	|	...	...	...	...	1928	2004	...	2301	...	...	0300
420	Valencia de Alcántara ES a.	...	|	...	...	|	...	...	|	|	...	|	|	...	...	...	...	...	|	...	|	...	...	0530
	Lisboa Sta Apolónia **691** PT a.	...	|	...	...	|	...	...	|	|	...	|	|	...	...	...	...	...	|	...	|	...	...	0800
401	Mérida a.	...	0751	...	...	0938	...	...	1245	1458	...	2006	2011	...	...	...	...	...	2101	...	0006	...	...	...
401	Mérida **678** d.	...	0755	0800	0900	0945	0945	1100	...	1503	1510	...	2023	2042	...	...	...	...	2113	...	...	...	...	...
461	**Badajoz 678** a.	...	0840	|	0946	1025	|	1146	...	1540	|	...	2115	|	...	...	...	...	2153	...	...	...	...	...
467	Zafra d.	0525	...	0901	...	...	1046	...	...	...	1604	...	...	2137	...	...	...	...	...	...	...	...	...	...
641	Sevilla a.	|	...	1244	...	...	1429	...	...	...	...	...	...	...	2	...	...	...	...	...	...	...	...	...
513	Fregenal de la Sierra d.	0626	...	...	...	...	...	...	...	...	...	...	...	...	1545	...	...	...	...	...	...	...	...	...
652	Huelva a.	0921	...	...	...	...	...	...	...	...	...	...	...	...	1840	...	...	...	...	...	...	...	...	...

	Hotel			TRD	TRD			Talgo								TRD		R-598	TRD				R-598	
	335			7021	7023			197								7027		7907	7025	7817	7817	8779	7909	
	✕		2	2	2	2	2	🍷	2	2	2	2	2	2	2	2	2	2	2	2	2	2	2	2
	L			①–⑤	⑥	①–⑤	①–⑤		①–⑤	⑥⑦	⑥⑦	⑥⑦					P		●	⑤⑦	⑦			⑧
Huelva d.	...	...	...	...	...	...	...	...	...	...	...	...	...	1200	...	...	...	...	...	...	...	...	...	1910
Fregenal de la Sierra d.	...	...	...	...	...	...	...	...	...	...	...	...	...	1455	...	...	...	...	...	...	...	...	...	2206
Sevilla d.	...	...	...	...	...	...	...	...	...	...	...	...	...	...	...	...	...	...	...	...	...	1515	...	|
Zafra d.	...	...	...	...	...	...	0655	...	...	0845	...	...	...	...	...	...	1402	...	...	...	...	1907	...	2306
Badajoz 678 d.	...	...	...	...	...	0700	|	0735	...	|	0855	...	...	...	1240	...	|	1420	...	...	...	|	1958	...
Mérida **678** a.	...	...	...	...	...	0748	0750	0808	...	0935	0943	...	...	...	1326	...	1452	1455	...	...	...	2008	2037	...
Mérida d.	...	...	...	0545	0620	...	...	0820	0905	...	...	0950	...	...	...	1335	...	1500	...	...	...	...	2045	...
Lisboa Sta Apolónia **691** PT d.	2200	...	...	|	|	...	...	|	|	...	...	|	...	...	...	|	...	|	...	...	...	...	|	...
Valencia de Alcántara ES d.	0230	...	...	|	|	...	...	|	|	...	...	|	...	...	...	|	...	|	...	...	...	...	|	...
Cáceres d.	0410	...	...	0646	0721	...	...	0925	1010	...	...	1055	...	...	...	1436	...	1602	...	...	1850	...	2155	...
Plasencia a.	|	...	...	0757	0835	...	...	|	...	...	...	...	...	...	...	1543	...	1702	...	...	|	...	2315	...
Plasencia d.	|	...	...	0800	0850	...	...	|	...	...	...	...	...	...	...	1545	...	1705	1911	1944	|	...	...	...
Talavera de la Reina d.	0615	...	0905	0922	1019	...	...	1125	...	...	...	...	1430	...	...	1710	...	1820	2031	2115	2115	...	...	...
Madrid Puerta de Atocha a.	0840c	...	1038	1055	1200	...	...	1251	...	...	...	...	1600	...	...	1845	...	1956	2212	2258	2258	...	...	...

L – LUSITANIA – 🛏 and (2) Madrid - Lisboa and v.v.
P – From / to Puertollano (Table **678**).
c – Madrid Chamartín.
△ – Via Ciudad Real (Table **678**).
● – Not ⑤⑦.
ES – Spain (Central European Time).
PT – Portugal (West European Time).

678 ALCÁZAR DE SAN JUAN - BADAJOZ

km								Arco		
			7042		7040		7804	697	8083	8027
		2	2	2	2	2	2	2	2	2
		①–⑤		⑥	①–⑥	Z		G	C	⑦V
	Madrid Pta de Atocha **667/71** d.	...	...	...	...	...	1328	...	...	...
	Albacete **667** d.	...	...	...	...	...	|	1330	1845	1958
0	**Alcázar de San Juan 671** d.	...	0750	...	1240	...	1459	1510	2008	2128
50	Manzanares **671** d.	...	0817	...	1307	...	1526	1538	2036	2155
114	Ciudad Real **680** d.	...	0855	...	1345	...	1610	1635	2114	2240
153	Puertollano **680** d.	...	...	...	...	1132	1645	1717	...	...
265	Cabeza del Buey d.	0610	...	0740	...	1316	1829	1910	...	...
392	Mérida **677** a.	0750	...	0924	...	1457	2011	2045	...	...
451	**Badajoz 677** a.	*0840*	...	*1025*	...	*1540*	2115	2145	...	...

			Arco					
	8024	8081	694	7041	7801		7043	
	2	2	2	2	2	2	2	2
	①V	C	G			Z	⑧	⑧
Badajoz 677 d.	...	...	0715	...	1240	*1420*	...	...
Mérida **677** d.	...	...	0756	...	1328	1508	...	205[illegible]
Cabeza del Buey d.	...	...	0927	...	1503	1645	...	223[illegible]
Puertollano **680** d.	...	...	1106	...	1643	1840	...	...
Ciudad Real **680** d.	0555	0920	1157	1445	1725	...	2150	...
Manzanares **671** d.	0633	1000	1244	1524	1808	...	2227	...
Alcázar de San Juan 671 a.	0658	1029	1315	1551	1834	...	2255	...
Albacete **667** a.	0819	1143	1449	|	|	...	...	...
Madrid Pta de Atocha **677/71** a.	...	...	...	1726r	2006	...	...	...

C – COSTA DE LA MANCHA – (2) Alacant - Ciudad Real and v.v.
G – GARCÍA LORCA – (2) Barcelona - Badajoz and v.v.
V – (2) València - Ciudad Real and v.v.
Z – To / from Zafra (Table **677**).
r – Madrid Atocha Cercanías.

679 MADRID - SEGOVIA, SALAMANCA and TOLEDO

2nd class

km		①–⑤					①–⑤				
0	**Madrid** Atocha C. d.	0602	0801	1001	1201	1401	1501	1601	...	1802	2002
8	Madrid Chamartín d.	0617	0815	1016	1216	1415	1516	1616	...	1816	2016
108	**Segovia** a.	0813	1005	1204	1402	1603	1710	1757	...	2003	2213

	①–⑤									
Segovia d.	0555	0655	0855	1055	1255	1455	1650	...	1855	2055
Madrid Chamartín a.	0738	0838	1036	1236	1436	1636	1836	...	2036	2235
Madrid Atocha C. a.	0752	0852	1050	1250	1450	1650	1850	...	2050	2249

km				TRD	TRD		TRD	TRD	TRD	TRD	TRD
				8901	8903		8905	8907	8913	8909	8911
									①–⑥		
0	**Madrid** Chamartín ◧ d.	...	...	0845	1100	...	1345	1545	1712	1945	2130
122	Ávila ◧ d.	0710	...	1002	1223	...	1505	1702	1830	2104	2249
233	**Salamanca** a.	0841	...	1105	1326	...	1613	1805	1937	2205	2350

	TRD	TRD	TRD		TRD			TRD	TRD	TRD
	8910	8900	8912		8902		8004	8904	8906	8908
			①–⑥							
Salamanca d.	0600	0745	0945	...	1245	1430	...	1550	1815	1953
Ávila ◧ d.	0705	0850	1055	...	1350	1602	1615	1655	1920	2058
Madrid Chamartín ◧ a.	0827	1008	1215	...	1515	...	1745	1815	2045	2220

km		AV	AV	AV	AV	AV	AV	AV	AV	AV	AV	AV	AV
		9512	9514	9518	9520	9522	9524	9526	9530	9534	9536	9538	9542
		①–⑤	①–⑤			⑥⑦					①–⑤		
0	**Madrid** △ d.	0650	0750	0920	1020	1050	1220	1350	1550	1750	1850	1950	2150
75	**Toledo** a.	0720	0820	0950	1050	1120	1250	1420	1620	1820	1920	2020	2220

	AV	AV	AV	AV	AV	AV	AV	AV	AV	AV	AV	AV
	9513	9515	9517	9519	9521	9525	9527	9531	9535	9537	9539	9543
	①–⑤	①–⑤	①–⑤							⑥⑦		
Toledo d.	0655	0730	0805	0925	1025	1225	1325	1525	1725	1825	1920	2120
Madrid △ a.	0725	0800	0835	0955	1055	1255	1355	1555	1755	1855	1955	2155

△ – Madrid Puerta de Atocha.
AV – ***Avant*** high-speed services. Single class. 🍷.
◧ – See also Tables **681**, **682**, **689**.

680 MADRID - PUERTOLLANO and CÓRDOBA - SEVILLA

For other high-speed trains between these points, see Table **651**

km		9712		9716		9720		9726	9728		9730	9732		9734		9736		9738	9788	9740		9742		9744
		①–⑥		⑧					①–⑤		①–⑥	⑤				⑧			①–⑤	⑧		①–⑥		⑧
0	**Madrid** Puerta de Atocha d.	0645	...	0810	...	1030	...	1330	1415	...	1530	1610	...	1725	...	1815	...	1915	1940	2025	...	2115	...	2235
171	Ciudad Real d.	0739	...	0904	...	1124	...	1424	1509	...	1624	1704	...	1819	...	1909	...	2009	2034	2119	...	2209	...	2329
210	**Puertollano** a.	0758	...	0923	...	1143	...	1443	1528	...	1643	1723	...	1838	...	1928	...	2028	2053	2138	...	2228	...	2348

	9713		9715	9765	9795		9717		9721		9725		9731		9733		9735	9737		9739		9741		9743
	①–⑤		①–⑥	①–⑤	⑧		①–⑥						①–⑥		①–⑤			⑤⑦				⑧		
Puertollano d.	0625	...	0700	0715	0745	...	0830	...	1000	...	1235	...	1530	...	1605	...	1730	1800	...	1905	...	2005	...	2130
Ciudad Real d.	0642	...	0717	0732	0802	...	0847	...	1017	...	1252	...	1547	...	1622	...	1747	1817	...	1922	...	2022	...	2147
Madrid Puerta de Atocha a.	0738	...	0813	0828	0858	...	0943	...	1113	...	1348	...	1643	...	1718	...	1843	1913	...	2018	...	2118	...	2243

km		9012	9016	9020		9026		9030	9034	9038	9042
		①–⑤	①–⑤			①–⑤			①–⑤		
0	**Córdoba** d.	0650	0805	1000	...	1300	...	1530	1730	1930	2130
126	**Sevilla** a.	0735	0850	1045	...	1345	...	1615	1815	2015	2215

	9013	9017	9019		9025		9031	9035	9039	9043
	①–⑤	①–⑤			①–⑤			①–⑤		
Sevilla d.	0650	0810	0930	...	1245	...	1530	1730	1945	2145
Córdoba a.	0735	0855	1015	...	1330	...	1615	1815	2030	2230

☛ All trains are ***Avant*** high-speed services: *Turista* and *Club* class; 🍷.

MADRID - ZAMORA - VIGO, PONTEVEDRA and A CORUÑA

For services to / from A Coruña via León, see Table **682**

km		2 ①–⑥	Hotel 851 🍴 A	2 ①–⑤	R-598 2000 2 ①–⑤	Hotel 851 🍴 B		R-598 2022 2	2	2 ①–⑤	R-598 2002 2	2	2 ①–⑤	2 Rb	2 ⑥	2 Rq	Estr 923 🍷 G	R-598 2004 2 ①–⑤	R-598 2006 2	2	R-598 2008 2	2 ①–⑤	2	2
0	**Madrid** Chamartín **682 689** d.	...	2230	...	...	2230	...	...	...	...	...	...	...	...	...	...	...	...	...	...	...	...	...	...
121	Ávila **682 689** d.	...	0003	...	...	0003	...	...	...	...	...	...	...	...	...	...	...	...	...	...	...	...	...	...
	Irún **689** d.	...	|	...	...	|	...	...	...	...	...	...	...	...	...	...	...	...	...	...	...	...	...	...
	Barcelona Sants **654** d.	...	|	...	...	|	...	...	...	...	...	...	...	...	...	...	2000	...	...	...	...	...	...	...
	Miranda de Ebro **682 689** d.	...	|	...	...	|	...	...	...	...	...	...	...	...	...	...	|	...	...	...	...	...	...	...
207	Medina del Campo **682 689** d.	...	0100	...	...	0100	...	...	...	...	...	...	...	...	...	...	|	...	...	...	...	...	...	...
297	**Zamora** d.	...	0150	...	...	0150	...	...	...	...	...	...	...	...	...	...	|	...	...	...	...	...	...	...
404	Puebla de Sanabria d.	...	0314	...	...	0314	...	...	...	...	...	...	0635	...	0745	...	|	...	...	...	...	...	...	...
547	**Ourense 682** d.	...	0520	...	...	0540	...	0655	...	...	...	...	0827	0841	0933	0944	1001	...	...	...	...	...	1425	...
641	Guillarei d.	...	|	...	...	0655	...	|	...	...	...	...	...	1014	...	1120	1133	...	...	...	...	...	|	...
	Vigo d.	...	|	0551	0630	|	...	|	0703	0810	0847	0915	...	|	...	|	|	1055	1155	1232	1343	1418	|	1530
666	Redondela d.	...	|	0604	|	0720	...	|	0714	0823	|	0926	...	1033	...	1140	1153	|	1204	1248	|	1430	|	1542
678	**Vigo** a.	...	|	|	|	0733s	...	|	|	|	|	|	...	1047	...	1151	1205	|	|	|	|	|	|	|
684	**Pontevedra** d.	...	|	0623	0654	0825	...	|	0731	0839	0914	0943	...	...	...	...	...	1118	1218	1311	1406	1451	|	1601
717	Vilagarcía de Arousa d.	...	|	0655	0721	...	...	|	0809	...	0938	1018	...	...	...	...	...	1147	1244	1343	1433	...	|	1632
677	Santiago de Compostela d.	0655	0723	0736	0756	...	...	0834	0900	...	1011	1107	...	...	...	...	...	1222	1322	1433	1510	...	1612	1717
751	**A Coruña** a.	0750	0824	...	0848	...	...	0920	1011	...	1056	1205	...	...	...	...	...	1310	1408	1525	1555	...	...	1814

	R-598 2010 2 ①–⑤	2	R-598 2012 2		R-598 2014 2	D 283 2🍷 Q	D 283 2🍷	2	2 ⑦	2 ①–⑤	R-598 2016 2	Talgo 151 🍷 ①–⑥	Talgo 129 🍷 K⑦	2 ⑦	R-598 2018 2	Talgo 129 🍷 H⑦	Talgo 151 🍷 ①–⑥	2 ⑦	2 L	2	Talgo 623 🍷 E	2 ⑧	Talgo 79 🍷 N	2 J
Madrid Chamartín **682 689** d.	...	...	...	...	...	...	...	...	...	...	...	1400	1400	...	...	1400	1400	...	...	...	...	...	1500	...
Ávila **682 689** d.	...	...	...	...	...	...	...	...	...	...	...	1521	1521	...	...	1521	1521	...	...	...	...	...	1621	...
Irún **689** d.	...	...	...	...	...	...	0845	...	...	...	...	|	|	...	...	|	|	...	...	...	...	...	|	...
Barcelona Sants **654** d.	...	...	...	...	...	...	|	...	...	...	...	|	|	...	...	|	|	...	...	...	0703	...	|	...
Miranda de Ebro **682 689** d.	...	...	...	...	...	1118	1118	...	...	...	...	|	|	...	...	|	|	...	...	...	1345	...	|	...
Medina del Campo **682 689** d.	...	...	...	...	...	|	|	...	...	...	...	1607	1607	...	...	1607	1607	...	...	...	|	...	1702	1757
Zamora d.	...	...	...	...	...	|	|	...	...	...	...	1656	1656	...	...	1656	1656	...	...	...	|	...	...	1902
Puebla de Sanabria d.	...	...	...	...	...	|	|	...	1750	...	...	1815	1815	...	...	1815	1815	...	...	...	|	...	...	2022
Ourense 682 d.	...	1535	...	...	...	1818	1830	...	1943	...	...	1959	1959	...	...	2009	2009	2017	2022	2039	2055	...	...	...
Guillarei d.	...	1659	...	...	...	1938	|	...	...	...	...	|	|	...	...	2120	2120	|	2145	|	|	...	...	...
Vigo d.	1515	|	1645	...	1815	|	|	1845	...	1928	1955	|	|	2020	2105	|	|	|	|	|	|	2230	...	...
Redondela d.	|	1720	|	...	|	1959	|	1857	...	1940	|	|	|	2031	2114	2140s	2140s	|	2208	|	2235	2244	...	...
Vigo a.	|	1733	|	...	|	2010	|	|	...	|	|	|	|	|	|	2154	2154	|	2224	|	2252	|	...	...
Pontevedra d.	1538	...	1709	...	1838	...	|	1916	...	1957	2020	|	|	2048	2129	2239	2239	|	...	|	...	2305	...	...
Vilagarcía de Arousa d.	1605	...	1736	...	1906	...	|	1949	...	...	2048	|	|	2124	2155	...	...	|	...	|	...	2337	...	...
Santiago de Compostela d.	1640	...	1810	...	1942	...	2010	2037	...	...	2120	2128	2128	2216	2234	...	...	2208	...	2231	...	0018z	...	...
A Coruña a.	1730	...	1856	...	2028	...	2108	2135	...	...	2205	2222	2222	...	2320	...	...	...	...	...	...	...	...	...

km		2 J	2 ①–⑥	8010 2 Vr	2 ①–⑤	2 ①–⑤	2 L	Talgo 620 🍷 F	R-598 2001 2 ①–⑤	2 ①–⑤	2 ⑥	R-598 2019 2	D 280 2🍷	D 280 2🍷 Q	Talgo 74 🍷 H⑥		R-598 2003 2 ①–⑤	Talgo 74 🍷 K⑥	2	R-598 2005 2 ①–⑤	Talgo 152 🍷 ⑧	R-598 2007 2	2	Talgo 152 🍷 ⑧
0	**A Coruña** d.	...	...	...	0536	...	...	...	0650	...	...	0755	0805	...	...	...	0830	0900	0930	1035	...	1145	1215	1250
74	Santiago de Compostela d.	...	0535z	...	0631	0645	...	...	0737	...	0812	0840	0904	...	...	...	0915	0954	1030	1120	...	1230	1308	1337
116	Vilagarcía de Arousa d.	...	0612	...	0719	|	...	...	0814	...	|	0914	|	...	...	...	0953	|	1109	1149	...	1302	1347	|
149	**Pontevedra** d.	...	0650	...	0800	|	...	...	0840	0855	|	0943	|	...	0845	...	1019	|	1143	1216	1235	1331	1430	|
	Vigo d.	...	|	...	|	|	0640	0735	|	|	|	|	|	0910	0930	...	|	|	|	|	1320	|	|	|
167	Redondela d.	...	0713	...	0823	|	0652	0746	0854	0919	|	|	|	0921	0941	...	|	|	1203	|	1331	1347	1449	|
179	**Vigo** a.	...	0725	...	0838	|	|	|	0905	0931	|	1009	|	|	|	...	1043	|	1218	1245	|	1359	1501	|
192	Guillarei d.	...	...	...	...	|	0714	|	...	...	|	...	|	0939	0959	...	...	|	...	...	1350	...	...	|
	Ourense 682 d.	...	...	...	...	0839	0841	0905	...	...	1002	...	1100	1100	1138	...	...	1138	...	...	1526	...	...	1526
	Puebla de Sanabria d.	0715	...	...	...	...	...	|	...	...	...	...	|	|	1320	...	...	1320	...	...	1708	...	...	1708
	Zamora d.	0832	...	...	...	...	...	|	...	...	...	...	|	|	1430	...	...	1430	...	...	1820	...	...	1820
	Medina del Campo **682 689** d.	0927	...	1030	...	...	...	|	...	...	...	...	|	|	1533	...	...	1533	...	...	1920	...	...	1920
	Miranda de Ebro **682 689** a.	...	...	|	...	...	...	1600	...	...	...	...	1740	1740	|	...	...	|	...	...	|	...	...	|
	Barcelona Sants **654** a.	...	...	|	...	...	...	2324	...	...	...	...	|	...	|	...	...	|	...	...	|	...	...	|
	Hendaye **689** a.	...	...	|	...	...	...	...	...	...	...	...	2035	...	|	...	...	|	...	...	|	...	...	|
	Ávila **682 689** d.	...	...	1115	...	...	...	...	...	...	...	...	...	...	1620	...	...	1620	...	...	2003	...	...	2003
	Madrid Chamartín **682 689** a.	...	...	1255	...	...	...	...	...	...	...	...	...	...	1752	...	...	1752	...	...	2132	...	...	2132

	2 ⑥	2 ①–⑤	R-598 2009 2	2 R	2	2 d	R-598 2011 2	2	2 ⑤	Estr 920 🍷 G	2 ⑤	R-598 2013 2	2	R-598 2015 2	2 ①–⑤	2	R-598 2023 2		Hotel 852 🍴 B	2	R-598 2017 2		Hotel 852 🍴 A	2 ⑧
A Coruña d.	...	...	1350	...	...	...	1450	1532	...	...	...	1700	...	1755	...	1835	1938	...	...	...	2036	...	2145	2225
Santiago de Compostela d.	...	...	1436	...	1450	...	1538	1625	1725	...	...	1745	...	1840	...	1930	2028	...	...	2045	2122	...	2235	2319
Vilagarcía de Arousa d.	...	...	1509	...	|	...	1607	1709	|	...	...	1814	...	1909	...	2012	|	...	...	2131	2154	...	|	...
Pontevedra d.	...	1507	1534	...	|	...	1637	1746	|	...	...	1839	...	1939	2028	2047	|	...	2130	2205	2221	...	|	...
Vigo d.	...	|	|	1437	|	...	|	|	|	1823	...	|	1923	|	|	|	|	...	2220u	|	|	...	|	...
Redondela d.	...	1524	|	1449	|	...	|	1802	|	1834	...	|	1935	|	2047	2110	|	...	2233	2222	|	...	|	...
Vigo a.	...	1540	1607	|	|	...	1703	1814	|	|	...	1910	|	2014	2100	2122	|	...	|	2242	2255	...	|	...
Guillarei d.	...	...	...	1511	|	...	...	...	|	1853	...	...	1957	...	...	...	|	...	2258	...	...	...	|	...
Ourense 682 d.	1530	...	...	1634	1634	1725	...	...	1915	2002	2010	...	2138	...	...	...	2200	...	0035	...	...	...	0035	...
Puebla de Sanabria d.	1738	...	...	...	...	1935	...	...	...	|	2215	...	...	...	...	...	...	...	0233	...	...	...	0233	...
Zamora d.	...	...	...	...	...	...	...	...	...	|	...	...	...	...	...	...	...	...	0400	...	...	...	0400	...
Medina del Campo **682 689** d.	...	...	...	...	...	...	...	...	...	|	...	...	...	...	...	...	...	...	0510	...	...	...	0510	...
Miranda de Ebro **682 689** a.	...	...	...	...	...	...	...	...	...	|	...	...	...	...	...	...	...	...	|	...	...	...	|	...
Barcelona Sants **654** a.	...	...	...	...	...	...	...	...	...	1108	...	...	...	...	...	...	...	...	|	...	...	...	|	...
Hendaye **689** a.	...	...	...	...	...	...	...	...	...	...	...	...	...	...	...	...	...	...	|	...	...	...	|	...
Ávila **682 689** d.	...	...	...	...	...	...	...	...	...	...	...	...	...	...	...	...	...	...	0557	...	...	...	0557	...
Madrid Chamartín **682 689** a.	...	...	...	...	...	...	...	...	...	...	...	...	...	...	...	...	...	...	0745	...	...	...	0745	...

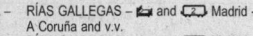

A – RÍAS GALLEGAS – 🛏 and (2) Madrid - A Coruña and v.v.
B – RÍAS GALLEGAS – 🛏 and (2) Madrid - Pontevedra and v.v.
E – FINISTERRE – ①③⑤. (12) Barcelona - Vigo.
F – FINISTERRE – ②④⑥. (12) Vigo - Barcelona.
G – GALICIA – 🛏, 🛌, (1) (reclining) Barcelona - Vigo and v.v.
H – (12) Alacant - Pontevedra and v.v.
J – (2) Valladolid - Puebla de Sanabria and v.v.
K – (12) Alacant - A Coruña and v.v.
L – (2) León - Vigo and v.v.
N – To Gijón (Table **682**).
Q – From / to Bilbao.
R – (2) Ponferrada - Vigo and v.v.
b – ①–⑤ only.
d – ①–④ and ⑦.
q – ⑥⑦ only.
r – ①–⑥ only.
s – Stops to set down only.
u – Stops to pick up only.
z – ① only

682 MADRID - LEÓN, FERROL and A CORUÑA

For services to / from A Coruña via Zamora, see Table **681**

km			Estr	R-598			Estr	Estr		Estr	Estr		Estr	7229		Talgo	Talgo	D	D					Talgo	Talgo
			751	2681			831	831		923	923		933	8009*	8101	131	61	283	283	8215	8001			623	623
		2		2	2	2	🍷	🍷	2	🍷	🍷	2		2	2	🍷	🍷	2🍷	2🍷	2	2	2	2	🍷	🍷
		①–⑤	A	①–⑤	①–⑤	①–⑤	C	C	⑥⑦	B	B	①–⑤	P	①–⑥				Q						F	G
0	**Madrid** Chamartín **681/9** d.	...	2210	...	...	...	2245	2245	...	...	...	...	...	...	...	0800	0900	...	...	...	1130	...	...	...	...
121	Ávila **681/9** d.	...	2336	...	...	...	0020	0020	...	...	...	...	...	...	...	0922	1020	...	...	...	1303	...	...	...	...
207	Medina del Campo **681/9** d.	...	0015	...	...	...	0110	0110	...	...	...	...	...	0655	...	1003	1102	...	...	...	1348	...	...	...	...
249	**Valladolid** C. Grande **689** d.	...	0037	...	...	...	0142	0142	...	...	...	...	...	0730	0935	1026	1124	...	...	1230	1411	...	1435	...	...
286	Venta de Baños **689** d.	...	0056	...	...	...	0305	0330	...	...	...	...	...	0757	1008	|	|	...	...	1303	1435	...	1506	...	...
	Barcelona Sants **654/5** d.	...	|	...	...	...	|	|	...	2000	2000	...	2200	|	|	|	|	...	...	|	|	...	|	0703	0703
	Irún **689** d.	...	|	...	...	...	|	|	...	|	|	...	|	|	|	|	|	...	0845	|	|	...	|	|	|
	Miranda de Ebro **689** d.	...	|	...	...	...	|	|	...	|	|	...	0544	|	|	|	|	1118	1118	|	|	...	|	1344	1344
	Burgos **689** d.	...	|	...	...	...	|	|	...	0343	0343	...	0654	|	|	|	|	1213	1213	|	|	...	|	1442	1442
297	Palencia **689** d.	...	0104	...	...	...	0319	0356	...	0430	0430	...	0753	0808	1020	1053	1151	1300	1300	1315	1445	...	1518	1531	1531
	Santander **684** a.	...	|	...	...	...	|	0737	...	|	|	...	|	|	1332	|	1435	|	|	|	|	...	1853	|	|
420	**León** a.	...	0148	...	...	...	0440	▬	...	0535	0535	...	0905	0920	...	1150	...	1405	1405	1435	1558	...	...	1637	1637
420	**León** d.	...	0204	...	...	...	0445	...	...	0540	0540	0710	0907	▬	...	1152	...	1407	1407	▬	▬	1610	...	1640	1640
	Gijón Cercanías **685** a.	...	|	...	...	...	0735j	2	...	|	|	|	1158	...	...	1415	...	|	|	...	...	|	...	|	|
472	Astorga d.	...	0235	...	...	...	▬	⑥⑦	...	0609	0609	0749	▬	...	...	▬	...	1444	1444	...	...	1642	...	1710	1710
548	Ponferrada d.	...	0336	...	0600	...	...	0700	...	0712	0712	0901	2	...	...	...	...	1543	1543	...	...	1751	...	1811	1811
658	Monforte de Lemos a.	...	0521	...	0743	...	...	0841	...	0850	0850	...	⑦	...	...	...	...	1715	1715	2	...	1931	...	1942	1942
658	Monforte de Lemos d.	...	0541	...	0748	0752	...	0844	0855	0910	0914	...	1123	...	...	...	...	1730	1730	1825	...	1934	...	1953	2009
705	Ourense **681** d.	...	|	...	0841	|	...	0944	|	1001	|	...	1209	...	...	...	...	1818	1830	|	...	2022	...	|	2055
836	**Vigo 681** a.	...	|	...	1047	|	2	1151	|	1205	|	...	...	...	...	...	...	2010	|	|	...	2224	...	|	2252
729	Lugo d.	...	0640	...	...	0852	⑥⑦	...	0956	...	1024	...	...	2	...	2	...	...	|	1924	2	...	...	2059	...
	Ferrol d.	0700	|	0905	...	|	0955	...	|	...	|	...	...	1430	...	1708	...	...	▲	|	2020	...	...	|	...
822	Betanzos-Infesta d.	0753	0759	0950	...	1012	1049	...	1124	...	1141	...	...	1530	...	1756	...	...	|	2057	2119	...	...	2216	...
865	**Ferrol** a.	|	0854	|	...	|	|	...	|	...	|	...	...	|	...	|	...	...	|	|	|	...	...	|	...
848	**A Coruña 681** a.	0820	...	1012	...	1037	1119	...	1150	...	1211	...	...	1556	...	1824	...	...	2110	2124	2147	...	...	2255	...

	Talgo		Talgo				Talgo			
	623	8003	79				77	8791	6791	8005
	🍷	2	🍷	2	2	2	🍷	2	2	2
	L		N		Y	Y	T	⑤	⑤	
Madrid Chamartín **681/9** d.	...	1430	1500	...	...	...	1630	1631c	1631c	1830
Ávila **681/9** d.	...	1553	1621	...	...	...	1752	1809	1809	2000
Medina del Campo **681/9** d.	...	1638	1703	...	...	...	1833	1855	1855	2045
Valladolid C. Grande **689** d.	...	1701	1725	1755	...	1810	1854	1918	1918	2108
Venta de Baños **689** d.	...	1725	|	1825	...	1843	|	1941	1941	2132
Barcelona Sants **654/5** d.	0703	|	|	|	...	|	|	|	|	|
Irún **689** d.	|	|	|	|	...	|	|	|	|	|
Miranda de Ebro **689** d.	1344	|	|	|	...	|	|	|	|	|
Burgos **689** d.	1442	|	|	|	...	|	|	|	|	|
Palencia **689** d.	1531	1735	1756	1836	...	1853	1924	1953	1957	2142
Santander **684** a.	|	|	|	|	...	2216	2200	|	2250	|
León a.	1637	1845	1858	2000	...	▬	...	2103	...	2252
León d.	1652	...	1900	...	2005	...	...	2104	...	...
Gijón Cercanías **685** a.	1930	...	2125	...	|	...	...	|	...	...
Astorga d.	...	...	...	...	2045	...	...	2145	...	...
Ponferrada d.	...	...	...	...	2155	2	...	2308	...	...
Monforte de Lemos a.	...	...	...	...	...	⑤	...	...	...	...
Monforte de Lemos d.	...	...	...	...	...	2138	...	...	...	...
Ourense **681** d.	...	...	...	...	...	2220	...	...	...	...
Vigo 681 a.	...	...	...	...	...	...	...	...	...	...
Lugo d.	...	...	...	...	...	...	...	...	...	...
Ferrol d.	...	...	...	...	...	...	...	...	...	...
Betanzos-Infesta d.	...	...	...	...	...	...	...	...	...	...
Ferrol a.	...	...	...	...	...	...	...	...	...	...
A Coruña 681 a.	...	...	...	...	...	...	...	...	...	...

				Talgo		Talgo		Talgo	Talgo
	8002			76		78		620	620
	2	2	2	🍷	2	🍷	2	🍷	🍷
		①–⑤	⑥	T	①–⑤	N		L	H
A Coruña 681 d.	...	...	...	...	0625	...	...	...	...
Ferrol d.	...	...	...	...	|	...	...	...	...
Betanzos-Infesta d.	...	...	...	...	0655	...	...	...	...
Ferrol a.	...	...	...	...	0748	...	...	...	...
Lugo d.	...	...	...	...	▬	...	...	...	...
Vigo 681 d.	...	...	...	...	...	...	0640	...	0735
Ourense **681** d.	...	...	0807	...	...	...	0843	...	0905
Monforte de Lemos a.	...	...	0849	...	...	...	0928	...	0945
Monforte de Lemos d.	...	...	▬	...	...	...	0933	...	1015
Ponferrada d.	...	0712	...	...	...	...	1114	...	1142
Astorga d.	...	0823	...	...	...	...	1224	...	1238
Gijón Cercanías **685** d.	...	|	...	...	...	0920	|	1030	|
León a.	...	0900	2	...	2	1139	1255	1255	1308
León d.	0710	...	0901	...	⑥⑦	1140	...	1321	1321
Santander **684** d.	|	...	|	0810	0818	|	...	|	|
Palencia **689** d.	0815	...	1025	1041	1140	1238	...	1423	1423
Burgos **689** d.	|	...	|	|	|	|	...	1507	1507
Miranda de Ebro **689** a.	|	...	|	|	|	|	...	1600	1600
Hendaye **689** a.	|	...	|	|	|	|	...	|	|
Barcelona Sants **654/5** a.	|	...	|	|	|	|	...	2324	2324
Venta de Baños **689** d.	0825	...	1035	|	1151	|	...	...	...
Valladolid Campo Grande **689** d.	0846	...	1107	1113	1219	1307	...	...	...
Medina del Campo **681 689** a.	0909	...	...	1134	...	1327	...	...	...
Ávila **681 689** a.	0954	...	...	1216	...	1409	...	...	...
Madrid Chamartín **681 689** a.	1128	...	...	1342	...	1540	...	...	...

	Talgo	R-598			D	D			Talgo		Talgo						Estr			Estr	Estr				Estr
	620	2682	8214		280	280			60		130	8104		8790		8008	930			920	920				752
	🍷	2	2	2	2🍷	2🍷	2	2	🍷	2	🍷	2	2	2	2	2	P	2	2	🍷	🍷	2	2	2	
	J	①–⑤				Q		⑥⑦		⑦		①–⑥	①–⑥	⑦					⑦	B	B				A
A Coruña 681 d.	0705	0725	...	0827	0800	...	...	1055	...	...	...	...	...	...	1440	...	...	...	...	...	1800	1840	1858	2029	...
Ferrol d.	|	|	...	|	|	...	...	|	...	...	...	...	...	...	|	...	...	...	...	...	|	|	|	|	2100
Betanzos-Infesta d.	0730	0752	...	0857	|	...	...	1125	...	...	...	...	...	...	1510	...	...	...	...	...	1828	1909	1927	2059	2155
Ferrol a.	|	0832	...	|	▲	...	...	1214	...	...	...	...	...	...	1559	...	...	...	...	...	|	|	2012	2147	|
Lugo d.	0853	▬	...	1022	|	...	...	▬	...	...	...	...	...	...	▬	...	...	...	...	...	1950	2036	▬	▬	2307
Vigo 681 d.	|	...	...	|	|	0910	...	...	...	...	...	...	...	...	...	...	...	1437	...	1823	|	|	...	...	|
Ourense **681** d.	|	...	...	|	1100	1100	...	...	...	...	...	...	...	...	...	...	...	1640	1740	2002	|	|	...	...	|
Monforte de Lemos a.	0956	...	...	1121	1140	1140	...	...	...	...	...	...	...	...	...	...	...	1726	1824	2045	2052	2137	Estr	...	0006
Monforte de Lemos d.	1015	...	...	▬	1150	1150	...	...	...	...	...	...	...	...	...	...	...	1731	▬	2110	2110	...	830	...	0026
Ponferrada d.	1142	...	...	...	1321	1321	...	...	...	...	...	...	1700	1700	...	...	...	1945	...	2247	2247	...	🍷	...	0203
Astorga d.	1238	...	...	...	1420	1420	...	...	...	...	...	...	1823	1823	...	...	...	2105	...	2348	2348	...	C	Estr	0302
Gijón Jovellanos **685** d.	|	**8004**	...	...	|	|	...	**8006**	...	...	1555	...	|	|	**8790**	...	1905	|	...	|	|	...	2230j	830	|
León a.	1308	2	...	...	1452	1452	...	2	...	...	1810	...	1901	1901	2	...	2126	2144	...	0020	0020	...	0109	🍷	0332
León d.	1321	1330	1500	...	1454	1454	...	1650	...	1745	1812	...	...	1905	⑦	2035	2128	▬	...	0025	0025	...	0112	C	0334
Santander **684** d.	|	|	|	...	|	|	1410	|	1545	|	|	1645	...	|	1715	|	|	...	...	|	|	...	|	2300	|
Palencia **689** d.	1423	1435	1622	...	1557	1557	1728	1755	1814	1854	1910	2017	...	2025	2025	2153	2240	...	...	0130	0130	...	0224	0229	0434
Burgos **689** d.	1507	|	|	...	1644	1644	|	|	|	|	|	|	...	|	|	|	2324	...	...	0217	0217	...	|	|	|
Miranda de Ebro **689** a.	1600	|	|	...	1740	1740	|	|	|	|	|	|	...	|	|	|	0018	...	...	|	|	...	|	|	|
Hendaye **689** a.	|	|	|	...	2035	...	|	|	|	|	|	|	...	|	|	|	|	...	...	|	|	...	|	|	|
Barcelona Sants **654/5** a.	2324	|	|	2	...	...	|	|	|	|	|	|	...	|	|	|	0900	**7726**	...	1108	1108	...	|	|	|
Venta de Baños **689** d.	...	1445	1633	⑦	...	...	1737	1805	|	1905	|	2028	...	2036	2036	2202	...	2	...	...	...	...	0330	0330	0445
Valladolid C. Grande **689** d.	...	1506	1705	1725	...	...	1805	1826	1845	1930	1938	2100	...	2100	2100	2230	...	2240	...	...	...	...	0400	0400	0507
Medina del Campo **681/9** a.	...	1529	...	1748	...	...	...	1849	1906	1953	1959	...	...	2127	2127	...	...	2313	...	...	...	...	0430	0430	0529
Ávila **681/9** a.	...	1614	...	1836	...	...	...	1934	1949	2036	2039	...	...	2212	2212	...	...	...	...	...	...	...	0540	0542	0616
Madrid Chamartín **681/9** a.	...	1745	...	2026d	...	...	...	2110	2120	2209d	2212	...	...	2341d	2341d	...	...	...	...	...	...	...	0735	0735	0800

A – ATLÁNTICO – ⑧. 🛏, ▬ and [1] Madrid - Ferrol and v.v.
B – GALICIA – 🛏, ▬ and [1] Barcelona - A Coruña and Vigo and v.v. 🍷 Barcelona - A Coruña and v.v.
C – COSTA VERDE – ⑧. 🛏 and [1] Madrid - Gijón and Santander and v.v.
F – FINISTERRE – ②④⑥⑦. [12] Barcelona - A Coruña.
G – FINISTERRE – ①③⑤. [12] Barcelona - Vigo.
H – FINISTERRE – ②④⑥. [12] Vigo - Barcelona.
J – FINISTERRE – ①③⑤⑦. [12] A Coruña - Barcelona.

L – LAGOS DE COVADONGA – [12] Barcelona - Gijón and v.v.
N – From / to Alacant.
P – PÍO BAROJA – ⑧. 🛏, ▬ and [12] Barcelona - Gijón and v.v.
Q – From / to Bilbao.
T – [12] Alacant - Santander and v.v.
Y – Not ⑤.

c – Starts from Madrid Atocha Cercanías (d. 1618).
d – Continues to Madrid Atocha Cercanías (a. 14–18 minutes later).

j – Gijón Jovellanos.
* – Number from Valladolid
▲ – Via Santiago (Table **681**).

683 LEÓN - BILBAO

FEVE narrow-gauge

León	La Vecilla	Cistierna	Guardo	Vado Cervera	Mataporquera	Espinosa	Balmaseda	**Bilbao** Concordia
1400 →	1445 →	1535 →	1636 →	1717 →	1801 →	1935 →	2042 →	2130
2145	← 2059	← 2018	← 1921	← 1841	← 1800	← 1623	← 1519	← 1430

PALENCIA - SANTANDER 684

km		*Estr* 831 C	2	2 8101	*Talgo* 61 🍷	2	2 B	*Talgo* 77 🍷L	2 8791 ⑤
	Madrid Chamartín **682 689** d.	2245	...	...	0900	*1130*	...	1630	1633
	Valladolid CG **682 689** d.	0142	...	0935	1124	1435	1810	1854	1919
0	**Palencia** d.	0356	...	1020	1151	1518	1855	1924	1957
98	Aguilar de Campoo d.	0521	...	1134	1251	1642	2003	2022	2104
110	Mataporquera **683** d.	0534	...	1144	|	1650	2013	|	2114
129	Reinosa § d.	0553	0855	1200	1316	1715	2036	2048	2129
188	Torrelavega § d.	0647	1001	1258	1405	1816	2140	2135	2224
218	**Santander** § a.	0737	1035	1332	1435	1853	2216	2200	2250

	2 8702 ①–⑤	*Talgo* 76 🍷L	2 ⑥⑦	2	2	*Talgo* 60 🍷	2 8104 ①–⑥	2 8790 ⑦	*Estr* 830 C
Santander § d.	...	0810	0818	1006	1410	1545	1645	1715	2300
Torrelavega § d.	...	0834	0854	1043	1447	1606	1721	1740	2329
Reinosa § d.	0715	0917	0957	1145	1548	1650	1822	1835	0035
Mataporquera **683** d.	0734	|	1013	...	1605	|	1838	1850	0052
Aguilar de Campoo d.	0744	0940	1022	...	1615	1714	1848	1857	0103
Palencia a.	0859	1040	1139	...	1727	1813	2016	2015	0224
Valladolid CG **682 689** a.	0943	1112	1219	...	1805	1844	2100	2058	0355
Madrid Chamartín **682 689** a.	*1255*	1342	*1540*	...	*2110*	2120	...	2341	0735

– Not ⑤. C – COSTA VERDE – Ⓑ. 🛏 and (1) Madrid - Santander and v.v. L – From / to Alacant. § – Additional local services operate.

LEÓN - OVIEDO - GIJÓN 685

km		*Estr* 831 C	2	*Estr* 933 P	*Talgo* 131 🍷	2	*Talgo* 623 🍷V	*Talgo* 79 🍷T	2 Ⓑ
	Barcelona Sants **682** d.	...	...	2200	...	...	0703	...	...
	Madrid Chamartín **682** d.	2245	...	|	0800	...	*1130*	1500	...
0	**León** d.	0445	...	0907	1152	1315	1652	1900	1940
109	Pola de Lena § a.	0620	0800	1048	|	1448	1822	2019	2120
140	**Oviedo** ▽ § a.	0657	0838	1116	1343	1523	1852	2044	2207
172	**Gijón** Cercanias § a.	0735j	0915	1158	1415	1553	1930	2125	2247

	2 ①–⑤	*Talgo* 78 🍷T	*Talgo* 620 🍷V	2	*Talgo* 130 🍷	2	*Estr* 930 P	2	*Estr* 830 C
Gijón Cercanias § d.	0655	0920	1030	1300	1555	1730	1905	2030	2230j
Oviedo ▽ § d.	0734	0950	1057	1336	1625	1806	1934	2106	2300
Pola de Lena § d.	0809	1021	1126	1418	|	1848	2004	2148	2334
León a.	1007	1139	1255	1558	1810	...	2126	...	0109
Madrid Chamartín **682** a.	...	1540	*1745*	*2110*	2212	...	|	...	0735
Barcelona Sants **682** a.	...	...	2324	...	...	...	0900	...	...

– COSTA VERDE – Ⓑ. 🛏 and (1) Madrid - Gijón and v.v.
– PÍO BAROJA – Ⓑ. 🛏, 🛌 (12) Barcelona - Gijón and v.v.
T – From / to Alacant.
V – COVADONGA.
j – Gijón Jovellanos.
§ – Additional local services operate between these stations.

▽ – **OVIEDO – AVILÉS** *31 km*
0515 Ⓐ, 0550 Ⓐ, 0620 Ⓐ, 0655 Ⓐ, 0720, 0820 and hourly until 2220. On Ⓐ also at 0750, 0850, 1250, 1350, 1450, 1750, 1850, 1950, 2050. On ⑥ also at 1350.

AVILÉS – OVIEDO Journey time: ± 38 minutes
0603 Ⓐ, 0645 Ⓐ, 0720 Ⓐ, 0745 Ⓐ, 0815, 0845 Ⓐ, 0915, 0945 Ⓐ, 1045, 1145, 1215, 1315 and hourly until 2315. On Ⓐ also at 1345, 1445, 1545, 1845, 1945, 2045, 2145. On ⑥ also at 1445.

SAN SEBASTIÁN - OVIEDO - FERROL 686

2nd class Narrow gauge

EuskoTren	Ⓐ									
San Sebastián ⊡ Amara d.	0547	0647*	0747	0847	0920	0947		1947	2020	2047
Zarautz d.	0620	0720*	0820	0920	0947	1020	and	2020	2047	2120
Eibar d.	0713	0813	0913	1013	1035	1113	hourly	2113	2136	2213
Durango d.	0742	0842	0942	1042	1101	1142	until	2142	2200	2242
Bilbao Bolueta ⊖ a.	0821	0921	1021	1121	1129	1221		2221	2231	...
Bilbao Atxuri § a.	0825	0925	1025	1125	1133	1225		2225	2235	...
FEVE	Ⓐ		Ⓐ			Ⓐ				
Bilbao Concordia ⊖ § d.	...	...	...	...	0802	...	...	1302	...	1930
Marrón d.	...	...	0720	...	0940	...	...	1434	...	2106
Santander a.	...	...	0828	...	1100	...	...	1558	...	2215
Santander ▽ d.	...	...	...	0910	...	...	...	1610	...	...
Torrelavega ▽ d.	...	...	...	0937	...	...	...	1638	...	...
Unquera d.	...	...	...	1044	...	...	...	1743	...	...
Llanes d.	0630	0755	...	1113	...	1430	...	1813	...	...
Ribadesella d.	0705	0832	...	1153	...	1507	...	1852	...	...
Oviedo a.	...	1029	...	1354	...	1707	...	2054	...	...
FEVE										
Oviedo △ d.	...	0747	1147	...	...	1447	...	1847	1947	...
Gijón Cercanías △ d.	0732	|	|	1132	1432	|	1832	|	|	2032
Avilés △ d.	0814	|	|	1218	1518	|	1918	|	|	2118
Pravia △ d.	0844	0846	1247	1248	1548	1552	1948	2000	2047	2148
Navia d.	—	1021	—	—	...	1728	...	2140	...	...
Tapia de Casariego d.	...	1044	...	...	...	1750	...	...	...	...
Ribadeo d.	0645	1112	...	1440	...	1817	...	...	...	...
Viveiro d.	0753	1221	Ⓐ	1547	...	1922	...	...	...	...
Ortigueira d.	0833	1300	1458	1630	...	2002	...	...	...	...
Ferrol a.	0947	1409	1610	1745	...	2109	...	...	...	...

FEVE								Ⓐ		
Ferrol d.	...	...	...	...	0810	1030	...	1345	1518	1845
Ortigueira d.	...	...	...	...	0922	1140	...	1457	1630	2001
Viveiro d.	...	...	...	...	1000	1220	...	—	1710	2041
Ribadeo d.	...	...	...	...	1110	1328	...	...	1818	2150
Tapia de Casariego d.	...	...	...	...	1134	—	...	...	1844	—
Navia d.	...	...	0640	...	1158	...	...	...	1907	...
Pravia △ d.	0645	0730	0829	0848	1331	1348	1630	1648	2047	2048
Avilés △ d.	0726	|	|	0928	|	1428	|	1728	|	2128
Gijón Cerçanías △ a.	0808	|	|	1008	|	1508	|	1808	|	2208
Oviedo △ a.	...	0829	0929	...	1428	...	1729	...	2148	...
FEVE		Ⓐ			Ⓐ		Ⓐ			
Oviedo d.	...	...	...	0905	1035	...	...	1535	...	1855
Ribadesella d.	...	0710	...	1100	1241	...	...	1735	...	2054
Llanes d.	...	0745	...	1139	1317	...	...	1814	...	2130
Unquera d.	...	...	...	1208	...	...	...	1843	...	...
Torrelavega ▽ d.	...	...	...	1316	...	...	...	1948	...	...
Santander ▽ a.	...	...	...	1346	...	...	...	2016	...	...
Santander d.	0800	...	...	1400	...	1900	2000	...	...	...
Marrón d.	0911	...	...	1514	...	2011	2106	...	...	...
Bilbao Concordia ⊖ § a.	1046	...	...	1646	...	2146	...	...	...	...
EuskoTren	Ⓐ									
Bilbao Atxuri § d.	...	0557*	0657	0757	0857	0934	0957		1957	2034
Bilbao Bolueta ⊖ d.	...	0601*	0701	0801	0901	0939	1001	and	2001	2039
Durango d.	0539	0641*	0741	0841	0941	1012	1041	hourly	2041	2112
Eibar d.	0613	0713*	0813	0912	1012	1035	1113	until	2113	2135
Zarautz d.	0708	0808	0908	1008	1108	1122	1208		2208	2222
San Sebastián ⊡ Amara a.	0739	0839	0939	1039	1139	1147	1239		2239	2247

⊡ – San Sebastián / Donostia.
⊖ – Metro interchange.
* – Ⓐ only.
§ – Bilbao Atxuri ⇆ Bilbao Concordia: ± *1000 m.* Bilbao Concordia is adjacent to Bilbao Abando (*Renfe*).
▽ – Additional trains run Santander - Torrelavega and v.v.
△ – Additional trains run Oviedo / Gijón - Pravia and v.v.

MADRID - LOGROÑO, PAMPLONA and IRÚN 687

High-speed services

km		*Alta* 601 ①–⑤		*Alta* 605		*Alta* 609		*Alta* 701 Ⓑ		*Alta* 801 Ⓑ
0	**Madrid** Pta de Atocha .. **650** d.	0715	...	0950	...	1405	...	1810	...	1930
64	Guadalajara - Yebes **650** d.	0743	...	|	...	1433	...	1838	...	|
221	Calatayud **650** d.	0839	...	|	...	1529	...	1934	...	|
361	Castejón de Ebro d.	1001	...	|	...	|	...	|	...	|
438	**Logroño** a.	|	...	|	...	|	...	2150	...	|
449	**Pamplona / Iruña** a.	1055	...	1320	...	1744	...	...	...	2301
544	Vitoria / Gasteiz a.	...	...	...	...	|	...	...	...	2352
588	San Sebastián / Donostia a.	...	...	...	...	1923	...	...	...	...
605	**Irún** a.	...	...	...	...	1941s	...	...	...	...
608	Hendaye a.	...	...	...	...	1946	...	...	...	...

	Alta 802 ①–⑥		*Alta* 702 ①–⑥		*Alta* 602 Ⓑ		*Alta* 606 Ⓑ		*Alta* 610
Irún d.	...	...	...	...	...	...	...	...	1705
San Sebastián / Donostia d.	...	...	...	...	...	...	...	...	1721
Vitoria / Gasteiz d.	0610	...	...	...	...	...	...	...	|
Pamplona / Iruña d.	0700	...	...	...	1220	...	1617	...	1900
Logroño d.	|	...	0800	...	|	...	|	...	|
Castejón de Ebro d.	0750	...	|	...	|	...	|	...	|
Calatayud **650** a.	0912	...	1015	...	|	...	1832	...	|
Guadalajara - Yebes **650** a.	1006	...	1109	...	|	...	1925	...	|
Madrid Pta de Atocha .. **650** a.	1037	...	1140	...	1543	...	1955	...	2234

s – Stops to set down only.
☛ All trains convey 🍷.

IRÚN - BILBAO - SANTANDER - GIJÓN 688

Turytrans ★

	▽ ①–⑥				▼	①–⑥			▼ Ⓑ		▽ Ⓑ			▼					▽ ⑤⑦			⑦		
Irún RENFE rail station d.	...	...	...	...	0645b	0745	0845	...	...	1100	...	...	1345	1445	...	1645	...	1830	...	...	2045	2115	...	2345
San Sebastián / Donostia d.	...	...	...	...	0710b	0810	0910	...	...	1125	...	...	1410	1510	...	1710	...	1855	...	...	2110	2140	...	0005
Bilbao TermiBus § d.	0600	0700	...	...	0830	0930	1030	...	1230	1330	1430	...	1530	1630	1730	1830	...	2030	2100	...	2230	2300	...	0130
Santander § d.	0715	0820	0830	...	0945	1100	1215	...	1345	1530	1545	...	1700	1745	1900	2000	...	2200	2215	...	2350	0020	...	0330
Oviedo d.	1000	...	1145	...	1200	...	|	...	1600	1845	1800	...	...	2000	2145	2300	...	...	0030	...	...	...	...	0630
Gijón a.	0930	...	1215	...	1230	...	1545	...	1630	1915	1830	...	...	2030	2215	2330	...	...	0100	...	...	...	...	0700

	①–⑥			①–⑥	▼	⑥			▽ ①–⑥			⑤⑦	▼		▼ Ⓑ					▽ Ⓑ		▽ ⑦		
Gijón d.	...	...	...	...	0715	...	...	0815	0915	...	1115	...	1315	...	1615	1515	...	1715	...	1915	2015	2115	...	2359
Oviedo d.	...	...	...	...	0745	...	...	0845	0945	...	1145	...	1345	...	1645	1545	...	1745	...	1945	2045	2145	...	0045
Santander § d.	0600	0700	...	0930	1000	0930	...	1200	1200	...	1500	1530	1600	1700	1900	1900	...	2030	...	2200	2340	2359	...	0330
Bilbao TermiBus § d.	0730	0840	...	1100	1115	1130	...	1400	1315	...	1630	1730	1715	1830	2015	2045	...	2200	...	2315	...	0115	...	0500
San Sebastián / Donostia a.	0840	1000	...	1210	1225	1240	...	1600	...	...	...	1840	1825z	1940	2125c	2155	...	2310	...	...	...	0225	...	0625
Irún RENFE rail station a.	0910	1030	...	1240	1255	1310	...	1630	...	...	...	1910	1855z	2010	2155c	2225	...	2340	...	...	...	0255	...	0645

– ①–⑤.
– Not ⑥.
c – ①–④ only.
z – ⑥ only.
▼ – *Clase Supra* luxury coach.
▽ – *Eurobús* luxury coach.
§ – Additional services operate Bilbao - Santander and v.v.
★ – Alsa Turytrans: ✆ +34 902 42 22 42 www.alsa.es
¶ – Services contiue to Hendaye SNCF station (a. 10 mins later).

For new high-speed services from Dec. 23/24, see page 540

689 MADRID and SALAMANCA - BILBAO and IRÚN

km △		Estr 310 🍷 S		6007 2 fN	2 ①–⑤	6001* 2	Estr 941 🍷 P	8401 2 ①–⑥	2 ①–⑥	TRD 8302 2 ①–⑤	Talgo 530 🍷 U	TRD 8314 2 ⑥	2 Y	8061 2	6003 2	Talgo 61 🍷 A	D 410 2🍷	D 410 2🍷	IC 203 🍷 ①–⑥	2	6021 6009* 2 N	Alta 609 🍷	2 ①–⑥
0	**Madrid** Chamartín **681 682** d.	...	...	...	...	...	...	...	...	...	...	...	...	0830	...	0900	...	...	1000	...	...	1405p	...
	Aranda de Duero d.	...	...	...	...	...	...	...	...	...	...	...	...	|	...	|	...	...	|	...	...	|	...
122	Ávila **681 682** d.	...	...	...	...	...	0548	...	0715	...	...	...	...	0953	...	1020	...	...	1121	...	...	|	...
**	**Salamanca** d.	0005	...	...	...	...	|	...	|	0715	0800	0813	...	|	...	|	1030	1030	|	...	...	|	...
207	Medina del Campo **681 682** d.	0057	...	...	...	...	0632	...	0803	0809	0850	0908	0928	1038	...	1102	1120	1120	1203	...	...	|	...
250	**Valladolid** Campo Grande **682** d.	0130	...	...	...	...	0657	0700	0827	0840	0918	0938	1000	1101	...	1124	1147	1147	1225	1230	...	|	...
286	Venta de Baños **682** d.	|	...	...	...	...	|	0733	...	...	|	...	...	1125	...	|	1211	1211	|	1303	...	|	...
298	Palencia **682** d.	|	...	...	...	...	|	0745	...	...	|	...	...	1138	...	1150	|	|	|	1313	...	⊡	...
371	**Burgos 682** d.	0254	...	...	...	...	0813	0842	...	...	1028	...	...	1226	...	...	1300	1300	1326	...	1400f	|	...
460	Miranda de Ebro **655** d.	0355	...	...	0725	0900	0913	...	...	...	1151	...	...	1330	...	...	1421	1440	1418	...	1501	|	1715
565	**Bilbao** Abando **655** a.	|	...	...	|	|	1118	...	...	...	|	...	...	|	...	...	|	1632	|	...	|	|	|
	Barcelona Sants **655** a.	|	...	...	|	|	...	...	...	...	1921	...	...	|	...	...	|	...	|	...	|	|	|
494	Vitoria / Gasteiz **655** d.	0424	...	0740	0751	0928	...	...	...	...	...	...	...	1402	1417	...	1459	...	1440	...	1530	|	1742
537	Altsasu **655** d.	|	...	0810n	...	0954	...	...	...	...	...	...	...	...	1445	...	1524	...	1505	...	1601n	|	...
624	**San Sebastián / Donostia 655** ... ▲ d.	0634	...	...	...	1110	...	...	...	...	...	...	...	...	1600	...	1640	...	1625s	...	...	1924	...
641	**Irún 655** ▲ a.	0658	...	...	...	1135	...	...	...	...	...	...	...	...	1623	...	1700	...	1650s	...	...	1941s	...
643	Hendaye **655** ▲ a.	0710	...	...	...	...	...	...	...	...	...	...	...	...	...	...	1707	...	1656	...	...	1946	...

	TRD 8306 2	D 280 2🍷 C	D 280 2 Z	8063 6005* 2	6011 2 N	IC 209 🍷 ⑦	6071 L2 ⑧	Talgo 201 🍷	TRD 8316 2 ⑦	8017 K2	2 ①–⑤	8065 2 ⑧	TRD 8312 2 ①–⑥	Estr 930 🍷 B	8719 2	TRD 8324 2 ⑦	2 ⑦	2	2 ⑤	8007 2 ⑧		Estr 205 🍷 V	Estr 205 🍷 X
Madrid Chamartín **681 682** d.	...	...	...	1330	...	1442	...	1605	...	...	...	1730	...	...	...	...	...	1932	1932	2030	...	2245	2245
Aranda de Duero d.	...	...	...	|	...	|	...	1812	...	...	...	|	...	...	...	...	...	|	|	|	...	|	|
Ávila **681 682** d.	...	...	...	1458	...	1611	...	|	...	...	...	1903	...	...	...	...	...	2125	2126	2153	...	0020	0020
Salamanca d.	1350	...	...	|	...	|	...	|	1700	...	...	|	2010	2025	...	2035	...	...	|	|	...	|	|
Medina del Campo **681 682** d.	1447	...	...	1543	...	1652	...	|	1753	...	1840	1948	2105	2117	...	2135	...	...	2218	2238	...	0110	0110
Valladolid Campo Grande **682** d.	1509	...	...	1606	...	1714	...	|	1825	1900	1915	2011	2135	2141	2200	2205	2210	...	2244	2301	...	0142	0142
Venta de Baños **682** d.	1533	...	...	1627	...	|	...	|	...	1921	...	2035	...	|	2233	...	2243	...	...	2325	...	0222	0222
Palencia **682** d.	1540	1557	1557	1640	...	|	...	|	...	1935	...	2048	...	2240	2243	...	2253	...	...	2342	...	|	|
Burgos 682 d.	...	1644	1644	1728	...	1821	...	1913	...	2023	...	2136	...	2324	...	...	...	...	...	...	...	0317	0317
Miranda de Ebro **655** d.	...	1750	1805	1828	...	1916	1958	2017	...	2125	...	2238	...	0043	...	...	...	...	...	...	...	0430	0530
Bilbao Abando **655** a.	...	|	1952	|	...	|	|	2159	...	...	...	|	...	|	...	...	...	...	...	...	...	|	0725
Barcelona Sants **655** a.	...	|	...	|	...	|	|	...	...	...	...	|	...	0845	...	...	...	...	...	...	...	|	...
Vitoria / Gasteiz **655** d.	...	1813	...	1900	1905	1937	2024	...	...	...	...	2308	...	...	...	...	...	...	...	...	...	0456	...
Altsasu **655** d.	...	1839	...	1929	1936n	1959	...	...	...	...	...	...	...	...	...	...	...	...	...	...	...	0523	...
San Sebastián / Donostia 655 ... ▲ d.	...	2005	...	2050	...	2123s	...	...	...	...	...	...	...	...	...	...	...	...	...	...	...	0652s	...
Irún 655 ▲ a.	...	2027s	...	2108	...	2146s	...	...	...	...	...	...	...	...	...	...	...	...	...	...	...	0717	...
Hendaye **655** ▲ a.	...	2035	...	...	...	2151	...	...	...	...	...	...	...	...	...	...	...	...	...	...	...	0725	...

km ▽		8000 2 ①–⑥	TRD 8300 2 ①–⑤	2 ①–⑤	Estr 933 🍷 B	8702 2 R	TRD 8304 2 ⑥	8010 2 ①–⑥	6070 K2 ①–⑤	8069 L2	2	6000 2 ①–⑥		6013 2 fN	IC 202 🍷	Talgo 200 🍷	D 283 2 Z	D 283 2🍷 C	TRD 8308 2		8012 2	2 ⑦	2 Y
0	**Irún 655** ▲ d.	...	...	...	...	...	...	...	...	...	...	0640	...	...	0815	...	...	0845	...	...	...	...	...
17	**San Sebastián / Donostia 655** ... ▲ d.	...	...	...	...	...	...	...	...	...	...	0657	...	...	0832	...	...	0902	...	...	...	...	...
104	Altsasu **655** d.	...	...	...	...	...	...	...	...	...	...	0814	...	0916n	0947	...	...	1017	...	...	...	...	...
147	Vitoria / Gasteiz **655** d.	...	...	...	...	...	...	0720	0810	...	...	0845	...	0948	1008	...	...	1040	...	...	1340	...	...
	Barcelona Sants **655** d.	...	...	...	2200	...	...	|	|	...	...	...	...	...	|	...	...	|	...	...	|	...	...
	Bilbao Abando **655** d.	...	...	...	|	...	...	|	|	...	...	...	...	...	|	0855	0915	|	...	...	|	...	...
180	Miranda de Ebro **682** d.	...	...	...	0544	...	...	0743	0835	0837	...	...	...	...	1029	1041	1118	1118	...	...	1403	...	...
270	**Burgos 682** d.	...	...	...	0654	...	...	0844	...	0943	...	...	...	...	1125	1141	1213	1213	...	...	1502	...	...
	Palencia **682** d.	0640	...	0733	0807	0900	...	0934	...	1037	...	...	...	...	|	|	1258	1258	1320	...	1552	...	...
	Venta de Baños **682** d.	0650	...	0744	|	0910	...	0944	...	1046	...	...	...	...	|	|	...	...	1329	...	1602	...	...
	Valladolid Campo Grande **682** d.	0711	0715	0815	0841	0943	0945	1005	...	1110	1130	...	...	...	1230	|	...	...	1353	...	1623	1725	1730
	Medina del Campo **681 682** d.	0735	0748	...	0908	...	1016	1030	...	...	1205	...	...	...	1253	|	...	...	1418	...	1648	1749	1756
	Salamanca a.	|	0846	...	0956	...	1116	|	...	...	...	...	...	...	|	|	...	...	1516	...	|	|	...
	Ávila **681 682** d.	0820	...	...	...	...	...	1115	...	...	...	...	...	...	1338	|	...	...	...	...	1733	1837	...
385	Aranda de Duero d.	|	...	...	...	...	...	|	...	...	...	...	...	...	|	1239	...	...	...	...	|	|	...
553	**Madrid** Chamartín **681 682** a.	0945	...	...	...	...	...	1255	...	...	...	...	...	...	1512	1450	...	...	...	...	1915	2028a	...

	2 ①–⑤		D 413 2	D 413 2🍷	TRD 8318 2 ⑦	Talgo 60 🍷 A	6002 2	2 ⑧	Alta 610 🍷	6015 2 N	8014 2	TRD 8310 2		8408 2 ⑧	Talgo 533 🍷 U		6017§ 2 N	Estr 940 🍷 Q	6004§ 2		Estr 313 🍷 T	Estr 204 🍷 X	Estr 204 🍷 W
Irún 655 ▲ d.	...	...	...	1320	...	...	1517	...	1705	...	...	...	...	...	...	...	...	...	1937	...	2200	...	2215
San Sebastián / Donostia 655 ... ▲ d.	...	...	...	1337	...	...	1535	...	1721	...	...	...	...	...	...	...	...	...	1956	...	2220	...	2237
Altsasu **655** d.	...	...	...	1448	...	...	1652	...	|	1713n	...	...	...	...	...	...	2015n	...	2114	...	|	...	2359
Vitoria / Gasteiz **655** d.	1430	...	...	1515	...	...	1721	...	|	1750	1755	...	...	1900	...	...	2055	...	2150	...	0015	...	0033
Barcelona Sants **655** d.	|	...	...	|	...	...	...	...	|	...	|	...	...	|	1230	...	|	...	|	...	|	...	|
Bilbao Abando **655** d.	|	...	1400	|	...	...	...	...	|	...	|	...	...	|	|	...	|	2035	|	...	|	2300	|
Miranda de Ebro **682** d.	1457	...	1602	1602	...	...	...	...	|	...	1816	...	...	1930	2005	...	2122	2214	2214	...	0040	0120	0120
Burgos 682 d.	...	...	1704	1704	...	...	...	...	|	...	1918	...	...	2035	2106	...	...	2313	...	...	0159	0220	0220
Palencia **682** d.	...	...	|	|	...	1814	...	...	⊡	...	2010	...	...	2130	|	...	...	|	...	...	|	|	|
Venta de Baños **682** d.	...	...	1748	1748	...	|	...	...	|	...	2019	...	...	2140	|	...	...	|	...	...	|	0330	0330
Valladolid Campo Grande **682** d.	...	...	1813	1813	1838	1845	...	1946	|	...	2041	2045	...	2210	2217	...	...	0022	...	...	0320	0400	0400
Medina del Campo **681 682** d.	...	...	1840	1840	1915	1907	...	2020	|	...	2105	2116	...	...	2240	...	...	0047	...	...	0353	0435	0435
Salamanca a.	...	...	1933	1933	2012	|	...	|	|	...	|	2211	...	...	2330	...	...	|	...	...	0448	|	|
Ávila **681 682** d.	...	...	...	...	...	1950	...	2110	|	...	2151	...	...	...	...	...	...	0134	...	...	...	0542	0542
Aranda de Duero d.	...	...	...	...	...	|	...	...	|	...	|	...	...	...	...	...	...	...	...	...	...	|	|
Madrid Chamartín **681 682** a.	...	...	...	...	...	2120	...	...	2234p	...	2327	...	...	...	...	...	...	...	...	...	...	0735	0735

A – [12] Madrid - Santander and v.v.
B – PÍO BAROJA – ⑤⑦. 🛏, 🛌 and [1] Salamanca - Barcelona and v.v.
C – [2] From / to A Coruña.
K – To Logroño.
L – From Logroño.
N – To / from Pamplona (Table **655**).
P – PICASSO – ⑦ (① from Ávila). 🛏, 🛌 and [12] Málaga - Bilbao (Table **671**).
Q – PICASSO – ⑤. 🛏, 🛌 and [12] Bilbao - Málaga (Table **671**).
R – ①–⑤. From Reinosa (Table **684**).
S – SUREX – 🛏, 🛌 and [12] Lisboa - Hendaye.
T – SUREX – 🛏, 🛌 and [12] Irún - Lisboa.
U – MIGUEL DE UNAMUNO – [12] Salamanca - Barcelona and v.v.
V – COSTA VASCA – 🛏, 🛌 and [1] Madrid - Hendaye.
W – COSTA VASCA – 🛏, 🛌 and [1] Irún - Madrid.
X – COSTA VASCA – ⑧. 🛏 and [1] Madrid - Bilbao and v.v.
Y – [2] Puebla de Sanabria - Valladolid and v.v.
Z – From / to Vigo.
a – Continues to Madrid Atocha (a. 2042).
f – ①–⑥.
n – Altsasu Pueblo.
p – Madrid Puerta de Atocha.
s – Stops to set down only.
⊡ – Runs via Pamplona (Table **655**).
* – Train number from Vitoria.
§ – Train number to Vitoria.
△ – Via Ávila.
▽ – Via Aranda.
** – Salamanca - Medina: *70 km.*

▲ – **SAN SEBASTIÁN - IRÚN** and v.v. ***Renfe Cercanías*** (suburban) service. *17 km.* Journey time: ± 23 minutes.

From San Sebastián: Approximately 2–3 trains each hour from 0630 until 2300.
From Irún: Approximately 2–3 trains each hour from 0522 until 2222.

▲ – **SAN SEBASTIÁN** (Amara) - **IRÚN** (Colón, near Renfe station) - **HENDAYE** (SNCF station) and v.v. ***EuskoTren*** (narrow-gauge) service. *22 km.* Journey time: ± 37 minutes.

From San Sebastián: 0000⑦, 0200⑦, 0400⑦, 0555Ⓐ, 0600⑦, 0615Ⓐ, 0645Ⓐ, 0715, 0745 and every 30 minutes until 2145; also at 1148©**n**, 2233©**n**.
From Hendaye (A): 0040⑦, 0240⑦, 0440⑦, 0640⑦, 0647Ⓐ, 0703Ⓐ, 0733Ⓐ, 0803, 0833 and every 30 minutes until 2233; also at 0849©**n**, 1949©**n**.

A – 4 minutes later from Irún.
n – Non-stop journey, not calling at Irún (journey time 27–29 minutes).

PORTUGAL

SEE MAP PAGE 321

Operator: CP – Comboios de Portugal (www.cp.pt).

Train categories: *Alfa Pendular* – *AP* – high-quality tilting express trains. *Intercidades* – *IC* – high-quality express trains linking the main cities of Portugal to Lisboa and Porto. *Interregional* – *IR* – 'semi-fast' links usually calling at principal stations only. *Regional* and *Suburbano* – local stopping trains (shown without train numbers).

Higher fares are payable for travel by *AP* and *IC* trains as well as the international **Sud Expresso** service (Lisboa - Hendaye / Irún - Lisboa), together with an additional supplement for travel by *AP* trains. Special fares apply to the **Lusitânia** *Hotel Train* service (Lisboa - Madrid and v.v.).

Services: All services shown with a train number convey first and second class accommodation (on *Alfa Pendular* trains termed, respectively, *Conforto* and *Turística*) unless otherwise indicated. *Regional* and *Suburbano* trains convey second-class seating only.

AP, *IC*, *IR* and international trains convey a buffet car (*carruagem-bar*) and there is an at-seat service of meals to passengers in 1st class on *AP* and certain *IC* trains. Sleeping- (🛏) and couchette (▬) cars are of the normal European types described on page 10.

Reservations: Reservations are compulsory for travel by *AP* and *IC* trains, also the *Sud Expresso* and *Lusitania*. Seat reservation is not normally available on other services.

Timings: Valid from **April 22, 2007**, with amendments to mid May. Amendments may come into effect at short notice.

LISBOA - COIMBRA - PORTO 690

Reservations compulsory on all *AP* and *IC* trains. For local trains Entroncamento - Coimbra / Coimbra - Aveiro / Aveiro - Porto see Table **699**

km		*AP* 121	*AP* 131	*IC* 521	*AP* 123	*IC* 511	*IC* 523	*AP* 182	*IC* 525	*AP* 125		*IC* 513	*AP* 133	*IC* 527	*AP* 135	311	*AP* 127	*IC* 621	*AP* 184	*IC* 515	*AP* 137	*IC* 529	*AP* 129	*IC* 531
		Ⓐ		①–⑥	①–⑥					⚒	⑤				Ⓑ h	S						Ⓑ		
			△		n	◇					z	◇	△		△	Ⓡ		☆		◇	△	h		
	Faro **697** d.	...	...	...	...	...	...	0655	...	...	...	...	...	...	...	..	...	...	1455	...	...	...	...	...
0	**Lisboa** Sta Apolónia ▷ d.	0600	0700	0730	0800	0830	0930	|	1130	1200	...	1328	1400	1530	1600	1606	1700	1730	|	1828	1900	1930	2000	2130
7	**Lisboa** Oriente ▷ d.	0609	0709	0739	0809	0839	0939	1009	1139	1209	...	1337	1409	1539	1609	1614	1709	1739	1809	1837	1909	1939	2009	2139
31	Vila Franca de Xira ▷ d.	|	|	0752	|	0852	0952	|	1152	|	...	1350	|	1552	|	|	|	1752	|	1850	|	1952	|	2152
75	Santarém ▷ d.	|	|	0815	0842	0917	1015	|	1215	|	...	1415	|	1615	|	|	|	1815	|	1915	|	2015	2042	2215
107	**Entroncamento** ▷ d.	|	|	0833	0900	0936	1033	|	1233	|	1358	1434	|	1633	|	1719	|	1833	|	1934	|	2033	2100	2233
131	Fátima ⊙ d.	|	|	|	|	0949	|	|	|	|	1414	1447	|	|	|	1733	|	|	|	1947	|	|	|	|
171	Pombal d.	|	|	0906	0929	1013	1109	|	1306	|	1438	1511	|	1706	|	1757	|	1909	|	2011	|	2106	2129	2309
199	Alfarelos d.	|	|	|	|	1027	|	|	1320	|	1456	1525	|	1720	|	|	|	|	|	2025	|	|	|	|
218	**Coimbra** B ▶ d.	0746	0846	0931	0952	1041	1134	1146	1333	1346	1510	1539	1546	1733	1746	1826	1846	1933	1946	2039	2046	2131	2152	2334
232	Pampilhosa d.	|	|	|	|	1053	|	|	1343	|	1521	1551	|	1743	|	1841	|	|	|	2051	|	|	|	|
273	Aveiro d.	0811	0911	1000	1016	...	1200	1211	1401	1411	1552	...	1611	1801	1811	...	1911	2000	2011	...	2111	2200	2216	0000
318	Espinho d.	|	|	1024	1037	...	1224	|	1423	|	1623	...	|	1823	|	...	|	2024	|	...	|	2224	2237	0024
334	Vila Nova de Gaia d.	0839	0939	1034	1047	...	1234	1239	1434	1439	1633	...	1639	1834	1839	...	1939	2034	2039	...	2139	2234	2247	0034
337	**Porto** Campanhã ▽ a.	0844	0944	1039	1052	...	1239	1244	1439	1444	1639	...	1644	1839	1844	...	1944	2039	2044	...	2144	2239	2252	0039

		AP 180	*AP* 130	*IC* 520	*AP* 120	*IN* 313	*IC* 510	*IC* 620	*AP* 122	*IC* 522	*AP* 124	*IC* 524	*AP* 132	*IC* 512	*IC* 526	*AP* 186	*AP* 126	*IC* 528	*AP* 128		*AP* 134	*IC* 514	*IC* 530	*AP* 136
	①–⑥			①–⑥	①–⑥	T			⚒	①–⑥	Ⓑ								Ⓑ	⑦				Ⓑ h
			△	n	n	Ⓡ	◇	☆			b		△	◇						◇	△	◇		△
Porto Campanhã ▽ d.	0123	0547	0647	0652	0745	...	...	0852	0947	1052	1147	1252	1347	...	1452	1547	1647	1652	1745	...	1847	...	1952	2047
Vila Nova de Gaia d.	0128	0552	0652	0657	0750	...	...	0857	0952	1057	1152	1257	1352	...	1457	1552	1652	1657	1750	...	1852	...	1957	2052
Espinho d.	0141	|	|	0708	0800	...	...	0908	|	1108	|	1308	|	...	1508	|	|	1708	1800	...	|	...	2008	|
Aveiro d.	0216	0621	0721	0732	0821	...	...	0931	1021	1131	1221	1331	1421	...	1529	1621	1721	1731	1821	...	1921	...	2031	2121
Pampilhosa d.	0247	|	|	|	|	0838	0907	|	|	1148	|	|	|	1507	1546	|	|	|	|	1853	|	2007	|	|
Coimbra B ▶ d.	0300	0645	0745	0800	0845	0851	0919	0957	1045	1158	1245	1357	1445	1519	1557	1645	1745	1757	1845	1907	1945	2019	2057	2145
Alfarelos d.	0315	|	|	|	|	|	0933	|	|	1211	|	|	|	1533	1610	|	|	|	|	1920	|	2033	|	|
Pombal d.	0334	|	|	0825	0908	0919	0948	1022	|	1225	|	1423	|	1548	1625	|	|	1823	1908	1937	|	2048	2123	|
Fátima ⊙ d.	0403	|	|	|	|	0942	1012	|	|	|	|	|	|	1612	|	|	|	1839	|	|	|	2112	|	|
Entroncamento ▷ d.	0421	|	|	0858	0938	0956	1025	1058	|	1258	|	1458	|	1625	1658	|	|	1858	1938	2019	|	2125	2158	|
Santarém ▷ d.	0445	|	|	0916	0957	|	1044	1116	|	1316	|	1516	|	1644	1716	|	|	1916	1957	2039	|	2144	2216	|
Vila Franca de Xira ▷ d.	0522	|	|	0938	|	|	1107	1138	|	1338	|	1538	|	1707	1738	|	|	1938	|	2113	|	2207	2238	|
Lisboa Oriente ▷ a.	0542	0822	0922	0952	1029	1054	1121	1152	1222	1352	1422	1552	1622	1721	1752	1822	1922	1952	2029	2131	2122	2221	2252	2322
Lisboa Sta Apolónia ▷ a.	0553	|	0930	1000	1038	1103	1130	1200	1230	1400	1430	1600	1630	1730	1800	|	1930	2000	2038	2141	2130	2230	2300	2330
Faro **697** a.	...	1156	...	...	...	...	...	...	...	...	...	...	...	...	...	2158	...	...	...	...	...	...	...	...

S – SUD EXPRESSO – see Table **692**.
b – Not public holidays.
h – Not Oct. 5.
n – Not Oct. 6.
z – Runs on ④ if ⑤ is a public holiday.
⊙ – Fátima station is *20* km from Fátima.
☆ – Lisboa - Porto - Guimarães and v.v. (Table **695a**).
◇ – Lisboa - Guarda and v.v. (Table **692**).
△ – Lisboa - Porto - Braga and v.v. (Table **695**).
▷ – For other fast trains see Table **691**, for local trains see Table **699**.
▽ – Local services run Porto Campanhã - Porto São Bento.
▶ – Local trains run Coimbra B - Coimbra and v.v. (journey 4 mins).

LISBOA - ABRANTES - ELVAS and COVILHÃ 691

km			*IC* 541			*IC* 543			*IC* 545	335
										L
0	**Lisboa** Sta Apolónia ▷ d.	...	0818	...	...	1318	1618	...	1918	2200
7	**Lisboa** Oriente ▷ d.	...	0826	...	...	1327	1627	...	1926	2209
31	Vila Franca de Xira ▷ d.	...	0843	...	...	1340	1644	...	1943	|
75	Santarém ▷ d.	...	0910	...	...	1406	1716	...	2010	|
107	**Entroncamento** ▷ d.	0746	0931	0949	1154	1424	1736	1845	2028	2317
135	Abrantes d.	0821	0958	1029	1224	1445	1809	1920	2055	2338
175	Torre das Vargens d.	|	|	1111	|	|	|	2002	|	|
240	Marvão Beirã 🏛 a.	|	|	*1218*v	|	|	|	*2112*v	|	0053
217	Portalegre ⊖ d.	|	|	1156	|	|	|	2047	|	▬
266	**Elvas** ⊙ a.	|	|	1248	|	|	|	2139	|	...
199	Ródão d.	0929	1049	...	1322	1536	1908	...	2146	...
229	Castelo Branco a.	0957	1112	...	1350	1559	1940	...	2209	⚒
229	Castelo Branco d.	*1009*	1128	...	*1442*	1616	*1948*	...	2225	0625
283	Fundaõ d.	*1110*	1207	...	*1550*	1654	*2049*	...	2303	0729
301	**Covilhã** a.	*1131*	1223	...	*1611*	1710	*2110*	...	2319	0750

	332			*IC* 540				*IC* 542	*IC* 544
	L	⚒							
Covilhã d.	...	*0425*	...	0714	*0847*	*1253*	...	1501	1805
Fundaõ d.	...	*0444*	...	0730	*0907*	*1313*	...	1517	1821
Castelo Branco a.	...	*0540*	...	0809	*1004*	*1410*	...	1555	1859
Castelo Branco d.	...	0544	...	0825	1017	1426	...	1611	1915
Ródão d.	...	0612	...	0849	1049	1454	...	1635	1939
Elvas ⊙ d.	...	|	0526	|	|	|	1431	|	|
Portalegre ⊖ d.	...	|	0619	|	|	|	1542	|	|
Marvão Beirã 🏛 d.	0502	|	*0558*v	|	|	|	*1503*v	|	|
Torre das Vargens d.	|	|	0711	|	|	|	1616	|	|
Abrantes d.	0617	0710	0746	0940	1148	1559	1651	1726	2031
Entroncamento ▷ d.	0650	0741	0820	1002	1221	1629	1725	1751	2052
Santarém ▷ d.	|	0806	...	1021	...	...	...	1809	2110
Vila Franca de Xira ▷ d.	|	0844	...	1047	...	...	...	1836	2136
Lisboa Oriente ▷ a.	0751	0902	...	1101	...	...	...	1851	2151
Lisboa Sta Apolónia ▷ a.	0800	0911	...	1111	...	...	...	1900	2200

L – LUSITANIA – 🛏 and (12) Madrid - Lisboa and v.v. (Table **48**). Ⓡ. Not Dec. 24, 31.
v – Change at Torre das Vargens.
▷ – For other fast trains see Table **690**, for local trains see Table **699**.
⊙ – *16 km* from Badajoz (no rail service across the border).
⊖ – Station is *10 km* from Portalegre.

COVILHÃ - GUARDA

km				
0	Covilhã d.	0751	1618	2112
46	Guarda a.	0906	1733	2227

Guarda d.	0728	1555	1830
Covilhã a.	0846	1714	1942

(LISBOA) - COIMBRA - GUARDA - VILAR FORMOSO 692

km			*IC* 511		*IC* 513		311		*IC* 515	
		⚒				Ⓑ	S			
	Lisboa Sta Apolónia **690** d.	...	0830	...	1328	...	1606	...	1828	...
	Lisboa Oriente **690** d.	...	0839	...	1337	...	1614	...	1837	...
0	**Coimbra** d.	*0704*	*1030*	*1200*	*1509*	*1602*	|	*1828*	*2029*	...
2	**Coimbra** B d.	0708	1041	1206	1539	1606	1826	1835	2039	...
16	Pampilhosa d.	0721	1054	1218	1552	1619	1842	1853	2052	...
51	Santa Comba Dão d.	0805	1120	1251	1620	1654	1909	1938	2118	...
83	Nelas d.	0835	1140	1319	1642	1726	1936	2010	2138	...
95	Mangualde d.	0845	1148	1330	1650	1736	1945	2020	2146	...
171	**Guarda** a.	0945	1240	1338	1746	1845	2040	2125	2239	...
218	Vilar Formoso 🏛 PT d.	...	*1345*	...	*1845*	*1933*	2125	...	...	...
220	Fuentes d'Oñoro 🏛 ES d.	...	...	...	...	...	2232	...	...	...
346	**Salamanca** a.	...	...	...	...	...	0005	...	...	...

			313	*IC* 510		*IC* 512			*IC* 514
	①	⚒	S				①–⑥	⑦	
Salamanca d.	...	...	0451	...	...	...	...	...	...
Fuentes d'Oñoro 🏛 ES d.	...	...	0636	...	...	...	...	...	...
Vilar Formoso 🏛 PT d.	...	...	0610	...	...	*1213*	...	...	*1710*
Guarda d.	0029	0500	0639	0722	1040	1322	1621	1621	1813
Mangualde d.	0126	0557	0734	0814	1148	1414	1739	1739	1908
Nelas d.	0134	0607	0743	0822	1157	1422	1751	1751	1916
Santa Comba Dão d.	0201	0638	0805	0841	1226	1441	1820	1820	1938
Pampilhosa d.	0230	0714	0838	0907	1305	1507	1853	1853	2007
Coimbra B a.	0242	0728	0849	0917	1319	1517	1905	1905	2017
Coimbra a.	*0307*	0734	|	*0925*	1324	*1525*	1910	*1918*	*2028*
Lisboa Oriente **690** a.	...	...	1054	1121	...	1721	...	2131	2221
Lisboa Sta Apolónia **690** a.	...	...	1103	1130	...	1730	...	2141	2230

S – SUD EXPRESSO – 🛏 1, 2 cl., ▬ 2 cl. and (2) Lisboa - Hendaye / Irún - Lisboa (Table **46**); ✕ Lisboa - Vilar Formosa and v.v. Ⓡ. Not Dec. 24, 31. Only for passengers making international journeys (unless space is available).

ES – Spain (Central European Time).
PT – Portugal (West European Time).

693 LISBOA - CALDAS DA RAINHA - FIGUEIRA DA FOZ / COIMBRA *Linha do Oeste*

km										IR 808				IR 902	IR 906				IR 908				
		⚒	Ⓒ	Ⓐ	Ⓐ	⑦	⑥v	Ⓐ	Ⓐ		Ⓐ	Ⓐ	Ⓒ			Ⓐ	Ⓐ	Ⓒ		Ⓐ	Ⓐ	⑦	
0	**Lisboa** Oriente ▷ d.	0507s	0555s	0538	...	...	...	0638	...	1014	...	...	...	1414	1614	1708	...	...	1820	1947	...	...	...
7	Entrecampos ▷ d.	0518	0606	0548	...	0713*	...	0648	...	1028	1044	...	1057*	1428	1628	1718	...	1743*	1831	1958	...	2043*	...
9	Sete Rios ▷ d.	0523	0611	0551	...	0717	...	0651	...	1033	1047	...	1101	1433	1633	1721	...	1747	1835	2001	...	2047	...
22	Agualva - Cacém ▷ d.	0539	0627	0611	...	0734	0734	0711	...	1051	1107	...	1117	1451	1651	1741	...	1803	1855	2021	...	2103	...
26	Mira Sintra - Meleças ⊙ d.	0544	0632	0616	0632	0739	0739	0716	0739	1056	1111	1122	1122	1456	1656	1746	1808	1808	1900	2026	2108	2108	...
72	Torres Vedras d.	0645	0738	...	0738	0845	0845	...	0845	1142	...	1222	1222	1542	1740	...	1911	1911	1947	...	2207	2207	...
95	Bombarral d.	0713	0802	...	0802	0913	0913	...	0913	1203	...	1247	1247	1603	1803	...	1937	1937	2008	...	2232	2232	...
114	**Caldas da Rainha** a.	0735	0824	...	0824	0935	0935	...	0935	1216	...	1309	1309	1616	1815	...	1959	1959	2021	...	2254	2254	...

				IR 804				IR 806	IR 900				IR 904										
	⑥v	Ⓐ	Ⓐ		Ⓒ	Ⓐ	Ⓐ			Ⓒ	Ⓐ	Ⓐ		Ⓒ	Ⓐ	Ⓐ		⑥	⑦	Ⓐ	Ⓐ	Ⓑ	
Caldas da Rainha d.	0510	0537	...	0701	0737	0737	...	0901	1109	1335	1335	...	1508	1737	1737	...	...	1856	1856	1856	...	2132	...
Bombarral d.	0531	0558	...	0715	0801	0801	...	0915	1122	1356	1356	...	1521	1802	1802	...	...	1917	1917	1917	...	2153	...
Torres Vedras d.	0557	0624	...	0739	0825	0825	...	0939	1144	1422	1422	...	1546	1827	1827	...	...	1945	1945	1945	...	2221	...
Mira Sintra - Meleças ⊙ d.	0707	0726	0731	0827	0929	0926	0935	1027	1231	1527	1526	1535	1636	1933	1932	1941	...	2048	2048	2047	2055	2324	...
Agualva - Cacém ▷ a.	0711	...	0735	0833	0935	...	0939	1033	1235	1533	...	1539	1643	1938	...	1945	...	2053	2053	...	2059	2329	...
Sete Rios ▷ a.	...	...	0756	0853	0955	...	1000	1053	1255	1554	...	1600	1703	1955	...	2006	...	2110	2110	...	2120	2348	...
Entrecampos ▷ a.	...	...	0759	0856	0959*	...	1002	1057	1259	1557*	...	1602	1706	1958*	...	2009	...	2115	2113*	...	2123	2353	...
Lisboa Oriente ▷ a.	...	...	0810	0905	...	...	...	1110	1310	...	...	...	1717	...	...	2020	...	2126s	...	...	...	0003s	...

km		IR 801			IR 803	Ⓑ
		⚒				
0	**Caldas da Rainha** d.	0620	0819	1322	1620	1858
13	São Martinho do Porto d.	0628	0832	1335	1628	1911
47	Marinha Grande d.	0659	0911	1414	1659	1950
57	Leiria d.	0710	0920	1423	1708	1959
104	Bifurcação de Lares ▽ a.	|	1012	1512	|	2050
111	**Figueira da Foz** a.	|	1024	1526	|	2100
118	Alfarelos ▽ d.	0800	...	...	1800	
138	**Coimba** B ▽ a.	0816	...	...	1817	...
140	**Coimbra** ▽ a.	0825	...	...	1827	...

		IR 800			IR 802
	⚒				Ⓑ
Coimbra ▽ d.	...	0851	...	...	1900
Comiba B ▽ d.	...	0903	...	...	1910
Alfarelos ▽ d.	...	0920	...	...	1928
Figueira da Foz d.	0618	|	1106	1604	|
Bifurcação de Lares ▽ d.	0632	|	1116	1612	|
Leiria d.	0711	1015	1206	1707	2022
Marinha Grande d.	0722	1025	1217	1718	2032
São Martinho do Porto d.	0758	1054	1252	1754	2101
Caldas da Rainha a.	0812	1104	1306	1808	2111

s – Lisboa **Santa Apolónia**.
v – Also public holidays (if fall on Mon - Fri).
▽ – See Table **693a** for connections to / from Coimbra.
▷ – Frequent suburban services (see Table **699**).
⊙ – Suburban services run Roma Areeiro - Entrecampos - Mira Sintra Meleças on Ⓐ (every 20 mins).
* – Terminal platforms (Entrecampos - Poente).

693a FIGUEIRA DA FOZ - COIMBRA

km		⚒	⚒	Ⓐ						Ⓐ							
0	**Figueira da Foz** d.	0632	0710	0741	0811	0910	1025	1118	1315	1410	1515	1615	1710	1815	1915	2010	2228
8	Bifurcação de Lares d.	0644	0721	0748	0822	0921	1036	1129	1326	|	1527	1626	1721	1826	1929	2021	2239
22	Alfarelos d.	0702	0740	0810	0842	0942	1054	1147	1346	1431	1546	1646	1741	1846	1949	2041	2258
42	**Coimbra** B a.	0730	0807	0828	0911	1010	1122	1215	1414	1459	1614	1714	1808	1914	2016	2110	2325
44	**Coimbra** a.	0739	0816	0837	0925	1019	1131	1224	1423	1508	1623	1723	1817	1923	2028	2121	2334

	⚒	⚒								Ⓐ		Ⓑ	Ⓐ				
Coimbra d.	0535	0642	0753	0912	0953	...	1251	1353	1451	1654	1706	1750	1835	1951	2232	0019	...
Coimbra B d.	0544	0652	0802	0923	1002	...	1259	1402	1500	1703	1715	1759	1846	2000	2231	0027	...
Alfarelos d.	0611	0719	0821	0949	1030	...	1326	1431	1526	1721	1742	1826	1907	2017	2258	0055	...
Bifurcação de Lares d.	0631	0738	0837	1007	1051	...	1344	1449	1545	|	1801	1845	|	2036	2316	0113	...
Figueira da Foz a.	0645	0750	0847	1018	1102	...	1355	1500	1556	1743	1812	1856	1928	2048	2327	0124	...

Figueira da Foz d.	0621*	1225*	1908*
Pampilhosa d.	0806	1409	2056
Coimbra B a.	0820	1424	2110
Coimbra B d.	0826	1425	*2133*
Comibra a.	0830	1429	*2137*

Coimbra d.	*0627*	1246	1928
Coimbra B a.	*0631*	1250	1932
Coimbra B d.	0651	1252	1934
Pampilhosa d.	0707	1309	1951
Figueira da Foz a.	0850*	1457*	2140*

* – By 🚌 Figueira - Cantanhede and v.v.

For main line trains calling at Alfarelos see Table **690**. Other trains: Coimbra - Alfarelos Table **699**, Figuerira da Foz - Bif. de Lares Table **693**.

694 PORTO - RÉGUA - POCINHO

km	*Numbered trains: IR*			861	863	867	869	873	877	961	
		Ⓐ									
0	**Porto** São Bento d.	0630	...	...	0915	...	1320	...	...	1920	...
3	**Porto** Campanhã d.	0635	...	0725	0920	1120	1325	1520	1715	1925	2156
12	Ermesinde d.	0647	...	0736	0929	1129	1334	1529	1726	1938	2206
50	Caíde d.	0723	0728	0810	1003	1203	1408	1603	1805	2012	2240
59	Livração ▷ d.	...	0741	0821	1012	1212	1417	1612	1813	2021	2254
64	Marco de Canaveses d.	...	0747	0827	1018	1218	1423	1618	1819	2028	2300
107	**Régua** ▷ a.	...	0842	0911	1104	1305	1510	1700	1902	2119	2356
	Pocinho a.	...	...	1037	...	...	...	...	2032	...	...

		862	864	866	870	874	878	962		
Pocinho d.	...	...	...	...	...	...	...	...	...	...
Régua ▷ d.	0608	0730	0848	1042	1247	1452	1702	1903	2033	...
Marco de Canaveses d.	0704	0815	0936	1131	1331	1536	1744	1945	2131	...
Livração ▷ d.	0711	0822	0943	1138	1338	1543	1751	1952	2138	...
Caíde d.	0729	0833	0954	1149	1349	1554	1803	2003	2154	2213
Ermesinde d.	0804	0905	1026	1220	1421	1626	1838	2039	...	2259
Porto Campanhã a.	0815	0915	1035	1230	1430	1635	1850	2049	...	2310
Porto São Bento a.	...	...	...	1235	...	...	1855	2055	...	2315

km	*Numbered trains: IR*	861		865		871	875		877		
	Porto Campanhã d.	0725	...	...	...	...	...	...	1715	...	...
0	**Régua** d.	0912	...	1115	...	1527	1727	...	1906	...	...
23	Pinhão d.	0940	...	1142	...	1555	1755	...	1933	...	...
36	Tua a.	0955	1006	1158	...	1610	1810	1816	1948	1955	...
90	Mirandela a.	|	1133	|	...	|	|	1944	|	2122	...
68	**Pocinho** a.	1037	...	1241	...	1654	1854	...	2032	...	...

	860		868	872	876			960		
				⚒	†					
Pocinho d.	0652	...	1114	1316	1531	...	...	1731	...	1905
Mirandela d.	|	0821	|	|	|	...	1637	|	1821	|
Tua d.	0733	0947	1159	1358	1615	...	1803	1815	1948	1951
Pinhaõ d.	0749	...	1215	1414	1631	...	...	1831	...	2006
Régua a.	0815	...	1241	1440	1658	...	...	1858	...	2032
Porto Campanhã a.	...	...	...	...	...	...	...	...	...	...

▷ NARROW-GAUGE BRANCHES

23 km	Ⓐ					Ⓐ		
Livração d.	0611	0715	0830	1220	1620	1820	2025	2100
Amarante a.	0638	0742	0857	1247	1647	1847	2052	2131
		Ⓐ					Ⓐ	
Amarante d.	0535	0641	0748	1105	1305	1715	1910	2102
Livração a.	0602	0708	0815	1132	1332	1742	1937	2129

26 km	①–⑤				
Régua d.	0706	0846	1120	1520	1920
Vila Real a.	0800	0939	1213	1613	2015
	①–⑤				
Vila Real d.	0700	0944	1351	1801	1915
Régua a.	0755	1038	1445	1855	2010

steam-hauled tourist train:
⑥ May 19 - Oct. 20, 2007.
Régua d. 1446 → Pinhão d. 1530 → Tua a. 1550.
Tua d. 1705 → Pinhão d. 1734 → Régua 1808.

695 PORTO - BRAGA

km								AP 131									AP 133					AP 135			AP 135	
		Ⓐ		Ⓐ		Ⓐ				Ⓐ		Ⓐ		Ⓐ		Ⓐ		Ⓐ		Ⓐ		Ⓑh	Ⓐ	b		b
	Lisboa ⊖ **690** d.	...	...	...	...	...	...	0700	...	...	...	...	...	...	...	...	1400	...	...	...	...	1600	...	...	1900	...
0	**Porto** São Bento ▷ d.	0625	0645	0725	0745	0825	0845	|	0945	1045	1145	1245	1345	1445	1545	1625	|	1725	1745	1825	1845	|	1925	1945	|	2245
3	**Porto** Campanhã ▷ d.	0630	0650	0730	0750	0830	0850	0946	0950	1050	1150	1250	1350	1450	1550	1630	1646	1730	1750	1830	1850	1846	1930	1950	2146	2250
12	Ermesinde ▷ d.	0642	0702	0742	0802	0842	0902	|	1002	1102	1202	1302	1402	1502	1602	1642	|	1742	1802	1842	1902	|	1942	2002	|	2302
26	Trofa ▷ d.	0659	0718	0759	0818	0859	0918	|	1018	1118	1218	1318	1418	1518	1618	1659	|	1759	1818	1859	1918	|	1959	2018	|	2318
35	Famalicão ▷ d.	0708	0729	0808	0829	0908	0929	1018	1029	1129	1229	1329	1429	1529	1629	1708	1718	1808	1829	1908	1929	1918	2008	2029	2218	2329
42	Nine ▷ d.	0713	0737	0813	0837	0913	0937	|	1037	1137	1237	1337	1437	1537	1637	1713	|	1813	1837	1913	1937	|	2013	2037	|	2337
57	**Braga** a.	0734	0758	0834	0858	0934	0958	1031	1058	1158	1258	1358	1458	1558	1658	1725	1731	1825	1858	1925	1958	1931	2025	2058	2231	2358

		AP 130											AP 132								AP 134				AP 136	
			Ⓐ		Ⓐ		Ⓐ			Ⓐ		Ⓐ		Ⓐ		Ⓐ		Ⓐ	Ⓐ			Ⓐ			Ⓑh	d
Braga d.	0530	0604	0608	0630	0705	0730	0805	0830	0930	1030	1130	1230	1304	1308	1330	1430	1530	1630	1708	1730	1804	1815	1830	1930	2004	2030
Nine ▷ d.	0550	|	0620	0650	0717	0750	0817	0859	0950	1050	1150	1250	|	1320	1350	1450	1550	1650	1720	1750	|	1827	1850	1950	|	2050
Famalicão ▷ d.	0558	0619	0626	0658	0723	0758	0823	0858	0958	1058	1158	1258	1319	1326	1358	1458	1558	1658	1726	1758	1819	1833	1858	1958	2019	2058
Trofa ▷ d.	0610	|-	0635	0710	0735	0810	0835	0910	1010	1110	1210	1310	|	1335	1410	1510	1610	1710	1735	1810	|	1842	1910	2010	|	2110
Ermesinde ▷ d.	0629	|	0649	0729	0749	0829	0849	0929	1029	1129	1229	1329	|	1349	1429	1529	1629	1729	1749	1829	|	1857	1929	2029	|	2129
Porto Campanhã ▷ a.	0641	0645	0701	0741	0801	0841	0901	0941	1041	1141	1241	1341	1345	1401	1441	1541	1641	1741	1801	1841	1845	1910	1941	2041	2045	2141
Porto São Bento ▷ a.	0645	|	0705	0745	0805	0845	0905	0945	1045	1145	1245	1345	|	1405	1445	1545	1645	1745	1805	1845	|	1915	1945	2045	|	2145
Lisboa ⊖ **690** a.	...	0930	...	...	...	...	...	...	...	...	...	...	1630	...	...	...	...	...	...	...	2130	...	...	...	2330	...

b – Additional journeys run at 2045 Ⓐ, 2145 Ⓐ.
d – One hour later on Ⓒ. Additional journey runs at 2230 Ⓐ.
h – Not Oct. 5.
⊖ – Lisboa Sta. Apolónia.
▷ – For other trains see Table **696**.

PORTO - GUIMARÃES 695a

60 km

							Ⓐ		Ⓐ	IC 621
Lisboa Sta Ap. **690** d.	...	...	...	...	...	...	...	...	...	...	1730
Porto São Bento ▷ d.	0615	0715	0815	1015	1215	1415	1615	1715	1815	1915	|
Porto Campanhã ▷ d.	0620	0720	0820	1020	1220	1420	1620	1720	1820	1920	2041
Ermesinde ▷ d.	0632	0732	0832	1032	1232	1432	1632	1732	1832	1932	|
Trofa ▷ d.	0650	0750	0850	1050	1250	1450	1650	1750	1850	1950	2101
Guimarães a.	0733	0833	0933	1133	1333	1533	1733	1833	1933	2033	2140

		IC 620							Ⓐ		b
Guimarães d.	0654	0743	0754	0854	0954	1154	1354	1554	1709	1809	2054
Trofa ▷ d.	0740	0825	0840	0940	1040	1240	1440	1640	1759	1859	2140
Ermesinde ▷ d.	0758	|	0858	0958	1058	1258	1458	1658	1819	1919	2158
Porto Campanhã ▷ a.	0810	0845	0910	1010	1110	1310	1510	1710	1831	1931	2210
Porto São Bento ▷ a.	0815	|	0915	1015	1115	1315	1515	1715	1835	1935	2215
Lisboa Sta Ap. **690** a.	...	1200	...	...	...	...	...	...	...	...	...

b – 10 - 15 mins later on Ⓐ. ▷ – See also Tables **695** and **696**. Additional trains: **Porto - Guimarães** 2015 Ⓒ, 2115 Ⓒ, 2215 Ⓐ; **Guimarães - Porto** 0554 Ⓐ, 1909 Ⓐ, 1954 Ⓒ.

PORTO - VIANA DO CASTELO - VALENÇA - VIGO 696

km		IR 851 Ⓐ	IN 421		IR 853	IR 855	IN 423		IR 857 Ⓐ	
0	**Porto** Campanhã ▷ d.	0555	0755	...	1245	1600	1755	...	1956	...
12	Ermesinde ▷ d.	0605	0807	...	1255	1610	1807	...	2007	...
23	Trofa ▷ d.	0618	0826	...	1310	1624	1827	...	2027	...
32	Famalicão ▷ d.	0629	0836	...	1321	1635	1837	...	2037	...
39	**Nine** ▷ d.	0636	0843	...	1328	1642	1844	...	2044	...
51	Barcelos d.	0646	0857	...	1338	1653	1854	...	2058	...
82	**Viana do Castelo** d.	0733	0935	...	1416	1729	1935	...	2134	...
116	Vila Nova de Cerveira d.	0807	1004	...	1445	1758	2010	...	2204	...
130	**Valença** 🏛 PT d.	0818	1017	...	1456	1810	2023	...	2215	...
134	Tui 🏛 ES d.	...	1135	...	...	...	2130	...	...	...
162	Redondela **681** d.	...	1159	...	...	...	2156	...	...	...
174	**Vigo 681** a.	...	1212	...	...	...	2208	...	...	...

	Ⓐ		IN 420	IR 850		IR 852	IR 854	IN 422	
Vigo 681 d.	...	...	0740	...	...	...	...	1944	...
Redondela **681** d.	...	...	0754	...	...	...	...	1957	...
Tui 🏛 ES d.	...	...	0830	...	...	...	...	2030	...
Valença 🏛 PT d.	0552	...	0737	0950	...	1412	1743	1940	...
Vila Nova de Cerveira d.	0605	...	0749	1003	...	1424	1757	1952	...
Viana do Castelo d.	0645	...	0821	1035	...	1457	1828	2023	...
Barcelos d.	0731	...	0858	1113	...	1534	1913	2059	...
Nine ▷ d.	0746	...	0913	1124	...	1546	1925	2111	...
Famalicão ▷ d.	0754	...	0921	1132	...	1554	1933	2119	...
Trofa ▷ d.	0805	...	0930	1141	...	1603	1942	2128	...
Ermesinde ▷ d.	0824	...	0946	1157	...	1619	1957	2144	...
Porto Campanhã ▷ a.	0835	...	0955	1210	...	1630	2010	2155	...

ADDITIONAL LOCAL TRAINS (see Table **695** for connections from / to Porto at Nine)

	Ⓐ	Ⓒ	Ⓐ		Ⓐ					Ⓑ §
Nine d.	0718	0742	0918	1100	1356	1455	...	1723	1855	2142
Barcelos d.	0733	0756	0932	1114	1410	1509	...	1736	1912	2156
Viana do Castelo a.	0820	0844	1020	1200	1456	1557	...	1823	1959	2242
Viana do Castelo d.	*0830*	*0846*	*1034*	...	...	*1605*	...	*1831*	...	...
Vila Nova de Cerveira d.	*0914*	*0930*	*1118*	...	...	*1649*	...	*1914*	...	...
Valença 🏛 d.	*0929*	*0945*	*1133*	...	...	*1704*	...	*1929*	...	...

	⚒ b	Ⓐ		Ⓐ	Ⓒ	Ⓐ			
Valença 🏛 d.	...	*0625*	...	*1100*	*1125*	...	*1505*	...	*1826*
Vila Nova de Cerveira d.	...	*0640*	...	*1119*	*1140*	...	*1520*	...	*1841*
Viana do Castelo a.	...	*0724*	...	*1203*	*1224*	...	*1604*	...	*1927*
Viana do Castelo d.	0510	0731	0934	1210	1228	1310	1607	1730	1932
Barcelos d.	0556	0818	1020	1256	1314	1409	1654	1820	2019
Nine a.	0610	0832	1034	1310	1328	1423	1708	1834	2033

b – 35 mins later on ⑥. § – Partly by 🚌. ▷ – See also Table **695**. ES – Spain (Central European Time). PT – Portugal (West European Time).

LISBOA - PINHAL NOVO - TUNES - FARO 697

km Δ				AP 180	IC 570		IC 572		IC 574	AP 186	IC 576 ⑤f
	Porto Campanhã **690** d.	...	...	0547	...	...	...	...	...	1547	...
	Coimbra B **690** d.	...	...	0645	...	...	...	...	...	1645	...
0	**Lisboa** Oriente ⊙ d.	...	...	0840	1020	...	1320	...	1720	1840	1920
7	Entrecampos ⊙ d.	...	...	0851	1030	...	1330	...	1730	1851	1930
18	Pragal ⊙ d.	...	...	|	1044	...	1344	...	1744	|	1944
47	**Pinhal Novo** ⊙ d.	...	0705	0931	1107	...	1407	1705	1807	1931	2007
60	Setúbal d.	...	0715	|	1115	...	1415	1714	1815	|	2016
110	Alcácer do Sal d.	...	0755	|	1157	...	1449	1754	1848	|	2050
134	Grândola d.	...	0811	|	1211	...	1503	1809	1909	|	2107
**	**Beja** d.	0755	|	|	|	1417	|	|	|	|	|
196	Funcheira d.	0851	0859	|	1244	1513	1539	1859	1944	|	2148
280	**Tunes** ▷ d.	...	1015	1126	1349	...	1648	2012	2046	2127	2250
285	Albufeira ▷ d.	...	1020	1133	1355	...	1654	2017	2052	2134	2256
302	Loulé ▷ d.	...	1035	1146	1408	...	1711	2032	2105	2147	2309
318	**Faro** ▷ a.	...	1049	1156	1420	...	1722	2046	2116	2158	2320

	AP 182			IC 670	IC 672		AP 184		IC 674	IC 676 ⑦
Faro ▷ d.	0655	0738	...	0905	1308	...	1455	1528	1700	1903
Loulé ▷ d.	0706	0753	...	0916	1319	...	1506	1544	1711	1914
Albufeira ▷ d.	0718	0807	...	0928	1331	...	1518	1558	1724	1926
Tunes ▷ d.	0726	0813	...	0935	1345	...	1525	1604	1731	1933
Funcheira d.	|	0918	0925	1047	1446	1518	|	1717	1832	2047
Beja a.	|	|	1023	|	|	1616	|	|	|	|
Grândola d.	|	1009	...	1122	1527	...	|	1809	1908	2122
Alcácer do Sal d.	|	1027	...	1136	1541	...	|	1825	1925	2139
Setúbal d.	|	1109	...	1213	1613	...	|	1917	2012	2213
Pinhal Novo ⊙ d.	0923	1120	...	1222	1622	...	1723	1927	2022	2222
Pragal ⊙ a.	|	...	...	1242	1642	...	|	...	2042	2242
Entrecampos ⊙ a.	0956	...	...	1256	1656	...	1756	...	2056	2256
Lisboa Oriente ⊙ a.	1004	...	...	1306	1705	...	1804	...	2106	2306
Coimbra B **690** a.	1146	...	...	...	...	...	1946	...	...	...
Porto Campanhã **690** a.	1244	...	...	...	...	...	2044	...	...	...

LOCAL TRAINS LAGOS - TUNES - FARO

			⚒		⚒						
0	**Lagos** d.	0611	0657	0819	0946	1219	1411	1624	1812	1920	2019
18	Portimão d.	0630	0715	0837	1004	1238	1430	1642	1830	1938	2037
29	Silves d.	0645	0730	0852	1020	1254	1445	1657	1850	1954	2053
42	Algoz d.	0701	0746	0909	1037	1312	1501	1717	1910	2014	2114
46	**Tunes** a.	0706	0751	0914	1043	1317	1506	1724	1915	2019	2119
46	**Tunes** ▷ d.	0707	0756	0916	1044	1320	1507	1730	1916	2021	...
52	Albufeira ▷ d.	0717	0807	0928	1051	1331	1520	1736	1926	2027	...
69	Loulé ▷ d.	0733	0823	0948	1112	1351	1544	1752	1946	2047	...
85	**Faro** ▷ a.	0753	0839	1003	1127	1406	1600	1808	2001	2103	...

		⚒				⚒					⑤f
Faro ▷ d.	0712	0916	1055	1319	1617	1731	1814	1914	2011	...	...
Loulé ▷ d.	0733	0933	1112	1336	1634	1752	1832	1931	2032	...	...
Albufeira ▷ d.	0749	0949	1132	1355	1654	1808	1848	1947	2052	...	...
Tunes ▷ a.	0755	0954	1137	1401	1659	1813	1853	1953	2057	...	...
Tunes d.	0756	0955	1139	1403	1701	1815	1854	1955	2058	2135	2300
Algoz d.	0802	1000	1144	1409	1707	1821	1859	2002	2103	2140	2305
Silves d.	0818	1020	1200	1426	1722	1836	1916	2019	2119	2156	2321
Portimão d.	0837	1034	1215	1446	1737	1851	1938	2037	2133	2210	2335
Lagos a.	0855	1052	1239	1504	1755	1909	1956	2055	2151	2229	2354

f – Also Mar. 20, Apr. 24; not Mar. 21, Apr. 25.
▷ – For additional trains see other section of table above or below.
⊙ – See Table **698** for other fast trains and Table **699** for local services.
** – Beja - Funcheira: *62 km*
Δ – Distances are via Setúbal (subtract *9* km for trains not serving Setúbal).

FARO - VILA REAL DE SANTO ANTÓNIO 697a

								Ⓐ				Ⓐ
0	**Faro** d.	0734	0925	1225	1427	1625	1730	1825	1925	2125	2215	2325
10	Olhão d.	0745	0941	1240	1438	1641	1741	1841	1941	2141	2226	2336
32	Tavira d.	0816	1010	1308	1505	1710	1810	1910	2010	2210	2254	0004
56	**Vila Real** § a.	0845	1039	1339	1535	1739	1839	1939	2039	2239	2323	0033

		Ⓐ								
Vila Real § d.	0547	0617	0716	0941	1141	1310	1541	1741	1841	2041
Tavira d.	0613	0648	0746	1013	1213	1340	1613	1813	1913	2113
Olhão d.	0637	0714	0813	1040	1241	1407	1640	1840	1940	2140
Faro a.	0648	0724	0824	1051	1252	1418	1651	1851	1951	2151

§ – Vila Real de Santo António. (± *1 500 m* from bus station / ferry terminal).

Additional journeys on Ⓐ:
Faro - Tavira 0758, 1025, 1130, 1323, 1525; Tavira - Faro 0913, 1119, 1312, 1513, 1711.

LISBOA - PINHAL NOVO - ÉVORA and BEJA 698

km				IC 690	IC 592		IC 694			IC 696	IC 594
0	**Lisboa** Oriente ⊙ d.	...	...	0810	0910	...	1410	...	...	1810	1910
7	Entrecampos ⊙ d.	...	...	0821	0921	...	1421	...	...	1821	1921
18	Pragal ⊙ d.	...	...	0835	0935	...	1435	...	...	1835	1935
	Barreiro d.	...	0644	|	|	...	|	...	...	|	|
47	**Pinhal Novo** ⊙ d.	...	0702	0859	0959	...	1459	...	...	1902	2002
88	Vendas Novas d.	...	0748	0927	1025	...	1525	...	...	1934	2034
	Évora d.	0622	|	|	|	1244	|	1523	1751	|	|
122	Casa Branca a.	0642	0814	0948	1046	1304	1546	1543	1811	1955	2055
122	Casa Branca d.	0647	0815	0949	1047	1309	1547	1552	1819	1956	2056
148	Évora a.	|	|	1007	|	|	1605	|	|	2014	|
185	**Beja** a.	0740	0910	...	1128	1406	...	1648	1911	...	2137

	IC 598	IC 590			IC 692			IC 698	IC 596	
Beja d.	...	0808	0915	1302	...	1621	1726	...	1920	1946
Évora d.	0644	|	|	|	1344	|	|	1844	|	|
Casa Branca a.	0701	0851	1007	1355	1401	1715	1816	1901	2001	2038
Casa Branca d.	0702	0852	1012	1404	1402	1720	1817	1902	2002	2043
Évora a.	|	|	1033	1424	|	1741	|	|	|	2103
Vendas Novas d.	0724	0914	...	...	1424	...	1843	1924	2024	...
Pinhal Novo ⊙ d.	0751	0951	...	...	1451	...	1931	1951	2051	...
Barreiro a.	|	|	...	...	|	...	1948	|	|	...
Pragal ⊙ a.	0812	1012	...	...	1512	...	...	2012	2112	...
Entrecampos ⊙ a.	0826	1026	...	...	1526	...	...	2026	2126	...
Lisboa Oriente ⊙ a.	0835	1036	...	...	1535	...	...	2036	2135	...

⊙ – See Table **697** for other fast trains and Table **699** for local services.

699 OTHER LOCAL SERVICES

LISBOA - ESTORIL - CASCAIS

26 km (Estoril 24 km)

																					*	*			
Lisboa Cais do Sodre .d.	Ⓐ	0530	every	0700	every	1000	every	1700	every	2030	every	2200	every	0130	Ⓒ	0530	every	0730	0800	every	1920	1940	2000	every	0130
Estoril .d.		0606	30	0728	15	1029	20	1729	15	2059	20	2236	30	0206		0606	30	0806	0829	20	1949	2016	2036	30	0206
Cascais .a.		0610	mins	0732	mins	1033	mins	1733	mins	2103	mins	2240	mins	0210		0610	mins	0810	0833	mins	1953	2020	2040	mins	0210

																				*	*			
Cascais .d.	Ⓐ	0530	0600	0630	0648	every	2048	2108	2130	every	0130	Ⓒ	0530	every	0700	every	0803	every	1903	1923	1943	2000	every	0130
Estoril .d.		0534	0604	0634	0652	15-20 ◧	2052	2112	2134	30	0134		0534	30	0707	20	0807	20	1907	1927	1947	2004	30	0134
Lisboa Cais do Sodre .a.		0610	0640	0703	0720	mins	2121	2141	2210	mins	0210		0610	mins	0743	mins	0836	mins	1936	1956	2023	2040	mins	0210

◧ – Every 15 minutes 0648 - 0948, every 20 minutes 1008 - 1648, every 15 minutes 1703 - 1948, every 20 minutes 2008 - 2108.

* – Every 30 mins 1900 - 2000 October - early May.

LISBOA - SINTRA

Rossio terminus is currently closed due to long-term work being carried out on the tunnel (see map on page 31) but is expected to reopen on Feb. 16, 2008. Rossio - Sintra = 27 km

Lisboa Oriente d.	Ⓐ	⊡		⊡		⊡	Ⓒ	...	0638	...	0708	at	2208		☆ 0008
Roma Areeiro d.		0602		2232		0132		0632	0646	0702	0716	these	2216		0016
Entrecampos d.		0604	every	2234	every	0134		0634	0648	0704	0718	mins	2218	every	0018
Sete Rios d.		0607	10 - 20	2237	30	0137		0637	0651	0707	0721	each	2221	30	0021
Agualva - Cacém d.		0627	mins	2257	mins	0157		0657	0711	0727	0741	hour	2241	mins	0041
Sintra a.		0641	△	2311		0211		0711	0725	0741	0755	until	2255		0055

Sintra d.	Ⓐ	0506		2156		0056	Ⓒ	0516	0532	0546	0602	at	2132		⊖ 2302
Agualva - Cacém d.		0519	every	2209	every	0109		0529	0545	0559	0615	these	2145	every	2315
Sete Rios d.		0540	10 - 20	2230	30	0130		0550	0606	0620	0636	mins	2206	30	2336
Entrecampos d.		0543	mins	2233	mins	0133		0553	0609	0623	0639	each	2209	mins	2339
Roma Areeiro d.		0545	▽	2235		0135		0555	0611	0625	0641	hour	2211		2341
Lisboa Oriente a.		⊙		⊙		⊙		...	0620	...	0650	until	2220		2350

△ – Every 10 mins 0602 - 0932, 1632 - 1952, every 20 mins 0932 - 1632, 1952 - 2232.

⊡ – Oriente - Roma Areeiro (journey 8 mins): 0538, 0608, 0638, every 10 mins to 0908, 0927, 0938, 0957, every 30 mins to 1627, every 10 mins to 1957, every 30 mins to 2327.

☆ – Also from Roma Areeiro 0046, 0116.

▽ – Every 10 mins 0506 - 0916, 1616 - 1956, every 20 mins 0916 - 1616, 1956 - 2156.

⊙ – Roma Areeiro - Oriente (journey 8 mins): 0541, 0611, 0641, every 10 mins to 0920, every 30 mins to1650, every 10 mins to 2020, every 30 mins to 2220, also 2350.

⊖ – Also to Roma Areeiro at 2332, 0002, 0032.

LISBOA - PINHAL NOVO - SETÚBAL

Operator: Fertagus. CP tickets not valid.

							Ⓒ				
Roma Areeiro d.	Ⓐ	0542		2242	2357	0042	Ⓒ	0642		2342
Entrecampos d.		0544	and	2244	2359	0044		0644	and	2344
Sete Rios d.		0548	every	2248	0003	0048		0648	every	2348
Pragal d.		0559	hour	2259	0014	0059		0659	hour	2359
Pinhal Novo d.		0627	until	2327	0042	0127		0727	until	0027
Setúbal a.		0640		2340	0055	0140		0740		0040

Setúbal d.	Ⓐ	0546	0656		1856	1926	2016		0016	Ⓒ	0556		2256
Pinhal Novo d.		0600	0710	and	1910	1940	2030	and	0030		0610	and	2310
Pragal d.		0629	0739	every	1939	2009	2059	every	0059		0639	every	2339
Sete Rios d.		0640	0750	hour	1950	2020	2110	hour	0110		0650	hour	2350
Entrecampos d.		0643	0753	until	1953	2023	2113	until	0113		0653	until	2353
Roma Areeiro a.		0645	0755		1955	2025	2115		0115		0655		2355

Additional journeys on Ⓐ: from Roma Areeiro 1812, 1912, 2012, from Setúbal 0626, 0726, 0826. *Fertagus* trains operate every 10 - 20 mins (30 evenings and Ⓒ) Roma Areeiro - Pragal - Coina.

Catamaran LISBOA - BARREIRO

Operator: Soflusa, Lisboa. Journey time: 20 minutes. *10 km*

From Lisboa Terreiro do Paço:

Ⓐ: 0545, 0610, 0640; every 5–10 minutes 0655–0920; 0945, 1005; every 30 minutes 1020–1550; 1615, 1630; every 10–15 minutes 1650–2040; 2105, 2130, 2200, 2230, 2300, 2330, 0000, 0030, 0100, 0130, 0230.

Ⓒ: 0545, 0610, 0640, 0710, 0740, 0805, 0830, 0855 and every 30 minutes until 2055, 2130, 2200, 2230, 2300, 2330, 0000, 0030, 0100, 0130, 0230.

From Barreiro Barcos:

Ⓐ: 0515, 0545, 0615; every 5–10 minutes 0630–0920; 0940, every 30 minutes 0950–1450; 1525, 1545, 1600; every 10–15 minutes 1620–2000; 2015, 2040, 2100, 2130, 2200, 2230, 2300, 2330, 0000, 0030, 0100, 0200.

Ⓒ: 0515, 0545, 0615, 0645, 0715, 0740, 0805, 0830, 0855 and every 30 minutes until 2025, 2100, 2130, 2200, 2230, 2300, 2330, 0000, 0030, 0100, 0200.

BARREIRO - SETÚBAL

km							
0	**Barreiro** d.	0549	and	2049	2154	and	0054
15	Pinhal Novo d.	0615	hourly	2115	2219	hourly	0119
28	**Setúbal** a.	0632	until	2132	2236	until	0136

Setúbal d.	0501	and	2301	0001
Pinhal Novo d.	0516	hourly	2316	0016
Barreiro a.	0542	until	2342	0042

Additional journeys on Ⓐ:
From Barreiro: 0619, 0719, 0819, 1719, 1819, 1919, 2019.
From Setúbal: 0631, 0731, 0831, 1731, 1831, 1931, 2031.

LISBOA - ENTRONCAMENTO - TOMAR

km																								
			Ⓐ	⚒		⚒		Ⓐ	Ⓐ		Ⓐ		Ⓐ			Ⓐ§		Ⓐ§				Ⓐ		
0	**Lisboa** Santa Apolónia ▷ d.	0017	0548	0648	0748	0848	0948	1048	1148	1248	1348	1448	1548	1618	1648	1718	1748	1818	1848	1948	2048	2148	2248	...
7	**Lisboa** Oriente ▷ d.	0025	0556	0656	0756	0856	0956	1056	1156	1256	1356	1456	1556	1627	1656	1726	1756	1826	1856	1956	2056	2156	2256	...
31	Vila Franca de Xira d.	0044	0615	0715	0815	0913	1015	1113	1215	1313	1415	1515	1615	1644	1715	1742	1815	1842	1915	2015	2115	2224	2313	...
75	Santarém d.	0123	0700	0800	0900	0952	1100	1153	1300	1352	1500	1554	1708	1716	1800	1821	1900	1920	2000	2100	2154	2301	2352	...
107	Entroncamento d.	0147	0724	0824	0923	1016	1124	1217	1324	1416	1524	1617	1731	1735	1824	1841	1923	1940	2024	2128	2217	2325	0016	...
130	**Tomar** a.	...	0755	0854	0950	...	1154	1243	...	1442	1554	1650	1758	...	1854	1902	1954	2001	2054	2155	2250	2351	0042	...

	⚒	Ⓐ	Ⓐ§		Ⓐ§	⚒	⚒	†		Ⓐ		⚒	†	Ⓐ		Ⓐ					Ⓐ		Ⓐ	
Tomar d.	...	0516	0557	0605v	0657	...	0737	...	0803	...	1010	1110	...	...	1316	...	1510	1610	1703	1803	1914	2002	...	2210
Entroncamento d.	0421	0543	0618	0632	0719	0741	0805	0804	0836	0924	1036	1142	1141	1236	1343	1436	1542	1637	1736	1836	1942	2036	2143	2242
Santarém d.	0445	0607	0638	0656	0739	0806	0829	0829	0900	0948	1100	1206	1206	1301	1407	1501	1606	1701	1800	1900	2006	2100	2204	2306
Vila Franca de Xira d.	0522	0644	0705	0741	0814	0844	0913	0913	0944	1029	1144	1244	1244	1344	1444	1544	1644	1744	1844	1944	2044	2144	2244	2343
Lisboa Oriente ▽ a.	0542	0703	0723	0802	0831	0902	0934	0934	1002	1048	1202	1302	1302	1402	1503	1602	1702	1802	1902	2002	2102	2202	2302	0002
Lisboa Santa Apolónia ▽ a.	0553	0711	0731	0811	0841	0911	0942	0942	1011	1057	1211	1311	1311	1411	1511	1611	1711	1811	1911	2011	2111	2211	2311	0010

▷ – Additional local trains Santa Apolónia - Oriente: every 30 mins 0536 - 0936, hourly 0936 - 1636, every 30 mins 1636 - 2036, hourly 2036 - 0036.

▽ – Additional local trains Oriente - Santa Apolónia: every 30 mins 0615 - 1015, hourly 1015 - 1715, every 30 mins 1715 - 2115, hourly 2115 - 0115.

v – ⚒ only.

§ – *IR* train.

ENTRONCAMENTO - COIMBRA

km													
		Ⓐ			⚒						Ⓐ		Ⓑ
0	**Entroncamento** d.	0442	0542	0659	0742	0842	1142	1242	1542	1742	1845	1959	2132
24	Fátima ⊙ d.	0503	0603	0720	0809	0903	1203	1309	1603	1809	1913	2020	2153
64	Pombal d.	0535	0635	0751	0842	0941	1235	1342	1635	1842	1945	2052	2225
91	Alfarelos d.	0558	0658	0815	0905	1004	1258	1405	1658	1905	2009	2120	2248
111	Coimbra B a.	0624	0718	0841	0925	1030	1318	1424	1718	1924	2032	2139	2314
111	Coimbra B d.	0631	*0735**	*0855*	0932	1035	*1334*	1430	*1734*	1935	*2100*	*2155*	2320
113	**Coimbra** a.	0635	*0739**	*0859*	0936	1039	*1338*	1434	*1738*	1939	*2104*	*2159*	2325

		Ⓐ					Ⓐ			Ⓑ
Coimbra d.	*0642**	0716	*0837*	*1030*	*1324*	1623	*1723*	*1808*	1914	2013
Coimbra B a.	*0646**	0720	*0841*	*1034*	*1328*	1627	*1727*	*1812*	1918	2017
Coimbra B d.	0650	0725	0853	1049	1333	1632	1735	1825	1925	2022
Alfarelos d.	0707	0747	0910	1116	1359	1658	1758	1858	1958	2049
Pombal d.	0731	0827	0934	1140	1430	1722	1831	1922	2022	2112
Fátima ‡ d.	0802	0900	1005	1212	1502	1754	1905	1954	2054	2152
Entroncamento a.	0824	0920	1032	1232	1522	1814	1928	2014	2114	2213

⊙ – Station is *20 km* from Fátima.

* – ⚒ only.

AVEIRO - COIMBRA

km													
					Ⓐ			Ⓐ					
0	**Aveiro** d.	0649	0749	0949	1049	1133	1223	1349	1449	1533	1749	1949	2149
41	Pampilhosa d.	0725	0825	1025	1126	1210	1300	1425	1525	1610	1825	2025	2226
55	Coimbra B a.	0740	0840	1040	1140	1224	1314	1440	1540	1624	1840	2040	2240
57	**Coimbra** a.	0745	0845	1046	1146	1230	1319	1446	1545	1632	1846	2046	2246

		⚒								
Coimbra d.	0635	0745	0845	1056	1338	1446	1638	1846	1946	2210
Coimbra B d.	0640	0750	0850	1101	1348	1451	1646	1850	1951	2215
Pampilhosa d.	0655	0805	0905	1116	1404	1505	1702	1905	2006	2231
Aveiro a.	0732	0843	0943	1153	1441	1543	1739	1943	2043	2308

Additional trains: **Aveiro - Coimbra**: 0549⚒, 0849Ⓐ, 1633Ⓐ, 1849Ⓐ, 2049Ⓐ. **Coimbra - Aveiro**: 0545Ⓐ, 1004Ⓐ, 1146Ⓐ, 1240Ⓐ, 1545Ⓐ, 1738Ⓐ, 2046Ⓐ.

Suburban trains run **Porto - Espinho - Aveiro** approx. hourly.

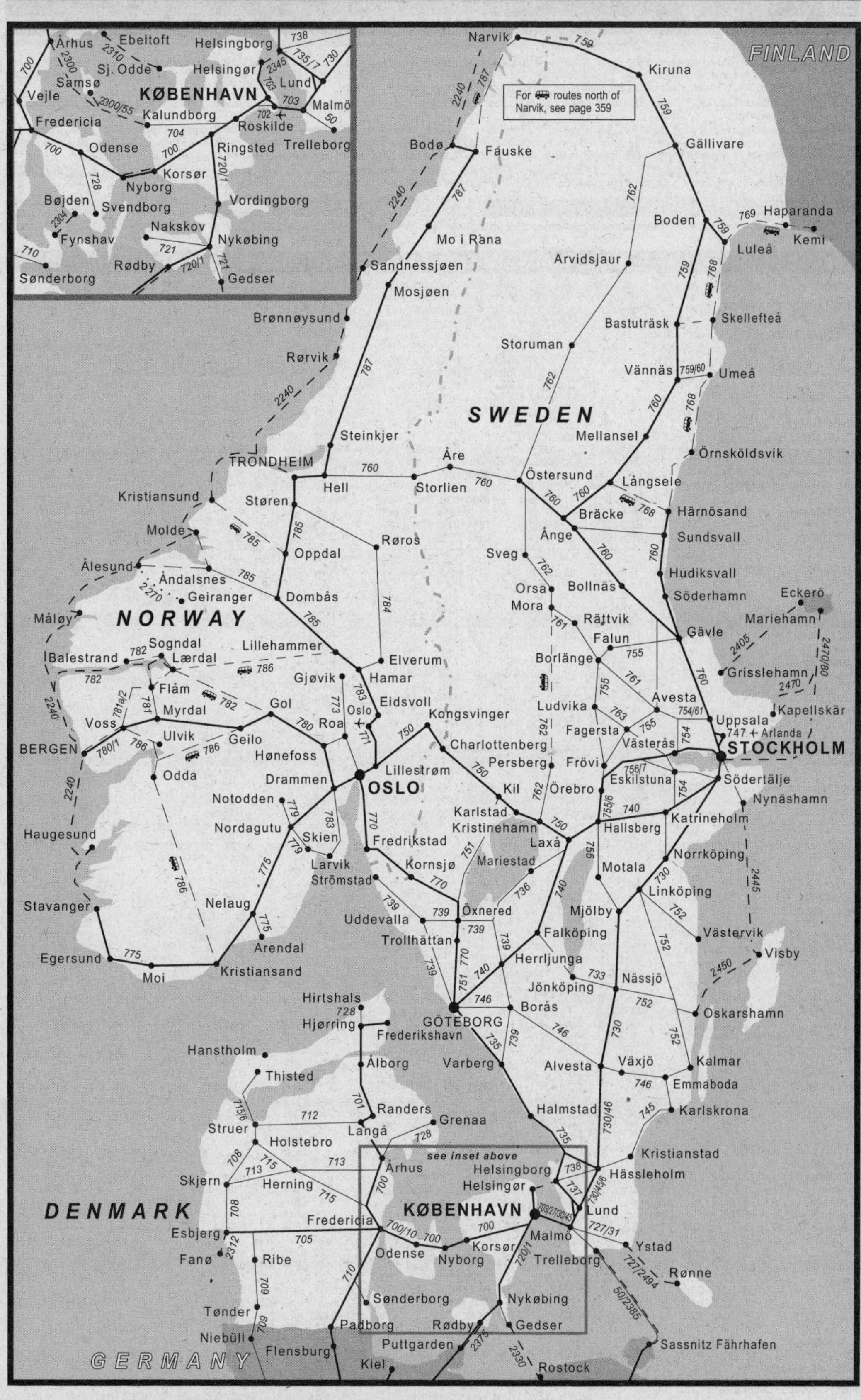
FINLAND
SWEDEN
NORWAY
DENMARK
GERMANY
KØBENHAVN
STOCKHOLM
OSLO
GÖTEBORG
TRONDHEIM
BERGEN
For routes north of Narvik, see page 359
see inset above
Narvik
Kiruna
Gällivare
Boden
Luleå
Haparanda
Kemi
Bodø
Fauske
Mo i Rana
Sandnessjøen
Mosjøen
Brønnøysund
Rørvik
Arvidsjaur
Bastuträsk
Skellefteå
Storuman
Vännäs
Umeå
Mellansel
Örnsköldsvik
Steinkjer
Hell
Storlien
Åre
Östersund
Långsele
Härnösand
Bräcke
Ånge
Sundsvall
Hudiksvall
Söderhamn
Kristiansund
Støren
Molde
Oppdal
Røros
Ålesund
Åndalsnes
Geiranger
Dombås
Måløy
Sveg
Orsa
Mora
Bollnäs
Rättvik
Falun
Gävle
Eckerö
Mariehamn
Grisslehamn
Kapellskär
Sogndal
Lærdal
Balestrand
Lillehammer
Elverum
Hamar
Gjøvik
Eidsvoll
Flåm
Myrdal
Gol
Voss
Ulvik
Geilo
Odda
Roa
Hønefoss
Drammen
Lillestrøm
Kongsvinger
Charlottenberg
Borlänge
Ludvika
Fagersta
Avesta
Uppsala
Arlanda
Västerås
Frövi
Persberg
Eskilstuna
Södertälje
Nynäshamn
Notodden
Nordagutu
Skien
Larvik
Strömstad
Fredrikstad
Kornsjø
Kil
Karlstad
Kristinehamn
Örebro
Laxå
Hallsberg
Katrineholm
Norrköping
Motala
Mariestad
Linköping
Mjölby
Västervik
Visby
Haugesund
Stavanger
Egersund
Moi
Nelaug
Arendal
Kristiansand
Uddevalla
Öxnered
Trollhättan
Falköping
Herrljunga
Jönköping
Nässjö
Borås
Oskarshamn
Hirtshals
Hjørring
Frederikshavn
Hanstholm
Ålborg
Thisted
Varberg
Alvesta
Växjö
Kalmar
Emmaboda
Karlskrona
Randers
Grenaa
Struer
Langå
Holstebro
Halmstad
Kristianstad
Århus
Skjern
Herning
Helsingborg
Helsingør
Hässleholm
Lund
Fredericia
Esbjerg
Malmö
Ystad
Odense
Nyborg
Korsør
Trelleborg
Fanø
Ribe
Rønne
Sønderborg
Nykøbing
Tønder
Padborg
Rødby
Gedser
Niebüll
Flensburg
Puttgarden
Sassnitz Fährhafen
Kiel
Rostock
Ebeltoft
Sj. Odde
Samsø
Vejle
Kalundborg
Roskilde
Ringsted
Vordingborg
Bøjden
Svendborg
Fynshav
Nakskov
Gedser

DENMARK

Operators: The principal operator is Danske Statsbaner (DSB). Arriva Tog (AT) operate many local services in Jutland.

Services: InterCity (*IC*) and InterCityLyn (*Lyn*) trains offer *Business* (1st class), *Standard* (2nd class), and on some services *Hvilepladser* ('quiet' seats) and *Familiepladser* ('family' seats). These services often consist of two or more portions for different destinations and care should be taken to join the correct portion. Other trains convey 1st and 2nd (standard) classes of accommodation unless otherwise shown. Øresund link services are strictly non-smoking.

Timings: Valid until **January 5, 2008** unless otherwise stated. Alterations may be made on and around the dates of public holidays (see **Holiday periods** below for known changes to schedules).

Reservations: Seat reservations (currently 20 DKK) are recommended for travel on *IC* and *Lyn* trains (especially at peak times) and may be purchased a maximum of two months and a minimum of 15 minutes before departure of the train from its *originating* station. Passengers may board the train without a reservation but are not guaranteed a seat. Reservations are also available on EuroCity (*EC*) trains. It is not possible to reserve seats on other types of train. Special reservation rules may apply during holiday periods.

Supplements: Supplements are payable for travel to and from Germany by EuroCity (*EC*) trains; also for journeys København – Høje Taastrup – Nykøbing Falster and v.v. by *EC* train. On DSB trains, a higher fare is payable for journeys in the Greater København area between 0100 and 0500 hours.

Holiday periods: DSB services will be amended as follows (e.g. Dec. 25⑥ means that a ⑥ service will operate on Dec. 25): Apr. 4⑤, 5⑥, 6⑥, 8⑥, 9⑦, May 3⑤, 4⑥, 16⑤, 17⑥, 27⑥, 28⑦, June 5⑥, Dec. 23⑥, 24⑥, 25⑥, 26⑦, 30, ⑥, 31⑥, Jan. 1⑦.
Arriva services will be amended as follows: Apr. 5⑦, 6⑦, 9⑦, May 4⑦, 17⑦, 28⑦, June 5⑥, Dec. 24⑦, 25⑦, 26⑦, 30, ⑦, 31⑦, Jan. 1⑦.

700 KØBENHAVN - ODENSE - FREDERICIA - ÅRHUS

km		*IC* 191 A	*IC* 805	*IC* 109 A ①–⑥	*Lyn* 11 F ①–⑥		*IC* 113 A ①–⑥	*IC* 917 S	*Lyn* 15 F ①–⑥	*IC* 117 A	*IC* 821 E	*Lyn* 19 F ①–⑥		*IC* 121 A	*IC* 925 S	*Lyn* 23 F ①–⑥	*IC* 125 A	*IC* 829 E	*Lyn* 27 F ①–⑥	*IC* 129 A	*IC* 933 S	*Lyn* 29 F ①–⑥	*IC* 133 A	*IC* 837 E
0	**København Lufthavn** d.	0011	0140	...	...	...	0440	...	...	0540	...	...	...	0640	...	...	0740	...	...	0840	...	...	0940	...
11	**København H 721** § d.	0030	0206	...	...	...	0500	0530**d**	0550	0600	0630	0650	...	0700	0730	0750	0800	0830	0850	0900	0930	0950	1000	1030
31	Høje Taastrup **721** § d.	0043	0221	...	...	...	0512	0543**d**	0602	0612	0643	0702	...	0712	0743	0802	0812	0843	0902	0912	0943	1002	1012	1043
42	Roskilde **721** § d.	0057	0233	...	...	...	0521	0552**d**	|	0621	0652	|	...	0721	0752	|	0821	0852	|	0921	0952	|	1021	1052
75	Ringsted **721** d.	0119	0255	...	...	...	0537	0607**d**	|	0637	0707	|	...	0737	0807	|	0837	0907	|	0937	1007	|	1037	1107
104	Slagelse d.	0138	0313	...	...	...	0552	0625**d**	|	0652	0725	|	...	0752	0825	|	0852	0925	|	0952	1025	|	1052	1125
119	Korsør d.	0148	0322	...	...	...	0601	0634**d**	|	0701	0734	|	...	0801	0834	|	0901	0934	|	1001	1034	|	1101	1134
143	Nyborg d.	0202	0336	0514**a**	...	...	0614	0647**d**	|	0714	0747	|	...	0814	0847	|	0914	0947	|	1014	1047	|	1114	1147
171	**Odense** a.	0217	0352	0528**a**	...	...	0628	0703**d**	0709	0728	0803	0809	...	0828	0903	0909	0928	1003	1009	1028	1103	1109	1128	1203
171	**Odense 729** d.	0220	0353	0531	0612	...	0631	0705	0712	0731	0805	0812	...	0831	0905	0912	0931	1005	1012	1031	1105	1112	1131	1205
221	Middelfart **710** d.	0248	0419	0557	|	...	0657	0730	|	0757	0830	|	...	0857	0930	|	0957	1030	|	1057	1130	|	1157	1230
231	**Fredericia** a.	0255	0428	0607	0643	...	0707	...	0743	0807	...	0843	...	0907	...	0943	1007	...	1043	1107	...	1143	1207	...
231	**Fredericia 705/10/5** d.	0257	...	0612	0646	...	0712	...	0746	0812	...	0846	...	0912	...	0946	1012	...	1046	1112	...	1146	1212	...
257	Vejle **715** d.	0313	...	0628	0702	...	0728	...	0802	0828	...	0902	...	0928	...	1002	1028	...	1102	1128	...	1202	1228	...
288	Horsens d.	0330	...	0645	0719	...	0745	...	0819	0845	...	0919	...	0945	...	1019	1045	...	1119	1145	...	1219	1245	...
317	Skanderborg **713** d.	0346	...	0700	0735	...	0800	...	0835	0900	...	0935	...	1000	...	1035	1100	...	1135	1200	...	1235	1300	...
340	**Århus 713** a.	0359	...	0715	0751	...	0815	...	0851	0915	...	0951	...	1015	...	1051	1115	...	1151	1215	...	1251	1315	...

	Lyn 41 F	*ICE* 386 ♦p	*EC* 386 ♦q	*IC* 137 A	*IC* 941 S	*Lyn* 43 F	*IC* 141 A	*IC* 845 E	*Lyn* 45 F	*IC* 145 A	*IC* 949 S	*Lyn* 47 F		*IC* 149 A	*IC* 853 E	*Lyn* 51 F Ⓑ	*IR* 1653 ⑤k	*IC* 153 A		*IC* 957 S	*Lyn* 55 F Ⓑ	*IR* 1655 ⑤k	*IC* 157 A	*IC* 861 E
København Lufthavn d.	...	...	...	1040	...	...	1140	...	...	1240	...	...	...	1340	...	...	...	1440	...	...	...	...	1540	...
København H 721 § d.	1050	...	...	1100	1130	1150	1200	1230	1250	1300	1330	1350	...	1400	1430	1450	1456	1500	...	1530	1550	1556	1600	1630
Høje Taastrup **721** § d.	1102	...	...	1112	1143	1202	1212	1243	1302	1312	1343	1402	...	1412	1443	1502	|	1512	...	1543	1602	|	1612	1643
Roskilde **721** § d.	|	...	...	1121	1152	|	1221	1252	|	1321	1352	|	...	1421	1452	|	|	1521	...	1552	|	|	1621	1652
Ringsted **721** d.	|	...	...	1137	1207	|	1237	1307	|	1337	1407	|	...	1437	1507	|	1532	1537	...	1607	|	1632	1637	1707
Slagelse d.	|	...	...	1152	1225	|	1252	1325	|	1352	1425	|	...	1452	1525	|	1547	1552	...	1625	|	1647	1652	1725
Korsør d.	|	...	...	1201	1234	|	1301	1334	|	1401	1434	|	...	1501	1534	|	|	1601	...	1634	|	|	1701	1734
Nyborg d.	|	...	...	1214	1247	|	1314	1347	|	1414	1447	|	...	1514	1547	|	|	1614	...	1647	|	|	1714	1747
Odense a.	1209	...	...	1228	1303	1309	1328	1403	1409	1428	1503	1509	...	1528	1603	1609	1622	1628	...	1703	1709	1722	1728	1803
Odense 729 d.	1212	...	...	1231	1305	1312	1331	1405	1412	1431	1505	1512	...	1531	1605	1612	1624	1631	...	1705	1712	1724	1731	1805
Middelfart **710** d.	|	...	...	1257	1330	|	1357	1430	|	1457	1530	|	...	1557	1630	|	|	1657	...	1730	|	|	1757	1830
Fredericia a.	1243	...	...	1307	...	1343	1407	...	1443	1507	...	1543	...	1607	...	1643	1659	1707	...	...	1743	1759	1807	...
Fredericia 705/10/5 d.	1246	1255	1300	1312	...	1346	1412	...	1446	1512	...	1546	...	1612	...	1646	1701	1712	...	...	1746	1801	1812	...
Vejle **715** d.	1302	1311	1315	1328	...	1402	1428	...	1502	1528	...	1602	...	1628	...	1702	1717	1728	...	...	1802	1817	1828	...
Horsens d.	1319	1327	1332	1345	...	1419	1445	...	1519	1545	...	1619	...	1645	...	1719	1735	1745	...	...	1819	1835	1845	...
Skanderborg **713** d.	1335	1343	1348	1400	...	1435	1500	...	1535	1600	...	1635	...	1700	...	1735	1751	1800	...	...	1835	1851	1900	...
Århus 713 a.	1351	1355	1402	1415	...	1451	1515	...	1551	1615	...	1651	...	1715	...	1751	1808	1815	...	...	1851	1908	1915	...

	Lyn 59 F Ⓑ	*IR* 1661 ⑤k		*IC* 161 A	*IC* 965 S	*Lyn* 63 Ⓑ	*IC* 165 A	*IC* 869 E	*Lyn* 65 Ⓑ		*EN* 483 Ⓡ ♦	*IC* 169 A	*IC* 973 S	*ICE* 380 ♦	*Lyn* 69 ⑦		*IC* 173 A	*IC* 877	*IC* 177	*IC* 981	*IC* 179	*IC* 885	*IC* 189	
København Lufthavn d.	...	...	...	1640	...	...	1740	...	...	...	...	1840	...	...	...	...	1940	...	2040	...	2140	...	2308	...
København H 721 § d.	1650	1656	...	1700	1730	1750	1800	1830	1850	...	1853	1900	1930	...	1950	...	2000	2030	2100	2130	2200	2230	2330	...
Høje Taastrup **721** § d.	1702	|	...	1712	1743	1802	1812	1843	1902	...	1907	1912	1943	...	2002	...	2012	2043	2112	2143	2212	2243	2343	...
Roskilde **721** § d.	|	|	...	1721	1752	|	1821	1852	|	...	|	1921	1952	...	|	...	2021	2052	2121	2152	2221	2252	2352	...
Ringsted **721** d.	|	1732	...	1737	1807	|	1837	1907	|	...	1931	1937	2007	...	|	...	2037	2107	2137	2207	2237	2307	0008	...
Slagelse d.	|	1747	...	1752	1825	|	1852	1925	|	...	|	1952	2025	...	|	...	2052	2125	2152	2225	2252	2325	0026	...
Korsør d.	|	|	...	1801	1834	|	1901	1934	|	...	|	2001	2034	...	|	...	2101	2134	2201	2234	2301	2334	0035	...
Nyborg d.	|	|	...	1814	1847	|	1914	1947	|	...	|	2014	2047	...	|	...	2114	2147	2214	2247	2314	2347	0048	...
Odense a.	1809	1822	...	1828	1903	1909	1928	2003	2009	...	2021	2028	2103	...	2109	...	2128	2203	2228	2303	2328	0003	0102	...
Odense 729 d.	1812	1824	...	1831	1905	1912	1931	2005	2012	...	...	2031	2105	...	2112	...	2131	2205	2231	2305	2331	0005	0107	...
Middelfart **710** d.	|	|	...	1857	1930	|	1957	2030	|	...	...	2057	2130	...	|	...	2157	2230	2257	2330	2357	0031	0132	...
Fredericia a.	1843	1859	...	1907	...	1943	2007	...	2043	...	...	2107	...	...	2143	...	2207	...	2307	...	0007	0039	0139	...
Fredericia 705/10/5 d.	1846	1901	...	1912	...	1946	2012	...	2046	...	...	2112	...	2106	2146	...	2212	...	2312	...	0012	...	0141	...
Vejle **715** d.	1902	1917	...	1928	...	2002	2028	...	2102	...	...	2128	...	2120	2202	...	2228	...	2328	...	0028	...	0157	...
Horsens d.	1919	1935	...	1945	...	2019	2045	...	2119	...	...	2145	...	2137	2219	...	2245	...	2345	...	0045	...	0214	...
Skanderborg **713** d.	1935	1951	...	2000	...	2035	2100	...	2135	...	...	2200	...	2153	2235	...	2300	...	0000	...	0100	...	0230	...
Århus 713 a.	1951	2008	...	2015	...	2051	2115	...	2151	...	...	2215	...	2207	2251	...	2315	...	0015	...	0115	...	0244	...

	IC 190 A	①–⑤	*Lyn* 2 ①–⑤	*IC* 800 ①–⑥	*IC* 802 ①–⑤	*IC* 804	*Lyn* 906 ①–⑤	*Lyn* 6 ①–⑤	*IC* 108 ①–⑥		*Lyn* 10 A ①–⑤	*IC* 908 S	*EN* 482 Ⓡ ♦	*IC* 112 A	*Lyn* 14 F ①–⑥	*IC* 812 E	*IC* 116 A	*ICE* 381 ♦		*Lyn* 18 F ①–⑥	*IC* 916 S	*IC* 120 A	*Lyn* 24 F ①–⑥	*IC* 820 E
Århus 713 729 d.	0154	...	0415	...	...	...	...	0548	0554**g**	...	0627	...	...	0654	0727	...	0754	0805	...	0827	...	0854	0927	...
Skanderborg **713** d.	0211	...	0430	...	...	...	...	0602	0609**g**	...	0641	...	...	0709	0741	...	0809	0819	...	0841	...	0909	0941	...
Horsens d.	0228	...	0444	...	...	...	...	0617	0624**g**	...	0656	...	...	0724	0756	...	0824	0835	...	0856	...	0924	0956	...
Vejle **715** d.	0246	...	0501	...	...	...	...	0634	0642**g**	...	0714	...	...	0742	0814	...	0842	0852	...	0914	...	0942	1014	...
Fredericia 715 a.	0301	...	0518	...	...	...	...	0651	0701**g**	...	0731	...	...	0801	0831	...	0901	0906	...	0931	...	1001	1031	...
Fredericia 705 710 d.	0306	0448	0522	0527	0540	0616	...	0653	0706	...	0736	...	...	0806	0836	...	0906	...	...	0936	...	1006	1036	...
Middelfart **710** d.	0315	0455	|	0535	0548	0624	0651	|	0715	...	|	0746	...	0815	|	0848	0915	...	...	|	0948	1015	|	1048
Odense a.	0342	0520	0553	0600	0615	0652	0716	0724	0743	...	0807	0813	...	0842	0907	0913	0942	...	...	1007	1013	1043	1107	1113
Odense 729 d.	0348	0524	0556	0602	0630	0702	0720	0729	0746	...	0810	0817	0822	0846	0910	0917	0946	...	...	1010	1017	1046	1110	1117
Nyborg d.	0404	0538	|	0616	0646	0716	0735	|	0802	...	|	0832	|	0902	|	0932	1002	...	...	|	1032	1102	|	1132
Korsør d.	0417	0551	|	0629	0659	0729	|	|	0815	...	|	0845	|	0915	|	0945	1015	...	...	|	1045	1115	|	1145
Slagelse d.	0426	0601	|	0639	0709	0739	0755	|	0825	...	|	0854	|	0925	|	0954	1025	...	...	|	1054	1125	|	1154
Ringsted **721** a.	0443	0618	|	0655	0726	0754	|	|	0838	...	|	0911	0916	0938	|	1011	1038	...	...	|	1111	1138	|	1211
Roskilde **721** § a.	0506	0640	|	0711	0744	0813	|	|	0855	...	|	0928	|	0955	|	1028	1055	...	...	|	1128	1155	|	1228
Høje Taastrup **721** § a.	0518	0648	0700	0719	0753	0823	|	0834	0904	...	0914	0937	0943	1004	1014	1037	1104	...	...	1114	1137	1204	1214	1237
København H 721 § a.	0536	0703	0715	0735	0810	0839	0844	0848	0919	...	0929	0953	0959	1019	1029	1053	1119	...	...	1129	1153	1219	1229	1253
København Lufthavn a.	0559	...	0739	...	...	...	...	...	0939	...	...	...	...	1039	...	...	1139	...	...	...	...	1239	...	...

FOR NOTES SEE FACING PAGE

ÅRHUS - FREDERICIA - ODENSE - KØBENHAVN 700

	IC 124	*Lyn* 26	*IC* 924	*IC* 128	*IR* 1658	*Lyn* 28	*IC* 828	*IC* 132		*Lyn* 40	*IC* 932	*IC* 136	*Lyn* 42	*IC* 836	*IC* 140	*Lyn* 87	*EC* 385	*iCE* 387	*IC* 940	*IC* 144	*Lyn* 46	*IC* 844	*IC* 148	*IR* 1650
	A	F	S	A		F	E	A		F	S	A	F	E	A	F			S	A	F	E	A	
		①–⑥			⑥z												♦m	♦p						⑤k
Århus 713 729 d.	0954	1027	...	1054	1058	1127	...	1154	...	1227	...	1254	1327	...	1354	1427	1413	1413	...	1454	1527	...	1554	1558
Skanderborg **713** d.	1009	1041	...	1109	1113	1141	...	1209	...	1241	...	1309	1341	...	1409	1441	1428	1429	...	1509	1541	...	1609	1614
Horsens d.	1024	1056	...	1124	1129	1156	...	1224	...	1256	...	1324	1356	...	1424	1456	1445	1445	...	1524	1556	...	1624	1633
Vejle **715** d.	1042	1114	...	1142	1148	1214	...	1242	...	1314	...	1342	1414	...	1442	1514	1505	1504	...	1542	1614	...	1642	1653
Fredericia 715 a.	1101	1131	...	1201	1205	1231	...	1301	...	1331	...	1401	1431	...	1501	1531	1521	1521	...	1601	1631	...	1701	1709
Fredericia 705 710 d.	1106	1136	...	1206	1210	1236	...	1306	...	1336	...	1406	1436	...	1506	1536	...	...	...	1606	1636	...	1706	...
Middelfart **710** d.	1115	|	1148	1215	|	|	1248	1315	...	|	1348	1415	|	1448	1515	|	...	...	1548	1615	|	1648	1715	...
Odense a.	1143	1207	1213	1243	1247	1307	1313	1343	...	1407	1413	1443	1507	1513	1543	1607	...	...	1613	1643	1707	1713	1743	...
Odense 729 d.	1146	1210	1217	1246	1250	1310	1317	1346	...	1410	1417	1446	1510	1517	1546	1610	...	...	1617	1646	1710	1717	1746	...
Nyborg d.	1202	|	1232	1302	1307	|	1332	1402	...	|	1432	1502	|	1532	1602	|	...	...	1632	1702	|	1732	1802	...
Korsør d.	1215	|	1245	1315	|	|	1345	1415	...	|	1445	1515	|	1545	1615	|	...	...	1645	1715	|	1745	1815	...
Slagelse d.	1225	|	1254	1325	1330	|	1354	1425	...	|	1454	1525	|	1554	1625	|	...	...	1654	1725	|	1754	1825	...
Ringsted **721** a.	1238	|	1311	1338	1345	|	1411	1438	...	|	1511	1538	|	1611	1638	|	...	...	1711	1738	|	1811	1838	...
Roskilde **721** § a.	1255	|	1328	1355	1404	|	1428	1455	...	|	1528	1555	|	1628	1655	|	...	...	1728	1755	|	1828	1855	...
Høje Taastrup **721** § a.	1304	1314	1337	1404	1413	1414	1437	1504	...	1514	1537	1604	1614	1637	1704	1714	...	...	1737	1804	1814	1837	1904	...
København H 721 § a.	1319	1329	1353	1419	1433	1429	1453	1519	...	1529	1553	1619	1629	1653	1719	1729	...	...	1753	1819	1829	1853	1919	...
København Lufthavn a.	1339	...	...	1439	...	...	...	1539	...	...	...	1639	...	...	1739	...	...	...	...	1839	...	...	1939	...

	Lyn 50	*IC* 948	*IC* 152	*IR* 1648	*Lyn* 54	*IC* 852		*IC* 156	*Lyn* 56	*IC* 956	*IC* 160	*IR* 1662	*Lyn* 60	*IC* 860		*IC* 164	*IC* 964	*IC* 168	*IC* 868		*IC* 172	*IC* 176		*IC* 180
	F	S	A		F	E		A	A	S	A		F	E		A	S	A	E		A	A		A
	⑧			⑦	⑧				⑧			⑤k	⑧											
Århus 713 729 d.	1627	...	1654	1658	1727	...	...	1754	1827	...	1854	1906	1927	...	...	1954	...	2054	...	...	2154	2254	...	2354
Skanderborg **713** d.	1641	...	1709	1713	1741	...	...	1809	1841	...	1909	1921	1941	...	...	2009	...	2109	...	...	2209	2309	...	0009
Horsens d.	1656	...	1724	1729	1756	...	...	1824	1856	...	1924	1938	1956	...	...	2024	...	2124	...	...	2224	2324	...	0024
Vejle **715** d.	1714	...	1742	1748	1814	...	...	1842	1914	...	1942	1957	2014	...	...	2042	...	2142	...	...	2242	2342	...	0042
Fredericia 715 a.	1731	...	1801	1804	1831	...	...	1901	1931	...	2001	2014	2031	...	...	2101	...	2201	...	...	2301	0001	...	0101
Fredericia 705 710 d.	1736	...	1806	1810	1836	...	...	1906	1936	...	2006	2016	2036	...	...	2106	...	2206	...	...	2306	0006	...	0106
Middelfart **710** d.	|	1748	1815	1819	|	1848	...	1915	|	1948	2015	2025	|	2048	...	2115	2148	2215	2248	...	2315	0015	...	0115
Odense a.	1807	1813	1843	1848	1907	1913	...	1943	2007	2013	2043	2053	2107	2113	...	2143	2213	2243	2313	...	2343	0043	...	0143
Odense 729 d.	1810	1817	1846	1850	1910	1917	...	1946	2010	2017	2046	2055	...	2117	...	2146	2217	2246	2317	...	2346	0049	...	...
Nyborg d.	|	1832	1902	1907	|	1932	...	2002	|	2032	2102	2112	...	2132	...	2202	2232	2302	2332	...	0002	0102	...	...
Korsør d.	|	1845	1915	|	|	1945	...	2015	|	2045	2115	2126	...	2145	...	2215	2245	2315	2345	...	0015	0115	...	...
Slagelse d.	|	1854	1925	1930	|	1954	...	2025	|	2054	2125	2137	...	2154	...	2225	2254	2325	2354	...	0025	0125	...	...
Ringsted **721** a.	|	1911	1938	1945	|	2011	...	2038	|	2111	2138	2153	...	2211	...	2238	2311	2338	0011	...	0038	0138	...	...
Roskilde **721** § a.	|	1928	1955	2004	|	2028	...	2055	|	2128	2155	2212	...	2228	...	2255	2328	2355	0028	...	0055	0155	...	...
Høje Taastrup **721** § a.	1914	1937	2004	2013	2014	2037	...	2104	2114	2137	2204	2221	...	2237	...	2304	2337	0004	0037	...	0104	0204	...	...
København H 721 § a.	1929	1953	2019	2033	2029	2053	...	2119	2129	2153	2219	2236	...	2253	...	2319	2353	0019	0053	...	0119	0219	...	...
København Lufthavn a.	...	...	2039	...	...	...	...	2139	...	...	2239	...	...	...	...	2339	...	0039	...	...	0139	0239	...	...

♦ – **NOTES** (LISTED BY TRAIN NUMBER)

380/1 – [12] and 🍷 Berlin - Hamburg - Århus and v.v.
385 – [12] and 🍷 Århus - Hamburg.
386 – [12] and 🍷 Hamburg - Århus.
387 – [12] and 🍷 Århus - Hamburg.
482 – *City Night Line* HANS CHRISTIAN ANDERSEN – 🛏 1, 2 cl., ▬ 2 cl., [2] and ✕ (Innsbruck, ⑥ Jan. 12 - Mar. 1 -) München - København; 🛏 1, 2 cl., ▬ 2 cl. (4/6 berth) and ✕ Basel - Frankfurt - København; 🛏 1, 2 cl., ▬ 2 cl., [2] and ✕ Amsterdam - Köln - København. Train for passengers making international journeys only.
483 – *City Night Line* HANS CHRISTIAN ANDERSEN – 🛏 1, 2 cl., ▬ 2 cl., [2] and ✕ København - München (- Innsbruck, ⑤ Jan. 11 - Feb. 29); 🛏 1, 2 cl., ▬ 2 cl. (4/6 berth) and ✕ København - Frankfurt - Basel; 🛏 1, 2 cl., ▬ 2 cl., [2] and ✕ København - Köln - Amsterdam. Train for passengers making international journeys only.

A – From/to Aalborg on some days (see Table **701**).
E – From/to Esbjerg (Table **705**).
F – From/to Frederikshavn on some days. A change of train may be necessary at Aalborg (see Table **701**).
S – From/to Sønderborg (Table **710**).

a – ①–⑤ only.
d – ①–⑥ only.
g – ⑥ only.
k – Not May 18.
m – Dec. 9 - Jan. 5.
p – Mar. 15 - Dec. 13, 2008.
q – Dec. 9 - Jan. 6.
z – Not Apr. 6 - 8, May 5, 19, 27, June 5, Dec. 23 - 25, 30, 31.
§ – *IC* and *Lyn* trains are not available for local journeys. Frequent local trains run between Roskilde and København.

ÅRHUS - AALBORG - FREDERIKSHAVN 701

2nd class only (*IC* & *Lyn* 1st & 2nd class)

km		*IC* 191				*Lyn* 7		*IC* 105		*Lyn* 9		*IC* 109	*Lyn* 11	*IC* 113	*Lyn* 15		*IC* 117	*Lyn* 19		*IC* 121	*Lyn* 23		*IC* 125	*Lyn* 27		*IC* 129	*Lyn* 29
			①–⑤		①–⑤	①–⑤	①–⑤		①–⑥	①–⑤	⑥		①–⑥		①–⑥	⑦		①–⑥	⑦		①–⑥	⑦		①–⑥	⑦		①–⑥
0	**Århus 712 729** d.	0405	...	...	0454	0533	...	0543	...	0633	0656	0722	0756	0822	0856	...	0922	0956	...	1022	1056	...	1122	1156	...	1222	1256
46	Langå **712** d.	|	...	...	0524	|	...	0610	...	|	0720	0749	|	0849	|	...	0949	|	...	1049	|	...	1149	|	...	1249	|
59	Randers d.	0438	...	...	0535	0606	...	0621	...	0706	0730	0800	0829	0900	0929	...	1000	1029	...	1100	1129	...	1200	1229	...	1300	1329
91	Hobro d.	0455	...	...	0554	0623	...	0638	...	0723	0746	0817	0846	0917	0946	...	1017	1046	...	1117	1146	...	1217	1246	...	1317	1346
140	**Aalborg** a.	0530	...	...	0635	0656	...	0718	...	0756	0824	0857	0919	0957	1019	...	1057	1119	...	1157	1219	...	1257	1319	...	1357	1419
140	**Aalborg** d.	...	0553	0626	...	...	0701	...	0726	0801	0826	...	0926	...	1026	1026	...	1126h	1126	...	1226h	1226	...	1326h	1326	...	1426v
188	Hjørring **729** d.	...	0645	0709	...	...	0747	...	0809j	0909	0909	...	1009	...	1109	1109	...	1209h	1209	...	1309h	1309	...	1409h	1409	...	1509v
225	**Frederikshavn** a.	...	0719	0737	...	...	0820	...	0837	0934	0934	...	1037	...	1134	1134	...	1237h	1237	...	1335h	1335	...	1437h	1437	...	1534v

		IC 133		*Lyn* 41	*IC* 137		*Lyn* 43	*IC* 141		*Lyn* 45	*IC* 145	*Lyn* 47	*IC* 149	*Lyn* 51		*IC* 153	*Lyn* 55		*IC* 157	*Lyn* 59		*IC* 161		*IC* 165	*IC* 169	*IC* 173
	⑦	z	⑤		⑥⑦	①–⑤		⑤–⑦	①–④					⑧	⑥		⑧	⑥		⑧	⑥					
Århus 712 729 d.	...	1322	1322	1356	1422	1422	1456	1522	1522	1556	1622	1656	1722	1756	...	1822	1856	...	1922	1956	...	2022	...	2122	2222	2322
Langå **712** d.	...	1349	1352	|	1449	1452	|	1549	1552	|	1649	|	1749	|	...	1849	|	...	1949	|	...	2049	...	2149	2249	2349
Randers d.	...	1400	1402	1429	1500	1502	1529	1600	1602	1629	1700	1729	1800	1829	...	1900	1929	...	2000	2029	...	2100	...	2200	2300	0000
Hobro d.	...	1417	1422	1446	1517	1522	1546	1617	1622	1646	1717	1746	1817	1846	...	1917	1946	...	2017	2046	...	2117	...	2217	2317	0017
Aalborg a.	...	1457	1504	1519	1557	1604	1619	1657	1704	1719	1757	1819	1857	1919	...	1957	2019	...	2057	2119	...	2157	...	2257	2357	0057
Aalborg d.	1426	...	...	1526t	...	...	1626v	...	...	1726	...	1826	...	1926	1926	...	2026	2026	...	2126	2126	...	2226	*2326*	*0026*	...
Hjørring **729** d.	1509	...	...	1609t	...	...	1709v	...	...	1809	...	1909	...	2009	2009	...	2109	2109	...	2209	2209	...	2309	*0009*	*0109*	...
Frederikshavn a.	1537	...	...	1637t	...	...	1734v	...	...	1837	...	1934	...	2037	2037	...	2132	2132	...	2237	2237	...	2334	*0037*	*0137*	...

	Lyn 10	*IC* 112	*Lyn* 14	*IC* 116	*Lyn* 18		*IC* 120	*Lyn* 24		*IC* 124		*Lyn* 26		*IC* 128		*Lyn* 28	*IC* 132	*Lyn* 40	*IC* 136	*Lyn* 42	*IC* 140	*Lyn* 87	*IC* 144	*Lyn* 46	*IC* 148	*Lyn* 50
	①–⑤	①–⑥	①–⑥		①–⑥	⑦		①–⑥	⑦	⑥⑦	①–⑤	①–⑥	①–⑤		⑦	①–⑥										
Frederikshavn d.	...	...	0439a	...	0542	0542	...	0639v	0639	...	..,	0742g	0745	...	0839	0839	...	0942	...	1039	...	1142h	...	1239	...	1342h
Hjørring **729** d.	...	...	0511a	...	0611	0611	...	0711v	0711	...	...	0811g	0816	...	0911	0911	...	1011	...	1111	...	1211h	...	1311	...	1411h
Aalborg a.	...	...	0555a	...	0655	0655	...	0755v	0755	...	...	0855g	0855	...	0951	0955	...	1055	...	1155	...	1255h	...	1355	...	1455h
Aalborg d.	0459	0510	0559	0610	0659	...	0710	0759	...	0810	0810	0859	...	0910	...	0959	1010	1059	1110	1159	1210	1259	1310	1359	1410	1459
Hobro d.	0529	0551	0629	0651	0729	...	0751	0829	...	0851	0854	0929	...	0951	...	1029	1051	1129	1151	1229	1251	1329	1351	1429	1451	1529
Randers d.	0547	0609	0647	0709	0747	...	0809	0847	...	0909	0916	0947	...	1009	...	1047	1109	1147	1209	1247	1309	1347	1409	1447	1509	1547
Langå **712** d.	|	0618	|	0718	|	...	0818	|	...	0918	0927	|	...	1018	...	|	1118	|	1218	|	1318	|	1418	|	1518	|
Århus 712 a.	0621	0647	0721	0747	0821	...	0847	0921	...	0947	1000	1021	...	1047	...	1121	1147	1221	1247	1321	1347	1421	1447	1521	1547	1621

	IC 152	*Lyn* 54		*IC* 156		*Lyn* 56		*IC* 160		*Lyn* 60		*IC* 164	*Lyn* 64		*IC* 168		*IC* 172		*IC* 176		*IC* 180		*IC* 184		*IC* 190	
		⑧	⑥	z	⑤	⑧	⑥	⑥⑦	①–⑤	⑧	⑥		m	⑤												
Frederikshavn d.	...	1439v	1439	...	...	1537p	1537	...	...	1639p	1639	...	1741y	1741	...	1839	...	1942	...	2039	...	2142	...	2239	...	...
Hjørring **729** d.	...	1511v	1511	...	...	1611p	1611	...	...	1711p	1711	...	1811y	1811	...	1911	...	2011	...	2111	...	2211	...	2311	...	...
Aalborg a.	...	1555v	1555	...	...	1655p	1655	...	...	1755p	1755	...	1855y	1855	...	1955	...	2055	...	2155	...	2255	...	2355	...	...
Aalborg d.	1510	1559	...	1610	1610	1659	...	1710	1710	1759	...	1810	1859	1859	1910	...	2010	...	2110	...	2210	...	2310	...	0010	...
Hobro d.	1551	1629	...	1651	1654	1729	...	1751	1754	1829	...	1851	1929	1929	1951	...	2051	...	2151	...	2251	...	2351	...	0051	...
Randers d.	1609	1647	...	1709	1716	1747	...	1809	1816	1847	...	1909	1947	1949	2009	...	2109	...	2209	...	2309	...	0009	...	0109	...
Langå **712** d.	1618	|	...	1718	1727	|	...	1818	1827	|	...	1918	|	|	2018	...	2118	...	2218	...	2318	...	0018	...	|	...
Århus 712 a.	1647	1721	...	1747	1800	1821	...	1847	1900	1921	...	1947	2021	2024	2047	...	2147	...	2247	...	2347	...	0047	...	0147	...

a – ①–⑤ only.
g – ⑥ only.
h – Connection on ⑤.
j – Depart 0812 on ①–⑤.
m – ①②③④⑦ only.
p – Connection on ⑤⑦.
t – Connection on ⑧.
v – Connection on ①–⑤.
y – Connection on ①–④.
z – ①②③④⑥⑦.

703 HELSINGØR - KØBENHAVN - KØBENHAVN LUFTHAVN (KASTRUP) ✈ - MALMÖ

km																					
											and at										
0	**Helsingør** § d.	0008j	0108j	0208j	0308j	...	...	0436	0456	0516	the same	1856	1916	1936	1952	and	2252	...	2312	2332	2352
43	Østerport ⊡ § d.	0051	0151	0251	0351	...	...	0514	0534	0554	minutes	1934	1954	2014	2034	every	2334	...	2354	0014	0034
46	**København H 700/20/1** ⊡ § d.	0103	0203	0303	0403	0434	0454	0523	0543	0603	past each	1943	2003	2023	2043	20	2343	...	0003	0023	0043
58	Køb Lufthavn (Kastrup) ✈ ⊡ a.	0116	0216	0316	0416	0443	0503	0536	0556	0616	hour	1956	2016	2036	2056	minutes	2356	...	0016	0036	0056
94	**Malmö C** a.	0138	0238	0338	0438	0455	0515	0558	0618	0638	until	2018	2038	2058	2118	until	0018	...	0038	...	...

										and at										
Malmö C d.	0022	0122	0222	0322	0422	...	...	0502	0522	0542	the same	1822	1842	1902	1922	and	2322	...	...	...	...
Køb Lufthavn (Kastrup) ✈ ⊡ d.	0044	0144	0244	0344	0444	0456	0504	0524	0544	0604	minutes	1844	1904	1924	1944	every	2344	...	0004	0024	...
København H 700/20/1 ⊡ § d.	0103	0203	0303	0403	0501	0511	0521	0541	0601	0621	past each	1901	1921	1941	2001	20	0001	...	0021	0041	...
Østerport ⊡ § a.	0111	0211	0311	0411	0509	0518	0529	0549	0609	0629	hour	1909	1929	1949	2009	minutes	0009	...	0029	0049	...
Helsingør § a.	0153j	0253j	0353j	0453j	0545	...	0605	0625	0645	0705	until	1945	2005	2025	2051	until	0051	...	0111	0131	...

j – ⑥⑦ only.

⊡ – Additional services operate Østerport - Kastrup and v.v.: Østerport depart 0524 and every 20 minutes until 2144; Kastrup depart 0516 and every 20 minutes until 2256.

§ – Additional services operate ①–⑤ København H - Helsingør and v.v.

704 KØBENHAVN - KALUNDBORG

km																											
		①–⑤	①–⑥	①–⑤	①–⑤	⑥⑦		①–⑤		①–⑤		①–⑤		①–⑤		①–⑤		①–⑤		①–⑤	①–⑤	⑥⑦	①–⑤	①–⑤	⑥⑦	①–⑤	①–⑤
0	**København H** d.	0450	0538	0641	0734	0734	0834	0853	0934	0953	1034	1053	1134	1153	1234	1253	1334	1353	1434	1453	1507	1534	1541	1607	1634	1642	1653
20	Høje Taastrup d.	0504	0554	0655	0749	0749	0849	0906	0949	1006	1049	1106	1149	1206	1249	1306	1349	1406	1449	1506	1524	1549	1556	1624	1649	1657	1705
31	Roskilde d.	0513	0606	0706	0803	0803	0903	0915	1003	1015	1103	1115	1203	1215	1303	1315	1403	1415	1503	1515	1535	1603	1605	1635	1703	1707	1715
67	Holbæk a.	0543	0638	0742	0838	0833	0933	0940	1033	1040	1133	1140	1233	1240	1333	1340	1433	1440	1533	1540	1606	1633	1635	1705	1733	1736	1741
67	Holbæk d.	0545	0702	0749	0840	0837g	0937c	0941	1037g	1041	1137c	1141	1237g	1241	1337c	1341	1437c	1441	1537c	1541	1608	1637	1637	1708	1737	1748	1742
111	Kalundborg a.	0630	0745	0830	0916	0912g	1012c	1016	1112g	1116	1212c	1216	1312g	1316	1412c	1416	1512c	1516	1612c	1616	1644	1712	1718	1744	1812	1824	1812

	①–⑤	⑥⑦	①–⑤	①–⑤							
København H d.	1707	1734	1742	1807	1834	1934	2034	2234	2334	0034	...
Høje Taastrup d.	1724	1749	1757	1824	1849	1949	2049	2249	2349	0049	...
Roskilde d.	1735	1803	1806	1835	1903	2003	2103	2303	0003	0103	...
Holbæk a.	1805	1833	1835	1905	1933	2033	2133	2333	0033	0133	...
Holbæk d.	1808	1837	1838	1906	1937	2037e	2137	2337	0037	0137	...
Kalundborg a.	1846	1912	1912	1944	2012	2112e	2212	0012	0112	0212	...

	①–⑤	①–⑥	①–⑤	⑥	①–⑤	①–⑤	①–⑤	①–⑤	⑥⑦	①–⑤	①–⑤
Kalundborg d.	0440	0504	0524	0557	0559	0617	0631	0657	0657	0729	0753
Holbæk a.	0510	0542	0601	0633	0643	0655	0701	0733	0733	0804	0833
Holbæk d.	0511	0543	0602	0634	0644	0717	0703	0734	0734	0805	0834
Roskilde a.	0541	0613	0634	0705	0716	0751	0735	0805	0805	0833	0905
Høje Taastrup a.	0555	0626	0643	0722	0726	0804	0744	0815	0818	0844	0917
København H a.	0611	0642	0659	0738	0743	0822	0801	0831	0835	0901	0933

	⑥⑦	①–⑤		①–⑤		①–⑤		①–⑤		①–⑤		①–⑤		①–⑤	⑥⑦	①–⑤	①–⑥	⑥⑦				⑤				
Kalundborg d.	0757g	0853	0857c	0953	0957g	1053	1057c	1153	1157g	1253	1257c	1353	1357c	1453	1457	...	1553	1557	1657	1757	1857	1957	1957e	2057	...	2300
Holbæk a.	0833g	0933	0937c	1033	1037g	1133	1137c	1233	1237g	1333	1337c	1433	1437c	1533	1537	...	1637	1637	1737	1838	1937	2033	2037e	2137	...	2337
Holbæk d.	0842	0934	0942	1034	1042	1134	1142	1234	1242	1334	1342	1434	1442	1542	1542	1610	1642	1642	1742	1842	1942	2034	2042	2142	2242	2342
Roskilde a.	0912	0959	1012	1059	1112	1159	1212	1259	1312	1359	1412	1459	1512	1612	1612	1643	1712	1712	1812	1912	2012	2059	2112	2212	2312	0012
Høje Taastrup a.	0925	1008	1025	1108	1125	1208	1225	1308	1325	1408	1425	1508	1525	1625	1625	1652	1725	1725	1825	1925	2025	2107	2125	2225	2325	0025
København H a.	0942	1023	1042	1123	1142	1223	1242	1323	1342	1423	1442	1523	1542	1642	1642	1708	1742	1742	1842	1942	2042	2123	2142	2242	2342	0042

c – ⑥⑦ only. e – ⑦ only. g – ⑥ only.

705 FREDERICIA - ESBJERG

2nd class only (*IC* & *Lyn* 1st & 2nd class)

km		*IC* 191										*IC* 821			*IC* 829		*IC* 861			*IC* 869				*IC* 877		
				①–⑤	①–⑥	①–⑤	①–⑤	①–⑤	⑥⑦	①–⑥																
	København 700 d.	0030	...	...	...	...	...	...	...	...	...	0630	...	...	0830		1630	...	...	1830	...	...	...	2030	...	...
	Odense 700 d.	0220	...	...	...	...	...	...	...	...	...	0805	...	...	1005		1805	...	...	2005	...	...	...	2205	...	...
	Middelfart 700 d.	0248	...	...	...	...	...	...	...	...	...	0831	...	...	1031	and in	1831	...	...	2031	...	...	...	2231	...	...
	Århus 700 d.	|	...	...	...	...	...	0613	...	0630	...	|	0730	0830	|	the same	|	1730	1830	|	...	1930	2030	|	2130	2230
0	**Fredericia 700/10** d.	0255	0315	0419	0528	0551	0618	0722	0722	0758	...	|	0858	0958	|	pattern	|	1858	1958	|	...	2058	2208	|	2308	0008
20	Kolding 710 d.	...	0331	0434	0544	0608	0634	0736	0738	0814	...	0847	0914	1014	1047	until	1847	1914	2014	2047	...	2114	2224	2247	2324	0024
33	Lunderskov 710 d.	...	0340	0443	0553	0618	0643	0744	0747	0823	...	|	0923	1023	|		|	1923	2023	|	...	2123	2233	|	2333	0033
44	Vejen d.	...	0348	0452	0602	0627	0651	0751	0756	0832	...	0901	0932	1032	1101		1901	1932	2032	2101	...	2132	2242	2301	2342	0042
72	Bramming 709 a.	...	0412	0515	0625	0653	0714	0812	0820	0856	...	0915	0956	1056	1115		1915	1956	2056	2115	...	2156	2306	2315	0006	0106
88	**Esbjerg** a.	...	0424	0528	0637	0705	0727	0824	0832	0908	...	0927	1008	1108	1127		1927	2008	2108	2127	...	2208	2318	2327	0018	0118

		Lyn 606				*IC* 812			*IC* 820			*IC* 828			*IC* 836			*IC* 844		*IC* 860			*IC* 868			*IC* 176
		①–⑤	①–⑤	①–⑥	①–⑤																					
Esbjerg d.	0541	0557	0615	0649	0715	0742	0749	0849	0942	0949	1049	1142	1149	1249	1342	1349	1449	1542		1942	1949	2049	2142	2149	2249	...
Bramming 709 d.	0553	0608	0632	0700	0729	0754	0800	0900	0954	1000	1100	1154	1200	1300	1354	1400	1500	1554		1954	2000	2100	2154	2200	2300	...
Vejen d.	0614	0625	0656	0725	0753	0813	0825	0925	1013	1025	1125	1213	1225	1325	1413	1425	1525	1613	and in	2013	2025	2125	2213	2225	2325	...
Lunderskov 710 d.	0621	|	0705	0733	0801	|	0833	0933	|	1033	1133	|	1242	1333	|	1433	1533	|	the same	|	2033	2133	|	2233	2333	...
Kolding 710 d.	0629	0641	0715	0743	0811	0831	0843	0943	1031	1043	1143	1231	1251	1343	1431	1443	1543	1631	pattern	2031	2043	2143	2231	2243	2343	...
Fredericia 700/10 a.	0643	|	0730	0759	0826	|	0859	0959	|	1059	1159	|	1307	1359	|	1459	1559	|	until	|	2059	2159	|	2259	2359	0006
Århus 700 a.	0801a	|	...	0934	...	|	1034	1134	|	1234	1334	|	1434	1534	|	1634	1734	|		|	2234	2334	|	0034	*0115*	|
Middelfart 700 a.	...	|	...	...	...	0848	...	...	1048	...	...	1248	...	...	1448	...	...	1648		2048	...	...	2248	...	...	0015
Odense 700 a.	...	0720	...	...	...	0913	...	...	1113	...	...	1313	...	...	1513	...	...	1713		2113	...	...	2313	...	...	0043
København 700 a.	...	0848	...	...	...	1053	...	...	1253	...	...	1453	...	...	1653	...	...	1853		2253	...	...	0053	...	...	0219

a – ①–⑤ only.

Additional services operate Fredericia - Esbjerg and v.v. on ①–⑤.

708 ESBJERG - SKJERN and SKJERN - STRUER

2nd class only. Operator: *AT*

km																								
										and each								⑥	†	⑥	⑥					
0	**Esbjerg 705** ⊗ d.	①-⑤	0432	0533	0621	0714	0828	0937	1027	train every	1737	1827	2023	2223	2337	Ⓒ	0527	0700	0736	0842	0936	and every	1936	2019	2136
17	Varde ⊗ d.		0450	0551	0645	0750	0848	0956	1048	two hours	1756	1848	2048	2242	2355		0545	0726	0754	0859	0954	two hours	1954	2039	2202
60	**Skjern 713** a.		0527	0628	0723	0832	0928	1032	1128	until	1832	1928	2128	2319	...		0622	0803	0831	...	1031	until	2031	...	2239

km																								
																⑥	†	⑥	†	⑥					
0	**Skjern 713** d.	①-⑤	0442	0533	0630	0724	0833	0933	1033		1733	1933	2133	...	Ⓒ	...	...	0637	0807	0837	1037		2037	...	2318
23	Ringkøbing a.		0500	0551	0651	0743	0854	0954	1054	and	1754	1954	2154	...		...	...	0655	0825	0855	1055	and every	2055	...	2336
23	Ringkøbing d.		0501	0554	0652	0744	0856	0956	1056	hourly	1756	1956	2203	...		0508	0652	0656	0826	0856	1056	two hours	2056	...	2337
71	Holstebro a.		0544	0634	0732	0824	0935	1035	1135	until	1835	2035	2242	...		0550	0735	0735	0905	0935	1135	until	2135	...	0016
71	Holstebro 715 d.		0548	0640	...	0849	0936	1036	1136		1836	2036	2243	...		0558	0736	0736	0917	0936	1136		2136	...	0017
86	**Struer 715** a.		0606	0657	...	0905	0949	1049	1149		1849	2049	2256	...		0612	0750	0750	0934	0950	1150		2150	...	0031

															⑥		†	⑥					
Struer 715 d.	①-⑤	0459	0525	0620	...	0832	0933		1633	1733	1933	2133	...	Ⓒ	0505	...	0633	0720	...	0920		1920	...	2133
Holstebro 715 a.		0513	0539	0638	...	0848	0949	and	1649	1749	1949	2149	...		0519	...	0647	0735	...	0934	and every	1934	...	2149
Holstebro d.		0514	0546	0656	0750	0849	0950	hourly	1650	1750	1950	2210	...		0520	...	0658	0736	...	0935	two hours	1935	...	2210
Ringkøbing a.		0553	0629	0739	0832	0932	1032	until	1732	1832	2032	2251	...		0559	...	0740	0815	...	1014	until	2014	...	2251
Ringkøbing d.		0555	0630	0744	0833	0933	1033		1733	1833	2033	2252	...		0600	...	0741	0816	...	1015		2015	...	2252
Skjern 713 a.		0615	0650	0803	0853	0953	1053		1754	1854	2054	2312	...		0620	...	0801	0836	...	1035		2035	...	2312

									and each							⑥	†	⑥					
Skjern 713 d.	①-⑤	0538	0631	0656	0804	0859	1002	1059	train every	1802	1859	2059	...	2320	Ⓒ	0623	0806	0840	...	1040	and every	2040	...	2320
Varde ⊗ d.		0619	0712	0743	0846	0935	1044	1135	two hours	1844	1935	2135	2221	2356		0703	0844	0917	1022	1117	two hours	2117	2222	2357
Esbjerg 705 ⊗ a.		0642	0734	0803	0905	0957	1103	1157	until	1903	1957	2157	2242	0015		0722	0903	0936	1041	1136	until	2136	2241	0016

⊗ – Additional services operate Esbjerg - Varde and v.v.

ESBJERG - RIBE - TØNDER - NIEBÜLL 709

Operator: *AT*. 2nd class only

km																							
		①-⑤													Ⓒ	⑥			and				
0	**Esbjerg 705** ⊗ d.		0513	0623	0702	0722	0807	0909	1007	and	1707	1907	2134	2309		0507	...	0707	every	1907	...	2007	2134	2309
16	Bramming **705** ⊗ d.		0528	0638	0719	0737	0821	0923	1021	hourly	1721	1921	2201	2323		0521	...	0721	two	1921	...	2021	2201	2323
33	Ribe ⊗ d.		0548	0658	0736	0756	0841	0941	1041	until	1741	1941	2219	2340		0541	...	0741	hours	1941	...	2040	2219	2340
80	**Tønder** a.		0640	0747	...	...	0931	1031	1131		1831	2031	2307	...		0631	...	0831	until	2031	...	...	2307	...

	①-⑤													Ⓒ	⑥	⑥			and				
Tønder d.		...	0609	0648	...	0831	0935	and	1835	...	2035	...	2311		...	0635	...	0835	every	2035	...	...	2311
Ribe ⊗ d.		0609	0701	0739	0823	0921	1023	hourly	1923	2023	2123	2223	2359		0623	0723	...	0923	two	2123	...	2223	2359
Bramming **705** ⊗ a.		0626	0718	0756	0840	0940	1040	until	1940	2040	2140	2240	0016		0640	0740	...	0940	hours	2140	...	2240	0016
Esbjerg 705 ⊗ a.		0646	0736	0811	0855	0955	1055		1955	2055	2155	2255	0031		0655	0755	...	0955	until	2155	...	2255	0031

km		Ⓐ	⚒				Ⓐ	Ⓒ	Ⓐ		h
0	**Tønder** ▲ ⊡ d.	0722	0834	1034	1234	1434	1534	1634	1734	1834	2034
17	Niebüll **821** ▲ ⊡ a.	0741	0853	1053	1253	1453	1553	1653	1753	1853	2053

	Ⓐ	⚒				Ⓐ	Ⓒ	Ⓐ		h
Niebüll **821** ▲ ⊡ d.	0701	0805	1005	1205	1405	1505	1605	1705	1805	2005
Tønder ▲ ⊡ a.	0719	0824	1024	1224	1424	1524	1624	1724	1824	2024

h – Mar. 31 - Oct. 28.

⊗ – Additional services operate Esbjerg - Ribe and v.v.

▲ – Bus service operates Niebüll - Tønder and v.v. up to 4 times daily on ⚒. Operator: Autokraft Niebüll. ✆ +49 0 46 61 87 75, fax +49 0 46 61 80 89.

⊡ – Operated by Nord-Ostsee-Bahn GmbH, Kiel. ✆ +49 (0) 180 10 180 11.

FREDERICIA - SØNDERBORG and FLENSBURG (- HAMBURG) 710

km		*IC*	*IC*	*IC*				*IC*		*IC*	*IC*	*ICE*		*IC*			*IC*			*IC*		*IC*				*IC*		*IC*
		191	**190**	**991**				**108**		**917**	**117**	**381**		**925**			**125**			**933**		**133**				**941**		**141**
					2	2	2		2				2			2		2	2		2		2		2		2	
						①–⑤		⑥				♦																
	København **700** d.	0030	...	...	...	...	...	...	...	0530d	0600	...	...	0730	...	...	0800	...	...	0930	...	1000	...	...	...	1130	...	1200
	Odense **700** d.	0220	...	...	...	...	...	...	...	0705	0731	...	...	0905	...	...	0931	...	...	1105	...	1131	...	...	...	1305	...	1331
	Århus **700** d.	|	0154	...	...	...	...	0554	0613a	|	|	0805	0730	|	...	0830	|	...	0930	|	1030	|	...	...	1130	|	1230	|
0	**Fredericia 700** d.	0255	0301	0310	0542	...	0624	0701	0722	|	0807	0908	0858	|	...	0958	1007	1019	1058	|	1158	1207	1219	...	1258	|	1358	1407
	Middelfart **700** d.	...	...	|	|	...	|	...	|	0731	▬	|	|	0931	...	|	...	|	|	1131	|	...	|	...	|	1331	|	...
20	Kolding **705** d.	...	...	0324	0556	...	0640	...	0736	0747	...	0920	0914	0947	...	1014	...	1033	1114	1147	1214	...	1233	...	1314	1347	1414	...
33	Lunderskov **705** d.	...	...	0331	0604	...	0649	...	0747	0754	...	|	0923	0954	...	1023	...	1042	1123	1154	1223	...	1242	...	1323	1354	1423	...
60	Vojens d.	...	...	0349	0625	...	0714	...	▬	0818	...	|	...	1018	...	...	...	1102	▬	1218	...	...	1302	...	▬	1418	...	...
95	Tinglev d.	...	...	0409	0648	0650	0739	...	...	0840	...	|	...	1040	...	...	...	1130	...	1240	...	...	1330	...	...	1440	...	...
136	**Sønderborg** a.	...	...	0445	0726	|	|	...	...	0917	...	|	...	1117	...	...	...	|	...	1317	...	...	|	...	...	1517	...	...
110	Padborg 🏛 **823** a.	...	...	...	...	0701	0750	...	0755	...	0945	1005	...	...	...	...	...	1141	1155	...	...	...	1341	...	1345	...	...	...
122	**Flensburg** 🏛 **823** a.	...	...	...	...	...	...	...	0806	...	0956	1021	...	...	...	...	...	...	1206	...	...	...	...	...	1356	...	...	...
302	*Hamburg Hbf* **823** a.	...	...	...	...	...	...	...	1014	...	1214	1230	...	...	...	...	...	...	1414	...	...	...	...	...	1614	...	...	...

			IC	*EC*	*ICE*		*IC*			*IC*			*IC*			*IC*		*IC*			*EN*		*IC*	*IC*				*IC*
			949	**385**	**387**		**149**			**957**			**157**			**965**		**165**			**483**		**973**	**173**				**981**
	2	2				2		2	2			2		2	2		2		2		Ⓡ	2			2	2	2	
				m	p																♦							
København **700** d.	...	...	1330	...	...	...	1400	...	...	1530	...	...	1600	...	...	1730	...	1800	...	...	1853	...	1930	2000	...	...	...	2130
Odense **700** d.	...	...	1505	...	...	...	1531	...	...	1705	...	...	1731	...	...	1905	...	1931	...	...	2023	...	2105	2131	...	...	...	2305
Århus **700** d.	...	1330	|	1413	1413	1430	|	...	1530	|	...	1630	|	...	1730	|	1830	|	...	...	|	1930	|	|	2030	...	2130	|
Fredericia 700 d.	1419	1458	|	1523	1525	1558	1607	1619	1658	|	...	1758	1807	1819	1858	|	1958	2007	2019	...	|	2058	|	2207	2208	2219	2308	|
Middelfart **700** d.	|	|	1531	|	|	|	...	|	|	1731	...	|	...	|	|	1931	|	...	|	...	|	|	2131	▬	|	|	|	2331
Kolding **705** d.	1433	1514	1547	1537	1538	1614	...	1633	1714	1747	...	1814	...	1833	1914	1947	2014	...	2033	...	2107	2114	2147	...	2224	2233	2324	2347
Lunderskov **705** d.	1442	1523	1554	|	|	1623	...	1642	1723	1754	...	1823	...	1842	1923	1954	2023	...	2042	...	|	2123	2154	...	2233	2242	2333	2354
Vojens d.	1502	▬	1618	|	|	...	...	1702	▬	1818	...	...	...	1902	▬	2018	...	...	2102	...	|	...	2218	2	...	2302	...	0013
Tinglev d.	1530	...	1640	|	|	...	...	1730	...	1840	...	...	...	1930	...	2040	...	...	2130	...	|	...	2240	2242	...	2330	...	0034
Sønderborg a.	|	...	1717	|	|	...	...	|	...	1917	...	...	...	|	...	2117	...	...	|	...	|	...	2317	|	...	|	...	0111
Padborg 🏛 **823** a.	1541	1545	...	1634	1634	...	...	1741	1745	...	...	...	...	1941	1945	...	...	...	2141	2145	2158	...	...	2252	...	2341	...	...
Flensburg 🏛 **823** a.	...	1556	...	1651	1651	...	...	...	1756	...	...	...	...	...	1956	...	...	...	...	2156	2230	...	...	...	...	...	...	...
Hamburg Hbf **823** a.	...	1814	...	1850	1850	...	...	...	2014	...	...	...	...	...	*2237z*	...	...	...	...	...	...	...	...	...	...	...	...	...

	Lyn		*IC*	*EN*			*IC*		*IC*				*IC*		*IC*			*ICE*	*EC*	*IC*		*IC*			*IC*		*IC*	
	906		**908**	**482**			**812**		**916**				**820**		**924**			**386**	**386**	**132**		**932**			**836**		**940**	
		2		Ⓡ		2		2		2		2		2		2					2			2		2		2
	①–⑤	①–⑤		♦		①–⑤												p	q									
Hamburg Hbf **823** d.	...	...	...	...	...	...	...	...	...	...	*0620z*	...	...	...	...	...	0843	0930	0930	...	...	...	1043	...	...	...	...	...
Flensburg 🏛 **823** d.	...	...	...	0548	0701	...	...	...	...	...	0901	...	...	...	...	...	1101	1126	1126	...	...	...	1301	...	...	...	...	...
Padborg 🏛 **823** d.	...	0529	...	0633	0712	0717	...	...	...	...	0912	0917	...	...	...	...	1112	1150	1142	...	...	...	1312	1317	...	...	...	...
Sønderborg d.	0505	|	0559	|	▬	|	...	...	0759	...	...	|	...	...	0959	...	...	|	|	...	...	1159	▬	|	...	...	1359	...
Tinglev d.	0545	0557v	0640	|	2	0731	...	...	0840	...	...	0931	...	...	1040	...	...	|	1154	...	...	1240	...	1331	...	...	1440	...
Vojens d.	0606	0624	0702	|	①–⑥	0756	...	...	0902	...	...	0956	...	...	1102	...	...	|	1218	...	...	1302	2	1356	...	...	1502	...
Lunderskov **705** d.	0625	0642	0721	|	0733	0815	...	0833	0921	0933	...	1015	...	1033	1121	1133	...	|	1237	...	1242	1321	1333	1415	...	1433	1521	1533
Kolding **705** d.	0635	0652	0731	0736	0743	0825	0831	0843	0931	0943	...	1025	1031	1043	1131	1143	...	1242	1246	...	1251	1331	1343	1425	1431	1443	1531	1543
Middelfart **700** a.	0650	|	0745	|	|	|	0848	|	0947	|	...	|	1048	|	1147	|	...	|	|	...	|	1347	|	|	1448	|	1547	|
Fredericia 700 a.	|	0707	|	|	0759	0839	|	0859	|	0959	...	1039	|	1059	|	1159	...	1254	1258	1306	1307	|	1359	1439	|	1459	|	1559
Århus **700** a.	|	...	|	|	0934	...	|	1034	|	1134	...	...	|	1234	|	1334	...	1355	1402	|	1434	|	1534	...	|	1634	|	1734
Odense **700** a.	0716	...	0813	0820	...	...	0913	...	1013	...	...	...	1113	...	1213	...	...		...	1343	...	1413	...	...	1513	...	1613	...
København **700** a.	0844	...	0953	0959	...	...	1053	...	1153	...	...	...	1253	...	1353	...	...		...	1519	...	1553	...	...	1653	...	1753	...

			IC		*IC*				*IC*		*IC*			*IC*		*ICE*	*IC*				*IC*			*IC*	*IC*	*IC*		*IC*
			844		**948**				**852**		**956**			**860**		**380**	**964**				**868**			**976**	**176**	**179**		**189**
		2		2		2		2		2			2		2			2		2		2	2				2	
																♦												
Hamburg Hbf **823** d.	1243	...	...	...	...	...	1443	...	...	...	...	1643	...	...	...	1730	...	...	1843	...	...	...	...	...	...	...	...	...
Flensburg 🏛 **823** d.	1501	...	...	...	...	...	1701	...	...	...	...	1901	...	...	...	1939	...	...	2101	...	...	...	...	...	...	...	...	...
Padborg 🏛 **823** d.	1512	1517	...		...	...	1712	1717	...	...	...	1912	1917	...	...	1955	...	...	2112	2117	...	...	2220	...	...	...	...	...
Sønderborg d.	...	|	...	...	1559	...	...	|	...	...	1759	▬	|	...	...	|	1959	...	...	|	...	...	|	2159	...	...	2337	...
Tinglev d.	...	1531	...	...	1640	...	...	1731	...	...	1840	...	1931	...	...	|	2040	...	...	2131	...	...	2231	2240	...	...	0014	...
Vojens d.	...	1556	...	...	1702	...	...	1756	...	...	1902	2	1956	...	...	|	2102	...	...	2156	...	...	...	2302	...	...	0034	...
Lunderskov **705** d.	...	1615	...	1633	1721	1733	...	1815	...	1833	1921	1933	2015	...	2033	|	2121	2133	...	2215	...	2233	...	2321	...	...	0051	...
Kolding **705** d.	...	1625	1631	1643	1731	1743	...	1825	1831	1843	1931	1943	2025	2031	2043	2051	2131	2143	...	2225	2231	2243	...	2331	...	...	0100	...
Middelfart **700** a.	...	|	1648	|	1747	|	...	|	1848	|	1947	|	|	2048	|	|	2147	|	...	|	2248	|	...	|	...	...	|	...
Fredericia 700 a.	...	1639	|	1659	|	1759	...	1839	|	1859	|	1959	2039	|	2059	2104	|	2159	...	2239	|	2259	...	2343	0006	0012	0114	0141
Århus **700** a.	...	...	|	1834	|	1934	...	...	|	2034	|	2134	...	|	2234	2207	|	2334	...	...	|	0034	...	...	|	0115	...	0244
Odense **700** a.	...	...	1713	...	1813	...	...	...	1913	...	2013	...	...	2113	...	...	2213	...	...	...	2313	...	...	...	0043	...	...	...
København **700** a.	...	...	1853	...	1953	...	...	...	2053	...	2153	...	...	2253	...	...	2353	...	...	...	0053	...	...	...	0219	...	...	...

♦ – **NOTES** (LISTED BY TRAIN NUMBER)

380 – 12 and 🍷 Berlin - Hamburg - Århus.

381 – 12 and 🍷 Århus - Hamburg - Berlin.

482 – *City Night Line* HANS CHRISTIAN ANDERSEN – 🛏 1, 2 cl., ▬ 2 cl., 2 and ✕ (Innsbruck, ⑥ Jan. 12 - Mar. 1 -) München - København; 🛏 1, 2 cl., ▬ 2 cl. (4/6 berth) and ✕ Basel - Frankfurt - København; 🛏 1, 2 cl., ▬ 2 cl., 2 and ✕ Amsterdam - Köln - København. Train for passengers making international journeys only.

483 – *City Night Line* HANS CHRISTIAN ANDERSEN – 🛏 1, 2 cl., ▬ 2 cl., 2 and ✕ København - München (- Innsbruck, ⑤ Jan. 11 - Feb. 29); 🛏 1, 2 cl., ▬ 2 cl. (4/6 berth) and ✕ København - Frankfurt - Basel; 🛏 1, 2 cl., ▬ 2 cl., 2 and ✕ København - Köln - Amsterdam. Train for passengers making international journeys only.

a – ①–⑤ only.
d – ①–⑥ only.
m – Dec. 9 - Jan. 5.
p – Mar. 15 - Dec. 13, 2008.
q – Dec. 9 - Jan. 6.
v – Arrive 0540.
z – Change at Neumünster (see Table **823**).

712 ÅRHUS - VIBORG - STRUER

2nd class only (**IC** & **Lyn** 1st & 2nd class). Operator: *AT*

km														*IC*725	*IC*1625											
		①–⑤	⑥	①–⑤	①–⑤	Ⓒ	①–⑤	⑥						①–⑤	⑥**p**		†**q**									
	København **700** ... d.	...	...	...	...	...	...	...	...	...	...	...	...	0800	0800	...	...	...	...	...	...	...	...	...	...	...
0	**Århus 700** ... ⊗ d.	...	0459	0518	0618	0627	0727	0727	...	0827	0927	1027	...	1127	1127	...	1127	1227	1327	1427	...	1527	1627	1727	1827	...
46	Langå **700** ... ⊗ a.	...	0530	0548	0649	0658	0758	0758	...	0858	0958	1058	...	1158	1158	...	1158	1258	1358	1458	...	1558	1658	1758	1858	...
46	Langå ... ⊗ d.	...	0534	0553	0653	0703	0802	0803	...	0903	1003	1103	...	1203	1203	...	1203	1303	1403	1503	...	1603	1703	1803	1903	...
86	Viborg ... ⊗ d.	0507	0611	0634	0728	0734	0833	0834	...	0934	1034	1134	...	1234	1234	...	1234	1334	1434	1534	...	1634	1734	1834	1934	...
116	Skive ... d.	0538	0635	0702	0753	0757	0856	0857	...	0957	1057	1157	...	1257	1257	...	1257	1357	1457	1557	...	1657	1757	1857	1957	...
148	**Struer** ... a.	0606	0703	0729	0818	0822	0925	0922	...	1025**d**	1125	1225**d**	...	1325	1322	...	1322	1425	1525	1625**b**	...	1722	1822**b**	1922	2022**a**	...

	*IC*757			*IC*765				
				⑤⑦**q**		**z**		
København **700** ... d.	1600	...	...	1800	...	...	...	...
Århus 700 ... ⊗ d.	1927	...	2027	2127	...	2127	2227	2327
Langå **700** ... ⊗ a.	1958	...	2058	2158	...	2158	2258	2358
Langå ... ⊗ d.	2003	...	2103	2203	...	2203	2303	0003
Viborg ... ⊗ d.	2034	...	2134	2234	...	2234	2334	0033
Skive ... d.	2057	...	2155	2257	...	2257	2357	...
Struer ... a.	2122	...	...	2322	...	2322	0022	...

											*IC*728	*IC*1628	
	①–⑤	①–⑤	⑥	①–⑤	①–⑤	①–⑤	Ⓒ	①–⑤	Ⓒ	①–⑤	①–⑤	⑥⑦	①–⑤
Struer ... d.	0440	0513	0539	0540	0610	0637	0637	0703	0737	0750	0837	0837	0859
Skive ... d.	0506	0539	0608	0607	0636	0703	0708	0729	0808	0828	0908	0908	0928
Viborg ... ⊗ d.	0532	0603	0633	0632	0702	0729	0733	0754	0833	0855	0933	0933	0955
Langå ... ⊗ a.	0605	0635	0703	0705	0735	0802	0803	0827	0903	0928	1002	1003	1028
Langå **700** ... ⊗ d.	0610	0640	0708	0710	0740	0806	0808	0832	0908	0932	1008	1008	1032
Århus 700 ... ⊗ a.	0642	0712	0740	0742	0812	0838	0840	0904	0940	1004	1040	1040	1104
København **700** ... a.	...	...	...	...	...	...	...	...	...	...	1419	1419	...

												*IC*752	*IC*1652							*IC*768					
	Ⓒ	①–⑤	Ⓒ	①–⑤	Ⓒ	①–⑤	Ⓒ	①–⑤	Ⓒ	①–⑤	⑥	⑦**q**	⑤**r**	①–⑤	Ⓒ	①–⑤	Ⓒ	①–⑤		⑧**q**	**y**				
Struer ... d.	0937**g**	0959	1037	1059	1137**g**	1159	1237	1259	1337	1359	1437	1437	1437	1459	1537**e**	1559	1637	1639	1737**b**	1837	1837	1937**a**	2037	...	2237
Skive ... d.	1008	1028	1108	1128	1208	1228	1308	1328	1408	1428	1508	1508	1508	1528	1608	1628	1708	1708	1808	1908	1908	2008	2108	2208	2308
Viborg ... ⊗ d.	1033	1055	1133	1155	1233	1255	1333	1355	1433	1455	1533	1533	1533	1555	1633	1655	1733	1733	1833	1933	1933	2033	2133	2233	2333
Langå ... ⊗ a.	1103	1128	1203	1228	1303	1328	1403	1428	1503	1528	1603	1603	1603	1628	1703	1728	1803	1803	1903	2003	2003	2103	2203	2303	0003
Langå **700** ... ⊗ d.	1108	1132	1208	1232	1308	1332	1408	1432	1508	1532	1608	1608	1608	1632	1708	1732	1808	1808	1908	2008	2008	2108	2208	2308	0008
Århus 700 ... ⊗ a.	1140	1204	1240	1304	1340	1404	1440	1504	1540	1604	1640	1640	1640	1704	1740	1804	1840	1840	1940	2040	2040	2140	2240	2340	0040
København **700** ... a.	...	...	...	...	...	...	...	...	...	...	...	2019	2019	...	...	...	...	...	...	0019	...	...	...	...	...

a – ①–⑤ only.
b – ⑧ only.
d – ①–⑥ only.
e – † only.
g – ⑥ only.
p – Also Apr. 5, 6, 8, May 4, 17, 27, Dec. 23 - 25, 30, 31.
q – Not Apr. 5, 6, 8, May 4, 17, 27, Dec. 23 - 25, 30, 31.
r – Also Apr. 4, May 3, 16.
y – Not when *IC*768 runs.
z – Not when *IC*765 runs.

⊗ – Additional services operate Århus - Viborg and v.v.

See **Table 715** below for direct services Struer - Herning - København and v.v.

713 ÅRHUS - HERNING - HOLSTEBRO - STRUER

2nd class only. Operator: *AT*

km																								
															⑥									
0	**Århus 700** ... ⊗ d.	①-⑤	0505	0617	0717	0842	0917	and at	1542	1617	1642	1842	2042	2142	2242	Ⓒ	0542	0742	and	1742	1842	1942	2042	2142	2242
23	Skanderborg **700** . ⊗ d.		0525	0637	0740	0905	0940	the same	1605	1640	1705	1905	2105	2205	2305		0605	0805	every	1805	1905	2005	2105	2205	2305
53	Silkeborg ... ⊗ d.		0600	0705	0808	0931	1008	minutes	1631	1708	1731	1931	2131	2231	2331		0631	0831	two	1831	1931	2031	2131	2231	2331
94	**Herning** ... ⊗ a.		0643	0742	0845	1014	1045	past	1714	1745	1814	2014	2214	2314	0014		0714	0914	hours	1914	2014	2114	2214	2314	0018
94	**Herning 715** ... d.		0658	0748	0848	...	1048	each hour	...	1748	1815	2015	2239	...	...		0750	0950	until	1950	...	...	2239	...	...
136	**Skjern** ... a.		0736	0827	0925	...	1125	until	...	1825	1852	2052	2316	...	...		0826	1027		2027	...	...	2316	...	...

																⑥	⑥	⑥	†	⑥					
Skjern ... d.	①-⑤	0604	0651	0740	0836	0936	1136	...	and at	1736	...	1855	2055	...	Ⓒ	...	...	0626	0809	0844	1044	and	2044	2317	...
Herning 715 ... a.		0639	0726	0817	0915	1015	1215	...	the same	1815	...	1931	2131	...		...	...	0702	0845	0919	1119	every	2119	2352	...
Herning ... ⊗ d.		0648	0727	0818	0918	1018	1218	1249	minutes	1818	1849	1949	2149	2249		0549	0649	0749	0849	0949	1149	two	2149	2353	...
Silkeborg ... ⊗ d.		0731	0806	0856	0956	1056	1256	1331	past	1856	1931	2031	2231	2331		0631	0731	0831	0931	1031	1231	hours	2231	0031	...
Skanderborg **700** .. ⊗ a.		0803	0840	0928	1028	1128	1328	1403	each hour	1928	2003	2103	2303	0003		0703	0800	0900	1000	1100	1300	until	2300	0100	...
Århus 700 ... ⊗ a.		0822	0859	0947	1047	1147	1347	1422	until	1947	2022	2122	2322	0022		0722	0822	0922	1022	1122	1322		2322	0123	...

⊗ – Additional services operate Århus - Herning and v.v.

715 FREDERICIA - STRUER - THISTED

2nd class only (**IC** & **Lyn** 1st & 2nd class)

km		*IC* **791**											*IC* **721**			*IC* **729**			*IC* **1637**	*IC* **737**				*IC* **745**	
			①–⑤	①–⑥	①–⑤		①–⑤	①–⑤		①–⑥	⑦	...							⑥⑦	①–⑤			①–④		①–⑤
	København **700** ... d.	0030	...	...	...	...	...	...	...	...	...	...	0700	...	...	0900	...	...	1100	1100	...	...	...	1300	...
	Odense **700** ... d.	0220	...	...	...	...	...	...	...	...	...	...	0831	...	...	1031	...	...	1231	1231	...	...	...	1431	...
0	**Fredericia 700** ... d.	0257	...	0508	...	...	0604	...	0704	0804	0804	...	0912	1004	...	1112	1204	...	1312	1312	...	1404	...	1512	...
26	Vejle **700** ... d.	0317	...	0528	...	...	0623	...	0734	0834	0834	...	0934	1034	...	1134	1233	...	1334	1334	...	1434	...	1534	...
99	Herning ... a.	0411	...	0632	...	...	0733	...	0834	0934	0934	...	1034	1134	...	1235	1335	...	1434	1434	...	1534	...	1634	...
99	Herning **713** ... d.	0412	0550	0643	0656	...	...	0754	0835	0935	...	...	1035	1135	...	1235	1335	...	1435	1435	...	1535	1609	1635	1709
140	Holstebro **708** ... d.	0447	0625	0718	0738	...	...	0834	0906	1006	...	...	1106	1206	...	1306	1406	...	1506	1506	...	1606	1649	1706	1749
155	**Struer 708** ... a.	0459	0638	0735	0756	...	...	0847	0919	1019	...	...	1119	1219	...	1319	1419	...	1519	1519	...	1619	1706	1719	1806
229	*Thisted* **716** ... a.	...	...	...	...	...	...	...	...	...	...	...	...	...	...	...	...	...	1640	1645	...	...	...	...	...

		IC **753**			*IC* **761**		*IC* **769**		*IC* **777**	
						⑧		⑧		
København **700** ... d.	...	1500	...	...	1700	...	1900	...	2100	...
Odense **700** ... d.	...	1631	...	...	1831	...	2031	...	2231	...
Fredericia 700 ... d.	1604	1712	1804	...	1912	2004	2112	2204	2312	...
Vejle **700** ... d.	1634	1734	1834	...	1934	2033	2134	2234	2334	...
Herning ... a.	1734	1834	1934	...	2034	2134	2234	2334	0034	...
Herning **713** ... d.	1735	1835	1935	...	2035	2135	2235	2335	0035	...
Holstebro **708** ... d.	1806	1906	2006	...	2106	2206	2306	0006	0106	...
Struer 708 ... a.	1819	1919	2019	...	2119	2219	2319	0019	0120	...
Thisted **716** ... a.	...	...	...	...	2240	...	...	...	...	...

	IC **708**			*Lyn* **710**					*IC* **716**	
	①–⑤		①–⑤	①–⑤	①–⑤	⑥	①–⑤	①–⑤		①–⑤
Thisted **716** ... d.	...	...	...	...	...	...	...	...	...	...
Struer 708 ... d.	0435	...	0514	0534	...	0545	0550	0610	0642	0704
Holstebro **708** ... d.	0451	...	0529	0547	...	0559	0606	0631	0702	0718
Herning **713** ... a.	0521	...	0605	0616	←	0630	0643	0710	0733	0746
Herning ... d.	0522	...	→	0617	0632	0632	0656	...	0738	...
Vejle **700** ... d.	0625	...	...	0708	0732	0731	0803	...	0834	...
Fredericia 700 ... a.	0642	...	...	0725	0752	0751	0823	...	0852	...
Odense **700** ... a.	0743	...	...	0807	...	...	...	...	0942	...
København **700** ... a.	0919	...	...	0929	...	...	...	...	1119	...

					IC **1624**	*IC* **724**			*IC* **732**		*IC* **740**			*IC* **748**				*IC* **756**		*IC* **764**				*IC* **776**	*IC* **176**
	①–⑤	①–⑤	⑥		⑥⑦	①–⑤									①–④							⑧			
Thisted **716** ... d.	...	...	...	...	0727	0728	...	...	...	...	...	...	...	...	...	...	...	...	...	1727	...	...	...	...	...
Struer 708 ... d.	0719	0741	0751	...	0851	0851	...	0951	1051	1151	1251	...	1351	1451	1502	1551	...	1651	1751	1851	...	1951	2051	2151	...
Holstebro **708** ... d.	0740	0800	0805	...	0905	0905	...	1005	1105	1205	1305	...	1405	1505	1522	1605	...	1705	1805	1905	...	2005	2105	2205	...
Herning **713** ... a.	0811	0835	0835	...	0935	0935	...	1035	1135	1235	1335	...	1435	1535	1558	1635	...	1735	1835	1935	...	2035	2135	2235	...
Herning ... d.	...	0836	0836	...	0936	0936	...	1036	1136	1236	1336	...	1436	1536	...	1636	...	1736	1836	1936	...	2036	2136	2236	...
Vejle **700** ... d.	...	0934	0934	...	1034	1034	...	1134	1234	1334	1434	...	1534	1634	...	1734	...	1834	1934	2034	...	2134	2234	2334	2342
Fredericia 700 ... a.	...	0952	0952	...	1052	1052	...	1152	1252	1352	1452	...	1552	1652	...	1752	...	1852	1952	2052	...	2152	2252	2352	0001
Odense **700** ... a.	...	...	...	...	1143	1143	...	...	1343	...	1543	...	...	1743	...	...	...	1943	...	2143	...	...	...	...	0043
København **700** ... a.	...	...	...	...	1319	1319	...	...	1519	...	1719	...	...	1919	...	...	...	2119	...	2319	...	...	...	...	0219

716 STRUER - THISTED

2nd class only (**IC** 1st & 2nd class). Operator: *AT* (**IC** trains: *DSB*)

km															*IC*1637		*IC*737						*IC*761		
		①–⑤	⑥	①–⑤	Ⓒ	①–⑤	Ⓒ	①–⑤	Ⓒ	①–⑤	Ⓒ	①–⑤	①–⑤		**Z**		**Y**		①–⑤	Ⓒ			**K**		
0	Struer ... d.	0449	0549	0549	0724	0802	0924	1024	1124	1228	1324	1331	1428	...	1524	...	1528	...	1650	1724	1924	...	2124	...	2328
74	Thisted ... a.	0609	0707	0726	0840	0918	1040	1140	1240	1345	1440	1450	1549	...	1640	...	1645	...	1820	1840	2040	...	2240	...	0043

					*IC*1624		*IC*724													*IC*764				
	①–⑤	⑥	①–⑤		**Z**		**Y**		①–⑤	Ⓒ	①–⑤	Ⓒ	①–⑤	Ⓒ	①–⑤	①–⑤	Ⓒ	①–⑤		**K**				
Thisted ... d.	0514	0520	0614	...	0727	...	0728	...	0822	0927	1027	1127	1155	1327	1354	1456	1527	1614	...	1727	...	1927	...	2209
Struer ... a.	0634	0636	0734	...	0846	...	0847	...	0943	1046	1146	1246	1314	1446	1514	1614	1646	1735	...	1846	...	2046	...	2326

K – From / to København (Table **715**).
Y – ①–⑤ only. From / to København (Table **715**).
Z – ⑥⑦ only. From / to København (Table **715**).

KØBENHAVN - RØDBY - PUTTGARDEN (- HAMBURG) 720

***EC* and *ICE* services only; all trains Ⓡ. For local trains see Table 721**

km		*ICE* 38 BY	*EC* 38 BX	*EC* 36 X	*EC* 36 Y	*EC* 34 R	*ICE* 32 Y	*EC* 32 X	*EC* 30 E	*EC* 30 D
0	**København H** d.	0745	0754	1138	1145	1345	1538	1538	1738	1738
20	Høje Taastrup ● d.	0757	0806	1152	1157	1357	1552	1551	1752	1751
64	Ringsted ● d.	0818	0829	1216	1218	1418	|	1618	1813	1818
91	Næstved ● d.	0832	0845	1234	1232	1432	1626	1636	1827	1834
147	Nykøbing (Falster) ● d.	0912	0916	1313	1312	1512	1712	1715	1913	1915
183	Rødby ▲ a.	0934	0937	1335	1335	1534	1734	1735	1935	1935
202	**Puttgarden** ▲ a.	1035	1035	1435	1435	1635	1835	1835	2035	2035
291	*Lübeck* **825** a.	1136	1136	1536	1536	1736	1936	1936	2136	2136
353	*Hamburg Hbf* **825** a.	1216	1216	1616	1616	1816	2016	2016	2216	2216

	EC 31 G	*EC* 31 F	*EC* 33 X	*ICE* 33 Y	*EC* 35 X	*EC* 35 Y	*ICE* 37 BX	*ICE* 37 BY	*EC* 39 R
Hamburg Hbf **825** d.	0725	0725	0928	0928	1328	1328	1728	1728	1928
Lübeck **825** d.	0807	0807	1007	1007	1407	1407	1807	1807	2007
Puttgarden ▲ d.	0910	0910	1110	1110	1510	1510	1910	1910	2110
Rødby ▲ d.	1007	1012	1207	1210	1607	1610	2007	2007	2213
Nykøbing (Falster) ● a.	1029	1034	1229	1230	1629	1632	2029	2029	2234
Næstved ● a.	1109	1118	1309	1318	1709	1718	2111	2118	2318
Ringsted ● a.	1126	1133	1326	1331	1726	|	2128	2133	2333
Høje Taastrup ● a.	1151	1155	1351	1355	1752	1755	2150	2155	2355
København H a.	1205	1209	1405	1409	1806	1809	2204	2209	0009

B – (12) and 🍷 København - Berlin Ost and v.v.
D – Dec. 9 - Jan. 5 (not Dec. 24, 31).
E – Mar. 14 - Oct. 26.
F – Mar. 15 - Oct. 27.
G – Dec. 9 - Jan. 5 (not Dec. 25, Jan. 1).

R – June 20 - Aug. 24.
X – Dec. 9 - Jan. 5.
Y – Jan. 6 - Dec. 13.

▲ – Through trains are conveyed by ⛴ Rødby - Puttgarden and v.v. ✕ on board ship. Passengers to/from Rødby or Puttgarden should leave or join the train on board the train-ferry. See **Table 2375** for other available sailings.
● – From København stops to pick up only; to København stops to set down only.

KØBENHAVN - NYKØBING - RØDBY and NAKSKOV 721

km		4207 ①–⑤	4213 ①–⑤	①–⑤	⑥⑦	①–⑤		①–⑤	⑦	①–⑥	1229 G			①–⑥		①–⑥		①–⑥			①–⑥	2245	1249 ①–⑥		①–⑤
0	**København H 700** § d.	...	...	0534	0534	0634	0704	0738	0804	0804	0842	...	0904	0942	1004	1042	1104	1142	...	1204	1242	1304	1342	1404	1420
20	Høje Taastrup **700** § d.	...	...	0548	0547	0647	0718	0752	0818	0818	0855	...	0918	0955	1018	1055	1118	1155	...	1218	1255	1318	1355	1418	|
31	Roskilde **700** § d.	...	...	0557	0557	0655	0727	0800	0827	0827	0904	...	0927	1004	1027	1104	1127	1204	...	1227	1304	1327	1404	1427	1444
64	Ringsted **700** § d.	...	...	0623	0623	0714	0751	|	0851	0851	0923	...	0951	1023	1051	1123	1151	1223	...	1251	1323	1351	1423	1451	1503
91	Næstved § d.	...	0558	0643	0700	0733	0810	0832	0910	0909	0939	...	1010	1039	1110	1139	1210	1239	...	1310	1339	1410	1439	1510	1523
118	Vordingborg d.	...	0618	0701	0718	0751	0828	0850	0928	...	0957	...	1028e	1057	1128e	1157	1228e	1257	...	1328e	1357	1428e	1457	1528e	1544
147	Nykøbing (Falster) ⊙ ⊡ d.	0503	0649	...	0742	0814	0854	0911	0951	...	1020	...	1053e	1120	1151e	1220	1253e	1320	...	1351e	1420	1453e	1521	1551e	1609
183	Rødby a.	0530	0713	...	...	...	...	...	...	...	...	...	...	...	...	...	...	...	...	...	...	1517e	1544	...	...

	①–⑤	⑥	⑥⑦	①–⑤	①–⑤	⑦	⑥⑦	4259 ①–⑤	①–⑤	⑦		⑥⑦	①–⑤	①–⑤	4287 F	1265 ⑦		⑥⑦	①–⑤	①–⑤	⑦		⑦	2273	
København H § **700** § d.	1442	1442	1504	1519	1534	1542	1604	1620	1638	1642	...	1704	1720	1734	1738	1742	...	1804	1819	1838	1842	1904	1942	2004	...
Høje Taastrup § **700** § d.	1455	1455	1518	1535	1548	1555	1618	1636	1654	1655	...	1718	1736	1748	1751	1755	...	1818	1835	1853	1855	1918	1955	2018	...
Roskilde § **700** § d.	1504	1504	1527	|	1600	1604	1627	|	1703	1704	...	1727	1745	1800	|	1804	...	1827	1844	1901	1904	1927	2004	2027	...
Ringsted § **700** § d.	1523	1523	1551	|	1624	1623	1651	|	1722	1723	...	1751	1805	1824	1818	1823	...	1851	1904	1924	1923	1951	2023	2051	...
Næstved § § d.	1539	1539	1610	1615	1643	1639	1710	1716	1741	1739	...	1810	1822	1843	1834	1839	...	1910	1923	1942	1939	2010	2039	2110	...
Vordingborg d.	1555	1557	1628	1633	1701	1657	1728g	1734	1759	1757	...	1828g	1841	1901	1853	1857	...	1928g	1942	...	1957	2028d	2057	2128d	...
Nykøbing (Falster) ⊙ ⊡ d.	1619	1619	1656	1658	1720	1720	1751g	1800	1828	1820	...	1851g	1903	1928	1914	1922	...	1951g	2007	...	2020	2051d	2120	2153d	...
Rødby a.	...	...	...	...	...	...	...	1830	...	...	...	...	...	...	1935	1945j	...	...	...	...	...	...	...	2222d	...

	1277 ⑦		⑦		⑦	⑦	①–⑥	⑦		
København H 700 § d.	2042	2104	2142	2204	2242	2304	2304	2342	...	0004
Høje Taastrup **700** § d.	2055	2118	2155	2218	2255	2318	2318	2355	...	0018
Roskilde **700** § d.	2104	2127	2204	2227	2304	2327	2327	0004	...	0027
Ringsted **700** § d.	2123	2151	2223	2251	2323	2351	0011r	0023	...	0051
Næstved § d.	2139	2210	2239	2310	2339	0009	0030	0039	...	0110
Vordingborg d.	2157	2228d	2257	2328d	2357	...	0047	0057	...	0128
Nykøbing (Falster) ⊙ ⊡ d.	2228	2251d	2320	2351d	0020	...	0109	0120	...	0151
Rødby a.	2249	...	...	...	...	...	...	...	...	...

	4204 ①–⑥	⑥⑦	①–⑤	①–⑤	①–⑤	⑥	4214 ①–⑤	①–⑤	①–⑤	⑥⑦
Rødby d.	0434a	...	...	...	...	...	0608	...	...	...
Nykøbing (Falster) ⊙ ⊡ d.	0457	0519	0524	0554	0614	0625	0633	0648	...	0716
Vordingborg d.	0520	0543	0545	0616	0635	0649	0657	0708	0720	0740
Næstved § d.	0538	0601	0604	0634	0652	0707	0714	0724	0739	0758
Ringsted **700** § d.	0556	0620	0624	0651	0712	0726	0733	|	0758	0817
Roskilde **700** § a.	0611	0643	0643	|	0731	0749	0749	0802	0821	0838
Høje Taastrup **700** § a.	0619	0656	0654	0714	0740	0757	0757	0811	0837	0848
København H 700 § a.	0634	0712	0711	0730	0757	0814	0814	0827	0853	0905

	①–⑤	4230 ①–⑤	⑥⑦	①–⑥		①–⑥			1216 ①–⑥	2242 ⑦	①–⑥	1220 H			①–⑥		①–⑥		①–⑥	⑦		①–⑤	⑥	①–⑤	⑦
Rødby d.	...	0724	...	...	...	...	...	...	0955p	1029q	...	...	...	...	...	...	...	...	...	...	...	...	...	...	...
Nykøbing (Falster) ⊙ ⊡ d.	0717	0748	0759e	0817	0854e	0920	0959e	...	1020	1056	...	1120	1159e	...	1220	1256e	1320	1359e	1420	1459	...	1520	1520	1557	1559
Vordingborg d.	0741	0814	0823e	0845	0923e	0943	1023e	...	1043	1123	...	1143	1223e	...	1243	1323e	1343	1423e	1443	1523	...	1543	1543	1624	1623
Næstved § d.	0800	0837	0842	0905	0942	1001	1042	...	1101	1142	1142	1201	1242	...	1301	1342	1401	1442	1501	1542	...	1601	1601	1642	1642
Ringsted **700** § d.	0819	0856	0901	0923	1001	1019	1101	...	1119	1201	1201	1219	1301	...	1319	1401	1419	1501	1519	1601	...	1619	1621	1701	1701
Roskilde **700** § a.	0838	0914	0923	0941	1023	1037	1123	...	1137	1223	1223	1237	1323	...	1337	1423	1437	1523	1537	1623	...	1637	1643	1723	1723
Høje Taastrup **700** § a.	0848	0925	0932	0950	1032	1046	1132	...	1146	1232	1232	1246	1332	...	1346	1432	1446	1532	1546	1632	...	1646	1651	1732	1732
København H 700 § a.	0905	0941	0948	1004	1048	1100	1148	...	1200	1248	1248	1300	1348	...	1400	1448	1500	1548	1600	1648	...	1700	1705	1748	1748

	2260 ⑥	1238 ⑧	⑦	⑥	⑦	①–⑤	⑥⑦		①–⑤	⑦	⑥⑦	4256 ①–⑤	①–⑤	⑦	⑥⑦		①–⑤	⑦		⑦		⑦		1268 ⑦	
Rødby d.	1554	1554	...	...	...	...	...	...	...	...	...	1846	...	...	...	...	...	...	...	...	...	...	2232d	2257	...
Nykøbing (Falster) ⊙ ⊡ d.	1620	1620	...	1714	1720	1721	1759g	...	1816	1820	1856g	1909	1915	1920	1959g	...	2015	2020	2059d	2120	2159d	2220	2259d	2320	...
Vordingborg d.	1645	1647	...	1742	1743	1750	1823g	...	1841	1843	1923g	...	1942	1943	2023g	...	2042	2043	2123d	2143	2223d	2243	2323d	2343	...
Næstved § d.	1704	1705	1742	1801	1801	1808	1842	...	1900	1901	1942	...	2000	2001	2042	...	2100	2101	2142	2201	2242	2301	2342	0001	...
Ringsted **700** § d.	1729	1722	1801	1820	1819	1827	1901	...	1919	1919	2001	...	2019	2019	2101	...	2119	2119	2201	2219	2301	2319	0001	0019	...
Roskilde **700** § a.	1751	1740	1823	1842	1837	1849	1923	...	1941	1937	2023	...	2041	2037	2123	...	2141	2137	2223	2237	2323	2337	0023	0037	...
Høje Taastrup **700** § a.	1800	1749	1832	1851	1846	1858	1932	...	1950	1946	2032	...	2050	2046	2132	...	2153	2146	2232	2246	2332	2346	0032	0046	...
København H 700 § a.	1816	1802	1848	1907	1900	1914	1948	...	2006	2000	2048	...	2106	2100	2148	...	2210	2200	2248	2300	2348	2400	0048	0100	...

F – ①–⑤ Jan. 8 - Mar. 29, Oct. 22 - Dec. 7.
G – ①–⑥. To Gedser (arrive 1044).
H – ①–⑥. From Gedser (depart 1058).

a – ①–⑤ only.
d – ①–⑥ only.
e – ⑦ only.

g – ⑥ only.
j – Jan. 7 - Mar. 25, Oct. 28 - Dec. 2.
p – Jan. 8 - Mar. 30, Oct. 22 - Dec. 8.
q – Jan. 7 - Mar. 25, Oct. 28 - Dec. 9.
r – Arrive 2350.

§ – Additional local services run between København - Næstved and v.v.
⊙ – Trains run approximately hourly (more frequent on ①–⑤) Nykøbing (Falster) - Nakskov and v.v., journey 45 minutes (A/S Lollandbanen).
⊡ – 🚌 connection Nykøbing (Falster) Railway Station - Gedser Market Place and v.v. *25 km*, journey 35 minutes.

Valid October 2, 2007 - January 5, 2008 KØBENHAVN - YSTAD - RØNNE 727

km				D	⑤⑦		E				🚌	🚌				X	F	G	Y	H			
0	**København H** d.	Oct. 2	0639	1007	1339	1707	2039	...	...	Nov. 5	0800	1745	...	...	Nov. 17	0639	1007	1339	1707	2039	...	...	...
11	Kastrup ✈ d.	to	0652	1020	1352	1720	2052	...	...	to	0820	1805	...	...	to	0652	1020	1352	1720	2052	...	...	...
76	**Ystad** a.	Nov. 4	0755	1132	1451	1825	2150	...	...	Nov. 16	0930	1915	...	...	Jan. 5	0755	1132	1451	1825	2150	...	...	...
	Ystad ⛴ d.	▶▶▶▶	*0830*	*1200*	*1530*	*1900*	*2230*	...	...	▶▶▶▶	*1000*	*1945*	...	...	▶▶▶▶	*0830*	*1200*	*1530*	*1900*	*2230*	...	...	...
	Rønne ⛴ a.		*0945*	*1315*	*1645*	*2015*	*2345*	...	...		*1230*	*2215*	...	...		*0945*	*1315*	*1645*	*2015*	*2345*	...	...	...

			D	⑤⑦		E				🚌	🚌				X	F	G	Y	H			
Rønne ⛴ d.	Oct. 2	*0645*	*1015*	*1345*	*1715*	*2045*	...	...	Nov. 5	*0645*	*1630*	...	...	Nov. 17	*0645*	*1015*	*1345*	*1715*	*2045*	...	...	...
Ystad ⛴ a.	to	*0800*	*1130*	*1500*	*1830*	*2200*	...	...	to	*0915*	*1900*	...	...	to	*0800*	*1130*	*1500*	*1830*	*2200*	...	...	...
Ystad d.	Nov. 4	0814	1144	1517	1845	2218	...	...	Nov. 16	0935	1920	...	...	Jan. 5	0814	1144	1517	1845	2218	...	...	...
Kastrup ✈ a.	▶▶▶▶	0919	1248	1619	1947	2319	...	...	▶▶▶▶	1040	2025	...	...	▶▶▶▶	0919	1248	1619	1947	2319	...	...	...
København H a.		0933	1302	1633	2001	2333	...	...		1100	2040	...	...		0933	1302	1633	2001	2333	...	...	...

D – Oct. 12, 13, 19 - 21 only.
E – ⑦ (not Nov. 4).
F – Dec. 22 - 31.
G – ⑤⑦ (also Dec. 26, Jan. 1; not Dec. 23, 28, 30, Jan. 4).

H – Dec. 21, 26, 28 only.
X – Not Dec. 31, Jan. 1.
Y – Not Dec. 24, 31.

728 BRANCH LINES in Denmark

2nd class only

ÅRHUS - GRENAA *69 km*

	①-⑥	①-⑥			and						
Århus.......d.	0514	0614	...	0714	hourly	2314	...	...	...	...	...
Grenaa.......a.	0626	0726	...	0828	until	0028	...	...	...	...	...

	①-⑤	①-⑤	①-⑥	①-⑥		and			and	
Grenaa.......d.	0502	0532	0632	0732	0832	hourly	1832	1933	hourly	2333
Århus.......a.	0614	0644	0744	0844	0945	until	1945	2045	until	0045

ODENSE - SVENDBORG *48 km*

Services are currently affected by engineering work

	①-⑥			①-⑤		①-⑥	and		①-⑥		and	
Odense.......d.	0535	0635	0735	0805	0835	0905	hourly	1535	1605	1635	hourly	2335
Svendborg....a.	0617	0717	0817	0846	0917	0946	until	1617	1646	1717	until	0017

	①-⑤	①-⑥			①-⑥	and		①-⑥		and		
Svendborg...d.	0523	0623	0723	0823	0853	hourly	1723	1753	1823	hourly	0023	...
Odense.......a.	0605	0705	0805	0905	0934	until	1805	1834	1905	until	0105	...

HJØRRING - HIRTSHALS

Nordjyske Jernbaner A/S 18 km Journey 22 minutes

From **Hjørring**:

①-⑤: 0456, 0552, 0616, 0646, 0714, 0746, 0816, 0912, 1012, and hourly until 1612, then 1642, 1712 **x**, 1742, 1812, 1912 **x**, 2112 **x**, 2312 **x**.

⑥: 0712, and hourly until 1412, then 1612, 1712, 1912, 2012, 2112, 2312.

⑦: 0812, 0912, 1112, 1212, 1312, 1412, 1612, 1712, 1812, 1912, 2012, 2112, 2312.

All services stop at Color Line station (19 minutes from Hjørring, 1 minute from Hirtshals) for Color Line sailings.

From **Hirtshals**:

①-⑤: 0523, 0618, 0648, 0713, 0748, 0818, 0844, and hourly until 1644, then 1714, 1744 **x**, 1814, 1844, 1944 **x**, 2144 **x**, 2338 **x**.

⑥: 0744, and hourly until 1444, then 1644, 1744, 1944, 2044, 2144, 2338.

⑦: 0844, 0944, 1144, 1244, 1344, 1444, 1644, 1744, 1844, 1944, 2044, 2144, 2338.

x – Not Dec. 24, 31.

Subject to alteration on and around holidays.

ICELAND

There are no railways in Iceland but bus services serve all major settlements (some are only served in summer, particularly in the eastern part of the country). Principal bus services enabling a circuit around the country are shown below - see the right hand column for operating dates of each journey. See www.bsi.is and www.austurleid.is for further information.

729 PRINCIPAL BUS SERVICES

Service to Aug. 31, 2008

Clockwise direction	*depart / arrive*	*Anti-clockwise direction*	*depart / arrive*	*Days of operation (applies to both directions)*
Reykjavík - Akureyri:	d. 0830 a. 1430 *	Akureyri - Reykjavík:	d. 0830 a. 1430 *	Daily May 1 - Sept. 30; ①-⑥ Oct. 1 - Apr. 30. * 1415 June 1 - Aug. 31.
	d. 1500 a. 2100		d. 1500 a. 2100	⑦ Oct. 1 - Apr. 30.
	d. 1700 a. 2300		d. 1700 a. 2300	⑤ Oct. 1 - Apr. 30, ⑤⑦ May 1 - June 14; daily June 15 - Aug. 31; ⑤⑦ Sept. 1 - 30.
Akureyri - Egilsstadir:	d. 0800 a. 1155	Egilsstadir - Akureyri:	d. 1300 a. 1645	Daily June 1 - Aug. 31. Limited winter service (4 per week ⊖).
Egilsstadir - Hofn:	d. 1330 a. 1700	Hofn - Egilsstadir:	d. 0830 a. 1210	Daily June 1 - Aug. 31. No winter service.
Hofn - Reykjavík:	d. 0830 a. 1655	Reykjavík - Hofn:	d. 0830 a. 1630	Daily June 1 - Sept. 15.
	d. 1200 a. 1905		d. 1230 a. 1930	②⑤⑦ Sept. 16 - May 31.

Blue Lagoon: departures several times per day from Reykjavík, also infrequent departures from Kevlavík Airport to Blue Lagoon.

Egilsstadir - Seydisfjördur (for Smyril ferry, Table **2295**) June 1 - Aug. 31: depart Egilsstadir 0915 Ⓐ, 1300 ③④, 1300 **b**, 1700 Ⓐ; depart Seydisfjördur 0820 Ⓐ, 0850 ③, 1220 ③④, 1220 **b**, 1620 Ⓐ. Winter service Sept. 1 2007 - May 31 2008: depart Egilsstadir 0920 Ⓐ, 1030 ⑥, 1125 ②, 1700 Ⓐ; depart Seydisfjördur 0820 Ⓐ, 0940 ⑥, 1030 ②, 1610 Ⓐ.

Reykjavík - Geysir: depart Reykjavík 0830 and 1230 June 1 - Aug. 31, arriving back at 1655 or 1855 (allows time for sightseeing at Gullfoss and Geysir en route). Also limited winter service.

b – ⑥⑦ July 1 - Aug. 6.   ⊖ – From Akureyri 0845 ②③, 1200 ⑦, 1300 ⑤, from Egilsstadir 1400 ②③, 1615 ⑦, 1715 ⑤.

SWEDEN

SEE MAP PAGE 339

Operators: Most services are operated by **Statens Järnvägar** - Swedish State Railways (*SJ*). There is, however, a number of other operators which run services shown within the European Timetable; these are indicated by their initials in the relevant table heading, or at the top of each train column where more than one operator runs services on the same route.
AEX – Arlanda Express (A-Train AB). *MER* – MerResor. *ST* – Svenska Tågkompaniet AB. *VEO* – Veolia Transport.
The Regional Public Transport Authority is responsible for many local services, known collectively as Länstrafik (*LT*). Those shown within these pages are abbreviated as follows: *Skåne* – Skånetrafiken. *V* – Västtrafik. *VTAB* – Värmlandstrafik.

Services: Trains convey first and second classes of accommodation, unless otherwise shown. The fastest trains are classified *X2000* (high-speed trains). Sleeping cars (🛏) are of two basic types with a range of supplements: older cars (those without showers) have one berth in first class, two or three berths in second class. Newer cars either have compartments with shower and WC (one or two berth, first class only) or have shower and WC available in the car (one or two berths in first class, two berths in second class). Couchette cars (▬) have six berths and are second class only. Refreshment services (✕, 🍸, Bistro or Shop) may be available for part of the journey only.

Timings: Valid **December 9, 2007 - June 14, 2008** except where indicated otherwise. Alterations may be made on and around the dates of public holidays.

Tickets: Through journeys between Länstrafik and Statens Järnvägar, Veolia Transport or Svenska Tågkompaniet are possible with a combined ticket known as 'Tågplus'. Similarly, Arlanda Express may be combined with Statens Järnvägar journeys. However, Veolia Transport and Svenska Tågkompaniet have their own fare structures and tickets cannot be combined with those of Statens Järnvägar.

Reservations: Seat reservation is compulsory on all *X2000* and night trains, and for through journeys to København (excluding local and *Skåne* services). Reserved seats are not labelled and, if occupied, must be claimed by presenting the seat ticket on the train.

Supplements: Special supplements are payable for travel on *X2000* high-speed trains.

730 STOCKHOLM - MALMÖ - KØBENHAVN

km				*X2000*	*X2000*		*X2000*				*X2000*				*X2000*	*X2000*		*X2000*	*X2000*			*X2000*	*X2000*	*X2000*
		67		**519**	**521**	**221**	**523**	**221**	**223**	**10223**	**525**	**223**	**10223**	**225**	**527**	**529**	**229**	**531**	**533**	**233**		**535**	**537**	**537**
		Ⓡ		Ⓡ✕	Ⓡ✕		Ⓡ✕				Ⓡ✕				Ⓡ✕	Ⓡ✕		Ⓡ✕	Ⓡ✕			Ⓡ✕	Ⓡ✕	Ⓡ✕
		♦		Ⓐz	⚒	Ⓐ	Ⓐz	Ⓐ	⑥x	⑥w		⑥x	⑥w	Ⓐ	⑤			Ⓑ				⑤†z	Ⓑ	⑥
0	**Stockholm** Central ‡ d.	...	...	0520	0620	0705	0720	...	0800	0800	0820	...	...	0815	0925	1020	1040	1120	1220	1240	...	1320	1420	1420
15	Flemingsberg ‡ d.	...	...	|	|	0716	0731	...	0811	0811	|	...	...	0826	|	1031	1051	|	|	1251	...	1331	1431	1431
36	Södertälje Syd ‡ d.	...	...	0538	0638	0727	|	...	0822	0822	0838	...	...	0843	|	|	1102	1138	1238	1302	...	|	|	|
	Katrineholm **740 754** d.	...	...	|	|	|	0815	←	|	|	|	←	←	|	|	|	|	|	|	|	...	|	|	|
103	Nyköping d.	...	...	|	|	0808	|	0810	0902	0902	|	0904	0911	0925	|	|	1142	|	|	1342	...	|	|	|
162	**Norrköping 754** a.	0528s	...	0633	0733	→	0836	0848	→	→	0933	0942	0953	1004	1035	1133	1225	1233	1333	1425	...	1433	1533	1533
162	**Norrköping** d.	|	...	0635	0735	...	0838	0850	...	...	0935	0944	0955	1007	1037	1135	1227	1235	1335	1427	...	1435	1535	1535
209	Linköping d.	0558s	...	0700	0800	...	0903	0916	...	...	1000	1010	1021	1033	1102	1200	1253	1300	1400	1453	...	1500	1600	1600
241	**Mjölby 755** d.	|	...	|	0815	...	|	...	...	...	1015	...	...	...	|	1215	...	|	1415	...	...	|	1615	1615
277	Tranås d.	|	...	0730	|	...	|	...	...	...	|	...	...	...	|	|	...	|	|	...	...	|	|	|
329	**Nässjö** d.	0659s	...	0753	0853	...	0953	...	...	...	1053	...	...	...	1153	1253	...	1353	1453	...	...	1553	1653	1653
416	Alvesta d.	0746s	...	0827	0927	...	1027	...	...	...	1127	...	...	...	1229	1327	...	1427	1527	...	...	1627	1727	1727
514	Hässleholm **745/6** a.	0841s	...	0902	1002	...	1102	...	...	...	1202	...	...	...	1304	1402	...	1502	1602	...	...	1702	1802	1802
581	Lund **745/6** § a.	0920s	...	0931	1031	...	1131	...	...	...	1231	...	...	...	1333	1431	...	1531	1631	...	...	1731	1831	1831
597	**Malmö 745/6** a.	0957	...	0946	1046s	...	1146	...	...	...	1246	...	...	...	1349	1446	...	1546	1646	...	...	1746	1846	1846s
597	**Malmö 703** d.	*1022*	...	...	|	...	...	...	...	...	...	...	...	...	...	...	...	...	...	...	...	...	...	|
633	København (Kastrup) ✈ **703** a.	*1043*	...	...	1119s	...	...	...	...	...	...	...	...	...	...	...	...	...	...	...	...	...	...	1919s
644	**København H 703** a.	*1057*	...	...	1133	...	...	...	...	...	...	...	...	...	...	...	...	...	...	...	...	...	...	1933

♦ – **NOTES** (LISTED BY TRAIN NUMBER)

67 – ⑤† Dec. 9 - 16; ①④⑤⑥† Dec. 17 - Jan. 5; ④⑤⑥† Jan. 6 - Feb. 3; ①④⑤⑥† Feb. 4 - Mar. 30; ④⑤⑥† Mar. 31 - Apr. 27; ⑤† Apr. 28 - June 14 (from Storlien): 🛏 1, 2 cl., ▬ 2 cl. and (2) Storlien - Malmö; ✕ Norrköping - Malmö. Runs as train **69** on some dates.

s – Stops to set down only.
w – Dec. 9 - Jan. 5.
x – Jan. 6 - June 14.
z – Not Dec. 24 - Jan. 5.

‡ – Most trains on this table do not convey passengers for local journeys between Stockholm and Södertälje Syd and v.v. Local trains run every 30 minutes Stockholm Central - Södertälje Hamn - Södertälje Centrum and v.v. (journey 42 mins). 🚌 Södertälje Syd - Södertälje Centrum runs every 30 minutes.

§ – From Malmö stops to pick up only, to Malmö stops to set down only. Frequent local trains run between Lund and Malmö.

STOCKHOLM - MALMÖ - KØBENHAVN — 730

	237 Ⓑ	235 ⑥	X2000 539 R ✕ Ⓑ	203 Q	X2000 541 R ✕	203 Q	241 Ⓑ	X2000 513 R ✕ ♦	241 Ⓑ	X2000 543 R ✕ Ⓑy		X2000 505 R ✕ Ⓑz	243 ⑥	263 Ⓐ	X2000 545 R ✕ ⚒	263 Ⓐ	X2000 555 R ✕ †	245 Ⓑ	X2000 547 R ✕ H	249 G	247 †z	251	1 R ♦	
Stockholm Central ‡ d.	1440	1440	1520	1545	1620	...	1640	1655	...	1720	...	1740	1740	1745	1820	...	1825	1840	1955	2040	2040	2145	2305	...
Flemingsberg ‡ d.	1451	1451	1531	|	|	...	1651	1706	...	1731	...	|	1751	1756	|	...	|	1851	|	2051	2051	2156	|	...
Södertälje Syd ‡ d.	1502	1502	|	1605	1638	...	1702	|	...	|	...	|	1803	1808	1838	...	|	1902	2013	2102	2103	2208	2330u	...
Katrineholm **740 754** d.	|	|	1615	|	|	...	|	|	←	|	...	|	|	|	|	←	|	|	|	|	|	|	|	...
Nyköping d.	1542	1547	|	|	|	...	1740	|	1742	|	...	|	1844	1847	|	1850	|	1942	|	2142	2143	2248	|	...
Norrköping 754 a.	1625	1627	1636	1710	1733	...	→	1808	1827	1833	...	1851	1922	→	1933	1928	1935	2025	2111	2220	2220	2326	0044	...
Norrköping d.	1627	1629	1638	1713	1735	...	...	1810	1829	1835	...	1853	1924	...	1935	1938j	1937	2027	2111	2220	2222	2328	0047	...
Linköping d.	1653	1655	1703	1742	1800	...	...	1838	1855	1900	...	|	1950	...	2000	2006j	2002	2053	2136	2246	2252	2354	0123	...
Mjölby 755 d.	...	...	|	1802	1815	...	...	|	...	|	...	|	...	...	2015	...	2017	...	...	...	...	...	|	...
Tranås d.	...	...	|	|	|	←	...	|	...	1929	...	|	...	...	|	...	|	...	...	...	...	...	|	...
Nässjö d.	...	...	1753	1900	1853	1900	...	1937	...	2004	...	|	...	...	2053	...	2055	...	...	...	...	...	|	...
Alvesta d.	...	...	1827	→	1927	1944	...	...	...	2038	...	|	...	...	2127	...	2130	...	...	...	...	...	|	...
Hässleholm **745/6** a.	...	...	1902	...	2002	2026	...	...	...	2112	...	2106	...	...	2202	...	2205	...	...	...	...	...	0500s	...
Lund **745/6** § a.	...	...	1931	...	2031	2102	...	...	...	2141	...	2134	...	...	2231	...	2234	...	...	...	...	...	0625s	...
Malmö 745/6 a.	...	...	1946s	...	2046	2117	...	...	...	2157	...	2149	...	...	2246	...	2249	...	...	...	...	...	0642	...
Malmö 703 d.	...	...	|	...	...	...	...	...	...	...	...	...	...	...	...	...	...	...	...	...	...	...	*0702*	...
København (Kastrup) ✈ **703** a.	...	...	2019s	...	...	...	...	...	...	...	...	...	...	...	...	...	...	...	...	...	...	...	*0723*	...
København H 703 a.	...	...	2033	...	...	...	...	...	...	...	...	...	...	...	...	...	...	...	...	...	...	...	*0737*	...

	218 Ⓐ	260 Ⓐz	270 Ⓐz	220 Ⓐ	X2000 520 R ✕ Ⓐz	222 Ⓐ	X2000 512 R ✕ ♦	224 ⑥		X2000 522 R ✕ Ⓐz	X2000 524 R ✕ Ⓐz	X2000 516 R ✕ ♦	226 Ⓑ	228 ⑥	X2000 526 R ✕		X2000 528 R ✕ ⚒	230	X2000 530 R ✕	X2000 532 R ✕ ⑤z	234 Ⓐz	232 †z	234 †v	X2000 534 R ✕
København H 703 d.	...	...	...	...	...	...	...	...	...	...	...	...	...	...	...	...	...	...	0831	...	...	...	...	...
København Kastrup ✈ **703** d.	...	...	...	...	...	...	...	...	...	...	...	...	...	...	...	...	...	...	0844u	...	...	...	...	...
Malmö 703 a.	...	...	...	...	...	...	...	...	...	...	...	...	...	...	...	...	...	...	|	...	...	...	...	...
Malmö 745/6 d.	...	...	...	...	...	...	...	...	...	0514	0614	...	...	...	0714	...	0814	...	0914u	1014	...	...	...	1114
Lund **745/6** § d.	...	...	...	...	...	...	...	...	...	0528	0628	...	...	...	0728	...	0828	...	0928	1028	...	...	...	1128
Hässleholm **745/6** d.	...	...	...	...	...	...	...	...	...	0557	0657	...	...	...	0757	...	0857	...	0957	1057	...	...	...	1157
Alvesta **746** d.	...	...	...	...	...	...	...	...	...	0634	0734	...	...	...	0834	...	0934	...	1034	1134	...	...	...	1234
Nässjö d.	...	...	...	...	...	...	0642	...	...	0708	0808	0808	...	...	0908	...	1008	...	1108	1208	...	...	...	1308
Tranås d.	...	...	...	...	...	...	0703	...	...	|	|	|	...	...	|	...	|	...	|	|	...	...	...	|
Mjölby 755 d.	...	...	...	...	...	...	|	...	...	0744	|	|	...	...	0944	...	|	...	1144	|	...	...	...	1344
Linköping d.	0506	0528e	0600	0615	0638	0700	0740	0755	...	0800	0900	0900	0905	0905	1000	...	1058	1105	1200	1300	1305	1305	1305	1400
Norrköping a.	0532	0554e	0626	0641	0700	0726	0802	0821	...	0822	0922	0922	0931	0931	1022	...	1120	1131	1222	1322	1331	1331	1331	1422
Norrköping 754 d.	0534	0556	0628	0643	0702	0728	0804	0823	...	0824	0924	0924	0933	0933	1024	...	1122	1133	1224	1324	1333	1333	1333	1424
Nyköping d.	0617	0645	|	0724	|	0808	|	0903	...	|	|	|	1013	1015	|	...	|	1213	|	|	1413	1415	1413	|
Katrineholm **740 754** a.	|	|	|	|	|	|	|	|	...	|	|	|	|	|	|	...	|	|	|	|	|	|	|	|
Södertälje Syd ‡ a.	0656	0725	0731	0805	0757	0847	|	0942	...	0919	|	|	1052	1055	1119	...	1217	1252	|	1419	1452	1455	1452	1519
Flemingsberg ‡ a.	0706	0736	0742	0816	0808	0857	0906	0952	...	|	1027	1027	1102	1106	|	...	1228	1302	1326	|	1502	1506	1502	|
Stockholm Central ‡ a.	0720	0750	0755	0830	0820	0910	0920	1005	...	0940	1040	1040	1115	1120	1140	...	1240	1315	1340	1440	1515	1520	1515	1540

	236 ⑥	X2000 502 R ✕ †	X2000 536 R ✕ Ⓐ	238 Ⓑ	X2000 518 R ✕ †	X2000 538 R ✕ ⚒		X2000 504 R ✕ ⑤z	X2000 540 R ✕ Ⓑ	244 ⑥	242 Ⓑ	X2000 542 R ✕		X2000 544 R ✕ Ⓑy	246 Ⓑ	204 ⑤†	206 ④x	X2000 546 R ✕	66 R ♦	X2000 548 R ✕ †z		X2000 550 R ✕ Ⓑz		2 R ♦
København H 703 d.	...	...	...	...	1231	1231	...	...	...	...	...	...	...	...	...	...	...	...	*1623*	...	...	...	...	*2223*
København Kastrup ✈ **703** d.	...	...	...	...	1244u	1244u	...	...	...	...	...	...	...	...	...	...	...	...	*1636*	...	...	...	...	*2236*
Malmö 703 a.	...	...	...	...	|	|	...	...	...	...	...	...	...	...	...	...	...	...	*1658*	...	...	...	...	*2258*
Malmö 745/6 d.	...	1212	1214	...	1314u	1314u	...	1344	1414	...	...	1514	...	1614	...	1617	1617	1714	1717	1814	...	1914	...	2308
Lund **745/6** § d.	...	1227	1228	...	1328	1328	...	1358	1428	...	...	1528	...	1628	...	1632	1632	1728	1734u	1828	...	1928	...	2323u
Hässleholm **745/6** d.	...	1257	1257	...	1357	1357	...	1427	1457	...	...	1557	...	1657	...	1708	1708	1757	1813u	1857	...	1957	...	2357u
Alvesta **746** d.	...	|	1334	...	1434	1434	...	|	1534	...	...	1634	...	1734	...	1802	1802	1834	1904u	1934	...	2034	...	|
Nässjö d.	...	|	1408	...	1508	1508	...	|	1608	...	...	1708	...	1808	...	1844	1844	1908	1949u	2008	...	2108	...	|
Tranås d.	...	|	|	...	|	|	...	|	|	...	...	|	...	|	...	|	|	|	|	|	...	|	...	|
Mjölby 755 d.	...	|	|	...	1544	1544	...	|	|	...	...	1744	...	|	...	|	|	1944	|	|	...	|	...	|
Linköping d.	1407	1452	1458	1503	1600	1600	...	1637	1658	1701	1705	1800	...	1858	1905	1941	1941	2000	2050u	2057	...	2157	...	0316s
Norrköping a.	1433	1514	1520	1529	1622	1622	...	1700	1720	1727	1731	1822	...	1920	1931	2009	2016	2022	|	2120	...	2219	...	0352s
Norrköping 754 d.	1435	1517	1522	1531	1624	1624	...	1702	1722	1729	1733	1824	...	1922	1933	2011	2018	2024	2125u	2122	...	2221	...	|
Nyköping d.	1516	|	|	1613	|	|	...	|	|	1810	1814	|	...	|	2013	|	|	|	...	|	...	|	...	|
Katrineholm **740 754** a.	|	|	|	|	|	|	...	|	1743	|	|	|	...	1943	|	|	|	|	...	|	...	|	...	|
Södertälje Syd ‡ a.	1556	|	|	1652	|	1719	...	|	|	1855	1857	1919	...	|	2052	|	|	2119	...	|	...	2316	...	0523s
Flemingsberg ‡ a.	1607	|	1626	1702	|	|	...	|	1827	1906	1907	|	...	2027	2102	|	|	|	...	|	...	2328	...	|
Stockholm Central ‡ a.	1620	1630	1640	1715	1735	1740	...	1815	1840	1920	1920	1940	...	2040	2115	2135	2158	2140	...	2235	...	2340	...	0555

♦ – **NOTES** (LISTED BY TRAIN NUMBER)

1 – Ⓑ (not Dec. 24 - Jan. 5: 🛏 1, 2 cl., 🛏 2 cl. and (2) Stockholm - Malmö.
2 – Ⓑ (not Dec. 24 - Jan. 5): 🛏 1, 2 cl., 🛏 2 cl. and (2) Malmö - Stockholm.
66 – ⑤† Dec. 9 - 16; ③④⑤⑥† Dec. 17 - Jan. 5; ③⑤⑥† Jan. 6 - Feb. 3; ③④⑤⑥† Feb. 4 - Mar. 30; ③⑤⑥† Mar. 31 - Apr. 27; ⑤† Apr. 28 - June 14: 🛏 1, 2 cl., 🛏 2 cl. and (2) Malmö - Storlien; ✕ and (Bio) Malmö - Stockholm.
512 – Ⓐ (not Dec. 24 - Jan. 5): (12) and ✕ Jönköping - Nässjö - Stockholm.
513 – Ⓑ (not Dec. 22 - Jan. 5): (12) and ✕ Stockholm - Nässjö - Jönköping.
516 – ⑥ (not Dec. 24 - Jan. 5): (12) and ✕ Jönköping - Nässjö - Stockholm.

G – ①②③④ (not Dec. 24 - Jan. 5).
H – ①②③④† Dec. 9 - 20, Mar. 2 - June 14.
Q – ⑤† Dec. 9 - Jan. 5; ④⑤† Jan. 6 - June 14.

e – ① only.
j – ⑤ (also ①②③④ Dec. 24 - Jan. 5).
s – Stops to set down only.
u – Stops to pick up only.
v – Dec. 24 - Jan. 5.
x – Jan. 6 - June 14.
y – Not Dec. 27 - Jan. 5.
z – Not Dec. 24 - Jan. 5.

‡ – Most trains on this table do not convey passengers for local journeys between Stockholm and Södertälje Syd and v.v. Local trains run every 30 minutes Stockholm Central - Södertälje Hamn - Södertälje Centrum and v.v. (journey 42 mins). 🚌 Södertälje Syd - Södertälje Centrum runs every 30 minutes.
§ – From Malmö stops to pick up only, to Malmö stops to set down only. Frequent local trains run between Lund and Malmö.

MALMÖ - YSTAD — 731

Operator: *Skåne*

65 km. Journey time: 45 minutes. 2nd class only

From **Malmö**:
0015②③④⑤⑥†, 0115©, 0545⚒, 0615Ⓐ, 0645Ⓐ, 0715, 0745Ⓐ, 0815, 0915, 1015, 1115, 1215, 1315, 1415, 1515, 1545Ⓐ, 1615, 1645Ⓐ, 1715, 1745Ⓐ, 1815, 1845Ⓐ, 1915, 2015, 2115, 2215, 2315.

From **Ystad**:
0508Ⓐ, 0538Ⓐ, 0608⚒, 0638Ⓐ, 0708⚒, 0738Ⓐ, 0808, 0838Ⓐ, 0908, 1008, 1108, 1208, 1308, 1408, 1508, 1608, 1638Ⓐ, 1708, 1738Ⓐ, 1808, 1838Ⓐ, 1908, 2008, 2108, 2208, 2308, 0008①⑥†.

733 SKÖVDE - JONKÖPING - NÄSSJÖ

°○ 2nd class only except where shown

km		Ⓐ	Ⓐ	ⒶSz	Ⓐ	⑥Sz	Ⓐ	⑥	Ⓐ	Ⓐ	Ⓐ		⑥	⑥		Ⓐ		Ⓐ	⚒		Ⓑx	Ⓑ		Ⓑ	Ⓑ		Ⓑ	⑥
0	**Skövde 740** ... d.	0450	...	...	0554	...	0628	0656	0658	0757	...	0854	0927	...	1054	...	1254	1357	...	1454	1552	...	1702	1800	...	1856	2100	...
	Göteborg .... d.	|	...	...	|	...	|	|	|	|	0657	|	|	0902	|	1102	|	|	1302y	|	|	1502	|	|	1707	|	|	...
30	Falköping **740**. d.	0508	0511	...	0616	...	0650	0716	0718	0815	0820	0916	0945	1020	1114	1220	1314	1415	1420	1514	1610	1616	1725	1818	1826	1916	2122	2251
100	Jönköping....... a.	...	0551	...	0707	...	0739	0756	0758	...	0902	1001	...	1100	1159	1301	1359	...	1500	1601	...	1702	1810	...	1911	2001	2208	2333
100	Jönköping....... d.	...	0553	0610	0710	0735	0742	0800	0802	...	0904	1010	...	1102	1201	1310	1407	...	1509	1607	...	1708	1812	...	1914	2015	2210	2335
143	**Nässjö 730** .... a.	...	0624	0637	0741	0802	0816	0838	0838	...	0942	1041	...	1139	1235	1341	1441	...	1548	1641	...	1741	1843	...	1945	2047	2241	0006

	Ⓐ	Ⓐ	Ⓐ	⑥	⚒	Ⓐ	⑥		Ⓐ			⑥		Ⓐ	Ⓐ		Ⓐ	Ⓑ	Ⓑ		Ⓑ	Ⓑ		ⒷSv		
Nässjö 730.............. d.	0518	0545	0702	0724	0824	...	...	0921	1017	...	1119	1208	1317	1420	...	1523	1553	1617	...	1721	1819	...	1921	1945	2122	...
Jönköping .... a.	0548	0622	0737	0759	0900	...	...	0953	1050	...	1152	1245	1350	1454	...	1559	1623	1658	...	1752	1851	...	1954	2012	2152	...
Jönköping .... d.	0551	0625	0740	0801	0904	...	...	1001	1102	...	1201	1302	1401	1501	...	1601	1632	1702	...	1754	1853	...	2003	...	2154	...
Falköping **740** .... a.	0632	0706	0833	0842	0945	0950	1015	1045	1143	...	1245	1342	1445	1543	1550	1646	1716	1742	1754	1842	1942	1953	2044	...	2235	2243
Göteborg.............. a.	|	|	|	|	1057	|	|	|	1257	...	|	1457	|	1657	|	|	|	1857	|	|	2057	|	|	...	...	|
Skövde 740.............. a.	0652	0740	0854	0902	...	1008	1033	1106	...	...	1306	...	1506	...	1608	1706	1738	...	1814	1902	...	2011	2106	...	...	2301

S – *X2000*: [12] and ✕ Stockholm - Nässjö - Jönköping and v.v. [R] and special supplement payable. Train numbers **512/3/6**.

v – Not Dec. 22 - Jan. 5.
x – 20 minutes earlier on †.
y – ⑤ Jan. 6 - June 14.
z – Not Dec. 24 - Jan. 5.

735 GÖTEBORG - MALMÖ - KØBENHAVN

km		Ⓐ	⚒	Ⓐ	Ⓐ	*X2000* 485 [R]✕ Ⓐ	Ⓐ	⚒	Ⓐ	*X2000* 491 [R]✕ ⑥y		*X2000* 487 [R]✕ ⑥x		Ⓐ		Ⓐ	*X2000* 429 [R]✕ †wS	*X2000* 489 [R]✕ A		Ⓐ	*X2000* 433 [R]✕ ⑥yS		Ⓐ	Ⓐ	Ⓐ	*X2000* 495 [R]✕ Ⓐ
	Oslo Sentral **770** .... d.	...	...	...	...	...	...	...	...	...	...	...	...	...	...	...	...	...	...	...	...	...	...	...	...	...
0	**Göteborg**................ d.	...	...	0555	0625	0655	0710	0740	0840	0930	0940	0955	...	1040	1140	1240	1330	1330	1335	1440	1530	1540	1610	1640	1710	1725
28	Kungsbacka .... d.	...	...	0613	0643	|	0728	0758	0857	|	0957	|	...	1057	1157	1257	|	|	1352	1457	|	1558	1628	1658	1728	|
76	Varberg .... d.	...	...	0635	0704	0730	0749	0819	0919	1003	1019	1030	...	1122	1219	1319	1400	1402	1415	1519	1600	1622	1657	1722	1750	1801
106	Falkenberg .... d.	...	...	0655	0722	|	0820	0837	0937	1021	1037	|	...	1137	1237	1337	1417	1417	1435	1537	1616	1636	1716	1737	1807	|
150	**Halmstad**................ d.	0600	0704	0716	0804	0807	0841	0904	1000	1043	1100	1103	1104	1200	1304	1404	1437	1437	1502	1602	1637	1704	1737	1804	1830	1836
*	Hässleholm .... a.	|	|	...	|	0859	▬	|	...	1137	→	1156	|	...	|	|	1530	1530	|	|	1730	|	...	|	...	1930
173	Laholm .... d.	0611	0715	...	0815	|	Ⓐ	0915	...	|	...	|	1115	...	1315	1415	|	|	1513	1613	|	1715	...	1815	...	|
185	Båstad .... d.	0619	0723	...	0823	|	←	0923	...	|	...	|	1124	...	1323	1423	|	|	1521	1621	|	1723	...	1823	...	|
210	Ängelholm .... d.	0640	0745	...	0845	|	0845	0945	...	|	...	|	1146	...	1345	1445	|	|	1546	1645	|	1745	...	1845	...	|
237	**Helsingborg** .... a.	0657	0804	...	→	|	0904	1004	...	|	...	|	1204	...	1404	1504	|	|	1604	1704	|	1804	...	1904	...	|
237	**Helsingborg 737** .... d.	0710	0810	...	...	|	0910	1010	...	|	...	|	1210	...	1410	1510	|	|	1610	1710	|	1810	...	1910	...	|
259	Landskrona **737**.......... d.	0722	0822	...	...	|	0922	1022	...	|	...	|	1222	...	1422	1522	|	|	1622	1722	|	1822	...	1922	...	|
290	Lund **737** .... a.	0737	0837	...	...	0925s	0937	1037	...	1203s	...	1226s	1237	...	1437	1537	1600s	1600s	1637	1737	1807s	1837	...	1937	...	2000s
306	**Malmö 737** .... a.	0752	0852	...	...	0943	0952	1052	...	1219	...	1242	1252	...	1452	1552	1615	1615	1652	1752	1827	1852	...	1952	...	2015
306	**Malmö 701** .... d.	0802	0902	...	...	*1002*	1002	1102	...	*1242*	...	*1302*	1302	...	1502	1602	*1642*	*1642*	1702	1802	*1842*	1902	...	2002	...	*2042*
342	København (Kastrup) ✈ **703**. a.	0823	0923	...	...	*1023*	1023	1123	...	*1303*	...	*1323*	1323	...	1523	1623	*1703*	*1703*	1723	1823	*1903*	1923	...	2023	...	*2103*
353	**København H 703**........ a.	0837	0937	...	...	*1037*	1037	1137	...	*1317*	...	*1337*	1337	...	1537	1637	*1717*	*1717*	1737	1837	*1917*	1937	...	2037	...	*2117*

		Ⓐ	Ⓐ	*X2000* 497 [R]✕ †v	Ⓐ	*X2000* 499 [R]✕ †w		Ⓐ	Ⓒ	Ⓐ
Oslo Sentral **770** ....d.	...	...	...	...	...	...	...	...	...	...
Göteborg ....d.	1740	1810	1840	1900	...	1930	1940	2040	2140	2240
Kungsbacka...........................d.	1758	1828	1858	|	...	|	1957	2057	2157	2257
Varberg ....d.	1819	1849	1919	1933	...	1959	2021	2121	2219	2319
Falkenberg ....d.	1838	1913	1937	|	...	2018	2037	2137	2237	2337
Halmstad ....d.	1904	1941	2004	2006	...	2040	2104	2200	2300	2400
Hässleholm ....a.	|	...	|	2100	←	2133	|	...	...	...
Laholm ....d.	1915	...	2015	|	2015	|	2115	...	...	...
Båstad..................................d.	1923	...	→	|	2023	|	2123	...	...	...
Ängelholm ....d.	1945	...	...	|	2045	|	2145	...	...	...
Helsingborg...........................a.	2004	...	...	|	2104	|	2204	...	...	...
Helsingborg 737.....................d.	2010	...	...	|	2110	|	2210	...	...	...
Landskrona **737**......................d.	2022	...	...	|	2122	|	2222	...	...	...
Lund **737** ....a.	2037	...	...	2127s	2137	2200s	2237	...	...	...
Malmö 737 ....a.	2052	...	...	2142	2152	2216	2252	...	...	...
Malmö 701 ....d.	2102	...	...	*2202*	2202	*2242*	2302	...	...	...
København (Kastrup) ✈ **703** ..a.	2123	...	...	*2223*	2223	*2303*	2323	...	...	...
København H 703.........a.	2137	...	...	*2237*	2237	*2317*	2337	...	...	...

	Ⓐ	Ⓐ	⚒	Ⓐ	Ⓐ	*X2000* 484 [R]✕ Ⓐ	⚒	†	*X2000* 488 [R]✕ ⑥y	Ⓐ	
København H 703......d.	...	...	...	...	0523	*0543*	0623	...	*0643*	...	0823
København (Kastrup) ✈ **703** d.	...	...	...	...	0536	*0556*	0636	...	*0656*	...	0836
Malmö 701 ....a.	...	...	...	...	0558	*0618*	0658	...	*0718*	...	0858
Malmö 737 ....d.	...	...	...	...	0608	0645	0708	...	0745	...	0908
Lund **737** ....d.	...	...	...	...	0622	0657u	0722	...	0759u	...	0922
Landskrona **737** ....d.	...	...	...	...	0638	|	0738	...	|	...	0938
Helsingborg 737...................a.	...	...	...	...	0650	|	0750	...	|	...	0950
Helsingborg ....d.	...	...	0554a	...	0657	|	0753	...	|	...	0953
Ängelholm ....d.	...	...	0613a	...	0717	|	0813	...	|	...	1013
Båstad.................................d.	...	...	0633a	...	0737	|	0837	...	|	...	1037
Laholm ....d.	...	...	0640a	...	0744	|	0844	...	|	...	1044
Hässleholm ....d.	...	...	|	...	|	0726	|	...	0828	...	→
Halmstad ....d.	0555	0625	0653	0723	0800	0816	0900	0900	0917	1000	...
Falkenberg ....d.	0615	0645	0713	0747	0820	|	0920	0920	0937	1020	...
Varberg ....d.	0632	0703	0729	0803	0837	0852	0937	0937	0955	1037	...
Kungsbacka...........................d.	0655	0724	0754	0825	0900	|	1000	1000	|	1100	...
Göteborg ....a.	0715	0745	0815	0845	0920	0929	1020	1020	1029	1120	...
Oslo Sentral **770** ....a.	...	...	...	...	...	...	...	...	...	...	...

	X2000 486 [R]✕ ⑥x		Ⓐ		Ⓐ	*X2000* 494 [R]✕ Ⓐy	*X2000* 440 [R]✕ †wS		*X2000* 490 [R]✕ Ⓐx		*X2000* 442 [R]✕ ⑥wS	Ⓐ	Ⓐ		*X2000* 492 [R]✕ Ⓒv		Ⓐ	Ⓐ		*X2000* 496 [R]✕ Ⓐ		Ⓐ	*X2000* 498 [R]✕ †	Ⓐ		Ⓑ
København H 703 ....d.	*0803*	...	...	1023	1123	*1143*	*1143*	1223	*1203*	...	1243	1323	...	1423	*1403*	...	...	1523	1623	*1603*	...	1723	*1703*	...	1823	2023
København (Kastrup) ✈ **703**.d.	*0816*	...	...	1036	1136	*1156*	*1156*	1236	*1216*	...	1256	1336	...	1436	*1416*	...	...	1536	1636	*1616*	...	1736	*1716*	...	1836	2036
Malmö 701 ....a.	*0838*	...	...	1058	1158	*1218*	*1218*	1258	*1238*	...	1318	1358	...	1458	*1438*	...	...	1558	1658	*1638*	...	1758	*1738*	...	1858	2058
Malmö 737 ....d.	0911	...	...	1108	1208	1245	1245	1308	1311	...	1345	1408	...	1508	1511	...	...	1608	1708	1711	...	1808	1811	...	1908	2108
Lund **737** ....d.	0925u	...	...	1122	1222	1259u	1259u	1322	1325u	...	1359u	1422	...	1522	1523u	...	...	1622	1722	1723u	...	1822	1825u	...	1922	2122
Landskrona **737** ....d.	|	...	...	1138	1238	|	|	1338	|	...	|	1438	...	1538	|	...	...	1638	1738	|	...	1838	|	...	1938	2140
Helsingborg 737...................a.	|	...	...	1150	1250	|	|	1350	|	...	|	1450	...	1550	|	...	...	1650	1750	|	...	1850	|	...	1950	2152
Helsingborg.......................d.	|	...	...	1153	1253	|	|	1353	|	...	|	1453	...	1553	|	...	...	1653	1753	|	...	1853	|	...	1953	2153
Ängelholm ....d.	|	...	...	1213	1313	|	|	1413	|	...	|	1513	...	1613	|	...	...	1713	1813	|	...	1913	|	...	2013	2213
Båstad.................................d.	|	←	...	1237	1336	|	|	1437	|	←	|	1535	...	1635	|	←	...	1737	1838	|	←	1937	|	←	2037	2237
Laholm ....d.	|	1044	...	1244	1343	|	|	1444	|	1444	|	1542	...	1642	|	1642	...	1744	1845	|	1845	1944	|	1944	2044	2244
Hässleholm ....d.	0952	|	...	|	|	1327	1327	→	1352	|	1427	|	...	→	1552	|	...	|	→	1752	|	→	1852	|	|	|
Halmstad ....d.	1043	1100	1156	1300	1356	1416	1416	...	1444	1458	1518	1556	1620	...	1646	1656	1744	1815f	...	1842	1900	...	1946	2000	2100	2256
Falkenberg ....d.	|	1120	1216	1320	1416	1436	1436	...	|	1517	1537	1616	1640	...	|	1716	1804	1835	...	|	1920	...	|	2020	2120	...
Varberg ....d.	1118	1137	1233	1337	1434	1453	1453	...	1519	1533	1554	1633	1657	...	1722	1733	1822	1853	...	1918	1937	...	2021	2037	2137	...
Kungsbacka...........................d.	|	1200	1256	1400	1456	|	|	...	|	1556	|	1656	1720	...	|	1756	1854	1918	...	|	2000	...	|	2100	2200	...
Göteborg ....a.	1150	1220	1315	1420	1515	1526	1526	...	1558	1615	1626	1715	1745	...	1755	1815	1915	1945	...	1956	2020	...	2055	2120	2220	...
Oslo Sentral **770** ....a.	...	...	...	...	...	...	...	...	...	...	...	...	...	...	...	...	...	...	...	...	...	...	...	...	...	...

♦ – **NOTES** (LISTED BY TRAIN NUMBER)

A – Daily Dec. 9 - Jan. 6; Ⓐ Jan. 7 - June 14.
S – [12] and ✕ Stockholm - Göteborg - Malmö and v.v.

a – Ⓐ only.
f – Arrive 1756.
s – Stops to set down only.
u – Stops to pick up only.
v – Dec. 9 - Jan. 6.
w – Jan. 7 - June 14.

x – Dec. 9 - Jan. 5.
y – Jan. 6 - June 14.
X2000 – High speed train. Special supplement payable.
* – Halmstad - Hässleholm: *91 km*.

Table 760 (continued from page 354)

STOCKHOLM - GÄVLE and v.v. (additional services):

	Ⓐq	Ⓐ	⑥	Ⓐ	⑥n	Ⓐ	†q	Ⓐq	Ⓐn	⑥	Ⓑq	Ⓑ
Stockholm C. .... d.	0728	0930	1128	1130	1325	1330	1528	1530	1616	1628	1730	1930
Arlanda C ✈........ ◧ d.	0749	0948	1147	1148	1343	1348	1547	1548	1638	1647	1748	1948
Uppsala **761** .... d.	0809	1009	1209	1209	1404	1409	1609	1608	1658	1709	1809	2009
Gävle 755 .... a.	0858	1054	1304	1258	1454	1454	1704	1658	1803	1804	1858	2058

	Ⓐ	Ⓐq	⚒	⚒q	Ⓐ	⑥n	Ⓑ	⑥	Ⓑ	†q	hq	
Gävle 755............ d.	0626	0732	0906	1102	1306	1306	1502	1556	1702	1856	1906	...
Uppsala 761 .... a.	0721	0830	0951	1151	1351	1351	1551	1651	1751	1951	1951	...
Arlanda C ✈.... ◧ a.	0739	0850	1009	1209	1409	1409	1609	1710	1809	2010	2009	...
Stockholm C....... a.	0800	0913	1030	1230	1430	1430	1630	1732	1830	2032	2030	...

FOR NOTES SEE PAGE 354

HALLSBERG - MARIESTAD - LIDKÖPING - HERRLJUNGA — 736

Operator: *V* 2nd class only

km		Ⓐ	Ⓐ	Ⓐ	⑥	Ⓐ	Ⓒ	Ⓐ	Ⓐ	†	Ⓐ	Ⓐ	⑥	Ⓒ	†	Ⓐ	⑥	Ⓐ	†	Ⓐ	⑥	Ⓐ	†	Ⓐ	†	Ⓐ
0	**Hallsberg 740** d.	...	...	...	...	...	...	0851	...	...	1045	...	...	1225	...	...	...	1441	...	...	1625	1637	...	...	1850	2014
30	Laxå **740** d.	...	...	...	...	...	...	0909	...	...	1103	...	...	1243	...	...	...	1458	...	...	1643	1747	...	...	1907	2032
92	Mariestad d.	...	0540	0650	...	0758	0835	1001	...	...	1151	...	1225	1331	1405	1435	1440	1552	1630	1705	1735	*1757*	1815	...	1958	2122
146	Lidköping a.	...	0620	0741	...	0854	0915	1049	...	...	...	...	1316	...	1453	1515	1520	1640	1710	1756	1823	*1845*	1903	...	2046	2210
146	Lidköping ▲ d.	0538	0622	*0756*	0800	0858	0915	...	1105	1205	...	1315	1318	...	1500	1518	1520	1715	1720	...	...	...	1905	2011	...	...
201	**Herrljunga ▲740** a.	0623	0702	*0844*	0847	0949	0957	...	1152	1252	...	1402	1405	...	1550	1600	1600	1802	1800	...	...	...	1954	2100	...	...
	Göteborg **740** a.	...	0757	...	...	...	1047	...	...	...	...	...	...	...	...	1647	1647	...	1847	...	...	...	...	...	...	...

	Ⓐ	Ⓐ	Ⓐ	Ⓐ	Ⓐ	Ⓒ	⑥	Ⓐ	Ⓐ	⑥	Ⓐ	†	Ⓐ	†	⑥	Ⓐ	†	Ⓐ	Ⓒ	Ⓐ	†	Ⓐ	⚒	Ⓐ	†	Ⓑ
Göteborg **740** d.	...	...	...	...	...	...	...	0932	...	1102	...	1132	...	...	...	...	...	...	...	...	...	...	1712	...	1912	...
Herrljunga ▲ 740 d.	...	...	0703	...	0911	...	0959	1018	...	1146	1159	1218	...	1302	...	1412	...	...	1600	1602	...	...	1802	1858	2000	2105
Lidköping ▲ a.	...	...	0753	...	1000	...	1046	1058	...	1225	1247	1300	...	1349	...	1500	...	...	1647	1649	...	...	1843	1945	2038	2152
Lidköping d.	0500	0530	...	0757	...	1018	1125	1058	...	1225	...	1300	1336	...	1352	...	1517	1542	...	1703	1712	...	1845	...	2045	...
Mariestad d.	0550	0621	...	0847	...	1111	1213	1138	1222	1305	...	1340	1426	...	1510	...	1607	1635	...	1752	1800	1802	1923	...	2125	...
Laxå **740** d.	0638	...	...	0935	...	1200	...	...	1311	...	...	...	1514	...	1601	...	1655	...	...	...	...	1851	...	...	...	...
Hallsberg 740 a.	0655	...	...	0954	...	1218	...	...	1330	...	...	...	1535	...	1619	...	1714	...	...	...	...	1909	...	...	...	...

▲ – Additional services available Lidköping - Herrljunga and v.v.

KØBENHAVN - KØBENHAVN LUFTHAVN (KASTRUP) ✈ - MALMÖ - HELSINGBORG — 737

Operator: *Skåne*

	Ⓐ2	Ⓐ2	Ⓐ2	Ⓐ	Ⓐ2	2	Ⓐ2	⚒	2	Ⓐ	2	Ⓐ	Ⓐ2	2		2	2	⚒	Ⓐ2	2		2	2	⚒	Ⓐ2	2	
København H **703** d.	...	...	...	0523	...	...	...	0623	...	...	...	0723	...	...	0823	...	...	0923	...	...	1023	...	...	1123	...	...	1223
Lufthavn (Kastrup) **703** d.	...	...	...	0536	...	...	...	0636	...	...	...	0736	...	...	0836	...	...	0936	...	...	1036	...	...	1136	...	...	1236
Malmö 703 735 d.	0437	0521	0537	0608	0621	0637	0703	0708	0721	0734	0737	0808	0821	0837	0908	0921	0937	1008	1021	1037	1108	1121	1137	1208	1221	1237	1308
Lund **735** d.	0451	0539	0551	0622	0639	0651	0717	0722	0739	0748	0751	0822	0839	0851	0922	0939	0951	1022	1039	1051	1122	1139	1151	1222	1239	1251	1322
Landskrona **735** d.	0515	|	0615	0638	|	0715	0745	0738	|	0804	0815	0840	|	0915	0938	|	1015	1040	|	1115	1138	|	1215	1238	|	1315	1338
Helsingborg 735 a.	0532	0627	0632	0650	0727	0732	0802	0750	0827	0818	0832	0852	0927	0932	0950	1027	1032	1052	1127	1132	1150	1227	1232	1250	1327	1332	1350

	2	2	⚒	Ⓐ2			2	Ⓐ	2	Ⓐ2	⚒	Ⓐ2	Ⓐ	2	Ⓐ2		2	Ⓐ	2	Ⓐ2	Ⓐ	Ⓐ2	2		2	2	Ⓐ2
København H **703** d.	...	...	1323	...	...	1423	...	...	...	...	1523	...	...	...	...	1623	...	...	...	...	1723	...	...	1823	...	...	...
Lufthavn (Kastrup) **703** d.	...	...	1336	...	...	1436	...	...	...	...	1536	...	...	...	...	1636	...	...	...	...	1736	...	...	1836	...	...	...
Malmö 703 735 d.	1321	1337	1408	1421	1437	1508	1521	1534	1537	1603	1608	1621	1634	1637	1703	1708	1721	1734	1737	1803	1808	1821	1837	1908	1921	1937	2017
Lund **735** d.	1339	1351	1422	1439	1451	1522	1539	1548	1551	1617	1622	1639	1648	1651	1717	1722	1739	1748	1751	1817	1822	1839	1851	1922	1939	1951	2039
Landskrona **735** d.	|	1415	1438	|	1515	1538	|	1604	1615	1645	1638	|	1704	1715	1745	1738	|	1804	1815	1845	1838	|	1915	1938	|	2015	|
Helsingborg 735 a.	1427	1432	1450	1527	1532	1550	1627	1618	1632	1702	1650	1727	1718	1732	1802	1750	1827	1818	1832	1902	1850	1927	1932	1950	2027	2032	2127

	2		2	2	Ⓐ2	2	⑤⑥	⚒2	⚒2	H
København H **703** d.	...	2023	...	...	...	...	2223	...	...	...
Lufthavn (Kastrup) **703** d.	...	2036	...	...	...	...	2236	...	...	...
Malmö 703 735 d.	2037	2108	2121	2137	2221	2237	2311	2321	2337	0100
Lund **735** d.	2051	2122	2139	2151	2239	2251	2325	2339	2351	0114
Landskrona **735** d.	2115	2140	|	2215	|	2315	2343	|	0015	0138
Helsingborg 735 a.	2132	2152	2227	2232	2327	2332	2355	0027	0032	0155

	Ⓐ2	Ⓐ2	2	Ⓐ	Ⓐ2	Ⓐ2	Ⓐ	⚒	Ⓐ	2	2	Ⓐ	Ⓐ2
Helsingborg 735 d.	0515	0533	0553	0610	0627	0633	0645	0653	0710	0727	0733	0745	0753
Landskrona **735** d.	0533	|	0611	0622	0645	|	0658	0711	0722	0745	|	0758	0811
Lund **735** d.	0558	0622	0636	0639	0710	0722	0716	0736	0739	0810	0822	0816	0836
Malmö 703 735 a.	0611	0639	0649	0652	0723	0739	0729	0749	0752	0823	0839	0829	0849
Lufthavn (Kastrup) **703** a.	...	...	...	0723	...	...	...	...	0823	...	...	...	...
København H **703** a.	...	...	...	0737	...	...	...	...	0837	...	...	...	...

	⚒	2	Ⓐ2	Ⓐ2	⚒	2	2		2	Ⓐ2	⚒	2	2		2	Ⓐ2	⚒	2	2		2	Ⓐ2	Ⓐ2	⚒	2	2	Ⓐ
Helsingborg 735 d.	0810	0827	0833	0853	0910	0927	0933	1010	1027	1033	1108	1127	1133	1210	1227	1233	1308	1327	1333	1410	1427	1433	1453	1510	1527	1533	1553
Landskrona **735** d.	0822	0845	|	0911	0922	0945	|	1022	1045	|	1120	1145	|	1222	1245	|	1320	1345	|	1422	1445	|	1511	1522	1545	|	1611
Lund **735** d.	0839	0910	0922	0936	0939	1010	1022	1039	1110	1122	1139	1210	1222	1239	1310	1322	1339	1410	1422	1439	1510	1522	1536	1539	1610	1622	1636
Malmö 703 735 a.	0852	0923	0939	0949	0952	1023	1039	1052	1123	1139	1152	1223	1239	1252	1323	1339	1352	1423	1439	1452	1523	1539	1549	1552	1623	1639	1649
Lufthavn (Kastrup) **703** a.	0923	...	...	...	1023	...	...	1123	...	...	1223	...	...	1323	...	...	1423	...	...	1523	...	...	...	1623	...	...	...
København H **703** a.	0937	...	...	...	1037	...	...	1137	...	...	1237	...	...	1337	...	...	1437	...	...	1537	...	...	...	1637	...	...	...

			Ⓐ2	Ⓐ	⚒	2	2	Ⓐ	Ⓐ2		2	Ⓐ2	Ⓐ	2	2		2	Ⓐ2	Ⓐ	2	2		2	Ⓐ2	⚒2	⚒2	
Helsingborg 735 d.	1610	1627	1633	1653	1710	1727	1733	1745	1753	1810	1827	1833	1910	1927	1933	2010	2027	2033	2110	2127	2133	2210	2227	2233	2327	2333	...
Landskrona **735** d.	1622	1645	|	1711	1722	1745	|	1758	1811	1822	1845	|	1922	1945	|	2022	2045	|	2122	2145	|	2222	2245	|	2345	|	...
Lund **735** d.	1639	1710	1722	1736	1739	1810	1822	1816	1836	1839	1910	1922	1939	2010	2022	2039	2110	2122	2139	2210	2222	2239	2310	2322	0010	0022	...
Malmö 703 735 a.	1652	1723	1739	1749	1752	1823	1839	1829	1849	1852	1923	1939	1952	2023	2039	2052	2123	2139	2152	2223	2239	2252	2323	2339	0023	0039	...
Lufthavn (Kastrup) **703** a.	1723	...	...	...	1823	...	...	...	...	1923	...	...	2023	...	...	2123	...	...	2223	...	...	2323	...	...	...	...	...
København H **703** a.	1737	...	...	...	1837	...	...	...	...	1937	...	...	2037	...	...	2137	...	...	2237	...	...	2337	...	...	...	...	...

H – ②③④⑤⑥† only.

HÄSSLEHOLM - HELSINGBORG — 738

Operator: *Skåne* Journey 55 – 65 minutes *77 km*

From **Hässleholm**: 0525Ⓐ, 0622⚒, 0722, 0822, and hourly until 2222, then 2322⚒.

From **Helsingborg**: 0536Ⓐ, 0636, 0736, and hourly until 2236, then 2336⚒.

VARBERG and GÖTEBORG - UDDEVALLA - STRÖMSTAD — 739

2nd class only except where shown

km		*V*									*V*		*V*			*V*				*X2000* **473**		*V*		*V*	
		Ⓐ	Ⓐ	Ⓐ	⚒	Ⓐ	Ⓒ	Ⓐ	Ⓒ	Ⓐ			Ⓐ	Ⓐ	Ⓐ	Ⓐ	†	Ⓐ	Ⓑ	**S**	⑥		Ⓑ	Ⓑ	
0	**Varberg 735** d.	...	...	0613	0705	...	0850**g**	0954	1050**e**	...	...	1250**g**	...	1347	1444	...	...	1544	1644	...	1659	...	1835	...	1952
84	Borås **746** a.	...	...	0727	0827	...	1000**g**	1105	1200**e**	...	...	1400**g**	...	1457	1558	...	...	1658	1758	...	1808	...	1951	...	2103
	Borås d.	...	0600	▬	0833	1003	1003	▬	1203	1203	...	1403	...	1503	1603	...	1603	1700	1802	...	1810	...	2000	...	...
127	Herrljunga **740** a.	...	0637	...	0910	1040	1040	...	1240	1240	...	1440	...	1540	1640	...	1640	1737	1839	...	1846	...	2037	...	...
	Herrljunga d.	...	0644	...	0918	▬	1118	...	▬	1318	...	1518	...	▬	...	...	1718	1742	...	1924	1919	...	2044	...	...
191	Vänersborg d.	...	0733	*V*	1004	...	1204	*V*	...	1404	...	1604	...	...	...	...	1808	1835	...	2004	2005	...	2130	...	...
195	Öxnered **750** d.	...	0739	⚒	1010	*V*	1210	⑤	*V*	1410	...	1610	...	*V*	...	...	1814	1841	...	|	2011	...	2136	...	...
	Göteborg ▲ d.	0640	|	0800	|	1030	|	1150	1305	|	1500	|	1610	1650	...	1730	|	|	...	|	|	1915	|	2105	...
217	Uddevalla C ▲ a.	0753	0755	0908	1026	1140	1226	1259	1414	1426	1610	1626	1721	1800	...	1839	1830	1857	...	2025	2027	2028	2152	2213	...
	Uddevalla C d.	...	...	0910	...	1143	...	...	1418**b**	...	1613	...	...	...	...	...	...	...	...	...	...	2035	...	...	...
309	**Strömstad** a.	...	...	1030	...	1307	...	...	1540**b**	...	1738	...	...	...	...	...	...	...	...	...	...	2155	...	...	...

km					*X2000* **472**	*V*	*V*	*V*		*V*		*V*	*V*		*V*			*V*		*V*		*V*		*V*	
		Ⓐ	⑥	Ⓐ	**T**	Ⓐ	Ⓐ	⚒	⚒	⑥	†	†	⚒	⚒		⑥	Ⓑ		Ⓑ		Ⓐ	Ⓑ			†
0	**Strömstad** d.	...	...	...	...	...	...	0635	...	...	...	...	...	...	1102	...	...	...	...	1435	...	1550	...	1802	...
92	Uddevalla C a.	...	...	...	...	...	...	0757	...	...	...	...	...	...	1222	...	...	...	...	1600	...	1712	...	1922	...
	Uddevalla C ▲ d.	...	...	0524	0540	0610	0645	0800	0803	0920	0933	0952	1038	1133	1225	1333	1333	1422	1533	1612	1633	1727	1737	1925	1933
180	**Göteborg** ▲ a.	...	...	|	|	0720	0800	0915	|	1030	|	1106	1148	|	1340	|	|	1535	|	1725	|	1844	|	2035	|
	Öxnered **750** d.	...	...	0540	|	...	▬	...	0819	...	0949	▬	▬	1149	▬	1349	1349	▬	1549	...	1649	▬	1753	▬	1949
	Vänersborg d.	...	...	0547	0559	...	...	...	0825	...	0955	...	...	1155	...	1355	1355	...	1555	...	1655	...	1759	...	1955
	Herrljunga **746** a.	...	...	0633	0643	...	...	...	0910	...	1040	⚒	†	1241	...	1444	1444	Ⓐ	1643	...	1741	Ⓐ	1845	Ⓐ	2042
	Herrljunga d.	0547	...	0647	...	...	...	...	0917	...	1117	1117	1317	1317	...	1512	1517	1617	1716	...	1748	1923	1923**c**	2050	2050
	Borås **746** a.	0626	...	0724	...	...	†	...	0954	...	1154	1154	1354	1354	Ⓐ	1548	1557	1657	1757	...	1829	1958	1958**c**	2125	2125
	Borås d.	0628	0727	0727	...	...	0900	...	1001	...	...	1200**a**	1400	1400**g**	1500	1550	1600	1700	1800	...	...	2000	...	...	2200
	Varberg 735 a.	0740	0837	0837	...	...	1010	...	1115	...	...	1310**a**	1510	1510**g**	1616	1659	1716	1811	1910	...	...	2115	...	...	2310

S – Ⓑ (not Dec. 22 - Jan. 5): (12) and ✕ Stockholm - Herrljunga - Uddevalla. 🅁 and special supplement payable.

T – Ⓐ (not Dec. 24 - Jan. 5): (12) and ✕ Uddevalla - Herrljunga - Stockholm. 🅁 and special supplement payable.

a – Ⓐ only.
b – Ⓑ only.
c – Ⓒ only.
e – † only.
g – ⑥ only.

▲ – Additional services available Göteborg - Uddevalla and v.v.

740 STOCKHOLM - HALLSBERG - GÖTEBORG

For Stockholm - Hallsberg - Karlstad / Oslo and v.v. services see Table 750

km		2 Ⓐ	2 Ⓐ	2 Ⓐ	2 Ⓐ	77 R ♦	117 Ⓐ	X2000 401 R✕ L	2 ⑥	X2000 421 R✕ Ⓐ	159 ⚒y	2 †	621 🍷 Ⓐz	X2000 423 R✕ Ⓐz	2 ⚒	X2000 415 R✕ †	X2000 425 R✕ ⚒	163 193		VEO 91 R ♦	X2000 427 R✕ ⚒	2 ⚒	X2000 429 R✕	167	2 ⚒	X2000 433 R✕
0	**Stockholm** C **730** d.	...	...	...	...	...	...	0600	...	0605	...	...	0630	0710	...	0810	0810	0706d	...	...	0915	...	1010	0906	...	1210
15	Flemingsberg ‡ d.	...	...	...	...	...	...	|	...	|	...	...	0641	0721	...	|	|	|	...	...	0926	...	|	|	...	|
36	Södertälje Syd ‡ d.	...	...	...	...	...	...	|	...	0623	...	...	0653	|	...	0828	0828	|	...	0817	0937	...	1028	|	...	1228
108	Flen **730** d.	...	...	...	...	...	...	|	...	|	...	...	0730	|	...	|	|	V	...	|	|	...	|	V	...	|
131	Katrineholm **730** d.	...	...	...	...	...	...	|	...	0706	...	...	0744	|	...	|	0906	|	...	|	|	...	1106	|	...	1306
197	**Hallsberg 755/6** a.	...	...	...	...	...	...	|	...	|	...	...	0818	0826	...	0926	|	|	...	|	|	...	|	|	...	|
	Örebro C **755/6** d.	...	...	...	...	0553c	0620	|	...	|	0710	...	...	|	...	|	|	0910	...	0951	|	...	|	1110	...	|
197	**Hallsberg** d.	...	...	...	...	0611s	0640	|	...	|	0733	...	...	0828	...	0928	|	0933	...	1011	|	...	|	1133	...	|
227	Laxå **736** d.	...	...	...	...	|	|	|	...	|	0748	...	...	|	...	|	|	0948	...	|	|	...	|	1148	...	|
272	Töreboda d.	...	...	...	...	|	|	|	...	|	0809	...	...	|	...	|	|	1009	...	|	|	...	|	1209	...	|
311	**Skövde** d.	0450	0600	0635	0653	0700s	0732	|	0732	0811	0832	0832	...	0914	...	1011	1011	1032	...	1117	1116	1132g	1211	1232	1332a	1413
341	Falköping d.	0508	0616	0651	0713	|	0748	|	0750	|	0850	0850	...	|	0950	|	|	1050	...	1139	|	1150	|	1250	1350	|
375	Herrljunga **736/9** d.	0528	0636	0708	0732	0738s	|	|	0808	0837	0908	0908	...	|	1008	|	|	1108	...	1200	|	1208	|	1308	1408	1439
	Borås a.	|	|	|	|	|	|	|	|	|	|	|	...	|	|	|	|	|	...	|	|	|	|	|	|	|
410	Alingsås a.	0549	0657	0729	0754	|	|	|	0829	|	0927	0928	...	|	1028	1046s	1046s	1127	...	1221s	|	1228	1246s	1327	1428	|
455	**Göteborg** a.	0617	0732	0802	0832	0837	0847	0852	0857	0917	0957	0957	...	1017	1057	1117	1117	1157	...	1252	1217	1257	1317	1357	1457	1517
	Oslo S **770** a.	...	...	...	...	...	...	...	...	...	...	...	...	...	...	...	...	...	...	...	...	...	...	...	...	...

	171	X2000 435 R✕ Ⓐ	2	X2000 437 R✕	175	X2000 439 R✕ Ⓑ	X2000 403 R✕ ⑤z	2	X2000 441 R✕ Ⓑx	X2000 411 R✕ M		179	Ⓐ	X2000 473 R✕ ♦	X2000 443 R✕ Ⓑ	X2000 405 R✕ Ⓑz	2 Ⓑ	Ⓐz	X2000 445 R✕	183	X2000 447 R✕ Ⓑz	2 ⑤⑥	X2000 449 R✕ Ⓑ	651 Ⓑ		VEO 7085 R ♦
Stockholm C **730** d.	1106	1315	...	1410	1306	1515	1530	...	1610	1610	...	1506	1625	1645	1710	1735	...	1800	1810	1706	1910	...	2010	2210	...	2308
Flemingsberg ‡ d.	|	1326	...	|	|	|	|	...	|	|	...	|	1636	|	|	|	...	1811	|	|	1921	...	|	2221	...	|
Södertälje Syd ‡ d.	|	|	...	1428	|	|	1548	...	1628	1628	...	|	1648	1705	1728	|	...	1823	1828	|	|	...	2028	2234	...	2333
Flen **730** d.	V	|	...	|	V	|	|	...	|	|	...	V	1726	|	|	|	...	1915	|	V	|	...	|	2315	...	|
Katrineholm **730** d.	|	|	...	1506	|	|	|	...	1706	1706	...	|	1740	|	|	|	...	1929	1906	|	2006	...	2106	2329	...	|
Hallsberg 755/6 a.	|	1431	...	|	|	1628	|	...	|	|	...	|	1817	1803	|	|	...	2004	|	|	|	...	2130	0003	...	0127s
Örebro C **755/6** d.	1310	|	...	|	1510	|	|	...	|	|	...	1710	...	|	|	|	...	...	|	1910	|	...	|	...	...	|
Hallsberg d.	1333	1433	...	|	1533	1630	|	...	|	|	...	1733	...	1805	|	|	...	...	|	1933	|	...	2132	...	...	|
Laxå **736** d.	1348	|	...	|	1548	|	|	...	|	|	...	1748	...	|	|	|	...	...	|	1948	|	...	|	...	...	|
Töreboda d.	1409	|	...	|	1609	|	|	...	|	|	...	1809	...	|	1853	|	...	...	|	2009	|	...	|	...	...	|
Skövde d.	1432	1516	1532c	1613	1632	1713	|	1732g	1811	1811	...	1832	...	1846	1910	|	...	...	2011	2032	2112	2137	2217	...	...	0238s
Falköping d.	1450	|	1550	|	1650	|	|	1750	|	|	...	1850	...	1901	|	|	1950	...	|	2050	|	2155	|	...	...	|
Herrljunga **736/9** d.	1508	|	1608	|	1708	1739	|	1808	|	1837	...	1908	...	1917	|	|	2008	...	2037	2108	|	2213	|	...	...	0352s
Borås a.	|	|	|	|	|	|	|	|	|	|	...	|	...	...	|	|	|	...	|	|	|	|	|	...	...	|
Alingsås a.	1527	|	1628	1648s	1727	|	|	1828	|	|	...	1927	...	...	1947s	|	2026	...	|	2127	2147s	2233	|	...	...	|
Göteborg a.	1557	1617	1657	1717	1757	1817	1822	1857	1917	1917	...	1957	...	...	2017	2022	2057	...	2117	2157	2217	2302	2317	...	...	0605
Oslo S **770** a.	...	...	...	...	...	...	...	...	...	...	...	...	...	...	...	...	...	...	...	...	...	...	...	...	...	...

	2 Ⓒ	618 Ⓐ	620 Ⓐ	X2000 420 R✕ Ⓐz	X2000 400 R✕ Ⓐz	X2000 472 R✕ ♦	164 ⚒	X2000 422 R✕ ⚒z	X2000 412 R✕ Ⓐw	624 ⑥	2 Ⓐ	X2000 424 R✕ Ⓐ	168		X2000 426 R✕ ⚒	X2000 416 R✕ †	2 ⚒	X2000 428 R✕ ⚒	172	X2000 430 R✕	2 Ⓐ	X2000 432 R✕ ⑤v	636 Ⓑz	636 †w	176	X2000 434 R✕
Oslo S **770** d.	...	...	...	...	...	...	...	...	...	...	...	...	...	...	...	...	...	...	...	...	...	...	...	...	...	...
Göteborg d.	0032	...	...	0512	0600	...	0602	0642	0642	...	0657	0742	0802	...	0842	0842	0902	0942	1002	1042	1102	1142	...	...	1202	1242
Alingsås d.	0059	...	...	0539u	|	...	0630	0707u	|	...	0730	0807u	0830	...	|	0907	0930	1007u	1030	1107u	1130	|	...	...	1230	|
Borås d.	|	...	...	|	|	...	|	|	|	...	|	|	|	...	|	|	|	|	|	|	|	|	...	...	|	|
Herrljunga **736/9** d.	0118	...	...	0553	|	0648	0653	|	0720	...	0750	|	0852	...	0920	|	0950	|	1052	|	1150	|	...	...	1252	1320
Falköping d.	0137	...	...	0609	|	0704	0711	|	|	...	0809	|	0911	...	|	|	1011	|	1111	|	1210	1231	...	...	1311	|
Skövde d.	0155	...	...	0627	|	0723	0729	0747	0747	...	...	0847	0929	...	0947	0947	1029a	1047	1129	1147	...	1249	...	...	1329	1347
Töreboda d.	...	...	...	|	|	0738	0747	|	|	...	...	|	0946	...	|	|	...	|	1146	|	...	|	...	...	1346	|
Laxå **736** d.	...	...	...	|	|	|	0809	|	|	...	...	|	1008	...	|	|	...	|	1208	|	...	|	...	...	1408	|
Hallsberg a.	...	...	...	0708	|	0808	0825	|	|	...	...	|	1025	...	|	|	...	|	1225	|	...	1333	...	...	1425	|
Örebro C **755/6** a.	...	...	...	|	|	|	0848	|	|	...	...	|	1048	...	|	|	...	|	1248	|	...	|	...	...	1448	|
Hallsberg 755/6 d.	...	0521	0623	0712	|	0810	|	|	|	0836	...	|	|	...	|	|	...	|	|	|	...	1335	1341	1341	|	|
Katrineholm **730** a.	...	0557	0658	0737	|	|	|	0851	0851	0911	...	|	|	...	1051	1051	...	|	|	1251	...	|	1416	1416	|	1451
Flen **730** a.	...	0611	0714	|	|	|	V	|	|	0924	...	|	V	...	|	|	...	|	V	|	...	|	1429	1429	V	|
Södertälje Syd ‡ a.	...	0649	0750	|	|	0909	|	0929	0929	1000	...	|	|	...	1129	1129	...	1224	|	1329	...	|	1505	1505	|	1529
Flemingsberg ‡ a.	...	0701	0801	0827	|	|	|	|	|	1011	...	1032	|	...	|	|	...	|	|	|	...	|	1516	1516	|	|
Stockholm C **730** a.	...	0715	0815	0840	0845	0930	1053	0950	0950	1025	...	1045	1253	...	1150	1150	...	1245	1453	1350	...	1450	1530	1530	1653	1550

	2 P	2 ⑤q	X2000 404 R✕ N	X2000 436 R✕ Ⓑ	180	X2000 438 R✕	2	X2000 440 R✕ Ⓑ	194 ⑤⑥†	184 G	X2000 406 R✕ L	X2000 442 R✕	2 Ⓐ	646 Ⓐz	VEO 92 R ♦	2 Ⓑ	X2000 444 R✕ Ⓑ	188	VEO 7080 R ♦	X2000 446 R✕	76 R ♦	150 Ⓑ	2	X2000 450 R✕ Ⓑz	2	2 j
Oslo S **770** d.	...	...	...	...	...	...	...	...	...	...	...	...	...	...	...	...	...	...	...	...	...	...	...	...	...	...
Göteborg d.	1302	1302	1312	1342	1402	1442	1502	1542	1602	1602	1612	1642	1627	...	1700	1707	1737	1802	1805	1842	1900	1907	2002	2042	2132	2302
Alingsås d.	1330	1330	|	1407u	1430	|	1530	1607u	1630	1630	|	|	1700	...	1733u	1737	1810u	1830	|	|	|	1934	2030	|	2200	2329
Borås d.	|	|	|	|	|	|	|	|	|	|	|	|	|	...	|	|	|	|	|	|	|	|	|	|	|	|
Herrljunga **736/9** d.	1350	1354	|	|	1452	|	1550	|	1652	1654	|	|	1732	...	1751	1758	|	1852	1900u	1920	1946u	1956	2050	|	2220	2349
Falköping d.	1409	1414	|	|	1511	|	1611	|	1711	1713	|	|	1754	...	1813	1818	|	1911	|	|	|	2017	2110	|	2243	0009
Skövde d.	...	...	1413	1447	1529	1543	1629g	1647	1729	1731	|	1748	1814	...	1831	...	1849	1929	1937u	1947	2017u	2039	2130	2145	2301	0029
Töreboda d.	...	...	|	|	1547	|	...	|	1747	1751	|	|	...	...	|	...	|	1946	|	|	|	2100j	2150b	|	...	...
Laxå **736** d.	...	...	|	|	1610	|	...	|	1809	1814	|	|	...	...	|	...	|	2008	|	|	|	2121j	...	|	...	...
Hallsberg a.	...	...	1454	|	1630	|	...	|	1825	1835	|	|	...	...	1925	...	1930	2025	|	|	2113u	2138j	...	2226	...	...
Örebro C **755/6** a.	...	...	|	|	1652	|	...	|	1848	1857	|	|	...	...	1945	...	|	2048	|	|	2132g	2200j	...	|	...	...
Hallsberg 755/6 d.	...	...	1456	|	|	|	...	|	|	|	|	|	...	1846	|	...	1932	|	2038u	|	...	...	...	2226	...	...
Katrineholm **730** d.	...	...	|	|	|	1646	...	|	|	|	|	1851	...	1921	|	...	|	|	|	2051	...	...	...	|	...	...
Flen **730** d.	...	...	|	|	V	|	...	|	V	V	|	|	...	1934	|	...	|	V	|	|	...	...	...	|	...	...
Södertälje Syd ‡ a.	...	...	|	1624	|	1724	...	|	|	|	|	1929	...	2010	2128	...	|	|	2234	2129	...	...	...	2326	...	...
Flemingsberg ‡ a.	...	...	|	|	|	|	...	1832	|	|	|	|	...	2021	...	...	2037	|	|	|	...	...	...	|	...	...
Stockholm C **730** a.	...	...	1615	1645	1853	1745	...	1845	2053	2108	1900	1950	...	2035	...	...	2050	2253	2258	2150	...	...	...	2346	...	...

♦ – **NOTES** (LISTED BY TRAIN NUMBER)

76 – Daily Dec. 9 - Apr. 27; Ⓑ Apr. 28 - June 14: 🛏 1, 2 cl., ▬ 2 cl. and [2] Göteborg - Storlien. Also conveys ✕ and [Bio].

77 – Daily Dec. 9 - Apr. 26; Ⓑ Apr. 27 - June 14: 🛏 1, 2 cl., ▬ 2 cl. and [2] Storlien - Stockholm - Göteborg. Also conveys ✕ and [Bio].

91 – 🛏 1, 2 cl., ▬ 2 cl., [2], ✕ and [Shop] Luleå - Göteborg.

92 – 🛏 1, 2 cl., ▬ 2 cl., [2], ✕ and [Shop] Göteborg - Luleå.

472 – Ⓐ (not Dec. 24 - Jan. 5): [12] and ✕ Uddevalla - Herrljunga - Stockholm.

473 – Ⓑ (not Dec. 22 - Jan. 5): [12] and ✕ Stockholm - Herrljunga - Uddevalla.

7080 – ③⑥ Dec. 29 - Jan. 5, Feb. 4 - Apr. 13: ▬ 2 cl., [2] and ✕ Göteborg - Stockholm - Storlien.

7085 – ④† Dec. 30 - Jan. 6, Feb. 4 - Apr. 13: ▬ 2 cl., [2] and ✕ Storlien - Stockholm - Göteborg.

G – ①②③④ only.
L – ①②③④ (not Dec. 24 - Jan. 5).
M – ⑥ (daily Dec. 22 - Jan. 5).
N – † Dec. 9-23; ⑤† Jan. 6 - June 14.
P – ⚒ Dec. 9 - Jan. 5; ①②③④⑥ Jan. 6 - June 14.
V – Via Västerås - see Table **756**.

a – Ⓐ only.
b – Ⓑ only.
c – Ⓒ only.
d – ⚒ only.
g – ⑥ only.
j – ①②③④† only.
q – Jan. 6 - June 14.

s – Stops to set down only.
u – Stops to pick up only.
v – Dec. 9 - 23.
w – Dec. 24 - Jan. 5.
x – Not Dec. 22 - Jan. 5.
y – Runs as train **157** on ⑥.
z – Not Dec. 24 - Jan. 5.

X2000 – High speed train. Special supplement payable.

‡ – Most trains on this table do not convey passengers for local journeys between Stockholm and Södertälje Syd or v.v. Local trains run every 30 minutes Stockholm Central - Södertälje Hamn - Södertälje Centrum and v.v. (journey 42 mins). 🚌 Södertälje Syd - Södertälje Centrum runs every 30 minutes.

[Bio] – Cinema / bistro car.
[Shop] – Bar / shop.

Operator: Skåne

KØBENHAVN - MALMÖ - KRISTIANSTAD - KARLSKRONA 745

For local services København - Kastrup ✈ - Malmö and v.v. see Table 703

km		Ⓐ	Ⓐ	⚒		Ⓐ	Ⓒ	Ⓐ		⚒	†	Ⓐ		⚒	†		Ⓐ				Ⓑ	⑥		Ⓑ	⑥
0	**København H 703/30** d.	...	...	0543	0643	0743	0743	0803	0843	0943	0943	1003	1043	1143	1143	...	1203	1243	1343	1443	1543	1543	1643	1743	1743
11	Kastrup ✈ 703/30 d.	...	...	0556	0656	0756	0756	0816	0856	0956	0956	1016	1056	1156	1156	...	1216	1256	1356	1456	1556	1556	1656	1756	1756
47	**Malmö 703** a.	...	...	0618	0718	0818	0818	0838	0918	1018	1018	1038	1118	1218	1218	...	1238	1318	1418	1518	1618	1618	1718	1818	1818
47	**Malmö 730/46** d.	...	0528	0628	0728	0828	0828	0848	0928	1028	1028	1048	1128	1228	1228	...	1248	1328	1428	1528	1628	1628	1728	1828	1828
63	Lund 730/46 d.	...	0542	0642	0742	0842	0842	0902	0942	1042	1042	1102	1142	1242	1242	...	1302	1342	1442	1542	1642	1642	1742	1842	1842
81	Eslöv 746 d.	...	0552	0652	0752	0852	0852	0912	0952	1052	1052	1112	1152	1252	1252	...	1312	1352	1452	1552	1652	1652	1752	1852	1852
130	Hässleholm 730/46 a.	...	0616	0716	0816	0916	0916	0936	1016	1116	1116	1136	1216	1316	1316	...	1336	1416	1516	1616	1716	1716	1816	1916	1916
130	Hässleholm d.	0516	0618	0718	0818	0918	0918	...	1018	1118	1118	...	1218	1318	1318	...	...	1418	1518	1618	1718	1718	1818	1918	1918
160	**Kristianstad** a.	0535	0637	0737	0837	0937	0937	...	1037	1137	1137	...	1237	1337	1337	...	...	1437	1537	1637	1737	1737	1837	1937	1937
160	**Kristianstad** d.	0546	0646	0746	0846	0946	...	...	1046	1146	...	...	1246	1346	...	...	...	1446	1546	1646	1746	...	1846	1946	...
191	Sölvesborg d.	0607	0707	0807	0907	1007	...	...	1107	1207	...	...	1307	1407	...	...	...	1507	1607	1707	1807	...	1907	2007	...
222	Karlshamn d.	0632	0732	0832	0932	1032	...	...	1132	1232	...	...	1332	1432	...	...	...	1532	1632	1732	1832	...	1932	2032	...
260	Ronneby d.	0700	0800	0900	1000	1100	...	...	1200	1300	...	...	1400	1500	...	...	...	1600	1700	1800	1900	...	2000	2100	...
290	**Karlskrona** a.	0722	0822	0922	1022	1122	...	...	1222	1322	...	...	1422	1522	...	...	...	1622	1722	1822	1922	...	2022	2122	...

	Ⓐ		Ⓑ	⑥	Ⓐ			⚒	Ⓒ	
København H 703/30 d.	1803	1843	1943	1943	2003	2043	2143	2243	0003	...
Kastrup ✈ 703/30 d.	1816	1856	1956	1956	2016	2056	2156	2256	0016	...
Malmö 703 a.	1838	1918	2018	2018	2038	2118	2218	2318	0038	...
Malmö 730/46 d.	1848	1928	2028	2028	2048	2128	2228	2328	0053	...
Lund 730/46 d.	1902	1942	2042	2042	2102	2142	2242	2342	0113	...
Eslöv 746 d.	1912	1952	2052	2052	2112	2152	2252	2352	0126	...
Hässleholm 730/46 a.	1936	2016	2116	2116	2136	2216	2316	0015	0155	...
Hässleholm d.	...	2018	2118	2118	...	2218	2318	0017	0157	...
Kristianstad a.	...	2037	2137	2137	...	2237	2337	0036	0216	...
Kristianstad d.	...	2046	2146	...	...	2246	...	...	...	...
Sölvesborg d.	...	2107	2207	...	...	2307	...	...	...	...
Karlshamn d.	...	2132	2232	...	...	2332	...	...	...	...
Ronneby d.	...	2200	2300	...	...	0000	...	...	...	...
Karlskrona a.	...	2222	2322	...	...	0022	...	...	...	...

	Ⓐ	Ⓐ	Ⓒ	⚒	†	Ⓐ	Ⓐ	⑥	y	w
Karlskrona d.	...	0438	...	0538	...	...	0638	...	0736	0738
Ronneby d.	...	0502	...	0602	...	...	0702	...	0802	0802
Karlshamn d.	...	0530	...	0630	...	...	0730	...	0830	0830
Sölvesborg d.	...	0552	...	0652	...	...	0751	...	0852	0852
Kristianstad a.	...	0614	...	0714	...	...	0814	...	0914	0914
Kristianstad d.	0520	0623	0623	0723	0723	...	0823	0823	0923	▬
Hässleholm a.	0541	0640	0640	0740	0740	...	0840	0840	0940	Ⓐ
Hässleholm 730/46 d.	0542	0642	0642	0742	0742	0824	0842	0842	0942	1024
Eslöv 746 d.	0607	0707	0707	0807	0807	0847	0907	0907	1007	1047
Lund 730/46 d.	0617	0717	0717	0817	0817	0857	0917	0917	1017	1059
Malmö 730/46 a.	0632	0732	0732	0832	0832	0912	0932	0932	1032	1112
Malmö 703 d.	0642	0742	0742	0842	0842	0922	0942	0942	1042	1122
Kastrup ✈ 703/30 d.	0703	0803	0803	0903	0903	0943	1003	1003	1103	1143
København H 703/30 a.	0717	0817	0817	0917	0917	0957	1017	1017	1117	1157

	w	Ⓐ	Ⓒ		Ⓐ	⚒	†		Ⓐ	⚒	†				Ⓑ	⑥		Ⓐ	Ⓑ	⑥		Ⓐ	Ⓑ	⑥	
Karlskrona d.	...	0838	...	0938	...	1038	...	1138	...	1238	...	1338	1438	1538	1638	...	1738	...	1838	...	1938	...	2038	...	2138
Ronneby d.	...	0902	...	1002	...	1102	...	1202	...	1302	...	1402	1502	1602	1702	...	1802	...	1902	...	2002	...	2102	...	2202
Karlshamn d.	...	0930	...	1030	...	1130	...	1230	...	1330	...	1430	1530	1630	1730	...	1830	...	1930	...	2030	...	2130	...	2230
Sölvesborg d.	...	0952	...	1052	...	1152	...	1252	...	1352	...	1452	1552	1652	1752	...	1852	...	1952	...	2052	...	2152	...	2252
Kristianstad a.	...	1014	...	1114	...	1214	...	1314	...	1414	...	1514	1614	1714	1814	...	1914	...	2014	...	2114	...	2214	...	2314
Kristianstad d.	0923	1023	1023	1123	...	1223	1223	1323	...	1423	1423	1523	1623	1723	1823	1823	1923	...	2023	2023	2123	...	2223	2223	2323
Hässleholm a.	0940	1040	1040	1140	...	1240	1240	1340	...	1440	1440	1540	1640	1740	1840	1840	1940	...	2040	2040	2140	...	2240	2240	2341
Hässleholm 730/46 d.	0942	1042	1042	1142	1224	1242	1242	1342	1424	1442	1442	1542	1642	1742	1842	1842	1942	2024	2042	2042	2142	2224	2242	2242	2342
Eslöv 746 d.	1007	1107	1107	1207	1247	1307	1307	1407	1447	1507	1507	1607	1707	1807	1907	1907	2007	2047	2107	2107	2207	2247	2307	2307	0005
Lund 730/46 d.	1017	1117	1117	1217	1259	1317	1317	1417	1459	1517	1517	1617	1717	1817	1917	1917	2017	2059	2117	2117	2217	2259	2317	2317	0015
Malmö 730/46 a.	1032	1132	1132	1232	1312	1332	1332	1432	1512	1532	1532	1632	1732	1832	1932	1932	2032	2112	2132	2132	2232	2312	2332	2332	0030
Malmö 703 d.	1042	1142	1142	1242	1322	1342	1342	1442	1522	1542	1542	1642	1742	1842	1942	1942	2042	2122	2142	2142	2242	2322	*0022*	*0022*	*0122*
Kastrup ✈ 703/30 a.	1103	1203	1203	1303	1343	1403	1403	1503	1543	1603	1603	1703	1803	1903	2003	2003	2103	2143	2203	2203	2303	2343	*0043*	*0043*	*0143*
København H 703/30 a.	1117	1217	1217	1317	1357	1417	1417	1517	1557	1617	1617	1717	1817	1917	2017	2017	2117	2157	2217	2217	2317	2357	*0057*	*0057*	*0157*

w – Dec. 9 - Jan. 5. y – Jan. 6 - June 14.

MALMÖ and GÖTEBORG - VÄXJÖ - KARLSKRONA and KALMAR 746

km		Ⓐ	Ⓐ	Ⓐ	⚒	Ⓐ		Ⓐ	Ⓒ	Ⓒ	Ⓐ	Ⓐ			Ⓐ	Ⓐ			Ⓐ	H	⑤	Ⓑ	Ⓑ			†
	København 730/45 d.	...	...	0603	0703	...	0903	1103	...	1103	...	...	...	1303	1403	...	...	1503	1603	...	...	1703	...	1903	2103	...
0	**Malmö 730/45** d.	...	0548	0648	0748	...	0948	1148	...	1148	...	...	...	1348	1448	...	...	1548	1648	...	...	1748	...	1948	2148	...
16	Lund 730/45 d.	...	0602	0702	0802	...	1002	1202	...	1202	...	...	...	1402	1502	...	...	1602	1702	...	...	1802	...	2002	2202	...
33	Eslöv 745 d.	...	0612	0712	0812	...	1012	1212	...	1212	...	...	...	1412	1512	...	...	1612	1712	...	...	1812	...	2012	2212	...
83	Hässleholm 730/45 d.	...	0639	0739	0839	...	1039	1239	...	1239	...	...	...	1439	1539	...	...	1639	1739	...	...	1839	...	2039	2239	...
134	Älmhult d.	...	0702	0802	0902	...	1102	1302	...	1302	...	...	...	1502	1602	...	...	1702	1802	...	...	1902	...	2102	2302	...
	Göteborg ▲ d.	...	|	|	|	0635	|	|	1050	|	1050	...	...	|	|	...	1450	|	|	1620	1620	|	1805	|	|	2120
	Borås ▲ d.	...	|	|	|	0745	|	|	1141	|	1141	...	...	|	|	...	1544	|	|	1728	1728	|	1909	|	|	2228
	Limmared d.	...	|	|	|	0814	|	|	1214	|	1214	...	...	|	|	...	1612	|	|	1757	1757	|	1937	|	|	2256
	Värnamo d.	...	|	|	|	0856	|	|	1254	|	1254	...	...	|	|	...	1653	|	|	1839	1839	|	2019	|	|	2338
181	Alvesta 730 a.	...	0721	0821	0921	0924	1121	1321	1323	1321	1323	...	...	1521	1621	...	1719	1721	1821	1904	1904	1921	2044	2123	2321	0003
181	Alvesta ▲ d.	0605	0722	0834	0934	0928	1134	1322	1325	1334	1334	...	...	1534	1626	1652	1721	1734	1826	1908	1908	1934	2046	2136	2322	0004
198	**Växjö** ▲ d.	0618	0733	0845	0946	0939	1144	1332	1336	1344	1344	...	...	1544	1647	1708	1733	1744	1837	1920	1932	1944	2058	2147	2333	0015
255	Emmaboda a.	0654	0806	...	1020	...	1220	1405	...	1420	1420	...	...	1620	...	1740	1807	1820	...	...	2005	2020	2130	2220	...	...
255	Emmaboda ● d.	0703	0807	...	1022	...	1222	1407	...	1422	1422	1423	...	1622	...	1742	1825	1822	...	...	2007	2022	2132	2222	...	...
	Karlskrona ● a.	|	|	...	|	...	|	|	...	|	1506	|	...	|	...	|	1909	|	...	...	|	|	|	|	...	...
283	Nybro d.	0724	0823	...	1037	...	1237	1422	...	1437	...	1438	...	1637	...	1757	...	1837	...	...	2022	2037	2147	2237	...	...
312	**Kalmar** a.	0740	0839	...	1053	...	1253	1438	...	1453	...	1454	...	1653	...	1813	...	1853	...	...	2038	2053	2203	2253	...	...

km		Ⓐ	Ⓐ	Ⓐ	Ⓐ	Ⓐ	⑥	⚒	†	⑥	Ⓐ					Ⓒ	Ⓐ	Ⓐ	Ⓐ	Ⓒ	G	⑤†	Ⓐ		Ⓑ	Ⓑ
	Kalmar d.	...	...	...	0535	0550	...	0708	...	0725	0803	0908	...	1108	1301	...	...	...	1448	1508	1549	1549	...	1708	...	1906
	Nybro d.	...	...	...	0551	0606	...	0724	...	0741	0822	0924	...	1124	1316	...	...	...	1507	1524	1605	1605	...	1724	...	1924
0	**Karlskrona** ● d.	...	...	...	|	|	...	|	...	|	|	|	0850	|	|	...	...	...	|	|	|	|	...	|	1733	|
57	Emmaboda ● a.	...	...	...	0605	0620	...	0738	...	0755	0836	0938	0935	1138	1333	...	...	...	1522	1538	1619	1619	...	1738	1817	1938
——	Emmaboda d.	...	...	...	0615	0627	...	0740	...	0756	0837	0940	0952	1140	1340	...	...	...	1540	1540	1621	1921	...	1740	1820	1940
	Växjö ▲ d.	0519	0537	0606	0649	0658	0720	0812	0812	0826	0909	1012	1025	1212	1412	1427	1427	1514	1612	1612	1653	1653	1721	1812	1853	2012
	Alvesta ▲ a.	0533	0548	0617	0702	0710	0731	0825	0825	0839	0922	1025	1038	1225	1425	1438	1438	1525	1625	1625	1706	1706	1732	1825	1906	2025
0	Alvesta 730 d.	0535	0550	0633	0704	0712	0733	0833	0833	0842	...	1033	1040	1233	1433	1440	1440	1533	1633	1633	...	1730	1733	1833	1908	2041
49	Värnamo d.	|	0617	|	0732	|	|	|	|	0909	...	|	1108	|	|	1507	1507	|	|	|	...	1758	|	|	1935	|
110	Limmared d.	|	0656	|	0815	|	|	|	|	0950	...	|	1150	|	|	1548	1548	|	|	|	...	1840	|	|	2021	|
149	Borås ▲ a.	|	0724	|	0843	|	|	|	|	1018	...	|	1219	|	|	1619	1619	|	|	|	...	1908	|	|	2049	|
222	**Göteborg** ▲ a.	|	0830	|	0937	|	|	|	|	1135	...	|	1320	|	|	1720	1735	|	|	|	...	2013	|	|	2145	|
	Älmhult d.	0555	...	0653	...	0732	0753	0853	0853	...	...	1053	...	1253	1453	...	...	1553	1653	1653	...	...	1753	1853	...	2100
	Hässleholm 730/45 a.	0618	...	0716	...	0755	0816	0916	0916	...	...	1116	...	1316	1516	...	...	1616	1716	1716	...	...	1816	1916	...	2122
	Eslöv 745 a.	0646	...	0746	...	0820	0846	0946	0946	...	...	1146	...	1346	1546	...	...	1646	1747	1747	...	...	1846	1946	...	2147
	Lund 730/45 a.	0657	...	0757	...	0831	0857	0957	0957	...	...	1157	...	1357	1557	...	...	1657	1757	1757	...	...	1857	1957	...	2158
	Malmö 730/45 a.	0712	...	0812	...	0846	0912	1012	1012	...	...	1212	...	1412	1612	...	...	1712	1812	1812	...	...	1912	2012	...	2213
	København 730/45 a.	0757	...	0857	...	0937	0957	1057	1057	...	...	1257	...	1457	1657	...	...	1757	1857	1857	...	...	1957	2057	...	2317

● – CONNECTING SERVICES **Emmaboda - Karlskrona and v.v.:**

	Ⓐ	🚌 Ⓐ	⑥	🚌 Ⓐ	⚒	🚌 ⚒	Ⓒ	🚌 Ⓑ	⑥	🚌 Ⓐ	🚌 Ⓑ	Ⓑ	🚌 Ⓐ
Emmaboda d.	0706	0741	0743	0840	1025	1229	1425	1629	1746	1747	2029	2135	2227
Karlskrona a.	0753	0836	0825	0935	1109	1324	1509	1724	1829	1842	2124	2217	2322

	Ⓐ	🚌 Ⓐ	⑥	🚌 Ⓐ	🚌 ⚒		🚌 Ⓑ	🚌 Ⓐ	🚌 Ⓑ	⑥	🚌 Ⓑ	Ⓑ	🚌 Ⓐ
Karlskrona a.	0528	0635	0650	0732	1035	1250	1435	1516	1635	1646	1835	1931	2117
Emmaboda d.	0611	0730	0735	0827	1130	1335	1530	1611	1730	1730	1930	2014	2212

G – ①②③④ only.
H – ①②③④† only.

▲ – Additional trains run Göteborg - Borås and v.v., and Alvesta - Växjö and v.v.

747 STOCKHOLM - STOCKHOLM ARLANDA ✈

Arlanda Express. Operator: A-Train AB (*AEX*)

Journey time: 20 minutes. All services stop at Arlanda Södra (17 minutes from Stockholm, 2 minutes from Arlanda Norra). Södra serves terminals 2, 3 and 4; Norra serves terminal 5.

From **Stockholm Central:** 0435, 0505, 0520, 0535, 0550, 0605, 0620, 0635, 0650 and at the same minutes past each hour until 2205, 2220, 2235, 2305, 2335, 0005, 0035.

From **Arlanda Norra:** 0505, 0535, 0550, 0605, 0620, 0635, 0650 and at the same minutes past each hour until 2205, 2220, 2235, 2250, 2305, 2335, 0005, 0035, 0105.

Minor alterations to schedules are possible at peak times

750 STOCKHOLM - HALLSBERG - KARLSTAD - OSLO

km		VTAB	VTAB	617	X2000 451	VTAB	625	VTAB	629	627	VTAB	VTAB	VTAB	633		X2000 455	VTAB	VTAB	637	VTAB	639	X2000 459	VTAB	647	VTAB	7
		2 Ⓐ	2 Ⓐ	Ⓐ	[R] 🍴 Ⓐ	2 Ⓐ	🍴 ⚒	2 Ⓐ	🍷 Ⓑ	⑥	2 Ⓒ	2 Ⓐ	2 Ⓐ	🍷 Ⓐ		[R] 🍴 Ⓑ	2 Ⓐ	2 Ⓐ		2 ⑥	Ⓑ	[R] 🍴 Ⓑ	2 †	🍷	2 Ⓑ	[R] ♦
0	**Stockholm** C **730/40** d.	...	...	...	0615	...	0830	...	1025	1025	...	...	...	1225	...	1415	...	...	1425	...	1525	1715	...	1915	...	2210
15	Flemingsberg **730/40**. d.	...	...	...	|	...	0841	...	1036	1036	...	...	...	1236	...	|	...	...	1436	...	1537	|	...	1926	...	2221u
36	Södertälje Syd **730/40**. d.	...	...	...	0633u	...	0853	...	1048	1048	...	...	...	1248	...	1433u	...	...	1448	...	1553	1733u	...	1938	...	2234u
108	Flen **730/40** d.	...	...	...	|	...	0930	...	1125	1128	...	...	...	1325	...	|	...	...	1525	...	1630	|	...	2014	...	2315u
131	Katrineholm **730/40** d.	...	...	...	0712	...	0944	...	1139	1143	...	...	...	1339	...	1511	...	...	1539	...	1644	1811	...	2028	...	2329u
197	**Hallsberg 740** a.	...	...	...	0736	...	1018	...	1213	1217	...	...	...	1413	...	1535	...	...	1613	...	1718	1835	...	2102	...	|
197	**Hallsberg** d.	...	...	0658	0738	...	1021	...	1216	1220	...	...	...	1416	...	1537	...	...	1616	...	1722	1837	...	2105	...	0055u
263	Degerfors d.	...	...	0734	0804	...	1051	...	1246	1249	...	...	...	1448	...	1605	...	...	1645	...	1802	1906	...	2135	...	|
289	Kristinehamn d.	...	...	0749	0822	...	1109	...	1304	1311	...	...	1450	1503	...	1623	...	1629	1713	...	1817	1920	...	2151	...	|
329	**Karlstad 751** a.	...	...	0820	0843k	...	1131	...	1329	1332	...	...	1515	1526	...	1641	...	1706	1740	...	1840	1941	...	2216	...	0239
329	**Karlstad** d.	0543	0641	0904	...	0934	1135	1246	...	...	1345	1427	1533	1559	...	...	1650	1712	1804b	1750	...	1945	1957	...	2220	0247
349	Kil d.	0556	0655	0917	...	0948	1149	1300	...	...	1359	1441	1547	1612	...	...	1704	1729	1818b	1804	...	2000	2011	...	2234	|
397	Arvika d.	0646	0746	...	...	1024	1217	1336	...	...	1435	1533	1624	...	...	...	1743	1807	1845b	1841	...	2026	2048	...	2311	|
432	Charlottenberg 🏛 a.	0708	0812	...	...	1046	1237	1400	...	...	1459	1559	1647	...	...	...	1806	1833	1905b	1907	...	...	2114	...	2337	|
474	Kongsvinger a.	...	...	...	...	1114	1307	...	...	...	...	...	1714	...	...	...	...	...	1934b	...	...	...	...	...	...	|
574	**Oslo** Sentral a.	...	...	...	...	1230	1436	...	...	...	...	...	1831	...	...	...	...	...	2103b	...	...	...	...	...	...	0600

	622	X2000 452	X2000 454	VTAB	VTAB	626	VTAB	VTAB	VTAB	630	VTAB	634	X2000 456	638	VTAB	642	VTAB	644	VTAB	X2000 458	VTAB	648	650	X2000 450	VTAB	VTAB	8
	Ⓐ	[R] 🍴 Ⓐ	[R] 🍴 ⑥	2 Ⓐ	2 Ⓐ	🍷 Ⓐ	2	2 ⑥	2 †		2 ⑥	🍴 ⑥	[R] 🍴 Ⓐ	🍷 Ⓑ	2 Ⓐ	Ⓑ	2 ⚒	🍷 ⑥	2 †	[R] 🍴 Ⓑ	2 Ⓐ	Ⓑ	Ⓑ	[R] 🍴 Ⓑ z	2 Ⓐ	2 Ⓐ	[R] ♦
Oslo Sentral d.	...	...	...	...	...	...	...	...	...	0727a	...	0928	...	...	...	...	1329a	...	...	...	...	1548	...	...	...	1929	2248
Kongsvinger d.	...	...	...	...	...	...	...	...	...	0849a	...	1047	...	...	...	...	1439a	...	...	...	...	1717	...	...	...	2052	|
Charlottenberg 🏛 d.	...	...	...	0620	0650	...	0720	0814	0834	0917a	1000	1115	...	...	1407	...	1510	...	1550	...	1625	1745	...	...	2022	2127	|
Arvika d.	...	0553	0631	0648	0715	...	0756	0839	0903	0940a	1028	1136	...	...	1432	...	1536	...	1617	...	1653	1807	...	...	2048	2155	|
Kil d.	...	0620	0656	0725	|	...	0837	0917	0939	1009a	1105	1210	...	1341a	1509	...	1610	...	1652	...	1730	1838	...	...	2121	2233	|
Karlstad 751 a.	...	0632	0712	0738	0754	...	0850	0930	0952	1022a	1118	1224	...	1400a	1522	...	1625	...	1705	...	1743	1853	...	...	2134	2246	0154
Karlstad d.	0604	0638	0715	0742	...	0820	...	...	...	1025	...	1226	1315	1420	...	1623	...	1632	...	1715	...	1858	2012	...	...	...	0304
Kristinehamn d.	0627	0657	0734	0809	...	0851	...	...	...	1049	...	1251	1334	1444	...	1654	...	1654	...	1735	...	1921	2034	...	...	...	|
Degerfors d.	0642	0710	0747	...	...	0906	...	...	...	1110	...	1308	1347	1505	...	1708	...	1708	...	1747	...	1936	2052	...	...	...	|
Hallsberg a.	0715	|	0815	...	...	0938	...	...	...	1140	...	1339	1416	1538	...	1741	...	1741	...	1817	...	2007	2125	...	...	...	0422s
Hallsberg 740 d.	0717	|	0817	...	...	0941	...	...	...	1142	...	1341	1418	1541	...	1745	...	1745	...	1819	...	2010	...	2226	...	...	|
Katrineholm **730/40** a.	0750	|	0841	...	...	1014	...	...	...	1215	...	1414	1442	1614	...	1821	...	1818	...	1843	...	2043	...	|	...	...	0555s
Flen **730/40** a.	0814	|	|	...	...	1028	...	...	...	1229	...	1428	|	1628	...	1835	...	1832	...	|	...	2059	...	|	...	...	0610s
Södertälje Syd **730/40** a.	0850	|	0919s	...	...	1104	...	...	...	1305	...	1509	1524s	1704	...	1911	...	1909	...	1924s	...	2141	...	2326s	...	...	0648s
Flemingsberg **730/40** a.	0902	|	|	...	...	1116	...	...	...	1317	...	1521	|	1716	...	1923	...	1921	...	|	...	2153	...	|	...	...	|
Stockholm C **730/40** a.	0915	0850	0940	...	...	1130	...	...	...	1330	...	1535	1545	1730	...	1935	...	1935	...	1945	...	2210	...	2346	...	...	0715

♦ – **NOTES** (LISTED BY TRAIN NUMBER)

7 – ④† Dec. 9-20, Jan. 3 - June 14: 🛏 1, 2 cl., 🛏 2 cl. and 🚃 Stockholm - Oslo.
8 – ④† Dec. 9-20, Jan. 3 - June 14: 🛏 1, 2 cl., 🛏 2 cl. and 🚃 Oslo - Stockholm.

a – Ⓐ only.
b – Ⓑ only.
k – Connects into train in previous column.
s – Stops to set down only.
u – Stops to pick up only.
z – Not Dec. 24 - Jan. 5.

X2000 – High speed train. Special supplement payable.

751 KARLSTAD - GÖTEBORG

km		Ⓐ	Ⓐ	⑥	Ⓐ	Ⓒ	⑥	†	Ⓐ	⚒	†	†	Ⓐ
0	**Karlstad 750** d.	...	0603	0646	0904	0904	1231	1310	1348	1559	1559	1753	1858
19	Kil d.	...	0621	0701	0919	0919	1246	1325	1402	1615	1615	1815	1912
70	Säffle d.	0520	0654	0732	0956	0951	1318	1357	1434	1646	1654	1846	1944
87	Åmål d.	0532	0707	0744	1007	1002	1329	1408	1445	1657	1706	1858	1955
128	Mellerud d.	0556	0733	0810	1033	1029	1355	1433	1510	1723	1731	1924	2021
169	Öxnered a.	0621	0800	0841	1056	1053	1420	1457	1533	1748	1754	1955	2044
179	Trollhättan a.	*0633*	0807	0853	1103	1103	1427	1505	1540	1802	1802	2003	2051
251	**Göteborg** a.	*0729*	0854	0949	1152	1152	1515	1551	1631	1853	1853	2050	2139

	Ⓐ	⑥	Ⓒ	Ⓐ	⑥	†	Ⓐ	⚒	†	Ⓑ	Ⓑ
Göteborg d.	0707	0807	1007	1107	1306	1407	1507	1707	1707	1807	1912
Trollhättan d.	0756	0856	1056	1156	1355	1453	1555	1751	1757	1857	2001
Öxnered d.	0805	0904	1104	1204	1403	1502	1604	1800	1804	1904	2008
Mellerud d.	0827	0926	1127	1226	1426	1524	1626	1821	1828	*1938*j	2033
Åmål d.	0852	0953	1152	1251	1451	1549	1651	1845	1854	*2010*j	2103
Säffle d.	0905	1013	1204	1304	1504	1601	1708	1858	1908	*2019*j	2117
Kil a.	0937	1046	1237	1339	1536	1635	1745	1940	1941	...	2150
Karlstad 750 a.	0959	1100	1258	1400	1551	1650	1759	1957	1957	...	2204

j – ①②③④† only.

752 SECONDARY LINES in South - East Sweden

2nd class only except where shown

km		Ⓐ‡	⑥‡	Ⓐ	⑥‡	†‡		Ⓐ‡	Ⓒ‡	Ⓐ	†‡		Ⓐ‡	
0	Västervik d.	0555	0710	0746	1010	1110	...	1236	1509	1612	1748	...	1939	...
116	Linköping a.	0740	0850	0926	1150	1250	...	1416	1649	1753	1933	...	2119	...

	Ⓐ	⑥‡	†‡	Ⓐ‡	⑥‡	†‡	Ⓐ		Ⓐ‡	⑥‡	†‡	Ⓐ‡
Linköping d.	0558	0813	1009	1012	1305	1408	1418	...	1717	1718	1821	2010
Västervik a.	0741	0955	1149	1152	1445	1548	1600	...	1902	1858	2002	2152

km		Ⓐ‡	Ⓐ‡	⑥‡		Ⓐ‡	†‡	⑥‡		†‡	⚒‡		‡	Ⓑ‡
0	Linköping d.	...	0608	...	...	0938	1005	1028	...	1300	1312	...	1712	1915
123	Hultsfred d.	0625	0805	0815	...	1113	1141	1204	...	1435	1450	...	1849	2052
159	Berga a.	0648	0828	0838	...	1136	1204	1227	...	1458	1513	...	1912	2115
159	Berga d.	0655	0833	0843	...	1141	1209	1232	...	1503	1521	...	1917	2120
235	Kalmar **746** a.	0755	0932	0942	...	1240	1308	1331	...	1602	1620	...	2016	2219

	Ⓐ‡	Ⓐ‡	⑥‡	†‡	⑥‡	Ⓐ‡	Ⓐ‡	†‡	⚒‡	‡	⑤‡	H‡
Kalmar **746** d.	...	0553	0741	0942	1036	1042	1247	1355	1423	1647	2020	2020
Berga a.	...	0651	0839	1040	1134	1140	1345	1453	1521	1745	2118	2118
Berga d.	...	0656	0844	1045	1139	1145	1350	1458	1526	1750	2123	2123
Hultsfred d.	0546	0720	0908	1109	1208	1209	1414	1522	1551	1814	2147	2146
Linköping a.	0723	0854	1045	1245	1348	1350	1550	1657	1735	1952	2321	...

km	*KLT* 🚌 service*	Ⓐ	Ⓐ	⑥	†	⑥	Ⓐ	Ⓒ	Ⓐ	†	⚒			Ⓑ
0	Berga d.	0655	0833	0845	1045	1138	1144	1230	1350	1500	1525	1748	1915	2120
29	Oskarshamn a.	0725	0903	0915	1115	1208	1214	1302	1420	1530	1555	1818	1945	2150

KLT 🚌 service*	Ⓐ	⑥	†		Ⓐ	†	⑥	Ⓐ		†	Ⓐ	Ⓐ
Oskarshamn d.	0620	0808	1010	...	1315	1425	1448	1607	...	1715	1840	2045
Berga a.	0650	0838	1040	...	1345	1455	1518	1636	...	1745	1910	2115

km	Operator: *MER*		Ⓐ				Ⓒ		Ⓐ				⑤†	
0	Nässjö d.	...	0703	...	0919	...	1316	...	1525	...	1721	...	1916	...
83	Hultsfred a.	...	0818	...	1037	...	1431	...	1639	...	1839	...	2030	...

Operator: *MER*		Ⓐ								⑤†		
Hultsfred d.	...	0628	...	0929	...	1327	...	1729	...	1923	...	...
Nässjö a.	...	0743	...	1043	...	1440	...	1845	...	2040	...	...

H – ①②③④† only.

‡ – Also conveys 1st class.

* – KLT 🚌 service is subject to confirmation.

754 NORRKÖPING - VÄSTERÅS - UPPSALA

2nd class only

km		Ⓐz	Ⓐ	Ⓐz	⚒	⚒			Ⓐz	Ⓑ	Ⓐz		Ⓑ
0	**Norrköping 730** d.	...	0633	0747	0832	1033	1233	1433	1533	1632	1736	1833	2033
48	Katrineholm **730** d.	...	0703	0813	0900	1100	1300	1500	1600	1700	1801	1900	2100
71	Flen **730** d.	...	0716	0826	0913	1113	1313	1513	1613	1713	1816	1913	2113
112	Eskilstuna d.	0552	0752	0908	0952	1152	1352	1552	1652	1752	1852	1952	2152
160	**Västerås** a.	0625	0825	0940	1025	1225	1425	1625	1725	1825	1925	2025	2225
160	**Västerås** d.	0627	0827	...	1027	1227	1427	1627b	1727	1827	...	2027y	...
199	Sala **761** a.	0653	0853	...	1053	1253	1453	1653b	1753	1853	...	2053y	...
	Uppsala **760/1** a.	...	...	...	...	...	...	...	1845	...	...	...	...

	Ⓐ	⚒			⚒	Ⓐz	Ⓑ		Ⓑ	Ⓐz	Ⓐ
Uppsala **760/1** d.	...	...	...	...	...	...	...	...	...	...	2113
Sala **761** d.	...	0707a	0907d	1107	1307	...	1507	1707b	1907	2107	2207
Västerås a.	...	0733a	0933d	1133	1333	...	1533	1733b	1933	2133	2233
Västerås d.	0535	0735	0935	1135	1335	1435	1535	1735	1935	2135	...
Eskilstuna d.	0609	0809	1009	1209	1409	1509	1609	1809	2009	2207	...
Flen **730** d.	0643	0844	1044	1244	1444	1544	1644	1844	2044	...	...
Katrineholm **730**. d.	0658	0900	1100	1300	1500	1557	1700	1900	2100	...	...
Norrköping 730 a.	0723	0925	1125	1325	1525	1622	1725	1925	2125	...	...

a – Ⓐ only.
b – Ⓑ only.
d – ⚒ only.
y – Ⓑ (not Ⓐ Dec. 24 - Jan. 5).
z – Not Dec. 24 - Jan. 5.

MJÖLBY - HALLSBERG - ÖREBRO - GÄVLE 755

Operator: *ST*

km		Ⓐ	Ⓐ	Ⓐ	Ⓐ	⚒	Ⓐ	⚒		⚒	†		⑥	Ⓐ	Ⓐ				Ⓐ	Ⓑ	Ⓑ	⑥	Ⓑ	Ⓑ	Ⓑ
0	**Mjölby 730** d.	...	...	...	...	...	0600	...	...	0812	...	1012	...	...	...	1212	...	1412	...	...	1612	1612	1812	...	2012
27	Motala d.	...	...	...	...	...	0617	...	...	0829	...	1029	...	...	...	1229	...	1429	...	...	1629	1629	1829	...	2029
96	**Hallsberg** a.	...	...	...	...	...	0659	...	...	0906	...	1106	...	...	...	1306	...	1506	...	...	1712	1712	1906	...	2111
	Hallsberg 756 ▲ d.	...	...	...	...	0516	0718	0812a	...	0924	...	1114	...	...	...	1314	...	1514	1638	...	1720	1720	1914	1943	2120
121	**Örebro C 756** ▲ a.	...	...	...	...	0535	0737	0831a	...	0943	...	1133	...	...	...	1333	...	1533	1657	...	1739	1739	1933	2002	2139
	Örebro C d.	...	...	...	...	0537	0748	0900	...	0947	...	1145	1300	1300	...	1342	...	1547	1700	1704	1747	...	1935	2018	...
146	Frövi d.	...	...	...	...	0553	0803	0914	...	1001	...	1159	1314	1314	...	1356	...	1603	1714	1718	1801	...	1951	2032	...
204	Kopparberg d.	...	...	...	...	0641	0848	|	...	1044	...	1300	|	|	...	1439	...	1658	1758	|	1846	...	2036	|	...
232	Grängesberg d.	...	...	...	...	0700	0913	|	...	1115	...	1318	|	|	...	1459	...	1718	1819	|	1907	...	2108	|	...
247	Ludvika d.	...	...	...	0625	0716	0926	|	...	1128	...	1330	|	|	...	1512	...	1730	1832	|	1920	...	2120	|	...
295	**Borlänge** a.	...	...	...	0707	0754	0956	|	...	1158	...	1400	|	|	...	1546	...	1759	1902	|	1950	...	2149	|	...
	Borlänge 761 d.	0520	0600	...	0709	0814	1013	|	...	1216	1216	1416	|	|	1508	1616	...	1810	1908	|	2016	...	2205	|	...
317	Falun **761** d.	0539	0632	...	0734	0832	1034	|	...	1235	1235	1435	|	|	1528	1634	...	1835	1927	|	2034	...	2221	|	...
	Fagersta d.	|	|	0600	|	|	|	1009	...	|	|	|	1404	1409	|	|	...	|	...	1803	|	...	...	2122	...
	Avesta Krylbo d.	|	|	0635	|	|	|	1038	...	|	|	|	1439	1436	|	|	...	|	...	1830	|	...	...	2150	...
371	Storvik d.	0619	0711	0717	0814	0911	1115	1119	...	1311	1311	1511	1519	1526	1613	1711	...	1918	...	1909	2111	...	...	2231	...
385	Sandviken d.	0629	0722	0728	0832	0922	1126	1131	...	1322	1322	1522	1530	1539	1627	1722	...	1929	...	1925	2122	...	...	2242	...
408	**Gävle 760** a.	0644	0736	0747	0847	0938	1141	1146	...	1337	1337	1537	1545	1554	1646	1744	...	1945	...	1940	2137	...	...	2256	...

	Ⓐ	Ⓐ	⚒	Ⓐ	⑥	Ⓐ	†	⑥	Ⓐ	⚒			†		Ⓐ		⑥	Ⓑ	Ⓐ	Ⓑ	Ⓑ	Ⓐ	Ⓑ	Ⓑ	Ⓑ
Gävle 760 d.	...	0417	...	...	0618	0618	...	...	0718	0812	0817d	...	1014	1022	1212	1222	1422	1422	1518	1612	1623	1722	1822	2022	2028
Sandviken d.	...	0436	...	...	0639	0639	...	...	0742	0828	0833d	...	1030	1039	1228	1239	1439	1439	1540	1628	1640	1739	1839	2039	2044
Storvik d.	...	0447	...	...	0649	0649	...	...	0752	0837	0848d	...	1040	1049	1238	1249	1449	1449	1550	1637	1649	1749	1851	2049	2054
Avesta Krylbo d.	...	0530	...	...	|	|	...	...	|	0920	|	...	1122	|	1325	|	|	|	|	1732	|	|	|	|	2149
Fagersta d.	...	0600	...	...	|	|	...	0745	|	0947	|	...	1148	|	1351	|	|	|	|	1802	|	|	|	|	2215
Falun **761** d.	...	|	0511e	0609	0726	0730	...	|	0830	|	0926d	...	|	1126	|	1326	1526	1526	1632	|	1726	1834	1927	2126	...
Borlänge 761 a.	...	|	0532e	0625	0743	0746	...	|	0848	|	0943d	...	|	1143	|	1343	1543	1543	1648	|	1743	1856	1943	2143	...
Borlänge d.	...	|	0533	0644	0800	0808	...	|	...	|	1000	...	|	1200	|	1400	...	1600	...	|	1800	...	2000	...	...
Ludvika d.	...	|	0610	0716	0831	0839	...	|	...	|	1032	...	|	1231	|	1431	...	1631	...	|	1831	...	2031	...	...
Grängesberg d.	...	|	0620	0727	0841	0851	...	|	...	|	1042	...	|	1242	|	1441	...	1640	...	|	1841	...	2041	...	...
Kopparberg d.	...	|	0640	0746	0900	0910	...	|	...	|	1103	...	|	1300	|	1504	...	1658	...	|	1905	...	2100	...	...
Frövi d.	0553	0644	0725	0834	0944	0953	...	0829	...	1036	1148	...	1231	1347	1435	1549	...	1744	...	1846	1951	...	2152	...	...
Örebro C a.	0609	0659	0740	0849	0959	1008	...	0844	...	1051	1209	...	1246	1402	1450	1604	...	1759	...	1901	2006	...	2210	...	...
Örebro C 756 ▲ d.	0613	0734	0815	0852	1015	1015	1015	...	...	...	1215	...	...	1416	...	1625	...	1815	...	1914	2022	...	2212	...	...
Hallsberg 756 ▲ a.	0632	0753	0835	0911	1036	1036	1036	...	...	...	1234	...	...	1435	...	1644	...	1837	...	1933	2041	...	2231	...	...
Hallsberg a.	0648	...	0845	...	1045	1045	1045	...	...	...	1245	...	...	1445	...	1651	...	1845	...	...	2048	...	...	...	...
Motala d.	0727	...	0927	...	1127	1127	1127	...	...	...	1328	...	...	1527	...	1733	...	1931	...	...	2133	...	...	...	...
Mjölby 730 a.	0743	...	0943	...	1143	1143	1143	...	...	...	1351	...	...	1544	...	1749	...	1947	...	...	2200	...	...	...	...

a – Ⓐ only. d – ⚒ only. e – ① only.

▲ – For additional services Hallsberg - Örebro and v.v. – see panel below Table **756**.

STOCKHOLM - VÄSTERÅS - ÖREBRO - HALLSBERG 756

km		159 Ⓐ	Ⓐz	163 ⚒	*VEO* 91 [R] ◆	Ⓐ	⚒z	167	Ⓐz	171	Ⓐz	175	Ⓐz	179	Ⓐz	Ⓐz	722 Ⓐ	183	Ⓐz	756 Ⓐz	Ⓑy	187	764 Ⓑ	Ⓐz	772	Gz	⑤⑥z
0	**Stockholm** C d.	...	0600	0706	...	0736	0806	0906	1006	1106	1206	1306	1406	1506	1536	1606	1636	1706	1736	1806	1806	1906	2006	2106	2206	2306	2336
72	Enköping d.	...	0637	0749	...	0819	0849	0949	1049	1149	1249	1349	1445	1549	1619	1645	1719	1749	1819	1849	1849	1949	2049	2149	2249	2349	0019
107	**Västerås** d.	0610	0654	0810	...	0837	0907	1010	1107	1210	1307	1410	1502	1610	1637	1702	1740	1810	1837	1910	1907	2010	2110	2207	2310	0007	0037
141	Köping d.	0629	0712	0829	...	...	...	1029	...	1229	...	1429	1518	1629	...	1718	1759	1829	...	1930	...	2029	2129	...	2329b	...	...
159	Arboga **757** d.	0641	0725	0841	...	...	...	1041	...	1241	...	1441	1531	1641	...	1731	1810	1841	...	1944	...	2041	2140	...	2340b	...	...
205	**Örebro** a.	0704	0746	0904	...	...	...	1104	...	1304	...	1504	1551	1704	...	1751	1835	1904	...	2016	...	2104	2205	...	0005b	...	...
205	**Örebro 755** ▲ d.	0710	...	0910	0951	...	...	1110	...	1310	...	1510	...	1710	...	...	1838	1910	...	2018	...	2107	2208	...	0008b	...	...
230	**Hallsberg 755** ▲ a.	0730	...	0930	1011	...	...	1130	...	1330	...	1530	...	1730	...	...	1858	1930	...	2038	...	2127	2228	...	0028b	...	...
	Göteborg a.	0957	...	1157	1252	...	...	1357	...	1557	...	1757	...	1957	...	...	...	2157	...	...	...	...	...	...	...	...	...

	Ⓐ	711 ⚒	Ⓐ	715 ⚒	Ⓐz	719 Ⓐ	719 ⑥	164 ⚒	723 †	Ⓐz	168	Ⓐz	172	Ⓑz	176	†z	Ⓐz	Ⓐz	180	Ⓐz	Ⓐz	194 ⑤⑥†	G	Ⓑz	*VEO* 92 [R] ◆	188	76 [R] ◆
Göteborg d.	...	...	...	...	...	...	...	0602	...	...	0802	...	1002	...	1202	...	...	...	1402	...	...	1602	1602	...	1700	1802	1900
Hallsberg 755 ▲ d.	...	0533a	...	0633a	...	...	0733	0828	0833	...	1028	...	1228	...	1428	...	...	...	1632	...	...	1828	1837	...	1926	2028	2113u
Örebro 755 ▲ a.	...	0553a	...	0653a	...	...	0753	0848	0853	...	1048	...	1248	...	1448	...	...	...	1652	...	...	1848	1857	...	1945	2048	|
Örebro d.	...	0556a	...	0656a	...	0756z	0756	0856	0856	...	1056	...	1256	...	1456	...	1605	...	1656	...	1803	1856	1900	...	...	2056	2132u
Arboga **757** d.	...	0620a	...	0720a	...	0820z	0820	0920	0920	...	1120	...	1320	...	1520	...	1628	...	1720	...	1828	1920	1925	...	...	2120	|
Köping d.	...	0631a	0658z	0731a	...	0831z	0831	0931	0931	...	1131	...	1331	...	1531	...	1641	...	1731	...	1841	1931	1936	...	...	2131	|
Västerås d.	0623	0653	0723	0753	0823	0853	0853	0953	0953	1053	1153	1253	1353	1453	1553	1653	1700	1723	1753	1823	1900	1953	1958	2053	...	2153	2228
Enköping d.	0640	0710	0740	0810	0840	0910	0910	1010	1010	1110	1210	1310	1410	1510	1610	1710	1714	1740	1810	1840	1914	2010	2015	2110	...	2210	...
Stockholm C a.	0723	0753	0823	0853	0923	0953	0953	1053	1053	1153	1253	1353	1453	1553	1653	1753	1753	1823	1853	1923	1953	2053	2108	2153	...	2253	...

G – ①②③④ only.
a – Ⓐ only.
b – Ⓑ only.
u – Stops to pick up only.
y – Dec. 24 - Jan. 5.
z – Not Dec. 24 - Jan. 5.
◆ – For days of running and composition see Tables **740/60**.
▲ – Additional services operate Hallsberg - Örebro. and v.v.

STOCKHOLM - ESKILSTUNA - ARBOGA 757

km		Ⓐ	Ⓐz	Ⓐ	⑥	Ⓐ	⑥	*VEO* 91 [R] ◆		Ⓐz		Ⓐz		Ⓐz		Ⓑ	Ⓐ		Ⓑz	H		Ⓑz	Ⓐz		Gz	*VEO* 7085 [R] ◆	⑤⑥z
0	**Stockholm** C d.	...	...	0625	...	0725	0750	...	0850	0950	1050	1150	1250	1350	1450	1550	1630	1650	1750	1750	1850	1950	2050	2150	2250	2308	2320
36	Södertälje Syd d.	...	...	0646	...	0746	0811	0817	0911	1011	1111	1211	1311	1411	1511	1611	1653	1711	1811	1811	1911	2011	2111	2211	2311	2333	2341
67	Läggesta ● d.	...	...	0705	...	0805	0830	|	0930	1030	1130	1230	1330	1430	1530	1630	1712	1730	1830	1830	1930	2030	2130	2230	2330	|	0000
83	Strängnäs d.	...	0619	0718	...	0817	0840	|	0940	1040	1140	1240	1340	1440	1540	1640	1726	1740	1840	1840	1940	2040	2140	2240	2340	|	0010
115	Eskilstuna d.	0542	0645	0800j	0800	0832	0855	0859	1000	1055	1200	1255	1400	1500	1600	1700	1742	1800	1900	1855	2000	2100	2155	2300	2355	0012	0025
141	Kungsör d.	0558	0659	0815	0815	...	...	|	1015	...	1215	...	1415	1515	1615	1715y	...	1815	1914a	...	2016	2115	...	2315a	...	|	...
159	**Arboga 756** a.	0611	0711	0826	0826	...	...	|	1026	...	1226	...	1426	1526	1626	1726y	...	1826	1926a	...	2032	2126	...	2326a	...	|	...
	Örebro **756** a.	...	...	...	...	...	...	0951	...	...	...	...	...	...	...	...	...	...	...	...	...	...	...	...	...	0108	...

	Ⓐ	Ⓐ	Ⓐz	Ⓐ	⑥	Ⓐ	Ⓐ	⑥	⚒	⚒	†	Ⓐz		Ⓐz		Ⓑz		Ⓐ	†z		H	Ⓐz			*VEO* 92 [R] ◆	*VEO* 7080 [R] ◆	
Örebro **756** d.	...	0525	...	...	...	...	...	...	...	...	...	...	...	...	...	...	...	...	...	...	...	...	...	...	1949	2059	...
Arboga 756 d.	...	0549	...	0625	...	...	0725	...	...	0934	...	...	1134	...	1334	1434a	1534	1634z	...	1734	...	1834	1934	...	|	|	2134
Kungsör d.	...	0558	...	0634	...	...	0734	...	...	0943	...	...	1143	...	1343	1443a	1543	1643z	...	1743	...	1843	1943	...	|	|	2143
Eskilstuna d.	0515	0616	0642	0655	0700	0715	0755	0805	0905	1005	1005	1105	1205	1305	1405	1505	1605	1705	1705	1802	1905	1905	2005	...	2039	2155u	2205
Strängnäs d.	0529	0632	|	0711	0714	0731	0809	0819	0919	1019	1019	1119	1219	1319	1419	1519	1619	1719	1719	1816	1919	1919	2019	...	|	|	2219
Läggesta ● d.	0538	0642	|	0721	0723	0741	0819	0828	0928	1028	1028	1128	1228	1328	1428	1528	1628	1728	1728	1825	1928	1928	2028	...	|	|	2228
Södertälje Syd d.	0558	0703	|	0742	0743	0801	0843	0848	0948	1048	1048	1148	1248	1348	1448	1548	1648	1748	1748	1845	1948	1948	2048	...	2131	2236	2248
Stockholm C a.	0620	0725	0735	0805	0805	0825	0905	0910	1010	1110	1110	1210	1310	1410	1510	1610	1710	1810	1810	1910	2010	2010	2110	...	...	2258	2310

G – ①②③④ only.
H – † Dec. 9 - 23; Ⓐ Dec. 24 - Jan. 5; † Jan. 6 - June 14.
a – Ⓐ only.
j – Arrive 0739.
y – Ⓐ (not Dec. 24 - Jan. 5).
z – Not Dec. 24 - Jan. 5.
◆ – For days of running and composition see Table **740/60**.
● – Summer only narrow gauge service operates Läggesta nedre - Mariefred. Operator: Östra Södermanlands Järnväg ✆ +46 (0)159 210 00, fax +46 (0)159 210 06.

759 NARVIK - KIRUNA - LULEÅ - UMEÅ

Operator: *VEO*

km		7005	97	7011	96	7007	92	95	91	93	7003	99	🚌
		♦	⚒🍷	Ⓐ🍷	2	†🍷	2	2🍷	♦	♦	♦	2m	z
0	**Narvik** d.	...	...	...	...	...	...	1050‡	...	1525	...	1922	1922
40	Riksgränsen 🏨 d.	...	...	...	...	...	...	1151	...	1614	...	2014	2014
47	Vassijaure ◇ d.	...	...	...	...	...	...	1200	...	1626	...	2023	2023
67	Björkliden d.	...	...	...	...	...	...	1226	...	1644	...	2043	2043
76	Abisko Östra d.	...	...	...	...	...	...	1240	...	1701	...	2056	2056
169	**Kiruna** d.	...	0600	...	...	0835	...	1411	...	1835	...	2217	2217
269	Gällivare **762** d.	...	0705	...	...	0949	...	1526	...	1947	...	...	...
437	**Boden 760** a.	0701	0858	...	...	1208	1224	1734	...	2145	2150	...	...
*	**Luleå 760 768** a.	0727	0923	0830	1143	|	1250	1815	1657	|	2215	...	...
437	**Boden 759** d.	...	...	0900	1207	1210	...	...	1750	2210	...	...	...
483	Älvsbyn d.	...	...	0926	...	1233	...	...	1819	2239	...	...	...
611	Bastuträsk **768** d.	...	...	1048	...	1349	...	...	1944	0002	...	...	...
722	Vännäs d.	...	...	1159	...	1520	...	...	|	0113	...	...	...
753	**Umeå 768** a.	...	...	1225	...	1546	...	...	2121	...	...	...	...

	🚌	90	7004	94	92	96		7012	98		7016	7006
	x	2t	♦	♦	♦	2🍷		Ⓐ🍷	🍷		†🍷	♦
Umeå d.	...	...	...	...	0844	...	...	1343	...	...	1734	...
Vännäs d.	...	...	...	0338	|	...	...	1409	...	...	1800	...
Bastuträsk **768** d.	...	...	...	0449	1015	...	...	1524	...	...	1912	...
Älvsbyn d.	...	...	...	0620	1141	...	...	1637	...	...	2040	...
Boden 759 a.	...	...	...	0646	1209	...	...	1701	...	...	2104	...
Luleå 760 768 d.	...	...	0616	|	1250	1143	...	1735	1640	...	2140	2112
Boden 760 d.	...	...	0641	0711	...	1224	...	...	1707	...	...	2138
Gällivare **762** d.	...	...	...	0914	...	1447	...	...	1913	...	...	...
Kiruna d.	0735	0735	...	1038	...	1608	...	...	2023	...	...	...
Abisko Östra d.	0852	0852	...	1147	...	1721	...	...	...	...	...	...
Björkliden d.	0905	0905	...	1206	...	1737	...	...	...	...	...	...
Vassijaure ◇ d.	0921	0921	...	1226	...	1756	...	...	...	...	...	...
Riksgränsen 🏨 d.	0931	0931	...	1236	...	1807	...	...	...	...	...	...
Narvik a.	1020	1020	...	1324	...	1915¶	...	...	...	...	...	...

760 UMEÅ and STORLIEN - GÄVLE - STOCKHOLM

km		*X2000* 561	*X2000* 563	*VEO* 93	*X2000* 567	*X2000* 565	*X2000* 571	*X2000* 575		10081	81	*X2000* 579	*X2000* 583	*X2000* 583		*X2000* 587	*VEO* 7085	85	85		77	77	*VEO* 91		67	87	
		R✕	R✕	R	R✕	R✕	R✕	R✕		✕	✕	R✕	R✕	R✕		R✕	🍷	✕	✕		R	R	R		R	R	
		Ⓐq	♦	♦		Ⓐn				ⒸZ	N	ⒷY	⑥n	M		Ⓑ	♦	S	r		A	C	♦		♦	♦	
	Umeå 768 d.	...	...	...	...	...	...	...	...	...	...	...	...	...	...	...	...	...	...	...	...	...	2139	...	...	...	...
	Vännäs d.	...	...	0113·	...	...	...	...	...	...	...	...	...	...	...	...	...	...	...	...	...	...	2208	...	...	...	...
	Långsele d.	...	...	0354	...	...	...	...	...	...	...	...	...	...	...	...	...	...	...	...	...	...	0048	...	...	...	...
0	**Storlien** 🏨 ▲ d.	...	...	|	...	...	...	...	...	...	...	...	...	...	...	...	1354	...	...	...	1700	1700	|	...	1800	...	...
48	• Duved ▲ d.	...	...	|	...	...	...	...	...	0912	0912	...	1223v	...	...	...	1435	1525c	1525h	...	1749	1749	|	...	1850u	2020	...
57	Åre ▲ d.	...	...	|	...	...	...	...	...	0929	0929	...	1240v	...	...	...	1448	1542	1542	...	1850	1850	|	...	1940u	2100u	...
162	**Östersund** ▲ a.	...	...	|	...	...	...	...	...	1039	1039	...	1341v	...	...	...	1550	1701	1701	...	2017	2017	|	...	2054	2215	...
162	**Östersund 762** ⊖ d.	...	...	|	0600j	0610	0807c	...	...	1054	1054	...	1350	...	...	...	1554	1707	1707	...	2043	2043	|	...	2100	2220	...
233	Bräcke ⊖ d.	...	...	0528	0637j	0646	0844c	...	...	1139	1139	...	1432	...	...	...	1642	1751	1751	...	2136	2136	|	...	|	|	...
263	Ånge ⊖ d.	...	...	0602	0656j	0706	0902c	...	...	|	|	...	1452	...	...	...	1711	1810	1810	...	2159	2159	0244	...	|	2328	...
432	Bollnäs d.	...	...	|	|	|	|	...	...	|	|	...	|	...	...	...	|	|	|	...	|	|	0450	...	|	|	...
	Härnösand **768** d.	...	0520a	|	|	|	|	...	...	|	|	1310a	|	...	...	...	|	|	|	...	|	|	|	...	|	|	...
	Sundsvall 768 ⊖ a.	...	0605a	0710	0804j	|	1007c	...	...	|	|	1401a	1605	...	...	...	|	|	|	...	2322	2322	|	...	2330	|	...
	Sundsvall d.	0510	0613	0720	0811	|	1011	1211	...	|	|	1406	1611	1611	...	1811	|	|	|	...	2322	2322	|	...	2340	|	...
	Hudiksvall d.	0558	0700	0823	0900	|	1100	1300	...	|	|	1500	1700	1700	...	1900	|	|	|	...	0030	0030	|	...	|	|	...
	Söderhamn d.	0627	0724	0900	0925	|	1125	1325	...	|	|	1526	1725	1725	...	1925	|	|	|	...	|	|	|	...	|	|	...
531	**Gävle 755** a.	0703	0803	0950	1003	0926	1203	1403	...	1504	1504	1603	1805	1805	...	2004	2037	2058	2058	...	0153	0153	0555	...	|	0426s	...
	Gävle ⊗ d.	0706	0806	0955	1006	0930	1206	1406	...	1507	1507	1606	1806	1806	...	2006	2042	2100	2100	...	0153	0153	0600	...	|	|	...
	Uppsala **761** ⊗ a.	0751	0851s	1100s	1051s	1021s	1251s	1451s	...	1559s	1630s	1651s	1851s	1851s	...	2051s	2156	2151	2151	...	0254	0254	0700	...	|	0546s	...
	Arlanda C ✈ ◧ ⊗ a.	0809	0909	|	1109	1039	1309	1509	...	1620	1650	1709	1909	1909	...	2109	|	2210	2210	...	0317	0317	|	...	|	0609s	...
	Stockholm C. ⊗ a.	0830	0930	1144	1130	1100	1330	1530	...	1643	1713	1730	1930	1930	...	2130	2236	2232	2232	...	0343	0343	0745s	...	0348s	0634	...
	Göteborg **740** a.	1217	...	...	...	...	...	...	...	...	...	...	...	...	...	...	0605	...	...	...	0837	|	1252	...	|	...	...
	Malmö **730** a.	...	...	...	...	...	...	...	...	...	...	...	...	...	...	...	...	...	...	...	...	0957	...	...	0957	...	...

km		*X2000* 560	10080	80	80	*X2000* 10564	*X2000* 568	*X2000* 572	*X2000* 576	84	*X2000* 578	10084	*X2000* 580	*X2000* 10580	*VEO* 94	*X2000* 10582	*X2000* 582	*X2000* 582	*X2000* 584	*X2000* 588		*VEO* 92	86	*VEO* 7080	66	76	76
		R✕	✕	✕	✕	R✕	R✕	R✕	R✕	✕	R✕		R✕	R✕	R	R✕	R✕	R✕	R✕	R✕		R	R	R	R	R	R
		Ⓐ	†r	⚒n	S	⚒Y	†	X		W	Ⓑn	⑤V	ⒷT	ⒷS	♦	ⒷS	Ⓑn	⑤v	Q	P		♦	♦	♦	♦	D	B
	Malmö **730** d.	...	...	...	...	...	...	...	...	...	...	...	...	...	...	...	...	...	...	...	...	...	...	...	1717	1717	...
	Göteborg **740** d.	...	...	...	...	...	...	...	...	...	...	...	...	...	...	...	...	...	...	1642	...	1700	...	1805	|	|	1900
0	**Stockholm C.** ⊗ d.	0630	0758	0758	0758	0830	1030	1230	1430	1358	1600	1616	1630	1630	1713	1700	1700	1700	1830	2000	...	2212u	2250	2315	2345u	2352u	2352u
39	Arlanda C ✈ ◧ ⊗ d.	0648	0817	0817	0817	0848	1048	1248	1448	1417	1618	1638	1648	1648	|	1718	1718	1718	1848	2018	...	|	2316	|	|	0020	0020
69	Uppsala **761** ⊗ d.	0709u	0839	0839	0839	0909u	1109u	1309u	1509u	1439u	1639u	1658	1709u	1709u	1759u	1739u	1739u	1739u	1909u	2039	...	2300	2342u	2355	|	0041u	0041u
182	**Gävle** ⊗ a.	0754	0933	0934	0934	0954	1154	1354	1554	1534	1726	1803	1754	1754	1852	1825	1825	1825	1954	2124	...	2355	|	0050	|	0145	0145
182	**Gävle 755** d.	0757	0935	0937	0937	0957	1157	1357	1557	1542	1728	1805	1757	1757	1857	1827	1827	1827	1957	2127	...	2359	0043u	0055	|	0145	0145
260	Söderhamn d.	0834	|	|	|	1034	1234	1436	1636	|	|	|	1834	1834	1953	1909	1909	1909	2034	2209	...	|	|	|	|	0240	0240
314	Hudiksvall d.	0900	|	|	|	1100	1300	1500	1700	|	|	|	1900	1900	2039	1937	1937	1937	2100	2235	...	|	|	|	|	|	|
402	**Sundsvall** a.	0949	|	|	|	1149	1346	1554	1749	|	|	|	1949	1949	2134	2030	2030	2030	2149	2324	...	|	|	0335	0354	0411	0411
——	**Sundsvall 768** ⊖ d.	...	|	|	|	1152a	...	...	1752g	|	|	|	1952	1952	2139	2033q	2033f	2033	...	...	...	|	|	0335	0358	0417	0417
*	Härnösand **768** a.	...	|	|	|	1243a	...	...	|	|	|	|	2040	|	|	2120q	|	|	...	...	...	|	|	|	|	|	|
	Bollnäs d.	...	|	|	|	...	...	...	|	|	|	|	...	|	|	...	|	|	...	...	...	0106	|	|	|	|	|
	Ånge ⊖ d.	...	|	1240	1240	...	...	...	1859g	|	2000	|	...	2100	2252	...	2141f	2141	...	...	...	0259	0424	0505	|	0530	0530
0	Bräcke ⊖ d.	...	1229	1257	1257	...	...	...	1914g	1847	2015	|	...	2120	2311	...	2157f	2157	...	...	...	|	|	0524	|	0553	0553
	Östersund 762 ⊖ a.	...	1310	1345	1345	...	...	...	1952g	1929	2100	2237	...	2216	|	...	2236f	2236	...	...	...	|	0526	0611	0629	0650	0650
	Östersund ▲ d.	...	1313	1348r	1348	...	...	...	...	1934	2105p	2240	...	...	|	...	...	2240	...	...	...	|	0600	0623	0642	0658	0658
	Åre ▲ d.	...	1420	1502r	1502	...	...	...	...	2108	2207p	2352	...	...	|	...	...	2342	...	...	...	|	0713s	0734	0752s	0831	0831
	Duved ▲ d.	...	1435	1513r	1513c	...	...	...	...	2123	2218p	2359	...	...	|	...	...	2355	...	...	...	|	0732	0747	0815s	0845	0845
	Storlien 🏨 ▲ a.	...	...	...	...	...	...	...	...	...	...	...	...	...	|	...	...	...	...	...	...	|	...	0825	0857	0935	0935
131	Långsele d.	...	...	...	...	...	...	...	...	...	...	...	...	...	0043	...	...	...	...	...	...	0520	...	...	...	...	...
341	Vännäs d.	...	...	...	...	...	...	...	...	...	...	...	...	...	0338	...	...	...	...	...	...	0800	...	...	...	...	...
372	**Umeå 768** a.	...	...	...	...	...	...	...	...	...	...	...	...	...	...	...	...	...	...	...	...	0826	...	...	...	...	...

♦ – **NOTES FOR TABLES 759/760** (LISTED BY TRAIN NUMBER)

66 – ③④⑤⑥† Dec. 17 - Jan. 5; ③⑤⑥ Jan. 6 - Feb. 3; ③④⑤⑥† Feb. 4 - Mar. 30; ③⑤⑥ Mar. 31 - Apr. 27: 🛏 1, 2 cl., ▬ 2 cl. and [2] Malmö - Stockholm (**76**) - Storlien; ✕ and [Bio] Malmö - Stockholm; ✕ Ånge - Storlien.

67 – ①④⑤⑥† Dec. 20 - Jan. 5; ④⑥† Jan. 6 - Feb. 3; ①④⑤⑥† Feb. 4 - Mar. 30; ④⑥† Mar. 31 - Apr. 27: 🛏 1, 2 cl., ▬ 2 cl. and [2] Storlien - Stockholm - Malmö; ✕ and [Bio] Storlien - Sundsvall; ✕ Norrköping - Malmö.

86 – ③⑥ Dec. 17 - Jan. 5; ⑥ Jan. 6 - Mar. 2; ③⑥ Mar. 3 - Apr. 27: ▬ 2 cl. and [2] (also 🛏 1, 2 cl. on ⑥) Stockholm - Duved; ✕ Östersund - Duved.

87 – † Dec. 17 - Apr. 27: 🛏 1, 2 cl., ▬ 2 cl. and [2] Duved - Stockholm; ✕ and [Bio] Duved - Ånge.

91/2 – 🛏 1, 2 cl., ▬ 2 cl., [2], ✕ and [Shop] Luleå - Stockholm - Göteborg and v.v.

93 – 🛏 1, 2 cl., ▬ 2 cl., [2], ✕ and [Shop] Narvik - Stockholm; 🛏 1, 2 cl., ▬ 2 cl. and [2] Luleå (**7006**) - Boden - Stockholm; [2] Narvik - Boden (**7003**) - Luleå.

94 – 🛏 1, 2 cl., ▬ 2 cl., [2], ✕ and [Shop] Stockholm - Narvik; 🛏 1, 2 cl., ▬ 2 cl. and [2] Stockholm - Boden (**7005**) - Luleå; [2] Luleå (**7004**) - Boden - Narvik.

563 – ⚒ Dec. 9 - Apr. 21 (not Dec. 24 - Jan. 5): [12] and ✕ (Härnösand Ⓐ -) Sundsvall - Stockholm.

7003/4 – [2] Narvik (**93/4**) - Boden - Luleå and v.v.

7005/6 – 🛏 1, 2 cl., ▬ 2 cl. and [2] Stockholm (**93/4**) - Boden - Luleå and v.v.

7080 – ③⑥ Dec. 29 - Jan. 5, Feb. 4 - Apr. 13: ▬ 2 cl., [2] and ✕ Göteborg - Stockholm - Storlien.

7085 – ④† Dec. 30 - Jan. 6, Feb. 4 - Apr. 13: ▬ 2 cl., [2] and ✕ Storlien - Stockholm - Göteborg.

A – Daily Dec. 9 - Apr. 26; Ⓑ Apr. 27 - June 14: 🛏 1, 2 cl., ▬ 2 cl. and [2] Storlien - Stockholm - Göteborg; ✕ and [Bio] Storlien - Sundsvall; ✕ Örebro - Göteborg.

B – Daily Dec. 9 - Apr. 27; Ⓑ Apr. 28 - June 14: 🛏 1, 2 cl., ▬ 2 cl. and [2] Göteborg - Stockholm - Storlien; ✕ and [Bio] Göteborg - Stockholm; ✕ Sundsvall - Storlien.

C – ⑤† Dec. 9 - 16; ⑤ Jan. 7 - Feb. 3, Mar. 31 - Apr. 26; ⑤† Apr. 27 - June 14: 🛏 1, 2 cl., ▬ 2 cl. and [2] Storlien - Stockholm (**69**) - Malmö; ✕ and [Bio] Storlien - Sundsvall.

D – ⑤† Dec. 9 - 16; † Jan. 6 - Feb. 3, Mar. 31 - Apr. 27; ⑤† Apr. 28 - June 14: 🛏 1, 2 cl., ▬ 2 cl. and [2] Malmö (**66**) - Stockholm - Storlien; ✕ Sundsvall - Storlien.

M – Daily Dec. 9 - Jan. 5; Ⓑ Jan. 6 - June 14.

N – ④⑤ Dec. 9 - Jan. 5; ⑤ Jan. 6 - Mar. 2; ④⑤ Mar. 3 - Apr. 27.

P – Ⓑ Dec. 9 - 21; ①②③④† Jan. 6 - June 14.

Q – Train **10584** on † (Sundsvall a. 2153).

S – Dec. 9 - Jan. 5. **T** – Jan. 6 - Apr. 20. **V** – Dec. 9 - Jan. 6.

W – ④⑤ Dec. 9 - Jan. 5; ④⑤⑥ Jan. 6 - Apr. 27.

X – Train **10572** on Ⓒ (Sundsvall a. 1549).

Y – Until Apr. 20. **Z** – Dec. 9 - Apr. 27.

a – Ⓐ only.
c – Ⓒ only.
f – ⑤ only.
g – ⑥ only.
h – † only.
j – Ⓐ Dec. 9 - Jan. 5.
m – Feb. 8 - May 31.
n – Jan. 6 - June 14.
p – ④ Feb. 4 - Apr. 27.
q – Not Dec. 24 - Jan. 5.
r – Jan. 6 - Apr. 27.
s – Stops to set down only.
t – Feb. 9 - June 1.
u – Stops to pick up only.
v – Feb. 4 - Apr. 27.
x – June 2 - 14. Riksgränsen stop is at hotel.
z – June 1 - 14. Riksgränsen stop is at hotel.

‡ – Depart 1057 from Jan. 6. ¶ – Arrive 1855 from Jan. 6. ◇ – Ticket point.
▲ – For Östersund - Storlien - Trondheim services see panel below.
⊖ – For Sundsvall - Östersund local services see panel below.
⊗ – For additional services Stockholm - Gävle and v.v. see panel on page 348.
◧ – From Stockholm stops to pick up only; to Stockholm stops to set down only.

SUNDSVALL - ÖSTERSUND and v.v. (local services):

Operator: *VEO*

		Ⓐ	Ⓐ	Ⓒ	Ⓐ	Ⓑ	Ⓑ
Sundsvall d.	0505	0744	1015	1406	1410	1632	2340
Ånge d.	0633	0856	1127	1518	1518	1746	0052
Bräcke d.	0648	0913	1144	1535	1535	1803	...
Östersund a.	0736	0957	1230	1616	1616	1849	...

	Ⓐ	Ⓐ	⚒	†	Ⓑ	Ⓑ	
Östersund d.	...	0755	1122	...	1325	1640	2041
Bräcke d.	...	0837	1213	...	1412	1727	2128
Ånge d.	0610	0855	1232	1232	1435	1748	2147
Sundsvall a.	0724	1003	1346	1346	1552	1902	2304

ÖSTERSUND - TRONDHEIM and v.v.:

Operator: *VEO*

km		2	2
0	**Östersund** d.	0800	1621
105	Åre d.	0921	1738
114	Duved d.	0929	1746
162	Storlien 🏨 a.	1007	1824
268	**Trondheim** a.	1156	2013

	2	2
Trondheim d.	0820	1640
Storlien 🏨 d.	1012	1832
Duved d.	1048	1908
Åre d.	1101	1921
Östersund a.	1213	2033

 [Bio] – Cinema/bistro car [Shop] – Bar/shop * – Sundsvall - Härnösand: *68 km*; Boden - Luleå: *36 km*

STOCKHOLM - BORLÄNGE - MORA 761

km																											
		ST	*ST*		*ST*		*ST*	*X2000*		*ST*	*ST*			*ST*				*ST*		*X2000*		*ST*	*X2000*				*ST*
				10		**40**		**592**	**16**			**20**	**44**		**22**	**24**	**46**		**58**	**596**	**28**		**590**	**48**	**36**		
								[R]												[R]			[R]				
		Ⓐ	Ⓐ	Ⓐz		Ⓐ	⑥	yz	Ⓒ	Ⓑ	⑥	Ⓑ	⑥	Ⓑ	Ⓐz	⚒	†	⚒	⑤	†z	Ⓐ		Ⓐz		Ⓑz	†w	Ⓑ
0	**Stockholm** C. **760** ..d.	...	...	0614	...	0744	...	0855	0944	...	...	1144	1144	...	1244	1344	1344	...	1444	1544	1544	...	1655	1744	1944	1944	...
37	Arlanda C ✈ ....◧ d.	...	...	0634	...	0804	...	0914	1004	...	...	1204	1204	...	1304	1404	1404	...	1504	1604	1604	...	1714	1804	2004	2004	...
66	Uppsala **754/60** ....d.	...	...	0656	...	0826	...	0935u	1026	...	...	1226	1226	...	1328	1426	1426	...	1526	1626	1626	...	1735u	1826	2026	2026	...
128	Sala ....d.	...	...	0744	...	0901	...	|	1100	...	...	1301	1301	...	|	1501	1501	...	1610	1701	1701	...	|	1901	2102	2102	...
161	Avesta Krylbo ....d.	...	0642	0803	...	0920	...	1022v	1120	...	...	1320	1320	...	1420	1520	1520	...	1639	1721v	1726	...	1820v	1920	2120	2120	...
226	**Borlänge** ....a.	...	0726	0851	...	1008	...	1058	1208	...	...	1408	1408	...	1504	1608	1608	...	1733	1753	1814	...	1858	2008	2208	2208	...
	Borlänge .... ● d.	0640	0728	0853	0900	1012	1020	1058	1210	1220	1220	1410	1412	1420	...	1610	1612	1623	1750	1753	1816	1822	1858	2012	2210	2210	2220
250	Falun **755** .... ● a.	|	0756	0911	|	|	|	1117	1228	|	|	1428	|	|	...	1628	|	|	1808	1813	1834	|	1918	|	2228	2228	|
269	Leksand ....d.	0709	...	...	0938	1052	1052	...	...	1252	1252	...	1452	1452	...	...	1650	1653	...	...	...	1852	...	2050	...	...	2250
289	Rättvik.......................d.	0725	...	...	0954	1112	1111	...	...	1308	1312	...	1513	1512	...	...	1709	1709	...	...	...	1909	...	2110	...	...	2304
329	**Mora** .... ♣ a.	0750	...	...	1017	1138	1135	...	...	1331	1335	...	1538	1535	...	...	1735	1733	...	...	...	1932	...	2137	...	...	2328
330	Mora Strand .... ♣ a.	0755	...	...	1022	...	1140	...	...	1336	1340	...	...	1540	...	...	...	1738	...	...	...	1937	...	...	...	...	2333

		ST	*X2000*		*ST*	*X2000*	*ST*			*ST*			*X2000*		*ST*		*ST*			*ST*		*ST*			*ST*		*ST*
	11		**591**	**41**		**595**		**43**	**19**		**23**		**593**	**45**		**27**		**31**	**59**		**47**		**35**	**49**		**39**	
			[R]			[R]							[R]														
	Ⓐz	Ⓐ	Ⓐz	Ⓐ	⑥	⑥z	Ⓑ	⑥	Ⓑz		⚒		yz	Ⓑ	⑥	⑥		Ⓑ	†	Ⓐ	⑥	Ⓑ	Ⓑ	†	⚒	Ⓐz	Ⓑ
Mora Strand.......... ♣ d.	...	0515	...	...	0627	...	0822	...	...	1027	...	...	...	...	1227	...	1427	...	...	...	...	1627	...	...	1827	...	2025
Mora .... ♣ d.	...	0520	...	0623	0632	...	0828	0827	...	1032	...	...	...	1222	1232	...	1432	...	...	...	1622	1632	...	1822	1832	...	2030
Rättvik .... d.	...	0543	...	0649	0655	...	0850	0853	...	1055	...	...	...	1247	1255	...	1455	...	...	...	1647	1654	...	1847	1853	...	2052
Leksand........................ d.	...	0557	...	0710	0711	...	0906	0912	...	1110	...	...	...	1310	1311	...	1511	...	...	...	1709	1708	...	1908	1908	...	2107
Falun **755**.......... ● d.	0521	|	0617	|	|	0732	|	|	0932e	|	1132	...	1235	|	|	1332	|	1532	1558	1632	|	|	1732	|	|	1932	|
Borlänge............. ● a.	0543	0630	0638	0748	0745	0750	0945	0950	0950e	1145	1150	...	1252	1348	1345	1349	1547	1550	1616	1648	1746	1740	1750	1944	1939	1950	2138
Borlänge..................... d.	0549	...	0640	0752	...	0752	...	0952	0952	...	1152	...	1254	1352	...	1352	...	1552	1628	1650	1752	...	1752	1952	...	1952	...
Avesta Krylbo .... d.	0634	...	0711v	0839	...	0835v	...	1039	1039	...	1239	...	1333v	1440	...	1439	...	1639	1719	1726	1839	...	1839	2039	...	2039	...
Sala............................. a.	0652	...	|	0859	...	0859	...	1059	1059	...	1259	...	|	1459	...	1459	...	1659	1737	...	1859	...	1859	2059	...	2059	...
Uppsala **754/60**.......... a.	0730	...	0802s	0934	...	0934s	...	1134	1134	...	1334	...	1434s	1534	...	1534	...	1734	1815	...	1934	...	1934	2134	...	2134	...
Arlanda C ✈..........◧ a.	0751	...	0821	0953	...	0953	...	1153	1153	...	1353	...	1453	1553	...	1553	...	1753	1836	...	1953	...	1953	2153	...	2157	...
Stockholm C. **761**.... a.	0813	...	0843	1016	...	1016	...	1216	1216	...	1416	...	1514	1616	...	1616	...	1816	1900	...	2016	...	2016	2216	...	2219	...

e – † only.
s – Stops to set down only.
u – Stops to pick up only.
v – Avesta **centrum** (not Krylbo).
w – Dec. 24 - Jan. 5.
y – ①②③④ only.
z – Not Dec. 24 - Jan. 5.
♣ – Local journeys are not permitted between Mora and Mora Strand.
● – Additional services operate Borlänge - Falun and v.v.
◧ – From Stockholm calls to pick up only; to Stockholm calls to set down only.

INLANDSBANAN 2007 service (Summer only) KRISTINEHAMN - MORA - ÖSTERSUND - GÄLLIVARE 762

km		B	A	🚌A	C
0	**Kristinehamn 750** .. d.	...	1055	...	...
40	Nykroppa .... d.	...	1140	1145	...
66	**Persberg** .... d.	...	...	1210	...
—	Vansbro .... d.	...	...	1400	...
0	**Mora 761** .... d.	0722	...	1505	1510
14	Orsa........................ d.	0736	...	...	1524
137	Sveg .... d.	1024	...	...	1810
321	**Östersund 760** .... a.	1401	...	...	2100

	🚌A	C	A	D
Östersund 760 ..... d.	...	0706	...	1447
Sveg .... d.	...	1034	...	1826
Orsa........................ d.	...	1307	...	2021
Mora 761 .... d.	1200	1320	...	2035
Vansbro .... d.	1315	...	...	...
Persberg .... d.	1530	...	...	...
Nykroppa .... d.	1555	...	1605	...
Kristinehamn 750 a.	...	...	1640	...

km		D	
0	**Östersund 760**....... d.	0725	...
115	Ulriksfors .... d.	0902	...
244	Vilhelmina .... d.	1142	...
312	Storuman.................. d.	1257	...
384	Sorsele .... d.	1422	...
473	Arvidsjaur................. d.	1554	...
646	Jokkmokk.................. d.	1925	...
746	**Gällivare 759** .... a.	2140	...

	E	
Gällivare 759 ....d.	0709	...
Jokkmokk...................d.	0905	...
Arvidsjaur ....d.	1253	...
Sorsele.......................d.	1423	...
Storuman....................d.	1526	...
Vilhelmina..................d.	1704	...
Ulriksfors ....d.	1905	...
Östersund 760 ....a.	2037	...

All rail services operated by Railbus.
A – ①–⑤ June 25 - Aug. 3.
B – June 18 - Sept. 2 (not June 22, 23).
C – June 25 - Aug. 5.
D – June 18 - Sept. 1 (not June 22, 23).
E – June 19 - Sept. 2 (not June 22, 23).

Operator: Inlandsbanan AB, Box 561, 831 27, Östersund.
✆ +46 (0)63 19 44 12, fax +46 (0)63 19 44 06.

Operator: *ST* 2nd class only VÄSTERÅS - LUDVIKA 763

km																							
		⚒	Ⓐ	Ⓐ		⑥	Ⓐ	⚒	†	Ⓐ			Ⓐ		Ⓐ			Ⓐ	Ⓐ	Ⓐ	Ⓑ	Ⓐ	
0	**Västerås**...................d.	0615	0715	0815	...	0815	0915	1015	1015	1115	...	1215	1315	1415	1515	1615	...	1715	1815	1915	2015	2115	...
80	Fagersta C...................d.	0714	0812	0916	...	0913	1012	1114	1112	1212	...	1312	1412	1514	1612	1714	...	1812	1914	2012	2114	2212	...
129	**Ludvika**.....................a.	0800	...	0957	...	...	...	1156	...	...	...	...	...	1556	...	1756	...	...	1956	...	2157	...	...

	Ⓐ	⚒	Ⓐ	⚒	Ⓐ		Ⓑ	⑥	Ⓐ	⚒	†		Ⓐ		Ⓐ			Ⓐ	Ⓑ		Ⓐ	Ⓐ	
Ludvika.......................d.	...	0604	...	0806	...	...	1005	...	...	1204	...	...	...	...	...	...	1604	...	1804	...	...	2004	...
Fagersta C ....d.	0548	0648	0748	0850	0948	...	1048	1048	1148	1248	1248	...	1348	1448	1548	...	1648	1748	1848	...	1948	2048	...
Västerås ....a.	0645	0745	0845	0945	1045	...	1145	1145	1245	1346	1343	...	1445	1545	1645	...	1745	1845	1945	...	2045	2147	...

Operator: *LT* 🚌 SUNDSVALL - UMEÅ - LULEÅ - HAPARANDA and northern road connections 768

		⊡		⊠			⊠					
Sundsvall .... ‡ d.	...	...	...	...	0810	1010	...	1210	1410	1610	1810	2010
Härnösand.... § a.	...	...	...	...	0855	1055	...	1255	1455	1655	1855	2055
Härnösand.... § d.	...	...	...	0745	0900	1100	1150	1300	1500	1700	1900	2100
Sollefteå.......d.	...	...	...	0950	|	|	1340	|	|	|	|	|
Långsele ......d.	...	...	...	*1010*	|	|	*1400*	|	|	|	|	|
Örnsköldsvik . § a.	...	...	...	—	1025	1225	—	1425	1625	1825	2025	2225
Umeå .... § a.	...	...	...	Ⓑ	1200	1400	...	1600	1800	2000	2205	2400
Umeå .... § d.	0535	...	0800	1000	1210	1410	⊡	1610	1810	2010	...	...
Skelleftea...... § a.	0745	0915	1015	1210	1405	1605	1810	1805	2005	2205	...	...
Bastuträsk....a.	|	1000	|	|	|	|	1900	|	|	|	...	...
Piteå............ § a.	0920	...	1140	1340	1525	1725	...	1925	2125	2325	...	...
Luleå........... § a.	1015	...	1240	1440	1620	1820	...	2020	2220	0020	...	...
Haparanda... § a.	1300	...	1530	1740	1845	2045	...	2245	...	...	...	...

		⊠			⊠		⊡					⊡	
Haparanda § d.	...	...	...	...	...	0520	...	0720	...	1120	1200	...	1610
Luleå .... § d.	...	...	...	0545	...	0750	...	0950	1150	1350	1500	...	1855
Piteå.......... § d.	...	...	...	0640	...	0845	...	1045	1245	1445	1605	...	1955
Bastuträsk d.	...	...	...	|	...	|	1020	|	|	|	|	1915	|
Skelleftea ..§ d.	...	...	...	0755	...	1000	1105	1200	1400	1600	1730	2000	2120
Umeå .... § a.	...	...	...	0950	...	1155	...	1355	1555	1755	1940	...	2330
Umeå .... § d.	0545	...	0805	1005	...	1205	...	1405	1605	1805	...	...	...
Örnsköldsvik § d.	0740	...	0940	1140	...	1340	...	1540	1740	1940	...	...	...
Långsele .. d.	|	*0850*	|	|	*1045*	|	...	|	|	|	...	...	...
Sollefteå ... d.	|	0920	|	|	1130	|	...	|	|	|	...	...	...
Härnösand . § a.	0905	1105	1105	1305	1340	1505	...	1705	1905	2105	...	...	...
Härnösand . § d.	0910	...	1110	1310	...	1510	...	1710	1910	2110	...	...	...
Sundsvall ‡ a.	0955	...	1155	1355	...	1555	...	1755	1955	2155	...	...	...

§ – Bus station.
⊡ – Operated by *VEO*. Subject to confirmation.
⊠ – Days of running are subject to confirmation – contact operator for details.
‡ – All buses originate / terminate at Sundsvall bus station (journey 5 – 10 minutes).

Information: Länstrafiken Norrbotten ✆ +46 020 47 00 47 🚌 LULEÅ - HAPARANDA and TORNIO - KEMI 769

Luleå - Haparanda valid August 20, 2007 - June 14, 2008; Tornio - Kemi valid August 9, 2007 - May 31, 2008

		Ⓐ	Ⓒ		Ⓐ	Ⓑ			Ⓐ		⑥	Ⓐ
Luleå Bus Station .... § d.	0830	1040	1050	1310	1345	1510	1630	1830	1930	2030	2230	2230
Haparanda Bus Station 🏢 . ▲ § d.	1050	1300	1310	1530	1630	1740	1845	2045	2150	2245	0045	0050

		Ⓐ		Ⓐ			Ⓐ	Ⓒ	Ⓐ		
Haparanda Bus Station 🏢 ▲ § d.	0520	0655	0720	0910	1120	1200	1335	1400	1415	1610	1810
Luleå Bus Station .... § a.	0740	0945	0940	1140	1340	1435	1600	1625	1700	1835	2035

	⚒	Ⓐ	Ⓐ	Ⓐ	⚒	Ⓐ		Ⓐ	Ⓐ	Ⓐ	⑥	x	Ⓐ	⑥	x	Ⓐ	⑥	Ⓑ	Ⓐ	⑥	Ⓐ	Ⓐ	Ⓐ	Ⓐ	x	Ⓐ	x	Ⓐ	Ⓐ
Tornio Bus Station 🏢..... ▲ ‡ d.	0525	0610	0705	0740	0810	0910	1005	1050	1130	1215	1235	1235	1310	1315	1340	1415	1440	1500	1505	1515	1605	1705	1710	1815	1900	1910	1915	1915	2135
Kemi Railway Station **790** .. ● ‡ a.	|	|	0800	|	|	|	|	|	|	|	|	|	1335	1351	1405	|	|	|	|	|	|	1741	1735	|	1925	1935	|	|	2205
Kemi Bus Station .... ● ‡ a.	0555	0650	0758	0810	0850	0950	1030t	1140	1205	1250	1310	1310	1334	1350	1410	1445	1515	1525	1545	1600	1645	1738	1735	1905	1930	1940	1950	1950	2200

	Ⓐ	Ⓐ	Ⓐ	Ⓐ	①–⑥	Ⓐ	Ⓐ	Ⓐ	⑥	Ⓐ	⑥	Ⓐ	Ⓐ	⚒	Ⓐ	Ⓐ	⑥	x	Ⓐ	Ⓐ	Ⓐ	①–④	⑤	Ⓐ	⑥⑦	Ⓐ	Ⓐ	Ⓐ	⑥
Kemi Bus Station .... ● ‡ d.	0615	0655	0750	0815	0920	0955	1040	1125	1125	1215	1310	1315	1345	1415	1430	1510	1510	1515	1530	1605	1610	1715	1725	1820	1850	1900	2010	2155	2245
Kemi Railway Station **790** .. ● ‡ d.	|	|	|	|	0930	|	|	|	|	|	|	|	|	1416	1432	1511	1520	1520	1535	|	|	|	|	1830	1851	|	|	|	|
Tornio Bus Station 🏢..... ▲ ‡ a.	0650	0745	0825	0850	1005	1040	1125	1150	1200	1250	1350	1355	1430	1450j	1500	1545	1555	1555	1610	1645	1648	1750	1800	1900	1925	1935	2045	2235	2315

j – 10 minutes later on ⑥.
t – 5 minutes later on ⑥⑦.
x – ⑦. However, runs on the last day only where there are two consecutive holidays.
‡ – Finnish time.
§ – Swedish time.
▲ – Walking distance between Haparanda Bus Station and Tornio Bus Station is approximately 800 metres.
● – Walking distance between Kemi Railway and Bus stations is approximately 200 metres.

NORWAY

SEE MAP PAGE 339

Operator: Norges Statsbaner (NSB).

Services: All trains convey second class seating accommodation. Many services, as identified in the notes, also convey *NSB Komfort* accommodation (see below). Sleeping-cars (🛏) have one-, two-, and three-berth compartments; passengers may reserve a berth in any category with either a first or second-class ticket. Most long distance express trains convey a bistro car (✕) serving hot and cold meals, drinks and snacks. 🍸 indicates that drinks and light refreshments are available from automatic vending machines.

Timings: NSB services are valid **Sept. 24**, 2007 - **Jan. 5**, 2008. Dec. 25, 26, Jan. 1 are Norwegian public holidays (trains marked ⚒ or Ⓐ do not run).

Reservations: Seat reservation is highly recommended on long-distance routes Oslo - Kristiansand - Stavanger (Table **775**), Oslo - Bergen (Table **780**), Oslo - Trondheim / Åndalsnes (Table **785**) and Trondheim - Bodø (Table **787**).

Supplements: A supplement is payable (75 NOK) to use *NSB Komfort* accommodation, a dedicated area provided on many trains with complimentary tea / coffee and newspapers.

770 OSLO - HALDEN - GÖTEBORG

Most trains convey *NSB Komfort* and 🍸

km	Norwegian train number	101	103	105	105	107	109	111	113	113	115	117	119	121	123	125	125	127	129	131	133	135		139
	Swedish train number	391			393					395							397	399						
		⊖	⚒	v	⑥e	⚒		⚒		Ⓑz	⚒		Ⓐr	Ⓐz	Ⓐr	z	⑥	Ⓑw	t	Ⓑw	z	Ⓑw		z
0	**Oslo** Sentral d.	0700	0800	0900	0900	1000	1100	1200	1300	1300	1400	1500	1530	1600	1632	1700	1700	1800	1900	2000	2100	2200	...	2359
60	Moss d.	0744	0843	0943	0943	1043	1143	1243	1343	1343	1443	1543	|	1644	|	1743	1743	1843	1943	2043	2143	2243	...	0050
94	Fredrikstad d.	0810	0910	1009	1009	1109	1209	1309	1410	1410	1509	1609	1637	1711	1739	1809	1809	1909	2010	2109	2209	2309	...	0117
109	Sarpsborg d.	0825	0925	1024	1024	1124	1224	1324	1425	1425	1523	1623	1653	1725	1753	1823	1823	1924	2025	2125	2223	2323	...	0130
137	**Halden** a.	0845	0945	1044	1044	1144	1244	1344	1445	1445	1543	1643	1719	1746	1818	1843	1843	1944	2045	2145	2243	2343	...	0150
137	**Halden** § d.	0851	...	...	1048	...	...	...	...	1450	...	...	...	...	...	...	1848	1953	...	...	...	...	...	...
268	Öxnered **751** d.	1005	...	...	1203	...	...	...	...	1605	...	...	...	...	...	...	2004	2108	...	...	...	...	...	...
278	Trollhättan **751** d.	1011	...	...	1209	...	...	...	...	1611	...	...	...	...	...	...	2011	2114	...	...	...	...	...	...
350	**Göteborg 751** a.	1055	...	...	1250	...	...	...	...	1654	...	...	...	...	...	...	2054	2157	...	...	...	...	...	...

Swedish train number							390			392					394					396		398	
Norwegian train number	100	102	104	106	108	110	112	112	114	116	116	118	120	122	124	124	126	128	130	132	132	134	136
	Ⓐz	Ⓐr	⚒	Ⓐr	v	⚒	⊖	v	⚒	⑥e		⚒		Ⓐz	Ⓑz		Ⓑw	t	Ⓑw	⑥	z	Ⓑw	z
Göteborg 751 d.	...	...	...	...	...	...	0645	...	...	0838	...	...	...	...	1244	...	...	...	...	1640	...	1750	...
Trollhättan **751** d.	...	...	...	...	...	...	0728	...	...	0923	...	...	...	...	1327	...	...	...	...	1723	...	1832	...
Öxnered **751** d.	...	...	...	...	...	...	0734	...	...	0929	...	...	...	...	1333	...	...	...	...	1729	...	1838	...
Halden § a.	...	...	...	...	...	...	0848	...	...	1042	...	...	...	...	1447	...	...	...	...	1846	...	1952	...
Halden d.	0500	0532	0558	0632	0658	0800	0900	0900	1000	1100	1100	1200	1300	1400	1500	1500	1600	1700	1800	1900	1900	2000	2100
Sarpsborg d.	0523	0553	0620	0652	0720	0822	0923	0923	1022	1122	1122	1222	1322	1423	1521	1521	1621	1723	1821	1922	1922	2023	2123
Fredrikstad d.	0537	0607	0634	0706	0734	0836	0937	0937	1037	1137	1137	1236	1337	1437	1535	1535	1635	1737	1835	1936	1936	2037	2137
Moss d.	0603	0633	0701	0732	0801	0903	1003	1003	1103	1203	1203	1303	1403	1503	1601	1601	1701	1803	1903	2003	2003	2103	2203
Oslo Sentral a.	0645	0715	0745	0815	0845	0945	1045	1045	1145	1245	1245	1345	1445	1545	1645	1645	1745	1845	1945	2045	2045	2145	2245

e – Also Dec. 24, 31.
r – Not Dec. 24 - Jan. 1.
t – Not Dec. 24.
v – Not Dec. 25, Jan. 1.
w – Not Dec. 24, 25, 31.
z – Not Dec. 24, 31.
⊖ – ①-⑤ (not Dec. 24, 25, 26, 31, Jan. 1).
§ – 🏛 at Kornsjø (*km169*).

771 OSLO - OSLO ✈ GARDERMOEN

See also Table **783**

Operated by NSB Gardermobanen AS.
Special fares apply.
✆ +47 23 15 90 00
fax +47 23 15 90 01.

Daily services (journey time: 22 minutes)
Trains call at Lillestrøm 10 minutes from Oslo
From Oslo Sentral every 20 minutes 0445 - 0005.
From Gardermoen every 20 minutes 0536 - 0036.

Additional services on Ⓑ (journey time: 19 minutes)
Non-stop services
From Oslo Sentral every 20 minutes: 0615 - 2215 on Ⓐ, 1215 - 2315 on ⑦.
From Gardermoen every 20 minutes: 0646 - 2246 on Ⓐ, 1246 - 2346 on ⑦.

773 OSLO - GJØVIK

All trains convey *NSB Komfort* and 🍸

km		b	v	c		d	Ⓐh	h	z	w	A	q
0	**Oslo** Sentral ‡ d.	0707	0907	1107	1307	1507	1613	1707	1907	2107	2307	0007
56	Roa ‡ d.	0805	1004	1203	1403	1605	1711	1809	2006	2205	0008	0107
70	Jaren ‡ d.	0821	1020	1219	1419	1621	1728	1824	2021	2220	0024	0123
99	Eina d.	0845	1044	1243	1442	1644	1755	1847	2044	2243	0047	0146
110	Raufoss d.	0855	1054	1253	1552	1654	1806	1957	2054	2253	0057	0156
122	**Gjøvik** a.	0905	1104	1303	1502	1704	1816	1907	2104	2303	0107	0206

	Ⓐh	▲	Ⓐh	b	f			h	w	z	r
Gjøvik d.	0433	0533	0633	0738	0937	1136	1333	1535	1734	1935	2134
Raufoss d.	0444	0544	0644	0749	0948	1147	1344	1546	1745	1946	2145
Eina d.	0454	0554	0654	0759	0958	1157	1354	1556	1756	1956	2155
Jaren ‡ d.	0517	0617	0717	0822	1021	1220	1418	1620	1823	2020	2219
Roa ‡ d.	0533	0633	0734	0838	1037	1236	1435	1637	1839	2037	2236
Oslo Sentral ‡ a.	0629	0731	0834	0935	1133	1334	1532	1734	1935	2134	2333

A – ①-⑤ (not Dec. 24, 31).
b – Not Dec. 24, 25, 26, Jan. 1.
c – Not Dec. 26.
d – Not Dec. 25.
f – Not Jan. 1.
h – Not Dec. 24.
q – Not Dec. 25, 26, Jan. 1.
r – Not Dec. 24, 26, 31.
v – Not Dec. 25, Jan. 1.
w – Not Dec. 24, 25, 31.
z – Not Dec. 24, 31.
▲ – Not Dec. 24, 25, Jan. 1. Runs 16 – 19 minutes later on ①-⑤.
‡ – Additional trains operate Oslo - Roa - Jaren and v.v.

775 OSLO - KRISTIANSAND - STAVANGER

km				73			77	79	81	81	
		769	771	773	773	775	777	779		781	705
		Ⓐz	⚒	⚒e		Ⓑw	y	z	w	⑤⑦f	Ⓑw
		✕□	✕□	✕□	✕□	✕□	✕□	✕□	✕□	✕□	♣✕
0	**Oslo** Sentral § d.	...	...	0711	...	...	1111	1507	1709	1709	2247
41	Drammen § d.	...	...	0748u	...	...	1148u	1546u	1745u	1745u	2337u
87	Kongsberg § d.	...	...	0821	...	...	1222	1621	1817	1817	0017
134	Nordagutu d.	...	...	0856	...	...	1256	1659	1851	1851	0053x
151	Bø d.	...	...	0910	...	...	1311	1713	1905	1905	0113
209	Neslandsvatn d.	...	...	0954	...	...	1355	1756	1950	1950	|
225	Gjerstad d.	...	...	1007	...	...	1408	1809	2003	2003	0213x
270	Nelaug ⊠ d.	...	...	1040	...	...	1441	1844	2036	2036	0247x
353	**Kristiansand** a.	...	...	1138	...	...	1542	1942	2134	2134	0354
353	**Kristiansand** d.	0520	0805	1146	1146	1415	1610	1950	...	2200	0413
465	Moi d.	0643	0928	1309	1309	1542	1741	2117	...	2330	0542x
514	Egersund ◇ d.	0725	1003	1348	1348	1620	1818	2155	...	0017	0622
573	Sandnes ◇ d.	0807	1046	1438	1438	1709	1909	2238	...	0058	0709s
587	**Stavanger** ◇ a.	0828	1105	1502	1502	1727	1927	2257	...	0113	0728

			776	778	780	782	784	784	786	
	70	72	76		80	82		84		706
	Ⓐz	⑥	⊖	Ⓐz	⊗	Ⓑ‡	z	⑤	Ⓑw	Ⓑw
	✕□	✕□	✕□	✕□	✕□	✕□	✕□	✕□	✕□	♣✕
Stavanger ◐ d.	...	...	0600	0855	1055	1355	1555	1555	1925	2219
Sandnes ◐ d.	...	...	0616u	0917u	1117u	1417u	1617u	1617u	1947u	2240u
Egersund ◐ d.	...	...	0704	1004	1205	1502	1705	1705	2029	2332
Moi d.	...	...	0739	1040	1242	1541	1742	1742	2105	0010
Kristiansand a.	...	...	0902	1205	1405	1709	1905	1905	2228	0138
Kristiansand d.	0530	0740	0910	...	1420	1717	...	1913	...	0215
Nelaug ⊠ d.	0626	0839	1009	...	1519	1815	...	|	...	0330x
Gjerstad d.	0656	0912	1044	...	1551	1848	...	|	...	0404x
Neslandsvatn d.	0709	0925	1056	...	1604	1901	...	|	...	|
Bø d.	0752	1013	1140	...	1646	1952	...	2131	...	0504
Nordagutu d.	0806	1028	1155	...	1701	2006	...	|	...	0519x
Kongsberg ¶ d.	0844	1104	1236	...	1737	2040	...	2218	...	0600
Drammen ¶ d.	0918s	1146s	1314s	...	1819s	2119s	...	2255s	...	0640s
Oslo Sentral ¶ a.	0956	1226	1358	...	1856	2156	...	2338	...	0726

Nelaug - Arendal

km		Ⓐz	⑥	⑦f	⚒		h	z		Ⓑw	
0	Nelaug d.	0630	0845	1015	1045	...	1522	1845	...	2040	...
36	Arendal a.	0705	0920	1050	1120	...	1557	1920	...	2115	...

	Ⓐz	⑥	d		h	Ⓑz	⑥		Ⓑw	
Arendal d.	0545	0800	0930	...	1435	1735	1800	...	1955	...
Nelaug a.	0620	0835	1005	...	1510	1810	1835	...	2030	...

d – Not Dec. 25.
e – Also Dec. 23.
f – Also Dec. 26, Jan. 1.
h – Not Dec. 24.
s – Stops to set down only.
u – Stops to pick up only.
v – Not Dec. 25, Jan. 1.
w – Not Dec. 24, 25, 31.
x – Stops on request.
y – Not Dec. 24, 25.
z – Not Dec. 24, 31.

♣ – Conveys 🛏 and 🛋. Reservation recommended.
⊖ – Not Dec. 25. On Jan. 1 runs Kristiansand - Oslo only.
⊗ – On Dec. 24 runs Stavanger - Kristiansand only.
‡ – Also Dec. 22; not Dec. 24, 25. On Dec. 31 runs Stavanger - Kristiansand only.
□ – Reservation recommended. Conveys *NSB Komfort*.
⊠ – See panel below main table for connections to / from Arendal.

§ – Additional local trains **Oslo** S - **Drammen** (39 – 42 minutes) - **Kongsberg** (79 – 86 minutes): 0617 ⚒, 0717 **v**, 0817 ⚒, 0917 **v**, 1017 **v**, 1117, 1217, 1317, 1417, 1517, 1617, 1717, 1817 **z**, 1917 **z**, 2017 **z**, 2117 **z**, 2217 **z** and 0017 **v**.

¶ – Additional local trains **Kongsberg** - **Drammen** (42 – 49 minutes) - **Oslo** S (81 – 88 minutes): 0457 Ⓐ**z**, 0554 ⚒, 0653 ⚒, 0750 ⚒, 0853 **v**, 0954 ⚒, 1053, 1150, 1253, 1353, 1453, 1550, 1650 **h**, 1751 **z**, 1853 **z**, 1954 Ⓐ**z**, 2053 **z** and 2253 **z**.

◇ – Additional local trains **Egersund** - **Sandnes** (51 – 55 minutes) - **Stavanger** (68 – 72 minutes): 0536 Ⓐ**z**, 0604 Ⓐ**z**, 0637 ⚒, 0706 Ⓐ**z**, 0736 ⚒, 0836 ⚒, 0936, 1036, 1136, 1236, 1336, 1438, 1536, 1604 Ⓐ**z**, 1636, 1736 **h**, 1836 **h**, 1936 **h**, 2036 **h**, 2136 **h**, 2236 **z** and 2336 **z**.

◐ – Additional local trains **Stavanger** - **Sandnes** (17 – 18 minutes) - **Egersund** (66 – 69 minutes): 0511 Ⓐ**z**, 0609 ⚒, 0711 ⚒, 0811 ⚒, 0911, 1011, 1111, 1211, 1311, 1411, 1441 Ⓐ**z**, 1511, 1541 Ⓐ**z**, 1611 **h**, 1711 **h**, 1811 **h**, 1911 **h**, 2011 **h**, 2111 **z**, 2211 **z**, 2311 Ⓑ**z** and 2341 **z**.

PORSGRUNN - NORDAGUTU - NOTODDEN 779

km		Ⓐz	Ⓐz	Ⓐz	Ⓐz	Ⓐz	🚌 ⑥	Ⓐz	Ⓐz	Ⓐz	
0	**Porsgrunn 783** d.	...	0639	0751	0951	*1115**	1220	1425	1551	1705	...
9	Skien **783** d.	0544	0648	0800	1000	1220	1235	1434	1600	1714	...
43	Nordagutu d.	0613	0723	0832	1034	1258e	1320	1508	1634	1748	...
62	**Notodden** a.	0632	0742	0851	1053	1317	1345	1527	1653	1807	...

	Ⓐz	Ⓐz	Ⓐz	Ⓐz		🚌 ⑥	Ⓐz	Ⓐz	Ⓐz	Ⓐz
Notodden d.	0644	0813	0955	1124	...	1350	1429	1555	1709	1847
Nordagutu d.	0704	0833	1015	1144	...	1415	1449	1615	1729	1907
Skien **783** d.	0734	0904	1044	1213	...	1500	1519	1645	1759	1939
Porsgrunn 783 a.	0743	0913	*1143**	*1241*	...	1515	1528	1658	*1843**	*2043**

e – Arrives 1250. z – Not Dec. 24, 31. * – By 🚌 to / from Skien. ☛ No service Skien - Nordagutu - Notodden and v.v. on ⑦.

OSLO - BERGEN 780

km		61 v ✕⊡		601 n ✕⊡	607 ⑦d R		603 ⑤f ✕⊡	63 n ✕⊡		605 Ⓑw ♣R	
0	**Oslo** Sentral d.	0811	...	1033	1227	...	1433	1607	...	2311	...
41	Drammen △ d.	0848	...	1115	1305	...	1512	1644	...	2354	...
112	Hønefoss d.	0938	...	1225	1414	...	1619	1737	...	0056	...
208	Nesbyen d.	1049	...	1341	1532	...	1745	1847	...	0228	...
225	Gol d.	1101	...	1354	1545	...	1800	1900	...	0239	...
250	Ål d.	1124	...	1419	1608	...	1832	1921	...	0305	...
275	Geilo d.	1145	...	1440	1630	...	1856	1942	...	0328	...
286	Ustaoset d.	1156	...	1452	1643	...	1906	1953	...	0341	...
324	Finse d.	1225	...	1524	1717	...	1937	2021	...	0417	...
354	**Myrdal** a.	1253	...	1550	1746	...	2004	2045	...	0445	...
354	**Myrdal 781** d.	1258	...	1554	1751	...	2006	2047	...	0445	...
403	**Voss 781** a.	1341	...	1637	1834	...	2049	2128	...	0532	...
443	Dale **781** ▽ a.	|	...	1709x	1903x	...	|	2156x	...	0609	...
480	Arna **781** ▽ a.	1441x	...	1740	1935	...	2155	2227x	...	0647	...
489	**Bergen 781** a.	1452	...	1752	1945	...	2204	2235	...	0657	...

	62 v ✕⊡		602 n ✕⊡		604 ⑤f R	604 ⑦d ✕⊡	64 n ✕⊡		606 Ⓑw ♣R	
Bergen 781 d.	0758	...	1028	...	1458	1458	1558	...	2258	...
Arna **781** △ d.	0806	...	1037	...	1506	1506	1606	...	2307	...
Dale **781** △ d.	0836x	...	1107x	...	1536x	1536x	|	...	2344x	...
Voss 781 d.	0907	...	1139	...	1607	1607	1710	...	0015	...
Myrdal 781 a.	0947	...	1220	...	1652	1652	1750	...	0101	...
Myrdal d.	0950	...	1225	...	1657	1657	1752	...	0105	...
Finse d.	1017	...	1254	...	1730	1730	1818	...	0138	...
Ustaoset d.	1046	...	1326	...	1800	1800	1845	...	0209	...
Geilo d.	1058	...	1339	...	1812	1812	1857	...	0222	...
Ål d.	1121	...	1400	...	1833	1833	1919	...	0245	...
Gol d.	1141	...	1423	...	1858	1858	1938	...	0309	...
Nesbyen d.	1152	...	1436	...	1909	1909	1949	...	0322	...
Hønefoss d.	1304	...	1554	...	2023	2023	2059	...	0445	...
Drammen ▽ d.	1353	...	1655	...	2126	2126	2151	...	0542	...
Oslo Sentral a.	1432	...	1732	...	2212	2212	2232	...	0626	...

R – Reservation recommended.
d – Also Dec. 26, Jan. 1.
f – Also Dec. 22.
n – Not Dec. 24, 31.
v – Not Dec. 25, Jan. 1.
w – Not Dec. 24, 25, 31.
x – Stops on request only.
♣ – Conveys 🛏, (2) and ✕.
⊡ – Reservation recommended. Conveys *NSB Komfort*.
△ – Trains stop to pick up ony.
▽ – Trains call to set down only.

MYRDAL - VOSS - BERGEN and MYRDAL - FLÅM 781

km		⑦c		Ⓐn	605 Ⓑw ✕◇	Ⓐ	Ⓐn	Ⓐn	⚒n	w	⚒n	Ⓐ	61 v ✕◇	w	Ⓐn	b	601 Ⓑn ✕◇	601 ⑥ ✕◇	Ⓑw	607 ⑦d ◇	⑦d	b	603 ⑤f ✕◇	⑤	63 n ✕◇
	Oslo Sentral **780** d.	...	...	...	2311	...	...	...	...	...	...	...	0811	...	...	...	1033	1033	...	1227	...	...	1433	...	1607
0	**Myrdal** d.	...	...	...	0445	...	...	...	...	...	1110	...	1258	...	...	...	1554	1554	...	1751	1825	...	2006	2015	2047
18	Mjølfjell d.	...	...	...	|	...	...	0742	...	...	1128	...	|	...	1515	...	|	1609x	...	|	1841	...	|	2030	|
49	**Voss** a.	...	...	...	0532	...	...	0816	...	...	1206	...	1341	...	1547	...	1637	1637	...	1834	1915	...	2049	2100	2128
49	**Voss** d.	...	...	0515	0537	0620	0720	0835	0835	1050	...	1250	1343	1435	1550	1550	1640	1640	1753	1836	1920	1920	2051	...	2130
89	Dale d.	0128	...	0543	0609	0649	0749	0907	0907	1122	...	1318	|	1503	1623	1623	1709z	1709z	1824	1903z	1950	1950	|	...	2156z
104	Vaksdal d.	0143	...	0559	0626	0705	0805	0927	0927	1140	...	1336	|	1522	1639	1639	|	|	1840	|	2009	2009	|	...	|
126	Arna ‡ d.	0200	...	0617	0647s	0727	0826	0946	0946	1157	...	1356	1441z	1543	1656	1656	1740s	1740s	1857	1935s	2026	2026	2155s	...	2227z
135	**Bergen** ‡ a.	0208	...	0625	0657	0735	0835	0954	0954	1205	...	1405	1452	1552	1704	1704	1752	1752	1905	1945	2034	2034	2204	...	2235

	⑦c		Ⓐn	Ⓐ	62 v ✕◇	⚒n	w	602 ⑦ ✕◇	602 A ✕◇	Ⓐn	g	Ⓑw	⑦d	604 ⑤f ◇	604 ⑦d ✕◇	Ⓐ	64 n ✕◇	Ⓐn	k	⑤	Ⓐn	w	Ⓑw	⑥	606 Ⓑw ✕◇
Bergen ‡ d.	0035	...	...	0658	0758	0840	0840	1028	1028	1110	1310	1310	1310	1458	1458	1510	1558	1610	1710	1710	1810	1928	2128	2258	2258
Arna ‡ d.	0044	...	...	0706	0806u	0848	0848	1037u	1037u	1118	1318	1318	1318	1506u	1506u	1518	1606u	1618	1718	1718	1818	1936	2136	2306	2307u
Vaksdal d.	0101	...	...	0726	|	0905	0905	|	|	1140	1336	1336	1336	|	|	1539	|	1639	1740	1740	1840	1953	2153	2324	2326x
Dale d.	0118	...	...	0748	0836x	0924	0924	1107y	1107y	1156	1352	1352	1352	1536y	1536y	1555	|	1655	1756	1756	1856	2009	2212	2341	2344x
Voss a.	...	...	...	0820	0905	0954	0954	1135	1135	1228	1424	1424	1424	1603	1603	1623	1708	1727	1825	1825	1932	2039	2240	0010	0013
Voss d.	...	...	0700	...	0907	0958	...	1139	1139	...	...	1432	1432	1607	1607	...	1710	...	...	1840	...	...	...	...	0015
Mjølfjell d.	...	...	0732	...	|	1032	...	1206x	|	...	...	1504	1506	|	|	...	|	...	...	1913	...	...	...	...	|
Myrdal a.	...	...	...	...	0947	1049	...	1220	1220	...	...	...	1525	1652	1652	...	1750	...	...	1928	...	...	...	...	0101
Oslo Sentral **780** a.	...	...	...	...	1432	...	...	1732	1732	...	...	...	...	2212	2212	...	2232	...	...	...	...	...	...	...	0626

Myrdal - Flåm ⊠

km		v				n		n			
0	Myrdal d.	0955	...	1300	...	1600	...	1755	...	...	...
20	Flåm a.	1040	...	1350	...	1645	...	1840	...	...	...

	v				n		n			
Flåm d.	0900	...	1130	...	1450	...	1700	...	...	...
Myrdal a.	0940	...	1210	...	1540	...	1740	...	...	...

A – ①–⑥ (not Dec. 24, 31).
b – Not Dec. 24, 25.
c – Also Jan. 1.
d – Also Dec. 26, Jan. 1.
f – Also Dec. 22.
g – Not Dec. 25.
k – Not Dec. 24, 25, 26.
n – Not Dec. 24, 31.
s – Stops to set down only.
u – Stops to pick up only.
v – Not Dec. 25, Jan. 1.
w – Not Dec. 24, 25, 31.
x – Stops on request.
y – Stops on request to pick up only.
z – Stops on request to set down only.
◇ – Reservation recommended. See also Table **780**.
‡ – Additional local services operate.
⊠ – **Myrdal - Flåm operator**: Flåm Utvikling AS ✆ + 47 57 63 21 00. 30 % discount available for rail pass holders.

Oct. 1, 2007 - Apr. 30, 2008 ⛴ FLÅM - GUDVANGEN and 🚌 GUDVANGEN - VOSS 781a

	⛴ A	🚌 A	⛴ B	🚌 B							
Flåm d.	1510	...	1510	...	...	...	...	...	...	...	...
Gudvangen a.	1650	...	1700	...	...	...	...	...	...	...	...
Gudvangen d.	...	1655	...	1745	...	...	...	...	...	...	...
Voss a.	...	1750	...	1905	...	...	...	...	...	...	...

	🚌	⛴									
Voss d.	1000	...	...	...	...	...	...	...	...	...	...
Gudvangen a.	1125	...	...	...	...	...	...	...	...	...	...
Gudvangen d.	...	1130	...	...	...	...	...	...	...	...	...
Flåm a.	...	1330	...	...	...	...	...	...	...	...	...

A – Nov. 1 - Apr. 1
B – Oct. 1 – 31 and Apr. 2 – 30.
🚌 operators : Sogn Billag ✆ +47 57 67 66 00. Tide ASA ✆ +47 05505.
⛴ operator : Fylkesbaatane i Sogn og Fjordane ✆ +47 57 75 70 00.

Oct. 1, 2007 - Apr. 30, 2008 ⛴ / 🚌 GOL and FLÅM - BALESTRAND - BERGEN 782

	⛴ Ⓐ	⛴ ⑥	🚌	🚌	⛴ ⑦	🚌	🚌	🚌	🚌 h	🚌 h	🚌
Gol skysstasjon d.	...	...	...	...	...	...	...	...	1320	...	1910
Sogndal d.	...	...	...	0805	...	...	1430	...	|	...	|
Kaupangersenteret d.	...	...	...	0820	...	...	1445	...	|	...	|
Øvre Årdal ◇ d.	*0535*e	...	0755	|	...	1440	|	1440	|	1840	|
Lærdal d.	*0605*e	...	0855	0855	...	1535	1535	|	1515	|	2105j
Kaupangersenteret d.	*0640*e	...	|	|	...	|	|	1550h	1550	1950	2140j
Sogndal ⊕ d.	0705	0705	|	|	1510	|	|	1605h	1615	2005	2205
Flåm d.	|	|	0940	0940	|	1620	1620	...	|	...	|
Leikanger d.	0730	0730	|	|	1535	|	|	...	1640	...	2230
Balestrand d.	0750	0750	|	|	1555	|	|	...	1730	...	2310
Voss a.	|	|	1055	1055	|	1730	1730	...	...	...	...
Bergen ⊡ a.	1140	1150	1235	1235	1940	1915	1915	...	...	...	...

	🚌	🚌	🚌	🚌	🚌	⛴ ⑥	🚌	🚌	⛴ Ⓑ	🚌	🚌 ⑤⑦
Bergen ⊡ d.	...	0905	0905	...	...	1415	1530	1530	1630	...	...
Voss d.	...	1050	1050	...	...	|	1720	1720	|	...	...
Balestrand d.	1005	|	|	1310	...	1820	|	|	2020	2120b	...
Leikanger d.	1045	|	|	1350	...	1835	|	|	2050	2200b	...
Flåm a.	|	1155	1155	|	...	|	1830	1830	|	|	...
Sogndal ⊕ d.	1130	|	|	1430	1430	1900	|	|	2120	2230	2230
Kaupangersenteret d.	1145	|	|	1445	1445	...	|	|	...	2245	2245
Lærdal a.	1225	1250	1250	1525	|	...	1915	1915	...	2325	|
Øvre Årdal ◇ a.	|	|	1345	|	1605	...	|	2030	...	|	0010
Kaupangersenteret a.	|	1320	...	|	...	...	1950	...	...	|	...
Sogndal a.	|	1335	...	|	...	...	2005	...	...	|	...
Gol skysstasjon a.	1420	...	...	1720	...	...	...	...	...	0120	...

b – Ⓑ.
e – By 🚌 to Sogndal. 10 minutes later until Dec. 31.
h – 10 – 15 minutes later from Jan. 1.
j – 10 minutes later until Dec. 31.
◇ – Øvre Årdal Farnes.
⊕ – 🚌: Sogndal skysstasjon. ⛴: Sogndal kai.
⊡ – 🚌: Bus station. ⛴: Strandkaiterminal.
🚌 operator : Sogn Billag ✆ +47 57 67 66 00.
⛴ operator : Fylkesbaatane i Sogn og Fjordane ✆ +47 57 75 70 00.

783 LILLEHAMMER - OSLO - SKIEN

All trains convey *NSB Komfort* and 🍷

km		Ⓐz	Ⓐz	Ⓐz	Ⓒr	Ⓐz	Ⓑp	⑥e	⚒	Ⓑp	⑥e	⚒		Ⓐz	Ⓐn	⑥e	Ⓑz	Ⓐz	⑦b	⚒z	†	Ⓑw	z	Ⓑw	z	Ⓑw‡	z‡
0	**Lillehammer** § d.	...	0402	0523	0523	0619	0718	0718	0820	0913	0913	1018	1110	1205	...	1315	1315	1408	1408	1512	1512	1611	1714	1811	1920	2007	...
58	**Hamar** § a.	...	0447	0608	0608	0704	0805	0805	0905	1003	1003	1104	1156	1257	...	1404	1404	1457	1457	1602	1602	1702	1803	1856	2006	2057	...
58	**Hamar** § d.	...	0450	0613	0613	0707	0807	0807	0907	1007	1007	1108	1208	1307	...	1408	1408	1500	1500	1605	1605	1707	1808	1908	2008	2108	...
117	Eidsvoll d.	...	0535	0657	0657	0757	0857	0857	0957	1057	1057	1157	1257	1357	...	1457	1457	1557	1557	1657	1657	1757	1857	1957	2057	2157	...
133	Oslo ✈ ● § d.	...	0546	0708	0708	0808	0908	0908	1008	1108	1108	1208	1308	1408	...	1508	1508	1608	1608	1708	1708	1808	1908	2008	2108	2208	...
164	Lillestrøm § d.	...	0601	0723	0723	0823	0923	0923	1023	1123	1123	1223	1323	1423	...	1523	1523	1623	1623	1723	1723	1823	1923	2023	2123	2223	...
185	**Oslo** Sentral § a.	...	0612	0734	0734	0834	0934	0934	1034	1134	1134	1234	1334	1434	...	1534	1534	1634	1634	1734	1734	1834	1934	2034	2134	2234	...
185	**Oslo** Sentral d.	0537	0643	0743	0743	0843	0943	0943	1043	1143	1143	1243	1343	1443	1511	1543	1543	1643	1643	1743	1743	1843	1943	2043	2143	2243	2343
225	Drammen d.	0616	0722	0822	0822	0922	1022	1022	1122	1222	1222	1322	1422	1522	1548	1622	1622	1722	1722	1822	1822	1922	2022	2122	2222	2322	0022
259	Holmestrand d.	0640	0746	0846	0846	0946	1046	1046	1146	1246	1246	1346	1446	1546	1610	1646	1646	1746	1746	1846	1846	1946	2046	2146	2246	2346	0046
273	Skoppum d.	0651	0757	0857	0857	0957	1057	1057	1157	1257	1257	1357	1457	1557	1625	1657	1657	1757	1757	1857	1857	1957	2057	2157	2257	2357	0057
289	Tønsberg d.	0718	0816	0916	0916	1016	1116	1116	1216	1316	1316	1416	1516	1616	1638	1716	1716	1816	1816	1916	1916	2016	2116	2216	2310	0010	0110
313	**Sandefjord** d.	0737	0837	0937	0937	1037	1137	1137	1237	1337	1337	1437	1537	1637	1659	1737	1737	1837	1837	1937	1937	2037	2137	2235	2329	0029	0129
332	Larvik a.	0750	0850	0950	0950	1050	1150	1150	1250	1350	1350	1450	1550	1650	1713	1750	1750	1850	1850	1950	1950	2050	2150	2248	2342	0042	0142
332	Larvik d.	0752*	0852	0955	1005*	1052*	1152*	1152	1252*	1352*	1352	1452*	1552*	1652*	1715	1752*	1758	1855	1852*	1955	1952*	2052*	2152	2250	2344	0044	0144
366	Porsgrunn **779** d.	0815*	0926	1030	1028*	1115*	1215*	1226	1315*	1415*	1426	1515*	1615*	1715*	1749	1815*	1833	1929	1915*	2031	2015*	2115*	2226	2323	0017	0117	0217
375	**Skien 779** a.	0833*	0934	1038	1046*	1133*	1233*	1234	1333*	1433*	1434	1533*	1633*	1733*	1757	1833*	1841	1937	1933*	2039	2033*	2133*	2234	2331	0025	0125	0225

	Ⓐz	⚒	Ⓐz	f	⚒	Ⓐz	Ⓒr	⚒	Ⓐz	Ⓒe	Ⓑw	⑥e	Ⓑz	⑦b	Ⓐz	⚒z	†	Ⓐz	⑦b	⚒z	†	Ⓑw	Ⓑz	⑥	⑥	Ⓑw	Ⓑz
Skien 779 d.	0343v	0443	0542	0633	0739	0825*	0839	0925*	1025*	1034	1125*	1225*	1233	1325*	1333	1425*	1440	1520*	1540	1620*	1640	1725*	1825*	1825*	...	1925*	2025
Porsgrunn **779** d.	0352v	0452	0551	0648	0749	0843*	0849	0943*	1043*	1044	1143*	1243*	1243	1343*	1343	1443*	1450	1543*	1550	1643*	1650	1743*	1843*	1843*	...	1943*	2043*
Larvik a.	0424v	0524	0624	0722	0822	0910*	0922	1010*	1110*	1116	1210*	1310*	1316	1410*	1416	1510*	1522	1610*	1622	1710*	1722	1810*	1910*	1910*	...	2010*	2110*
Larvik d.	0426v	0526	0626	0724	0824	0924	0924	1024	1124	1124	1224	1324	1324	1424	1424	1524	1524	1624	1624	1724	1724	1824	1924	1924	...	2024	2124
Sandefjord d.	0441	0541	0641	0739	0839	0939	0939	1039	1139	1139	1239	1339	1339	1439	1439	1539	1539	1639	1639	1739	1739	1839	1939	1939	...	2039	2139
Tønsberg d.	0501	0601	0701	0801	0901	1001	1001	1101	1201	1201	1301	1401	1401	1501	1501	1601	1601	1701	1701	1801	1801	1901	2001	2001	...	2101	2201
Skoppum d.	0513	0613	0713	0813	0913	1013	1013	1113	1213	1213	1313	1413	1413	1513	1513	1613	1613	1713	1713	1813	1813	1913	2013	2013	...	2113	2213
Holmestrand d.	0524	0624	0724	0824	0924	1024	1024	1124	1224	1224	1324	1424	1424	1524	1524	1624	1624	1724	1724	1824	1824	1924	2024	2024	...	2124	2224
Drammen d.	0551	0651	0751	0851	0951	1051	1051	1151	1251	1251	1351	1451	1451	1551	1551	1651	1651	1751	1751	1851	1851	1951	2051	2051	...	2151	2251
Oslo Sentral a.	0630	0732	0828	0928	1028	1128	1128	1230	1328	1328	1428	1528	1528	1628	1628	1728	1728	1828	1828	1928	1928	2028	2128	2128	...	2228	2329
Oslo Sentral § d.	0637	0737	0837	0937	1037	1137	1137	1237	1337	1337	1437	1537	1537	1637	1637	1737	1737	1837	1837	1937	1937	2037	2137	...	2307	...	...
Lillestrøm § d.	0649	0749	0849	0949	1049	1149	1149	1249	1349	1349	1449	1549	1549	1649	1649	1749	1749	1849	1849	1949	1949	2049	2149	...	2319	...	...
Oslo ✈ ● § d.	0705	0805	0905	1005	1105	1205	1205	1305	1405	1405	1505	1605	1605	1705	1705	1805	1805	1905	1905	2005	2005	2105	2205	...	2335	...	...
Eidsvoll d.	0716	0816	0916	1016	1116	1216	1216	1316	1416	1416	1516	1616	1616	1716	1716	1816	1816	1916	1916	2016	2016	2116	2216	...	2346	...	...
Hamar § a.	0759	0903	0959	1059	1159	1259	1259	1402	1459	1459	1559	1703	1703	1759	1759	1859	1859	2004	2004	2059	2059	2204	2259	...	0028	...	...
Hamar § d.	0806	0905	1004	1106	1202	1302	1302	1405	1502	1502	1602	1705	1705	1806	1806	1901	1901	2008	2008	2101	2101	2206	2304	...	0030	...	...
Lillehammer § a.	0855	0950	1053	1154	1256	1353	1353	1457	1549	1549	1649	1750	1750	1900	1900	1955	1955	2100	2100	2151	2151	2251	2349	...	0116	...	...

b – Also Dec. 26, Jan. 1.
e – Also Dec. 24, 31.
f – Not Dec. 25, Jan. 1.
n – Not Dec. 24 - Jan. 1.
p – Not Dec. 24, 25, 31, Jan. 1.
r – Also Dec. 24, 31; not Dec. 25, Jan. 1.
v – On ②–⑤ until Nov. 2 by 🚌 to Sandefjord.
w – Not Dec. 24, 25, 31.
z – Not Dec. 24, 31.
* – By 🚌.
§ – See also Table **785**.
● – Oslo Lufthavn Gardermoen. See also Table **771**.
‡ – Subject to alteration south of Drammen on ①–④ until Nov. 1 (by 🚌 for part of journey).

784 HAMAR - RØROS - TRONDHEIM

km		Ⓐz	⑥	Ⓐ	⚒z	Ⓑ	⑤	Ⓐz	Ⓒ	z	Ⓑw	Ⓑq
0	**Hamar** d.	...	...	0808	1009	1209	1209	...	...	1608	1811	2014
32	Elverum d.	...	...	0831	1034	1234	1234	...	...	1633	1834	2039
64	Rena d.	...	...	0853	1059	1256	1256	...	...	1655	1859	2101
120	Koppang d.	...	...	0935	1141	1338	1338	...	...	1737	1941	2143
273	**Røros** a.	...	...	1130	1335	1529	1529	...	...	1930	2131	2334
273	**Røros** d.	0510	0705	...	...	...	1535	1535	1630	1935	...	...
384	Støren d.	0643	0835	...	...	...	1709	1709	1802	2106	...	...
435	**Trondheim** a.	0735	0930	...	...	...	1800	1800	1855	2200	...	...

	Ⓐz	⚒	Ⓐz		⑤⑥†		Ⓑw	†	z	Ⓐz	⑦b
Trondheim d.	...	...	0540	0950	0950	...	...	1350	...	1615	2040
Støren d.	...	...	0644	1041	1041	...	...	1444	...	1709	2132
Røros a.	...	...	0815	1212	1212	...	...	1615	...	1845	2303
Røros d.	0427	0617	0824	...	1218	1218	1411	1622	1622	...	...
Koppang d.	0617	0807	1017	...	1417	1417	1606	1817	1817	...	...
Rena d.	0659	0852	1059	...	1459	1459	1654	1859	1859	...	...
Elverum d.	0721	0914	1121	...	1521	1521	1716	1921	1921	...	...
Hamar a.	0746	0939	1146	...	1546	1546	1741	1946	1946	...	...

b – Also Dec. 26, Jan. 1.
q – Not Dec. 23, 24, 25, 31.
w – Not Dec. 24, 25, 31.
z – Not Dec. 24, 31.

785 OSLO - LILLEHAMMER - ÅNDALSNES and TRONDHEIM

km		407	41	2341	313	2343	45	2345	47	2347	329	405
		①–⑤	v	v	Ⓐ	Ⓐz	z	z	Ⓑw	Ⓑw	Ⓑw	Ⓑw
		n R	R	R		R	R	R	R	R		R
		🍴⊡	🍴⊡	🍷	🍷⊡	🍷	🍴⊡	🍷	🍴⊡	🍷	🍷⊡	🍴♣
0	**Oslo** Sentral § d.	...	0807	...	1037	...	1450	...	1607	...	1837	2305
21	Lillestrøm § d.	...	0819u	...	1049	...	1505u	...	1619u	...	1849	2327u
52	Oslo ✈ ● § d.	...	0833u	...	1105	...	1524u	...	1633u	...	1905	2346u
127	**Hamar** § d.	...	0929	...	1202	...	1619	...	1730	...	2008	0045
185	**Lillehammer** § d.	...	1014	...	1256	1301	1702	...	1814	...	2103	0139
243	Ringebu d.	...	1056	...	...	1344	1744	...	1856	...	2145	0234
267	Vinstra d.	...	1112	...	...	1404	1801	...	1913	...	2202	0256
298	Otta d.	...	1136	...	...	1429	1823	...	1941	...	2226	0324
344	Dombås d.	...	1208	1215	...	1500	1854	1856	2013	2014	2258	0406
458	**Åndalsnes** a.	...	|	1332	...	1630	|	2012	|	2130	...	|
430	Oppdal d.	0650	1308	...	...	...	1952	...	2112	...	...	0515
502	Støren d.	0740	1359	...	...	...	2042	...	2203	...	...	0613
553	**Trondheim** a.	0835	1448	...	...	...	2125	...	2250	...	...	0700

🚌	v	v		Ⓐz	Ⓐz		z	z		Ⓑw‡	Ⓑw‡
Åndalsnes d.	1345	1345	...	1640	1700	...	2015	2025	...	2135	2135
Molde a.	1510	|	...	|	1820	...	2135	|	...	2255	|
Ålesund a.	...	1555	...	1850	...	...	...	2235	...	...	2345

🚌	⚒		Ⓐ		v		⑤⑦		Ⓑw		
Oppdal d.	0530	...	1020	...	1315	...	1810	...	2130	...	...
Kristiansund a.	0905	...	1430	...	1635	...	2130	...	0040	...	...

	308	2340	316	2342	42	2344	44	2346	46	406
	⚒	Ⓐz		v	v	Ⓑw	Ⓑw	z	z	Ⓑw
		R		R	R	R	R	R	R	R
	🍷⊡	🍷	🍷⊡	🍷	🍴⊡	🍷	🍴⊡	🍷	🍴⊡	🍴♣
Trondheim d.	...	...	...	...	0825	...	1405	...	1610	2305
Støren d.	...	...	...	...	0909	...	1449	...	1653	2355
Oppdal d.	...	...	...	...	1003	...	1541	...	1748	0100
Åndalsnes d.	...	0742	...	0933	|	1500	|	1718	|	|
Dombås d.	0525	0904	...	1055	1102	1621	1646	1839	1849	0210
Otta d.	0556	0934	...	...	1133	...	1716	...	1923	0247
Vinstra d.	0619	0957	...	...	1154	...	1738	...	1945	0314
Ringebu d.	0636	1013	...	...	1212	...	1759	...	2001	0332
Lillehammer 783 d.	0718	1058	1110	...	1257	...	1845	...	2045	0420
Hamar 783 d.	0807	...	1208	...	1350	...	1929	...	2129	0512
Oslo ✈ ● **783** d.	0908	...	1308	...	1443s	...	2014s	...	2214s	0606s
Lillestrøm **783** d.	0923	...	1323	...	1501s	...	2031s	...	2231s	0626s
Oslo Sentral **783** a.	0934	...	1334	...	1513	...	2042	...	2242	0643

🚌	Ⓐz		v	v		Ⓑw	Ⓑw		z	z
Ålesund d.	...	...	0705	...	...	...	1235	...	...	1455
Molde d.	0620	...	|	0800	...	1305	|	...	1530c	|
Åndalsnes a.	0740	...	0920	0920	...	1425	1450	...	1655	1710

🚌	⚒		Ⓐ			z		⑤⑦		Ⓑw
Kristiansund d.	0630	...	1040	...	...	1400	...	1635	...	2050
Oppdal a.	0945	...	1420	...	...	1725	...	2010	...	0010

R – Reservation recommended.
c – 1535 on ⑥⑦.
n – Not Dec. 24 - Jan. 1.
s – Stops to set down only.
u – Stops to pick up only.
v – Not Dec. 25, Jan. 1.
w – Not Dec. 24, 25, 31.
z – Not Dec. 24, 31.
♣ – Conveys 🛏 and [2].
⊡ – Conveys *NSB Komfort*.
§ – See also Table **783**.
‡ – By Taxi (only available for passengers from train **2347**). Runs on request only – please inform the on train staff.
● – Oslo Lufthavn Gardermoen (see also Table **771**).

786 SOUTHWEST NORWAY 🚌 LINKS

BERGEN - TRONDHEIM (Operator: NOR-WAY Bussekspress ✆ +47 815 44 444)
Bergen d. 1630 → Trondheim a. 0645.
Trondheim d. 2000 → Bergen a. 0945.

BERGEN - ÅLESUND (Operator: NOR-WAY Bussekspress ✆ +47 815 44 444)
Bergen d. 0800 → Ålesund a. 1735 (1720 on ⑥).
Ålesund d. 1100 → Bergen a. 2020.

BERGEN - LILLEHAMMER (Operator: NOR-WAY Bussekspress ✆ +47 815 44 444)
Bergen d. 0905 → Voss d. 1050 → Flåm d. 1155 → Lillehammer a. 1755.
Lillehammer d. 1010 → Flåm d. 1620 → Voss a. 1730 → Bergen a. 1915.

BERGEN - KRISTIANSAND (Operator: NOR-WAY Bussekspress ✆ +47 815 44 444)
Bergen d. 0730 → Odda d. 1110 → Haukeli a. 1300, d. 1440 → Kristiansand a. 1850.
Kristiansand d. 0845 → Haukeli a. 1300, d. 1440 → Odda a. 1635 → Bergen a. 2000.

BERGEN - ODDA ★ 🚌/⛴ *Journey time: 3 hrs 20 m – 3 hrs 50 m.*
From Bergen at 0730, 0910 Ⓐ, 1130, 1300 Ⓐ, 1340 ⑥, 1430, 1610 Ⓑ, 1730 Ⓑ and 2030 Ⓑ.
From Odda at 0535 ⚒, 0610 Ⓐ, 0930, 1230, 1540 ⑦, 1550 ①–⑥, 1635 and 2035 Ⓑ.

GEILO - ODDA ★ *Journey time: 3 hrs 25 m – 3 hrs 50 m. Summer services only.*
From Geilo at 1150 **B**. From Odda at 0720 ①–⑥ **B** and 1230 Ⓑ **A**.

VOSS - ULVIK ★ *Journey time: 50 – 65 minutes.*
From Voss at 0845 Ⓐ, 1005 **D**, 1140 Ⓐ, 1530 Ⓐ **e**, 1645 ⑥ **C**, 1650 ⑦, 1735 Ⓑ and 2135 Ⓑ.
From Ulvik at 0725 Ⓐ, 0855 ①–⑥, 0855 ⑦ **C**, 1410 Ⓐ **e**, 1525 Ⓑ, 1525 ⑥ **C** and 1810 Ⓑ.

A – July 1 - Aug. 12.
B – July 1 - Sept. 9.
C – Until Sept. 30.
D – Daily until Sept. 30; ⑥ from Oct. 6.
e – Also ⑥ from Oct. 6.
★ – Operator: Tide ASA ✆ +47 05505.

TRONDHEIM - BODØ and NARVIK 787

km		1781	1783	475		473	473	1785	471	1789		479	477
		Ⓐn	Ⓐz	w	🚌	⚒	Ⓐz	Ⓐn	d	Ⓐz	🚌	Ⓑn	Ⓑp
		🍷	🍷	NR	◇	🍷	🍷R	🍷	✕R	🍷	◇	🍷R	🍷R
0	**Trondheim** .... § d.	...	...	2335	...	...	...	...	0740	...	...	...	1558
33	Værnes ✈ ‡ ... § d.	...	...	0005	...	...	...	...	0815u	...	...	...	1632u
34	Stjørdal .... § d.	...	...	0010	...	...	...	...	0820u	...	...	...	1637u
126	Steinkjer .... § d.	...	...	0129	...	...	...	...	0944u	...	...	...	1800u
220	Grong .... d.	...	...	0238	...	...	...	...	1053	...	...	...	1907
406	Mosjøen .... d.	...	...	0458	...	0650	0650	...	1308	...	...	1645	2119
498	Mo i Rana .... d.	...	...	0608	...	0753	0800	...	1418	...	...	1746	2222
648	Rognan .... d.	0542	0642	0802	...	...	0954	...	1613	1740	...	1936	...
	Bodø ⊖ .... d.	|	|	|	0700	...	|	...	|	|	1615	|	...
674	Fauske .... a.	0603	0703	0825	0815	...	1014	...	1635	1800	1730	1956	...
674	Fauske .... d.	0603	0703	0830	0855	...	1016	1415	1645	1808	1810	2001	...
	Narvik ⊡ ...... a.	|	|	|	1330	...	|	|	|	|	2300	|	...
729	**Bodø** .... a.	0642	0742	0910	...	...	1055	1455	1725	1847	...	2040	...

	478	470	1792		472	1786	1788	474		476
	c	Ⓐn	A	🚌	d	Ⓐz	Ⓐz	Ⓑg	🚌	w
	🍷R	🍷	🍷	◇	✕R	🍷	🍷	🍷R	◇	NR
Bodø .... d.	...	0748	0748	...	1220	1505	1605	1727	...	2100
Narvik ⊡ ... d.	...	|	|	0700	|	|	|	|	1610	|
Fauske .... a.	...	0828	0828	1200	1257	1551	1643	1806	2110	2138
Fauske .... d.	...	0828	0828	1215	1300	...	1645	1807	2125	2142
Bodø ⊖ ..... a.	...	|	|	1325	|	...	|	|	2240	|
Rognan .... d.	...	0848	0848	...	1322	...	1705	1832	...	2204
Mo i Rana ...... d.	0820	1032	...	...	1530	...	...	2017	...	0003
Mosjøen .... d.	0927	1135	...	...	1640	...	...	2117	...	0205*
Grong .... d.	1146	...	...	...	1904	...	...	...	...	0426
Steinkjer ..... § d.	1248s	...	...	...	2012s	...	...	...	...	0540
Stjørdal .... § d.	1404r	...	...	...	2133r	...	...	...	...	0704
Værnes ✈ ‡ § d.	1406r	...	...	...	2135r	...	...	...	...	0706
Trondheim . § a.	1439	...	...	...	2210	...	...	...	...	0740

Local services Trondheim - Steinkjer and v.v.

km	▶	Ⓐz	⚒z				Ⓐn	v	Ⓑe	z	z	z	Ⓑw
0	**Trondheim** .... d.	0610	0710	0910	1110	1310	1439	1510	1538	1710	1910	2110	2310
31	Hell ● .... d.	0644	0744	0944	1144	1344	1513	1544	1613	1744	1944	2144	2344
33	Værnes ✈ ‡ ● .. d.	0646	0746	0946	1146	1346	1515	1546	1615	1746	1946	2146	2346
34	Stjørdal .... d.	0652	0752	0952	1152	1352	1520	1552	1620	1752	1952	2152	2349
126	**Steinkjer** .... a.	0816	0916	1116	1319	1516	1644	1716	1744	1916	2116	2316	0107

▶	Ⓐn	b	b				v	z	Ⓐn	z
Steinkjer .... d.	0600	0728	0925	1128	1328	1528	1728	1928	2028	2134
Stjørdal .... d.	0720	0852	1052	1252	1452	1652	1852	2052	2152	2254
Værnes ✈ ‡ ● d.	0722	0854	1054	1254	1454	1654	1854	2054	2154	2256
Hell ● .... d.	0725	0857	1057	1257	1457	1657	1857	2057	2157	2259
Trondheim .... a.	0805	0935	1135	1335	1535	1735	1935	2135	2231	2335

A – Runs on Dec. 27, 28 only.
N – Conveys 🛏, 2 and ✕.
R – Reservation recommended.

b – Not Dec. 25, Jan. 1.
c – Not Dec. 24, 25, 31, Jan. 1.
d – Not Dec. 25.
e – Not Dec. 24, 25, 27, 28, 30, 31.
g – Not Dec. 24, 25, 26, 31.
n – Not Dec. 24 - Jan. 1.

p – Also Dec. 22; not Dec. 24, 25, 31.
r – Stops on request to set down only.
s – Stops to set down only.
u – Stops to pick up only.
v – Not Dec. 24.
w – Not Dec. 24, 25, 31.
z – Not Dec. 24, 31.

* – Arrives 0110.
● – Trains stop on request.

⊡ – Bus station.
⊖ – Bodø Busstorget.
◇ – Operator: Ofotens Bilruter. ✆ +47 76 92 35 00.
§ – See also panel below main table.
‡ – Station for Trondheim Airport.

▶ – **Additional services** Trondheim - Stjørdal - Steinkjer and v.v.:
From Trondheim at 0510 Ⓐ **n**, 0810 Ⓐ **n**, 1010 Ⓐ **n**, 1210 Ⓐ **z**, 1410 Ⓐ **z**, 1610 Ⓐ **z** and 1810 Ⓐ **n**.
From Steinkjer at 0528 Ⓐ **z**, 0628 Ⓐ **z**, 0657 Ⓐ **n**, 0828 Ⓐ **z**, 1028 Ⓐ **n**, 1228 Ⓐ **n**, 1428 Ⓐ **z**, 1628 Ⓐ **n** and 1828 Ⓐ **z**.

LAPLAND 🚌 LINKS 789

Narvik – Tromsø – Alta

Operator: T

km		①–⑤			Ⓑ	Ⓑ			⑦		
0	**Narvik** .... d.	0520	...	...	1300	1300	...	1530*	1835*	...	...
181	Nordkjosbotn .... d.	0820	...	...	1615	1615	...	1845	2150	...	...
252	Tromsø .... d.	0925	...	1600	|	1725	...	1945	2250	...	...
241	Lyngseidet .... d.	...	...	1745	1745	...	...	...	...	...	...
465	**Alta** .... a.	...	...	2230	2230	...	...	...	...	...	...

km		①–⑤					⚒	Ⓐ	⑥		⑦	⑦	⑦
0	**Alta** .... d.	...	...	...	...	...	1045	1045	1045	...	...	1410	1410
224	Lyngseidet .... d.	...	...	...	...	...	1545	1545	1545	...	...	1910	1910
293	Tromsø .... d.	0620	...	1030	...	1600	|	1725	1800	...	2020	|	2045
	Nordkjosbotn .... d.	0735	...	1135	...	1705	1705	...	...	...	2125	2125	...
	Narvik .... a.	1030‡	...	1445‡	...	2010	2010	...	...	...	0015	0015	...

Alta – Hammerfest – Karasjok – Kirkenes

Operator: F

km		①–⑤	⑦	①–⑤	①–⑤	①③	⑤⑦	①–④	①–④	⑥	⑤⑦	⑤⑦
0	**Alta** .... d.	...	...	0635	...	...	...	1430	...	1445	1500	...
	Hammerfest .. d.	...	...	|	0710	...	...	|	1505	|	|	1540
87	Skaidi .... d.	...	...	0810z	0810	...	...	1615	1615	1610	1645	1645
	Hammerfest .. a.	...	...	0900	|	...	...	1705	|	1700	1745	|
112	Olderfjord .... d.	...	...	...	0845	...	...	...	1650	...	...	1720
174	Lakselv .... d.	...	...	...	1010	...	...	...	1755	...	...	1835
248	Karasjok .... d.	...	...	...	1125	1200	1410	...	1910	...	...	1950
429	Tanabru .... d.	0830	1130	...	...	1500	1715	...	...	...	...	...
571	**Kirkenes** .... a.	1050	1350	...	...	1720	1935	...	...	...	...	...

km		①–⑤	①–⑤	⑥	K	①–④	①–④		⑤⑦	⑤⑦	Ⓑ
	Kirkenes .... d.	...	...	...	0805	...	...	...	...	...	1510
	Tanabru .... d.	...	...	...	1035	...	...	...	...	...	1800
	Karasjok .... d.	0525	...	...	1310	1350	...	...	1430	...	...
	Lakselv .... d.	0725	...	...	...	1520	...	...	1605	...	...
	Olderfjord .... d.	0845	...	...	...	1650	...	...	1720	...	...
0	Hammerfest ... d.	|	0810	1015	...	|	1615	...	|	1635	...
57	Skaidi .... d.	0915	0915	1110	...	1720	1720	...	1750	1750	...
	Hammerfest ... a.	1010	|	|	...	1815	|	...	1845	|	...
144	**Alta** .... a.	...	1035	1220	...	...	1840	...	...	1915	...

Rovaniemi – Muonio – Tromsø

km			A	C
0	**Rovaniemi** rail station d.	1110	1110	1110
157	Kittilä .... d.	1335	1335	1335
238	Muonio .... d.	1505	1505	1505
327	Karesuvanto .... d.	...	1625	1625
440	Kilpisjärvi ⊡ .... FI d.	...	1755	1755
535	Nordkjosbotn .... NO d.	...	...	1830
608	**Tromsø** .... a.	...	...	1930

		B	D
Tromsø .... d.	...	...	0730
Nordkjosbotn .... NO d.	...	...	0830
Kilpisjärvi ⊡ .... FI d.	...	1110	1110
Karesuvanto .... d.	...	1245	1245
Muonio .... d.	1415	1415	1415
Kittilä .... d.	1545	1545	1545
Rovaniemi rail station a.	1745	1745	1745

Rovaniemi – Karasjok – Nordkapp

Operator: E

km			H
0	**Rovaniemi** rail station ... d.	1110	1110
130	Sodankylä .... d.	1345	1345
305	Ivalo .... d.	1620	1620
345	Inari .... FI d.	1655	1655
461	Karasjok, Rica Hotel NO a.	1755	1755
536	Lakselv, Statoil .... a.	...	1925
735	**Nordkapp** .... a.	...	2220

		J
Nordkapp .... d.	...	0100
Lakselv, Statoil .... d.	...	0815
Karasjok, Rica Hotel . NO d.	0920	0920
Inari .... FI d.	1215	1215
Ivalo .... d.	1320	1320
Sodankylä .... d.	1555	1555
Rovaniemi rail station ..... a.	1735	1735

A – ⑤⑥ Mar. 21 - May 9.
B – ⑥⑦ Mar. 22 - May 10.
C – June 1 - Sept. 22.
D – June 2 - Sept. 23.

H – June 1 - Aug. 24.
J – June 2 - Aug. 25.
K – ①③⑤⑦.

c – From Norwegian Consulate.
q – ③④⑤⑦ (daily June 1 - Sept. 21).
v – ①④⑤⑥ (daily June 1 - Sept. 22).
z – Arrives 0805.

* – Calls 7 minutes later at rail station.
‡ – Calls 5 minutes earlier at rail station.
⊡ – Trekking centre (Retkeilykeskus).
◆ – Runs one hour later on ⑥⑦.

FI – Finland (East European Time).
NO – Norway (Central European Time).
RU – Russia (Moskva Time).

Rovaniemi – Karasjok, Tanabru, Kirkenes and Murmansk

Operator:	G	G	S	G/M	E	P		E	G/L	G
		◆		①③⑤		①–⑥			Ⓑ	①–⑤
Rovaniemi rail station .. d.	0820	...	...	...	1110	1520	...	1705	2010	2300
Sodankylä .... d.	1020	...	...	...	1345	1730	...	1915	2200	0105
Ivalo .... FI d.	1250	1300	...	1530	1620	1935	...	2130	0015	0310
Inari .... FI d.	...	1340	...	|	1655	...	...	2205	...	...
Karasjok .... NO a.	...	...	...	|	1755	...	...	|	...	...
Tanabru .... NO a.	...	...	...	|	...	...	...	2355q	...	...
Kirkenes, Europris ... NO d.	...	...	1500	|	...	...	...	...	...	...
Murmansk .... RU a.	...	...	2100	2300	...	...	...	...	...	...

Operator:	G	E	G	G/L	E	S		G/M	G	G
	①–⑤		①–⑤	①–⑥				①③⑤		
Murmansk .... RU d.	...	...	...	...	...	0700c	...	0830	...	...
Kirkenes .... NO d.	...	...	...	...	...	1100	...	|	...	...
Tanabru .... NO d.	...	0330v	...	...	...	...	...	|	...	...
Karasjok .... NO d.	...	|	...	...	0920	...	...	|	...	...
Inari .... FI d.	...	0715	1105	...	1215	...	...	|	1415	...
Ivalo .... FI d.	0615	0815	1140	1215	1320	...	...	1400	1450	1615
Sodankylä .... d.	0900	1040	...	1500	1555	...	...	...	...	1845
Rovaniemi rail station .. a.	1045	1220	...	1705	1735	...	...	...	...	2030

Operators: *E* – Eskelisen Lapin Linjat. *F* – FFR Connex. *G* – Gold Line. *L* – Liikenne O. Niemelä. *M* – Murmanskavtotrans. *P* – Pikakuljetus Rovaniemi. *S* – Pasvikturist AS. *T* – TIRB.

FINLAND

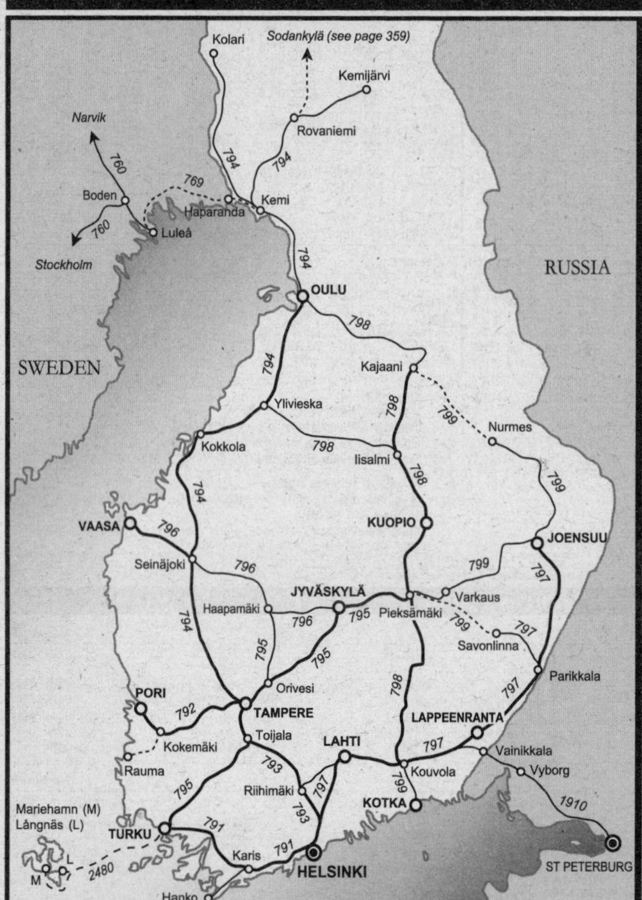

Operator: VR – VR-Yhtymä Oy (www.vr.fi).

Tickets and train types: For all except purely local journeys, tickets are always sold for travel by a specific train or combination of trains. There are four different pricing-scales, corresponding to each of the following train types (in descending order of cost):

- **S 220 Pendolino** (e.g. *S* **123**) – high-speed tilting trains (220 km/h), with 1st (*Business*) and 2nd class seats, all reservable.
- **InterCity** (e.g. *IC* **124**) – quality fast trains between major centres, with 1st and 2nd class seats, all reservable.
- **Express**, *pikajunat* (train number only shown, e.g. **128**) – other fast trains, with 2nd class seats, all reservable.

  Night expresses – all trains in Table **790** and those marked ★ in other tables – convey sleeping-cars and 2nd class seats only; see also **Services**, below.
- **Regional**, *taajamajunat* (no train number shown) – stopping-trains, normally with 2nd class seats only, non-reservable.

  S 220, InterCity and Express tickets – if purchased before the train's departure – include an allocated reserved seat.

Services: ✗ indicates a train with a restaurant car (which may be self-service).

Trains marked 🍸 convey a buffet car.

Complimentary light meals are served to holders of Plus and Business Plus tickets.

A supplement is payable for travel in sleeping-cars (🛏) in addition to the appropriate **Regional** fare – 2nd class for a berth in a 2- or 3-person cabin, 1st class for occupancy of a single-berth cabin. Sleeper supplements cost up to 50% more on peak nights in mid-winter. Seated passengers on night express trains pay the 2nd class **Express** fare.

Timings: Timings are valid from **December 8, 2007** to **May 31, 2008**.

In these tables Ⓐ = ①–⑤, ⚒ = ①–⑥.

Changes to the normal pattern of services are likely to occur on and around the dates of public holidays – check timings locally if planning to travel at these times.

790 🛏 Summary of Sleeper Trains 🛏

	263 A		265		267 ⑤J		269 E		933	273
Helsinki d.	1852	...	1930	...	2030	...	2130	...	...	2230
Turku d.	|	...	|	...	|	...	|	...	2105	|
Tampere d.	2136	...	2211	...	2308	...	2359	...	0115	0115
Oulu a.	0437	...	0501	...	0630	...	0605	...	0727	0727
Kolari a.	0930	...	|	...	|	....	1045	...	|	|
Rovaniemi a.	...	...	0753	...	0932	...	...	...	1041	1041

	262 B	264 ⑦J		266	266		270 D	272 H		274
Rovaniemi d.	...	1717	...	1800	1800	...	...	...	...	2110
Kolari d.	1615	|	...	|	|	...	1830	1830	...	|
Oulu d.	2050	2031	...	2140	2140	...	2320	2320	...	2355
Tampere a.	0326	0349	...	0405	0405	...	0537	0610	...	0548
Turku a.	|	|	...	|	0755	...	|	|	...	|
Helsinki a.	0606	0630	...	0654	...	...	0806	0937	...	0837

A – ④–⑥ Dec. 20 - Jan. 4; ⑤ Feb. 1 - Apr. 25.
B – ⑤⑥ Dec. 21 - Jan. 5; ⑥ Feb. 9 - Apr. 26.
D – ⑥ Dec. 15 - Jan. 26; ⑤⑥ Feb. 1 - May 3.
E – ③⑤⑥ Dec. 12 - Jan. 30; daily Jan. 31 - May 3.
H – ④⑦ Dec. 9 - Jan. 31; ①②③④⑦ Feb. 3 - May 4.
J – Also ⑥ Feb. 16 - Apr. 19.

791 HELSINKI - HANKO and TURKU

km		121	Ⓐ		*S* 123 ⚒	*IC* 125	*S* 127 ⚒	*S* 129	⚒	*IC* 131	155 ⑦	*S* 133 ⚒	135		*IC* 137	*IC* 139	*S* 141		143	*IC* 145 N	157 ⑤	Ⓑ	147	*S* 149	*IC* 151 N	*IC* 153
0	**Helsinki** d.	0546	0608	...	0738	0903	1009	1103	1133	1203	1303	1309	1403	1433	1503	1603	1709	1733	1803	1903	1903	1933	2003	2109	2203	2303
3	Pasila d.	0552	0613	...	0745	0909	1015	1109	1138	1209	1309	1315	1409	1438	1509	1609	1715	1738	1809	1909	1909	1938	2009	2115	2209	2309
87	Karis a.	0643	*0735*y	0743	0832	1001	1101	1201	1239	1301	1401	1401	1501	1539	1601	1701	1801	1839	1901	2001	2001	2039	2101	2201	2301	0004
137	**Hanko** a.	|	...	0823	|	*1050*	|	|	...	*1350*	|	|	*1550*	...	|	*1750*	|	...	*1950*	|	|	...	*2250*	|	|	|
138	Salo d.	0712	...	...	0857	1030	1130	1230	...	1330	1430	1430	1530	...	1630	1730	1830	...	1930	2030	2030	...	2130	2230	2330	0033
194	**Turku** a.	0742	...	...	0925	1100	1158	1300	...	1400	1500	1458	1600	...	1700	1800	1858	...	2000	2100	2100	...	2200	2258	2400	0103
197	Turku satama a.	0752	...	...	...	...	...	...	...	...	...	...	...	...	1712d	...	1912e	...	2012	...	...	...	...	...	...	...

	Ⓐ	*IC* 122 Ⓐ	Ⓐ	*IC* 124	⚒	⑦	*S* 126 ⚒	*IC* 128 Ⓐ	130		*S* 132 ⚒	134	*IC* 136	⚒	*S* 138	*IC* 140	*IC* 142		156 ⑦	*S* 144 ⚒	146	*IC* 148		*IC* 150	*S* 152	154
Turku satama d.	...	...	...	...	...	...	...	...	0830	...	...	...	...	...	...	...	...	...	...	...	...	1745d	...	...	1945e	2045
Turku d.	...	0546	...	0638	...	...	0743	0800	0855	...	1002	1100	1200	...	1302	1400	1500	...	1600	1602	1700	1800	...	1900	2002	2100
Salo d.	...	0618	...	0710	...	...	0813	0830	0932	...	1032	1132	1232	...	1332	1432	1532	...	1632	1632	1732	1832	...	1932	2032	2132
Hanko d.	...	|	...	*0640*	...	...	|	|	*0910*	...	|	|	*1210*	...	|	*1410*	|	...	*1610*	*1610*	|	*1810*	...	|	|	*2110*
Karis d.	0600	0645	0650	0737	0752	0800	0836	0900	1000	...	1057	1200	1300	1304	1357	1500	1600	1615	1700	1700	1800	1900	1918	2000	2100	2200
Pasila a.	0707	0736	0752	0826	0853	0916	0921	0951	1051	...	1142	1251	1351	1407	1442	1551	1651	1722	1751	1751	1851	1951	2022	2051	2138	2251
Helsinki a.	0712	0742	0758	0832	0858	0921	0927	0957	1057	...	1148	1257	1357	1412	1448	1557	1657	1727	1757	1757	1857	1957	2027	2057	2157	2257

N – Not ⑤⑥.
d – Dec. 9-19.
e – Dec. 20 - May 31.
y – Change at Kirkkonummi.
☛ Helsinki - Karis also at 1533 Ⓐ, 1633 Ⓐ. *IC* trains convey 🍸. Other numbered trains convey ✗.

792 TAMPERE - RAUMA and PORI

km		⚒							
0	**Tampere** d.	0807	...	1215	1415	1615	1815	...	2205
97	Kokemäki a.	0912	...	1320	1531	1723	1923	...	2310
144	**Rauma** 🚌 a.	|	...	|	|	*1825*r	*2025*x	...	|
135	**Pori** a.	0937	...	1345	1556	1748	1948	...	2335

	⚒								
Pori d.	0520	0715	...	1015	...	1415	1615	1815	...
Rauma 🚌 d.	|	|	...	|	...	|	*1530*r	*1730*x	...
Kokemäki d.	0545	0740	...	1040	...	1441	1640	1840	...
Tampere a.	0650	0850	...	1145	...	1545	1747	1945	...

r – Not ⑥.
x – ⑤⑦ only.

HELSINKI - TAMPERE 793

km			IC161	S41	IC83	IC43	IC165	IC85		S45	IC47	IC169	IC171		S87	IC49		IC173	S89	IC175		S53	IC55	S91	IC177	IC57
				✕	✕	✕	🍷	🍷		✕	✕	✕	🍷		✕	✕		🍷	✕	✕		✕	✕	✕	🍷	✕
		Ⓐ	Ⓐ	⚒			⚒								b				d							⑥
0	**Helsinki** ..... 797 d.	0519	0606	0630	0706	0730	0806	0906	0919	0930	1006	1106	1206	1219	1230	1306	...	1406	1430	1506	1519	1530	1606	1630	1706	1730
3	Pasila .... 797 d.	0524	0612	0636	0712	0736	0812	0912	0924	0936	1012	1112	1212	1224	1236	1312	...	1412	1436	1512	1524	1536	1612	1636	1712	1736
16	Tikkurila ⊙ . 797 d.	0532	0622	0646	0722	0746	0822	0922	0932	0946	1022	1122	1222	1232	1246	1322	...	1422	1446	1522	1532	1546	1622	1646	1722	1746
71	Riihimäki..... 797 d.	0613	0652	|	0752	|	0852	0952	1013	|	1052	1152	1252	1313	|	1352	...	1452	|	1552	1613	|	1652	|	1752	|
108	Hämeenlinna .....d.	0636	0711	|	0811	|	0911	1011	1036	|	1111	1211	1311	1336	|	1411	...	1511	|	1611	1636	|	1711	|	1811	|
147	Toijala ....d.	0659	0731	|	0831	|	0931	1031	1059	|	1131	1231	1331	1359	|	1431	...	1531	|	1631	1659	|	1731	|	1831	|
187	**Tampere** ....a.	0722	0752	0756	0852	0902	0952	1052	1122	1056	1152	1252	1352	1422	1356	1452	...	1552	1556	1652	1722	1656	1752	1756	1852	1902

	IC179	S59	IC181	265	IC93		IC185	269	IC187	273	
	🍷	✕	🍷	✕	✕		✕	✕	🍷	✕	
				★			N	★c		★	
Helsinki ..... 797 d.	1806	1830	1906	1930	2006	...	2100	2130	2206	2230	...
Pasila .... 797 d.	1812	1836	1912	1937	2012	...	2106	2137	2212	2237	...
Tikkurila ⊙ . 797 d.	1822	1846	1922	1948	2022	...	2116	2148	2222	2248	...
Riihimäki..... 797 d.	1852	|	1952	2026	2052	...	2152	2226	2252	2326	...
Hämeenlinna......d.	1911	|	2011	2052	2111	...	2211	2252	2311	2352	...
Toijala...............d.	1931	|	2031	|	2131	...	2231	|	2331	0019	...
Tampere ....a.	1952	1956	2055	2142	2152	...	2255	2340	2352	0046	...

	264	266	IC160	270	IC162	274	S80	S40	IC164	S82	S42
	✕	✕		✕	✕	✕	✕	✕	🍷	✕	✕
	★c	★	Ⓐ	★c	Ⓐ	★	Ⓐ	Ⓐ	⚒	⚒	⚒
Tampere..................d.	0402	0440	0533	0548	0604	0611	0657	0702	0707	0757	0802
Toijala.......................d.	0434	0507	0554	0615	0626	0638	|	|	0728	|	|
Hämeenlinna...............d.	0502	0534	0615	0642	0647	0705	|	|	0749	|	|
Riihimäki .... 797 d.	0531	0600	0635	0708	0707	0732	|	|	0809	|	|
Tikkurila ⊙ .... 797 a.	0610	0635	0702	0746	0737	0820	0810	0815	0837	0910	0915
Pasila .... 797 a.	0622	0647	0711	0758	0746	0831	0819	0824	0846	0919	0924
Helsinki........... 797 a.	0630	0654	0717	0806	0752	0837	0825	0830	0852	0925	0930

	IC166	S84	IC44	IC188	S46	IC168	IC170	IC48		IC174	IC176	IC50		S52	IC88	IC180		IC54	S90	IC182	S56	IC184	IC58	S60	IC186	S94
	🍷	✕	✕	🍷	✕	🍷	🍷	✕		✕	✕	✕		✕	🍷	🍷		✕	✕	🍷	✕	🍷	✕	✕	✕	✕
		E	⚒	⑦	⚒																			Ⓑ		
Tampere ....d.	0807	0902	0907	0907	1002	1007	1107	1207	1237	1307	1407	1507	1537	1602	1607	1707	1737	1807	1902	1907	2002	2007	2107	2202	2207	2302
Toijala...............d.	0828	|	0928	0928	|	1028	1128	1228	1300	1328	1428	1528	1600	|	1628	1728	1800	1828	|	1928	|	2028	2128	|	2228	2321
Hämeenlinna......d.	0849	|	0949	0949	|	1049	1149	1249	1323	1349	1449	1549	1623	|	1649	1749	1823	1849	|	1949	|	2049	2149	|	2249	2339
Riihimäki .... 797 d.	0909	|	1009	1009	|	1109	1209	1309	1352	1409	1509	1609	1652	|	1709	1809	1852	1909	|	2009	|	2109	2209	|	2309	2356
Tikkurila ⊙ . 797 a.	0937	1015	1037	1037	1115	1137	1237	1337	1428	1437	1537	1637	1728	1715	1737	1837	1928	1937	2015	2037	2115	2137	2237	2315	2337	0021
Pasila .... 797 a.	0946	1024	1046	1046	1124	1146	1246	1346	1436	1446	1546	1646	1736	1724	1746	1846	1936	1946	2024	2046	2124	2146	2246	2324	2346	0030
Helsinki ..... 797 a.	0952	1030	1052	1052	1130	1152	1252	1352	1441	1452	1552	1652	1741	1730	1752	1852	1941	1952	2030	2052	2130	2152	2252	2330	2352	0036

E – ①–⑥ Dec. 10 - May 3.
N – Not ⑤⑥.
b – Dec. 9 - May 4.
c – For days of running see Table **790**.
d – Ⓑ Dec. 9 - May 4; daily from May 5.
★ – Conveys 🚗. For through cars see Table **790**.

TAMPERE - OULU, KOLARI and ROVANIEMI 794

km		273	🚌		S41		🚌	🚌	IC43	701	🚌	S45	IC47	703	IC49	IC49	413	S53	IC55	IC57	S59	263	265		267	269
		✕			✕				✕	L✕		✕	✕	J✕	✕	✕	✕	✕	✕	V✕	✕	✕	✕		✕	✕
		★	Ⓐ		⚒		⚒	Ⓐ							Ⓑ		⑤			Ⓑ		★c	★	F	★c	★c
	Helsinki **793** ...d.	2230	...	...	0630	...	...	...	0730	...	...	0930	1006	...	1306	1306	*1406*	1530	1606	1730	1830	1852	1930	...	2030	2130
0	**Tampere** ....d.	0115	...	...	0800	...	...	...	0907	...	...	1100	1200	...	1500	1500	1600	1700	1804	1907	2000	2136	2211	...	2308	2359
75	Parkano...............d.	0211	...	...	|	...	...	...	0952	...	...	|	1238	...	1544	1544	1643	1738	1842	1952	|	|	2309	...	|	|
159	Seinäjoki.............d.	0310	...	...	0921	...	...	...	1032	...	...	1215	1331	...	1631	1631	1738	1818	1933	2034	2122	2356	0021	...	0200	0208
292	Kokkola ....d.	0450	...	0632	1037	...	...	...	1157	...	...	1329	1502	...	1802	1802	1914	1947	2104	...	2237	0146	0230	...	0412	0345
371	Ylivieska ....d.	0548	...	0730	1125	...	...	...	1246	...	...	1418	1553	...	1858	1858	...	2033	2159	...	2323	0319	0340	...	0511	0443
493	**Oulu**..................a.	0727	...	0850	1232	...	...	...	1359	...	...	1524	1712	...	2013	2013	...	2139	2319	...	0030	0437	0501	...	0630	0605
493	**Oulu**..................d.	0755	...	...	...	1255	...	...	...	1407	...	...	...	1727	2023	...	...	...	...	...	...	0505	0522	...	0635	0622
599	Kemi....................a.	0909	...	...	...	1402	...	1432	...	1507	...	...	...	1826	2123	...	...	...	...	...	...	0620	0630	...	0746	0736
808	**Kolari** ....a.	|	...	...	...	|	...	1810	...	|	...	...	...	|	|	...	...	...	...	...	...	0930	|	...	|	1045
713	**Rovaniemi** ....a.	1041	1135	...	...	1523	1535	...	...	1629	1640	...	...	1946	2244	...	...	...	...	...	...	...	0753	0810	0932	...
796	Kemijärvi ....a.	...	1250	...	...	...	1650	...	...	...	1820	...	...	...	...	...	...	...	...	...	...	...	0940t	0920	...	...

	S40	S42	IC44	S46	IC48	🚌	🚌	IC50	IC50	S52	🚌	708	IC54	🚌	710	S56	IC58	S60		264	262	266	270	272		274
	✕	✕	V✕	✕	✕			✕	✕	✕		J✕	✕		P✕	✕	✕	✕		✕	✕	✕	✕	✕		✕
	Ⓐ	⚒	⚒	⚒		Ⓐ	Ⓐ	⚒			⚒							Ⓑ		★c	★c	★	★c	★c	F	★
Kemijärvi............d.	...	...	...	...	...	...	0525	...	...	...	0840	...	...	1115	...	...	...	...	...	...	...	...	...	...	1930	1905t
Rovaniemi ....d.	...	...	...	...	...	...	0645	0715	...	...	0950	1007	...	1230	1250	...	...	...	1630	1717	...	1800	...	...	2040	2110
Kolari ....d.	...	...	...	...	...	0415	...	|	...	...	...	|	...	...	|	...	...	...	|	|	1615	|	1830	1830	...	|
Kemi....................d.	...	...	...	...	...	0725	...	0837	...	...	...	1125	...	...	1410	...	...	...	1753	1855	1914	1942	2131	2131	...	2234
Oulu....................a.	...	...	...	...	...	...	...	0937	...	...	...	1225	...	...	1519	...	...	...	1859	2023	2032	2058	2243	2243	...	2343
Oulu....................d.	...	...	...	0530	0650	...	...	0945	0945	1115	...	...	1245	...	...	1525	1555	1730	1905	2031	2050	2140	2320	2320	...	2355
Ylivieska ....d.	...	...	...	0639	0811	...	...	1100	1100	1228	...	...	1400	...	...	1633	1712	1836	2031	2218	2234	2322	0043	0043	...	0123
Kokkola ....d.	...	0516	*0540*	0725	0903	...	...	1157	1157	1323	...	...	1503	...	...	1720	1803	1922	2125	2316	2329	0018	0203	0203	...	0228
Seinäjoki.............d.	0540	0640	0738	0843	1038	...	...	1338	1338	1443	...	...	1638	...	...	1843	1938	2043	...	0115	0122	0205	0351	0351	...	0410
Parkano...............d.	0618	0718	0816	|	1116	...	...	1416	1416	|	...	...	1716	...	...	|	2017	|	...	|	|	0315	|	|	...	|
Tampere ....a.	0655	0755	0859	0955	1159	...	...	1453	1453	1555	...	...	1759	...	...	1955	2059	2155	...	0349	0326	0405	0537	0610	...	0548
Helsinki **793** ...a.	0830	0930	1052	1130	1352	...	...	1652	1652	1730	...	...	1952	...	...	2130	2252	2330	...	0630	0606	0654	0806	0937	...	0837

*FOR NOTES, SEE TABLE **795** BELOW.*

TURKU - TAMPERE - PIEKSÄMÄKI 795

km		S81	IC905	IC83		909	IC85	911	S87	IC917	S89		921	923	S91	IC927		IC931	IC93	933
		✕	🍷	✕			🍷	✕	✕	✕	✕		✕		✕	✕		🍷	✕	★
		ⒶK									Ⓑ					K	Ⓑ			
0	Turku satama ....d.	...	...	...	...	0836	...	...	...	...	...	...	...	...	...	...	...	...	...	2050
3	**Turku**...............d.	...	0705	...	...	0905	...	1005	...	1305	...	...	1505	1605	...	1805	...	2005	...	2105
69	Loimaa ....d.	...	0744	...	...	0944	...	1044	...	1344	...	...	1544	1644	...	1844	...	2044	...	2147
	Helsinki **793** ...d.	0630q	|	0706	...	|	0906	*1006*r	1230	*1306*r	1430	...	*1530*r	|	1630	*1830*r	...	|	2006	|
131	Toijala ....d.	|	0825	0831	...	1025	1031	1125	|	1425	|	...	1625	1725	|	1925	...	2125	2131	2234
171	**Tampere** ....a.	0756	0847	0852	...	1047	1052	1147	1356	1447	1556	...	1647	1747	1756	1947	...	2147	2152	2300
171	**Tampere** ....d.	0805	...	0905	1005	...	1105	1205	1405	1505	1605	1615	1705	...	1805	2005	2015	...	2205	...
213	Orivesi...............d.	|	...	0930	1031	...	|	1230	|	1530	|	1641	1730	...	1832	2030	2041	...	2232	...
285	Haapamäki.....a.	|	...	|	1124	...	|	|	|	|	|	1734	|	...	|	|	2134	...	|	...
269	Jämsä ....d.	0858	...	1006	...	...	1205	1306	1500	1606	1656	...	1806	...	1906	2106	...	...	2307	...
326	Jyväskylä............a.	0924	...	1041	...	...	1235	1341	1527	1641	1727	...	1836	...	1941	2136	...	...	2337	...
406	**Pieksämäki**........a.	1012	...	1136	...	...	...	1436	...	1736	1815	...	1935	...	2030	2233	...	...	...	...

	904	S80	906		S82	S84	910	IC912	916		IC922	IC88	IC924	928	S90		IC92	IC58	IC934	S94
	★	✕			✕	✕		✕	✕		✕	🍷	🍷	✕	✕		✕	✕	🍷	✕
		Ⓐ	A	⚒	⚒	⚒K	⚒													
Pieksämäki.......d.	...	...	...	...	0530	0643	...	...	0924	...	1224	...	...	1524	...	...	1827	...	...	2049
Jyväskylä...........d.	...	0530	...	...	0630	0730	...	0822	1022	...	1322	1425	...	1622	1735	...	1922	...	...	2136
Jämsä ....d.	...	0557	...	...	0657	0757	...	0856	1054	...	1354	1458	...	1654	1804	...	1954	...	...	2204
Haapamäki.....d.	...	|	...	0621	|	|	...	|	|	1221	|	|	...	|	|	1821	|	...	...	|
Orivesi ....d.	...	|	...	0717	|	|	...	0931	1129	1317	1429	|	...	1729	|	1917	2029	...	...	|
Tampere ....a.	...	0650	...	0742	0750	0847	...	0955	1153	1342	1453	1553	...	1753	1853	1942	2053	...	...	2253
Tampere ....d.	0556	0657	0711	...	0757	0902	0911	1011	1211	...	1511	1607	1611	1811	1902	...	...	2107	2111	2302
Toijala................d.	0623	|	0735	...	|	|	0935	1035	1235	...	1535	1628	1635	1835	|	...	...	|	2135	|
Helsinki **793**.....a.	|	0825	|	...	0925	1030	|	*1130*r	*1352*r	...	*1652*r	1752	|	*1952*r	2030	...	...	2252	|	0036
Loimaa ....d.	0709	...	0813	...	...	...	1013	1113	1313	...	1613	...	1713	1916	...	...	...	...	2215	...
Turku................a.	0755	...	0850	...	...	...	1055	1150	1355	...	1655	...	1750	1955	...	...	...	...	2252	...
Turku satama ....a.	0807	...	...	...	...	...	...	...	...	...	...	...	...	*2012*	...	...	...	...	...	...

NOTES FOR TABLES 794 and 795:

A – Ⓐ (Ⓑ Feb. 11 - Apr. 27).
F – Until Feb. 29.
J – From / to Kajaani.
K – To / from Kuopio.
L – From Kouvola (on ⚒) and Kuopio.
P – To Pieksämäki.
V – From / to Vaasa.

c – For days of running see Table **790**.
q – Train **41** Helsinki - Tampere.
r – Change at Tampere.
t – From Mar. 1.

★ – Conveys 🚗. For through cars see Table **790**.

☛ Services between Tampere and Pieksämäki are subject to alteration from May 5.

796 JYVÄSKYLÄ - SEINÄJOKI - VAASA

km		⚒	⚒							IC57 ✕ ®	
0	Jyväskylä d.	...	0733	...	...	1033	...	...	1633	...	...
78	Haapamäki d.	...	0844	...	...	1144	...	...	1744	...	...
151	Alavus d.	...	0953	...	...	1253	...	...	1853	...	...
196	Seinäjoki a.	...	1025	...	...	1325	...	...	1925	...	...
	Helsinki 794 d.	0630	|	0730	...	1006	1306	1530	1606	1730	1830
196	Seinäjoki d.	0930	1038	1038	...	1338	1638	1822	1943	2052	2125
270	Vaasa a.	1032	1136	1136	...	1440	1736	1920	2045	2144	2223

	⚒	IC44 ✕ ⚒	⑦						®		®
Vaasa d.	0545	0622	0740	0922	...	1222	1330	1522	1806	1806	1935
Seinäjoki a.	0634	0720	0838	1020	...	1320	1428	1620	1908	1908	2033
Helsinki 794 a.	0930	1052	...	1352	...	1652	1730	1952	|	2252	2330
Seinäjoki d.	...	...	...	1034	...	...	...	1634	1934	...	...
Alavus d.	...	...	...	1107	...	...	...	1707	2007	...	...
Haapamäki d.	...	...	...	1215	...	...	...	1815	2114	...	...
Jyväskylä a.	...	...	...	1327	...	...	...	1927	2219	...	...

797 HELSINKI - KOUVOLA - SAVONLINNA and JOENSUU

km		⚒	⚒	⚒	S1 ✕	IC71 ✕		IC3 ✕			IC105 🍷	IC5 ✕		IC109 🍷	S7 ✕	IC77 ✕	IC77 ✕ ®	Ⓐ	IC111 🍷 ®			IC11 ✕	S79 ✕	IC113 ✕		IC115 🍷
0	Helsinki 793 d.	...	0519	...	0712	0800	...	1000	1019	...	1112	1300	1319	1412	1512	1600	1600	1625	1712	1741	...	1800	1912	2012	...	2212
3	Pasila 793 d.	...	0524	...	0718	0806	...	1006	1024	...	1118	1306	1324	1418	1518	1606	1606	1631	1718	1746	...	1806	1918	2018	...	2118
16	Tikkurila ⊙ 793 d.	...	0532	...	0728	0816	...	1016	1032	...	1128	1316	1332	1428	1528	1616	1616	1641	1728	1755	...	1816	1928	2028	...	2128
*	Riihimäki 793 d.	...	0608	0613	0713	0813	0913	1013	1108	1113	|	1313	1413	|	1513	1613	1613	|	1713	|	1813	|	1913	2013	2113	2213
104	Lahti d.	...	...	0650	0802	0902	0954	1102	...	1155	1208	1402	1450	1508	1602	1702	1702	1729	1808	1841	1850	1902	2002	2108	2154	2308
166	Kouvola a.	...	...	0730	0835	0935	...	1135	...	1235	1240	1435	1530	1540	1635	1735	1735	1808	1843	...	1930	1935	2035	2140	...	2343
166	Kouvola d.	...	...	...	0838	...	...	1138	...	...	...	1438	...	...	1639	...	1743	...	...	...	...	1938	...	2143	...	...
252	Lappeenranta a.	...	...	...	0921	...	...	1221	...	...	...	1521	...	...	1722	...	1826	...	...	...	...	2021	...	2226	...	...
288	Imatra a.	...	...	...	0947	...	...	1247	...	...	...	1547	...	...	1745	...	1852	...	...	...	...	2052	...	2252	...	...
352	Parikkala a.	0733	...	...	1028	...	...	1328	...	...	...	1628	...	...	|	...	1933	...	...	...	...	2133	...	...	...	...
411	Savonlinna a.	0827	...	...	1127	...	...	1427	...	...	...	1727	...	...	|	...	2035	...	...	...	...	2232	...	...	...	...
482	Joensuu a.	...	...	...	1145	...	...	1445	...	...	...	1745	...	...	1929	...	2050	...	...	...	...	2250	...	...	...	...

	⚒	Ⓐ	⑥	IC102 🍷 ⚒		IC104 ✕ ⚒	IC106 🍷 ⑦	S2 ✕ ⚒		IC4 ✕	IC4 ✕ ⚒	IC108 ✕ ⚒	IC74 ✕	IC6 ✕	IC110 🍷 ⑦		IC112 🍷 ⚒	IC68 ✕ ⑦	S8 ✕	S76 ✕		IC114 🍷	IC10 ✕	IC116 🍷 ®	IC78 ✕	IC12 ✕
Joensuu d.	...	...	...	...	...	...	...	0521	...	...	0610	...	...	0910	...	...	...	...	1210	...	...	...	1510	...	...	1810
Savonlinna d.	...	...	...	...	...	...	...	0535	...	...	0555r	...	...	0928	...	...	...	...	1228	...	...	...	1528	...	...	1821
Parikkala d.	...	...	...	...	...	...	...	0634	...	...	0728	...	...	1028	...	...	...	...	1328	...	...	...	1628	...	...	1933
Imatra d.	...	...	...	...	...	0609	...	0712	...	0809	0809	...	...	1109	...	...	...	...	1409	...	...	...	1709	...	...	2014
Lappeenranta d.	...	...	...	...	...	0635	...	0735	...	0835	0835	...	...	1135	...	...	...	...	1435	...	...	...	1740	...	...	2040
Kouvola a.	...	...	...	...	...	0718	...	0818	...	0918	0918	...	...	1218	...	...	...	...	1518	...	...	...	1823	...	...	2123
Kouvola d.	0500	...	...	0620	0635a	0720	0720	0825	0830	0925	0925	1037	1125	1225	1320	...	1420	1420	1525	1625	1630	1720	1825	1925	2025	2125
Lahti d.	0541	0549	0628	0654	0717	0754	0754	0900	0911	1000	1000	1112	1200	1300	1354	1406	1454	1454	1600	1700	1711	1754	1900	2000	2100	2200
Riihimäki 793 a.	|	0630	0708	0746	|	0846	0846	|	0946	1046	1046	|	1246	1346	|	1446	1546	1546	1646	|	1746	1846	1946	2046	2146	2246
Tikkurila ⊙ 793 a.	0628	...	...	0732	0807	0832	0832	0932	1028	1044	1044	1150	1244	1344	1432	...	1532	1532	1632	1732	1828	1832	1944	2044	2144	2244
Pasila 793 a.	0636	...	...	0741	0816	0841	0841	0941	1036	1054	1054	1159	1254	1354	1441	...	1541	1541	1641	1741	1836	1841	1954	2054	2154	2254
Helsinki 793 a.	0641	...	...	0748	0821	0848	0848	0948	1041	1100	1100	1206	1300	1400	1448	...	1548	1548	1648	1748	1841	1848	2000	2100	2200	2300

a – ①–⑤. r – By 🚌. * – Riihimäki - Lahti: *59 km*. ⊙ – For Helsinki ✈ Vantaa.

798 KOUVOLA - KUOPIO - OULU

km		⚒	⚒	701 R✕ ⚒	701 R✕	S81 ✕ Ⓐ V	IC71 ✕	703 R✕	705 ✕		707 ✕	707 ✕ ®	S7‡ ✕	🚌 ▲ Ⓐ	IC77 ✕	709 ✕ ®	🚌 ⑦	S79 ✕	S79 ✕ ®	IC927 T✕
	Helsinki 797 d.	...	...	...	...	0630j	0800	...	1112	...	1412	1412	1512	...	1600	1712	...	1912	1912	...
0	Kouvola d.	...	...	0632	...	|	0948	...	1245	...	1548	1548	1644	...	1751	1848	...	2042	2042	...
113	Mikkeli d.	...	...	0747	...	|	1058	...	1356	...	1700	1700	1744	...	1905	1959	...	2139	2139	...
184	Pieksämäki d.	...	...	0846	...	1014	1146	...	1446	...	1746	1746	1826	...	1953	2046	...	2219	2219	2235
273	Kuopio d.	...	...	0947	0947	1101	1247	...	1547	...	1843	1847	1913	1930	2050	2138	2145	2309	2312	2325
358	Iisalmi d.	...	0545	1048	1048	...	1348	...	1648	1650	...	1948	...	2052	2148	...	2305	...	0007	...
512	Ylivieska a.	...	0725	|	|	...	|	...	|	1830	...	|	...	|	|	...	|	...	|	...
441	Kajaani a.	...	|	1140	1140	...	1440	...	1739	|	...	2041	...	2210	2240	...	0015	...	0054	...
441	Kajaani d.	0620	|	1144	1144	...	...	1512	1746	|	...	2143	...	...	...	...	...	...	...	...
484	Paltamo d.	0652	|	1215	1215	...	...	1543	1818	|	...	2216	...	...	...	...	...	...	...	...
633	Oulu a.	0834	0850	1355	1355	...	...	1724	1954	2013	...	2349	...	...	...	...	...	...	...	...

	700 ✕ ⚒	S70 ✕ ⚒	S84 ✕ ⚒V	IC72 ✕ ⚒	IC74 ✕		704 ✕ ⚒	IC68 ✕ ⑦		S76 ✕	706 ✕	708 R✕		IC78 ✕	710 R✕	S94 ✕ V	714 ✕		®	®
Oulu d.	...	...	...	...	...	...	0712	...	...	...	1005	1237	1245	...	1529	...	...	...	1905	2018
Paltamo d.	...	...	...	...	...	...	0849	...	...	...	1146	1415	|	...	1705	...	...	...	|	2151
Kajaani a.	...	...	...	...	...	...	0917	...	...	...	1216	1446	|	...	1742	...	...	...	|	2222
Kajaani d.	...	0400	...	...	0620	...	0920	...	...	...	1220	...	|	1520	1748	...	...	...	|	...
Ylivieska d.	...	|	...	...	|	...	|	...	...	...	|	...	1425	|	|	...	...	...	2036	...
Iisalmi d.	...	0448	...	...	0715	...	1015	...	...	...	1315	...	1605	1615	1843	...	...	...	2216	...
Kuopio d.	0415	0545	0555	0635	0820	...	1120	1120	...	1350	1420	...	...	1720	1951	...	...	...	...	...
Pieksämäki d.	0513	0638	0641	0727	0919	...	1217	1217	...	1441	1518	...	...	1822	2044	2049	2108	...	...	...
Mikkeli d.	0600	0721	|	0813	1006	...	1304	1304	...	1522	1605	...	...	1908	...	|	2204	...	...	...
Kouvola a.	0709	0815	|	0916	1109	...	1407	1407	...	1615	1710	...	...	2011	...	|	2313	...	...	...
Helsinki 797 a.	0848	0948	1030j	1100	1300	...	1548	1548	...	1748	1848	...	...	2200	...	0036j	...	...	...	...

R – To / from Rovaniemi.
T – Until May 4. From Turku.
V – Until May 4.
j – Via Tampere (Table **795**).
‡ – Train **75** from Kouvola.
▲ – Serves bus, not rail stations.

799 OTHER BRANCH LINES

km		⚒									®
	Helsinki 797 d.	...	0712	...	1112	...	1319	...	1600	...	2012
0	Kouvola d.	0630	0845	...	1245	...	1535	...	1747	...	2147
52	Kotka satama a.	0715	0930	...	1330	...	1620	...	1832	...	2232

	⚒									®
Kotka satama d.	0726	...	1026	...	1426	1626	...	1926	...	2240
Kouvola a.	0812	...	1112	...	1512	1712	...	2012	...	2326
Helsinki 797 a.	0948	...	1300	...	1648	1848	...	2200	...	...

km						🚌 ⑦	🚌 ⚒			®	🚌 ®
0	Pieksämäki d.	1148	...	1448	...	1755	1755	1829	...	2050	2240
49	Varkaus d.	1223	...	1522	...	1825	1830	1903	...	2125	2315
183	Joensuu a.	1353	...	1653	...	...	...	2035	...	2258	...

	🚌 ⚒		🚌 Ⓐ	🚌 ⚒				🚌 ⚒		®
Joensuu d.	...	0700	...	0910	...	1218	...	...	1605	1828
Varkaus d.	0600	0836	1100	1120	...	1357	...	1700	1743	2007
Pieksämäki a.	0630	0909	1135	1155	...	1430	...	1735	1815	2039

km			🚌 ⑤⑦	🚌 ⑦	🚌 ⚒				🚌 ®	🚌 ⑦	
0	Joensuu d.	1150	1210	1315	1405	...	1810	...	2115	2310	...
104	Lieksa d.	1311	|	|	|	...	1931	...	|	|	...
160	Nurmes d.	1356	1405	1505	1615	...	2016	...	2335	0135	...
274	Kajaani a.	...	1600	1640	1805	...	...	...	...	...	...

	🚌 ⚒			🚌 ®		🚌	🚌			🚌 ⑤⑦
Kajaani d.	...	...	...	...	...	1040	...	...	...	1800
Nurmes d.	...	...	0650	...	...	1235	...	...	1550	1945
Lieksa d.	0510	...	0736	1005	...	|	1250	...	1636	|
Joensuu a.	0645	...	0855	1150	...	1430	1435	...	1755	2140

🚌 **PIEKSÄMÄKI – SAVONLINNA**: 1020 ⚒, 1520, 1830 ⑤⑦, 2100 ⑦. 🚌 **SAVONLINNA – PIEKSÄMÄKI**: 0655 ⚒, 1230, 1530 ⑤⑦, 1800 ⑦. Journey time ± 2 hours; *123 km*.

GERMANY

Operator: Principal operator is Deutsche Bahn Aktiengesellschaft (DB). Many regional services are run by independent operators – these are specified in the table heading (or by footnotes for individual trains).

Services: Trains convey first- and second-class seating accommodation unless otherwise shown (by '2' in the column heading, a footnote or a general note in the table heading). Overnight sleeping car (🛏) and couchette (▬) trains do not necessarily convey seating accommodation - refer to individual footnotes for details. Any light refreshment service on overnight trains (🍸) may only be available to couchette and sleeping car passengers. Descriptions of sleeping and couchette cars appear on page 10.

There are various categories of trains in Germany. The type of train is indicated by the following letter codes above each column (or by a general note in the table heading):

ICE	**InterCity Express**	German high-speed (230 – 320 km/h) train. Higher fares payable.
EC	**EuroCity**	International express train.
IC	**InterCity**	Internal express train.
THA	**Thalys**	International high-speed train. Special fares.
TGV	**Train à Grande Vitesse**	French high-speed (320 km/h) train.
IRE	**InterRegio Express**	Regional express train.
RE	**Regional Express**	Semi-fast train.
RB	**Regional Bahn**	Stopping train.
S-Bahn		Suburban stopping train.
CNL	**City Night Line**	Quality overnight express train. Most services convey *Deluxe* sleeping cars (1/2 berth) with en-suite shower and WC, *Economy* sleeping cars (1/2/4 berth), couchettes (4/6 berth) and reclining seats. *Talgo* type trains operate on the routes München - Hamburg / Berlin and convey *Deluxe* sleeping cars, special 2 berth couchettes (*Kajütte*) and reclining seats. Most trains convey ✕. Reservation compulsory. See also page 10.
EN	**Euro Night**	International overnight express train. See also page 10.
D	**Durchgangszug**	Or **Schnellzug** – other express train (day or night).

Other operators:

ALX	**Arriva-Länderbahn-Express**	Operated by Arriva / Regentalbahn AG - Die Länderbahn. Runs trains on the route Hof - Regensburg - München - Oberstdorf / Lindau.
X	**InterConnex**	Long-distance routes operated by Veolia Verkehr GmbH. **DB tickets are not valid.**

Timings: Valid **December 9**, 2007 - **June 14**, 2008 (except where shown otherwise in the table heading).

Many long distance trains operate on selected days only for part of the journey. These are often indicated in the train composition footnote by showing the dated journey segment within brackets. For example '12 Leipzig - Hannover (- Dortmund ⑦)' means that the train runs daily (or as shown in the column heading) between Leipzig and Hannover, but only continues to Dortmund on Sundays. Additional footnotes / symbols are often used to show more complex running dates, e.g. '12 (München ⊡ -) Nürnberg - Hamburg' means that the train runs only on dates in note ⊡ between München and Nürnberg, but runs daily (or as shown in the column heading) between Nürnberg and Hamburg.

International overnight trains that are not intended for internal German journeys are not usually shown in the German section. Please refer to the International section for details of these services.

Engineering work may occasionally disrupt services at short notice (especially at weekends and during holiday periods), so it is advisable to check timings locally before travelling. The locations of known service alterations are summarised in the shaded panel below.

Supplements: A 'Sprinter' supplement (€16 in first class, €11 in second class) is payable for travel by limited stop *ICE-Sprinter* services. Special 'global' fares are payable for international journeys on *Thalys* trains. Special overnight 'global' fares (*SparNight*) are available on *CNL* and certain *EN* services – other tickets are also accepted on payment of a special supplement (*Aufpreis*), which varies depending on the journey and type of accommodation required. Please note that it is no longer possible for single travellers to book a berth in a shared sleeping compartment on *CNL* trains. However, holders of 2nd class tickets are now able to book a *CNL Economy* single berth compartment.

Reservations: Reservation is compulsory for travel by *CNL*, *Thalys* and any other trains marked Ⓡ. Seat reservations are also available (€3.50) on *ICE*, *EC* and *IC* trains.

Holidays: Dec. 25, 26, Jan. 1, Mar. 21, 24, May 1, 12 and Oct. 3 are German national public holidays (trains marked ⚒ or Ⓐ do not run). In addition there are other regional holidays as follows: May 22 – Fronleichnam (Corpus Christi), Aug. 15 – Mariä Himmelfahrt (Assumption), Oct. 31 – Reformationstag (Reformation Day), Nov. 1 – Allerheiligen (All Saints Day) and Nov. 19 Buß und Bettag (Repentance Day). On these days the regional service provided is usually that applicable on ⑦ (please refer to individual footnotes for details).

ENGINEERING WORK SUMMARY

- **Hamburg**: Dec. 24 - Jan. 1. Services between Hamburg and Hannover / Bremen are subject to alteration. Most Bremen line trains and *ICE* trains via Hannover will start from / terminate at Hamburg **Harburg** (situated to the south of Hamburg). Most *IC* trains will be suspended between Hannover and Hamburg, together with a number of early morning/late evening *ICE* trains. A limited number of services will continue to operate from / to Hamburg Hbf but with earlier departures / later arrivals. Trains to / from Kiel and Westerland will use a diversionary route calling at Hamburg Harburg. Please confirm timings before travelling.
- **Stuttgart**: From May 16. Early morning services via Stuttgart (approximately 0000 - 0400) will be diverted, not calling at Stuttgart Hbf.
- **Mainz**: ⑥⑦ from May 17. Earlier departures / later arrivals possible at Mainz Hbf (by up to 4 minutes). Services from / to Wiesbaden also subject to alteration.
- **Magdeburg**: Services via Magdeburg are subject to alteration from May 25. Some services will call at Magdeburg Buckau instead of Magdeburg Hbf.

Local services OFFENBURG - BASEL 912

Temporarily relocated from page 423

	†w		Ⓐe	Ⓒz	Ⓐe	Ⓐe	⚒	Ⓐe	⚒r																Ⓐe	
Offenburg .... d.	0045	...	0428	...	...	0525	0549	0634	0707	...	0807	0907	1007	1107	1204	1307	1404	1507	1607	1707	1807	1907	2007	2034	...	2242
Freiburg (Brsg) Hbf ..... a.	0128	...	0528	...	...	0625	0649	0729	0756	...	0855	0955	1056	1156	1250	1355	1450	1555	1656	1755	1856	1955	2055	2133	...	2341
Freiburg (Brsg) Hbf ..... d.	0129	...	0529	0608	0609	0628	0711	0734	0815	0815	0915	1015	1115	1215	1315	1415	1515	1615	1715	1815	1915	2015	...	2135	2235	2343
Basel Bad Bf .... a.	0217	...	0625	0711	0703	0733	0806	0813	0911	0911	1011	1111	1211	1311	1412	1511	1611	1711	1812	1911	2011	2111	...	2240	2340	0046

		Ⓐe	⚒r	Ⓐe												Ⓐe		Ⓐe		Ⓒk	Ⓒz					⑥k
Basel Bad Bf .... d.	0519	0549	...	0625	0634	0748	0848	0948	1048	1148	1248	1348	1448	1548	1648	1726	1748	1826	1848	1848	...	1948	...	2126	2258	2348
Freiburg (Brsg) Hbf ..... a.	0615	0645	...	0718	0736	0847	0944	1044	1144	1244	1344	1444	1544	1644	1744	1823	1844	1923	1944	1944	...	2044	...	2219	0003	0050
Freiburg (Brsg) Hbf ..... d.	0626	0656	0656	0720	0803	0903	1003	1103	1203	1307	1403	1507	1603	1703	1803	1825	1907	1925	...	2003	2026	...	2125	2225	0017	...
Offenburg .... a.	0719	0744	0744	0814	0851	0953	1053	1153	1253	1353	1450	1553	1650	1751	1850	1921	1953	2021	...	2050	2122	...	2221	2318	0113	...

e – Not Dec. 24, 31, May 22.
k – Also Dec. 24, 31.
r – Not May 22.
w – Also May 22..
z – Also Dec. 24, 31, May 22.

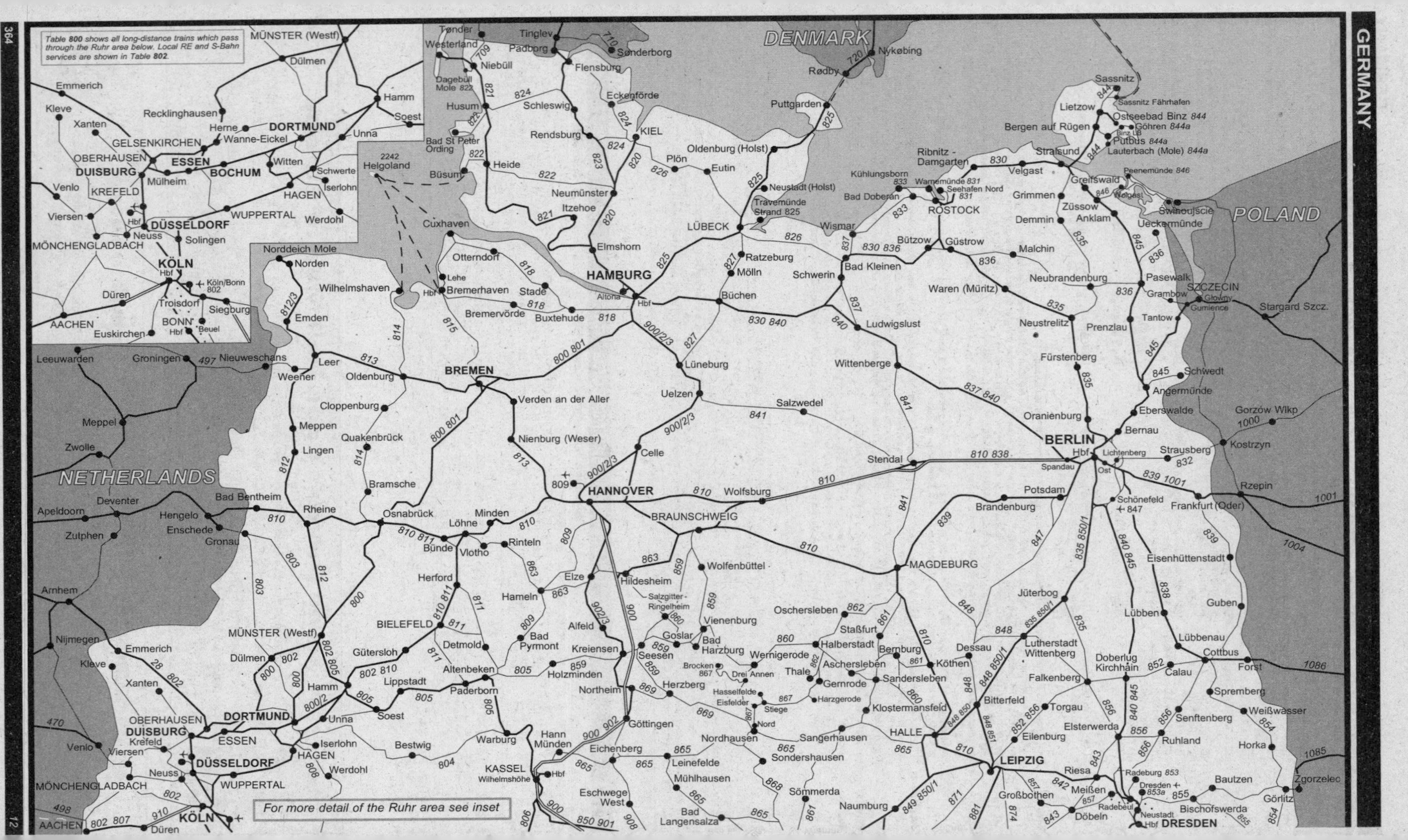

Table 800 shows all long-distance trains which pass through the Ruhr area below. Local RE and S-Bahn services are shown in Table 802.
DENMARK
POLAND
NETHERLANDS
HAMBURG
BERLIN
HANNOVER
BREMEN
KIEL
LÜBECK
ROSTOCK
MAGDEBURG
LEIPZIG
DRESDEN
HALLE
BRAUNSCHWEIG
KÖLN
DÜSSELDORF
DORTMUND
ESSEN
DUISBURG
BOCHUM
WUPPERTAL
MÜNSTER (Westf)
BIELEFELD
KASSEL
SZCZECIN
For more detail of the Ruhr area see inset

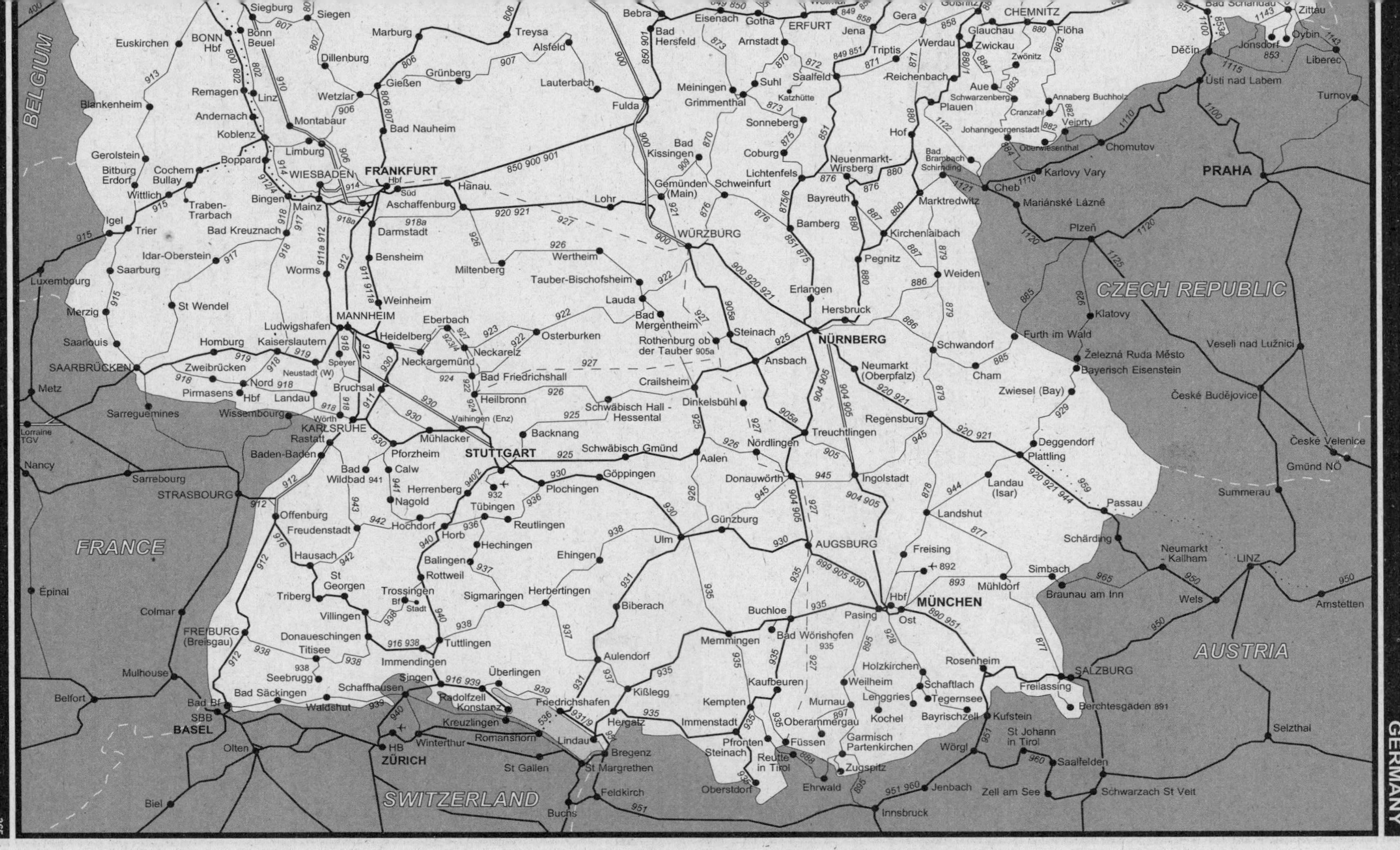
CZECH REPUBLIC
AUSTRIA
SWITZERLAND
FRANCE
BELGIUM
PRAHA
Zittau
Oybin
Jonsdorf
Liberec
Turnov
Děčín
Ústí nad Labem
Chomutov
Karlovy Vary
Mariánské Lázně
Plzeň
Cheb
Klatovy
Železná Ruda Město
Bayerisch Eisenstein
Veseli nad Lužnici
České Budějovice
České Velenice
Gmünd NÖ
Summerau
LINZ
Amstetten
Wels
Neumarkt - Kallham
Selzthal
SALZBURG
Berchtesgaden
Schwarzach St Veit
Saalfelden
Zell am See
St Johann in Tirol
Kufstein
Wörgl
Jenbach
Innsbruck
CHEMNITZ
Flöha
Glauchau
Zwickau
Zwönitz
Aue
Annaberg Buchholz
Vejprty
Cranzahl
Oberwiesenthal
Johanngeorgenstadt
Schwarzenberg
Werdau
Plauen
Reichenbach
Gera
Triptis
Jena
ERFURT
Gotha
Eisenach
Arnstadt
Saalfeld
Katzhütte
Suhl
Meiningen
Grimmenthal
Sonneberg
Coburg
Lichtenfels
Hof
Neuenmarkt-Wirsberg
Bayreuth
Bamberg
Marktredwitz
Bad Brambach
Schirnding
Kirchenlaibach
Pegnitz
Weiden
Schwandorf
Cham
Furth im Wald
Zwiesel (Bay)
Deggendorf
Plattling
Passau
Schärding
Braunau am Inn
Simbach
Mühldorf
Landau (Isar)
Landshut
Freising
MÜNCHEN
Hbf
Ost
Pasing
Regensburg
Neumarkt (Oberpfalz)
NÜRNBERG
Hersbruck
Erlangen
Ingolstadt
Treuchtlingen
Ansbach
Steinach
Rothenburg ob der Tauber
Dinkelsbühl
Nördlingen
Donauwörth
AUGSBURG
Günzburg
Ulm
Aalen
Crailsheim
Schwäbisch Hall - Hessental
Schwäbisch Gmünd
Göppingen
Plochingen
STUTTGART
Backnang
Heilbronn
Bad Friedrichshall
Neckarelz
Osterburken
Lauda
Bad Mergentheim
Tauber-Bischofsheim
Wertheim
Miltenberg
WÜRZBURG
Schweinfurt
Bad Kissingen
Gemünden (Main)
Lohr
Fulda
Bad Hersfeld
Bebra
Lauterbach
Alsfeld
Treysa
Marburg
Gießen
Grünberg
Bad Nauheim
FRANKFURT
Süd
Hanau
Aschaffenburg
Darmstadt
Bensheim
Weinheim
MANNHEIM
Heidelberg
Eberbach
Neckargemünd
WIESBADEN
Mainz
Worms
Ludwigshafen
Kaiserslautern
Neustadt (W)
Speyer
Bruchsal
KARLSRUHE
Landau
Wörth
Pirmasens
Nord
Zweibrücken
Homburg
SAARBRÜCKEN
Saarlouis
Merzig
St Wendel
Idar-Oberstein
Bad Kreuznach
Bingen
Boppard
Koblenz
Andernach
Remagen
BONN Hbf
Bonn Beuel
Siegburg
Siegen
Dillenburg
Wetzlar
Limburg
Montabaur
Linz
Cochem Bullay
Traben-Trarbach
Wittlich
Trier
Saarburg
Igel
Luxembourg
Bitburg Erdorf
Gerolstein
Blankenheim
Euskirchen
Metz
Sarreguemines
Wissembourg
Sarrebourg
STRASBOURG
Nancy
Lorraine TGV
Épinal
Colmar
Mulhouse
Belfort
Rastatt
Baden-Baden
Pforzheim
Mühlacker
Vaihingen (Enz)
Calw
Bad Wildbad
Herrenberg
Nagold
Hochdorf
Horb
Tübingen
Reutlingen
Hechingen
Balingen
Rottweil
Trossingen
Villingen
St Georgen
Triberg
Hausach
Offenburg
Freudenstadt
FREIBURG (Breisgau)
Donaueschingen
Titisee
Seebrugg
Immendingen
Tuttlingen
Sigmaringen
Herbertingen
Ehingen
Biberach
Aulendorf
Memmingen
Buchloe
Kaufbeuren
Kempten
Immenstadt
Oberstdorf
Pfronten Steinach
Reutte in Tirol
Füssen
Ehrwald
Zugspitz
Garmisch Partenkirchen
Murnau
Oberammergau
Weilheim
Kochel
Lenggries
Tegernsee
Schaftlach
Holzkirchen
Bayrischzell
Rosenheim
Freilassing
Bad Wörishofen
Kißlegg
Hergatz
Lindau
Bregenz
Feldkirch
Buchs
St Margrethen
Friedrichshafen
Überlingen
Radolfzell
Konstanz
Kreuzlingen
Romanshorn
St Gallen
Winterthur
ZÜRICH
HB
Singen
Schaffhausen
Waldshut
Bad Säckingen
BASEL
Bad Bf
SBB
Olten
Biel

800 KOBLENZ - KÖLN - DORTMUND - HAMBURG

km		ICE	IC	ICE	ICE	IC	CNL	IC	ICE	IC	IC	IC	IC	ICE	ICE	IC	CNL	CNL	ICE	ICE	ICE	ICE	ICE	IC	IC
		949	2020	841	1028	2243	408	60408	541	2214	2314	2145	2355	853	843	2331	40408	318	808	1035	828	553	543	2212	21
		①g		①g	Ⓐm	①–⑥	🅁		①–⑥	L		①–⑥	①g	①–⑥		⊡	🅁	🅁		①–④	①–⑤	①–⑥			①–
				✕	🍷	e B	✕♦		h✕	🍷	🍷♦	e🍷	🍷♦	e✕	✕	N🍷	✕♦	✕♦	K✕	b⚡ 🍷	a🍷	e✕	✕	🍷♦	e
	*Basel SBB 🏛 **912*** d.	...	...	...	...	...	2207	...	...	...	...	...	...	...	...	...	2207	...	2326		...	...	...	...	...
	*Karlsruhe Hbf **912*** d.	...	...	...	...	...	0010	...	...	...	...	...	...	...	...	...	0010	...	0133	...	...	...	...	...	...
	*München Hbf **904 930*** d.	...	...	...	...	...	|	...	...	...	...	...	...	...	...	...	|	2242	|	...	...	...	...	...	...
	*Stuttgart Hbf **930*** d.	...	...	...	...	...	|	...	...	...	...	...	...	...	...	...	|	0126x	|	...	...	...	...	...	...
	*Nürnberg Hbf **920*** d.	...	...	...	...	...	|	...	...	...	...	...	...	...	...	...	|	|	|	...	...	...	...	...	...
	*Frankfurt (Main) Hbf **910/2*** d.	...	2314	...	...	...	|	...	...	...	...	...	...	...	...	...	|	|	0315	...	0449	...	...	...	...
	Frankfurt Flughafen ✈ § d.	...	2329	...	...	...	|	...	...	...	...	...	...	...	...	...	|	|	0349‡	...	0502	...	...	...	...
	*Mainz Hbf **912*** d.	...	2347	...	...	...	|	...	...	...	...	...	...	...	...	...	|	|	0408	...	|	...	...	...	...
0	**Koblenz** Hbf d.	...	0103	...	...	...	|	...	...	...	...	...	...	...	...	...	|	|	0503	...	|	0547	...	0606v	...
18	Andernach d.	...	0116	...	...	...	|	...	...	...	...	...	...	...	...	...	|	|	|	...	|	|	...	0619v	...
39	Remagen d.	...	0129	...	...	...	|	...	...	...	...	...	...	...	...	...	|	|	|	...	|	|	...	0631v	...
59	**Bonn** Hbf d.	...	0142	...	...	...	|	...	...	...	...	...	...	...	...	...	0520s	0521s	0544	...	|	0625	...	0645v	...
	Köln/Bonn Flughafen ✈ d.	...	|	...	...	...	|	...	...	...	...	...	...	...	...	...	|	|	|	...	0609	|	...	|	...
93	**Köln** Hbf a.	...	0205	...	...	...	|	...	...	...	...	...	...	...	...	...	0545s	0545s	0605	...	|	0646	...	0705v	...
93	**Köln** Hbf d.	0155	0210	0329	...	...	|	...	0429	0511	0511	0513	...	0549	0529	0542	|	|	0609	0616	|	0649	0626	0710	07
94	**Köln** Messe/Deutz d.	|	|	|	...	...	|	...	|	|	|	|	...	|	|	|	|	|	|	|	0622	|	|	|	|
	Solingen Hbf d.	|	|	|	...	...	|	...	|	|	|	0531	...	|	|	|	|	|	|	|	|	|	|	|	073
	Wuppertal Hbf d.	|	|	|	...	...	|	...	|	|	|	0543	...	0617	|	|	|	|	|	|	|	0717	|	|	074
	Hagen Hbf d.	|	|	|	...	...	|	...	|	|	|	0601	...	0635	|	|	|	|	|	|	|	0735	|	|	080
133	**Düsseldorf** Hbf d.	0219	0234	0353	...	...	|	...	0453	0534	0534	|	0546	|	0553	0609	0613s	0613s	0633	0639u	0645	|	0653	0734	|
140	Düsseldorf Flughafen ✈ d.	|	0241	0401	...	...	|	...	0501	|	|	|	0553	|	0600	0616	|	|	|	|	|	|	0700	|	|
157	**Duisburg** Hbf d.	0233	0251	0411	...	...	|	...	0511	0547	0547	|	0604	|	0610	0626	0628s	0628s	0646	0651u	0705	|	0710	0747	|
165	Oberhausen Hbf d.	|	|	|	...	...	|	...	|	|	|	|	|	|	|	0633f	0637	0637	|	|	|	|	|	|	|
167	Mülheim (Ruhr) Hbf d.	0241	0258	|	...	...	|	...	|	|	|	|	|	|	|	|	...	...	|	|	|	|	|	|	|
176	**Essen** Hbf d.	0249	0306	0424	...	...	|	...	0524	0600	0600	|	0618	|	0624	|	...	...	0700	0703u	0717	|	0724	0800	|
	Gelsenkirchen Hbf d.	|	|	|	...	...	|	...	|	|	|	|	|	|	|	0645	...	...	|	|	...	|	|	|	|
	Wanne-Eickel Hbf d.	|	|	|	...	...	|	...	|	|	|	|	|	|	|	0651	...	...	|	|	...	|	|	|	|
	Recklinghausen Hbf d.	|	|	|	...	...	|	...	|	|	|	|	|	|	|	0659	...	...	|	|	...	|	|	|	|
192	Bochum Hbf d.	0301	0317	0435	...	...	|	...	0535	0611	0611	|	0629	|	0635	|	...	...	0711	|	...	|	0735	0811	|
210	**Dortmund** Hbf a.	0311	0327	0445	...	...	0515	...	0545	0621	0621	0620	0639	|	0646	|	...	...	0721	|	...	|	0746	0821	082
210	**Dortmund** Hbf **805** d.	0314	0330	0448	...	...	|	0523	0548	0625	0625	0628	0644	|	0648	|	...	...	0725	|	...	|	0748	0825	082
	Hamm (Westf) **805** a.	0330	0353	0504	...	...	|	|	0606	|	|	0643	0702	0702	0707	|	...	...	|	|	...	0802	0807	|	084
	Hamm (Westf) **810** d.	0332	0355	0506	...	...	|	|	0611	|	|	0645	0707	0711	0711	|	...	...	|	|	...	0811	0811	|	084
	*Hannover Hbf **810*** a.	0458	|	0628	...	...	|	|	0728	|	|	0818	|	0828	0828	|	...	...	|	|	...	0928	0928	|	101
	*Leipzig Hbf **810*** a.	|	|	|	...	...	|	|	|	|	|	1120	|	|	|	|	...	...	|	|	...	|	|	|	132
	*Berlin Hbf **810*** a.	0655	|	0821	...	...	|	|	0908	|	|	...	1322	1010	1010	|	...	...	|	|	...	1108	1108	|	..
266	Münster (Westf) Hbf **801** d.	...	0418	...	...	0538	0555s	0557	...	0657	0657	...	...	...	...	0727	...	...	0757	|	...	...	...	0857	...
316	Osnabrück Hbf **801** d.	...	0453	...	...	0601	0622s	0624	...	0723	0723	...	...	...	...	...	...	...	0823	|	...	...	...	0923	...
438	**Bremen** Hbf **801** d.	...	0555	...	0717	...	0722r	0724r	...	0817	0817	...	...	...	...	...	...	...	0917	|	...	...	...	1017	...
553	**Hamburg** Hbf **801** a.	...	0651	...	0812	...	0832r	0832r	...	0912	0912	...	...	...	...	...	...	...	1012	0946	...	...	...	1112	...
560	**Hamburg** Altona a.	...	0706	...	0827	...	0853r	0853r	...	0927	...	...	...	...	...	...	...	...	...	1001	...	...	...	...	...

	ICE	IC	ICE	ICE	IC	ICE	IC	IC	ICE	ICE	ICE	ICE	ICE	IC	IC	ICE	IC	ICE	ICE	IC	IC	IC	ICE	ICE	IC
	826	2357	855	845	2333	616	2320	2120	824	555	545	545	226	2310	2141	822	2157	857	847	431	431	2247	614	928	82
							R	©	①–⑥		①–⑥									①–⑥					①–
	🍷	🍷	T✕	✕	N🍷	🍷	🍷	🍷♦	e D 🍷	✕	✕	✕	🍷♦	🍷♦	🍷	🍷	🍷♦	✕	✕	e♥	♥	B	🍷	✕	a🍷
*Basel SBB 🏛 **912*** d.	...	...	...	...	...	...	...	...	...	...	...	...	...	...	...	...	...	...	...	...	...	...	...	...	...
*Karlsruhe Hbf **912*** d.	...	...	...	...	...	...	...	...	...	...	...	...	...	...	...	...	...	...	...	...	...	...	...	...	...
*München Hbf **904 930*** d.	...	...	...	...	...	0317p	...	...	...	...	...	...	...	...	...	0451g	...	...	...	...	...	...	0523	...	055
*Stuttgart Hbf **930*** d.	...	...	...	...	...	0551	...	...	...	...	...	...	...	...	...	|	...	...	...	...	...	...	0751	...	|
*Nürnberg Hbf **920*** d.	...	...	...	...	...	|	...	...	...	...	...	...	...	...	...	0600	...	...	...	...	...	...	|	0530	070
*Frankfurt (Main) Hbf **910/2*** d.	0548	...	...	...	...	|	0542	0542	0702	...	...	...	0728	0638	...	0810	...	...	...	...	...	...	|	0742	09
Frankfurt Flughafen ✈ § d.	0607	...	...	...	...	0709	0558	0558	0714	...	...	...	0743	0658	...	0824	...	...	...	...	...	...	0909	0758	092
*Mainz Hbf **912*** d.	|	...	...	...	...	|	0618	0618	|	...	...	...	|	0717	...	|	...	...	...	...	...	...	|	0820	|
Koblenz Hbf d.	|	...	0643	...	...	|	0712	0712	|	...	...	...	|	0812	...	|	...	...	...	0843	...	...	|	0912	|
Andernach d.	|	...	0657	...	...	|	|	|	|	...	...	...	|	|	...	|	...	...	...	0856	...	...	|	|	|
Remagen d.	|	...	|	...	...	|	|	|	|	...	...	...	|	|	...	|	...	...	...	0908	...	...	|	|	|
Bonn Hbf d.	|	...	0722	...	...	|	0744	0744	|	0825e	...	...	|	0844	...	|	...	...	...	0922	...	...	|	0944	|
Köln/Bonn Flughafen ✈ d.	|	...	|	0713	...	|	|	|	|	|	0813	...	|	|	...	|	...	...	...	|	...	...	|	|	|
Köln Hbf a.	|	...	0742	|	...	0805	0805	0805	|	0846e	|	...	0840	0905	...	|	...	...	...	0942	...	...	1005	1005	|
Köln Hbf d.	|	0719g	0749	|	0748	0811	0811	0811	|	0849	|	...	0848	0911	0913	|	0905	0949	...	0948	0948	...	1011	1011	|
Köln Messe/Deutz d.	0717	|	|	0730	|	|	|	|	0824	|	0830	...	|	|	|	0917	|	|	...	|	|	...	|	|	101
Solingen Hbf d.	|	|	|	|	|	|	0830	0830	|	|	|	...	|	|	0931	|	|	|	...	|	|	...	|	|	|
Wuppertal Hbf d.	|	|	0817	|	|	|	0843	0843	|	0917	|	...	|	|	0943	|	|	1017	...	|	|	...	|	1043	|
Hagen Hbf d.	|	|	0835	|	|	|	0901	0901	|	0935	|	...	|	|	1001	|	|	1035	...	|	|	...	|	1101	|
Düsseldorf Hbf d.	0740	0746	|	0753	0812	0834	|	|	0846	|	0853	0853	0915	0934	|	0939	0946	|	0953	1012	1012	...	1034	|	103
Düsseldorf Flughafen ✈ d.	|	0753	|	0800	|	|	|	|	|	|	0900	0900	|	|	|	|	0953	|	1000	|	|	...	|	|	|
Duisburg Hbf d.	0753	0804	|	0810	0826	0847	|	|	0905	|	0910	0910	0927	0947	|	0951	1004	|	1010	1026	1026	...	1047	|	105
Oberhausen Hbf d.	|	|	|	|	0833f	|	|	|	|	|	|	|	0933	|	|	|	|	|	|	1033f	1033f	...	|	|	|
Mülheim (Ruhr) Hbf d.	|	|	|	|	|	|	|	|	|	|	|	...	|	|	|	|	|	|	|	|	|	...	|	|	|
Essen Hbf d.	0806	0818	|	0824	|	0859	|	|	0918	|	0924	0924	...	1000	|	1002	1018	|	1024	|	|	...	1059	|	110
Gelsenkirchen Hbf d.	...	|	|	|	0845	|	|	|	...	|	|	|	...	|	|	...	|	|	|	1045	1045	...	|	|	...
Wanne-Eickel Hbf d.	...	|	|	|	0851	|	|	|	...	|	|	|	...	|	|	...	|	|	|	1051	1051	...	|	|	...
Recklinghausen Hbf d.	...	|	|	|	0859	|	|	|	...	|	|	|	...	|	|	...	|	|	|	1059	1059	...	|	|	...
Bochum Hbf d.	...	0829	|	0835	|	0911	|	|	...	|	0935	0935	...	1011	|	...	1029	|	1035	|	|	...	1111	|	...
Dortmund Hbf a.	...	0839	|	0846	|	0921	0920	0920	...	|	0946	0946	...	1021	1020	...	1039	|	1046	|	|	...	1121	1120	...
Dortmund Hbf **805** d.	...	0842	|	0848	|	...	0926	0926	...	|	0948	0948	...	1025	1028	...	1042	|	1048	|	|	...	...	1126	...
Hamm (Westf) **805** a.	...	0902	0902	0907	|	...	|	|	...	1002	1007	1007	...	|	1043	...	1102	1102	1107	|	|	...	...	|	...
Hamm (Westf) **810** d.	...	0907	0911	0911	|	...	|	|	...	1011	1011	1011	...	|	1045	...	1107	1111	1111	|	|	...	...	|	...
*Hannover Hbf **810*** a.	...	|	1028	1028	|	...	|	|	...	1128	1128	1128	...	|	1218	...	|	1228	1228	|	|	...	...	|	...
*Leipzig Hbf **810*** a.	...	|	|	|	|	...	|	|	...	|	|	|	...	|	1520	...	|	|	|	|	|	...	...	|	...
*Berlin Hbf **810*** a.	...	1522	1210	1210	|	...	|	|	...	1308	1308	1308	...	|	...	...	1722	1410	1410	|	|	...	...	|	...
Münster (Westf) Hbf **801** d.	...	...	...	...	0927	...	0957	0957	...	...	...	...	...	1057	...	...	...	...	...	1127	1127	1138	...	1157	...
Osnabrück Hbf **801** d.	...	...	...	...	...	...	1023	1023	...	...	...	...	...	1123	...	...	...	...	...	...	...	1201	...	1223	...
Bremen Hbf **801** d.	...	...	...	...	...	...	1117	1117	...	...	...	...	...	1217	...	...	...							1317	...
Hamburg Hbf **801** a.	...	...	...	...	...	...	1212	1213	...	...	...	...	...	1312	...	...	...							1412	...
Hamburg Altona a.	...	...	...	...	...	...	1226	...	...	...	...	...	...	...	...	...	...							1427	...

*See Table **802** for Rhein - Ruhr local RE and S-Bahn services*

♦ – **NOTES** (LISTED BY TRAIN NUMBER)

226 – ICE INTERNATIONAL – 🚃12 and 🍷 Frankfurt - Arnhem - Utrecht - Amsterdam.
318 – POLLUX – 🛏 1, 2 cl., 🛏 2 cl., 🚃2 (reclining) and ✕ (Garmisch ⑥ **A** -) München - Amsterdam.
408 – KOMET – 🛏 1, 2 cl., 🛏 2 cl., 🚃2 (reclining) and ✕ (Brig ⑥ **A** -) Zürich - Hamburg
2120 – © from Mar. 15. FEHMARN – 🚃12 and 🍷 Frankfurt - Hamburg - Lübeck - Puttgarden.
2157 – 🚃12 and 🍷 Köln - Kassel - Erfurt - Halle - Berlin (- Stralsund Ⓑ **q**). Train number **2257** on ⑥ **c**.
2212 – RÜGEN – 🚃12 and 🍷 Koblenz - Hamburg - Rostock - Stralsund - Ostseebad Binz.
2310 – NORDFRIESLAND – 🚃12 and 🍷 Frankfurt - Köln - Westerland.
2314 – From Mar. 15. DEICHGRAF – 🚃12 and 🍷 Köln - Westerland.
2355 – STRELASUND – 🚃12 and 🍷 Düsseldorf - Kassel - Erfurt - Halle - Berlin - Ostseebad Binz.
40408 – PEGASUS – 🛏 1, 2 cl., 🛏 2 cl., 🚃2 (reclining) and ✕ Zürich - Amsterdam.

A – ⑥ Dec. 22 - Mar. 29.
B – To Berlin (Table **810**).
D – From Darmstadt Hbf (d. 0637).
K – To Kiel (Table **820**).
L – Until Mar. 14.
N – To Norddeich Mole (Table **812**).

R – Daily to Mar. 14; Ⓐ from Mar. 17.
T – From Trier (Table **915**).

a – Not Dec. 24, 25, 26, 31, Jan. 1, Mar. 21, 24, May 12.
b – Not Dec. 24 - Jan. 1, Mar. 24, May 1, 12, 22.
c – Also Dec. 24, 25, 31, Mar. 21, 23, May 11.
e – ①–⑥ (not Dec. 25, 26, Jan. 1, Mar. 22, 24, May 12).

f – Not Mar. 29 - May 25; not ⑥⑦ May 31 - June 15.
g – ① (also Dec. 27, Jan. 2, Mar. 25, May 13; not Dec. 24, 31, Mar. 24, May 1
h – Not Dec. 24, 25, 26, 31, Jan. 1, Mar. 22, 24, May 12.

m – Not Dec. 24 - Jan. 1.
p – 0324 on ⑥ (also Dec. 24, 31, May 22).
q – Not Dec. 24, 25, 31, Mar. 21, 23, May 11.
r – On © Bremen Hbf a. 0715, d. 0717, Hamburg Hbf a. 0812, Altona a. 0826.

s – Stops to set down on
u – Stops to pick up only.
v – Not Dec. 25, Jan. 1.
x – Until May 15.

♥ – 🚃12 and 🍷 (Luxembourg ①–⑥ **e** -) Köln - Münster - Emden. Runs with train number **331** and continues to Norddeich Mole on ①②③④ to Mar. 13 (not Dec. 20, 22, 26, 27, 29, Jan. 1, 2, 3, 5).
⊡ – ① to Mar. 10 (also Jan. 2; not Dec. 24, 31); ①④⑤⑥⑦ from Mar. 15.
⚡ – 🅁 and 'Sprinter' supplement payable.
§ – Frankfurt Flughafen Fernbahnhof. See also Tables **910** and **912**.
‡ – Frankfurt Flughafen ✈ Regionalbahnhof.

KOBLENZ - KÖLN - DORTMUND - HAMBURG 800

	ICE 557	*ICE* 547 ①–⑤	*ICE* 547	*IC* 1818 ①–⑤	*IC* 1818 ⑤v	*ICE* 128	*IC* 1818 ⑤v	*IC* 2116	*IC* 2049	*IC* 2359 ⑤⑦r	*ICE* 859	*ICE* 849	*IC* 433	*ICE* 612	*ICE* 926 ①⑦	*ICE* 1026 ②–⑥	*ICE* 726 ①–⑥	*ICE* 559	*ICE* 549	*ICE* 126 E	*IC* 2114	*IC* 2047 ⑧c	*IC* 2151	*ICE* 951	*ICE* 941
	✕	✕	✕	t🍷	🍷	A🍷	🍷	🍷♦	🍷	🍷♦	✕	✕	🍷♦	🍷	✕♦	✕♦	e🍷	✕	✕	A🍷	🍷	🍷	🍷	✕	✕
Basel SBB 🚌 **912** d.	...	...	...	...	...	...	...	...	...	...	...	...	...	...	...	...	...	...	...	...	...	...	...	...	...
Karlsruhe Hbf **912** d.	...	...	...	...	...	...	...	...	...	...	...	...	...	...	...	...	...	...	...	...	...	...	...	...	...
München Hbf **904 930** d.	...	...	...	...	...	...	...	...	...	...	...	...	...	0723	0614z	...	0755	...	...	...	...	...	...	...	...
Stuttgart Hbf **930** d.	...	...	...	0714	0714	...	...	0737	...	...	...	...	...	0951	|	...	|	...	...	...	0937	...	...	...	...
Nürnberg Hbf **920** d.	...	...	...	|	|	...	...	|	...	...	...	...	...	|	0729	0729	0900	...	...	...	|	...	...	...	...
Frankfurt (Main) Hbf **910/2** d.	...	...	...	|	|	0928	...	|	...	...	...	...	...	|	0942	0942	1110	...	...	1128	|	...	...	...	...
Frankfurt Flughafen + § d.	...	...	...	|	|	0943	...	|	...	...	...	...	...	1109	0958	0958	1124	...	...	1143	|	...	...	...	...
Mainz Hbf **912** d.	...	...	...	0848	0848	|	...	0920	...	...	...	...	...	|	1020	1020	|	...	...	|	1120	...	...	...	...
oblenz Hbf d.	...	...	...	0943	0943	|	...	1012	...	...	...	...	1043	|	1112	1112	|	...	...	|	1212	...	...	...	...
dernach d.	...	...	...	0956	0956	|	...	|	...	...	...	...	1056	|	|	|	|	...	...	|	|	...	...	...	...
emagen d.	...	...	...	|	|	|	...	|	...	...	...	...	1108	|	|	|	|	...	...	|	|	...	...	...	...
nn Hbf d.	...	...	...	1022	1022	|	...	1044	...	...	...	...	1122	|	1144	1144	|	1223e	...	|	1244	...	...	...	...
Köln/Bonn Flughafen + d.	...	1012	...	|	|	|	...	|	...	...	...	...	|	|	|	|	|	|	1212	|	|	...	...	...	...
öln Hbf a.	...	|	...	1042	1042	1040	...	1105	...	...	...	...	1142	1205	1205	1205	|	1242e	|	1240	1305	...	...	...	...
öln Hbf d.	1049	|	...	...	1045	1048	...	1111	1113	1120	1149	...	1148	1211	1211	1211	|	1249	|	1248	1311	1313	...	1349	...
öln Messe/Deutz d.	|	1030	...	...	|	|	...	|	|	|	|	...	|	|	|	|	1217	|	1230	|	|	|	...	|	...
Solingen Hbf d.	|	|	...	...	|	|	...	|	1131	|	|	...	|	|	|	|	|	|	|	|	|	1331	...	|	...
Wuppertal Hbf d.	1117	|	...	...	|	|	...	|	1143	|	1217	...	|	|	1243	1243	|	1317	|	|	|	1343	...	1417	...
Hagen Hbf d.	1135	|	...	...	|	|	←	|	1201	|	1235	...	|	|	1301	1301	|	1335	|	|	|	1401	...	1435	...
isseldorf Hbf d.	|	1053	1053	...	1106	1113	1117	1134	|	1146	|	1153	1212	1234	|	|	1239	|	1253	1314	1334	|	1346	|	1353
isseldorf Flughafen + d.	|	1100	1100	...	→	|	|	|	|	1153	|	1200	|	|	|	|	|	|	1300	|	|	|	1353	|	1400
iisburg Hbf d.	|	1110	1110	...	...	1126	1131	1147	|	1204	|	1210	1226	1247	|	|	1251	|	1310	1328	1347	|	1404	|	1410
Oberhausen Hbf d.	|	|	|	...	...	1133	|	|	|	|	|	|	1233f	|	|	|	|	|	|	1333	|	|	|	|	|
ilheim (Ruhr) Hbf d.	|	|	|	...	...	...	1138	|	|	|	|	|	|	|	|	|	|	|	|	...	|	|	|	|	|
ssen Hbf d.	|	1124	1124	...	...	...	1146	1200	|	1218	|	1224	|	1259	|	|	1302	|	1324	...	1400	|	1418	|	1424
Gelsenkirchen Hbf d.	|	|	|	...	...	...	|	|	|	|	|	|	1245	|	|	|	...	|	|	...	|	|	|	|	|
Wanne-Eickel Hbf d.	|	|	|	...	...	...	|	|	|	|	|	|	1251	|	|	|	...	|	|	...	|	|	|	|	|
Recklinghausen Hbf d.	|	|	|	...	...	...	|	|	|	|	|	|	1259	|	|	|	...	|	|	...	|	|	|	|	|
ochum Hbf d.	|	1135	1135	...	...	...	1157	1211	|	1229	|	1235	|	1311	|	|	...	|	1335	...	1411	|	1429	|	1435
ortmund Hbf a.	|	1146	1146	...	...	...	1207	1221	1220	1239	|	1246	|	1321	1320	1320	...	|	1346	...	1421	1420	1439	|	1446
ortmund Hbf **805** d.	|	1148	1148	...	...	...	1210	1225	1228	1242	|	1248	|	...	1326	1326	...	|	1348	...	1425	1428	1442	|	1448
Hamm (Westf) **805** a.	1202	1207	1207	...	...	...	1232	|	1243	1302	1302	1307	|	...	|	|	...	1402	1407	...	|	1443	1502	1502	1507
Hamm (Westf) **810** d.	1211	1211	1211	...	...	...	1234	|	1245	1307	1311	1311	|	...	|	|	...	1411	1411	...	|	1445	1507	1511	1511
Hannover Hbf **810** a.	1328	1328	1328	...	...	...	1359	|	1418	|	1428	1428	|	...	|	|	...	1528	1528	...	|	1618	|	1628	1628
Leipzig Hbf **810** a.	|	|	|	...	...	...	|	|	1720	|	|	|	|	...	|	|	...	|	|	...	|	1920	|	|	|
Berlin Hbf **810** a.	1508	1508	1508	...	...	...	1550	|	...	1922	1610	1610	|	...	|	|	...	1708	1708	...	|	...	2124	1810	1810
inster (Westf) Hbf **801** d.	...	...	...	...	...	...	...	1257	...	...	...	...	1327	...	1357	1357	...	...	...	...	1457	...	...	...	...
snabrück Hbf **801** d.	...	...	...	...	...	...	...	1323	...	...	...	...	...	...	1423	1423	...	...	...	...	1523	...	...	...	...
emen Hbf **801** d.	...	...	...	...	...	...	...	1417	...	...	...	...	...	...	1517	1517	...	...	...	...	1617	...	...	...	...
amburg Hbf **801** a.	...	...	...	...	...	...	...	1512	...	...	...	...	...	...	1612	1612	...	...	...	...	1712	...	...	...	...
amburg Altona a.	...	...	...	...	...	...	...	...	...	...	...	...	...	...	...	...	...	...	...	...	1727	...	...	...	...

	IC 435	*IC* 2249	*ICE* 610	*IC* 2028	*ICE* 722	*ICE* 651	*ICE* 641	*ICE* 124	*IC* 1926 ⑦w	*IC* 2010 ⑤v	*IC* 2112	*IC* 2045	*IC* 2153	*ICE* 953 ⑧q	*ICE* 943	*IC* 2014 ①–⑤	*IC* 2004 ⑦	*IC* 2006 ⑥	*IC* 1908 ⑦	*ICE* 518	*IC* 2026	*ICE* 628	*ICE* 653 n	*ICE* 643 n	*IC* 2012
	🍷♦	♦	🍷	🍷♦	🍷	✕	✕	🍷A			🍷	🍷♦	🍷♦	✕	✕	🍷♦	🍷♦	🍷♦	🍷♦	🍷	🍷	🍷	✕	✕	🍷♦
Basel SBB 🚌 **912** d.	...	...	...	...	...	...	...	...	...	...	...	...	...	...	...	...	...	...	...	...	...	...	...	...	...
Karlsruhe Hbf **912** d.	...	...	...	...	...	...	...	...	...	...	...	...	...	...	...	...	1221	1221	...	...	...	...	...	...	...
München Hbf **904 930** d.	...	...	0923	...	0956	...	...	...	...	...	...	...	...	...	...	...	|	|	...	1123	...	1156	...	...	...
Stuttgart Hbf **930** d.	...	...	1151	...	|	...	...	...	...	1114	1137	...	...	...	...	1209	|	|	...	1351	...	|	...	...	1314
Nürnberg Hbf **920** d.	...	...	|	0928	1101	...	...	...	...	|	|	...	...	...	...	|	|	|	...	|	...	1301	...	...	|
Frankfurt (Main) Hbf **910/2** d.	...	...	|	1144	1310	...	...	1328	1215	|	|	...	...	...	...	|	|	|	...	|	1344	1510	...	...	|
Frankfurt Flughafen + § d.	...	...	1309	1159	1324	...	...	1343	1228	|	|	...	...	...	...	|	|	|	...	1509	1358	1524	...	...	|
Mainz Hbf **912** d.	...	...	|	1220	|	...	...	|	1248	1248	1320	...	...	...	...	1342	1342	1342	...	|	1420	|	...	...	1448
oblenz Hbf d.	1243	...	|	1312	|	...	...	|	1343	1343	1412	...	...	...	...	1443	1443	1443	...	|	1512	|	...	...	1543
dernach d.	1256	...	|	|	|	...	...	|	1356	1356	|	...	...	...	...	1456	1456	1456	...	|	|	|	...	...	1556
emagen d.	1308	...	|	|	|	...	...	|	1408	1408	|	...	...	...	...	1508	1508	1508	...	|	|	|	...	...	1608
nn Hbf d.	1322	...	|	1344	|	1425	...	|	1422	1422	1444	...	...	...	...	1522	1522	1522	...	|	1544	|	...	...	1622
Köln/Bonn Flughafen + d.	|	...	|	|	|	|	...	|	|	|	|	...	...	...	...	|	|	|	...	|	|	|	...	1612	|
öln Hbf a.	1342	...	1405	1405	|	1446	...	1440	1442	1442	1505	...	...	...	...	1542	1542	1542	...	1605	1605	|	...	|	1642
öln Hbf d.	1348	...	1411	1411	|	1449	...	1448	1445	1445	1511	1513	...	1549	...	1548	1548	1548	1539	1611	1611	|	1649	|	1648
öln Messe/Deutz d.	|	...	|	|	1417	|	...	|	|	|	|	|	...	|	...	|	|	|	|	|	|	1617	|	1630	|
Solingen Hbf d.	|	...	|	1430	|	|	...	|	|	|	|	1531	...	|	...	|	|	|	|	|	1630	|	|	|	|
Wuppertal Hbf d.	|	...	|	1443	|	1517	...	|	|	|	|	1543	...	1617	...	|	|	|	|	|	1643	|	1717	|	|
Hagen Hbf d.	|	...	|	1501	|	1535	...	|	|	|	|	1601	...	1635	...	|	|	|	|	|	1701	|	1735	|	|
üsseldorf Hbf d.	1412	...	1434	|	1439	|	1453	1514	1518	1518	1534	|	1546	|	1553	1612	1612	1612	1617	1634	|	1639	|	1653	1714
üsseldorf Flughafen + d.	|	...	|	|	|	|	1500	|	|	|	|	|	1553	|	1600	|	|	|	|	|	|	|	|	1700	|
uisburg Hbf d.	1426	...	1447	|	1451	|	1510	1528	1532	1532	1547	|	1604	|	1610	1626	1626	1626	1630	1647	|	1651	|	1710	1727
Oberhausen Hbf d.	1433f	...	|	|	|	|	|	1533	|	|	|	|	|	|	|	1633f	1633f	1633f	|	|	|	|	|	|	|
ülheim (Ruhr) Hbf d.	|	...	|	|	|	|	|	...	|	|	|	|	|	|	|	|	|	|	|	|	|	|	|	|	1734
ssen Hbf d.	|	...	1459	|	1502	|	1524	...	1544	1544	1600	|	1618	|	1624	|	|	|	1643	1659	|	1702	|	1724	1742
Gelsenkirchen Hbf d.	1445	...	|	|	...	|	|	...	|	|	|	|	|	|	|	1645	1645	1645	|	|	|	...	|	|	|
Wanne-Eickel Hbf d.	1451	...	|	|	...	|	|	...	|	|	|	|	|	|	|	1651	1651	1651	|	|	|	...	|	|	|
Recklinghausen Hbf d.	1459	...	|	|	...	|	|	...	|	|	|	|	|	|	|	1659	1659	|	|	|	|	...	|	|	|
ochum Hbf d.	|	...	1511	|	...	|	1535	...	1555	1555	1611	|	1629	|	1635	|	|	|	|	1711	|	...	|	1735	1753
ortmund Hbf a.	|	...	1521	1520	...	|	1546	...	1605	1605	1621	1620	1639	|	1646	|	|	1707	1700	1721	1720	...	|	1746	1805
ortmund Hbf **805** d.	|	...	...	1526	...	|	1548	...	1608	1608	1625	1628	1642	|	1648	|	|	...	1702	...	1726	...	|	1748	→
Hamm (Westf) **805** a.	|	...	...	|	...	1602	1607	...	1628	1632	|	1643	1702	1702	1707	|	|	...	|	...	|	...	1802	1807	...
Hamm (Westf) **810** d.	|	...	...	|	...	1611	1611	...	1631	1634	|	1645	...	1711	1711	|	|	...	|	...	|	...	1811	1811	...
Hannover Hbf **810** a.	|	...	...	|	...	1728	1728	...	1759	1759	|	1818	...	1828	1828	|	|	...	|	...	|	...	1928	1928	...
Leipzig Hbf **810** a.	|	...	...	|	...	|	|	...	|	|	|	2120b	...	|	|	|	|	...	|	...	|	...	|	|	...
Berlin Hbf **810** a.	|	...	...	|	...	1908	1908	...	1951	1952	|	...	...	2010	2010	|	|	...	|	...	|	...	2108	2108	...
ünster (Westf) Hbf **801** d.	1529	1538	...	1557	...	...	...	...	...	...	1657	...	...	...	...	1727	1727	...	1741	...	1757	...	...	...	...
snabrück Hbf **801** d.	...	1601	...	1623	...	...	...	...	...	...	1723	...	...	...	...	...	...	...	1813	...	1823	...	...	...	...
emen Hbf **801** d.	...	...	...	1717	...	...	...	...	...	...	1817								1907	...	1917	...	...	...	...
amburg Hbf **801** a.	...	...	...	1812	...	...	...	...	...	...	1912								2006	...	2012	...	...	...	...
amburg Altona a.	...	...	...	1826	...	...	...	...	...	...	1927								...	...	2026	...	...	...	...

*See Table **802** for Rhein-Ruhr local RE and S-Bahn services*

– **NOTES** (LISTED BY TRAIN NUMBER)

33/5 – 🚃12 and 🍷 Luxembourg - Trier - Koblenz - Emden - Norddeich Mole.
26 – ①⑦ (also Dec. 26, 27, Jan. 1, 2, Mar. 25, May 13; not Dec. 24, 31, Mar. 24, May 12). 🚃12 and ✕ (München ①**z** -) Nürnberg - Frankfurt - Köln - Kiel.
026 – ②–⑥ (also Dec. 24, 31, Mar. 24, May 12; not Dec. 26, 27, Jan. 1, 2, Mar. 25, May 13). 🚃12 and ✕ Regensburg - Nürnberg - Frankfurt - Köln - Kiel.
908 – ⑦ (also Jan. 1, Mar. 24, May 12; not Dec. 23, 30, Mar. 23, May 11). 🚃12 Köln - Westerland.
004 – ⑦ (also Dec. 26, Jan. 1, Mar. 21, 24, May 1, 12, 22; not Dec. 23, 30, Mar. 23, May 11). BODENSEE – 🚃12 and 🍷 Konstanz - Karlsruhe - Emden.
006 – ⑥ (also Dec. 23, 25, 30, 31, Mar. 23, May 11). BODENSEE – 🚃12 and 🍷 Konstanz - Dortmund.
012 – ALLGÄU – 🚃12 and 🍷 Oberstdorf - Ulm - Köln - Hannover (- Leipzig ⑤⑦**r**).
014 – ①–⑤ (not Dec. 24, 25, 26, 31, Jan. 1, Mar. 21, 24, May 1, 12, 22). 🚃12 and 🍷 Stuttgart - Emden.
028 – 🚃12 and 🍷 Passau - Regensburg - Frankfurt - Köln - Hamburg.
045 – 🚃12 and 🍷 Köln - Hannover - Magdeburg (- Leipzig ⑧**b**).
116 – 🚃12 and 🍷 Stuttgart - Köln - Hamburg - Stralsund. On Dec. 25, Jan. 1 starts from Köln Hbf.
153 – 🚃12 and 🍷 Düsseldorf - Kassel - Erfurt - Halle.
249 – 🚃12 and 🍷 Münster - Osnabrück - Hannover - Berlin.
359 – 🚃12 and 🍷 Köln - Kassel - Erfurt - Halle - Berlin - Stralsund.

A – To Amsterdam (Table **28**).
E – From Mar. 14.

b – ⑧ (not Dec. 24, 25, 31, Mar. 23, May 11).
c – Also Dec. 29, Mar. 22, May 3; not Mar. 21, May 1.
e – ①–⑥ (not Dec. 25, 26, Jan. 1, Mar. 22, 24, May 12).
f – Not Mar. 29 - May 25; not ⑥⑦ May 31 - June 15.
n – Not Dec. 24, 31.
q – Not Dec. 24, 25, 31, Mar. 21, 23, May 11.
r – Also Dec. 26, Jan. 1, Mar. 20, 24, Apr. 30, May 12; not Dec. 23, 30, Mar. 21, 23, May 2, 11.
t – Not Dec. 24, 25, 26, 31, Jan. 1, Mar. 21, 24, May 1, 2, 12, 22, 23.
v – Also Mar. 20, Apr. 30, May 21; not Mar. 21, May 2, 23.
w – Also Dec. 26, Jan. 1, Mar. 24, May 12; not Dec. 23, 30, Mar. 23, May 11.
z – ① (not Dec. 24, 31, Mar. 24, May 12).

§ – Frankfurt Flughafen Fernbahnhof. See also Tables **910** and **912**.

800 KOBLENZ - KÖLN - DORTMUND - HAMBURG

		ICE 506	EC 100	EC 102	IC 2012	IC 2155	ICE 122	ICE 955	ICE 945	IC 437	ICE 516	IC 2024	ICE 624	ICE 655	ICE 645	ICE 645	IC 118	EC 6	EC 6	ICE 804	IC 2041	ICE 104	ICE 622	ICE 957	ICE 947	ICE 43
			N	⑦w		⑦w		Ⓑq						n	Ⓑn	n			Ⓑq	①–⑥	⑦w	n		Ⓑq		Ⓑ
		🍷	🍴♦	🍴♦	🍷♦	🍷♦	A🍷	🍴	🍴	🍷♦	🍷	🍷	🍷	🍴	🍴	🍴	🍷♦	🍴♦	🍴♦	z🍷	🍷	🍷♦	🍷	🍴	🍴	🍷♦
*Basel SBB 🏛 **912***	d.	1312	1218	1218	...	...	...	...	...	...	...	...	...	...	...	...	...	1418	1418	...	...	1512	...	...	...	...
*Karlsruhe Hbf **912***	d.	1500	1412	1412	...	...	...	...	...	...	...	...	...	...	...	...	...	1612	1612	...	...	1700	...	...	...	...
*München Hbf **904 930***	d.	|	|	|	...	...	...	...	...	...	1323	...	1356	...	...	...	...	|	|	...	...	|	1455	...	...	...
*Stuttgart Hbf **930***	d.	|	|	|	...	...	...	...	...	...	1551	...	|	...	...	...	1512	|	|	...	...	|	|	...	...	...
*Nürnberg Hbf **920***	d.	|	|	|	...	...	...	...	...	...	|	...	1501	...	...	...	|	|	|	...	...	|	1600	...	...	...
*Frankfurt (Main) Hbf **910/2***	d.	|	|	|	...	...	1628	...	...	...	|	1542	1710	...	...	...	|	|	|	...	...	|	1810	...	...	...
Frankfurt Flughafen ✈ §	d.	1609	|	|	...	...	1643	...	...	...	1709	1558	1724	...	...	...	|	|	|	...	...	1809	1824	...	...	...
*Mainz Hbf **912***	d.	|	1520	1520	...	...	|	...	...	...	|	1620	|	...	...	...	1648	1720	1720	...	...	|	|	...	...	...
Koblenz Hbf	d.	|	1612	1612	...	...	|	...	...	1643	|	1712	|	...	...	...	1743	1812	1812	...	...	|	|	...	...	184
Andernach	d.	|	|	|	...	...	|	...	...	1656	|	|	|	...	...	...	1756	|	|	...	...	|	|	...	...	185
Remagen	d.	|	|	|	...	...	|	...	...	1708	|	|	|	...	...	...	1808	|	|	...	...	|	|	...	...	190
Bonn Hbf	d.	|	1644	1644	...	...	|	...	...	1722	|	1744	|	...	...	...	1822	1844	1844	...	...	|	|	...	...	192
Köln/Bonn Flughafen ✈	d.	|	|	|	...	...	|	...	...	|	|	|	|	...	1812	...	|	|	|	...	...	|	|	...	...	|
Köln Hbf	a.	1705	1705	1705	...	...	1740	...	...	1742	1805	1805	|	...	|	...	1842	1905	1905	...	...	1905	|	...	...	194
Köln Hbf	d.	1711	1711	1711	...	...	1748	1749	...	1745	1811	1811	|	1849	|	...	1848	1911	1911	1913	1913	1917	|	1949	...	194
Köln Messe/Deutz	d.	|	|	|	...	...	|	|	...	|	|	|	1817	|	1830	...	|	|	|	|	|	|	1922	|	...	|
Solingen Hbf	d.	1729	|	|	...	...	|	|	...	|	1829	|	|	|	|	...	|	|	|	1931	1931	|	|	|	...	|
Wuppertal Hbf	d.	1743	|	|	...	...	|	1817	...	|	1843	|	|	1917	|	...	|	|	|	1943	1943	|	|	2017	...	|
Hagen Hbf	d.	1801	|	|	...	...	|	1835	...	|	1901	|	|	1935	|	...	|	|	|	2001	2001	|	|	2035	...	|
Düsseldorf Hbf	d.	|	1734	1734	...	1746	1813	|	1753	1817c	|	1834	1839	|	1853	1853	1913	1934	1934	|	|	1940	1944	|	1953	201
Düsseldorf Flughafen ✈	d.	|	|	|	...	1753	|	|	1800	|	|	|	|	|	1900	1900	|	|	|	|	|	|	|	|	2000	|
Duisburg Hbf	d.	|	1747	1747	...	1804	1826	|	1810	1830	|	1847	1851	|	1910	1910	1926	1947	1947	|	|	1953	1957	|	2010	202
Oberhausen Hbf	d.	|	|	|	...	|	1833	|	|	1837f	|	|	|	|	|	|	|	|	|	|	|	1958	|	|	|	203
Mülheim (Ruhr) Hbf	d.	|	|	|	...	|	...	|	|	|	|	|	|	|	|	|	|	|	|	|	|	...	|	|	|	|
Essen Hbf	d.	|	1800	1800	...	1818	...	|	1824	|	|	1900	1904	|	1924	1924	1938	2000	2000	|	|	...	2013	|	2024	|
Gelsenkirchen Hbf	d.	|	|	|	...	|	...	|	|	1849	|	|	|	|	|	|	1948	|	|	|	|	...	|	|	|	204
Wanne-Eickel Hbf	d.	|	|	|	...	|	...	|	|	|	|	|	|	|	|	|	|	|	|	|	|	...	|	|	|	205
Recklinghausen Hbf	d.	|	|	|	...	|	...	|	|	1900	|	|	|	|	|	|	1959	|	|	|	|	...	|	|	|	|
Bochum Hbf	d.	|	1811	1811	...	1829	...	|	1835	|	|	1911	1916	|	1935	1935	|	2011	2011	|	|	...	2027	|	2035	|
Dortmund Hbf	a.	1820	1821	1821	←	1839	...	|	1846	|	1920	1921	1929	|	1946	1946	|	2021	2021	2020	2020	...	2038	|	2046	210
Dortmund Hbf **805**	d.	...	1825	1825	1828	1842	...	|	1848	|	...	1925	...	|	1948	1948	|	...	2025	...	2028	...	...	|	2048	...
Hamm (Westf) **805**	a.	...	|	|	1843	1902	...	1902	1907	|	...	|	...	2002	2007	2007	|	...	|	...	2043	...	...	2102	2107	...
Hamm (Westf) **810**	d.	...	|	|	1845	...	...	1911	1911	|	...	|	...	2011	2011	2011	|	...	|	...	2045	...	...	2111	2111	...
*Hannover Hbf **810***	a.	...	|	|	2018	...	...	2028	2028	|	...	|	...	2128	2128	2128	|	...	|	...	2218	...	...	2228	2228	...
*Leipzig Hbf **810***	a.	...	|	|	2323r	...	...	|	|	|	...	|	...	|	|	|	|	...	|	...	...	...	...	|	|	...
*Berlin Hbf **810***	a.	...	|	|	...	...	...	2221	2221	|	...	|	...	2308	2308	2308	|	...	|	...	...	...	...	0020	0020	...
Münster (Westf) Hbf **801**	d.	...	1857	1857	...	...	...	...	...	1929	...	1957	...	...	...	...	2029	...	2057	...	...	...	...	...	...	...
Osnabrück Hbf **801**	d.	...	1923	1923	...	...	...	...	...	...	...	2023	...	...	...	...	...	...	2123	...	...	...	...	...	...	...
Bremen Hbf **801**	d.	...	2017	2017	...	...	...	...	...	...	...	2117	...	...	...	...	...	...	2220	...	...	...	...	...	...	...
Hamburg Hbf **801**	a.	...	2112	2112	...	...	...	...	...	...	...	2212	...	...	...	...	...	...	2314	...	...	...	...	...	...	...
Hamburg Altona	a.	...	2126	...	...	...	...	...	...	...	...	2226	...	...	...	...	...	...	2328	...	...	...	...	...	...	...

		ICE 26	ICE 514	ICE 710	ICE 1820	ICE 1826	ICE 120	ICE 657	ICE 647	EC 114	IC 2318	IC 2318	ICE 502	ICE 528	ICE 1828	ICE 910	ICE 24	ICE 512	ICE 526	EN 347	IC 2018	IC 2110	ICE 500	ICE 524	ICE 22	ICE 920
				Ⓑq	⑦v	⑥k	Ⓑt	⑦w	⑦w		n	Ⓑq		Ⓑn	⑥	n		n	Ⓑq	🅁	⑦w	Ⓑq	n			d
		P🍴	🍷	E🍷	🍷	🍷	A🍷	🍴	🍴	🍴♦	🍴	🍴	🍷	🍷	G🍷	🍷	P🍴	🍷	🍷	🍷♦		🍷	🍷	🍷	P🍴	🍷
*Basel SBB 🏛 **912***	d.	...	...	...	...	...	...	...	...	...	...	...	1712	...	...	...	...	...	...	...	...	...	1912	...	...	...
*Karlsruhe Hbf **912***	d.	...	...	...	...	...	...	...	...	...	...	...	1901	...	...	...	...	...	...	...	...	...	2101	...	...	...
*München Hbf **904 930***	d.	...	1523	...	1556	1556	...	...	...	1440	...	...	|	1651	1655	...	...	1723	1756	...	1613	...	|	1855	...	...
*Stuttgart Hbf **930***	d.	...	1751	...	|	|	...	...	...	1713	1741	1741	|	|	|	...	...	1951	|	...	1914	1937	|	|	...	...
*Nürnberg Hbf **920***	d.	1528	|	...	1701	1701	...	...	...	|	|	|	|	1800	1800	...	1728	|	1901	...	|	|	|	2000	1928	...
*Frankfurt (Main) Hbf **910/2***	d.	1742	|	...	1910	1910	1928	...	...	|	|	|	|	2010	2010	2016	1942	|	2110	...	|	|	|	2210	2146	231
Frankfurt Flughafen ✈ §	d.	1758	1909	...	1924	1924	1943	...	...	|	|	|	2009	2024	2024	2031	1958	2109	2124	...	|	|	2209	2224	2159	232
*Mainz Hbf **912***	d.	1821	|	...	|	|	|	...	...	1848	1920	1920	|	|	|	|	2020	|	|	...	2048	2120	|	|	2220	|
Koblenz Hbf	d.	1912	|	...	|	|	|	...	...	1943	2012	2012	|	|	|	|	2112	|	|	...	2143	2212	|	|	2312	|
Andernach	d.	|	|	...	|	|	|	...	...	1956	|	|	|	|	|	|	|	|	|	...	2156	|	|	|	|	|
Remagen	d.	|	|	...	|	|	|	...	...	2008	|	|	|	|	|	|	|	|	|	...	2208	|	|	|	|	|
Bonn Hbf	d.	1945	|	...	|	|	|	2025	...	2022	2044	2044	|	|	|	|	2144	|	|	...	2222	2244	|	|	2344	|
Köln/Bonn Flughafen ✈	d.	|	|	1948	|	2027	|	|	...	|	|	|	|	|	|	2139	|	|	|	...	|	|	|	2330	|	|
Köln Hbf	a.	2005	2005	|	|	2040	2040	2046	...	2042	2105	2105	2105	|	|	|	2205	2205	|	...	2242	2305	2312	|	0005	|
Köln Hbf	d.	2011	2011	|	|	2048	2048	2049	...	2045	...	2111	2111	|	|	|	2211	2211	|	2228	2245	...	2317	|	0011x	|
Köln Messe/Deutz	d.	|	|	2003	2017	|	|	|	...	|	...	|	|	2118	2117	2152	|	|	2223	|	|	...	|	2345	|	003
Solingen Hbf	d.	2030	|	|	|	|	|	|	...	|	...	|	2129	|	|	|	2230	|	|	2300	|	...	|	|	|	|
Wuppertal Hbf	d.	2043	|	|	|	|	|	2117	...	|	...	|	2143	|	|	|	2243	|	|	2314	|	...	|	|	|	|
Hagen Hbf	d.	2101	|	|	|	|	|	2135	...	|	...	|	2201	|	|	|	2301	|	|	2334	|	...	|	|	|	|
Düsseldorf Hbf	d.	|	2034	2027	2039	2113	2113	|	2053	2117c	...	2134	|	2139	2139	2213	|	2234	2244	2202*	2309	...	2340	0006	0036x	005
Düsseldorf Flughafen ✈	d.	|	|	|	|	|	|	|	2100	|	...	|	|	|	|	|	|	|	|	|	2316	...	|	|	|	|
Duisburg Hbf	d.	|	2047	2051	2056	2126	2126	|	2110	2130	...	2147	|	2151	2151	2226	|	2247	2256	2147*	2326	...	2353	0019	0049x	011
Oberhausen Hbf	d.	|	|	|	|	|	2133	|	|	|	...	|	|	|	|	|	|	|	|	2139*	|	...	|	|	|	|
Mülheim (Ruhr) Hbf	d.	|	|	|	|	|	...	|	|	|	...	|	|	|	|	|	|	|	|	|	2334	...	|	|	|	|
Essen Hbf	d.	|	2059	2104	2114	2138	...	|	2124	2143	...	2200	|	2204	2204	2238	|	2259	2309	|	2342	...	0005	0031	0101x	012
Gelsenkirchen Hbf	d.	|	|	|	|	|	...	|	|	|	...	|	|	|	|	|	|	|	|	|	|	...	|	|	|	|
Wanne-Eickel Hbf	d.	|	|	|	|	|	...	|	|	|	...	|	|	|	|	|	|	|	|	|	|	...	|	|	|	|
Recklinghausen Hbf	d.	|	|	|	|	|	...	|	|	|	...	|	|	|	|	|	|	|	|	|	|	...	|	|	|	|
Bochum Hbf	d.	|	2111	2115	2126	2148	...	|	2135	2154	...	2211	|	2216	2216	2249	|	2311	2326	|	2353	...	0016	0042	0111x	013
Dortmund Hbf	a.	2120	2121	2130	2137	2159	...	|	2146	2205	...	2221	2220	2228	2228	2300	2320	2321	2336	2354	0004	...	0026	0052	0122x	014
Dortmund Hbf **805**	d.	...	2125	2132w	...	...	...	|	2148	...	...	2225w	2228	...	...	...	...	2325	...	2356	...	...	...	...	...	...
Hamm (Westf) **805**	a.	...	|	2147w	...	...	...	2202	2207	...	...	|	2248	...	...	...	...	|	...	0012	...	...	...	...	...	...
Hamm (Westf) **810**	d.	...	|	2149w	...	...	...	2211	2211	...	...	|	2250	...	...	...	...	|	...	0014	...	...	...	...	...	...
*Hannover Hbf **810***	a.	...	|	2317w	...	...	...	2328	2328	...	...	|	0026	...	...	...	...	|	...	|	...	...	...	...	...	...
*Leipzig Hbf **810***	a.	...	|	...	...	...	...	|	|	...	...	|	...	...	...	...	...	|	...	|	...	...	...	...	...	...
*Berlin Hbf **810***	a.	...	|	...	...	...	...	0111	0111	...	...	|	...	...	...	...	...	|	...	|	...	...	...	...	...	...
Münster (Westf) Hbf **801**	d.	...	2201	...	...	...	...	...	...	...	...	2254w	...	...	...	...	...	2357	...	0422	...	...	...	...	...	...
Osnabrück Hbf **801**	d.	...	2227	...	...	...	...	...	...	...	...	...	...	...	...	...	...	...	...	...	...	...	...	...	...	...
Bremen Hbf **801**	d.	...	2323	...	...	...	...	...	...	...	...	...	...	...	...	...	...	...	...	...						
Hamburg Hbf **801**	a.	...	0021	...	...	...	...	...	...	...	...	...	...	...	...	...	...	...	...	...						
Hamburg Altona	a.	...	0035	...	...	...	...	...	...	...	...	...	...	...	...	...	...	...	...	...						

*See Table **802** for Rhein-Ruhr local RE and S-Bahn services*

♦ – **NOTES** (LISTED BY TRAIN NUMBER)

6 – 🚃12 and 🍴 Chur - Zürich - Basel - Karlsruhe - Dortmund (- Hamburg Ⓑ**q**).
100/2 – 🚃12 and 🍴 Chur - Zürich - Basel - Köln - Hamburg (- Kiel ⑦**w**).
104 – ICE INTERNATIONAL – 🚃12 and 🍷 Basel - Köln - Arnhem - Utrecht - Amsterdam.
114 – WÖRTHERSEE – 🚃12 and 🍴 Klagenfurt - Villach - Salzburg - Dortmund.
118 – 🚃12 and 🍷 Innsbruck - Bregenz - Lindau - Ulm - Stuttgart - Münster.
347 – JAN KIEPURA – 🛏 1,2 cl., 🛌 2 cl. and 🚃2 Amsterdam - Köln - Warszawa (Table **24**); 🛏 1,2 cl. Amsterdam - Köln - Moskva (Table **24**); 🛏 1,2 cl., 🛌 2 cl. and 🚃2 (*CNL* **40347**) Amsterdam - Köln - København (Table **22**); 🛏 1,2 cl., 🛌 2 cl. and 🚃2 (*CNL* **379** – KOPERNIKUS) Amsterdam - Köln - Dresden - Praha (Table **28**). For overnight journeys only.
437 – 🚃12 and 🍷 Luxembourg - Trier - Koblenz - Emden.
439 – 🚃12 and 🍷 Luxembourg - Trier - Koblenz - Dortmund.
2012 – ALLGÄU – 🚃12 and 🍷 Oberstdorf - Ulm - Köln - Hannover (- Leipzig ⑤⑦**r**).
2155 – 🚃12 and 🍷 Düsseldorf - Kassel - Erfurt.

c – Arrives 11 minutes earlier.
d – Not Dec. 24, 31, Mar. 21, May 10.
f – Not Mar. 29 - May 25; not ⑥⑦ May 31 - June 15.
k – Also Dec. 24, 25, 31, Mar. 23, May 11.
n – Not Dec. 24, 31.
q – Ⓑ (not Dec. 24, 25, 31, Mar. 21, 23, May 11).
r – ⑤⑦ (also Dec. 26, Jan. 1, Mar. 20, 24, Apr. 30, May 12; not Dec. 23, 30, Mar. 21, 23, May 2, 11).
t – Not Dec. 24, 25, 31, Mar. 23, May 11.
v – Also Dec. 26, Jan. 1, Mar. 21, 24, May 12; not Mar. 23, May 11.
w – ⑦ (also Dec. 26, Jan. 1, Mar. 24, May 12; not Dec. 23, 30, Mar. 23, May 11
x – Not Dec. 25, Jan. 1.
z – Not Dec. 24, 25, 26, 31, Jan. 1, Mar. 22, 24, May 12.

A – To Amsterdam (Table **28**).
E – From Wiesbaden (Table **910**).
G – From Garmisch (d. 1518).
N – ①–⑥ (also Dec. 23, 30, Mar. 23, May 11; not Dec. 26, Jan. 1, Mar. 24, May 12).
P – 🚃12 and 🍴 Wien - Passau - Regensburg - Dortmund.

***** – Calls before Köln.
§ – Frankfurt Flughafen Fernbahnhof ✈. See also Tables **910** and **912**.

HAMBURG - DORTMUND - KÖLN - KOBLENZ 800

km		*ICE* 523	*ICE* 948	*ICE* 23	*ICE* 711	*EN* 346	*ICE* 525	*ICE* 501	*IC* 2319	*EC* 115	*ICE* 813	*ICE* 527	*ICE* 25	*ICE* 513	*ICE* 815	*IC* 438	*ICE* 529	*ICE* 529	*ICE* 503	*EC* 7	*EC* 7	*IC* 119	*ICE* 646	*ICE* 656	*ICE* 621
		①-⑥	①g		①-⑥	R	v	v	①-⑥		①-⑤	①-⑥			①-⑥	①-⑥	⑥⑦			①-⑥			①-⑤	①-⑤	
		e🍷		W✕	e◆	🍷◆	🍷	🍷	e✕	✕◆	d🍷	r◆	W✕	🍷	e🍷	e◆	h🍷	🍷	🍷	e◆	✕◆	🍷◆	d✕	d✕	🍷
	Hamburg Altona d.	...	...	...	...	...	...	...	...	...	...	...	...	...	...	...	...	...	...	0427	...	...	...	...	...
	Hamburg Hbf **801** d.	...	...	...	...	...	...	...	...	...	...	...	...	...	...	...	...	...	...	0441	...	...	...	...	...
	Bremen Hbf **801** d.	...	...	...	...	...	...	...	...	...	...	...	...	...	...	...	...	...	...	0540	...	...	...	...	...
	Osnabrück Hbf **801** d.	...	...	...	...	...	...	...	...	...	...	...	...	...	...	...	...	...	...	0637	...	...	...	...	...
	Münster (Westf) Hbf **801** d.	...	...	...	...	...	...	...	0504g	...	...	...	...	0601	...	0631	...	...	...	0704	...	0727	...	...	...
	Berlin Hbf **810** d.	...	0037	...	...	0032	...	...	|	...	...	...	...	|	...	|	...	...	...	|	...	|	0428	0428	...
	Leipzig Hbf **810** d.	...	|	...	...	|	...	...	|	...	...	...	...	|	...	|	...	...	...	|	...	|	|	|	...
	Hannover Hbf **810** d.	...	0231	...	...	|	...	...	|	...	...	0410g	...	|	...	|	...	...	0540	|	...	|	0621	0621	...
	Hamm (Westf) a.	...	0359	...	...	0425	...	...	|	...	...	0548g	...	|	...	|	...	...	0712	|	...	|	0748	0748	...
0	Hamm (Westf) **805** d.	...	0401	...	...	0427	...	...	|	...	...	0551g	...	|	...	|	...	...	0714	|	...	|	0752	0754	...
	Dortmund Hbf **805** a.	...	0418	...	...	0448	...	...	0533g	...	...	0610g	...	0633	...	|	...	...	0732	0733	...	|	0809	|	...
	Dortmund Hbf d.	0401	0421	0433v	0437	0459	0523	0537	0538	0552	0559	0623	0636	0638	0653	|	0723	...	0737	0738	0738	|	0812	|	...
	Bochum Hbf d.	0413	0433	0444v	0450	|	0535	|	0549	0605	0611	0635	|	0649	0704	|	0735	...	|	0749	0749	|	0825	|	...
	Recklinghausen Hbf d.	|	|	|	|	|	|	|	|	|	|	|	|	|	|	0700	|	...	|	|	|	0757	|	|	...
	Wanne-Eickel Hbf d.	|	|	|	|	|	|	|	|	|	|	|	|	|	|	0709f	|	...	|	|	|	0806	|	|	...
	Gelsenkirchen Hbf d.	|	|	|	|	|	|	|	|	|	|	|	|	|	|	0715c	|	...	|	|	|	0812	|	|	...
	Essen Hbf d.	0423	0444	0455v	0500	|	0551	|	0600	0616	0623	0651	|	0700	0715	|	0753	0753	|	0800	0800	0823	0836	|	0840
	Mülheim (Ruhr) Hbf d.	|	|	|	|	|	|	|	|	0624	|	|	|	|	|	|	|	|	|	|	|	0831	|	|	|
	Oberhausen Hbf d.	|	|	|	|	0732*	|	|	|	|	|	|	|	|	|	0727f	|	|	|	|	|	|	|	|	|
	Duisburg Hbf d.	0437	0457	0508v	0513	0715*	0605	|	0613	0632	0637	0703	|	0713	0729	0735	0808	0808	|	0813	0813	0838	0849	|	0855
	Düsseldorf Flughafen ✈ d.	|	0507	|	|	|	|	|	|	|	|	|	|	|	|	|	|	|	|	|	|	|	0859	|	|
	Düsseldorf Hbf d.	0453	0515	0523v	0529	0654*	0622	|	0627	0650	0654	0722	|	0727	0748	0752	0822	0822	|	0827	0827	0852	0908	|	0913
48	**Hagen** Hbf d.	|	|	|	|	0523	|	0557	|	|	|	|	0657	|	|	|	|	|	0757	|	|	|	|	0824	|
75	Wuppertal Hbf d.	|	|	|	|	0541	|	0614	|	|	|	|	0714	|	|	|	|	|	0814	|	|	|	|	0841	|
93	Solingen Hbf d.	|	|	|	|	|	|	0626	|	|	|	|	0727	|	|	|	|	|	0826	|	|	|	|	|	|
120	**Köln** Messe/Deutz a.	0513	|	|	0548	|	0642	|	|	|	0716	0742	|	|	0808	|	0842	0842	|	|	|	|	0928	|	0935
121	**Köln** Hbf a.	|	0540	0546v	|	0614	|	0646	0649	0714	|	|	0746	0749	|	0815	|	|	0846	0850	0850	0915	|	0909	|
	Köln Hbf d.	|	0543	0553	|	...	|	0654	0653	0718	|	|	0753	0754	|	0818	|	|	0854	0853	0853	0918	|	...	|
	Köln/Bonn Flughafen ✈ a.	0528	0604	|	0609	...	|	|	|	|	|	|	|	|	0819	|	|	|	|	|	|	|	0942	...	|
	Bonn Hbf d.	|	...	0614	...	...	|	|	0714	0737	|	|	0814	|	...	0837	|	|	|	0914	0914	0937	...	...	|
	Remagen d.	|	...	|	...	...	|	|	|	0751	|	|	|	|	...	0851	|	|	|	|	|	0951	...	...	|
	Andernach d.	|	...	|	...	...	|	|	|	0803	|	|	|	|	...	0903	|	|	|	|	|	1003	...	...	|
	Koblenz Hbf a.	|	...	0646	...	...	|	|	0746	0815	|	|	0846	|	...	0916	|	|	|	0946	0946	1015	...	...	|
	Mainz Hbf **912** a.	|	...	0738	...	...	|	|	0837	0911	|	|	0938	|	...	...	|	|	|	1037	1037	1111	...	...	|
	Frankfurt Flughafen ✈ § a.	0634	...	0759	...	...	0734	0751	|	|	0827	0834	0959	0851	0926	...	0934	0934	0951	|	|	|	...	...	1034
	Frankfurt (Main) Hbf **910/2** a.	0648	...	0813	...	...	0748	|	|	|	0841	0848	1013	|	0941	...	0948	0948	|	|	|	|	...	...	1048
	Nürnberg Hbf **920** a.	0859	...	1028	...	...	0959	|	|	|	...	1059	1228	|	...	...	1159	1159	|	|	|	|	...	...	1259
	Stuttgart Hbf **930** a.	|	...	...	...	...	|	|	1018	1046	...	|	...	1008	...	...	|	|	|	|	|	1246	...	...	|
	München Hbf **904 930** a.	1004	...	...	...	...	1104	|	...	1317	...	1204	...	1231	...	...	1304	1304	|	|	|	...	...	...	1404
	Karlsruhe Hbf **912** a.	...	...	...	...	...	...	0859	...	...	...	...	...	...	...	...	...	...	1059	1147	1147	...	...	...	...
	Basel SBB 🚌 **912** a.	...	...	...	...	...	...	1047	...	...	...	...	...	...	...	...	...	...	1247	1337	1337	...	...	...	...

	ICE 1034	*ICE* 121	*ICE* 515	*ICE* 27	*IC* 2005	*IC* 2007	*IC* 2015	*ICE* 946	*ICE* 956	*ICE* 105	*EC* 101	*IC* 2013	*ICE* 644	*ICE* 654	*ICE* 625	*IC* 2025	*ICE* 517	*IC* 2248	*IC* 436	*ICE* 944	*ICE* 954	*IC* 2156	*IC* 2044	*IC* 2113	*ICE* 123
	①-④	①-⑥			⑤⑥	X	①-④	①-⑥	①-⑥	v								①-⑥		①-⑥	①-⑥				
	t✓	r A	🍷	W✕	🍷◆	🍷	b◆	e✕	e✕	🍷◆	✕◆	🍷◆	✕	✕	🍷	🍷	🍷	e B	🍷◆	e✕	e✕	🍷◆	🍷	🍷	A🍷
Hamburg Altona d.	0556	...	0523	...	...	...	...	...	...	...	0632	...	...	...	...	0732	...	...	...	...	...	...	...	0832	...
Hamburg Hbf 801 d.	0611	...	0537	...	...	...	...	...	...	...	0646	...	...	...	...	0746	...	...	...	...	...	...	...	0846	...
Bremen Hbf 801 d.	|	...	0637	...	...	...	...	...	...	...	0744	...	...	...	...	0844	...	...	...	...	...	...	...	0944	...
Osnabrück Hbf 801 d.	|	...	0732	...	...	...	...	...	...	...	0837	...	...	...	...	0937	...	1000	...	...	...	...	...	1037	...
Münster (Westf) Hbf 801 d.	|	...	0801	...	0831	...	0831	...	...	...	0904	...	...	...	...	1004	...	1024	1032	...	...	...	...	1104	...
Berlin Hbf **810** d.	|	...	|	...	|	...	|	0538	0538	...	|	...	0651	0651	...	|	...	...	|	0748	0748	...	...	|	...
Leipzig Hbf **810** d.	|	...	|	...	|	...	|	|	|	...	|	0437k	|	|	...	|	...	...	|	|	|	...	0640	|	...
Hannover Hbf **810** d.	|	...	|	...	|	...	|	0731	0731	...	|	0740	0831	0831	...	|	...	...	|	0931	0931	...	0940	|	...
Hamm (Westf) a.	|	...	|	...	|	...	|	0848	0848	...	|	0912	0948	0948	...	|	...	...	|	1048	1048	...	1112	|	...
Hamm (Westf) **805** d.	|	...	|	...	|	...	|	0852	0854	...	|	0914	0952	0954	...	|	...	...	|	1052	1054	1056	1114	|	...
Dortmund Hbf **805** a.	|	...	0833	...	|	...	|	0909	|	...	0933	0932	1009	|	...	1033	...	...	|	1109	|	1115	1132	1133	...
Dortmund Hbf d.	|	...	0837	0838	|	0852	|	0912	|	...	0938	0952	1012	|	...	1036	1038	...	|	1112	|	1118	1137	1138	...
Bochum Hbf d.	|	...	|	0849	|	|	|	0925	|	...	0949	1003	1025	|	...	|	1049	...	|	1125	|	1130	|	1149	...
Recklinghausen Hbf d.	|	...	|	|	0900	|	0900	|	|	...	|	|	|	|	...	|	|	...	1101	|	|	|	|	|	...
Wanne-Eickel Hbf d.	|	...	|	|	0909f	0909f	0909f	|	|	...	|	|	|	|	...	|	|	...	1110	|	|	|	|	|	...
Gelsenkirchen Hbf d.	|	...	|	|	0915c	0915c	0915c	|	|	...	|	|	|	|	...	|	|	...	1116	|	|	|	|	|	...
Essen Hbf d.	0853s	...	|	0900	|	|	|	0936	|	...	1000	1014	1036	|	1053	|	1100	...	|	1136	|	1141	|	1200	...
Mülheim (Ruhr) Hbf d.	|	...	|	|	|	|	|	|	|	...	|	1022	|	|	|	|	|	...	|	|	|	|	|	|	...
Oberhausen Hbf d.	|	0900	|	|	0927f	0927f	0927f	|	|	1000	|	|	|	|	|	|	|	...	1128f	|	|	|	|	|	1226
Duisburg Hbf d.	|	0908	|	0913	0935	0935	0935	0949	|	1008	1013	1032	1049	|	1108	|	1113	...	1135	1149	|	1155	|	1213	1235
Düsseldorf Flughafen ✈ d.	|	|	|	|	|	|	|	0959	|	|	|	|	1059	|	|	|	|	...	|	1159	|	1206	|	|	|
Düsseldorf Hbf d.	0915s	0922	|	0927	0949	0949	0949	1005	|	1022	1027	1050	1108	|	1122	|	1127	...	1149	1205	|	1212	|	1227	1248
Hagen Hbf d.	|	|	0857	|	|	|	|	...	0924	|	|	|	|	1024	|	1057	|	...	|	...	1124	...	1157	|	|
Wuppertal Hbf d.	|	|	0914	|	|	|	|	...	0941	|	|	|	|	1041	|	1114	|	...	|	...	1141	...	1214	|	|
Solingen Hbf d.	|	|	0926	|	|	|	|	...	|	|	|	|	|	|	|	1127	|	...	|	...	|	...	1226	|	|
Köln Messe/Deutz a.	|	0943	|	|	|	|	|	...	|	|	|	|	1128	|	1142	|	|	...	|	...	|	...	|	|	|
Köln Hbf a.	0941	|	0946	0949	1012	1012	1012	...	1009	1045	1049	1112	|	1109	|	1146	1149	...	1212	...	1209	...	1245	1249	1312
Köln Hbf d.	...	|	0954	0953	1018	1018	1018	...	...	1054	1053	1118	|	1112e	|	1153	1154	...	1218	...	...	...	...	1253	1320
Köln/Bonn Flughafen ✈ a.	...	|	|	|	|	|	|	...	...	|	|	|	1142	|	|	|	|	...	|	...	...	...	...	|	|
Bonn Hbf d.	...	|	|	1014	1037	1037	1037	...	...	|	1114	1137	...	1132e	|	1214	|	...	1237	...	...	...	...	1314	|
Remagen d.	...	|	|	|	1051	1051	1051	...	...	|	|	1151	...	...	|	|	|	...	1251	...	...	...	...	|	|
Andernach d.	...	|	|	|	1103	1103	1103	...	...	|	|	1203	...	...	|	|	|	...	1303	...	...	...	...	|	|
Koblenz Hbf a.	...	|	|	1046	1115	1115	1115	...	...	|	1146	1215	...	...	|	1246	|	...	1316	...	...	...	...	1346	|
Mainz Hbf **912** a.	...	|	|	1138	1213	1213	1213	...	...	|	1237	1311	...	...	|	1338	|	...	...	...	...	...	...	1437	|
Frankfurt Flughafen ✈ § a.	...	1043	1051	1159	|	|	|	...	...	1151	|	|	...	...	1234	1359	1251	...	...	...	...	...	...	|	1414
Frankfurt (Main) Hbf **910/2** a.	...	1102	|	1213	|	|	|	...	...	|	|	|	...	...	1248	1413	|	...	...	...	...	...	...	|	1430
Nürnberg Hbf **920** a.	...	...	|	1428	|	|	|	...	...	|	|	|	...	...	1459	...	|	...	...	...	...	...	...	|	...
Stuttgart Hbf **930** a.	...	...	1208	...	|	|	1358	...	...	|	|	1446	...	...	|	...	1408	...	...	...	...	...	...	1622	...
München Hbf **904 930** a.	...	...	1431	...	|	|	...	...	...	|	|	...	...	...	1604	...	1631	...	...						
Karlsruhe Hbf **912** a.	...	...	...	...	1335	1335	...	...	...	1259	1347	...	...	...	...	...	...	...	...						
Basel SBB 🚌 **912** a.	...	...	...	...	...	...	...	...	...	1447	1537	...	...	...	...	...	...	...	...						

See Table 802 for Rhein-Ruhr local RE and S-Bahn services

◆ – NOTES (LISTED BY TRAIN NUMBER)

– [12] and ✕ (Hamburg ①-⑥ e -) Dortmund - Karlsruhe - Basel - Zürich - Chur.
01 – [12] and ✕ Hamburg - Köln - Karlsruhe - Basel - Zürich - Chur. Train number **103** on ⑥.
05 – ICE INTERNATIONAL – [12] and 🍷 Amsterdam - Utrecht - Arnhem - Basel.
15 – WÖRTHERSEE – [12] and ✕ Dortmund - Salzburg - Villach - Klagenfurt.
19 – [12] and 🍷 Münster - Ulm - Linau - Bregenz - Innsbruck.
46 – JAN KIEPURA – 🛏 1, 2 cl., 🛌 2 cl. and [2] Warszawa - Köln - Amsterdam (Table **24**); 🛏 1, 2 cl. Moskva - Köln - Amsterdam (Table **24**); 🛏 1, 2 cl., 🛌 2 cl. and [2] (*CNL* **40483**) København - Köln - Amsterdam (Table **22**); 🛏 1, 2 cl., 🛌 2 cl. and [2] (*CNL* **378** – KOPERNIKUS) Praha - Dresden - Köln - Amsterdam (Table **28**). For overnight journeys only.
36 – [12] and 🍷 Emden - Münster - Koblenz - Trier - Luxembourg.
38 – [12] and 🍷 Münster - Koblenz - Trier - Luxembourg.
27 – WETTERSTEIN – [12] and 🍷 (Hannover ① g -) Dortmund - München (- Garmisch ⑥).
11 – [12] and 🍷 Dortmund - Wiesbaden (Table **910**).
005 – ⑤⑥ (also Mar. 20, Apr. 30, May 21). BODENSEE – [12] and 🍷 Emden - Konstanz.
013 – ALLGÄU – [12] and 🍷 (Leipzig ①⑥ **k** -) (Magdeburg ①-⑥ **e** -) Hannover - Köln - Oberstdorf.
015 – [12] and 🍷 Emden - Stuttgart.
156 – [12] and 🍷 Erfurt - Kassel - Düsseldorf.

A – From Amsterdam (Table **28**).
B – From Berlin (Table **810**).
W – [12] and ✕ Dortmund - Regensburg - Passau - Linz - Wien.
X – Runs on Dec. 24, 25, 30, 31, Mar. 23, May 11 only. To Konstanz (Table **916**).

b – Not Dec. 24, 25, 26, 31, Jan. 1, Mar. 20, 24, Apr. 30, May 12, 21.
c – 3 minutes earlier Mar. 29 - May 24 (also ⑥ from May 31).
d – Not Dec. 24, 25, 26, 31, Jan. 1, Mar. 21, 24, May 12.
e – ①-⑥ (not Dec. 25, 26, Jan. 1, Mar. 22, 24, May 12).
f – Not Mar. 29 - May 25; not ⑥⑦ May 31 - June 15.
g – ① (also Dec. 27, Jan. 2, Mar. 25, May 13; not Dec. 24, 31, Mar. 24, May 12).
h – Also Dec. 24, 25, 26, 31, Jan. 1, Mar. 21, 24, May 12.
k – ①⑥ (also Dec. 27, Jan. 2, Mar. 21, 26, May 1, 13; not Dec. 24, 31, Mar. 22, 24, May 3, 12).
r – Not Dec. 25, 26, Jan. 1, Mar. 24, May 12.
s – Stops to set down only.
t – Not Dec. 24 - Jan. 1, Mar. 24, May 1, 12, 22.
v – Not Dec. 25, Jan. 1.
* – Arrival times. Calls after Köln.
✓ – R and 'Sprinter' supplement payable. ✕.
§ – Frankfurt Flughafen Fernbahnhof ✈. See also Tables **910** and **912**.

Warning! Hamburg area alterations Dec. 24 - Jan. 1 (see page 363)

800 HAMBURG - DORTMUND - KÖLN - KOBLENZ

	IC 2011	IC 1811	ICE 642	ICE 652	ICE 629	IC 2027	ICE 519	IC 434	ICE 942	ICE 952	IC 2154	IC 2046	IC 2115	ICE 125	IC 1819	IC 2017	IC 2017	ICE 640	ICE 650	ICE 723	IC 2029	IC 2329	IC 2246	IC 432	IC 432
	⑤t	⑦w								n		①–⑥.			①–④	⑦w	⑤t			⑧q		⑥			⑧q
		🍷	✕	✕	🍷	🍷	🍷	🍷♦	✕	✕	🍷	e🍷	🍷♦	A🍷	v🍷	🍷	🍷	✕	✕	🍷	🍷♦	🍷♦	♦	🍷♦	🍷♦
Hamburg Altona d.	...	...	...	...	...	0932	...	...	...	...	...	...	...	...	...	...	...	...	...	...	1132	...	...	...	...
Hamburg Hbf **801** d.	...	...	...	...	...	0946	...	...	...	...	...	...	1046	...	...	...	...	...	...	...	1146	1146	...	...	...
Bremen Hbf **801** d.	...	...	...	...	...	1044	...	...	...	...	...	...	1144	...	...	...	...	...	...	...	1244	1244	...	...	...
Osnabrück Hbf **801** d.	...	...	...	...	...	1137	...	...	...	...	...	...	1237	...	...	...	...	...	...	...	1337	1337	1400	...	...
Münster (Westf) Hbf **801** d.	...	...	...	...	...	1204	...	1232	...	...	...	...	1304	...	...	...	...	...	...	...	1404	1404	1424	1431	1431
Berlin Hbf **810** d.	...	...	0851	0851	...	|	...	|	0948	0948	0640	...	|	...	...	1010	...	1051	1051	...	|	|	▬	|	|
Leipzig Hbf **810** d.	...	...	|	|	...	|	...	|	|	|	|	0840	|	...	...	|	...	|	|	...	|	|	...	|	|
Hannover Hbf **810** d.	...	...	1031	1031	...	|	...	|	1131	1131	|	1140	|	...	...	1158	1158	1231	1231	...	|	|	*ICE*	|	|
Hamm (Westf) a.	...	...	1148	1148	...	|	...	|	1248	1248	1252	1312	|	...	...	1323	1323	1348	1348	...	|	|	**611**	|	|
Hamm (Westf) **805** d.	...	...	1152	1154	...	|	...	|	1252	1254	1256	1314	|	...	...	1325	1325	1352	1354	...	|	|		|	|
Dortmund Hbf **805** a.	...	...	1209	|	...	1233	...	|	1309	|	1315	1332	1333	...	...	1347	1347	1409	|	...	1433	1433	🍷	|	|
Dortmund Hbf d.	1152	1152	1212	|	...	1236	1238	|	1312	|	1318	1337	1338	...	...	1352	1352	1412	|	...	1436	1436	1438	|	|
Bochum Hbf d.	1203	1203	1225	|	...	|	1249	|	1325	|	1330	|	1349	...	...	1403	1403	1425	|	...	|	|	1449	|	|
Recklinghausen Hbf d.	|	|	|	|	...	|	|	1301	|	|	|	|	|	...	...	|	|	|	|	...	|	|	|	1500	1500
Wanne-Eickel Hbf d.	|	|	|	|	...	|	|	1310	|	|	|	|	|	...	...	|	|	|	|	...	|	|	|	1509f	1509f
Gelsenkirchen Hbf d.	|	|	|	|	...	|	|	1316	|	|	|	|	|	...	...	|	|	|	|	...	|	|	|	1515c	1515c
Essen Hbf d.	1214	1214	1236	|	1253	|	1300	|	1336	|	1341	|	1400	...	...	1414	1414	1436	|	1453	|	|	1500	|	|
Mülheim (Ruhr) Hbf d.	1222	1222	|	|	|	|	|	|	|	|	|	|	|	...	...	1422	1422	|	|	|	|	|	|	|	|
Oberhausen Hbf d.	|	|	|	|	|	|	|	1328f	|	|	|	|	|	1426	...	|	|	|	|	|	|	|	|	1527f	1527f
Duisburg Hbf d.	1230	1230	1249	|	1308	|	1313	1335	1349	|	1355	|	1413	1434	...	1429	1429	1449	|	1508	|	|	1513	1534	1534
Düsseldorf Flughafen ✈ d.	|	|	1259	|	|	|	|	|	1359	|	1406	|	|	|	...	|	|	1459	|	|	|	|	|	|	|
Düsseldorf Hbf d.	1251	1251	1305	|	1322	|	1327	1349	1408	|	1412	|	1427	1448	...	1451	1451	1505	|	1522	|	|	1527	1549	1549
Hagen Hbf d.	|	|	...	1224	|	1257	|	|	|	1324	...	1357	|	|	...	|	|	...	1424	|	1457	1457	|	|	|
Wuppertal Hbf d.	|	|	...	1241	|	1314	|	|	|	1341	...	1414	|	|	...	|	|	...	1441	|	1514	1514	|	|	|
Solingen Hbf d.	|	|	...	|	|	1327	|	|	|	|	...	1426	|	|	...	|	|	...	|	|	1527	1527	|	|	|
Köln Messe/Deutz a.	|	|	...	|	1342	|	|	|	|	|	...	|	|	|	...	|	|	...	|	1542	|	|	|	|	|
Köln Hbf a.	1315	1315	...	1309	|	1346	1349	1412	|	1409	...	1445	1450	1512	...	1515	1515	...	1509	|	1546	1546	1549	1612	1612
Köln Hbf d.	1318	1318	...	1312	|	1353	1354	1418	|	...	...	...	1453	1520	1518	1518	1518	...	...	|	1553	1553	1554	...	1618
Köln/Bonn Flughafen ✈ a.	|	|	...	|	|	|	|	|	1445	...	...	...	|	|	|	|	|	...	...	|	|	|	|	...	|
Bonn Hbf d.	1337	1337	...	1332	|	1414	|	1437	...	...	...	...	1514	|	1537	1537	1537	...	...	|	1614	1614	|	...	1637
Remagen d.	1351	1351	...	...	|	|	|	1451	...	...	...	...	|	|	1551	1551	1551	...	...	|	|	|	|	...	1651
Andernach d.	1403	1403	...	...	|	|	|	1503	...	...	...	...	|	|	1603	1603	1603	...	...	|	|	|	|	...	1703
Koblenz Hbf a.	1415	1415	...	...	|	1446	|	1516	...	...	...	...	1546	|	1615	1615	1615	...	...	|	1646	1646	|	...	1716
Mainz Hbf **912** a.	1511	1511	...	...	|	1538	|	...	...	...	...	...	1637	|	1711	1711	1711	...	...	|	1738	1738	|	...	...
Frankfurt Flughafen ✈ § a.	|	|	...	...	1434	1559	1451	...	...	...	...	...	|	1614	|	|	|	...	...	1634	1759	1759	1651	...	...
Frankfurt (Main) Hbf **910/2** a.	|	|	...	...	1448	1613	|	...	...	...	...	...	|	1630	|	|	|	...	...	1648	1813	1813	|	...	...
Nürnberg Hbf **920** a.	|	|	...	...	1659	...	|	...	...	...	...	...	|	...	|	|	|	...	...	1859	2028	2028	|	...	...
Stuttgart Hbf **930** a.	1646	1646	...	...	|	...	1608	...	...	...	...	...	1822	...	1846	1846	1846	...	...	|	...	...	1808	...	...
München Hbf **904 930** a.	...	...	...	...	1804	...	1831	...	...	...	...	...	...	...	...	...	2128	...	...	2004	...	...	2031	...	...
Karlsruhe Hbf **912** a.	...	...	...	...	...	...	...	...	...	...	...	...	...	...	...	...	...	...	...	...	...	...	...	...	...
Basel SBB 🚌 **912** a.	...	...	...	...	...	...	...	...	...	...	...	...	...	...	...	...	...	...	...	...	...	...	...	...	...

	ICE 940	ICE 950	IC 2152	ICE 725	ICE 725	IC 2048	IC 2311	ICE 127	IC 2019	ICE 548	ICE 548	ICE 558	ICE 727	ICE 927	ICE 1027	ICE 613	IC 430	ICE 848	ICE 858	IC 2150	ICE 729	IC 2140	IC 2213	IC 1842	IC 1946
		n	⑤⑦k	⑦w				G	⑤⑦	⑧		n	⑧q		⑤				n					⑤r	⑦w
	✕	✕	🍷♦	🍷	🍷	🍷	🍷♦	A🍷	k	✕	✕	✕	🍷	✕♦	✕♦	🍷	🍷♦	✕	✕	🍷♦	🍷	🍷	🍷♦	🍷	🍷
Hamburg Altona d.	...	...	...	...	...	...	...	...	...	...	...	...	...	...	...	...	...	...	...	...	...	...	...	...	...
Hamburg Hbf **801** d.	...	...	...	...	...	...	1246	...	...	...	...	...	...	1346	1346	...	...	...	...	...	...	...	1446	...	...
Bremen Hbf **801** d.	...	...	...	...	...	...	1344	...	...	...	...	...	...	1444	1444	...	...	...	...	...	...	...	1544	...	...
Osnabrück Hbf **801** d.	...	...	...	...	...	...	1437	...	...	...	...	...	...	1537	1537	...	...	...	...	...	...	...	1637	...	...
Münster (Westf) Hbf **801** d.	...	...	...	...	...	...	1504	...	...	...	...	...	...	1603	1603	...	1631	...	...	...	...	...	1704	...	...
Berlin Hbf **810** d.	1148	1148	0840	...	...	...	|	...	1209	1251	1251	1251	...	|	|	...	|	1348	1348	1040	...	...	|	1409	1409
Leipzig Hbf **810** d.	|	|	|	...	...	1040	|	...	|	|	|	|	...	|	|	...	|	|	|	|	...	1240	|	|	|
Hannover Hbf **810** d.	1331	1331	|	...	...	1340	|	...	1358	1431	1431	1431	...	|	|	...	|	1531	1531	|	...	1540	|	1558	1558
Hamm (Westf) a.	1448	1448	1452	...	...	1512	|	...	1523	1548	1548	1548	...	|	|	...	|	1648	1648	1652	...	1712	|	1724	1725
Hamm (Westf) **805** d.	1452	1454	1456	...	...	1514	|	...	1525	1552	1552	1554	...	|	|	...	|	1652	1654	1656	...	1714	|	1726	1727
Dortmund Hbf **805** a.	1509	|	1515	...	...	1532	1533	...	1547	1609	1609	|	...	1633	1633	...	|	1709	|	1715	...	1732	1733	1748	1749
Dortmund Hbf d.	1512	|	1518	1522	...	1537	1538	...	1552	1612	1612	|	...	1636	1636	1638	|	1712	|	1718	...	1737	1738	1752	1752
Bochum Hbf d.	1525	|	1530	1536	...	|	1549	...	1603	1625	1625	|	...	|	|	1649	|	1725	|	1730	...	|	1749	1803	1803
Recklinghausen Hbf d.	|	|	|	|	...	|	|	...	|	|	|	|	...	|	|	|	1700	|	|	|	...	|	|	|	|
Wanne-Eickel Hbf d.	|	|	|	|	...	|	|	...	|	|	|	|	...	|	|	|	1709f	|	|	|	...	|	|	|	|
Gelsenkirchen Hbf d.	|	|	|	|	...	|	|	...	|	|	|	|	...	|	|	|	1715c	|	|	|	...	|	|	|	|
Essen Hbf d.	1536	|	1541	1553	1553	|	1600	...	1614	1636	1636	|	1653	|	|	1700	|	1736	|	1741	1753	|	1800	1814	1814
Mülheim (Ruhr) Hbf d.	|	|	|	|	|	|	|	...	1622	|	|	|	|	|	|	|	|	|	|	|	|	|	|	1822	1822
Oberhausen Hbf d.	|	|	|	|	|	|	|	1626	|	|	|	|	|	|	|	|	1727f	|	|	|	|	|	|	|	|
Duisburg Hbf d.	1549	|	1555	1608	1608	|	1613	1634	1630	1649	1649	|	1708	|	|	1713	1735	1749	|	1755	1808	|	1813	1830	1830
Düsseldorf Flughafen ✈ d.	1559	|	1606	|	|	|	|	|	|	1659	1659	|	|	|	|	|	|	1759	|	1807	|	|	|	|	|
Düsseldorf Hbf d.	1605	|	1612	1622	1622	|	1627	1648	1651j	1710	1710	|	1722	|	|	1727	1749	1805	|	1815	1821	|	1827	1851	1851
Hagen Hbf d.	...	1524	...	|	|	1557	|	|	|	|	...	1624	|	1657	1657	|	|	...	1724	...	|	1757	|	|	|
Wuppertal Hbf d.	...	1541	...	|	|	1614	|	|	|	|	...	1641	|	1714	1714	|	|	...	1741	...	|	1814	|	|	|
Solingen Hbf d.	...	|	...	|	|	1626	|	|	|	|	...	|	|	|	|	|	|	...	|	...	|	1826	|	|	|
Köln Messe/Deutz a.	...	|	...	1642	1642	|	|	|	|	1728	...	|	1742	|	|	|	|	...	|	...	1841	|	|	|	|
Köln Hbf a.	...	1609	...	|	|	1645	1649	1712	1715	|	...	1709	|	1746	1746	1749	1812	...	1809	...	|	1845	1849	1915	1915
Köln Hbf d.	...	...	...	|	|	...	1653	1720	1718	|	...	...	|	1753	1753	1754	1818	...	...	...	|	...	1853	...	1918
Köln/Bonn Flughafen ✈ a.	...	...	...	|	|	...	|	|	|	1742	...	...	|	|	|	|	|	...	...	...	|	...	|	...	|
Bonn Hbf d.	...	...	...	|	|	...	1714	|	1737	...	...	...	|	1814	1814	|	1837	...	...	...	|	...	1914	...	1937
Remagen d.	...	...	...	|	|	...	|	|	1751	...	...	...	|	|	|	|	1851	...	...	...	|	...	|	...	1951
Andernach d.	...	...	...	|	|	...	|	|	1803	...	...	...	|	|	|	|	1903	...	...	...	|	...	|	...	2003
Koblenz Hbf a.	...	...	...	|	|	...	1746	|	1815	...	...	...	|	1846	1846	|	1916	...	...	...	|	...	1946	...	2015
Mainz Hbf **912** a.	...	...	...	|	|	...	1837	|	1911	...	...	...	|	1938	1938	|	...	...	...	...	|	...	2037	...	2111
Frankfurt Flughafen ✈ § a.	...	...	...	1734	1734	...	...	1814	|	...	...	...	1834	1959	1959	1851	...	...	...	...	1935	...	|	...	|
Frankfurt (Main) Hbf **910/2** a.	...	...	...	1748	1748	...	...	1830	|	...	...	...	1848	2013	2013	|	...	...	...	...	1948	...	|	...	|
Nürnberg Hbf **920** a.	...	...	...	1959	1959	...	...	...	|	...	...	...	2059	2224	2224	|	...	...	...	...	2159	...	|	...	|
Stuttgart Hbf **930** a.	...	...	...	|	|	...	...	...	2046	...	...	...	|	|	...	2008	...	...	...	...	|	...	2222	...	|
München Hbf **904 930** a.	...	...	...	2104	2104							...	2208	2348	...	2231	...	...	...	...	2304	...	...	...	|
Karlsruhe Hbf **912** a.	...	...	...	...	...							...	...	...	...	...	...	...	...	...	...	...	...	...	2224
Basel SBB 🚌 **912** a.	...	...	...	...	...							...	...	...	...	...	...	...	...	...	...	...	...	...	...

*See Table **802** for Rhein-Ruhr local RE and S-Bahn services*

♦ – **NOTES** (LISTED BY TRAIN NUMBER)

430 – NORDERNEY – 🚃 and 🍷 Norddeich Mole - Emden - Koblenz - Trier - Luxembourg.
432 – 🚃 and 🍷 Norddeich Mole - Emden - Köln (- Luxembourg ⑧**q**).
434 – 🚃 and 🍷 Norddeich Mole - Emden - Koblenz - Trier - Luxembourg.
927 – ①②③④⑥⑦ (not Dec. 23, Mar. 23, May 11). 🚃 and ✕ Kiel - Köln - Frankfurt - München.
1027 – ⑤ (also Dec. 23, Mar. 23, May 11). 🚃 and ✕ Kiel - Köln - Frankfurt - Regensburg.
2029 – Daily until June 13. 🚃 and 🍷 Hamburg - Köln - Frankfurt - Regensburg - Passau.
2115 – 🚃 and 🍷 Stralsund - Hamburg - Köln - Stuttgart. On Dec. 24, 31 terminates at Köln Hbf.
2150 – 🚃 and 🍷 (Stralsund ①–⑥**e** -) Berlin - Halle - Erfurt - Kassel - Düsseldorf. Train number **2250** on ⑦ (also Dec. 25, 26, Jan. 1, Mar. 22, 24, May 12).
2152 – 🚃 and 🍷 (Berlin ⑤**r** -) Halle - Erfurt - Kassel - Düsseldorf.
2213 – RÜGEN – 🚃 and 🍷 Ostseebad Binz - Stralsund - Rostock - Hamburg - Köln - Stuttgart.
2246 – 🚃 and 🍷 Berlin - Hannover - Osnabrück - Münster.
2311 – NORDFRIESLAND – 🚃 and 🍷 Westerland - Hamburg - Köln - Heidelberg. On Dec. 24, 31 terminates at Köln Hbf.
2329 – ⑥ from June 14. LÜBECKER BUCHT – 🚃 and 🍷 Puttgarden - Lübeck - Hamburg - Köln - Frankfurt - Regensburg - Passau.

A – From Amsterdam (Table **28**).
G – From Mar. 14.

c – 3 minutes **earlier** Mar. 29 - May 25 (also ⑥⑦ May 31 - June 15).
e – Not Dec. 25, 26, Jan. 1, Mar. 22, 24, May 12.
f – Not Mar. 29 - May 25; not ⑥⑦ May 31 - June 15.
j – Arrives 1642.
k – Also Dec. 26, Jan. 1, Mar. 20, 24, Apr. 30, May 12; not Dec. 23, 30, Mar. 21, 23, May 2, 11.
n – Not Dec. 24, 31.
q – Not Dec. 24, 25, 31, Mar. 21, 23, May 11.
r – Also Mar. 20, Apr. 30; not Mar. 21, May 2.
t – Also Mar. 20, Apr. 30, May 21; not Mar. 21, May 2, 23.
v – Not Dec. 24, 25, 26, 31, Jan. 1, Mar. 20, 24, Apr. 30, May 1, 12, 21, 22.
w – Also Dec. 26, Jan. 1, Mar. 24, May 12; not Dec. 23, 30, Mar. 23, May 11.
§ – Frankfurt Flughafen ✈ Fernbahnhof. See also Tables **910** and **912**.

HAMBURG - DORTMUND - KÖLN - KOBLENZ 800

	ICE 129	ICE 546	ICE 546	ICE 556	ICE 556	ICE 929	IC 615	IC 2244	IC 2332	ICE 846	ICE 856	IC 2356	ICE 617	ICE 607	IC 2142	IC 2215	IC 2315	ICE 227	IC 1909	ICE 544	ICE 744	ICE 554	ICE 619	IC 2321	IC 2121
	A🍷	✕	①–⑥ z✕	✕	①–⑤ d✕	✕	n 🍷	B	M 🍷	✕	T✕	🍷♦	⑦w 🍷	①–⑥ v🍷	⑧q 🍷	H 🍷	🍷♦	A🍷	⑦ 🍷♦	①–⑥ z✕	⑦w ✕	✕	🍷	D 🍷	Ⓒ 🍷♦
Hamburg Altona d.	...	...	...	...	...	1532	...	...	...	...	...	...	...	...	...	1632	...	...	...	...	...	...	...	1732	...
Hamburg Hbf **801** d.	...	...	...	...	...	1546	...	...	...	...	...	...	...	...	...	1646	1646	...	1705	...	...	...	...	1746	1746
Bremen Hbf **801** d.	...	...	...	...	...	1644	...	...	...	...	...	...	...	...	...	1744	1744	...	1800	...	...	...	...	1844	1844
Osnabrück Hbf **801** d.	...	...	...	...	...	1737	...	1800	...	...	...	...	...	...	...	1837	1837	...	1856	...	...	...	...	1937	1937
Münster (Westf) Hbf **801** d.	...	...	...	...	...	1803	...	1824	1832	...	...	...	...	...	...	1904	1904	...	1927	...	...	...	...	2004	2004
Berlin Hbf **810** d.	...	1451	1451	1451	1451	|	...	...	|	1548	1548	1240	...	...	...	|	|	...	|	1651	1651	1651	...	|	|
Leipzig Hbf **810** d.	...	|	|	|	|	|	...	...	|	|	|	|	...	...	1440	|	|	...	|	|	|	|	...	|	|
Hannover Hbf **810** d.	...	1631	1631	1631	1631	|	...	...	|	1731	1731	|	...	...	1740	|	|	...	|	1831	1831	1831	...	|	|
Hamm (Westf) a.	...	1748	1748	1748	1748	|	...	...	|	1848	1848	1852	...	...	1912	|	|	...	|	1948	1948	1948	...	|	|
Hamm (Westf) **805** d.	...	1752	1752	1754	1754	|	...	...	|	1852	1854	1856	...	...	1914	|	|	...	|	1952	1952	1954	...	|	|
Dortmund Hbf **805** a.	...	1809	1809	|	|	1833	...	...	|	1909	|	1915	...	...	1932	1933	1933	...	|	2009	2009	|	...	2033	2033
Dortmund Hbf d.	...	1812	1812	|	|	1836	1838	...	|	1912	|	1918	1923	1923	1937	1938	1938	...	|	2012	2012	|	2037	2038	2038
Bochum Hbf d.	...	1825	1825	|	|	|	1849	...	|	1925	|	1930	1936	1936	|	1949	1949	...	|	2025	2025	|	|	2049	2049
Recklinghausen Hbf d.	...	|	|	|	|	|	|	...	1901	|	|	|	|	|	|	|	|	...	2000	|	|	|	|	|	|
Wanne-Eickel Hbf d.	...	|	|	|	|	|	|	...	1910	|	|	|	|	|	|	|	|	...	|	|	|	|	|	|	|
Gelsenkirchen Hbf d.	...	|	|	|	|	|	|	...	1916	|	|	|	|	|	|	|	|	...	2011	|	|	|	|	|	|
Essen Hbf d.	...	1836	1836	|	|	|	1900	...	|	1936	|	1941	1949	1949	|	2000	2000	...	2022	2036	2036	|	|	2100	2100
Mülheim (Ruhr) Hbf d.	...	|	|	|	|	|	|	...	|	|	|	|	|	|	|	|	|	...	|	|	|	|	|	|	|
Oberhausen Hbf d.	1826	|	|	|	|	|	|	...	|	|	|	|	|	|	|	|	|	2026	|	|	|	|	|	|	|
Duisburg Hbf d.	1834	1849	1849	|	|	|	1913	...	1938	1949	|	1955	2005	2005	|	2013	2013	2034	2037	2049	2049	|	|	2113	2113
Düsseldorf Flughafen ✈ d.	|	1859	1859	|	|	|	|	...	|	1959	|	2007	|	|	|	|	|	|	|	2059	2059	|	|	|	|
Düsseldorf Hbf d.	1848	1908	1908	|	|	|	1927	...	1954	2008	|	2015	2022	2022	|	2027	2027	2048	2054	2110	2108	|	|	2127	2127
Hagen Hbf d.	|	...	|	1824	1824	1857	|	...	|	|	1924	...	|	|	1957	|	|	|	|	|	|	2024	2057	|	|
Wuppertal Hbf d.	|	...	|	1841	1841	1914	|	...	|	|	1941	...	|	|	2014	|	|	|	|	|	|	2041	2114	|	|
Solingen Hbf d.	|	...	|	|	|	|	|	...	|	|	|	...	|	|	2026	|	|	|	|	|	|	|	2126	|	|
Köln Messe/Deutz a.	|	...	1931	|	|	|	|	...	|	|	|	...	2042	2042	|	|	|	|	|	|	2131	|	|	|	|
Köln Hbf a.	1912	...	|	1909	1909	1946	1949	...	2019	2034	2009	...	|	|	2045	2049	2049	2112	2119	2133	|	2109	2146	2149	2149
Köln Hbf d.	1920	...	|	1912q	1912	1953	1954	...	...	...	2018	...	|	|	...	2053	2053	2120	...	...	|	...	2154	2153	2153
Köln/Bonn Flughafen ✈ a.	|	...	1944	|	|	|	|	...	...	...	|	...	|	|	...	|	|	|	...	...	2144	...	|	|	|
Bonn Hbf d.	|	...	...	1932q	1937	2014	|	...	...	...	2041	...	|	|	...	2114	2114	|	...	...	...	...	|	2214	2214
Remagen d.	|	...	...	...	|	|	|	...	...	...	|	...	|	|	...	|	|	|	...	...	...	...	|	|	|
Andernach d.	|	...	...	...	|	|	|	...	...	...	|	...	|	|	...	|	|	|	...	...	...	...	|	|	|
Koblenz Hbf a.	|	...	...	...	2011	2046	|	...	...	...	2115	...	|	|	...	2146	2146	|	...	...	...	...	|	2246	2246
Mainz Hbf **912** a.	|	...	...	...	...	2140	|	...	...	...	...	...	|	|	...	2238	2238	|	...	...	...	...	|	2338	2338
Frankfurt Flughafen ✈ § a.	2014	...	...	...	...	2159	2051	...	...	...	...	...	2146	2151	...	2259	2259	2218	...	...	...	...	2256	2359	2359
Frankfurt (Main) Hbf **910/2** a.	2030	...	...	...	...	2213	|	...	...	...	...	...	|	|	...	|	|	2234	...	...	...	...	2310	0013	0013
Nürnberg Hbf **920** a.	...	...	...	...	...	0037	|	...	...	...	...	...	|	|	...	|	|	...	...	...	...	...	...	...	...
Stuttgart Hbf **930** a.	...	...	...	...	...	...	2208	...	...	...	...	...	2324	|	...	0051t	0051t	...	...	...	...	...	...	...	...
München Hbf **904 930** a.	...	...	...	...	...	...	0035	...	...	...	...	...	...	|	...	...	...	...	...	...	...	...	...	...	...
Karlsruhe Hbf **912** a.	...	...	...	...	...	...	...	...	...	...	...	...	...	2300	...	...	...	...	...	...	...	...	...	...	...
Basel SBB **912** a.	...	...	...	...	...	...	...	...	...	...	...	...	...	0106	...	...	...	...	...	...	...	...	...	...	...

	IC 2330	ICE 844	ICE 854	ICE 854	IC 2354	IC 2144	IC 2307	ICE 542	ICE 552		CNL 319	CNL 40319	ICE 809	ICE 842	ICE 852	IC 2352	IC 2146	IC 60409	CNL 409	IC 2309	ICE 540	ICE 540	ICE 840	IC 2240	IC 2021
	N 🍷	✕	⑧q ✕	⑦y ✕	⑦w 🍷	⑧q 🍷	🍷	✕	✕		Ⓡ ✕♦	Ⓡ ✕♦	K✕	✕	⑦w ✕	⑦w 🍷♦	⑦w 🍷		Ⓡ ✕♦	⑦w 🍷	⊡ ✕	⑤⑥ j✕	⑦w	⑦w B	
Hamburg Altona d.	...	...	...	...	...	...	1832	...	...	...	...	...	...	...	...	...	...	2008	2008	2032	...	...	...	...	2232
Hamburg Hbf **801** d.	...	...	...	...	...	...	1846	...	...	...	...	...	1946	...	...	...	...	2024	2024	2046	...	...	...	...	2246
Bremen Hbf **801** d.	...	...	...	...	...	...	1944	...	...	...	...	...	2044	...	...	...	...	2130	2130u	2144	...	...	...	...	2347
Osnabrück Hbf **801** d.	...	...	...	...	...	...	2037	...	...	...	...	...	2137	...	...	...	...	2231	2231u	2241	...	...	...	2359	0047
Münster (Westf) Hbf **801** d.	2032	...	...	...	...	...	2104	...	...	...	...	...	2203	...	...	...	...	2301	2301u	2306	...	...	...	0024	0115
Berlin Hbf **810** d.	|	1748	1748	1748	1440	...	|	1851	1851	...	...	...	|	1948	1948	1640	...	|	|	|	2105	2105	2149	...	|
Leipzig Hbf **810** d.	|	|	|	|	|	1640	|	|	|	...	...	...	|	|	|	|	1840	|	|	|	|	|	|	...	|
Hannover Hbf **810** d.	|	1931	1931	1931	|	1940	|	2031	2031	...	...	...	|	2131	2131	|	2140	|	|	|	2300	2300	2340	...	|
Hamm (Westf) a.	|	2048	2048	2048	2052	2110	|	2148	2148	...	...	...	|	2248	2248	2252	2310	|	|	|	0023	0023	0109	...	0135
Hamm (Westf) **805** d.	|	2052	2054	2054	2056	2112	|	2152	2154	...	...	...	|	2252	2254	2256	2312	|	|	|	0025	0025	0111	...	0137
Dortmund Hbf **805** a.	|	2109	|	|	2115	2132	2133	2209	|	...	...	...	2233	2309	|	2315	2332	2333	|	2336	0042	0047	0127	...	0154
Dortmund Hbf d.	|	2112	|	|	2118	2137	2138	2212	|	...	...	...	2238	2312	|	2318	2337	...	2338u	...	0044	0049	0130	...	0203
Bochum Hbf d.	|	2125	|	|	2130	|	2149	2225	|	...	...	...	2250	2325	|	2330	|	...	|	...	0056	0102	0142	...	0215
Recklinghausen Hbf d.	2101	|	|	|	|	|	|	|	|	...	...	...	|	|	|	|	|	...	|	...	|	|	|	...	|
Wanne-Eickel Hbf d.	2110	|	|	|	|	|	|	|	|	...	...	...	|	|	|	|	|	...	|	...	|	|	|	...	|
Gelsenkirchen Hbf d.	2116	|	|	|	|	|	|	|	|	...	...	...	|	|	|	|	|	...	|	...	|	|	|	...	|
Essen Hbf d.	|	2136	|	|	2141	|	2200	2236	|	...	...	...	2300	2336	|	2341	|	...	|	...	0106	0113	0153	...	0228
Mülheim (Ruhr) Hbf d.	|	|	|	|	|	|	|	|	|	...	...	...	|	|	|	|	|	...	|	...	|	|	|	...	|
Oberhausen Hbf d.	2128f	|	|	|	|	|	|	|	|	...	2248	2248	|	|	|	|	|	...	|	...	|	|	|	...	|
Duisburg Hbf d.	2135	2151	|	|	2156	|	2213	2249	|	...	2256u	2256u	2313	2349	|	2355	|	...	|	...	0119	0127	0206	...	0241
Düsseldorf Flughafen ✈ d.	|	2201	|	|	2208	|	|	2259	|	...	|	|	|	2359	|	0006	|	...	|	...	0129	0139	0216	...	0252
Düsseldorf Hbf d.	2149	2209	|	|	2216	|	2227	2307	|	...	2312u	2312u	2327	0007	|	0014	|	...	|	...	0138	0147	0224	...	0302
Hagen Hbf d.	|	|	2124	2124	|	2157	|	|	2224	...	|	|	|	|	2324	|	2357	...	|	...	|	|	|	...	|
Wuppertal Hbf d.	|	|	2141	2141	|	2214	|	|	2241	...	|	|	|	|	2341	|	0014	...	|	...	|	|	|	...	|
Solingen Hbf d.	|	|	|	|	|	2226	|	|	|	...	|	|	|	|	|	|	0026	...	|	...	|	|	|	...	|
Köln Messe/Deutz a.	|	|	|	|	|	|	|	|	|	...	|	|	|	|	|	|	|	...	|	...	|	|	|	...	|
Köln Hbf a.	2212	2231	2209	2209	2240	2245	2249	2329	2309	...	|	|	2349	0029	0009	0035	0045	...	|	...	0201	0209	0246	...	0336
Köln Hbf d.	...	...	...	2218	...	...	2253	...	2318q	...	2346u	2346u	2353	...	...	...	...	...	|	...	0214	...	...	...	0352
Köln/Bonn Flughafen ✈ a.	...	...	...	|	...	...	|	...	|	...	|	|	|	...	...	...	...	...	|	...	0226	...	...	...	0404
Bonn Hbf d.	...	...	...	2237	...	...	2314	...	2338q	...	0007u	0007u	0014	...	...	...	...	...	|	...	...	...	...	...	|
Remagen d.	...	...	...	|	...	...	2328	...	...	...	|	|	|	...	...	...	...	...	|	...	...	...	...	...	|
Andernach d.	...	...	...	|	...	...	2341	...	...	...	|	|	|	...	...	...	...	...	|	...	...	...	...	...	|
Koblenz Hbf a.	...	...	...	2311	...	...	2354	...	...	...	|	|	0046	...	...	...	...	...	|	...	...	...	...	...	0512
Mainz Hbf **912** a.	...	...	...	...	...	...	...	...	...	...	|	|	0141	...	...	...	...	...	|	...	...	...	...	...	0627
Frankfurt Flughafen ✈ § a.	...	...	...	...	...	...	...	...	...	...	|	|	0202r	...	...	...	...	...	|	...	...	...	...	...	0646
Frankfurt (Main) Hbf **910/2** a.	...	...	...	...	...	...	...	...	...	...	|	|	0217	...	...	...	...	...	|	...	...	...	...	...	0702
Nürnberg Hbf **920** a.	...	...	...	...	...	...	...	...	...	...	|	|	|	...	...	...	...	...	|	...	...	...	...	...	...
Stuttgart Hbf **930** a.	...	...	...	...	...	...	...	...	...	...	0419x	|	|	...	...	...	...	...	|	...	...	...	...	...	...
München Hbf **904 930** a.	...	...	...	...	...	...	...	...	...	...	0716	|	|	...	...	...	...	...	|	...	...	...	...	...	...
Karlsruhe Hbf **912** a.	...	...	...	...	...	...	...	...	...	...	...	0437	0337	...	...	...	...	...	0437	...	...	...	...	...	...
Basel SBB **912** a.	...	...	...	...	...	...	...	...	...	...	...	0654	0548	...	...	...	...	...	0654	...	...	...	...	...	...

See Table **802** for Rhein-Ruhr local RE and S-Bahn services

♦ – NOTES (LISTED BY TRAIN NUMBER)

319 – POLLUX – 🛏 1,2 cl., 🛏 2 cl., 💺 (reclining) and ✕ Amsterdam - München (Amsterdam - München - Garmisch on ⑤ Dec. 21 - Mar. 28).
409 – KOMET – 🛏 1,2 cl., 🛏 2 cl., 💺 (reclining) and ✕ Hamburg - Basel - Zürich (Hamburg - Zürich - Brig on ⑤ Dec. 21 - Mar. 28).
1909 – ⑦ (also Jan. 1, Mar. 24, May 12; not Dec. 23, 30, Mar. 23, May 11). 💺 and 🍷 (Ostseebad Binz on dates in Table **830** -) Rostock - Hamburg - Köln.
2121 – Ⓒ from Mar. 15. FEHMARN – 💺 and 🍷 Puttgarden - Lübeck - Köln - Frankfurt.
2315 – From Mar. 15. DEICHGRAF – 💺 and 🍷 Westerland - Köln - Stuttgart.
2352 – 💺 and 🍷 Stralsund - Berlin - Halle - Erfurt - Kassel - Köln.
2356 – STRELASUND – 💺 and 🍷 Stralsund - Berlin - Halle - Erfurt - Kassel - Düsseldorf.
40319 – PEGASUS – 🛏 1,2 cl., 🛏 2 cl., 💺 (reclining) and ✕ Amsterdam - Zürich.

A – From Amsterdam (Table **28**).
B – From Berlin (Table **810**).
D – Daily to Mar. 14; Ⓐ from Mar. 17.
H – Until Mar. 14.
K – From Kiel (Table **820**).

M – 💺 and 🍷 (Norddeich Mole ⊖ -) Emden - Köln. Train number **2334** on dates in note ⊖.
N – ⑦ to Mar. 9 (also Jan. 1; not Dec. 23, 30). ③–⑦ from Mar. 14. From Norddeich Mole (Table **812**).
T – To Trier (Table **915**).

d – Not Dec. 24, 25, 26, 31, Jan. 1, Mar. 21, 24, May 12.
f – Not Mar. 29 - May 25; not ⑥⑦ May 31 - June 15.
j – Also Dec. 23, 24, 25, 30, 31, Mar. 20, 23, Apr. 30, May 11, 21.
n – Not Dec. 24, 31.
q – ⑧ (not Dec. 24, 25, 31, Mar. 21, 23, May 11).
r – Frankfurt Flughafen ✈ Regionalbahnhof.
t – 0040 on ①⑦. 0145 from May 17.
u – Stops to pick up only.
v – Also Dec. 23, 30, Mar. 23, May 11; not Dec. 24, 26, 31, Jan. 1, Mar. 24, May 12.
w – Also Dec. 26, Jan. 1, Mar. 24, May 12; not Dec. 23, 30, Mar. 23, May 11.
x – Until May 15.
y – Also Dec. 26, Jan. 1, Mar. 24, May 12; not Mar. 23, May 11.
z – Also Dec. 23, 30, Mar. 23, May 11; not Dec. 26, Jan. 1, Mar. 24, May 12.

⊡ – ①②③④⑦ (not Dec. 23, 24, 25, 30, 31, Mar. 20, 23, Apr. 30, May 11, 21).
⊖ – ①②③④⑥ to Mar. 13 (not Dec. 20, 22, 26, 27, 29, Jan. 1, 2, 3, 5).
§ – Frankfurt Flughafen Fernbahnhof. See also Tables **910** and **912**.

801 Local services MÜNSTER - OSNABRÜCK - BREMEN - HAMBURG

See Table **800** for fast trains

Münster (Westf) Hbf - **Osnabrück** Hbf and v.v. Operated by WestfalenBahn. Journey time: 36 minutes.
From Münster (Westf) Hbf at 0504 Ⓐ **n**, 0604 ⚒, 0634 Ⓐ **n**, 0704, 0733 Ⓐ **n** 0804, 0904 and hourly until 1604, then 1634 Ⓐ **n**, 1704, 1734 Ⓐ **n**, 1804, 1904, 2004, 2104, 2204 and 2306.
From Osnabrück Hbf at 0519 Ⓐ **n**, 0549 Ⓐ **n**, 0619 ⚒, 0719, 0749 Ⓐ **n**, 0819, 0919 and hourly until 1619, then 1649 Ⓐ **n**, 1719, 1744 Ⓐ **n**, 1819, 1919, 2019, 2119, 2219 and 2319.

Osnabrück Hbf - **Bremen** Hbf and v.v. *RE* services. Journey time: 74 minutes. Certain trains continue to / start from Bremerhaven (see Table **815**).
From Osnabrück Hbf at 0418 ¶ ⚒, 0538 ⚒, 0638 ⚒, 0738, 0838, 0938, 1038, 1138, 1238 ⚒, 1338 Ⓑ **n**, 1438, 1538, 1638, 1738, 1838, 1938 Ⓑ **n**, 2038 and 2138.
From Bremen Hbf 0506 ⚒, 0606 ⚒, 0706 ⚒, 0806, 0906, 1006, 1106, 1206, 1306, 1406, 1506, 1606 ⚒, 1706, 1806 Ⓑ **n**, 1906, 2006 Ⓑ **n**, 2106 and 2253.

Bremen Hbf - **Hamburg** Hbf and v.v. *metronom* (operated by metronom Eisenbahngesellschaft mbH). Journey time: 73 – 79 minutes.
Subject to alteration Dec. 24 - Jan. 1 (trains terminate at / start from Hamburg Harburg).
From Bremen Hbf at 0513, 0618 **v**, 0645 ⚒, 0728 **x**, 0828 **r**, 0928, 1028, 1128, 1228, 1328, 1428 **x**, 1528, 1628, 1728, 1828 **z**, 1928 **z**, 2028 **n**, 2128 **n** and 2228 **n**.
From Hamburg Hbf at 0015 ⑦, 0515 ⚒, 0615 **v**, 0716 **w**, 0816, 0915 **x**, 1015 **r**, 1115, 1215 **x**, 1315, 1415, 1515, 1615, 1715, 1815 **z**, 1915 **t**, 2015 **n**, 2115 **n**, 2215 † and 2315 **n**.

n – Not Dec. 24, 31.
r – Not Jan. 1.
t – Not Dec. 24.
v – Not Dec. 25, Jan. 1.
w – Not Dec. 25, 26, Jan. 1.
x – Not Dec. 25.
z – Not Dec. 31.
¶ – Arrives Bremen 0548.

802 RHEIN – RUHR LOCAL SERVICES

RE / RB services

Services in this table (pages 372 – 374) are shown route by route. Sub-headings indicate the route number and principal stations served.

RE1 Aachen - Köln - Düsseldorf - Duisburg - Dortmund - Hamm ⊡ *RE6* Düsseldorf - Duisburg - Dortmund - Bielefeld - Minden ⊡

km																				n					⑤⑥t
0	**Aachen** Hbf **807 910** d.	...	...	...	...	0449e	...	0549	...	0649	...		...	1749	...	1849	...	1949	...	2049	2149	2249	2349	2349
31	Düren **807** d.	...	...	...	...	0515e	...	0615	...	0715	...		...	1815	...	1915	...	2015	...	2115	2215	2315	0015	0015
70	**Köln** Hbf **807 910** a.	...	...	...	...	0542e	...	0642	...	0742	...		...	1842	...	1942	...	2042	...	2142	2242	2342	0042	0042
70	**Köln** Hbf ♥ d.	...	...	...	...	0551	...	0651	...	0751	...		...	1851	...	1951	...	2051	...	2151	2251	2351	...	0051
83	Leverkusen Mitte d.	...	...	...	...	0605	...	0705	...	0805	...	and at	...	1905	...	2005	...	2105	...	2205	2305	0005	...	0105
110	**Düsseldorf** Hbf d.	0423c	...	0523	...	0623	0654e	0723	0754r	0823	0854		1854	1923	...	2023	...	2123	...	2223	2323	0023	...	0123
117	Düsseldorf Flughafen ✈ d.	0429c	...	0529	...	0629	0702e	0729	0802r	0829	0902	the same	1902	1929	...	2029	...	2129	...	2229	2329	0029	...	0129
134	**Duisburg** Hbf d.	0439	...	0539	...	0639	0715e	0739	0815r	0839	0915		1915	1939	...	2039	...	2139	...	2239	2339	0039	...	0139
144	Mülheim (Ruhr) Hbf d.	0445	...	0545	...	0645	0721e	0745	0821r	0845	0921	minutes	1921	1945	...	2045	...	2145	...	2245	2345	0045	...	0145
153	**Essen** Hbf d.	0453	...	0553	...	0653	0729e	0753	0829r	0853	0929		1929	1953	...	2053	...	2153	...	2253	2353	0053	...	0153
169	Bochum Hbf d.	0505	...	0605	...	0705	0743e	0805	0843r	0905	0943	past each	1943	2005	...	2105	...	2205	...	2305	0005	0105	...	0205
187	**Dortmund** Hbf d.	0517	0555	0617	0655	0717	0755	0817	0855	0917	0955		1955	2017	2055	2117	2155	2217	2255	2317	0017	0117	...	0217
218	**Hamm** (Westf) **810** d.	0546	0615	0640	0715	0745	0815	0840	0915	0945	1015	hour until	2015	2040	2115	2145	2215	2245	2322	2345	0045	0145	...	0245
268	Gütersloh Hbf **810** d.	...	0649	...	0749	...	0849	...	0949	...	1049		2049	...	2149	...	2249	...	2354	...	...	...	...	...
285	**Bielefeld** Hbf **810** a.	...	0658	...	0758	...	0858	...	0958	...	1058		2058	...	2158	...	2258	...	0008	...	...	...	...	...
299	Herford **810** a.	...	0707r	...	0807	...	0907	...	1007	...	1107		2107	...	2207r	...	2307b	...	...	...	...	...	...	...
309	Löhne **810** a.	...	0713r	...	0813	...	0913	...	1013	...	1113		2113	...	2213r	...	2313b	...	...	...	...	...	...	...
315	Bad Oeynhausen **810** a.	...	0718r	...	0818	...	0918	...	1018	...	1118		2118	...	2218r	...	2318b	...	...	...	...	...	...	...
330	**Minden** (Westf) **810** a.	...	0730r	...	0830	...	0930	...	1030	...	1130		2130	...	2230r	...	2330b	...	...	...	...	...	...	...

	Ⓐe				⚒r																			⑤⑥t
Minden (Westf) **810** d.	...	...	...	...	0528e	...	0628r	...	0728r	...	0828	...		1728	...	1828	...	1928	...	2028	...	2128	...	...
Bad Oeynhausen **810** d.	...	...	...	...	0539e	...	0639r	...	0739r	...	0839	...		1739	...	1839	...	1939	...	2039	...	2139	...	...
Löhne **810** d.	...	...	...	...	0544e	...	0644r	...	0744r	...	0844	...		1744	...	1844	...	1944	...	2044	...	2144	...	...
Herford **810** d.	...	...	...	...	0551e	...	0651r	...	0751r	...	0851	...		1751	...	1851	...	1951	...	2051	...	2151	...	...
Bielefeld Hbf **810** d.	...	...	...	...	0600	...	0700	...	0800	...	0900	...	and at	1800	...	1900	...	2000	...	2100	...	2200	...	...
Gütersloh Hbf **810** d.	...	...	...	...	0609	...	0709	...	0809	...	0909	...		1809	...	1909	...	2009	...	2109	...	2209	...	...
Hamm (Westf) d.	...	0416	0516	0616	0644	0720	0744	0816	0844	0920	0944	1016	the same	1844	1920	1944	2016	2044	2116	2144	2216	2244	2316	2316
Dortmund Hbf d.	...	0445	0545	0645	0706	0745	0806	0845	0906	0945	1006	1045		1906	1945	2004	2045	2104	2145	2204	2245	2304	2345	2345
Bochum Hbf d.	...	0456	0556	0656	0719	0756	0819	0856	0919	0956	1019	1056	minutes	1919	1956	...	2056	...	2156	...	2256	...	2356	2356
Essen Hbf d.	...	0509	0609	0709	0732	0809	0832	0909	0932	1009	1032	1109		1932	2009	...	2109	...	2209	...	2309	...	0009	0009
Mülheim (Ruhr) Hbf d.	...	0516	0616	0716	0738	0816	0838	0916	0938	1016	1038	1116	past each	1938	2016	...	2116	...	2216	...	2316	...	0016	0016
Duisburg Hbf d.	...	0524	0624	0724	0748	0824	0848	0924	0948	1024	1048	1124		1948	2024	...	2124	...	2224	...	2324	...	0021	0024
Düsseldorf Flughafen ✈ d.	...	0532	0632	0732	0757	0832	0857	0932	0957	1032	1057	1132	hour until	1957	2032	...	2132	...	2232	...	2332	...	...	0032
Düsseldorf Hbf d.	...	0540	0640	0740	0805	0840	0905	0940	1005	1040	1105	1140		2005	2040	...	2140	...	2240	...	2340	...	...	0040
Leverkusen Mitte d.	...	0555	0655	0755	...	0855	...	0955	...	1055	...	1155		...	2055	...	2155	...	2255	...	2355	...	...	0055
Köln Hbf ★ a.	...	0611	0711	0811	...	0911	...	1011	...	1111	...	1211		...	2111	...	2211	...	2311	...	0011	...	...	0111
Köln Hbf **807 910** d.	0517	0617	0717	0817	...	0917	...	1017	...	1117	...	1217		...	2117	...	2217	...	2317	...	0017	...	...	0117
Düren **807** d.	0541	0641	0741	0841	...	0941	...	1041	...	1141	...	1241		...	2141	...	2241	...	2341	...	0041	...	...	0141
Aachen Hbf **807 910** a.	0609	0709	0809	0909	...	1009	...	1109	...	1209	...	1309		...	2209	...	2309	...	0009	...	0109	...	...	0209

RE2 Mönchengladbach - Duisburg - Essen - Gelsenkirchen - Münster ⊡ *RB33* Aachen - Mönchengladbach - Duisburg ⊡ *RB42* Essen - Münster

km		Ⓐe	⚒r			⚒r																		
0	**Aachen** Hbf d.	...	*0413*	...	*0513*	*0513*	...	0538r	*0613*	...	0638		*1813*	...	1838	*1913*	...	1938	*2013*	...	2038	*2113*	...	2238
62	**Mönchengladbach** Hbf d.	...	0521	...	0621	0621	...	0637	0721	...	0737		1921	...	1937	2021	...	2037	2121	...	2137	2221	...	2337
71	Viersen d.	...	0531	...	0631	0631	...	0645	0731	...	0745	and at	1931	...	1945	2031	...	2045	2131	...	2145	2231	...	2345
86	Krefeld Hbf d.	...	0542	...	0642	0642	...	0659	0742	...	0759		1942	...	1959	2042	...	2059	2142	...	2159	2242	...	2359
107	**Duisburg** Hbf d.	...	0601	...	0701	0701	...	0724	0801	...	0824	the same	2001	...	2024	2101	...	2124	2201	...	2224	2301	...	0024
117	Mülheim (Ruhr) Hbf d.	...	0607	...	0707	0707	...	...	0807	...	...		2007	...	...	2107	...	...	2207	...	...	2307	...	...
126	**Essen** Hbf d.	0515	0615	0648	0713	0715	0748	...	0815	0848	...	minutes	2015	2048	...	2115	2148	...	2215	2248	...	2313	2348	...
134	Gelsenkirchen Hbf d.	0524	0624	0656	...	0724	0756	...	0824	0856	...		2024	2056	...	2124	2156	...	2224	2256	...	...	2356	...
139	Wanne-Eickel Hbf d.	0529	0629	0701	...	0729	0801	...	0829	0901	...	past each	2029	2101	...	2129	2201	...	2229	2301	...	...	0001	...
149	Recklinghausen Hbf d.	0537	0637	0709	...	0737	0809	...	0837	0909	...		2037	2109	...	2137	2209	...	2237	2309	...	...	0009	...
164	Haltern am See d.	0549	0649	0719	...	0749	0819	...	0849	0919	...	hour until	2049	2119	...	2148	2219	...	2248	2319	...	...	0019	...
177	Dülmen **803** d.	0559	0659	0728	...	0759	0828	...	0859	0928	...		2059	2128	...	...	2228	...	...	2328	...	...	0028	...
206	**Münster** (Westf) Hbf a.	0621	0721	0749	...	0821	0849	...	0921	0949	...		2121	2149	...	...	2249	...	...	2349	...	...	0049	...

	⚒r	⚒r	⚒r	⚒r																				
Münster (Westf) Hbf d.	0411	...	0511	0537e	...	...	0611	0637r	...	0711	0737r	...	0811	0837	...	0911		2037	...	2111	...	...	2211	2311
Dülmen **803** d.	0432	...	0532	0558e	...	...	0632	0658r	...	0732	0758r	...	0832	0858	...	0932		2058	...	2132	...	...	2232	2332
Haltern am See d.	0441	0508	0541	0608	...	...	0641	0708	...	0741	0808	...	0841	0908	...	0941	and at	2108	...	2141	2208	...	2241	2341
Recklinghausen Hbf d.	0451	0521	0551	0621	...	...	0651	0721	...	0751	0821	...	0851	0921	...	0951		2121	...	2151	2221	...	2251	2351
Wanne-Eickel Hbf d.	0500	0529	0600	0629	...	...	0700	0729	...	0800	0829	...	0900	0929	...	1000	the same	2129	...	2200	2229	...	2300	0000
Gelsenkirchen Hbf d.	0504	0534	0604	0634	...	...	0704	0734	...	0804	0834	...	0904	0934	...	1004		2134	...	2204	2234	...	2304	0004
Essen Hbf d.	0515	0545	0615	0645	0645	...	0714	0745	...	0814	0845	...	0914	0945	...	1014	minutes	2145	...	2214	2245	...	2314	0014
Mülheim (Ruhr) Hbf d.	...	0551	...	0651	0651	...	...	0751	...	...	0851	...	...	0951	...	...		2151	...	...	2251	...	...	...
Duisburg Hbf d.	...	0559	...	0659	0659	0736	...	0759	0836	...	0859	0936	...	0959	1036	...	past each	2159	2236	...	2259	2336	...	...
Krefeld Hbf d.	...	0619	...	0719	0719	0800	...	0819	0900	...	0919	1000	...	1019	1100	...		2219	2300	...	2319	0000	...	...
Viersen d.	...	0633	...	0733	0733	0813	...	0833	0913	...	0933	1013	...	1033	1113	...	hour until	2233	2313	...	2333	0013	...	...
Mönchengladbach Hbf a.	...	0642	...	0742	0742	0820	...	0842	0920	...	0942	1020	...	1042	1120	...		2242	2320	...	2342	0020	...	...
Aachen Hbf a.	...	*0745*	...	*0845*	*0845*	0920	...	*0945*	1020	...	*1045*	1120	...	*1145*	1220	...		*2345*	0020	...	*0045*	...	...	...

RE3 Düsseldorf - Duisburg - Gelsenkirchen - Dortmund - Hamm ⊡

km											
0	**Düsseldorf** Hbf d.	0545e	0645r	0745	0845		1745	1845	1945		2345
7	Düsseldorf Flughafen ✈ d.	0553e	0653r	0753	0853		1753	1853	1953		2353
24	**Duisburg** Hbf a.	0603e	0703r	0803	0903	and	1803	1903	2003	and	0003
24	**Duisburg** Hbf d.	0610*	0710*	0810*	0910*		1810*	1910*	2010*		0010*
32	Oberhausen Hbf d.	0617*	0717*	0817*	0917*	hourly	1817*	1917*	2017*	hourly	0017*
48	Gelsenkirchen Hbf d.	0629	0729	0829	0929		1829	1929	2029		0029
53	Wanne-Eickel Hbf d.	0634	0734	0834	0934	until	1834	1934	2034	until	0034
57	Herne d.	0638	0738	0838	0938		1838	1938	2038		0038
78	**Dortmund** Hbf a.	0657	0757	0857	0957		1857	1957	2057		0057
109	**Hamm** (Westf) Hbf a.	0730e	0830e	0930e	1030r		1930r	2030e	*2145*		*0145*

Hamm (Westf) Hbf d.	0529e	0629e	0729e	0829r		1729r	1829e	*1920*	*2016*	*2116*
Dortmund Hbf d.	0603	0703	0803	0903		1803	1903	2003	2103	2203
Herne d.	0620	0720	0820	0920	and	1820	1920	2020	2120	2220
Wanne-Eickel Hbf d.	0624	0724	0824	0924		1824	1924	2024	2124	2224
Gelsenkirchen Hbf d.	0629	0729	0829	0929	hourly	1829	1929	2029	2129	2229
Oberhausen Hbf d.	0643	0743	0843	0943		1843	1943	2043	2144	2243
Duisburg Hbf a.	0648	0748	0848	0948	until	1848	1948	2048	2150	2248
Duisburg Hbf d.	0652	0752	0852	0952		1852	1952	2052	2152	2252
Düsseldorf Flughafen d.	0702	0802	0902	1002		1902	2002	2102	2202	2302
Düsseldorf Hbf a.	0710	0810	0910	1010		1910	2010	2110	2210	2310

b – Ⓑ (not Dec. 24, 31).
c – Ⓒ (also Dec. 24, 31, May 22).
e – Ⓐ (not Dec. 24, 31, May 22).
n – Not Dec. 24, 31.
r – ⚒ (not May 22).
t – Also Dec. 23, 24, 25, 30, 31, Mar. 20, 23, Apr. 30, May 11, 21.
* – 3 minutes earlier Mar. 29 - May 25.
⊡ – See note and shaded panel on page 373.
♥ – Trains also call at Köln Messe/Deutz (3 minutes after Köln Hbf).
★ – Trains also call at Köln Messe/Deutz (5 minutes before Köln Hbf).

RE4 **Aachen - Mönchengladbach - Düsseldorf - Wuppertal - Dortmund** ⊡ *RE13* **Venlo - Mönchengladbach - Düsseldorf - Wuppertal - Hamm** ⊡

km			⚒r	⚒r	Ⓐe	⚒r		⚒r												z		z		z
0	**Aachen** Hbf **497** ....d.	0253	0413	...	...	...	0513	...	0613	...	0713	...		...	1713	...	1813	...	1913	...	2013	...	2113	...
14	Herzogenrath **497** ....d.	0307	0427	...	...	...	0527	...	0627	...	0727	...		...	1727	...	1827	...	1927	...	2027	...	2127	...
58	Rheydt Hbf ....d.	0341	0503	...	...	...	0603	...	0703	...	0803	...		...	1803	...	1903	...	2003	...	2103	...	2203	...
	Venlo 🏛 ....d.	|	|	0504	0504	...	|	0604	|	0704t	|	0804	and at	1704	|	1804	|	1904	|	2004	|	2104	|	2204
	Kaldenkirchen ....d.	|	|	0510	0510	...	|	0610	|	0710	|	0810		1710	|	1810	|	1910	|	2010	|	2110	|	2210
	Viersen ....d.	|	|	0527	0527	...	|	0627	|	0727	|	0827	the same	1727	|	1827	|	1927	|	2027	|	2127	|	2227
62	**Mönchengladbach** Hbf d.	0349	0510	0545j	0545j	...	0610	0645j	0710	0745j	0810	0845j		1745j	1810	1845j	1910	1945j	2010	2045j	2110	2145j	2210	2235
79	Neuss Hbf ....d.	0403	0524	0557	0557	...	0624	0657	0724	0757	0824	0857	minutes	1757	1824	1857	1924	1957	2024	2057	2124	2157	2224	...
90	**Düsseldorf** Hbf ....a.	0413	0534	0608	0608	...	0634	0708	0734	0808	0834	0908		1808	1834	1908	1934	2008	2034	2108	2134	2208	2234	...
90	**Düsseldorf** Hbf ....d.	f	0540e	...	0614	0640	0640h	0714	0740	0814	0840	0914	past each	1814	1840	1914	1940	2014	2040	...	2140	*2240*	2240h	...
117	**Wuppertal** Hbf ....d.	...	0602e	...	0631	0702	0702h	0731	0802	0831	0902	0931		1831	1902	1931	2002	2031	2102	...	2202	*2302*	2302h	...
144	**Hagen** Hbf.................d.	...	0630e	...	0658	0730	0730h	0758	0830	0858	0930	0958	hour until	1858	1930	1955	2030	2055	2130	...	2230	*2330*	2330h	...
159	Witten.........................d.	...	0641e	...	|	0741	0741h	|	0841	|	0941	|		|	1941	...	2041	...	2141	...	2241	*2341*	2341h	...
175	**Dortmund** Hbf..............d.	...	0651e	...	|	0751	0751h	|	0851	|	0951	|		|	1951	...	2051	...	2151	...	2251	*2351*	2351h	...
	Schwerte (Ruhr).......d.	...	...	...	0708	...	...	0808e	...	0908r	...	1008		1908	...	...	...	...	...	...	...	...	...	...
	Unna..........................d.	...	...	...	0720	...	...	0820e	...	0920r	...	1020		1920	...	...	...	...	...	...	...	...	...	...
	Hamm (Westf) ....d.	...	...	...	0734	...	...	0834e	...	0934r	...	1034		1934	...	...	...	...	...	...	...	...	...	...

km		⚒r																						
0	**Hamm** (Westf) ....d.	...	...	...	0622e	...	0722e	...	0822e	...	0922r	...	1022		...	1722	...	...	1822	...	1922	...	...	...
19	Unna..........................d.	...	...	...	0635e	...	0735e	...	0835e	...	0935r	...	1035		...	1735	...	...	1835	...	1935	...	...	...
35	Schwerte (Ruhr).......d.	...	...	...	0648e	...	0748e	...	0848e	...	0948r	...	1048		...	1748	...	...	1848	...	1948	...	...	...
	Dortmund Hbf..............d.	...	...	0609e	|	0709r	|	0809	|	0909	|	1009	|	and at	1709	|	...	1809	|	1909	|	2009	2109	2209
	Witten.........................d.	...	...	0619e	|	0719r	|	0819	|	0919	|	1019	|		1719	|	...	1819	|	1919	|	2019	2119	2219
48	**Hagen** Hbf.................d.	...	0602e	0632e	0702r	0732r	0802	0832	0902	0932	1002	1032	1102	the same	1732	1802	...	1832	1902	1932	2002	2032	2132	2232
75	**Wuppertal** Hbf ....d.	...	0626e	0658e	0726r	0758r	0826	0858	0926	0958	1026	1058	1126		1758	1826	...	1858	1926	1958	2026	2058	2158	2258
102	**Düsseldorf** Hbf ....a.	...	0645e	0719e	0745r	0819r	0845	0919	0945	1019	1045	1119	1145	minutes	1819	1845	...	1919	1945	2019	2045	2119	2219	2319
102	**Düsseldorf** Hbf ....d.	0622	0648r	0722	0748	0822	0848	0922	0948	1022	1048	1122	1148		1822	1848	1922	1922h	1948	2022	2048	2122	2222	2322
113	Neuss Hbf ....d.	0636	0701r	0736	0801	0836	0901	0936	1001	1036	1101	1136	1201	past each	1836	1901	1936	1936h	2001	2036	2101	2136	2236	2336
130	**Mönchengladbach** Hbf d.	0649	0725j	0749	0825j	0849	0925j	0949	1025j	1049	1125j	1149	1225j		1849	1925j	1949	1949h	2025j	2049	2125j	2149	2249	2349
139	Viersen ....d.	|	0733	|	0833	|	0933	|	1033	|	1133	|	1233	hour until	|	1933	|	|	2033z	|	2133z	|	|	|
157	Kaldenkirchen ....d.	|	0752	|	0852	|	0952	|	1052	|	1152	|	1252		|	1952	|	|	2052z	|	2152z	|	|	|
167	**Venlo** 🏛 ....a.	|	0757	|	0857	|	0957	|	1057	|	1157	|	1257		|	1957	|	|	2057z	|	2157z	|	|	|
	Rheydt Hbf ....d.	0654	...	0754	...	0854	...	0954	...	1054	...	1154	...		1854	...	1954	1954h	...	2054	...	2154	2254	2354
	Herzogenrath **497** ....d.	0729	...	0829	...	0929	...	1029	...	1129	...	1229	...		1929	...	2029	2029h	...	2129	...	2229	2329	0029
	Aachen Hbf **497** ....a.	0745	...	0845	...	0945	...	1045	...	1145	...	1245	...		1945	...	2045	2045h	...	2145	...	2245	2345	0045

RE5 **Koblenz - Bonn - Köln - Düsseldorf - Duisburg - Emmerich** ⊡ *RB26* **Koblenz - Bonn - Köln**

km				Ⓐe	⚒r																			⊠	
0	**Koblenz** Hbf **800** ....d.	...	...	0516	0616	...	0716	0816	0916	1016	1116	1216	1316	1416	1516	1616	1716	1816	1916	2016	...		0526		2326
18	Andernach **800** ....d.	...	...	0526	0626	...	0726	0826	0926	1026	1126	1226	1326	1426	1526	1626	1726	1826	1926	2026	...		0543		2343
29	Bad Breisig ....d.	...	...	0533	0633	...	0733	0833	0933	1033	1133	1233	1333	1433	1533	1633	1733	1833	1933	2033	...		0553		2353
39	Remagen **800** ....d.	...	...	0542	0642	...	0742	0842	0942	1042	1142	1242	1342	1442	1542	1642	1742	1842	1942	2042	...		0611j		0011j
59	**Bonn** Hbf **800** ....d.	...	...	0601	0701	...	0801	0901	1001	1101	1201	1301	1401	1501	1601	1701	1801	1901	2001	2101	...		0631	and	0031
93	**Köln** Hbf **800**..............a.	...	...	0628	0728	...	0828	0928	1028	1128	1228	1328	1428	1528	1628	1728	1828	1928	2028	2128	...		0702		0102
93	**Köln** Hbf .... ♥d.	...	0631r	0631	0731	...	0831	0931	1031	1131	1231	1331	1431	1531	1631	1731	1831	1931	2031	2131	*2251*	also	...	hourly	...
106	Leverkusen Mitte ....d.	...	0645r	0645	0745	...	0845	0945	1045	1145	1245	1345	1445	1545	1645	1745	1845	1945	2045	2145	*2305*		...		...
133	**Düsseldorf** Hbf ....d.	...	0703r	0703	0803	...	0903	1003	1103	1203	1303	1403	1503	1603	1703	1803	1903	2003	2103	2203	*2323*		...	until	...
140	Düsseldorf Flughafen ✈ d.	...	0710r	0710	0810	...	0910	1010	1110	1210	1310	1410	1510	1610	1710	1810	1910	2010	2110	2210	*2329*		...		...
157	**Duisburg** Hbf..............d.	0620	0720	0720	0820	0820	0920	1020	1120	1220	1320	1420	1520	1620	1720	1820	1920	2020	2120	2220	2344		...		...
165	Oberhausen Hbf ....d.	0628	0728	0728	0828	0828	0928	1028	1128	1228	1328	1428	1528	1628	1728	1828	1928	2028	2128	2228	2352		...		...
192	Wesel ....d.	0659	0755	0754	0855	0855	0955	1055	1155	1255	1355	1455	1555	1655	1755	1855	1955	2055	2155	2255	0022		...		...
226	**Emmerich** ....a.	0725	0821	0821	0925	0925	1021	1125	1221	1325	1421	1525	1621	1725	1821	1925	2021	2125	2227	2327	...		...		...

	Ⓐe	⚒r		⚒r																				❖	
mmerich ....d.	...	0433e	0533	0533	0636	0740	0836	0940	1036	1140	1236	1340	1436	1540	1636	1740	1836	1940	2036	2140	2234		...		...
esel ....d.	...	0506e	0606	0606	0706	0806	0906	1006	1106	1212	1306	1412	1506	1612	1706	1812	1906	2012	2106	2206	2307		...		...
berhausen Hbf ....d.	...	0534e	0634	0634	0734	0834	0934	1034	1134	1234	1334	1434	1534	1634	1734	1834	1934	2034	2134	2234	2335		...		...
uisburg Hbf..............d.	...	0542	0640	0642	0742	0842	0942	1042	1142	1242	1342	1442	1542	1642	1742	1842	1942	2042	2140	2240	2341		...		...
üsseldorf Flughafen ✈ .d.	...	0551	▬	0651	0751	0851	0951	1051	1151	1251	1351	1451	1551	1651	1751	1851	1951	2051	*2202*	*2302*	...		...		...
üsseldorf Hbf ....d.	...	0558	...	0658	0758	0858	0958	1058	1158	1258	1358	1458	1558	1658	1758	1858	1958	2058	*2210*	*2310*	...		...	and	...
everkusen Mitte ....d.	...	0614	...	0714	0814	0914	1014	1114	1214	1314	1414	1514	1614	1714	1814	1914	2014	2114	...	...	...		...		...
öln Hbf ....★a.	...	0629	...	0729	0829	0929	1029	1129	1229	1329	1429	1529	1629	1729	1829	1929	2029	2129	...	...	...	also	...	hourly	...
öln Hbf **800**...............d.	0532	0632	0732	0732	0832	0932	1032	1132	1232	1332	1432	1532	1632	1732	1832	1932	2032	...	...	...	...		0556		2256
onn Hbf **800**..............d.	0558	0658	0758	0758	0858	0958	1058	1158	1258	1358	1458	1558	1658	1758	1858	1958	2058	...	...	...	...		0627	until	2327
emagen **800**...............d.	0615	0715	0815	0815	0915	1015	1115	1215	1315	1415	1515	1615	1715	1815	1915	2015	2115	...	...	...	...		0654j		2354j
ad Breisig....................d.	0623	0723	0823	0823	0923	1023	1123	1223	1323	1423	1523	1623	1723	1823	1923	2023	2123	...	...	...	...		0703		0003
ndernach **800** ....d.	0630	0730	0830	0830	0930	1030	1130	1230	1330	1430	1530	1630	1730	1830	1930	2030	2130	...	...	...	...		0713		0013
oblenz Hbf **800**.........a.	0642	0742	0842	0842	0942	1042	1142	1242	1342	1442	1542	1642	1742	1842	1942	2042	2142	...	...	...	...		0731		0031

RE7 **Krefeld - Köln - Wuppertal - Hagen - Hamm - Münster (- Rheine: Table 812)** ⊡

km		Ⓐe									
0	**Krefeld** Hbf ....d.	...	...	0535r	0635		1935	2035	2135	2235	2335
19	Neuss Hbf ....d.	...	...	0553r	0653		1953	2053	2153	2253	2353
57	**Köln** Hbf ....a.	...	...	0618r	0718	and	2018	2118	2218	2318	0018
57	**Köln** Hbf .... ♥d.	...	0521e	0621r	0721		2021	2121	2221	*2352*	*0052*
85	Solingen Hbf.................d.	...	0543e	0643r	0743	hourly	2043	2143	2243	*0020*	*0120*
103	**Wuppertal** Hbf ....d.	...	0556e	0656r	0756		2056	2156	2256	*0037*	*0137*
130	**Hagen** Hbf..................d.	0521	0621	0721	0821	until	2121	2221	2321	...	...
143	Schwerte (Ruhr) ....d.	0531	0631	0731	0831		2131	2231	2331	...	...
159	Unna ....d.	0543	0643	0743	0843		2143	2243	2343	...	...
178	**Hamm** (Westf) ....d.	0559	0659	0759	0859		2159	2259	0006j	...	...
214	**Münster** (Westf) Hbf...d.	0622	0722	0822	0922		2229	2329	0036v	...	...

	Ⓐe	⚒r	⚒k							
Münster (Westf) Hbf .d.	...	...	...	0529e	0634		2034	...	...	2134
Hamm (Westf)..........d.	...	...	0501	0604	0701		2101	...	...	2201
Unna..........................d.	...	...	0514	0614	0714		2114	...	...	2214
Schwerte (Ruhr) ....d.	...	...	0526	0626	0726	and	2126	...	...	2226
Hagen Hbf..................d.	0439	...	0539	0639	0739	hourly	2139	...	...	2237
Wuppertal Hbf.........d.	0504	...	0604	0704	0804		2204	*2221*	2321	...
Solingen Hbf.................d.	0515	...	0615	0715	0815		2215	*2238*	2338	...
Köln Hbf...............★a.	0538	...	0638	0738	0838	until	2238	*2305*	0005	...
Köln Hbf....................d.	0543	0543	0643	0743	0843		2243	2343	...	...
Neuss Hbf....................d.	0607	0607	0707	0807	0907		2307	0007	...	...
Krefeld Hbf ....a.	0625	0625	0725	0825	0925		2325	0025	...	...

RE10 **Düsseldorf - Krefeld - Kleve**

km		⚒r	Ⓐe			Ⓐe				
0	**Düsseldorf** Hbf ....d.	0609	0639	0709		1939	2009	2109	2209	2309
27	**Krefeld** Hbf ....d.	0637	0707	0737	and at	2007	2037	2137	2237	2337
57	Geldern ....d.	0702	0732	0802	the same	2032	2102	2202	2302	0002
66	Kevelaer.......................d.	0709	0739	0809	minutes	2039	2109	2209	2309	0009
72	Weeze...........................d.	0715	0745	0815	past each	2045	2115	2215	2315	0015
79	Goch ....d.	0721	0751	0821	hour until	2051	2121	2221	2321	0021
92	**Kleve** ....a.	0734	0804	0834		2104	2134	2234	2334	0034

	⚒r		Ⓐe		Ⓐe				
Kleve..........................d.	0525	0618	0648		1748	1818	1918		2218
Goch.............................d.	0538	0635	0705	and at	1805	1835	1935		2235
Weeze...........................d.	0545	0645	0715	the same	1815	1845	1945	and	2245
Kevelaer.......................d.	0551	0651	0721	minutes	1821	1851	1951	hourly	2251
Geldern........................d.	0558	0658	0728	past each	1828	1858	1958	until	2258
Krefeld Hbf ....d.	0626	0726	0756	hour until	1856	1926	2026		2326
Düsseldorf Hbf ....a.	0652	0752	0822		1922	1952	2052		2352

– Ⓐ (not Dec. 24, 31, May 22).
– To Düsseldorf Flughafen Terminal ✈ (a. 0425).
– ⑥ (also Dec. 24, 31).
– Arrives 8 – 10 minutes earlier.
– ⚒ (May 22); runs daily Köln - Krefeld.

n – Not Dec. 24, 31.
r – ⚒ (not May 22).
t – ①–⑥ only.
v – Not Dec. 25, Jan. 1.
z – Not Dec. 31.

⊠ – On Dec. 25, Jan. 1 the 0526 and 0626 from Koblenz do not run. On Dec. 24, 31 the 2026, 2126, 2226 and 2326 from Koblenz do not run.
❖ – On Dec. 25, Jan. 1 the 0556 from Köln Hbf terminates at Remagen. On Dec. 24, 31 the 1956, 2056, 2156 and 2256 from Köln Hbf terminate at Remagen.
⊡ – See shaded panel for a summary of the principal Rhein – Ruhr *RE* routes.
♥ – Trains also call at Köln Messe/Deutz (3 minutes after Köln Hbf).
★ – Trains also call at Köln Messe/Deutz (4 minutes before Köln Hbf).

	RE1	*RE2*	*RE3*	*RE4*	*RE5*	*RE6*	*RE7*	*RE13*	*RB33*
Aachen Hbf	●	...	...	●	...	...	...	...	●
Köln Hbf	●	...	...	|	●	...	●	...	|
Mönchengladbach Hbf	|	●	...	●	|	...	|	●	●
Düsseldorf Hbf	●	|	●	●	●	●	|	●	|
Duisburg Hbf	●	●	●	|	●	●	|	|	●
Essen Hbf	●	●	|	|	...	●	|	|	...
via Gelsenkirchen	|	●	●	|	...	|	|	|	...
via Wuppertal and Hagen	|	|	|	●	...	|	●	●	...
Dortmund Hbf	●	|	●	●	...	●	|	|	...
Hamm (Westf)	●	|	●	...	...	●	●	●	...
Münster (Westf) Hbf	...	●	...	...	...	...	●	...	...

802 RHEIN – RUHR LOCAL SERVICES

RE / RB services

RB8 / 27 Mönchengladbach - Köln - Königswinter - Koblenz

km		Ⓐe	⚒r	⚒r m		⚒r m						▲						Ⓑn m				
0	**Mönchengladbach** ⊖ d.	0440	0503e	0540	0603e	0640	0703e	0740	0803e	0840	...		1340	...	1440	1503e		1740	1803e	1840	1903e	1940	2040	2140
3	Rheydt Hbf ⊖ d.	0444	0507e	0544	0607e	0644	0707e	0744	0807e	0844	...		1344	...	1444	1507e		1744	1807e	1844	1907e	1944	2044	2144
22	Grevenbroich ⊖ d.	0502	0528e	0602	0628e	0702	0728e	0802	0828e	0902	...	and at	1402	...	1502	1528e	and at	1802	1828e	1902	1928e	2002	2102	2202
56	**Köln** Hbf ⊖ a.	0535	0600e	0635	0700e	0735	0800e	0835	0900e	0935	...		1435	...	1535	1600e		1835	1900e	1935	2000e	2035	2135	2235
56	**Köln** Hbf **807** ♥ d.	0538	0601j	0638	0701j	0738	0801j	0838	0901j	0938	1001j	the same	1438	1501j	1538	1601j	the same	1838	1901j	1938	2001j	2101	2201	2301
71	Köln/Bonn Flughafen ✈ d.	0550	|	0650	|	0750	|	0850	|	0950	|		1450	|	1550	|		1850	|	1950	|	|	|	|
83	Troisdorf **807** d.	0601	0623	0701	0723	0801	0823	0901	0923	1001	1023	minutes	1501	1523	1601	1623	minutes	1901	1923	2001	2023	2123	2223	2323
92	**Bonn** Beuel d.	0611	0633	0711	0733	0811	0833	0911	0933	1011	1033		1511	1533	1611	1633		1911	1933	2011	2033	2133	2233	2333
100	Königswinter d.	0620	0643	0720	0743	0820	0843	0920	0943	1020	1043	past each	1520	1543	1620	1643	past each	1920	1943	2020	2043	2143	2243	2343
105	Bad Honnef d.	0626	0649	0726	0749	0826	0849	0926	0949	1026	1049		1526	1549	1626	1649		1926	1949	2026	2049	2149	2249	2349
115	Linz (Rhein) d.	0637	0702	0735	0802	0835	0902	0935	1002	1035	1102	hour until	1535	1602	1635	1702	hour until	1935	2002	2035	2102	2202	2302	0002
122	Bad Hönningen d.	0642	0709	0740	0809	0840	0909	0940	1009	1040	1109		1540	1609	1640	1709		1940	2009	2040k	2109n	2209n	2309n	...
138	Neuwied d.	0655	0724	0752	0824	0852	0924	0952	1024	1052	1124		1552	1624	1652	1724		1952	2024	2052k	2124n	2224n	2324n	...
◊153	**Koblenz** Hbf a.	0716	0740	0816	0840	0913	0940	1013	1040	1113	1140		1613	1640	1713	1740		2013	2040	2113k	2140n	2240n	2340n	...

	⚒r			Ⓐe m		Ⓐe m	⑥q m		⚒r m													Ⓑn m		
Koblenz Hbf d.	...	...	0515r	0536	0618r	0637	0648	0718	0748	0818	0848		1218	1248	1318	1348	1418		1818	1848	1918	1948	2018	2118r
Neuwied d.	...	...	0532r	0558	0632r	0658	0708	0732	0808	0832	0908		1232	1306	1332	1408	1432		1832	1908	1932	2008	2032	2132r
Bad Hönningen d.	...	...	0546r	0612	0646r	0712	0719	0746	0819	0846	0919	and at	1246	1317	1346	1419	1446	and at	1846	1919	1946	2019	2046	2146r
Linz (Rhein) d.	0453	...	0553	0619	0653	0719	0724	0753	0824	0853	0924		1253	1322	1353	1424	1453		1853	1924	1953	2024	2053	2153
Bad Honnef d.	0503	...	0603	0629	0703	0729	0733	0803	0833	0903	0933	the same	1303	1333	1403	1433	1503	the same	1903	1933	2003	2033	2103	2203
Königswinter d.	0509	...	0609	0635	0709	0735	0739	0809	0839	0909	0939		1309	1339	1409	1439	1509		1909	1939	2009	2039	2109	2209
Bonn Beuel d.	0518	...	0618	0646	0718	0746	0749	0818	0849	0918	0949	minutes	1318	1349	1418	1449	1518	minutes	1918	1949	2018	2049	2118	2218
Troisdorf **807** d.	0528	...	0628	0659	0728	0759	0759	0828	0859	0928	0959		1328	1359	1428	1459	1528		1928	1959	2028	2059	2128	2228
Köln/Bonn Flughafen ✈ d.	|	...	|	0708	|	0808	0808	|	0908	|	1008	past each	|	1408	|	1508	|	past each	|	2008	|	2108	|	|
Köln Hbf **807** ★ a.	0553	...	0653	0722	0753	0822	0822	0853	0922	0953	1022		1353	1422	1453	1522	1553		1953	2022	2053	2122	2153	2253
Köln Hbf ⊖ d.	0559e	0625	0659e	0725	0759e	0825	0825	...	0925	...	1025	hour until	...	1425	1459e	1525	1559e	hour until	1959e	2025	...	2125	2225	2325
Grevenbroich ⊖ d.	0630e	0655	0730e	0755	0830e	0855	0855	...	0955	...	1055		...	1455	1530e	1555	1630e		2030e	2055	...	2155	2255	2355
Rheydt Hbf ⊖ d.	0651e	0715	0751e	0815	0851e	0915	0915	...	1015	...	1115		...	1515	1551e	1615	1651e		2051e	2115	...	2215	2315	0015
Mönchengladbach ⊖ a.	0656e	0720	0756e	0820	0856e	0920	0920	...	1020	...	1120		...	1520	1556e	1620	1656e		2056e	2120	...	2220	2320	0020

S-Bahn 13 Köln - Köln/Bonn Flughafen ✈ - Troisdorf

				Ⓒz		Ⓒz	Ⓐe		Ⓐe	Ⓒz	Ⓐe			Ⓐe	Ⓒz	Ⓐe							
Köln Hbf d.	0011	0041	0241	0241	0341	0341	0421	0441	0501	0511	0521	0541	and at the same	2001	2011	2021	2041	2111	2141	2211	2241	2311	2341
Köln Messe/Deutz d.	0013	0043	0243	0243	0343	0343	0423	0443	0503	0513	0523	0543	minutes past	2003	2013	2023	2043	2113	2143	2213	2243	2313	2343
Köln/Bonn Flughafen ✈ d.	0026	0056	0255	0256	0355	0356	0436	0456	0516	0526	0536	0556	each hour until	2016	2026	2036	2056	2126	2156	2226	2256	2326	2356
Troisdorf a.	0036	0108	...	0308	...	0408	0448	0508	0528	0536	0548	0608		2028	2036	2048	2108	2136	2208	2236	2308	2336	0008

					Ⓒz		Ⓒz		Ⓐe	Ⓒz	Ⓐe			Ⓐe	Ⓒz	Ⓐe							
Troisdorf d.	0023	0053	0123	...	0303	...	0403	...	0513	0523	0533	0553	and at the same	2013	2023	2033	2053	2123	2153	2223	2253	2323	2353
Köln/Bonn Flughafen ✈ d.	0034	0104	0134	...	0314	0314	0414	0414	0524	0534	0544	0604	minutes past	2024	2034	2044	2104	2134	2204	2234	2304	2334	0004
Köln Messe/Deutz a.	0046	0116	0146	...	0326	0326	0426	0426	0536	0546	0556	0616	each hour until	2036	2046	2056	2116	2146	2216	2246	2316	2346	0016
Köln Hbf a.	0049	0119	0149	...	0329	0329	0429	0429	0539	0549	0559	0619		2039	2049	2059	2119	2149	2219	2249	2319	2349	0019

RB 59 Dortmund - Unna - Soest

km		v		⚒r	Ⓐe	⚒r	Ⓐe		Ⓐe		Ⓐe			Ⓐe		Ⓐe			n				
0	**Dortmund** Hbf **805** d.	0007	...	0507	0537	0607	0637	0707	0737	0807	0837	and at the same	1807	1837	1907	1937	2007	2107	2207	2307	...	...	...
23	Unna d.	0032	...	0532	0602	0632	0702	0732	0802	0832	0902	minutes past	1832	1902	1932	2002	2032	2132	2232	2332	...	...	...
53	**Soest 805** a.	0056	...	0556	0626	0656	0726	0756	0826	0856	0926	each hour until	1856	1926	1956	2026	2056	2156	2256	2356	...	...	...

	w		⚒r	Ⓐe	⚒r	Ⓐe		Ⓐe		Ⓐe			Ⓐe		Ⓐe			n			
Soest 805 d.	0002	...	0502	0532	0602	0632	0702	0732	0802	0832	and at the same	1802	1832	1902	1932	2002	2102	2202	2302	...	...	...
Unna d.	0027	...	0527	0557	0627	0657	0727	0757	0827	0857	minutes past	1827	1857	1927	1957	2027	2127	2227	2327	...	...	...
Dortmund Hbf **805** a.	0051	...	0551	0621	0651	0721	0751	0821	0851	0921	each hour until	1851	1921	1951	2021	2051	2151	2251	2351	...	...	...

RB 53 Dortmund - Schwerte - Iserlohn

km		Ⓐe	Ⓐe	Ⓐe		Ⓐe		Ⓐe			Ⓐe		Ⓐe		Ⓐe		Ⓐe		Ⓐe		Ⓐe	n	n	x
0	**Dortmund** Hbf d.	0523	0553	0623	0653	0723	0753	0823	0853	and at the same	1523	1553	1623	1653	1723	1753	1823	1853	1923	1953	2023	2053	2153	2323
18	Schwerte (Ruhr) d.	0545	0615	0645	0715	0745	0815	0842	0915	minutes past	1542	1615	1645	1715	1745	1815	1842	1915	1942	2015	2042	2115	2215	2344
38	**Iserlohn** a.	0608	0638	0708	0738r	0808	0838	...	0938	each hour until	...	1638	1708	1738	1808	1838	...	1938	...	2038	...	2138	2238	...

	Ⓐe	Ⓐe	Ⓐe		Ⓐe		Ⓐe		Ⓐe			Ⓐe		Ⓐe		Ⓐe		Ⓐe		Ⓐe			n
Iserlohn d.	...	0523	...	0617e	0647	0717r	0747	0817	...	0917	and at the same	...	1617	1647	1717	1747	1817	...	1917	...	2017	2117	2217
Schwerte (Ruhr) d.	0520	0550	0620	0650	0720	0750	0820	0850	0920	0950	minutes past	1620	1650	1720	1750	1820	1850	1920	1950	2020	2050	2150	2250
Dortmund Hbf a.	0539	0609	0639	0709	0739	0809	0839	0909	0939	1009	each hour until	1639	1709	1739	1809	1839	1909	1939	2009	2039	2109	2209	2309

RB31 **Duisburg - Moers - Xanten and v.v.** (45 km, journey time: 45 minutes)

From Duisburg Hbf at: 0556 ⚒ r, 0710 ⚒ r, 0810, 0910 and hourly until 2310.
From Xanten at: 0500 ⚒ r, 0600 ⚒ r, 0700, 0800 and hourly until 2200.
Trains call at Moers 18 minutes from Duisburg, 28 minutes from Xanten.

OTHER USEFUL S-BAHN LINKS

Services operate every 20 minutes (every 30 minutes evenings and weekends)

Service	*Route (journey time in minutes)*
S 3	Oberhausen Hbf - Mülheim Hbf (8) - Essen Hbf (17).
S 7	Düsseldorf Flughafen Terminal ✈ - Düsseldorf Hbf (12) - Solingen Hbf (34)
S 9	Essen Hbf - Wuppertal Hbf (47).

e – Ⓐ (not Dec. 24, 31, May 22).
j – 2 minutes later on Ⓐ**e**.
k – Linz - Koblenz only on ✝ (also May 22).
m – Runs daily Mönchengladbach - Köln and v.v.
n – Not Dec. 24, 31.
q – Also Dec. 24, 31.
r – ⚒ (not May 22).

v – Not Dec. 25, Jan. 1.
w – Not Dec. 25.
x – Not Dec. 24, 31, Mar. 20, 21.
z – Also Dec. 24, 31, May 22.

♥ – Trains also call at Köln Messe/Deutz (3 minutes after Köln Hbf).

★ – Trains also call at Köln Messe/Deutz (4 – 5 minutes before Köln Hbf).
◊ – Via Koblenz-Lützel (*159 km* via Koblenz-Ehrenbreitstein).
▲ – On Ⓐ**e** the 1040 and 1140 departures from Mönchengladbach depart Linz 2 minutes later, Bad Hönningen 4 minutes later, Neuwied 5 minutes later and arrive Koblenz 5 minutes later.
⊖ – Additional trains Mönchengladbach Hbf - Köln Hbf and v.v.
From Mönchengladbach Hbf at 0440 ⑥ **q**, 2240 and 2340.
From Köln Hbf at 0025, 0525 ⚒ **r** and 1635 Ⓐ **e**.

803 DORTMUND and MÜNSTER - ENSCHEDE

2nd class only

km	△	①-⑤ e	①-⑥ k		①-⑥ k					⑦ w
0	**Dortmund** Hbf d.	0552	0652	...	0752	0852		1852	1952	1952
44	Dülmen **802** d.	0640	0740	...	0840	0940	and	1940	2040	2040
61	Coesfeld (Westf) d.	0705	0801	0901	0901	1001	hourly	2001	2053	2101
96	Gronau (Westf) d.	0739	0839	0939	0939	1039	until	2039	...	2139
103	**Enschede** a.	0750	0850	0950	0950	1050		2050	...	2150

△	①-⑤ e	①-⑥ k	①-⑥ k	①-⑥ k					
Enschede d.	...	...	0556e	0656	0756		1856	1956	2056
Gronau (Westf) d.	...	0525e	0621	0708	0821	and	1921	2007	2107
Coesfeld (Westf) d.	0506	0603	0703	0803	0903	hourly	2003	...	...
Dülmen **802** d.	0520	0617	0717	0817	0917	until	2017	...	...
Dortmund Hbf a.	0607	0707	0807	0907	1007		2107	...	...

km	♥	①-⑤ e	①-⑤ e	①-⑥ t	①-⑥					⑤⑥ d
0	**Münster** (Westf) Hbf d.	0506	0606	...	0708	...	0808	and	2208	2308
56	Gronau (Westf) d.	0604	0709	0709	0809	0809	0909	hourly	2309	0009
63	**Enschede** a.	0620	0720	0720	0820	0820	0920	until	2320n	0020

♥	①-⑥ k	①-⑤ e	⑥ q	①-⑥ t					⑤⑥ d
Enschede d.	...	0626	0626	0726	...	0826	and	2126	2226
Gronau (Westf) d.	0542	0645	0645	0745	0745	0845	hourly	2145	2245
Münster (Westf) Hbf a.	0643	0746	0746	0846	0846	0946	until	2246	2346

d – Also Dec. 25, Mar. 23, Apr. 30, May 11, 21; not Mar. 21.
e – ①-⑤ (not Dec. 24, 25, 26, 31, Jan. 1, Mar. 21, 24, May 1, 12, 22).
k – Not Dec. 25, 26, Jan. 1, Mar. 21, 24, May 1, 12, 22.

n – Not Dec. 25, Jan. 1.
q – Also Dec. 24, 31.
t – Not Dec. 25, 26, Jan. 1, Mar. 24, May 1, 12.

w – Also Dec. 25, 26, Jan. 1, Mar. 24, May 1, 12.
△ – Operated by Prignitzer Eisenbahn GmbH.
♥ – Operated by DB (*RB* services).

HAGEN - KASSEL — 804

RE services

km		⚒r	Ⓐt	⑥k	⚒r	Ⓐt	⑥k															Ⓒw	n	
0	**Hagen** Hbf **802** d.	...	0509	...	...	0604	0613	0713	0813	0913	1013	1113	1213	1313	1413	1513	1613	1713	1813	1913	2013	2013	2113	2213
14	Schwerte (Ruhr) **802** d.	...	0519	...	...	0617	0623	0723	0823	0923	1023	1123	1223	1323	1423	1523	1623	1723	1823	1923	2023	2023	2123	2223
57	Arnsberg (Westf) d.	...	0549	...	...	0649	0656	0756	0856	0956	1056	1156	1256	1356	1456	1556	1656	1756	1856	1956	2056	2056	2156	2256
77	Meschede d.	...	0606	...	...	0708	0715	0815	0915	1015	1115	1215	1315	1415	1515	1615	1715	1815	1915	2015	2115	2115	2215	2315
86	Bestwig d.	...	0613	0623	...	0716	0723	0823	0923	1023	1123	1223	1323	1423	1523	1623	1723	1823	1923	2023	2122	2123	2222	2322
100	Brilon Wald d.	...	0628	0639	...	0734	0739	0839	0939	1039	1139	1239	1339	1439	1539	1639	1739	1839	1939	2039	...	2139	...	...
152	Warburg (Westf) a.	...	0714	0720	...	0820	0820	0920	1020	1120	1220	1320	1420	1520	1620	1720	1820	1920	2020	2120	...	2220	...	...
152	Warburg (Westf) **805** d.	0601	0720	0721	0801	...	...	0921	...	1121	...	1321	...	1521	...	1721	...	1921	...	*2141*	...	...	...	...
205	**Kassel** Hbf a.	0656	0759	0759	0856	...	...	0959	...	1159	...	1359	...	1559	...	1759	...	1959	...	*2236*	...	...	...	...
209	**Kassel** Wilhelmshöhe **805** a.	...	0809	0809	...	...	...	1009	...	1209	...	1409	...	1609	...	1809	...	2009	...	...	...	...	...	...

	⚒r	⚒r	⚒r		Ⓐt	⑥k		Ⓐt															⚒r	†w
Kassel Wilhelmshöhe **805** d.	...	...	...	...	...	...	...	...	...	0748	...	0948	...	1148	...	1348	...	1548	...	1748	...	1948	...	...
Kassel Hbf d.	...	...	...	...	*0527*	*0527*	...	0629	...	0758	...	0958	...	1158	...	1358	...	1558	...	1758	...	1958	2029	2259
Warburg (Westf) **805** a.	...	...	...	...	*0620*	*0620*	...	0725	...	0835	...	1035	...	1235	...	1435	...	1635	...	1835	...	2035	2123	2353
Warburg (Westf) d.	...	...	0531z*	...	0631	0638	...	...	0738r	0838	0938	1038	1138	1238	1338	1438	1538	1638	1738	1838	1938	2038	...	...
Brilon Wald d.	...	...	0621	...	0718	0721	...	...	0821r	0921	1021	1121	1221	1321	1421	1521	1621	1721	1821	1921	2021	2121	...	...
Bestwig d.	0436	0536	0636	0636	0736	0736	0736	...	0836	0936	1036	1136	1236	1336	1436	1536	1636	1736	1836	1936	2036	2136	...	...
Meschede d.	0443	0543	0643	0643	0743	0743	0743	...	0843	0943	1043	1143	1243	1343	1443	1543	1643	1743	1843	1943	2043	2143n	...	...
Arnsberg (Westf) d.	0503	0603	0703	0703	0803	0803	0803	...	0903	1003	1103	1203	1303	1403	1503	1603	1703	1803	1903	2003	2103	2203n	...	...
Schwerte (Ruhr) **802** d.	0535	0635	0735	0735	0835	0835	0835	...	0935	1035	1135	1235	1335	1435	1535	1635	1735	1835	1935	2035	2135	2235n	...	...
Hagen Hbf **802** a.	0546	0646	0746	0746	0846	0846	0846	...	0946	1046	1146	1246	1346	1446	1546	1646	1746	1846	1946	2046	2145	2246n	...	...

k – Also Dec. 24, 31.
n – Not Dec. 24, 31.
r – ⚒ (not May 22).
t – Ⓐ (not Dec. 24, 31, May 22).
w – Also May 22.
z – 0538 on ⑥ (also Dec. 24, 31).

DORTMUND and MÜNSTER - PADERBORN - KASSEL — 805

RE/RB services except where shown

km					*IC* 2355				*IC* 2357				*IC* 2157				*IC* 2359				*IC* 2151				*IC* 2153
		Ⓐt	⑥k		v O 🍷	Ⓐt	Ⓒz		🍷	Ⓐt	Ⓒz		§ 🍷	Ⓐt	Ⓒz		⑤⑦ b 🍷	Ⓐt	Ⓒz		🍷	Ⓐt	Ⓒz		🍷
	Köln Hbf **800** d.	...	...	...	...	...	...	...	0719g	...	...	...	0905	...	...	...	1120	...	...	...	...	...	...	...	...
	Düsseldorf Hbf **800** d.	...	...	...	0546g	...	...	...	0746	...	...	...	0946	...	...	...	1146	...	...	...	1346	...	...	...	1546
0	**Dortmund** Hbf **802** d.	...	...	...	0644	...	...	...	0842	...	...	...	1042	...	...	...	1242	...	...	...	1442	...	...	...	1642
	Münster (Westf) Hbf **802** d.	0509	0509	0634	|	0709	0709	0834	|	0909	0909	1034	|	1109	1109	1234	|	1309	1309	1434	|	1509	1509	1634	|
31	Hamm (Westf) **802** a.	0537	0537	0659	0702	0737	0737	0859	0902	0937	0937	1059	1102	1137	1137	1259	1302	1337	1337	1459	1502	1537	1537	1659	1702
31	Hamm (Westf) d.	0546	0552	...	0707	0746	0752	...	0907	0946	0952	...	1107	1146	1152	...	1307	1346	1352	...	1507	1546	1552	...	1707
57	Soest **802** d.	0602	0608	...	0722	0802	0808	...	0922	1002	1008	...	1122	1202	1208	...	1322	1402	1408	...	1522	1602	1608	...	1722
77	Lippstadt d.	0614	0620	...	0733	0814	0820	...	0933	1014	1020	...	1133	1214	1220	...	1333	1414	1420	...	1533	1614	1620	...	1733
109	**Paderborn** Hbf **809 811** ⊖ d.	0642	0642	...	0749	0842	0842	...	0949	1042	1042	...	1149	1242	1242	...	1349	1442	1442	...	1549	1642	1642	...	1749
126	Altenbeken **809 811** ⊖ d.	0654	0654	...	0804	0854	0854	...	1004	1054	1054	...	1204	1254	1254	...	1404	1454	1454	...	1604	1654	1654	...	1804
163	Warburg (Westf) **804** d.	0716	0716	...	0826	0916	0916	...	1026	1116	1116	...	1226	1316	1316	...	1426	1516	1516	...	1626	1716	1716	...	1826
220	**Kassel** Wilhelmshöhe **804** a.	*0809*	*0809*	...	0857	*1009*	*1009*	...	1057	*1209*	*1209*	...	1257	*1409*	*1409*	...	1457	*1609*	*1609*	...	1658	*1809*	*1809*	...	1857
	Erfurt Hbf **850** a.	...	...	...	1029	...	...	...	1229	...	...	...	1429	...	...	...	1629	...	...	...	1829	...	...	...	2029
	Halle (Saale) Hbf **850** a.	...	...	...	1158	...	...	...	1358	...	...	...	1558	...	...	...	1758	...	...	...	1958	...	...	...	2201
	Berlin Hbf **850** a.	...	...	...	1322	...	...	...	1522	...	...	...	1722	...	...	...	1922	...	...	...	2124	...	...	...	...
	Stralsund **845** a.	...	...	...	1623	...	...	...	...	...	...	...	2040q	...	...	...	2223	...	...	...	...	...	...	...	...

					IC 2155						
	Ⓐt	Ⓒz			⑦w 🍷						v
Köln Hbf **800** d.	...	...	...	...	...	...	...	...	...	...	...
Düsseldorf Hbf **800** d.	...	...	...	...	1746	...	...	...	...	...	...
Dortmund Hbf **802** d.	...	...	...	...	1842	...	...	...	...	...	...
Münster (Westf) Hbf **802** d.	1709	1709	1809	1834	|	1909	*2034*	*2134*	2209	2311	...
Hamm (Westf) **802** a.	1737	1737	1837	1859	1902	1937	*2059*	*2159*	2237	2339	...
Hamm (Westf) d.	1746	1752	1846	...	1907	1952	2107	2207	2307	...	0007
Soest **802** d.	1802	1808	1902	...	1922	2008	2123	2223	2323	...	0023
Lippstadt d.	1814	1820	1914	...	1933	2020	2135	2235	2335	...	0035
Paderborn Hbf **809 811** ⊖ d.	1842	1842	1939	...	1949	2058j	2200	2300	0002	...	0100
Altenbeken **809 811** ⊖ d.	1854	1854	...	...	2004	2110	...	...	0014c	...	...
Warburg (Westf) **804** d.	1916	1916	...	...	2026	2133	...	...	0035c	...	...
Kassel Wilhelmshöhe **804** a.	*2009*	*2009*	...	...	2057	*2236*h	...	...	...	...	...
Erfurt Hbf **850** a.	...	...	...	...	2231	...	...	...	...	...	...
Halle (Saale) Hbf **850** a.	...	...	...	...	...	...	...	...	...	...	...
Berlin Hbf **850** a.	...	...	...	...	...	...	...	...	...	...	...
Stralsund **845** a.	...	...	...	...	...	...	...	...	...	...	...

								IC 2156	
	⚒r		Ⓐt	Ⓒz		Ⓒz	Ⓐt	🍷	
Stralsund **845** d.	...	...	...	...	...	...	...	...	...
Berlin Hbf **850** d.	...	...	...	...	...	...	...	...	...
Halle (Saale) Hbf **850** d.	...	...	...	...	...	...	...	...	...
Erfurt Hbf **850** d.	...	...	...	...	...	...	...	0727	...
Kassel Wilhelmshöhe **804** d.	...	...	...	...	...	*0748*	*0748*	0900	...
Warburg (Westf) **804** d.	...	...	0624	0639k	...	0839	0839	0933	...
Altenbeken **809 811** ⊖ d.	...	...	0647	0702k	...	0902	0902	0956	...
Paderborn Hbf **809 811** ⊖ d.	0513	0621	0721y	0717	0821	0917	0921	1010	...
Lippstadt d.	0536	0644	0744	0736	0844	0936	0944	1026	...
Soest **802** d.	0548	0656	0756	0749	0856	0949	0956	1037	...
Hamm (Westf) a.	0606	0714	0814	0806	0914	1006	1014	1052	...
Hamm (Westf) **802** d.	0620	0720	0820	0820	0920	1020	1020	1056	1059
Münster (Westf) Hbf **802** a.	0648	0748	0848	0848	0948	1048	1048	|	1122
Dortmund Hbf **802** a.	...	...	...	...	...	...	...	1115	...
Düsseldorf Hbf **800** a.	...	...	...	...	...	...	...	1212	...
Köln Hbf **800** a.	...	...	...	...	...	...	...	...	...

			IC 2154				*IC* 2152				*IC* 2150				*IC* 2356				*IC* 2354			*IC* 2352			
	Ⓒz	Ⓐt	🍷		Ⓒz	Ⓐt	⑤⑦ b 🍷		Ⓒz	Ⓐt	‡ 🍷		Ⓒz	Ⓐt	O 🍷		Ⓒz	Ⓐt	n 🍷			⑦w 🍷			n
Stralsund **845** d.	...	...	...	...	...	...	...	...	...	...	0739e	...	...	...	0939	...	...	...	...	...	...	1339	...	...	...
Berlin Hbf **850** d.	...	...	0640	...	...	...	0840f	...	...	...	1040	...	...	...	1240	...	...	...	1440	...	...	1640	...	...	...
Halle (Saale) Hbf **850** d.	...	...	0759	...	...	...	0959	...	...	...	1159	...	...	...	1359	...	...	...	1559	...	...	1759	...	...	...
Erfurt Hbf **850** d.	...	...	0927	...	...	...	1127	...	...	...	1327	...	...	...	1527	...	...	...	1727	...	...	1927	...	...	...
Kassel Wilhelmshöhe **804** d.	*0948*	*0948*	1100	...	*1148*	*1148*	1300	...	*1348*	*1348*	1500	...	*1548*	*1548*	1700	...	*1748*	*1748*	1900	...	*1948*	2100	...	...	...
Warburg (Westf) **804** d.	1039	1039	1133	...	1239	1239	1333	...	1439	1439	1533	...	1639	1639	1733	...	1839	1839	1933	...	2039	2133	...	...	...
Altenbeken **809 811** ⊖ d.	1102	1102	1156	...	1302	1302	1356	...	1502	1502	1556	...	1702	1702	1756	...	1902	1902	1956	...	2102	2156	...	...	...
Paderborn Hbf **809 811** ⊖ d.	1117	1121	1210	...	1317	1321	1410	...	1517	1521	1610	...	1717	1721	1810	...	1917	1921	2010	...	2116	2210	...	2216	2308
Lippstadt d.	1136	1144	1226	...	1336	1344	1426	...	1536	1544	1626	...	1736	1744	1826	...	1936	1944	2026	...	2139	2226	...	2239	2332
Soest **802** d.	1149	1156	1237	...	1349	1356	1437	...	1549	1556	1637	...	1749	1756	1837	...	1949	1956	2037	...	2151	2237	...	2251	2344
Hamm (Westf) a.	1206	1214	1252	...	1406	1414	1452	...	1606	1614	1652	...	1806	1814	1852	...	2006	2014	2052	...	2208	2252	...	2308	0001
Hamm (Westf) **802** d.	1220	1220	1256	1259	1420	1420	1456	1459	1620	1620	1656	1659	1820	1820	1856	1859	2020	2020	2056	2059	...	2256	2259	...	*0006*
Münster (Westf) Hbf **802** a.	1248	1248	|	1322	1448	1448	|	1522	1648	1648	|	1722	1848	1848	|	1922	2048	2048	|	2122	...	|	2329	...	*0036*
Dortmund Hbf **802** a.	...	...	1315	...	...	...	1515	...	...	...	1715	...	...	...	1915	...	...	...	2115	...	...	2315	...	...	...
Düsseldorf Hbf **800** a.	...	...	1412	...	...	...	1612	...	...	...	1815	...	...	...	2015	...	...	...	2214	...	...	0012	...	...	...
Köln Hbf **800** a.	...	...	...	...	...	...	...	...	...	...	...	...	...	...	...	...	...	...	2240w	...	...	0035	...	...	...

Paderborn - Holzminden ⊡

km		Ⓐt	⚒r	Ⓐt	⚒r					Ⓒz	
0	**Paderborn** Hbf d.	0453	0553	0607	0653	0753	and	2053	2206	2315	...
17	Altenbeken d.	0507	0606	0621	0707	0807	hourly	2107	2219	2329	...
66	**Holzminden** a.	0553	0658*	0720	0753	0853	until	2153	2302	0012	...

	Ⓐt	⚒r	Ⓐt	⚒r					Ⓒz
Holzminden d.	0450	0604	0618	0704	0804	and	2204	...	2316
Altenbeken d.	0537	0651	0707	0754	0851	hourly	2251	...	0001
Paderborn Hbf a.	0551	0705	0720	0807	0905	until	2304	...	0015

O – To/from Ostseebad Binz (Table **844**).
b – Also Dec. 26, Jan. 1, Mar. 20, 24, Apr. 30, May 12; not Dec. 23, 30, Mar. 21, 23, May 2, 11.
c – ⑥⑦ (also Dec. 26, Mar. 24, May 1, 12, 22; not Mar. 22).
e – ①–⑥ (not Dec. 25, 26, Jan. 1, Mar. 22, 24, May 12).
f – ⑤ (also Mar. 20, Apr. 30; not Mar. 21, May 2).
g – ① (also Dec. 27, Jan. 2, Mar. 25, May 13; not Dec. 24, 31, Mar. 24, May 12).
h – Kassel **Hbf**.
j – Arrives 2044.
k – ⑥ (also Dec. 24, 31).
n – Not Dec. 24, 31.
q – Ⓑ (not Dec. 24, 25, 31, Mar. 21, 23, May 11).
r – Not May 22.
t – Not Dec. 24, 31, May 22.
v – Not Dec. 25, Jan. 1.
w – ⑦ (also Dec. 26, Jan. 1, Mar. 24, May 12; not Dec. 23, 30, Mar. 23, May 11).
y – Arrives 0700.
z – Also Dec. 24, 31, May 22.
* – 0651 on ⑥.
§ – Train number **2257** on ⑥ (also Dec. 24, 25, 31, Mar. 21, 23, May 11).
‡ – Train number **2250** on ⑦ (also Dec. 25, 26, Jan. 1, Mar. 22, 24, May 12).
⊖ – See panel below for Holzminden connections.
⊡ – Operated by Nord West Bahn (2nd class only).

806 FRANKFURT - GIESSEN - KASSEL

See Table **900** for faster *ICE* services Frankfurt - Kassel - Hannover - Hamburg and v.v.

Most services in this table will not run north of Hannover Dec. 24 - Jan. 1

km		*RE* 4120	*RE* 4100	*IC* 2378	*RE* 4122	*RE* 4102	*IC* 2376	*RE* 4104	*IC* 2374	*RE* 4106	*IC* 2372	*RE* 4108	*IC* 2370	*IC* 2186	*RE* 4110	*IC* 2278	*RE* 4112	*IC* 2276	*RE* 4114	*IC* 2274	*IC* 2270	*IC* 2194	*RE* 4116/8	*IC* 2272	*RE* 2503
		†c	⚒s	①–⑥ p🍷	Ⓐe	Ⓒz	🍷		🍷		🍷		T 🍷	⑤⑦f 🍷		🍷		🍷		①–⑤ g🍷	⑥b A	⑦w S🍷		⑦w	
	Konstanz **916** d.	...	...	...	...	...	...	...	...	...	...	...	0938	0938	...	...	...	...	...	...	...	...	...	...	...
	Karlsruhe Hbf **912** d.	...	...	...	...	...	0647r	...	0854	...	1054	...	1253	1253	...	1454	...	1654	...	1854	...	...	...	...	...
	Heidelberg Hbf **912** d.	...	...	...	...	...	0724r	...	0924	...	1124	...	1324	1324	...	1524	...	1724	...	1924	...	1924	...	2124	...
0	**Frankfurt (Main)** Hbf **807** d.	0509	0522	0623	0718	0722	0823	0922	1023	1122	1223	1322	1423	1423	1522	1623	1722	1823	1922	2023	2023	2023	2122	2223	2228
34	Friedberg (Hess) **807** d.	0532	0545	0646	0745	0745	0846	0945	1046	1145	1246	1345	1446	1446	1545	1646	1745	1846	1945	2046	2046	2046	2145	2246	2251
38	Bad Nauheim **807** d.	0536	|	|	|	|	|	|	|	|	|	|	|	|	|	|	|	|	|	|	|	|	|	|	2255
66	**Gießen 807** d.	0604	0604	0705	0804	0804	0905	1004	1105	1204	1305	1404	1505	1505	1604	1705	1804	1905	2004	2105	2105	2105	2204	2305	2322
96	Marburg (Lahn) d.	0621	0621	0721	0821	0821	0921	1021	1121	1221	1321	1421	1521	1521	1621	1721	1821	1921	2021	2121	2121	2121	2221	2321	2350
118	Stadtallendorf d.	0636	0636	|	0836	0836	|	1036	|	1236	|	1436	|	|	1636	|	1836	|	2036	|	|	|	2236	|	0009
138	Treysa d.	0651	0651	0746	0851	0851	0946	1051	1146	1251	1346	1451	1546	1546	1651	1746	1851	1946	2051	2146	2146	2146	2251	2346	0026
166	Wabern d.	0707	0707	0804	0907	0907	1004	1107	1204	1307	1404	1507	1604	1604	1707	1804	1907	2004	2107	2204	2204	2204	2307k	0004	...
196	**Kassel** Wilhelmshöhe ‡ a.	0727	0727	0826	0927	0927	1026	1127	1226	1327	1426	1527	1626	1626	1727	1826	1927	2028	2127	2226	2226	2226	2327k	0026	...
200	**Kassel** Hbf ‡ a.	0734	0734	|	0934	0934	|	1134	|	1334	|	1534	|	|	1734	|	1934	|	2135	...	...	2234	2334k	...	...
	Hannover Hbf **902** a.	...	...	0956	...	...	1156	...	1356	...	1556	...	1756	1756	...	1956	...	2156f	...	...	...	...	...	...	...
	Hamburg Hbf **902** a.	...	...	1127	...	...	1327	...	1530	...	1732	...	1927	1928	...	2127	...	2326w	...	...	...	...	...	...	...
	Stralsund **830** a.	...	...	...	...	...	1642	...	...	...	2041	...	...	2230	...	...	...	...	...	...	...	...	...	...	...

	RE 25045	*RE* 4121	*RE* 4101	*IC* 2273	*RE* 4123	*RE* 4103	*IC* 2275	*RE* 25007	*RE* 4105	*IC* 2277	*RE* 4107	*IC* 2279	*RE* 4109	*IC* 2371	*RE* 4111	*RE* 4125	*IC* 2373	*RE* 4113	*IC* 2375	*RE* 4115	*IC* 2377	*RE* 4117	*IC* 2379	*IC* 1999	*RE* 4119
		Ⓐe	⑥m	①–⑥ h🍷	Ⓐe	Ⓒz	①–⑤ d S 🍷			🍷		🍷		🍷	Ⓒz	Ⓐe	🍷		🍷		O 🍷		⑤v 🍷	⑦w B	
Stralsund **830** d.	...	...	...	...	...	...		...	...	...	...	0529r	...	...	...	...	0915	...	...	...	1327	...	1515	...	...
Hamburg Hbf **902** d.	...	...	...	...	...	...	...	...	...	0626r	...	0828	...	1028	...	...	1228	...	1428	...	1628	...	1828	...	...
Hannover Hbf **902** d.	...	...	...	...	...	...	0600	...	...	0800r	...	1000	...	1200	...	...	1400	...	1600	...	1800	...	2000	2101	...
Kassel Hbf ‡ d.	...	0401	0423	...	0613	0615	|	...	0823	|	1023	|	1223	|	1423	1423	|	1623	|	1823	|	2023	|	|	2221
Kassel Wilhelmshöhe ‡ d.	...	0406	0429	0530	0619	0621	0730	...	0829	0930	1029	1130	1229	1330	1429	1429	1530	1629	1730	1829	1930	2029	2130	2203	2227
Wabern d.	...	0424	0448	0552	0644	0646	0752	...	0848	0952	1048	1152	1248	1352	1448	1448	1552	1648	1752	1848	1952	2048	2152	2225	2250
Treysa d.	...	0440	0505	0610	0705	0705	0810	0815	0905	1010	1105	1210	1305	1410	1505	1505	1610	1705	1810	1905	2010	2105	2210	2243	2309
Stadtallendorf d.	...	0455	0519	|	0719	0719	|	0829	0919	|	1119	|	1319	|	1519	1519	|	1719	|	1919	|	2119	|	2259	2323
Marburg (Lahn) d.	0408	0512	0535	0635	0735	0735	0835	0849	0935	1035	1135	1235	1335	1435	1535	1535	1635	1735	1835	1935	2035	2135	2235	2313	2339
Gießen 807 d.	0439	0536	0553	0653	0753	0753	0853	0922	0953	1053	1153	1253	1353	1453	1553	1553	1653	1753	1853	1953	2053	2153	2253	2331	0006
Bad Nauheim **807** d.	0505	0554	|	|	|	|	|	0939	|	|	|	|	|	|	|	|	|	|	|	|	|	|	2309	2350	0029
Friedberg (Hess) **807** d.	0510	0600	0612	0712	0812	0812	0912	0942	1012	1112	1212	1312	1412	1512	1612	1612	1712	1812	1912	2012	2112	2212	2314	2356	0034
Frankfurt (Main) Hbf **807** a.	0536	0625	0634	0733	0836	0834	0933	1007	1034	1133	1234	1333	1434	1533	1634	1637	1733	1834	1933	2034	2133	2234	2336	0019	0057
Heidelberg Hbf **912** a.	...	...	...	0830	...	...	1030	...	...	1230	...	1430	...	1630	...	...	1830	...	2032q	...	2230t	...	...	...	...
Karlsruhe Hbf **912** a.	...	...	...	0902	...	...	...	...	...	1302	...	1502	...	1702	...	...	1902	...	2106a	...	2304t	...	...	...	...
Konstanz **916** a.	...	...	...	...	...	...	...	...	...	...	...	...	...	2015	...	...	...	...	...	...	...	...	...	...	...

A – From Saarbrücken (Table **919**).
B – From Berlin (Table **810**).
O – From Ostseebad Binz (Table **844**).
S – From / to Stuttgart (Table **930**).
T – ①②③④⑥ (also Dec. 23, 30, Mar. 21, 23, May 2, 11; not Dec. 26, Jan. 1, Mar. 20, 24, Apr. 30, May 12).
a – ①–⑤ (also Dec. 23, 30; not Dec. 24, 25, 26, 31, Jan. 1, Mar. 21, 24, May 12).
c – Also May 22.
d – Not Dec. 24, 25, 26, 31, Jan. 1, Mar. 21, 24, May 12.
e – Not Dec. 24, 31, May 22.
f – ⑤⑦ (also Dec. 26, Jan. 1, Mar. 20, 24, Apr. 30, May 12; not Dec. 23, 30, Mar. 21, 23, May 2, 11).
g – Also Dec. 23, 30; not Dec. 24, 25, 26, 31, Jan. 1, Mar. 24, May 2, 12.
h – Not Dec. 25, 26, Jan. 1, Mar. 24, May 1, 12.
k – ⑤⑥† (also Dec. 24, 31, May 22).
m – Also Dec. 24, 31.
p – Not Dec. 25, 26, 29, Jan. 1, Mar. 22, 24, May 12.
q – ⑧ (not Dec. 24, 25, 31, Mar. 21, 23, May 11).
r – ①–⑥ (not Dec. 25, 26, Jan. 1, Mar. 22, 24, May 12).
s – Not May 22.
t – ⑤⑦ (also Dec. 26, Jan. 1, Mar. 20, 24, Apr. 30, May 12, 21; not Dec. 23, 30, Mar. 21, 23, May 2, 11, 23).
v – Also Mar. 20, Apr. 30; not Dec. 28, Mar. 21, May 2.
w – ⑦ (also Dec. 26, Jan. 1, Mar. 24, May 12; not Dec. 23, 30, Mar. 23, May 11).
z – Also Dec. 24, 31, May 22.
‡ – See Tables **804** / **901** for other local services Kassel Hbf - Kassel Wilhelmshöhe and v.v.

807 AACHEN - KÖLN - SIEGEN - GIESSEN - FRANKFURT

RE / *RB* services

km																									
					⑥m	Ⓐe		Ⓐe		⚒r															
0	**Aachen** Hbf **802 910** d.	...	...	...	...	...	...	...	...	0510e	...	0610e	...	0710e	...	0810r	...	0910	1010	...	1110	...	1210	...	1310
31	Düren **802** d.	...	...	...	...	...	...	...	...	0544e	...	0644e	...	0744e	...	0844r	...	0944	1044	...	1144	...	1244	...	1344
70	**Köln** Hbf **802 910** a.	...	...	...	...	...	...	...	...	0612e	...	0712e	...	0812e	...	0912r	...	1012	1112	...	1212	...	1312	...	1412
70	**Köln** Hbf **802 910** d.	...	...	...	0341	...	...	0431	...	0623	...	0723	...	0823	...	0923	...	1023	1123	...	1223	...	1323	...	1423
91	Troisdorf **802** d.	...	...	...	0409	...	...	0454	...	0640	...	0740	...	0840	...	0940	...	1040	1140	...	1240	...	1340	...	1440
95	Siegburg/Bonn **910** d.	...	...	...	0414	...	...	0459	...	0645	...	0745	...	0845	...	0945	...	1045	1145	...	1245	...	1345	...	1445
102	Hennef (Sieg) d.	...	...	...	0420	...	...	0506	...	0650	...	0750	...	0850	...	0950	...	1050	1150	...	1250	...	1350	...	1450
114	Eitorf d.	...	...	...	0431	...	...	0517	...	0659	...	0759	...	0859	...	0959	...	1059	1159	...	1259	...	1359	...	1459
136	Au (Sieg) d.	...	...	...	0509	0515	...	0545	...	0717	...	0817	...	0917	...	1017	...	1117	1217	...	1317	...	1417	...	1517
142	Wissen (Sieg) d.	...	...	...	0516	0522	...	0552	...	0722	...	0822	...	0922	...	1022	...	1122	1222	...	1322	...	1422	...	1522
154	Betzdorf (Sieg) d.	...	...	...	0530	0536	...	0606	...	0732	...	0832	...	0932	...	1032	...	1132	1232	...	1332	...	1432	...	1532
171	**Siegen** a.	...	...	...	0555	0601	...	0631	...	0752	...	0852	...	0952	...	1052	...	1152	1252	...	1352	...	1452	...	1552
		Ⓐe	Ⓐe	◧	⚒r	Ⓐe	⑥m	Ⓐe		⑥m		|		Ⓐe		|			|		Ⓒz		|		
171	**Siegen** d.	...	0457	...	0559	0606	0644	0654	...	0802	...	0854	...	1002	...	1054	...	1202	1254	...	1402	...	1454	...	1602
203	Dillenburg d.	0424	0527	0531r	0623	0633	0718	0728	0733	0827	0833r	0918	0933	1027	1033r	1118	1133	1227	1318	1333	1427	1433r	1518	1533	1627
209	Herborn d.	0432	0532	0539r	0628	0643	0723	0734	0740	0833	0840r	0923	0940	1033	1040r	1123	1140	1233	1323	1340	1433	1440r	1523	1540	1633
231	Wetzlar **906** d.	0454	0552	0601r	0648	0709	0737	0752	0802	0848	0902r	0937	1002	1048	1102r	1137	1202	1248	1337	1402	1448	1502r	1537	1602	1648
244	**Gießen 906** a.	0505	|	0611r	0658	0722	0747	0802	0814	0858	0914r	0947	1014	1058	1114r	1147	1214	1258	1347	1414	1458	1514r	1547	1614	1658
244	**Gießen 806** d.	0514	|	0619	0705	*0728*	*0753*	0809	0822	0905	0922	*0953*	1022	1105	1122	*1153*	1222	1305	*1353*	1422	1505	1522	*1553*	1622	1705
272	Bad Nauheim **806** d.	0538	|	0638	0723	*0755*	|	0826	0839	0926	0939	|	1039	1126	1139	|	1239	1326	|	1439	1526	1539	|	1639	1726
276	Friedberg (Hess) **806** d.	0542	|	0642	0728	*0800*	*0812*	0830	0842	0930	0942	*1012*	1042	1130	1142	*1212*	1242	1330	*1412*	1442	1530	1542	*1612*	1642	1730
310	**Frankfurt** (Main) Hbf **806** a.	0607	0640	0707	0755	*0826*	*0834*	0855	0907	0953	1007	*1034*	1107	1153	1207	*1234*	1307	1353	*1434*	1507	1553	1607	*1637*q	1707	1753

											t
Aachen Hbf **802 910** d.	1410	...	1510	1610	1710	...	1810	1910	...	...	...
Düren **802** d.	1444	...	1544	1644	1744	...	1844	1944	...	...	...
Köln Hbf **802 910** a.	1512	...	1612	1712	1812	...	1912	2012	...	...	...
Köln Hbf **802 910** d.	1523	...	1623	1723	1823	...	1923	2023	2123	2223	2323
Troisdorf **802** d.	1540	...	1640	1740	1840	...	1940	2040	2140	2240	2340
Siegburg/Bonn **910** d.	1545	...	1645	1745	1845	...	1945	2045	2145	2245	2345
Hennef (Sieg) d.	1550	...	1650	1750	1850	...	1950	2050	2150	2250	2350
Eitorf d.	1559	...	1659	1759	1859	...	1959	2059	2159	2259	2359
Au (Sieg) d.	1617	...	1717	1817	1917	...	2017	2117	2217	2317	0017
Wissen (Sieg) d.	1622	...	1722	1822	1922	...	2022	2122	2224	2324	0024
Betzdorf (Sieg) d.	1632	...	1732	1832	1932	...	2032	2132	2238	2338	0038
Siegen a.	1652	...	1752	1852	1952	...	2052	2152	2300	2400	0100
	|			|	▬		|	▬	|		
Siegen d.	1654	...	1802	1854	...	...	2054	...	2307	...	...
Dillenburg d.	1718	1733	1827	1918	1933	2027e	2118	2233e	2331	...	...
Herborn d.	1723	1740	1833	1923	1940	2035e	2123	2240e	2336	...	...
Wetzlar **906** d.	1737	1802	1848	1937	2002	2057e	2137	2302e	2350	...	...
Gießen 906 a.	1747	1814	1858	1947	2014	2108e	2147	2314e	2400	...	...
Gießen 806 d.	*1753*	1822	1905	*1953*	2022	2117	*2153*	2322	*0006*	...	...
Bad Nauheim **806** d.	|	1839	1926	|	2039	2140	|	2345	*0029*	...	...
Friedberg (Hess) **806** d.	*1812*	1842	1930	*2012*	2042	2143	*2212*	2349	*0034*	...	...
Frankfurt (Main) Hbf **806** a.	*1834*	1907	1953	*2034*	2107	2209	*2234*	0011	*0057*	...	...

			⚒r		Ⓐe	Ⓐe		⚒r	
Frankfurt (Main) Hbf **806** d.	...	...	*0522*	...	...	0630	*0718*k	0802	0850
Friedberg (Hess) **806** d.	...	...	*0545*	...	*0620*	0659	*0745*	0827	0915
Bad Nauheim **806** d.	...	...	|	...	*0624*	0703	|	0832	0919
Gießen 806 a.	...	...	*0603*	...	*0648*	0725	*0803*	0853	0935
Gießen 906 d.	...	...	0613	...	0652	0740	0809	0909	0940
Wetzlar **906** d.	...	...	0622	...	0703	0750	0818	0918	0950
Herborn d.	...	...	0635	...	0727	0812	0833	0932	1012
Dillenburg d.	...	...	0640	...	0736	0823	0839	0937	1023
Siegen a.	...	...	0705	...	0804	...	0906	1000	...
	⚒r		|		d		|	d	
Siegen d.	0454	0608	0707	0707	0808	...	0908	1008	...
Betzdorf (Sieg) d.	0515	0626	0726	0726	0826	...	0926	1026	...
Wissen (Sieg) d.	0527	0636	0736	0736	0836	...	0936	1036	...
Au (Sieg) d.	0535	0642	0742	0742	0842	...	0942	1042	...
Eitorf d.	0556	0659	0759	0759	0859	...	0959	1059	...
Hennef (Sieg) d.	0609	0709	0809	0809	0909	...	1009	1109	...
Siegburg/Bonn **910** d.	0614	0714	0814	0814	0914	...	1014	1114	...
Troisdorf **802** d.	0619	0719	0819	0819	0919	...	1019	1119	...
Köln Hbf **802 910** a.	0637	0737	0837	0837	0937	...	1037	1137	...
Köln Hbf **802 910** d.	0647e	0747e	0847r	...	0947	...	1047	1147	...
Düren **802** d.	0714e	0814e	0914r	...	1014	...	1114	1214	...
Aachen Hbf **802 910** a.	0749e	0849e	0949r	...	1049	...	1149	1249	...

d – Daily from Siegen.
e – Ⓐ (not Dec. 24, 31, May 22).
k – *0722* on Ⓒz.
m – Also Dec. 24, 31.
q – *1634* on Ⓒz.
r – ⚒ (not May 22).
t – Not Dec. 24.
z – Also Dec. 24, 31, May 22.
◧ – Change trains at Gießen on ⑥m. Departs Gießen 0622 on Ⓒz.

FRANKFURT - GIESSEN - SIEGEN - KÖLN - AACHEN 807

RE / RB services

				Ⓒz			Ⓑn				n		Ⓑn	Ⓐe	Ⓐe	Ⓒz					Ⓑn			Ⓐe	◇	
Frankfurt (Main) Hbf **806**	d.	*0922*	0952	1002	1052	*1122*	1202	1252	*1322*	1402	1452	*1522*	1601	1701	1630	1652	*1722*	1801	1852	*1922*	2002	2052	*2122*	2152	2228	*2326*
Friedberg (Hess) **806**	d.	*0945*	1015	1027	1115	*1145*	1227	1315	*1345*	1427	1515	*1545*	1626	|	1656	1715	*1745*	1826	1915	*1945*	2027	2115	*2145*	2215	2251	*2348*
Bad Nauheim **806**	d.	|	1019	1032	1119	|	1232	1319	|	1432	1519	|	1631	|	1700	1719	|	1831	1919	|	2032	2119	|	2219	2255	|
Gießen 806	a.	*1003*	1035	1053	1135	*1203*	1253	1335	*1403*	1453	1535	*1603*	1659	|	1725	1735	*1803*	1859	1935	*2003*	2053	2135	*2203*	2242	2318	*0010*
Gießen 906	d.	1009	1040r	1109	1140	1209	1309	1340	1409	1509	1540	1609	1709	|	1740	1740	1809	1909	1940	2009	2109	2140	2209	2248	2324	0030
Wetzlar **906**	d.	1018	1050r	1118	1150	1218	1318	1350	1418	1518	1550	1618	1718	1750	1755	1750	1818	1918	1950	2018	2118	2150	2218	2258	2335	0041
Herborn	d.	1033	1112r	1132	1212	1233	1332	1412	1433	1532	1612	1633	1732	1807	1817	1812	1833	1932	2012	2033	2132	2212	2233	2320	2357	0102
Dillenburg	d.	1039	1123r	1137	1223	1239	1337	1423	1439	1537	1623	1639	1737	1812	1825	1823	1839	1937	2023	2039	2137	2223	2239	2328	0005	0111
Siegen	a.	1106	...	1200	...	1306	1400	...	1506	1600	...	1706	1800	1839	...	...	1906	2000	...	2106	2200	...	2306	—	...	...
		|		d		|	d		|			|	d				|	◐ |		|	t		Ⓐe	⑥		
Siegen	d.	1108	...	1208	...	1308	1408	...	1508	1608	...	1708	1808	...	...	...	1908	2008	...	2108	2208	...	2313	2359	...	...
Betzdorf (Sieg)	d.	1126	...	1226	...	1326	1426	...	1526	1626	...	1726	1826	...	...	...	1926	2026	...	2126	2226	...	2336	0022	...	...
Wissen (Sieg)	d.	1136	...	1236	...	1336	1436	...	1536	1636	...	1736	1836	...	...	...	1936	2036	...	2136	2236	...	2348	0034	...	...
Au (Sieg)	d.	1142	...	1242	...	1342	1442	...	1542	1642	...	1742	1842	...	...	...	1942	2042	...	2142	2242	...	2357	0043	...	...
Eitorf	d.	1159	...	1259	...	1359	1459	...	1559	1659	...	1759	1859	...	...	...	1959	2059	...	2159	2259	...	...	...	...	...
Hennef (Sieg)	d.	1209	...	1309	...	1409	1509	...	1609	1709	...	1809	1909	...	...	...	2009	2109	...	2209	2309	...	...	...	...	...
Siegburg/Bonn **910**	d.	1214	...	1314	...	1414	1514	...	1614	1714	...	1814	1914	...	...	...	2014	2114	...	2214	2314	...	...	...	...	...
Troisdorf **802**	d.	1219	...	1319	...	1419	1519	...	1619	1719	...	1819	1919	...	...	...	2019	2119	...	2219	2319	...	...	...	...	...
Köln Hbf **802 910**	a.	1237	...	1337	...	1437	1537	...	1637	1737	...	1837	1937	...	...	...	2037	2137	...	2237	2337	...	...	...	...	...
Köln Hbf **802 910**	d.	1247	...	1347	...	1447	1547	...	1647	1747	...	1847	1947	...	...	...	*2047*e	...	...	...	...	...	...	...	...	...
Düren **802**	d.	1314	...	1414	...	1514	1614	...	1714	1814	...	1914	2014	...	...	...	*2114*e	...	...	...	...	...	...	...	...	...
Aachen Hbf **802 910**	a.	1349	...	1449	...	1549	1649	...	1749	1849	...	1949	2049	...	...	...	*2149*e	...	...	...	...	...	...	...	...	...

d – Daily from Siegen.
e – Ⓐ (not Dec. 24, 31, May 22).
n – Not Dec. 24, 31.
t – Not Dec. 24.
r – ⚒ (not May 22).
z – Also Dec. 24, 31, May 22.
◐ – Change trains at Siegen on Ⓒ (also Dec. 24, 31, May 22).
◇ – Change trains at Gießen on ①–④ (not Dec. 25, 26, Jan. 1, Mar. 24, May 1, 12, 22).

ESSEN - HAGEN - SIEGEN 808

ABELLIO Rail NRW

km																									
		Ⓒz	Ⓐe	Ⓐe	Ⓐe	Ⓐe	Ⓒz	Ⓐe	Ⓒz		Ⓐe	Ⓒz			Ⓐe	Ⓒz		Ⓐe	Ⓒz		Ⓐe	Ⓒz			
0	**Essen** Hbf ⊡ d.	...	...	...	...	...	...	0634	0634k	...	0734	0734	...	and at the same minutes past each hour until	1734	1734	...	1834	1834	...	1934	1934	...	...	...
16	Bochum Hbf ⊡ d.	...	...	...	...	...	...	0647	0647k	...	0747	0747	...		1747	1747	...	1847	1847	...	1947	1947	...	...	...
30	Witten Hbf ⊡ d.	...	...	...	...	...	...	0657	0657k	...	0757	0757	...		1757	1757	...	1857	1857	...	1957	1957	...	...	...
45	**Hagen** Hbf ⊡ a.	...	...	...	...	...	...	0709	0709k	...	0809	0809	...		1809	1809	...	1909	1909	...	2009	2009	...	...	...
45	**Hagen** Hbf d.	0024	...	...	...	0609	0615	0715	0715	0740	0815	0815	0840		1815	1815	1840	1915	1915	1940	2015	2015	2114	2214	2314
75	Altena (Westf) d.	0050	...	...	...	0635	0640	0740	0740	0806	0840	0840	0906		1840	1840	1906	1940	1940	2006	2040	2040	2140	2240	2340
84	Werdohl d.	0059	...	...	...	0644	0649	0749	0749	0815	0849	0849	0915		1849	1849	1915	1949	1949	2015	2049	2049	2149	2249	2349
106	Finnentrop d.	0116	0402	0502	0602	0702	0706	0807	0806	0832	0907	0906	0932		1907	1906	1932	2007	2006	2032	2106	2106	2206	2306	0006
119	Altenhundem d.	0129	0415	0515	0613	0714	0718	0818	0819	0845	0918	0918	0945		1918	1918	1945	2018	2019	2045	2119	2118	2219	2319	0019
141	Kreuztal d.	0152	0438	0539	0632	0738	0739	0837	0839	0908	0937	0939	1008		1937	1939	2008	2037	2039	2108	2142	2139	2242	2342	0042
152	**Siegen** a.	0203	0450	0550	0642	0749	0749	0847	0849	0919	0947	0949	1019		1947	1949	2019	2047	2049	2119	2153	2149	2253	2353	0053

	Ⓐe	⑥k	Ⓐe	Ⓒz	Ⓐe	Ⓐe	Ⓒz	⚒r	Ⓐe	Ⓒz			Ⓐe	Ⓒz		Ⓐe	Ⓒz		Ⓐe	Ⓒz				n
Siegen d.	0402	...	0506	0510k	0543	0612	0612	0636	0712	0712	0743	and at the same minutes past each hour until	1712	1712	1743	1812	1812	1843	1912	1912	2011	...	2211	2311
Kreuztal d.	0413	...	0517	0521k	0556	0622	0622	0648	0722	0722	0755		1722	1722	1755	1822	1822	1855	1922	1922	2022	...	2222	2323
Altenhundem d.	0436	...	0541	0542k	0618	0641	0643	0711	0741	0742	0818		1741	1742	1818	1841	1843	1918	1941	1942	2045	...	2246	2347
Finnentrop d.	0453	0453	0553	0555	0631	0653	0655	0729	0753	0755	0831		1753	1755	1831	1853	1855	1931	1953	1955	2105	2205	2305	2359
Werdohl d.	0511	0510	0611	0611	0648	0710	0711	0747	0810	0811	0848		1810	1811	1848	1910	1911	1948	2010	2011	2122	2223	2322	
Altena (Westf) d.	0520	0519	0619	0620	0657	0719	0720	0755	0819	0820	0857		1819	1820	1857	1919	1920	1957	2019	2020	2131	2231	2331	
Hagen Hbf a.	0546	0546	0646	0646	0723	0746	0746	0823	0846	0846	0923		1846	1846	1923	1946	1946	2023	2046	2046	2158	2258	2358	
Hagen Hbf ⊡ d.	...	...	0650	0650	...	0750	0750	...	0850	0850	...		1850	1850	...	1950	1950	...	...	...	...	...	...	...
Witten Hbf ⊡ d.	...	...	0702	0702	...	0802	0802	...	0902	0902	...		1902	1902	...	2002	2002	...	...	...	...	...	...	...
Bochum Hbf ⊡ d.	...	...	0714	0714	...	0814	0814	...	0914	0914	...		1914	1914	...	2014	2014	...	...	...	...	...	...	...
Essen Hbf ⊡ a.	...	...	0729	0729	...	0829	0829	...	0929	0929	...		1929	1929	...	2029	2029	...	...	...	...	...	...	...

Additional services Essen - Hagen and v.v.

	⚒r									
Essen Hbf d.	0508	0608	0708	and hourly until	1908	2008	2108	2208	2308	...
Bochum Hbf d.	0522	0622	0722		1922	2022	2122	2222	2322	...
Witten Hbf d.	0532	0632	0732		1932	2032	2132	2232	2332	...
Hagen Hbf a.	0546	0646	0746		1946	2046	2146	2246	2346	...

	⚒r									
Hagen Hbf d.	0517	0617	0717	and hourly until	1917	2017	2117	2217	2317	...
Witten Hbf d.	0531	0631	0731		1931	2031	2131	2231	2331	...
Bochum Hbf d.	0541	0641	0741		1941	2041	2141	2241	2341	...
Essen Hbf a.	0556	0656	0756		1956	2056	2156	2256	2356	...

e – Not Dec. 24, 31, May 22.
k – ⑥ (also Dec. 24, 31).
n – Not Dec. 24, 31.
r – Not May 22.
z – Also Dec. 24, 31, May 22.
⊡ – See also panel below main table.

PADERBORN - HAMELN - HANNOVER - HANNOVER FLUGHAFEN ✈ 809

S-Bahn 5

km																										
							⑥z		⚒	†				⚒	†				⚒	†				⚒	†
0	**Paderborn** Hbf **805 811** d.	...	...	...	...	0512e	...	...	0615	...	...	0715	...	0815	...	...	0915	...	1015	...	...	1115	...	1215	...
17	Altenbeken **805 811** d.	...	...	...	...	0524e	...	...	0627	...	...	0727	...	0827	...	...	0927	...	1027	...	...	1127	...	1227	...
56	Bad Pyrmont d.	...	...	0505r	...	0602e	0605	0635e	0702	0705	0735e	0802	...	0902	0905	...	1002	...	1102	1105	...	1202	...	1302	1305
75	Hameln a.	...	...	0519r	...	0616e	0619	0649e	0716	0719	0749e	0816	...	0916	0919	...	1016	...	1116	1119	...	1216	...	1316	1319
75	Hameln d.	0420e	0450e	0520	0550r	0620	0620	0650r	0720	0720	0750r	0820	0850r	0920	0920	0950r	1020	1050r	1120	1120	1150r	1220	1250r	1320	1320
133	**Hannover** Hbf a.	0503e	0533e	0603	0633r	0703	0703	0733r	0803	0803	0833r	0903	0933r	1003	1003	1033r	1103	1133r	1203	1203	1233r	1303	1333r	1403	1403
133	**Hannover** Hbf d.	0505	0535	0605	0635	0705	0705	0735	0805	0805	0835	0905	0935	1005	1005	1035	1105	1135	1205	1205	1235	1305	1335	1405	1405
148	**Hannover** Flughafen ✈ a.	0522	0552	0622	0652	0722	0722	0752	0822	0822	0852	0922	0952	1022	1022	1052	1122	1152	1222	1222	1252	1322	1352	1422	1422

				⚒	†				⚒	†				Ⓐe	Ⓒz				Ⓐe	Ⓒz					♥
Paderborn Hbf **805 811** d.	...	1315	...	1415	...	...	1515	...	1615	...	...	1715	...	1815	...	...	1915	...	2015	...	...	2115	...	...	...
Altenbeken **805 811** d.	...	1327	...	1427	...	...	1527	...	1627	...	...	1727	...	1827	...	...	1927	...	2027	...	...	2127	...	...	...
Bad Pyrmont d.	1335e	1402	...	1502	1505	...	1602	1635e	1702	1705	...	1802	1835e	1902	1905	...	2002	...	2102	2105	...	2202	...	2305	2305
Hameln a.	1349e	1416	...	1516	1519	...	1616	1649e	1716	1719	...	1816	1849e	1916	1919	...	2016	...	2116	2119	...	2216	...	2319	2319
Hameln d.	1350r	1420	1450r	1520	1520	1550r	1620	1650r	1720	1720	1750e	1820	1850e	1920	1920	1950e	2020	2050e	2120	2120	...	2220	...	2320	2320
Hannover Hbf a.	1433r	1503	1533r	1603	1603	1633r	1703	1733r	1803	1803	1833e	1903	1933e	2003	2003	2033e	2103	2133e	2203	2203	...	2303	...	0003	0003
Hannover Hbf d.	1435	1505	1535	1605	1605	1635	1705	1735	1805	1805	1835	1905	1935	2005	2005	2035	2105	2135	2205	2205	2235	2305	2335	...	0005
Hannover Flughafen ✈ a.	1452	1522	1552	1622	1622	1652	1722	1752	1822	1822	1852	1922	1952	2022	2022	2052	2122	2152	2222	2222	2252	2322	2352	...	0022

		△	Ⓐe	⚒		⚒					†	⚒				†	⚒				†	⚒			
Hannover Flughafen ✈ d.	0006	0036	...	...	0506	0536	0536	0606	0636	0706	0736	0736	0806	0836	0906	0936	0936	1006	1036	1106	1136	1136	1206	1236	1306
Hannover Hbf a.	0023	0053	...	...	0523	0553	0553	0623	0653	0723	0753	0753	0823	0853	0923	0953	0953	1023	1053	1123	1153	1153	1223	1253	1323
Hannover Hbf d.	...	0100	0455	...	0525e	0555	...	0625r	0655	0725r	0755	0755	0825r	0855	0925r	0955	0955	1025r	1055	1125r	1155	1155	1225r	1255	1325r
Hameln a.	...	0144	0540	...	0610e	0640	...	0710r	0740	0810r	0840	0840	0910r	0940	1010r	1040	1040	1110r	1140	1210r	1240	1240	1310r	1340	1410r
Hameln d.	...	...	...	0544	0611e	0644	...	0711e	0744	...	0841	0844	...	0944	...	1041	1044	...	1144	...	1241	1244	1311e	1344	...
Bad Pyrmont d.	...	...	...	0600	0625e	0700	...	0725e	0800	...	0855	0900	...	1000	...	1055	1100	...	1200	...	1255	1300	1325e	1400	...
Altenbeken **805 811** d.	...	...	...	0633	...	0733	...	...	0833	...	...	0933	...	1033	...	...	1133	...	1233	...	...	1333	...	1433	...
Paderborn Hbf **805 811** a.	...	...	...	0647	...	0747	...	...	0847	...	...	0947	...	1047	...	...	1147	...	1247	...	...	1347	...	1447	...

	†	⚒				†					Ⓒz	Ⓐe				Ⓒz	Ⓐe								
Hannover Flughafen ✈ d.	1336	1336	1406	1436	1506	1536	1536	1606	1636	1706	1736	1736	1806	1836	1906	1936	1936	2006	2036	2106	2136	2206	2236	2306	2336
Hannover Hbf a.	1353	1353	1423	1453	1523	1553	1553	1623	1653	1723	1753	1753	1823	1853	1923	1953	1953	2023	2053	2123	2153	2223	2253	2323	2353
Hannover Hbf d.	1355	1355	1425r	1455	1525r	1555	1555	1625r	1655	1725r	1755	1755	1825e	1855	1925e	1955	1955	2025e	2055	2125e	2155	...	2255	...	2355
Hameln a.	1440	1440	1510r	1540	1610r	1640	1640	1710r	1740	1810r	1840	1840	1910e	1940	2010e	2040	2040	2110e	2140	2210e	2240	...	2340	...	0040
Hameln d.	1441	1444	...	1544	1611e	1641	1644e	...	1744	1811e	1841	1844	...	1944	...	2041	2044	...	2146	...	2241	...	2341	...	...
Bad Pyrmont d.	1455	1500	...	1600	1625e	1655	1700e	...	1800	1825e	1855	1900	...	2000	...	2055	2100	...	2200	...	2255	...	2355	...	...
Altenbeken **805 811** d.	...	1533	...	1633	...	...	1733e	...	1833	...	...	1933	...	2033	...	...	2133	...	2233	...	...	...	...	...	...
Paderborn Hbf **805 811** a.	...	1547	...	1647	...	...	1747e	...	1847	...	...	1947	...	2047	...	...	2147	...	2247	...	...	...	...	...	...

e – Ⓐ (not Dec. 24, 31).
r – ⚒ only.
z – Also Dec. 24, 31.
♥ – ⑤⑥⑦ (also Dec. 25, 26, 31, Jan. 1, Mar. 24, Apr. 30, May 1, 12).
△ – ①⑥⑦ (also Dec. 26, 27, Jan. 1, 2, Mar. 25, May 1, 2, 13).

Warning! Services via Magdeburg are subject to alteration from May 25

810 HAMM and BAD BENTHEIM - HANNOVER - BERLIN and LEIPZIG

km	km		EN 347	ICE 1741	ICE 949	ICE 649	IC 2031	CNL 1243	RE 14201	ICE 841	ICE 841	IC 2147	RE 14003	IC 2243	ICE 541	ICE 541	ICE 974	IC 2033	RE 14203	ICE 1092	IC 2145	ICE 843	ICE 853	ICE 696	IC 2145
			[R]	①–⑤	①g	①–⑤	①–⑥	[R]	⚒H	①g	①–⑥	①–⑤	⚒H	①–⑥	①–⑥					①–⑤	①–⑥		①–⑥	①g	①–⑥
			🍷♦	d R		d✕	e	✕♦		✕	e✕	d🍷		e M 🍷	h✕	✕	✕♦	🍷		d D ⚡✕	e🍷	✕	e✕	L✕	e🍷
		Bonn Hbf **800** d.	...	...	...	...	...	...	...	...	...	...	...	...	...	...	...	...	...	...	...	...	...	...	...
		Köln/Bonn Flughafen ✈ **800** d.	...	...	...	...	...	...	...	...	...	...	...	...	...	...	...	...	...	...	...	...	...	...	...
		Köln Hbf **800** d.	2228	...	0155	...	...	...	...	0329	...	...	...	...	0429	...	...	...	...	...	0513	0529	0549	...	...
		Wuppertal Hbf **800** d.	2314	...	|	...	...	...	...	|	...	...	...	...	|	...	...	...	...	...	0543	|	0617	...	...
		Hagen Hbf **800** d.	2334	...	|	...	...	...	...	|	...	...	...	...	|	...	...	...	...	...	0601	|	0635	...	...
		Düsseldorf Hbf **800 802** d.	2202	...	0219	...	...	...	...	0353	...	...	...	...	0453	...	...	...	...	...	|	0553	|	...	...
		Dortmund Hbf **800 802** d.	2356	...	0314	...	...	...	...	0448	...	...	...	...	0548	...	...	...	...	...	0628	0648	|	...	...
0		**Hamm** (Westf) **802** d.	0014	...	0332	...	...	...	...	0506	...	...	...	...	0611	...	...	...	...	...	0645	0711	0711	...	...
50		Gütersloh Hbf **802** d.	|	...	0352	...	...	...	...	0526	...	...	...	...	|	...	...	...	...	...	0705	|	|	...	...
67		**Bielefeld** Hbf **802** d.	0043	...	0403	...	...	...	0424	0537	...	...	...	...	0638	...	...	...	0624	...	0717	0737	0737	...	...
81		Herford **802** d.	|	...	0413	...	...	...	0433	|	...	...	...	...	|	...	...	...	0633	...	0727	|	|	...	...
		Amsterdam Centraal **22** ⊡ d.	|	...	|	...	...	...	|	|	...	...	...	...	|	...	...	...	|	...	|	|	|	...	...
		Bad Bentheim **811** 🏛 d.	|	...	|	...	...	...	|	|	...	...	...	...	|	...	...	...	|	...	|	|	|	...	...
		Rheine **811** d.	|	...	|	...	...	...	|	|	...	...	...	...	|	...	...	...	|	...	|	|	|	...	...
		Osnabrück Hbf **811** d.	|	...	|	...	...	...	|	|	...	...	0516	0603	|	...	...	...	|	...	|	|	|	...	...
		Bünde (Westf) **811** d.	|	...	|	...	...	...	|	|	...	...	0540	0626	|	...	...	...	|	...	|	|	|	...	...
91		Löhne (Westf) **802** d.	|	...	|	...	...	...	0440	|	...	...	0550	|	|	...	...	...	0640	...	|	|	|	...	...
97		Bad Oeynhausen **802** d.	|	...	|	...	...	...	0445	|	...	...	0555	0639	|	...	...	...	0645	...	0737	|	|	...	...
112		Minden (Westf) **802** d.	|	...	0430	...	...	...	0507t	0600	...	...	0607	0649	|	...	...	...	0707t	...	0749	|	|	...	...
		Basel SBB **912** d.	|	...	|	...	...	2107	|	|	...	...	|	|	|	...	...	...	|	...	|	|	|	...	...
		Stuttgart Hbf **930** d.	|	...	|	...	...	|	|	|	...	...	|	|	|	...	...	...	|	...	|	|	|	...	...
		Frankfurt (Main) Hbf **900** d.	|	...	|	...	...	0055x	|	|	...	...	|	|	|	...	0510g	...	|	0614	|	|	|	...	...
		Oldenburg (Oldb) Hbf **813** d.	|	...	|	...	...	|	|	|	...	...	|	|	|	...	|	0535e	|	|	|	|	|	...	...
		Bremen Hbf **813** d.	|	...	|	...	...	|	|	|	...	...	|	|	|	...	|	0609	|	|	|	|	|	...	...
177		**Hannover** Hbf a.	|	...	0458	...	...	0537s	0550	0628	...	...	0650	0718	0728	...	|	0714	0750	|	0818	0828	0828	...	←
177		**Hannover** Hbf d.	|	...	0501	0527	0536	|	0555	0631	0631	0636	0655	0721	0731	0731	|	0736	0755	|	→	0831	0831	...	0836
212		Peine d.	|	...	|	|	|	|	0624	|	|	|	0724	|	|	|	|	|	0824	|	...	|	|	...	|
238	0	**Braunschweig** Hbf ‡ d.	|	...	|	0601	0610	|	0641	|	|	0711	0741	|	|	|	0800	0810	0841	|	...	|	|	0900	0911
274		Helmstedt ‡ d.	|	...	|	|	0632	|	*0720*a	|	|	|	...	|	|	|	|	0832	▬	|	...	|	|	|	|
322		**Magdeburg** Hbf ‡ a.	|	...	|	|	0658	|	...	|	|	0757	...	|	|	|	|	0858	...	|	...	|	|	|	0957
324		**Magdeburg** Hbf ‡ d.	|	0626	|	|	0703	|	...	|	|	0803	...	|	|	|	|	0903	...	|	...	|	|	|	1003
372		Köthen ‡ d.	|	0655	|	|	0732	|	...	|	|	0832	...	|	|	|	|	|	...	|	...	|	|	|	1032
408		**Halle (Saale)** Hbf ‡ d.	|	0718	|	|	0755	|	...	|	|	0855	...	|	|	|	|	0953	*EC*	|	...	|	|	|	1055
426		Leipzig/Halle Flughafen ✈ ‡ a.	|	0729	|	|	0806	|	...	|	|	0906	...	|	|	|	|	1004	**241**	|	...	|	|	|	1106
446		**Leipzig** Hbf ‡ a.	|	0743	|	|	0820	|	...	|	|	0920	...	|	|	|	|	1018	①–⑥	|	...	|	|	|	1120
	32	Wolfsburg d.	|	...	0534	0620	...	0646s	...	0705	0705	...	...	0756	|	|	0818	...	w♦	|	...	0905	0905	0918	...
	107	Stendal **838** d.	|	...	0605	0648	...	|	...	0734	0734	...	...	0826	|	|	|	...	0848	|	...	|	|	|	...
	141	Rathenow **838** d.	|	...	|	|	...	|	...	|	|	...	...	0843	|	|	|	...	|	|	...	|	|	|	...
	199	**Berlin** Spandau **838** a.	|	...	0641	0722	...	0752	...	0807	0807	...	...	0907	0853	0853	0911	...	0923	0938	...	0956	0956	1009	...
	215	**Berlin** Hbf **838** a.	0422	...	0655	0736	...	0810	...	0821	0821	...	...	0921	0908	0908	0925	...	0937	0952	...	1010	1010	1023	...
	220	**Berlin** Ostbahnhof **838** a.	0434	...	0706	0748	...	0820	...	0832	0832	...	...	0932	0919	0919	0936	...	0946	1002	...	1021	1021	1034	...

	RE 14005	IC 2245	ICE 543	ICE 553	ICE 972	IC 2035	RE 14205	IC 2143	ICE 845	ICE 855	ICE 694	IC 2143	RE 14007	IC 141	ICE 545	ICE 555	ICE 976	IC 2037	RE 14207	IC 2141	ICE 847	ICE 857	ICE 692	IC 2141	RE 14009
		¶		①–⑥				①–⑥				①–⑥													
		🍷	✕	e A	✕♦	🍷		e🍷	✕	✕♦	✕	e🍷		🍷	✕	✕	✕	🍷♦		🍷	✕	✕	✕	🍷	
Bonn Hbf **800** d.	...	...	...	0625	...	...	...	...	...	0722	...	...	...	...	...	0825e	...	...	...	...	...	...	...	...	...
Köln/Bonn Flughafen ✈ **800** d.	...	...	...	|	...	...	...	...	0713	|	...	...	...	...	0813p	|	...	...	...	...	...	...	...	...	...
Köln Hbf **800** d.	...	...	0626	0649	...	...	...	0713	|	0749	...	...	...	...	|	0849	...	...	...	0913	...	0949	...	...	...
Wuppertal Hbf **800** d.	...	...	|	0717	...	...	...	0743	|	0817	...	...	...	...	|	0917	...	...	...	0943	...	1017	...	...	...
Hagen Hbf **800** d.	...	...	|	0735	...	...	...	0801	|	0835	...	...	...	...	|	0935	...	...	...	1001	...	1035	...	...	...
Düsseldorf Hbf **800 802** d.	...	...	0653	|	...	...	...	|	0753	|	...	...	...	...	0853	|	...	...	...	|	0953	|	...	...	...
Dortmund Hbf **800 802** d.	...	...	0748	|	...	...	...	0828	0848	|	...	...	...	...	0948	|	...	...	...	1028	1048	|	...	...	...
Hamm (Westf) **802** d.	...	...	0811	0811	...	...	...	0845	0911	0911	...	...	...	...	1011	1011	...	...	...	1045	1111	1111	...	...	...
Gütersloh Hbf **802** d.	...	...	|	|	...	...	...	0905	|	|	...	...	...	...	|	|	...	...	...	1105	|	|	...	...	...
Bielefeld Hbf **802** d.	...	...	0838	0838	...	...	0824	0917	0937	0937	...	...	...	...	1038	1038	...	...	1024	1117	1137	1137	...	...	...
Herford **802** d.	...	...	|	|	...	...	0833	0927	|	|	...	...	...	...	|	|	...	...	1033	1127	|	|	...	...	...
Amsterdam Centraal **22** ⊡ d.	...	...	|	|	...	...	|	|	|	|	...	...	...	0658z	|	|	...	...	|	|	|	|	...	...	...
Bad Bentheim **811** 🏛 d.	*0557*a	0721e	|	|	...	...	|	|	|	|	...	...	*0757*r	0931v	|	|	...	...	|	|	|	|	...	...	*0957*r
Rheine **811** d.	0638	0735e	|	|	...	...	|	|	|	|	...	...	0838	0945v	|	|	...	...	|	|	|	|	...	...	1038
Osnabrück Hbf **811** d.	0716	0806k	|	|	...	...	|	|	|	|	...	...	0916	1012v	|	|	...	...	|	|	|	|	...	...	1116
Bünde (Westf) **811** d.	0738	0826	|	|	...	...	|	|	|	|	...	...	0938	|	|	|	...	...	|	|	|	|	...	...	1138
Löhne (Westf) **802** d.	0750	|	|	|	...	...	0840	|	|	|	...	...	0950	|	|	|	...	...	1040	|	|	|	...	...	1150
Bad Oeynhausen **802** d.	0755	0839	|	|	...	...	0845	0937	|	|	...	...	0955	|	|	|	...	...	1045	1137	|	|	...	...	1155
Minden (Westf) **802** d.	0807	0849	|	|	...	...	0907t	0949	|	|	...	...	1007	1049v	|	|	...	...	1107t	1149	|	|	...	...	1207
Basel SBB **912** d.	|	|	|	|	...	...	|	|	|	|	...	...	|	|	|	|	0608	...	|	|	|	|	...	...	|
Stuttgart Hbf **930** d.	|	|	|	|	...	...	|	|	|	|	0651	...	|	|	|	|	|	...	|	|	|	|	0851	...	|
Frankfurt (Main) Hbf **900** d.	|	|	|	|	0713	...	|	|	|	|	0813	...	|	|	|	|	0913	...	|	|	|	|	1013	...	|
Oldenburg (Oldb) Hbf **813** d.	|	|	|	|	|	0735	|	|	|	|	|	...	|	|	|	|	|	0935	|	|	|	|	|	...	|
Bremen Hbf **813** d.	|	|	|	|	|	0809	|	|	|	|	|	...	|	|	|	|	|	1009	|	|	|	|	|	...	|
Hannover Hbf a.	0850	0918	0928	0928	|	0914	0950	1018	1028	1028	|	←	1050	1118v	1128	1128	|	1114	1150	1218	1228	1228	|	←	1250
Hannover Hbf d.	0855	0921	0931	0931	|	0936	0955	→	1031	1031	|	1036	1055	1121	1131	1131	|	1136	1155	→	1231	1231	|	1236	1255
Peine d.	0924	|	|	|	|	|	1024	...	|	|	|	|	1124	|	|	|	|	|	1224	...	|	|	|	|	1324
Braunschweig Hbf ‡ d.	0941	|	|	|	1000	1010	1041	...	|	|	1100	1111	1141	|	|	|	1200	1210	1241	...	|	|	1300	1311	1341
Helmstedt ‡ d.	...	|	|	|	|	1032	...	...	|	|	|	|	...	|	|	|	|	1232	...	...	|	|	|	|	▬
Magdeburg Hbf ‡ a.	...	|	|	|	|	1058	...	...	|	|	|	1157	...	|	|	|	|	1258	...	...	|	|	|	1357	...
Magdeburg Hbf ‡ d.	...	|	|	|	|	1103	...	...	|	|	|	1203	...	|	|	|	|	1303	...	...	|	|	|	1403	...
Köthen ‡ d.	...	|	|	|	|	|	...	...	|	|	|	1232	...	|	|	|	|	|	...	...	|	|	|	1432	...
Halle (Saale) Hbf ‡ d.	...	|	|	|	|	1153	...	...	|	|	|	1255	...	|	|	|	|	1353	...	...	|	|	|	1455	*IC*
Leipzig/Halle Flughafen ✈ ‡ a.	...	|	|	|	|	1204	...	...	|	|	|	1306	...	|	|	|	|	1404	...	...	|	|	|	1506	**1931**
Leipzig Hbf ‡ a.	...	|	|	|	|	1218	...	...	|	|	|	1320	...	|	|	|	|	1418	...	...	|	|	|	1520	⑤f
Wolfsburg d.	...	0956	|	|	1018	...	...	...	1105	1105	|	...	...	1156	|	|	1218	...	...	...	1305	1305	|	...	U
Stendal **838** d.	...	1026	|	|	|	...	...	...	|	|	|	...	...	1226	|	|	|	...	...	...	|	|	|	...	1412
Rathenow **838** d.	...	1043	|	|	|	...	...	...	|	|	|	...	...	1243	|	|	|	...	...	...	|	|	|	...	|
Berlin Spandau **838** a.	...	1107	1053	1053	1111	...	...	...	1156	1156	1205	...	...	1307	1253	1253	1311	...	...	...	1356	1356	1405	...	1450
Berlin Hbf **838** a.	...	1121	1108	1108	1125	...	...	...	1210	1210	1219	...	...	1321	1308	1308	1325	...	...	...	1410	1410	1419	...	1459
Berlin Ostbahnhof **838** a.	...	1132	1119	1119	1136	...	...	...	1221	1221	1230	...	...	1332	1319	1319	1336	...	...	...	1421	1421	1430	...	...

♦ – **NOTES** (LISTED BY TRAIN NUMBER)

241 – WAWEL – (12) and ✕ Hamburg - Uelzen - Berlin - Cottbus - Forst 🏛 - Wrocław - Kraków.
347 – JAN KIEPURA – 🛏 1, 2 cl., ▬ 2 cl. and (2) Amsterdam - Köln - Warszawa (Table **24**); 🛏 1, 2 cl. Amsterdam - Köln - Moskva (Table **24**); 🛏 1, 2 cl., ▬ 2 cl. and (2) (*CNL* **379** – KOPERNIKUS) Amsterdam - Köln - Dresden - Praha (Table **28**).
855 – (12) and ✕ Trier - Koblenz - Berlin.
972 – (12) and ✕ (Basel Bad. Bf ①**g** -) Karlsruhe - Mannheim - Frankfurt - Berlin.
974 – (12) and ✕ (Frankfurt ①**g** -) Kassel - Berlin.
1243 – BERLINER – 🛏 1, 2 cl., ▬ 2 cl., (2) (reclining) and ✕ Zürich - Berlin. Also calls at Berlin Zoo (a. 0803).
2037 – (12) and 🍷 Norddeich Mole - Emden - Oldenburg - Leipzig.

k – 0803 on ⑦ (also Dec. 25, 26, Jan. 1, Mar. 22, 24, May 12).
p – ①–⑥ only.
r – ⚒ only.
s – Stops to set down only.
t – Arrives 10 minutes earlier.
v – Not Dec. 25, Jan. 1.
w – Not Dec. 25, 26, 31, Jan. 1, Mar. 22, 24, May 12.
x – Frankfurt (Main) **Süd**.
z – Not Dec. 25, Jan. 1. Amsterdam **Zuid**.

A – (12) and ✕ Koblenz Hbf (d. 0547) - Berlin.
D – From Darmstadt Hbf (d. 0543).
H – Runs daily Hannover - Braunschweig.
L – From Kassel (Table **900**).
M – From Münster (Table **800**).
R – To Dresden (Table **842**).
U – From Uelzen (Table **841**).

a – Ⓐ (not Dec. 24, 31).
d – Not Dec. 24, 25, 26, 31, Jan. 1, Mar. 21, 24, May 12.
e – ①–⑥ (not Dec. 25, 26, Jan. 1, Mar. 22, 24, May 12).
f – Also Mar. 20, Apr. 30; not Dec. 28, Mar. 31, May 2.
g – ① (also Dec. 27, Jan. 2, Mar. 25, May 13; not Dec. 24, 31, Mar. 24, May 12).
h – Not Dec. 24, 25, 26, 31, Jan. 1, Mar. 22, 24, May 12.

¶ – Train number **2345** on ⑦ (also Dec. 25, 26, Jan. 1, Mar. 22, 24, May 12).
⚡ – [R] and 'Sprinter' supplement payable.
‡ – See panel on page 379 for additional local services.
⊡ – Amsterdam timings are subject to alteration on Apr. 30.

HAMM and BAD BENTHEIM - HANNOVER - BERLIN and LEIPZIG 810

	IC 2247	*ICE* 547	*ICE* 557	*ICE* 278	*IC* 2039	*RE* 14209	*IC* 1818	*IC* 2049	*ICE* 849	*ICE* 859	*ICE* 690	*IC* 2049	*RE* 14011	*IC* 143	*ICE* 549	*ICE* 559	*ICE* 372	*IC* 2131	*IC* 2239	*RE* 14211	*IC* 2047	*ICE* 941	*ICE* 951	*ICE* 108	*IC* 2047
							⑤f												R		Ⓑk				
	M🍷	✕	✕	A✕	🍷		T🍷	🍷	✕	✕	✕	🍷		S🍷	✕	✕	A✕	L🍷	🍷		🍷	✕	✕	✕	🍷
Bonn Hbf **800** d.	...	...	...	...	...	...	1022	...	...	...	...	...	...	...	...	1223**e**	...	...	...	...	...	...	...	...	...
Köln/Bonn Flughafen ✈ **800** d.	...	1012**a**	...	...	...	...	|	...	...	...	...	...	...	...	1212	|	...	...	...	...	...	...	...	...	...
Köln Hbf **800** d.	...	|	1049	...	...	...	1045	1113	...	1149	...	...	...	...	|	1249	...	...	...	...	1313	...	1349	...	...
Wuppertal Hbf **800** d.	...	|	1117	...	...	...	|	1143	...	1217	...	...	...	...	|	1317	...	...	...	...	1343	...	1417	...	...
Hagen Hbf **800** d.	...	|	1135	...	...	...	|	1201	...	1235	...	...	...	...	|	1335	...	...	...	...	1401	...	1435	...	...
Düsseldorf Hbf **800 802** d.	...	1053	|	...	...	...	1117	|	1153	|	...	...	...	...	1253	|	...	...	...	...	|	1353	|	...	...
Dortmund Hbf **800 802** d.	...	1148	|	...	...	...	1210	1228	1248	|	...	...	...	...	1348	|	...	...	...	...	1428	1448	|	...	...
Hamm (Westf) **802** d.	...	1211	1211	...	...	...	1234	1245	1311	1311	...	...	...	...	1411	1411	...	...	...	...	1445	1511	1511	...	...
Gütersloh Hbf **802** d.	...	|	|	...	...	...	1255	1305	|	|	...	...	...	...	|	|	...	...	...	...	1505	|	|	...	...
Bielefeld Hbf **802** d.	...	1238	1238	...	...	1224	1306	1317	1337	1337	...	...	...	...	1438	1438	...	...	...	1424	1517	1537	1537	...	...
Herford **802** d.	...	|	|	...	...	1233	1315	1327	|	|	...	...	...	...	|	|	...	...	...	1433	1527	|	|	...	...
Amsterdam Centraal **22** ⊡ d.	...	|	|	...	...	|	|	|	|	|	...	...	...	1057	|	|	...	...	...	|	|	|	|	...	...
Bad Bentheim **811** 🏛 d.	...	|	|	...	...	|	|	|	|	|	...	...	*1157*r	1331	|	|	...	...	...	|	|	|	|	...	...
Rheine **811** d.	...	|	|	...	...	|	|	|	|	|	...	...	1238	1345	|	|	...	...	...	|	|	|	|	...	...
Osnabrück Hbf **811** d.	1203	|	|	...	...	|	|	|	|	|	...	...	1316	1412	|	|	...	...	...	|	|	|	|	...	...
Bünde (Westf) **811** d.	1226	|	|	...	...	|	|	|	|	|	...	...	1338	|	|	|	...	...	...	|	|	|	|	...	...
Löhne (Westf) **802** d.	|	|	|	...	...	1240	|	|	|	|	...	...	1350	|	|	|	...	...	...	1440	|	|	|	...	...
Bad Oeynhausen **802** d.	1239	|	|	...	...	1245	|	1337	|	|	...	...	1355	|	|	|	...	...	...	1445	1537	|	|	...	...
Minden (Westf) **802** d.	1249	|	|	...	...	1307**t**	|	1349	|	|	...	...	1407	1449	|	|	...	...	...	1507**t**	1549	|	|	...	...
Basel SBB **912** d.	|	|	|	0812	...	|	|	|	|	|	...	...	|	|	|	|	1012	...	...	|	|	|	|	...	...
Stuttgart Hbf **930** d.	|	|	|	|	...	|	|	|	|	|	1051	...	|	|	|	|	|	...	...	|	|	|	|	1251	...
Frankfurt (Main) Hbf **900** d.	|	|	|	1113	...	|	|	|	|	|	1213	...	|	|	|	|	1313	...	...	|	|	|	|	1413	...
Oldenburg (Oldb) Hbf **813** d.	|	|	|	|	1135	|	|	|	|	|	|	...	|	|	|	|	|	1335	...	|	|	|	|	|	...
Bremen Hbf **813** d.	|	|	|	|	1209	|	|	|	|	|	|	...	|	|	|	|	|	1409	...	|	|	|	|	|	...
Hannover Hbf a.	1318	1328	1328	|	1314	1350	1359	1418	1428	1428	|	←	1450	1518	1528	1528	|	1514	...	1550	1618	1628	1628	|	←
Hannover Hbf d.	1321	1331	1331	|	1336	1355	1402	→	1431	1431	|	1436	1455	1521	1531	1531	|	1536	...	1555	→	1631	1631	|	1636
Peine d.	|	|	|	|	|	1424	|	...	|	|	|	|	1524	|	|	|	|	|	...	1624	...	|	|	|	|
Braunschweig Hbf ‡ d.	|	|	|	1400	1410	1441	|	...	|	|	1500	1511	1541	|	|	|	1600	1610	...	1641	...	|	|	1700	1711
Helmstedt ‡ d.	|	|	|	|	1432	...	|	...	|	|	|	|	...	|	|	|	|	1632	...	...	...	|	|	|	|
Magdeburg Hbf ‡ a.	|	|	|	|	1458	...	|	...	|	|	|	1557	...	|	|	|	|	1658	...	...	...	|	|	|	1757
Magdeburg Hbf ‡ d.	|	|	|	|	1503	...	|	...	|	|	|	1603	...	|	|	|	|	1700	1704	...	...	|	|	|	1803
Köthen ‡ d.	|	|	|	|	|	...	|	...	|	|	|	1632	...	|	|	|	|	|	1732	...	...	|	|	|	1832
Halle (Saale) Hbf ‡ d.	|	|	|	|	1553	...	|	...	|	|	|	1655	...	|	|	|	|	|	1755	...	...	|	|	|	1855
Leipzig/Halle Flughafen ✈ ‡ a.	|	|	|	|	1604	...	|	...	|	|	|	1706	...	|	|	|	|	|	1806	...	...	|	|	|	1906
Leipzig Hbf ‡ a.	|	|	|	|	1618	...	|	...	|	|	|	1720	...	|	|	|	|	|	1820	...	...	|	|	|	1920
Wolfsburg d.	1356	|	|	1418	...	...	1437	...	1505	1505	|	...	...	1556	|	|	1618	|	...	...	...	1705	1705	|	...
Stendal **838** d.	1426	|	|	|	...	...	|	...	|	|	|	...	...	1626	|	|	|	|	...	...	...	|	|	|	...
Rathenow **838** d.	1443	|	|	|	...	...	|	...	|	|	|	...	...	1643	|	|	|	|	...	...	...	|	|	|	...
Berlin Spandau **838** a.	1507	1453	1453	1511	...	...	1540	...	1556	1556	1605	...	...	1707	1653	1653	1711	|	...	...	...	1756	1756	1805	...
Berlin Hbf **838** a.	1521	1508	1508	1526	...	...	1550	...	1610	1610	1619	...	...	1717	1708	1708	1725	1826	...	...	...	1810	1810	1819	...
Berlin Ostbahnhof **838** a.	1532	1519	1519	1537	...	...	...	...	1621	1621	1630	...	...	...	1719	1719	1736	1838	...	...	...	1821	1821	1829	...

	RE 14013	*IC* 2449	*ICE* 641	*ICE* 651	*ICE* 272	*IC* 2133	*RE* 14213	*IC* 1926	*IC* 2010	*IC* 2045	*ICE* 943	*ICE* 953	*ICE* 596	*IC* 2045	*RE* 14015	*IC* 145	*ICE* 643	*ICE* 653	*ICE* 276	*IC* 2135	*RE* 14215	*ICE* 1090	*IC* 2012	*ICE* 945	*ICE* 955
								⑦w	⑤f			Ⓑq					n	n				Ⓑq			Ⓑq
		M🍷	✕	✕	A✕	🍷		F	T	🍷	✕	✕	✕	🍷		🍷	✕	✕	A✕	N🍷		✕⚡	G🍷	✕	✕
Bonn Hbf **800** d.	...	...	...	1425	...	...	...	1422	1422	...	...	...	...	...	...	...	...	...	...	...	...	...	1622	...	...
Köln/Bonn Flughafen ✈ **800** d.	...	...	...	|	...	...	...	|	|	...	...	...	...	...	...	...	1612	...	...	...	...	...	|	...	...
Köln Hbf **800** d.	...	...	...	1449	...	...	...	1445	1445	1513	...	1549	...	...	...	...	|	1649	...	...	...	...	1648	...	1749
Wuppertal Hbf **800** d.	...	...	...	1517	...	...	...	|	|	1543	...	1617	...	...	...	...	|	1717	...	...	...	...	|	...	1817
Hagen Hbf **800** d.	...	...	...	1535	...	...	...	|	|	1601	...	1635	...	...	...	...	|	1735	...	...	...	...	|	...	1835
Düsseldorf Hbf **800 802** d.	...	...	1453	|	...	...	...	1518	1518	|	1553	|	...	...	...	...	1653	|	...	...	...	...	1714	1753	|
Dortmund Hbf **800 802** d.	...	...	1548	|	...	...	...	1608	1608	1628	1648	|	...	...	...	...	1748	|	...	...	...	...	1828	1848	|
Hamm (Westf) **802** d.	...	...	1611	1611	...	...	...	1631	1634	1645	1711	1711	...	...	...	...	1811	1811	...	...	...	...	1845	1911	1911
Gütersloh Hbf **802** d.	...	...	|	|	...	...	...	1655	1655	1705	|	|	...	...	...	...	|	|	...	...	...	...	1905	|	|
Bielefeld Hbf **802** d.	...	...	1638	1638	...	...	1624	1706	1706	1717	1737	1737	...	...	...	...	1838	1838	...	...	1824	...	1917	1937	1937
Herford **802** d.	...	...	|	|	...	...	1633	1715	1715	1727	|	|	...	...	...	...	|	|	...	...	1833	...	1927	|	|
Amsterdam Centraal **22** ⊡ d.	...	...	|	|	...	...	|	|	|	|	|	|	...	...	...	1458**z**	|	|	...	...	|	...	|	|	|
Bad Bentheim **811** 🏛 d.	*1357*	...	|	|	...	...	|	|	|	|	|	|	...	...	*1557*	1731	|	|	...	...	|	...	|	|	|
Rheine **811** d.	1438	...	|	|	...	...	|	|	|	|	|	|	...	...	1638	1745	|	|	...	...	|	...	|	|	|
Osnabrück Hbf **811** d.	1516	1603	|	|	...	...	|	|	|	|	|	|	...	...	1716	1812	|	|	...	...	|	...	|	|	|
Bünde (Westf) **811** d.	1538	1626	|	|	...	...	|	|	|	|	|	|	...	...	1738	|	|	|	...	...	|	...	|	|	|
Löhne (Westf) **802** d.	1550	|	|	|	...	...	1640	|	|	|	|	|	...	...	1750	|	|	|	...	...	1840	...	|	|	|
Bad Oeynhausen **802** d.	1555	1639	|	|	...	...	1645	|	|	1737	|	|	...	...	1755	|	|	|	...	...	1845	...	1937	|	|
Minden (Westf) **802** d.	1607	1649	|	|	...	...	1707**t**	|	|	1749	|	|	...	...	1807	1849	|	|	...	...	1907**t**	...	1949	|	|
Basel SBB **912** d.	|	|	|	|	1212	...	|	|	|	|	|	|	...	...	|	|	|	|	1412	...	|	...	|	|	|
Stuttgart Hbf **930** d.	|	|	|	|	|	...	|	|	|	|	|	|	1451	...	|	|	|	|	|	...	|	1651	|	|	|
Frankfurt (Main) Hbf **900** d.	|	|	|	|	1513	...	|	|	|	|	|	|	1613	...	|	|	|	|	1713	...	|	1813	|	|	|
Oldenburg (Oldb) Hbf **813** d.	|	|	|	|	|	1535	|	|	|	|	|	|	|	...	|	|	|	|	|	1735	|	|	|	|	|
Bremen Hbf **813** d.	|	|	|	|	|	1609	|	|	|	|	|	|	|	...	|	|	|	|	|	1809	|	|	|	|	|
Hannover Hbf a.	1650	1718	1728	1728	|	1714	1750	1759	1759	1818	1828	1828	|	←	1850	1918	1928	1928	|	1914	1950	|	2018	2028	2028
Hannover Hbf d.	1655	1721	1731	1731	|	1736	1755	1802	1802	→	1831	1831	|	1836	1855	1921	1931	1931	|	1936	1955	|	→	2031	2031
Peine d.	1724	|	|	|	|	|	1824	|	|	...	|	|	|	|	1924	|	|	|	|	|	2024	|	...	|	|
Braunschweig Hbf ‡ d.	1741	|	|	|	1800	1810	1841	|	|	...	|	|	1900	1911	1941	|	|	|	2000	2010	2041	|	...	|	|
Helmstedt ‡ d.	...	|	|	|	|	1832	...	|	|	...	|	|	|	|	...	|	|	|	|	2032	...	|	...	|	|
Magdeburg Hbf ‡ d.	...	|	|	|	|	1858	...	|	|	...	|	|	|	1957	...	|	|	|	|	2058	...	|	...	|	|
Magdeburg Hbf ‡ d.	...	|	|	|	|	1903	...	|	|	...	|	|	|	2003**b**	...	|	|	|	|	2103	...	|	...	|	|
Köthen ‡ d.	...	|	|	|	|	|	...	|	|	...	|	|	|	2032**b**	...	|	|	|	|	2132	...	|	...	|	|
Halle (Saale) Hbf ‡ d.	...	|	|	|	|	1953	...	|	|	...	|	|	|	2055**b**	...	|	|	|	|	2155	...	|	...	|	|
Leipzig/Halle Flughafen ✈ ‡ a.	...	|	|	|	|	2004	...	|	|	...	|	|	|	2106**b**	...	|	|	|	|	2206	...	|	...	|	|
Leipzig Hbf ‡ a.	...	|	|	|	|	2018	...	|	|	...	|	|	|	2120**b**	...	|	|	|	|	2220	...	|	...	|	|
Wolfsburg d.	...	1756	|	|	1818	...	...	1837	1837	...	1905	1905	|	...	...	1956	|	|	2018	...	...	|	...	2105	2105
Stendal **838** d.	...	1826	|	|	|	...	...	|	|	...	|	|	|	...	...	2026	|	|	|	...	...	|	...	2134	2134
Rathenow **838** d.	...	1843	|	|	|	...	...	|	|	...	|	|	|	...	...	2043	|	|	|	...	...	|	...	|	|
Berlin Spandau **838** a.	...	1907	1853	1853	1911	...	...	1940	1940	...	1956	1956	2005	...	...	2107	2053	2053	2111	...	...	2137	...	2206	2206
Berlin Hbf **838** a.	...	1921	1908	1908	1925	...	...	1951	1952	...	2010	2010	2019	...	...	2121	2108	2108	2125	...	...	2147	...	2221	2221
Berlin Ostbahnhof **838** a.	...	1932	1919	1919	1936	...	...	...	...	...	2021	2021	2030	...	...	2132	2119	2119	2136	...	...	2156	...	2231	2231

A – From Interlaken via Bern (Table **560**).
F – From Frankfurt (Table **912**).
G – ALLGÄU – (12) and 🍷 Oberstdorf - Stuttgart - Köln - Hannover (- Leipzig ⑤⑦ **p**).
L – OSTFRIESLAND – (12) and 🍷 Emden - Magdeburg - Berlin (- Cottbus Ⓑ **q**). Also calls at Brandenburg Hbf (a. 1740), Potsdam Hbf (a. 1759) and Berlin Wannsee (a. 1808).
M – From Münster (Table **800**).
N – From Norddeich Mole on dates in Table **813**.
R – Ⓑ (daily to Mar. 14). From Warnemünde via Rostock and Schwerin on ⑤⑦ from Mar. 14 (Tables **830**, **837** and **841**).
S – To Szczecin (Table **845**).
T – From Stuttgart (Tables **800/912**).

a – ①–⑤ only.
b – Ⓑ (not Dec. 24, 25, 31, Mar. 23, May 11).
e – ①–⑥ (not Dec. 25, 26, Jan. 1, Mar. 22, 24, May 12).
f – Also Mar. 20, Apr. 30, May 21; not Mar. 21, May 2, 23.
k – Also Dec. 29, Mar. 22, May 3; not Mar. 21, May 1.
m – Also Dec. 24, 31.
n – Not Dec. 24, 31.
p – Also Dec. 26, Jan. 1, Mar. 20, 24, Apr. 30, May 12; not Dec. 23, 30, Mar. 21, 23, May 2, 11.
q – Not Dec. 24, 25, 31, Mar. 21, 23, May 11.
r – ⚒ only.
s – Also Dec. 24, 31; not May 1.
t – Arrives 10 minutes earlier.
v – Also May 1; not Dec. 24, 31.
w – Also Dec. 26, Jan. 1, Mar. 24, May 12; not Dec. 23, 30, Mar. 23, May 11.
z – Amsterdam **Zuid**.

⚡ – 🅁 and 'Sprinter' supplement payable.
⊡ – Amsterdam timings are subject to alteration on Apr. 30.
‡ – See below for additional *RE*/*RB* services:

	Ⓐn			Ⓐn		Ⓐn
Braunschweig Hbf d.	0617	0717	then hourly on Ⓐn,	2017	2117**n**	2217
Helmstedt d.	0644	0744	every **two** hours	2044	2144	2244
Magdeburg Hbf a.	0726	0826	on Ⓒ**m** until	2126	2226	2326

	Ⓐn	Ⓐn	Ⓐv	Ⓒs			
Magdeburg Hbf d.	0413	0507	0555	0607	0707	and	2207
Köthen d.	0447	0547	0635	0647	0747	hourly	2247
Halle (Saale) Hbf a.	0515	0615	0702	0715	0815	until	2315

Halle (Saale) Hbf d.	0442	0522	and at the same	2222	2244	2324
Leipzig/Halle Flughafen ✈ d.	0454	|	minutes past	|	2256	2336
Leipzig Hbf a.	0508	0559	each hour until	2259	2310	2351

810 HAMM and BAD BENTHEIM - HANNOVER - BERLIN and LEIPZIG

	IC	ICE	RE	IC	IC	ICE	ICE	ICE	IC	RB	RE	IC	ICE	ICE	ICE	RE	ICE	RE	ICE	ICE	ICE	ICE	RE	ICE	RB
	2012	594	14017	147	147	645	655	872	2137	36041	14217	2041	947	957	592	14019	710	14219	647	657	970	1743	14221	502	29783
	⑤⑦p	⑥h			⑤⑦j	n	n		Ⓑq	x		⑦w		Ⓑq			⑦w		⑦w	⑦w	⑦w	⑦w			n
	🍷♦	✕		🍷	🍷	✕	✕	✕				🍷	✕	✕	✕		B 🍷		✕	✕	✕			🍷♦	
Bonn Hbf **800** d.																				2025					
Köln/Bonn Flughafen ✈ **800** d.						1812b																			
Köln Hbf **800** d.							1849					1913		1949			2003d			2049				2111	
Wuppertal Hbf **800** d.							1917					1943		2017						2117				2143	
Hagen Hbf **800** d.							1935					2001		2035						2135				2201	
Düsseldorf Hbf **800 802** d.						1853							1953				2027		2053						
Dortmund Hbf **800 802** d.						1948						2028	2048				2132		2148					2228	
Hamm (Westf) **802** d.						2011	2011					2045	2111	2111			2149		2211	2211				2250	
Gütersloh Hbf **802** d.												2105					2209							2310	
Bielefeld Hbf **802** d.						2038	2038				2024	2117	2137	2137			2220	2224	2238	2238				2320	2327
Herford **802** d.											2033	2127						2233						2330	2336
Amsterdam Centraal **22** ⊡ d.				1658z	1658z																				
Bad Bentheim **811** 🏛 d.			*1757*b	1928	1928											*1957*a									
Rheine **811** d.			1838	1942	1942											2038									
Osnabrück Hbf **811** d.			1916	2009	2009											2116									
Bünde (Westf) **811** d.			1938	2029	2029											2138									
Löhne (Westf) **802** d.			1950								2040					2150		2240							2343
Bad Oeynhausen **802** d.			1955								2045	2137				2155		2245							2348
Minden (Westf) **802** d.			2007	2049	2049						2107t	2149				2207	2247	2257						2346	2359
Basel SBB **912** d.								1612													1812				
Stuttgart Hbf **930** d.		1651													1851										
Frankfurt (Main) Hbf **900** d.		1813						1913							2013						2113				
Oldenburg (Oldb) Hbf **813** d.									1935																
Bremen Hbf **813** d.									2009																
Hannover Hbf a.	←		2050	2118	2118	2128	2128		2114		2150	2218	2228	2228		2250	2317		2328	2328				0026	
Hannover Hbf d.	2036		2055		2121	2131	2131		2136		2155		2231	2231		2255			2331	2331		2350	0011		
Peine d.			2124						2157		2224					2324							0038		
Braunschweig Hbf ‡ d.	2111	2100	2141					2200	2213		2241				2300	2341					2359	0026	0055		
Helmstedt ‡ d.									2236														*0130*v		
Magdeburg Hbf ‡ a.	2157								2302													0114	*0212*v		
Magdeburg Hbf ‡ d.	2203									2308															
Köthen ‡ d.	2235									2348															
Halle (Saale) Hbf ‡ d.	2258									0016															
Leipzig/Halle Flughafen ✈ ‡ a.	2309																								
Leipzig Hbf ‡ a.	2323									*0133*															
Wolfsburg d.		2118			2156			2218					2305	2305	2318				0005	0005	0018				
Stendal **838** d.					2226								2334	2334											
Rathenow **838** d.					2243																				
Berlin Spandau **838** a.		2211			2307	2253	2253	2311					0006	0006	0012				0057	0057	0110				
Berlin Hbf **838** a.		2226			2321	2308	2308	2325					0020	0020	0027				0111	0111	0124				
Berlin Ostbahnhof **838** a.		2237			2332	2319	2319	2336					0031	0031	0038				0122	0122	0135				

km		EN	ICE	ICE	RE	ICE	ICE	ICE	RE	IC	IC	ICE	RE	IC	ICE	ICE	ICE	IC	ICE	RE	IC	ICE	ICE	ICE	IC
		346	948	527	14002	503	656	646	14202	2136	146	375	14004	2013	593	956	946	2013	1091	14204	2134	277	654	644	2248
		Ⓡ	①g	①g	⚒		①–⑤	①–⑤	⚒H	①–⑤		①–⑤		①–⑥	⑥⑦	①–⑥	①–⑥		①–⑤						①–⑥
		🍷♦		♦		🍷♦	k✕	k✕		k	🍷	k A		e♦	s✕	e✕	e✕	🍷♦	k ⚡		🍷♦	A✕	✕	✕	e M
0	**Berlin** Ostbahnhof **838** d.	0022	0027				0417	0417				0422			0523	0528	0528		✕			0622	0640	0640	0628
5	**Berlin** Hbf **838** d.	0032	0037				0428	0428				0433			0534	0538	0538		0608			0633	0651	0651	0638
21	**Berlin** Spandau **838** d.		0051				0442	0442				0447			0548	0552	0552		0618			0647	0705	0705	0652
79	Rathenow **838** d.																								0716
113	Stendal **838** d.		0125				0517	0517								0626	0626								0734
188	Wolfsburg d.		0155				0546	0546				0540			0640	0655	0655					0740			0805
	Leipzig Hbf ‡ d.													0437y							0540k				
	Leipzig/Halle Flughafen ✈ ‡ d.													0450y							0553k				
	Halle (Saale) Hbf ‡ d.													0503y							0606k				
	Köthen ‡ d.													0526y							0628k				
	Magdeburg Hbf ‡ a.													0556y							0656k				
	Magdeburg Hbf ‡ d.									0500				0600							0700				
	Helmstedt ‡ d.									0528				0628						0646a	0728				
	Braunschweig Hbf ‡ d.				0420				0520	0551		0558	0620	0650	0658					0720	0751	0758			
	Peine d.				0437				0537	0606			0637							0737					
263	**Hannover** Hbf a.		0228		0505		0618	0618	0605	0627			0705	0723		0728	0728	←		0805	0823		0828	0828	0837
263	**Hannover** Hbf d.		0231	0410	0509	0540	0621	0621	0609	0645	0640		0709	→		0731	0731	0740		0809	0845		0831	0831	0840
	Bremen Hbf **813** a.									0751											0951				
	Oldenburg (Oldb) Hbf **813** a.									0822											1022				
	Frankfurt (Main) Hbf **900** a.											0844			0944				0942			1044			
	Stuttgart Hbf **930** a.														1108				1108						
	Basel SBB **912** a.											1147										1347			
328	Minden (Westf) **802** d.		0302	0447	0555	0612	0651	0651	0702		0712		0752					0812		0902t					0912
343	Bad Oeynhausen **802** d.				0607				0714				0804					0822		0914					0922
349	Löhne (Westf) **802** d.				0611				0719				0811							0919					
359	Bünde (Westf) **811** d.				0622						0731		0821												0935
396	**Osnabrück** Hbf **811** d.				0648						0752		0848												0958
444	Rheine **811** d.				0723						0820		0923												
465	Bad Bentheim **811** 🏛 a.				*0803*						0833		*1003*r												
647	*Amsterdam Centraal* **22** ⊡ a.										1101z														
	Herford **802** d.		0320	0504		0632	0710	0710	0727									0833		0927					
	Bielefeld Hbf **802** d.	0356	0330	0514		0641	0720	0720	0736							0822	0822	0842		0936			0922	0922	
	Gütersloh Hbf **802** d.		0340	0524		0651												0852							
	Hamm (Westf) **802** a.	0425	0359	0548		0712	0748	0748								0848	0848	0912					0948	0948	
	Dortmund Hbf **800 802** a.	0448	0418	0610		0732		0809									0909	0932						1009	
	Düsseldorf Hbf **800 802** a.	0654	0513	0719				0905									1005	1045						1105	
	Hagen Hbf **800** a.	0521				0755	0822									0922							1022		
	Wuppertal Hbf **800** a.	0539				0812	0839									0939							1039		
	Köln Hbf **800** a.	0614	0540	0742d		0846	0909									1009		1112					1109		
	Köln/Bonn Flughafen ✈ **800** d.		0604					0942																1142	
	Bonn Hbf **800** a.																	1135					1132e		

♦ – **NOTES** (LISTED BY TRAIN NUMBER)

346 – JAN KIEPURA – 🛏 1, 2 cl., ▬ 2 cl. and (2) Warszawa - Köln - Amsterdam (Table **24**); 🛏 1, 2 cl. Moskva - Köln - Amsterdam (Table **24**); 🛏 1, 2 cl., ▬ 2 cl. and (2) (*CNL* **378** – KOPERNIKUS) Praha - Dresden - Köln - Amsterdam (Table **28**).
502/3 – (12) and 🍷 Basel - Karlsruhe - Köln - Hannover and v.v.
527 – WETTERSTEIN – (12) and ✕ Hannover - Köln - Frankfurt - Nürnberg - München.
2012 – ALLGÄU – (12) and 🍷 Oberstdorf - Köln - Hannover (- Leipzig ⑤⑦**p**).
2013 – ALLGÄU – (12) and 🍷 (Leipzig ①⑥**y** -) (Magdeburg ①–⑥**e** -) Hannover - Köln - Oberstdorf.
2134 – (12) and 🍷 (Leipzig ①–⑤**k** -) Magdeburg - Oldenburg - Emden.

A – To Interlaken via Bern (Table **560**).
B – From Wiesbaden (Table **910**).
H – Runs daily Braunschweig - Hannover.
M – To Münster (Table **800**). Conveys 🍷.

a – Ⓐ (not Dec. 24, 31).
b – Ⓑ (not Dec. 24, 31).
d – Köln **Messe/Deutz**.
e – ①–⑥ (not Dec. 25, 26, Jan. 1, Mar. 22, 24, May 12).
g – Also Dec. 27, Jan. 2, Mar. 25, May 13; not Dec. 24, 31, Mar. 24, May 12.
h – Also Dec. 24, 25, 31, Mar. 21, 23, May 11.
j – Also Dec. 26, Jan. 1, Mar. 20, 24, Apr. 30, May 12; not Dec. 23, 28, 30, Mar. 21, 23, May 11.
k – ①–⑤ (not Dec. 24, 25, 26, 31, Jan. 1, Mar. 21, 24, May 12).
n – Not Dec. 24, 31.
p – Also Dec. 26, Jan. 1, Mar. 20, 24, Apr. 30, May 12; not Dec. 23, 30, Mar. 21, 23, May 2, 11.
q – Not Dec. 24, 25, 31, Mar. 21, 23, May 11.
r – ⚒ only.
s – Also Dec. 24, 25, 26, 31, Jan. 1, Mar. 21, 24, May 12.
t – Arrives 9–10 minutes earlier.
v – ⑦ only.
w – Also Dec. 26, Jan. 1, Mar. 24, May 12; not Dec. 23, 30, Mar. 23, May 11.
x – Not Dec. 24, 25, 31.
y – ①⑥ (also Dec. 27, Jan. 2, Mar. 21, 26, May 1, 13; not Dec. 24, 31, Mar. 22, 24, May 3, 12).
z – Amsterdam **Zuid**.

⚡ – Ⓡ and 'Sprinter' supplement payable.
‡ – See panels on pages 379 and 381 for additional local services.
⊡ – Amsterdam timings are subject to alteration on Apr. 30.

LEIPZIG and BERLIN - HANNOVER - BAD BENTHEIM and HAMM 810

	RE 14006	*IC* 2044	*ICE* 595	*ICE* 954	*ICE* 944	*IC* 2044	*RE* 14206	*IC* 2238	*IC* 2132	*ICE* 875	*ICE* 652	*ICE* 642	*IC* 144	*RE* 14008	*IC* 2046	*ICE* 597	*ICE* 952	*ICE* 942	*IC* 2046	*IC* 2017	*IC* 2017	*RE* 14208	*IC* 2130	*ICE* 373	*ICE* 650
				①–⑥	①–⑥			R							①–⑥		n		①–⑥	⑦w	⑤f				
		🍷	✕	e✕	e✕	🍷		🍷	O🍷	✕	✕	✕	S🍷		e🍷	✕	✕	✕	e🍷	T🍷	L🍷		🍷	A✕	✕
Berlin Ostbahnhof **838** d.	...	...	0726	0738	0738	...	...	...	0721	0821	0840	0840	...	...	...	0926	0938	0938	...	...	...	...	...	1022	1040
Berlin Hbf **838** d.	...	...	0737	0748	0748	...	...	...	0732	0832	0851	0851	0839	...	...	0937	0948	0948	...	1010	...	...	...	1033	1051
Berlin Spandau **838** d.	...	...	0751	0802	0802	...	...	...	|	0846	0905	0905	0849	...	...	0951	1002	1002	...	1019	...	...	...	1047	1105
Rathenow **838** d.	...	...	|	|	|	...	...	...	|	|	|	|	0913	...	...	|	|	|	...	|	...	...	...	|	|
Stendal **838** d.	...	...	|	|	|	...	...	...	|	|	|	|	0935	...	...	|	|	|	...	|	...	...	...	|	|
Wolfsburg d.	...	...	|	0855	0855	...	...	...	|	0940	|	|	1005	...	...	|	1055	1055	...	1121	...	...	...	1140	|
Leipzig Hbf ‡ d.	...	0640	|	|	|	...	...	0740	|	|	|	|	|	...	0840	|	|	|	...	|	...	...	0942	|	|
Leipzig/Halle Flughafen ✈ ‡ d.	...	0653	|	|	|	...	...	0753	|	|	|	|	|	...	0853	|	|	|	...	|	...	...	0955	|	|
Halle (Saale) Hbf ‡ d.	...	0706	|	|	|	...	...	0806	|	|	|	|	|	...	0906	|	|	|	...	|	...	...	1008	|	|
Köthen ‡ d.	...	0728	|	|	|	...	...	0828	|	|	|	|	|	...	0928	|	|	|	...	|	...	...	|	|	|
Magdeburg Hbf ‡ a.	...	0756	|	|	|	...	...	0854	0857	|	|	|	|	...	0956	|	|	|	...	|	...	...	1056	|	|
Magdeburg Hbf ‡ d.	...	0800	|	|	|	...	...	...	0900	|	|	|	|	...	1000	|	|	|	...	|	...	...	1100	|	|
Helmstedt ‡ d.	...	|	|	|	|	...	...	...	0928	|	|	|	|	...	|	|	|	|	...	|	...	...	1128	|	|
Braunschweig Hbf ‡ d.	0820	0850	0858	|	|	...	0920	...	0951	0958	|	|	|	1020	1050	1058	|	|	...	|	...	1120	1151	1158	|
Peine d.	0837	|	|	|	|	...	0937	...	|	|	|	|	|	1037	|	|	|	|	...	|	...	1137	|	|	|
Hannover Hbf a.	0905	0923	|	0928	0928	←	1005	...	1023	|	1028	1028	1037	1105	1123	|	1128	1128	←	1155	...	1205	1223	|	1228
Hannover Hbf d.	0909	→	|	0931	0931	0940	1009	...	1045	|	1031	1031	1040	1109	→	|	1131	1131	1140	1158	1158	1209	1245	|	1231
Bremen Hbf **813** a.	|	...	|	|	|	|	|	...	1151	|	|	|	|	|	...	|	|	|	|	|	|	|	1351	|	|
Oldenburg (Oldb) Hbf **813** a.	|	...	|	|	|	|	|	...	1222	|	|	|	|	|	...	|	|	|	|	|	|	|	1422	|	|
Frankfurt (Main) Hbf **900** a.	|	...	1144	|	|	|	|	...	...	1244	|	|	|	|	...	1344	|	|	|	|	|	|	...	1444	|
Stuttgart Hbf **930** a.	|	...	1308	|	|	|	|	...	...	|	|	|	|	|	...	1508	|	|	|	|	|	|	...	|	|
Basel SBB **912** a.	|	...	...	|	|	|	|	...	...	1547	|	|	|	|	...	...	|	|	|	|	|	|	...	1747	|
Minden (Westf) **802** d.	0952	...	...	|	|	1012	1102t	...	...	...	|	|	1112	1152	...	...	|	|	1212	|	|	1302t	...	...	|
Bad Oeynhausen **802** d.	1004	...	...	|	|	1022	1114	...	...	...	|	|	|	1204	...	...	|	|	1222	|	|	1314	...	...	|
Löhne (Westf) **802** d.	1011	...	...	|	|	|	1119	...	...	...	|	|	|	1211	...	...	|	|	|	|	|	1319	...	...	|
Bünde (Westf) **811** d.	1021	...	...	|	|	|	|	...	...	...	|	|	|	1221	...	...	|	|	|	|	|	|	...	...	|
Osnabrück Hbf **811** d.	1048	...	...	|	|	|	|	...	...	...	|	|	1150	1248	...	...	|	|	|	|	|	|	...	...	|
Rheine **811** d.	1123	...	...	|	|	|	|	...	...	...	|	|	1217	1323	...	...	|	|	|	|	|	|	...	...	|
Bad Bentheim **811** 🏛 a.	*1203*r	...	...	|	|	|	|	...	...	...	|	|	1230	*1403*	...	...	|	|	|	|	|	|	...	...	|
Amsterdam Centraal **22** ⊡ a.	...	...	...	|	|	|	|	...	...	...	|	|	1501z	...	...	...	|	|	|	|	|	|	...	...	|
Herford **802** d.	...	...	...	|	|	1033	1127	...	...	...	|	|	...	...	...	...	|	|	1233	1244	1244	1327	...	...	|
Bielefeld Hbf **802** d.	...	...	...	1022	1022	1042	1136	...	...	...	1122	1122	...	...	...	...	1222	1222	1242	1253	1253	1336	...	...	1322
Gütersloh Hbf **802** d.	...	...	...	|	|	1052	...	...	...	...	|	|	...	...	...	...	|	|	1252	1303	1303	...	...	...	|
Hamm (Westf) **802** a.	...	...	...	1048	1048	1112	...	...	...	...	1148	1148	...	...	...	...	1248	1248	1312	1323	1323	...	...	...	1348
Dortmund Hbf **800 802** a.	...	...	...	|	1109	1132	...	...	...	...	|	1209	...	...	...	...	|	1309	1332	1347	1347	...	...	...	|
Düsseldorf Hbf **800 802** a.	...	...	...	|	1205	|	...	...	...	...	|	1305	...	...	...	...	|	1405	|	1442	1442	...	...	...	|
Hagen Hbf **800** a.	...	...	...	1122	...	1155	...	...	...	...	1222	...	...	...	...	...	1322	|	1355	|	|	...	...	...	1422
Wuppertal Hbf **800** a.	...	...	...	1139	...	1212	...	...	...	...	1239	...	...	...	...	...	1339	|	1412	|	|	...	...	...	1439
Köln Hbf **800** a.	...	...	...	1209	...	1245	...	...	...	...	1309	...	...	...	...	...	1409	|	1445	1515	1515	...	...	...	1509
Köln/Bonn Flughafen ✈ **800** d.	...	...	...	...	...	...	...	...	...	...	|	...	...	...	...	...	...	1445	...	|	|	...	...	...	...
Bonn Hbf **800** a.	...	...	...	...	...	...	...	...	...	...	1332	...	...	...	...	...	...	...	...	1535	1535	...	...	...	...

	ICE 640	*IC* 2246	*RE* 14010	*IC* 2048	*ICE* 109	*ICE* 950	*ICE* 940	*IC* 2048	*IC* 2019	*RE* 14210	*IC* 2038	*ICE* 279	*ICE* 558	*ICE* 548	*IC* 142	*RE* 14012	*IC* 2140	*ICE* 691	*ICE* 858	*ICE* 848	*IC* 2140	*IC* 1946	*IC* 1842	*RE* 14212	*IC* 2036
						n			⑤⑦c				n						n			⑦w	⑤v		
	✕	M🍷		🍷	✕	✕	✕	🍷	T		🍷	A✕	✕	✕	🍷		🍷	✕	✕	✕	🍷	K🍷	🍷		N🍷
Berlin Ostbahnhof **838** d.	1040	1028	...	...	1126	1138	1138	...	...	...	...	1222	1240	1240	1228	...	...	1326	1338	1338	...	...	...	...	...
Berlin Hbf **838** d.	1051	1038	...	...	1137	1148	1148	...	1209	...	...	1233	1251	1251	1238	...	...	1337	1348	1348	...	1409	1409	...	...
Berlin Spandau **838** d.	1105	1052	...	...	1151	1202	1202	...	1219	...	...	1247	1305	1305	1252	...	...	1351	1402	1402	...	1419	1420	...	...
Rathenow **838** d.	|	1116	...	...	|	|	|	...	|	...	...	|	|	|	1316	...	...	|	|	|	...	|	|	...	...
Stendal **838** d.	|	1135	...	...	|	|	|	...	|	...	...	|	|	|	1335	...	...	|	|	|	...	|	|	...	...
Wolfsburg d.	|	1205	...	...	|	1255	1255	...	1321	...	...	1340	|	|	1405	...	...	|	1455	1455	...	1521	1521	...	...
Leipzig Hbf ‡ d.	|	|	...	1040	|	|	|	...	|	...	1142	|	|	|	|	...	1240	|	|	|	...	|	|	...	1342
Leipzig/Halle Flughafen ✈ ‡ d.	|	|	...	1053	|	|	|	...	|	...	1155	|	|	|	|	...	1253	|	|	|	...	|	|	...	1355
Halle (Saale) Hbf ‡ d.	|	|	...	1106	|	|	|	...	|	...	1208	|	|	|	|	...	1306	|	|	|	...	|	|	...	1408
Köthen ‡ d.	|	|	...	1128	|	|	|	...	|	...	|	|	|	|	|	...	1328	|	|	|	...	|	|	...	|
Magdeburg Hbf ‡ a.	|	|	...	1156	|	|	|	...	|	...	1256	|	|	|	|	...	1356	|	|	|	...	|	|	...	1456
Magdeburg Hbf ‡ d.	|	|	...	1200	|	|	|	...	|	...	1300	|	|	|	|	...	1400	|	|	|	...	|	|	...	1500
Helmstedt ‡ d.	|	|	...	|	|	|	|	...	|	...	1328	|	|	|	|	...	|	|	|	|	...	|	|	...	1528
Braunschweig Hbf ‡ d.	|	|	1220	1250	1258	|	|	...	|	1320	1351	1358	|	|	|	1420	1450	1458	|	|	...	|	|	1520	1551
Peine d.	|	|	1237	|	|	|	|	...	|	1337	|	|	|	|	|	1437	|	|	|	|	...	|	|	1537	|
Hannover Hbf a.	1228	1237	1305	1323	|	1328	1328	←	1355	1405	1423	|	1428	1428	1437	1505	1523	|	1528	1528	←	1554	1554	1605	1623
Hannover Hbf d.	1231	1240	1309	→	|	1331	1331	1340	1358	1409	1445	|	1431	1431	1440	1509	→	|	1531	1531	1540	1558	1558	1609	1645
Bremen Hbf **813** a.	|	|	|	...	|	|	|	|	|	|	1551	|	|	|	|	|	...	|	|	|	|	|	|	|	1751
Oldenburg (Oldb) Hbf **813** a.	|	|	|	...	|	|	|	|	|	|	1622	|	|	|	|	|	...	|	|	|	|	|	|	|	1822
Frankfurt (Main) Hbf **900** a.	|	|	|	...	1544	|	|	|	|	|	...	1644	|	|	|	|	...	1744	|	|	|	|	|	|	...
Stuttgart Hbf **930** a.	|	|	|	...	1708	|	|	|	|	|	...	|	|	|	|	|	...	1908	|	|	|	|	|	|	...
Basel SBB **912** a.	|	|	|	...	...	|	|	|	|	|	...	1947	|	|	|	|	...	...	|	|	|	|	|	|	...
Minden (Westf) **802** d.	|	1312	1352	...	...	|	|	1412	|	1502t	...	...	|	|	1512	1552	...	...	|	|	1612	|	|	1702t	...
Bad Oeynhausen **802** d.	|	1322	1404	...	...	|	|	1422	|	1514	...	...	|	|	|	1604	...	...	|	|	1622	|	|	1714	...
Löhne (Westf) **802** d.	|	|	1411	...	...	|	|	|	|	1519	...	...	|	|	|	1611	...	...	|	|	|	|	|	1719	...
Bünde (Westf) **811** d.	|	1335	1421	...	...	|	|	|	|	|	...	...	|	|	|	1621	...	...	|	|	|	|	|	|	...
Osnabrück Hbf **811** d.	|	1358	1448	...	...	|	|	|	|	|	...	...	|	|	1550	1648	...	...	|	|	|	|	|	|	...
Rheine **811** d.	|	...	1523	...	...	|	|	|	|	|	...	...	|	|	1617	1723	...	...	|	|	|	|	|	|	...
Bad Bentheim **811** 🏛 a.	|	...	*1603*	...	...	|	|	|	|	|	...	...	|	|	1630	*1803*q	...	...	|	|	|	|	|	|	...
Amsterdam Centraal **22** ⊡ a.	|	...	...	...	...	|	|	|	|	|	...	...	|	|	1901	...	...	...	|	|	|	|	|	|	...
Herford **802** d.	|	...	...	...	...	|	|	1433	1444	1527	...	...	|	|	...	...	...	...	|	|	1633	1644	1644	1727	...
Bielefeld Hbf **802** d.	1322	...	...	...	...	1422	1422	1442	1453	1536	...	...	1522	1522	...	...	...	...	1622	1622	1642	1653	1653	1736	...
Gütersloh Hbf **802** d.	|	...	...	...	...	|	|	1452	1503	...	...	...	|	|	...	...	...	...	|	|	1652	1703	1703	...	...
Hamm (Westf) **802** a.	1348	...	...	...	...	1448	1448	1512	1523	...	...	...	1548	1548	...	...	...	...	1648	1648	1712	1725	1724	...	...
Dortmund Hbf **800 802** a.	1409	...	...	...	...	|	1509	1532	1547	...	...	...	|	1609	...	...	...	...	|	1709	1732	1749	1748	...	...
Düsseldorf Hbf **800 802** a.	1505	...	...	...	...	|	1605	|	1642	...	...	...	|	1705	...	...	...	...	|	1805	|	1842	1842	...	...
Hagen Hbf **800** a.	...	...	...	...	...	1522	...	1555	|	...	...	...	1622	|	...	...	...	...	1722	...	1755	|	|	...	...
Wuppertal Hbf **800** a.	...	...	...	...	...	1539	...	1612	|	...	...	...	1639	|	...	...	...	...	1739	...	1812	|	|	...	...
Köln Hbf **800** a.	...	...	...	...	...	1609	...	1645	1715	...	...	...	1709	|	...	...	...	...	1809	...	1845	1915	1915	...	...
Köln/Bonn Flughafen ✈ **800** d.	...	...	...	...	...	...	...	...	|	...	...	...	...	1742b	...	...	...	...	...	...	...	|	...	...	...
Bonn Hbf **800** a.	...	...	...	...	...	...	...	...	1735	...	...	...	...	...	...	...	...	...	...	...	...	1935	...	...	...

A – To Interlaken via Bern (Table **560**).
K – To Karlsruhe (Tables **800**/**912**).
L – To München via Stuttgart (Tables **800**/**912**/**930**).
M – To Münster (Table **800**).
N – 🚃12 and 🍷 Leipzig - Emden - Norddeich Mole.
O – OSTFRIESLAND – 🚃12 and 🍷 (Cottbus ①–⑥ **e** -) Berlin - Oldenburg (- Norddeich Mole ♠). Also calls at Berlin Wannsee (d. 0748), Potsdam Hbf (d. 0756) and Brandenburg Hbf (d. 0815).
R – ①–⑥ (daily to Mar. 15). To Warnemünde via Schwerin and Rostock on ⑤⑥ from Mar. 14 (Tables **841**, **837** and **830**).
S – From Szczecin (Table **845**).
T – To Stuttgart (Tables **800**/**912**).

b – Ⓑ only.
c – Also Dec. 26, Jan. 1, Mar. 20, 24, Apr. 30, May 12; not Dec. 23, 30, Mar. 21, 23, May 2, 11.
e – Not Dec. 25, 26, Jan. 1, Mar. 22, 24, May 12.
f – Also Mar. 20, Apr. 30, May 21; not Mar. 21, May 2, 23.
j – 0530 on ⑥.
m – Also Dec. 24, 31.
n – Not Dec. 24, 31.
q – Ⓑ (not Dec. 24, 31).
r – ⚒ only.
t – Arrives 9 minutes earlier.
v – Also Mar. 20, Apr. 30; not Mar. 21, May 2.
w – Also Dec. 26, Jan. 1, Mar. 24, May 12; not Dec. 23, 30, Mar. 23, May 11.
x – Not Dec. 24, 25, 31.
z – Amsterdam **Zuid**.

♠ – ⑤⑦ to Mar. 9 (also Dec. 20, 22, 26, 27, 29, Jan. 1, 2, 3, 5); daily from Mar. 14.
⊡ – Amsterdam timings are subject to alteration on Apr. 30.

⊖ – 12–13 minutes later on ⑦**w**.
‡ – See below for additional *RE*/*RB* services.

Leipzig Hbf d.	0451	0505	and at the same	2205	2251	2338
Leipzig/Halle Flughafen ✈ d.	0507	|	minutes past	|	2307	2353
Halle (Saale) Hbf a.	0518	0541	each hour until	2241	2318	0004

	Ⓐn						x
Halle (Saale) Hbf d.	0443	0543	0643	and	2043	2143	2243
Köthen d.	0512	0612	0712	hourly	2112	2212	2312
Magdeburg Hbf a.	0551	0651	0751	until	2151	2251	2351

		Ⓐn				⚒n	n⊖
Magdeburg Hbf d.	0533j	0633	0733	then hourly on Ⓐ**n**,	1933	2033	2200
Helmstedt d.	0615	0715	0815	every **two** hours	2015	2115	2243
Braunschweig Hbf a.	0642	0742	0842	on Ⓒ**m** until	2042n	2142	2310

810 LEIPZIG and BERLIN - HANNOVER - BAD BENTHEIM and HAMM

	ICE 879	ICE 556	ICE 546	IC 2244	RE 14014	IC 2142	ICE 693	ICE 856	ICE 846	IC 2142	RE 14214	IC 2034	ICE 977	ICE 554	ICE 544	ICE 744	IC 140	EC 240	ICE 695	IC 2144	ICE 854	ICE 844	IC 2144	ICE 1093	RE 14216
						⑧q				⑧q					①-⑥	⑦w		⑧b	⑥c	⑧q	⑧q		⑧q	⑧q	
	✕	Q✕	✕	M🍷		🍷	✕	✕◆	✕	🍷		🍷	✕	✕	p✕	✕	🍷	✕◆	✕	🍷	H✕	✕	🍷	✕⟋	
Berlin Ostbahnhof **838** d.	1422	1440	1440	1428	...	...	1526	1538	1538	...	...	...	1622	1640	1640	1640	1628	1724	1724	...	1738	1738	...	1754	...
Berlin Hbf **838** d.	1433	1451	1451	1438	...	...	1537	1548	1548	...	...	...	1633	1651	1651	1651	1638	1735	1735	...	1748	1748	...	1804	...
Berlin Spandau **838** d.	1447	1505	1505	1452	...	...	1551	1602	1602	...	...	...	1647	1705	1705	1705	1652	1751	1751	...	1802	1802	...	1818	...
Rathenow **838** d.	|	|	|	1516	...	...	|	|	|	...	...	...	|	|	|	|	1716	|	|	...	|	|	...	|	...
Stendal **838** d.	|	|	|	1535	...	...	|	|	|	...	...	...	|	|	|	|	1735	1824	|	...	|	|	...	|	...
Wolfsburg d.	1540	|	|	1605	...	...	|	1655	1655	...	...	...	1740	|	|	|	1805	▬	|	...	1855	1855	...	|	...
Leipzig Hbf ‡ d.	|	|	|	|	...	1440	|	|	|	...	...	1542	|	|	|	|	|	...	|	1640	|	|	...	|	...
Leipzig/Halle Flughafen ✈ ‡ d.	|	|	|	|	...	1453	|	|	|	...	...	1555	|	|	|	|	|	...	|	1653	|	|	...	|	...
Halle (Saale) Hbf ‡ d.	|	|	|	|	...	1506	|	|	|	...	...	1608	|	|	|	|	|	...	|	1706	|	|	...	|	...
Köthen ‡ d.	|	|	|	|	...	1528	|	|	|	...	...	|	|	|	|	|	|	*RE*	|	1728	|	|	...	|	...
Magdeburg Hbf ‡ a.	|	|	|	|	...	1556	|	|	|	...	...	1656	|	|	|	|	|	**14016**	|	1756	|	|	...	|	...
Magdeburg Hbf ‡ d.	|	|	|	|	...	1600	|	|	|	...	...	1700	|	|	|	|	|		|	1800	|	|	...	|	...
Helmstedt ‡ d.	|	|	|	|	...	|	|	|	|	...	...	1728	|	|	|	|	|	|	|	|	|	|	...	|	...
Braunschweig Hbf ‡ d.	1558	|	|	|	1620	1650	1658	|	|	...	1720	1751	1758	|	|	|	|	1820	1858	1850	|	|	...	|	1920
Peine d.	|	|	|	|	1637	|	|	|	|	...	1737	|	|	|	|	|	|	1837	|	|	|	|	...	|	1937
Hannover Hbf a.	|	1628	1628	1637	1705	1723	|	1728	1728	←	1805	1823	|	1828	1828	1828	1837	1905	|	1923	1928	1928	←	|	2005
Hannover Hbf d.	|	1631	1631	1640	1709	→	|	1731	1731	1740	1809	1845	|	1831	1831	1831	1840**n**	1909	|	→	1931	1931	1940	|	2009
Bremen Hbf **813** a.	|	|	|	|	|	...	|	|	|	|	|	1951	|	|	|	|	|	|	|	...	|	|	|	|	|
Oldenburg (Oldb) Hbf **813** a.	|	|	|	|	|	...	|	|	|	|	|	2022	|	|	|	|	|	|	|	...	|	|	|	|	|
Frankfurt (Main) Hbf **900** a.	1844	|	|	|	|	...	1944	|	|	|	|	...	2044	|	|	|	|	|	2142	...	|	|	|	2142	|
Stuttgart Hbf **930** a.	|	|	|	|	|	...	2108	|	|	|	|	...	|	|	|	|	|	|	2308	...	|	|	|	2308	|
Basel SBB **912** a.	2147	|	|	|	|	...	...	|	|	|	|	...	2355	|	|	|	|	|	...	...	|	|	|	...	|
Minden (Westf) **802** d.	...	|	|	1712	1752	...	...	|	|	1812	1902**t**	...	...	|	|	|	1912**n**	1952	...	...	|	|	2012	...	2102**t**
Bad Oeynhausen **802** d.	...	|	|	1722	1804	...	...	|	|	1822	1914	...	...	|	|	|	|	2004	...	...	|	|	2022	...	2114
Löhne (Westf) **802** d.	...	|	|	|	1811	...	...	|	|	|	1919	...	...	|	|	|	|	2011	...	...	|	|	|	...	2119
Bünde (Westf) **811** d.	...	|	|	1735	1821	...	...	|	|	|	|	...	...	|	|	|	|	2021	...	...	|	|	|	...	|
Osnabrück Hbf **811** d.	...	|	|	1758	1848	...	...	|	|	|	|	...	...	|	|	|	1950**n**	2048	...	...	|	|	|	...	|
Rheine **811** d.	...	|	|	...	1923	...	...	|	|	|	|	...	...	|	|	|	2017**n**	2123	...	...	|	|	|	...	|
Bad Bentheim **811** 🏛 a.	...	|	|	...	*2003***a**	...	...	|	|	|	|	...	...	|	|	|	2030**n**	*2203***a**	...	...	|	|	|	...	|
Amsterdam Centraal **22** ⊡ a.	...	|	|	...	...	...	...	|	|	|	|	...	...	|	|	|	2301**z**	...	...	...	|	|	|	...	|
Herford **802** d.	...	|	|	...	...	...	...	|	|	1833	1927	...	...	|	|	|	...	...	...	...	|	|	2032	...	2127
Bielefeld Hbf **802** d.	...	1722	1722	...	...	...	...	1822	1822	1842	1936	...	...	1922	1922	1922	...	...	...	...	2022	2022	2041	...	2136
Gütersloh Hbf **802** d.	...	|	|	...	...	...	...	|	|	1852	...	...	...	|	|	|	...	...	...	...	|	|	2051	...	...
Hamm (Westf) **802** a.	...	1748	1748	...	...	...	...	1848	1848	1912	...	...	...	1948	1948	1948	...	...	...	...	2048	2048	2110	...	...
Dortmund Hbf **800 802** a.	...	|	1809	...	...	...	...	|	1909	1932	...	...	...	|	2009	2009	...	...	...	...	|	2109	2132	...	...
Düsseldorf Hbf **800 802** a.	...	|	1905	...	...	...	...	|	2005	|	...	...	...	|	2105	2105	...	...	...	...	|	2207	|	...	...
Hagen Hbf **800** a.	...	1822	|	...	...	...	...	1922	|	1955	...	...	...	2022	|	|	...	...	...	...	2122	|	2155	...	...
Wuppertal Hbf **800** a.	...	1839	|	...	...	...	...	1939	|	2012	...	...	...	2039	|	|	...	...	...	...	2139	|	2212	...	...
Köln Hbf **800** a.	...	1909	|	...	...	...	...	2009	2034	2045	...	...	...	2109	2133	|	...	...	...	...	2209	2231	2245	...	...
Köln/Bonn Flughafen ✈ **800** d.	...	|	1944**p**	...	...	...	...	|	...	...	...	...	...	...	...	2144	...	...	...	...	|	...	...	...	...
Bonn Hbf **800** a.	...	1932**q**	...	...	...	...	...	2039	...	...	...	...	...	...	...	...	...	...	...	...	2235**v**	...	...	...	...

	IC 2032	ICE 971	ICE 552	ICE 542	IC 2242	RE 14018	IC 1999	IC 2146	ICE 697	ICE 852	ICE 842	ICE 832	ICE 862	IC 2146	IC 1932	IC 1930	IC 2030	ICE 973	IC 2240	ICE 540	ICE 1740	ICE 1740	CNL 1242	ICE 840	ICE 850
					◇		⑦w	⑧q		⑦w		B	⑤f	⑦w	⑦w	⑦w		⑦w	⑦w		A	⑦w	🅁	⑦w	⑦w
	🍷	✕◆	✕	✕	🍷		◆	🍷	✕◆	✕	✕	✕	✕	🍷	◆	E		✕◆	M🍷	✕	D	D	✕◆	✕	✕
Berlin Ostbahnhof **838** d.	...	1822	1840	1840	1828	...	...	...	1926	1938	1938	1938	1938	...	...	...	...	2021	2025	2054	...	...	2117	2138	2138
Berlin Hbf **838** d.	...	1833	1851	1851	1838	...	1909	...	1937	1948	1948	1948	1948	...	...	2014	...	2032	2035	2105	...	...	2126	2149	2149
Berlin Spandau **838** d.	...	1847	1905	1905	1852	...	1919	...	1951	2002	2002	2002	2002	...	2009	2029	...	2046	2049	2120	...	...	2145	2203	2203
Rathenow **838** d.	...	|	|	|	1916	...	|	...	|	|	|	|	|	...	|	|	...	|	2113	|	...	...	|	|	|
Stendal **838** d.	...	|	|	|	1935	...	|	...	|	|	|	|	|	...	|	2110	...	|	2134	2152	...	...	|	2230	2230
Wolfsburg d.	...	1940	|	|	2005	...	2021	...	|	2055	2055	2055	2055	...	|	▬	...	2140	2205	2221	...	...	2252**u**	2300	2300
Leipzig Hbf ‡ d.	1742	|	|	|	|	...	|	1840	|	|	|	|	|	...	|	...	1940	|	|	|	2010	2010	|	|	|
Leipzig/Halle Flughafen ✈ ‡ d.	1755	|	|	|	|	...	|	1853	|	|	|	|	|	...	|	...	1953	|	|	|	2024	2024	|	|	|
Halle (Saale) Hbf ‡ d.	1808	|	|	|	|	...	|	1906	|	|	|	|	|	...	|	...	2006	|	|	|	2037	2037	|	|	|
Köthen ‡ d.	|	|	|	|	|	...	|	1928	|	|	|	|	|	...	|	*RE*	2028	|	|	|	2059	2059	|	|	|
Magdeburg Hbf ‡ a.	1856	|	|	|	|	...	|	1956	|	|	|	|	|	...	|	**14218**	2056	|	|	|	2127	2127	|	|	|
Magdeburg Hbf ‡ d.	1900	|	|	|	|	...	|	2000	|	|	|	|	|	...	|		2100	|	|	|	▬	2200	|	|	|
Helmstedt ‡ d.	1928	|	|	|	|	...	|	|	|	|	|	|	|	...	|		2128	|	|	|	...	|	|	|	|
Braunschweig Hbf ‡ d.	1951	1958	|	|	|	2020	|	2050	2058	|	|	|	|	...	|	2120	2151	2158	|	|	*RE*	2249	|	|	|
Peine d.	|	|	|	|	|	2037	|	|	|	|	|	|	|	...	|	2137	|	|	|	|	**14020**	|	|	|	|
Hannover Hbf a.	2023	|	2028	2028	2037	2105	2055	2123	|	2128	2128	2128	2128	←	2142	2205	2223	|	2237	2256	⑧	2321	|	2335	2335
Hannover Hbf d.	2045	|	2031	2031	2040	2109	2101	→	|	2131	2131	2145	2145	2140	2145	2209	...	|	2240	2300	2309	...	2352**u**	2340	2345
Bremen Hbf **813** a.	2151	|	|	|	|	|	|	...	|	|	|	2244	2247	|	2244	|	...	|	|	|	|	...	|	|	0044
Oldenburg (Oldb) Hbf **813** a.	2222**q**	|	|	|	|	|	|	...	|	|	|	...	2328	|	2315	|	...	|	|	|	|	...	|	|	0123
Frankfurt (Main) Hbf **900** a.	...	2244	|	|	|	|	0019	...	2344**k**	|	|	...	...	|	...	|	...	0058	|	|	|	...	0400**x**	|	...
Stuttgart Hbf **930** a.	...	...	|	|	|	|	...	...	...	|	|	...	...	|	...	|	...	...	|	|	|	...	|	|	...
Basel SBB **912** a.	...	...	|	|	|	|	...	...	...	|	|	...	...	|	...	|	...	...	|	|	|	...	0755	|	...
Minden (Westf) **802** d.	...	...	|	|	2112	2152	...	...	...	|	|	...	...	2212	...	2302**t**	...	...	2312	|	2352	...	...	0011	...
Bad Oeynhausen **802** d.	...	...	|	|	2122	2204	...	...	...	|	|	...	...	2222	...	2314	...	...	2322	|	...	...	...	|	...
Löhne (Westf) **802** d.	...	...	|	|	|	2211	...	...	...	|	|	...	...	|	...	2319	...	...	|	|	...	...	...	|	...
Bünde (Westf) **811** d.	...	...	|	|	2135	2221	...	...	...	|	|	...	...	|	...	|	...	...	2335	|	...	...	...	|	...
Osnabrück Hbf **811** d.	...	...	|	|	2157	2246	...	...	...	|	|	...	...	|	...	|	...	...	2358	|	...	...	...	|	...
Rheine **811** d.	...	...	|	|	2227**q**	*2346*	...	...	...	|	|	...	...	|	...	|	...	...	...	|	...	...	...	|	...
Bad Bentheim **811** 🏛 a.	...	...	|	|	2240**q**	...	...	...	...	|	|	...	...	|	...	|	...	...	...	|	...	...	...	|	...
Amsterdam Centraal **22** ⊡ a.	...	...	|	|	...	...	...	...	...	|	|	...	...	|	...	|	...	...	...	|	...	...	...	|	...
Herford **802** d.	...	...	|	|	...	...	...	...	...	|	|	...	...	2232	...	2327	...	...	...	2344	...	...	...	0029	...
Bielefeld Hbf **802** d.	...	...	2122	2122	...	...	...	...	...	2222	2222	...	...	2241	...	2336	...	...	...	2354	...	...	...	0039	...
Gütersloh Hbf **802** d.	...	...	|	|	...	...	...	...	...	|	|	...	...	2251	...	...	...	...	...	0004	...	...	...	0049	...
Hamm (Westf) **802** a.	...	...	2148	2148	...	...	...	...	...	2248	2248	...	...	2310	...	...	...	...	...	0023	...	...	...	0109	...
Dortmund Hbf **800 802** a.	...	...	|	2209	...	...	...	...	...	|	2309	...	...	2332	...	...	...	...	...	0042**r**	...	...	...	0127	...
Düsseldorf Hbf **800 802** a.	...	...	|	2305	...	...	...	...	...	|	0005	...	...	|	...	...	...	...	...	0136**r**	...	...	...	0222	...
Hagen Hbf **800** a.	...	...	2222	|	...	...	...	...	...	2322	|	...	...	2355	...	...	...	...	...	|	...	...	...	|	...
Wuppertal Hbf **800** a.	...	...	2239	|	...	...	...	...	...	2339	|	...	...	0012	...	...	...	...	...	|	...	...	...	|	...
Köln Hbf **800** a.	...	...	2309	2329	...	...	...	...	...	0009	0029	...	...	0045	...	...	...	...	...	0201**r**	...	...	...	0246	...
Köln/Bonn Flughafen ✈ **800** d.	...	...	|	...	...	...	...	...	...	...	...	...	...	...	...	...	...	...	...	0226**r**	...	...	...	...	...
Bonn Hbf **800** a.	...	...	2338**q**	...	...	...	...	...	...	...	...	...	...	...	...	...	...	...	...	...	...	...	...	...	...

◆ – **NOTES** (LISTED BY TRAIN NUMBER)

240 – WAWEL – 1,2 cl. and ✕ Kraków - Forst 🏛 - Cottbus - Berlin - Uelzen - Hamburg.
697 – 1,2 cl. and ✕ Berlin - Kassel (- Frankfurt ⑤–⑦ **k**).
856 – 1,2 cl. and ✕ Berlin - Koblenz - Trier.
971/3 – 1,2 cl. and ✕ Berlin - Mannheim - Karlsruhe.
1242 – BERLINER – 1,2 cl. sleeper, 2 cl. couchette, 1,2 cl. (reclining) and ✕ Berlin - Karlsruhe - Basel - Zürich. Also calls at Berlin Zoo (d. 2134).
1932 – 1,2 cl. Stralsund - Bernau - Berlin Spandau - Bremen - Oldenburg.
1999 – 1,2 cl. Berlin - Kassel - Gießen - Frankfurt.

A – ①②③④⑦ (not Dec. 23, 24, 25, 30, 31, Mar. 20, 23, May 11).
B – ①②③④⑥ (also Dec. 23, 30, Mar. 21, 23, May 2, 11; not Dec. 26, Jan. 1, Mar. 20, 24, Apr. 30, May 12).
D – From Dresden (Table **842**).
E – To Uelzen (Table **841**).
H – To Koblenz Hbf (a. 2311) on ⑦**v**.
M – To Münster (Table **800**).

Q – To Koblenz Hbf (a. 2011) on ①–⑤ (not Dec. 24, 25, 26, 31, Jan. 1, Mar. 21, 24, May 12).

a – Ⓐ (not Dec. 24, 31).
b – Not Dec. 24, 25, 30, 31, Mar. 21, 23, May 11.
c – Also Dec. 24, 25, 31, Mar. 21, 23, May 11.
f – Also Mar. 20, Apr. 30; not Mar. 21, May 2.
k – ⑤–⑦ (also Dec. 26, Jan. 1, Mar. 20, 24, Apr. 30, May 1, 12, 21, 22; not Dec. 23, 30, Mar. 22, 23, May 2, 3, 23, 24).
n – Not Dec. 24, 31.
p – ①–⑥ (also Dec. 23, 30, Mar. 23, May 11; not Dec. 26, Jan. 1, Mar. 24, May 12).
q – ⑧ (not Dec. 24, 25, 31, Mar. 21, 23, May 11).
r – On ⑥⑦ (also Dec. 24, 25, 26, 31, Jan. 1, Mar. 21, 24, May 1, 12, 22) arrives Dortmund 0047, Düsseldorf 0145 and terminates at Köln Hbf, a. 0209.

t – Arrives 9 minutes earlier.
u – Stops to pick up only.
v – ⑦ (also Dec. 26, Jan. 1, Mar. 24, May 12; not Mar. 23, May 11).
w – Also Dec. 26, Jan. 1, Mar. 24, May 12; not Dec. 23, 30, Mar. 23, May 11.
x – Frankfurt (Main) **Süd**.
z – Not Dec. 24, 31. Amsterdam **Zuid**.

◇ – Not Dec. 24, 25, 31. Train number **2342** on ⑥ (also Mar. 21, 23, May 11).
⟋ – 🅁 and 'Sprinter' supplement payable.
‡ – See panel on page 381 for additional local services.
⊡ – Amsterdam timings are subject to alteration on Apr. 30.

BIELEFELD - PADERBORN and RHEINE — 811

Nord West Bahn; Westfalenbahn

Bielefeld Hbf - **Paderborn** Hbf via Hövelhof (*44 km*). Operated by Nord West Bahn. Journey time: 61 – 75 minutes. On Dec. 24, 31 services run as on ⑥. On May 22 services run as on ⑦.
From Bielefeld at 0432 Ⓐ, 0528 Ⓐ, 0539 ⑥, 0616 Ⓐ, 0639 ⑥, 0739 ⚒, 0839 ⚒, 0939, 1039 ⚒, 1139, 1239 ⚒, 1339, 1439 ⚒, 1539, 1639 ⚒, 1739, 1839 Ⓐ, 1939, 2039 Ⓐ, 2139 and 2239 Ⓐ.
From Paderborn at 0504 Ⓐ, 0513 ⑥, 0604 Ⓐ, 0613 ⑥, 0628 Ⓐ, 0714 ⚒, 0813 ⚒, 0913, 1013 ⚒, 1113, 1213 ⚒, 1313, 1413 ⚒, 1513, 1613 ⚒, 1713, 1813 Ⓐ, 1913, 2013 Ⓐ, 2113 and 2213 Ⓐ.

km	⊖	⚒t								F	
0	**Bielefeld** Hbf d.	0750	0850	1050	1250	1450	1650	1850	2050	2250	...
11	Oerlinghausen d.	0803	0903	1103	1303	1503	1703	1903	2103	2303	...
31	Detmold d.	0820	0920	1120	1320	1520	1720	1920	2120	2320	...
60	Altenbeken a.	...	0946	1146	...	1546	1746	1946	...	2345	...

⊖	Ⓐe	⚒t								
Altenbeken d.	0610	0713e	0813	1013	1213	...	1613	1813	2013	...
Detmold d.	0637	0740	0840	1040	1240	1440	1640	1840	2040	2240
Oerlinghausen d.	0655	0801	0901	1101	1301	1501	1701	1901	2101	2301
Bielefeld Hbf a.	0706	0812	0912	1112	1312	1512	1712	1912	2112	2312

km	⊡	Ⓐe	⚒t					Ⓒ	⊖F	
	Bielefeld Hbf **810** d.	0509	0609	0709		2109	2209	2209	2250	...
0	Herford d.	0530	0633	0733	and	2133	2233	2233	|	...
28	Detmold d.	0559	0702	0802	hourly	2202	2258	2302	2320	...
57	Altenbeken ‡ a.	0624	0727	0827	until	2227	...	2327	2345	...
74	**Paderborn** Hbf ‡ a.	0638	0741	0841		2241	...	2341	2358	...

⊡	Ⓐ	⚒						⊖F	
Paderborn Hbf ‡ d.	...	0518	...	0621		2121	...	2232	...
Altenbeken ‡ d.	...	0530	...	0633	and	2133	...	2245	...
Detmold d.	0458	0558	...	0701	hourly	2201	...	2322	...
Herford a.	0524	0624	...	0727	until	2227	...	2350	...
Bielefeld Hbf **810** a.	0548	0648	...	0748		2248	...	0007	...

km	⊡	⚒	⚒																	
0	**Bielefeld** Hbf d.	0509	0609	0709	0809	0909	1009	1109	1209	1309	1409	1509	1609	1709	1809	1909	2009	2109	2209	2309
14	Herford a.	0520	0620	0720	0820	0920	1020	1120	1220	1320	1420	1520	1620	1720	1820	1920	2020	2120	2220	2320
14	Herford **810** d.	0533	0633	0733	0833	0933	1033	1133	1233	1333	1433	1533	1633	1733	1833	1933	2033	2133	2233	2333
28	Bünde (Westf) **810** d.	0546	0646	0746	0846	0946	1046	1146	1246	1346	1446	1546	1646	1746	1846	1946	2046	2146	2246	2346
65	**Osnabrück** Hbf **810** d.	0614	0714	0814	0914	1014	1114	1214	1314	1414	1514	1614	1714	1814	1914	2014	2114	2214	2314	0012
113	**Rheine 810** a.	0646	0746	0846	0946r	1046	1146	1246	1346	1446	1546	1646	1746b	1846	1946a	2046	2146a	2246	2346	...
134	Bad Bentheim **810** a.	0703	0803	0903	1003r	1103	1203r	1303	1403	1503	1603	1703	1803b	1903	2003a	2103	2203a	2303	...	...

⊡	⚒	⚒																	
Bad Bentheim **810** d.	...	...	0557a	0657r	0757r	0857	0957r	1057	1157r	1257	1357	1457	1557	1657	1757b	1857	1957a	2057	2157a
Rheine 810 d.	...	0514	0614a	0714r	0814	0914	1014r	1114	1214	1314	1414	1514	1614	1714	1814b	1914	2014a	2114	2214a
Osnabrück Hbf **810** d.	0448	0548	0648	0748	0848	0948	1048	1148	1248	1348	1448	1548	1648	1748	1848	1948	2048	2148	2248
Bünde (Westf) **810** d.	0513	0613	0713	0813	0913	1013	1113	1213	1313	1413	1513	1613	1713	1813	1913	2013	2113	2213	2313
Herford **810** a.	0527	0627	0727	0827	0927	1027	1127	1227	1327	1427	1527	1627	1727	1827	1927	2027	2127	2227	2327
Herford d.	0537	0637	0737	0837	0937	1037	1137	1237	1337	1437	1537	1637	1737	1837	1937	2037	2137	2237	2337
Bielefeld Hbf a.	0548	0648	0748	0848	0948	1048	1148	1248	1348	1448	1548	1648	1748	1848	1948	2048	2148	2248	2348

F – ⑤⑥† (also Dec. 24, 31, May 22).

a – Ⓐ (not Dec. 24, 31).
b – Ⓑ (not Dec. 24, 31).
e – Not Dec. 24, 31, May 22.
r – ⚒ only.
t – Not May 22.

‡ – See also Tables **805/9**.
⊖ – 2nd class only. Operated by Nord West Bahn.
⊡ – Operated by WestfalenBahn.

MÜNSTER - EMDEN - NORDDEICH — 812

RE services except where shown

km						*IC* 2331			*IC* 2333			*IC* 331	*IC* 431				*IC* 433			*IC* 435			*IC* 2014	*IC* 2004	*IC* 2036
		Ⓐn	⚒	⚒		A 🍷			🍷			G L🍷	E 🍷◆	Ⓒw	Ⓐn		L🍷			L🍷			①–⑤ 🍷◆	⑦ ◆	🍷◆
	Köln Hbf **800** d.	...	...	...	...	0542	...	...	0748	...	...	0948	0948	...	...	...	1148	...	...	1348	...	...	1548	1548	...
0	**Münster** (Westf) Hbf. § d.	0502	...	0602	0702	0731	0805	0905	0931	1005	1105	1131	1131	1205	1205	1305	1331	1405	1505	1531	1605	1705	1731	1731	...
39	Rheine § d.	0534	0534	0634	0734	0756	0834	0934	0956	1034	1134	1156	1156	1234	1234	1334	1356	1434	1534	1556	1634	1734	1756	1756	...
70	Lingen (Ems) d.	0556	0556	0656	0756	0815	0856	0956	1015	1056	1156	1215	1215	1256	1256	1356	1415	1456	1556	1615	1656	1756	1815	1815	...
91	Meppen d.	0611	0611	0711	0811	0829	0911	1011	1029	1111	1211	1229	1229	1311	1329h	1411	1429	1511	1611	1629	1711	1811	1829	1829	...
137	Papenburg (Ems) d.	0643	0643	0743	0843	0856	0943	1043	1056	1143	1243	1256	1256	1343	1403	1443	1456	1543	1643	1656	1743	1843	1856	1856	...
154	Leer (Ostfriesl) **813** d.	0656	0656	0756	0856	0909	0956	1056	1109	1156	1256	1309	1309	1356	1416	1456	1509	1556	1656	1709	1756	1856	1909	1909	1925
180	**Emden** Hbf **813** a.	0713	0713	0813	0913	0925	1013	1113	1125	1213	1313	1325	1325	1413	1433	1513	1525	1613	1713	1725	1813	1913	1925	1925	1942
180	**Emden** Hbf **813** d.	0735	0735	0843	...	0928	1043	...	1142	1243	...	1328	1341	1443	1443	...	1527	1643	...	1728	1843	...	...	...	1945
209	Norden **813** d.	0810	0810	0907	...	0953	1107	...	1206	1307	...	1353	1409	1507	1507	...	1550	1707	...	1753	1907	...	...	...	2008
214	**Norddeich 813** a.	0816	0816	0913	...	0959	1113	...	1212	1313	...	1359	1415	1513	1513	...	1557	1713	...	1759	1913	...	...	...	2015
215	**Norddeich Mole 813** a.	0820	0820	0918	...	1004	1118	...	1218	1318	...	1404	1421	1518	1518	...	1604	1718	...	1804	1918	...	...	...	2021

			IC 437						
			L🍷		Ⓑn	n	¶	¶ v	
Köln Hbf **800** d.	...	...	1745	...	...	...	...	...	...
Münster (Westf) Hbf. § d.	1805	1905	1931	2005	2105	2205	2311	0011	...
Rheine § d.	1834	1934	1956	2034	2134	2234	2343	0043	...
Lingen (Ems) d.	1856	1956	2015	2056	2156	2256	...	...	...
Meppen d.	1911	2011	2029	2111	2211	2311	...	...	...
Papenburg (Ems) d.	1943	2043	2056	2143	2243	2343	...	...	...
Leer (Ostfriesland) **813** d.	1956	2056	2109	2156	2256	2356	...	...	...
Emden Hbf **813** a.	2013	2113	2125	2213	2313	0013	...	...	...
Emden Hbf **813** d.	2043	...	...	2243	...	...	...	...	...
Norden **813** d.	2107	...	...	2307	...	...	...	...	...
Norddeich 813 a.	2113	...	...	2313	...	...	...	...	...
Norddeich Mole 813 a.	...	...	...	...	...	...	...	...	...

					IC 2015	*IC* 2005				*IC* 2037	*IC* 436
	Ⓐn	⚒	⚒	⚒	①–④ ◆	⑤⑥ ◆	⚒	†		🍷◆	L🍷
Norddeich Mole 813 d.	...	...	...	...	...	...	...	...	...	0737	...
Norddeich 813 d.	...	...	...	0532	...	...	...	...	0642	0740	...
Norden **813** d.	...	...	...	0538	...	...	...	...	0648	0747	...
Emden Hbf **813** a.	...	...	...	0602	...	...	...	...	0716	0812	...
Emden Hbf **813** d.	...	0450	0550	0604	0634	0634	0642	0650	0750	0814	0834
Leer (Ostfriesland) **813** d.	...	0506	0606	0620	0653	0653	0658	0706	0806	0831	0853
Papenburg (Ems) d.	...	0516	0616	...	0704	0704	0709	0716	0816	...	0904
Meppen d.	...	0550	0650	...	0731	0731	0750	0750	0850	...	0931
Lingen (Ems) d.	...	0604	0704	...	0744	0744	0804	0804	0904	...	0944
Rheine § d.	0528	0628	0728	...	0804	0804	0828	0828	0928	...	1004
Münster (Westf) Hbf § a.	0554	0654	0756	...	0829	0829	0856	0856	0956	...	1029
Köln Hbf **800** a.	...	...	...	...	1012	1012	...	...	...	...	1212

			IC 434				*IC* 432				*IC* 430			*IC* 2332	*IC* 2334			*IC* 2330							
			L🍷			Ⓐn	🍷◆	Ⓐn	Ⓒw		L🍷			E 🍷	G 🍷			B 🍷			Ⓑn	¶		n	¶ n
Norddeich Mole 813 d.	...	0840	0951	...	1040	...	1136	...	...	1240	1354	...	1440	1539	1558	...	1640	1754	...	1840	...	...	2040	...	...
Norddeich 813 d.	...	0842	0955	...	1042	...	1139	...	...	1242	1402	...	1442	1542	1602	...	1642	1802	...	1842	...	...	2042	...	...
Norden **813** d.	...	0848	1009	...	1048	...	1146	...	...	1248	1409	...	1448	1549	1609	...	1648	1809	...	1848	...	...	2048	...	...
Emden Hbf **813** a.	...	0916	1031	...	1116	...	1215	...	...	1316	1431	...	1516	1611	1631	...	1716	1831	...	1916	...	...	2116	...	...
Emden Hbf **813** d.	0850	0950	1034	1050	1150	1224	1234	...	1250	1350	1434	1450	1550	1634	1634	1650	1750	1834	1850	1950	2050	...	2118	2214	...
Leer (Ostfriesland) **813** d.	0906	1006	1053	1106	1206	1241	1253	...	1306	1406	1453	1506	1606	1653	1653	1706	1806	1853	1906	2006	2106	...	2135	2229	...
Papenburg (Ems) d.	0916	1016	1104	1116	1216	1251	1304	←	1316	1416	1504	1516	1616	1704	1704	1716	1816	1904	1916	2016	2116	...	...	2239	...
Meppen d.	0950	1050	1131	1150	1250	1325	1331	1337	1350	1450	1531	1550	1650	1731	1731	1750	1850	1931	1950	2050	2150	...	...	2313	...
Lingen (Ems) d.	1004	1104	1144	1204	1304	→	1344	1351	1404	1504	1544	1604	1704	1744	1744	1804	1904	1944	2004	2104	2204	...	...	2327	...
Rheine § d.	1028	1128	1204	1228	1327	...	1404	1428j	1428	1528	1604	1628	1728	1804	1804	1828	1928	2004	2028	2128	2228	2252	...	2349	2352
Münster (Westf) Hbf § a.	1056	1156	1229	1256	1356	...	1429	1456	1456	1556	1629	1656	1756	1829	1829	1856	1956	2029	2056	2156	2256	2325	...	...	0025
Köln Hbf **800** a.	...	...	1412	...	...	...	1612	...	...	...	1812	...	...	2019	2019	...	...	2212	...	...	...	...	...	...	...

	⚒r							¶	¶
Köln Hbf **802** d.	...	0621r	...	0821	each train	...	1821	...	...
Münster (Westf) Hbf d.	0722	0824	0922	1024	runs every **two** hours	1922	2024	2136	2236
Rheine a.	0749	0851	0949	1051	until	1949	2051	2208	2308

	¶⚒r	Ⓐe			¶					
Rheine d.	0452	0606	0617	0706	0752	0906	1010	each train	1906	2010
Münster (Westf) Hbf a.	0525	0632	0650	0732	0825	0932	1036	runs every **two** hours	1932	2036
Köln Hbf **802** a.	...	0838	...	0938	...	1138	...	until	2138	...

◆ – **NOTES** (LISTED BY TRAIN NUMBER)

431 – BORKUM – [12] and 🍷 (Luxembourg ★ -) Köln - Emden.
432 – [12] and 🍷 Emden - Köln (- Luxembourg Ⓑ **q**).
2004 – ⑦ (also Dec. 26, Jan. 1, Mar. 21, 24, May 1, 12, 22; not Dec. 23, 30, Mar. 23, May 11). BODENSEE – [12] and 🍷 Konstanz - Karlsruhe - Köln - Emden.
2005 – ⑤⑥ (also Mar. 20, Apr. 30, May 21). BODENSEE – [12] and 🍷 Emden - Köln - Karlsruhe - Konstanz.
2014 – ①–⑤ (not Dec. 24, 25, 26, 31, Jan. 1, Mar. 21, 24, May 1, 12, 22). [12] and 🍷 Stuttgart - Koblenz - Köln - Emden.
2015 – ①–④ (not Dec. 24, 25, 26, 31, Jan. 1, Mar. 20, 24, Apr. 30, May 12, 21). [12] and 🍷 Emden - Köln - Koblenz - Stuttgart.
2036/7 – [12] and 🍷 Leipzig - Magdeburg - Hannover - Bremen - Norddeich Mole and v.v.

A – ① to Mar. 10 (also Jan. 2; not Dec. 24, 31); ①④⑤⑥⑦ from Mar. 15.
B – ⑦ to Mar. 9 (also Jan. 1; not Dec. 23, 30). ③–⑦ from Mar. 14.
E – ⑤⑦ to Mar. 9 (also Dec. 20, 22, 26, 27, 29, Jan. 1, 2, 3, 5); daily from Mar. 14.
G – ①②③④⑥ to Mar. 13 (not Dec. 20, 22, 26, 27, 29, Jan. 1, 2, 3, 5).
L – From / to Luxembourg (Table **915**).

e – Not Dec. 24, 31, May 22.
h – Arrives 1310.
j – Arrives 1417.
n – Not Dec. 24, 31.
q – Not Dec. 24, 25, 31, Mar. 21, 23, May 11.
r – ⚒ (not May 22).
v – Not Dec. 25, Jan. 1.
w – Also Dec. 24, 31.

★ – ⑤ to Mar. 7 (also Dec. 20, 22, 27, 29, Jan. 2, 3, 5); ①–⑥ from Mar. 14 (not Mar. 22, 24, May 12).
¶ – Operated by WestfalenBahn.
§ – See panel below main table for additional trains.

813 NORDDEICH - EMDEN - BREMEN - HANNOVER

RB/RE services except where shown

km				ICE 531 ①g ✕	ICE 531 ①–⑤ d✕		IC 2033 🍷			ICE 533 ①–⑥ e✕		IC 1987 ⑥t A🍷		IC 2035 🍷		ICE 535 ✕		IC 2037 🍷		ICE 537 ✕			IC 2039 🍷		ICE 539 ✕
			Ⓐn			⚒n																			
0	**Norddeich Mole 812** d.	...	...	...	...	...	...	...	...	...	...	...	...	...	...	...	...	0737	...	...	0840	...	...	...	...
1	**Norddeich 812** d.	...	...	...	...	...	...	...	...	...	...	...	0532r	...	...	...	0642	0740	...	...	0842	0922	...	...	...
6	Norden **812** d.	...	...	...	...	...	...	...	...	...	...	...	0538r	...	...	...	0648	0747	...	...	0848	0928	...	...	...
35	**Emden** Hbf **812** d.	...	...	...	...	0418	...	...	0518	...	...	...	0604	...	...	...	0718	0814	...	...	0918	1018	...	...	...
61	Leer (Ostfriesland) **812** a.	...	...	...	...	0435	...	...	0535	...	...	...	0620	...	...	...	0735	0831	...	...	0935	1035	...	...	...
61	Leer (Ostfriesland) d.	...	...	...	...	0442	...	...	0542	...	...	...	0632	...	...	...	0742	0841	...	...	0942	1042	...	...	...
101	Bad Zwischenahn d.	...	...	...	...	0510	...	...	0613	...	...	...	0707	...	...	...	0813	0918	...	...	1013	1113	...	...	...
116	**Oldenburg** (Oldb) a.	...	...	...	...	0521	...	...	0623	...	...	...	0719	...	...	...	0823	0930	...	...	1023	1123	...	...	...
116	**Oldenburg** (Oldb) d.	...	0409	0446	...	▬	0535e	...	0635	0642	...	...	...	0735	...	...	0835	0935	...	...	1035	...	1135	...	...
147	Delmenhorst d.	...	0438	|	...	...	0553e	...	0654	|	...	...	...	0753	...	...	0854	0953	...	...	1054	...	1153	...	...
161	**Bremen** Hbf a.	...	0451	0512	...	...	0603e	...	0705	0709	←	...	...	0803	...	...	0905p	1003	...	...	1105p	...	1203	...	...
161	**Bremen** Hbf d.	0418	...	0514	0514	0518	0609	0618	→	0714	0718	0737	...	0809	0818	0914	0918	1009	1018	1114	1118	...	1209	1218	1314
196	Verden (Aller) d.	0443	...	|	|	0543	0629	0643	...	|	0743	|	...	0829	0843	|	0943	1029	1043	|	1143	...	1229	1243	|
227	Nienburg (Weser) d.	0504	...	|	|	0604	0647	0705	...	|	0804	|	...	0847	0904	|	1004	1047	1104	|	1204	...	1247	1304	|
283	**Hannover** Hbf a.	0538	...	0614	0614	0638	0714	0738	...	0814	0838	0846	...	0914	0938	1014	1038	1114	1138	1214	1238	...	1314	1338	1414
	Magdeburg Hbf **810** a.	...	...	|	|	...	0858	...	...	|	...	|	...	1058	...	|	...	1258	...	|	...	...	1458	...	|
	Berlin Hbf **810** a.	...	...	|	|	...	|	...	...	|	...	|	...	|	...	|	...	|	...	|	...	...	|	...	|
	Leipzig Hbf **810** a.	...	...	|	|	...	1018	...	...	|	...	|	...	1218	...	|	...	1418	...	|	...	...	1618	...	|
	Nürnberg Hbf **900** a.	...	...	0928	0928	...	...	...	...	|	...	1232	...	...	...	1329	...	...	...	|	...	...	...	...	|
	München Hbf **900** a.	...	...	1040	1040	...	...	...	...	1303	...	...	...	...	...	1443	...	...	...	1708	...	...	...	...	1903

		IC 2131 B🍷		ICE 631 ✕			IC 2133 🍷		ICE 633 ✕		IC 2135 □ 🍷	IC 2135 🍷		ICE 635 ✕	ICE 635 ⑦w ✕			IC 2137 ⑧q		ICE 637 ⑦w ✕					n
Norddeich Mole 812 d.	1040	*1136*	...	...	1240	...	...	...	...	1440	1539	...	...	...	...	1640	...	...	...	...	1840	...	...	2040	...
Norddeich 812 d.	1042	*1139*	...	...	1242	...	...	...	...	1442	1542	...	...	...	...	1642	...	...	...	...	1842	...	...	2042	...
Norden **812** d.	1048	*1146*	...	...	1248	...	...	...	...	1448	1549	...	...	...	...	1648	...	...	...	...	1848	...	...	2048	...
Emden Hbf **812** d.	1118	1219	...	...	1318	1418	...	...	...	1518	1619	...	...	...	...	1718	1818	...	...	...	1918	...	2018	2118	...
Leer (Ostfriesland) **812** a.	1135	1236	...	...	1335	1435	...	...	...	1535	1636	...	...	...	...	1735	1835	...	...	...	1935	...	2035	2135	...
Leer (Ostfriesland) d.	1142	1242	...	...	1342	1442	...	...	...	1542	1641	...	...	...	...	1742	1842	...	...	...	1942	...	2042	2142	...
Bad Zwischenahn d.	1213	1321	...	...	1413	1513	...	...	...	1613	1718	...	...	...	...	1813	1913	...	...	...	2013	...	2113	2213	...
Oldenburg (Oldb) a.	1223	1331	...	...	1423	1523	...	...	...	1623	1730	...	...	...	...	1823	1923	...	...	...	2023	...	2123	2223	...
Oldenburg (Oldb) d.	1235	1335	...	...	1435	...	1535	...	...	1635	1735	1735	...	...	...	1835	...	1935	...	...	2035	*2109*	2137	2235	2340
Delmenhorst d.	1254	1353	...	...	1454	...	1553	...	...	1654	1753	1753	...	...	...	1854	...	1953	...	...	2054	*2138*	2204	2254	0009
Bremen Hbf a.	1305p	1403	...	...	1505p	...	1603	...	...	1705p	1803	1803	...	...	...	1905p	...	2004	...	...	2105p	*2151*	2221	2305	0022
Bremen Hbf d.	1318	1409	1418	1514	1518	...	1609	1618	1714	1718	1809	1809	1818	1914	1914	1918	...	2009	2018	2114	2118	2218	...	2311	...
Verden (Aller) d.	1343	1429	1443	|	1543	...	1629	1643	|	1743	1829	1829	1843	|	|	1943	...	2029	2043	|	2143	2243	...	2343	...
Nienburg (Weser) d.	1404	1447	1504	|	1604	...	1647	1704	|	1804	1847	1847	1904	|	|	2004	...	2047	2104	|	2204	2304	...	0004	...
Hannover Hbf a.	1438	1514	1538	1614	1638	...	1714	1738	1814	1838	1914	1914	1938	2014	2014	2038	...	2114	2138	2214	2238	2338	...	0038	...
Magdeburg Hbf **810** a.	...	1658	...	|	...	...	1858	...	|	...	2058	2058	...	|	|	...	...	2302	...	|	...	...	...	...	...
Berlin Hbf **810** a.	...	1826	...	|	...	...	|	...	|	...	|	|	...	|	|	...	...	...	...	|	...	...	...	...	...
Leipzig Hbf **810** a.	...	...	...	|	...	...	2018	...	|	...	2220	2220	...	|	|	...	...	...	...	|	...	...	...	...	...
Nürnberg Hbf **900** a.	...	...	...	|	...	...	...	...	|	...	...	...	...	2324	2324	...	...	...	...	|	...	...	...	...	...
München Hbf **900** a.	...	...	...	2103	...	...	...	...	2308	...	...	...	...	...	0056	...	...	...	...	...	...	...	...	...	...

	⚒n				IC 2136 ①–⑥ e			ICE 636 ①–⑤ d✕		IC 2134 🍷		ICE 634 ✕		IC 2132 C🍷	IC 2132 □ C🍷		ICE 632 ✕		IC 2130 🍷			ICE 630 ✕		IC 2038 🍷	
München Hbf **900** d.	...	...	...	...	...	...	...	...	...	...	...	0517a	...	...	...	...	0652	...	...	...	...	0916	...	...	...
Nürnberg Hbf **900** d.	...	...	...	...	...	...	...	...	...	...	...	0631	...	...	...	...	|	...	...	...	...	1032	...	...	...
Leipzig Hbf **810** d.	...	...	...	...	...	...	...	...	...	0540a	...	|	...	...	...	...	|	...	0942	...	...	|	...	1142	...
Berlin Hbf **810** d.	...	...	...	...	...	...	...	...	...	|	...	|	...	0732	0732	...	|	...	|	...	...	|	...	|	...
Magdeburg Hbf **810** d.	...	...	...	...	0500a	...	...	...	...	0700	...	|	...	0900	0900	...	|	...	1100	...	...	|	...	1300	...
Hannover Hbf d.	...	...	0521	0617	0645	...	0721	0745	0821	0845	0921	0945	1021	1045	1045	1121	1145	1221	1245	...	1321	1345	1421	1445	...
Nienburg (Weser) d.	...	...	0555	0655	0713	...	0755	|	0855	0913	0955	|	1055	1113	1113	1155	|	1255	1313	...	1355	|	1455	1513	...
Verden (Aller) d.	...	...	0615	0715	0730	...	0816	|	0915	0930	1015	|	1115	1130	1130	1215	|	1315	1330	...	1415	|	1515	1530	...
Bremen Hbf a.	...	...	0640	0740	0751	...	0840	0844p	0939	0951	1039	1044p	1139	1151	1151	1239	1244p	1340	1351	...	1440	1444p	1539	1551	...
Bremen Hbf d.	0444	0543	0654	...	0755	...	0854	...	...	0955	1054	...	...	1155	1155	1254	...	...	1355	...	1454	...	...	1555	...
Delmenhorst d.	0457	0556	0704	...	0806	...	0904	...	...	1006	1104	...	...	1206	1206	1304	...	...	1406	...	1504	...	...	1606	...
Oldenburg (Oldb) a.	0525	0623	0723	...	0822	...	0923	...	...	1022	1123	...	...	1222	1222	1323	...	...	1422	...	1523	...	...	1622	...
Oldenburg (Oldb) d.	0532	0626	0732	...	...	0832	0932	...	...	1032	1132	...	...	...	1224	1332	...	...	...	1432	1532	...	...	...	1632
Bad Zwischenahn d.	0545	0638	0745	...	...	0845	0945	...	...	1044	1145	...	...	...	1236	1345	...	...	...	1445	1545	...	...	...	1645
Leer (Ostfriesland) a.	0614	0706	0814	...	...	0914	1014	...	...	1115	1214	...	...	...	1307	1414	...	...	...	1514	1614	...	...	...	1714
Leer (Ostfriesland) **812** d.	0625	0715	0825	...	...	0925	1025	...	...	1120	1225	...	...	...	1319	1425	...	...	...	1521	1625	...	...	...	1721
Emden Hbf **812** d.	0643	0735	0843	...	...	0942	1043	...	...	1137	1243	...	...	...	1341	1443	...	...	...	1538	1643	...	...	...	1738
Norden **812** d.	0707	0810	0907	...	...	...	1107	...	...	*1206*	1307	...	...	...	1409	1507	...	...	...	...	1707	...	...	...	...
Norddeich 812 a.	0713	0816	0913	...	...	...	1113	...	...	*1212*	1313	...	...	...	1415	1513	...	...	...	...	1713	...	...	...	...
Norddeich Mole 812 a.	0717	0820	0918	...	...	...	1118	...	...	*1218*	1318	...	...	...	1421	1518	...	...	...	...	1718	...	...	...	...

		ICE 538 ✕		IC 2036 🍷	IC 1986 ⑥t A🍷		ICE 536 ✕		IC 2034 🍷		ICE 776 ⑧q F✕			IC 2032 🍷	⑧n	D	ICE 832 H ✕	ICE 862 ⑤f ✕	IC 1932 ⑦w R		ICE 732 ✕	ICE 732 ⑦w ✕		ICE 850 ⑦w ✕	
München Hbf **900** d.	...	1052	...	...	...	...	1252	...	...	...	...	...	...	...	...	...	...	...	...	...	1820	1820	...	...	...
Nürnberg Hbf **900** d.	...	|	...	...	1318	...	|	...	...	...	...	...	...	...	...	...	...	...	...	...	1933	1933	...	...	...
Leipzig Hbf **810** d.	...	|	...	1342	|	...	|	...	1542	...	...	...	...	1742	...	...	...	...	...	...	|	|	...	...	...
Berlin Hbf **810** d.	...	|	...	|	|	...	|	...	|	...	...	...	...	|	...	...	1948	1948	2009s	...	|	|	...	2149	...
Magdeburg Hbf **810** d.	...	|	...	1500	|	...	|	...	1700	...	...	...	...	1900	...	...	|	|	|	...	|	|	...	|	...
Hannover Hbf d.	1521	1545	1621	1645	1702	1721	1745	1821	1845	1920	1949	...	2020	2045	...	2120	2145	2145	2145	2220	2251	2251	2320	2345	0020
Nienburg (Weser) d.	1555	|	1655	1713	1730	1755	...	1855	1913	1954	|	...	2054	2113	...	2154	|	|	|	2254	|	|	2354	|	0054
Verden (Aller) d.	1615	|	1715	1730	1750	1815	...	1915	1930	2015	|	...	2115	2130	...	2215	|	|	|	2315	|	|	0015	|	0115
Bremen Hbf a.	1639	1644p	1739	1751	1811	1839	1844p	1939	1951	2039	2048	←	2140	2151	...	2240	2244p	2247	2244	2339	2348	2348	0039	0044	0139
Bremen Hbf d.	1654	...	...	1755	...	1854	...	...	1955	→	2050a	2056	...	2155q	...	2254	...	2258	2247	...	...	2352	...	0046	...
Delmenhorst d.	1704	...	...	1806	...	1904	...	...	2006	▬	|	2106	...	2206q	...	2304	...	|	2258	...	...	|	...	|	...
Oldenburg (Oldb) a.	1723	...	...	1822	...	1923	...	...	2022	...	2115a	2125	...	2222q	...	2323	...	2328	2315	...	...	0017	...	0123	...
Oldenburg (Oldb) d.	1732	...	...	1832	...	1932	...	...	...	2032	...	2132	...	...	2232	2332	...	...	...	...	...	...	...	...	...
Bad Zwischenahn d.	1745	...	...	1844	...	1945	...	...	...	2045	...	2145	...	...	2245	2345	...	...	...	...	...	...	...	...	...
Leer (Ostfriesland) a.	1814	...	...	1915	...	2014	...	...	...	2114	...	2214	...	...	2314	0014	...	...	...	...	...	...	...	...	...
Leer (Ostfriesland) **812** d.	1825	...	...	1925	...	2025	...	...	...	2121	...	2225	...	...	2321	0025	...	...	...	...	...	...	...	...	...
Emden Hbf **812** d.	1843	...	...	1945	...	2043	...	...	...	2138	...	2243	...	...	2338	0041	...	...	...	...	...	...	...	...	...
Norden **812** d.	1907	...	...	2008	...	2107	...	...	...	...	...	2307	...	...	...	...	...	...	...	...	...	...	...	...	...
Norddeich 812 a.	1913	...	...	2015	...	2113	...	...	...	...	...	2313	...	...	...	...	...	...	...	...	...	...	...	...	...
Norddeich Mole 812 a.	1918	...	...	2021	...	...	...	...	...	...	...	...	...	...	...	...	...	...	...	...	...	...	...	...	...

A – ROTTALER LAND – (12) and 🍷 Passau - Regensburg - Bremen - Hamburg and v.v.
B – OSTFRIESLAND – (12) and 🍷 Emden - Magdeburg - Berlin (- Cottbus ⑧q).
C – OSTFRIESLAND – (12) and 🍷 (Cottbus ①–⑥e -) Berlin - Oldenburg (- Norddeich Mole □).
D – Daily Hannover - Bremen - Oldenburg; ⑥ only Oldenburg - Emden.
F – (12) and ✕ (Darmstadt ①–⑤a -) Frankfurt - Hannover - Bremen (- Oldenburg ①–⑤a).
H – ①②③④⑥ (also Dec. 23, 30, Mar. 21, 23, May 2, 11; not Dec. 26, Jan. 1, Mar. 20, 24, Apr. 30, May 12).
R – From Stralsund (Table **845**).

a – ①–⑤ (not Dec. 24, 25, 26, 31, Jan. 1, Mar. 21, 24, May 12).
d – Not Dec. 24, 25, 26, 31, Jan. 1, Mar. 21, 24, May 12.
e – ①–⑥ (not Dec. 25, 26, Jan. 1, Mar. 22, 24, May 12).

f – Also Mar. 20, Apr. 30; not Mar. 21, May 2.
g – Also Dec. 27, Jan. 2, Mar. 25, May 13; not Dec. 24, 31, Mar. 24, May 12.
n – Not Dec. 24, 31.
p – Connects with train in previous column.
q – ⑧ (not Dec. 24, 25, 31, Mar. 21, 23, May 11).
r – ⚒ only.
s – Berlin **Spandau**.
t – Not Dec. 29.
w – Also Dec. 26, Jan. 1, Mar. 24, May 12; not Dec. 23, 30, Mar. 23, May 11.

□ – ⑤⑦ to Mar. 9 (also Dec. 20, 22, 26, 27, 29, Jan. 1, 2, 3, 5); daily from Mar. 14.

OSNABRÜCK - OLDENBURG - WILHELMSHAVEN 814

NordWestBahn

km																									
		⚒	Ⓐ	⚒D		Ⓐ										B							⚒		†
0	**Osnabrück** Hbf d.	...	0442	0602	...	0626	0702	0802	0902	1002	1102	1202	1302	1402	1502	...	1602	1702	1802	1902	2002	2102	...	2253	2253
20	Bramsche d.	...	0500	0617	...	0641	0717	0817	0917	1017	1117	1217	1317	1417	1517	...	1617	1717	1817	1917	2017	2117	...	2313	2313
50	Quakenbrück d.	...	0539	0640	...	0710	0740	0840	0940	1040	1140	1240	1340	1440	1540	...	1640	1740	1840	1940	2040	2140	...	2341	2341
72	Cloppenburg d.	...	0556	0656	...	0742	0756	0856	0956	1056	1156	1256	1356	1456	1556	...	1656	1756	1856	1956	2056	2156	...	2358	2358
113	**Oldenburg** (Oldb) a.	...	0629	0729	...	0819	0829	0929	1029	1129	1229	1329	1429	1529	1629	...	1729	1829	1929	2029	2129	2229	...	0032	0032
113	**Oldenburg** (Oldb) d.	0535	0635	0735	0735	...	0835	0935	1035	1135	1235	1335	1435	1535	1635	1706	1735	1835	1935	2035	2135	2235	2335	...	0039
143	Varel (Oldb) d.	0558	0658	0758	0758	...	0858	0958	1058	1158	1258	1358	1458	1558	1658	1729	1758	1858	1958	2058	2158	2258	2358	...	0103
165	**Wilhelmshaven** a.	0618	0718	0818	0818	...	0918	1018	1118	1218	1318	1418	1518	1618	1718	1748	1818	1918	2018	2118	2218	2318	0018	...	0122

	Ⓐ		Ⓐ	⚒	Ⓐ					⑥	Ⓑ		Ⓐ										©A		
Wilhelmshaven d.	...	0444	...	0544	*0613*	0644	0744	0844	0944	*1013*	1044	1144	...	1244	1344	1444	1544	1644	1744	1844	1944	2044	2044	2144	2244
Varel (Oldb) d.	...	0502	...	0602	*0631*	0702	0802	0902	1002	1102	1102	1202	...	1302	1402	1502	1602	1702	1802	1902	2002	2102	2102	2202	2302
Oldenburg (Oldb) a.	...	0525	...	0625	*0653*	0725	0825	0925	1025	1125	1125	1225	...	1325	1425	1525	1625	1725	1825	1925	2025	2125	2125	2225	2325
Oldenburg (Oldb) d.	0412	0529	0546	0629	0657	0729	0829	0929	1029	1129	1129	1229	1246	1329	1429	1529	1629	1729	1829	1929	2029	...	2129	2229	...
Cloppenburg d.	0444	0606	0631	0706	0733	0806	0906	1006	1106	1206	1206	1306	1332	1406	1506	1606	1706	1806	1906	2006	2106	...	2206	2301	...
Quakenbrück d.	0459	0621	0651	0721	0750	0821	0921	1021	1121	1221	1221	1321	1352	1421	1521	1621	1721	1821	1921	2021	2121	...	2221	2321	...
Bramsche d.	0522	0641	0710	0741	0810	0841	0941	1041	1141	1241	1241	1341	1412	1441	1541	1641	1741	1841	1941	2041	2141	...	2241	2341	...
Osnabrück Hbf a.	0540	0657	0727	0757	0827	0857	0957	1057	1157	1257	1257	1357	1427	1457	1557	1657	1757	1857	1957	2057	2157	...	2257	2357	...

A – From Apr. 12. B – From Bremen Hbf (d. 1631). D – Daily from Apr. 7. **Operator**: NordWestBahn GmbH, Alte Poststr. 9, 49074 Osnabrück. ✆ +49 (0) 1805 60 01 61.

BREMEN - BREMERHAVEN - CUXHAVEN 815

RE/RB services

km																								
			©v	⚒			Ⓐn	©d			Ⓐn			Ⓐn			Ⓐn	©d			Ⓐn			Ⓐn
	Osnabrück Hbf 800 801 d.	...	...	...	0538r	...	0638	...	0738	...	...	0938	...	...	1138	...	...	...	1338b	...	1438	1538	...	1638
0	**Bremen** Hbf d.	0004	0045	0534	0656	0734	0756	0757	0856	0934	...	1056	1134	...	1256	1334	...	1357	1456	1534	1556	1656	1734	1756
21	Osterholz-Scharmbeck d.	0022	0102	0552	0710	0752	0810	0811	0910	0952	...	1110	1152	...	1310	1352	...	1411	1510	1552	1610	1710	1752	1810
63	**Bremerhaven** Hbf d.	0057	0140	0627	0732	0827	0832	0837	0932	1027	1036	1132	1227	1236	1332	1427	1436	1437	1532	1627	1632	1732	1827	1832
66	**Bremerhaven** Lehe d.	0101	0144	0632	0736	0832	0836	0842	0936	1032	1041	1136	1232	1241	1336	1432	1441	1442	1536	1632	1636	1736	1832	1836
106	**Cuxhaven** a.	...	...	*0727*	*0827*	...	*0927*	0921	*1027*	...	1127	*1227*	...	1327	*1427*	...	1527	1521	*1627*	...	*1727*	*1827*	...	*1927*

			Ⓐn		Ⓑn			Ⓐn	†	
Osnabrück Hbf 800 801 d.	1738	...	...	...	1938	...	...	...	...	...
Bremen Hbf d.	1856	1934	...	2034	2056	...	2134	...	2157g	2234
Osterholz-Scharmbeck d.	1910	1952	...	2052	2110	...	2152	...	2211g	2252
Bremerhaven Hbf d.	1932	2027	2036	2127	2132	2136	2227	2236	2238	2327
Bremerhaven Lehe d.	1936	2032	2041	2132	2136	2141	2232	2241	2243	2332
Cuxhaven a.	*2027*	...	2127	...	...	2227	...	2327	2324	...

	⚒	⚒	Ⓐn	⚒		⚒	Ⓐn		
Cuxhaven d.	...	...	*0509*	...	...	0639	...	...	*0739*
Bremerhaven Lehe d.	0407	0528	0554	0623	0628	0720	0723	0728	0823
Bremerhaven Hbf d.	0412	0533	0559	0628	0633	0724	0728	0733	0828
Osterholz-Scharmbeck d.	0457	0608	0634	0650	0708	...	0750	0808	0850
Bremen Hbf a.	0505	0626	0656	0703	0726	...	0803	0826	0903
Osnabrück Hbf 800 801 a.	...	...	...	0820	...	...	0920	...	1020

	Ⓐn			©d	Ⓐn			Ⓐn			Ⓐn			©d	Ⓐn			Ⓐn			Ⓐn		Ⓐn	⑤⑥
Cuxhaven d.	*0839*	...	*0939*	1033	1039	...	*1139*	1239	...	*1339*	1439	...	*1539*	1633	*1639*	...	*1739*	1839	...	*1939*	2039	*2139*	2239	...
Bremerhaven Lehe d.	0923	0928	1023	1112	1120	1128	1223	1320	1328	1423	1520	1528	1623	1712	1723	1728	1823	1920	1928	2023	2120	2228	2320	2328
Bremerhaven Hbf d.	0928	0933	1028	1118	1124	1133	1228	1324	1333	1428	1524	1533	1628	1718	1728	1733	1828	1924	1933	2028	2124	2233	2324	2333
Osterholz-Scharmbeck d.	0950	1008	1050	1143	...	1208	1250	...	1408	1450	...	1608	1650	1743	1750	1808	1850	...	2008	2050	2155f	2308	...	0008
Bremen Hbf a.	1003	1026	1103	1158	...	1226	1303	...	1426	1503	...	1626	1703	1758	1803	1826	1903	...	2026	2103	2210f	2326	...	0026
Osnabrück Hbf 800 801 a.	1120	...	1220	...	...	...	1420	...	...	1620	...	...	1820	...	1920	...	2020	...	...	2220	...	...	...	...

b – Ⓑ (not Dec. 24, 31). d – From Mar. 29. f – ⑤ from Mar. 28 (also Apr. 30). g – † from Mar. 30 (not May 11). n – Not Dec. 24, 31. v – Not Dec. 25, Jan. 1. r – ⚒ only.

HAMBURG - CUXHAVEN and BREMERHAVEN 818

metronom; EVB

Hamburg - Buxtehude - Cuxhaven ⊖

km																									
		Ⓐn‡	⚒	‡	Ⓐn‡	Ⓐg	⚒	⚒	w	⚒	c	⚒		⚒		⚒	b	⚒b	b	m	n	n	n	‡	‡
0	**Hamburg** Hbf § d.	0448	...	0528	0558	...	...	0707	0807	0907	1007	1107	1207d	1307	1407	1506	1607	1707	1807	1907	2007	2107	2207	2328	0028
12	**Hamburg** Harburg § d.	0501	...	0541	0611	0624	...	0724	0824	0924	1024	1124	1224d	1324	1424	1524	1624	1724	1824	1924	2024	2124	2224	2341	0041
33	**Buxtehude** § d.	0525	...	0605	0635	0638	...	0738	0838	0938	1038	1138	1238d	1338	1438	1538	1638	1738	1838	1938	2038	2138	2238	0005	0105
54	Stade § d.	0545	0550	0625	...	0656	0656	0756	0856	0956	1056	1156	1256	1356	1456	1556	1656	1756	1856	1956	2056	2156	2256	0025	0125
102	Otterndorf d.	...	0632	...	...	0738	0738	0838	0938	1038	1138	1238	1338	1438	1538	1638	1738	1838	1938	2038	2138	2238	2338	...	...
116	**Cuxhaven** a.	...	0644	...	...	0750	0750	0850	0950	1050	1150	1250	1350	1450	1550	1650	1750	1850	1950	2050	2150	2250	2350	...	...

	⚒	Ⓐ	⚒	†v	‡	⚒	c	d	e	⚒		⚒b	b	⚒b		⚒b	n	n	©	Ⓐb	‡	©	Ⓐn	‡
Cuxhaven d.	0511	0551	0611	0638	...	0651	0811	0911	1011	1111	1211	1311	1411	1511	1611	1711	1811	1911	2011	2039	...	2211	2239	...
Otterndorf d.	0523	0603	0623	0650	...	0703	0823	0923	1023	1123	1223	1323	1423	1523	1623	1723	1823	1923	2023	2051	...	2223	2251	...
Stade § d.	0606	0646	0706	0732	0737	0746	0906	1006	1106	1206	1306	1406	1506	1606	1706	1806	1906	2006	2106	2133	2137	2306	2333	2337
Buxtehude § d.	0621	0701	0721	...	0756	0801	0921	1021	1121	1221	1321	1421	1521	1621	1721n	1821	1921	2021	2121	...	2156	2321	...	2356
Hamburg Harburg § a.	0637	0717	0737	...	0820	0817	0937	1037	1137	1237	1337	1437	1537	1637	1737n	1837	1937	2037	2137	...	2220	2337	...	0020
Hamburg Hbf § a.	0656	0737	0758	...	0834	0837	0958	1058	1158	1258	1358	1458	1558	1658	1758n	1858	1958	2058	2158	...	2234	2354	...	0034

Buxtehude - Bremerhaven △

km																									
		⚒		Ⓐ	Ⓐ	©	⚒		⚒		⚒	Ⓐ		©	⚒	Ⓐn		⚒n	Ⓐn		Ⓐn	⚒n	©		n
0	**Buxtehude** d.	...	0533a	0642	0722	0742	0842	0942	1042	1142	1242	...	1342	1342	1447	...	1547	1647	...	1747	1847	1847	1947	1947	2147
39	Bremervörde a.	...	0625a	0727	0825	0825	0925	1025	1125	1225	1325	...	1425	1425	1530	...	1630	1730	...	1830	1930	1930	2030	2030	2230
39	Bremervörde d.	0535	0635	0735	0835	0835	...	1035	...	1235	...	1335	...	1435	...	1535	1635	...	1735	1835	1935	...	2035	...	...
78	**Bremerhaven** Hbf a.	0621	0721	0821	0921	0921	...	1121	...	1321	...	1421	...	1521	...	1621	1721	...	1821	1921	2021	...	2121	...	...

	Ⓐ	⚒	†	⚒		⚒	Ⓐ	©	⚒	Ⓐ	©	⚒		⚒n		Ⓐn	⚒n		Ⓐn		©	⚒n	†	⑥	Ⓐn
Bremerhaven Hbf d.	...	0539a	...	0639	0739	0839a	...	0939	1039a	...	1139	1239a	1339	...	1539	1639	...	1739	1839	1939	1939	2039	2139	2239	2339
Bremervörde a.	...	0620a	...	0720	0820	0920a	...	1020	1120a	...	1220	1320a	1420	...	1620	1720	...	1820	1920	2020	2020	2120	2220	2320	0020
Bremervörde d.	0530	0630	0635	0730	0830z	0930	1030	1030z	1130	1230	1230z	1330	1435	1535	1635	...	1735	1835	1935	...	2035	...	...	...	...
Buxtehude a.	0614	0714	0719	0814	0914z	1014	1114	1114z	1214	1314	1314z	1414	1519	1619	1719	...	1819	1919	2019	...	2119	...	...	...	...

a – Ⓐ only.
b – Not Dec. 24.
c – Not Dec. 25.
d – Not Jan. 1.
e – Not Dec. 25, 26.
g – Not Dec. 27.
m – Not Dec. 24, 25, 26.
n – Not Dec. 24, 31.
v – Not Dec. 25, 26, Jan. 1.
w – Not Dec. 25, Jan. 1.
z – 5 minutes later on †.
‡ – Hamburg S-Bahn (2nd class only).
§ – Additional S-Bahn trains operate.
⊖ – Operated by metronom Eisenbahngesellschaft mbH. Most trains start from / terminate at Hamburg Harburg Dec. 24 - Jan. 1.
△ – Operated by Eisenbahnen und Verkehrsbetriebe Elbe-Weser GmbH (EVB).

HAMBURG - KIEL 820

RE services except where shown

ICE services are subject to alteration Dec. 24 - Jan. 1

km										ICE 808	ICE 76	ICE 926	ICE 74	ICE 1508	ICE 774	EC 102
											x	1026		Ⓑq	Ⓑq	⑦w
		v	⚒				n			B ✕	Z ✕	A ✕	Z ✕	M ✕	S ✕	C ✕
0	**Hamburg** Hbf 823 d.	0028	0520	0620	and	2220	2323	...	also	1015	1538	1615	1738	1844	2040	2115
37	Elmshorn 823 d.	0059	0552	0650	hourly	2250	2353	...		|	|	|	|	|	|	|
73	Neumünster 823 d.	0132	0618	0716	until	2316	0019	...		1103	1626	1704	1828	1932	2128	2203
111	**Kiel** Hbf a.	0157	0638	0736		2336	0039	...		1121	1644	1722	1846	1951	2147	2221

										ICE 773	ICE 73	ICE 1509	ICE 927		ICE 677	ICE 809
										①-⑥		①-⑥	1027		x	
	⑥k	Ⓐn		v				n		e S ✕	Z ✕	e M ✕	A ✕		K ✕	B ✕
Kiel Hbf d.	0355	0406	0521	0621	0721	and	2221	2321	also	0612	0712	0810	1238	...	1712	1838
Neumünster 823 d.	0420	0426	0542	0642	0742	hourly	2242	2342		0631	0730	0828	1257	...	1730	1857
Elmshorn 823 d.	0453	0458	0609	0709	0809	until	2309	0009		|	|	|	|		|	|
Hamburg Hbf 823 a.	0527	0530	0637	0737	0837		2337	0037		0720	0820	0914	1343	...	1819	1943

A – (12) Nürnberg - Frankfurt - Köln - Kiel and v.v.
B – (12) Basel - Karlsruhe - Frankfurt - Köln - Kiel and v.v.
C – (12) Chur - Zürich - Basel - Karlsruhe - Köln - Kiel.
K – (12) Kiel - Hannover - Frankfurt - Karlsruhe.
M – (12) München - Nürnberg - Leipzig - Berlin - Kiel and v.v.
S – (12) Kiel - Hannover - Frankfurt - Stuttgart and v.v.
Z – (12) Kiel - Hannover - Frankfurt - Karlsruhe - Basel - Zürich and v.v.

e – Not Dec. 25, 26, Jan. 1, Mar. 22, 24, May 12.
k – Also Dec. 24, 31.
n – Not Dec. 24, 31.
q – Not Dec. 24, 25, 31, Mar. 21, 23, May 11.
v – Not Dec. 25, Jan. 1.
w – Also Dec. 26, Jan. 1, Mar. 24, May 12; not Dec. 23, 30, Mar. 23, May 11.
x – Not Dec. 24 - Jan. 1.

821 HAMBURG - WESTERLAND

DB; NOB

km		◇	◇	◇	◇	◇	◇	◇	◇	◇	◇	◇	*IC* 2314	◇	◇	*IC* 2074	*IC* 2072	◇	◇	*IC* 2310	◇	◇	*IC* 2170	◇	◇
			Ⓐ		Ⓒ		Ⓐ					S	S	W		⑥⑦	①–⑤								
													🍷			D✕	D✕			F🍷			J🍷		
	Köln Hbf **800** d.	...	...	...	...	...	...	...	...	...	...	...	0511	...	...	...	...	...	...	0911	...	...	...	...	...
	Berlin Hbf **840** d.	...	...	...	...	...	...	...	...	...	...	...	|	...	...	0822	0822	...	...	|	...	...	...	...	...
	Hamburg Hbf **820** d.	...	...	...	...	...	*0500‡*	...	*0620**	*0720**	*0820**	*0843**	0915	*0920**	*1020**	1048	1048	*1120**	*1220**	1315	*1335‡*	*1420**	1448	*1520**	*1620*
0	**Hamburg** Altona d.	...	...	...	...	...	0524	...	0633	0733	0833	0907	|	0933	1033	|	|	1133	1233	|	1358	1433	|	1533	1633
30	Elmshorn **820** d.	...	...	...	...	...	0545	...	0655	0755	0855	0932	|	0955	1055	|	|	1155	1255	|	1420	1455	|	1555	1655
64	Itzehoe a.	...	...	...	...	...	0610	...	0719	0817	0917	0956	1001	1019	1119	1140	1140	1219	1319	1401	1445	1519	1541	1619	1719
64	Itzehoe d.	...	0454	...	0536	...	0610	...	0720	0818	0918	0957	1016	1020	1120	1142	1142	1220	1320	1416	1446	1520	1543	1620	1720
123	Heide (Holst) a.	...	0540	...	0622	...	0656	...	0756	0856	0956	1033	1053	1056	1156	1219	1219	1256	1356	1453	1525	1556	1620	1656	1756
123	Heide (Holst) d.	...	0549	...	0623	...	0702	...	0802	0902	1002	1034	1055	1102	1202	1221	1221	1302	1402	1455	1527	1602	1622	1702	1802
157	Husum a.	...	0615	...	0649	...	0728	...	0828	0929	1029	1058	1118	1128	1228	1243	1243	1328	1428	1518	1555	1628	1644	1728	1828
157	Husum d.	0600	...	0630	...	0700	0730	0730	0830	0930	1030	1100	1120	1130	1230	1245	1245	1330	1430	1520	1600	1630	1657	1730	1830
197	Niebüll a.	0628	...	0658	...	0728	0758	0758	0858	0958	1058	1128	1146	1158	1258	1311	1311	1358	1458	1546	1628	1658	1724	1758	1858
197	Niebüll d.	0631	...	0701	...	0731	0801	0801	0901	1001	1101	1131	1201	1201	1301	1331	1331	1401	1501	1601	1631	1701	1731	1801	1901
237	**Westerland** (Sylt) a.	0705	...	0735	...	0805	0835	0835	0937	1035	1135	1207	1234	1235	1337	1404	1406	1435	1535	1634	1705	1735	1804	1835	1935

	◇	◇	◇	*IC* 1908	◇	◇	◇	◇		
				⑦d			n	m	n ‡	v
Köln Hbf **800** d.	...	...	...	1539	...	...	...	...	...	...
Berlin Hbf **840** d.	...	...	...	|	...	...	...	...	...	...
Hamburg Hbf **820** d.	*1720**	*1820**	*1920**	2009	*2020**	*2120**	...	*2220**	2340	...
Hamburg Altona d.	1733	1833	1933	|	2033	2133	...	2233	2352	0002
Elmshorn **820** d.	1755	1855	1955	|	2055	2155	...	2255	...	0029
Itzehoe a.	1819	1919	2019	2054	2119	2219	...	2317	...	0058
Itzehoe d.	1820	1920	2020	2106	2120	2220	...	2318	...	...
Heide (Holst) a.	1856	1956	2056	2143	2206	2306	...	0006	...	...
Heide (Holst) d.	1902	2002	2102	2145	2207	2307	...	0007	...	...
Husum a.	1928	2028	2128	2210	2233	2333	...	0035	...	...
Husum d.	1930	2030	2130	2219	2235**n**	...	2336	...	...	...
Niebüll a.	1958	2058	2158	2244	2303**n**	...	0004	...	...	...
Niebüll d.	2001	2101	2201	2247	2304**n**	...	0005	...	...	...
Westerland (Sylt) a.	2035	2135	2235	2314	2337**n**	...	0037	...	...	...

	◇		◇	◇	◇	◇	◇	◇	◇	◇
	v		Ⓐ	Ⓐ		Ⓒv	Ⓐ			
Westerland (Sylt) d.	0100	...	...	0423	...	0522	0522	...	0622	0722
Niebüll a.	0130	...	...	0453	...	0559	0559	...	0659	0759
Niebüll d.	0131	...	...	0454	...	0600	0601	...	0701	0801
Husum a.	0201	...	...	0522	...	0628	0629	...	0729	0829
Husum d.	...	...	0425	...	0525	...	0631	0631	0731	0831
Heide (Holst) a.	...	...	0450	...	0550	...	0656	0656	0756	0856
Heide (Holst) d.	...	...	0452	...	0552	...	0702	0702	0802	0902
Itzehoe a.	...	...	0538	...	0638	...	0738	0738	0838	0938
Itzehoe d.	...	...	0539	...	0639	...	0739	0739	0839	0939
Elmshorn **820** d.	...	...	0604	...	0704	...	0804	0804	0904	1004
Hamburg Altona a.	...	...	0626	...	0726	...	0826	0826	0926	1026
Hamburg Hbf **820** a.	...	...	*0637**	...	*0737**	...	*0837**	*0837**	*0937**	*1037*
Berlin Hbf **840** a.	...	...	...	...	...	...	...	...	...	...
Köln Hbf **800** a.	...	...	...	...	...	...	...	...	...	...

	◇	*IC* 2311	◇	◇	◇	*IC* 2171	*IC* 2181	◇	◇	*IC* 2315	◇	◇	◇	*IC* 2073	*IC* 2075	◇	◇	◇	◇	◇		◇	◇	◇	◇
					A	⑤–⑦	①–④		W	S	S			①–⑤	⑥⑦					n	n		n		v
		H🍷				L🍷	N🍷			G🍷				D✕	D✕										
Westerland (Sylt) d.	0822	0926	0952	1022	1122	1156	1156	1222	1322	1326	1352	1422	1522	1552	1552	1622	1722	1822	1922	2022	...	2122	...	2255	0000
Niebüll a.	0859	0959	1029	1059	1159	1229	1229	1259	1359	1359	1429	1459	1559	1629	1629	1659	1759	1859	1959	2059	...	2159	...	2326	0030
Niebüll d.	0901	1013	1031	1101	1201	1245	1245	1301	1401	1413	1431	1501	1601	1643	1643	1701	1801	1901	2001	2101	...	2201	...	2331	0031
Husum a.	0929	1039	1059	1129	1229	1310	1310	1329	1429	1439	1459	1529	1629	1707	1707	1729	1829	1929	2029	2129	...	2229	...	0001	0101
Husum d.	0931	1041	1101	1131	1231	1312	1312	1331	1431	1441	1501	1531	1631	1709	1709	1731	1831	1931	2031	2131	...	...	2244	...	...
Heide (Holst) a.	0956	1102	1129	1156	1256	1333	1333	1356	1456	1502	1527	1556	1656	1733	1733	1756	1856	1956	2056	2156	...	...	2309	...	...
Heide (Holst) d.	1002	1104	1131	1202	1302	1335	1335	1402	1502	1504	1529	1602	1702	1735	1735	1802	1902	2002	2102	2202	...	...	2313	...	...
Itzehoe a.	1038	1141	1206	1238	1338	1412	1412	1438	1538	1541	1605	1638	1738	1812	1812	1838	1938	2038	2147	2247	...	...	0001	...	...
Itzehoe d.	1039	1157	1207	1239	1339	1414	1414	1439	1539	1557	1606	1639	1739	1814	1814	1839	1939	2039	2148	2248	2323	...	...	...	...
Elmshorn **820** d.	1104	|	1230	1304	1404	|	|	1504	1604	|	1629	1704	1804	|	|	1904	2004	2104	2214	2314	2353	...	...	...	...
Hamburg Altona a.	1126	|	1252	1326	1426	|	|	1526	1626	|	1651	1726	1826	|	|	1926	2026	2126	2235	2335	0020	...	...	...	...
Hamburg Hbf **820** a.	*1137**	1243	*1311‡*	*1337**	*1437**	1511	1511	*1537**	*1637**	1643	*1711‡*	*1737**	*1837**	1909	1909	*1937**	*2037**	*2137**	*2252***r**	*0001‡*	*0037**	...	...	...	...
Berlin Hbf **840** a.	...	|	...	...	...	...	...	...	...	|	...	...	...	2123	2123	...	...	...	...	...	...	...	...	...	...
Köln Hbf **800** a.	...	1649	...	...	...	...	...	...	...	2049	...	...	...	...	...	...	...	...	...	...	...	...	...	...	...

A – Daily until Mar. 14; Ⓐ from Mar. 17.
D – SYLTER STRAND. From / to Dresden on dates in Table **840**.
F – NORDFRIESLAND – (12) and 🍷 Frankfurt - Koblenz - Köln - Westerland.
G – DEICHGRAF – (12) and 🍷 Westerland - Köln - Mainz - Heidelberg - Stuttgart.
H – NORDFRIESLAND – (12) and 🍷 Westerland - Köln - Mainz - Heidelberg.
J – WATTENMEER – (12) and 🍷 (Frankfurt ⑥⑦ **c** -) Hannover - Westerland.
L – ⑤–⑦ (also Dec. 24, 25, 26, 31, Jan. 1, Mar. 20, 24, Apr. 30, May 12).
WATTENMEER – (12) and 🍷 Westerland - Hannover - Frankfurt.
N – ①–④ (not Dec. 24, 25, 26, 31, Jan. 1, Mar. 20, 24, Apr. 30, May 12).
WATTENMEER – (12) and 🍷 Westerland - Hannover - Göttingen.
S – From Mar. 15.
W – Until Mar. 14.

a – Ⓐ only.
c – Also Dec. 24, 31, Mar. 21, May 1; not Dec. 30, Mar. 23.
d – Also Jan. 1, Mar. 24, May 12; not Dec. 23, 30, Mar. 23, May 11.
m – Not Dec. 24, 31, Mar. 15.
n – Not Dec. 24, 31.
r – *2258* Dec. 24 – 31.
v – Not Dec. 25, Jan. 1.

* – Change trains at Elmshorn.
‡ – S-Bahn connection Hamburg Hbf - Hamburg Altona and v.v.
◇ – Operated by Nord-Ostsee-Bahn GmbH.

822 SCHLESWIG-HOLSTEIN BRANCH LINES

Neumünster - Heide - Büsum ⊠

km		⚒		⚒	⑥		Ⓐ													k	k		n		n
0	Neumünster d.	...	...	...	0537	...	0537	...	0737	...	0937	...	1137	...	1337	...	1537	...	1737	...	1937	...	...	...	2137
63	Heide a.	...	...	...	0646	...	0710	...	0846	...	1046	...	1246	...	1446	...	1646	...	1846	...	2046	...	...	...	2246
63	Heide d.	0451	...	0601	0701	0701	...	0801	0901	1001	1101	1201	1301	1401	1501	1601	1701	1801	1901**k**	2001	2101	...	2211	...	...
87	Büsum a.	0517	...	0627	0727	0727	...	0827	0927	1027	1127	1227	1327	1427	1527	1627	1727	1827	1927**k**	2027	2127	...	2237	...	...

	⚒	⚒		⚒	⑥														k	k	k		n	
Büsum d.	...	0521	...	0631	0631	...	0731	0831	0931	1031	1131	1231	1331	1431	1531	1631	1731	1831	1931	2031	2131	...	2241	...
Heide a.	...	0547	...	0657	0657	...	0757	0857	0957	1057	1157	1257	1357	1457	1557	1657	1757	1857	1957	2057	2157	...	2307	...
Heide d.	0517	...	...	...	0717	0717	...	0917	...	1117	...	1317	...	1517	...	1717	...	1917	...	2117	...	...	2318	...
Neumünster a.	0625	...	...	...	0825	0825	...	1025	...	1225	...	1425	...	1625	...	1825	...	2025	...	2225	...	...	0026	...

Husum - Bad St Peter Ording ◇

km		⑥	Ⓐn				n	n	n	n
0	Husum d.	0430	0437	0537	and	1837	1937	2037	2137	2237
21	Tönning d.	0455	0502	0602	hourly	1902	2002	2102	2202	2302
43	Bad St Peter Ording a.	0521	0528	0628	until	1928	2028	2128	2228	2328

	⑥	Ⓐn				n	n	n	n
Bad St Peter Ording d.	0527	0534	0634	and	1934	2034	2134	2234	2334
Tönning d.	0558	0605	0705	hourly	2005	2105	2205	2305	0005
Husum a.	0617	0624	0724	until	2024	2124	2224	2324	0024

Niebüll - Dagebüll Mole ⊡

km	*Until Mar. 14*	Ⓐ	🚌 Ⓒ	⚒		🚌 Ⓐ		n			🚌 ★	⑤⑦f
	Niebüll d.	...	...	...	...	...	...	...	...	1701	...	...
0	Niebüll neg d.	0635	0705	0805	0905	1035	1135	1320	1410	1710	1805	1910
14	Dagebüll Mole a.	0654	0720	0824	0924	1055	1154	1335	1429	1729	1825	1929

Until Mar. 14	Ⓐ	🚌 Ⓒ			🚌 Ⓐ		n			🚌 ★	⑤⑦
Dagebüll Mole d.	0705	0725	0830	0930	1100	1200	1340	1435	1730	1835	1935
Niebüll neg a.	0724	0740	0849	0949	1120	1219	1355	1454	1749	1855	1954
Niebüll a.	...	...	0855	0955	...	1225	...	...	...	...	...

km	*From Mar. 15*	◐										
	Niebüll d.	...	...	...	...	...	1148	1313	...	1548	...	1738
0	Niebüll neg ‡ d.	0635	0805	0905	1035	1135	1205	1325	1410	1605	1710	1805
14	Dagebüll Mole ‡ a.	0654	0824	0924	1054	1150	1220	1340	1425	1624	1729	1824

From Mar. 15	Ⓐ	🚌 Ⓒ	⚒								
Dagebüll Mole d.	0705	0725	0830	0935	1105	1155	1320	1435	1635	1735	1835
Niebüll neg a.	0724	0740	0849	0954	1124	1226	1351	1454	1654	1754	1854
Niebüll a.	...	...	0855	1000	...	1232	1357	1500	...	...	...

f – Also Dec. 26, Jan. 1.
k – Not Dec. 24.
n – Not Dec. 24, 31.

★ – ①②③④⑥ (not Dec. 24, 26, Jan. 1).
◐ – By 🚌 on Ⓒ (Niebüll d. 0705, Dagebüll Mole a. 0720).
⊠ – Operator: Schleswig-Holstein-Bahn GmbH.
◇ – Operator: Nord-Ostsee-Bahn GmbH.

⊡ – Operator: Norddeutsche Eisenbahngesellschaft Niebüll GmbH ✆ +49 (0) 4661 9808 90. Please check rail pass validity. Niebüll neg station is situated a short distance from the Niebüll DB station forecourt. Timings are subject to confirmation.

HAMBURG - NEUMÜNSTER - FLENSBURG - PADBORG 823

RE / RB services except where shown

km			CNL							EC	ICE									ICE						IC
			482							386	386									380						1970
		①–⑥	[R]	⚒	⑥m	Ⓐn				L	K														n	⑦w
		v	C ✕							A	A 🍷									B 🍷						F 🍷
0	Hamburg Hbf 820 d.	2323p	...	...	0520	0520	0620	0720	0843	0930	0930	0920	1043	1120	1243	1320	1443	1520	1643	1730	1720	1849	1920	2050	2120	2235
37	Elmshorn 820 d.	2353p	...	...	0552	0552	0650	0750	0910	│	│	0950	1110	1150	1310	1350	1510	1550	1710	│	1750	1917	1950	2117	2150	│
73	Neumünster 820 d.	0033	0443	0533	0633	0657	0733	0833	0933	1022	1022	1033	1133	1233	1333	1433	1533	1633	1733	1822	1833	1942	2033	2142	2233	2322
112	Rendsburg 824 d.	0103	│	0603	0703	0727	0803	0903	1003	1048	1048	1103	1203	1303	1403	1503	1603	1703	1803	1851	1903	2013	2103	2213	2303	2348
136	Schleswig 824 d.	0120	│	0620	0720	0744	0820	0920	1019	1104	1104	1120	1219	1320	1419	1520	1619	1720	1819	1907	1920	2029	2120	2229	2320	0004
174	Flensburg a.	0150	0546	0650	0750	0814	0850	0950	1044	1124	1124	1150	1244	1350	1444	1550	1644	1750	1844	1928	1950	2054	2150	2254	2350	0026
174	Flensburg 710 d.	...	│	0701	...	...	0901	...	1101	1126	...	...	1301	...	1501	...	1701	...	1901	...	...	2101	...	...	...	...
186	Padborg 🏛 710 a.	...	0559	0711	...	...	0911	...	1111	1137	...	...	1311	...	1511	...	1711	...	1911	...	...	2111	...	...	...	...
	København H 710 a.	...	0959	...	...	...	...	...	...	...	...	...	...	...	...	...	...	...	...	...	...	...	...	...	...	...

						IC		ICE		IC						EC	ICE							CNL	
						1973		381		1971						385	387							483	
	⚒	⚒				v	⑥r				⑤z						J	K							[R]	⑧n
									B 🍷		F						A	A 🍷							C ✕	
København H 710 d.	...	...	...	...	...	...	...	...	...	...	...	...	...	...	...	...	...	...	...	...	...	...	...	...	1853	...
Padborg 🏛 710 d.	...	...	...	...	0755	...	...	0945	...	...	...	1155	...	1345	...	1545	1640	...	...	1745	...	1945	...	2145	2218	...
Flensburg 710 a.	...	...	...	...	0807	...	...	0957	...	...	...	1207	...	1357	...	1557	1651	...	...	1757	...	1957	...	2157	│	...
Flensburg d.	0408	0508	0613	0706	0813	0908	0923	1013	1023	1108	1201	1213	1308	1413	1508	1613	1653	1653	1708	1813	1908	2008	2108	...	2232	2308
Schleswig 824 d.	0437	0537	0638	0735	0838	0937	0945	1038	1045	1137	1223	1238	1337	1438	1537	1638	1715	1715	1737	1838	1937	2037	2137	...	│	2337
Rendsburg 824 d.	0457	0557	0655	0755	0855	0957	1003	1055	1101	1157	1241	1255	1357	1455	1557	1655	1733	1733	1757	1855	1957	2057	2157	...	│	2357
Neumünster 820 a.	0526	0626	0723	0823	0923	1026	1029	1123	1129	1226	1306	1323	1428	1523	1626	1723	1757	1757	1826	1923	2026	2126	2226	...	2335	0026
Elmshorn 820 a.	0607	0707	0745	0907	0945	1107	│	1145	│	1307	1337	1345	1507	1545	1707	1745	│	│	1907	1945	2107	2207	2307	...	...	...
Hamburg Hbf 820 a.	0637	0737	0814	0937	1014	1137	1125	1214	1232	1337	1408	1414	1537	1614	1737	1814	1850	1850	1937	2014	2137	2237	2337	...	...	...

A – 🚃12 Hamburg - Fredericia - Århus and v.v.
B – 🚃12 and 🍷 Berlin - Hamburg - Fredericia - Århus and v.v.
C – Overnight train from / to München (see Table **900**), Basel (train number **40353/50483** – see Table **912**) and Amsterdam via Köln (train number **40347/40483** – see Tables **22** and **800**). For overnight journeys only.
F – From / to Berlin (Table **840**).
J – Until Jan. 5.
K – From Mar. 15.
L – Until Jan. 6.
m – Also Dec. 24, 31.
n – Not Dec. 24, 31.
p – Previous night.
r – Also Mar. 21, May 1; not Dec. 29, Mar. 22, May 3.
v – Not Dec. 25, Jan. 1.
w – Also Dec. 26, Jan. 1, Mar. 24, May 12; not Dec. 23, 30, Mar. 23, May 11.
z – Also Mar. 20, Apr. 30; not Mar. 21, May 2.

KIEL - HUSUM and FLENSBURG 824

RB services

km		A		⚒n					n	t	n	n
0	Kiel Hbf △ d.	0003	...	0345	0503	and	1903	2003	2103	2203	2303
40	Rendsburg 823 d.	0034	...	0434e	0534	hourly	1934	2034	2134	2234	2334
65	Schleswig 823 d.	0052	...	0452	0552	until	1952	2052	2152	2252	2352
102	Husum a.	0124	...	0524	0624		2024	2124	2224	2324	0024

	⚒n				t	n	n		⑧q
Husum △ d.	0435	0535	and	1935	2035	2135	2235	...	2335
Schleswig 823 d.	0508	0608	hourly	2008	2108	2208	2308	...	0008
Rendsburg 823 d.	0528	0628	until	2028	2128	2228	2328	...	0028
Kiel Hbf a.	0558	0658		2058	2158	2258	2358	...	0058

km		Ⓐn	⚒					n	n	n	
0	Kiel Hbf d.	0407	0519	...	0642	and	2042	2142	2242	2342	...
29	Eckernförde d.	0432	0555	...	0709	hourly	2109	2209	2309	0011	...
50	Süderbrarup d.	0450	0614	...	0729	until	2129	2229	2329	0029	...
81	Flensburg a.	0521	0641	...	0756		2156	2256	2356	0056	...

	⚒	v					n		n
Flensburg d.	0446	0546	...	0703	and	2103	2203	...	2322
Süderbrarup d.	0513	0613	...	0730	hourly	2130	2230	...	2351
Eckernförde d.	0532	0632	...	0749	until	2149	2249	...	0011
Kiel Hbf a.	0602	0702	...	0816		2216	2316	...	0038

A – ①–⑥ (not Dec. 25, 26, Jan. 1).
e – Arrives 0415.
n – Not Dec. 24, 31.
q – Not Dec. 24, 25, 31.
t – Not Dec. 24.
v – Not Dec. 25, Jan. 1.
△ – Kiel - Husum operator: Nord-Ostsee-Bahn GmbH. ✆ +49 (0) 180 10 180 11.

HAMBURG - LÜBECK - PUTTGARDEN 825

RB / RE services except where shown

km						EC				ICE*						IC				EC				EC			
						31				33						2120			35				337			
						L										©D							●			
						R				R						F			R				R			
0	Hamburg Hbf d.	0505	0605	...	0705	0725	0805	...	0905	0928	1005	...	1105	1205	...	1229	...	1305	1328	1405	...	1505	1528	1605	...	1705
40	Bad Oldesloe d.	0531	0631	...	0731	│	0831	...	0931	│	1031	...	1131	1231	...	│	...	1331	│	1431	...	1531	│	1631	...	1731
63	Lübeck Hbf a.	0550	0650	...	0750	│	0850	...	0950	│	1050	...	1150	1250	...	1312	...	1350	│	1450	...	1550	│	1650	...	1750
		v				│				│				E	E	│	©D		│				│			
63	Lübeck Hbf d.	0611	0711	0711	0811	0807u	0911	0911	1011	1007u	1111	1111	1211	1311	1311	1314	1318	1411	1407u	1511	1511	1611	1607u	1711	1711	1811
93	Neustadt (Holst) a.	0651	0751	│	0851	│	0951	│	1051	│	1153	│	1251	1353	│	│	1401	1451	│	1553	│	1651	│	1753	│	1851
115	Oldenburg (Holst) d.	...	...	0811	...	0839	...	1011	...	1039	...	1211	...	...	1411	1410	...	...	1439	...	1611	...	1639	...	1811	...
151	Puttgarden 🏛 a.	...	...	0839	...	0904	...	1039	...	1104	...	1239	...	...	1439	1435	...	...	1504	...	1639	...	1704	...	1839	...
	København H 720 a.	...	...	...	...	1211e	...	...	...	1411e	...	...	...	...	...	...	...	...	1811e	...	...	...	2011	...	...	...

	ICE										
	37										
										v	
	B R										
Hamburg Hbf d.	1728	1805	...	1905	2005	...	2105	2205	2326	0026	...
Bad Oldesloe d.	│	1831	...	1931	2031	...	2131	2231	2352	0052	...
Lübeck Hbf a.	1805	1850	...	1950	2050	...	2150	2250	0011	0111	...
	│					⑧q	n	n			
Lübeck Hbf d.	1807	1911	1911	2011	2111	2111	2211	2311	...	...	...
Neustadt (Holst) a.	│	1953	│	2051	2149	2149	2245	2345	...	...	...
Oldenburg (Holst) d.	1839	...	2011	...	...	2220	...	0014	...	...	...
Puttgarden 🏛 a.	1904	...	2039	...	...	2248	...	0042	...	...	...
København H 720 a.	2211e	...	...	...	...	...	...	...	...	...	...

											IC
											2329
			⚒		⚒		v	v			⑥C
											P
København H 720 d.	...	...	...	...	...	...	...	...	...	...	...
Puttgarden 🏛 d.	...	...	...	...	0521	...	0622	...	...	...	0907
Oldenburg (Holst) d.	...	...	...	...	0547	...	0648	...	...	...	0933
Neustadt (Holst) d.	...	...	0517	...	0617	0617	│	0709	0821	0917	│
Lübeck Hbf a.	...	...	0550	...	0650	0650	0750	0750	0855	0950	1037
	v										│
Lübeck Hbf d.	0413	0507	...	0607	...	0707	...	0807	0907	1007	1043
Bad Oldesloe d.	0432	0527	...	0627	...	0727	...	0827	0927	1027	│
Hamburg Hbf a.	0513	0553	...	0653	...	0753	...	0853	0953	1053	1121

			ICE				EC				EC		IC						ICE*				EC			
			38				338				36		2121						32				30			
							●						©D	ⒶE									H			n
			B R				R				R		F						R				R			
København H 720 d.	...	...	0742j	...	...	...	0942	...	...	...	1142k	...	...	...	...	...	...	...	1538	...	...	...	1738	...	...	...
Puttgarden 🏛 d.	0922	...	1042	...	1122	...	1242	...	1322	...	1442	...	1507	1522	...	...	1722	...	1842	...	1922	...	2042	...	2113	...
Oldenburg (Holst) d.	0948	...	1106	...	1148	...	1306	...	1348	...	1506	...	1533	1548	...	...	1748	...	1906	...	1948	...	2106	...	2139	...
Neustadt (Holst) d.	│	1013	│	1113	│	1213	│	1313	│	1413	│	1513	│	│	1613g	1713	│	1813	│	1913	│	2013	│	2113	2213	2313
Lübeck Hbf a.	1055	1055	1136	1155	1255	1255	1336s	1355	1455	1455	1536s	1555	1629	1655	1655	1755	1855	1855	1936s	1955	2055	2055	2136s	2155	2248	2348
			│				│				│		│						│				│			v
Lübeck Hbf d.	...	1107	1138	1207	...	1307	│	1407	...	1507	│	1607	1634	...	1707	1807	...	1907	│	2007	...	2107	│	2207	2307	0007
Bad Oldesloe d.	...	1127	│	1227	...	1327	│	1427	...	1527	│	1627	│	...	1727	1827	...	1927	│	2027	...	2127	│	2227	2327	0027
Hamburg Hbf a.	...	1153	1216	1253	...	1353	1416	1453	...	1553	1616	1653	1724	...	1753	1853	...	1953	2016	2053	...	2153	2216	2253	2353	0053

Lübeck - Travemünde

km		Ⓐn						
0	Lübeck Hbf d.	0601	0701	0801	and	2001	2101	2201
18	Travemünde Skandinavienkai ⊡ a.	0618	0718	0818	hourly	2018	2118	2218
21	Travemünde Strand a.	0623	0723	0823	until	2023	2123	2223

	Ⓐn							
Travemünde Strand d.	0630	0730	...	0830	and	2030	2130	2230
Travemünde Skandinavienkai ⊡ d.	0636	0736	...	0836	hourly	2036	2136	2236
Lübeck Hbf a.	0653	0753	...	0853	until	2053	2153	2253

B – From / to Berlin (Table **840**).
C – From June 14.
D – From Mar. 15.
E – Ⓐ (daily to Mar. 14).
F – FEHMARN – 🚃12 Frankfurt - Köln - Hamburg - Puttgarden and v.v.
H – Dec. 9 - Jan. 5 (not Dec. 24, 31) and from Mar. 14.
L – Dec. 9 - Jan. 5 (not Dec. 25, Jan. 1) and from Mar. 15.
P – LÜBECKER BUCHT – 🚃12 Puttgarden - Hamburg - Köln - Frankfurt - Passau.
R – [R] for journeys to / from Denmark.
e – 5–7 minutes earlier until Jan. 5.
g – 1621 on © from Mar. 15.
j – 0754 until Jan. 5.
k – 1138 until Jan. 5.
n – Not Dec. 24, 31.
q – Not Dec. 24, 25, 31, Mar. 20, 23, Apr. 30, May 11.
s – Stops to set down only.
u – Stops to pick up only.
v – Not Dec. 25, Jan. 1.
● – ⑤⑥ May 30 - June 7; daily June 13 - Aug. 24.
⊡ – For sailings to / from Trelleborg (Table **2390**) and Helsinki (Table **2485**).
* – Train classification *EC* until Jan. 5.

826 KIEL - LÜBECK - BAD KLEINEN

RE / RB services

km			v	ⒶS				S				S			P			nN				n	n	n
0	**Kiel** Hbf d.	...	0444	...	...	0544	0644	...		1344	1444	...	1544	1644	...	1744	1844	...	1944	2044	2144	...	2244	2344
33	Plön d.	...	0515	...	...	0616	0716	...	each train	1416	1516	...	1616	1716	...	1816	1916	...	2016	2116	2216	...	2316	0016
47	Eutin d.	...	0529	...	...	0630	0730	...	runs every	1430	1530	...	1630	1730	...	1830	1930	...	2030	2130	2230	...	2330	0030
80	**Lübeck** Hbf a.	...	0556	...	...	0656	0756	...	**two** hours	1456	1556	...	1656	1756	...	1856	1956	...	2056	2156	2256	...	2358	0058
80	**Lübeck** Hbf d.	0504	...	0601	...	0704	...	0801	until	1504	...	1601	1704	...	1801	1904	...	2001	2104	...	...	2301	...	...
119	Grevesmühlen d.	0539	...	0638	...	0741	...	0838		1541	...	1638	1741	...	1838	1941	...	2038	2141	...	...	2338	...	...
142	**Bad Kleinen** a.	0553	...	0656	...	0755	...	0856		1555	...	1656	1755	...	1856	1955	...	2056	2155	...	...	2356	...	...

	v		w	⚒	Ⓐ		Ⓐ		N				S				nS				nS	n		n
Bad Kleinen d.	...	...	...	...	0432	...	0519	0602	0704	...	...	0802	0904	...		1802	1904	...	...	2002	2104	...	2202	...
Grevesmühlen d.	...	...	...	...	0446	...	0541	0617	0722	...	...	0817	0922	...	each train	1817	1922	...	...	2017	2122	...	2221	...
Lübeck Hbf a.	...	...	...	...	0525	...	0622	0654	0756	...	...	0854	0956	...	runs every	1854	1956	...	...	2054	2156	...	2256	...
Lübeck Hbf d.	0019	...	0400	0500	...	0603	...	0703	...	0803	...	0903	...	1003	**two** hours	1903	...	2003	...	2103	...	2201	...	2301
Eutin d.	0049	...	0428	0528	...	0628	...	0728	...	0828	...	0928	...	1028	until	1928	...	2028	...	2128	...	2229	...	2329
Plön d.	0105	...	0443	0544	...	0644	...	0744	...	0844	...	0944	...	1044		1944	...	2044	...	2144	...	2244	...	2344
Kiel Hbf a.	0145	...	0515	0615	...	0715	...	0815	...	0915	...	1015	...	1115		2015	...	2115	...	2215	...	2315	...	0015

N – To / from Neubrandenburg (Table **836**).
P – To Pasewalk (Table **836**).
S – To / from Szczecin (Table **836**).
n – Not Dec. 24, 31.
v – Not Dec. 25, Jan. 1.
w – Not Dec. 25.

827 LÜBECK - BÜCHEN - LÜNEBURG

RB services

km	-	Ⓐn									n
0	**Lübeck** Hbf d.	0508	0608	0706	0805	0905		1905	2005	2105	2311
22	Ratzeburg d.	0529	0628	0723	0821	0921	each train	1921	2021	2121	2326
31	Mölln (Lauenburg) d.	0537	0635	0734	0834	0934	runs every	1934	2034	2134	2337
50	Büchen a.	0550	0648	0746	0846	0946	**two** hours	1946	2046	2147	2352
50	Büchen d.	0600	0655	0801	0904	1001	until	2001	2104	2201n	...
79	**Lüneburg** a.	0622	0718	0823	0926	1023		2023	2126	2223n	...

	Ⓐn	Ⓐn	Ⓒt							n
Lüneburg d.	0528	0628	0628	0728	0830	0933		1933	2030	2245
Büchen a.	0551	0651	0651	0751	0852	0955	each train	1955	2052	2308
Büchen d.	0558	0652	0708	0811	0911	1011	runs every	2011	2111	2323
Mölln (Lauenburg) d.	0610	0704	0732	0828	0928	1028	**two** hours	2028	2128	2336
Ratzeburg d.	0617	0711	0739	0835	0935	1035	until	2035	2135	2344
Lübeck Hbf a.	0632	0732	0754	0850	0950	1050		2050	2150	2400

n – Not Dec. 24, 31.
t – Also Dec. 24, 31.

830 HAMBURG - ROSTOCK - STRALSUND

RE services except where shown

km	See note ⊠		Ⓐ			*IC* **2184** ①g	Ⓐn	Ⓐn			*IC* **2182** ①–⑥ e H			*IC* **2180** 🍷♦	*IC* **2238** 🍷♦			*IC* **2212** 🍷♦			*IC* **2376** A 🍷			*IC* **2116** T 🍷	*IC* **1961** ⑤f
	Hamburg Altona d.	...	...	...	...	0528	...	...	...	...	...	...	...	...	...	...	...	...	...	...	...	...	...	...	1522
0	**Hamburg** Hbf d.	...	...	...	...	0541	0526	...	0630	...	0744	0830	...	0944	...	1028	...	1117	1228	...	1344	1428	...	1517	1544
47	Büchen d.	...	...	0502a	...	|	0559j	...	0656	...	|	0856	...	|	...	1056	...	|	1302	...	|	1456	...	|	|
123	**Schwerin** Hbf a.	...	...	0549a	...	0635	0652	...	0749	...	0835	0949	...	1035	...	1142	...	1209	1349	...	1435	1542	...	1609	1635
123	**Schwerin** Hbf **836 837** d.	...	...	0551	...	0639	...	0712	0751	...	0837	0951	...	1037	1056	1151	...	1215	1351	...	1437	1551	...	1615	1637
140	Bad Kleinen **836 837** d.	...	...	0602	...	|	...	0728	0802	...	0850	1002	...	1050	1109	1202	...	|	1402	...	1450	1602	...	|	1650
181	Bützow **836** d.	...	...	0629	...	0717	...	0759	0829	...	0917	1029	...	1117	1136	1229	...	1254	1429	...	1517	1629	...	1654	1717
211	**Rostock** Hbf a.	...	...	0652	...	0736	...	0821	0852	...	0936	1052	...	1136	1155	1252	...	1313	1452	...	1536	1652	...	1713	1736
211	**Rostock** Hbf d.	0454	0553	...	0700	0746	...	...	...	0900	0946	...	1100	1146	...	...	1300	1318	...	1500	1546	...	1700	1718	1746r
240	Ribnitz-D'garten West d.	0516	0618	...	0724	0813	...	...	...	0922	1007	...	1122	1219	...	...	1322	1340	...	1522	1607	...	1722	1739	1808r
265	Velgast d.	0541	0637	...	0742	0839	...	...	...	0941	1027	...	1143	1239	...	...	1341	1401	...	1542	1628	...	1741	1800	1828r
283	**Stralsund** a.	0556	0655	...	0757	0851	...	...	...	0956	1039	...	1157	1251	...	...	1357	1420	...	1557	1642	...	1756	1827	1842r
	Ostseebad Binz **844** a.	|	|	...	|	0938	...	...	...	|	1131	...	|	...	...	...	|	1516	...	|	...	...	|	...	1938r
	Sassnitz **844** a.	0655	0755	...	0855	...	...	...	...	1055	...	...	1255	...	...	...	1455	...	...	1655	...	...	1855	...	...

See note ⊠			*IC* **2372** A 🍷			*IC* **2188** ①–④ m	*IC* **2186** ⑤⑦h 🍷♦		*IC* **1937** ⑦w	
Hamburg Altona d.	...	...	...	...	...	1922	...	...	2131	...
Hamburg Hbf d.	1630	...	1744	1830	...	1944	1944	2028	2146	2249
Büchen d.	1656	...	|	1856	...	|	|	2056	2210	2317
Schwerin Hbf a.	1749	...	1835	1942	...	2035	2035	2142	2242	0002
Schwerin Hbf **836 837** d.	1751	...	1837	1951	...	2037	2037	2151	2244	0003
Bad Kleinen **836 837** d.	1802	...	1850	2002	...	2050	2050	2202	2257	0013
Bützow **836** d.	1829	...	1917	2029	...	2117	2117	2229	2324	0040
Rostock Hbf a.	1852	...	1936	2052	...	2136	2136	2252	2343	0102
Rostock Hbf d.	...	1900	1946	...	2100	...	2141	...	...	...
Ribnitz-Damgarten West d.	...	1922	2007	...	2122	...	2202	...	...	...
Velgast d.	...	1941	2029	...	2141	...	2218	...	...	...
Stralsund a.	...	1956	2041	...	2156	...	2230	...	...	...
Ostseebad Binz **844** a.	...	|	...	...	|	...	...	...	...	...
Sassnitz **844** a.	...	2055	...	...	2255	...	...	...	...	...

See note ⊠		*IC* **2189** Ⓐn		Ⓐ	*IC* **2279** ①–⑥ e A			*IC* **2115** T 🍷		
Sassnitz **844** d.	...	...	...	0403	...	0505	...	...	0705	...
Ostseebad Binz **844** d.	...	...	...	|	...	|	...	...	|	...
Stralsund d.	...	...	...	0455	0529	0600	...	0728	0800	...
Velgast d.	...	...	...	0509	0543	0615	...	0743	0815	...
Ribnitz-Damgarten West d.	...	...	...	0525	0556	0633	...	0757	0832	...
Rostock Hbf a.	...	...	...	0547	0616	0654	...	0817	0854	...
Rostock Hbf d.	...	0500	0507	...	0625	...	0704	0825	...	0904
Bützow **836** d.	...	0521	0528	...	0644	...	0725	0844	...	0925
Bad Kleinen **836 837** d.	...	0547	0554	...	0711	...	0751	|	...	0951
Schwerin Hbf **836 837** a.	...	0559	0604	...	0722	...	0801	0920	...	1001
Schwerin Hbf d.	0504	0604	0615	...	0724	...	0813	0924	...	1013
Büchen d.	0555	0636	0702	...	|	...	0900	|	...	1100
Hamburg Hbf a.	0623	0701	0728	...	0816	...	0930	1016	...	1130
Hamburg Altona a.	...	0720	...	...	...	...	...	...	...	...

See note ⊠	*IC* **2373** A 🍷			*IC* **2213** T 🍷			*IC* **2239** 🍷♦	*IC* **2377** 🍷♦	*IC* **1909** ⑦z K 🍷			*IC* **2379** ⑥G 🍷♦	*IC* **2379** E 🍷♦			*IC* **2183** ⑦w H	*IC* **2183** ⑤⑦ h 🍷			*IC* **2185** ⑦w H					
Sassnitz **844** d.	...	0905	...	...	1105	...	...	...	...	1305	...	...	...	1505	...	...	...	...	...	...	1905	...	...	2103	...
Ostseebad Binz **844** d.	...	|	...	1027	|	...	...	1230	1220t	|	...	...	...	|	...	1622	...	1706	...	...	|	...	...	|	...
Stralsund d.	0915	1000	...	1128	1200	...	...	1327	1334t	1400	...	1500	1515	1600	...	1715	1715	1800	...	1915	2000	...	...	2200	...
Velgast d.	0929	1015	...	1143	1215	...	...	1341	1401t	1415	...	1521	1532	1615	...	1729	1729	1815	...	1929	2015	...	...	2216	...
Ribnitz-Damgarten West d.	0950	1032	...	1158	1233	...	...	1355	1416t	1432	...	1545	1550	1632	...	1750	1750	1833	...	1950	2032	...	...	2232	...
Rostock Hbf a.	1016	1054	...	1218	1254	...	...	1415	1438t	1454	...	1610	1616	1654	...	1817	1817	1854	...	2016	2054	...	...	2254	...
Rostock Hbf d.	1025	...	1104	1243	...	1304	1357	1425	1443	...	1504	1625	1625	...	1704	1825	1825	...	1904	2025	...	2104	...	...	2304
Bützow **836** d.	1044	...	1125	1303	...	1325	1418	1444	1507	...	1526	1644	1644	...	1725	1844	1844	...	1925	2044	...	2125	...	...	2325
Bad Kleinen **836 837** d.	1111	...	1151	|	...	1351	1445	1511	|	...	1552	1711	1711	...	1751	|	|	...	1951	2111	...	2151	...	...	2351
Schwerin Hbf **836 837** a.	1122	...	1201	1337	...	1401	1455	1522	1541	...	1603	1722	1722	...	1801	1922	1922	...	2001	2122	...	2201	...	...	0001
Schwerin Hbf d.	1124	...	1213	1339	...	1405	...	1524	1558	...	1605	1724	1724	...	1805	1924	1924	...	2005	2124	...	...	2211	...	...
Büchen d.	|	...	1300	|	...	1500	...	|	|	...	1700	|	|	...	1906	|	|	...	2106	|	...	...	2314	...	...
Hamburg Hbf a.	1216	...	1330	1430	...	1528	...	1616	1655	...	1728	1816	1816	...	1934	2016	2016	...	2134	2217	...	...	*0018*v	...	...
Hamburg Altona a.	...	...	...	...	...	...	...	...	...	...	...	...	...	...	...	...	...	...	...	...	...	...	...	...	...

♦ – **NOTES** (LISTED BY TRAIN NUMBER)

2180 – 🚃12 (Kassel ①–⑤ **d** -) Hannover - Hamburg - Stralsund.
2186 – SCHWARZWALD – 🚃12 Konstanz - Karlsruhe - Frankfurt - Hannover - Hamburg - Stralsund.
2212 – RÜGEN – 🚃12 Koblenz - Köln - Ostseebad Binz.
2238 – ⑤⑥ from Mar. 14. WARNOW – 🚃12 Leipzig - Halle - Magdeburg - Stendal - Rostock - Warnemünde (a. 1228).
2239 – ⑤⑦ from Mar. 14. WARNOW – 🚃12 Warnemünde (d. 1332) - Rostock - Stendal - Magdeburg - Halle - Leipzig. On Mar. 21 Warnemünde d. 1317, Rostock Hbf d. 1335, Bützow d. 1356, Bad Kleinen d. 1423, Schwerin Hbf a. 1434.
2377 – ARKONA – 🚃12 Ostseebad Binz - Hamburg - Hannover - Frankfurt (- Karlsruhe: Table **911**).
2379 – 🚃12 Stralsund - Hamburg - Hannover (- Göttingen ⑤⑦ **h**) (- Frankfurt ⑤ **f**).

A – 🚃12 and 🍷 Stralsund - Hamburg - Hannover - Frankfurt - Karlsruhe and v.v.
E – Daily to Mar. 14; Ⓑ from Mar. 16 (also Mar. 22, May 3; not Mar. 21, May 1).
G – ⑥ from Mar. 15 (also Mar. 21, May 1; not Mar. 22, May 3).
H – From / to Hannover (Table **904**). Conveys 🍷.
K – To Köln (Table **800**).
T – To / from Stuttgart via Köln (Table **800**).

a – Ⓐ only.
d – Not Dec. 24, 25, 26, 31, Jan. 1, Mar. 21, 24, May 12.
e – Not Dec. 25, 26, Jan. 1, Mar. 22, 24, May 12.
f – Also Mar. 20, Apr. 30; not Mar. 21, May 2.
g – Also Dec. 27, Jan. 2, Mar. 25, May 13; not Dec. 24, 31, Mar. 24, May 12.
h – Also Dec. 26, Jan. 1, Mar. 20, 24, Apr. 30, May 12; not Dec. 23, 30, Mar. 21, 23, May 2, 11.
j – 0554 on ① (also Dec. 27, Jan. 2, Mar. 25, May 13).
m – Not Dec. 24, 25, 26, 31, Jan. 1, Mar. 20, 24, Apr. 30, May 12.
n – Not Dec. 24, 31.
r – ⑤ from Apr. 11 (also Mar. 20, Apr. 30; not May 2).
t – ⑦ from Apr. 13 (also Mar. 24, May 12; not May 11).
v – Change trains at Aumühle (a. 2333, d. *2346*).
w – Also Dec. 26, Jan. 1, Mar. 24, May 12; not Dec. 23, 30, Mar. 23, May 11.
z – Also Jan. 1, Mar. 24, May 12; not Dec. 23, 30, Mar. 23, May 11.

⊠ – Dec. 24 - Jan. 1 services which normally run from / to Hannover and beyond will start from / terminate at Hamburg Hbf and may operate with a different train number. Earlier departures from Hamburg also possible.

ROSTOCK - WARNEMÜNDE and SEEHAFEN NORD — 831

S-Bahn

Rostock Hbf - Rostock Seehafen Nord and v.v. *12 km.* Journey time: 18 minutes. **Rostock Überseehafen ferry terminal** is situated just over 1 km from Seehafen Nord station.
From Rostock Hbf at 0434 Ⓐ, 0534 Ⓐ, 0634, 0734 Ⓐ, 0834, 0934, 1034, 1134, 1234, 1334, 1434, 1534, 1634, 1734, 1834, 1934, 2034 and 2134.
From Rostock Seehafen Nord at 0506 Ⓐ, 0603 Ⓐ, 0706, 0806 Ⓐ, 0906, 1006, 1106, 1206, 1303, 1403, 1503, 1603, 1703, 1806, 1906, 2006, 2106 and 2206.

Rostock Hbf - Warnemünde and v.v. *13 km.* Journey time: 21 minutes. **From Rostock Hbf** on Ⓐ **e** at 0001, 0401, 0431, 0446, 0501, 0516, 0531, 0546, 0556 and every 10 minutes until 0816, 0831 and every 15 minutes until 1416, 1426 and every 10 minutes until 1716, 1731 and every 15 minutes until 2016, 2036, 2101, 2141, 2201, 2231 and 2301. **From Rostock** on © **z** at 0001, 0431, 0501, 0531, 0601, 0631, 0701, 0716, 0731, 0801, 0816 and every 15 minutes until 2016, 2036, 2101, 2141, 2201, 2231 and 2301. **From Warnemünde** on Ⓐ **e** at 0037, 0407, 0432, 0507, 0522, 0532 and every 10 minutes until 0822, 0837 and every 15 minutes until 1422, 1432 and every 10 minutes until 1722, 1737 and every 15 minutes until 2037, 2107, 2137, 2207, 2237 and 2307.
From Warnemünde on © **z** at 0037, 0432, 0507, 0532, 0552, 0607, 0637, 0707, 0737, 0752 and every 15 minutes until 2037, 2107, 2137, 2207, 2237 and 2307.

e – Not Dec. 24, 27, 28, 31. z – Also Dec. 24, 27, 28, 31.

BERLIN - KOSTRZYN — 832

Niederbarnimer Eisenbahn (2nd class only)

km									
0	**Berlin** Lichtenberg ..... d.	0534	0634	then each train	1934	2034	...	...	...
23	Strausberg ..... d.	0552	0652	runs every	1952	2052	...	...	...
80	**Kostrzyn** 🏛 ..... a.	0655	0746	**two** hours until	2055	2146	...	...	...

Kostrzyn 🏛 ..... d.	0500	...	0555	0702	then each train	1955	2102	...
Strausberg ..... d.	0611	...	0711	0811	runs every	2111	2211	...
Berlin Lichtenberg ... a.	0628	...	0728	0828	**two** hours until	2128	2228	...

Warning! Subject to alteration Jan. 12, 13, Feb. 23, 24

WISMAR - ROSTOCK — 833

RE services

km			Ⓐ								
0	**Wismar** ..... d.	0442	0542	...	0642	and	2042	...	...	...	...
22	Neubukow ..... d.	0511	0611	...	0711	hourly	2111	...	...	...	...
41	Bad Doberan ▲ ..... d.	0530	0630	...	0730	until	2130	...	2231	...	
57	**Rostock** Hbf ..... a.	0551	0651	...	0751		2151	...	2251	...	

	Ⓐ									
Rostock Hbf ..... d.	0412	0509	0606	0704	0806	and	2006	...	2206	
Bad Doberan ▲ ..... d.	0432	0532	0632	0732	0832	hourly	2032	...	2225	
Neubukow ..... d.	0451	0551	0651	0751	0851	until	2051	...	...	
Wismar ..... a.	0515	0615	0715	0815	0915		2115	...	...	

▲ – **BAD DOBERAN - OSTSEEBAD KÜHLUNGSBORN WEST.** All services worked by steam locomotive. 2nd class only. Journey time: 40 minutes.
Operator: Mecklenburgische Bäderbahn Molli GmbH, Am Bahnhof, 18209 Bad Doberan. ✆ +49 (0) 38203 4150, Fax +49 (0) 38203 41512. **Service until Apr. 25.**
From **Bad Doberan** at 0835 Ⓐ **e**, 1035, 1235, 1435 and 1640. From **Ostseebad Kühlungsborn West** at 0643 Ⓐ **e**, 0935, 1135, 1342 and 1535.

ROSTOCK and STRALSUND - BERLIN - LUTHERSTADT WITTENBERG — 835

RE services

km			◐	Ⓐ					ICE 1001 AM		◐		ICE 1003 GM					◐			X 80004 L				◐
	Warnemünde **831** ..... d.	...	...	...	...	...	...	...	...	...	...	...	0902k	...	...	...	...	...	...	...	1415	...	...	...	...
0	**Rostock** Hbf ..... d.	...	...	0437	...	...	...	0633	0724	...	...	0833	0924	...	...	1033	...	...	1233	...	1432	...	1453	...	...
34	Güstrow ..... d.	...	...	0502	...	...	...	0658	|	...	...	0858	|	...	...	1058	...	...	1258	...	1457	...	|	...	...
85	Waren (Müritz) ..... d.	...	...	0534	...	...	...	0734	0810	...	...	0934	1010	...	...	1134	...	...	1334	...	1529	...	1536	...	...
	Stralsund ..... d.	...	...	|	...	0502	0602e	|	|	0702	0802	|	|	0902	1002	|	1102	1202	|	1302	|	1402	|	1502	1602
	Grimmen ..... d.	...	...	|	...	0523	0623e	|	|	0723	0823	|	|	0923	1023	|	1123	1223	|	1323	|	1423	|	1523	1623
	Demmin ..... d.	...	...	|	...	0546	0646e	|	|	0746	0846	|	|	0946	1046	|	1146	1246	|	1346	|	1446	|	1546	1646
	Neubrandenburg ..... d.	0427	0527	|	...	0632	0730	|	|	0830	0930	|	|	1030	1130	|	1230	1330	|	1430	|	1530	|	1630	1730
121	**Neustrelitz** Hbf ..... a.	0455	0556	0558	...	0659	0757	0758	0833	0858	0956	0958	1033	1058	1156	1158	1258	1356	1358	1458	1551	1556	1600	1658	1756
121	**Neustrelitz** Hbf ..... d.	0502	...	0602	...	0702	...	0802	0835	0902	...	1002	1035	1102	...	1202	1302	...	1402	1502	1553	...	1602	1702	...
141	Fürstenberg (Havel) ..... d.	0516	...	0616	...	0716	...	0816	|	0916	...	1016	|	1116	...	1216	1316	...	1416	1516	|	...	1616	1716	...
162	Gransee ..... d.	0531	...	0631	...	0731	...	0831	|	0931	...	1031	|	1131	...	1231	1331	...	1431	1531	|	...	1631	1731	...
191	Oranienburg ..... d.	0550	...	0650	...	0750	...	0850	|	0950	...	1050	|	1150	...	1250	1350	...	1450	1550	|	...	1650	1750	...
223	**Berlin** Hbf ..... a.	0615	...	0715	...	0815	...	0915	0942	1015	...	1115	1142	1215	...	1315	1415	...	1515	1615	1702	...	1715	1815	...
223	**Berlin** Hbf ..... △ d.	0617	...	0717	0717	0817	...	0917	0953	1017	...	1117	1153	1217	...	1317	1417	...	1517	1617	...	...	1717	1817	...
276	Luckenwalde ..... d.	0655	...	0753	0753	0855	...	0953	|	1055	...	1153	|	1255	...	1353	1455	...	1553	1655	...	...	1753	1855	...
289	Jüterbog ..... d.	0703	...	0801	0801	0903	...	1001	|	1103	...	1201	|	1303	...	1401	1503	...	1601	1703	...	...	1801	1903	...
	Falkenberg (Elster) ..... a.	0748	...	|	|	0948	...	|	|	1148	...	|	|	1347	...	|	1548	...	|	1748	...	...	|	1948	...
321	**Lutherstadt Wittenberg** △ a.	...	...	0830	0830	...	...	1030	1034	...	...	1230	1234	...	...	1430	...	...	1630	...	...	...	1830	...	...

			©r				◐ Ⓑ			◐
Warnemünde **831** ..... d.	...	...	1816	...	...	...	...	...	...	...
Rostock Hbf ..... d.	1633	...	1835	...	1833	...	...	2033	...	...
Güstrow ..... d.	1658	...	|	...	1858	...	...	2058	...	...
Waren (Müritz) ..... d.	1734	...	1923	...	1934	...	...	2134	...	...
Stralsund ..... d.	|	1702	|	1802	|	1902	2002	|	2102	...
Grimmen ..... d.	|	1723	|	1823	|	1923	2023	|	2123	...
Demmin ..... d.	|	1746	|	1846	|	1946	2046	|	2146	...
Neubrandenburg ..... d.	|	1830	|	1930	|	2030	2130	|	2229	2252
Neustrelitz Hbf ..... a.	1758	1858	1947	1956	1958	2058	2156	2158	▬	2327
Neustrelitz Hbf ..... d.	1802	1902	1948	...	2002	2102	...	2202	...	▬
Fürstenberg (Havel) ..... d.	1816	1916	2001	...	2016	2116	...	2216	...	...
Gransee ..... d.	1831	1931	|	...	2031	2131	...	2231	...	...
Oranienburg ..... d.	1850	1950	2033	...	2050	2150	...	2250	...	...
Berlin Hbf ..... a.	1915	2015	2059	...	2115	2215	...	2315	...	v H
Berlin Hbf ..... △ d.	1917	2017	...	...	2117	2217	...	...	2319	0017
Luckenwalde ..... d.	1953	2055	...	...	2156	2300	...	...	0003	0100
Jüterbog ..... d.	2001	2103	...	...	2204	2308	...	...	0010	0108
Falkenberg (Elster) ..... a.	|	2148	...	...	|	2351	...	...	...	|
Lutherstadt Wittenberg .. △ a.	2030	...	...	...	2233	...	...	...	...	0124c

km		Ⓐ	◐		H			©r		◐
	Lutherstadt Wittenberg △ d.	...	...	...	0526	...	...	...	0726	...
0	**Falkenberg** (Elster) ..... d.	...	...	...	|	...	0609	...	|	...
49	Jüterbog ..... d.	...	...	0453	0554	...	0653	...	0754	...
62	Luckenwalde ..... d.	...	...	0500	0602	...	0700	...	0802	...
115	**Berlin** Hbf ..... △ a.	...	...	0538	0638	...	0738	...	0838	...
115	**Berlin** Hbf ..... d.	0443	...	0543	0643	...	0743	0823	0843	...
147	Oranienburg ..... d.	0508	...	0608	0708	...	0808	0848	0908	...
176	Gransee ..... d.	0526	...	0627	0726	...	0827	|	0926	...
197	Fürstenberg (Havel) ..... d.	0541	...	0641	0741	...	0841	0919	0941	...
218	**Neustrelitz** Hbf ..... a.	0555	...	0655	0755	...	0855	0932	0955	...
218	**Neustrelitz** Hbf ..... d.	0604	0601	0700	0801	0803	0900	0935	1001	1003
253	**Neubrandenburg** ..... d.	|	0633	0733	|	0833	0933	|	|	1033
295	Demmin ..... d.	|	0709	0809	|	0909	1009	|	|	1109
319	Grimmen ..... d.	|	0729	0829	|	0929	1029	|	|	1129
342	**Stralsund** ..... a.	|	0751	0851	|	0951	1051	|	|	1151
	Waren (Müritz) ..... d.	0630	...	...	0830	...	...	0959	1030	...
	Güstrow ..... d.	0701	...	...	0901	...	...	|	1101	...
	Rostock Hbf ..... a.	0724	...	...	0924	...	...	1045	1124	...
	Warnemünde **831** ..... a.	...	...	...	...	...	...	1112	...	...

				X 80003 J			◐						◐ Ⓑd		ICE 1000 BM		Ⓑd			◐ Ⓑ		⊡		⑤⑥	
Lutherstadt Wittenberg .. △ d.	...	0926	...	...	...	1126	...	...	1326	...	...	1526	...	...	1722	1726	...	...	1926	...	...	...	2126	...	...
Falkenberg (Elster) ..... d.	0809	|	...	...	1009	|	...	1209	|	...	1409	|	...	1609	|	|	...	1809	|	...	2009	2009	|	...	2211
Jüterbog ..... d.	0853	0954	...	...	1053	1154	...	1253	1354	...	1453	1554	...	1653	|	1754	...	1853	1954	...	2053	2053	2154	...	2253
Luckenwalde ..... d.	0900	1002	...	...	1100	1202	...	1300	1402	...	1500	1602	...	1700	|	1802	...	1900	2002	...	2100	2100	2202	...	2300
Berlin Hbf ..... △ a.	0938	1038	...	...	1138	1238	...	1338	1438	...	1538	1638	...	1738	1805	1838	...	1938	2038	...	2138	2138	2244	...	2344
Berlin Hbf ..... d.	0943	1043	...	1058	1143	1243	...	1343	1443	...	1543	1643	...	1743	1812	1843	...	1943	2043	...	...	2143	...	2246	...
Oranienburg ..... d.	1008	1108	...	|	1208	1308	...	1408	1508	...	1608	1708	...	1808	|	1908	...	2008	2108	...	...	2208	...	2309	...
Gransee ..... d.	1027	1126	...	|	1227	1326	...	1427	1526	...	1627	1726	...	1827	|	1926	...	2027	2126	...	...	2227	...	2328	...
Fürstenberg (Havel) ..... d.	1041	1141	...	|	1241	1341	...	1441	1541	...	1641	1741	...	1841	|	1941	...	2041	2141	...	...	2241	...	2341	...
Neustrelitz Hbf ..... a.	1055	1155	...	1205	1255	1355	...	1455	1555	...	1655	1755	...	1855	1919	1955	...	2055	2155	...	...	2255	...	2355	...
Neustrelitz Hbf ..... d.	1100	1158	1203	1207	1300	1401	1403	1500	1601	1603	1700	1801	1803	1900	1921	2001	2003	2100	2201	2203	...	2303	...	2356	...
Neubrandenburg ..... d.	1133	|	1233	|	1333	|	1433	1533	|	1633	1733	|	1833	1933	|	|	2033	2133	|	2229	...	2330	...	0023	...
Demmin ..... d.	1209	|	1309	|	1409	|	1509	1609	|	1709	1809	|	1909	2009	|	|	2109	2209	|	...	...	...	...	...	...
Grimmen ..... d.	1229	|	1329	|	1429	|	1529	1629	|	1729	1829	|	1929	2029	|	|	2129	2229	|	...	...	...	...	...	...
Stralsund ..... a.	1251	|	1351	|	1451	|	1551	1651	|	1751	1851	|	1951	2051	|	|	2151	2251	|	...	...	...	...	...	...
Waren (Müritz) ..... d.	...	1222	...	1231	...	1430	...	...	1630	...	...	1830	...	...	1947	2030	...	...	2230	...	...	...	...	...	...
Güstrow ..... d.	...	|	...	1301	...	1501	...	...	1701	...	...	1901	...	...	|	2101	...	...	2301	...	...	...	...	...	...
Rostock Hbf ..... a.	...	1306	...	1324	...	1524	...	...	1724	...	...	1924	...	...	2030	2124	...	...	2324	...	...	...	...	...	...
Warnemünde **831** ..... a.	...	...	...	1357	...	...	...	...	...	...	...	...	...	...	2044f	...	...	...	...	...	...	...	...	...	...

A – ①–⑤ (not Dec. 24, 25, 26, 31, Jan. 1, Mar. 21, 24, May 12).
B – ⑧ (not Dec. 24, 25, 31, Mar. 21, 23, May 11).
G – ⑥ (also Dec. 24, 31, Mar. 21; not Mar. 22).
H – To / from Halle (Table **848**) on © (not Dec. 25).
J – From Leipzig Hbf (d. 0926). Operated by Veolia Verkehr GmbH. **DB tickets not valid.**
L – To Leipzig Hbf (a. 1833). Operated by Veolia Verkehr GmbH. **DB tickets not valid.**

M – 🚃12 and ✕ (Warnemünde -) Rostock - Berlin - Leipzig - Nürnberg - München and v.v.

d – Runs daily Neustrelitz - Neubrandenburg.
c – © (not Dec. 25).
e – ①–⑥ only.
f – ⑤ from Mar. 14 (also Mar. 20; not Mar. 21).
k – ⑥ from Mar. 15 (also Mar. 21; not Mar. 22).

r – Not Dec. 25 - Jan. 1.
v – Not Dec. 25.

⊡ – ①②③④⑦.
△ – See Tables **850/1** for other *ICE* / *IC* services Berlin - Lutherstadt Wittenberg and v.v.
◐ – Operated by Ostseeland Verkehr GmbH.

836 LÜBECK and SCHWERIN - PASEWALK - SZCZECIN and UECKERMÜNDE

DB (*RE* services); OLA ‡

See Table **826** for complete service Lübeck - Bad Kleinen and v.v. (including stops at Grevesmühlen).

km			‡	Ⓐ		‡	Ⓐ	Ⓒ	‡		‡		‡Ⓐ	‡		‡		‡		‡		‡	‡⑤f		‡⑦
0	**Lübeck** Hbf d.	...	...	...	...	...	0601	...	...	0801	...	1001	...	...	1201	...	1401	...	1601	...	1801	...	...	2001n	...
	Schwerin Hbf **830/7** d.	...	...	0440	...	*0551*	|	0638	*0751*	|	*0951*	|	...	*1151*	|	*1351*	|	*1551*	|	*1751*	|	*1951*	*1951*	|	*2151*
62	Bad Kleinen **830/7** d.	...	...	0459	...	*0602*	0703	0703	*0802*	0903	*1002*	1057	...	*1202*	1303	*1402*	1503	*1602*	1703	*1802*	1903	*2002*	*2002*	2103	*2202*
103	Bützow **830** d.	...	...	0532	...	0632	0736	0736	0832	0936	1032	1138j	...	1232	1336	1432	1538	1632	1736	1832	1936	2032	2032	2136	2232
117	Güstrow a.	...	...	0541	...	0641	0745	0745	0841	0945	1041	1147	...	1241	1345	1441	1547	1641	1745	1841	1945	2041	2041	2145	2241
117	Güstrow d.	...	...	0558	...	0704	0758	0758	0904	0958	1104	1158	...	1304	1358	1504	1558	1704	1758	1904	1958	2104	2104	2158	2304
146	Teterow d.	...	...	0623	...	0730	0823	0823	0930	1023	1130	1223	...	1330	1423	1530	1623	1730	1823	1930	2023	2130	2130	2223	2330
160	Malchin d.	...	0535a	0634	...	0740	0834	0834	0940	1034	1140	1234	...	1340	1434	1540	1634	1740	1834	1940	2034	2141	2141	2234	2340
204	**Neubrandenburg** a.	...	0611a	0708	...	0825	0908	0908	1025	1108	1225	1308	...	1425	1508	1625	1708	1825	1908	2025	2108	2226	2226	2308	0013
204	**Neubrandenburg** d.	0513a	0612	0712	0712	0832	0912	0912	1032	1112	1232	1312	...	1432	1512	1632	1712	1832	1912	2032	2132	...	2232	...	...
257	**Pasewalk** a.	0558a	0701	0801	0801	0916	1001	1001	1116	1201	1316	1401	...	1516	1601	1716	1801	1916	2001	2116	2218	...	2315	...	...
257	**Pasewalk** ◐ d.	0602	0721	0802	0802	0921	1002	1002	1121	1202	1321	1402	1404	1521	1602	1721	1802	1930	2002	2121n	...	...	2328	...	...
287	Ueckermünde ◐ a.	|	0753	|	|	0953	|	|	1153	|	1353	|	1435	1553	|	1753	|	2001	|	2153n	...	...	|	...	...
284	Grambow d.	0625	...	0826	0826	...	1026	1026	...	1226	...	1426	...	...	1626	...	1826	...	2026	...	...	...	2351	...	...
294	Szczecin Gumience 🏛 d.	0635	...	0836	0836	...	1036	1035	...	1240	...	1441	...	...	1640	...	1836	...	2036	...	...	...	0002	...	...
299	**Szczecin** Głowny a.	0641	...	0842	0842	...	1042	1042	...	1245	...	1446	...	...	1646	...	1842	...	2042	...	...	...	0007	...	...

	‡⑥k	‡	Ⓐ	‡	Ⓐ		‡	‡Ⓐ		‡		‡		‡		‡	‡Ⓐ		‡		‡		‡	‡⑦	
Szczecin Głowny d.	0013	...	...	...	0451	...	...	...	0653	...	0853	...	1053	...	1253	...	...	1453	...	1653	...	1853	...	...	2053
Szczecin Gumience 🏛 d.	0020	...	...	...	0501	...	...	...	0701	...	0901	...	1101	...	1301	...	...	1501	...	1701	...	1901	...	...	2101
Grambow d.	0030	...	...	...	0512	...	...	...	0712	...	0912	...	1112	...	1312	...	...	1512	...	1712	...	1912	...	...	2111
Ueckermünde ◐ d.	|	...	...	...	|	...	0555a	0656	|	0803	|	1003	|	1203	|	1403	1453	|	1603	|	1803	|	2007	2007	|
Pasewalk ◐ a.	0053	...	...	...	0535	...	0627a	0728	0735	0834	0935	1034	1135	1234	1335	1438	1527	1535	1634	1735	1834	1935	2039	2039	2135
Pasewalk d.	0053	...	...	...	0541	...	0643	...	0741	0843	0941	1043	1141	1243	1341	1443	...	1541	1643	1741	1843	1941	2043	2043	2141
Neubrandenburg a.	0135	...	...	...	0628	...	0728	...	0828	0928	1028	1128	1228	1328	1428	1528	...	1628	1728	1828	1928	2028	2128	2128	2231
Neubrandenburg d.	...	...	0446	0528	0637	0637	0736	...	0838	0936	1038	1136	1238	1336	1438	1536	...	1638	1736	1838	1936	2038	...	2136	...
Malchin d.	...	...	0519	0609	0716	0716	0809	...	0916	1009	1116	1209	1316	1409	1516	1609	...	1716	1809	1916	2009	2116	...	2209	...
Teterow d.	...	...	0531	0624	0731	0731	0824	...	0931	1024	1131	1224	1331	1424	1531	1624	...	1731	1824	1931	2024	2131	...	2224	...
Güstrow a.	...	...	0556	0649	0756	0756	0849	...	0956	1049	1156	1249	1356	1449	1556	1649	...	1756	1849	1956	2049	2156	...	2249	...
Güstrow d.	...	0508	0604	0708	0804	0804	0908	...	1004	1108	1204	1308	1404	1508	1604	1708	...	1804	1908	2004	2108	2204	...	2308	...
Bützow **830** d.	...	0517	0616	0718	0816	0816	0918	...	1016	1118	1216	1318	1425j	1518	1616	1718	...	1816	1918	2016	2118	2216	...	2318	...
Bad Kleinen **830/7** a.	...	*0553*	0649	*0750*	0849	0849	*0950*	...	1049	*1150*	1249	*1350*	1459	*1552*	1649	*1750*	...	1849	*1950*	2049	*2150*	2249	...	*2350*	...
Schwerin Hbf **830/7** a.	...	*0604*	|	*0801*	|	|	*1001*	...	|	*1201*	|	*1401*	|	*1603*	|	*1801*	...	|	*2001*	|	*2201*	2302	...	*0001*	...
Lübeck Hbf a.	...	...	0756	...	0956	0956	...	...	1156	...	1356	...	1556	...	1756	...	...	1956n	...	2156n	...	...	...	...	...

a – Ⓐ only.
f – Also Mar. 20; not Mar. 21.
j – Arrives 11 minutes earlier.
k – Also Mar. 21; not Mar. 22.
n – Not Dec. 24, 31.
‡ – Operated by Ostseeland Verkehr (OLA).
◐ – Additional trains Pasewalk - Ueckermünde and v.v. (operated by Ostseeland Verkehr): **From Pasewalk** at 0515 ⚒ and 0609 Ⓐ. **From Ueckermünde** at 2203 **n**.

837 WISMAR - SCHWERIN - BERLIN

RE services except where shown

km		Ⓐ		⚒	Ⓐ							Ⓐ			*IC* 2239 L🍷				Ⓐn							
0	**Wismar** d.	0430	...	0539	...	0644	0741	0844	0942	1044	1142	...	1244	1332	...	...	1444	1532	...	1644	1732	1844	1932	...	2044	2140
16	Bad Kleinen a.	0447	...	0554	...	0659	0757	0859	0957	1059	1157	...	1259	1347	...	...	1459	1547	...	1659	1747	1859	1947	...	2059	2155
16	Bad Kleinen **830/6** d.	0448	...	0557	...	0701	0758	0901	0958	1101	1158	...	1301	1358	1445k	...	1501	1558	...	1701	1758	1901	1958	...	2101	2157
32	**Schwerin** Hbf **830/6** a.	0500	...	0609	...	0713	0810	0913	1010	1113	1210	...	1313	1410	1455k	...	1513	1610	...	1713	1810	1913	2010	...	2113	2209
32	**Schwerin** Hbf d.	...	0518	0610	0657	0714	0818	0914	1018	1114	1218	1248	1314	1418	1457	...	1514	1618	1657	1714	1818	1914	2018	...	2114	▬
72	Ludwigslust **840** d.	...	0549	0649*	0721	0746	0849	0946	1049	1146	1249	1312	1346	1449	1523	...	1546	1649	1726	1746	1849	1946	2049	...	2151	...
116	Wittenberge **840** d.	...	0616	0716	◇	...	0916	...	1116	...	1316	◇	...	1517	1541	1616	...	1716	◇	...	1916	◇	...	2116	2214	2249
167	Neustadt (Dosse) d.	...	0647	0747	|	...	0947	...	1147	...	1347	|	...	1547	...	1647	...	1747	|	...	1947	|	...	2147	|	2324
207	Nauen d.	...	0710	0810	|	...	1010	...	1210	...	1410	|	...	1610	...	1710	...	1810	|	...	2010	|	...	2210	|	2347
229	**Berlin** Spandau **840** d.	...	0726	0826	◇	...	1026	...	1226	...	1429	|	...	1626	...	1726	...	1826	◇	...	2026	◇	...	2226	◇	0003
241	**Berlin** Hbf **840** a.	...	0736	0836	◇	...	1036	...	1236	...	1439	◇	...	1636	...	1736	...	1836	◇	...	2036	◇	...	2235	◇	0013z

		⚒			Ⓐ			*IC* 2238 R🍷								Ⓐ			Ⓐn							
Berlin Hbf **840** d.	0420	0523	...	0725	◇	...	0826	...	...	0923	...	1122	...	1322	...	◇	1521	...	◇	1723	◇	...	1923	2025	2123	2223
Berlin Spandau **840** d.	0430	0532	...	0735	◇	...	0835	...	...	0932	...	1132	...	1332	...	|	1531	...	◇	1732	◇	...	1932	2035	2132	2232
Nauen d.	0446	0546	...	0749	|	...	0849	...	...	0946	...	1146	...	1346	...	|	1547	...	|	1746	|	...	1946	2049	2146	2246
Neustadt (Dosse) d.	0511	0611	...	0814	|	...	0914	...	...	1011	...	1211	...	1411	...	|	1612	...	|	1811	|	...	2011	2114	2211	2311
Wittenberge **840** d.	0544	0648	...	0844	◇	...	0944	1014	...	1044	...	1244	...	1444	...	◇	1644	...	◇	1844	◇	...	2041	2144	2241	2341
Ludwigslust **840** d.	0609	0713	0812	0909	0938	1012	...	1033	...	1109	1212	1309	1412	1509	1612	1639	1709	1812	1830	1909	2030	2109	...	2209	...	...
Schwerin Hbf a.	0644	0743	0844	0938	1004	1044	...	1054	...	1138	1244	1338	1444	1538	1644	1705	1738	1844	1854	1938	2104	2138	...	2240	...	...
Schwerin Hbf **830/6** d.	0647	0745	0847	0945	...	1047	...	1056	...	1145	1247	1345	1447	1545	1647	...	1745	1847	...	1945	2105	2145	...	*2249*	...	...
Bad Kleinen **830/6** a.	0659	0757	0859	0957	...	1059	...	1107	←	1157	1259	1357	1459	1557	1659	...	1757	1859	...	1957	2117	2157	...	*2302*	...	...
Bad Kleinen d.	0701	0804	0901	1004	...	→	...	...	1112	1204	1301	1404	1501	1604	1701	...	1804	1901	...	2004	2118	2204	...	*2303*	...	...
Wismar a.	0717	0819	0916	1019	...	...	...	...	1127	1219	1316	1419	1516	1619	1716	...	1819	1916	...	2019	2133	2219	...	*2318*	...	...

L – ⑤⑦ from Mar. 14. WARNOW – [12] Warnemünde - Rostock - Stendal - Magdeburg - Leipzig.
R – ⑤⑥ from Mar. 14. WARNOW – [12] Leipzig - Magdeburg - Stendal - Rostock - Warnemünde.
k – 21–22 minutes **earlier** on Mar. 21.
n – Not Dec. 24, 31.
z – Berlin **Zoo**.
* – Arrives 0639.
◇ – See Table **840** for *ICE*, *EC* or *IC* connection.

838 STENDAL - BERLIN - LÜBBEN - COTTBUS

RE services except where shown

km								*EC* 241 n B✕											*IC* 2131 Ⓑq E							
0	**Stendal 810** d.	...	0446	*0522*r	*0616*	...	0805	0848j	...	...	*1005*	...	*1205*	...	*1405*	...	*1605*	...	...	*1805*	...	*2005*n	...	*2219*k	...
34	Rathenow **810** d.	0405a	0503	0605	0705	0805	0831	|	0905	1005	1107	1205	1307	1405	1507	1605	1707	...	1805	1907	2005	2105	2205	2305	...
92	**Berlin** Spandau **810** d.	0448a	0548	0648	0749	0848	...	0925j	0949	1049	1149	1248	1349	1448	1549	1648	1749	...	1848	1949	2048	2148	2248	2346	...
104	**Berlin** Zoo d.	0457a	0557	0657	0758	0857	...	|	0958	1058	1158	1257	1358	1457	1558	1657	1758	...	1857	1958	2057	2157	2257	2355	0034
108	**Berlin** Hbf **810** d.	0503a	0603	0703	0803	0903	...	0940	1003	1104	1203	1303	1403	1503	1603	1703	1803	1831	1903	2003	2103	2203	2303	2400	0040
113	**Berlin** Ostbahnhof **810** d.	0513	0613	0713	0813	0913	...	0949	1013	1114	1213	1313	1413	1513	1613	1713	1813	1842	1913	2013	2113	2213	2313	...	0049
146	Königs Wusterhausen d.	0539	0639	0739	0839	0939	...	|	1039	1139	1239	1338	1439	1539	1639	1739	1839	|	1939	2039	2139	2239	2339	...	0113
192	Lübben (Spreewald) d.	0608	0708	0808	0909	1008	...	1044	1108	1208	1308	1408	1508	1608	1708	1808	1908	1934	2010	2108	2218	2318	0018	...	0150
203	Lübbenau (Spreew) d.	0617	0715	0815	0916	1015	...	1053	1115	1215	1315	1415	1515	1619	1715	1815	1915	1944	2017	2115	2225	2326	0026	...	0158
233	**Cottbus** a.	0646	0745	0845	0945	1045	...	1112	1145	1245	1345	1445	1545	1645	1745	1845	1945	2004	2045	2142	2251	...	0049	...	0218

	Ⓐ	⚒r			*IC* 2132 ①–⑥ e N											*EC* 240 c A✕									
Cottbus d.	...	...	0418	0515	0557	0615	0715	0815	0915	1015	1115	1215	1315	1415	1515	1559	1615	1715	1815	1915	2015	2112	...	2313	...
Lübbenau (Spreew) d.	...	...	0442	0542	0617	0642	0742	0842	0942	1042	1142	1242	1342	1442	1542	1619	1642	1742	1842	1942	2042	2135	...	2336	0042
Lübben (Spreewald) d.	...	...	0449	0549	0626	0649	0749	0849	0949	1049	1149	1249	1349	1449	1549	1628	1649	1749	1849	1949	2049	2142	...	2343	0049
Königs Wusterhausen d.	...	...	0519	0619	|	0719	0819	0919	1019	1119	1219	1319	1419	1519	1619	|	1719	1819	1919	2019	2119	2221	...	0023	0119
Berlin Ostbahnhof **810** d.	...	...	0548	0648	0721	0748	0848	0948	1048	1148	1248	1348	1448	1548	1648	1724	1748	1848	1948	2048	2148	2248	...	0048	0149
Berlin Hbf **810** d.	...	...	0600	0700	0728	0800	0900	1000	1100	1200	1300	1400	1500	1600	1700	1735	1800	1900	2000	2100	2200	2300	0016	0100	0200a
Berlin Zoo d.	0505	...	0605	0705	...	0805	0905	1005	1105	1205	1305	1405	1505	1605	1705	|	1805	1905	2005	2105	2205	2306	0021	0104	0204a
Berlin Spandau **810** d.	0514	...	0613	0715	...	0815	0915	1015	1115	1215	1315	1415	1515	1615	1715	1751b	1815	1915	2015	2115	2215	2315	0029	...	...
Rathenow **810** a.	0552	0555	0654	0754	...	0849	0955	1049	1154	1249	1354	1449	1554	1654	1754	|	1854	1954	2054	2156	2249	2356	0102	...	...
Stendal 810 a.	...	0621	*0749*	...	...	*0949*	...	*1149*	...	*1349*	...	*1549*	...	*1749*	...	1824b	*1949*	...	*2145*n	...	...	0013	...	...	...

A – WAWEL – [12] and ✕ Kraków - Katowice - Wrocław - Forst 🏛 - Cottbus - Berlin Hbf (- Hamburg Ⓑ **b**).
B – WAWEL – [12] and ✕ (Hamburg ①–⑥ **j** -) Berlin Hbf - Cottbus - Forst 🏛 - Wrocław - Katowice - Kraków.
E – OSTFRIESLAND – [12] and 🍷 Emden - Bremen - Hannover - Magdeburg - Cottbus.
N – OSTFRIESLAND – [12] and 🍷 Cottbus - Magdeburg - Hannover - Bremen - Oldenburg (- Norddeich Mole: Table **813**).
a – Ⓐ only.
b – Ⓑ (not Dec. 24, 25, 30, 31, Mar. 21, 23, May 11).
c – Not Dec. 24, 31.
e – ①–⑥ (not Dec. 25, 26, Jan. 1, Mar. 22, 24, May 12).
j – ①–⑥ (not Dec. 25, 26, 31, Jan. 1, Mar. 22, 24, May 12).
k – Not Dec. 24, 25, 31.
n – Not Dec. 25, 31.
q – Ⓑ (not Dec. 24, 25, 31, Mar. 21, 23, May 11).
r – ⚒ (not Dec. 24, 31).

RE services MAGDEBURG - BERLIN - FRANKFURT (ODER) - COTTBUS 839

km														P🍷					S★					
0	**Magdeburg** Hbf ... d.	...	...	...	0458v	...	0604	...	0706	...	and at the same minutes past each hour until	1606	...	1700	1706	...	1806	...	1853	1906	2006	2104	2204	*2317*
79	**Brandenburg** Hbf ... d.	0421	0459	0521	0559	0621r	0659	0721r	0759	0821		1659	1721	1742	1759	1821	1859	1921	|	1959	2059	2156	2256	0021
114	Potsdam Hbf ... d.	0450	0521	0551	0621	0651	0721	0753	0821	0851		1721	1751	1801	1821	1851	1921	1951	2007	2020	2121	2222	2322	0049
123	Berlin Wannsee ... d.	0457	0528	0558	0628	0658	0728	0802	0828	0858		1728	1758	1810	1828	1858	1928	1958	2015	2026	2128	2228	2328	0055
138	**Berlin** Zoo ... d.	0509	0540	0610	0640	0710	0740	0814	0840	0910		1740	1810	|	1840	1910	1940	2010	2031	2040	2140	2240	2340	0106t
142	**Berlin** Hbf ... d.	0514	0547	0617	0647	0717	0746	0819	0847	0917		1747	1817	1831	1847	1917	1947	2017	|	2047	2147	2247	2347	0112t
147	**Berlin** Ostbahnhof **1001** ... d.	0524	0557	0627	0657	0727	0756	0828	0857	0927		1757	1827	1842	1857	1927	1957	2027	2048	2057	2157	2257	2357	0121t
194	Fürstenwalde (Spree) ... d.	*0606*	0631	0706	0731	0806	0831	0906	0931	1006		1831	1906	|	1931	2006	2031	2106	...	2135	2235	2335	0035	...
228	**Frankfurt (Oder) 1001** ... a.	*0628*	0700	0724	0800	0824	0900	0924	1000	1024		1900	1924	⊖	2000	2024	2100	2124	...	2204	2304	0004	0104	...
	Cottbus (see below) ... a.	...	...	...	...	...	...	...	...	...		...	...	2004b	...	2129	...	2251	...	2314	0025	...	...	...

	Ⓒ							T★	N🍷															⑤⑥f
Cottbus (see below) ... d.	...	...	...	...	0341	...	0440	...	0557e	0511	0541	...	...	and at the same minutes past each hour until										
Frankfurt (Oder) 1001 ... d.	...	...	0352	...	0452	0534	0555	...	⊖	0634	0655	0734	0755		1834	1855	1934	1955	2031	2127	2225	...	2325	2325
Fürstenwalde (Spree) ... d.	...	...	0422	...	0522	0553	0627	...	|	0653	0727	0753	0827		1853	1927	1953	2027	2053	2153	2253	...	2353	2353
Berlin Ostbahnhof **1001** ... d.	0131		0501	0531	0601	0631	0701	0706	0721	0731	0801	0831	0901		1931	2001	2031	2101	2131	2231	2329	2332	0031	0031
Berlin Hbf ... d.	0143		0513	0543	0613	0643	0713	|	0732	0743	0813	0843	0913		1943	2013	2043	2113	2143	2243	...	2343	0043	0043
Berlin Zoo ... d.	0149		0519	0549	0619	0649	0719	0725	|	0749	0819	0849	0919		1949	2019	2049	2118	2149	2249	...	2349	0049	0049
Berlin Wannsee ... d.	0200		0530	0600	0630	0700	0730	0736	0748	0800	0830	0900	0930		2000	2030	2100	...	2200	2300	...	0000	0100	0100
Potsdam Hbf ... d.	0207		0538	0607	0637	0707	0738	0744	0756	0807	0838	0907	0938		2007	2038	2107	...	2207	2307	...	0007	0107	0107
Brandenburg Hbf ... d.	0236		0557	0636	0657	0736	0757	|	0815	0836	0857	0936	0957		2036	2057	2137	...	2236	2337	...	0036	0136	0137
Magdeburg Hbf ... a.	...	...	0653	...	0753	...	0853	0903	0857	...	0953	...	1053		...	2153	2238	...	...	0030	...	...	...	0223

km		Ⓐ	Ⓐ				B	B	M	M
0	**Frankfurt (Oder)** ... d.	0404	0434	0534	and hourly until	1934	2026	2131	2206	2306
23	Eisenhüttenstadt ... d.	0424	0454	0554		1954	2047	2151	2227	2327
48	Guben ... d.	0446	0516	0616		2016	2104	2214	2249	2349
86	**Cottbus** ... a.	0521	0551	0651		2051	2129	2251	2314	0025

	M	M	B	M	Ⓐ					
Cottbus ... d.	0341	0440	0511	0541	0608	0708	and hourly until	1908	2108	2308
Guben ... d.	0406	0508	0549	0606	0644	0744		1944	2144	2345
Eisenhüttenstadt ... d.	0427	0529	0610	0627	0705	0805		2005	2204	0005
Frankfurt (Oder) ... a.	0448	0550	0631	0648	0725	0825		2025	2223	0025

B – From / to Brandenburg (see main table).
M – From / to Magdeburg (see main table).
N – *IC* **2132**. To Norddeich Mole (Tables **810** / **813**).
P – *IC* **2131**. From Emden (Tables **813** / **810**).
S – ⑤⑥† (also Dec. 31, Mar. 20, Apr. 30).
T – ⑥⑦ (also Dec. 26, Jan. 1, Mar. 21, 24, May 1, 12).

b – Ⓑ (not Dec. 24, 25, 31, Mar. 21, 23, May 11).
e – ①–⑥ (not Dec. 25, 26, Jan. 1, Mar. 22, 24, May 12).
f – Also Dec. 25, 31, Mar. 20, 23, Apr. 30, May 11.

r – 4 minutes later on Ⓐ.
t – 4–6 minutes later on ① (also Dec. 27, Jan. 2, Mar. 25, May 13).
v – Not Dec. 24, 25, 31. On Ⓐ depart *0446* and change trains at Genthin (a. *0527*, d. 0538).
★ – *Harz-Berlin-Express.* [2] Berlin - Halberstadt - Thale and v.v. (Table **862**). Operated by Veolia Verkehr Sachsen-Anhalt GmbH.
⊖ – Via Lübben (Table **838**).

HAMBURG - BERLIN - DRESDEN 840

km		*CNL* 379	*EC* 171	*ICE* 1607	*ICE* 907	*EC* 173	*ICE* 1507	*ICE* 901	*EC* 175	*ICE* 1509	*ICE* 903	*ICE* 1511	*EC* 177	*ICE* 913	*ICE* 38 381	*EC* 371	*ICE* 1513	*ICE* 905	*IC* 1971	*ICE* 1515	*EC* 179	*ICE* 911	*IC* 2071	*ICE* 1517	*ICE* 1017	*ICE* 909
				①g	②–⑥	◐	①–⑥			①–⑥								n	⑤f	n				Ⓑq	Ⓑq	
		♦	✕♦	✕M	p✕	✕♦	eM	✕	✕♦	e♦	✕	✕M	✕♦	✕	🍷A	✕♦	✕M	✕	Q	✕M	✕♦	✕	✕	✕M	✕♦	✕
0	**Hamburg** Altona ... d.	...	...	0546	0546	0622u	0703	0742	0820	...	0951	1042	...	1151	...	...	1303	1351	...	1442	...	1551	1619	1703	1703	1751
7	**Hamburg** Hbf **830** ... d.	...	...	0600	0600	0640	0718	0805	0844	0918	1005	1103	...	1205	1239	...	1318	1405	1411	1503	...	1605	1644	1718	1718	1805
54	Büchen **830** ... d.	...	...	|	|	|	|	|	0907	|	|	|	...	|	|	...	|	|	1433	|	...	|	1707	|	|	|
122	Ludwigslust **837** ... d.	...	...	0644	0644	0734	|	|	0934	|	|	|	...	|	1325	...	|	|	1459	|	...	|	1734	|	|	1847
167	Wittenberge **837** ... d.	...	...	0700	0700	0752	|	|	0952	|	|	|	...	|	1344	...	|	|	|	|	...	|	1752	|	|	|
280	**Berlin** Spandau **837** .. d.	...	...	0739	0739	0834	|	0936	1035	|	1136	|	...	1336	|	...	|	1536	1554	|	...	1736	1835	|	|	1938
292	**Berlin** Hbf **837** ... a.	...	...	0747	0747	0843	0851	0944	1043	1054	1144	1239	...	1344	1436	...	1454	1544	1604	1639	...	1744	1843	1851	1851	1947
292	**Berlin** Hbf ... d.	0453o	0646	0753	...	0846	0858	...	1046	1059	...	1258	1246	...	...	1446	1458	...	...	1658	1646	...	1846	1858	1858	...
	Leipzig Hbf **851** ... a.	|	‡	0905	...	|	1005	...	|	1205	...	1405	‡	...	...	|	1605	...	...	1805	‡	...	‡	2005	2005	...
485	**Dresden** Neustadt ... a.	0657	0844	...	...	1044	...	...	1244	...	...	...	1444	...	...	1644	...	...	...	...	1844	...	2044	...	...	...
489	**Dresden** Hbf ... a.	0705	0854	...	...	1052	...	...	1252	...	...	...	1452	...	...	1653	...	...	...	...	1852	...	2052	...	...	...

	ICE 909	*ICE* 1519	*IC* 2073	*IC* 2075	*IC* 2075	*ICE* 701	*ICE* 1621	*ICE* 1521	*ICE* 703	*ICE* 705*
	⑦w	Ⓑq	①–⑤	⑦m	⑥⑦	⑦w	⑤f	⑦w	①–⑥	⑤⑦
	✕	✕	T✕	T✕	T✕	✕	✕	✕	z✕	c✕
Hamburg Altona ... d.	1751	1903	...	...	...	1951	1951	...	2103	2151
Hamburg Hbf **830** ... d.	1805	1918	1922	1922	1922	2005	2005	2121	2121	2205
Büchen **830** ... d.	|	|	1945	1945	1945	|	|	|	|	|
Ludwigslust **837** ... d.	1847	|	2011	2011	2011	|	|	2205	2205	|
Wittenberge **837** ... d.	|	|	2030	2030	2030	|	|	2222	2222	|
Berlin Spandau **837** .. d.	1938	2049	2115	2115	2115	2134	2136	2301	2258	2334
Berlin Hbf **837** ... a.	1947	2057	2123	2123	2123	2144	2144	2310	2312	2348
Berlin Hbf ... d.	1951	2100	2127y	2127	...	...	2153	2313	...	...
Leipzig Hbf **851** ... a.	2105	2210	|	|	...	...	2306	0024	...	...
Dresden Neustadt ... a.	...	...	2324y	2324	...	...	...	...	...	...
Dresden Hbf ... a.	...	...	2334y	2334	...	...	...	...	...	...

	ICE 702	*ICE* 904	*ICE* 1518	*ICE* 708	*ICE* 1616	*IC* 2072	*IC* 2074	*IC* 2074	*IC* 2070	*ICE* 906	*ICE* 1614	*ICE* 1614
		①–⑤	①–⑤	⑥⑦	①–⑥	①–⑤	⑥x	⑥⑦			①–⑥	
	✕	d✕	aR	t✕	e✕	T✕	T✕	T✕	✕	✕	eN	✕
Dresden Hbf ... d.	...	...	✕	...	...	0604j	0604	...	0703	...	...	...
Dresden Neustadt .. d.	...	...	...	...	...	0612j	0612	...	0712	...	...	...
Leipzig Hbf **851** ... d.	...	...	0548	...	0651	‡	‡	...	‡	...	0851	...
Berlin Hbf ... a.	...	...	0714	...	0805	0819j	0819	...	0912	...	1005	...
Berlin Hbf **837** ... d.	0518	0558	0718	0718	0818	0822	0822	0822	...	0919	1018	1018
Berlin Spandau **837** d.	0528	0608	0728	0728	0828	0831	0831	0831	...	|	1028	1028
Wittenberge **837** ... d.	0608	0644	|	|	|	0914	0914	0914	...	|	|	|
Ludwigslust **837** ... d.	0625	0701	|	|	|	0934	0934	0934	...	|	|	|
Büchen **830** ... d.	|	|	|	|	|	1001	1001	1001	...	|	|	|
Hamburg Hbf **830** .. a.	0707	0746	0857	0857	0957	1023	1023	1023	...	1052	1157	1157
Hamburg Altona ... a.	...	0759	0914	0917	1013	...	...	...	...	1115	1213	1213

	EC 178	*ICE* 1514	*ICE* 1714	*ICE* 1724	*ICE* 902	*ICE* 1512	*EC* 176	*ICE* 900	*ICE* 1510	*EC* 370	*ICE* 37 380	*ICE* 908	*ICE* 1508	*EC* 174	*ICE* 706	*ICE* 1006	*ICE* 1506	*EC* 172	*ICE* 1604	*IC* 1970	*EC* 170	*ICE* 1504	*ICE* 704	*ICE* 1502	*ICE* 912	*CNL* 378
		①–⑤	⑥k	⑦s		Ⓑq			Ⓑq			n	Ⓑq		Ⓑq	⑥h	⑤⑦	◧	Ⓑq	⑦w		⑤–⑦	①–④	①–⑥	⑦w	
	✕♦	aM	✕M	✕N	✕	✕M	✕♦	✕	✕M	✕♦	🍷B	✕	✕♦	✕♦	✕	✕M	cM	✕♦	✕M	🍷Q	✕♦	vM	r✕	bM	✕	♦
Dresden Hbf ... d.	0903	...	...	...	...	...	1103	...	...	1303	...	...	...	1503	...	...	...	1703	...	...	1903	...	...	...	...	2123
Dresden Neustadt ... d.	0912	...	...	...	...	...	1112	...	...	1312	...	...	...	1512	...	...	...	1712	...	...	1912	...	...	...	...	2131
Leipzig Hbf **851** ... d.	|	0951	0951	0951	...	1151	|	...	1351	‡	...	...	1551	|	...	1651	1751	|	1851	...	‡	1951	...	2151	...	|
Berlin Hbf ... a.	1113	1100	1100	1100	...	1300	1313	...	1500	1513	...	...	1700	1713	...	1805	1900	1913	2005	...	2112	2101	...	2300	...	2350o
Berlin Hbf **837** ... d.	...	1118	1118	1118	1218	1303	1318	1418	1503	...	1522	1618	1703	1718	1818	1818	1903	1918	2018	2018	...	2118	2118	2303	2303	...
Berlin Spandau **837** .. d.	...	|	|	|	1228	|	1328	1427	|	...	|	1628	|	1728	1828	1828	|	1928	2028	2031	...	2128	2128	|	|	...
Wittenberge **837** ... d.	...	|	|	|	|	|	1409	|	|	...	1614	|	|	1809	|	|	|	2009	|	2114	...	|	|	|	|	...
Ludwigslust **837** ... d.	...	|	|	|	|	|	1427	|	|	...	1633	|	|	1827	|	|	|	2027	|	2134	...	|	|	|	|	...
Büchen **830** ... d.	...	|	|	|	|	|	1455	|	|	...	|	|	|	1855	|	|	|	2055	|	|	...	|	|	|	|	...
Hamburg Hbf **830** ... a.	...	1254	1254	1254	1357	1439	1518	1557	1639	...	1717	1757	1839	1918	1957	1957	2040	2120	2157	2223	...	2257	2257	0036	0036	...
Hamburg Altona ... a.	...	1313	1313	1313	1414	1505	1539	...	1700	...	...	1819	...	1935	2013	2013	2057	2136	2213	...	...	2313	...	0052	0052	...

♦ – **NOTES** (LISTED BY TRAIN NUMBER)

170/1 – [12] and ✕ Budapest - Bratislava - Praha - Děčín - Berlin and v.v.
172/3 – VINDOBONA – [12] and ✕ Wien - Břeclav - Praha - Děčín - Berlin - Hamburg and v.v.
174/5 – [12] and ✕ Budapest - Bratislavav - Praha - Děčín - Berlin - Hamburg and v.v.
176 – [12] and ✕ Praha - Děčín - Berlin - Hamburg.
177 – [12] and ✕ Berlin - Děčín - Praha - Wien.
178/9 – [12] and ✕ Praha - Děčín - Berlin and v.v.
370 – [12] and ✕ Wien - Břeclav - Praha - Děčín - Berlin - Stralsund ⊖.
371 – [12] and ✕ Stralsund ⊖ - Berlin - Děčín - Praha.
378/9 – KOPERNIKUS – 🛏 1, 2 cl., 🛏 2 cl. and [2] (Ⓡ) Praha - Berlin - Köln - Amsterdam and v.v. Conveys [2] (**60378/9**) Praha - Berlin and v.v.
1017 – [12] and ✕ Hamburg - Berlin - Erfurt (- Frankfurt ⑦**w**).
1508/9 – [12] and ✕ München - Nürnberg - Jena - Leipzig - Kiel and v.v.

A – [12] (38) København - Puttgarden - Hamburg - Berlin; [12] (381) Århus - Flensburg - Hamburg - Berlin.
B – [12] (37) Berlin - Hamburg - Puttgarden - København; [12] (380) Berlin - Hamburg - Flensburg - Århus.
M – [12] and ✕ Hamburg - Leipzig - Jena - Nürnberg - München and v.v.
N – [12] and ✕ Nürnberg - Jena - Leipzig - Hamburg.

Q – To / from Flensburg (Table **823**).
R – From München on dates in Table **851**.
T – To / from Westerland (Table **821**).

a – Not Dec. 24, 25, 26, 31, Jan. 1, Mar. 21, 24, May 12.
b – Also Dec. 23, 30, Mar. 23, May 11; not Dec. 24, 25, 26, 31, Jan. 1, Mar. 24, May 12.
c – Also Dec. 26, Jan. 1, Mar. 20, 24, Apr. 30, May 12; not Dec. 23, 30, Mar. 21, 23, May 2, 11.
d – Not Dec. 24–31, Jan. 1, Mar. 21, 24, May 12.
e – Not Dec. 25, 26, Jan. 1, Mar. 22, 24, May 12.
f – Also Mar. 20, Apr. 30; not Mar. 21, May 2.
g – Also Dec. 27, Jan. 2, Mar. 25, May 13; not Dec. 24, 31, Mar. 24, May 12.
h – Also Dec. 24, 25, 31, Mar. 21, 23, May 11.
j – Not Dec. 25, 26, Jan. 1, Mar. 24, May 12.
k – Also Dec. 24, 31, Mar. 21; not Mar. 22.
m – Not Mar. 23, May 11.
n – Not Dec. 24, 31.
o – Berlin **Ostbahnhof**.
p – Not Dec. 25, 26, 27, Jan. 1, 2, Mar. 25, May 13.

q – Not Dec. 24, 25, 31, Mar. 21, 23, May 11.
r – Not Dec. 24, 25, 26, 31, Jan. 1, Mar. 20, 24, Apr. 30, May 1, 12.
s – Also Dec. 25, 26, Jan. 1, Mar. 22, 24, May 12.
t – Also Dec. 24, 25, 26, 31, Jan. 1, Mar. 21, 24, May 12.
u – 0615 on ⑥.
v – Also Dec. 24, 25, 26, 31, Jan. 1, Mar. 20, 24, Apr. 30, May 1, 12.
w – Also Dec. 26, Jan. 1, Mar. 24, May 12; not Dec. 23, 30, Mar. 23, May 11.
x – Not Mar. 22.
y – Not Dec. 24, 25, 31, Mar. 21.
z – Also Dec. 23, 30, Mar. 23, May 11; not Dec. 26, Jan. 1, Mar. 24, May 12.

⊖ – To / from Ostseebad Binz on dates in Table **844**.
* – Train number **1623** on ⑤ (also Mar. 20, Apr. 30).
‡ – Also calls at Elsterwerda (see Table **843**).
◧ – On Dec. 24, 31 terminates at Berlin Hbf.
◐ – On Dec. 25, Jan. 1 starts from Berlin Hbf.

841 MAGDEBURG - STENDAL - UELZEN and WITTENBERGE

RE / RB services except where shown

km										IC 2238																
		⚒n	Ⓐn		Ⓐn	Ⓒz			①–⑥ t		⑤⑥ DR	⑤⑥ D	G													
0	Magdeburg Hbf ... d.	0359	...	0509	0602	0604	0609	0709	0756	0809	0902	0856	0904	0909	1009	1104*	1109	1209	1304*	1309	1409	1504*	1509	1609	1704*	1709
58	Stendal ... a.	0441	...	0558	0641	0643	0657	0757	0833	0858	0938	0932	0943	0958	1058	1143	1158	1258	1343	1358	1458	1543	1558	1658	1743	1758
58	Stendal ... d.	0450	0459	0559	0644	0644	0659a	0759	0834	...	0940	0944	0944	0959	...	1144	1159	1259a	1344	1359	1509a	1544	1559	1659a	1744	1759
113	**Wittenberge** ... a.	|	0540	0640	|	|	0740a	0840	0909	...	1012	|	|	1040	...	|	1240	1340a	|	1440	1551a	|	1640	1740a	|	1840
116	Salzwedel ... d.	0536	...	...	0714	0720	...	...	...	...	...	1014	1014	...	...	1214	...	...	1414	...	...	1614	...	...	1814	...
167	**Uelzen** ... a.	0608	...	...	0745	0751	...	...	...	...	...	1045	1045	...	...	1245	...	...	1445	...	...	1645	...	...	1845	...

	EC 240					IC 1930					
	Ⓑq W					⑦w B		Ⓑm	n	r	⑥k
Magdeburg Hbf ... d.	...	1809	1904*	1909	2009	...	2109	...	2214	2324	2324
Stendal ... a.	...	1858	1943	1958	2058	...	2158	...	2303	0009	0009
Stendal ... d.	1826	1859b	1944	1959	...	2123	2159r	2212	...	...	0019
Wittenberge ... a.	|	1940b	|	2040	...	|	2240r	|	...	...	|
Salzwedel ... d.	1853	...	2014	...	...	2152	...	2251	...	...	0056
Uelzen ... a.	1929	...	2045n	...	...	2216	...	...	...	...	...

										EC 241	
	Ⓐn		Ⓐn		①–⑥ t	v		⚒n		①–⑥ eW	
Uelzen ... d.	...	...	...	...	...	...	...	0620	...	0756	...
Salzwedel ... d.	...	...	0501	...	0536	0601	...	0655	...	0820	...
Wittenberge ... d.	...	...	|	0516a	|	|	0616a	|	0716	|	0816a
Stendal ... a.	...	...	0541	0555a	0607	0641	0655a	0724	0755	0846	0855a
Stendal ... d.	0355	0457	0543	0557	0609	0645	0657	0725	0757	...	0857
Magdeburg Hbf ... a.	0444	0544	0622	0644	0650x	0726	0744	0802	0844	...	0944

									IC 1931					IC 2239												
			①–⑥ t						⑤f B					⑤⑦ DR								Ⓑb			Ⓐn	
Uelzen ... d.	0825	...	...	...	...	1102	...	...	1250	1302	...	...	1502	...	...	...	1702	...	...	1902	...	...	...	2103	...	...
Salzwedel ... d.	0904	...	...	...	...	1134	...	...	1323	1334	...	...	1534	...	...	...	1734	...	...	1934	*1955*	...	...	2134	2231	...
Wittenberge ... d.	|	0916	1016	...	1116	|	...	1316	|	|	1416a	1516	|	1543	1616a	1716	|	1816a	1916	|	|	2035	2116	|	|	2248r
Stendal ... a.	0944	0955	1055	...	1155	1207	...	1355	1410	1405	1455a	1555	1607	1615	1655a	1755	1807	1855a	1955	2007	*2039*	2109	2155	2210	2314	2327r
Stendal ... d.	...	0957	1057	1057	1157	1211	1257	1357	...	1411	1457	1557	1609	1617	1657	1757	1811	1857	1957	2011	2057	2110	...	2211	...	2331
Magdeburg Hbf ... a.	...	1044	1144	1144	1244	1253	1344	1444	...	1453	1544	1644	1650	1653	1744	1844	1853	1944	2044	2053	2144	2153	...	2259	...	0018

B – From / to Berlin (Table **810**).
D – From Mar. 14.
G – ①②③④⑦ (daily to Mar. 13).
R – WARNOW – ⟨12⟩ and 🍷 Leipzig - Halle - Magdeburg - Schwerin - Rostock - Warnemünde and v.v.
W – WAWEL – ⟨12⟩ and ✕ Kraków - Wrocław - Forst 🏛 - Cottbus - Berlin - Hamburg and v.v.

a – Ⓐ (not Dec. 24, 31).
b – Ⓑ (not Dec. 23, 24, 25, 30, 31, Mar. 23, May 11).
e – Not Dec. 25, 26, 31, Jan. 1, Mar. 22, 24, May 12.
f – Also Mar. 20, Apr. 30; not Dec. 28, Mar. 21, May 2.
k – Also Dec. 23, 30, Mar. 21, 23, May 11.
m – Not Dec. 23, 24, 25, 30, 31, Mar. 21, 23, May 11.
n – Not Dec. 24, 31.
q – Not Dec. 24, 25, 30, 31, Mar. 21, 23, May 11.
r – Not Dec. 24, 25, 31.

t – Not Dec. 24, 25, 26, 31, Jan. 1, Mar. 24, May 12.
v – Not Dec. 25, 26, Jan. 1.
w – Also Dec. 26, Jan. 1, Mar. 24, May 12; not Dec. 23, 30, Mar. 23, May 11.
x – 0655 from May 26.
z – Also Dec. 24, 31.
* – 2 minutes **earlier** from May 25.

842 LEIPZIG - DRESDEN

km		RE 17441	CNL 353	D 60353	RE 17443	RE 17445	CNL 459	IC 61459	RE 17447	ICE 1741	RE 17449	ICE 1553	RE 17451	ICE 1543	RE 17453	ICE 1555	RE 17455	ICE 1545	ICE 1745	RE 17457	ICE 1557	ICE 1597	RE 17459
		w	Ⓡ P	L	⚒		Ⓡ R✕	F	⚒	①–⑥ eM		①–⑤ dE	⚒	✕		✕	⚒	①–⑥ e✕	⑦c ✕		①–⑥ eS	⑦k W	⚒
	Frankfurt Flughafen Fernbf ✈ 850 d.	...	...	...	...	...	...	...	...	...	...	...	...	...	...	...	...	0811	...	...	...	0901	...
	Frankfurt (Main) Hbf 850 d.	...	2219z	...	...	...	0055z	...	...	...	...	0517g	...	0618e	...	0720	...	◇	0822	...	0921	0921	...
0	**Leipzig** Hbf ... d.	...	0429	0429	0458	0558	|	0651	0658	0751	0758	0851	0858	0951	0958	1051	1058	1151	1151	1158	1251	1251	1258
26	Wurzen ... d.	...	|	|	0519	0619	|	|	0719	|	0819	|	0919	|	1019	|	1119	|	|	1219	|	|	1319
53	Oschatz ... d.	...	|	|	0538	0638	|	|	0738	|	0838	|	0938	|	1038	|	1138	|	|	1238	|	|	1338
66	Riesa ... d.	0448	0504	0504	0548	0648	0720	0722	0748	0824	0848	0924	0948	1024	1048	1124	1148	1224	1224	1248	1324	1324	1348
102	Coswig **843 856 857** ... d.	0517	|	|	0617	0717	|	|	0817	|	0917	|	1017	|	1117	|	1217	|	|	1317	|	|	1417
116	**Dresden** Neustadt **856 857** ... a.	0532	0536	0536	0632	0732	0754	0754	0832	0854	0932	0954	1032	1054	1132	1154	1232	1254	1254	1332	1354	1354	1432
120	**Dresden** Hbf **843 856 857** ... a.	0539	0551	0551	0639	0739	0803	0803	0839	0902	0939	1002	1039	1102	1139	1202	1239	1302	1302	1339	1402	1402	1439

	X 82661	ICE 1547	RE 17461	ICE 1559	RE 17463	ICE 1549	RE 17465	ICE 1651	RE 17467	ICE 1641	RE 17469	ICE 1653	RE 17471	ICE 1643	RE 17473	ICE 1655	ICE 1645	RE 17475	ICE 1657	RE 17477	RE 17479	◧	◧
	⚒ G▲	✕		W✕		✕		W✕		✕		n W✕	Ⓑ	n ✕		Ⓑq W✕	n ✕		⑤⑦f W✕	A	⑤⑦t	Ⓐ	Ⓒ
Frankfurt Flughafen Fernbf ✈ 850 d.	...	1011	...	1102	...	1211	...	1302	...	1411	...	1502	...	1611	...	1702	1811	...	1902	...	...	...	...
Frankfurt (Main) Hbf 850 d.	...	◇	...	1119	...	◇	...	1319	...	◇	...	1520	...	◇	...	1720	|	...	1919	...	...	...	...
Leipzig Hbf ... d.	1320	1351	1358	1451	1458	1551	1558	1651	1658	1751	1758	1851	1858	1951	1958	2051	2151	2158	2256	2258	2304	0010	0120
Wurzen ... d.	|	|	1419	|	1519	|	1619	|	1719	|	1819	|	1919	|	2019	|	|	2219	|	2319	2326	0038	0151
Oschatz ... d.	1400	|	1438	|	1538	|	1638	|	1738	|	1838	|	1938	|	2038	|	|	2238	|	2338	2345	0057	0211
Riesa ... d.	1416	1424	1448	1524	1548	1624	1648	1724	1748	1824	1848	1924	1948	2024	2048	2124	2224	2248	2329	2348	2358	...	...
Coswig **843 856 857** ... d.	1439	|	1517	|	1617	|	1717	|	1817	|	1917	|	2017	|	2117	|	|	2317	|	0017	0028	...	...
Dresden Neustadt **856 857** ... a.	1455	1454	1532	1554	1632	1654	1732	1754	1832	1854	1932	1954	2032	2054	2132	2154	2254	2332	2400	0032	0041	...	...
Dresden Hbf **843 856 857** ... a.	...	1502	1539	1602	1639	1702	1739	1802	1839	1902	1939	2002	2039	2102	2139	2202	2302	2339	0008	0039	0049	...	...

	◧	◧	RE 17440	ICE 1644	RE 17442	ICE 1654	RE 17444	ICE 1642	RE 17446	X 82662	ICE 1652	X 82662	RE 17448	ICE 1640	RE 17450	ICE 1650	RE 17452	ICE 1548	RE 17454	ICE 1558	RE 17456	ICE 1546	RE 17458
	Ⓐ	†	⚒	①–⑥ m✕		①–⑥ eW	⚒	v ✕		⚒ G▲	W✕	⚒ G▲	⚒	✕		W✕	⚒	✕		W✕	⚒	✕	
Dresden Hbf **843 856 857** ... d.	...	...	0412	0443	0521	0555	0621	0655	0721	...	0755	...	0821	0855	0921	0955	1021	1055	1121	1155	1221	1255	1321
Dresden Neustadt **856 857** ... d.	...	...	0419	0451	0528	0603	0628	0703	0728	0800	0803	←	0828	0903	0928	1003	1028	1103	1128	1203	1228	1303	1328
Coswig **843 856 857** ... d.	...	...	0431	|	0540	|	0640	|	0740	0818	|	0821	0840	|	0940	|	1040	|	1140	|	1240	|	1340
Riesa ... d.	...	...	0501	0524	0610	0634	0710	0734	0810	→	0834	0846	0910	0934	1010	1034	1110	1134	1210	1234	1310	1334	1410
Oschatz ... d.	0407	0500	0510	|	0619	|	0719	|	0819	...	|	0858	0919	|	1019	|	1119	|	1219	|	1319	|	1419
Wurzen ... d.	0425	0519	0530	|	0639	|	0739	|	0839	...	|	|	0939	|	1039	|	1139	|	1239	|	1339	|	1439
Leipzig Hbf ... a.	0453	0548	0553	0557	0703	0707	0801	0807	0901	...	0907	0931	1001	1007	1101	1107	1201	1207	1301	1307	1401	1407	1501
Frankfurt (Main) Hbf 850 a.	...	...	...	|	...	1037	...	◇	...	...	1237	...	...	◇	...	1437	...	◇	...	1637	...	◇	...
Frankfurt Flughafen Fernbf ✈ 850 a.	...	...	...	0948	...	1056	...	1148	...	...	1256	...	...	1348	...	1456	...	1548	...	1656	...	1748	...

	ICE 1556	RE 17460	ICE 1544	ICE 1744	RE 17462	ICE 1554	ICE 1594	RE 17464	ICE 1542	RE 17466	ICE 1552	RE 17468	ICE 1740	RE 17470	ICE 1550	RE 17472	IC 61458	CNL 458		RE 17474	CNL 352	D 60352	RE 17476
	W✕		①–⑥ h✕	⑦v ✕		n W✕	Ⓑq S✕		Ⓑq ✕		n ✕		Ⓑb H	Ⓑ	⑦v ✕		F	Ⓡ R✕		n	Ⓡ P	L	r
Dresden Hbf **843 856 857** ... d.	1355	1421	1455	1455	1521	1555	1555	1621	1655	1721	1755	1821	1855	1921	1955	2021	2054	2054	...	2221	2256	2256	2321
Dresden Neustadt **856 857** ... d.	1403	1428	1503	1503	1528	1603	1603	1628	1703	1728	1803	1828	1903	1928	2003	2028	2103	2103	...	2228	2303	2303	2328
Coswig **843 856 857** ... d.	|	1440	|	|	1540	|	|	1640	|	1740	|	1840	|	1940	|	2040	|	|	...	2240	|	|	2340
Riesa ... d.	1434	1510	1534	1534	1610	1634	1634	1710	1734	1810	1834	1910	1934	2010	2034	2110	2135	2135	...	2310	2336	2336	0010
Oschatz ... d.	|	1519	|	|	1619	|	|	1719	|	1819	|	1919	|	2019	|	2119	|	|	...	2319	|	|	...
Wurzen ... d.	|	1539	|	|	1639	|	|	1739	|	1839	|	1939	|	2039	|	2139	|	|	...	2339	|	|	...
Leipzig Hbf ... a.	1507	1601	1607	1607	1701	1707	1707	1801	1807	1901	1907	2001	2004	2101	2107	2201	2208	|	...	0001	0009	0009	...
Frankfurt (Main) Hbf 850 a.	1837	...	1940	◇	...	2037	2037	...	2146	...	2254	...	...	...	0051	...	...	0400z	...	...	0654z	...	...
Frankfurt Flughafen Fernbf ✈ 850 a.	1856	...	...	1948	...	2056	...	...	...	...	...	...	...	...	...	...	...	...	...	...	...	...	...

A – ①②③④⑥ (also Dec. 23, 30, Mar. 21, 23, May 11; not Dec. 24, 26, 31, Jan. 1, Mar. 20, 24, Apr. 30, May 12).
E – ⟨12⟩ and ✕ (Frankfurt ① g -) Eisenach - Dresden.
F – From / to Fulda (Table **850**).
G – To / from Görlitz (Table 855). Operated by Veolia Verkehr GmbH.
H – ⟨12⟩ Dresden - Leipzig (- Magdeburg ①②③④⑦ a) (- Hannover ⑦).
L – ⟨12⟩ Leipzig - Praha and v.v.
M – ⟨12⟩ (Magdeburg ①–⑤ d -) Leipzig - Dresden.
P – JOHANNES KEPLER – 🛏 1, 2 cl., ▬ 2 cl. and ⟨2⟩ Praha - Děčín - Bad Schandau - Dresden - Karlsruhe - Basel and v.v.
R – SEMPER – 🛏 1, 2 cl., ▬ 2 cl., ⟨2⟩ (reclining) and ✕ Dresden - Karlsruhe - Basel - Zürich and v.v.
S – ⟨12⟩ and ✕ Saarbrücken - Mannheim - Frankfurt - Dresden and v.v.
W – From / to Wiesbaden (Table 912).

a – Not Dec. 23, 24, 25, 30, 31, Mar. 20, 23, May 11.
b – Not Dec. 23, 24, 25, 30, 31, Mar. 21, 23, May 11.
c – Also Dec. 26, Mar. 22, 24, May 12.
d – Not Dec. 24, 25, 26, 31, Jan. 1, Mar. 21, 24, May 12.
e – ①–⑥ (not Dec. 25, 26, Jan. 1, Mar. 22, 24, May 12).
f – Also Dec. 26, Jan. 1, Mar. 20, 24, Apr. 30; not Dec. 23, 30, Mar. 21, 23, May 11.
g – ① (also Dec. 27, Jan. 2, Mar. 25, May 13; not Dec. 24, 31, Mar. 24, May 12).
h – Also Dec. 23, 30, Mar. 23, May 11; not Dec. 26, Jan. 1, Mar. 24, May 12.
k – Also Dec. 25, 26, Jan. 1, Mar. 22, 24, May 12.
m – Not Dec. 24, 25, 26, 31, Jan. 1, Mar. 22, 24, May 12.
n – Not Dec. 24, 31.

q – Not Dec. 24, 25, 31, Mar. 21, 23, May 11.
r – Not Dec. 24, 25, 31.
t – Also Dec. 26, Jan. 1, Mar. 20, 24, Apr. 30, May 12; not Dec. 23, 30, Mar. 21, 23, May 11.
v – Also Dec. 26, Jan. 1, Mar. 24, May 12; not Dec. 23, 30, Mar. 23, May 11.
w – Not Dec. 25, 26, Jan. 1.
x – Not Dec. 25, Jan. 1.
z – Frankfurt (Main) **Süd**.
▲ – DB tickets not valid.
◇ – See Table **850** for connection from / to Frankfurt (Main) Hbf.
◧ – S-Bahn.

843 (BERLIN -) ELSTERWERDA - CHEMNITZ and DRESDEN

RE / RB services except where shown

See Tables **851 / 874** for Berlin - Chemnitz via Leipzig. See Table **840** for direct *EC* and *IC* services Berlin - Dresden and v.v.

km																									
					Ⓐ	Ⓐ	*EC* 171 ✕						*EC* 177 ✕				Ⓐ		*EC* 179 ✕		V 🍷	*IC* 2071 ✕			n
0	**Berlin** Zoo d.	...	...	...	...	...	...	...	...	...	...	...	...	...	...	...	...	...	...	...	1750	...	...	...	...
4	**Berlin** Hbf 845 d.	...	...	...	0426	...	0646	...	0731	...	0931	...	1246	...	1331	...	1431	...	1646	...	|	1846	...	1931	...
9	**Berlin** Ostbahnhof d.	...	...	...	|	...	|	...	|	...	|	...	|	...	|	...	|	...	|	...	1805	|	...	|	...
28	Berlin Schönefeld ✈ d.	...	...	...	|	...	|	...	|	...	|	...	|	...	|	...	|	...	|	...	1822	|	...	|	...
141	**Elsterwerda 845** d.	...	0452a	0602a	0626	0702	0805	0810	0931	1002	1131	1202	1406	1413	1531	1602	1631	1702a	1805	1813	|	2004	2013	2130	2216
165	Riesa a.	...	0517a	0627a	...	0727	...	0838	...	1027	...	1227	...	1438	...	1627	...	1727a	...	1838	1955	...	2039	...	2241
165	Riesa d.	0440	0540	0640	...	0740	...	0840	...	1040	...	1240	...	1440	...	1640	...	1740	...	1840	1956	...	2040n	...	2250
191	Döbeln Hbf d.	0504	0604	0704	...	0804	...	0904	...	1104	...	1304	...	1504	...	1704	...	1804	...	1904	2014	...	2104n	...	2313
232	**Chemnitz** Hbf a.	0547	0652	0747	...	0847	...	0947	...	1147	...	1347	...	1547	...	1747	...	1847	...	1947	2045	...	2147n	...	2355

		Ⓐ		*IC* 2072 G✕		*IC* 2070 ✕	V 🍷						*EC* 370 ✕				Ⓐ				*EC* 170 ✕	Ⓑ	n	Ⓐ	n
Chemnitz Hbf d.	0407	...	0507	...	0607	...	0642	0807	...	1007	...	1207	...	1406	...	1507	...	1607	...	1807	...	1907	2007	2109	2207
Döbeln Hbf d.	0449	...	0549	...	0649	...	0721	0849	...	1049	...	1249	...	1449	...	1549	...	1649	...	1849	...	1949	2049	2151	2249
Riesa a.	0514	...	0614	...	0714	...	0740	0914	...	1114	...	1314	...	1514	...	1614	...	1714	...	1914	...	2014	2114	2216	2314
Riesa d.	0514a	...	0620a	...	0716	...	0742	0931	...	1131	...	1316	...	1516	...	1631a	...	1731	...	1916	...	2031a	2131c	2231	...
Elsterwerda 845 d.	0536a	0539	0642a	0654	0738	0749	|	0953	1026	1153	1226	1338	1349	1538	1626	1653a	1725	1753	1826	1938	1949	2053a	2153c	2254	...
Berlin Schönefeld ✈ a.	...	|	...	|	...	|	0909	...	|	...	|	...	|	...	|	...	|	...	|	...	|	...	...	...	...
Berlin Ostbahnhof a.	...	|	...	|	...	|	0927	...	|	...	|	...	|	...	|	...	|	...	|	...	|	...	...	...	...
Berlin Hbf 845 a.	...	0728	...	0819	...	0912	|	...	1228	...	1428	...	1513	...	1828	...	1928	...	2028	...	2112	...	...	...	...
Berlin Zoo a.	...	...	...	...	...	...	1007	...	...	...	...	...	...	...	...	...	...	...	...	...	...	...	...	...	...

Elsterwerda - Dresden

km		Ⓐ	Ⓐ	Ⓐ						⑥⑦
0	Elsterwerda-Biehla d.	0440	0541	0640	0740	0940	and every two hours until	2140	2340	2340
2	**Elsterwerda** d.	0445	0545	0645	0745	0945		2145	2343	2345
41	Coswig 842 856/7 d.	0525	0625	0725	0825	1025		2225	...	0025
59	**Dresden** Hbf 842 856/7 a.	0547	0647	0747	0847	1047		2247	...	0047

		Ⓐ					
Dresden Hbf 842 856/7 d.	0510	0610	0710	0910	and every two hours until	1910	2110
Coswig 842 856/7 d.	0534	0634	0734	0934		1934	2134
Elsterwerda a.	0613	0713	0813	1013		2013	2213
Esterwerda-Biehla a.	0619	0719	0819	1019		2019	2219

G – ①–⑥ (not Dec. 25, 26, Jan. 1, Mar. 22, 24, May 12). Train number **2074** on ⑥.
V – *VOGTLAND-EXPRESS.* From / to Plauen (Table **880**). Operated by Vogtlandbahn. 2nd class only. **DB tickets not valid.**

a – Ⓐ only.
c – Ⓒ only.
n – Not Dec. 24, 31.

844 STRALSUND - OSTSEEBAD BINZ / SASSNITZ

RE / RB services except where shown

km																									
		Ⓐ			Ⓐ	Ⓐ					*IC* 2184 ①g H		A		A	*IC* 2182 ①–⑥ e♦		A		A		A		A	*IC* 2212 ♦
	Rostock Hbf **830** d.	...	...	0454	...	0553	...	...	0700	...	0746	...	...	0900	...	0946	...	...	1100	...	...	...	1300	...	1318
0	**Stralsund** d.	0504	...	0604	...	0704	0704	...	0804	...	0853	0904	...	1004	...	1041	1102	...	1204	...	1304	...	1404	...	1424
29	Bergen auf Rügen d.	0533	...	0633	...	0733	0733	...	0833	...	0919	0933	...	1033	...	1107	1131	...	1233	...	1333	...	1433	...	1450
39	Lietzow (Rügen) d.	0542	...	0642	0644	0742	0742	0744	0842	0844	|	0942	0944	1042	1044	|	1140	1144	1242	1244	1342	1344	1442	1444	|
	Ostseebad Binz a.	|	...	|	0657	|	|	0757	|	0857	0938	0955	|	|	1057	1131	1153	|	|	1257	1355	|	|	1457	1516
51	**Sassnitz** a.	0556	...	0655	...	0755	0755	...	0855	...	...	...	0957	1055	...	...	...	1157	1255	...	...	1357	1455	...	...

		A		A	*IC* 2355 ♦					*EC* 370 ♦		*IC* 1961 ⑤ ♦												Ⓑ
Rostock Hbf **830** d.	...	...	1500	...	...	...	...	1700	...	...	...	1746	...	...	1900	...	...	...	...	...	2100	...	...	...
Stralsund d.	1502	...	1604	...	1628	1704	...	1804	...	1829	...	1852	1904	...	2004	...	2104	...	...	...	2204	...	...	2311
Bergen auf Rügen d.	1531	...	1633	...	1654	1733	...	1833	...	1853	...	1918	1933	...	2033	...	2133	...	←	...	2233	...	...	2339
Lietzow (Rügen) d.	1540	1544	1642	1644	|	1742	1744	1842	1844	|	...	|	1942	1944	2042	2044	2141	2144	2146	...	2242	2244	...	...
Ostseebad Binz a.	1553	|	|	1657	1719	1755	|	|	1857	1919	...	1938	1955	|	|	2057	→	|	2158	...	|	2257	...	...
Sassnitz a.	...	1557	1655	...	...	...	1757	1855	...	...	...	...	...	1957	2055	...	...	2157	...	...	2255	...	...	...

km																									
		Ⓐ			Ⓐ	⚒					*IC* 2356 ①–⑥ e♦	A		A		*IC* 2213 ♦		*EC* 371 ♦	A		A		*IC* 1909 ⑦ ♦		*IC* 2377 ♦
	Sassnitz d.	0403	...	0505	...	0605	...	0705	...	0805	...	...	0905	1003	...	...	...	...	...	1105	1203	...	...	...	...
0	**Ostseebad Binz** d.	|	...	|	0603	|	0703	|	0803	|	0843	0903	|	|	1006	1027	...	1042	1103	|	|	1206	1220	...	1230
12	Lietzow (Rügen) d.	0417	...	0520	0616	0620	0716	0720	0816	0820	|	0916	0920	1017	1020	|	...	|	1116	1120	1217	1220	|	...	|
22	Bergen auf Rügen d.	0425	...	0528	...	0628	...	0728	...	0828	0910	...	0928	...	1028	1056	...	1108	...	1128	...	1228	1244	...	1258
51	**Stralsund** a.	0454	...	0557	...	0657	...	0757	...	0857	0933	...	0957	...	1057	1119	...	1130	...	1157	...	1257	1312	...	1321
	Rostock Hbf **830** a.	0547	...	0654	...	...	...	0854	...	...	...	...	1054	...	...	1218	...	...	...	1254	...	...	1438	...	1415

	A		A		A		A		*IC* 2183 ⑦w ♦					*IC* 1952 ⑦w ♦										
Sassnitz d.	...	1305	1403	...	...	1505	1603	...	...	...	1703	...	...	...	1803	...	...	1905	2003	...	...	2103	2203	...
Ostseebad Binz d.	1303	|	|	1406	1503	|	|	1606	1622	...	|	1706	...	1757	|	1806	1903	|	|	2006	2103	|	|	2206
Lietzow (Rügen) d.	1316	1320	1417	1420	1516	1520	1617	1620	|	...	1717	1720	...	|	1817	1820	1916	1920	2017	2020	2116	2120	2217	2220
Bergen auf Rügen d.	...	1328	...	1428	...	1528	...	1628	1643	...	...	1728	...	1817	...	1828	...	1928	...	2028	...	2128	...	2228
Stralsund a.	...	1357	...	1457	...	1557	...	1657	1709	...	...	1757	...	1844	...	1858	...	1957	...	2057	...	2157	...	2257
Rostock Hbf **830** a.	...	1454	...	...	...	1654	...	...	1817	...	...	1854	...	...	...	...	...	2054	...	...	...	2254	...	...

♦ – **NOTES** (LISTED BY TRAIN NUMBER)

370 – Daily Dec. 21 - Jan. 5; ⑤⑥ from Mar. 14 (also Mar. 20, 23, Apr. 30, May 1, 11). (12) Wien - Praha - Berlin - Ostseebad Binz.
371 – Daily Dec. 22 - Jan. 6; ⑥⑦ from Mar. 15 (also Mar. 21, 24, May 1, 2, 12). (12) Ostseebad Binz - Berlin - Praha.
1909 – ⑦ from Apr. 13 (also Mar. 24, May 12; not May 11). (12) Ostseebad Binz - Hamburg - Köln.
1952 – (12) Ostseebad Binz - Berlin.
1961 – ⑤ from Apr. 11 (also Mar. 20, Apr. 30; not May 2). (12) Hamburg - Ostseebad Binz.
2182/3 – (12) and 🍷 Hannover - Hamburg - Ostseebad Binz and v.v.
2212 – RÜGEN – (12) and 🍷 Koblenz - Köln - Hamburg - Ostseebad Binz.
2213 – RÜGEN – (12) and 🍷 Ostseebad Binz - Hamburg - Köln - Stuttgart.
2355 – STRELASUND – (12) and 🍷 (Düsseldorf ① **m** -) Dortmund - Kassel - Erfurt - Halle - Berlin - Ostseebad Binz.
2356 – STRELASUND – (12) and 🍷 Ostseebad Binz - Berlin - Halle - Erfurt - Kassel - Düsseldorf.
2377 – ARKONA – (12) and 🍷 Ostseebad Binz - Hamburg - Hannover - Frankfurt (- Karlsruhe on dates in Table **911**).

A – Ⓐ (daily from Apr. 28).
H – From Hamburg (Table **830**).
e – Not Dec. 25, 26, Jan. 1, Mar. 22, 24, May 12.
g – Also Dec. 27, Jan. 2, Mar. 25, May 13; not Dec. 24, 31, Mar. 24, May 12.
m – Also Dec. 27, Jan. 2, Mar. 25, May 13; not Dec. 24, 31, Mar. 24, May 12.
w – Also Dec. 26, Jan. 1, Mar. 24, May 12; not Dec. 23, 30, Mar. 23, May 11.

844a BERGEN AUF RÜGEN - PUTBUS - LAUTERBACH and RÜGENSCHE KLEINBAHN

OLA ★

km		Ⓐ	Ⓒk		z			z	
0	**Bergen** auf Rügen d.	0536	0636	0736	0836	each train runs every **two** hours until	1736	1836	1936
10	**Putbus** a.	0545	0645	0745	0845		1745	1845	1945
12	**Lauterbach** (Mole) a.	0550	0650	0750	...		1750	...	1950

	Ⓐ	Ⓒk		z			z	
Lauterbach (Mole) d.	0605	0705	0805	...	each train runs every **two** hours until	1805	...	2005
Putbus d.	0612	0712	0812	0912		1812	1912	2012
Bergen auf Rügen a.	0621	0721	0821	0921		1821	1921	2021

RÜGENSCHE KLEINBAHN: Rügensche Kleinbahn GmbH, Binzer Straße 12, 18581 Putbus. ✆ + 49 (0) 3 8301 801 12. Fax + 49 (0) 3 8301 801 15. All services worked by steam locomotive.

km	*2007 service*		A				A			A	z
0	**Lauterbach** (Mole) d.	...	...	0901z	1101z	1301z	...	1501z	1701z	1901z	2101
2	**Putbus** a.	...	...	0908z	1108z	1308z	...	1508z	1708z	1908z	2108
2	**Putbus** d.	0748	0854	0948	1148	1348	...	1548	1748	1948	...
14	Binz Lokalbahn ▲ ‡ d.	0820	0925	1020	1220	1420	1525	1620	1820	2020	...
22	Sellin (Rügen) Ost ‡ d.	0848	0953	1048	1248	1448	1553	1648	1848	2048	...
27	**Göhren** (Rügen) ‡ a.	0902	1007	1102	1302	1502	1607	1702	1902	2102	...

2007 service		A			A		A			A
Göhren (Rügen) ‡ d.	0935	1029	1135	1335	1429	1535	1629	1735	1935	2135
Sellin (Rügen) Ost. ‡ d.	0952	1047	1152	1352	1447	1552	1647	1752	1952	2152
Binz Lokalbahn ▲ ‡ d.	1020	1112	1220	1420	1512	1620	1715	1820	2020	2220
Putbus a.	1046	...	1246	1446	...	1646	1741	1846	2046	2246
Putbus d.	1050z	...	1250z	1450z	...	1650z	...	1850z	2050z	...
Lauterbach (Mole) a.	1056z	...	1256z	1456z	...	1656z	...	1856z	2056z	...

A – May 1 - Oct. 3.
k – Not Dec. 25, 26, Jan. 1.
z – May 31 - Sept. 8.
★ – Ostseeland Verkehr GmbH.
▲ – 2½ km from Ostseebad Binz DB station.
‡ – **Additional trains** Binz - Göhren and v.v. May 1 - Oct. 3. From Binz Lokalbahn at 1125 and 1325. From Göhren at 1229.

845 ELSTERWERDA - BERLIN - STRALSUND

RE/RB services except where shown

km																								
															IC 2351				*IC* 2353				*IC* 2355	
						Ⓐ		⑥⑦	Ⓐ	Ⓒ		Ⓐ		⑥⑦			①–⑤		‡					
								Z	◧2	◧2					H 🍷				K 🍷				G 🍷	
0	**Elsterwerda 840** d.	...	...	0415j	...	0539	...	...	...	...	0626	0725	...	...	...	0826	...	...	...	1026	...	...	...	1226
20	Doberlug-Kirchhain d.	...	...	0444	...	0554	...	...	...	...	0644	0744	...	...	...	0844	...	...	...	1044	...	...	...	1244
140	**Berlin** Hbf **840** a.	...	...	0628	...	0728	...	...	p	...	0832	0928	...	...	...	1028	...	...	...	1228	...	...	...	1428
140	**Berlin** Hbf d.	...	0529	0631	...	0731	0731	0811	0759	0759	0833	0931	0931	...	0938	1031	...	1131	1138	1231	...	1331	1338	1431
166	Bernau (b. Berlin) d.	...	0547	0650	...	0750	0750	0832	0836	0840	0852	0950	0950	...	0959	1050	...	1150	1159	1250	...	1350	1359	1450
188	Eberswalde Hbf d.	0505	0601	0705	...	0805	0805	0847	0850	0855	0906	1005	1005	...	1014	1105	...	1205	1214	1305	...	1405	1414	1505
214	Angermünde a.	0525	0621	0725	...	0825	0825	0903	0905	0910	0925	1025	1025	...	1030	1125	...	1225	1230	1325	...	1425	1430	1525
214	Angermünde d.	0532	0632	0732	0734	0832	0832	0906	0912	0912	0932	1032	1032	1034	1032	1132	1134	1232	1232	1332	1334	1432	1432	1532
237	Schwedt (Oder) a.	|	0654	|	|	0854	0854	|	|	|	|	1054	1054	|	|	|	|	1254	|	|	|	1454	|	|
	Tantow (ticket point) d.	|	...	|	0807	...	...	|	0938	0938	|	...	...	1107	|	|	1207	...	|	|	1407	...	|	|
	Szczecin Gumience 🏛 d.	|	...	|	0824	...	...	|	0956	0956	|	...	...	1124	|	|	1224	...	|	|	1424	...	|	|
	Szczecin Głowny a.	|	...	|	0829	...	...	|	1001	1001	|	...	...	1129	|	|	1229	...	|	|	1429	...	|	|
251	Prenzlau d.	0600	...	0800	...	...	...	0930	...	...	1000	...	...	...	1055	1200	...	...	1255	1400	...	...	1455	1600
276	**Pasewalk** a.	0616	...	0816	...	...	...	|	...	...	1016	...	...	...	1108	1216	...	...	1308	1416	...	...	1508	1616
276	**Pasewalk** d.	0620	...	0822	...	...	...	|	...	...	1022	...	...	...	1110	1222	...	...	1310	1422	...	...	1510	1622
319	Anklam d.	0650	...	0851	...	...	...	|	...	...	1051	...	...	...	1136	1251	...	...	1336	1452	...	...	1536	1651
335	Züssow **846** d.	0703	...	0905	...	...	...	1019	...	...	1105	...	...	...	1148	1305	...	...	1348	1505	...	...	1548	1705
353	Greifswald **846** d.	0722	...	0922	...	...	...	1031	...	...	1122	...	...	...	1201	1322	...	...	1401	1522	...	...	1601	1722
384	**Stralsund 846** a.	0744	...	0943	...	...	...	1054	...	...	1143	...	...	...	1223	1343	...	...	1423	1544	...	...	1623	1743

			EC 370				*IC* 143			*IC* 2157					*IC* 2359								
					⑦w	①–⑥	n	Ⓐ		Ⓑq			Ⓐ		⑤⑦		⑤⑥	Ⓐ		⑦r	⑤–⑦		①–⑥	
			B ✕			t	A			L 🍷					f L		v				b		d	
Elsterwerda 840 d.	...	...	1349	1426	...	...	...	1525	...	...	1626	...	1725	...	...	1826	1826	1925	...	...	...	2034	...	...
Doberlug-Kirchhain d.	...	...	|	1444	...	...	...	1544	...	...	1644	...	1744	...	...	1844	1844	1944	...	...	...	2052	...	...
Berlin Hbf **840** a.	...	...	1513	1628	...	...	...	1728	...	...	1828	...	1928	...	...	2028	2028	2129	...	...	...	2230	...	...
Berlin Hbf d.	...	1531	1536	1631	...	...	1729	1737	1737	1751	1831	...	1931	1931	1938	2031	2031	2131	2131	...	...	2231	...	2331
Bernau (b. Berlin) d.	...	1550	1558	1650	...	...	1750	1756	1756	1812	1850	...	1950	1950	1959	2050	2050	2150	2150	...	...	2250	...	2350
Eberswalde Hbf d.	...	1605	1613	1705	...	...	1805	1811	1811	1827	1905	...	2005	2005	2014	2105	2105	2205	2205	...	...	2305	...	0009
Angermünde a.	...	1625	1630	1725	...	...	1820	1830	1830	1842	1925	...	2025	2025	2030	2125	2125	2225	2225	...	...	2325	...	...
Angermünde d.	1534	1632	1632	1732	1742	1754	1839	1832	1832	1844	1932	1954	2032	2032	2032	2132	2132	2232	2232	2232	2234	2332	2332	...
Schwedt (Oder) a.	|	1654	|	|	|	|	|	1854	1854	|	|	|	2054	2054	|	|	|	2254	2254	|	|	2354	|	...
Tantow (ticket point) d.	1607	...	|	|	1826	1833	|	...	...	|	|	2033	...	...	|	|	|	...	...	|	2311	...	|	...
Szczecin Gumience 🏛 d.	1624	...	|	|	1843	1850	1932	...	...	|	|	2050	...	...	|	|	|	...	...	|	2328	...	|	...
Szczecin Głowny a.	1637	...	|	|	1853	1900	1938	...	...	|	|	2100	...	...	|	|	|	...	...	|	2333	...	|	...
Prenzlau d.	...	...	1655	1800	...	...	...	...	...	1907	2000	...	...	...	2055	2200	2200	...	...	2300	...	...	0000	...
Pasewalk a.	...	...	1709	1816	...	...	...	...	...	1920	2016	...	...	...	2108	2216	2216	...	...	2316	...	...	0016	...
Pasewalk d.	...	...	1710	1822	...	...	...	...	...	1922	2022	...	...	...	2110	...	2222	...	...	2317	...	...	...	...
Anklam d.	...	...	1736	1851	...	...	...	...	...	1947	2054	...	...	...	2136	...	2251	...	...	2349	...	...	...	...
Züssow **846** d.	...	...	1748	1905	...	...	...	...	...	2002	2109	...	...	...	2148	...	2305	...	...	0002	...	...	...	...
Greifswald **846** d.	...	...	1800	1922	...	...	...	...	...	2019	2124	...	...	...	2201	...	2322	...	...	0018	...	...	...	...
Stralsund 846 a.	...	...	1821	1943	...	...	...	...	...	2040	2145	...	...	...	2223	...	2343	...	...	0040	...	...	...	...

km																								
											IC 144			*IC* 2150				*IC* 2356				*EC* 371		
		Ⓐ	Ⓒ	Ⓐ	①h			Ⓐ			z			①–⑥										Ⓐ
											A			e D				E 🍷				C ✕		
	Stralsund 846 d.	...	...	...	0319	...	...	...	...	0416	...	...	0616	0739	...	...	0816	0939	...	1016	...	1139	...	...
	Greifswald **846** d.	...	...	...	0354	...	...	...	...	0438	...	...	0638	0759	...	...	0838	0959	...	1038	...	1159	...	...
	Züssow **846** d.	...	...	...	0407	...	...	...	...	0455	...	...	0655	0813	...	...	0855	1013	...	1055	...	1213	...	...
	Anklam d.	...	...	...	0418	...	...	...	...	0507	...	...	0707	0825	...	...	0907	1025	...	1107	...	1225	...	...
	Pasewalk a.	...	...	...	0441	...	...	...	...	0535	...	...	0735	0848	...	...	0935	1048	...	1135	...	1248	...	...
	Pasewalk d.	...	...	...	0442	0442	...	...	...	0544	...	...	0744	0850	...	...	0944	1050	...	1144	...	1250	...	...
	Prenzlau d.	...	...	...	0458	0458	...	...	...	0600	...	...	0800	0906	...	...	1000	1106	...	1200	...	1306	...	...
0	**Szczecin** Głowny d.	...	...	...	|	|	...	...	0517	|	0611	...	|	|	...	0912	|	|	...	|	1221	|	...	...
5	Szczecin Gumience 🏛 d.	...	...	...	|	|	...	...	0525	|	0620	...	|	|	...	0919	|	|	...	|	1232	|	...	...
24	Tantow (ticket point) d.	...	...	...	|	|	...	...	0541	|	0638u	...	|	|	...	0940	|	|	...	|	1249	|	...	...
	Schwedt (Oder) d.	...	...	...	|	|	0506	0506	|	|	|	0706	|	|	0906	|	|	|	1106	|	|	|	1306	1306
64	Angermünde a.	...	...	...	0526	0526	0528	0528	0613	0628	0705	0728	0828	0928	0928	1011	1028	1128	1128	1228	1321	1328	1328	1328
	Angermünde d.	...	...	0435	...	...	0533	0533	...	0635	0720	0735	0835	0930	0935	...	1035	1130	1135	1235	...	1330	1335	1335
	Eberswalde Hbf d.	...	0451	0456	...	...	0554	0554	...	0656	0744	0756	0856	0947	0956	...	1056	1147	1156	1256	...	1347	1356	1356
	Bernau (b. Berlin) d.	...	0511	0511	...	...	0611	0611	...	0711	0800	0811	0911	1002	1011	...	1111	1202	1211	1311	...	1403	1411	1411
	Berlin Hbf a.	...	0529	0529	...	...	0629	0629	...	0729	0821	0829	0929	1023	1029	...	1129	1223	1229	1329	...	1424	1429	1429
	Berlin Hbf **840** d.	0426	0531	0531	...	...	...	0631	...	0731	...	...	0931	...	...	...	1131	...	...	1331	...	...	...	1431
	Doberlug-Kirchhain d.	0556	0712	0712	...	...	...	0815	...	0912	...	...	1112	...	...	...	1312	...	...	1512	...	...	...	1615
	Elsterwerda 840 a.	0626	0731	0731	...	...	...	0831	...	0931	...	...	1131	...	...	...	1331	...	...	1531	...	...	...	1631

			IC 2352					*IC* 2350					*IC* 1932				*IC* 1952							
					Ⓐ					Ⓐ		⑦w	⑦w	①–⑥			⑦w		⑥⑦		⑤–⑦			
			N 🍷					R 🍷					S	t	⊡		T	△2	Z		b			●
Stralsund 846 d.	1216	...	1339	...	...	1416	...	1539	...	...	1616	...	1710	...	...	1816	1853	...	1915	...	...	2016	...	2301
Greifswald **846** d.	1238	...	1359	...	...	1438	...	1559	...	...	1638	...	1730	...	...	1838	1914	...	1937	...	...	2038	...	2325
Züssow **846** d.	1255	...	1413	...	...	1455	...	1613	...	...	1655	...	|	...	...	1855	|	...	1956	...	...	2055	...	2340
Anklam d.	1307	...	1425	...	...	1507	...	1625	...	...	1707	...	1752	...	...	1907	1938	...	|	...	...	2107	...	...
Pasewalk a.	1335	...	1448	...	...	1535	...	1648	...	...	1735	...	1815	...	...	1935	2003	...	|	...	...	2135	...	...
Pasewalk d.	1344	...	1450	...	...	1544	...	1650	...	...	1744	...	1817	...	...	1944	2005	...	|	...	...	2144	...	...
Prenzlau d.	1400	...	1506	...	...	1600	...	1706	...	...	1800	...	1833	...	...	2000	2021	...	2043	...	...	2200	...	...
Szczecin Głowny d.	|	1422	|	...	...	|	1626	|	...	...	|	1755	|	1807	...	|	|	2009	|	...	2126	|	...	...
Szczecin Gumience 🏛 d.	|	1433	|	...	...	|	1633	|	...	...	|	1802	|	1814	...	|	|	2016	|	...	2133	|	...	...
Tantow (ticket point) d.	|	1449	|	...	...	|	1649	|	...	...	|	1818	|	1830	...	|	|	2032	|	...	2149	|	...	...
Schwedt (Oder) d.	|	|	|	1506	1506	|	|	|	1706	1706	|	|	|	|	1906	|	|	|	|	2106	|	|	2306	...
Angermünde a.	1428	1521	1528	1528	1528	1628	1721	1728	1728	1728	1828	1850	1855	1902	1928	2028	2043	2057	2108	2128	2221	2228	2328	...
Angermünde d.	1435	...	1530	1535	1535	1635	...	1730	1735	1735	1835	...	1857	...	1935	2035	2045	2058	2109	2135	...	2235	2335	...
Eberswalde Hbf d.	1456	...	1547	1556	1556	1656	...	1747	1756	1756	1856	...	1914	...	1956	2056	2102	2114	2126	2156	...	2256	2356	...
Bernau (b. Berlin) d.	1511	...	1602	1611	1611	1711	...	1802	1811	1811	1911	...	1927	...	2011	2111	2117	2132	2142	2211	...	2311	0011	...
Berlin Hbf a.	1529	...	1623	1629	1629	1729	...	1823	1829	1829	1929	...	*2015*g	...	2029	2129	2136	2206	2204	2229	...	2329	0028	...
Berlin Hbf **840** d.	1531	...	...	...	1631	1731	...	...	...	1831	1931	...	...	...	...	2131	...	...	...	...	...	...	...	...
Doberlug-Kirchhain d.	1712	...	...	...	1815	1912	...	...	...	2010	2110	...	...	...	...	2312	...	...	...	...	...	...	...	...
Elsterwerda 840 a.	1731	...	...	...	1831	1931	...	...	...	2026	2130	...	...	...	...	2331	...	...	...	...	...	...	...	...

A – [12] Amsterdam - Berlin - Angermünde - Szczecin and v.v.
B – [12] and ✕ Wien - Praha - Dresden - Stralsund (- Ostseebad Binz ⊖).
C – [12] and ✕ (Ostseebad Binz ⊖ -) Stralsund - Dresden - Praha.
D – [12] and 🍷 Stralsund - Halle - Erfurt - Kassel - Düsseldorf.
E – STRELASUND – [12] and 🍷 (Ostseebad Binz ①–⑥ **e** -) Stralsund - Berlin - Halle - Erfurt - Kassel - Düsseldorf.
G – STRELASUND – [12] and 🍷 (Düsseldorf ① **m** -) Dortmund - Kassel - Erfurt - Halle - Berlin - Ostseebad Binz.
H – [12] and 🍷 Halle - Berlin - Stralsund.
K – [12] and 🍷 (Kassel ① **m** -) Erfurt - Halle - Berlin - Stralsund.
L – [12] and 🍷 Köln - Kassel - Erfurt - Halle - Berlin - Stralsund.
N – [12] and 🍷 Stralsund - Berlin - Halle - Erfurt (- Köln ⑦ **w**).
R – [12] and 🍷 Stralsund - Berlin - Halle - Erfurt (- Fulda - Würzburg ⑦ **w**).
S – [12] Stralsund - Berlin Gesundbrunnen (a. 1943) - Berlin Spandau (a. 1955) - Hannover - Bremen - Oldenburg.
T – From Ostseebad Binz (Table **844**).
Z – Ⓒ from Apr. 26 (also Mar. 21–24).

b – Also Dec. 24, 25, 26, Jan. 1, Mar. 24, May 1, 12, 22.
d – Also Mar. 23, May 11; not Mar. 24, May 12.
e – Not Dec. 25, 26, Jan. 1, Mar. 22, 24, May 12.
f – Also Dec. 26, Jan. 1, Mar. 20, 24, Apr. 30, May 12; not Dec. 23, 30, Mar. 21, 23, May 2, 11.
g – Change at Berlin Gesundbrunnen (a. 1943, d. *2011*).
h – Also Mar. 25, May 13; not Mar. 24, May 12.
j – 0426 on Ⓒ (also Dec. 24, 31).
m – Also Dec. 27, Jan. 2, Mar. 25, May 13; not Dec. 24, 31, Mar. 24, May 12.
n – Not Dec. 23, 24, 25, 31, Mar. 22, 23.
p – From Potsdam Hbf (d. 0725).
q – Not Dec. 24, 25, 31, Mar. 21, 23, May 11.
r – Also Mar. 24, May 12; not Mar. 23, May 11.
t – Also Dec. 23, 30, Mar. 23, May 11; not Dec. 26, Jan. 1, Mar. 24, May 12.
u – Stops to pick up only.
v – Also Dec. 24, 25, 31, Mar. 20, 23, Apr. 30, May 11.

w – Also Dec. 26, Jan. 1, Mar. 24, May 12; not Dec. 23, 30, Mar. 23, May 11.
z – Not Dec. 24, 25, 26, Jan. 1, Mar. 23, 24.

‡ – Train number **2253** on ⑦ (also Dec. 25, 26, Jan. 1, Mar. 22, 24, May 12).
⊖ – See Table **844** for running dates.
◧ – Also calls at Berlin Zoo (d. 0753) and Berlin Ostbf (d. 0811).
△ – Also calls at Berlin Ostbf (a. 2155) and Berlin Zoo (a. 2213). On Ⓐ (not Dec. 24, 31) continues to Potsdam Hbf (a. 2232).
⊡ – On ⑦ from May 25 Angermünde d. 1929, Eberswalde d. 1949, Bernau d. 2004, Berlin Hbf a. 2024.
● – Not Dec. 24, 31. Operated by Usedomer Bäderbahn.

STRALSUND - ZÜSSOW - ŚWINOUJŚCIE — 846

Usedomer Bäderbahn (2nd class only) — *Service until May 18*

km		Ⓐ						❖	n	n	n
	Stralsund 845 d.	0522	...	...	0722v	...	0922		1922	...	2122
	Greifswald **845** d.	0547	...	...	0747v	...	0947	then	1947	...	2147
0	Züssow **845** d.	0607	...	0707	0807	0907	1007	hourly from	2007	2107	2207
18	Wolgast d.	0630	0630	0730	0830	0930	1030	Züssow	2030	2130	2230
28	Zinnowitz ▲ d.	0648	0648	0748	0848	0948	1048	and every	2048	2151	2248
55	Seebad Heringsdorf d.	0730	0730	0830	0930	1030	1130	two hours	2130	2230	2330
57	Seebad Ahlbeck d.	0734	0734	0834	0934	1034	1134	from	2134	2234	2334
59	Ahlbeck Grenze § a.	0737	0737	0837	0937	1037	1137	Stralsund	2137	2237	2337
60	**Świnoujście** ⊖ a.	...	...	...	...	...	...		...	...	...

	Ⓐe	©d						n	n	n
Świnoujście ⊖ d.	...	...	...	...		...	...	...	...	...
Ahlbeck Grenze § d.	0556	0620	0720	0820	then	1620	1720	1820	1920	2020
Seebad Ahlbeck d.	0600	0624	0724	0824	hourly to	1624	1724	1824	1924	2024
Seebad Heringsdorf d.	0609	0633	0733	0833	Züssow	1633	1733	1833	1933	2033
Zinnowitz ▲ d.	0648	0711	0811	0911	and every	1711	1811	1911	2011	2111
Wolgast d.	0733j	0733	0833	0933	two hours	1733	1833	1929	2033	2133
Züssow **845** d.	0757	0757	0852	0957	to	1757	1852n	1949	2052	2157
Greifswald **845** d.	0813	0813	...	1013	Stralsund	1813n	...	2004	...	2213
Stralsund 845 a.	0840	0840	...	1038		1838n	...	2028	...	2238

d – Daily Dec. 22 - Jan. 6, Feb. 2–17, Mar. 15–26, May 9–13.
e – Not Dec. 24 - Jan. 4, Feb. 4–15, Mar. 17–26, May 9–13.
j – Arrives 0703.
n – Not Dec. 24, 31.
v – Not Dec. 25, Jan. 1.
⊖ – Świnoujście Centrum. Services should commence during the currency of this timetable.

▲ – **Zinnowitz - Peenemünde** and v.v. (12 km, 14 minutes): **From Zinnowitz** at 0431Ⓐ, 0512Ⓐ, 0612**v**, 0659Ⓐ**e**, 0712©**d**, 0812, 0912 and hourly until 2112. **From Peenemünde** at 0452Ⓐ, 0530Ⓐ, 0630**v**, 0717Ⓐ**e**, 0730©**d**, 0830, 0930 and hourly until 2130. Last trains on Dec. 24, 31: From Zinnowitz at 1712. From Peenemünde at 1730.

❖ – Last trains on Dec. 24, 31: From Stralsund at 1522. From Züssow at 1707.

§ – Ahlbeck Grenze station is located at the Polish frontier. Allow approximately 45 minutes to walk between the border and Świnoujście town centre / harbour area. Alternatively, bus number 9 operates to / from the town centre, connecting with most trains. Through rail services to / from central Świnoujście should commence during the currency of this timetable. A frequent ferry service operates from the harbour to the Polish mainland and Świnoujście PKP station.

BERLIN SCHÖNEFELD ✈ - BERLIN - DESSAU — 847

RE services

km		Ⓐe																		Ⓐ					
0	**Berlin** Schönefeld ✈ ‡ d.	0425	0525e	0625r	0725	0825	0925	1026	1125	1225	1325	1425	1525	1625	1725	1825	1925	2025	2125	2225	...		0655		2255
19	**Berlin** Ostbahnhof ‡ d.	0443	0543	0643	0743	0843	0943	1043	1143	1243	1343	1443	1543	1643	1743	1843	1943	2043	2143	2243	...		0713	and	2313
24	**Berlin** Hbf ‡ d.	0456	0556	0656	0756	0856	0956	1056	1156	1256	1356	1456	1556	1656	1756	1856	1956	2056	2156	2256	...	also	0726	hourly	2326
28	**Berlin** Zoo ‡ d.	0502	0602	0702	0802	0902	1002	1102	1202	1302	1402	1502	1602	1702	1802	1902	2002	2102	2202	2300	...		0732	until	2332
	Berlin Spandau ‡ a.	|	|	|	|	|	|	|	|	|	|	|	|	|	|	|	|	|	|	...	...		0741		2341
43	**Berlin** Wannsee d.	0515	0615	0715	0815	0915	1015	1115	1215	1315	1415	1515	1615	1715	1815	1915	2015	2115	2215	...	...		...		...
95	Belzig d.	0603	0703	0803	0901	1003	1101	1203	1303	1403	1503	1603	1703	1803	1901	2003	2101	2203	2303	...	...		...		...
139	Roßlau (Elbe) **848** d.	0636	0736e	0836	...	1036	...	1236c	1336a	1436	1536a	1636	1736a	1836	...	2036	...	2236	2336q	...	...		...		...
144	**Dessau** Hbf **848** a.	0643	0743e	0843	...	1043	...	1243c	1343a	1443	1543a	1643	1743a	1843	...	2043	...	2243	2343q	...	...		...		...

	Ⓐe																	Ⓐ							
Dessau Hbf **848** d.	...	...	0517t	0617a	0717	0817e	0917c	1017a	1117c	...	1317	1417a	1517	1617a	1717	1817a	1917c	2017	2117c	2317	...		...		...
Roßlau (Elbe) **848** d.	...	...	0524t	0624a	0724	0824e	0924c	1024a	1124c	...	1324	1424a	1524	1624a	1724	1824a	1924c	2024	2124c	2324	...		...		...
Belzig d.	0402	0502	0602	0702	0802	0902	1002	1102	1202	1302	1402	1502	1602	1702	1802	1902	2002	2102	2202	0002	...		...		...
Berlin Wannsee d.	0448	0548	0648	0749	0848	0948	1048	1148	1248	1348	1448	1548	1648	1748	1848	1948	2048	2148	2248	0048	...		...		...
Berlin Spandau ‡ d.	|	|	|	|	|	|	|	|	|	|	|	|	|	|	|	|	|	|	|	|	...		0517		2118
Berlin Zoo ‡ d.	0501	0601	0701	0802	0901	1001	1101	1201	1301	1401	1501	1601	1701	1801	1901	2001	2101	2201	2301	0101	...		0528	and	2129
Berlin Hbf ‡ d.	0507	0607	0707	0808	0907	1007	1107	1207	1307	1407	1507	1607	1707	1807	1907	2007	2107	2207	2307	0107	...	also	0534	hourly	2134
Berlin Ostbahnhof ‡ d.	0518	0618	0718	0818	0918	1018	1118	1218	1318	1418	1518	1618	1718	1818	1918	2018	2118	2218	2316	0116	...		0545	until	2145
Berlin Schönefeld ✈ ‡ a.	0536	0636r	0736	0836	0936	1036	1136	1236	1336	1436	1536	1636	1736	1836	1936	2036	2136	2236	...	...	...		0602		2202

a – Ⓐ only.
c – © only.
e – Ⓐ (not Dec. 24, 31).
q – † only.
r – ⚒ only.
t – ①–⑥ only.
‡ – S-Bahn trains also operate early morning to late evening (every 20 minutes – route **S9** – journey time approximately 40 minutes Berlin Schönefeld ✈ - Berlin Hbf and v.v.).

MAGDEBURG - DESSAU - LEIPZIG and HALLE — 848

RE / *RB* services

See Tables **850** and **851** for other *ICE* and *IC* services Lutherstadt Wittenberg - Bitterfeld - Halle / Leipzig and v.v.

km		©z	©z					v				Ⓐe													
0	**Magdeburg** Hbf d.	...	...	...	...	...	...	0513	...	...	0613r	0633	...	0712	...	0813	...	...	0912	...	1012	...	...	1112	...
56	Roßlau (Elbe) **847** d.	...	...	...	...	...	...	0605	...	...	0705r	0718	...	0805	...	0858	...	...	1005	...	1058	...	...	1205	...
61	**Dessau** Hbf **847** a.	...	...	...	...	...	...	0613	...	...	0713r	0726	...	0813	...	0906	...	...	1013	...	1106	...	...	1213	...
		B						|			|	d				|				...	|				
61	**Dessau** Hbf d.	0159	...	0452	...	0552	...	0614	0652	...	0714	0752	...	0852	...	0914	0952	...	1052	...	1114	1152	...	1252	...
	Lutherstadt Wittenberg d.	0129	...	|	0446	|	0546	|	|	0646	|	|	0746	|	0846	|	|	0946	|	1046	|	|	1146	|	1246
87	Bitterfeld a.	0215	...	0515	0516	0615	0616	0631	0715	0716	0731	0815	0816	0915	0916	0931	1015	1016	1115	1116	1131	1215	1216	1315	1316
87	Bitterfeld d.	0215	0220	0520	0520	0620	0620	0632	0720	0720	0732	0820	0820	0920	0920	0932	1020	1020	1120	1120	1132	1220	1220	1320	1320
	Halle (Saale) Hbf a.	0234	|	0548	|	|	0645	|	0745	|	|	|	0845	0945	|	|	|	1045	1145	|	|	|	1245	1345	|
120	**Leipzig** Hbf a.	...	0249	...	0549	0649	...	0658	...	0749	0758	0849	...	...	0949	0958	1049	...	...	1149	1158	1249	...	...	1349

								Ⓐe			Ⓐe													n
Magdeburg Hbf d.	1212	...	...	1312	...	1412	...	1512	1542	...	1612	1640	...	1712	...	1812	...	1912	2012	...	...	...	2112	...	2321
Roßlau (Elbe) **847** d.	1258	...	...	1405	...	1458	...	1605	1630	...	1658	1722	...	1805	...	1858	...	2005	2052	...	...	...	2205	...	0015
Dessau Hbf **847** a.	1306	...	...	1413	...	1506	...	1613	1638	...	1706	1729	...	1813	...	1906	...	2013	2059	...	...	...	2213	...	0022
	|					|		▬	d		|	d			...	|		▬	|						
Dessau Hbf d.	1314	1352	...	1452		1514	1552	...	1652		1714	1752	...	1852	...	1914	1952	...	2102	...	2152	...	2252	...	...
Lutherstadt Wittenberg d.	|	|	1346	|	1446	|	|	1546	|	1646	|	|	1746	|	1846	|	|	1946	|	2054	|	2146	|	2246	...
Bitterfeld a.	1331	1415	1416	1515	1516	1531	1615	1616	1715	1716	1731	1815	1816	1915	1916	1931	2015	2016	2126	2123	2215	2216	2315	2316	...
Bitterfeld d.	1332	1420	1420	1520	1520	1532	1620	1620	1720	1720	1732	1820	1820	1920	1920	1932	2020	2020	2128	2131	2220	2220	2320	2320	...
Halle (Saale) Hbf a.	|	|	1445	1545	|	|	|	1645	1745	|	|	|	1845	1945	|	|	|	2045	|	2156	2245	|	|	2345	...
Leipzig Hbf a.	1358	1449	...	...	1549	1558	1649	...	...	1749	1758	1849	...	...	1949	1958	2049	...	2158	...	...	2249	2349	...	...

		Ⓐw	Ⓐw	©z				⚒r																	
Leipzig Hbf d.	...	...	0411	...	...	...	0511	0539e	0611	...	...	0711	0801	0811	...	...	0911	1001	1011	...	...	1111	1201	1211	...
Halle (Saale) Hbf d.	...	0415	|	0427	...	0515	|	*0543*e	|	0615	0715	|	|	|	0815	0915	|	|	|	1015	1115	|	|	|	1215
Bitterfeld a.	...	0439	0439	0451	...	0539	0539	0607e	0639	0639	0739	0739	0826	0839	0839	0939	0939	1025	1039	1039	1139	1139	1225	1239	1239
Bitterfeld d.	...	0443	0443	0452	...	0543	0543	0615e	0643	0643	0743	0743	0828	0843	0843	0943	0943	1027	1043	1043	1143	1143	1227	1243	1243
Lutherstadt Wittenberg a.	...	|	0515	0524	...	0615	|	|	0715	|	0815	|	|	0915	|	1015	|	|	1115	|	1215	|	|	1315	|
Dessau Hbf a.	...	0509	...	R	...	...	0609	0639e	...	0709	...	0809	0846	...	0909	...	1009	1046	...	1109	...	1209	1246	...	1309
	v	Ⓐe					Ⓐe	|					|					|					|		
Dessau Hbf **847** d.	0434	*0517*	...	...	0542	...	*0617*	0642	...	0742	...	...	0851	...	0942	...	...	1051	...	1142	...	...	1251	...	1342
Roßlau (Elbe) **847** d.	0442	0531	...	...	0550	...	0629	0649	...	0750	...	...	0858	...	0950	...	...	1058	...	1150	...	...	1258	...	1350
Magdeburg Hbf a.	0537	0620	...	...	0645	...	0720	0745	...	0845	...	...	0945	...	1045	...	...	1145	...	1245	...	...	1345	...	1445

																							n		
Leipzig Hbf d.	...	1311	1401	1411	...	...	1511	1601	1611	...	...	1711	1801	1811	...	...	1911	2001	2011	...	...	2111	2211	...	2312
Halle (Saale) Hbf d.	1315	|	|	|	1415	1515	|	|	|	1615	1715	|	|	|	1815	1915	|	|	|	2015	2115	|	|	2315	|
Bitterfeld a.	1339	1339	1425	1439	1439	1539	1539	1625	1639	1639	1739	1739	1825	1839	1839	1939	1939	2025	2039	2039	2139	2139	2237	2339	2339
Bitterfeld d.	1343	1343	1427	1443	1443	1543	1543	1627	1643	1643	1743	1743	1827	1843	1843	1943	1943	2027	2043	2043	2143	2143	2237	2343	2343
Lutherstadt Wittenberg a.	1415	|	|	1515	|	1615	|	|	1715	|	1815	|	|	1915	|	2015	|	|	2115	|	2215	|	|	0015	|
Dessau Hbf a.	...	1409	1446	...	1509	...	1609	1646	...	1709	...	1809	1846	...	1909	...	2009	2046	...	2109	...	2209	2255	...	0009
		Ⓐe	|					|					|				|					|		
Dessau Hbf **847** d.	...	1423	1451	...	1542	...	...	1651	...	1742	...	...	1851	...	1942	...	...	2048	...	...	...	...	2256	...	...
Roßlau (Elbe) **847** d.	...	1431	1458	...	1550	...	...	1658	...	1750	...	...	1858	...	1950	...	...	2055	...	...	...	...	2304	...	...
Magdeburg Hbf a.	...	1531	1545	...	1645	...	...	1745	...	1845	...	...	1945	...	2045	...	...	2145	...	...	...	...	2358	...	...

Dessau - Lutherstadt Wittenberg - Falkenberg ⊠

km		v									
0	**Dessau** Hbf **847** d.	0511e	0711	0911	1011	1311	1511	1611	1711	1911	2111
5	Roßlau (Elbe) **847** d.	0518e	0718	0918	1018	1318	1518	1618	1718	1918	2118
37	Lutherstadt Wittenberg a.	0549e	0749	0949	1049	1349	1549	1649	1749	1949	2149
37	Lutherstadt Wittenberg d.	0551	0751	...	1051	1351	1551	1651e	1751	1951	2151b
91	**Falkenberg** (Elster) a.	0640	0840	...	1140	1440	1640	1749e	1840	2040	2240b

	⚒r							n		n
Falkenberg (Elster) d.	0521	0614e	0723	0923	1223	1523	1721	1814e	1923	2123
Lutherstadt Wittenberg a.	0609	0709e	0810	1010	1310	1610	1810	1910e	2010	2210
Lutherstadt Wittenberg d.	0611	0711	0811	1011	1311	1611	1811	1911	2011	2211
Roßlau (Elbe) **847** d.	0643	0743	0843	1043	1343	1643	1843	1943	2043	2243
Dessau Hbf **847** a.	0650	0750	0850	1050	1350	1650	1850	1950	2050	2250

B – From Berlin (Table **835**). Calls at Dessau after Lutherstadt Wittenberg.
R – To Rostock (Table **835**).
b – ,Ⓑ (not Dec. 23, 24, 25, 30, 31, Mar. 23, May 11).
d – Daily from Dessau.
e – Ⓐ (not Dec. 24, 31).
n – Not Dec. 24, 25, 31.
r – ⚒ (not Dec. 24, 31).
v – Not Dec. 25, 26, Jan. 1.
w – Also Dec. 25.
z – Not Dec. 25.
⊠ – Additional journeys Dessau - Lutherstadt Wittenberg and v.v. **From Dessau** at 0611**v**, 0811, 1111, 1211, 1411, 1811 and 2011⚒**r**. **From Lutherstadt Wittenberg** at 0406Ⓐ**e**, 0511**v**, 0911, 1111, 1211, 1411, 1511 and 1711.

849 Local services LEIPZIG and HALLE - EISENACH and SAALFELD *RB services*

See Tables **850** and **851** for faster *IC* and *ICE* services

km																								
		v		Ⓐn		Ⓐn				Ⓐn	Ⓒk													Ⓐn
0	**Halle** (Saale) Hbf d.	...	...	0422	...	...	0522	...	0622	...	...	0722	...	0822	...	0922	...	1022	...	1122	...	1222	...	...
32	Weißenfels d.	...	...	0453	...	...	0553	...	0653	...	...	0753	...	0853	...	0953	...	1053	...	1153	...	1253	...	...
46	Naumburg (Saale) Hbf d.	...	...	0503	0503	...	0603	0613	0703	0707	0713	0803	...	0903	0913	1003	...	1103	1113	1203	...	1303	1313	...
59	Großheringen d.	...	...	0513	0513	0520	0613	|	0713	|	|	0813	0822	0913	|	1013	1022	1113	|	1213	1222	1313	|	...
	Jena Paradies d.	0434	...	|	|	0546	|	0648	|	0742	0748	|	0848	|	0948	|	1048	|	1148	|	1248	|	1348	1428
	Göschwitz (Saale) d.	0439	...	|	|	0552	|	0654	|	0754c	0754	|	0854	|	0954	|	1054	|	1154	|	1254	|	1354	1434
	Rudolstadt (Thür) d.	0509	...	|	|	0619	|	0721	|	0821	0821	|	0921	|	1021	|	1121	|	1221	|	1321	|	1421	1504
	Saalfeld (Saale) a.	0519	...	|	|	0628	|	0730	|	0830	0830	|	0930	|	1030	|	1130	|	1230	|	1330	|	1430	1514
87	Weimar d.	...	...	0538	0538	...	0640	...	0742	...	...	0840	...	0940	...	1040	...	1140	...	1240	...	1340	...	...
108	**Erfurt** Hbf d.	...	...	0557	0557	...	0659	...	0801	...	...	0859	...	1001	...	1059	...	1201	...	1259	...	1401	...	...
136	Gotha d.	...	...	0624	0624	...	0724	...	0827	...	...	0924	...	1027	...	1124	...	1227	...	1324	...	1427	...	...
165	**Eisenach** a.	...	...	0647	0647	...	0747	...	0850	...	...	0947	...	1050	...	1147	...	1250	...	1347	...	1450	...	...

			Ⓐn			Ⓐn			Ⓐn										t		n	n	n
Halle (Saale) Hbf d.	1322	...	...	1422	...	...	1522	...	...	1622	...	1722	...	1822	...	1922	...	2022	...	*2122	...	2222	2330
Weißenfels d.	1353	...	...	1453	...	...	1553	...	...	1653	...	1753	...	1853	...	1953	...	2053	...	2153	...	2253	0006
Naumburg (Saale) Hbf d.	1403	...	...	1503	1513	...	1603	...	...	1703	1713	1803	...	1903	1913	2003	...	2103	2113	2203	...	2303	0016
Großheringen d.	1413	1422	...	1513	|	...	1613	1622	...	1713	|	1813	1822	1913	|	2013	2022	2113	|	2213	2222	2313	0026
Jena Paradies d.	|	1448	1528	|	1548	1628	|	1648	1728	|	1748	|	1848	|	1948	|	2048	|	2148	|	2248	|	|
Göschwitz (Saale) d.	|	1454	1534	|	1554	1634	|	1654	1734	|	1754	|	1854	|	1954	|	2054	|	2154	|	2254	|	|
Rudolstadt (Thür) d.	|	1521	1602	|	1621	1704	|	1721	1802	|	1821	|	1921	|	2021	|	2121	|	2221	|	2321	|	|
Saalfeld (Saale) a.	|	1530	1612	|	1630	1714	|	1730	1812	|	1830	|	1930	|	2030	|	2132	|	2232	|	2330	|	|
Weimar d.	1440	...	...	1540	...	...	1640	...	...	1740	...	1840	...	1940	...	2040	...	2140	...	2243	...	2340	0051
Erfurt Hbf d.	1459	...	...	1601	...	...	1659	...	...	1801	...	1859	...	2001	...	2101	...	2201	...	2307	...	2359	0108
Gotha d.	1524	...	...	1627	...	...	1724	...	...	1827	...	1924	...	2027	...	2126	...	2227	...	2339n	...	0025	...
Eisenach a.	1547	...	...	1650	...	...	1747	...	...	1850	...	1947	...	2050	...	2149	...	2250	...	0002v	...	0049	...

km																								
		r	Ⓐn		Ⓐn	v	Ⓐ				Ⓐn													
	Eisenach d.	...	0402	...	...	...	...	0506z	...	0606	...	...	0706	...	0810	...	0906	...	1010	...	1106	...	1210	...
	Gotha d.	...	0427	...	...	...	...	0531z	...	0631	...	...	0731	...	0835	...	0931	...	1035	...	1131	...	1235	...
	Erfurt Hbf d.	0405	0451	0451	...	...	...	0558	...	0700	...	...	0800	...	0900	...	1000	...	1100	...	1200	...	1300	...
	Weimar d.	0437	0509	0509	...	...	...	0620	...	0720	...	...	0820	...	0920	...	1020	...	1120	...	1220	...	1320	...
0	**Saalfeld** (Saale) d.	|	|	|	0437	0509	0509	|	0620	|	0650	0724	|	0824	|	0930	|	1024	|	1130	|	1224	|	1330
10	Rudolstadt (Thür) d.	|	|	|	0446	0518	0518	|	0629	|	0659	0733	|	0833	|	0939	|	1033	|	1139	|	1233	|	1339
42	Göschwitz (Saale) d.	|	|	|	0520	0544	0544	|	0656	|	0726	0801	|	0901	|	1005	|	1101	|	1205	|	1301	|	1405
47	**Jena** Paradies d.	|	|	|	0525	0549	0549	|	0702	|	0730	0806	|	0906	|	1011	|	1106	|	1211	|	1306	|	1411
75	Großheringen d.	0500	0533	0533	|	|	|	0644	0728	0744	...	|	0844	0932	0944	|	1044	1132	1144	|	1244	1332	1344	|
	Naumburg (Saale) Hbf d.	0510	0545	0545	0558	0622	0625	0654	...	0754	...	0839	0854	...	0954	1046	1054	...	1154	1246	1254	...	1354	1446
	Weißenfels d.	0521	0557	0557	...	...	0636	0705	...	0805	...	...	0905	...	1005	...	1105	...	1205	...	1305	...	1405	...
	Halle (Saale) Hbf a.	0553	0629	0629	...	...	0707	0737	...	0837	...	...	0937	...	1037	...	1137	...	1237	...	1337	...	1437	...

						Ⓐn											⊡	⑤⑥	n	n	n	n	n
Eisenach d.	1306	...	1410	...	1506	...	...	1610	...	1706	...	1810	...	1906	...	2010	...	...	2106	...	...	...	2220
Gotha d.	1331	...	1435	...	1531	...	...	1635	...	1731	...	1835	...	1931	...	2035	...	...	2131	2231	...	...	2246
Erfurt Hbf d.	1400	...	1500	...	1600	...	...	1700	...	1800	...	1900	...	2000	...	2100	...	...	2200	2250	2300	...	2310
Weimar d.	1420	...	1520	...	1620	...	...	1720	...	1820	...	1920	...	2020	...	2120	...	...	2220	...	2320	...	...
Saalfeld (Saale) d.	|	1424	|	1530	|	1546	1624	|	1730	|	1824	|	1930	|	2024	|	2134	2134	|	...	|	2234	...
Rudolstadt (Thür) d.	|	1433	|	1539	|	1556	1633	|	1739	|	1833	|	1939	|	2033	|	2143	2143	|	...	|	2243	...
Göschwitz (Saale) d.	|	1501	|	1605	|	1623	1701	|	1805	|	1901	|	2005	|	2101	|	2209	2209	|	...	|	2309	...
Jena Paradies d.	|	1506	|	1611	|	1627	1706	|	1811	|	1906	|	2011	|	2106	|	2215	2215	|	...	|	2314	...
Großheringen d.	1444	1532	1544	|	1644	...	1732	1744	|	1844	1932	1944	|	2044	2132	2144	2240	|	2244	...	2344	...	...
Naumburg (Saale) Hbf d.	1454	...	1554	1646	1654	...	...	1754	1846	1854	...	1954	2045	2054	...	2154	...	2249	2254	...	2354	...	...
Weißenfels d.	1505	...	1605	...	1705	...	...	1805	...	1905	...	2005	...	2105	...	2205	...	...	2305	...	0005	...	...
Halle (Saale) Hbf a.	1537	...	1637	...	1737	...	...	1837	...	1937	...	2037	...	2137	...	2237	...	...	2337	...	0037	...	...

Leipzig - Weißenfels and v.v. ⊠

From Leipzig Hbf at 0425 Ⓐ, 0445 Ⓒ, 0524 Ⓐ, 0619 Ⓐ, 0648 Ⓒ, 0748 Ⓐ, 0848, 0948 Ⓐ, 1048, 1148 Ⓐ, 1248, 1348 Ⓐ, 1448, 1548 Ⓐ, 1648, 1748 Ⓐ, 1848, 1948 Ⓐ, 2048 and 2321.
From Weißenfels at 0426, 0526 Ⓐ, 0626, 0726 Ⓐ, 0826, 0926 Ⓐ, 1026, 1126 Ⓐ, 1226, 1326 Ⓐ, 1426, 1526 Ⓐ, 1626, 1726 Ⓐ, 1826, 1926 Ⓐ, 2026 and 2233.

Eisenach - Bebra and v.v. ❖

From Eisenach at 0452 Ⓐ, 0530 Ⓐ, 0614 ⚒, 0712 ⚒, 0812, 0912 ⚒, 1012, 1112 Ⓐ, 1212, 1331 Ⓐ, 1412 ⚒, 1414 †, 1512 Ⓐ, 1612, 1712 Ⓐ, 1812, 1912 Ⓐ, 2012, 2112 Ⓐ and 2212 Ⓒ.
From Bebra at 0506 Ⓐ, 0606 ⚒, 0659 Ⓐ, 0706 Ⓒ, 0723 Ⓐ, 0806 ⑥, 0906, 1006 Ⓐ, 1106, 1206 Ⓐ, 1306 Ⓒ, 1315 Ⓐ, 1418 Ⓐ, 1506, 1606 Ⓐ, 1706, 1806 Ⓐ, 1906, 2006 Ⓐ and 2118.

c – Arrives 0747.
k – Also Dec. 24, 31.
n – Not Dec. 24, 31.
r – Not Dec. 25.
t – Not Dec. 24.
v – Not Dec. 25, Jan. 1.
z – Not Dec. 25, 26, Jan. 1.
⊡ – ①②③④⑦ (not Dec. 24).
⊠ – Journey 40–46 minutes.
❖ – Journey 35–41 minutes. 2nd class only. Operated by CANTUS Verkehrsgesellschaft. On Dec. 24, 31 services run as on ⑥.

850 BERLIN and LEIPZIG - EISENACH - KASSEL and FRANKFURT

Alternative regional services: Table **835** Berlin - Lutherstadt Wittenberg. Table **848** Lutherstadt Wittenberg - Halle. Table **849** Leipzig / Halle - Erfurt - Eisenach - Bebra.

km		*IC*	*IC*	*ICE*‡	*ICE*‡	*ICE*	*ICE*	*IC*	*ICE*	*IC*	*ICE*	*IC*	*ICE*	*IC*	*IC*	*ICE*	*IC*	*ICE*	*IC*	*ICE*	*IC*	*ICE*	*IC*	*ICE*	*IC*
		1950	**1950**	**1646**	**1646**	**1656**	**1644**	**2156**	**1654**	**2154**	**1642**	**2154**	**1652**	**2152**	**2152**	**1640**	**2152**	**1650**	**2150**	**1548**	**2150**	**1558**	**2356**	**1546**	**2356**
		①g	①-⑤	①g	①-⑤	①-⑥	①-⑥				v			①-⑥	b		⑤⑦		◧		◧				
			h	🍷	d🍷	e✕	z✕	🍷	✕	🍷	✕	🍷	✕	e🍷	🍷	✕	r🍷	✕	🍷	✕	🍷	✕	⊖🍷	✕	⊖🍷
	Stralsund **845** d.	...	...	...	...	...	...	...	...	...	...	...	...	...	...	...	...	...	0739e	...	...	...	0939	...	...
	Berlin Hbf **851** d.	0042	...	...	...	...	...	...	...	0640	...	...	...	0840	...	...	...	...	1040	...	...	...	1240	...	...
	Lutherstadt Wittenberg **851** d.	0124	...	...	...	...	...	...	...	0721	...	...	...	0921	...	...	...	...	1121	...	...	...	1321	...	...
	Bitterfeld **851** d.	0141	...	...	...	...	...	...	...	0738	...	...	...	0938	...	...	...	...	1138	...	...	...	1338	...	...
	Dresden Hbf **842** d.	|	...	...	...	...	0443	...	0555e	|	0655	...	0755	|	...	0855	...	0955	|	1055	...	1155	|	1255	...
0	**Leipzig** Hbf **851** d.	0234*	...	0401	...	0501	0601	...	0716	|	0811	...	0916	|	...	1011	...	1116	|	1211	...	1316	|	1411	...
	Halle (Saale) Hbf d.	0203*	...	|	...	|	|	...	|	0759	|	...	|	0959	0959	|	...	|	1159	|	...	|	1359	|	...
40	Weißenfels d.	|	...	|	...	|	|	...	|	0825	|	...	|	1025	1025	|	...	|	1225	|	...	|	1425	|	...
54	Naumburg (Saale) Hbf **851** d.	|	...	0436	...	0538	0640	...	|	0835	|	...	|	1035	1035	|	...	|	1235	|	...	|	1435	|	...
95	Weimar **858** d.	0335	...	0500	...	0602	0704	...	0808	0900	0906	...	1008	1100	1100	1106	...	1208	1300	1306	...	1408	1500	1506	...
117	**Erfurt** Hbf **858** a.	0351	...	0516	...	0616	0719	...	0821	0917	0921	←	1021	1117	1117	1121	←	1221	1317	1321	←	1421	1517	1521	←
117	**Erfurt** Hbf **858** d.	0353	...	0518	0518	0618	0721	0727	0823	→	0923	0927	1023	→	→	1123	1127	1223	→	1323	1327	1423	→	1523	1527
144	Gotha **858** d.	0411	...	0536	0536	0636	0737	0743	0841	...	|	0943	1041	...	...	|	1143	1241	...	|	1343	1441	...	|	1543
173	**Eisenach** d.	0426	...	0553	0553	0652	0753	0759	0857	...	0953	0959	1057	...	...	1153	1159	1257	...	1353	1359	1457	...	1553	1559
	Bebra **901** d.	0503	0503	|	|	|	|	0823	|	...	|	1023	|	...	...	|	1223	|	...	|	1423	|	...	|	1623
	Kassel Wilhelmshöhe **901** a.	|	|	|	|	|	|	0858	|	...	|	1058	|	...	...	|	1258	|	...	|	1458	|	...	|	1658
	Düsseldorf Hbf **800** a.	|	|	|	|	|	|	1212	|	...	|	1412	|	...	...	|	1612	|	...	|	1815	|	...	|	2015
230	Bad Hersfeld **901** d.	0514	0514	0620	0620	0720	0820	...	|	...	1020	...	|	...	...	1220	...	|	...	1420	...	|	...	1620	...
272	Fulda **900/1** d.	0541	0541	0644	0644	0744	0844	...	0944	...	1044	...	1144	...	...	1244	...	1344	...	1444	...	1544	...	1644	...
353	Hanau Hbf **900/1** d.	0623	0623	|	|	|	|	...	|	...	|	...	|	...	...	|	...	|	...	|	...	|	...	|	...
372	**Frankfurt** (Main) Süd a.	|	|	0737	0737	|	0935	...	|	...	1135	...	|	...	...	1335	...	|	...	1535	...	|	...	1735	...
376	**Frankfurt** (Main) Hbf **900/1** a.	0642	0642	*0745*f	*0745*f	0837	|	...	1037	...	*1144*f	...	1237	...	...	*1344*f	...	1437	...	*1544*f	...	1637	...	*1744*f	...
	Frankfurt Flughafen ✈ § a.	...	...	0750	0750	0856	0948	...	1056	...	1148	...	1256	...	...	1348	...	1456	...	1548	...	1656	...	1748	...
	Mainz Hbf **912** ● a.	...	...	...	...	0916	...	...	1110	...	...	...	1316	...	...	...	...	1516	...	...	...	1716	...	...	...
	Wiesbaden Hbf **912** ● a.	...	...	...	...	0932	...	...	1132	...	...	...	1332	...	...	...	...	1532	...	...	...	1732	...	...	...

b – Not Dec. 23, 25, 30, Mar. 22, 23, May 11.
d – Not Dec. 24, 25, 26, 31, Jan. 1, Mar. 21, 24, May 1, 12.
e – ①-⑥ (not Dec. 25, 26, Jan. 1, Mar. 22, 24, May 12).
f – Change trains at Fulda (see Table **900**).
g – Also Dec. 27, Jan. 2, Mar. 25, May 13; not Dec. 24, 31, Mar. 24, May 12.
h – Not Dec. 24, 25, 26, 31, Jan. 1, Mar. 21, 24, May 1, 12, 22.
r – Also Dec. 26, Jan. 1, Mar. 20, 24, Apr. 30, May 12; not Dec. 23, 30, Mar. 21, 23, May 2, 11.
v – Not Dec. 25, Jan. 1.
z – Not Dec. 24, 25, 26, 31, Jan. 1, Mar. 22, 24, May 12.
⊖ – From Ostseebad Binz (Table **844**) on ①-⑥ **e**.
◧ – Train number **2250** on ⑦ (also Dec. 25, 26, Jan. 1, Mar. 22, 24, May 12).
* – Calls at Halle before Leipzig.
§ – Frankfurt Flughafen Fernbahnhof.
‡ – Train category *IC* Leipzig - Erfurt - Eisenach, *ICE* Eisenach - Frankfurt.
● – Timings at Mainz and Wiesbaden are subject to alteration on ⑥⑦ from May 17.

FRANKFURT and KASSEL - EISENACH - LEIPZIG and BERLIN 850

Alternative regional services: Table **835** Berlin - Lutherstadt Wittenberg. Table **848** Lutherstadt Wittenberg - Halle. Table **849** Leipzig / Halle - Erfurt - Eisenach - Bebra.

	ICE 1556	IC 2252	IC 2354	ICE 1544	ICE 1744	IC 2354	ICE 1554	ICE 1594	IC 1958	IC 1954	IC 2352	ICE 1542	IC 2352	ICE 1552	IC 2419	IC 2350	IC 2350	ICE 1017	ICE 1017	ICE 1717	IC 2350	ICE 1550	IC 61458	CNL 458	CNL 352
		⑦w		①–⑥	⑦w	n	n	⑧q	⑦w	⑦w		⑧q	⑦w	n	①–④		⑦w	⑦w	⑧q	⑥t	⑦w	⑦w		R	R
	✗	T🍷	B🍷	h✗	✗	B🍷	✗	S✗			🍷	✗	🍷	✗	m	🍷	L🍷	H✗	H✗	✗	L🍷	✗		A✗	E
Stralsund **845** d.	...	...	...	...	...	...	...	...	...	...	1339	...	...	...	...	1539	1539	...	...	...	...	...	...	...	...
Berlin Hbf **851** d.	...	...	1440	...	...	...	...	...	...	...	1640	...	...	...	1730	1840	1840	1858	1858	1858	...	...	...	...	...
Lutherstadt Wittenberg **851** d.	...	...	1521	...	...	...	...	...	...	...	1721	...	...	...	1821	1921	1921	|	|	|	...	...	...	...	...
Bitterfeld **851** d.	...	...	1538	...	...	...	...	...	...	...	1738	...	...	...	1837	1939	1939	|	|	|	...	...	...	...	...
Dresden Hbf **842** d.	1355	...	|	1455	1455	...	1555	1555	...	...	|	1655	...	1755	|	|	|	|	|	|	...	1955	2054	2054	2256
Leipzig Hbf **851** d.	1516	1543	|	1611	1611	...	1716	1716	...	1743	|	1811	...	1916	|	|	|	2011	2011	2011	...	2112	2218	2218	0054
Halle (Saale) Hbf d.	|	|	1559	|	|	...	|	|	1654	|	1759	|	...	|	1856	2002	2002	|	|	|	...	|	|	|	|
Weißenfels d.	|	|	1625	|	|	...	|	|	1718	|	1825	|	...	|	...	2025	2025	|	|	|	...	|	|	|	|
Naumburg (Saale) Hbf **851** d.	|	1618	1635	|	|	...	|	|	1729	1818	1835	|	...	1949	...	2035	2035	2047	2047	2047	...	2146	2254	2254u	|
Weimar **858** d.	1608	1645	1700	1706	1706	...	1808	1808	1758	1845	1900	1906	...	2012	...	2103	2103	2111	2111	2111	...	2209	2320	2320u	|
Erfurt Hbf **858** a.	1621	1704	1717	1721	1721	←	1822	1822	1816	1904	1917	1921	←	2027	...	2119	2119	2126	2126	2126	...	2223	2336	|	|
Erfurt Hbf **858** d.	1623	1706	→	1723	1723	1727	1824	1824	1818	1906	→	1923	1927	2029	...	...	2121	2128	...	...	...	2225	2338	2338u	|
Gotha **858** d.	1641	1730	...	|	|	1743	1841	1841	|	1930	...	|	1943	2046	...	...	2139	2145	...	...	←	2243	2356	2356u	|
Eisenach d.	1657	1746	...	1753	1753	1759	1857	1857	1901	1946	...	1953	1959	2102	...	...	2153	2201	...	...	2205	2259	0013	0013u	|
Bebra **901** d.	|	|	...	|	|	1823	|	|	|	|	...	|	2023	|	...	...	→	|	...	...	|	|	|	|	|
Kassel Wilhelmshöhe **901** a.	|	|	...	|	|	1858	|	|	|	|	...	|	2058	|	...	...	...	|	...	...	|	|	|	|	|
Düsseldorf Hbf **800** a.	|	|	...	|	|	2214w	|	|	|	|	...	|	0012	|	...	...	...	|	...	...	|	|	|	|	|
Bad Hersfeld **901** d.	|	|	...	1820	1820	...	|	|	|	|	...	2020	...	|	...	...	...	|	...	...	2234	2326	0108	|	|
Fulda **900/1** d.	1744	1838	...	1844	1844	...	1944	1944	1953	2038	...	2044	...	2159*	...	...	...	2252	...	...	2301	2351	0137	|	0513y
Hanau Hbf **900/1** d.	|	|	...	|	|	...	|	|	|	|	...	2125	...	2240	...	...	...	2335	...	...	...	0034	...	|	|
Frankfurt (Main) Süd a.	|	|	...	|	1935	...	|	|	2044	2131	...	2137	...	|	...	...	...	|	...	...	...	0044	...	0400	0654
Frankfurt (Main) Hbf **900/1** a.	1837	1932	...	1940	*1944*f	...	2037	2037	2052	|	...	2146	...	2254	...	...	...	2349	...	...	...	0051	...	...	...
Frankfurt Flughafen + § a.	1856	...	...	...	1948	...	2056	...	...	2142	...	...	...	...	...	...	...	...	...	...	...	...	...	...	...
Mainz Hbf **912** ● a.	1916	...	...	...	...	...	2116	...	...	2202	...	...	...	...	...	...	...	...	...	...	...	...	...	...	...
Wiesbaden Hbf **912** ● a.	1932	...	...	...	...	...	2132	...	...	...	...	...	...	...	...	...	...	...	...	...	...	...	...	...	...

km		IC 2216	CNL 459	IC 61459	ICE 1516	IC 2351	ICE 1553	IC 2253	ICE 1724	IC 2253	IC 2353	IC 2353	ICE 1543	IC 2353	ICE 1555	IC 2355	ICE 1545	ICE 1745	IC 2355	ICE 1557	ICE 1597	IC 2357	ICE 1547	IC 2357	ICE 1559
		①–⑤	R		v		①–⑤	⑦k	⑦k	⑦k	①g	①–⑥	①–⑥	①–⑥			①–⑥	⑦c		①–⑥	⑦k				
		a	A✗		✗	🍷	a✗	🍷	H✗	🍷	🍷	e🍷	e✗	e🍷	✗	D🍷	e✗	✗	D🍷	e S ✗	✗	🍷	✗	🍷	✗
	Wiesbaden Hbf **912** ● d.	...	...	...	...	...	...	...	...	...	...	...	...	...	...	...	...	...	...		0831	...	...	...	1024
	Mainz Hbf **912** ● d.	...	...	...	...	...	...	...	...	...	...	...	...	...	...	...	...	...	...	...	0842	...	...	...	1042
0	**Frankfurt** Flughafen + § d.	...	...	...	...	...	...	...	...	...	...	...	...	...	...	...	0811	...	...	...	0901	...	1011	...	1102
	Frankfurt (Main) Hbf **900/1** d.	...	...	...	...	...	0517g	...	...	...	...	...	0618	...	0720	...	*0813*f	0822	...	0921	0921	...	*1013*f	...	1119
11	**Frankfurt** (Main) Süd d.	...	0055	...	...	...	|	...	...	...	...	...	|	...	|	...	0822	|	...	|	|	...	1022	...	|
—	Hanau Hbf **900/1** d.	...	|	...	...	...	|	...	...	...	...	...	0634	...	|	...	|	|	...	|	|	...	|	...	|
	Fulda **900/1** d.	...	|	0341	...	...	0612g	...	...	...	...	...	0715	...	0813	...	0915	0915	...	1013	1013	...	1115	...	1213
	Bad Hersfeld **901** d.	...	|	|	...	...	0636g	...	...	...	...	...	0739	...	|	...	0939	0939	...	|	|	...	1139	...	|
	Düsseldorf Hbf **800** d.	...	|	|	...	...	|	...	...	...	...	...	|	...	|	0546g	|	|	...	|	|	0746	|	...	|
0	**Kassel** Wilhelmshöhe **901** d.	...	|	|	...	...	|	...	...	...	0700	...	|	...	|	0900	|	|	...	|	|	1100	|	...	|
54	Bebra **901** d.	...	|	|	...	...	|	...	...	...	0736	...	|	...	|	0936	|	|	...	|	|	1136	|	...	|
99	**Eisenach** d.	...	0446s	0451	0602a	...	0703	...	...	...	0759	...	0806	...	0901	0959	1006	1006	...	1101	1101	1159	1206	...	1301
128	Gotha **858** d.	...	0506s	0508	0617a	...	0719	...	...	...	0814	...	|	...	0917	1014	|	|	...	1117	1117	1214	|	...	1317
155	**Erfurt** Hbf **858** a.	...	0523s	0523	0633a	...	0734	...	...	...	0829	...	0835	...	0932	1029	1035	1035	...	1132	1132	1229	1235	...	1332
155	**Erfurt** Hbf **858** d.	...	|	0525	0635	...	0736	0827	...	...	0831	0831	0837	←	0934	1031	1037	1037	←	1134	1134	1231	1237	←	1334
177	Weimar **858** d.	...	0540s	0542	0652	...	0753	0845	...	←	0848	0848	0853	0859	0951	1048	1053	1053	1059	1151	1151	1248	1253	1259	1351
218	Naumburg (Saale) Hbf **851** d.	...	0606s	0608	0715	...	|	0908	0914	0923	→	→	|	0925	|	→	|	|	1125	|	|	→	|	1325	|
232	Weißenfels d.	...	|	|	|	...	|	→	|	0935	...	...	|	0935	|	...	|	|	1135	|	|	...	|	1335	|
264	**Halle** (Saale) Hbf d.	0639	|	|	|	0801	|	...	|	1001	...	...	|	1001	|	...	|	|	1201	|	|	...	|	1401	|
	Leipzig Hbf **851** a.	|	0641	0641	0748	|	0846	...	0946	|	...	...	0946	|	1042	...	1146	1146	|	1242	1242	...	1346	|	1442
	Dresden Hbf **842** a.	|	0803	0803	|	|	1002	...	|	|	...	...	1102	|	1202	...	1302	1302	|	1402	1402	...	1502	|	1602
294	Bitterfeld **851** d.	|	...	...	|	0820	...	...	|	1020	...	...	...	1020	...	...	...	...	1220	...	...	...	...	1420	...
331	Lutherstadt Wittenberg **851** d.	0714	...	...	|	0836	...	...	|	1036	...	...	...	1036	...	...	...	...	1236	...	...	...	...	1436	...
429	**Berlin** Hbf **851** a.	0755	...	...	0905	0922	...	...	1100	1122	...	...	...	1122	...	...	...	...	1322	...	...	...	...	1522	...
	Stralsund **845** a.	...	...	...	...	1223	...	...	...	1423	...	...	...	1423	...	...	...	...	1623	...	...	...	...	...	...

	IC 2157	ICE 1549	IC 2157	ICE 1651	IC 2359	ICE 1641	IC 2359	IC 2259	ICE 1653	IC 2151	ICE 1643	IC 2151	IC 1959	IC 2204	ICE 1655	IC 2153	ICE 1645	IC 2153	ICE 1657	IC 2155	ICE 1747	ICE 1647	ICE 1659	ICE 1659	CNL 353
	◧		◧		⑤⑦		⑤⑦	Y					⑤x	①–④	⑧q		n		n	⑦w	⑦w	①–⑥	⑧b	⑤⑦	R
	🍷	✗	🍷	✗	p🍷	✗	p🍷	🍷	✗	🍷	✗	🍷	🍷	¶	✗	🍷	✗	🍷	✗	🍷	✗	j✗	✗	‡✗	E
Wiesbaden Hbf **912** ● d.	...	...	...	1224	...	...	...	...	1424	...	...	...	...	...	1624	...	...	...	1824	...	...	...	2024	2024	...
Mainz Hbf **912** ● d.	...	...	...	1242	...	...	...	...	1442	...	...	...	...	...	1642	...	...	...	1842	...	...	...	2042	2042	...
Frankfurt Flughafen + § d.	...	1211	...	1302	...	1411	...	...	1502	...	1611	...	...	...	1702	...	1811	...	1902	...	2013	...	2102	2102	...
Frankfurt (Main) Hbf **900/1** d.	...	*1213*f	...	1319	...	*1413*f	...	...	1520	...	*1613*f	...	1615	1617	1720	...	|	...	1919	...	|	2022	2119	2119	...
Frankfurt (Main) Süd d.	...	1222	...	|	...	1422	...	...	|	...	1622	...	|	|	|	...	1822	...	|	...	2025	|	|	|	2219
Hanau Hbf **900/1** d.	...	|	...	|	...	|	...	...	|	...	|	...	|	1637	|	...	|	...	|	...	2037	2037	|	|	|
Fulda **900/1** d.	...	1315	...	1413	...	1515	...	...	1613	...	1715	...	1721	1721	1813	...	1915	...	2013	...	2118	2118	2213	2213	0047r
Bad Hersfeld **901** d.	...	1339	...	|	...	1539	...	...	|	...	1739	...	1749	1749	|	...	1939	...	|	...	2142	2142	|	|	|
Düsseldorf Hbf **800** d.	0946	|	...	|	1146	|	...	...	|	1346	|	...	|	|	|	1546	|	...	|	1746	|	|	|	|	|
Kassel Wilhelmshöhe **901** d.	1300	|	...	|	1500	|	...	...	|	1700	|	...	|	|	|	1900	|	...	|	2100	|	|	|	|	|
Bebra **901** d.	1336	|	...	|	1536	|	...	...	|	1736	|	...	|	1800	|	1936	|	...	|	2136	|	|	|	|	|
Eisenach d.	1359	1406	...	1503	1559	1606	...	...	1703	1759	1806	...	|	...	1901	1959	2006	...	2101	2159	2210	2210	2301	2301	|
Gotha **858** d.	1414	|	...	1518	1614	|	...	...	1718	1814	|	...	1831	...	1917	2014	|	...	2117	2214	2227	2227	2317	2317	|
Erfurt Hbf **858** a.	1429	1435	...	1533	1629	1635	...	...	1733	1829	1835	...	1852	...	1932	2029	2035	...	2132	2231	2242	2242	2332	2332	|
Erfurt Hbf **858** d.	1431	1437	←	1535	1631	1637	←	1631	1735	1831	1837	←	1855	...	1934	2031	2037	←	2134	...	2246	2246	...	2334	|
Weimar **858** d.	1448	1453	1459	1551	1648	1653	1659	1659	1751	1848	1853	1859	1912	...	1951	2048	2053	2059	2151	...	2302	2302	...	2351	|
Naumburg (Saale) Hbf **851** d.	→	|	1525	|	→	|	1725	1725	|	→	|	1925	1938	...	|	→	|	2128	2213	...	2325	2325	...	0014	|
Weißenfels d.	...	|	1534	|	...	|	1734	1734	|	...	|	1935	1948	...	|	...	|	2138	|	...	|	|	...	|	|
Halle (Saale) Hbf d.	...	|	1601	|	...	|	1801	1801	|	...	|	2001	|	...	|	...	|	2201	|	...	2356	2356	...	|	|
Leipzig Hbf **851** a.	...	1546	|	1642	...	1746	|	|	1842	...	1946	|	2018	...	2042	...	2146	...	2245	...	0031	0031	...	0046	0348
Dresden Hbf **842** a.	...	1702	|	1802	...	1902	|	|	2002n	...	2102n	|	...	...	2202	...	2302	...	0008z	...	...	...	...	...	0551
Bitterfeld **851** d.	...	...	1620	...	...	...	1820	1820	...	...	...	2020	...	...	...	...	...	...	...	...	...	...	...	...	...
Lutherstadt Wittenberg **851** d.	...	...	1636	...	...	...	1836	1836	...	...	...	2036	...	...	...	...	...	...	...	...	...	...	...	...	...
Berlin Hbf **851** a.	...	...	1722	...	...	...	1922	1922	...	...	...	2124	...	...	...	...	...	...	...	...	...	...	...	...	...
Stralsund **845** a.	...	...	2040q	...	...	...	2223	...	...	...	...	...	...	...	...	...	...	...	...	...	...	...	...	...	...

- **A** – SEMPER – 🛏 1,2 cl., 🛏 2 cl., (2) (reclining) and ✗ Dresden - Karlsruhe - Basel - Zürich and v.v.
- **B** – (12) and 🍷 Berlin - Kassel - Dortmund (- Köln ⑦**w**).
- **D** – STRELASUND – (12) and 🍷 (Düsseldorf ①**g** -) Dortmund - Kassel - Berlin - Ostseebad Binz. On Dec. 25, Jan. 1 starts from Erfurt.
- **E** – JOHANNES KEPLER – 🛏 1,2 cl., 🛏 2 cl. and (2) Praha - Dresden - Karlsruhe - Basel and v.v.
- **H** – From / to Hamburg (Table **840**).
- **L** – To Gemünden (a. 2332) and Würzburg (a. 2356).
- **S** – From / to Saarbrücken (Table **919**).
- **T** – To Stuttgart (Tables **911** and **930**).
- **Y** – ①②③④⑥ (also Mar. 21, May 2; not Dec. 25, 26, Jan. 1, Mar. 20, 22, 24, Apr. 30, May 12).
- **a** – ①–⑤ (not Dec. 24, 25, 26, 31, Jan. 1, Mar. 21, 24, May 12).
- **b** – Not Dec. 23, 24, 25, 30, 31, Mar. 21, 23, May 11.
- **c** – Also Dec. 26, Mar. 22, 24, May 12.
- **e** – ①–⑥ (not Dec. 25, 26, Jan. 1, Mar. 22, 24, May 12).
- **f** – Change trains at Fulda (see Table **900**).
- **g** – ① (also Dec. 27, Jan. 2, Mar. 25, May 13; not Dec. 24, 31, Mar. 24, May 12).
- **h** – Also Dec. 23, 30, Mar. 23, May 11; not Dec. 26, Jan. 1, Mar. 24, May 12.
- **j** – Also Dec. 23, 30, Mar. 23, May 11; not Dec. 24, 26, 31, Jan. 1, Mar. 24, May 12.
- **k** – Also Dec. 25, 26, Jan. 1, Mar. 22, 24, May 12.
- **m** – Not Dec. 24, 25, 26, 31, Jan. 1, Mar. 20, 24, May 12.
- **n** – Not Dec. 24, 31.
- **p** – Also Dec. 26, Jan. 1, Mar. 20, 24, Apr. 30, May 12; not Dec. 23, 30, Mar. 21, 23, May 2, 11.
- **q** – ⑧ (not Dec. 24, 25, 31, Mar. 21, 23, May 11).
- **r** – Arrives 2314.
- **s** – Stops to set down only.
- **t** – Also Dec. 25, Mar. 21, 23, May 11.
- **u** – Stops to pick up only.
- **v** – Not Dec. 25, Jan. 1.
- **w** – ⑦ (also Dec. 26, Jan. 1, Mar. 24, May 12; not Dec. 23, 30, Mar. 23, May 11).
- **x** – Also Mar. 20, Apr. 30; not Mar. 21, May 2.
- **y** – Arrives 0431.
- **z** – Leipzig - Dresden on ⑤⑦ (also Dec. 26, Jan. 1, Mar. 20, 24, Apr. 30; not Dec. 23, 30, Mar. 21, 23, May 11).
- **‡** – Also Dec. 26, Jan. 1, Mar. 20, 24, Apr. 30, May 12; not Dec. 23, 30, Mar. 21, 23, May 11.
- **¶** – Not Dec. 24, 25, 26, 31, Jan. 1, Mar. 20, 24, Apr. 30, May 1, 12, 22.
- ***** – Arrives 2152.
- **◧** – From Köln (Table **800**). Train number **2257** on ⑥ (also Dec. 24, 25, 31, Mar. 21, 23, May 11).
- **§** – Frankfurt Flughafen Fernbahnhof.
- **●** – Timings at Mainz and Wiesbaden are subject to alteration on ⑥⑦ from May 17.

Warning! Hamburg area alterations Dec. 24 - Jan. 1 (see page 363)

851 BERLIN - LEIPZIG - SAALFELD - NÜRNBERG

Alternative regional services: Table **835** Berlin - Lutherstadt Wittenberg. Table **848** Lutherstadt Wittenberg - Leipzig. Table **849** Leipzig / Halle - Saalfeld. Table **875** Lichtenfels - Nürnberg.

km		*RB*	*ICE*	*RB*	*ICE*	*ICE*	*ICE*	*ICE*	*RE*	*ICE*	*IC*	*ICE*	*RE*	*ICE*	*ICE*	*X*	*IC*	*IC*	*ICE*	*RE*	*ICE*	*IC*	*ICE*	*RE*	*ICE*
		16841	**1501**	**16843**	**1603**	**1644**	**1503**	**1703**	**3481**	**1605**	**2154**	**1505**	**3483**	**1607**	**1727**	**80002**	**2152**	**2152**	**1507**	**3485**	**1001**	**2150**	**1509**	**3487**	**1003**
		Ⓐ x	①–⑤		①–⑤	①–⑥	①–⑥	⑦ v		①–⑥				① g	②–⑦		①–⑥	¶				**2250**			
			t ✕		d ✕	e n	e ✕			e ✕	⊖	✕		✕	k ✕	△	e ⊖	⊖	G ✕		R ✕	⊖	K ✕		R ✕
	Hamburg Hbf **840** d.	...	...	...	...	...	...	...	...	...	...	...	...	0600	...	...	...	...	0718**e**	...	...	...	0918**e**	...	...
0	**Berlin** Hbf **850** d.	...	...	...	...	...	...	...	...	0549	0640	0652	...	0753	0753	0757	0840	...	0858**e**	...	0953	1040	1059	...	1153
98	Lutherstadt Wittenberg **850** d.	...	...	...	...	...	...	...	...	0633	0721	0736	...	0836	0836	|	0921	...	|	...	1036	1121	|	...	1236
135	Bitterfeld **850** d.	...	...	...	...	...	...	...	...	0649	0738	|	...	|	|	|	0938	...	|	...	|	1138	|	...	|
168	**Leipzig** Hbf a.	...	...	...	...	...	...	...	...	0705	|	0805	...	0905	0905	0916	|	...	1005**e**	...	1105	|	1205	...	1305
168	**Leipzig** Hbf **850** d.	...	...	...	0501	0601	...	0607	...	0711	|	0816	...	0911	0911	...	|	...	1016	...	1111	|	1216	...	1311
	Halle (Saale) Hbf **850** d.	...	...	...	|	|	0603	|	...	|	0759	|	...	|	|	...	0959	0959	|	...	|	1159	|	...	|
222	Naumburg (Saale) Hbf **850** d.	...	...	...	0545	0638	0645	0645	...	|	0833	0851	...	|	|	...	1033	1033	1051	...	|	1233	1251	...	|
261	**Jena** Paradies d.	...	...	...	0608	...	0711	0711	...	0806	...	0918	...	1006	1006	...	...	...	1118	...	1206	...	1318	...	1406
308	**Saalfeld** (Saale) d.	0433	...	0525	0634	...	0741	0741	0752	|	...	0946	0952	|	|	...	...	...	1146	1152	|	...	1346	1352	|
372	Kronach d.	0532	...	0627	|	...	|	|	0841	|	...	|	1041	|	|	...	...	...	|	1241	|	...	|	1441	|
395	Lichtenfels d.	0555	0628	0649	0729	...	0831	0831	0853	0926	...	|	1053	1126	1126	...	...	...	|	1253	1326	...	|	1453	1526
427	**Bamberg** d.	...	0647	...	0746	...	0848	0848	...	0943	...	|	...	1143	1143	...	...	...	|	...	1343	...	|	...	1543
465	Erlangen d.	...	0708	...	|	...	0907	0907	...	1003	...	|	...	1203	1203	...	...	...	|	...	1403	...	|	...	1603
481	Fürth (Bay) Hbf a.	...	|	...	|	...	|	|	...	|	...	|	...	|	|	...	...	...	|	...	|	...	|	...	|
489	**Nürnberg** Hbf a.	...	0725	...	0820	...	0925	0925	...	1020	...	1125	...	1220	1220	...	...	...	1325	...	1420	...	1525	...	1620
	München Hbf **904** a.	...	0839	...	0937	...	1111**d**	...	...	1137	...	1239	...	1412	1412	...	...	...	1439	...	1612	...	1639	...	1812

	IC	*ICE*	*RE*	*ICE*	*IC*	*ICE*	*RE*	*ICE*	*IC*	*ICE*	*RE*	*X*	*ICE*	*ICE*	*IC*	*ICE*	*ICE*	*RE*	*ICE*	*ICE*	*ICE*	*EN*	*ICE*	*CNL*	*ICE*
	2356	**1511**	**3489**	**1613**	**2354**	**1513**	**3491**	**1615**	**2352**	**1515**	**3493**	**80004**	**1617**	**1617**	**2350**	**1717**	**1517**	**3495**	**909**	**1619**	**1519**	**429**	**1621**	**1201**	**1521**
														⑤⑦		⑥ j	n		⑦ w	①–⑥	Ⓑ q	🅁	⑤ a	🅁	⑦ w
	⊖	✕		✕	⊖	✕		✕	⊖	n ✕		R △	✕	c ✕	⊖	D ✕	✕		✕	z ✕	✕	B 🍷	✕	P ✕	✕
Hamburg Hbf **840** d.	...	1103	...	...	...	1318	...	...	...	1503	...	...	...	...	...	...	1718**q**	...	1805	...	1918	...	2005	...	2121
Berlin Hbf **850** d.	1240	1258	...	1353	1440	1458	...	1553	1640	1658	...	1706	1753	1753	1840	1858	1858	...	1951	1953	2100	2056	2153	2214	2313
Lutherstadt Wittenberg **850** d.	1321	|	...	1436	1521	|	...	1636	1721	|	...	|	1836	1836	1921	|	|	...	2036	2036	2140	2215	2238	|	2354
Bitterfeld **850** d.	1338	|	...	|	1538	|	...	|	1738	|	...	|	|	|	1939	|	|	...	|	|	|	|	|	|	|
Leipzig Hbf a.	|	1405	...	1505	|	1605	...	1705	|	1805	...	1833	1905	1905	|	2005	2005	...	2105	2105	2210	2258	2306	|	0024
Leipzig Hbf **850** d.	|	1416	...	1511	|	1616	...	1711	|	1816	...	...	...	1911	|	2011	2011	...	...	...	...	2316	...	|	...
Halle (Saale) Hbf **850** d.	1359	|	...	|	1559	|	...	|	1759	|	...	...	...	|	2002	|	|	...	...	...	...	|	...	0049**u**	...
Naumburg (Saale) Hbf **850** d.	1433	1451	...	|	1633	1651	...	|	1833	1851	...	...	...	|	2033	2043	2052	...	...	...	...	2354	...	|	...
Jena Paradies d.	...	1518	...	1606	...	1718	...	1806	...	1918	...	...	...	2006	...	...	2117	...	...	...	...	0022	...	|	...
Saalfeld (Saale) d.	...	1546	1552	|	...	1746	1752	|	...	1946	1952	...	...	|	...	...	2146	2152	...	...	...	0057	...	|	...
Kronach d.	...	|	1641	|	...	|	1841	|	...	|	2041	...	...	|	...	...	|	2247	...	...	...	|	...	|	...
Lichtenfels d.	...	|	1653	1726	...	|	1853	1926	...	|	2053	...	...	2126	...	...	2236	2310	...	...	...	|	...	|	...
Bamberg d.	...	|	...	1743	...	|	...	1943	...	2051	...	...	...	2143	...	...	2253	...	...	...	...	|	...	|	...
Erlangen d.	...	|	...	1803	...	|	...	2003	...	|	...	...	...	2203	...	...	2315	...	...	...	...	|	...	|	...
Fürth (Bay) Hbf a.	...	|	...	|	...	|	...	|	...	|	...	...	...	|	...	...	|	...	...	...	...	|	...	0424**s**	...
Nürnberg Hbf a.	...	1725	...	1820	...	1925	...	2020	...	2125	...	...	...	2220	...	...	2334	...	...	...	...	0253	...	|	...
München Hbf **904** a.	...	1840	...	2012	...	2039	...	2215	...	2241	...	...	...	2337**w**	...	...	0049	...	...	...	...	...	...	0642	...

	CNL	*EN*	*ICE*	*ICE*	*ICE*	*ICE*	*RB*	*ICE*	*X*	*RE*	*ICE*	*ICE*	*ICE*	*IC*	*ICE*	*RE*	*ICE*	*IC*	*ICE*	*RE*	*ICE*	*ICE*	*IC*	*ICE*	*RE*
	1200	**428**	**1518**	**1518**	**1616**	**1516**	**16842**	**1614**	**80003**	**3480**	**1724**	**1514**	**1714**	**2253**	**1612**	**3482**	**1512**	**2355**	**1610**	**3484**	**1510**	**1710**	**2357**	**1608**	**3486**
	🅁	🅁	① g	①–⑤	①–⑥		①–⑥	①–⑥			⑦ v	①–⑤	⑥ r	**2353**	①–⑥		§				Ⓑ q	⑥ h			
	N ✕	A 🍷		d ✕	e ✕	E ✕		e ✕	R △		✕	d ✕	✕	⊖	e ✕		✕	⊖	✕		✕	✕	⊖	✕	
München Hbf **904** d.	2301	...	0013	...	...	...	...	...	...	...	...	0433	0516	...	0531	...	0722	...	0743	...	0921**d**	...	...	0944	...
Nürnberg Hbf d.	|	0145	0222	...	...	...	...	0521	...	...	0627	0635	0635	...	0737	...	0835	...	0937	...	1036	1036	...	1137	...
Fürth (Bay) Hbf d.	0109**u**	|	|	...	...	...	...	|	...	...	|	|	|	...	|	...	|	...	|	...	|	|	...	|	...
Erlangen d.	|	|	0241	...	...	...	...	0540	...	...	0647	|	|	...	0757	...	|	...	0957	...	|	|	...	1157	...
Bamberg d.	|	|	0302	...	...	...	...	0601	...	...	0707	|	|	...	0816	...	|	...	1016	...	|	|	...	1216	...
Lichtenfels d.	|	|	0320	...	...	...	0543	0621	...	0704	0724	|	|	...	0833	0904	|	...	1033	1104	|	|	...	1233	1304
Kronach d.	|	|	|	...	...	...	0607	|	...	0716	|	|	|	...	|	0916	|	...	|	1116	|	|	...	|	1316
Saalfeld (Saale) d.	|	0337	0415	...	...	...	0710	0717	...	0808	0815	0815	0815	...	|	1008	1015	...	|	1208	1215	1215	...	|	1408
Jena Paradies d.	|	0408	0442	...	...	...	...	0744	...	...	0842	0842	0842	...	0953	...	1042	...	1153	...	1242	1242	...	1353	...
Naumburg (Saale) Hbf **850** d.	|	0435	0505	...	...	0715	...	0808	...	...	0914	0907	0907	0923	|	...	1107	1125	|	...	1307	1307	1325	|	...
Halle (Saale) Hbf **850** a.	0500**s**	|	|	...	...	|	...	|	...	...	|	|	|	0958	|	...	|	1158	|	...	|	|	1358	|	...
Leipzig Hbf **850** a.	|	0529	0539	...	...	0748	...	0842	...	...	0946	0942	0942	|	1046	...	1142	|	1246	...	1342	1342	|	1446	...
Leipzig Hbf d.	|	0557	0548	0548	0651	0757	...	0851	0926	...	0951	0951	0951	|	1051	...	1151	|	1251	...	1351	1351	|	1451	...
Bitterfeld **850** d.	|	|	0612	0612	0710	|	...	|	|	...	|	|	|	1020	|	...	|	1220	|	...	|	|	1420	|	...
Lutherstadt Wittenberg **850** d.	|	0643	0631	0631	|	|	...	0922	|	...	|	|	|	1036	1122	...	|	1236	1322	...	|	|	1436	1522	...
Berlin Hbf **850** a.	0748	0801	0714	0714	0805	0905	...	1005	1050	...	1100	1100	1100	1122	1206	...	1300	1322	1407	...	1500	1500	1522	1606	...
Hamburg Hbf **840** a.	...	...	0857	0857	0957	...	...	1157	...	...	1254	1254	1254	...	...	...	1439**q**	...	...	...	1639	...	...	...	...

	ICE	*ICE*	*IC*	*ICE*	*ICE*	*RE*	*ICE*	*ICE*	*IC*	*ICE*	*X*	*RE*	*ICE*	*ICE*	*IC*	*ICE*	*RE*	*ICE*	*ICE*	*IC*	*ICE*	*RE*	*ICE*	*ICE*	*RB*
	1508	**1708**	**2157**	**1000**	**1006**	**3488**	**1506**	**1706**	**2259**	**1604**	**80005**	**3490**	**1504**	**1702**	**2151**	**1602**	**3492**	**1722**	**1502**	**2153**	**1600**	**3494**	**1500**	**1647**	**1686**
	Ⓑ q	⑥ h	**2257**	Ⓑ q	⑥ h		⑤⑦	T	**2359**	n ‡			⑤–⑦	①–④		Ⓑ q		⑦ w	①–⑥		⑤⑦		n	**1747**	⑥
	L ✕	G ✕	⊖	R ✕	✕		y ✕	✕	¶ ⊖	✕	△		f ✕	m ✕	⊖	✕		✕	z ✕	⊖	b ✕		✕	n	
München Hbf **904** d.	1122	1122	...	1132	1132	...	1322	1322	...	1340	...	...	1522	1522	...	1622	...	1722	1722	...	1744	...	1922	...	...
Nürnberg Hbf d.	1235	1235	...	1337	1337	...	1435	1435	...	1537	...	...	1636	1636	...	1738	...	1836	1836	...	1937	...	2036	...	...
Fürth (Bay) Hbf d.	|	|	...	|	|	...	|	|	...	|	...	...	|	|	...	|	...	|	|	...	|	...	|	...	...
Erlangen d.	|	|	...	1357	1357	...	|	|	...	1557	...	...	|	|	...	1757	...	|	|	...	1957	...	2054	...	...
Bamberg d.	|	|	...	1416	1416	...	|	|	...	1616	...	...	|	|	...	1816	...	|	|	...	2016	...	2113	...	...
Lichtenfels d.	|	|	...	1433	1433	1504	|	|	...	1633	...	1704	|	|	...	1833	1904	|	|	...	2033	2103	2131	...	2212
Kronach d.	|	|	...	|	|	1516	|	|	...	|	...	1716	|	|	...	|	1916	|	|	...	|	2116	|	...	2236
Saalfeld (Saale) d.	1415	1415	...	|	|	1608	1615	1615	...	|	...	1808	1815	1815	...	|	2008	2015	2015	...	2127	2208	2225	...	2340
Jena Paradies d.	1442	1442	...	1555	1555	...	1642	1642	...	1755	...	...	1842	1842	...	1953	...	2042	2042	...	2155	...	2251	...	...
Naumburg (Saale) Hbf **850** d.	1507	1507	1525	|	|	...	1707	1707	1725	|	...	...	1907	1907	1925	|	...	2107	2107	2128	2219	...	2315	2325	...
Halle (Saale) Hbf **850** a.	|	|	1558	|	|	...	|	|	1758	|	...	...	|	|	1958	|	...	|	|	2201	|	...	|	2354	...
Leipzig Hbf **850** a.	1542	1542	|	1646	1646	...	1742	1742	|	1846	...	...	1942	1942	|	2046	...	2142	2142	...	2251	...	2348	...	...
Leipzig Hbf d.	1551	1551	|	1651	1651	...	1751	1751	|	1851	1854	...	1951	1951	|	2051	...	2151	2151	...	2257	...	...	...	...
Bitterfeld **850** d.	|	|	1620	|	|	...	|	|	1820	|	|	...	|	|	2020	|	...	|	|	...	|	...	...	...	...
Lutherstadt Wittenberg **850** d.	|	|	1636	1722	1722	...	|	|	1836	1922	|	...	|	|	2036	2122	...	|	|	...	2328	...	...	...	...
Berlin Hbf **850** a.	1700	1700	1722	1805	1805	...	1900	1900	1922	2005	2015	...	2101	2101	2124	2205	...	2259	2300	...	0010	...	...	...	...
Hamburg Hbf **840** a.	1839	...	...	...	1957	...	2040	...	...	2157**q**	...	...	2257	...	...	...	...	...	0036	...	...	...	...	...	...

A – DONAU-SPREE KURIER – 🛏 1, 2 cl., ▬ 2 cl. and (2) Wien - Linz - Passau - Berlin. Also calls at Berlin Schönefeld Flughafen ✈ (a. 0732), Berlin Ostbahnhof (a. 0750), Berlin Zoo (a. 0809) and Berlin Wannsee (a. 0824).
B – SPREE-DONAU-KURIER – 🛏 1, 2 cl., ▬ 2 cl. and (2) Berlin - Passau - Linz - Wien. Also calls at Berlin Wannsee (d. 2030), Berlin Zoo (d. 2048), Berlin Ostbahnhof (d. 2106) and Berlin Schönefeld Flughafen ✈ (d. 2125).
D – To Erfurt (Table **850**).
E – Daily except Dec. 25, Jan. 1. (2) and ✕ (Eisenach ①–⑤ **d** -) Erfurt - Leipzig - Berlin.
G – To / from Garmisch (Table **865**) on ⑥ (also Mar. 21; not Mar. 22).
K – From Kiel on ①–⑥ **e** (Table **820**). Train number **1709** on ⑦ **v**.
L – To Kiel (Table **820**).
N – PLUTO – 🛏 1 cl., ▬ 2 cl., (2) (reclining) and ✕ München - Berlin. Also calls at Augsburg Hbf (d. 2344), Potsdam Hbf (a. 0701), Berlin Wannsee (a. 0715), Berlin Zoo (a. 0736), Berlin Ostbahnhof (a. 0758) and Berlin Lichtenberg (a. 0813).
P – PLUTO – 🛏 1 cl., ▬ 2 cl., (2) (reclining) and ✕ Berlin - München. Also calls at Berlin Lichtenberg (d. 2150), Berlin Ostbahnhof (d. 2204), Berlin Zoo (d. 2221), Berlin Wannsee (d. 2253), Potsdam Hbf (d. 2304) and Augsburg Hbf (a. 0555).

R – To / from Rostock on dates in Table **835**.
T – ①②③④⑥ (also Dec. 23, 30, Mar. 21, 23, May 2, 11; not Dec. 26, Jan. 1, Mar. 20, 24, Apr. 30, May 12).

a – Also Mar. 20, Apr. 30; not Mar. 21, May 2.
b – Also Dec. 26, Jan. 1, Mar. 20, 24, Apr. 30, May 12, 21; not Dec. 23, 30, Mar. 21, 23, May 2, 11, 23.
c – Also Dec. 26, Jan. 1, Mar. 20, 24, Apr. 30, May 12; not Dec. 23, 30, Mar. 21, 23, May 2, 11.
d – ①–⑤ (not Dec. 24, 25, 26, 31, Jan. 1, Mar. 21, 24, May 12).
e – ①–⑥ (not Dec. 25, 26, Jan. 1, Mar. 22, 24, May 12).
f – Also Dec. 24, 25, 26, 31, Jan. 1, Mar. 20, 24, Apr. 30, May 1, 12.
g – Also Dec. 27, Jan. 2, Mar. 25, May 13; not Dec. 24, 31, Mar. 24, May 12.
h – Also Dec. 24, 25, 31, Mar. 21, 23, May 11.
j – Also Dec. 25, Mar. 21, 23, May 11.
k – Also Dec. 24, 31, Mar. 24, May 12; not Dec. 27, Jan. 2, Mar. 25, May 13.
m – Not Dec. 24, 25, 26, 31, Jan. 1, Mar. 20, 24, Apr. 30, May 1, 12.

n – Not Dec. 24, 31.
q – Ⓑ (not Dec. 24, 25, 31, Mar. 21, 23, May 11).
r – Also Dec. 24, 31, Mar. 21; not Mar. 22.
s – Stops to set down only.
t – Not Dec. 24, 25, 26, 31, Jan. 1, Mar. 21, 24, May 1, 12, 22.
u – Stops to pick up only.
v – Also Dec. 25, 26, Jan. 1, Mar. 22, 24, May 12.
w – ⑦ (also Dec. 26, Jan. 1, Mar. 24, May 12; not Dec. 23, 30, Mar. 23, May 11).
x – Not Dec. 24, 31, May 22.
y – Also Dec. 26, Jan. 1, Mar. 20, 24, Apr. 30, May 12; not Dec. 23, 30, Mar. 21, 23, May 2, 11.
z – Also Dec. 23, 30, Mar. 23, May 11; not Dec. 24, 25, 26, 31, Jan. 1, Mar. 24, May 12.

¶ – Not Dec. 23, 25, 30, Mar. 22, 23, May 11.
§ – Train number **1712** on ⑥ **h**.
‡ – Train number **1704** on ⑥ **j**.
⊖ – See Table **850** for further details.
△ – *InterConnex*. Operated by Veolia Verkehr GmbH. **DB tickets are not valid.**

COTTBUS - LEIPZIG — 852

RE / RB services

km			⚒									
0	**Cottbus**	d.	0458	0658	0758	0858	1058	1158		1858	1958	2305
24	Calau (Niederl)	d.	0515	0715	0816	0915	1115	1216	each	1915	2016	2324
46	Finsterwalde	d.	0529	0729	0831	0929	1129	1231	train	1929	2031	2339
56	Doberlug-Kirchhain	d.	0537	0737	0840	0937	1137	1240	runs	1937	2040	2346
79	Falkenberg (Elster)	a.	0555	0755	0906	0955	1155	1306	every	1955	2106	0012
79	Falkenberg (Elster) 856	d.	0556	0756	...	0956	1156	...	two	1956	...	...
97	Torgau **856**	d.	0610	0810	...	1010	1210	...	hours	2010	...	...
124	Eilenburg **856**	d.	0639	0839	...	1039	1239	...	until	2039	...	...
149	**Leipzig** Hbf **856**	a.	0700	0900	...	1100	1300	...		2100	...	...

			⚒								
Leipzig Hbf **856**	d.	*0607*	0707	...	0907	1107	...	each	...	1907	2107
Eilenburg **856**	d.	*0628*	0728	...	0928	1128	...	train	...	1928	2129
Torgau **856**	d.	*0649*	0749	...	0949	1149	...	runs	...	1949	2151
Falkenberg (Elster) **856**	a.	*0705*	0803	...	1003	1203	...	runs	...	2003	2205
Falkenberg (Elster)	d.	0726	0804	0850	1004	1204	1250	every	1850	2004	2206
Doberlug-Kirchhain	d.	0749	0820	0917	1020	1220	1317	two	1917	2020	2221
Finsterwalde	d.	0756	0827	0925	1027	1227	1325	hours	1925	2027	2229
Calau (Niederl)	d.	0812	0841	0944	1041	1241	1344	until	1944	2041	2242
Cottbus	a.	0831	0859	1003	1059	1259	1403		2003	2059	2300

STEAM TRAINS IN SACHSEN — 853

km			Ⓐe							A	
	Dresden Hbf (S-Bahn) **857**	d.	*0430*	...	*0800*	*1000*	*1230*	*1400*	*1630*	*1800*	...
0	Radebeul Ost	d.	0456	...	0826	1026	1256	1426	1656	1826	...
8	Moritzburg	d.	0525	...	0853	1055	1323	1455	1723	1853	...
16	Radeburg	a.	0546	...	...	1116	...	1516	...	...	...

		Ⓐe								A
Radeburg	d.	0611	...	...	...	1139	...	1539	...	...
Moritzburg	d.	0634	...	0903	...	1203	1333	1603	1733	1903
Radebeul Ost	a.	0701	...	0930	...	1230	1400	1630	1800	1930
Dresden Hbf (S-Bahn) **857**	a.	*0728*	...	*0958*	...	*1258*	*1428*	*1658*	*1828*	*1958*

km					🍷	C	🍷	C	🍷	🍷	🍷	C	🍷	C		C	🍷	C	C		🍷	🍷	🍷	🍷	🍷	🍷
0	Zittau	d.	High season	0839	0922	1001	1118	...	1221	...	...	...	1520	...	1601	...	...	1729	...	Low season	0922	...	...	1325	...	...
9	Bertsdorf	d.	★	0910	0953	1033	1149	1149	1253	1253	1344	1344	1552	1552	1632	1638	1728	1804	1922	●	0953	1040	1127	1356	1447	1548
12	Kurort Oybin	a.	→	|	1005	|	1201	|	1305	|	1356	|	1604	|	|	1650	1740	|	1934	→	1005	|	1139	1408	|	1600
13	Kurort Jonsdorf	a.		0922	...	1045	...	1201	...	1305	...	1356	...	1604	1644	...	...	1816	...		...	1051	...	...	1458	...

				🍷	C	🍷	C	🍷	🍷	C		C	🍷	🍷	C		C	C		🍷	🍷	🍷	🍷	🍷	🍷
Kurort Jonsdorf	d.	High season	0938	...	1114	...	1235	...	1316	1408	...	1614	...	1659	...	...	1855	...	Low season	...	1102	...	...	1515	...
Kurort Oybin	d.	★	|	1019	|	1215	|	1316	|	|	1408	|	1618	|	1714	1752	|	1946	●	1016	|	1149	1420	|	1618
Bertsdorf	d.	→	0956	1031	1126	1227	1247	1328	1328	1420	1421	1626	1631	1711	1727	1804	1907	1959	→	1028	1114	1201	1431	1527	1631
Zittau	a.		1030	1100	...	...	...	...	1357	...	1450	...	1659	...	1758	1833	...	2027		...	...	1229	...	...	1659

Operators: Radebeul service – BVO Bahn GmbH, Betriebsleitung Lößnitzgrundbahn, Am Bahnhof 1, 01468 Moritzburg. ✆ +49 (0) 35207 89290. Fax: + 49 (0) 35207 89291.
Zittau service – SOEG - Sächisch Oberlausitzer Eisenbahngesellschaft mbH, Bahnhofstraße 41, 02763 Zittau. ✆ +49 (0) 3583 516461. Fax: + 49 (0) 3583 516462.

A – From Mar. 21.
C – ⑥⑦ from May 3 (also Mar. 21 – 24, May 1, 2, 12).
e – Not Dec. 24 - Jan. 2, Feb. 4 – 15, Mar. 20 – 28, May 2, 13.
★ – High season: Dec. 22 - Jan. 13, Feb. 2 – 17 and from Mar. 15.
● – Low season: Dec. 9 – 21, Jan. 14 - Feb. 1 and Feb. 18 - Mar. 14.

SEUSSLITZ - DRESDEN - BAD SCHANDAU - SCHMILKA — 853a

March 20 - November 2, 2008

Special dates: May 1 "Steamship Parade", May 15 "Riverboat - Shuffle", Aug. 16 "Steamship - Fest". Contact the operator for service details on these dates.

		A	B		A		A	A	A		A	B	A
Seußlitz	d.	...	...	...	...	...	...	...	...	...	...	...	1315
Meißen	d.	...	...	...	...	...	...	...	...	...	...	1300	1445
Radebeul	d.	...	...	...	...	...	...	...	...	...	...	1445	1630
Dresden	d.	...	0830	0900	...	1000	1030	1200	1330	1400	1600	1615	1800
Pillnitz	d.	...	1020	1050	...	1130	1200	1330	1500	1530	1730	...	...
Pirna	d.	0930	1130	1200	...	...	1300	...	1600	...	...	...	...
Königstein	d.	1130	1400	1430	1445	...	1500	...	1800	...	...	...	...
Bad Schandau	d.	1215	...	...	1530	...	1600	...	1845	...	...	...	...
Schmilka	a.	1300	...	...	1615	...	...	...	...	...	...	...	...

		A	B		A	A		A	B		A	A	A
Schmilka	d.	...	...	...	...	...	...	1315	...	...	...	...	1630
Bad Schandau	d.	...	...	...	0930	...	...	1345	...	...	...	1630	1700
Königstein	d.	...	...	...	1000	...	...	1415	1430	1500	...	1700	1730
Pirna	d.	...	...	...	1115	...	...	...	1600	1630	...	1815	1845
Pillnitz	d.	...	...	1145	1200	1345	1545	...	1645	1715	1745	1900	...
Dresden	d.	0945	1045	1245	1300	1445	1645	...	1800	1830	1845	2000	...
Radebeul	d.	1045	1145	...	...	...	...	...	...	...	...	...	...
Meißen	d.	1145	1245	...	...	...	...	...	...	...	...	...	...
Seußlitz	a.	1245	...	...	...	...	...	...	...	...	...	...	...

A – Apr. 26 - Oct. 19.
B – ④⑤⑥ Apr. 26 - Oct. 18.
⊡ – Dresden Terrassenufer.

Operator: Sächsische Dampfschiffahrts GmbH & Co. Conti Elbschiffahrts KG.
Hertha-Lindner Straße 10, D-01067 Dresden. ✆ +49 (0) 351 866 090, Fax +49 (0) 351 866 09 88.

COTTBUS - GÖRLITZ - ZITTAU — 854

LausitzBahn ★ (2nd class only)

km			Ⓐ	Ⓐ	Ⓐ								Ⓐ											⑤⑥	Ⓐ		
0	**Cottbus**	d.	...	...	0452	...	0552	0652	0752	0852	0952	1052	1052	1152	1252	1352	1452	1552	1652	1752	1852	1914	2052	2052	2152	...	2308
24	Spremberg	d.	...	...	0511	...	0611	0711	0811	0911	1011	1110	1111	1211	1311	1411	1511	1611	1711	1811	1911	1932	2111	2111	2211	...	2327
42	Weißwasser	d.	...	0428	0530	0530	0630	0730	0830	0930	1030	...	1130	1230	1330	1430	1530	1630	1730	1830	1930	...	2130	2130	2228	...	2347
72	Horka	d.	...	0449	0551	0551	0650	0751	0850	0951	1050	...	1151	1250	1351	1450	1551	1650	1751	1850	1954	...	2158	2158	2249	...	0005
93	**Görlitz**	a.	...	0504	0607	0607	0707	0807	0907	1007	1107	...	1207	1307	1407	1507	1607	1707	1807	1905	2009	...	2213	2213	2307	...	0019
93	**Görlitz**	d.	0413	0513	0613	0613	0713	0813	0913	1013	1113	...	1213	1313	1413	1513	1613	1713	1810	1906	2013	...	...	2214	...	...	...
127	**Zittau**	a.	0456	0556	0656	0656	0756	0856	0956	1056	1156	...	1256	1356	1456	1556	1656	1756	1848	1949	2051	...	...	2257	...	...	...
	Liberec **1143**	a.	...	...	...	...	...	...	...	...	...	...	...	...	...	...	...	...	...	...	...	...	...	...	...	...	...

		Ⓐ		Ⓒ	Ⓐ							Ⓐ														Ⓐ
Liberec **1143**	d.	...	...	...	...	...	...	...	...	...	...	...	...	...	...	...	...	...	...	...	...	...	...	...	...	...
Zittau	d.	...	...	...	0405	...	0505	0605	0705	0805	0905	1005	...	1105	1205	1305	1405	1505	1605	1705	...	1858	...	2102	...	2206
Görlitz	a.	...	...	...	0442	...	0542	0642	0742	0842	0942	1042	...	1142	1242	1342	1442	1542	1642	1742	...	1935	...	2139	...	2243
Görlitz	d.	0338	...	0438	0447	...	0551	0651	0751	0851	0951	1051	...	1151	1251	1351	1451	1551	1651	1751	...	1938	...	2142	...	2251
Horka	d.	0351	...	0451	0509	...	0608	0709	0808	0909	1008	1109	...	1208	1309	1408	1509	1608	1709	1808	...	1953	...	2157	...	2309
Weißwasser	d.	0414	...	0514	0531	...	0631	0731	0831	0931	1031	1131	...	1231	1331	1431	1531	1631	1731	1831	...	2013	...	2226	...	2331
Spremberg	d.	0427	...	0527	0544	...	0644	0744	0844	0944	1044	1144	1144	1244	1344	1444	1544	1644	1744	1844	1938	2027	...	2239	...	...
Cottbus	a.	0446	...	0546	0608	...	0708	0808	0908	1008	1108	1208	1208	1308	1408	1508	1608	1708	1808	1908	1957	2045	...	2258	...	...

★ – LausitzBahn GmbH, Zittauer Straße 71/73, 02826 Görlitz.

GÖRLITZ and ZITTAU - DRESDEN — 855

RE / RB services

km			R	v			⚒L																		n	n	
	Zgorzelec **1085**	d.	...	...	...	...	...	...	...	*0814*	...	*1018*	...	...	...	...	1420	...	*1614*	...	*1818*	...	...	...	...	...	...
0	**Görlitz**	d.	...	...	0548	...	0649	0710	...	0836	...	1036	...	1236	...	...	1436	...	1636	...	1836	...	1910	...	2110	...	2310
24	Löbau (Sachs)	d.	...	...	0603	...	0704	0729	...	0851	...	1051	...	1251	...	...	1451	...	1651	...	1851	...	1929	...	2129	...	2329
46	Bautzen	d.	...	...	0616	...	0720	0747	...	0904	...	1104	...	1304	T	...	1504	...	1704	...	1904	...	1947	T	2147	...	2347
	Liberec **1143**	d.	...	...	|	...	|	|	...	|	0803	|	...	|	1203	...	|	...	|	1603	|	...	|	2003n	|	...	|
	Zittau	d.	0349	0514	|	0550	|	|	0718	|	0838	|	1038	|	1238	1335	|	1518	|	1638	|	1838	|	2038	|	2135	|
	Neugersdorf	d.	0412	0534	|	0613	|	|	0738	|	0903	|	1103	|	1303	1403	|	1538	|	1703	|	1903	|	2103	|	2204	|
	Ebersbach (Sachs)	d.	0417	0543	|	0618	|	|	0743	|	0908	|	1108	|	1308	1408	|	1543	|	1708	|	1908	|	2108	|	2209	|
65	Bischofswerda	d.	0502	0616	0628	0702	0732	0803	0816	0916	0944	1116	1144	1316	1344	1502	1516	1616	1716	1744	1916	1944	2003	2144	2203	2302	0000
102	Dresden Neustadt	a.	0538	0643	0655	0738	0755	0837	0842	0944	1012	1144	1212	1344	1412	1538	1544	1642	1744	1812	1944	2012	2038	2212	2238	2338	0038
106	**Dresden** Hbf	a.	0545	0651	0701	0745	*0810*	0844	0850	0950	1020	1150	1220	1350	1420	1545	1550	1650	1750	1820	1950	2020	2044	2220	2244	2345	0044

km			R													⚒L										n	n
0	**Dresden** Hbf	d.	0412	0512	0612	0710	0736	0805	0910	0936	1005	1136	1205	1336	1405	*1447*	1536	1605	1736	1805	1936	2005	2012	2110	2204	2312	2336
4	Dresden Neustadt	d.	0419	0519	0619	0719	0743	0812	0919	0943	1012	1143	1212	1343	1412	1500	1543	1612	1743	1812	1943	2012	2019	2119	2211	2319	2343
41	Bischofswerda	d.	0456	0556	0659	0756	0816	0841	0956	1016	1041	1216	1241	1413	1441	1527	1616	1641	1816	1841	2016	2041	2100	2156	2238	2356	0012
79	Ebersbach (Sachs)	d.	0540	|	0744	|	0850	|	|	1050	|	1250	|	1449	|	|	1650	|	1850	|	2050	|	2149	|	2313	|	0046
83	Neugersdorf	d.	0544	|	0748	|	0854	|	|	1054	|	1254	|	1453	|	|	1654	|	1854	|	2054	|	2153	|	2317	|	0050
105	**Zittau**	a.	0606	|	0816	|	0913	|	|	1113	|	1313	|	1512	|	|	1713	|	1913	|	2113	|	2216	|	2336	|	0109
	Liberec **1143**	a.	...	|	...	|	0953	|	|	...	|	1353	|	...	|	|	1753	|	...	|	2153n	|	...	|	...	|	...
	Bautzen	d.	...	0611	...	0811	T	0853	1011	...	1053	...	1253	...	1453	1539	T	1653	...	1853	...	2053	...	2211	...	0011	...
	Löbau (Sachs)	d.	...	0629	...	0829	...	0906	1029	...	1106	...	1306	...	1506	1553	...	1706	...	1906	...	2106	...	2229	...	0029	...
	Görlitz	a.	...	0648	...	0848	...	0921	1048	...	1121	...	1321	...	1521	1607	...	1721	...	1921	...	2121	...	2248	...	0048	...
	Zgorzelec **1085**	a.	...	...	...	...	...	*0937*	...	...	*1137*	...	1333	...	...	...	...	*1737*	...	*1937*	...	...	...	...	...	...	...

L – Operated by Lausitzbahn. To / from Leipzig (Table **842**). Conveys 🍷. DB tickets are not valid Dresden - Leipzig and v.v.
R – ①–⑥ (not Dec. 24, 25, 26, 31, Jan. 1, Mar. 24, May 12).
T – To / from Tanwald on ⑥⑦ (also Czech holidays). See Table **1141**.
n – Not Dec. 24, 31.
v – Not Dec. 25, Jan. 1.

856 DRESDEN - COTTBUS and LEIPZIG - RUHLAND

RE services

km	km																							
					v																	n	t
	0	**Dresden** Hbf 842 843 857 d.	...	...	0540	...	...	0645	0740	...	⊠	...	1645	1740	...	...	1845	1940	...	...	2045	...	2140	...
	4	**Dresden** Neustadt 842 857 d.	...	...	|	...	...	0652	|	...		...	1652	|	...	...	1852	|	...	...	2052	...	|	...
	18	Coswig 842 843 857 d.	...	...	0604	...	...	0705	0804	...	each train	...	1705	1804	...	...	1905	2004	...	...	2105	...	2204	...
0		**Leipzig** Hbf 852 d.	...	...	|	...	0607	|	|	...		1607	|	|	...	1807	|	|	...	2007	|	...	|	2316
25		Eilenburg 852 d.	...	...	|	...	0628	|	|	...	runs every	1628	|	|	...	1828	|	|	...	2028	|	...	|	2340
52		Torgau 852 d.	...	...	|	...	0649	|	|	...		1649	|	|	...	1849	|	|	...	2050	|	...	|	0000
70		Falkenberg (Elster) 852 d.	0409a	...	|	0609a	0708	|	|	0809a	two hours	1708	|	|	1809e	1908	|	|	2009e	2108	|	...	|	0015
94		Elsterwerda-Biehla ◇ d.	0432a	E	|	0632a	0735	|	|	0832a		1735	|	|	1832e	1935	|	|	2032e	2135	|	...	|	...
120	73	Ruhland a.	0453a	0600	0656	0653a	0756	0757	0856	0853a	until	1756	1757	1856	1853e	1956	1957	2056	2053e	2156	2157	...	2250	...
	73	Ruhland d.	0506	0601	...	0706	...	0802	...	0906		...	1802	...	1906	...	2002	...	2106	...	2202	...	...	...
	86	Senftenberg d.	0517	0612	...	0717	...	0812	...	0917		...	1812	...	1917	...	2012	...	2117	...	2212	2352	...	...
	120	**Cottbus** 852 a.	0549	0645	...	0749	...	0842	...	0949		...	1842	...	1949	...	2042	...	2149	...	2242	0021	...	...

		v																					n	
Cottbus 852 d.	0416	...	0515	...	0608	...	0715	...	0808	...	⊡	1513	...	1608	...	1715	...	1808	...	1915	...	2008	...	2208
Senftenberg d.	0446	...	0544	...	0641	...	0744	...	0841	...		1544	...	1641	...	1744	...	1841	...	1944	...	2041	...	2241
Ruhland a.	0457	...	0554	...	0652	...	0753	...	0852	...	each train	1553	...	1652	...	1753	...	1852	...	1953	...	2052	...	2252
Ruhland d.	0506a	0502	0600	0601	0706a	0702	0800	0801	0906a	0902		1600	1601	1706e	1702	1800	1801	1906e	1902	2000	2001	2106e	2102	2253
Elsterwerda-Biehla ◇ d.	0530a	|	|	0624	0730a	|	|	0824	0930a	|	runs every	|	1624	1730e	|	|	1824	1930e	|	|	2024	2130e	|	L
Falkenberg (Elster) 852 d.	0551a	|	|	0651	0751a	|	|	0854	0951a	|		|	1654	1751e	|	|	1854	1951e	|	|	2054	2151e	|	...
Torgau 852 d.	...	|	|	0707	...	|	|	0910	...	|	two hours	|	1710	...	|	|	1910	...	|	|	2110	...	|	...
Eilenburg 852 d.	...	|	|	0733	...	|	|	0939	...	|		|	1739	...	|	|	1939	...	|	|	2139	...	|	...
Leipzig Hbf 852 a.	...	|	|	0754	...	|	|	1000	...	|	until	|	1800	...	|	|	2000	...	|	|	2203	...	|	...
Coswig 842 843 857 d.	...	0554	0652	...	...	0754	0852	...	...	0954		1652	...	...	1754	1852	...	...	1954	2052	...	...	2154	...
Dresden Neustadt 842 857 a.	...	|	0708	...	...	|	0908	...	...	|		1708	...	...	|	1908	...	...	|	2108	...	...	|	...
Dresden Hbf 842 843 857 a.	...	0617	0715	...	...	0817	0915	...	...	1017		1715	...	...	1817	1915	...	...	2017	2115	...	...	2217	...

E – From Elsterwerda (d. 0536).
L – To Elsterwerda (a. 2320).
a – Ⓐ only.
e – Ⓐ (not Dec. 24, 31).
n – Not Dec. 24, 31.
t – Not Dec. 31.
v – Not Dec. 25, Jan. 1.
◇ – See Table **843** for connections from / to Elsterwerda.
⊠ – The 1209 and 1409 from Falkenberg run daily throughout. The 1609 from Falkenberg does not run on Dec. 24, 31 between Falkenberg and Ruhland.
⊡ – The 1208 and 1408 from Cottbus run daily throughout.

857 BAD SCHANDAU - DRESDEN - MEISSEN - LEIPZIG

RB / S-Bahn services

km	S-Bahn																							
																t		n		n		n	t	
0	**Bad Schandau** 1100 ⊡ d.	...	0508r	0538a	0608	0638	0708	0738	0808	0839	0908	...	and at	1808	...	1908	1938*	2008	...	2108	...	2208	2310	0010
4	Königstein d.	...	0515r	0545a	0615	0645	0715	0745	0815	0845	0915	0945	the same	1815	1845	1915	1945	2015	...	2115	...	2215	2115	0015
23	Pirna d.	0435	0535r	0605	0635	0705	0735	0805	0835	0905	0935	1005	minutes	1835	1905	1935	2005	2035	2105	2135	2205	2235	2335	0035
40	**Dresden** Hbf 842/3 856 1100 d.	0500	0600	0630	0700	0730	0800	0830	0900	0930	1000	1030	past each	1900	1930	2000	2030	2100	2130	2200	2230	2300	0000	0058
44	**Dresden** Neustadt 842 856 d.	0507	0607	0637	0707	0737	0807	0837	0907	0937	1007	1037	hour until	1907	1937	2007	2037	2107	2137	2207	2237	2307	0008	...
50	Radebeul Ost d.	0516	0616	0646	0716	0746	0816	0846	0916	0946	1016	1046		1916	1946	2016	2046	2116	2146	2216	2246	2316	0017	...
58	Coswig 842/3 856 d.	0528	0628	0658	0728	0758	0828	0858	0928	0958	1028	1058		1928	1958	2028	2058	2128	2158	2228	2258	2328	0028	...
68	**Meißen** a.	0537	0637	0707	0737	0807	0837	0907	0937	1007	1037	1107		1937	2007	2037	2107	2137	2207	2237	2307	2337	0037	...

S-Bahn																							
		r	r												n		n	t					r	
Meißen d.	...	0450	0520	0550	0620	0650	0720	0750		1820	1850	1920	1950	2020	2050	2120	2150	2220	2250	2320	...	...	0020	...
Coswig 842/3 856 d.	0430v	0500	0530	0600	0630	0700	0730	0800	and at	1830	1900	1930	2000	2030	2100	2130	2200	2230	2300	2330	...	...	0031	...
Radebeul Ost d.	0440v	0510	0540	0610	0640	0710	0740	0810	the same	1840	1910	1940	2010	2040	2110	2140	2210	2240	2310	2340	...	...	0042	...
Dresden Neustadt 842 856 d.	0450v	0520	0550	0620	0650	0720	0750	0820	minutes	1850	1920	1950	2020	2050	2120	2150	2220	2250	2320	2350	...	...	0051	...
Dresden Hbf 842/3 856 1100 d.	0500	0530	0600	0630	0700	0730	0800	0830	past each	1900	1930	2000	2030	2100	2130	2200	2230	2300	2330	2358	0015	...	0059	0103
Pirna d.	0524	0554	0624	0654	0724	0754	0824	0854	hour until	1924	1954	2024	2053	2124	2153	2224	2253	2324	2353	...	0039	...	...	0126
Königstein a.	0541	0611a	0641	0711	0741	0811	0840	0911		1940	2011	2041	...	2141	...	2241	...	2341	...	...	0056	...	...	...
Bad Schandau 1100 ⊡ a.	0546	0616a	0656	0716	0746	0816	...	0916		...	2016	2046	...	2146	...	2246	...	2346	...	...	0101	...	...	...

km											
0	**Meißen** d.	...	...	0713a	0913	1113	1313	1513	1713	1913	2113
21	Nossen d.	...	0554a	0754	0954	1154	1354	1554	1754	1954	2154
29	Roßwein d.	...	0604a	0804	1004	1204	1404	1604	1804	2004	2204
40	Döbeln Hbf d.	0526	0626	0826	1026	1226	1426	1626	1826	2026	2226
53	Leisnig d.	0539	0639	0839	1039	1239	1439	1639	1839	2039	2239
68	Großbothen d.	0557	0657	0857	1057	1257	1457	1657	1857	2057	2257
75	Grimma ob Bf d.	0604	0704	0904	1104	1304	1504	1704	1904	2104	2304
106	**Leipzig** Hbf a.	0641	0741	0938	1136	1336	1541	1741	1936	2136	2336

	Ⓐ										
Leipzig Hbf d.	...	0615	0815	1015	1215	1415	1615	1815	1915	2115	2317
Grimma ob Bf d.	...	0648	0848	1048	1248	1448	1648	1848	1948	2148	2350
Großbothen d.	...	0656	0856	1056	1256	1456	1656	1856	1956	2156	2357
Leisnig d.	...	0710	0910	1110	1310	1510	1710	1910	2010	2210	0011
Döbeln Hbf d.	0524	0724	0924	1124	1324	1524	1724	1924	2024	2224	0024
Roßwein d.	0537	0737	0937	1137	1337	1537	1737	1937	2037a	2237	...
Nossen d.	0548	0748	0948	1148	1348	1548	1748	1948	2047a	2247	...
Meißen a.	0614	0814	1014	1214	1414	1614	1814	2014	...	...	...

a – Ⓐ only.
n – Not Dec. 24, 31.
r – Not Jan. 1.
t – Not Dec. 31.
v – Not Dec. 25, Jan. 1.
* – From Mar. 21.
⊡ – A frequent ferry services links the railway station with Bad Schandau town centre. Depart Bad Schandau, Bahnhof 0700 and every 30 minutes until 2100 (10 minute journey). Depart Bad Schandau, Elbkai 0655 and every 30 minutes until 2055 (5 minute journey). **Operator**: Oberelbische Verkehrsgesellschaft Pirna - Sebnitz mbH (OVPS), ✆ +49 (0) 3501 7920.

857a DRESDEN - DRESDEN FLUGHAFEN ✈

S-Bahn

km						
0	**Dresden** Hbf d.	0417	0447	and at the same	2247	2317
4	**Dresden** Neustadt d.	0425	0455	minutes past	2255	2325
15	**Dresden** Flughafen ✈ a.	0440	0510	each hour until	2310	2340

Dresden Flughafen ✈ d.	0446	0516	0548	and at the same	2116	2146	2216	2248	2316	2346
Dresden Neustadt a.	0459	0529	0601	minutes past	2129	2159	2229	2301	2329	2359
Dresden Hbf a.	0508	0538	0610	each hour until	2138	2208	2238	2310	2339	0007

858 CHEMNITZ / ZWICKAU - GERA - ERFURT

RB / RE services

km																								
		⚒n		Ⓐe	⚒n	⚒n		▶			▶		▶		▶		▶		▶	L		n▶	n	n
0	**Chemnitz** Hbf 880 d.	...	...	...	▶	0626	...	...	0826	...	...	1026	...	1226	...	1426	...	1626	...	1826	...	...	2026	...
32	Glauchau (Sachs) 880 d.	...	...	...	...	0654	...	...	0854	0927c	...	1054	...	1254	...	1454	...	1654	...	1854	1927c	...	2054	...
	Zwickau (Sachs) Hbf 881 d.	...	...	...	0648	|	...	0848	|	|	1048	|	1248	|	1448	|	1648	|	1848	|	|	2048	|	...
	Werdau 881 d.	...	...	...	0656	|	...	0856	|	|	1056	|	1256	|	1456	|	1656	|	1856	|	|	2056	|	...
48	Gößnitz 881 a.	...	...	...	0711	0716	...	0911	0916	0949c	1111	1116	1311	1316	1511	1516	1711	1716	1911	1916	1949c	2111	2116	...
48	Gößnitz d.	...	...	...	▬	0724	...	▬	0924	0950c	▬	1124	▬	1324	▬	1524	▬	1724	▬	1924	1950c	▬	2124	...
83	**Gera** Hbf a.	...	...	...	...	0756	...	...	0956	1025c	...	1156	...	1356	...	1556	...	1756	...	1956	2025c	n	2156	...
83	**Gera** Hbf d.	0444	0556	0623	0702	0802	0802	0902	1002	1033	1102	1202	1302	1402	1502	1602	1702	1802	1902	2002	2033	2133	2202	2341
123	Göschwitz (Saale) d.	0517	0623	0651	0730	0830	0830	0930	1030	1109	1130	1230	1330	1430	1530	1630	1730	1830	1930	2030	2109	2213	2230	0017
128	Jena West d.	0522	0628	0658	0736	0836	0836	0936	1036	1115	1136	1236	1336	1436	1536	1636	1736	1836	1936	2036	2115	2218	2236	0023
151	Weimar 850 d.	0545	0646	0722	0752	0852	0852	0952	1052	1137	1152	1252	1352	1452	1552	1652	1752	1852	1952	2052	2137	2240	2252	0048
172	**Erfurt** Hbf 850 a.	0601	0703	0737	0808	0908	0908	1008	1108	*1157*	1208	1308	1408	1508	1608	1708	1808	1908	2008	2108	*2157*	*2303*	2308	*0108*
	Göttingen 865 a.	...	0852	...	...	1052	1052	...	1252	...	...	1452	...	1652	...	1852	...	2052	...	...	...	...	...	...

	v	⚒n	⚒n	⑥	Ⓒc	Ⓐe																n	n	v
Göttingen 865 d.	...	...	...	...	...	...	...	0603a	0707	...	0907	...	1107	...	1307	...	1507	...	1707	...	1907	...	...	...
Erfurt Hbf 850 d.	0438e	...	...	*0558*	...	0607	0649	0749	0849	0949	1049	1149	1249	1349	1449	1549	1649	1749	1849	1949	2049	2149	*2300*	0011
Weimar 850 d.	0456	...	...	0619	...	0627	0707	0807	0907	1007	1107	1207	1307	1407	1507	1607	1707	1807	1907	2007	2107	2207	2323	0030
Jena West d.	0517	...	...	0642	...	0654	0724	0824	0924	1024	1124	1224	1324	1424	1524	1624	1724	1824	1924	2024	2124	2224	2345	0052
Göschwitz (Saale) d.	0521	...	...	0647	...	0703	0729	0829	0929	1029	1129	1229	1329	1429	1529	1629	1729	1829	1929	2029	2129	2229	2350	0057
Gera Hbf a.	0554	...	...	0723	...	0741	0756	0856	0956	1056	1156	1256	1356	1456	1556	1656	1756	1856	1956	2056	2156	2256	0025	...
Gera Hbf d.	...	0600	...	0731	0731	...	0800	▬	1000	▬	1200	▬	1400	▬	1600	▬	1800	▬	2000n	▬	...	...	...	...
Gößnitz a.	...	0630	◀	0810	0810	...	0831	◀	1031	◀	1231	◀	1431	◀	1631	◀	1831	◀	2031n	n◀	...	...	...	...
Gößnitz 881 d.	...	0635	0639	0811	0811	...	0835	0839	1035	1039	1235	1239	1435	1439	1635	1639	1835	1839	2035n	2039	...	...	...	...
Werdau 881 d.	...	0650	|	|	|	...	0850	|	1050	|	1250	|	1450	|	1650	|	1850	|	2050n	|	...	...	...	...
Zwickau (Sachs) Hbf 881 a.	...	0658	|	|	|	...	0858	|	1058	|	1258	|	1458	|	1658	|	1858	|	2058n	|	...	...	...	...
Glauchau (Sachs) 880 d.	...	...	0703	0832	0832	...	...	0903	...	1103	...	1303	...	1503	...	1703	...	1903	...	2103	...	...	...	...
Chemnitz Hbf 880 a.	...	...	0730	*0901*	*0901*	...	...	0930	...	1130	...	1330	...	1530	...	1730	...	1930	...	2130	...	...	...	...

L – To Leinefelde (Table **865**).
a – Ⓐ only.
c – Ⓒ (also Dec. 24, 31).
e – Ⓐ (not Dec. 24, 31).
n – Not Dec. 24, 31.
v – Not Dec. 25, Jan. 1.
▶ – Attached to train in the next column at Gößnitz.
◀ – Detached from train in previous column at Gößnitz.

RB services — HOLZMINDEN and HERZBERG - GOSLAR - BAD HARZBURG - BRAUNSCHWEIG — 859

km		Ⓐn	Ⓐ	Ⓐ	Ⓐ	Ⓐ	Ⓒ	Ⓐ	⑥	Ⓐ											g			g
0	**Holzminden** d.	...	...	...	*0530e*	...	...	0629	0654	0710	...	0759	...	...	0959	...	...	1159	...	...	...	1359	...	...	1559
44	**Kreiensen** a.	...	...	...	*0604e*	...	...	0703	0728	0744	...	0833	...	...	1033	...	...	1233	...	...	...	1433	...	...	1633
44	**Kreiensen** d.	0457	0535	...	0646	...	0657	...	0746	0746	...	0846	...	...	1046	...	...	1246	...	1346	...	1446	...	...	1646
50	Bad Gandersheim d.	0502	0540	...	0651	...	0702	...	0751	0751	...	0851	...	...	1051	...	...	1251	...	1351	...	1451	...	...	1651
	Herzberg (Harz) d.	|	|	0534	|	0634	|	...	|	|	0734	|	0834r	0934	|	1034r	1134	|	1234r	|	1334	|	1434a	1534	|
	Osterode (Harz) Mitte d.	|	|	0547	|	0647	|	...	|	|	0747	|	0847r	0947	|	1047r	1147	|	1247r	|	1347	|	1447a	1547	|
64	Seesen d.	0513	0551	0613	0702	0713	0713	...	0802	0802	0813	0902	0913	1013	1102	1113	1213	1302	1313	1402	1413	1502	1513	1613	1702
	Salzgitter-Ringelheim d.	0529	|	0629	|	0729	0729	...	|	|	0829	|	0929	1029	|	1129	1229	|	1329	|	1429	|	1529	1629	|
87	Goslar **860** a.	|	0610	|	0721	|	|	...	0821	0821	|	0921	|	|	1121	|	|	1321	|	1421	|	1521	|	|	1721
98	**Bad Harzburg 860** a.	|	0634	|	0738	|	|	...	0840	0840	|	0934	|	|	1134	|	|	1338	|	1440	|	1534	|	|	1738
	Braunschweig Hbf a.	0551	...	0651	...	0751	0751	...	...	...	0851	...	0951	1051	...	1151	1251	...	1351	...	1451	...	1551	1651	...

						Ⓐn	n	n	n	†	n
Holzminden d.	...	1654a	...	1754f	...	*1834*	...	1959	...	2034	...
Kreiensen a.	...	1728a	...	1828f	...	*1908*	...	2033	...	2108	...
Kreiensen d.	...	1749	...	1846	...	1938	...	2046	...	...	2138
Bad Gandersheim d.	...	1755	...	1851	...	1943	...	2051	...	...	2143
Herzberg (Harz) d.	1634a	|	1734	|	1834a	|	1934	|	2034e	...	|
Osterode (Harz) Mitte d.	1647a	|	1747	|	1847a	|	1947	|	2047e	...	|
Seesen d.	1713	1806	1813	1902	1913	1954	2013	2102	2113	...	2154
Salzgitter-Ringelheim d.	1729	|	1829	|	1929	...	2029	|	2129	...	...
Goslar **860** a.	|	1824	|	1921	|	...	|	2121	|	...	...
Bad Harzburg 860 a.	|	1840	|	1934	|	...	|	2134	|	...	...
Braunschweig Hbf a.	1751	...	1851	...	1951	...	2051	...	2151	...	...

km		Ⓐn	Ⓐn	Ⓐ	Ⓐ	⚒		⚒		k
0	**Braunschweig** Hbf d.	0504	...	0604	...	...	0704	...	0804	...
	Bad Harzburg 860 d.	|	...	|	0618	...	|	0714	|	0820
	Goslar **860** d.	|	...	|	0631	...	|	0731	|	0833
31	Salzgitter-Ringelheim d.	0529	...	0629	|	...	0729	|	0829	|
52	Seesen d.	0545	0550	0645	0650	...	0745	0751	0845	0851
71	Osterode (Harz) Mitte d.	0607	|	0707	|	...	0807	|	0907r	|
83	**Herzberg** (Harz) a.	0621	|	0721	|	...	0821	|	0921r	|
	Bad Gandersheim d.	...	0600	...	0700	...	...	0802	...	0902
	Kreiensen a.	...	0607	...	0707	...	...	0809	...	0909
	Kreiensen d.	...	*0627*	...	0708	0754	...	...	...	0923
	Holzminden a.	...	*0700*	...	0742	0828	...	...	...	0957

			k								Ⓐ				Ⓐ					n	Ⓐn	n	n	†	n
Braunschweig Hbf d.	0904	1004	...	1104	1204	...	1304	...	1404	...	...	1504	1604	...	...	1704	...	1804	...	1904	...	2004	...	...	2204
Bad Harzburg 860 d.	|	|	1020	|	|	1220	|	1323	|	1420	...	|	|	1620	...	|	1723	|	1820	|	...	|	2020	...	|
Goslar **860** d.	|	|	1033	|	|	1233	|	1341	|	1433	...	|	|	1633	...	|	1741	|	1833	|	...	|	2033	...	|
Salzgitter-Ringelheim d.	0929	1029	|	1129	1229	|	1329	|	1429	|	...	1529	1629	|	...	1729	|	1829	|	1929	...	2029	|	...	2229
Seesen d.	0945	1045	1051	1145	1245	1251	1345	1359	1445	1451	...	1545	1645	1651	...	1745	1759	1845	1851	1945	1959	2045	2051	...	2249
Osterode (Harz) Mitte d.	1007	1107r	|	1207	1309r	|	1407	|	1507a	|	...	1607	1707a	|	...	1807	|	1907a	|	2007	|	2107e	|	...	|
Herzberg (Harz) a.	1021	1121r	|	1221	1325r	|	1421	|	1521a	|	...	1621	1721a	|	...	1821	|	1921a	|	2021	|	2121e	|	...	|
Bad Gandersheim d.	...	...	1102	...	...	1302	...	1410	...	1502	...	...	...	1702	...	...	1810	...	1902	...	2010	...	2102	...	2300
Kreiensen a.	...	...	1109	...	...	1309	...	1416	...	1509	...	...	...	1709	...	...	1816	...	1909	...	2016	...	2109	...	2307
Kreiensen d.	...	...	1123	...	...	1323	...	...	...	1523	1649	...	...	1723c	1749	...	1829e	...	1923n	...	...	...	2123	2238	...
Holzminden a.	...	...	1157	...	...	1357	...	...	...	1557	1723	...	...	1757c	1823	...	1902e	...	1957n	...	...	...	2157	2312	...

GOSLAR and BAD HARZBURG - BRAUNSCHWEIG

km		Ⓐ	⚒	⚒	⚒													n	n	n
0	**Goslar 860** d.	0445	0523a	0627	...	0801	*0828*r	1001	...	1201	...	1401	*1428*	1601	...	1801	*1828*	2001	...	2201
	Bad Harzburg 860 d.	|	0541	|	0651	*0802*	0851	*1002*	1051	*1202*	1251	*1402*	1451	*1602*	1651	*1802*	1851	*2002*	2051	*2202*
13	Vienenburg **860** d.	0457	0556	0639	0701	0813	0901	1013	1101	1213	1301	1413	1501	1613	1701	1813	1901	2013	2101	2213
40	Wolfenbüttel d.	0522	0621	0702	0725	0836	0925	1036	1125	1236	1325	1436	1525	1636	1725	1836	1925	2036	2125	2236
52	**Braunschweig** Hbf a.	0531	0630	0712	0734	0846	0934	1046	1134	1246	1334	1446	1534	1646	1734	1846	1934	2046	2134	2246

km		Ⓐ												Ⓐ		n	n	n	n	Ⓑn
0	**Braunschweig** Hbf d.	0513	0626	0713	0826	0913	1026	1113	1226	1313	1426	1513	1626	1639	1713	1826	1913	2026	2113	2220
12	Wolfenbüttel d.	0523	0636	0723	0836	0923	1036	1123	1236	1323	1436	1523	1636	1650	1723	1836	1923	2036	2123	2230
39	Vienenburg **860** d.	0547	0702	0747	0902	0947	1102	1147	1302	1347	1502	1547	1702	1715	1747	1902	1947	2102	2147	2254
47	**Bad Harzburg 860** a.	*0559*	0711	*0759*	0911	*0959*	1111	*1159*	1311	*1359*	1511	*1559*	1711	|	*1759*	1911	*1959*	2111	*2159*	|
58	**Goslar 860** a.	0600	...	0800	...	1000	...	1200	*1338*	1400	...	1600	*1738*	1728	1800	...	2000	...	2200	2307

a – Ⓐ only.
c – Ⓒ only.
e – Ⓐ (not Dec. 24, 31).
f – 5 minutes later on Ⓒ.
g – Change trains at Kreiensen on †.
k – Change trains at Kreiensen on ⑥.
n – Not Dec. 24, 31.
r – ⚒ only.

DB (*RE* services); *Harz Elbe Express* ◇ — HANNOVER - BAD HARZBURG - HALLE — 860

km		Ⓐ	Ⓒv	Ⓐ			Ⓐ	Ⓐ	Ⓒv	⚒	⚒		⚒													
0	**Hannover** Hbf d.	...	...	...	...	...	...	...	...	...	...	...	0547	0637	...	0747	0837	...	0947	1037	...	1147	1237	...	1347	1437
36	**Hildesheim** Hbf d.	...	...	...	...	...	...	...	...	...	...	...	0614	0702	...	0814	0902	...	1014	1102	...	1214	1302	...	1414	1502
70	Salzgitter-Ringelheim d.	...	...	...	...	...	...	...	...	...	...	...	0643	0724	...	0843	0924	...	1043	1124	...	1243	1324	...	1443	1524
89	Goslar **859** d.	...	...	...	...	...	0523	0557	...	0627	...	...	0658	0736	...	0858	0936	...	1058	1136	...	1258	1336	...	1458	1536
100	**Bad Harzburg 859** a.	...	...	...	...	...	0535	|	...	|	...	...	0711	0748	...	0911	0948	...	1111	1148	...	1311	1348	...	1511	1548
100	**Bad Harzburg 859** d.	...	...	...	...	...	0541	|	...	|	0651	...	...	0802	*0851*	...	1002	*1051*	...	1202	*1251*	...	1402	*1451*	...	1602
108	Vienenburg **859** d.	...	...	...	...	...	0548	0607	...	0638	0658	0705	...	0810	0905	...	1010	1105	...	1210	1305	...	1410	1505	...	1610
124	Ilsenburg d.	...	...	...	0448a	0535	...	0620	0621	...	...	0718	...	0821	0918	...	1021	1118	...	1221	1318	...	1421	1518	...	1621
133	Wernigerode d.	...	...	...	0500a	0547	...	0632	0635	...	...	0730	...	0830	0930	...	1030	1130	...	1230	1330	...	1430	1530	...	1630
157	**Halberstadt** a.	...	...	...	0519a	0605	...	0651	0651	...	...	0748	...	0845	0948	...	1045	1148	...	1245	1348	...	1445	1548	...	1645
157	**Halberstadt** d.	0340	0406	0441	0524	m	...	0701	0701	...	...	0801	...	0901	1001	...	1101	1201	...	1301	1401	...	1501	1601	...	1701
190	Aschersleben d.	0408	0435	0509	0553	...	...	0718	0718	...	...	0829	...	0918	1029	...	1118	1229	...	1318	1429	...	1518	1629	...	1718
201	Sandersleben (Anh) d.	0422	0449	0528	0606	...	...	0725	0725	...	...	0845	...	0925	1045	...	1125	1245	...	1325	1445	...	1525	1645	...	1725
219	Könnern ⊡ d.	0437	0504	0543	0620	...	...	0736	0735	...	...	0859	...	0936	1059	...	1136	1259	...	1336	1459	...	1536	1659	...	1736
248	**Halle** (Saale) Hbf a.	0507	0534	0616	0653	...	...	0754	0752	...	...	0929	...	0954	1129	...	1154	1329	...	1354	1529	...	1554	1729	...	1754

						n	n	n	n	n	n	v
Hannover Hbf d.	...	1547	1637	...	1747	1837	...	1947	2037	2147	2305	0014
Hildesheim Hbf d.	...	1614	1702	...	1814	1902	...	2014	2102	2214	2341	0049
Salzgitter-Ringelheim d.	...	1643	1724	...	1843	1924	...	2043	2124	2243	...	...
Goslar **859** d.	...	1658	1736	...	1858	1936	...	2058	2136	2257	...	...
Bad Harzburg 859 a.	...	1711	1748	...	1911	1948	...	2111	2148	...	...	...
Bad Harzburg 859 d.	*1651*	▬	1802	*1851*	...	2002	*2051*	...	2202	...	...	...
Vienenburg **859** d.	1705	...	1810	1905	...	2010	2105	...	2210	...	...	...
Ilsenburg d.	1718	...	1821	1918	...	2021	2118	...	2221	...	...	...
Wernigerode d.	1730	...	1830	1930	...	2030	2130	...	2229	...	...	...
Halberstadt a.	1748	...	1845	1948	...	2045	2148	...	2245	...	...	...
Halberstadt d.	...	1801	1901	2001	...	2101	2201	...	2301	...	...	...
Aschersleben d.	...	1829	1918	2029	...	2118	2229	...	2318	...	...	...
Sandersleben (Anh) d.	...	1845	1925	2045	...	2125	2242	...	...	...	...	...
Könnern ⊡ d.	...	1859	1936	2059	...	2136	2255	...	...	...	...	...
Halle (Saale) Hbf a.	...	1929	1954	2129	...	2154	2315	...	...	...	...	...

	Ⓐn	Ⓐn	Ⓐ			Ⓐ		Ⓐ	
Halle (Saale) Hbf d.	...	...	...	...	...	...	...	0513	0602v
Könnern ⊡ d.	...	...	...	...	...	...	...	0545	0621v
Sandersleben (Anh) d.	...	...	...	...	...	...	...	0605	0632v
Aschersleben d.	...	...	0434	...	...	0500	...	0619	0641
Halberstadt a.	...	...	0453	...	...	0529	...	0648	0658
Halberstadt d.	...	...	0500	...	...	...	0545	...	0710
Wernigerode d.	...	...	0519	...	...	...	0604	...	0731
Ilsenburg d.	...	...	0532	...	...	...	0620	...	0740
Vienenburg **859** d.	...	...	0551	...	...	...	0633	...	0751
Bad Harzburg 859 a.	...	...	0559	...	...	...	*0711*	...	0759
Bad Harzburg 859 d.	...	...	0610	...	0642	...	...	...	0810
Goslar **859** d.	...	0457	0624	0624	0657	...	...	...	0824
Salzgitter-Ringelheim d.	...	0511	0635	0635	0711	...	...	...	0835
Hildesheim Hbf d.	0515	0543	0658	0658	0745	...	...	...	0858
Hannover Hbf a.	0550	0609	0721	0721	0812	...	...	...	0921

					◧											n			n		n	n		v	b t	n
Halle (Saale) Hbf d.	...	0623	0805	...	0831	1005	...	1031	1205	...	1231	1405	...	1431	1605	...	1631	1805	...	1831	...	2005	2031	...	2206	2331
Könnern ⊡ d.	...	0700*	0821	...	0859	1021	...	1059	1221	...	1259	1421	...	1459	1621	...	1659	1821	...	1859	...	2021	2059	...	2234	2359
Sandersleben (Anh) d.	...	0714	0832	...	0913	1032	...	1113	1232	...	1313	1432	...	1513	1632	...	1713	1832	...	1913	...	2032	2113	...	...	0013
Aschersleben d.	...	0729	0839	...	0928	1039	...	1128	1239	...	1328	1439	...	1528	1639	...	1728	1839	...	1928	...	2039	2128	...	...	0025
Halberstadt a.	...	0757	0856	...	0956	1056	...	1156	1256	...	1356	1456	...	1556	1656	...	1756	1856	...	1956	...	2056	2156	m	...	*0101*
Halberstadt d.	...	0808	0910	...	1008	1110	...	1208	1310	...	1408	1510	...	1608	1710	...	1808	1910	...	2008	...	2110	2208	0021	...	...
Wernigerode d.	...	0830	0931	...	1030	1131	...	1230	1331	...	1431	1531	...	1630	1731	...	1830	1931	...	2030	...	2131	2230	0041	...	...
Ilsenburg d.	...	0841	0940	...	1041	1140	...	1241	1340	...	1443	1540	...	1641	1740	...	1841	1940	...	2041	...	2140	2240	0053	...	...
Vienenburg **859** d.	...	0854	0951	...	1054	1151	...	1254	1351	...	1455	1551	...	1654	1751	...	1854	1951n	...	2054	...	2151	...	...	...	...
Bad Harzburg 859 a.	...	*0911*	0959	...	*1111*	1159	...	*1311*	1359	...	*1511*	1559	...	*1711*	1759	...	*1911*	1959n	...	*2111*n	...	2159	...	...	...	...
Bad Harzburg 859 d.	0846	...	1010	1046	...	1210	1246	...	1410	1446	...	1610	1646	...	1810	1846	...	2010n	2046	...	...	2210	...	...	...	...
Goslar **859** d.	0901	...	1024	1101	...	1224	1301	...	1424	1501	...	1624	1701	...	1824	1901	...	2024n	2101	...	...	2222	...	...	...	...
Salzgitter-Ringelheim d.	0915	...	1035	1115	...	1235	1315	...	1435	1515	...	1635	1715	...	1835n	1915	...	2035n	2115	...	...	...	...	...	...	...
Hildesheim Hbf d.	0945	...	1058	1145	...	1258	1345	...	1458	1545	...	1658	1745	...	1858n	1945	...	2058n	2145	...	2315	...	...	...	...	...
Hannover Hbf a.	1012	...	1121	1212	...	1321	1412	...	1521	1612	...	1721	1812	...	1921n	2012	...	2122n	2212	...	2350	...	...	...	...	...

a – Ⓐ only.
b – To Bernburg (a. 2300).
m – To / from Magdeburg (Table **862**).
n – Not Dec. 24, 31.
t – Not Dec. 31.
v – Not Dec. 25, Jan. 1.
* – Arrives 0649.
◧ – Change trains at Halberstadt on Ⓒ.

◇ – *Harz Elbe Express* (*HEX*). Operated by Veolia Verkehr Sachsen-Anhalt GmbH.

⊡ – **Könnern - Bernburg** and v.v. (*16 km*, journey 25 – 28 minutes) ◇: **From Könnern** at 0545 Ⓐ, 0655 ⚒, 0829, 1029, 1229, 1429, 1629, 1829, 2032, 2235 **t**. **From Bernburg** at 0511 Ⓐ, 0549 ⑥, 0624 Ⓐ, 0704 †, 0729 ⚒, 0904, 1104, 1304, 1504, 1704, 1904.

861 MAGDEBURG - SANGERHAUSEN - ERFURT and DESSAU - ASCHERSLEBEN
RE / RB services

Magdeburg - Erfurt and Aschersleben

km			⚒n	Ⓐn	Ⓒz	Ⓐn	Ⓐn	w		⑥								Ⓐn	Ⓒz	Ⓐn					t		
0	**Magdeburg** Hbf	d.	...	...	...	0404	0511	0611	0711	0711	0811	0911	1011	1111	1211	1311	1411	1457g	1511	1532	1611	1711	1811	1911	2011	2111	2244
37	Staßfurt	d.	...	...	...	0436	0552	0643	0749	0749	0843	0949	1043	1149	1243	1349	1443	1537	1549	1606	1643	1749	1843	1949	2043	2149	2326
44	Güsten	d.	...	...	...	0443	0559	0649	0758	0802	0849	0956	1049	1156	1249	1356	1449	1544	1556	1613	1649	1756	1849	1956	2053	2156	2334
	Aschersleben	a.	...	...	...	0455	0611	|	0809	|	|	1007	|	1207	|	1407	|	|	1607	1624	|	1807	|	2007	|	2207	2345
60	Sandersleben	d.	...	...	...	▬	▬	0702	▬	0815	0902	▬	1102	▬	1302	▬	1502	1557	▬	▬	1702	▬	1902	▬	2105	...	...
66	Hettstedt	d.	...	...	...	...	...	0709	...	0822	0909	...	1109	...	1309	...	1509	1604	...	...	1709	...	1909	...	2112	...	...
75	Klostermansfeld	d.	...	...	...	Ⓐn	...	0719	...	0832	0919	...	1119	...	1319	...	1519	1614	Ⓐn	Ⓒz	1719	...	1919	n	2122	...	...
97	**Sangerhausen**	d.	0408	0514	0545	0629	0648	0740	0840	0900	0940	1040	1140	1240	1340	1440	1540	1633	1638	1640	1740	1840	1940	2040	2143	...	...
142	Sömmerda	d.	0449	0549	0629	0703	0730	0829	0929	...	1029	1129	1229	1329	1429	1529	1629	...	1729	1729	1829	1929	2029	2129	...	...	...
167	**Erfurt** Hbf	a.	0510	0608	0651	0720	0751	0851	0951	...	1051	1151	1251	1351	1451	1552	1653	...	1751	1751	1851	1951	2053	2151	...	...	...

		Ⓐn	Ⓐn	Ⓒz	Ⓐn	Ⓐn	Ⓐn	w	v										Ⓐn		⑥	Ⓐn			t		n
Erfurt Hbf	d.	...	...	...	...	...	0458	...	0610	0707	0807	0907	1007	1107	1207	1307	1407	1507	1541	1607	...	1641	1707	1807	1907	2007	2207
Sömmerda	d.	...	...	...	...	...	0520	...	0636	0729	0829	0929	1029	1129	1229	1329	1429	1529	1600	1629	...	1700	1729	1829	1929	2029	2229
Sangerhausen	d.	...	...	...	0514	...	0617	0617	0731	0817	0916	1017	1116	1217	1316	1417	1516	1617	1644	1720j	1739	1737	1817	1916	2017	2116	2314
Klostermansfeld	d.	...	...	...	0534	...	0637	0637	▬	0837	▬	1037	▬	1237	▬	1437	▬	1637	...	▬	1758	...	1837	▬	2037	▬	...
Hettstedt	d.	...	...	...	0544	...	0647	0647	...	0847	...	1047	...	1247	...	1447	...	1647	...	...	1812	...	1847	...	2047	...	...
Sandersleben	d.	...	...	...	0551	...	0654	0654	...	0854	...	1054	...	1254	...	1454	...	1654	...	...	1820	...	1854	...	2054	...	...
Aschersleben	d.	0448	0531	0548	|	0621	|	|	0748	|	0948	|	1148	|	1348	|	1544f	|	...	1748	|	...	|	1948	|	2148	...
Güsten	d.	0500	0543	0600	0604	0633	0706	0706	0800	0906	1000	1106	1200	1306	1400	1506	1556f	1706	...	1800	1832	...	1906	2000	2108	2200	...
Staßfurt	d.	0509	0552	0609	0612	0644	0714	0714	0809	0914	1009	1114	1209	1314	1409	1514	1609	1714	...	1809	1844	...	1914	2009	2115	2209	...
Magdeburg Hbf	a.	0543	0626	0643	0641	0717	0743	0743	0843	0943	1043	1143	1243	1343	1443	1543	1643	1743	...	1843	1913	...	1943	2043	2144	2248	...

Dessau - Aschersleben

km			Ⓐn	C	Ⓐn		Ⓐn		Ⓒz	Ⓐn			Ⓐn					Ⓐn	Ⓒz					t			t
0	**Dessau** Hbf	d.	0419	0458	0527	0603	0650	...	0711	0731	0803	0903	1003	1103	1203	1303	1403	1503	1503	1603	1703	1803	1903	2003	2103	...	2303
21	Köthen	a.	0442	0521	0555	0625	0715	...	0734	0752	0825	0926	1025	1126	1225	1326	1425	1526	1526	1625	1726	1825	1926	2025	2126	...	2326
21	Köthen	d.	0456	0522	0555	0627	0716	...	0735	0753	0827	0935	1027	1135	1227	1335	1427	1531	1535	1627	1735	1827	1935	2035	2135	...	2327
42	Bernburg	d.	0517	0545	0616	0649	0737	...	0757	0815	0849	0957	1049	1157	1249	1357	1449	1553	1557	1649	1757	1849	1957	2052	2157	...	2349
54	Güsten	d.	0527	0555	0626	0700	0747	0758	0808	0825	0900	1008	1100	1208	1300	1408	1500	1603	1608	1700	1808	1900	2008	2102	2208	...	0000
66	**Aschersleben**	a.	0538	0607	0635	0712	...	0809	0820	0834	0912	1020	1112	1220	1312	1420	1512	1611	1620	1712	1820	1912	2020	2113	2220	...	0012

		w	Ⓐn	Ⓒz	Ⓐn		Ⓒz		Ⓐn			Ⓐn					Ⓐn	Ⓒz	Ⓐn						t	t	t
Aschersleben	d.	0436	0517	0558	0558	0647	0739	0748	...	0847	0939	1047	1139	1247	1339	1447	1535	1539	...	1647	1739	1847	1938	...	2045	...	2138
Güsten	d.	0448	0529	0609	0609	0659	0751	0759	0805	0859	0951	1059	1151	1259	1351	1459	1551	1551	...	1659	1751	1859	1950	...	2056	2111	2150
Bernburg	d.	0500	0541	0619	0619	0711	0803	...	0815	0911	1003	1111	1203	1311	1403	1511	1603	1603	...	1711	1803	1911	2002	...	...	2122	2202
Köthen	a.	0521	0603	0638	0638	0734	0826	...	0834	0934	1026	1134	1226	1334	1426	1534	1626	1626	...	1734	1826	1934	2023	...	...	2141	2223
Köthen	d.	0523	0604	0640	0640	0735	0835	...	0835	0935	1035	1135	1235	1335	1435	1535	1635	1635	1651	1735	1827	1935	2035	...	...	2142	2224
Dessau Hbf	a.	0546	0631	0702	0706	0757	0857	...	0857	0957	1057	1157	1257	1357	1457	1557	1657	1657	1718	1757	1846	1957	2057	...	...	2204	2246

C – ⑥⑦ (also Dec. 24, 31, Mar. 21, 24, May 1, 12).
f – 4 minutes later on Ⓒ (also Dec. 24, 31).
g – 1453 from May 26.
j – 1716 on Ⓒ (also Dec. 24, 31).
n – Not Dec. 24, 31.
t – Not Dec. 24, 25, 31.
v – Not Dec. 25, Jan. 1.
w – Not Dec. 25, 26, Jan. 1.
z – Also Dec. 24, 31.

862 MAGDEBURG - HALBERSTADT - THALE
HEX ◇

km			v	Ⓐ					B				Ⓒ	Ⓐ		Ⓒ	Ⓐ								n L
0	**Magdeburg** Hbf	d.	...	0446	...	0555v	0709	0809	0909	1009	1044	1209	1244	1309	1409	1444	1509	1609	1709	1809	1909	2009	2106	...	2213	2314
39	Oschersleben (Bode)	d.	...	0520	...	0634v	0741	0841	0941	1041	1120	1241	1323	1341	1441	1523	1541	1641	1741	1841	1941	2042	2143	...	2254	2354
59	**Halberstadt**	a.	...	0539	...	0656v	0757	0857	0957	1057	1142	1257	1345	1357	1457	1545	1557	1657	1757	1857	1957	2057	2204	...	2315	0015
59	**Halberstadt**	d.	0500	...	0612	0706	0806	0906	1006	1106	1206	1306	1406	1406	1506	1606	1606	1706	1806	1906	2006	2106	2206	...	2317n	...
77	Quedlinburg	a.	0516	...	0627	0723	0823	0923	1023	1123	1223	1323	1423	1423	1523	1623	1623	1723	1823	1923	2023	2123	2223	...	2338n	...
77	Quedlinburg	d.	0519	...	0629	0730	0830	0930	1030	1130	1230	1330	1430	1430	1530	1630	1630	1730	1830	1930	2030	2130	2230	...	2339n	...
87	**Thale** Hbf	a.	0531	...	0641	0742	0842	0942	1042	1142	1242	1342	1442	1442	1542	1642	1642	1742	1842	1942	2042	2142	2242	...	2350n	...

		Ⓐ	v		L			Ⓐ	Ⓒ					Ⓐ	Ⓒ				A			n			n
Thale Hbf	d.	...	...	0505v	...	0616	0716	0816	0816	0916	1016	1116	1216	1316	1316	1416	1516	1616	1716	1816	1916	2016	...	2116	2216
Quedlinburg	a.	...	...	0517v	...	0628	0728	0828	0828	0928	1028	1128	1228	1328	1328	1428	1528	1628	1728	1828	1928	2028	...	2128	2228
Quedlinburg	d.	...	...	0517v	...	0633	0733	0833	0833	0933	1033	1133	1233	1333	1333	1433	1533	1633	1733	1833	1933	2033	...	2133	2233
Halberstadt	a.	...	...	0538v	...	0649	0749	0849	0849	0949	1049	1149	1249	1349	1349	1449	1549	1649	1749	1849	1949	2049	...	2149	2249
Halberstadt	d.	0350	0450	0541	0613	0701	0801	0901	0912	1001	1101	1212	1301	1401	1412	1501	1601	1701	1801	1901	2012	2101	...	2204n	...
Oschersleben (Bode)	d.	0407	0512	0602	0628	0716	0816	0916	0933	1016	1116	1233	1316	1416	1433	1516	1616	1716	1816	1916	2033	2116	...	2225n	...
Magdeburg Hbf	a.	0440	0549	0646	0658	0742	0842	0942	1014	1042	1142	1314	1342	1442	1514	1543	1643	1742	1842	1942	2112	2146	...	2306n	...

A – To Berlin (Table **839**) on ⑤⑥† (also Dec. 31, Mar. 20, Apr. 30).
B – From Berlin (Table **839**) on ⑥⑦ (also Dec. 26, Jan. 1, Mar. 21, 24, May 1, 12).
L – To / from Ilsenburg (Table **860**).
n – Not Dec. 24, 31.
v – Not Dec. 25, Jan. 1.
◇ – *Harz Elbe Express*. Operated by Veolia Verkehr Sachsen-Anhalt GmbH.

863 LÖHNE - HAMELN - HILDESHEIM - BRAUNSCHWEIG
DB (RB services); eurobahn ★

km			⚒	Ⓐn	⚒	⚒		Ⓐn							Ⓒz	Ⓐn					Ⓐn						Ⓑn
	Bielefeld Hbf **810**	d.	...	*0524*	...	*0624*	...	*0724*	...	*0824*	*0924*e	*1024*	*1124*e	*1224*	*1224*	...	*1324*e	*1424*	*1524*e	*1624*	*1724*	...	*1824*	*1924*k	...	*2024*	*2024*
	Herford **810**	d.	...	*0533*	...	*0633*	...	*0733*	...	*0833*	*0933*e	*1033*	*1133*e	*1233*	*1233*	...	*1333*e	*1433*	*1533*e	*1633*	*1733*	...	*1833*	*1933*k	...	*2033*	*2033*
0	**Löhne** (Westf)	d.	...	0545	...	0645	...	0745	...	0845	0945e	1045	1145e	1245	1245	...	1345e	1445	1545e	1645	1745	...	1845	1945	...	2048	2048
12	Vlotho	d.	...	0559	...	0659	...	0759	...	0859	0959e	1059	1159e	1259	1259	...	1359e	1459	1559e	1659	1759	...	1859	1959	...	2059	2059
29	Rinteln	d.	...	0610	...	0710	...	0810	...	0910	1010e	1110	1210e	1310	1310	...	1410e	1510	1610e	1710	1810	...	1910	2010	...	2110	2110
53	**Hameln**	d.	0528	0628	0628	0728	0728	0828	0828	0928	1028	1128	1228	1327	1328	1337	1428	1528	1628	1728	1828	1828	1928	2028	2028	2127	2128
82	Elze	a.	0553	0653	0653	0753	0753	0852	0852	0953	1052	1153	1252	...	1353	1402	1452	1553	1652	1753	1852	1852	1953	2052	2052	...	2153
82	Elze	d.	0602	0702	0702	0802	0802	0907	0907	1002	1107	1202	1307	...	1402	1403	1507	1602	1707	1802	1907	1907	2002	2107	2107	...	2202
100	**Hildesheim** Hbf	a.	0620	0720	0720	0820	0820	0925	0925	1020	1125	1220	1325	...	1420	1422	1525	1620	1725	1820	1925	1925	2020	2125	2125	...	2220

		Ⓐn	⚒	⚒	Ⓐn			Ⓐn			Ⓐn			Ⓐn			Ⓐn			Ⓐn			Ⓐn			Ⓑn
Hildesheim Hbf	d.	...	0537	0634	0634	0737	0834	0834	0937	1034	1034	1137	1234	1234	1337	1434	1434	1537	1634	1634	1737	1834	1834	1937	2034	2137
Elze	a.	...	0553	0650	0650	0753	0850	0850	0953	1050	1050	1153	1250	1250	1353	1450	1450	1553	1650	1650	1753	1850	1850	1953	2050	2153
Elze	d.	...	0602	0702	0702	0802	0902	0902	1004	1102	1102	1202	1302	1302	1402	1502	1502	1602	1702	1702	1802	1902	1902	2002	2102	2202
Hameln	d.	0529	0629	0727	0729	0829	0927	0929	1029	1127	1129	1229	1327	1329	1429	1527	1529	1629	1727	1729	1829	1927	1929	2029	2127	2227
Rinteln	d.	0546	0646	...	0746	0846	...	0946	1046	...	1146	1246	...	1346	1446	...	1546	1646	...	1746	1846	...	1946	2046	...	...
Vlotho	d.	0602	0702	...	0802	0902	...	1002	1102	...	1202	1302	...	1402	1502	...	1602	1702	...	1802	1902	...	2002	2102	...	...
Löhne (Westf)	a.	0613	0713	...	0813	0913	...	1013	1113	...	1213	1313	...	1413	1513	...	1613	1713	...	1813	1913	...	2013	2113	...	...
Herford **810**	a.	*0626*	*0725*	...	*0826*	*0925*	...	*1026*	*1125*	...	*1226*	*1325*	...	*1426*	*1525*	...	*1626*	*1725*	...	*1826*	*1925*	...	*2026*	*2125*	...	...
Bielefeld Hbf **810**	a.	*0636*	*0736*	...	*0836*	*0936*	...	*1036*	*1136*	...	*1236*	*1336*	...	*1436*	*1536*	...	*1636*	*1736*	...	*1836*	*1936*	...	*2036*	*2136*	...	...

Hildesheim - Braunschweig

km					◇			◇	◇		◇	◇		◇	◇		◇		◇		◇	◇		◇		◇	◇
			Ⓐn			⚒												Ⓐn		n			n	q	n		
0	**Hildesheim** Hbf	d.	0559	0659	0734	0759	0859	0934	1034	1059	1134	1234	1259	1334	1434	1459	1534	1559	1634	1659	1734	1834	1900	1934	2059	2134	2234
43	**Braunschweig** Hbf	a.	0645	0745	0758	0845	0945	0958	1058	1145	1158	1258	1345	1358	1458	1545	1558	1645	1658	1745	1758	1858	1951	1958	2145	2158	2258

				◇		◇	◇		◇	◇		◇	◇		◇		◇		◇		◇			◇		◇	
		⚒	Ⓐn													Ⓐ				Ⓐn		⚒n	†		n		Ⓒ
Braunschweig Hbf	d.	0615	0646	0758	0815	0858	0958	1015	1058	1158	1215	1258	1358	1415	1458	1515	1558	1615	1658	1715	1758	1815	1817	1958	2015	2058	2215
Hildesheim Hbf	a.	0651	0724	0823	0856	0923	1023	1056	1123	1223	1256	1323	1423	1456	1523	1556	1623	1656	1723	1756	1823	1856	1856	2023	2056	2123	2256

e – Ⓐ (not Dec. 24, 31).
k – Not May 22.
n – Not Dec. 24, 31.
q – Not Dec. 24, 25, 31, Mar. 23, May 11.
z – Also Dec. 24, 31.
◇ – *ICE* train (see Table **900**).
★ – Löhne - Hildesheim operated by **eurobahn** Rhenus Keolis GmbH & Co. KG.

CANTUS Verkehrsgesellschaft (2nd class only) — GÖTTINGEN - KASSEL local services — 864

For fast trains Göttingen - Kassel Wilhelmshöhe and v.v. see Tables **900** (*ICE* services) and **904** (*IC* services).

km		Ⓐn	⑥k	⚒		⚒		⚒			Ⓒk	Ⓐe			Ⓐe	Ⓒk	Ⓑn	Ⓐe	Ⓒk	Ⓑn	⚒	Ⓑn	Ⓐn		Ⓒk	Ⓐn
0	**Göttingen 908** d.	0455	0457	0614	0714	0814	0914	1018	1114	1218	1314	1332	1418	1514	1614	1618	1714	1814	1818	1914	2014	2118	2214	...	2335	2335
20	Eichenberg **908** a.	0509	0511	0628	0728	0828	0928	1032	1128	1232	1328	1346	1432	1528	1628	1632	1728	1828	1832	1928	2028	2132	2228	...	2350	2352
20	Eichenberg **865** d.	0513	0513	0633	0733	0833	0933	1033	1133	1233	1333	1349	1433	1533	1633	1633	1733	1833	1833	1933	2033	2133	2237	...	2354	...
43	Hann Münden **865** d.	0534	0534	0653	0753	0853	0953	1053	1153	1253	1353	1409	1453	1553	1653	1653	1753	1853	1853	1953	2053	2153	2258	...	0015	...
67	**Kassel** Hbf **865** ⊡ a.	0554	0554	0713	0813	0913	1013	1113	1213	1313	1413	1430	1513	1613	1713	1713	1813	1913	1913	2013	2113	2213	2319	...	0036	...

	Ⓐn	⑥k	Ⓐn	Ⓐn	†	⑥k	⚒	†	⚒	⚒						Ⓑn	Ⓒk	Ⓐn		Ⓒk	Ⓐn	Ⓑn	⚒		Ⓐn	Ⓒk
Kassel Hbf **865** ⊡ d.	0425	0545	0545	0625	0645	0645	0745	0845	0845	0945	1045	1145	1245	1345	1445	1545	1645	1645	1745	1845	1845	1945	2045	2145	2245	2347
Hann Münden **865** d.	0446	0605	0605	0645	0705	0705	0805	0905	0905	1005	1105	1205	1305	1405	1505	1605	1705	1705	1805	1905	1905	2005	2105	2205	2305	0006
Eichenberg **865** a.	0505	0626	0626	0706	0726	0726	0826	0926	0926	1026	1126	1226	1326	1426	1526	1626	1726	1726	1826	1926	1926	2026	2126	2226	2326	0026
Eichenberg **908** d.	0508	0627	0632	0707	0727	0732	0832	0927	0932	1032	1127	1232	1327	1432	1527	1632	1727	1732	1832	1927	1932	2032	2132	2227	2327	0027
Göttingen 908 a.	0522	0640	0645	0721	0740	0745	0845	0940	0945	1045	1140	1245	1340	1445	1540	1645	1740	1745	1845	1940	1945	2045	2145	2240	2340	0040

k – Also Dec. 24, 31. **n** – Not Dec. 24, 31. ⊡ – See Tables **804**, **806** and **901** for connecting trains to / from Kassel Wilhelmshöhe.

DB (*RE* / *RB* services); EIB ◇ — ERFURT and HALLE - LEINEFELDE - KASSEL and GÖTTINGEN — 865

km		⚒	◇ Ⓐ	⚒		◇ Ⓐ	v			◇		G		◇	◇	A		◇	◇	A		◇	◇	A
0	**Erfurt** Hbf **849 850** d.	...	...	...	0429y	...	...	...	0557	...	...	0711	...	...	0811	0911	...	...	1011	1111	...	...	1211	1311
27	Gotha **849 850** d.	...	...	...	0504	0539	...	...	0621	0636	...	0737	...	0839	|	0937	...	1039	|	1137	...	1239	|	1337
48	Bad Langensalza d.	...	0452	...	0515	0602	...	...	—	0654	...	0749	...	0856	0902	0949	...	1056	1102	1149	...	1256	1302	1349
67	Mühlhausen (Thür) d.	...	0509	...	0529	0617	...	...	...	0714	...	0802	...	—	0918	1002	...	—	1118	1202	...	—	1318	1402
	Halle (Saale) Hbf ◧ d.	...	|	...	|	|	0421	...	...	|	0521	|	0650	...	|	|	0850	...	|	|	1050	...	|	|
	Lutherstadt Eisleben ◧ d.	...	|	...	|	|	0504	...	...	|	0604	|	0727	...	|	|	0927	...	|	|	1127	...	|	|
	Sangerhausen ◧ d.	...	|	0413a	|	|	0527	...	...	|	0628	|	0746	...	|	|	0946	...	|	|	1146	...	|	|
	Nordhausen ◧ a.	...	|	0452a	|	|	0606	...	...	|	0709	|	0820	...	|	|	1020	...	|	|	1220	...	|	|
	Nordhausen d.	...	|	0459	|	|	...	0621	0649	|	...	|	0821	0851	|	|	1021	1051	|	|	1221	1251	|	|
94	**Leinefelde** a.	...	0535	0542	0547	0641	...	0655	0733	0741	...	0818	0855	0937	0941	1018	1055	1137	1141	1218	1255	1337	1341	1418
94	**Leinefelde** d.	0421	0536	0554	0548	...	...	0656	...	0742	...	0820	0856	...	0942	1020	1056	...	1142	1220	1256	...	1342	1420
110	Heilbad Heiligenstadt d.	0436	0551	0608	0559	...	...	0706	...	0758	...	0831	0906	...	0958	1031	1106	...	1158	1231	1306	...	1358	1431
	Göttingen a.	|	|	|	0625	...	...	|	...	|	...	0852	|	...	|	1052	|	...	|	1252	|	...	|	1452
125	Eichenberg **864** d.	0450	0605	0622	...	...	...	0718	...	0812	...	...	0918	...	1012	...	1118	...	1212	...	1318	...	1412	...
148	Hann Münden **864** a.	*0533*	0626	*0652*	...	...	...	0736	...	0831	...	...	0936	...	1031q	...	1136	...	1231a	...	1336	...	1431b	...
172	**Kassel** Hbf **864** a.	*0554*	0649	*0713*	...	...	...	0753c	...	|	...	...	0953c	...	|	...	1153c	...	|	...	1353c	...	|	...
176	**Kassel** Wilhelmshöhe **864** a.	...	...	...	...	...	...	0754a	...	0850	...	...	0954a	...	1050q	...	1154a	...	1250a	...	1355a	...	1450b	...

		◇	◇	A		◇	◇	A	n			◇ n	◇ n	A	n		◇ n	◇ n	Ⓐn	nA	j		◇ n	◇ n
Erfurt Hbf **849 850** d.	...	...	1411	1511	...	...	1611	1711	...	...	...	...	1811	1911	...	...	...	2011	...	2111	...	...	...	2215
Gotha **849 850** d.	...	1439	|	1537	...	1639	|	1737	...	...	...	1839	|	1937	...	...	2039	|	...	2137	...	...	2239	|
Bad Langensalza d.	...	1456	1502	1549	...	1656	1702	1749	...	...	...	1856	1902	1949	...	...	2056	2102	...	2150	...	...	2256	2312
Mühlhausen (Thür) d.	...	—	1518	1602	...	—	1718	1802	...	...	...	—	1918	2002	...	...	...	2118	...	2205	...	...	...	2330
Halle (Saale) Hbf ◧ d.	1250	...	|	|	1450	...	|	|	1608	...	1650	...	|	|	1850	1921	...	|	...	|	2101	2221	...	|
Lutherstadt Eisleben ◧ d.	1327	...	|	|	1527	...	|	|	1643	...	1727	...	|	|	1927	2004	...	|	...	|	2140	2304	...	|
Sangerhausen ◧ d.	1346	...	|	|	1546	...	|	|	1705	...	1746	...	|	|	1946	2027	...	|	...	|	2201	2327	...	|
Nordhausen ◧ a.	1420	...	|	|	1620	...	|	|	1739	...	1820	...	|	|	2020	2106	...	|	...	|	2235	0006	...	|
Nordhausen d.	1421	1451	|	|	1621	1651	|	|	...	1751	1821	1851	|	|	2021	2110n	...	|	...	|	2237	...	...	|
Leinefelde a.	1455	1537	1541	1618	1655	1737	1741	1819	...	1836	1855	1937	1941	2018	2055	2153n	...	2141	...	2222	2321	...	...	2347
Leinefelde d.	1455	...	1542	1620	1656	...	1742	1820	...	1837	1856	...	1942	2020	2056	...	...	2159k	...	...	...	...	...	...
Heilbad Heiligenstadt d.	1505	...	1558	1631	1706	...	1758	1831	...	1851	1906	...	1958	2031	2106	...	...	2214k	...	...	...	...	...	...
Göttingen a.	|	...	|	1652	|	...	|	1852	...	...	|	...	|	2052	|	...	...	|	...	...	...	...	...	...
Eichenberg **864** d.	1518	...	1612	...	1718	...	1812	...	...	...	1918	...	2012	...	2118	...	...	2228k	2237	...	...	...	...	...
Hann Münden **864** a.	1536	...	1631a	...	1736	...	1831	...	...	...	1936	...	2031g	...	2136	...	...	...	2257	...	...	...	...	...
Kassel Hbf **864** a.	1553c	...	|	...	1753c	...	|	...	...	...	1953d	...	|	...	2153	...	...	...	2319	...	...	...	...	...
Kassel Wilhelmshöhe **864** a.	1554a	...	1650a	...	1754a	...	1850	...	...	...	1954e	...	2050g	...	...	...	...	...	...	...	...	...	...	...

km		⚒	x	v	v	Ⓐ		◇	◇	ⒶG	Ⓐ	Ⓒ	◇ Ⓐ	A	◇			A	◇			A	◇	
0	**Kassel** Wilhelmshöhe **864** d.	...	...	...	...	...	...	...	...	...	...	...	...	...	...	...	0804a	...	0909	...	1004a	...	1109q	...
	Kassel Hbf **864** d.	...	...	...	...	...	...	...	...	...	0602	0605	...	...	0657a	...	0805c	...	|	...	1005c	...	|	...
23	Hann Münden **864** d.	...	...	...	...	...	...	...	...	...	0618	0621	...	...	0718a	...	0821	...	0927	...	1021	...	1127q	...
46	Eichenberg **864** d.	...	...	...	0510r	0532	...	...	...	...	0636	0640	...	...	0741a	...	0840	...	0949	...	1040	...	1149	...
	Göttingen d.	...	...	...	|	|	...	...	...	0603	|	|	...	0707	|	...	|	0907	|	...	|	1107	|	...
61	Heilbad Heiligenstadt d.	*0411*a	...	0451e	0524r	0546	...	...	...	0631	0649	0652	...	0730	0757a	...	0852	0930	1003	...	1052	1130	1203	...
77	**Leinefelde** a.	*0427*a	...	0502e	0539r	0600	...	...	...	0641	0659	0702	...	0742	0812a	...	0902	0942	1018	...	1102	1142	1218	...
77	**Leinefelde** d.	0432	...	0503	0539	0601	...	0608a	...	0642	0703	0703	0708	0743	0821	0823	0903	0943	1021	1023	1103	1143	1221	1223
119	**Nordhausen** a.	0514	...	|	0620	0642	...	|	...	|	0736	0736	|	|	|	0907	0936	|	|	1107	1136	|	|	1307
119	**Nordhausen** ◧ d.	0516	0516	|	0622	...	0646	|	...	|	0737	0737	|	|	|	—	0937	|	|	—	1137	|	|	—
157	Sangerhausen ◧ d.	0557	0557	|	0655	...	0726	|	...	|	0811	0811	|	|	|	...	1011	|	|	...	1211	|	|	...
179	Lutherstadt Eisleben ◧ d.	0616	0616	|	0713	...	0748	|	...	|	0830	0830	|	|	|	...	1030	|	|	...	1230	|	|	...
217	**Halle** (Saale) Hbf ◧ d.	0655	0655	|	0753	...	0834	|	...	|	0909	0909	|	|	|	◇	1109	|	|	◇	1309	|	|	◇
—	Mühlhausen (Thür) d.	...	...	0525	...	...	...	0636	...	0659	...	...	0731	0800	0844		...	1000	1044		...	1200	1244	
0	Bad Langensalza a.	...	...	0536	...	...	...	0652	0658	0708	...	...	0747	0810	0859	0902	...	1010	1059	1102	...	1210	1259	1302
	Gotha **849 850** a.	...	...	0551	...	...	...	|	0716	0720	...	...	0810	0822	|	0920	...	1022	|	1120	...	1222	|	1320
38	**Erfurt** Hbf **849 850** a.	...	...	0617	...	...	...	0747	...	0745	...	...	...	0847	0958	...	...	1047	1158	...	...	1247	1358	...

		A	◇	Ⓒz	Ⓐt	Ⓐw		A	◇			A	◇			G	◇		n	n	◇ n	n	◇ n	n
Kassel Wilhelmshöhe **864** d.	1204a	...	1309a	...	...	...	1404a	...	1509b	...	1604a	...	1709a	...	1804a	...	1909	...	2004e	...	...	...	2109g	...
Kassel Hbf **864** d.	1205c	...	|	...	1318	...	1405c	...	|	...	1605c	...	|	...	1805c	...	|	...	2005c	...	...	...	|	...
Hann Münden **864** d.	1221	...	1327a	...	1340	...	1421	...	1527b	...	1621	...	1727a	...	1821	...	1927	...	2021	...	...	...	2127g	...
Eichenberg **864** d.	1240	...	1349	...	1402	1412	1440	...	1549	...	1640	...	1749	...	1840	...	1949	...	2040	...	...	...	2149	...
Göttingen d.	|	1307	|	...	...	|	|	1507	|	...	|	1707	|	...	|	1907	|	...	|	...	...	2107	|	...
Heilbad Heiligenstadt d.	1252	1330	1403	...	...	1426	1452	1530	1603	...	1652	1730	1803	...	1852	1930	2003	...	2052	...	...	2131	2203	...
Leinefelde a.	1302	1342	1418	...	...	1440	1502	1542	1618	...	1702	1742	1818	...	1902	1942	2018	...	2102	...	...	2142	2217	...
Leinefelde d.	1303	1343	1421	1423	...	1441	1503	1543	1621	1623	1703	1743	1821	1823	1903	1943	2021	2028	2103	...	2108	2143	2227	2230
Nordhausen a.	1336	|	|	1507	...	1525	1536	|	|	1707	1736	|	|	1907	1936	|	|	2110	2136	...	|	|	|	2311
Nordhausen ◧ d.	1337	|	|	—	...	...	1537	|	|	—	1737	|	|	—	1937n	|	|	—	...	2144	|	|	|	...
Sangerhausen ◧ d.	1411	|	|	...	...	...	1611	|	|	...	1811	|	|	...	2011n	|	|	...	...	2226	|	|	|	...
Lutherstadt Eisleben ◧ d.	1430	|	|	...	...	...	1630	|	|	...	1830	|	|	...	2030n	|	|	...	...	2248	|	|	|	...
Halle (Saale) Hbf ◧ d.	1509	|	|	◇	...	...	1709	|	|	◇	1909	|	|	◇	2110n	|	|	◇	...	2334	|	|	|	...
Mühlhausen (Thür) d.	...	1400	1444		...	...	...	1600	1644		...	1800	1844	n	...	2000	2044	n	...	...	2134	2200	2250	...
Bad Langensalza a.	...	1410	1459	1502	...	...	...	1610	1659	1702	...	1810	1859	1902	...	2010	2059	2102	...	...	2149	2210	2305	...
Gotha **849 850** a.	...	1422	|	1520	...	...	...	1622	|	1720	...	1822	|	1920	...	2022	|	2120	...	...	|	2222	2333	...
Erfurt Hbf **849 850** a.	...	1447	1558	...	...	...	...	1647	1758	...	...	1847	1958	...	...	2047	2154	...	...	...	2244	2250	2359	...

A – From / to Chemnitz and Zwickau (Table **858**).
G – From / to Gera (Table **858**).

a – Ⓐ only.
b – Ⓑ only.
c – Ⓒ only.
d – Ⓒ (also Dec. 24, 31).
e – Ⓐ (not Dec. 24, 31).
g – ⑤⑥† only.

j – Not Dec. 24, 25, 31.
k – Not Dec. 24, 25, 26, 31, Jan. 1.
n – Not Dec. 24, 31.
q – † only.
r – ⚒ only.
t – Not Dec. 24, 31, May 22.
v – Not Dec. 25, Jan. 1.
w – Not Dec. 24 - Jan. 4, Feb. 4 – 8, Mar. 25 – 28, May 13 – 16.
x – Not Dec. 25, 26, Jan. 1.

y – 0438 on Ⓒ (also Dec. 24, 27, 28, 31, May 2).
z – Ⓒ (daily Dec. 22 - Jan. 6, Feb. 2 – 10, Mar. 21 – 30, May 10 – 18).

◇ – Operated by Erfurter Industriebahn GmbH (2nd class only).
◧ – See panel below for additional services Halle - Nordhausen and v.v.

Halle (Saale) Hbf d.	0721	and every	1721
Lutherstadt Eisleben d.	0804	**two** hours	1804
Sangerhausen d.	0827	until	1827
Nordhausen d.	0906		1906

Nordhausen d.	0844	and every	2044
Sangerhausen d.	0926	**two** hours	2126
Lutherstadt Eisleben d.	0948	until	2148
Halle (Saale) Hbf a.	1034		2234

867 HARZER SCHMALSPURBAHNEN

2nd class only

Nordhausen - Wernigerode: *Die Harzquerbahn*; Eisfelder Talmühle - Stiege - Alexisbad - Quedlinburg: *Die Selketalbahn*; Drei Annen Hohne - Brocken: *Die Brockenbahn*

Winter service: November 5, 2007 - April 25, 2008

km		v	🚂🍷	C🚂	🚂	🚂🍷	r🚂	r🚂	r🚂	L🚂	n	
0	**Wernigerode** § d.	0710	0910	1025	1140	...	1240	1440	...	1540	1610	...
15	Drei Annen Hohne a.	0747	0947	1102	1217	...	1327	1517	...	1634	1647	...
15	Drei Annen Hohne d.	0802	1000	1115	1232	1230	1345	1532	1545	1645	1702	...
20	Schierke d.	|	1019	1134	|	1249	1405	|	1604	1716	|	...
34	**Brocken** a.	|	1049	1204	|	1319	1435	|	1634	1746	|	...
19	Elend d.	0814	▬	▬	1244	▬	▬	1544	...	...	1714	...
28	Sorge d.	0833	...	...	1303	...	...	1603	...	...	1733	...
31	Benneckenstein d.	0842	...	🚌	1312	...	...	1612	...	...	1742	...
44	Eisfelder Talmühle a.	0911	Ⓒv	Ⓐ	1341	...	🚌	1641	...	...	1811	...
44	Eisfelder Talmühle d.	...	0923	*0923*	...	1357		1655	...	...	...	1829
50	Ilfeld d.	...	0941	0941	...	1412	1441	1711	...	...	...	1844
61	**Nordhausen** Nord § a.	...	1010	1010*	...	1440e	1510*	1740	...	...	...	1910

	v	🚂🍷	🚂🍷	C🚂	🚂🍷		r🚂	J🚂	K🚂	L🚂	n
Nordhausen Nord § d.	*0829*	...	1014	...	...	1314	...	...	...	...	*1744**
Ilfeld d.	*0858*	...	1039	...	...	1339	...	...	...	...	*1809*
Eisfelder Talmühle a.	*0912*	...	1053	...	...	1353	...	...	...	...	*1823*
Eisfelder Talmühle d.	0931	...	1101	...	...	▬	1401	...	...	...	1831
Benneckenstein d.	1001	...	1131	...	...	...	1431	...	...	...	1901
Sorge d.	1009	...	1139	...	...	🚂	1439	...	...	...	1909
Elend d.	1028	...	1158	...	...	r	1458	...	...	...	1928
Brocken d.	|	1101	|	1216	1333	1445	|	1644	1716	1756	|
Schierke d.	|	1138	|	1253	1408	1516	|	1715	1747	1827	|
Drei Annen Hohne a.	1039	1149	1209	1304	1419	1527	1509	1726	1758	1838	1939
Drei Annen Hohne d.	1108	...	1238	1338	1438	...	1538	1738	1808	1845	1940
Wernigerode § a.	1148	...	1318	1418	1518	...	1618	1818	1848	1922	2018

km		v	v	🚂			n	r🚂	n	n	n	n
0	**Quedlinburg** § △ d.	0830	...	1030v	1130v	...	...	*1430*	1630	...	1730	2030
8	**Gernrode** △ d.	0847	...	1047	1147	...	...	1447	1647	...	1747	2045
18	Mägdesprung d.	0920	...	1120	1221	...	...	1520	1720	...	1821	▬
	Harzgerode d.	|	0928	|	|	1328	1528	|	|	1828	|	...
23	Alexisbad a.	0935	0938	1135	1238	1338	1538	1535	1735	1838	1836	n🚂
23	Alexisbad d.	▬	0942	*1142*	*1242*	1342	▬	1542	1742	...	1842	1842
26	**Harzgerode** a.	...	|	*1151*	*1251*	|	...	|	1751	...	|	1851
26	Silberhütte d.	...	0954	...	...	1354	...	1554	▬	...	1854	...
30	Straßberg (Harz) d.	...	1007	...	...	1407	...	1607	...	...	1907	...
35	Güntersberge d.	...	1016	...	...	1416	...	1616	...	...	1916	...
	Hasselfelde d.	1001	|	...	...	|	1500	|	1746	...	|	...
44	Stiege a.	1021	1031	...	...	1431	1520	1631	1806	...	1931	...
44	Stiege d.	...	1032	...	...	1432	1531	1632	1807	...	1932	...
48	**Hasselfelde** a.	...	|	...	...	1451	|	1651	|	...	|	...
53	Eisfelder Talmühle d.	...	1056	...	...	...	1553	...	1829	...	1956	...
59	Ilfeld d.	...	1111	...	...	...	1611	...	1844	...	2012	...
70	**Nordhausen** Nord § a.	...	1140	...	...	...	1640	...	1910	...	2040	...

	v	v			🚂	r		n	n🚂	n	n🚂
Nordhausen Nord § d.	0629	...	0829	...	...	...	1114	1614	...	...	...
Ilfeld d.	0658	...	0858	...	...	...	1139	1639	...	...	...
Eisfelder Talmühle d.	0715	...	0916	...	...	...	1200	1700	...	...	...
Hasselfelde d.	|	0800	|	1001	...	...	|	|	1701	...	...
Stiege a.	0736	0820	0937	1021	...	...	1220	1720	1721	...	...
Stiege d.	0737	0821	0938	1037	...	...	1235	1723	1737	...	...
Hasselfelde a.	0756	|	0957	|	...	...	|	1742	|	...	...
Güntersberge d.	▬	0836	▬	1053	...	...	1253	▬	1753	...	...
Straßberg (Harz) d.	...	0846	...	1103	...	...	1302	...	1802	...	...
Silberhütte d.	...	0858	...	1115	...	...	1315	n	1815	...	...
Harzgerode d.	...	|	...	|	...	*1228*	|	1528	|	1828	1928
Alexisbad a.	...	0910	v	1127	...	*1238*	1327	1538	1827	1838	1938
Alexisbad d.	...	0914	0956	1142	1156	1256	1342	1556	1842	1856	1956
Harzgerode a.	...	0924	|	1151	|	|	1351	|	1851	|	|
Mägdesprung d.	v	...	1011	...	1222	1311	...	1611	...	1911	2011
Gernrode △ d.	0759	...	1059f	...	1259	1359f	...	1659f	...	1959f	2043
Quedlinburg § △ a.	0815	...	1115	...	1315r	1415	...	1715	...	2015	...

C – ⑥⑦ (daily Dec. 22 - Feb. 24 and from Mar. 8).
J – Nov. 6 - Jan. 25 and from Mar. 8 (not Dec. 24).
K – Jan. 26 - Mar. 7.
L – From Mar. 8.
e – Ⓒ (also during school holidays).
f – Arrives 16 minutes earlier.
n – Not Dec. 24, 31.

r – Not Dec. 24.
v – Not Jan. 1.
🚂 – Steam train.
🚌 – Nordhausen Stadtbahn.
* – Nordhausen **Bahnhofsplatz**.
§ – Adjacent to DB station.

△ – Additional services Quedlinburg - Gernrode and v.v.
From Quedlinburg at 1330 🚂 r. **From Gernrode** at 0959 🚂 v and 1559 n.

☛ Additional 🚌 services run Nordhausen - Ilfeld and v.v.

Operator: Harzer Schmalspurbahnen GmbH, Friedrichstrasse 151, 38855 Wernigerode.
✆ + 49 (0) 3943 558 151. Fax + 49 (0) 3943 558 148.

868 ERFURT - NORDHAUSEN

RE / RB services

km		Ⓐn	⚒n																n
0	**Erfurt** Hbf d.	...	0445	0604	0703	0806	0903	1006	1103	1206	1303	1406	1503	1606	1703	1806	1903	2006	2126
27	Straußfurt d.	...	0514	0628	0730	0828	0930	1028	1130	1228	1330	1428	1530	1628	1730	1828	1930	2028	2156
60	Sondershausen d.	0444	0552	0658	0810	0858	1010	1058	1210	1258	1410	1458	1610	1658	1810	1858	2010	2058	2229
80	**Nordhausen** a.	0508	0614	0719	0833	0919	1033	1119	1233	1319	1433	1519	1633	1719	1833	1919	2033	2119	2253

	Ⓐn	⚒n																n
Nordhausen d.	0414	0525	0633	0728	0834	0928	1034	1128	1234	1328	1434	1528	1634	1728	1834	1928	...	2125
Sondershausen d.	0441	0553	0659	0753	0859	0953	1059	1153	1259	1353	1459	1553	1659	1753	1859	1953	...	2145
Straußfurt d.	0514	0627	0731	0829	0931	1029	1131	1229	1331	1429	1531	1629	1731	1829	1931	2029	...	2214
Erfurt Hbf a.	0540	0653	0752	0854	0952	1054	1152	1254	1352	1454	1552	1654	1752	1854	1952	2054	...	2236

n – Not Dec. 24, 31.

869 NORDHAUSEN - GÖTTINGEN

RB services

km		⚒	v												r	n	n	Ⓑn
0	**Nordhausen** d.	0538	0638	0738	0838	0938	1038	1138	1238	1338	1438	1538	1638	1738	1838	1938	2038	2142
20	Walkenried d.	0603	0703	0803	0903	1003	1103	1203	1303	1403	1503	1603	1703	1803	1903	2003	2103	2203
23	Bad Sachsa d.	0608	0708	0808	0908	1008	1108	1208	1308	1408	1508	1608	1708	1808	1908	2008	2108	2208
37	Bad Lauterberg ⊡ d.	0619	0719	0819	0919	1019	1119	1219	1319	1419	1519	1619	1719	1819	1919	2019	2119	2219
43	Herzberg (Harz) d.	0626	0726	0826	0926	1026	1126	1226	1329	1426	1526	1626	1726	1826	1926	2026	2126	2226
70	Northeim (Han) **904** a.	0650	0750	0850	0950	1050	1150	1250	1353	1450	1550	1650	1750	1850	1950	2050	2150	2250
90	**Göttingen 904** a.	0715	0808	0915	1008	1115	1208	1315	1411	1515	1608	1715	1808	1920	2008	2120j	2208	2308

	⚒n	⚒	v												r	n	n	Ⓒ
Göttingen 904 d.	*0407*	0538	0638	0749	0838	0949	1038	1149	1238	1349	1438	1549	1638	1749	1838	1949	2038k	2149
Northeim (Han) **904** d.	0506	0606	0706	0806	0906	1006	1106	1206	1306	1406	1506	1606	1706	1806	1906	2006	2106	2206
Herzberg (Harz) d.	0530	0630	0730	0830	0930	1030	1130	1230	1330	1430	1530	1630	1730	1830	1930	2030	2130	2230
Bad Lauterberg ⊡ d.	0536	0636	0736	0836	0936	1036	1136	1236	1336	1436	1536	1636	1736	1836	1936	2036	2136	2236
Bad Sachsa d.	0547	0647	0747	0847	0947	1047	1147	1247	1347	1447	1547	1647	1747	1847	1947	2047	2147	2247
Walkenried d.	0552	0652	0752	0852	0952	1052	1152	1252	1352	1452	1552	1652	1752	1852	1952	2052	2205	2252
Nordhausen a.	0615	0715	0815	0915	1015	1115	1215	1315	1415	1515	1615	1715	1815	1915	2015	2115	2227	2315

j – 2108 on ①②③④⑥ (also Dec. 23, 30, Mar. 21, 23, May 2, 11; not Dec. 26, Jan. 1, Mar. 20, 24, Apr. 30, May 12).
k – 2049 on ①②③④⑥ (also Dec. 23, 30, Mar. 21, 23, May 2, 11; not Dec. 26, Jan. 1, Mar. 20, 24, Apr. 30, May 12).
n – Not Dec. 24, 31.
r – Not Dec. 24.
v – Not Dec. 25, Jan. 1.

⊡ – Bad Lauterberg im Harz Barbis

870 ERFURT - MEININGEN - SCHWEINFURT - WÜRZBURG

DB (*RE* services); *STB*; *EIB*

km					Ⓐ ▽			▽		▽		▽		▽		▽		▽		▽		Ⓒ	n ▽	n	n ▽
0	**Erfurt** Hbf **872** d.	...	...	...	0410	...	0539	0643	0739	0843	0939	1043	1139	1243	1339	1443	1539	1643	1739	1843	1939	1939	2043	2220	2343
23	Arnstadt Hbf **872** d.	...	...	...	0433	...	0558	0706	0800	0906	1000	1106	1200	1306	1400	1506	1600	1706	1800	1906	2000	2000	2106	2239	0006
31	Plaue (Thür) d.	...	...	...	0442	...	0604	0717	0806	0917	1006	1117	1206	1317	1406	1517	1606	1717	1806	1917	2006	2006	2117	2246	0017
37	Gräfenroda d.	...	...	...	0447	...	0611	0722	0811	0922	1011	1122	1211	1322	1411	1522	1611	1722	1811	1922	2011	2011	2122	2251	0022
53	Oberhof (Thür) d.	...	...	...	0502	...	0624	0738	0824	0938	1024	1138	1224	1338	1424	1538	1624	1738	1824	1938	2024	2024	2138	2303	0038
58	Zella-Mehlis d.	...	...	...	0508	...	0631	0744	0831	0944	1031	1144	1231	1344	1431	1544	1631	1744	1831	1944	2031	2031	2144	2309	0044
64	Suhl d.	...	...	...	0517	...	0639	0751	0839	0951	1039	1151	1239	1351	1439	1551	1639	1751	1839	1951	2039	2039	2151	2318	0051
84	Grimmenthal **873** a.	...	...	...	0539	...	0656	0810	0855	1010	1055	1210	1255	1410	1455	1610	1655	1810	1855	2010	2055	2055	2210	2333	0110
92	**Meiningen 873** a.	...	...	...	0547	...	*0711*	0819	*0911*	1019	*1111*	1219	*1312*	1419	*1511*	1619	*1711*	1819	*1911*	2019	2103	2103	2219	2340	0119
		Ⓐ	Ⓐe ◇	Ⓒz ◇		Ⓐe ◇	|	▬ ◇	|	▬ ◇	|	▬ ◇	|	▬ ◇	|	▬ ◇	|	▬ ◇	|	▬ ◇	Ⓐ ◇	|			...
	Meiningen 873 d.	0430	0530	0540j	...	0608	*0647*	0741	*0847*	0944	*1047*	1144	*1247*	1341	*1447*	1544	*1647*	1744	*1847*	1944	2107	2109	...	...	...
84	Grimmenthal **873** d.	|	|	|	...	|	0700	|	0900	|	1100	|	1300	|	1500	|	1700	|	1900	|	|	|	...	...	...
99	Rentwertshausen d.	0448	0549	0557	...	0623	0708	0801	0908	1001	1108	1201	1308	1401	1508	1601	1708	1801	1908	2001	2123	2125	...	...	...
110	Mellrichstadt d.	0456	0556	0604	...	0632	0716	0809	0916	1009	1116	1209	1316	1409	1516	1609	1716	1809	1916	2009	2130	2133	...	...	...
124	Bad Neustadt (Saale) d.	0504	0605	0613	...	0641	0724	0818	0924	1018	1124	1218	1324	1418	1524	1618	1724	1818	1924	2018	2140	2140	...	...	...
134	Münnerstadt d.	0512	0615	0624	...	0649	0731	0827	0931	1027	1131	1227	1331	1427	1531	1627	1731	1827	1931	2027	2149	2149	...	...	...
149	Ebenhausen (Unterfr) d.	0527	0633	0639	...	0701	0743	0841	0943	1041	1143	1241	1343	1441	1543	1641	1743	1841	1943	2041	2201	2201	...	...	...
163	**Schweinfurt** Hbf **876** a.	0538	0643	0649	...	0716	0753	0852	0953	1052	1153	1252	1354	1452	1553	1652	1753	1852	1953	2052	2212	2212	...	...	...
206	**Würzburg** Hbf **876** a.	*0618*e	*0719*	...	...	*0801*	0825	*0923*	1025	*1123*	1225	*1323*	1425	*1523*	1625	*1723*	1824	*1923*	2025	*2151*g	*2253*	*2254*	...	...	...

e – Not Dec. 24, 31, May 22.
g – *2123* on Ⓒ (also Dec. 24, 31, May 22).
j – 0530 on Dec. 24, 31, May 22.
n – Not Dec. 24, 31.
z – Also Dec. 24, 31, May 22.
▽ – Operated by Süd Thüringen Bahn (STB; 2nd class only).
◇ – Operated by Erfurter Industriebahn (EIB; 2nd class only).

DB (*RE* services); *STB*; *EIB* — WÜRZBURG - SCHWEINFURT - MEININGEN - ERFURT — 870

			Ⓐ ◇	Ⓐe	©z	Ⓐe ◇	©z ◇		◇		◇		Ⓐe ◇	©z ◇		◇		◇		◇		Ⓐe ◇	⚒r ◇	†w ◇
Würzburg Hbf **876** ● d.	...	...	...	0507	0504k	0602	0602	0725g	0836	0933	1036	1133	1209	1236	1333	1436	1533	1636	1733	1836	1933	2036	2139f	2144
Schweinfurt Hbf **876** ● d.	...	...	...	0550	0558	0649	0705	0805	0906	1005	1106	1205	1253	1306	1405	1506	1605	1706	1805	1906	2005	2106	2224	2233
Ebenhausen (Unterf) ● d.	...	...	...	0603	0611	0703	0720	0817	0920	1017	1120	1217	1304	1320	1417	1520	1617	1720	1817	1920	2017	2120	2238	2248
Münnerstadt d.	...	...	...	0614	0622	0714	0731	0826	0931	1026	1131	1226	1315	1331	1426	1531	1626	1731	1826	1931	2026	2131	2249	2301
Bad Neustadt (Saale) d.	...	...	...	0623	0631	0725	0740	0833	0940	1033	1140	1233	1324	1340	1433	1540	1633	1740	1833	1940	2033	2140	2258	2310
Mellrichstadt d.	...	...	...	0631	0639	0734	0749	0841	0949	1041	1149	1241	1333	1349	1441	1549	1641	1749	1841	1949	2041	2149	2307	2319
Rentwertshausen d.	...	...	0548	0641	0648	0742	0801	0850	1001	1050	1201	1250	1342	1401	1450	1601	1650	1801	1850	2001	2050	2158	2315	2328
Grimmenthal **873** a.	...	...	|	0649	0659	|	|	0858	|	1058	|	1258	|	|	1458	|	1658	|	1858	|	2100	|	|	|
Meiningen 873 a.	...	...	0603	0711	0711	0757	0816	0911	1016	1111	1216	1311	1357	1416	1511	1616	1711	1816	1911	2016	2114	2213	2330	2345
	①-⑥	v	Ⓐ ▽			▬			▬ ▽		▬ ▽		▬ ▽			▬ ▽		▬ ▽		n▽		▬ n▽		
Meiningen 873 d.	0342	0510	0611	0647	0647	0736	...	0847	0936	1047	1136	1247	1336	...	1447	1536	1647	1736	1847	1936	2047	2136	...	...
Grimmenthal **873** d.	0348	0516	0628	0700	0702	0744	...	0902	0944	1102	1144	1302	1344	...	1502	1544	1702	1744	1902	1944	2102	2144	...	...
Suhl d.	0404	0532	0652	0722	0722	0807	...	0922	1007	1122	1207	1322	1407	...	1522	1607	1722	1807	1922	2007	2122	2207	...	...
Zella-Mehlis d.	0412	0541	0659	0730	0730	0815	...	0930	1015	1130	1215	1330	1415	...	1530	1615	1730	1815	1930	2015	2130	2215	...	...
Oberhof (Thür) d.	0418	0547	0705	0737	0737	0821	...	0937	1021	1137	1221	1337	1421	...	1537	1621	1737	1821	1937	2021	2137	2221	...	...
Gräfenroda d.	0430	0558	0724	0748	0748	0838	...	0948	1036	1148	1236	1348	1436	...	1548	1636	1748	1836	1948	2036	2148	2236	...	...
Plaue (Thür) d.	0435	0603	0729	0753	0753	0844	...	0953	1045	1153	1245	1353	1445	...	1553	1645	1753	1845	1953	2045	2153	2245	...	...
Arnstadt Hbf **872** d.	0443	0611	0737	0800	0800	0853	...	1000	1053	1200	1253	1400	1453	...	1600	1653	1800	1853	2000	2053	2200	2253	...	...
Erfurt Hbf **872** a.	0503	0629	0759	0816	0816	0914	...	1016	1114	1216	1314	1416	1514	...	1616	1714	1816	1914	2016	2114	2216	2314	...	...

e – Not Dec. 24, 31, May 22.
f – *2144* on ⑥ (also Dec. 24, 31).
g – 0733 on © (also Dec. 24, 31, May 22).
k – ⑥ (also Dec. 24, 31).
r – Not May 22.
v – Not Dec. 25, Jan. 1.
w – Also May 22.
z – Also Dec. 24, 31, May 22.
▽ – Operated by Süd Thüringen Bahn (STB; 2nd class only).
◇ – Operated by Erfurter Industriebahn (EIB; 2nd class only).
● – Trains between Würzburg, Schweinfurt and Ebenhausen are often combined with a service to Bad Kissingen. Passengers should take care to join the correct portion for their destination.

RE / *RB* services — LEIPZIG - GERA - HOF and SAALFELD — 871

km																											
		Ⓐe	⚒n	v				⑥H		R					R					R					n	n	n
0	**Leipzig** Hbf d.	...	...	...	0455e	0627	0711	0827	0827	...	0911	1027	1111	1227	...	1311	1427	1511	1627	...	1711	1827	1911	2027	...	2118	2306
45	Zeitz d.	...	0445e	...	0545e	0704	0804	0904	0904	...	1004	1104	1204	1304	...	1404	1504	1604	1704	...	1804	1904	2004	2104	...	2204	2357
72	**Gera** Hbf a.	...	0515e	...	0617e	0726	0830	0926	0926	...	1030	1126	1230	1326	...	1430	1526	1630	1726	...	1830	1926	2030	2126	...	2230	0024
72	**Gera** Hbf d.	0434	0517	0609	0630	0745	0840	0936	0945	1009	1041	1145	1241	1347	1409	1440	1544	1641	1749	1809	1840	1945	2042	...	2132	2253	...
84	Weida d.	0500	0531	0622	0644	0758	0853	0947	1003	1021	1054	1203	1254	1403	1421	1455	1602	1654	1802	1821	1855	2003	2055	...	2146	2307	...
	Hof Hbf a.	|	|	0746	|	|	|	|	|	1139	|	|	|	|	1539	|	|	|	|	1939	|	|	|	...	...	|	...
99	Triptis d.	0512	0546	...	0657	0814	0911	|	1016	...	1110	1216	1310	1416	...	1510	1616	1710	1816	...	1910	2016	2109	...	...	2320	...
108	Neustadt (Orla) d.	0520	0555	...	0704	0822	0917	|	1024	...	1117	1224	1317	1424	...	1517	1624	1717	1824	...	1917	2024	2116	...	...	2328	...
139	**Saalfeld** (Saale) a.	0552	0628	...	0731	0854	0940	1035	1054	...	1140	1254	1340	1454	...	1540	1654	1740	1854	...	1940	2054	2140	...	...	2357	...

km																											
		⚒n	Ⓐe	⚒n					R						R					R		⑥L				n	n
	Saalfeld (Saale) d.	...	...	0506	...	0618	0721	0819	...	0904	1019	1104	1219	...	1304	1419	1504	1619	...	1704	1729	1819	1904	2019	...	2141	2229
	Neustadt (Orla) d.	...	...	0537	...	0649	0752	0850	...	0940	1049	1140	1249	...	1340	1449	1540	1649	...	1740	|	1849	1940	2049	...	2208	2258
	Triptis d.	...	...	0546	...	0659	0801	0858	...	0949	1057	1149	1257	...	1349	1457	1549	1657	...	1749	|	1857	1949	2056	...	2216	2307
0	**Hof** Hbf d.	...	...	...	...	|	|	|	0822	|	|	|	|	1221	|	|	|	|	1621	|	|	|	|	|	2034	|	|
72	Weida d.	...	0451	0558	...	0712	0816	0911	0930	1002	1110	1202	1310	1335	1402	1510	1602	1709	1737	1802	1821	1910	2002	2110	2147	2228	2322
84	**Gera** Hbf a.	...	0506	0611	...	0724	0828	0924	0940	1015	1123	1215	1323	1346	1415	1523	1615	1722	1747	1815	1829	1923	2015	2123	2159	2240	2335
	Gera Hbf ◐ d.	0452	0532	...	0630	...	0830	...	...	1030	...	1230	...	...	1430	...	1630	...	...	1830	1830	...	2030	...	...	2242	...
	Zeitz ◐ d.	0524	0601	...	0654	...	0854	...	...	1054	...	1254	...	...	1454	...	1654	...	...	1854	1854	...	2054	...	...	2310	...
	Leipzig Hbf ◐ a.	0614	0646	...	0729	...	0929	...	...	1129	...	1329	...	...	1529	...	1729	...	...	1929	1929	...	2129	...	...	2354	...

H – ⑥ from Apr. 26. To Rottenbach (a. 1055), Obstfelderschmiede (a. 1123) and Katzhütte (a. 1141).
L – ⑥ from Apr. 26. From Katzhütte (d. 1617), Obstfelderschmiede (d. 1635) and Rottenbach (d. 1703).
R – To / from Regensburg (Table **879**).
e – Ⓐ (not Dec. 24, 31).
n – Not Dec. 24, 31.
v – Not Dec. 25, Jan. 1.
◐ – Additional journeys Gera - Zeitz - Leipzig: From Gera Hbf at 0712, 0912 and every **two** hours until 1912.

RE / *RB* services — ERFURT - SAALFELD and ROTTENBACH - KATZHÜTTE — 872

km		⚒n				C			n	n
0	**Erfurt** Hbf **870** d.	0455	0637	0739	0838	then each train runs every **two** hours until	1939	2038	2143	2252
23	Arnstadt Hbf **870** d.	0518	0655	0802	0900		2002	2100	2211	2311
38	Stadtilm d.	0537	0708	0816	0913		2016	2113	2225	2326
54	Rottenbach d.	0554	0721	0835	0925		2035	2125	2244	2339
62	Bad Blankenburg d.	0601	0728	0842	0932		2042	2132	2251	2346
70	**Saalfeld** (Saale) a.	0609	0736	0850	0940		2050	2140	2259	2354

	⚒n								n	n
Saalfeld (Saale) d.	0506	0612	0705	0819	0907	then each train runs every **two** hours until	2019	2107	2228
Bad Blankenburg d.	0513	0619	0712	0826	0914		2026	2114	2235
Rottenbach d.	0521	0626	0723	0833	0927		2033	2127	2242
Stadtilm d.	0536	0639	0737	0846	0941		2046	2141	2255
Arnstadt Hbf **870** a.	0550	0653	0751	0858	0955		2058	2155	2307
Erfurt Hbf **870** a.	0613	0718	0816	0918	1016		2118	2216	2325

km		Ⓐ			A			⑤⑦f	
0	Rottenbach d.	0544	0641	0730	then each train runs every **two** hours until	1841	1930	2041	...
15	Obstfelderschmiede ¶ a.	0610	0705	0754		1905	1954	2105	...
25	Katzhütte a.	0628	0723	0812		1923	2012	2123	...

	Ⓐ				B			⑤⑦f
Katzhütte d.	0538	...	0635	0746	then each train runs every **two** hours until	1835	1946	2035
Obstfelderschmiede ¶ d.	0557	...	0653	0804		1853	2004	2053
Rottenbach a.	0622	...	0717	0828		1917	2029	2117

A – On ⑥ from Apr. 26 the 1041 and 1641 from Rottenbach run 18–19 minutes later.
B – On ⑥ from Apr. 26 the 1035 and 1635 from Katzhütte run 18–19 minutes **earlier**.
C – On ⑥ from Apr. 26 Saalfeld a. 1055 (not 1050).
f – Also Mar. 24, May 12; not Mar. 23, May 11.
n – Not Dec. 24, 31.
¶ – Station for the *Oberweißbacher Bergbahn* to Lichtenhain and Cursdorf.

Süd Thüringen Bahn (2nd class only) — EISENACH - MEININGEN - SONNEBERG — 873

km																									
		Ⓐ	Ⓐ	Ⓐ		v								©	Ⓐ		©	Ⓐ				n	n	n	n
0	**Eisenach** d.	...	0404	0447	...	0609	0715	0815	0915	1015	1115	1215	1315	1415	1415	1515	1615	1615	1715	1815	1915	2015	2115	2221	2310
27	Bad Salzungen d.	...	0431	0515	...	0641	0741	0841	0941	1041	1141	1241	1341	1441	1441	1541	1641	1641	1741	1841	1941	2041	2141	2251	2334
41	Wernshausen d.	...	0446	0530	...	0657	0757	0857	0957	1057	1157	1257	1357	1457	1457	1557	1657	1657	1757	1857	1957	2057	2157	2305	...
61	**Meiningen** a.	...	0504	0547	...	0714	0814	0914	1014	1114	1214	1314	1414	1514	1514	1614	1714	1714	1814	1914	2014	2114	2214	2322	...
61	**Meiningen 870** d.	0423	0549	0620	0620	0720	0820	0920	1020	1120	1220	1320	1420	1520	1520	1620	1720	1720	1820	1920n	2020n	2120	...	...	...
68	Grimmenthal **870** d.	0430	0556	0631	0631	0731	0831	0931	1031	1131	1231	1331	1431	1531	1539k	1631	1731	1739k	1831	1931n	2031n	2131	...	...	...
82	Themar d.	0447	0609	0644	0644	0744	0844	0944	1044	1144	1244	1344	1444	1544	1552	1644	1744	1752	1844	1944n	2044n	2144	...	...	...
94	Hildburghausen d.	0459	0621	0700	0700	0800	0900	1000	1100	1200	1300	1400	1500	1600	1603	1700	1800	1803	1900	2000n	2100n	2156	...	...	...
109	**Eisfeld** d.	0514	0643	0716	0716	0814	0916	1014	1116	1214	1316	1414	1516	1614	1618	1716	1814	1818	1916	2014n	2114n	2211	...	...	...
141	**Sonneberg** (Thür) Hbf a.	0558	0727	0800	0800	...	1000	...	1200	...	1400	...	1600	...	...	1800	...	...	2000	...	...	...	...	...	...

	Ⓐ	Ⓐ	Ⓐ	Ⓐ		Ⓐ											©	Ⓐ		©	Ⓐ			n
Sonneberg (Thür) Hbf d.	...	...	...	...	...	...	...	0600	...	0802	...	1002	...	1202	...	1402	...	...	1602	...	1630	1802	...	2002
Eisfeld d.	...	...	0420	...	...	0540	...	0645	0745	0845	0945	1045	1145	1245	1345	1445	1545	1545	1645	1745	1745r	1845	1945	2045
Hildburghausen d.	...	...	0435	...	...	0555	...	0659	0759	0859	0959	1059	1159	1259	1359	1459	1559	1604	1659	1759	1804	1859	1959	2059
Themar d.	...	...	0446	...	...	0610	...	0711	0811	0911	1011	1111	1211	1311	1411	1511	1611	1616	1711	1811	1816	1911	2011	2111
Grimmenthal **870** d.	...	...	0500	...	...	0628	...	0729	0829	0929	1029	1129	1229	1329	1429	1529	1629	1629	1729	1829	1829	1929	2029	2129
Meiningen 870 a.	...	...	0506	...	...	0635	...	0735	0835	0935	1035	1135	1235	1335	1435	1535	1635	1635	1735	1835	1835	1935	2035	2135
Meiningen d.	...	0428	...	0512	0552	0639	0639	0739	0839	0939	1039	1139	1239	1339	1439	1539	1639	1639	1739	1839	1839	1939n	2039n	2139
Wernshausen d.	...	0447	...	0530	0609	0657	0657	0757	0857	0957	1057	1157	1257	1357	1457	1557	1657	1657	1757	1857	1857	1957n	2057n	2157
Bad Salzungen d.	0414	0500	...	0543	0622	0711	0711	0811	0911	1011	1111	1211	1311	1411	1511	1611	1711	1711	1811	1911	1911	2011n	2111n	2211
Eisenach a.	0442	0525	...	0607	0647	0740	0740	0840	0940	1040	1140	1240	1340	1440	1540	1640	1740	1740	1840	1940	1940	2040n	2140n	2237

k – Arrives 12 minutes earlier.
n – Not Dec. 24, 31.
r – Arrives 1713.
v – Not Dec. 25, 26, Jan. 1.

RE services — LEIPZIG - CHEMNITZ — 874

km		v	①-⑥					n
0	**Leipzig** Hbf d.	0527	0632	0732	and hourly until	2132	...	2338
33	Bad Lausick d.	0551	0651	0751		2151	...	0002
44	Geithain d.	0559	0659	0759		2159	...	0010
66	Burgstädt d.	0613	0713	0813		2213	...	0024
81	**Chemnitz** Hbf a.	0625	0725	0825		2225	...	0036

	v	①-⑥				n
Chemnitz Hbf d.	0425	0533	0633	and hourly until	2033	2247
Burgstädt d.	0437	0545	0645		2045	2259
Geithain d.	0451	0600	0700		2100	2313
Bad Lausick d.	0458	0608	0708		2108	2321
Leipzig Hbf a.	0521	0626	0726		2126	2352

n – Not Dec. 24, 31.
v – Not Dec. 25, Jan. 1.

875 NÜRNBERG - COBURG - SONNEBERG

RE / RB services except where shown

See Table **851** for faster *ICE* services Nürnberg - Erlangen - Bamberg - Lichtenfels and v.v.

km		Ⓐe	Ⓐe																					Ⓐe	
0	**Nürnberg** Hbf **851** ‡ d.	...	0429	0553	...	0651	0745	0840	...	0847	0945	1040	...	1046	1145	1149	1240	...	1246	1345	1440	...	1446	1545	1614	1640
8	Fürth (Bay) Hbf ‡ d.	...	0438	0601	...	0659	0753	0848	...	0854	0953	1048	...	1054	1153	1158	1248	...	1254	1353	1448	...	1454	1553	1622	1648
24	Erlangen **851** ‡ d.	...	0455	0613	...	0719	0806	0900	...	0913	1006	1100	...	1112	1206	1215	1300	...	1312	1406	1500	...	1512	1606	1635	1700
39	Forchheim (Oberfr) ‡ d.	...	0508	0621	...	0733	0816	0908	...	0927	1016	1108	...	1126	1216	1229	1308	...	1326	1416	1508	...	1526	1616	1646	1708
62	**Bamberg 851** ‡ a.	...	0532	0636	...	0752	0831	0924	...	0948	1031	1124	...	1148	1231	1250	1324	...	1348	1431	1524	...	1548	1631	1702	1724
62	**Bamberg 851 876** d.	0450	0538	0638	0741	0754	0838	0926	0941	0954	1038	1126	1141	1154	1238	1252	1326	1341	1354	1438	1526	1541	1554	1638	1717	1726
	Schweinfurt Hbf **876** a.	|	|	|	|	|	|	0955	|	|	|	1155	|	|	|	|	1355	|	|	|	1555	|	|	|	|	1755
94	Lichtenfels **851 876** a.	0520	0610	0656	0800	0822	0856	...	1000	1023	1056	...	1200	1223	1256	1317	...	1400	1423	1456	...	1600	1623	1656	1746	...
94	Lichtenfels d.	0524	0622	0702	0810	0839	0906	...	1010	1039	1106	...	1210	1239	1306	1336e	...	1410	1439	1506	...	1610	1639	1706	1754	...
114	**Coburg** a.	0553	0645	0722	0833	0906	0930	...	1029	1106	1130	...	1229	1306	1330	1403e	...	1429	1506	1530	...	1629	1706	1730	1814	...
114	**Coburg** d.	0554	0701	0724	0835	...	0932	...	1032	...	1132	...	1232	...	1332	...	...	1434	...	1532	...	1632	1707q	1732	...	...
135	**Sonneberg** (Thür) Hbf a.	0621	0725	0745	0857	...	0954	...	1054	...	1154	...	1254	...	1354	...	...	1456	...	1554	...	1654	1739q	1754	...	...

Nürnberg Hbf **851** ‡ d.	...	1646	1745	1840	...	1945	2040	...	2145	2253	2355
Fürth (Bay) Hbf ‡ d.	...	1654	1753	1848	...	1953	2048	...	2154	2307	0005
Erlangen **851** ‡ d.	...	1712	1806	1900	...	2006	2101	...	2214	2325	0023
Forchheim (Oberfr) ‡ d.	...	1726	1816	1908	...	2016	2112	...	2228	2338	0038
Bamberg 851 ‡ a.	...	1749	1831	1924	...	2031	2128	...	2248	2358	0059
Bamberg 851 876 d.	1741	1754	1838	1926	1941	2038	2138c	2141	2252	0020	...
Schweinfurt Hbf **876** a.	|	|	|	1955	|	|	2216c	|	|	|	...
Lichtenfels **851 876** a.	1800	1823	1856	...	2000	2056	...	2205	2319	0047	...
Lichtenfels d.	1810	1839	1906	...	2010	2109	...	2212	2321	...	...
Coburg a.	1829	1906	1929	...	2029	2126	...	2238	2341	...	...
Coburg d.	1832	...	1932	...	2032	...	...	2239	...	...	...
Sonneberg (Thür) Hbf a.	1854	...	1954	...	2054	...	...	2301	...	...	...

	Ⓐe	Ⓐe	Ⓒz	Ⓐe			Ⓐe	Ⓒz		
Sonneberg (Thür) Hbf d.	0433	...	...	0518	0612	...	0648	0656	...	0732e
Coburg a.	0456	...	...	0542	0634	...	0721	0721	...	0800e
Coburg d.	0457	0518	0518	0543	0636	0649e	0724	0732	...	0802e
Lichtenfels a.	0519	0539	0539	0604	0656	0714e	0749	0753	...	0823e
Lichtenfels **851 876** d.	0520	0542	0542	0605	0702	0736	0800	0800	...	0840
Schweinfurt Hbf **876** d.	|	|	|	|	|	|	|	|	0803	|
Bamberg 851 876 a.	0549	0612	0612	0632	0722	0806	0819	0819	0834	0908
Bamberg 851 ‡ d.	0551	0618	0628	0635	0727	0809	...	...	0836	0910
Forchheim (Oberfr) ‡ d.	0606	0634	0643	0650	0744	0831	...	...	0851	0932
Erlangen **851** ‡ d.	0616	0646	0656	0715v	0756	0846	...	...	0900	0945
Fürth (Bay) Hbf ‡ d.	0628	0701	0709	0727	0808	0903	...	...	0912	1002
Nürnberg Hbf **851** ‡ a.	0637	0708	0717	0734	0817	0912	...	...	0921	1011

Sonneberg (Thür) Hbf d.	0807	...	0907	...	1007	...	1107	...	1207	...	1303	...	1407	...	1507	...	1607	...	1707	...	1807	...	1907	2007	...	2140
Coburg a.	0829	...	0929	...	1029	...	1129	...	1229	...	1325	...	1429	...	1529	...	1629	...	1729	...	1829	...	1929	2029	...	2203
Coburg d.	0835	0858	0932	...	1035	1058	1132	...	1235	1258	1332	...	1435	1458	1532	...	1635	1658	1732	...	1835	1858	1932	2037	2134	2204
Lichtenfels a.	0852	0920	0951	...	1052	1120	1151	...	1252	1320	1351	...	1452	1520	1551	...	1652	1720	1751	...	1852	1920	1951	2054	2153	2225
Lichtenfels **851 876** d.	0902	0936	1000	...	1102	1136	1200	...	1302	1337	1400	...	1502	1536	1600	...	1702	1736	1800	...	1902	1936	2000	2102	2200	2314
Schweinfurt Hbf **876** d.	|	|	|	1003	|	|	|	1203	|	|	|	1403	|	|	|	1603	|	|	|	1803	|	|	|	|	|	|
Bamberg 851 876 a.	0922	1006	1019	1034	1122	1206	1219	1234	1322	1406	1419	1434	1522	1606	1619	1634	1722	1806	1819	1834	1922	2006	2019	2127	2224	2342
Bamberg 851 ‡ d.	0930	1009	...	1036	1130	1209	...	1236	1326	1409	...	1436	1530	1609	...	1636	1730	1809	...	1836	1930	2009	...	2130	...	2343
Forchheim (Oberfr) ‡ d.	0944	1030	...	1051	1144	1230	...	1251	1346	1430	...	1451	1544	1630	...	1651	1744	1830	...	1851	1944	2030	...	2144	...	0004
Erlangen **851** ‡ d.	0956	1045	...	1101	1156	1245	...	1301	1356	1445	...	1501	1556	1645	...	1701	1756	1845	...	1901	1956	2052t	...	2156	...	0018
Fürth (Bay) Hbf ‡ d.	1008	1104	...	1113	1208	1304	...	1313	1408	1504	...	1513	1608	1704	...	1713	1808	1904	...	1913	2008	2113	...	2209	...	0036
Nürnberg Hbf **851** ‡ a.	1017	1112	...	1121	1217	1312	...	1321	1417	1512	...	1521	1617	1712	...	1721	1817	1912	...	1921	2017	2120	...	2217	...	0043

b – Not May 22. Departs 0614 on Dec. 24, 31, Mar. 22.
c – Ⓒ (also Dec. 24, 31, May 22). On † (also May 22) departs Bamberg 2148, Schweinfurt a. 2221.
e – Ⓐ (not Dec. 24, 31, May 22).
q – ①–④ (not Dec. 24, 25, 26, 31, Jan. 1, Mar. 24, May 1, 12, 22).

r – Not May 22.
t – Arrives 2044.
v – Arrives 0701.
z – Also Dec. 24, 31, May 22.

‡ – Additional *RB* services Nürnberg - Bamberg and v.v.:
From Nürnberg Hbf at 0106, 0618 ⚒ **b**, 0750, 0950, 1350, 1518 Ⓐ **e**, 1550, 1715 Ⓐ **e**, 1750, 1845, 1950 and 2047.
From Bamberg at 0356 Ⓐ **e**, 0444 ⚒ **r**, 0505, 0543 Ⓒ **z**, 0605 Ⓒ **z**, 0707, 1110, 1310, 1510, 1654 Ⓐ **e**, 1710, 1910 and 2210.
See Table **921** for additional trains Nürnberg - Fürth and v.v.

876 WÜRZBURG - BAMBERG - HOF

RE / RB services

km		Ⓐe		2	⑥k	Ⓐt								
0	**Würzburg** Hbf ◇ d.	...	...	...	0504	0507	...	...	0602	...	...	0725g	...	...
43	Schweinfurt Hbf ◇ d.	...	...	...	0538	0543	...	...	0636	...	...	0803	...	...
68	Haßfurt ◇ d.	...	...	...	0556	0600	...	...	0653	...	...	0817	...	...
100	**Bamberg** ◇ a.	...	...	...	0620	0625	...	...	0719	...	...	0834	...	...
100	**Bamberg 851 875** d.	...	0450e	...	...	...	0638	0638	...	0741	0741	0836	0838	0838
	Nürnberg Hbf **875** a.	...	|	...	...	...	|	|	...	|	|	0921	|	|
132	Lichtenfels **851 875** d.	0436	0550	...	...	...	0700	0700	...	0802	0802	...	0900	0900
162	Kulmbach d.	0505	0618	...	...	...	0718	0718	...	0821	0821	...	0918	0918
174	Neuenmarkt-Wirsberg a.	0519	0632	...	...	...	0727	0727	...	0833	0833	...	0927	0927
174	Neuenmarkt-Wirsberg d.	0520	0633	0637	...	...	0729	0733	...	0835	0837	...	0929	0933
196	**Bayreuth** Hbf a.	0548	|	0700	...	...	|	0752	...	0856	|	...	|	0955
203	Münchberg **880** d.	...	0657	...	...	...	0754	...	...	...	0900	...	0954	...
216	Schwarzenbach d.	...	0709	...	...	...	0804	...	...	...	0909	...	1004	...
227	**Hof** Hbf **880** a.	...	0720	...	...	...	0816	...	...	...	0920	...	1014	...

							⊠				
Würzburg Hbf ◇ d.	0809	0836	0836	0933	...	...		1609	1636	1636	1733
Schweinfurt Hbf ◇ d.	0842	0903	0903	1003	...	...		1642	1703	1703	1803
Haßfurt ◇ d.	0858	0918	0918	1017	...	...		1658	1718	1718	1817
Bamberg ◇ a.	0923	0936	0936	1034	...	...	each	1723	1736	1736	1834
Bamberg 851 875 d.	...	0941	0941	1036	1038	1038	train	...	1741	1741	1836
Nürnberg Hbf **875** a.	...	|	|	1121	|	|	runs	...	|	|	1921
Lichtenfels **851 875** d.	...	1002	1002	...	1100	1100	every	...	1802	1802	...
Kulmbach d.	...	1021	1021	...	1118	1118	**two**	...	1821	1821	...
Neuenmarkt-Wirsberg a.	...	1033	1033	...	1127	1127	hours	...	1833	1833	...
Neuenmarkt-Wirsberg d.	...	1035	1037	...	1129	1133	until	...	1835	1837	...
Bayreuth Hbf a.	...	1056	|	...	|	1155		...	1856	|	...
Münchberg **880** d.	...	...	1100	...	1154	...		...	...	1900	...
Schwarzenbach d.	...	...	1109	...	1204	...		...	...	1909	...
Hof Hbf **880** a.	...	...	1120	...	1214	...		...	...	1920	...

Würzburg Hbf ◇ d.	...	...	1809	1836	1836	1933	...	2009	2036	2036	...
Schweinfurt Hbf ◇ d.	...	...	1842	1903	1903	2003	...	2042	2103	2103	...
Haßfurt ◇ d.	...	...	1858	1918	1918	2017	...	2058	2118	2118	...
Bamberg ◇ a.	...	...	1923	1936	1936	2034	...	2123	2136	2136	...
Bamberg 851 875 d.	1838	1838	...	1941	1941	...	2038	...	2141	2141	...
Nürnberg Hbf **875** a.	|	|	...	|	|	...	|	...	|	|	...
Lichtenfels **851 875** d.	1900	1900	...	2002	2002	...	2107	...	2206	2206	2316
Kulmbach d.	1918	1918	...	2021	2021	...	2134	...	2226	2226	2340
Neuenmarkt-Wirsberg a.	1927	1927	...	2033	2033	...	2148	...	2238	2238	2353
Neuenmarkt-Wirsberg d.	1929	1933	...	2035	2037	...	2148	...	2240	2242	2354
Bayreuth Hbf a.	|	1955	...	2056	|	...	2207	...	2300	|	0016
Münchberg **880** d.	1954	...	...	...	2100	...	...	...	...	2305	...
Schwarzenbach d.	2004	...	...	...	2109	...	...	...	...	2314	...
Hof Hbf **880** a.	2014	...	...	...	2120	...	...	...	...	2324	...

	2Ⓐe	Ⓐe			⚒r						
Hof Hbf **880** d.	...	...	0525	...	...	0638	...	...	...	0744	...
Schwarzenbach d.	...	...	0533	...	...	0647	...	...	...	0752	...
Münchberg **880** d.	...	...	0543	...	...	0656	...	...	...	0803	...
Bayreuth Hbf d.	0452	...	|	0550	...	|	0703	...	0801	|	...
Neuenmarkt-Wirsberg a.	0513	...	0606	0610	...	0721	0725	...	0823	0828	...
Neuenmarkt-Wirsberg d.	0520	...	0613	0613	...	0728	0728	...	0830	0830	...
Kulmbach d.	0532	...	0622	0622	...	0738	0738	...	0838	0838	...
Lichtenfels **851 875** d.	0601	...	0650j	0650j	...	0800	0800	...	0857	0857	...
Nürnberg Hbf **875** d.	|	...	|	|	...	|	|	...	|	|	0840
Bamberg 851 875 a.	0632	...	0717e	0717e	...	0819	0819	...	0922	0922	0924
Bamberg ◇ d.	...	0644	...	...	0726	0824	0824	0838	...	...	0926
Haßfurt ◇ d.	...	0708	...	...	0741	0841	0841	0900	...	...	0941
Schweinfurt Hbf ◇ d.	...	0727	...	...	0755	0856	0856	0918	...	...	0955
Würzburg Hbf ◇ a.	...	0801	...	...	0825	0923	0923	0951	...	...	1025

							★														⑥k	Ⓐe	†w					
Hof Hbf **880** d.	0841	...	...	...	0944	...		1640	...	...	...	1744	...	1841	...	1941	...	...	...	...	2041	...	...	...	2237
Schwarzenbach d.	0849	...	...	...	0952	...		1648	...	...	...	1752	...	1849	...	1950	...	...	...	...	2049	...	...	...	2248
Münchberg **880** d.	0858	...	...	...	1003	...		1659	...	...	...	1803	...	1858	...	2002	...	...	...	...	2058	...	...	...	2301
Bayreuth Hbf d.	|	0903	...	1001	|	...	each	|	1703	...	1801	|	...	|	1903	|	2003	...	...	...	|	2103	...	2211	|
Neuenmarkt-Wirsberg a.	0921	0925	...	1023	1028	...	train	1721	1725	...	1823	1828	...	1921	1925	2025	2029	...	...	...	2121	2125	...	2232	2323
Neuenmarkt-Wirsberg d.	0928	0928	...	1030	1030	...	runs	1728	1728	...	1830	1830	...	1928	1928	▬	2030	...	...	...	2128	2128	...	2232	▬
Kulmbach d.	0938	0938	...	1038	1038	...	every	1738	1738	...	1838	1838	...	1938	1938	...	2038	...	...	...	2138	2138	...	2245	...
Lichtenfels **851 875** d.	1000	1000	...	1057	1057	...	**two**	1800	1800	...	1857	1857	...	2000	2000	...	2057	...	...	...	2200	2200	...	2305	...
Nürnberg Hbf **875** d.	|	|	...	|	|	1040	hours	|	|	...	|	|	1840	|	|	...	|	2040	...	2040	|	|	...	|	...
Bamberg 851 875 a.	1019	1019	...	1122	1122	1124	until	1819	1819	...	1922	1922	1924	2019	2019	Ⓑn	2127	2128	...	2128	2224	2224	...	2342	⑤⑥¶
Bamberg ◇ d.	1024	1024	1038	...	...	1126		1824	1824	1838	...	...	1926	2024z	2024z	2038	...	2138	2145	2148	...	...	2240	...	2347
Haßfurt ◇ d.	1041	1041	1100	...	...	1141		1841	1841	1900	...	...	1941	2041z	2041z	2100	...	2159	2201	2205	...	...	2303	...	0010
Schweinfurt Hbf ◇ d.	1056	1056	1118	...	...	1155		1856	1856	1918	...	...	1955	2056z	2056z	2118	...	2218	2219	2222	...	...	2323	...	0028
Würzburg Hbf ◇ a.	1123	1123	1151	...	...	1225		1923	1923	1951	...	...	2025	2123z	2123z	2151	...	2251	2253	2254	...	...	2357	...	0102

e – Ⓐ (not Dec. 24, 31, May 22).
g – 0733 on Ⓒ (also Dec. 24, 31, May 22).
j – Arrives 0642.
k – Also Dec. 24, 31.

n – Not Dec. 24, 31.
r – Not May 22.
w – Also May 22.
z – Ⓒ (also Dec. 24, 31, May 22).

¶ – ⑤⑥ (also Mar. 23, May 11; runs daily Bamberg - Schweinfurt).
⊠ – The 1209 Würzburg - Bamberg runs only on Ⓒ (daily Dec. 22 - Jan. 6, Feb. 2 - 10, Mar. 15 - 30, May 10 - 25).
★ – Hof Hbf d. 1141 / 1541 (not 1144 / 1544; also departs Schwarzenach 2 minutes earlier, Münchberg 1 minute earlier).

◇ – Additional trains Würzburg - Bamberg and v.v.

	Ⓒz	Ⓐe		
Würzburg Hbf **870** d.	2139	2139	2300	...
Schweinfurt Hbf **870** d.	2205	2217	2334	...
Haßfurt d.	2219	2233	2350	...
Bamberg a.	2237	2257	0015	...

	Ⓒz	Ⓐe		
Bamberg d.	0447	0500	0617	0702
Haßfurt d.	0508	0521	0633	0725
Schweinfurt Hbf **870** d.	0527	0545	0650	0743
Würzburg Hbf **870** a.	0600	0618	0719	0816

LANDSHUT - MÜHLDORF - SALZBURG 877

RB services

km		Ⓐe	⚒r								
0	**Landshut** (Bay) Hbf d.	...	0609	...	0839	1039	1238	1439	1639	1839	2039
55	Mühldorf (Oberbay) a.	...	0714	...	0930	1130	1329	1531	1730	1930	2130
55	Mühldorf (Oberbay) d.	0609	0743	0743	0942	1143	1343	1543	1743	1943	2146n
120	Freilassing **890/1** a.	0713	0841	0841	1041	1241	1442	1641	1841	2041	2239n
126	**Salzburg** Hbf **890/1** a.	*0725*	0850	0850	1050	*1315*	1450	1650	1849	*2116*	2247n

	Ⓐe	⚒r								n
Salzburg Hbf **890/1** d.	*0511*	...	*0709*	0911	1110	*1314*	1510	1710	1912	...
Freilassing **890/1** d.	0531	...	0720	0919	1120	1324	1520	1720	1920	...
Mühldorf (Oberbay) a.	0624	...	0814	1013	1214	1416	1614	1814	2015	...
Mühldorf (Oberbay) d.	...	0633	0830	1030	1229	1430	1630	1830	2030	2151
Landshut (Bay) Hbf a.	...	0723	0924	1124	1323	1524	1724	1923	2123	2246

e – Not Dec. 24, 31, May 22.
n – Not Dec. 24, 31.
r – Not May 22.

MÜNCHEN - REGENSBURG 878

DB (*RE* services); *ALX*

km				*ALX*		*ALX*		*ALX*		*ALX*		*ALX*			*ALX*	*ALX*		*ALX*			*ALX*			*ALX*	*ALX*
		Ⓒz	Ⓐe		N	P	N		N		N		N	Ⓐe	P	Ⓑ	N		⑥	N			⑥h	Ⓑq	x
0	**München** Hbf **944** d.	0536	0544	0644	0743	0844	0943	1044	1143	1244	1343	1444	1543	1623	1644	1644	1743	1844	1904	1943	2044	...	2244	2244	2355
42	Freising **944** d.	0604	0609	0708	0808	0908	1008	1108	1208	1308	1408	1508	1608	1648	1708	1708	1808	1908	1929	2008	2108	...	2310	2310	0019
76	Landshut (Bay) Hbf **944** d.	0628	0645	0732	0833	0932	1033	1132	1233	1332	1433	1532	1632	1714	1732	1732	1832	1932	1953	2032	2132	...	2335	2335	0041
99	Neufahrn (Niederbay) d.	0644	0702	0748	0849	0948	1049	1148	1249	1348	1449	1547	1649	1731	1748	1748	1849	1948	2011	2049	2148	...	2352	2352	0057
138	**Regensburg** Hbf a.	0711	0733	0812	0914	1012	1114	1212	1314	1412	1514	1612	1714	1758	1811	1811	1914	2012	2038	2121	2211	...	0024	0028	0122
	Schwandorf **879 885** a.	...	...	0846	...	1047	...	1246	...	1446	...	1647	...	...	1848	1848	...	2046	...	...	2252	...	...	...	...
	Hof Hbf **879** a.	...	...	1018	...	...	...	1418	...	...	...	1818	...	...	...	2025	...	2220	...	...	...	...	...	...	...

	ALX	*ALX*					*ALX*			*ALX*		*ALX*		*ALX*		*ALX*		*ALX*		*ALX*					
	Ⓐe		Ⓐe	⑥t	Ⓒz	Ⓐe		⑥	N		N		N	P	N		N		N			AN		P	N
Hof Hbf **879** d.	...	...	...	...	...	...	0536r	...	...	0740	...	0940	...	...	...	1340	...	...	...	1740	...	...	...	...	...
Schwandorf **879 885** d.	...	0501r	...	...	...	...	0709	...	...	0907	...	1108	...	1311	...	1508	...	1709	...	1911	...	...	...	2121	...
Regensburg Hbf d.	0443	0547	0600	0603	0643	0700	0746	0831	0844	0946	1044	1146	1243	1346	1444	1546	1644	1746	1843	1947	2044	2044	...	2157	2244
Neufahrn (Niederbay) d.	0509	0611	0626	0637	0709	0727	0811	0857	0911	1010	1111	1210	1310	1411	1511	1611	1711	1811	1910	2010	2117	2117	...	2220	2315
Landshut (Bay) Hbf **944** d.	0527	0628	0646	0657	0729	0746	0827	0916	0930	1027	1130	1227	1329	1427	1530	1627	1730	1827	1929	2027	2134	2135	2144	2236	2334
Freising **944** d.	0549	0649	0709	0728	0751	0809	0848	0937	0953	1048	1153	1248	1351	1449	1550	1649	1750	1849	1951	2048	...	2156	2209	2257	2356
München Hbf **944** a.	0615	0716	0737	0759	0820	0836	0916	1004	1020	1116	1221	1316	1421	1519	1620	1719	1820	1919	2017	2116	...	2221	2236	2321	0021

A – ⑤⑥† (also Dec. 24, 31, May 22).
N – To / from Nürnberg (Table **921**).
P – [12] München - Schwandorf - Furth im Wald 🚌 - Praha and v.v. See also Tables **57** and **885**.
e – Not Dec. 24, 31, May 22.
h – Also Dec. 24, 25, 31, Mar. 23, May 11.
q – Not Dec. 24, 25, 31, Mar. 23, May 11.
r – ①–⑥ only.
t – Also Dec. 24, 31.
x – Not Dec. 31.
z – Also Dec. 24, 31, May 22.
ALX – *Arriva-Länderbahn-Express* Operated by Arriva / Regentalbahn AG - Die Länderbahn. Conveys 🍷.

REGENSBURG - HOF 879

DB (*RE* services); *ALX*; Vogtlandbahn

km						*ALX*				*ALX*			*ALX*			*ALX*			*ALX*			*ALX*		*ALX*	
		Ⓐe 2	G	Ⓐe	2		2	G	2		⑤f	2		G	2			2	ⒷJ	2	2		2		2
	München Hbf **878** d.	...	...	...	...	0644	...	...	...	1044	...	...	1244	...	...	1444	...	...	1644	...	...	1844	...	2044	...
0	**Regensburg** Hbf **885** d.	...	0623	0729	0730z	0821	0931	1030	1130	1221	1321	1331	1421	1430	1528	1621	1737	1723	1821	*1833*	1929	2021	2131	2221	...
42	Schwandorf **885** a.	...	0650	0756	0759z	0846	1000	1057	1159	1246	1348	1400	1446	1457	1557	1647	1758	1752	1848	*1900*	1958	2046	2200	2252	...
42	Schwandorf d.	0505	0652	...	0801	0847	1001	1059	1201	1247	1349	1401	...	1459	1601	1648	1759	1802	1856	1902	2006	2047	2202	...	2305
86	Weiden (Oberpf) a.	0544	0719	...	0841	0913	1041	1123	1241	1313	1418	1441	...	1522	1641	1713	1823	1841	1921	1941	2046	2113	2242	...	2344
86	Weiden (Oberpf) d.	0551	0720	...	0851	0914	1051	1123	1251z	1314	1419	1451	...	1523	1651	1714	1824	1851	1922	1951e	2051	2114	2251	...	...
137	Marktredwitz **880** a.	0634	0755	...	0934	0950	1134	1157	1334z	1350	1456	1534	...	1557	1734	1750	1907	1934	1959	2034e	2134	2152	2334	...	...
179	**Hof** Hbf **880** a.	0710	0819	...	1010	1018	1210	1219	1410z	1418	*1524*	1610	...	1619	1810	1818	1930	2010	2025	2110e	2210	2220	0010	...	...

	ALX			*ALX*		*ALX*		*ALX*					*ALX*			*ALX*		*ALX*							
	①–⑥	Ⓒz 2	Ⓐe 2	H			2		2	G	2	Ⓐe 2		2	G		2		2	⑦w	G	2		Ⓐe 2	
Hof Hbf **880** d.	...	...	...	0536	0642	0740	0748	0940	0948	1144	1148	...	1340	1348	1544	...	1548	1740	1748	...	1944	1948	...	2048	...
Marktredwitz **880** d.	...	...	...	0604	0708	0807	0824	1007	1024	1206	1224	...	1407	1424	1606	...	1624	1808	1824	1905	2006	2024	...	2124	...
Weiden (Oberpf) a.	...	...	...	0641	0741	0840	0905	1040	1105	1237	1305	...	1441	1505	1637	...	1705	1841	1905	1941	2037	2105	...	2205	...
Weiden (Oberpf) d.	0414e	0508	0541	0642	0742	0841	0914	1041	1114	1238	1314z	1322	1442	1514	1638	...	1714	1842	1914	1942	2038	2114z	...	2217	...
Schwandorf a.	0454e	0548	0621	0708	0809	0906	0954	1107	1154	1300	1354z	1400	1507	1554	1700	...	1754	1909	1952	2008	2100	2154z	...	2255	...
Schwandorf **885** d.	0501	0552	0622	0709	0810	0907	1002	1108	1202	1301	1402z	1402	1508	1606	1702	1709	1804	1911	2006k	2009	2100	...	2206	...	2303
Regensburg Hbf **885** a.	0536	0621	0653	0736	0837	0936	1033	1136	1233	1330	1433z	1433	1536	1637	1730	1736	1835	1937	2037k	2037	2130	...	2237	...	2332
München Hbf **878** a.	0716	...	...	0916	...	1116	...	1316	...	...	...	...	1719	...	...	1919	...	2116	...	...	...	...	...	...	...

G – To / from Gera (Table **871**).
H – ①–⑥ (daily Schwandorf - München).
J – Runs daily München - Schwandorf.
e – Ⓐ (not Dec. 24, 31, May 22).
f – Also Mar. 20, Apr. 30, May 21; not Mar. 21, May 2, 23.
k – On ⑦**w** Schwandorf d. 1953, Regensburg a. 2027.
w – Also Mar. 24, May 12; not Mar. 23, May 11.
z – Ⓒ (also Dec. 24, 31, May 22).
ALX – *Arriva-Länderbahn-Express* Operated by Arriva / Regentalbahn AG - Die Länderbahn. Conveys 🍷.

NÜRNBERG - HOF - DRESDEN 880

IRE / *RE* / *RB* services

km		Ⓐn		B🍷		L	Ⓐn			⚒										Ⓐn					
0	**Nürnberg** Hbf ● d.	...	...	...	...	...	...	0548	0548	0643	0648	0648	0748	0748	0843	0848	0848	0948	0948	1043	1048	1048	1148	1148	1243
28	Hersbruck (r Pegnitz) ● d.	...	...	...	...	...	...	0606	0606	|	0706	0706	0806	0806	|	0906	0906	1006	1006	|	1106	1106	1206	1206	|
67	Pegnitz ● a.	...	...	...	...	...	...	0627	0627	|	0727	0727	0827	0827	|	0927	0927	1027	1027	|	1127	1127	1227	1227	|
67	Pegnitz d.	...	...	...	...	...	...	0629	0635	|	0729	0733	0829	0835	|	0929	0933	1029	1035	|	1129	1133	1229	1235	|
	Bayreuth Hbf **876** d.	...	...	...	...	...	0519	|	0654	|	|	0754	|	0854	0932	|	0954	|	1054	1132	|	1154	|	1254	1332
	Münchberg **876** d.	...	...	...	...	...	0554	|	...	|	|	...	|	...	1005	|	...	|	...	1205	|	...	|	...	1405
94	Kirchenlaibach d.	...	...	...	...	...	|	0643	...	|	0743	...	0843	...	|	0943	...	1043	...	|	1143	...	1243	...	|
125	Marktredwitz **879** d.	...	...	...	...	...	|	0702	...	0800t	0812	...	0902	...	|	1012	...	1102	...	|	1212	...	1302	...	|
167	**Hof** Hbf **876 879** a.	...	...	...	...	...	0618	0724	...	0823	...	...	0924	...	1023	...	...	1124	...	1223	...	...	1324	...	1423
167	**Hof** Hbf **881** d.	0428	...	...	0527	0602	0628	0728	...	0828	...	...	0928	...	1028	...	...	1128	...	1228	...	...	1328	...	1428
215	Plauen (Vogtl) ob Bf **881** d.	0457	...	0507r	0557	0631	0657	0756	...	0857	...	...	0956	...	1057	...	...	1156	...	1257	...	...	1356	...	1457
240	Reichenbach (Vogtl) ob Bf **881** d.	0512	...	0535	0611	0648	0712	0810	...	0912	...	...	1010	...	1112	...	...	1210	...	1312	...	...	1410	...	1512
263	**Zwickau** (Sachs) Hbf d.	0528	0534v	0557	0628	0703	0728	0828	...	0928	...	...	1028	...	1128	...	...	1228	...	1328	...	...	1428	...	1528
279	Glauchau (Sachs) **858** d.	0538	0551v	0609	0637	...	0738	0837	...	0938	...	...	1037	...	1138	...	...	1237	...	1338	...	...	1437	...	1538
311	**Chemnitz** Hbf **858** d.	0605	0631	0635	0704	...	0805	0904	...	1005	...	...	1104	...	1205	...	...	1304	...	1405	...	...	1504	...	1605
324	Flöha d.	0616	0644	...	0716	...	0816	0916	...	1016	...	...	1116	...	1216	...	...	1316	...	1416	...	...	1516	...	1616
350	Freiberg (Sachs) d.	0633	0708	...	0733	...	0833	0933	...	1033	...	...	1133	...	1233	...	...	1333	...	1433	...	...	1533	...	1633
390	**Dresden** Hbf a.	0703	0751	...	0805	...	0903	1005	...	1103	...	...	1205	...	1303	...	...	1405	...	1503	...	...	1605	...	1703

					Ⓐn																			⑥	
Nürnberg Hbf ● d.	1248	1248	1348	1348	1443	1448	1448	1548	1548	1643	1648	1648	1748	1748	1843	1848	1848	1948	1948	2050	2148	2148	2250	2250	0012
Hersbruck (r Pegnitz) ● d.	1306	1306	1406	1406	|	1506	1506	1606	1606	|	1706	1706	1806	1806	|	1906	1906	2006	2006	2109	2206	2206	2309	2309	0031
Pegnitz ● a.	1327	1327	1427	1427	|	1527	1527	1627	1627	|	1727	1727	1827	1827	|	1927	1927	2027	2027	2130	2227	2227	2330	2330	0052
Pegnitz d.	1329	1333	1429	1435	|	1529	1533	1629	1635	|	1729	1733	1829	1835	|	1929	1933	2029	2035	2131	2229	2233	2331	2331	0054
Bayreuth Hbf **876** d.	|	1354	|	1454	1532	|	1554	|	1654	1732	|	1754	|	1854	1932	|	1954	|	2054	2151	2250	|	2351	2352	0113
Münchberg **876** d.	|	...	|	...	1605	|	...	|	...	1805	|	...	|	...	2005	|	▬	|	▬	...	...	|	...	0041	...
Kirchenlaibach d.	1343	...	1443	...	|	1543	...	1643	...	|	1743	...	1843	...	|	1943	...	2043	...	...	...	2252	...	|	...
Marktredwitz **879** d.	1412	...	1502	...	|	1612	...	1702	...	|	1812	...	1902	...	|	2012	...	2102	...	...	...	2315	...	|	...
Hof Hbf **876 879** a.	...	...	1524	...	1623	...	...	1724	...	1823	...	...	1924	...	2022	▬	...	2124	n 2	...	...	2341	...	0103	...
Hof Hbf **881** d.	...	...	1528	...	1628	...	...	1728	...	1828	...	...	1928	...	2029	...	...	...	2225	...	...	...	...	...	...
Plauen (Vogtl) ob Bf **881** d.	...	...	1556	...	1657	...	...	1756	...	1857	...	...	1956	...	2057	...	*2141*n	...	2304	...	...	...	...	...	...
Reichenbach (Vogtl) ob Bf **881** d.	...	...	1610	...	1712	...	...	1810	...	1912	...	...	2010	...	2112	...	*2207*n	...	...	...	...	...	...	...	...
Zwickau (Sachs) Hbf d.	...	...	1628	...	1728	...	...	1828	...	1928	...	...	2028	...	2128	2134	2234	...	...	...	...	...	...	...	...
Glauchau (Sachs) **858** d.	...	...	1637	...	1738	...	...	1837	...	1938	...	...	2037	...	2138	2151	2251	...	...	...	...	...	...	...	...
Chemnitz Hbf **858** d.	...	...	1704	...	1805	...	...	1904	...	2005	...	...	2104	...	2205	2231	2331	...	...	...	...	...	...	...	...
Flöha d.	...	...	1716	...	1816	...	...	1916	...	2016	...	...	2116	...	2216c	2244	2344	...	...	...	...	...	...	...	...
Freiberg (Sachs) d.	...	...	1733	...	1833	...	...	1933	...	2033	...	...	2133	...	2233c	2308	0007	...	...	...	...	...	...	...	...
Dresden Hbf a.	...	...	1805	...	1903	...	...	2005	...	2103	...	...	2205	...	2303c	2351	...	...	...	...	...	...	...	...	...

B – *VOGTLAND-EXPRESS*. To Berlin (Table **843**). Operated by Vogtlandbahn. **DB tickets are not valid**.
L – To Leipzig (Table **881**).
c – Ⓒ (also Dec. 24, 31, Mar. 20, Apr. 30).
n – Not Dec. 24, 31.
r – 0515 on Ⓒ (also Dec. 24, 31).
t – Arrives 0749.
v – Not Dec. 25, Jan. 1.
● – Most trains between Nürnberg and Pegnitz convey portions for two separate destinations. Passengers should take care to join the correct portion for their destination.

880 DRESDEN - HOF - NÜRNBERG *IRE / RE services*

km			Ⓐe		v					①m	⚒										Ⓐn				
0	**Dresden** Hbf	d.	...	...	...	...	...	...	...	...	0457	...	0556	...	...	...	0657	0756	...	...	...	0857	...	0956	...	...
40	Freiberg (Sachs)	d.	...	...	...	...	...	...	...	...	0527	...	0629	...	...	...	0727	0829	...	...	...	0927	...	1029	...	...
66	Flöha	d.	...	...	...	...	...	...	...	...	0545	...	0645	...	...	...	0745	0845	...	...	...	0945	...	1045	...	...
79	**Chemnitz** Hbf **858**	d.	...	...	...	0412	...	...	...	...	0559	0559	0658	...	...	...	0759	0858	...	...	...	0959	...	1058	...	...
111	Glauchau (Sachs) **858**	d.	...	...	...	0446	...	...	...	...	0622	0622	0721	...	...	...	0822	0921	...	...	...	1022	...	1121	...	...
127	**Zwickau** (Sachs) Hbf	d.	...	...	...	0502	0519	...	...	...	0633	0633	0733	...	...	...	0833	0933	...	...	...	1033	...	1133	...	...
150	Reichenbach (Vogtl) ob Bf **881**	d.	...	...	...	▬	0534	...	...	...	0649	0649	0749	...	...	...	0849	0949	...	...	...	1049	...	1149	...	...
175	Plauen (Vogtl) ob Bf **881**	d.	...	...	...	...	0550	...	...	...	0705	0705	0804	...	...	...	0905	1004	...	...	...	1105	...	1204	...	...
223	**Hof** Hbf **881**	a.	...	...	...	...	0628	...	...	...	0734	0734	0834	...	...	...	0934	1034	...	...	...	1134	...	1234	...	...
223	**Hof** Hbf **876 879**	d.	...	0420	0528q	...	0630	...	...	...	0737	0737	0837	...	...	...	0937	1037	...	...	...	1137	...	1237	...	...
	Marktredwitz **879**	d.	...	0442	0548	...	0656	...	0738	...	|	|	0900	...	0939	...	|	1100	...	1139	...	|	...	1300	1331t	...
	Kirchenlaibach	d.	...	0506	0605	...	0711	...	0812	...	|	|	0916	...	1012	...	|	1116	...	1212	...	|	...	1316	1412	...
247	Münchberg **876**	d.	...	|	|	...	|	...	|	...	0753	0753	|	...	|	...	0953	|	...	|	...	1153	...	|	|	...
295	**Bayreuth** Hbf **876**	d.	0504	|	|	0606	|	0713	|	0812	0827	0827	|	0912	|	1014	1027	|	1112	|	1214	1227	1305	|	|	1414
322	Pegnitz	a.	0523	0527	0624	0628	0730	0734	0830	0834	|	|	0932	0936	1029	1034	|	1132	1136	1229	1234	|	1326	1333	1429	1434
322	Pegnitz	d.	0529	0529	0630	0630	0737	0737	...	0834	|	|	0939	0939	1037	1037	|	1139	1139	1237	1237	|	1336	1336	1437	1437
361	Hersbruck (r Pegnitz)	d.	0551	0551	0653	0653	0758	0758	...	0856	|	|	1001	1001	1059	1059	|	1201	1201	1259	1259	|	1358	1358	1459	1459
389	**Nürnberg** Hbf	a.	0607	0607	0710	0710	0815	0815	...	0912	0919	0919	1017	1017	1115	1115	1119	1217	1217	1315	1315	1319	1414	1414	1515	1515

							Ⓐn								Ⓑn						Ⓒk		B 🍷	⑤f		z
Dresden Hbf	d.	1057	1156	...	...	...	1257	1356	...	...	...	1457	1556	...	1657	...	...	1756	...	1857	1857	1956	...	2057	2107	2207a
Freiberg (Sachs)	d.	1127	1229	...	...	...	1327	1429	...	...	...	1527	1629	...	1727	...	...	1829	...	1927	1927	2029	...	2127	2151	2251
Flöha	d.	1145	1245	...	...	...	1345	1445	...	...	...	1545	1645	...	1745	...	...	1845	...	1945	1945	2045	...	2145	2215	2315
Chemnitz Hbf **858**	d.	1159	1258	...	...	...	1359	1458	...	...	...	1559	1658	...	1759	...	...	1858	...	1959	1959	2058	2050	2159	2234	2334
Glauchau (Sachs) **858**	d.	1222	1321	...	...	...	1422	1521	...	...	...	1622	1721	...	1822	...	...	1921	...	2022	2022	2121	2125	2222	2308n	0008
Zwickau (Sachs) Hbf	d.	1233	1333	...	...	...	1433	1533	...	...	...	1633	1733	...	1833	...	...	1933	...	2033	2033	2132	2144r	2233	2324n	0024
Reichenbach (Vogtl) ob Bf **881**	d.	1249	1349	...	...	...	1449	1549	...	...	...	1649	1749	...	1849	...	...	1949	...	2049	2049	*2209*	2200r	2249	...	...
Plauen (Vogtl) ob Bf **881**	d.	1305	1404	...	...	...	1505	1604	...	...	...	1705	1804	...	1905	...	...	2004	...	2105	2105	*2236*	2217r	2308	...	...
Hof Hbf **881**	a.	1334	1434	...	...	...	1534	1634	...	...	...	1734	1834	...	1934	...	...	2034	...	2134	2134	...	...	2336	...	...
Hof Hbf **876 879**	d.	1337	1437	...	...	...	1537	1637	...	...	...	1737	1837	...	1937	...	...	2037	...	▬	2137	...	...	...	...	...
Marktredwitz **879**	d.	|	1500	...	1539	...	|	1700	...	1739	...	|	1900	...	|	1939	...	2100	...	...	|	...	...	...	...	...
Kirchenlaibach	d.	|	1516	...	1612	...	|	1716	...	1812	...	|	1916	...	|	2012	...	2116	...	...	|	...	...	...	...	...
Münchberg **876**	d.	1353	|	...	|	...	1553	|	...	|	...	1753	|	...	1953	|	...	|	...	...	2153	...	...	...	...	...
Bayreuth Hbf **876**	d.	1427	|	1512	|	1614	1627	|	1712	|	1814	1827	|	1912	2027	|	2014	|	2116	2213	2233	...	...	...	...	...
Pegnitz	a.	|	1532	1536	1629	1634	|	1732	1736	1829	1834	|	1932	1936	|	2029	2034	2132	2136	2233	|	...	...	...	...	...
Pegnitz	d.	|	1539	1539	1637	1637	|	1739	1739	1837	1837	|	1939	1939	|	2037	2037	2139	2139	2234	|	...	...	...	...	...
Hersbruck (r Pegnitz)	d.	|	1601	1601	1659	1659	|	1801	1801	1959	1859	|	2001	2001	|	2108	2108	2201	2201	2256	|	...	...	...	...	...
Nürnberg Hbf	a.	1519	1617	1617	1715	1715	1719	1817	1817	1915	1915	1919	2017	2017	2119	2124	2124	2217	2217	2312	2325	...	...	...	...	...

B – *VOGTLAND-EXPRESS*. From Berlin (Table **843**). Operated by Vogtlandbahn. **DB tickets are not valid**.
a – Ⓐ only.
e – Not Dec. 24, 31, May 22.
f – Also Mar. 20; not Mar. 21.
k – Also Dec. 24, 31.
m – Also Jan. 2, Mar. 25, May 13; not Dec. 24, 31, Mar. 24, May 12.
n – Not Dec. 24, 31.
q – † (also May 22).
r – On ①②③④⑦ (not Dec. 23, 24, 25, 30, 31, Mar. 20, 23, Apr. 30, May 11) departs Zwickau 2148, Reichenbach 2209, arrives Plauen 2236.
t – 1339 on Ⓒ (also Dec. 24, 31, May 12).
v – Not Dec. 25, Jan. 1.
z – On Dec. 24, 31 terminates at Chemnitz.

881 ZWICKAU and PLAUEN - LEIPZIG *RE / RB services*

km			w	w	①–⑥		①–⑤	H																n
	Plauen (Vogtl) ob Bf **880**	d.	...	...	...	*0457*e	...	0631	*0657*e	...	0851	...	...	1051	...	...	1251	...	...	1451	...	...	1651	...
	Reichenbach (Vogtl) ob Bf **880**	d.	...	...	...	*0512*e	...	0648	*0712*e	...	0917	...	...	1117	...	...	1317	...	...	1517	...	...	1717	...
0	**Zwickau** (Sachs) Hbf **858 880**	d.	0337	...	0510	0537	0611	0713	0737	0811	|	0937	1011	|	1137	1211	|	1337	1411	|	1537	1611	|	1737
9	Werdau **858**	d.	0350	...	0520	0550	0620	0721	0750	0820	0928	0950	1020	1128	1150	1220	1328	1350	1420	1528	1550	1620	1728	1750
29	Gößnitz **858**	d.	0409	...	0535	0609	0635	0736	0809	0835	0943	1009	1035	1143	1209	1235	1343	1409	1435	1543	1609	1635	1743	1809
45	Altenburg	d.	0424	0524	0551	0624	0651	0751	0824	0851	0958	1024	1051	1158	1224	1251	1358	1424	1451	1558	1624	1651	1758	1824
89	**Leipzig** Hbf	a.	0522	0622	0632	0722	0732	0833	0922	0932	1041	1122	1132	1241	1322	1332	1441	1522	1532	1641	1722	1732	1841	1922

				n	n	A	n	n	
Plauen (Vogtl) ob Bf **880**	d.	...	1851	...	...	*2057*	...	...	...
Reichenbach (Vogtl) ob Bf **880**	d.	...	1917	...	...	*2112*	...	...	...
Zwickau (Sachs) Hbf **858 880**	d.	1811	|	1937	2011	2137	...	...	...
Werdau **858**	d.	1820	1928	1950	2020	2150	...	...	...
Gößnitz **858**	d.	1835	1943	2009	2035	2209	...	...	...
Altenburg	d.	1851	1958	2024	2051	2224	2224	2324	...
Leipzig Hbf	a.	1932	2041	2122	2132	2322	2322	0022	...

km			v		①–⑤	Ⓐ				
0	**Leipzig** Hbf	d.	0016	...	0425	0434	0534	0626	0712	0734
44	Altenburg	d.	0111	...	0509	0529	0631	0709	0801	0831
60	Gößnitz **858**	d.	...	...	0522	0545	0647	0722	0814	0847
80	Werdau **858**	d.	...	...	0538	0604	0706	0739	0830	0906
	Zwickau (Sachs) Hbf **858 880**	a.	...	...	0547	0614	0716	0747	|	0916
97	Reichenbach (Vogtl) ob Bf **880**	a.	...	...	...	*0648*	*0748*	...	0842	*0948*
122	Plauen (Vogtl) ob Bf **880**	a.	...	...	...	*0704*	*0803*	...	0910	*1003*

															Ⓑ				n	n		n		n
Leipzig Hbf	d.	0826	0912	0934	1027	1112	1134	1227	1312	1334	1427	1512	1534	1627	1727	1734	1827	1912	1934	2027	2112	2134	...	2227
Altenburg	d.	0909	1001	1031	1109	1201	1231	1309	1401	1431	1509	1601	1631	1709	1809	1831	1909	2001	2031	2109	2201	2231	...	2309
Gößnitz **858**	d.	0922	1014	1047	1122	1214	1247	1322	1414	1447	1522	1614	1647	1722	1822	1847	1922	2014	2047	2122	2214	2247	...	2322
Werdau **858**	d.	0939	1030	1106	1139	1230	1306	1339	1430	1506	1539	1630	1706	1739	1839	1906	1939	2030	2106	2139	2230	2306	...	2339
Zwickau (Sachs) Hbf **858 880**	a.	0947	|	1116	1147	|	1316	1347	|	1516	1547	|	1716	1747	1847	1916	1947	|	2116	2147	|	2316	...	2346
Reichenbach (Vogtl) ob Bf **880**	a.	...	1042	*1148*	...	1242	*1348*	...	1442	*1548*	...	1642	*1748*	...	...	*1948*	...	2042	*2208*	...	2242	...	...	...
Plauen (Vogtl) ob Bf **880**	a.	...	1110	*1203*	...	1310	*1403*	...	1510	*1603*	...	1710	*1803*	...	...	*2003*	...	2110	*2236*	...	2310	...	...	...

A – ①②③④⑦ (not Dec. 24, 31).
H – From Hof (Table **880**).
e – Ⓐ (not Dec. 24, 31).
n – Not Dec. 24, 31.
v – Not Dec. 25, Jan. 1.
w – Not Jan. 1.

882 CHEMNITZ - VEJPRTY - CHOMUTOV DB (*RB* services); ČD

km					⑥⑦c						n	n
0	**Chemnitz** Hbf **880**	d.	0538	0738	0838	0938	1138	1338	1538	1738	1838	2038
13	Flöha **880**	d.	0549	0749	0849	0949	1149	1349	1549	1749	1849	2049
31	Zschopau	d.	0609	0809	0907	1009	1209	1409	1609	1809	1909	2109
57	Annaberg-Buchholz Unt.	d.	0645	0845	0940	1045	1245	1445	1645	1845	1945	2145
64	Cranzahl ⊖	d.	0658	0859	0957	1059	1258	1459	1659	1858	2005	2158
74	Bärenstein (Annab)	d.	...	0912	1010	1112	...	1512	1712	...	...	...
75	Vejprty 🛃	a.	...	0914	1012	1114	...	1514	1714	...	...	...
75	Vejprty 🛃	d.	...	...	1018	...	...	...	*1725*c	...	...	...
133	Chomutov	a.	...	...	1145	...	...	...	*1852*c	...	...	...

								⑥⑦c		n	n
Chomutov	d.	...	...	*0803*c	...	...	...	1507	...	...	...
Vejprty 🛃	a.	...	...	*0930*c	...	...	...	1634	...	...	...
Vejprty 🛃	d.	...	...	0940	1140	...	1540	1638	1740	...	...
Bärenstein (Annab)	d.	...	...	0942	1142	...	1542	1640	1742	...	...
Cranzahl ⊖	d.	0555	0755	0955	1155	1355	1555	1700	1755	1948	2055
Annaberg Buchholz Unt.	d.	0608	0808	1008	1208	1408	1608	1710	1808	2008	2108
Zschopau	d.	0646	0846	1046	1246	1446	1646	1744	1846	2046	2146
Flöha **880**	a.	0709	0909	1109	1309	1509	1709	1809	1909	2109	2209
Chemnitz Hbf **880**	a.	0721	0921	1121	1321	1521	1721	1819	1921	2121	2221

⊖ – **Cranzahl - Kurort Oberwiesenthal** *Fichtelbergbahn* (17 km, narrow gauge steam) Journey: 60 minutes. Operator: BVO Bahn GmbH, Bahnhofstraße 7, 09484 Kurort Oberwiesenthal.
From **Cranzahl** at 0914 Ⓐ, 1006 Ⓒ, 1114 **k**, 1314, 1514 **k**, 1702 Ⓐ, 1714 Ⓒ, 1805 Ⓒ **k**.
From **Kurort Oberwiesenthal** at 0805 Ⓐ, 0845 Ⓐ **k**, 0858 Ⓒ, 0937 Ⓒ **k**, 1045 Ⓐ, 1144 Ⓒ, 1245 Ⓐ **k**, 1344 Ⓒ **k**, 1445 Ⓐ, 1544 Ⓒ, 1645 Ⓒ **k**

c – ⑥⑦ (also Dec. 25, 26, Jan. 1, Mar. 24, May 1).
k – Not Mar. 31 - Apr. 30.
n – Not Dec. 24, 31.

883 CHEMNITZ - AUE *RB services*

km				Ⓐ	Ⓒ							n	n
0	**Chemnitz** Hbf	d.	0610	0710	0810	0910	1110	1310	1510	1710	1910	2114	2248
27	Thalheim	d.	0657	0751	0851	0957	1157	1357	1557	1757	1957	2203	2329
36	Zwönitz	d.	0710	0804	0902	1010	1210	1410	1610	1810	2010	2216	2341
47	Lößnitz unt Bf.	d.	0721	0815	|	1021	1221	1421	1621	1821	2021	2227	2353
51	**Aue** (Sachs)	a.	0727	0821	0916	1027	1227	1427	1627	1827	2027	2233	2359

		v	Ⓐ								n	Ⓒ	n
Aue (Sachs)	d.	0406	0528	0626	0818t	0926	1126	1326	1526	1726	1926	2037	2132
Lößnitz unt Bf	d.	0412	0534	0632	0824t	0932	1132	1332	1532	1732	1932	2043	2138
Zwönitz	d.	0424	0546	0644	0836t	0944	1144	1344	1544	1744	1944	2055	2150
Thalheim	d.	0436	0558	0658	0858	0958	1158	1358	1558	1758	1958	2107	2202
Chemnitz Hbf	a.	0514	0640	0740	0940	1040	1240	1440	1640	1840	2040	2145	2241

n – Not Dec. 24, 31.
t – 10 minutes later on Ⓐ.
v – Not Dec. 25, Jan. 1.

884 ZWICKAU - JOHANNGEORGENSTADT - KARLOVY VARY

DB; ČD (2nd class only)

km		Ⓐ					n	n	©	n
0	**Zwickau** (Sachs) Hbf d.	0506	0606	and	1906	2006	2106	2206	2206	2306
27	Aue (Sachs) d.	0538	0638	hourly	1938	2038	2138	2238	2238	2338
37	Schwarzenberg (Erzg) d.	0557	0657	until	1957	2057	2157	2251	2257	2351c
56	**Johanngeorgenstadt** a.	0622	0722		2022	2122n	2222	...	2322	...

	v						n	n	©
Johanngeorgenstadt d.	0431a	0531v	0631	and	1931	2031	2131	2231
Schwarzenberg (Erzg) d.	0455	0555	0655	hourly	1955	2055	2155	2255
Aue (Sachs) d.	0508	0608	0708	until	2008	2108	2208	2308
Zwickau (Sachs) Hbf a.	0540	0640	0740		2040n	2140	2240	2340

km	▶	Ⓐ	v	D			©	Ⓐ		x	n
0	**Johanngeorgenstadt** d.	...	0727	1032	1245	...	1432	1432	1537c	1735	2047
1	Potučky 🚍 d.	0608	0731	1039	1250	...	1437	1437	1541	1740	2051
28	Nejdek d.	0707	0819	1130	1347	1420	1525	1540	1635	1836	2225
44	**Karlovy Vary** a.	0736	0846	1156	1414a	1446	1551	1606	1701	1902	2250
47	**Karlovy Vary** dolní a.	0742	0854	1202	1420a	1458	1557	1613	1712	1908	2256

▶	©v	v	D		Ⓐ	©	x	n	n
Karlovy Vary dolní d.	0504	0541a	0745	0952	1233	1300	1448	1755	2103
Karlovy Vary d.	0513	0547a	0751	0958	1240	1307	1454	1801	2110
Nejdek d.	0539	0626	0819	1026	1308	1337	1526	1830	2138
Potučky 🚍 d.	...	0718	0908	1118	1358	1424	1618	1918	2308k
Johanngeorgenstadt a.	...	0720	0910	1120	1400	1426	1620	1920	...

D – © (also May 12); runs daily Dec. 22 - Mar. 24.
a – Ⓐ only.
c – © only.
k – Not Dec. 24 - 31.
n – Not Dec. 24, 31.
v – Not Dec. 25, Jan. 1.
x – Not Dec. 24.
▶ – Czech holiday dates apply (see page 2).

885 REGENSBURG - SCHWANDORF - FURTH IM WALD - PLZEŇ

DB (*RE* / *RB* services); ČD

km		2	2 Ⓐe		451	2			2	2 x	455 ‡🍷	2	2 ©z	2 ⑥⑦c	2	‡	453	2			2	2	457 ‡🍷	2	2	2
	München Hbf 878 d.	...	...	...	...	...	...	...	...	...	0844	...	...	...	...	1244	...	...	...	...	...	...	1644	...	...	...
0	**Regensburg** Hbf 879 d.	...	*0527*	0623	...	*0729*	0832	...	*0931*	...	1021	*1130*	*1230*	...	*1331*	1421	...	*1528*	1633	...	...	*1737*	1821	*1929*	*2031*	*2221*
	Nürnberg Hbf 886 d.	...	|	|	0540	|	|	0753	|	...	|	|	|	...	|	|	1340	|	|	1553	...	|	|	|	|	|
42	**Schwandorf** 879 d.	...	0559	0650	0655	0803	0900	0905	1004	...	1056	1203	1305	...	1405	1446	1456	1602	1700	1705	...	1804	1856	2003	2107	2306
90	Cham (Oberpf) d.	...	0639	▬	0726	0839	▬	0940	1039	...	1124	1239	1339	...	1439	▬	1524	1639	...	1740	...	1839	1924	2041	2142	2341
109	**Furth im Wald** 🚍 a.	...	0656	2	0740	0856	2 x	0956	1056	...	1139	1256	1356	...	1456	2	1539	1657	...	1758	...	1856	1939	2058	2159	2358r
109	**Furth im Wald** 🚍 d.	...	...	*0703*	0749	...	0906	...	...	1103	1149	...	...	1402	...	1516	1549	...	...	...	1806	...	1949	...	...	...
131	Domažlice d.	0606	...	0731	0810	...	0930	...	...	1127	1210	...	...	1426	...	1540	1610	...	...	...	1835	...	2010	...	...	...
190	**Plzeň** Hlavní a.	0731	...	0852	0857	...	*1055*v	...	...	*1252*	1257	...	...	*1555*	...	...	1657	...	...	...	1955	...	2057	...	...	...
	Praha Hlavní 1120 a.	...	...	...	1045	...	...	...	...	...	1445	...	...	...	...	...	1845	...	...	...	...	...	2245	...	...	...

	2 Ⓐe	2	Ⓐn	©z		2	450	2 x	2		2 x	2	454 ‡🍷	2 ⑥⑦c	2 ©z	2	2	2	452	2	2	2	2	456 ‡🍷	2	2 x
Praha Hlavní 1120 d.	...	...	...	...	...	...	0516	...	...	...	...	...	0916	...	...	...	...	...	1316	...	...	...	...	1716	...	...
Plzeň Hlavní d.	...	...	...	...	...	...	0700	*0705*	...	...	*0808*	...	1100	*1105*	...	...	*1208*	...	1500	*1510*a	...	...	...	1900	...	2252
Domažlice d.	...	0528	...	...	...	...	0746	0828	...	...	1028	...	1146	1228	...	...	1428	...	1546	1636	...	...	...	1946	...	0005
Furth im Wald 🚍 a.	...	0552	...	...	...	...	0811	0852	...	...	1052	...	1211	1252	...	...	1452	...	1611	1700	...	...	...	2011	...	...
Furth im Wald 🚍 d.	0445	...	0556	0600	...	0701k	0821	▬	0901	1002	▬	1102	1221	...	1301	1401	...	1502	1621	▬	1704	1801	*1902*	2021	2104	...
Cham (Oberpf) d.	0500	...	0612	0616	...	0726	0835	‡	0917	1017	...	1124	1235	...	1317	1417	...	1524	1635	‡	1718	1817	1928	2037	2120	...
Schwandorf 879 a.	0536	...	0648	0648	0653	0759	0903	0907	0955	1055	1100	1157	1303	...	1357	1455	...	1559	1703	1709	1757	1855	2001	2105	2158	...
Nürnberg Hbf 886 a.	|	...	0806	0821	|	|	1009	|	|	1221	|	|	|	...	|	|	...	|	1809	|	|	|	|	|	|	...
Regensburg Hbf 879 a.	*0621*	...	...	...	0722	*0834*	...	0936	*1033*	...	1129	*1233*	1337	...	*1433*	*1529*	...	*1637*	...	1736	*1835*	*1929*	*2037*	2148	*2237*	...
München Hbf 878 a.	...	...	...	...	...	...	...	1116	...	...	...	...	1519	...	...	...	...	...	...	1919	...	...	...	2321	...	...

a – Ⓐ only.
c – Also Dec. 26, May 22.
e – Not Dec. 24, 31, May 22.
k – ⚒ (not May 22). Departs *0705* on ⑥ (also Dec. 24, 31).
r – ⑤⑥ only.
v – ①–⑥ (not Dec. 24, 25, 26, Jan. 1, Mar. 24).
x – Not Dec. 24, 25, 31.
z – Also Dec. 24, 31, May 22.
‡ – *ALX* in Germany (operated by Arriva / Regentalbahn AG - Die Länderbahn).

886 NÜRNBERG - SCHWANDORF and WEIDEN

RE services

Nürnberg - Schwandorf

km		Ⓐe	P								P			Ⓐe		Ⓐe										
0	**Nürnberg** Hbf ◧ d.	0434	0540	0648	0753	0848	0936	1048	1136	1248	1340	1353	1448	1536	1553	1636	1653	1736	1753	1848	1953	2050	2153	2250	...	0012
28	Hersbruck (r Pegnitz) ◧ d.	0449	|	0712	0812	0912	0951	1112	1151	1312	|	1412	1512	1551	1612	1651	1712	1751	1812	1912	2012	2112	2212	2312	...	0029
68	Amberg d.	0532	0630	0743	0843	0943	1028	1143	1228	1341	1431	1443	1543	1629	1643	1731	1744	1828	1843	1943	2043	2143	2246	2347	...	0101
94	**Schwandorf** a.	0551	0647	0757	0857	0957	1044	1157	1243	1357	1450	1457	1557	1644	1657	1746	1759	1843	1857	1957	2057	2157	2301	0001	...	...
	Furth im Wald 885 a.	...	0740	...	0956	...	...	...	...	...	1539	...	...	...	1758	...	...									

	Ⓐe	⚒r	†w	Ⓐe	⚒r	†w	Ⓐe	©z		P									P							
Furth im Wald 885 d.	...	...	...	...	...	...	0556	0600	...	0821	...	...	1002	...	...	...	...	...	1621	...	...	...	...	...	...	...
Schwandorf d.	0400	0513	0516	0544	0557	0609	0701	0709	0809	0904	0911	1009	1109	1209	1309	1409	1509	1609	1704	1711	1809	1909	2009	2113	2209	2309
Amberg d.	0416	0529	0532	0602	0615	0628	0718	0724	0824	0921	0929	1024	1124	1224	1326	1424	1524	1626	1721	1729	1824	1924	2024	2130	2224	2326
Hersbruck (r pegnitz) d.	|	0606	0606	|	0648	0706	0750	0806	0907	|	1007	1107	1206	1307	1406	1507	1606	1707	|	1806	1907	2006	2108	2206	2306	...
Nürnberg Hbf a.	0516	0621	0621	0656	0706	0723	0806	0821	0923	1009	1022	1123	1221	1323	1421	1523	1621	1723	1809	1821	1923	2021	2124	2221	2321	...

Nürnberg - Weiden

km		Ⓐe								
0	**Nürnberg** Hbf ◧ d.	0434	0535	0625	0737	0836	and	2036	2250	...
28	Hersbruck (r Pegnitz) ◧ d.	0449	0551	0643	0752	0851	hourly	2051	2312	...
97	**Weiden** (Oberpf) a.	0541	0645	0745	0845	0945	until	2145	0007	...

	Ⓐe	⚒r			✣				
Weiden (Oberpf) d.	0415	0505	0612	0710	and	1809	1910	2010	2213
Hersbruck (r Pegnitz) d.	0515	0606	0706	0806	hourly	1907	2006	2108	2306
Nürnberg Hbf a.	0548	0621	0723	0821	until	1923	2021	2124	2321

P – To / from Praha (Table 885).
e – Not Dec. 24, 31, May 22.
r – Not May 22.
w – Also May 22.
z – Also Dec. 24, 31, May 22.
✣ – Certain trains depart Weiden at 09 minutes past the hour.
◧ – Certain trains from Nürnberg and Hersbruck convey portions for two separate destinations. Passengers should take care to join the correct portion for their destination.

887 BAYREUTH - WEIDEN

RB services

km		Ⓐe	Ⓐe			Ⓐe					Ⓐe			Ⓐe			Ⓐe		Ⓐe		Ⓐe		Ⓑn			
0	**Bayreuth** Hbf d.	0441	0544	0615	0716	0818	0818	0918	1018	1118	1218	1218	1318	1418	1418	1518	1618	1618	1644	1718	1818	1818	1918	1918	2018	2226
19	Kirchenlaibach a.	0458	0601	0632	0739	0839	0839	0939	1039	1139	1239	1239	1339	1439	1439	1539	1639	1639	1701	1739	1839	1839	1939	1939	2039	2246
19	Kirchenlaibach d.	*0532*	...	0655	0746	0846	...	0946	...	1146	1246	...	1346	1446	...	1546	1646	...	...	1746	1846	...	1946			
59	**Weiden** a.	*0607*	...	0725	0817	0917	...	1017	...	1219	1317	...	1417	1517	...	1617	1717	...	...	1817	1917	...	2017			

	Ⓐe	Ⓐe	⚒r	Ⓐe	Ⓑn		Ⓐe					Ⓐe			Ⓐe			Ⓐe			Ⓐe				©z	
Weiden d.	0429	0524	...	0631	...	0731	0831	...	0931	...	1131	1231	...	1331	1431	...	1531	1631	...	1731	1831	...	1931	...	2131	...
Kirchenlaibach a.	0501	0557	...	0707	...	0808	0908	...	1008	...	1208	1308	...	1408	1508	...	1608	1708	...	1808	1908	...	2008	...	2203	...
Kirchenlaibach d.	0509	0608	0651	0717	0717	0819	0919	0919	1019	1119	1219	1319	1319	1419	1519	1519	1619	1719	1719	1819	1919	1919	2019	2119	...	2208
Bayreuth Hbf a.	0525	0629	0707	0734	0734	0836	0936	0936	1036	1136	1236	1336	1336	1436	1536	1536	1636	1736	1736	1836	1936	1936	2036	2136	...	2224

e – Not Dec. 24, 31, May 22.
n – Not Dec. 24, 31.
r – Not May 22.
z – Also Dec. 24, 31, May 22.

888 KEMPTEN - REUTTE IN TIROL - GARMISCH-PARTENKIRCHEN

RB services; 2nd class only

km										
0	**Kempten** (Allgäu) Hbf d.	...	0717	0917	1017	1117	1317	1517	1717	1917
18	Oy-Mittelberg d.	...	0749	0948	1048	1148	1348	1549	1748	1948
24	Nesselwang d.	...	0800	0959	1059	1159	1359	1600	1759	1959
31	Pfronten-Ried d.	...	0813	1013	1113	1213	1413	1613	1813	2013
33	**Pfronten-Steinach** 🚍 d.	...	0820	1020	1130	1220	1420	1620	1820	2020
38	Vils 🚍 d.	...	0827	1033	1137	1227	1427	1627	1844	2027
48	**Reutte in Tirol** a.	...	0842	1048	1152	1242	1442	1642	1859	2042
	Change trains									
48	**Reutte in Tirol** d.	0700	0903	1103		1303	1500h	1703	1903	
68	Lermoos d.	0726	0929	1129		1329	1527	1729	1929	
71	Ehrwald Zugspitzbahn 🚍 d.	0731	0934	1134		1334	1533	1734	1934	
93	**Garmisch**-Partenkirchen a.	0756	0959	1201		1359	1559	1759	1959	

					⑥⑦c	A			
Garmisch-Partenkirchen d.	...	0804	1004	1204	1404	1438	1604	1804	2006
Ehrwald Zugspitzbahn 🚍 d.	...	0829	1029	1229	1429	1503	1629	1829	2031
Lermoos d.	...	0833	1033	1233	1433	1507	1633	1833	2035
Reutte in Tirol a.	...	0859	1059	1259	1459	1536	1700	1859	2100
Change trains					d				
Reutte in Tirol d.	0717	0917	1105	1317	1517	...	1717	1917	2105
Vils 🚍 d.	0731	0931	1119	1331	1531	...	1731	1931	2119
Pfronten-Steinach 🚍 d.	0739	0939	1128	1339	1539	...	1739	1939	2139
Pfronten-Ried d.	0745	0945	1145	1345	1545	...	1745	1945	2145
Nesselwang d.	0801	1001	1201	1401	1601	...	1801	2001	2206
Oy-Mittelberg d.	0813	1013	1213	1413	1613	...	1813	2012	2218
Kempten (Allgäu) Hbf a.	0846	1045	1245	1445	1645	...	1845	2045	2251

A – ①–⑤ (not Dec. 25, 26, Jan. 1, Mar. 24, May 1, 12, 22).
c – Also Dec. 25, 26, Jan. 1, Mar. 24, May 1, 12, 22.
d – Runs daily from Reutte.
h – 1503 on ⑥⑦c.

890 MÜNCHEN - SALZBURG

km			*EN*		*RB*	*RB*	*RB*	*RB*	*IC*	*RB*	*IC*	*RE*	*EC*	*RB*	*IC*	*RE*	*EC*	*RB*	*IC*	*RB*	*EC*	*RB*	*IC*	*IC*
			265		**30061**	**30063**	**30001**	**30003**	**111**	**30007**	**2291**	**30009**	**63**	**30011**	**2293**	**30013**	**113**	**30015**	**2295**	**30017**	**115**	**30019**	**2083**	**2297**
					Ⓐe	Ⓐe	Ⓐe				①–⑥													
		⊖	🍷♦						♦		r		✕♦		🍷♦		✕♦		🍷		✕♦		🍷♦	🍷
	Frankfurt Hbf **911** d.	...	...	...	...	...	...	...	...	...	...	...	...	...	...	...	...	...	0820	...	...	...	...	1020
	Stuttgart Hbf **930** d.	...	...	...	...	...	...	...	...	...	0553	...	...	...	0758	...	...	...	0958	...	1054	...	...	1158
0	**München** Hbf **951** d.	0318	...	...	...	...	0552	0639	0726	0742	0825	0848	0927	0942	1022	1048	1126	1142	1222	1242	1327	1342	...	1422
10	München Ost **951** d.	0326	0345	...	...	...	0601	0647	|	0750	|	0856	|	0950	1031	1056	|	1150	1231	1250	|	1350	1414	1431
65	Rosenheim **951** d.	...	|	...	0542	...	0641	0731	|	0831	0901	0931	|	1030	1101	1131	|	1230	1301	1331	|	1430	1444	1501
82	Bad Endorf d.	...	|	...	0554	...	0653	0742	|	0849	|	0943	|	1049	|	1142	|	1249	|	1342	|	1449	1457	|
90	Prien am Chiemsee d.	...	|	...	0601	...	0701	0750	|	0856	0918	0950	|	1056	1118	1150	|	1256	1318	1350	|	1456	1504	1518
118	Traunstein d.	...	|	...	0625	0656	0725	0814	0831	0917	0937	1014	|	1117	1137	1214	|	1319	1337	1415	|	1519	1526	1537
147	Freilassing **891** d.	...	|	...	0645	0719	0745	0834	0850	0938	0956	1035	|	1138	1156	1235	|	1339	1356	1435	|	1540	1546	1556
153	**Salzburg** Hbf **891** 🛃 a.	...	0509	...	0652	0725	0752	0841	0858	0947	1002	1042	1054	1147	1203	1241	1254	1347	1403	1442	1454	1547	...	1603
	Wien Westbahnhof **950** a.	...	0835	...	...	...	...	...	...	...	...	...	1338	...	...	...	...	...	...	...	...	...	...	...

	RE	*EC*	*RB*	*IC*	*RE*	*RE*	*ICE*	*RB*	*RE*	*IC*	*RE*	*IC*	*RB*	*IC*	*RE*	*RB*	*RE*		*D*	*EN*		*RB*	*RB*	*RB*
	30021 30051	**69**	**30023**	**2299**	**30025**	**30027**	**117**	**30029**	**30031**	**2391**	**30033**	**2265**	**30035**	**391**	**30037**	**30039**	**30041**		**297**	**269**		**30043 30045**	**30043**	**30067**
					Ⓐe			Ⓒz	Ⓐe	Ⓑq		Ⓑq											⑤⑥f	Ⓐe
		✕		🍷			✕			🍷		🍷♦		🍷♦					🍷♦	🍷♦		m		
Frankfurt Hbf **911** d.	...	...	...	1220	...	...	...	...	...	1420	...	...	...	1620	...	...	...	...	...	...	...	...	...	...
Stuttgart Hbf **930** d.	...	...	...	1358	...	...	...	...	...	1558	...	1653	...	1758	...	...	...	...	...	...	...	...	...	...
München Hbf **951** d.	1446	1526	1542	1622	1626	1648	1723	1740	1759	1822	1846	1922	1942	2024	2047	2149	2246	...	2345	2345	...	2350	2350	...
München Ost **951** d.	1455	|	1550	1631	1636	1657	|	1749	1807	1831	1854	1931	1950	2034	2055	2157	2254	...	|	|	...	2359	2359	...
Rosenheim **951** d.	1531	|	1630	1701	1708	1731	|	1838	1838	1901	1931	2003	2030	2104	2132	2237	2331	...	0026	0026	...	0037	0038	0045
Bad Endorf d.	1543	|	1649	|	1720	1743	|	1850	1850	|	1942	2015	2049	2116	2143	2249	2342	...	|	|	...	...	0050	0058
Prien am Chiemsee d.	1550	|	1656	1718	1727	1750	|	1857	1857	1918	1950	2023	2056	2124	2151	2256	2350	...	|	|	...	...	0057	0105
Traunstein d.	1615	|	1719	1737	1752	1815	|	1921	1921	1937	2014	2042	2119	2143	2214	2319	0014	...	|	|	...	...	0120	0129
Freilassing **891** d.	1639	|	1740	1756	1813	1838	|	1942	1942	1956	2035	2101	2140	2201	2235	2339	0034	...	|	|	...	...	0141	0151
Salzburg Hbf **891** 🛃 a.	1647	1654	1747	1803	...	1844	1858	1949	1949	2003	2042	2109	2147	2209	*2247*n	2345	*0047*	...	0121	0121	...	...	0147	...
Wien Westbahnhof **950** a.	...	1935	...	...	...	...	2142	...	...	...	...	...	...	...	...	...	...	...	...	0555	...	...	...	...

	RB		*EN*	*D*		*RB*	*RE*	*IC*	*RE*	*RB*	*RE*	*IC*	*RB*	*RE*	*IC*	*RB*	*ICE*	*RE*	*IC*	*IC*	*RB*	*EC*	*RE*	*IC*
	30000		**268**	**296**		**30002**	**30004**	**2392**	**30006**	**30010**	**30008**	**2264**	**30012**	**30014**	**390**	**30016**	**116**	**30018**	**2082**	**2298**	**30020**	**68**	**30022**	**2296**
	Ⓐe					Ⓐp		①–⑥	Ⓐe	Ⓒz	Ⓐe	①–⑥	Ⓐe		①–⑥									
			🍷♦	🍷♦				r🍷				r♦			r♦		✕		🍷♦	🍷		✕		🍷
Wien Westbahnhof **950** d.	...	...	2345	...	...	...	...	...	...	...	...	...	...	...	...	...	0614	...	...	...	...	0822	...	...
Salzburg Hbf **891** 🛃 d.	...	...	0428	0428	...	...	*0511*v	0547	...	0607	*0611*	0646	...	0709	0753	0817	0903	0918	...	0957	1011	1103	1118	1153
Freilassing **891** d.	0414	...	|	|	...	0452	0522	0555	0607	0618	0622	0654	0658	0725	0801	0824	|	0925	0942	1005	1019	|	1125	1201
Traunstein d.	0434	...	|	|	...	0512	0543	0613	0628	0637	0650	0712	0718	0745	0819	0845	|	0945	1000	1023	1039	|	1145	1219
Prien am Chiemsee d.	0458	...	|	|	...	0535	0607	0631	0652	0708	0708	0730	0741	0809	0837	0909	|	1009	1021	1041	1103	|	1209	1237
Bad Endorf d.	0505	...	|	|	...	0542	0615	0639	0700	0715	0715	0738	0748	0816	|	0916	|	1016	1029	|	1110	|	1216	1245
Rosenheim **951** d.	0520	...	0529	0529	...	0558	0630	0654	0716	0730	0729	0754	0803	0831	0857	0931	|	1031	1044	1101	1130	|	1231	1300
München Ost **951** a.	0558	...	0603	0603	...	0636	0702	0722	0747	0807	0758	0821	0840	0902	0924	1008	|	1102	1112	|	1207	|	1308	|
München Hbf **951** a.	0608	...	0615	0615	...	0646	0713	0733	0800	0817	0808	0832	0854	0913	0934	1019	1031	1112	...	1136	1217	1231	1318	1334
Stuttgart Hbf **930** a.	...	...	...	...	...	...	...	1000	...	...	...	1107	...	...	1200	...	...	...	...	1400	...	...	...	1600
Frankfurt Hbf **911** a.	...	...	...	...	...	...	...	1140	...	...	...	...	...	...	1340	...	...	...	...	1540	...	...	...	1740

	RB	*EC*	*RE*	*IC*	*RB*	*EC*	*RB*	*IC*	*RB*	*IC*	*RE*	*RB*	*EC*	*RE*	*RB*		*IC*	*RE*		*RB*		*EN*		
	30024	**114**	**30028**	**2294**	**30030**	**112**	**30032**	**2292**	**30034**	**2290**	**30036**	**30038**	**62**	**30040**	**30042**		**110**	**30044**		**30070**		**264**		
																				n				
		✕♦		🍷		✕♦		🍷♦		🍷♦			✕♦				♦					🍷♦	⊖	
Wien Westbahnhof **950** d.	...	...	...	...	...	...	...	...	...	...	...	...	1622	...	...	...	...	...	...	...	...	2035	...	...
Salzburg Hbf **891** 🛃 d.	1211	1302	1314	1353	1411	1503	1518	1553	1611	1653	1718	1812	1903	1918	2013	...	2104	2118	...	2258	...	2342	...	...
Freilassing **891** d.	1219	|	1325	1401	1420	|	1525	1601	1619	1701	1725	1819	|	1925	2020	...	|	2125	...	2304	...	|	...	...
Traunstein d.	1239	|	1345	1419	1440	|	1545	1619	1639	1719	1745	1839	|	1945	2040	...	|	2145	...	2326	...	|	...	...
Prien am Chiemsee d.	1303	|	1409	1437	1503	|	1609	1637	1703	1737	1809	1903	|	2009	2110	...	|	2209	...	2351	...	|	...	...
Bad Endorf d.	1310	|	1416	|	1510	|	1616	|	1710	|	1816	1910	|	2016	2117	...	|	2216	...	...	...	|	...	...
Rosenheim **951** d.	1330	|	1431	1457	1530	|	1631	1657	1730	1757	1831	1930	|	2031	2131	...	|	2231	...	...	...	|	...	...
München Ost **951** a.	1407	|	1502	1524	1607	|	1708	1724	1807	1824	1902	2007	|	2102	2208	...	|	2302	...	...	...	0108	0115	...
München Hbf **951** a.	1417	1430	1513	1534	1616	1632	1718	1734	1817	1834	1912	2017	2034	2112	2219	...	2232	2312	...	...	...	...	0123	...
Stuttgart Hbf **930** a.	...	1705	...	1800	...	...	...	2000	...	2106q	...	...	...	...	...	...	...	...	...	...	...	...	...	...
Frankfurt Hbf **911** a.	...	...	...	1940	...	...	...	...	...	...	...	...	...	...	...	...	...	...	...	...	...	...	...	...

♦ – **NOTES** (LISTED BY TRAIN NUMBER)

62/3 – [12] and ✕ Budapest - Hegyeshalom 🛃 - Wien - München and v.v.

110/1 – [12] Klagenfurt - Villach - München and v.v.; [12] Beograd (**210/1**) - Vinkovci - Zagreb - Dobova 🛃 - Ljubljana - Jesenice 🛃 - Villach - München and v.v.

112/3 – [12] and ✕ Klagenfurt - Villach - München and v.v.; [12] Zagreb (**212/3**) - Dobova 🛃 - Ljubljana - Jesenice 🛃 - Villach - München and v.v.

114/5 – WÖRTHERSEE – [12] and ✕ Klagenfurt - Villach - München - Stuttgart - Heidelberg - Mannheim - Koblenz - Köln - Dortmund and v.v.

264/5 – ORIENT EXPRESS – 🛏 1, 2 cl., 🛌 2 cl., [2] and 🍷 Wien - Karlsruhe - Strasbourg and v.v.

268/9 – KÁLMÁN IMRE – 🛏 1, 2 cl., 🛌 2 cl., [2] and 🍷 Budapest - Wien - München and v.v. 🛏 1, 2 cl. Bucureşti - Timişoara - Budapest - München and v.v.

296 – LISINSKI – 🛏 1, 2 cl., 🛌 2 cl. and [2] Zagreb - Dobova 🛃 - Ljubljana - Jesenice 🛃 - Villach - München; [2] Beograd (**418**) - Vinkovci (**748**) - Zagreb (**296**) - München. Dec. 9–20, Jan. 1–6, Mar. 14–29, Apr. 30 - Sept. 19 (from Rijeka) conveys 🛌 2 cl. (also 🛏 1, 2 cl. Apr. 30 - Sept. 19) Rijeka (**480**) - Ljubljana (**296**) - München.

297 – LISINSKI – 🛏 1, 2 cl., 🛌 2 cl. and [2] München - Villach - Jesenice 🛃 - Ljubljana - Dobova 🛃 - Zagreb; [2] München - Zagreb (**741**) - Vinkovci (**419**) - Beograd. Dec. 9–21, Jan. 2–7, Mar. 15–30, May 1 - Sept. 20 (from München) conveys 🛌 2 cl. (also 🛏 1, 2 cl. May 1 - Sept. 20) München - Ljubljana (**481**) - Rijeka.

390 – [12] and 🍷 Linz - Salzburg - Frankfurt.

391 – [12] and 🍷 Frankfurt - Salzburg (- Linz Ⓑq).

2082/3 – KÖNIGSEE – [12] and 🍷 Berchtesgaden - Augsburg - Hamburg and v.v. See Table **900** for timings to / from Hamburg.

2264/5 [12] and 🍷 Salzburg - München - Karlsruhe and v.v.

2290 – [12] and 🍷 Salzburg - München (- Karlsruhe Ⓑq).

2292/3 – [12] and 🍷 Salzburg - Stuttgart - Mannheim - Saarbrücken and v.v.

e – Not Dec. 24, 31, May 22.
f – Also Dec. 23, 24, 25, 30, Mar. 20, 23, Apr. 30, May 11, 21.
m – Not Dec. 31.
n – Not Dec. 24, 31.
p – Not May 22.
q – Ⓑ (not Dec. 24, 25, 31, Mar. 21, 23, May 11).
r – Not Dec. 25, 26, Jan. 1, Mar. 22, 24, May 12.
v – ①–⑤ (not Dec. 24, 25, 26, 31, Jan. 1, Mar. 24, May 1, 12, 22).
z – Also Dec. 24, 31, May 22.

⊖ – S-bahn route **8**.

891 (SCHWARZACH -) SALZBURG - BERCHTESGADEN

RB services (2nd class only)

km																									
		Ⓐe		Ⓐe	Ⓒz					Ⓐe	Ⓒz	Ⓐe	Ⓐe	Ⓒz			H						n	n	Ⓒr
	Schwarzach-St Veit ◐ d.	*0453*	...	0623	0623t	0723	0823	0923	1023	...	1123	...	...	1223	1323	1423	...	1523	1623	1723	1823	1923	2023	2123	2223
	Bischofshofen ◐ d.	*0509*	...	0639	0639t	0739	0839	0939	1039	...	1139	...	...	1239	1339	1439	...	1539	1639	1739	1839	1939	2039	2139	2239
0	**Salzburg** Hbf **890** ◐ d.	*0611*	*0709*	0742	0742t	0842	0942	1042	1142	*1211*	1242	...	*1314*	1342	1442	1542	...	1642	1742	1845	1942	2042	2142	2242	2346
6	Freilassing **890** a.	*0618*	*0715*	0749	0749t	0849	0950	1049	1149	*1217*	1249	...	*1320*	1349	1449	1549	...	1649	1749	1852	1949	2049	2149	2249	2353
6	Freilassing d.	0634	0720	0759	0759	0853	0959	1051	1159	1239	1251	1251	1351	1359	1451	...	1600	1651	1800	1854	1959	2104	2203	2251	2355
21	Bad Reichenhall d.	0652	0741	0817	0817	0908	1017	1109	1217	1256	1309	1314	1418	1418	1509	...	1619	1709	1818	1912	2017	2121	2220	2309	0011
39	**Berchtesgaden** Hbf a.	0727	0810	0855	0902	0945	1051	1138	1251	...	1338	1342	1447	1447	1538	...	1650	1743	1852	1941	2051	2150	2250	2338	...

	Ⓐe	⑥k	Ⓐe		Ⓐe		zH	eH						Ⓒz	Ⓐe						Ⓐe				n
Berchtesgaden Hbf d.	*0510**	0620	0621	0709	0816	...	0827	0837	...	0910	1016	1102	1216	1302	1324	1411	1502	1613	1708	...	...	1817	1905	2016	2214
Bad Reichenhall d.	0546	0650	0656	0740	0847	0847	0910	0910	...	0940	1046	1136	1246	1336	1356	1445	1536	1647	1740	...	1817	1849	1939	2046	2247
Freilassing a.	0602	0706	0713	0756	0907	0907	0928	0928	...	0957	1106	1156	1306	1353	1414	1506	1556	1707	1759	...	1833	1912	1956	2103	2307
Freilassing **890** d.	0608	0708	*0719*	0808	0908	0908	...	...	0938	1008	1108	1208	1308	1408	1417	1508	1608	1708	...	1808	*1838*	1917	2008	2108	2308
Salzburg Hbf **890** ◐ a.	0616	0715	*0725*	0815	0916	0916	...	...	0947	1016	1115	1216	1315	1416	1424	1515	1616	1716	...	1815	*1844*	1924	2015	2116	2315
Bischofshofen ◐ a.	0719	0819	...	0919	1019	1019	...	...	...	1119	1219	1319	1419	1519	...	1619	1719	1819	...	1919	...	...	2119	2219	0019
Schwarzach-St Veit ◐ a.	0736	0836	...	0936	1036	1036	...	...	...	1136	1236	1336	1436	1536	...	1636	1736	1836	...	1936	...	...	2136	2236	...

H – *IC* **2082/3**: KÖNIGSSEE – [12] Berchtesgaden - Hamburg and v.v. Train category *RE* Berchtesgaden - Freilassing and v.v.

e – Ⓐ (not Dec. 24, 31, May 22).

k – Also Dec. 24, 31.
n – Not Dec. 24, 31.
r – Also May 22.
t – Not Mar. 21.

z – Ⓒ (also Dec. 24, 31, May 22).

* – By 🚌 to Bad Reichenhall.
◐ – For other services see Tables **970** / **980**.

FLUGHAFEN MÜNCHEN ✈ (S-Bahn services S1, S8) 892

2nd class only

km		S8		S8	S1	S8	S1	S8	S1	S8		S1	S8	S1	S8	S1	S8	S8	S8	S8
0	**München** Pasing d.	0309	and every 20 minutes until	0449	...	0509	...	0529	...	0549	and at the same minutes past each hour until	...	2249	...	2309	...	2329	2349	0009	0029
7	**München** Hbf (low level) d.	0318		0458	0505	0518	0525	0538	0545	0558		2245	2258	2305	2318	2325	2338	2358	0018	0038
11	**München** Ost d.	0327		0507	|	0527	|	0547	|	0607		|	2307	|	2327	|	2347	0007	0027	0047
44	**München Flughafen** Terminal ✈ a.	0357		0537	0546	0557	0606	0617	0626	0637		2326	2337	2346	2357	0006	0017	0037	0057	0117

km ◐		S8		S8	S1	S8	S1	S8	S1	S8		S8	S1	S8	S1	S8	S1	S8	S8	S8
0	**München Flughafen** Terminal ✈ d.	0402	and every 20 minutes until	0542	0551	0602	0611	0622	0631	0642	and at the same minutes past each hour until	2322	2331	2342	2351	0002	0011	0022	0042	0102
	München Ost a.	0433		0613	|	0633	|	0653	|	0713		2353	|	0013	|	0033	|	0053	0113	0133
41	**München** Hbf (low level) a.	0443		0623	0636	0643	0656	0703	0716	0723		0003	0016	0023	0036	0043	0056	0103	0123	0143
	München Pasing a.	0452		0632	...	0652	...	0712	...	0732		0014	...	0032	...	0054	...	0112	0132	0152

◐ – Via Neufahrn (b Freising).

☛ Many **S1** trains from München Hbf are combined with a Freising service - travel in the rear portion for the Airport.

MÜNCHEN - MÜHLDORF - SIMBACH 893

km			⚒r									Ⓐe	Ⓒz	Ⓐe	Ⓒz	Ⓐe		Ⓐe	Ⓒz		Ⓐe					
0	**München** Hbf d.	...	...	0707	0807z	0907	1009	1107	1207	1307	1407	1507	1507	...	1607	1618	1707	1727	...	1807	...	1907	2028	2129	2228	2336
10	**München** Ost d.	...	0616	0717	0817	0917	1018	1117	1217	1317	1417	1518	1518	1539	1617	1638	1718	1740	...	1817	1840	1916	2038	2139	2238	2345
85	**Mühldorf** (Oberbay) a.	...	0723	0816	0919	1016	1119	1216	1317	1417	1517	1620	1618	1646	1717	1732	1819	1828	...	1918	1934	2021	2142	2238	2333	0044
		⚒r	d									|	Ⓒz	Ⓐe		d		|			|			n		
85	**Mühldorf** (Oberbay) d.	0637	0737	0842	0937	1037	1136	1227	1337	1437	1536	1626	1637	1655	...	1737	...	1831	1837	1936	1936	2030	2146	2246	...	...
98	Neuötting d.	0647	0747	0853	0948	1047	1146	1237	1347	1447	1546	1638	1647	1711	...	1747	...	1843	1847	1946	1946	2041	2157	2257	...	...
124	**Simbach** (Inn) 🚌 **965** a.	0714	0813	0924	1013	1116	1212	1258	1413	1513	1612	1700	1713	1731	...	1813	...	1905	1913	2013	2013	2101	2217	2317	...	...

		Ⓐe	⑥k	Ⓐe	Ⓐe	Ⓒz												Ⓐe	Ⓒz			Ⓒz			n
Simbach (Inn) 🚌 **965** d.	...	0507	0547	0554	0648	0648	0749	0900	0949	1051	1148	1300	1349	1449	...	1548	...	...	1631	1649	...	1749	1849	1949	2106	2222
Neuötting d.	...	0528	0607	0616	0711	0711	0810	0921	1010	1112	1209	1321	1410	1510	...	1609	...	...	1658	1710	...	1810	1910	2010	2126	2242
Mühldorf (Oberbay) a.	...	0540	0619	0628	0724	0724	0822	0932	1021	1125	1220	1333	1421	1521	...	1620	...	...	1709	1721	...	1821	1921	2022	2138	2257
	①–⑥	Ⓐe	Ⓒz	|	|	Ⓒz								Ⓐe	Ⓒz		Ⓒz	Ⓐe					Ⓒz			
Mühldorf (Oberbay) d.	0522	0545	0623	0637	0730	0729	0830	0937	1030	1137	1228	1339	1428	1539	1540	...	1628	1628	...	...	1737	1830	1939	2029	2146	...
München Ost a.	0625	0640	0724	0723	0823	0826	0927	1045	1125	1245	1325	1445	1526	1646	1645	...	1725	1746	...	...	1846	1926	2044	2126	2247	...
München Hbf a.	0636	...	0737	0737	0836	0837	0938	1055	1140	1255	1338	1455	1539	1656	1656	...	1739	...	...	...	1856	1938	2054	2137	2257	...

d – Daily from Mühldorf. **e** – Not Dec. 24, 31, May 22. **k** – Also Dec. 24, 31. **n** – Not Dec. 24, 31. **r** – Not May 22. **z** – Ⓒ (also Dec. 24, 31, May 22).

MÜNCHEN - GARMISCH - INNSBRUCK 895

DB; ÖBB (2nd class only in Austria)

km							*CNL* **319** ⑥**A**					*ICE* **527** ⑥**W**				*ICE* **1507** ⑥**K**		*ICE* **787** ⑥**H**						n	n	n
			Ⓐe																							
0	**München** Hbf d.	...	0537	...	0630	0732	0734	0832	0932	1032	1132	1209	1232	1332	1432	1445	1532	1547	1632	1732	1832	1932	2032	2132	2232	2333
7	München Pasing d.	...	0544	...	0638	0739	|	0839	0939	1039	1139	|	1239	1339	1439	|	1539	|	1639	1739	1839	1939	2039	2139	2240	2340
40	Tutzing d.	...	0609	...	0701	0801	|	0901	1001	1101	1201	|	1301	1401	1501	|	1601	|	1701	1801	1901	2001	2101	2201	2301	0001
54	Weilheim (Oberbay) d.	...	0631	...	0711	0813	0828	0911	1011	1111	1211	|	1311	1411	1511	|	1611	|	1711	1812	1911	2012	2111	2212	2312	0011
75	Murnau d.	...	0650	...	0729	0832	0851	0930	1031	1130	1230	|	1331	1430	1530	|	1630	|	1730	1830	1930	2030	2130	2230	2330	0030
101	**Garmisch**-Partenk. a.	...	0717	...	0759	0857	0923	0959	1057	1157	1256	1342	1357	1456	1557	1622	1658	1721	1757	1857	1957	2056	2157	2255	2356	0056
101	**Garmisch**-Partenk. d.	0630	0727	...	0804	0900j	...	1004	1100	1204	1300	...	1404	1500	1604	...	1700h	...	1804	1900	2004	2100	2200	2300	0000	0057g
118	**Mittenwald** 🚌 d.	0654	0754	0826	0826	0922j	...	1026	1122	1226	1322	...	1426	1522	1626	...	1722h	...	1826	1922	2026	2122	2222	2322	0022	0118g
125	Scharnitz ⊡ d.	0702	...	0834	0834b	...	...	1034	...	1234	...	...	1434	...	1634	...	...	...	1834	...	2034	...	...	...	...	...
135	Seefeld in Tirol ⊡ d.	0716	...	0846	0846b	...	...	1046	...	1246	...	...	1446	...	1646	...	...	...	1846	...	2046	...	...	...	...	...
160	**Innsbruck** Hbf ⊡ a.	0753	...	0922	0922b	...	...	1122	...	1322	...	...	1522	...	1722	...	...	...	1922	...	2122	...	...	...	...	...

								ICE **1708** ⑥**K**		*ICE* **788** ⑥**H**					L		*ICE* **1828** ⑥**W**						*CNL* **318** ⑥**A**	n		n
	⚒r	Ⓐe	Ⓒz	Ⓐe																						
Innsbruck Hbf ⊡ d.	...	...	...	...	...	0634	...	...	0838	...	...	1038	...	1238c	1304	...	...	1438	...	1638	...	1838	...	...	2038	...
Seefeld in Tirol ⊡ d.	...	...	...	...	...	0715	...	...	0915	...	...	1115	...	1315c	1345	...	...	1515	...	1715	...	1915	...	...	2115	...
Scharnitz ⊡ d.	...	...	...	...	...	0727	...	...	0927	...	...	1127	...	1327c	1357	...	...	1527	...	1727	...	1927	...	...	2127	...
Mittenwald 🚌 d.	...	...	0537	0553	0621k	0737	0837	...	0937	...	1037	1136	1237	1337	1406	1437z	...	1537	1637	1737	1837	1937	...	2037	2137	2237
Garmisch-Partenk. a.	...	...	0559	0615	0649k	0759	0859	...	0959	...	1059	1158	1259	1359	1433y	1459z	...	1559	1659	1759	1859	1959	...	2059	2159	2259
Garmisch-Partenk. d.	0504	0557	0604	0623	0657k	0804	0904	0925	1004	1035	1104	1206	1308	1404	...	1504	1518	1604	1704	1804	1904	2004	2035	2104	2204n	2304
Murnau d.	0530	0624	0631	0651	0730	0831	0931	|	1031	|	1131	1230	1333	1430	...	1530	|	1630	1731	1830	1930	2030	2106	2130	2230n	2330
Weilheim (Oberbay) d.	0548	0648	0649	0716	0749	0849	0949	|	1049	|	1148	1249	1349	1449	...	1548	|	1649	1750	1849	1949	2049	2129	2148	2249n	2348
Tutzing d.	0559	0700	0700	0729	0800	0900	1000	|	1100	|	1200	1300	1400	1500	...	1600	|	1700	1800	1900	2000	2100	|	2200	2300n	0000
München Pasing a.	0622	0722	0722	0753	0821	0919	1020	|	1119	|	1219	1319	1420	1519	...	1620	|	1720	1820	1919	2019	2119	|	2219	2319n	0019
München Hbf a.	0629	0729	0729	0800	0828	0927	1027	1059	1128	1211	1228	1327	1427	1527	...	1630	1646	1727	1827	1927	2027	2127	2220	2226	2326n	0027

München - Tutzing - Kochel ⊗

km		⊗	Ⓐ	Ⓐ	Ⓐ	Ⓐ	Ⓐ	Ⓐ	Ⓐ	Ⓐ	Ⓐ	Ⓐ	Ⓐ	Ⓐ	Ⓐ	Ⓐ	Ⓐ	Ⓐ	Ⓐ	Ⓐ	⊗	Ⓒ	Ⓒ		Ⓒ
0	**München** Hbf d.	Ⓐ	0640	0757	*0832*	*0932*	*1032*	*1132*	*1232*	*1332*	1446	1546	1646	1746	*1832*	*1932*	*2032*	*2132*	*2232*	*2333*	Ⓒ	*0630*	*0732*	and hourly until	*2333*
7	München Pasing d.		0647	0805	*0839*	*0939*	*1039*	*1139*	*1239*	*1339*	1453	1553	1653	1754	*1839*	*1939*	*2039*	*2139*	*2240*	*2340*		*0638*	*0739*		*2340*
40	Tutzing d.		0715	0831	0905	1005	1105	1205	1310	1420	1519	1620	1720	1820	1905	2005	2105	2205	2305	0006		0705	0805		0006
75	**Kochel** a.		0748	0904	0936	1036	1136	1236	1348	1453	1553	1653	1753	1853	1936	2036	2136	2236	2336	0038		0736	0836		0038

	⊗	Ⓐ	Ⓐ	Ⓐ	Ⓐ	Ⓐ	Ⓐ	Ⓐ	Ⓐ	Ⓐ	Ⓐ	Ⓐ	Ⓐ	Ⓐ	Ⓐ	Ⓐ	Ⓐ	Ⓐ	Ⓐ	Ⓐ	⊗	Ⓒ	Ⓒ		Ⓒ
Kochel d.	Ⓐ	0517	0602	0638	0726	0813	0913	1013	1113	1213	1300	1403	1503	1603	1703	1803	1913	2013	2113	2213	Ⓒ	0618	0713	and hourly until	2313
Tutzing a.		0550	0636	0710	0808	0852	0952	1052	1152	1252	1333	1440	1540	1645	1745	1845	1952	2052	2152	2252		0652	0752		2352
München Pasing a.		0614	0700	0741	0832	*0919*	*1020*	*1119*	*1219*	*1319*	*1359*	1503	1604	1712	*1820*	*1919*	*2019*	*2119*	*2219*	*2319*		*0722*	*0821*		*0019*
München Hbf a.		0621	0707	0750	0839	*0927*	*1027*	*1128*	*1228*	*1327*	*1405*	1511	1612	1720	*1827*	*1927*	*2027*	*2127*	*2226*	*2326*		*0729*	*0828*		*0027*

A – ⑥ Dec. 22 - Mar. 29. POLLUX – 🛏 1, 2 cl., 🛌 2 cl. and (2.) Garmisch - Köln - Amsterdam and v.v. Ⓡ. For overnight journeys only.
H – WERDENFELSERLAND – (12.) and ✕ Hamburg - Hannover - Nürnberg - Garmisch and v.v.
K – ⑥ (also Mar. 21; not Mar. 22). KARWENDEL – (12.) and ✕ Berlin - Leipzig - Nürnberg - Garmisch and v.v.
L – ①–⑤ (not Dec. 25, 26, Jan. 1, Mar. 24, May 1, 12, 22).
W – WETTERSTEIN – (12.) Dortmund - Köln - Frankfurt - Nürnberg - Garmisch and v.v.

b – ⑥⑦ (also Dec. 24, 25, 26, 31, Jan. 1, Mar. 21, 24, May 1, 12, 22).
c – ⑥⑦ (also Dec. 25, 26, Jan. 1, Mar. 24, May 1, 12, 22).
e – Ⓐ (not Dec. 24, 31, May 22).
g – ① (also Dec. 27, Jan. 2, Mar. 25, May 13; not Dec. 24, 31, Mar. 24, May 12).

h – On Ⓒ (also Dec. 24, 31, May 22) Garmisch d. 1704, Mittenwald a. 1731.
j – On Ⓒ (also May 22) change trains at Garmisch (d. *0904*, Mittenwald a. *0925*).
k – On Ⓒ (also Dec. 24, 31, May 22) Mittenwald d. 0633, Garmisch a. 0700, d. 0704.
n – Not Dec. 24, 31.
r – Not May 22.
y – Not Dec. 24, 31, Mar. 21.
z – Ⓒ (also Dec. 24, 31, May 22).

⊡ – Additional ÖBB trains Scharnitz - Seefeld - Innsbruck and v.v.
From Scharnitz at 0634, 0734, 0934, 1303 ⚒, 1534, 1734, 1934 Ⓐ and 2130.
From Innsbruck Hbf at 0738, 1208 ⚒, 1408, 1538, 1738 Ⓐ and 1938.

⊗ – On Dec. 24, 31, May 22 services run as on Ⓒ. Last services on Dec. 24, 31: From Tutzing at 2105 (*2032* from München Hbf). From Kochel at 2013.

A rack railway operates between Garmisch-Partenkirchen and the Zugspitz mountain: departures at 0815 and hourly to 1415, returning from Bf Zugspitzplatt at 0930 and hourly to 1630. All trains call at Eibsee (30 minutes from Garmisch, 49 minutes from Zugspitzplatt). Service may be suspended in bad weather conditions – please check locally before travelling. Cable cars run between Eibsee and Zugspitzgipfel (Eibsee-Seilbahn) and between Zugspitzplatt and Zugspitzgipfel summit (Gletscherbahn). **Operator**: Bayerische Zugspitzbahn AG ✆ + 49 (0) 88 21 7970.

MURNAU - OBERAMMERGAU 897

RB services

km		Ⓐe	Ⓐe						Ⓐe	Ⓒz	Ⓐe	Ⓒz									n	n
0	**Murnau** d.	0602	0644	0742	0842	0942	1042	1142	1235	1242	1320	1342	1442	1542	1642	1742	1842	1942	2042	2142	2335
12	Bad Kohlgrub d.	0620	0706	0801	0901	1001	1101	1201	1253	1301	1338	1401	1501	1601	1701	1801	1901	2001	2101	2201	2353
20	Unterammergau d.	0634	0720	0815	0915	1015	1115	1215	1307	1315	1352	1415	1515	1615	1715	1815	1915	2015	2115	2215	0007
24	**Oberammergau** a.	0639	0725	0820	0920	1020	1120	1220	1312	1320	1357	1420	1520	1620	1720	1820	1920	2020	2120	2220	0012

	Ⓐe		Ⓐe					Ⓐe	Ⓒz	Ⓐe	Ⓒz								n	n
Oberammergau d.	0559	0648	0740	0840	0940	1040	1140	1232	1240	1317	1340	1440	1540	1640	1740	1840	1940	2040	2140	2244
Unterammergau d.	0603	0652	0744	0844	0944	1044	1144	1236	1244	1321	1344	1444	1544	1644	1744	1844	1944	2044	2144	2248
Bad Kohlgrub d.	0621	0705	0802	0902	1002	1102	1202	1254	1302	1339	1402	1502	1602	1702	1802	1902	2002	2102	2202	2302
Murnau a.	0639	0724	0820	0920	1020	1120	1220	1313	1320	1358	1420	1520	1620	1720	1820	1920	2020	2120	2220	2321

e – Not Dec. 24, 31, May 22.
n – Not Dec. 24, 31.
z – Also Dec. 24, 31, May 22.

900 NÜRNBERG and FRANKFURT - HAMBURG

See Table **901** for local services Frankfurt - Fulda - Kassel. See Table **904** for other *IC* services Frankfurt - Gießen - Kassel - Göttingen - Hannover - Hamburg.

km		*ICE* 990 ⑦w	*IC* 2176 ①–⑤ h	*CNL* 1288 [R] ✕◆	*CNL* 1200 [R] ✕◆	*CNL* 1243 [R] ✕◆	*IC* 2182 ①–⑥ e🍷	*EN* 490 492 [R]◆	*IC* 2174 Ⓐn 🍷	*ICE* 988 ①–⑥ e✕	*ICE* 974 ①g ✕	*ICE* 974 ✕	*ICE* 678 ✕◆	*ICE* 1092 ①–⑤ a D	*ICE* 888 ①–⑤ a✕	*ICE* 696 ①g ✕	*ICE* 676 ①–⑥ e✕	*ICE* 684 ✕	*ICE* 634 ✕	*ICE* 972 ✕	*ICE* 674 ✕	*ICE* 886 ✕	*ICE* 694 ✕
	Zürich HB **510** d.	...	...	...	...	1944	...	...	...	...	...	...	...	⚡✕	...	...	...	...	...	...	...	...	...
	Basel SBB **912** d.	...	...	...	...	2107	...	...	...	...	...	...	...	...	...	...	...	...	...	...	...	...	...
	Karlsruhe Hbf **912** d.	...	...	...	...	2305	...	...	...	...	...	...	...	...	...	...	...	...	...	0559	0651	...	...
	Ulm Hbf **930** d.	2204	...	...	...	|	...	...	...	...	...	...	...	...	...	...	...	...	...	|	|	...	...
	Stuttgart Hbf **930** d.	2305	...	...	...	|	...	...	...	...	...	...	...	...	...	...	0509	...	...	|	|	...	0651
	Mannheim Hbf **912** d.	2351	...	...	...	0005	...	...	...	...	...	...	...	...	...	...	0601	...	...	0631	0716	...	0731
	Frankfurt Flughafen Fernbf ✈ d.	0029	...	...	...	|	...	...	...	...	...	...	0539	...	...	...	0642	...	...	|	|	...	|
	Frankfurt (Main) Hbf **850** d.	0055	...	...	...	0055x	...	...	...	0504	0510	...	0555	0614	...	...	0658	...	...	0713	0758	...	0813
	Hanau Hbf **850** d.	0112	...	...	...	|	...	...	...	0520	0526	...	0611	|	...	...	|	...	...	0729	|	...	0829
	München Hbf **904** d.	|	...	2254	2301	|	...	...	...	|	|	...	|	|	...	...	|	0517a	0517a	|	|	0620	|
	Augsburg Hbf **904** d.	|	...	2339	2344	|	...	...	...	|	|	...	|	|	...	...	|	|	|	|	|	|	|
0	**Nürnberg** Hbf **920 921** d.	|	...	|	|	|	...	0131	...	|	|	...	|	|	0534	...	|	0631	0631	|	|	0733	|
102	**Würzburg** Hbf **920 921** d.	|	...	|	|	|	...	0228	...	|	|	...	|	|	0632	...	|	0730	0730	|	|	0832	|
195	Fulda **850** d.	0158	...	|	|	|	...	|	...	0604	0609	...	|	|	0707	...	|	0803	0803	0811	|	0904	0911
285	**Kassel** Wilhelmshöhe d.	|	...	|	|	|	...	|	...	0636	0643	0643	0723	|	0739	0744	0823	0836	0836	0844	0923	0937	0944
330	Göttingen d.	0325	...	|	|	|	...	0508	0548	0657	0703	0703	0743	|	0759	0805	0843	0856	0856	0903	0943	0957	1004
	Hildesheim Hbf d.	|	...	|	|	|	...	|	|	|	0734	0734	|	|	|	0834	|	|	|	0934	|	|	1034
	Braunschweig Hbf a.	|	...	|	|	|	...	|	|	|	0758	0758	|	|	|	0858	|	|	|	0958	|	|	1058
430	**Hannover** Hbf a.	0421	...	0527s	|	0537s	...	0613	0656	0732	|	|	0817	|	0832	|	0917	0932	0932	|	1017	1032	|
430	**Hannover** Hbf d.	0424	0511	|	|	|	0555	0617	0659	0736	|	|	0820	|	0836	|	0920	0936	0945	|	1020	1036	|
	Berlin Hbf **810** a.	|	|	|	0748	0810	|	|	|	|	0925	0925	|	0952	|	1023	|	|	|	1125	|	|	1219
	Bremen Hbf **813** a.	|	|	0642	...	...	|	|	|	|	...	...	|	...	|	...	|	|	1044	...	|	|	...
608	**Hamburg** Hbf a.	0543	0644	0755	...	...	0728	0750	0828	0854	...	...	0935	...	0954	...	1035	1054	...	...	1135	1154	...
615	**Hamburg** Altona a.	...	0658	0811	...	...	...	0806	0843	0908	...	...	0950	...	1008	...	1050	1108	...	...	1150	1208	...

	ICE 672 ✕	*RE* 34604	*ICE* 682 ✕	*ICE* 632 ✕	*ICE* 976 ✕	*ICE* 78 ✕	*ICE* 882 ✕	*ICE* 692 ✕	*IC* 2170 ⑥⑦ 🍷◆	*ICE* 670 ✕	*ICE* 680 ✕	*ICE* 630 ✕	*ICE* 278 R✕	*ICE* 76 K✕	*ICE* 880 ✕	*ICE* 690 ✕	*ICE* 578 ✕	*RE* 34612	*ICE* 588 ✕	*ICE* 538 ✕	*ICE* 372 R✕	*ICE* 74 K✕	*ICE* 788 G✕
Zürich HB **510** d.	...	...	...	...	...	0554	...	...	...	...	...	...	...	0802	...	...	...	...	...	...	...	1002	...
Basel SBB **912** d.	...	...	...	...	0608	0704	...	...	...	...	...	...	0812	0904	...	...	...	...	...	...	1012	1104	...
Karlsruhe Hbf **912** d.	...	...	...	...	0800	0851	...	...	...	...	...	...	1000	1051	...	...	...	...	...	...	1200	1251	...
Ulm Hbf **930** d.	...	...	...	...	|	|	...	0751	...	...	...	...	|	|	...	0951	...	...	...	...	|	|	...
Stuttgart Hbf **930** d.	0727	...	...	...	|	|	...	0851	...	0927	...	...	|	|	...	1051	1127	...	...	...	|	|	...
Mannheim Hbf **912** d.	0806	...	...	...	0831	0916	...	0931	...	1006	...	...	1031	1116	...	1131	1206	...	...	...	1231	1316	...
Frankfurt Flughafen Fernbf ✈ d.	0842	...	...	...	|	|	...	|	...	1042	...	...	|	|	...	|	1242	...	...	...	|	|	...
Frankfurt (Main) Hbf **850** d.	0858	...	...	...	0913	0958	...	1013	1017	1058	...	...	1113	1158	...	1213	1258	...	...	...	1313	1358	...
Hanau Hbf **850** d.	|	...	...	...	0929	|	...	1029	1038	|	...	...	1129	|	...	1229	|	...	...	...	1329	|	...
München Hbf **904** d.	|	...	0652	0652	|	|	0820	|	|	|	0916	0916	|	|	1020	|	|	...	1052	1052	|	|	1220
Augsburg Hbf **904** d.	|	...	0733	0733	|	|	|	|	|	|	|	|	|	|	|	|	|	...	1133	1133	|	|	|
Nürnberg Hbf **920 921** d.	|	0805	|	|	|	|	0933	|	|	|	1032	1032	|	|	1133	|	|	1205	|	|	|	|	1333
Würzburg Hbf **920 921** d.	|	0919	0930	0930	|	|	1032	|	|	|	1130	1130	|	|	1232	|	|	1319	1330	1330	|	|	1432
Fulda **850** d.	|	...	1003	1003	1011	|	1104	1111	1122	|	1203	1203	1211	|	1304	1311	|	...	1403	1403	1411	|	1504
Kassel Wilhelmshöhe d.	1023	...	1036	1036	1044	1123	1137	1144	1159	1223	1236	1236	1244	1323	1337	1344	1423	...	1436	1436	1444	1523	1537
Göttingen d.	1043	...	1056	1056	1103	1143	1157	1204	1219	1243	1256	1256	1303	1343	1357	1404	1443	...	1456	1456	1503	1543	1557
Hildesheim Hbf d.	|	...	|	|	1134	|	|	1234	|	|	|	|	1334	|	|	1434	|	...	|	|	1534	|	|
Braunschweig Hbf a.	|	...	|	|	1158	|	|	1258	|	|	|	|	1358	|	|	1458	|	...	|	|	1558	|	|
Hannover Hbf a.	1117	...	1132	1132	|	1217	1232	|	1258	1317	1332	1332	|	1417	1432	|	1517	...	1532	1532	|	1617	1632
Hannover Hbf d.	1120	...	1136	1145	|	1220	1236	|	1301	1320	1336	1345	|	1420	1436	|	1520	...	1536	1545	|	1620	1636
Berlin Hbf **810** a.	|	...	|	|	1325	|	|	1419	|	|	|	|	1526	|	|	1619	|	...	|	|	1725	|	|
Bremen Hbf **813** a.	|	...	|	1244	...	|	|	...	|	|	|	1444	...	|	|	...	|	...	|	1644	...	|	|
Hamburg Hbf a.	1235	...	1254	...	...	1335	1353	...	1431	1435	1454	...	...	1535	1554	...	1635	...	1653	...	...	1735	1755
Hamburg Altona a.	1249	...	1308	...	...	1350	1408	...	...	1450	1510	...	...	...	1608	...	1650	...	1707	...	...	...	1809

	ICE 108 ✕	*IC* 2082 🍷◆	*IC* 1986 ⑥ 🍷◆	*ICE* 576 ✕	*RE* 34616	*ICE* 586 ✕	*ICE* 536 ✕	*ICE* 272 R✕	*ICE* 72 ✕	*ICE* 786 ✕	*ICE* 596 ✕	*ICE* 774 ⑧q K✕	*ICE* 574 ⑥t ✕	*ICE* 584 ✕	*ICE* 276 d R✕	*ICE* 776 ⑧q ✕◆	*ICE* 70 ✕	*ICE* 784 ✕	*ICE* 1090 ⑧q ⚡✕	*ICE* 594 ⑥t ✕	*IC* 1978 A	*ICE* 572 ✕	*ICE* 582 ✕
Zürich HB **510** d.	...	...	...	...	...	...	...	...	1202	...	...	...	...	...	...	...	...	...	...	...	...	...	...
Basel SBB **912** d.	...	...	...	...	...	...	...	1212	1304	...	...	...	...	...	1412	...	1504	...	...	...	...	...	...
Karlsruhe Hbf **912** d.	...	...	...	...	...	...	...	1400	1451	...	...	...	...	...	1600	...	1651	...	...	...	...	...	...
Ulm Hbf **930** d.	1151	...	...	...	...	...	...	|	|	...	1351	...	...	...	|	...	|	...	1551	1551	...	...	...
Stuttgart Hbf **930** d.	1251	...	...	1327	...	...	...	|	|	...	1451	1527	1527	...	|	...	|	...	1651	1651	...	1727	...
Mannheim Hbf **912** d.	1331	...	...	1406	...	...	...	1431	1516	...	1531	1606	1606	...	1631	...	1716	...	1731	1731	...	1806	...
Frankfurt Flughafen Fernbf ✈ d.	|	...	...	1442	...	...	...	|	|	...	|	1642	1642	...	|	...	|	...	|	|	...	1842	...
Frankfurt (Main) Hbf **850** d.	1413	...	...	1458	...	...	...	1513	1558	...	1613	1658	1658	...	1713	1716	1758	...	1813	1813	1822	1858	...
Hanau Hbf **850** d.	1429	...	...	|	...	...	...	1529	|	...	1629	|	|	...	1729	1741	|	...	|	1829	1838	1914	...
München Hbf **904** d.	|	1114o	...	|	...	1252	1252	|	|	1420	|	|	|	1516	|	|	|	1616	|	|	|	|	1716
Augsburg Hbf **904** d.	|	1230	...	|	...	1333	1333	|	|	|	|	|	|	|	|	|	|	|	|	|	|	|	|
Nürnberg Hbf **920 921** d.	|	|	1318	|	1405	|	|	|	|	1533	|	|	|	1632	|	|	|	1734	|	|	|	|	1832
Würzburg Hbf **920 921** d.	|	1440	1419	|	1519	1530	1530	|	|	1632	|	|	|	1730	|	|	|	1831	|	|	|	|	1930
Fulda **850** d.	1511	1518	1524	|	...	1603	1603	1611	|	1704	1711	|	|	1803	1811	|	|	1907r	|	1911	1921	|	2003
Kassel Wilhelmshöhe d.	1544	1554	1601	1623	...	1636	1636	1644	1723	1737	1744	1823	1823	1836	1844	1850	1923	1940	|	1944	1959	2026	2036
Göttingen d.	1604	1615	1622	1643	...	1656	1656	1703	1743	1757	1804	1843	1843	1856	1903	1912	1943	1959	|	2005	2021	2045	2056
Hildesheim Hbf d.	1634	|	|	|	...	|	|	1734	|	|	1834	|	|	|	1934	|	|	|	|	2034	|	|	|
Braunschweig Hbf a.	1658	|	|	|	...	|	|	1758	|	|	1858	|	|	|	1958	|	|	|	|	2058	|	|	|
Hannover Hbf a.	|	1654	1659	1717	...	1732	1732	|	1817	1832	|	1917	1917	1932	|	1946	2017	2032	|	|	2100	2118	2132
Hannover Hbf d.	|	1658	1702	1720	...	1736	1745	|	1820	1836	|	1920	1920	1936	|	1949	2020	2036	|	|	2105	2121	2136
Berlin Hbf **810** a.	1819	|	|	|	...	|	|	1925	|	|	2019	|	|	|	2125	|	|	|	2147	2226	2251	|	|
Bremen Hbf **813** a.	...	|	1811	|	...	|	1844	...	|	|	...	|	|	|	...	2048	|	|	...	...	...	|	|
Hamburg Hbf a.	...	1829	1905	1835	...	1854	...	...	1935	1954	...	2037	2037	2053	...	...	2138	2155	...	...	...	2241	2254
Hamburg Altona a.	...	1843	1920	1900	...	1909	...	...	1950	2009	...	...	2051	2111	...	...	2153	2209	...	...	...	2255	2309

◆ – **NOTES** (LISTED BY TRAIN NUMBER)

490/2 – HANS ALBERS – 🛏 1, 2 cl., 🛌 2 cl., (2) and 🍷 Wien - Linz - Passau - Regensburg - Hamburg. Conveys (2) (*D* **60490/2**) Nürnberg - Hamburg (reservation not required).

678 – (12) and ✕ Wiesbaden Hbf (d. 0500) - Mainz Hbf (d. 0511) - Frankfurt - Hamburg.

776 – (12) and ✕ (Darmstadt Hbf, d. 1647 ①–⑤ **a** -) Frankfurt - Bremen (- Oldenburg ①–⑤ **a**).

1200 – PLUTO – 🛏 1 cl., 🛌 2 cl., (2) (reclining) and ✕ München - Berlin. For other stops see Table **851**.

1243 – BERLINER – 🛏 1, 2 cl., 🛌 2 cl., (2) (reclining) and ✕ Zürich - Berlin.

1288 – METEOR – 🛏 1 cl., 🛌 2 cl., (2) (reclining) and ✕ München - Hamburg. Also calls at München Pasing (d. 2303).

1986 – ROTTALER LAND – (12) and 🍷 Passau - Hamburg. Also calls at Gemünden (d. 1447). Terminates at Hannover on Dec. 29.

2082 – KÖNIGSSEE – (12) and 🍷 Berchtesgaden - Hamburg; (12) Oberstdorf (**2084**) - Augsburg (**2082**) - Hamburg. Also calls at Treuchtlingen, Gunzenhausen, Ansbach and Steinach (Table **905a**). Does not run Hannover - Hamburg Dec. 24 – 31.

2170 – From Frankfurt on ⑥⑦ (also Dec. 24, 31, Mar. 21, May 1; not Dec. 30, Mar. 23); runs daily from Hannover (see also Table **902**). WATTENMEER – (12) and 🍷 Frankfurt - Hannover - Hamburg - Westerland.

A – ④⑤⑦ (also Dec. 26, Jan. 1, Mar. 19, 24, Apr. 29, 30, May 12; not Dec. 23, 28, 30, Mar. 21, 23, May 1, 2, 11). Train number **1878** on ⑦ (also Dec. 26, Jan. 1, Mar. 24, May 12). Runs 7 – 9 minutes later Fulda - Berlin on ④ (also Mar. 19, Apr. 29, 30; not May 22).

D – From Darmstadt Hbf (d. 0543).

G – From Garmisch-Partenkirchen (d. 1035) on ⑥.

K – To Kiel (Table **820**).

R – From Interlaken via Bern (Table **560**).

a – ①–⑤ (not Dec. 24, 25, 26, 31, Jan. 1, Mar. 21, 24, May 12).

d – Not Dec. 24, 25, 31, Mar. 23, May 11.

e – Not Dec. 25, 26, Jan. 1, Mar. 22, 24, May 12.

g – Also Dec. 27, Jan. 2, Mar. 25, May 13; not Dec. 24, 31, Mar. 24, May 12.

h – Not Dec. 24 - Jan. 1, Mar. 21, 24, May 12.

m – Not Dec. 24, 31, Mar. 24, May 12.

n – Not Dec. 24 - Jan. 1.

o – München **Ost**.

q – Not Dec. 24, 25, 31, Mar. 21, 23, May 11.

r – Arrives 1902.

s – Stops to set down only.

t – Also Dec. 24, 25, 31, Mar. 21, 23, May 11.

w – Also Jan. 1, Mar. 24, May 12; not Dec. 23, 30, Mar. 23, May 11.

x – Frankfurt (Main) **Süd**.

⚡ – [R] and 'Sprinter' supplement payable.

NÜRNBERG and FRANKFURT - HAMBURG 900

See Table **901** for local services Frankfurt - Fulda - Kassel and v.v. See Table **904** for other *IC* services Frankfurt - Gießen - Kassel - Göttingen - Hannover - Hamburg and v.v.

		ICE	ICE	ICE	ICE	ICE	ICE	ICE	ICE	ICE	ICE	ICE	ICE	ICE	ICE	ICE	ICE	IC	ICE	ICE	ICE	CNL	D	ICE
		872	**374**	**782**	**732**	**592**	**782**	**732**	**570**	**524**	**580**	**580**	**580**	**980**	**876**	**870**	**970**	**1976**	**590**	**598**	**698**	**482**	**50482**	**780**
			⑤⑦r						⑦w		H	⑥⑦	⑦v	⑤j	⑥h	①–⑤	⑦w	⑦w	⑥b	⑦q	⑤f		Ⓡ	⑦§
		✕	A✕	✕	L✕	✕	✕	L✕	✕	🍷	✕	k✕	✕	✕	✕	n✕	✕		✕	✕	✕	✕♦	●	✕
Zürich HB **510**	d.	...	...	...	...	...	...	...	...	...	...	...	...	...	...	...	...	...	...	...	...	...	...	...
Basel SBB **912**	d.	1612	1704	...	...	...	...	...	...	...	...	...	...	...	1812	1812	1812	...	...	...	...	...	...	...
Karlsruhe Hbf **912**	d.	1801	1851	...	...	...	...	...	...	...	...	...	...	...	2000	2000	2000	...	...	...	...	...	...	...
Ulm Hbf **930**	d.	|	|	...	...	1751	...	...	...	...	...	...	...	...	|	|	|	...	1951	1951	1951	...	...	...
Stuttgart Hbf **930**	d.	|	|	...	...	1851	...	...	1927	...	...	...	...	...	|	|	|	2009	2051	2051	2051	...	...	...
Mannheim Hbf **912**	d.	1831	1916	...	...	1931	...	...	2006	...	...	...	...	...	2031	2031	2031	|	2131	2131	2131	...	...	...
Frankfurt Flughafen Fernbf ✈	d.	|	|	...	...	|	...	...	2042	...	...	...	...	...	|	|	|	|	|	|	|	...	...	...
Frankfurt (Main) Hbf **850**	d.	1913	1958	...	...	2013	...	...	2058	...	...	...	...	...	2113	2113	2113	2157	2222	2222	2222	...	...	...
Hanau Hbf **850**	d.	1929	|	...	...	2029	...	...	|	...	...	...	...	...	2129	2129	2129	2212	2238	2238	2238	...	...	...
München Hbf **904**	d.	|	|	1820	1820	|	...	...	|	1855	1850	1850	1850	1850	|	|	|	|	|	|	|	1900*	1900*	2020
Augsburg Hbf **904**	d.	|	|	|	|	|	...	...	|	|	1931	1931	1931	1931	|	|	|	|	|	|	|	|	|	|
Nürnberg Hbf **920 921**	d.	|	|	1933	1933	|	...	...	|	2000	|	|	|	|	|	|	|	|	|	|	|	2135	2135	2140
Würzburg Hbf **920 921**	d.	|	|	2032	2032	|	...	...	|	2054	2131	2131	2131	2131	|	|	|	|	|	|	|	2233	2233	2236
Fulda **850**	d.	2011	|	2104	2104	|	...	...	|	...	2205	2205	2205	2205	2211	2211	2211	2256	2323	2323	2323	2340u	2340	2311
Kassel Wilhelmshöhe	d.	2044	2121	2137	2137	2141	←	←	2223	...	...	2237	2237	2237	2244	2244	2244	2332	2353	2356	0033	...	|	2342
Göttingen	d.	2103	2143	2155	2155	2201	2205	2205	2243	...	...	2256	2256	2258	2305	2305	2303	2352	...	0046	...	...	|	...
Hildesheim Hbf	d.	2134	|	→	→	2234	|	|	|	...	...	|	|	|	|	|	2334	|	...	|	...	...	|	...
Braunschweig Hbf	a.	2158	|	...	...	2258	|	|	|	...	...	|	|	|	|	|	2358	|	...	|	...	...	|	...
Hannover Hbf	a.	|	2217	...	...	|	2239	2239	2317	...	...	2332	2332	2357	2341	0003	|	0051	...	0144	...	...	|	...
Hannover Hbf	d.	|	2220	...	...	|	2244	2251	2320	...	...	...	2336	...	2345	0006	|	...	...	...	...	...	|	...
Berlin Hbf **810**	a.	2325	|	...	...	0027	|	|	|	...	...	...	|	...	|	|	0124	...	...	...	...	...	0422	...
Bremen Hbf **813**	a.	...	|	...	...	...	|	2348	|	...	...	...	|	...	|	|	...	...	...	...	...	...	...	...
Hamburg Hbf	a.	...	2344	...	...	...	0003	...	0037	...	...	...	0103	...	0118	0134	...	...	...	...	...	...	...	...
Hamburg Altona	a.	...	2358	...	...	...	0018	...	0058	...	...	...	0118	...	0132	0148	...	...	...	...	...	...	...	...

km			ICE	CNL	346	ICE	ICE	ICE	ICE	ICE	ICE	ICE	ICE	ICE	ICE	ICE	ICE	ICE	ICE	ICE	ICE	ICE	ICE	RE
			5	**483**	**483**	**591**	**591**	**599**	**781**	**781**	**375**	**531**	**581**	**571**	**1071**	**593**	**1091**	**783**	**783**	**71**	**277**	**533**	**583**	**34613**
			①g		Ⓡ	①–⑤	①–⑥	⑦d	①⑥	①–⑥	①–⑤	①–⑤		①–⑥	①–⑤	⑥⑦	①–⑤	⑥c				①–⑥		
			A	✕♦	●	a✕	m✕	✕	‡✕	e✕	tA ✕	tE ✕	✕	e✕	⊡✕	z✕	t⸝ ✕	✕	✕	✕	A✕	eN ✕	✕	
	Hamburg Altona	d.	...	...	...	0303	...	...	...	...			0443	0505	0551	...		0551	...	0605	...		0645	...
	Hamburg Hbf	d.	0024	...	...	0317	...	...	...	...	...	...	0457	0519	0607	...	...	0605	...	0619	...	...	0659	...
	Bremen Hbf **813**	d.	|	...	...	|	...	...	...	...	...	0514	|	|	|	...	...	|	...	|	...	0714	|	...
	Berlin Hbf **810**	d.	|	...	0032	|	...	...	...	...	0433	|	|	|	|	0534	0608	|	...	|	0633	|	|	...
	Hannover Hbf	a.	0147	...	|	0459	...	...	...	...	|	0614	0623	0638	0719	|	|	0723	...	0738	|	0814	0823	...
	Hannover Hbf	d.	0150	...	|	0518	0518	...	0526	...	|	0626	0626	0641	0722	|	|	0726	0726	0741	|	0826	0826	...
0	**Braunschweig** Hbf	d.	|	...	|	|	|	...	|	...	0558	|	|	|	|	0658	|	|	|	|	0758	|	|	...
43	Hildesheim Hbf	d.	|	...	|	|	|	...	|	...	0625	|	|	|	|	0725	|	|	|	|	0825	|	|	...
121	Göttingen	d.	0247	...	|	0555	0555	...	0603	...	0655	0703	0703	0717	|	0755	|	0803	0803	0817	0855	0903	0903	...
166	**Kassel** Wilhelmshöhe	d.	|	...	|	0615	0615	0615	0623	...	0715	0723	0723	0737	|	0815	|	0826	0826	0837	0915	0923	0923	...
256	Fulda **850**	d.	0418	0450x	0450s	0647	0647	0647	0655	0655	0747	0756	0756	|	|	0847	|	0859	0859	|	0947	0956	0956	...
	Würzburg Hbf **920 921**	d.	|	0536x	0534s	|	|	|	0729	0729	|	0831	0831	|	|	|	|	0931	0931	|	|	1031	1031	1040
	Nürnberg Hbf **920 921**	a.	|	0646p	0646p	|	|	|	0824	0824	|	0928	0928	|	|	|	|	1024	1024	|	|	|	|	1155
	Augsburg Hbf **904**	a.	|	|	|	|	|	|	|	|	|	|	|	|	|	|	|	|	|	|	|	1222	1222	...
	München Hbf **904**	a.	|	0857	0857	|	|	|	0941	0941	|	1040	1040	|	|	|	|	1141	1141	|	|	1303	1303	...
337	Hanau Hbf **850**	d.	0506	...	...	0731	0731	0731	...	...	0829	...	...	|	|	0929	|	...	...	|	1029	...	...	...
360	**Frankfurt** (Main) Hbf **850**	a.	0529	...	...	0745	0745	0745	...	...	0844	...	...	0900	0928	0944	0942	...	...	1000	1044	...	...	...
	Frankfurt Flughafen Fernbf ✈ §	a.	0550	...	...	|	|	|	...	...	|	...	...	0916	...	|	|	...	...	|	|	...	...	...
	Mannheim Hbf **912**	a.	0625	...	...	0828	0828	0828	...	...	0928	...	...	0953	...	1028	1028	...	...	1042	1128	...	...	...
	Stuttgart Hbf **930**	a.	|	...	...	0908	0908	0908	...	...	|	...	...	1033	...	1108	1108	...	...	|	|	...	...	...
	Ulm Hbf **930**	a.	|	...	...	1006	1006	1006	...	...	|	...	...	...	...	1206	1206	...	...	|	|	...	...	...
	Karlsruhe Hbf **912**	a.	0653	...	...	...	...	...	...	...	0959	...	...	...	...	...	...	...	...	1107	1159	...	...	...
	Basel SBB **912**	a.	0847	...	...	...	...	...	...	...	1147	...	...	...	...	...	...	...	...	1255	1347	...	...	...
	Zürich HB **510**	a.	...	...	...	...	...	...	...	...	...	...	...	...	...	...	...	...	...	...	...	...	...	...

		ICE	ICE	IC	IC	ICE	ICE	ICE	ICE	ICE	ICE	ICE	IC	ICE	ICE	ICE	ICE	ICE	ICE	RE	ICE	ICE	ICE	ICE
		573	**773**	**1987**	**2083**	**595**	**785**	**73**	**875**	**535**	**585**	**575**	**1979**	**597**	**787**	**75**	**373**	**537**	**587**	**34621**	**577**	**109**	**789**	**77**
		⑦y	①–⑥	⑥△	△								⑤⑦											
		✕	eK ✕	🍷♦	🍷♦	✕	✕	K✕	✕	✕	✕	✕	¶	✕	G✕	✕	A✕	✕	✕		✕	✕	✕	✕
Hamburg Altona	d.	0709		0621	0714	...	0749	...	...	...	0847	0909	0914	...	0946	1009	...	...	1047	...	1109	...	1146	1209
Hamburg Hbf	d.	0724	0724	0635	0728	...	0803	0824	...	...	0901	0924	0928	...	1001	1024	...	...	1101	...	1124	...	1201	1224
Bremen Hbf **813**	d.	|	|	0737	|	...	|	|	...	0914	|	|	|	...	|	|	...	1114	|	...	|	...	|	|
Berlin Hbf **810**	d.	|	|	|	|	0737	|	|	0832	|	|	|	|	0937	|	|	1033	|	|	...	|	1137	|	|
Hannover Hbf	a.	0838	0838	0846	0858	|	0923	0938	|	1014	1023	1038	1056	|	1121	1138	|	1214	1223	...	1238	|	1321	1338
Hannover Hbf	d.	0841	0841	0849	0901	|	0926	0941	|	1026	1026	1041	1059	|	1126	1141	|	1226	1226	...	1241	|	1326	1341
Braunschweig Hbf	d.	|	|	|	|	0858	|	|	0958	|	|	|	|	1058	|	|	1158	|	|	...	|	1258	|	|
Hildesheim Hbf	d.	|	|	|	|	0925	|	|	1025	|	|	|	|	1125	|	|	1225	|	|	...	|	1325	|	|
Göttingen	d.	0917	0917	0929	0943	0955	1003	1017	1055	1103	1103	1117	1140	1155	1203	1217	1255	1303	1303	...	1317	1355	1403	1417
Kassel Wilhelmshöhe	d.	0937	0937	0951	1005	1015	1023	1037	1115	1123	1123	1137	1203	1215	1223	1237	1315	1323	1323	...	1337	1415	1423	1437
Fulda **850**	d.	|	|	1028	1043	1047	1056	|	1147	1156	1156	|	1240	1247	1256	|	1347	1356	1356	...	|	1447	1456	|
Würzburg Hbf **920 921**	d.	|	|	1118	1121	|	1129	|	|	1231	1231	|	|	|	1329	|	|	1431	1431	1440	|	|	1529	|
Nürnberg Hbf **920 921**	a.	|	|	1232	|	|	1224	|	|	1329	1329	|	|	|	1424	|	|	|	|	1555	|	|	1624	|
Augsburg Hbf **904**	a.	|	|	...	1328	|	|	|	|	|	|	|	|	|	|	|	|	1625	1625	...	|	|	|	|
München Hbf **904**	a.	|	|	...	1412o	|	1339	|	|	1443	1443	|	|	|	1539	|	|	1708	1708	...	|	|	1738	|
Hanau Hbf **850**	d.	|	|	...	...	1129	...	|	1229	...	...	|	|	1329	...	|	1429	...	...	...	|	1529	...	|
Frankfurt (Main) Hbf **850**	a.	1100	1100	...	...	1144	...	1200	1244	...	...	1300	1336	1344	...	1400	1444	...	...	...	1500	1544	...	1600
Frankfurt Flughafen Fernbf ✈	a.	1116	1116	...	...	|	...	|	|	...	...	1316	...	|	...	|	|	...	...	...	1516	|	...	|
Mannheim Hbf **912**	a.	1153	1153	...	...	1228	...	1242	1328	...	...	1353	...	1428	...	1442	1528	...	...	...	1553	1628	...	1642
Stuttgart Hbf **930**	a.	1233	1233	...	...	1308	...	|	|	...	...	1433	...	1508	...	|	|	...	...	...	1632	1708	...	|
Ulm Hbf **930**	a.	...	...	...	...	1406	...	|	|	...	...	...	...	1606	...	|	|	...	...	...	...	1806	...	|
Karlsruhe Hbf **912**	a.	...	...	...	...	...	...	1307	1359	...	...	...	...	...	...	1507	1559	...	...	...	...	...	...	1707
Basel SBB **912**	a.	...	...	...	...	...	...	1455	1547	...	...	...	...	...	...	1655	1747	...	...	...	...	...	...	1855
Zürich HB **510**	a.	...	...	...	...	...	...	1600	...	...	...	...	...	...	...	1800	...	...	...	...	...	...	...	2000

♦ – **NOTES** (LISTED BY TRAIN NUMBER)

482 – HANS CHRISTIAN ANDERSEN – 🛏 1, 2 cl., ▬ 2 cl. and [2] München - Ingolstadt Hbf (d. 1948*) - Flensburg - København (Table **50**). Ⓡ for overnight journeys.

483 – HANS CHRISTIAN ANDERSEN – 🛏 1, 2 cl., ▬ 2 cl. and [2] København - Flensburg - Ingolstadt Hbf (a. 0807) - München (Table **50**). Ⓡ for overnight journeys.

1987 – ROTTALER LAND – [12] and 🍷 Hamburg - Passau. Also calls at Gemünden (d. 1057).

2083 – KÖNIGSSEE – [12] and 🍷 Hamburg - Berchtesgaden; [12] Hamburg - Augsburg (**2085**) - Oberstdorf. Also calls at Steinach, Ansbach, Gunzenhausen and Treuchtlingen (Table **905a**).

A – From / to Interlaken via Bern (Table **560**).
E – From Oldenburg (d. 0446) on ① **g**.
G – To Garmisch (a. 1721) on ⑥.
H – ①②③④⑥⑦ (also Mar. 21; not Mar. 20).
K – From Kiel (Table **820**).
L – To Oldenburg on ⑦ **w** (Table **813**).
N – From Oldenburg (d. 0642).

a – Not Dec. 24 - Jan. 1, Mar. 21, 24, May 1, 12.
b – Also Mar. 21.
c – Also Mar. 21; not Mar. 22.
d – Also Mar. 24, May 12.
e – Not Dec. 25, 26, Jan. 1, Mar. 22, 24, May 12.
f – Also Mar. 20, Apr. 30; not Mar. 21.
g – Also Dec. 27, Jan. 2, Mar. 25, May 13; not Dec. 24, 31, Mar. 24, May 12.
h – Also Dec. 23, 25, 30, Mar. 21, 23, May 11.
j – Also Mar. 20; not Mar. 21.
k – Also Dec. 26, Jan. 1, Mar. 21, 24, May 12; not Mar. 23, May 11.
m – Not Dec. 24, 25, 26, 31, Mar. 24, May 12.
n – Not Dec. 25, 26, Jan. 1, Mar. 21, 24, May 12.
o – München **Ost**.
p – ②–⑦ (also Mar. 24, May 12; not Dec. 27, Jan. 2, Mar. 25, May 13).
q – Also Dec. 26, Jan. 1, Mar. 24, May 12; not Mar. 23, May 11.
r – Also Dec. 26, Jan. 1, Mar. 20, 24, Apr. 30, May 12, 21; not Dec. 23, 30, Mar. 21, 23, May 2, 11, 23.
s – 15 – 19 minutes later on dates in note **x**.
t – Not Dec. 24, 25, 26, 31, Jan. 1, Mar. 21, 24, May 12.
u – Stops to pick up only.
v – Also Jan. 1, Mar. 24, May 12; not Dec. 23, 30, Mar. 23, May 11.
w – Also Dec. 26, Jan. 1, Mar. 24, May 12; not Dec. 23, 30, Mar. 23, May 11.
x – On ①⑦ (also Dec. 25, 26, 27, Jan. 1, 2, Mar. 22, 25, May 13) Fulda a. 0509, Würzburg d. 0551. Calls at Fulda to set down only.
y – Also Dec. 25, 26, Jan. 1, Mar. 22, 24, May 12.
z – Also Dec. 24, 25, 26, 31, Jan. 1, Mar. 21, 24, May 12.

* – On © München Hbf d. 1916, Ingolstadt Hbf d. 2011.
● – 🛏 1, 2 cl. and ▬ 2 cl. München - Warszawa and v.v.; 🛏 1, 2 cl. München - Moskva and v.v. For overnight journeys only. See Table **24**.
△ – Does not run Hamburg - Hannover Dec. 25 - Jan. 1.
§ – Also Mar. 24, May 12; not Dec. 23, 30, Mar. 23, May 11.
‡ – Also Dec. 27, Jan. 2, Mar. 25, May 13; not Mar. 22, 24, May 12.
¶ – Also Mar. 20, 24, Apr. 30, May 12; not Dec. 23 – 30, Mar. 21, 23, May 2, 11.
⊡ – ①–⑤ (not Dec. 24 - Jan. 1, Mar. 21, 24, May 12). To Darmstadt Hbf (a. 0949). Note ⸝ applies for journeys to Frankfurt and Darmstadt.
⸝ – Ⓡ and 'Sprinter' supplement payable.

900 HAMBURG - FRANKFURT and NÜRNBERG

See Table **904** for other *IC* services Hamburg - Hannover - Göttingen - Kassel - Gießen - Frankfurt. See Table **901** for local services Kassel - Fulda - Frankfurt.

	ICE 279	*ICE* 539	*ICE* 589	*RE* 34625	*ICE* 579	*ICE* 691	*ICE* 881	*ICE* 79	*ICE* 879	*ICE* 631	*ICE* 681	*RE* 34629	*ICE* 671	*IC* 2171	*ICE* 693	*ICE* 883	*ICE* 673	*ICE* 977	*ICE* 633	*ICE* 683	*RB* 35091	*ICE* 675	*ICE* 695
														⑤–⑦									⑥k
	✕♦	✕	✕		✕	✕	✕	✕	✕	✕	✕		✕	🍷♦	✕	✕	✕	✕	✕	✕		✕	✕
Hamburg Altona d.	...	...	1247	...	1309	...	1346	1409	...	...	1447	...	1509	...	...	1546	1609	...	...	1647	...	1709	...
Hamburg Hbf d.	...	...	1301	...	1324	...	1401	1424	...	...	1501	...	1524	1528	...	1603	1624	...	...	1701	...	1724	...
Bremen Hbf **813** d.	...	1314	|	...	|	...	|	|	...	1514	|	...	|	|	...	|	|	...	1714	|	...	|	...
Berlin Hbf **810** d.	1233	|	|	...	|	1337	|	|	1433	|	|	...	|	|	1537	|	|	1633	|	|	...	|	1735
Hannover Hbf a.	|	1414	1423	...	1438	|	1521	1538	|	1614	1623	...	1638	1658	|	1723	1738	|	1814	1823	...	1838	|
Hannover Hbf d.	|	1426	1426	...	1441	|	1526	1541	|	1626	1626	...	1641	1702	|	1726	1741	|	1826	1826	...	1841	|
Braunschweig Hbf d.	1358	|	|	...	|	1458	|	|	1558	|	|	...	|	|	1658	|	|	1758	|	|	...	|	1858
Hildesheim Hbf d.	1425	|	|	...	|	1525	|	|	1625	|	|	...	|	|	1725	|	|	1825	|	|	...	|	1925
Göttingen d.	1455	1503	1503	...	1517	1555	1603	1617	1655	1703	1703	...	1717	1742	1755	1803	1817	1855	1903	1903	...	1917	1955
Kassel Wilhelmshöhe d.	1515	1523	1523	...	1537	1615	1623	1637	1715	1723	1723	...	1737	1803	1815	1823	1837	1915	1923	1923	...	1937	2015
Fulda **850** d.	1547	1556	1556	...	|	1647	1656	|	1747	1756	1756	...	|	1840	1847	1856	|	1947	1956	1956	...	|	2047
Würzburg Hbf **920 921** d.	|	1631	1631	1640	|	|	1729	|	|	1831	1831	1840	|	|	|	1929	|	|	2031	2031	2036	|	|
Nürnberg Hbf **920 921** a.	|	|	|	1755	|	|	1824	|	|	|	|	1955	|	|	|	2024	|	|	|	|	2153	|	|
Augsburg Hbf **904** a.	|	1822	1822	...	|	|	|	|	|	2022	2022	...	|	|	|	|	|	|	2222	2222	...	|	|
München Hbf **904** a.	|	1903	1903	...	|	|	1938	|	|	2103	2103	...	|	|	|	2138	|	|	2308	2308	...	|	|
Hanau Hbf **850** d.	1629	...	...	...	|	1729	...	|	1829	...	...	...	|	1925	1929	...	|	2029	...	...	...	|	|
Frankfurt (Main) Hbf **850** a.	1644	...	...	...	1700	1744	...	1800	1844	...	...	...	1900	1950	1944	...	2000	2044	...	...	...	2100	2142
Frankfurt Flughafen Fernbf ✈ a.	|	...	...	...	1716	|	...	|	|	...	...	...	1916	...	|	...	|	|	...	...	...	2116	|
Mannheim Hbf **912** a.	1728	...	...	...	1753	1828	...	1842	1928	...	...	...	1953	...	2028	...	2042	2128	...	...	...	2153	2228
Stuttgart Hbf **930** a.	|	...	...	...	1833	1908	...	|	|	...	...	...	2033	...	2108	...	|	|	...	...	...	2248	2308
Ulm Hbf **930** a.	|	...	...	...	...	2006	...	|	|	...	...	...	...	...	2206	...	|	|	...	...	...	...	...
Karlsruhe Hbf **912** a.	1759	...	...	...	...	...	...	1907	1959	...	...	...	...	...	...	...	2107	2159	...	...	...	...	...
Basel SBB **912** a.	1947	...	...	...	...	...	...	2055	2147	...	...	...	...	...	...	...	2300w	2355	...	...	...	...	...
Zürich HB **510** a.	...	...	...	...	...	...	...	2200	...	...	...	...	...	...	...	...	...	...	...	...	...	...	...

	ICE 1093	*ICE* 885	*ICE* 677	*ICE* 971	*ICE* 635	*ICE* 685	*ICE* 635	*ICE* 685	*ICE* 1517	*IC* 1999	*ICE* 697	*ICE* 697	*ICE* 887	*IC* 2350	*ICE* 973	*ICE* 1687	*ICE* 973	*EN* 491 493	*ICE* 889	*CNL* 1242	*CNL* 1201	*CNL* 1289	*IC* 2185
	⑧q						⑦w	⑦w	n	⑦w		⑤–⑦		⑦w	⑦w	⑦v	⑦w		⑧q	Ⓡ	Ⓡ	Ⓡ	⑥⑦
	✕⚡	✕	✕♦	✕	✕	✕	✕	✕	✕		✕	f✕	✕♦	♦	✕	✕	✕	Ⓡ♦	✕	✕♦	✕♦	✕♦	d
Hamburg Altona d.	...	1746	...	...	...	1847	...	1847	...	...	...	...	1946	...	...	2047	...	2018	2113	...	...	2146	...
Hamburg Hbf d.	...	1803	1824	...	...	1901	...	1901	...	...	...	...	2001	...	...	2101	...	2033	2127	...	...	2202	2228
Bremen Hbf **813** d.	...	|	|	...	1914	|	1914	|	...	...	...	...	|	...	...	|	...	|	|	...	...	2324	|
Berlin Hbf **810** d.	1804	|	|	1833	|	|	|	|	...	1909	1937	1937	|	1840	2032	|	...	|	|	2126	2214	|	|
Hannover Hbf a.	|	1923	1938	|	2014	2023	2014	2023	...	2055	|	|	2121	|	|	2218	...	2223	2256	|	|	|	2357
Hannover Hbf d.	|	1926	1941	|	2026	2026	2026	2026	...	2101	|	|	2126	|	|	2221	...	2226	...	2352u	|	0046u	...
Braunschweig Hbf d.	|	|	|	1958	|	|	|	|	...	|	2058	2058	|	|	2158	|	...	|	...	|	|	|	...
Hildesheim Hbf d.	|	|	|	2025	|	|	|	|	...	|	2125	2125	|	|	2225	|	...	|	...	|	|	|	...
Göttingen d.	|	2003	2017	2055	2103	2103	2103	2103	...	2142	2155	2155	2203	|	2255	2302	...	2325	...	|	|	|	...
Kassel Wilhelmshöhe d.	|	2026	2037	2115	2123	2123	2123	2123	...	2203	2213	2215	2223	|	2315	2322	←	|	...	|	|	|	...
Fulda **850** d.	|	2059	|	2147	2156	2156	2156	2156	...	|	...	2247	2255	2305	2346	2357	2358	|	...	|	|	|	...
Würzburg Hbf **920 921** d.	|	2134	|	|	2231	2231	2231	2231	...	|	...	|	|	2356	→	0032	|	0207	...	|	|	|	...
Nürnberg Hbf **920 921** a.	|	2228	|	|	2324	2324	2324	2324	2338	⊡	...	|	|	...	...	0126	|	0307	...	|	|	|	...
Augsburg Hbf **904** a.	|	|	|	|	...	...	|	|	|	|	...	|	|	...	...	...	|	...	...	|	0555	0622	...
München Hbf **904** a.	|	2341	|	|	...	...	0056	0056	0049	|	...	|	|	...	...	...	|	...	...	|	0642	0705	...
Hanau Hbf **850** d.	|	...	|	2229	...	...	...	...	...	|	...	2329	2340	...	...	...	0040	...	...	|	...	...	...
Frankfurt (Main) Hbf **850** a.	2142	...	2200	2244	...	...	...	...	...	0019	...	2344	2356	...	...	...	0058	...	...	0400x	...	...	...
Frankfurt Flughafen Fernbf ✈ a.	|	...	|	|	...	...	...	...	...	...	...	...	0016	...	...	...	0122	...	...	|	...	...	...
Mannheim Hbf **912** a.	2228	...	2242	2341	...	...	...	...	...	...	...	...	...	...	...	...	0200	...	...	0443	...	...	...
Stuttgart Hbf **930** a.	2308	...	|	|	...	...	...	...	...	...	...	...	...	...	...	...	|	...	...	|	...	...	...
Ulm Hbf **930** a.	...	...	|	|	...	...	...	...	...	...	...	...	...	...	...	...	|	...	...	|	...	...	...
Karlsruhe Hbf **912** a.	...	...	2307	0013	...	...	...	...	...	...	...	...	...	...	...	...	0238	...	...	0540	...	...	...
Basel SBB **912** a.	...	...	...	...	...	...	...	...	...	...	...	...	...	...	...	...	...	...	...	0755	...	...	...
Zürich HB **510** a.	...	...	...	...	...	...	...	...	...	...	...	...	...	...	...	...	...	...	...	0918	...	...	...

♦ – **NOTES** (LISTED BY TRAIN NUMBER)

279 – [12] and ✕ Berlin - Basel - Bern - Interlaken.
491/3 – HANS ALBERS – 🛏 1, 2 cl., ▬ 2 cl., [2] and 🍷 Hamburg - Passau - Linz - Wien. Conveys [2] (*D* **60491/3**) Hamburg - Nürnberg (reservation not required).
677 – [12] and ✕ Kiel - Hamburg - Karlsruhe.
887 – [12] and ✕ Hamburg - Frankfurt - Mainz Hbf (a. 0044) - Wiesbaden Hbf (a. 0057).
1201 – PLUTO – 🛏 1 cl., ▬ 2 cl., [2] (reclining) and ✕ Berlin - München. For other stops see Table **851**.
1242 – BERLINER – 🛏 1, 2 cl., ▬ 2 cl., [2] (reclining) and ✕ Berlin - Zürich.
1289 – METEOR – 🛏 1 cl., ▬ 2 cl., [2] (reclining) and ✕ Hamburg - München.
2171 – ⑤–⑦ (also Dec. 24, 25, 26, 31, Jan. 1, Mar. 20, 24, Apr. 30, May 12). WATTENMEER – [12] and 🍷 Westerland - Hamburg - Frankfurt.
2350 – [12] Stralsund - Berlin - Halle - Erfurt - Fulda - Gemünden (a. 2332) - Würzburg.

d – Also Jan. 1, Mar. 24, May 12; not Dec. 23, 29, 30, Mar. 23, May 11.
f – Also Dec. 26, Jan. 1, Mar. 20, 24, Apr. 30, May 1, 12, 21, 22; not Dec. 23, 30, Mar. 22, 23, May 2, 2, 23, 24.
k – Also Dec. 24, 25, 31, Mar. 21, 23, May 11.
n – Not Dec. 24, 31.
q – Not Dec. 24, 25, 31, Mar. 21, 23, May 11.
u – Stops to pick up only.
v – Also Jan. 1, Mar. 24, May 12; not Dec. 23, 30, Mar. 23, May 11.
w – ⑦ (also Dec. 26, Jan. 1, Mar. 24, May 12; not Dec. 23, 30, Mar. 23, May 11).
x – Frankfurt (Main) **Süd**.

⊡ – Via Gießen (Table **806**).
⚡ – Ⓡ and 'Sprinter' supplement payable.

901 Local services FRANKFURT - FULDA - KASSEL

RE | *RB* services

Other *ICE* | *IC* services: Table **850** for Bebra - Kassel Wilhelmshöhe and v.v., also Frankfurt - Fulda - Bad Hersfeld and v.v. Table **900** for Frankfurt - Fulda - Kassel Wilhelmshöhe and v.v.

Frankfurt - Fulda

km								
0	**Frankfurt** (Main) Hbf d.	0526	0626	0726	and hourly until	2326	...	...
10	Offenbach (Main) Hbf d.	0538	0638	0738		2338	...	...
23	Hanau Hbf d.	0548	0648	0748		2348	...	...
104	**Fulda** a.	0649	0749	0849		0049	...	...

		ⒶB		ⒶB						
Fulda d.	0401	0438	0516	0600	0608	0708	0808	0908	and hourly until	2308
Hanau Hbf d.	0500	0538	0616	0656	0709	0809	0909	1009		0009
Offenbach (Main) Hbf d.	0509	0547	0625	|	0717	0817	0922	1017		0017
Frankfurt (Main) Hbf a.	0520	0559	0636	0716	0728	0828	0932	1028		0028

Fulda - Kassel ♠

km		Ⓐe	Ⓐe	Ⓐe	†w	⚒r	Ⓐe																		Ⓐe
0	**Fulda 908** d.	...	...	0548	0610	0616	...	0719	0819	*0900*	1019	*1100*	1219	*1300*	1419	*1500*	1619	*1700*	1819	*1900*	2019	...	2221	2259	2356
42	Bad Hersfeld **908** d.	...	0521	0616	0639	0644	0714	0748	0848	0944	1048	1145	1248	1345	1448	1543	1648	1744	1848	1945	2048	2145	2250	2329	0026
56	Bebra **908** d.	0437	0535	0627	0650	0657	0727	0757	0857	0957	1057	1157	1257	1357	1457	1557	1657	1757	1857	1957	2059	2157	2301	2340	0038
62	Rotenburg (Fulda) d.	0443	0541	0634	0656	0704	0734	0804	0904	1004	1104	1204	1304	1404	1504	1604	1704	1804	1904	2004	2105	2204	...	...	...
84	Melsungen d.	0504	0600	0653	0715	0723	0753	0823	0923	1023	1123	1223	1323	1423	1523	1623	1723	1823	1923	2023	2124	2223	...	...	...
110	**Kassel** Wilhelmshöhe § a.	0531	0617	0713	0741	0742	0813	0842	0942	1042	1142	1242	1342	1442	1542	1642	1742	1842	1942	2042	2143	2243	...	...	...
114	**Kassel** Hbf § a.	0536	0623	0718	0747	0748	0818	0849	0949	1049	1149	1249	1349	1449	1549	1649	1749	1849	1949	2053	2153	2253	...	...	...

		ⒶB	Ⓐe	ⒶB	⚒r	Ⓒd	Ⓐe		†w	⚒r														A	⑦c
Kassel Hbf § d.	...	...	...	...	0506	0606	0629	0659	0806	0810	0910	1010	1110	1210	1310	1410	1510	1610	1710	1810	1910	2010	2105j	2309	2329
Kassel Wilhelmshöhe § d.	...	...	...	...	0510	0614	0633	0704	0814	0814	0914	1014	1114	1214	1314	1414	1514	1614	1714	1814	1914	2014	2114	2315	2334
Melsungen d.	...	...	...	...	0530	0634	0651	0731	0834	0834	0934	1034	1134	1234	1334	1434	1534	1634	1734	1834	1934	2034	2134	2343	2359
Rotenburg (Fulda) d.	...	...	...	...	0549	0652	0709	0751	0852	0852	0952	1052	1152	1252	1352	1452	1552	1652	1752	1852	1952	2052	2152	0001	0018
Bebra **908** d.	0315	0359	0425	0522	0558	0700	0717	0800	0900	0900	1000	1100	1200	1300	1400	1500	1600	1700	1801	1900	2000	2100	2201	0008	0024
Bad Hersfeld **908** d.	0325	0409	0437	0531	0608	0709	0726	0810	0909	0909	1010	1109	1211	1309	1411	1510	1610	1709	1811	1909	2010	2109	2210	...	...
Fulda 908 a.	0355	0436	0507	0558	0638	0738	0755	*0853*	0938	0938	*1053*	1138	*1253*	1338	*1453*	1538	*1653*	1738	*1853*	1938	*2053*	2138	2240	...	...

A – ①–⑥ (also Mar. 23, May 11; not Dec. 26, Jan. 1, Mar. 21, 24, May 1, 12, 22).
B – Ⓐ (not Dec. 24, 31, May 22). [12] Bebra - Fulda - Frankfurt.
c – Also Dec. 26, Jan. 1, Mar. 21, 24, May 1, 12, 22; not Mar. 23, May 11.
d – Also Dec. 24, 31, May 22.
e – Not Dec. 24, 31, May 22.
j – 2110 on Ⓐ**e**.
r – Not May 22.
w – Also May 22.
§ – See also Tables **804** and **806**.
♠ – Most services are operated by CANTUS Verkehrsgesellschaft (2nd class only).

IC services KASSEL - HANNOVER - HAMBURG 902

See Table **900** for faster *ICE* trains Karlsruhe - Frankfurt - Kassel - Göttingen - Hannover - Hamburg and v.v. See Table **903** for other regional services operated by *metronom*.

km		*IC* 2176	*IC* 2182	*IC* 2174	*IC* 2180	*IC* 2180		*IC* 2378	*IC* 2376	*IC* 2170	*IC* 2170	*IC* 2374	*IC* 1972	*IC* 2372	*IC* 2082	*IC* 2370	*IC* 2186	*EC* 240	*IC* 1988	*IC* 2278	*IC* 1980	*IC* 2276	*IC* 2276	*IC* 1982
		①-⑤	①-⑥	Ⓐ n	①-⑤					⑥⑦ c			⑤ r			Y	⑤⑦ j	Ⓑ w	⑦ z		⑦ z	⑤⑦ j	⑦ z	⑦ z
		a	e O	◧	d ◧	◧		◧	◧	S	S	◧		⊕	◐ B	K	◐ K	A		◐				
			🍷	🍷	🍷	🍷		🍷	🍷	🍷	🍷	🍷		🍷	🍷	🍷	🍷	🍴		🍷		🍷	🍷	
	Karlsruhe Hbf **912** d.	...	...	...	...	...	...	...	0647e	...	...	0854	...	1054	...	1253	1253	...	...	1454	...	1654	1654	...
	Frankfurt (Main) Hbf **806** d.	...	...	...	...	...	...	0623g	0823	1017	...	1023	1207	1223	...	1423	1423	...	...	1623	...	1823	1823	...
0	**Kassel** Wilhelmshöhe d.	...	...	...	0623	...	...	0828	1028	1159	...	1228	1356	1428	1554	1628	1628	...	1754	1828	1950	2030	2030	...
45	**Göttingen** d.	...	...	0548	0645	...	...	0850	1050	1219	...	1250	1417	1450	1615	1650	1650	...	1815	1850	2013	2051	2051	...
65	Northeim (Han) d.	...	...	0600	0658	...	...	0902	1102	|	...	1302	|	1502	|	1702	1702	...	|	1902	|	2103	2103	...
84	Kreiensen d.	...	...	0613	0712	...	...	0916	1116	|	...	1316	|	1516	|	1716	1716	...	|	1916	|	2116	2116	...
103	Alfeld (Leine) d.	...	...	0626	0725	...	...	0929	1129	|	...	1329	|	1529	|	1729	1729	...	|	1929	|	2129	2129	...
120	Elze (Han) d.	...	...	0637	0737	...	...	|	|	|	...	|	|	|	|	|	|	...	|	|	|	|	|	...
153	**Hannover** Hbf a.	...	...	0656	0756	...	...	0956	1156	1258	...	1356	1455	1556	1654	1756	1756	...	1855	1956	2052	2156	2156	...
153	**Hannover** Hbf d.	0511	0555	0659	0759	0759	...	0959	1159	1301	1301	1359	1459	1559	1658	1759	1759	...	1858	1959	2055	...	2159	2259
194	Celle d.	0532	0619	0719	0819	0819	...	1019	1219	1321	1321	1419	1519	1619	1719	1820	1820	...	1918	2019	2117	...	2219	2319
246	Uelzen d.	0557	0643	0743	0843	0843	...	1043	1243	1344	1344	1443	1542	1643	1743	1843	1843	1937	1943	2043	2143	...	2242	2345
259	Bad Bevensen d.	|	|	|	0852	0852	...	|	|	|	|	1452	|	1652	|	|	|	|	|	|	|	...	|	|
282	Lüneburg d.	0615	0700	0800	0904	0904	...	1100	1300	1403	1403	1504	1559	1704	1759	1900	1900	1953	2000	2100	2159	...	2259	0001
331	**Hamburg** Hbf a.	0644	0728	0828	0932	0932	...	1127	1327	1431	1431	1530	1628	1732	1829	1927	1928	2027	2032	2127	2227	...	2326	0028
338	**Hamburg** Altona a.	0658	|	0843	|	|	...	1141	|	...	...	1544	1643	|	1843	...	|	2042	2046	2143	2241	...	2340	0043
	Rostock Hbf **830** a.	...	0936	...	1136	1136	...	...	1536	...	...	...	...	1936	...	...	2136	...	...	...	...	...	...	...
	Stralsund **830** a.	...	1039	...	1251	1251	...	...	1642	...	...	...	...	2041	...	...	2230	...	...	...	...	...	...	...

	IC 2275	*IC* 2179	*IC* 2277	*EC* 241	*IC* 2083	*IC* 2279	*IC* 1979	*IC* 2371		*IC* 2373	*IC* 1981	*IC* 2375	*IC* 2171	*IC* 2181	*IC* 2377	*IC* 2173	*IC* 2379	*IC* 2379	*IC* 2379	*IC* 2175	*IC* 2183	*ICE* 889	*IC* 2185	*IC* 2185
	①-⑤	Ⓐ	①-⑥	①-⑥			⑤⑦				⑤⑦		⑤-⑦	①-④		Ⓑ b		⑤⑦ j	⑤ ‡	T	⑦ z	Ⓑ q	⑦ z	⑥⑦
	d G	¶	e ◧	v A	B ◧	◧	u	◧ K		◧	t	◧	h S	m S	⊕ O		⊕	⊕	⊕		O			y
	🍷		🍷	🍴	🍷	🍷		🍷		🍷		🍷	🍷	🍷	🍷	🍷	🍷	🍷	🍷	🍷	🍷	🍴		
Stralsund **830** d.	...	...	...	...	...	0529e	...	...	...	0915	...	...	...	...	1327	...	1515*	1515	1515	...	1715	...	1915	...
Rostock Hbf **830** d.	...	...	...	...	...	0625e	...	...	...	1025	...	...	...	...	1425	...	1625	1625	1625	...	1825	...	2025	...
Hamburg Altona d.	...	0510	0610	0641	0714	|	0914	1014	...	|	1314	1414	...	...	|	1714	|	|	|	1914	|	2113	|	...
Hamburg Hbf d.	...	0524	0626	0703	0728	0828	0928	1028	...	1228	1328	1428	1528	1528	1628	1728	1828	1828	1828	1928	2028	2127	2228	2228
Lüneburg d.	...	0553	0656	0734	0757	0857	0957	1057	...	1257	1357	1457	1557	1557	1657	1758	1857	1857	1857	1958	2058	2156	2257	2257
Bad Bevensen d.	...	0605	|	|	|	|	|	|	...	|	|	|	1609	1609	|	1809	|	|	|	|	|	|	|	|
Uelzen d.	...	0614	0713	0754	0813	0914	1014	1114	...	1314	1414	1514	1618	1618	1714	1817	1914	1914	1914	2016	2115	2214	2314	2314
Celle d.	...	0637	0736	...	0839	0937	1037	1137	...	1337	|	1537	1640	1640	1737	1841	1937	1937	1937	2040	2139	2237	2337	2337
Hannover Hbf a.	...	0656	0756	...	0858	0956	1056	1156	...	1356	1453	1556	1658	1658	1756	1906	1956	1956	1956	2101	2200	2256	2357	2357
Hannover Hbf d.	0600	...	0800	...	0901	1000	1059	1200	...	1400	1456	1600	1702	1702	1800	...	...	2000	2000	...	...	...	...	...
Elze (Han) d.	|	...	|	...	|	|	|	|	...	|	|	|	|	1722	|	...	...	|	|	...	...	...	...	...
Alfeld (Leine) d.	0629	...	0829	...	|	1029	|	1229	...	1429	|	1629	|	1733	1829	...	...	2029	2029	...	...	...	...	...
Kreiensen d.	0642	...	0842	...	|	1042	|	1242	...	1442	|	1642	|	1746	1842	...	...	2042	2042	...	...	...	...	...
Northeim (Han) d.	0656	...	0856	...	|	1056	|	1256	...	1456	|	1656	|	1759	1856	...	...	2056	2056	...	...	...	...	...
Göttingen d.	0710	...	0910	...	0943	1110	1140	1310	...	1510	1536	1710	1742	1811	1910	...	...	2108	2110	...	...	...	...	...
Kassel Wilhelmshöhe a.	0728	...	0928	...	1003	1128	1201	1328	...	1528	1557	1728	1801	...	1928	...	...	...	2128	...	...	...	...	...
Frankfurt (Main) Hbf **806** a.	0933	...	1133	...	...	1333	1336	1533	...	1733	...	1933	1950	...	2133	...	...	...	2336	...	...	...	...	...
Karlsruhe Hbf **912** a.	...	...	1302	...	...	1502	...	1702	...	1902	...	2106p	...	...	2304f	...	...	...	...	...	...	...	...	...

A – WAWEL – (12) and 🍴 Kraków - Cottbus - Berlin - Stendal - Hamburg and v.v.
B – KÖNIGSSEE – (12) and 🍷 Berchtesgaden - München - Augsburg - Hamburg and v.v.; (12) Oberstdorf - Augsburg - Hamburg and v.v.
G – To Stuttgart (Table **930**).
K – From / to Konstanz (Table **916**).
O – To / from Ostseebad Binz (Table **844**).
S – To / from Westerland (Table **821**).
T – ①②③④⑦ (not Dec. 23–31, Mar. 20, 23, May 11).
Y – ①②③④⑥ (also Dec. 23, 30, Mar. 21, 23, May 2, 11; not Dec. 26, Jan. 1, Mar. 20, 24, Apr. 30, May 12). Terminates at Hannover Dec. 23–31.

a – Not Dec. 24 - Jan. 1, Mar. 21, 24, May 12.
b – Also Mar. 22; not Dec. 24 - Jan. 1, Mar. 21.
c – Also Dec. 24, 31, Mar. 21, May 1; not Dec. 30, Mar. 23.
d – Not Dec. 24, 25, 26, 31, Jan. 1, Mar. 21, 24, May 12.
e – ①-⑥ (not Dec. 25, 26, Jan. 1, Mar. 22, 24, May 12).
f – ⑤⑦ (also Dec. 26, Jan. 1, Mar. 20, 24, Apr. 30, May 12, 21; not Dec. 23, 30, Mar. 21, 23, May 2, 11, 23).
g – ①-⑥ (not Dec. 25, 26, 29, Jan. 1, Mar. 22, 24, May 12).
h – Also Dec. 24, 25, 26, 31, Jan. 1, Mar. 20, 24, Apr. 30, May 12.

j – Also Dec. 26, Jan. 1, Mar. 20, 24, Apr. 30, May 12; not Dec. 23, 30, Mar. 21, 23, May 2, 11.
m – Not Dec. 24, 25, 26, 31, Jan. 1, Mar. 20, 24, Apr. 30, May 12.
n – Not Dec. 24, 31.
p – ①-⑤ (also Dec. 23, 30; not Dec. 24, 25, 26, 31, Jan. 1, Mar. 21, 24, May 12).
q – Not Dec. 24, 25, 31, Mar. 21, 23, May 11.
r – Also Mar. 20, Apr. 30; not Dec. 28, Mar. 21, May 2.
t – Also Mar. 20, 24, May 12; not Dec. 23, 28, 30, Mar. 21, 23, May 11.
u – Also Mar. 20, 24, Apr. 30, May 12; not Dec. 23, 28, 30, Mar. 21, 23, May 2, 11.
v – Not Dec. 25, 26, 31, Jan. 1, Mar. 22, 24, May 12.
w – Not Dec. 24, 25, 30, 31, Mar. 21, 23, May 11.
y – Also Jan. 1, Mar. 24, May 12; not Dec. 23, 29, 30, Mar. 23, May 11.
z – Also Jan. 1, Mar. 24, May 12; not Dec. 23, 30, Mar. 23, May 11.

* – 1500 on ⑥ from Mar. 15 (also Mar. 21, May 1; not Mar. 22, May 3).
◐ – Does not run north of Hannover Dec. 24–31.
◧ – Does not run north of Hannover Dec. 25 - Jan. 1.
⊕ – Does not run north of Hannover Dec. 24 - Jan. 1.
¶ – Not Dec. 24 - Jan. 1.
‡ – Also Mar. 20, Apr. 30; not Mar. 21, May 2. On Dec. 28 does not run Kassel - Frankfurt.

metronom Local services GÖTTINGEN - HANNOVER - UELZEN - HAMBURG 903

Services below are operated by ***metronom***. For *ICE* services see Table **900**. For *IC* services see Table **902**.

Certain trains do not run on Dec. 24, 25, 26, 31, Jan. 1. All services to / from Hamburg are subject to alteration Dec. 24 - Jan. 1

		⚒		⚒	†	⚒			⊖			⊖											⚒	Ⓑ	⚒	†
Göttingen d.	...	...	...	0407	0502	*0502*	0607	0707	0812	0907	1012	1107	1212	1307	1412	1507	1612	1707	1812	1907	...	2012	...	2107	2207	2207
Northeim (Han) d.	...	...	...	0420	0515	*0515*	0620	0720	0825	0920	1025	1120	1225	1320	1425	1520	1625	1720	1825	1920	...	2025	...	2120	2220	2220
Kreiensen d.	...	...	...	0433	0533	*0533*	0633	0733	0838	0933	1038	1133	1238	1333	1438	1533	1638	1733	1838	1933	...	2038	...	2133	2233	2233
Alfeld (Leine) d.	...	...	...	0446	0546	*0546*	0646	0746	0851	0946	1051	1146	1251	1346	1451	1546	1651	1746	1851	1946	...	2051	...	2146	2246	2246
Elze (Han) d.	...	...	...	0458	0558	*0558*	0658	0758	0903	0958	1103	1158	1303	1358	1503	1558	1703	1758	1903	1958	...	2103	...	2158	2258	2258
Hannover Hbf a.	...	...	...	0521	0627	*0627*	0728	0828	0926	1028	1126	1227	1326	1428	1526	1628	1726	1828	1926	2028	...	2126	...	2228	2321	2321
Hannover Hbf d.	...	...	...	0540	0640	0640	0740	0840	0940	1040	1140	1240	1340	1440	1540	1640	1740	1840	1940	2040	...	*2140*	2140	2248	2340	2351
Celle d.	...	0506	...	0606	0706	0706	0806	0906	1006	1106	1206	1306	1406	1506	1606	1706	1806	1906	2006	2106	...	*2206*	2206	2316	0006	0019
Uelzen a.	...	0536	...	0637	0737	0737	0837	0937	1037	1137	1237	1337	1437	1537	1637	1737	1837	1937	2037	2137	...	*2237*	2237	...	0039	0047
	⚒	⚒	⚒	d		|		⚒	|											†	⚒		|			
Uelzen d.	0501	0540	0628	0702	...	0800	0900	1001	1100	1200	1300	1400	1500	1600	1700	1800	1900	2000	2100	2200	2200	...	2300	...	...	...
Bad Bevensen d.	0510	0549	0636	0710	...	0809	0909	1009	1109	1209	1309	1409	1509	1609	1709	1809	1909	2009	2109	2209	2209	...	2309	...	...	...
Lüneburg d.	0524	0603	0651	0728	...	0828	0928	1028	1128	1228	1328	1428	1528	1628	1728	1828	1928	2028	2128	2228	2234	...	2323	...	...	...
Hamburg Hbf a.	0556	0635	0723	0802	...	0902	1002	1102	1202	1302	1402	1502	1602	1702	1802	1902	2001	2102	2203	2301	2320	...	2358	...	...	...

				Ⓐ	Ⓒ	⚒			⚒		⚒		⚒												†	⚒
Hamburg Hbf d.	...	...	...	0544	0554	0650	...	0754	0857	0954	1057	1157	1257	1357	1457	1554	1656	1754	1857	1957	...	2057	2155	2255	2355	2355
Lüneburg d.	...	...	...	0617	0627	0723	...	0827	0933	1033	1133	1233	1333	1433	1533	1627	1733	1827	1933	2033	...	2130	2228	2328	0028	0041
Bad Bevensen d.	...	...	...	0632	0645	0742	...	0846	0949	1048	1149	1248	1349	1448	1549	1646	1749	1846	1949	2049	...	2146	2243	2343	0043	0055
Uelzen a.	...	...	...	0641	0653	0750	...	0854	0957	1056	1157	1256	1357	1456	1557	1654	1757	1854	1957	2057	...	2157	2251	2352	0052	0104
	⚒	⊖		Ⓐ	Ⓒ	|	†		d	⊖	d		d							†	Ⓐ					
Uelzen d.	0413	0513	0609	0651	0709	0809	0809	0909	1009	1109	1209	1309	1409	1509	1609	1709	1809	1909	*2009*	2109	2128	2217	...	...	...	...
Celle d.	0447	0547	0647	0747	0747	0847	0847	0947	1047	1147	1247	1347	1447	1547	1647	1747	1847	1947	*2047*	2149	2201	2251	...	...	...	...
Hannover Hbf a.	0514	0614	0714	0814	0814	0914	0914	1014	1114	1214	1314	1414	1514	1614	1714	1814	1914	2014	*2114*	2214	2226	2317	...	...	...	...
Hannover Hbf d.	0530	0633	0717e	0833	0833	*0933*	0933	1033	1130	1233	1330	1433	1530	1633	1730	1833	1930	2033	2133	2237	2237	2330	...	...	...	...
Elze (Han) d.	0558	0655	0758	0855	0855	*1001*	1001	1055	1158	1255	1358	1455	1558	1655	1758	1855	1958	2055	2201	2258	2258	2358	...	...	...	...
Alfeld (Leine) d.	0610	0706	0810	0906	0906	*1013*	1013	1106	1210	1306	1410	1506	1610	1706	1810	1906	2010	2106	2213	2310	2310	0010	...	...	...	...
Kreiensen d.	0623	0719	0823	0919	0919	*1026*	1026	1119	1223	1319	1423	1519	1623	1719	1823	1919	2023	2119	2226	2323	2323	0023	...	...	...	...
Northeim (Han) d.	0637	0734	0837	0934	0934	*1040*	1040	1134	1237	1334	1437	1534	1637	1734	1837	1934	2037	2134	2240	2337	2337	0037	...	...	...	...
Göttingen d.	0649	0746	0849	0946	0946	*1052*	1052	1146	1249	1346	1449	1546	1649	1746	1849	1946	2049	2146	2252	2349	2349	0049	...	...	...	...

d – Runs daily from Uelzen. e – 0730 on Ⓒ. ⊖ – Change trains at Hannover Hbf on ⚒.

904 MÜNCHEN - NÜRNBERG fast services *ICE and IC services*

See Table **905** for regional services

km		ICE 1518	ICE 1514	ICE 822	ICE 1714	ICE 684	ICE 1612	ICE 820	ICE 926	ICE 886	ICE 728	ICE 682	ICE 1512 1712	ICE 1610	ICE 726	ICE 882	ICE 724	ICE 680	ICE 1510	ICE 1608	ICE 722	ICE 880	ICE 588	ICE 720	ICE 1508 1708
		①g	①–⑤	①g	⑥s	①–⑤	①–⑥	①–⑤	①y						①–⑥				①–⑤						
			d	E		d⊖	e	E				⊖			eE			⊖	d		E		⊖		F
		✕	✕	🍷	✕	✕	✕	🍷	✕	✕	🍷	✕	✕	✕	🍷	✕	🍷	✕	✕	✕	🍷	✕	✕	🍷	✕
0	**München** Hbf 930 d.	0013	0433	0451	0516	0517	0531	0551	0614	0620	0651	0652	0722	0743	0755	0820	0855	0916	0921	0944	0956	1020	1052	1055	1122
	München Pasing 930 d.	0021	0441	|	|	|	0539	|	|	|	|	0700	|	0751	|	|	|	|	|	0952	|	|	1101	|	|
	Augsburg Hbf 930 d.	0054	0515	|	|	|	0614	|	|	|	|	0733	|	0824	|	|	|	|	|	1024	|	|	1133	|	|
	Donauwörth d.	0112	0533	|	|	|	0634	|	|	|	|	0752	|	|	|	|	|	|	|	|	|	|	|	|	|
	Treuchtlingen d.	0132	0553	|	|	|	0654	|	|	|	|	|	|	|	|	|	|	|	|	|	|	|	|	|	|
81	**Ingolstadt** Hbf d.	|	|	0529	0554	0557	|	0630	|	0659	0729	|	0800	|	|	0859	|	|	1000	|	|	1059	|	|	1200
171	**Nürnberg** Hbf a.	0219	0626	0557	0626	0628	0727	0658	0726	0730	0757	|	0832	0926	0857	0930	0957	1023	1032	1127	1058	1130	|	1157	1232
	Würzburg Hbf **900 920** a.	|	|	0654	|	0727	|	0754	0825	0828	0854	0927	|	|	0954	1028	1054	1127	|	|	1154	1228	1327	1254	|
	Frankfurt (Main) Hbf **920** a.	|	|	0805	|	|	|	0905	0936	|	1005	|	|	|	1105	|	1205	|	|	|	1305	|	|	1405	|
	Köln Hbf **910** a.	|	|	0914k	|	|	|	1014k	1205	|	1140	|	|	|	1214k	|	1340	|	|	|	1414k	|	|	1540	|
	Berlin Hbf **851** a.	0714	1100	...	1100	|	1206	...	...	|	...	|	1300	1407	...	|	...	|	1500	1606	...	|	|	...	1700
	Hamburg Hbf **900** a.	0857	...	...	...	1054	...	...	...	1154	...	1254	...	...	...	1353	...	1454	...	...	...	1554	1653	...	...

	ICE 1000 1006	ICE 628	ICE 788	ICE 586	ICE 626	ICE 1506 1706	ICE 1604 1704	ICE 624	ICE 786	ICE 622	ICE 584	ICE 1504 1702	IC 2206	ICE 1820	ICE 620	ICE 1826	ICE 784	ICE 1602	ICE 1700	IC 2200	ICE 528	ICE 1828	ICE 582	ICE 1502 1722	ICE 1600
														⑦c	①–⑤	⑥p		⑧q	①–④	⑤	⑧n	⑥			⑧q
	R	E	G	⊖			n	D		D				D	d	D			‡	◐	D	T		¶	
	✕	🍷	✕	✕	🍷	✕	✕	🍷	✕	🍷	✕	✕	🍷	🍷	🍷	🍷	✕	✕	✕		🍷	🍷	✕	✕	✕
München Hbf 930 d.	1132	1156	1220	1252	1255	1322	1340	1356	1420	1455	1516	1522	1532	1556	1556	1556	1616	1622	1637	1637	1651	1655	1716	1722	1744
München Pasing 930 d.	1140	|	|	1301	|	|	|	|	|	|	|	|	1540	|	|	|	|	|	|	|	|	|	|	|	|
Augsburg Hbf 930 d.	1213	|	|	1333	|	|	1419	|	|	|	|	|	1614	|	|	|	|	|	1715	1715	|	|	|	|	1822
Donauwörth d.	1232	|	|	|	|	|	|	|	|	|	|	|	1635	|	|	|	|	|	1735	1735	|	|	|	|	1842
Treuchtlingen d.	1255	|	|	|	|	|	|	|	|	|	|	|	1656	|	|	|	|	|	1756*	1756	|	|	|	|	|
Ingolstadt Hbf d.	|	|	1259	|	|	1400	|	|	1459	|	|	1600	|	|	|	|	1659	|	|	|	1729	|	|	1800	|
Nürnberg Hbf a.	1327	1258	1330	|	1357	1432	1523	1458	1530	1557	1623	1632	1734	1658	1658	1658	1730	1735	1828	1831	1757	1757	1823	1832	1928
Würzburg Hbf **900 920** a.	|	1354	1428	1527	1454	|	|	1554	1628	1654	1727	|	...	1754	1754	1754	1828	|	...	...	1854	1854	1927	|	|
Frankfurt (Main) Hbf **920** a.	|	1505	|	|	1605	|	|	1705	|	1805	|	|	...	1905	1905	1905	|	|	...	...	2005	2005	|	|	|
Köln Hbf **910** a.	|	1614k	|	|	1731	|	|	1814k	|	1914k	|	|	...	2014k	2031	2040	|	|	...	...	2114k	2114k	|	|	|
Berlin Hbf **851** a.	1805	...	|	|	...	1900	2005	...	|	...	|	2101	...	...	...	...	|	2205	...	...	...	...	|	2300	0010b
Hamburg Hbf **900** a.	...	...	1755	1854	...	...	...	...	1954	...	2053	...	...	...	...	...	2155	...	...	...	...	...	2254	...	...

	ICE 526	ICE 782	ICE 980	ICE 580	ICE 524	ICE 1500	ICE 522	ICE 780	ICE 1824	ICE 520	ICE 922	ICE 1822
	⑧q		⑤j					⑦u	⑦w	①–⑥	①–⑥	⑦w
	D	⊖	H	Q	D	L		A		r	r	
						n	n					
	🍷	✕	✕	✕	🍷	✕	🍷	✕	✕	✕	✕	✕
München Hbf 930 d.	1756	1820	1850	1850	1855	1922	1951	2020	2053	2056	2255	2255
München Pasing 930 d.	|	|	1858	1858	|	|	|	|	|	|	|	|
Augsburg Hbf 930 d.	|	|	1931	1931	|	|	|	|	|	|	|	|
Donauwörth d.	|	|	1951	1951	|	|	|	|	|	|	|	|
Treuchtlingen d.	|	|	2011	2011	|	|	|	|	|	|	|	|
Ingolstadt Hbf d.	|	1859	|	|	|	2000	2029	2059	|	|	2333	2333
Nürnberg Hbf a.	1858	1930	|	|	1957	2032	2057	2130	2158	2158	0002	0004
Würzburg Hbf **900 920** a.	1954	2028	2129	2129	2054	...	2154	2234	2254	2254	...	0101
Frankfurt (Main) Hbf **920** a.	2105	|	...	|	2205	...	2300f	...	0013	0012	...	0214
Köln Hbf **910** a.	2219k	|	...	|	2341k	...	...	...	...	...	...	...
Berlin Hbf **851** a.	...	|	...	|	...	...	...	...	...	...	...	...
Hamburg Hbf **900** a.	...	0003	...	0103	...	...	...	...	...	...	...	...

	ICE 1701	ICE 823	ICE 981	ICE 985	ICE 983	ICE 827	ICE 1601	ICE 1501
	①–⑤		①–⑤	①–⑤	①–⑤	①–⑤	①–⑤	①–⑥
	z		a	a	a	a	a	eN
		🍷		✕	✕	🍷	✕	✕
Hamburg Hbf **900** d.	...	...	...	...	...	...	...	...
Berlin Hbf **851** d.	...	...	...	...	...	...	...	...
Köln Hbf **910** d.	...	...	...	...	...	...	...	...
Frankfurt (Main) Hbf **920** d.	...	...	...	...	...	...	...	...
Würzburg Hbf **900 920** d.	...	...	...	...	...	...	...	...
Nürnberg Hbf d.	0412	0601	...	0627	...	0701	0618	0728
Ingolstadt Hbf d.	|	0630	...	0701	...	0730	|	0801
Treuchtlingen d.	0445	|	...	|	0623	|	0653	|
Donauwörth d.	0506	|	0609	|	0647	|	0713	|
Augsburg Hbf 930 a.	0530	|	0628	|	0705	|	0730	|
München Pasing 930 a.	0601	|	0702	|	0738	|	0801	|
München Hbf 930 a.	0612	0707	0712	0739	0748	0807	0812	0839

	ICE 521	IC 2201	ICE 1603	ICE 781	ICE 523	ICE 581	ICE 1503	ICE 525	ICE 1605	ICE 783	ICE 527	ICE 1505	ICE 583	ICE 529	ICE 785	ICE 1607 1727	ICE 621	ICE 1507	ICE 585	ICE 623	ICE 787	ICE 625	ICE 1001	ICE 1509 1709	ICE 627
			①–⑤	①–⑥	①–⑥		①–⑤	x	①–⑥		①–⑥														
			dL	eM	eD	⊖	dJ	D	e	Y	tD		⊖	D			E	Z	⊖		G	E	R		
	🍷	🍷	✕	✕	🍷	✕	✕	🍷	✕	✕	G🍷	✕	✕	🍷	✕	✕	🍷	✕	✕	🍷	✕	🍷	✕	✕	🍷
Hamburg Hbf **900** d.	...	...	...	...	...	0457	...	...	...	0605h	...	...	0659	...	0803	...	...	...	0901	...	1001	...	...	...	...
Berlin Hbf **851** d.	...	...	...	...	...	|	...	...	0549	|	...	0652	|	...	|	0753	...	0858e	|	...	|	...	0953	1059	...
Köln Hbf **910** d.	0420	...	...	...	0518k	|	...	0644k	|	|	0744k	|	|	0844k	|	|	0944k	|	|	1020	|	1144k	|	|	1220
Frankfurt (Main) Hbf **920** d.	0551	...	...	...	0654	|	...	0754	|	|	0854	|	|	0954	|	|	1054	|	|	1154	|	1254	|	|	1354
Würzburg Hbf **900 920** d.	0705	...	...	0729	0805	0831	...	0905	|	0931	1005	|	1031	1105	1129	|	1205	|	1231	1305	1329	1405	|	|	1505
Nürnberg Hbf d.	0802	0718	0823	0827	0902	0931	0931	1002	1023	1027	1102	1128	|	1202	1227	1229	1302	1328	1332	1402	1427	1502	1429	1528	1602
Ingolstadt Hbf d.	|	|	|	0901	|	1003	|	|	|	1101	|	1201	|	|	1301	|	|	1401	|	|	1501	|	|	1601	|
Treuchtlingen d.	|	0753	|	|	|	|	|	|	|	|	|	|	|	|	|	|	|	|	|	|	|	|	|	|	|
Donauwörth d.	|	0814	|	|	|	|	|	|	|	|	|	|	|	|	|	|	|	|	|	|	|	|	|	|	|
Augsburg Hbf 930 a.	|	0832	|	|	|	|	1032	|	|	|	|	|	1222	|	|	1334	|	|	|	|	|	|	1531	|	|
München Pasing 930 a.	|	0905	|	|	|	|	|	|	|	|	|	|	1253	|	|	|	|	|	|	|	|	|	1601	|	|
München Hbf 930 a.	0904	0916	0937	0941	1004	1040	1111	1104	1137	1141	1204	1239	1303	1304	1339	1412	1404	1439	1443	1504	1539	1604	1612	1639	1704

	ICE 587	ICE 789	ICE 629	ICE 1003	ICE 1511	ICE 589	ICE 721	ICE 881	ICE 723	ICE 1613	ICE 1513	ICE 681	ICE 725	ICE 883	ICE 727	ICE 1615	ICE 1515	ICE 683	ICE 729	ICE 1617	ICE 885	ICE 927	ICE 821	ICE 1517	ICE 685
									⑧q						⑧q		n			⑦w		⊡	⑤⑦	n	⑦w
	⊖		E	R		⊖			E			⊖	E		E			⊖	E				§		⊖
	✕	✕	🍷	🍷	✕	✕	🍷	✕	🍷	✕	✕	✕	🍷	✕	🍷	✕	✕	✕	🍷	✕	✕	✕	🍷	✕	
Hamburg Hbf **900** d.	1101	1201	...	...	...	1301	...	1401	...	...	...	1501	...	1603	...	...	...	1701	...	...	1803	...	...	...	1901
Berlin Hbf **851** d.	|	|	...	1153	1258	|	...	|	...	1353	1458	|	...	|	...	1553	1658	|	...	1753	|	...	...	1858	|
Köln Hbf **910** d.	|	|	1344k	|	|	|	1428	|	1544k	|	|	|	1644k	|	1744k	|	|	|	1845k	|	|	1753	1928	|	|
Frankfurt (Main) Hbf **920** d.	|	|	1454	|	|	|	1554	|	1654	|	|	|	1754	|	1854	|	|	|	1954	|	|	2018	2054	|	|
Würzburg Hbf **900 920** d.	1431	1529	1605	|	|	1631	1705	1729	1805	|	|	1831	1905	1929	2005	|	|	2031	2105	|	2134	2130	2205	|	2231
Nürnberg Hbf d.	|	1627	1702	1629	1728	|	1802	1827	1902	1829	1928	|	2002	2027	2102	2029	2129	|	2202	2224	2231	2235	2303	2338	2342
Ingolstadt Hbf d.	|	1701	|	|	1801	|	|	1901	|	|	2001	|	|	2101	2132	|	2202	|	|	2258	2304	2311	|	0012	0019
Treuchtlingen d.	|	|	|	|	|	|	|	|	|	|	|	|	|	|	|	|	|	|	|	|	|	|	|	|	|
Donauwörth d.	1608	|	|	|	|	|	|	|	|	1917	|	|	|	|	|	2117	|	|	|	|	|	|	|	|	|
Augsburg Hbf 930 a.	1625	|	|	1731	|	1822	|	|	|	1934	|	2022	|	|	|	2134	|	2222	|	|	|	|	|	|	|
München Pasing 930 a.	1656	|	|	1801	|	1853	|	|	|	|	|	2053	|	|	|	2206	|	2253	|	|	|	|	|	|	|
München Hbf 930 a.	1708	1738	1804	1812	1840	1903	1904	1938	2004	2012	2039	2103	2104	2138	2208	2215	2241	2308	2304	2337	2341	2348	0005	0049	0056

A – To Kassel (Table **900**).
D – To / from Dortmund (Table **800**).
E – To / from Essen (Table **800**).
F – From Garmisch (d. 0925) on ⑥ **h**.
G – To / from Garmisch on ⑥ (Table **895**).
H – To Hannover (Table **900**).
J – From Halle (Table **851**).
L – To / from Leipzig (Table **851**).
M – 🛏 and ✕ (Hannover ①⑥ **m** -) Fulda - München.
N – From Lichtenfels (Table **851**) on ①–⑤ **a**.
Q – ①②③④⑥⑦ (also Mar. 21; not Mar. 20). 🛏 and ✕ München - Fulda (- Hannover ⑥⑦ **c**) (- Hamburg ⑦ **v**).
R – To / from Rostock on dates in Table **835**.
T – From Garmisch (d. 1518).
Y – 🛏 and ✕ (Hamburg ⑥ **h** -) Hannover - München.
Z – 🛏 and ✕ (Berlin ①–⑥ **e** -) Leipzig - München (- Garmisch ⑥ **h**).

a – Not Dec. 24, 25, 26, 31, Jan. 1, Mar. 21, 24, May 1, 12, 22.
b – Nürnberg - Berlin on ⑤⑦ (also Dec. 26, Jan. 1, Mar. 20, 24, Apr. 30, May 12, 21; not Dec. 23, 30, Mar. 21, 23, May 2, 11, 23).
c – Also Dec. 26, Jan. 1, Mar. 21, 24, May 12; not Mar. 23, May 11.
d – Not Dec. 24, 25, 26, 31, Jan. 1, Mar. 21, 24, May 12.
e – ①–⑥ (not Dec. 25, 26, Jan. 1, Mar. 22, 24, May 12).
f – Frankfurt (Main) **Süd**.
g – Also Dec. 27, Jan. 2, Mar. 25, May 13; not Dec. 24, 31, Mar. 24, May 12.
h – ⑥ (also Mar. 21; not Mar. 22).
j – Also Mar. 20; not Mar. 21.
k – Köln **Messe/Deutz**.
m – Also Dec. 27, Jan. 2, Mar. 25, May 13; not Mar. 22, 24, May 12.
n – Not Dec. 24, 31.
p – Also Dec. 24, 25, 31, Mar. 23, May 11.
q – Not Dec. 24, 25, 31, Mar. 21, 23, May 11.
r – Also Dec. 23, 30, Mar. 23, May 11; not Dec. 26, Jan. 1, Mar. 24, May 12.
s – Also Dec. 24, 31, Mar. 21; not Mar. 22.
t – Not Dec. 25, 26, Jan. 1, Mar. 24, May 12.
u – Also Mar. 24, May 12; not Dec. 23, 30, Mar. 23, May 11.
v – Also Jan. 1, Mar. 24, May 12; not Dec. 23, 30, Mar. 23, May 11.
w – Also Dec. 26, Jan. 1, Mar. 24, May 12; not Dec. 23, 30, Mar. 23, May 11.
x – Not Dec. 25, Jan. 1.
y – Not Dec. 24, 31, Mar. 24, May 12.
z – Not Dec. 24 – 28, 31, Jan. 1, Mar. 21, 24, May 1, 12, 22.
* – Not May 1, 22.
¶ – Not Dec. 24, 25, 31.
‡ – Not Dec. 24, 25, 26, 31, Jan. 1, Mar. 20, 24, Apr. 30, May 12.
§ – Also Dec. 26, Jan. 1, Mar. 20, 24, Apr. 30, May 12, 21; not Dec. 23, 30, Mar. 23, May 11.
◐ – Also Mar. 20, Apr. 30; not Mar. 21, May 2.
⊡ – ①②③④⑥⑦ (not Dec. 23, Mar. 23, May 11).
⊖ – Conveys 🛏 München - Hannover - Bremen and v.v. (Tables **900** / **813**).

RE / RB services — Regional services MÜNCHEN - NÜRNBERG — 905

See Table 904 for *ICE* and *IC* services

km		⑥2			Ⓐe2	Ⓐe	Ⓒz	Ⓒz	⚒c							⚒e2						⚒e2				
0	**München** Hbf 930 d.	...	...	0504	...	0526	...	...	...	0626	0704	0705	0729	...	...	...	0829	0905	0905	0929	...	...	1029	1105	1105	1126
7	München Pasing 930 d.	...	...	|	...	|	...	...	K	|	0711	|	|	...	L	...	|	|	0912	|	...	...	|	|	1112	|
62	**Augsburg** Hbf 930 d.	0518	...	|	0526	|	...	0616	0718	|	0751	|	|	0828	0918	0928	|	|	0951	|	1028	1122	|	|	1151	|
103	Donauwörth d.	0558	...	|	0609	|	...	0658	0739	|	0834	|	|	0858	0939	0958	|	|	1034	|	1058	1159	|	|	1238	|
	Pfaffenhofen (Ilm) d.	|	...	0529	|	0602	...	|	|	0702	...	0730	0805	|	|	|	0905	0930	...	1005	|	|	1105	1130	...	1205
	Ingolstadt Hbf a.	|	...	0548	|	0625	...	|	|	0724	...	0749	0827	|	|	|	0927	0949	...	1027	|	|	1127	1149	...	1227
	Ingolstadt Hbf d.	|	0529	0602	|	0628	0628	|	|	0726	...	0804	0830	|	|	|	0930	1004	...	1030	|	|	1130	1204	...	1230
	Kinding (Altmühltal) d.	|	|	0618	|	|	|	|	|	|	...	0820	|	|	|	|	|	1020	...	|	|	|	|	1220	...	|
	Allersberg (Rothsee) d.	|	|	0632	|	|	|	|	|	|	...	0834	|	|	|	|	|	1034	...	|	|	|	|	1234	...	|
	Eichstätt Bahnhof d.	|	0556	|	|	0656	0656	|	|	0756	...	|	0856	|	|	|	0956	|	...	1056	|	|	1156	|	...	1256
137	**Treuchtlingen** a.	0620	0620	|	0630	0720	0720	0720	|	0820	...	|	0920	0920	|	1020	1020	|	...	1120	1120	1221	1220	|	...	1320
137	**Treuchtlingen** d.	...	0626	|	*0635*	*0725*	...	0725	|	0826	...	|	...	0925	|	...	1026	|	...	...	1125	...	1226	|	...	...
146	Weißenburg (Bay) d.	...	0632	|	*0641*	*0732*	...	0732	|	0832	...	|	...	0932	|	...	1032	|	...	...	1132	...	1232	|	...	...
199	**Nürnberg** Hbf a.	...	0718	0645	*0722*	*0817*	...	0817	0826	0917	...	0849	...	1017	1026	...	1117	1047	...	...	1217	...	1317	1247	...	...

		Ⓐe2							Ⓐe						Ⓐe		⑥⑦S		Ⓐe							
München Hbf 930 d.	...	...	1229	1305	1305	1329	...	...	...	1429	1502	1505	1529	...	*1616*	1626	1701	1705	1709	1726	...	...	1829	1902	1905	1926
München Pasing 930 d.	...	...	|	|	1312	|	...	L	...	|	1509	|	|	...	*1623*	|	|	|	1716	|	...	L	|	1909	|	|
Augsburg Hbf 930 d.	1218	1306	|	|	1351	|	1428	1518	1528	|	1552	|	|	1627	1727	|	1741	|	1800	|	1827	1918	|	1955	|	|
Donauwörth d.	1258	1359j	|	|	1433	|	1458	1539	1558	|	1640	|	|	1658	1758	|	1803	|	1847	|	1858	1939	|	2041	|	|
Pfaffenhofen (Ilm) d.	|	|	1305	1330	...	1405	|	|	|	1505	...	1530	1605	|	|	1703	...	1730	...	1805	|	|	1905	...	1930	2002
Ingolstadt Hbf a.	|	|	1327	1349	...	1427	|	|	|	1527	...	1549	1627	|	|	1725	...	1749	...	1828	|	|	1927	...	1949	2025
Ingolstadt Hbf d.	|	|	1330	1404	...	1430	|	|	|	1530	...	1604	1630	|	|	1731	...	1804	...	1830	|	|	1930	...	2004	2031
Kinding (Altmühltal) d.	|	|	|	1420	...	|	|	|	|	|	...	1620	|	|	|	|	...	1820	...	|	|	|	|	...	2020	|
Allersberg (Rothsee) d.	|	|	|	1434	...	|	|	|	|	|	...	1634	|	|	|	|	...	1834	...	|	|	|	|	...	2034	|
Eichstätt Bahnhof d.	|	|	1356	|	...	1456	|	|	|	1556	...	|	1656	|	|	1758	...	|	...	1856	|	|	1956	...	|	2056
Treuchtlingen a.	1320	1421	1420	|	...	1520	1520	|	1620	1620	...	|	1720	1720	1820	1820	...	|	...	1920	1920	|	2020	...	|	2120
Treuchtlingen d.	1325	...	1426	|	...	...	1525	|	...	1626	...	|	...	1725	...	1826	...	|	...	...	1925	|	2026	...	|	...
Weißenburg (Bay) d.	1332	...	1432	|	...	...	1532	|	...	1632	...	|	...	1732	...	1832	...	|	...	...	1932	|	2032	...	|	...
Nürnberg Hbf a.	1417	...	1517	1447	...	...	1617	1628	...	1717	...	1648	...	1817	...	1917	...	1847	...	...	2017	2026	2117	...	2047	...

		†w	Ⓐe2					n
München Hbf 930 d.	...	...	...	2025	2108	2109	2126	2226	2325
München Pasing 930 d.	...	L	...	|	2115	|	|	|	|
Augsburg Hbf 930 d.	2027	2118	2128	|	2156	|	|	|	|
Donauwörth d.	2058	2139	2158	|	2239	|	|	|	|
Pfaffenhofen (Ilm) d.	|	|	|	2105r	|	2134	2202	2302	0001
Ingolstadt Hbf a.	|	|	|	2128r	|	2153	2224	2325	0024
Ingolstadt Hbf d.	|	|	|	2131	|	2158	2225	—	...
Kinding (Altmühltal) d.	|	|	|	|	|	2214	|	...	...
Allersberg (Rothsee) d.	|	|	|	|	|	2228	|	...	...
Eichstätt Bahnhof d.	|	|	|	2157	|	|	2253	...	...
Treuctlingen a.	2120	|	2220	2220	2301	|	2317	...	...
Treuchtlingen d.	2125	|	...	2226	...	|	...	2322	...
Weißenburg (Bay) d.	2132	|	...	2232	...	|	...	2328	...
Nürnberg Hbf a.	2217	2226	...	2317	...	2241	...	0011	...

km	km		Ⓐe		Ⓒz		⑥2	Ⓐe	Ⓐe	Ⓐe	Ⓒz	Ⓒz	Ⓐe
0	0	**Nürnberg** Hbf d.	...	0510	...	0438	...	...	0610	*0528*	0539	...	0557
	53	Weißenburg (Bay) d.	...	|	...	0522	...	...	|	*0610*	0623	...	0638
	62	**Treuchtlingen** a.	...	|	...	0530	...	...	|	*0617*	0630		0645
	62	**Treuchtlingen** d.	0450	|	...	0532	0540	0541	|	0631	0635	0635	0646
	91	Eichstätt Bahnhof d.	0514	|	...	0559	|	|	|	0657	|	0659	|
25		Allersberg (Rothsee) d.	|	0523	...	|	|	|	0623	|	|	|	|
59		Kinding (Altmühltal) d.	|	0538	...	|	|	|	0638	|	|	|	|
90	118	**Ingolstadt** Hbf a.	0532	0554	...	0624	|	|	0655	0722	|	0725	|
90	118	**Ingolstadt** Hbf d.	0533	0603	...	0633	|	|	0704	0733	|	0733	|
121	149	Pfaffenhofen (Ilm) d.	0555	0621	...	0656	|	|	0724	0756	|	0756	|
		Donauwörth d.	|	|	0515	|	0602	0613t	|	|	0658	|	0716t
		Augsburg Hbf 930 d.	|	|	0606	|	0632	0647	|	|	0730	|	0756t
		München Pasing 930 a.	|	|	0642	|	...	0722	|	|	...	|	0834
171	199	**München** Hbf 930 a.	0633	0648	0651	0735	...	0731	0752	0835	...	0835	0843

		⑥⑦S		Ⓒz2			Ⓐe				⑥m						⚒e2	Ⓒz						Ⓐe2		
Nürnberg Hbf d.	0710	...	0629q	...	0738	...	0835	...	0910	0839	0935	0939	...	...	1110	1038	...	1134	1138	...	...	1310	1238	...	1338	...
Weißenburg (Bay) d.	|	...	0715	...	0822	...	|	...	|	0923	|	1023	...	...	|	1122	...	|	1222	...	...	|	1322	...	1422	...
Treuchtlingen a.	|	...	0725	...	0830	...	0905	...	|	0930	|	1030	...	...	|	1130	...	|	1230	...	...	|	1330	...	1430	...
Treuchtlingen d.	|	...	0735	0735	0835	0835	0906	...	|	0935	|	1035	1035	...	|	1135	1135	|	1235	1240	...	|	1335	1335	1435	1435
Eichstätt Bahnhof d.	|	...	0759	|	|	0859	|	...	|	0959	|	|	1059	...	|	1159	|	|	|	1304	...	|	1359	|	|	1459
Allersberg (Rothsee) d.	0723	...	|	|	|	|	|	...	0924	|	|	|	|	...	1123	|	|	|	|	|	...	1323	|	|	|	|
Kinding (Altmühltal) d.	0738	...	|	|	|	|	|	...	0939	|	|	|	|	...	1138	|	|	|	|	|	...	1338	|	|	|	|
Ingolstadt Hbf a.	0755	...	0825	|	|	0925	|	...	0956	1025	|	|	1125	...	1155	1225	|	|	|	1333	...	1355	1425	|	|	1525
Ingolstadt Hbf d.	0806	...	0831	|	|	0931	|	...	1007	1031	|	|	1131	...	1204	1231	|	|	|	1335	...	1409	1431	|	|	1531
Pfaffenhofen (Ilm) d.	0826	...	0855	|	|	0955	|	...	1028	1055	|	|	1155	...	1224	1255	|	|	|	1356	...	1429	1455	|	|	1555
Donauwörth d.	|	0752	|	0757	0857	|	0924	0917	|	|	1022	1057	|	1120	|	|	1159	1222	1257	|	1320	|	|	1358	1457	|
Augsburg Hbf 930 d.	|	0824	|	0827	0928	|	0945	1008	|	|	1042	1129	|	1206	|	|	1236	1242	1326	|	1406	|	|	1428	1529	|
München Pasing 930 a.	|	|	|	...	...	|	...	1043	|	|	L	...	|	1242	|	|	...	L	...	|	1443	|	|	...	...	|
München Hbf 930 a.	0853	0902	0933	...	...	1035	...	1052	1054	1133	...	...	1233	1251	1252	1335	...	...	...	1434	1452	1453	1535	...	...	1633

				Ⓐe												Ⓐe						Ⓐe	†w			
Nürnberg Hbf d.	1508	...	1438	1534	1538	...	...	1708	1638	1734	1738	...	...	1910	1838	...	1938	...	...	2110	2038	...	2134	2138	...	2233
Weißenburg (Bay) d.	|	...	1522	|	1622	...	...	|	1722	|	1822	...	...	|	1922	...	2022	...	...	|	2122	...	|	2222	...	|
Treuchtlingen a.	|	...	1530	|	1630	...	...	|	1730	|	1830	...	...	|	1930	...	2030	...	...	|	2130	...	2204	2230	...	2303
Treuchtlingen d.	|	...	1535	|	1635	1635	...	|	1735	|	1835	1835	...	|	1935	1935	2035	2035	...	|	2135	2135	2205	2235	2235	2305
Eichstätt Bahnhof d.	|	...	1559	|	|	1659	...	|	1759	|	|	1859	...	|	1959	|	|	2059	...	|	2159	|	|	|	2259	|
Allersberg (Rothsee) d.	1521	...	|	|	|	|	...	1721	|	|	|	|	...	1923	|	|	|	|	...	2123	|	|	|	|	|	|
Kinding (Altmühltal) d.	1536	...	|	|	|	|	...	1736	|	|	|	|	...	1938	|	|	|	|	...	2138	|	|	|	|	|	|
Ingolstadt Hbf a.	1553	...	1625	|	|	1725	...	1753	1825	|	|	1925	...	1955	2025	|	|	2125	...	2155	2225	|	|	|	2325	|
Ingolstadt Hbf d.	1604	...	1631	|	|	1731	...	1804	1831	|	|	1931	...	2004	2031	|	|	2135	...	2205	2231	|	|	|	2332	|
Pfaffenhofen (Ilm) d.	1624	...	1655	|	|	1755	...	1824	1855	|	|	1955	...	2024	2055	|	|	2159	...	2225	2255	|	|	|	2356	|
Donauwörth d.	|	1520	|	1621	1657	|	1707	|	|	1821	1857	|	1920	|	|	1958	2057	|	2120	|	|	2159	2224	2258	|	2326
Augsburg Hbf 930 d.	|	1606	|	1641	1729	|	1758	|	|	1842	1928	|	2006	|	|	2105j	2129	|	2206	|	|	2236	2245	2329	|	2348
München Pasing 930 a.	|	1643	|	L	...	|	1842	|	|	L	...	|	2042	|	|	2141	...	|	2242	|	|	...	K	...	|	...
München Hbf 930 a.	1652	1653	1732	...	...	1833	1851	1852	1933	...	...	2033	2051	2052	2133	2150	...	2237	2252	2253	2333	...	...	...	0034	...

K – From / to Kempten (Table **935**).
L – From / to Lindau and Oberstdorf (Table **935**).
S – [12] Stuttgart - Schwäbisch Gmünd - Aalen - München and v.v.
c – Not May 22.
e – Not Dec. 24, 31, May 22.
j – Arrives 13 – 15 minutes earlier.
m – Also Dec. 24, 31.
n – Not Dec. 31.
q – 0633 on Ⓒ (also Dec. 24, 31, May 22).
r – 4 minutes earlier on † (also Dec. 24, 31).
t – Arrives 7 – 9 minutes earlier.
w – Also May 22.
z – Also Dec. 24, 31, May 22.

RB services (except trains A and B) — TREUCHTLINGEN - WÜRZBURG — 905a

km		⚒r	Ⓒz	Ⓐe	Ⓐe	Ⓒz	Ⓐe	⑥k						Ⓐe	A🍷										Ⓒz	Ⓐe
0	**Treuchtlingen** d.	...	0506	0515	0612	0625	*0701*	0725	0825	0925	1025	1125	1225	1305	1308	1325z	1425	1525	1625	1725	1825	1925	2025	2125	2225	2225
24	Gunzenhausen d.	...	0519	0528	0626	0639	*0716*	0739	0839	0939	1039	1139	1239	1318	1324	1339z	1439	1539	1639	1739	1839	1939	2039	2139	2239	2239
51	Ansbach a.	...	0539	0548	0646	0659	*0739*	0759	0859	0959	1059	1159	1259	1339	1342	1359z	1500	1559	1659	1759	1859	1959	2059	2200	2259	2301
51	Ansbach d.	0443	0541	0607	0702	0710	0811	0811	0910	1010	1110	1210	1310	...	1344	1410	1510	1610	1710	1810	1910	2010	2110	2200e	2300	...
83	Steinach (b Rothenb) ◐ d.	0504	0602	0628	0723	0731	0832	0832	0931	1031	1131	1231	1331	...	1404	1431	1531	1631	1731	1831	1931	2031	2131	2221e	2321	...
140	**Würzburg** Hbf a.	0550	0647	0716	0809	0816	0917	0917	1016	1116	1216	1316	1416	...	1438	1519	1615	1715	1816	1916	2016	2116	2216	2306e	0006	...

	⚒r	Ⓒz	Ⓐe	Ⓐe	Ⓒz	Ⓐe2					B🍷	Ⓒz	Ⓐe				⑤f								
Würzburg Hbf d.	0437	0531	0541	0632	0641	0710	0741	0841	0941	1041	1121	1141	1141	1241	1341	1441	1511	1541	1641	1741	1841	1941	2041	2141	2241
Steinach (b Rothenb) ◐ d.	0520	0615	0625	0716	0725	0755	0825	0925	1025	1125	1154	1225	1225	1327	1425	1525	1555	1625	1725	1825	1925	2025	2125	2225	2325
Ansbach a.	0542	0637	0646	0737	0746	0818	0846	0946	1046	1146	1215	1246	1246	1347	1446	1546	1617	1646	1746	1846	1946	2046	2146	2246	2347
Ansbach d.	0544	0655	0711	0754	0754	...	0854	0954	1054	1154	1217	1254	1315	1354	1454	1554	1620	1654	1754	1854	1954	2054	2154	2254	2354
Gunzenhausen d.	0603	0715	0732	0815	0815	...	0915	1015	1115	1215	1234	1315	1335	1415	1515	1615	1640	1715	1815	1915	2015	2115	2215	2315	0015
Treuchtlingen a.	0617	0730	0746	0830	0830	...	0930	1030	1130	1230	1250	1330	1349	1430	1530	1630	1655	1730	1830	1930	2030	2130	2230	2330	0030

◐ – Local trains **STEINACH BEI ROTHENBURG - ROTHENBURG OB DER TAUBER** and v.v. 2nd class only *12 km* Journey time: 14 minutes.
From Steinach (b Rothenb) at 0524 Ⓐ**e**, 0619 Ⓒ**z**, 0631 Ⓐ**e**, 0727 Ⓐ**e**, 0735 Ⓒ**z**, 0836, 0935, 1035, 1135, 1235 Ⓒ**z**, 1245 Ⓐ**e**, 1335, 1435, 1535, 1635 Ⓒ**z**, 1645 Ⓐ**e**, 1735, 1835, 1935, 2035.
From Rothenburg ob der Tauber at 0445 Ⓐ**e**, 0606 Ⓐ**e**, 0657 Ⓐ**e**, 0706 Ⓒ**z**, 0806, 0906, 1006, 1106, 1206, 1309, 1406, 1506, 1606, 1706, 1806, 1906, 2006.

A – *IC* **2082**. KÖNIGSSEE – [12] and 🍷 Berchtesgaden - München Ost - Augsburg - Würzburg - Hannover - Hamburg; [12] Oberstdorf (**2084**) - Augsburg (**2082**) - Hamburg.
B – *IC* **2083**. KÖNIGSSEE – [12] and 🍷 Hamburg - Hannover - Würzburg - Augsburg - München Ost - Berchtesgaden; [12] Hamburg - Augsburg (**2085**) - Oberstdorf.
e – Ⓐ (not Dec. 24, 31, May 22).
f – Also Mar. 20, Apr. 30; not Mar. 21.
k – Also Dec. 24, 31.
r – Not May 22.
z – Ⓒ (also Dec. 24, 31, May 22).

906 GIESSEN - KOBLENZ; LIMBURG - FRANKFURT and WIESBADEN

DB (RE/RB services); VEC★

Gießen - Limburg - Koblenz △ ⊠

km											
			Ⓐ		⚒						†
0	Gießen 807 d.	...	0523	0618	0717	...	0823	0918		1918	2023	2118
13	Wetzlar 807 d.	...	0533	0628	0727	...	0833	0927		1927	2033	2127
36	Weilburg d.	...	0558	0655	0744	...	0859	0944		1944	2059	2144
65	Limburg (Lahn) a.	...	0635	0731	0809	...	0935	1009	and	2009	2135	2209
			◧	◧	|		◧	|	every	|	◧	|
		⚒	d		|			|	two	|	⚒	|
65	Limburg (Lahn) d.	0545	0645	0745	0810	0845	0945	1010	hours	2010	2145	2210
68	Diez d.	0549	0649	0749	0814	0849	0949	1014	until	2014	2149	2214
91	Nassau (Lahn) d.	0615	0715	0815	0834	0915	1015	1034		2034	2215	2234
99	Bad Ems d.	0624	0724	0824	0842	0924	1024	1042		2042	2224	2242
112	Niederlahnstein § d.	0643	0743	0843	0856	0943	1043	1056		2056	2243	2256
117	Koblenz Hbf § a.	0653	0753	0853	0905	0953	1053	1105		2105	2253	2305

	Ⓐ						n			n	
Koblenz Hbf § d.	0504	0656	0856		1656	1806	1856	1906	2006	2106	2317
Niederlahnstein § d.	0514	0702	0903		1703	1814	1903	1914	2014	2114	2323
Bad Ems d.	0532	0716	0718		1718	1832	1918	1932	2032	2132	2339
Nassau (Lahn) d.	0541	0726	0725	and	1725	1844	1925	1941	2044	2141	2348
Diez d.	0608	0746	0745	every	1745	1909	1945	2008	2109	2208	0013
Limburg (Lahn) a.	0613	0749	0749	two	1749	1913	1949	2013	2113	2213	0017
	◧	|	|	hours	|	◧	|	◧			
	⚒¶	|	|	until	|	Ⓐ	|				
Limburg (Lahn) d.	0618	0750	0750		1750	1923	1950t	2023	...	...	...
Weilburg d.	0657	0816	0816		1816	1959	2016t	2059	...	...	...
Wetzlar 807 d.	0722	0833	0833		1833	2027	2033t	2127	...	...	...
Gießen 807 a.	0733	0843	0843		1843	2037	2043t	2137	...	...	...

Limburg - Niedernhausen - Frankfurt and Wiesbaden ⊠

km																										
		⚒	Ⓐ	Ⓐ	⑥	Ⓐ	Ⓐ	Ⓒ	Ⓐ	Ⓐ	Ⓐ	⚒	Ⓐ			Ⓐ			Ⓐ		Ⓐ	Ⓒ	Ⓐ		Ⓐ	Ⓒ
0	Limburg (Lahn) d.	0418	0448	0518	0518	0555	0608	0618	0623	0638	0655	0718	0755	0818	0918	0955	1018	1118	1155	1218	1318	1318	1355	1418	1518	1518
21	Bad Camberg d.	0442	0512	0542	0542	0614	0633	0642	0644	0703	0714	0742	0814	0842	0942	1014	1042	1142	1214	1242	1342	1342	1414	1442	1542	1542
30	Idstein d.	0451	0521	0551	0552	0621	0644	0651	0651	0714	0721	0751	0821	0851	0952	1021	1051	1152	1221	1251	1351	1352	1421	1451	1551	1552
38	Niedernhausen ‡ a.	0457	0527	0557	0559	0627	0651	0657	0657	0721	0727	0757	0827	0857	0959	1027	1057	1159	1227	1257	1357	1359	1427	1457	1557	1559
	Wiesbaden Hbf a.	|	0555	0625	0625	0655	0714	0725k	|	0744	|	0825	0857	0925	1025	|	1125	1225	|	1325	1425	1425	|	1525	1627	1625
70	Frankfurt (Main) Hbf ‡ a.	0528	0558	0628	...	0658	...	0728	0728	...	0758	0828	0858	0928	...	1058	1128	...	1258	1328	1428	...	1458	1528	1628	...

	Ⓐ		Ⓐ	Ⓐ	Ⓒ	Ⓐ					
Limburg (Lahn) d.	1555	1618	1655	1718	1718	1755	1818	1918	2018	2118	2218
Bad Camberg d.	1614	1642	1714	1742	1742	1814	1842	1942	2042	2141	2241
Idstein d.	1621	1651	1721	1751	1752	1821	1851	1952	2052	2151	2251
Niedernhausen ‡ a.	1627	1657	1727	1757	1759	1827	1857	1959	2059	2157	2257
Wiesbaden Hbf a.	|	1727	1757	1827	1825	1857	1925	2025b	...	...	...
Frankfurt (Main) Hbf ‡ a.	1658	1728	1758	1828	...	1858	1928	...	...	...	...

km										
			Ⓐ	Ⓒ	Ⓐ	Ⓐ	Ⓒ	Ⓐ		Ⓐ
	Frankfurt (Main) Hbf ‡ d.	...	0600	0630	0643	0730	...	...	0830	0857
0	Wiesbaden Hbf d.	0531j	0601	0634k	0650	0720	0736k	0801	0834r	|
20	Niedernhausen ‡ d.	0601	0631	0701	0718	0801	0801	0831	0901	0931
28	Idstein d.	0608	0638	0708	0725	0808	0808	0838	0908	0938
37	Bad Camberg d.	0617	0647	0717	0734	0817	0817	0847	0917	0945
58	Limburg (Lahn) a.	0640	0710	0740	0800	0840	0840	0910	0940	1003

			Ⓐ			Ⓐ	Ⓐ	Ⓒ		Ⓐ		Ⓐ	Ⓒ	Ⓐ	Ⓐ	Ⓐ	Ⓒ	Ⓐ		Ⓐ	Ⓐ	Ⓒ				
Frankfurt (Main) Hbf ‡ d.	...	1030	1100	...	1230	1300	1330	...	1430	1500	...	1600	1630	...	1700	1730	...	1800	1830	1900	1930	...	2030	...	...	...
Wiesbaden Hbf d.	0936	1034	|	1136	1234	|	1334	1336	1434	1501	1536	1604	1634	1636	1704	1734	1736	1804	1834	|	1934	1936	2034a	...	...	...
Niedernhausen ‡ d.	1001	1101	1131	1201	1301	1331	1401	1401	1501	1531	1601	1631	1701	1701	1731	1801	1801	1831	1901	1931	2001	2001	2101	2201	2301	0001
Idstein d.	1008	1108	1138	1208	1308	1338	1408	1408	1508	1538	1608	1638	1708	1708	1738	1808	1808	1838	1908	1938	2008	2008	2108	2208	2308	0008
Bad Camberg d.	1017	1117	1145	1217	1317	1345	1417	1417	1517	1545	1617	1645	1717	1717	1745	1817	1817	1845	1917	1945	2017	2017	2117	2217	2317	0017
Limburg (Lahn) a.	1040	1140	1203	1240	1340	1403	1440	1440	1540	1603	1640	1703	1740	1740	1803	1840	1840	1903	1940	2003	2040	2040	2140	2240	2340	0040

a – Ⓐ.
b – Ⓑ.
d – Runs daily from Limburg.
j – ⚒ only. 0536 on ⑥.
k – ⑥ only.
n – Not Dec. 24, 31.
r – ⚒ only.

t – † only.
¶ – Runs 2–5 minutes later on ⑥.
◧ – Change trains at Limburg.
★ – Vectus Verkehrsgesellschaft mbH.
△ – Additional stopping trains operate.
§ – See also Table **914**.

⊠ – On Dec. 24, 31 services run as on ⑥. On May 22 services run as on ⑦.

‡ – **Additional S-Bahn *S2* services** Frankfurt - Niedernhausen and v.v. Journey time 35 minutes.
From Frankfurt (Main) Hbf (underground platforms): On ⚒ every 30 minutes 0522–2322; on † hourly 0522–1222, then every 30 minutes 1252–2322.
From Niedernhausen: On ⚒ every 30 minutes 0433–2303; on † hourly 0503–1203, then every 30 minutes 1233–2303.

907 GIESSEN - FULDA

RE/RB services

On Dec. 24, 31 services run as on ⑥. On May 22 services run as on ⑦.

km																											
		⚒A	⑥	Ⓐ	⑥	Ⓐ	Ⓒ	Ⓒ	Ⓐ	Ⓒ	⑥	Ⓐ	Ⓐ	Ⓒ	Ⓒ	Ⓐ	Ⓐ	Ⓒ	⑥	Ⓐ	Ⓒ	Ⓒ	Ⓐ	Ⓐ	Ⓒ	Ⓐ	Ⓒ
0	Gießen d.	...	0619	0621	0743	0843	0848	0943	1043	1048	1143	1143	1241	1248	1343	1343	1443	1448	1543	1643	1648	1743	1744	1843	1848	2043	2045
23	Grünberg d.	...	0650	0703	0806	0906	0920	1005	1108	1120	1205	1210	1308	1322	1406	1411	1508	1520	1606	1706	1720	1806	1808	1913	1922	2110	2117
60	Alsfeld d.	0555	0739	0741	0838	0937	1004	1037	1138	1204	1239	1257	1338	1405	1438	1453	1538	1604	1638	1740	1806	1839	1908j	1959	2003	2148	2155
79	Lauterbach d.	0613	0757	0801	0900	0951	1022	1059	1152	1223	1300	1316	1353	1424	1500	1516	1555	1623	1700	1803	1825	1854	1926	2018	2021	...	...
106	Fulda a.	0641	0825	0826	0929	1016	1058f	1128	1217	1258	1329	1349	1417	1458h	1529	1554	1620	1658	1729	1833	1852	1924	1954	2049	2049	...	...

	Ⓐ	⑥	Ⓐ	⑥	⑥	Ⓐ	Ⓒ	Ⓒ	Ⓐ	⑥	Ⓒ	Ⓐ	Ⓒ	Ⓒ	Ⓐ	⑥	Ⓒ	Ⓐ	Ⓐ	Ⓒ	Ⓒ	Ⓐ	Ⓐ	Ⓒ	Ⓐ	Ⓐ	†
Fulda d.	...	...	0501	0558	0710	0728	0832	0915	0936	1032	1115	1136	1232	1315	1321	1432	1515	1526	1605	1632	1715	1736	1819	1910	1938	2035	2125
Lauterbach d.	...	...	0534	0632	0738	0757	0857	0943	1005	1057	1143	1206	1257	1343	1354	1458	1543	1558	1638	1657	1743	1802	1847	1939	2019	2103	2153
Alsfeld d.	0503	0548	0603v	0653	0804	0813	0913	1005	1021	1113	1205	1221	1313	1406	1413	1514	1605	1617	1704	1713	1807	1819	1907	2004	2038	2122	2212
Grünberg d.	0541	0625	0636	0735	0847	0844	0944	1047	1050	1144	1247	1251	1346	1447	1451	1545	1647	1647	1747	1744	1849	1849	1945	2042	...	...	...
Gießen a.	0606	0651	0709	0805	0912	0914	1014	1112	1114	1212	1312	1314	1412	1512	1512	1612	1712	1714	1814	1812	1914	1914	2011	2109	...	...	...

A – Runs 17–18 minutes later on ⑥.
f – 1049 on †.
h – 1452 on †.
j – Arrives 1852.
v – Arrives 0553.

908 GÖTTINGEN - BEBRA - FULDA

CANTUS Verkehrsgesellschaft (2nd class only)

km										
		Ⓐn	⚒		⚒					
0	Göttingen 864 d.	0455	0614	0714	0814	0914		1914	2014	2214
20	Eichenberg 864 d.	0511	0630	0730	0830	0930	and	1930	2030	2230
35	Bad Sooden-Allendorf d.	0521	0639	0739	0839	0939	every	1939	2039	2239
46	Eschwege West d.	0529	0647	0747	0847	0947	two	1947	2047	2247
81	Bebra a.	0553	0712	0812	0912	1012	hours	2012	2111	2312
81	Bebra 901 d.	0558r	0717e	0814	1000r	1014	until	2014	2201	...
95	Bad Hersfeld 901 a.	0608r	0726e	0824	1010r	1024		2024	2210	...
137	Fulda 901 a.	0638r	0755e	0853	...	1053		2053	2240	...

	Ⓐn	Ⓐn		⚒				Ⓐn		
Fulda 901 d.	...	0548r	0700	0719	0900		1700	1732r	1900	...
Bad Hersfeld 901 d.	0521r	0616r	0729	0748	0929	and	1729	1801r	1929	1945
Bebra 901 a.	0531r	0626r	0741	0756	0941	every	1741	1811r	1941	1956
Bebra d.	0545	0645	0745	0845	0945	two	1745	1845	1945	2045
Eschwege West d.	0609	0709	0809	0909	1009	hours	1809	1909	2009	2109
Bad Sooden-Allendorf d.	0617	0717	0817	0917	1017	until	1817	1917	2017	2117
Eichenberg 865 d.	0632	0732	0832	0932	1032		1832	1932	2032	2132
Göttingen 865 a.	0645	0745	0845	0945	1045		1845	1945	2045	2145

e – Ⓐ (not Dec. 24, 31, May 22).
n – Not Dec. 24, 31.
r – Not May 22.

909 GEMÜNDEN - BAD KISSINGEN - SCHWEINFURT - WÜRZBURG

DB (RB services); EIB ★

km																									
		Ⓐe	Ⓐe				Ⓐe							Ⓒz	Ⓐe							Ⓐe	Ⓐe		
0	Gemünden (Main) d.	...	...	0621e	0704	...	0749	0904	...	...	1104	...	...	1304	1313	...	1504	...	1606e	1706	...	1806	...	1906	2104
28	Hammelburg d.	0544	0623	0658e	0736	...	0822	0936	...	...	1136	...	...	1336	1358	...	1536	...	1659e	1737	...	1837	1901	1937	2136
47	Bad Kissingen a.	0611	0653	0722e	0800	...	0845	1000	...	...	1200	...	...	1400	1421	...	1600	...	1723e	1800	...	1900	1923	2000	2200
		Ⓐe	|	|	|		d	|			|			d	d		|		|	|		|	d	|	|
47	Bad Kissingen d.	0621	0708	0728	0805	0826	0928	1005	1026	1128	1205	1226	1328	1405	1426	1528	1605	1626	1728	1805	1826	1907	1928	2005	2225
56	Ebenhausen (Unterf) 870 d.	0633	0718	0743	0815	0841	0943	1015	1041	1143	1215	1241	1343	1415	1441	1543	1614	1641	1743	1815	1841	1917	1943	2015	2235
70	Schweinfurt Hbf 870 876 a.	0643	0730	0753	0826	0852	0953	1026	1052	1153	1226	1252	1353	1426	1452	1553	1625	1652	1753	1826	1852	1928	1953	2026	2246
113	Würzburg Hbf 870 876 a.	0719	0816	0825	...	0923	1025	...	1123	1225	...	1323	1425	...	1523	1625	...	1723	1824	...	1923	...	2025	2151y	2357

		Ⓐe								Ⓐe	Ⓒz												⚒r	†w	
Würzburg Hbf 870 876 ● d.	...	0507	0602f	...	0725v	0836	0933	1036	1133	...	1236	1236	1333	1436	...	1533	1636	1646e	1733	1836	...	1933	2036	2109	2139
Schweinfurt Hbf 870 876 ● d.	0515	0550	0705	0731	0805	0931	1005	1131	1205	1230	1306	1331	1405	1506	1531	1605	1706	1731	1805	1906	1931	2005	2106	2149	2224
Ebenhausen (Unter) 870 d.	0527	0605	0718	0744	0815	0944	1015	1144	1215	1242	1317	1344	1415	1517	1544	1615	1718	1744	1815	1917	1944	2015	2117	2202	2236
Bad Kissingen a.	0537	0615	0727	0755	0825	0955	1025	1155	1225	1252	1327	1355	1425	1527	1555	1625	1727	1755	1825	1927	1955	2025	2127	2212	2246
		|	Ⓐe	|		|		|		|	|	†w	Ⓐe	|	|	|	Ⓐe	|	Ⓐe		|			|	|
Bad Kissingen d.	0545	0624	0732	0801z	...	1001	...	1201	...	1257	1332k	1401	1434	1532e	1601z	1631e	1732	1801z	1831	...	2001	...	...	2219	2251p
Hammelburg d.	0612t	0648	0823j	0823z	...	1023	...	1223	...	1322	1358k	1423	1458	1558e	1623z	1653e	1758	1823z	1857	...	2023	...	...	2240	2312p
Gemünden (Main) a.	0648t	0735	0854	0854z	...	1054	...	1254	...	1354	1429k	1454	1535	1635e	1654z	1735e	1835	1854z	...	...	2054	...	...	2311	2343p

d – Runs daily from Bad Kissingen.
e – Ⓐ (not Dec. 24, 31, May 22).
f – 0624 on Ⓐ (not Dec. 24, 31, May 22).
j – Arrives 0757.
k – ⑥ (also Dec. 24, 31).
p – ⑥ only.

r – Not May 22.
t – On Ⓒ (also Dec. 24, 31, May 22) departs Hammelburg 0609, arrives Gemünden 0639.
v – 0733 on Ⓒ (also Dec. 24, 31, May 22).
w – Also May 22.
y – 2123 on Ⓒ (also Dec. 24, 31, May 22).

z – Ⓒ (also Dec. 24, 31, May 22).

★ – Erfurter Industriebahn (2nd class only).
● – Trains between Würzburg, Schweinfurt and Ebenhausen are often combined with a service to Meiningen or Erfurt. Passengers should take care to join the correct portion for their destination.

AACHEN - KÖLN - FRANKFURT via the high-speed line — 910

See Tables **800**/**912** for services via Bonn and Koblenz.

km		ICE 521		ICE 523		ICE 511	ICE 711	ICE 811	ICE 525	ICE 501	ICE 713	ICE 813	ICE 527	ICE 513		ICE 815	ICE 529	ICE 503	ICE 11	ICE 621	ICE 121	ICE 515	ICE 623
				①–⑥			①–⑥	Ⓑq	v	v	①–⑤	①–⑤	①–⑥			①–⑥					①–⑥		
		🍷		e🍷		🍷	e🍷	🍷	🍷	🍷	d🍷	d🍷	rG	🍷		e🍷	🍷	H🍷	🍷	🍷	r🍷	J🍷	🍷
	Münster (Westf) Hbf **800** d.	...	...	...	...	...	...	...	...	...	...	...	...	0601	...	...	...	...	...	...	...	0801	...
	Dortmund Hbf **800** d.	...	...	0401	...	...	0437	...	0523	0537	...	0559	0623	0638	...	0653	0709c	0737	...	...	...	0837	...
	Essen Hbf **800** d.	...	...	0423	...	...	0500	...	0551	|	...	0623	0651	0700	...	0715	0753	|	...	0840	...	|	...
	Amsterdam Centraal **28** ⊡ d.	...	...	|	...	...	|	...	|	|	...	|	|	|	...	|	|	|	...	|	0704	|	...
	Düsseldorf Hbf **800** d.	...	...	0453	...	...	0529	...	0622	|	...	0654	0722	0727	...	0748	0822	|	...	0913	0922	|	...
	Brussels Midi/Zuid **21 400** d.	...	...	|	...	...	|	...	|	|	...	|	|	|	...	|	|	|	0659	|	|	|	...
	Aachen Hbf **802 807** d.	...	...	|	...	...	|	...	|	|	...	|	|	|	...	|	|	|	0839	|	|	|	...
	Köln Hbf **802 807** a.	...	...	|	...	...	|	...	|	0646	...	|	|	0749	...	|	|	0846	0915	|	|	0946	...
0	**Köln** Hbf **802 807** d.	0420	...	|	...	0554	|	0619	|	0654	0658	|	|	0754	...	|	|	0854	0920	|	|	0954	1020
1	**Köln** Messe/Deutz **802** d.	|	...	0518	...	|	0600	|	0644	|	|	0720	0744	|	...	0810	0844	|	|	0944	0951	|	|
	Köln/Bonn Flughafen ✈ **802** ⊖ d.	|	...	0530	...	|	0611	|	|	|	0710	|	|	|	...	0821	|	|	|	|	|	|	|
25	Siegburg/Bonn **807** ▲ ⊖ d.	0437	...	0543	...	0611	|	0636	|	0711	|	0736	|	0811	...	0833	|	0911	|	|	|	1011	1037
88	Montabaur d.	0458	...	0604	...	|	0638	0657	|	|	0738	0757	|	|	...	0855	|	|	|	|	|	|	1058
110	Limburg Süd d.	0511	...	0615	...	|	0649	0707	|	|	0749	0807	|	|	...	0906	|	|	|	|	|	|	1109
	Wiesbaden Hbf a.	|	...	|	...	|	0711	|	|	|	0811	|	|	|	...	|	|	|	|	|	|	|	|
	Mainz Hbf a.	|	...	|	...	|	...	|	|	|	0830	|	|	|	...	|	|	|	|	|	|	|	|
169	**Frankfurt** Flughafen Fernbf ✈ a.	0533	...	0634	...	0651	...	0727	0734	0751	...	0827	0834	0851	...	0926	0934	0951	1014	1034	1043	1051	1128
180	**Frankfurt** (Main) Hbf a.	0546	...	0648	...	|	...	0741	0748	|	...	0841	0848	|	...	0941	0948	|	1030	1048	1102	|	1142
	Nürnberg Hbf **920** a.	0759	...	0859	...	|	...	...	0959	|	...	...	1059	|	...	...	1159	|	...	1259	...	|	1359
	Mannheim Hbf **912** a.	|	...	|	...	0724	...	...	|	0824	...	...	|	0924	...	...	|	1024	...	|	...	1124	|
	Karlsruhe Hbf **912** a.	|	...	|	...	|	...	...	|	0859	...	...	|	|	...	...	|	1059	...	|	...	|	|
	Basel SBB **912** a.	|	...	|	...	|	...	...	|	1047	...	...	|	|	...	...	|	1247	...	|	...	|	|
	Stuttgart Hbf **930** a.	|	...	|	...	0808	...	...	|	...	...	...	|	1008	...	...	|	...	...	|	...	1208	|
	München Hbf **904 930** a.	0904	...	1004	...	1031	...	...	1104	...	...	...	1204	1231	...	...	1304	...	...	1404	...	1431	1504

	THA 9409	ICE 105	ICE 505		ICE 625	ICE 517	ICE 627	THA 9417	ICE 507	ICE 123	ICE 629	ICE 519	ICE 15	ICE 721	ICE 509	ICE 125	ICE 723	THA 9429	ICE 611	ICE 915	ICE 725	THA 9433	ICE 601
		v															Ⓑq			n			
	ⓇP	🍷	🍷		🍷	🍷	🍷	ⓇP	🍷	🍷	🍷	🍷	🍷	🍷	🍷	🍷	🍷	ⓇP	🍷	🍷	🍷	ⓇP	🍷
Münster (Westf) Hbf **800** d.	...	...	...	...	...	...	...	...	...	...	...	...	...	...	...	...	...	...	...	...	...	...	...
Dortmund Hbf **800** d.	...	...	...	...	...	1038	...	...	...	...	...	1238	...	...	...	...	...	...	1438	...	1522w	...	...
Essen Hbf **800** d.	...	...	...	...	1053	1100	...	...	...	...	1253	1300	...	...	...	...	1453	...	1500	...	1553	...	...
Amsterdam Centraal **28** ⊡ d.	...	0804	...	...	|	|	...	...	...	1034	|	|	...	...	...	1234	|	...	|	...	|	...	...
Düsseldorf Hbf **800** d.	...	1022	...	...	1122	1127	...	...	...	1248	1322	1327	...	...	...	1448	1522	...	1527	...	1622	...	...
Brussels Midi/Zuid **21 400** d.	0825	|	...	...	|	|	...	1025	...	|	|	|	1159	...	...	|	|	1325	|	...	|	1425	...
Aachen Hbf **802 807** d.	1005	|	...	...	|	|	...	1205	...	|	|	|	1339	...	...	|	|	1505	|	...	|	1605	...
Köln Hbf **802 807** a.	1045	1045	...	...	|	1149	...	1245	...	1312	|	1349	1415	...	...	1512	|	1545	1549	...	|	1645	...
Köln Hbf **802 807** d.	...	1054	1054	...	|	1154	1220	...	1254	1320	|	1354	1420	1428	1454	1520	|	...	1554	1620	|	...	1654
Köln Messe/Deutz **802** d.	...	|	|	...	1144	|	|	...	|	|	1344	|	|	|	|	|	1544	...	|	|	1644	...	|
Köln/Bonn Flughafen ✈ **802** ⊖ d.	...	|	|	...	|	|	|	...	|	|	|	|	|	1441	|	|	|	...	|	|	|	...	|
Siegburg/Bonn **807** ▲ ⊖ d.	...	1111	1111	...	|	1211	1237	...	1311	|	|	1411	1436	|	1511	|	|	...	1611	1636	|	...	1711
Montabaur d.	...	|	|	...	|	|	1258	...	|	|	|	|	|	1509	|	|	|	...	|	1657	|	...	|
Limburg Süd d.	...	|	|	...	|	|	1309	...	|	|	|	|	1502	|	|	|	|	...	|	1707	|	...	|
Wiesbaden Hbf a.	...	|	|	...	|	|	|	...	|	|	|	|	|	|	|	|	|	...	|	|	|	...	|
Mainz Hbf a.	...	|	|	...	|	|	|	...	|	|	|	|	|	|	|	|	|	...	|	|	|	...	|
Frankfurt Flughafen Fernbf ✈ a.	...	1151	1151	...	1234	1251	1328	...	1351	1414	1434	1451	1522	1534	1551	1614	1634	...	1651	1727	1734	...	1751
Frankfurt (Main) Hbf a.	...	|	|	...	1248	|	1344	...	|	1430	1448	|	1540	1548	|	1630	1648	...	|	1741	1748	...	|
Nürnberg Hbf **920** a.	...	|	|	...	1459	|	1559	...	|	...	1659	|	...	1759	|	...	1859	...	|	...	1959	...	|
Mannheim Hbf **912** a.	...	1224	1224	...	|	1324	|	...	1424	...	|	1524	...	|	1624	...	|	...	1724	...	|	...	1824
Karlsruhe Hbf **912** a.	...	1259	1259	...	|	|	|	...	1459	...	|	|	...	|	1659	...	|	...	|	...	|	...	1859
Basel SBB **912** a.	...	1447	1447	...	|	|	|	...	1647	...	|	|	...	|	1847	...	|	...	|	...	|	...	2047
Stuttgart Hbf **930** a.	...	...	...	...	|	1408	|	...	...	...	|	1608	...	|	...	...	|	...	1808	...	|	...	...
München Hbf **904 930** a.	...	...	...	...	1604	1631	1704	...	...	...	1804	1831	...	1904	...	...	2004	...	2031	...	2104	...	...

	ICE 715	ICE 127	ICE 727	ICE 613	ICE 917	ICE 729	ICE 603	ICE 129	ICE 821	ICE 821	THA 9445	ICE 615	ICE 17		ICE 617	ICE 607	ICE 605	ICE 227		THA 9453	ICE 619		ICE 919
	n	L	Ⓑq		Ⓑq					⑤⑦f		n			⑦w	①–⑥	⑦w						n
	🍷	🍷	🍷	🍷	🍷	🍷	🍷	🍷	🍷	🍷	ⓇP	🍷	🍷		🍷	k🍷	🍷	🍷		ⓇP	🍷		🍷
Münster (westf) Hbf **800** d.	...	...	...	...	...	...	...	...	...	...	...	...	...	...	...	...	...	...	...	...	...	...	...
Dortmund Hbf **800** d.	...	...	...	1638	...	...	...	...	...	...	...	1838	...	...	1923	1923	...	...	...	...	2037	...	...
Essen Hbf **800** d.	...	...	1653	1700	...	1753	...	...	...	...	...	1900	...	...	1949	1949	...	...	...	...	|	...	...
Amsterdam Centraal **28** ⊡ d.	...	1434	|	|	...	|	...	1634	...	...	...	|	...	...	|	|	...	1834	...	...	|	...	...
Düsseldorf Hbf **800** d.	...	1648	1722	1727	...	1821	...	1848	...	...	...	1927	...	...	2022	2022	...	2048	...	...	|	...	...
Brussels Midi/Zuid **21 400** d.	...	|	|	|	...	|	...	|	...	...	1725	|	1759	...	|	|	...	|	...	1925	|	...	...
Aachen Hbf **802 807** d.	...	|	|	|	...	|	...	|	...	...	1905	|	1939	...	|	|	...	|	...	2105	|	...	...
Köln Hbf **802 807** a.	...	1712	|	1749	...	|	...	1912	...	...	1945	1949	2015	...	|	|	...	2112	...	2145	2146	...	...
Köln Hbf **802 807** d.	1707	1720	|	1754	1820	|	1854	1920	1928	1928	...	1954	2020	...	|	|	2054	2120	...	...	2154	...	2254
Köln Messe/Deutz **802** d.	|	|	1744	|	|	1845	|	|	|	|	...	|	|	...	2044	2044	|	|	...	...	|	...	|
Köln/Bonn Flughafen ✈ **802** ⊖ d.	|	|	|	|	|	|	|	|	|	|	...	|	|	...	|	|	|	|	...	...	|	...	2307
Siegburg/Bonn **807** ▲ ⊖ d.	|	|	|	1811	1836	|	1911	|	|	|	...	2011	|	...	|	2100	2111	|	...	...	2211	...	|
Montabaur d.	1738	|	|	|	1857	|	|	|	2002	2002	...	|	|	...	2116	2120	|	|	...	...	|	...	2334
Limburg Süd d.	1749	|	|	|	1907	|	|	|	2014	2014	...	|	|	...	2126	2131	|	|	...	...	|	...	2345
Wiesbaden Hbf a.	1811	|	|	|	|	|	|	|	|	|	...	|	|	...	|	|	|	|	...	...	|	...	|
Mainz Hbf a.	...	|	|	|	|	|	|	|	|	|	...	|	|	...	|	|	|	|	...	...	|	...	|
Frankfurt Flughafen Fernbf ✈ a.	...	1814	1834	1851	1927	1935	1951	2014	2034	2034	...	2051	2114	...	2146	2151	2151	2218	...	...	2256	...	0010
Frankfurt (Main) Hbf a.	...	1830	1848	|	1941	1948	|	2030	2048	2048	...	|	2130	...	|	|	|	2234	...	...	2310	...	0023
Nürnberg Hbf **920** a.	...	...	2059	|	...	2159	|	...	2259	2259	...	|	...	...	|	|	|	...	...	...	...	...	...
Mannheim Hbf **912** a.	...	...	|	1924	...	|	2024	...	...	|	...	2124	...	...	|	2224	2224	...	...	...	...	...	...
Karlsruhe Hbf **912** a.	...	...	|	|	...	|	2100	...	...	|	...	|	...	...	|	2300	2300	...	...	...	...	...	...
Basel SBB **912** a.	...	...	|	|	...	|	2300z	...	...	|	...	|	...	...	|	0106	0058b	...	...	...	...	...	...
Stuttgart Hbf **930** a.	...	...	|	2008	...	|	...	...	...	|	...	2208	...	...	2324	...	...	...	...	...	...	...	...
München Hbf **904 930** a.	...	...	2208	2231	...	2304	...	...	...	0005	...	0035	...	...	...	...	...	...	...	...	...	...	...

G – (12) and 🍷 (Hannover ①g -) Dortmund - München (- Garmisch ⑥).
H – From Hannover (Table **810**).
J – From Hamburg (Table **800**).
L – From Mar. 14.
P – (12) and 🍷 Paris - Brussels - Liège - Köln.

b – Basel **Badischer Bahnhof**.
c – ⑥⑦ (also Dec. 24, 25, 26, 31, Jan. 1, Mar. 21, 24, May 12).
d – Not Dec. 24, 25, 26, 31, Jan. 1, Mar. 21, 24, May 12.
e – Not Dec. 25, 26, Jan. 1, Mar. 22, 24, May 12.
f – Also Dec. 26, Jan. 1, Mar. 20, 24, Apr. 30, May 12, 21; not Dec. 23, 30, Mar. 23, May 11.
g – Also Dec. 27, Jan. 2, Mar. 25, May 13; not Dec. 24, 31, Mar. 24, May 12.
k – Also Dec. 23, 30, Mar. 23, May 11; not Dec. 24, 26, 31, Jan. 1, Mar. 24, May 12.
n – Not Dec. 24, 31.
q – Not Dec. 24, 25, 31, Mar. 21, 23, May 11.
r – Not Dec. 25, 26, Jan. 1, Mar. 24, May 12.
v – Not Dec. 25, Jan. 1.
w – ⑦ (also Dec. 26, Jan. 1, Mar. 24, May 12; not Dec. 23, 30, Mar. 23, May 11).
z – 2253 on ⑦ (also Dec. 26, Jan. 1, Mar. 24, May 12; not Dec. 23, 30, Mar. 23, May 11).
⊡ – Amsterdam timings are subject to alteration on Apr. 30.

⊖ – For local connections Köln/Bonn Flughafen - Siegburg/Bonn see Tables **802** (Köln/Bonn Flughafen - Troisdorf) and **807** (Troisdorf - Siegburg/Bonn).

▲ – Light-rail services operate Bonn Hbf - Siegburg/Bonn and v.v. Journey time: 25 minutes. Operator: Elektrische Bahnen der Stadt Bonn und des Rhein-Sieg-Kreises (SSB). On May 22 services run as on †.

Departures from Bonn Hbf

On Ⓐ: 0016, 0046, 0133, 0418, 0438, 0458, 0518, 0528, 0543 and every 10 minutes until 1953, 2013, 2032, 2046 and every 15 minutes until 2246, 2316, 2346.

On ⑥: 0016, 0046, 0133, 0416 and every 30 minutes until 0746, 0801, 0816, 0831, 0846, 0856, 0906, 0916, 0925, 0932 and every 10 minutes until 1602, 1616, 1626, 1646 and every 15 minutes until 2246, 2316, 2346.

On †: 0016, 0046, 0133, 0511, 0541, 0616 and every 30 minutes until 1016, 1031 and every 15 minutes until 2246, 2316, 2346.

Departures from Siegburg/Bonn

On Ⓐ: 0022, 0052, 0122, 0202, 0454, 0514, 0534, 0554 and every 10 minutes until 1934, 1952, 2002, 2012, 2022 and every 15 minutes until 2222, 2232, 2252, 2302, 2322, 2352.

On ⑥: 0022, 0052, 0122, 0202, 0452 and every 30 minutes until 0752, 0814, 0834, 0854 and every 10 minutes until 1424, 1438 and every 10 minutes until 1538, 1552, 1602, 1612, 1622, 1632, 1642, 1652 and every 15 minutes until 2222, 2232, 2252, 2322, 2352.

On †: 0022, 0052, 0122, 0202, 0552 and every 30 minutes until 1052, 1107 and every 15 minutes until 2222, 2232, 2252, 2322, 2352.

910 FRANKFURT - KÖLN - AACHEN via the high-speed line

See Tables **800**/**912** for services via Koblenz and Bonn.

km		ICE 828 ①-⑤ d 🍷	RE 4852 ①-⑤ x	THA 9416 M R P	ICE 826 🍷	◇	THA 9418 ⑦c R P	ICE 716 ①-⑤ d 🍷	ICE 616 🍷	ICE 824 ①-⑥ e D	ICE 16 🍷	ICE 226 🍷	ICE 604 🍷	ICE 822 🍷	ICE 812 ⑧q 🍷	ICE 614 🍷	THA 9428 R P	ICE 820 ①-⑤ d 🍷	ICE 128 🍷	ICE 602 🍷	ICE 728 🍷	ICE 612 🍷	THA 9436 R P
	München Hbf **904 930** d.	...	...	...	...	...	...	...	0317z	🍷	...	...	...	0451g	...	0523	...	0551	...	...	0651	0723	...
	Stuttgart Hbf **930** d.	...	...	...	...	...	...	...	0551	...	...	...	...	|	...	0751	...	|	...	...	|	0951	...
	Basel SBB **912** d.	...	...	...	...	...	...	...	|	...	...	...	0516b	|	...	|	...	|	...	0712	|	|	...
	Karlsruhe Hbf **912** d.	...	...	...	...	...	...	...	|	...	...	...	0700	|	...	|	...	|	...	0901	|	|	...
	Mannheim Hbf **912** d.	...	...	...	...	...	...	...	0635	...	...	...	0735	|	...	0835	...	|	...	0935	|	1035	...
	Nürnberg Hbf **920** d.	...	...	...	...	...	...	...	|	...	...	...	|	0600	...	|	...	0701	...	|	0800	|	...
	Frankfurt (Main) Hbf d.	0449	...	...	0548	...	...	...	|	0702	0728	0728	|	0810	0816	|	...	0910	0928	|	1010	|	...
	Frankfurt Flughafen Fernbf ✈ d.	0502	...	...	0607	...	...	...	0709	0714	0743	0743	0809	0824	0831	0909	...	0924	0943	1009	1024	1109	...
0	**Mainz** Hbf d.	|	...	...	|	...	...	0609	|	|	|	|	|	|	|	|	...	|	|	|	|	|	...
10	**Wiesbaden** Hbf d.	|	...	...	|	...	...	0628	|	|	|	|	|	|	|	|	...	|	|	|	|	|	...
65	Limburg Süd d.	0521	...	...	0626	...	...	0649	|	0733	|	|	|	|	0850	|	...	|	|	|	1044	|	...
87	Montabaur d.	0532	...	...	0637	...	...	0700	|	0744	|	|	|	|	0901	|	...	|	|	|	1056	|	...
150	Siegburg/Bonn **807** ▲ ⊖ d.	0559	0614	...	0659	...	...	|	0749	0806	|	|	0849	|	0923	0949	...	|	|	1049	1118	1149	...
166	Köln/Bonn Flughafen ✈ **802** ⊖ a.	0607	|	...	|	...	...	0726	|	|	|	|	|	|	|	|	...	|	|	|	1126	|	...
180	**Köln** Messe/Deutz **802** a.	0619	0633	...	0714	0727	...	|	|	0822	|	|	|	0914	|	|	...	1014	|	|	|	|	...
181	**Köln** Hbf **802 807** a.	|	0637	...	|	0729	...	0740	0805	|	0840	0840	0905	|	0940	1005	...	|	1040	1105	1140	1205	...
181	**Köln** Hbf **802 807** d.	|	0647	0713	|	...	0739	...	0811	|	0844	0848	...	|	...	1011	1013	|	1048	...	...	1211	1213
251	**Aachen** Hbf **802 807** a.	|	0749	0752	|	...	0815	...	|	|	0916	|	...	|	...	|	1052	|	|	...	...	|	1252
	Brussels Midi/Zuid **21 400** a.	|	...	0935	|	...	1000	...	|	|	1101	|	...	|	...	|	1235	|	|	...	...	|	1435
	Düsseldorf Hbf **800** a.	0643	...	...	0740	...	...	...	0832	0844	...	0913	...	0937	...	1032	...	1037	1111	...	...	1232	...
	Amsterdam Centraal **28** ⊡ a.	|	...	...	|	...	...	...	|	|	...	1125	...	|	...	|	...	|	1325	...	...	|	...
	Essen Hbf **800** a.	0717	...	...	0806	...	...	...	0857	0918	...	...	...	1002	...	1057	...	1102	...	...	...	1257	...
	Dortmund Hbf **800** a.	...	...	...	...	...	...	...	0921	...	...	...	...	...	...	1121	...	...	...	...	...	1321	...
	Münster (Westf) Hbf **800** a.	...	...	...	...	...	...	...	...	...	...	...	...	...	...	...	...	...	...	...	...	...	...

	ICE 726 ①-⑥ e 🍷	ICE 126 L 🍷	ICE 600 🍷	ICE 724 🍷	ICE 610 🍷	ICE 722 🍷	ICE 14 🍷	ICE 124 🍷	ICE 508 🍷	THA 9448 R P	ICE 720 🍷	ICE 518 🍷	ICE 628 🍷	ICE 810 🍷	ICE 506 🍷	THA 9456 R P	ICE 626 🍷	ICE 122 🍷	ICE 712 n 🍷	ICE 516 🍷	THA 9460 R P	ICE 624 🍷	ICE 916 ①-⑤ d 🍷
München Hbf **904 930** d.	0755	...	...	0855	0923	0956	...	...	...	...	1055	1123	1156	...	...	...	1255	...	...	1323	...	1356	...
Stuttgart Hbf **930** d.	|	...	...	|	1151	|	...	...	...	...	|	1351	|	...	...	...	|	...	...	1551	...	|	...
Basel SBB **912** d.	|	...	0912	|	|	|	...	...	1112	...	|	|	|	...	1312	...	|	...	...	|	...	|	...
Karlsruhe Hbf **912** d.	|	...	1100	|	|	|	...	...	1300	...	|	|	|	...	1500	...	|	...	...	|	...	|	...
Mannheim Hbf **912** d.	|	...	1135	|	1235	|	...	...	1335	...	|	1435	|	...	1535	...	|	...	...	1635	...	|	...
Nürnberg Hbf **920** d.	0900	...	|	1000	|	1101	...	...	|	...	1200	|	1301	...	|	...	1400	...	...	|	...	1501	...
Frankfurt (Main) Hbf d.	1110	1128	|	1210	|	1310	1328	1328	|	...	1410	|	1510	1517	|	...	1610	1628	...	|	...	1710	1717
Frankfurt Flughafen Fernbf ✈ d.	1124	1143	1209	1224	1309	1324	1343	1343	1409	...	1424	1509	1524	1532	1609	...	1623	1643	...	1709	...	1724	1732
Mainz Hbf d.	|	|	|	|	|	|	|	|	|	...	|	|	|	|	|	...	|	|	1622	|	...	|	|
Wiesbaden Hbf d.	|	|	|	|	|	|	|	|	|	...	|	|	|	|	|	...	|	|	1645	|	...	|	|
Limburg Süd d.	|	|	|	1244	|	|	|	|	|	...	1444	|	|	1551	|	...	1642	|	1706	|	...	|	1751
Montabaur d.	|	|	|	1256	|	|	|	|	|	...	1456	|	|	1602	|	...	1653	|	1717	|	...	|	1802
Siegburg/Bonn **807** ▲ ⊖ d.	|	|	1249	1318	1349	|	|	|	1449	...	1518	1549	|	1623	1649	...	1714	|	1738	1749	...	|	1823
Köln/Bonn Flughafen ✈ **802** ⊖ a.	|	|	|	1326	|	|	|	|	|	...	1527	|	|	|	|	...	|	|	1747	|	...	|	|
Köln Messe/Deutz **802** a.	1214	|	|	|	|	1414	|	|	|	...	|	|	1614	|	|	...	|	|	|	|	...	1814	|
Köln Hbf **802 807** a.	|	1240	1305	1340	1405	|	1440	1440	1505	...	1540	1605	|	1640	1705	...	1731	1740	1801	1805	...	|	1840
Köln Hbf **802 807** d.	|	1248	...	...	1411	|	1444	1448	...	1513	...	1611	|	...	1711	1713	...	1748	...	1811	1813	|	...
Aachen Hbf **802 807** a.	|	|	...	...	|	|	1516	|	...	1552	...	|	|	...	|	1752	...	|	...	|	1852	|	...
Brussels Midi/Zuid **21 400** a.	|	|	...	...	|	|	1701	|	...	1735	...	|	|	...	|	1935	...	|	...	|	2035	|	...
Düsseldorf Hbf **800** a.	1237	1311	...	...	1432	1437	...	1511	...	...	...	1632	1637	...	|	...	...	1811	...	|	...	1837	...
Amsterdam Centraal **28** ⊡ a.	|	1525	...	...	|	|	...	1725	...	...	...	|	|	...	|	...	...	2025	...	|	...	|	...
Essen Hbf **800** a.	1302	...	...	...	1457	1502	...	...	...	...	...	1657	1702	...	|	...	...	...	...	|	...	1902	...
Dortmund Hbf **800** a.	...	...	...	...	1521	...	...	...	...	...	...	1721	...	...	1820	...	...	...	...	1920	...	1929	...
Münster (Westf) Hbf **800** a.	...	...	...	...	...	...	...	...	...	...	...	...	...	...	...	...	...	...	...	...	...	...	...

	ICE 504 🍷	ICE 104 n 🍷	ICE 622 🍷	ICE 914 ⑧q 🍷	ICE 10 🍷	ICE 914 ⑧q 🍷	ICE 710 ⑧q J 🍷	ICE 514 A 🍷	ICE 1820 ⑦v 🍷	ICE 620 ①-⑤ d 🍷	ICE 1826 ⑥t 🍷	ICE 120 ⑧r 🍷	ICE 502 H 🍷	ICE 528 ⑧n 🍷	ICE 1828 ⑥ G 🍷	ICE 910 n 🍷	ICE 512 n 🍷	ICE 526 ⑧q 🍷		ICE 500 n 🍷	ICE 524 🍷	ICE 1810 ⑦v 🍷	ICE 920 k 🍷
München Hbf **904 930** d.	...	...	1455	...	...	...	...	1523	1556	1556	1556	...	...	1651	1655	...	1723	1756	...	...	1855	1923	...
Stuttgart Hbf **930** d.	...	...	|	...	...	...	...	1751	|	|	|	...	...	|	|	...	1951	|	...	...	|	2151	...
Basel SBB **912** d.	1512	1512	|	...	...	...	...	|	|	|	|	...	1712	|	|	...	|	|	...	1912	|	|	...
Karlsruhe Hbf **912** d.	1700	1700	|	...	...	...	...	|	|	|	|	...	1901	|	|	...	|	|	...	2101	|	|	...
Mannheim Hbf **912** d.	1735	1735	|	...	...	...	...	1835	|	|	|	...	1935	|	|	...	2035	|	...	2135	|	2231	...
Nürnberg Hbf **920** d.	|	|	1600	...	...	...	...	|	1701	1701	1701	...	|	1800	1800	...	|	1901	...	|	2000	|	...
Frankfurt (Main) Hbf d.	|	|	1810	1816	1828	...	...	|	1910	1910	1910	1928	|	2010	2010	2016	|	2110	...	|	2210	|	2310
Frankfurt Flughafen Fernbf ✈ d.	1809	1809	1824	1831	1843	...	...	1909	1924	1923	1924	1943	2009	2024	2024	2031	2109	2124	...	2209	2224	2304	2324
Mainz Hbf d.	|	|	|	|	|	...	...	|	|	|	|	|	|	|	|	|	|	|	...	|	|	|	|
Wiesbaden Hbf d.	|	|	|	|	|	...	1848	|	|	|	|	|	|	|	|	|	|	|	...	|	|	|	|
Limburg Süd d.	|	|	|	1850	|	←	1909	|	|	1942	1942	|	|	|	|	2050	|	|	...	|	2243	|	2343
Montabaur d.	|	|	|	1859	|	1907	1920	|	|	1953	1953	|	|	|	|	2101	|	|	...	|	2254	|	2354
Siegburg/Bonn **807** ▲ ⊖ d.	1849	1849	|	→	1923	1929	|	1949	|	2014	2014	|	2049	|	|	2128	2149	|	...	2254	2320	2349	0020
Köln/Bonn Flughafen ✈ **802** ⊖ a.	|	|	|	...	|	1937	1946	|	|	|	2027	|	|	|	|	2137	|	|	...	|	2328	|	|
Köln Messe/Deutz **802** a.	|	|	1914	...	|	|	1958	|	2014	|	|	|	|	2114	2114	2150	|	2219	...	|	2341	|	0034
Köln Hbf **802 807** a.	1905	1905	|	...	1940	1956	|	2005	|	2031	2040	2040	2105	|	|	|	2205	|	...	2312	|	0005	|
Köln Hbf **802 807** d.	...	1917	|	...	1944	...	|	2011	|	...	2048	2048	2111	|	|	|	2211	|	...	2317	|	...	|
Aachen Hbf **802 807** a.	...	|	|	...	2016	...	|	|	|	...	|	|	|	|	|	|	|	|	...	|	|	...	|
Brussels Midi/Zuid **21 400** a.	...	|	|	...	2201	...	|	|	|	...	|	|	|	|	|	|	|	|	...	|	|	...	|
Düsseldorf Hbf **800** a.	...	1938	1942	...	...	...	2025	2032	2037	...	2111	2111	|	2137	2137	2211	2232	2242	...	2338	0004	...	0057
Amsterdam Centraal **28** ⊡ a.	...	2155	|	...	...	...	|	|	|	...	|	2325	|	|	|	|	|	|	...	|	|	...	|
Essen Hbf **800** a.	...	...	2008	...	...	...	2102	2057	2108	...	2136	...	|	2202	2202	2236	2257	2307	...	0003	0029	...	0122
Dortmund Hbf **800** a.	...	...	2038	...	...	...	2130	2121	2137	...	2159	...	2220	2228	2228	2300	2321	2336	...	0026	0052	...	0146
Münster (Westf) Hbf **800** a.	...	...	...	...	...	...	...	2157	...	...	...	...	...	...	...	...	2357	...	...	...	...	...	...

A – To Hamburg (Table **800**).
D – From Darmstadt Hbf (d. 0637).
G – From Garmisch (Table **895**).
H – To Hannover (Table **810**).
J – To Hannover on ⑦**w** (Table **810**).
L – From Mar. 14.
M – ①-⑥ (not Dec. 25, 26, Jan. 1, Mar. 24, May 1, 12).
P – 12 and 🍷 Köln - Liège - Brussels - Paris.

b – Basel **Badischer Bahnhof**.
c – Also Dec. 25, 26, Jan. 1, Mar. 24, May 1, 12.
d – Not Dec. 24, 25, 26, 31, Jan. 1, Mar. 21, 24, May 12.
e – Not Dec. 25, 26, Jan. 1, Mar. 22, 24, May 12.
g – ① (also Dec. 27, Jan. 2, Mar. 25, May 13; not Dec. 24, 31, Mar. 24, May 12).
k – Not Dec. 24, 31, Mar. 21, May 10.
n – Not Dec. 24, 31.
q – Not Dec. 24, 25, 31, Mar. 21, 23, May 11.
r – Not Dec. 24, 25, 31, Mar. 23, May 11.
t – Also Dec. 24, 25, 31, Mar. 23, May 11.
v – Also Dec. 26, Jan. 1, Mar. 21, 24, May 12; not Mar. 23, May 11.
w – Also Dec. 26, Jan. 1, Mar. 24, May 12; not Dec. 23, 30, Mar. 23, May 11.
x – Not Dec. 24, 25, 26, 31, Jan. 1, Mar. 21, 24, May 1, 12, 22.
z – 0324 on ⑥⑦ (also Dec. 24, 31, May 22).

⊡ – Amsterdam timings are subject to alteration on Apr. 30.
◇ – S-Bahn connection.
⊖ – For local connections Siegburg/Bonn - Köln/Bonn Flughafen see Tables **807** (Siegburg/Bonn - Troisdorf) and **802** (Troisdorf - Köln/Bonn Flughafen).
▲ – Frequent light-rail services operate from/to Bonn Hbf. See page 419.

FRANKFURT - DARMSTADT - HEIDELBERG - KARLSRUHE — 911

See Table **912** for *ICE* services via Mannheim. See Table **911a** for other local services.

Most services in this table will not run north of Hannover Dec. 24 - Jan. 1

km		*IC*		*ICE*	*IC*	*IC*	*ICE*	*IC*	*IC*	*IC*	*IC*	*IC*	*IC*	*IC*	*IC*	*IC*	*IC*	*IC*	*IC*	*IC*	*IC*		*IC*	*IC*	*ICE*
		1591		**181**	**2273**	**2295**	**1071**	**2275**	**2297**	**2277**	**2299**	**2279**	**2391**	**2371**	**391**	**2373**	**2395**	**2375**	**2375**	**2252**	**2397**		**2377**	**2177**	**617**
		v		★	①–⑥		①–⑤	①–⑤									Ⓑq	Ⓑq	①–⑤	⑦w			⑤⑦r	Ⓑq	⑦w
		◧		Z🍴	h🍷	🍷	a⚡	d🍷	🍷	🍷	🍷	🍷	🍷	N🍷	L🍷	🍷	🍷	🍷	m🍷	R🍷	🍷		🍷		C🍷
	Stralsund **830** d.	...	...	...	...	...	...	...	...	...	...	0529e	...	...	...	0915	...	...	...	...	...	...	1327	...	...
	Hamburg Hbf **800 902** d.	...	...	...	...	...	0607	...	...	0626e	...	0828	...	1028	...	1228	...	1428	1428	...	...	...	1628	...	...
	Hannover Hbf **902** d.	...	...	...	...	...	0722	0600	...	0800e	...	1000	...	1200	...	1400	...	1600	1600	...	...	...	1800	...	...
	Kassel Wilhelmshöhe **806** d.	...	...	...	0530	...	|	0730	...	0930	...	1130	...	1330	...	1530	...	1730	1730	...	...	...	1930	...	...
0	**Frankfurt** (Main) Hbf d.	0007	...	0618	0738	0820	0934	0938	1020	1138	1220	1338	1420	1538	1620	1738	1820	1938	1938	1955	2020	...	2138	2154	...
28	Darmstadt Hbf d.	|	...	0636	0755	0837	0949	0955	1037	1155	1237	1355	1437	1555	1637	1755	1837	1955	1955	2013	2037	...	2155	2211	2215
50	Bensheim d.	◐	...	|	0807	0850	...	1007	1050	1207	1250	1407	1450	1607	1650	1807	1850	2007	2007	2025	2050	...	2207	|	|
64	Weinheim (Bergstr) d.	|	...	|	0817	0900	...	1017	1100	1217	1300	1417	1500	1617	1700	1817	1900	2017	2017	2036	2100	...	2217	|	|
87	**Heidelberg** Hbf ‡ d.	0119	...	0717t	0832	0914	...	1032	1114	1232	1314	1432	1514	1632	1714	1832	1914	2032	2032	2052	2114	...	2232	2243	2248
120	Bruchsal **930** ‡ d.	0139	...	|	0849	|	...	|	|	1249	|	1449	|	1649	|	1849	|	...	2052	|	|	...	2249	2303	|
	Stuttgart Hbf **930** a.	0236	...	0757	|	0953	...	1123	1153	|	1353	|	1553	|	1753	|	1953	...	|	2146	2154	...	|	|	2324
	München Hbf **930** a.	0505g	...	...	|	1217	...	...	1417	|	1617	|	1817q	|	2017	|	2221	...	|	...	...	...	|	|	...
	Salzburg Hbf **890** a.	...	...	...	|	1403	...	...	1603	|	1803	|	2003q	|	2209	|	...	...	|	...	...	...	|	|	...
141	**Karlsruhe** Hbf **930** ‡ a.	...	...	...	0902	...	...	...	...	1302	...	1502	...	1702	...	1902	...	...	2106	...	...	...	2304	2322	...

	ICE	*IC*	*ICE*	*ICE*	*IC*	*IC*	*IC*	*IC*	*IC*	*IC*	*IC*	*IC*	*IC*	*IC*	*IC*	*IC*	*ICE*	*IC*	*IC*	*IC*	*IC*	*IC*	*IC*	*IC*	*ICE*
	808	**1590**	**1092**	**824**	**2172**	**2396**	**2376**	**2394**	**2374**	**2392**	**2372**	**390**	**2370**	**2186**	**2298**	**2278**	**776**	**2296**	**2276**	**2294**	**2194**	**2274**	**1976**	**2272**	**180**
		v	①–⑤	①–⑥	①–⑥	①–⑥	①–⑥	①–⑥					J	⑤⑦f			①–⑤				⑦w	①–⑤	⑦w	⑦w	
	A🍴	◧	dB	eE	e	e🍷	e🍷	e🍷	🍷	🍷	🍷	L🍷	N🍷	N🍷	🍷	🍷	dO	🍷	🍷	🍷	🍷	k🍷		🍷	Z🍴
Karlsruhe Hbf **930** ‡ d.	0133	...	⚡	...	0615	...	0647	...	0854	...	1054	...	1253	1253	...	1454	...	...	1654	...	...	1854	...	...	...
Salzburg Hbf **890** d.	|	...	...	...	|	...	|	...	|	0547e	|	0753e	|	|	0957	|	...	1153	|	1353	...	|	...	...	...
München Hbf **930** d.	|	0033g	...	...	|	...	|	0515	|	0739e	|	0939	|	|	1141	|	...	1339	|	1539	...	|	...	...	...
Stuttgart Hbf **930** d.	|	0305	...	...	|	0603	|	0805	|	1005	|	1205	|	|	1405	|	...	1605	|	1805	1837	|	2009	...	2205
Bruchsal **930** ‡ d.	0148	0407	...	...	0633	|	0703	|	0907	|	1107	|	1307	1307	|	1507	...	|	1707	|	|	1907	|	...	|
Heidelberg Hbf ‡ d.	0210	0428	...	...	0654	0658	0724	0847	0924	1047	1124	1247	1324	1324	1447	1524	...	1647	1724	1847	1924	1924	2050	2124	2248
Weinheim (Bergstr) d.	|	|	...	...	|	0714	0739	0901	0939	1101	1139	1301	1339	1339	1501	1539	...	1701	1739	1901	1939	1939	2104	2139	|
Bensheim d.	◐	◐	...	...	◐	0729	0749	0910	0949	1110	1149	1310	1349	1349	1510	1549	...	1710	1749	1910	1949	1949	2114	2149	|
Darmstadt Hbf d.	|	|	0543	0637	|	0743	0802	0924	1002	1124	1202	1324	1402	1402	1524	1602	1647	1724	1802	1924	2002	2002	2127	2202	2322
Frankfurt (Main) Hbf a.	0308	0535	0600	0656	0752	0800	0818	0940	1018	1140	1218	1340	1418	1418	1540	1618	1710	1740	1818	1940	2018	2018	2143	2218	2339
Kassel Wilhelmshöhe **806** a.	|	...	...	...	...	...	1026	...	1226	...	1426	...	1626	1626	...	1826	1848	...	2028	...	2226	2226	2330	0026	...
Hannover Hbf **902** a.	|	...	...	...	...	...	1156	...	1356	...	1556	...	1756	1756	...	1956	1946	...	2156f	...	...	...	0051	...	...
Hamburg Hbf **902** a.	1012	...	...	...	...	...	1327	...	1530	...	1732	...	1927	1928	...	2127	...	...	2326w	...	...	...	...	...	...
Stralsund **930** a.	...	...	...	...	...	...	1642	...	...	...	2041	...	...	2230	...	...	...	...	...	...	...	...	...	...	...

A – (12) and 🍴 Basel - Köln - Kiel.
B – (12) and 🍴 Darmstadt - Berlin.
C – (12) and 🍷 Dortmund - Köln - Stuttgart.
E – (12) and 🍷 Darmstadt - Köln - Essen.
J – ①②③④⑥ (also Dec. 23, 30, Mar. 21, 23, May 2, 11; not Dec. 26, Jan. 1, Mar. 20, 24, Apr. 30, May 12).
L – From / to Linz on dates in Table **950**.
N – To / from Konstanz (Table **916**).
O – To Oldenburg (Table **813**).
R – From Leipzig (Table **850**).
Z – From / to Zürich (Table **940**).

a – Not Dec. 24 - Jan. 1, Mar. 21, 24, May 12.
d – Not Dec. 24, 25, 26, 31, Jan. 1, Mar. 21, 24, May 12.
e – ①–⑥ (not Dec. 25, 26, Jan. 1, Mar. 22, 24, May 12).
f – ⑤⑦ (also Dec. 26, Jan. 1, Mar. 20, 24, Apr. 30, May 12; not Dec. 23, 30, Mar. 21, 23, May 2, 11).
g – ① (also Dec. 27, Jan. 2, Mar. 25, May 13; not Dec. 24, 31, Mar. 24, May 12).
h – Not Dec. 25, 26, Jan. 1, Mar. 24, May 1, 12.
k – Also Dec. 23, 30; not Dec. 24, 25, 26, 31, Jan. 1, Mar. 24, May 2, 12.
m – Also Dec. 23, 30; not Dec. 24, 25, 26, 31, Jan. 1, Mar. 21, 24, May 12.
q – Ⓑ (not Dec. 24, 25, 31, Mar. 21, 23, May 11).
r – Also Dec. 26, Jan. 1, Mar. 20, 24, Apr. 30, May 12, 21; not Dec. 23, 30, Mar. 21, 23, May 2, 11, 23.

t – Arrives 0710.
v – Not Dec. 25, Jan. 1.
w – ⑦ (also Dec. 26, Jan. 1, Mar. 24, May 12; not Dec. 23, 30, Mar. 23, May 11).
★ – ①–⑥ (not Dec. 24, 25, 31, Jan. 1, Mar. 24, May 12).
◧ – Subject to alteration in the Stuttgart area from May 16.
◐ – Via Mannheim (Table **912**).
‡ – See also panel below main table.
⚡ – Ⓡ and 'Sprinter' supplement payable.

RE / RB / S-Bahn services Local services FRANKFURT and MAINZ - MANNHEIM - KARLSRUHE — 911a

Frankfurt - Darmstadt - Heidelberg and Mannheim

	⚒r	Ⓐe		Ⓐe			⚒					Ⓐe				Ⓐe	Ⓒz	Ⓐe						
Frankfurt (Main) Hbf **911/2** d.	0511	0506	0606	0630	0710	0706	0810	0806	0913	0906		1810	1806	1913	1906	2010	2006	2029	2113	2106	2206	2306	2318	0006
Darmstadt Hbf **911** d.	|	0530	0630	0653	|	0730	|	0830	|	0930	this pattern	|	1830	|	1930	|	2030	2054	|	2130	2230	2330	|	0030
Bensheim **911** d.	◐	0552	0658	0709	◐	0752	◐	0858	◐	0952	runs every	◐	1858	◐	1952	◐	2058	2109	◐	2152	2254	2355	◐	0055
Weinheim (Bergstr) **911** d.	|	0608	0713	0722	|	0808	|	0913	|	1008	**two** hours	|	1913	|	2008	|	2113	2122	|	2208	2310	0010	|	0110
Mannheim Friedrichsfeld d.	|	0621	0727	0733	|	0818	|	0927	|	1018	until	|	1927	|	2018	|	2127	2132	|	2218	2324	0024	|	0124
Mannheim Hbf **912** a.	0621	*0644*	*0743*z	0743	0820	*0842*	0920	*0942*	1020	*1042*		1920	*1942*	2020	*2042*	2120	*2143*	*2143*	2220	*2242*	*2343*	|	0025	0138
Heidelberg Hbf **911** a.	...	0631	0738	...	...	0827	...	0939	...	1027		...	1939	...	2027	...	2139	2141	...	2227	2335	0035	...	...

	Ⓐe		Ⓐe		⚒r				⚒					Ⓐe				Ⓐe				Ⓐe		
Heidelberg Hbf **911** d.	0424	0525	...	0625	...	0728	...	0821	...	0928	...		1821	...	1928	...	2021	...	2128	...	2221	...	2325	...
Mannheim Hbf **912** d.	|	*0516*r	0536	*0612*	0638	*0716*t	0738	*0816*	0838	*0916*	0938	this pattern	*1816*	1838	*1916*	1938	*2016*	2038	*2116*	2138	*2216*	2238	*2316*	0009
Mannheim Friedrichsfeld d.	0434	0534	|	0634	|	0737	|	0832	|	0938	|	runs every	1832	|	1938	|	2032	|	2138	|	2232	|	2335	|
Weinheim (Bergstr) **911** d.	0448	0549	◐	0648	◐	0749	◐	0845	◐	0949	◐	**two** hours	1845	◐	1949	◐	2045	◐	2149	◐	2245	◐	2349	◐
Bensheim **911** d.	0503	0603	|	0703	|	0803	|	0900	|	1003	|	until	1900	|	2003	|	2100	|	2203	|	2300	|	0004	|
Darmstadt Hbf **911** d.	0531	0630	|	0730	|	0830	|	0930	|	1030	|		1930	|	2030	|	2130	|	2230	|	2330	|	0029	|
Frankfurt (Main) Hbf **911/2** a.	0550	0648	0645	0748	0747	0848	0845	0948	0947	1048	1045		1948	1947	2048	2045	2148	2147	2248	2245	2348	2347	0048	0132

Mannheim - Heidelberg - Karlsruhe

S-Bahn	v			Ⓒz	Ⓐe					❖		
Mannheim Hbf d.	0005	...	0459	0529	0544	0647	0729*	0829	0929	and	2129	2236
Heidelberg Hbf d.	0022	...	0518	0548	0603	0707	0748	0848	0948	hourly	2148	2253
Bruchsal d.	0048	...	0544	0623	0630	0733	0817	0922	1018	until	2218	2319
Karlsruhe Hbf a.	0106	...	0601	0642	0648	0750	0832	0936	1032		2232	0032

S-Bahn	v		⚒r							
Karlsruhe Hbf d.	0012	0333	0436	0534	0620	0654	0728	and	2228	2328
Bruchsal d.	0026	0350	0453	0558	0638	0713	0743	hourly	2243	2343
Heidelberg Hbf d.	0054	0418	0522	0634	0708	0744	0814	until	2314	0014
Mannheim Hbf a.	0112	0434	0538	0652	0725r	0802	0829		2330	0029

Mainz - Worms - Mannheim

km		Ⓐe	Ⓐe	Ⓐe	⚒r	v	⚒r	v	Ⓐe		Ⓐe						Ⓐe			Ⓐe			Ⓐe	Ⓒz		Ⓐe
0	**Mainz** Hbf **912** d.	0456	0545	0552	...	0621	0656	0722	0813	0752	0819	...	0851	1013	0952	1051	1213	1152	1252	1413	1352	1451	1613	1613	1552	1628
46	Worms Hbf a.	0540	0614	0633	...	0706	0740	0805	0839	0835	0903	...	0935	1039	1035	1135	1239	1235	1335	1439	1435	1535	1639	1639	1635	1716
46	Worms Hbf d.	0541	0615	0635	0635	0712	0746	0818	0840	0848	0916	0916	0948	1040	1048	1148	1240	1249	1348	1440	1448	1548	1640	1640	1648	1717
67	Ludwigshafen Hbf a.	0557	0632	0652	0652	0730	0804	0834	0856	0908	0936	0936	1008	1056	1108	1208	1256	1308	1408	1456	1508	1608	1654	1656	1708	1736
70	**Mannheim** Hbf **912** a.	0603	g	0658	0658	0737	0811	0841	k	0914	0942	0942	1014	k	1114	1214	k	1314	1414	k	1514	1614	1701	k	1714	1742

	Ⓐe					Ⓑm		n	n	n	v
Mainz Hbf **912** d.	1719	1651	1813	1752	1851	2013	1952	2052	2152	2317	0022
Worms Hbf a.	1745	1735	1839	1835	1935	2039	2035	2135	2240	0000	0105
Worms Hbf d.	1746	1749	1840	1848	1948	2040	2048	2148	2241	0001	...
Ludwigshafen Hbf a.	1800	1808	1855	1908	2008	2056	2108	2208	2300	0017	...
Mannheim Hbf **912** a.	g	1814	k	1914	2014	k	2114	2214	2306	0024	...

	⚒r	⚒r	Ⓐe	⚒r	⚒r	Ⓐe		⚒r	Ⓐe		Ⓐe
Mannheim Hbf **912** d.	...	0427	0500	...	0532	0550	...	0619	g	0650	g
Ludwigshafen Hbf d.	...	0436	0507	...	0543	0558	...	0625	0655	0659	0750
Worms Hbf a.	...	0454	0525	...	0601	0615	...	0644	0712	0718	0804
Worms Hbf d.	0417	0455	0526	0526	0605	0620	0620	0653	0714	0724	0805
Mainz Hbf **912** a.	0504	0538	0609	0609	0648	0706	0706	0736	0748	0807	0835

	Ⓒz	Ⓐe		Ⓐe						Ⓐe			Ⓐe								n	Ⓐe	n	n		v
Mannheim Hbf **912** d.	0744	0748	0844	k	0944	1044	k	1144	1244	k	1344	1444	k	1544	1644	k	1744	1844	k	1944	2044	k	2144	2248	...	0011
Ludwigshafen Hbf d.	0750	0755	0850	0904	0950	1050	1104	1150	1250	1304	1350	1450	1504	1550	1650	1704	1750	1850	1904	1950	2050	2104	2150	2253	...	0017
Worms Hbf a.	0816	0816	0914	0919	1014	1114	1119	1214	1311	1319	1414	1514	1519	1614	1714	1719	1814	1914	1919	2014	2114	2119	2209	2312	...	0039
Worms Hbf d.	0825	0825	0925	0920	1025	1125	1120	1225	1324	1320	1425	1525	1520	1625	1725	1720	1825	1925	1920	2025	2125	2120	2225	2313	...	...
Mainz Hbf **912** a.	0908	0908	1008	0947	1108	1208	1147	1308	1408	1347	1508	1608	1547	1708	1808	1747	1908	2008	1947	2108	2207	2147	2308	2358	...	...

e – Not Dec. 24, 31, May 22.
g – To / from Gemersheim (Table 918).
k – To / from Karlsruhe via Germersheim (Table **918**).
m – Not Dec. 24, 25, 26, 31, Jan. 1, Mar. 21, 23, 24, May 1, 12, 22.

n – Not Dec. 24, 31.
r – ⚒ (not May 22).
t – 0720 on Ⓐe.
v – Not Dec. 25, Jan. 1.

z – Ⓒ (also Dec. 24, 31, May 22).
* – Change at Heidelberg on Ⓒz.
◐ – Via Biblis.

❖ – Timings at Bruchsal and Karlsruhe may vary by up to 5 minutes on certain journeys.

912 (KÖLN -) KOBLENZ - FRANKFURT - MANNHEIM - KARLSRUHE - BASEL

km	km		IC 1591	ICE 973	IC 60319	ICE 809	CNL 40319	CNL 409	EN 264	CNL 458	CNL 1242	IC 60458	ICE 275	ICE 678	ICE 991	ICE 1593	ICE 5	ICE 5	TGV 9578	IC 2021	ICE 511	ICE 271	CNL 352	ICE 23	IC 2317
		See note ●	x	⑦w			🅁	🅁		🅁	🅁				①–⑥	⑦y	①m		⊡🅁				🅁		①–⑥
			✣		✣2	✕K	✕♦	✕♦	🍷♦	✕♦	✕♦		Z✕	♦	¶✕	✕	✕♦	✕♦	J🍷	⊖	🍷	Z✕	✕♦	Q✕	e
		Berlin Hbf **810** d.	...	2032	...	...	...	...	...	...	2126	...	...	...	...	...	...	...	...	...	...	...	...	...	...
		Hamburg Hbf **800 900** d.	...	|	...	1946	...	2024	...	...	|	...	...	...	...	...	0024	...	...	2246	...	...	...	...	...
		Dortmund Hbf **800** d.	...	|	...	2238	...	2338	...	...	|	...	...	...	...	...	|	...	...	0203	...	...	...	0433x	...
0		*Köln Hbf* **800 910** d.	...	|	...	2353	2346	|	...	...	|	...	...	...	...	...	|	...	...	0352	0554	...	...	0553	...
34		*Bonn Hbf* **800** d.	...	|	...	0014	0007	|	...	...	|	...	...	...	...	...	|	...	...	|	|	...	...	0614	...
93		**Koblenz** Hbf **914** d.	...	|	0102	0048	|	|	...	...	|	...	...	...	...	...	|	...	...	0530	|	...	...	0648	...
154		Bingen (Rhein) Hbf **914** d.	...	|	|	0124	|	|	...	...	|	...	...	...	...	...	|	...	...	0609	|	...	...	|	...
		Wiesbaden Hbf d.	...	|	|	|	|	|	...	...	|	...	...	0500	0522	0524	|	...	...	|	|	...	...	|	0733
184		**Mainz** Hbf **914** a.	...	|	0155	0141	|	|	...	...	|	...	...	0509	0536	0536	|	...	...	0627	|	...	...	0738	0744
184		**Mainz** Hbf **911a** d.	...	|	0157	0143	|	|	...	...	|	...	...	0511	0540	0540	|	...	...	0629	|	...	...	0740	0746
	0	**Frankfurt** (Main) Hbf ◇ d.	0007	0109	|	|	|	|	...	...	|	0402z	...	|	|	|	0538	0538	...	|	|	0650	0659z	|	|
210		**Frankfurt** Flughafen Fernbf ✈ a.	0023	0122	|	0202‡	|	|	...	...	|	|	...	0537	|	|	0550	0550	...	0646	0651	|	|	0759	|
210		**Frankfurt** Flughafen Fernbf ✈ d.	0028	0127	|	0205‡	|	|	...	...	|	|	...	0539	|	|	0555	0555	...	0648	0654	|	|	0801	|
221		**Frankfurt** (Main) Hbf a.	|	|	|	0217	|	|	...	...	|	|	...	0550	|	|	|	|	...	0702	|	|	|	0813	|
—	78	**Mannheim** Hbf **911a 919** a.	0104	0200	0241	0300	|	|	...	0443s	0443s	0443	...	...	0622	0622	0625p	0625p	...	...	0724	0728p	0750	...	0824
	78	**Mannheim** Hbf **911a** d.	0106	0202	0243	0302	|	|	...	|	|	0445	...	...	0630	0630	0627	0627	...	...	0733	0736	0752	...	0826
		Heidelberg Hbf **911 911a** d.	0119	|	|	|	|	|	...	0458s	0458s	0500	...	...	|	|	|	|	...	...	|	|	|	...	0838
		Stuttgart Hbf **930** a.	0236	|	0419	|	|	|	...	|	|	|	...	...	0707	0709	|	|	...	...	0808	|	|	...	0923
		München Hbf **930** a.	0505g	|	0716	|	|	|	...	|	|	|	...	...	0931	...	|	|	...	...	1031	|	|	...	...
0	138	**Karlsruhe** Hbf **911 911a 916** d.	...	0238	...	0337	0437s	0437s	0532	0540s	0540s	0543	0556	...	...	...	0657	0657	0731	...	...	0801	0831	...	...
31	169	Baden-Baden **916** d.	...	...	...	0358	0458s	0458s	0554	|	|	|	0612	...	...	...	0713	0713	|	...	...	|	|	...	...
	209	Offenburg **916** ★ d.	...	...	...	0416	0519s	0519s	|	0620s	0620s	0622	0629	...	...	...	0730	0730	|	...	...	0829	0903	...	...
84		**Strasbourg** ★ a.	...	...	...	|	|	|	0643	|	|	|	|	...	...	...	|	|	0812	...	...	|	|	...	...
	272	**Freiburg** (Brsg) Hbf ★ d.	...	...	...	0452	0556s	0556s	...	0653s	0653s	0655	0702	...	...	...	0802	0802	...	...	...	0901	0941	...	...
	333	**Basel** Bad. Bf 🏛 ★ a.	...	...	...	0537	0643	0643	...	0746	0746	0746	0737	...	...	...	0837	0837	...	...	...	0936	1027	...	...
	338	**Basel** SBB a.	...	...	...	0548	0654	0654	...	0755	0755	0755	0747	...	...	...	0847	0847	...	...	...	0947	1037	...	...

	ICE 591	ICE 591	ICE 599	ICE 501	TGV 9576	IC 2319	ICE 1597	ICE 1597	ICE 513	ICE 375	EC 115	ICE 571	ICE 593	ICE 1091	ICE 503	ICE 25	ICE 71	EC 7	ICE 1559	ICE 515	ICE 277	IC 119	ICE 773	ICE 573	ICE 595
See note ●	①–⑤	①–⑥	⑦	x		①–⑥	n	⑦c				①–⑥	⑥⑦	①–⑤									①–⑥	⑦c	
	u✕	G✕	N✕	🍷	🅁♦	e✕	E	D✕	M🍷	B✕	✕♦	e✕	b✕	a✕	H🍷	Q✕	✕	✕♦	D✕	🍷	B✕	🍷♦	e K ✕	✕	✕
Berlin Hbf **810** d.	...	...	...	...	...	...	...	...	...	0433a	...	...	0534	0608*	...	...	...	...	...	...	0633	...		...	0737
Hamburg Hbf **800 900** d.	0317	...	...	...	...	...	...	...	...	|	...	0519	|	|	...	...	0619	0441e	...	0537	|	...	0724	0724	|
Dortmund Hbf **800** d.	|	...	...	0537	...	0538	...	...	0638	|	0552	|	|	|	0737	0636	|	0738	...	0837	|	...	|	|	|
Köln Hbf **800 910** d.	|	...	...	0654	...	0653	...	...	0754	|	0718	|	|	|	0854	0753	|	0853	...	0954	|	0918	|	|	|
Bonn Hbf **800** d.	|	...	...	|	...	0714	...	...	|	|	0737	|	|	|	|	0814	|	0914	...	|	|	0937	|	|	|
Koblenz Hbf **914** d.	|	...	...	|	...	0748	...	...	|	|	0817	|	|	|	|	0848	|	0948	...	|	|	1017	|	|	|
Bingen (Rhein) Hbf **914** d.	|	...	...	|	...	|	...	...	|	|	0852	|	|	|	|	|	|	|	...	|	|	1052	|	|	|
Wiesbaden Hbf d.	|	...	...	|	...	|	...	0831	|	|	|	|	|	|	|	|	|	|	1024	|	|	|	|	|	|
Mainz Hbf **914** a.	|	...	...	|	...	0837	...	0840	|	|	0911	|	|	|	|	0938	|	1037	1035	|	|	1111	|	|	|
Mainz Hbf **911a** d.	|	...	...	|	...	0839	0842	0842	|	|	0913	|	|	|	|	0940	|	1039	1042	|	|	1113	|	|	|
Frankfurt (Main) Hbf ◇ d.	0750	0750	0750	|	...	|	|	|	|	0850	|	0905	0950	0950	|	|	1005	|	|	|	1050	|	1105	1105	1150
Frankfurt Flughafen Fernbf ✈ a.	|	|	|	0751	...	|	0859	0859	0851	|	|	0916	|	|	0951	0959	|	|	1100	1051	|	|	1116	1116	|
Frankfurt Flughafen Fernbf ✈ d.	|	|	|	0754	...	|	0901	0901	0854	|	|	0920	|	|	0954	1001	|	|	1102	1054	|	|	1120	1120	|
Frankfurt (Main) Hbf a.	|	|	|	|	...	|	0913	0913	|	|	|	|	|	|	|	1013	|	|	1114	|	|	|	|	|	|
Mannheim Hbf **911a 919** a.	0828	0828	0828	0824p	...	0921	...	...	0924	0928p	0952	0953	1028	1028	1024p	...	1042	1121	...	1124	1128p	1152	1153	1153	1228
Mannheim Hbf **911a** d.	0831	0831	0831	0836	...	0923	...	...	0933	0936	0954	0955	1031	1031	1036	...	1044	1123	...	1133	1136	1154	1155	1155	1231
Heidelberg Hbf **911 911a** d.	|	|	|	|	...	0936	...	...	|	|	1006	|	|	|	|	...	|	|	...	|	|	1206	|	|	|
Stuttgart Hbf **930** a.	0908	0908	0908	|	...	1018	...	...	1008	|	1046	1033	1108	1108	|	...	|	|	...	1208	|	1246	1233	1233	1308
München Hbf **930** a.	1131	1131	1131	|	...	...	...	...	1231	|	1317	...	1331	1331	|	...	|	|	...	1431	|	...	...	...	1531
Karlsruhe Hbf **911 911a 916** d.	...	...	...	0901	0931	...	...	...	...	1001	...	...	...	...	1101	...	1109	1149	...	...	1201	...	...	...	...
Baden-Baden **916** d.	...	...	...	0917	|	...	...	...	...	|	...	...	...	...	|	...	1125	1206	...	...	|	...	...	...	...
Offenburg **916** ★ d.	...	...	...	|	|	...	...	...	...	1029	...	...	...	...	1129	...	|	|	...	...	1229	...	...	...	...
Strasbourg ★ a.	...	...	...	|	1013	...	...	...	...	|	...	...	...	...	|	...	|	|	...	...	|	...	...	...	...
Freiburg (Brsg) Hbf ★ d.	...	...	...	1002	...	...	...	...	...	1101	...	...	...	...	1201	...	1210	1255	...	...	1301	...	...	...	...
Basel Bad. Bf 🏛 ★ a.	...	...	...	1037	...	...	...	...	...	1136	...	...	...	...	1236	...	1246	1329	...	...	1336	...	...	...	...
Basel SBB a.	...	...	...	1047	...	...	...	...	...	1147	...	...	...	...	1247	...	1255	1337	...	...	1347	...	...	...	...

	ICE 105	ICE 27	ICE 73	TGV 9574	IC 2005	IC 2015	EC 101	ICE 1651	ICE 517	ICE 875	IC 2013	ICE 575	ICE 597	ICE 507	IC 2025	ICE 75	IC 2113	ICE 1653	ICE 519	ICE 373	IC 2011	IC 1811	ICE 577	ICE 109	ICE 509
See note ●					⑤⑥	①–④															⑤f	⑦w			
	🍷♦	Q✕	✕♦	🅁J	🍷♦	🍷♦	✕♦	D✕	🍷	✕	🍷♦	✕	✕	🍷	🍷	Z✕	🍷	D✕	🍷	B✕		🍷	✕	Y✕	🍷
Berlin Hbf **810** d.	...	...	...	...	...	...	...	...	...	0832	...	...	0937	...	...	...	...	...	...	1033	...	...	...	1137	...
Hamburg Hbf **800 900** d.	...	...	0824	...	...	...	0646	...	...	|	...	0924	|	...	0746	1024	0846	...	...	|	...	...	1124	|	...
Dortmund Hbf **800** d.	...	0838	|	...	...	...	0938	...	1038	|	0952	|	|	...	1036	|	1138	...	1238	|	1152	1152	|	|	...
Köln Hbf **800 910** d.	1054	0953	|	...	1018	1018	1053	...	1154	|	1118	|	|	1254	1153	|	1253	...	1354	|	1318	1318	|	|	1454
Bonn Hbf **800** d.	|	1014	|	...	1037	1037	1114	...	|	|	1137	|	|	|	1214	|	1314	...	|	|	1337	1337	|	|	|
Koblenz Hbf **914** d.	|	1048	|	...	1117	1117	1148	...	|	|	1217	|	|	|	1248	|	1348	...	|	|	1417	1417	|	|	|
Bingen (Rhein) Hbf **914** d.	|	|	|	...	|	|	|	...	|	|	1252	|	|	|	|	|	|	...	|	|	1452	1452	|	|	|
Wiesbaden Hbf d.	|	|	|	...	|	|	|	1224	|	|	|	|	|	|	|	|	|	1424	|	|	|	|	|	|	|
Mainz Hbf **914** a.	|	1138	|	...	1213	1213	1237	1235	|	|	1311	|	|	|	1338	|	1437	1435	|	|	1511	1511	|	|	|
Mainz Hbf **911a** d.	|	1140	|	...	1217	1217	1239	1242	|	|	1313	|	|	|	1340	|	1439	1442	|	|	1513	1513	|	|	|
Frankfurt (Main) Hbf ◇ d.	|	|	1205	...	|	|	|	|	|	1250	|	1305	1350	|	|	1405	|	|	|	1450	|	|	1505	1550	|
Frankfurt Flughafen Fernbf ✈ a.	1151	1159	|	...	|	|	|	1300	1251	|	|	1316	|	1351	1359	|	|	1500	1451	|	|	|	1516	|	1551
Frankfurt Flughafen Fernbf ✈ d.	1154	1201	|	...	|	|	|	1302	1254	|	|	1320	|	1354	1401	|	|	1502	1454	|	|	|	1520	|	1554
Frankfurt (Main) Hbf a.	|	1213	|	...	|	|	|	1314	|	|	|	|	|	|	1413	|	|	1515	|	|	|	|	|	|	|
Mannheim Hbf **911a 919** a.	1224p	...	1242	...	1307	1307	1321	...	1324	1328p	1352	1353	1428	1424p	...	1442	1521	...	1524	1528p	1552	1552	1553	1628	1624p
Mannheim Hbf **911a** d.	1236	...	1244	...	1309	1312	1323	...	1333	1336	1354	1355	1431	1436	...	1444	1523	...	1533	1536	1554	1554	1555	1631	1636
Heidelberg Hbf **911 911a** d.	|	...	|	...	|	|	|	...	|	|	1406	|	|	|	...	|	1536	...	|	|	1606	1606	|	|	|
Stuttgart Hbf **930** a.	|	...	|	...	|	1358	|	...	1408	|	1446	1433	1508	|	...	|	1622	...	1608	|	1646	1646	1632	1708	|
München Hbf **930** a.	|	...	|	...	|	...	|	...	1631	|	...	...	1731	|	...	|	...	...	1831	|	...	...	...	1931	|
Karlsruhe Hbf **911 911a 916** d.	1301	...	1309	1331	1338	...	1349	...	...	1401	...	...	...	1501	...	1509	...	...	...	1601	...	...	...	...	1701
Baden-Baden **916** d.	|	...	1325	|	1356	...	1406	...	...	|	...	...	...	|	...	1525	...	...	...	|	...	...	...	...	|
Offenburg **916** ★ d.	1329	...	|	|	1415	...	|	...	...	1429	...	...	...	1529	...	|	...	...	...	1629	...	...	...	...	1729
Strasbourg ★ a.	|	...	|	1412	...	...	|	...	...	|	...	...	...	|	...	|	...	...	...	|	...	...	...	...	|
Freiburg (Brsg) Hbf ★ d.	1401	...	1410	...	...	...	1455	...	...	1501	...	...	...	1601	...	1610	...	...	...	1701	...	...	...	...	1801
Basel Bad. Bf 🏛 ★ a.	1436	...	1446	...	...	...	1529	...	...	1536	...	...	...	1636	...	1646	...	...	...	1736	...	...	...	...	1836
Basel SBB a.	1447	...	1455	...	...	...	1537	...	...	1547	...	...	...	1647	...	1655	...	...	...	1747	...	...	...	...	1847

♦ – **NOTES** (LISTED BY TRAIN NUMBER) for pages 422 and 423

5 – [12] and ✕ (Hamburg ①**m** -) Frankfurt - Basel - Bern - Interlaken.
7 – [12] and ✕ (Hamburg ①–⑥**e** -) Dortmund - Basel - Zürich - Chur.
60 – [12] and ✕ München - Stuttgart - Strasbourg.
73 – [12] and ✕ Kiel - Hamburg - Basel - Zürich.
101 – [12] and ✕ Hamburg - Köln - Basel - Zürich - Chur. Train number **103** on ⑥.
105 – ICE INTERNATIONAL – [12] and 🍷 Amsterdam - Utrecht - Arnhem - Basel; conveys [12] (*ICE* **505**) Köln - Basel.
115 – WÖRTHERSEE – [12] and ✕ Dortmund - Salzburg - Villach - Klagenfurt.
119 – [12] and 🍷 Münster - Stuttgart - Ulm - Lindau - Bregenz - Innsbruck.
264 – ORIENT EXPRESS – 🛏 1, 2 cl., ▬ 2 cl., [2] and 🍷 Wien - Salzburg - München Ost - Karlsruhe - Basel - Bern - Interlaken.
352 – JOHANNES KEPLER – 🛏 1,2 cl., ▬ 2 cl. and [2] Praha - Dresden - Leipzig - Basel; ✕ Fulda - Basel. Conveys 🛏 1, 2 cl., ▬ 2 cl. and ✕ (*CNL* **50483** – AURORA) København - Basel. For Warszawa and Moskva cars see Table **24**.
409 – KOMET – 🛏 1, 2 cl., ▬ 2 cl., [2] (reclining) and ✕ Hamburg - Zürich (- Brig on dates in Table **73**).
458 – SEMPER – 🛏 1, 2 cl., ▬ 2 cl., [2] (reclining) and ✕ Dresden - Leipzig - Zürich.
678 – [12] and ✕ Wiesbaden - Frankfurt - Hamburg.
927 – ①②③④⑥⑦ (not Dec. 23, Mar. 23, May 11). [12] and ✕ Kiel - Köln - Frankfurt - Nürnberg - München.
929 – [12] and ✕ Hamburg - Köln - Frankfurt - Nürnberg.
1027 – ⑤ (also Dec. 23, Mar. 23, May 11). [12] and ✕ Kiel - Köln - Frankfurt - Nürnberg - Regensburg.
1242 – BERLINER – 🛏 1, 2 cl., ▬ 2 cl., [2] (reclining) and ✕ Berlin - Hannover - Zürich.
1655 – [12] and ✕ Wiesbaden - Frankfurt (- Dresden Ⓑ **q**).
1657 – [12] and ✕ Wiesbaden - Leipzig (- Dresden on dates in Table **842**).
1659 – [12] and ✕ Wiesbaden - Frankfurt (- Erfurt - Leipzig on dates in Table **850**).
2005 – ⑤⑥ (also Dec. 24, 25, 30, 31, Mar. 20, 23, Apr. 30, May 11, 21). BODENSEE – [12] and 🍷 Emden - Münster - Karlsruhe - Konstanz. On Dec. 24, 25, 30, 31, Mar. 23, May 11 runs with train number **2007** and starts from Dortmund (see Table **800**).

NOTES CONTINUED ON NEXT PAGE →

(KÖLN -) KOBLENZ - FRANKFURT - MANNHEIM - KARLSRUHE - BASEL 912

See note ●	*IC* 2027	*ICE* 77	*TGV* 9572	*IC* 2115	*ICE* 1655	*ICE* 611	*ICE* 279	*IC* 1819	*IC* 2017	*IC* 2017	*ICE* 579	*ICE* 691	*ICE* 601	*IC* 2029	*ICE* 79	*TGV* 9570	*IC* 2311	*ICE* 1657	*ICE* 613	*ICE* 879	*EC* 60	*IC* 2019	*ICE* 671	*ICE* 693	*ICE* 603
			C	n				①–④	⑤f	⑦w						A	n	n				⑤⑦			
	🍷	Z✕	Ⓡ J	S🍷	✕◆	🍷	B✕	r🍷	H🍷	🍷	✕	✕	🍷	🍷◆	Z✕	Ⓡ J	L🍷	✕◆	🍷	✕	✕◆	t	✕	✕	🍷
Berlin Hbf **810** d.	...	...	...	...	...	...	1233	...	...	1010	...	1337	...	...	...	...	...	...	...	1433	...	1209	...	1537	...
Hamburg Hbf **800 900** d.	0946	1224	...	1046	...	...	|	...	...	|	1324	|	...	1146	1424	...	1246	...	...	|	...	|	1524	|	...
Dortmund Hbf **800** d.	1236	|	...	1338	...	1438	|	...	1352	1352	|	|	...	1436	|	...	1538	...	1638	|	...	1552	|	|	...
Köln Hbf **800 910** d.	1353	|	...	1453	...	1554	|	1518	1518	1518	|	|	1654	1553	|	...	1653	...	1754	|	...	1718	|	|	1854
Bonn Hbf **800** d.	1414	|	...	1514	...	|	|	1537	1537	1537	|	|	|	1614	|	...	1714	...	|	|	...	1737	|	|	|
Koblenz Hbf **914** d.	1448	|	...	1548	...	|	|	1617	1617	1617	|	|	|	1648	|	...	1748	...	|	|	...	1817	|	|	|
Bingen (Rhein) Hbf **914** d.	|	|	...	|	...	|	|	|	1652	1652	|	|	|	|	|	...	|	...	|	|	...	|	|	|	|
Wiesbaden Hbf d.	|	|	...	|	1624	|	|	|	|	|	|	|	|	|	|	...	|	1824	|	|	...	|	|	|	|
Mainz Hbf **914** a.	1538	|	...	1637	1635	|	|	1711	1711	1711	|	|	|	1738	|	...	1837	1835	|	|	...	1911	|	|	|
Mainz Hbf **911a** d.	1540	|	...	1639	1642	|	|	1713	1713	1713	|	|	|	1740	|	...	1839	1842	|	|	...	1913	|	|	|
Frankfurt (Main) Hbf ◇ d.	|	1605	...	|	|	|	1650	|	|	|	1705	1750	|	|	1805	...	|	|	|	1850	...	|	1905	1950	|
Frankfurt Flughafen Fernbf ✈ a.	1559	|	...	|	1700	1651	|	|	|	|	1716	|	1751	1759	|	...	|	1900	1851	|	...	|	1916	|	1951
Frankfurt Flughafen Fernbf ✈ d.	1601	|	...	|	1702	1654	|	|	|	|	1720	|	1754	1801	|	...	|	1902	1854	|	...	|	1920	|	1954
Frankfurt (Main) Hbf a.	1613	|	...	|	1715	|	|	|	|	|	|	|	|	1813	|	...	|	1914	|	|	...	|	|	|	|
Mannheim Hbf **911a 919** a.	...	1642	...	1721	...	1724	1728p	1752	1752	1752	1753	1828	1824p	...	1842	...	1921	...	1924	1928p	...	1952	1953	2028	2024p
Mannheim Hbf **911a** d.	...	1644	...	1723	...	1733	1736	1754	1754	1754	1755	1831	1836	...	1844	...	1923	...	1933	1936	...	1954	1955	2031	2036
Heidelberg Hbf **911 911a** d.	...	|	...	1736	...	|	|	1806	1806	1806	|	|	|	...	|	...	1935	...	|	|	...	2006	|	|	|
Stuttgart Hbf **930** a.	...	|	...	1822	...	1808	|	1846	1846	1846	1833	1908	|	...	|	...	...	...	2008	|	...	2046	2033	2108	|
München Hbf **930** a.	...	|	...	...	...	2031	|	...	2128	...	...	2134	|	...	|	...	...	...	2231	|	...	...	...	2331	|
Karlsruhe Hbf **911 911a 916** d.	...	1709	1731	...	...	...	1801	...	...	...	...	...	1901	...	1909	1931	...	...	...	2001	2006	...	...	...	2100
Baden-Baden **916** d.	...	1725	|	...	...	...	|	...	...	...	...	...	|	...	1925	|	...	...	...	|	2024	...	...	...	→
Offenburg **916** ★ d.	...	|	|	...	...	...	1829	...	...	...	...	...	1929	...	|	|	...	...	...	2029	|	...	...	...	...
Strasbourg ★ a.	...	|	1812	...	...	...	|	...	...	...	...	...	|	...	|	2012	...	...	...	|	2101	...	...	...	...
Freiburg (Brsg) Hbf ★ d.	...	1810	...	...	...	...	1901	...	...	...	...	...	2001	...	2010	...	...	...	...	2101	...	...	...	...	...
Basel Bad. Bf 🏛 ★ a.	...	1846	...	...	...	...	1936	...	...	...	...	...	2036	...	2046	...	...	...	...	2136	...	...	...	...	...
Basel SBB a.	...	1855	...	...	...	...	1947	...	...	...	...	...	2047	...	2055	...	...	...	...	2147	...	...	...	...	...

See note ●	*ICE* 603	*ICE* 927	*ICE* 1027	*ICE* 673	*ICE* 673	*ICE* 603	*IC* 2213	*ICE* 1659	*ICE* 615	*ICE* 977	*ICE* 675	*IC* 1946	*ICE* 617	*ICE* 607	*ICE* 605	*ICE* 695	*ICE* 1093	*ICE* 677	*ICE* 607	*ICE* 605	*IC* 929	*IC* 2315	*ICE* 971	*IC* 2321	*IC* 2121
	⑦w		⑤		⑦w	①–⑥			n			⑦w	⑦w	①–⑥	⑦w	⑥k	Ⓑq		①–⑥	⑦w				F	ⒸR
	🍷	✕◆	✕◆	✕	✕	h🍷	🍷◆	◆	🍷	✕	✕	🍷	🍷	v🍷	🍷	✕	✕	K✕	v🍷	🍷	✕◆	T🍷	✕	🍷	🍷
Berlin Hbf **810** d.	...	...	...	...	...	...	...	...	...	1633	...	1409	...	...	...	1735	1804*	...	...	...	...	...	1833	...	...
Hamburg Hbf **800 900** d.	...	1346	1346	1624	1624	...	1446	...	...	|	1724	|	...	...	...	|	|	1824	...	...	1546	1646	|	1746	1746
Dortmund Hbf **800** d.	...	1636	1636	|	|	...	1738	...	1838	|	|	1752	1923	1923	...	|	|	|	...	...	1836	1938	|	2038	2038
Köln Hbf **800 910** d.	1854	1753	1753	|	|	...	1853	...	1954	|	|	1918	2044d	2044d	2054	|	|	|	...	...	1953	2053	|	2153	2153
Bonn Hbf **800** d.	|	1814	1814	|	|	...	1914	...	|	|	|	1937	|	|	|	|	|	|	...	...	2014	2114	|	2214	2214
Koblenz Hbf **914** d.	|	1848	1848	|	|	...	1948	...	|	|	|	2017	|	|	|	|	|	|	...	...	2048	2148	|	2248	2248
Bingen (Rhein) Hbf **914** d.	|	|	|	|	|	...	|	...	|	|	|	|	|	|	|	|	|	|	...	...	2123	|	|	|	|
Wiesbaden Hbf d.	|	|	|	|	|	...	|	2024	|	|	|	|	|	|	|	|	|	|	...	...	|	|	|	|	|
Mainz Hbf **914** a.	|	1938	1938	|	|	...	2037	2035	|	|	|	2111	|	|	|	|	|	|	...	...	2140	2238	|	2338	2338
Mainz Hbf **911a** d.	|	1940	1940	|	|	...	2039	2042	|	|	|	2113	|	|	|	|	|	|	...	...	2142	2240	|	2340	2340
Frankfurt (Main) Hbf ◇ d.	|	|	|	2005	2005	...	|	|	|	2050	2105	|	|	|	|	2150	2150	2205	...	...	|	|	2300	|	|
Frankfurt Flughafen Fernbf ✈ a.	1951	1959	1959	|	|	...	|	2100	2051	|	2116	|	2146	2151	2151	|	|	|	...	...	2159	2259	|	2359	2359
Frankfurt Flughafen Fernbf ✈ d.	1954	2001	2001	|	|	...	|	2102	2054	|	2120	|	2149	2154	2154	|	|	|	...	...	2201	2301	|	0001	0001
Frankfurt (Main) Hbf a.	|	2013	2013	|	|	...	|	2114	|	|	|	|	|	|	|	|	|	|	...	...	2213	|	|	0013	0013
Mannheim Hbf **911a 919** a.	2024	|	...	2042	2042	...	2121	...	2124	2128p	2153	2152p	|	2224	2224	2228p	2228p	2242	...	...	...	2336	2341	...	...
Mannheim Hbf **911a** d.	2036	|	...	2044	2044	...	2123	...	2133	2136	2157	2158	|	2236	2236	2231	2231	2244	...	...	...	2346	2349	...	...
Heidelberg Hbf **911 911a** d.	|	|	...	|	|	...	2136	...	|	|	2210	|	2248	|	|	|	|	|	...	...	...	2359	|	...	...
Stuttgart Hbf **930** a.	|	|	...	|	|	...	2222	...	2208	|	2248	|	2324	|	|	2308	2308	|	...	...	...	0051j	|	...	...
München Hbf **930** a.	|	2348	...	|	|	←	...	...	0035	|	...	|	...	|	|	...	...	|	←	←	...	...	|	...	...
Karlsruhe Hbf **911 911a 916** d.	2102	...	...	2107	2111	2111	...	...	...	2201	...	2224	...	2300	2300	...	...	2307	2314	2314	...	...	0013	...	...
Baden-Baden **916** d.	2118	...	...	...	2127	2127	...	...	...	2218	...	...	...	→	→	...	...	...	2330	2330	...	...	...	...	...
Offenburg **916** ★ d.	2135	...	...	...	2145	2145	...	...	...	2239	...	...	...	...	...	...	...	...	2350	2350	...	...	...	...	...
Strasbourg ★ a.	|	...	...	...	|	|	...	...	...	|	...	...	...	...	...	...	...	...	|	|	...	...	...	...	...
Freiburg (Brsg) Hbf ★ d.	2208	...	...	...	2217	2217	...	...	...	2311	...	...	...	...	...	...	...	...	0022	0022	...	...	...	...	...
Basel Bad. Bf 🏛 ★ a.	2243	...	...	...	2252	2252	...	...	...	2346	...	...	...	...	...	...	...	...	0058	0058	...	...	...	...	...
Basel SBB a.	2253	...	...	...	2300	2300	...	...	...	2355	...	...	...	...	...	...	...	...	0106	...	...	...	...	...	...

◆ – **NOTES** (CONTINUED FROM PREVIOUS PAGE)

2013 – ALLGÄU – (12) and 🍷 (Leipzig ♠ -) (Magdeburg ①–⑥ **e** -) Hannover - Dortmund - Ulm - Oberstdorf.
2015 – ①–④ (not Dec. 24, 25, 26, 31, Jan. 1, Mar. 20, 24, May 12). (12) and 🍷 Emden - Münster - Stuttgart.
2029 – (12) and 🍷 Hamburg - Frankfurt - Nürnberg - Regensburg - Passau. On ⑥ from June 14 starts from Puttgarden (Table **825**) and runs with train number **2329**.
2213 – (12) and 🍷 Ostseebad Binz - Stralsund - Rostock - Hamburg - Köln - Stuttgart.
9576 – (12) and 🍷 München - Stuttgart - Strasbourg - Paris.
40319 – PEGASUS – 🛏 1, 2 cl., ▬ 2 cl., (2) (reclining) and ✕ Amsterdam - Zürich.

A – ①–⑤ (not Dec. 25, Jan. 1, Mar. 24, May 12).
B – (12) and ✕ Berlin - Basel - Bern - Interlaken.
C – ⑥⑦ (also Dec. 25, Jan. 1, Mar. 24, May 12).
D – (12) and ✕ Wiesbaden - Leipzig - Dresden.
E – Train number *IC* **2197** on ⑥ (also Mar. 21, May 1; not Mar. 22, May 3).
F – Daily to Mar. 14; Ⓐ from Mar. 17.
G – ①–⑥ (not Dec. 24, 25, 26, 31, Mar. 24, May 12). From Hannover (Table **900**).
H – From Hannover (Table **810**).
J – (12) and 🍷 Stuttgart - Strasbourg - Paris.
K – From Kiel (Table **820**).
L – From Westerland (Table **821**).
M – From Münster (Table **800**).
N – ⑦ (also Mar. 24, May 12). From Kassel (Table **900**).
Q – (12) and ✕ Dortmund - Nürnberg - Passau - Linz - Wien.
R – Ⓒ from Mar. 15. From Puttgarden (Table **825**).
S – From Stralsund (Table **830**).
T – From Westerland from Mar. 15 (Table **821**). Train number **2215** until Mar. 14.
Y – To Innsbruck (Table **951**).
Z – To Zürich (Table **510**).

a – ①–⑤ (not Dec. 24, 25, 26, 31, Jan. 1, Mar. 21, 24, May 12).
b – Also Dec. 24, 25, 26, 31, Jan. 1, Mar. 21, 24, May 12.
c – Also Dec. 25, 26, Jan. 1, Mar. 22, 24, May 12.
d – Köln **Messe/Deutz**.
e – ①–⑥ (not Dec. 25, 26, Jan. 1, Mar. 22, 24, May 12).
f – Also Mar. 20, Apr. 30, May 21; not Mar. 21, May 2, 23.
g – ① (also Dec. 27, Jan. 2, Mar. 25, May 13; not Dec. 24, 31, Mar. 24, May 12).
h – Also Dec. 23, 30, Mar. 23, May 11; not Dec. 26, Jan. 1, Mar. 24, May 12.
j – 0040 on ①⑦. 0145 from May 17.
k – Also Dec. 24, 25, 31, Mar. 21, 23, May 11.
m – Also Jan. 2, Mar. 25, May 13; not Dec. 24, 31, Mar. 24, May 12.
n – Not Dec. 24, 31.
p – Connects with train in previous column.
q – Not Dec. 24, 25, 31, Mar. 21, 23, May 11.
r – Not Dec. 24, 25, 26, 31, Jan. 1, Mar. 20, 24, Apr. 30, May 1, 12, 21, 22.
s – Stops to set down only.
t – Also Dec. 26, Jan. 1, Mar. 20, 24, Apr. 30, May 12; not Dec. 23, 30, Mar. 21, 23, May 2, 11.
u – Not Dec. 24 - Jan. 1, Mar. 21, 24, May 1, 12.
v – Also Dec. 23, 30, Mar. 23, May 11; not Dec. 24, 26, 31, Jan. 1, Mar. 24, May 12.
w – Also Dec. 26, Jan. 1, Mar. 24, May 12; not Dec. 23, 30, Mar. 23, May 11.
x – Not Dec. 25, Jan. 1.
y – Also Dec. 24, 25, 31, Jan. 1, Mar. 24, May 12.
z – Frankfurt (Main) **Süd**.

⊡ – ①–⑥ (not Dec. 25, Jan. 1, Mar. 24, May 12).
¶ – Not Dec. 24, 25, 31, Jan. 1, Mar. 24, May 12.
✣ – Subject to alteration in the Stuttgart area from May 16.
♠ – See Table **810**.
⊖ – Also calls at Boppard Hbf (d. 0543).
* – Ⓡ and 'Sprinter' supplement payable for journeys from Berlin.
‡ – Frankfurt Flughafen Regionalbahnhof.
● – Services via Mainz are subject to alteration on ⑥⑦ from May 17.
◇ – See also Tables **911** (services to Karlsruhe via Darmstadt and Heidelberg), **911a** (local services) and **919** (services to Saarbrücken via Mannheim).
★ – See panel below for local services Offenburg - Strasbourg and v.v. See page 363 for additional local trains Offenburg - Freiburg - Basel and v.v.
⊠ – Operated by DB (*RB* services) / Ortenau-S-Bahn GmbH. German holiday dates apply.

Local services Offenburg - Strasbourg and v.v.

km	⊠																										
			Ⓐ		Ⓐ		Ⓐ	Ⓒ	Ⓐ	Ⓒ		Ⓐ	Ⓐ	Ⓒ		Ⓐ		Ⓐ		Ⓐ	Ⓐ		Ⓐ				n
0	Offenburg d.	0632	0704	0734	0804	0834	0904	1004	1034	1206	1234	1304	1334	1403	1434	1504	1604	1634	1704	1734	1805	1834	1904	2004	2104	...	2304
21	Kehl 🏛 d.	0652	0722	0752	0822	0852	0922	1022	1052	1224	1252	1322	1352	1422	1452	1522	1622	1652	1722	1757	1822	1852	1922	2022	2122	...	2322
29	Strasbourg a.	0705	0734	0804	0834	0904	0934	1034	1104	1236	1304	1334	1404	1434	1504	1534	1634	1704	1734	1809	1834	1904	1934	2034	2134	...	2334

⊠																										
		Ⓐ		Ⓐ	Ⓐ							Ⓐ		Ⓐ		Ⓐ			Ⓐ	Ⓐ						x
Strasbourg d.	0622	0723	0750	0823	0853	0923	...	1049	...	1253	1323	1423	1453	1523	1623	1653	1723	1751	1823	1853	1923	2023	...	2153	...	0005
Kehl 🏛 d.	0634	0734	0804	0834	0904	0934	...	1104	...	1304	1334	1434	1504	1534	1634	1704	1737	1804	1834	1904	1934	2034	...	2204	...	0016
Offenburg a.	0652	0752	0822	0852	0922	0952	...	1122	...	1322	1352	1452	1522	1552	1652	1722	1755	1822	1852	1922	1952	2052	...	2222	...	0034

912 BASEL - KARLSRUHE - MANNHEIM - FRANKFURT - KOBLENZ (- KÖLN)

km		IC	IC	IC	IC	ICE	IC	RE	ICE	ICE	ICE	IC	ICE	ICE	ICE	IC	IC	ICE	ICE	IC	EC	ICE	ICE	ICE	IC
	See note ●	1590	1590	2320	2120	676	2310	4732	972	972	616	2172	674	694	604	1816	928	778	672	1818	61	976	614	1656	2116
		①g	x	F	©R	①–⑥			①g			①–⑥				①–⑥		①–⑥		①–⑤				①–⑥	x
		✣	✣	🍷	🍷	e✕	🍷♦		✕	✕	🍷	e	✕	✕	🍷	⊡	✕♦	e✕	✕	a🍷	✕♦	✕	🍷	e♦	S🍷
	Basel SBB d.	...	...	...	...	...	...	...	...	...	...	...	...	...	...	...	...	...	...	...	...	0608	...	...	...
	Basel Bad. Bf ★ d.	...	...	...	...	...	...	...	0413	...	...	...	...	...	0516	...	...	0545	...	...	...	0616	...	...	...
	Freiburg (Brsg) Hbf ★ d.	...	...	...	...	...	...	...	0448	...	...	...	...	...	0552	...	...	0623	...	...	...	0652	...	...	...
0	**Strasbourg** ★ d.	...	...	...	...	...	...	...	|	...	...	...	...	...	|	...	...	|	...	...	0654	|	...	...	...
29	Offenburg **916** ★ d.	...	...	...	...	...	...	0450	0521	...	...	...	...	...	0626	...	...	0656	...	...	|	0725	...	...	...
—	Baden-Baden **916** d.	...	...	...	...	...	...	0517	0537	...	...	...	...	...	0643	...	...	0714	...	...	0732	0743	...	...	...
	Karlsruhe Hbf **911 911a 916** d.	...	...	...	...	...	...	0543	0559	0559	...	0615	0651	...	0700	...	...	0736	...	...	0752	0800	...	...	...
	München Hbf **930** d.	0033	...	...	...	...	...	...	|	|	0317v	|	|	...	|	...	...	|	...	...	...	|	0523	...	...
	Stuttgart Hbf **930** d.	0305	0305	...	...	0509	...	...	|	|	0551	|	|	0651	|	0633	...	|	0727	0714	...	|	0751	...	0737
	Heidelberg Hbf **911 911a** d.	0428	0428	...	...	0547	...	...	|	|	|	0654	|	|	|	0720	...	|	|	0755	...	|	|	...	0825
	Mannheim Hbf **911a** a.	0438	0438	...	...	0559	...	...	0622	0622	0626p	0709	0714	0728	0723p	0731	...	0800	0804	0806	...	0822	0826p	...	0837
0	**Mannheim** Hbf **911a 919** d.	0440	0440	...	...	0601	...	...	0631	0631	0635	0711	0716	0731	0735	0733	...	...	0806	0808	...	0831	0835	...	0839
	Frankfurt (Main) Hbf d.	|	|	0542	0542	|	0638	...	|	|	|	|	|	|	|	|	0742	...	|	|	...	|	|	0842	|
72	**Frankfurt** Flughafen Fernbf ✈ a.	0512	0512	0555	0555	0638	0656	...	|	|	0706	|	|	|	0806	|	0755	...	0838	|	...	|	0906	0856	|
	Frankfurt Flughafen Fernbf ✈ d.	0517	0517	0558	0558	0642	0658	...	|	|	0709	|	|	|	0809	|	0758	...	0842	|	...	|	0909	0859	|
	Frankfurt (Main) Hbf ◇ a.	0535	0535	|	|	0652	|	...	0708	0708	|	0752	0752	0808	|	|	|	...	0853	|	...	0908	|	|	|
	Mainz Hbf **911a** a.	...	...	0616	0616	|	0714	...	|	|	|	...	|	|	|	0813	0816	...	|	0846	...	|	|	0916	0918
	Mainz Hbf **914** d.	...	...	0618	0618	|	0717	...	|	|	|	...	|	|	|	...	0820	...	|	0848	...	|	|	0922	0920
	Wiesbaden Hbf a.	...	...	|	|	|	|	...	|	|	|	...	|	|	|	...	|	...	|	|	...	|	|	0932	|
	Bingen (Rhein) Hbf **914** d.	...	...	0635	0635	|	|	...	|	|	|	...	|	|	|	...	|	...	|	|	...	|	|	...	|
	Koblenz Hbf **914** a.	...	...	0710	0710	|	0810	...	|	|	|	...	|	|	|	...	0910	...	|	0941	...	|	|	...	1010
	Bonn Hbf **800** a.	...	...	0742	0742	|	0842	...	|	|	|	...	|	|	|	...	0942	...	|	1020	...	|	|	...	1042
	Köln Hbf **800 910** a.	...	...	0805	0805	|	0905	...	|	|	0805	...	|	|	0905	...	1005	...	|	1042	...	|	1005	...	1105
	Dortmund Hbf **800** a.	...	...	0920	0920	|	1021	...	|	|	0921	...	|	|	...	...	1120	...	|	1207f	...	|	1121	...	1221
	Hamburg Hbf **800 900** a.	...	...	1212	1213	1035	1312	...	|	|	...	...	1135	|	...	...	1412	...	1235	|	...	|	...	...	1512
	Berlin Hbf **810** a.	...	...	...	...	...	...	...	1125	1125	...	...	...	1219	...	...	...	...	...	1550f	...	1325	...	...	...

	ICE	ICE	ICE	ICE	ICE	ICE	ICE	ICE	ICE	IC	IC	TGV	ICE	ICE	ICE	IC	IC	ICE	ICE	ICE	ICE	IC	IC	IC	IC
See note ●	926	1026	78	602	692	670	278	612	1654	2114	2028	9571	76	600	690	1926	2010	578	372	610	1652	2112	2006	2004	2014
	①⑦	②–⑥														⑦w	⑤f						⑥	⑦	①–⑤
	✕♦	✕♦	Z✕	🍷	✕	✕	B✕	🍷	✕♦	🍷	🍷♦	®J	✕♦	🍷	✕			✕	B✕	🍷	D✕	🍷	🍷♦	🍷♦	🍷♦
Basel SBB d.	...	...	0704	0712	...	...	0812	...	...	...	...	...	0904	0912	...	...	...	...	1012	...	...	...	...	...	...
Basel Bad. Bf ★ d.	...	...	0713	0721	...	...	0822	...	...	...	...	...	0913	0922	...	...	...	...	1022	...	...	...	...	...	...
Freiburg (Brsg) Hbf ★ d.	...	...	0749	0756	...	...	0857	...	...	...	...	...	0949	0957	...	...	...	...	1057	...	...	...	...	...	...
Strasbourg ★ d.	...	...	|	|	...	...	|	...	...	...	...	0947	|	|	...	...	...	...	|	...	...	...	...	...	...
Offenburg **916** ★ d.	...	...	|	0828	...	...	0930	...	...	...	...	|	|	1030	...	...	...	...	1130	...	...	...	1139	1139	...
Baden-Baden **916** d.	...	...	0834	0844	...	...	|	...	...	...	...	|	1034	|	...	...	...	...	|	...	...	...	1202	1202	...
Karlsruhe Hbf **911 911a 916** d.	...	...	0851	0901	...	...	1000	...	...	...	...	1025	1051	1100	...	...	...	...	1200	...	...	...	1221	1221	...
München Hbf **930** d.	0614‡	...	|	|	0625	...	|	0723	...	...	...	...	|	|	0823	...	...	...	|	0923	...	...	|	|	...
Stuttgart Hbf **930** d.	|	...	|	|	0851	0927	|	0951	...	0937	...	...	|	|	1051	...	1114	1127	|	1151	...	1137	|	|	1209
Heidelberg Hbf **911 911a** d.	|	...	|	|	|	|	|	|	...	1025	...	...	|	|	|	...	1155	|	|	|	...	1225	|	|	|
Mannheim Hbf **911a** a.	|	...	0914	0924	0928p	1004	1022	1026p	...	1037	...	...	1114	1123	1128p	...	1206	1204	1222	1226p	...	1237	1252	1252	1256
Mannheim Hbf **911a 919** d.	|	...	0916	0935	0931	1006	1031	1035	...	1039	...	...	1116	1135	1131	...	1209	1206	1231	1235	...	1239	1258	1258	1258
Frankfurt (Main) Hbf d.	0942	0942	|	|	|	|	|	|	1042	|	1144	...	|	|	|	1215	|	|	|	|	1242	|	|	|	|
Frankfurt Flughafen Fernbf ✈ a.	0955	0955	|	1006	|	1038	|	1106	1056	|	1157	...	|	1206	|	1226	|	1238	|	1306	1256	|	|	|	|
Frankfurt Flughafen Fernbf ✈ d.	0958	0958	|	1009	|	1042	|	1109	1059	|	1159	...	|	1209	|	1228	|	1242	|	1309	1259	|	|	|	|
Frankfurt (Main) Hbf ◇ a.	|	|	0953	|	1008	1053	1108	|	|	|	|	...	1153	|	1208	|	|	1253	1308	|	|	|	|	|	|
Mainz Hbf **911a** a.	1016	1016	|	|	|	|	|	|	1110	1118	1216	...	|	|	|	1246	1246	|	|	|	1316	1318	1340	1340	1340
Mainz Hbf **914** d.	1020	1020	|	|	|	|	|	|	1122	1120	1220	...	|	|	|	1248	1248	|	|	|	1322	1320	1342	1342	1342
Wiesbaden Hbf a.	|	|	|	|	|	|	|	|	1132	|	|	...	|	|	|	|	|	|	|	|	1332	|	|	|	|
Bingen (Rhein) Hbf **914** d.	|	|	|	|	|	|	|	|	...	|	|	...	|	|	|	1306	1306	|	|	|	...	|	|	|	|
Koblenz Hbf **914** a.	1110	1110	|	|	|	|	|	|	...	1210	1310	...	|	|	|	1341	1341	|	|	|	...	1410	1441	1441	1441
Bonn Hbf **800** a.	1142	1142	|	|	|	|	|	|	...	1242	1342	...	|	|	|	1420	1420	|	|	|	...	1442	1520	1520	1520
Köln Hbf **800 910** a.	1205	1205	|	1105	|	|	|	1205	...	1305	1405	...	|	1305	|	1442	1442	|	|	1405	...	1505	1542	1542	1542
Dortmund Hbf **800** a.	1320	1320	|	...	|	|	|	1321	...	1421	1520	...	|	...	|	1605	1605	|	|	1521	...	1621	1707	...	...
Hamburg Hbf **800 900** a.	1612	1612	1335	...	|	1435	|	...	...	1712	1812	...	1535	...	|	|	|	1635	|	...	...	1912	...	...	...
Berlin Hbf **810** a.	...	...	...	...	1419	...	1526	...	...	...	...	...	...	...	1619	1951	1952	...	1725	...	...	...	...	...	...

	IC	ICE	ICE	ICE	ICE	IC	ICE	ICE	ICE	EC	IC	TGV	ICE	ICE	ICE	ICE	ICE	IC	ICE	ICE	ICE	EC	ICE	ICE	ICE
See note ●	2026	74	508	108	576	2012	272	518	1650	100	2024	9573	72	506	596	774	574	118	276	516	1558	6	70	104	504
																⑧q	⑥t								
	🍷	✕♦	🍷	Y✕	✕	🍷♦	B✕	🍷	D✕	✕♦	🍷	®J	Z✕	🍷	✕	K✕	✕	🍷♦	B✕	🍷	D✕	✕♦	✕	🍷♦	🍷
Basel SBB d.	...	1104	1112	...	...	...	1212	...	...	1218	...	...	1304	1312	...	...	...	...	1412	...	...	1418	1504	1512	1512
Basel Bad. Bf ★ d.	...	1113	1122	...	...	...	1222	...	...	1227	...	...	1313	1322	...	...	...	...	1422	...	...	1427	1513	1522	1522
Freiburg (Brsg) Hbf ★ d.	...	1149	1157	...	...	...	1257	...	...	1304	...	...	1349	1357	...	...	...	...	1457	...	...	1504	1549	1557	1557
Strasbourg ★ d.	...	|	|	...	...	...	|	...	...	|	...	1347	|	|	...	...	...	...	|	...	...	|	|	|	|
Offenburg **916** ★ d.	...	|	1230	...	...	...	1330	...	...	|	...	|	|	1430	...	...	...	...	1530	...	...	|	|	1630	1630
Baden-Baden **916** d.	...	1234	|	...	...	...	|	...	...	1352	...	|	1434	|	...	...	...	...	|	...	...	1552	1634	|	|
Karlsruhe Hbf **911 911a 916** d.	...	1251	1300	...	...	...	1400	...	...	1412	...	1425	1451	1500	...	...	...	...	1600	...	...	1612	1651	1700	1700
München Hbf **930** d.	...	|	|	1023	...	...	|	1123	...	|	...	...	|	|	1223	...	...	...	|	1323	...	|	|	|	|
Stuttgart Hbf **930** d.	...	|	|	1251	1327	1314	|	1351	...	|	...	...	|	|	1451	1527	1527	1512	|	1551	...	|	|	|	|
Heidelberg Hbf **911 911a** d.	...	|	|	|	|	1355	|	|	...	|	...	...	|	|	|	|	|	1555	|	|	...	|	|	|	|
Mannheim Hbf **911a** a.	...	1314	1323	1328p	1404	1406	1422	1426p	...	1437	...	...	1514	1523	1528p	1604	1604	1606	1622	1626p	...	1637	1714	1723	1723
Mannheim Hbf **911a 919** d.	...	1316	1335	1331	1406	1408	1431	1435	...	1439	...	...	1516	1535	1531	1606	1606	1608	1631	1635	...	1639	1716	1735	1735
Frankfurt (Main) Hbf d.	1344	|	|	|	|	|	|	|	1442	|	1542	...	|	|	|	|	|	|	|	|	1642	|	|	|	|
Frankfurt Flughafen Fernbf ✈ a.	1356	|	1406	|	1438	|	|	1506	1456	|	1555	...	|	1606	|	1638	1638	|	|	1706	1656	|	|	1806	1806
Frankfurt Flughafen Fernbf ✈ d.	1358	|	1409	|	1442	|	|	1509	1459	|	1558	...	|	1609	|	1642	1642	|	|	1709	1659	|	|	1809	1809
Frankfurt (Main) Hbf ◇ a.	|	1353	|	1408	1453	|	1508	|	|	|	|	...	1553	|	1608	1653	1653	|	1708	|	|	|	1753	|	|
Mainz Hbf **911a** a.	1416	|	|	|	|	1446	|	|	1516	1518	1616	...	|	|	|	|	|	1646	|	|	1716	1718	|	|	|
Mainz Hbf **914** d.	1420	|	|	|	|	1448	|	|	1522	1520	1620	...	|	|	|	|	|	1648	|	|	1722	1720	|	|	|
Wiesbaden Hbf a.	|	|	|	|	|	|	|	|	1532	|	|	...	|	|	|	|	|	|	|	|	1732	|	|	|	|
Bingen (Rhein) Hbf **914** d.	|	|	|	|	|	1506	|	|	...	|	|	...	|	|	|	|	|	1706	|	|	...	|	|	|	|
Koblenz Hbf **914** a.	1510	|	|	|	|	1541	|	|	...	1610	1710	...	|	|	|	|	|	1741	|	|	...	1810	|	|	|
Bonn Hbf **800** a.	1542	|	|	|	|	1620	|	|	...	1642	1742	...	|	|	|	|	|	1820	|	|	...	1842	|	|	|
Köln Hbf **800 910** a.	1605	|	1505	|	|	1642	|	1605	...	1705	1805	...	|	1705	|	|	|	1842	|	1805	...	1905	|	1905	1905
Dortmund Hbf **800** a.	1720	|	...	|	|	1805	|	1721	...	1821	1921	...	|	1820	|	|	|	...	|	1920	...	2021	|	...	...
Hamburg Hbf **800 900** a.	2012	1735	...	|	1835	...	|	...	...	2112	2212	...	1935	...	|	2037	2037	...	|	...	...	2314q	2138	...	...
Berlin Hbf **810** a.	...	...	...	1819	...	...	1925	...	...	...	...	...	...	...	2019	...	...	...	2125j	...	...	...	...	...	...

♦ – **NOTES** (LISTED BY TRAIN NUMBER)

6 – [12] and ✕ Chur - Zürich - Basel - Dortmund (- Hamburg ⑧ **q**).

61 – [12] and ✕ Strasbourg - Stuttgart - München.

74/6 – [12] and ✕ Zürich - Basel - Hamburg - Kiel.

100 – [12] and ✕ Chur - Zürich - Dortmund - Hamburg (- Kiel ⑦ **w**). Train number **102** on ⑦ **w**.

104 – [12] and 🍷 Basel - Köln - Amsterdam.

114 – WÖRTHERSEE – [12] and ✕ Klagenfurt - Villach - Salzburg - Dortmund.

118 – [12] and 🍷 Innsbruck - Bregenz - Lindau - Ulm - Münster.

265 – ORIENT EXPRESS – 🛏 1, 2 cl., ▬ 2 cl., [2] and 🍷 Strasbourg - Salzburg - Wien.

353 – JOHANNES KEPLER – 🛏 1, 2 cl., ▬ 2 cl. and [2] Basel - Leipzig - Dresden - Praha; ✕ Basel - Fulda. Conveys 🛏 1, 2 cl., ▬ 2 cl. and ✕ (*CNL* **40353** – AURORA) Basel - København. For Warszawa and Moskva cars see Table **24**.

408 – KOMET – 🛏 1, 2 cl., ▬ 2 cl., [2] (reclining) and ✕ (Table **73**: Brig -) Zürich - Hamburg.

459 – SEMPER – 🛏 1, 2 cl., ▬ 2 cl., [2] (reclining) and ✕ Zürich - Leipzig - Dresden.

926 – ①⑦ (also Dec. 26, 27, Jan. 1, 2, Mar. 25, May 13; not Dec. 24, 31, Mar. 24, May 12). [12] and ✕ (München ①‡ -) Nürnberg - Frankfurt - Köln - Kiel.

928 – [12] and ✕ Nürnberg - Frankfurt - Köln - Hamburg.

1026 – ②–⑥ (also Dec. 24, 31, Mar. 24, May 12; not Dec. 26, 27, Jan. 1, 2, Mar. 25, May 13). [12] and ✕ Regensburg - Nürnberg - Frankfurt - Köln - Kiel.

1243 – BERLINER – 🛏 1, 2 cl., ▬ 2 cl., [2] (reclining) and ✕ Zürich - Berlin.

1654 – [12] and ✕ (Dresden ①–⑥ **e** -) Leipzig - Wiesbaden.

1656 – [12] and ✕ Leipzig - Wiesbaden.

2004 – ⑦ (also Dec. 26, Jan. 1, Mar. 21, 24, May 1, 12, 22; not Dec. 23, 30, Mar. 23, May 11). BODENSEE – [12] and 🍷 Konstanz - Münster - Emden.

2006 – ⑥ (also Dec. 23, 25, 30, 31, Mar. 23, May 11). BODENSEE – [12] and 🍷 Konstanz - Dortmund.

2012 – ALLGÄU – [12] and 🍷 Oberstdorf - Ulm - Stuttgart - Köln - Dortmund - Hannover (- Leipzig on dates in Table **810**).

2014 – ①–⑤ (not Dec. 24, 25, 26, 31, Jan. 1, Mar. 21, 24, May 1, 12, 22). [12] and 🍷 Stuttgart - Münster - Emden.

2028 – [12] and 🍷 Passau - Regensburg - Nürnberg - Frankfurt - Hamburg.

2310 – NORDFRIESLAND – [12] and 🍷 Frankfurt - Westerland.

9575 – [12] and 🍷 Paris - Strasbourg - Stuttgart - München.

40408 – PEGASUS – 🛏 1, 2 cl., ▬ 2 cl., [2] (reclining) and ✕ Zürich - Amsterdam.

NOTES CONTINUED ON NEXT PAGE →

BASEL - KARLSRUHE - MANNHEIM - FRANKFURT - KOBLENZ (- KÖLN) 912

See note ●	*ICE* **1090**	*ICE* **594**	*IC* **2316**	*ICE* **26**	*ICE* **572**	*EC* **114**	*ICE* **1556**	*ICE* **872**	*ICE* **514**	*IC* **2318**	*TGV* **9575**	*ICE* **374**	*ICE* **374**	*ICE* **24**	*ICE* **502**	*ICE* **592**	*ICE* **570**	*IC* **2018**	*ICE* **1554**	*ICE* **876**	*ICE* **870**	*ICE* **970**	*ICE* **512**	*IC* **2110**	*CNL* **353**
	Ⓑq	⑥t	Ⓑq							n			⑤⑦h				⑦w	⑦w	n	⑥k	①–⑤	⑦w	n	Ⓑq	R
	✕	✕		Q✕	✕	✕◆	D✕	✕	🍷	✕	R◆	B✕	B✕	Q✕	H🍷	✕	✕		D✕	✕	d✕	✕	M🍷	🍷	✕◆
Basel SBB ... d.	...	...	...	...	...	...	...	1612	...	...	...	1704	1704	...	1712	...	...	...	...	1812	1812	1812	...	...	1804
Basel Bad. Bf ... ★ d.	...	...	...	...	...	...	...	1621	...	...	...	1713	1713	...	1721	...	...	...	...	1822	1822	1822	...	...	1817
Freiburg (Brsg) Hbf ... ★ d.	...	...	...	...	...	...	...	1656	...	...	...	1749	1749	...	1756	...	...	...	...	1857	1857	1857	...	...	1904
Strasbourg ... ★ d.	...	...	...	...	...	...	...	|	...	...	1747	|	|	...	|	...	...	...	...	|	|	|	...	...	|
Offenburg **916** ... ★ d.	...	...	...	...	...	...	...	1728	...	...	|	|	|	...	1828	...	...	...	...	1930	1930	1930	...	...	1937
Baden-Baden **916** ... d.	...	...	...	...	...	...	...	1744	...	...	|	1834	1834	...	1844	...	...	...	...	|	|	|	...	...	|
Karlsruhe Hbf **911 911a 916** d.	...	...	...	...	...	...	...	1801	...	...	1825	1851	1851	...	1901	...	...	...	...	2000	2000	2000	...	...	2018
München Hbf **930** ... d.	1423	1423	...	...	...	1440	...	|	1523	...	...	|	|	...	|	1623	...	1613	...	|	|	|	1723	...	|
Stuttgart Hbf **930** ... d.	1651	1651	1636	...	1727	1713	...	|	1751	1741	...	|	|	...	|	1851	1927	1914	...	|	|	|	1951	1937	|
Heidelberg Hbf **911 911a** d.	|	|	1720	...	|	1755	...	|	|	1825	...	|	|	...	|	|	|	1955	...	|	|	|	|	2025	|
Mannheim Hbf **911a** ... a.	1728p	1728p	1736	...	1804	1806	...	1823	1826p	1837	...	1914	1914	...	1924	1928p	2004	2006	...	2022	2022	2022	2026p	2037	2057
Mannheim Hbf **911a 919** ... d.	1731	1731	1738	...	1806	1808	...	1831	1835	1839	...	1916	1916	...	1935	1931	2006	2008	...	2031	2031	2031	2035	2039	2116
Frankfurt (Main) Hbf ... d.	|	|	|	1742	|	|	1842	|	|	|	...	|	|	1942	|	|	|	|	2042	|	|	|	|	|	|
Frankfurt Flughafen Fernbf ✈ a.	|	|	|	1755	1838	|	1856	|	1906	|	...	|	|	1955	2006	|	2038	|	2056	|	|	|	2106	|	|
Frankfurt Flughafen Fernbf ✈ d.	|	|	|	1758	1842	|	1859	|	1909	|	...	|	|	1958	2009	|	2042	|	2059	|	|	|	2109	|	|
Frankfurt (Main) Hbf ◇ ... a.	1808	1808	|	|	1853	|	|	1908	|	|	...	1953	1953	|	|	2008	2053	|	|	2108	2108	2108	|	|	2217y
Mainz Hbf **911a** ... a.	|	|	1819	1815	|	1846	1916	|	|	1918	...	...	|	2016	|	|	|	2046	2116	|	|	|	|	2118	...
Mainz Hbf **914** ... d.	|	|	1821	1821	|	1848	1922	|	|	1920	...	...	|	2020	|	|	|	2048	2122	|	|	|	|	2120	...
Wiesbaden Hbf ... a.	|	|	1833	|	|	|	1932	|	|	|	...	...	|	|	|	|	|	|	2132	|	|	|	|	|	...
Bingen (Rhein) Hbf **914** ... d.	|	|	...	|	|	1906	...	|	|	|	...	...	|	|	|	|	|	|	...	|	|	|	|	|	...
Koblenz Hbf **914** ... a.	|	|	...	1910	|	1941	...	|	|	2010	...	...	|	2110	|	|	|	2141	...	|	|	|	|	2210	...
Bonn Hbf **800** ... a.	|	|	...	1943	|	2020	...	|	|	2042	...	...	|	2142	|	|	|	2220	...	|	|	|	|	2242	...
Köln Hbf **800 910** ... a.	|	|	...	2005	|	2042	...	|	2005	2105	...	...	|	2205	2105	|	|	2242	...	|	|	|	2205	2305	...
Dortmund Hbf **800** ... a.	|	|	...	2120	|	2205	...	|	2121	2221q	...	...	|	2320	2220	|	|	0004	...	|	|	|	2321	...	...
Hamburg Hbf **800 900** ... a.	|	|	...	...	2241	...	...	|	0021	...	...	...	2345	...	...	|	0037	...	...	0118	0134	|	...	...	...
Berlin Hbf **810** ... a.	2147*	2226	...	...	...	...	...	2325	...	...	...	...	...	...	...	0027	...	...	...	...	...	0124	...	...	...

See note ●	*TGV* **9577**	*ICE* **500**	*ICE* **590**	*ICE* **698**	*ICE* **598**	*IC* **1896**	*ICE* **22**	*ICE* **270**	*ICE* **510**	*ICE* **1810**	*IC* **2020**	*ICE* **887**	*IC* **60459**	*ICE* **990**	*ICE* **990**		*CNL* **459**	*CNL* **1243**	*EN* **265**	*RE* **4752**	*RB* **18650**	*CNL* **408**	*CNL* **40408**	*ICE* **808**	*IC* **60318**
	Ⓑb	n	♠	⑤§	⑦m	⑦w			①–⑥	⑦m					⑦s		R	R				R	R		
	RJ	🍷	✕	✕	N✕	🍷	Q✕	Z✕	z🍷	🍷	⊙	G		✕			✕◆	✕◆	🍷◆			✕◆	✕◆	K✕	✣2
Basel SBB ... d.	...	1912	...	...	...	...	...	2012	...	...	...	...	2107	...	...	...	2107	2107	...	...	...	2207	2207	2326	...
Basel Bad. Bf ... ★ d.	...	1921	...	...	...	...	...	2022	...	...	...	...	2121	...	...	...	2121u	2121u	...	*2126*	...	2219u	2219u	2334	...
Freiburg (Brsg) Hbf ... ★ d.	...	1956	...	...	...	...	...	2057	...	...	...	...	2158	...	...	...	2158u	2158u	...	*2225*	...	2257u	2257u	0014	...
Strasbourg ... ★ d.	1947	|	...	...	...	...	...	|	...	...	...	...	|	...	...	...	|	|	2220	|	...	|	|	|	...
Offenburg **916** ... ★ d.	|	2028	...	...	...	...	...	2130	...	...	...	...	2230	...	...	...	2230u	2230u	|	2323	...	2331u	2331u	0049	...
Baden-Baden **916** ... d.	|	2044	...	...	...	...	...	|	...	...	...	...	|	...	...	...	|	|	2307	2347	...	2351u	2351u	0113	...
Karlsruhe Hbf **911 911a 916** d.	2025	2101	...	...	...	...	...	2200	...	...	...	...	2305	...	...	...	2305u	2305u	2324	0005	0015	0010u	0010u	0133	...
München Hbf **930** ... d.	...	|	1823	1823	1823	...	...	|	1923	1923	...	...	|	2039	2039	...	|	|	...	...	|	|	|	|	2242
Stuttgart Hbf **930** ... d.	...	|	2051	2051	2051	2035	...	|	2151	2151	...	...	|	2305	2305	...	|	|	...	...	|	|	|	|	0126
Heidelberg Hbf **911 911a** d.	...	|	|	|	|	2120	...	|	|	|	...	...	2334	|	|	...	2334u	2334u	...	...	|	|	|	0210	|
Mannheim Hbf **911a** ... a.	...	2124	2128p	2128p	2128p	2131	...	2222	2228p	2228p	...	...	2346	2342	2342	...	|	|	...	...	0108	|	|	0222	0247
Mannheim Hbf **911a 919** ... d.	...	2135	2131	2131	2131	2135	...	2235	2231	2231	...	...	...	2351	2351	...	0005u	0005u	...	...	...	|	|	0224	0249
Frankfurt (Main) Hbf ... d.	...	|	|	|	|	|	2146	|	|	|	2314	0003	...	|	|	...	...	|	...	...	...	|	|	0315	|
Frankfurt Flughafen Fernbf ✈ a.	...	2206	|	|	|	|	2157	|	2303	2302	2327	0016	...	0023	0023	...	...	|	...	...	...	|	|	0330r	|
Frankfurt Flughafen Fernbf ✈ d.	...	2209	|	|	|	|	2159	|	2313	2204	2329	0027	...	0029	0029	...	...	|	...	...	...	|	|	0349r	|
Frankfurt (Main) Hbf ◇ ... a.	...	|	2208	2208	2208	|	|	2315	2325	|	|	|	...	0042	0042	...	...	|	...	...	...	|	|	|	|
Mainz Hbf **911a** ... a.	...	|	...	...	...	2213	2217	...	...	|	2345	0044	...	...	|	...	...	|	...	...	...	|	|	0406	0332
Mainz Hbf **914** ... d.	...	|	...	...	...	2220	2220	...	...	|	2347	0046	...	...	|	...	...	|	...	...	...	|	|	0408	0334
Wiesbaden Hbf ... a.	...	|	...	...	...	2233	|	...	...	|	|	0057	...	...	|	...	...	|	...	...	...	|	|	|	|
Bingen (Rhein) Hbf **914** ... d.	...	|	...	...	...	...	|	...	...	|	0006	...	...	...	|	...	...	|	...	...	...	|	|	0425	|
Koblenz Hbf **914** ... a.	...	|	...	...	...	...	2310	...	...	|	0045	...	...	...	|	...	...	|	...	...	...	|	|	0501	0426
Bonn Hbf **800** ... a.	...	|	...	...	...	...	2342	...	...	|	0140	...	...	...	|	...	...	|	...	...	...	|	0521	0534	...
Köln Hbf **800 910** ... a.	...	2312	...	...	...	...	0005	...	...	0005	0205	...	...	...	|	...	...	|	...	...	...	|	0545	0605	...
Dortmund Hbf **800** ... a.	...	0026	...	...	...	...	0122x	...	...	...	0327	...	...	...	|	...	...	|	...	...	...	0515	...	0721	...
Hamburg Hbf **800 900** ... a.	...	...	...	...	...	...	...	...	...	...	0651	...	...	...	0543	...	...	|	...	...	...	0832c	...	1012	...
Berlin Hbf **810** ... a.	...	...	...	...	...	...	...	...	...	...	...	...	...	...	...	...	...	0810	...	...	...	...	...	...	...

NOTES (CONTINUED FROM PREVIOUS PAGE)

B – From Interlaken via Bern (Table **560**).
D – (12) and ✕ Dresden - Leipzig - Wiesbaden.
F – Daily to Mar. 14; Ⓐ from Mar. 17.
G – From Hamburg (Table **900**).
H – To Hannover (Table **810**).
J – (12) and 🍷 Paris - Strasbourg - Stuttgart.
K – To Kiel (Table **820**).
M – To Münster (Table **800**).
N – To Hannover (Table **900**).
Q – (12) and ✕ Wien - Passau - Regensburg - Nürnberg - Dortmund.
R – © from Mar. 15. To Puttgarden (Table **825**).
S – To Stralsund (Table **830**).
Y – From Innsbruck (Table **951**).
Z – From Zürich (Table **510**).
a – Not Dec. 24, 25, 26, 31, Jan. 1, Mar. 21, 24, May 1, 2, 12, 22, 23.
b – Not Dec. 24, 31, Mar. 23, May 11.
c – 0812 on ©.
d – Not Dec. 25, 26, Jan. 1, Mar. 21, 24, May 12.
e – Not Dec. 25, 26, Jan. 1, Mar. 22, 24, May 12.
f – ⑤ (also Mar. 20, Apr. 30, May 21; not Mar. 21, May 2, 23).
g – ① (also Dec. 27, Jan. 2, Mar. 25, May 13; not Dec. 24, 31, Mar. 24, May 12).
h – ⑤⑦ (also Jan. 1, Mar. 20, 24, Apr. 30, May 12, 21; not Dec. 23, 28, 30, Mar. 21, 23, May 2, 11, 23).
j – Not Dec. 24, 25, 31, Mar. 23, May 11.
k – Also Dec. 23, 25, 30, Mar. 21, 23, May 11.
m – Also Dec. 26, Jan. 1, Mar. 24, May 12; not Mar. 23, May 11.
n – Not Dec. 24, 31.
p – Connects with train in previous column.
q – Ⓑ (not Dec. 24, 25, 31, Mar. 21, 23, May 11).
r – Frankfurt Flughafen Regionalbahnhof.
s – Also Jan. 1, Mar. 24, May 12; not Dec. 23, 30, Mar. 23, May 11.
t – Also Dec. 24, 25, 31, Mar. 21, 23, May 11.
u – Stops to pick up only.
v – 0324 on ⑥⑦ (also Dec. 24, 31, May 22).
w – Also Dec. 26, Jan. 1, Mar. 24, May 12; not Dec. 23, 30, Mar. 23, May 11.
x – Not Dec. 25, Jan. 1.
y – Frankfurt (Main) **Süd**.
z – Also Mar. 23, May 11; not Dec. 25, 26, Jan. 1, Mar. 24, May 12.
‡ – ① (not Dec. 24, 31, Mar. 24, May 12).
§ – ⑤ (also Mar. 20, Apr. 30; not Mar. 21). To Kassel (Table **900**).
⊡ – ①–⑥ (not Dec. 24, 25, 26, 31, Jan. 1, Mar. 22, 24, May 12). Train number **2218** on ⑥ (also Mar. 21, May 1; not May 3).
♠ – ①②③④⑥ (also Mar. 21, 23, May 11; not Dec. 24, 26, 31, Jan. 1, Mar. 20, 24, Apr. 30, May 12). To Kassel on ⑥ (Table **900**).
⊙ – Also calls at Boppard Hbf (d. 0032).
✣ – Subject to alteration in the Stuttgart area from May 16.
● – Services via Mainz are subject to alteration on ⑥⑦ from May 17.
* – R and 'Sprinter' supplement payable for journeys to Berlin.
◇ – See also Tables **911** (services from Karlsruhe via Heidelberg and Darmstadt), **911a** (local services) and **919** (services from Saarbrücken via Mannheim).
★ – See note on page 423.

KÖLN - GEROLSTEIN - TRIER 913

RE / RB services

km																										
		Ⓐe	⚒r				†w	⚒r										©z		n		⑤⑥f	†w	⚒r	Ⓐe	
0	**Köln** Hbf ... d.	...	...	...	0611	0721	0811	0821	0921	1021	1121	1221	1321	1421	1521	1621	1721	1721	...	1821	1921	1921	2011	2027	2027	2211
40	Euskirchen ... d.	...	...	...	0659	0759	0859	0859	0959	1059	1159	1259	1359	1459	1559	1659	1759	1759	...	1859	1959	1959	2059	2110	2110	2259
55	Mechernich ... d.	...	...	...	0710	0810	0910	0909	1010	1109	1210	1309	1410	1509	1610	1709	1810	1810	...	1909	2010	2010	2110	2121	2121	2310
64	Kall ... d.	...	...	...	0720	0818	0920	0917	1018	1117	1218	1317	1418	1517	1618	1717	1818	1818	...	1917	2018	2018	2120	2131	2131	2320
80	Blankenheim ... d.	...	...	...	0736	0834	0936	0933	1034	1133	1234	1333	1434	1533	1634	1733	1834	1834	...	1933	2034	2034	2136	2147	2147	2336
93	Jünkerath ... d.	...	...	0654e	0750	0848	0950	0947	1048	1147	1248	1347	1448	1547	1648	1747	1848	1848	...	1947	2048	2048	2150	2201	2201	2350
112	**Gerolstein** ... a.	...	...	0712e	0807	0903	1007	1006	1103	1206	1303	1406	1503	1606	1703	1806	1903	1903	...	2006	2103	2103	2207	2223	2223	0007
112	**Gerolstein** ... d.	0449	0600	0713	0818	0904	1018	1018	1104	1218	1304	1418	1504	1618	1704	1818	...	1904	1913	2018	...	2104	2233	...	2233	...
142	Bitburg-Erdorf ... d.	0522	0633	0746	0859	0933	1059	1059	1132	1259	1332	1459	1532	1659	1734	1859	...	1932	1946	2059	...	2134	2307	...	2307	...
181	**Trier** Hbf ... a.	0607	0719	0839	0940	1009	1140	1140	1209	1340	1409	1540	1609	1740	1809	1940	...	2009	2039	2140	...	2210	2349	...	2349	...

	⚒r	⑥k	Ⓐe	⚒r	⑥k	⚒r	†w	⚒r		g									Ⓑn	⑥k		†w	⚒e	n	A	⑤⑥
Trier Hbf ... d.	...	...	...	...	0528	...	0528v	0556	0759	0816	0959	1016	1159	1216	1329j	1416	1559	1616	1759	1759	1816	1959	2028	2028	2216	2328
Bitburg-Erdorf ... d.	...	...	...	...	0606	...	0606v	0656	0834	0858	1033	1058	1234	1258	1433	1458	1634	1658	1833	1833	1858	2034	2118	2118	2308	0013
Gerolstein ... a.	...	...	...	...	0642	...	0642v	0731	0859	0932	1059	1132	1259	1332	1459	1532	1659	1732	1859	1859	1932	2059	2159	2159	2343	0048
Gerolstein ... d.	0445	0545	0555	0618	0644	0644	0644	0737	0900	0945	1100	1145	1300	1345	1500	1545	1700	1745	1900	1900	1945	2100	2202	...	...	...
Jünkerath ... d.	0502	0602	0612	0635	0709	0709	0709	0810	0915	1010	1115	1210	1315	1410	1515	1610	1715	1810	1915	1915	2008	2115	2223	...	...	...
Blankenheim ... d.	0516	0616	0623	0649	0725	0725	0725	0824	0927	1024	1127	1224	1327	1424	1527	1624	1727	1824	1927	1927	2022	2127	2237	...	...	...
Kall ... d.	0533	0633	0639	0705	0742	0742	0742	0840	0942	1040	1142	1240	1342	1440	1542	1640	1742	1840	1942	1942	2039	2142	2254	...	...	...
Mechernich ... d.	0541	0641	0646	0714	0749	0749	0751	0847	0949	1047	1149	1247	1349	1447	1549	1647	1749	1847	1949	1949	2048	2149	2303	...	...	...
Euskirchen ... d.	0557	0659	0657	0729	0801	0801	0807	0901	1001	1101	1201	1300	1400	1501	1601	1701	1801	1901	2001	2007	2107	2207	2314	...	...	...
Köln Hbf ... a.	0639	0739	0739	0812	0839	0839	0851	0939	1039	1139	1239	1339	1439	1539	1639	1739	1839	1939	2039	2051	2151	2251	2354	...	...	...

A – ①②③④⑦ (not Dec. 24, 31.
e – Ⓐ (not Dec. 24, 31, May 22).
f – Also Dec. 24, 31.
g – Change trains at Gerolstein on Ⓐ **e**.
j – 1359 on © (also Dec. 24, 31, May 22).
k – Also Dec. 24, 31.
n – Not Dec. 24, 31.
r – Not May 22.
v – Not Dec. 25, Jan. 1.
w – Also May 22.
z – Also Dec. 24, 31, May 22.

914 Local services KOBLENZ - WIESBADEN / MAINZ - FRANKFURT

RE / RB services

Koblenz - St Goarshausen - Wiesbaden - Frankfurt (*Rechte Rheinstrecke*)

km		Ⓐe	⚒r	Ⓐe	Ⓐe		Ⓐe	Ⓒz						Ⓐe					Ⓐe			Ⓐe				
0	**Koblenz** Hbf **906** d.	...	...	0438	0508	0555	0652	0710	0755	0910	0955	1110	1155	1225	1310	1355	1510	1555	1638	1710	1755	1810	1910	2010	...	2210
5	Niederlahnstein **906** d.	...	...	0444	0514	0601	0658	0716	0801	0916	1001	1116	1201	1231	1316	1401	1516	1601	1644	1716	1801	1816	1916	2016	...	2216
11	Braubach d.	...	...	0451	0521	0608	0705	0722	0808	0922	1008	1122	1208	1237	1322	1408	1522	1608	1651	1722	1808	1822	1922	2022	...	2222
23	Kamp-Bornhofen d.	...	...	0502	0532	0618	0716	0733	0818	0933	1018	1133	1218	1248	1333	1418	1533	1618	1702	1733	1818	1833	1933	2033	...	2233
35	St Goarshausen d.	...	...	0514	0544	0630	0728	0744	0830	0944	1030	1144	1230	1259	1344	1430	1544	1630	1714	1744	1830	1844	1944	2044	...	2244
46	Kaub d.	...	...	0522	0552	0640	0738	0753	0840	0953	1040	1153	1240	1308	1353	1440	1553	1640	1722	1753	1840	1853	1953	2053	...	2253
52	Lorch d.	...	...	0529	0559	0645	0744	0759	0845	0959	1045	1159	1245	1314	1359	1445	1559	1645	1729	1759	1845	1859	1959	2059	...	2259
64	Rüdesheim d.	0440	0510	0540	0610	0655	0755	0810	0855	1010	1055	1210	1255	1340	1410	1455	1610	1655	1740	1810	1855	1910	2010	2110	...	2310
94	**Wiesbaden** Hbf a.	0514	0544	0614	0644	0724	0824	0844	0924	1044	1124	1244	1324	1414	1444	1524	1644	1724	1814	1844	1924	1944	2044	2144	...	2344
94	**Wiesbaden** Hbf d.	0520	0550	0632	0658	0732	0832	0850	0932	1050	1132	1250	1332	1432	1450	1532	1650	1732	1832	1850	1932	1950	2050	2150	...	2350
135	**Frankfurt** (Main) Hbf a.	0614*	0644*	0705	0735	0805	0905	0944*	1005	1144*	1205	1344*	1405	1505	1544*	1605	1744*	1805	1905	1944*	2005	2044*	2144*	2244*	...	0044*

	Ⓐe	⚒r	⚒r						Ⓐe	Ⓒz	Ⓐe				Ⓐe			Ⓐe	Ⓐe					†w		
Frankfurt (Main) Hbf d.	...	...	0512*	0612*	0753	0812*	0953	1012*	1053	1153	1153	1212*	1353	1412*	1523	1553	1623e	1653	1723	1753	1823e	1953	2012*	2112*	2112*	2242*
Wiesbaden Hbf a.	...	...	0555	0655	0828	0855	1028	1055	1128	1228	1228	1255	1428	1455	1558	1628	1658e	1728	1758	1828	1858e	2028	2055	2155	2155	2325
Wiesbaden Hbf d.	...	0521e	0612	0712	0836	0912	1036	1112	1150	1236	1236	1312	1436	1512	1612	1636	1712	1742	1812	1836	1912	2036	2112	2212	2212	2342
Rüdesheim d.	...	0554e	0644	0744	0902	0944	1102	1144	1224	1302	1302	1344	1502	1544	1644	1702	1744	1814	1844	1902	1944	2102	2144	2244	2244	0015
Lorch d.	...	0604e	0654	0754	0910	0954	1110	1154	1234	1310	1310	1354	1510	1554	1654	1710	1754	1824	1854	1910	1954	2110	2154	2254	...	...
Kaub d.	0513	0613	0701	0801	0916	1001	1116	1201	1241	1316	1318	1401	1516	1601	1701	1716	1801	1831	1901	1916	2001	2116	2201	2301	...	...
St Goarshausen d.	0522	0622	0709	0809	0925	1009	1125	1209	1254	1325	1327	1409	1525	1609	1709	1725	1809	1839	1909	1925	2009	2125	2209	2309	...	...
Kamp-Bornhofen d.	0533	0633	0720	0820	0935	1020	1135	1220	1305	1335	1337	1420	1535	1620	1720	1735	1820	1850	1920	1935	2020	2135	2220	2320	...	...
Braubach d.	0545	0645	0732	0832	0946	1032	1146	1232	1317	1346	|	1432	1546	1632	1732	1746	1832	1902	1932	1946	2032	2146	2232	2332	...	...
Niederlahnstein **906** d.	0553	0653	0739	0839	0953	1039	1153	1239	1324	1353	1353	1439	1553	1639	1739	1753	1839	1909	1939	1953	2039	2153	2239	2339	...	...
Koblenz Hbf **906** a.	0600	0701	0746	0846	1001	1046	1201	1246	1331	1401	1401	1446	1601	1646	1746	1801	1846	1918	1946	2001	2046	2201	2246	2346	...	...

Koblenz - Bingen - Mainz - Frankfurt (*Linke Rheinstrecke*) ⊠

km		Ⓐe	⚒h	Ⓐe		⚒r															Ⓐe	◇		n◐	n	n
0	**Koblenz** Hbf d.	0448	0551	0607	0651	0707	0751	0851	0902	0951	1051	1102	1151	1251	1302	1351	1451	1502	1551	1651	1702	1751	1851	1951	2051	2151
19	Boppard Hbf d.	0504	0607	0621	0707	0721	0807	0907	0921	1007	1107	1121	1207	1307	1321	1407	1507	1521	1607	1707	1721	1807	1907	2007	2107	2207
24	Boppard-Bad Salzig d.	0508	0611	|	0711	|	0811	0911	|	1011	1111	|	1211	1311	|	1411	1511	|	1611	1711	|	1811	1911	2011	2111	2211
34	St Goar d.	0517	0620	|	0720	|	0820	0920	|	1020	1120	|	1220	1320	|	1420	1520	|	1620	1720	|	1820	1920	2020	2120	2220
41	Oberwesel d.	0523	0626	0635	0726	0735	0826	0926	0935	1026	1126	1135	1226	1326	1335	1426	1526	1535	1626	1726	1735	1826	1926	2026	2126	2226
47	Bacharach d.	0528	0631	|	0731	|	0831	0931	|	1031	1131	|	1231	1331	|	1431	1531	|	1631	1731	|	1831	1931	2031	2131	2231
61	Bingen (Rhein) Hbf a.	0541	0644	0647	0744	0747	0844	0944	0947	1044	1144	1147	1244	1344	1347	1444	1544	1547	1644	1744	1747	1844	1943	2044	2144	2244
61	Bingen (Rhein) Hbf d.	0542	0652	0648	0752	0748	0855	0952	0948	1055	1155	1148	1255	1352	1348	1455	1552	1548	1655	1752	1748	1852	1944	2052	2158	2252
62	Bingen (Rhein) Stadt d.	0545	0655	|	0755	|	0858	0955	|	1058	1158	|	1258	1355	|	1458	1555	|	1658	1755	|	1855	1946	2055	2201	2255
73	Ingelheim d.	0555	0707	0656	0807	0756	0910	1007	0956	1110	1210	1156	1310	1407	1356	1510	1607	1556	1710	1807	1756	1907	1958	2107	2213	2307
91	**Mainz** Hbf d.	0610	0727	0710	0828	0810	0929	1027	1010	1129	1229	1210	1329	1427	1410	1529	1627	1610	1729	1827	1810	1927	2021	2127	2233	2327
119	Frankfurt Flughafen ‡ a.	0634	...	0735	0851e	0834	...	...	1036	...	...	1236	...	...	1436	...	...	1634	...	...	1836	...	...	...	...	...
130	**Frankfurt** (Main) Hbf a.	0649	...	0751	0904e	0849	...	...	1049	...	...	1249	...	...	1449	...	...	1649	...	...	1849	...	...	...	...	...

	⚒r		Ⓐe		⊖	⚒r		⊡									Ⓒb¶	Ⓐe			Ⓒzb	Ⓐe		n	n	⑤⑥
Frankfurt (Main) Hbf d.	...	...	0706	...	...	0908	...	...	1108	...	...	1308	...	...	1508	...	...	1608	1708	1658e	...	1808	1858e	...	...	
Frankfurt Flughafen ‡ d.	...	...	0720	...	...	0923	...	...	1123	...	...	1323	...	...	1523	...	...	1623	1723	1709e	...	1823	1909e	...	...	
Mainz Hbf d.	0530e	0624	0751	0724	0830	0951	0930	1030	1151	1130	1230	1351	1330	1430	1551	1530	1630	1652	1751	1730	1830	1852	1930	2030	2130	2330
Ingelheim d.	0549e	0643	0803	0743	0847	1003	0949	1049	1203	1149	1247	1403	1348	1447	1603	1549	1647	|	1803	1749	1847	1904	1949	2049	2149	2349
Bingen (Rhein) Stadt d.	0601e	0657	|	0803	0859	|	1003	1103	|	1203	1305	|	1401	1459	|	1603	1659	|	|	1803	1859	|	2001	2107	2203	0000
Bingen (Rhein) Hbf a.	0604e	0659	0811	0806	0903	1011	1006	1106	1211	1206	1308	1411	1403	1501	1611	1606	1701	1712	1811	1806	1901	1912	2004	2110	2206	0003
Bingen (Rhein) Hbf d.	0608	0709	0811	0814	0909	1011	1014	1109	1211	1214	1309	1411	1414	1511	1611	1614	1709	1713	1811	1814	1914	1913	2009	2110	2209	0011
Bacharach d.	0620	0721	|	0826	0921	|	1026	1121	|	1226	1321	|	1426	1524	|	1626	1721	1725	|	1826	1926	1925	2021	2122	2221	0023
Oberwesel d.	0625	0726	0823	0831	0926	1023	1031	1126	1223	1231	1326	1423	1431	1529	1623	1631	1726	1730	1823	1831	1931	1930	2026	2127	2226	0028
St Goar d.	0631	0732	|	0837	0932	|	1037	1132	|	1237	1332	|	1437	1535	|	1637	1732	1736	|	1837	1937	1936	2032	2133	2232	0034
Boppard-Bad Salzig d.	0640	0741	|	0846	0941	|	1046	1141	|	1246	1341	|	1446	1543	|	1646	1741	1744	|	1846	1946	1944	2041	2142	2241	0043
Boppard Hbf d.	0645	0746	0838	0850	0946	1038	1050	1146	1238	1250	1346	1438	1450	1548	1638	1650	1746	1750	1838	1850	1950	1950	2046	2146	2246	0047
Koblenz Hbf a.	0702	0803	0852	0907	1003	1052	1107	1203	1252	1307	1403	1452	1507	1605	1652	1707	1803	1807	1852	1907	2007	2007	2103	2203	2303	0104

b – Runs daily Mainz - Bingen Hbf.
e – Ⓐ (not Dec. 24, 31, May 22).
h – ⚒ (not May 22); runs daily Bingen Hbf - Mainz.
n – Not Dec. 24, 31.
r – Not May 22.
w – Also May 22.
z – Also Dec. 24, 31, May 22.

◇ – Runs 2–3 minutes later Bingen Hbf - Mainz on ⑤⑦ (also Dec. 26, Jan. 1, Mar. 20, 24, Apr. 30, May 12).
◐ – Runs 2–3 minutes later Bingen Hbf - Mainz on ⑦ (also Dec. 26, Jan. 1, Mar. 24, May 12).
⊡ – Runs 4–5 minutes later Bingen Hbf - Koblenz on ⑦ (also Dec. 26, Jan. 1, Mar. 24, May 12; not Dec. 23, 30, Mar. 23, May 11).

⊖ – Runs 4–5 minutes later Bingen Hbf - Koblenz on Ⓐe.
¶ – Runs 4–5 minutes later Bingen Hbf - Koblenz from May 17.
* – Underground platforms.
‡ – Frankfurt Flughafen Regionalbahnhof ✈.
⊠ – See Table **912** for long-distance *EC / IC / ICE* services. See Table **917a** for other S-Bahn services Mainz - Frankfurt Flughafen ✈ - Frankfurt (Main) Hbf and v.v.

914a ⛴ KÖLN - KOBLENZ - MAINZ

2008 service; KD (see shaded panel)

◐		A	A⛴	K	D	B	D	①E	A	D	G
750	**Köln** (Rheingarten) d.	...	...	...	...	...	...	...	...	0930	0930
1600	**Bonn** d.							0800	...	1230	1230
1300	Bad Godesberg d.							0830	...	1300	1300
900	Königswinter Fähre d.	...	...	...	...	...	...	0845	...	1330	1330
750	Bad Honnef (Rhein) d.	...	...	...	...	...	...	0905	...	1350	1350
400	Remagen d.	...	...	...	...	...	...	0940	...	1420	1420
750	Linz am Rhein d.	...	...	...	...	...	...	1000	...	1450	1450
1500	Bad Breisig d.	...	...	...	0800	...	...	1030	...	1520t	▬
400	Bad Hönningen d.	...	...	...	0805	...	...	1035	...	1525t	...
1200	Andernach d.	...	...	...	0850	...	...	1120	...	...	...
1500	Neuwied d.	...	...	...	0910	...	...	1140	...	...	...
2200	**Koblenz** ⊙ a.	...	...	...	1040	...	...	1300	...	...	L
2200	**Koblenz** ⊙ d.	...	0900	0945	1100	...	...	1310	1400	...	1810
600	Winningen (Mosel) a.	...	|	1055	|	...	...	1420	|	...	|
800	Cochem (Mosel) a.	...	|	1500	|	...	...	...	|	...	|
750	Niederlahnstein d.	...	0930	...	1130	...	...	...	1430	...	1835
150	Oberlahnstein d.	...	0940	...	1140	...	...	...	1440	...	1845
450	Braubach d.	...	1005	...	1205	...	...	...	1505	...	1910
400	**Boppard** d.	0900	1100	...	1300	...	1400	...	1600	...	2000
400	Kamp-Bornhofen d.	0910	1110	...	1310	...	1410	...	1610	...	...
300	Bad Salzig d.	0925	1125	...	1325	...	1425	...	1625	...	...
450	**St Goarshausen** ★ d.	1010	1210	...	1410	1410	1510	...	1710	...	...
250	**St Goar** ★ d.	1020	1220	...	1420	1420	1520	...	1720	...	...
450	Oberwesel d.	1050	1250	...	1450	1450	1550	...	1750	...	...
900	Kaub d.	1105	1305	...	1505	1505	1605	...	1805	...	...
600	Bacharach d.	1130	1330	...	1530	1530	1630	...	1830	...	...
900	Assmannshausen d.	1230	1430	...	1630	1630	1730	...	1930	...	...
400	**Bingen** (Rhein) d.	1300	1500	...	1700	1700	1800	...	2000	...	...
900	**Rüdesheim** (Rhein) d.	1315	1515	...	1715	1715	1815	...	2015	...	...
1500	Wiesbaden-Biebrich d.	...	...	...	1905	1905z	2005r	...	...	...	...
1600	**Mainz** (Am Rathaus) a.	...	...	...	1930	1930z	2030r	...	...	...	...

A special service operates on "Rhein in Flammen" days

	J	A	D‡	①E	D	B	L	B	K	A⛴
Mainz (Am Rathaus) d.	...	...	0845	...	0945r	0945z	...	...	...	...
Wiesbaden-Biebrich d.	...	...	0905	...	1005r	1005z	...	...	...	...
Rüdesheim (Rhein) d.	...	0915	1015	...	1115	1115	1415	1415	...	1615
Bingen (Rhein) d.	...	0930	1030	...	1130	1130	1430	1430	...	1630
Assmannshausen d.	...	0945	1045	...	1145	1145	1445	1445	...	1645
Bacharach d.	...	1015	1115	...	1215	1215	1515	1515	...	1715
Kaub d.	...	1025	1125	...	1225	1225	1525	1525	...	1725
Oberwesel d.	...	1035	1135	...	1235	1235	1535	1535	...	1735
St Goar ★ d.	...	1055	1155	...	1255	1255	1555	1555	...	1755
St Goarshausen ★ d.	...	1105	1205	...	1305	1305	1605	1605	...	1805
Bad Salzig d.	...	1130	1230	...	1330	...	1630	1630	...	1830
Kamp-Bornhofen d.	...	1140	1240	...	1340	...	1640	1640	...	1840
Boppard d.	...	1150	1250	...	1350	...	1650	1650	...	1850
Braubach d.	...	1220	1320	...	...	...	1720	...	...	1920
Oberlahnstein d.	...	1240	1340	...	...	...	1740	...	...	1940
Niederlahnstein d.	...	1250	1350	...	...	...	1750	...	...	1950
Cochem (Mosel) d.	...	|	|	...	...	...	|	...	1540	|
Winningen (Mosel) d.	...	|	|	1600	...	...	|	...	1845	|
Koblenz ⊙ a.	...	1310	1410	1700	...	...	1810	...	2000	2010
Koblenz ⊙ d.	...	...	1430	1705	...	...	...	...	...	...
Neuwied d.	...	...	1520	1750	...	...	...	...	...	...
Andernach d.	...	...	1540	1805	...	...	...	...	...	...
Bad Hönningen d.	...	...	1615‡	1830	...	...	...	...	...	...
Bad Breisig d.	...	...	1620	1840						
Linz am Rhein d.	1450	...	1650	1905						
Remagen d.	1500	...	1700	1915						
Bad Honnef (Rhein) d.	1525	...	1725	1940						
Königswinter Fähre d.	1540	...	1740	2000						
Bad Godesberg d.	1545	...	1745	2010						
Bonn d.	1615	...	1815	2030						
Köln (Rheingarten) a.	1800	...	2000	...						

Köln-Düsseldorfer Deutsche Rheinschiffahrt AG, Frankenwerft 35, D-50667 Köln.
✆ +49 (0) 221 20 88 319
Fax +49 (0) 221 20 88 345

A – Mar. 21 - Oct. 26.
B – Mar. 21 - Apr. 25 and Oct. 6 – 26.
D – Apr. 26 - Oct. 5.
E – ① May 26 - Sept. 29.
G – ①⑤⑥⑦ Mar. 21 - Apr. 25; ①⑤⑥⑦ Oct. 6 – 26.
J – ①⑤⑥⑦ Mar. 21 - Apr. 26; ⑤⑥ May 2 - Oct. 4; ①⑤⑥⑦ Oct. 6 – 26.
K – ①⑤⑥⑦ Apr. 26 - June 10; daily June 20 - Oct. 5.

L – ①⑤⑥⑦ Mar. 21 - Apr. 21; daily Apr. 25 - Oct. 6; ①⑤⑥⑦ Oct. 10 – 26.
r – July and August only.
t – ①②③④⑦ only.
z – ①⑤⑥⑦ only.

⛴ – Operated by paddlesteamer *Goethe* Apr. 26 - Oct. 5.
⊙ – Koblenz (Konrad-Adenauer-Ufer).
‡ – Change ships at Bad Hönningen on ①②③④⑦.
◐ – Distance in metres from rail station to river landing stage.
★ – A passenger ferry links St Goar and St Goarshausen. Frequent trips 0600 (0800 on †) to 2100 (2300 May 1 - Sept. 30). Operator: Rheinschiffahrt Goar. ✆ + 49 (0) 6771 26 20. Fax + 49 (0) 6771 24 04.

KOBLENZ - TRIER - LUXEMBOURG and SAARBRÜCKEN — 915

RE / RB services except where shown

km																					IC 438				
			⑥p	Ⓐt	Ⓐt	Ⓐt K	Ⓐt	N	K	Ⓐt	⚒r	⚒r			Ⓐt M	⑥p	⚒r				①–⑥ e🍷				K
	Norddeich Mole 812	d.	...	...	...	...	...	...	...	...	...	...	...	...	...	...	...	...	...	...	...	...	...	...	...
	Emden Hbf 812	d.	...	...	...	...	...	...	...	...	...	...	...	...	...	...	...	...	...	...	...	...	...	...	...
	Münster (Westf) Hbf 800	d.	...	...	...	...	...	...	...	...	...	...	...	...	...	...	...	...	...	...	0631	...	...	...	...
	Köln Hbf 800 802	d.	...	...	...	...	...	...	...	...	...	...	...	...	...	...	...	...	...	...	0818	...	...	...	...
0	**Koblenz** Hbf	d.	...	...	...	...	...	...	...	...	...	0559	...	...	0622	0631	0722	...	0731	0822	0924	...	0931	1022	1122
47	Cochem (Mosel)	d.	...	...	...	...	...	...	...	0540	...	0634	...	...	0724	0724	0758	...	0824	0858	0958	...	1024	1058	1158
59	Bullay ◧	d.	...	...	...	...	...	...	...	0554	...	0643	...	...	0735	0735	0807	...	0835	0907	1008	...	1035	1107	1207
76	Wittlich Hbf	d.	...	...	...	...	0515	...	...	0609	...	0656	...	...	0750	0750	0820	...	0850	0920	1023	...	1050	1120	1220
112	**Trier** Hbf	a.	...	...	...	...	0552	...	...	0647	...	0728	...	...	0830	0830	0847	...	0930	0947	1049	...	1130	1147	1247
112	**Trier** Hbf ⊙	d.	0357	0413	0524	0529	...	0621	0636t	...	0701	0730	0730	0801r	0834	...	...	0901	...	0949	1056	1101	...	1149	1249
	Luxembourg ⊙	a.	|	|	|	|	...	|	|	...	|	|	|	|	|	...	...	|	...	|	1139	|	...	|	|
135	Saarburg	d.	0422	0433	0542	0554	...	0640	0703t	...	0726	0748	0748	0826r	0853	...	...	0926	...	1007	...	1126	...	1207	1307
161	Merzig (Saar)	d.	0449	0451	0600	0621	...	0701	0729	...	0751	0808	0808	0851	0911	...	...	0951	...	1026	...	1151	...	1226	1329
173	Dillingen (Saar)	d.	0500	0502	0610	0632	...	0710	0738	...	0802	0816	0816	0902	0919	...	...	1002	...	1034	...	1202	...	1234	1340
177	Saarlouis Hbf	d.	0504	0506	0614	0635	...	0714	0741	...	0805	0820	0820	0905	0923	...	...	1005	...	1038	...	1205	...	1238	1343
190	Völklingen	d.	0515	0518	0625	0645	...	0722	0750	...	0816	0830	0830	0916	0931	...	...	1016	...	1046	...	1216	...	1246	1351
200	**Saarbrücken** Hbf	a.	0528	0529	0634	0656	...	0731	0759	...	0827	0840	0840	0927	0939	...	...	1027	...	1054	...	1227	...	1254	1400

			IC 436					IC 434				IC 432					IC 430						ICE 856		
			🍷		Ⓒz	Ⓐt		🍷	L			Ⓑq 🍷	Ⓐt K				🍷	Ⓐt K	n	n	n	n	✖B	n	⑤⑥† s
Norddeich Mole 812	d.	...	...	...	...	...	...	0954	...	...	...	1136	...	...	...	...	1354	...	...	...	...	...	...	...	...
Emden Hbf 812	d.	...	0834	...	...	...	...	1034	...	...	...	1234	...	...	...	...	1434	...	...	...	...	...	...	...	...
Münster (Westf) Hbf 800	d.	...	1032	...	...	...	...	1232	...	...	...	1431	...	...	...	...	1631	...	...	...	...	...	...	...	...
Köln Hbf 800 802	d.	...	1218	...	...	...	...	1418	...	...	...	1618	...	...	...	...	1818	...	...	...	...	...	2009	...	...
Koblenz Hbf	d.	1222	1324	...	1331	1335	1422	1524	...	1531	1622	1724	...	...	1731	1822	1924	...	...	1931	2022	...	2123	2222	2318
Cochem (Mosel)	d.	1258	1358	...	1424	1426	1458	1558	...	1624	1658	1758	...	...	1824	1858	1958	...	...	2024	2058	...	2158	2258	0009
Bullay ◧	d.	1307	1408	...	1435	1437	1507	1608	...	1635	1707	1808	...	...	1835	1907	2008	...	...	2035	2107	...	2208	2307	0022
Wittlich Hbf	d.	1320	1423	...	1450	1452	1520	1623	...	1650	1720	1823	...	...	1850	1920	2023	...	...	2050	2120	...	2223	2320	0038
Trier Hbf	a.	1347	1449	...	1530	1532	1547	1649	...	1730	1747	1849	...	...	1930	1947	2049	...	...	2130	2147	...	2253	2352	0116
Trier Hbf ⊙	d.	1349	1456	1501	...	...	1549	1656	1654	...	1749	1851	1854	1901	...	1949	2051	2055	2101	...	2149	2253	...	...	...
Luxembourg ⊙	a.	|	1539	|	...	...	|	1743	|	...	|	1934	|	|	...	|	2134	|	|	...	|	|	...	...	...
Saarburg	d.	1407	...	1526	...	...	1607	...	1712	...	1807	...	1912	1926	...	2007	...	2114	2126	...	2207	2319	...	...	...
Merzig (Saar)	d.	1426	...	1551	...	...	1626	...	1729	...	1826	...	1929	1951	...	2026	...	2131	2151	...	2226	2343	...	...	...
Dillingen (Saar)	d.	1434	...	1602	...	...	1634	...	1737	...	1834	...	1937	2002	...	2034	...	2138	2202	...	2234	2352	...	...	...
Saarlouis Hbf	d.	1438	...	1605	...	...	1638	...	1740	...	1838	...	1940	2005	...	2038	...	2142	2205	...	2238	2356	...	...	...
Völklingen	d.	1446	...	1616	...	...	1646	...	1748	...	1846	...	1948	2016	...	2046	...	2149	2216	...	2246	0005	...	...	...
Saarbrücken Hbf	a.	1454	...	1627	...	...	1654	...	1756	...	1854	...	1956	2027	...	2054	...	2200	2227	...	2254	0014	...	...	...

				ICE 855						IC 431§					IC 433				IC 435						IC 437
		Ⓐt		✖B	Ⓐt	v	Ⓐt	Ⓒz	Ⓐt	①–⑥ e🍷	v	⚒r		v	🍷			K	🍷			K		K	🍷
Saarbrücken Hbf	d.	...	...	...	0434	...	0522	0535	0550	...	...	0625	0703	0733	...	...	0905	1001	...	...	1105	1201	1303	1401	...
Völklingen	d.	...	...	...	0441	...	0532	0542	0557	...	...	0635	0710	0743	...	...	0912	1008	...	...	1112	1208	1310	1408	...
Saarlouis Hbf	d.	...	...	...	0450	...	0542	0551	0608	...	...	0646	0719	0753	...	...	0921	1016	...	...	1121	1218	1319	1416	...
Dillingen (Saar)	d.	...	...	...	0453	...	0545	0555	0611	...	...	0649	0722	0757	...	...	0924	1019	...	...	1124	1222	1322	1419	...
Merzig (Saar)	d.	...	...	...	0507	...	0556	0603	0621	...	...	0700	0731	0807	...	...	0933	1027	...	...	1133	1231	1331	1427	...
Saarburg	d.	...	...	...	0533	...	0621	0633	0642	...	...	0727	0750	0833	...	...	0951	1045	...	...	1151	1250	1350	1445	...
Luxembourg ⊙	d.	...	...	...	|	...	|	|	|	0620	...	|	|	|	0824	...	|	|	1024	...	|	|	|	|	1424
Trier Hbf ⊙	a.	...	...	...	0559	...	0648	0659	0702	0707	...	0758	0810	0859	0907	...	1010	1104	1107	...	1210	1310	1410	1504	1507
Trier Hbf	d.	0355	...	0500	...	0612	...	...	...	0709	0721	...	0812	...	0909	0921	1012	...	1109	1121	1212	1312	1412	...	1509
Wittlich Hbf	d.	0418	...	0525	...	0636	...	...	...	0734	0758	...	0836	...	0934	0958	1036	...	1134	1158	1236	1336	1436	...	1534
Bullay ◧	d.	0431	...	0540	...	0650	...	...	...	0749	0814	...	0850	...	0949	1014	1050	...	1149	1214	1250	1350	1450	...	1549
Cochem (Mosel)	d.	0440	...	0551	...	0659	...	...	...	0759	0825	...	0859	...	0959	1025	1059	...	1159	1225	1259	1359	1459	...	1559
Koblenz Hbf	a.	0520	...	0629	...	0738	...	...	...	0835	0920	...	0938	...	1035	1120	1138	...	1235	1320	1339	1437	1538	...	1635
Köln Hbf 800 802	a.	...	...	0742	...	...	...	...	...	0942	...	...	...	...	1142	...	...	...	1342	...	...	...	...	...	1742
Münster (Westf) Hbf 800	a.	...	...	...	...	...	...	...	...	1127	...	...	...	...	1327	...	...	...	1529	...	...	...	...	...	1929
Emden Hbf 812	a.	...	...	...	...	...	...	...	...	1325	...	...	...	...	1525	...	...	...	1725	...	...	...	...	...	2125
Norddeich Mole 812	a.	...	...	...	...	...	...	...	...	1404g	...	...	...	...	1604	...	...	...	1804	...	...	...	...	...	...

						IC 439																			
					Ⓐt K	Ⓑq D🍷		Ⓐt M			K	†s K	Ⓑn				n	n		n	⑤f	n	⑥⑦	n	Ⓑn
Saarbrücken Hbf	d.	...	1505	1533	1601	...	...	1619	1633	1703	1801	1801	...	...	1905	2003	...	2033	2116	...	2116	2234	...	2319	2344
Völklingen	d.	...	1512	1543	1608	...	...	1626	1643	1710	1808	1808	...	...	1912	2010	...	2043	2123	...	2123	2241	...	2329	2354
Saarlouis Hbf	d.	...	1521	1553	1616	...	...	1638	1653	1719	1816	1816	...	...	1921	2020	...	2053	2131	...	2131	2251	...	2339	0006
Dillingen (Saar)	d.	...	1524	1557	1619	...	...	1641	1657	1722	1819	1819	...	...	1924	2024	...	2057	2135	...	2135	2254	...	2343	0009
Merzig (Saar)	d.	...	1533	1607	1627	...	...	1651	1707	1731	1827	1827	...	...	1933	2033	...	2107	2144	...	2144	2304	...	2352	0020
Saarburg	d.	...	1551	1633	1645	...	...	1716	1733	1750	1846	1846	...	...	1952	2054	...	2133	2205	...	2205	2326	...	...	0041
Luxembourg ⊙	d.	...	|	|	|	1624	...	|	|	|	|	|	...	...	|	|	...	|	|	...	|	|	...	...	|
Trier Hbf ⊙	a.	...	1610	1659	1704	1707	...	1744	1759	1810	1907	1907	...	...	2011	2116	...	2159	2227	...	2227	2352	...	...	0101
Trier Hbf	d.	1521	1612	...	...	1709	1721	...	...	1812	...	1912	1912	1921	2012n	...	2131	...	...	2242	2242	...	0001	...	...
Wittlich Hbf	d.	1558	1636	...	...	1734	1758	...	...	1836	...	1936	1936	1958	2036n	...	2206	...	...	2319	2319	...	0038	...	...
Bullay ◧	d.	1614	1650	...	...	1749	1814	...	...	1850	...	1950	1950	2014	2050n	...	2218	...	...	2335	2335	...	0053	...	...
Cochem (Mosel)	d.	1625	1659	...	...	1759	1825	...	...	1859	...	1959	1959	2025	2059n	...	2227	...	...	2347	2348	...	0107	...	...
Koblenz Hbf	a.	1720	1738	...	...	1835	1920	...	...	1938	...	2038	2038	2120n	2138n	...	2306	...	...	...	0042	...	...	...	...
Köln Hbf 800 802	a.	...	...	...	...	1942	...	...	...	...	...	...	...	...	...	...	...	...	...	...	...	...	...	...	...
Münster (Westf) Hbf 800	a.	...	...	...	...	...	...	...	...	...	...	...	...	...	...	...	...	...	...	...	...	...	...	...	...
Emden Hbf 812	a.	...	...	...	...	...	...	...	...	...	...	...	...	...	...	...	...	...	...	...	...	...	...	...	...
Norddeich Mole 812	a.	...	...	...	...	...	...	...	...	...	...	...	...	...	...	...	...	...	...	...	...	...	...	...	...

Complete service Trier - Luxembourg and v.v.

km	🛃 at Igel		①–⑤ d	①–⑤ d	①–⑥ d	⑦ w	①–⑤ d				①–⑥ e‡				‡		‡	①–⑤ d		Ⓑ q‡	⑥ m		‡	n	①–⑤ a	n
0	**Trier** Hbf	d.	0534	0624	0641	0707	0724	0752	0857	0952	1056	1152	1257	1352	1456	1552	1656	1726	1752	1851	1857	1952	2051	2152	2257	2357
51	**Luxembourg**	a.	0633	0717	0745	0808	0817	0845	0941	1045	1139	1245	1345	1445	1539	1645	1743	1815	1845x	1934	1941	2041	2134	2241	2341	0041

🛃 at Wasserbillig		①–⑤ d	①–⑥ e‡	①–⑤ d		‡		‡				‡		Ⓑ q‡	⑥ m	①–⑤ d	⑥⑦ w	①–⑤ d	①–⑤ d	⑥⑦ w	①–⑤ d		n	n	①–⑤ a	n
Luxembourg	d.	0517	0620	0635	0717	0824	0917	1024	1117	1217	1317	1424	1517	1624	1624	1715	1717	1741	1815	1817	1841	1915y	2017	2115y	2152	2252
Trier Hbf	a.	0606	0707	0734	0806	0907	1006	1107	1206	1306	1406	1507	1606	1707	1707	1804	1806	1832	1904	1904	1932	2006	2106	2206	2256	2356

◧ – **BULLAY - TRABEN-TRARBACH** and v.v. *13 km* Journey time: 19 minutes. **Operator**: Trans Regio Deutsche Regionalbahn GmbH.
From Bullay at 0550⚒r, 0705⚒r, 0817, 0917 and hourly until 1917n, 2017n, 2117n. **From Traben-Trarbach** at 0621⚒r, 0745⚒r, 0845, 0945 and hourly until 1945n, 2045n, 2145n.

B – 🚌(12) Trier - Hannover - Berlin and v.v.
D – To Dortmund (Table 800).
K – To / from Kaiserslautern (Table 919).
L – To Kaiserslautern (Table 919) on ⚒r.
M – To / from Mannheim (Table 919).
N – To Mannheim (Table 919) on Ⓐt.
a – Not Dec. 24, 25, 26, 31, Jan. 1, Mar. 24, May 1, 12.
d – Not Dec. 25, 26, Jan. 1, Mar. 24, May 1, 12.
e – Not Dec. 25, 26, Jan. 1, Mar. 22, 24, May 12.
f – Not Mar. 21.
g – ①②③④⑥ Dec. 10 - Mar. 13 (not Dec. 20, 22, 25, 26, 27, 29, Jan. 1, 2, 3, 5).
m – Also Dec. 24, 25, 31, Mar. 21, 23, May 11.
n – Not Dec. 24, 31.
p – Also Dec. 24, 31.
q – Not Dec. 24, 25, 31, Mar. 21, 23, May 11.
r – ⚒ (not May 22).
s – Also May 22.
t – Ⓐ (not Dec. 24, 31, May 22).
v – Not Dec. 25, Jan. 1.
w – Also Dec. 25, 26, Jan. 1, Mar. 24, May 1, 12.
x – 1853 May 5 - June 1.
y – 3 minutes earlier May 5 - June 1.
z – Also Dec. 24, 31, May 22.
⊙ – See also panel below main table.
‡ – *IC* train (see main Table).
§ – Train number **331** on ①②③④⑥ Dec. 10 - Mar. 13 (not Dec. 20, 22, 25, 26, 27, 29, Jan. 1, 2, 3, 5).

916 KARLSRUHE - OFFENBURG - KONSTANZ

IRE / RE services except where shown

km													IC 2005 ⑤⑥ 🍷N				IC 2371 🍷B	IC 2364 ①–⑤ d S					†w	⚒r ◐	R
			⚒r	Ⓐe	Ⓒz																				
0	**Karlsruhe** Hbf **912 943**	d.	...	...	0500k	0608	0704	0810	0910	1010	1110	1210	1310	1338	1410	1510	1610	1714	1734	1810	1910	...	2010	2116	2116	2221
23	Rastatt **943**	d.	...	...	0513k	0619	0719	0823	0923	1023	1123	1223	1323	|	1423	1523	1623	1728	1747	1823	1923	...	2023	2129	2129	2240
31	Baden-Baden **912**	d.	...	...	0519k	0626	0727	0830	0930	1030	1130	1230	1330	1356	1430	1530	1630	1735	1754	1830	1930	...	2030	2136	2136	2247
71	**Offenburg 912 942**	d.	...	0523	0554k	0658	0759	0859	0959	1059	1159	1259	1359	1418	1459	1559	1659	1753	1813	1859	1959	...	2104	2205	2205	2323j
104	Hausach **942**	d.	...	0548	0619k	0723	0818	0921	1018	1121	1218	1321	1418	1439	1521	1618	1721	1813	...	1921	2018	...	2128	2229	2229	2348
114	Hornberg (Schwarzw)	d.	...	0556	0627k	0731	0826	0930	1026	1129	1225	1330	1426	1448	1530	1626	1730	1821	...	1930	2026	...	2136	2236	2236	2356
127	Triberg	d.	...	0609	0640k	0744	0839	0944	1039	1144	1238	1344	1439	1503	1544	1639	1744	1835	...	1944	2039	...	2149	2249	2249	0009
142	St Georgen (Schwarzw)	d.	...	0625	0655k	0759	0854	0958	1054	1158	1253	1359	1454	1520	1559	1654	1759	1850	...	1959	2054	...	2203	2303	2303	0023
157	Villingen (Schwarzw) **938**	d.	0553	0636	0705	0808	0904	1009	1104	1209	1303	1409	1504	1532	1609	1704	1809	1901	...	2009	2104	...	2213	2312	2312	0032
171	Donaueschingen **938**	d.	0603	0654j	0714	0818	0913	1018	1113	1218	1313	1419	1513	1543	1618	1713	1819	1913	...	2019	2113	...	2222	2322	2326	...
190	Immendingen **938**	d.	0619	0706	0726	0828	|	1029	|	1229	|	1429	|	|	1629	|	1829	|	...	2029	2124	...	2234	2334	2339	...
206	Engen **940**	d.	0633	0719	0738	0841	|	1042	|	1242	|	1442	|	|	1642	|	1842	|	...	2042	|	2149	2247	|	...	...
220	**Singen 940**	a.	0645	0733	0748	0850	0943	1050	1143	1250	1343	1450	1543	1615	1650	1743	1850	1943	...	2050	2143	2202	2300	2353	...	...
220	**Singen 939**	d.	0651	0735	0752	0853	0953	1053	1153	1253	1353	1453	1553	1618	1653	1753	1853	1953	...	2053	2155b	2212	2301	2354	...	...
230	Radolfzell **939**	d.	0703	0746	0800	0900	1000	1100	1200	1300	1400	1500	1600	1628	1700	1800	1900	2001	...	2100	2202b	2222	2308	0001	...	...
250	**Konstanz**	a.	0725	0810	0816	0916	1016	1116	1216	1316	1416	1516	1616	1644	1716	1816	1916	2015	...	2116	2217b	2245	2327	0016	...	...

		IC 2365 ①–⑤ d S	⚒r	⚒r	⚒r		◐			IC 2004 ⑦ 🍷E	IC 2006 ⑥ 🍷D	IC 2370 ¶ 🍷A									†w			⑤f	g
Konstanz	d.	...	...	0441	0502e	0526r	0638	0735	0838	0909	0909	0938	1038	1138	1238	1338	1438	1538	1638	1738	1838	1938	2038	2124	2124	2321
Radolfzell **939**	d.	...	...	0503	0516e	0541r	0657	0758j	0855	0924	0924	0957j	1055	1158j	1255	1358j	1455	1558j	1655	1758j	1855	1958j	2055	2147	2147	2347
Singen 939	a.	...	...	0512	0522e	0547r	0704	0805	0902	0932	0932	1004	1102	1205	1302	1405	1502	1605	1702	1805	1902	2005	2102	2156	2156	2356
Singen 940	d.	...	...	0516	0530	0558	0706	0816	0905	0940	0940	1015	1105	1216	1305	1416	1505	1616	1705	1816	1905	2016	2105	2157	2157	0000
Engen **940**	d.	...	...	0529	0539	|	0716	|	0914	|	|	|	1114	|	1314	|	1514	|	1714	|	1914	|	2114	2211	2211	0013
Immendingen **938**	d.	...	...	...	0552	0620	0729	|	0928	|	|	|	1128	|	1328	|	1528	|	1728	|	1928	|	2127	2224	2224	—
Donaueschingen **938**	d.	...	0505	...	0603	0630	0741	0845	0939	1015	1015	1045	1139	1245	1339	1445	1539	1645	1739	1845	1939	2045	2139	2237	2237	...
Villingen (Schwarzw) **938**	d.	...	0535	...	0612	0641	0751	0855	0949	1026	1026	1055	1149	1255	1349	1455	1549	1655	1749	1855	1949	2055	2149	2248	2253	...
St Georgen (Schwarzw)	d.	...	0544	...	0620	0650	0800	0903	0958	1036	1036	1104	1158	1303	1358	1503	1558	1703	1758	1903	1958	2103	2158	—	2302	...
Triberg	d.	...	0558	...	0635	0705	0814	0918	1012	1052	1052	1120	1212	1318	1412	1518	1612	1718	1812	1918	2012	2118	2212	...	2316	ICE
Hornberg (Schwarzw)	d.	...	0612	...	0648	0718	0829	0928	1024	1107	1107	1134	1224	1328	1424	1528	1624	1728	1827	1928	2024	2131	2227	...	2331	808
Hausach **942**	d.	...	0621	...	0657	0727	0837	0939	1035	1116	1116	1143	1235	1339	1435	1539	1635	1739	1835	1939	2035	2139	2235	...	2339	
Offenburg 912 942	d.	0558	0657j	...	0718	0752	0902t	1002	1102	1139	1139	1204	1302	1402	1502	1602	1702	1802	1902	2002	2102	2202	2300	2323	0004	0049
Baden-Baden **912**	d.	0617	0724	...	...	0819	0928t	1028	1128	1202	1202	1221	1328	1428	1528	1628	1728	1828	1928	2028	2128	2228	...	2347	...	0113
Rastatt **943**	d.	0624	0731	...	...	0826	0934t	1034	1134	|	|	1229	1334	1434	1534	1634	1734	1834	1934	2034	2134	2234	...	2353	...	|
Karlsruhe Hbf **912 943**	a.	0635	0748	...	...	0839	0948t	1048	1148	1219	1219	1242	1348	1448	1548	1648	1748	1848	1948	2048	2148	2248	...	0005	...	0131

A – SCHWARZWALD – 🚃 Konstanz - Frankfurt - Hamburg (- Stralsund ⑤⑦ **h**).
B – SCHWARZWALD – 🚃 Hamburg - Frankfurt - Konstanz.
D – ⑥ (also Dec. 23, 25, 30, 31, Mar. 23, May 11). BODENSEE – 🚃 Konstanz - Karlsruhe - Köln - Dortmund.
E – ⑦ (also Dec. 26, Jan. 1, Mar. 21, 24, May 1, 12, 22; not Dec. 23, 30, Mar. 23, May 11). BODENSEE – 🚃 Konstanz - Karlsruhe - Köln - Münster - Emden.
N – ⑤⑥ (also Dec. 24, 25, 30, 31, Mar. 20, 23, Apr. 30, May 11, 21). BODENSEE – 🚃 Emden - Münster - Köln - Karlsruhe - Konstanz. On Dec. 24, 25, 30, 31, Mar. 23, May 11 runs with train number **2007** and starts from Dortmund (Table **800**).

R – ⑤ (not May 21); runs daily Karlsruhe - Hausach.
S – To / from Stuttgart (Table **930**).
b – Ⓑ (not Dec. 24, 31).
d – Not Dec. 24, 25, 26, 31, Jan. 1, Mar. 21, 24, May 12.
e – Ⓐ (not Dec. 24, 31, May 22).
f – Not May 21.
g – Not Dec. 25, 26, Jan. 1, Mar. 21, 24, May 1, 12, 22.
h – Also Dec. 26, Jan. 1, Mar. 20, 24, Apr. 30, May 12; not Dec. 23, 30, Mar. 21, 23, May 2, 11.

j – Arrives 7 – 10 minutes earlier.
k – ⑥ (also Dec. 24, 31).
r – ⚒ (not May 22).
t – 4 – 5 minutes later on Ⓐ **e**.
w – Also May 22.
z – Also Dec. 24, 31, May 22.
¶ – Train number **2186** on ⑤⑦ **h**.
◐ – Change trains at Offenburg on Ⓐ **e**.

917 FRANKFURT - MAINZ - IDAR OBERSTEIN - SAARBRÜCKEN

RB / RE services

km			v	Ⓐe	Ⓐe	⚒r	⚒r	v										⑤f			⊖			n	Ⓐe	n
0	**Frankfurt** (Main) Hbf	‡ d.	...	...	...	...	...	...	0724	0825	0908r	1025	1108	1225	1308	1425	1508	1531	1625	1708	1734	1825	1858e	2025	2225	...
11	Frankfurt Flughafen ✈ §	‡ d.	...	...	...	...	...	...	0738	0838	0923r	1038	1123	1238	1323	1438	1523	|	1638	1723	|	1838	1909e	2038	2238	...
39	**Mainz** Hbf	‡ d.	...	...	0510	...	b	0655	|	0900	1000	1100	1155	1300	1355	1500	1555	1606	1700	1755	1806	1900	1955	2100	2200	2305
80	Bad Kreuznach	d.	...	0501	0542	...	0632e	0737	0826	0926	1026	1126	1224	1326	1424	1526	1624	1643	1726	1824	1843	1926	2024	2126	2326	2344
102	Bad Sobernheim	d.	...	0523	0603	...	0654	0755	0845	0944	1044	1144	1244	1344	1444	1544	1644	1706	1744	1844	1906	1944	2044	2144	2344	0007
117	Kirn	d.	...	0540	0619	...	0712	0805	0854	0954	1054	1154	1254	1354	1454	1554	1654	1725	1754	1854	1925	1954	2054	2154	2354	0023
131	Idar-Oberstein	d.	...	0558	0635	0635	0729	0816	0905	1005	1105	1205	1305	1405	1505	1605	1705	1743	1805	1905	1943	2005	2105	2205	0005	0040
155	Türkismühle	d.	0543	0628	0704	0704	0759	0837	0926	1026	1126	1226	1326	1426	1526	1626	1726	...	1826	1926	...	2026	2126	2226	0026	...
170	St Wendel	d.	0600	0653	0723	0723	0818	0850	0938	1038	1138	1238	1338	1438	1538	1638	1738	...	1838	1938	...	2038	2138	2238	0038	...
179	Ottweiler (Saar)	d.	0608	0700	0733	0733	0826	0858	0945	1045	1145	1245	1345	1445	1545	1645	1745	...	1845	1945	...	2045	2145	2245	0045	...
184	Neunkirchen (Saar)	d.	0615	0707	0740	0740	0833	0905	0952	1052	1152	1252	1352	1452	1552	1652	1752	...	1852	1952	...	2052	2152	2252	0052	...
205	**Saarbrücken** Hbf	a.	0642	0724	0801	0801	0854	0924	1010	1110	1210	1310	1412	1510	1612	1710	1812	...	1910	2012	...	2110	2212	2310	0110	...

		Ⓐe	Ⓐe	⚒r	v		⚒r													n	n	n	Ⓑn	Ⓐe	n	n
Saarbrücken Hbf	d.	0348	...	0446	0546	...	0652	0750	0852	0950	1052	1150	1252	1350	1452	1550	1652	1750	1850	1934	...	2036	2106	...	2136	2236
Neunkirchen (Saar)	d.	0404	...	0504	0602	...	0708	0808	0908	1008	1108	1208	1308	1408	1508	1608	1708	1808	1908	2002	...	2108	2134	...	2214	2314
Ottweiler (Saar)	d.	0410	...	0510	0608	...	0713	0813	0913	1013	1113	1213	1313	1413	1513	1613	1713	1813	1913	2009	...	2115	2141	...	2221	2321
St Wendel	d.	0417	...	0517	0616	...	0721	0821	0921	1021	1121	1221	1321	1421	1521	1621	1721	1821	1921	2020	...	2125	2151	2202	2233	2331
Türkismühle	d.	0428	...	0528	0627	...	0732	0832	0932	1032	1132	1232	1332	1432	1532	1632	1732	1832	1932	2037	...	2141		2222	2253	2347
Idar-Oberstein	d.	0449	...	0549	0649	...	0752	0852	0952	1052	1152	1252	1352	1452	1552	1652	1752	1852	1952	2103	...	...		2251	...	...
Kirn	d.	0500	0505	0600	0700	...	0803	0903	1003	1103	1203	1303	1403	1503	1603	1703	1803	1903	2003	2117	...	...		...	...	...
Bad Sobernheim	d.	0509	0523	0610	0710	...	0812	0912	1012	1112	1212	1312	1412	1512	1612	1712	1812	1912	2012	2131	k	...		...	...	...
Bad Kreuznach	d.	0529	0547	0631	0731	...	0831	0933	1031	1133	1231	1333	1431	1533	1631	1733	1831	1933	2033	2153	2240	...		...	...	...
Mainz Hbf	‡ a.	0557	0636	0657	0756	...	0858	1004	1058	1204	1258	1404	1458	1604	1658	1804	1858	2004	2104	2220	2317	...		...	...	...
Frankfurt Flughafen ✈ §	‡ a.	0621	|	|	0821	...	0933t	1036	1133t	1236	1333t	1436	1537	1634	1735	1836e	1933x	...	...	...						
Frankfurt (Main) Hbf	‡ a.	0636	0724	0745	0836	...	0947t	1049	1147t	1249	1347t	1449	1554	1649	1752	1849e	1947x	...	...	...						

b – From Bingen (Table **918**).
e – Ⓐ (not Dec. 24, 31, May 22).
f – Not Mar. 21.
k – From Kaiserslautern (Table **918**).

n – Not Dec. 24, 31.
r – ⚒ (not May 22).
t – 4 – 5 minutes later on † (also May 22).
v – Not Dec. 25, Jan. 1.

x – On ⑦ from May 4 (also ⑤ from May 30) Frankfurt Flughafen a. 1938, Frankfurt Hbf a. 2001.
⊖ – ①–④ (not Dec. 24, 25, 26, 31, Jan. 1, Mar. 24, May 1, 12, 22).
‡ – See also Tables **912** and **917a**.
§ – Frankfurt Flughafen Regionalbahnhof ✈.

917a FRANKFURT - FRANKFURT FLUGHAFEN ✈ - MAINZ - WIESBADEN

S-Bahn 8 / 9

See note ⊠		⚒	†	⚒	⚒		⚒		⚒	†	⚒	⚒		†	⚒		†	⚒			†	⚒		†	⚒
Frankfurt (Main) Hbf ▽	d.	0417	0447	0447	0502	0517	0532	and at	1232	1247	1247	1302	1317	1331*	1332	1347	1401*	1402	1417	and at	2001*	2002	2017	2031*	2032
Frankfurt Flughafen ✈	d.	0429	0459	0459	0514	0529	0544	the same	1244	1259	1259	1314	1329	1344	1344	1359	1412	1414	1429	the same	2012	2014	2029	2044	2044
Mainz Hbf	d.	0456	|	0526	|	0556	|	minutes	|	|	1326	|	1356	|	|	1426	...	|	1456	minutes	...	|	2056	|	|
Mainz-Kastel	d.	|	0524	|	0539	|	0609	past each	1309	1324	|	1339	|	1409	1409	|	...	1439	|	past each	...	2039	|	2109	2109
Wiesbaden Hbf	a.	0507	0533	0537	0548	0607	0618	hour until	1318	1333	1337	1348	1407	1418	1418	1437	...	1448	1507	hour until	...	2048	2107	2118	2118

See note ⊠											
Frankfurt (Main) Hbf ▽	d.	2047	2117	2131*	2147	2217	2231*	2247	2317	2331*	0017
Frankfurt Flughafen ✈	d.	2059	2129	2144	2159	2229	2244	2259	2329	2344	0029
Mainz Hbf	d.	2126	2156	|	2226	2256	|	2326	2356	|	0056
Mainz-Kastel	d.	|	|	2209	|	|	2309	|	|	0009	|
Wiesbaden Hbf	a.	2137	2207	2218	2237	2307	2318	2337	0007	0018	0107

See note ⊠			⚒	†	⚒		⚒		⚒	†	⚒
Wiesbaden Hbf	d.	0350	0420	0427	0442	0450	0512	and at	1120	1127	1142
Mainz-Kastel	d.	|	|	0435	0450	|	0520	the same	|	1135	1150
Mainz Hbf	d.	0402	0432	|	|	0502	|	minutes	1132	|	|
Frankfurt Flughafen ✈	d.	0432	0502	0502	0517	0532	0547	past each	1202	1202	1217
Frankfurt (Main) Hbf	a.	0443	0513	0513	0528	0543	0558	hour until	1213	1213	1228

See note ⊠			⚒				⚒	†		⚒	†													Ⓐn	Ⓒk	
Wiesbaden Hbf	d.	1150	1212	1220	1242	1250	1312	...	and at	1912	...	1920	1942	1950	2020	2042	2050	2120	2142	2150	2220	2242	2250	2320	2327	2350
Mainz-Kastel	d.	|	1220	|	1250	|	1320	...	the same	1920	...	|	1950	|	|	2050	|	|	2150	|	|	2250	|	|	2335	|
Mainz Hbf	d.	1202	|	1232	|	1302	|	...	minutes	|	...	1932	|	2002	2032	|	2102	2132	|	2202	2232	|	2302	2332	|	0002
Frankfurt Flughafen ✈	d.	1232	1247	1302	1317	1332	1347	1347	past each	1947	1947	2002	2017	2032	2102	2117	2132	2202	2217	2232	2302	2317	2332	0002	0002	0032
Frankfurt (Main) Hbf	a.	1243	1258	1313	1329	1343	1358	1359	hour until	1958	1959	2013	2029	2043	2113	2129	2143	2213	2229	2243	2313	2329	2343	0013	0013	0043

k – Also Dec. 24, 31.
n – Not Dec. 24, 31.

⊠ – On May 22 services run as on ⑦. Certain services via Mainz Kastel are subject to alteration Dec. 23, Jan. 12, 13, 19, 20, 26, 27, Mar. 13 – 29.

▽ – From the underground platforms, except where shown by note *.
* – Departs from the main station (not underground platforms).

RHEINLAND-PFALZ LOCAL SERVICES

Pirmasens - Saarbrücken

km		Ⓐe	Ⓐe	⚒r	v					n
0	**Pirmasens Hbf** d.	0515	0547	0629	0732p	0832	and hourly until	1832	1932	2032
7	Pirmasens Nord d.	0522	0602	0641	0743	0843		1843	1943	2043
31	Zweibrücken Hbf d.	0554	0641	0713	0811	0911		1911	2011	2111
67	**Saarbrücken Hbf** a.	0634	0722	0754	0850	0952		1951	2050	2148

	v	Ⓐe	v					n	n
Saarbrücken Hbf d.	0603	0616	0705	0807	and hourly until	1807	1908	2007	2115
Zweibrücken Hbf d.	0643	0712	0745	0846		1846	1946	2046	2156
Pirmasens Nord a.	0717	0740	0816	0916		1916	2016	2116	2223
Pirmasens Hbf a.	0730e	0758	0826	0926		1926	2026	2128	2232

Pirmasens - Neustadt (Weinstr)

km		Ⓐe	⚒r	⚒r	Ⓐe	v	Ⓐe	v													n				
0	**Pirmasens Hbf** d.	0446	0547	0629		0641	0702	...	0801	0901	1001	1101	1201	1301	1401	1501	1601	1701	1801	1901	2001	...	...	...	...
7	Pirmasens Nord d.	0457	0558	0636	0639	0648	0709	0719	0819	0919	1019	1119	1219	1319	1419	1519	1619	1719	1819	1919	2019	...	...	...	...
55	**Landau** (Pfalz) Hbf a.	0550	0658	...	0737	...	...	0818	0918	1018	1118	1218	1318	1418	1518	1618	1718	1817	1918	2018	2118	...	...	...	...
73	**Neustadt** (Weinstr) Hbf. a.	0618	0723	...	0758	...	...	0844	0944	1044	1144	1244	1344	1444	1544	1644	1744	1844	1944	2044	2156	...	...	...	...

	Ⓐe	Ⓐe	⚒r	⑥g			†B	A							Ⓒz	Ⓐe		†w	⑥g	Ⓐe	n	n		
eustadt (Weinstr) Hbf d.	0511	0554	0616	...	0717r	0816	0916	0916	1016	1116	1216	1316	1416	1516	1616	1618	1716	1816	1816	1818	1916	2016	...	...
andau (Pfalz) Hbf d.	0533	0620	0635	0645	0741	0841	0941	0941	1041	1141	1241	1341	1441	1541	1641	1641	1741	1839	1841	1841	1941	2041	...	...
rmasens Nord a.	0636	0717	...	0742	0840	0940	1040	1040	1140	1240	1340	1440	1540	1640	1740	1740	1840	1940	1940	1940	2040	2137	...	...
rmasens Hbf a.	0658	0730	...	0818	0858	0958	1058	1058	1158	1258	1358	1458	1558	1658	1758	1758	1858	1958	1958	1958	2058	2151	...	...

Bingen - Kaiserslautern - Pirmasens

km		Ⓐe	⚒r	Ⓐe	⚒r	⑥g	v	Ⓐe	v													n	†w	n
0	**Bingen** (Rhein) Hbf d.	...	...	0516	0552	0552	...	0612	0651	0756	0855	0956	1055	1156	1255	1356	1455	1556	1655	1756	1855	1956	2102	2102	...
16	Bad Kreuznach d.	...	0508e	0536	0613	0613	...	0631	0711	0817	0916	1017	1116	1217	1316	1417	1516	1617	1716	1817	1916	2029t	2121	2132	...
43	Rockenhausen d.	...	0535e	0612	0640	0640	...	s	0738	0855	0955	1055	1155	1255	1355	1455	1555	1655	1755	1854	1955	2057	...	2200	...
79	**Kaiserslautern** Hbf a.	...	0612e	0649	0718	0718	...	...	0819	0929	1034	1128	1234	1331	1434	1531	1634	1731	1834	1931	2034	2138	...	2237	...
79	**Kaiserslautern** Hbf d.	0530	0630	...	...	0735	0735	...	0835	0935	1035	1135	1235	1335	1435	1535	1635	1735	1835	1935	2040n	...	...	...	2249
108	Pirmasens Nord a.	0601	0704	...	...	0806	0806	...	0906	1006	1106	1206	1306	1406	1506	1606	1706	1806	1906	2006	2111n	...	...	...	2320
115	**Pirmasens** Hbf a.	0610	0719	...	...	0818	0818	...	0918	1018	1118	1218	1318	1418	1518	1618	1718	1818	1918	2018	2119n	...	...	...	2328

	⚒r	⚒r	⚒r	Ⓐe	⚒r	vk	Ⓐe	⑥g	†d														n	Ⓒw	n
rmasens Hbf d.	...	...	0537	0614	...	0641	0732	0732	0741	...	0841	0941	1041	1141	1241	1341	1441	1541	1641	1741	1841	1941	2041	2041	...
rmasens Nord d.	...	...	0545	0622	...	0651	0750	0750	0750	...	0850	0950	1050	1150	1250	1350	1450	1550	1650	1750	1850	1950	2050	2050	...
aiserslautern Hbf a.	...	...	0618	0658	...	0722	0823	0823	0823	...	0923	1023	1123	1223	1323	1423	1523	1623	1723	1823	1923	2023	2128	2128	...
aiserslautern Hbf d.	0523	0606	0640e	...	0715	0737	...	...	...	0830	0924	1030	1124	1230	1324	1430	1524	1638	1724	1838	1924	2024n	...	2139	2139
ockenhausen d.	0556	0647	0713e	...	0751	0815	...	...	...	0900	1001	1100	1201	1300	1401	1500	1601	1710	1801	1909	2001	2101n	...	2209	2209
ad Kreuznach d.	0642	0716	0743e	...	0822	0843	...	...	...	0942	1043	1142	1242	1342	1443	1542	1643	1744	1845	1943	2040	2132n	...	2239	2239
ingen (Rhein) Hbf a.	0701	0735	0802e	...	0842	0902	...	...	...	1001	1102	1201	1301	1401	1502	1601	1702	1803	1904	2002	2059	2151n	...	◇	◇

Neustadt (Weinstr) - Karlsruhe and Wissembourg

km		Ⓐe	Ⓐe	Ⓐe	Ⓐe	⚒r	⚒r	⚒r	Ⓐe	Ⓒz							A	†B		A	†B			Ⓐe	Ⓒz
0	**Neustadt** (Weinstr) Hbf. d.	0430	...	0511	...	0529	0616	...	0658	0703b	0736	0809	0836	0910	0936	1010	1036	1044	1110	1136	1145	1210	1236	1307	1310
18	Landau (Pfalz) Hbf d.	0448	...	0536	...	0554	0636	...	0712	0723	0758	0823	0858	0923	0958	1023	1058	1058	1123	1158	1159	1223	1258	1320	1323
31	Winden (Pfalz) d.	0502	0505	0551	0555	0601	0652	0658	0721	0731	0808	0831	0908	0931	1008	1031	1108	1108	1131	1208	1208	1231	1308	1331	1331
47	**Wissembourg** a.	|	0521	|	0615	|	|	0718	|	|	0828	|	0928	|	1028	|	1128	1128	|	1228	1228	|	1328	|	|
44	Wörth (Rhein) d.	0517	...	0605	...	0617	0708	...	0736	0744	...	0844	...	0944	...	1044	...	...	1144	...	...	1244	...	1344	1344
58	**Karlsruhe** Hbf a.	0530	...	...	...	0635	0726	...	0752	0754	...	0854	...	0954	...	1054	...	...	1154	...	...	1254	...	1354	1354

						n		n	n	n	n
eustadt (Weinstr) Hbf d.	1336	1410	and at the same minutes past each hour until	1836	1908	1936	2010	2105	2138	2221	2321
andau (Pfalz) Hbf d.	1358	1423		1858	1923	1958	2023	2123	2158	2241	2341
inden (Pfalz) d.	1408	1431		1908	1931	2008	2031	2131	2229	...	...
Wissembourg a.	1428	|		1928	|	2029	|	|	|	...	...
örth (Rhein) d.	...	1444		...	1944	...	2044	2143	2243	...	...
arlsruhe Hbf a.	...	1454		...	1954	...	2054	2154	2256	...	...

	Ⓐe	Ⓐe	⚒r	⚒r	Ⓒz	Ⓐe	⑥g	Ⓐe
Karlsruhe Hbf d.	0431	...	0602	...	0707	0714	...	...
Wörth (Rhein) d.	0447	...	0618	...	0717	0735	...	...
Wissembourg d.	|	0527	|	0623e	|	|	0733	0733
Winden (Pfalz) d.	0502	0547	0630	0650	0728	0747	0753	0757
Landau (Pfalz) Hbf d.	0519	0609	0644	0702	0736	0757	0802	0806
Neustadt (Weinstr) Hbf a.	0542	0628	0705	0723	0754	0810	0824	0826

	Ⓐe	Ⓒz						Ⓐe	Ⓒz	†B	A		†B	A							n	n	⑥	n	n
arlsruhe Hbf d.	0802	0806	...	0907	and at the same minutes past each hour until	1507	...	1603	1607	...	...	1705	...	...	1807	...	1907	...	2007	...	2106	...	2206	2315
örth (Rhein) d.	0817	0816	...	0917		1517	...	1617	1617	...	...	1717	...	...	1817	...	1917	...	2017	...	2117	...	2217	2326
Wissembourg d.	|	|	0833	|		|	1533	|	|	1633	1633	|	1732	1732	|	1833	|	1932	|	2033	|	2203	|	|
inden (Pfalz) d.	0829	0829	0853	0929		1529	1553	1629	1629	1653	1653	1729	1753	1753	1829	1853	1929	1953	2029	2053	2128	2224	2228	2338
andau (Pfalz) Hbf d.	0838	0839	0902	0938		1538	1602	1638	1638	1702	1702	1738	1802	1802	1838	1902c	1938	2002	2038	2102	2136	...	2236	2352
eustadt (Weinstr) Hbf a.	0851	0852	0924	0951		1551	1624	1651	1651	1714	1724	1751	1816	1824	1851	1926	1951	2024	2051	2124	2156	...	2255	0011

Wörth and Karlsruhe - Speyer - Mannheim - Heidelberg

km	km			Ⓐe	Ⓐe	Ⓐe	⚒r	Ⓐe	Ⓐe	Ⓐe	Ⓒz		Ⓐe	Ⓒz	Ⓐe										Ⓐe
0		**Wörth** (Rhein) d.	...	...	0534	...	...	0622	...	0651	0718	...	0736	...	...	0818	...	0918	...	...	1018	...	1118	...	...
	0	**Karlsruhe** Hbf ⊠ d.	...	...	|	...	...	|	...	|	|	...	|	...	0808	|	...	|	...	1008	|	...	|	...	1208
27	38	Germersheim d.	0412e	0525	0605	0619	...	0651	0717	0725	0748	...	0810	0813	0838	0849	0913	0949	1013	1038	1049	1113	1149	1213	1238
41		Speyer Hbf d.	0426	0541	0621	0631	0635g	0707	0727	0738	0802	0802	0824	0826	0847	0902	0926	1002	1026	1047	1102	1126	1202	1226	1247
61		Ludwigshafen Hbf d.	0451	0607	0648	0651	0700	0732	0748	0811	0820	0820	0847	0848	0903	0921	0948	1021	1048	1103	1121	1148	1221	1248	1303
64		**Mannheim** Hbf ⊡ a.	0456	0625	0658	m	0705	0747	m	0817	0825	0825	0853	0853	m	0926	0953	1026	1053	m	1126	1153	1226	1253	m
81		**Heidelberg** Hbf ⊡ a.	0516	0646	0713	...	0723	0816	...	...	0844	0844	0916	0916	...	0944	1016	1044	1116	...	1144	1216	1244	1316	...

					Ⓐe														Ⓐe		n	n	n	n	n
örth (Rhein) d.	1218	...	1318	...	...	1418	...	1518	...	...	1618	...	1718	...	...	1818	...	1918	...	2018n	...	2119	2219	...	...
Karlsruhe Hbf ⊠ d.	|	...	|	...	1408	|	...	|	...	1608	|	...	|	...	1808	|	...	|	2008	|	...	|	|	2225	...
ermersheim d.	1249	1313	1349	1413	1438	1449	1513	1549	1613	1638	1649	1713	1749	1813	1838	1849	1913	1949	2038	2049	2121	2202	2251	2308	2322y
peyer Hbf d.	1302	1326	1402	1426	1447	1502	1526	1602	1626	1647	1702	1726	1802	1826	1847	1902	1926	2002	2047	2102	2137	2217	2303	...	2335y
udwigshafen Hbf d.	1321	1348	1421	1448	1503	1521	1548	1621	1648	1703	1721	1748	1821	1848	1903	1921	1948	2021	2103	2120	2200	2242	2328	...	2359
annheim Hbf ⊡ a.	1326	1353	1426	1453	m	1526	1553	1626	1653	m	1726	1753	1826	1853	m	1926	1953	2026	m	2125	2205	2248	2333	...	0004
eidelberg Hbf ⊡ a.	1344	1416	1444	1516	...	1544	1616	1644	1716	...	1744	1816	1844	1916	...	1944	2016	2044	...	2144	...	2313	2353	...	0021

	Ⓐe		Ⓐe	Ⓐe	Ⓐe	Ⓒz	Ⓐe		⚒r			Ⓐe										Ⓐe			Ⓒz
eidelberg Hbf ⊡ d.	0504	0534r	0605	...	...	0634	0645	...	0708	0744	0814	...	0844	0914	0944	1014	...	1044	1114	1144	1214	...	1244	1314	1344
annheim Hbf ⊡ d.	0526	0554	0624	m	0633	0654	0706	...	0730	0804	0831	m	0904	0931	1004	1031	m	1104	1131	1204	1231	m	1304	1331	1404
udwigshafen Hbf d.	0532	0614	0629	0636	0638	0701	0714	...	0738	0810	0837	0858	0910	0937	1010	1037	1058	1110	1137	1210	1237	1258	1310	1337	1410
peyer Hbf d.	0555	0639	...	0655	0705	0726x	0741	0741	0804	0831	0856	0913	0931	0956	1031	1056	1113	1131	1156	1231	1256	1313	1331	1356	1431
ermersheim a.	0609	0653	...	0709	0719	0740x	0755	0812	0818	0844	0908	0921	0944	1008	1044	1108	1121	1144	1208	1244	1308	1321	1344	1408	1444
Karlsruhe Hbf ⊠ a.	|	|	...	0754	|	...	...	|	...	...	|	0952	...	|	...	|	1152	...	|	...	|	1352	...	|	...
örth (Rhein) a.	0647	0729	...	...	0748	...	...	0840	...	...	0940	...	...	1040	...	1140	...	...	1240	...	1340	...	...	1440	...

	Ⓐe		Ⓐe			Ⓒz	Ⓐe		Ⓒz	Ⓐe			Ⓐe	Ⓒz	Ⓐe						n	Ⓑq	n	n	
eidelberg Hbf ⊡ d.	1347	1414	...	1444	1514	1544	1547	1614	...	...	1644	1714	...	1744	1747	1814	...	1844	1914	1944	2014	...	2114*	2214	2314
annheim Hbf ⊡ d.	1404	1431	m	1504	1531	1604	1604	1631	m	1644	1704	1731	m	1804	1804	1831	m	1904	1931	2004	2031	m	2136	2236	2336
udwigshafen Hbf d.	1410	1437	1458	1510	1537	1610	1610	1637	1658	1657	1710	1737	1801	1810	1810	1837	1856	1910	1937	2010	2037	2057	2143	2243	2343
peyer Hbf d.	1431	1456	1513	1531	1556	1631	1631	1656	1713	1723	1733	1756	1818	1831	1831	1856	1915	1931	1956	2031	2056	2113	2205	2311	0008
ermersheim a.	1444	1508	1521	1544	1608	1644	1644	1708	1721	1738	1745	1808	1830	1844	1844	1908	1923	1944	2008	2044	2108	2121	2218	2324	0021
Karlsruhe Hbf ⊠ a.	...	|	1552	...	|	...	...	|	1752	|	...	|	...	...	...	|	1952	...	|	...	|	2152e	...	...	...
örth (Rhein) a.	...	1540	...	...	1640	...	...	1740	...	1814	...	1840	...	...	...	1940	...	...	2040n	...	2140	...	...	...	...

– ⚒ (not May 22; daily until May 3).
– † from May 4 (also May 22).
– 0710 on ⑥ (also Dec. 24, 31).
– 1907 on ⑥⑦ (also May 1, 12, 22).
– Also May 22; not Dec. 25, Jan. 1.
– Ⓐ (not Dec. 24, 31, May 22).
– ⑥ (also Dec. 24, 31).

k – Change trains at Kaiserslautern on Ⓐ (not May 22).
m – To / from Mainz (Table **912a**).
n – Not Dec. 24, 31.
p – Change trains at Pirmasens Nord on ⑥**g**.
q – Not Dec. 24, 25, 26, 31, Jan. 1, Mar. 21, 23, 24, May 1, 12, 22.
r – ⚒ (not May 22).
s – To Saarbrücken (Table **917**).

t – Arrives 2016.
v – Not Dec. 25, Jan. 1.
w – Also May 22.
x – Change trains at Schifferstadt (a. 0713, d. 0717).
y – Change trains at Schifferstadt (a. 2345, d. 2348).
z – Also Dec. 24, 31, May 22.

* – Change trains at Mannheim on ①–⑥.
◇ – To Mainz (Table **917**).
⊡ – See also Tables **911a** and **923**.
⊠ – Additional connections available via Wörth (see Neustadt - Karlsruhe table above).

918a WIESBADEN - MAINZ - DARMSTADT - ASCHAFFENBURG

RB service

km		⚒r	⚒r	Ⓐe	2	Ⓐe		2		2		2		2		Ⓐe	2	Ⓐe						
0	**Wiesbaden** Hbf d.	...	0539	0602	0639	0702	0739	0839	0939	1039	1139	1239	1339	1439	1539	1602	1639	1702	1739	1839	1939	2039	2139	2239	233
10	**Mainz** Hbf d.	...	0549	|	0649	|	0749	0849	0949	1049	1149	1249	1349	1449	1549	|	1649	|	1749	1849	1949	2049	2149	2249	234
43	Darmstadt Hbf a.	...	0623	0643	0723	0743	0823	0923	1023	1123	1223	1323	1423	1523	1623	1643	1723	1743	1823	1923	2023	2123	2223	2323	002
43	Darmstadt Hbf d.	0452	0632	0703	0732	0800	0832r	0932	1032r	1132	1232r	1332	1432r	1532	1632r	1659	1732	1800	1832e	1932	2032e	2132e	...	...
87	**Aschaffenburg** Hbf a.	0535	0712	0744	0812	0841	0912r	1012	1112r	1212	1312r	1412	1512r	1612	1712r	1741	1812	1841	1912e	2012	2112e	2212e	...	...

	Ⓐe	Ⓐe		Ⓐe		Ⓐe			2		2		2		Ⓐe	2	Ⓐe		Ⓐe	2	Ⓐe		2		
Aschaffenburg Hbf d.	...	0510	0542r	0606	0640r	0716	0746	0846r	0946	1046r	1146	1246r	1346	1446r	1516	1546	1616	1646r	1716	1746	1816	1846e	1946	2046e	...
Darmstadt Hbf a.	...	0552	0623r	0652	0727r	0759	0827	0927r	1027	1127r	1227	1327r	1427	1527r	1559	1627	1659	1727r	1759	1827	1859	1927e	2027	2127e	...
Darmstadt Hbf d.	0434	0606	0634	0706	0734	0806	0834	0935	1035	1135	1235	1335	1435	1535	1606	1634	1706	1735	1806	1834	1906	1934	2035	2135	223
Mainz Hbf d.	0512	|	0712	|	0811	|	0911	1011	1111	1211	1311	1411	1511	1611	|	1711	|	1811	|	1911	|	2011	2111	2211	231
Wiesbaden Hbf a.	0525	0655	0725	0755	0825	0855	0925	1025	1125	1225	1325	1425	1525	1625	1655	1725	1755	1825	1855	1925	1955	2025	2125	2225	232

e – Ⓐ (not Dec. 24, 31, May 22). r – ⚒ (not May 22).

919 SAARBRÜCKEN - MANNHEIM (- FRANKFURT)

RE / RB / S-Bahn services except where shown

km				IC 2051 ①–⑤ d🍷	⚒r	IC 2293 A🍷	IC 2053 ①–⑤ d S	ICE 1557 ①–⑥ e D		v	Ⓐa				ICE 9551 T R✕		Ⓐa K				ICE 9553 R✕				
	Paris Est **390** d.	...	...	...	...	...	...	...	...	...	...	...	...	...	0658	...	...	...	...	...	0909k	...	...	...	...
	Trier Hbf **915** d.	...	...	...	...	...	...	...	...	0529a	0621	...	0636a	...	|	...	0834	...	...	...	|	...	...	...	...
0	**Saarbrücken** Hbf d.	...	...	0440	...	0535	0621	0646	...	0658	0740	...	0802	...	0900	0904	0940	...	1002	...	1100	1104	...	1202	...
31	Homburg (Saar) Hbf d.	...	...	0503	0541	0558	0644	0708	...	0727	0804	...	0827	0854	|	0927	1004	...	1027	1054	|	1127	1154	1227	125
67	**Kaiserslautern** Hbf a.	...	...	0527	0612	0622	0703	0727	...	0754	0825	...	0854	0924	0935	0954	1025	...	1054	1124	1135	1154	1224	1254	132
			Ⓐa	|	|	|	|	|		◧	|		◧	|	|	◧	|		◧	|	|	◧	|	◧	|
67	**Kaiserslautern** Hbf d.	0354	0456	0529	0614	0624	0705	0729	0733	0758	0826	0830	0858	0928	0937	0958	1026	1030	1058	1128	1137	1158	1228	1258	132
100	Neustadt (Weinstr) Hbf d.	0423	0527	0553	0651	0648	0729	0752	0805	0830	0850	0905	0930	1005	|	1030	1050	1105	1130	1205	|	1230	1305	1330	140
128	Ludwigshafen Hbf **911a 918** d.	0451	0554	0612	0720	0705	0746	|	0828	0857	|	0928	0957	1028	|	1057	|	1128	1157	1228	|	1257	1328	1357	142
131	**Mannheim** Hbf **911a 918** a.	0456	0559	0616	0725	0709	0751	0810	0834	0903	0910	0934	1003	1034	1016	1103	1110	1134	1203	1234	1216	1303	1334	1403	143
131	**Mannheim** Hbf **911a 918** ▽ d.	0459	0606	0619	0729	...	0754	0812	0837	0907	*0929*	0937	1007	1037	1020	1107	*1129*	1137	1207	1237	1220	1307	1337	1407	143
	Heidelberg Hbf **911a 918** a.	0516	0623	|	0744	...	0804	|	0853	0923	*0944*	0953	1023	1053	|	1123	*1144*	1153	1223	1253	|	1323	1353	1423	145
	Osterburken **923** a.	...	M	|	0923	...	...	|	1023	...	...	1123	...	1223	|	...	...	1323	...	1423	|	...	1523	...	162
191	Darmstadt Hbf ▽ a.	...	...	0653	...	...	...	0845	...	...	...	...	...	...	|	...	...	...	...	...	|	...	...	...	...
219	**Frankfurt** (Main) Hbf ▽ a.	...	...	0712	...	...	...	0903	...	...	...	...	...	...	1058	...	...	...	...	...	1258	...	...	...	...

	IC 2055 Ⓑq S🍷			K		ICE 9555 R✕						IC 2057 Ⓑm	IC 2270 ⑥ L			M	ICE 9557 Ⓑt R✕			n	ICE 9559 R✕	n	n	n	n
Paris Est **390** d.	...	...	...	...	...	1309	...	...	...	...	...	...	...	...	...	...	1709	...	...	...	1905	...	...	...	...
Trier Hbf **915** d.	...	...	...	1249	...	|	...	...	...	...	...	...	...	...	1654r	...	|	...	...	1854a	|	...	...	2055a	...
Saarbrücken Hbf d.	1249	1302	...	1402	...	1500	1504	...	1602	...	1702	1741	1741	...	1802	...	1900	1904	...	2002	2100	...	2104	2202	230
Homburg (Saar) Hbf d.	1313	1327	1354	1427	1454	|	1527	1554	1627	1654	1727	1805	1805	1752	1827	1854	|	1927	1954	2027	|	...	2127	2227	232
Kaiserslautern Hbf a.	1335	1354	1424	1454	1524	1535	1554	1624	1654	1724	1754	1826	1826	1822	1854	1924	1935	1954	2024	2054	2135	...	2158	2258	000
	|	◧	|	◧	|	|	◧	|	◧	|	◧	|	|	|	◧	|	|	◧	|	◧	|		◧n	◧n	◧v
Kaiserslautern Hbf d.	1337	1358	1428	1458	1528	1537	1558	1628	1658	1728	1758	1828	1828	1832	1858	1928	1937	1958	2028	2058	2137	2141	2232*	2302	000
Neustadt (Weinstr) Hbf d.	1401	1430	1505	1530	1605	|	1630	1705	1730	1805	1830	1852	1852	1905	1930	2005	|	2030	2105	2130	|	2210	2300*	2330	003
Ludwigshafen Hbf **911a 918** d.	|	1457	1528	1557	1628	|	1657	1728	1757	1828	1857	|	|	1928	1957	2028	|	2057	2128	2200	|	2242	2328	2359	010
Mannheim Hbf **911a 918** a.	1419	1503	1534	1603	1634	1616	1704	1734	1805	1834	1903	1910	1910	1934	2003	2034	2016	2103	2134	2205	2216	2248	2333	0004	010
Mannheim Hbf **911a 918** ▽ d.	1424	1507	1537	1607	1637	1620	1707	1737	1807	1837	1907	1912	1912	1937	2007	2037	2020	2107	2137	2207	2220	2257	2337	0005	011
Heidelberg Hbf **911a 918** a.	1435	1523	1553	1623	1653	|	1723	1753	1823	1853	1923	|	|	1953	2023	2053	|	2123	2153	2223	|	2313	2353	0021	013
Osterburken **923** a.	...	...	1723	...	1823	|	...	1923	...	2023	...	|	|	2123	...	...	|	...	2333	...	|	0043c	M	...	...
Darmstadt Hbf ▽ a.	...	...	...	...	...	|	...	...	...	...	...	1944	1944	...	...	...	|	...	...	...	|	...	...	...	...
Frankfurt (Main) Hbf ▽ a.	...	...	...	...	...	1658	...	...	...	...	...	2004	2004	...	...	...	2058	...	...	...	2258	...	...	...	...

	⚒r		ICE 9558 T R✕	Ⓐa		Ⓐa				IC 2058 ①–⑤ d		ICE 9556 R✕								Ⓐa		ICE 9554 R✕			
Frankfurt (Main) Hbf ▽ d.	...	...	0600	...	...	...	...	...	...	0749	...	0901f	...	...	...	...	...	...	...	...	...	1301f	...	...	...
Darmstadt Hbf ▽ d.	...	...	|	...	...	...	...	...	...	0812	...	|	...	...	...	...	...	...	...	...	...	|	...	...	...
Osterburken **923** d.	...	M	|	M	...	0513	0536y	0606a	0636z	|	0706a	|	0736	...	0836	...	0936	...	1036	...	...	|	1136	...	123
Heidelberg Hbf **911a 918** d.	...	0534r	|	0622	0634	0645	0705	0735	0805	|	0835	|	0905	0935	1005	1035	1105	1135	1205	*1214*	1235	|	1305	1335	140
Mannheim Hbf **911a 918** ▽ a.	...	0552r	0636	0637	0652	0703	0720	0751	0821	0847	0851	0937	0921	0951	1021	1051	1121	1151	1221	*1229*	1251	1337	1321	1351	142
Mannheim Hbf **911a 918** d.	0425	0554	0640	0644	0654	0706	0721	0756	0826	0849	0856	0941	0926	0956	1026	1056	1126	1156	1226	1248	1256	1341	1326	1356	142
Ludwigshafen Hbf **911a 918** d.	0432	0600	|	0651	0701	0714	0727	0803	0832	|	0903	|	0932	1003	1032	1103	1132	1203	1232	|	1303	|	1332	1403	143
Neustadt (Weinstr) Hbf d.	0506	0632	|	0715	0732	0745	0802	0832	0857	0908	0932	|	1002	1032	1100	1132	1200	1232	1300	1309	1332	|	1402	1432	150
Kaiserslautern Hbf a.	0534	0659	0720	0743	0759	0812	0829	0859	0925	0930	0959	1020	1029	1059	1128	1159	1228	1259	1328	1330	1359	1420	1429	1459	152
	◧v	◧v	|		◧		|	◧		|	◧	|	|	◧K	|	◧	|	◧	|	|	◧	|	|	◧	|
Kaiserslautern Hbf d.	0556	0703	0722	...	0803	...	0833	0903	...	0932	1003	1022	1033	1103	1133	1203	1233	1303	1333z	1332	1403	1422	1433	1503	1533
Homburg (Saar) Hbf d.	0624	0743	|	...	0831	...	0904	0933	...	0954	1031	|	1104	1131	1204	1231	1304	1331	1405z	1355	1431	|	1504	1531	1605
Saarbrücken Hbf a.	0657	0816	0758	...	0857	...	...	0958	...	1016	1055	1059	...	1157	...	1258	...	1400	...	1418	1455	1459	...	1557	...
Trier Hbf **915** a.	...	...	|	...	...	...	...	1104	...	...	...	|	...	1310	...	...	...	1504	...	...	...	|	...	1704a	...
Paris Est **390** a.	...	...	0950	...	...	...	...	...	...	...	...	1249h	...	...	...	...	...	...	...	...	...	1649	...	...	...

	Ⓐe		IC 2056 ①–⑤ d S				IC 2054 ①–⑥ e🍷		ICE 9552 R✕				IC 2052 Ⓑq S🍷		ICE 9550 Ⓑt R✕				IC 2292 A🍷		ICE 1594 Ⓑq D✕	n	n	IC 2050 ⑦w S	n
Frankfurt (Main) Hbf ▽ d.	...	...	...	...	...	...	1554	...	1701f	...	...	...	...	...	1901	...	...	...	...	...	2054	...	...	...	...
Darmstadt Hbf ▽ d.	...	...	...	...	...	...	1611	...	|	...	...	...	...	...	|	...	...	...	...	...	2111	...	...	...	...
Osterburken **923** d.	...	...	...	1336	...	1436	|	...	|	1536	...	1636	...	...	|	1736	...	1836	...	...	|	...	2036	...	...
Heidelberg Hbf **911a 918** d.	*1414*	1435	1520	1505	1535	1605	|	1635	|	1705	1735	1805	...	1835	|	1905	1935	2005	...	2035	|	2114	2205	2255	231
Mannheim Hbf **911a 918** ▽ a.	*1429*	1451	1537	1521	1551	1621	1646	1651	1737	1721	1751	1821	...	1851	1937	1921	1951	2021	...	2051	2147	2130	2221	2306	233
Mannheim Hbf **911a 918** d.	1448	1456	1539	1526	1556	1626	1648	1656	1741	1726	1756	1826	1848	1856	1941	1926	1956	2026	2050	2056	2149	2136	2236	2308	233
Ludwigshafen Hbf **911a 918** d.	|	1503	|	1532	1603	1632	1654	1703	|	1732	1803	1832	1854	1903	|	1932	2003	2032	|	2103	|	2143	2243	|	234
Neustadt (Weinstr) Hbf d.	1509	1532	1558	1602	1632	1700	1710	1732	|	1802	1832	1900	1910	1932	|	2002	2032	2100	2109	2132	2208	2214	2314	2327	001
Kaiserslautern Hbf a.	1530	1559	1619	1629	1659	1728	1731	1759	1820	1829	1859	1928	1931	1959	2020	2029	2059	2128	2131	2159	2229	2241	2341	2349	004
	|	◧	|	|	◧J	|	|	◧	|	|	◧		|	◧n	|	|	◧n		|	◧n	|		◧b	|	
Kaiserslautern Hbf d.	1532	1603	1621	1633	1703	1733p	1733	1803	1822	1833	1903	...	1933	2003	2022	2033n	2103	...	2133	2205	2231	...	2348	2351	...
Homburg (Saar) Hbf d.	1555	1631	1643	1704	1731	1806p	1755	1831	|	1904	1931	...	1956	2031	|	2104n	2131	...	2155	2233	2252	...	0019	0012	...
Saarbrücken Hbf a.	1618	1657	1705	...	1757	...	1816	1855	1859	...	1957	...	2019	2055	2059	...	2157	...	2218	2259	2313	...	0051	0033	...
Trier Hbf **915** a.	1744	...	...	...	1907	...	...	...	|	...	2116y	...	...	...	|	...	...	...	...	...	...	...	...	...	...
Paris Est **390** a.	...	...	...	...	...	...	...	...	2053g	...	...	...	...	...	2253	...	...	...	...	...	...	...	...	...	...

A – [12] and 🍷 Salzburg - München - Stuttgart - Saarbrücken and v.v.
D – [12] and ✕ Dresden - Leipzig - Frankfurt - Saarbrücken and v.v.
J – To Koblenz (Table **915**) on † (also May 22).
K – From / to Koblenz (Table **915**).
L – ⑥ (not Dec. 29, Mar. 22, May 3). To Kassel (Table **806**).
M – To / from Mosbach (Table **923**).
S – To / from Stuttgart (Table **930**).
R – 🅁 for journeys to / from France.
T – ①–⑥ (not Dec. 25, Jan. 1, Mar. 24, May 12).

a – Ⓐ (not Dec. 24, 31, May 22).
b – Not Dec. 24, 31. Runs 7 minutes later on ⑦w.
c – The morning of ⑦ (also Dec. 26, Mar. 21, 24, May 1, 12, 22).
d – Not Dec. 24, 25, 26, 31, Jan. 1, Mar. 21, 24, May 12.
e – Not Dec. 25, 26, Jan. 1, Mar. 22, 24, May 12.
f – 1–2 minutes earlier on ⑥⑦ from May 17.
g – 2057 on ⑥ (also Dec. 24, 31, Mar. 23, May 11).
h – 1253 on ⑦ (also Dec. 25, Jan. 1, Mar. 24, May 12).
k – 0901 on ⑦ (also Dec. 25, Jan. 1, Mar. 24, May 12).
m – Also Dec. 29, Mar. 22, May 3.
n – Not Dec. 24, 31.
p – ⑦ (also Dec. 25, 26, Jan. 1, Mar. 22, 24, May 12).
q – Not Dec. 24, 25, 31, Mar. 21, 23, May 11.
r – ⚒ (not May 22).
t – Not Dec. 24, 31, Mar. 23, May 11.
v – Not Dec. 25, Jan. 1.
w – Also Dec. 26, Jan. 1, Mar. 24, May 12; not Dec. 23, 30, Mar. 23, May 11.
y – ⑥ (also Dec. 24, 31).
z – Ⓒ (also Dec. 24, 31, May 22).

* – On ⑤⑥ passengers to Heidelberg and beyond should change trains at Schifferstadt (a. 2314, d. 2317).
◧ – Change trains at Kaiserslautern.
▽ – Other services Mannheim - Frankfurt and v.v.: *ICE* services see Table **912**. Local *RE / RB* trains see Table **911a**.

FRANKFURT FLUGHAFEN ✈ - FRANKFURT - NÜRNBERG - PASSAU 920

For other regional trains see Table **921** below.

km		*ICE* **521**	*ICE* **21**	*ICE* **523**	*ICE* **525**	*ICE* **23**		*ICE* **527**		*ICE* **529**	*ICE* **25**	*IC* **1987**	*ICE* **621**	*ICE* **623**	*ICE* **27**	*ICE* **625**	*ICE* **627**	*ICE* **29**	*ICE* **629**	*ICE* **721**	*ICE* **229**	*ICE* **723**	*ICE* **725**	*IC* **2029***	*ICE* **727**
				①–⑥	v			①–⑥				⑥										Ⓑq			Ⓑq
		🍷	🍴	e🍷	🍷	🍴		dG		🍷	🍴	🍷	🍷	🍷	🍴	🍷	🍷	🍴	🍷	🍷	🍴	🍷	🍷	🍷	🍷
	Hamburg Hbf **800 900** d.	...	...	...	...	...	...	🍷	...	...	...	0635z	...	...	...	...	...	...	...	...	...	...	...	1146	...
	Dortmund Hbf **800** d.	...	...	0401	0523	0433v	...	0623	...	0723c	0636	|	...	...	0838	...	...	...	...	...	...	...	1522w	1436	...
	Wuppertal Hbf **800** d.	...	...	|	|	|	...	|	...	|	0714	|	...	...	|	...	...	...	...	...	...	...	|	1514	...
	Essen Hbf **800** d.	...	...	0423	0551	0455v	...	0651	...	0753	|	|	0840	...	0900	1053	...	...	1253	...	...	1453	1553	|	1653
	Düsseldorf Hbf **800** d.	...	...	0453	0622	0523v	...	0722	...	0822	|	|	0913	...	0927	1122	...	...	1322	...	...	1522	1622	|	1722
	Köln Hbf **800 910** d.	0420	...	|	|	0553	...	|	...	|	0753	|	|	1020	0953	|	1220	...	|	1428	...	|	|	1553	|
	Köln Messe/Deutz **910** d.	|	...	0518	0644	|	...	0744	...	0844	|	|	0944	|	|	1144	|	...	1344	|	...	1544	1644	|	1744
	Bonn Hbf **800** d.	|	...	|	|	0614	...	|	...	|	0814	|	|	|	1014	|	|	...	|	|	...	|	|	1614	|
	Koblenz Hbf **912** d.	|	...	|	|	0648	...	|	...	|	0848	|	|	|	1048	|	|	...	|	|	...	|	|	1648	|
	Mainz Hbf **912** d.	|	...	|	|	0740	...	|	...	|	0940	|	|	|	1140	|	|	...	|	|	...	|	|	1740	|
0	**Frankfurt** Flughafen ✈ § d.	0535	...	0637	0737	0801	...	0837	...	0937	1001	|	1037	1130	1201	1237	1330	...	1437	1537	...	1637	1737	1801	1837
11	**Frankfurt** (Main) Hbf **850** d.	0551	0622	0654	0754	0818	...	0854	...	0954	1021	|	1054	1154	1221	1254	1354	1416	1454	1554	1621	1654	1754	1818	1854
35	Hanau Hbf **850** d.	|	0638	|	|	0835	...	|	...	|	1038	|	|	|	1238	|	|	1439	|	|	1638	|	|	1835	|
57	Aschaffenburg Hbf d.	0624	0652	0724	0824	|	...	0924	...	1024	|	|	1124	1224	|	1324	1424	|	1524	1624	|	1724	1824	1849	1924
36	**Würzburg** Hbf a.	0703	0731	0803	0903	0925	...	1003	...	1103	1131	1116	1203	1303	1331	1403	1503	1531	1603	1703	1731	1803	1903	1931	2003
36	**Würzburg** Hbf **900** d.	0705	0734	0805	0905	0934	...	1005	...	1105	1134	1118	1205	1305	1334	1405	1505	1534	1605	1705	1734	1805	1905	1934	2005
38	**Nürnberg** Hbf **900** a.	0759	0828	0859	0959	1028	...	1059	...	1159	1228	1232	1259	1359	1428	1459	1559	1628	1659	1759	1828	1859	1959	2028	2059
38	**Nürnberg** Hbf d.	0802	0831	0902	1002	1031	...	1102	...	1202	1231	1235	1302	1402	1431	1502	1602	1631	1702	1802	1831	1902	2002	2031	2102
	München Hbf **904** a.	0904	|	1004	1104	|	...	1204	...	1304	|	|	1404	1504	|	1604	1704	|	1804	1904	|	2004	2104	|	2208
39	**Regensburg** Hbf a.	...	0922	...	...	1122	...	...	...	...	1322	1335	...	...	1522	...	...	1722	...	...	1922	...	...	2131	...
39	**Regensburg** Hbf d.	...	0924	...	...	1124	...	...	...	...	1324	1337	...	...	1524	...	...	1724	...	...	1924	...	...	2133	...
79	Straubing d.	...	|	...	...	|	...	...	...	...	|	1400	...	...	|	...	...	|	...	...	|	...	...	2155	...
04	Plattling **944** d.	...	0958	...	...	1158	...	...	...	...	1358	1414	...	...	1558	...	...	1758	...	...	1958	...	...	2210	...
56	**Passau** Hbf 🏨 **944** a.	...	1026	...	...	1226	...	...	...	...	1426	1443	...	...	1626	...	...	1826	...	...	2026	...	...	2242	...
	Linz Hbf **950** a.	...	1145	...	...	1345	...	...	...	...	1545	...	...	...	1745	...	...	1945	...	...	2145	...	...	...	...
	Wien Westbahnhof **950** a.	...	1326	...	...	1526	...	...	...	...	1726	...	...	...	1926	...	...	2126	...	...	2326	...	...	...	...

	ICE **729**	*ICE* **927**	*ICE* **1027**	*IC* **2165**	*RB* **32149**	*ICE* **821**	*ICE* **821**	*ICE* **929**	*CNL* **313**	*EN* **491**	*EN* **493**	*EN* **429**	
		A	⑤h	⑦w	Ⓐt		⑤⑦f		🅁	T🅁	Y🅁	🅁	
	🍷	🍴	🍴	K🍷		🍷	🍷	🍴	N🍴	L🍷	L🍷	R🍷	
Hamburg Hbf **800 900** d.	...	1346	1346	...	...	...	...	1546	...	2033	2033	...	...
Dortmund Hbf **800** d.	...	1636	1636	...	...	...	...	1836	...	|	|	...	...
Wuppertal Hbf **800** d.	...	1714	1714	...	...	...	...	1914	...	|	|	...	...
Essen Hbf **800** d.	1753	|	|	...	...	...	...	|	...	|	|	...	...
Düsseldorf Hbf **800** d.	1821	|	|	...	...	...	...	|	1935	|	|	...	...
Köln Hbf **800 910** d.	|	1753	1753	...	...	1928	1928	1953	2006	|	|	...	...
Köln Messe/Deutz **910** d.	1845	|	|	...	...	|	|	|	|	|	|	...	...
Bonn Hbf **800** d.	|	1814	1814	...	...	|	|	2014	2035	|	|	...	...
Koblenz Hbf **912** d.	|	1848	1848	...	...	|	|	2048	2115	|	|	...	...
Mainz Hbf **912** d.	|	1940	1940	...	...	|	|	2142	2212	|	|	...	...
ankfurt Flughafen ✈ § d.	1937	2001	2001	...	...	2037	2037	2201	|	|	|	...	...
ankfurt (Main) Hbf **850** d.	1954	2018	2018	...	...	2054	2054	2218	2247	|	|	...	...
anau Hbf **850** d.	|	2035	2035	...	...	|	|	2235	|	|	|	...	...
schaffenburg Hbf d.	2024	2049	2049	...	...	2124	2124	2249	|	|	|	...	...
ürzburg Hbf a.	2103	2128	2128	...	...	2203	2203	2341	|	0205	0205	...	...
ürzburg Hbf **900** d.	2105	2130	2130	...	...	2205	2205	2343	|	0207	0207	...	...
irnberg Hbf **900** a.	2159	2224	2224	...	...	2259	2259	0037	|	0307	0307	...	...
irnberg Hbf d.	2202	2235	2235	2240	2249	...	2303	...	|	0319	0323	0323	...
München Hbf **904** a.	2304	2348	|	|	|	...	0005	...	|	|	|	|	...
egensburg Hbf a.	...	...	2337	2342	0015	...	...	...	|	0418	0427	0427	...
egensburg Hbf d.	...	...	...	2344	0029	...	...	...	|	0420	0430	0430	...
raubing d.	...	...	...	0008	0101	...	...	...	|	|	|	|	...
attling **944** d.	...	...	...	0022	0119	...	...	...	|	|	|	|	...
assau Hbf 🏨 **944** a.	...	...	...	0054	...	...	...	...	|	0525	0532	0532	...
Linz Hbf **950** a.	...	...	...	...	...	...	...	...	0644	0650	0658	0658	...
Wien Westbahnhof **950** a.	...	...	...	...	...	...	...	...	0835	0902	0907	0907	...

K – 🚃12 and 🍷 Karlsruhe - Stuttgart - Nürnberg - Passau.
L – HANS ALBERS – 🛏 1, 2 cl., 🛌 2 cl. and 🚃2 Hamburg - Hannover - Wien. Conveys 🚃2 (*D* **60491/3**) Hamburg - Nürnberg (reservation not required).
N – DONAU-KURIER – 🛏 1, 2 cl., 🛌 2 cl., 🚃2 and 🍴 Amsterdam - Utrecht - Arnhem - Salzburg (a. 0510) - Wien.
R – SPREE-DONAU-KURIER – 🛏 1, 2 cl., 🛌 2 cl. and 🚃2 Berlin - Leipzig - Saalfeld - Wien. See also Table **851**.
T – Daily Dec. 21 - Jan. 6 and Mar. 14–30; ⑤–⑦ from Apr. 4 (also Apr. 30, May 1, 12, 21, 22).
Y – Daily Dec. 9–20 and Jan. 7 - Mar. 13; ①–④ from Mar. 31 (not Apr. 30, May 1, 12, 21, 22).

c – ⑥⑦ (also Dec. 24, 25, 26, 31, Jan. 1, Mar. 21, 24, May 12).
d – Not Dec. 25, 26, Jan. 1, Mar. 24, May 12.
e – Not Dec. 25, 26, Jan. 1, Mar. 22, 24, May 12.
f – Also Dec. 26, Jan. 1, Mar. 20, 24, Apr. 30, May 12, 21; not Dec. 23, 30, Mar. 23, May 11.
h – Also Dec. 23, Mar. 23, May 11.
q – Not Dec. 24, 25, 31, Mar. 21, 23, May 11.
t – Not Dec. 24, 31, May 22.
v – Not Dec. 25, Jan. 1.
w – ⑦ (also Dec. 26, Jan. 1, Mar. 24, May 12; not Dec. 23, 30, Mar. 23, May 11).
z – Starts from Hannover on Dec. 29 (see Table **900**).

***** – Train number **2329** on ⑥ from June 14.
§ – Frankfurt Flughafen Fernbahnhof.

– ①②③④⑥⑦ (not Dec. 23, Mar. 23, May 11).
G – To Garmisch on ⑥ (a. 1342).

RE / RB services Local trains FRANKFURT - WÜRZBURG - NÜRNBERG - REGENSBURG - PASSAU 921

For faster *ICE / IC* trains see Table **920** above.

km			©z	Ⓐe	†w	⚒r	Ⓐe	©z								©z	Ⓐe		©z	Ⓐe			⑦d	A		⊠
0	**Frankfurt** (Main) Hbf d.	...	*0442*k	*0442*	*0530*	0634	*0726*	0730	0834	0930	1034	1130	1234	1330	1434	1530	1534	1634	1730	1734	1834	1930	2034	2034	2130	2236
4	**Frankfurt** (Main) Süd d.	...	*0448*k	*0448*	*0536*	0640	*0733*	0736	0840	0936	1040	1136	1240	1336	1440	1536	1540	1640	1736	1740	1840	1936	2040	2040	2136	2242
10	Offenbach (Main) Hbf d.	...	|	|	|	0645	*0738*	|	0845	|	1046	|	1245	|	1445	|	1545	1645	|	1745	1845	|	2045	2045	|	2248
24	Hanau Hbf d.	...	*0513*k	*0513*	*0614*	0659	0759	0759	0859	0959	1059	1159	1259	1359	1459	1559	1559	1659	1759	1759	1859	1959	2059	2059	2159	2259
46	Aschaffenburg Hbf d.	0500	0602	0611	0710	0717	0817	0817	0917	1017	1117	1217	1317	1417	1517	1617	1617	1717	1817	1817	1917	2017	2117	2128	2221	2322
84	Lohr Bahnhof d.	0531	0632	0642	0741	0744	0844	0844	0944	1044	1144	1244	1344	1444	1544	1644	1644	1744	1844	1844	1944	2044	2144	2200	2253	2354
96	Gemünden (Main) d.	0543	0645	0654	0752	0800	0900	0900	1000	1100	1200	1300	1400	1500	1556	1700	1656	1756	1900	1858	2000	2100	2156	2212	2304	0007
109	Karlstadt (Main) d.	0553	0654	0703	0802	0808	0908	0908	1008	1108	1208	1308	1408	1508	1606	1708	1706	1806	1908	1908	2008	2108	2204	2220	2314	0016
136	**Würzburg** Hbf a.	0617	0718	0718	0824	0824	0924	0924	1024	1124	1224	1324	1424	1524	1622	1724	1722	1822	1924	1924	2024	2124	2220	2236	2336	0040

km			2⚒r	Ⓐe							⑥♥									2Ⓐe	2		2		2	
0	**Würzburg** Hbf d.	...	...	0511	0557	0638	0741	0840	0940	1040	1118	1140	1240	1340	1440	1540	1640	1740	1840	...	1946	2036	...	...	...	2255
23	Kitzingen d.	...	...	0526	0616	0653	0800	0900	1000	1100	|	1200	1300	1400	1500	1600	1700	1800	1900	...	2006	2054	...	...	...	2314
61	Neustadt (Aisch) Bf d.	0457	0525	0552	0641	0719	0825	0925	1025	1125	1204j	1225	1325	1425	1525	1625	1725	1825	1925	2010	...	2117	2143	...	2310	2338
94	Fürth (Bay) Hbf d.	0528	0556	0619	0705	0741	0848	0948	1048	1148	|	1248	1348	1448	1548	1648	1748	1848	1948	2041	...	2142	2224	...	2342	0008
102	**Nürnberg** Hbf a.	0537	0605	0627	0714	0750	0855	0955	1055	1155	1232	1255	1355	1455	1555	1655	1755	1855	1955	2050	...	2153	2234	...	2350	0017

	⚒r	△												Ⓐe	©z			⊙								
ürnberg Hbf d.	...	0529e	0656	0736	...	...	0936	...	...	1136	...	...	1336	...	...	...	1536	...	1635e	1736	...	...	1936	...	...	2136
eumarkt (Oberpf) d.	0452	0554e	0719	0757	0801	0902e	0957	1001	1102e	1157	1201	1302e	1357	...	1401	1501e	1557	1601	1702e	1757	1801	1902e	1957	2001	...	2157
egensburg Hbf a.	0549	0649e	0759	0839	0857	0959e	1039	1057	1159e	1239	1257	1359e	1439	...	1457	1557e	1639	1657	1759e	1839	1857	1959e	2039	2057	...	2239
egensburg Hbf d.	0551	0651	0801	0844	0859	1001	1044	1059	1201	1243	1259	1401	1444	1457	1459	1559	1644	1658	1801	1843	1859	2001	2044f	2059	2200	2244
München Hbf **878** a.	|	|	|	1020	|	|	1221	|	|	1421	|	|	1620	|	|	|	1820	|	|	2017	|	|	2221f	|	|	0021
raubing d.	0620	0721	0829	...	0928	1028	...	1128	1228	...	1328	1428	...	1528	1528	1628	...	1728	1828	...	1928	2028	...	2128	2229	...
attling a.	0637	0739	0846	...	0945	1045	...	1145	1245	...	1345	1445	...	1546	1545	1645	...	1745	1846	...	1945	2045	...	2145	2246	...
attling **944** d.	*0644*	0802	*0900*	...	*1004*	*1059*	...	1204	*1259*	...	*1404*q	*1459*	...	*1604*	1604	*1659*	...	1804	*1859*	...	*2004*e	*2101*	...	*2221*	*2305*n	...
assau Hbf **944** a.	*0718*	0837	*0937*	...	*1041*	*1136*	...	1241	*1336*	...	*1441*q	*1536*	...	*1641*	1641	*1736*	...	1841	*1936*	...	*2041*e	*2137*	...	*2258*	*2341*n	...

– ①–⑥ (not Dec. 25, 26, Jan. 1, Mar. 24, May 12).
– Also Dec. 25, 26, Jan. 1, Mar. 24, May 12.
– Ⓐ (not Dec. 24, 31, May 22).
– ⑤–⑦ (also Dec. 24, 25, 26, 31, Jan. 1, Mar. 24, May 1, 12, 22).
– Arrives 1155.

k – ⑥ (also Dec. 24, 31).
n – Not Dec. 24, 31.
q – 17 minutes later on ⑥.
r – Not May 22.
w – Also May 22.
z – Also Dec. 24, 31, May 22.

♥ – *IC* **1987**: 🚃12 Hamburg - Passau.
⊠ – Runs daily Frankfurt - Gemünden; ⑤⑥ only Frankfurt - Würzburg.
△ – Change trains at Plattling on © (also Dec. 24, 31, May 22).
⊙ – Change trains at Plattling on Ⓐ (not Dec. 24, 31, May 22).

Warning! Hamburg area alterations Dec. 24 - Jan. 1 (see page 363)

920 PASSAU - NÜRNBERG - FRANKFURT - FRANKFURT FLUGHAFEN ✈

For other regional trains see Table **921** below.

	ICE 928	ICE 822	ICE 820	IC 2162	ICE 1026	ICE 926	ICE 728	ICE 726	IC 2028	ICE 724	ICE 722	ICE 228	ICE 720	ICE 628	IC 1986	ICE 28	ICE 626	ICE 624	ICE 26	ICE 622	ICE 620	ICE 1820	ICE 1826	ICE 24	ICE 528
			①–⑤	①g	②–⑥	①⑦		①–⑥							⑥						①–⑤	⑦c	⑥p		Ⓑr
	✕	🍷	d🍷	K🍷	m✕	b✕	🍷	e🍷	🍷	🍷	🍷	✕	🍷	🍷	🍷	✕	🍷	🍷	✕	🍷	d🍷	🍷	🍷	✕	🍷
Wien Westbahnhof **950** d.	...	...	...	...	...	...	...	...	...	...	...	0640	...	...	...	0840	...	...	1040	...	...	...	...	1240	...
Linz Hbf **950** d.	...	...	...	...	...	...	...	...	...	...	...	0816	...	...	...	1016	...	...	1216	...	...	...	...	1416	...
Passau Hbf 🏛 **944** d.	...	...	...	0512	...	...	...	...	0719	...	...	0931	...	...	1102	1131	...	...	1331	...	...	...	...	1531	...
Plattling **944** d.	...	...	...	0544	...	...	...	...	0752	...	...	1000	...	...	1133	1200	...	...	1400	...	...	...	...	1600	...
Straubing d.	...	...	...	0558	...	...	...	...	0806	...	...	|	...	...	1147	|	...	...	|	...	...	...	...	|	...
Regensburg Hbf a.	...	...	...	0619	...	...	...	...	0826	...	...	1031	...	...	1207	1231	...	...	1431	...	...	...	...	1631	...
Regensburg Hbf d.	...	...	...	0621	0622	...	...	...	0828	...	...	1033	...	...	1209	1233	...	...	1433	...	...	...	...	1633	...
München Hbf **904** d.	...	0451g	0551	|	|	0614j	0651	0755	|	0855	0956	|	1055	1156	|	|	1255	1356	|	1455	1556	1556	1556	|	165
Nürnberg Hbf a.	...	0557g	0658	0721	0721	0726j	0757	0857	0925	0957	1058	1125	1157	1258	1315	1325	1357	1458	1525	1557	1658	1658	1658	1725	175
Nürnberg Hbf **900** d.	0530	0600	0701	...	0729	0729	0800	0900	0928	1000	1101	1128	1200	1301	1318	1328	1400	1501	1528	1600	1701	1701	1701	1728	180
Würzburg Hbf **900** a.	0625	0654	0754	...	0825	0825	0854	0954	1023	1054	1154	1225	1254	1354	1417	1425	1454	1554	1625	1654	1754	1754	1754	1825	185
Würzburg Hbf d.	0627	0656	0756	...	0827	0827	0856	0956	1025	1056	1156	1227	1256	1356	1419	1427	1456	1556	1627	1656	1756	1756	1756	1827	185
Aschaffenburg Hbf d.	0708	0737	0837	...	|	|	0937	1037	|	1137	1237	|	1337	1437	|	|	1537	1637	|	1737	1837	1837	1837	|	193
Hanau Hbf **850** d.	|	|	|	...	0920	0920	|	|	1120	|	|	|	|	|	|	1520	|	|	1720	|	|	|	|	1920	|
Frankfurt (Main) Hbf **850** a.	0736	0805	0905	...	0936	0936	1005	1105	1136	1205	1305	1340	1405	1505	|	1536	1605	1705	1736	1805	1905	1905	1905	1936	200
Frankfurt Flughafen ✈ § a.	0755	0821	0921	...	0955	0955	1021	1121	1157	1221	1321	...	1421	1521	|	...	1621	1721	1755	1821	1921	1921	1921	1955	202
Mainz Hbf **912** a.	0816	|	|	...	1016	1016	|	|	1216	|	|	...	|	|	|	...	|	|	1815	|	|	|	|	2016	|
Koblenz Hbf **912** a.	0910	|	|	...	1110	1110	|	|	1310	|	|	...	|	|	|	...	|	|	1910	|	|	|	|	2110	|
Bonn Hbf **800** a.	0942	|	|	...	1142	1142	|	|	1342	|	|	...	|	|	|	...	|	|	1943	|	|	|	|	2142	|
Köln Messe/Deutz **910** a.	|	0914	1014	...	|	|	|	1214	|	|	1414	...	|	1614	|	...	|	1814	|	1914	|	2014	|	|	211
Köln Hbf **800 910** a.	1005	|	|	...	1205	1205	1140	|	1405	1340	|	...	1540	|	|	...	1731	|	2005	|	2031	|	2040	2205	|
Düsseldorf Hbf **800** a.	|	0937	1037	...	|	|	...	1237	|	...	1437	...	...	1637	|	...	...	1837	|	1942	...	2037	2111	|	213
Essen Hbf **800** a.	|	1002	1102	...	|	|	...	1302	|	...	1502	...	...	1702	|	...	...	1902	|	2008	...	2108	2136	|	220
Wuppertal Hbf **800** a.	1041	...	...	...	1241	1241	...	...	1441	...	...	...	...	...	|	...	...	|	2041	|	...	|	|	2241	|
Dortmund Hbf **800** a.	1120	...	...	...	1320	1320	...	...	1520	...	...	...	...	...	|	...	...	1929	2120	2038	...	2137	2159	2320	222
Hamburg Hbf **800 900** a.	1412	...	...	...	1612	1612	...	...	1812	...	...	...	...	...	1905h	...	...	...	...	...	...	...	...	...	...

	ICE 1828	ICE 526	ICE 22	ICE 524	ICE 522	ICE 20	ICE 1824	ICE 520	ICE 1822	EN 428	EN 492	EN 490	CNL 312
	⑥	Ⓑq			n		⑦w	①–⑥	⑦w	🅁	T🅁	Y🅁	🅁
	G🍷	🍷	✕	🍷	🍷	✕	✕	t🍷	✕	M🍷	L🍷	L🍷	N✕
Wien Westbahnhof **950** d.	...	...	1440	...	...	1640	...	...	...	1952	1952	1957	2035
Linz Hbf **950** d.	...	...	1616	...	...	1816	...	...	...	2151	2151	2156	2220
Passau Hbf 🏛 **944** d.	...	...	1731	...	...	1931	...	...	...	2305	2305	2312	|
Plattling **944** d.	...	...	1800	...	...	2000	...	...	...	|	|	|	|
Straubing d.	...	...	|	...	...	|	...	...	...	2349	2349	|	|
Regensburg Hbf a.	...	...	1831	...	...	2032	...	...	...	0011	0011	0017	|
Regensburg Hbf d.	...	...	1833	...	...	2034	...	...	...	0013	0013	0019	|
München Hbf **904** d.	1655	1756	|	1855	1951	|	2053	2056	2255	|	|	|	|
Nürnberg Hbf a.	1757	1858	1925	1957	2057	2124	2158	2158	0004	0117	0117	0121	|
Nürnberg Hbf **900** d.	1800	1901	1928	2000	2100	2127	2201	2201	0007	...	0131	0131	|
Würzburg Hbf **900** a.	1854	1954	2025	2054	2154	2227	2254	2254	0101	...	0226	0226	|
Würzburg Hbf d.	1856	1956	2027	2056	2156	2229	2301	2301	0103	...	0228	0228	|
Aschaffenburg Hbf d.	1937	2037	|	2137	2237	2310	2343	2343	0143	...	|	|	|
Hanau Hbf **850** d.	|	|	2120	|	|	2324	2356	2356	0157	...	|	|	|
Frankfurt (Main) Hbf **850** a.	2005	2105	2136	2205	2300z	2339	0013	0012	0214	...	|	|	0600
Frankfurt Flughafen ✈ § a.	2021	2121	2157	2221	2315	...	...	...	...	...	|	|	|
Mainz Hbf **912** a.	|	|	2217	|	...	...	...	...	...	...	|	|	0632r
Koblenz Hbf **912** a.	|	|	2310	|	...	...	...	...	...	...	|	|	0744
Bonn Hbf **800** a.	|	|	2342	|	...	...	...	...	...	...	|	|	0817
Köln Messe/Deutz **910** a.	2114	2219	|	2341	...	...	...	...	...	...	|	|	|
Köln Hbf **800 910** a.	|	|	0005	|	...	...	...	...	...	...	|	|	0842
Düsseldorf Hbf **800** a.	2137	2242	0034x	0004	...	...	...	...	...	...	|	|	0909
Essen Hbf **800** a.	2202	2307	0059x	0029	...	...	...	...	...	...	|	|	...
Wuppertal Hbf **800** a.	|	|	|	|	...	...	...	...	...	...	|	|	...
Dortmund Hbf **800** a.	2228	2336	0122x	0052	...	...	...	...	...	...	|	|	...
Hamburg Hbf **800 900** a.	...	...	...	...	...	...	...	...	...	...	0750	0750	...

G – From Garmisch (d. 1518).
K – 🚃12 and 🍷 Passau - Nürnberg - Stuttgart - Karlsruhe.
L – HANS ALBERS – 🛏 1, 2 cl., 🛌 2 cl. and 🚃2 Wien - Hannover - Hamburg. Conveys 🚃2 (*D* **60490/2**) Nürnberg - Hamburg (reservation not required).

M – DONAU-SPREE-KURIER – 🛏 1, 2 cl., 🛌 2 cl. and 🚃2 Wien - Saalfeld - Leipzig - Berlin. See also Table **851**.
N – DONAU-KURIER – 🛏 1, 2 cl., 🛌 2 cl., 🚃2 and ✕ Wien - Salzburg (d. 2342) - Arnhem - Utrecht - Amsterdam.
T – Daily Dec. 9 – 19 and Jan. 6 - Mar. 12; ①②③⑦ from Mar. 30 (not Apr. 29, 30, May 11, 20, 21).
Y – Daily Dec. 20 - Jan. 5 and Mar. 13 – 29; ④–⑥ from Apr. 3 (also Apr. 29, 30, May 11, 20, 21).

b – Also Dec. 26, 27, Jan. 1, 2, Mar. 25, May 13; not Dec. 24, 31, Mar. 24, May 12.
c – Also Dec. 26, Jan. 1, Mar. 21, 24, May 12; not Mar. 23, May 11.
d – Not Dec. 24, 25, 26, 31, Jan. 1, Mar. 21, 24, May 12.
e – Not Dec. 25, 26, Jan. 1, Mar. 22, 24, May 12.
g – ① (also Dec. 27, Jan. 2, Mar. 25, May 13; not Dec. 24, 31, Mar. 24, May 12).
h – Terminates at Hannover on Dec. 29 (see Table **900**).
j – ① (not Dec. 24, 31, Mar. 24, May 12).
m – Also Dec. 24, 31, Mar. 24, May 12; not Dec. 26, 27, Jan. 1, 2, Mar. 25, May 13.
n – Not Dec. 24, 31.
p – Also Dec. 24, 25, 31, Mar. 23, May 11.
q – Not Dec. 24, 25, 31, Mar. 21, 23, May 11.
r – 0645 on ©.
t – Also Dec. 23, 30, Mar. 23, May 11; not Dec. 26, Jan. 1, Mar. 24, May 12.
w – Also Dec. 26, Jan. 1, Mar. 24, May 12; not Dec. 23, 30, Mar. 23, May 11.
x – Not Dec. 25, Jan. 1.
z – Frankfurt (Main) **Süd**.

§ – Frankfurt Flughafen Fernbahnhof.

921 Local trains PASSAU - REGENSBURG - NÜRNBERG - WÜRZBURG - FRANKFURT

RE / RB services

For faster *ICE / IC* trains see Table **920** above.

	⚒r												⊙			⊙					©z	Ⓐe				
Passau Hbf **944** d.	0438	0549	0604f	...	...	0821	0912	...	1021	1112	...	1221	1312	...	1421	1512	...	1621	1712	...	1821*	1821	1912	...	2023	...
Plattling **944** a.	0514	0625	0640f	...	...	0856	0948	...	1056	1148	...	1256	1348	...	1456	1548	...	1656	1748	...	1856*	1856	1948	...	2058	...
Plattling d.	0521	0630	0704	0804z	...	0904	1004	...	1104	1204	...	1304	1404	...	1504	1604	...	1704	1804	...	1903	1904	2004	...	2104	2204
Straubing d.	0538	0646	0723	0823	...	0923	1023	...	1123	1223	...	1323	1423	...	1523	1623	...	1723	1823	...	1920	1923	2023	...	2123	2223
München Hbf **878** d.	|	|	|	|	0743	|	|	0943	|	|	1143	|	|	1343	|	|	1543	|	|	1743	|	|	|	1943	|	|
Regensburg Hbf a.	0609	0716	0752	0851	0914	0951	1051	1114	1151	1252	1314	1352	1451	1514	1551	1652	1714	1751	1851	1914	1948	1953	2053	2121	2151	2251
Regensburg Hbf d.	...	0720	0755e	0853	0919	0953e	1053	1120	1153e	1253z	1320	1353e	1453	1520	1553e	1654	1720	1753e	1853	1920	1950	2025	2053z	2125	...	2253
Neumarkt (Oberpf) d.	...	0802	0854e	0950	1002	1050e	1150	1202	1250e	1350z	1402	1450e	1550	1602	1650e	1752	1802	1850e	1950	2002	2031	2129	2150z	2209	...	2351
Nürnberg Hbf a.	...	0825	...	...	1027	...	...	1225	...	...	1425	...	...	1627	...	...	1827	...	...	2025	2053	...	...	2231	...	0026

			⚒r													Ⓐe				2	2		2			
Nürnberg Hbf d.	0041	...	0448	0543	0607	0706	0805	0904	1005	1105	1205	1305	1405	1505	1605	1623	1705	1805	1905	...	2010	2104	2210	...	2335	...
Fürth (Bay) Hbf d.	0050	...	0457	0552	0615	0714	0813	0912	1013	1113	1213	1313	1413	1513	1613	1631	1713	1813	1913	...	2019	2112	2219	...	2345	...
Neustadt (Aisch) Bf d.	0120	...	0525	0621	0635	0734	0834	0934	1034	1134	1234	1334	1434	1534	1634	1702	1734	1834	1934	...	2049	2141	2249	...	0013	...
Kitzingen d.	...	...	0549	...	0659	0758	0858	0958	1058	1158	1258	1358	1458	1558	1658	1728	1758	1858	1958	2056	...	2204	...	...	0036	...
Würzburg Hbf a.	...	...	0609	...	0719	0819	0919	1019	1119	1219	1319	1419	1519	1619	1719	1751	1819	1919	2019	2116	...	2224	...	...	0056	...

	Ⓐe			©z	⑥m	Ⓐe								©z	Ⓐe							†w	⚒r	⑥d	⑦c	A
Würzburg Hbf d.	0424	0517	...	0611	0611	0635	0735	0835	0935	1035	1135	1235	1335	1435	1435	1535	1635	1735	1835	1935	2035	2136	2139	2139	2305	2316
Karlstadt (Main) d.	0446	0541	...	0633	0633	0650	0750	0850	0950	1050	1150	1250	1350	1450	1450	1550	1650	1750	1850	1950	2050	2153	2201	2201	2327	2338
Gemünden (Main) d.	0458	0553	...	0645	0645	0705	0805	0905	1005	1105	1205	1305	1405	1505	1505	1605	1705	1805	1905	2005	2105	2205	2212	2212	2338	2349
Lohr Bahnhof d.	0508	0603	...	0654	0654	0715	0815	0915	1015	1115	1215	1315	1415	1515	1515	1615	1715	1815	1915	2015	2115	2215	2222	2222	2348	2359
Aschaffenburg Hbf d.	0542	0640	0717	0726	0743	0744	0844	0944	1044	1144	1244	1344	1444	1544	1544	1644	1744	1844	1944	2044	2144	2244	2255	2313	0020	0031
Hanau Hbf d.	0604	0704r	0802	...	0804	0804	0904	1003	1104	1203	1304	1403	1504	1603	1604	1704	1803	1904	2003	2104	2203	2303	...	0001n	...	...
Offenbach (Main) Hbf d.	0612	0712r	|	...	0812	0812	0912	|	1112	|	1312	|	1512	|	1612	1712	|	1912	|	2112	|	|	...	|	...	...
Frankfurt (Main) Süd a.	0616	0716r	0825	...	0816	0816	0916	1025	1116	1225	1316	1425	1516	1625	1616	1716	1825	1915	2025	2116	2225	2325	...	0025	...	...
Frankfurt (Main) Hbf a.	0624	0724r	0832	...	0826	0826	0924	1032	1124	1232	1324	1432	1524	1632	1628	1724	1832k	1924	2032	2124	2232	2332	...	0032	...	...

A – ①–⑥ (also Dec. 23, 30, Mar. 23, May 11; not Mar. 24, May 12).
c – Also Mar. 24, May 12; not Dec. 23, 30, Mar. 23, May 11.
d – Runs daily Aschaffenburg - Frankfurt.
e – Ⓐ (not Dec. 24, 31, May 22).
f – 11 minutes later on © (also Dec. 24, 31, May 22).
k – 1840 on ⑦ (also Dec. 26, Jan. 1, Mar. 24, May 12; not Dec. 23, 30, Mar. 23, May 11).
m – Also Dec. 24, 31.
n – Arrives 2338.
r – ⚒ (not May 22).
w – Also May 22.
z – © (also Dec. 24, 31, May 22).
* – Through service from Apr. 26 (Passau d. 1830, Plattling a. 1901).
⊙ – Change trains at Plattling on Ⓐ (not Dec. 24, 31, May 22).

WÜRZBURG - HEILBRONN - STUTTGART — 922

RE services

km		Ⓐe	Ⓐe	Ⓐe		Ⓐe		Ⓐe					†w		Ⓑn		
0	**Würzburg** Hbf d.	...	...	...	0637	...	0837	0937	1037	1237	1437	1637	1736	1837	1936	2037	2137
43	Lauda d.	...	0532	...	0710	0719	0910	1010	1110	1310	1510	1710	1806	1910	2006	2110	2206
78	Osterburken d.	0502	0600	0611	0733	0802	0933	1033	1133	1333	1533	1733	1830	1933	2030	2133	2230
94	Möckmühl d.	0519	...	0628	0745	0819	0945	1045	1145	1345	1545	1745	1842	1945	2042	2145	2242
116	Bad Friedrichshall ⊖ d.	0544	...	0654	0801	0844	1001	1101	1201	1401	1601	1801	1858	2001	2058	2201	2258
127	**Heilbronn** Hbf **924** d.	0559	...	0712	0812	0856	1012	1112	1212	1412	1612	1812	1909	2012	2107	2210	2307
140	Lauffen (Neckar) **924** d.	0610	...	|	|	0904	|	|	|	|	|	|	|	|	2116	2218	2316
180	**Stuttgart** Hbf **924** a.	0651	...	0747	0853	0943	1053	1150	1253	1453	1653	1853	1949	2053	2155	2253	2353

	Ⓐe	†w	Ⓐe	⑥k						†w	Ⓐe		†w	Ⓐe			⑥⑦C
Stuttgart Hbf **924** d.	0452	0456	0558	0559	0705	0907	1107	1307	1504	1605	1632	1704	1805	1809	1907	2031	2315
Lauffen (Neckar) **924** d.	0527	0532	|	0635	0739	|	|	|	|	|	|	|	|	|	|	2106	2352
Heilbronn Hbf **924** d.	0538	0544	0642	0647	0750	0947	1147	1347	1547	1647	1710	1747	1847	1844	1947	2117	0011
Bad Friedrichshall ⊖ d.	0549	0554	0650	0657	0800	0957	1157	1357	1557	1657	1721	1757	1857	1854	1957	2126	0024
Möckmühl d.	0605	0610	0713	0713	0816	1013	1213	1413	1613	1713	1755	1813	1913	1918	2013	2142	0048
Osterburken d.	0616	0622	0727	0727	0828	1027	1227	1427	1627	1727	1813	1827	1927	1930	2027	2154	0106
Lauda d.	0643	0650	0750	0750	0851	1050	1250	1450	1650	1750	...	1850	1950	1954	2050	2218	...
Würzburg Hbf a.	0722	0722	0822	0822	0922	1122	1322	1522	1722	1822	...	1922	2022	2024	2122	2247	...

C – ⑥⑦ (also Dec. 26, Jan. 1, Mar. 24, May 1, 12, 22; not Dec. 23, 30, Mar. 23, May 11). On ⑥ change trains at Heilbronn.

e – Not Dec. 24, 31, May 22.
k – Also Dec. 24, 31.
n – Not Dec. 24, 31.
w – Also May 22.

⊖ – Bad Friedrichshall-Jagstfeld. See also Table **924**.

MANNHEIM - EBERBACH - OSTERBURKEN — 923

S-Bahn

km		Ⓐe	Ⓐe	⚒r	⚒r	Ⓐe										n	⑥t	n
	Kaiserslautern Hbf 919 d.	...	...	...	...	0456	...	0614r	0733	0830	0928		1832	1928	2028	2141	2141	2232*
0	**Mannheim** Hbf **924** ¶ d.	0422	...	0459j	...	0606	0637q	0729	0837	0937	1037		1937	2037	2137	2257	2257	2337
17	**Heidelberg** Hbf **924** ¶ d.	0442	...	0555	...	0625	0655	0755	0855	0955	1055	and	1955	2055	2200	2315	2315	2355
28	Neckargemünd **924** d.	0456	...	0609	...	0639	0709	0809	0909	1009	1109		2009	2109	2214	2329	2329	0009
34	Neckarsteinach d.	0502	...	0615	...	0645	0715	0815	0915	1015	1115	hourly	2015	2115	2220	2335	2335	0015
41	Hirschhorn (Neckar) d.	0509	...	0622	...	0652	0722	0822	0922	1022	1122		2022	2122	2227	2342	2342	0022
50	Eberbach **924** d.	0516	...	0629	...	0713f	0729	0829	0929	1029	1129	until	2029	2129	2234	2349	2349	0029
69	Mosbach-Neckarelz **924** d.	0535	0623	0648	0710	0734	0748	0848	0948	1048	1148		2048	2148	2258	0008	0008	0048
72	Mosbach (Baden) d.	0539	0627	0652	0714	0739	0752	0852	0952	1052	1152		2052	2152	2302	0012	0012	0052
101	**Osterburken** a.	0612	0658	...	0752v	...	0823	0923	1023	1123	1223		2123	...	2333	...	0043	...

	⚒r	Ⓐe	Ⓐe	⑥k	⚒r	Ⓐe	Ⓒz		Ⓐe		Ⓐe							
Osterburken d.	...	...	0513	0536	...	0606	0636	...	0644	...	0706	...	0736		1836	1936	2036	2206
Mosbach (Baden) d.	0435	0510	0543	0605	0605	0635	0705	0705	0718	...	0735	...	0805		1905	2005	2105	2235
Mosbach-Neckarelz **924** d.	0440	0528g	0550	0610	0610	0640	0710	0710	0724	0729	0740	0740r	0810	and	1910	2010	2110	2240
Eberbach **924** d.	0459	0547	0609	0629	0629	0659	0729	0729	...	0743	0759	0759	0829		1929	2029	2129	2259
Hirschhorn (Neckar) d.	0506	0554	0616	0636	0636	0706	0736	0736	...	|	0806	0806	0836	hourly	1936	2036	2136	2306
Neckarsteinach d.	0512	0600	0622	0642	0642	0712	0742	0742	...	|	0812	0812	0842		1942	2042	2142	2312
Neckargemünd **924** d.	0519	0607	0629	0649	0649	0719	0749	0749	...	|	0819	0819	0849	until	1949	2049	2149	2319
Heidelberg Hbf **924** ¶ a.	0533	0620	0643	0703	0703	0733	0803	0803	...	0808	0833	0833	0903		2003	2103	2203	2333
Mannheim Hbf **924** ¶ a.	0552	0637	0703	0720	0720	0751	0821	0821	...	0824	0851	0851	0921		2021	2121	2221	2355
Kaiserslautern Hbf 919 a.	0659	0743	0812	0829	0829	0859	0925	0925	...	...	0959	0959	1029		2128	...	2341n	...

e – Ⓐ (not Dec. 24, 31, May 22).
f – Arrives 0658.
g – Arrives 0514.
j – 0529 on ⑥ (also Dec. 24, 31).
k – Also Dec. 24, 31.
n – Not Dec. 24, 31.
q – ⑥ (also Dec. 24, 31). On † (also May 22) depart 0616. On Ⓐ (not Dec. 24, 31, May 22) depart 0629.
r – ⚒ (not May 22).
t – Also Dec. 25, Mar. 20, 23, Apr. 30, May 11, 21.
v – 0744 on ⑥ (also Dec. 24, 31).
z – Also Dec. 24, 31, May 22.

* – On ⑤⑥ change trains at Schifferstadt (a. 2314, d. 2317).
¶ – See also Tables **911a**, **918**, **919**.

MANNHEIM - HEILBRONN - STUTTGART — 924

RE / RB services

km		Ⓐe	Ⓐe	Ⓒz	Ⓐe	Ⓐe		Ⓐe	Ⓐe	Ⓐe		Ⓐe	Ⓐe	Ⓐe											
0	**Mannheim** Hbf **923** ¶ d.	...	...	...	...	...	...	0459	...	0626	...	0734	0700	...	0759	0834	...	0859	0934	0959	1034	...	1059	1134	1159
17	**Heidelberg** Hbf **923** ¶ d.	...	...	...	...	...	...	0542	...	0642	...	0749	0720	...	0821	0849	...	0921	0949	1021	1049	...	1121	1149	1221
29	Neckargemünd **923** d.	...	...	...	...	...	...	0554	...	|	...	|	0733	...	0833	|	...	0933	|	1033	|	...	1133	|	1233
49	Sinsheim (Elsenz) d.	...	...	...	0503	...	...	0625	...	0713	...	|	0759	...	0858	0919	...	0959	|	1058	1119	...	1159	|	1258
72	Bad Wimpfen d.	...	...	...	0535	...	...	0657	...	0737	...	|	0834*	...	▬	0937	...	1034	|	▬	1137	...	1234	|	▬
	Eberbach **923** d.	...	...	...	|	...	...	|	...	|	...	0814	|	...	...	|	...	|	1014	...	|	...	|	1214	...
	Mosbach-Neckarelz **923** d.	...	...	...	|	0552	0618r	|	0651	|	0752	0828	|	...	0852	|	0952	|	1028	1052	|	1152	|	1228	1252
75	Bad Friedrichshall-J. ◐ **922** d.	...	...	...	0544	0612	0638r	0703	0711	0742	0812	0841	0838*	0844	0912	0942	1012	1038	1042	1112	1142	1212	1238	1242	1312
86	**Heilbronn** Hbf **922** a.	...	...	...	0557	0625	0651r	0718	0724	0752	0825	0851	...	0854	0925	0952	1025	...	1051	1125	1152	1225	...	1251	1325
86	**Heilbronn** Hbf **922** d.	0435	0536	0554	0559	0627	0653	...	0725	0756	0826	0856	...	0856	0926	0956e	1026	...	1056f	1126	1156e	1226	...	1256f	1326
99	Lauffen (Neckar) **922** d.	0445	0545	0604	0610	0636	0704	...	0736	0804	0837	0904	...	0904	0937	1004e	1037	...	1104f	1137	1204e	1237	...	1304f	1337
139	**Stuttgart** Hbf **922** a.	0525	0625	0643	0651	0718	0743	...	0815	0843	0915	0943	...	0943	1015	1043e	1115	...	1143f	1215	1243e	1315	...	1343f	1415

			◇										⊡								n	n	n	n	A
	Mannheim Hbf **923** ¶ d.	1234	...	1259	1334	1359	1434	...	1459	1534	1559	1634	...	1659	1734	1759	1834	...	1859	1934	1959*	2034	2107	2142	2253	...
	Heidelberg Hbf **923** ¶ d.	1249	...	1321	1349	1421	1449	...	1521	1549	1621	1649	...	1721	1749	1821	1849	...	1921	1949	2021	2049	2128	2157	2305	2309
	Neckargemünd **923** d.	|	...	1333	|	1433	|	...	1533	|	1633	|	...	1733	|	1833	|	...	1933	|	2033	|	2145	|	|	2325
	Sinsheim (Elsenz) d.	1319	...	1359	|	1458	1519	...	1559	|	1658	1719	...	1759	|	1858	1919	...	1959	|	2058	2119	2212	|	|	2352
	Bad Wimpfen d.	1337	...	1434	|	▬	1537	...	1634	|	▬	1737	...	1834	|	▬	1937	...	2034	|	▬	2139	...	|	|	...
	Eberbach **923** d.	|	...	|	1414	...	|	...	|	1614	...	|	...	|	1814	...	|	...	|	2014	...	|	...	2223	2331	...
	Mosbach-Neckarelz **923** d.	|	1352	|	1428	1452	|	1552	|	1628	1652	|	1752	|	1828	1852	|	1952	|	2028	2052	|	...	2238	2345	...
	Bad Friedrichshall-J. ◐ **922** d.	1342	1412	1438	1442	1512	1542	1612	1638	1642	1712	1742	1812	1838	1842	1912	1942	2012	2038	2042	2112	2144	...	2251	2357	...
	Heilbronn Hbf **922** a.	1352	1425	...	1451	1525	1552	1625	...	1651	1725	1752	1825	...	1851	1925	1952	2025	...	2051	2125	2154	...	2300	0007	...
	Heilbronn Hbf **922** d.	1356e	1426	...	1456f	1526	1556e	1626	...	1656f	1726	1756e	1826	...	1856e	1926	2012	2026	...	2107b	2126	2210	...	2307	...	...
	Lauffen (Neckar) **922** d.	1404e	1437	...	1504f	1537	1604e	1637	...	1704f	1737	1804e	1837	...	1904e	1937	|	2037	...	2116b	2137	2218	...	2316	...	...
	Stuttgart Hbf **922** a.	1443e	1515	...	1543f	1615	1643e	1715	...	1745f	1815	1843e	1915	...	1943e	2015	2053	2115	...	2155b	2215	2253	...	2353	...	...

km		Ⓐe	Ⓐe	Ⓐe	⚒r	Ⓐe		Ⓐe	Ⓐe	⑥k		Ⓐe													
0	**Stuttgart** Hbf **922** d.	...	...	...	...	0452	...	0545	0558	0559	...	...	0705	0745	0809g	...	0845	0915e	0945	1009g	...	1045	1115e	1145	1209g
40	Lauffen (Neckar) **922** d.	...	...	...	...	0527	...	0623	|	0635	0649e	...	0739	0822	0844g	...	0922	0953e	1022	1044g	...	1122	1153e	1223	1244g
53	**Heilbronn** Hbf **922** a.	...	...	...	...	0538	...	0633	0640	0646	0659e	...	0748	0832	0854g	...	0932	1001e	1032	1054g	...	1132	1201e	1233	1254g
53	**Heilbronn** Hbf **922** d.	...	0456	0500	0529	0543	0622	0634	0642	0647	0700	...	0805	0834	0905	...	0934	1005	1034	1105	...	1134	1205	1234	1305
64	Bad Friedrichshall-J. ⊖ **922** d.	...	0504	0515	0543	0554	0637	0647	0650	0657	0710	0718	0816	0847	0915	0918	0947	1016	1047	1115	1118	1147	1216	1247	1315
82	Mosbach-Neckarelz **923** d.	...	0518	|	0604	|	|	0704	...	...	0729	|	|	0906	0929	|	1006	|	1106	1129	|	1206	|	1306	1329
101	Eberbach **923** d.	...	0532	|	▬	|	|	...	...	...	0743	|	|	▬	0943	|	...	|	▬	1143	|	...	|	▬	1343
	Bad Wimpfen d.	...	|	0518		0558	0640	...	...	...	|	0721	0820	...	|	0921	...	1020	...	|	1121	...	1220	...	|
	Sinsheim (Elsenz) d.	0509	|	0549	0550	0621	0714	...	...	...	|	0759	0839	0859	|	0959	...	1039	1059	|	1159	...	1239	1259	|
123	Neckargemünd **923** d.	0534	|	0614	0614	|	0741	...	...	...	|	0824	|	0924	|	1024	...	|	1124	|	1224	...	|	1324	|
135	**Heidelberg** Hbf **923** ¶ a.	0548	0557	0629	0629	0648	0759	...	...	...	0808	0838	0908	0938	1008	1038	...	1108	1138	1208	1238	...	1308	1338	1408
152	**Mannheim** Hbf **923** ¶ a.	0621	0614	0652	0652	0706	0829	...	...	...	0824	0902	0924	1002	1024	1102	...	1124	1202	1224	1302	...	1324	1402	1424

		★					♥									n			n	n	n		n			v
	Stuttgart Hbf **922** d.	...	1245	1315e	1345	1409g	...	1445	1515e	1545	1609g	...	1645	1716e	1745	1813	...	1845	1915e	...	1945	2031	...	2115	2315	0015
	Lauffen (Neckar) **922** d.	...	1323	1353e	1422	1444g	...	1522	1553e	1622	1644g	...	1722	1753e	1823	1850	...	1922	1953e	...	2022	2106	...	2153	2352	0051
	Heilbronn Hbf **922** a.	...	1333	1401e	1432	1454g	...	1532	1601e	1632	1654g	...	1732	1801e	1833	1901	...	1932	2001e	...	2032	2115	...	2203	0004	0102
	Heilbronn Hbf **922** d.	...	1334	1405	1434	1505	...	1534	1605	1634	1705	...	1734	1805	1834	1905	...	1934	2005	...	2059	2117	...	2204	▬	...
	Bad Friedrichshall-J. ⊖ **922** d.	1318	1347	1416	1447	1515	1518	1547	1616	1647	1715	1718	1747	1816	1847	1915	1918	1947	2016	...	2111	2126	2144	2217	...	...
	Mosbach-Neckarelz **923** d.	|	1406	|	1506	1529	|	1606	|	1706	1729	|	1806	|	1906	1929	|	2006	|	...	2129	...	|	2236	...	...
	Eberbach **923** d.	|	...	|	▬	1543	|	...	|	▬	1743	|	...	|	▬	1943	|	...	|	...	2143	...	|	▬	...	...
	Bad Wimpfen d.	1321	...	1420	...	|	1521	...	1620	...	|	1721	...	1820	...	|	1921	...	2020	...	|	...	2147	A	B 🚌	...
	Sinsheim (Elsenz) d.	1359	...	1439	1459	|	1559	...	1639	1659	|	1759	...	1839	1859	|	1959	...	2039	2059	|	...	2216	2223	2223	...
	Neckargemünd **923** d.	1424	...	|	1524	|	1624	...	|	1724	|	1824	...	|	1924	|	2024	...	|	2124	|	...	...	2247	2258	...
	Heidelberg Hbf **923** ¶ a.	1438	...	1508	1538	1608	1638	...	1708	1738	1808	1838	...	1908	1938	2008	2038	...	2108	2138	2208	...	...	2304	2320	...
	Mannheim Hbf **923** ¶ a.	1502	...	1524	1602	1624	1702	...	1724	1802	1824	1902	...	1924	2002	2024	2102	...	2124	2224	2224	...	...	2330	2355	...

A – Until Mar. 2 (not Dec. 24, 31).
B – From Mar. 3.
b – Ⓑ (not Dec. 24, 31).
e – Ⓐ (not Dec. 24, 31, May 22).
f – 3–6 minutes later on Ⓒ (also Dec. 24, 31, May 22).
g – 4–7 minutes later on Ⓐ (not Dec. 24, 31, May 22).

k – Also Dec. 24, 31.
n – Not Dec. 24, 31.
r – ⚒ (not May 22).
v – Not Dec. 25, Jan. 1.
z – Also Dec. 24, 31, May 22.

⊖ – Bad Friedrichshall-Jagstfeld.

* – Change trains at Steinsfurt (a. 0803, d. 0807).
◇ – On Ⓐe change trains at Steinsfurt (a. 1403, d. 1407).
⊡ – On Ⓐe change trains at Steinsfurt (a. 1803, d. 1807).
★ – On Ⓐe change trains at Steinsfurt (a. 1347, d. 1351).
♥ – On Ⓐe change trains at Steinsfurt (a. 1547, d. 1551).
¶ – See also Tables **911a**, **918**, **919**.

GERMANY

925 STUTTGART - BACKNANG / AALEN - NÜRNBERG

RE services except where shown

km			RE	IC			IC			IC				IC				IC			IC			IC		
			4199	2061			2063			2065				2067				2069			2161			2163		
		Ⓐe	⑥⑦	①–⑤			v					Ⓒz	Ⓐe			Ⓒz	Ⓐe							Ⓑq		
			M	d	2		🍷			🍷				🍷				🍷			🍷			🍷		
	Karlsruhe Hbf 930 .. d.	...	...	...	...	...	0706	...	...	0906	...	...	...	1106	...	...	...	1306	...	...	1506	...	...	1706	...	...
0	**Stuttgart** Hbf ‡ d.	0540	0548	0605	0620e	0640	0807	0822	0840	1007	1022	1040	1040	1207	1222	1240	1240	1407	1422	1440	1607	1619h	1640	1807	1819h	1840
31	Backnang d.	0609	|	|	|	0706	|	|	0906	|	|	1106	1106	|	|	1306	1311	|	|	1506	|	|	1706	|	|	1906
73	Schwäbisch H-H ⊡ a.	0653	|	|	|	0759	|	|	0957g	|	|	1157	1149	|	|	1357	1349	|	|	1557	|	|	1757g	|	|	1957g
73	Schwäbisch H-H ⊡ d.	0654	|	|	|	0759	|	|	0959	|	|	1159	1159	|	|	1359	1359	|	|	1559	|	|	1759	|	|	1959
	Schwäbisch Gmünd ‡ d.	|	0632	0642	0705e	|	0842	0905	|	1040	1105	|	|	1240	1305	|	|	1440	1505	|	1640	1705	|	1840	1905	|
	Aalen ‡ d.	|	0651	0659	0728	|	0859	0925	|	1057	1125	|	|	1257	1325	|	|	1457	1525	|	1657	1725	|	1857	1925	|
	Ellwangen d.	|	...	0710	0749	|	0910	0948	|	1108	1148	|	|	1308	1348	|	|	1508	1548	|	1708	1748	|	1908	1948	|
100	Crailsheim d.	0713	...	0726	0812	0818	0926	1011	1018	1125	1211	1218	1218	1325	1411	1418	1418	1525	1611	1618	1725	1811	1818	1925	2011	2018
146	Ansbach d.	0756c	...	0751	...	0851	0951	...	1051	1151	...	1251	1256	1351	...	1451	1456	1551	...	1651	1751	...	1851	1951	...	2051
190	**Nürnberg** Hbf a.	0841	...	0818	...	0925	1018	...	1125	1217	...	1325	1341	1417	...	1525	1541	1617	...	1725	1817	...	1925	2017	...	2125

			IC				IC				
			2165				2167				
	Ⓒz	Ⓐe	⑤⑦f		①–⑥	⑦	⑦w		Ⓒm	Ⓐe	
			P 🍷				🍷				
Karlsruhe Hbf 930 .. d.	...	...	1906	...	...	...	2106	...	...	...	...
Stuttgart Hbf ‡ d.	1945u	1958	2007	2022	2058	2108	2207	2222	2245u	2258	2358
Backnang d.	2021	2025	|	|	2125	2138	|	|	2325	2325	0026
Schwäbisch H-H ⊡. a.	2055	2102	|	|	2202	2221	|	|	0002	0002	0102
Schwäbisch H-H ⊡. d.	2059	2103	|	|	2203	2223	|	|	0003	0003	0103
Schwäbisch Gmünd ‡ d.	|	|	2040	2105	|	|	2240	2305	|	|	|
Aalen ‡ d.	|	|	2057	2125	|	|	2257	2325	|	|	|
Ellwangen d.	|	|	2108	2152	|	|	2308	2354	|	|	|
Crailsheim d.	2121	2121	2125	2208	2222	2241	2325	0010	0021	0021	0121
Ansbach d.	...	...	2151	...	...	...	2351	...	...	...	...
Nürnberg Hbf a.	...	...	2217	...	...	...	0017	...	...	...	...

km						IC					
						2164					
		Ⓐe	Ⓐe	Ⓒz	Ⓐe	①–⑤	Ⓐe	Ⓒz	Ⓐe	Ⓒz	Ⓐe
						d 🍷					
0	**Nürnberg** Hbf d.	...	...	...	...	0537	...	...	...	...	0614
44	Ansbach d.	...	...	...	...	0604	...	...	...	...	0707c
90	Crailsheim d.	0452	0517	0552	0556	0632	0635	0635	0650	0651	0742
111	Ellwangen d.	|	0533	|	|	0648	|	|	0710	0712	|
127	**Aalen** ‡ d.	|	0600	|	|	0701	|	|	0733	0735	|
152	Schwäbisch Gmünd ‡ d.	|	0621	|	|	0718	|	|	0752	0754	|
	Schwäbisch H-H ⊡ a.	0510	|	0610	0614	|	0653	0653	|	|	0800
	Schwäbisch H-H ⊡ d.	0511	|	0611	0618	|	0654	0702	|	|	0803
	Backnang d.	0551	|	0651	0705	|	0736	0737	|	|	0851
203	**Stuttgart** Hbf ‡ a.	0618	0713	0718	0735	0753	0803	0815	0843	0838	0918
	Karlsruhe Hbf 930 .. a.	...	...	...	...	0853	...	...	...	...	...

			IC			IC			IC				IC			IC			IC	RE			IC			IC
			2162			2160			2068				2066			2064			2062	4198			2060			1968
	Ⓒz		①–⑥							Ⓐe	Ⓒz								n	⑥⑦			⑤⑦f			⑦w
			r P			🍷			🍷				🍷			🍷			🍷	M			🍷		2	
Nürnberg Hbf d.	0635	...	0741	0833h	...	0941	1035	...	1141	1213	1235	...	1341	1435	...	1541	1635	...	1741	...	1835	...	1941	2035	...	2141
Ansbach d.	0707	...	0807	0907	...	1007	1107	...	1207	1310c	1307	...	1407	1507	...	1607	1707	...	1807	...	1907	...	2007	2107	...	2207
Crailsheim d.	0742	0752	0835	0942	0952	1035	1142	1152	1235	1343	1342	1352	1435	1543	1552	1635	1742	1752	1835	...	1942	1952	2035	2142	2146	2235
Ellwangen d.	|	0812	0851	|	1012	1051	|	1212	1251	|	|	1412	1451	|	1612	1651	|	1812	1851	...	|	2012	2051	|	2208	2251
Aalen ‡ d.	|	0835	0903	|	1035	1103	|	1235	1303	|	|	1435	1503	|	1635	1703	|	1835	1903	1911	|	2035	2103	|	2224	2303
Schwäbisch Gmünd ‡ d.	|	0854	0920	|	1054	1120	|	1254	1320	|	|	1454	1520	|	1654	1720	|	1854	1920	1927	|	2054	2120	|	2243n	2320
Schwäbisch H-H ⊡. a.	0800	|	|	1000	|	|	1200	|	|	1400	1400	|	|	1601	|	|	1801	|	|	|	2000	|	|	2200	|	|
Schwäbisch H-H ⊡. d.	0803	|	|	1003	|	|	1203	|	|	1403	1403	|	|	1603	|	|	1803k	|	|	|	2003	|	|	2203	|	|
Backnang d.	0851	|	|	1051	|	|	1251	|	|	1451	1451	|	|	1651	|	|	1851	|	|	|	2051	|	|	2251	|	|
Stuttgart Hbf ‡ a.	0918	0938	0953	1118	1138	1153	1318	1338	1353	1518	1518	1538	1553	1719	1743j	1753	1918	1938	1953	2008	2118	2138	2153	2318	2329n	2355
Karlsruhe Hbf 930 .. a.	...	...	1053	...	...	1253	...	...	1453	...	...	...	1653	...	...	1853	...	...	2053	...	...	...	2253	...	...	...

M – 🚌12 Stuttgart - Donauwörth - München and v.v.
P – To / from Passau on dates in Table **920**.
c – Arrives 7–10 minutes earlier.
d – Not Dec. 24, 25, 26, 31, Jan. 1, Mar. 21, 24, May 12.
e – Ⓐ (not Dec. 24, 31, May 22).
f – Also Dec. 26, Jan. 1, Mar. 20, 24, May 12; not Dec. 23, 30, Mar. 21, 23, May 11.
g – 7–8 minutes earlier on Ⓐ (not Dec. 24, 31, May 22).
h – 2–3 minutes later on Ⓒ (also Dec. 24, 31, May 22).
j – 1738 on Ⓒ (also Dec. 24, 31, May 22).

k – 1806 on Ⓐ (not Dec. 24, 31, May 22).
m – Also Dec. 31, May 22.
n – Not Dec. 24, 31.
q – Not Dec. 24, 25, 31, Mar. 21, 23, May 11.
r – Not Dec. 25, 26, Jan. 1, Mar. 22, 24, May 12.
u – From the S-Bahn (underground) platforms.
v – Not Dec. 25, Jan. 1.
w – Also Dec. 26, Jan. 1, Mar. 24, May 12; not Dec. 23, 30, Mar. 23, May 11.
z – Also Dec. 24, 31, May 22.

⊡ – Schwäbisch Hall-Hessental.

‡ – Additional *RE* trains Stuttgart - Schwäbisch Gmünd - Aalen and v.v. **From Stuttgart** Hbf at 0032 **v**, 0507 Ⓐ **e**, 0528 Ⓐ **e**, 0650 Ⓐ **e**, 0719 Ⓐ **e**, 0722 Ⓒ **z**, 0922, 1122, 1322, 1522, 1549 Ⓐ **e**, 1649 Ⓐ **e**, 1719 Ⓐ **e**, 1722 Ⓒ **z**, 1749 Ⓐ **e**, 1849 Ⓐ **e**, 1922, 2122 and 2332. **From Aalen** at 0426 Ⓐ **e**, 0503 Ⓐ **e**, 0518 Ⓐ **e**, 0533 Ⓐ **e**, 0535 Ⓒ **z**, 0627 Ⓐ **e**, 0635 Ⓒ **z**, 0706 Ⓐ **e**, 0805 Ⓐ **e**, 0935, 1135, 1335, 1535, 1708 Ⓐ **e**, 1735, 1805 Ⓐ **e**, 1935 and 2135.

926 HEILBRONN / ASCHAFFENBURG - CRAILSHEIM and AALEN - DONAUWÖRTH / ULM

RE / *RB* services

Aschaffenburg - Lauda - Crailsheim ⊠

km		Ⓐe								
0	**Aschaffenburg** Hbf d.	...	...	0652	0923	1123	1323	1523	1723	1923c
38	Miltenberg d.	...	...	0745r	0959	1159	1359	1559	1759	2000
69	Wertheim d.	...	0625e	0823r	1035	1235	1435	1635	1835	2036
93	Tauberbischofsheim d.	0559	0651e	0901	1101	1301	1501	1701	1901	2100
100	**Lauda** a.	0608	0701e	0906	1106	1306	1506	1706	1906	2106
100	**Lauda** d.	0613	0713	0913	1113	1313	1513	1713	1913	2113p
110	Bad Mergentheim d.	0625	0725	0925	1125	1325	1525	1725	1925	2125p
169	**Crailsheim** a.	0729	0829	1031	1231	1431	1631	1831	2029	...

	Ⓐe	Ⓒz	Ⓐe			Ⓒg	Ⓐt				
Crailsheim d.	...	...	0524	0737	0930	1128	1128	1328	1528	1728	1935
Bad Mergentheim d.	0513	0610	0645	0835	1034	1234	1234	1434	1634	1834	2035
Lauda a.	0524	0621	0657	0844	1044	1244	1244	1444	1644	1844	2045
Lauda d.	0528	0622	0702	0854	1053	1253	1253	1453	1653	1853	...
Tauberbischofsheim d.	0536	0630	0712	0900	1059	1259	1259	1459	1659	1859	...
Wertheim d.	0559	0705	0738	0921	1121	1321	1326	1521	1721	1921	...
Miltenberg d.	0645	0745	...	0959	1159	1359	...	1559	1759	2000	...
Aschaffenburg Hbf a.	0730	0828	...	1038	1238	1438	...	1638	1838	2038f	...

Heilbronn - Crailsheim ⊠

km		Ⓐe	Ⓒz	Ⓐe		Ⓒz	Ⓐe	Ⓒz	Ⓐe
0	**Heilbronn** Hbf d.	0550*	0803	0805	and every	1803	1805	2003	2005
54	Schwäbisch Hall d.	0642	0851	0852	**two** hours	1851	1852	2051	2052
61	Schwäbisch Hall-H ⊡ d.	0649	0859	0859	until	1859	1859	2059	2058
88	**Crailsheim** a.	0712	0921	0921		1921	1921	2121	2121

			Ⓐe	Ⓒz		Ⓐe	Ⓒz		
Crailsheim d.	0635	...	0838	0838	and every	1838	1838	...	2038
Schwäbisch Hall-H ⊡ d.	0658	...	0858	0900	**two** hours	1858	1900	...	2106j
Schwäbisch Hall d.	0705	...	0905	0906	until	1905	1906	...	2113
Heilbronn Hbf a.	0751	...	0951	0952		1951	1952	...	2216‡

Aalen - Donauwörth

km		Ⓐe	Ⓒz	Ⓐe	Ⓐe		⑥⑦§		①–⑤			Ⓐe		Ⓐe		Ⓐe		Ⓐe		Ⓐe		Ⓐe			n	
0	**Aalen** d.	...	0531	...	0626	...	0653	...	0735	...	...	0835h	0935	1035h	1135	1235h	1335	1435h	1535	1635h	1736	1835h	1935	...	2035x	...
39	Nördlingen d.	0538	0615	0638	0708	...	0724	...	0815	0815	...	0915	1015	1115	1220	1315	1415	1515	1615	1715	1815	1915	2015	...	2115	...
68	**Donauwörth** a.	0604	0646	0708	0738	...	0751	...	0846	0846	...	0946	1046	1146	1249	1346	1446	1546	1646	1746	1846	1946	2046	...	2146	...

	Ⓐe		Ⓐe		Ⓐe	Ⓒz		Ⓐe		Ⓐe		Ⓐe		Ⓐe		Ⓐe			⑥⑦§	Ⓐe			Ⓐe		n
Donauwörth d.	...	...	0550	...	0657	0707	...	0804	0904	1004	1104	1204	1304	1404	1504	1604	1704	...	1807	1804	...	1904	2004	...	2104
Nördlingen d.	0535	...	0642b	...	0744b	0744	...	0844j	0944j	1044j	1144j	1244j	1344j	1444j	1544j	1644j	1744j	...	1836	1844j	...	1944j	2044j	...	2134
Aalen a.	0619	...	0722	...	0826	0825	...	0925h	1025	1125h	1225	1325h	1425	1525h	1625	1725h	1825	...	1910	1925h	...	2025	2125h	...	2215

Aalen - Ulm

km		2Ⓐe	2⑥k	Ⓐe	2Ⓐe	2Ⓒz	2Ⓐe	2	2	Ⓐe	2	2		2		2		2	2		2	2		2	2	2
0	**Aalen** d.	0501	0524	0554	0625	0633	0702	0733	0833	0908	0933	1033	1108	1133	1308	1333	1508	1533	1633	1708	1733	1833	1908	1933	2039	2133
23	Heidenheim d.	0524	0547	0617	0647	0659	0725	0756	0859	0924	0957	1059	1124	1157	1324	1357	1524	1557	1659	1724	1757	1859	1924	1957	2107	2157
73	**Ulm** Hbf a.	0621	0644	0709	0745	0744	0756	0844	0945	0956	1044	1145	1156	1245	1356	1445	1556	1644	1745	1756	1844	1945	1956	2041	2151	2254

	2Ⓐe	2Ⓐe	2Ⓐe	2Ⓒz	2Ⓐe	2Ⓒz	Ⓐe	2	2		2	2		2	2		2	2		2	2		2	2	2	2
Ulm Hbf d.	0437	0548	0559	0614	0648	0712	0803	0812	0912	1003	1012	1112	1203	1212	1312	1403	1412	1512	1603	1612	1712	1803	1812	1912	2012	2218
Heidenheim d.	0527	0630	0657	0658	0759	0759	0835	0859	0959	1035	1059	1159	1235	1259	1359	1435	1459	1559	1635	1659	1759	1835	1859	1959	2058	2310
Aalen a.	0554	0651	0724	0721	0824	0824	0851	0924	1023	1051	1124	1223	1251	1324	1423	1451	1524	1623	1651	1724	1824	1851	1924	2024	2121	2333

b – Arrives 18 minutes earlier.
c – 1928 on Ⓒ (also Dec. 24, 31, May 22).
e – Ⓐ (not Dec. 24, 31, May 22).
f – On ①–④ (not Dec. 24, 25, 26, 31, Jan. 1, Mar. 20, 24, Apr. 30, May 1, 12, 21, 22) change trains at Miltenberg (d. 2034, Aschaffenburg Hbf a. 2125).
g – Crailsheim - Wertheim on Ⓒ (daily Dec. 22 - Jan. 6, Feb. 2–10, Mar. 15–30, May 10–25). Wertheim - Aschaffenburg daily.
h – Not Dec. 24 - Jan. 4.

j – Arrives 8–11 minutes earlier.
k – Also Dec. 24, 31.
n – Not Dec. 24, 31.
p – † (also May 22).
r – 12–14 minutes later on Ⓐ **e**.
t – Not Dec. 24 - Jan. 4, Feb. 4–8, Mar. 17–28, May 12–23.
x – Not Dec. 27, 28, Jan. 2, 3, 4.

z – Also Dec. 24, 31, May 22.

§ – 🚌12 Stuttgart - Schwäbisch Gmünd - Donauwörth - München and v.v. (see also Tables **905** and **925**).
* – Change trains at Öhringen (a. 0614, d. 0618).
‡ – Change trains at Öhringen (a. 2136, d. 2138).
⊠ – 2nd class only.
⊡ – Schwäbisch Hall-Hessental.

German national public holidays are on Dec. 25, 26, Jan. 1, Mar. 21, 24, May 1, 12, Oct. 3

Reservation is recommended

ROMANTISCHE STRASSE (EUROPABUS 🚌 2007) 927

	B	R			
Frankfurt (Main) Hbf (Mannheimerstraße, DTG office) ... d.	...	0800	...	...	...
Würzburg Hbf (Busbahnhof) ... d.	...	1000	...	...	...
Mannheim Hbf ... d.	0750	|	...	...	...
Heidelberg Hbf ... d.	0825	|	...	...	...
Neckargemünd (Bahnhof) ... d.	0840**z**	|	...	...	...
Eberbach (Neckaranlagen) ... d.	0910**z**	|	...	...	...
Mosbach-Neckarelz ... d.	0930**z**	|	...	...	...
Heilbronn (Hinter der Harmonie) ... d.	1020	|	...	...	...
Rothenburg ob der Tauber (Schranenplatz) ... a.	1145	1215	...	...	...
Rothenburg ob der Tauber (Schranenplatz) ... d.	1230	1245	...	...	...
Rothenburg ob der Tauber (Bahnhof) ... d.	1235**z**	1250**x**	...	...	...
Nürnberg (Adcom-Center) ... a.	1435	|	...	...	...
Feuchtwangen (Marktplatz) ... d.	...	1320	...	...	...
Dinkelsbühl (Schweinemarkt) ... a.	...	1340	...	...	...
Dinkelsbühl (Schweinemarkt) ... d.	...	1410	...	...	...
Nördlingen (Rathaus) ... d.	...	1505	...	...	...
Donauwörth (Pfarrkirche) ... d.	...	1535**x**	...	...	...
Augsburg Hbf ... d.	...	1620	...	...	...
Schwangau (Tourist information) ... d.	...	1920**x**	...	...	...
Hohenschwangau ... d.	...	1930	...	...	...
Füssen (Bahnhof) ... a.	...	1935	...	...	...
München (Arnulfstraße, Starnberger Bahnhof) ... a.	...	2115	...	...	...

	B	R			
München (Arnulfstraße, Starnberger Bahnhof) ... a.	...	0815	...	...	...
Füssen (Bahnhof) ... d.	...	1010	...	...	...
Hohenschwangau ... d.	...	1040	...	...	...
Schwangau (Tourist information) ... d.	...	1045**x**	...	...	...
Augsburg Hbf ... d.	...	1410	...	...	...
Donauwörth (Pfarrkirche) ... d.	...	1455**x**	...	...	...
Nördlingen (Rathaus) ... d.	...	1545	...	...	...
Dinkelsbühl (Schweinemarkt) ... a.	...	1615	...	...	...
Dinkelsbühl (Schweinemarkt) ... d.	...	1635	...	...	...
Feuchtwangen (Marktplatz) ... d.	...	1655	...	...	...
Nürnberg (Adcom-Center) ... d.	1500	|	...	...	...
Rothenburg ob der Tauber (Bahnhof) ... d.	1640**z**	1725**x**	...	...	...
Rothenburg ob der Tauber (Schranenplatz) ... a.	1645	1730	...	...	...
Rothenburg ob der Tauber (Schranenplatz) ... d.	1745	1800	...	...	...
Heilbronn (Hinter der Harmonie) ... d.	1900	|	...	...	...
Mosbach-Neckarelz ... d.	1950**z**	|	...	...	...
Eberbach (Neckaranlagen) ... d.	2010**z**	|	...	...	...
Neckargemünd (Bahnhof) ... d.	2035**z**	|	...	...	...
Heidelberg Hbf ... a.	2100	|	...	...	...
Mannheim Hbf ... a.	2130	|	...	...	...
Würzburg Hbf (Busbahnhof) ... a.	...	1930	...	...	...
Frankfurt (Main) Hbf (Mannheimerstraße, DTG office) ... a.	...	2100	...	...	...

B – *Die Burgenstraße*: Daily May 1 - Sept. 30.
R – *Romantische Straße*: Daily Apr. 1 - Oct. 31.
x – Stops only on request: ✆ 0171 653 23 40 or 0171 651 24 71 (before 1000).
z – Stops only on request: ✆ 0171 620 09 01 or 0171 620 09 02 (before 0830).

Operator: Deutsche Touring GmbH, Am Römerhof 17, 60486 Frankfurt (Main).
Information and reservations: ✆ +49 (0) 69 7903 230 Fax +49 (0) 69 7903 219.

60% discount available for holders of the Eurail and German Rail passes.

Bayerische Oberlandbahn GmbH

MÜNCHEN - BAYRISCHZELL, LENGGRIES and TEGERNSEE 928

On Dec. 24, 31, May 22 services run as on Ⓒ

km		Ⓐ	Ⓒ		ⒸB		Ⓒ																n	n		
0	**München** Hbf ... d.	0631	0642	0742	0802	0842	0901	0942	...	1042	1142	1242	...	1342	1442	1542	1642	1742	1842	1942	2042	2142	2242	2342	...	...
37	Holzkirchen ... d.	0701	0709	0809	0829	0909	0929	1009	...	1109	1209	1309	...	1409	1509	1609	1709	1809	1909	2009	2109	2209	2309	0009	...	...
61	Schliersee ... d.	0733	0737	0837	0856	0937	0956	1037	...	1137	1237	1337	...	1437	1537	1637	1737	1837	1937	2037	2137	2237	2333	0037	...	...
78	**Bayrischzell** ... a.	0756	0800	0900	...	1000	...	1100	...	1200	1300	1400	...	1500	1600	1700	1800	1900	2000	2100	2200	2300	...	0100	...	...

km		Ⓐ	Ⓒ		ⒸB		Ⓒ		ⒸA			Ⓒ	Ⓐ										n	n		
0	**München** Hbf ... d.	0631	0642	0742	0802	0842	0901	0942	1002	1042	1142	1242	1242	1342	1442	1542	1642	1742	1842	1942	2042	2142	2242	2342	...	...
37	Holzkirchen ... d.	0704	0711	0811	0831	0911	0931	1011	1031	1111	1211	1311	1311	1411	1511	1611	1711	1811	1911	2011	2111	2211	2311	0011	...	...
47	Schaftlach ... d.	0719	0723	0823	0845	0923	0945	1023	1045	1123	1223	1323	1327	1423	1523	1623	1723	1823	1923	2023	2123	2223	2323	0023	...	...
57	Bad Tölz ... d.	0733	0734	0834	0856	0934	0956	1034	1056	1134	1234	1334	1338	1434	1534	1634	1734	1834	1934	2034	2134	2234	2334	0034	...	...
67	**Lenggries** ... a.	0744	0745	0845	0907	0945	1007	1045	1107	1145	1245	1345	1349	1445	1545	1645	1745	1845	1945	2045	2145	2245	2345	0045	...	...

km		Ⓐ	Ⓒ						ⒸA			Ⓒ	Ⓐ										n	n		
0	**München** Hbf ... d.	0631	0642	0742	...	0842	...	0942	1002	1042	1142	1242	1242	1342	1442	1542	1642	1742	1842	1942	2042	2142	2242	2342	...	...
37	Holzkirchen ... d.	0704	0711	0811	...	0911	...	1011	1031	1111	1211	1311	1311	1411	1511	1611	1711	1811	1911	2011	2111	2211	2311	0011	...	...
47	Schaftlach ... d.	0718	0724	0824	...	0924	...	1024	1048	1124	1224	1324	1326	1424	1524	1624	1724	1824	1924	2024	2124	2224	2324	0024	...	...
59	**Tegernsee** ... a.	0738	0743	0843	...	0943	...	1043	1107	1143	1243	1343	1345	1443	1543	1643	1743	1843	1943	2043	2143	2243	2343	0043	...	...

	Ⓐ	Ⓐ			Ⓐ	Ⓐ	Ⓒ						Ⓐ				ⒸB		ⒸB		ⒸA				n	n
Bayrischzell ... d.	0455	...	0607	...	...	0703	0707	0807	0907	1007	1107	1207	...	1307	1407	1507	...	1607	...	1707	...	1807	1907	2007	...	2207
Schliersee ... d.	0523	0555	0635	...	0705	0731	0735	0835	0935	1035	1135	1235	1312	1335	1435	1535	1611	1635	1711	1735	1811	1835	1935	2035	2135	2235
Holzkirchen ... d.	0550	0622	0702	...	0731	0802	0802	0902	1002	1102	1202	1302	1342	1402	1502	1602	1641	1702	1741	1802	1841	1902	2002	2102	2202	2302
München Hbf ... a.	0616	0649	0729	...	0800	0829	0829	0929	1029	1129	1229	1329	1412	1429	1529	1629	1711	1729	1809	1829	1909	1929	2029	2129	2229	2329

	Ⓐ	Ⓐ	Ⓐ	Ⓒ	Ⓐ	Ⓐ	Ⓒ										ⒸB		Ⓒ		ⒸA				n	n
Lenggries ... d.	0511	0547	0619	0621	0653	0721	0721	0821	0921	1021	1121	1221	...	1321	1421	1521	1600	1621	1700	1721	1800	1821	1921	2021	2121	2221
Bad Tölz ... d.	0522	0558	0630	0634	0705	0735	0734	0834	0934	1034	1134	1234	...	1334	1434	1534	1611	1634	1711	1734	1811	1834	1934	2034	2134	2234
Schaftlach ... d.	0538	0610	0646	0650	0717	0748	0750	0850	0950	1050	1150	1250	...	1350	1450	1550	1624	1650	1724	1750	1824	1850	1950	2050	2150	2250
Holzkirchen ... d.	0550	0622	0702	0702	0731	0802	0802	0902	1002	1102	1202	1302	...	1402	1502	1602	1641	1702	1741	1802	1841	1902	2002	2102	2202	2302
München Hbf ... a.	0616	0649	0729	0729	0800	0829	0829	0929	1029	1129	1229	1329	...	1429	1529	1629	1711	1729	1811	1829	1909	1929	2029	2129	2229	2329

	Ⓐ		Ⓐ	Ⓒ	Ⓐ🚌	Ⓐ	Ⓒ						Ⓐ	Ⓒ					ⒸA						n	n
Tegernsee ... d.	0517	...	0624	0627	0645	0723	0727	0827	0927	1027	1127	1227	1307	1327	1427	1527	...	1627	1703	1727	...	1827	1927	2027	2127	2227
Schaftlach ... a.	0535	...	0643	0647	0705	0742	0747	0847	0947	1047	1147	1247	1325	1347	1447	1547	...	1647	1723	1747	...	1847	1947	2047	2147	2247
Holzkirchen ... a.	0548	...	0656	0700	...	0757	0800	0900	1000	1100	1200	1300	1339	1400	1500	1600	...	1700	1737	1800	...	1900	2000	2100	2200	2300
München Hbf ... a.	0616	...	0729	0729	...	0829	0829	0929	1029	1129	1229	1329	1412	1429	1529	1629	...	1729	1811	1829	...	1929	2029	2129	2229	2329

A – From Mar. 30. B – Until Mar. 29. n – Not Dec. 24, 31.

DB (2nd class only); ČD

PLATTLING - BAYERISCH EISENSTEIN - PLZEŇ 929

km				Ⓐe	⑥	⑥⑦h																			
0	**Plattling** ... d.	...	...	0520	0558	...	0659	0805	0905	1005	1105	...	1205	1305	...	1405	1505	...	1605	1705	1805	1905	2005	2105	2308
9	Deggendorf Hbf ... d.	...	...	0532	0613	...	0709	0815	0915	1015	1115	...	1215	1315	...	1415	1515	...	1615	1715	1815	1915	2015	2115	2318
33	Gotteszell ... d.	...	...	0554	0631	...	0734	0833	0933	1033	1133	...	1233	1333	...	1433	1533	...	1633	1733	1833	1933	2033	2133	2336
48	Regen ... d.	...	...	0607	0643	...	0747	0846	0946	1046	1146	...	1246	1346	...	1446	1546	...	1646	1746	1846	1946	2046	2146	2349
58	Zwiesel (Bay) ... d.	...	...	0616	0653	0658	0758	0858	0958	1058	1158	...	1258	1358	...	1458	1558	...	1658	1758	1858	1958	2058	2155	2358
72	**Bayerisch Eisenstein** 🏛 ... a.	...	...	▬	▬	0711	0811	0911	1011	1111	1211	...	1311	1411	...	1511	1611	...	1711	1811	1911	2011	2111	...	...
			2w		2	|	⊕	|	⊕2k	|	|		▬	|		⊕2	|		▬	|	⊕2n	▬			
72	**Bayerisch Eisenstein** ☆ 🏛 d.	...	0410	...	*0555*a	0713	0840	0917	1040	1117j	1213h	1240	...	1413	...	1518	1613j	1640	...	1813j	1935	...	...	...	...
76	Železná Ruda Město ... d.	...	0417	...	*0601*a	0719	0850	0923	1050	1123j	1219h	1250	...	1419	...	1528	1619j	1650	...	1819j	1942	...	...	...	...
79	Špičák ... d.	...	0422	①–⑥	*0606*a	0723	0901	0927	1101	1127j	1223h	1302	...	1423	...	1536	1623j	1658	...	1823j	1947	...	...	...	...
131	**Klatovy** ... a.	2v	0518	r	*0708*a	...	0956	...	1153	...	...	1352	2	...	2	1626	...	1752	...	...	2042	2n	...	...	...
131	**Klatovy** ... d.	0358	*0527*a	0606	0806	...	1006	...	1206	...	...	1406	1446	...	1606	1646	...	1806	1846	...	...	2046	...	...	...
141	Švihov u Klatov ... d.	0410	*0538*a	0615	0815	...	1015	...	1215	...	...	1415	1458	...	1615	1658	...	1815	1858	...	...	2058	...	...	...
170	**Plzeň** Hlavni ... a.	0500	*0627*a	0656	0856	...	1056	...	1256	...	...	1456	1547	...	1656	1747	...	1856	1947	...	...	2147	...	...	...
	Praha Hlavní **1120** ... a.	...	...	0845	...	...	1245	...	...	...	...	1645	...	...	...	...	...	2045	...	...	...	...	...	...	...

				2		2	2k		2				2			2Ⓐ		2n			2n	2	2m	Ⓑq	2n
Praha Hlavní **1120** ... d.	...	...	...	...	...	...	...	...	...	0716	...	...	...	...	1116	...	...	...	...	1516	...	...	...	1916	...
Plzeň Hlavni ... d.	...	...	...	...	...	0520	0702	...	0810	0902	...	...	*1102*	...	1302	...	...	*1502*	...	1702	...	1810	*1910*	2102	2251
Švihov u Klatov ... d.	...	...	...	...	...	0615	0743	...	0859	0943	...	...	*1143*	...	1343	...	...	*1546*	...	1743	...	1859	*1959*	2143	2339
Klatovy ... a.	...	...	...	...	...	0627	0752	...	0911	0952	...	...	*1152*	...	1352	...	...	*1555*	...	1752	...	1911	*2011*	2152	2351
Klatovy ... d.	...	...	...	0431	...	0651	0802	...	0921	1002	...	...	1202	...	1402	1459	...	1628	...	...	1810	▬	2020	...	...
Špičák ... d.	...	...	...	0527	0728h	0741	0902	0932	1018	1102	1132j	1228h	1301	1428	1502	1601	1628j	1725	1828j	...	1905	...	2118	...	...
Železná Ruda Město ... d.	...	...	...	0533	0732h	0746	0909	0936	1024	1109	1136j	1232h	1306	1432	1509	1605	1632j	1730	1832j	...	1910	...	2123	...	...
Bayerisch Eisenstein ☆ 🏛 . a.	...	...	...	0538	0738h	0753	0915	0942	1030	1115	1142j	1238h	1313	1438	1515	1611	1638j	1737	1838j	...	1916	...	2129	...	...
		Ⓐe	Ⓒz		|	⊕		|	⊕		|	|	⊕	|	⊕		|	⊕	|		⊕		⊕		
Bayerisch Eisenstein 🏛 ... d.	...	...	...	...	0742	0842	...	0943	1042	...	1143	1242	1342	1442	1542	...	1642	1742	1842	...	1942	2042	2142	...	...
Zwiesel (Bay) ... d.	0530	0622	0655	...	0757	0857	...	0957	1057	...	1157	1257	1357	1456	1557	...	1657	1757	1857	...	1957	2057	2156	...	...
Regen ... d.	0540	0632	0705	...	0807	0907	...	1007	1107	...	1207	1307	1407	1506	1607	...	1707	1807	1907	...	2007	2107	2205	...	...
Gotteszell ... d.	0555	0645	0720	...	0820	0920	...	1020	1120	...	1220	1320	1420	1520	1620	...	1720	1820	1920	...	2020	2120	2217	...	...
Deggendorf Hbf ... d.	0612	0710	0738	...	0844	0942	...	1042	1142	...	1242	1342	1442	1542	1642	...	1742	1842	1942	...	2042	2142	2234	...	...
Plattling ... a.	0623	0720	0748	...	0854	0952	...	1052	1152	...	1252	1352	1452	1552	1652	...	1752	1852	1952	...	2052	2152	2243	...	...

a – Ⓐ only.
e – Not Dec. 24, 31, May 22.
h – ⑥⑦ Dec. 9 - Mar. 2.
j – Dec. 9 - Mar. 2.
k – Change trains at Klatovy on Ⓐ.
m – Not Dec. 24, 25, 31.
n – Not Dec. 24, 31.
q – Not Dec. 23, 24, 25, 31, Mar. 23.
r – Not Dec. 24, 25, 26, Jan. 1, Mar. 24.
v – Not Dec. 25, Jan. 1.
w – Not Dec. 25, 26, Jan. 1.
z – Also Dec. 24, 31, May 22.
☆ – Železná Ruda-Alžbětín in Czech.
⊕ – Change trains.

930 MANNHEIM and KARLSRUHE - STUTTGART - MÜNCHEN

km ●	km ●		IC 1591	IC 1591	CNL 319	IC 60319	RE 4161	IC 2095	IC 2095	RE 4199	IC 2361	IC 2291	CNL 261	IC 2363	ICE 699	ICE 699	IRE 4219 4221	IRE 4901	IC 1899 1991	ICE 991	ICE 1593	IC 2365	IC 2367	IC 2293	IRE 4223
			v	①g	Ⓡ	K		①g	Ⓐy	⑥⑦	Ⓐy	①-⑥	Ⓡ	①-⑥	⑦u			Ⓐn		①-⑥	⑦m	①-⑤	①-⑤		
			◧	◧	◧♦	◧2					♀	e♀	♀♦	‡	✕	✕	F		Ⓐr	✕♦	W✕	aO	a♀	A♀	L
		Köln Hbf **800 910** d.	...	...	2346	...	...	...	...	...	...	...	...	...	...	...	...	...	...	...	...	...	...	...	...
		Frankfurt (Main) Hbf **911/2** d.	0007	0007	|	...	...	...	...	...	...	...	...	...	...	...	...	...	...	...	...	...	...	...	...
		Frankfurt Flughafen ✈ **912** d.	0028	0028	|	...	...	...	...	...	...	...	...	...	...	...	...	...	...	...	...	...	...	...	...
	0	**Mannheim** Hbf d.	0106	0106	|	0243	...	...	...	...	...	...	...	...	...	...	...	...	0557	0630	0630	...	...	0712	...
		Heidelberg Hbf ★ d.	0119	0119	|	|	...	...	...	...	...	...	...	...	...	...	...	...	0615	|	|	...	...	|	...
0		**Karlsruhe** Hbf d.	|	|	|	|	...	...	...	...	0457	...	0455s	0559	0607	...	...	0601	|	|	|	0637	0659	|	...
		Pforzheim Hbf d.	|	|	|	|	...	...	...	...	|	...	0538s	|	|	...	...	0624	|	|	|	|	|	|	...
21		Bruchsal ★ d.	0139	0139	|	|	...	...	...	...	0514	...	|	0617	0621	...	...	|	|	|	|	0654	0719	|	...
		Mühlacker ★ d.	|	|	|	|	...	...	...	...	|	...	|	|	|	...	...	0632	|	|	|	|	|	|	...
58	78	Vaihingen (Enz) ★ d.	0207	0207	|	|	...	...	...	...	0531	...	|	|	|	...	...	0639	|	|	|	|	|	|	...
87	107	**Stuttgart** Hbf ★ a.	0236	0236	0419s	0419	...	...	...	...	0546	...	0611s	0648	0648	...	...	0656	0700	0707	0709	0724	0750	0754	...
	107	**Stuttgart** Hbf **936** ★ d.	...	0241	|	0438	...	0503	...	0548	...	0553	|	...	0656	0656	0659	...	...	0712	▬	...	...	0758	0802
	129	Plochingen **936** ★ d.	...	|	0452s	0454	...	0518	...	|	...	0609	|	...	|	|	0713	...	...	|	*RE*	...	...	|	0816
	149	Göppingen ★ d.	...	|	0505s	0507	...	0531	...	|	...	0621	0650s	...	|	|	0725	...	...	|	**4165**	...	...	|	0827
	168	Geislingen (Steige) ★ d.	...	|	0520s	0521	...	0544	...	✣	...	|	|	...	|	|	0737	...	...	|		...	...	|	0840
	201	**Ulm** Hbf **945** ★ d.	...	0337	0543s	0545	0550	0609	0609	|	...	0655	0725s	...	0755	0755	0759	...	...	0808	0812	...	...	0855	0902
	225	Günzburg **945** d.	...	0355	0600s	0602	0612	0626	0626	|	...	0711	|	...	|	|	...	...	...	|	0832	...	...	0910	...
	287	**Augsburg** Hbf **904 905** d.	...	0426	0634s	0636	0715	0658	0658	0824	...	0741	0811s	...	0839	0839	...	...	...	0852	0918	...	...	0941	...
	342	München Pasing **904 905** a.	...	0455	|	|	0753	0729	0729	|	...	0811	|	...	0911	0911	...	...	...	0921	0955	...	...	|	...
	349	**München** Hbf **904 905** a.	...	0505	0716	0716	0803	0741	0741	0902	...	0820	0858	...	0921	0921	...	...	...	0931	1003	...	...	1017	...
		Salzburg Hbf **890** 🏛 a.	...	...	...	...	...	...	...	...	...	1002	...	...	...	...	...	...	...	...	...	...	...	1203	...

	ICE 181	IC 2063	ICE 511	IC 2053	EC 61	IRE 4903	ICE 777	ICE 591	RE 4169	IC 2317	IC 2295	IRE 4225	IC 2065	ICE 513	IC 2319	ICE 571	EC 115	IRE 4905	TGV 9571	ICE 1091	RE 4171	IC 2275	IC 2297	IRE 4227	IC 2067
	①-⑥	v		①-⑤			①-⑥	x		①-⑥					①-⑥	①-⑥				§		①-⑤			
	✕♦	N♀	♀	aA	✕♦		e✕	✕♦		eW	♀	L	N♀	M♀	e♦	eH	✕♦		P♀	B✕		a♦	♀	L	N♀
Köln Hbf **800 910** d.	...	...	0554	...	...	...	...	...	...	...	...	...	...	0754	0653	✕	0718	...	...	...	...	...	...	...	...
Frankfurt (Main) Hbf **911/2** d.	0618	...	|	...	...	...	...	0750	...	...	0820	...	...	|	|	0905	|	...	...	0950	...	0938	1020	...	...
Frankfurt Flughafen ✈ **912** d.	|	...	0654	...	...	...	...	|	...	...	|	...	...	0854	|	0920	|	...	...	|	...	|	|	...	...
Mannheim Hbf d.	|	...	0733	0754	...	...	0818	0831	...	0826	|	...	...	0933	0923	0955	0954	...	...	1031	...	|	|	...	...
Heidelberg Hbf ★ d.	0717	...	|	0806	...	...	|	|	...	0838	0914	...	...	|	0936	|	1006	...	...	|	...	1032	1114	...	...
Karlsruhe Hbf d.	|	0706	|	|	0806	0805	|	|	...	|	|	...	0906	|	|	|	|	1005	1026	|	...	|	|	...	1106
Pforzheim Hbf d.	|	0727	|	|	|	0826	|	|	...	|	|	...	0927	|	|	|	|	1026	|	|	...	|	|	...	1127
Bruchsal ★ d.	|	|	|	|	0819	|	|	|	...	|	|	...	|	|	|	|	|	|	|	|	...	|	|	...	|
Mühlacker ★ d.	|	0737	|	|	|	0834	|	|	...	|	|	...	0937	|	|	|	|	1034	|	|	...	|	|	...	1137
Vaihingen (Enz) ★ d.	|	0746	|	|	|	0841	0848	|	...	0905	|	...	0946	|	|	|	|	1041	|	|	...	1105	|	...	1146
Stuttgart Hbf ★ a.	0757	0803	0808	0846	0849	0858	0905	0908	...	0923	0953	...	1003	1008	1018	1033	1046	1058	1103	1108	...	1123	1153	...	1203
Stuttgart Hbf **936** ★ d.	...	...	0812	...	0853	...	...	0912	...	...	0958	1002	...	1012	...	...	1054	...	...	1112	...	...	1158	1202	...
Plochingen **936** ★ d.	...	...	|	...	0909	...	...	|	...	...	|	1016	...	|	...	...	1109	...	...	|	...	...	|	1216	...
Göppingen ★ d.	...	...	|	...	0921	...	...	|	...	...	|	1027	...	|	...	...	1121	...	...	|	...	...	|	1227	...
Geislingen (Steige) ★ d.	...	...	|	...	|	...	...	|	...	...	|	1040	...	|	...	...	|	...	...	|	...	...	|	1240	...
Ulm Hbf **945** ★ d.	...	...	0908	...	0955	...	...	1008	1012	...	1055	1102	...	1108	...	...	1155	...	...	1208	1212	...	1255	1302	...
Günzburg **945** d.	...	...	|	...	|	...	...	|	1032	...	1110	...	...	|	...	...	|	...	...	|	1232	...	1310	...	...
Augsburg Hbf **904 905** d.	...	...	0952	...	1038	...	...	1052	1118	...	1141	...	...	1152	...	...	1238	...	...	1252	1318	...	1341	...	...
München Pasing **904 905** a.	...	...	1021	...	1107	...	...	1121	1155	...	|	...	...	1221	...	...	1307	...	...	1321	1354	...	|	...	...
München Hbf **904 905** a.	...	...	1031	...	1117	...	...	1131	1203	...	1217	...	...	1231	...	...	1317	...	...	1331	1403	...	1417	...	...
Salzburg Hbf **890** 🏛 a.	...	...	...	...	...	...	...	...	...	...	1403	...	...	...	...	...	1454	...	...	...	...	...	1603	...	...

	ICE 515	ICE 773	IC 119	IC 2369	IC 119	IRE 4907	ICE 595	RE 4173	IC 2299	IRE 4229	IC 2015	IC 2069	ICE 517	ICE 575	IC 2013	IC 2263	IRE 4909	TGV 9573	ICE 597	IC 2055	IC 2391	IC 2391	IRE 4231	IC 2161	ICE 519
											①-④					Ⓑc				Ⓑq		Ⓑq			
	H♀	✕♦	♀♦	♀	♀♦		B✕		♀	L	♀♦	N♀	D♀	H✕	♀♦	♀		P♀	B✕	A♀	♀	♀	L	N♀	D♀
Köln Hbf **800 910** d.	0954	...	0918	...	...	...	...	...	...	...	1018	...	1154	...	1118	...	...	...	...	...	...	...	...	...	1354
Frankfurt (Main) Hbf **911/2** d.	|	1105	|	...	...	...	1150	...	1220	...	|	...	|	1305	|	...	...	...	1350	...	1420	1420	...	...	|
Frankfurt Flughafen ✈ **912** d.	1054	1120	|	...	...	...	|	...	|	...	|	...	1254	1320	|	...	...	...	|	...	|	|	...	...	1454
Mannheim Hbf d.	1133	1155	1154	...	...	...	1231	...	|	...	1312	...	1333	1355	1354	...	...	...	1431	1424	|	|	...	...	1533
Heidelberg Hbf ★ d.	|	|	1206	...	...	...	|	...	1314	...	|	...	|	|	1406	...	...	...	|	1437	1514	1514	...	...	|
Karlsruhe Hbf d.	|	|	|	1206	...	1205	|	...	|	...	|	1306	|	|	|	1406	1405	1426	|	|	|	|	...	1506	|
Pforzheim Hbf d.	|	|	|	|	...	1226	|	...	|	...	|	1327	|	|	|	|	1426	|	|	|	|	|	...	1527	|
Bruchsal ★ d.	|	|	|	1219	...	|	|	...	|	...	|	|	|	|	|	1419	|	|	|	|	|	|	...	|	|
Mühlacker ★ d.	|	|	|	|	...	1234	|	...	|	...	|	1337	|	|	|	|	1434	|	|	|	|	|	...	1537	|
Vaihingen (Enz) ★ d.	|	|	|	|	...	1241	|	...	|	...	|	1346	|	|	|	|	1441	|	|	1505	|	|	...	1546	|
Stuttgart Hbf ★ a.	1208	1233	1246	1249	←	1258	1308	...	1353	...	1358	1403	1408	1433	1446	1449	1458	1503	1508	1523	1553	1553	...	1603	1608
Stuttgart Hbf **936** ★ d.	1212	...	→	1253	1257	...	1312	...	1358	1402	...	...	1412	...	1454	...	...	...	1512	▬	...	1558	1602	...	1612
Plochingen **936** ★ d.	|	...	...	1309	|	...	|	...	|	1416	...	...	|	...	1509	...	...	...	|	*RE*	...	|	1616	...	|
Göppingen ★ d.	|	...	...	1321	1327	...	|	...	|	1427	...	...	|	...	|	...	...	...	|	**4175**	...	|	1627	...	|
Geislingen (Steige) ★ d.	|	...	...	|	1340	...	|	...	|	1440	...	...	|	...	|	...	...	...	|		...	|	1640	...	|
Ulm Hbf **945** ★ d.	1308	...	...	1355	1401	...	1408	1412	1455	1502	...	...	1508	...	1558	...	...	...	1608	1612	...	1655	1702	...	1708
Günzburg **945** d.	|	...	...	|	...	...	|	1432	1510	...	...	...	|	...	...	...	...	...	|	1632	...	1710	...	...	|
Augsburg Hbf **904 905** d.	1352	...	...	1438	...	...	1452	1518	1541	...	...	...	1552	...	...	...	...	...	1652	1719	...	1741	...	...	1752
München Pasing **904 905** a.	1421	...	...	1507	...	...	1521	1554	|	...	...	...	1621	...	...	...	...	...	1721	1756	...	|	...	...	1821
München Hbf **904 905** a.	1431	...	...	1516	...	...	1531	1603	1617	...	...	...	1631	...	...	...	...	...	1731	1804	...	1817	...	...	1831
Salzburg Hbf **890** 🏛 a.	...	...	...	...	...	...	...	...	1803	...	...	...	...	...	...	...	...	...	...	...	...	2003	...	...	...

	IC 2113	ICE 577	IC 2011	IC 2265	IRE 4233	IRE 4911	ICE 109	RE 4177	IC 391	IRE 4235	IC 2163	ICE 611	IC 2115	ICE 579	IC 2267	IC 1819	IC 2017	IC 2017	IRE 4913	ICE 691	TGV 9575	IC 2395	IRE 4237	IC 2165	ICE 613
			⑤⑦		Ⓐy						Ⓑq		n			①-④	⑦w	⑤f				Ⓑq			
	H♀	H✕	¶D	♀	L		✕♦		Y♀	L	N♀	D♀	♀♦	H✕	♀	k♀	B♀	R♀		B✕	♀♦	♀	F	♀♦	D♀
Köln Hbf **800 910** d.	1253	...	1318	...	...	...	...	...	...	...	...	1554	1453	...	...	1518	1518	1518	...	...	...	...	...	...	1754
Frankfurt (Main) Hbf **911/2** d.	|	1505	|	...	...	...	1550	...	1620	...	...	|	|	1705	...	|	|	|	...	1750	...	1820	...	...	|
Frankfurt Flughafen ✈ **912** d.	|	1520	|	...	...	...	|	...	|	...	...	1654	|	1720	...	|	|	|	...	|	...	|	...	...	1854
Mannheim Hbf d.	1523	1555	1554	...	...	...	1631	...	|	...	...	1733	1723	1755	...	1754	1754	1754	...	1831	...	|	...	...	1933
Heidelberg Hbf ★ d.	1536	|	1606	...	...	...	|	...	1714	...	...	|	1736	|	...	1806	1806	1806	...	|	...	1914	...	...	|
Karlsruhe Hbf d.	|	|	|	1606	...	1605	|	...	|	...	1706	|	|	|	1806	|	|	|	1805	|	1826	|	...	1906	|
Pforzheim Hbf d.	|	|	|	|	...	1626	|	...	|	...	1727	|	|	|	|	|	|	|	1826	|	|	|	...	1927	|
Bruchsal ★ d.	|	|	|	1619	...	|	|	...	|	...	|	|	|	|	1819	|	|	|	|	|	|	|	...	|	|
Mühlacker ★ d.	|	|	|	|	...	1634	|	...	|	...	1737	|	|	|	|	|	|	|	1834	|	|	|	...	1937	|
Vaihingen (Enz) ★ d.	1605	|	|	|	...	1641	|	...	|	...	1746	|	1805	|	|	|	|	|	1841	|	|	|	...	1946	|
Stuttgart Hbf ★ a.	1622	1632	1646	1649	...	1658	1708	...	1753	...	1803	1808	1822	1833	1849	1846	1846	1846	1858	1908	1903	1953	...	2003	2008
Stuttgart Hbf **936** ★ d.	...	...	...	1653	1702	...	1712	...	1758	1802	...	1812	...	...	1853	...	...	1858	...	1912	1918n	1958	2002	...	2012
Plochingen **936** ★ d.	...	...	...	1709	1716	...	|	...	|	1816	...	|	...	...	1909	...	...	1915	...	|	|	|	2016	...	|
Göppingen ★ d.	...	...	...	1721	1727	...	|	...	|	1827	...	|	...	...	1921	...	...	|	...	|	|	|	2027	...	|
Geislingen (Steige) ★ d.	...	...	...	|	1740	...	|	...	|	1840	...	|	...	...	|	...	...	1938	...	|	|	|	2040	...	|
Ulm Hbf **945** ★ d.	...	...	...	1755	1802	...	1808	1812	1854	1902	...	1908	...	...	1955	...	...	2002	...	2008	2016n	2055	2102	...	2108
Günzburg **945** d.	...	...	...	|	...	...	|	1832	1909	...	...	|	...	...	|	...	...	|	...	|	|	2110	...	...	|
Augsburg Hbf **904 905** d.	...	...	...	1838	...	...	1852	1918	1941	...	...	1952	...	...	2038	...	...	2047	...	2052	2100n	2141	...	...	2152
München Pasing **904 905** a.	...	...	...	1907	...	...	1921	1955	|	...	...	2021	...	...	2107	...	...	2118	...	2124	|	2212	...	...	2221
München Hbf **904 905** a.	...	...	...	1916	...	...	1931	2003	2017	...	...	2031	...	...	2116	...	...	2128	...	2134	2140n	2221	...	...	2231
Salzburg Hbf **890** 🏛 a.	...	...	...	2109q	...	...	...	...	2209	...	...	...	...	...	...	...	...	...	...	...	...	...	...	...	...

♦ – NOTES (LISTED BY TRAIN NUMBER)

61 – [12] and ✕ Strasbourg - Karlsruhe - München.

109 – [12] and ✕ Berlin - Frankfurt - München - Kufstein 🏛 - Innsbruck.

115 – WÖRTHERSEE – [12] and ✕ Dortmund - Villach - Klagenfurt.

119 – [12] and ♀ Münster - Ulm - Lindau - Bregenz - Innsbruck.

181 – ①-⑥ (not Dec. 24, 25, 31, Jan. 1, Mar. 24, May 12). [12] and ✕ Frankfurt - Singen - Schaffhausen - Zürich.

261 – 🛏 1, 2 cl., ▬ 2 cl., [2] and ♀ Paris - München (Table **30**).

264/5 – ORIENT EXPRESS – 🛏 1, 2 cl., ▬ 2 cl., [2] and ♀ Wien - Linz - Salzburg - Strasbourg and v.v.

312/3 – DONAU-KURIER – 🛏 1, 2 cl., ▬ 2 cl., [2] and ✕ Wien - Linz - Amsterdam and v.v,

319 – POLLUX – 🛏 1, 2 cl., ▬ 2 cl., [2] (reclining) and ✕ Amsterdam - München (- Garmisch on dates in Table **895**).

591 – [12] and ✕ (Hamburg on dates in Table **900** -) Kassel - Frankfurt - München. Train number **599** on ⑦ (also Mar. 24, May 12).

NOTES CONTINUE ON NEXT PAGE →

MANNHEIM and KARLSRUHE - STUTTGART - MÜNCHEN 930

	ICE 671	*IC* 2019	*IC* 2269	*IC* 2269	*IC* 2269	*IRE* 4915	*TGV* 9577	*ICE* 693	*RE* 37043	*RB* 19371	*IC* 2252	*IC* 2397	*IC* 2167	*ICE* 615	*IC* 2213	*RB* 19375	*ICE* 675	*IC* 1967	*ICE* 1093	*ICE* 617	*RB* 19379	*RE* 19125	*CNL* 313	*EN* 265	*IC* 2315
		⑤⑦t	⑧q	♣	⑦w		⑧j				⑦w		⑧q	n				⑤	⊖	⑦w			[R]		
	H✕	B	🍷	🍷	🍷		P🍷	B✕			T🍷	🍷	🍷◆	D🍷	🍷◆		H✕	◐	B✕	D🍷			✕◆	🍷◆	◧◆
Köln Hbf **800 910** d.	...	1718	...	...	...	...	...	...	...	...	...	...	...	1954	1853	...	...	...	...	2044d	...	...	2006	...	2053
Frankfurt (Main) Hbf **911/2**. d.	1905	|	...	...	...	...	...	1950	...	...	1955	2020	...	|	|	...	2105	...	2150	|	...	...	2247	...	|
Frankfurt Flughafen ✈ **912** d.	1920	|	...	...	...	...	...	|	...	...	|	|	...	2054	|	...	2120	...	|	2149	...	...	|	...	2301
annheim Hbf d.	1955	1954	...	...	...	...	...	2031	...	...	|	|	...	2133	2123	...	2157	...	2231	|	...	...	2332	...	2346
eidelberg Hbf ★ d.	|	2006	...	...	...	...	...	|	...	...	2052	2114	...	|	2136	...	2210	...	|	2248	...	...	|	...	2359
Karlsruhe Hbf d.	|	|	2006	2006	2006	2005	2026	|	...	...	|	|	2106	|	|	...	|	2205	|	|	...	2318	|	0022	|
Pforzheim Hbf d.	|	|	|	|	|	2026	|	|	...	...	|	|	2127	|	|	...	|	2226	|	|	...	2340	|	|	|
uchsal ★ d.	|	|	2019	2019	2019	|	|	|	...	...	|	|	|	|	|	...	|	|	|	|	...	|	|	|	|
ühlacker ★ d.	|	|	|	|	|	2034	|	|	...	...	|	|	2137	|	|	...	|	2235	|	|	...	2352	|	|	|
aihingen (Enz) ★ d.	|	|	|	|	|	2041	|	|	...	...	2128	|	2146	|	2205	...	|	2244	|	|	...	0000	|	|	|
uttgart Hbf ★ a.	2033	2046	2049	2049	2049	2058	2103	2108	...	...	2146	2154	2203	2208	2222	...	2248	2301	2308	2324	...	0036	|	|	0051b
uttgart Hbf **936** ★ d.	...	...	...	2053	2053	...	...	2112	...	2132	...	...	...	2212	...	2232	...	...	...	...	2332	...	|	|	...
ochingen **936** ★ d.	...	...	...	2108	2108	...	...	|	...	2151	...	...	...	|	...	2252	...	...	...	...	2352	...	|	|	...
öppingen ★ d.	...	...	...	2120	2120	...	...	|	...	2208	...	...	...	|	...	2311	...	...	...	...	0013	...	|	|	...
eislingen (Steige) ★ d.	...	...	...	2132	2132	...	...	|	...	2231	...	...	...	|	...	2339	...	...	...	...	0038	...	|	|	...
m Hbf **945** ★ d.	...	...	...	2153	2155	...	...	2208	*2212*	2302	...	...	...	2308	...	0004	...	...	...	...	0103	...	|	|	...
ünzburg **945** d.	...	...	...	...	2212	...	...	|	*2231*	...	...	...	...	|	...	...	...	...	...	...	...	...	|	|	...
ugsburg Hbf **904 905** d.	...	...	...	...	2242	...	...	2252	2343	...	...	...	...	2356	...	...	...	...	...	...	...	...	|	|	...
ünchen Pasing **904 905** a.	...	...	...	...	2310	...	...	2321	0018	...	...	...	...	0025	...	...	...	...	...	...	...	...	|	|	...
ünchen Hbf **904 905** a.	...	...	...	...	2320	...	...	2331	0026	...	...	...	...	0035	...	...	...	...	...	...	...	...	|	|	...
Salzburg Hbf **890** 🏛 a.	...	...	...	...	...	...	...	...	...	...	...	...	...	...	...	...	...	...	...	...	...	...	0509	0509	...

km ●	km		*IC* 1590	*IC* 1590	*EN* 264	*CNL* 312	*ICE* 676	*RB* 19202	*IC* 2360	*ICE* 616	*IC* 2396	*IC* 1816	*RB* 19208	*ICE* 694	*TGV* 9578	*IC* 2268	*IC* 2268	*IC* 2268	*IC* 1818	*RE* 19106	*ICE* 672	*IC* 2116	*IRE* 19228	*ICE* 614	*IC* 2164
			①g	v		[R]	①–⑥		①–⑤		①–⑥	①–⑥			①–⑥	①g	①–⑤	①–⑥	Ⓐr	19130		v	Ⓐy		
			◧	◧	🍷◆	✕◆	eH✕		a🍷	D🍷	e🍷	⊠		B✕	hP	🍷	a🍷	e🍷	🍷		H✕	🍷◆		D🍷	🍷◆
		Salzburg Hbf **890** 🏛 d.	...	...	2342	2342	...	...	...	...	...	...	...	...	...	...	...	...	...	...	...	...	...	...	...
		München Hbf **904 905** d.	0033	...	|	|	...	...	...	0317*	...	...	...	...	...	0426	...	...	...	...	...	...	...	0523	...
		München Pasing **904 905** d.	0041	...	|	|	...	...	...	0325*	...	...	...	...	...	0434	...	...	...	...	...	...	...	0531	...
		Augsburg Hbf **904 905** d.	0114	...	|	|	...	...	...	0357*	...	...	...	...	...	0513	...	...	...	...	...	...	...	0604	...
		Günzburg **945** d.	0144	...	|	|	...	...	...	|	...	...	...	...	...	0544	...	...	...	...	...	...	...	|	...
		Ulm Hbf **945** ★ d.	0202	...	|	|	...	0411	...	0440*	...	...	0455	...	...	0602	0602	...	...	...	...	...	0613	0651	...
		Geislingen (Steige) ★ d.	|	...	|	|	...	0436	...	|	...	...	0528	...	...	0625	0625	...	...	...	...	...	0644	|	...
		Göppingen ★ d.	|	...	|	|	...	0458	...	|	...	...	0553	...	...	0639	0639	...	...	...	...	...	0709	|	...
		Plochingen **936** ★ d.	|	...	|	|	...	0518	...	|	...	...	0612	...	...	0651	0651	...	...	...	...	...	0722	|	...
		Stuttgart Hbf **936** ★ a.	0300	...	|	|	...	0538	...	0537*	...	...	0632	...	...	0707	0707	...	...	...	...	...	0738	0747	...
0	*0*	**Stuttgart** Hbf ★ d.	0305	0305	|	|	0509	...	0545	0551	0603	0633	...	0651	0654	0711	0711	0711	0714	0717	0727	0737	...	0751	0801
29	*39*	Vaihingen (Enz) ★ d.	0336	0336	|	|	|	...	0603	|	0620	0650	...	|	|	|	|	|	|	0750	|	0755	...	|	0816
	47	Mühlacker ★ d.	|	|	|	|	|	...	0611	|	|	|	...	|	|	|	|	|	|	0759	|	|	...	|	0823
	79	Bruchsal ★ d.	0407	0407	|	|	|	...	|	|	|	|	...	|	|	0740	0740	0740	|	|	|	|	...	|	|
	60	Pforzheim Hbf d.	|	|	|	|	|	...	0622	|	|	|	...	|	|	|	|	|	|	0813	|	|	...	|	0834
	86	**Karlsruhe** Hbf a.	|	|	0423	|	|	...	0645	|	|	|	...	|	0729	0753	0753	0753	|	0838	|	|	...	|	0853
92		**Heidelberg** Hbf ★ a.	0426	0426	...	|	0545	...	...	|	0647	0718	...	|	...	...	...	...	0753	...	|	0823	...	|	...
109		**Mannheim** Hbf a.	0438	0438	...	0515	0559	...	...	0626	|	0731	...	0728	...	...	...	...	0806	...	0804	0837	...	0826	...
		Frankfurt Flughafen ✈ **912**. a.	0512	0512	...	|	0638	...	...	0706	|	...	...	|	...	...	...	...	|	...	0838	|	...	0906	...
		Frankfurt (Main) Hbf **911/2** a.	0535	0535	...	0600	0652	...	...	|	0800	...	...	0808	...	...	...	...	|	...	0853	|	...	|	...
		Köln Hbf **800 910** a.	...	...	...	0842	...	...	...	0805	...	...	...	...	...	...	...	...	1042	...	...	1105	...	1005	...

	IRE 4222	*IRE* 4220	*IC* 2394	*RE* 4160	*TGV* 9576	*ICE* 692	*IRE* 4902	*IC* 2266	*ICE* 670	*IC* 2114	*ICE* 612	*IC* 2162	*IRE* 4224	*IC* 2392	*RE* 4162	*ICE* 690	*IRE* 4904	*IC* 2264	*IC* 2010	*ICE* 578	*IC* 2112	*ICE* 610	*IC* 2160	*IRE* 4226	*IC* 390
	Ⓐy	Ⓒ◇	①–⑥					①–⑥				①–⑥		①–⑥					⑤f						
	F	F	e🍷		🍷◆	B✕		⊙🍷	H✕	H🍷	D🍷	e◆	L	e🍷		B✕		🍷	B	H✕	H🍷	D🍷	N🍷	F	Y🍷
Salzburg Hbf **890** 🏛 d.	...	...	...	...	...	...	...	...	...	...	...	...	...	0547	...	...	...	0646e	...	...	...	...	...	...	0753e
ünchen Hbf **904 905** d.	...	...	0515	0539	0620v	0625	...	0640	...	...	0723	...	...	0739	0749	0823	...	0841	...	...	...	0923	...	...	0939
ünchen Pasing **904 905** d.	...	...	0523	0546	|	0634	...	0648	...	...	0731	...	...	|	0756	0831	...	0849	...	...	...	0931	...	...	|
ugsburg Hbf **904 905** d.	...	...	0556	0631	0657v	0707	...	0721	...	...	0804	...	...	0817	0836	0904	...	0921	...	...	...	1004	...	...	1017
ünzburg **945** d.	...	...	0629	0715	|	|	...	|	...	...	|	...	...	0849	0920	|	...	|	...	...	...	|	...	...	1049
m Hbf **945** ★ d.	0654	0655	0700	0736	0742v	0751	...	0805	...	...	0851	...	0855	0905	0942	0951	...	1005	...	...	...	1051	...	1055	1105
eislingen (Steige) ★ d.	0717	0717	0722	...	|	|	...	|	...	...	|	...	0917	|	▬	|	...	|	...	...	...	|	...	1117	|
öppingen ★ d.	0729	0728	|	...	|	|	...	0839	...	...	|	...	0928	|	*IC*	|	...	1039	...	...	...	|	...	1128	|
ochingen **936** ★ d.	|	0739	0746	...	|	|	...	0851	...	...	|	...	0939	|	**2392**	|	...	1051	...	...	...	|	...	1139	|
uttgart Hbf **936** ★ a.	0756	0756	0800	...	0842v	0847	...	0907	...	...	0947	...	0956	1000	🍷	1047	...	1107	...	...	...	1147	...	1156	1200
uttgart Hbf ★ d.	...	...	0805	...	0854	0851	0900	0911	0927	0937	0951	1001	...	1005	1005	1051	1059	1111	1114	1127	1137	1151	1201	...	1205
aihingen (Enz) ★ d.	...	...	|	...	|	|	0916	|	|	0955	|	1016	...	|	|	|	1115	|	|	|	1155	|	1216	...	|
ühlacker ★ d.	...	...	|	...	|	|	0921	|	|	|	|	1023	...	|	|	|	1121	|	|	|	|	|	1223	...	|
uchsal ★ d.	...	...	|	...	|	|	|	0940	|	|	|	|	...	|	|	|	|	1139	|	|	|	|	|	...	|
Pforzheim Hbf d.	...	...	|	...	|	|	0930	|	|	|	|	1034	...	|	|	|	1130	|	|	|	|	|	1234	...	|
Karlsruhe Hbf a.	...	...	|	...	0929	|	0953	0953	|	|	|	1053	...	|	|	|	1153	1153	|	|	|	|	1253	...	|
eidelberg Hbf ★ a.	...	...	0845	...	...	|	...	...	|	1023	|	...	...	1045	1045	|	...	...	1153	|	1223	|	...	...	1245
annheim Hbf a.	...	...	|	...	...	0928	...	...	1004	1037	1026	...	...	|	|	1128	...	...	1206	1204	1237	1226	...	...	|
Frankfurt Flughafen ✈ **912** a.	...	...	|	...	...	|	...	...	1038	|	1106	...	...	|	|	|	...	...	|	1238	|	1306	...	...	|
Frankfurt (Main) Hbf **911/2**. a.	...	...	0940	...	...	1008	...	...	1053	|	|	...	...	1140	1140	1208	...	...	|	1253	|	|	...	...	1340
Köln Hbf **800 910** a.	...	...	...	...	...	...	...	...	...	1305	1205	...	...	...	...	...	...	...	1442	...	1505	1405	...	...	...

– **NOTES** (LISTED BY TRAIN NUMBER)

3 – [12] (Kiel ①–⑥ **e** -) Hamburg - Stuttgart. Train number **573** on ⑦ (also Dec. 25, 26, Jan. 1, Mar. 22, 24, May 12).
1 – ①–⑥ (not Dec. 24, 25, 31, Jan. 1, Mar. 24, May 12). [12] and ✕ Wiesbaden - Mainz - München.
013 – ALLGÄU – [12] (Leipzig on dates in Table **810** -) (Magdeburg ①–⑥ **e** -) Hannover - Dortmund - Oberstdorf.
015 – ①–④ (not Dec. 24, 25, 26, 31, Jan. 1, Mar. 20, 24, Apr. 30, May 12, 21). [12] and 🍷 Emden - Münster - Stuttgart.
15/6 – [12] and 🍷 Stralsund - Hamburg - Köln - Stuttgart and v.v.
162 – [12] and 🍷 (Passau ① **g** -) Nürnberg - Stuttgart - Karlsruhe.
164 – Daily except Dec. 25, 26, Jan. 1. [12] and 🍷 (Nürnberg ①–⑤ **a** -) Stuttgart - Karlsruhe.
165 – Daily except Dec. 24, 25, 31. [12] and 🍷 Karlsruhe - Stuttgart (- Nürnberg ⑤⑦ **z**) (- Passau ⑦ **w**).
167 – [12] and 🍷 Karlsruhe - Stuttgart (- Nürnberg ⑦ **w**).
213 – RÜGEN – [12] and 🍷 Ostseebad Binz - Stralsund - Hamburg - Köln - Stuttgart.
275 – [12] and 🍷 Hannover - Kassel - Gießen - Frankfurt - Stuttgart.
315 – [12] and 🍷 (from Mar. 15: Westerland -) Hamburg - Dortmund - Stuttgart. Train number **2215** until Mar. 14.
319 – [12] and ✕ (Münster ① **g** -) Dortmund - Stuttgart.
575/6 – [12] and 🍷 Paris - Strasbourg - München and v.v. [R] for international journeys.

– From Saarbrücken (Table **919**).
– From / to Berlin (Tables **810** / **900**).
– From / to Dortmund (Table **800**).
– To / from Friedrichshafen (Table **931**).
– From / to Hamburg (Table **800** or **900**).
– From Koblenz (Table **912**).
– To / from Lindau (Table **931**).
– From Münster (Table **800**).
– To / from Nürnberg (Table **925**).
– From Offenburg (Table **916**).
– [12] and 🍷 Paris - Strasbourg - Stuttgart and v.v. [R] for international journeys.
– From Hannover (Table **810**).
– From Leipzig (Table **850**).
– [12] Wiesbaden - Mainz - Stuttgart.
– From / to Linz on dates in Table **950**.

a – ①–⑤ (not Dec. 24, 25, 26, 31, Jan. 1, Mar. 21, 24, May 12).
b – 0040 on ①⑦.
c – Not Dec. 23, 24, 25, 30, 31, Mar. 21, 23, May 11.
d – Köln **Messe/Deutz**.
e – ①–⑥ (not Dec. 25, 26, Jan. 1, Mar. 22, 24, May 12).
f – Also Mar. 20, Apr. 30, May 21; not Mar. 21, May 2, 23.
g – Also Dec. 27, Jan. 2, Mar. 25, May 13; not Dec. 24, 31, Mar. 24, May 12.
h – Not Dec. 25, Jan. 1, Mar. 24, May 12.
j – Not Dec. 24, 31, Mar. 23, May 11.
k – Not Dec. 24, 25, 26, 31, Jan. 1, Mar. 20, 24, Apr. 30, May 1, 12, 21, 22.
m – Also Dec. 24, 25, 31, Jan. 1, Mar. 24, May 12.
n – Not Dec. 24, 31.
q – ⑧ (not Dec. 24, 25, 31, Mar. 21, 23, May 11).
r – Not Dec. 24, 31, May 2, 22, 23.

s – Stops to set down only.
t – Also Dec. 26, Jan. 1, Mar. 20, 24, Apr. 30, May 12; not Dec. 23, 30, Mar. 21, 23, May 2, 11.
u – Also Dec. 26, Jan. 1, Mar. 24, May 12; not Dec. 23, 30.
v – Not Dec. 25, Jan. 1.
w – Also Dec. 26, Jan. 1, Mar. 24, May 12; not Dec. 23, 30, Mar. 23, May 11.
x – Not Dec. 24, 25, 26, 31.
y – Not Dec. 24, 31, Jan. 1, May 22.
z – Also Dec. 26, Jan. 1, Mar. 20, 24, May 12; not Dec. 23, 30, Mar. 21, 23, May 11.

◇ – Also Dec. 24, 31, May 22.
◐ – Also Mar. 20; not Mar. 21.
‡ – Not Dec. 25, 26, Jan. 1, Mar. 22, 24, May 1, 12, 22.
¶ – ⑤⑦ (also Dec. 26, Jan. 1, Mar. 20, 24, Apr. 30, May 12, 21; not Dec. 23, 30, Mar. 21, 23, May 2, 11, 23). Train number **1811** on ⑦ **w**.
⊠ – ①–⑥ (not Dec. 24, 25, 26, 31, Jan. 1, Mar. 22, 24, May 12). To Mainz Hbf (a. 0813). Train number **2218** on ⑥ (also Mar. 21, May 1; not May 3).
♣ – ①②③④⑦ (not Dec. 23, 24, 25, 30, 31, Mar. 20, 23, May 11).
* – 7–11 minutes later on ⑥⑦ (also Dec. 24, 31, May 22).
§ – Train number **593** on ⑥⑦ (also Dec. 24, 25, 26, 31, Jan. 1, Mar. 21, 24, May 12).
⊖ – Train number **695** on ⑥ (also Dec. 24, 25, 31, Mar. 21, 23, May 11)
◧ – Subject to alteration in the Stuttgart area from May 16.
⊙ – Runs daily Stuttgart - Karlsruhe.
✣ – Via Schwäbisch Gmünd (Table **925**).
★ – See panel on page 438 for additional *RE* services.
● – Via the high-speed line.

930 MÜNCHEN - STUTTGART - KARLSRUHE and MANNHEIM

	RE 4164	*IC* 2014 ①-⑤ ♀♦	*ICE* 108 ✕♦	*TGV* 9574 P♀	*IRE* 4906	*IC* 2262 ①-⑤ t♀	*IC* 2012 ♀♦	*ICE* 576 H✕	*ICE* 518 D♀	*IC* 2068 N♀	*IRE* 4228 L	*IC* 2298 ♀	*RE* 4166	*IC* 2056 ①-⑤ tA	*ICE* 596 B✕	*IRE* 4908	*IC* 118 ♀♦	*IC* 2368 ♀	*IC* 118 ♀♦	*ICE* 774 ✕♦	*ICE* 516 D♀	*IC* 2066 N♀	*IRE* 4230 L	*IC* 2296 ♀	*IC* 2316 ⑧q W
Salzburg Hbf 890 🚌 d.	...	...	...	...	...	...	...	...	...	...	...	0957	...	...	...	...	...	...	...	...	...	...	...	1153	...
München Hbf 904 905 d.	0950	...	1023	...	...	...	...	...	1123	...	...	1141	1149	...	1223	...	...	1241	...	...	1323	...	...	1339	...
München Pasing 904 905 d.	0957	...	1032	...	...	...	...	...	1132	...	...	|	1156	...	1231	...	...	1249	...	...	1331	...	...	|	...
Augsburg Hbf 904 905 d.	1036	...	1104	...	...	...	...	...	1204	...	...	1217	1236	...	1304	...	...	1321	...	...	1404	...	...	1417	...
Günzburg 945 d.	1121	...	|	...	...	...	...	...	|	...	...	1249	1321	...	|	...	...	|	...	...	|	...	...	1449	...
Ulm Hbf 945 ★ d.	1142	...	1151	...	...	...	1157	...	1251	...	1255	1305	1342	...	1351	...	1356	1405	...	...	1451	...	1455	1505	...
Geislingen (Steige) ★ d.	...	...	|	...	...	...	|	...	|	...	1317	|	...	...	|	...	1420	|	...	...	|	...	1517	|	...
Göppingen ★ d.	...	...	|	...	...	...	1235	...	|	...	1329	|	...	...	|	...	1433	|	...	...	|	...	1528	|	...
Plochingen 936 ★ d.	...	...	|	...	...	...	1249	...	|	...	1339	|	...	...	|	...	|	1449	...	...	|	...	1539	|	...
Stuttgart Hbf 936 ★ a.	...	...	1247	...	...	...	1305	...	1347	...	1356	1400	...	...	1447	...	1458	1503	←	...	1547	...	1556	1600	...
Stuttgart Hbf ★ d.	...	1209	1251	1254	1259	1311	1314	1327	1351	1401	...	1405	...	1434	1451	1459	→	1508	1512	1527	1551	1601	...	1605	1636
Vaihingen (Enz) ★ d.	...	1226	|	|	1315	|	|	|	|	1416	...	|	...	1451	|	1515	...	|	|	|	|	1616	...	|	|
Mühlacker ★ d.	...	|	|	|	1321	|	|	|	|	1423	...	|	...	|	|	1521	...	|	|	|	|	1623	...	|	|
Bruchsal ★ d.	...	|	|	|	|	1340	|	|	|	|	...	|	...	|	|	|	...	1537	|	|	|	|	...	|	|
Pforzheim Hbf d.	...	|	|	|	1330	|	|	|	|	1434	...	|	...	|	|	1530	...	|	|	|	|	1634	...	|	|
Karlsruhe Hbf a.	...	|	|	1329	1353	1353	|	|	|	1453	...	|	...	|	|	1553	...	1550	|	|	|	1653	...	|	|
Heidelberg Hbf ★ a.	...	|	|	...	...	...	1353	|	|	...	...	1445	...	1518	|	...	...	...	1553	|	|	...	...	1645	1718
Mannheim Hbf a.	...	1256	1328	...	...	...	1406	1404	1426	...	...	|	...	1537	1528	...	...	...	1606	1604	1626	...	...	|	1736
Frankfurt Flughafen ✈ 912 a.	...	|	|	...	...	...	|	1438	1506	...	...	|	...	...	|	...	...	...	|	1638	1706	...	...	|	...
Frankfurt (Main) Hbf 911/2 a.	...	|	1408	...	...	...	|	1453	|	...	...	1540	...	...	1608	...	...	...	|	1653	|	...	...	1740	...
Köln Hbf 800 910 a.	...	1542	...	...	...	...	1642	...	1605	...	...	...	...	...	...	...	...	...	1842	...	1805	...	...	...	...

	IC 2364 ①-⑤ tO ♀	*RE* 4168	*ICE* 1090 ‡ B✕	*TGV* 9572 ⑥⑦c P♀	*IRE* 4910	*IRE* 4232 Ⓐy L	*IC* 2260 ⑧q ♀	*EC* 114 ✕♦	*ICE* 572 H✕	*IC* 2362 ①-⑤ r♀	*IC* 2318 n ✕♦	*ICE* 514 H♀	*IC* 2052 ⑧q A♀	*IC* 2064 N♀	*IRE* 4234 L	*IC* 2294 ♀	*IC* 2194 ⑦w T♀	*RE* 4170	*ICE* 592 B✕	*TGV* 9570 ①-⑤ dP	*IRE* 4912	*IC* 2018 ⑦w D	*EC* 60 S✕	*ICE* 570 ⑦w H✕	*IC* 2110 ⑧q ♀
Salzburg Hbf 890 🚌 d.	...	...	...	...	...	...	...	1302	...	...	...	...	...	...	...	1353	...	...	...	...	...	...	...	...	...
München Hbf 904 905 d.	...	1349	1423	...	...	...	...	1440	...	...	...	1523	...	...	...	1539	...	1549	1623	...	...	1613	1642	...	...
München Pasing 904 905 d.	...	1357	1431	...	...	...	...	1448	...	...	...	1531	...	...	...	|	...	1556	1631	...	...	1621	1650	...	...
Augsburg Hbf 904 905 d.	...	1436	1504	...	...	...	...	1521	...	...	...	1604	...	...	...	1617	...	1636	1704	...	...	1653	1722	...	...
Günzburg 945 d.	...	1521	|	...	...	...	...	|	...	...	...	|	...	...	...	1649	...	1722	|	...	...	1728	|	...	...
Ulm Hbf 945 ★ d.	...	1542	1551	...	...	1555	...	1605	...	...	...	1651	...	...	1655	1705	...	1742	1751	...	...	1757	1805	...	...
Geislingen (Steige) ★ d.	...	...	|	...	...	1618	...	|	...	...	...	|	...	...	1717	|	...	...	|	...	...	1820	|	...	...
Göppingen ★ d.	...	...	|	...	...	1630	...	1639	...	...	...	|	...	...	1728	|	...	...	|	...	...	|	1839	...	...
Plochingen 936 ★ d.	...	...	|	...	...	1641	...	1651	...	...	...	|	...	...	1739	|	...	...	|	...	...	|	1851	...	...
Stuttgart Hbf 936 ★ a.	...	...	1647	...	...	1656	...	1705	...	...	...	1747	...	...	1756	1800	...	...	1847	...	...	1858	1907	...	...
Stuttgart Hbf ★ d.	1641	...	1651	1654	1659	...	1708	1713	1727	1734	1741	1751	1757	1801	...	1805	1837	...	1851	1854	1859	1914	1911	1927	1937
Vaihingen (Enz) ★ d.	|	...	|	|	1715	...	|	|	|	|	|	|	|	1816	...	|	1855	...	|	|	1915	|	|	|	1955
Mühlacker ★ d.	|	...	|	|	1721	...	|	|	|	|	|	|	|	1823	...	|	|	...	|	|	1921	|	|	|	|
Bruchsal ★ d.	1714	...	|	|	|	...	1737	|	|	1804	|	|	|	|	...	|	|	...	|	|	|	|	1939	|	|
Pforzheim Hbf d.	|	...	|	|	1730	...	|	|	|	|	|	|	|	1834	...	|	|	...	|	|	1930	|	|	|	|
Karlsruhe Hbf a.	1732	...	|	1729	1753	...	1753	|	|	1821	|	|	|	1853	...	|	|	...	|	1929	1953	|	1953	|	|
Heidelberg Hbf ★ a.	...	...	|	...	...	...	...	1753	|	...	1823	|	|	...	...	1845	1922	...	|	...	...	1953	...	|	2023
Mannheim Hbf a.	...	...	1728	...	...	...	...	1806	1804	...	1837	1826	1845	...	...	|	|	...	1928	...	...	2006	...	2004	2037
Frankfurt Flughafen ✈ 912 a.	...	...	|	...	...	...	...	|	1838	...	|	1906	...	...	...	|	|	...	|	...	...	|	...	2038	|
Frankfurt (Main) Hbf 911/2 a.	...	...	1808	...	...	...	...	|	1853	...	|	|	...	...	...	1940	2018	...	2008	...	...	|	...	2053	|
Köln Hbf 800 910 a.	...	...	...	...	...	...	...	2042	...	...	2105	2005	...	...	...	...	...	...	...	...	...	2242	...	...	2305

	ICE 512 n M♀	*IC* 2062 n N♀	*IRE* 4236 L	*IC* 2292 A♀	*IC* 1976 ⑦w ♦	*RE* 4198 ⑥⑦	*IC* 1896 ⑦w ♀♦	*RE* 4172	*ICE* 590 ⊡ ✕	*IRE* 4914	*IC* 2290 ⑧q ♀	*ICE* 510 ①-⑥ z♀	*ICE* 1810 ⑦v ♀	*IC* 2060 ⑧q N♀	*IRE* 4238 ©j L	*ICE* 180 ✕♦	*IC* 2050 ⑦w A	*RE* 19124 19196	*RE* 19380 19382 g	*ICE* 990 ⊖✕	*CNL* 260 Ⓡ ♀♦	*IC* 2090 ⑦w ♀	*RB* 37226	*IC* 60318 K ◧2	*CNL* 318 Ⓡ ◧♦
Salzburg Hbf 890 🚌 d.	...	...	...	1553	...	...	...	...	...	...	1653	...	...	...	...	...	...	...	...	...	...	...	...	...	...
München Hbf 904 905 d.	1723	...	...	1739	...	1701	...	1749	1823	...	1839	1923	1923	...	...	...	...	...	...	2039	2053	2136	*2151*	2242	2240
München Pasing 904 905 d.	1731	...	...	|	...	|	...	1756	1831	...	|	1931	1931	...	...	...	...	...	...	|	|	2144	*2158*	|	|
Augsburg Hbf 904 905 d.	1804	...	...	1817	...	1741	...	1836	1904	...	1917	2004	2004	...	...	...	...	...	...	2117	2133u	2217	2243	2320	2320
Günzburg 945 d.	|	...	...	1849	...	|	...	1924	|	...	1949	|	|	...	...	...	...	...	...	|	|	2248	2338	2353	2353
Ulm Hbf 945 ★ d.	1851	...	1855	1905	...	|	...	1945	1951	...	2005	2051	2051	...	2055	...	...	...	2103	2204	2220u	2304	2359	0010	0010
Geislingen (Steige) ★ d.	|	...	1917	|	...	✣	...	...	|	...	|	|	|	...	2117	...	...	...	2133	|	|	2327	▬	0034	0034
Göppingen ★ d.	|	...	1928	|	...	|	...	...	|	...	2039	|	|	...	2128	...	...	...	2150	|	2256u	2340	*RE*	0048	0048
Plochingen 936 ★ d.	|	...	1939	|	...	|	...	...	|	...	2051	|	|	...	2139	...	...	...	2205	|	|	2353	**19128**	0102	0102
Stuttgart Hbf 936 ★ a.	1947	...	1956	2000	...	2008	...	...	2047	...	2106	2147	2147	...	2156	...	...	...	2224	2300	|	0008		0116	|
Stuttgart Hbf ★ d.	1951	2001	...	2005	2009	...	2035	...	2051	2059	2111	2151	2151	2201	...	2205	2209	2217	...	2305	2331u	...	0019	0126	0126
Vaihingen (Enz) ★ d.	|	2016	...	|	|	...	2052	...	|	2115	|	|	|	2216	...	|	2225	2252	...	|	|	...	0052	|	|
Mühlacker ★ d.	|	2023	...	|	|	...	|	...	|	2121	|	|	|	2223	...	|	|	2300	...	|	|	...	0100	|	|
Bruchsal ★ d.	|	|	...	|	|	...	|	...	|	|	2140	|	|	|	...	|	|	|	...	|	|	...	|	|	|
Pforzheim Hbf d.	|	2034	...	|	|	...	|	...	|	2130	|	|	|	2234	...	|	|	2313	...	|	2359u	...	0113	|	|
Karlsruhe Hbf a.	|	2053	...	|	|	...	|	...	|	2153	2153	|	|	2253	...	|	|	2338	...	|	0054u	...	0136	|	|
Heidelberg Hbf ★ a.	|	...	...	|	2048	...	2118	...	|	...	...	|	|	...	...	2246	2253	...	...	|	...	...	...	|	|
Mannheim Hbf a.	2026	...	...	2048	|	...	2131	...	2128	...	...	2228	2228	...	...	|	2306	...	...	2342	...	...	...	0247	|
Frankfurt Flughafen ✈ 912 a.	2106	...	...	...	2143	...	...	...	|	...	...	2303	2302	...	...	|	...	...	...	0023	...	...	...	...	|
Frankfurt (Main) Hbf 911/2 a.	|	...	...	...	...	...	...	...	2208	...	...	2325	|	...	...	2339	...	...	...	0042	...	...	...	...	|
Köln Hbf 800 910 a.	2205	...	...	...	...	...	...	...	...	...	...	...	0005	...	...	...	...	...	...	...	...	...	...	...	0545

♦ – NOTES (LISTED BY TRAIN NUMBER)

108 – 🛏12 and ✕ Innsbruck - Kufstein 🚌 - München - Frankfurt - Berlin.
114 – WÖRTHERSEE – 🛏12 and ✕ Klagenfurt - Villach - Salzburg - Dortmund.
118 – 🛏12 and ♀ Innsbruck - Bregenz - Lindau - Ulm - Münster.
180 – 🛏12 and ✕ Zürich - Schaffhausen - Singen - Stuttgart - Frankfurt.
260 – 🛏 1,2 cl., ▬ 2 cl., 🛏2 and ♀ München - Paris (Table **30**).
318 – POLLUX – 🛏 1,2 cl., ▬ 2 cl., 🛏2 (reclining) and ✕ (Garmisch ♣ -) München - Amsterdam.
774 – 🛏12 and ✕ Stuttgart - Hamburg (- Kiel ⑧q). Train number **574** on ⑥ (also Dec. 24, 25, 31, Mar. 21, 23, May 11).
1896 – 🛏12 and ♀ Stuttgart - Wiesbaden.
1976 – 🛏12 Stuttgart - Frankfurt - Hannover.
2012 – ALLGÄU – 🛏12 and ♀ Oberstdorf - Ulm - Dortmund - Hannover (- Leipzig on dates in Table **810**).
2014 – ①-⑥ (not Dec. 24, 25, 26, 31, Jan. 1, Mar. 21, 24, May 1, 12, 22). 🛏12 and ♀ Stuttgart - Emden.
2318 – 🛏12 and ✕ Stuttgart - Köln (- Dortmund ⑧q) (- Münster ⑦w).

q – Not Dec. 24, 25, 31, Mar. 21, 23, May 11.
r – Not Dec. 24, 25, 26, 31, Jan. 1, Mar. 21, 24, May 2, 12, 23.
t – Not Dec. 24, 25, 26, 31, Jan. 1, Mar. 21, 24, May 12.
u – Stops to pick up only.
v – Also Dec. 26, Jan. 1, Mar. 24, May 12; not Mar. 23, May 11.
w – Also Dec. 26, Jan. 1, Mar. 24, May 12; not Dec. 23, 30, Mar. 23, May 11.
y – Not Dec. 24, 31, May 22.
z – Also Mar. 23, May 11; not Dec. 25, 26, Jan. 1, Mar. 24, May 12.

♣ – ⑥ Dec. 22 - Mar. 29.
✣ – Via Schwäbisch Gmünd (Table **925**).
‡ – Train number **594** on ⑥ (also Dec. 24, 25, 31, Mar. 21, 23, May 11).
◧ – Subject to alteration in the Stuttgart area from May 16.
⊖ – Conveys 🛏12 München - Frankfurt - Hannover - Hamburg on ⑦ (also Jan. 1, Mar. 24, May 12; not Dec. 23, 30, Mar. 23, May 11).
⊡ – Train number **698** on ⑤ (also Mar. 20, Apr. 30; not Mar. 21). Train number **598** on ⑦ (also Dec. 26, Jan. 1, Mar. 24, May 12; not Mar. 23, May 11). To Kassel / Hannover on dates in Table **900**.

A – To Saarbrücken (Table **919**).
B – To Berlin (Table **900**).
D – To Dortmund (Table **800**).
H – To Hamburg (Table **800** or **900**).
K – To Koblenz (Table **912**).
L – From Lindau (Table **931**).
M – To Münster (Table **800**).
N – From Nürnberg (Table **925**).
O – To Offenburg (Table **916**).
P – 🛏12 and ♀ Stuttgart - Strasbourg - Paris. Ⓡ for international journeys.
S – To Strasbourg (Table **912**).
T – To Kassel (Table **806**).
W – To Wiesbaden (Table **912**).

c – Also Dec. 25, Jan. 1, Mar. 24, May 12.
d – Not Dec. 25, Jan. 1, Mar. 24, May 12.
g – Runs 5-10 minutes later on ©j.
j – Also Dec. 24, 31, May 22.

m – Also Dec. 24, 31, May 22; not Dec. 25, Jan. 1.
n – Not Dec. 24, 31.

★ – Additional *RE* services Heidelberg - Stuttgart - Ulm and v.v.

	©					
Heidelberg Hbf d.	0611	0811	1011	and	2011	...
Bruchsal d.	0632	0833	1033	every	2033	...
Mühlacker d.	0655	0859	1059	**two**	2059	...
Vaihingen (Enz) d.	0705	0907	1107	hours	2107	...
Stuttgart Hbf a.	0738	0939	1139	until	2139	...

Stuttgart Hbf d.	0619	0819	1019	1219	1419	1617	1819	2018
Vaihingen (Enz) d.	0650	0850	1050	1250	1450	1650	1850	2050
Mühlacker d.	0700	0859	1059	1259	1459	1659	1859	2059
Bruchsal d.	0727	0929	1129	1329	1529	1729	1929	2129
Heidelberg Hbf a.	0747	0948	1148	1348	1548	1748	1948	2156

	Ⓐy	©m				
Stuttgart Hbf d.	0622	0632	0832	and	2032	...
Plochingen d.	0645	0651	0851	every	2051	...
Göppingen d.	0659	0705	0905	**two**	2105	...
Geislingen (Steige) d.	0719	0723	0923	hours	2123	...
Ulm Hbf a.	0749	0747	0947	until	2147	...

	Ⓐy	Ⓐy	©j					
Ulm Hbf d.	0523	0706	0710	0810	1010	and	2010	2242
Geislingen (Steige) d.	0555	0732	0738	0833	1033	every	2033	2308
Göppingen d.	0609	0751	0758	0850	1050	**two**	2050	2323
Plochingen d.	0623	0805	0815	0905	1105	hours	2105	2340
Stuttgart Hbf a.	0643	0824	0832	0924	1124	until	2124	2400

IRE/RE services (except trains C and D) ULM - LINDAU 931

km			F	B			B			B			B	C 🍷		B			B						2
	Stuttgart Hbf 930	d.	...	...	...	0659j	0802	...	...	1002	...	...	1202	...	1257	1402	...	...	1602	...	1702e	1802	...	2002	...	...
0	Ulm Hbf	d.	0550	0709k	0806	0812	0912	1006	1012	1112	1206	1212	1312	1406	1411	1512	1606	1612	1712	1806	1812	1912	2012	2112	2212	2317
37	Biberach (Riß)	d.	0619	0735	0827	0835	0935	1027	1035	1135	1227	1235	1335	1427	1433	1535	1627	1635	1735	1827	1835	1935	2035	2139	2238	2346
62	Aulendorf	d.	0639	0754	|	0854	0954	|	1053	1154	|	1253	1354	1441	1451	1553	1641	1654	1753	|	1854	1954	2054	2157	2258	0004
84	Ravensburg	d.	0653	0807	0853	0907	1007	1053	1106	1207	1253	1306	1407	1455	1505	1606	1655	1707	1806	1853	1907	2007	2107	2211	2311	0018
95	Meckenbeuren	d.	0700	0814	|	0915	1015	|	1113	1215	|	1313	1415	|	1513	1614	|	1714	1814	|	1915	2015	2115	2218	2319	0025
99	Friedrichshafen Flughafen ✈	d.	0705	|	0902	|	|	1102	1117	|	1302	1317	|	1504	|	|	1706	1718	|	1902	|	2019	|	2223	2323	|
103	Friedrichshafen Stadt ▲	a.	0714	0823	0908	0924	1024	1108	1123	1224	1308	1324	1424	1510	1521	1624	1711	1724	1824	1908	1924	2027	2124	2231	2329	0033
103	Friedrichshafen Stadt 939	d.	0729	0829	...	0930	1034	...	1130	1230	...	1329	1429	...	1535	1634	...	1730	1834	...	1930	2034	2131	2237	2339	...
127	Lindau Hbf 939	a.	0751	0853	...	0951	1056	...	1151	1256	...	1351	1452	...	1554	1656	...	1751	1856	...	1952	2100	2154	2309	0013	...

		Ⓒz	Ⓐe			F	B			B		D 🍷	B			B			B			B		B	2	2
Lindau Hbf 939	d.	...	0513	0559	0706t	0806	...	0902	1006	...	1104	1202	...	1305	1405	...	1504	1603	...	1703	1806	...	1903	2012	2103	2142
Friedrichshafen Stadt 939	a.	...	0544	0622	0726	0826	...	0923	1026	...	1126	1219	...	1326	1426	...	1526	1624	...	1725	1827	...	1925	2034	2124	2219
Friedrichshafen Stadt ▲	d.	0522	0549	0628	0732	0832	0850	0932	1032	1050	1133	1233	1250	1333	1432	1450	1532	1631	1650	1733	1832	1845	1933	2046	2128	2231
Friedrichshafen Flughafen ✈	d.	|	|	0632	|	0837	0855	|	1036	1055	|	|	1256	|	1437	1456	|	1636z	1655	|	1836	1850	|	|	|	2236
Meckenbeuren	d.	0530	|	0637	0739	0841	|	0940	1040	|	1140	1241	|	1340	1441	|	1540	1639	|	1740	1840	|	1940	2053	2135	2240
Ravensburg	d.	0538	0601	0645	0747	0848	0904	0948	1048	1104	1148	1250	1305	1348	1448	1505	1549	1647	1704	1748	1848	1901	1948	2100	2142	2248
Aulendorf	d.	0554	|	0659	0803	0902	|	1003	1102	|	1203	1306	|	1403	1502	|	1603	1701	|	1803	1902	1915	2003	2113	2156	2303
Biberach (Riß)	d.	0612	0627	0719	0821	0919	0930	1021	1119	1130	1220	1322	1331	1421	1519	1531	1621	1719	1730	1821	1919	1930	2021	2130	2212	2321
Ulm Hbf	a.	0644	0650	0745	0845	0945	0953	1045	1145	1153	1245	1345	1353	1445	1545	1553	1645	1745	1753	1845	1945	1953	2045	2155	2237	2355
Stuttgart Hbf 930	a.	0756	0756	...	0956	...	...	1156	...	...	1356	1458	...	1556	1656e	...	1756	...	...	1956	...	...	2156z	...	...	...

B – To/from Basel Bad Bf (Table 939).
C – IC 119: (12) and 🍷 Münster - Köln - Stuttgart - Lindau - Bregenz - Innsbruck.
D – IC 118: (12) and 🍷 Innsbruck - Bregenz - Lindau - Stuttgart - Köln - Münster.
F – Change trains at Friedrichshafen Stadt on Ⓐ e.

e – Ⓐ (not Dec. 24, 31, May 22).
j – 0702 on Ⓒ z.
k – 0712 on Ⓐ e.
t – 0703 on Ⓐ e (change trains at Friedrichshafen).

z – Ⓒ (also Dec. 24, 31, May 22).

▲ – Regular services operate to/from Friedrichshafen Hafen.

S-Bahn 2/3 FLUGHAFEN STUTTGART - ECHTERDINGEN ✈ 932

S-Bahn **Stuttgart Hbf** (underground platforms) - **Stuttgart Flughafen** ✈ and v.v. (*20 km*, journey 27 minutes). On Dec. 24, 31 services run as on ⑥. On May 22 services run as on ⑦.

From Stuttgart Hbf at 0455 Ⓐ, 0515 Ⓐ, 0525, 0545 Ⓑ, 0555 ⚒, 0615 Ⓐ, 0625, 0645 Ⓑ, 0655 ⚒, 0715 Ⓐ, 0725, 0745 Ⓐ, 0755, 0815 Ⓐ, 0825, 0845 Ⓐ, 0855, 0915, 0925, 0945, 0955 and then at 15, 25, 45, and 55 minutes past each hour until 1715, 1725, 1745, 1755, 1815 Ⓐ, 1825, 1845 Ⓐ, 1855, 1915 Ⓐ, 1925, 1945 Ⓐ, 1955, 2015 Ⓐ, 2025, 2045 Ⓐ, 2055, 2115 Ⓐ, 2125, 2155 (not Dec. 24), 2225, 2255 (not Dec. 24), 2325, 2355 (not Dec. 24) and 0025.

From Stuttgart Flughafen ✈ at 0508, 0518 Ⓐ, 0538 ⚒, 0548 Ⓑ, 0608, 0618 Ⓐ, 0638 ⚒, 0648 Ⓑ, 0708, 0718 Ⓐ, 0738 ⚒, 0748 Ⓑ, 0808, 0818 Ⓐ, 0838, 0848 Ⓐ, 0908, 0918 Ⓐ, 0938, 0948, 1008, 1018, 1038, 1048 and then at 08, 18, 38 and 48 minutes past each hour until 1748, 1808, 1818, 1838, 1848 Ⓐ, 1908, 1918 Ⓐ, 1938, 1948 Ⓐ, 2008, 2018 Ⓐ, 2038, 2048 Ⓐ, 2108, 2118 Ⓐ, 2138 (not Dec. 24), 2148 Ⓐ, 2208, 2238 (not Dec. 24), 2308, 2338 (not Dec. 24) and 0008.

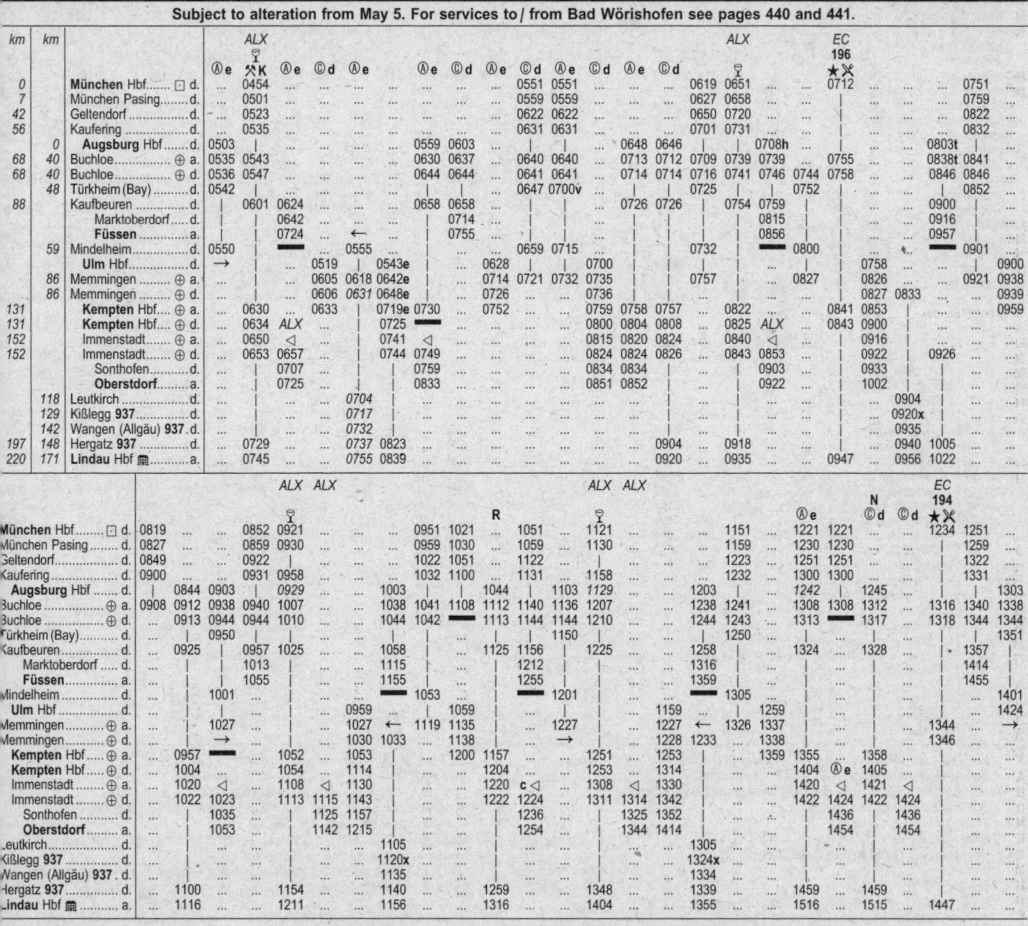

RE/RB services except where shown MÜNCHEN, AUGSBURG and ULM - OBERSTDORF and LINDAU 935

Subject to alteration from May 5. For services to/from Bad Wörishofen see pages 440 and 441.

km	km			Ⓐe	ALX 🍷 ⚒K	Ⓐe	Ⓒd	Ⓐe		Ⓐe	Ⓒd	Ⓐe	Ⓒd	Ⓐe	Ⓒd	Ⓐe	Ⓒd		ALX 🍷			EC 196 ★✕					
0		München Hbf ⊡	d.	...	0454	...	...	...	...	...	...	...	0551	0551	...	...	...	0619	0651	...	...	0712	...	...	...	0751	...
7		München Pasing	d.	...	0501	...	...	...	...	...	...	...	0559	0559	...	...	...	0627	0658	...	...	|	...	...	...	0759	...
42		Geltendorf	d.	...	0523	...	...	...	...	...	...	...	0622	0622	...	...	...	0650	0720	...	...	|	...	...	...	0822	...
56		Kaufering	d.	...	0535	...	...	...	...	...	...	...	0631	0631	...	...	...	0701	0731	...	...	|	...	...	...	0832	...
	0	Augsburg Hbf	d.	0503	|	...	...	...	...	0559	0603	...	|	|	...	0648	0646	|	|	0708h	...	|	...	...	0803t	|	...
68	40	Buchloe ⊕	a.	0535	0543	...	...	...	...	0630	0637	...	0640	0640	...	0713	0712	0709	0739	0739	...	0755	...	...	0838t	0841	...
68	40	Buchloe ⊕	d.	0536	0547	...	...	...	...	0644	0644	...	0641	0641	...	0714	0714	0716	0741	0746	0744	0758	...	...	0846	0846	...
	48	Türkheim (Bay)	d.	0542	|	...	...	...	...	|	|	...	0647	0700v	...	|	|	0725	|	|	0752	|	...	...	|	0852	...
88		Kaufbeuren	d.	|	0601	0624	...	...	...	0658	0658	...	|	|	...	0726	0726	|	0754	0759	|	|	...	...	0900	|	...
		Marktoberdorf	d.	|	|	0642	...	...	...	|	0714	...	|	|	...	|	|	|	|	0815	|	|	...	...	0916	|	...
		Füssen	a.	|	|	0724	...	←	...	|	0755	...	|	|	...	|	|	|	|	0856	|	|	...	...	0957	|	...
	59	Mindelheim	d.	0550	|	▬	...	0555	...	|	...	...	0659	0715	...	|	|	0732	|	▬	0800	|	...	...	▬	0901	...
		Ulm Hbf	d.	→	|	...	0519	|	0543e	|	...	0628	|	|	0700	|	|	|	|	...	|	|	0758	...	...	|	0900
	86	Memmingen ⊕	a.	...	|	...	0605	0618	0642e	|	...	0714	0721	0732	0735	|	|	0757	|	...	0827	|	0826	...	...	0921	0938
	86	Memmingen ⊕	d.	...	|	...	0606	0631	0648e	|	...	0726	...	...	0736	|	|	...	|	...	...	|	0827	0833	...	...	0939
131		Kempten Hbf ⊕	a.	...	0630	...	0633	|	0719e	0730	...	0752	...	...	0759	0758	0757	...	0822	...	...	0841	0853	|	...	...	0959
131		Kempten Hbf ⊕	d.	...	0634	ALX	...	|	0725	▬	...	...	...	...	0800	0804	0808	...	0825	ALX	...	0843	0900	|	...	...	...
152		Immenstadt ⊕	a.	...	0650	◁	...	|	0741	◁	...	...	...	...	0815	0820	0824	...	0840	◁	...	|	0916	|	...	...	...
152		Immenstadt ⊕	d.	...	0653	0657	...	|	0744	0749	...	...	...	...	0824	0824	0826	...	0843	0853	...	|	0922	|	0926	...	...
		Sonthofen	d.	...	|	0707	...	|	|	0759	...	...	...	...	0834	0834	|	...	|	0903	...	|	0933	|	|	...	...
		Oberstdorf	a.	...	|	0725	...	|	|	0833	...	...	...	...	0851	0852	|	...	|	0922	...	|	1002	|	|	...	...
	118	Leutkirch	d.	...	|	...	...	0704	|	...	...	...	...	...	...	...	|	...	|	...	...	|	...	0904	|	...	...
	129	Kißlegg 937	d.	...	|	...	...	0717	|	...	...	...	...	...	...	...	|	...	|	...	...	|	...	0920x	|	...	...
	142	Wangen (Allgäu) 937	d.	...	|	...	...	0732	|	...	...	...	...	...	...	...	|	...	|	...	...	|	...	0935	|	...	...
197	148	Hergatz 937	d.	...	0729	...	...	0737	0823	...	...	...	...	...	...	...	0904	...	0918	...	...	|	...	0940	1005	...	...
220	171	Lindau Hbf	a.	...	0745	...	...	0755	0839	...	...	...	...	...	...	...	0920	...	0935	...	...	0947	...	0956	1022	...	...

						ALX 🍷	ALX						R			ALX 🍷	ALX					Ⓐe		N Ⓒd	Ⓒd	EC 194 ★✕		
München Hbf ⊡	d.	0819	...	...	0852	0921	...	...	...	0951	1021	...	1051	...	1121	...	...	...	1151	...	1221	1221	...	...	1234	1251	...
München Pasing	d.	0827	...	...	0859	0930	...	...	...	0959	1030	...	1059	...	1130	...	...	...	1159	...	1230	1230	...	...	|	1259	...
Geltendorf	d.	0849	...	...	0922	|	...	...	...	1022	1051	...	1122	...	|	...	...	...	1223	...	1251	1251	...	...	|	1322	...
Kaufering	d.	0900	...	...	0931	0958	...	...	...	1032	1100	...	1131	...	1158	...	...	...	1232	...	1300	1300	...	...	|	1331	...
Augsburg Hbf	d.	|	0844	0903	|	0929	...	...	1003	|	|	1044	|	1103	1129	...	...	1203	|	...	1242	|	1245	...	|	|	1303
Buchloe ⊕	a.	0908	0912	0938	0940	1007	...	...	1038	1041	1108	1112	1140	1136	1207	...	...	1238	1241	...	1308	1308	1312	...	1316	1340	1338
Buchloe ⊕	d.	...	0913	0944	0944	1010	...	...	1044	1042	▬	1113	1144	1144	1210	...	...	1244	1243	...	1313	▬	1317	...	1318	1344	1344
Türkheim (Bay)	d.	...	|	0950	|	|	...	...	|	|	...	|	|	1150	|	...	...	|	1250	...	|	...	|	...	|	|	1351
Kaufbeuren	d.	...	0925	|	0957	1025	...	...	1058	|	...	1125	1156	|	1225	...	...	1258	|	...	1324	...	1328	...	|	1357	|
Marktoberdorf	d.	...	|	|	1013	|	...	...	1115	|	...	|	1212	|	|	...	...	1316	|	...	|	...	|	...	|	1414	|
Füssen	a.	...	|	|	1055	|	...	...	1155	|	...	|	1255	|	|	...	...	1359	|	...	|	...	|	...	|	1455	|
Mindelheim	d.	...	|	1001	...	|	...	...	▬	1053	...	|	▬	1201	|	...	...	▬	1305	...	|	...	|	...	|	...	1401
Ulm Hbf	d.	...	|	|	...	|	...	0959	...	|	1059	|	...	|	|	...	1159	...	|	1259	|	...	|	...	|	...	1424
Memmingen ⊕	a.	...	|	1027	...	|	...	1027	←	1119	1135	|	...	1227	|	...	1227	←	1326	1337	|	...	|	...	1344	...	→
Memmingen ⊕	d.	...	|	→	...	|	...	1030	1033	...	1138	|	...	→	|	...	1228	1233	...	1338	|	...	|	...	1346	...	...
Kempten Hbf ⊕	a.	...	0957	▬	...	1052	...	1053	|	...	1200	1157	...	...	1251	...	1253	|	...	1359	1355	...	1358	...	|	...	...
Kempten Hbf ⊕	d.	...	1004	...	...	1054	...	1114	|	...	...	1204	...	...	1253	...	1314	|	...	...	1404	Ⓐe	1405	...	|	...	...
Immenstadt ⊕	a.	...	1020	◁	...	1108	◁	1130	|	...	...	1220	c ◁	...	1308	◁	1330	|	...	...	1420	◁	1421	◁	|	...	...
Immenstadt ⊕	d.	...	1022	1023	...	1113	1115	1143	|	...	...	1222	1224	...	1311	1314	1342	|	...	...	1422	1424	1422	1424	|	...	...
Sonthofen	d.	...	|	1035	...	|	1125	1157	|	...	...	|	1236	...	|	1325	1352	|	...	...	|	1436	|	1436	|	...	...
Oberstdorf	a.	...	|	1053	...	|	1142	1215	|	...	...	|	1254	...	|	1344	1414	|	...	...	|	1454	|	1454	|	...	...
Leutkirch	d.	...	|	...	...	|	...	...	1105	...	...	|	...	...	|	...	...	1305	...	...	|	...	|	...	|	...	...
Kißlegg 937	d.	...	|	...	...	|	...	...	1120x	...	...	|	...	...	|	...	...	1324x	...	...	|	...	|	...	|	...	...
Wangen (Allgäu) 937	d.	...	|	...	...	|	...	...	1135	...	...	|	...	...	|	...	...	1334	...	...	|	...	|	...	|	...	...
Hergatz 937	d.	...	1100	...	...	1154	...	...	1140	...	...	1259	...	...	1348	...	...	1339	...	...	1459	...	1459	...	|	...	...
Lindau Hbf	a.	...	1116	...	...	1211	...	...	1156	...	...	1316	...	...	1404	...	...	1355	...	...	1516	...	1515	...	1447	...	...

K – Runs daily from Kempten.
N – From Nürnberg (Table 905).
R – From Nürnberg (Table 905) on ⑥ d.
c – Not Dec. 25.
d – Also Dec. 24, 31.
e – Ⓐ (not Dec. 24, 31).
h – 0711 on Ⓐ (not Dec. 24, 31).

t – On Ⓐ (not Dec. 24, 31) Augsburg d. 0812, Buchloe a. 0843.
v – Arrives 0647.
x – Arrives 6–10 minutes earlier.
★ – (12) and ✕ München - Bregenz - St Gallen - Zürich (Table 75).

◁ – Detached from train in previous column at Immenstadt.
⊡ – Most trains in Table 935 use platforms 27–36 at München Hbf (minimum connecting time from other services is 10 minutes).
⊕ – Many services connect at Buchloe, Memmingen, Kempten and Immenstadt (connecting trains may be found in preceding columns). Minimum connectional time is 3 minutes.
ALX – *Arriva-Länderbahn-Express*. Operated by Arriva/Regentalbahn AG - Die Länderbahn.

935 MÜNCHEN, AUGSBURG and ULM - OBERSTDORF and LINDAU

RE / RB services except where shown

Subject to alteration from May 5. For services to / from Bad Wörishofen see panel below and on page 441.

	ALX 🍷	ALX			IC 2085 H					Ⓐe			ALX 🍷	ALX	RE 2013 A🍷				R		EC 192 ★✕			ALX 🍷	ALX	
München Hbf ⊡ d.	1321	...	...	...	...	1351	...	1421	...	...	...	1451	1521	...	...	...	1551	1619	...	...	1632	...	1651	1721	...	...
München Pasing d.	1330	...	...	...	...	1359	...	1430	...	...	...	1459	1530	...	...	...	1559	1630	...	...	|	...	1659	1730	...	...
Geltendorf d.	|	...	...	...	...	1422	...	1451	...	...	...	1522	|	...	...	...	1622	1651	...	...	|	...	1723	|	...	...
Kaufering d.	1358	...	...	...	...	1432	...	1500	...	...	...	1531	1558	...	...	...	1632	1700	...	...	|	...	1732	1758	...	...
Augsburg Hbf d.	*1327*	...	...	...	1356	|	1403	|	1444	...	1503	|	*1518*	...	...	1603	|	|	1644	...	|	1703	|	*1729*	...	...
Buchloe ⊕ a.	1407	...	...	...	|	1441	1438	1509	1512	...	1538	1540	1607	...	...	1638	1641	1708	1712	...	1716	1737	1741	1807	...	...
Buchloe ⊕ d.	1410	...	...	...	|	1443	1444	▬	1513	...	1544	1543	1609	...	...	1644	1643	▬	1713	...	1718	1744	1742	1809	...	...
Türkheim (Bay) d.	|	...	...	...	|	1454	|	...	|	...	1550	|	|	...	...	|	1650	...	|	...	|	1751	|	|	...	...
Kaufbeuren d.	1424	...	...	...	1438	|	1458	...	1527	...	|	1557	1625	...	...	1659	|	...	1725	...	|	|	1758	1823	...	...
Marktoberdorf d.	|	...	...	...	|	|	1516	...	|	...	|	1613	|	...	...	1716	|	...	|	...	|	|	1815	|	...	...
Füssen a.	|	...	...	...	|	|	1557	...	|	...	|	1656	|	...	...	1757	|	...	|	...	|	|	1856	|	...	...
Mindelheim d.	|	...	...	...	|	1504	...	...	|	...	1600	...	|	...	...	▬	1701	...	|	...	|	1802	...	|	...	...
Ulm Hbf d.	|	...	1413	...	|	|	...	1459	|	...	|	...	|	...	1607	...	|	1659	|	...	|	|	...	|	...	1813
Memmingen ⊕ a.	|	...	1441	←	|	1524	...	1530	|	...	1628	...	|	...	1636	←	1722	1729	|	...	1744	1826	...	|	...	1841
Memmingen ⊕ d.	|	...	1442	1445	|	...	...	1531	|	...	→	...	|	...	1638	1645	▬	1730	|	...	1746	→	...	|	...	1842
Kempten Hbf ⊕ a.	1451	...	1505	|	1510	...	...	1557	1557	...	...	...	1651	...	1701	|	...	1753	1757	...	|	...	...	1851	...	1912
Kempten Hbf ⊕ d.	1453	...	1508	|	1513	...	...	...	1604	...	...	...	1653	...	1703	|	...	...	1804	...	|	...	...	1853	...	1914
Immenstadt ⊕ a.	1508	◁	1524	|	1529	...	...	...	1620	◁	...	...	1709	◁	1718	|	...	...	1820	◁	|	...	...	1909	◁	1930
Immenstadt ⊕ d.	1513	1515	1542	|	1547	...	...	...	1622	1624	...	...	1711	1719	1733	|	1727	...	1822	1823	|	...	...	1915	1916	1938
Sonthofen d.	|	1525	1551	|	1558	...	...	...	|	1635	...	...	|	1729	1742	|	|	...	|	1835	|	...	...	1925	|	|
Oberstdorf a.	|	1541	1610	|	1618	...	...	...	|	1654	...	...	|	1745	1802	|	|	...	|	1853	|	...	...	1941	|	|
Leutkirch d.	|	...	...	1510	...	...	...	...	|	...	...	...	|	...	...	1710	|	...	|	...	|	...	...	...	|	|
Kißlegg **937** d.	|	...	...	1520	...	...	...	...	|	...	...	...	|	...	...	1720	|	...	|	...	|	...	...	...	|	|
Wangen (Allgäu) **937** d.	|	...	...	1535	...	...	...	...	|	...	...	...	|	...	...	1732	|	...	|	...	|	...	...	...	|	|
Hergatz **937** d.	1554	...	...	1542	...	...	...	...	1659	...	...	...	1748	...	...	1740	1806	...	1859	...	|	...	...	...	1952	2015
Lindau Hbf 🏛 a.	1611	...	...	1559	...	...	...	...	1716	...	...	...	1804	...	...	1756	1824	...	1916	...	1847	...	...	...	2008	2032

					N		EC 190 ★✕			ALX 🍷									ALX 🍷			Ⓐe	†		e Q	
München Hbf ⊡ d.	...	1751	...	1821	...	...	1834	...	1851	1921	...	...	1951	...	...	2039	...	...	2141	...	...	...	...	2251	...	2353
München Pasing d.	...	1759	...	1830	...	...	|	...	1859	1930	...	...	1959	...	...	2046	...	...	2149	...	...	...	...	2259	...	0001
Geltendorf d.	...	1823	...	1851	...	...	|	...	1922	|	...	...	2022	...	...	2109	...	...	2210	...	...	...	...	2323	...	0023
Kaufering d.	...	1832	...	1900	...	...	|	...	1931	1958	...	...	2032	...	...	2119	...	...	2219	...	...	...	...	2333	...	0033
Augsburg Hbf d.	...	|	1803	|	1845	...	|	1903	|	*1940*	...	2003	|	...	2045	|	...	2147	|	...	...	...	...	|	2309	|
Buchloe ⊕ a.	...	1842	1838	1909	1912	...	1916	1938	1940	2007	...	2038	2041	...	2122	2128	...	2220	2228	...	←	...	...	2342	2345	0042
Buchloe ⊕ d.	...	1844	1845	▬	1917	...	1918	1944	1944	2011	...	2044	2044	...	2131	2130	...	→	2233	...	2237	...	...	2348	2350	...
Türkheim (Bay) d.	...	1851	|	...	|	...	|	1951	|	|	...	|	2051	...	2137	|	...	...	|	...	2243	...	...	2355	|	...
Kaufbeuren d.	...	|	1859	...	1931	...	|	|	1956	2027	...	2058	|	...	|	2144	2149	...	2248	2253	|	...	...	|	0004	...
Marktoberdorf d.	...	|	1916	...	|	...	|	|	2011	|	...	2116	|	...	|	|	2205	...	|	2310	|	...	...	|	|	...
Füssen a.	...	|	1957	...	|	...	|	|	2055	|	...	2157	|	...	|	|	2245	...	|	2349	|	...	...	|	|	...
Mindelheim d.	...	1859	...	...	|	...	|	2000f	...	|	...	▬	2059	...	2146	|	▬	...	|	▬	2251	...	...	0003	|	...
Ulm Hbf d.	...	|	...	1859	|	...	|	|	...	|	2013	...	|	2059	|	|	...	2213	|	...	|	...	2314	|	|	...
Memmingen ⊕ a.	←	1920	...	1931	|	...	1944	2023f	...	|	2041	...	2122	2130	2207	|	...	2251	|	...	2312	...	2353	0029	|	...
Memmingen ⊕ d.	1845	▬	...	1932	|	...	1946	...	...	|	2042	2046	...	2133	...	|	...	2252	|	...	...	2317	2355	...	|	...
Kempten Hbf ⊕ a.	|	...	...	1958	2003	...	|	...	...	2054	2107	|	...	2159	...	2213	...	2322	2316	...	...	|	0021	...	0035	...
Kempten Hbf ⊕ d.	|	...	...	...	2004	...	|	...	...	2103	2109	|	...	...	...	2214	...	2323	2327	...	...	|	...	...	...	...
Immenstadt ⊕ a.	|	◁	...	...	2020	◁	|	...	...	2118	2126	|	...	...	...	2231	...	2339	2343	←	...	|	...	...	...	...
Immenstadt ⊕ d.	|	1943	...	...	2024	2029	|	...	...	2129	2131	|	...	...	...	2232	2236	→	2344	2349	...	|	...	...	...	...
Sonthofen d.	|	1952	...	...	|	2039	|	...	...	|	2141	|	...	...	...	|	2245	...	|	2358	...	|	...	...	...	...
Oberstdorf a.	|	2010	...	...	|	2103	|	...	...	|	2159	|	...	...	...	|	2304	...	|	0017	...	|	...	...	...	...
Leutkirch d.	1910	...	...	...	|	...	|	...	...	|	...	2112	...	...	...	|	...	...	|	...	...	2344	...	...	...	...
Kißlegg **937** d.	1920	...	...	...	|	...	|	...	...	|	...	2124	...	...	...	|	...	...	|	...	...	2354	...	...	...	...
Wangen (Allgäu) **937** d.	1933	...	...	...	|	...	|	...	...	|	...	2135	...	...	...	|	...	...	|	...	...	0005	...	...	...	...
Hergatz **937** d.	1938	...	...	...	2104	...	|	...	...	2206	...	2141	...	...	...	2311	...	...	0021	...	...	0010	...	...	...	...
Lindau Hbf 🏛 a.	1957	...	...	...	2120	...	2047	...	...	2223	...	2159	...	...	...	2328	...	...	0038	...	...	...	...	...	...	...

km	km		ALX ⚒🍷	Ⓐe		Ⓐe	Ⓐe	N Ⓐe	Ⓐe		Ⓐe	Ⓒz			ALX 🍷	⑥	Ⓐe			N						
		Lindau Hbf 🏛 d.	...	...	...	...	...	...	...	...	...	...	...	0529	...	0603	*0602*	...	...	0638	0703t	...	...	0803	0726	...
		Hergatz **937** d.	...	...	...	...	...	...	...	...	...	...	...	0546	...	0619	0621	...	...	0657	0723t	...	...	0819	0743	...
		Wangen (Allgäu) **937** d.	...	...	...	...	...	...	...	...	...	...	...	|	...	0624	0626	...	...	|	0728t	...	...	0826	|	...
		Kißlegg **937** d.	...	...	...	*0518*	...	...	...	...	...	...	...	|	...	0636	0636	...	...	|	0739t	...	...	0838	|	...
		Leutkirch d.	...	...	...	*0526*	...	...	...	...	...	...	...	|	...	0645	0645	...	...	|	0747t	...	...	0847	|	...
	0	**Oberstdorf** d.	...	...	...	|	0503	...	...	...	...	...	0552	|	...	|	|	...	0705	|	|	...	...	|	|	0751
	13	Sonthofen d.	...	...	...	|	0522	...	...	...	...	...	0610	|	...	|	|	...	0727	|	|	...	...	|	|	0809
	21	Immenstadt ⊕ a.	...	...	...	|	0531	...	...	...	...	...	0621	0624	...	|	|	...	0738	0738	|	...	...	|	0819	0820
	21	Immenstadt ⊕ d.	...	...	...	|	0539	...	...	...	...	...	▷	0627	...	|	|	...	▶	0741	|	...	...	|	▷	0830
	46	**Kempten** Hbf ⊕ a.	...	...	...	|	0555	...	...	...	...	...	▬	0644	...	|	|	...	▬	0757	|	...	...	|	...	0847
	46	**Kempten** Hbf ⊕ d.	0446	...	0542	|	0557	0605	...	...	...	...	...	0647	0649	|	|	...	...	0758	|	0800	...	|	...	0854
	81	Memmingen ⊕ a.	|	...	|	*0551*	0628	|	...	...	...	...	Ⓐe	0713	|	0711	0711	...	...	|	0813	0826	...	0914	...	0917
	81	Memmingen ⊕ d.	|	0532	|	0600	0632	|	...	...	0622	0636	0652	0715	|	...	...	0738	...	|	0814	0828	0838	→	...	0918
	133	**Ulm** Hbf a.	|	|	|	|	0725	|	...	...	|	|	|	0745	|	...	...	|	...	|	|	0858	|	▬	...	0945
		Mindelheim d.	|	0554	|	0621	...	|	...	...	0644	0659	0715	...	|	...	...	0800	...	|	0831	...	0901	...	...	...
0		**Füssen** d.	|	|	|	|	...	|	...	0551	|	|	|	...	|	...	...	|	0703	|	|	...	|	0805	...	...
31		Marktoberdorf d.	|	|	|	|	...	|	...	0638	|	|	|	...	|	...	...	|	0751	|	|	...	|	0851	...	...
43		Kaufbeuren d.	0521	|	0616	|	...	0635	...	0652	|	|	|	...	0720	...	...	|	0805	0830	|	...	|	0905	...	...
		Türkheim (Bay) d.	|	0602	|	0631	...	|	...	|	0653	0706	0724	...	|	...	...	0809	|	|	|	...	0910	|	...	...
63		Buchloe ⊕ a.	0532	0609	0629	0637	...	0648	...	0707	0700	0713	0730	...	0731	...	...	0816	0817	0842	0843	...	0917	0917	...	...
63		Buchloe ⊕ d.	0534	0610	0631	0640	...	0649	0652	0722z	0713	0714	0735	...	0733	...	...	0823	0820	0849	0847	...	0920	0922	...	...
103		**Augsburg** Hbf a.	|	*0647*	|	0712	...	0716	|	0757z	|	|	0812	...	|	...	...	0856	|	0916	|	...	|	0957	...	...
		Kaufering d.	0542	0618	0640	...	...	...	0700	...	0721	0723	...	...	0741	...	...	...	0828	...	0859	...	0928	...	...	...
		Geltendorf d.	|	0628	0650	...	...	...	0710	...	0731	0732	...	...	|	...	...	...	0837	...	0909	...	0937	...	...	...
		München Pasing a.	0610	0652	0716	...	...	...	0734	...	0756	0753	...	...	0810	...	...	...	0858	...	0929	...	0958	...	...	...
		München Hbf ⊡ a.	0618	0700	0724	...	...	...	0745	...	0804	0801	...	...	0818	...	...	...	0908	...	0937	...	1007	...	...	...

A – ALLGÄU – 🚃12 (*IC* **2013**) (Leipzig - Magdeburg on dates in Table **810** -) Hannover - Dortmund - Köln - Stuttgart - Ulm (*RE* **2013**) - Oberstdorf.
H – NEBELHORN – 🚃12 Hamburg (**2083**) - Augsburg (**2085**) - Oberstdorf. See Table **900** for timings from Hamburg.
N – From / to Nürnberg (Table **905**).
Q – From Nürnberg on † (Table **905**).
R – From Nürnberg (Table **905**) on Ⓐ (not Dec. 24, 31).

e – Not Dec. 24, 31.
f – On Ⓐ (not Dec. 24, 31) Mindelheim d. 2006, Memmingen a. 2027.
t – 3–4 minutes later on Ⓐ (not Dec. 24, 31).
z – Ⓒ (also Dec. 24, 31).

★ – 🚃12 and ✕ München - Bregenz - St Gallen - Zürich (Table **75**).
◁ – Detached from train in previous column at Immenstadt.
▷ – Attached to train in the next column at Immenstadt.
▶ – On Ⓒ attached to train in the next column at Immenstadt (change trains on Ⓐ).
♥ – 16 minutes later on Ⓒ (also Dec. 24, 31).
⊡ – Most trains in Table **935** use platforms 27–36 at München Hbf (minimum connecting time from / to other services is 10 minutes).
⊕ – Many services connect at Buchloe, Memmingen, Kempten and Immenstadt (connecting trains may be found in preceding columns). Minimum connectional time is 3 minutes.

ALX – *Arriva-Länderbahn-Express*. Operated by Arriva / Regentalbahn AG - Die Länderbahn.

km		♥	Ⓐe	Ⓒz	Ⓐe	Ⓐe				Ⓐe	Ⓒz											Ⓐe	Ⓒz			
0	**Augsburg** Hbf d.	...	...	0729	0733	0803	0929	...	1129	...	...	1327	...	1518	1546	...	...	1729	...	...	...	1940	1940	...	...	...
40	Buchloe d.	...	...	0800	0820	0851	1000	1120	1200	1253	1323	1400	1523	1600	1620	...	1723	1800	1837	...	1923	2011	2020	...	...	...
48	Türkheim (Bay) d.	0658	0727	0812	0827	0858	1012	1130	1212	1300	1330	1412	1530	1612	1631	1702	1730	1812	1844	1910	1930	2018	2031	2144	2246	2358
53	**Bad Wörishofen** a.	0704	0733	0818	0833	0905	1018	1136	1218	1306	1336	1418	1536	1618	1637	1708	1736	1818	1850	1916	1936	2024	2037	2151	2252	0004

RE / RB services except where shown — LINDAU and OBERSTDORF - ULM, AUGSBURG and MÜNCHEN — 935

Subject to alteration from May 5. For services from / to Bad Wörishofen see panel below and on page 440.

	ALX	ALX			EC 191							IC 2084			IC 2012	ALX	ALX			EC 193						
		🍷			★🍴		Ⓐe	Ⓒz				H			A 🍷		🍷			★🍴						
Lindau Hbf ... d.	...	0747	...	...	0912	...	0842	0842	...	...	...	...	1003	0926	...	...	0956	...	...	1112	...	1042	...	...	1206	...
Hergatz 937 ... d.	...	0804	...	...	|	...	0900	0900	...	...	...	...	1019	0944	...	...	1013	...	...	|	...	1059	...	...	1222	...
Wangen (Allgäu) 937 . d.	...	|	...	...	|	...	|	|	...	...	...	...	1028	|	...	...	|	...	...	|	...	|	...	...	1228	...
Kißlegg 937 ... d.	...	|	...	...	|	...	|	|	...	...	...	...	1038	|	...	...	|	...	...	|	...	|	...	...	1238	...
Leutkirch ... d.	...	|	...	...	|	...	|	|	...	...	...	...	1047	|	...	...	|	...	...	|	...	|	...	...	1248	...
Oberstdorf ... d.	0802	|	...	...	|	0900	|	|	...	...	...	0927	|	|	0951	1017	|	...	...	|	1104	|	...	...	|	1143
Sonthofen ... d.	0820	|	...	...	|	0922	|	|	...	...	...	0952	|	|	1012	1034	|	...	...	|	1124	|	...	...	|	1208
Immenstadt ... ⊕ a.	0835	0840	...	...	|	0933	0937	0937	...	...	...	1000	|	1024	1020	1042	1048	...	...	|	1135	1138	...	...	|	1218
Immenstadt ... ⊕ d.	▷	0851	...	...	|	▷	0940	0940	...	...	...	1015	|	1025	1036	▷	1056	...	...	|	▷	1141	...	...	|	1234
Kempten Hbf ... ⊕ a.	...	0905	...	...	|	...	0956	0956	...	...	...	1030	|	1042	1052	...	1111	...	...	|	...	1157	...	...	|	1250
Kempten Hbf ... ⊕ d.	...	0907	...	...	|	...	0958	0958	1003	...	...	1043	|	...	1054	...	1113	...	...	|	...	1158	1201	...	|	1254
Memmingen ... ⊕ a.	...	|	←	...	1012	...	|	|	1027	...	...	|	1113	...	1113	...	|	←	...	1212	...	|	1227	...	1314	1317
Memmingen ... ⊕ d.	...	|	0934	...	1014	...	|	|	1028	1031	...	|	→	...	1124	...	|	1134	...	1214	...	|	1228	1240	→	1318
Ulm Hbf ... a.	...	|	|	...	|	...	|	|	1058	|	...	|	...	...	1154	...	|	|	...	|	...	|	1258	|	▬	1345
Mindelheim ... d.	...	|	1002	...	|	...	|	|	▬	1102	...	|	...	...	...	...	|	1202	...	|	...	|	▬	1302	...	...
Füssen ... d.	...	|	|	0907	|	...	|	|	...	|	1005	|	...	...	...	...	|	|	1105	|	...	|	...	|	1205	...
Marktoberdorf ... d.	...	|	|	0954	|	...	|	|	...	|	1050	|	...	...	...	...	|	|	1153	|	...	|	...	|	1251	...
Kaufbeuren ... d.	...	0933	|	1008	|	...	1031	1036	...	|	1104	1116	...	...	...	...	1139	|	1207	|	...	1236	...	|	1305	...
Türkheim (Bay) ... d.	...	|	1011	|	|	...	|	|	...	1111	|	|	...	...	...	...	|	1211	|	|	...	|	...	1309	|	...
Buchloe ... ⊕ a.	...	0947	1017	1019	1041	...	1044	1048	...	1117	1116	1129	...	...	...	...	1154	1217	1218	1241	...	1248	...	1317	1321	...
Buchloe ... ⊕ d.	...	0955	1022	1020	1043	...	1051	1050	1051	1119	1121	1131	...	...	...	...	1155	1222	1220	1243	...	1250	1251	1325	1322	...
Augsburg Hbf ... a.	...	*1018*	1057	|	|	...	|	1116	|	|	1155	1158	...	...	...	...	*1230*	1257	|	|	...	1316	|	|	1357	...
Kaufering ... d.	...	1003	...	1028	|	...	1100	...	1100	1128	...	...	...	...	...	...	1203	...	1228	|	...	...	1300	1337	...	...
Geltendorf ... d.	...	|	...	1037	|	...	1109	...	1109	1137	...	...	...	...	...	...	|	...	1237	|	...	...	1310	1347	...	...
München Pasing ... a.	...	1029	...	1058	|	...	1129	...	1129	1158	...	...	...	...	...	...	1229	...	1258	|	...	...	1329	1410	...	...
München Hbf ... ⊡ a.	...	1038	...	1107	1128	...	1138	...	1138	1207	...	...	...	...	...	...	1238	...	1307	1328	...	...	1338	1417	...	...

	ALX	ALX								ALX	ALX			EC 195							ALX	ALX				
		🍷			N						🍷			★🍴								🍷			N	
Lindau Hbf ... d.	...	1156	...	...	1242	...	...	1403	...	...	1356	...	...	1512	...	1442	...	...	1606	...	...	1556	...	...	1642	...
Hergatz 937 ... d.	...	1213	...	...	1259	...	...	1419	...	...	1412	...	...	|	...	1459	...	...	1622	...	...	1613	...	...	1659	...
Wangen (Allgäu) 937 . d.	...	|	...	...	|	...	...	1428	...	...	|	...	...	|	...	|	...	...	1628	...	...	|	...	...	|	...
Kißlegg 937 ... d.	...	|	...	...	|	...	...	1440	...	...	|	...	...	|	...	|	...	*1556*e	1640	...	...	|	...	...	|	...
Leutkirch ... d.	...	|	...	...	|	...	...	1450	...	...	|	...	...	|	...	|	...	*1605*e	1650	...	...	|	...	...	|	...
Oberstdorf ... d.	1217	|	...	1304	|	...	...	|	1345	1417	|	...	...	|	1504	|	...	|	|	1557	1619	|	...	1658	|	...
Sonthofen ... d.	1235	|	...	1324	|	...	...	|	1406	1437	|	...	...	|	1524	|	...	|	|	1621	1635	|	...	1717	|	...
Immenstadt ... ⊕ a.	1243	1248	...	1334	1337	...	...	|	1418	1445	1448	...	...	|	1534	1537	...	|	|	1636	1642	1648	...	1729	1737	...
Immenstadt ... ⊕ d.	▷	1256	...	▷	1340	...	...	|	1441	▷	1456	...	...	|	▷	1540	...	|	|	1644	▷	1656	...	1735	1740	...
Kempten Hbf ... ⊕ a.	...	1311	...	▬	1357	...	...	|	1457	...	1510	...	...	|	...	1556	...	|	|	1700	...	1711	...	1750	1755	...
Kempten Hbf ... ⊕ d.	...	1313	...	...	1359	1400	...	|	1506	...	1512	...	...	|	...	1559	1559	|	|	1702	...	1713	...	▬	1758	1759
Memmingen ... ⊕ a.	...	|	←	...	|	1420	...	1524	1530	...	|	←	...	1612	...	|	1622	*1631*e	1724	1727	...	|	←	...	|	1820
Memmingen ... ⊕ d.	...	|	1330	...	|	1421	1440	→	1531	...	|	1535	...	1614	...	|	1623	1640	→	1731	...	|	1725t	...	|	1821
Ulm Hbf ... a.	...	|	|	...	|	1458	|	▬	1559	...	|	|	...	|	...	|	1658	|	▬	1758	...	|	|	...	|	1858
Mindelheim ... d.	...	|	1402	...	|	▬	1504	...	...	...	|	1601	...	|	...	|	▬	1701	...	...	...	|	1801	...	|	▬
Füssen ... d.	...	|	|	1306	|	...	|	1405k	...	...	|	|	1507	|	...	|	...	|	1605	...	...	|	|	1705	|	...
Marktoberdorf ... d.	...	|	|	1355	|	...	|	1451	...	...	|	|	1554	|	...	|	...	|	1651	...	...	|	|	1751	|	...
Kaufbeuren ... d.	...	1339	|	1408	1430	...	|	1505	...	...	1538	|	1607	|	...	1636	...	|	1704	...	...	1739	|	1805	1828	...
Türkheim (Bay) ... d.	...	|	1411	|	|	...	1511	|	...	...	|	1610	|	|	...	|	...	1710	|	...	...	|	1810	|	|	...
Buchloe ... ⊕ a.	...	1353	1417	1419	1442	...	1519	1517	...	...	1553	1616	1618	1641	...	1648	...	1716	1720c	...	...	1753	1816	1817	1842	...
Buchloe ... ⊕ d.	...	1355	1423	1420	1449	1449	1520	1522	...	...	1555	1622	1620	1643	...	1650	1651	1720	1723	...	...	1754	1820	1819	1849	1850
Augsburg Hbf ... a.	...	*1431*	1457	|	1516	|	|	1557	...	...	*1630*	1657	|	|	...	1717	|	|	1757	...	...	*1830*	1856	|	1916	|
Kaufering ... d.	...	1403	...	1428	...	1459	1528	...	...	...	1603	...	1628	|	...	...	1700	1728	...	...	...	1802	...	1828	...	1859
Geltendorf ... d.	...	|	...	1437	...	1509	1537	...	...	...	|	...	1637	|	...	...	1710	1737	...	...	...	|	...	1837	...	1910
München Pasing ... a.	...	1429	...	1458	...	1529	1558	...	...	...	1629	...	1658	|	...	...	1729	1758	...	...	...	1829	...	1858	...	1929
München Hbf ... ⊡ a.	...	1437	...	1507	...	1537	1607	...	...	...	1638	...	1707	1728	...	...	1738	1807	...	...	...	1837	...	1907	...	1938

				ALX	ALX												EC 197	ALX	ALX			ALX				ALX
					🍷	Ⓐe	Ⓒz		R	Ⓒz	Ⓐe	2					★🍴		🍷					2		
Lindau Hbf ... d.	...	...	1725	...	1755	1802	1802	...	1842	...	...	...	1932	...	2009	...	2016	...	2030	...	...	2138	...	...	...	2338
Hergatz 937 ... d.	...	...	1742	...	1812	1818	1818	...	1859	...	...	...	1948	...	2029	...	|	...	2047	...	...	2155	...	...	...	2354
Wangen (Allgäu) 937 . d.	...	...	|	...	|	1828	1828	...	|	...	...	...	|	...	2034	...	|	...	|	...	...	|	...	...	...	|
Kißlegg 937 ... d.	...	...	|	...	|	1840	1840	...	|	...	...	...	|	...	2044	...	|	...	|	...	...	|	...	...	...	|
Leutkirch ... d.	...	...	|	...	|	1850	1850	...	|	...	...	...	|	...	2053	...	|	...	|	...	...	|	...	...	...	|
Oberstdorf ... d.	...	1734	|	1817	|	|	|	1904	|	...	...	1948	|	...	|	...	|	2051	|	...	2200	|	...	...	2310	|
Sonthofen ... d.	...	1808	|	1838	|	|	|	1923	|	...	...	2011	|	...	|	...	|	2110	|	...	2219	|	...	...	2329	|
Immenstadt ... ⊕ a.	...	1818	1821	1846	1848	|	|	1934	1937	...	...	2020	2025	...	|	...	|	2119	2122	...	2227	2230	...	...	2337	0030
Immenstadt ... ⊕ d.	...	▷	1825	▷	1856	|	|	▷	1940	...	...	▬	2026	...	|	...	|	▷	2132	...	▬	2231	...	...	2344	0031
Kempten Hbf ... ⊕ a.	...	▬	1841	...	1911	|	|	▬	1956	...	...	...	2043	...	|	...	2120	▬	2149	...	...	2248	...	...	2400	0047
Kempten Hbf ... ⊕ d.	...	...	1852	...	1913	|	|	Ⓐe	1959	1959	2005	...	▬	2047	|	2108	2122	...	2150	2203	...	▬	2259	2300	...	...
Memmingen ... ⊕ a.	...	...	1916	...	|	1927	1927	←	|	2020	2028	...	...	|	2124	2130v	|	...	|	2229	...	...	|	2325	...	...
Memmingen ... ⊕ d.	1836	...	1932	...	|	→	1931	1945	|	2021	2030	2046	...	|	...	2131v	|	2142	|	2230	2258	...	|	2328	...	...
Ulm Hbf ... a.	|	...	2000	...	|	▬	|	|	|	2058	2131	|	...	|	...	2159v	|	|	|	2315	|	...	|	0001	...	...
Mindelheim ... d.	1859	...	...	...	|	...	2001	2006	|	▬	...	2112	...	|	...	...	|	2210	|	...	2326	...	|	▬	...	...
Füssen ... d.	|	1805	...	...	|	1905	|	|	|	...	...	|	2003	|	...	...	|	|	|	...	|	2222	|	...	...	...
Marktoberdorf ... d.	|	1850	...	...	|	1952	|	|	|	...	...	|	2049	|	...	...	|	|	|	...	|	2308	|	...	...	...
Kaufbeuren ... d.	|	1904	...	...	1939	2006	|	|	2031	...	...	|	2102	2117	...	...	|	|	2219	...	|	2322	2331	...	...	...
Türkheim (Bay) ... d.	1909	|	...	...	|	|	2011	2020	|	...	...	2119	...	|	...	...	|	2218	|	...	2334	...	|	...	...	...
Buchloe ... ⊕ a.	1916	1916	...	...	1953	2017	2017	2026	2043	...	...	2125	...	2130	...	...	2204	2225	2232	...	2341	...	2345	←	...	...
Buchloe ... ⊕ d.	1920	1922	...	...	1955	2020z	2022	2027	2048	2050	...	2134	...	2141	...	...	2206	2241	2233	...	→	...	2346	2348	...	...
Augsburg Hbf ... a.	|	1957	...	...	*2030*	|	2056	2103	2116	|	...	|	...	2214	...	...	|	2316	|	...	...	...	|	0021	...	...
Kaufering ... d.	1928	...	...	...	2003	2028z	...	...	...	2059	...	2143	...	...	...	...	|	...	2241	...	...	...	2356	...	...	...
Geltendorf ... d.	1937	...	...	...	|	2037z	...	...	...	2109	...	2152	...	...	...	...	|	...	2250	...	...	...	0006	...	...	...
München Pasing ... a.	1958	...	...	...	2029	2058z	...	...	...	2129	...	2214	...	...	...	...	|	...	2311	...	...	...	0029	...	...	...
München Hbf ... ⊡ a.	2007	...	...	...	2038	2107z	...	...	...	2138	...	2221	...	...	...	...	2245	...	2319	...	...	...	0039	...	...	...

A – ALLGÄU – (12) and 🍷 Oberstdorf - Ulm - Stuttgart - Köln - Dortmund - Hannover (- Leipzig on dates in Table **810**).
H – NEBELHORN – (12) Oberstdorf - Augsburg (**2082**) - Hamburg. See Table **900** for timings to Hamburg.
N – To Nürnberg (Table **905**).
R – To Nürnberg (Table **905**) on ✝.

c – 1717 on Ⓒ (also Dec. 24, 31).
e – Ⓐ (not Dec. 24, 31).
k – Change trains at Marktoberdorf on Ⓐ (not Dec. 24, 31).
t – 1730 on Ⓒ (also Dec. 24, 31).

v – On Ⓐ (not Dec. 24, 31) Memmingen a. 2132, d. 2138, Ulm a. 2222.
z – Ⓒ (also Dec. 24, 31).

★ – (12) and 🍴 Zürich - St Gallen - Bregenz - München (Table **75**).
▷ – Attached to train in the next column at Immenstadt.
⊡ – Most trains in Table **935** use platforms 27 – 36 at München Hbf (minimum connecting time to other services is 10 minutes).
⊕ – Many services connect at Buchloe, Memmingen, Kempten and Immenstadt (connecting trains may be found in preceding columns). Minimum connectional time is 3 minutes.

ALX – Arriva-Länderbahn-Express. Operated by Arriva / Regentalbahn AG - Die Länderbahn.

	Ⓐe	Ⓐe	Ⓐe	Ⓒz	Ⓐe		Ⓐe					Ⓐe	Ⓒz									Ⓒ	Ⓐe			
Bad Wörishofen ... d.	0544	0613	0643	0656	0711	0740	0848	0921	1023	1141	1223	1324	1341	1423	1541	1623	1651	1741	1823	1855	1941	2023	2029	2108	2208	2324
Türkheim (Bay) ... a.	0551	0620	0650	0703	0718	0746	0854	0928	1029	1147	1229	1330	1347	1430	1548	1629	1657	1748	1829	1902	1947	2029	2035	2115	2215	2331
Buchloe ... a.	...	...	...	...	...	0757	0905	0935	1037	1158	1237	1337	1358	1437	1557	1637	...	1757	1836	...	1957	2037	2043	...	...	...
Augsburg Hbf ... a.	...	...	...	...	...	0830z	0942	1018	...	1230	...	1431	1431	...	1630	...	...	1830	...	...	2030	...	...	...	...	...

936 STUTTGART - TÜBINGEN - HORB

IRE / RE services

km		Ⓐh	2	Ⓐe					
0	**Stuttgart** Hbf **930 937** .. d.	0520	0532e	0616	0722	0822	and	2322	0044
22	Plochingen **930** .... d.	0539	0557	0638	0741	0844	hourly	2344	0104
35	Nürtingen .... d.	0552	0610	0652	0755	0855	until	2355	0116
57	Reutlingen Hbf **937** ...... d.	0609	0629	0709	0812	0912		0012	0133
71	**Tübingen** Hbf **937** ...... a.	0620	0644	0722	0823	0923		0023	0147

			Ⓒz	Ⓐe		Ⓒz	Ⓐe				
Tübingen Hbf **937** .... d.	0535	0628	0730	0737	0837	0932	0937	1037	and	2137	2236
Reutlingen Hbf **937** .... d.	0546	0638	0740	0748	0848	0943	0948	1048	hourly	2148	2250
Nürtingen .... d.	0602	0655	0757	0804	0904	0959	1004	1104	until	2204	2307
Plochingen **930** .... d.	0618	0705*	0818	0818	0918	1018	1018	1118		2219	2319
Stuttgart Hbf **930 937** a.	0638	0723*	0838	0838	0938	1038	1038	1138		2238	2338

TÜBINGEN - HORB 32 *km* 2nd class only Journey time: 30 – 39 minutes

From **Tübingen** Hbf at 0535 Ⓐ **e**, 0633, 0802, 0835, 1004, 1035, 1204, 1235, 1303 Ⓐ **e**, 1333 Ⓐ **e**, 1404 Ⓒ **z**, 1435, 1604, 1635, 1703 Ⓐ **e**, 1804, 1835, 1933 Ⓐ **e**, 2006, 2036, 2133 Ⓒ **z**, 2236.
From **Horb** at 0455 Ⓐ **e**, 0619 Ⓐ **e**, 0648, 0730 Ⓐ **e**, 0750 Ⓒ **z**, 0817 Ⓐ **e**, 0848, 0922, 1048, 1123, 1248, 1322, 1420 Ⓐ **e**, 1448, 1524, 1648, 1722, 1817 Ⓐ **e**, 1846, 1922, 2048, 2122, 2249 Ⓒ **z**.

e – Ⓐ (not Dec. 24, 31, May 22). **h** – Not Dec. 24 - Jan. 4, May 22. **z** – Also Dec. 24, 31, May 22. * – 4 – 5 minutes later on Ⓒ (also Dec. 24, 31, May 22).

937 STUTTGART - TÜBINGEN - AULENDORF - HERGATZ

DB (IRE / RB services); HzL

km		⑥k	Ⓐe	2Ⓐe	2Ⓐe	2Ⓒz	Ⓐe‡		Ⓒz‡	Ⓐe‡		‡	2	‡		‡		‡		‡§		‡	2		†q	‡
0	**Stuttgart** Hbf **936** ..... d.	...	...	...	...	...	...	...	...	0616	0816	0822	1016	1022	1216	1222	1416	1422	1616	1622	1816	1822	...	2016	...	2122
57	Reutlingen **936** .... d.	...	...	...	...	...	...	...	...	0709	0849	0912	1049	1112	1249	1312	1449	1512	1649	1712	1849	1912	...	2049	...	2212
71	**Tübingen** Hbf **936** .... d.	...	...	...	...	...	0546	0658	0725	0727	0900	0928	1100	1128	1300	1328	1500	1528	1700	1728	1900	1928	...	2100	...	2234
96	Hechingen .... d.	...	...	...	...	...	0616	0718	0749	0753	0919	0952	1119	1152	1320	1352	1519	1552	1719	1752	1918	1952	...	2119	...	2257
113	Balingen (Württ) .... d.	...	...	...	...	...	0637	0731	0808	0808	0932	1006	1132	1206	1335	1406	1535	1610	1732	1807	1930	2009	...	2133	...	2312
131	Albstadt-Ebingen .... d.	...	...	...	...	...	0659	0743	0829	0829	0945	1029	1145	1229	1347	1429	1547	1629	1745	1830	1945	2030	...	2150	...	2331
158	**Sigmaringen** .... a.	...	...	...	...	...	0723	0808	0853	0853	1009	1054	1209	1254	1411	1454	1610	1654	1809	1854	2009	2054	...	2211	...	2355q
158	**Sigmaringen 938** ..... d.	...	...	0540	0645	0653	0726	0809	0901	0901	1010	1059	1210	1303	1412	1500	1611	1701	1810	1901	2010	...	2111	2213	2235	...
175	Herbertingen **938** ...... d.	...	...	0555	0708	0710	0743	0822	0917	0917	1024	1112	1225	1318	|	1516	1624	1717	1825	1916	2025	...	2130	2228	2250	...
177	Herbertingen Ort .... d.	...	...	0558	0711	0712	...	0825	0920	0920	1027	1115	1227	1321	1426	1518	1627	1719	1828	1919	2027	...	2132	2231	|	...
184	Bad Saulgau .... d.	...	...	0609	0724	0727	...	0832	0927	0927	1033	1127	1234	1327	1432	1527	1633	1727	1834	1928	2034	...	2138	2237	2258	...
203	**Aulendorf** .... d.	...	...	0625	0741	0743	...	0848	0943	0943	1049	1143	1249	1343	1448	1543	1649	1742	1850	1943	2049	...	2153	2252	2312	...
	Change trains					d				d					2Ⓐe		Ⓐe						2		|	
203	**Aulendorf** .... d.	0556	0556	...	...	0808	...	...	...	1008	...	1208	...	1408	1515	1608	1715	1808	...	2013	...	...	2208	...	2313	...
213	Bad Waldsee .... d.	0604	0613	...	...	0816	...	...	...	1016	...	1216	...	1416	1524	1616	1724	1816	...	2021	...	...	2216	...	2322	...
233	Kißlegg **935** .... a.	0620	0632	...	...	0835	...	...	...	1035	...	1235	...	1435	1549	1635	1749	1835	...	2040	...	...	2235	...	2341	...
246	Wangen (Allgäu) **935** a.	0651	0647	...	...	0850	...	...	...	1050	...	1250	...	1450	...	1650	...	1850	...	2056	...	...	2250	...	...	...
252	**Hergatz 935** .... a.	0656	0653	...	...	0855	...	...	...	1055	...	1255	...	1455	...	1655	...	1855	...	2101	...	...	2255	...	...	...

	Ⓐe	Ⓐe‡	Ⓒz‡	Ⓐe	⑥k		Ⓐe	Ⓒz											2⑤v					2		
Hergatz 935 .... d.	...	...	...	0533	...	...	0659	0701	...	0902	...	1102	...	1302	...	1502	...	1702	1818	...	1902	...	...	2106	...	...
Wangen (Allgäu) **935** . d.	...	...	...	0538	...	...	0704	0706	...	0907	...	1107	...	1307	...	1507	...	1707	1828	...	1907	...	...	2111	...	...
Kißlegg **935** .... d.	...	0518	...	0552	0631	...	0719	0722	...	0922	...	1122	...	1322	...	1522	...	1722	1841	...	1922	...	...	2126	...	...
Bad Waldsee .... d.	...	0534	...	0616	0647	...	0737	0740	...	0940	...	1140	...	1340	...	1540	...	1740	1857	...	1940	...	...	2144	...	...
Aulendorf .... a.	...	0542	...	0624	0655	...	0745	0748	...	0948	...	1148	...	1348	...	1548	...	1748	1905	...	1948	...	...	2151	...	...
Change trains		|		Ⓐe	|			d‡		‡		‡	2	‡		‡		‡			2	‡	2	2Ⓐe	2†q	2
Aulendorf .... d.	...	0553	...	0633	0705	0705	...	0812	0907	1012	1108	1212	1308	1412	1511	1612	1707	1812	...	1910	2012	...	2118	2201	2201	2313
Bad Saulgau .... d.	...	0608	...	0650	0721	0721	...	0832	0926	1033	1124	1234	1328	1433	1527	1633	1726	1834	...	1927	2035	...	2139	2217	2217	2330
Herbertingen Ort .... d.	...	0614	...	0656	0727	0727	...	0837	0931	1039	1130	1239	1334	1439	1533	1639	1731	1839	...	1933	2041	...	2145	2223	2223	2336
Herbertingen **938** .... d.	...	0617	...	0702	0731	0731	...	0840	0935	1044	1134	1244	1338	1444	1537	1643	1736	1844	...	1936	2046	...	2148	2229	2229	2339
Sigmaringen 938 .... a.	...	0630	...	0719	0746	0746	...	0856	0948	1058	1147	1258	1349	1458	1549	1656	1749	1858	...	1948	2102	...	2205	2244	2256	2355
Sigmaringen .... d.	0545	0634	0657	...	0747	0747	...	0900	0949	1100	1149	1303	1350	1500	1550	1700	1750	1910	...	1949	▬	2106	...	...	...	...
Albstadt-Ebingen .... d.	0608	0703	0722	...	0806	0806	...	0924	1010	1124	1210	1327	1410	1528	1609	1724	1811	1934	...	2008	...	2130	...	...	...	...
Balingen (Württ) .... d.	0620	0734	0746	...	0823	0823	...	0949	1023	1149	1223	1350	1423	1550	1625	1749	1823	1954	...	2025	...	2149	...	...	...	...
Hechingen .... d.	0634	0752	0804	...	0836	0836	...	1007	1036	1207	1236	1407	1436	1607	1637	1807	1840	2009	...	2037	...	2205	...	...	...	...
Tübingen Hbf **936** ..... a.	0653	0815	0828	...	0857	0857	...	1030	1057	1230	1257	1430	1457	1630	1657	1830	1857	2032	...	2059	2137	2229	...	...	...	...
Reutlingen **936** .... a.	0707	0847	0847	...	0908	0908	...	1047	1108	1247	1308	1447	1508	1647	1708	1847	1908	2047	...	2108f	2147	2249	...	...	...	...
Stuttgart Hbf **936** ...... a.	0743	0938	0938	...	0943	0943	...	1138	1143	1338	1343	1538	1543	1738	1743	1938	1943	2138	...	2143f	2238	2338	...	...	...	...

d – Daily from Aulendorf.
e – Not Dec. 24, 31, May 22.
f – ⑤⑥† (also Dec. 24, 31, May 22).
k – Also Dec. 24, 31.
q – † (also May 22).
v – Also Mar. 20, Apr. 30, May 21; not Mar. 21.
z – Also Dec. 24, 31, May 22.
§ – Change trains at Sigmaringen on Ⓐ **e**.
‡ – 2nd class only. Operated by Hohenzollerischen Landesbahnen (HzL) Tübingen - Sigmaringen and v.v.

938 ULM and ROTTWEIL - NEUSTADT (Schwarzw) - FREIBURG

DB (RE / RB services); HzL

km		Ⓒz	Ⓐe	‡Ⓐe	2Ⓐe		Ⓒz	Ⓐe			2		2		2		2		2		2		2	2†w	‡Ⓒw
0	**Ulm** Hbf .... d.	...	...	...	...	...	0554	0554	...	0810	0915	1014	1115	1214	1316	1414	1515	1614	1715	1814	1916	2024	2112	2112	...
16	Blaubeuren .... d.	...	...	...	...	...	0605	0609	...	0822	0930	1025	1130	1225	1330	1425	1530	1625	1730	1825	1931	2036	2131	2131	...
34	Ehingen (Donau) .... d.	...	...	...	...	...	0624	0628	...	0835	0943	1038	1142	1238	1344	1438	1542	1638	1742	1838	1944	2053	2147	2147	...
65	Riedlingen .... d.	...	...	...	...	...	0651	0656	...	0900	1004	1058	1207	1258	1404	1458	1603	1658	1803	1858	2004	2119	2209	2209	...
76	Herbertingen **937** .... d.	...	...	...	...	...	0658	0708	...	0907	1012	1112j	1214	1305	1411	1505	1611	1706	1810	1906	2012	2128	2216	2216	...
93	**Sigmaringen 937** .... a.	...	...	...	...	...	0713	0723	...	0920	1027	1125	1228	1322	1428	1520	1628	1721	1828	1921	2029	2142	2233	2233	...
93	**Sigmaringen** .... d.	...	...	...	...	...	0716	0733	...	0930	▬	1130	▬	1330	▬	1530	▬	1730	▬	1930	▬	▬	▬	2239	...
135	Tuttlingen .... d.	...	...	...	...	...	0816t	0816	...	1016j	...	1216j	...	1416j	...	1616j	...	1816j	...	2016j	...	...	...	2314	...
145	Immendingen **916** .... d.	...	...	...	...	...	0824	0824	...	1024	...	1224	...	1424	...	1624	...	1824	...	2024	‡	...	‡Ⓐe	2323	...
	Rottweil .... §d.	...	...	0558	0700	...	|	|	0911	|	1111	|	1311	|	1511	|	1711	|	1911	|	2119	...	2157	|	2253
	Trossingen Bahnhof ▲ .. §d.	...	...	0608	0713	...	|	|	0920	|	1120	|	1320	|	1520	|	1720	|	1920	|	2129	...	2208	|	2302
	Villingen (Schwarzw) **916** §d.	0605	0620	0629	0733	0738	|	|	0938	|	1138	|	1338	|	1538	|	1738	|	1938	|	2145	2213	2244x	|	2322
164	Donaueschingen **916** .... §d.	0616	0642	0645	...	0750	0848j	0848j	0950	1048j	1150	1248j	1350	1448j	1550	1648j	1750	1848j	1950	2048j	...	2221	2301	2336	2339
204	**Neustadt** (Schwarzw) .... a.	0656	0727	...	...	0826	0926	0926	1026	1126	1226	1326	1426	1526	1626	1726	1826	1926	2026	2126	...	...	...	...	...

km		2⑥k	2Ⓐe	‡⚒r	Ⓐe	‡Ⓒz	Ⓒz	Ⓐe														⚒r	†w	‡Ⓒw	
0	**Neustadt** (Schwarzw) .... d.	...	...	...	...	...	...	0629	0732	0832	0932	1032	1132	1232	1330	1432	1532	1632	1732	1832	1932	2032	2032	2032	2202
40	Donaueschingen **916** .... §d.	...	...	0505	0520	0715	0720	0719	0810	0919j	1010	1119j	1210	1319j	1410	1519j	1610	1719j	1810	1919j	2010	2108	2119h	2122	2241
54	Villingen (Schwarzw) **916** §d.	...	...	0525	|	0736	|	|	0822	|	1022	|	1222	|	1422	|	1622	|	1822	|	2022	2118	|	2146	2259
69	Trossingen Bahnhof ▲ .. §d.	...	...	0541	|	0752	|	|	0835	|	1035	|	1235	|	1435	|	1635	|	1835	|	2035p	2143e	|	2201	...
81	**Rottweil** .... §a.	...	...	0552	|	0802	|	|	0844	|	1044	|	1244	|	1444	|	1644	|	1844	|	2044p	2153e	|	2211	...
	Immendingen **916** .... d.	...	...	▬	0534	▬	0734	0740j	...	0934	▬	1134	▬	1334	▬	1534	▬	1734	▬	1934	...	...	2134	...	...
	Tuttlingen .... d.	...	...	...	0542	...	0751h	0751	...	0947j	...	1147j	...	1347j	...	1547j	...	1747j	...	1947j	...	...	2156v	...	...
	Sigmaringen .... a.	...	...	2Ⓒz	0622	...	0825	0825	...	1022	...	1222	2	1422	2	1622	2	1822	2	2022	...	...	2231	...	...
	Sigmaringen 937 .... d.	0520	0534	0617	0633	0726	0835	0835	...	1030	1130	1230	1323	1430	1525	1629	1723	1832	1923	2032	...	...	2235	...	...
	Herbertingen **937** .... d.	0533	0547	0632	0646	0743	0851	0851	...	1045	1145	1245	1339	1445	1538	1645	1738	1846	1939	2047	...	...	2249	...	...
	Riedlingen .... d.	0541	0555	0644	0653	0751	0858	0858	...	1058	1151	1258	1346	1458	1545	1658	1745	1859	1946	2054	...	...	...	...	...
	Ehingen (Donau) .... d.	0602	0617	0706	0715	0814	0917	0917	...	1117	1211	1317	1411	1517	1611	1717	1810	1919	2012	2113	...	...	...	...	...
	Blaubeuren .... d.	0619	0633	0725	0732	0833	0930	0930	...	1130	1226	1330	1426	1530	1626	1730	1830	1931	2025	2131	...	...	...	...	...
	Ulm Hbf .... a.	0637	0645	0742	0744	0845	0942	0942	...	1142	1238	1342	1438	1542	1637	1742	1843	1943	2042	2143	...	...	...	...	...

km		Ⓐe	🚌e	⚒r	🚌e	Ⓐe	Ⓐe	Ⓐe	Ⓒw	Ⓒz	Ⓑn								🚌n	🚌n			🚌n	
0	**Neustadt** (Schwarzw) d.	0531	...	0600	...	0631	0657	...	0701	0708	0731	0801	...	0831	...	and at the same	...	2031	...	2040	2131	...	...	2223
	Seebrugg .... d.	|	0503	|	0558	|	|	0641	|	|	|	|	...	|	0839	minutes past	1939	|	2024	|	|	...	2153	|
5	Titisee .... d.	0538	0531	0607	0626	0638	0703	0708	0708	0715	0738	0808	...	0838	0908	each hour until	2008	2038	2052	2056	2138	...	2221	2230
36	**Freiburg** (Brsg) Hbf .. a.	0617	...	0645	...	0719	...	0748	0748	...	0818	0848	...	0918	0948		2048	2118	...	2148	2218	...	...	2314

km		Ⓐe	Ⓐe	🚌r	Ⓐe	Ⓒz	Ⓒz	Ⓐe	Ⓐe								🚌			🚌n			🚌n	
0	**Freiburg** (Brsg) Hbf ... d.	...	0540	...	0640	0640	...	0710	...	0742	0810	0840	and at the same	1810	1840	1910	...	1940	2010	...	2110	2226	...	2325
31	Titisee .... d.	0610	0617	0628	0719	0722	0724	0749	0752	0819	0849	0919	minutes past	1849	1919	1949	1953	2019	2049	2053	2149	2302	2306	0001
50	**Seebrugg** .... a.	0635	|	0659	|	0748	|	|	0818	|	0915	|	each hour until	1915	|	|	2024	|	|	2124	|	|	2337	|
	Neustadt (Schwarzw) a.	...	0623	...	0725	...	0730	0755	...	0825	...	0925		...	1925	1955	...	2025	2055	...	2155	2308	...	0007

e – Ⓐ (not Dec. 24, 31, May 22).
h – Arrives 10 minutes earlier.
j – Arrives 6 – 9 minutes earlier.
k – Also Dec. 24, 31.
n – Not Dec. 24, 31.
p – ①②③④⑦ (not Dec. 23, 24, 25, 30, 31, Mar. 20, 23, Apr. 30, May 21).
r – ⚒ (not May 22).
t – Arrives 0750.
v – Arrives 2141.
w – Also May 22.
x – Arrives 2224.
z – Also Dec. 24, 31, May 22.

‡ – Operated by Hohenzollerischen Landesbahnen (HzL). 2nd class only.
▲ – Regular services operate to / from Trossingen Stadt (operated by HzL). Journey time: 5 minutes.
§ – **Additional trains** (operated by HzL) Rottweil - Donaueschingen and v.v. Journey time: 47 – 54 minutes. **From Rottweil** at 0646 Ⓐ **e**, 0748 Ⓒ **z**, 0754 Ⓐ **e**, 0952, 1152, 1352, 1552, 1651 Ⓐ **e**, 1754 and 1952. **From Donaueschingen** at 0546 Ⓐ **e**, 0618 ¶ Ⓐ **e**, 0902 ¶ Ⓒ **z**, 0915 Ⓐ **e**, 1115, 1315 Ⓒ **z**, 1317 Ⓐ **e**, 1515, 1618 Ⓐ **e**, 1715 and 1915. Trains marked ¶ have a journey time of 64 – 66 minutes.

LINDAU - SCHAFFHAUSEN - BASEL — 939

IRE / RB services

km		r	Ⓐe		2	Ⓐe	U	2	Ⓐe	U	2	Ⓐe	U	2	Ⓐe	U	2	Ⓐe	U	2	U	2	Ⓐe	2	2	2
0	**Lindau** Hbf **931** d.	...	...	0641t	0703j	...	0833	0902	...	1030	1104	...	1231	1305	...	1432	1504	...	1635	1703	1831	1903	...	2012	...	2142
24	Friedrichshafen Stadt a.	...	...	0700t	0726	...	0906	0923	...	1103	1126	...	1306	1326	...	1506	1526	...	1709	1725	1905	1925	...	2034	...	2219
24	Friedrichshafen Stadt d.	0436e	...	0704t	0739	...	0914	0938	...	1114	1138	...	1313	1338	...	1513	1538	...	1714	1740	1915	1933	...	2035	...	2240
58	Überlingen d.	0514e	...	0730	0813	...	0934	1012	...	1134	1212	...	1334	1412	...	1534	1612	...	1734	1814	1934	2010	...	2113	...	2315
83	Radolfzell a.	0537e	...	0749	0843	...	0951	1043	...	1151	1243	...	1351	1443	...	1551	1643	...	1751	1843	1951	2043	...	2139	...	2340
83	Radolfzell **916** d.	0541v	0637	0752	0847	...	0953	1047	...	1153	1247	...	1353	1447	...	1553	1647	...	1753	1847	1953	2047	2055	2140	2147	2341
93	**Singen 916** a.	0547v	0647	0758	0856	...	1000	1056	...	1200	1256	...	1400	1456	...	1600	1656	...	1800	1856	2000	2056	2102	2148	2156	2349
93	**Singen 940** d.	0552	0651	0802	...	0902	1002	...	1102	1202	...	1302	1402	...	1502	1602	...	1702	1802	▬	2002	...	2106	▬	2206	...
112	**Schaffhausen** ⊞ **940** d.	0605	0709	0815	...	0915	1015	...	1115	1215	...	1315	1415	...	1515	1615	...	1715	1815	...	2015	...	2126	...	2302f	...
131	Erzingen (Baden) ⊞ d.	0625	0729	0829	...	0929	1029	...	1129	1229	...	1329	1429	...	1529	1629	...	1729	1829	2	2029	...	2140	Ⓒz	2328	...
151	Waldshut d.	0640	0742	0842	...	0942	1042	...	1142	1242	...	1344	1442	...	1542	1642	...	1742	1842	1915	2042	...	2155	2234	2346k	...
174	Bad Säckingen d.	0654	0755	0855	...	0955	1055	...	1155	1255	...	1356	1455	...	1555	1655	...	1755	1854	1937	2055	...	2217	2256	...	...
191	Rheinfelden (Baden) d.	0704	0805	0905	...	1005	1105	...	1205	1305	...	1405	1505	...	1605	1705	...	1805	1905	1952	2105	...	2232	2311	...	...
206	**Basel** Bad Bf a.	0715	0816	0916	...	1016	1116	...	1216	1316	...	1416	1516	...	1616	1716	...	1816	1916	2007	2116	...	2248	2326	...	...

	2Ⓒz	2Ⓐe	2	U	2	Ⓐe	U	2	Ⓐe	U	2	Ⓐe	U	2	Ⓐe	U	2	Ⓐe	U	Ⓐe	2	U	Ⓐe	2		2n
Basel Bad Bf d.	...	...	0456e	0637	...	0743	0843	...	0943	1043	...	1143	1243	...	1343	1443	...	1543	1643	1743	...	1843	1943	1947	2143	2258
Rheinfelden (Baden) d.	...	...	0512e	0646	...	0751	0851	...	0951	1051	...	1151	1251	...	1351	1451	...	1551	1651	1751	...	1851	1951	2001	2151	2312
Bad Säckingen d.	...	...	0530e	0656	...	0801	0901	...	1001	1101	...	1201	1301	...	1401	1501	...	1601	1701	1801	...	1901	2001	2017	2201	2328
Waldshut d.	...	...	0556	0712	...	0815	0915	...	1015	1115	...	1215	1315	...	1415	1515	...	1615	1715	1815	...	1915	2015	2039	2215	2350
Erzingen (Baden) ⊞ d.	...	0532	0625	0729	...	0829	0929	...	1029	1129	...	1229	1329	...	1429	1529	...	1629	1729	1829	...	1929	2029	▬	2231	...
Schaffhausen ⊞ **940** d.	0527	0556	0651	0742	...	0842	0942	...	1042	1142	...	1242	1342	...	1442	1542	...	1642	1742	1842	...	1942	2042	...	2249	...
Singen 940 a.	0546	0617	0708	0756	...	0856	0956	...	1056	1156	...	1256	1356	...	1456	1556	...	1656	1756	1856	...	1956	2056	2	2305	...
Singen 916 d.	0608	0621	0723	0758	0853	0903	0958	1053	1103	1158	1253	1303	1358	1453	1503	1558	1653	1703	1758	...	1903	1958	...	2103	2306	...
Radolfzell **916** a.	0615	0628	0732	0804	0859	0912	1004	1059	1112	1204	1259	1312	1404	1459	1512	1604	1659	1712	1804	...	1912	2004	...	2112	2316	...
Radolfzell d.	0616	0629	...	0806	0914	...	1006	1114	...	1206	1314	...	1406	1514	...	1606	1714	...	1806	...	1918	2006	...	2118	2317	...
Überlingen d.	0640	0656	...	0824	0942	...	1024	1142	...	1224	1342	...	1424	1542	...	1624	1742	...	1824	...	1955	2025	...	2141	2342	...
Friedrichshafen Stadt a.	0720	0738	...	0843	1022	...	1043	1222	...	1243	1422	...	1443	1622	...	1643	1827	...	1843	...	2030	2044	...	2216	0020	...
Friedrichshafen Stadt d.	0729	0743	...	0847	1034	...	1047	1230	...	1247z	1429	...	1447	1634	...	1647	1834	...	1848	...	2034	2052	...	2237	...	...
Lindau Hbf **931** a.	0751	0817	...	0922	1056	...	1123	1256	...	1324z	1452	...	1522	1656	...	1722	1856	...	1922	...	2100	2126	...	2309	...	...

U – From / to Ulm (Table **931**).
e – Ⓐ (not Dec. 24, 31, May 22).
f – Arrives 2224.
j – 0706 on Ⓒ**z** (change trains at Friedrichshafen).
k – Not Mar. 21. Change trains at Erzingen on ①②③④⑦.
n – Not Dec. 24, 31.
r – Change trains at Radolfzell and Singen.
t – 6–7 minutes later on Ⓒ**z**.
v – ⚒ (not May 22).
z – Ⓒ (also Dec. 24, 31, May 22).

STUTTGART - SINGEN - SCHAFFHAUSEN - ZÜRICH — 940

km				EC 173 ✕ A	‡ Ⓐe	Ⓒz		Ⓐe	ICE 181 ✕ F	EC 175 ✕ L		ICE 183 ✕		ICE 185 ✕		ICE 187 ✕		ICE 281 ✕	CIS 157 ✕ M		ICE 283 ✕		ICE 285 ✕			⑤⑥
0	**Stuttgart** Hbf **942** d.	...	...	...	0518	0618	...	0618	0804	...	0818	1004	1018	1204	1218	1404	1418	1604	...	1618	1804	1818	2004	2018	2225	2225
26	Böblingen **942** d.	...	...	...	0538	0638	...	0638	|	...	0838	|	1038	|	1238	|	1440	|	...	1638	|	1838	|	2038	2245	2245
42	Herrenberg **942** d.	...	...	...	0547	0650	...	0650	|	...	0850	|	1050	|	1250	|	1450	|	...	1650	|	1850	|	2050	2259	2259
57	Eutingen im Gäu **942** d.	...	...	...	0600	0705	...	0705	|	...	0907	|	1107	|	1307	|	1507	|	...	1707	|	1907	|	2105	2314	2314
67	Horb d.	...	...	...	0608	0713	...	0717	0842	...	0917	1042	1117	1242	1317	1442	1517	1642	...	1717	1842	1917	2042	2114	2322	2322
110	Rottweil d.	...	...	...	0641	0744	...	0751	0909	...	0951	1109	1151	1309	1351	1509	1551	1709	...	1751	1909	1951	2113	2146	2353	2353
138	Tuttlingen d.	...	...	...	0720	0805	...	0818j	0926	...	1014	1126	1214	1326	1414	1526	1614	1726	...	1814	1926	2014	2130	▬	0014	0014
157	Engen **916** d.	...	...	...	0736	0822	...	0835	|	...	1030	|	1230	|	1430	|	1630	|	...	1830	|	2030	|	...	0029	0029
172	**Singen 916** a.	...	...	...	0746	0833	...	0844	0948	...	1040	1148	1240	1348	1440	1548	1640	1748	...	1840	1948	2040	2151	...	0039	0039
172	**Singen 939** d.	0552	0633	0734	0751	...	0834v	0906	0954	...	▬	1154	▬	1354	▬	1554	▬	1754	...	▬	1954	▬	2156	...	...	0050
191	**Schaffhausen** ⊞ **939** a.	0603	0654	0753	0806	...	0853	0924	1007	...	...	1207	...	1407	...	1607	...	1807	...	...	2007	...	2209	...	...	0107
191	**Schaffhausen** ⊞ **531** d.	0607	0707	0809	⊕	...	0909	...	1009	1016	1109	1209	1309	1409	1509	1609	1709	1809	1816	1909	2009	2109	2211	2309	...	...
219	Bülach d.	0630	0730	0830	...	...	0930	...	1030	1039	1130	1230	1330	1430	1530	1630	1730	1830	1839	1930	2030	2130	2231	2330	...	...
239	**Zürich** HB a.	0647	0748	0847	...	...	0948	...	1048	1055	1148	1248	1348	1448	1548	1648	1748	1848	1855	1948	2048	2148	2248	2348	...	...

			Ⓐe				ICE 284 ✕		ICE 282 ✕		ICE 280 ✕		ICE 186 ✕		CIS 154 ✕ T	ICE 184 ✕		ICE 182 ✕			EC 174 ✕ A	ICE 180 ✕ F				
Zürich HB d.	0015	...	...	0504	...	0614	0714	0814	0914	1014	1114	1214	1314	1414	1505	1514	1614	1705	1714	1814	1905	1914	2014	2114	2214	2314
Bülach d.	0039	...	...	0531	...	0631	0731	0831	0931	1031	1131	1231	1331	1431	1525	1531	1631	1725u	1731	1831	1925	1931	2031	2131	2231	2331
Schaffhausen ⊞ **531** a.	0107	...	...	0610	...	0656	0750	0852	0950	1052	1150	1252	1350	1452	1547	1550	1654	1750	1754	1854	1950	1951	2052	2152	2252	2352
Schaffhausen ⊞ **939** d.	0113c	...	0527	0628	0651	0710	0752	▬	0952	▬	1152	▬	1352	▬	▬	1552	▬	1752	1804	▬	...	1953	2104	▬	▬	...
Singen 939 a.	0131c	...	0546	0647	0708	0729	0805	...	1005	...	1205	...	1405	...	...	1605	...	1805	1824	...	...	2005	2124	Ⓒz	...	...
Singen 916 d.	▬	...	0551	▬	0714k	...	0810	0919	1010	1119	1210	1319	1410	...	1519	1610	1719	1810	...	1919	...	2010	▬	2129	...	...
Engen **916** d.	...	...	0600	...	0724k	...	|	0928	|	1128	|	1328	|	...	1528	|	1728	|	...	1928	...	|	...	2139	...	...
Tuttlingen d.	Ⓐe	...	0616	...	0739k	...	0831	0945	1031	1145	1231	1346	1431	Ⓐe	1545	1631	1745	1831	...	1945	...	2031	...	2153	...	...
Rottweil d.	0508	0603	0641	0703z	0810	...	0848	1010	1048	1210	1248	1410	1448	1508	1610	1648	1811	1848	...	2010	...	2048	n	2215	...	...
Horb d.	0543	0642	0711	0743	0846	...	0918	1046	1118	1246	1318	1446	1518	1543	1646	1718	1846	1918	...	2046	...	2114	2146	2246	Ⓐe	...
Eutingen im Gäu **942** d.	0555	0655	|	0756	0857	...	|	1057	|	1257	|	1457	|	1556	1657	|	1857	|	...	2057	...	|	2159	2256	2256	...
Herrenberg **942** d.	0611	0711	0727	0811	0912	...	|	1111	|	1311	|	1511	|	1611	1711	|	1911	|	...	2111	...	|	2212	2310	2310	...
Böblingen **942** d.	0622	0722	0737	0822	0922	...	|	1122	|	1322	|	1522	|	1622	1722	|	1922	|	...	2122	...	|	2230	2322	2330	...
Stuttgart Hbf **942** a.	0642	0742	0757	0842	0942	...	0956	1142	1156	1342	1356	1542	1556	1642	1742	1756	1942	1956	...	2142	...	2156	2255	2342	2355	...

A – CISALPINO CANALETTO – [12] and ✕ Schaffhausen - Zürich - Lugano - Chiasso ⊞ - Milano - Venezia and v.v.
F – To / from Frankfurt (Table **911**).
L – CISALPINO CINQUE TERRE – [12] and ✕ Schaffhausen - Zürich - Lugano - Chiasso ⊞ - Milano - Genova - Livorno.
M – [12] and ✕ Schaffhausen - Lugano - Milano.
T – [12] and ✕ Trieste - Milano - Lugano - Schaffhausen.
c – ⑥⑦ only.
e – Not Dec. 24, 31, May 22.
j – Arrives 0811.
k – 6–7 minutes later on Ⓒ**z**.
n – Not Dec. 24, 31.
u – Stops to pick up only.
v – 0838 on Ⓒ**z**.
z – Ⓒ (also Dec. 24, 31, May 22).
‡ – Operated by Hohenzollerischen Landesbahnen between Rottweil and Singen.
⊕ – Connects at Schaffhausen with train *EC* **173**.

PFORZHEIM - HORB and BAD WILDBAD — 941

RB services (2nd class only)

km		Ⓐe	Ⓒvz	Ⓐe	Ⓐe	Ⓐe	Ⓒvz	⚒d				⑥k	Ⓐe		Ⓒz	Ⓐe		†w	Ⓐe		†w	Ⓐe	x	⊡	x
0	**Horb** d.	0500	0529	0551	0616	0649	0656	0751	0853	0953	1053	1131	1153	1253	1331	1353	1453	1531	1553	1653	1731	1753	1853	1934	2119
15	Hochdorf (b. Horb) d.	0510	0540	0601	0628	0700	0707	0802	0904	1004	1104	1148r	1204	1304	1348r	1404	1504	1548r	1604	1704	1748r	1804	1904	1954r	2130
25	Nagold d.	0519	0549	0610	0637	0710	0716	0814	0913	1013	1113	1213j	1213	1314	1413j	1413	1513	1613j	1613	1714	1813j	1813	1913	2013r	2140
34	Wildberg (Württ) d.	0527	0557	0618	0645	0718	0724	0822	0921	1021	1121	1221	1221	1321	1421	1421	1521	1621	1621	1722	1821	1821	1921	2021	2148
45	Calw d.	0539	0609	0629	0658	0730	0736	0833	0933	1033	1133	1233	1233	1333	1433	1433	1533	1633	1633	1733	1833	1833	1933	2033	2159
52	Bad Liebenzell d.	0547	0618	0642	0706	0744r	0744	0843	0944	1044	1144	1244	1244	1345r	1445r	1445r	1545r	1645r	1645r	1745r	1845r	1845r	1944	2041	2209
71	**Pforzheim** Hbf a.	0608	0640	0706	0726	0806	0806	0905	1005	1105	1205	1306	1306	1405	1506	1506	1606	1706	1706	1806	1906	1906	2006	2102	2230

	Ⓐe	Ⓐe	⑥k	v	Ⓐe	Ⓒvz	v	Ⓐe	⑥k		Ⓐe	⑥k		Ⓐe	Ⓒz		Ⓐe	Ⓒz		Ⓐe	Ⓑn		Ⓑn	x	x
Pforzheim Hbf d.	0447	0638	0656	0754	0853	0853	0953	1053	1053	1153	1253	1253	1353	1453	1453	1553	1653	1653	1753	1823	1853	1953	2051	2148	2345
Bad Liebenzell d.	0508	0711r	0718	0816	0915	0915	1016	1116	1116	1216	1316	1316	1416	1516	1516	1616	1716	1716	1816	1845	1916	2016	2113	2208	0007
Calw d.	0515	0719	0726	0823	0923	0923	1023	1123	1123	1223	1323	1323	1423	1523	1523	1623	1723	1723	1823	1852	1923	2023	2120	2216	0014
Wildberg (Württ) d.	0528	0731	0738	0835	0935	0935	1035	1136	1136	1235	1335	1335	1435	1535	1535	1635	1735	1735	1835	1904	1935	2035	2131	2227	0026
Nagold d.	0541	0740	0750	0843	0943	0951r	1043	1145	1158j	1243	1343	1358j	1443	1543	1558j	1643	1743	1758j	1843	1914	1943	2043	2139	2236	0034
Hochdorf (b. Horb) d.	0550	0751	0811j	0853	0953	1011j	1053	1154	1212r	1253	1353	1412r	1453	1553	1613r	1653	1753	1813r	1853	1923	1953	2053	2155r	2252r	0046
Horb a.	0602	0803	0823	0905	1005	1023	1105	1206	1224	1305	1405	1424	1505	1605	1625	1705	1805	1825	1905	1935	2004	2105	2207	2304	0057

S-Bahn service **S6 Pforzheim** Hbf - **Bad Wildbad** Bf. *23 km.* 2nd class only. Journey time: 26–34 mins. Trains continue to / start from Bad Wilbad Kurpark (additional journey time 3–4 mins).
From Pforzheim Hbf at 0517 Ⓐ**e**, 0612 Ⓐ**e**, 0647 ⚒**d**, 0705 Ⓐ**e**, 0747, 0847, 0947, 1047, 1147, 1227 Ⓐ**e**, 1247, 1317 Ⓐ**e**, 1347, 1447, 1547, 1617 Ⓐ**e**, 1647, 1717 Ⓐ**e**, 1747, 1817 Ⓐ**e**, 1847, 1917 Ⓐ**e**, 1947, 2047, 2147, 2217, 2317 and 0017. **From Bad Wildbad** Bf at 0509 Ⓐ**e**, 0536 Ⓐ**e**, 0605 Ⓐ**e**, 0639 ⚒**d**, 0701 Ⓐ**e**, 0739, 0809 Ⓐ**e**, 0839, 0909 Ⓐ**e**, 0939, 1039, 1139, 1219 Ⓐ**e**, 1239 Ⓒ**z**, 1309 Ⓐ**e**, 1339, 1439, 1539, 1609 Ⓐ**e**, 1639, 1709 Ⓐ**e**, 1739, 1809 Ⓐ**e**, 1839, 1939, 2039, 2139, 2255 and 2355.

d – Not May 22.
e – Not Dec. 24, 31, May 22.
j – Arrives 11–16 minutes earlier.
k – Also Dec. 24, 31.
n – Not Dec. 24, 31.
r – Arrives 5–10 minutes earlier.
v – Not Dec. 25, Jan. 1.
w – Also May 22.
x – Not Dec. 24.
z – Also Dec. 24, 31, May 22.
⊡ – ①②③④⑦ (also Mar. 21; not Dec. 24, 31).

942 STUTTGART - FREUDENSTADT - OFFENBURG

DB (RE/RB services); OSB★; 2nd class only

km		Ⓒz					Ⓒz	Ⓐe																Ⓒz	Ⓐe
0	**Stuttgart** Hbf 940 d.	2335p	...	...	...	0618	0718	0718	0818	0918	1018	...	1118	1218	1318	1418	1518	1618	1718	1818	1918	2018	2118	2225	2225
26	Böblingen 940 d.	2359p	...	...	...	0638	0738	0738	0838	0938	1038	...	1138	1238	1338	1440	1538	1638	1738	1838	1938	2038	2138	2245	2245
42	Herrenberg 940 d.	0017	...	...	...	0650	0747	0747	0850	0947	1050	...	1147	1250	1347	1450	1547	1650	1747	1850	1947	2050	2147	2259	2317
57	**Eutingen im Gäu** 940 d.	0040	...	...	...	0709	0802	0809	0909	1004f	1109	...	1204f	1309	1404f	1509	1604f	1709	1804f	1909	2009	2109	2209	2319	2334
62	Hochdorf (b. Horb) d.	0045	...	...	...	0714	0806	0814	0914	1010f	1114	...	1210f	1314	1410f	1514	1610f	1714	1810f	1914	2014	2114	2214	2324	2338
87	**Freudenstadt** Hbf a.	0109	...	...	...	0740	0831	0840	0940	1040	1140	...	1240	1340	1440	1540	1640	1740	1840	1940	2040	2140	2240	2348	0002
	Change trains		Ⓐe	Ⓒvz	Ⓐe	Ⓐe	Ⓒz	Ⓐe	Ⓐe		Ⓐe	Ⓐe	Ⓒz									Ⓐe			
87	**Freudenstadt** Hbf ★ d.	...	0533	0636	0640	0743	0834	0843	0943	1043	1143	1220	1243	1343	1443	1543	1643	1743	1843	1943	2043	2143	...	...	...
103	Alpirsbach ★ d.	...	0550	0654	0657	0800	0851	0900	1000	1100	1200	1237	1300	1400	1500	1600	1700	1800	1900	2000	2100	2200	...	...	...
112	Schiltach ★ d.	...	0601	0705	0708	0811	0902	0911	1011	1111	1211	1254	1311	1411	1511	1611	1711	1811	1911	2011	2111	2211	...	...	...
122	Wolfach ★ d.	...	0612	0716	0719	0822	0913	0922	1022	1122	1222	1305	1322	1422	1522	1622	1722	1822	1922	2022	2122	2222	...	...	...
126	Hausach 916 ★ d.	...	0616	0720	0730	0827	0927r	0927	1027	1127	1227	1310	1327	1427	1527	1627	1727	1827	1927	2027	2126	2226	...	...	...
159	**Offenburg** 916 ★ a.	...	0647	0746	0759	0854	0954	0954	1054	1154	1254	1340	1354	1454	1554	1654	1754	1854	1954	2054	2158q	2300	...	...	...

		Ⓐe		Ⓐe		Ⓐe	Ⓒz	Ⓐe		Ⓐe		Ⓐe	Ⓒz								Ⓐe			n
Offenburg 916 ★ d.	...	0446	...	0558	...	0702	0704	0804	0904	1004	1104	1159	1204	1304	1404	1504	1604	1704	1804	1904	2004	...	...	2226
Hausach 916 ★ d.	...	0521	...	0627	...	0730	0735	0831	0931	1031	1131	1231	1231	1331	1431	1531	1631	1731	1831	1931	2031	...	...	2253
Wolfach ★ d.	...	0526	...	0632	...	0735	0740	0836	0936	1036	1136	1236	1236	1336	1436	1536	1636	1736	1836	1936	2036	...	...	2258
Schiltach ★ d.	...	0537	...	0643	...	0747	0752	0847	0947	1047	1147	1248	1248	1347	1447	1547	1647	1747	1847	1947	2047	...	...	2309
Alpirsbach ★ d.	...	0550	...	0700	...	0800	0804	0900	1000	1100	1200	1300	1300	1400	1500	1600	1700	1800	1900	2000	2100	...	...	2321
Freudenstadt Hbf ★ a.	...	0607	...	0717	...	0817	0821	0917	1017	1117	1217	1317	1317	1417	1517	1617	1717	1817	1917	2017	2117	...	...	2338
Change trains	Ⓐe	Ⓐe	Ⓒz	d	Ⓒz	Ⓐe		d		d			d								d	Ⓒz	Ⓐe	
Freudenstadt Hbf d.	0519	0615	0619	0719	0808	0819	...	0919	1019	1119	1219	...	1319	1419	1519	1619	1719	1819	1919	2019	2119	2219	2219	...
Hochdorf (b. Horb) d.	0543	0640	0644	0744	0836	0844	...	0944	1044	1144	1244	...	1344	1444	1544	1644	1744	1844	1948	2044	2151	2247	2247	...
Eutingen im Gäu 940 a.	0548	0645	0649	0749	0840	0849	...	0949	1049	1150	1249	...	1350	1449	1550	1649	1750	1849	1953	2049	2155	2251	2251	...
Herrenberg 940 a.	0610	0710	0710	0810	0911	0911	...	1010	1110	1210	1310	...	1410	1510	1610	1710	1810	1910	2010	2110	2212	2310	2310	...
Böblingen 940 a.	0621	0721	0721	0821	0921	0922	...	1021	1121	1221	1321	...	1421	1521	1621	1721	1821	1921	2021	2121	...	2321	2330	...
Stuttgart Hbf 940 a.	0642	0742	0742	0842	0942	0942	...	1042	1142	1242	1342	...	1442	1542	1643	1742	1842	1942	2042	2142	...	2342	2355	...

d – Daily from Freudenstadt.
e – Ⓐ (not Dec. 24, 31, May 22).
f – 4–5 minutes later on Ⓐe.
n – Not Dec. 24, 31.
p – Previous night. Departs from the underground platforms at Stuttgart Hbf.
q – † (also May 22).
r – Arrives 0917.
v – Not Dec. 25, Jan. 1.
z – Also Dec. 24, 31, May 22.
★ – Freudenstadt - Offenburg operated by Ortenau-S-Bahn GmbH.

943 KARLSRUHE - FREUDENSTADT

S-Bahn (2nd class only)

km		Ⓐe	⑥k	Ⓐe	Ⓒz	Ⓐe	Ⓐe	Ⓒz	†w					A	B	A								
	Karlsruhe Bahnhofsvorplatz d.	0508	0513	0538	0613	...	...	0713	...	0813z	0913	...	1013	1113	...	1213	Train A	...	1813	1913	2013	2113	2213	2315
0	**Karlsruhe** Hbf 916 d.	|	|	|	|	0611	0707	|	0806	0810e	|	1010	|	|	1210	|	runs	1810	|	|	|	|	|	|
24	Rastatt 916 d.	0533	0538	0609	0638	0634	0738	0738	0829	0838	0938	1029	1038	1138	1229	1238	hourly	1829	1838	1938	2038	2138	2238	2340
40	Gernsbach Bf d.	0601	0600	0640	0700	0701	0800	0800	0844	0900	1000	1044	1100	1200	1244	1300	and	1844	1900	2000	2100	2200	2300	0000
51	Forbach (Schwarzw) d.	0626	0618	0658	0718	0718	0818	0818	0900	0918	1018	1100	1118	1218	1300	1318	train B	1900	1918	2018	2118	2218	2318	0018
61	Schönmünzach d.	0638	0631	0710	0731	0733	0829	0831	0911	0931	1031	1111	1131	1231	1311	1331	runs every	1911	1931	2031	2131	2231	2331	0032
74	Baiersbronn Bf d.	0654	0648	0725	0748	0752	0847	0848	0922	0948	1048	1122	1148	1248	1322	1348	two hours	1922	1948	2048	2145	2245	2345	0046
79	**Freudenstadt** Stadt a.	0701	0656	0733	0756	0759	0854	0856	0929	0956	1056	1129	1156	1256	1329	1356	until	1929	1956	2056	2152	2252	2352	0054
82	**Freudenstadt** Hbf a.	0708	0707	0738	0805	0809	0906	0907	0937	1007	1107	1137	1215r	1307	1337	1407		1937	2007	2107	2158	2258	2357	0059

	Ⓐe	Ⓐe	Ⓒz		Ⓐe		⑥k	A	A	B							†w						Ⓒz	D
Freudenstadt Hbf d.	0448	0533	0602	0653	0720	0745t	0824	0853	0953	1023	Train A	1453	1553	1623	1653	1753	1823	1853	1953	2053	2202	2302	2359	0005
Freudenstadt Stadt d.	0455	0541	0607	0703	0733	0803	0830	0903	1003	1030	runs	1503	1603	1630	1703	1803	1830	1903	2003	2103	2208	2308	0010	0010
Baiersbronn Bf d.	0502	0547	0615	0710	0740	0810	0837	0910	1010	1037	hourly	1510	1610	1637	1710	1810	1837	1910	2010	2110	2216	2316	0018	0018
Schönmünzach d.	0518	0605	0629	0728	0751	0828	0849	0928	1028	1049	and	1528	1628	1649	1728	1828	1849	1928	2028	2128	2230	2330	0032	0032
Forbach (Schwarzw) d.	0530	0620	0640	0741	0801	0840	0901	0940	1040	1101	train B	1540	1640	1701	1740	1840	1901	1940	2040	2140	2242	2342	0044	0044
Gernsbach Bf d.	0546	0640	0700	0800	0816	0900	0916	1000	1100	1116	runs every	1600	1700	1716	1800	1900	1916	2000	2100	2200	2300	0000	0103	0103
Rastatt 916 d.	0604	0705	0722	0822	0830	0922	0930	1022	1122	1130	two hours	1622	1722	1730	1822	1922	1930	2022	2122	2222	2322	0022	0122	0122
Karlsruhe Hbf 916 a.	0622	0727	|	|	0849	|	0949	|	|	1149	until	|	|	1749	|	|	1949	|	|	|	|	|	|	|
Karlsruhe Bahnhofsnorplatz a.	...	...	0747	0847	...	0947	...	1047	1147	...		1647	1747	...	1847	1947	...	2047	2147	2247	2347	0047	0147	0147

A – Train runs hourly.
B – Train runs every two hours.
D – ②–⑥ (not Dec. 25, 26, 27, Jan. 1, 2, Mar. 22, 25, May 2, 13, 23).
e – Ⓐ (not Dec. 24, 31, May 22).
k – Also Dec. 24, 31.
r – 1207 on Ⓒz.
t – 0753 on Ⓒz.
w – Also May 22.
z – Ⓒ (also Dec. 24, 31, May 22).

944 MÜNCHEN - PASSAU

RE / RB services

km		①–⑥	†w	⑥k									⊡										Ⓐe		⑤	n
0	**München** Hbf 878 d.	...	0536	0612	0717	0805	...	0924	1005	...	1124	1205	...	1323	1343	1405f	...	1524	1603t	...	1724	1803t	...	1924	2024	2124
42	Freising 878 d.	...	0604	0648	0749	0833	...	0949	1033	...	1149	1233	...	1347	1408	1433	...	1549	1631	...	1749	1832	...	1949	2052	2149
76	Landshut (Bay) Hbf 878 d.	0536	0655	0711	0814	0903	...	1014	1104	...	1214	1312	...	1414	1431	1504	...	1614	1703	...	1814	1902	...	2013	2127	2214
121	Landau (Isar) d.	0622	0730	0742	0845	0938	...	1045	1135	...	1245	1341	...	1445	...	1538	...	1645	1736	...	1845	1936	...	2046	2202	2244
139	Plattling 920/1 d.	0637	0744	0756	0858	0952	1004	1057	1150	1204	1257	1354	1404	1457	...	1552	1604	1657	1750	1804	1857	1950	2004	2059	2215	2303
191	**Passau** Hbf 920/1 🏨 a.	0718	0837	0837	0937	1026*	1041	1136	1226*	1241	1336	1426*	1441	1536	...	1626*	1641	1736	1826*	1841	1936	2026*	2041	2137	2258	2341

	2⚒r	Ⓐe	Ⓒz	Ⓐe													Ⓒz	Ⓐe								n
Passau Hbf 920/1 🏨 d.	0438	0604	0615	0644	0719*	0821	0912	0931*	1021	1112	1131*	1221	1312	1331*	1421	1512	1531*	1531*	1621	1712	1731*	1821	1912	1931*	2023	2208
Plattling 920/1 d.	0516	0642	0653	0727	0801	0901	0948	1005	1058	1148	1205	1258	1348	1405	1458	1548	1605	1605	1658	1748	1805	1858	1948	2005	2100	2247
Landau (Isar) d.	0531	0655	0707	0742	0817	0913	...	1019	1109	...	1219	1309	...	1419	1509	...	1619	1619	1709	...	1819	1909	...	2019	2111	2258
Landshut (Bay) Hbf 878 d.	0605	0729	0747	0813	0900	0946	...	1058	1146	...	1258	1346	...	1458	1546	...	1658	1700	1745	...	1858	1945	...	2058	2144	2328
Freising 878 a.	0628	0748	0808	0847	0927	1008	...	1127	1208	...	1327z	1409	...	1527	1608	...	1727	1728	1808	...	1927	2008	...	2127	2208	2355
München Hbf 878 a.	0701	0820	0836	0916	0959	1036	...	1159	1236	...	1359z	1436	...	1559	1641	...	1759	1820	1840	...	1959	2040	...	2156	2236	0021

e – Not Dec. 24, 31, May 22.
f – ⑤⑥† (also Dec. 24, 31, May 22).
k – Also Dec. 24, 31.
n – Not Dec. 24, 31.
r – Not May 22.
t – 2 minutes later on Ⓒz.
w – Also May 22.
z – Ⓒ (also Dec. 24, 31, May 22).
* – ICE or IC connection.
⊡ – 17 minutes later on ⑥.

945 REGENSBURG - DONAUWÖRTH - ULM

RB services (2nd class only)

On Dec. 24, 31, May 22 services run as on Ⓒ

km		Ⓒ	Ⓐ	Ⓐ	Ⓐ	Ⓒ	Ⓐ	Ⓒ	Ⓐ	Ⓐ	Ⓒ	Ⓐ	Ⓐ	Ⓒ	Ⓐ	Ⓐ	Ⓒ	Ⓐ	Ⓐ	Ⓒ	Ⓐ	Ⓐ	Ⓒ	Ⓐ	Ⓐ	
0	**Regensburg** Hbf d.	...	...	0512	0615	0644	0744	0844	0844	0944	1044	1044	1144	1244	1244	1344	1444	1444	1544	1644	1644	1744	1844	1844	1944	2044
46	Neustadt (Donau) d.	...	...	0557	0657	0731	0831	0931	0931	1031	1131	1131	1231	1331	1331	1431	1531	1531	1631	1731	1731	1831	1931	1931	2031	2131
74	**Ingolstadt** Hbf a.	...	...	0622	0719	0752	0852	0952	0952	1052	1152	1152	1252	1352	1352	1452	1552	1552	1652	1752	1752	1852	1952	1952	2052	2152
74	**Ingolstadt** Hbf d.	0607	0607	0701	0808	0807	0907	1007	1007	1107	1207	1207	1308	1407	1407	1507	1607	1607	1707	1807	1807	1907	2007	2007	2107	2207c
95	Neuburg (Donau) d.	0620	0624	0720	0826	0826	0926	1026	1026	1126	1226	1226	1326	1426	1426	1526	1626	1626	1726	1826	1826	1926	2026	2026	2126	2226c
127	**Donauwörth** a.	0648	0656	0747	0853	0853	0953	1053	1053	1154	1253	1253	1354	1453	1453	1553	1653	1653	1753	1853	1853	1953	2053	2053	2153	2253c
127	**Donauwörth** d.	0702	0712	0802	0902	0902	1002	1102	1102	1202	1302	1302	1402	1502	1502	1602	1702	1702	1802	1902	1902	2002	2102n	2102	...	...
153	Dillingen (Donau) d.	0726	0730	0825	0930	0926	1025	1126	1130	1225	1326	1330	1425	1526	1530	1625	1726	1730	1825	1925	1933	2025	2126n	2133	...	...
176	Günzburg 930 a.	0745	0748	0843	0947	0945	1043	1145	1147	1243	1345	1347	1443	1545	1547	1643	1745	1747	1843	1944	1953	2043	2145n	2152	...	...
200	**Ulm** Hbf 930 a.	0809	0816	0942*	1017	1009	1142*	1209	1217	1317*	1409	1417	1542*	1609	1617	1717*	1809	1822	1945*	2009	2017	2145	2211n	2252	...	...

	Ⓐ	Ⓒ	Ⓐ	Ⓒ	Ⓐ	Ⓐ	Ⓒ	Ⓐ	Ⓐ	Ⓒ	Ⓐ	Ⓐ	Ⓒ	Ⓐ	Ⓐ	Ⓒ	Ⓐ	Ⓐ	Ⓒ	Ⓐ	Ⓐ	Ⓒ	Ⓐ	Ⓐ	Ⓒ	Ⓐ
Ulm Hbf 930 ‡ d.	...	...	0456	0550	0550*	0744	0748	0818*	0944	0947	1012*	1144	1147	1244*	1344	1347	1412*	1544	1547	1644*	1744	1747	1836*	1944	1947	2020*
Günzburg 930 ‡ d.	...	...	0519	0616	0553	0804	0804	0913	1004	1004	1113	1204	1204	1313	1404	1404	1513	1604	1604	1713	1804	1804	1912	2004	2004	2113
Dillingen ‡ d.	...	...	0538	0633	0710	0827	0822	0930	1027	1022	1130	1227	1223	1330	1427	1422	1530	1628	1622	1730	1827	1822	1930	2027	2024	2130
Donauwörth ‡ a.	...	...	0603	0653	0737	0850	0848	0953	1050	1047	1153	1250	1248	1353	1450	1447	1553	1652	1647	1753	1850	1847	1953	2051	2049	2153
Donauwörth d.	0504	0512	0617	0703	0803	0903	0903	1003	1103	1103	1203	1303	1303	1403	1503	1503	1603	1703	1703	1803	1903	1903	2003	2103	2103n	...
Neuburg (Donau) d.	0531	0536	0649	0737	0837	0937	0937	1037	1137	1137	1237	1337	1337	1437	1537	1537	1637	1737	1737	1837	1937	1937	2037	2137	2131n	...
Ingolstadt Hbf a.	0548	0555	0707	0755	0855	0955	0955	1055	1155	1155	1255	1355	1355	1455	1555	1555	1655	1755	1755	1855	1955	1955	2055	2154	2148n	...
Ingolstadt Hbf d.	0600	0605	0724	0805	0905	1005	1005	1105	1205	1205	1306	1405	1405	1505	1605	1605	1705	1805	1805	1905	2005	2005	...	...	...	...
Neustadt (Donau) d.	0620	0627	0743	0831	0931	1031	1027	1131	1231	1227	1331	1431	1427	1531	1631	1627	1731	1831	1831	1931	2031	2027	...	...	...	...
Regensburg Hbf a.	0707	0712	0824	0912	1012	1112	1112	1212	1312	1312	1412	1512	1512	1612	1712	1712	1812	1912	1912	2012	2112	2112	...	...	...	...

c – Ⓒ (not Dec. 24, 31).
n – Not Dec. 24, 31.
‡ – **Additional trains.** On Ⓒ n: Ulm Hbf d. 2200 → Günzburg d. 2218 → Dillingen d. 2235 → Donauwörth a. 2300. On Ⓐ: Ulm Hbf d. 2212 → Günzburg d. 2236 → Dillingen d. 2253 → Donauwörth a. 2317.
* – Earlier arrival / later departure possible by IC train (Table 930).

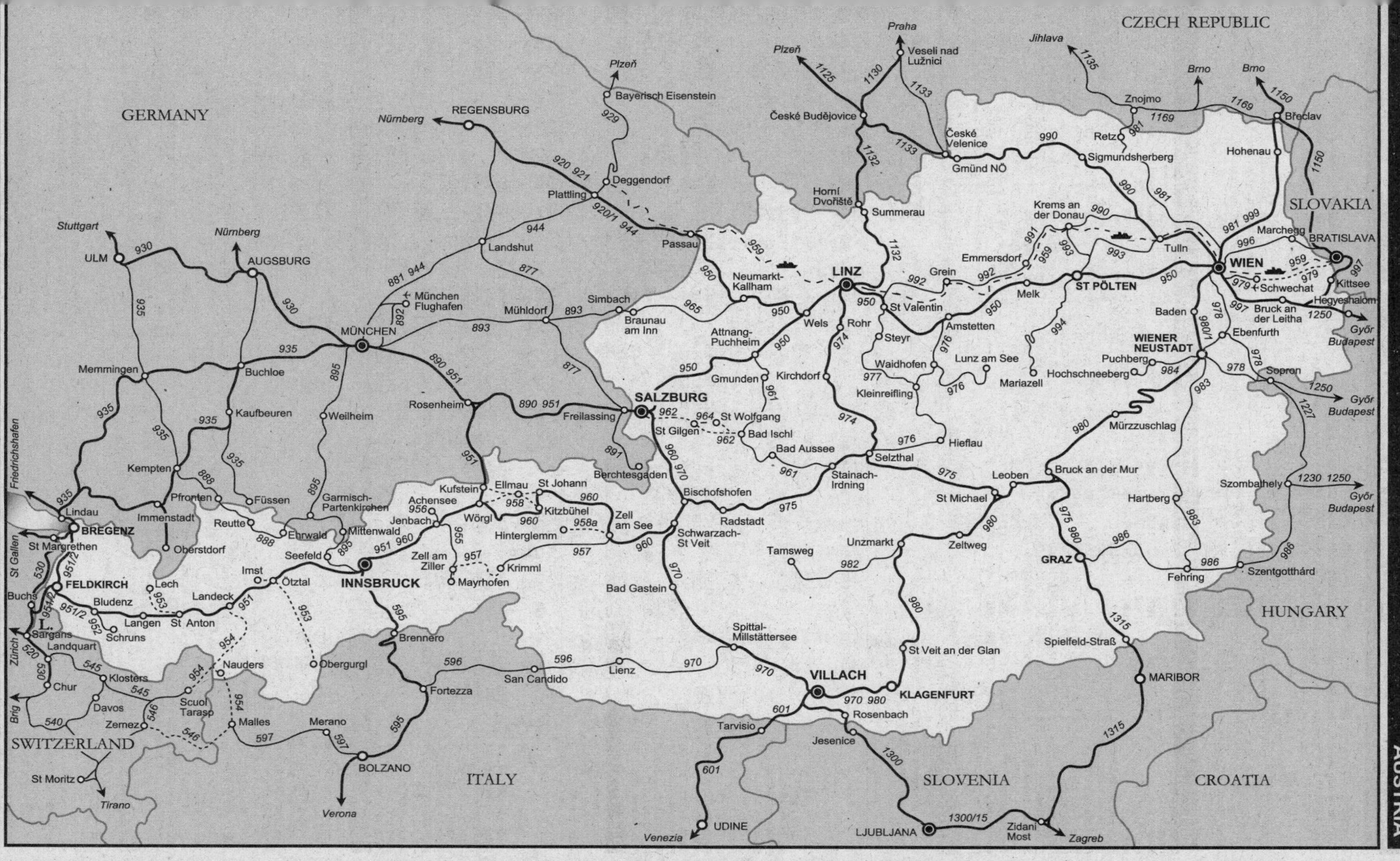
CZECH REPUBLIC
SLOVAKIA
HUNGARY
CROATIA
SLOVENIA
ITALY
SWITZERLAND
GERMANY
WIEN
ST PÖLTEN
LINZ
SALZBURG
INNSBRUCK
GRAZ
KLAGENFURT
VILLACH
BREGENZ
FELDKIRCH
WIENER NEUSTADT
BRATISLAVA
MARIBOR
LJUBLJANA
UDINE
BOLZANO
MÜNCHEN
AUGSBURG
ULM
REGENSBURG
Praha
Brno
Jihlava
Plzeň
Győr
Budapest
Zagreb
Venezia
Verona
Tirano
Zürich
Brig
St Gallen
Friedrichshafen
Stuttgart
Nürnberg
Břeclav
Znojmo
Retz
Hohenau
Marchegg
Kittsee
Hegyeshalom
Bruck an der Leitha
Schwechat
Ebenfurth
Sopron
Szombathely
Szentgotthárd
Baden
Tulln
Sigmundsherberg
Gmünd NÖ
České Velenice
Veseli nad Lužnici
České Budějovice
Summerau
Horní Dvořiště
Krems an der Donau
Melk
Emmersdorf
Grein
Amstetten
St Valentin
Steyr
Waidhofen
Kleinreifling
Hieflau
Lunz am See
Mariazell
Puchberg
Hochschneeberg
Mürzzuschlag
Bruck an der Mur
Leoben
St Michael
Zeltweg
Unzmarkt
Tamsweg
St Veit an der Glan
Rosenbach
Jesenice
Tarvisio
Spielfeld-Straß
Fehring
Hartberg
Zidani Most
Wels
Rohr
Kirchdorf
Selzthal
Stainach-Irdning
Bad Aussee
Bad Ischl
Gmunden
Attnang-Puchheim
St Wolfgang
St Gilgen
Neumarkt-Kallham
Passau
Braunau am Inn
Simbach
Bischofshofen
Radstadt
Schwarzach-St Veit
Bad Gastein
Spittal-Millstättersee
Lienz
San Candido
Fortezza
Brennero
Zell am See
Krimml
Hinterglemm
Kitzbühel
St Johann
Ellmau
Wörgl
Kufstein
Jenbach
Achensee
Zell am Ziller
Mayrhofen
Seefeld
Mittenwald
Garmisch-Partenkirchen
Ehrwald
Reutte
Füssen
Pfronten
Ötztal
Imst
Obergurgl
Landeck
Nauders
Scuol Tarasp
Malles
Merano
St Anton
Lech
Langen
Schruns
Bludenz
Buchs
Sargans
St Margrethen
Lindau
Landquart
Chur
Klosters
Davos
Zernez
St Moritz
Oberstdorf
Immenstadt
Kempten
Memmingen
Buchloe
Kaufbeuren
Weilheim
Rosenheim
Freilassing
Berchtesgaden
Mühldorf
Landshut
Plattling
Deggendorf
Bayerisch Eisenstein
München Flughafen

AUSTRIA

Operator: Except where otherwise stated, rail services are operated by Österreichische Bundesbahnen (**ÖBB**).

Timings: Valid **December 9, 2007 - December 13, 2008** unless stated otherwise in individual tables. See page 2 for public holiday dates.

Services: Trains convey both first- and second-class seating unless footnotes show otherwise or there is a '2' in the train column. Overnight sleeping car (🛏) or couchette (▬) trains do not necessarily convey seating accommodation - refer to individual footnotes for details. Descriptions of sleeping and couchette cars appear on page 10.

Train categories:

ICE	**InterCity Express**	German high-speed train.
ÖEC	**ÖBB-EuroCity**	Quality international or internal express train.
ÖIC	**ÖBB-InterCity**	Quality internal express train.
EC	**EuroCity**	Quality international express train.
IC	**InterCity**	Internal or international express train.
D	**Schnellzug**	Ordinary fast train.
REX	**Regional Express**	Semi-fast regional train.
EZ	**Erlebniszug**	Semi-fast regional train running through tourist areas.
EN	**EuroNight**	Quality overnight express train. Special fares payable.

Local stopping trains (second-class only) are shown with no category / train number.

Reservations: Seats may be reserved on all express trains (*ICE, ÖEC, ÖIC, EC, IC, EN, D*).

950 WIEN - SALZBURG and PASSAU

km ♣		2 ⚒	*REX* **1654** 2 ⚒	2	*IC* **390** ①–⑥ e◆	2 ⚒	2 Ⓐ	*REX* **1782** 2 Ⓐ	2 ⚒	*ÖIC* **540** 🍷	*REX* **1784** 2 Ⓒ	*ICE* **562** ✕	*ICE* **116** ✕	2 ⚒	2	*ICE* **228** ✕ G	*ÖIC* **542** 🍷	2	*ÖEC* **662** ✕ F	*ÖEC* **160** ✕ ◆	2	*ÖIC* **690** 🍷 ◆	*EZ* **1996** ✕2 ⒸS	*EZ* **5914** ✕2	*ÖEC* **68** ✕	*ICE* **28** ✕ G
0	**Wien** Westbahnhof ... d.	...	...	...	...	...	0415	...	*0452*	0540	...	0614	0614	...	0610	0640	0644	...	0657	0740	...	0744	◇	◧	0822	0840
6	**Wien** Hütteldorf ● ... d.	...	...	...	...	...	0423	...	*0500*	0548	...	|	|	...	0622	|	0652	...	|	|	...	0752	0734	0808	|	|
61	**St Pölten** Hbf ... d.	...	...	...	...	0433	0529	...	0602	0625	...	0656	0656	...	0718	0722	0729	...	|	0822	...	0829	0836	0908	|	0922
	Melk ... d.	...	...	...	...	0457	0546	...	0626	|	...	|	|	←	0742	|	|	←	|	|	...	|	0853	0924	|	|
93	Pöchlarn ... d.	...	...	...	...	0504	0553	...	0632	|	...	|	|	0633	0748	|	|	0749	|	|	...	|	0900	0930	|	|
104	Ybbs an der Donau ... d.	...	...	...	...	0517	0600	...	→	|	...	|	|	0646	→	|	|	0800	|	|	...	|	0909	→	|	|
121	Amstetten ... d.	...	...	*0428*v	...	0535	0615	0623	...	0653	...	|	|	0703	...	|	0757	0817	|	|	...	0857	0921	...	|	|
158	St Valentin **977** ... d.	...	...	*0510*	...	0613	k	0647	...	0710	...	|	|	0739	...	|	0814	0840	|	|	...	0914	...	...	|	|
183	**Linz** Hbf **977** ... a.	...	...	*0535*	...	0638	...	0709	...	0725	...	0745	0745	*0803*	...	0813	0829	*0908*	|	0913	...	0929	...	...	0950	1013
183	**Linz** Hbf ... d.	*0457*	0510	0547	0626	...	...	0712	...	0728	0737	0747	0747	...	...	0816	0832	...	|	0916	0920	0932	...	...	0953	1016
208	**Wels** Hbf ... ‡ d.	0524	0527	0616	0640	...	...	0730	...	0742	0755	|	|	...	...	0830	0850	...	|	0930	0938	0946	...	...	|	1030
	Neumarkt-Kallham ‡ d.	0552	|	0647	|	...	...	0758	...	|	0821	|	|	...	...	|	|	...	|	|	1007	|	...	...	|	|
	Schärding ... d.	0625	|	0722	|	...	...	0828	...	|	0851	|	|	...	...	|	|	...	|	|	1043	|	...	...	|	|
	Passau Hbf 🏛 ... a.	0638	|	0736	|	...	...	0843	...	|	0906	|	|	...	...	0924	|	...	|	|	1056	|	...	...	|	1124
238	Attnang-Puchheim ... d.	...	0550	...	0658	...	...	...	...	0758	...	|	|	...	...	...	0907	...	|	|	...	1002	...	...	|	...
243	Vöcklabruck ... d.	...	0555	...	0704	...	...	...	...	0804	...	|	|	...	...	...	0913	...	|	|	...	1008	...	...	|	...
308	**Salzburg** Hbf ... a.	...	0648	...	0750	...	...	...	...	0848	...	0853	0853	...	...	...	0955	...	0948	1027	...	1050	...	...	1058	...
	München Hbf **890** .. a.	...	...	...	0934	...	...	...	...	...	...	|	1031	...	...	...	...	...	|	|	...	...	...	...	1231	...
	Innsbruck Hbf **951** .. a.	...	...	...	...	...	...	...	...	...	...	1044	...	...	...	...	...	...	1143	1230	...	...	...	...	...	...
	Bregenz **951** ... a.	...	...	...	...	...	...	...	...	...	...	1312	...	...	...	...	...	...	...	...	...	...	...	...	...	...

	ÖIC **544** 🍷 A	*EZ* **5914** ✕2	*REX* **1614** 2	*ÖEC* **162** ✕ ◆	*EZ* **5914** ✕2	*ÖIC* **546** 🍷	*REX* **1616** 2	*ICE* **26** ✕ H	*REX* **1786** 2	*ÖIC* **548** 🍷	*REX* **1618** 2	*ÖEC* **564** ✕	2	*ÖIC* **640** 🍷	*REX* **1622** 2	*ICE* **24** ✕ H	*REX* **1788** 2 Ⓐn	*ÖIC* **642** 🍷	*REX* **1624** 2	*ÖEC* **566** ✕	*EZ* **5924** ✕2	*ÖIC* **644** 🍷	*REX* **1626** 2	*ICE* **22** ✕ H	*REX* **1792** 2	*ÖIC* **646** 🍷
Wien Westbahnhof ... d.	0830	...	0904	0940	...	0944	1004	1040	...	1044	1104	1140	...	1144	1204	1240	...	1244	1304	1340	...	1344	1404	1440	...	1444
Wien Hütteldorf ● ... d.	0838	...	0912	|	...	0952	1012	|	...	1052	1112	|	...	1152	1212	|	...	1252	1312	|	...	1352	1412	|	...	1452
St Pölten Hbf ... d.	0916	...	0959	1022	...	1029	1059	1122	...	1129	1159	1222	...	1229	1259	1322	...	1329	1359	1422	...	1429	1459	1522	...	1529
Melk ... d.	|	←	1017	|	...	|	1117	|	...	|	1217	|	...	|	1317	|	...	|	1417	|	...	|	1517	|	...	|
Pöchlarn ... d.	|	0938	1023	|	...	|	1123	|	...	|	1223	|	...	|	1323	|	...	|	1423	|	...	|	1523	|	...	|
Ybbs an der Donau ... d.	|	0949	1032	|	...	|	1132	|	...	|	1232	|	...	|	1332	|	...	|	1432	|	...	|	1532	|	...	|
Amstetten ... d.	0952	1003	1044	|	...	1057	1144	|	...	1157	1244	|	...	1257	1344	|	...	1357	1444	|	...	1457	1544	|	...	1557
St Valentin **977** ... d.	1012	1043	...	|	...	1114	...	|	...	1214	...	|	1243	1314	...	|	...	1414	...	|	...	1514	...	|	...	1614
Linz Hbf **977** ... a.	1029	1105	...	1113	...	1129	...	1213	...	1229	...	1313	1308	1329	...	1413	...	1429	...	1513	...	1529	...	1613	...	1629
Linz Hbf ... d.	1032	1107	...	1116	←	1132	...	1216	1220	1232	...	1316	1320	1332	...	1416	1420	1432	...	1516	1520	1532	...	1616	1620	1632
Wels Hbf ... ‡ d.	1048	1124	...	1130	1133	1146	...	1230	1238	1246	...	1330	1338	1346	...	1430	1438	1446	...	1530	1539	1546	...	1630	1638	1646
Neumarkt-Kallham ‡ d.	|	→	...	|	1202	|	...	|	1303	|	...	|	1407	|	...	|	1503	|	...	|	1608	|	...	|	1705	|
Schärding ... d.	|	...	...	|	1236	|	...	|	1335	|	...	|	1443	|	...	|	1535	|	...	|	1643	|	...	|	1745	|
Passau Hbf 🏛 ... a.	|	...	...	|	1250	|	...	1324	1348	|	...	|	1456	|	...	1524	1548	|	...	|	1656	|	...	1724	1758c	|
Attnang-Puchheim ... d.	1106	...	...	|	...	1202	...	...	...	1302	...	|	...	1402	...	...	...	1502	...	|	...	1602	...	...	...	1702
Vöcklabruck ... d.	1112	...	...	|	...	1208	...	...	...	1308	...	|	...	1408	...	...	...	1508	...	|	...	1608	...	...	...	1708
Salzburg Hbf ... a.	1154	...	...	1227	...	1250	...	...	...	1350	...	1427	...	1450	...	...	...	1550	...	1627	...	1650	...	...	...	1750
München Hbf **890** ... a.	...	...	...	|	...	...	...	...	...	...	...	|	...	...	...	...	...	...	...	|	...	...	...	...	...	...
Innsbruck Hbf **951** .. a.	...	...	...	1430	...	...	...	...	...	...	...	1632	...	...	...	...	...	...	...	1830	...	...	...	...	...	...
Bregenz **951** ... a.	...	...	...	...	...	...	...	...	...	...	...	...	...	...	...	...	...	...	...	2105	...	...	...	...	...	...

	REX **1794** 2 Ⓐ	*REX* **1628** 2	*ÖEC* **568** ✕	2	*IC* **692** 🍷 ◆	*REX* **1630** 2	*ÖEC* **62** ✕ B	*ICE* **20** ✕ G	2 Ⓐ	*ÖIC* **740** 🍷	*REX* **1634** 2	*ÖEC* **844** ✕ Ⓑ	*ÖEC* **660** ✕	2	*IC* **742** 🍷	*REX* **1636** 2	*ICE* **766** ✕ Ⓑr	2	*ÖIC* **744** 🍷	*REX* **1638** 2	*ÖEC* **768** ✕	*REX* **1694** 2 Ⓐ	*REX* **1696** 2 Ⓒ	*ÖIC* **746** 🍷	*EN* **428** R ◆	*EN* **490** R ◆
Wien Westbahnhof ... d.	...	1504	1540	...	1544	1604	1622	1640	...	1644	1704	1722	1740	...	1744	1804	1822	...	1844	1904	1922	...	...	1944	1952	1957
Wien Hütteldorf ● ... d.	...	1512	|	...	1552	1612	|	|	...	1652	1712	|	|	...	1752	1812	|	...	1852	1912	|	...	...	1952	2000	2005
St Pölten Hbf ... d.	...	1559	1622	...	1629	1659	1704	1722	...	1729	1759	1804	1822	...	1829	1904	|	...	1929	2004	|	...	...	2029	2040	2045
Melk ... d.	...	1617	|	...	|	1717	|	|	...	|	1817	|	|	...	|	1922	|	...	|	2022	|	...	...	|	|	|
Pöchlarn ... d.	...	1623	|	...	|	1723	|	|	...	|	1823	|	|	...	|	1928	|	...	|	2028	|	...	...	|	|	|
Ybbs an der Donau ... d.	...	1632	|	...	|	1732	|	|	...	|	1832	|	|	...	|	1937	|	...	|	2037	|	...	...	|	|	|
Amstetten ... d.	...	1644	|	...	1657	1744	|	|	...	1757	1844	1831	|	...	1857	1949	|	...	1957	2049	|	...	...	2057	2114	2119
St Valentin **977** ... d.	...	...	|	...	1714	...	|	|	...	1814	...	|	|	...	1914	...	|	...	2014	...	|	...	...	2114	|	|
Linz Hbf **977** ... a.	...	...	1713	...	1729	...	1752	1813	...	1829	...	1858	1913	...	1929	...	1950	...	2029	...	2050	...	...	2129	2148	2153
Linz Hbf ... d.	1636	...	1716	1720	1732	...	1754	1816	1820	1832	...	...	1916	1920	1932	...	1953	2020t	2032	...	2053	2115	2115	...	2151	2156
Wels Hbf ... ‡ d.	1654	...	1730	1738	1746	...	|	1830	1838	1846	...	...	1930	1938	1946	...	|	2038	2046	...	|	2134	2134	...	2208	2213
Neumarkt-Kallham ‡ d.	1715	...	|	1807	|	...	|	|	1907	|	...	...	|	2007	|	...	|	2107	|	...	|	|	|	...	|	|
Schärding ... d.	1745	...	|	1843	|	...	|	|	1943	|	...	...	|	2043	|	...	|	2143	|	...	|	|	|	...	2250	2255
Passau Hbf 🏛 ... a.	1758	...	|	1856	|	...	|	1924	1956	|	...	...	|	2056	|	...	|	2156	|	...	|	|	|	...	2302	2307
Attnang-Puchheim ... d.	...	...	|	...	1802	...	|	...	...	1902	...	...	|	...	2002	...	|	...	2102	...	|	2200	2208	...	...	...
Vöcklabruck ... d.	...	...	|	...	1808	...	|	...	...	1908	...	...	|	...	2008	...	|	...	2108	...	|	2204	2212	...	...	...
Salzburg Hbf ... a.	...	...	1827	...	1850	...	1858	...	...	1950	...	...	2027	...	2050	...	2058	...	2150	...	2158	2305	2313	...	...	...
München Hbf **890** ... a.	...	...	|	...	...	...	2034	...	...	...	...	...	|	...	...	...	|	...	...	...	...	...	...	...	...	...
Innsbruck Hbf **951** .. a.	...	...	2030	...	...	...	...	...	...	...	...	...	2230	...	...	...	2259	...	...	...	...	...	...	...	...	...
Bregenz **951** ... a.	...	...	2305	...	...	...	...	...	...	...	...	...	0056	...	...	...	...	...	...	...	...	...	...	...	...	...

◆ – **NOTES** (LISTED BY TRAIN NUMBER)

160 – VORARLBERG – [12] and ✕ Wien - Buchs 🏛 - Zürich.

162 – TRANSALPIN – [1] (observation car), [12] and ✕ Wien - Buchs 🏛 - Zürich - Basel.

390 – [12] and 🍷 Linz - München - Stuttgart - Frankfurt.

428 – DONAU-SPREE-KURIER – 🛏 1,2 cl., ▬ 2 cl. and [2] Wien - Leipzig - Berlin.

490 – HANS ALBERS – 🛏 1,2 cl., ▬ 2 cl. and [2] Wien - Nürnberg - Hannover - Hamburg. Dec. 9 – 19, Jan. 6 - Mar. 12, Oct. 5 - Dec. 13 (also ①②③⑦ Mar. 30 - Apr. 28, May 4 – 7, ①②③⑦ May 12 – 19, ①②③⑦ May 25 - June 25 and ①②③⑦ Sept. 7 – 30) runs with train number **492** in the timings of train **428** (in previous column).

690 – [12] and 🍷 Wien - Salzburg - Klagenfurt; on ⑤⑥⑦ (also Mar. 24, May 1, 12, 22, Dec. 8) conveys [12] Wien - Schwarzach (*D* **840**) - Zell am See - Wörgl.

692 – [12] and 🍷 Wien - Salzburg - Villach.

A – Conveys [12] Wien - Attnang-Puchheim - Stainach-Irdning (Table **961**).
B – From Budapest (Table **1250**).
F – To Feldkirch (Table **951**).
G – [12] and ✕ Wien - Passau 🏛 - Regensburg - Nürnberg - Frankfurt.
H – [12] and ✕ Wien - Passau 🏛 - Regensburg - Nürnberg - Frankfurt - Köln - Dortmund.

R – 🅁 for journeys to Germany.
S – To Bischofshofen via Selzthal (Tables **975** and **977**).

c – Ⓒ only.
e – Not Dec. 25, 26, Jan. 1, Mar. 22, 24, May 12.
k – To Kleinreifling (Table **976**).
n – Not Dec. 24, 31.
r – Not Dec. 23, 24, 25, 30, 31, Mar. 23, May 11, Aug. 15.
t – *1957* on †.
v – Change trains at St Valentin and Linz.

◇ – From Wien Südbf (d. 0712) and Wien Meidling (d. 0721).
◧ – From Wien Südbf (d. 0746) and Wien Meidling (d. 0753).
♣ – Via high-speed alignments.
‡ – See also Table **965**.
● – See note on page 447 for local connections.

PASSAU and SALZBURG - WIEN 950

	EN 264	IC 748		D 207		EN 466	REX 1642	EN 246	EN 268	REX 1644
	[R] ♦	🍷 V	2 ⚒	♦	2 n	♦	2	♦	♦	2 n
Wien Westbahnhof d.	2035	2040	...	...	...	2125	2129	2220	2345	2350
Wien Hütteldorf ● d.	2043	2048	...	...	...	|	2136	|	|	2358
St Pölten Hbf d.	2120	2125	...	...	2133	2209	2221	2305	0030	0048
Melk d.	|	|	...	...	2157	|	2239	|	|	0106
Pöchlarn d.	|	|	...	...	2204	|	2245	|	|	0112
Ybbs an der Donau d.	|	|	...	...	2217	|	2254	|	|	0120
Amstetten d.	|	2154	...	...	2233	2239	2306	2339	0104	0133
St Valentin **977** d.	|	2213	...	...	...	|	...	0000	0126	...
Linz Hbf 977 a.	2217	2229	...	...	...	2311	...	0017	0143	...
Linz Hbf d.	2220	2232	...	2246	...	2314	...	0020	0146	...
Wels Hbf ‡ d.	2234	2246	2250	2303	...	2329	...	0037	0203	...
Neumarkt-Kallham ‡ d.	|	|	2319	|	...	|	...	|	|	...
Schärding d.	|	|	2353	|	...	|	...	|	|	...
Passau Hbf 🏛 a.	|	|	...	|	...	|	...	|	|	...
Attnang-Puchheim d.	|	2305	...	2323	...	|	...	0056	0222	...
Vöcklabruck d.	|	2311	...	2328	...	|	...	|	|	...
Salzburg Hbf a.	2333	2352	...	0014	...	0032	...	|	0309	...
München Hbf **890** a.	0108o	...	...	...	...	|	...	|	0615	...
Innsbruck Hbf **951** a.	...	...	...	...	...	0237	...	0451	...	...
Bregenz **951** a.	...	...	...	...	...	...	...	0754	...	...

km ♥		REX 1603	EN 269	REX 1605		REX 1607	ÖIC 843	REX 1613		EN 247	REX 1615	REX 1783
		2	♦	2 Ⓐ	2 ⚒	2 Ⓐ	🍷	2 ⚒	2 ⚒	♦	2 ⚒	2 Ⓐ
	Bregenz **951** d.	...	...	...	...	...	...	...	...	2144	...	...
	Innsbruck Hbf **951** d.	...	...	...	...	...	...	...	...	0042	...	...
	München Hbf **890** d.	...	2345	...	...	...	...	...	...	|	...	...
	Salzburg Hbf d.	...	0218	...	...	...	...	...	...	|	...	...
	Vöcklabruck d.	...	|	...	...	...	...	...	...	|	...	...
	Attnang-Puchheim d.	...	0306	...	...	...	...	...	...	0455	...	...
0	**Passau** Hbf 🏛 d.	...	|	...	...	...	...	...	...	|	...	0415
14	Schärding d.	...	|	...	...	...	...	...	0401	|	...	0429
52	Neumarkt-Kallham ‡ d.	...	|	...	...	...	...	...	0435	|	...	0457
81	**Wels** Hbf ‡ d.	...	0325	...	...	...	...	...	0503	0514	...	0522
106	**Linz** Hbf a.	...	0340	...	...	...	...	...	0524	0528	...	0538
106	**Linz** Hbf **977** d.	...	0342	...	...	...	0455	...	...	0531	...	...
131	St Valentin **977** d.	...	0402	...	0418	...	0513	0510	...	0550	0526	...
170	Amstetten d.	0415	0425	0443	0455	0511	0532	0540	...	0611	0614	...
187	Ybbs an der Donau d.	0428	|	0456	0512	0524	|	0553	...	|	0627	...
200	Pöchlarn d.	0435	|	0503	0525	0531	|	0600	...	|	0636	...
209	Melk d.	0442	|	0510	0532	0538	|	0607	...	|	0643	...
233	**St Pölten** Hbf d.	0504	0500	0532	0554	0600	0606	0630	...	0645	0705	...
288	**Wien** Hütteldorf ● a.	0551	0546	0617	...	0643	0647	0718	...	0723	0750	...
294	**Wien** Westbahnhof a.	0600	0555	0626	...	0653	0657	0728	...	0732	0759	...

	ÖIC 845	EN 467		D 206		IC 849	EN 265		EN 491	EN 429	ÖEC 541		ÖEC 847	REX 1787	REX 1663	ICE 767	REX 1617		ÖIC 543	REX 1619	ÖIC 545	REX 1623		IC 547	ÖEC 561	REX 1625
	🍷 Ⓐ	♦	2	♦	2	🍷 V	[R] ♦	2	R ♦	R ♦	✕	2	✕ ①-⑥	2 Ⓐn	2	✕ N	2	2 ⚒	🍷	2	🍷	2	2	🍷 ♦	✕	2
Bregenz **951** d.	...	...	...	...	...	...	...	...	...	...	...	...	...	...	...	...	...	...	...	...	...	...	...	...	0500	...
Innsbruck Hbf **951** d.	...	0227	...	...	...	...	...	...	...	...	...	...	...	...	...	0500	...	...	...	...	...	...	...	...	0730	...
München Hbf **890** d.	...	|	...	...	...	...	0345o	...	...	...	...	...	...	...	...	|	...	...	...	...	...	...	...	...	|	...
Salzburg Hbf d.	...	0436	...	0441	...	0500	0526	...	...	...	0600	...	...	...	0605	0700	...	...	0708	...	0808	...	...	0908	0934	...
Vöcklabruck d.	...	|	...	|	...	0545	|	...	...	...	|	...	...	...	0703	|	...	...	0751	...	0851	...	...	0951	|	...
Attnang-Puchheim d.	...	|	...	0528	...	0551	|	...	...	...	0644	...	...	...	0712	|	...	...	0757	...	0857	...	...	0957	|	...
Passau Hbf 🏛 d.	...	|	...	|	0430c	|	|	...	0530	0536	|	0543	...	0630	|	|	...	0645	|	...	|	...	0807	|	|	...
Schärding d.	...	|	...	|	0443	|	|	...	0543	0549	|	0557	...	0643	|	|	...	0659	|	...	|	...	0820	|	|	...
Neumarkt-Kallham ‡ d.	...	|	...	|	0519	|	|	...	|	|	|	0635	...	0710	|	|	...	0735	|	...	|	...	0856	|	|	...
Wels Hbf ‡ d.	0529	0539	...	0547	0550	0613	0629	...	0633	0643	|	0707	...	0732	0736	|	...	0805	0814	...	0914	...	0925	1014	1033	...
Linz Hbf a.	0543	0554	...	0602	0614	0627	0644	...	0650	0658	0708	0726	...	0750	0758	0804	...	0821	0827	...	0927	...	0941	1027	1045	...
Linz Hbf **977** d.	0545	0557	...	...	...	0630	0647	...	0656	0701	0710	...	0742	...	...	0806	...	...	0830	...	0930	...	...	1030	1048	...
St Valentin **977** d.	0601	|	0611	...	...	0648	|	...	|	|	|	...	0800	...	...	|	...	...	0848	k	0948	...	...	1048	|	...
Amstetten d.	0620	0632	0651	...	...	0707	|	...	0739	0744	|	...	0817	...	...	|	0809	...	0905	0909	1005	1009	...	1105	|	1109
Ybbs an der Donau d.	|	|	0707	...	...	|	|	←	|	|	|	...	|	...	...	|	0821	...	|	0921	|	1021	...	|	|	1121
Pöchlarn d.	|	|	0719	...	...	|	|	0720	|	|	|	...	|	...	...	|	0830	...	|	0930	|	1030	...	|	|	1130
Melk d.	|	|	→	...	...	|	|	0727	|	|	|	...	|	...	...	|	0836	...	|	0936	|	1036	...	|	|	1136
St Pölten Hbf d.	0650	0709	...	...	...	0738	0747	0751	0813	0818	|	...	0845	...	...	|	0903	...	0933	0957	1033	1057	...	1133	1143	1157
Wien Hütteldorf ● a.	0728	0754	...	...	...	0821	0826	...	0853	0858	|	...	0921	...	...	|	0951	...	1009	1046	1109	1146	...	1209	1219	1246
Wien Westbahnhof a.	0737	0803	...	...	...	0830	0835	...	0902	0908	0840	...	0930	...	...	0935	1000	...	1018	1055	1118	1155	...	1218	1228	1255

	ÖIC 549		ICE 21	ÖEC 63	REX 1627	IC 693	ÖEC 563	REX 1629	ÖIC 643		ICE 23	REX 1633	ÖIC 645	EZ 5921	ÖEC 565	REX 1635	ÖIC 647		ICE 25	REX 1637	ÖIC 745	REX 1793	ÖEC 163	REX 1639	ÖIC 15649	ÖIC 649
	🍷	2	✕ G	✕ B	2	🍷 ♦	✕	2	🍷	2	✕ H	2	🍷	✕2	✕	2	🍷	2	✕ H	2	🍷	2 Ⓐn	✕ ♦	2	🍷 ⑦z	🍷 A
Bregenz **951** d.	...	...	...	...	...	...	0650	...	...	...	...	...	...	...	...	...	...	...	...	...	...	...	...	...	...	...
Innsbruck Hbf **951** d.	...	...	...	...	...	...	0930	...	...	...	...	...	...	...	1130	...	...	...	...	...	...	...	1330	...	...	...
München Hbf **890** d.	...	...	...	0927	...	...	|	...	...	...	...	...	...	...	|	...	...	...	...	...	...	...	|	...	...	...
Salzburg Hbf d.	1008	...	...	1100	...	1108	1134	...	1208	...	...	...	1308	...	1334	...	1408	...	...	...	1508	...	1534	...	1603	1603
Vöcklabruck d.	1051	...	...	|	...	1151	|	...	1251	...	...	...	1351	...	|	...	1451	...	...	...	1551	...	|	...	1646	1646
Attnang-Puchheim d.	1057	...	...	|	...	1157	|	...	1257	...	...	...	1357	...	|	...	1457	...	...	...	1557	...	|	...	1652	1657
Passau Hbf 🏛 d.	|	1007	1035	|	...	|	|	...	|	1207	1235	...	|	1310	|	...	|	1407	1435	...	|	1510	|	...	|	|
Schärding d.	|	1020	|	|	...	|	|	...	|	1220	|	...	|	1324	|	...	|	1420	|	...	|	1524	|	...	|	|
Neumarkt-Kallham ‡ d.	|	1056	|	|	...	|	|	...	|	1256	|	...	|	1356	|	...	|	1456	|	...	|	1556	|	...	|	|
Wels Hbf ‡ d.	1114	1125	1133	|	...	1214	1233	...	1314	1325	1333	...	1414	1423	1433	...	1514	1525	1533	...	1614	1625	1633	...	1709	1714
Linz Hbf a.	1127	1141	1145	1204	...	1227	1245	...	1327	1341	1345	...	1427	1441	1445	...	1527	1541	1545	...	1627	1641	1645	...	1722	1727
Linz Hbf **977** d.	1130	...	1148	1206	...	1230	1248	...	1330	...	1348	...	1430	...	1448	...	1530	...	1548	...	1630	...	1648	...	1725	1730
St Valentin **977** d.	1148	...	|	|	...	1248	|	...	1348	...	|	...	1448	...	|	...	1548	...	|	...	1648	...	|	...	1743	1748
Amstetten d.	1205	...	|	|	1209	1305	|	1309	1405	...	|	1409	1505	...	|	1509	1605	...	|	1609	1705	...	|	1709	1800	1805
Ybbs an der Donau d.	|	...	|	|	1221	|	|	1321	|	...	|	1421	|	...	|	1521	|	...	|	1621	|	...	|	1721	|	|
Pöchlarn d.	|	...	|	|	1230	|	|	1330	|	...	|	1430	|	...	|	1530	|	...	|	1630	|	...	|	1730	|	|
Melk d.	|	...	|	|	1236	|	|	1336	|	...	|	1436	|	...	|	1536	|	...	|	1636	|	...	|	1736	|	|
St Pölten Hbf d.	1233	...	1243	1258	1303	1333	1343	1357	1433	...	1443	1457	1533	...	1543	1557	1633	...	1643	1657	1733	...	1743	1757	1828	1833
Wien Hütteldorf ● a.	1309	...	|	|	1353	1409	1419	1446	1509	...	|	1546	1609	...	1619	1646	1709	...	|	1746	1809	...	1819	1846	1904	1909
Wien Westbahnhof a.	1318	...	1326	1338	1402	1418	1428	1455	1518	...	1526	1555	1618	...	1628	1655	1718	...	1726	1755	1818	...	1828	1855	1913	1918

♦ – **NOTES** (LISTED BY TRAIN NUMBER)

161 – VORARLBERG – [12] and ✕ Zürich - Buchs 🏛 - Wien and v.v.

163 – TRANSALPIN – [1] (observation car), [12] and ✕ Basel - Zürich - Buchs 🏛 - Wien.

206 – [12] Salzburg - Linz - Summerau 🏛 - Praha; couchette 1, 2 cl. and sleeper 2 cl. Zürich (**467**) - Salzburg (**206**) - Praha; sleeper 2 cl. Venezia (**239**) - Udine (**236**) - Salzburg (**206**) - Praha.

207 – [12] Praha - Summerau 🏛 - Salzburg; couchette 1, 2 cl. and sleeper 2 cl. Praha - Salzburg (**466**) - Zürich; sleeper 2 cl. Praha - Salzburg (**237**) - Venezia.

246/7 – couchette 1, 2 cl., sleeper 2 cl. and [2] Wien - Innsbruck - Feldkirch - Bregenz and v.v.

264/5 – ORIENT-EXPRESS – couchette 1, 2 cl., sleeper 2 cl. and [2] Wien - Karlsruhe - Strasbourg and v.v.; conveys couchette 1, 2 cl., sleeper 2 cl., [2] (reclining) and ✕ (*City Night Line* **312/3** [R] Special fares – DONAU-KURIER) Wien - Mannheim - Frankfurt - Köln - Dortmund and v.v. (see Table **66**).

268/9 – KÁLMÁN IMRE – couchette 1, 2 cl., sleeper 2 cl. and [2] Budapest - München and v.v.; couchette 1, 2 cl. Bucureşti - Budapest - München and v.v.

391 – [12] and 🍷 Frankfurt - Stuttgart - München - Linz.

429 – SPREE-DONAU-KURIER – couchette 1, 2 cl., sleeper 2 cl. and [2] Berlin - Leipzig - Wien.

466/7 – WIENER WALZER – sleeper 2 cl. and [2] Budapest - Wien - Zürich and v.v.; couchette 1, 2 cl., sleeper 2 cl. and [2] Wien - Zürich and v.v. [R] for journeys to / from Switzerland.

491 – HANS ALBERS – couchette 1, 2 cl., sleeper 2 cl. and [2] Hamburg - Hannover - Nürnberg - Wien. Dec. 9–21, Jan. 8 - Mar. 14, Oct. 7 - Dec. 13 (also ②–⑤ Apr. 1–30, May 6–9, ②–⑤ May 14–21, ②–⑤ May 27 - June 27 and ②–⑤ Sept. 9 - Oct. 2) runs with train number **493** in the timings of train **429** (in next column).

691/3 – [12] and 🍷 Klagenfurt - Villach - Salzburg - Wien.

A – ①–⑥ (also Dec. 23, 30, Mar. 23, May 11, Dec. 7; not Dec. 26, Jan. 1, Mar. 24, May 12, Dec. 8). Conveys [12] Stainach-Irdning - Attnang-Puchheim - Wien (Table **961**).

B – To Budapest (Table **1250**).

F – From Feldkirch (Table **951**).

G – [12] and ✕ Frankfurt - Nürnberg - Regensburg - Passau 🏛 - Wien.

H – [12] and ✕ Dortmund - Köln - Frankfurt - Nürnberg - Regensburg - Passau 🏛 - Wien.

J – Conveys [12] Innsbruck (**1511**) - Wörgl - Schwarzach - Salzburg (**741**) - Wien.

N – ①–⑥ (not Dec. 24, 25, 26, 31, Jan. 1, Mar. 24, May 12, Aug. 16).

R – [R] for journeys to / from Germany.

S – From Bischofshofen via Selzthal (Tables **975** and **977**).

T – From Stainach-Irdning (Table **961**).

V – [12] Salzburg - Wien and v.v.; conveys couchette 1, 2 cl., sleeper 2 cl. and [2] (*EN* **236/7** [R] – ALLEGRO DON GIOVANNI) Venezia - Udine - Tarvisio - Villach - Salzburg - Wien and v.v. (Table **88**).

c – © only.

k – From Kleinreifling (Table **976**).

n – Not Dec. 24, 31.

o – München **Ost**.

q – Not Dec. 24, 25, 31, Mar. 21, 23, May 11.

z – Also Dec. 26, Jan. 1, Mar. 24, May 12, Dec. 8; not Dec. 23, 30, Mar. 23, May 11, Dec. 7.

⊖ – To Wien Meidling (a. 2028) and Wien Südbf (a. 2035).

★ – To Wien Meidling (a. 2158) and Wien Südbf (a. 2206).

♥ – Via original alignments.

‡ – See also Table **965**.

● – S-Bahn trains operate every 10 – 15 minutes to / from Wien Heiligenstadt (journey time: 21 minutes). See panel below for Wien S-Bahn links to / from other Wien stations.

WIEN S-Bahn	Ⓐ		Ⓐ		Ⓐ					
Hütteldorf d.	0551	0621	0651	0721	0751	0821	0921		2321	2351
Meidling **981** a.	0602	0632	0702	0732	0802	0832	0932	and	2332	0002
Südbahnhof **981** a.	0610	0640	0710	0740	0810	0840	0940	hourly	2340	0010
Mitte **981** a.	0615	0645	0715	0745	0815	0845	0945	until	2345	0015
Praterstern **981** a.	0619	0649	0719	0749	0819	0849	0949		2349	0019

WIEN S-Bahn		Ⓐ		Ⓐ		Ⓐ				
Praterstern **981** d.	0512	0539	0612	0639	0712	0739	0809	0909		2309
Mitte **981** d.	0516	0543	0616	0643	0716	0743	0813	0913	and	2313
Südbahnhof **981** d.	0523	0550	0623	0650	0723	0750	0820	0920	hourly	2320
Meidling **981** d.	0533	0558	0633	0658	0733	0758	0828	0928	until	2328
Hütteldorf a.	0545	0609	0645	0709	0746	0811	0839	0939		2339

950 PASSAU and SALZBURG - WIEN

	IC 749		ICE 27	ÖEC 69	REX 1641	EZ 1997	ÖIC 741	ÖIC 15741	EZ 5927	ÖEC 569	REX 1645	REX 1645	EZ 5927	ÖIC 743	ICE 29	ÖEC 663	ICE 117		ÖIC 691	ÖEC 161	ÖIC 747	ICE 229	REX 1649		ICE 661	IC 391
	T🍷 ⑦z	2	✕ H	✕	2	S✕ ©	🍷 Ⓐ	🍷 ©J	✕2	✕	2 n	2 †	✕2	🍷	✕ G	F✕	✕	2	🍷 ♦	✕ ♦	🍷	✕ G	2	2	✕	Ⓑq ♦
Bregenz **951** d.	...	...	...	...	...	...	...	...	...	1246	...	...	...	...	...	...	...	...	...	...	...	...	...	...	1646	...
Innsbruck Hbf **951** d.	...	...	...	...	...	...	...	...	...	1530	...	...	...	...	...	1702	...	...	...	1730	...	...	...	...	1930	...
München Hbf **890** d.	...	...	...	1526	...	...	...	...	...	|	...	...	...	...	...	|	1723	...	...	|	...	...	...	...	|	2024
Salzburg Hbf d.	...	...	...	1700	...	...	1705	1708	...	1734	...	...	...	1808	...	1858	1904	...	1908	1934	2008	...	...	...	2132	2215
Vöcklabruck d.	...	...	...	|	...	...	1749	|	...	|	...	...	...	1851	...	|	|	...	1951	|	2051	...	...	...	|	2301
Attnang-Puchheim d.	1657	...	...	|	...	...	1755	1755	...	|	...	...	...	1857	...	|	|	...	1957	|	2057	...	...	...	|	2307
Passau Hbf 🏛 d.	|	1607	1635	|	...	...	|	|	1710	|	...	...	...	|	1835	|	|	1846	|	|	|	2035	...	2107	|	|
Schärding d.	|	1620	|	|	...	...	|	|	1724	|	...	...	...	|	|	|	|	1859	|	|	|	|	...	2120	|	|
Neumarkt-Kallham ‡ d.	|	1656	|	|	...	...	|	|	1756	|	...	...	...	|	|	|	|	1932	|	|	|	|	...	2156	|	|
Wels Hbf ‡ d.	1714	1725	1733	|	...	...	1813	1813	1823	1833	...	...	...	1914	1933	|	|	1959	2014	2033	2114	2133	...	2223	2229	2325
Linz Hbf a.	1727	1741	1745	1804	...	...	1828	1828	1841	1845	...	...	←	1927	1945	|	2008	▬	2027	2045	2127	2145	...	...	2241	2342
Linz Hbf **977** d.	1730	...	1748	1806	...	...	1831	1831	→	1848	...	...	1853	1930	1948	|	2010	...	2030	2048	2130	2148	...	...	2243	...
St Valentin **977** d.	1748	...	|	|	...	...	1850	1850	...	|	...	...	1921	1948	|	|	|	2	2048	|	2148	|	...	...	|	...
Amstetten d.	1805	...	|	|	1809	1850	1911	1911	...	|	1920	1920	1958	2005	|	|	|	2023	2105	|	2205	|	2209	...	|	...
Ybbs an der Donau d.	|	...	|	|	1821	|	|	|	...	|	1933	1933	2010	|	|	|	|	2040	|	|	|	|	2221	...	|	...
Pöchlarn d.	|	...	|	|	1830	|	|	|	...	|	1943	1943	2019	|	|	|	|	2053	|	|	|	|	2230	...	|	...
Melk d.	|	...	|	|	1836	|	|	|	...	|	1949	1949	2027	|	|	|	|	2100	|	|	|	|	2236	...	|	...
St Pölten Hbf d.	1833	...	1843	|	1903	1929	1948	1948	...	1943	2009	2011	2047	2033	2043	|	2102	2122	2133	2143	2233	2243	2257	...	2335	...
Wien Hütteldorf ● a.	1909	...	|	|	1953	2015	2026	2026	...	2019	...	2100	2147	2109	|	|	|	...	2209	2219	2309	|	2348	...	|	...
Wien Westbahnhof a.	1918	...	1926	1935	2002	⊖	2035	2035	...	2028	...	2109	★	2118	2126	2147	2142	...	2218	2228	2318	2326	2357	...	0015	...

← FOR NOTES SEE PREVIOUS PAGE

951 SALZBURG and MÜNCHEN - INNSBRUCK - BREGENZ - LINDAU

km		EN 466		D 15464	EN 464	EN 246		REX 1540	ÖEC 760	REX 5151			ÖEC 164	REX 1864	IC 118	EC 81			REX 1502	ICE 562	EC 85	ÖEC 662	REX 5179	REX 5570		ÖEC 160
		♦	2	L	♦	♦	2	2	✕	2 ⚒	2	2	✕	2	🍷 ♦	✕R V	2	2	2	✕	✕R ♦	✕	2	2	2	✕
	Wien Westbf **950** d.	2125	...	...	...	2220	...	...	...	...	...	...	...	...	...	...	...	...	...	0614	...	0657	...	...	...	0740
	Linz Hbf **950** d.	2314	...	...	...	0020	...	...	...	...	...	...	...	...	...	...	...	...	...	0747	...	|	...	...	...	0916
0	**Salzburg** Hbf d.	0044	...	...	...	|	...	...	...	...	...	...	0622	...	...	...	...	...	...	0856	...	0953	...	...	...	1031
	München Hbf **890** d.	|	...	...	...	|	...	...	...	...	...	...	|	...	...	0730	...	*0742*	...	|	0932	|	...	...	*0942*	|
	München Ost **890** d.	|	...	...	...	|	...	...	...	...	...	...	|	...	...	0740	...	*0750*	...	|	0941	|	...	...	*0950*	|
	Rosenheim **890** d.	|	...	...	...	|	...	...	...	...	...	0609k	|	...	...	0812	...	0835	...	|	1013	|	...	...	1035	|
120	Kufstein 🏛 d.	|	...	...	...	|	...	*0511*	...	0554	...	0647	0738	...	...	0834	...	0906	...	|	1035	|	...	...	1109	1145
134	Wörgl **960** d.	|	...	0255	...	|	...	0531	...	0610	...	0701	0749	...	...	0845	...	0920	1000	|	1046	|	...	...	1123	1156
159	Jenbach **960** d.	|	...	|	...	0429	...	0551	...	0630	...	0723	0806	...	...	0859	...	0942	1017	|	1100	|	...	...	1145	1210
193	**Innsbruck** Hbf **960** a.	0237	...	0337	...	0451	...	0617	...	0654	...	0757	0830	...	...	0920	...	1016	1040	1044	1121	1143	...	...	1218	1230
193	**Innsbruck** Hbf d.	0241	...	0345	0402	0455	0552	...	0638	▬	0722	...	0839	...	0910	...	0952	...	...	1046	...	1146	1213	...	...	1239
239	Ötztal d.	|	...	|	|	0521	0647	...	0705	...	0811	...	0903	...	0934	...	1044	...	...	1110	...	|	1251	...	...	1303
248	Imst-Pitztal d.	|	...	|	|	0532	0704	...	0714	...	0822	...	0912	...	0943	...	1059	...	...	|	...	|	1304	...	...	1312
265	Landeck-Zams d.	|	...	0439	0453	0547	0718	...	0728	...	0837	...	0927	...	0957	...	1113	...	...	1130	...	|	1318	...	...	1327
293	St Anton am Arlberg d.	|	...	0505	0518	0612	▬	...	0751	...	...	...	0951	...	1020	...	...	...	...	1152	...	|	▬	...	...	1351
304	Langen am Arlberg d.	|	...	0516	0529	0623	...	...	0801	...			1001	...	1031	...	...	...	...	1203	...	|	...	...	...	1401
329	Bludenz ⊖ d.	0427	...	0555	0615	0703	2	...	0828	2	...	...	1028	...	1057	...	...	...	...	1228	...	|	2	1330	...	1428
350	**Feldkirch** ⊖ a.	0440	...	0609	0631	0717	P		0840				1040	...	1109	...	...	...	...	1240	...	1332		1345	...	1440
350	**Feldkirch** ⊖ d.	0446	0458	0646	0646	0721	0747	...	0844	0846	...	...	1042	1046	1110	...	...	...	...	1244	...	...	1341	1346	...	1442
369	**Buchs** 🏛 ⊖ a.	0502	|	0702	0702	|	0808	...	|	0909	...	...	1058	|	|	...	...	...	...	|	...	...	1358	|	...	1458
	Zürich HB **520** a.	0620	|	0820	0820	|	...	...	|	...	...	...	1220	|	|	...	...	...	...	|	...	...	...	|	...	1620
375	Dornbirn ⊖ d.	...	0527	...	...	0742	...	...	0903	...	...	...	...	1108	1132	...	...	...	...	1303	...	...	...	1408	...	...
387	**Bregenz** 🏛 ⊖ a.	...	0542	...	...	0754	...	...	0912	...	...	...	...	1115	1140	...	...	...	...	1312	...	...	...	1415	...	...
397	**Lindau** Hbf 🏛 ⊖ a.	...	0555	...	...	*0828*r	...	...	*0952*	...	...	...	...	1128	1151	...	...	...	...	*1339*	...	...	...	1428	...	...

	EC 87		ÖEC 162	EC 89	REX 1878		ÖEC 564	ÖEC 668	EC 83		D 1281	ÖEC 566	ÖEC 189			ÖEC 568		ICE 109			ÖEC 660		CNL 389	ICE 766		
	✕R ♦	2	✕ ♦	✕R ♦	2	2	✕	✕ ♦	✕R V	2	⑥G	✕	✕R V	2 ⑥⑦c	2 N	✕	2 ⚒¶	✕ ♦	2	2 ⑧¶	✕	2	✕R ♦	✕ ⑧m	2	2
Wien Westbf **950** d.	...	...	0940	...	...	...	1140	...	...	...	...	1340	...	...	...	1540	...	...	...	...	1740	...	...	1822	...	...
Linz Hbf **950** d.	...	...	1116	...	...	...	1316	...	...	...	...	1516	...	...	...	1716	...	...	...	...	1916	...	...	1953	...	...
Salzburg Hbf d.	...	...	1231	...	...	...	1431	...	...	...	...	1631	...	...	...	1831	...	...	...	...	2030	...	...	2100	...	...
München Hbf **890** d.	1130	*1142*	|	1331	...	*1342*	|	...	1530	*1542*	1600	|	1731	*1740*	*1753*	|	*1846*	1936	...	*1942*	|	*2047*	2103	|	...	...
München Ost **890** d.	1140	*1150*	|	1341	...	*1350*	|	...	1540	*1550*	|	|	1741	*1749*	*1802*	|	*1854*	1945	...	*1950*	|	*2055*	|	|	...	...
Rosenheim **890** d.	1212	1234	|	1413	...	1436	|	...	1612	1634	1641	|	1812	1835	*1835*	|	1935	|	...	2036	|	2135	2143	|	←	...
Kufstein 🏛 d.	1234	1306	1345	1435	...	1506	1545	...	1634	1706	1714	1745	1834	1909	1909	1945	2006	2035	...	2106	2145	2203	2209	2216	2221	...
Wörgl **960** d.	1245	1320	1356	1446	...	1520	1556	1550	1645	1720	1723	1756	1845	1920	1920	1956	2020	2045	...	2120	2156	→	2220	2225	2235	...
Jenbach **960** d.	1259	1342	1410	1500	...	1542	1610	1605	1659	1742	...	1810	1859	1942	1942	2010	2042	2059	...	2142	2210	...	2234	2239	2255	...
Innsbruck Hbf **960** a.	1320	1416	1430	1521	...	1616	1632	1626	1720	1816	...	1830	1920	2016	2016	2030	2116	2120	...	2216	2230	...	2255	2259	2321	...
Innsbruck Hbf d.	▬	...	1439	▬	1539	▬	...	1639	▬	...	...	1839	▬	...	...	2039	...	...	2152	...	2233	...	...	...	...	2330
Ötztal d.	...	...	1503	...	1607	...	...	1703	...	...	...	1903	...	...	...	2103	...	...	2241	...	2300	...	...	...	...	0019
Imst-Pitztal d.	...	...	|	...	1619	...	...	1712	...	...	...	1912	...	...	...	2112	...	...	2259	...	2309	...	...	...	...	0029
Landeck-Zams d.	...	...	1527	...	1634	...	...	1727	...	...	...	1927	...	...	...	2127	...	...	2313	...	2323	...	...	...	...	0044
St Anton am Arlberg d.	*REX*	...	1551	*REX*	1656	...	...	1751	*IC*	...	...	1951	...	...	...	2151	...	...	...	...	2345	...	...	...	...	...
Langen am Arlberg d.	**1860**	...	1601	**1862**	1706	...	...	1801	**168**	...	...	2001	...	...	...	2201	...	...	...	...	2356	...	...	...	...	...
Bludenz ⊖ d.	2	...	1628	2	1732	2	...	1828		...	...	2028	2	...	...	2228	...	...	...	...	0021	...	...	...	...	...
Feldkirch ⊖ a.		...	1640		1744	A	...	1840		...	...	2040		...	...	2240	...	...	...	...	0032	...	...	...	...	...
Feldkirch ⊖ d.	1446	...	1642	1646	1745	1800	...	1844	1846	...	...	2042	2048	...	...	2242	...	...	...	...	0033	...	...	...	...	...
Buchs 🏛 ⊖ a.	|	...	1658	|	|	1822	...	|	1902	...	...	|	2111	...	...	|	...	...	...	...	|	...	...	...	...	...
Zürich HB **520** a.	|	...	1820	|	|	...	...	|	2020	...	...	|	...	...	...	|	...	...	...	...	|	...	...	...	...	...
Dornbirn ⊖ d.	1508	...	...	1708	1806	...	...	1903	...	...	...	2056	...	...	...	2256	...	...	...	...	0048	...	...	...	...	...
Bregenz 🏛 ⊖ a.	1515	...	...	1715	1815	...	...	1915	...	...	...	2105	...	...	...	2305	...	...	...	...	0056	...	...	...	...	...
Lindau Hbf 🏛 ⊖ a.	1528	...	...	1728	1826	...	...	*1929*	...	...	...	*2122*	...	...	...	*2325*	...	...	...	...	...	...	...	...	...	...

♦ – **NOTES** (LISTED BY TRAIN NUMBER)

84/5 – MICHELANGELO – [12] and ✕ Roma - Verona - Brennero 🏛 - München and v.v.

86/7 – TIEPOLO – [12] and ✕ Venezia - Verona - Brennero 🏛 - München and v.v.

88/9 – LEONARDO DA VINCI – [12] and ✕ Milano - Verona - Brennero 🏛 - München and v.v.

108/9 – [12] and ✕ Innsbruck - München - Stuttgart - Frankfurt - Berlin and v.v.

118/9 – [12] and 🍷 Innsbruck - Lindau - Ulm - Stuttgart - Köln - Münster and v.v.

162/3 – TRANSALPIN – [1] (observation car), [12] and ✕ Wien - Zürich - Basel and v.v.

246/7 – 🛏 1,2 cl., 🛌 2 cl. and [2] Wien - Bregenz and v.v.

388/9 – *City Night Line.* 🛏 1,2 cl., 🛌 2 cl., [2] and ✕ Roma - Firenze - Verona - Brennero 🏛 - München and v.v.; 🛏 1,2 cl., 🛌 2 cl. and [2] Venezia (**358/63**) - Verona - München and v.v.

464 – ZÜRICHSEE – 🛏 1,2 cl., 🛌 2 cl. and [2] Graz - Bruck a. d. Mur - Selzthal - Schwarzach - Zürich. Conveys daily from Schwarzach (except when train **L** runs) 🛏 1,2 cl.*, 🛌 2 cl.* and [2] Beograd (**414**) - Zagreb - Ljubljana - Villach - Schwarzach (**464**) - Zürich.

465 – ZÜRICHSEE – 🛏 1,2 cl., 🛌 2 cl. and [2] Zürich - Schwarzach - Selzthal - Bruck a. d. Mur - Graz. Conveys daily (except when train **J** runs) 🛏 1,2 cl.*, 🛌 2 cl.* and [2] Zürich - Schwarzach (**415**) - Villach - Ljubljana - Zagreb - Beograd.

466/7 – WIENER WALZER – 🛌 2 cl. and [2] Budapest - Wien - Zürich and v.v.; 🛏 1,2 cl., 🛌 2 cl. and [2] Wien - Zürich and v.v.; 🛏 1,2 cl. and 🛌 2 cl. Praha (**207/6**) - Salzburg - Zürich and v.v. Ⓡ for journeys to / from Switzerland.

668/9 – [12] and ✕ Graz - Selzthal - Bischofshofen - Kitzbühel - Bregenz and v.v.

A – ①–⑤ (not Dec. 25, 26, Jan. 1, Mar. 24, May 12).

G – ⑥ Dec. 22 - Mar. 22, June 21 - Aug. 23 (also Jan. 2). To Zell am See (Table **960**).

H – ⑥ Dec. 29 - Mar. 22, June 28 - Aug. 30 (also Jan. 2, 6, Mar. 24). From Zell am See (Table **960**).

J – Daily Dec. 9 - Jan. 6, Mar. 13–25 (also Feb. 15, 16, 22, 23); ⑤⑥⑦ Mar. 28 - June 22 (also May 1, 12, 21); daily June 26 - Sept. 7; ⑤⑥⑦ Sept. 12 - Oct. 31. 🛏 1,2 cl.*, 🛌 2 cl.* and [2] Zürich (**465**) - Feldkirch (**15465**) - Schwarzach (**415**) - Villach - Ljubljana - Zagreb - Beograd.

L – From Wörgl daily Dec. 9 - Jan. 7, Mar. 14–26 (also Feb. 16, 17, 23, 24); ①⑥⑦ Mar. 29 - June 23 (also May 2, 13, 22); daily June 27 - Sept. 8; ①⑥⑦ Sept. 13 - Nov. 1. 🛏 1,2 cl.*, 🛌 2 cl.* and [2] Beograd (**414**) - Zagreb - Ljubljana - Villach - Schwarzach (**15464**) - Feldkirch (**464**) - Zürich.

N – ①–⑤ (not Dec. 24, 25, 26, 31, Jan. 1, Mar. 21, 24, May 1, 12, 22, Aug. 15, Oct. 3).

P – ①–⑥ (not Dec. 25, 26, Jan. 1, Mar. 24, May 12).

Q – ①–⑥ (not Dec. 24, 25, 26, 31, Jan. 1, Mar. 24, May 12, Aug. 16).

R – Ⓡ for journeys to / from Italy.

V – To / from Verona (Table **595**).

b – Also Dec. 26, Jan. 1, Mar. 24, May 12, Dec. 8; not Dec. 23, 30, Mar. 23, May 11, Dec. 7.

c – Also Dec. 24, 25, 26, 31, Jan. 1, Mar. 21, 24, May 1, 12, 22, Aug. 15, Oct. 3.

k – ①–⑥ (not Dec. 25, 26, Jan. 1, Mar. 21, 24, May 1, 12, 22, Aug. 15, Oct. 3, Nov. 1).

m – Not Dec. 23, 24, 25, 30, 31, Mar. 23, May 11, Aug. 15.

n – Not Dec. 24, 31.

q – Not Mar. 21, Oct. 3.

r – ⚒ only.

⊖ – See Table **952** for other local services.

* – 🛏 1,2 cl. and 🛌 2 cl. from / to Zagreb.

¶ – Runs daily München - Kufstein.

LINDAU - BREGENZ - INNSBRUCK - MÜNCHEN and SALZBURG 951

km		CNL	ICE	REX			REX	ÖEC		ICE	REX		ÖEC	D		REX	ÖEC	IC	ÖEC	ÖEC		REX	ÖEC			ÖEC
		388	767	5100			5152	561		108	5176		563	1280		1879	188	169	669	565		1863	163			569
		✕R	✕	2	2	2	2	✕	2	✕	2	2	✕		2	2	✕R		✕	✕	2	2	✕	2	2	✕
		♦	Q	⚒			⚒			♦	⚒	A		⑥H			V		♦				♦			
	Lindau Hbf ⊖ d.	...	...	...	...	...	...	...	...	...	...	...	*0633*	...	...	0727	...	...	*0824*	...	...	1030	...	...	...	*1229*
	Bregenz ⊖ d.	...	...	...	...	...	...	0500	...	...	...	...	0650	...	...	0740	...	...	0841	...	...	1043	...	...	...	1246
	Dornbirn ⊖ d.	...	...	...	...	...	...	0509	...	...	...	...	0700	...	...	0750	...	...	0852	...	...	1052	...	...	...	1257
	Zürich HB **520** d.	...	...	...	...	...	...	|	...	...	...	...	|	...	...	|	...	0740	|	...	...	|	0940	...	...	|
	Buchs ⊖ d.	...	...	...	...	...	...	|	...	...	...	0602	|	...	0748	|	...	0856	|	...	...	|	1102	...	1254	|
	Feldkirch ⊖ a.	...	...	...	...	...	...	0522	...	...	...	0624	0717	...	0812	0814	...	0912	0910	...	...	1113	1118	...	1316	1315
	Feldkirch ⊖ d.	...	...	...	...	...	...	0524	...	...	...	▬	0720	...	▬	0815	...	...	0920	...	...	▬	1120	...	▬	1320
	Bludenz ⊖ d.	...	...	...	...	...	...	0538	...	...	...	...	0735	...	...	0830	...	...	0935	...	...	...	1135	...	...	1335
	Langen am Arlberg d.	...	...	...	...	...	...	|	...	...	...	...	0801	...	...	0854	...	...	1001	...	...	...	1202	...	...	1401
	St Anton am Arlberg d.	...	...	...	...	...	...	0613	...	...	...	...	0812	...	...	0905	...	...	1012	...	...	...	1213	...	...	1412
	Landeck-Zams d.	...	...	0420	*0453*	...	0557	0636	...	...	0723	...	0835	...	...	0929	...	...	1035	...	...	*EC*	1240	...	*EC*	1435
	Imst-Pitztal d.	...	...	0436	*0509*	...	0613	0650	...	...	0741	...	0848	...	...	0944	...	...	1048	...	...	**88**	|	...	**82**	1448
	Ötztal d.	...	...	0446	*0519*	...	0624	0700	...	...	0752	2	0858	...	...	0953	...	...	1058	...	...	✕R	1303	...	✕R	1458
	Innsbruck Hbf a.	...	...	0534	*0607*	...	0654	0726	...	...	0825		0921	...	...	1026	...	...	1121	...	...	♦	1326	...	V	1521
0	**Innsbruck** Hbf **960** d.	0434	0500	0536	0623	0642	0702	0730	0742	0824	...	0842	0930	...	0942	...	1037	...	1135	1130	1142	1237	1330	1343	1437	1530
4	Jenbach **960** d.	|	0519	0602	0648	0716	0729	0750	0816	0843	...	0916	0950	...	1016	...	1058	...	1155	1150	1216	1258	1350	1416	1458	1550
9	Wörgl **960** d.	0514	0534	0622	0710	0739	0749	0805	0839	0858	...	0939	1005	1035	1039	...	1114	...	1209	1205	1239	1314	1405	1439	1514	1605
3	Kufstein d.	0530	0544	0637	0721	0754	0802	0816	0856	0909	...	0954	1016	1046	1054	...	1125	...	...	1216	1254	1325	1416	1454	1525	1616
7	Rosenheim **890** a.	0551	|	0708q	...	0824	...	|	0924	|	...	1023	|	1115	1123	...	1144	...	...	|	1324	1344	|	1523	1544	|
2	**München** Ost **890** a.	|	|	...	...	*0902*	...	|	*1008*	0956	...	*1102*	|	|	*1207*	...	1215	...	...	|	*1407*	1415	|	*1607*	1615	|
2	**München** Hbf **890** a.	0630	|	...	...	*0913*	...	|	*1019*	1007	...	*1112*	|	1154	*1217*	...	1226	...	...	|	*1417*	1427	|	*1616*	1626	|
	Salzburg Hbf a.	...	0657	...	...	...	...	0929	...	...	...	...	1129	...	...	...	...	...	...	1329	...	...	1529	...	...	1729
	Linz Hbf **950** a.	...	0804	...	...	...	...	1045	...	...	...	...	1245	...	...	...	...	...	...	1445	...	...	1645	...	...	1845
	Wien Westbf **950** a.	...	0935	...	...	...	...	1228	...	...	...	...	1428	...	...	...	...	...	...	1628	...	...	1828	...	...	2028

		REX	ÖEC	REX	ÖEC		REX	EC		IC	IC	ICE		EC	REX	ÖEC			ÖEC	REX	EN		EN	D	REX	EN
		1861	663	5162	161		5190	86		119	15661	661		80	1869	165			765	1549	247		465	15465	5589	467
	2	2	✕	2	✕	2	2	✕R	2	🍷	2🍷	✕	2	✕R	2	✕	2	2	✕	2		2			2	
				Ⓑ				♦		♦	⑦b			V			n	A			♦		♦	J		♦
dau Hbf ⊖ d.	...	1415	...	...	...	...	...	...	...	1605	...	*1625*	...	...	1830	...	...	...	*2030*	...	*2127*	2203	...	...	2332	...
genz ⊖ d.	...	1428	...	...	...	...	...	...	...	1616	...	1646	...	...	1843	...	...	...	2055	...	2144	2216	...	...	2344	...
nbirn ⊖ d.	...	1436	...	...	...	...	...	...	...	1625	...	1657	...	...	1853	...	...	...	2104	...	2153	2232	...	...	2356	...
ürich HB **520** d.	...	|	...	...	1340	...	...	...	...	|	...	|	...	...	|	1740	...	...	|	...	|	|	2140	2140	|	2240
uchs ⊖ d.	...	|	...	...	1502	...	...	...	1602	|	...	|	...	...	|	1902	...	2055	|	...	|	|	2259	2259	|	0005
dkirch ⊖ a.	...	1457	...	...	1518	...	...	...	1624	1648	...	1715	...	...	1914	1918	...	2117	2118	...	2212	2302	2314	2314	0017	0020
dkirch ⊖ d.	...	1506	1502	...	1520	...	...	...	*1633*	1650	...	1720	...	...	▬	1920	...	▬	2120	...	2220	2303	2332	2344	...	0022
denz ⊖ d.	...	1526	|	...	1535	...	...	...	*1653*	1704	...	1735	...	...	...	1935	...	...	2135	...	2240	2323	2348	0004	...	0039
gen am Arlberg d.	...	▬	|	...	1601	...	...	...	...	1736	...	1801	...	...	...	2001	...	...	2201	...	2308	...	0020	0035	...	|
Anton am Arlberg d.	...	...	|	...	1612	...	...	...	...	1748	...	1812	...	...	...	2012	...	...	2212	...	2319	...	0031	0047	...	|
deck-Zams d.	...	*EC*	|	...	1635	...	1721	...	...	1810	1828	1835	...	...	...	2035	...	...	2235	...	2346	...	0055	0110	...	|
t-Pitztal d.	...	**84**	|	...	1648	...	1740	...	...	1823	1842	1848	...	...	...	2048	...	...	2248	...	|	...	|	|	...	|
tal d.	...	✕R	|	...	1658	...	1751	...	...	1833	1852	1858	...	...	2	2058	...	2	2258	...	0009	...	|	|	...	|
sbruck Hbf a.	...	♦	1650	...	1721	...	1826	...	...	1856	1917	1921	...	...		2121			2325	...	0034	...	0140	0154	...	0224
sbruck Hbf **960** d.	1542	1637	1702	1708	1730	1742	...	1837	...	...	1920	1930	1942	2037	2042	2130	...	2230	...	2342	0042	...	0143	0158	...	0227
bach **960** d.	1616	1658	|	1736	1751	1816	...	1858	...	...	1940	1950	2016	2058	2116	2150	...	2302	...	0016	0105	...	|	|	...	|
rgl **960** d.	1639	1714	|	1800	1806	1839	...	1914	...	...	1955	2005	2039	2114	2139	2205	...	2325	...	0038	0123	...	0216	0233	...	|
stein d.	1654	1725	|	1810	1816	1854	...	1925	...	...	2006	2016	2054	2125	2154	2216	2254	2338	...	...	|	...	...	...	...	|
osenheim **890** a.	1723	1744	|	...	|	1924	...	1944	...	...	|	|	2123	2144	2223	|	2322	...	...	...	|	...	...	...	...	|
ünchen Ost **890** a.	*1807*	1815	|	...	|	*2007*	...	2015	...	...	|	|	*2208*	2214	*2302*	|	...	...	...	...	|	...	...	...	...	|
ünchen Hbf **890** a.	*1817*	1826	|	...	|	*2017*	...	2026	...	...	|	|	*2219*	2226	*2312*	|	...	...	...	...	|	...	...	...	...	|
zburg Hbf a.	...	...	1853	...	1929	...	...	...	...	...	2120	2129	...	...	...	2329	...	...	...	...	|	...	...	...	...	0424
inz Hbf **950** a.	...	...	|	...	2045	...	...	...	...	...	...	2241	...	...	...	...	...	...	...	...	0528	...	...	...	...	0554
ien Westbf **950** a.	...	...	2147	...	2228	...	...	...	...	...	...	0015	...	...	...	...	...	...	...	...	0732	...	...	...	...	0803

FOR NOTES SEE PREVIOUS PAGE

VORARLBERG LOCAL SERVICES 952

d class only (except where shown); see also Table **951**

km														*EC* 191					*EC* 193							
		Ⓐ	A			A				⚒	P			Z✕					Z✕							
	Schruns ▣ d.	...	...	...	...	...	...	0625a	...	0703	...	...	...	...	...	...	...	...	...	...	...	...	...	...	...	...
	Bludenz ▣ d.	0506	...	...	0603	*0607*	...	0650	0659	0728	...	...	0737	...	*0828*	0837	...	0937	...	*1028*	...	1137	...	1237	...	*1307*a
	Feldkirch d.	0528	0530	...	0618	0633	...	0710	0714	0746	0747	...	0758	...	0846	0858	...	0958	...	1046	...	1158	...	1258	...	1341
	Buchs a.	|	0552	...	|	0655	...	|	0737	|	0808	...	|	...	0909	|	...	|	...	|	...	|	...	|	...	1358
	Dornbirn d.	0557	▬	...	0639	...	...	0736	...	0808	...	...	0827	...	...	0927	...	1027	...	1108	...	1231	...	1327	...	...
0	St Margrethen d.	|	...	0633	|	...	0723	|	...	|	...	0819	|	0842	...	|	0933	|	1042	|	1154	|	1310	|	1333	...
2	**Bregenz** d.	0613	0613	0645	0650	...	0739	0748	...	0816	...	0835	0843	0855	...	0943	0949	1043	1055	1116	1208	1247	1327	1342	1348	...
2	**Lindau** Hbf a.	0625	0625	...	0659	...		0759	...	0828	...	...	0855	0905	...	0952	...	1055	1105	1128	*1225*r	1259	1339	...	1358	...

			EC 195															*EC* 197								
			Z✕												A			Z✕								
chruns ▣ d.	1307	...	...	...	...	...	...	...	...	...	1635	...	...	...	...	...	...	...	...	...	...	...	...	...	...	...
denz ▣ d.	1330	1337	...	*1428*	1437	...	*1507*a	1600	...	*1628*	1700	*1707*a	...	1732	*1737*	...	1837	...	1937	...	*2028*	2037	2137	...	2237	2337
dkirch d.	1346	1358	...	1446	1458	...	1535	1616	...	1646	1716	1730	...	1745	1800	...	1858	...	1958	...	2048	2058	2158	...	2258	2358
uchs a.	|	|	...	|	|	...	1557	|	...	|	|	1753	...	|	1822	...	|	...	|	...	2111	|	|	...	|	|
nbirn d.	1408	1427	...	1508	1527	...	...	1638	...	1708	1738	...	...	1806	...	...	1927	...	2027	...	...	2127	2227	...	2327	0027
t Margrethen d.	|	|	1442	|	|	1533	...	|	1638	|	|	...	1754	|	...	1833	|	1942	|	2033	...	|	|	2256	|	|
genz d.	1416	1443	1455	1516	1542	1548	...	1646	1701	1716	1746	...	1808	1816	...	1848	1942	1955	2042	2048	...	2142	2242	2313	2342	0042
dau Hbf a.	1428	1455	1505	1528	...	1558	...	1658	...	1728	1758	...	...	1826	...	1858	...	2005	...	2058	...	...	...	2323	...	...

															EC 196											
	Ⓐ	A	⚒				A	⚒							Z✕						⚒	P				
dau Hbf d.	...	...	...	...	...	0650	...	...	...	0727	...	0759	*0824*	0903	0955	...	1030	1100	...	...	1200	...	...	...	1229	1330
genz d.	0516	...	0546	0607	0616	0703	...	0711	...	0740	0750	0813	0850	0916	1006	1016	1043	1111	1116	1208	1213	...	1216	...	1242	1343
t Margrethen a.	|	...	|	0620	|	0719	...	|	...	|	0803	|	0903	|	1018	|	|	1124	|	1224	|	...	|	...	1258	|
nbirn d.	0532	...	0602	...	0632	...	...	0722	...	0750	...	0822	...	0932	...	1032	1052	...	1132	...	1222	...	1232	...	...	1352
uchs d.	|	0602	|	...	|	...	0717	|	0748	|	...	|	...	|	...	|	|	...	|	...	|	1227	|	1254	...	|
dkirch d.	0601	0624	0632	...	0703	...	0742	0745	0812	0815	...	0844	...	1003	...	1103	1113	...	1203	...	1244	1250	1303	1316	...	1414
denz ▣ a.	0621	...	0652	...	0723	...	...	0800	...	0828	...	0859	...	1023	...	1123	*1132*	...	1223	...	1259	...	1323	*1332*	...	1427
chruns ▣ a.	0645	...	...	...	...	...	...	...	...	...	...	0922v	...	...	...	...	...	...	1256	...	...	...	...	...	...	1457

			EC 194														*EC* 192					*EC* 190				
			Z✕							A							Z✕				A	Z✕				
dau Hbf d.	1400	1415	1456	1501	...	1533	...	1625	...	...	1703	1729	...	1800	...	1830	1855	1903	*1933*a	2001	...	2056	...	2127	2203	2332
genz d.	1411	1428	1507	1513	...	1546	1608	1638	...	...	1716	1742	...	1811	1816	1843	1906	1916	1950	2012	...	2107	2116	2147	2216	2344
t Margrethen a.	1424	|	1519	|	...	|	1624	1654	...	...	|	|	...	1824	|	|	1918	|	2003	|	...	2119	|	2203	|	|
nbirn d.	...	1436	...	1522	...	1602	...	...	...	...	1732	1752	...	...	1832	1853	...	1932	...	2022	...	...	2132	...	2232	2356
uchs d.	...	|	...	|	1602	|	...	...	1702	1733	|	|	1803	...	|	|	...	|	...	|	2055	...	|	...	|	|
dkirch d.	...	1506	...	1544	1624	1633	...	...	1724	1755	1803	1814	1825	...	1903	1914	...	2003	...	2044	2117	...	2203	...	2303	0017
denz ▣ a.	...	1526	...	1559	...	1653	...	...	*1753*a	...	1823	1832	*1853*a	...	1923	*1932*	...	2023	...	2059	*2132*	...	2223	...	2323	*0035*
chruns ▣ a.	...	...	...	1623	...	...	...	...	...	...	...	...	...	...	...	...	...	...	...	...	...	...	...	...	...	...

①–⑤ (not Dec. 25, 26, Jan. 1, Mar. 24, May 12).
①–⑥ (not Dec. 25, 26, Jan. 1, Mar. 24, May 12).

Z – (12) and ✕ Zürich - St Gallen - Lindau - München and v.v. See also Table **75**.

a – Ⓐ only.
r – ⚒ only.

v – ⑦ Dec. 9 - Mar. 9 (daily Dec. 23 - Jan. 6, Feb. 10–17 and Mar. 16–24).

- Complete service **Bludenz - Schruns** and v.v. (*12 km*, journey 20 minutes). Operated by Montafonerbahn AG ✆ +43 (0) 5556 9000.
From Bludenz at 0540 Ⓐ, 0625 ⚒, 0703, 0737, 0803, 0833, 0937, 1037, 1137, 1204 ⚒, 1235, 1307 ⚒, 1337, 1437, 1537, 1603, 1635, 1707, 1737, 1804, 1837, 1937, 2037, 2137, 2237.
From Schruns at 0512 Ⓐ, 0540 ⚒, 0625, 0703, 0737, 0803, 0903, 1003, 1105, 1137 ⚒, 1204, 1235 ⚒, 1307, 1337, 1505, 1537, 1603, 1635, 1707, 1737, 1804, 1903, 2003, 2103, 2203.

953 🚌 IMST - ÖTZTAL - OBERGURGL and ST ANTON - LECH ÖBB-Postb

km	🚌 Route 4194			Ⓐ	Ⓒ								Ⓐ	Ⓒ	Ⓐ	Ⓒ				Ⓐ	Ⓒ		
0	**Imst** (Postamt)	d.	0615	0640	0655	...	0755	0855	0955	1055	1140	...	1235	1255	1325	1355	...	1455	1555	1645	1655	...	1800	19
13	**Ötztal** (Bahnhof)	a.	0629	0654	0709	...	0809	0909	1009	1109	1154	...	1249	1309	1339	1409	...	1509	1609	1659	1709	...	1814	19
13	**Ötztal** (Bahnhof)	d.	0630	0700	0715	...	0815	0915	1015	1115	1200	...	1250	1315	1345	1415	...	1515	1615	1705	1715	...	1815	19
21	Oetz (Posthotel Kassel)	d.	0644	0714	0729	...	0829	0929	1029	1129	1214	...	1304	1329	1359	1429	...	1529	1629	1719	1729	...	1829	19
54	Sölden (Postamt)	d.	0732	0802	0817	...	0917	1017	1117	1217	1317	...	1352	1417	1447	1517	...	1617	1717	1807	1817	...	1917	20
58	Zwieselstein (Gh Neue Post)	d.	0740	0810	0825	...	0925	1025	1125	1225	1325	...	1400	1425	1455	1525	...	1625	1725	1815	1825	...	1925	20
68	**Obergurgl** (Zentrum)	a.	0755	0825	0840	...	0940	1040	1140	1240	1340	...	1415	1440	1510	1540	...	1640	1740	1830	1840	...	1940	20

🚌 Route 4194		Ⓐ	Ⓒ	Ⓐ		Ⓐ	Ⓒ				Ⓐ	Ⓒ	Ⓐ	Ⓒ	Ⓐ	Ⓒ	Ⓐ	Ⓒ					
Obergurgl (Zentrum)	d.	...	...	...	...	0645	0710	0815	0915	1015	1100	1115	1200	1215	1255	1315	1355	1415	...	1515	1615	1715	1815	19
Zwieselstein (Gh Neue Post)	d.	0520	0545	0555	...	0700	0725	0830	0930	1030	1115	1130	1215	1230	1310	1330	1410	1430	...	1530	1630	1730	1830	19
Sölden (Postamt)	d.	0530	0555	0605	...	0710	0735	0840	0940	1040	1125	1140	1225	1240	1320	1340	1420	1440	...	1540	1640	1740	1840	19
Oetz (Posthotel Kassel)	d.	0615	0640	0650	...	0800	0825	0930	1030	1130	1215	1230	1315	1330	1410	1430	1510	1530	...	1630	1730	1830	1930	20
Ötztal (Bahnhof)	a.	0627	0652	0702	...	0812	0837	0942	1042	1142	1227	1242	1327	1342	1422	1442	1522	1542	...	1642	1742	1842	1942	20
Ötztal (Bahnhof)	d.	...	0705	0705	...	0815	0840	0945	1045	1145	1230	1245	1330	1345	1425	1445	1525	1545	...	1645	1745	1845	1945	20
Imst (Postamt)	a.	...	0720	0720	...	0830	0855	1000	1100	1200	1245	1300	1345	1400	1440	1500	1540	1600	...	1700	1800	1900	2000	21

🚌 Route **4248**: **ST ANTON AM ARLBERG - LECH** *20 km* Journey time: 38–46 minutes

From St Anton Bahnhof: 0755, 0855, 0955, 1225, 1455, 1555, 1655 and 1755 ⊙.

From Lech Postamt: 0849, 1049, 1249 ⊙, 1449, 1649 and 1749.

Winter service: **Valid Dec. 9 - Apr. 20.**

☛ All services call at St Christoph am Arlberg and Zürs.

⊙ – Dec. 15 - Apr. 13 only.

954 🚌 LANDECK - NAUDERS - SCUOL and MALLES Valid until June 20, 20

		⚒		⚒					⚒										⚒						
Landeck-Zams (Bahnhof) **951**	d.	...	0650	...	0750	...	0950	...	1050	...	1150	...	...	1250	...	1350	...	...	...	1650	...	...	1750	1855	
Ried im Oberinntal (Postamt)	d.	...	0718	...	0818	...	1018	...	1118	...	1218	...	...	1318	...	1418	...	...	...	1718	...	...	1818	1923	
Martina (posta) 🛃	d.	...	|	...	0900	0901	|	...	1200	1201	1300	1301	...	1400	1401	1500	1501	...	...	1800	1801	...	|	|	
Scuol-Tarasp (staziun) **546**	a.	...	|	...	|	0928	|	...	|	1228	|	1328	...	|	1428	|	1528	...	...	|	1828	...	|	|	
Nauders (Postamt)	d.	...	0758	0847	0913	...	1058	1132	1213	...	1313	...	1332	1413	...	1513	...	1532	1732	1813	...	1832	1858	2005	
Reschenpass / Passo di Resia 🛃	d.	0740	...	0855	...	...	...	1140	...	...	...	...	1340	...	...	...	...	1540	1740	...	...	1840	...	2013	20
Resia	d.	0744	...	0859	...	...	...	1144	...	...	...	...	1344	...	...	...	...	1544	1744	...	...	1844	...	...	20
Malles Stazione **597**	a.	0816	...	0931	...	...	...	1216	...	...	...	...	1416	...	...	...	...	1616	1816	...	...	1916	...	...	20

			⚒					⚒	†						⚒		†			⚒					
Malles Stazione **597**	d.	...	0758	...	...	...	...	0942	1042	...	...	1242	...	...	1342	...	1442	...	...	1642	...	...	1720	...	19
Resia	d.	...	0830	...	...	...	...	1014	1114	...	...	1319	...	...	1414	...	1514	...	...	1714	...	...	1752	...	20
Passo di Resia / Reschenpass 🛃	d.	...	0834	...	...	...	...	1018	1118	...	...	1323	...	...	1418	...	1518	...	...	1718	...	...	1756	...	20
Nauders (Postamt)	d.	0605	0842	...	0845	...	0945	1026	1126	...	1145	1331	...	1345	1426	1458	1526	...	1543	1726	...	1745	1804	1816	
Scuol-Tarasp (staziun) **546**	d.	|	...	0830	|	0930	|	...	...	1130	|	...	1330	|	...	|	...	1530	|	...	1730	|	...	|	
Martina (posta) 🛃	d.	|	...	0858	0900	0958	1000	...	...	1158	1200	...	1358	1400	...	|	...	1558	1600	...	1758	1800	...	|	
Ried im Oberinntal (Postamt)	d.	0648	...	...	0942	...	1042	...	...	...	1242	...	...	1442	...	1543	...	...	1642	...	...	1842	...	1857	
Landeck-Zams (Bahnhof) **951**	a.	0715	...	...	1009	...	1109	...	...	...	1309	...	...	1509	...	1610	...	...	1709	...	...	1909	...	1924	

Operators: Landeck – Scuol-Tarasp and v.v.: Bundesbus, Postautostelle, A-6500 Landeck: ✆ +43 (0) 5442 64 422.
Auto da posta, Agentura Scuol, CH-7550 Scuol: ✆ +41 (0) 81 86 41 683, Fax +41 (0) 81 86 49 148.

Malles – Nauders and v.v.: SAD – Servizi Autobus Dolomiti, Via Conciapelli 60, I-39100 Bolzano: ✆ +39 0471 97 12 59, Fax +39 0471 97 00 42.

955 JENBACH - MAYRHOFEN 2nd class only Narrow gauge ZV

km									🚂A								🚂B							
0	**Jenbach** Zillertalbahn §	d.	0652	0722	0822	0852	0922	1022	1047	1122	1152	1222	1322	1422	1452	1522	1516	1622	1722	1752	1822	...	...	...
11	Fügen-Hart △	d.	0709	0740	0840	0910	0940	1040	1118	1140	1210	1240	1340	1440	1510	1540	1548	1640	1740	1810	1840	...	...	...
13	Uderns	d.	0713	0745	0845	0915	0945	1045	1123	1145	1215	1245	1345	1445	1515	1545	1554	1645	1745	1815	1845	...	...	...
17	Kaltenbach-Stumm	d.	0720	0752	0852	0922	0952	1052	1133	1152	1222	1252	1352	1452	1522	1552	1606	1652	1752	1822	1852	...	...	...
21	Aschau im Zillertal △	d.	0727	0759	0859	0929	0959	1059	1142	1159	1229	1259	1359	1459	1529	1559	1613	1659	1759	1829	1859	...	...	...
25	**Zell am Ziller**	d.	0736	0806	0906	0936	1006	1106	1150	1206	1236	1306	1406	1506	1536	1606	1620	1706	1806	1836	1906	...	...	...
32	**Mayrhofen**	a.	0748	0818	0918	0948	1018	1118	1205	1218	1248	1318	1418	1518	1548	1618	1635	1718	1818	1848	1918	...	...	...

										🚂A							🚂B					
Mayrhofen	d.	0547	0642	0755	0835	0935	1005	1035	1135	1235	1248	1305	1335	1435	1535	1605	1635	1705	1735	1835	...	...	...
Zell am Ziller	d.	0559	0655	0807	0852	0952	1022	1052	1152	1252	1305	1322	1352	1452	1552	1622	1652	1721	1752	1852	...	...	...
Aschau im Zillertal △	d.	0606	0702	0813	0859	0959	1029	1059	1159	1259	1314	1329	1359	1459	1559	1629	1659	1729	1759	1859	...	...	...
Kaltenbach-Stumm	d.	0612	0708	0819	0907	1007	1037	1107	1207	1307	1323	1337	1407	1507	1607	1637	1707	1737	1807	1907	...	...	...
Uderns	d.	0618	0714	0824	0914	1014	1044	1114	1214	1314	1333	1344	1414	1514	1614	1644	1714	1746	1814	1914	...	...	...
Fügen-Hart △	d.	0623	0719	0829	0919	1019	1049	1119	1219	1319	1339	1349	1419	1519	1619	1649	1719	1753	1819	1919	...	...	...
Jenbach Zillertalbahn §	a.	0640	0736	0846	0936	1036	1106	1136	1236	1336	1401	1406	1436	1536	1636	1706	1736	1820	1836	1936	...	...	...

A – Daily Dec. 25 - Jan. 6, Mar. 21–24 and May 3 - Oct. 19 (also ③ Jan. 9 - Mar. 19).
B – Daily May 31 - Sept. 7 (also ⑤⑥ Sept. 12 - Oct. 4).

🚂 – Steam train. Special fares apply.
§ – Adjacent to ÖBB station.

* – **Operator**: Zillertaler Vehrkehrsbetriebe, Austraf
A-6200 Jenbach. ✆ +43 (0) 5244 606 0.

956 JENBACH - ACHENSEE *Achenseebahn* 2nd class or

Narrow gauge rack railway operated by steam locomotives. Special fares apply. **Service May 31 - October 5, 2008***.

km										
0	**Jenbach** Achensee-Bahnhof §	d.	0840	1015	1055	1210	1345	1455	1645	...
5	Maurach	d.	0915	1050	1130	1245	1420	1530	1720	...
7	**Achensee** Seespitz-Bahnstation	a.	0925	1100	1140	1255	1430	1540	1730	...

Achensee Seespitz-Bahnstation	d.	0930	1110	1225	1400	1510	1555	...	17
Maurach	d.	0937	1117	1232	1407	1517	1602	...	17
Jenbach Achensee-Bahnhof §	a.	1010	1150	1305	1440	1550	1635	...	18

§ – Adjacent to ÖBB station.

Operator: Achenseebahn AG, A-6200 Jenbach: ✆ +43 (0) 5244 62243, Fax +43 (0) 5244 622435

* – Service May 1–30 and October 6–26: **Jenbach** → **Achensee** at 1105, 1305, 1505; **Achensee** → **Jenbach** at 1200, 1400, 1600.

957 MAYRHOFEN - (🚌) - KRIMML - ZELL AM SEE 2nd class or

km	🚌 *Routes* **4094/670**		🚌 *June 7 - Oct. 5, 2008 (summer service only)*							
				A				A		
0	**Mayrhofen** Bahnhof	d.	0830	...	...	...	...	...	...	1830
8	Zell am Ziller Bahnhof	d.	0852	...	1112	...	1332	...	1612	1847
28	**Gerlos** Gasthaus Oberwirt	d.	0927	...	1147	...	1407	...	1647	1920
37	Königsleiten Sessellift	d.	0940	0955	1200	...	1420	1655	1700	...
50	Krimml Wasserfälle	d.	...	1028	...	...	...	1728	...	...
53	**Krimml** Bahnhof	a.	...	1034	...	...	...	1734	...	...

🚌 *Routes* **4094/670**		🚌 *June 7 - Oct. 5, 2008 (summer service only)*							
			A					A	
Krimml Bahnhof	d.	...	0835	...	...	...	...	1518	
Krimml Wasserfälle	d.	...	0842	...	...	...	...	1532	
Königsleiten Sessellift	d.	...	0905	0950	1200	...	1450	1555	17
Gerlos Gasthaus Oberwirt	d.	0700	...	1003	1213	...	1503	...	17
Zell am Ziller Bf	a.	0734	...	1036	1246	...	1536	...	18
Mayrhofen Bahnhof	a.	0750	...	...	...	...	...	...	18

Train (narrow gauge) / 🚌 : KRIMML - ZELL AM SEE ⊡

km			⚒🚌	Ⓐ🚌	Ⓒ		⑥n	🚌	Ⓒ		Ⓐ🚌	Ⓐ		🚌		⚒🚌	Ⓐ		🚌	Ⓐ		Ⓐ🚌	Ⓐ🚌		🚌	Ⓐ
	Krimml Wasserfälle	d.	0443	0543	0525*	...	0548*	0633	0728*	...	0808	...	0928*	1008	1128*	1208	1228*	1328*	1408	1428*	1528*	1608	1708	1728*	1808	19
0	**Krimml** Bahnhof	d.	0449	0549	0531*	...	0554*	0639	0734*	...	0814	0834*	0934*	1014	1134*	1214	1234*	1334*	1414	1434*	1534*	1614	1714	1734*	1814	19
24	Mittersill	d.	|	|	0608	0608	0632	|	0814	0814	|	0914	1014	|	1214	|	1326	1414	|	1514	1614	|	|	1814	|	
53	**Zell am See**	a.	0558	0658	0703	0703	0729	0800	0908	0908	0935	1008	1108	1135	1308	1335	1426	1508	1535	1608	1708	1735	1835	1908	1935	20

		Ⓐ🚌		Ⓐ🚌	🚌		Ⓐ🚌	⚒🚌		Ⓐ	🚌		Ⓐ		🚌		Ⓑw	†🚌	n🚌	Ⓐ🚌		Ⓒ🚌	Ⓐ🚌	b🚌	🚌
Zell am See	d.	0607	0626	0720	0820	0849	0920	1020	1049	1149	1220	1249	1349	1449	1620	1649	1749	...	1750	1820	1849	...	1920	1950	20
Mittersill	a.	|	0720	|	|	0943	|	|	1143	1243	|	1356	1443	1543	|	1743	1843	1845	|	1857	1943	1945	1957	|	
Krimml Bahnhof	a.	0718	0754*	0834	0938	1018*	1038	1138	1218*	1318*	1338	1411z	1518*	1618*	1738	1818*	...	1918	1908	1933	...	2018	2033	2100	21
Krimml Wasserfälle	a.	0727	0804*	...	0947	1027*	1047	1147	1227*	1327*	1347	1420z	1527*	1627*	1747	1827*	...	1927	1917	1942	...	2027	2042	2108	22

A – July 5 - Sept. 28. Subject to confirmation.
b – Ⓑ (also Nov. 1; not Dec. 24, 31).
n – ⑥ (also Dec. 24, 31; not Nov. 1).

w – Not Dec. 24, 25, 31, Jan. 5, Mar. 23, Apr. 30, May 11, 21, Aug. 14, Oct. 31, Dec. 7.
z – By 🚌 from Uttendorf-Stubachtal (a. 1327, d. 1330).

* – By 🚌 to / from Mittersill.
⊡ – Runs year round (rail services currently replaced by 🚌 between Krimml and Mittersill). On Dec. 24, 31 services run as on ⑥.

WÖRGL - ELLMAU - KITZBÜHEL and ST JOHANN — 958

BB-Postbus routes **4006**, **4060**, **4902**

	Ⓐ	⑥k	⚒	⚒	⚒	⚒	⚒			⚒		Ⓐ	⚒	Ⓑm	⚒		⚒	✝	⚒	Ⓐ	⚒	⑥k	Ⓐ	Ⓑm
örgl Bahnhof ... d.	0550	...	...	0645	0740	...	0845	...	...	1120	...	1210	1210	...	...	...	1400	...	1615	...	1720	...	1825	...
Kufstein Bahnhof ... d.	*0545*	*0545*	...	|	*0735*	...	|	*0845*	1110	|	1210	|	|	...	...	1350	|	...	*1620*	...	*1720*	1800	|	*1830*
l (Dorf) ... d.	0610	0612	...	0705	0802	...	0917	0917	1137	1140	1240	1240	1240	1240	...	1414	1430	1545	1645	...	1750	1824	1855	1855
heffau (Gh zum Wilder Kaiser) ... d.	0617	0619	...	...	0809	...	0927	0927	...	1147	...	1247	1247	1247	...	...	1439	1552	1653	...	1800	...	1903	1903
nau (Dorf) ... d.	0626	0628	0630	...	0818	0900	0942	0942	...	1203	...	1303	1303	1303	1315	...	1456	1604	1706	1715	1815	...	1914	1914
Kitzbühel Bahnhof ... a.	|	|	0654t	...	|	0924t	|	|	...	|	...	|	...	|	1345	...	|	|	|	1745	|	...	|	|
Johann in Tirol Bahnhof ... a.	0644	0646	...	...	0836	...	1002	1002	...	1225	...	1325	...	1325	...	...	1516	1627	1730	...	1835	...	1930	1930

	⚒	Ⓐ	⚒	✝	⚒	⚒			⚒		⚒	Ⓐ	⑥		⚒		⚒	Ⓐ	Ⓑ	Ⓐ	⚒	Ⓐ	Ⓐ	Ⓐ
Johann in Tirol Bahnhof ... d.	0535	0535	0730	0750	...	0840	...	1055	1055	...	...	1230	...	1330	1330	...	1550	...	1700	1700	1740	...	...	1850
Kitzbühel Bahnhof ... d.	|	|	|	|	0800	|	...	|	|	...	1215	|	...	|	|	...	|	1620	|	|	|	...	1815	|
nau (Dorf) ... d.	0552	0552	0748	0812	0830	0902	...	1117	1117	...	1245	1257	1303	1352	1352	...	1612	1650	1722	1722	1759	...	1843	1909
heffau (Gh zum Wilder Kaiser) ... d.	0559	0559	0755	0818	...	0908	...	1123	1123	...	...	1303	1309	1358	1358	...	1618	...	1728	1728	1805	...	...	1915
l (Dorf) ... d.	0612	0615	0805	0832	...	0925	0925	1137	1140	1240	...	1320	1323	1412	1415	1545	1635	...	1742	1745	1817	1855	...	1924
Kufstein Bahnhof ... a.	*0640*	|	*0830*	...	...	|	0950	*1202*	|	1305	...	*1355*	|	*1445*	|	1615	*1715*	...	...	*1812*	*1850*	|	...	*1945*
örgl Bahnhof ... a.	...	0645	0835	...	...	0955	...	...	1210	...	...	1350	1350	...	1445	...	1705	...	...	1808	...	1915	...	...

- Not Nov. 1. **m** – Also Nov. 1. **t** – 6–7 minutes later on ⑥.

ZELL AM SEE - HINTERGLEMM — 958a

BB-Postbus Route **680**

km		⚒	E	E		E		E		A		A		A	E
0	**Zell am See** Bahnhof ... d.	0610p	0655	0820	0920	1020	1120	1220	1320	1420	1520	1620	1720	1820	1920
20	Saalbach Schattberg ... a.	0637	0724	0852	0952	1052	1152	1252	1352	1452	1552	1652	1752	1852	1952
23	**Hinterglemm** Ellmauweg ... a.	0643	0731	0859	0959	1059	1159	1259	1359	1459	1559	1659	1759	1859	1959

	⚒	⚒		E		E		E		A		A	E	A	
nterglemm Ellmauweg ... d.	0621	0657	0755	0920	1020	1120	1220	1320	1420	1520	1620	1720	1820	1913	...
albach Schattberg ... d.	0628	0703	0805	0930	1030	1130	1230	1330	1430	1530	1630	1730	1830	1918	...
l am See Bahnhof ... a.	0700	0735	0839	1004	1104	1204	1304	1404	1504	1604	1704	1804	1904	1944p	...

A – Ⓐ (daily Dec. 9 - Apr. 4 and June 9 - Oct. 3); not Dec. 24, 31.
E – ⚒ (daily Dec. 9 - Apr. 5 and June 9 - Oct. 4).

p – Zell am See Postplatz (not Bahnhof).

Information: ✆ +43 (0) 6542 5444.

Danube shipping: BUDAPEST - BRATISLAVA - WIEN - LINZ - PASSAU — 959

008 service

Hydrofoil services. 🍷.	V	W	B	R	V	V	Z	T	
	[R]♠	[R]♠	[R]◇	⊙	[R]♠	[R]♠	⊙	[R]♠	
en Reichsbrücke ▲ ... d.	...	...	0900	0945	...	...	1815	...	...
en Schwedenplatz ▲ .. d.	0830	0900	|	|	1230	1630	|	2030	...
atislava ... d.	0945	1015	1030u	1115	1345	1745	1945	2145	...
dapest § ... a.	...	...	1430	...	...	...	...	...	...

	Z	V	B	V	R	W	V		T
	⊙	[R]♠	[R]◇	[R]♠	⊙	[R]♠	[R]♠		[R]♠
Budapest § ... d.	...	...	0900	...	...	...	...	...	...
Bratislava ... d.	0715	1030	1330s	1430	1600	1700	1830	...	2230
Wien Schwedenplatz ... a.	|	1145	|	1545	|	1815x	1945	...	2345
Wien Reichsbrücke ▲ ... a.	0900	...	1530	...	1745	...	...	...	...

All sailings convey ✕	④A	J	C	⑦N	D	⑦E	K	D	D
	⊖	⊡	◐	⊖	◐	[R]◐	⊡	◐	◐
en Reichsbrücke ▲ ... d.	...	...	...	0730n	...	0835	...	...	...
lln ... d.	...	...	...	0950n	...	1120	...	...	...
ems an der Donau ... d.	0830	1010	1015	1220	1300	1355	1540	1545	...
rnstein ... d.	0900	1040	1050	1250	1330	1430	1610	1620	...
itz an der Donau ... d.	0955	1140	1145	1345	1420	...	1705	1715	1725
elk ... a.	1120	1300	1315	1510	1540	...	1820	...	1840
ein ... d.	1430	...	...	1820	...	...	...	...	...
nz Nibelungenbrücke ... a.	1830	...	...	2220	...	...	...	...	...

	K	D	C	J	⑥N	③A	⑦F	D	D
	⊡	◐	◐	⊡	⊖	⊖	[R]◐	◐	◐
Linz Nibelungenbrücke ... d.	...	...	...	...	0900	0900	...	...	...
Grein ... d.	...	...	...	...	1200	1200	...	...	...
Melk ... d.	0825	1100	1350	1350	1440	1440	...	1615	...
Spitz an der Donau ... d.	0915	1150	1440	1445	1520	1520	...	1705	1720
Dürnstein ... d.	0940	1210	1510	1515	1600	1600	1640	...	1740
Krems an der Donau ... d.	1005	1240	1530	1535	1620	1620	1700	...	1800
Tulln ... d.	...	...	...	...	1820q	...	1855	...	...
Wien Reichsbrücke ▲ ... a.	...	...	...	...	2030q	...	2100	...	...

All sailings convey ✕	G	M	L
	⊖	⊖	⊖
nz Nibelungenbrücke ... d.	...	*0945*r	1420
hlögen ... d.	...	1425	1755
ernzell ... d.	1440	1615	1935
ssau Liegestelle 11 🏛 d.	1545	1715	2040
ggendorf ... a.	2035	...	...

	L	M	G
	⊖	⊖	⊖
ggendorf ... d.	...	...	0945
ssau Liegestelle 11 🏛 d.	0900	1200	1345
ernzell ... d.	0945	1245	1435
hlögen ... a.	1105	1410	...
nz Nibelungenbrücke ... a.	1405	*1750*r	...

– July 2 - Aug. 28.
– Daily Apr. 26 - Oct. 5.
– Daily Apr. 5 - Oct. 26.
– Daily Apr. 19 - Sept. 28.
– ⑦ May 11 - Sept. 21 (also June 21; not June 1, 15, 22, July 6, Aug. 3, Sept. 4).
– ⑦ May 11 - Sept. 21 (not June 1, 15, July 6, 27, Aug. 3, Sept. 4).

G – ①②③④⑥⑦ Apr. 26 - Oct. 12.
J – Daily Apr. 12 - Oct. 26.
K – Daily May 3 - Oct. 5.
L – ②–⑦ Apr. 26 - Oct. 5 (also ⑥⑦ Oct. 11–26).
M – Mar. 22 - Oct. 12.
N – Apr. 26 - Oct. 5.
R – ③–⑦ Apr. 25 - Oct. 28.
T – Daily May 1 - Sept. 29.
V – Daily Mar. 29 - Nov. 2.
W – © Mar. 1–24; daily May 31 - Nov. 2.
Z – ③–⑦ May 30 - Sept. 1 (also ⑥ May 5–26 and ⑥ Sept. 8–29).

n – Not June 22.
q – Not June 21.
r – ②–⑦ Apr. 26 - Oct. 12. Change ships at Schlögen.
s – Calls to set down only.
u – Calls to pick up only.
x – 1830 on © Mar. 1–24.

§ – Nemzetközi hajóállomás (International shipping terminal).

▲ – DDSG operates Wien cruises Schwedenplatz - Reichsbrücke and v.v. Daily Apr. 1 - Oct. 31. **From Schwedenplatz** (duration 1 hr 55 m) at 1030, 1400 (also 1130, 1500 Apr. 26 - Sept. 28). **From Reichsbrücke** (duration 1 hr 20 m) at 1230, 1600 (also 1330, 1700 Apr. 26 - Sept. 28).

Operators:
⊡ – Brandner Schiffahrt GmbH, Ufer 50, A-3313 Wallsee.
Services are subject to alteration on June 21.
✆ +43 (0) 7433 25 90 21, Fax +43 (0) 7433 25 90 25.
◐ – DDSG Blue Danube Schiffahrt GmbH, Handelskai 265, A-1020 Wien.
✆ +43 (0)1 588 80, Fax +43 (0)1 588 80 440.
⊖ – Wurm und Köck, Höllgasse 26, D-94032 Passau.
✆ +49 (0) 851 929292, Fax +49 (0) 851 35518.
⊙ – SPaP - LOD – Slovenská Plavba a Prístavy - Lodná Osobná Doprava a.s., Fajnorovo nábrežie 2, 811 02 Bratislava. Reservation recommended.
2008 timings not yet available (2007 timings shown).
Bratislava: ✆ +421 2 529 32 226, Fax +421 2 529 32 231.
◇ – Operator: MAHART PassNave, H-1056 Budapest, Belgrád rakpart.
Check-in 60 minutes before departure.
Budapest: ✆ +36 1 4844 005, Fax +36 1 266 4201.
Wien (DDSG): ✆ +43 (0)1 588 80, Fax +43 (0)1 588 80 440.
♠ – *Twin City Liner*. Central Danube GmbH, Handelskai 265, A-1020 Wien.
Check-in 30 minutes before departure.
✆ +43 (0)1 588 80. Internet booking: www.twincityliner.com

SALZBURG - SCHWARZACH - INNSBRUCK — 960

km		*D* 15464	*EN* 464	*REX* 1540			*REX* 1500	*IC* 511		*REX* 1520			*ÖEC* 790	*REX* 1502	*D* 1280	*REX* 1522	*ÖIC* 111	*REX* 1504	*REX* 1524		*IC* 512	*ÖIC* 690	*REX* 1506	*IC* 690 / *D* 840	
				2	2	2	2	🍷	2	2	2	2	✕	2		2	🍷	2	2	2	🍷	🍷	2	C	2
		B	A		⚒	⚒			⚒	Ⓐn	⚒		K		⑥E	P	M		Ⓐn			K		⑤–⑦	
	Wien Westbahnhof **950** ... d.	...	...	...	...	...	...	...	...	...	...	...	...	...	...	...	...	...	...	...	...	0744t	...	0744t	...
0	**Salzburg** Hbf **951 970 975** .. d.	...	...	...	...	...	...	0525	...	0604	...	0618	0704	...	...	0804	0904	...	1004	1018	...	1104	...	1104	...
29	Golling-Abtenau **970** ... d.	...	...	...	...	...	...	|	*0526*	0629	...	0656	0729	...	...	0829	0929	...	1029	1056	...	1129	...	1129	...
	Graz Hbf **975** ... d.	...	2135	...	...	...	...	|	|	|	...	|	|	...	...	|	|	...	|	|	0835	|	...	|	...
53	**Bischofshofen 970 975** ... d.	...	0108	...	...	...	0521	0604	0621	0653	...	0721	0753	...	...	0853	0953	...	1053	1121	1149	1153	...	1153	...
61	St Johann im Pongau **970** ... d.	...	|	...	...	...	0531	▬	0630	0701	...	0730	0801	...	...	0901	1001	...	1101	1130	|	1201	...	1201	...
67	**Schwarzach - St Veit 970** ... a.	...	0121	...	...	...	0536	...	0636	0707	...	0736	0807	...	...	0907	1007	...	1107	1136	1201	1207	...	1207	...
67	**Schwarzach - St Veit** ... d.	0101	0145	...	...	...	0544	...	0637	0709	...	0737	...	0811	...	0909	▬	1011	1109	▬	1202	...	1210	1222	...
99	**Zell am See** ... d.	|	|	...	...	...	0620	...	0713	0743	...	0813	...	0843	0853	0943	...	1043	1143	2	1232	...	1245	1256	...
113	Saalfelden ... a.	|	|	...	...	...	0632	2	0725	0751	...	0825	...	0851	0901	0951	2	1051	1151	⚒	1241	...	1253	1305	...
113	Saalfelden ... d.	|	|	0416	0506	0600	0638		...	...	0806	...	...	0852	0902	...		1052	...	1206	1242	...	...	1306	...
148	St Johann in Tirol ... d.	|	|	0445	0543	0637	0710	0743	...	...	0843	...	...	0921	0935	...	1043	1121	...	1243	1311	...	...	1335	1343
157	**Kitzbühel** ... d.	|	|	0453	0552	0646	0718	0752	...	...	0852	...	...	0929	0944	...	1052	1129	...	1252	1319	...	...	1342	1352
166	Kirchberg in Tirol ... d.	|	|	0503	0603	0657	0728	0803	...	...	0903	...	...	0938	0955	...	1103	1138	...	1303	|	...	...	1351	1403
192	Wörgl ... a.	0244	|	0529	0633	0727	0754	0833	...	...	0933	...	...	0959	1023	...	1133	1159	...	1333	1349	...	...	1412	1433
192	Wörgl **951** ... d.	0255	|	0531	*0638*	0733a	0755	*0845*	...	...	...	...	...	1000	...	...	*1156*	1200	...	...	1350	...	...	*1420*	*1446*
217	Jenbach **951** ... d.	|	|	0551	*0659*	0754a	0812	*0859*	...	...	...	...	...	1017	...	...	*1210*	1215	...	...	1405	...	...	*1442*	*1500*
251	**Innsbruck** Hbf **951** ... a.	0337	0358	0617	*0729*	...	0835	*0920*	...	...	...	...	...	1040	...	...	*1230*	1235	...	...	1425	...	...	*1516*	*1521*

– ZÜRICHSEE – 🛏 1, 2 cl., ▬ 2 cl. and ⟦2⟧ Graz - Buchs 🏛 - Zürich. Conveys from Schwarzach (except when train **B** runs) 🛏 1, 2 cl.*, ▬ 2 cl.* and ⟦2⟧ Beograd (**414**) - Zagreb - Ljubljana - Villach - Schwarzach (**464**) - Zürich.
– From Schwarzach daily Dec. 9 - Jan. 7, Mar. 14–26 (also Feb. 16, 17, 23, 24); ①⑥⑦ Mar. 29 - June 23 (also May 2, 13, 22); daily June 27 - Sept. 8; ①⑥⑦ Sept. 13 - Nov. 1. 🛏 1, 2 cl.*, ▬ 2 cl.* and ⟦2⟧ Beograd (**414**) - Zagreb - Ljubljana - Villach - Schwarzach (**15464**) - Feldkirch (**464**) - Buchs 🏛 - Zürich.
– ⑤–⑦ (also Mar. 24, May 1, 12, 22, Dec. 8). ⟦12⟧ Wien (**690**) - Schwarzach (**840**) - Wörgl.
– ⑥ Dec. 29 - Mar. 22, ⑥ June 28 - Aug. 30 (also Jan. 2, 6, Mar. 24). To München (Table **951**).
– To Klagenfurt (Table **970**).

M – ⟦12⟧ München - Villach - Klagenfurt.
P – Ⓐ (daily Mar. 31 - Oct. 31).

a – Ⓐ only.
n – Not Dec. 24, 31.
t – Departure at 0822 possible by changing trains at Salzburg (see Table **950**).
***** – 🛏 1, 2 cl. and ▬ 2 cl. from Zagreb.

960 SALZBURG - SCHWARZACH - INNSBRUCK

	REX 1526		ÖEC 668	ÖEC 113	REX 1508	REX 1528		EC 115	REX 1510			REX 1530		REX 1512		REX 1532		REX 1554	IC 610	IC 692		REX 1534			
	2 Ⓐn	2	✕ B	✕ M	2	2 Ⓐn	2 Ⓐ	✕ D	2	2	2	2 Ⓐn	2 ⚒	2	2	2 Ⓐn	2	2 Ⓐn	🍷	🍷 L	2	2 Ⓑ	2	2	2
Wien Westbahnhof **950** .... d.	...	...	...	...	...	...	...	...	...	...	...	...	...	...	...	...	...	...	...	1544t	...	...	...	...	...
Salzburg Hbf **951 970 975** .. d.	1204	1218	...	1304	...	1404	...	1504	...	...	1518	1604	...	1704	...	1804	1818	1834	...	1904	...	2004	2118	2218	2318
Golling-Abtenau **970** .... d.	1229	1256	...	1329	...	1429	...	1529	...	...	1556	1629	...	1729	...	1829	1856	1902	...	1929	...	2029	2156	2256	2356
Graz Hbf **975** .... d.	|	|	1035	|	...	|	...	|	...	...	|	|	...	|	...	|	|	|	1635	|	...	|	|	|	|
Bischofshofen 970 975 ...... d.	1253	1321	1349	1353	...	1453	...	1553	...	...	1621	1653	...	1753	...	1853	1921	1927	1949	1953	...	2053	2221	2321	0021
St Johann im Pongau **970**.... d.	1301	1330	|	1401	...	1501	...	1601	...	...	1630	1701	...	1801	...	1901	1930	1936	|	2001	...	2101	2230	2330	0030z
Schwarzach - St Veit 970.... a.	1307	1336	1401	1407	...	1507	...	1607	...	...	1636	1707	...	1807	...	1907	1936	1941	2001	2007	...	2107	2236	2336	0036z
Schwarzach - St Veit.......... d.	1309	▬	1402	▬	1410	1509	...	...	1611	...	1637	1709	...	1809	...	1909	...	▬	2002	...	2010	2109	2237	2353	...
Zell am See .... d.	1343	...	1432	...	1445	1543	...	...	1643	...	1713	1743	...	1843	...	1943	...	...	2032	...	2046	2143	2313	0029	...
Saalfelden .... a.	1351	2	1441	2	1453	1551	...	...	1651	...	1725	1751	...	1851	...	1951	...	2	2041	...	2058	2153	2325	0041	...
Saalfelden .... d.	...	⚒	1442		...	...	1601	...	1652	...	...	...	1806	1852	...	...	...		2042	...	...	...	...	...	...
St Johann in Tirol .... d.	...	1443	1511	1543	...	...	1638	...	1721	1743	...	...	1843	1921	1943	...	...	2043	2111	...	...	...	...	...	...
Kitzbühel .... d.	...	1452	1519	1552	...	...	1647	...	1729	1752	...	...	1852	1929	1952	...	...	2052	2119	...	...	...	...	...	...
Kirchberg in Tirol .... d.	...	1503	|	1603	...	...	1658	...	1738	1803	...	...	1903	1938	2003	...	...	2103	|	...	...	...	...	...	...
Wörgl.............................. a.	...	1533	1549	1633	...	...	1728	...	1759	1833	...	...	1933	1959	2033	...	...	2133	2149	...	...	...	...	...	...
Wörgl **951**........................ d.	...	...	1550	*1645*	...	...	*1735*	...	1800	*1845*	...	...	*1956*	2000	*2045*	...	...	...	2150	...	...	...	...	...	...
Jenbach **951**...................... d.	...	...	1605	*1659*	...	...	*1755*	...	1815	*1859*	...	...	*2010*	2015	*2059*	...	...	...	2205	...	...	...	...	...	...
Innsbruck Hbf **951**............. a.	...	...	1626	*1720*	...	...	*1823*	...	1835	*1920*	...	...	*2030*	2035	*2120*	...	...	...	2225	...	...	...	...	...	...

	EN 465		D 15465		REX 1501	REX 1521	REX 1503	IC 791			REX 1523			REX 1505	IC 693	IC 515		REX 1525		REX 1507	EC 114		REX 1527	REX 1509	ÖEC 112
	G	2 ⚒	F	2 ⚒	2	2 ⚒	2	🍷 K	2 ⚒	2	2 Ⓐn	2	2 ⚒	2	🍷 K	🍷	2 ⚒	2 P	2	2	✕ D	2 ⚒	2 Ⓐn	2	✕ M
Innsbruck Hbf **951**............. d.	0143	...	0158	...	...	...	*0500e*	...	...	...	...	*0536v*	*0623*	...	...	0735	...	...	*0824*	0925	...	*0930*	...	...	...
Jenbach **951**...................... d.	|	...	|	...	...	...	*0519e*	...	...	...	...	*0602v*	*0648*	...	...	0755	0801a	...	*0843*	0945	...	*0950*	...	...	...
Wörgl **951**........................ a.	0216	...	0233	...	...	...	*0533e*	...	...	...	...	*0621v*	*0708*	...	...	0809	0823a	...	*0857*	0958	...	*1003*	...	...	...
Wörgl.............................. d.	0217	...	0234	...	...	...	0545	...	0600	...	...	0627	0715	...	...	0810	0827	...	0927	0959	...	1027	...	...	...
Kirchberg in Tirol .... d.	|	...	|	...	...	...	0611	...	0631	...	...	0658	0746	...	...	|	0858	...	0958	1021	...	1058	...	...	...
Kitzbühel .... d.	|	...	|	...	...	...	0620	...	0642	...	...	0709	0757	...	...	0840	0909	...	1009	1029	...	1109	...	...	...
St Johann in Tirol .... d.	|	...	|	...	...	...	0628	...	0651	...	...	0717	0806	...	...	0848	0917	...	1017	1037	...	1117	...	...	...
Saalfelden .... a.	|	...	|	...	...	...	0659	...	0727	...	...	...	0842	...	...	0917	▬	...	...	1106	...	...	...	...	...
Saalfelden .... d.	|	...	|	...	0459	0607	0707	...	...	0734	0807	...	...	0906	...	0918	...	1007	...	1107	...	...	1207	1306	...
Zell am See .... d.	|	...	|	...	0508	0617	0717	...	...	0746	0817	...	...	0916	...	0929	2	1017	...	1117	...	...	1218	1316	...
Schwarzach - St Veit.......... a.	0355	...	0414	...	0541	0649	0749	...	...	0821	0849	...	...	0949	...	0958		1049	...	1149	...	...	1250	1349	...
Schwarzach - St Veit 970.... d.	0400	...	...	0453	0542	0652	...	0752	...	0823	0852	...	...	...	0952	0959	1023	1052	...	...	1152	...	1252	...	1352
St Johann im Pongau **970**.... d.	|	...	...	0458	0548	0658	...	0758	...	0828	0858	...	...	...	0958	|	1028	1058	...	...	1158	...	1258	...	1358
Bischofshofen 970 975 ...... d.	0413	0439	...	0509	0557	0708	...	0808	...	0839	0908	...	...	...	1008	1013	1039	1108	...	...	1208	...	1308	...	1408
Graz Hbf **975** .... a.	0737	|	...	|	|	|	...	|	...	|	|	...	...	...	|	1325	|	|	...	...	|	...	|	...	|
Golling-Abtenau **970** .... d.	...	0503	...	0533	0619	0730	...	0830	...	0903	0930	...	...	...	1030	...	1103	1130	...	...	1230	...	1330	...	1430
Salzburg Hbf **951 970 975** .. a.	...	0540	...	0610	0645	0755	...	0855	...	0940	0955	...	...	...	1055	...	1140	1155	...	...	1255	...	1355	...	1455
Wien Westbahnhof **950** .... a.	...	...	...	...	...	...	...	...	...	...	...	...	...	...	1418r	...	...	...	...	...	...	...	...	...	...

		ÖEC 669		REX 1529		REX 1511	REX 1531	REX 1513	ÖIC 691		IC 613			REX 1533	REX 1545		D 1281	REX 1515	ÖIC 110				REX 1517	REX 1519	REX 1549
	2	✕ B	2 ⚒	2 Ⓐn	2	C	2 Ⓐn	2	🍷 K	2	🍷	2	2 ⚒	2 Ⓐn	2	2 ⚒	⑥E	2	🍷 M	2	2	2	2	2	2
Innsbruck Hbf **951**............. d.	*1037*	1135	...	...	*1237*	1320	...	...	...	*1437*	1535	...	...	...	*1612a*	...	...	1724	...	...	*1730*	*1837*	1925	*2130*	2342
Jenbach **951**...................... d.	*1058*	1155	...	...	*1258*	1342	...	...	...	*1458*	1555	...	...	...	*1641a*	...	...	1746	...	...	*1751*	*1858*	1945	*2150*	0016
Wörgl **951**........................ a.	*1112*	1209	...	...	*1312*	1358	...	...	...	*1512*	1609	...	...	...	*1701a*	...	...	1759	...	...	*1804*	*1912*	1958	*2203*	0038
Wörgl.............................. d.	1127	1210	1227	...	1327	1359	*1427*	...	...	1527	1610	...	1627	...	1706	...	1735	1800	...	...	1827	1927	1959	2208	0039
Kirchberg in Tirol .... d.	1158	|	1258	...	1358	1421	*1458*	...	...	1558	|	...	1658	...	1732	...	1805	1822	...	...	1858	1958	2026	2235	0104
Kitzbühel .... d.	1209	1240	1309	...	1409	1429	*1509*	...	...	1609	1640	...	1709	...	1741	...	1816	1830	...	...	1909	2009	2035	2244	0113
St Johann in Tirol .... d.	1217	1248	1317	...	1417	1437	*1518*	...	...	1617	1648	...	1718	...	1750	...	1825	1838	...	...	1917	2017	2043	2252	0121
Saalfelden .... a.	...	1317	▬	...	...	1506	*1554*	...	...	...	1717	...	1754	...	1826	...	1856	1907	...	...	...	...	2113	2322	0151
Saalfelden .... d.	...	1318	...	1407	...	1507	1607	1706	...	...	1718	1734	...	1807	...	1834v	1857	1908	...	1934	...	...	2114	▬	...
Zell am See .... d.	...	1329	2	1418	...	1517	1617	1716	...	...	1729	1746	...	1817	...	1846v	1906	1918	...	1946	...	...	2126	2	...
Schwarzach - St Veit.......... a.	...	1358		1450	...	1549	1649	1749	...	...	1758	1821	...	1849	...	1921v	...	1950	...	2021	...	...	2201		...
Schwarzach - St Veit 970.... d.	...	1359	1423	1452	...	1553	1652	...	1752	...	1759	1823	...	1852	...	1923	...	...	1953	2023	...	...	*2223*	2323	...
St Johann im Pongau **970**.... d.	...	|	1428	1458	...	1559	1658	...	1758	...	|	1828	...	1858	...	1928	...	...	1959	2028	...	...	*2228*	2328	...
Bischofshofen 970 975 ...... d.	...	1413	1439	1508	...	1608	1708	...	1808	...	1813	1839	...	1908	...	1939	...	...	2009	2039	...	...	*2239*	2337	...
Graz Hbf **975** .... a.	...	1725	|	|	...	|	|	...	|	...	2125	|	...	|	...	|	...	...	|	|	...	...	|	...	...
Golling-Abtenau **970** .... d.	...	...	1503	1530	...	1630	1730	...	1830	...	...	1903	...	1930	...	2003	...	...	|	2103	...	...	*2303*	...	...
Salzburg Hbf **951 970 975** .. a.	...	...	1540	1555	...	1655	1755	...	1855	...	...	1940	...	1955	...	2040	...	...	2048	2140	...	...	*2340*	...	...
Wien Westbahnhof **950** .... a.	...	...	...	...	...	...	...	...	2218q	...	...	...	...	...	...	...	...	...	...	...	...	...	...	...	...

B – To / from Bregenz (Table **951**).
C – [2] Innsbruck - Salzburg; on Ⓒ conveys [12] Innsbruck - Salzburg (*ÖIC* **15741**) - Wien.
D – WÖRTHERSEE – [12] and ✕ Klagenfurt - München - Dortmund and v.v.
E – ⑥ Dec. 22 - Mar. 22, ⑥ June 21 - Aug. 23 (also Jan. 2). From München (Table **951**).
F – From Zürich daily Dec. 9 - Jan. 6, Mar. 13 – 25 (also Feb. 15, 16, 22, 23); ⑤⑥⑦ Mar. 28 - June 22 (also May 1, 12, 21); daily June 26 - Sept. 7; ⑤⑥⑦ Sept. 12 - Oct. 31. 🛏 1, 2 cl.*, ▬ 2 cl.* and [2] Zürich (**465**) - Buchs 🏛 - Feldkirch (**15465**) - Schwarzach (**415**) - Villach - Ljubljana - Zagreb - Beograd.
G – ZÜRICHSEE – 🛏 1, 2 cl., ▬ 2 cl. and [2] Zürich - Buchs 🏛 - Graz. Conveys daily from Zürich (except when train **F** runs) 🛏 1, 2 cl.*, ▬ 2 cl.* and [2] Zürich (**465**) - Schwarzach (**415**) - Villach - Ljubljana - Zagreb - Beograd.
K – From Klagenfurt (Table **970**).
L – To Villach (Table **970**).
M – [12] Klagenfurt - München and v.v.
P – Ⓐ (daily Mar. 31 - Oct. 31).
a – Ⓐ only.
e – ①-⑥ (not Dec. 24, 25, 26, 31, Jan. 1, Mar. 24, May 12, Aug. 16).
n – Not Dec. 24, 31.
q – Arrival at 2142 possible by changing trains at Salzburg (see Table **950**).
r – Arrival at 1338 possible by changing trains at Salzburg (see Table **950**).
t – Departure at 1622 possible by changin trains at Salzburg (see Table **950**).
v – ⚒ only.
z – Bischofshofen - Schwarzach on † only.
* – 🛏 1, 2 cl. and ▬ 2 cl. to Zagreb.

961 ATTNANG-PUCHHEIM - STAINACH-IRDNING

2nd class only

km		⚒							E										
0	**Attnang-Puchheim** ....d.	...	...	0605	0713	0818	0913	1015	1113	1215	1313	1415	1513	1615	1711	1815	1913	2015	2115
12	**Gmunden**..........................d.	...	...	0623	0731	0838	0928	1036	1128	1236	1328	1436	1528	1636	1728	1836	1928	2033	2133
17	Altmünster am Traunsee .....d.	...	...	0629	0736	0844	0934	1041	1134	1241	1334	1441	1534	1641	1734	1841	1934	2039	2140
22	Traunkirchen.......................d.	...	...	0634	0742	0849	0940	1047	1140	1247	1340	1447	1540	1647	1740	1847	1940	2044	2145
27	Ebensee Landungsplatz ......d.	...	...	0643	0750	0857	0946	1055	1146	1255	1346	1455	1546	1655	1746	1855	1946	2052	2153
44	**Bad Ischl** ....d.	...	...	0706	0816	0922	1005	1120	1205	1320	1405	1520	1605	1720	1805	1920	2005	2115	2217
54	Bad Goisern.........................d.	...	...	0720	0829	0934	1016	1133	1216	1333	1416	1533	1616	1733	1816	1933	2016	2128	...
64	Hallstatt ⊡ ....d.	...	...	0733	0842	0949	1027	1148	1227	1348	1427	1549	1627	1749	1827	|	|	|	...
67	Obertraun-Dachsteinhöhlen .d.	...	...	0737	0846	0952	1031	1151	1231	1351	1431	1552	1631	1752	1831	1953	2033	2145	...
78	**Bad Aussee** ....d.	0504	0641	0758t	0900	...	1043	...	1243	...	1443	...	1643	...	1843	2005	2045	2157	...
93	Bad Mitterndorf ....d.	0521	0658	0815	0919	...	1101	...	1300	...	1500	...	1701	...	1901	2023	...	...	...
108	**Stainach-Irdning**..............a.	0539	0716	0830	0936	...	1117	...	1316	...	1516	...	1718	...	1918	2039	...	...	...

			⚒									G						Ⓒ	
Stainach-Irdning................ d.	...	...	...	0605v	0725	0841	...	1042	...	1242	...	1442	...	1642	...	1843	1930	1930	2049
Bad Mitterndorf .... d.	...	...	...	0622v	0742	0859	...	1100	...	1259	...	1459	...	1700	...	1900	1946	1946	2107
Bad Aussee........................ d.	...	0500	0601	0647r	0758	0916	...	1116	...	1316	...	1516	...	1716	...	1917	2004	2018	2124
Obertraun-Dachsteinhöhlen.. d.	...	0512	0613	0700	0810	0928	1007	1128	1206	1328	1406	1528	1606	1728	1806	1929	...	2032	...
Hallstatt ⊡ .... d.	...	|	|	0704	0814	0932	1010	1132	1209	1332	1409	1532	1609	1732	1809	|	...	|	...
Bad Goisern .... d.	...	0528	0630	0720	0829	0943	1024	1143	1224	1343	1424	1543	1624	1743	1825	1944	...	2049	...
Bad Ischl .... d.	0441	0541	0643	0733	0842	0954	1037	1154	1237	1354	1437	1554	1637	1754	1838	1954	...	2102	...
Ebensee Landungsplatz....... d.	0503	0604	0710	0758	0906	1015	1104	1215	1304	1415	1504	1615	1704	1815	1904	2015	...	2127	...
Traunkirchen........................ d.	0511	0611	0718	0806	0914	1022	1112	1222	1312	1422	1512	1622	1712	1822	1913	2022	...	2134	...
Altmünster am Traunsee...... d.	0516	0616	0724	0812	0920	1027	1118	1227	1318	1427	1518	1627	1718	1827	1919	2028	...	2140	...
Gmunden............................. d.	0522	0622	0730	0818	0929	1033	1129	1233	1329	1433	1529	1633	1729	1833	1929	2034	...	2145	...
Attnang-Puchheim .... a.	0539	0639	0747	0836	0947	1047	1147	1247	1347	1447	1547	1647	1747	1850	1947	2051	...	2203	...

E – Conveys [12] Wien (**544**) - Attnang-Puchheim - Stainach
G – Conveys [12] Stainach - Attnang-Puchheim (**649/749**) - Wien.

r – Arrives 0640.
t – Arrives 0750.
v – ⚒ only.

⊡ – Connecting ⛴ services operate Hallstatt Bahnhof - Hallstatt Zentrum and v.v. **Operator**: Hallstättersee-Schifffahrt Hemetsberger KE ✆ +43 (0)6134 8228.

Routes 150, 2560 — SALZBURG and ST WOLFGANG - STROBL - BAD ISCHL — 962

Route **150**: Salzburg - Bad Ischl and v.v.

km																									
		⚒	⚒		Ⓐn	⑥k		⚒		⑥k	Ⓐn	Ⓒw	Ⓐn	⚒		Ⓐn	Ⓒw	Ⓐn	Ⓐn		Ⓐn		Ⓐn	†	⚒
0	**Salzburg** Hbf ▲ .... d.	...	0555	...	0625	0645	0815	0915	1015	1115	1115	1215	1215	1315	1415	1515	1615	1625	1725	1815	1845	1915	2015	2115	2230
32	St Gilgen (Busbahnhof) d.	0600	0645	0645	0740	0740	0910	1010	1110	1210	1220	1310	1315	1410	1510	1610	1710	1710	1810	1910	1935	2010	2104	2205	2315
45	Strobl (Busbahnhof) ..... d.	0618	0703	0703	0758	0758	0928	1028	1128	1228	1238	1328	1333	1428	1528	1628	1728	1728	1828	1928	...	2027	...	2221	2331
57	**Bad Ischl** Bahnhof ...... a.	0640	0725	0725	0820	0820	0950	1050	1150	1250	1300	1350	1355	1450	1550	1650	1750	1750	1850	1950	...	2045	...	2240	2350

	Ⓐn	⚒	Ⓐn	Ⓐn	⑥k	Ⓐn	Ⓒw	⚒				⑥k	Ⓐn	Ⓒw	Ⓐn	⑥k	Ⓐn		⚒		Ⓐn		Ⓐn	
ad Ischl Bahnhof .... d.	...	0500	...	...	...	0608	0608	0642	0745	0923	1022	1122	1122	1222	1222	1322	1330	1422	1522	1622	1722	1822	1922	2022
robl (Busbahnhof) .... d.	...	0518	0548	0615	...	0629	0629	0705	0808	0945	1045	1145	1145	1245	1245	1345	1355	1445	1545	1645	1745	1845	1945	2045
Gilgen (Busbahnhof).......... d.	0515	0535	0605	0630	0635	0645	0645	0730	0828	1005	1105	1205	1220	1305	1315	1405	1415	1505	1605	1705	1805	1905	2005	2101
alzburg Hbf ▲ .... a.	0553	0619	0649	0719	0719	0730	0735	0822	0920	1057	1157	1257	1305	1357	1405	1457	1507	1557	1657	1757	1853	1953	2053	...

Route **2560**: St Wolfgang - Bad Ischl and v.v.

km																							
		Ⓐ	⚒	⚒			Ⓐ	Ⓒ				Ⓒ	Ⓐ					Ⓐ					
0	**St Wolfgang** Schafbergbahnhof ‡ ◐ d.	0505	0600	0648	0743	...	0903	0913	1013	1113	1213	1313	1318	1413	1513	1613	1713	1713	1813	1913	2013	...	...
7	Strobl (Busbahnhof) .... d.	0518	0613	0703	0757	...	0918	0927	1028	1127	1228	1327	1333	1428	1527	1628	1727	1728	1827	1927	2027	...	...
19	**Bad Ischl** Bahnhof .... a.	0540	0640	0730*	...	...	0945	...	1055	...	1255	...	1358	1455	...	1655	...	1752	...	...	...	...	...

	Ⓐ	⚒	⚒	†	⚒				⚒		†	⚒	Ⓐ			Ⓐ			Ⓐ		Ⓒ	Ⓐ	
ad Ischl Bahnhof .... d.	...	0642	...	0825	0922	...	...	1120	1215	...	...	...	1415	...	1520	1620	...	1720	1815	...	...	...	...
robl (Busbahnhof) .... d.	0630	0707	0808	|	0945	0945	1045	1145	1245	1245	1328	1355	1445	1445	1545	1645	1645	1745	1845	1846	1930	1945	2045
Wolfgang Schafbergbahnhof ‡ ◐ a.	0645	0722	0823	0859	1000	1000	1100	1200	1300	1300	1340	1410	1500	1500	1600	1700	1700	1800	1900	1900	1945	2000	2100

– Also Dec. 24, 31; not Nov. 1.
– Not Dec. 24, 31.
– Also Dec. 24, 31.
– All services also call at St Wolfgang Markt.
– All services also call at Mirabellplatz.

* – On Ⓐ (not Dec. 24 - Jan. 4, Feb. 18 – 22, Mar. 17 – 25, May 13, July 7 - Sept. 5) change at Bad Ischl Schröpferplatz and arrive 0735.
‡ – The **Schafbergbahn** narrow-gauge steam rack railway operates **St Wolfgang - Schafbergspitze** (*6 km*). Services operate subject to demand (minimum 20 passengers) and weather conditions permitting **April 26 - November 2**. 2nd class only. Special fares payable. **Journey time**: 40 minutes each way. **Information**: ✆ +43 (0) 6138 2232 0.

☛ 🚌 **information**: ✆ Bad Ischl +43 (0) 6132 23113 / Salzburg +43 (0) 662 4660 334.

April 26 - November 2, 2008 — STROBL - ST GILGEN (WOLFGANGSEE) — 964

trobl Schiffstation ⊡ .... d.	...	0850	1000	1130	1300	1430	1600	1730	1855
Wolfgang Markt .... d.	...	0915	1030	1200	1330	1500	1630	1800	1910
Wolfgang Schafbergbahnhof ‡ .. d.	0815	0923	1040	1210	1340	1510	1640	1810	1920
Gilgen Schiffstation ● .... a.	0840	0950	1115	1245	1415	1545	1715	1845	...

St Gilgen Schiffstation ● .... d.	...	0845	1000	1130	1300	1430	1600	1730	1855
St Wolfgang Schafbergbahnhof ‡ d.	0822	0917	1038	1208	1338	1508	1638	1808	1935a
St Wolfgang Markt .... d.	0830	0925	1050	1220	1350	1520	1650	1820	1925
Strobl Schiffstation ⊡ .... a.	0845	0950	1115	1245	1415	1545	1715	1845	...

– Arrival time (calls after St Wolfgang Markt).
– See note under Table **962**.

⊡ – Approximately 400 metres from Strobl Busbahnhof.
● – Approximately 500 metres from St Gilgen Busbahnhof.

2nd class only — LINZ - BRAUNAU - SIMBACH — 965

km																					
		⚒	Ⓐ	⚒			Ⓐ	Ⓒ			⚒	Ⓐ			Ⓐn	Ⓐ	Ⓒ	Ⓐ			
0	**Linz** Hbf **950** .... d.	0457	...	...	0547	...	0712	0737	0920	1107	1220	1220	1320	1520	1620	1640	1720	1720	...	1920	2115
25	**Wels** Hbf **950** .... d.	0524	...	...	0616	0621	0730	0755	0938	1133	1238	1238	1338	1539	1638	1701	1738	1738	...	1938	2136
54	Neumarkt-Kallham **950** d.	0551	0553	0620	0643	0651	0811	0832	1011	1203	1311	1311	1411	1609	1707	1734	1808	1808	...	2011	2205
76	Ried im Innkreis.......... d.	...	0613	0641	...	0714	0832	0853	1032	1225	1337	1337	1434	1630	1729	1753	1830	1834	...	2032	2225
13	**Braunau** am Inn.......... a.	...	...	0717	...	0740	0905	0926	1105	1258	1411	1411	1512	1702	1806	1821	1902	1911	...	2107	...
15	**Simbach** (Inn) 🚌 **893** .. a.	...	...	...	...	0744	0909	0930	1109	1302c	...	1415	1516	1706c	1811	...	...	...	...	...	...

	⚒	Ⓐ	⑥k	†	Ⓐ	⚒	†				⚒	Ⓒ	Ⓐ			Ⓐn	†	⑥k	Ⓐ		
mbach (Inn) 🚌 **893** .. d.	...	...	...	...	...	...	...	0753c	0953	1143	...	1350	1451	1523	...	...	1751	1751	1819	...	...
raunau am Inn.......... d.	...	0512	0512	...	...	0630	0630	0757	0957	1147	1259	1354	1455	1526	1554	1715	1755	1755	1824	...	1957
ed im Innkreis.......... d.	0456	0550	0550	0612	0620	0712	0712	0832	1032	1232	1334	1432	1532	...	1632	1806	1831	1831	1859	...	2032
eumarkt-Kallham **950**.a.	0514	0610	0610	0630	0638	0731	0731	0851	1051	1251	1352	1451	1551	...	1651	1826	1851	1851	1918	1932	2051
els Hbf **950** .... a.	0547	0636	0636	0705	0715	0803	0803	0923	1123	1323	1420	1523	1620n	...	1723	1857	1921	...	...	1959	2122
nz Hbf **950** .... a.	0614	0654	0658	0726	0745	0821	0827	0941	1141	1341	1441	1541	1641n	...	1741	1927	1945	...	...	2027	2145

c – Ⓒ only.
k – Not Nov. 1.
n – Not Dec. 24, 31.

SALZBURG and LIENZ - VILLACH - KLAGENFURT — 970

km		D 297	EN 237		ÖEC 732		D 415	ÖIC 532		REX 1561			REX 1563	REX 1563	ÖIC 534			ÖEC 790	ÖEC 536			ÖIC 111		EC 32	
			R		✕	2		🍷	2	2	2	2	2	2	🍷	2	2	✕	✕	2	2	🍷	2	🍷	2
		♦	♦	⚒	⚒	Ⓐ	♦			⚒	Ⓐ	⚒		⚒			Ⓐ				⚒	♦			Ⓐ
0	**Salzburg** Hbf **960 975** .... d.	0138	0138	...	...	...	...	...	...	...	...	...	...	...	...	...	...	0704	...	...	...	0904	...	...	...
29	Golling-Abtenau **960**............ d.	|	|	...	...	...	...	...	...	...	...	...	...	...	...	...	...	0729	...	...	...	0929	...	...	...
53	**Bischofshofen 960 975** ...... d.	|	|	...	...	...	...	...	...	...	...	...	...	...	...	...	...	0753	...	...	...	0953	...	...	...
61	St Johann im Pongau **960**... d.	|	|	...	...	...	...	...	...	...	...	...	...	...	...	...	...	0801	...	...	...	1001	...	...	...
67	**Schwarzach - St Veit 960** ... a.	0227	0227	...	...	...	...	...	...	...	...	...	...	...	...	...	...	0807	...	...	...	1007	...	...	...
67	**Schwarzach - St Veit**.......... d.	0229	0229	...	...	...	0430	...	...	...	...	...	...	...	...	...	...	0810	...	...	...	1010	...	...	...
86	Bad Hofgastein .... d.	|	|	...	...	...	0447	...	...	...	...	...	...	...	...	...	...	0829	...	...	...	1029	...	...	...
97	Bad Gastein........................... d.	|	|	...	...	...	0502	...	...	...	...	...	...	...	...	...	...	0842	...	...	...	1042	...	...	...
113	Mallnitz-Obervellach ⊠ .... d.	|	|	...	...	...	0518	...	...	...	...	0643	...	...	...	...	...	0856	...	...	...	1056	...	...	...
	Lienz 596......................... d.	|	|	...	...	...	|	...	...	0520	...	|	0628	0628	...	0736	0736	|	...	0923	0923	|	1017	...	...
146	Spittal-Millstättersee .... a.	|	|	...	...	...	0544	...	...	0623	...	0716	0721	0721	...	0831	0831	0923	...	1026	1026	1122	1118x	...	...
146	Spittal-Millstättersee .... d.	|	|	0500	...	...	0546	...	0553v	0635	0639	...	...	0723	0731	...	0834	0925	...	...	1033	1124	1135	...	1236
182	**Villach** Hbf .... a.	0356	0356	0532	...	←	0609	...	0627v	0659	0716	...	...	0747	0804	...	0908	0948	...	...	1106	1147	1209	...	1310
182	**Villach** Hbf **980**................... d.	...	...	→	0537	0545	...	0620	0630	0709	0730	...	...	0750	0820	...	0920	0950	1020	...	1120	1150	...	1220	1335
198	Velden am Wörthersee **980**. d.	...	...	...	|	0601	...	0631	0646	|	0746	...	...	0801	0831	...	0936	1001	1031	...	1136	1201	...	1231	1351
207	Pörtschach am W'see **980** .. d.	...	...	...	|	0609	...	0637	0654	|	0754	...	...	|	0837	...	0944	1008	1037	...	1144	1208	...	1237	1359
220	**Klagenfurt** Hbf **980** .... a.	...	...	...	0559	0624	...	0646	0707	0734	0809	...	...	0816	0846	...	0957	1020	1046	...	1157	1220	...	1246	1414
	Bruck a. d. Mur **980** .... a.	...	...	...	0753	...	...	0859	0952	...	...	...	...	...	1059	...	...	...	1259	...	...	...	...	1459	...
	Wien Südbahnhof **980** ..... a.	...	...	...	0942	...	...	1102	...	...	...	...	...	...	1302	...	...	...	1502	...	...	...	...	1702	...

	ÖIC 690		IC 630					ÖEC 113	ÖEC 530		ÖEC 30	EC 115		ÖIC 632		REX 1565			EC 315		IC 738			IC 692	IC 796 1567
	🍷	2	✕	2	2	2	2	✕	✕	2	R ✕	✕	2	🍷	2	2	2	2	✕	2	🍷	2	2	🍷	§
	W				⚒	Ⓐ	Ⓐ	♦	S			♦	Ⓐ			†	⚒		♦		⑦z		†	W	
alzburg Hbf **960 975** .... d.	1104	...	...	...	...	...	...	1304	...	...	...	1504	...	...	...	...	...	...	1713	...	...	...	...	1904	2104
olling-Abtenau **960** .... d.	1129	...	...	...	...	...	...	1329	...	...	...	1529	...	...	...	...	...	...	|	...	...	...	...	1929	2129
ischofshofen 960 975 ...... d.	1153	...	...	...	...	...	...	1353	...	...	...	1553	...	...	...	...	...	...	1758	...	...	...	...	1953	2153
t Johann im Pongau **960**.... d.	1201	...	...	...	...	...	...	1401	...	...	...	1601	...	...	...	...	...	...	1806	...	...	...	...	2001	2201
chwarzach - St Veit 960.... a.	1207	...	...	...	...	...	...	1407	...	...	...	1607	...	...	...	...	...	...	1812	...	...	...	...	2007	2207
chwarzach - St Veit........... d.	1210	...	...	...	...	...	...	1410	...	...	...	1610	...	...	...	...	...	...	1813	...	...	...	...	2010	2210
ad Hofgastein .... d.	1229	...	...	...	...	...	...	1429	...	...	...	1629	...	...	...	...	...	...	1832	...	...	...	...	2029	2229
ad Gastein.......................... d.	1242	...	...	...	...	...	...	1442	...	...	...	1642	...	...	...	...	...	...	1845	...	...	...	...	2042	2242
allnitz-Obervellach ⊠......... d.	1256	...	...	...	1406r	1406r	...	1456	...	1606	...	1656	...	...	...	...	1802r	...	1859	...	...	...	...	2056	2256
Lienz 596......................... d.	|	1216	...	1316	|	|	1416	|	1504	|	...	|	1616	...	1716	1738	|	1818	|	...	...	1918	2018	|	|
pittal-Millstättersee.............. a.	1322	1319x	...	1419	1436r	1436r	1519	1522	1549	1636	...	1722	1719x	...	1819	1825	1831r	1919	1925	...	...	2017	2117	2122	2322
pittal-Millstättersee.............. d.	1324	1333	...	...	1440	1440	...	1524	1551	1641	...	1723	1731	...	...	1827	1832	...	1926	...	...	2031	...	2124	2323
illach Hbf.......................... a.	1347	1407	...	...	1514	1514	...	1547	1613	1714	...	1746	1805	...	...	1856	1906	...	1949	...	...	2105	...	2149	2347
illach Hbf **980** .... d.	1350	...	1420	...	...	1520	...	1550	1620	1720a	1742	1750	...	1820	...	1858	...	...	...	1954	2005	2110	...	2154	2349
elden am Wörthersee **980**.. d.	1401	...	1431	...	...	1536	...	1601	1631	1736a	|	1801	...	1831	...	1910	...	...	...	2010t	|	2125	...	2209	0005
örtschach am W'see **980** ... d.	1408	...	1437	...	...	1544	...	1608	1637	1744a	|	1808	...	1837	...	1916	...	...	...	2016t	|	2133	...	2217	0011
lagenfurt Hbf **980** .... a.	1420	...	1446	...	...	1557	...	1620	1646	1757a	1804	1820	...	1846	...	1927	...	...	...	2027t	2028	2146	...	2230	0026
Bruck a. d. Mur **980**........... a.	...	...	1659	...	...	...	...	...	1859	...	1956	...	...	2059	...	...	...	...	...	...	2232	...	...	...	...
Wien Südbahnhof **980** ...... a.	...	...	1902	...	...	...	...	...	2102	...	2144	...	...	2302	...	...	...	...	...	...	0025	...	...	...	...

FOR NOTES SEE NEXT PAGE →

970 KLAGENFURT - VILLACH - SALZBURG and LIENZ

km		D 296 ♦	EN 236 Ⓡ ♦	2 ⚒	2	1568 IC 791 ⊖ †	IC 791 H 🍷 ⚒	2 Ⓐ	2	IC 693 🍷 W	2 ⚒	2	EC 114 ✗ ♦	2	ÖEC 31 Ⓡ✗	2	ÖEC 531 ✗ S	ÖEC 112 ✗ ♦	2	2 ⚒	2 ⚒	IC 533 ✗	2	2	EC 314 ✗ ♦
	Wien Südbahnhof **980** d.	...	...	...	...	...	...	...	...	...	...	...	...	...	0630	...	0657	...	...	...	...	0857	...	...	...
	Bruck a. d. Mur **980** d.	...	...	...	...	...	...	...	...	...	...	...	...	0702	0818	...	0901	...	...	...	...	1101	...	...	...
	Klagenfurt Hbf **980** d.	...	...	...	...	0525	0525	0602	0622	0736	0802	...	0936	0941	1013	...	1113	1126	...	1202	...	1313	...	1326	...
	Pörtschach am W'see **980** d.	...	...	...	...	0540	0540	0616	0638	0750	0816	...	0950	0956	|	...	1122	1140	...	1216	...	1322	...	1341	...
	Velden am Wörthersee **980** d.	...	...	...	...	0547	0547	0624	0645	0757	0824	...	0957	1004	|	...	1128	1147	...	1224	...	1328	...	1349	...
	Villach Hbf **980** a.	...	...	...	...	0606	0606	0640	0700	0808	0840	...	1008	1020	1034	...	1139	1158	...	1240	...	1339	...	1405	...
	Villach Hbf d.	0145	0145	0528	...	0609	0611	0655	0710t	0811	0848	...	1011	...	...	1056v	1145	1211	...	1245	...	...	1345	...	1411
	Spittal-Millstättersee a.	|	|	0601	...	0633	0633	0729	0736	0833	0922	...	1033	...	...	1129v	1208	1233	...	1320	...	...	1420	...	1433
0	Spittal-Millstättersee d.	|	|	0603r	0624	0634	0635	...	0738	0835	0926	0926	1035	...	...	1142	1211	1235	1242	1328r	1342	...	→	...	1435
68	**Lienz 596** a.	|	|	|	0727	|	|	...	0833	|	1027	1026	|	...	...	1245	1256	|	1345	|	1445	...	...	...	|
	Mallnitz-Obervellach ⊠ d.	|	|	0633r	...	0703	0703	...	...	0903	...	...	1103	...	...	...	...	1303	...	1358r	...	...	...	...	1503
	Bad Gastein d.	|	|	...	...	0718	0718	...	...	0918	...	...	1118	...	...	...	...	1318	...	...	...	...	...	...	1518
	Bad Hofgastein d.	|	|	...	...	0729	0729	...	...	0929	...	...	1129	...	...	...	...	1329	...	...	...	...	...	...	1529
	Schwarzach - St Veit a.	0314	0314	...	...	0747	0747	...	...	0947	...	...	1147	...	...	...	...	1347	...	...	...	...	...	...	1547
	Schwarzach - St Veit 960 d.	0317	0317	...	...	0752	0752	...	...	0952	...	...	1152	...	...	...	...	1352	...	...	...	...	...	...	1548
	St Johann im Pongau **960** d.	|	|	...	...	0758	0758	...	...	0958	...	...	1158	...	...	...	...	1358	...	...	...	...	...	...	1554
	Bischofshofen 960 975 d.	|	|	...	...	0808	0808	...	...	1008	...	...	1208	...	...	...	...	1408	...	...	...	...	...	...	1603
	Golling-Abtenau **960** d.	|	|	...	...	0830	0830	...	...	1030	...	...	1230	...	...	...	...	1430	...	...	...	...	...	...	|
	Salzburg Hbf **960 975** a.	0405	0405	...	...	0855	0855	...	...	1055	...	...	1255	...	...	...	...	1455	...	...	...	...	...	...	1648

	2	2	2 ⚒	ÖIC 535 🍷	2	ÖIC 691 🍷 W	2	REX 1757 2 ⚒	2 Ⓐ	EC 33 🍷	2 ⚒	ÖIC 110 🍷 ♦	2	2 Ⓐ	2 ⚒	ÖIC 539 🍷	2	ÖEC 797 ✗	2	ÖEC 631 ✗	2 Ⓑ	🚌 ⑤f	ÖEC 633 ✗	2	D 414 ♦
Wien Südbahnhof **980** d.	...	...	...	1057	...	...	...	...	...	1257	...	...	...	...	...	1457	...	...	...	1657	...	...	1827	...	...
Bruck a. d. Mur **980** d.	...	...	...	1301	...	...	...	...	...	1501	...	...	...	...	...	1701	...	...	...	1901	...	...	2018	...	...
Klagenfurt Hbf **980** d.	...	1402v	...	1513	...	1536	...	1620a	...	1713	...	1726	...	1819	...	1913	...	1936	...	2113	...	...	2215	2218	...
Pörtschach am W'see **980** d.	...	1416v	...	1522	...	1550	...	1631a	...	1722	...	1740	...	1831	...	1922	...	1950	...	2122	...	...	|	2232	...
Velden am Wörthersee **980** d.	...	1424v	...	1528	...	1557	...	1637a	...	1728	...	1747	...	1839	...	1928	...	1957	...	2128	...	...	|	2239	...
Villach Hbf **980** a.	...	1440v	...	1539	...	1608	...	1652a	...	1739	...	1758	...	1851	...	1939	...	2008	...	2139	...	...	2236	2255	...
Villach Hbf d.	...	1445	...	...	1545	1611	...	1654	...	...	1746	1811	...	1857	1857	...	1954	2011	...	...	2145	...	...	...	2300
Spittal-Millstättersee a.	←	1520	...	...	1620	1633	←	1727	...	...	1821	1833	←	1930	1930	...	2028	2033	←	...	2217	...	...	...	2323
Spittal-Millstättersee d.	1442	1528	1542	...	→	1635	1642	1728	1742	...	→	1835	1842	...	...	...	→	2035	2042	...	...	2240	...	...	2325
Lienz 596 a.	1546	|	1645	...	...	|	1746	|	1847	...	...	|	1947	...	...	...	...	|	2143	...	...	0005	...	...	|
Mallnitz-Obervellach ⊠ d.	...	1558	...	...	...	1703	...	1756	...	...	...	1903	...	...	...	...	...	2103	...	...	...	...	...	...	2359
Bad Gastein d.	...	...	...	...	...	1718	...	...	...	...	...	1918	...	...	...	...	...	2118	...	...	...	...	...	...	0014
Bad Hofgastein d.	...	...	...	...	...	1729	...	...	...	...	...	1929	...	...	...	...	...	2129	...	...	...	...	...	...	0025
Schwarzach - St Veit a.	...	...	...	...	...	1747	...	...	...	...	...	1947	...	...	...	...	...	2147	...	...	...	...	...	...	0042
Schwarzach - St Veit 960 d.	...	...	...	...	...	1752	...	...	...	...	...	1953	...	...	...	...	...	2148	...	...	...	...	...	...	...
St Johann im Pongau **960** d.	...	...	...	...	...	1758	...	...	...	...	...	1959	...	...	...	...	...	2154	...	...	...	...	...	...	...
Bischofshofen 960 975 d.	...	...	...	...	...	1808	...	...	...	...	...	2009	...	...	...	...	...	2204	...	...	...	...	...	...	...
Golling-Abtenau d.	...	...	...	...	...	1830	...	...	...	...	...	|	...	...	...	...	...	|	...	...	...	...	...	...	...
Salzburg Hbf **960 975** a.	...	...	...	...	...	1855	...	...	...	...	...	2048	...	...	...	...	...	2248	...	...	...	...	...	...	...

♦ – **NOTES** (LISTED BY TRAIN NUMBER)

110 – [12] and 🍷 Klagenfurt - München; [12] Beograd (**210**) - Zagreb - Ljubljana - Villach (**110**) - München.
111 – [12] and 🍷 München - Klagenfurt; [12] München - Villach (**211**) - Ljubljana - Zagreb - Beograd.
112 – [12] and ✗ Klagenfurt - München; [12] Zagreb (**212**) - Ljubljana - Villach (**112**) - München.
113 – [12] and ✗ München - Klagenfurt; [12] München - Villach (**213**) - Ljubljana - Zagreb.
114/5 – WÖRTHERSEE – [12] and ✗ Klagenfurt - München - Stuttgart - Köln - Dortmund and v.v.
236 – ALLEGRO DON GIOVANNI – 🛏 1,2 cl., ▬ 2 cl. and [2] Venezia (**239**) - Udine (**236**) - Salzburg (d. 0500) - Wien; ▬ 2 cl. Venezia (**239**) - Udine (**236**) - Salzburg (**206**) - Summerau 🏛 - Praha.
237 – ALLEGRO DON GIOVANNI – 🛏 1,2 cl., ▬ 2 cl. and [2] Wien - Salzburg (a. 2352) - Udine - Venezia; ▬ 2 cl. Praha (**207**) - Summerau 🏛 - Salzburg (**237**) - Venezia.
296 – LISINSKI – 🛏 1,2 cl., ▬ 2 cl. and [2] Zagreb - Ljubljana - Villach - Salzburg - München; [2] Beograd (**418**) - Vinkovci (**748**) - Zagreb (**296**) - München; Dec. 9–20, Jan. 1–6, Mar. 14–29, Apr. 30 - Sept. 19 (from Rijeka) conveys ▬ 2 cl. Rijeka (**480**) - Ljubljana (**296**) - München; Apr. 30 - Sept. 19 (from Rijeka) conveys 🛏 1,2 cl. Rijeka (**480**) - Ljubljana (**296**) - München.
297 – LISINSKI – 🛏 1,2 cl., ▬ 2 cl. and [2] München - Salzburg - Villach - Ljubljana - Zagreb; [2] München - Zagreb (**741**) - Vinkovci (**419**) - Beograd; Dec. 9–21, Jan. 2–7, Mar. 15–30, May 1 - Sept. 20 (from München) conveys ▬ 2 cl. München - Ljubljana (**481**) - Rijeka; May 1 - Sept. 20 (from München) conveys 🛏 1,2 cl. München - Ljubljana (**481**) - Rijeka.
314/5 – AGRAM – [12] and ✗ Zagreb - Ljubljana - Villach - Salzburg and v.v.
414 – [2] Beograd - Zagreb - Ljubljana - Villach - Schwarzach (**464/15464**) - Feldkirch (**464**) - Zürich; 🛏 1,2 cl. and ▬ 2 cl. Zagreb - Villach - Schwarzach (**464/15464**) - Feldkirch (**464**) - Zürich.
415 – [2] Zürich (**465**) - Feldkirch (**465/15465**) - Schwarzach (**415**) - Villach - Ljubljana - Zagreb - Beograd; 🛏 1,2 cl. and ▬ 2 cl. Zürich (**465**) - Feldkirch (**465/15465**) - Schwarzach (**415**) - Villach - Zagreb.

H – [12] and 🍷 Klagenfurt (*REX* **1568**) - Villach (*IC* **791**) - Salzburg.
K – ⑥ until June 14 (also Dec. 25, 26, Jan. 6, Mar. 24, May 4, 9, 12, 22, 25 ⓒ June 21 - Sept. 14.
L – June 21 - Sept. 13.
N – ⑦ June 22 - Sept. 14 (also May 4, 9, 12, 22, 25, Aug. 15).
R – ⑥ until Sept. 13 (also Dec. 25, 26, Jan. 6, Mar. 24, May 22).
S – From / to Sillian on ⑥ (Table **596**).
W – From / to Wien Westbahnhof (Table **950**).

a – Ⓐ only.
f – Also Apr. 30, May 21, Aug. 14; not Aug. 15.
r – Not July 7 - Sept. 6.
t – 5–6 minutes **earlier** on †.
v – ⚒ only.
x – Connects with train in previous column.
z – Also Dec. 26, Jan. 1, Mar. 24, May 12, Dec. 8; not Dec. 23, 30, Mar 2 May 11, Dec. 7.

§ – *IC* **796** to Villach, *REX* **1567** from Villach (on ⑥, also Dec. 24, 25, 31, Mar. 23, Apr. 30, May 11, 21, Aug. 14, Oct. 31, Dec. 7, *IC* **796** to Schwarzach, *REX* **1567** from Schwarzach).
⊖ – *REX* **1568** to Schwarzach. *IC* **791** from Schwarzach.
⊠ – For car-carrying trains through the Tauern Tunnel, see panel below.
◐ – *11 km* north of Mallnitz.

TAUERN TUNNEL CAR-CARRYING TRAINS *Autoschleuse Tauernbahn* Böckstein ◐ - Mallnitz-Obervellach and v.v. For notes see above. Transit time: 11 minute

Passengers without cars are also conveyed ✆ Böckstein +43 (0) 6434 2436 32 or Mallnitz-Obervellach +43 (0) 4784 600 390

From Böckstein at 0620, 0650 ⑥ **L**, 0720, 0750 ⑥ **R**, 0820, 0850 **K** and at 20 and 50 **K** minutes past each hour until 1620, 1650 **K**, then 1720, 1750 ⑦ **N**, 1820, 1853 ⑦ **N**, 1920, 2020, 2120, 222

From Mallnitz-Obervellach at 0550, 0650, 0720 ⑥ **R**, 0750, 0820 **K**, 0850 and at 20 **K** and 50 minutes past each hour until 1620 **K**, 1650, then 1720 ⑦ **N**, 1750, 1820 ⑦ **N**, 1850, 1950, 2050, 215

974 LINZ - SELZTHAL

2nd class only except where shown

km		⚒	⚒	IC 501 ¶		REX 3903		REX 3905		EC 101 ✗A	REX 3907		REX 3909			IC 601 ¶			Ⓐ	REX 3913			Ⓐn	Ⓑr	⚒n
0	**Linz** Hbf d.	0506	0535	0614	0634	0759	0836	0959	1036	1110	1200	1236	1359	1436	1536	1614	...	1636	1709	1802	1836	1936	2036	2138	231
28	Rohr - Bad Hall d.	0540	0608	|	0708	0823	0908	1023	1111	|	1222	1310	1423	1511	1610	|	...	1711	1750	1825	1908	2010	2109	2211	235
32	Kremsmünster d.	0545	0614	|	0713	0827	0912	1027	1116	|	1226	1314	1427	1516	1614	|	←	1715	1754	1830	1912	2015	2113	2215	235
51	Kirchdorf a. d. Krems d.	0604	0632	0652	0731	0843	0934	1041	1135	1146	1241	1332	1441	1536	1632	1652	1705	1734	1813	1844	1934	2034	2129	2232	001
68	Hinterstoder d.	0627	...	|	0752	0906	...	1104	...	|	1304	...	1505	...	→	|	1728	...	1834	1905	1954	2055	...	...	...
82	Windischgarsten d.	0643	...	0722	...	0920	...	1118	...	|	1318	...	1519	...	...	1722	1742	...	1851	1919	2008	2109	...	...	...
87	Spital am Pyhrn d.	0649	...	|	...	0926	...	1124	...	|	1324	...	1531	...	...	|	1749	...	1857	1926	2014	2115	...	...	...
104	**Selzthal 975** a.	0705	...	0742	...	0943	...	1141	...	1233	1341	...	1548	...	...	1742	1805	...	1913	1943	2031	2131	...	...	...
	Graz Hbf **975** a.	...	...	0925	...	...	...	|	...	1400	...	...	...	...	...	1925	...	...	...	|	...	...	...	...	...
111	Liezen **975** a.	...	...	...	...	...	...	1151	...	...	...	...	...	...	...	...	...	...	...	1952a	...	...	...	...	...

	⚒	Ⓐ	Ⓐ	⚒	⚒		REX 3900 ⚒			IC 500 ¶			REX 3906				REX 3910	EC 100 ✗A		REX 3912		IC 600 ¶		⚒	
Liezen **975** d.	...	...	...	...	...	...	...	...	...	...	...	...	...	...	1205	...	...	...	...	...	...	...	...	...	2005
Graz Hbf **975** d.	...	...	...	...	...	...	...	...	...	0635	...	...	...	...	|	...	...	1349	...	...	...	1635	...	...	|
Selzthal 975 d.	...	...	0423	...	...	...	0539	0620	...	0816	0827	...	1016	...	1220	...	1417	1517	...	1615	...	1816	1827	...	201
Spital am Pyhrn d.	...	...	0441	...	...	...	0557	0637	...	|	0845	...	1033	...	1239	...	1435	|	...	1632	...	|	1844	...	203
Windischgarsten d.	...	...	0448	...	...	...	0603	0643	...	0837	0851	...	1040	...	1245	...	1441	|	...	1638	...	1837	1851	...	204
Hinterstoder d.	...	...	0501	...	...	...	0617	0658	0758	|	0905	...	1054	...	1303	...	1455	|	...	1652	...	|	1905	...	205
Kirchdorf a. d. Krems d.	0422	0458	0524	0524	0555	0624	0641	0724	0824	0907	0928	1020	1117	1230	1326	1422	1517	1605	1624	1715	1825	1907	1927	2026	211
Kremsmünster d.	0438	0516	0545	0545	0614	0645	0701	0743	0843	|	0946	1043	1133	1247	1345	1444	1531	|	1645	1731	1844	|	1946	2044	213
Rohr - Bad Hall d.	0443	0520	0549	0549	0618	0650	0707	0749	0849	|	0951	1048	1138	1251	1349	1449	1536	|	1650	1735	1848	|	1951	2049	214
Linz Hbf a.	0517	0554	0625	0625	0653	0728	0735	0825	0925	0944	1025	1125	1202	1325	1425	1525	1601	1649	1725	1800	1925	1944	2025	2125	221

A – JÓŽE PLEČNIK – [12] and ✗ Ljubljana - Spielfeld Straß 🏛 - Graz - Linz - Summerau 🏛 - České Budějovice - Praha and v.v.

a – Ⓐ only.
n – Not Dec. 24, 31.

r – Also Nov. 1.
¶ – Also conveys [1].

SALZBURG - BISCHOFSHOFEN - SELZTHAL - GRAZ 975

km		REX 1991	EN 465	REX 1995	REX 1752		REX 4471	IC 511	IC 501 511		REX 4473	REX 1700	ÖEC 151	IC 513	ÖIC 534		REX 4475	REX 1702	ÖIC 111	IC 515	ÖEC 536	EC 101	REX 4477	REX 1704	ÖEC 557
		2 ⚒	Z	2 ⚒	2 ⚒	2 Ⓐ	2 ⚒	🍷		2	2	2	✕	🍷	🍷	2 Ⓐ	2	2	🍷	🍷	✕	✕ P	2	2	✕
0	**Salzburg** Hbf **960 970** d.	...	...	...	...	...	...	0525	...	...	...	...	...	0715	...	...	...	...	0904	...	...	...	...	...	...
	Innsbruck Hbf **960** d.	...	0143	...	...	...	...	|	...	...	...	...	...	|	...	...	...	...	|	0735	...	...	...	...	...
53	**Bischofshofen 960 970** a.	...	0412	...	...	...	...	0604	...	...	...	...	...	0800	...	...	...	...	0951	1011	...	...	...	...	...
53	**Bischofshofen** d.	...	0413	...	...	...	...	0611	...	...	...	...	...	0813	...	...	...	...	▬	1013	...	...	...	...	...
77	Radstadt d.	...	|	...	...	...	...	0634	...	...	...	...	...	0836	...	...	...	...	...	1036	...	...	1109	...	...
94	Schladming d.	...	0451	0500	...	0606	...	0650	...	0700	...	...	...	0852	...	...	0931	...	...	1052	...	...	1131	...	...
33	**Stainach-Irdning** d.	0427	0522	0541	...	0647	...	0723	...	0741	...	...	...	0922	...	...	1012	...	...	1122	...	...	1212	...	...
45	Liezen d.	0438	|	0553	...	0659	...	0734	...	0756	0826	...	...	0933	...	1005	1026	...	...	1133	...	...	1226	...	...
	Linz Hbf **974** d.	|	|	|	...	|	...	|	0614	|	|	...	...	|	...	|	|	...	...	|	...	1110	|	...	...
52	**Selzthal** a.	0444	0539	0559	...	0706	...	0741	0742	0802	0832	...	...	0940	...	1012	1032	...	...	1140	...	1233	1232	...	...
52	**Selzthal** d.	0451	0548	0606	...	▬	0715	0750	0750	▬	0838	...	...	0950	...	1034	1038	...	...	1150	...	1234	1238	...	...
	Kleinreifling **976** a.	|	|	|	...	...	|	|	|	...	|	...	...	|	...	1150	|	...	...	|	...	|	|	...	...
58	Stadt Rottenmann d.	0458	|	0613	...	ÖEC	0722	0757	0757	ÖIC	0844	...	...	0957	...	...	1044	...	...	1157	...	|	1244	...	...
69	Trieben d.	0506	|	0621	...	**732**	0730	0805	0805	**532**	0852	...	...	1005	...	...	1052	...	ÖEC	1205	...	|	1252	...	...
15	St Michael a.	0540	0625	0655	...	✕	0804	0830	0830	🍷	0927	...	...	1030	...	...	1127	...	**555**	1230	...	|	1327	...	...
15	St Michael **980** d.	0541	0626	0656	0659	⚒	*0812*	0831	0831		...	0932	...	1031	...	...	...	1132	✕	1231	...	|	...	1332	...
25	Leoben Hbf **980** d.	0551	0636	0713	0707	0743	*0826*	0841	0841	0848	...	0940	...	1041	1048	...	...	1140		1241	1248	1317	...	1340	...
41	**Bruck** a. d. Mur **980** a.	*0618*a	0647	0725	|	0753	...	|	|	0859	...	0952	0959	|	1059	...	...	1152	1159	|	1259	|	...	1352	1359
	Wien Südbahnhof **980** a.	|	|	|	|	0942	...	|	|	1102	...	*1202*	|	|	1302	...	...	*1402*	|	|	1502	|	...	*1602*	|
95	**Graz** Hbf **980** a.	0645	0737	0813	0759	...	...	0925	0925	...	...	...	1034	1125	...	...	...	...	1234	1325	...	1400	...	...	1434

	IC 517	EC 32	REX 4481	REX 1706	ÖEC 113	ÖEC 669	IC 630	EZ 1997		REX 4483	REX 1708	EC 159	IC 611	IC 601 611	ÖEC 530		REX 4487	REX 1710	EC 315	IC 613	ÖIC 632	REX 4489	ÖEC 655	IC 615	🚌
	🍷	🍷	2 Ⓑ	2	✕	✕ B	✕	2✕ Ⓒ	2 Ⓐ	2	2	✕	🍷		✕	2 Ⓐ	2	2	✕	🍷	🍷	2 Ⓑ	✕	🍷	
Salzburg Hbf **960 970** d.	1115	...	...	...	1304	...	...	*1318*	...	...	...	...	1515	...	...	...	...	...	1713	...	...	...	...	1915	*2104*
Innsbruck Hbf **960** d.	|	...	...	...	|	1135	...	|	...	...	...	...	|	...	...	...	...	...	|	1535	...	...	...	|	|
Bischofshofen 960 970 a.	1155	...	...	...	1351	1411	...	*1419*	...	...	...	...	1555	...	...	...	...	...	1755	1811	...	...	...	1955	*2151*
Bischofshofen d.	1213	...	...	...	▬	1413	...	1426	...	...	...	...	1613	...	...	...	...	...	▬	1813	...	...	...	2013	2202
Radstadt d.	1236	...	1309	...	...	1436	...	1452	...	...	...	...	1636	...	...	...	1709c	...	...	1836	...	...	...	2036	2243
Schladming d.	1252	...	1331	...	...	1452	...	1509	...	1531	...	...	1652	...	...	...	1731	...	...	1852	...	1931	...	2052	...
Stainach-Irdning d.	1322	...	1412	...	...	1522	...	1545	...	1612	...	...	1722	...	...	...	1812	...	...	1922	...	2012	...	2122	...
Liezen d.	1333	...	1426	...	...	1533	...	1558	1605	1626	...	...	1733	...	...	1805	1825	...	...	1933	...	2026	...	2133	...
Linz Hbf **974** d.	|	...	|	...	...	|	...	|	|	|	...	...	|	1614	...	|	|	...	...	|	...	|	...	|	...
Selzthal a.	1340	...	1432	...	...	1540	...	1605	1612	1632	...	...	1740	1742	...	1812	1831	...	...	1940	...	2032	...	2140	...
Selzthal d.	1350	...	1438	...	...	1550	...	1623	1624	1638	...	...	1750	1750	...	1820	1838	...	...	1950	...	2038	...	2150	...
Kleinreifling **976** a.	|	...	|	...	...	|	...	1745	1743	|	...	...	|	|	...	1939	|	...	...	|	...	|	...	|	...
Stadt Rottenmann d.	1357	...	1444	...	...	1557	...	|	...	1644	...	...	1757	1757	...	...	1844	...	...	1957	...	2044	...	2157	...
Trieben d.	1405	...	1452	...	IC	1605	...	|	...	1652	...	...	1805	1805	...	...	1852	...	ÖIC	2005	...	2052	...	2205	...
St Michael a.	1430	...	1527	...	**559**	1630	...	✣	...	1727	...	...	1830	1830	...	...	1927	...	**653**	2030	...	2127	...	2230	...
St Michael **980** d.	1431	...	...	1532	🍷	1631	...	|	...	...	1733	...	1831	1831	...	...	...	1932	🍷	2031	...	2132	...	2231	...
Leoben Hbf **980** d.	1441	1448	...	1540		1641	1648	|	...	...	1741	...	1841	1841	1848	...	...	1940		2041	2048	2140	...	2241	...
Bruck a. d. Mur **980** a.	|	1459	...	1552	1559	|	1659	|	...	...	1753	1759	|	|	1859	...	...	1952	1959	|	2059	2152	2159	|	...
Wien Südbahnhof **980** a.	|	1702	...	*1802*	|	|	1902	2035	...	...	*2002*	|	|	|	2102	...	...	*2144*	|	|	2302	*0002*	|	|	...
Graz Hbf **980** a.	1525	...	...	...	1634	1725	...	...	...	...	...	1834	1925	1925	...	...	...	...	2034	2125	...	...	2234	2325	...

km				REX 4470	REX 1703	IC 510 500	IC 510	ÖIC 550	REX 4474		ÖEC 531	IC 512	IC 552	REX 1707	REX 4476	EZ 1996	IC 533	ÖEC 668	EC 158	REX 1709	REX 4478	ÖIC 535	IC 514	REX 1711	EC 100
		2 ⚒	2	2 ⚒	2		🍷	🍷	2	2 Ⓐ	✕	🍷	🍷	2	2 Ⓑ	2✕ Ⓒ	✕	✕ B	✕	2	2	🍷	🍷	2	✕ P
0	**Graz** Hbf **980** d.	...	...	*0422*	...	0635	0635	0726	...	...	...	0835	0926	...	...	...	...	1035	1126	...	...	...	1235	...	1349
	Wien Südbahnhof **980** d.	...	...	|	...	|	|	|	*0557*	...	0657	|	|	*0757*	...	0712	0857	|	|	*0957*	...	1057	|	*1157*	|
	Bruck a. d. Mur **980** d.	...	...	0515	0702	|	|	0801	0808	...	0901	|	1001	1008	...	|	1101	|	1201	1208	...	1301	|	1408	|
68	Leoben Hbf **980** d.	...	...	0532	0712	0720	0720	...	0821	...	0911	0920	▬	1021	...	|	1111	1120	▬	1221	...	1311	1320	1421	1437
78	St Michael **980** a.	...	...	0547	▬	0728	0728	...	0828	...	...	0928	...	1028	...	✣	...	1128	...	1228	...	...	1328	1428	|
78	St Michael d.	...	...	0600	...	0729	0729	...	0831	...	...	0929	...	...	1031	|	...	1129	...	...	1231	...	1329	...	|
24	Trieben d.	...	...	0636	...	0756	0756	...	0906	...	...	0956	...	...	1106	|	...	1156	...	...	1306	...	1356	...	|
35	Stadt Rottenmann d.	...	...	0644	...	0804	0804	...	0914	...	...	1004	...	...	1114	|	...	1204	...	...	1314	...	1404	...	|
	Kleinrefling **976** d.	...	...	|	2	|	|	...	|	0824	...	|	...	...	|	1037	...	|	...	...	|	...	|	...	|
41	**Selzthal** a.	...	...	0650	Ⓐ	0810	0810	...	0920	0942	...	1010	...	...	1120	1156	...	1210	...	...	1320	...	1410	...	1516
41	**Selzthal** d.	0544	...	...	0749	0816	0818	...	0926	0944	...	1018	...	...	1126	1157	...	1218	...	...	1326	...	1418	...	1517
	Linz Hbf **974** a.	|	...	...	|	0944	|	...	|	|	...	|	...	...	|	|	...	|	...	...	|	...	|	...	1649
48	Liezen d.	0552	...	...	0756	...	0825	...	0934	0951	...	1025	...	...	1134	1204	...	1225	...	...	1334	...	1425	...	...
60	**Stainach-Irdning** d.	0604	...	...	0808	...	0836	...	0946	...	...	1036	EC	...	1146	1216	...	1236	ÖEC	...	1348	...	1436	...	...
99	Schladming d.	0646	0650	...	0850	...	0909	...	1029	...	...	1109	**114**	...	1229	1252	...	1309	**112**	...	1429	...	1509	...	...
216	Radstadt d.	...	0708	...	...	...	0926	...	1052	...	...	1126	✕	...	1252	1308	...	1326	✕	...	...	...	1526	...	...
240	**Bischofshofen** a.	...	0736	...	...	...	0948	...	...	...	...	1148		...	...	1334	...	1348		...	...	...	1548	...	...
240	**Bischofshofen 960 970** d.	...	*0739*	...	...	...	0956	...	...	...	...	1149	1208	...	...	*1339*	...	1349	1408	...	...	...	1556	...	...
	Innsbruck Hbf **960** a.	...	|	...	...	...	|	...	...	...	...	1425	|	...	...	|	...	1626	|	...	...	...	|	...	...
293	**Salzburg** Hbf **960 970** a.	...	*0840*	...	...	...	1044	...	...	...	...	...	1255	...	...	*1440*	...	...	1455	...	...	...	1644	...	...

		REX 4482		REX 4482	EC 33	IC 518	ÖEC 558	REX 1713	REX 4484		REX 1992	ÖIC 539	IC 610 600	IC 610	REX 4486	REX 4486	ÖEC 156	REX 1735	REX 4488	ÖEC 631	IC 612	ÖEC 150	REX 1737	REX 4490	EN 464
	2 Ⓒ	2 Ⓐ	2 Ⓐ	2 Ⓐ	🍷	🍷	✕	2	2 Ⓑ	2 Ⓐ	2 Ⓐ	🍷		🍷	2	2 Ⓑ	✕	2	2	✕	🍷	✕	2	2	Z
Graz Hbf **980** d.	...	...	...	...	...	1435	1526	...	...	...	*1601*	...	1635	1635	...	...	1726	...	...	...	1835	1926	...	...	2135
Wien Südbahnhof **980** d.	...	...	...	...	1257	|	|	*1357*	...	...	|	1457	|	|	...	...	|	*1557*	...	1657	|	|	*1757*	...	|
Bruck a. d. Mur **980** d.	...	...	...	...	1501	|	1601	1608	...	...	|	1701	|	|	...	1711	1801	1808	...	1901	|	2001	2008	...	2227
Leoben Hbf **980** d.	...	...	...	...	1511	1520	...	1621	...	...	1654	1711	1720	1720	1725	1725	...	1821	...	1911	1920	...	2034	...	2240
St Michael **980** a.	...	...	...	...	...	1528	...	1628	...	...	1703	...	1728	1728	1733	1733	...	1828	...	...	1928	...	2041	...	2248
St Michael d.	1431	1431	...	...	...	1529	...	...	1631	...	1706	...	1729	1729	1734	1734	...	...	1831	...	1929	...	...	2051	2250
Trieben d.	1510	1510	...	...	...	1556	...	...	1706	...	1743	...	1756	1756	1809	1809	...	...	1906	...	1956	...	...	2126	|
Stadt Rottenmann d.	1517	1517	...	...	...	1604	...	...	1714	...	1751	...	1804	1804	1817	1817	...	...	1914	...	2004	...	...	2134	|
Kleinrefling **976** d.	|	|	1419	...	...	|	...	...	|	1626	|	...	|	|	|	|	...	...	|	...	|	...	...	|	|
Selzthal a.	1522	1522	1541	←	...	1610	...	...	1720	1743	1757	...	1810	1810	1823	1823	...	...	1920	...	2010	...	...	2140	2327
Selzthal d.	1527	→	1544	1551	...	1618	...	...	1726	1745	...	...	1816	1818	▬	1832	...	...	1926	...	2018	...	...	2147	2339
Linz Hbf **974** a.	|	...	|	|	...	|	...	...	|	|	...	...	1944	|	...	|	...	...	|	...	|	...	...	|	|
Liezen d.	1535	...	1551	1558	...	1625	...	...	1734	1752	...	...	...	1825	...	1838	...	...	1934	...	2025	...	...	2154	|
Stainach-Irdning d.	1547	...	...	1612	...	1636	...	...	1746	...	...	...	...	1836	ÖIC	1848	...	...	1946	...	2036	...	...	2206	2356
Schladming d.	1630	...	...	1650	...	1709	...	...	1828	...	...	...	...	1909	**110**	1925	...	...	2028	...	2109	...	...	2248	0028
Radstadt d.	1652	...	...	...	...	1726	...	...	...	...	...	...	...	1926	🍷	...	...	...	...	...	2126	...	...	...	|
Bischofshofen a.	...	...	...	...	...	1748	...	...	...	...	...	...	...	1948		...	...	...	...	...	2148	...	...	...	0106
Bischofshofen 960 970 d.	...	...	...	...	...	1756	...	...	...	...	...	...	...	1949	2009	...	...	...	...	...	2156	...	...	...	0108
Innsbruck Hbf **960** a.	...	...	...	...	...	|	...	...	...	...	...	...	...	2225	|	...	...	...	...	...	|	...	...	...	0358
Salzburg Hbf **960 970** a.	...	...	...	...	...	1844	...	...	...	...	...	...	...	...	2048	...	...	...	...	...	2244	...	...	...	...

– To / from Bregenz (Table **951**).
– JÓŽE PLEČNIK – 12 and ✕ Ljubljana - Maribor - Spielfeld Straß - Graz - Linz - Summerau - Praha and v.v.
– ZÜRICHSEE – 1, 2 cl., 2 cl. and 2 Graz - Innsbruck - Feldkirch - Buchs - Zürich and v.v.

a – Ⓐ only.
c – Ⓒ only.
✣ – Via Amstetten (Tables **976** and **950**).

976 AMSTETTEN - KLEINREIFLING - SELZTHAL

2nd class only

km		⚒	W	⑥k	Ⓐ	Ⓒ	⚒	ⒸB	Ⓐ			⚒	Ⓐ		⑥k	Ⓐ		n	Ⓐ	Ⓐ		Ⓒp	Ⓐn	Ⓐ	Ⓑq	
0	**Amstetten** d.	0449	0626	0704	0722	0759	0900	0929	1000	1100	1200	1300	1322	1400	1500	1500	...	1600	1622	1700	...	1800	1800	1822	1900	2000
23	Waidhofen a. d. Ybbs. d.	0526	0706	0735	0751	0830	0928	1007	1028	1129	1230	1329	1354	1430	1530	1530	...	1630	1653	1730	...	1826	1830	1853	1931	2028
47	**Kleinreifling** a.	0554	0743	...	...	0855	0955	1036	...	1154	1257	1354	...	1457	1557	*1610*f	...	1657	...	1757	...	1853	1857	...	1959	...
		Ⓐ	ⒶL			|		|		Ⓐ		ⒶL					L			|					ⒷG	
47	**Kleinreifling** d.	0619	0824	...	...	0856	...	1037	...	1244	...	1419	...	...	...	...	1626	...	...	1817	1817	...	...	...	2002	...
82	Hieflau d.	0657	0903	...	...	0941	...	1115	...	1323	...	1500	...	...	...	...	1705	...	...	1859	1859	...	...	...	2039	...
105	Admont d.	0724	0928	...	...	1007	...	1143	...	1347	...	1527	...	...	...	...	1729	...	...	1924	1924	...	...	...	...	...
119	**Selzthal** a.	0738	0942	...	...	1021	...	1156	...	1403	...	1541	...	...	...	...	1743	...	...	1938	1938	...	...	...	...	...

	⚒	⚒	Ⓐ		H	⑥k	Ⓐ	W	Ⓐ	Ⓐ	Ⓒ		⚒	ⒶL	⚒	Ⓒ	⚒	Ⓐ	Ⓒ	Ⓐ	Ⓐn	ⒸB	ⒶL	†	Ⓑr	L
Selzthal d.	...	...	...	...	...	...	0550	...	...	0822	0834	...	...	1034	...	1234	...	1421	...	...	...	1623	1624	...	...	1820
Admont d.	...	...	...	...	...	...	0604	...	...	0836	0849	...	...	1048	...	1248	...	1435	...	...	...	1638	1639	...	...	1834
Hieflau d.	...	...	...	...	0536	...	0629	...	...	0903	0914	...	...	1113	...	1313	...	1500	...	...	...	1705	1705	...	...	1900
Kleinreifling a.	...	...	...	...	0614	...	0718	...	...	0940	0950	...	...	1150	...	1350	...	1540	...	...	...	1745	1743	...	...	1939
					d									d		d		Ⓐ				|	|			n
Kleinreifling d.	...	...	0514	0605k	0635	...	...	0802	...	...	...	0959	1102k	1159	1302	1359	1502	*1545*e	1602	...	1702	1756	1802	1902	...	2004
Waidhofen a. d. Ybbs.. d.	0456	0531	0548	0634	0710	0746	...	0830	0930	...	...	1030	1130	1230	1330	1430	1530	1630	1630	1703	1731	1825	1831	1931	1931	2032
Amstetten a.	0524	0559	0616	0701	0738	0814	...	0858	0958	...	...	1058	1158	1258	1358	1458	1558	1658	1658	1732	1758	1848	1858	1958	1958	2100

Waidhofen a. d. Ybbs - Lunz am See

km	*Narrow gauge*	ⒸN	Ⓐ	Ⓒ				Ⓐ		Ⓒ
0	Waidhofen a. d. Ybbs. d.	0832	0932	1012	...	1432	...	1632	...	1833
54	Lunz am See a.	1000	1105	1145	...	1605	...	1759	...	2000

Narrow gauge	Ⓐz		Ⓐz	ⒶA	Ⓒ	ⒸV	Ⓐ	Ⓒ		Ⓐ	Ⓒ
Lunz am See d.	0547	...	*0755*x	0750	0827	1009	1147	1248	...	1626	1645
Waidhofen a. d. Ybbs a.	0722	...	0925	0925	1003	1156	1326	1427	...	1759	1822

A – Dec. 24 - Jan. 4, Mar. 17–25 and July 7 - Aug. 29 (also May 13).
B – 2 and ✕ Wien Südbf - Selzthal - Bischofshofen and v.v.
G – Ⓑ (not Dec. 24, 25, 31, Mar. 23, May 11, Dec. 7). From Linz (Table **977**).
H – ①–⑥ (not Dec. 25, 26, Jan. 1, Mar. 24, May 12, Dec. 8). To Linz (Table **977**).
L – To / from Liezen (Table **975**).
N – Ⓒ May 1 - Oct. 26. Change trains at Gstadt (a. 0843, d. 0846).
V – May 1 - Oct. 26.
W – From / to Wien (Table **950**).
d – Daily from Kleinreifling.
e – Change trains at Weyer (a. *1552*, d. 1610).
f – Change trains at Weyer (a. 1549, d. *1602*).
k – ⑥ (not Nov. 1).
n – Not Dec. 24, 31.
p – Also Dec. 24, 31.
q – Also Nov. 1; not Dec. 24, 31.
r – Also Nov. 1.
x – By 🚌 to Großhollenstein (a. *0837*), then train (d. 0841).
z – Not Dec. 24 - Jan. 4, Mar. 17–25, May 13, July 7 - Aug. 29.

977 LINZ - KLEINREIFLING

2nd class only

km		⚒	⚒					⚒		Ⓐ	Ⓐ		Ⓐ		Ⓐe		Ⓐ		Ⓐe		Ⓐ		Ⓐe	H			
0	**Linz** Hbf **950**... d.	0441	0517	0618	0652	0753	*0830*	0849	0953	*1030*	*1130*	*1153*	1221	1253	*1330*	1353	1421	1453	*1530*	1553	1621	1653	*1730*	1753	*1853*	1953	2153
25	St Valentin **950** d.	0516	0549	0649	0722	0820	0853	0920	1020	1053	1153	1220t	1253	1320	1353	1420	1451	1520	1552	1620	1650	1720	1753	1820	1923	2020	2220
45	Steyr d.	0540	0614	0715	0748	0848	0913	0947	1047	1113	1213	1247	1313	1347	1413	1447	1518	1547	1614	1647	1712	1747	1814	1847	1948	2046	2244
47	Garsten d.	0543	0617	0718	0752	0851	0917	0949	1051	1117	1216	1251	1316	1351	1415	1451	1522	1550	1619	1651	1717	1751	1817	1851	1951	2050	2247
91	**Kleinreifling**... a.	0644	...	...	0849	...	1008	...	1146c	1209	...	1347c	1409	1450a	...	1546c	1615	...	1711	1746c	1810	1844a	...	1947	...	2143	...

		Ⓐ	⚒	⚒	H				Ⓐ		⚒	Ⓐ			Ⓐ			Ⓐe		Ⓐ		Ⓐe				Ⓐe
Kleinreifling d.	...	0441	0518	...	0615	...	0747	...	0954	1014c	...	1154	1213c	...	1354	1413c	...	...	1617	...	1714a	...	1814	1919e	2024	...
Garsten d.	0438	0535	0607	0637	0711	0809	0842	0931	1043	1109	1208	1243	1309	1409	1443	1509	1609	1652	1709	1744	1809	1844	1909	2010	2118	2324
Steyr d.	0443	0540	0613	0641	0715	0814	0847	0936	1048	1114	1213	1248	1314	1414	1448	1514	1614	1657	1714	1748	1814	1848	1914	2014	2122	2327
St Valentin **950** a.	0506	0606	0637	0704	0741	0838	0906	1002	1106	1140	1240	1306	1338	1440	1506	1540	1640	1719	1740	1806	1840	1906	1940	2039	2144	2352
Linz Hbf **950** a.	0535	0627	0659	0730	0803	0908	*0929*	1041	*1129*	1208	*1308*	*1329*	1408	1508	*1529*	1608	1708	...	1808	1845	*1929*	*1929*	2008	2102	2211	*0017*

H – To / from Hieflau on dates in Table **976**.
a – Ⓐ only.
c – Ⓒ only.
e – Ⓐ (not Dec. 24, 31).
t – 1223 on Ⓒ.

978 WIEN and WIENER NEUSTADT - SOPRON

ÖBB, GySEV ● (2nd class only except where shown)

km		Ⓐn	Ⓐn	D✗	⚒			F	B✗	⚒	⚒	S		⚒	⚒S			⚒	⚒	Ⓐn	V		Ⓐn	Ⓐn
0	**Wien** Südbahnhof ▽ **980/1**... d.	*0454*	*0519*	0619	...	*0657*	0654	0727	0754	*0757*	0750	*0857*	0900	*0957*	1000	*1057*	1100	*1157*	1200	*1227*	*1257*	1300	*1327*	*1357*
	Wiener Neustadt Hbf **980/1** d.	0600	0615	0700	0706	0737	|	0803	0832	0837	|	0933	|	1037	|	1133	|	1233	|	1305	1333	|	1405	1432
42	Ebenfurth d.	|	0626	|	|	|	0741	|	|	|	0839	|	0939	|	1039	|	1139	|	1239	|	|	1339	|	|
74	**Sopron** 🏛 a.	0626	0711	0726	0756	0815	0816	0829	0857	0915	0916	1015	1016	1115	1116	1215	1216	1315	1316	1342	1415	1416	1442	1457

	Ⓐn	Ⓐn	S		Ⓐn	F		Ⓐn	⚒			Ⓐn	Ⓐn	Ⓒ	S	Ⓐn	Ⓐn	Ⓑq				Ⓑq		S
Wien Südbahnhof ▽ **980/1**.... d.	1400	*1427*	*1457*	1500	*1527*	*1538**	*1557*	1600	1654	*1657*	1700	*1727*	1754	*1738**	*1757*	1800	*1817**	*1857*	*1857*	1900	*1957*	*1957*	*2057*	*2057*
Wiener Neustadt Hbf **980/1** . d.	|	1505	1537	|	1605	1632	1637	|	1732	1737	|	1805	1832	1832	1837	|	1905	1932	1937	|	2033	2035	2135	2137
Ebenfurth d.	1439	|	|	1539	|	|	|	1639	|	|	1739	|	|	|	|	1839	|	|	|	1939	|	2046	2146	|
Sopron 🏛 a.	1516	1542	1615	1616	1642	1657	1715	1716	1757	1815	1816	1842	1857	1858	1915	1916	1942	1957	2015	2016	2115	2123	2222	2220

km	km		Ⓐn	Ⓐn	Ⓐn	Ⓐn	Ⓐn	Ⓐn	Ⓐn	S		Ⓐn	⚒				S	F	⚒		Ⓒ			⚒
0	0	**Sopron** 🏛 d.	0415	0416	0437	0446	0502	0513	0515	0539	0539	0602	0624	0639	0702	0740	0742	0802	0840	0842	0900	0940	0941	1040
32		Ebenfurth d.	0459	|	0521	|	|	0557	|	|	0623	|	0709	|	|	0825	|	|	0923	|	|	1023	|	1123
45	33‡	**Wiener Neustadt** Hbf **980/1** a.	|	0453	|	0523	0529	|	0556	0621	|	0629	|	0722	0729	|	0823	0829	|	0921	0927	|	1022	|
		Wien Südbahnhof △ **980/1**... a.	0533	*0535*	0558	...	0608	0630	*0636*	...	0659	0706	0742	...	0806	0858	*0908*	...	0956	*1002*	*1002*	1056	*1102*	1156

	⚒	⚒S	†		⚒	V			Ⓐn	S			Ⓐn	V		S	Ⓐn	Ⓐn	S	Ⓒ	C✗	Ⓐn		B✗
Sopron 🏛 d.	1041	1140	1140	1141	1240	1241	1340	1343	1440	1443	1540	1543	1640	1643	1740	1743	1843	1840	1943	1940	2027	2041	...	2205
Ebenfurth d.	|	1223	1223	|	1323	|	1423	|	1523	|	1623	|	1723	|	1823	|	|	1920	|	2020	|	|	...	|
Wiener Neustadt Hbf **980/1** . a.	1122	|	|	1222	|	1322	|	1422	|	1522	|	1622	|	1722	|	1822	1922	1929	2023	2029	2053	2122	...	2231
Wien Südbahnhof △ **980/1**.... a.	*1202*	1256	1256	*1302*	1356	*1402*	1456	*1502*	1556	*1602*	1656	*1702*	1756	*1802*	1856	*1902*	*2002*	2020*	*2102*	2120*	2133	*2202*	...	2305

B – Conveys 12 Wien - Csorna - Budapest and v.v. (Table **1240**).
C – *IC* **982**: CORVINUS – 12 and ✕ Pécs - Szombathely - Wien. Also calls at Baden (a. 2110).
D – *IC* **981**: CORVINUS – 12 and ✕ Wien - Szombathely - Pécs. Also calls at Baden (d. 0642).
F – To / from Fehring via Szombathely (Tables **1227** / **986**).
S – To / from Szombathely (Table **1227**).
V – 2 Wiener Neustadt - Sopron - Szombathely - Szentgotthárd - Graz and v.v. (Tables **1227** / **986**).
n – Not Dec. 24, 31.
q – Not Dec. 24, 25, 31, Mar. 23, May 11, Dec. 7.
* – Suburban platforms 21 / 22.
‡ – Via Mattersburg.
▽ – Trains call at Wien Meidling 6 minutes later.
△ – Trains call at Wien Meidling 7 minutes earlier.
● – GySEV / ROeEE: Győr-Sopron-Ebenfurti Vasút / Raab-Oedenburg-Ebenfurter Eisenbahn.
✗ – Supplement payable in Hungary. Ⓡ for journey from Hungary.

979 FLUGHAFEN WIEN ✈ Schwechat

CAT ★; S-Bahn (2nd class only)

km		★	★	★		★	★																
0	**Wien** Praterstern d.	*CAT*	...	...	and	...	...	...	S-Bahn	0451	0521	0551	0618	0651	0721	0748	0818	0851	0921	and	2151	2221	2321
2	**Wien** Mitte d.	→	0538	0608	every	2308	2338	...	→	0455	0525	0555	0622	0655	0725	0752	0822	0855	0925	every	2155	2225	2325
	Wien Südbahnhof ◧ d.		|	|	30	|	|	...		*0455*	*0525*	*0555*	*0621*	*0655*	*0725*	*0751*	*0821*	*0855*	*0925*	30	*2155*	*2225*	*2324*
3	**Wien** Rennweg d.		|	|	minutes	|	|	...		0459	0529	0559	0626	0659	0729	0756	0826	0859	0929	minutes	2159	2229	2329
21	**Flughafen Wien** ✈... a.		0554	0624	until	2324	2354	...		0521	0551	0621	0648	0721	0751	0820	0848	0921	0951	until	2221	2251	2351

km		★	★	★		★	★				⚒			⚒									
0	**Flughafen Wien** ✈... d.	*CAT*	0605	0635	and	2335	0005	...	S-Bahn	0539	0547	0609	0639	0648	0709	0739	0809	0839	0909	and	2239	2309	0009
18	**Wien** Rennweg a.	→	|	|	every	|	|	...	→	0600	0603	0630	0700	0703	0730	0800	0830	0900	0930	every	2300	2330	0030
20	**Wien** Südbahnhof ◧ a.		|	|	30	|	|	...		*0604*	*0607*	*0634*	*0704*	*0707*	*0734*	*0804*	*0834*	*0904*	*0934*	30	*2304*	*2334*	*0034*
	Wien Mitte a.		0621	0651	minutes	2351	0021	...		0604	0607	0634	0704	0707	0734	0804	0834	0904	0934	minutes	2304	2334	0034
	Wien Praterstern a.		...	...	until	...	...	...		0608	0611	0638	0708	0711	0738	0808	0838	0908	0938	until	2308	2338	0038

★ – *City Airport Train (CAT).* Non-stop service with special fares.
◧ – Suburban platforms 21 / 22. Change trains at Rennweg (cross platform).

🚌 *Vienna Airport Lines*: **Wien Westbahnhof** – Wien Südbahnhof – **Flughafen Wien** ✈ and v.v.
🚌 From **Wien Westbahnhof** at 0500, 0530 and every 30 minutes until 2230, 2300. Journey time: 35 minutes (from Wien Westbahnhof), 20 minutes (from Wien Südbahnhof).
🚌 From **Flughafen Wien** ✈ at 0600, 0630 and every 30 minutes until 2330, 2359. Journey time: 20 minutes (to Wien Südbahnhof), 40 minutes (to Wien Westbahnhof).

🚌 ÖBB-Bahn Bus / SAD Bratislava: **Bratislava**, AS Mlynské nivy (bus station) – **Flughafen Wien** ✈ and v.v. Ⓡ (✆ +43 (0) 810 222 333). Journey time: 60 minutes. Subject to alteration on Dec. 24, 25, 26, 31, Jan. 1.
🚌 From **Bratislava** AS Mlynské nivy at 0515, 0600, 0700 and hourly until 2000. 🚌 From **Flughafen Wien** ✈ at 0800, 0830, 0930, 1040, 1130, 1230 and hourly until 2230.

WIEN - BRUCK AN DER MUR - GRAZ and VILLACH 980

km		REX 1753			REX 4001			REX 1703	EN 465	ÖEC 157	REX 4474	ÖEC 31	REX 1705	ÖEC 531	REX 1911	ÖEC 151	REX 1707	IC 533	REX 1913	ÖEC 555	REX 1709	ÖIC 535	REX 1915	ÖEC 557
	2	2	2	2	2	2	2	2	2	✕	2	🅁✕	2	✕		✕	2	✕		✕	2	🍷		✕
		Ⓐ	⚒	⚒	⚒					♦		♦		♦		♦								
0	**Wien** Südbahnhof ★d.	...	...	...	...	...	...	...	...	0557	...	0630	...	0657	...	0757	...	0857	...	0957	...	1057	...	1157
4	**Wien** Meidling ● ★d.	...	...	...	...	...	...	...	...	0604	...	|	...	0704	...	0804	...	0904	...	1004	...	1104	...	1204
48	**Wiener Neustadt** Hbf ★d.	...	...	...	...	...	...	...	...	0631	...	|	...	0731	...	0831	...	0931	...	1031	...	1131	...	1231
103	Semmering ★d.	...	...	...	...	...	...	...	...	|	...	|	...	|	...	0914	...	|	...	|	...	|	...	|
117	Mürzzuschlag ★d.	...	...	0424	...	0534	...	...	0614r	...	0731	...	|	...	0831	...	0931	...	1031	...	1131	...	1231	...	1331
	Graz Hbf 975 ◇d.	...	...	|	*0422**	|	*0530*	0611	|	...	|	*0726*	|	...	*0821*	...	|	*0926*	*1021*	...	|	*1126*	*1221*	...	|
158	**Bruck** an der Mur a.	...	...	0507	*0509*	0617	*0608*	0658	0657r	...	0757	*0801*	0816	...	0857	...	0957	*1001*	1057	...	1157	*1201*	1257	...	1357
158	**Bruck** an der Mur 975 d.	...	0440	0509	*0515*	0619	0632	...	0702	0702	0759	0808	0818	...	0901	0902	0959	1008	1101	1102	1159	1208	1301	1302	1359
212	**Graz** Hbf a.	...	|	0556	|	0700	|	...	|	0737	0834	|	|	...	|	0937	1034	|	|	1137	1234	|	|	1337	1434
174	Leoben Hbf 975 d.	...	0454	▬	*0532*	...	0647	...	0714	▬	▬	0821	|	...	0913	...	▬	1021	1113	▬	...	1221	1313	▬	...
◧	St Michael 975 a.	...	0502	...	*0547*	...	0655	...	|	...	...	0828	|	...	|	...	...	1028	|	...	...	1228	|	...	...
◧	St Michael d.	...	0510	...	0552	...	0702	...	|	...	...	...	|	0838	|	...	...	1034	|	...	...	1234	|	...	...
205	Knittelfeld d.	...	0531	...	0612	...	0722	...	0733	...	...	...	|	0853	0932	...	...	1049	1132	...	...	1249	1332	...	...
213	Zeltweg d.	...	0540	...	0620	...	0730	...	0740	...	...	...	|	0900	0940	...	...	1056	1140	...	...	1256	1340	...	...
220	Judenburg d.	...	0548	2	0628	...	...	...	0748	...	...	...	|	0908	0949	...	...	1104	1149	2	...	1304	1349	2	...
239	Unzmarkt d.	...	0606	⚒	0644	...	...	...	0803	EC	REX	...	|	0923	1003	...	2	1119	1203	⚒	...	1319	1403	⚒	...
276	Friesach d.	0525	0643	0643	...	...	...	...	0838	114	1703	...	|	0956	1033	...	⚒	1157	1233	1309	...	1354	1433	1509	...
309	St Veit an der Glan d.	0558	0719	0719	...	...	...	...	0911	✕	2	...	|	*1043*	1059	...	1215	*1243*	1259	1341	...	1427	1459	1541	...
329	**Klagenfurt** Hbf ◇a.	0617	0739	0739	...	...	...	...	0931	...	←	...	1012	*1102*	1111	...	1234	*1302*	1311	1400	...	1445	1511	1600	...
329	**Klagenfurt** Hbf 970 d.	0622	0741	0741	...	...	...	...	→	0936	0941	...	1013	...	1113	...	1236	...	1313	1402	...	1447	1513	1602	...
342	Pörtschach am W'see 970 d.	0638	0756	0756	...	...	...	...	...	0950	0956	...	|	...	1122	...	1251	...	1322	1416	...	1501	1522	1616	...
351	Velden am Wörthersee 970 d.	0645	0804	0804	...	...	...	...	...	0957	1004	...	|	...	1128	...	1259	...	1328	1424	...	1509	1528	1624	...
367	**Villach** Hbf 970 a.	0700	0820	0820	...	...	...	...	...	1008	1020	...	1034	...	1139	...	1315	...	1339	1440	...	1525	1539	1640	...

	REX 1711		EC 33	REX 1917	IC 559	REX 1713	REX 1759	ÖIC 539	REX 1919	EC 159	REX 1715	ÖEC 631	REX 1921	ÖIC 653	REX 1737	ÖEC 633	REX 1737		EN 235		ÖEC 655	EN 1237	EN 1239	IC 657	D 1459
	2	2	🍷		🍷	2		🍷		✕	2	✕		🍷	2	✕	2	2	🍷	2	✕	🅁	🅁	🍷	2
			♦				Ⓐ			♦	⚒							Ⓑ	♦	Ⓑ		⑤♦	♦		⑤♦
Wien Südbahnhof ★d.	...	...	1257	...	1357	...	...	1457	...	1557	...	1657	...	1757	...	1827	...	...	1915	...	1957	2005	2005	2057	2205
Wien Meidling ● ★d.	...	...	1304	...	1404	...	...	1504	...	1604	...	1704	...	1804	...	1834	...	...	|	...	2004	|	|	2104	|
Wiener Neustadt Hbf ★d.	...	...	1331	...	1431	...	...	1531	...	1631	...	1731	...	1831	...	|	...	...	1952	...	2031	2043	2043	2131	2236
Semmering ★d.	...	...	|	...	|	...	...	|	...	|	...	|	...	|	...	|	...	...	|	...	|	|	|	2216	|
Mürzzuschlag ★d.	...	...	1431	...	1531	...	...	1631	...	1731	...	1831	...	1931	...	|	...	...	2054	...	2131	|	|	2231	2334
Graz Hbf 975 ◇d.	*1326*	...	*1421*	...	|	*1526*	1601	*1621*	...	|	1733	*1821*	...	|	*1926*	|	...	*2021*	*2021*	...	|	*2126*	*2126*	|	|
Bruck an der Mur a.	*1401*	...	1457	...	1557	*1601*	|	1657	...	1757	...	1857	...	1957	*2001*	2016	...	*2056*	2122	...	2157	2205	2205	2304	2359
Bruck an der Mur 975 d.	1408	...	1501	1502	1559	1608	|	1701	1702	1759	*1808*	1901	1902	1959	2008	2018	...	2101	2124	...	2159	2207	2207	2306	0000
Graz Hbf a.	|	...	|	1537	1634	|	|	|	1737	1834	|	|	1937	2034	|	|	←	|	|	...	2234	|	|	2343	0035
Leoben Hbf 975 d.	1421	...	1513	...	▬	1621	1650	1713	▬	...	1829	1913	...	...	2020	2029	2034	2117	2139	...	...	2221	2221	...	...
St Michael 975 a.	1428	...	|	...	...	1628	|	|	...	...	1836	|	...	...	→	|	2041	2126	|	...	...	|	|	...	...
St Michael d.	1434	...	|	...	...	1634	|	|	...	...	1843	|	...	...	...	|	2049	2132	|	←	...	|	|	...	...
Knittelfeld d.	1449	...	1532	...	...	1649	1711	1732	...	...	1901	1932	...	...	...	|	2104	2152	2201	2206	...	|	|	...	...
Zeltweg d.	1456	...	1540	...	...	1656	1718	1740	...	...	1908	1940	...	...	...	|	2111	→	|	2214	...	|	|	...	...
Judenburg d.	1504	...	1549	...	2	1704	1726	1749	...	...	1916	1949	...	...	...	|	2119	...	|	2222	...	|	|	...	...
Unzmarkt d.	1519	...	1603	...	Ⓐ	1719	1739	1803	...	...	1931	2003	...	...	...	|	2133	...	|	2238	...	|	|	...	...
Friesach d.	1557	1603	1633	...	1724	1754	...	1833	...	...	2005	2033	...	...	...	|	▬	...	2258	...	...	|	|	...	...
St Veit an der Glan d.	...	1635	1659	...	1759	1827	...	1859	2	...	2037	2059	...	...	...	|	2	...	|	...	...	|	|	...	...
Klagenfurt Hbf ◇a.	...	1654	1711	...	1817	1845	...	1911	Ⓑ	...	...	2111	...	...	...	2214	...	...	2333	...	...	0012	0012	...	...
Klagenfurt Hbf 970 d.	...	1656	1713	...	1819	1847	...	1913	2015	...	...	2113	...	...	...	2215	2218	...	2335	...	...	0014	0014	...	...
Pörtschach am W'see 970 d.	...	1710	1722	...	1831	1901	...	1922	2030	...	...	2122	...	...	...	|	2232	...	|	...	...	|	|	...	...
Velden am Wörthersee 970 d.	...	1718	1728	⚒	1839	1909	...	1928	2038	...	...	2128	...	...	...	|	2239	...	|	...	...	|	|	...	...
Villach Hbf 970 a.	...	1734	1739	...	1851	1925	...	1939	2055	...	...	2139	...	...	...	2236	2255	...	2358	...	...	0038	0038	...	...

	D 1458	IC 658		EN 1236	EN 1238	ÖEC 656	REX 1750	EN 234	REX 1752	REX 1754	REX 1756		ÖEC 732		REX 1910	ÖIC 532	REX 1700	IC 552	REX 1912	ÖIC 534		REX 1702	EC 158		ÖEC 536
	2	🍷	2	🅁	🅁	✕	2	2	2	2	2	2	✕	2		🍷	2	🍷		🍷	2	2	✕	2	✕
	♦		Ⓐ	♦	♦	⚒	⚒	♦	⚒	⚒	†	Ⓐ	⚒	Ⓐ									♦	Ⓐ	
Villach Hbf 970 d.	...	...	...	0349	0349	...	...	0416	...	...	...	0517	0537	...	...	0620	0630	...	...	0820	0830	...	...	0920	1020
Velden am Wörthersee 970 d.	...	...	...	|	|	...	...	|	...	...	...	0532	|	...	...	0631	0646	...	...	0831	0846	...	...	0936	1031
Pörtschach am W'see 970 d.	...	...	...	|	|	...	...	|	...	...	...	0540	|	...	...	0637	0654	...	...	0837	0854	...	...	0944	1037
Klagenfurt Hbf 970 a.	...	...	...	0413	0413	...	...	0438	...	...	...	0553	0559	...	...	0646	0707	...	...	0846	0907	...	...	0957	1046
Klagenfurt Hbf ◇d.	...	...	...	0415	0415	...	...	0439	...	...	...	→	0600	0603	...	0648	0709	...	...	0848	0909	...	...	0959	1048
St Veit an der Glan d.	...	...	...	|	|	...	...	|	...	0518	...	▬	0614	0622	...	0703	0730	...	...	0903	0930	...	...	1019	1103
Friesach d.	...	...	...	|	|	...	...	|	...	0544	...	...	|	0654	...	0728	0804	...	...	0928	1002	1007	...	▬	1128
Unzmarkt d.	...	...	0445	|	|	...	0534	|	0600	0623	0639	...	|	▬	...	0759	0841	...	...	0959	...	1041	...	...	1159
Judenburg d.	...	...	0501	|	|	...	0548	|	0618	0638	0654	...	|	...	...	0813	0856	...	...	1013	...	1056	...	...	1213
Zeltweg d.	...	...	0509	|	|	...	0556	|	0626	0646	0702	...	|	...	...	0821	0904	...	...	1021	...	1104	...	...	1221
Knittelfeld d.	...	...	0518	|	|	...	0602	|	0633	0654	0708	...	|	ÖIC	...	0828	0910	...	...	1028	...	1110	...	REX	1228
St Michael a.	...	...	0538	|	|	...	...	|	0652	|	0724	...	|	550	...	|	0925	...	...	|	...	1125	...	1914	|
St Michael 975 d.	...	...	0548	|	|	...	...	|	0659	|	0730	2	|	🍷	...	|	0932	...	...	|	...	1132	...	...	|
Leoben Hbf 975 d.	...	...	0603	0611	0611	...	0623	0628	0707	0718	0738	⚒	0743	...	...	0848	0940	...	...	1048	...	1140	...	...	1248
Graz Hbf d.	0413	0530	|	|	|	0631	|	|	|	|	|	0654	|	0726	0821	|	|	0926	1021	|	...	|	1126	1221	|
Bruck an der Mur 975 a.	0452	0608	0618	0624	0624	|	|	0639	|	0731	0750	0741	0753	0801	0856	0859	0952	1001	1056	1059	...	1152	1201	1256	1259
Bruck an der Mur d.	0454	0610	|	0626	0626	|	|	0641	|	*0734*	*0759*	...	0755	0803	...	0903	*0959*	1003	...	1103	...	*1159*	1203	...	1303
Graz Hbf 975 ◇a.	|	|	*0645v*	|	|	|	0715	*0737*	0759	*0813*	*0834*	...	*0834*	|	...	*0937*	*1034*	|	...	*1137*	...	*1234*	|	...	*1337*
Mürzzuschlag ★d.	0534	0645	...	|	|	|	...	0708	...	...	...	...	|	0830	...	0930	...	1030	...	1130	...	...	1230	...	1330
Semmering ★d.	|	0657	...	|	|	|	...	|	...	...	...	...	|	|	...	|	...	|	...	|	...	...	|	...	|
Wiener Neustadt Hbf ★d.	0637	0746	...	0757	0757	|	...	0806	...	...	...	...	|	0931	...	1031	...	1131	...	1231	...	...	1331	...	1431
Wien Meidling ● ★a.	0712	0816	...	0832	0845	0846	...	|	...	...	...	...	0936	0955	...	1055	...	1155	...	1255	...	...	1355	...	1455
Wien Südbahnhof ★a.	0720	0822	...	0839	0855	0851	...	0852	...	...	...	...	0942	1002	...	1102	...	1202	...	1302	...	...	1402	...	1502

♦ – NOTES (LISTED BY TRAIN NUMBER)

0/1 – ALLEGRO JOHANN STRAUSS – [12] and ✕ Venezia - Udine - Tarvisio 🛃 - Wien and v.v.

2/3 – ALLEGRO STRADIVARI – [12] and 🍷 Venezia - Udine - Tarvisio 🛃 - Wien and v.v.

50/1 – EMONA – [12] and ✕ Ljubljana - Maribor - Spielfeld-Straß 🛃 - Wien and v.v.; [2] Rijeka (**482/3**) - Ljubljana - Wien and v.v.

56/7 – ZAGREB – [12] and ✕ Zagreb - Maribor - Spielfeld-Straß 🛃 - Wien and v.v.

58/9 – CROATIA – [12] and ✕ Zagreb - Maribor - Spielfeld-Straß 🛃 - Wien and v.v.; conveys on dates in Table 89a ▬ 2 cl. Split (**824/5**) - Zagreb - Wien and v.v.

34/5 – ALLEGRO TOSCA – 🛏 1, 2 cl., ▬ 2 cl. and [2] Roma - Venezia - Wien and v.v.; 🛏 1, 2 cl. and ▬ 2 cl. Milano - Venezia - Wien and v.v. 🅁 for journeys from / to Italy. See also Table **88**.

30/1 – [12] and ✕ (⑥ Sillian -) Lienz - Villach - Wien and v.v.

236 – Fom Villach on ⑦ Mar. 16 - Sept. 28 (previous night from Roma). ALLEGRO ROSSINI – 🛏 1, 2 cl., ▬ 2 cl. and [2] Roma - Firenze - Wien.

237 – ⑤ Mar. 14 - Sept. 26. ALLEGRO ROSSINI – 🛏 1, 2 cl., ▬ 2 cl. and [2] Wien - Venezia - Firenze - Roma.

238 – From Villach on Dec. 23, 26, 29, 30, 31, Jan. 3 – 7, Mar. 18, 25, May 2, 13, 23, Nov. 2, Dec. 8 (previous night from Roma). 🛏 1, 2 cl., ▬ 2 cl. and [2] Roma - Firenze - Venezia - Wien.

239 – Dec. 21, 23, 27, 28, 29, Jan. 1 – 5, Mar. 16, 23, Apr. 30, May 11, 21, Oct. 31, Dec. 5. 🛏 1, 2 cl., ▬ 2 cl. and [2] Wien - Venezia - Firenze - Roma.

458 – ⑦ June 15 - Aug. 24 (previous night from Koper / Rijeka). ISTRIA – ▬ 2 cl. and [2] Koper - Ljubljana - Wien; ▬ 2 cl. and [2] Rijeka (**480**) - Ljubljana - Wien.

459 – ⑤ June 13 - Aug. 22. ISTRIA – ▬ 2 cl. and [2] Wien - Ljubljana - Koper; ▬ 2 cl. and [2] Wien - Ljubljana (**481**) - Rijeka.

B – Ⓑ (not Aug. 15). By 🚌 on ⑤ (departs Klagenfurt 2035, St Veit 2105, arrives Friesach 2142).

c – © only.
e – Change trains at Leoben (d. *2241*).
r – Change trains at Bruck a. d. Mur on ⚒.
v – Change trains at St Michael (d. *0541*).
z – Also Dec. 26, Jan. 1, Mar. 24, May 12, Dec. 8; not Dec. 23, 30, Mar. 23, May 11, Dec. 7.

* – Change trains at Bruck an der Mur and St Michael.
¶ – Train number **15654** July 4 - Aug. 3.
★ – See Table **981** for other regional services.
◧ – Leoben - St Michael is *10 km*. St Michael - Knittelfeld is *22 km*.
⊠ – Daily Villach - Friesach; ①②③④⑦ Friesach - Bruck a. d. Mur - Graz.
● – See panel on page 447 for S-Bahn trains from / to Wien Hütteldorf. U-bahn line **U6** provides a direct link Wien Spittelau - Westbahnhof - Meidling.
◇ – Additional express 🚌 services Graz - Klagenfurt and v.v. *ÖBB IC Bus*. Rail tickets valid. 🅁. 1st and 2nd class. 🍷 in 1st class. Journey time: 2 hours 5 minutes. **From Graz** Hbf at 0710, 0910, 1110, 1310, 1510, 1710 and 1900. **From Klagenfurt** Hbf at 0630, 0830, 1030, 1230, 1430, 1630 and 1830.

980 VILLACH and GRAZ - BRUCK AN DER MUR - WIEN

	REX 1704	ÖEC 556		EC 32	REX 1706	ÖEC 558		IC 630		REX 1708	ÖEC 156		ÖEC 530	REX 1710	ÖEC 30		ÖEC 150	REX 1922	ÖIC 632	REX 1720	REX 1712		IC 738		
	2	X	2 ⚒	🍷 ♦	2	X	2 ⚒	X	2	2	X ♦	2 Ⓐ	X ♦	2	🅁X ♦	2 Ⓐ	X ♦		🍷	2 ⊗	2 †	2 ⚒	🍷 ⑦z	2 B	2
Villach Hbf **970** d.	...	...	1120	1220	1230	...	1300	1420	1425	...	...	1520	1620	1630	1742	1720	...	...	1820	1830	1954	1954	2005	...	2154
Velden am Wörthersee **970** d.	...	...	1136	1231	1246	...	1316	1431	1441	...	...	1536	1631	1646	│	1736	...	...	1831	1846	2005	2010	│	...	2209
Pörtschach am W'see **970** d.	...	...	1144	1237	1254	...	1324	1437	1449	...	...	1544	1637	1654	│	1744	...	...	1837	1854	2011	2016	│	...	2217
Klagenfurt Hbf **970** a.	...	...	1157	1246	1307	...	1337	1446	1502	...	...	1557	1646	1707	1804	1757	...	...	1846	1907	2022	2027	2028	...	2230
Klagenfurt Hbf ◇ d.	1109	...	1159	1248	1309	...	1339	1448	1504	...	...	1559	1648	1709	1805	1808	...	...	1848	1909	▬	...	2030	2034	2231
St Veit an der Glan d.	1130	...	1220	1303	1330	...	1400	1503	1525	...	...	1620	1703	1730	│	1829	...	...	1903	1930	...	...	2046	2054	2251
Friesach d.	1207	...	1252	1328	1404	...	1432	1528	1557	1604	...	1652	1728	1804	│	1901	...	...	1928	2004	...	...	│	2126	2323
Unzmarkt d.	1241	...	▬	1359	1441	...	▬	1559	...	1641	...	▬	1759	1841	│	▬	...	...	1959	2044	...	...	│	▬	▬
Judenburg d.	1256	...	...	1413	1456	...	...	1613	...	1656	...	...	1813	1856	│	...	...	...	2013	2057	...	...	│	...	...
Zeltweg d.	1304	...	...	1421	1504	...	...	1621	...	1704	...	...	1821	1904	│	...	...	...	2021	2105	...	...	│	...	...
Knittelfeld d.	1310	...	REX	1428	1510	...	REX	1628	...	1710	...	REX	1828	1910	│	...	...	...	2028	2112	IC	...	2201	...	...
St Michael a.	1325	...	**1916**	│	1525	...	**1918**	│	...	1725	...	**1920**	│	1925	│	...	...	...	│	2127	**654**	...	│	...	...
St Michael **975** d.	1332	...		│	1532	...		│	...	1733	...		│	1932	│	ÖIC	...	...	│	2140	🍷	...	│	2	2
Leoben Hbf **975** d.	1340	...		1448	1540	...		1648	...	1741	...		1848	1940	│	**653**	...	...	2048	2148	¶	...	2221	⚒	
Graz Hbf d.	│	1326	1421	│	│	1526	1621	│	...	│	1726	1821	│	│	│	🍷	1926	2021	│	│	2126	...	│	2305	0005
Bruck an der Mur **975** a.	1352	1401	1456	1459	1552	1601	1656	1659	...	1753	1801	1856	1859	1952	1956		2001	2056	2059	2158	2201	...	2232	2353	0053
Bruck an der Mur d.	1359	1403	...	1503	1559	1603	...	1703	...	1759	1803	...	1903	...	1958	1959	2003	...	2103	2206	2203	...	2234	2354	0055c
Graz Hbf **975** ◇ a.	1434	│	...	1537	1634	│	...	1737	...	1834	│	...	1937	...	│	2034	│	...	2153	2253	│	...	2325e	│	│
Mürzzuschlag ★ d.	...	1430	...	1530	...	1630	...	1730	...	...	1830	...	1930	...	│	...	2032	...	2130	...	2230	...	│	0038	0139c
Semmering ★ d.	...	│	...	│	...	1643	...	│	...	...	│	...	│	...	│	...	│	...	2142	...	│	...	│	...	...
Wiener Neustadt Hbf ★ d.	...	1531	...	1631	...	1731	...	1831	...	...	1931	...	2031	...	│	...	2131	...	2231	...	2331	...	│	...	...
Wien Meidling ● ★ a.	...	1555	...	1655	...	1755	...	1855	...	...	1955	...	2055	...	│	...	2155	...	2255	...	2355	...	0019	...	...
Wien Südbahnhof ★ a.	...	1602	...	1702	...	1802	...	1902	...	...	2002	...	2102	...	2144	...	2202	...	2302	...	0002	...	0025	...	...

← FOR NOTES SEE PREVIOUS PAGE

981 Local trains BŘECLAV and ZNOJMO - WIEN - WIENER NEUSTADT - MÜRZZUSCHLAG
2nd class only

km		Ⓐe	Ⓐ	Ⓒ	Ⓐe	⚒		Ⓐe	⊡					ⒸX		ⒸX		⚒							
0	**Břeclav** 🏛 **999** d.	...	...	...	...	...	...	...	...	0532	...	...	...	...	0632	...	...	0725	...	0832	...	...	...	1032	...
18	Hohenau 🏛 **999** d.	...	...	...	...	0452	...	0529	...	0553	...	★	...	...	0653	...	★	0753	★	0853	★	...	...	1053	★
	Šatov 🏛 **995** ★ d.	...	...	...	...	│	...	│	...	│	...	0543z	...	...	│	...	0659k	│	0804k	│	0909	...	...	│	1109
	Retz 🏛 d.	...	...	...	0418	│	0513k	│	...	│	0536k	0553	0619k	...	│	...	0715k	│	0819	│	0919	...	1019k	│	1119
	Hollabrunn d.	...	...	...	0445	│	0541k	│	...	│	0604k	0622	0646k	...	│	...	0746k	│	0846	│	0946	...	1046k	│	1146
	Stockerau d.	...	...	...	0502	│	0558k	│	...	│	0631k	0643	0703k	...	│	...	0803k	│	0903	│	1003	...	1103k	│	1203
83	**Wien** Praterstern d.	...	...	...	0527	0557	0627	0635	...	0657	0703	0715	0727k	...	0757	...	0827	0857	0927	0957	1027	1057	1127	1157	1227
85	**Wien** Mitte d.	...	...	...	0531	0601	0631	0640	...	0701	0709	0719	0731k	...	0801	...	0831	0901	0931	1001	1031	1101	1131	1201	1231
88	**Wien** Südbahnhof ▲ **999** d.	0438	0542	0542	0538	0608	0638	0647	...	0708	0715	0726	0738k	B	0808	0814	0838	0908	0938	1008	1038	1108	1138	1208	1238
92	**Wien** Meidling ● **980** d.	0444	0549	0549	0545	0616	0646	0655	...	0716	0725	0733	0746	0809	0816	0822	0846	0916	0946	1016	1046	1116	1146	1216	1246
114	Baden d.	0502	0609	0609	...	0635	0705	│	...	0735	0742	...	0805	0826	0835	0842	0905	0935	1005	1035	1105	1135	1205	1235	1305
136	**Wiener Neustadt** Hbf **980** a.	0522	0624	0624	...	0654	0724	0727	...	0754	0757	...	0824	0842	0854	0857	0924	0954	1024	1054	1124	1154	1224	1254	1324
136	**Wiener Neustadt** Hbf **980** d.	0525	0635	0635	...	0704	...	0735	0735	0805a	...	...	0835	0845	0905a	0900	0935	0959a	1035	...	1135	1205a	1235	...	1335
170	Payerbach-Reichenau d.	0600	0708	0708	...	0734	...	0806	0809	0836a	...	...	0906	0912	0936a	0930	1006	1029a	1106	...	1206	1236a	1306	...	1406
191	Semmering **980** d.	0626	0734	...	...	...	...	...	0837	...	...	...	...	0937	...	0958	1037	...	...	...	1237	...	1337a	...	1437
205	**Mürzzuschlag 980** a.	0642	0748	...	...	...	...	...	0855	...	...	...	...	0955	...	1016	1055	...	...	...	1255	...	1355a	...	1455

		ⒸX																	⚒						
Břeclav 🏛 **999** d.	...	...	...	1232	...	1332k	...	1432	...	...	...	1632	...	...	1732	...	1832	...	...	...	...	...	...	...	...
Hohenau 🏛 **999** d.	...	...	...	1253	★	1353k	...	1453	★	1553k	...	1653	★	...	1753	...	1853	★	1953a	...	...	2053	...	...	...
Šatov 🏛 **995** ★ d.	...	...	...	│	1309	│	...	│	1509	│	...	│	1709	...	│	...	│	1909v	│	...	...	│	...	...	...
Retz 🏛 d.	...	...	1219k	│	1319	│	1419k	│	1519	│	1619k	│	1719	...	│	1819a	│	1919	│	2019	...	│	...	...	...
Hollabrunn d.	...	...	1246k	│	1346	│	1446k	│	1546	│	1646k	│	1746	...	│	1846a	│	1946	│	2046	...	│	...	...	...
Stockerau d.	...	...	1303k	│	1403	│	1503k	│	1603	│	1703k	│	1803	...	│	1903a	│	2003	│	2103	...	│	...	...	...
Wien Praterstern d.	1257	...	1327	1357	1427	1457	1527	1557	1627	1657	1727	1757	1827	...	1857	1927	1957	2027	2057	2127	2142	2157	2242	2342	0044
Wien Mitte d.	1301	...	1331	1401	1431	1501	1531	1601	1631	1701	1731	1801	1831	...	1901	1931	2001	2031	2101	2131	2146	2201	2246	2346	0048
Wien Südbahnhof ▲ **999** d.	1308	...	1338	1408	1438	1508	1538	1608	1638	1708	1738	1808	1838	1857	1908	1938	2008	2038	2108	2138	2153	2208	2253	2353	0055
Wien Meidling ● **980** d.	1316	...	1346	1416	1446	1516	1546	1616	1646	1716	1746	1816	1846	1904	1916	1946	2016	2046	2116	2146	2203	2216	2303	0003	0103
Baden d.	1335	...	1405	1435	1505	1535	1605	1635	1705	1735	1805	1835	1905	│	1935	2005	2035	2105	2135	2205	2217	2235	2317	0017	0120
Wiener Neustadt Hbf **980** a.	1354	...	1424	1454	1524	1554	1624	1654	1724	1754	1824	1854	1924	1927	1954	2024	2054	2124	2154	2224	2228	2254	2328	0028	0136
Wiener Neustadt Hbf **980** d.	...	1400	1435	...	1535	...	1635	...	1735	...	1835	...	...	1930	1956	2035	2056h	2135	...	...	2229	...	2330	0029	...
Payerbach-Reichenau d.	...	1428	1506	...	1606	...	1706	...	1806	...	1909	...	...	2002	2026	2106	2126h	2206	...	...	2300	...	0002	0100	...
Semmering **980** d.	...	1455	1537e	...	1637	...	1737a	...	1837	...	1947	...	...	2027	...	...	...	...	...	...	2325	...	0027	...	...
Mürzzuschlag 980 a.	...	1512	1555e	...	1655	...	1755a	...	1855	...	2004	...	...	2043	...	...	...	...	...	...	2341	...	0041	...	...

km			⚒	Ⓐe	Ⓒt			Ⓐ	Ⓒt		Ⓐe		⑥t		⚒		⚒								
	Mürzzuschlag 980 d.	...	...	0358	0413	...	...	0456	0508	...	0523	...	0557	...	0618e	...	0656	...	...	...	0903	...	...	...	1103
	Semmering **980** d.	...	...	0413	0428	...	...	0511	0523	...	0538	...	0612	...	0633e	...	0711	...	...	...	0917	...	...	...	1117
	Payerbach-Reichenau d.	0402	...	0442	0457	...	0531k	0542	0557	0557e	0612	0629	0644	...	0704	...	0748	0819	0847	0932a	0954	...	1054	1132a	1154
	Wiener Neustadt Hbf **980** a.	0431	...	0514	0529	...	0558k	0614	0628	0628e	0644	0658	0718	...	0739	...	0817	0850	0925	1003a	1025	...	1125	1203a	1225
	Wiener Neustadt Hbf **980** d.	0433	0503	0516	0531	0533	0603	0616	0631	0633	0646	0703	0719	0733	0749	0803	0819	0900	0935	1005	1035	1105	1135	1205	1235
	Baden d.	0453	0523	│	│	0553	0623	│	│	0653	│	0723	0738	0753	0807	0823	0839	0919	0954	1024	1054	1124	1154	1224	1254
0	**Wien** Meidling ● **980** d.	0515	0545	0548	0600s	0615	0645	0648	0659	0715	0716s	0745	0755s	0815	0825s	0845	0859	0945	1015	1045	1115	1145	1215	1245	1315
4	**Wien** Südbahnhof ▲ **999** d.	0521k	0551	0555	0608	0621	0651	0655	0706	0721	0723	0751	0803	0821	0833	0851	0906	0951	1021	1051	1121	1151	1221	1251	1321
7	**Wien** Mitte d.	0528k	0558	0601	...	0628	0658	0701	0713	0728	...	0758	...	0828	...	0858	0913	0958	1028	1058	1128	1158	1228	1258	1328
9	**Wien** Praterstern d.	0532k	0602	0605	...	0632	0702	0705	0716	0731	...	0802	...	0832	...	0902	0916	1002	1032	1102	1132	1202	1232	1302	1332
34	Stockerau d.	│	0630	0641	...	│	0728	0741	...	...	...	0828	...	│	...	0928	...	1028k	│	1128	│	1228k	│	1328	│
60	Hollabrunn d.	│	0647	...	...	│	0745	...	...	...	...	0845	...	│	...	0945	...	1045k	│	1145	│	1245k	│	1345	│
90	Retz 🏛 a.	│	0713	...	...	│	0811	...	...	...	...	0911	...	│	...	1011	...	1111k	│	1211	│	1311k	│	1411	│
96	Šatov 🏛 **995** ★ a.	│	0723	...	...	│	0826	...	...	...	...	...	...	│	...	1021	...	...	│	1221	│	...	│	1421	│
	Hohenau 🏛 **999** a.	0637k	★	...	...	0737	★	...	...	...	...	...	...	0937	...	★	...	...	1137	★	1237k	...	1337	★	1437k
	Břeclav 🏛 **999** a.	0657k	...	...	...	0757	...	...	...	...	...	...	...	0957	...	...	...	...	1157	...	1257k	...	1357	...	...

		ⒸX									ⒸX	Ⓐe			ⒸX		⚒								
Mürzzuschlag 980 d.	...	1203	1203e	...	1303	...	1403e	...	1503	...	1605	...	1603a	...	1649	1703	...	...	...	1903	...	...	...	...	...
Semmering **980** d.	...	1217	1217e	...	1317	...	1417e	...	1517	...	1620	...	1617a	...	1707	1717	...	...	...	1917	...	...	...	...	...
Payerbach-Reichenau d.	...	1254	1254e	...	1354	...	1454	...	1554	1626e	1649	...	1654	1726e	1734	1754	...	1854	...	1954	2044	2154e	...	...	...
Wiener Neustadt Hbf **980** a.	...	1325	1325e	...	1425	...	1525	...	1625	1656e	1717	...	1725	1756e	1757	1825	...	1925	...	2025	2125	2225e	...	...	...
Wiener Neustadt Hbf **980** d.	1305	...	1335	1405	1435	1505	1535	1605	1635	1705	1719	1719	1735	1805	1809	1835	1905	1935	2005	2035	2135	2233	...	2241	2342
Baden d.	1324	...	1354	1424	1454	1524	1554	1624	1654	1724	1735	1738	1754	1824	│	1854	1924	1954	2024	2054	2154	│	...	2308	0014
Wien Meidling ● **980** d.	1345	...	1415	1445	1515	1545	1615	1645	1715	1745	1803	1807	1815	1845	1846	1915	1945	2015	2045	2115	2215	2259s	2304	2341	0047
Wien Südbahnhof ▲ **999** d.	1351	...	1421	1451	1521	1551	1621	1651	1721	1751	1808	1813	1821	1851	B	1921	1951	2021	2051	2121	2221	2305	2311	2348	0054
Wien Mitte d.	1358	...	1428	1458	1528	1558	1628	1658	1728	1758	...	1820	1828	1858	...	1928	1958	2028	2058	2128	2228	...	2317	2355	0100
Wien Praterstern d.	1402	...	1432	1502	1532	1602	1632	1702	1732	1802	...	1826	1832	1902	...	1932	2002	2032	2102	2131	2232	...	2321	2358	0103
Stockerau d.	1428k	...	│	1528	│	1628a	│	1728	│	1828	...	1902	│	1928	...	│	2028e	│	2127	...	│	...	2346	...	...
Hollabrunn d.	1445k	...	│	1545	│	1645a	│	1745	│	1845	...	1925	│	1945	...	│	2045e	│	2152	...	│	...	0006	...	...
Retz 🏛 a.	1511k	...	│	1611	│	1711a	│	1811	│	1911	...	1953	│	2011	...	│	2111e	│	2218	...	│	...	0032	...	...
Šatov 🏛 ★ a.	...	...	│	1621	│	...	│	1821v	│	...	...	...	│	2021v	...	│	...	│	...	...	│	...	...	...	...
Hohenau 🏛 **999** a.	...	...	1537	★	1637	...	1737	★	1837a	...	...	...	1937	★	...	2037b	...	2137	...	...	2337	...	...	...	...
Břeclav 🏛 **999** a.	...	...	1557	...	1657	...	1757	...	...	...	...	...	...	...	...	...	...	2157	...	...	...	...	...	...	...

B – From / to Bratislava (Table **997**).
a – Ⓐ only.
b – Ⓑ (not Dec. 24, 25, 31, Mar. 23, May 11, Dec. 7).
e – Ⓐ (not Dec. 24, 31).
h – † only.
k – ⚒ only.

s – Stops to set down only.
t – Also Dec. 24, 31.
v – Not Dec. 24, 25, 31.
w – Not Dec. 25, 26, Jan. 1, Mar 24, May 1.
z – ①–⑤ (not Dec. 24 - Jan. 1, Mar. 24, May 1, 8, Oct. 28, Nov. 17).
⊡ – Change trains at Payerbach on ⚒.

● – See panel on page 447 for S-Bahn trains from / to Wien Hütteldorf. U-bahn line **U6** provides a direct link Wien Spittelau - Westbahnhof - Meidling.
▲ – Cross-City services (via Wien Mitte) use suburban platforms 21 / 22 (allow 10 minutes to / from the main station). Services starting from / terminating at Wien Südbahnhof use platforms 11 – 19.
★ – **Znojmo** - **Šatov** and v.v. (*11 km*, journey 17 minutes). Services may be operated by 🚌. From **Znojmo** at 0524 ①–⑤ **z**, 0640 ①–⑥ **w**, 0745, 0850, 1050, 1250, 1450, 1650 **v** and 1850 **v**. From **Šatov** at 0551 ①–⑤ **z**, 0725 ①–⑥ **w**, 0828, 1023, 1223, 1423, 1623, 1823 **v** and 2023 **v**.

UNZMARKT - TAMSWEG 982

2nd class only Narrow gauge *Murtalbahn*

km			Ⓐ	E🚌		B🚂	Ⓐ	©🚌		A🚂	©	ⒶG	Ⓐh	B🚂	Ⓐ	©🚌		🚌
0	**Unzmarkt**	d.	...	0620	0805	...	1005	1005	1205	...	*1405**	1405	1405	...	1605	1605	1805	2005
27	Murau-Stolzalpe	d.	0625	0654	0850	1000	1050	1055	1250	1340	1450	1450	1500	1600	1650	1655	1850	2045
34	St Lorenzen	d.	0637	0700	0901	1020	1101	1105	1301	1400	1501	1501	1511	|	1701	1705	1900	...
44	Stadl an der Mur	d.	0655	0712	0916	1050	1116	1119	1316	1435	1516	1516	1526	1649	1716	1719	1914	...
65	**Tamsweg**	a.	0730	0735	0950	1138	1150	1145	1350	1523	1550	1550	1600	1735	1750	1745	1945	...

			Ⓐ	⑥🚌	©🚌		Ⓐ	©🚌	B🚂	©	Ⓐh	ⒶG	†	⚒	A🚂	Ⓐ	©🚌	🚌
Tamsweg	d.	0620	0810	0810	...	1010	1210	1215	1305	1400	1400	1410	1605	1610	1705	1810	1815	...
Stadl an der Mur	d.	0655	0843	0837	...	1043	1243	1237	1355	1433	1433	1443	1638	1643	1800	1843x	1837	...
St Lorenzen	d.	0711	0900	|	...	1100	1300	|	|	1450	1450	1500	1654	1700	1822	1859	1852	...
Murau-Stolzalpe	d.	0724	0911	0911	0911	1111	1311	1311	1430	1500	1511	1511	1705	1711	1835	1910	1911	1911
Unzmarkt	a.	0757	0950	0950	0950	1150	1350	1350	...	*1550**	1550	1550	1743	1750	...	...	1950	1950

A – ② June 24 - Sept. 2.
B – ③ June 25 - Sept. 3.
E – ⑥ (not Nov. 1).
G – Dec. 24 - Jan. 4, Feb. 18 – 22, Mar. 17 – 25, July 7 - Sept. 5 (also May 13).
h – Not Dec. 24 - Jan. 4, Feb. 18 – 22, Mar. 17 – 25, May 13, July 7 - Sept. 5.
x – Stops on request.
* – By 🚌.
🚂 – Steam train. 🍷. Special fares apply.
Operator: Steiermärkische Landesbahnen.

(WIEN -) WIENER NEUSTADT - FEHRING 983

2nd class only

km						⚒	⚒	Ⓐ🚌			⚒	
	Wien Südbf **980/1**	d.	*0619*	*0826*	*1008**	...	1227	...	1427	1627	*1808**	*2057*
	Wien Meidling **980/1**	d.	*0625*	*0832*	*1016*	...	1233	...	1433	1633	*1816*	*2104*
0	**Wiener Neustadt** Hbf	d.	0704	0901	1101	...	1301	...	1501	1701	1901	2133
55	Friedberg	d.	0759	0954	1157	...	1357	...	1557	1758	1957	2238
82	Hartberg	d.	0832	1027	1230	1335	1430	1435	1631	1833	2028	2312k
113	Fürstenfeld	d.	0902	1058	...	1407	...	1519	1704	1912	2103	...
133	**Fehring**	a.	0928	1123	...	1435	...	1553	1731	1939	2128	...
	Graz Hbf **986**	a.	1030	1230	...	*1603*a	...	*1721*	*1856*	*2121*	*2235*	...

		Ⓐn	Ⓐ	⚒		†	⚒				
Graz Hbf **986**	d.	...	...	...	*0614*	*0809*	*1007*	...	...	1519	1743
Fehring	d.	...	0510	0624	0819	1015	1218	...	1423g	1623	1844
Fürstenfeld	d.	...	0539	0653	0846	1042	1247	...	1450g	1650	1912
Hartberg	d.	0434	0611	0726	0920	1117	1317	1319	1522	1722	1943
Friedberg	d.	0510	0651	0802	1002	1202	...	1401	1601	1800	2019
Wiener Neustadt Hbf	a.	0559	0750	0856	1056	1256	...	1456	1658	1858	2126
Wien Meidling **980/1**	a.	0628	*0828*	0927a	1127	*1343*	...	*1543*	1726	1927	*2155*
Wien Südbf **980/1**	a.	0636	*0835*	0934a	1134	*1350**	...	*1550**	1733	1933	*2202*

a – Ⓐ only. g – † only. k – ①②③④⑦ (not Dec. 24, 25, 31, Mar. 23, Apr. 30, May 11, 21, Aug. 14, Dec. 7). n – Not Dec. 24, 31. * – Wien Südbahnhof platforms 21 / 22.

WIENER NEUSTADT - PUCHBERG am Schneeberg - HOCHSCHNEEBERG 984

2nd class only

WIENER NEUSTADT - PUCHBERG am Schneeberg *28 km.* Journey time: 44 – 48 minutes.
From Wiener Neustadt at 0038 † (not Dec. 25), 0736, 0836 **A**, 0936, 1036 **E**, 1136, 1236 **E**, 1336, 1436 **E**, 1536, 1636, 1736, 1836 Ⓑ **w**, 1936, 2036 Ⓑ **w**, 2136 and 2238 Ⓑ **w**.
From Puchberg at 0455 Ⓐ **n**, 0525 Ⓐ **n**, 0555 ⚒, 0625 Ⓐ **n**, 0637 © **k**, 0647 Ⓐ **n**, 0737, 0836, 0937 © **G**, 1035 ©, 1037 Ⓐ, 1137 **E**, 1235 ©, 1237 Ⓐ, 1337 **E**, 1435 ©, 1437 Ⓐ, 1537 **E**, 1637, 1735 ©, 1737 Ⓐ, 1837, 1937 Ⓑ **w** and 2037 ⑤⑥ **r**.

PUCHBERG am Schneeberg - **HOCHSCHNEEBERG** *Schneebergbahn* (narrow-gauge rack railway). *9 km* Journey time: 50 minutes.
Services run **Apr. 26 - Oct. 26, 2008** subject to demand and weather conditions. **Operator**: NÖ Schneebergbahn GmbH, Bahnhofplatz 1, A-2734 Puchberg. ✆ +43 (0) 2636 3661.
From Puchberg at 0900, 1015 🚂 † **H**, 1100, 1330 and 1530. **From Hochschneeberg** at 1000, 1200, 1430, 1445 🚂 † **H** and 1630. Additional trains operate when there is sufficient demand.

A – Ⓐ (daily Apr. 27 - Oct. 31).
E – ⚒ (daily Apr. 21 - Oct. 31).
G – May 1 - Oct. 26.
H – † July 6 - Aug. 31. Steam train (supplement).
k – Also Dec. 24, 31.
n – Not Dec. 24, 31.
r – Also Dec. 24, 25, 31, Mar. 23, Apr. 30, May 11, 21, Aug. 14, Dec. 7.
w – Not Dec. 23, 24, 25, 30, 31, Mar. 23, May 11, Dec. 7.

GRAZ - SZENTGOTTHÁRD - SZOMBATHELY 986

ÖBB, GySEV ●; 2nd class only

km				S	A✗		S		S	⚒				W			N	©			Ⓐ	n		Ⓑ	n		
0	**Graz** Hbf	d.	...	...	0614	...	0805c	1007	1144	1236	...	1330	...	1519	...	1632	1743	...	1803	1858	1858	...	2011	2011	...	2130	2304
30	Gleisdorf	d.	...	...	0651	...	0846	1047	1220	1309	...	1405	...	1551	...	1705	1815	...	1841	1936	1936	...	2047	2047	...	2205	2339
62	Fehring	d.	...	0505	0726	...	0920	1126	1257	1350	...	1439	...	1620	1627	1735	1842	1846	1919	2010	2011	...	2123	2137	...	2239	0011
82	Szentgotthárd 🏛	a.	...	0528	0744	...	0943	1147	1319	1412	...	1502	...	...	1649	1758	...	1907	1942	...	2033	...	...	2200	...	...	...
82	Szentgotthárd 🏛	d.	0408	0535	0753	0835	0947	1151	1344	...	1434	...	1610	...	1700	1819	...	...	1952	...	...	2105	...	...	2232	...	...
110	Körmend	d.	0444	0611	0826	0911	1023	1227	1421	...	1510	...	1647	...	1736	1855	...	...	2032	...	...	2142	...	...	2309	...	...
146	**Szombathely**	a.	0518	0645	0855	0945	1059	1300	1458	...	1544	...	1721	...	1810	1930	...	...	2106	...	...	2216	...	...	2343	...	...

		⚒	Ⓐ	©	†	⚒	⚒				N	S	W			⚒					S		S	B✗		n	n
Szombathely	d.	...	...	...	...	0408	...	0454	0620	0713	...	0948	...	...	1035	...	1150	1320	...	1434	1548	1636	1819	2000	2042	2152	2230
Körmend	d.	...	...	...	...	0445	...	0531	0659	0748	...	1023	...	...	1110	...	1228	1355	...	1511	1623	1711	1857	2030	2118	2229	2309
Szentgotthárd 🏛	a.	...	...	...	...	0520	...	0606	0734	0824	...	1057	...	...	1145	...	1303	1431	...	1546	1658	1747	1932	2102	2153	2304	2344
Szentgotthárd 🏛	d.	...	0411	...	...	...	0532	0620	0746	...	...	1059	...	...	...	1255	...	1437	1536	...	1711	*1817*	1945	2116	...	...	...
Fehring	d.	0408	0439	0453	0552	...	0558	0643	0809	...	0929	1121	1124	1210	...	1323	...	1500	1600	...	1735	*1839*	2007	2137	...	...	...
Gleisdorf	d.	0443	0507	0533	0626	...	0627	0715	0846	...	1002	...	1155	1244	...	1405	...	1529b	1639	...	1815	...	*2048*	2205	...	...	...
Graz Hbf	a.	0518	0541	0605	0702	...	0702	0746	0921	...	1030	...	1230	1321	...	1441	...	1603b	1721	...	1856	...	*2121*	2235	...	...	...

A – 🚃2 Graz (*ER* **4760**) - Szentgotthárd (*IC* **917**) Györ - Budapest.
B – 🚃2 Budapest (*IC* **916**) - Györ - Szentgotthárd (*ER* **4761**) - Graz.
N – 🚃2 Wiener Neustadt - Hartberg - Fehring - Graz and v.v.
S – To / from Wiener Neustadt via Sopron (Tables **1227** / **978**).
W – 🚃2 Wien - Hartberg - Fehring - Graz and v.v.
b – Fehring - Graz daily except ⑥.
c – 0809 on †.
n – Not Dec. 24, 31.
✗ – Ⓡ and supplement payable in Hungary.
● – GySEV: Györ-Sopron-Ebenfurti Vasút.

WIEN - GMÜND and KREMS AN DER DONAU 990

2nd class only

km			⚒	⚒	†	P				ⒶV	©V	Ⓐ												Ⓐ			C
0	**Wien** Franz-Josefs-Bf	d.	0500	0554	0617	0622	0651	0725	0751	✗	✗	0825	0924	0951	1029	1051	1151	1229	1251	1351	1429	1451	1551	1555	1619	1651	1659
1	Wien Spittelau ●	d.	0502	0557	0620	0625	0654	0728	0754	◧	◐	0827	0926	0954	1032	1054	1154	1232	1254	1354	1432	1454	1554	1558	1623	1654	1702
3	Wien Heiligenstadt △	d.	0506	0600	0624	0628	0658	0731	0758	|	|	0831	0930	0958	1035	1058	1158	1235	1258	1358	1435	1458	1558	1601	1626	1658	1705
33	Tulln	d.	0537	0621	0644	0649	0723	0752	0819	0850	0850	0857	0954	1019	1056	1119	1219	1256	1319	1419	1456	1519	1619	1624	1649	1719	|
44	Absdorf-Hippersdorf	d.	0549	0632	0656	0700	0732	0802	0829	|	|	0906	1006	1029	1106	1129	1229	1306	1329	1429	1506	1529	1629	|	1706	1729	|
75	**Krems** a. d. Donau	a.	0638	0714	0722	|	0803	|	0855	0927	0927	0935	|	1054	|	1154	1254	|	1354	1454	|	1554	1654	|	|	1758	|
79	Eggenburg	d.	...	...	...	0726	...	0832	...	...	...	▬	1044	...	1135	▬	...	1335	...	▬	1535	...	...	|	1735	...	1756
89	**Sigmundsherberg**	d.	...	...	...	0735	...	0840	...	...	...	...	1053	...	1144	...	...	1344	...	...	1544	...	...	1701	1744	...	1804
121	Göpfritz	d.	...	...	...	0759	...	0905	...	...	...	⚒	...	...	1209	Ⓐ	...	1409	...	Ⓐ	1609	...	...	1726	1813	...	1830
138	Schwarzenau	d.	...	...	...	0814	...	0920	...	...	...	1136	...	...	1224	1304	...	1424	...	1536	1624	...	...	1741	1827	...	1845
162	**Gmünd** NÖ	a.	...	...	...	0836	...	0943	...	...	...	1158	...	...	1246	1327	...	1446	...	1558	1646	...	...	1804	1850	...	1907

					Ⓐ					Ⓑz	
Wien Franz-Josefs-Bf	d.	1750	1755	1851	1857	1921	1951	2029	2051	2058	2151
Wien Spittelau ●	d.	1753	1759	1854	1900	1923	1954	2032	2054	2101	2154
Wien Heiligenstadt △	d.	1757	1803	1858	1903	1927	1958	2035	2058	2104	2158
Tulln	d.	1818	1824	1919	|	1952	2019	2056	2119	2128	2219
Absdorf-Hippersdorf	d.	1829	1833	1929	|	2005	2029	2111	2129	2139	2229
Krems a. d. Donau	a.	1855	|	1955	|	|	2054	|	2203	|	2256
Eggenburg	d.	...	1903	...	2001	2043	...	2139	...	2206	...
Sigmundsherberg	d.	...	1911	...	2012	2052	...	2148	...	2214	...
Göpfritz	d.	...	1937	...	2041	...	...	2213	...	...	...
Schwarzenau	d.	...	1953	...	2056	...	...	2228	...	...	...
Gmünd NÖ	a.	...	2016	...	2118	...	...	2250	...	...	...

		Ⓐ	⚒	⚒	Ⓐ	†	Ⓐ	⚒	Ⓐ		Ⓐ	©
Gmünd NÖ	d.	...	0346	...	...	...	0419	...	...	...	...	0514
Schwarzenau	d.	...	0408	...	...	...	0441	...	...	...	*0527*	0536
Göpfritz	d.	...	0422	...	...	...	0457	...	...	...	*0541*	0551
Sigmundsherberg	d.	...	0447	...	...	0505	0522	0529	...	...	0616	0616
Eggenburg	d.	...	0456	...	...	0514	|	0538	...	...	0625	0625
Krems a. d. Donau	d.	0426	|	0452	0522	|	|	|	0559	0614	|	|
Absdorf-Hippersdorf	d.	0457	|	0530	|	0549	|	0615	0631	0649	0654	0654
Tulln	d.	0506	0533	0539	|	0557	|	0624	0642	0658	0703	0703
Wien Heiligenstadt △	d.	0527	0554	0605	0615	0622	0619	0646	0706	0720	0724	0724
Wien Spittelau ●	d.	0531	0558	0609	0619	0625	0623	0650	0710	0724	0728	0728
Wien Franz-Josefs-Bf	a.	0533	0600	0611	0621	0627	0625	0653	0712	0727	0730	0730

		Ⓐ	⚒						Ⓑz	C				⚒			Ⓐ			Ⓐ	V✗					P	
Gmünd NÖ	d.	0531	...	0616	...	...	...	...	...	0913	...	...	1113	1202	...	1313	1340	...	1513	1616	...	...	1735	...	...	1930	...
Schwarzenau	d.	0553	...	0639	...	...	...	...	...	0937	...	...	1136	1223	...	1336	1402	...	1536	1639	...	...	1758	...	...	1952	...
Göpfritz	d.	0605	...	0653	...	...	...	...	...	0951	...	...	1151	▬	...	1351	▬	...	1551	▬	...	...	1812	...	...	2007	...
Sigmundsherberg	d.	0630	...	0717	...	...	...	0907	...	1017	...	...	1217	...	...	1417	...	...	1617	...	...	...	1837	...	...	2033	...
Eggenburg	d.	|	...	0726	...	...	...	0917	...	1025	...	...	1225	...	...	1425	...	...	1625	...	...	...	1846	...	...	2042	...
Krems a. d. Donau	d.	|	0644	|	0726	0815	0903	|	1003	|	1103	1201	|	1303	1401	|	1503	1601	|	1701	1715	1803	|	1903	2001	|	2103
Absdorf-Hippersdorf	d.	|	0721	0754	0759	0853	0928	0955	1028	1054	1128	1228	1254	1328	1428	1454	1528	1628	1656	1728	1753	1828	1920	1928	2028	2111	2128
Tulln	d.	|	0730	0803	0807	0901	0937	1003	1037	1103	1137	1237	1303	1337	1437	1503	1537	1637	1705	1737	1801	1837	1929	1937	2037	2120	2137
Wien Heiligenstadt △	d.	0729	0755	0824	0829	0922	0958	1028	1058	1124	1158	1258	1324	1358	1458	1524	1558	1658	1726	1758	|	1858	1950	1958	2058	2142	2158
Wien Spittelau ●	d.	0732	0759	0827	0833	0926	1001	1032	1101	1127	1201	1301	1327	1401	1501	1527	1601	1701	1729	1801	★	1901	1954	2001	2101	2145	2201
Wien Franz-Josefs-Bf	a.	0735	0801	0830	0835	0928	1004	1034	1104	1130	1204	1304	1330	1404	1504	1530	1604	1704	1732	1804	...	1904	1956	2004	2104	2147	2204

C – To / from České Budějovice (Table **1133**).
P – To / from Plzeň (Tables **1133** and **1125**).
V – Mar. 15 - Oct. 26. To / from St Valentin (Tables **991/2**).
z – Also Nov. 1.
◧ – From Wien Südbahnhof d. 0741.
◐ – From Wien Südbahnhof d. 0758.
★ – To Wien Handelskai a. 1832 (also Wien Südbahnhof on © a. 1902).
● – Direct U-bahn links: Line **U4** – Wien Mitte - Spittelau. Line **U6** – Wien Meidling - Westbahnhof - Spittelau.
△ – S-Bahn trains run every 15 – 20 minutes from / to Wien Hütteldorf (journey time: 21 minutes).

991 KREMS an der Donau - SPITZ an der Donau - EMMERSDORF an der Donau

2nd class only

km		Ⓐ	⚒	Ⓐ	⚒	E		W✕					ⒶB	A✕	D		E	E	L✕	B	E	Ⓐ		
0	**Krems** an der Donau d.	0423	0458	0607	0645	0805	0901	0936	...	1059	1201	1301	1334	1334	1401	1501	1601	1636	1700	1701	1801	1836	1901	2001
7	Dürnstein-Oberloiben d.	0433	0509	0619	0707	0814	0912	0947	...	1110	1212	1312	1346	1346	1412	1513	1612	1649	1711	1712	1812	1849	1912	2012
13	Weißenkirchen d.	0440	0516	0627	0714	0821	0919	0955	...	1119	1219	1319	1353	1354	1419	1520	1619	1656	1719	1719	1819	1856	1919	2019
18	**Spitz** an der Donau d.	0447	0530	0635	0721	0828	0927	1004	...	1127	1227	1327	1402	1403	1427	1527	1627	1704	1728	1727	1827	1903	1927	2027
26	Aggsbach Markt d.	...	0550	...	...	...	...	1026	...	...	...	...	1422	1424	...	...	...	...	1749	...	...	...	...	...
34	**Emmersdorf** an der Donau a.	...	0559	...	...	...	...	1036	...	...	...	...	...	...	...	...	...	...	1800	...	...	...	...	...

	Ⓐ	Ⓐ	⚒	Ⓐ	⑥z	⚒	⚒	E		L✕				D	A✕	ⒶB		ⒶB	W✕		E	Ⓐ		
Emmersdorf an der Donau d.	...	...	...	0611	0618	...	...	...	...	1039	...	...	...	...	...	...	...	...	1554	...	...	...	...	...
Aggsbach Markt d.	...	...	...	0621	0628	...	...	...	...	1049	...	...	...	...	1435	1436	...	...	1604	...	...	...	...	...
Spitz an der Donau d.	0454	0527	0604	0642	0651	0651	0729	0832	0931	1110	1131	1231	1331	1431	1457	1457	1531	1632	1633	1731	1832	1910	1931	2031
Weißenkirchen d.	0502	0535	0612	0649	0659	0659	0737	0840	0939	1119	1139	1239	1339	1439	1505	1505	1539	1640	1641	1739	1840	1920	1939	2039
Dürnstein-Oberloiben d.	0509	0542	0619	0657	0706	0706	0744	0847	0946	1129	1146	1246	1346	1446	1513	1513	1546	1647	1649	1746	1848	1927	1946	2046
Krems an der Donau a.	0520	0553	0630	0705	0717	0717	0755	0856	0957	1140	1157	1257	1357	1457	1524	1524	1557	1658	1659	1757	1859	1938	1957	2057

A – Mar. 15 - Oct. 26.
B – To Mar. 14 and from Oct. 27.
D – ⚒ (daily Mar. 10 - Oct. 31).
E – Ⓐ (daily Mar. 10 - Oct. 31).
L – Mar. 15 - Oct. 26. From / to Linz (Table **992**).
W – Mar. 15 - Oct. 26. 🚌 Wien - St Valentin and v.v. (Tables **990/2**).
z – Not Nov. 1.

992 EMMERSDORF an der Donau - GREIN - ST VALENTIN and LINZ

2nd class only

km		⚒	Ⓐ	⚒	Ⓐ			⚒		Ⓐ			⚒		W✕	⚒		⚒	Ⓐ	Ⓒ	Ⓐ			K✕
0	**Emmersdorf** an der Donau d.	...	...	...	...	...	...	...	...	...	...	...	...	...	1039	...	...	...	...	...	...	...	...	1801
37	St Nikola-Struden d.	...	...	0531	...	0559	0632	0701	0804	0839	0923	...	1036	1136	1136	1236	1336	1436	1536	1536	1634	1736	1836	1903
43	Grein-Bad Kreuzen d.	0406	0443	0541	0602	0613	0643	0712	0815	0851	0946	...	1046	1146	1146	1246	1346	1446	1546	1546	1646	1746	1846	1916
81	**St Valentin** a.	0459	0535	0634	|	0705	|	0805	0909	0941	1037	...	1137	1237	1237	1337	1437	1538	|	1637	1736	1837	1937	|
99	**Linz** Hbf a.	*0535*	*0605*	*0659*	0704	*0725*	0758	*0829*	*0929*	*1029*	*1105*	...	*1208*	*1308*	*1308*	*1408*	*1508*	*1608*	1701	*1708*	*1808*	*1929*	*2008*	2023

	⚒	Ⓐ	⚒				K✕			Ⓐ		⚒		W✕		Ⓐ	⚒	Ⓐ		Ⓐ	⚒	Ⓐ		
Linz Hbf d.	...	*0517*	*0618*	*0652*	...	0824	0824	...	*0930*	*1030*	*1130*	*1230*	*1330*	*1330*	*1430*	*1453*	*1530*	1602	*1630*	1702	*1730*	1802	*1831*	*1930*
St Valentin d.	0504	0548	0648	0718	...	|	|	...	0951	1051	1151	1251	1351	1351	1451	1523	1551	|	1651	|	1751	|	1851	1951
Grein-Bad Kreuzen d.	0610	0643	0743	0815	...	0933	0933	...	1046	1146	1246	1346	1446	1446	1546	1615	1646	1715	1746	1815	1845	1916	1946	2045
St Nikola-Struden a.	0619	0653	0752	0826	...	0943	0943	...	1055	1155	1255	1355	1455	1455	1557	...	1655	...	1755	1824	...	1925	1957	2054
Emmersdorf an der Donau a.	...	...	...	...	...	...	1038	...	...	...	...	...	...	1553	...	...	...	...	...	...	...	...	...	...

K – Mar. 15 - Oct. 26. To / from Krems a. d. Donau (Table **991**).
W – Mar. 15 - Oct. 26. 🚌 Wien - Krems - St Valentin and v.v. (Tables **990/1**).

993 ST PÖLTEN - KREMS and TULLN

2nd class only

km		⚒	Ⓐ	Ⓐ	⚒	⚒	⚒	†		Ⓐ												Ⓐ			
0	**St Pölten** Hbf d.	0428	0451	0603	0608	0634	0708	0716	0737	...	0838	...	0935	...	1037	1135	...	1237	1335	...	1437	1514	1535	...	1637
11	Herzogenburg d.	0443	0506	0611	0640	0647	0728	0728	0751	0753	0847	0849	0950	0952	1046	1150	1152	1246	1350	1352	1446	1526	1550	1552	1646
	Tulln a.	0529	|	|	0734	|	|	|	0835	|	|	0935	1035	|	|	1235	|	|	1435	|	|	|	1635	|	|
30	**Krems** an der Donau a.	...	0537	0639	...	0718	0755	0755	...	0825	0913	...	...	1024	1110	...	1224	1310	...	1424	1510	1555	...	1624	1712

	Ⓐ				Ⓐ				Ⓑ	
St Pölten Hbf d.	1714	1735	...	1837	...	1935	...	2041	2140	...
Herzogenburg d.	1726	1750	1752	1847	1849	1951	1952	2058	2150	...
Tulln a.	|	1835	|	|	1935	2035	|	|	|	
Krems an der Donau a.	1755	...	1825	1911	...	...	2023	2128	2219	...

km		Ⓐn	Ⓐ	Ⓐn	⚒	⚒		⚒	⚒	⚒
	Krems an der Donau d.	0433	0454	...	0540	0603	0615	...	0640	...
0	Tulln d.	|	|	0502	|	|	|	0625	|	0705
38	Herzogenburg d.	0506	0527	0545	0611	0631	0647	0708	0714	0739
49	**St Pölten** Hbf a.	0523	0542	0558	0626	0642	0704	0717	0723	0747

														†	⚒						Ⓐ		Ⓑ		Ⓑ
Krems an der Donau d.	0719	0816	...	0947	1034	...	1147	1234	...	1347	1434	...	1547	1633	1636	...	1747	1835	...	...	...	1942	2016	...	2047
Tulln d.	|	|	0809	|	|	1007	|	|	1207	|	|	1407	|	|	|	1607	|	|	1807	...	1907	|	|	2007	|
Herzogenburg d.	0751	0845	0910	1013	1105	1110	1213	1305	1310	1413	1505	1510	1613	1705	1705	1710	1813	1906	1910	...	1951	2013	2042	2057	2119
St Pölten Hbf a.	0806	...	0925	1021	...	1125	1221	...	1325	1421	...	1525	1621	...	...	1725	1821	...	1925	...	2005	2021	2056	2111	2127

n – Not Dec. 24, 31.

994 ST PÖLTEN - MARIAZELL

Narrow gauge 2nd class only

km			r	P🚂	C				Ⓐ	Ⓒ
0	**St Pölten** Hbf d.	0733	0835	0935	1034	...	1336	1638	1949	2048
12	Ober Grafendorf d.	0756	0857	1009	1053	...	1355	1658	2008	2107
31	Kirchberg a. d. Pielach d.	0831	0933	1045	1126	...	1430	1732	2044	2141
43	Frankenfels d.	0851	0954	|	1147	...	1451	1753	2105	2202
48	Laubenbachmühle d.	0900	1005	|	1156	...	1501	1803	2114	2211
57	Winterbach ● d.	0916	1022	|	1210	...	1517	1819	...	...
67	Gösing d.	0936	1042	|	1226	1416	1535	1836	...	...
80	Mitterbach ● d.	1001	1107	|	1250	1441	1559	1900	...	...
84	**Mariazell** a.	1008	1114	1251	1259	1448	1605	1906	...	...

				ⒶE	⚒			P🚂	Ⓒr	Ⓐ	Ⓒ
Mariazell d.	...	0758	1153	1302	...	1333	1501	1606	1657	1659	1804
Mitterbach ● d.	...	0804	1159	1308	...	1339	1507	|	1703	1705	1810
Gösing d.	...	0829	1228	1332	...	1405	1534	|	1730	1730	1836
Winterbach ● d.	...	0844	1245	1347	...	...	1551	|	1746	1746	1851
Laubenbachmühle d.	0648	0901	1300	1402	1402	...	1606	|	1802	1803	1907
Frankenfels d.	0657	0911	1309	1410	1410	...	1615	|	1811	1812	1916
Kirchberg a. d. Pielach d.	0720	0933	1330	1431	1431	...	1636	1751	1832	1834	1937
Ober Grafendorf d.	0755	1008	1406	1508	1508	...	1712	1836	1906	1907	2011
St Pölten Hbf a.	0815	1026	1428	1527	1527	...	1733	1855	1925	1925	2029

C – Ⓒ (daily May 1 - Oct. 26).
E – May 2 - Oct. 24.
P – Runs on May 4, June 1, July 6, Aug. 3, Sept. 7 and Oct. 5 only. PANORAMIC 760. Conveys 🚃 and ✕. Steam train with special fares.
r – Conveys ✕ on Ⓒ May 1 - Oct. 26.
● – Trains stop on request.

996 WIEN - BRATISLAVA via Marchegg

km																			2	2	2
0	**Wien** Südbahnhof d.	0528	0628	0728	0828	0928	1028	1128	1228	1328	1428	1528	1628	1728	1828	1928	2028	2128	2228	2324*	0024*
47	Marchegg 🛃 d.	0616	0704	0816	0904	1016	1104	1216	1304	1416	1504	1616	1704	1816	1904	2016	2104	2216	2304	0016	0116
53	Devínska Nová Ves 🛃 a.	0623	0711	0823	0911	1023	1111	1223	1311	1423	1511	1623	1711	1823	1911	2023	2111	2223	2311	0023	0123
66	**Bratislava** Hlavná a.	0637	0725	0837	0925	1037	1125	1237	1325	1437	1525	1637	1725	1837	1925	2037	2125	2237	2325	0037	0137

	①–⑤																		2	2	2
Bratislava Hlavná d.	0445	0550	0700	0750	0900	0950	1100	1150	1300	1350	1500	1550	1700	1750	1900	1950	2100	2150	2300	2350	0050
Devínska Nová Ves 🛃 d.	0502	0604	0714	0804	0914	1004	1114	1204	1314	1404	1514	1604	1714	1804	1914	2004	2114	2204	2314	0004	0104
Marchegg 🛃 d.	0512	0614	0722	0814	0922	1014	1122	1214	1322	1414	1522	1614	1722	1814	1922	2014	2122	2214	2322	0014	0114
Wien Südbahnhof a.	0558	0658	0758	0858	0958	1058	1158	1258	1358	1458	1558	1658	1758	1858	1958	2058	2158	2258	2358	0103*	0203*

* – From / to suburban platforms 21 / 22.

997 WIEN - BRATISLAVA via Bruck an der Leitha

km		2	2Ⓐ	2Ⓒ	2	2	2	*IC* 405 K✕	2	2	2	2	2	2	2	*IC* 403 K✕	2	2	2	2Ⓒ	2	2	2	*IC* 407 ✕	2
0	**Wien** Südbahnhof **1250** d.	0112	0512	0512	0612	0712	0812	...	0912	1012	1116	1212	1312	1412	1512	...	1612	1712	1812	✕	1912	2012	2112	...	2312
	Wien Westbahnhof **1250** d.	|	|	|	|	|	|	0814	|	|	|	|	|	|	|	1536	|	|	|	m	|	|	|	2150	|
	Wien Meidling d.	|	|	|	|	|	|	0829	|	|	|	|	|	|	|	1550	|	|	|	1848	|	|	|	2205	|
41	Bruck an der Leitha **1250** d.	0139	0536	0539	0639	0739	0843	0902	0939	1039	1143	1239	1339	1439	1539	1626	1639	1739	1839	1928	1939	2039	2139	2237	2339
69	Kittsee 🛃 d.	0205	0553	0606	0659	0805	0909	0919	1005	1105	1209	1305	1405	1505	1605	1645	1705	1805	1905	1946	2005	2105	2205	2254	0005
74	**Bratislava** - Petržalka 🛃 a.	0210	0559	0613	0705	0810	0914	0925	1010	1110	1214	1310	1410	1510	1610	1651	1710	1810	1910	1953	2010	2110	2210	2300	0010
92	**Bratislava** Hlavná a.	...	...	...	...	...	...	0955	...	...	...	...	...	...	...	1721	...	...	...	...	...	...	...	2330	...

km		2Ⓒ	*IC* 400 ✕	2	2A	2Ⓒ	2	2	2	2	*IC* 402 K✕	2	2	2	2	2	2	2	*IC* 404 K✕	2	2	2	2	2Ⓒ	2
0	**Bratislava** Hlavná d.	...	...	...	...	✕	...	...	...	...	1052	...	...	...	...	...	...	...	1812	...	...	...	...	...	...
18	**Bratislava** - Petržalka 🛃 d.	0456	0547	0600	0637	0651	0740	0843	0940	1040	1122	1144	1240	1340	1440	1540	1640	1740	1842	1858	1940	2040	2140	2245	2340
23	Kittsee 🛃 d.	0502	|	0606	0642	0659	0746	0849	0946	1046	1128	1150	1246	1346	1446	1546	1646	1746	1848	1904	1946	2046	2146	2253	2346
51	Bruck an der Leitha **1250** d.	0528	0608	0631	0701	0730	0820	0917	1014	1114	1146	1218	1314	1414	1514	1614	1714	1814	1906	1933	2014	2114	2214	2325	0014
89	**Wien** Meidling a.	|	0645	|	|	0807	|	|	|	|	1217	|	|	|	|	|	|	|	1938	|	|	|	|	|	|
104	**Wien** Westbahnhof **1250** a.	|	0701	|	|	m	|	|	|	|	1232	|	|	|	|	|	|	|	1954	|	|	|	|	|	|
	Wien Südbahnhof **1250** a.	0555	...	0659	0727	...	0846	0945	1040	1140	...	1245	1340	1440	1540	1640	1740	1840	...	2000	2040	2140	2240	2358	0040

A – Ⓐ (not Dec. 24, 31).
K – From / to Košice (Table **1180**).
m – To / from Mürzzuschlag (Table **981**).

WIEN - BŘECLAV 999

See also Table 981

km		EC 370 H ⚡	D 270 B	EC 104 S ⚡	EC 172 V ⚡	D 272 B	EC* 72 🍷⚡	EC 102 P ⚡	EC* 74 🍷⚡	D 274 B	EC 70 ✕⚡	D 202 W	202 224 C
0	**Wien** Südbahnhof .... d.	0608	0732	0908	1004	1232	1333	1433	1533	1732	1833	2233	2233
71	Hohenau 🏛 .... d.	0655	0817	0955	1051	1317	1420	1520	1620	1817	1920	2320	2320
89	**Břeclav** 🏛 .... a.	0708	0830	1008	1104	1330	1433	1533	1633	1830	1933	2333	2333
	Praha Hlavní **1150** .... a.	|	...	...	|	...	|	...	|	...	2310	...	0621
	Praha Holešovice **1150** .... a.	1025	...	...	1425	...	1732	...	1932	...	...	...	...

	D 203 W	225 203 C	EC 71 ✕⚡	D 271 B	EC* 73 🍷⚡	EC 103 P ⚡	EC* 75 🍷⚡	D 273 B	EC 173 V ⚡	EC 105 S ⚡	D 275 B	EC 177 L ⚡
Praha Holešovice **1150** .... d.	...	...	...	...	0823	...	1023	...	1333	...	...	1733
Praha Hlavní **1150** .... d.	...	2206	0500	...	|	...	|	...	|	...	...	|
řeclav 981 🏛 .... d.	0457	0457	0823	1025	1123	1223	1323	1525	1658	1723	2025	2058
ohenau **981** 🏛 .... d.	0510	0510	0836	1038	1136	1236	1336	1538	1711	1736	2038	2111
ien Südbahnhof **981** .... a.	0603	0603	0928	1130	1228	1328	1428	1630	1803	1828	2130	2203

B – To / from Brno (Table **1150**).
C – 🛏 1, 2 cl. Wien - Přerov - Praha and v.v.
H – [12] and ✕ Wien - Dresden - Berlin - Stralsund.
L – [12] and ✕ Berlin - Dresden - Praha - Wien.
P – POLONIA – [12] and ✕ Wien - Ostrava - Petrovice - Warszawa and v.v.; [2] Wien - Petrovice - Kraków and v.v.
S – SOBIESKI – [12] and ✕ Wien - Ostrava - Warszawa and v.v.
V – [12] and ✕ Wien - Dresden - Berlin - Hamburg and v.v.
W – CHOPIN – 🛏 1, 2 cl., ▬ 2 cl. and [2] Wien - Warszawa and v.v.; conveys 🛏 1, 2 cl. (also ▬ 2 cl. Apr. 30 - Sept. 28 from Wien, Apr. 29 - Sept. 27 from Kraków) Wien - Kraków and v.v.; 🛏 1, 2 cl. Wien - Moskva and v.v.

* – Classified *SC* in Czech Republic (higher supplement).
⚡ – Supplement payable in Czech Republic.

POLAND

perator: Polskie Koleje Państwowe (PKP).

ervices: All trains convey first and second class seating, **except** where shown otherwise in footnotes or by '2' in the train column, or where the footnote shows sleeping and/or couchette cars only. Descriptions of sleeping (🛏) and couchette (▬) cars appear on page 10. As shown in the individual tables, Russian/Ukrainian sleeping car services cannot be used for journeys in or between Poland and Germany unless seating cars are also conveyed. Note that train numbers often change en route by one or two digits. In station names, Gł. is short for Główny or Główna, meaning main station.

mings: Valid from **December 9, 2007 - June 14, 2008**. Many trains, including long-distance and express services, do not run over the Christmas and Easter periods. A number of long-distance trains running only in high summer (particularly to coastal resorts) are not shown due to lack of space.

ckets: A higher fare is payable for travel by all *EC*, *IC*, *Ex*, and *IR* trains. Special fares are payable on *TLK* (Tanie Linie Kolejowe / cheap railway lines) trains.

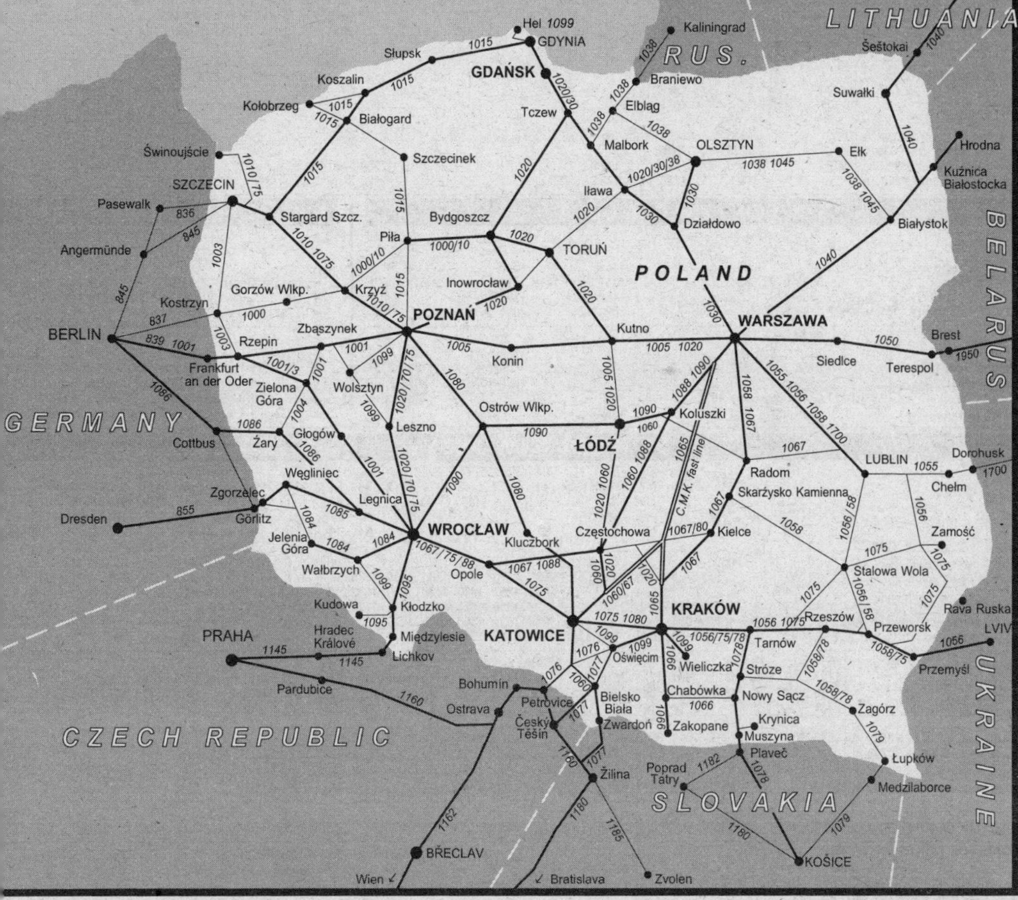

KOSTRZYN - KRZYŻ - PIŁA - BYDGOSZCZ 1000

km		82106 A	◇	81102 F	◇	◇ q	◇	◇ q	88100	81102	◇	◇ q	81704 j
0	**Kostrzyn** .... d.	...	0547	...	0836	...	1122	...	1401	...	1626	...	...
43	Gorzów Wlkp. ..... d.	0459	0631	...	0922	...	1205	...	1447	...	1710	...	...
03	Krzyż .... a.	0604	0723	...	1015	...	1257	...	1538	...	1802	...	...
03	Krzyż **1010** .... d.	...	...	0757	...	1025	...	1433	...	1548	...	1932	0140
61	**Piła 1010** .... a.	...	...	0900	...	1116	...	1524	...	1652	...	2023	0240
48	**Bydgoszcz 1010** a.	...	...	1024	...	...	...	...	...	1817	...	...	0410
	Warszawa ▲... a.	...	...	1410	...	...	...	...	...	2220	...	...	0810

	◇ q	◇	◇	◇	18102	88101	◇	18102 F	28106 A	◇	18704 k	◇
Warszawa ▲... d.	...	...	...	...	0700	...	...	1500	...	...	2200	...
Bydgoszcz 1010 d.	...	...	...	...	1051	...	...	1901	...	...	0142	...
Piła 1010 .... d.	0638	...	0915	...	1214	...	...	2025	...	...	0306	...
Krzyż **1010** .... a.	0729	...	1006	...	1312	...	...	2122	...	...	0403	...
Krzyż .... d.	...	0826	...	1214	...	1323	1810	...	2136	...	...	0528
Gorzów Wlkp. ..... d.	...	0921	...	1310	...	1417	1904	...	2240	2300	...	0632
Kostrzyn .... a.	...	1002	...	1350	...	1458	1944	...	...	2340	...	0722

– [12] Gorzów Wlkp. - Poznań - Kraków - Zamość and v.v.
– [12] Szczecin - Krzyż - Warszawa - Lublin and v.v.
– Not Dec. 25, Mar. 24.

k – Not Dec. 24, Mar. 23.
q – To / from Chojnice.

◇ – Stopping train. 2nd class only.
▲ – Warszawa Centralna (Table **1020**).

1001 BERLIN - POZNAŃ and WROCŁAW

See Table **56** for train **246/247** Berlin - Moskva / St Petersburg and train **1248/1249** Berlin - Saratov (these are not available for journeys Germany - Poland or v.v.)

km		2 ◇ H	73100 73101 ✕ F	2 ◇	Ex 7111/0 ®✕ Z	EN® 347 71008 J	70243 70244 2	EC 41 ✣ By	75103 75102 ✕ D	EC 241 ®✕ M	2 ◇	2 ◇	EC 45 ✣ Bk	70245 70246 2	7644 ◇ 2	◇ 2	TLK 7116 ✕® Zh	◇	5883 2 ◇	EC 47 ✣ Bk	5885 2 ◇	EC 49 ✣ Nk	7648 2 ◇	345 72002 A	345 83704 ®🍸 Y	70241 70242
	Berlin Hauptbahnhof **839** .. d.	...	...	...	...	...	...	0629	...	0940	...	...	1229	...	...	...	...	1347	...	1629	...	1826	...	...	...	...
0	**Berlin** Ostbahnhof **839** ...... d.	...	...	...	...	...	...	0640	...	0949	...	...	1240	...	...	...	...	1357	...	1640	...	1838	...	2138q	2138q	...
82	Frankfurt an der Oder **839** . a.	...	...	...	...	...	...	0736	...	|	...	...	1336	...	...	...	...	1500	...	1736	...	1936	...	|	|	...
82	Frankfurt an der Oder 🏛 ... d.	...	...	...	...	...	...	0739	...	◐	...	...	1339	...	...	...	...	...	1519	1739	1910	1939	...	|	|	...
93	Kunowice 🏛 .... d.	...	...	...	...	...	...	|	...	|	...	...	|	...	...	...	...	...	1534	|	1924	|	...	|	|	...
105	Rzepin .... a.	...	...	...	...	...	...	0755	...	|	...	...	1355	...	...	...	...	...	1544	1755	1934	1956	...	|	|	...
105	Rzepin **1003** .... d.	...	...	0455	...	0601s	...	0805	...	|	...	...	1405	...	...	1445	...	...	1554	1805	1948	2006	...	2347u	2347u	...
176	**Zielona Góra 1003** .... d.	...	0518	0623	...	|	...	|	...	|	...	1239	|	...	1429	|	...	...	|	|	|	|	1832	|	|	...
229	Glogów .... d.	...	0628	0735	...	|	...	|	...	|	...	1354	|	...	1554	|	...	...	|	|	|	|	1946	|	|	...
**	**Zielona Góra** .... d.	...	|	|	0531	|	0611	|	0937	|	...	|	|	1410	|	|	1512	...	|	|	2117	|	|	|	|	2349
180	Zbąszynek **1099** .... d.	0353	|	|	0638	|	0719	|	1101	|	1204	|	1443	1522	|	1550	1624	...	1652	|	...	2052	|	|	|	0056
186	Zbąszyń **1099** .... d.	0359	|	|	|	|	0725	|	1107	|	1210	|	|	1529	|	...	1632	...	1658	|	...	|	|	|	|	0102
261	**Poznań** Gł. .... a.	0510	|	|	0730	0739	0830	0932	1200	|	1320	|	1532	1623	|	...	1730	...	1805	1932	...	2145	|	0138	0138	0153
329*	**Wrocław** Gł. .... a.	...	0856	1004	|	|	...	|	...	1524	...	1620	|	...	1823	...	|	...	...	|	...	...	2215	|	0439	...
	Katowice **1075** .... a.	...	1210	...	|	|	...	|	...	1815	...	...	|	...	...	...	|	...	...	|	...	...	...	|	0729	...
	Kraków **1075** .... a.	...	1355	...	|	|	...	|	...	1944	...	...	|	...	...	...	|	...	...	|	...	...	...	|	0858	...
	Warszawa Centralna **1005**. a.	...	...	...	1054	1040	...	1235	...	...	...	...	1835	...	...	...	2120	...	...	2235	...	...	...	0550	...	...
	Warszawa Wschodnia **1005** a.	...	...	...	1110	1052	...	1247	...	...	...	...	1847	...	...	...	2132	...	...	2247	...	...	...	0602	...	...

	EC 48 ✣ Pk	77243 77244 2	TLK 1717/6 ®✕ Zh	EC 46 ✣ Bk	6741 ◇ 2	EC 44 ✣ Bk	6743 ◇ 2	EC 240 ®✕ M	77223 ◇ 2	57105 57104 ✕ D	6745 ◇ 2	77245 ◇ 2	6747 ◇ 2	◇ 2	EC 40 ✣ Bb	77231 ◇ 2	6749 ◇ 2	Ex 1711/0 ®✕ Z	EN® 346 17009 J	37100 37101 ✕ F	77241 ◇ 2	344 27003 A	38705 344 ®🍸 Y			
Warszawa Wschodnia **1005** d.	...	...	0543	0713	...	1113	...	...	...	...	...	...	...	...	1613	...	...	1713	1742	...	...	2317	...	...	...	...
Warszawa Centralna **1005** d.	...	...	0555	0725	...	1125	...	...	...	...	...	...	...	...	1625	...	...	1725	1755u	...	...	2330	...	...	...	...
Kraków **1075** .... d.	...	...	|	|	...	|	...	0731	...	...	...	...	...	...	|	...	...	|	|	1517	...	|	2005	...	...	...
Katowice **1075** .... d.	...	...	|	|	...	|	...	0854	...	...	...	...	...	...	|	...	...	|	|	1656	...	|	2140	...	...	...
Wrocław Gł. .... d.	...	...	|	|	0528	|	0943	1136	...	...	1243	...	1443	...	|	...	1643	|	|	2002	...	|	0025	...	...	...
Poznań Gł. .... d.	0601	0620	0944	1020	|	1420	|	|	1440	1535	|	1640	|	...	1920	1933	|	2040	2105u	|	0300	0330	0330	...	...	...
Zbąszyń **1099** .... d.	|	0728	1038	|	|	|	|	|	1546	1630	|	1736	|	...	|	2040	|	|	|	|	0353	|	|	...	...	...
Zbąszynek **1099** .... d.	0654	0737	1045	|	|	1506	|	|	1552	1645	|	1743	|	...	|	2047	|	2134	|	|	0401	|	|	...	...	...
Zielona Góra .... a.	|	0847	1202	|	|	|	|	|	...	1800	|	1853	|	...	|	...	|	2245	|	|	0512	|	|	...	...	...
Glogów .... d.	|	...	...	|	0803	|	1218	|	...	...	1507	...	1718	...	|	...	1916	...	|	2228	...	|	|	...	...	...
Zielona Góra 1003 .... d.	|	...	...	|	0915	|	1331	|	...	...	1620	...	1833	1915	|	...	2030	...	|	2338	...	|	|	...	...	...
Rzepin **1003** .... a.	0744	...	...	1144	...	1544	...	|	...	...	...	...	...	2043	2044	...	2157	...	|	...	...	0503s	0503s	...	...	...
Rzepin .... d.	0754	...	...	1154	...	1554	...	|	...	...	...	...	...	...	2054	...	...	...	2244u	...	...	|	|	...	...	...
Kunowice 🏛 .... d.	|	...	...	|	...	|	...	|	...	...	...	...	...	...	|	...	...	...	...	...	...	|	|	...	...	...
Frankfurt an der Oder 🏛 ... a.	0813	...	...	1213	...	1613	...	◐	...	...	...	...	...	...	2113	...	...	...	...	...	...	|	|	...	...	...
Frankfurt an der Oder **839** d.	0816	...	...	1216	...	1616	...	|	...	...	...	...	...	...	2116	...	...	...	...	...	...	|	|	...	...	...
Berlin Ostbahnhof **839** ..... a.	0915	...	...	1315	...	1715	...	1721	...	...	...	...	...	...	2209	...	...	...	...	...	...	0714q	0714q	...	...	...
Berlin Hauptbahnhof **839**.. a.	0926	...	...	1326	...	1726	...	1731	...	...	...	...	...	...	2220	...	...	...	...	...	...	...	...	...	...	...

1003 SZCZECIN - ZIELONA GÓRA

km		◇ 2	◇2 V	◇ 2	◇2 V		◇ 2		◇ 2	◇2 ⑧	◇ 2	◇ 2	◇ 2	◇ 2	◇ 2	84500 E
0	**Szczecin** Gł. .... d.	...	...	...	0600	...	0845	...	1145	...	1445	1545	...	1745	2045	2133
104	Kostrzyn .... d.	...	0523	0708	0831	...	1116	...	1417	1540	1715	1817	...	2019	2316	0001
136	Rzepin **1001** .... d.	0455	0605	0751	...	...	...	...	1456	1621	...	1856	1948	...	...	|
207	**Zielona Góra 1001** . a.	0622	0735	0917	...	...	...	...	1623	1747	...	2024	2117	...	...	0155

	◇2 f	◇ 2	48501 Q	◇ 2	◇ 2	◇ 2		◇2 ①–⑥	◇ 2		◇ 2	◇2 V	◇2 W		◇ 2	◇ 2
Zielona Góra 1001 ..d.	...	...	0156	...	0622	...	...	1100	...	...	...	1440	1525	...	1915	2032
Rzepin **1001** ....d.	...	...	|	...	0750	...	...	1229	...	...	...	1608	1656	...	2048	2157
Kostrzyn ....d.	0320	0430	0349	0630	0831	1030	...	1311	1330	...	1530	...	1757	...	2131	...
Szczecin Gł. ....a.	0520	0630	0536	0830	1030	1230	...	...	1530	...	1730	...	1958	...	...	...

1004 ZIELONA GÓRA - ŻAGAŃ

km		m 2 ◇	w 2 ◇	2 ◇	w 2 ◇	①–⑤ 2 ◇	V 2 ◇	
0	**Zielona Góra** d.	0625	1055	...	1532	...	1915	...
54	Żary .... d.	0737	1203	1208	1641	1716	2024	...
67	Żagań .... a.	0752	...	1223	...	1731	2039	...

	2 ◇	2 ◇	V 2 ◇	V 2 ◇	⑧ 2 ◇	w 2 ◇	V 2 ◇	X 2 ◇
Żagań .... d.	0441	...	0520	...	1250	...	...	...
Żary .... d.	0453	0458	0532	0752	1302	1315	1718	1914
Zielona Góra a.	...	0607	...	0901	...	1423	1827	2022

1005 POZNAŃ - WARSZAWA

For other trains Warszawa - Wrocław and v.v. see Table 1090

km		TLK 7114 7115 ®✕ ph	IC 7100 ® ✕ H	IC 6103 6102 ®✕ K	Ex 7110 ® ✕ Z	EN 347 71008 ® J	IC 8102 ® ✕ R	IC 6105/4 ® ✕ H	EC 41 ® ✕ By	TLK 8210 ® 🍸 §	Ex/IC 6113 61403 ® ✕	Ex 8110 81412 ® ✕	Ex 7112 ® ✕ H	EC 45 ® ✕ Bk	IC 6107 6106 ®✕ v	TLK 7116 ® ✕ Zh	81100 81101 gh	IC 8100 81402 ®✕ L	EC 47 ® ✕ Bk	81202 81203 G	345 72002 A	TLK 83704 81704 Sj		
	Szczecin Gł. **1010** ....d.	...	...	...	...	...	0531	...	...	0845	...	1103	...	...	...	...	1513	1603	...	2300	...	2315	...	...
	Wrocław Gł. **1070** ....d.	...	...	0500	...	...	|	0630	...	|	1030	|	...	...	1430	...	|	|	...	|	...	|	...	...
0	**Poznań** Gł. ....d.	0527	0635	0705	0735	0739s	|	0835	0935	1135	1235	1335	1435	1535	1635	1735	1755	1835	1935	0200	0208	|	...	...
100	Konin ....d.	0646	|	|	0850	0838s	|	|	1032	1257	1330	1430	1530	1632	|	1857	1946	|	2032	0326	|	|	...	...
179	Kutno **1020** ....d.	0739	|	|	0939	0923s	0944	1019	1122	1356	1422	1529	1624	1722	|	1954	2039	2020	2122	0429	0419	0634	...	...
306	**Warszawa** Centralna **1020** ...a.	0905	0926	1005	1054	1040s	1058	1135	1235	1525	1540	1645	1740	1835	1935	2120	...	2135	2235	0605	0550	0810	...	...
311	**Warszawa** Wschodnia **1020** .a.	0927	0937	1022	1110	1052	1114	1147	1247	1542	1552	1657	1752	1847	1947	2132	...	2147	2247	0617	0602	0822	...	...

	TLK 1717 1716 ®✕ Zh	IC 1801 18401 ®🍸 U	EC 46 ® ✕ Bk	18100 18101 gh	IC 1607 1606 ®✕ h	Ex 1713 ® ✕ H	TLK 2810 ® 🍸 §	EC 44 ® ✕ Bk		Ex 1811 18411 ® ✕	Ex/IC 1613 16403 ® ✕	IC 1701 ® ✕ H	IC 1603/2 ® ✕ L	EC 40 ® ✕ Bb	IC 1803 ® ✕ T	Ex 1711 ® ✕ Z	EN 346 17008 ®✕ J	IC 1605/4 ® ✕ H	TLK 1714 1715 ®✕ ph	TLK 18705 38705 ® Sr	18202 18203 G	344 27003 A		
Warszawa Wschodnia **1020** .d.	0543	0608	0713	...	0813	0913	0943	1113	...	1308	1413	1513	1558	1613	1643	1713	1742	1813	1823	2149	2243	2317	...	...
Warszawa Centralna **1020**....d.	0555	0625	0725	...	0825	0925	0955	1125	...	1325	1425	1525	1615	1625	1655	1725	1755u	1825	1855	2200	2255	2330	...	...
Kutno **1020** ....d.	0723	0744	0842	0852	|	1043	1125	1242	...	1444	1543	|	|	1742	1812	1843	1913u	1942	2026	2329	0027	0055	...	...
Konin ....d.	0812	|	0921	0941	|	1124	1213	1321	...	1525	1625	|	|	1821	|	1927	1955u	|	2113	|	0117	|	...	...
Poznań Gł. ....a.	0940	0924	1017	1102	1117	1230	1335	1417	...	1632	1729	1820	1908	1917	|	2038	2105u	2120	2233	|	0238	0300	...	...
Wrocław Gł. **1070** ....a.	...	|	...	|	1333	...	|	...	...	|	1943	...	2123	...	|	...	...	2333	...	|	|	...	...	...
Szczecin Gł. **1010** ....d.	...	1156	...	1337	...	...	1617	...	...	1900	...	...	...	...	2222	...	...	...	...	0617	0533	...	...	...

NOTES FOR TABLES 1001 - 1005

A – 🛏 1,2 cl. and ▬ 2 cl. Berlin - Warszawa and v.v. For other cars see Tables **51**, **56**.
B – BERLIN WARSZAWA EXPRESS – [12] and ✕ ®, Berlin - Warszawa and v.v. Special fares apply.
D – [12] and ✕ Zielona Góra - Poznań - Bydgoszcz - Gdynia and v.v.
E – June 21 - Aug. 30: ▬ 2 cl. and [12] Świnoujście - Szczecin - Katowice.
F – [12] and ✕ Zielona Góra - Wrocław - Przemyśl and v.v.
G – [12] Szczecin - Warszawa - Terespol and v.v.
H – ①–⑤ (not Dec. 24 - Jan. 1, Mar. 24, May 1, 2, 22, 23).
J – JAN KIEPURA – 🛏 1,2 cl. Amsterdam / Basel / München - Warszawa - Moskva and v.v. (journey 2 nights). 🛏 1,2 cl., ▬ 2 cl., [2] and ✕ Amsterdam - Köln - Warszawa and v.v.; see Table **24**.
K – ①–⑥ (not Dec. 25, 26, Jan. 1, Mar. 24, May 2, 3, 24).
L – ⑧ (not Dec. 24, 25, 31, Mar. 23, May 1, 2, 22, 23).
M – WAWEL – [12] and ✕ (Hamburg ◧) - Berlin - Wrocław - Katowice - Kraków and v.v.
N – ⑤⑦ (also Jan. 1, Mar. 20, 24, Apr. 30, May 12; not Dec. 30, Mar. 21, 23, May 2, 11).
P – ①⑥ (also Jan. 2, Mar. 21, 25, May 1, 13; not Dec. 31, Mar. 22, 24, May 3, 12).
Q – June 20 - Aug. 29: ▬ 2 cl. and [12] Katowice - Szczecin - Świnoujście.
R – ①–⑥ (not Dec. 24, 25, 26, 31, Jan. 1, Mar. 24, May 2, 3, 23, 24).
S – 🛏 1,2 cl. and ▬ 2 cl. Świnoujście - Szczecin - Warszawa and v.v.
T – ⑧ (not Dec. 23, 24, 25, 30, 31, Mar. 23, May 1, 2, 22, 23).
U – ①–⑥ Dec. 24, 25, Jan. 1, Mar. 24, May 2, 23).
V – ①–⑤ (not Dec. 25, 26, Jan. 1, Mar. 24, May 1, 22).
W – ①–⑥ (also Dec. 23, 30, Feb. 10, 17, Mar. 23; not Dec. 22, Jan. 1, Feb. 9, Mar. 20, 25, May 1, 22).
X – ⑥⑦ (also Dec. 25, 26, Jan. 1, Mar. 24, May 1, 22).
Y – 🛏 1,2 cl. and ▬ 2 cl. Berlin - Poznań - Kraków and v.v.
Z – [12] and ✕ Zielona Góra - Poznań - Warszawa and v.v.

b – Not Dec. 24, Jan. 12, 13, Feb. 23, 24.
f – Not Dec. 25, 26, Jan. 1, Mar. 23, 24.
g – To / from Łódź Kaliska.
h – Not Dec. 25, Mar. 23.
j – Not Dec. 25, Mar. 24.
k – Not Jan. 12, 13, Feb. 23, 24, see note ✣.
m – To Legnica.
p – To / from Białystok.
q – Berlin **Lichtenberg**.
r – Not Dec. 24, Mar. 23.
s – Stops to set down only.

u – Stops to pick up only.
v – Not Dec. 24, 25, Mar. 23.
w – To / from Jelenia Góra.
y – Not Dec. 25, Jan. 12, 13, Feb. 23, 24.

◇ – Stopping train.
* – Via Zielona Góra.
§ – To / from Lublin.
◧ – For dates of running see Table **56**.
◐ – 🏛 between Berlin and Wrocław is Forst / Zasieki ticketing point is Forst.
** – Zielona Góra - Zbąszynek: *58 km.*
✣ – Services on Jan. 12, 13, Feb. 23, 24 are shown in special Table on page 75.

SWINOUJSCIE - SZCZECIN - POZNAŃ 1010

km																								
				82106	IC	84104	82102	83100	TLK		83104	Ex	84102	TLK		81102		81100	IC		83200	81202	81704	TLK
		2	2	83107	8102	84105	82103	83101	8210	2	83105	8110/1	84103	8310	2	81103	2	81101	8100	86102	83512	81203	81705	83704
		◇	◇		R ✕			✕	R ✕	◇	✕	81412		83412	◇		◇		R 🍷					83705
				G	Q	g	F	Pr	k		P	R ✕	f	R ✕		✕	q	Lr	M	2	B	A	j	Kp
	Świnoujście d.	...	...	...	...	...	...	...	...	...	...	0915x	...	...	...	...	...	...	...	1550y	...	...	...	2122
0	**Szczecin** Gł. **1015** d.	...	...	...	0531	0555	0607	0755	0845	...	0955	1103	1145	1255	...	1400	...	1513	1603	1755	2047	2300	...	2315
15	Szczecin Dąbie **1015** d.	...	...	...	0544	0610	0623	0809	0901	...	1010	1117	1200	1309	...	1415	...	1529	1617	1809	2102	2315	...	2330
40	Stargard Szczeciński **1015** d.	...	...	...	0601	0631	0642	0830	0920	...	1029	1135	1220	1327	...	1434	...	1549	1635	1828	2125	2336	...	2351
130	Krzyż **1000** d.	0525	0621	0626	0654	0733	0757	0930	1022	1025	1131	1230	1319	1425	1433	1548	1630	1650	1730	1928	2230	0039	0140	0101
	Piła **1000** d.	0616	0712	|	|	|	0910	|	|	1116	|	|	|	|	1527	1704	1721	|	|	|	|	|	0304	|
	Bydgoszcz **1000** a.	...	*0906*	|	|	|	1024	|	|	*1255*	|	|	|	|	*1717*	1817	...	|	|	|	|	|	0410	|
213	**Poznań** Gł. a.	...	...	0730	|	0835	|	1035	1126	...	1235	1326	1420	1530	...	|	...	1752	1826	2031	2325	0145	|	0200
	Wrocław Gł. **1070** a.	...	...	1005	|	1105	|	1305	|	...	1505	|	...	1805	...	|	...	...	|	2256	0215	|	|	0439
	Warszawa Cent. **1005** a.	...	...	|	1058	...	1410	|	1525	...	|	1645	...	|	...	2220	...	...	2135	...	|	0605	0810	|
	Kraków Gł. **1075, 1080** a.	...	...	1455	...	...	...	1755	...	...	2000	...	...	2248	...	...	...	...	...	...	0737	...	...	0920

	38200	68101		IC	18100	48102	18102	TLK		TLK		48104		Ex		38105	38100		IC	28103	28106	18203	18704	TLK
	38511	38501	2	1801	18101	48103	18103	3811	2	2810	2	48105		1811	2	38104	38101		1803	28103	28107	18203	18705	38704
			◇	R 🍷			✕	38411	◇	R ✕	◇		2	18411	◇	✕	✕	2	R ✕	✕				38705
	B	2		R	Lr	f		R ✕	O	k	q	g	◇	R ✕	O	P	Pr	◇	J	F	G	A	p	Kp
Kraków Gł. **1075, 1080** d.	2153	...	...	...	...	...	...	0553	...	...	...	...	...	...	...	0953	1153	...	...	...	1253	...	...	2007
Warszawa Cent. **1005** d.	|	...	...	0625	...	...	0700	|	...	0955	...	...	...	1325	...	|	|	...	1655	1500	|	2255	2200	|
Wrocław Gł. **1070** d.	0320	0535	...	|	...	...	|	1035	...	|	...	1235	...	|	...	1435	1635	...	|	|	1735	|	|	0038
Poznań Gł. d.	0600	0802	...	0933	1105	1207	|	1256	...	1345	...	1459	...	1641	...	1705	1902	...	|	|	2012	0254	|	0320
Bydgoszcz **1000** d.	|	|	*0740*r	|	|	|	1051	|	*1145*	|	...	|	...	|	*1545*	|	|	*1743*	|	1901	|	|	0142	|
Piła **1000** d.	|	|	0915	|	|	|	1214	|	1315	|	1450	|	1550	|	1734	|	|	1955	|	2025	|	|	0306	|
Krzyż **1000** d.	0703	0901	1006	1029	1204	1306	1327	1355	1405	1445	1540	1558	1640	1733	1824	1807	2005	2046	2058	2135	2112	0355	0403	0415
Stargard Szczeciński **1015** d.	0812	1001	...	1122	1303	1405	1426	1454	...	1551	...	1701	...	1826	...	1910	2105	...	2148	2233	...	0456	...	0535
Szczecin Dąbie **1015** a.	0831	1020	...	1140	1321	1423	1445	1513	...	1602	...	1719	...	1845	...	1928	2124	...	2207	2250	...	0516	...	0600
Szczecin Gł. **1015** a.	0848	1036	...	1156	1337	1439	1502	1528	...	1617	...	1736	...	1900	...	1944	2139	...	2222	2307	...	0533	...	0617
Świnoujście a.	...	1239y	...	...	...	...	...	...	...	...	...	...	...	2053v	...	...	...	...	...	...	...	...	...	0814

km												
		◇2	◇	◇		◇2		◇2	◇	◇	◇	◇2
		b	2	2		r		N	2	2	2	Kp
0	**Świnoujście** d.	0516	0716	0850	...	1132	...	1423	1532	1720	1940	2122
101	Szczecin Dąbie a.	0658	0846	1033	...	1301	...	1605	1714	1848	2126	2329
116	**Szczecin** Gł. a.	0717	0903	1050	...	1317	...	1622	1729	1906	2143	2310

	◇	◇2	◇		◇2		◇2	◇		◇	◇
	2	Kj	2		r		N	2		2	2
Szczecin Gł. d.	0510	0625	0840	...	1140	...	1440	1540	...	1840	2040
Szczecin Dąbie d.	0527	|	0857	...	1156	...	1457	1557	...	1856	2057
Świnoujście a.	0711	0814	1042	...	1328	...	1630	1742	...	2041	2228

A – [12] Szczecin - Poznań - Warszawa - Terespol and v.v.
B – 🛏 1, 2 cl., ▬ 2 cl., [12] and ✕ Szczecin - Poznań - Kraków - Przemyśl and v.v.
F – [12] Szczecin - Warszawa - Lublin and v.v.
G – [12] Gorzów Wlkp - Krzyż - Poznań - Kraków - Zamość and v.v.
H – 🛏 1, 2 cl., ▬ 2 cl., [2] and ✕ Świnoujście - Szczecin - Warszawa and v.v.
J – ⑧ (not Dec. 23, 24, 25, 30, 31, Mar. 23, May 1, 2, 22, 23).
K – 🛏 1, 2 cl., ▬ 2 cl., [2] and ✕ Świnoujście - Kraków and v.v.
L – [12] Szczecin - Poznań - Kutno - Łódź and v.v.
M – ⑧ (not Dec. 24, 25, 31, Mar. 23, May 1, 22).
N – ①–⑤ (not Dec. 24 - Jan. 1, Mar. 24, May 1, 2, 22, 23).
O – ①–⑤ (not Dec. 24 - Jan. 1, Jan. 28 - Feb. 8, Mar. 20–25, May 1, 2, 22, 23).
P – [12] and ✕ Szczecin - Poznań - Kraków - Przemyśl and v.v.
Q – ①–⑥ (not Dec. 24, 25, 26, 31, Jan. 1, Mar. 24, May 2, 3, 23, 24).
R – ①–⑥ (not Dec. 24, 25, Jan. 1, Mar. 24, May 2, 23).
b – Not Dec. 25, 26, Jan. 1, Mar. 23, 24.
f – To / from Katowice.
g – To / from Bielsko Biała.
j – Not Dec. 25, Mar. 24.
k – To / from Lublin.
p – Not Dec. 24, Mar. 23.
q – Not Dec. 24, 25, 31, Mar. 22, 23, May 1, 2, 3, 22, 23, 24
r – Not Dec. 25, Mar. 23.
v – Apr. 29 - Sept. 29.
x – Apr. 28 - Sept. 30.
y – June 21 - Aug. 30.
◇ – Stopping train.

SZCZECIN - KOSZALIN - GDYNIA - GDAŃSK 1015

km																									
		Ex			85102	TLK		Ex		81112	48101	TLK		85102		38103				83202	TLK		78101		81200
		8114	48201		85103	8116		83414		81113	48100	81414		85103		38102	◇		85120	83203	83702		78102		81201
		R ✕		2	✕	R ✕	2	R ✕	◇2	✕		R ✕	2	✕	2	✕	①–⑤	2	2	✕	R ✕	2		2	
		G	C	◇	O	Vh	◇	J	h	E	Ph	Y	◇	Oh	◇	M	b	◇	k	S	Q	◇	h	◇	A
0	**Szczecin** Gł. § d.	...	...	...	0600	...	...	...	0735	1030	...	...	1235	1355	...	...	1405	1535	1705	...	...	...	...	1935	2030
15	Szczecin Dąbie § d.	...	...	...	0616	...	...	...	0753	1045	...	...	1249	1410	...	...	1420	1549	1721	...	...	...	...	1952	2045
40	Stargard Szczeciński § d.	...	...	0459	0634	...	...	...	0819	1105	...	...	1310	1430	...	...	1444	1616	1739	...	...	...	...	2020	2110
*231	**Poznań** Gł. d.	...	0104	|	|	...	0521	...	|	|	1059	...	|	|	1231	1403	|	|	|	...	...	1630	1830	|	|
*135	Piła d.	...	0258	|	|	...	0717	...	|	|	1245	...	|	|	1430	1547	|	|	|	...	...	1815	2028	|	|
*64	Szczecinek d.	...	0354	|	|	...	0826	...	|	|	1342	...	|	|	1536	1646	|	|	|	...	...	1909	2129	|	|
151	Białogard a.	...	0446	0635	0809	...	0926	...	1004	1235	1434	...	1455	1603	1637	1744	1628	1802	1910	...	...	2011	2222	2200	2244
151	Białogard ▶ d.	...	0448	0644	0809	...	0929	...	1005	1237	1435	...	1502	1604	1644	1745	1642	1803	1911	...	...	2017	2225	2200	2245
187	Kołobrzeg ▶ a.	...	0520	|	|	...	1005	...	|	|	|	...	|	|	1724	1814	|	|	|	...	...	|	|	|	|
**43	Kołobrzeg d.	0316	...	|	|	0745	...	0945	|	|	|	1427	|	|	...	...	|	|	|	1949	2026	|	|	|	|
175	**Koszalin** d.	0357	...	0709	0826	0836	...	1029	1041	1254	1453	1512	1524	1625	...	...	1704	1824	1929	2041	2143	2034	2242	2224	2307
242	Słupsk d.	0441	...	...	0916	0934	...	1114	1133	1340	1553	1622	1628	1711	...	...	...	1927	2016	2130	2238	...	2335	...	2351
294	Lębork d.	0518	...	...	0950	1008	...	1157	...	1414	...	1715	...	1751	...	...	...	...	2051	2218	2315	...	...	...	0025
353	**Gdynia** Gł. **1020, 1030** a.	0559	...	...	1035	1056	...	1240	...	1516	...	1800	...	1847	...	...	...	...	2139	2305	0001	...	...	...	0109
353	**Gdynia** Gł. **1020, 1030** d.	0604	...	...	1045	1104	...	1252	...	1526	...	1804	...	1851	...	...	...	...	2143	2325	0018	...	...	...	0112
362	Sopot **1020** a.	0615	...	...	1055	1114	...	1303	...	1536	...	1815	...	1900	...	...	...	...	2153	2336	0029	...	...	...	0121
374	**Gdańsk** Gł. **1020, 1030** a.	0631	...	...	1111	1131	...	1321	...	1553	...	1831	...	1916	...	...	...	...	2210	2354	0045	...	...	...	0138
	Warszawa C. **1030** a.	1105	...	...	...	1611	...	1800	...	...	...	2313	...	...	...	...	...	...	...	0450	0520	...	...	...	...

				87101		38202	TLK		83102		58101	84101			TLK		18113	87421		TLK		58103	TLK	Ex	18201
				87102	2	38203	38703	58121	83103	◇	58102	84100			18415	◇	18112	87420		1817	84200	58104	1817	1815	18200
	2	2	2		◇	✕	✕	2	✕	①–⑤	✕		◇2	2	R ✕	①–⑤	✕		2	R ✕		✕	R ✕	R ✕	
	◇	◇	◇	h	h	S	Q	k	M	b	Oh	Pg	h	◇	Z	b	E		◇	Th	C	O	K	H	B
Warszawa C. **1030** d.	...	...	...	...	...	2325	0034	...	...	...	...	...	...	...	0555	...	...	...	...	1055	...	...	1255	1555	...
Gdańsk Gł. **1020, 1030** d.	...	...	...	...	...	0420	0519	0614	...	...	0933	...	...	...	1046	...	1324	...	...	1534	...	1645	1736	2028	0209
Sopot **1020** d.	...	...	...	...	...	0438	0534	0628	...	...	0949	...	...	...	1101	...	1340	...	...	1548	...	1701	1752	2044	0224
Gdynia Gł. **1020, 1030** a.	...	...	...	...	...	0448	0546	0638	...	...	0959	...	...	...	1112	...	1350	...	...	1600	...	1711	1804	2057	0235
Gdynia Gł. **1020, 1030** d.	...	...	...	...	...	0518	0601	0641	...	...	1010	...	...	...	1125	...	1405	...	...	1608	...	1715	1812	2100	0238
Lębork d.	...	...	...	...	...	0635	0711	0733	...	...	1101	...	...	...	1213	...	1456	...	...	1657	...	1809	1855	2145	0328
Słupsk d.	...	...	0522	0505	...	0723	0817	0809	...	...	1136	1206	1240	...	1300	1423	1537	...	1734	1742	...	1844	1935	2218	0403
Koszalin d.	0433	...	0617	0549	...	0814	0913	0855	...	1120	1219	1300	1339	...	1355	1525	1623	1638	1829	1846	...	1928	2035	2304	0459
Kołobrzeg a.	|	...	|	|	...	0859	1018	|	...	|	|	|	|	...	1440	|	|	|	|	1939	...	|	2125	2348	|
Kołobrzeg ▶ d.	|	...	|	|	0810	...	...	|	1021	|	|	|	|	1431	...	|	|	|	|	...	1836	|	...	...	|
Białogard ▶ a.	0451	...	0637	0613	0844	...	...	0912	1051	1142	1236	1320	1402	1511	...	1546	1640	1705	1851	...	1914	1945	...	...	0516
Białogard d.	0451	0521	0637	0626	0845	...	...	0913	1052	1143	1238	1326	1403	1511	...	1547	1641	1706	1852	...	1915	1946	...	...	0525
Szczecinek d.	|	0621	|	0721	0951	...	...	|	1146	|	|	1426	|	1617	...	|	|	1808	|	...	2020	|	...	...	|
Piła d.	|	0727	|	0818	1052	...	...	|	1244	|	|	1540	|	1731	...	|	|	1911	|	...	2123	|	...	...	|
Poznań Gł. a.	|	0930	|	1010	1257	...	...	|	1435	|	|	1735	|	1936	...	|	|	2110	|	...	2317	|	...	...	|
Stargard Szczeciński § d.	0645	...	0815	...	...	...	...	1045	...	1345	1415	...	1545	...	...	1745	1823	...	2045	...	...	2121	...	...	0726
Szczecin Dąbie § a.	0708	...	0839	...	...	...	...	1104	...	1409	1433	...	1609	...	...	1808	1840	...	2108	...	...	2139	...	...	0748
Szczecin Gł. § a.	0724	...	0856	...	...	...	...	1121	...	1425	1448	...	1625	...	...	1824	1856	...	2124	...	...	2155	...	...	0807

A – Dec. 9 - Jan. 2 (not Dec. 24), Jan. 12 - Feb. 25, Mar. 20–22, 24–26, Apr. 26 - Nov. 12: ▬ 2 cl. and [12] Szczecin - Białystok.
B – Dec. 9 - Jan. 1 (not Dec. 24), Jan. 11 - Feb. 24, Mar. 19–22, 24, 25, Apr. 25 - Nov. 11: ▬ 2 cl. and [12] Białystok - Szczecin.
C – Dec. 9 - Feb. 23 (not Dec. 24, 25, 31), Mar. 19 - Nov. 10 (not Mar. 22, 23) from Katowice; Dec. 9 - Feb. 24 (not Dec. 24, 25, 31), Mar. 20 - Nov. 11 (not Mar. 22, 23) from Kołobrzeg: [12] Katowice - Kołobrzeg and v.v.
E – [12] and ✕ Szczecin - Gdańsk - Białystok and v.v.
G – ①–⑥ (not Dec. 25, 26, Jan. 1, Mar. 24, May 2, 23).
H – ⑧ (not Dec. 24, 25, 31, Mar. 23, May 1, 22).
J – June 22 - Aug. 31.
K – June 21 - Aug. 30.
M – [12] and ✕ Kraków - Poznań - Kołobrzeg and v.v.
O – [12] and ✕ Szczecin - Gdańsk - Olsztyn and v.v.
P – [12] Katowice - Wrocław - Poznań - Słupsk and v.v.
Q – From Kołobrzeg Apr. 26 - Sept. 27: 🛏 1, 2 cl., ▬ 2 cl., [2] and ✕ Kołobrzeg - Warszawa - Katowice (arrive 1000) - Kraków (1155); from Kraków Apr. 25 - Sept. 26: 🛏 1, 2 cl., ▬ 2 cl., [2] and ✕ Kraków (depart 1822) - Katowice (depart 2015) - Warszawa - Kołobrzeg.
S – 🛏 1, 2 cl., ▬ 2 cl., [12] and ✕ Kołobrzeg - Warszawa - Kielce - Kraków and v.v.
T – Dec. 9 - June 19 and Sept. 1 - Dec. 13.
V – Dec. 9 - June 20 and Sept. 2 - Dec. 13.
Y – ⑦ (also Dec. 26, Jan. 1, Mar. 24, May 2, 23; not Mar. 23).
Z – ⑥ (also Dec. 24, 31, May 1, 22).
b – Not Dec. 24 - Jan. 1, Mar. 24, May 1, 2, 22, 23.
g – Not Dec. 24, Mar. 22.
h – Not Dec. 25, Mar. 23.
k – To / from Malbork.
* – Distance from Białogard.
** – Distance from Koszalin.
§ – See also Table **1010**.
◇ – Stopping train.

▶ – Other local trains: From Białogard: 0549 **h**, 0643, 1240 **h**, 1438 ①–⑤ **b**, 1551, 1857 **h**, 2230. From Kołobrzeg: 0540 **h**, 0700 ①–⑤ **b**, 1157, 1526, 1627, 1849, 2040.

▲ – Frequent local trains run between Gdynia and Gdańsk; See also tables 1020 and 1030.

1020 GDYNIA - BYDGOSZCZ - ŁÓDŹ, POZNAŃ, KATOWICE and KRAKÓW

km		TLK 81704	52100 52101	TLK 5112	51118 51119	56100 56101		54100 54101	56104 56105	57102 57103	82102 82103	53102 53103		53104 53105	57104 57105	56112 56113	54102 54103	16116 16117	52102 52103	56102 56103	81102 81103	51112 51113	57106 57107	54200 54201	56200 56201	
		🅁🍷 Sg	①–⑥ JP	🅁🍷 F	Mk	✕		✕ ①–⑥	q	✕ k	NP	k	◇	B	✕ H	p	✕ ⑧	z	P	✕	R		✕ b	C	A	
0	**Gdynia** Gł. **1030** d.	...	...	...	...	0453	...	0645	...	0701	...	0836	...	...	1040	...	1218	...	...	1447	...	1620	1724	2045	2110	...
9	Sopot **1030** d.	...	...	...	...	0503	...	0655	...	0711	...	0846	...	...	1050	...	1229	...	...	1457	...	1630	1734	2057	2121	...
21	**Gdańsk** Gł. **1030** d.	...	...	...	...	0522	...	0713	...	0731	...	0903	...	...	1107	...	1249	...	...	1518	...	1646	1752	2117	2140	...
53	Tczew **1030** d.	...	...	...	...	0554	...	0740	...	0758	...	0934	...	...	1134	...	1320	...	...	1548	...	1715	1824	2149	2222	...
181	**Bydgoszcz** Gł. d.	0425	0530	0633	0714	0734	...	0920	...	0940	1030	1127	1220	1230	1315	...	1504	...	1530	1730	1825	1906	2003	2345	0007	...
	Olsztyn d.	|	|	|	|	|	...	|	0620	|	|	|	|	|	|	...	|	1253	|	|	|	|	|	|	|	...
	Iława d.	|	|	|	|	|	...	|	0718	|	|	|	|	|	|	...	|	1358	|	|	|	|	|	|	|	...
232	**Toruń** Gł. d.	0521	0630	0734	|	|	...	1020	0902	|	1128	1228	|	1332	|	1306	|	1546	1630	|	1922	2008	|	0049	|	...
287	Włocławek d.	0559	0709	0814	|	|	...	1100	|	|	1207	1306	|	1409	|	|	|	|	1708	|	2000	2048	|	0130	|	...
227	Inowrocław d.	|	|	|	0753	0815	...	|	0944	1020	|	|	1317	|	1355	1346	1543	1625	|	1809	|	|	2043	|	0051	...
342	Kutno d.	0634	0745	0853	0951	|	...	1134	|	|	1243	1342	|	1444	|	|	1751	|	1743	|	2043	2127	|	0209	|	...
410	**Łódź** Kaliska a.	|	|	|	|	|	...	1306	|	|	|	1518	|	|	|	|	1928	|	|	|	|	2256	|	0356	|	...
469	**Warszawa** Cent a.	0810	0910	1020	1115	|	...	|	|	|	1410	|	|	1611	|	|	|	|	1910	|	2220	...	|	|	|	...
474	**Warszawa** Wsch. a.	0822	0922	1032	1127	|	...	|	|	|	1422	|	|	1622	|	|	|	|	1922	|	2232	...	|	|	|	...
283	Gniezno d.	...	...	...	...	0904	...	|	1035	1110	...	|	1414	...	1446	1449	|	1715	...	1855	...	...	2135	|	0139	...
334	**Poznań** Gł. a.	...	...	...	...	0958	...	|	1135	1225	...	|	1517	...	1532	|	|	1820	...	1945	...	...	2225	|	0230	...
	Wrocław **1070** a.	...	...	...	...	1225	...	|	1405	...	...	|	...	...	...	1902	|	2050	...	2211	...	...	...	|	0510	...
483	**Częstochowa Osobowa** ▲ d.	...	...	...	...	...	...	1521	...	...	...	1724	...	...	...	...	2148	...	...	...	...	...	...	0625	...	...
526	Zawiercie ▲ d.	...	...	...	...	...	...	1556	...	...	...	1758	...	...	...	...	2220	...	...	...	...	...	...	0705	...	...
561	Sosnowiec Gł. ▲ d.	...	...	...	...	...	...	1624	...	...	...	|	...	...	...	...	2250	...	...	...	...	...	...	0739	...	...
569	**Katowice** ▲ a.	...	...	...	...	...	...	1635	...	...	...	|	...	...	...	...	2302	...	...	...	...	...	...	0751	...	...
615	**Kraków** Gł. a.	...	...	...	...	...	...	...	...	...	...	1952	...	...	...	...	...	...	...	...	...	...	...	...	...	...

	75100 75101	30101	15112 15113	18102 18103	65101 65100		45100 45101	61117 61116	25100 25101	75102 75103	35102 35103	65113 65112	35104 35105	75104 75105		28103 28102	65105 65104	45102 45103	TLK 1513	15118 15119	65102 65103	25102 25103	TLK 18705	65201 65200	45200 45201	
	✕			R	✕		✕ ①–⑥	z	P	✕ H	k	p	B	✕ k		NP		✕ ⑧	🅁🍷 G	Mk	✕	⑧ KP	🅁🍷 Sh	A	C	
Kraków Gł. d.	...	...	...	...	...	...	...	...	...	...	0711	...	...	...	...	...	...	...	...	...	...	...	...	...	...	...
Katowice ▲ d.	...	...	...	...	...	...	0515	...	...	...	|	...	...	...	...	...	...	1240	...	...	...	...	...	...	2225	...
Sosnowiec Gł. ▲ d.	...	...	...	...	...	...	0527	...	...	...	|	...	...	...	...	...	...	1252	...	...	...	...	...	...	2237	...
Zawiercie ▲ d.	...	...	...	...	...	...	0556	...	...	...	0859	...	...	...	...	...	...	1322	...	...	...	...	...	...	2309	...
Częstochowa Osobowa ▲ d.	...	...	...	...	...	...	0632	...	...	...	0936	...	...	...	...	...	...	1358	...	...	...	...	...	...	2357	...
Wrocław **1070** d.	...	...	...	...	0635	...	|	0815	...	...	|	1035	...	...	...	...	1335	|	...	...	1535	...	...	0005	|	...
Poznań Gł. d.	0541	...	...	...	0857	...	|	1050	...	1205	|	1305	...	1451	...	...	1607	|	...	...	1812	...	...	0248	|	...
Gniezno d.	0625	...	...	...	0940	...	|	1135	...	1247	|	1341	...	1614	...	...	1650	|	...	...	1854	...	...	0334	|	...
Warszawa Wsch d.	|	...	...	0648	|	...	|	|	0838	|	|	|	1238	|	...	1448	|	|	1543	1626	|	1833	2149	|	|	...
Warszawa Cent d.	|	...	...	0700	|	...	|	|	0855	|	|	|	1300	|	...	1500	|	|	1600	1700	|	1900	2200	|	|	...
Łódź Kaliska d.	|	...	0604	|	|	...	0856	|	|	|	1159	|	|	|	...	|	|	1613	|	|	|	|	|	|	0205	...
Kutno d.	|	...	0738	0832	|	...	1034	|	1030	|	1327	|	1429	|	...	1631	|	1753	1728	1829	|	2031	2329	|	0344	...
Inowrocław d.	0721	0745	|	|	1030	...	1205	1228	|	1342	|	1431	|	1704	...	|	1744	|	|	2014	1947	|	|	0429	|	...
Włocławek d.	|	|	0815	0906	|	...	|	|	1104	|	1403	|	1504	|	...	1706	|	1826	1800	|	|	2105	0004	|	0422	...
Toruń Gł. d.	|	0830	0855	0947	|	...	|	1308	1145	|	1443	1520	1544	|	...	1753	1824	1906	1842	|	|	2145	0045	|	0512	...
Iława d.	|	0946	|	|	|	...	|	1432	|	|	|	...	|	|	...	|	1946	|	|	|	|	|	|	|	|	...
Olsztyn a.	|	1039	|	|	|	...	|	1530	|	|	|	...	|	|	...	|	2043	|	|	|	|	|	|	|	|	...
Bydgoszcz Gł. d.	0812	...	1003	1041	1124	...	1310	...	1239	1434	1558	...	1640	1756	...	1850	...	2017	1936	2105	2042	2238	0135	0528	0630	...
Tczew **1030** d.	1027	...	1220	...	1345	...	1529	...	...	1649	1822	...	...	2016	...	...	...	2236	...	...	2259	...	...	0758	0849	...
Gdańsk Gł. **1030** a.	1052	...	1254	...	1414	...	1558	...	...	1717	1850	...	...	2044	...	...	...	2302	...	...	2326	...	...	0826	0917	...
Sopot **1030** a.	1109	...	1309	...	1431	...	1615	...	...	1734	1907	...	...	2101	...	...	...	2319	...	...	2344	...	...	0844	0936	...
Gdynia Gł. **1030** a.	1120	...	1319	...	1443	...	1626	...	...	1745	1918	...	...	2114	...	...	...	2331	...	...	2357	...	...	0857	0949	...

A – (12) (also 🛏 1, 2 cl. on certain dates) Gdynia - Wrocław and v.v. Conveys 🛏 1, 2 cl. Kaliningrad / Gdynia - Poznań - Berlin and v.v. See Table **51**.
B – (12) Bydgoszcz - Warszawa - Lublin - Przemyśl / Zamość and v.v.
C – Not Dec. 24, 31, Mar. 1, 8, 15, 22, 29, Apr. 5, 12, 19, May 10, 17, 24, 31: 🛏 1, 2 cl., ▬ 2 cl. and (12) Gdynia - Katowice - Bielsko Biała and v.v.
F – ①–⑥ (not Dec. 24, 25, 26, 31, Jan. 1, Mar. 24, May 2, 3, 23, 24).
G – ⑧ (not Dec. 23, 24, 25, 30, 31, Mar. 23, May 1, 2, 22, 23).
H – (12) and ✕ Gdynia - Zielona Góra and v.v.
J – ①–⑥ (not Dec. 25, 26, Jan. 1, Mar. 24).
K – ⑧ (not Dec. 24, 25, 31, Mar. 23).
M – To / from Białystok (Table **1040**).
N – From / to Gorzów and Szczecin.
P – To / from Lublin.
R – From / to Kostrzyn and Szczecin.
S – From / to Świnoujście.
b – Not Dec. 24, 25, 31, Mar. 22, 23.
g – Not Dec. 25, Mar. 24.
h – Not Dec. 24, Mar. 23.
k – Not Dec. 25, Mar. 23.
p – From / to Grudziądz.
q – Not Dec. 25, Jan. 1, Mar. 23.
z – From / to Ełk / Suwałki.
◇ – Stopping train.
▲ – For additional trains see Table **1060**.

1030 GDYNIA - GDAŃSK - WARSZAWA

km		52105 52104	TLK 5210	IC ✕ 5306	53100 53101	Ex 8114	IC 5302	56110 56111	7 55000	Ex 54410	Ex 5310	TLK 8116	54112 54113	Ex 5312 83414	Ex 5410	TLK 54414	IC 5300	51104	IC 5100	TLK 5114 81414	TLK 53702	83202 83203	
		T k	🅁 U b	🅁 F	m	🅁✕ X	🅁✕	h w	A	🅁✕ ⑥f	🅁✕ H	🅁✕ V h	g	🅁 p	🅁✕ t	🅁✕ ⑦d t	🅁 ✕		🅁✕	R q	🅁 Z p	B	
0	**Gdynia** Gł. **1038** ▲ d.	...	0405	0505	...	0604	0653	...	0735	0753	0852	1104	...	1252	1352	...	1452	...	1652	1804	1856	2325	...
9	Sopot **1038** ▲ d.	...	0415	0515	...	0615	0704	...	0746	0804	0903	1114	...	1303	1504	...	1504	...	1704	1815	1907	2337	...
21	**Gdańsk** Gł. **1038** ▲ d.	...	0435	0535	...	0635	0725	...	0804	0825	0925	1135	...	1325	1425	...	1525	...	1725	1835	1926	2357	...
53	Tczew **1038** d.	...	0459	|	...	0705	|	...	0843	0858	0958	1203	...	1358	1458	...	|	...	1758	1905	1958	0028	...
72	Malbork **1038** d.	...	0520	|	...	0721	0816	...	0900	0916	1016	1221	...	1416	1516	...	1616	...	1816	1923	2016	0048	...
**	**Olsztyn 1020 1038** d.	0515	|	|	0645	|	|	0830	...	|	|	|	1309	|	|	1553	|	1656	|	|	|	|	...
141	Iława **1020 1038** d.	|	0609	|	|	0801	0901	0927	...	1001	1101	1310	|	1501	1601	|	1659	|	1901	2011	2103	0138	...
201	Działdowo d.	0630	0648	|	0815	0841	|	1006	...	1041	1141	1353	1420	1541	|	1716	|	1808	|	2053	2145	0221	...
251	Ciechanów d.	0705	0718	|	0849	|	|	1041	...	|	|	1428	1454	|	1712	1749	|	1842	|	2127	2222	0258	...
345	**Warszawa** Wschodnia a.	0840	0852	0940	1025	1053	1140	1218	...	1245	1345	1603	1629	1745	1845	1930	1940	2016	2143	2303	2359	0440	...
350	**Warszawa** Centralna a.	0850	...	0956	1035	1105	1155	1230	...	1300	1400	1611	1637	1800	1901	1949	1956	2025	2152	2313	0015	0450	...
	Katowice **1060** a.	...	...	|	|	...	|	...	...	1550	|	...	2044	|	2150	2308	|	...	...	...	0408	|	...
	Kraków Gł. **1065** a.	...	...	1300	1610	...	1500	...	...	...	1700	...	...	2100	...	...	2300	...	...	...	0605	1045	...

	TLK 1515 18415	IC 1501	15101 15100	IC 3500 3501	TLK 45414	TLK 1817	45110 45111	Ex 4511	Ex 3513 38415	Ex 3511	65110 65111	Ex 1815	IC 3507	8 55002	35100 35101	TLK 2510	Ex 45411	25104 25105	IC 3503	38203 38202	TLK 35702		
	S q	🅁 ✕		🅁✕	🅁✕ ⑥y t	🅁✕ F h	g	🅁✕ t	🅁 p	🅁✕ H	h w	🅁✕ W	🅁✕ C	A	r	🅁 U b	🅁✕ ⑦j	Y k	🅁 ✕	B	🅁 Z p		
Kraków Gł. **1065** d.	...	...	...	0555	...	...	...	...	0955	1155	...	...	1355	...	1212	...	...	...	1555	1812	2253	...	...
Katowice **1060** d.	...	...	...	|	0530	...	0650	0900	|	|	...	...	|	...	|	...	1500	...	|	|	0045	...	...
Warszawa Centralna d.	0555	0655	0700	0855	0900	1055	1111	1155	1255	1455	1510	1555	1655	...	1710	...	1755	1910	1855	2325	0455	...	...
Warszawa Wschodnia d.	0605	0705	0712	0910	0917	1104	1120	1210	1310	1510	1519	1605	1710	...	1719	1810	1810	1918	1910	2334	0512	...	...
Ciechanów d.	0745	|	0851	|	1057	1242	1302	1349	|	|	1700	|	|	...	1901	1945	|	2100	|	0118	0656	...	...
Działdowo d.	0818	|	0927	|	1131	1316	1337	|	1512	1721	1737	1809	|	...	1945	2015	2012	2137	|	0155	0733	...	...
Iława **1020 1038** d.	0858	0950	|	1155	|	1355	|	1458	1557	1758	1818	1848	|	...	|	2058	2055	|	2149	0237	0814	...	...
Olsztyn 1020 1038 a.	|	|	1036	|	1240	|	1451	|	|	|	1913	|	|	...	2054	|	|	2246	|	|	|	...	...
Malbork **1038** d.	0947	1035	...	1240	...	1445	...	1544	1643	1843	...	1934	|	2117	...	2144	2143	...	2235	0329	0901	...	...
Tczew **1038** d.	1005	1052	...	|	...	1503	...	1601	1700	1900	...	1954	|	2142	...	2201	2201	...	2253	0348	0919	...	...
Gdańsk Gł. **1038** ▲ a.	1043	1125	...	1329	...	1531	...	1634	1733	1934	...	2025	2115	2209	...	2231	2231	...	2323	0418	0950	...	...
Sopot **1038** ▲ a.	1101	1144	...	1347	...	1548	...	1653	1752	1952	...	2044	2132	2226	...	2249	2249	...	2341	0437	1009	...	...
Gdynia Gł. **1038** ▲ a.	1112	1157	...	1400	...	1600	...	1706	1804	2005	...	2057	2144	2237	...	2304	2304	...	2356	0448	1020	...	...

A – (2) Gdynia - Malbork - Kaliningrad and v.v. Conveys Berlin - Kaliningrad cars and v.v.; see Tables **51 / 1038**.
B – 🛏 1, 2 cl., ▬ 2 cl., (12) and ✕ Kołobrzeg - Gdynia - Warszawa - Kielce - Kraków and v.v.
C – ⑧ (not Dec. 24, 25, 31, Mar. 23, May 1, 2, 23).
F – ①–⑥ (not Dec. 25, 26, Jan. 1, Mar. 24, May 2, 3, 24).
H – To / from Przemyśl (Tables **1058 / 1075**).
R – ⑤⑦ (also Dec. 26, Jan. 1, Mar. 24, Apr. 30, May 21; not Mar. 23).
S – ①⑥ (also Dec. 24, 27, 31, Jan. 2, Mar. 25, May 1, 22; not Dec. 24, 31, Mar. 24).
T – ①–⑥ (not Dec. 25, 31, Mar. 22).
U – ①–⑤ (not Dec. 24, 25, 26, 31, Jan. 1, Mar. 24, May 1, 2, 22, 23).
V – From / to Kołobrzeg.
W – To Kołobrzeg on ⑧ (not Dec. 24, 25, 31, Mar. 23, May 1, 22). **15415** on ⑥.
X – From Kołobrzeg on ①–⑥ (not Dec. 25, 26, Jan. 1, Mar. 24, May 2, 23). **51414** on ⑦.
Y – ⑧ (not Dec. 25, 31, Mar. 23).
Z – 🛏 1, 2 cl., ▬ 2 cl. and (2) Gdynia - Zakopane and v.v.
b – To / from Lublin.
d – Also Mar. 24, May 2, 23; not Mar. 23.
f – Also Dec. 31, May 1, 22.
g – To / from Racibórz.
h – Not Dec. 25, Mar. 23.
j – Also Jan. 1, Mar. 24, May 2, 23; not Mar. 23.
k – To / from Kielce.
m – Not Dec. 26, 31, May 1, 3.
p – Not Dec. 24, 25, Mar. 23.
q – To / from Kołobrzeg on dates in Table **1015**.
r – Not Dec. 27, Jan. 1, May 2, 4.
t – To / from Gliwice.
w – To / from Wrocław.
y – Also May 1, 22.
** – Olsztyn - Działdowo: *84 km*.
▲ – Frequent local trains run between **Gdynia** and **Gdańsk**.

GDYNIA - GDAŃSK - OLSZTYN and KALININGRAD 1038

km		70140 70141 k	55000 7 A 2	51114 51115 🍷	85102 85103 E 🍴	70142 70143 h	5410	55007 17 2	81112 81113 🍴	85102 85103 g	81200 81201 C	
	Szczecin Gł. **1015** d.	...	...	...	0600	...	...	...	1030	1355	2030	...
0	**Gdynia** Gł. **1030** d.	0535	0735	0720	1045	1230	1352	...	1526	1851	0112	...
9	Sopot **1030** d.	0543	0746	0730	1056	1239	1404	...	1537	1901	0122	...
21	**Gdańsk** Gł. **1030** d.	0558	0804	0748	1114	1255	1425	...	1556	1919	0141	...
53	Tczew **1030** d.	0629	0843	0820	1144	1327	1458	...	1627	1947	0212	...
72	Malbork **1030** ▲ d.	0648	0914	0838	1202	1346	1515	1558	1650	2005	0231	...
101	Elbląg ▲ d.	|	0942	0901	1225	|	...	1622	1716	2028	0254	...
156	Braniewo 🛃 a.	|	1036	|	|	|	...	1710	|	|	|	...
219	**Kaliningrad** § a.	|	1516	|	|	|	...	...	|	|	|	...
	Iława d.	0747	...	|	|	1445	...	...	|	|	|	...
200	**Olsztyn** a.	0842	...	1030	1348	1548	...	...	1848	2152	0422	...
471	*Białystok* **1045** a.	...	...	1504	...	...	...	...	2325	...	0851	...

	58101 58102 g	70120 70121	55006 18 2	18113 18112 🍴	58103 58104 G 🍴	15115 15114 🍷	55002 8 B 2	70122 70123	18201 18200 D		
Białystok **1045** d.	...	...	...	0600	...	1213	...	...	1907	...	...
Olsztyn d.	0641	0812	...	1036	1406	1650	...	1932	2328	...	...
Iława d.	|	0925	...	|	|	|	...	2033	|	...	...
Kaliningrad § d.	|	|	...	|	|	|	1844	|	|	...	...
Braniewo 🛃 d.	|	|	1100	|	|	|	1950	|	|	...	...
Elbląg ▲ d.	0810	|	1145	1206	1531	1826	2040	|	0054	...	...
Malbork **1030** ▲ d.	0838	1019	1210	1231	1555	1854	2117	2127	0118	...	...
Tczew **1030** d.	0859	1038	...	1251	1612	1913	2142	2146	0139	...	...
Gdańsk Gł. **1030** a.	0930	1107	...	1319	1645	1941	2209	2215	0206	...	...
Sopot **1030** a.	0948	1122	...	1339	1701	1958	2226	2232	0223	...	...
Gdynia Gł. **1030** a.	0959	1133	...	1350	1711	2010	2237	2243	0235	...	...
Szczecin Gł. **1015** a.	1448	...	...	1856	2155	...	...	...	0807	...	...

A – Conveys 🛏 1, 2 cl. Berlin (**345**) (previous night) - Frankfurt an der Oder 🛃 (**72002**) - Poznan (**65200**) - Gniezno (**65201**) - Tczew (**55001**) - Braniewo 🛃 (**7**) - Kaliningrad (Tables **51** / **1030**).
B – Conveys 🛏 1, 2 cl. Kaliningrad (**8**) - Braniewo 🛃 (**55002/3**) - Tczew (**56200**) - Gniezno (**56201**) - Poznan (**344**) - Frankfurt an der Oder 🛃 - Berlin (Tables **51** / **1030**).
C – Dec. 9 - Jan. 2, Jan. 12 - Feb. 25, Mar. 20–22, 24–26, Apr. 26 - Nov. 12 (not Dec. 24): ▬ 2 cl. and [12] Szczecin - Białystok.
D – Dec. 9 - Jan. 1, Jan. 11 - Feb. 24, Mar. 19–22, 24, 25, Apr. 25 - Nov. 11 (not Dec. 24): ▬ 2 cl. and [12] Białystok - Szczecin.
E – June 20 - Aug. 30 conveys [2] Szczecin - Suwałki (arrive 1904).
G – June 21 - Aug. 31 conveys [2] Suwałki (depart 0850) - Szczecin.
g – Not Dec. 25, Mar. 23.
h – Not Dec. 24, 25, Mar. 23, May 3.
k – Not Dec. 24, 25, 26, 31, Mar. 24, May 2, 3.
§ – Moskva time (2 hours ahead of Polish time, 1 hour ahead of Kaliningrad time).
▲ – Additional local trains run Malbork - Elbląg and v.v. Journey 30 mins.

PKP, BCh, LG WARSZAWA - BIAŁYSTOK - VILNIUS 1040

km		79821 2	77641 2	138 2	31502 31503 L	77621 2	15107	77623 ①–⑤ 2	91001 910	194 2	TLK 7114/5 hp	79823 2 q	15119 b	77625 2	134 2	61105 61104 S	77627 2	31106 31107 Nq	77629 ⑧ 2	79111 79112 T	77101	79825 2	77103 ⑧ h	140 2 j	41114 41115 P	🚌 99928 A	142 2t	
0	**Warszawa** Centralna d.	...	...	...	0255	...	...	...	0720	...	0920	...	1120	...	...	1320	...	1520	...	1620	1720	...	1820	...	2020	2300	...	...
5	**Warszawa** Wschodnia d.	...	...	...	0319	...	0639	...	0729	...	0929	...	1129	...	...	1329	...	1529	...	1629	1729	...	1829	...	2029	|	...	...
184	**Białystok** a.	...	...	...	0538	...	0849	...	0955	...	1147	...	1347	...	...	1547	...	1747	...	1847	1947	...	2047	...	2247	|	...	...
184	**Białystok** d.	0508	...	...	0549	0655	▬	0900	1010	...	...	1200	...	1435	...	1620	1550	...	1755	1903	...	2007	...	2230	...	0200	...	...
225	Sokółka d.	0555	0643	...	0655	0738	...	0948	1055	...	...	1242	...	1523	...	1708	1637	...	1838	1941	...	2050	...	2313	...	|	...	...
324	**Suwałki** d.	0728	|	...	0847	|	...	|	1242	...	...	1417	...	|	...	1848	|	...	|	2104	...	2227	...	|	...	|	...	...
377	Šeštokai 🛃 ◐ § a.	...	|	...	...	|	...	|	1448	1503	...	...	...	|	...	...	|	...	|	▬	...	...	...	|	...	|	...	...
471	**Kaunas 1810** § a.	...	|	...	...	|	...	|	...	1634	...	...	...	|	...	...	|	...	|	...	...	...	...	|	...	0720	...	...
575	**Vilnius** § a.	...	|	...	...	|	**136**	|	...	1749	...	...	...	|	...	...	|	...	┐	**144**	...	...	...	|	...	0900	...	...
241	Kuźnica Białostocka a.	...	0700	...	...	0755	2t	1005	...	...	...	...	...	1540	...	...	1654	...	1855	2t	...	...	...	2330	...	...	...	...
241	Kuźnica Białostocka 🛃 d.	...	...	0715	...	...	1135	...	...	...	...	...	...	...	1635	...	...	...	...	1900	...	...	...	0025	...	...	0341	...
268	Hrodna 🛃 ‡ a.	...	...	0910	...	...	1330	...	...	...	...	...	...	...	1830	...	...	...	...	2101	...	...	...	0220	...	...	0536	...

	77110 ①–⑥ g	139 2 t	77620 ①–⑥ 2	14114 14115 P	77622 2	79100 79101 T	77640 2	79820 2	77112	77624 2	141 2 t	79822 2	13106 13107 Nf	137 2	16104 16105 S	77626 ①–⑥ 2	15118 15119 bh	77628 2	TLK 1715/4 hp	135 2 t	77642 2	193 2 W	91002 910	51106	133 2	13502 13503 L	🚌 99927 B	143 2t
Hrodna 🛃 ‡ d.	...	0340	...	...	...	...	...	...	...	...	0759	...	...	1005	...		...	...	...	1450	...	...	...	...	1950	...	...	2234
Kuźnica Białostocka 🛃 a.	...	0335	...	...	...	...	...	...	...	...	0800	...	...	1000	...	...	...	...	...	1445	...	...	...	...	1945	...	...	2229
Kuźnica Białostocka d.	...	...	0420	...	0520	...	0615	...	...	0719	...	...	...	...	...	1220	...	1430	...	▬	1615	...	...	...	2030	...	...	...
Vilnius § d.	...	...	|	...	|	...	|	...	...	|	...	...	...	...	...	|	...	|	...	**79824**	|	1147	...	...	|	...	2200	...
Kaunas 1810 § d.	...	...	|	...	|	...	|	...	...	|	...	...	...	...	...	|	...	|	...	2	|	1303	...	...	|	...	2330	...
Šeštokai 🛃 ◐ § d.	...	...	|	...	|	...	|	...	...	|	...	...	...	...	...	|	...	|	...	q	|	1438	1508	...	|	...	|	...
Suwałki d.	...	...	|	...	|	0429	|	0500	...	|	...	0739	...	...	0918	|	...	|	...	1430	|	...	1538	...	|	2046	|	...
Sokółka d.	...	...	0437	...	0537	0558	0631	0638	...	0739	...	0914	...	...	1059	1242	...	1447	...	1604	1632	...	1707	...	2047	2238	|	...
Białystok a.	...	...	0524	...	0620	0642	...	0723	...	0820	...	0953	...	...	1140	1325	...	1529	...	1650	...	...	1749	...	2130	2325	0220	...
Białystok d.	0505	...	...	0605	...	0705	...	...	0805	...	...	...	1005	...	1205	...	1405	...	1605	...	...	...	1805	2010	...	2345	|	...
Warszawa Wschodnia a.	0721	...	...	0821	...	0921	...	...	1021	...	...	...	1221	...	1421	...	1621	...	1821	...	...	...	2021	2222	...	0203	|	...
Warszawa Centralna a.	0732	...	...	0830	...	0930	...	...	1030	...	...	...	1235	...	1431	...	1633	...	1830	...	...	...	2030	...	...	0220	0500	...

A – ①③⑤ (daily June 14 - Sept. 13) 🚌 run by PKP InterCity.
B – ②④⑥ (daily June 15 - Sept. 14) 🚌 run by PKP InterCity.
L – From Kraków Apr. 25 - May 3, June 20 - Aug. 29; from Suwałki Apr. 26 - May 4, June 21 - Aug. 30: [12] Kraków - Warszawa - Suwałki and v.v.
N – [12] Kraków - Warszawa - Białystok and v.v.
P – [12] Bielsko Biała - Warszawa - Białystok and v.v.
S – [12] Wrocław - Warszawa - Suwałki and v.v.
T – ①–⑤ (not Dec. 25, 26, Jan. 1, Mar. 24, May 1, 22: [12] Łódź - Warszawa - Suwałki and v.v.
W – Dec. 9 - May 24.
b – From / to Bydgoszcz (Table **1020**).
f – Not Dec. 24, 25, 31, Mar. 22.
g – Not Dec. 25, Mar. 24.
h – Not Dec. 25, Mar. 23.
j – Not Dec. 23–26, 30, 21, Jan. 4, 6, Mar. 22, 23.
k – From / to Szczecin.
p – From / to Poznań.
q – Not Dec. 25, 26, Jan. 1, Mar. 23, 24.
t – Not Dec. 24–27, 31, Jan. 1, 5, 6, 7, Mar. 23, 24.
§ – Lithuanian time (Polish time + 1 hour).
‡ – Belarus time (Polish time + 1 hour).
◧ – 🛃 at Szypliszki (Poland) / Kalvarija (Lithuania).
◐ – 🛃 at Trakiszki / Mockava; ticketing point is Mockava.

OLSZTYN - EŁK - BIAŁYSTOK 1045

km		◇ 2	81201 Z	◇ 2	◇ 2	◇ 2	51114 W	◇ 2 E	◇ 2	◇ 2	51106 H	61117 A	◇ 2	81112 G	
0	**Olsztyn** d.	...	0422	...	0900	0953	1041	...	1305	...	...	1540	1607	1856	...
120	Giżycko d.	...	0624	...	1114	|	1237	...	1517	...	...	1739	1821	2051	...
167	Ełk a.	...	0715	...	1209	1315	1325	...	1608	...	...	1833	1912	2149	...
	Ełk d.	0543	0729	0742	...	...	1339	1410	...	1613	1838	...	...	2200	...
271	**Białystok** a.	0723	0851	0926	...	...	1504	1546	...	1752	1955	...	...	2325	...

	◇ 2	◇ 2	18113 G	◇ 2	◇ 2	16116 A	15107 H	15115 W	◇ 2	◇ 2	◇ 2	◇ 2 E	◇ 2	18201 Z
Białystok d.	...	0527	0600	...	...	...	0907	1213	1410	...	...	1653	1813	1907
Ełk a.	...	0710	0726	...	...	...	1027	1337	1558	...	...	1831	1956	2033
Ełk d.	0459	...	0738	0750	0913	0941	...	1350	...	1612	1615	...	...	2047
Giżycko d.	0549	...	0838	|	1004	1037	...	1439	...	1703	|	...	...	2137
Olsztyn a.	0800	...	1026	1115	1221	1242	...	1640	...	1925	1941	...	...	2324

A – [12] Wrocław - Poznań - Olsztyn - Ełk - Suwałki and v.v.
E – ①–⑤ (Not Dec. 25, 26, Jan. 1, Mar. 24, May 1, 22).
G – [12] and 🍴 Szczecin - Olsztyn - Ełk - Białystok and v.v.
H – To / from Warszawa.
W – From / to Gdynia.
Z – From / to Szczecin on dates in Table **1038**.
◇ – Stopping train.

WARSZAWA - BREST 1050

km		◇ D2	◇ P2	D 2	◇ 2	81203 B	2	209 A	◇ 2	◇ P2	31111 p	D 2	12 ⊠	◇ 2	◇ 2	D 2	10103 P	10 ⊠	10105	D 2	◇ 2	◇ 2	104 ⊠	◇ 2	2	247 1249		
0	**Warszawa** Centralna d.	...	...	...	...	0610	...	...	0846r	...	1115	...	...	...	...	...	1530	1625	1730	...	1836r	...	2025	2041r	2241r	2335	...	...
5	**Warszawa** Wschodnia d.	...	...	...	...	0629	...	...	0855	...	1124	...	1208	...	...	...	1538	1635	1738	...	1845	...	2037	2050	2250	2351	...	...
93	Siedlce d.	...	...	...	*0645*	0731	...	...	1030	...	1231	...	1321	*1300*	*1440*	...	1640	1736	1846	...	2021	...	2149	2226	0025	⊠	...	...
121	Łuków d.	0545	0640	...	0735	0757	...	1057	*1116*	1130	1252	...	|	1430	1530	...	1701	1758	1908	...	2051	2100	2215	2256	...	|	...	...
173	Biała Podlaska d.	0649	0743	...	0838	0858	...	|	...	1233	1350	...	|	1533	1633	...	1756	1852	2015	...	...	2203	2312	...	...	|	...	...
210	Terespol 🛃 a.	0743	0838	0905	0932	0950	1126	1237	...	1327	1442	1520	1525	1627	1728	1733	1845	1938	2111	2200	...	2257	0003	...	...	0245	...	...
217	**Brest** 🛃 ‡ a.	...	...	1036	...	...	1308	1504	...	...	...	1656	1741	...	...	1909	...	2144	...	2336	...	...	0222	...	...	0516	...	...
	Moskva **1950** a.	...	...	...	...	...	...	0824	...	...	...	...	1059	...	...	...	...	1210	...	...	...	...	...	...	...	2035	...	...

	246 1248	◇ 2	◇ h2	103 ⊠	◇ 2	10122 E	◇ 2	10104 P	2	◇ 2	◇ 2	9 ⊠	D 2	◇ 2	D 2	◇ P2	11 ⊠	13111 gp	10522 ⑦k	208 A	D 2	◇ 2	2	D 2	18202 B	◇ 2	◇ 2	
Moskva **1950** d.	0800	...	...	...	...	...	...	...	...	...	...	1920	...	...	...	...	2109	...	...	2344	...	...	...	...	...	...	...	...
Brest 🛃 ‡ d.	2115	...	...	0240	...	...	...	...	0750	...	...	0837	1003	...	1203	...	1250	...	...	1440	1632	...	...	1832	...	...	...	...
Terespol 🛃 d.	2113	...	...	0238	...	0337	...	0510	0708	0629	...	0835	0923	0937	1121	1130	1248	1310	1510	1438	1550	1607	...	1751	1900	1930	...	...
Biała Podlaska d.	|	...	...	0337	...	0440	...	0608	...	0728	...	0927	...	1036	...	1229	|	1410	1612	|	...	1706	...	...	2004	2029	...	...
Łuków d.	⊠	...	0345	0435	0501	0553	...	0707	...	0833	*1035*	1021	...	1141	...	1334	|	1509	1720	1639	...	1811	...	...	2101	2135	...	...
Siedlce d.	|	0342	0418	0500	0534	0613	0651	0730	...	...	1154	1042	...	...	...	...	1504	1532	1740	...	...	*2018*	2031	...	2122	*2220*	2223	...
Warszawa Wschodnia a.	0033	0516	0551	0611	0649	0716	0825	0831	...	...	1328	1133	...	...	...	...	1611	1633	1839	...	...	...	2205	...	2218	...	2357	...
Warszawa Centralna a.	0045	0525r	0600r	0620	0658r	0724	0834r	0840	...	...	1337r	1145	...	...	...	...	...	1641	1850	...	...	...	2215r	...	2251	...	0006r	...

A – VLTAVA – 🛏 1, 2 cl. Moskva - Praha and v.v. (for additional cars see Table **95**).
B – [12] Szczecin - Terespol and v.v.
D – ①–⑤ (not Dec. 24, 25, 26, 31, Jan. 1, 5, 6, 7, Mar. 23, Apr. 4, May 1, 2, 3, 22, 23, 24).
E – ①–⑤ (not Dec. 25, 26, Jan. 1, Mar. 21, 24, May 1, 2, 3, 22, 23, 24).
P – ①–⑤ (not Dec. 24, 25, 26, Jan. 1, Mar. 24, May 1, 2, 22, 23).
g – Not Dec. 24, 25, 31, Mar. 22.
h – Not Jan. 22, 23, 24, 25.
k – Also Dec. 26, Jan. 1, Mar. 24; not Mar. 23.
p – From / to Kraków.
r – Warszawa **Śródmieście** (adjacent to Centralna).
⊠ – Conveys only sleeping car passengers to / from Brest and points east thereof. For composition and days of running see **International** section (Tables **24** / **56** / **94**).
◇ – Stopping train.
‡ – Belarus time (Polish time + 1 hour).

1055 WARSZAWA - LUBLIN - CHEŁM

For Warszawa - Lublin - Yahodyn - Kyïv sleeping car services, see Table **1700**

km		13108 13109	*TLK* 5210/1	52100 52101	12101 12102	82102 82103	*TLK* 8210/1	53104 53105	12105 12104	52102 52103	68 13210 13211	
			R ✕				R ✕					
		C	J	F		Q	Q	K	⑧g	b		
0	**Warszawa** Centralna d.	0715	...	0915	1215	1415	1535	1615	1815	1915	2115	...
5	**Warszawa** Wschodnia d.	0724	0903	0924	1224	1424	1544	1624	1824	1924	2124	...
125	Puławy Miasto d.	0906	1100	1109	1410	1613	1726	1812	2009	2113	2318	...
175	**Lublin** a.	0946	1137	1147	1446	1650	1805	1849	2045	2150	2359	...
175	**Lublin** d.	*1028*	...	*1228*	*1528*f	*1728*	*1828*f	*1928*f	2058	*2228*	...	...
249	Chełm a.	*1142*	...	*1342*	*1642*f	*1844*	*1942*f	*2042*f	2213	*2342*	...	...

	67 31211 31210	25100 25101	*TLK* 2810/1	21122 21102	35104 35105	28102 28103	21104 21105	*TLK* 2510/1	25102 25103	31108 31109	
			R ✕	①–⑥				R ✕			
		b	Q	h	K	Q		J	Sb	C	
Chełm d.	...	*0449*	*0549*	0649	*0749*f	*1049*	*1249*f	*1349*	...	*1647*f	...
Lublin a.	...	*0602*	*0702*	0802	*0902*f	*1202*	*1402*f	*1502*	...	*1800*f	...
Lublin d.	0405	0615	0715	0815	1010	1215	1415	1525	1605	1920	...
Puławy Miasto d.	0445	0653	0754	0852	1047	1254	1453	1603	1643	2000	...
Warszawa Wschodnia a.	0638	0836	0940	1032	1236	1446	1643	1757	1825	2151	...
Warszawa Centralna a.	0650	0846	0951	1045	1245	1455	1655	...	1840	2200	...

FOR NOTES SEE TABLE 1058

1056 PRZEMYŚL - LVIV

km		75 760	73101 51/107	51 73101	35 ⊠✣	
		G	B	D	V	
	Warszawa C. **1058** d.	...	...	...	...	...
	Kraków Gł. **1075** d.	...	1330	1330	2128	...
0	**Przemyśl** d.	1814	1924	1924	0120	...
13	Medyka 🏛 d.	|	|	|	|	...
20	Mostiska II 🏛 ‡ d.	2102	2222	2222	0327	...
98	**Lviv** ‡ a.	2224	2346	2346	0448	...
	Chernivtsi **1720** a.	0350	|	|	|	...
	Kyïv **1750** a.	...	|	1024	1438	...
	Odesa **1750** a.	...	1220	...	...	...

	36 ⊠✣	108/52 37100	51/52 37100	76	
	T	B	D	G	
Odesa **1750** d.	...	1700	...	...	...
Kyïv **1750** d.	2241	|	2041	...	...
Chernivtsi **1720** d.	|	|	|	0810	...
Lviv ‡ d.	0835	0718	0718	1356	...
Mostiska II 🏛 ‡ d.	1028	0937	0937	1620	...
Medyka 🏛 d.	|	|	|	|	...
Przemyśl a.	1003	0935	0935	1606	...
Kraków Gł. **1075** a.	1350	1535	1535	...	...
Warszawa C. **1058** a.	...	...	...	...	...

WARSZAWA - RAVA RUSKA - LVIV

	13109 22109	82101 22105
		K
Warszawa Cent. d.	*0715*	1615
Warszawa Wsch. d.	*0724*	1624
Lublin a.	*0946*	1835
Lublin d.	0958	1908
Zawada d.	1215	2120
Zamość a.	1228	2132
Hrebenne 🏛 a.	...	...
Rava Ruska ‡ a.	...	...
Lviv ‡ a.	...	...

	22104 35105	22108 31108
	K	
Lviv ‡ d.	...	...
Rava Ruska ‡ d.	...	...
Hrebenne 🏛 d.	...	...
Zamość d.	0715	1622
Zawada d.	0738	1647
Lublin a.	0940	1845
Lublin d.	1010	*1920*
Warszawa Wsch. a.	1236	*2151*
Warszawa Cent. a.	1245	*2200*

FOR NOTES SEE TABLE 1058

1058 WARSZAWA and LUBLIN - PRZEMYŚL

km		13109 13108		*Ex* 5311	53104 53105	34200	*Ex* 1309		13210 13211	
		C		R A	K		R P			
0	**Warszawa** Centralna d.	0715	...	...	1615	...	...	...	2115	...
5	**Warszawa** Wschodnia d.	0724	...	1353	1624	...	1653	...	2124	...
	Warszawa Centralna d.	|	...	1405	|	...	1705	...	|	...
175	**Lublin** d.	1000	...	|	1905	...	|	...	0025	...
278	Stalowa Wola Rozwadów d.	1147	...	k	2053	...	k	...	0228	...
	Rzeszów **1075** d.	|	...	1917	|	...	2225	...	|	...
353	Przeworsk **1075** d.	1321	...	1954	2215	2247	2300	...	|	...
	Rzeszów **1075** a.	|	...	|	|	2319	|	...	0425	...
	Zagórz **1078** a.	|	...	|	|	...	|	...	...	...
368	Jarosław **1075** d.	1335	...	2008	2229	...	2313	...	...	...
403	**Przemyśl 1075** a.	1408	...	2038	2258	...	2344	...	...	...

	Ex 3108	35104 35105	◇	*Ex* 3510		31108 31109		31210 31211	
	R P	K	2	R A		C			
Przemyśl 1075 d.	0410	0603	...	0820	...	1452	...	...	...
Jarosław **1075** d.	0437	0630	...	0846	...	1522	...	...	...
Zagórz **1078** d.	|	|	...	|	...	|	...	...	...
Rzeszów **1075** d.	|	|	0740	|	...	|	...	2321	...
Przeworsk **1075** d.	0450	0643	0824	0859	...	1536	...	|	...
Rzeszów **1075** d.	0527	|	...	0936	...	|	...	|	...
Stalowa Wola Rozwadów d.	k	0819	...	k	...	1719	...	0138	...
Lublin d.	|	1010	...	|	...	1920	...	0405	...
Warszawa Centralna a.	1050	|	...	1450	...	|	...	|	...
Warszawa Wschodnia a.	1106	1236	...	1502	...	2151	...	0643	...
Warszawa Centralna a.	...	1245	...	...	...	2200	...	0650	...

A – (12) and ✕ Gdynia - Warszawa - Kraków - Przemyśl and v.v.
B – From Wrocław Dec. 26, 27, Jan. 1–12; from Odesa Dec. 27, 28, Jan. 2–13: ▬ 2 cl. Wrocław - Kraków - Odesa and v.v.
C – (12) Warszawa - Przemyśl and v.v.
D – 🛏 2 cl. Wrocław - Kraków - Przemyśl - Kyïv and v.v.
F – ①–⑥ (not Dec. 25, 26, Jan. 1, Mar. 24): (12) Bydgoszcz - Warszawa - Lublin and v.v.
G – 🛏 2 cl. Przemyśl – Chernivtsi and v.v.
J – ①–⑤ (not Dec. 24, 25, 26, 31, Jan. 1, Mar. 24, May 1, 2, 22, 23): (12) and ✕ Gdynia - Warszawa - Lublin and v.v.
K – (12) Bydgoszcz - Warszawa - Przemyśl / Zamość and v.v.
P – (12) and ✕ Warszawa - Kraków - Przemyśl and v.v.
Q – (12) Szczecin - Warszawa - Lublin and v.v.
S – ⑧ (not Dec. 24, 25, 31, Mar. 23)
T – ✣ JÓZEF CHEŁMOŃSKI ②④⑥: 🛏 2 cl. Kyïv - Kraków.
V – ✣ JÓZEF CHEŁMOŃSKI ③⑤⑦: 🛏 2 cl. Kraków - Kyïv.
b – From / to Bydgoszcz.
f – ①–⑤ (not Dec. 25, 26, Jan. 1, Mar. 24, May 1, 2, 22, 23).
g – Not Dec. 25, 31; daily from Apr. 26.
h – Not Dec. 26, Jan. 1; daily from Apr. 27.
k – Via Kraków (Tables **1065** and **1075**).
⊠ – Only for sleeping car passengers to / from Lviv and beyond.
‡ – Ukrainian (East European) time.
◇ – Stopping train.
✣ – Subject to confirmation. When train runs, a change of train may be necessary at the border.

1060 WARSZAWA - KATOWICE - GLIWICE and BIELSKO BIAŁA

km		54200 54201	*EC*103 14000	14121	13101	*IC* 1601	*IC* 1405 14411	*Ex* 1411	*EC*106 14005	14114 14115	*EC*105 14002	*IC* 1407	*Ex* 54411 14403	54100 54101	*Ex* 1415	53102 53103	*IC* 1401	54112 54113	*IC* 1609	*IC* 1403	*Ex* 5411	54102 54103	*TLK* 54415	203 14011		
		⑧	R ✕			R ✕	R ✕	R ✕	R ✕		R ✕	R ✕		✕	R ✕		R ✕		R ✕	R ✕	R ✕	✕ ⑧	✕q ⑦h			
		A	H		M	P			J	G	E	V	Q		R	k	b	gq		V				C		
	Gdynia Gł. **1030** d.	2045	...	...	...	...	...	...	...	...	...	...	0753e	0545	...	0836	...	...	...	...	1352	1218	...	...	...	...
0	**Warszawa** Wschodnia § d.	|	0548	...	...	0623	0658	0758	0858	0823	1043	1258	1253	|	1458	|	1553	1630	1658	1758	1853	|	1942	2053	...	...
5	**Warszawa** Centralna § d.	◐	0600	...	...	0635	0710	0810	0910	0845	1100	1310	1310	◐	1510	◐	1610	1645	1710	1810	1910	◐	2010	2105	...	...
*194	**Łódź** Fabryczna d.	0356r	|	...	0647	|	|	|	|	|	|	|	|	1310r	|	1518r	|	|	|	|	|	1933r	|	|	...	...
*167	Koluszki § d.	|	|	...	|	|	|	|	|	0959	|	|	|	|	|	|	|	1800	|	|	|	|	|	|	...	...
*128	Piotrków Trybunalski § d.	0515	|	0704	|	|	|	|	|	1030	|	|	|	1421	|	1623	|	1829	|	|	|	2042	|	|	...	...
*43	**Częstch Ob**¶ **1020** § d.	0625	|	0814	|	|	|	|	|	1133	|	|	|	1521	|	1724	|	1930	|	|	|	2148	|	|	...	...
259	Zawiercie **1020** d.	0705	|	0851	|	|	0910	1010	|	1208	|	1510	1510	1556	1710	1758	1810	2004	1910	2010	2110	2222	2227	|	...	...
294	Sosnowiec Gł. **1020** d.	0739	0819	0924	|	|	0937	1037	1136	1237	1319	1537	1537	1624	1737	|	1837	2032	1937	2037	2137	2250	2255	|	...	...
302	**Katowice 1020** a.	0751	0830	0935	|	0911	0950	1050	1147	1249	1330	1550	1550	1635	1750	|	1850	2044	1950	2050	2150	2302	2308	2347	...	...
	Kraków Gł. a.	|	...	...	1029	|	|	|	...	|	...	|	|	...	|	1952	|	...	|	|	|	...	|	...	...	...
	Gliwice **1075** a.	|	...	...	...	0944	1024c	|	...	|	...	1624c	|	...	1824	...	|	...	2024	|	2224	...	2341	...	...	...
	Wrocław Gł. **1075** a.	|	...	...	...	1150	...	|	...	|	...	...	|	...	...	...	|	...	2230	|	...	...	...	...	...	...
357	**Bielsko Biała 1077** a.	0929	...	...	...	...	...	1207	...	1413	...	...	1707	...	...	...	2007	...	...	2207	...	...	...	...	...	...

	202 41010	45100 45101	*TLK* 45414	*IC* 4102	45110 45111	*IC* 6108	*IC* 4100	*Ex* 4510	35102 35103	*Ex* 4114	*IC* 4104	*IC* 41402	45102 45103	*EC*104 41002	*Ex* 45410	41115 41114	*EC*107 41004	*Ex* 4110	*IC* 4106 41410	31100	70016	*EC*102 41000	*IC* 6100	45200 45201		
		✕ ①–⑥	✕q ⑥j	R ✕		R ✕	R ✕	R ✕		R ✕	R ✕	R ✕	✕ ⑧	R ✕	R ✕		R ✕	R 🍸	R ✕			R ✕	R ✕	⑧		
	C			V	gq		K		k	L	V	Q		E	S	G	J			N		H	T	A		
Bielsko Biała 1077 d.	...	...	...	0447	...	...	0647	...	...	...	...	1047	...	...	1347	1434	...	1547	...	...	...	...	...	2105	...	...
Wrocław Gł. **1075** d.	...	...	...	|	...	0424	|	...	...	...	...	|	...	...	|	|	...	|	...	...	...	...	1735	|	...	...
Gliwice **1075** d.	...	...	0442	|	...	0623	|	0823	...	0923	1123	|	...	...	|	|	...	|	1723c	...	...	...	1931	|	...	...
Kraków Gł. d.	...	...	|	|	...	|	|	|	0711	|	|	|	|	|	|	|	...	|	|	1836	...	...	|	|	...	...
Katowice 1020 d.	0423	0515	0530	0600	0650	0700	0800	0900	|	1000	1200	1200	1240	1400	1500	1550	1600	1700	1800	|	1830	1935	2006	2225	...	...
Sosnowiec Gł. **1020** d.	|	0527	0542	0612	0702	0712	0812	0912	|	1012	1212	1212	1252	1412	1512	1602	1612	1712	1812	|	1841	1947	|	2237	...	...
Zawiercie **1020** d.	|	0556	0617	0640	0731	0740	0840	0940	0859	1040	1240	1240	1322	|	1540	1631	|	1740	1840	|	1913	|	|	2309	...	...
Częstch Ob¶ **1020** § d.	|	0632	|	|	0808	|	|	|	0936	|	|	|	1358	|	|	1708	|	|	|	|	1948	|	|	2347	...	...
Piotrków Trybunalski § d.	|	0751	|	|	0916	|	|	|	1050	|	|	|	1508	|	|	1814	|	|	|	|	...	|	|	0058	...	...
Koluszki § d.	|	|	|	|	0943	|	|	|	|	|	|	|	|	|	|	1842	|	|	|	|	...	|	|	|	...	...
Łódź Fabryczna a.	|	0853r	|	|	|	|	|	|	1156r	|	|	|	1608r	|	|	|	|	|	|	2211	...	|	|	0202r	...	...
Warszawa Centralna § a.	0705	◐	0845	0845	1102	0945	1045	1145	◐	1245	1445	1445	◐	1640	1745	2000	1840	1945	2045	...	...	2215	2245	◐	...	...
Warszawa Wschodnia § a.	0717	|	0907	0857	1118	0957	1057	1202	|	1257	1457	1457	|	1652	1802	2027	1852	1957	2057	...	...	2227	2257	|	...	...
Gdynia Gł. **1030** a.	...	1626	...	...	...	...	...	1706	1918	...	...	...	2331	...	2304	...	...	...	...	...	...	...	...	0949	...	...

A – ⑧ (daily Dec. 9 - Feb. 29; also Apr. 26, May 3; not Dec. 24, 31): 🛏 1, 2 cl., ▬ 2 cl. and (12) Gdynia - Katowice - Bielsko Biała and v.v.
C – CHOPIN – 🛏 1, 2 cl. and ▬ 2 cl. Warszawa - Wien and v.v. 🛏 1, 2 cl. and ▬ 2 cl. Warszawa - Praha and v.v. 🛏 1, 2 cl., ▬ 2 cl. and (2) Warszawa - Bratislava - Budapest and v.v.
E – SOBIESKI – (12) and ✕ Warszawa - Katowice - Zebrzydowice 🏛 - Břeclav - Wien and v.v.
G – (12) Białystok - Warszawa - Bielsko Biała and v.v.
H – POLONIA – (12) and ✕ Warszawa - Zebrzydowice 🏛 - Wien and v.v.
J – PRAHA – (12) and ✕ Warszawa - Zebrzydowice 🏛 - Praha and v.v.
K – ①–⑥ (not Dec. 25, 26, Jan. 1, Mar. 24, May 2, 23).
L – ①–⑥ (not Dec. 24, 25, 26, 31, Jan. 1, Mar. 24, May 2, 3, 23, 24).
M – ①–⑥ (not Dec. 25, Mar. 24).
N – ⑧ (not Dec. 24, Mar. 23).
P – ①–⑥ (not Dec. 24, 25, Jan. 1, Mar. 24, May 2, 23).
Q – ⑥⑦ (also Dec. 24 – Jan. 1, Mar. 24, May 1, 2, 22, 23).
R – ⑧ (not Dec. 23, 24, 25, 30, 31, Mar. 23, May 1, 2, 22, 23).
S – ⑦ (also Jan. 1, Mar. 24, May 2, 23; not Mar. 23).
T – ⑧ (not Dec. 25, 31, Mar. 23, May 1, 22).
V – ①–⑤ (not Dec. 24 - Jan. 1, Mar. 24, May 1, 2, 22, 23).
b – Not Dec. 24, 25, Mar. 23.
c – ①–⑤ (not Dec. 24 - Jan. 1, Mar. 24, May 1, 2, 22, 23).
e – ⑥ (also Dec. 31, May 1, 22).
g – To / from Racibórz.
h – Also Mar. 24, May 2, 23; not Mar. 23.
j – Also May 1, 22.
k – Not Dec. 25, Mar. 23.
q – From / to Olsztyn.
r – Łódź **Kaliska**.
x – ⑤ only.
◇ – Stopping train.
* – Distance from Zawiercie.
◐ – Via Bydgoszcz (Table **1020**).
¶ – Full name is Częstochowa Osobowa.
§ – For Warszawa - Częstochowa see Table **1088**.

WARSZAWA - KRAKÓW 1065

Via CMK high-speed line ▲

For trains via Kielce (including night trains) see Table **1067**

km	*For slow trains see* **1067**	*Ex*	*IC*	*Ex*	*EC*	*IC*	*IC*	*IC*	*Ex*	*Ex*	*Ex*	*IC*	*Ex*	*Ex*	*Ex*	*IC*
		1311	**1301**	**1313**	**383**	**5307**	**1305**	**5303**	**1319**	**5311**	**1315**	**1303**	**1309**	**5313**	**1317**	**5301**
		13411		**13413**	**13001**	**1307**		**5302**		**5310**	**13415**		**3309**	**83415**		**5300**
		R✕	R✕	R✕	R✕	R✕	R✕	R✕	R✕	R✕	R✕	R✕	R✕	R✕	R✕	R✕
		K	D	Z	A		C		G	E	FZ		B	f	G	
	Gdynia Gł. **1030** d.	...	...	...	...	0505j	...	0653	...	0852	...	...	...	1252	...	1452
0	**Warszawa** Wschodnia d.	0553	0653	0748	0853	0948	1048	1148	1253	1353	1453	1548	1653	1753	1848	1948
5	**Warszawa** Centralna d.	0605	0705	0805	0905	1005	1105	1205	1305	1405	1505	1605	1705	1805	1905	2005
297	**Kraków** Gł. a.	0900	1000	1100	1200	1300	1400	1500	1600	1700	1800	1900	2001	2100	2200	2300

	IC	*IC*	*Ex*	*Ex*	*Ex*	*Ex*	*Ex*	*Ex*	*IC*	*IC*	*Ex*	*IC*	*IC*	*EC*	*Ex*	*Ex*
	3500	**3102**	**3108**	**3114**	**3512**	**3116**	**3510**	**3118**	**3506**	**3106**	**3100**	**3502**	**3104**	**382**	**3112**	**3110**
	3501		**3308**		**38414**		**3511**		**3507**		**31414**	**3503**		**31000**	**31412**	**31410**
	R✕	R✕	R✕	R✕	R✕	R✕	R✕	R✕	R✕	R✕	R✕	R✕	R✕	R✕	R✕	R✕
			B	M	f	G	E	L	R	⑥k	Zh		⑧g	A	Z	K
Kraków Gł. d.	0555	0655	0755	0855	0955	1055	1155	1255	1355	1355	1455	1555	1655	1755	1855	1955
Warszawa Centralna a.	0850	0950	1050	1150	1250	1350	1450	1550	1650	1650	1750	1850	1950	2049	2150	2250
Warszawa Wschodnia a.	0902	1007	1106	1207	1302	1402	1502	1612	1702	1702	1807	1902	2002	2101	2202	2302
Gdynia Gł. **1030** a.	1400	...	...	...	1804	...	2005	...	2144	...	...	2356	...	...	...	...

A – JÓZEF BEM – [12] and ✕ Warszawa - Kraków - Košice - Budapest and v.v.
B – Conveys [12] Warszawa - Przemyśl / Nowy Sącz and v.v.; for dates of running see Table **1078**.
C – ①–⑥ (also Feb. 24; not Dec. 25, Jan. 1, May 2, 23).
D – ①–⑥ (not Dec. 24, 25, Jan. 1, Feb. 23, Mar. 24, May 2, 3, 23, 24).
E – [12] Gdynia - Kraków - Przemyśl and v.v.
F – ①–⑤ (not Dec. 24–30, Jan. 1, Mar. 24, May 1, 22).
G – ①–⑤ (not Dec. 24 – Jan. 1, Mar. 24, May 1, 2, 22, 23).
K – Conveys [12] Warszawa - Krynica / Rzeszów and v.v.; for dates of running see Table **1078**.
L – ①–⑤ (not Dec. 25 – Jan. 1, Mar. 24, May 1, 22).
M – ②–⑤ (not Dec. 25 – Jan. 2, Mar. 25, May 1, 2, 22, 23).
R – ⑧ (not Dec. 24, 25, 31, Mar. 23, May 1, 2, 23).
Z – Conveys [12] Warszawa - Kraków - Zakopane and v.v.; for dates of running see Table **1066**.
f – Not Dec. 24, 25, Mar. 23.
g – Also Feb. 23; not Dec. 24, 31, May 1, 22.
h – Not Dec. 25, Mar. 23, May 2, 23.
j – ①–⑥ (not Dec. 25, 26, Jan. 1, Mar. 24, May 2, 3, 24).
k – Also May 1, 2, 23.
▲ – Ticketing route is via Idzikowice.

KRAKÓW and KATOWICE - ZAKOPANE 1066

Ex trains convey ✕

km		**13201**	◇	**73500**	◇	*TLK*	◇		*Ex*	*Ex***1313**	◇	*Ex*	**13104**	*TLK*	◇		◇	*Ex*✕	**43127**	◇		
			2		2	**53702**	2		**13403**	**13413**	2	**13401**	**13504**	**33411**	2		2	**13415**		2		
		L		Q		RFg			G	RK		H	L	⑥j				RR	h			
	Warszawa Cent **1065 1067** d.	2140	...	...	...	0019	...	...	0610	0805	...	0815	0650	...	...	...	...	1505	...	...	...	...
	Katowice **1060** d.	|	...	...	...	0426	...	...	|	|	...	|	|	...	...	...	...	|	...	...	...	...
0	**Kraków** Gł. d.	0316	...	0326	0506	0615	0748	...	0930	1104	1123	1132	1225	1310	1444	...	1624	1805	1830	2219	...	...
5	Kraków Płaszów d.	0340	...	0352	0520	0641	0800	...	0952	1121	1136	1154	1248	1333	1457	...	1638	1827	1842	2232	...	...
68	Sucha Beskidzka d.	0513	0525	0539	0656	0830	0925	...	1108	1241	1259	1316	1430	1509	1624	...	1808	1956	2006	2358	...	...
103	Chabówka a.	0551	0607	0617	0745	0911	1007	...	1141	1314	1345	1414	1508	1549	1709	...	...	2029	2048	...	...	...
	Chabówka d.	0603	0608	0634	0759	0921	1021	...	1151	1324	1358	1425	1520	1602	1722	...	...	2039	2102	...	...	...
126	Nowy Targ d.	0637	0653	0707	0830	0951	1052	...	1234	1352	1435	1502	1552	1656	1753	...	...	2107	2131	...	...	...
147	**Zakopane** a.	0659	0718	0731	0855	1015	1117	...	1306	1411	1505	1521	1623	1716	1818	...	...	2126	2154	...	...	...

	◇	◇	**34126**		◇	*Ex*✕	*TLK*	**31104**	◇	◇	*Ex*	*Ex***3112**	*Ex*	◇		*TLK*	◇		**31200**	**37500**		
	2	2	**34127**		2	**31414**	**33410**	**31504**	2	2	**31402**	**31412**	**31400**	2		**35702**	2					
			k			RX	⑦f	L			J	RK	H			RFg			L	P		
Zakopane d.	...	...	0530	...	...	1136	1200	1217	1230	1425	1438	1545	1657	1717	...	1900	1930	...	2127	2210	...	...
Nowy Targ d.	...	...	0551	...	...	1156	1220	1239	1252	1447	1504	1604	1721	1739	...	1926	1952	...	2154	2233	...	...
Chabówka a.	...	...	0621	...	...	1222	1246	1305	1323	1518	1537	1631	1752	1813	...	1952	2027	...	2220	2259	...	...
Chabówka d.	...	...	0634	...	...	1232	1256	1316	1346	1531	1550	1641	1801	1826	...	2003	2032	...	2232	2311	...	...
Sucha Beskidzka d.	0440	0615	0719	...	1127	1325	1345	1411	1438	1620	1637	1725	1843	1912	...	2108	2114	...	2322	0004	...	...
Kraków Płaszów a.	0605	0735	0834	...	1256	1431	1506	1525	1602	1742	1758	1832	2008	2038	...	2215	...	...	0040	0118	...	...
Kraków Gł. a.	0618	0748	0846	...	1314	1450	...	1605	1615	1757	1821	1850	2034	2051	...	2238	...	...	0104	0141	...	...
Katowice **1060** a.	...	...	...	...	...	|	...	|	...	...	|	|	|	...	...	0029	...	...	|	...	...	...
Warszawa Cent **1065 1067** a.	...	...	...	...	...	1750	...	2105	...	...	2145	2150	2351	...	...	0450	...	...	0615	...	...	...

F – 🛏 1, 2 cl., 🛏 2 cl. and [2] R Zakopane - Kraków - Katowice - Gdynia and v.v.
G – Dec. 26 - Jan. 2, Feb. 9, 10, 11, 16, 17, 21, 22, 23, 24, May 1, 4, 22, 25.
H – Dec. 26, 27, 28, 29, Jan. 1, 2, Feb. 9, 10, 11, 16, 17, 22, 23, 24.
J – Dec. 26, 27, 28, 29, 30, Jan. 1, 2, Feb. 9, 10, 11, 16, 17, 21, 22, 23, 24, May 1, 4, 22, 25.
L – For dates of running see Table **1067**.
K – ⑥⑦ (daily Dec. 9 - Feb. 24, Mar. 20–25, Apr. 30 - Sept. 30; also Nov. 11).
P – Dec. 24, 27–31, Jan. 2, Jan. 28 - Feb. 25, Apr. 28 - May 5, May 24, 25, 26: [12] Zakopane - Kraków - Łódź - Poznań (Table **1080**).
Q – From Poznań on Dec. 22, 23, 26–30, Jan. 26 - Feb. 23, Apr. 26 - May 3, May 22, 23, 24: [12] Poznań - Łódź - Kraków - Zakopane (Table **1080**).
R – ⑤ (also Dec. 31, Apr. 30, May 21).
X – ⑦ (also Jan. 1, Feb. 23, Mar. 24, May 1, 22; not Mar. 23).
f – Also Dec. 28, Jan. 1, Mar. 24, May 2, 23; not Mar. 23.
g – Not Dec. 24, 25, Mar. 23.
h – From Częstochowa (depart 1532).
j – Also Dec. 27, 31, May 1, 22.
k – To Częstochowa (arrive 1137).
◇ – Stopping train.

WARSZAWA and LUBLIN - KIELCE - KRAKÓW 1067

km	*For fast trains to Kraków see Table* **1065**			**83202**	**23100**	**13504**	**52104**		**53100**		**26102**	**13106**		**13102**	**23102**	**12114**	**13110**		**12112**	**26200**	**13200**		**13503**		
			◇	**83203**	**23101**	**13505**	**52105**		**53101**		**26103**	**13107**		**13103**	**23103**	**12115**	**13111**		**12113**	**26201**	**13201**		**13502**		
		◇	2				T			◇							f	◇							
		2	b	A			w		Mg	2	h	Q			V	C	St	2		J	B		K		
0	**Warszawa** Wschodnia d.	...	...	0442	...	0628	0843	...	1028	...	...	1228	...	1433	...	1538	1634	1728	1838	...	2127	...	0213	...	...
5	**Warszawa** Centralna d.	...	...	0455	...	0650	0900	...	1050	...	...	1250	...	1450	...	1550	1650	1740	1850	...	2140	...	0225	...	...
	Lublin d.	...	...	|	0550	|	|	...	|	...	1235	|	...	|	1620	|	|	|	|	2155	|	...	|	...	...
108	Radom d.	...	...	0659	0739	0847	1048	...	1235	...	1409	1438	...	1641	1813	1741	1840	1924	2038	2344	2330	...	0407	...	...
149	Skarżysko Kamienna d.	...	...	0750	0826	0933	1132	...	1324	...	1452	1525	...	1728	1900	1827	1926	2017	2123	0028	0017	...	0451	...	...
193	Kielce d.	0535	0605	0833	0915	1015	1210	...	1407	1430	1542	1606	...	1814	1946	...	2010	...	2201	0119	0109	...	0529	...	...
	Katowice a.	0905	|	|	|	|	...	...	|	|	|	|	...	|	|	...	|	...	...	0329	|	...	|	...	...
	Częstochowa Stradom d.	...	|	|	|	|	...	...	|	|	1743	|	...	|	|	...	|	...	...	...	|	...	|	...	...
	Wrocław Gł. a.	...	|	|	|	|	...	...	|	|	2050	|	...	|	|	...	|	...	...	...	|	...	|	...	...
325	**Kraków** Gł. a.	...	0830	1045	1114	1215	...	...	1610	1652	...	1811	...	2011	2146	...	2211	...	...	...	0312	...	0727	...	...
330	Kraków Płaszów a.	...	...	1103	1126	1233	...	...	1642	...	...	...	...	2031	2159	...	2223	...	...	...	0324	...	0738	...	...
	Zakopane **1066** a.	...	...	...	...	1623x	...	...	...	...	...	...	...	...	...	...	...	...	...	...	0659	...	...	...	...

		21110			**31110**	**32100**	**31102**		**31106**	**62102**		**35100**		**25104**	**31104**	**32102**	**38202**		**31502**		**31200**	**62200**			
		21111		**21114**	**31111**	**32101**	**31103**		**31107**	**62103**		**35101**		**25105**	**31504**	**32103**	**35502**	◇	**31503**		**31201**	**62201**			
	◇		◇					◇			◇			Y				2							
	2	C	2		Rf	W		2	Q	h	2	Md		w			A	j	K		B	J			
Zakopane **1066** d.	...	...	...	...	...	...	...	...	...	...	...	...	...	...	1217x	...	...	...	...	...	2127	...	...	...	...
Kraków Płaszów d.	...	...	...	...	0553	0703	0753	...	...	...	...	1156	...	...	1557	...	1757	...	2132	...	0055	...	...	...	...
Kraków Gł. d.	...	...	...	...	0611	0720	0812	...	1012	...	1030	1212	...	...	1612	1654	1812	1910	2200	...	0109	...	...	...	...
Wrocław Gł. d.	...	...	...	...	|	|	|	...	|	0715	|	|	...	...	|	|	|	|	|	...	|	...	...	...	...
Częstochowa Stradom d.	...	...	...	...	|	|	|	...	|	0958	|	|	...	...	|	|	|	|	|	...	|	...	...	...	...
Katowice d.	...	...	...	...	|	|	|	0751	|	|	|	|	...	...	|	|	|	|	|	...	|	0132	...	...	...
Kielce d.	...	...	*0541*	0632	0806	0939	1008	1120	1211	1224	1250	1412	...	1613	1809	1930	2015	2131	2359	...	0311	0404	...	...	...
Skarżysko Kamienna d.	0426	0518	0636	0712	0846	1019	1049	...	1251	1304	...	1453	...	1652	1850	2012	2058	...	0038	...	0352	0443	...	...	...
Radom d.	0510	0549	0720	0746	0919	1054	1127	...	1325	1337	...	1526	...	1726	1926	2045	2137	...	0113	...	0427	0525	...	...	...
Lublin a.	|	|	|	|	|	1224	|	...	|	1506	...	|	...	|	|	2218	|	...	|	...	|	0655	...	...	...
Warszawa Centralna a.	0710	0740	0920	0935	1106	...	1315	...	1505	...	...	1705	...	1905	2105	...	2320	...	0250	...	0615	...	...	...	...
Warszawa Wschodnia a.	0732	0747	0932	0952	1122	...	1332	...	1527	...	...	1717	...	1917	2117	...	2332	...	0302	...	0627	...	...	...	...

A – 🛏 1, 2 cl., 🛏 2 cl. and [12] Kołobrzeg - Warszawa - Kraków and v.v.
B – From Warszawa Dec. 20 - Jan. 1, Jan. 25 - Feb. 23, Apr. 25 - May 3; from Zakopane Dec. 21 - Jan. 2, Jan. 26 - Feb. 24, Apr. 26 - May 4: [12] Warszawa - Zakopane and v.v.
C – ①–⑤ (not Dec. 24, 25, 26, 31, Jan. 1, Mar. 24, Apr. 30, May 1, 21, 22).
J – [12] Lublin - Katowice and v.v.; To Wrocław and Jelenia Góra on June 22 - Sept. 1 (one day later from Jelenia Góra).
K – From Suwałki Apr. 26 - May 4, June 21 - Aug. 30; from Kraków Apr. 25 - May 3, June 20 - Aug. 29: [12] Suwałki - Warszawa - Kraków and v.v.
M – [12] Olsztyn - Warszawa - Kraków and v.v.
Q – From / to Białystok: to Białystok (not Dec. 25, 26, Jan. 1, Mar. 23) and from Białystok (not Dec. 24, 25, 31, Mar. 22).
R – Conveys daily (not Dec. 22, 23, 25, 26, 29, Jan. 1, Mar. 20, 23) 🛏 1, 2 cl. Kraków - Moskva.
S – Conveys daily (not Dec. 23, 24, 26, 27, 30, Jan. 2, Mar. 21, 24) 🛏 1, 2 cl. Moskva - Kraków.
T – ①–⑥ (not Dec. 25, 31, Mar. 22).
V – ⑧ (not Dec. 24, 25, 31, Mar. 23).
W – ①–⑥ (not Dec. 25, 26, Jan. 1, Mar. 24).
Y – ⑧ (not Dec. 25, 31, Mar. 23).
b – Not Dec. 26, Mar. 24.
d – Not Dec. 27, Jan. 1, May 2, 4.
f – From / to Terespol.
g – Not Deć. 26, 31, May 1, 3.
h – Not Dec. 24, 25, 31, May 23.
j – Not Dec. 25, May 23.
t – Not Dec. 24, 25, 31, Mar. 22.
v – Not Dec. 25, 26, Jan. 1, Mar. 23.
x – Dec. 21 - Jan. 2, Jan. 26 - Feb. 24, Apr. 26 - May 4.
w – From / to Olsztyn.
◇ – Stopping train.

1070 POZNAŃ - WROCŁAW

FOR NOTES SEE TABLE 1075

km		345		TLK						IC	56104			TLK	56112	Ex/IC	84101	16116	IC		86102	IC	83200		
		83704	56200	7310	7620	82106	84104	56100	83100	1607/6	56105	83104	83102	83412	56113	1613/2	84100	16117	1603/2	56102	86502	1605/4	83512		
				R✕					✕	✕		R✕	✕	8310		✕			✕	✕	m	✕	✕		
		D	E		h	A	mb	n	mg	Vg	jq	m	B	R✕	p	V	Gd	e	LV	n	2	CV	S		
0	Poznań Gł. d.	0220	0245	0540	0636	0740	0840	0958	1040	1120	1135	1240	1440	1540	1635	1732	1740	1820	1911	1950	2034	2123	2340	...	...
69	Leszno d.	0314	0343	0636	0735	0838	0935	1055	1138	1208	1233	1338	1538	1637	1733	1819	1836	1916	1959	2046	2131	2210	0042	...	...
165	Wrocław Gł. a.	0433	0510	0800	0857	1005	1105	1225	1305	1333	1405	1505	1703	1805	1905	1943	2005	2050	2123	2211	2256	2333	0215	...	...

	38200	IC	68103	IC	65101			Ex/IC	TLK	65113					IC	38104		38100			TLK		38705		
	38201	6103/2	68503	6105/4	65100	61117	48101	6113/2	38411	65112	2	38102	48105	65105	6107/6	38105	27101	38101	28106	6722	3711	65201	344		
	✕	✕	m	✕	✕			R✕	3811		◇	✕	✕		✕	✕	✕				R🍷				
	S	MV	2	CV	n	e	Gg	V	R✕	p	w	B	mb	qc	Vf	m	n	mg	A	h		E	D		
Wrocław Gł. d.	0320	0500	0535	0630	0635	0815	0835	1030	1035	1035	1040	1135	1235	1335	1430	1435	1535	1635	1735	1935	2035	0005	0025	...	...
Leszno d.	0446	0615	0700	0745	0759	0942	1000	1145	1158	1201	1220	1303	1400	1501	1545	1600	1700	1800	1900	2100	2155	0134	0142	...	...
Poznań Gł. a.	0555	0702	0755	0832	0854	1037	1054	1232	1253	1300	1333	1358	1454	1557	1632	1657	1755	1857	1956	2157	2250	0230	0255	...	...

1075 WROCŁAW - KATOWICE - KRAKÓW - PRZEMYŚL

km		43100	63100		TLK	73100	82106	84104	63102	Ex	83100	EC 241	Ex	83104	35	63110	83102	TLK	84101	63200	83200	TLK	345	
		43101	63101	32111	7310	73101	83107	84105	63103	5311	83101	73000	1309	83105	33011	63111	83103	8310	84100	63201	83514	83704	83704	
		✕	✕		R✕	✕			✕	R✕	✕	R🍷	R✕	R✕			✕	83410			✕	✕		
		y		g	Z	J	A	mb		K	g	Wt	T		P		B	R✕	Gd	N	S	Yk	D	
	Świnoujście **1010** d.	...	...	...	...	...	...	...	...	...	...	...	...	...	...	...	...	1101v	...	...	...	2122	...	...
	Szczecin Gł. **1010** d.	...	...	...	...	...	...	...	...	...	0755	...	...	0955	...	...	...	1255	...	...	2047	2305	...	...
	Poznań Gł. **1070** d.	...	...	...	0540	...	0740	0840	...	...	1040	...	...	1240	...	...	1440	1540	1740	...	2340	0220	0220	...
0	**Wrocław** Gł. **1088** d.	...	0615	...	0815	0915	1015	1115	1215	...	1315	1537	...	1515	...	1615	1715	1820	2015	2215	0228	0443	0443	...
42	Brzeg **1088** d.	...	0652	...	0852	0951	1052	1152	1252	...	1352	|	...	1552	...	1652	1751	1851	2052	2252	0309	0514	0514	...
82	Opole Gł. **1088** d.	...	0724	...	0923	1024	1124	1224	1324	...	1424	1638	...	1624	...	1723	1832	1923	2124	2324	0348	0538	0538	...
162	Gliwice **1060** d.	0636	0837	...	1037	1137	1237	1337	1437	...	1537	1743	...	1737	...	1837	1947	2037	2237	0037	0505	0703	0703	...
190	**Katowice 1060** a.	0710	0910	...	1110	1210	1310	1410	1510	...	1610	1815	...	1810	...	1910	2020	2110	2310	0111	0540	0729	0729	...
190	**Katowice** ▲ d.	0715	0915	...	1115	1215	1315	...	1515	...	1615	1818	...	1823	...	1915	2025	2115	...	0121	0555	0731	0731	...
268	**Kraków** Gł. ▲ a.	0856	1056	...	1255	1355	1455	...	1655	...	1755	1944	...	2000	...	2055	2203	2248	...	0302	0737	0858	0858	...
268	**Kraków** Gł. **1078** d.	0916	1108	...	1319	1405	1500	...	...	1710	1810	...	2011	2015	2128	...	...	...	...	0306	0743	...	...	...
273	Kraków Pł ✣ **1078** d.	0927	1117	...	1328	1414	1509	...	...	1718	1819	...	2020	2025	|	...	...	...	...	0329	0811	...	...	...
346	Tarnów **1078** d.	1029	1217	...	1425	1517	1609	...	...	1814	1921	...	2123	2128	2228	...	...	...	...	0429	0916	...	...	...
379	Dębica d.	1058	1245	...	1453	1546	1647	...	...	1839	1949	...	2149	2156	2256	...	...	...	...	0455	0943	...	...	...
426	Rzeszów **1058** d.	1137	1332	1347	1529	1628	|	...	...	1915	2029	...	2223	2236	2333	...	...	...	...	0533	1023	...	...	...
463	Przeworsk **1058** d.	1213	1411	1427	1615	1708	|	...	...	1953	2109	...	2259	2315	|	...	...	...	...	0610	1104	...	...	...
478	Jarosław **1058** d.	1227	1426	1443	1630	1723	|	...	...	2007	2124	...	2313	2329	|	...	...	...	...	0626	1119	...	...	...
**	Zamość a.	|	|	1840	|	|	2210	...	...	|	|	...	|	|	|	...	...	...	...	|	|	...	...	...
513	**Przemyśl 1058** a.	1258	1456	...	1705	1758	...	...	...	2038	2156	...	2344	0002	0050	...	...	...	...	0700	1153	...	...	...

	48100	TLK	38102	EC 240	48104	Ex	36102	38104	38100	Ex	28106	36	37100		TLK	36110		36100	34100	TLK	38705	38200	36200	
	48101	3811	38103	37001	48105	3108	36103	38105	38101	3510	38107	33012	37101	51	3710	36111	23110	36101	34101	38705	344	38201	36201	
		38411	✕	R🍷		R✕		✕	✕	R✕			✕	R🍷	R🍷			✕	✕	✕		✕		
	Gg	R✕	B	Wr	mb	T	g		g	K	A	Q	J	U			g		y	Yk	D	S	N	
Przemyśl 1058 d.	...	...	...	...	...	0410	...	0612	0758	0839	...	1038	1125	1205	1158	...	...	1358	1557	...	...	1745	2203	...
Zamość d.	...	...	...	...	...	|	...	|	|	|	0545	|	|	|	|	...	1005	|	|	...	...	|	|	...
Jarosław **1058** d.	...	...	...	...	...	0437	...	0642	0828	0906	|	|	1155	1238	1226	...	1416	1428	1626	...	...	1816	2232	...
Przeworsk **1058** d.	...	...	...	...	...	0450	...	0655	0841	0917	|	|	1209	1249	1239	...	1431	1440	1638	...	...	1829	2245	...
Rzeszów **1058** d.	...	...	...	...	...	0527	...	0733	0919	0949	|	1147	1249	1325	1319	...	1509	1529	1713	...	...	1908	2322	...
Dębica d.	...	...	...	...	...	0601	...	0811	0957	1022	1109	1222	1327	1401	1354	...	...	1607	1752	...	...	1947	2359	...
Tarnów **1078** d.	...	...	...	...	...	0637	...	0838	1025	1048	1136	1249	1354	1428	1422	...	...	1633	1820	...	...	2015	0026	...
Kraków Pł ◧ **1078** d.	...	...	...	...	...	0737	...	0940	1128	1140	1237	|	1459	1528	1536	...	...	1734	1925	...	...	2140	0140	...
Kraków Gł. **1078** a.	...	...	...	...	...	0745	...	0948	1136	1147	1245	1350	1507	1535	1544	...	...	1741	1932	...	...	2148	0148	...
Kraków Gł. ▲ d.	...	0553	0653	0731	...	...	0853	0953	1153	...	1253	...	1517	1545	1553	1653	...	1753	1945	2007	2007	2153	0153	...
Katowice ▲ a.	...	0729	0829	0852	...	...	1029	1129	1329	...	1429	...	1651	1715	1729	1829	...	1929	2118	2142	2142	2329	0329	...
Katowice 1060 d.	0534	0734	0834	0854	0934	...	1034	1134	1334	...	1434	...	1656	1720	1734	1834	...	1934	2123	2146	2146	2345	0349	...
Gliwice **1060** d.	0607	0807	0907	0924	1007	...	1107	1207	1407	...	1507	...	1728	1750	1807	1907	...	2007	2157	2219	2219	0024	0423	...
Opole Gł. **1088** d.	0718	0917	1018	1030	1118	...	1218	1318	1518	...	1618	...	1841	1859	1919	2018	...	2118	...	2331	2331	0145	0535	...
Brzeg **1088** d.	0746	0945	1046	|	1146	...	1246	1346	1546	...	1646	...	1910	1927	1948	2046	...	2146	...	2358	2358	0218	0606	...
Wroclaw Gł. **1088** a.	0825	1025	1125	1132	1225	...	1325	1425	1625	...	1725	...	1950	2003	2025	2125	...	2224	...	0035	0035	0300	0646	...
Poznań Gł. **1070** a.	1054	1253	1358	...	1454	...	...	1357	1857	...	1956	...	...	...	2250	...	...	...	...	0255	0255	0555	...	...
Szczecin Gł. **1010** a.	...	1528	...	...	...	...	...	1944	2139	...	...	...	...	...	...	...	...	...	...	0617	...	0848	...	...
Świnoujście **1010** a.	...	1721o	...	...	...	...	...	...	...	...	...	...	...	...	...	...	...	...	...	0814	...	...	...	...

NOTES FOR TABLES 1070 and 1075

A – [12] Gorzów Wlkp - Krzyż - Poznań - Zamość and v.v.
B – [12] and ✕ Kołobrzeg - Poznań - Kraków and v.v.
C – ①–⑤ (not Dec. 24 - Jan. 1, Mar. 24, May 1, 2, 22, 23).
D – 🛏 1, 2 cl., ▬ 2 cl. and 🍷 Berlin - Wrocław - Kraków and v.v. (not Dec. 24).
E – [12] Gdynia - Poznań - Wrocław and v.v.
G – [12] Słupsk - Poznań - Wrocław - Katowice and v.v.
J – [12] and ✕ Zielona Góra - Wrocław - Przemyśl and v.v. From Wrocław Dec. 26, 27, Jan. 1–12; from Odesa Dec. 27, 28, Jan. 2–13: ▬ 2 cl. Wrocław - Kraków - Odesa and v.v.
K – [12] and ✕ Gdynia - Warszawa - Kraków - Przemyśl and v.v. (Table **1030**).
L – ⑧ (not Dec. 24, 25, 31, Mar. 23, May 1, 2, 22, 23).
M – ①–⑥ (not Dec. 25, 26, Jan. 1, Mar. 24, May 2, 3, 24).
N – [12] Wrocław - Przemyśl and v.v. From/to Jelenia Góra on dates in Table **1084**.
P – ✣ JÓZEF CHEŁMOŃSKI ③⑤⑦: 🛏 2 cl. Kraków - Kyïv.
Q – ✣ JÓZEF CHEŁMOŃSKI ②④⑥: 🛏 2 cl. Kyïv - Kraków.
S – Conveys 🛏 1, 2 cl., ▬ 2 cl., [12] and ✕.

T – [12] and ✕ Warszawa - Kraków - Przemyśl and v.v.
U – 🛏 2 cl. Kyïv - Przemyśl - Kraków - Wrocław and 🛏 1, 2 cl. Kyïv - Kraków - Praha.
V – [12] and ✕ R Warszawa - Poznań - Wrocław and v.v.
W – WAWEL – [12] and 🍷 Berlin - Wrocław - Kraków and v.v. For dates from/to Hamburg see Table **56**.
Y – Conveys 🛏 1, 2 cl., ▬ 2 cl., [2] and ✕.
Z – [12] Poznań - Wrocław - Przemyśl. Conveys 🛏 2 cl. Wrocław - Kraków - Przemyśl - Kyïv and 🛏 1, 2 cl. Praha - Kraków - Kyïv.

b – To/from Bielsko Biała.
c – Not Dec. 25, 31, Mar. 23.
d – Not Dec. 24, Mar. 22.
e – From/to Ełk and Suwałki.
f – Not Dec. 24, 25, Mar. 23.
g – Not Dec. 25, Mar. 23.
h – To/from Jelenia Góra.
j – Not Dec. 25, Jan. 1, Mar. 23.
k – Not Dec. 24, Mar. 23.
m – From/to Szczecin.
n – From/to Bydgoszcz and Gdynia (Table **1020**).

o – June 21 - Aug. 30.
p – From/to Toruń and Grudziądz.
q – To/from Toruń and Olsztyn (Table **1020**).
r – Not Dec. 24, 31
t – Not Dec. 25, 31.
v – June 22 - Aug. 31.
w – To/from Kudowa Zdrój (Table **1095**).
y – Conveys [12] Gliwice - Kraków - Rzeszów - Zagórz and v.v. on dates in Table **1078**.
z – To/from Zamość.

◧ – Full name is Kraków **Płaszów**.
◇ – Stopping train.
** – Dębica - Zamość: *– 207 km*.
▲ – Additional trains run Katowice - Kraków and v.v. (Journey time: 80–100 minutes).
✣ – Subject to confirmation. When train runs, a change of train may be necessary at the border.

1076 KATOWICE and KRAKÓW - OSTRAVA

km		EC	EC 108	EC	EC	EC		200			203
		108	EC 103	103	106	105	208	203	200	203	200
		✕⁄	✕	✕⁄	✕⁄	✕⁄					
		§	§	§	§	§	V	K	W	C	S
	Warszawa Cent. **1060** d.	...	...	0600	0910	1100	...	...	...	2105	2105
0	**Katowice** d.	...	...	0832	1150	1332	2240	...	...	2352	2352
	Kraków Gł. **1099** d.	0700	0700	|	|	|	|	2225	2225	|	|
	Oświecim **1099** d.	0818	0818	|	|	|	|	2347	2347	|	|
74	Zebrzydowice 🛃 d.	0919	0919	0943	1304	1443	2352	0048	0048	0103	0103
94	Bohumín 🛃 **1160** a.	0938	0938	1002	1324	1502	0015	0109	0109	0121	0121
	Bohumín 🛃 **1160** d.	0950	1014	1014	1350	1514	0033	0213	0220	0213	0220
102	**Ostrava** Hlavní **1160** a.	0959	1022	1022	1359	1522	0043	0222	0229	0222	0229
	Praha Hlavní **1160** a.	1400	|	|	1800	|	0503	|	0645	|	0645
	Wien Südbf **995** a.	...	1328	1328	...	1828	...	0603	...	0603	...

	201		202			EC	EC	EC	EC 102	EC
	202	201	202	201	209	104	107	102	EC 109	109
						✕⁄	✕⁄	✕⁄	✕	✕⁄
	S	W	C	K	V	§	§	§	§	§
Wien Südbf **995** d.	...	...	2233	2233	...	0908	...	1433	1433	...
Praha Hlavní **1160** d.	2124	2124	|	|	2256	|	1006	|	|	1406
Ostrava Hlavní **1160** d.	0135	0135	0204	0204	0300	1213	1404	1747	1747	1802
Bohumín 🛃 **1160** a.	0144	0144	0213	0213	0323	1221	1412	1755	1755	1810
Bohumín 🛃 **1160** d.	0251	0307	0251	0307	0333	1234	1434	1813	1826	1826
Zebrzydowice 🛃 d.	0315	0331	0315	0331	0357	1256	1456	1834	1848	1848
Oświecim **1099** a.	|	0437	|	0437	|	|	|	|	1948	1948
Kraków Gł. **1099** a.	|	0622	|	0622	|	|	|	|	2119	2119
Katowice a.	0418	...	0418	...	0500	1355	1556	1932	...	...
Warszawa Cent. **1060** a.	0705	...	0705	...	...	1640	1840	2215	...	...

C – CHOPIN – 🛏 1, 2 cl., ▬ 2 cl. and [2] Warszawa - Wien and v.v. Conveys 🛏 1, 2 cl., ▬ 2 cl. and [2] Warszawa - Bratislava - Budapest and v.v. Conveys 🛏 1, 2 cl. Moskva - Wien/Budapest and v.v.
K – 🛏 1, 2 cl. (also ▬ 2 cl. Apr. 29 - Sept. 27 from Kraków; Apr. 30 - Sept. 28 from Wien) Kraków - Wien and v.v. 🛏 1, 2 cl. and ▬ 2 cl. Kraków - Bratislava - Budapest and v.v.
S – 🛏 1, 2 cl., ▬ 2 cl. and [2] Warszawa - Praha and v.v.
V – VLTAVA – 🛏 1, 2 cl. Moskva - Terespol - Katowice - Praha and v.v. For additional cars see Table **95**.
W – SILESIA – 🛏 1, 2 cl., ▬ 2 cl. and [2] Kraków - Praha and v.v.

⁄ – Supplement payable.
§ – R in Poland.

TRAIN NAMES:

EC **104/105** SOBIESKI.
EC **106/107** PRAHA.
EC **102/103** POLONIA.
EC **108/109** COMENIUS.

KATOWICE and KRAKÓW - ŽILINA 1077

km		413	2221	415	335	417	3921	2223	4411	419
		◇	◇	◇	34009	◇	◇	◇	333	◇
		2	2p	2	f	2p	2	2	y	2p
0	**Katowice 1060** d.	0505	0648	0711	...	1210	...	...	1513	1735
	Kraków Gł. **1099** d.	|	|	|	0640	|	...	...	|	|
	Oświecim **1099** d.	|	|	|	0807	|	...	...	|	|
	Bielsko Biała 1060 d.	0632	|	0844	0922	1338	...	1417	1632	1901
	Zywiec d.	0730	|	0932	1001	1424	...	|	1711	1944
	Zwardoń 🏛 d.	0835	|	1044	1121	1528	1548	|	1827	2053
	Cieszyn 🏛 d.	...	0857	...	|	...	|	1545	|	...
89	Český Těšín 🏛 **1160** d.	...	0910	...	|	...	|	1550	|	...
127	Čadca 🏛 **1160** d.	...	...	...	1153	...	1646	...	1857	...
158	**Žilina 1160** a.	...	...	...	1232	...	1728	...	1927	...

km		414	418	2222	332	424	2224	3950	426	334	
		◇	◇	◇	4412	◇	◇	◇	◇	43008	
		2	2q	2	g	2	2p	2	2p	f	
0	**Žilina 1160** d.	...	...	...	0850	...	...	1346	...	1603	...
31	Čadca 🏛 **1160** d.	...	...	...	0921	...	...	1430	...	1639	...
	Český Těšín 🏛 **1160** d.	...	...	0952	|	...	1603	|	...	|	...
	Cieszyn 🏛 d.	...	...	0959	|	...	1616	|	...	|	...
52	Zwardoń 🏛 d.	0418	0623	|	1007	1406	|	1508	1558	1733	...
89	Zywiec d.	0525	0729	|	1107	1522	|	...	1712	1839	...
110	**Bielsko Biała 1060** d.	0606	0820	1120	1145	1606	|	...	1752	1917	...
142	Oświecim **1099** a.	|	|	...	|	|	|	...	|	2026	...
207	**Kraków** Gł. **1099** a.	|	|	...	|	|	|	...	|	2210	...
	Katowice 1060 a.	0730	0941	...	1253	1730	1818	...	1915	...	...

f – Not Dec. 24, 25, 26, Jan. 1, Mar. 23, 24.
g – Not Dec. 24, 25, 26, Jan. 1, Mar. 22, 23.
p – Not Dec. 25, Mar. 23.
q – Not Dec. 26, Mar. 24.
y – Not Dec. 24, 25, 26, 31, Mar. 22, 23.
◇ – Stopping train.

TRAIN NAMES: **333 / 332** GORAL **335 / 334** SKALNICA

KRAKÓW - ZAGÓRZ and KRYNICA 1078

km					13211	63200		13201	623	53505	53505				43100	43100	*Ex*	*Ex*		*EC*	*EX*				633
					30511	63201	621	33201	2 ◇	33519	33503	33101	121		43101	33511	13411	3311	66121	383	33401	627			2
		2	2	2			2		①–⑤					2			🅁 ✕	🅁 ✕	2	✕	✕	2		2	◇
		◇	◇	◇	A		◇	P	j	H	H	◇	◇	◇	h	Vh	G	D	◇	F	R	◇	N	◇	T
	Warszawa Cent. **1065** d.	...	...	...	2115	...	...	2140	...	0105	0105	...	...	...	...	...	0605	0605	...	0905	0905	...	...	...	...
	Katowice **1075** d.	...	...	...	|	0121	...	|	...	|	|	...	...	...	0715	0715	|	|	...	|	|	...	...	...	...
0	**Kraków** Gł. **1075** d.	...	...	...	|	0306	...	0316	...	0440	0440	0645	0736	...	0916	0916	0904	0904	1034	1210	1210	...	...	...	...
5	Kraków Płaszów **1075** d.	...	...	...	|	0329	...	0346	...	0510	0510	0652	0744	...	0927	0927	0921	0921	1042	|	|	...	...	...	...
78	Tarnów **1075** d.	...	...	...	|	0429	0431	0443	0506	0614	0614	0749	0901	...	1029	1029	1020	1018	1200	1311	1311	...	...	...	1415
136	Stróze d.	...	...	...	|	|	0548	0600	0641	0749	0751	0902	|	...	|	|	1121	|	1312	1413	1413	1436	...	...	1534
**	Rzeszów d.	...	0440	...	0505	0531	|	|	|	|	|	|	1016	...	1135	1155	|	1117	|	|	|	|	...	...	|
182	Jasło d.	0430	0634	0653	0730	▬	|	|	|	|	0920	|	▬	1213	...	1407	|	...	|	|	|	|	...	1543	|
205	Krosno d.	0513	...	0746	0815	...	|	|	|	|	1005	|	...	1256	...	1500	|	...	|	|	|	|	...	1636	|
244	Sanok d.	0626	...	0900	0929	...	|	|	|	|	1126	|	...	1410	...	1640	|	...	|	|	|	|	...	1752	|
251	**Zagórz** a.	0638	...	0913	0943	...	|	|	|	|	1140	|	...	1423	...	1654	|	...	|	|	|	|	...	1805	|
167	**Nowy Sącz** d.	...	...	...	...	N	0628	0641	0723	0837	...	0946	N	...	...	...	1200	...	1356	1452	1452	1533	...	...	1614
	Krynica d.	...	...	...	...	0752	...	|	...	|	...	|	1043	...	...	...	|	...	|	|	|	|	1719	...	...
217	Muszyna d.	...	...	...	...	0815	...	0756x	...	0954x	...	1102	1102	...	...	...	1314x	...	1524	1600	1608	1701	1737	...	...
228	**Krynica** a.	...	...	...	...	|	...	0813	...	1012	...	1119	|	...	...	...	1331	...	1546	|	1630	1718	|	...	...
231	**Plaveč** 🏛 a.	...	...	...	...	0839	...	...	...	...	...	...	1126	...	...	...	...	...	...	1620	...	...	1801	...	...
	Košice **1196** a.	...	...	...	...	...	...	...	...	...	...	...	...	...	...	...	...	...	...	1800	...	...	...	...	...

	TLK				*Ex*			*Ex*	*Ex*	381
	7310		631	2223	5311	66131	66133	1309	1309	539
	🅁	2	2		🅁 ✕	2	2	🅁 ✕	3309	🍷
	✕	◇	◇	◇	E	◇	◇	J	L 🅁	C
Warszawa Cent. **1065** d.	...	...	...	...	1405	...	...	1705	1705	...
Katowice **1075** d.	1115	...	...	...	|	...	...	|	|	...
Kraków Gł. **1075** d.	1319	...	*1430*	1629	1710	1745	1935	2011	2011	2245
Kraków Płaszów **1075** d.	1328	...	*1438*	1637	1718	1753	1944	2020	2020	2254
Tarnów **1075** d.	1425	...	1552	1732	1814	1909	2104	2123	2132	2353
Stróze d.	|	...	1709	1854	|	2024	2221	|	2231	0057
Rzeszów d.	1529	1533	|	|	1915	|	...	2223	|	|
Jasło d.	...	1730	|	|	...	|	...	...	|	|
Krosno d.	...	...	|	|	...	|	...	...	|	|
Sanok d.	...	...	|	|	...	|	...	...	|	|
Zagórz a.	...	...	|	|	...	|	...	...	|	|
Nowy Sącz d.	...	...	1751	1934	...	2105	...	...	2309	0136
Krynica d.	...	...	|	...	...	...	...	...	...	|
Muszyna d.	...	...	1905	...	...	...	...	...	...	0304
Krynica a.	...	...	1923	...	...	...	...	...	...	|
Plaveč 🏛 a.	...	...	...	...	...	...	...	...	...	0325
Košice **1196** a.	...	...	...	...	...	...	...	...	...	0511

		Ex	*Ex*				38104		6026	*Ex*
	6022	3108	3308	2222	66120		38105	6024	2	3510
	2	🅁 ✕	3108		2	2		2	◇	🅁 ✕
	◇	J	🅁	◇	◇	◇		◇	T	E
Košice **1196** d.	...	...	M	...	...	...	...	...	...	...
Plaveč 🏛 d.	...	...	...	...	...	...	...	...	...	...
Krynica d.	...	...	...	...	0443	...	...	0609	...	...
Muszyna d.	...	...	...	...	0506	...	...	0632	...	...
Krynica a.	...	...	...	...	|	...	...	|	...	...
Nowy Sącz d.	0416	...	0446	0551	0617	...	...	0743	0822	...
Zagórz d.	|	...	|	|	|	...	...	...	|	...
Sanok d.	|	...	|	|	|	...	...	...	|	...
Krosno d.	|	...	|	|	|	...	...	...	|	...
Jasło d.	|	...	|	|	|	0444	...	...	|	...
Rzeszów d.	|	0527	|	|	|	0642	0733	...	|	0936
Stróze d.	0457	|	0523	0630	0658	...	|	...	0904	|
Tarnów **1075** d.	0612	0637	0637	0739	0817	...	0838	...	1015	1037
Kraków Płaszów **1075** a.	...	0736	0736	0834	0933	...	0939	...	...	1132
Kraków Gł. **1075** a.	...	0745	0745	0842	0942	...	0948	...	...	1140
Katowice **1075** a.	...	|	|	...	...	...	1129	...	...	|
Warszawa Cent. **1065** a.	...	1050	1050	...	...	...	...	...	...	1450

					6030		*EC*	*Ex*				34100	33512	*Ex*	*Ex*	2							33200	30512	538
	2	6028		2	2 ◇		382	33402	6032	2		34101	34100	3310	31410	◇	33102	2	33500	33504		6036	31200	31210	380
	◇	2		◇	①–⑤		✕	✕	2	◇	2			🅁 ✕	🅁 ✕	①–⑤		◇	35504	35504		2			🍷
		◇	N		j	N	F	S	◇		◇	h	Wh	D	G	j	◇		K	K	N	◇	Q	B	C
Košice **1196** d.	...	...	...	...	...	...	1155	...	...	...	...	...	...	...	...	...	...	...	...	...	...	...	...	...	2254
Plaveč 🏛 d.	...	...	0900	...	...	1145	1330	...	...	...	...	...	...	...	...	...	...	...	...	...	1811	...	...	...	0104
Krynica d.	...	...	|	...	...	|	|	1332	1341	...	...	...	...	...	1528	...	1611	...	...	1725	|	1834	2029	...	|
Muszyna d.	...	...	0926	...	...	1211	1402	1402	1414	...	...	...	...	...	1553x	...	1634	...	...	1751	1837	1907	2055	...	0135
Krynica a.	...	...	0943	...	...	1228	|	|	|	...	...	...	...	...	|	...	|	...	...	|	1854	|	|	...	|
Nowy Sącz d.	...	1123	▬	...	1407	...	1507	1507	1531	...	...	...	...	...	1655	...	1745	...	...	1901	...	2017	2201	...	0245
Zagórz d.	0611	|	...	0955	|	...	|	|	|	1252	...	...	1217	...	|	1355	|	...	1552	|	...	|	|	1903	|
Sanok d.	0629	|	...	1007	|	...	|	|	|	1304	...	...	1230	...	|	1412	|	...	1610	|	...	|	|	1917	|
Krosno d.	0750	|	2	1120	|	...	|	|	|	1435	...	...	1355	...	|	1535	|	...	1732	|	...	|	|	2030	|
Jasło d.	0834	|	◇	1203	|	...	|	|	|	1518	1524	...	1450	...	|	1619	|	...	1822	|	...	|	|	2121	|
Rzeszów d.	...	|	1220	...	|	...	|	|	|	▬	1710	1713	1713	1733	|	...	|	1942	|	|	...	|	|	2321	|
Stróze d.	...	1204	|	...	1448	...	1544	1544	1612	2 ◇	...	|	|	|	1732	...	1825	|	1950	1950	...	2058	2240	|	0323
Tarnów **1075** d.	...	1327	1337	...	1607	...	1647	1647	1728	1800	...	1820	1820	1832	1834	...	1939	2106	2049	2049	...	2222	2343	|	0433
Kraków Płaszów **1075** a.	...	...	1453	...	...	...	|	|	...	1919	...	1923	1923	1927	1930	...	2033	2225	2140	2140	...	...	0040	|	0532
Kraków Gł. **1075** a.	...	...	1501	...	...	...	1745	1745	...	1928	...	1932	1932	1950	1950	...	2040	2233	2205	2205	...	...	0104	|	0540
Katowice **1075** a.	...	...	...	...	...	...	|	|	...	...	...	2118	2118	|	|	...	...	...	|	|	...	...	|	|	...
Warszawa Cent. **1065** a.	...	...	...	...	...	...	2049	2049	...	...	...	...	...	2250	2250	...	...	...	0137	0137	...	...	0615	0650	...

A – ⑤ (also Dec. 22, 23, 25–31, Jan. 11 - Feb. 23, Apr. 25 - May 2, May 21): [12] Warszawa - Zagórz.
B – ⑦ (also Dec. 22, 24, 26–31, Jan. 1, Jan. 12 - Feb. 24, Mar. 24, Apr. 26 - May 3, May 24; not Mar. 23): [12] Zagórz - Warszawa.
C – June 19 - Aug. 31 from Kraków; June 20 - Sept 1 from Budapest: CRACOVIA – 🛏 1, 2 cl., ▬ 2 cl. and [12] Kraków - Košice - Budapest and v.v. [2] Kraków - Košice - Lökösháza and v.v.
D – ①–⑤ (not Dec. 25 – Jan. 1, Mar. 24, May 1, 22).
E – [12] and ✕ Gdynia - Warszawa - Kraków - Rzeszów - Przemyśl and v.v.
F – JÓZEF BEM – [12] and 🍷 Warszawa - Kraków - Košice - Budapest and v.v.
G – ⑥⑦ (also Dec. 25 – Jan. 1, Mar. 24, May 1, 22).
H – June 22 - Sept. 1 from Gdynia: [12] Gdynia - Warszawa - Kraków - Zagórz / Krynia.
J – [12] and ✕ Warszawa - Kraków - Rzeszów - Przemyśl and v.v.
K – June 23 - Sept. 2: [12] Zagórz / Krynia - Kraków - Warszawa - Gdynia.
L – ⑧ (not Dec. 24, 25, 31, Mar. 23, May 1, 2, 22).
M – ①–⑥ (not Dec. 25, 26, Jan. 1, Mar. 24, May 2, 3, 23).
N – Jan. 15 - Feb. 23, Apr. 26 - May 4, June 20 - Sept. 14.
P – Dec. 20 - Jan. 1, Jan. 25 - Feb. 23, Apr. 25 - May 3: [12] Warszawa - Krynica.
Q – Dec. 21 - Jan. 2, Jan. 26 - Feb. 24, Apr. 26 - May 4: [12] Krynica - Warszawa.
R – Dec. 31, Feb. 9, 21, 23.
S – Jan. 1, Feb. 10, 22, 24.
T – Not Dec. 25, 26, Jan. 1, Mar. 23, 24, May 22, Nov. 11.
V – Dec. 21, 22, 25, 26, 30, 31, Jan. 1, Apr. 30, May 1, 2, 3, 22, 23, 24, June 21 - Aug. 30.
W – Dec. 22, 23, 26, 27, 31, Jan. 1, 2, May 1, 2, 3, 4, 23, 24, 25, June 22 - Aug. 31.
h – From / to Gliwice.
j – Not Dec. 25, 26, Jan. 1, Mar. 24, May 1, 22.
v – *0900* on ©.
x – Arrives 10 minutes earlier.
◇ – Stopping train.
** – Rzeszów - Jasło: *71 km*.

ZAGÓRZ - ŁUPKÓW - MEDZILABORCE - HUMENNÉ 1079

km			X	W	h		X	W	A	
		2 ◇	2 ◇	2 ◇	2 ◇	2 ◇	2 ◇	2 ◇	2 ◇	2 ◇
	Jasło d.	0430	...	...	...	1213	...	...	...	...
0	**Zagórz** d.	0638	0641	...	...	1423	1435	...	...	...
48	Łupków 🏛 d.	...	0828	0854	...	...	1624	1640	...	...
63	Medzilaborce Mesto 🏛 d.	...	...	0913	0957	...	...	1659	1805	2014
65	Medzilaborce **1194** d.	...	...	0916	1005	...	...	1702	1811	2019
106	Humenné **1194** a.	...	...	...	1115	...	...	...	1912	2129

		W	X	f		W	X		
	2 ◇	2 ◇	2 ◇	2 ◇	2 ◇	2 ◇	2 ◇	⑦f	
Humenné d.	0623	...	...	...	1434	...	...	...	...
Medzilaborce d.	0732	0749	...	...	1601	1603	...	...	...
Medzilaborce Mesto 🏛 d.	...	0754	...	...	...	1610	...	...	...
Łupków 🏛 d.	...	0814	0839	...	...	1631	1644	...	...
Zagórz a.	...	...	1029	1217	...	...	1834	1903	...
Jasło a.	...	...	...	1440	...	...	...	2109	...

A – ⑧ (not Dec. 30, Mar. 23). W – ⑤⑥⑦ June 20 - Aug. 31. X – ⑤⑥⑦ June 27 - Aug. 31. f – See Note **B** in Table **1078**. h – Not Dec. 23, 24, 25. ◇ – Stopping train.

1080 POZNAŃ - OSTRÓW - KATOWICE - KRAKÓW

For other trains Poznań - Katowice - Kraków (via Wrocław) see Table **1075**

km		◇ 2	◇ 2	◇ 2 w	◇ 2	◇ 2 y	84102 84103 p	73500 73501 k	◇ 2	84200 Q		
	Szczecin Gł. **1010**..d.	...	...	...	...	...	1145	...	...	...	...	...
0	**Poznań** Gł. ....d.	0626	...	1042	...	...	1425	1824	1842	2320	...	...
67	Jarocin ....d.	0735	...	1148	...	...	1518	1921	1947	0019	...	...
114	Ostrów Wlkp ⊠ **1090**.d.	0822	...	1240	...	...	1556	2010	2039	0101	...	...
160	Kępno ....d.	0914	...	1320	...	...	1632	|	2123	0139	...	...
201	Kluczbork ....d.	1000	1031	1407	1431	1642	|	|	...	0219	...	...
252	Lubliniec ....d.	...	1134	...	1535	1754	|	|	...	0318	...	...
302	Bytom ....d.	...	1256	...	1656	1917	1940	|	...	0440	...	...
320	**Katowice** ....a.	...	1324	...	1724	1945	2008	|	...	0510	...	...
398	**Kraków** Gł. ....a.	...	...	...	...	...	...	0321	...	...	...	...

	37500 k	◇ 2	48102 48103 p	◇ 2 y	◇ 2	◇ 2	◇ 2 w	◇ 2	◇ 2 y	48201 P			
Kraków Gł. ....d.	0146	...	...	...	...	...	...	...	...	...	...	...	...
Katowice ....d.	|	...	0615	0947	...	1154	...	...	1804	1903	...	...	...
Bytom ....d.	|	...	0645	1016	...	1224	...	...	1833	1935	...	...	...
Lubliniec ....d.	|	...	|	1136	...	1336	...	...	1951	2053	...	...	...
Kluczbork ....d.	|	...	|	1226	1249	1426	1447	...	2042	2146	...	...	...
Kępno ....d.	|	...	0930	...	1342	...	1532	...	...	2228	...	...	...
Ostrów Wlkp. ⊠ **1090** d.	0849	0925	1019	...	1427	...	1618	1623	...	2309	...	...	...
Jarocin ....d.	0936	1017	1058	...	1513	...	...	1719	...	2353	...	...	...
Poznań Gł. ....a.	1034	1125	1202	...	1632	...	...	1834	...	0059	...	...	...
Szczecin Gł. **1010**..a.	...	...	1439	...	...	...	...	...	...	...	...	...	...

P – Not Dec. 24, 25, 31, Feb. 24 - Mar. 18, Mar. 22, 23: (12) Katowice - Poznań - Kołobrzeg.
Q – Not Dec. 24, 25, 31, Feb. 25 - Mar. 19, Mar. 22, 23: (12) Kołobrzeg - Poznań - Katowice.
k – To / from Zakopane on dates in Table **1066**.
p – Not Dec. 25, Mar. 23.
w – Not Dec. 24, 25, 31, Mar. 22, 23, May 1, 2, 3, 22, 23, 24.
y – Not Dec. 25, 26, Jan. 1, Mar. 23, 24, May 1, 3, 4, 22.
⊠ – Full name is Ostrów Wielkopolski.
◇ – Stopping train.

1084 WĘGLINIEC - JELENIA GÓRA - WAŁBRZYCH - WROCŁAW

km		◇ 2	◇ 2	◇ 2	◇ 2	◇ 2	◇ 2 T	◇ 2	◇ 2	◇ 2	◇ 2	68504 E	◇ 2 g	◇ 2 p	◇ 2 ⑦	64500 B	◇ 2	◇ 2	63200 J	◇ 2 g	61200 A	65502 R		
0	Węgliniec ....d.	...	...	...	...	...	0554	0801	...	...	...	...	1300	...	...	...	1544		...	1747	...	...	...	...
74	**Jelenia Góra** ....d.	...	...	...	0553	0709	0743	0934	0953	1153	1353	1335	1431	1553	1653	1727	1731	1809	1827	1930	2009	2116	...	...
121	Wałbrzych Gł. ....d.	...	0522	0622	0722	0833	0922	...	1122	1322	1522	1458	...	1722	1822	1850	...	1936	1957	...	2135	2237	...	...
151	Jaworzyna Śląska ....d.	0524	0624	0724	0824	0933	1024	...	1224	1424	1624	1551	...	1823	1924	...	...	2037	2059	...	2238	2331	...	...
200	**Wrocław** Gł. ....a.	0628	0730	0830	0930	1030	1130	...	1330	1529	1730	1647	...	1920	2029	...	...	2141	2200	...	2340	0044	...	...

	◇ 2	56503 Q	◇ 2 T	16201 A	◇ 2	◇ 2	◇ 2 g	36200 K	46501 G	◇ 2 p		◇ 2 h	86504 F	◇ 2	◇ 2 k	◇ 2	◇ 2	◇ 2	◇ 2	◇ 2	◇ 2	◇ 2	◇ 2	
Wrocław Gł. ....d.	...	0315	...	0528	0537	0637	...	0700	...	0910	...	...	1112	1137	...	1337	...	1537	1637	1749	1858	2037	2237	...
Jaworzyna Śląska ....d.	...	0411	...	0624	0641	0733	...	0801	...	1007	...	...	1208	1241	...	1440	...	1641	1739	1843	1959	2139	2339	...
Wałbrzych Gł. ....d.	...	0507	0600	0718	0735	0826	...	0852	0951	1100	...	...	1305	1335	...	1534	...	1737	1832	1936	2051	2232		...
Jelenia Góra ....a.	0557	0635	0730	0845	0908	0953	1027	1022	1123	1222	...	1439	1434	1503	1635	1712	1831	1911	...	2058	...	...	...	...
Węgliniec ....a.	0738	...	...	...	...	...	1159	...	...	...	...	1609	...	...	1812	...	2003	...	...	...	...	...	...	...

A – (12) (also ▬ 2 cl. from Jelenia Góra June 23 - Sept. 2; from Warszawa June 22 - Sept. 1): Jelenia Góra - Warszawa and v.v. (Tables **1088** / **1090**).
B – June 23 - Sept. 2: (12) Jelenia Góra - Lublin (Table **1067**).
E – June 23 - Sept. 2: (12) Jelenia Góra - Wrocław - Szczecin (Table **1010**).
F – June 22 - Sept. 1: (12) Szczecin - Wrocław - Jelenia Góra (Table **1010**).
G – June 22 - Sept. 1: (12) Lublin - Jelenia Góra (Table **1067**).
J – To Przemyśl on Dec. 22, 23, 26–30, Jan. 1, Jan. 12 - Feb. 24, Apr. 26 - May 4, May 22–25 (Table **1075**).
K – From Przemyśl on Dec. 22, 23, 26–30, Jan. 1, Jan. 12 - Feb. 24, Apr. 26 - May 4, May 22–25 (Table **1075**).
Q – June 22 - Sept. 1: ▬ 2 cl. and (12) Gdynia - Jelenia Góra, (Table **1020**).
R – June 23 - Sept. 2 (12) (also ▬ 2 cl. June 23 - Sept. 1): Jelenia Góra - Gdynia (Table **1020**).
T – ①–⑤ (not Dec. 25, 26, Jan. 1, Mar. 24, May 1, 22).
g – From / to Zielona Góra.
h – To Zielona Góra on ①–⑤ (not Dec. 25, 26, Jan. 1, Mar. 24, May 1, 22).
k – To Zielona Góra on ⑥⑦ (also Dec. 25, 26, Jan. 1, Mar. 24, May 1, 22).
p – To / from Poznań.
◇ – Stopping train.

1085 GÖRLITZ - WROCŁAW

km		520 ◇ A	66100	61102 61103	2	2	524 ◇	2	2 A	526 ◇	2	2
	Dresden Hbf **855**.....d.	...	...	...	0805	1005	...	1205	...	...	1510	1805
	Görlitz ▦ ....a.	...	...	...	0921	1121	...	1321	...	...	1648	1921
					501	**5515** ◇		|			**5517** ◇	**503**
0	**Görlitz** ▦ ....d.	...	...	...	0931	1131	...	1327	...	...	1731	1931
2	Zgorzelec ▦ ....d.	...	0613	0755	0938	1138	...	1333	1512	...	1738	1938
30	Węgliniec ....d.	...	0652	0834	1010	1218	...	...	1540	1553	1818	2010
55	Bolesławiec ....d.	0514	0710	0852	1029	1239	1414	...	...	1614	1839	2028
99	Legnica ....d.	0557	0745	0923	1059	1318	1457	...	...	1655	1919	2100
165	**Wrocław** Gł. ....a.	0715	0848	1023	1207	1435	1615	...	...	1815	2035	2207
	Warszawa C. **1090**.a.	...	...	1700	...	...	...	...	...	...	...	...

	5502 ◇	502	521 ◇	◇	2	5504 ◇	523 ◇ A	504	16102 16103	527 ◇	66101
Warszawa C. **1090**.. d.	...	...	...	...	...	...	...	...	1045	...	...
Wrocław Gł. ....d.	0516	0744	0952	...	...	1312	1452	1544	1732	1852	2012
Legnica ....d.	0633	0854	1111	...	...	1433	1612	1656	1835	2012	2120
Bolesławiec ....d.	0710	0924	1153	1158	...	1511	1653	1725	1905	2052	2150
Węgliniec ....d.	0743	0954	...	1222	...	1542	...	1755	1933	2114	2219
Zgorzelec ▦ ....d.	0814	1018	...	1250	1420	1614	...	1818	2001	...	2243
Görlitz ▦ ....a.	0820	1024	...	...	1426	1620	...	1824	...	...	...
	2	2			|	2		2			
Görlitz ▦ ....d.	0836	1036	...	...	1436	1636	...	1836	...	...	...
Dresden Hbf. **855**.. a.	0950	1150	...	...	1550	1750	...	1950	...	...	...

B – ①–⑤ (not not Dec. 25, 26, Jan. 1, Mar. 24, May 1, 22).
◇ – Stopping train.

1086 BERLIN - WROCŁAW

km		◇ 2	◇ 2	①–⑤ ◇ 2	f ◇ 2	61102 w	*EC* 241 Aq	◇ 2	⑦ ◇ 2	①–⑥ ◇ 2	◇ 2	①–⑤ ◇ 2	◇ 2
	Berlin Hbf. 838 ......d.	...	...	...	...	...	0940	...	...	...	...	...	...
	Cottbus **854** ....d.	...	0606	...	...	...	1123	...	...	...	1606	...	1726
0	Forst ▦ ....d.	...	0628	0632	...	...	1154	...	...	...	1628	1632	1752
14	Tuplice ....d.	...	...	0651	...	...	|	...	1615	...	▬	1649	1811
35	Záry ....d.	...	...	0717	0737	...	1235	1519	1645	1733	2	1716	1837
48	Zagań ....d.	0610	...	0735	0752	...	1255	1534	1708	1748	◇	1731	1855
122	Legnica ....d.	0757	...	...	0916	0923	1426	...	1833	1910	1919	...	...
188	**Wrocław** Gł. ....a.	0915	...	...	...	1023	1534	...	...	...	2035	...	...
	Katowice **1075**......a.	...	...	...	...	...	1815	...	...	...	...	...	...
	Kraków Gł. **1075**...a.	...	...	...	...	...	1944	...	...	...	...	...	...

	①–⑤ ◇ 2	◇ 2	D ◇ 2	◇ 2	◇ 2	◇ 2	*EC* 240 Ap	①–⑤ ◇ 2	①–⑤ ◇ 2	◇ 2	◇ 2	◇ 2
Kraków Gł. **1075** d.	...	...	...	...	...	...	0731	...	...	...	...	...
Katowice **1075**....d.	...	...	...	...	...	...	0854	...	...	...	...	...
Wrocław Gł. ....d.	...	...	...	...	0744	...	1136	...	...	1352	1755	...
Legnica ....d.	...	...	0527	...	0852	0925	1257	...	...	1525	1910	1915
Zagań ....d.	0503	...	0706	0820	▬	1053	1426	1458	...	1656	...	2044
Záry ....d.	0526	...	...	0835	◇	1106	1443	1510	1533	▬	...	2056
Tuplice ....d.	0552	...	...	0900	2	1128	|	...	1558	2 ◇	...	...
Forst ▦ ....d.	0610	0634	...	0918	0934	...	1527	...	1615	1634	...	...
Cottbus **854** ....a.	...	0655	...	...	0955	...	1547	...	...	1655	...	...
Berlin Hbf. 838 ....a.	...	...	...	...	...	...	1731	...	...	...	...	...

A – WAWEL – (12) and 🍷 Berlin - Wrocław - Kraków and v.v. Ⓡ ⚡. For dates from / to Hamburg see Table **56**.
D – ①–⑤ (not Dec. 24 - Jan. 1, Jan. 28 - Feb. 8, Mar. 20–25, May 1, 2, 22, 23).
f – From Zielona Góra.
p – Not Dec. 24, 31
q – Not Dec. 25, 31.
w – To Warszawa (Table **1085**).
⚡ – Supplement payable.
◇ – Stopping train.

1088 WARSZAWA - CZĘSTOCHOWA - WROCŁAW

§ – For other trains Warszawa - Wrocław (via Łódź) and additional trains Warszawa - Skierniewice - Koluszki see Table **1090**

km		16107 16106 ✕	14114 14115 T	56110 56111 p		16110 16111 Ⓑ f	54112 54113 pg	14104 ①–⑤ j	16201 16200 A	.
0	**Warszawa** Wschodnia ....§ d.	0633	0823	1223	...	1533	1630	1828	2228	...
5	**Warszawa** Centralna ....§ d.	0645	0845	1245	...	1545	1645	1845	2245	...
71	Skierniewice ....§ d.	0733	0934	1333	...	1638	1734	1933	2338	...
111	Koluszki **1060** ....§ d.	0759	0959	1358	...	1702	1800	1959	0005	...
150	Piotrków Trybunalski **1060**........d.	0828	1030	1427	...	1730	1829	2028	0038	...
235	Częstochowa Osobowa **1060**...d.	0930	1130	1530	...	1830	1927	2127	0146	...
275	Lubliniec ....d.	1030	...	1633	...	1934	...	...	0250	...
330	Opole Gł **1075** ....d.	1128	...	1730	...	2028	...	...	0350	...
370	Brzeg **1075** ....d.	1156	...	1757	...	...	...	...	0419	...
412	**Wrocław** Gł **1075** ....a.	1235	...	1835	...	...	...	...	0500	...

	41104 ①–⑤ k	61110 ①–⑤ h	45112 45113 pg	65110 65111 p		41114 41115 T	61106 61107	61200 61201 A	
Wrocław Gł **1075**..........d.	...	...	...	0910	...	...	1621	0001	...
Brzeg **1075** ....d.	...	...	...	0944	...	...	1658	0038	...
Opole Gł **1075** ....d.	...	0520	...	1021	...	...	1728	0111	...
Lubliniec ....d.	...	0617	...	1122	...	...	1823	0211	...
Częstochowa Osobowa **1060** d.	0608	0703	0808	1208	...	1708	1908	0258	...
Piotrków Trybunalski **1060**.....d.	0717	0810	0916	1315	...	1814	2014	0410	...
Koluszki **1060** ....§ d.	0745	0837	0943	1343	...	1842	2042	0441	...
Skierniewice ....§ d.	0809	0903	1007	1408	...	1907	2107	0506	...
Warszawa Centralna..........§ a.	0900	0955	1102	1500	...	2000	2200	0600	...
Warszawa Wschodnia ....§ a.	0912	1012	1118	1517	...	2027	2212	0612	...

A – (12) (also ▬ 2 cl. from Warszawa June 22 - Sept. 1; from Jelenia Góra June 23 - Sept. 2): Jelenia Góra - Warszawa - Jelenia Góra - and v.v. (Tables **1084** / **1090**).
T – (12) Białystok - Warszawa - Częstochowa - Katowice - Bielsko Biała and v.v.
f – Not Dec. 24.
g – To / from Racibórz.
h – Not Dec. 25, 26, Jan. 1, Mar. 24.
j – Not Dec. 24, 25, 31, Mar. 24, May 1, 22, 23.
k – Not Dec. 25, 26, 31, Mar. 24, May 1, 2, 22, 23.
p – From / to Olsztyn.

WARSZAWA - ŁÓDŹ - WROCŁAW — 1090

See Table **1005** for the through trains Warszawa - Wrocław via Poznań (also Łódź - Poznań via Kutno).

km		16109 16108 ①–⑥ b	22500 22501 ①–⑤ g	22100 22101	22102 22103 f	16100 16500 q	22502 22503 ①–⑤ g	22104 22105	79100 79101 B	22504 22505 ①–⑤ g	16102 16103 y	22106 22107	22506 22507 ①–⑤ k	22108 22109	16104 16105 S	22508 22509 ①–⑤ k	22110 22111	22510 22511 ①–⑤ g	2200 2201 ①–⑤ h	16112 17112 Ⓑj	22514 22515 ①–⑤ g	22112 22113	22516 22517 ①–⑤ g	22114 22115	16200 16201 A
0	**Warszawa** Wschodnia **1088** d.	...	0538	0603	0708	0733	0808	0908	0923	1008	1018	1108	1208	1308	1423	1408	1508	1608	1703	1733	1808	1908	2008	2108	2228
5	**Warszawa** Centralna **1088** d.	...	0550	0620	0720	0745	0820	0920	0950	1020	1045	1120	1220	1320	1445	1420	1520	1620	1715	1745	1820	1920	2020	2120	2245
71	Skierniewice **1088** d.	...	0637	0707	0807	0835	0907	1007	1037	1107	1133	1207	1307	1407	1534	1507	1607	1708	|	1838	1907	2007	2107	2207	2338
111	Koluszki **1088** d.	...	0658	0728	0828	0900	0928	1028	1100	1128	1159	1228	1328	1428	1600	1528	1628	1733	|	1902	1931	2028	2128	2228	0005
132	Łódź Widzew d.	...	0713	0743	0843	0918	0943	1043	1118	1143	1216	1243	1343	1443	1620	1543	1643	1750	1835	1925	1946	2043	2143	2243	|
138	**Łódź** Fabryczna a.	...	0720	0750	0850	|	0950	1050	1125	1150	|	1250	1350	1450	|	1550	1650	1758	1842	|	1953	2050	2150	2250	|
147	**Łódź** Kaliska d.	0600	...	...	...	0953	...	...	...	...	1250	...	...	...	1655	...	...	...	...	1959	...	...	...	...	|
260	Kalisz d.	0749	...	...	...	1145	...	...	...	...	1440	...	...	...	1847	...	...	...	...	2149	...	...	...	...	◐
284	Ostrów Wielkopolski **1080** d.	0819	...	...	...	1218	...	...	...	...	1511	...	...	...	1930	...	...	...	...	2218	...	...	...	...	|
390	**Wrocław** Gł. a.	1000	...	...	...	1406	...	...	...	...	1716	...	...	...	2116	...	...	...	...	0004p	...	...	...	...	0500
	Jelenia Góra **1084** a.	...	...	...	...	...	...	...	...	...	...	...	...	...	...	...	...	...	...	...	...	...	...	...	0845

	33501 33500 ①–⑤ g	33101 33100 f	3301 ①–⑤ h	33103 33102	33503 33502 ①–⑤ g	71112 71113 ①–⑥ b	33105 33104	33505 33504 ①–⑤ k	33107 33106	61104 61105 ✕ S	33507 33506 ①–⑤ k	61102 61103 y	33109 33108	33509 33508 ①–⑤ k	79111 79110 B	33111 33110	33511 33510 ①–⑤ g	33113 33112	33513 33512 ①–⑤ g	33115 33114	61100 61500 q	33117 33116	61109 61108 Ⓑd	61200 61201 A	
Jelenia Góra **1084** d.	...	...	...	...	...	...	...	...	...	...	...	...	...	...	...	...	...	...	...	...	...	...	...	2009	...
Wrocław Gł. d.	...	...	...	...	...	...	...	...	...	0640	...	1045	...	...	...	...	...	...	...	...	1447	...	1750	0001	...
Ostrów Wielkopolski **1080** d.	...	...	...	...	...	0540	...	...	...	0838	...	1237	...	...	...	...	...	...	...	...	1636	...	1930	|	...
Kalisz d.	...	...	...	...	...	0602	...	...	...	0902	...	1300	...	...	...	...	...	...	...	...	1659	...	1952	◐	...
Łódź Kaliska d.	...	...	...	...	...	0803	...	...	...	1105	...	1501	...	...	...	...	...	...	...	...	1901	...	2135	|	...
Łódź Fabryczna d.	0457	0549	0630	0657	0757	|	0857	0957	1057	|	1157	|	1257	1357	1415	1457	1557	1657	1757	1857	|	2057	...	|	...
Łódź Widzew d.	0505	0558	0639	0705	0805	0823	0905	1005	1105	1128	1205	1521	1305	1405	1423	1505	1605	1705	1805	1905	1923	2105	...	|	...
Koluszki **1088** d.	0521	0616	|	0721	0821	0845	0921	1021	1121	1146	1221	1545	1321	1421	1444	1521	1621	1721	1821	1921	1945	2121	...	0441	...
Skierniewice **1088** d.	0542	0641	|	0742	0842	0909	0942	1042	1142	1211	1242	1610	1342	1442	1509	1542	1642	1742	1842	1942	2010	2142	...	0506	...
Warszawa Centralna **1088** a.	0630	0730	0800	0830	0930	1000	1030	1130	1230	1300	1330	1700	1430	1530	1600	1630	1730	1830	1930	2030	2100	2230	...	0600	...
Warszawa Wschodnia **1088** a.	0642	0742	0812	0842	0942	1017	1042	1141	1242	1327	1342	1712	1442	1547	1627	1642	1742	1842	1942	2042	2112	2242	...	0612	...

A – [12] (also ▬ 2 cl. from Warszawa June 22 - Sept. 1; from Jelenia Góra June 23 - Sept. 2): Warszawa - Jelenia Góra and v.v. (Tables **1084**/**1088**).
B – ①–⑤ (not Dec. 25, 26, Jan. 1, Mar. 24, May 1, 22): [12] Suwałki - Warszawa - Łódź and v.v.
S – [12] Suwałki - Warszawa - Wrocław and v.v.
b – Not Dec. 25, 26, Jan. 1, Mar. 24.
d – Not Dec. 24, 25, 31, Mar. 23.
f – Not Dec. 25, 26, 29, 30, Jan. 1, Mar. 22, 23, 24, May 1, 3, 4, 22, 24, 25.
g – Not Dec. 25, 26, Jan. 1, Mar. 24, May 1, 22.
h – Also Dec. 24, 25, 26, 31, Jan. 1, Mar. 24, May 1, 2, 22, 23.
j – Not Dec. 24, 25, 31, Mar. 23, May 23.
k – Not Dec. 24, 25, 26, Jan. 1, Mar. 21, 24, May 1, 2, 22, 23.
p – ⑥ (also May 1, 22; not May 3, 24).
q – Not Dec. 25, Mar. 23.
y – To/from Zgorzelec.
◐ – Via Częstochowa (Table **1088**).

WROCŁAW - KŁODZKO - LICHKOV — 1095

km		16201 66501 A	2 ◇ B	2 ◇	2 ◇	2 ◇ f	2 ◇	16100 66511 C	2 ◇ B	2 ◇	2 ◇ p	2 ◇ q
	Warszawa C. **1090** d.	2250	...	...	...	...	...	0745	...	...	...	...
0	**Wrocław** Gł. d.	0525	0535	0635	0925	1135	1335	1432	1435	1535	1745	1835
72	Kamieniec Ząbkowicki d.	0637	0653	0755	1054	1255	1455	1538	1556	1653	1908	1953
94	Kłodzko Gł. a.	0659	0720	0820	1122	1320	1520	1559	1621	1720	1933	2020
	Kłodzko Gł. d.	0711	0722	0830	1137	1322	1522	1613	1622	1722	1945	2022
138	**Kudowa Zdrój** a.	0938	|	1040	1359	|	|	1829	|	|	2156	|
130	Międzylesie a.	...	0810	...	...	1406	1605	...	1712	1805	...	2105
	Międzylesie ▦ d.	...	...	...	...	...	...	...	...	...	...	...
139	**Lichkov** ▦ a.	...	...	...	...	...	...	...	...	...	...	...
	Praha Hlavní **1145** a.	...	...	...	...	...	...	...	...	...	...	...

	2 ◇ B	2 ◇ q	2 ◇ p	2 ◇ f	66510 61101 C	2 ◇	2 ◇ f	2 ◇	2 ◇ f	66500 61200 A
Praha Hlavní **1145** d.	...	...	...	...	...	...	...	...	...	...
Lichkov ▦ d.	...	...	...	...	...	...	...	...	...	...
Międzylesie ▦ a.	...	...	...	...	...	...	...	...	...	...
Międzylesie d.	0553	0653	...	1053	...	...	1541	...	1852	...
Kudowa Zdrój d.	|	|	0624	|	1042	1200	|	1515	|	1958
Kłodzko Gł. a.	0636	0736	0835	1137	1253	1418	1633	1726	1936	2210
Kłodzko Gł. d.	0638	0738	0847	1138	1305	1433	1638	1738	1938	2222
Kamieniec Ząbkowicki d.	0702	0802	0911	1203	1326	1458	1703	1802	2003	2242
Wrocław Gł. a.	0818	0918	1025	1318	1430	1618	1818	1918	2118	2351
Warszawa C. **1090** a.	...	...	...	...	2100	...	...	...	...	0600

A – Dec. 22, 23, 24, 26–31, Jan. 1, 2, Jan. 26 - Feb. 24, Mar. 21, 22, 24, 25, Apr. 26 - May 4. From Warszawa June 21 - Sept. 1; from Kudowa Zdrój June 22 - Sept. 2: ▬ 2 cl. and [12] Warszawa - Wrocław - Kudowa Zdrój and v.v.
B – ①–⑤ (not Dec. 25, 26, Jan. 1, Mar. 24, May 1, 22).
C – Dec. 22, 23, 24, 26–31, Jan. 1, 2, Jan. 26 - Feb. 24, Mar. 21, 22, 24, 25, Apr. 26 - May 4.
f – Not Dec. 25, Mar. 23.
p – From/to Poznań (Table **1070**).
q – From/to Ostrów Wlkp.
◇ – Stopping train.

POLISH LOCAL RAILWAYS — 1099

2nd class only

Certain trains Wolsztyn - Poznań and Wolsztyn - Leszno are hauled by steam locomotive - for details see www.parowozy.com.pl

km		⚒	Ⓐ								
0	Zbąszyń d.	...	...	...	0800	...	1226	1532	...	1914	...
22	Wolsztyn d.	0512	0601	...	0828	...	1255	1600	...	1942	...
69	**Leszno** a.	0610	0710	...	0927	...	1356	1709	...	2040	...

						Ⓐ			⚒	
Leszno d.	0625	...	1026	...	1402	1543	1735	...	2050	...
Wolsztyn d.	0721	...	1122	...	1458	1644	1830	...	2146	...
Zbąszyń a.	0749	...	1206	...	1526	...	1859	...	...	...

km											
0	**Wolsztyn** d.	0527	0802	...	1009	1135	...	1603	...	1959	...
81	**Poznań** Gł. a.	0717	0949	...	1143	1320	...	1742	...	2140	...

	Ⓐ								
Poznań Gł. d.	0526	0728	0923	1314	...	1530	...	1723	1930
Wolsztyn a.	0706	0906	1118	1448	...	1715	...	1856	2104

KRAKÓW - TRZEBINIA - OŚWIĘCIM (for Auschwitz) *65 km*. Journey time: 77–90 mins (from Kraków), 90–111 mins (from Oświęcim). Additional services by changing at Trzebinia.
From **Kraków Główny**: 0640 **c**, 0700 (*EC*108), 0915, 1105 **d**, 1440, 1507 Ⓐ, 1544 Ⓐ, 1920, 2225, 2305.
From **Oświęcim**: 0320, 0444, 0502 Ⓐ, 0658 **d**, 0808, 1120, 1640 Ⓐ, 1949 (*EC*109), 2027 **e**.

KRAKÓW - SKAWINA - OŚWIĘCIM (for Auschwitz). *70 km*. Journey time: 106–110 mins (from Kraków), 111–118 mins (from Oświęcim).
From **Kraków Główny**: 0425, 1306 Ⓐ, 1435, 1525, 1740.
From **Oświęcim**: 0355, 0542, 0735 Ⓐ, 1539, 1739.

KATOWICE - OŚWIĘCIM. *33 km*. Journey time: 56–62 mins. From **Katowice**: 0534 Ⓐ, 0700, 1434, 1534, 1855. From **Oświęcim**: 0521 Ⓐ, 0621, 0821, 1538, 1821.

KRAKÓW - WIELICZKA (for Salt Mine). *15 km*. Journey time: 26 mins.
From **Kraków Główny**: 0514, 0550 Ⓐ, 0625, 0752, 0908, 1024, 1204, 1344, 1440, 1535, 1704, 1845, 2110.
From **Wieliczka Rynek**: 0545, 0623 Ⓐ, 0657, 0825, 0942, 1056, 1238, 1420, 1515, 1618, 1735, 1920, 2147.

WAŁBRZYCH - KŁODZKO. *51 km*.
June 23 - Sept. 2, 2007: Kłodzko Gł. dep. 0822, arr. Wałbrzych Gł. 0949 (**46501**).
June 23 - Sept. 2, 2007: Wałbrzych Gł. dep. 1851; arr. Kłodzko Gł. 2012 (**64500**).

KRAKÓW - WADOWICE (Birth place of Pope John Paul II) *62 km*. From **Kraków**: 0855 **n**, 1005, 1255 **g n**, 1655 **g n**. From **Wadowice**: 0749, 1030 **g n**, 1430 **g n**, 1530 **k n**, 1830 **g n**. Journey time 80–85 minutes. Special fares payable.

GDYNIA - HEL *77 km*. Local services only.
Dec. 9 - June 20 and Sept. 1 - Dec. 13. Journey time 96–109 mins.
From **Gdynia Gł.**: 0540, 0702, 1034, 1232, 1341, 1516, 1636, 1838, 2035.
From **Hel**: 0436, 0624, 0749, 0948, 1231, 1432, 1632, 1834.

June 21 - Aug. 31. Journey time 114–147 mins
From **Gdynia Gł.**: 0349, 0434 **r**, 0502 **r**, 0539, 0701, 0834, 0931, 1114, 1201, 1252 [R], 1337, 1516, 1642, 1820 Ⓑ **x**, 1948.
From **Hel**: 0408, 0638, 0836, 1000 ①–⑥ **z**, 1043, 1202, 1322, 1435, 1508 [R], 1621, 1746, 1818 **r**, 1904 **r**, 1947 **r**, 2037, 2102 **r**.

c – Not Dec. 24, 25, 26, Jan. 1, Mar. 23, 24.
d – Not Dec. 25, 26, Jan. 1, Mar. 23, 24.
e – Not Dec. 24, 25, 26, 31, Jan. 1, Mar. 22, 23, 24.
g – May 1 - Sept. 30.
k – Dec. 9 - Apr. 30.
n – Not Jan. 3, 31, Feb. 28, Mar. 27, Apr. 24, May 23.
r – Not Aug. 31.
x – Ⓑ (not Aug. 14).
z – ①–⑥ June 23 - Aug. 30 (not Aug. 15).

CZECH REPUBLIC

Services: Operator: České Dráhy (ČD). All daytime trains convey first and second classes of travel unless otherwise shown by '2' at the top of the column or by a note (which may be in the table heading). Overnight sleeping car (🛏) or couchette (▬) trains do not necessarily convey seating accommodation and individual footnotes should be checked carefully.

Timings: Valid **December 9, 2007 - December 13, 2008**. Timetable amendments may take place from March 3 and June 15. There is a reduced service on the evening of Dec. 24, 31 and the morning of Dec. 25, Jan. 1 (these alterations are partially shown in the tables but cannot be shown in detail for space reasons, particularly for local trains).

Reservations: It is possible to reserve seats on most Express trains.

Supplements: Supplements (60 Kč) are payable on all *EC* and *IC* trains. SuperCity (*SC*) trains are operated by tilting *Pendolino* units and a supplement of 200 Kč is payable.

Station names: hlavní = main; západ = west; východ = east; horní = upper; dolní = lower; starý = old; město = town; předměstí = suburban; nádraží = station.

1100 PRAHA - ÚSTÍ NAD LABEM - DĚČÍN - DRESDEN

km	Praha - Ústí : see also **1110**	420	◇	*EC* 178	770	*EC* 176	772	*EC* 370	774	*EC* 174	776	*EC* 172	778	970	697	*EC* 170	782	972	784	378	*EN* 352	786	788
		◆		✕ ◆		✕ ◆		✕ ◆		✕ ◆		✕ ◆		Ⓐ	2	✕ ◆			Ⓐ	◆	◆	⊕	⊗
0	**Praha** hlavní ▷ d.	0515	...	0625	...	0825	...	...	...	...	...	...	...	...	...	...	...	...	...	1850	2025	...	...
0	**Praha** Masarykovo d.	|	...	|	0652	|	0852	...	1052	...	1252	...	1452	1552	...	...	1652	1752	...	|	|	2052	2325
3	**Praha** Holešovice ▷ d.	0526	...	0636	|	0836	|	1036	|	1236	|	1436	|	|	...	1636	|	|	1836	1902	2036	|	|
27	Kralupy nad Vltavou d.	0547	...	|	0717	|	0917	|	1117	|	1317	|	1517	1617	...	|	1717	1817	|	1923	|	2117	2350
66	Roudnice nad Labem d.	0609	...	|	0743	|	0943	|	1143	|	1343	|	1543	1643	...	|	1743	1843	|	1946	|	2143	0014
84	Lovosice d.	0621	...	|	0758	|	0958	|	1158	|	1358	|	1558	1658	...	|	1758	1858	|	1958	|	2158	0027
106	**Ústí nad Labem** hlavní ▷ a.	0639	...	0739	0815	0939	1015	1139	1215	1339	1415	1539	1615	1715	...	1739	1815	1915	1939	2015	2139	2215	0043
106	**Ústí nad Labem** hlavní ▶ d.	...	0700	0740	0817	0940	1017	1140	1217	1340	1417	1540	1617	...	1727	1740	1817	*1927*	1940	2016	2140	2217	0045
129	**Děčín** ▶ a.	...	0728	0756	0833	0956	1033	1156	1233	1356	1433	1556	1633	...	1744	1756	1833	*1944*	1956	2035	2156	2233	0104
129	**Děčín** 🏛 ⊖ d.	...	...	0758	...	0958	...	1158	...	1358	...	1558	...	...	...	1758	...	...	...	2038	2158	...	...
151	Bad Schandau 🏛 ⊖ **857** d.	...	...	0818	...	1018	...	1218	...	1418	...	1618	...	...	...	1818	...	...	...	2056	2215	...	...
191	**Dresden** Hbf **857** a.	...	...	0846	...	1046	...	1246	...	1446	...	1646	...	...	...	1846	...	...	...	2121	2245	...	...

	771	773	775	*EN* 353	◇	971	379	688	973	779	*EC* 171	781	*EC* 173	783	*EC* 175	785	*EC* 177	787	*EC* 371	789	*EC* 179	◇	421
	⊖		Ⓐ	◆	Ⓐ	△ ⊖	◆	2			✕ ◆		✕ ◆		✕ ◆		✕ ◆		✕ ◆	⊗	✕ ◆	⊕	◆
Dresden Hbf **857** d.	...	...	...	0608	...	...	0710	...	...	...	0910	...	1110	...	1310	...	1510	...	1710	...	1910	...	...
Bad Schandau 🏛 ⊖ **857** d.	...	...	...	0638	...	...	0738	...	...	...	0940	...	1140	...	1340	...	1540	...	1740	...	1940	...	...
Děčín 🏛 ⊖ a.	...	...	...	0653	...	...	0757	...	...	...	0957	...	1157	...	1357	...	1557	...	1757	...	1957	...	...
Děčín ▶ d.	0422	0522	0622	0659	0702	...	0759	0818	...	0922	0959	1122	1159	1322	1359	1522	1559	1722	1759	1922	1959	2028	...
Ústí nad Labem hlavní ▶ a.	0438	0538	0638	0714	0729	...	0814	0836	...	0938	1014	1138	1214	1338	1414	1538	1614	1738	1814	1938	2014	2055	...
Ústí nad Labem hlavní ▷ d.	0440	0540	0640	0715	...	0740	0815	...	0840	0940	1015	1140	1215	1340	1415	1540	1615	1740	1815	1940	2015	...	2115
Lovosice d.	0458	0558	0658	|	...	0758	|	...	0858	0958	|	1158	|	1358	|	1558	|	1758	|	1958	|	...	2134
Roudnice nad Labem d.	0513	0613	0713	|	...	0813	|	...	0913	1013	|	1213	|	1413	|	1613	|	1813	|	2013	|	...	2146
Kralupy nad Vltavou d.	0539	0639	0739	|	...	0839	|	...	0939	1039	|	1239	|	1439	|	1639	|	1839	|	2039	|	...	2211
Praha Holešovice ▷ a.	|	|	|	0818	...	0859	0918	...	|	|	1118	|	1318	|	1518	|	1718	|	1918	|	2118	...	2230
Praha Masarykovo a.	0604	0704	0804	...	...	...	|	...	1004	1104	...	1304	...	1504	...	1704	...	1904	|	2104	|	...	|
Praha hlavní ▷ a.	...	...	...	...	...	...	0933	...	...	...	...	...	...	...	...	...	...	...	1931	...	2132	...	2242

ADDITIONAL LOCAL TRAINS DĚČÍN - DRESDEN AND V.V.

2nd class

					⑥⑦	E			
Děčín 🏛 ⊖ d.	...	0637	0900	...	1300	1606	1700	1900	...
Bad Schandau a.	...	0701	0933	...	1333	1628	1733	1933	...
Bad Schandau **857** d.	...	*0708*	*0938*r	...	*1338*r	1629	*1738*r	*1938*r	...
Dresden Hbf **857** a.	...	*0758*	*1028*r	...	*1428*r	1705	*1828*r	*2028*r	...

			E			⑥⑦			
Dresden Hbf **857** d.	...	*0630*	0820	*0830*	...	*1230*	*1630*	*1830*	...
Bad Schandau **857** a.	...	*0716*	0854	*0916*	...	*1316*	*1716*	*1916*	...
Bad Schandau d.	...	0719	0855	0950	...	1350	1752	1952	...
Děčín 🏛 ⊖ a.	...	0753	0917	1024	...	1424	1824	2024	...

◆ – NOTES (LISTED BY TRAIN NUMBERS)

170/1 – HUNGARIA – 🚃12 Budapest - Bratislava - Praha - Dresden - Berlin and v.v.
172/3 – VINDOBONA – 🚃12 Wien - Praha - Dresden - Berlin - Hamburg (⊙) and v.v.
174/5 – JAN JESENIUS – 🚃12 Budapest - Bratislava - Praha - Dresden - Berlin - Hamburg and v.v.
176 – 🚃12 Praha - Dresden - Berlin - Hamburg.
177 – 🚃12 Berlin - Dresden - Praha - Brno - Wien.
178/9 – 🚃12 Praha - Dresden - Berlin and v.v.
352/3 – JOHANNES KEPLER – 🚃12 Praha - Leipzig and v.v.; 🛏 1, 2 cl., ▬ 2 cl., 🚃2 (®) Praha - Leipzig - Frankfurt - Karlsruhe - Basel and v.v.
370 – 🚃12 Wien - Brno - Praha - Dresden - Berlin - Stralsund (- Binz ◐).
371 – 🚃12 (Binz ◐) - Stralsund - Hamburg - Berlin - Dresden - Praha.
378/9 – KOPERNIKUS – 🚃2 Praha - Dresden - Berlin and v.v. For 🛏 1, 2 cl., ▬ 2 cl., 🚃2 Praha - Berlin - Dortmund - Köln - Amsterdam and v.v. (®) see Table **22**.

420/1 – EXCELSIOR – 🛏 1, 2 cl., ▬ 2 cl., 🚃12 Cheb - Karlovy Vary - Ústí nad Labem - Praha - Žilina - Košice and v.v.

E – ⑥⑦ Mar. 22 - Nov. 2.
r – 30 minutes later Dec. 9 - Mar. 20.
◐ – Stralsund - Binz and v.v. on dates in Table **844**.
▶ – Ústí nad Labem - Děčín : see also Table **1115** and foot of Table **1110**.
▷ – For other non-stop trains Praha - Ústí nad Labem and v.v. see Table **1110**.
△ – From Chomutov (Table **1110**). Train **1571** on ©.
⊖ – Routeing point for international tickets = Schöna.
⊙ – Berlin - Hamburg not Dec. 24, 31. Hamburg - Berlin not Dec. 25, Jan. 1.

⊕ – Not Dec. 24, 31.
⊗ – Not Dec. 24, 25, 31.
⊖ – Not Dec. 25, Jan. 1.
◇ – Stopping train, 2nd class only.

Other local services:
Praha Masarykovo - Roudnice nad Labem : approx every 2 hours.
Roudnice nad Labem - Ústí : every 1 - 2 hours.

LOVOSICE - LITOMĚŘICE - ČESKÁ LÍPA 1102

Local trains, 2nd class

km										
0	**Lovosice 1100** d.	0601	0801	1001	1201	1401	1601	1801	2001	2210
8	Litoměřice horní d.	0614	0814	1014	1214	1414	1614	1814	2014	2222
50	**Česká Lípa** a.	0719	0924	1124	1324	1524	1724	1924	2124	...

			Ⓐ									
Česká Lípa d.	...	0359	...	0626	0834	1034	1234	1434	1634	1834	2034
Litoměřice horní d.	0010	0505	0505	0740	0940	1140	1340	1540	1740	1940	2140
Lovosice 1100 a.	0022	0518	0518	0753	0953	1153	1353	1553	1753	1953	2153

Also: Lovosice - Litoměřice horní: 0502, 0646 Ⓐ, 0701 Ⓐ, 0719, 0836, 0936, 1032, 1136, 1232, 1301 Ⓐ, 1336, 1436, 1501 Ⓐ, 1536, 1635, 1701 Ⓐ, 1736, 1836, 1901, 1936, 2032, 2137, 2259.
Litoměřice horní - Lovosice: 0437 Ⓐ, 0528, 0558 Ⓐ, 0630 Ⓐ, 0703 Ⓐ, 0757, 0839, 0908, 0958, 1108, 1158, 1258, 1358, 1439 Ⓐ, 1458, 1558, 1639 Ⓐ, 1658, 1758, 1839, 1858, 1958, 2115.

PRAHA - KLADNO - CHOMUTOV 1105

2nd class only

km	*See also Table* **1110**	**1130**	**1890**	◇	**1892**	**1894**	**1132**	**1896**	**1134**	**1898**	◇
						Ⓐ			⊗	Ⓑ d	⊕
0	**Praha** Masarykovo d.	0717	0947	1145	1307	1409	1509	1618	1711	1938	2049
31	Kladno d.	0805	1026	1237	1345	1449	1547	1701	1748	2020	2138
64	Lužná u Rakovnika a.	0839	1104	1325	1420	1524	1624	1741	1822	2057	2223
73	**Rakovník** a.	*0855*	1117	1347	1434	1540	*1638*	1754	*1852*	2110	2236
64	Lužná u Rakovnika d.	0840	...	...	...	...	1625	...	1824	...	...
105	Žatec **1126** d.	0923	...	...	...	...	1712	...	1912	...	...
128	**Chomutov** **1126** a.	0948	...	...	...	...	1741	...	1935	...	...
134	Jirkov a.	1001	...	...	...	...	...	...	1946	...	...

	1131	**1891**	**1135**	◇	**1893**	**1895**	**1133**	**1897**	**1535**	◇
	Ⓐ	Ⓐ							E	⊕
Jirkov d.	0448	...	0636	...	...	...	1350	...	...	...
Chomutov **1126** d.	0504	...	0702	...	...	...	1408	...	1803	...
Žatec **1126** d.	0529	...	0726	...	...	...	1436	...	1832	...
Lužná u Rakovnika a.	0616	...	0812	...	...	...	1521	...	1916	...
Rakovník d.	|	0608	*0756*	0926	1148	1319	*1509*	1641	*1903*	1903
Lužná u Rakovnika d.	0623	0623	0813	0940	1200	1332	1525	1654	1918	1932
Kladno d.	0705	0705	0851	1028	1236	1413	1603	1736	1953	2023
Praha Masarykovo a.	0744	0744	0926	1122	1316	1457	1639	1819	2028	2110

E – ⑤⑥⑦ (also holidays; not Dec. 24, 25).
d – Not Dec. 23 - 26, 30, Mar. 23, May 1, 8, July 5, Oct. 26, Nov. 16.
⊕ – Not Dec. 24, 31.
⊗ – Not Dec. 24, 25, 31.
◇ – Stopping train.

PRAHA - ÚSTI NAD LABEM - CHOMUTOV - KARLOVY VARY - CHEB 1110

For other trains Praha - Ústí nad Labem and v.v. see Table **1100**. For other trains Praha - Chomutov and v.v. (via Kladno) see Table **1105**

km		**1690**		**1692**	**420**	**604**		**608**				**610**	**1694**		**612**		**1696**	**614**		**1698**	**616**		**618**		
			◇				◇		◇	◇			◇		◇			◇			◇		◇	◇
		⊖		Ⓐ	E	m	Ⓐ			Ⓐ		Ⓐ	Ⓐ				Ⓐ			Ⓐ		⊗	⊕	⊕	
0	**Praha** hlavní ▷ d.	...	...	...	0515	0725	...	...	...	...	...	...	...	...	...	...	...	...	...	...	...	...	...	...
3	**Praha** Holešovice ▷ d.	...	...	...	0526	0736	...	0936	...	...	1136	...	...	1336	...	...	1536	...	...	1736	...	1936	...	...
106	**Ústí nad Labem** hlavní ▷ a.	...	...	...	0639	0839	...	1039	...	...	1239	...	...	1439	...	...	1639	...	...	1839	...	2039	...	...
106	**Ústí nad Labem** hlavní d.	0048	...	0441	0645	0845	...	1045	...	...	1245	1344	...	1445	...	1544	1645	...	1744	1845	...	2045	...	2222
123	Teplice v Čechách d.	0109	...	0502	0703	0903	...	1103	...	...	1303	1404	...	1503	...	1604	1703	...	1804	1903	...	2103	...	2243
152	**Most** d.	0138	...	0531	0731	0931	...	1131	...	...	1331	1431	...	1531	*1612*	1631	1731	*1808*	1831	1931	...	2131	...	2323
177	**Chomutov** a.	0158	...	0552	0751	0951	...	1151	...	...	1351	1451	...	1551	*1632*	1651	1751	*1832*	1851	1951	...	2151	...	2343
177	**Chomutov** d.	▬	0527	▬	0753	0953	...	1153	...	...	1353	▬	...	1553	*1634*	...	1753	*1834*	...	1953	...	▬	*2156*	...
196	Klášterec nad Ohři d.	◇	0544	...	0809	1009	...	1209	1217	...	1409	...	1534	1609	1657	...	1809	1857	...	2009	...	...	2220	...
236	**Karlovy Vary** ⊙ a.	Ⓐ	0629	◇	0847	1047	...	1247	1302	...	1447	◇	1619	1647	1742	...	1847	1942	...	2047	...	◇	2304	...
236	**Karlovy Vary** ⊙ d.	0536	0631	0742	0850	1050	1200	1250	1316	1418	1450	1517	1622	1650	1744	...	1850	2000	...	2050	2115	2220	...	...
262	Sokolov d.	0604	0700	0816	0913	1113	1229	1313	1343	1446	1513	1546	1650	1713	1813	...	1913	2029	...	2113	2141	2245	...	...
291	**Cheb** a.	0639	0735	0851	0941	1141	1302	1341	1418	1521	1541	1621	1725	1741	1848	...	1941	2104	...	2141	2218	2319	...	...

	1691	**619**		**1693**	**1695**		**609**		**611**	**613**		**617**			**615**			**605**		**421**				
				△		◇		◇			◇		◇	◇		◇	◇		◇	E	◇	◇	◇	◇
	⊖	Ⓐ	Ⓐ	⊖	Ⓐ	⊖							Ⓐ	Ⓒ		Ⓐ		m z			Ⓐ	⊕	⊕	v
Cheb d.	...	...	0342	...	...	0533	0615	0708	0815	1015	1107	1215	1233	1314	1415	1432	1540	1615	1715	1815	...	...	2005	2203
Sokolov d.	...	...	0414	...	...	0614	0643	0750	0843	1043	1143	1243	1309	1350	1443	1508	1616	1643	1751	1843	...	...	2041	2240
Karlovy Vary ⊙ a.	...	...	0441	...	...	0641	0705	0817	0905	1105	1210	1305	1336	1417	1505	1535	1643	1705	1818	1905	...	...	2107	2304
Karlovy Vary ⊙ d.	...	...	0446	...	...	0650	0707	...	0907	1107	1221	1307	...	1421	1507	1537	1649	1707	*1821*	1907	2024	...	...	2308
Klášterec nad Ohři d.	...	...	0533	...	...	0735	0744	...	0944	1144	1304	1344	...	1504	1544	1622	1735	1744	*1904*	1944	2107	2110	...	2351
Chomutov a.	...	...	0550	...	...	...	0759	...	0959	1159	*1322*	1359	...	*1522*	1559	...	...	1759	...	1959	...	2126	...	0005
Chomutov d.	0324	0458	...	0625	0701	...	0801	...	1001	1201	*1324*	1401	...	*1524*	1601	...	...	1801	...	2001	...	2130	...	...
Most d.	0347	0523	...	0646	0722	...	0823	...	1023	1223	*1347*	1423	...	*1544*	1623	...	...	1823	...	2023	...	2153	...	...
Teplice v Čechách d.	0418	0550	...	0713	0751	...	0850	...	1050	1250	...	1450	...	...	1650	...	...	1850	...	2050	...	2226	...	...
Ústí nad Labem hlavní a.	0438	0608	...	0733	0812	...	0908	...	1108	1308	...	1508	...	...	1708	...	...	1908	...	2108	...	2248	...	...
Ústí nad Labem hlavní ▷ d.	...	0615	...	0740	...	...	0915	...	1115	1315	...	1515	...	...	1715	...	...	1915	...	2115	...	...	...	...
Praha Holešovice ▷ a.	...	0718	...	0859	...	...	1018	...	1218	1418	...	1618	...	...	1818	...	...	2018	...	2230	...	...	...	...
Praha hlavní ▷ a.	...	...	...	...	...	...	...	...	...	...	...	...	...	...	...	...	...	2035	...	2242	...	...	...	...

km	*via Louny (2 cl.)*	**1712**	**1710**
		Ⓒ n	Ⓑ h
0	**Praha** Masarykovo d.	0704	1628
27	Kralupy nad Vltavou d.	0731	1654
47	Slaný d.	0758	1729
90	Louny d.	0845	1817
115	**Most** a.	0913	...

via Louny (2 cl.)	**1711**	**1713**
	⚒	Ⓒ n
Most d.	...	1640
Louny d.	0535	1708
Slaný d.	0624	1758
Kralupy nad Vltavou a.	0659	1826
Praha Masarykovo a.	0728	1855

Local trains (2 cl.)			
Děčín d.	0528	and	2028
Ústí nad Labem hlavní a.	0555	hourly	2055
Ústí nad Labem hlavní d.	0557	⊡	2057
Teplice v Čechách d.	0618	until	2118
Most a.	0652		2152

Local trains (2 cl.)			
Most d.	0503	and	2003
Teplice v Čechách d.	0536	hourly	2036
Ústí nad Labem hlavní a.	0558	⊖	2058
Ústí nad Labem hlavní d.	0600	until	2100
Děčín a.	0628		2128

E – EXCELSIOR – 🛏 1, 2 cl., 🛌 2 cl., (12) Cheb - Ústí nad Labem - Praha - Žilina - Košice and v.v.
h – Not Dec. 23 - 25, 31, Mar. 23, July 5, Nov. 16.
m – Conveys 🛏 1, 2 cl. Cheb - Praha (**375/4**) - Bratislava (**811/0**) - Zvolen - Banská Bystrica and v.v.; 🛏 1, 2 cl. Cheb - Praha (**209/8**) - Moskva and v.v.
n – Not Dec. 24.
v – Not Dec. 24 - 31.
z – To Havlíčkův Brod on Ⓑ (Table **1151**).
▷ – For other non-stop trains Praha - Ústí nad Labem and v.v. see Table **1100**.
△ – Train **1571** on Ⓒ.
⊙ – Known locally as Karlovy Vary horní (upper).
◇ – Stopping train. 2nd class only.
⊕ – Not Dec. 24, 31.
⊗ – Not Dec. 24, 25, 31.
⊖ – Not Dec. 25, Jan. 1.
⊡ – Also Děčín - Ústí at 2128, 2228.
⊖ – Also Ústí - Děčín at 0450, 0523, 2230.

ÚSTÍ NAD LABEM - DĚČÍN - ČESKÁ LIPA - LIBEREC 1115

2nd class

km		**1993**	**689**	◇	**691**	◇	**693**	**695**	**697**	◇	**699**
		⊖		◧		◧				◧	⊗
0	**Ústí nad Labem** hl. § d.	...	0727	...	0927	...	1327	1527	1727	...	1927
23	**Děčín** § a.	...	0744	...	0944	...	1344	1544	1744	...	1944
23	**Děčín** d.	0506	0747	0841	0947	1041	1347	1547	1747	1841	1947
54	Česká Lipa a.	0549	0823	0930	1023	1130	1423	1623	1823	1930	2023
54	Česká Lipa d.	0555	0830	*0945*	1030	*1145*	1430	1630	1830	*1945*	2030
113	**Liberec** a.	0720	0946	*1120*	1146	*1320*	1546	1746	1946	*2120*	2146

	◇	**688**	**690**	◇	**692**	**694**	**696**	**698**	◇	◇
	⚒			◐				⊗	◐ ⊕	◐ ⊕
Liberec d.	0450	0632	0832	1051	1232	1432	1632	1832	1851	2051
Česká Lipa a.	0616	0737	0937	1227	1337	1537	1737	1937	2027	2227
Česká Lipa d.	*0630*	0739	0939	*1230*	1339	1539	1739	1939	*2030*	*2230*
Děčín a.	*0715*	0815	1015	*1315*	1415	1615	1815	2015	*2115*	*2315*
Děčín § d.	...	0818	1018	...	1418	1618	1818	2018	...	...
Ústí nad Labem hl. § a.	...	0836	1036	...	1436	1636	1836	2036	...	...

§ – See also Table **1100** and foot of Table **1110**.
◇ – Stopping train. 2nd class.
◧ – Every 2 hours 0841 - 2041.
◐ – Every 2 hours 0651 - 2051.
⊕ – Not Dec. 24, 31.
⊗ – Not Dec. 24, 25, 31.
⊖ – Not Dec. 25, Jan. 1.

DĚČÍN - VARNSDORF / RUMBURK 1116

Local trains, 2nd class

km							Ⓐ				
0	**Děčín** d.	0616	0816	1016	1216	1416	1616	1703	1816	2016	2241	...
50	Rybniště a.	0735	0935	1135	1335	1535	1735	1834	1929	2135	2347	...
61	Varnsdorf a.	*0755*	*0958*	*1158*	*1358*	*1558*	*1758*	|	*1948*	*2156*	|	...
61	**Rumburk** a.	0749	0949	1149	1349	1549	1749	1854	1949	2149	2400	...

	Ⓐ								b	
Rumburk d.	0410	0621	0825	1025	1225	1425	1625	1825	...	2025
Varnsdorf d.	*0403*	*0615*	*0815*	*1005*	*1218*	*1415*	*1605*	*1812*	2005	|
Rybniště d.	0427	0636	0839	1039	1239	1439	1639	1839	2022	2041
Děčín a.	0538	0746	0946	1146	1346	1546	1746	1946	...	2146

b – On ⑥ depart 1951, arrive 2008.

KARLOVY VARY - MARIÁNSKÉ LÁZNĚ 1118

Operator: Viamont. 2nd class

km										
0	**Karlovy Vary** dolní △ d.	0622	0900	1100	1300	1500	1700	1910	2100	...
33	Bečov nad Teplou d.	0652	0932	1134	1332	1532	1732	1941	2134	...
53	**Mariánské Lázně** a.	0739	1019	1221	1419	1619	1819	2028	2221	...

Mariánské Lázně d.	0602	0827	1045	1227	1427	1627	1850	2045	...
Bečov nad Teplou d.	0652	0917	1133	1315	1515	1715	1941	2133	...
Karlovy Vary dolní △ a.	0724	0949	1205	1349	1549	1749	2013	2205	...

△ – Lower station (not main station).

1120 PRAHA - PLZEŇ - CHEB - FRANTIŠKOVY LÁZNĚ

km			1650	376	450		752	850	754		454	756	852	758	452	760		854	762	456	764	856	766	858	
			⚒q	G	N			z			M		z		N			k		M	△	k⊗	⊕	⊗	
0	**Praha** hlavní	d.	0016	0416	0516	...	0616	0716	0816	...	0916	1016	1116	1216	1316	1416	...	1516	1616	1716	1816	1916	2016	2216	...
4	Praha Smíchov	d.	0024	0424	0524	...	0624	0724	0824	...	0924	1024	1124	1224	1324	1424	...	1524	1624	1724	1824	1924	2024	2224	...
43	Beroun	d.	0054	0454	0554	...	0654	0754	0854	...	0954	1054	1154	1254	1354	1454	...	1554	1654	1754	1854	1954	2054	2254	...
52	Zdice	d.	0103	|	|	...	0702	|	0902	...	|	|	|	|	|	1502	...	|	1702	|	1902	|	|	|	...
91	Rokycany	d.	0138	0535	0631	...	0735	0835	0935	...	1031	1135	1235	1335	1431	1535	...	1635	1735	1831	1935	2035	2135	2335	...
114	**Plzeň** hlavní	a.	0159	0554	0650	...	0754	0854	0954	...	1050	1154	1254	1354	1450	1554	...	1654	1754	1850	1954	2054	2154	2354	...
114	**Plzeň** hlavní	d.	...	0605	0700	...	0805	...	1005	...	1100	1205	...	1405	1500	1605	...	...	1805	1900	2005	...	2205	...	...
	Furth im Wald 🚌 **885**	a.	...	|	0811	...	|	...	|	...	1211	|	...	|	1611	|	...	...	|	2011	|	...	|	...	...
147	Stříbro	d.	...	0641	...	...	0841	...	1041	...	...	1241	...	1441	...	1641	...	...	1841	...	2041	...	2241	...	...
190	Mariánské Lázně	d.	...	0724	...	...	0924	...	1124	...	...	1324	...	1524	...	1724	...	...	1924	...	2124	...	2324	...	...
220	**Cheb**	a.	...	0758	...	...	0958	...	1158	...	...	1358	...	1558	...	1758	...	...	1958	...	2158	...	2358	...	...
220	**Cheb**	▶ d.	...	0801	...	...	1001	...	1201	...	...	1401	...	...	...	1801	...	...	...	...	...	...	...	...	...
227	**Františkovy Lázně**	▶ a.	...	0808	...	...	1008	...	1208	...	...	1408	...	...	...	1808	...	...	...	...	...	...	...	...	...

		1651	851		751	853	753	451		755	855	757	455		759	857	761	453		763	859	765	457	377	
		⚒q	☆		⊖	k	⊖	N			z		M			z		N			k⊗		M	G	
Františkovy Lázně	▶ d.	...	...	...	...	...	...	...	...	...	...	0953	...	...	1153	...	1353	...	...	1553	...	1753	...	1953	...
Cheb	▶ a.	...	...	...	...	...	...	...	...	...	...	1000	...	...	1200	...	1400	...	...	1600	...	1800	...	2000	...
Cheb	d.	...	...	...	0407	...	0607	...	...	0807	...	1007	...	...	1207	...	1407	...	...	1607	...	1807	...	2007	...
Mariánské Lázně	d.	...	...	...	0440	...	0640	...	...	0840	...	1040	...	...	1240	...	1440	...	...	1640	...	1840	...	2040	...
Stříbro	d.	...	...	...	0521	...	0721	...	...	0921	...	1121	...	...	1321	...	1521	...	...	1721	...	1921	...	2121	...
Furth im Wald 🚌 **885**	d.	...	...	...	|	...	|	0749	...	|	...	|	1149	...	|	...	|	1549	...	|	...	|	1949	|	...
Plzeň hlavní	a.	...	...	...	0551	...	0751	0857	...	0951	...	1151	1257	...	1351	...	1551	1657	...	1751	...	1951	2057	2151	...
Plzeň hlavní	d.	0335	0508	...	0608	0708	0808	0908	...	1008	1108	1208	1308	...	1408	1508	1608	1708	...	1808	1908	2008	2108	2208	...
Rokycany	d.	0355	0527	...	0627	0727	0827	0927	...	1027	1127	1227	1327	...	1427	1527	1627	1727	...	1827	1927	2027	2127	2227	...
Zdice	d.	0434	0559	...	0659	|	0859	|	...	|	|	1259	|	...	1459	|	1659	|	...	1859	|	|	|	|	...
Beroun	d.	0444	0608	...	0708	0808	0908	1008	...	1108	1208	1308	1408	...	1508	1608	1708	1808	...	1908	2008	2108	2208	2308	...
Praha Smíchov	a.	0513*	0637	...	0737	0837	0937	1037	...	1137	1237	1337	1437	...	1537	1637	1737	1837	...	1937	2037	2137	2237	2337	...
Praha hlavní	a.	0521*	0645	...	0745	0845	0945	1045	...	1145	1245	1345	1445	...	1545	1645	1745	1845	...	1945	2045	2145	2245	2345	...

G – GALILEO GALILEI – [12] and ▬ 2 cl. Františkovy Lázně - Plzeň - Praha - Brno - Bratislava - Budapest and v.v.; [2] Františkovy Lázně - Plzeň - Praha (**420/1**) - Žilina - Košice and v.v.; 🛏 1, 2 cl. and ▬ 2 cl. Plzeň - Praha (**420/1**) - Žilina - Košice and v.v.
M – [12] Praha - Plzeň - Furth im Wald - Regensburg - München and v.v. (Table **57**).
N – [12] Praha - Schwandorf - Nürnberg and v.v. (Table **57**).
k – To/from Klatovy (Table **929**).
q – Also May 1, 8, Oct. 28.

r – Not Dec. 23 - 25, 31, Mar. 23, July 5, Nov. 16.
z – To/from Klatovy and Železná Ruda (Table **929**).
⊕ – Not Dec. 24, 31.
⊗ – Not Dec. 24, 25, 31.
⊖ – Not Dec. 25, Jan. 1.
☆ – Not Dec. 25, 26, Jan. 1.
△ – Plzeň - Cheb: not Dec. 24, 31.

* – On ⑥ change at Beroun (arrive Smíchov 0532, Praha hlavní 0540).
▶ – Additional local trains (see also Table **1122**):
From Cheb: 0507 Ⓐ, 0556, 0647 Ⓐ, 0818, 1018, 1218, 1423 Ⓑ r, 1526, 1626, 1818, 2018, 2228.
From Františkovy Lázně: 0517, 0631 Ⓐ, 0722, 0828 Ⓐ, 0936, 1136, 1336, 1536 Ⓑ r, 1736, 1936, 2136.

1121 CHEB - MARKTREDWITZ - NÜRNBERG

27 km *		⊖	⊖	⊖		⊖	⊖		⊖	⊖	⊖		⊖
		C	A		C							C	
Cheb	d.	0622	0651	0822	0902	1022	1222	1302	1422	1622	1822	1902	2022
Schirnding 🚌	d.	0636	0705	0836	0916	1036	1240	1316	1436	1636	1836	1916	2036
Marktredwitz	a.	0648	0717	0848	0929	1048	1251	1329	1448	1648	1851	1929	2048
Nürnberg **880**	a.	*0815*	*0912z*	*1017*	1115	*1217*	*1414*	1515	*1617*	*1817*	*2017*	2124	*2217*

		⊖		⊖	⊖		⊖	⊖	⊖		⊖	⊖
			C							C		
Nürnberg **880**	d.	*0548*	0648	*0748*	*0948*	1048	*1148*	*1348*	*1548*	1648	*1748*	*1948*
Marktredwitz	d.	0710r	0828	0910	1110	1228	1310	1510	1710	1828	1910	2110
Schirnding 🚌	d.	0723r	0840	0923	1123	1240	1326	1523	1723	1840	1923	2123
Cheb	a.	0735r	0854	0938	1135	1254	1338	1535	1735	1854	1938	2135

A – ①–⑤ (not Dec. 24 - 26, 31, Jan. 1, Mar. 21 - 24, May 1, 12, 22, Oct. 3).
C – ⑥⑦ (also Dec. 24 - 26, 31, Jan. 1, Mar. 21 - 24, May 1, 12, 22, Oct. 3).
r – On dates in note **A** runs 28 minutes later.
z – Change at Marktredwitz and Pegnitz.
⊖ – Operator: Vogtlandbahn GmbH.
* – Cheb - Schirnding = 13 km; Cheb - Marktredwitz = 27 km.

1122 CHEB - FRANTIŠKOVY LÁZNĚ - PLAUEN - ZWICKAU

Local trains 1, 2 class

km											
0	**Cheb**	▶ d.	0609	0809	1009	1209	1409	1609	1809	2009	...
9	**Františkovy Lázně**	▶ d.	0617	0817	1017	1217	1417	1617	1817	2017	...
27	Bad Brambach 🚌	**881** d.	0639	0839	1039	1239	1439	1639	1839	2039	...
76	**Plauen**	**880/1** d.	0741	0941	1141	1341	1541	1741	1941	2141	...
101	Reichenbach (Vogtl)	**880/1** a.	0806	1006	1206	1406	1606	1806	2006	2206	...
124	**Zwickau** (Sachs)	**880/1** a.	0836	1036	1236	1436	1636	1836	2036	2227	...

Zwickau (Sachs)	**880/1** d.	...	0719	0919	1119	1319	1519	1719	1919
Reichenbach (Vogtl)	**880/1** d.	0555	0754	0954	1154	1354	1554	1754	1954
Plauen	**880/1** d.	0622	0823	1023	1223	1423	1623	1823	2023
Bad Brambach 🚌	**881** d.	0723	0923	1123	1323	1523	1723	1923	2123
Františkovy Lázně	▶ d.	0745	0945	1145	1345	1545	1745	1945	2145
Cheb 1110	▶ a.	0752	0952	1152	1352	1552	1752	1952	2152

▶ – See also Table **1120**.
Operator: Vogtlandbahn GmbH.

1124 MOST - BEROUN - PŘÍBRAM - PISEK - CESKÉ BUDEJOVICE

2nd class only

km			890	892			894	894	896		
					◇	◇		n	v	◇	◇
0	**Most**	d.	...	0606	...	...	...	...	...	...	...
73	Rakovník	d.	...	0803	...	...	...	...	...	...	...
	Praha hlavní **1120**	d.	*0616*	*0816*	*0926*	...	*1216*	*1416*	*1616*	*1726*	...
117	**Beroun**	**1120** d.	0659	0859	1023	...	1259	1459	1659	1823	...
126	Zdice	**1120** d.	0710	0910	1033	1036	1310	1510	1710	1833	1836
156	Příbram	d.	0740	0940	...	1115	1340	1540	1740	...	1915
216	Pisek	d.	0845	1045	...	...	1445	1645	1845	...	...
229	Protivín	**1125** d.	0903	1103	...	...	1503	1703	1903	...	...
266	**Ceské Budejovice**	**1125** a.	0938	1138	...	...	1538	1738	1938	...	...

		891	895					897	893	899
		⊖		◇	◇	◇	◇			n
Ceské Budejovice	**1125** d.	...	0626	...	...	...	...	1226	1426	1626
Protivín	**1125** d.	0500	0700	...	...	...	...	1300	1500	1700
Pisek	d.	0514	0714	...	...	...	...	1314	1514	1714
Příbram	d.	0623	0823	0941	...	1141	...	1423	1623	1823
Zdice	**1120** d.	0655	0855	1015	1028	1215	1228	1455	1655	1855
Beroun	**1120** a.	0703	0903	...	1039	...	1239	1503	1703	1903
Praha Hlavní **1120**	a.	*0745*	*0945*	...	*1140*	...	*1340*	*1545*	*1745*	*1945*
Rakovník	a.	...	...	...	...	...	...	...	...	1758
Most	a.	...	...	...	...	...	...	...	...	1949

n – Not Dec. 24.
v – Not Dec. 23 - 25, 31.
⊖ – Not Dec. 24 - 26, Jan. 1.
◇ – Stopping train (runs approx every 2 hours).

1125 PLZEŇ - ČESKÉ BUDĚJOVICE

km				667	363	665	661	663	361	913	911
			Ⓐ	⊖	G			B	W		⊕
0	**Plzeň** hlavní	d.	...	0603	0803	1003	1203	1403	1603	1803	2003
34	Nepomuk	d.	...	0632	0832	1032	1232	1432	1632	1832	2032
59	Horaždovice předměstí	d.	0542	0652	0852	1052	1252	1452	1652	1852	2052
76	Strakonice	d.	0604	0707	0907	1107	1307	1507	1707	1907	2107
99	Protivín	**1124** d.	0633	0726	0926	1126	1326	1526	1726	1926	2126
136	**České Budějovice**	**1124** a.	0720	0756	0956	1156	1356	1556	1756	1956	2156
	Brno **1135**	a.	...	1237	...	1637	1837	2037			

		910	660	360	662	912	664	362	666	
		⊖	J	W	B			G	⊕	2
Brno **1135**	d.	...	...	...	0716	...	1120	...	1520	...
České Budějovice	**1124** d.	0602	0802	1002	1202	1402	1602	1802	2002	2109
Protivín	**1124** d.	0633	0833	1033	1233	1433	1633	1833	2033	2153
Strakonice	d.	0652	0852	1052	1252	1452	1652	1852	2052	2218
Horaždovice předměstí	d.	0710	0910	1110	1310	1510	1710	1910	2110	...
Nepomuk	d.	0730	0930	1130	1330	1530	1730	1930	2130	...
Plzeň hlavní	a.	0758	0958	1158	1358	1558	1758	1958	2158	...

B – [12] Plzeň - Brno - Ostrava - Bohumín and v.v.
G – [12] Plzeň - Gmünd and v.v.
J – From Jihlava (Table **1137**).
W – [12] Plzeň - Gmünd - Wien FJB and v.v.
⊖ – Not Dec. 25, Jan. 1.
⊕ – Not Dec. 24, 31.

1126 PLZEŇ - CHOMUTOV - MOST

km			1190		1192		1194		1196		1490
									⊕		†e
0	**Plzeň** hlavní	d.	0605	...	1005	...	1405	...	1605	...	2005
59	Blatno u Jesenice	d.	0710	...	1110	...	1510	...	1710	...	2110
107	Žatec	▷ d.	0802	...	1202	...	1602	...	1802	...	2202
130	Chomutov	**1110** a.	0827	...	1227	...	1627	...	1827	...	2227
155	**Most**	**1110** a.	0850	...	1250	...	1650	...	1850	...	2250

		1191	1491		1193		1195		1197		1493
		Ⓐ	Ⓒ						⊕		†e
Most	**1110** d.	0505	0705	...	0905	...	1305	...	1705	...	1905
Chomutov	**1110** d.	0528	0728	...	0928	...	1328	...	1728	...	1928
Žatec	▷ d.	0553	0753	...	0953	...	1353	...	1753	...	1953
Blatno u Jesenice	d.	0646	0846	...	1046	...	1446	...	1846	...	2046
Plzeň hlavní	a.	0754	0954	...	1154	...	1554	...	1954	...	2154

e – Not Dec. 23 - 30, Mar. 23, May 1, 8, July 5, Oct. 26, Nov. 16.
⊕ – Not Dec. 24, 31.
▷ – Žatec - Chomutov: see also Table **1105**.

PRAHA - TÁBOR - ČESKÉ BUDĚJOVICE 1130

km		1831	*Ex* 101	631	1835	633	635	637	639	641	643	207	645	647	1531	649
		⊙	J		⚒				Ⓐ			S		⊕	†e	⊗
0	**Praha** hlavní d.	0021	0611	0711	0807	0911	1111	1311	1411	1511	1611	1711	1811	1911	2011	2111
49	Benešov u Prahy d.	0112	0706	0806	0909	1006	1206	1406	1506	1606	1706	1806	1906	2006	2106	2206
103	**Tábor** d.	0200	0750	0858	1020	1058	1258	1458	1558	1658	1758	1858	1952	2057	2154	2254
130	Veselí nad Lužnicí **1135** d.	0229	0817	0929	...	1129	1329	1529	1629	1729	1829	1929	2024	2124	2224	2324
169	**České Budějovice** **1135** a.	0300	0850	1004	...	1204	1404	1604	1704	1804	1904	2004	2055	2155	2255	2355

	630	1830	632	634	636	206	638	640	642	644	646	1530	648	*Ex* 100	1836	
	Ⓐ	⚒	⊖			S						†e	⊗	J	⊗	
České Budějovice **1135** d.	0401	...	0501	0601	0701	0854	0954	1154	1354	1454	1554	1654	1754	1906	2105	...
Veselí nad Lužnicí **1135** d.	0433	0447	0533	0633	0733	0927	1027	1227	1427	1527	1627	1727	1827	1942	2147	...
Tábor d.	0511	0524	0609	0707	0812	1001	1101	1301	1501	1601	1701	1801	1901	2015	2217	...
Benešov u Prahy d.	0556	0626	0656	0756	0856	1056	1156	1356	1556	1656	1756	1856	1956	2059	2305	...
Praha hlavní a.	0653	0727	0753	0853	0953	1153	1253	1453	1653	1753	1853	1953	2053	2155	2357	...

J – JÓŽE PLEČNIK – [12] and ✕ Praha - Linz - Graz - Ljubljana and v.v.
S – [12] Praha - Linz - Salzburg and v.v.; 🛏 1, 2 cl., ▬ 2 cl. Praha - Linz - Innsbruck - Zürich and v.v.; ▬ 2 cl. Praha - Linz - Salzburg - Venezia and v.v.
e – Not Dec. 23 - 30, Mar. 23, May 1, 8, July 5, Oct. 26, Nov. 16.
⊕ – Not Dec. 24, 31.
⊗ – Not Dec. 24, 25, 31.
⊖ – Not Dec. 25, Jan. 1.
⊙ – Not Dec. 25, 26, Jan. 1.

ČESKÉ BUDĚJOVICE - LINZ 1132

2nd class (except trains **J** and **S**)

km				*Ex* 101		1931			1933	207
				J					⊕	S
	Praha hlavní **1130** d.	...	...	0611	...	...	...	...	...	1711
0	**České Budějovice** d.	0533	...	0902	1010	1209	*1409*	...	1811	2030
57	Horní Dvořiště 🏛 d.	0654	...	0957	1132	1313	1519	...	1917	2136
64	Summerau 🏛 a.	0703	...	1006	1141	1322	1528	...	1926	2145
64	Summerau d.	...	0715	1010	...	1336	...	1535	1933	2147
73	Freistadt d.	...	0724	1019	...	1345	...	1544	1941	2156
126	**Linz** Hbf a.	...	0825	1106	...	1443	...	1643	2045	2244

	206	1936			1930			*EC* 100	1932
	S					Ⓐ		J	⊗
Linz Hbf d.	0614	*0721*	1035	...	1308	1408	...	1654	1830
Freistadt d.	0705	*0821*	1142	...	1405	1514	...	1741	1924
Summerau a.	0714	*0830*	1151	...	1414	1523	...	1749	1932
Summerau 🏛 d.	0717	0833	...	1205	1426	*1552*	...	1751	1942
Horní Dvořiště 🏛 d.	0728	0843	...	1216	1437	*1601*	1641	1802	1953
České Budějovice a.	0820	0946	...	1328	1549	...	1749	1854	2100
Praha hlavní **1130** a.	1153	...	...	...	...	...	...	2155	...

J – JÓŽE PLEČNIK – [12] and ✕ Praha - Linz - Graz - Ljubljana and v.v. *Ex* in Czech Republic, *EC* in Austria.
S – [12] Praha - Linz - Salzburg and v.v. See Table **1130** for portions to / from Zürich and Venezia.
⊕ – Not Dec. 24, 31.
⊗ – Not Dec. 24, 25, 31.

ČESKÉ BUDĚJOVICE - ČESKÉ VELENICE - GMÜND 1133

2nd class only

km							1761			363												361				
		Ⓐ	Ⓐ	⊖	⊖	Ⓐb	⊖	F					Ⓐ	Ⓐ			Ⓐ			Ⓐ	Ⓐ		Ⓐ	⊕		Ⓐ
	Plzeň **1125** d.	...	...	...	...	...	...	...	...	0803	...	...	...	...	...	...	...	...	...	...	...	1603	...	...	...	...
0	**České Budějovice** d.	...	0508	0626	...	...	0801	...	...	1009	1132	...	1333	...	...	1500	...	1627	...	1727	...	1809	...	1910	...	2115
*55	Veselí nad Lužnicí d.	0439	|	|	0602	0655	|	0847	0942	|	|	1139	|	1345	1445	|	1545	|	1651	|	1744	|	1845	|	1945	|
*34	Třeboň d.	0516	|	|	0627	0728	|	0913	1008	|	|	1206	|	1409	1508	|	1608	|	1715	|	1807	|	1908	|	2011	|
50	České Velenice a.	0605	0607	0724	0723	0814	0856	1002	1049	1059	1230	1251	1430	1453	1555	1602	1655	1727	1802	1835	1847	1859	1948	2014	2059	2215
50	České Velenice 🏛 d.	...	0609	...	0727r	...	0858	1005r	...	1103	1240r	1259	1433	...	...	1604	...	1728	...	...	...	1901	...	...	*2106*r	...
52	**Gmünd NÖ** 🏛 a.	...	0613	...	0731r	...	0902	1009r	...	1107	1244r	1303	1437	...	...	1608	...	1732	...	...	...	1905	...	...	*2110*r	...
	Wien FJB **990** a.	...	*0830*	...	...	...	1130	...	...	*1330*	...	*1530*	...	...	...	...	...	*1956*	...	...	...	2147	...	...	...	...

								360												362			1760			
	⊖	⚒		Ⓐb	Ⓐ		Ⓒ		Ⓐ	Ⓐ	...	Ⓐ	Ⓒ		Ⓐ	Ⓐ			Ⓐ			Ⓐ	⊕	⊕	⊕	Ⓐ
Wien FJB **990** d.	...	...	...	...	...	...	...	0622	...	...	...	...	*1029*	*1029*	...	...	*1229*	...	...	*1429*	...	...	1659	...	...	...
Gmünd NÖ 🏛 d.	...	...	...	0625r	...	0743r	...	0850	...	*1020*	...	1206	1250	1250r	1329	...	1449	...	...	1655	...	...	1917	...	2122r	...
České Velenice 🏛 a.	...	...	...	0629r	...	0747r	...	0854	...	*1024*	...	1210	1254	1254r	1333	...	1453	...	...	1659	...	...	1921	...	2126r	...
České Velenice d.	0517	0616	0621	0637	0728	0750	0759	0901	0902	1032	1104	1235	1257	1307	1338	1353	1456	1500	1612	1701	1704	1907	1923	2017	2127	2218
Třeboň d.	0604	|	0702	0724	0814	|	0848	|	0946	|	1145	|	|	1348	|	1445	|	1545	1654	|	1746	1948	|	2058	|	2259
Veselí nad Lužnicí a.	0630	|	0724	...	0839	|	0918	|	1011	|	1207	|	|	1411	|	1512	|	1612	1718	|	1810	2013	|	2120	|	2321
České Budějovice a.	...	0714	...	...	...	0849	...	0949	...	1130	...	1330	1351	...	1441	...	1549	...	...	1749	...	...	2019	...	2222	...
Plzeň **1125** a.	...	...	...	...	...	...	...	1158	...	...	...	...	...	...	...	...	...	...	...	1958	...	...	...	...	...	...

F – Ⓒ (daily June 28 - Aug. 31), also Dec. 27 - Jan. 2, Feb. 1, 25 - 29, Mar. 20, 21, Oct. 27 - 29.
b – Not Dec. 27 - Jan. 2, Feb. 1, 25 - 29, Mar. 20, 21, June 30 - Aug. 29, Oct. 27 - 29.
r – Ⓐ only.
* – Distance from České Velenice.
⊕ – Not Dec. 24, 31.
⊖ – Not Dec. 25, Jan. 1.

ČESKÉ BUDĚJOVICE - JIHLAVA - BRNO 1135

km		1661	925	925	923	667	1663	665	661	663	921
		⚒	Ⓐ	⑥			Ⓐ			B⊕	k⊗
	Plzeň **1125** d.	...	...	...	...	0603	...	1003	1203	1403	...
0	**České Budějovice** d.	...	0408	...	0608	0808	...	1208	1408	1608	1808
39	Veselí nad Lužnicí ▷ d.	...	0445	...	0643	0843	...	1245	1443	1643	1843
65	Jindřichův Hradec ▷ d.	...	0516	...	0716	0916	...	1316	1516	1716	1916
117	Kostelec u Jihlavy d.	...	0616	...	0816	1016	...	1416	1616	1816	2016
132	**Jihlava** a.	...	0634	...	0834	1034	...	1434	1634	1834	2034
132	**Jihlava** d.	0531	0640	0640	0840	1040	1237x	1440	1640	1840	...
161	Okříšky d.	0604	0710	0710	0910	1110	1310	1510	1710	1910	...
173	Trebíč d.	0620	0727	0727	0927	1127	1327	1527	1727	1927	...
236	**Brno** hlavní a.	0732	0837	0837	1037	1237	1437	1637	1837	2037	...

	660	◇	920	662	◇	664	922	666	924	926
	Ⓐ	Ⓐ	k⊙	B					⊕	Ⓑh
Brno hlavní d.	...	0326	...	0716	0939	1120	1320	1520	1720	1920
Trebíč d.	...	0505	...	0834	1125	1232	1432	1632	1832	2037
Okříšky d.	...	0522	...	0848	1142	1246	1446	1646	1846	2052
Jihlava a.	...	0600	...	0918	1221z	1318	1518	1718	1918	2119
Jihlava d.	0524	...	0724	0924	...	1324	1524	1724	1924	...
Kostelec u Jihlavy d.	0542	...	0742	0942	...	1342	1542	1742	1942	...
Jindřichův Hradec ▷ d.	0645	...	0845	1045	...	1445	1645	1845	2045	...
Veselí nad Lužnicí ▷ d.	0716	...	0916	1116	...	1516	1716	1916	2116	...
České Budějovice a.	0748	...	0948	1148	...	1548	1748	1948	2148	...
Plzeň **1125** a.	0958	...	...	1358	...	1758	...	2158	...	...

CONNECTIONS OKŘÍŠKY - ZNOJMO

km											
		⚒			Ⓐ	Ⓒ	Ⓐ	Ⓒ	Ⓐ		
0	Okříšky d.	0607	0915	1120	1250	1313	1415	1514	1615	1715	1915
32	Moravské Budějovice a.	0644	0952	1155	1325	1350	1450	1549	1655	1752	1953
70	Znojmo a.	0732	1038	1238	...	1446	*1549*	*1645*	1750	1846	2038

	Ⓐ		⑥		Ⓐ	Ⓒ	Ⓐ			d
Znojmo d.	*0532*	*0642*c	0901	1101	...	1301	1358	1501	1701	1855
Moravské Budějovice d.	0625	0805	0955	1158	1331	1403	1457	1601	1804	1938
Okříšky a.	0704	0840	1030	1238	1405	1438	1537	1641	1838	2011

JIHLAVA - KOSTELEC U JIHLAVY - TELČ - SLAVONICE §

	Ⓐ			Ⓐ	Ⓒ	Ⓐ		Ⓐ	Ⓒ	Ⓐ		Ⓐ
Jihlava d.	*0535*	*0733*	*0941*	1052	*1202*	*1225*	*1350*	*1455*	*1550*	*1644*	*1837*	*2009*
Kostelec u J. a.	*0555*	*0759*	*1002*	1116	*1223*	*1245*	*1410*	*1518*	*1610*	*1708*	*1857*	*2033*
Kostelec u J. d.	0636	0819	1023	1121	1227	1310	1419	1527	1619	1713	1905	2037
Telč a.	0713	0857	1100	1158	1304	1352	1500	1604	1656	1750	1942	2112
Slavonice a.	...	0954r	1154r	1254	1358	1451	1604	...	1753	1855	2039	...

	Ⓐ	Ⓒ	Ⓐ	Ⓒ	Ⓐ		Ⓐ	Ⓒ	Ⓐ	Ⓒ	Ⓐ	Ⓒ
Slavonice d.	0703	0808	0842	*1006*	*1040*	...	...	1409	1502	1607	1712	1802
Telč d.	0803	0900	0935	1140	1204	1329	1438	1502	1609	1659	1814	1851
Kostelec u J. a.	0844	0938	1013	1218	1242	1406	1515	1539	1647	1738	1852	1935
Kostelec u J. d.	0849	*0942*	*1016*	*1258*	*1258*	*1416*	*1520*	*1616*	*1650*	*1816*	*1901*	*1942*
Jihlava a.	0911	*1006*	*1034*	*1321*	*1321*	*1434*	*1546*	*1634*	*1721*	*1834*	*1922*	*2003*

B – [12] Plzeň - Brno - Ostrava - Bohumin and v.v. Conveys (not Dec. 24, 31) 🛏 1, 2 cl. České Budějovice - Přerov (**422/3**) - Košice and v.v.
c – 0701 on Ⓒ.
d – To Jihlava (arrive 2106).
h – Not Dec. 23 - 25, 31, Mar. 23, July 5, Nov. 16.
k – To / from Havlíčkův Brod (Table **1137**).
r – Ⓒ only.
x – ⑤ (Ⓐ to June 30 / from Sept. 1), not Dec. 31.
z – ⑤⑥⑦ (daily to June 30 / from Sept. 1).
▷ – Additional trains Veselí nad Lužnicí - Jindřichův Hradec and v.v.: From Veselí nad Lužnicí 0750, 0933, 1041, 1210, 1410, 1546, 1730, 1942, 2148, 2247 Ⓐ; from Jindřichův Hradec 0718, 0952, 1135, 1407, 1548, 1748, 2113. Journey 35 minutes.
◇ – Stopping train. 2nd class.
⊕ – Not Dec. 24, 31.
⊗ – Not Dec. 24, 25, 31.
⊙ – Not Dec. 25, 26, Jan. 1.
§ – Kostelec - Telc *23 km*, Kostelec - Slavonice *53 km*.

HAVLÍČKŮV BROD - JIHLAVA 1137

2nd class

km					920		1183										1181			607				
			Ⓐ		▽		△					Ⓐ			Ⓐr		△	Ⓐr		P⊕				
0	Havlíčkův Brod d.	0449	0603	0647	0658	0805	0854	...	1005	1215	...	1311	1404	...	1511	1603	1651	1713	1805	1859	...	2005	2210	...
27	Jihlava a.	0518	0633	0718	0722	0835	0917	...	1035	1249	...	1346	1433	...	1545	1633	1719	1747	1835	1921	...	2034	2238	...

	606					1180									1514		1182				921			
	P⊖	Ⓐr		⚒b		△				Ⓐn		Ⓐ		Ⓐr	†v		△				▽			
Jihlava d.	0532	0605	0653	0729	...	0843	0923	...	1122	1227	1323	1436	1522	1608	1621	...	1647	1723	1810	1923	2036	2242	...	...
Havlíčkův Brod a.	0555	0644	0734	0752	...	0913	0954	...	1152	1256	1353	1505	1553	1643	1645	...	1711	1754	1844	1953	2059	2311	...	...

P – [12] Praha - Havlíčkův Brod - Jihlava and v.v.
b – Not Dec. 15, 22 - 29, Jan. 2 - 5, 12, 19, 26, Feb. 1, 2, 9, 16, 23, Mar. 1, 8, 15, 20 - 22.
n – Not Dec. 27 - 31, June 30 - Aug. 29.
r – Not Dec. 27 - 31.
v – Not Dec. 23 - 30, Mar. 23, May 1, 8, July 5, Oct. 26, Nov. 16. To Praha Holesoviče (arrive 1857).
⊕ – Not Dec. 24, 31.
⊖ – Not Dec. 25, Jan. 1.
△ – To / from Pardubice (Table **1142**).
▽ – To / from České Budějovice (Table **1135**).

1140 PRAHA - MLADÁ BOLESLAV - TURNOV - TANWALD

2nd class only

km			940	942		944	1140	946	1142		
								⊕	⊗	⊕	Ⓑh
0	**Praha** hlavní	d.	0528	0715	0915	1127	1315	1515	1715	1915	2103	2103
34	Neratovice	d.	0621	0751	0951	1211	1351	1551	1751	1951	2147	2147
40	Všetaty	d.	0630	0759	0959	1223	1359	1559	1759	1959	2154	2154
72	**Mladá Boleslav**	a.	0708	0829	1029	1302	1429	1629	1829	2029	2232	2232
72	**Mladá Boleslav**	d.	0716r	0833	1033	...	1433	1633	1833	2032	...	2235
88	Mnichovo Hradiště	d.	0743r	0857	1057	...	1457	1657	1857	2051	...	2256
102	**Turnov**	a.	0806r	0912	1112	...	1512	1712	1912	2110	...	2314
	Liberec **1142**	a.	...	*0958*	*1158*	...	*1558*	*1758*	*1958*	*2158*	...	*2358*
102	**Turnov**	d.	...	0919	1119	...	1519	...	1919	...	...	...
116	Železný Brod	a.	...	0935	1135	...	1535	...	1935	...	...	...
133	**Tanwald**	a.	...	1004	1204	...	1604	...	2004	...	...	...

		1141	941	1143		943	945	1847	947	949	
		Ⓐ	⊖				⚒	†e			
Tanwald	d.	...	0545	...	...	1145	1345a	...	1545c	1751	...
Železný Brod	d.	...	0620	...	...	1220	1420a	...	1620c	1820	...
Turnov	a.	...	0636	...	...	1236	1436a	...	1636c	1836	...
Liberec **1142**	d.	*0400*	*0602*	*0802*	...	*1202*	*1402*	*1431*	*1602*	*1802*	*2002*
Turnov	d.	0443	0643	0843	1032	1243	1443	1530	1643	1843	2048
Mnichovo Hradiště	d.	0502	0656	0856	1054	1256	1456	1545	1656	1856	2109
Mladá Boleslav	a.	0524	0714	0914	1112	1314	1514	1604	1714	1914	2128
Mladá Boleslav	d.	0526	0723	0923	1121	1323	1523	1605	1723	1923	2132
Všetaty	d.	0556	0757	0957	1202	1357	1557	1644	1757	1957	2210
Neratovice	d.	0603	0803	1003	1212	1403	1603	1651	1803	2003	2216
Praha hlavní	a.	0639	0839	1039	1253	1439	1638	1730	1839	2039	2255

a – Ⓐ only (also Dec. 24).
c – Ⓒ only (not Dec. 24).
e – Not Dec. 23 - 30, Mar. 23, May 1, 8, July 5, Oct. 26, Nov. 16.
h – Not Dec. 23 - 25, 31, Mar. 23, July 5, Nov. 16.
⊕ – Not Dec. 24, 31.
⊗ – Not Dec. 24, 25, 31.
⊖ – Not Dec. 25, Jan. 1.

1141 LIBEREC - TANWALD - HARRACHOV

km						Ⓒd					Ⓒd	
0	**Liberec**	d.	0628	0828	0908	0957	1108	1308	1508	1628	1757	1908
12	Jablonec nad Nisou	d.	0656	0856	0936	1016	1136	1336	1536	1656	1816	1936
27	Tanwald	a.	0732	0932	1012	1052	1212	1412	1612	1732	1852	2012
27	Tanwald	d.	*0734*	0935r	1019	*1101*	1219	1419	1624	*1739*	*1855*	2015v
39	**Harrachov**	a.	*0755*	1003r	1045	*1125*	1246	1444	1649	*1804*	*1921*	2040v

					Ⓒd					Ⓒd	
Harrachov	d.	...	*0757*	*0855*z	*1024*	1104	*1255*	1456	*1707*	*1821*	*1941*
Tanwald	a.	...	*0820*	*0920*z	*1058*	1138	*1324*	1524	*1735*	*1849*	*2009*
Tanwald	d.	0702	0822	0942	1102	1142	1342	1542	1742	1902	2022
Jablonec nad Nisou	d.	0737	0858	1018	1137	1218	1418	1618	1818	1937	2100
Liberec	a.	0756	0924	1044	1156	1244	1444	1644	1844	1956	2124

d – To / from Dresden (Table **1143**).
r – Ⓒ only.
v – ⑤⑥ only.
z – Ⓒ (daily Dec. 9 - Mar. 30, May 31 - Sept. 28).

Note: trains run approx every 40 mins Liberec - Tanwald and v.v.

1142 LIBEREC - TURNOV - HRADEC KRÁLOVÉ - PARDUBICE

2nd class

km			981	983	985	987	989	991	993	995	997
										⊗	⊗
0	**Liberec**	d.	0400	0602	0802	1002	1202	1402	1602	1802	2002
38	Turnov	d.	0439	0642	0842	1042	1242	1442	1642	1842	2042
52	Železný Brod	d.	0456	0700	0900	1100	1300	1500	1700	1900	2100
76	Stará Paka	d.	0525	0727	0927	1127	1327	1527	1727	1927	2127
107	Dvůr Králové nad Labem	d.	0600	0800	1000	1200	1400	1600	1800	2000	2200
122	Jaroměř **1145**	d.	0621	0821	1021	1221	1421	1621	1821	2021	2221
139	**Hradec Králové** **1145**	a.	0635	0837	1037	1237	1437	1637	1837	2037	2237
139	**Hradec Králové** ▶	d.	0643	0840	1040	1240	1440	1640	1840	2040	2240
159	Pardubice-Rosice	a.	0658	0858	1058	1258	1458	1658	1858	2058	2257
161	**Pardubice** ▶	a.	0702	0902	1102	1302	1502	1702	1902	2102	2301

		980	982	984	986	988	990	992	994	996
		☆								⊗
Pardubice ▶	d.	0455	0655	0855	1055	1255	1455	1655	1855	2055
Pardubice-Rosice	d.	0500	0700	0900	1100	1300	1500	1700	1900	2100
Hradec Králové ▶	a.	0519	0719	0919	1119	1319	1519	1719	1919	2119
Hradec Králové **1145**	d.	0523	0723	0923	1123	1323	1523	1723	1923	2123
Jaroměř **1145**	d.	0542	0742	0942	1142	1342	1542	1742	1942	2142
Dvůr Králové nad Labem	d.	0559	0759	0959	1159	1359	1559	1759	1959	2159
Stará Paka	d.	0631	0831	1031	1231	1431	1631	1831	2031	2234
Železný Brod	d.	0700	0900	1100	1300	1500	1700	1900	2100	2301
Turnov	d.	0721	0921	1121	1321	1521	1721	1921	2121	2319
Liberec	a.	0758	0958	1158	1358	1558	1758	1958	2158	2358

km			1183			1181	
0	**Pardubice**	d.	0655	*0925*	*1325*	1455	*1725*
2	Pardubice-Rosice	d.	0705	0930	1333	1503	1732
11	Chrudim	d.	0725	0943	1354	1520	1745
92	**Havlíčkův Brod**	a.	0853	1148	1553	1649	1920
	Jihlava **1137**	a.	0917	...	...	1719	...

		1886	1180			1182
Jihlava **1137**	d.	...	0843	...	...	1647
Havlíčkův Brod	d.	0506	0915	1214	1410	1714
Chrudim	d.	0651	1041	1408	1637	1842
Pardubice-Rosice	a.	0704	1055	1424	1654	1855
Pardubice	a.	0715	1108	1439	1709	1908

▶ – Additional trains **Hradec Kralové - Pardubice** and v.v. Journey 20 - 30 minutes. *Subject to alteration Dec. 23 - Jan. 1.*
From Hradec Kralové: 0056, 0439 Ⓐ, 0505 and hourly to 2105 (also 0530 Ⓐ, 0743, 0930, 1130, 1330, 1530, 1730, 2209).
From Pardubice: 0129, 0425 Ⓐ, 0525 and hourly to 2125 (also 0608 Ⓐ, 0808, 1009, 1209, 1409, 1609, 1809, 2253).

⊗ – Not Dec. 24, 25, 31.
☆ – Not Dec. 25, 26, Jan. 1.

1143 LIBEREC - ZITTAU - VARNSDORF

Local trains, 2nd class

km						⊖				⊖				⊖					⊖	⊖				
			Ⓐ	Ⓒ	Ⓐ	Ⓐ				①–⑤		▽	⑥⑦	①–⑤					①–⑤				▽	
0	**Liberec**	d.	0451	0626	0629	0729	0803	...	0929	1050	...	1203	1229	1329	1459	...	1603	1629	1729	...	1829	...	2003	...
27	Zittau 🏛	a.	0530	0700	0706	0802	0832	...	1018	1123	...	1232	1306	1402	1541	...	1632	1708	1805	...	1907	...	2032	...
27	Zittau	d.	0531	0708	0708	...	0838	...	1023	*1126*	...	1238	1307	*1411*	1543	...	1638	1709	...	1815	1908	...	2038	...
	Dresden Hbf **855**	a.	|	|	|	...	1020	...	|	|	...	1420	|	|	|	...	1820	|	...	|	|	...	2220	...
45	**Varnsdorf** 🏛	a.	0551	0728	0728	...	...	...	1043	*1148*	...	...	1327	*1439*	1603	...	...	1729	...	1837	1928	...	...	...

			⊖	⊖					⊖	⊖			⊖	⊖				⊖	⊖					
		Ⓐ	Ⓐ	Ⓐ				▽		①–⑤		⑥⑦	①–⑤	①–⑤					①–⑤			▽		
Varnsdorf 🏛	d.	0420	0554	...	0617	...	0827	...	0919	...	...	1102	1225	...	...	...	1446	1519	...	...	1627	...	1847	...
Dresden Hbf **855**	d.	|	|	...	|	...	|	0736	|	...	...	|	|	...	1136	...	|	|	...	...	|	1536	|	1936
Zittau	a.	0439	0617	...	0636	...	0846	0913	0942	...	...	1121	1248	...	1313	...	1505	1542	...	...	1646	1713	1906	2113
Zittau 🏛	d.	0440	...	0619	0637	...	0847	0919	...	0947	...	1122	...	1250	1319	...	1517	...	1547	...	1647	1719	1918	2119
Liberec	a.	0521	...	0653	0727	...	0927	0953	...	1022	...	1158	...	1325	1353	...	1557	...	1624	...	1727	1753	1957	2153

⊖ – Operator: Railtrans.
▽ – To / from Tanwald on Ⓒ (Table **1141**).

1145 PRAHA - HRADEC KRÁLOVÉ - TRUTNOV / LETOHRAD

km			791	651	⊖	793	653	953	1953	955	957	1955	655	959	1957	657	⊖	795	659	961	1959	963	965	967	969
			⚒	⊖																				⊕	⊗
0	**Praha** hlavní	d.	0511	0611	...	0711	0811	0911	...	1011	1111	...	1211	1311	...	1411	...	1511	1611	1711	...	1811	1911	2011	2211
35	Lysá nad Labem **1147**	d.	0544	0644	...	0744	0844	0944	...	1044	1144	...	1244	1344	...	1444	...	1544	1644	1744	...	1844	1944	2044	2244
50	Nymburk **1147**	d.	0556	0656	...	0756	0856	0956	...	1056	1156	...	1256	1356	...	1456	...	1556	1656	1756	...	1856	1956	2056	2256
57	Poděbrady **1147**	d.	0602	0702	...	0802	0902	1002	...	1102	1202	...	1302	1402	...	1502	...	1602	1702	1802	...	1902	2002	2102	2302
89	Chlumec nad Cidlinou	d.	0630	0730	...	0830	0930	1030	...	1130	1230	...	1330	1430	...	1530	...	1630	1730	1830	...	1930	2030	2130	2328
116	**Hradec Králové**	a.	0651	0751	...	0851	0951	1051	...	1151	1251	...	1351	1451	...	1551	...	1651	1751	1851	...	1951	2051	2151	2349
116	**Hradec Králové** **1142**	d.	0705	0804	...	0905	1004	...	1105	*1204*	...	1305	1404	...	1505	1604	...	1705	1804	...	1905	*2002*	...	*2202*	...
133	Jaroměř **1142**	d.	|	0821	...	|	1021	...	|	*1221*	...	|	1421	...	|	1621	...	|	1821	...	|	*2021*	...	*2221*	...
185	**Trutnov**	a.	|	0921	...	|	1120	...	|	*1321*	...	|	1520	...	|	1720	...	|	1921	...	|	*2121*	...	*2331*	...
137	Týniště nad Orlicí	d.	0732	...	...	0932	...	...	1131	...	...	1331	...	...	1531	...	...	1732	...	...	1931	...	...	...	...
	Ústí nad Orlici **1150/60**	d.	|	...	0945	|	...	...	|	...	...	|	...	...	|	...	1635	|	...	...	|	...	...	...	...
178	Letohrad	d.	0829	...	1005	1028	...	...	1234	...	...	1428	...	...	1633	...	1655	1828	...	...	2023	...	...	...	...
199	**Lichkov** 🏛	a.	...	...	...	...	...	...	...	...	...	...	...	...	...	...	...	...	...	...	...	...	...	...	...
	Wrocław Gl **1095** ❖	a.	...	...	...	...	...	...	...	...	...	...	...	...	...	...	...	...	...	...	...	...	...	...	...

		950	952	1950	954	650	1952	956	1783	958	⊖	790	652	1954	960	654	1956	962	964	1958	966	656	792	⊖	658
		⊙	⊖																					⊕	⊕
Wrocław Gl **1095** ❖	d.	...	...	...	...	...	...	...	...	...	...	...	...	...	...	...	...	...	...	...	...	...	...	...	...
Lichkov 🏛	d.	...	...	...	...	...	...	...	...	...	...	...	...	...	...	...	...	...	...	...	...	...	...	...	...
Letohrad	d.	...	...	0535	...	...	0737	...	...	...	0857	0939	...	1132	...	...	1332	...	...	1530	...	...	1739	1740	...
Ústí nad Orlici **1150/60**	a.	...	...	|	...	...	|	...	...	...	0917	|	...	|	...	...	|	...	...	|	...	...	|	1803	...
Týniště nad Orlicí	d.	...	...	0630	...	...	0832	...	...	...	...	1032	...	1232	...	...	1432	...	...	1632	...	...	1832	...	...
Trutnov	d.	...	...	|	...	0640	|	...	0841	...	...	|	1041	|	...	1241	|	...	*1440*	|	...	1640	|	...	1840
Jaroměř **1142**	d.	...	...	|	...	0741	|	...	0941	...	...	|	1141	|	...	1341	|	...	*1541*	|	...	1741	|	...	1941
Hradec Králové **1142**	a.	...	...	0653	...	0755	0853	...	0955	...	...	1054	1155	1253	...	1355	1453	...	*1555*	1653	...	1755	1854	...	1955
Hradec Králové	d.	0508	0608	...	0708	0808	...	0908	...	1008	...	1108	1208	...	1308	1408	...	1508	1608	...	1708	1808	1908	...	2008
Chlumec nad Cidlinou	d.	0529	0629	...	0729	0829	...	0929	...	1029	...	1129	1229	...	1329	1429	...	1529	1629	...	1729	1829	1929	...	2029
Poděbrady **1147**	d.	0554	0654	...	0754	0854	...	0954	...	1054	...	1154	1254	...	1354	1454	...	1554	1654	...	1754	1854	1954	...	2054
Nymburk **1147**	d.	0601	0701	...	0801	0901	...	1001	...	1101	...	1201	1301	...	1401	1501	...	1601	1701	...	1801	1901	2001	...	2101
Lysá nad Labem **1147**	d.	0612	0712	...	0812	0912	...	1012	...	1112	...	1212	1312	...	1412	1512	...	1612	1712	...	1812	1912	2012	...	2112
Praha hlavní	a.	0645	0745	...	0845	0945	...	1045	...	1145	...	1245	1345	...	1445	1545	...	1646	1745	...	1845	1945	2045	...	2145

⊕ – Not Dec. 24, 31.
⊗ – Not Dec. 24, 25, 31.
⊖ – Not Dec. 25, Jan. 1.
⊙ – Not Dec. 25, 26, Jan. 1.
⊖ – Local trains run approx 15 times daily.
❖ – Service Lichkov - Wrocław is currently suspended.

Děčín - Ústí: see Table 1100

DĚČÍN - ÚSTÍ NAD LABEM - MĚLNÍK - KOLÍN 1147

km		2Ⓐ	2	2Ⓒ		2	2	2	2	
0	**Děčín** hlavní d.	0424	0602	0802	...	1202	1402	1602	1802	...
3	Děčín východ d.	0429	0607	0807	...	1207	1407	1607	1807	...
28	**Ústí n. Labem** Střekov. a.	0503	0641	0841	...	1241	1441	1641	1841	...

	2Ⓐ	2	2Ⓒ		2	2	2	2		
Ústí n. Labem Střekov. d.	0519	0653	0914	...	1314	1514	1714	1914	...	...
Děčín východ a.	0552	0727	0947	...	1347	1547	1747	1947	...	...
Děčín hlavní a.	0557	0732	0957	...	1357	1557	1757	1957	...	...

km		711	713	715	717	719	721	723	725	◇
		⚒							⊕	⊕
0	**Ústí n. Labem** západ d.	0445	0645	0845	1045	1245	1445	1645	1845	2003
2	**Ústí n. Labem** Střekov. d.	0450	0650	0850	1050	1250	1450	1650	1850	2008
27	Litoměřice město d.	0510	0710	0910	1110	1310	1510	1710	1910	2030
63	**Mělník** d.	0538	0738	0938	1138	1338	1538	1738	1938	2103
73	Všetaty d.	0546	0746	0946	1146	1346	1546	1746	1946	2112
85	Stará Boleslav d.	0555	0755	0955	1155	1355	1555	1755	1955	2124
96	Lysá nad Labem **1145** d.	0604	0804	1004	1204	1404	1604	1804	2004	2135
111	Nymburk **1145** d.	0616	0816	1016	1216	1416	1616	1816	2016	...
118	Poděbrady **1145** d.	0623	0823	1023	1223	1423	1623	1823	2023	...
134	**Kolín** d.	0636	0836	1036	1236	1436	1636	1836	2036	...

	◇	◇	710	712	714	716	718	720	722	724
	⊖								⊕	Ⓑh
Kolín d.	...	...	0715	0915	1115	1315	1515	1715	1915	2115
Poděbrady **1145** d.	...	...	0729	0929	1129	1329	1529	1729	1929	2129
Nymburk **1145** d.	...	...	0739	0939	1139	1339	1539	1739	1939	2139
Lysá nad Labem **1145** d.	0605	0704	0751	0951	1151	1351	1551	1751	1951	2151
Stará Boleslav d.	0615	0713	0758	0958	1158	1358	1558	1758	1958	2158
Všetaty d.	0632	0734	0808	1008	1208	1408	1608	1808	2008	2208
Mělník d.	0641	0748	0816	1016	1216	1416	1616	1816	2016	2216
Litoměřice město d.	0716	0824	0845	1045	1245	1445	1645	1845	2045	2245
Ústí n. Labem Střekov a.	0736	0845	0903	1103	1303	1503	1703	1903	2103	2303
Ústí n. Labem západ a.	0741	0850	0909	1109	1309	1509	1709	1909	2109	2309

km		2Ⓐ	2	2		2	2	2	2⊗	
0	Rumburk d.	0453	...	0656	...	...	1257	...	1657	...
45	Česka Lipá d.	0552	0602	0802	...	1202	1402	1602	1802	...
99	Mladá Boleslav d.	...	0718	0918	...	1318	1518	1718	1918	...
129	Nymburk a.	...	0744	0944	...	1344	1544	1744	1944	...

		2Ⓐ	2	2		2	2	2	2⊗	
Nymburk d.	...	...	0804	1004	...	1404	1604	1804	2004	...
Mladá Boleslav a.	...	...	0829	1029	...	1429	1629	1829	2029	...
Česka Lipá a.	...	0518	0934	1134	...	1534	1734	1934	2134	...
Rumburk a.	...	0619	1039	...	...	1639	...	2040	...	...

h – Not Dec. 23-25, 31, Mar. 23, July 5, Nov. 16. ⊕ – Not Dec. 24, 31. ⊗ – Not Dec. 24, 25, 31. ⊖ – Not Dec. 25, Jan. 1.

PRAHA - PARDUBICE - BRNO - BŘECLAV - BRATISLAVA 1150

km			*EC*	*IC•*	*Ex*		*EC*	*SC**		*Ex*	*SC**	*EC*		*Ex*	*EC*		*Ex*	*EC*	*Ex*		*EC*	*SC**	*Ex*		*EN•*
		235	71	131	573	271	279	73	277	575	75	171	273	577	173	233	579	175	571	275	177	135	569	375	377
			✕	🍷			✕	🍷			🍷	✕			✕	2		✕			✕	🍷			
			b	♦b	⚒r			Ⓡ	★		Ⓡ	♦			♦			♦			♦	Ⓡ	⊕	♦	♦
	Praha Holešovice d.	...	...	...	0633	...	0733	0823	...	0933	1023	1133	...	1233	1333	...	1433	1533	1633	...	1733	1823	1933	...	...
0	**Praha** hlavni ▷ d.	...	0500	...	|	...	|	|	0753	|	|	|	...	|	|	...	|	|	|	...	|	|	|	2153	0030
62	Kolín ▷ d.	...	0542	...	|	...	0812	|	0846	|	|	1212	...	|	1412	...	|	1612	|	...	1812	|	|	2246	|
154	**Pardubice** ▷ d.	...	0605	...	0736	...	0836	0921	|	1036	1121	1236	...	1336	1436	...	1536	1636	1736	...	1836	1921	2036	|	0146
164	Česká Třebová ▷ d.	...	0640	...	|	...	0911	|	⊡	|	|	1311	...	|	1511	...	|	1711	|	...	1911	|	|	⊡	|
255	**Brno** hlavní a.	...	0741	...	0915	...	1015	1049	1134	1215	1249	1415	...	1515	1615	...	1715	1815	1915	...	2015	2049	2215	0129	0329
255	**Brno** hlavní d.	0517	0743	...	...	0938	1017	1051	1140	...	1251	1417	1438	...	1617	...	...	1817	...	1938	2017	2051	...	0135	0335
314	**Břeclav** a.	0555	0814	...	...	1015	1049	1121	1217	...	1321	1449	1515	...	1649	...	...	1849	...	2015	2049	2121	...	0210	0410
314	**Břeclav** d.	0559	0823	0833	...	1025	1052	1123	1220	...	1323	1452	1525	...	1658	1659	...	1852	...	2025	2058	2123	...	0224	0450
	Wien Süd **981 999** a.	|	0928	|	...	1130	|	1228	|	...	1428	|	1630	...	1803	|	...	|	...	2130	2203	|	...	|	|
332	Kúty 🏛 d.	0615	...	0849	...	...	1106	...	1234	...	...	1506	...	...	...	1715	...	1906	...	...	...	2137	...	0240	0504
396	**Bratislava** Hlavná a.	0659	...	0930	...	...	1142	...	1318	...	...	1542	...	...	...	1759	...	1942	...	...	...	2213	...	0324	0541
	Budapest Keleti **1170** a.	...	...	1232	...	...	1432	...	...	...	...	1832	...	...	...	...	...	2232	...	...	...	...	...	0703	0832

	Ex	*SC**		*EC*	*Ex*		*EC*	*Ex*	*EC*	*Ex*	*EC*		*SC**	*Ex*			*SC**	*EC*	*Ex*			*IC•*	*EC*	*EN•*	
	568	134	232	370	570	270	174	572	172	574	170	272	72	576	276	2014	74	278	578	234	274	130	70	376	374
		🍷	2	✕			✕		✕		✕		🍷			◇	🍷	✕				🍷	✕		
	⚒r	Ⓡ		♦			♦		♦		♦		Ⓡ		★		Ⓡ		⊕			♦d	d	♦	♦
Budapest Keleti **1170** d.	...	...	...	...	...	...	0530	...	...	...	0930	...	...	...	...	...	...	1330	...	...	...	1530	...	2000	1940
Bratislava Hlavná d.	...	0542	0608	...	...	...	0815	...	...	...	1215	...	...	...	1444	1450	...	1615	...	1708	...	1840	...	2251	2344
Kúty 🏛 d.	...	0620	0654	...	...	...	0853	...	...	...	1253	...	...	...	1530	1613	...	1653	...	1754	...	1921	...	2330	0102
Wien Süd **981 999** d.	...	|	|	0608	...	0732	|	...	1004	...	|	1232	1333	...	|	|	1533	|	...	|	1732	|	1833	|	|
Břeclav a.	...	0632	0708	0708	...	0830	0905	...	1104	...	1305	1330	1433	...	1542	1630	1633	1705	...	1807	1830	1933	1933	2342	0115
Břeclav d.	...	0635	...	0717	...	0839	0908	...	1113	...	1308	1339	1435	...	1544	...	1635	1708	...	1810	1839	...	1950	0002	0140
Brno hlavní a.	...	0705	...	0748	...	0917	0940	...	1144	...	1340	1417	1505	...	1621	...	1705	1740	...	1848	1917	...	2021	0036	0215
Brno hlavní d.	0543	0707	...	0750	0843	...	0943	1043	1146	1243	1343	...	1507	1543	1624	...	1707	1743	1843	...	...	...	2023	0038	0225
Česká Třebová ▷ d.	|	|	...	|	|	...	1048	|	1248	|	1448	...	|	|	⊡	...	|	1848	|	...	...	...	2125	|	⊡
Pardubice ▷ d.	0722	0834	...	0924	1022	...	1122	1222	1322	1422	1522	...	1634	1722	|	...	1834	1922	2022	...	...	...	2200	0217	|
Kolín ▷ d.	|	|	...	|	|	...	1144	|	1344	|	1544	...	|	|	1911	...	|	1944	|	...	...	...	2224	|	0518
Praha hlavni ▷ a.	|	|	...	|	|	...	|	|	|	|	|	...	|	|	2004	...	|	2033	2128	...	...	...	2310	0332	0614
Praha Holešovice a.	0825	0932	...	1025	1125	...	1225	1325	1425	1525	1625	...	1732	1825	...	...	1932	...	...	...	...	...	...	...	...

SLOWER TRAINS PRAHA - ČESKÁ TŘEBOVÁ - BRNO △

km		1973	1975	865	867	869	871	1977	873	875	877	879
		⊙	Ⓐ					Ⓐ				⊗
0	**Praha** hlavní ▷ d.	...	...	0538	0738	0938	1138	*1238*	1338	1538	1738	2038
62	Kolín ▷ d.	...	...	0631	0831	1031	1231	*1331*	1431	1631	1831	2131
104	**Pardubice** ▷ d.	...	...	0706	0906	1106	1306	*1400*	1506	1706	1906	2206
139	Choceň ▷ d.	...	...	0724	0924	1124	1324	*1418*	1524	1724	1924	2224
154	Ústí nad Orlicí ▷ d.	...	...	0738	0938	1138	1338	*1432*	1538	1738	1938	2238
164	**Česká Třebová** ▷ a.	...	...	0747	0947	1147	1347	*1441*	1547	1747	1947	2247
164	**Česká Třebová** d.	0551	0651	0800	1000	1200	1400	1451	1600	1800	2000	...
181	Svitavy d.	0603	0703	0812	1012	1212	1412	1503	1612	1812	2012	...
208	Letovice d.	0630	0730	0830	1030	1230	1430	1530	1630	1830	2030	...
233	Blansko d.	0650	0750	0850	1050	1250	1450	1550	1650	1850	2050	...
255	**Brno** hlavní a.	0712	0812	0912	1112	1312	1512	1612	1712	1912	2112	...

	860	862	864	866	868	870	872	874	876	878
	⚒r	Ⓐ	⚒z					△	△	
Brno hlavní d.	...	...	0446	0646	0846	1046	1246	1446	1646	1846
Blansko d.	...	...	0509	0709	0909	1109	1309	1509	1709	1909
Letovice d.	...	...	0527	0727	0927	1127	1327	1527	1727	1927
Svitavy d.	...	0456	0544	0744	0944	1144	1344	1544	1744	1944
Česká Třebová a.	...	0507	0556	0756	0956	1156	1356	1556	1756	1956
Česká Třebová ▷ d.	0350	0509	0609	0809	1009	1209	1409	1609	1809	2009
Ústí nad Orlicí ▷ d.	0359	0518	0618	0818	1018	1218	1418	1618	1818	2018
Choceň ▷ d.	0412	0531	0631	0831	1031	1231	1431	1631	1831	2031
Pardubice ▷ d.	0435	0554	0656	0856	1056	1256	1456	1656	1856	2056
Kolín ▷ d.	0505	0624	0725	0925	1125	1325	1525	1725	1925	2125
Praha hlavní ▷ a.	0601	0719	0819	1019	1219	1419	1619	1819	2019	2219

♦ – **NOTES** (LISTED BY TRAIN NUMBERS)

130/1 – MORAVIA – [12] 🍷 Bohumin - Ostrava - Břeclav - Bratislava - Budapest and v.v.
170/1 – HUNGARIA – [12] ✕ Berlin - Dresden - Praha - Budapest and v.v.
172/3 – VINDOBONA – [12] ✕ Hamburg - Berlin - Dresden - Praha - Wien and v.v.
174/5 – JÁN JESENIUS – [12] ✕ Hamburg - Berlin - Dresden - Praha - Budapest and v.v.
177 – [12] ✕ Berlin - Dresden - Praha - Wien.
370 – [12] ✕ Wien - Praha - Dresden - Berlin - Stralsund (- Binz on dates in Table **844**).
374/5 – PANNONIA – 🛏 1, 2 cl., ▬ 2 cl., [12] Praha - Bratislava - Györ - Budapest - Lőkösháza and v.v.; [2] Praha - Budapest - Bucureşti and v.v. (also 🛏 1, 2 cl. on dates in Table **60**); 🛏 1, 2 cl. Cheb (**604/5**) - Karlovy Vary - Praha - Bratislava (**811/0**) - Zvolen - Banská Bystrica and v.v. For ▬ Praha - Varna / Burgas and v.v. (summer only) see Table **60**. Train number **733/2** in Hungary.
376/7 – GALILEO GALILEI – [12] and ▬ 2 cl. Františkovy Lázně - Cheb - Plzeň - Praha - Brno - Bratislava - Budapest and v.v. For other cars conveyed between Břeclav and Budapest see Tables **95** and **99**.

b – Conveys [2] Praha (**71**) - Břeclav (**131**) - Budapest.
d – Conveys [2] Budapest (**130**) - Břeclav (**70**) - Praha.
e – † (not Dec. 23-30, Mar. 23, May 1, 8, July 5, Oct. 26, Nov. 16).
h – Not Dec. 23-25, 31, Mar. 23, July 5, Nov. 16.
r – ⚒ (also May 1, 8, Oct. 28).
z – Runs daily from Česká Třebová.
★ – Praha - Bratislava and v.v. Conveys June 20 - Sept. 5: 🛏 1, 2 cl., ▬ 2 cl. [2] Praha - Split, returning next day (train number **1202/3** JADRAN).
▷ – See also Table **1160**.
△ – Additional journeys Brno - Česká Třebová: 1346 Ⓐ, 1546 Ⓑ, 1746 Ⓑ (trains **1970/2/4**).
◇ – Stopping train. 2nd class.
⊡ – Via Havlíčkův Brod (Table **1151**).
* – Pendolino tilting train. Classified *EC* in Austria.

⊕ – Not Dec. 24, 31.
⊗ – Not Dec. 24, 25, 31.
⊖ – Not Dec. 25, Jan. 1.
⊙ – Not Dec. 25, 26, Jan. 1.
• – *Ex* in Slovakia.

SELECTED TRAIN NAMES:
70/71 – ANTONÍN DVOŘÁK
72/73 – JOHANN GREGOR MENDEL
74/75 – SMETANA
134/5 – SLOVENSKÁ STRELA
276/7 – SLOVAN
278/9 – JAROSLAV HAŠEK

For fast trains see Table 1150

PRAHA - HAVLIČKŮV BROD - BRNO 1151

km		673	277	675	677	679	681	607	683	685	605	375
		⊖	★					⊕		⊕	Ⓑh	♦
0	**Praha** hlavni d.	0549	0753	0953	1153	1353	1553	1653	1753	1853	2053	2153
62	Kolín d.	0646	0846	1046	1246	1446	1646	1746	1846	1946	2146	2246
73	Kutná Hora d.	0658	0858	1058	1258	1458	1658	1758	1858	1958	2158	2258
82	Čáslav d.	0708	0908	1108	1308	1508	1708	1807	1908	2008	2208	2308
136	**Havlíčkův Brod** d.	0802	1002	1202	1402	1602	1802	1857	2002	2102	2259	0002
	Jihlava **1137** a.	|	|	|	|	|	|	1921	|	|	...	|
169	Ždár nad Sázavou d.	0829	1029	1229	1429	1629	1829	...	2029	2129e	...	0027
257	**Brno** hlavní a.	0934	1134	1334	1534	1734	1934	...	2134	2234e	...	0129

	374	606	670	672	674	676	678	680	276	682
	♦	⊖	⊖						★	⊕
Brno hlavní d.	0225	...	0524r	0624	0824	1024	1224	1424	1624	1824
Ždár nad Sázavou d.	0331	...	0632r	0732	0932	1132	1332	1532	1732	1932
Jihlava **1137** d.	|	0532	|	|	|	|	|	|	|	|
Havlíčkův Brod d.	0403	0558	0658	0758	0958	1158	1358	1558	1758	1958
Čáslav d.	0456	0650	0750	0850	1050	1250	1450	1650	1850	2050
Kutná Hora d.	0506	0659	0759	0859	1059	1259	1459	1659	1859	2059
Kolín d.	0518	0711	0811	0911	1111	1311	1511	1711	1911	2111
Praha hlavni a.	0614	0805	0904	1005	1205	1405	1605	1805	2004	2205

FOR NOTES SEE TABLE 1150 ABOVE

1160 PRAHA - OLOMOUC - OSTRAVA - ŽILINA

FASTEST TRAINS (calling only at points shown). See below for other services. *SC (SuperCity)* trains are named *SC PENDOLINO* and are operated by tilting trains.

km		*SC* 501	*SC* 503	*IC* 517	*SC* 505	*SC* 507	*SC* 509	*IC* 519	*SC* 511	
		R Y	R Y	X	R Y	R Y	R Y	X	R Y	
							⊕	⑧n	⑦v	
0	**Praha** Holešovice .... d.	0523	0923	1123	1323	1523	1723	1923	2023	...
104	Pardubice .... d.	0621	1021	1225	1421	1621	1821	2025	2121	...
252	**Olomouc** .... d.	0740	1140	1353	1540	1740	1940	2153	2240	...
353	Ostrava Svinov .... a.	0827	1227	1445	1627	1827	2027	2245	2327	...
358	**Ostrava** hlavní .... a.	0835	1235	1454	1635	1835	2035	2254	2335	...
366	Bohumín .... a.	...	...	1505	...	...	...	2305	...	...

	IC 518	*SC* 500	*SC* 502	*SC* 504	*SC* 506	*IC* 516	*SC* 508	*SC* 510	
	X	R Y	R Y	R Y	R Y	X	R Y	R Y	
	⚒q	⊖						⑦v	
Bohumín .... d.	0350	...	...	...	...	1450	...	...	...
Ostrava hlavní .... d.	0401	0520	0720	0920	1320	1501	1720	1920	...
Ostrava Svinov .... d.	0410	0528	0728	0928	1328	1510	1728	1928	...
Olomouc .... d.	0505	0617	0817	1017	1417	1605	1817	2017	...
Pardubice .... d.	0630	0734	0934	1134	1534	1730	1934	2134	...
Praha Holešovice .... a.	0735y	0832	1032	1232	1632	1832	2032	2232	...

OTHER TRAINS. *SEE ABOVE FOR FASTEST TRAINS PRAHA - OSTRAVA*

km		421	2903	*Ex* 141	625	*IC* 583	705	*Ex* 127	*EC* 143	627	*Ex* 525	*EC* 107	*EC* 145	707	*Ex* 121	*EC* 147	629	*Ex* 523	433	*EC* 109	703	*Ex* 129	*IC* 541	623
			2	X	X	X	X	X	X		X	X	X	X	X	X	X	X	2	X	X		Y	X
		♦					L		‡		V	♦	♦‡	L	§			L		♦	V			
0	**Praha** hlavní .... △ d.	0006	...	0406	0433	0606	0638	0706	0806	0838	0906	1006	1006	1038	1106	1206	1238	1306	...	1406	1438	1506	1606	1638
62	Kolín .... △ d.	0058	...	0455	0526	0655	0731	0755	0855	0931	0955	1055	1055	1131	1155	1255	1331	1355	...	1455	1531	1555	1655	1731
104	**Pardubice** .... △ d.	0126	...	0519	0555	0719	0800	0823	0923	1000	1023	1123	1123	1200	1219	1319	1400	1423	...	1519	1600	1623	1719	1800
139	Choceň .... △ d.	0147	...	|	0613	|	0818	|	|	1018	|	|	|	1218	|	|	1418	|	...	|	1618	|	|	1818
154	Ústí nad Orlicí .... △ d.	0201	...	|	0627	|	0832	|	|	1032	|	|	|	1232	|	|	1432	|	...	|	1632	|	|	1832
164	Česká Třebová .... △ d.	0212	...	0555	0644	0755	0843	0859	0959	1043	1059	1159	1159	1243	1300	1355	1443	1459	...	1555	1643	1659	1755	1843
206	Zábřeh na Moravé .... d.	|	...	0620	0713	0820	0913	|	|	1113	|	|	|	1309	|	1420	1513	|	...	1620	1713	|	1820	1913
252	**Olomouc** .... a.	0309	...	0654	0749	0854	0949	0954	1054	1149	1154	1254	1254	1345	1355	1454	1549	1554	...	1654	1749	1754	1854	1949
252	**Olomouc** .... d.	0312	...	0657	0752	0857	0952	0957	1057	1152	1157	1257	1257	1348	1357	1457	1552	1557	...	1657	1752	1757	1857	1952
274	Přerov .... a.	|	...	|	0806	|	1006	|	|	|	1211	|	|	1402	|	|	|	1611	...	|	1806	|	|	|
274	Přerov .... ▷ d.	|	...	|	0831	|	*1026*	|	|	|	*1226*	|	|	*1426*	|	|	|	*1626*	...	|	*1826*	|	|	|
303	Hranice na Moravě .... ▷ d.	0344	...	0725	0854	0925	*1044*	1027	1125	1227	*1244*	1325	1325	*1444*	1427	1525	1627	*1644*	...	1725	*1844*	1827	1925	2027
353	Ostrava Svinov .... ▷ d.	0420	0540	0753	|	1001	*1118*	|	1153	|	*1318*	1355	1404	*1518*	|	1553	|	*1718*	1720	1753	*1918*	|	|	|
358	**Ostrava** hlavní .... ▷ d.	0429	0549	0802	|	1010	*1127*	|	1202	|	*1327*	1404	|	*1527*	|	1602	|	*1727*	1712*	1802	*1927*	|	|	|
	Ostrava Vitkovice .... d.	|	|	|	|	|	|	|	|	|	|	|	1412	|	|	|	|	|	1727	|	|	|	2002	|
366	Bohumín .... ▷ a.	0438	0557	0810	|	1019	*1135*	|	1210	|	*1335*	1412	|	*1535*	|	1610	|	*1735*	|	1810	*1935*	|	|	|
366	Bohumín .... d.	0439	0558	0820	|	...	...	|	1220	|	...	1434	|	...	|	1620	|	...	1702*	...	...	|	|	|
	Katowice **1076** .... a.	|	|	|	|	...	...	|	|	|	...	1556	|	...	|	|	|	...	|	...	...	|	|	|
381	Karviná hlavní .... d.	0450	0611	0832	|	...	...	|	1232	|	...	...	|	...	|	1632	|	...	|	...	...	|	|	|
397	Český Těšín .... **1077** d.	0509	0628	0851	|	...	...	|	1251	|	...	...	1443	...	|	1651	|	...	1803	...	...	|	2033	|
435	Čadca .... **1077** d.	0603	0724	0943	|	...	...	|	1343	|	...	...	1535	...	|	1743	|	...	1902	...	...	|	...	|
329	Valašské Meziříčí .... d.	|	|	|	0919	...	...	1051	|	1252	...	...	|	...	1451	|	1652	...	|	...	...	1851	...	2052
348	**Vsetín** .... d.	|	|	|	0935	...	...	1109	|	1308	...	...	|	...	1509	|	1708	...	|	...	...	1909	...	2108
339	Horní Lideč .... d.	|	|	|	...	...	...	1128	|	...	...	...	|	...	1528	|	...	...	|	...	...	1928	...	...
394	Púchov .... **1180** d.	|	|	|	...	...	...	1151	|	...	...	...	|	...	1551	|	...	...	|	...	...	1951	...	...
△439	**Žilina** .... **1180** a.	0633	*0815*	1013	...	...	...	1228	1413	...	...	...	1605	...	1628	1813	...	...	1932	...	...	2028	...	...
	Košice **1180** .... a.	0950	...	...	...	...	...	...	...	...	...	...	...	...	1921	...	...	...	...	...	...	...	...	...

	Ex 521	*IC* 581	621	701	423	201	225	209	
	X	X	X					⊠	
	Y⊕		B	⑧n	♦K	♦	♦W	♦	
Praha hlavní .... △ d.	1706	1806	1838	1938	2006	2124	2206	2256	...
Kolín .... △ d.	1755	1855	1931	2031	2057	2214	2300	2347	...
Pardubice .... △ d.	1823	1923	2000	2106	2124	2241	2330	0014	...
Choceň .... △ d.	|	|	2018	2124	|	|	|	|	...
Ústí nad Orlicí .... △ d.	|	|	2032	2138	|	|	|	|	...
Česká Třebová .... △ d.	1859	1959	2043	2149	2203	2324	0011	|	...
Zábřeh na Moravé .... d.	|	|	2108	2213	|	2350	0039	|	...
Olomouc .... a.	1954	2054	2144	2246	2304	0023	0112	0151	...
Olomouc .... d.	1957	2057	2147	2249	2308	0026	0115	0154	...
Přerov .... a.	2011	|	|	2304	|	|	0131	|	...
Přerov .... ▷ d.	*2026*	|	|	...	|	|	0148	|	...
Hranice na Moravě .... ▷ d.	*2044*	2125	2221	...	2338	0057	|	|	...
Ostrava Svinov .... ▷ d.	*2118*	2201	|	...	0017	0126	|	0251	...
Ostrava hlavní .... ▷ d.	*2127*	2210	|	...	0026	0135	|	0300	...
Ostrava Vitkovice .... d.	|	|	|	...	|	|	|	|	...
Bohumín .... ▷ a.	*2135*	2219	|	...	0035	0144	|	0310	...
Bohumín .... d.	...	2222	|	...	0119	0251	|	...	...
Katowice **1076** .... a.	...	|	|	...	|	0418	|	...	...
Karviná hlavní .... d.	...	2233	|	...	0130	...	|	...	...
Český Těšín .... **1077** d.	...	2250	|	...	0149	...	|	...	...
Čadca .... **1077** d.	...	...	|	...	0250	...	|	...	...
Valašské Meziříčí .... d.	...	...	2246	...	|	...	0233	...	...
Vsetín .... d.	...	...	2302	...	|	...	0253	...	...
Horní Lideč .... d.	...	...	...	...	|	...	0315	...	...
Púchov .... **1180** d.	...	...	...	...	|	...	0339	...	...
Žilina .... **1180** a.	...	...	...	...	0320	...	0416	...	...
Košice **1180** .... a.	...	...	...	...	0650	...	0754	...	...

	208	224	200	700	422	620	*Ex* 520	*IC* 580	622
	⊠					X	X	X	X
	♦	♦W	♦	⚒q	♦K	D	Z⊖		
Košice **1180** .... d.	...	2022	...	...	2222	...	...	...	...
Žilina .... **1180** d.	...	2354	...	...	0132	...	...	...	...
Púchov .... **1180** d.	...	0032	...	...	|	...	...	...	...
Horní Lideč .... d.	...	0100	...	...	|	...	...	...	...
Vsetín .... d.	...	0120	...	...	|	0440	...	...	0639
Valašské Meziříčí .... d.	...	0139	...	...	|	0458	...	...	0656
Čadca .... **1077** d.	...	|	...	...	0205	|	...	...	|
Český Těšín .... **1077** d.	...	|	...	...	0259	|	...	0517	|
Karviná hlavní .... d.	...	|	...	...	0315	|	...	0533	|
Katowice **1076** .... d.	...	|	2352	...	|	|	...	|	|
Bohumín .... a.	...	|	0121	...	0326	|	...	0544	|
Bohumín .... ▷ d.	0033	|	0220	...	0358	|	...	0545	|
Ostrava Vitkovice .... d.	|	|	|	...	|	|	...	|	|
Ostrava hlavní .... ▷ d.	0045	|	0231	...	0409	|	...	0556	|
Ostrava Svinov .... ▷ d.	0055	|	0240	...	0418	|	...	0604	|
Hranice na Moravě .... ▷ d.	|	|	0307	...	0456	0524	...	0636	0724
Přerov .... ▷ a.	|	0220	|	...	|	|	...	|	|
Přerov .... d.	|	0250	|	0452	|	|	0550	|	|
Olomouc .... a.	0151	0306	0337	0506	0526	0557	0604	0704	0757
Olomouc .... d.	0155	0309	0340	0509	0529	0600	0607	0707	0800
Zábřeh na Moravé .... d.	|	0346	0416	0542	0601	0646	|	0739	0846
Česká Třebová .... △ d.	|	0413	0443	0606	0628	0712	0706	0806	0912
Ústí nad Orlicí .... △ d.	|	|	0452	|	|	0721	|	|	0921
Choceň .... △ d.	|	|	0506	|	|	0734	|	|	0934
Pardubice .... △ d.	0341	0454	0528	0643	0707	0756	0743	0843	0956
Kolín .... △ d.	0409	0524	0554	0708	0735	0825	0808	0908	1025
Praha hlavní .... △ a.	0503	0621	0645	0800	0829	0919	0900	0959	1119

	Ex 522	*IC* 540	702	432	*Ex* 128	*EC* 108	624	440	1604 *EC*144	*EC* 144	704	*Ex* 120	*EC* 106	626	*Ex* 524	*EC* 142	706	*Ex* 126	*IC* 582	628	*Ex* 140	2912	420	
	X	Y	X	2		X	X		X	X	X	X	X		X	X	X	X	X	X		2		
	V		L			♦				♦‡	L	§	♦		V	‡	L						♦	
Košice **1180** .... d.	...	...	...	...	...	...	...	...	...	...	...	0839	...	...	...	...	...	...	...	...	...	...	1822	...
Žilina .... **1180** d.	...	...	...	0637	0735	...	...	0842	...	0942	...	1135	...	...	...	1342	...	1535	...	...	1742	...	2137	...
Púchov .... **1180** d.	...	...	...	|	0812	...	...	|	...	|	...	1212	...	...	...	|	...	1612	...	...	|	...	|	...
Horní Lideč .... d.	...	...	...	|	0837	...	...	|	...	|	...	1237	...	...	...	|	...	1637	...	...	|	...	|	...
Vsetín .... d.	...	...	...	|	0854	...	1025	|	...	|	...	1254	...	1440	...	|	...	1654	...	1825	|	...	|	...
Valašské Meziříčí .... d.	...	...	...	|	0911	...	1043	|	...	|	...	1311	...	1458	...	|	...	1711	...	1843	|	...	|	...
Čadca .... **1077** d.	...	...	...	0710	|	...	|	0915	...	1015	...	|	...	|	...	1415	...	|	...	|	1815	2038	2210	...
Český Těšín .... **1077** d.	...	0728	...	0801	|	...	|	1008	...	1112	...	|	...	|	...	1507	...	|	...	|	1907	2142	2301	...
Karviná hlavní .... d.	...	|	...	|	|	...	|	1024	...	|	...	|	...	|	...	1523	...	|	...	|	1923	2200	2317	...
Katowice **1076** .... d.	...	|	...	|	|	...	|	|	...	|	...	|	1150	|	...	|	...	|	...	|	|	|	|	...
Bohumín .... a.	...	|	...	0857*	|	...	|	1035	...	|	...	|	1324	|	...	1534	...	|	...	|	1934	2215	2328	...
Bohumín .... ▷ d.	*0623*	|	*0823*	|	|	0950	|	...	1134	|	*1223*	|	1350	|	*1423*	1550	*1623*	|	1745	|	1950	*2218*	2329	...
Ostrava Vitkovice .... d.	|	0802	|	0831	|	|	|	...	|	1145	|	|	|	|	|	|	|	|	|	|	|	|	|	...
Ostrava hlavní .... ▷ d.	*0633*	|	*0833*	0847*	|	1001	|	...	1144	|	*1233*	|	1401	|	*1433*	1601	*1633*	|	1756	|	2001	*2228*	2340	...
Ostrava Svinov .... ▷ d.	*0641*	|	*0841*	0837	|	1010	|	...	1210z	1210z	*1241*	|	1410	|	*1441*	1610	*1641*	|	1804	|	2010	*2235*	2349	...
Hranice na Moravě .... ▷ d.	*0714*	0836	*0914*	...	0936	1036	1108	...	1236	1236	*1314*	1336	1436	1524	*1514*	1636	*1714*	1736	1836	1908	2036	...	0025	...
Přerov .... ▷ a.	*0731*	|	*0931*	...	|	|	1127	...	|	|	*1331*	|	|	|	*1531*	|	*1731*	|	|	1927	|	...	|	...
Přerov .... d.	0750	|	0943	...	|	|	1143	...	|	|	1343	|	|	|	1554	|	1743	|	|	1943	|	...	|	...
Olomouc .... a.	0804	0904	0957	...	1004	1104	1157	...	1304	1304	1357	1404	1504	1557	1608	1704	1757	1804	1904	1957	2104	...	0056	...
Olomouc .... d.	0807	0907	1000	...	1007	1107	1200	...	1307	1307	1400	1407	1507	1600	1611	1707	1800	1807	1907	2000	2107	...	0059	...
Zábřeh na Moravé .... d.	|	0939	1046	...	|	1139	1246	...	1339	1339	1446	|	1539	1646	|	1739	1846	|	1939	2036	2139	...	|	...
Česká Třebová .... △ d.	0906	1006	1112	...	1106	1206	1312	...	1406	1406	1512	1506	1606	1712	1706	1806	1912	1906	2006	2106	2206	...	0154	...
Ústí nad Orlicí .... △ d.	|	|	1121	...	|	|	1321	...	|	|	1521	|	|	1721	|	|	1921	|	|	2115	|	...	|	...
Choceň .... △ d.	|	|	1134	...	|	|	1334	...	|	|	1534	|	|	1734	|	|	1934	|	|	2128	|	...	|	...
Pardubice .... △ d.	0943	1043	1156	...	1143	1243	1356	...	1443	1443	1556	1543	1643	1756	1743	1843	1956	1943	2043	2150	2243	...	0235	...
Kolín .... △ d.	1008	1108	1225	...	1208	1308	1425	...	1508	1508	1625	1608	1708	1825	1808	1908	2025	2008	2108	2219	2308	...	0303	...
Praha hlavní .... △ a.	1100	1159	1319	...	1300	1400	1519	...	1600	1600	1719	1700	1800	1919	1900	1959	2119	2100	2159	2312	2359	...	0355	...

FOR NOTES SEE FOOT OF NEXT PAGE

FOR FASTEST TRAINS SEE TOP OF PAGE

BRNO - PŘEROV - OSTRAVA - BOHUMÍN 1161

km		202	731	831	733	833	735	EC 104		737	837	739	839	741	EC 102	841	743	843	745	IC 130	1539	663	
		♦	⊖					♦			Ⓐ				♦			Ⓑn	⊕	♦	†e	R⊕	
0	**Brno** hlavní ... 1164 d.	...	0503	0603	0703	0803	0903	...	...	1103	1203	1303	1403	1503	...	1603	1703	1803	1903	...	2003	2103	...
45	Vyškov na Moravě ... 1164 d.	...	0543	0643	0743	0843	0943	...	...	1143	1243	1343	1443	1543	...	1643	1743	1843	1943	...	2043	2141	...
	Wien Südbahnhof **999** ... d.	2233	|	|	|	|	|	0908	...	|	|	|	|	|	1433	|	|	|	|	...	|	|	...
	Břeclav **1162** ... d.	0005	|	|	|	|	|	1019	...	|	|	|	|	|	1552	|	|	|	|	1945	|	|	...
88	**Přerov** ... a.	0105	0623	0723	0823	0923	1023	1119	...	1223	1323	1423	1523	1623	1651	1723	1823	1923	2023	2045	2123	2223	...
88	**Přerov** ... ▽ d.	0110	0626	0725	0826	0926	1026	1120	...	1226	1326	1426	1526	1626	1652	1726	1826	1926	2026	2047	2126	2226	...
117	Hranice na Moravě ... ▽ d.	|	0644	|	0844	|	1044	|	...	1244	|	1444	|	1644	|	|	1844	|	2044	2105	|	2244	...
167	Ostrava Svinov ... ▽ a.	0153	0716	0809	0916	1009	1116	1202	...	1316	1409	1516	1609	1716	1735	1809	1916	2009	2116	2131	2209	2316	...
172	**Ostrava** hlavní ... ▽ a.	0202	0725	0819	0925	1019	1125	1211	...	1325	1419	1525	1619	1725	1745	1819	1925	2019	2125	2140	2219	2325	...
180	Bohumín ... ▽ a.	0213	0735	0829	0935	1029	1135	1221	...	1335	1429	1535	1629	1735	1755	1829	1935	2029	2135	2150	2229	2335	...

	203	662	1600	830	IC 131	730	832	732		EC 103	734	836	736	838	738	EC 105	840	740	842	742	1538	744	
	♦	R⊖	⑥	⚒q	♦	⊖				♦		Ⓐ				♦					†e	⊕	
Bohumín ... ▽ d.	0213	0423	0453	0538	0610	0623	0738	0823	...	1014	1023	1138	1223	1338	1423	1514	1538	1623	1738	1823	1938	2023	...
Ostrava hlavní ... ▽ d.	0224	0433	0503	0548	0620	0633	0748	0833	...	1024	1033	1148	1233	1348	1433	1524	1548	1633	1748	1833	1948	2033	...
Ostrava Svinov ... ▽ d.	0233	0441	0511	0556	0629	0641	0756	0841	...	1032	1041	1156	1241	1356	1441	1532	1556	1641	1756	1841	1956	2041	...
Hranice na Moravě ... ▽ d.	|	0514	|	|	0654	0714	|	0914	...	|	1114	|	1314	|	1514	|	|	1714	|	1914	|	2114	...
Přerov ... ▽ a.	0315	0531	0558	0637	0711	0731	0837	0931	...	1111	1131	1237	1331	1437	1531	1611	1637	1731	1837	1931	2037	2131	...
Přerov ... d.	0330	0539	...	0639	0713	0739	0839	0939	...	1113	1139	1239	1339	1439	1539	1613	1639	1739	1839	1939	2039	2139	...
Břeclav **1162** ... a.	0430	|	...	|	0814	|	|	|	...	1214	|	|	|	|	|	1714	|	|	|	|	|	|	...
Wien Südbahnhof **999** ... a.	0603	|	...	|	...	|	|	|	...	1328	|	|	|	|	|	1828	|	|	|	|	|	|	...
Vyškov na Moravě ... 1164 d.	...	0618	...	0718	...	0818	0918	1018	...	...	1218	1318	1418	1518	1618	...	1718	1818	1918	2018	2118	2218	...
Brno hlavní ... 1164 d.	...	0701	...	0757	...	0857	0957	1057	...	...	1257	1357	1457	1557	1657	...	1757	1857	1957	2057	2155	2255	...

FOR NOTES SEE BELOW

OLOMOUC - UHERSKÉ HRADIŠTĚ - LUHAČOVICE / BŘECLAV 1162

km		203	1820	928	IC 131	800	◇	802	705	EC 103	804	Ex 525	806	707	808	EC 105	Ex 523	810	703	812	Ex 521	814	◇
		♦W	⊖	✕	♦				✕	♦		✕		✕		♦	✕		✕	⊕	Y⊕	⊕	⊕
	Praha hlavní **1160** ... d.	...	...	...	...	...	...	...	0638	...	...	0906	...	1038	...	...	1306	...	1438	...	1706	...	...
0	**Olomouc** ... 1160 d.	...	0500a	0532	0632	0720	0752	0920	0952	1032	1120	1157	1320	1348	1520	1532	1557	1720	1752	1920	1957	2120	2157
22	Přerov ... 1160 a.	...	0519a	0552	0652	0734	0806	0934	1006	1052	1134	1211	1334	1402	1534	1552	1611	1734	1806	1934	2011	2134	2217
22	Přerov ... d.	0330	0536	0605	0713	0736	0828	0936	1009	1113	1136	1215	1336	1409	1536	1613	1617	1736	1810	1936	2015	2136	2228
37	Hulín ... d.	|	0548	0617	|	0748	0845	0948	1021	|	1148	1226	1348	1421	1548	|	1628	1748	1821	1948	2026	2148	2247
50	Otrokovice ... ★ d.	0347	0559	0626	0731	0758	0858	0958	1031	1131	1158	1236	1358	1431	1558	1631	1637	1758	1831	1958	2034	2158	2300
68	**Staré Město u Uherské Hradiště** .. a.	0357	0608	0637	0740	0807	0913	1007	1042	1140	1207	1246	1407	1442	1607	1640	1647	1807	1842	2007	...	2207	2316
68	**Staré Město u Uherské Hradiště** .. d.	0358	0610	0647	0742	0809	0914	1009	1053	1142	1209	1300	1409	1452	1609	1642	1657	1809	1853	2009	...	2209	...
73	Uherské Hradiště ... ⊖ d.	|	|	0658	|	|	|	|	1100	|	|	1307	|	1502	|	|	1704	|	1900	|	...	|	...
75	Kunovice ... d.	|	|	0704	|	|	|	|	1104	|	|	|	|	1507	|	|	1708	|	|	|	...	|	...
87	Veseli nad Moravou ... a.	|	|	|	|	|	|	|	|	|	|	1326	|	|	|	|	|	|	1919	|	...	|	...
90	Uherský Brod ... d.	|	|	0719	|	|	|	|	1119	|	|	...	|	1524	|	|	1723	|	...	|	...	|	...
104	**Luhačovice** ... a.	|	|	0740	|	|	|	|	1139	|	|	...	|	1547	|	|	1743	|	...	|	...	|	...
102	Hodonin ... d.	0416	0631	...	0800	0831	0954	1031	...	1200	1231	...	1431	...	1631	1700	...	1831	...	2031	...	2231	...
122	**Břeclav** ... a.	0430	0647	...	0814	0845	1015	1045	...	1214	1245	...	1445	...	1645	1714	...	1845	...	2045	...	2245	...

	202	Ex 520	801	Ex 522	803	◇	702	805	EC 104	807	704	809	◇	Ex 524	811	EC 102	706	813	◇	929	815	IC 130	1821
	♦W	Z⊖	⊖	✕			✕		♦		✕			✕		♦	✕			✕	⊕	♦	⊕
Břeclav ... d.	0005	...	0532	...	0713	0754	...	0911	1019	1111	...	1311	1346	...	1511	1552	...	1711	1746	...	1911	1945	2109
Hodonin ... d.	0019	...	0546	...	0727	0815	...	0925	1033	1125	...	1325	1407	...	1525	1606	...	1725	1807	...	1925	1959	2125
Luhačovice ... d.	|	...	|	...	|	|	0806	|	|	|	1206	|	|	...	|	|	1606	|	|	1806	|	|	|
Uherský Brod ... d.	|	...	|	...	|	|	0827	|	|	|	1227	|	|	...	|	|	1627	|	|	1827	|	|	|
Veseli nad Moravou ... d.	|	...	|	0642	|	|	|	|	|	|	|	|	|	1445	|	|	|	|	|	|	|	|	|
Kunovice ... d.	|	...	|	|	|	|	0841	|	|	|	1241	|	|	|	|	|	1641	|	|	1841	|	|	|
Uherské Hradiště ... ⊖ d.	|	...	|	0657	|	|	0846	|	|	|	1246	|	|	1501	|	|	1646	|	|	1846	|	|	|
Staré Město u Uherské Hradiště ... a.	0036	...	0605	0704	0746	0847	0853	0944	1050	1144	1253	1344	1441	1507	1544	1623	1653	1744	1841	1853	1944	2016	2144
Staré Město u Uherské Hradiště ... d.	0037	...	0606	0717	0747	0848	0907	0946	1051	1146	1307	1346	1444	1518	1546	1624	1707	1746	1844	1907	1946	2017	2146
Otrokovice ... ★ d.	0048	0529	0618	0729	0758	0905	0919	0958	1102	1158	1319	1358	1500	1530	1558	1634	1719	1758	1900	1919	1958	2028	2158
Hulín ... d.	|	0539	0628	0738	0808	0918	0929	1008	|	1208	1329	1408	1515	1539	1608	|	1729	1808	1915	1928	2008	|	2208
Přerov ... a.	0105	0549	0639	0748	0818	0933	0940	1018	1119	1218	1340	1418	1530	1550	1618	1651	1740	1818	1930	1938	2018	2045	2220
Přerov ... 1160 d.	...	0550	0641	0750	0820	...	0943	1020	1143	1220	1343	1420	1536a	1554	1620	1705	1743	1820	...	1943	2020	2105	2245
Olomouc ... 1160 a.	...	0604	0655	0804	0834	...	0957	1034	1157	1234	1357	1434	1555a	1608	1634	1724	1757	1834	...	1957	2034	2124	2304
Praha hlavní **1160** ... a.	...	0900	...	1100	...	...	1319	...	...	...	1719	...	...	1900	...	...	2119	...	...	2312	...	...	...

FOR NOTES SEE BELOW

BRNO - PROSTĚJOV - OLOMOUC - JESENIK 1164

km		903	1701	909	931	933	905	907	935	1707	937
			©							⊕	c
0	**Brno** hlavní ... 1161 d.	0516	...	0719	0919	1119	1319	1519	1719	...	1919
45	Vyškov na Moravé . 1161 d.	0600	...	0800	1000	1200	1400	1600	1800	...	2000
61	Nezamyslice ... d.	0619	...	0819	1019	1219	1419	1619	1819	...	2019
80	Prostějov ... d.	0635	...	0835	1035	1235	1435	1635	1835	...	2035
100	**Olomouc** ... a.	0651	...	0851	1051	1251	1451	1651	1851	...	2051
100	**Olomouc** ... 1160 d.	0658	0746	0854	...	1258	1454	1654	...	1858	...
146	Zábřeh na Moravé .. 1160 d.	0740	0826	0940	...	1340	1540	1740	...	1940	...
176	Hanušovice ... d.	0810	0900	1013	...	1410	1610	1812	...	2012	...
212	**Jesenik** ... a.	0915	1011	1125	...	1515	1715	1916	...	2114	...

	1646	930	902	904	932	934	906	1704	908	1436
	⚒							©		†e
Jesenik ... d.	...	...	0633	0838	...	1241	1438	1546	1639	...
Hanušovice ... d.	...	...	0747	0947	...	1345	1547	1652	1747	...
Zábřeh na Moravé . 1160 d.	...	...	0827	1027	...	1423	1627	1725	1827	...
Olomouc ... 1160 a.	...	...	0900	1100	...	1501	1700	1803	1900	...
Olomouc ... d.	0600	0707	0907	1107	1307	1507	1707	...	1907	2107
Prostějov ... d.	0616	0725	0925	1125	1325	1525	1725	...	1925	2125
Nezamyslice ... d.	0637	0742	0939	1139	1339	1539	1739	...	1939	2139
Vyškov na Moravé 1161 d.	0659	0801	1001	1201	1401	1601	1801	...	2001	2157
Brno hlavní ... 1161 a.	0739	0838	1038	1238	1438	1638	1838	...	2038	2231

♦ – **NOTES FOR TABLES 1160/1161/1162/1164** (LISTED BY TRAIN NUMBER)

102/3 – POLONIA – (12) ✕ Wien Süd - Břeclav - Katowice - Warszawa and v.v.; (2) Wien Süd - Petrovice (**108/9**) - Kraków and v.v.

104/5 – SOBIESKI – (12) ✕ Wien Süd - Břeclav - Katowice - Warszawa and v.v.

106/7 – PRAHA – (12) ✕ Praha - Ostrava - Katowice - Warszawa and v.v.

108/9 – COMENIUS – (12) ✕ Praha - Ostrava - Kraków and v.v.

130/1 – MORAVIA – (12) 🍸 Budapest - Bratislava - Břeclav - Ostrava - Bohumin and v.v.

144/5 – DETVAN – (12) Praha - Ostrava Svinov - Žilina - Zvolen and v.v.

200/1 – SILESIA – 🛏 1, 2 cl., ▬ 2 cl. (12) Praha - Kraków and v.v.; 🛏 1, 2 cl., ▬ 2 cl. (2) Praha - Bohumín (**202/3**) - Warszawa and v.v.; (2) Praha - Ostrava - Bohumín and v.v.; 🛏 1, 2 cl. Praha - Kraków - Przemysl - Lviv - Kyïv and v.v.

202/3 – CHOPIN – 🛏 1, 2 cl., ▬ 2 cl., (2) Wien Süd - Warszawa and v.v.; 🛏 1, 2 cl. Wien - Bohumín (**200/1**) - Kraków and v.v. (also ▬ 2 cl. from Wien Apr. 30 - Sept. 28, from Kraków Apr. 29 - Sept. 27); 🛏 1, 2 cl. Wien - Bohumín (**208/9**) - Minsk - Moskva and v.v.; 🛏 1, 2 cl., ▬ 2 cl., (2) Budapest (**376/7**) - Bratislava - Břeclav (**202/3**) - Warszawa and v.v.; 🛏 1, 2 cl., ▬ 2 cl. Budapest (**376/7**) - Bratislava - Břeclav (**202/3**) - Bohumín (**201/0**) - Kraków and v.v.; 🛏 1, 2 cl. Budapest (**376/7**) - Bratislava - Břeclav (**202/3**) - Bohumín (**208/9**) - Minsk - Moskva and v.v.

208/9 – VLTAVA – 🛏 1, 2 cl. Praha - Ostrava - Minsk - Moskva and v.v. (also Praha - Minsk on ②④⑦, Minsk - Praha on ①③⑥); 🛏 1, 2 cl. Cheb (**605/4**) - Karlovy Vary - Praha (**209/8**) - Moskva and v.v. Conveys on dates in Table **95**, 🛏 1, 2 cl. Praha - Brest - St Peterburg and v.v.

224/5 – ŠÍRAVA – 🛏 1, 2 cl., ▬ 2 cl., (12) Praha - Žilina - Košice - Humenné and v.v.; 🛏 1, 2 cl. Praha - Žilina (**1846/7**) - Banská Bystrica and v.v.

420/1 – EXCELSIOR – 🛏 1, 2 cl., ▬ 2 cl., (12) Cheb - Karlovy Vary - Praha - Žilina - Košice and v.v.; 🛏 1, 2 cl., ▬ 2 cl. Plzeň (**377/6**) - Praha - Žilina - Košice and v.v.; (2) Františkovy Lázně (**377/6**) - Plzeň - Praha - Žilina - Košice and v.v.

422/3 – CASSOVIA – (12) and ✕ Praha - Ostrava - Bohumín and v.v.; 🛏 1, 2 cl., ▬ 2 cl., (2) Praha - Bohumnín - Žilina - Košice and v.v.

B – Daily to Olomouc (not Dec. 24, 31); Ⓑ **n** to Vsetín.

D – ⚒**q** from Vsetín; daily (not Dec. 25, Jan. 1) from Olomouc.

K – Conveys (not Dec. 24, 31) 🛏 1, 2 cl. České Budějovice (**662/3**) - Brno - Bohumín (**422/3**) - Žilina - Košice and v.v.

L – To/from Luhacovice (Table **1162**).

R – ROŽMBERK – (12) Bohumin - Ostrava - Přerov - Brno - Jihlava - České Budějovice - Plzeň and v.v.

V – (12) Praha - Přerov - Veseli nad Moravou and v.v. (Table **1162**).

W – Conveys 🛏 1, 2 cl. Praha (**225/4**) - Přerov (**203/2**) - Břeclav - Wien and v.v.

Y – (12) Praha - Přerov - Zlín střed (arrive 2056).

Z – (12) Zlín střed (depart 0502) - Přerov - Praha.

a – Ⓐ only.

c – Not Dec. 24

e – Not Dec. 23 - 30, Mar. 23, May 1, 8, July 5, Oct. 26, Nov. 16.

n – Not Dec. 23 - 25, 31, Mar. 23, July 5, Nov. 16.

q – Also May 1, 8, Oct. 28.

v – † (also Dec. 21, Jan. 2, Mar. 21, Apr. 30, May 7, June 27, Oct. 24, 31, Nov. 14; not Dec. 23 - 30, Mar. 23, May 1, 8, July 5, Oct. 26, Nov. 16).

y – Praha **hlavní**.

z – Arrive 1152.

★ – Connection to **Zlín** by local train (1 - 2 per hour) or trolleybus (every 10 minutes), *11 km*.

⊕ – Not Dec. 24, 31.

⊖ – Not Dec. 25, Jan. 1.

⊖ – Connecting trains run to/from Staré Město u Uherské Hradiště (journey 7 mins).

◇ – Local train, 2nd class.

△ – See also Table **1150**.

▷ – See also Table **1161**.

▽ – See also Table **1160**.

⊠ – For international journeys only.

▵ – *466 km* via Ostrava.

‡ – Classified *Ex* in Slovakia.

§ – Classified *EC* in Slovakia.

• – Via Ostrava-Svinov.

1166 OLOMOUC / JESENIK - OPAVA - OSTRAVA
2nd class only

km		881 ⊖	819	1629	883	821	823	885	825	827	887	829 ⊕
0	**Olomouc** d.	...	0709	0903	...	1109	1309	...	1509	1709	...	1909
64	Bruntál d.	...	0832	1032	...	1232	1432	...	1632	1832	...	2032
• 58	**Jesenik** d.	0535	|	|	0935	|	|	1335	*1518**	|	1735	|
• 17	Tremešná ve Slez. △ d.	0643	|	|	1043	|	|	1443	*1641**	|	1843	|
87	Krnov d.	0708	0908	1057	1108	1308	1508	1508	1708	1908	1908	2057
116	Opava východ ▶ d.	0746	0946	...	1146	1346	1546	1546	1746	1946	1946	*2137*
144	**Ostrava** Svinov ▶ a.	0806	1006	...	1206	1406	1606	1606	1806	2006	2006	...

	880	820	822	882	1628	824	884	826	828	886 ⊕
Ostrava Svinov ▶ d.	0612	0612	0812	1012	*1012*	1212	1412	1412	1612	1812
Opava východ ▶ d.	0634	0634	0836	1036	*1036*	1236	1434	1434	1636	1836
Krnov d.	0711	0710	0910	1111	1110	1310	1511	1510	1710	1911
Tremešná ve Slez. △ a.	0727	|	*0929**	1127	|	|	1527	|	*1729**	1927
Jesenik a.	0834	|	*1054**	1234	|	|	1635	|	*1855**	2038
Bruntál d.	...	0739	0939	...	1139	1339	...	1539	1739	...
Olomouc a.	...	0852	1052	...	1301	1452	...	1652	1852	...

⊕ – Not Dec. 24, 31.
⊖ – Not Dec. 25, Jan. 1.
• – Distance from Krnov.
△ – Station for narrow gauge line to Osoblaha (6 - 7 trains per day, *20 km*).
* – Local train, change at Krnov.
▶ – Local trains **Opava - Ostrava** (journey 32 - 40 minutes):
From Opava východ: 0333, 0430, 0528, 0551, 0633, 0730 and hourly to 2030, 2140, 2240, 2342.
From Ostrava Svinov: 0030, 0445, 0543, 0648, 0745 and hourly to 1945, 2012, 2048, 2153, 2212, 2254.

1168 BRNO - UHERSKÉ HRADIŠTĚ - TRENČIANSKA TEPLÁ
2nd class only

km		◇	1721 d	1723	◇	1725	1727	1729 b	1731	1733 ⊕	1735 ⊗
0	**Brno** hlavní d.	...	0734	0931	...	1131	1331	1531	1731	1931	2131
67	Kyjov d.	...	0841	1038	...	1238	1438	1638	1838	2038	2234
90	Veselí nad Moravou d.	...	0907	1107	...	1307	1507	1707	1907	2113	2300
104	**Kunovice** a.	...	0924	1126	...	|	1520	1724	1927	2130	▬
106	Uherské Hradiště a.	...	*0931*	*1132*	...	1328	*1526*	*1734*	*1934*	*2135*	...
	Staré Město u Uh. H ▷ d.	*0720*	*0916*	*1116*	1253	▬	*1452*	*1718*	*1916*	*2059*a	...
	Uherské Hradiště ▷ d.	0745	*0923*	*1123*	1300	...	*1502*	*1724*	*1925*	*2123*	...
104	**Kunovice** ▷ d.	0750	0928	1129	1305	...	1521	1730	1931	2131	...
119	Uherský Brod ▷ d.	0812	0947	1153	1327	...	1541	1756	1952	2151	...
132	Bojkovice d.	0835	1007	1214	1359	...	1601	1821	2012	2212	...
160	Bylnice a.	0918	1045	1301	1440	...	1642	1902	...	2250	...
165	Vlárský průsmyk a.	0925	1101	*1328*	1448	Ⓑz	...	1917	...	...	...
165	Vlárský průsmyk 🏛 d.	...	*1106*c	...	...	1450	...	*1956*	...	...	0703
175	**Trenčianska Teplá** a.	...	*1123*c	...	...	1512	...	*2017*	...	...	0720

	1722	1724	1726	1728 d	◇ ⑦e	1730 d	1732 n	◇ Ⓐ	1734 ⊙	1736 ⊗b
Trenčianska Teplá d.	...	*0643*	...	*0952*c	1246	...	...	*1343*	...	*1911*
Vlárský průsmyk 🏛 a.	...	*0700*	...	*1011*c	1306	...	...	*1403*	...	*1929*
Vlárský průsmyk d.	...	0702	...	1042	...	1309	...	1407	...	1931
Bylnice d.	0539	0710	...	1105	...	1321	...	1415	...	1939
Bojkovice d.	0622	0750	...	1142	...	1400	...	1513	1747	2018
Uherský Brod ▷ d.	0644	0811	...	1203	...	1422	...	1540	1808	2038
Kunovice ▷ a.	0702	0830	...	1222	...	1442	...	1603	1827	2056
Uherské Hradiště ▷ a.	*0710*	*0835*	...	1226	...	*1449*	...	1607	*1832*	*2102*
Staré Město u Uh. H ▷ a.	*0737*	*0843*r	...	*1239*	...	*1507*r	...	*1639*	*1839*	*2141*r
Uherské Hradiště d.	*0658*	*0824*	*1034*	1238	...	*1435*	*1634*	...	*1822*	*2051*
Kunovice d.	0704	0832	|	|	...	1444	1642	...	1831	2057
Veselí nad Moravou d.	0719	0906	1106	1306	...	1506	1706	...	1906	2112
Kyjov d.	0743	0934	1134	1334	...	1534	1734	...	1934	2140
Brno hlavní a.	0844	1039	1239	1439	...	1639	1839	...	2039	2245

a – Ⓐ only.
b – Change at Bojkovice on Ⓐ.
c – June 28 - Aug. 31.
d – Change at Bylnice.
e – Also Jan. 1, Mar. 24, Nov. 17; not Dec. 23, 30, Mar. 23, Oct. 26, Nov. 16.
n – Change at Veselí nad Moravou on ⚒.
r – Change at Kunovice and Uherské Hradiště.
z – Not Dec. 23 - 26, 30, Mar. 21, 23, May 1, 8, Aug. 29, Sept. 1, 15, Oct. 26, Nov. 16.
◇ – Stopping train, 2nd class.
▷ – See also Table **1162**.
⊕ – Not Dec. 24, 31.
⊗ – Not Dec. 24, 25, 31.
⊙ – Not Dec. 24.

1169 OTHER LOCAL SERVICES
2nd class

BŘECLAV - ZNOJMO *69 km* Journey 90 - 100 minutes
From Břeclav: every 2 hours 0655 - 1855, also 1155 Ⓐ, 1355 Ⓐ, 1555 Ⓑ*, 1755 Ⓑ*, 2055 Ⓑ*.
From Znojmo: every 2 hours 0655 - 1855, also 0558 Ⓐ, 1155 Ⓐ, 1355 Ⓐ, 1555 Ⓑ*, 1755 Ⓑ*.

BRNO - ZNOJMO *89 km* Journey 2 hours Change at Hrušovany nad Jevišovkou
From Brno: 0646, 0846, 1046, 1246, 1446, 1646, 1946 Ⓑ*.
From Znojmo: 0658, 0855, 1055, 1258, 1458, 1658, 1858 Ⓒ.

ČESKÉ BUDĚJOVICE - ČESKÝ KRUMLOV *31 km* Journey 60 - 65 mins
To May 16 / from Sept. 15:
From České Bud. 0526 Ⓒ, 0539 Ⓐ, 0802, 1034, 1223, 1506, 1713, 1909, 2209 ⑦ **e**, 2246 Ⓐ.
From Český Krumlov 0541 Ⓐ, 0601 Ⓒ, 0616 Ⓐ, 0805 Ⓒ, 0838 Ⓐ, 1228, 1441, 1755, 2003.
May 17 - Sept. 14:
From České Bud. 0539, 0742, 0914, 1034, 1220, 1448, 1716, 1909, 2209 Ⓒ, 2246 Ⓐ.
From Český Krumlov 0541, 0637 ⚒, 0838, 1037 **d**, 1228, 1448, 1647, 1801, 2003, 2142 ⑥.

CHOCEŇ - LITOMYŠL *24 km* Journey 55 minutes
From Choceň: 0520 Ⓐ, 0638, 0945, 1242, 1516, 1643, 1738 Ⓐ, 1845, 1937 Ⓐ, 2141 Ⓐ.
From Litomyšl: 0649 Ⓐ, 0729 Ⓒ, 0822 Ⓐ, 1122, 1403, 1522 Ⓑ*, 1619, 1831, 2026, 2233 Ⓐ.

HULIN - KROMĚŘÍŽ *8 km* Journey 8 minutes
1 - 2 trains per hour, connecting with trains in Table **1162**.
Trains also run Kroměříž - Kojetin for connections to / from Brno.

PRAHA - KARLŠTEJN *33 km* Journey 43 minutes
From Praha hlavní: hourly 0526 - 2326 (every 30 mins 1426 - 1726). From Karlštejn: hourly 0557 - 2257 (every 30 mins 1357 - 1857). Trains continue to / from Beroun (9 mins to Beroun).

d – Not June 28, July 5, 12.
e – Not Dec. 23, Mar. 23, Nov. 16.
* – Not Dec. 23 - 25, 31, Mar. 23, July 5, Nov. 16.

SLOVAKIA

Operator: National railway company is Železničná spoločnosť Slovensko (ŽSSK) on the network of Železnice Slovenskej Republiky (ŽSR).

Services: All trains convey first and second class seating, **except** where shown otherwise in footnotes or by '2' in the train column, or where the footnote shows sleeping and/or couchette cars only. Descriptions of sleeping (🛏) and couchette (▬) cars appear on page 10.

Timings: Valid **December 9, 2007 - December 13, 2008**. Scheduled holiday variations are shown in the relevant tables. However, certain local trains may be cancelled during the period **Dec. 24 - Jan. 1** and these cancellations may not be shown in the tables.

Reservations: It is possible to reserve seats on most Express trains.

Supplements: A higher level of fares applies to travel by *EC* and *IC* trains.

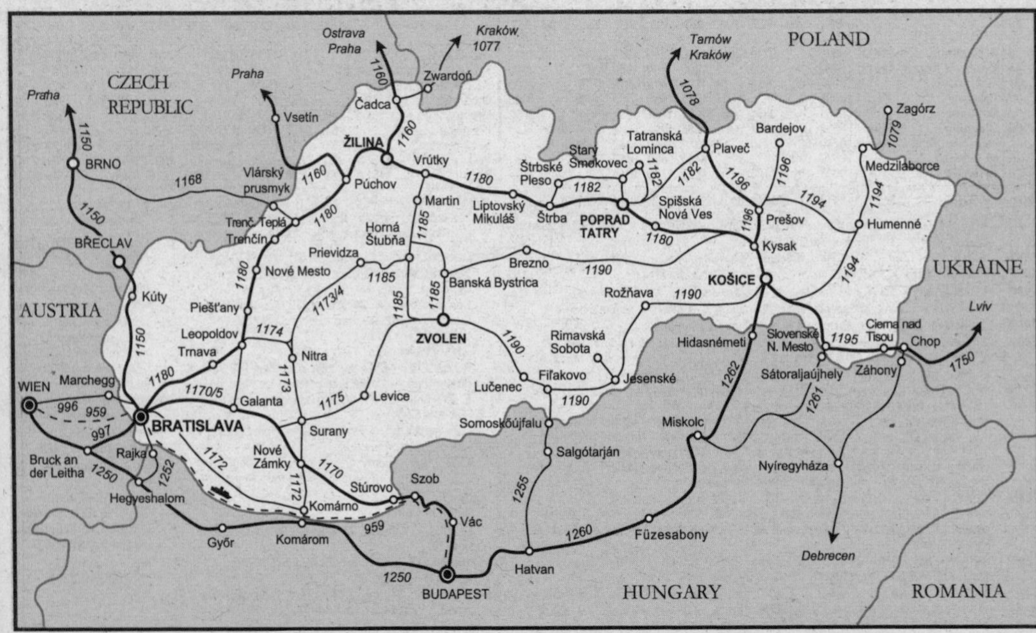

BRATISLAVA - ŠTÚROVO - BUDAPEST 1170

For slower services Bratislava - Budapest via Rajka and Györ see Table **1250**. Hourly local trains run Szob - Budapest (see note ★).

km			375		EN*		IC*		EC						EC					1831		EC		
		◇	732	2137	377	◇	131	◇	279	◇	2133	◇	871	◇	171	◇	873	875	2121	1833	◇	175	◇	◇
		★		2			🍷		✕		2				✕	★	2	2	2			✕		
			P		G		M			Ⓐb			ⒶK		H		⚒	ⒶK		n		J		
	Praha Hlavní **1150** d.	...	2153	...	0030	...	...	...	0733h	...	...	...	...	...	1133h	...	...	...	...	...	...	1533h	...	...
	Brno Hlavní **1150** d.	...	0135	...	0335	...	...	...	1017	...	...	...	...	...	1417	...	...	...	...	...	...	1817	...	...
	Břeclav **1150** 🏛 d.	...	0224	...	0450	...	0833	...	1052	...	...	...	...	...	1452	...	...	...	...	...	...	1852	...	...
0	**Bratislava Hlavná 1175** d.	...	0356	...	0544	0729	0940	1045	1145	1242	...	1342	1421	...	1545	...	1621	1715	...	1821	1842	1945	2056	2300
49	Galanta **1175** d.	...	|	...	|	0831	1009	1136	|	1337	...	1436	1456	←	|	...	1656	1756	...	1856	1935	|	2150	2354
91	Nové Zámky **1175** d.	...	|	0522	0638	0915	1034	1220	1238	1421	1440	1519	1524	1529	1638	...	1726	1824	1841	1924	2020	2038	2234	0037
135	Štúrovo a.	...	|	0605	0704	...	1100	...	1304	...	1523	→	...	1612	1704	...	1801	...	1924	...	...	2104	▬	...
135	Štúrovo 🏛 d.	...	◐	0628	0709	...	1109	...	1309	...	1533	...	...	...	1709	...	...	...	1935	...	...	2109	★	...
150	Szob 🏛 ★ d.	0625	|	0655	|	...	|	...	|	...	1555	...	...	...	|	1755	...	...	2000	...	...	|	2200	...
163	Nagymaros-Visegrád ¶ ★ d.	0641	|	0711	|	...	|	...	|	...	1611	...	...	...	|	1811	...	...	2016	...	...	|	2216	...
180	Vác ★ d.	0658	|	0728	0746	...	1146	...	1346	...	1628	...	...	...	1746	1828	...	...	2033	...	...	2146	2233	...
214	**Budapest Nyugati** ★ a.	0734	|	0754	|	...	|	...	|	...	1654	...	...	...	|	1854	...	...	2118	...	...	|	2318	...
214	**Budapest Keleti** a.	...	0703	...	0832	...	1232	...	1432	...	...	...	...	...	1832	...	...	...	...	...	...	2232	...	...

					EC				EC				EC		IC*					EN*	733		
	876	872	870	◇	2110	174	878		2112	170	◇	◇	◇	278	◇	130	2136	1874	2136	◇	376	374	◇	◇
	2	2	2		2	✕	2	★	2	✕			★	✕		🍷	2		2				★	★
	Ⓐ		ⒶK			J	⚒			H						M		⑦W			G	P		
udapest Keleti d.	...	...	...	...	...	0530	...	...	...	0930	...	...	...	1330	...	1530	...	...	...	...	2000	1940	...	...
Budapest Nyugati ★ d.	...	...	...	...	0440	|	...	0705	0805	|	...	...	1205	|	...	|	1705	...	...	...	|	|	2105	2140
ác ★ d.	...	...	...	...	0527	0612	...	0732	0832	1012	...	...	1232	1412	...	1612	1732	...	...	...	2042	|	2132	2227
agymaros-Visegrád ¶ ★ d.	...	...	...	...	0543	|	...	0748	0848	|	...	...	1248	|	...	|	1748	...	...	...	|	|	2148	2243
zob 🏛 ★ d.	...	...	...	...	0600	|	...	0803	0905	|	...	...	1303	|	...	|	1805	...	...	...	|	|	2203	2258
túrovo 🏛 a.	...	...	...	...	0614	0648	...	...	0918	1048	...	...	...	1448	...	1648	1818	...	←	...	2117	◐	...	...
túrovo d.	0342	0456	...	...	0628	0653	...	...	0928	1053	...	*1250*	...	1453	...	1657	→	1821	1840	...	2120	|	...	...
ové Zámky **1175** d.	0417	0530	0630	0635	0712	0720	0830	...	1011	1120	1137	1346	...	1520	1537	1724	...	1849	1924	1944	2148	|	...	...
alanta **1175** d.	0448	0600	0700	0719	...	|	0900	...	...	|	1223	1432	...	|	1621	1749	...	1918	...	2028	|	|	...	...
ratislava Hlavná 1175 a.	0525	0635	0735	0807	...	0812	0935	...	...	1212	1317	1527	...	1612	1714	1818	...	1953	...	2123	2241	2320	...	...
Břeclav **1150** 🏛 a.	...	...	...	...	...	0905	...	...	...	1305	...	...	...	1705	...	1933	...	...	...	...	2342	0115	...	...
Brno Hlavní **1150** a.	...	...	...	...	...	0940	...	...	...	1340	...	...	...	1740	...	...	...	...	...	...	0036	0215	...	...
Praha Hlavní **1150** a.	...	...	...	...	...	1225h	...	...	...	1625h	...	...	...	2033	...	...	...	...	...	...	0332	0614	...	...

– GALILEO GALILEI – [12] and ▬ 2 cl. Františkovy Lázně - Cheb - Plzeň - Praha - Bratislava - Budapest and v.v.; 🛏 1, 2 cl., ▬ 2 cl., [2] Warszawa (**202/3**) - Břeclav - Budapest and v.v.; 🛏 1, 2 cl., ▬ 2 cl. Kraków (**200/1**) - Břeclav - Budapest and v.v.; 🛏 1, 2 cl. Moskva - Katowice - Břeclav - Bratislava - Budapest and v.v.

– HUNGARIA – [12] ✕ Berlin - Dresden - Praha - Bratislava - Budapest and v.v.

– JÁN JESENIUS – [12] ✕ Hamburg - Berlin - Dresden - Praha - Budapest and v.v.

– [2] Bratislava - Komárno and v.v.

– MORAVIA – [12] 🍷 Bohumín - Ostrava - Břeclav - Bratislava - Budapest and v.v.

– PANNONIA – 🛏 1, 2 cl., ▬ 2 cl., [12] Praha - Bratislava - Györ - Budapest - Lökösháza and v.v.; [2] Praha - Budapest - Bucureşti and v.v. (also 🛏 1, 2 cl. on dates in Table **60**); 🛏 1, 2 cl. Cheb - Praha - Bratislava - Banská Bystrica and v.v. For ▬ 2 cl. Praha - Varna / Burgas and v.v. (summer only) see Table **60** in summer editions.

W – ⑦ to June 22 / from Sept. 7 (also Jan. 1, Mar. 24, Sept. 1, 15, Nov. 17; not Dec. 23, 30, Mar. 23, Sept. 14, Nov. 16).

b – Not Dec. 22 - Jan. 6, June 30 - Aug. 28.

h – Praha **Holešovice**.

n – Not Dec. 22 - 25, 29 - 31, Mar. 21 - 23, Aug. 29, 31, Sept. 14, Nov. 16.

◐ – Via Rajka 🏛 and Györ (Table **1250**).

◇ – Stopping train. 2nd class.

¶ – A ferry operates across the river to Visegrád.

* – Classified *Ex* in Slovakia.

★ – **Budapest Nyugati - Vác - Szob**:
From Budapest 0540, 0705 and hourly to 2105, also 2140, 2240, 2340.
From Szob 0455, 0625, 0655 and hourly to 1855, also 2000, 2100, 2200, 2300.

OTHER TRAIN NAMES: **278/9** – JAROSLAV HAŠEK

2nd class BRATISLAVA - KOMÁRNO 1172

km					Ⓐ	Ⓐ	Ⓐ	Ⓐd	Ⓐ		d
0	Bratislava Hlavná d.	0605	1036	1311	1413z	1421	1601	1635	1715	...	2053
5	Bratislava Nové Mesto d.	0624	1050	1320	1423	|	1610	1650	|	1738	2109
42	Dunajská Streda d.	0733	1149	1425	1528	|	1653	1749	|	1847	2210
‡29	Nové Zamky ▶ d.	|	|	|	|	1530	|	|	1828	|	|
94	Komárno ▶ a.	0839	1255	1531	1639	1557	1748	1852	1854	1958	2314

	Ⓐ	Ⓐd	Ⓐ			Ⓐ	Ⓐ		d	
omárno ▶ d.	0420	0502	0559	0622	0913	...	1313	...	1717	1900
Nové Zamky ▶ d.	|	|	0630	|	|	...	|	...	|	|
unajská Streda d.	0531	0626	|	0732	1020	1128	1422	1613	1849	2010
ratislava Nové Mesto a.	0614	0726	|	0831	1124	1230	1524	1722	1950	2108
ratislava Hlavná a.	0623	0735	0735	0842	1134	1245	1537	...	2001	2117

– Additional local trains Nové Zamky - Komárno and v.v., journey 27 - 29 minutes:
rom Nové Zamky: 0500, 0647, 0734 Ⓐ, 0828, 1130, 1305 Ⓐ, 1430, 1645, 1727, 1828, 1935.
rom Komárno: 0644, 0732 Ⓐ, 0844, 1257, 1358 Ⓐ, 1440, 1540, 1642 Ⓐ, 1800, 1859 Ⓐ, 2018.

– Ⓒ only.
– Not Dec. 22 - Jan. 6.
– Not Mar. 21 - 24.
– ⑦ only.
– Not July 1 - Aug. 31.

u – Not Dec. 24 - Jan. 6, June 28 - Aug. 31.
z – Not June 22 - Sept. 7.
⊖ – Change at Šurany (10 km from Nové Zamky).
‡ – Distance from Komárno.

2nd class NOVÉ ZAMKY - PRIEVIDZA 1173

km			Ⓐ		⚒		Ⓐ		Ⓑ⊖		h⊖	h
0	Nové Zamky d.	0534	0639	0847	...	1258	...	1433	1532	1736	1840	2052
36	Nitra a.	0627	0732	0939	...	1346	...	1534	1628	1826	1941	2140
36	Nitra d.	0639	0805	0940c	1231	*1348*r	1420	1535	1644	1827	1942	*2217*
69	Topoľčany a.	0732	0902	1031c	1329	*1442*r	1516	1634	1754	1921	2034	*2313*

		Ⓐ			⚒			Ⓐ		Ⓒ	Ⓐ	⚒
Topoľčany d.	0537	0623	0739	1111	...	1418	1542	...	1658	1828	*1857*	2012
Nitra a.	0631	0727	0846	1206	...	1519	1635	...	1800	1937	*2008*	2109
Nitra d.	0640	...	0849	1208	1424	1538	1636	1711	1832	1946	2047	...
Nové Zamky a.	0726	...	0936	1257	1515	1624	1721	1804	1916	2031	2142	...

km		Ⓐ	Ⓒ	Ⓐ	Ⓐu	Ⓐ	Ⓒ	Ⓐ	Ⓒ	Ⓐ		Ⓐs
0	Topoľčany § d.	0645	0741	0905	1203	1342	1350	1448	1500	1526	1705	1932
44	Prievidza § a.	0802	0847	1025	1319	1447	1507	1608	1620	1646	1819	2042

		Ⓐ			Ⓐu	Ⓐ	Ⓒ	Ⓐ		⚒	⑦	Ⓐ
Prievidza § d.	0605	0654	0959	1216	1255	1342	1430	1440	1544	1847	1958	2228
Topoľčany § a.	0726	0811	1108	1316	1414	1520	1533	1608	1657	2004	2119	2338

← FOR OTHER NOTES SEE TABLE **1172**

§ – See also Table **1174**.

2nd class BRATISLAVA - NITRA and PRIEVIDZA 1174

km		1725	1735			1721		1733	1723		1727	
		F	G	⚒		G	Ⓐ	Ⓐn	Ⓐn	Ⓐ	⑦e	⚒
	Bratislava Petržalka d.	0635	0635	...	...	...	...	...	...	...	...	...
	Brat. Nové Mesto d.	0650	0650	...	...	...	...	...	...	...	...	...
0	**Bratislava Hl. 1180** d.	|	|	*0823*	*1015*	1250	*1255*	1530	1647	*1747*	1753	*1947*
46	Trnava **1180** d.	0730	0730	*0916*	*1114*	1327	*1400*	1604	1727	*1819*	1826	*2019*
63	Leopoldov **1180** a.	0742	0742	*0930*	*1128*	1339	*1415*	1616	1739	*1830*	1838	*2030*
63	Leopoldov d.	0750	0750	0952	1206	1349	1420	1624	1749	1835	1850	2036
87	Zbehy d.	0813	0813	1026	1238	1413	1451	|	1823	1907	1914	2112
98	**Nitra** a.	*0836*	0832	1045	1301	*1452*	1510	1708	|	1926	|	2130
114	Topoľčany **1173** d.	0839	...	...	...	1439	...	...	1853	...	1952	...
158	**Prievidza 1173** a.	0937	...	...	...	1533	...	...	1956	...	2055	...

	1732	1722							1720		
	Ⓐn	⚒n	F		Ⓐ		Ⓐ				b
Prievidza 1173 d.	...	0516	...	...	...	...	...	...	1640	...	...
Topoľčany **1173** d.	...	0614	...	...	...	...	...	...	1735	...	...
Nitra d.	0527	|	0742	0912	1103	1231r	1428	1525	*1737*a	1844	2042
Zbehy d.	|	|	0757	0932	1123	1257	1454	1545	1800	1909	2110
Leopoldov a.	0607	0704	0827	1009	1157	1330	1527	1617	1823	1941	2141
Leopoldov **1180** d.	0615	0718	...	*1012*	1159	1331	*1546*	*1620*	1831	*1946*	*2146*
Trnava **1180** a.	0628	0731	...	*1027*	1219	1351	*1557*	*1635*	1842	*1957*	*2157*
Bratislava Hl. 1180 a.	0707	0807	...	*1119*	*1319*	*1430*	*1630*	*1726*	|	*2030*	*2229*
Brat. Nové Mesto a.	...	...	...	...	...	...	...	...	1919	...	...
Bratislava Petržalka a.	...	...	...	...	...	...	...	...	1934	...	...

– Ⓒ (daily June 30 - Aug. 28).
– Ⓐ (not June 30 - Aug. 28).
– Ⓐ only.

b – Not Dec. 24 - 26, Jan. 1.
e – Also Dec. 26, Mar. 24, May 1, 8, Aug. 29; not Dec. 9, Mar. 23.
n – Not Dec. 31.

r – Change at Lužianky.

1175 BRATISLAVA - LEVICE - ZVOLEN

km		◇	811	831	803	803	805	805	*Ex*	1831	801
						1803		1805	531	1833	
		Ⓐ	H	b		y	m	Ⓑ	Ⓑ	2	Ⓑ
								z	x	w	Ph
0	**Bratislava Hlavná 1170** d.	...	0621	0951	1221	1221	1521	1521	1654	1821	2346
49	Galanta **1170** d.	...	0656	1026	1256	1256	1556	1556	|	1856	0021
*10	Nové Zámky **1170** ▶ d.	0508	*0659*	|	*1258*	*1258*	*1532*	*1532*	*1736*	1933	|
89	Šurany ▶ d.	0519	0726	1057	1326	1326	1626	1626	1749	1943	0052
131	Levice d.	0620	0813	1140	1408	1408	1708	1708	1826	2023	0138
198	Hronská Dúbrava **1185** d.	0801	0916	1242	1511	1511	1811	1811	|	2129	|
209	**Zvolen** osob. **1185** a.	0810	0926	1252	1521	1521	1821	1821	1929	2148	0248
	Banská Bystrica **1185** a.	*0903*	0955	1322	1548	|	1855	|	1950	...	|
	Košice **1190** a.	...	1359	...	...	1910	...	2211	...	...	0634
	Prešov **1183** a.	...	...	...	...	1959	...	...	...	...	0717

	1830	*Ex*	804	1804	802	1802	832	1530	810	80
		530		804		802				
	Ⓐ	R	m	n		c	b	⑦	H	Ⓑ
	2							e		Ph
Prešov **1183** d.	...	...	...	...	...	0830	...	...	...	222
Košice **1190** d.	...	...	...	0558	...	0916	...	...	1506	230
Banská Bystrica **1185** d.	...	0539	0850	|	1206	|	1501	*1751*	1908	|
Zvolen osob. **1185** d.	...	0559	0935	0935	1251	1251	1534	1826	1934	030
Hronská Dúbrava **1185** d.	...	|	0945	0945	1301	1301	1544	1840	1944	|
Levice d.	0533	0704	1048	1048	1407	1407	1645	1945	2048	041
Šurany ▶ d.	0614	0740	1128	1128	1448	1448	1729	2031	2128	045
Nové Zámky **1170** ▶ a.	|	*0819*	|	|	|	|	*1816*	|	*2142*a	|
Galanta **1170** d.	0647	0805	1200	1200	1522	1522	1800	2102	2200	052
Bratislava Hlavná 1170 a.	0727	0835	1235	1235	1556	1556	1835	2138	2235	060

H – HOREHRONEC – 🚃 Bratislava - Banská Bystrica - Košice and v.v.; 🛏 1, 2 cl. Cheb (**605/4**) - Karlovy Vary - Praha (**375/4**) - Bratislava (**810/1**) - Banská Bystrica and v.v.
P – POL'ANA – 🛏 1, 2 cl. and 🚃.
R – ①–⑥ (not Dec. 24 - 29, 31, Jan. 1, Mar. 22, 24, Sept. 1, 15, Nov. 17).

a – Ⓐ only.
b – Not Dec. 24, 25, 31.
c – Not Dec. 25, 26, Jan. 1, Mar. 23.
e – Also Dec. 26, Jan. 1, Mar. 24, Sept. 1, 15, Nov. 17; not Dec. 23, 30, Mar. 23, Aug. 31, Sept. 14, Nov. 16.
h – Not Dec. 23 - 28, 30, 31, Mar. 21, 23, Aug. 29, 31, Sept. 14, Nov. 16.
m – Not Dec. 24, 25, 31, Jan. 1, Mar. 22, 23.
n – ①–⑥ (not Dec. 24 - 26, 31, Jan. 1, Mar. 22 - 24, Sept. 1, 15, Nov. 17).
w – Not Dec. 22 - 25, 29 - 31, Mar. 21 - 23, Aug. 29, 31, Sept. 14, Nov. 16.
x – Not Dec. 23 - 28, 30, 31, Mar. 21, 23, Aug. 31 Sept. 14, Nov. 16.
y – Not Dec. 24, 25, 31, Mar. 22.
z – Not Dec. 23 - 25, 31, Jan. 1, Mar. 21, 23, Aug 31, Sept. 14, Nov. 16.

◇ – Stopping train. 2nd class only.
▶ – Local trains run 10 - 12 times per day.
* – Distance from Šurany.

1180 BRATISLAVA - ŽILINA - KOŠICE

km		423	1421	225	701	421		*IC* 501	601	603	605	*IC* 405	605	607	*IC* 511	*EC* 121	609	707	1507	611	*IC* 403	703		705	615
							2	✕ R	✕	✕	✕	✕ R	✕	✕	✕ R	✕	✕			✕	✕ R		2		
		♦Z	♦	♦	R	♦		n	u		♦		♦		Ⓑh		⊖△	Ⓐb	⑤d	v		y	⚒t	Z	♦
	Wien Westbf **997** d.	...	...	...	...	...	...	...	...	...	...	0814	...	...	...	...	...	...	...	...	1536	...	...	...	...
	Bratislava Petržalka d.	...	...	...	...	...	...	...	...	...	...	0935	...	...	...	...	...	...	...	...	1701	...	...	...	...
0	**Bratislava Hl. 1174** d.	...	...	...	...	...	0427	0540	0547	0747	0947	1000	...	1147	1312	...	1347	1447	1515	1547	1731	1747	...	1947	234
46	Trnava **1174** d.	...	...	...	0400	...	0520	0609	0619	0819	1019	1040	...	1219	|	...	1419	1519	1546	1619	|	1819	...	2019	001
64	Leopoldov **1174** d.	...	...	...	0423	...	0536	|	0632	0832	1032	|	...	1232	|	...	1432	1532	|	1632	|	1832	...	2032	003
81	Piešťany d.	...	...	...	0435	...	0555	|	0644	0844	1044	|	...	1244	|	...	1444	1544	|	1644	|	1844	...	2044	004
99	Nové Mesto nad Váhom d.	...	...	...	0453	...	0623	|	0702	0902	1102	|	...	1302	|	...	1502	1602	|	1702	|	1902	...	2102	010
123	**Trenčín** d.	...	...	...	0522	...	0653	0712	0730	0930	1130	1144	...	1330	1440	...	1530	1630	1647	1730	|	1930	...	2130	013
131	Trenčianska Teplá d.	...	...	...	0530	...	...	|	0738	0938	1138	|	...	1338	|	...	1538	1638	|	1738	|	1938	...	2138	013
	Praha Hlavní **1160** d.	2006	2144	2206	|	0006	...	|	|	|	|	|	...	|	|	1106	|	|	|	|	|	|	...	|	|
158	Púchov **1160** d.	|	|	0339	0552	|	...	|	0757	0957	1156	|	...	1357	|	1551	1557	1657	1712	1757	|	1959	...	2159	015
203	**Žilina 1160** a.	0320	0405	0416	0631	0633	...	0806	0834	1034	1233	1238	←	1434	1534	1628	1634	1734	1745	1834	1948	2038	...	2238	023
203	**Žilina 1185** d.	0340	0409	0440	...	0640	...	0809	0840	1040	→	1241	1245	1440	1537	1631	1640	...	1748	1840	1951	2040	...	2251r	024
224	Vrútky **1185** d.	0359	0428	0459	...	0659	...	|	0859	1059	...	|	1304	1459	|	|	1659	...	|	1859	|	2057	2108	2310r	025
242	Kral'ovany d.	0414	0442	0514	...	0714	...	|	0914	1114	...	|	1319	1514	|	|	1714	...	|	1914	|	m	2130	2324r	031
260	Ružomberok d.	0431	0459	0531	...	0731	...	|	0931	1131	...	|	1336	1531	|	|	1731	...	1831	1931	|	▬	2155	2341r	033
286	Liptovský Mikuláš d.	0450	0520	0550	...	0750	...	0906	0950	1150	...	1338	1355	1550	1635	1728	1750	...	1849	1950	2048	...	2226	2358r	035
325	Štrba d.	0519	0548	0618	...	0819	...	|	1019	1219	...	|	1424	1619	|	1756	1819	...	|	2019	|	2	2305	...	041
344	**Poprad-Tatry** d.	0535	0606	0639	...	0835	...	0947	1035	1235	...	1418	1440	1635	1717	1811	1835	...	1930	2035	2128	2245	2324	...	043
370	Spišská Nová Ves d.	0555	0627	0659	...	0856	...	|	1055	1255	...	|	1500	1655	1737	1831	1855	...	1949	2055	|	2314	...	...	045
410	Margecany d.	0622	0656	0726	...	0922	...	|	1124	1324	...	|	1527	1722	|	|	1922	...	|	2122	|	2358	...	...	052
429	Kysak **1183** § a.	0637	0711	0741	...	0937	...	1041	1139	1339	...	1511	1544	1737	1814	1908	1937	...	2026	2137	2222	...	...	...	053
445	**Košice 1183** a.	0650	0724	0754	...	0950	...	1053	1152	1352	...	1523	1555	1750	1827	1921	1950	...	2038	2150	2234	...	...	...	055

	706	614	700	702	1510	600	*IC* 402	602	604	*EC* 120	604	606	704	608	*IC* 404	608	610	1506	1508	612	*IC* 500	420	224	1420	422
	⊖				①	✕	✕ R	✕	✕	✕	✕	✕		✕	✕ R	✕	✕		2	✕	✕ R				⊖
	Z	♦	Ⓐb	x	g	P			♦▽		♦		Ⓑk				v	⑦e	⑦e	v	z	♦	♦	♦	♦Z
Košice 1183 d.	...	0022	...	...	...	0416	0534	0622	0815	0839	...	1022	...	1210	1244	...	1420	1513	...	1624	1722	1822	2022	2040	222
Kysak **1183** d.	...	0035	...	...	...	0429	0546	0635	0828	0852	...	1035	...	1223	1257	...	1433	1526	...	1637	1735	1835	2035	2053	223
Margecany d.	...	0051	...	...	...	0445	|	0651	0844	|	...	1051	...	1239	|	...	1449	|	...	1653	|	1851	2051	2108	225
Spišska Nová Ves d.	...	0120	...	...	...	0514	|	0720	0913	0932	...	1120	...	1308	|	...	1520	1605	...	1722	|	1920	2120	2136	232
Poprad-Tatry d.	...	0142	...	...	...	0536	0641	0742	0935	0952	...	1142	...	1330	1351	...	1542	1625	...	1744	1831	1942	2149	2157	234
Štrba d.	...	0158	...	...	...	0552	|	0758	0951	1007	...	1158	...	1346	|	...	1558	|	...	1759	|	1958	2205	2213	235
Liptovský Mikuláš d.	...	0226	...	...	0515	0622	0722	0826	1019	1035	...	1226	...	1414	1431	...	1626	1706	...	1827	1912	2026	2233	2242	002
Ružomberok d.	...	0246	...	...	0537	0643	|	0846	1039	|	...	1246	...	1434	|	...	1646	1727	...	1847	|	2046	2253	2302	|
Kral'ovany d.	...	0303	...	m	0555	0659	|	0903	1056	|	...	1303	...	1451	|	...	1703	|	...	1903	|	2103	2310	2318	|
Vrútky **1185** d.	...	0318	...	0504	0612	0713	|	0918	1111	|	...	1318	...	1506	|	...	1718	|	...	1918	|	2118	2325	2333	|
Žilina 1185 a.	...	0334	...	0526	0628	0729	0819	0934	1127	1132	←	1334	...	1522	1527	←	1734	1808	...	1934	2009	2134	2341	2349	012
Žilina 1160 d.	0240	0340	0440	0540	0640	0740	0822	0940	→	1135	1140	1340	1440	→	1530	1540	1740	1812	1840	1940	2012	2137	2354	0003	013
Púchov **1160** d.	0320	0420	0520	0620	0720	0820	|	1020	...	1212	1220	1420	1520	...	|	1621	1820	|	1920	2020	|	|	0032	|	|
Praha Hlavní **1160** a.	|	|	|	|	|	|	|	|	...	1700	|	|	|	...	|	|	|	|	|	|	|	0355	0621	0631s	082
Trenčianska Teplá d.	0342	0440	0542	0641	0742	0841	|	1040	...	...	1240	1440	1541	...	|	1640	1840	|	1941	2040	|	▬	...	...	...
Trenčín d.	0349	0448	0549	0649	0750	0849	|	1048	...	...	1248	1448	1548	...	1624	1648	1848	1909	1948	2048	2107	...	...	...	...
Nové Mesto nad Váhom d.	0417	0517	0618	0718	0818	0918	|	1117	...	...	1317	1517	1618	...	|	1717	1917	|	2020	2117	|	...	...	...	...
Piešťany d.	0433	0533	0634	0734	0834	0934	|	1133	...	...	1333	1533	1634	...	|	1733	1933	|	2037	2133	|	2	...	...	...
Leopoldov **1174** d.	0446	0546	0647	0747	0847	0947	|	1146	...	...	1346	1546	1647	...	|	1746	1946	|	2050	2146	|	2212	...	...	...
Trnava **1174** d.	0459	0559	0700	0800	0900	1000	|	1159	...	...	1359	1559	1701	...	1726	1759	1959	2010	2103	2158	2209	2240	...	...	...
Bratislava Hl. 1174 a.	0530	0630	0731	0831	0934	1031	1040	1230	...	...	1430	1630	1732	...	1755	1830	2030	2040	2136	2229	2238	2328	...	...	...
Bratislava Petržalka a.	...	...	...	...	...	...	1112	...	...	...	...	...	...	...	1832	...	...	...	...	...	...	...	...	...	...
Wien Westbf **997** a.	...	...	...	...	...	...	1232	...	...	...	...	...	...	...	1954	...	...	...	...	...	...	...	...	...	...

♦ – NOTES (LISTED BY TRAIN NUMBERS)

224/5 – ŠÍRAVA – 🛏 1, 2 cl., ▬ 2 cl. 🚃 Praha - Košice - Humenné and v.v.
420/1 – EXCELSIOR – 🛏 1, 2 cl., ▬ 2 cl., 🚃 Cheb - Karlovy Vary - Ústí nad Labem - Praha - Žilina - Košice and v.v.; 🛏 1, 2 cl., ▬ 2 cl. Plzeň (**377/6**) - Praha (**421/0**) - Žilina - Košice and v.v.; 🚃 Františkovy Lázně (**377/6**) - Cheb - Plzeň - Praha - Žilina - Košice and v.v.
422/3 – CASSOVIA – 🛏 1, 2 cl., ▬ 2 cl., 🚃 Praha - Žilina - Košice and v.v. Conveys (not Dec. 24, 31) 🛏 1, 2 cl. České Budějovice (**663/2**) - Brno - Žilina - Košice and v.v.
604/5 – DARGOV – 🚃 and ✕ Bratislava - Košice (**1901/4**) - Humenné and v.v.; 🚃 Bratislava - Košice - Čierna nad Tisou and v.v.
614/5 – ZEMPLÍN – 🛏 1, 2 cl., ▬ 2 cl., 🚃 Bratislava - Košice - Humenné and v.v. Not Dec. 24, 31 from Bratislava or Humenné.
1420/1 – Dec. 20 - 23, Jan. 1, 2, Mar. 20, 21, 24, 25, Apr. 29, 30, May 6, 7, ④⑤ June 26 - Aug. 22, also Aug. 29, 30, Oct. 23, 24, 30, 31, Nov. 1, 2. 🛏 1, 2 cl., ▬ 2 cl., 🚃 Praha - Žilina - Košice and v.v.

P – ①–⑥ (not Dec. 22, 24 - 29, 31, Jan. 1, Mar. 22, 24, Sept. 1, 15, Nov. 17).
R – ①–⑥ (not Dec. 24 - Jan. 1).
Z – Also conveys 🛏 1, 2 cl. Bratislava (**705/6**) - Žilina (**423/2**) - Košice and v.v. Not Dec. 24, 31.

b – Not Dec. 27, 28, 31.
d – Also Mar. 20, Aug. 28; not Dec. 28, Mar. 21, Aug. 29.
e – Also Jan. 1, Mar. 24, Sept. 1, 15, Nov. 17; not Dec. 23, 30, Mar. 23, Aug. 31, Sept. 14, Nov. 16.
g – Also Jan. 2, Mar. 25, Sept. 2, 16, Nov. 18; not Dec. 24, 31, Mar. 24, Sept. 1, 15, Nov. 1
h – Not Dec. 23 - 28, 30, 31, Jan. 1, Mar. 21, 23, Aug. 31, Sept. 14, Nov. 16.
k – Not Dec. 24 - Jan. 1.
m – To / from Martin (Table **1185**).
n – Not Dec. 23 - 31, Jan. 1, Mar. 22 - 24, May 1, 8, Sept. 1, 15.
r – ⑤ (also Mar. 20, Aug. 28; not Mar. 21, Aug. 29).
s – Praha **Smíchov**.
t – Not Dec. 31, July 5. Runs daily to Liptovský Mikuláš.
u – Not Dec. 25, Jan. 1.
v – Not Dec. 24, 31.
x – Not Dec. 24, 25, 31, Jan. 1.
y – Not Dec. 23, 24, 30, 31.
z – Not Dec. 22 - 31, Mar. 21 - 23, Apr. 30, May 7, Aug. 31, Sept. 14.

§ – Most trains set down only.
⊖ – Also conveys 🛏 1, 2 cl. Wien - Bratislava - Košice - Chop - Lviv / Kyïv and v.v. (Table 9
△ – Conveys on ①②④⑥ 🛏 1, 2 cl. Žilina - Košice - Chop - Moskva (journey 2 nights).
▽ – Conveys on ②④⑥⑦ (from Moskva) 🛏 1, 2 cl. Moskva - Chop - Košice - Žilina (journey nights).

2nd class only

LOCAL LINES IN POPRAD TATRY AREA 1182

km		Ⓐd		Ⓐd			f	Ⓐd				
0	**Poprad Tatry** .. d.	0343	0504	0542	0711	0959	1144	1410	1458	1544	1840	2151
8	Studený Potok . d.	0357	0517	0602	0733	1014	1156	1423	1511	1559	1853	2204
14	Kežmarok .... d.	0406	0539	0611	0743	1023	1206	1435	1520	1610	1903	2214
44	Stará Lubovňa . d.	0452	0622	0653	0826	1106	1250	1526	1610	1723**r**	1947	2256
60	**Plaveč** .... a.	0509	0640	0711	0843**c**	1123	1308	...	1628	1741	2005	2314

		Ⓐd		Ⓐ	Ⓒ		f	Ⓐd		Ⓑ	
Plaveč .... d.	0433	0532	0734	0858	0901	1159	1437	...	1704	1857	2206
Stará Lubovňa d.	0454	0550	0753	0921	0921	1218	1456	1537	1721	1915	2225
Kežmarok .... d.	0537	0636	0840	1002	1002	1302	1548	1637	1803	2000	2310
Studený Potok d.	0547	0647	0849	1012	1012	1311	1557	1647	1812	2009	2319
Poprad Tatry . a.	0600	0700	0903	1025	1025	1325	1610	1700	1826	2023	2332

km				Ⓐd			Ⓒ		Ⓐ		f	N	Ⓒ	Ⓐd	Ⓐ						h			
0	**Poprad Tatry** .... d.	0504	...	0542	...	0749	0950	0959	...	1106	1144	...	...	1410	...	1458	...	1544	...	1708	1756	2037	2151	...
8	Studený Potok .... d.	0516	0518	0602	0604	0802	1003	1011	1013	1118	1156	1158	1314	1422	1425	1510	1513	1556	1600	1721	1814	2050	2203	2206
17	**Tatranská Lomnica** .... a.	...	0529	...	0616	0814	1015	...	1025	1131	...	1210	1327	...	1438	...	1525	...	1612	1733	1825	2102	...	2219

				Ⓐd	Ⓒ	Ⓐ		Ⓒ		N	Ⓒ		Ⓐ			f		h						
Tatranská Lomnica .... d.	0534	...	0633	...	0633	0835	...	0856	1030	1140	1256	...	1336	1456	1543	...	1623	1750	...	1839	...	2146	2248	...
Studený Potok .... a.	0545	0547	0645	0647	0645	0847	0849	0908	1041	1152	1308	1311	1348	1508	1555	1557	1635	1802	1812	1851	...	2158	2300	...
Poprad Tatry .... a.	...	0600	...	0700	0700	...	0903	0922	1055	...	...	1325	...	...	...	1610	1649	...	1826	1907	...	...	2313	...

Poprad Tatry - Starý Smokovec (journey 25 minutes, *13* km, narrow gauge): 0418, 0515, 0618, 0658, 0745, 0837**N**, 0910, 1010, 1100, 1155**S**, 1242, 1338, 1430, 1525, 1618, 1722, 1814, 1907, 2001, 2055**S**, 2148, 2246**h**. Most continue to Štrbské Pleso (see below).

Starý Smokovec - Štrbské Pleso (journey 40 - 45 minutes, *16* km, narrow gauge): 0539, 0643, 0735, 0812, 0904**N**, 0938, 1038, 1127, 1221**S**, 1319, 1410, 1457, 1550, 1644, 1752, 1842, 1932, 2033, 2128**S**, 2219. Most journeys start from Poprad Tatry (see above).

Starý Smokovec - Tatranská Lomnica (14 mins, *6* km, nar. gauge): 0500, 0541, 0710, 0815, 0903**N**, 0942, 1042, 1140, 1311, 1418**N**, 1501, 1552, 1647, 1734**a**, 1844**h**, 2034, 2130.

Štrbské Pleso - Štrba (journey 17 - 18 minutes, *5* km, rack railway): 0528, 0617, 0724, 0823, 0923, 1119, 1320, 1435, 1536, 1551**R**, 1640, 1728, 1812**S**, 1930, 2140, 2235.

Starý Smokovec - Poprad Tatry (journey 25 minutes, *13* km, narrow gauge): 0447, 0538, 0706, 0734, 0902, 0938**S**, 1001, 1128, 1250, 1347, 1417**S**, 1458, 1551, 1645, 1733**b**, 1841, 1933, 2027, 2120, 2216, 2311**N**. Most journeys start from Štrbské Pleso (see below).

Štrbské Pleso - Starý Smokovec (journey 40 - 45 minutes, *16* km, narrow gauge): 0459, 0627, 0651, 0820, 0852**S**, 0921, 1046, 1206, 1303, 1328**S**, 1418, 1505, 1558, 1651**a**, 1800, 1849, 1940, 2041, 2136, 2226**N**. Most journeys continue to Poprad Tatry (see above).

Tatranská Lomnica - Starý Smokovec (14 mins, *6* km, nar. gauge): 0519, 0624, 0730**z**, 0841, 0922**N**, 1020, 1106, 1229, 1330**N**, 1440, 1527, 1619, 1710**b**, 1820, 1913**h**, 2104, 2151.

Štrba - Štrbské Pleso (journey 15 minutes, *5* km, rack railway): 0442, 0600, 0648, 0802, 0852, 1010**R**, 1028, 1230, 1401, 1512, 1612**S**, 1622, 1708, 1832, 2025, 2209.

N – Dec. 9 - Mar. 30, June 1 - Sept. 15.
R – Dec. 9 - Mar. 30, June 1 - Sept. 30.
S – June 1 - Sept. 15.
a – Štrbské Pleso - Tatranská Lomnica.
b – Tatranská Lomnica - Poprad Tatry.
c – Ⓒ only.
d – Not Dec. 24 - 31.
f – Not Dec. 22 - Jan. 1.
h – Not Dec. 24, 25, 31.
r – Arrive 1658.
z – 0749 on ⑥† (daily June 28 - Aug. 31), also Dec. 24 - Jan. 7, Feb. 1, Mar. 3 - 7, 20 - 25.

ŽILINA - VRÚTKY - MARTIN - BANSKÁ BYSTRICA - ZVOLEN 1185

km		◇ Ⓐ	◇	**1847** 2 P	◇ Ⓐ	◇ Ⓒ	◇ Ⓒ	◇ Ⓐ	◇ Ⓒ	◇ Ⓐ	◇ Ⓐ	**1841** 2 n	◇	◇ Ⓐ	◇ Ⓐ	◇	*Ex* **145** D	**1843** 2 m	◇	◇	◇	**1845** Ⓑ 2h	**703** B k	◇ ⑦	◇ ①–⑥ b
0	**Žilina 1180** .... d.	*0340*	0446	0553	0622	*0640*	*0840*	*0840*	*1040*	1053	...	1333	*1245*	...	*1447*	*1525*	1619	1740	...	*1745*	*1844*	1956	2040	...	*2135*
21	Vrútky **1180** .... a.	*0357*	0509	0611	0647	*0657*	*0857*	*0857*	*1057*	1116	...	1349	*1302*	...	*1509*	*1546*	1635	1756	...	*1808*	*1906*	2012	2057	...	*2158*
21	Vrútky .... d.	0436	0510	0613	0648	0728	0924	0931	1120	1120	...	1351	1328	1430	1514	1554	1636	1758	...	1825	1924	2014	2059	2121	2220
28	**Martin** .... d.	0446	0519	0620	0658	0738	0934	0941	1130	1130	...	1358	1337	1441	1525	1604	1644	1805	...	1834	1935	2021	2106	2131	2230
51	Diviaky .... d.	0514	0548	|	0727	0806	1003	1010	1158	1158	1208	|	1421	1512	1556	1630	|	|	1831	1904	2002	|	...	2158	2257
52	Turčianske Teplice ...... d.	0517	0551	0638	0731	0809	1006	1013	1201	1201	1211	1415	1424	1516	1600	1634	1704	1822	1834	1907	2006	2039	...	2201	2300
61	Horná Štubňa .... a.	|	0603	|	0743	0821	|	1025	1213	|	1223	|	1436	1528	|	1645	|	|	1849	|	2018	|	...	2213	2312
99	**Prievidza** .... a.	|	*0714***r**	|	*0845*	*0927*	|	*1140*	*1323*	|	*1323*	|	1540	*1648*	|	*1756*	|	|	1945	|	*2117*	|	...	...	...
61	Horná Štubňa .... d.	|	0603	|	...	...	|	...	1223	|	1223	|	...	...	|	1646	|	|	...	|	2022	|	...	...	...
80	Kremnica .... d.	|	0629	|	...	...	|	...	1248	|	1248	|	...	...	|	1709	|	|	...	|	2048	|	...	...	...
106	Hronská Dúbrava § .. d.	|	0707	|	...	...	|	...	1319	|	1319	|	...	...	|	1743	|	|	...	|	2121	|	...	...	...
97	**Banská Bystrica** .... a.	0616	|	0727	...	...	1049	...	|	1254	|	1455	...	...	1655	|	1749	1905	...	2009	|	2118	...	...	...
97	**Banská Bystrica** ... ▶ d.	*0629*	|	0732	...	...	...	...	|	1258	|	*1501*	...	...	*1717*	|	1751	*1908*	...	*2012*	|	2120	...	...	...
*118	**Zvolen** osob. .... ▶ a.	*0653*	0717	0757	...	...	...	...	1329	1329	1329	*1525*	...	...	*1750*	1752	1812	*1931*	...	*2045*	2131	2143	...	...	...

	702 B m	◇	◇ Ⓐ	**1840** 2 n	◇ Ⓐ	◇ Ⓒ	*Ex* **144** D	◇	◇ Ⓐ	◇ Ⓐ	◇ Ⓒ	◇ Ⓒ	◇ Ⓐ	◇ Ⓒ	**1842** 2 m	◇ Ⓐ	◇	**1844** Ⓑ 2h	◇ s	◇	◇	◇	◇ d	◇	**1846** 2 P	◇ Ⓒ n
Zvolen osob. .... ▶ d.	...	...	0414	0521	0617	0617	0740	...	1029	1044	1055	...	...	*1257*	...	1425	*1526*	...	1530	...	1633	*1813*	1826**c**	1911	...
Banská Bystrica .... ▶ a.	...	...	|	0549	|	|	0800	...	|	1113	|	...	...	*1322*	...	|	*1548*	...	|	...	1708	*1844*	|	1943	...
Banská Bystrica .... d.	...	...	|	0551	|	|	0802	...	|	1115	|	...	...	1333	...	|	1551	...	|	...	1719	1907	|	1955	...
Hronská Dúbrava § ... d.	...	...	0425	|	0627	0627	|	...	1040	|	1105	...	...	|	...	1436	|	...	1541	...	|	|	1843	|	...
Kremnica .... d.	...	...	0512	|	0700	0735**x**	|	...	1117	|	1139	...	...	|	...	1512	|	...	1617	...	|	|	1922	|	...
Horná Štubňa .... a.	...	...	0550	|	0724	0801	|	...	1142	|	1204	...	...	|	...	1537	|	...	1642	...	|	|	1948	|	...
Prievidza .... d.	...	...	*0441*	|	*0610*	*0643*	|	0856	*1037*	|	|	...	*1215*	|	*1328*	*1436***z**	|	1509	|	1653	|	|	*1838*	|	2122
Horná Štubňa .... d.	...	0506	0551	|	0725	0802	|	0954	1143	|	1205	1250	1330	|	1430	1538	|	1639	1647	1749	|	|	1951	|	2249
Turčianske Teplice ...... d.	...	0517	0601	0630	0735	0811	0847	1004	1153	1203	1215	1300	1339	1413	1441	1548	1631	...	1657	1757	1814	1953	2002	2040	2258
Diviaky .... d.	...	0521	0604	|	0737	0814	|	1007	1156	1207	1219	1303	1342	|	1444	1550	|	...	1700	1800	1816	1955	2007	|	2301
Martin .... d.	0455	0549	0630	0647	0803	0841	0905	1036	...	1234	1246	1331	1409	1433	1514	1617	1648	...	1730	...	1843	...	2034	2058	...
Vrútky .... a.	0503	0558	0639	0653	0812	0850	0912	1045	...	1243	1255	1340	1418	1439	1523	1626	1654	...	1739	...	1852	...	2044	2105	...
Vrútky **1180** .... d.	0504	*0604*	*0644*	0655	0813	*0855*	0914	*1053*	...	*1306*	*1306*	*1346*	...	1441	*1553*	...	1656	...	1740	...	*1857*	...	...	2107	...
Žilina 1180 .... a.*	0526	*0624*	*0706*	0710	0836	*0915*	0929	*1113*	...	*1328*	*1328*	*1408*	...	1504	*1613*	...	1712	...	1803	...	*1920*	...	...	2125	...

▶ – *Full service* : ⊖	**1840** 2n	◇	◇ Ⓐ	◇	◇ Ⓐ	*Ex* **144** D	◇	**811**	◇ Ⓐ	◇	**831** b	◇ f	◇	◇ Ⓐ	**803**	◇	◇ g	◇	**805** e	**1846**	*Ex* **531** Ⓑy	◇	◇	◇ ⑤⑦v	◇ ⚒
Zvolen .... d.	0521	0557	0619	0655	0714	0740	0828	0931	1044	1157	1257	1334	1413	1506	1526	1633	1713	1813	1828	1911	1932	2008	2112	2153	2218
Banská Bystrica .... a.	0549	0627	0653	0727	0745	0800	0903	0955	1113	1231	1322	1402	1447	1537	1548	1708	1746	1844	1855	1943	1950	2037	2140	2224	2250

	◇	*Ex* **530** R	◇ Ⓐ	◇	◇ Ⓐ	**1847** 2	◇	**804** e	◇ u	◇	◇ Ⓐ	**802**	◇ Ⓐ	◇	◇	**832** b	◇ Ⓐ	◇	◇ g	◇ f	*Ex* **145** D	◇	**810**	◇	**1845** Ⓑh
Banská Bystrica .... d.	0441	0539	0603	0629	0702	0732	0817	0850	0921	1036	1116	1206	1258	1339	1422	1501	1514	1550	1622	1717	1751	1830	1908	2012	2120
Zvolen .... a.	0510	0556	0637	0653	0732	0757	0846	0916	0950	1103	1144	1232	1329	1410	1452	1526	1544	1622	1652	1750	1812	1902	1931	2045	2143

B – [12] Bratislava - Žilina - Martin and v.v.
D – DETVAN – [12] and ✕ Praha - Ostrava Svinov - Zvolen and v.v.
P – Conveys 🛏 1, 2 cl. Praha (**224/5**) - Žilina - Banská Bystrica and v.v.
R – ①–⑥ (not Dec. 24 - 29, 31, Jan. 1, Mar. 22, 24, Sept. 1, 15, Nov. 17).
b – Not Dec. 24, 25, 31.
c – ①–⑥ (not Dec. 26, Jan. 1, Mar. 24, Sept. 1, 15, Nov. 17).
d – Not Dec. 24 - 26, 31, Mar. 21 - 23, Aug. 31, Sept. 14, Nov. 16.
e – Not Dec. 24, 25, 31, Jan. 1, Mar. 22, 23.
f – Not Dec. 24 - 31.
g – Not Dec. 24 - 31, Jan. 1, Mar. 21, 24, Aug. 29, Sept. 1, 15, Nov. 17.
h – Not Dec. 23 - 25, 31, Mar. 21, 23.
k – Not Dec. 23, 24, 30, 31.
m – Not Dec. 24, 25, 31, Jan. 1.
n – Not Dec. 23 - 25, 31, Mar. 21 - 23.
r – ⚒ only.

s – Depart Prievidza 1545 on Ⓐ.
u – Not Dec. 24 - Jan. 1.
v – Also Dec. 26, Mar. 24, Aug. 28, Sept. 1, 15, Nov. 17; not Mar. 23, Aug. 29, 31, Sept. 14, Nov. 16.
x – Arrive 0700.
y – Not Dec. 23 - 28, 30, 31, Mar. 21, 23, Aug. 31, Sept. 14, Nov. 16.
z – Ⓑ only.
▶ – For complete service see panel below main table.
◇ – Stopping train. 2nd class.
⊖ – Also from Zvolen 0432 **g**; from Banská Bystrica 2141, 2227 **f**. Certain trains run to / from Bratislava (Table **1175**).
* – *117* km via Kremnica.
§ – Junction for Banská Štiavnica (5 - 6 trains per day, journey 30 minutes). See also Table **1175**.

1190 ZVOLEN / BANSKÁ BYSTRICA - KOŠICE

km		1823 Ⓐ 2		1829 Ⓒ 2s	◇ Ⓑ	◇	811 H	◇	1803 2△ n	1805 2▽ Ⓑv	801 Ⓑ h◧
	Bratislava Hlavná **1175** d.	...	...	...	...	...	0621	...	1221	1521	2346
0	**Zvolen** osob. d.	0601	*0815*	0933	...	*1000*a	0931	1317	1540	1844	0300
54	Lučenec **1255** d.	0650	0924	1018	...	*1114*a	|	1433	1630	1935	0350
70	Fiľakovo **1255** d.	0703	0943	1031	...	1150	|	1452	1644	1948	0404
98	Jesenské d.	0731	...	1058	1115	1231	⊙	...	1712	2017	0432
109	Rimavská Sobota a.	*0813*	...	|	1133	1249	|	...	*1743*	*2038*	*0508*a
161	Rožňava d.	0827	...	1157	...	...	|	...	1811	2116	0533
233	**Košice** a.	0922	...	1252	...	...	1359	...	1910	2211	0634
	Prešov **1196** a.	...	...	1338**z**	...	...	...	...	1959	...	0717

	◇ Ⓐ	1804 2▽ P	1802 2△ u	◇	◇ Ⓐ	◇	810 H	1822 2 s		800 Ⓑ h◧
Prešov **1196** d.	...	...	0830	...	...	...	...	1459**z**	...	2224
Košice d.	...	0558	0916	...	...	...	1506	1535	...	2306
Rožňava d.	...	0655	1012	...	...	...	|	1627	...	0008
Rimavská Sobota d.	...	*0706*	*1031*	*1308*	...	1436**a**	|	*1647*	...	|
Jesenské d.	...	0752	1110	1333	...	1456**a**	⊙	1725	...	0106
Fiľakovo **1255** d.	*0650*	0819	1138	1411	1415	1558	|	1751	1836	0134
Lučenec **1255** d.	0718	0833	1152	...	1440	1616	|	1805	1853	0148
Zvolen osob. a.	0823	0923	1239	...	1551	1737	1931	1859	2001	0246
Bratislava Hlavná **1175** a.	...	1235	1556	...	...	...	2235	...	...	0600

km		◇	◇	811 H	◇	◇ E	607	◇ F	◇	◇	◇
0	**Zvolen** 1185 d.	0557	...	0931	1157	...	...	...	*1526*	...	...
21	**Banská Bystrica** 1185 d.	0630	...	1008	1241	...	...	...	1616	...	...
64	Brezno d.	0727	...	1054	1348	1410	...	*1410*	1727	1833	...
107	Červená Skala a.	0823	...	1141	...	1516	...	*1516*	▬	1924	...
107	Červená Skala d.	...	0829	1142	...	1520	...	1543	...	...	1926
135	Dedinky d.	...	0901*	1213	...	1550*	...	1613*	...	...	1956*
192	Gelnica d.	...	1028	1311	...	1708	...	1759	...	...	2107
200	Margecany a.	...	1040	1319	...	1719	...	1812	◇	...	2119
200	Margecany 1180 d.	...	*1124*	1331	...	...	1722	...	1842	...	*2122*
219	Kysak 1180 a.	...	*1139*	1346	...	...	1737	...	1914	...	*2137*
235	**Košice** 1180 a.	...	*1152*	1359	...	...	1750	...	1931	...	*2150*

	◇	◇	◇	◇	◇	810 H	◇ F	◇ Ⓑk	420	◇ Ⓑ
Košice 1180 d.	...	...	*0844*	...	...	1506	...	...	1822	...
Kysak 1180 d.	...	...	*0902*	...	...	1519	...	...	1835	...
Margecany 1180 a.	...	...	*0924*	...	...	1533	...	...	1849	...
Margecany d.	0524	...	0927	...	...	1541	1613	...	▬	1858
Gelnica d.	0536	...	0939	...	...	1550	1626	...	...	1910
Dedinky d.	0707	...	1058*	...	...	1653	1749	...	...	2105
Červená Skala a.	0738	...	1129	...	...	1722	1820	...	...	...
Červená Skala d.	...	0838	...	1258	...	1723	...	1823	◇	...
Brezno d.	...	0930	...	1351	1418	1808	...	1927	1945	...
Banská Bystrica 1185 a.	...	1034	...	...	1528	1854	...	...	2040	...
Zvolen 1185 a.	...	1103	...	...	1622	1931	...	...	...	...

E – Ⓒ (daily June 28 - Sept. 1).
F – Ⓐ (not June 28 - Sept. 1).
H – HOREHRONEC – [12] Bratislava - Zvolen - Brezno - Košice and v.v.
P – ①–⑥ (not Dec. 24 - 26, 31, Jan. 1, Mar. 22, 24, Sept. 1, 15, Nov. 17).
a – Ⓐ only.
h – Not Dec. 23 - 28, 30, 31, Mar. 21, 23, Aug. 29, 31, Sept. 14, Nov. 16.
k – Not Dec. 23 - 26, 31, Jan. 1, Mar. 21, 23, Aug. 29, 31, Sept. 14, Nov. 16.
n – Not Dec. 24, 25, 31, Mar. 22.
s – Not Dec. 23 - 25, Mar. 21 - 23, Sept. 14.
u – Not Dec. 25, 26, Jan. 1, Mar. 23.
v – Not Dec. 23 - 25, 31, Jan. 1, Mar. 21, 23, Aug. 31, Sept. 14, Nov. 16.
z – ⑦ (also Dec. 26, Jan. 1, Mar. 24, Sept. 1, 15, Nov. 17; not Dec. 23, Mar. 23, Aug. 31, Sept. 14, Nov. 16).
◧ – POL'ANA – [couchette] 1, 2 cl. and [12].
◇ – Stopping train. 2nd class.
△ – [2] Bratislava (**803/2**) - Zvolen (**1803/2**) - Košice - Prešov and v.v.
▽ – [2] Bratislava (**805/4**) - Zvolen (**1805/4**) - Košice and v.v.
⊙ – Via Banská Bystrica and Brezno (see lower panel).
* – Request stop.

1194 KOŠICE / PREŠOV - HUMENNÉ - MEDZILABORCE

2nd class

km			615 Z	225 S	8907 n	8909	1907	1901 B	1903 u	1905	
	Bratislava **1180** d.	...	2347	...	...	...	...	0947	...	...	...
0	**Košice** d.	...	0615	0815	1107	1414	1527	1638	1848	2243	...
68	Trebišov d.	...	0700	0900	1154	1504	1613	1723	1937	2331	...
88	Michalovce d.	...	0733	0933	1229	1542	1654	1756	2009	0002	...
112	**Humenné** a.	...	0801	1001	1301	1622	1726	1817	2030	0023	...

	1906 P	1904 B	8904 n	8906	8908	1902 u	224 S	614 Z	
Humenné d.	0340	0524	0627	1012	1207	1536	1821	2230	...
Michalovce d.	0402	0547	0703	1042	1246	1557	1844	2254	...
Trebišov d.	0434	0620	0736	1116	1326	1628	1919	2329	...
Košice a.	0519	0707	0820	1202	1409	1712	2003	0013	...
Bratislava **1180** a.	...	1430	...	...	...	...	...	0630	...

km							Ⓐr				
0	Prešov d.	0332	0428	0559	0835	1158	1436	1514	1703	1902	2010
70	Humenné a.	0517	0610	0733	1008	1334	1554	1653	1843	2102	2148

Humenné d.	0407	0548	0738	1139	1440	1630	1754	2038	...
Prešov a.	0542	0725	0916	1314	1631	1821	1933	2219	...

km					n		Ⓐ	⑦e		n	
0	Humenné d.	0623	0821	1016	1308	1434	1627	1646	1820	2033	2227
105	Medzilaborce a.	0732	0931	1134	1425	1601	1753	1755	1935	2142	2333
107	Medzilaborce mesto a.	0738r	0937	...	...	1607	1759	1801	1941	2148	...

						n	c	Ⓑe	
Medzilaborce mesto d.	0407	0601	0741r	0957	...	1419	1614	1805	2014
Medzilaborce d.	0412	0605	0806	1005	1158	1431	1617	1811	2019
Humenné a.	0520	0721	0918	1115	1305	1533	1729	1912	2129

B – Conveys [12] and ✕ Bratislava (**604/5**) - Žilina - Košice - Humenné and v.v.
P – ①–⑥ (not Dec. 24 - 26, Jan. 1, Mar. 21, 22, 24, May 1, 8, July 5, Aug. 29, Sept. 1, 15, Nov. 17).
S – ŠIRAVA – [couchette] 1, 2 cl., [sleeper] 2 cl. and [12] Praha - Humenné and v.v.
Z – ZEMPLÍN – [couchette] 1, 2 cl., [sleeper] 2 cl., [12] Bratislava - Košice - Humenné and v.v. Not Dec. 24, 31 from Bratislava or Humenné.
c – Runs 7 - 12 minutes later on ⑦**e**.
e – Also Jan. 1, Mar. 24, Sept. 1, 15, Nov. 17; not Dec. 30, Mar. 23, Aug. 31, Sept. 14, Nov. 16.
n – Not Dec. 23 - 25, Mar. 21 - 23.
r – Ⓐ (not Dec. 24 - Jan. 7, Feb. 1, Mar. 3 - 7, 20 - 25, June 28 - Aug. 31).
u – Not Dec. 23 - 25, 31, Mar. 21 - 23.

1195 KOŠICE - ČIERNA NAD TISOU - CHOP

km		◇	◇	◇ n	◇	◇ n	605 b	◇ Ⓐ	◇	◇ ⊖△	◇
0	**Košice** d.	0517	0733	1000	1205	1435	1614	1646	1857	2007	2300
62	Slovenské Nové Mesto d.	0622	0840	1106	1311	1541	1704	1755	2002	2116	0012
95	Čierna nad Tisou a.	0700	0917	1143	1350	1618	1733	1833	2040	2156	0050
95	Čierna nad Tisou 🏛 d.	...	...	...	...	*1634*	...	...	...	*2220*	...
105	**Chop** 🏛 ⊕ a.	...	...	...	...	*1820*	...	...	...	*0006*	...

	◇	◇ △	604 b	◇	◇	◇ ⑦ u	◇ ①–⑥ d	◇	◇ n	◇ ⊖
Chop 🏛 ⊕ d.	...	*0428*	...	...	...	...	...	...	...	*1950*
Čierna nad Tisou 🏛 a.	...	*0434*	...	...	...	...	...	...	...	*1956*
Čierna nad Tisou d.	0313	0452	0615	0713	1000	1303	1340	1515	1828	2020
Slovenské Nové Mesto d.	0353	0531	0644	0751	1039	1342	1418	1553	1906	2058
Košice a.	0501	0640	0729	0854	1145	1448	1521	1706	2016	2200

b – From / to Bratislava (Table **1180**).
d – Also Dec. 23, 30, Mar. 23, Aug. 31, Sept. 14, Nov. 16; not Jan. 7, Mar. 24, 25, Sept. 1, 15, Nov. 17.
n – Not Dec. 23 - 25, Mar. 21 - 23.
u – Also Jan. 7, Mar. 24, 25, Sept. 1, 15, Nov. 17; not Dec. 23, 30, Mar. 23, Aug. 31, Sept. 14, Nov. 16.
⊕ – East European time (one hour ahead).
◇ – Stopping train. 2nd class.
⊖ – Also conveys [couchette] 1, 2 cl. Wien - Bratislava - Žilina - Košice - Lviv (- Kyïv on dates in Table **96**) and v.v.
△ – Conveys [couchette] 1, 2 cl. Košice - Chop - Moskva and v.v. (Žilina - Košice - Moskva and v.v. on dates in Table **1180**).

1196 KOŠICE - PREŠOV - PLAVEČ

km		◇ Ⓐ	◇	◇ Ⓐ	801 ①–⑥ Pn	◇ Ⓒ	◇	◇	2 u	382 J	◇ ①–⑥ d	1829 ⑦ 2q	◇	◇ Ⓐ	◇	◇	◇	◇	◇	1803 ⊖z	◇ Ⓐ	2 Ⓑ h	◇ Ⓑ h	◇	380 C	◇
0	**Košice** 1180 d.	0428	0524	0640	0649	0702	0745	0932	1035	1155	1249	1300	...	1425	1456	1601	1732	1812	...	1930	2027	...	2205	...	2254	2314
16	Kysak 1180 d.	0446	0551	0706	0701	0720	0758	0950	1050	1207	1307	1315	1400	1439	1515	1619	1750	1832	1912	1943	2047	2140	2227	2227	2307	2332
33	**Prešov** a.	0515	0617	0728	0717	0742	0825	1017	1107	1223	1331	1338	1429	1508	1537	1641	1812	1857	1935	1959	2109	2200	2257	2257	2323	2358
88	Plaveč a.	...	...	...	...	...	...	1130	...	1319	...	...	...	...	1702	...	...	2012	...	...	...	...	...	...	0024	...

	◇ Ⓐ	381 C	◇	◇	◇ Ⓐ	◇		1802 ⊖v	◇	◇	2	◇ Ⓐ	◇ Ⓐ	◇ Ⓒ	◇ ①–⑥ d	1822 ⑦ 2q	◇	◇	383 J	2	◇	◇	◇ Ⓑ h	◇	800 Ⓑ Pb	◇ Ⓐ
Plaveč d.	...	0345	...	0441	...	...	...	...	...	...	...	1219	...	1250	...	...	...	...	1635	...	...	1808	1808	...	...	
Prešov d.	0400	0442	0519	0552	0634	0801	...	0830	0954	1140	1230	1333	1405	1405	1433	1459	1553	1653	1731	1815	1833	1938	1938	2202	2224	2303
Kysak 1180 a.	0423	0459	0542	0617	0657	0824	...	0847	1017	1203	1246	1358	1428	1428	1454	1516	1616	1720	1747	1831	1901	2005	2005	2225	|	2330
Košice 1180 a.	0440	0511	0600	0635	0718	0849	...	0859	1035	1216	...	1417	1446	1446	1511	1530	1634	1738	1800	...	1915	...	2019	2243	2251	2347

C – CRACOVIA – June 20 - Sept. 1. [sleeper] 1, 2 cl. and [2] București - Miskolc - Košice - Kraków and v.v.; [sleeper] 2 cl. and [2] Keszthely - Budapest - Košice - Kraków and v.v.
J – JOSEF BEM – [12] and ✕ Budapest - Warszawa and v.v.
P – POL'ANA – [couchette] 1, 2 cl. and [12] Bratislava - Košice - Prešov and v.v. (Table **1175**).
b – Not Dec. 23 - 28, 30, 31, Mar. 21, 23, Aug. 29, 31, Sept. 14, Nov. 16.
d – Also Dec. 23, Mar. 23, Aug. 31, Sept. 14, Nov. 16; not Dec. 26, Jan. 1, Mar. 24, Sept. 1, 15, Nov. 17.
h – Not Dec. 23 - 25, Mar. 21, 23, Aug. 31, Sept. 14, Nov. 16.
n – Not Dec. 24 - 29, 31, Jan. 1, Mar. 22, 24, Aug. 30, Sept. 1, 15, Nov. 17.
q – Also Dec. 26, Jan. 1, Mar. 24, Sept. 1, 15, Nov. 17.; not Dec. 23, Mar. 23, Aug. 31, Sept. 14, Nov. 16. To / from Zvolen (Table **1190**).
s – Not Dec. 23 - 25, 31, Mar. 21, 23, Aug. 29 - 31, Sept. 14, Nov. 16.
u – Not Dec. 23 - 31, Jan. 1, Mar. 22 - 24, May 1, 8, Sept. 1, 15.
v – Not Dec. 25, 26, Jan. 1, Mar. 23.
x – Change at Kapušany pri Prešove.
z – Not Dec. 24, 25, 31, Mar. 22.
⊖ – To / from Bratislava via Zvolen (Table **1175**).
◇ – Stopping train. 2nd class.

PREŠOV - BARDEJOV *45* km, 70 - 75 mins.
From Prešov: 0332**x**, 0559**x**, 0758, 1158**x**, 1514**x**, 1646, 1902**x**, 2041Ⓑ**s**, 2302Ⓑ**sx**.
From Bardejov: 0514, 0720, 1213, 1437, 1653, 2050Ⓑ**h**, 2226.

HUNGARY

Operator: Magyar Államvasutak (MÁV), except the lines from Sopron to Győr and Szombathely which are operated by Győr - Sopron - Ebenfurthi Vasút (GySEV).

Services: All trains convey first and second class seating, **except** where shown otherwise in footnotes or by '2' in the train column, or where the footnote shows sleeping- and/or couchette cars only. Descriptions of sleeping- (🛏) and couchette (🛏) cars appear on page 10. Certain international services, as indicated in the tables, cannot be used for internal journeys in Hungary, whilst others generally convey dedicated carriages for internal journeys, which may be made without reservation.

Timings: Valid **December 9, 2007 - June 14, 2008.** Christmas cancellations of long-distance trains are shown in the tables but some local trains may not run on the evening of Dec. 24, 31 or on Dec. 25, Jan. 1, and these cancellations are generally **not** shown in the tables.

Reservations: Most **Domestic** InterCity (*IC*) and all InterPici (*IP*) trains have **compulsory** reservation, as shown by 🅁 in the tables. *IC* trains require a supplement of 520 HUF which includes the reservation fee. The price of the supplement may be reduced on certain journeys or on certain dates. Passengers having passes which include the supplement (e.g. Eurail) have to pay only the reservation fee of 130 HUF. For domestic journeys on **International** *EC*/*IC*/*EN* trains, the supplement is 390 HUF, but seat reservation is not possible. For international journeys on these trains the supplement does not apply (unless shown) but seat reservation is possible (and is **compulsory** on certain trains where shown).

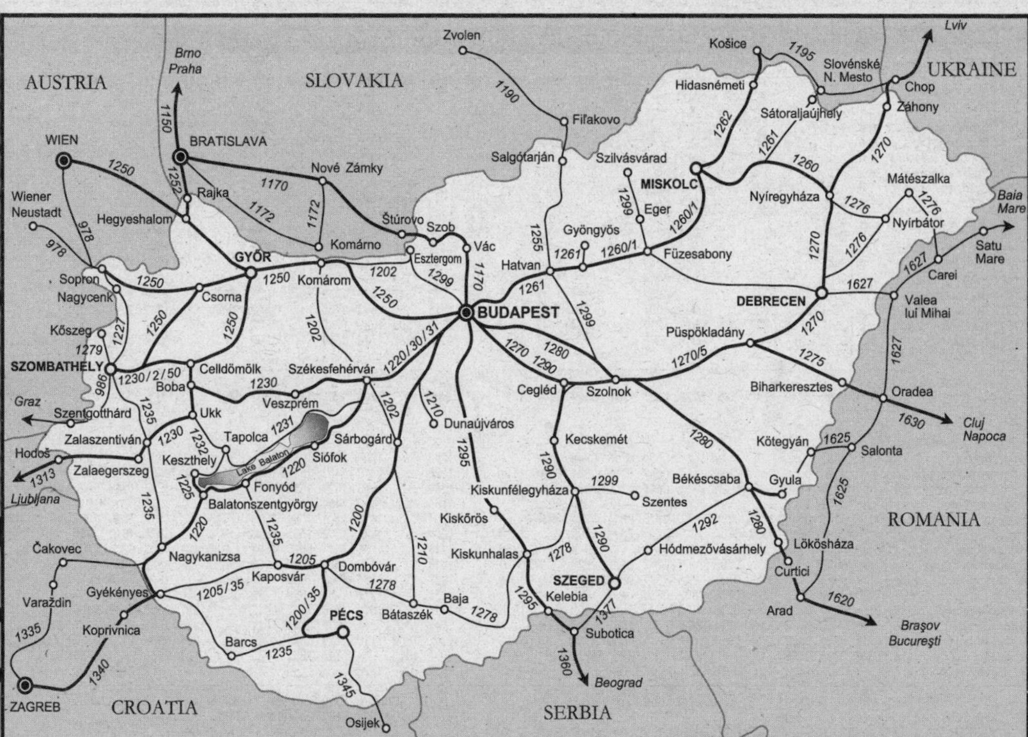

BUDAPEST - DOMBÓVÁR - PÉCS 1200

km		8010	*IC* 800	8002	*IC* 802	*IC* 804	8204	*IC* 814	8006	*IC* 806	*IC* 828	*IC* 816	*IC* 808	4018
			🅁✕		🅁✕	🅁✕	2	🅁✕		🅁✕	🅁	🅁✕	🅁✕	
		2		2	S				2		n			2
	Budapest Keleti .... § d.	...	0630	...	0930	1230	...	1430	...	1630	...	1745	1930	...
0	**Budapest** Déli .... § d.	...	|	0730	|	|	1245	|	1530	|	1700	|	|	2050
4	Budapest Kelenföld .... § d.	...	0649	0737	0948	1247	1252	1447	1537	1648	1707	1802	1947	2057
84	Sárbogárd .... § d.	0341	0756	0855	1052	1349	1412	1556	1651	1750	1809	1906	2050	2225
164	Dombóvár .... a.	0458	0849	1000	1140	1437	1524	1643	1801	1836	1856	2002	2138	...
164	Dombóvár **1235** .... d.	0508	0850	1001	1141	1438	*1548*	1644	1807	1838	...	2003	2139	...
209	Szentlőrinc .... d.	0606	0927	1049	1214	1511	*1644*	1717	1857	1911	...	2036	2214	...
228	**Pécs 1235** .... a.	0627	0941	1105	1228	1525	*1709*	1730	1917	1924	...	2050	2229	...

	8009	*IC* 807	*IC* 829	*IC* 817	8007	*IC* 805	*IC* 815	8203	*IC* 803	*IC* 801	18001	*IC* 811	1821	
		🅁✕	🅁	🅁✕		🅁✕	🅁🍷	2	🅁✕	🅁✕	2	🅁✕		2
	2		n							S	⑦		⑦	Ⓑ
Pécs 1235 ....d.	0453	0615	...	0655	...	0855	1155	*1214*	1355	1555	1745	1855	...	2255
Szentlőrinc......................d.	0508	0630	...	0710	...	0911	1220	*1247*	1409	1609	1802	1911	...	2314
Dombóvár **1235** ....a.	0546	0703	...	0742	...	0944	1256	*1338*	1442	1641	1852	1943	...	0003
Dombóvár.........................d.	0548	0705	0716	0743	0733	0946	1257	1359	1444	1644	1858	1944	1947	...
Sárbogárd.................. § d.	0651	0755	0809	0832	0901	1035	1349	1538	1533	1733	2011	2033	2049	...
Budapest Kelenföld ...... § a.	0800	0855	0906	0936	1011	1137	1447	1651	1632	1845	2136	2142	2150	...
Budapest Déli .... § a.	0808	|	0913	|	1018	|	|	1658	|	|	2143	|	2158	...
Budapest Keleti .... § a.	...	0913	...	0953	...	1153	1503	...	1649	1903	...	2158	...	...

S – To/from Sarajevo (Table **92a**). **n** – To/from Nagykanizsa (Table **1205**). § – See also **1210**.

2nd class LOCAL TRAINS 1202

90 km							
Győr **1250** .... d.	*0431*	0631	...	1131	...	*1531*	*1831*
Komárom **1250** .. d.	0535	0704	...	1204	...	1635	1930
Almásfüzitő .... d.	0552	0715	0720	1215	1240	1650	1945
Esztergom .... a.	0726	...	0840	...	1403	1807	2107
	⚒						
Esztergom .... d.	0525	0745	...	1333	1433	1850	2133
Almásfüzitő .... a.	0659	0911	0939	1456	1556	2013	2256
Komárom **1250** .. a.	*0751*	...	0951	1511	1611	2030	2311
Győr **1250** .... a.	*0827*	...	1027	*1627*	*1727*	*2127*	...
82 km							
Komárom .... d.	0450	0805	...	1130	1605	2005	...
Székesfehérvár ... a.	0628	0938	...	1305	1741	2138	...
Székesfehérvár ... d.	0400	0600	...	1115	1515	1815	...
Komárom .... a.	0532	0732	...	1247	1647	1947	...
39 km	*Subject to confirmation*						Ⓑ
Székesfehérvár ... d.	0530	0757	1044	1435	1702	1923	2312
Sárbogárd .... a.	0640	0854	1147	1541	1802	2025	0013
Sárbogárd........... d.	0454	0657	0900	1150	1542	1810	2043
Székesfehérvár ... a.	0557	0756	1003	1251	1645	1913	2145

DOMBÓVÁR - KAPOSVÁR - GYÉKÉNYES - NAGYKANIZSA 1205

For other services Budapest - Nagykanisza and v.v. (via Fonyód) see Table **1220**

km				*IP* 822			*IP* 824		*IP* 1824	8204	*IP* 826	*IC* 828	
		2	2	🅁	2	2	🅁	2	🅁		🅁	🅁	2
				2			2		2		2		Ⓑ
	Budapest Déli **1200** . d.	...	...	...	...	...	...	...	...	1245	...	1700	...
0	**Dombóvár** .... d.	0345	0619	0853	1028	1152	1300	1347	1447	1532	1650	1857	2147
2	Dombóvár alsó .... ◐ d.	0349	0623	|	1032	1155	|	1351	|	1540	|	|	2151
31	**Kaposvár**............ ◐ a.	0441	0719	0934	1124	1251	1345	1443	1532	1624	1736	1937	2243
31	**Kaposvár**............ ◐ d.	0452	0722	0938	1127	...	*1351*	1447	1551	1626	...	1939	2246
71	Somogyszob .... d.	0612	0825	1024	1238	...	*1500*	1552	1640	1711	...	2022	2343
101	Gyékényes .... ◐ a.	0650	0906	1056	1314	...	*1542*	1629	1713	1750	...	2054	0021
130	**Nagykanizsa**........ ◐ a.	...	1003	...	1350	...	*1616*	...	...	*1916*	...	2125	...

	IC 829		*IP* 825	8203	*IP* 1825		*IP* 823		*IP* 821	
	🅁	2	🅁	2	🅁	2	🅁	2	🅁	2
			2		2	Ⓑ	2△		◇	
Nagykanizsa ...... ◐ d.	0447	...	...	*1052*	...	...	...	1438	...	1702
Gyékényes .... ◐ d.	0513	0530	...	*1124*	1223	1413	...	1513	1722	1753
Somogyszob.......... d.	0547	0613	...	*1201*	1302	1453	...	1552	1756	1829
Kaposvár .... ◐ a.	0631	0708	...	*1256*	1348	1547	...	1648	1846	1924
Kaposvár .... ◐ d.	0633	0735	1208	1303	1354	...	1600	1649	1853	1944
Dombóvár alsó .. ◐ d.	|	0834	|	|	|	...	|	1741	|	2044
Dombóvár............ a.	0715	0837	1248	1345	1439	...	1640	1744	1940	2047
Budapest Déli **1200**. a.	0913	...	...	1658	...	...	...	...	...	...

◐ – See also Table **1235**. ◇ – On ⑦ train **1821** (not 🅁) to Budapest Déli, arrive 2158. △ – On ⑦ to June 8/from Aug. 31 train *IC* **1823** to Budapest Déli, arrive 1903.

1210 BUDAPEST - BAJA

km		*IP*® 830	4200					8006 8346	4206	*IP*® 838	4008 8348
		2		2	2	2	2	2		2	2
0	**Budapest** Déli **1200** . d.	*0630*k	0645	*0730*	...	*1245*	...	1530	1610	*1700*	1910
4	Budapest Kelenföld... d.	*0649*	0653	*0737*	...	*1252*	...	1537	1618	*1707*	1917
80	Dunaújváros .... a.	|	0800	|	...	|	...	|	1726	|	|
	Sárbogárd **1200** .... a.	*0750*	...	*0854*	...	*1411*	...	1646	...	*1808*	2027
	Sárbogárd .... d.	0810	...	0900	1150	1418	...	1700	...	1815	2053
149	Szekszárd................ d.	0910	...	1025	1305	1536	1640	1832	...	1916	2211
168	Bátaszék **1278**.......... a.	0941	...	1100	...	...	1715	1916	...	1947	2246
188	**Baja 1278**................ a.	1000	...	1123	...	...	1738	1938	...	2005	2309

		IP® 839	4227	8347 8007				*IP*® 833	4201	8341 4001
	2	2	2	2	2	2	2	2c		2
Baja 1278 ....d.	...	0551	...	0609	*0854*	...	1310	1538	...	1812
Bátaszék **1278** ....d.	...	0610	...	0633	0946	1200	1332	1558	...	1834
Szekszárd ....d.	0527	0642	...	0720	1024	1236	1412	1630	...	1922
Sárbogárd...............a.	0642	0741	...	0839	1139	1405	1527	1728	...	2036
Sárbogárd **1200** .....d.	*0651*	*0755*	...	0901	...	*1413*	*1533*	*1733*	...	2055
Dunaújváros..............d.	|	|	0834	|	...	|	|	|	1810	|
Budapest Kelenföld ...a.	*0800*	*0855*	0951	1011	...	*1540*	*1632*	*1845*	1921	2206
Budapest Déli **1200**..a.	*0808*	*0913*k	0958	1018	...	*1548*	*1649*k	*1903*k	1928	2213

c – On ⑦ (not June 15 - Aug. 24) numbered *IC* **1833** and runs through to Budapest Déli, arrive 1834.
k – Budapest Keleti.
See Tables 1295/1278 for Budapest - Baja train via Kiskunhalas

1220 BUDAPEST - SIÓFOK - FONYÓD - NAGYKANIZSA

km		8530	8642	8510	8720	*IC* 840 *IC* 200	852	8752	8802	8502	8644	5209	8514	854	1854	8504	8726	856 204	8806	*IC* 846	8518	*EN* 240	8508	8768	8728
		2	2	2	2	✕		2			2		2		⑤		2	M		®✕	2			2	2
			d			K	b		P	b		A			b			⊖	Q	b⊕		V			⊕
*	**Budapest** Keleti ..... ◧ d.	...	...	...	...	0605	...	...	...	...	...	1015	...	...	...	...	...	1500	...	1605	...	1700	...	...	...
0	**Budapest** Déli......... ◧ d.	...	...	0345	0455	|	0655	...	...	0745	...	|	...	1255	1320	1345	1420	|	...	|	...	|	1845	2020	2120
4	Budapest Kelenföld .. ◧ d.	...	...	0352	0502	0622	0702	...	...	0753	...	1031	...	1303	1329	1352	1427	1517	...	1624	...	1717	1852	2027	2127
67	**Székesfehérvár** ..... ◧ a.	...	...	0514	0622	0720	0800	...	...	0857	...	1134	...	1402	1427	1454	1547	1616	...	1724	...	1815	1958	2149	2247
67	**Székesfehérvár** ....d.	...	...	0525	0624	0723	0802	...	...	0900	...	1136	1240	1404	1430	1457	1600	1619	...	1727	...	1818	1959	2150	2250
115	Siófok.........................d.	0345	...	0624	0723	0804	0848	0901	...	1005	...	1221	1343	1446	1518	1600	1653	1701	...	1809	1812	1901	2100	2247	2349
130	Balatonföldvár..............d.	0407	...	0647	...	0819	0906	0924	...	1027	...	1242	1406	1503	1543	1622	...	1720	...	1824	1833	1917	2123	...	...
146	Balatonlelle..................d.	0428	...	0711	...	0834	0929	0945	...	1050	...	1302	1427	1523	1605	1643	...	1739	...	1840	1853	1938	2144	...	...
149	Balatonboglár ....d.	0433	...	0716	...	|	0934	0950	...	1055	...	1307	1432	1528	1610	1648	...	1744	...	|	1858	|	2150	...	...
157	**Fonyód** ....a.	0442	...	0725	...	0846	0942	1000	...	1105	...	1315	1442	1536	1618	1658	...	1752	...	1852	1907	1949	2200	...	...
157	**Fonyód** ....d.	0500	0630	0730	...	0849	0944	...	1006	1107	1205	1317	1446	1539	1621	1702	...	1754	1817	1854	1910	1952	2201	...	...
165	Balatonfenyves ....d.	0510	0644	0740	...	|	0952	...	1017	1117	1215	1325	1455	1547	1628	1712	...	1804	1827	|	1920	|	2211	...	...
181	Balatonszentgyörgy.....a.	0531	0704	0805	...	0909	1007	...	1040	1138	1235	1342	1516	1603	1643	1736	...	1819	1848	1916	1940	2012	2232	...	...
181	Balatonszentgyörgy.....d.	0547	0705	0807	...	0911	1011	...	1043	1142	1236	1346	1518	1605	1647	1740	...	1822	1856	1920	1942	2014	2233	...	...
221	**Nagykanizsa**..............a.	0638	n	0852	...	0946	1048	...	n	1227	n	1434	1605	1642	1728	1830	...	1900	n	1955	2027	2049	2318	...	...
352	*Zagreb* **1335 1340**...a.	...	...	...	...	1201	...	...	...	...	...	...	...	...	...	...	...	2222	...	...	...	2305	...	...	...

	8719	8509	8649	8747	*IC* 849	8727	8537	*EN* 241	8507	8807	8715		205 855		5208	853	1853	8503	8801		851	*IC* 201 *IC* 841	8511		8531
	2		2	2	®✕	2	2				2	2	N	2			⑦			2		✕		2	2
			d		b⊗			V		Q		Ⓐ	b⊖		A		b		P		b	K			
Zagreb **1335 1340**....d.	...	...	...	...	...	...	...	0456	...	...	...	...	0720	...	...	...	...	...	...	...	...	1546	...	...	...
Nagykanizsa...............d.	...	0320	n	...	0540	...	0525	0713	0745	n	...	...	1050	...	1300	1355	1440	1500	n	...	1700	1804	1832	...	2035
Balatonszentgyörgy......a.	...	0405	0535	...	0616	...	0612	0748	0831	0901	...	...	1128	...	1345	1433	1518	1546	1718	...	1738	1845	1917	...	2124
Balatonszentgyörgy......d.	...	0410	0545	...	0629	...	0645	0751	0832	0910	...	...	1140	...	1355	1437	1529	1549	1719	...	1748	1848	1920	...	2126
Balatonfenyves ....d.	...	0431	0607	...	|	...	0709	|	0856	0930	...	...	1156	...	1412	1454	1547	1610	1741	...	1804	|	1943	...	2146
Fonyód ....a.	...	0440	0617	...	0650	...	0718	0811	0905	0939	...	...	1203	...	1419	1501	1554	1619	1751	...	1811	1909	1952	...	2155
Fonyód ....d.	...	0443	▬	0630	0652	...	0731	0813	0908	...	1010	...	1204	...	1421	1503	1557	1623	...	...	1818	1912	1955	...	2201
Balatonboglár...............d.	...	0454	...	0641	|	...	0742	|	0918	...	1021	...	1213	...	1431	1511	1605	1633	...	...	1827	|	2006	...	2211
Balatonlelle..................d.	...	0459	...	0646	0705	...	0747	0826	0923	...	1026	...	1218	...	1436	1515	1610	1638	...	...	1832	1924	2011	...	2216
Balatonföldvár..............d.	...	0520	2	0708	0720	...	0807	0846	0945	...	1048	...	1237	...	1455	1538	1633	1657	...	...	1856	1940	2032	...	2237
Siófok.........................d.	0400	0544	0627	0728	0735	0802	0834	0903	1008	...	1130	...	1255	...	1517	1557	1659	1722	...	1820	1919	1956	2059	...	2259
Székesfehérvár...........a.	0458	0642	0724	...	0818	0859	...	0941	1103	...	1230	...	1336	...	1602	1636	1742	1815	...	1927	2000	2036	2156	...	...
Székesfehérvár....... ◧ d.	0500	0645	0730	...	0821	0900	...	0943	1106	...	...	1235	1341	1345	1604	1639	1744	1817	...	1935	2003	2038	2200	2245	...
Budapest Kelenföld.. ◧ a.	0618	0750	0850	...	0921	1019	...	1043	1211	...	...	1356	1441	1506	1710	1739	1840	1916	...	2056	2101	2137	2320	0008	...
Budapest Déli......... ◧ a.	0628	0758	0858	...	|	1028	...	|	1218	...	...	1403	|	1513	|	1748	1851	1923	...	2103	2108	|	2328	0015	...
Budapest Keleti ...... ◧ a.	...	...	...	...	0938	...	...	1058	...	...	...	...	1458	...	1728	...	...	...	...	...	...	2153	...	...	...

A – [12] Sátoraljaújhely - Miskolc - Budapest - Nagykanizsa / Keszthely and v.v.
K – KVARNER – [12] Budapest - Zagreb and v.v.
M – MAESTRAL – [12] Budapest - Murakeresztúr (**204**) - Zagreb. Conveys June 6 - Sept. 12 🛏 1, 2 cl. and [2] Budapest - Split (also ▬ 2 cl. on ⑤).
N – MAESTRAL – [12] Zagreb (**205**) - Murakeresztúr - Zagreb. Conveys June 7 - Sept. 13 🛏 1, 2 cl. and [2] Split - Budapest (also ▬ 2 cl. on ⑥).
P – [12] Pécs - Fonyód - Tapolca - Celldömölk and v.v.
Q – [12] Pécs - Fonyód - Tapolca - Celldömölk - Szombathely and v.v.
V – VENEZIA – 🛏 1, 2 cl., ▬ 2 cl., [2] Venezia - Zagreb - Budapest and v.v.; [12] and ✕ Gyékényes - Nagykanizsa - Budapest and v.v. For Venezia - Bucureşti portion see Table **1280**; for weekly 🛏 Venezia - Moskva see Table **97**. Special fares payable for international journeys.
W – ⑥⑦ (also Dec. 25, 26, Jan. 1, Mar. 24, May 1, 12, 22). [2] Keszthely - Szombathely (*IC* **981/2**) - Wien and v.v. Runs daily June 7 - 20 as train *IC* **1874/5**.

b – Conveys [12] Budapest - Keszthely and v.v. (Table **1225**).
c – To / from Celldömölk (Table **1232**).
d – [2] Fonyód - Keszthely - Tapolca and v.v.
k – Budapest **Keleti**.
n – To / from Keszthely (Table **1225**).
***** – Keleti - Kelenföld : *13 km.*
⊖ – Conveys on dates in Table **97**, 🛏 1, 2 cl. Moskva / Kyïv (**15/6**) - Budapest - Zagreb and v.v.
◧ – See also Tables **1230/31**.
⊕ – Not Dec. 24, 31.
⊗ – Not Dec. 25, Jan. 1.

1225 BALATONSZENTGYÖRGY - KESZTHELY - TAPOLCA

km					8642			852 862	8802		8502 9644	8644		5209		9606		19804	1854 1864		8806	*IC* 846 *IC* 876				
		2	2	2	2	2	2			2		2	2		2	2	2	2	2	2		2®	2	2	2	2
		Ⓐ		c	d				P				c	A		c		W	⑤		Q	⊕				
	Budapest Déli **1220** .. d.	...	...	...	...	...	...	0655	...	...	0745	...	...	1015k	...	...	...	...	1320	...	...	1605k	...	...	...	...
0	**Balatonszentgyörgy** ... d.	...	0538	...	0705	0814	0915	1018	1043	1141	1150	1236	...	1352	1440	...	1610	...	1655	1743	1856	1929	1947	2113	2150	2235
10	Keszthely .... a.	...	0550	...	0717	0827	0927	1029	1054	1153	1203	1248	...	1404	1452	...	1621	...	1706	1755	1907	1940	1959	2125	2202	2247
10	Keszthely .... d.	0415	...	0630	0722	0828	...	...	1056	1154	...	...	1350	...	...	1509	1640	1701	...	*1800*	1910	...	2000	...	*2207*	...
35	**Tapolca** .... a.	0448	...	0708	0754	0902	...	...	1128	1227	...	...	1421	...	...	1544	1713	1725	...	*1832*	1941	...	2033	...	*2240*	...

		8649		*IC* 879 *IC* 849			8807			19807		865 855		9655 5208		9605	1863 1853			8801	863 851					
	2	2	2	2®	2	2		2	2	2	2		2		2	2	2	2	2			2	2	2	2	2
		d	Ⓐ	⊗			Q			W	c			A		c	⑦			P		c				
Tapolca..........................d.	...	0450	0530	...	...	0645	0819	...	0946	1028	1039	...	1250	...	...	1430	...	...	1522	1627	...	1726	...	*1945*	2059	...
Keszthely.........................a.	...	0522	0602	...	...	0720	0847	...	1019	1051	1114	...	1323	...	...	1500	...	...	1558	1659	...	1756	...	*2020*	2130	...
Keszthely.........................d.	0353	0523	...	0607	0628	0721	0850	0950	1030	...	...	1118	...	1330	1405	...	1505	1530	...	1707	1725	1807	1830	2055	2131	2215
Balatonszentgyörgy.....a.	0405	0535	...	0618	0640	0734	0901	1002	1042	...	...	1129	...	1342	1416	...	1516	1542	...	1718	1736	1818	1842	2107	2143	2227
Budapest Déli **1220** ....a.	...	...	...	0938k	...	...	...	...	...	...	...	1458k	...	1728k	...	...	1851	...	...	...	2108	...	...	...	...	...

FOR NOTES SEE TABLE 1220 ABOVE

1227 SOPRON - SZOMBATHELY

Operated by GySEV

km			*IC* 981									
		2	C	2	2	2	2	2v	2	2	2	2
	Wien Süd **978** .....d.	...	0619	0727	...	1000r	...	...	...	...	...	...
	W. Neustadt **978** ..d.	...	0700	0803	0933	|	...	1333	1537	1632	1837	2137
0	**Sopron**.....................d.	0701	0742	0840	1028	1128	1322	1428	1628	1702	1926	2235
38	Bük...........................d.	0745	0822	0923	1116	1218	1404	1518	1716	1748	2010	2320
62	**Szombathely**..........a.	0807	0841	0945	1140	1240	1424	1540	1738	1810	2032	2342

										IC 982
	2		2	2	2	2	2v	2	2	C
Szombathely.........d.	0620	0648	1015	1117	1310	1424	1517	1617	1817	1920
Bük...........................d.	0643	0713	1040	1141	1332	1446	1540	1640	1840	1940
Sopron.....................a.	0727	0754	1127	1228	1416	1527	1627	1727	1926	2017
W. Neustadt **978** . a.	0823	0829	|	1322	1522	...	1722	1822	2023	2053
Wien Süd **978**.....a.	...	...	1256r	...	...	...	...	...	...	2133

C – CORVINUS *IC* **981/2** – [12] and ✕ Wien - Pécs and v.v. Conveys [2] Wien - Keszthely and v.v. on dates in Table **1232**.
r – ⚒ only.
v – To / from Graz (Table **986**).

Additional trains: Sopron - Szombathely 0340, 0442, 0602; Szombathely - Sopron 0402, 0524, 2045, 2226.

BUDAPEST - SZÉKESFEHÉRVÁR - ZALAEGERSZEG and SZOMBATHELY 1230

Trains *IC* **950 / 1 / 4 / 5** run non-stop Boba - Zalaegerszeg and v.v.

km			900		9002		*IC* 955		9006	*IC*	
		900	959	9002	39215	904	246	9006	9501	951	908
					2	2	C		2	🅁✗	
0	**Budapest** Déli ◧ d.	0600	0600	0900	0900	1200	1250	1500	1500	1705	1800
4	B'pest Kelenföld ◧ d.	0607	0607	0907	0907	1207	1258	1507	1507	1712	1807
67	**Székesfehérvár** ◧ a.	0704	0704	1006	1006	1304	1357	1605	1605	1809	1904
67	**Székesfehérvár** ... d.	0707	0707	1009	1009	1307	1400	1608	1608	1812	1907
90	Várpalota d.	0725	0725	1026	1026	1325	|	1626	1626	|	1925
112	Veszprém d.	0756	0756	1050	1050	1347	1438	1650	1650	1849	1949
148	Ajka d.	0826	0826	1123	1123	1421	1507	1724	1724	1920	2020
181	Boba d.	0857	0904	1151	1200	1448	1540	1759	1807	1953	2046
	Zalaegerszeg ◐ a.	|	1000	|	1313	|	1630	|	1904	2044	|
191	Celldömölk d.	0908	...	1208	...	1501	...	1810	...	...	2056
236	**Szombathely** a.	0941	...	1252	...	1541	...	1855	...	...	2130

		IC			9502		247			9506		958
	969	950	909	9007	9007	9005	*IC* 954	9005	903	903	901	901
	2	🅁✗			2		C					2
Szombathely d.	0532	...	0614	0900	...	1248	...	...	1550	...	1815	...
Celldömölk d.	0605	...	0652	0948	...	1320	...	...	1626	...	1851	...
Zalaegerszeg ◐ d.	|	0530	|	|	0852	|	1238	←	|	1525	|	1755
Boba d.	0613	0634	0700	1009	1009	1329	1339	1342	1645	1645	1910	1910
Ajka d.	...	0700	0724	1043	1043	→	1405	1423	1709	1709	1939	1939
Veszprém d.	...	0734	0752	1118	1118	...	1441	1502	1743	1743	2017	2017
Várpalota d.	...	|	0815	1141	1141	...	|	1527	1806	1806	2039	2039
Székesfehérvár a.	...	0809	0840	1158	1158	...	1515	1553	1827	1827	2059	2059
Székesfehérvár ◧ d.	...	0812	0842	1201	1201	...	1518	1555	1830	1830	2102	2102
B'pest Kelenföld ◧ a.	...	0912	0942	1302	1302	...	1617	1657	1937	1937	2202	2202
Budapest Déli ◧ a.	...	0918	0948	1308	1308	...	1623	1703	1943	1943	2208	2208

CELLDÖMÖLK - BOBA - ZALAEGERSZEG

km				959		39215			9501			
		2	2	B	2	2B	2	2	2B	2	2	2⑥
0	**Celldömölk** 1232 d.	*0548*	*0723*	0843	*1035*	1135	...	*1554*	1747	1843	1955	2140
10	Boba 1232 d.	*0602*	*0734*	0904	*1051*	1200	...	*1610*	1807	1903	2009	2155
28	Ukk 1232 a.	*0625*	*0751*	0920	*1113*	1227	...	*1639*	1824	1926	2036	2216
28	Ukk d.	0627	0819	0921	1118	1228	1535	1655	1825	1933	2037	2217
59	Zalaszentiván a.	0707	0855	0950	1153	1302	1611	1735	1854	2010	2114	2253
59	Zalaszentiván d.	0709	0902	0951	1154	1303	1613	1740	1855	2015	2127	2257
68	**Zalaegerszeg** a.	0719	0912	1000	1204	1313	1622	1750	1904	2024	2136	2307

	9500		9502				9506		958		
	2	2	2B	2	2	2	2B	2	2B	2	2
Zalaegerszeg d.	0455	0658	0852	1020	1346	1425	1525	1640	1755	1845	2053
Zalaszentiván a.	0504	0708	0900	1030	1356	1435	1534	1649	1805	1853	2103
Zalaszentiván d.	0505	0710	0901	1032	1357	1438	1535	1652	1806	1856	2128
Ukk a.	0534	0746	0937	1108	1434	1515	1610	1731	1844	1931	2206
Ukk 1232 d.	0536	*0754*	0938	...	*1510*	...	1611	1732	1845	1932	...
Boba 1232 a.	0552	*0816*	0959	...	*1532*	...	1628	1757	1901	1952	...
Celldömölk 1232 a.	0603	*0830*	1019	...	*1545*	...	1655	1816	1914	2008	...

B – Conveys (2) Budapest - Boba - Zalaegerszeg and v.v. (see upper table).
C – CITADELLA – (12) Budapest - Hodoš (**246/7**) - Ljubljana and v.v.
◧ – See also Tables **1220** and **1231**.
◐ – See lower table.

BUDAPEST - SZÉKESFEHÉRVÁR - BALATONFÜRED - TAPOLCA 1231

km			*IC*						*IC*		
		9730	972	9702	9704	974	9714	9706	978	9708	9728
		2	🅁✗				2		🅁✗		2⑥
0	**Budapest** Déli ◧ d.	*0345*	0620	0700	0940	1215	*1320*	1520	1715	1810	*2120*
4	Budapest Kelenföld ◧ d.	*0352*	0627	0707	0947	1222	*1327*	1528	1722	1817	*2127*
67	**Székesfehérvár** ◧ a.	*0514*	0725	0809	1050	1320	*1449*	1631	1820	1919	*2247*
67	**Székesfehérvár** d.	0520	0735	0825	1100	1330	1453	1645	1832	1930	2300
117	Balalatonalmádi d.	0624	0827	0928	1206	1431	1556	1753	1925	2040	0007
132	**Balatonfüred** d.	0646	0842	0951	1230	1447	1619	1812	1940	2101	0027
157	Révfülöp d.	0729	0909	1034	1319	1513	1708	1848	2006	2139	...
168	Badacsonytomaj d.	0744	0920	1053	1334	1524	1722	1903	2017	2153	...
170	Badacsony d.	0747	|	1056	1337	1527	1725	1907	|	2156	...
184	**Tapolca** a.	0806	0933	1114	1354	1540	1741	1926	2032	2215	...

		IC						*IC*		
	9709	977	9725	9705	975	9703	9701	971	9711	9751
		🅁✗	2					🅁✗	2	2
Tapolca d.	0430	0610	0830	1030	1230	1430	1630	1845	1808	2058
Badacsony d.	0450	|	0851	1049	1244	1450	1650	|	1828	2118
Badacsonytomaj d.	0453	0626	0854	1052	1248	1454	1653	1902	1831	2122
Révfülöp d.	0508	0637	0911	1108	1259	1512	1707	1913	1850	2138
Balatonfüred d.	0548	0702	0952	1148	1324	1552	1748	1939	1945x	2217
Balatonalmádi d.	0608	0717	1012	1207	1340	1611	1808	1954	2006	2237r
Székesfehérvár a.	0713	0812	1115	1311	1433	1714	1912	2043	2117	2343r
Székesfehérvár ◧ d.	0725	0826	...	1325	1445	1725	1925	2055	*2200*	...
B'pest Kelenföld ◧ a.	0826	0926	...	1433	1545	1830	2031	2154	*2320*	...
Budapest Déli ◧ a.	0833	0933	...	1443	1553	1838	2038	2203	*2328*	...

r – ⑥ only.
x – Arrive 1927.
◧ – See also Tables **1220** and **1230**.

SZOMBATHELY - UKK - TAPOLCA 1232

km		9609	8807	9617	19807	9625	9605	8801	9623	9603		
		2		2	W	2	2		2	2		2
0	**Szombathely** d.	...	0632	...	0853	*0900*	*1136*	*1422*	*1430*	*1627*	...	...
45	Celldömölk a.	...	0713	...	0930	*0946*	*1221*	*1455*	*1515*	*1711*	...	...
45	Celldömölk 1230 d.	0508	0723	0855	0931	1031	1317	1458	1554	1726	*1843*	...
55	Boba 1230 d.	0519	0734	0911	|	1051	1335	1511	1610	1737	*1903*	...
73	Ukk 1230 a.	0535	0751	0933	|	1113	1356	1533	1639	1756	*1926*	...
73	Ukk d.	0538	0753	0934	|	1114	1357	1534	1640	1800	1950	2220
81	Sümeg d.	0548	0802	0947	1009	1129	1406	1547	1656	1811	2005	2234
101	**Tapolca** a.	0605	0818	1012	1026	1158	1425	1614	1718	1829	2030	2300
	Keszthely 1225 a.	...	0847	1114	1051	...	1500	1659	1756	...	...	...
	Pécs 1235 ◧ a.	...	1349	...	...	...	...	2128	...	...	...	...

	9622	9602	8802	9614	9606	9626	19804		8806	9608	
	2	2		2	2	2	W	2		2	2
Pécs 1235 ◧ d.	...	...	0715	...	...	...	...	...	1410	...	...
Keszthely 1225 d.	...	...	1056	1350	1509	...	1701	...	1910	...	...
Tapolca d.	0715	0945	1130	1429	1546	1630	1728	1745	1944	2040	2100
Sümeg d.	0740	1008	1153	1456	1608	1654	1748	1810	2004	2058	2126
Ukk a.	0752	1016	1204	1509	1616	1705	|	1821	2012	2106	2140
Ukk 1230 d.	0754	1017	1205	1510	1618	*1732*	|	*1845*	2013	2107	...
Boba 1230 a.	0817	1036	1225	1534	1638	*1802*	|	*1906*	2031	2128	...
Celldömölk 1230 a.	0830	1047	1237	1545	1648	*1816*	1832	*1914*	2040	2139	...
Celldömölk d.	*0834*	...	*1300*	*1628*	*1659*	...	1833	...	2101	*2145*	...
Szombathely a.	*0916*	...	*1337*	*1713*	*1734*	...	1910	...	2143	*2223*	...

W – ⑥⑦ (also Dec. 25, 26, Jan. 1, Mar. 24, May 1, 12, 22). (2) Keszthely - Szombathely (*IC* **981/2**) - Wien and v.v. Runs daily June 7 - 20 as train *IC* **1874 / 5**.

◧ – For faster trains Pécs - Szombathely and v.v. see Table **1235**.

Additional journeys:
Tapolca 0430 - Ukk 0513 - Celldömölk 0557.
Celldömölk 0548 - Ukk 0628 - Tapolca 0706.

SZOMBATHELY - NAGYKANIZSA - PÉCS 1235

km		9800	2	*IC* 981	2	2	2	2	8906	2	*IC* 986	2
				C					2		🅁B	⑥k
	Wien Süd 978 d.	...	...	0619	...	...	...	...	...	...	...	...
	Győr 1250 d.	...	...	|	...	...	...	...	...	...	1835	...
	Celldömölk 1250 d.	...	...	|	...	...	...	...	...	...	|	...
0	**Szombathely** d.	0526	0713	0852	1119	1330r	1443	1620	1756	1911	2012	2205
49	Zalaszentiván a.	0604	0810	0931	1217	1427r	1543	1721	1846	2008	2053	2301
49	Zalaszentiván d.	*0628*	*0813*	*0935*	*1257*	*1441*	1555	*1740*	*1855*	2020	2105	*2304*
58	**Zalaegerszeg** a.	*0638*	*0823*	*0944*	*1307*	*1451*	1605	*1750*	*1904*	2030	2115	*2314*
		|	|	|	|	2	2	|	|	2		|
	Zalaegerszeg d.	*0540r*	*0846*	*0852*	*1138*	1429	1541	*1710*	*1845*	1948	...	*2245*
	Zalaszentiván a.	*0551r*	*0856*	*0900*	*1148*	1439	1551	*1719*	*1854*	1958	...	*2255*
49	Zalaszentiván d.	0605	0903x	0932	1225	1440	1554	1722	1858	2014	...	2306
102	**Nagykanizsa** a.	0647	1002x	1016	1327	1537	1655	1825	1939	2116	...	0005
	Pécs ⊗ a.	1050	...	1234	...	...	...	...	...	2223	...	...

	2	*IC* 987	8907	2	2	2	19803	2	*IC* 982	2	9803
		🅁B	2		Ⓐ		⑦		C		
Pécs ⊗ d.	...	...	0525	...	...	...	...	...	1535	...	1640
Nagykanizsa d.	0705	...	0810	1155	...	1455	1516	1634	1744	1903	2037
Zalaszentiván a.	0804	...	0856	1255	...	1554	1609	1738	1828	2003	2123
Zalaszentiván d.	0813	...	*0902*	1257	...	*1613*	*1613*	|	*1830*	*2015*	*2127*
Zalaegerszeg a.	0823	...	*0912*	1307	...	*1622*	*1622*	|	*1839*	*2024*	*2136*
	▬		▬	▬		|	|	|	|	|	|
Zalaegerszeg d.	0524	0750	*0846*	1138	*1425*	*1541*	*1541*	*1710*	*1815*	*1948*	*2053*
Zalaszentiván a.	0534	0759	*0856*	1148	*1435*	*1551*	*1551*	*1719*	*1824*	*1958*	*2103*
Zalaszentiván d.	0546	0811	0859	1200	1445	1623	1616	1739	1829	2018	2124
Szombathely a.	0651	0850	0943	1256	1541	1721	1704	1838	1908	2119	2204
Celldömölk 1250 a.	...	|	...	...	...	...	...	...	|	...	...
Győr 1250 a.	...	1025	...	...	...	...	...	...	|	...	...
Wien Süd 978 a.	...	...	...	...	...	...	...	...	2133	...	...

km		8920	8209	9800	8912	*IC* 981	8807	8924	8225	8926	8801	8906
		2	2		2	C		2	2	2	P	2
	Szombathely ⊗ d.	...	...	0526	...	0852	0632	...	...	...	...	1756
0	**Nagykanizsa** d.	*0417*	0417	0657	0724	1018	|	*1052*	1438	...	...	1942
29	Gyékényes d.	0500	0453	0743	0805	1045	n	1130	1512	1610	...	2019
84	Barcs d.	0616	|	|	0919	1133	|	1256	...	1728	...	2120
114	Szigetvár d.	0657	|	|	0959	1201	|	1336	...	1808	...	2154
	Fonyód ▶ d.	|	|	|	|	|	1005	|	...	|	1816	|
	Kaposvár ▶ d.	|	0624	0908	|	|	1132	|	...	|	1951	|
	Dombóvár alsó d.	|	0720	0952	|	|	1227d	|	...	|	2034	|
129	Szentlőrinc d.	0717	0833	1035	1017	1220	1331	1356	...	1828	2112	2209
148	**Pécs** a.	0740	0847	1050	1036	1234	1349	1423	...	1847	2128	2223

	8907	8802	8927	8923	*IC* 982	8806	8911	8236	9803	8951	8969
	2	P	2	2	C		2	2		2	2⑥
Pécs d.	0525	0715	0648	1250	1535	1410	1602	...	1640	2010	2247
Szentlőrinc d.	0541	0730	0718	1314	1549	1429	1626	...	1657	2038	2306
Dombóvár alsó d.	|	0809	|	|	|	1549d	|	...	1741	|	|
Kaposvár ▶ d.	|	0857	|	|	|	1656	|	1658	1823	|	|
Fonyód ▶ a.	|	1005	|	|	|	1815	|	...	|	|	|
Szigetvár d.	0558	...	0740	1337	1604	|	1647	|	|	2058	2326
Barcs d.	0636	...	0818	1425	1631	|	1727	|	|	2140	0005
Gyékényes a.	0735	...	0920	1527	1720	n	1828	1843	1953	...	...
Nagykanizsa a.	0807	...	*1003*	*1616*	1743	|	1916	1937	2028	...	...
Szombathely ⊗ a.	0943	...	...	...	1908	2143	...	...	2204	...	...

B – (12) and ✗ Budapest - Szombathely - Zalaegerszeg and v.v.
C – CORVINUS – (12) and ✗ Wien Süd - Pécs and v.v.
P – (12) Celldömölk - Tapolca - Fonyód - Pécs and v.v.

d – Also calls at Dombóvár (train **8807** at 1241, **8806** at 1545).
k – Also runs on ⑥ Szombathely - Zalaegerszeg (a. 2323).
n – Via Tapolca / Kesthely (Tables **1232/25**).
r – Ⓐ only.

x – On June 8 - Sept. 16 d. 0840, a. 0952.
⊗ – See other section of the table.

▶ – Local trains **Fonyód - Kaposvár** and v.v. (2nd class, journey approx. 70 minutes):
From Fonyód 0308Ⓐ, 0450, 0730, 1137, 1300Ⓐ, 1449, 1640, 2000.
From Kaposvár 0315Ⓐ, 0503, 0735, 1005Ⓐ, 1315, 1453, 1825, 2246⑥.

1250 BUDAPEST - GYÖR - SOPRON / SZOMBATHELY / WIEN

See below main table for additional slower services. For other services Budapest - Szombathely see Table 1230.

km		739 346 ✕ D	IC910 IC930 R	IC 910 R✕	EC 42 ✕	EC 46 ✕	IC912 IC932 R	IC 912 R✕	EC 48 ✕		EC 62 ✕ M	IC914 IC934 R	IC 914 R✕	IC793 IC344 ✕ A	IC 946 R	IC916 IC936 R	IC 916 R✕ G	IC916 IC986 R	EC 44 ✕	EN 466 ✕ W	IC918 IC938 R ⊙	IC 918 ✕	EC 40 ✕	EN 268 K
0	**Budapest** Keleti d.	0555	0610	0610	0710	0910	1010	1010	1110	...	1310	1410	1410	1510	1610	1705	1705	1705	1710	1805	1905	1905	1910	2020
13	Budapest Kelenföld d.	0610	0625	0625	0725	0925	1025	1025	1125	...	1325	1425	1425	1525	1625	1720	1720	1720	1725	1820	1920	1920	1925	2035
75	Tatabánya d.	|	0700	0700	|	|	1100	1100	|	...	|	1500	1500	|	1700	1755	1755	1755	|	|	1955	1955	|	|
141	**Györ** a.	0721	0739	0739	0836	1036	1139	1139	1236	...	1436	1539	1539	1636	1739	1834	1834	1834	1836	1931	2034	2034	2036	2146
141	**Györ** d.	0722	0744	0744	0837	1037	1140	1140	1237	...	1437	1544	1544	1637	1741	1835	1835	1835	1837	1932	2035	2035	2037	2147
172	Csorna d.	|	0809	0819	|	|	1209	1219	|	...	|	1609	1619	|	|	1859	1907	1907	|	|	2059	2107	|	|
226	**Sopron** 🛃 a.	|	0846	|	|	|	1246	|	|	...	|	1646	|	|	|	1940	|	|	|	|	2136	|	|	|
244	**Szombathely** a.	|	...	0908	|	|	...	1308	|	...	|	...	1708	|	|	...	1956	1956	|	|	...	2156	|	|
302	Zalaegerszeg **1235** a.	|	...	...	|	|	...	...	|	...	|	...	...	|	|	...	|	2115	|	|	...	...	|	|
	Graz **986** a.	|	...	...	|	|	...	...	|	...	|	...	...	|	|	...	2235	...	|	|	...	...	|	|
188	Hegyeshalom 🛃 d.	0755	...	...	0906	1106	...	...	1306	...	1506	...	...	1706	1811	...	...	...	1906	2003	...	...	2106	2216
219	Bruck an der Leitha **996** d.	0815	...	...	0927	1127	...	...	1327	...	|	...	...	1727	...	...	...	...	1927	2023	...	...	2124	2237
272	**Wien** Westbahnhof a.	0857	...	...	1008	1208	...	...	1408	...	1608	...	...	1808	...	...	...	...	2008	2105	...	...	2208	2322

	IC 949 R	EC 43 ✕	IC939 IC919 R✕	IC 919 R✕	EN 269 K	EC 41 ✕	EN 467 ✕ W	IC937 IC917 R ⊙	IC 917 R G	IC987 IC917 R	IC345 IC794 ✕ A		EC 47 ✕	IC935 IC915 R	IC 915 R✕	EC 63 ✕ M	IC933 IC913 R	IC 913 R✕	EC 45 ✕		EC 49 ✕	IC931 IC911 R	IC 911 R✕	347 738 ✕ D
Wien Westbahnhof d.	...	0525	...	...	0625	0752	0825	...	...	...	0952	...	1152	...	...	1352	...	...	1552	...	1752	...	...	1948
Bruck an der Leitha **996** d.	...	0607	...	...	0707	0839	0907	...	...	...	1034	...	1234	...	...	|	...	...	1635	...	1834	...	...	2032
Hegyeshalom 🛃 d.	0555	0630	...	...	0730	0900	0930	...	...	...	1057	...	1257	...	...	1457	...	...	1657	...	1857	...	...	2057
Graz **986** d.	|	|	...	...	|	|	|	...	0614	...	|	...	|	...	...	|	...	...	|	...	|	...	...	|
Zalaegerszeg **1235** d.	|	|	...	...	|	|	|	...	|	0750	|	...	|	...	...	|	...	...	|	...	|	...	...	|
Szombathely d.	|	|	...	0605	|	|	|	...	0905	0905	|	...	|	...	1305	|	...	1505	|	...	|	...	1853	|
Sopron 🛃 d.	|	|	0615	|	|	|	|	0915	|	|	|	...	|	1315	|	|	1515	|	|	...	|	1915	|	|
Csorna d.	|	|	0705	0705	|	|	|	1005	1005	1005	|	...	|	1405	1405	|	1605	1605	|	...	|	2005	2005	|
Györ a.	0625	0658	0725	0725	0758	0927	0958	1025	1025	1025	1125	...	1325	1425	1425	1525	1625	1625	1725	...	1925	2025	2025	2125
Györ d.	0628	0659	0728	0728	0759	0928	0959	1028	1028	1028	1127	...	1327	1428	1428	1527	1628	1628	1727	...	1927	2028	2028	2127
Tatabánya d.	0705	|	0805	0805	|	|	|	1105	1105	1105	|	...	|	1505	1505	|	1705	1705	|	...	|	2105	2105	|
Budapest Kelenföld a.	0741	0809	0841	0841	0909	1038	1109	1141	1141	1141	1237	...	1437	1541	1541	1637	1741	1741	1837	...	2037	2141	2141	2237
Budapest Keleti a.	0758	0823	0858	0858	0923	1053	1123	1158	1158	1158	1253	...	1453	1558	1558	1653	1758	1758	1853	...	2053	2158	2158	2253

SLOWER SERVICES BUDAPEST - GYÖR - SZOMBATHELY / SOPRON

See above for faster services

km		2	2	2⚒	920	920	2	992	2	922	2	9304	2	2Ⓐ	924	924	2	9306	2	928	928	733 P	2	2	2
0	**Budapest** Keleti d.	...	...	...	0540	0540	...	0740	...	0940	...	1140	...	...	1340	1340	...	1540	...	1740	1740	1940	...	2125d	2225d
13	Budapest Kelenföld d.	...	...	...	0555	0555	...	0755	...	0955	...	1155	...	...	1355	1355	...	1555	...	1755	1755	1956	...	2133	2233
75	Tatabánya d.	...	...	...	0635	0635	...	0835	...	1035	...	1235	...	...	1435	1435	...	1635	...	1835	1835	2036	...	2223	2323
84	Tata d.	...	...	...	0644	0644	...	0844	...	1044	...	1244	...	...	1444	1444	...	1644	...	1844	1844	2045	...	2234	2334
104	Komárom d.	...	...	...	0704	0704	...	0857	...	1057	...	1257	...	...	1457	1457	...	1657	...	1857	1857	2100	...	2257	2351
141	**Györ** a.	...	...	...	0734	0734	...	0927	...	1127	...	1327	...	...	1527	1527	...	1727	...	1927	1927	2130	...	2327	...
141	**Györ** d.	0410	0555	0645	0751	0756	0856	0937	1003	1141	1153	*1330*	1355	1450	1539	1556	1614	*1746*	1850	1942	1956	...	2240	...	...
213	Celldömölk a.	|	|	|	0854	|	1027	|	1131	1246	|	*1455*	|	|	1645	|	1743	*1924*	|	2048	|	...	|	...	...
258	**Szombathely** ▷ a.	|	|	|	...	|	...	|	...	1337	|	...	|	|	1734	|	...	...	|	...	|	...	|	...	...
172	Csorna d.	0436	0622	0721	...	0826	...	1004	...	...	1224	...	1426	1521	...	1627	...	...	1923	...	2026	...	2308	...	...
226	**Sopron** 🛃 a.	0530	0717	0813	...	0910	...	1047	...	...	1313	...	1512	1615	...	1710	...	...	2015	...	2110	...	2355	...	...

	2	732 P	9307	2⚒	929	999	2	2	9305	995	925	2	2	9303	993	923	2	2	921	991	2	2	2	2	2
Sopron 🛃 d.	0345	...	...	0450	...	0605	0745	...	...	1100	...	1145	...	...	1435	...	1556	...	...	1810	...	...	1945	...	2230
Csorna d.	0435	...	...	0542	...	0649	0841	...	...	1144	...	1241	...	...	1519	...	1654	...	...	1856	...	...	2040	...	2323
Szombathely ▷ d.	|	...	...	|	...	|	|	...	...	|	1023	|	...	...	|	1422	|	...	1728	|	...	...	|	...	|
Celldömölk d.	|	...	...	|	0610	|	|	0740	...	|	1107	|	1140	*1247*	|	1505	|	1702	1812	|	*1840*	1940	|	...	|
Györ a.	0505	...	...	0612	0716	0715	0910	0916	...	1210	1219	1310	1312	*1419*	1543	1615	1720	1835	1919	1920	*2023*	2109	2110	...	2348
Györ d.	...	0529	0557	...	0731	0731	...	...	1031	1231	1231	...	...	1431	1631	1631	...	...	1931	1931	2031	...	...	2131	...
Komárom d.	...	0548	0627	...	0802	0802	...	...	1102	1302	1302	...	...	1502	1702	1702	...	...	2002	2002	2104	...	...	2204	...
Tata d.	...	0601	0640	...	0815	0815	...	...	1115	1315	1315	...	...	1515	1715	1715	...	...	2015	2015	2122	...	...	2222	...
Tatabánya d.	...	0609	0651	...	0824	0824	...	...	1124	1324	1324	...	...	1524	1724	1724	...	...	2024	2024	2131	...	...	2231	...
Budapest Kelenföld a.	...	0647	0730	...	0902	0902	...	...	1202	1402	1402	...	...	1602	1802	1802	...	...	2102	2102	2225	...	...	2325	...
Budapest Keleti a.	...	0703	0748	...	0918	0918	...	...	1218	1418	1418	...	...	1618	1818	1818	...	...	2118	2118	2233d	...	...	2333d	...

LOCAL TRAINS GYÖR - WIEN

2nd class

Györ d.	0443	0643	0743	0943	1143	1343	1543	1743	1943	2138
Mosonmagyaróvár d.	0511	0711	0811	1011	1211	1411	1611	1811	2011	2211
Hegyeshalom a.	0519	0719	0819	1019	1219	1419	1619	1819	2019	2219
Hegyeshalom 🛃 d.	0532	0732	0824	1024	1224	1424	1624	1824	2024	2224
Bruck an der Leitha d.	0558	0758	0851	1051	1251	1451	1651	1851	2051	2251
Wien Südbahnhof a.	0626	0826	0920	1120	1320	1520	1720	1920	2120	2320

Wien Südbahnhof d.	0540	0640	0840	1040	1240	1440	1640	1840	2040	2140
Bruck an der Leitha d.	0611	0711	0911	1109	1309	1509	1709	1909	2109	2209
Hegyeshalom 🛃 a.	0635	0735	0935	1135	1335	1535	1735	1935	2135	2235
Hegyeshalom d.	0640	0740	0940	1140	1340	1540	1740	1940	2140	2240
Mosonmagyaróvár d.	0650	0750	0950	1150	1350	1550	1750	1950	2150	2250
Györ a.	0716	0816	1016	1216	1416	1616	1816	2016	2216	2316

A – AVALA – [12] and ✕ Wien - Budapest - Beograd and v.v.

D – DACIA – [12] and ✕ Budapest - Wien and v.v.; 🛏 1, 2 cl., ▬ 2 cl. and [2] Bucureşti - Budapest - Wien and v.v.; 🛏 1, 2 cl. and ▬ 2 cl. Beograd - Budapest - Wien and v.v.; 🛏 1, 2 cl. Sofiya - Beograd - Budapest - Wien and v.v.

G – [12] Budapest - Szombathely and v.v.; [2] Budapest - Szombathely - Graz and v.v.

K – KÁLMÁN IMRE – 🛏 1, 2 cl., ▬ 2 cl., [2] Budapest - Wien - München and v.v.; 🛏 1, 2 cl. Bucureşti - Timişoara - Budapest - Wien - München and v.v.; [12] Timişoara - Budapest - Wien and v.v.; ✕ Bucureşti - Timişoara - Budapest - Wien and v.v.

M – [12] and ✕ Budapest - Wien - München and v.v.

P – PANNONIA – 🛏 1, 2 cl., ▬ 2 cl. and [12] Praha - Bratislava - Györ - Budapest - Lökösháza and v.v.; [2] Praha - Budapest - Bucureşti and v.v. (also 🛏 1, 2 cl. on dates in Table 60).

W – WIENER WALZER – [12] and ✕ Budapest - Wien and v.v.; ▬ 2 cl., [2] Budapest - Wien - Zürich and v.v.

d – Budapest **Déli**.

▷ – For services via Székesfehérvár see Table **1230**.

⊙ – To / from Wien Süd (Table **978**).

* – Train **733/2** in Hungary.

OTHER TRAIN NAMES:

40/41 LÉHAR FERENC / LEHÁR
42/43 LISZT FERENC / FRANZ LISZT
44/45 BARTÓK BÉLA
46/47 SEMMELWEIS IGNAC / IGNAZ SEMMELWEIS
48/49 CSÁRDÁS

1252 GYÖR - BRATISLAVA

km		2	2	2	2	2	2	2	2	374* P
	Budapest Keleti **1250** d.	...	...	...	...	...	...	...	...	1940
0	**Györ** **1250** d.	0543	0843	1043	1243	1443	1643	1843	2043	2134
36	Mosonmagyaróvár **1250** d.	0611	0911	1111	1311	1511	1711	1911	2111	2159
47	Hegyeshalom **1250** d.	0640	0922	1122	1322	1522	1722	1922	2122	2208
60	Rajka a.	0655	0937	1137	1337	1537	1737	1937	2137	2218
60	Rajka 🛃 d.	...	*0947*	...	*1347*	...	*1747*	...	...	2235
79	Bratislava Petržalka a.	...	*1006*	...	*1406*	...	*1806*	...	...	2257
96	**Bratislava** Hlavná a.	...	...	...	...	...	...	...	...	2320

	375* P	9307	2	2	2	2	2	2	2
Bratislava Hlavná d.	0356	...	...	...	...	...	...	...	...
Bratislava Petržalka d.	0417	...	*0754*	...	*1154*	...	*1554*	...	*1954*
Rajka 🛃 a.	0437	...	*0812*	...	*1212*	...	*1612*	...	*2012*
Rajka d.	0449	0500	0822	1025	1225	1422	1625	1822	2025
Hegyeshalom **1250** d.	0500	0513	0840	1040	1240	1440	1640	1840	2040
Mosonmagyaróvár **1250** d.	0508	0523	0850	1050	1250	1450	1650	1850	2050
Györ **1250** a.	0527	0552	0916	1116	1316	1516	1716	1916	2116
Budapest Keleti **1250** a.	0703	0748	...	...	...	...	...	...	...

FOR NOTES SEE TABLE 1250 ABOVE

Local trains Rajka - Bratislava Petržalka are subject to confirmation

2nd class — BUDAPEST - SALGÓTARJÁN - FIL'AKOVO — 1255

km								586			
0	**Budapest Keleti** ◇ d.	...	*0705*	*0905*	*1105*	*1305*	*1505*	1630	*1705*	*1905*	*2105*
67	Hatvan ◇ d.	0410	0810	1010	1210	1410	1610	1733	1810	2010	2210
126	**Salgótarján** d.	0547	0947	1147	1347	1547	1747	1905	1947	2147	2340
132	Somoskőújfalu 🏛 a.	0557	0957	1157	1357	1557	1757	1915	1957	2157	2350
132	Somoskőújfalu d.	*0620*	*1008*	...	...	...	*1814*	...	...	...	...
146	**Fil'akovo** a.	*0638*	*1027*	...	...	...	*1833*	...	...	...	...

		589								
Fil'akovo d.	*0546*	...	...	*0946*	...	...	...	*1752*	...	...
Somoskőújfalu a.	*0605*	...	...	*1005*	...	...	...	*1811*	...	...
Somoskőújfalu 🏛 d.	0610	0635	0817	1017	1217	1417	1617	1817	2017	2217
Salgótarján d.	0621	0646	0828	1028	1228	1428	1628	1828	2028	2228
Hatvan ◇ a.	0750	0812	0950	1150	1350	1550	1750	1950	2150	2350
Budapest Keleti ◇ a.	*0857*	0932	*1057*	*1257*	*1457*	*1657*	*1857*	*2057*	*2257*	...

◇ – See also Table **1261**.

On Ⓐ trains run Hatvan - Salgótarján hourly 0310 - 2210, returning 0228, 0328, 0428, 0528, 0621, 0721, 0828 and hourly to 2228.

Fast trains — BUDAPEST - MISKOLC - NYÍREGYHÁZA — 1260

For slower trains Budapest - Miskolc see Table **1261**. Most *IC* trains continue beyond Debrecen to / from Budapest Nyugati. For trains Budapest - Debrecen - Nyiregyháza see Table **1270**

km		*IC*		*IC*	*IC*		*IC*	*EC*		*IC*	*IC*		*IC*	*IC*		*IC*	*IC*		*IC*	*IC*		*IC*	*IC*		*IC*	
		560	**532**	**659**	**500**		**657**	**382**		**564**	**512**		**655**	**504**		**566**	**514**		**653**	**506**		**568**	**536**		**508**	
		Ⓡ✕		Ⓡ✕	Ⓡ✕	2	Ⓡ✕	✕	2	Ⓡ✕	Ⓡ✕	2	Ⓡ✕	Ⓡ✕	2	Ⓡ✕	Ⓡ✕	2	Ⓡ✕	Ⓡ✕	2	Ⓡ✕	✕	2	Ⓡ✕	2
			R					**B**															**H** ⊖			
0	**Budapest** Keleti ▶ d.	...	0535	...	0635	...	0735	0835	...	0935	1035	...	1135	1235	...	1335	1435	...	1535	1635	...	1735	1835	...	1935	...
126	Füzesabony ▶ d.	...	0659	...	0758	...	0858	0958	...	1058	1158	...	1258	1358	...	1458	1558	...	1658	1758	...	1858	1958	...	2058	...
183	**Miskolc** ▶ a.	...	0732	...	0832	...	0932	1032	...	1132	1232	...	1332	1432	...	1532	1632	...	1732	1832	...	1932	2032	...	2132	...
183	**Miskolc** d.	0630	...	0735	...	*0839*	0934	...	*1039*	1134	...	*1239*	1334	...	*1439*	1534	...	*1639*	1734	...	*1839*	1934	...	*2039*	...	2139
221	Szerencs d.	0656	...	0800	...	0918	0959	...	1118	1159	...	1318	1359	...	1518	1559	...	1718	1759	...	1918	1959	...	2118	...	2218
239	Tokaj d.	0708	...	0812	...	0936	1011	...	1136	1211	...	1336	1411	...	1536	1611	...	1736	1811	...	1936	2011	...	2136	...	2236
271	**Nyíregyháza** a.	0733	...	0835	...	1017	1034	...	1217	1234	...	1417	1434	...	1617	1634	...	1817	1834	...	2017	2034	...	2217	...	2317
	Debrecen **1270** a.	0806	...	0906	...	...	1106	...	...	1306	...	...	1506	...	...	1706	...	...	1906	...	...	2108	...	...	...	...

		IC		*IC*	*IC*		*IC*	*IC*		*IC*	*IC*		*IC*	*IC*		*IC*	*IC*			*IC*	*IC*		*EC*	*IC*		
	529	**519**		**537**	**569**		**517**	**650**		**507**	**567**		**505**	**652**		**515**	**565**	**533**		**503**	**654**		**383**	**563**		
		Ⓡ✕	2	✕	Ⓡ✕	2	Ⓡ✕	Ⓡ✕	2	Ⓡ✕	Ⓡ✕	2	Ⓡ✕	Ⓡ✕	2	Ⓡ✕	Ⓡ✕		2	Ⓡ✕	Ⓡ✕	2	✕	Ⓡ✕	2	2
				H ⊖														**R**					**B**			
Debrecen **1270** d.	...	...	...	...	0654	...	...	0854	...	...	1054	...	...	1254	...	...	1454	...	...	...	1654	...	...	1854	...	...
Nyíregyháza d.	*0343*	0526	0543	...	0726	0743	...	0926	0943	...	1126	1143	...	1326	1343	...	1526	...	1543	...	1726	1743	...	1926	1943	2043
Tokaj d.	*0418*	0550	0623	...	0750	0823	...	0950	1023	...	1150	1223	...	1350	1423	...	1550	...	1623	...	1750	1823	...	1950	2023	2123
Szerencs d.	0447	0602	0642	...	0802	0842	...	1002	1042	...	1202	1242	...	1402	1442	...	1602	...	1642	...	1802	1842	...	2002	2042	2215
Miskolc a.	0521	0626	*0721*	...	0826	*0921*	...	1026	*1121*	...	1226	*1321*	...	1426	*1521*	...	1626	...	*1721*	...	1826	*1921*	...	2026	*2121*	2249
Miskolc ▶ d.	0533	0628	...	0728	0828	...	0928	1028	...	1128	1228	...	1328	1428	...	1528	1628	1650	...	1728	1828	...	1928	...	...	...
Füzesabony ▶ d.	0618	0703	...	0803	0903	...	1003	1103	...	1203	1303	...	1403	1503	...	1603	1703	1725	...	1803	1903	...	2003	...	...	...
Budapest Keleti ▶ a.	0757	0827	...	0927	1027	...	1127	1227	...	1327	1427	...	1527	1627	...	1727	1827	1852	...	1927	2027	...	2127	...	...	...

B – BEM JÓZSEF – [12] Budapest - Košice - Warszawa and v.v.

H – HERNÁD / HORNÁD – [12] Budapest - Miskolc - Košice and v.v. Conveys June 21 - Aug. 31: [12] Keszthely - Budapest - Miskolc - Košice and v.v.

R – RÁKÓCZI – [12] Budapest - Hidasnémeti (**7202/3**) - Košice and v.v.

⊖ – Reservation compulsory for international journeys.

▶ – For slower services see Table **1261**.

Slower trains — BUDAPEST - MISKOLC - SÁTORALJAÚJHELY — 1261

For fast trains Budapest - Miskolc - Szerencs see Table **1260**. For faster journeys use *IC* train (Table **1260**) and change at Füzesabony (for Eger) or Szerencs (for Sátoraljaújhely)

km					**5500**	**5200**	**5510**	**520**	**5502**	**522**	**5512**	**524**	**5504**	**526**	**5506**	**528**	**5516**	**5208**	**1578**	**5508**	**5008**	**5518**	**5108**	
		2	2	2														**K**	**C**					2
0	**Budapest** Keleti ▶ d.	...	...	...	0505	0605	0705	0805	0905	1005	1105	1205	1305	1405	1505	1605	1705	1805	...	1905	2005	2105	2205	2240
67	Hatvan d.	...	...	*0505*	0600	0700	0800	0900	1000	1100	1200	1300	1400	1500	1600	1700	1800	1900	1940	2000	2100	2200	2300	2355
87	Vámosgyörk ⊡ d.	...	...	*0521*	0616	0715	0816	0915	1016	1115	1216	1315	1416	1515	1616	1715	1816	1915	1952	2016	2115	2216	2315	0011
126	Füzesabony ▶ a.	...	...	*0557*	0652	0742	0852	0942	1052	1142	1252	1342	1452	1542	1652	1742	1852	1942	2014	2052	2142	2252	2342	0047
126	Füzesabony ▶ d.	...	...	0605	0707	0744	0907	0944	1107	1144	1307	1344	1507	1544	1707	1744	1907	1944	2015	2107	2144	2307	2344	...
143	**Eger** ⊙ a.	...	...	|	0724	|	0924	|	1124	|	1324	|	1524	|	1724	|	1924	|	|	2124	|	2324	|	...
139	Mezőkövesd d.	...	...	0617	▬	0754	▬	0954	▬	1154	▬	1354	▬	1554	▬	1754	▬	1954	2024	▬	2154	...	2354	...
183	**Miskolc** ▶ a.	...	...	0658	2	0826	2	1026	2	1226	2	1426	2	1626	2	1826	2	2026	2052	2	2226	...	0026	...
183	**Miskolc** ▶ d.	*0539*	0639	...	*0739*	0839	*0939*	1039	*1139*	1239	*1339*	1439	*1539*	1639	*1739*	1839	*1939*	2039	...	*2139*	...	...	...	...
221	Szerencs ▶ d.	0615	0715	...	0815	0915	1015	1115	1215	1315	1415	1515	1615	1715	1815	1915	2015	2115	...	2227	...	...	...	...
257	Sárospatak a.	0702	0802	...	0902	1002	1102	1202	1302	1402	1502	1602	1702	1802	1902	2002	2102	2202	...	2308	...	...	...	...
267	**Sátoraljaújhely** 🏛 a.	0711	0811	...	0911	1011	1111	1211	1311	1411	1511	1611	1711	1811	1911	2011	2111	2211	...	2317	...	...	...	...
269	Slovenské Nové Mesto a.	...	...	...	...	1020	...	...	...	...	1520	...	...	...	...	2020	...	...	...	...	...	...	...	...

	5009	**5509**	**529**	**5519**	**1577**	**5209**		**527**		**525**		**5205**		**523**		**521**		**5201**						
		2			**D**	**K**	2		2		2		2		2		2		2	2	2	2	2	2
Slovenské Nové Mesto d.	...	...	...	...	...	0540	...	...	...	...	1040	...	...	...	...	1540	...	...	...	...	...	...	2040	...
Sátoraljaújhely 🏛 d.	...	...	0349	...	...	0549	0649	0749	0849	0949	1049	1149	1249	1349	1449	1549	1649	1749	...	1849	1949	...	2049	...
Sárospatak d.	...	...	0403	...	...	0603	0703	0803	0903	1003	1103	1203	1303	1403	1503	1603	1703	1803	...	1903	2003	...	2103	...
Szerencs ▶ d.	...	...	0447	...	...	0647	0745	0847	0945	1047	1145	1247	1345	1447	1545	1647	1745	1847	...	1945	2047	...	2145	*2215*
Miskolc ▶ a.	...	...	0521	...	...	0721	*0821*	0921	*1021*	1121	*1221*	1321	*1421*	1521	*1621*	1721	*1821*	1921	...	*2021*	2121	...	...	*2249*
Miskolc ▶ d.	0325	...	0533	...	0703	0733	▬	0933	▬	1133	▬	1333	▬	1533	▬	1733	▬	1933	2002	▬	...	2202	...	2302
Mezőkövesd d.	0406	...	0605	...	0731	0805	...	1005	...	1205	...	1405	...	1605	...	1805	...	2005	2044	...	...	2244	...	2344
Eger ⊙ d.	|	0436	|	0636	|	|	0836	|	1036	|	1236	|	1436	|	1636	|	1836	|	|	2036	...	|	...	|
Füzesabony ▶ a.	0417	0453	0614	0653	0739	0814	0853	1014	1053	1214	1253	1414	1453	1614	1653	1814	1853	2014	2055	2053	...	2255	...	2355
Füzesabony ▶ d.	0418	0502	0618	0709	0740	0818	0909	1018	1109	1218	1309	1418	1509	1618	1709	1818	1909	2018	...	2109	...	...	...	...
Vámosgyörk ⊡ d.	0455	0538	0646	0745	0803	0846	0945	1046	1145	1246	1345	1446	1545	1646	1745	1846	1945	2046	...	2145	...	...	...	...
Hatvan d.	0511	0555	0702	0802	0814	0902	1002	1102	1202	1302	1402	1502	1602	1702	1802	1902	2002	2102	...	2202	...	...	...	...
Budapest Keleti ▶ a.	0617	0712	0757	0857	...	0957	1057	1157	1257	1357	1457	1557	1657	1757	1857	1957	2057	2157	...	2257	...	...	...	...

C – CRACOVIA – from Bucureşti June 22 - Aug. 31: 🛏 1, 2 cl. and [2] Bucureşti - Lökösháza - Košice - Kraków. From Keszthely June 21 - Aug. 31: [2] Keszthely - Budapest - Košice - Kraków.

D – CRACOVIA – from Kraków June 23 - Aug. 31: 🛏 1, 2 cl. and [2] Kraków - Košice - Lökösháza - Bucureşti. From Kraków June 20 - Aug. 30: [2] Kraków - Košice - Budapest - Keszthely.

K – [12] Sátoraljaújhely - Miskolc - Budapest - Nagykanizsa / Keszthely and v.v.

▶ – For faster trains see Table **1260**.

⊡ – Connecting trains **Vámosgyörk - Gyöngyös** and v.v. (journey 16 mins):
From Vámosgyörk : 0530, 0620 and hourly to 1920 (not 1020), also 2120.
From Gyöngyös : 0555 and hourly to 1955 (not 1055), also 2155.

⊙ – Full service **Füzesabony - Eger** and v.v. (journey 17 minutes):
From Füzesabony : 0422, 0507, 0607, 0636, 0707 and hourly to 2307.
From Eger : 0336 and hourly to 2236.

MISKOLC - KOŠICE — 1262

km			**532**		*EC*				*IC*	**1578**
			7202		**382**				**536**	**380**
		2		2		2	2	2	⊖	
			R		**B**				**H**	**C**
	Budapest Keleti **1260/1** d.	...	0535	...	0835	...	...	...	1835	...
	Füzesabony **1260/1** d.	0505	0659	0805	0958	1205	1405	1605	1958	2015
0	**Miskolc** d.	0606	0734	0906	1034	1306	1506	1706	2034	2055
61	Hidasnémeti a.	0713	0828	1013	1122	1413	1613	1813	2122	2142
61	Hidasnémeti 🏛 d.	...	0838	...	1132	...	1625	...	2132	2209
87	**Košice** a.	...	0912	...	1152	...	1700	...	2152	2229

	381	*IC*				**7203**		*EC*	
	1577	**537**				**533**		**383**	
		⊖	2	2	2		2		2
	D	**H**				**R**		**B**	
Košice d.	0540	0605	...	1040	...	1454	...	1805	...
Hidasnémeti 🏛 a.	0600	0625	...	1115	...	1529	...	1825	...
Hidasnémeti d.	0614	0635	0947	1147	1347	1535	1647	1835	2147
Miskolc a.	0700	0726	1055	1255	1455	1626	1755	1926	2255
Füzesabony **1260/1** a.	0739	0802	1155	1355	1555	1724	1855	2002	2355
Budapest Keleti **1260/1** a.	...	0927	...	...	...	1852	...	2127	...

B – BEM JÓSEF – [12] and ✕ Budapest - Košice - Kraków - Warszawa and v.v. (Table **99**). Classified *EC* in Hungary, *Ex* in Slovakia.

C – CRACOVIA – from Bucureşti June 22 - Aug. 31: 🛏 1, 2 cl. and [2] Bucureşti - Lökösháza - Košice - Kraków. From Keszthely June 21 - Aug. 31: [2] Keszthely - Budapest - Košice - Kraków.

D – CRACOVIA – from Kraków June 23 - Aug. 31: 🛏 1, 2 cl. and [2] Kraków - Košice - Lökösháza - Bucureşti. From Kraków June 20 - Aug. 30: [2] Kraków - Košice - Budapest - Keszthely.

H – HERNÁD / HORNÁD – [12] Budapest - Miskolc - Košice and v.v. Conveys June 21 - Aug. 31: [12] Keszthely - Budapest - Miskolc - Košice and v.v.

R – RÁKÓCZI.

⊖ – Reservation compulsory for international journeys.

1270 BUDAPEST - DEBRECEN - NYÍREGYHÁZA - ZÁHONY - CHOP

For trains to/from Romania see Table **1275**

km		IC 569	IC 650	IC 622	IC 567	IC 612	IC 652	IC 604	IC 565	IC 614	IC 654	IC 624	IC 563	IC 626	IC 616	628 16	IC 608
		R ✕	R ✕	R ✕	R ✕	R ✕	R ✕	R ✕	R ✕	R ✕	R ✕	R ✕	R ✕	R ✕	R ✕		R ✕
		◇	◇		◇		◇		◇		◇		◇			T	
0	**Budapest** Nyugati .. ◧ d.	...	0620	0720	0820	0920	1020	1120	1220	1320	1420	1520	1620	1720	1820	1815k	1920
11	Köbánya Kispest ... ◧ d.	...	0635	0735	0835	0935	1035	1135	1235	1335	1435	1535	1635	1735	1835	|	1935
18	Ferihegy ✈ ... ◧ d.	...	0642	0742	0842	0942	1042	1142	1242	1342	1442	1542	1642	1742	1842	|	1942
73	Cegléd ... ◧ d.	...	0717	0817	0917	1017	1117	1217	1317	1417	1517	1617	1717	1817	1917	|	2017
100	**Szolnok** ... ◧ d.	...	0736	0836	0936	1036	1136	1236	1336	1436	1536	1636	1736	1836	1936	1939	2036
177	Püspökladány ... d.	...	0823	0923	1023	1123	1223	1323	1423	1523	1623	1723	1823	1923	2023	2033	2123
201	Hajdúszoboszló ... d.	...	0839	0939	1039	1139	1239	1339	1439	1539	1639	1739	1839	1939	2039	2050	2139
221	**Debrecen** ... a.	...	0852	0952	1052	1152	1252	1352	1452	1552	1652	1752	1852	1952	2052	2102	2152
221	**Debrecen** ... d.	0654	0854	0954	1054	1154	1254	1354	1454	1554	1654	1757	1854	1954	2054	2105	2154
270	**Nyíregyháza** ... a.	0724	0924	1024	1124	1224	1324	1424	1524	1624	1724	1827	1924	2024	2124	2136	2224
270	**Nyíregyháza** ... d.	0737	...	1029	...	...	...	...	...	...	...	1829	...	2026	...	2139	...
313	Kisvárda ... d.	0821	...	1111	...	...	...	...	...	...	...	1900	...	2053	...	2211	...
335	Záhony 🏛 ... ▶ a.	0848	...	1129	...	...	...	...	...	...	...	1918	...	2111	...	2230	...
341	**Chop** 🏛 ... ⊙ ▶ a.	...	...	1316	...	...	...	...	...	...	...	...	...	...	...	0058	...

SLOWER TRAINS — Debrecen - Záhony : hourly 0434 - 1934 (*connections available from IC at Nyíregyháza*).

Budapest Nyugati d.	...	0500	0625	E	1625	1825	2025	2225
Köbánya Kispest d.	...	0515	0640	V	1640	1840	2040	2240
Ferihegy d.	...	0525	0647	E	1647	1847	2047	2247
Cegléd d.	...	0624	0724	R	1724	1924	2124	2324
Szolnok d.	...	0649	0749	Y	1749	1949	2149	2349
Püspökladány d.	0655	0755	0855		1855	2055	2255	0052
Hajdúszoboszló d.	0714	0814	0914	2	1914	2114	2314	—
Debrecen a.	0730	0830	0930		1930	2130	2330	...
Debrecen d.	0734	0834	0934	H	1934	2134	...	...
Nyíregyháza a.	0819	0919	1019	O	2019	2219	...	2
Nyíregyháza d.	0837	0937	1037	U	2037	...	...	2252
Kisvárda d.	0921	1021	1121	R	2121	...	...	2336
Záhony a.	0948	1048	1148	S	2148	...	...	0003
Chop a.	...	...	...		...	...	...	...

	IC 609	15 629	IC 627	IC 560	IC 659	IC 607	IC 657	IC 605	IC 564	IC 615	IC 655	IC 623	IC 566	IC 621	IC 621	IC 653	IC 568
	R ✕		R ✕	R ✕	R ✕	R ✕	R ✕	R ✕	R ✕	R ✕	R ✕	R ✕	R ✕	R ✕	R ✕	R ✕	R ✕
		T		◇	◇		◇		◇		◇		◇		⑦	◇	◇
Chop 🏛 ... ⊙ ▶ d.	...	0500	0610	...	...	...	...	...	...	...	...	1435	...	...	...	...	...
Záhony 🏛 ... ▶ d.	...	0518	0540	...	...	...	...	...	...	...	...	1431	...	...	1631	...	1912
Kisvárda ... d.	...	0538	0559	...	...	...	...	...	...	...	...	1450	...	...	1650	...	1940
Nyíregyháza ... a.	...	0611	0626	...	...	...	...	...	...	...	...	1519	...	...	1719	...	2023
Nyíregyháza ... d.	0536	0614	0628	0736	0836	0936	1036	1136	1236	1336	1436	1536	1636	1736	1736	1836	2036
Debrecen ... a.	0606	0647	0658	0806	0906	1006	1106	1206	1306	1406	1506	1606	1706	1806	1806	1906	2108
Debrecen ... d.	0608	0650	0708	0808	0908	1008	1108	1208	1308	1408	1508	1608	1708	1808	1808	1908	...
Hajdúszoboszló ... d.	0622	0705	0722	0822	0922	1022	1122	1222	1322	1422	1522	1622	1722	1822	1822	1922	...
Püspökladány ... d.	0638	0721	0738	0838	0938	1038	1138	1238	1338	1438	1538	1638	1738	1838	1838	1938	...
Szolnok ... ◧ d.	0724	0827	0824	0924	1024	1124	1224	1324	1424	1524	1624	1725	1824	1924	1924	2024	...
Cegléd ... ◧ d.	0744	|	0844	0944	1044	1144	1244	1344	1444	1544	1644	1744	1844	1944	1944	2044	...
Ferihegy ✈ ... ◧ d.	0821	|	0921	1021	1121	1221	1321	1421	1521	1621	1721	1821	1921	2021	2021	2121	...
Köbánya Kispest ... ◧ a.	0827	|	0927	1027	1127	1227	1327	1427	1527	1627	1727	1827	1927	2027	2027	2127	...
Budapest Nyugati .. ◧ a.	0842	0947k	0942	1042	1142	1242	1342	1442	1542	1642	1742	1842	1942	2042	2042	2142	...

SLOWER TRAINS — Záhony - Debrecen : hourly 0712 - 2012 (*connections available into IC at Nyíregyháza*).

Chop d.	...	...	...	...		...	...	...
Záhony d.	...	0412	0558	0812	E	1612	1712	2012
Kisvárda d.	...	0440	0626	0840	V	1640	1740	2040
Nyíregyháza a.	...	0523	0710	0923	E	1723	1823	2123
Nyíregyháza d.	...	0541	0741	0941	R	1741	1841	2141
Debrecen a.	...	0626	0826	1026	Y	1826	1926	2226
Debrecen d.	0422	0630	0830	1030		1830	1930	—
Hajdúszoboszló d.	0439	0647	0847	1047	2	1847	1947	...
Püspökladány d.	0458	0708	0908	1108		1908	2008	2
Szolnok d.	0604	0814	1014	1214	H	2014	2124	2227
Cegléd d.	0632	0839	1039	1239	O	2039	2152	2252
Ferihegy d.	0723	0916	1116	1316	U	2116	2249	2349
Köbánya Kispest a.	0729	0922	1122	1322	R	2122	2259	2359
Budapest Nyugati a.	0744	0937	1137	1337	S	2137	2314	0014

T – TISZA/TISSA – 2 Budapest - Chop and v.v.; 🛏 2 cl. Budapest - Kyïv/Moskva and v.v. 🛏 2 cl. Beograd - Budapest - Kyïv/Moskva and v.v. For other 🛏 see Table **97**.

k – Budapest **Keleti**.
◧ – Also **1290** Budapest - Cegléd; **1280** Budapest - Szolnok.
⊙ – Ukrainian (East European) time, one hour ahead.
◇ – To/from Miskolc (Table **1260**).

▶ – Other connections Záhony - Chop :

Záhony . d.	0800	1531	2000	Chop . ⊙ d.	1015	1435	1755
Chop ⊙ a.	0918	1648	2117	Záhony .. a.	0932	1352	1712

1275 BUDAPEST - BIHARKERESZTES - ORADEA

km ☆		6412 411 2	2	6414 413 2	2	684 S⊖	644 365 A⊖	2	2	646 407 C⊖
0	**Budapest Keleti** ... ▷ d.	...	...	...	...	1215	1315	...	...	1715
100	Szolnok ... ▷ d.	...	...	...	...	1341	1441	...	...	1841
177	Püspökladány ... ▷ d.	0845	1056	1225	1340	1440	1556	1700	1825	1956
228	Biharkeresztes ... a.	0939	1143	1312	1427	...	1636	1752	1920	2043
228	Biharkeresztes 🏛 ... d.	0955	...	1327	...	...	1702	...	...	2105
241	Episcopia Bihor 🏛 ... ⊙ a.	1110	...	1442	...	...	1817	...	...	2220
241	Episcopia Bihor ... ⊙ d.	1125	...	1500	...	...	1832	...	...	2235
247	**Oradea** ... ⊙ a.	1133	...	1508	...	...	1845	...	...	2243
	Cluj Napoca **1630** ... ⊙ a.	...	...	...	...	...	2128	...	...	0117

	406 649 C⊖	2	689 S⊖	364 647 A⊖	2	412 6425 2	2	414 6423 2	2
Cluj Napoca **1630** ... ⊙ d.	0222	...	...	0548	...	...	...	...	...
Oradea ... ⊙ d.	0450	...	...	0822	...	1322	...	1717	...
Episcopia Bihor ... ⊙ a.	0458	...	...	0830	...	1330	...	1725	...
Episcopia Bihor 🏛 ... ⊙ d.	0520	...	...	0845	...	1345	...	1745	...
Biharkeresztes 🏛 ... a.	0435	...	...	0800	...	1300	...	1700	...
Biharkeresztes ... d.	0458	0700	...	0825	0948	1325	1432	1715	1900
Püspökladány ... ▷ a.	0544	0749	0752	0906	1035	1416	1519	1802	1947
Szolnok ... ▷ a.	0650	...	0849	1019	...	...	...	...	...
Budapest Keleti ... ▷ a.	0817	...	1017	1147	...	...	...	...	...

A – ADY ENDRE – 12 Budapest - Cluj Napoca and v.v.
C – CORONA – 🛏 1, 2 cl., ▬ 1, 2 cl. and 12 Budapest - Cluj Napoca - Deda - Braşov and v.v.; ▬ 2 cl. and 2 Budapest - Deda - Târgu Mureş and v.v.

S – SZAMOS – 12 Budapest - Debrecen - Satu Mare - Baia Mare and v.v. (Table **1627**).
⊙ – Romanian (East European) time.

⊖ – R for international journeys.
▷ – For connections Budapest **Nyugati** - Püspökladány see Table **1270**.

1276 DEBRECEN and NYÍREGYHÁZA - MÁTÉSZALKA

2nd class

km									△			Ⓑ
0	**Debrecen** ... d.	0510	0715	0915	1115	1315	1515	1715	1807	1920	2120	2245
58	Nyírbátor ... d.	0631	0836	1036	1236	1436	1636	1836	1910	2041	2241	0005
78	**Mátészalka** ... a.	0655	0900	1100	1300	1500	1700	1900	1928	2105	2306	0031

			▽								
Mátészalka ... d.	0410	0455	0530	0703	0903	1103	1303	1503	1703	1903	2109
Nyírbátor ... d.	0434	0519	0550	0727	0927	1127	1327	1527	1727	1933	2133
Debrecen ... a.	0556	0639	0652	0845	1045	1245	1445	1645	1852	2052	2250

km		⚒								Ⓑ	Ⓑ	
0	**Nyíregyháza** ... d.	0528	0825	1025	1225	1425	1625	1825	2038	2235	...	...
38	Nyírbátor ... d.	0703	1000	1200	1400	1553	1753	1953	2206	2355	0005	...
58	**Mátészalka** ... a.	0730	1022	1222	1423	1623	1816	2015	2228	...	0031	...

								⑦	⚒		Ⓑ
Mátészalka ... d.	0440	0530	...	0734	0935	1135	1334	1528	1535	1722	1950
Nyírbátor ... d.	0505	0549	0555	0759	0959	1159	1359	1559	1559	1759	2016
Nyíregyháza .. a.	0625	...	0715	0920	1120	1320	1520	1720	1720	1920	2136

△ – *IC* **624/638** from Budapest Nyugati, depart 1520, R.
▽ – *IC* **639/627** to Budapest Nyugati, arrive 0942, R.

Local trains Mátészalka - Tiborszállás 🏛 - Carei : from Mátészalka 0540, 1405 (arrive 0755, 1535 Romanian time); from Carei 0920, 1805 (arrive Mátészalka 0950, 1822 Hungarian time).

1277 DEBRECEN - FÜZESABONY

2nd class

km											
0	**Debrecen** ... d.	0529	0729	0929	1129	1329	1529	1729	1929	2045	2240
42	Hortobágy ... d.	0617	0815	1015	1215	1415	1615	1815	2015	2136	2330
73	Tiszafüred ... d.	0659	0859	1059	1259	1459	1659	1859	2059	2212	0005
103	**Füzesabony** ... a.	0732	0932	1132	1332	1532	1732	1932	2132	2252	...

Füzesabony ... d.	0422	0622	0822	1022	1222	1422	1622	1822	2022	2200
Tiszafüred ... d.	0501	0701	0901	1101	1301	1501	1701	1901	2056	2235
Hortobágy ... d.	0537	0737	0937	1137	1337	1537	1737	1937	2139	...
Debrecen ... a.	0628	0828	1028	1228	1428	1628	1828	2028	2224	...

1278 DOMBÓVAR - BAJA - KISKUNFÉLEGYHÁZA - SZEGED

2nd class

km			B								7808
	Pécs **1200** ... d.	...	...	...	...	...	...	...	...	...	1624
0	**Dombóvár** ... △ d.	...	...	...	...	...	...	...	...	...	1748
60	Bátaszék **1210** ... △ d.	...	0500	...	0638	0930	1241	1355	...	1534	1850
80	**Baja 1210** ... a.	...	0522	...	0659	0949	1301	1415	...	1600	1907
80	**Baja** ... d.	...	0553	...	0703	1003	1303	1417	...	1603	1908
156	Kiskunhalas ... a.	...	0705	...	0822	1122	1422	1540	...	1722	2022
156	Kiskunhalas ... d.	0640	...	0742	0840	1142	1432	...	1544	1742	2036
202	Kiskunfélegyháza ... ◧ a.	0722	...	0823	0924	1223	1516	...	1624	1823	2114
262	**Szeged** ... ◧ a.	...	...	...	...	...	...	...	...	...	2234

		7809							B	
Szeged ... ◧ d.	...	0510	...	...	...	...	...	...	...	...
Kiskunfélegyháza ... ◧ d.	...	0637	0838	0939	1239	1410	1539	1639	1839	2046
Kiskunhalas ... a.	...	0718	0919	1020	1320	1451	1622	1720	1920	2126
Kiskunhalas ... d.	0538	0738	...	1038	1338	1456	1638	...	1938	2138
Baja ... a.	0656	0852	...	1153	1453	1621	1753	...	2052	2252
Baja 1210 ... d.	0702	0854	...	1155	1502	1622	1755	...	...	...
Bátaszék **1210** ... △ a.	0723	0915	...	1216	1523	1642	1816	...	...	...
Dombóvár ... △ a.	...	1022	...	...	...	...	...	...	...	...
Pécs **1200** ... a.	...	1144	...	...	...	...	...	...	...	...

B – 2 Baja - Köbánya Kispest and v.v. (train **796/797**).
a – Dombóvár **alsó**.
◧ – See also Table **1290**.
△ – For local trains Dombóvár - Bátaszék see panel on right.

	Ⓐ			Ⓑ		Ⓐ
Dombóvár ... d.	0425	0720	1030	1445	1549	2116
Bátaszék ... a.	0545	0845	1145	1555	1704	2230

					Ⓐ
Bátaszék ... d.	0455	0728	1223	1615	1951
Dombóvár ... a.	0612	0845	1340	1734a	2108

1279 SZOMBATHELY - KOSZEG

2nd class

From **Szombathely**: 0448 ⚒, 0554, 0713, 0823, 0955, 1140, 1314, 1418, 1523, 1626, 1745, 1915, 2015, 2230.
From **Köszeg**: 0410 ⚒, 0520, 0628, 0750, 0858, 1040, 1214, 1345, 1452, 1555, 1658, 1819, 1945, 2049, 2302 Ⓑ.

18 km, journey time 25-30 minutes

BUDAPEST - BÉKÉSCSABA - LÖKÖSHÁZA - ARAD 1280

km				740		732			*IC* 730		744		*IC* 734	*IC* 734			*IC* 746				*EN*	736		738
				451	7400	375	7302		75		453		355	355		7404	79		7306		371	455	7408	347
		2	2	⊖		⊖			✕	2	⊖		⊖	⊖	2		⊖	2			⊖	⊖		⊖
					G	P			T				M	N			K				W			D
0	**Budapest** Keleti **1270** d.	...	...	0545	0645	0745	0845	...	0945	...	1145	...	1245	1245	...	1445	1545	...	1645	...	1745	1845	1945	2325
100	Szolnok **1270** d.	0445	0545	0708	0811	0908	1011	...	1108	1155	1308	...	1408	1408	1445	1611	1708	1645	1811	...	1908	2012	2111	0049
141	Mezötúr d.	0527	0635	0735	0838	0935	1038	...	1135	1235	1335	...	1435	1435	1534	1638	1735	1740	1838	...	1935	2039	2138	|
159	Gyoma d.	0551	0651	0748	0851	0948	1051	...	1151	1251	1348	...	1451	1451	1553	1651	1753	1800	1851	...	1948	2052	2151	|
196	**Békéscsaba** a.	0622	0722	0812	0922	1012	1122	...	1215	1322	1416	...	1515	1515	1624	1732	1817	1831	1922	...	2012	2116	2222	0155
196	**Békéscsaba** d.	...	0724	0820	*0936*	1015	1125	...	1220	1325	1426	...	1520	1520	1656	...	1820	1835	1933	...	2020	2120	...	0200
225	Lökösháza a.	...	0748	0840	*1000*	1035	1152	...	1240	1352	1446	...	1540	1540	1728	...	1840	1859	1955	...	2040	2140	...	0220
225	Lökösháza 🏛 d.	...	...	0901	...	1101	...	...	1301	...	1501	...	1601	1601	...	...	1901	...	...	...	2101	2201	...	0240
236	Curtici 🏛 ⊙ d.	...	...	1028	...	1228	...	...	1428	...	1635	...	1738	1738	...	...	2028	...	...	...	2228	2328	...	0407
253	**Arad** ⊙ a.	...	...	1046	...	1246	...	...	1446	...	1653	...	1756	1756	...	...	2046	...	...	...	2246	2346	...	0425
	Timişoara **1625** ⊙ a.	...	...	...	...	|	...	...	1534	...	...	...	|	|	...	...	2134	...	...	...	|	...	...	|
	Târgu Mureş **1630** ⊙ a.	...	...	...	...	|	...	...	...	...	...	...	2330	|	...	...	...	...	...	...	|	...	...	|
	Bucureşti Nord **1620** ⊙ a.	...	...	...	...	2316	...	...	...	...	...	...	...	0515z	...	...	...	...	...	...	0843	...	...	1402

	346	*EN*					78			454		354	354		452				374	74			456	
	739	370	7309				*IC* 747	7307		737		*IC* 735	*IC* 735		745		7303		733	*IC* 731	7401		7301	
	2 ⊖	⊖		2	2		⊖		2	⊖		⊖	⊖	2	⊖	2			⊖	⊖		2	⊖	2
	D	W					K					M	N						P	T				
Bucureşti Nord **1620** ⊙ d.	1645	1850	...	...	...	...	...	...	...	...	...	...	2358z	...	...	...	...	...	0630	...	...	...	...	...
Târgu Mureş **1630** ⊙ d.	|	|	...	...	...	...	...	...	...	...	...	0523	|	...	...	...	...	...	|	...	...	...	...	...
Timişoara **1625** ⊙ d.	|	|	...	...	...	...	0530	...	...	...	...	|	|	...	...	...	...	...	|	1600	...	...	...	...
Arad ⊙ d.	0208	0416	...	...	...	...	0618	...	...	0918	...	1103	1103	...	1315	...	...	...	1618	1648	...	...	1848	...
Curtici 🏛 ⊙ a.	0223	0431	...	...	...	...	0633	...	...	0933	...	1118	1118	...	1330	...	...	...	1633	1703	...	...	1903	...
Lökösháza 🏛 a.	0205	0400	...	...	...	...	0600	...	...	0900	...	1100	1100	...	1300	...	...	...	1600	1630	...	...	1842	...
Lökösháza d.	0225	0420	0456	0555	0655	...	0620	0656	0755	0915	...	1120	1120	...	1320	1355	1456	...	1620	1650	...	1755	1900	...
Békéscsaba a.	0245	0440	0519	0619	0719	...	0640	0719	0819	0935	...	1140	1140	...	1340	1419	1519	...	1640	1710	...	1819	1923	...
Békéscsaba d.	0250	0445	0525	0630	0730	...	0645	0725	0830	0940	...	1145	1145	1230	1345	1430	1530	...	1645	1715	1733	1832	1930	2018
Gyoma d.	|	0514	0602	0706	0820	...	0714	0802	0906	1014	...	1214	1214	1320	1414	1506	1606	...	1714	1739	1809	1908	2006	2054
Mezötúr d.	|	0527	0615	0736	0836	...	0727	0815	0922	1027	...	1227	1227	1340	1427	1522	1619	...	1727	1752	1822	1923	2019	2109
Szolnok **1270** d.	0357	0557	0648	0815	0915	...	0757	0848	1001	1055	...	1257	1257	1419	1457	1601	1653	...	1757	1827	1853	...	2053	...
Budapest Keleti **1270** a.	0517	0717	0812	...	...	...	0917	1012	...	1217	...	1417	1417	...	1617	...	1817	...	1917	1947	2017	...	2217	...

BÉKÉSCSABA - GYULA ◇

2nd class

km	◇	G										
0	Békéscsaba d.	0934	1144	1221	1344	1444	1540	1644	1736	1821	1931	2042
16	Gyula a.	0949	1200	1237	1400	1500	1556	1700	1752	1837	1947	2058

◇											
Gyula d.	0501	0601	0701	0901	1001	1101	1301	1501	1601	1701	1801
Békéscsaba a.	0517	0617	0717	0917	1017	1117	1317	1517	1617	1717	1817

D – DACIA – 🛏 1,2 cl., ▬ 2 cl. and [2] Wien - Budapest - Bucureşti and v.v.; [2] Budapest - Bucureşti and v.v.

G – [12] Budapest - Gyula.

K – KÖRÖS / CRIS – [12] and ✕ Budapest - Arad - Timişoara and v.v.

M – MAROS / MUREŞ – [12] Budapest - Arad - Targu Mureş and v.v.

N – MAROS / MUREŞ – 🛏 1,2 cl. Venezia (**240/1**) - Budapest - Arad - (**625/6**) Bucureşti and v.v. (also [2] on ②③④⑥⑦ from Venezia, ①②④⑤⑦ from Bucureşti).

P – PANNONIA – [12] and ✕ Budapest - Bucureşti and v.v.; 🛏 1,2 cl., ▬ 2 cl. and [12] Praha - Budapest - Lökösháza and v.v.; [2] Praha - Budapest - Bucureşti and v.v. (also 🛏 1,2 cl. on dates in Table **60**).

T – TRAIANUS – [12] Wien (**268/9**) - Budapest - Timişoara and v.v.; ✕ Wien - Budapest - Timişoara (- Bucureşti) and v.v.; 🛏 1,2 cl. München - Wien - Timişoara (- Bucureşti) and v.v.

W – ISTER – 🛏 1,2 cl., ▬ 1,2 cl., [2] and ✕ Budapest - Bucureşti and v.v.; 🛏 1,2 cl. Budapest - Bucureşti (**463/2**) - Sofija and v.v.

z – Train **625 / 626** (in [12] change at Arad).

⊙ – Romanian (East European) time.

◇ – Also at 0544, 0644, 0744, 0944, 2234 from Békéscsaba, 1911, 1957, 2101 from Gyula.

⊖ – 🅁 for international journeys (and domestic journeys in Romania).

BUDAPEST - KECSKEMÉT - SZEGED 1290

km			*IC*	*IC*	*IC*		*IC*	*IC*			
			710	760	702		756	766	7008	7108	
		2	🅁✕	🅁✕	🅁✕		🅁✕	🅁✕			2
0	**Budapest** Nyugati § d.	0400	0550	0650	0750		1750	1850	1950	2050	2135
11	Köbánya Kispest § d.	0415	0605	0705	0805	and	1805	1905	2005	2105	2150
18	Ferihegy ✈ § d.	0425	0612	0712	0812	hourly	1812	1912	2012	2113	2200
73	Cegléd § d.	0522	0647	0747	0847	until	1847	1947	2047	2152	2257
106	**Kecskemét** d.	0604	0711	0811	0911		1911	2011	2111	2217	2329
131	Kiskunfélegyháza d.	0629	0729	0829	0929		1929	2029	2129	2234	2352
191	**Szeged** a.	0715	0815	0915	1015		2015	2115	2215	2323	...

		IC	*IC*	*IC*	*IC*		*IC*	*IC*		
	7009	709	719	707	717		753	763	7001	7101
		🅁✕	🅁✕	🅁✕	🅁✕		🅁✕	🅁✕		
Szeged d.	0440	0544	0642	0742	0842		1742	1842	1942	2042
Kiskunfélegyháza d.	0528	0630	0730	0830	0930	and	1830	1930	2030	2130
Kecskemét d.	0545	0647	0747	0847	0947	hourly	1847	1947	2047	2147
Cegléd § d.	0612	0715	0815	0915	1015	until	1915	2015	2117	2219
Ferihegy ✈ § d.	0702	0751	0851	0951	1051		1951	2051	2156	2302
Köbánya Kispest § a.	0709	0757	0857	0957	1057		1957	2057	2203	2309
Budapest Nyugati § a.	0724	0812	0912	1012	1112		2012	2112	2219	2324

§ – For additional trains see Table **1270**.

Note : on this line only, all *IC* trains have designated carriages for the use of passengers without seat reservations.

SZEGED - BÉKÉSCSABA 1292

2nd class

km												
0	**Szeged** d.	0620	0720	0920	1120	1320	1420	1520	1620	1720	1820	1920
31	Hódmezövásárhely d.	0703	0759	0959	1159	1359	1503	1559	1703	1759	1903	1959
62	Orosháza d.	0728	0829	1029	1229	1429	1528	1629	1728	1829	1928	2029
97	**Békéscsaba** a.	0807	0914	1111	1311	1511	1607	1711	1807	1911	2007	2111

Békéscsaba d.	0743	0943	1143	1343	1443	1543	1643	1743	1846	1943
Orosháza d.	0830	1030	1230	1430	1530	1630	1730	1830	1930	2030
Hódmezövásárhely d.	0900	1100	1300	1500	1600	1700	1800	1900	2000	2100
Szeged a.	0937	1137	1337	1537	1637	1737	1837	1937	2033	2137

Additional trains : from Szeged 0520, from Békéscsaba 0543, 0646.

BUDAPEST - KISKUNHALAS - KELEBIA 1295

km						*IC* 794					790
		792	7900	7902	7904	*IC* 345	7906	796	798	7908	341
		N	2	2	2	A	2	C	2		B
0	**Budapest Keleti** d.	0700	...	...	...	1320	...	...	...	2055	2325
0	Köbánya Kispest d.	|	0856	1056	1256	|	1456	1656	1856	|	|
61	Kunszentmiklós-Tass d.	0801	1001	1201	1405	1419	1601	1801	2001	2201	|
107	Kiskörös d.	0854	1054	1255	1454	1502	1654	1854	2054	2251	|
134	Kiskunhalas a.	0925	1125	1326	1526	1530	1725	1925	2125	2322	0139
163	**Kelebia** 🏛 a.	1002	1202	1402	1601	1610	1802	*1958*	2202	...	0215
	Beograd **1360** a.	...	...	...	...	2043	...	...	...	...	0639

	340					*IC* 344				
	799	7909	797	7907	795	*IC* 793	7905	7903	791	7901
	B	2	C	2	2	A	2	2	N	2
Beograd **1360** d.	2200	...	...	...	...	0645	...	...	...	...
Kelebia 🏛 d.	0220	0459	*0648*	0848	1048	1125	1248	1448	1659	1848
Kiskunhalas d.	0250	0531	0731	0931	1131	1157	1330	1531	1731	1931
Kiskörös d.	|	0604	0804	1004	1204	1226	1403	1604	1804	2004
Kunszentmiklós-Tass d.	|	0655	0855	1055	1254	1313	1455	1655	1855	2055
Köbánya Kispest a.	|	0751	0951	1151	1356	|	1551	1751	|	2151
Budapest Keleti a.	0503	...	...	...	...	1409	...	...	1953	...

A – AVALA – [12] and ✕ Wien - Budapest - Beograd and v.v. Conveys 🛏 2 cl. Moskva / Kyïv - Budapest - Beograd and v.v. (Table **97**).

B – BEOGRAD – for composition see Table **1360**.

C – [2] Köbánya Kispest - Kiskunhalas - Baja and v.v.

N – [2] Budapest - Kelebia - Novi Sad and v.v.

OTHER LOCAL SERVICES 1299

Most trains 2nd class only

BUDAPEST - ESZTERGOM *53 km*, journey 95 - 105 mins.
From **Budapest** Nyugati : 0610, 0720, 0820, 0852 Ⓐ, 0920 and hourly to 2320 (also on Ⓐ at 1352, 1452, 1552, 1652, 1752, 1852).
From **Esztergom** : 0330, 0413, 0455, 0532 Ⓐ, 0548 Ⓐ, 0605, 0637 Ⓐ, 0705, 0728 Ⓐ, 0809 and hourly to 2209 (also at 1232 Ⓐ).

BUDAPEST - MAGYAR VASÚTTÖRTÉNETI PARK (Hungarian Railway Museum)
Vintage diesel shuttle service, ②–⑦ Mar. 1 - Nov. 2. *5 km*, journey 18 mins, special fares.
From Budapest Nyugati : 0945, 1045, 1345, 1545.
From Museum : 1315, 1515.

BUDAPEST - SZENTENDRE *21 km*, journey time 38 minutes.
HÉV suburban trains from Budapest Batthyány tér, every 10 - 20 minutes (30 - 40 evenings).

EGER - SZILVÁSVÁRAD *34 km*, journey time 65 minutes.
From **Eger** : 0446, 0746, 0946, 1346, 1446, 1746, 1946.
From **Szilvásvárad** : 0510, 0600, 0910, 1110, 1510, 1710, 1910.
Via Szilvásvárad-Szalajkavölgy (for the forest railway).

HATVAN - SZOLNOK *68 km*, journey 71 - 73 minutes
From **Hatvan** : 0400, 0515 Ⓐ, 0615 and hourly (two-hourly on Ⓒ) until 2215.
From **Szolnok** : 0315, 0433, 0533 Ⓐ, 0633 and hourly (two-hourly on Ⓒ) until 2033, 2133.

KISKUNFÉLEGYHÁZA - CSONGRÁD - SZENTES *39 km*, journey time 55 minutes
From **Kiskunfélegyháza** : 0632, 0932, 1232, 1432, 1632, 1832, 2032 ⑤, 2132.
From **Szentes** : 0509, 0828, 1130, 1330, 1530, 1730, 1930 ⑤ (calls Csongrád 18 mins later).

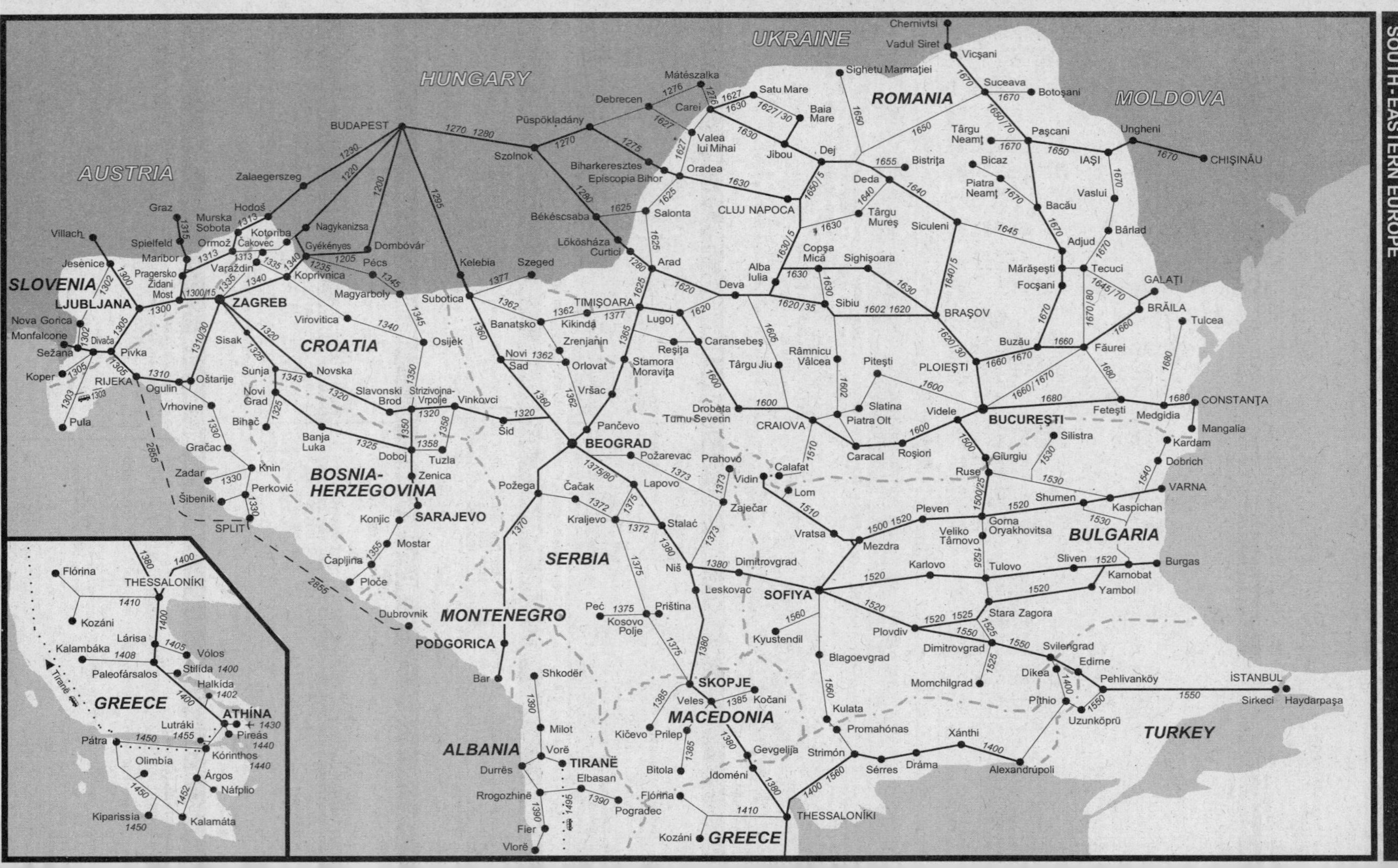
UKRAINE
HUNGARY
ROMANIA
MOLDOVA
AUSTRIA
SLOVENIA
CROATIA
BOSNIA-HERZEGOVINA
SERBIA
MONTENEGRO
BULGARIA
ALBANIA
MACEDONIA
GREECE
TURKEY
BUDAPEST
CHIŞINĂU
LJUBLJANA
ZAGREB
CLUJ NAPOCA
TIMIŞOARA
BRAŞOV
GALAŢI
BRĂILA
PLOIEŞTI
BUCUREŞTI
CONSTANŢA
BEOGRAD
SARAJEVO
PODGORICA
SOFIYA
VARNA
SKOPJE
TIRANË
THESSALONÍKI
İSTANBUL
ATHÍNA
RIJEKA
SPLIT

SLOVENIA, CROATIA and BOSNIA-HERZEGOVINA

Operators: Slovenske Železnice (SŽ); Hrvatske Željeznice (HŽ); Željeznice Federacije Bosne i Hercegovine (ŽFBH) and Željeznice Republike Srpske (ŽRS).

Services: All trains convey first and second class seating, **except** where shown otherwise in footnotes or by '2' in the train column, or where the footnote shows sleeping and / or couchette cars only. Descriptions of sleeping (🛏) and couchette (▬) cars appear on page 10. Travel on *ICS* trains in Slovenia requires compulsory reservation and payment of a special fare; second class, second plus and first class plus accommodation is conveyed.

Timings: Timings valid from **December 9, 2007**. However, readers should note that domestic services in the Bosnian Federation are subject to alteration, and are advised to check locally before travelling.

Tickets: A supplement is payable for travel by internal express trains. Reservation of seats is possible on most express trains.

SŽ, HŽ, ÖBB — VILLACH - JESENICE - LJUBLJANA - ZAGREB — 1300

km		EN 241 ◆	2	2 Ⓐ	297 ◆	2	2	2 ⚒	2 Ⓐ	2 Ⓐ	415 ◆	2 Ⓐ	2	2 Ⓐ	2	2 Ⓐ	2 Ⓐ		2 Ⓐ	IC 211 ✕ ◆	431 ①–⑤	2	2	2 Ⓐ	2 Ⓑ	EC 213 ◆
	München Hbf **890** .. d.	...	...	...	2345	...	...	...	...	...	...	...	...	...	...	...	...	...	...	0726	...	...	...	...	...	1126
	Salzburg Hbf **970** ... d.	...	...	...	0138	...	...	...	...	...	...	...	...	...	...	...	...	...	...	0904	...	...	...	...	...	1304
0	**Villach** Hbf. ... d.	...	...	...	0408	...	...	0518	...	...	0626	...	...	...	...	...	...	...	...	1204	...	...	...	...	...	1555
1	Villach Westbf. ... d.	...	...	...	|	...	...	0522	...	...	|	...	...	...	...	...	...	...	...	|	...	...	...	...	...	|
25	Rosenbach ... d.	...	...	...	0432	...	...	0548	...	...	0653	...	...	...	...	...	...	...	...	1227	...	...	...	...	...	1618
38	**Jesenice** ▦ a.	...	...	...	0445	...	...	0601	...	...	0707	...	...	...	...	...	...	...	...	1241	...	...	...	...	...	1632
38	**Jesenice 1302** ... d.	...	...	0440	0508	...	0532	...	0608	0628	0732	...	0738	...	...	...	1110	...	...	1255	...	1420	...	1525	...	1647
51	Lesce-Bled ... d.	...	...	0454	0521	...	0548	...	0622	0642	0745	...	0752	...	...	...	1124	...	...	1308	...	1436	...	1541	...	1700
74	Kranj ... d.	...	...	0520	0543	...	0614	...	0649	0708	0805	...	0816	...	...	...	1148	...	...	1329	...	1500	...	1605	...	1721
102	**Ljubljana** ... a.	...	...	0553	0605	...	0650	...	0724	0742	0828	...	0849	...	...	...	1220	...	...	1353	...	1535	...	1642	...	1742
102	**Ljubljana 1315** ... d.	0200	0550	...	0615	0655	...	...	...	...	0835	0845	...	0950	1050	1150	...	...	1350	1408	1540	...	1545	...	1650	1745
166	Zidani Most **1315** ... d.	0254	0655	...	0712	0802	...	...	...	...	0930	0955	...	1055	1155	1255	...	...	1455	1505	1642	...	1655	...	1755	1840
182	Sevnica **1315** ... d.	0310	0715	...	0728	0821	...	...	...	...	0945	1013	...	1114	1214	1314	...	...	1514	1521	1658	...	1714	...	1814	1855
215	Dobova **1315** ▦ d.	0349	0742	...	0805	0849	...	...	...	...	1024	1042	...	1142	1242	1342	...	...	1542	1603	1745	...	1742	...	1842	1935
245	**Zagreb 1315** ... a.	0418	...	...	0834	...	...	...	...	...	1053	...	...	...	...	...	...	...	...	1632	1814	...	...	...	...	2004
	Beograd **1320** ... a.	...	...	...	1533	...	...	...	...	...	1720	...	...	...	...	...	...	...	...	2247	...	...	...	...	...	...

	2 Ⓐ	2	2	IC 311	2	411 ◆		2 N	EC 315 ✕ ◆
München Hbf **890** ... d.	...	...	...	...	...	...	...	...	...
Salzburg Hbf **970** ... d.	...	...	...	...	...	...	...	...	1713
Villach Hbf. ... d.	...	...	...	1804	...	...	...	...	1957
Villach Westbf. ... d.	...	...	...	|	...	...	...	...	|
Rosenbach ... d.	...	...	...	1829	...	...	...	...	2020
Jesenice ▦ a.	...	...	...	1842	...	...	...	...	2034
Jesenice 1302 ... d.	...	1750	...	1854	1910	...	...	2020	2047
Lesce-Bled ... d.	...	1804	...	1906	1924	...	...	2034	2101
Kranj ... d.	...	1834	...	1926	1948	...	...	2059	2121
Ljubljana ... a.	...	1911	...	1948	2023	...	...	2132	2142
Ljubljana 1315 ... d.	1750	...	1850	...	...	2105	...	...	2145
Zidani Most **1315** ... d.	1855	...	1955	...	...	2204	...	...	2241
Sevnica **1315** ... d.	1914	...	2014	...	...	2220	...	...	2257
Dobova **1315** ▦ d.	1942	...	2042	...	...	2300	...	...	2334
Zagreb 1315 ... a.	...	...	...	...	...	2329	...	...	0003
Beograd **1320** ... a.	...	...	...	...	...	0623	...	...	...

	2 Ⓐ	2 ⚒	2 Ⓐ	630 ①–⑥	2 Ⓒ N	632 2 Ⓐ	2	IC 310	410 ◆	2	2	EC 212 ◆	2 Ⓐ
Beograd **1320** ... d.	...	...	...	...	...	...	...	...	2215	...	...	...	...
Zagreb 1315 ... d.	...	...	...	...	...	...	...	...	0530	...	...	0750	...
Dobova **1315** ▦ d.	...	...	...	0452	...	0545	0600	...	0614	0705	...	0836	1005
Sevnica **1315** ... d.	...	...	...	0526	...	0610	0631	...	0642	0733	...	0858	1033
Zidani Most **1315** ... d.	...	...	...	0547	...	0625	0700	...	0657	0753	...	0913	1053
Ljubljana 1315 ... a.	...	...	...	0647	...	0719	0803	...	0750	0856	...	1006	1156
Ljubljana ... d.	0448	...	0615	...	0650	...	...	0805	...	...	0945	1012	...
Kranj ... d.	0520	...	0649	...	0719	...	...	0835	...	...	1017	1034	...
Lesce-Bled ... d.	0548	...	0714	...	0753	...	...	0857	...	...	1041	1056	...
Jesenice 1302 ... a.	0602	...	0728	...	0810	...	...	0910	...	...	1055	1109	...
Jesenice ▦ d.	...	0637	...	...	...	...	...	0923	...	...	...	1121	...
Rosenbach ... d.	...	0651	...	...	...	...	...	0937	...	...	...	1136	...
Villach Westbf. ... a.	...	0719	...	...	...	...	...	|	...	...	...	|	...
Villach Hbf. ... a.	...	0724	...	...	...	...	...	1000	...	...	...	1158	...
Salzburg Hbf **970** a.	...	...	...	...	...	...	...	...	...	...	...	1455	...
München Hbf **890** a.	...	...	...	...	...	...	...	...	...	...	...	1632	...

	EC 314 ✕ ◆	2	2	2 Ⓐ	2 Ⓐ	2	2	2	IC 210 ✕ ◆	2 Ⓐ		2 Ⓐ	2 Ⓐ	2	2	2	2 Ⓑ	2 Ⓐ	2 Ⓐ	2	414 ◆	2 Ⓑ	2 Ⓐ	296 ◆	2 Ⓑ	EN 240 ◆
Beograd **1320** ... d.	...	...	...	...	...	...	...	...	0620	...	...	...	...	...	...	...	...	...	...	...	1045	...	...	1320	...	...
Zagreb 1315 ... d.	0944	...	...	...	...	...	...	...	1315	...	...	...	...	...	...	...	...	...	...	...	1810	...	...	2105	...	2335
Dobova **1315** ▦ d.	1027	...	1105	...	1211	...	1305	...	1402	1406	...	...	...	1511	...	1611	...	1705	...	1806	1856	1911	2005	2154	2211	0040
Sevnica **1315** ... d.	1049	...	1135	...	1239	...	1334	...	1426	1434	...	...	...	1539	...	1640	...	1733	...	1834	1919	1939	2033	2219	2239	0104
Zidani Most **1315** ... d.	1104	...	1155	...	1300	...	1400	...	1442	1500	...	...	...	1600	...	1700	...	1800	...	1855	1935	2000	2100	2234	2300	0119
Ljubljana 1315 ... a.	1202	...	1303	...	1403	...	1503	...	1539	1603	...	...	...	1703	...	1803	...	1903	...	1958	2031	2103	2203	2328	0003	0212
Ljubljana ... d.	1205	1255	...	1336	...	1441	...	1530	1600	...	...	1620	1703	...	1742	...	1853	...	2004	...	2035	...	...	2350	...	...
Kranj ... d.	1227	1329	...	1412	...	1516	...	1605	1624	...	...	1658	1738	...	1814	...	1926	...	2037	...	2059	...	...	0013	...	...
Lesce-Bled ... d.	1248	1354	...	1436	...	1541	...	1631	1646	...	...	1726	1804	...	1838	...	1954	...	2102	...	2125	...	...	0034	...	...
Jesenice 1302 ... a.	1304	1408	...	1450	...	1555	...	1646	1705	...	...	1740	1818	...	1852	...	2008	...	2116	...	2139	...	...	0048	...	...
Jesenice ▦ d.	1316	...	...	...	...	...	...	...	1722	...	...	...	...	...	...	...	...	...	...	...	2155	...	...	0054	...	...
Rosenbach ... d.	1330	...	...	...	...	...	...	...	1736	...	...	...	...	...	...	...	...	...	...	...	2209	...	...	0108	...	...
Villach Westbf. ... a.	|	...	...	...	...	...	...	...	|	...	...	...	...	...	...	...	...	...	...	...	|	...	...	|	...	...
Villach Hbf. ... a.	1352	...	...	...	...	...	...	...	1758	...	...	...	...	...	...	...	...	...	...	...	2231	...	...	0130	...	...
Salzburg Hbf **970** ... a.	1648	...	...	...	...	...	...	...	2048	...	...	...	...	...	...	...	...	...	...	...	...	...	...	0405	...	...
München Hbf **890** ... a.	...	...	...	...	...	...	...	...	2232	...	...	...	...	...	...	...	...	...	...	...	...	...	...	0615	...	...

◆ – **NOTES** (LISTED BY TRAIN NUMBER)

- **210/1** – SAVA – [12] Beograd - Villach (**110/1**) - München and v.v.; ✕ Beograd - Jesenice and v.v.
- **212/3** – MIMARA – [12] Zagreb - Villach (**112/3**) - München and v.v.
- **240/1** – VENEZIA – For days of running and composition – see Table **1305**.
- **296/7** – LISINSKI – 🛏 1, 2 cl., ▬ 2 cl. and [2] Zagreb - Salzburg (**268/9**) - München and v.v.; [2] Beograd (**418/9**) - Vinkovci (**741/8**) - Zagreb - München and v.v. Also conveys: 🛏 1, 2 cl., ▬ 2 cl. and [2] Rijeka (**480/1**) - Ljubljana - München and v.v. on dates in Table **1305**.
- **314/5** – AGRAM – [12] and ✕ Zagreb - Salzburg and v.v.
- **410/1** – For days of running and composition – see Table **1320**.
- **414/5** – For days of running and composition – see Table **1320**.

N – Conveys on Ⓒ: [2] Nova Gorica - Jesenice - Ljubljana and v.v.

SŽ 2nd class only — JESENICE - NOVA GORICA - SEŽANA — 1302

km		Ⓐ	m	k	Ⓐ	N		Ⓐ	Ⓐ	Ⓐ		Ⓑ	
0	**Jesenice 1300** .. d.	...	0410	0410	0612	0818	1115	...	...	1435	1653	...	1900
10	Bled Jezero ... d.	...	0426	0426	0628	0834	1130	...	...	1451	1708	...	1916
28	Bohinjska Bistrica d.	...	0447	0447	0655	0910	1151	...	...	1513	1729	...	1938
56	Most na Soči ... d.	...	0524	0524	0731	0947	1228	...	...	1605	1804	...	2014
89	Nova Gorica ... a.	...	0608	0608	0816	1030	1309	...	...	1645	1843	...	2053
89	Nova Gorica ... d.	0455	0616	...	0913	...	...	1410	1530	...	...	1845	...
130	**Sežana 1305** ... a.	0557	0721	...	1013	...	...	1510	1630	...	...	1944	...

	Ⓐ		Ⓐ			j		Ⓐ	Ⓒ N	Ⓑ	h	Ⓑ
Sežana 1305 ... d.	...	...	0515	0638a	1018a	...	1427a	1632	...	...	2000	2045
Nova Gorica ... a.	...	...	0613	0730a	1110a	...	1522a	1724	...	...	2051	2137
Nova Gorica ... d.	0320	0528	...	0735	1115	1414	1524	...	1804	1928	2100	...
Most na Soči ... d.	0400	0609	...	0818	1158	1456	1604	...	1851	2016	2141	...
Bohinjska Bistrica d.	0452	0652	...	0901	1251	1540	1644	...	1939	2058	2225	...
Bled Jezero ... d.	0513	0713	...	0923	1313	1600	1712	...	1959	2119	2247	...
Jesenice 1300 ... a.	0530	0729	...	0940	1330	1616	1729	...	2014	2135	2303	...

N – Conveys on Ⓒ: [2] Ljubljana - Jesenice - Nova Gorica and v.v.
a – Ⓐ only.
h – Ⓒ June 15 - Aug. 24.
j – Not Ⓒ June 26 - Aug. 29.
k – ⑥ Dec. 15 - June 14, Aug. 30 - Dec. 13.
m – Ⓐ (daily June 15 - Aug. 24).

HŽ, SŽ 2nd class only — DIVAČA and RIJEKA - PULA — 1303

km			🚌	k	1472 L	🚌		Ⓐ	🚌 j	Ⓐ	🚌 m		🚌	
0	**Divača 1305** ... d.	...	...	...	0840	...	...	...	...	...	...	*1505*a	...	...
12	Hrpelje-Kozina ... d.	...	...	...	0857	...	...	...	...	...	...	*1520*a	...	...
48	Buzet ▦ ... d.	...	...	0716	0944	...	1120	1310	...	...	...	1600	...	...
	Rijeka 1305/10 . d.	...	0600	|	|	1030	|	|	1425	...	1520	|	1920	...
61	Lupoglav ... d.	0455	0640	0734	1000	1110	1138	1327	1505	1507	1600	1617	2000	2012
135	**Pula** ... a.	0622	...	0909	1116	...	1308	1458	...	1647	...	1752	...	2140

	k	🚌		🚌	Ⓐ			🚌	Ⓐ	Ⓐ	1473 L		🚌
Pula ... d.	0505	...	0923	...	...	1318	1425	...	1530	1720	1802	1930	...
Lupoglav ... a.	0642	0645	1054	1115	1240	1459t	1601	1605	1710	1853	1925	2106	2110
Rijeka 1305/10 . a.	|	0725	|	1155	|	|	...	1645	...	...	|	...	2150
Buzet ▦ ... d.	0704	...	1113	...	1258	1528	...	...	...	...	1950	...	...
Hrpelje-Kozina .. d.	...	...	...	...	...	*1644*a	...	...	...	...	2037	...	...
Divača 1305 ... a.	...	...	...	...	...	*1657*a	...	...	...	...	2049	...	...

L – ISTRA – Apr. 26 - May 4, June 28 - Aug. 31: [2] Ljubljana - Pula and v.v.
a – Ⓐ only.
j – Ⓐ (not June 20 - Aug. 31).
k – Ⓑ (daily June 22 - Aug. 31).
m – Ⓒ (daily June 20 - Aug. 31).
t – Depart 1510.

1305 LJUBLJANA - RIJEKA, KOPER and MONFALCONE

SŽ, HŽ

km		EN									ICS		IC		EC							IC		IC				
		240	1459					481	1605	1472	1011		503		60					483		552		509				
		♦⊖	♦🅁	2Ⓐ	2Ⓐp	2	2	♦	n	♦	♦🅁	2Ⓐ	♦	2	🅁⊖ ♦	2Ⓐ	2Ⓐ	2	2Ⓐ	♦	2	Ⓐ	2Ⓐ		2	2Ⓐ	2m	2Ⓐ
	Maribor **1315** ... d.	...	0148	...	...	...	...	...	0345	...	0540	...	0650	...	...	...	...	...	...	...	...	...	...	...	...	...	...	...
0	**Ljubljana** ... d.	0222	0412	0430	...	...	0555	0620	0633	0710	0740	0808	0930	...	1035	1042	1210	1320	1433	1455	1540	1609	1653	1810	1850	1940	2040	2225
67	Postojna ... d.	0318	0506	0535	...	...	0700	0718	0730	0804	0830	0913	1024	...	1125	1147	1315	1425	1538	1554	1646	1704	1759	1911	1955	2047	2144	2330
80	Pivka ... d.	|	0519	0548	...	*0555*a	0714	0730	0742	0817	0842	0926	1038	...	|	1200	1329	1438	1551	1608	1659	1716	1812	1923	2008	2101	2157	2342
	Ilirska Bistrica ... 🛃 d.	|	|	|	...	0632	|	0758	|	|	|	|	|	...	|	|	|	|	|	1632	|	|	|	|	|	|	|	...
	Šapjane ... 🛃 d.	|	|	|	...	0651	|	0822	|	|	|	|	|	...	|	|	|	|	|	1656	|	|	|	|	|	|	|	...
	Rijeka 1310 ... a.	|	|	|	...	0726	|	0851	|	|	|	|	|	...	|	|	|	|	|	1725	|	|	|	|	|	|	|	...
104	Divača **1303** ... d.	0353	0542	0613	0615	...	0739	...	0805	0840	0904	0951	1101	1108	|	1224	1353	1503	1616	...	1723	1739	1837	1947	2033	2125	2221	...
116	Hrpelje-Kozina § .. d.	|	0557	|	0630	...	|	...	0818	0852	0915	|	1114	|	|	|	|	|	|	...	1736	|	|	1959	|	|	|	...
153	**Koper** § ... a.	|	0642	|	0706	...	|	...	0850	...	0945	|	1150	|	|	|	|	|	|	...	1810	|	|	2032	|	|	|	...
	Sežana ... a.	0402	...	0623	...	...	0749	...	...	...	...	1001	...	1118	1203	1234	1403	1513	1626	...	...	1749	1847	...	2043	2135	2231	...
113	Sežana ... 🛃 d.	0420	...	...	...	...	...	...	...	...	...	...	...	...	1208	...	...	...	...	...	...	...	...	...	...	...	...	...
117	Villa Opicina ⊗ ... 🛃 a.	0428	...	...	...	...	...	...	...	...	...	...	...	...	1215	...	...	...	...	...	...	...	...	...	...	...	...	...
150	**Monfalcone 605/6** .. a.	0542	...	...	...	...	...	...	...	...	...	...	...	...	1255	...	...	...	...	...	...	...	...	...	...	...	...	...
	Venezia SL **605** .. a.	0716	...	...	...	...	...	...	...	...	...	...	...	...	1421	...	...	...	...	...	...	...	...	...	...	...	...	...

km								IC									IC		ICS		EC							EN
								508					482				502		1024		61			1473	1604	480	1458	241
		2	2Ⓐ	2m	2Ⓐ	2	2		2Ⓐ	2Ⓐ	2	2Ⓐ	♦	2Ⓐp	2Ⓐ	2	♦	2Ⓐ	♦🅁	2	🅁⊖ ♦	2Ⓑ	2	♦	n	♦	♦🅁	♦⊖
	Venezia SL **605** .. d.	...	...	...	...	...	...	...	...	...	...	...	...	...	...	...	...	...	...	...	1546	...	...	...	...	...	...	2127
	Monfalcone 605/6 .. d.	...	...	...	...	...	...	...	...	...	...	...	...	...	...	...	...	...	...	...	1707	...	...	...	...	...	...	2300
	Villa Opicina ⊗ ... 🛃 d.	...	...	...	...	...	...	...	...	...	...	...	...	...	...	...	...	...	...	...	1750	...	...	...	...	...	...	2348
	Sežana ... 🛃 a.	...	...	...	...	...	...	...	...	...	...	...	...	...	...	...	...	...	...	...	1758	...	...	...	...	...	...	2355
	Sežana ... d.	...	0440	0515	0600	...	0629	...	0923	1042	...	1252	...	...	1425	1520	...	1652	...	1732	1805	1952	...	...	...	...	...	0015
	Koper § ... d.	...	|	|	|	...	|	0555	|	|	1003	|	...	1328	|	|	1445	|	1640	|	|	|	1910	...	2013	...	2215	|
	Hrpelje-Kozina § .. d.	...	|	|	|	...	|	0630	|	|	1037	|	...	1416	|	|	1520	|	1711	|	|	|	1945	2037	2049	...	2251	|
	Divača **1303** ... d.	...	0451	0526	0611	...	0638	0643	0934	1052	1100	1303	...	1429	1436	1529	1533	1703	1723	1742	|	2002	2007	2050	2103	...	2305	|
0	**Rijeka 1310** ... d.	...	|	|	|	0520	▬	|	|	...	|	|	1257	...	|	...	|	|	|	|	|	...	|	|	|	2045	|	|
28	Šapjane ... 🛃 d.	...	|	|	|	0606	2Ⓐ	|	|	...	|	|	1340	...	|	...	|	|	|	|	|	...	|	|	|	2128	|	|
40	Ilirska Bistrica .. 🛃 d.	...	|	|	|	0618	0629	|	|	...	|	|	1401	...	|	...	|	|	|	|	|	...	|	|	|	2200	|	|
56	Pivka ... d.	0425	0515	0551	0635	...	0646	0706	0958	...	1125	1327	1417	...	1500	...	1556	1727	1744	1806	|	...	2031	2113	2126	2216	2329	|
	Postojna ... d.	0438	0529	0604	0648	...	0659	0719	1011	...	1138	1340	1429	...	1514	...	1610	1740	1755	1820	1843	...	2044	2125	2138	2228	2342	0057
	Ljubljana ... a.	0541	0634	0708	...	...	0802	0818	1114	...	1240	1444	1525	...	1617	...	1704	1843	1843	1923	1932	...	2143	2219	2235	2322	0035	0151
	Maribor **1315** ... a.	...	...	...	...	...	...	...	...	...	...	...	...	...	...	...	1952	...	2037	...	...	...	...	...	0116	...	0259	...

♦ – NOTES (LISTED BY TRAIN NUMBER)

60/1 – CASANOVA – [12] and 🍷 Ljubljana - Venezia Santa Lucia and v.v.

240/1 – VENEZIA – 🛏 1,2 cl., 🛌 2 cl. and [2] Budapest - Zagreb - Ljubljana - Venezia and v.v.; 🛏 1,2 cl. (also [2] on ①②④⑤⑦ from Bucureşti, ②③④⑥⑦ from Venezia) Bucureşti (**625/6**) - Vinţu de Jos (**354/5**) - Lőkösháza (**734/5**) - Budapest - Venezia and v.v.; 🛌 2 cl. Beograd (**412/3**) - Zagreb - Venezia and v.v. Conveys on dates in Table **97**: 🛏 1,2 cl. Moskva (**15/6**) - Budapest - Venezia and v.v.

480/1 – OPATIJA – [2] Rijeka - Ljubljana and v.v.; [2] (also 🛏 1,2 cl. Apr. 30 - Sept. 19, and 🛌 2 cl. Dec. 9-20, Jan. 1-6, Mar. 14-29, Apr. 30 - Sept. 19 (from Rijeka, one day later from München) Rijeka - Ljubljana (**296/7**) - Salzburg (**268/9**) - München and v.v. Conveys ⑥ June 14 - Aug. 23 (from Rijeka), ⑤ June 13 - Aug. 22 (from Wien): 🛌 2 cl. and [2] Rijeka - Ljubljana (**1458/9**) - Wien and v.v.

482/3 – LJUBLJANA – [2] Rijeka - Ljubljana and v.v.; [2] Rijeka - Ljubljana (**150/1**) - Wien and v.v.

502/3 – POHORJE – [12] and ✕ Koper - Maribor and v.v.; [12] Koper - Pragersko (**516/7**) - Hodoš and v.v.

1011/24 – Ⓒ June 15 - Aug. 24: [12] and 🍷 Maribor - Koper and v.v.

1458/9 – ⑥ June 14 - Aug. 23 (from Koper and Rijeka), ⑤ June 13 - Aug. 22 (from Wien): 🛌 2 cl. and [2] Koper - Wien and v.v.; 🛌 2 cl. and [2] Rijeka - Ljubljana (**480/1**) - Wien and v.v.

1472/3 – ISTRA – Apr. 26 - May 4, June 28 - Aug. 31: [2] Ljubljana - Pula and v.v.

a – Ⓐ only.

m – Ⓐ (daily June 21 - Aug. 31).

n – June 21 - Aug. 30.

p – Not Dec. 24, 27, 28, 31, Feb. 25-29, Apr. 28-30, June 26 - Aug. 29, Oct. 27-30.

⊖ – 🅁 and special fares payable for journeys to / from Italy.

§ – 🚌 service (hourly 0630 – 1930) on ⚒ Koper - Trieste and v.v. An irregular 🚌 service also operates Trieste - Hrpelje-Kozina and v.v.

⊗ – 🚋 service (every 20 minutes 0700 – 1940) Villa Opicina - Trieste (Piazza Oberdan) and v.v. Operator: Trieste Trasporti S.p.A. Villa Opicina tram terminus is ±20 minutes walk from railway station.

1310 RIJEKA - ZAGREB

2nd class only except where shown HŽ

km		1901		703				701			IC 501		
											🅁 🍷		
		L		T	Ⓑ						R		
0	**Rijeka 1305** ... d.	0020	*0430*	0545	...	*0730*	...	1115	1335	1520	1655	...	1945
61	Delnice ... d.	0134	*0549*	0656	...	*0851*	...	1225	1455	1649	1759	...	2111
90	Moravice ... d.	0231	0630	0740	0808	0943	1140	1315	1549	1725	1832	1843	2147
120	Ogulin **1330** ... d.	0310	0706	0813	0846	1017	1217	1346	1625	...	1901	1922	...
176	Karlovac **1330** ... d.	0410	0817	0905	0950	1133	1323	1439	1735	...	1947	2032	...
229	**Zagreb 1330** ... a.	0448	0910	0941	1043	1224	1411	1514	1831	...	2020	2124	...
	Osijek **1340** ... a.	1132	...	1435	...	...	...	...	...	...	...	...	...

	1984	IC 500			700				702	
		🅁 🍷								
	M	R					Ⓐ	Ⓐ	T	
Osijek **1340** ... d.	1936	...	...	...	...	...	...	...	1205	...
Zagreb 1330 ... d.	0110	0650	0634	0807	1245	1332	1427	1529	1715	1720
Karlovac **1330** ... d.	0151	0723	0735	0906	1324	1426	1528	1629	1752	1814
Ogulin **1330** ... d.	0250	0812	0847	1016	1419	1538	1647	1735	1844	1921
Moravice ... d.	0333	0841	0917	1058	1500	1608	1718	1805	1928	1953
Delnice ... d.	0406	0914	...	1135	1535	*1648*	...	...	2003	*2046*
Rijeka 1305 ... a.	0516	1015	...	1253	1643	*1809*	...	...	2111	*2203*

L – June 22 - Aug. 31: [2] Rijeka - Zagreb; [2] Rijeka - Zagreb (**413**) - Vinkovci; [2] Rijeka - Zagreb (**783**) - Osijek; 🛌 1,2 cl. and [2] Rijeka - Zagreb (**205**) - Murakeresztúr (**855**) - Budapest.

M – June 20 - Aug. 29 (from Osijek, one day later from Zagreb): [2] Osijek - Zagreb - Rijeka; [2] Vinkovci (**412**) - Zagreb - Rijeka; 🛌 1,2 cl. and [2] (from Budapest, one day later from Zagreb) Budapest (**856**) - Murakeresztúr (**204**) - Zagreb - Rijeka.

R – RIJEKA – [12] and 🍷 Zagreb - Rijeka and v.v.

T – [12] Osijek - Zagreb - Rijeka and v.v.

1313 MARIBOR - ČAKOVEC, MURSKA SOBOTA and ZALAEGERSZEG

2nd class only except where shown SŽ, MÁV

km										IC												IC			IC		
										247							640				1642	518			516		
		Ⓐ	Ⓐ	S	Ⓐ	Ⓐ	Ⓐ	Ⓒ	Ⓐ	C	Ⓐ	Ⓐ	g	Ⓐ	Ⓐ	Ⓐ	H	Ⓐ			y	P		Ⓐ	M	Ⓐ	Ⓐ
	Ljubljana **1315** ... d.	...	...	...	...	...	...	...	...	0740	...	...	...	...	...	...	1245	...	...	...	1345	1515	...	...	1725	...	...
0	**Maribor 1315** ... d.	...	...	...	...	...	0700	0700	...	|	...	1034	1225	1225	1325	1425	|	...	1525	...	|	|	...	1832	|	...	2205
19	Pragersko **1315** ... d.	...	...	...	...	0617	|	0731	...	0954	...	1104	1257	1257	|	|	1510	...	|	...	1604	1722	...	|	1944	...	2236
37	Ptuj ... d.	...	...	...	...	0646	0747	0756	...	1008	...	1133	1320	1324	1407	1507	1525	...	1612	...	1634	1737	...	1920	1958	...	2302
59	Ormož ... d.	...	...	0449	0531	0709	0810	0819	0815	1026	1055	1157	1345	1349	1433	1529	1546j	1545	1636	1640	1704	1755	1800	1945	2020	2024	2326
	Središče ... 🛃 d.	...	...	0503	|	...	|	|	0826	|	|	▬	|	|	1444	▬	|	1556	|	1654	|	|	1811	...	|	2035	...
	Čakovec 1335 ... a.	...	...	0513	|	...	|	|	...	|	|	...	|	|	▬	①–⑤	|	...	|	1704	|	|	▬	...	|	...	...
98	**Murska Sobota** ... d.	0310	0510	▬	0624	...	0857	0906	...	1105	1141	...	1432	1435	...	1510	1630	...	1722	...	1753	1837	...	...	2115	...	...
127	Hodoš ... a.	0339	0545	...	...	...	...	...	...	1131	...	...	1459x	...	...	1540	1658	...	...	...	...	1905	...	...	2149	...	...
127	Hodoš ... 🛃 d.	*0345*	*0548*	0715	...	...	...	...	...	1141	...	1300	...	...	1535	...	...	...	...	...	...	...	1930	...	...	...	...
174	**Zalaegerszeg** ... a.	*0449*	*0655*	0819	...	...	...	...	...	1226	...	1404	...	...	1635	...	...	...	...	...	...	...	2032	...	...	...	...
	Budapest D **1230** .. a.	...	...	...	...	...	...	...	...	1623	...	...	...	...	...	...	...	...	...	...	...	...	...	...	...	...	...

km			IC			IC																IC				
			519			517															1641		246				
			P	S	Ⓐ	M	Ⓐ	Ⓐ		Ⓐ	Ⓐ		Ⓐ	Ⓐ	Ⓐ	g	Ⓐ	Ⓐ		①–⑤	g		C		x		Ⓐ
	Budapest D **1230** .. d.	...	...	...	...	...	...	...	...	...	...	...	...	...	...	...	...	...	...	...	...	...	1250	...	...	...	...
	Zalaegerszeg ... d.	...	...	...	...	...	*0425*	...	0535	...	...	1135	...	...	...	...	...	...	1340	...	...	...	1642	1720	...	2057	...
	Hodoš ... 🛃 a.	...	...	...	...	...	*0530*	...	0640	...	...	1241	...	...	...	...	...	...	1449	...	...	...	1727	1823	...	2200	...
	Hodoš ... d.	...	0420	...	...	0505	0557	...	...	...	...	▬	...	...	...	...	...	...	▬	1553	1700x	...	1740	...	...	▬	2220
	Murska Sobota ... d.	...	0449	...	...	0540	0628	...	...	...	*0935*	...	1210	...	1457	1457	...	...	...	1624	1725	...	1803	...	1931	...	2248
0	**Čakovec 1335** ... d.	...	|	0525	...	|	|	...	...	...	|	...	|	...	|	|	...	...	1713	...	|	...	|	...	|	...	...
12	Središče ... 🛃 d.	0430	|	0538	...	|	|	...	...	1030	|	Ⓐ	|	1510	|	|	1604	...	1726	...	|	1827	|	...	|	...	...
22	Ormož ... d.	0442	0526	0549	0553	0627	0715	0718	...	1041	1049	1208	1258	1521	1544	1544	1615	1710	1738	...	1811	1838	1843	...	2017	...	...
	Ptuj ... d.	0507	0542	...	0618	0645	...	0746	...	...	1113	1233	1322	...	1614	1614	...	1736	...	...	1837	...	1903	...	2042	x	...
	Pragersko **1315** ... d.	0539	0609	...	0655	0717	...	0818	...	...	1144	|	1352	...	1645	1645	...	1758	...	...	1909	...	1927	...	2103	2112	...
	Maribor 1315 ... a.	0602	|	...	0717	|	...	0840	...	...	1207	1318	1415	...	1709	1709	...	...	...	...	|	...	|	...	...	2133	...
	Ljubljana **1315** ... a.	...	0812	...	...	0925	...	...	...	...	...	...	...	...	...	...	...	...	...	...	2114	...	2130	...	...	...	...

C – CITADELLA – [12] Budapest - Ljubljana and v.v.

H – [2] and ✕ Ljubljana (**506**) - Pragersko - Hodoš.

M – MURA – [12] Koper (**502/3**) - Pragersko - Hodoš and v.v.

P – PTUJ – Ⓐ: [2] Ljubljana - Hodoš and v.v.

S – ①–⑤ (not Dec. 25, 26, Jan. 1, 2, Feb. 8, Mar. 24, May 1, 2, June 25, Aug. 15, Oct. 31).

g – ⑦ Dec. 9 - June 22, Aug. 31 - Dec. 7 (also Jan. 2, Mar. 24; not Dec. 23, 30, Mar. 23, Apr. 27, Oct. 26).

j – Arrive 1541.

x – Subject to confirmation.

y – ⑤ Dec. 14 - June 20, Sept. 5 - Dec. 12 (also Feb. 7; not Dec. 28, Feb. 8, May 2, Oct. 31).

LJUBLJANA and ZAGREB - MARIBOR - GRAZ — 1315

SŽ, HŽ, ÖBB

km					ICS	IC	IC	ICS	EC		IC	IC			EC	ICS	IC	EC	ICS	IC	IC	ICS	ICS	ICS			
		1458			12	247	158	14	100		154	506		1642	156	20	518	150	22	502	152	1124	1024	26		604	1604
		R	2	2	R		✕	R	✕	2			2		✕	R	2	✕	R			R	R	R	2		
		♦		Ⓐ		♦	♦		♦			♦		y			♦	♦	Ⓐ	♦		t	♦			w	v
	Rijeka 1305 d.	2045	...	...	...	...	...	...	...	...	...	...	...	...	...	...	...	1257	...	...	...	...	...	...	...	...	...
0	**Ljubljana 1300** d.	0050	...	...	0545	0740	...	0830	1018	1050	....	1245	1250	1345	...	1445	1515	1600	1645	1725	...	1845	1845	1945	2050	2225	2245
*	**Zagreb 1300** d.	|	...	...	|	|	0725	|	|	|	...	|	|	|	1335	|	|	|	|	|	...	|	|	|	|	|	|
	Dobova 1300 🛃 d.	|	...	...	|	|	0808	|	|	|	...	|	|	|	1420	|	|	|	|	|	...	|	|	|	|	|	|
	Sevnica 1300 d.	|	...	...	|	|	0834	|	|	|	...	|	|	|	1444	|	|	|	|	|	...	|	|	|	|	|	|
64	Zidani Most 1300 d.	|	0500	0556	0630	0838	|	0914	1113	1200	...	1342	1400	1443	|	1530	1608	1654	1730	1824	...	1930	1930	2030	2200	2334	2349
89	Celje d.	0206	0525	0622	0650	0905	0912	0934	1138	1225	...	1409	1425	1510	1520	1550	1635	1719	1750	1850	...	1950	1950	2050	2225	0001	0016
137	Pragersko 1313 d.	|	0612	0711	0722	0944	0953	1004	1218	1311	...	1455	1512	1550	1601	1622	1720	1758	1822	1935	...	2022	2022	2122	2312	0045	0100
156	**Maribor 1313** a.	0259	0631	0730	0736	...	1009	1016	1233	1331	...	1513	1533	...	1617	1637	...	1813	1837	1952	...	2037	2037	2137	2333	0102	0116
156	**Maribor** d.	0304	...	...	...	...	1021	...	1242	...	1414	...	...	...	1621	...	...	1819	...	...	2015	...	...	...	...	...	...
172	Spielfeld-Straß 🛃 a.	0323	...	...	...	...	1039	...	1300	...	1432	...	...	...	1638	...	...	1837	...	...	2032	...	...	...	...	...	...
172	Spielfeld-Straß 🛃 d.	0335	...	...	...	...	1051	...	1312	...	1447	...	...	...	1651	...	...	1849	...	...	2045	...	...	...	...	...	...
219	**Graz Hbf** a.	0410	...	...	...	...	1124	...	1347	...	1520	...	...	...	1724	...	...	1922	...	...	2119	...	...	...	...	...	...
	Wien Südbf 980 a.	0720	...	...	...	...	1402	...	...	...	...	...	...	...	2002	...	...	2202	...	...	...	...	...	...	...	...	...

					ICS	ICS	IC	IC	IC	ICS		EC		EC	ICS	EC			IC	ICS			IC	ICS	EC	
	1459	605	1605	607		11	1011	519	503	153	13		157		151	17	101		1611	155	21	1615	1641	246	23	159	
	R			2	2	R	R	2			R	2	✕	2	✕	R	✕	2	2		R	2	2		R	✕	2
	♦	w	v	Ⓐ		x	♦	♦	♦			Ⓐ			♦		♦		g		Ⓐ	g	g	♦		♦	Ⓑ
Wien Südbf 980 d.	2205	...	...	...	...	...	...	...	...	...	...	...	0557	...	0757	...	...	...	...	...	...	...	...	...	...	1557	...
raz Hbf d.	0037	...	...	...	...	...	...	...	...	0655	...	...	0836	...	1036	...	1402	...	...	1540	...	...	...	...	...	1837	...
pielfeld-Straß 🛃 a.	0111	...	...	...	...	...	...	...	...	0728	...	...	0909	...	1109	...	1435	...	...	1613	...	...	...	...	...	1909	...
pielfeld-Straß 🛃 d.	0125	...	...	...	...	...	...	...	...	0740	...	...	0921	...	1121	...	1447	...	...	1626	...	...	...	...	...	1921	...
laribor a.	0143	...	...	...	...	...	...	...	...	0756	...	...	0937	...	1139	...	1504	...	...	1647	...	...	...	...	...	1938	...
laribor 1313 d.	0148	0345	0345	0440	0515	0540	0540	...	0650	...	0817	0915	0944	1015	1150	1245	1514	1520	1620	...	1650	1800	...	...	1945	1955	2220
ragersko 1313 d.	|	0402	0402	0457	0535	0555	0555	0609	0717	...	0831	0935	1000	1035	1206	1259	1530	1539	1639	...	1703	1817	1909	1927	1959	2011	2240
elje d.	0240	0450	0450	0545	0621	0633	0633	0652	0759	...	0906	1023	1041	1123	1245	1335	1610	1623	1724	...	1735	1859	1950	2006	2035	2049	2326
idani Most 1300 d.	0119	0516	0516	0610	0645	0654	0654	0718	0825	...	0925	1047	|	1147	1310	1354	1635	1647	1750	...	1754	1926	2015	2031	2054	|	...
Sevnica 1300 d.	|	|	|	|	...	|	|	|	|	...	|	...	1120	...	|	|	|	...	|	...	|	|	|	|	|	2125	...
Dobova 1300 🛃 d.	|	|	|	|	...	|	|	|	|	...	|	...	1200	...	|	|	|	...	|	...	|	|	|	|	|	2204	...
Zagreb 1300 a.	|	|	|	|	...	|	|	|	|	...	|	...	1229	...	|	|	|	...	|	...	|	|	|	|	|	2233	...
jubljana 1300 a.	0357	0616	0616	0712	...	0738	0738	0812	0925	...	1009	...	...	...	1410	1438	1732	...	1845	...	1838	2025	2114	2130	2138	...	...
Rijeka 1305 a.	0851	...	...	...	...	...	...	...	...	...	...	...	...	...	1725	...	...	...	...	...	...	...	...	...	...	...	...

DDITIONAL SERVICES MARIBOR - ZIDANI MOST and v.v.: 2nd class only

	Ⓐ	Ⓐ	Ⓐ	Ⓐ	Ⓐ	Ⓐ	Ⓐ		Ⓐ		Ⓐ	Ⓐ		Ⓑ
laribor d.	0420	0615	0715	0755	1115	1215	1315	1415	1615	1715	1815	1920	2015	2100
ragersko d.	0440	0635	0735	0814	1135	1235	1335	1435	1635	1735	1835	1938	2035	2119
elje d.	0528	0723	0823	0910	1223	1323	1423	1523	1723	1823	1923	2023	2123	2207
idani Most d.	0552	0747	0847	0934	1247	1347	1447	1547	1747	1847	1947	2047	2147	2232

		Ⓐ	Ⓐ	Ⓐ	Ⓐ	Ⓐ	Ⓐ			Ⓐ	Ⓑ	Ⓑ	Ⓐ
Zidani Most d.	0700	0800	0918	1000	1100	1300	1500	1600	1700	1800	1900	2000	2100
Celje d.	0725	0825	0943	1025	1125	1325	1525	1625	1725	1825	1925	2025	2125
Pragersko d.	0811	0912	1030	1112	1209	1412	1612	1712	1812	1912	2012	2112	2212
Maribor a.	0831	0933	1050	1133	1228	1433	1633	1733	1833	1933	2033	2133	2233

♦ – **NOTES** (LISTED BY TRAIN NUMBER)

00/1 – JÓŽE PLEČNIK – [12] and ✕ Ljubljana - Praha and v.v.
50/1 – EMONA – [12] and ✕ Ljubljana - Wien and v.v.; [2] Rijeka (**482/3**) - Ljubljana - Wien and v.v.
58/9 – CROATIA – [12] and ✕ Zagreb - Wien and v.v. Conveys ⑦ June 15 - Aug. 24 (from Split), ⑥ June 14 - Aug. 23 (from Wien): 🛏 2 cl. Split (**824/5**) - Zagreb - Wien and v.v.
46/7 – CITADELLA – [12] Budapest - Ljubljana and v.v.
02/3 – POHORJE – [12] and ✕ Koper - Maribor and v.v.; [12] Koper - Pragersko (**516/7**) - Hodoš and v.v.
06 – [12] Ljubljana - Maribor; [2] and ✕ Ljubljana - Pragersko (**640**) - Hodoš.
18/9 – PTUJ – Ⓐ: [2] Ljubljana - Hodoš and v.v.
011/24 – © June 15 - Aug. 24: [12] and 🍷 Maribor - Koper and v.v.
458/9 – ⑥ June 14 - Aug. 23 (from Koper and Rijeka), ⑤ June 13 - Aug. 22 (from Wien): 🛏 2 cl. and [2] Koper - Wien and v.v.; 🛏 2 cl. and [2] Rijeka - Ljubljana (**480/1**) - Wien and v.v.

g – ⑦ Dec. 9 - June 22, Aug. 31 - Dec. 7 (also Jan. 2, Mar. 24; not Dec. 23, 30, Mar. 23, Apr. 27, Oct. 26).
t – ⑦ Dec. 9 - June 8, Aug. 31 - Dec. 7 (also Jan. 2, Mar. 24; not Dec. 23, 30, Mar. 23, Apr. 27).
v – June 21 - Aug. 30.
w – Not June 21 - Aug. 30.
x – Not © June 15 - Aug. 24.
y – ⑤ Dec. 14 - June 20, Sept. 5 - Dec. 12 (also Feb. 7; not Dec. 28, Feb. 8, May 2, Oct. 31).
* – Zagreb - Celje : *104 km.*

ZAGREB - VINKOVCI - BEOGRAD — 1320

SŽ, HŽ, ŽS

km								IC	IC		
		413	741	419	415	743	745	211	551	747	411
		✕			✕			✕	R 🍷		
		♦	♦	♦	♦			♦			♦
	Ljubljana 1300 d.	...	...	...	0835	...	...	1408	...	...	2105
0	**Zagreb** d.	0603	0900	...	1110	1320	1523	1648	1820	2057	0015
105	Novska d.	0740	1032	...	1247	1453	1700	1823	|	2234	0148
191	Slavonski Brod d.	0836	1128	...	1344	1549	1756	1918	2036	2336	0243
224	Strizivojna-Vrpolje 1350 d.	0854	1145	...	1402	1606	1813	1935	2054	2357	0300
	Osijek 1350 a.	|	|	...	|	|	|	|	2140	|	|
256	**Vinkovci** d.	0929	1205	1227	1432	1626	1833	2007	...	0022	0337
288	Šid 🛃 d.	1035	...	1350	1537	...	...	2112	...	...	0445
407	**Beograd** a.	1213	...	1533	1720	...	...	2247	...	...	0623

			IC			IC					
	410	740	550	742	744	210	746	414	418	748	412
			R 🍷			✕		✕			✕
	♦					♦		♦	♦	♦	♦
Beograd d.	2215	...	...	...	...	0620	...	1045	1320	...	1540
Šid 🛃 d.	0102	...	...	...	...	0903	...	1334	1603	...	1828
Vinkovci d.	0150	0306	...	0605	0742	0958	1242	1440	1706	1725	1938
Osijek 1350 d.	|	|	0525	|	|	|	|	|	...	|	|
Strizivojna-Vrpolje 1350 d.	0210	0332	0611	0625	0802	1018	1302	1500	...	1750	1958
Slavonski Brod d.	0227	0354	0628	0644	0820	1036	1320	1517	...	1812	2016
Novska d.	0323	0458	|	0743	0915	1130	1417	1611	...	1912	2109
Zagreb a.	0455	0639	0847	0918	1053	1304	1557	1748	...	2050	2240
Ljubljana 1300 a.	0750	...	...	...	...	1539	...	2031	...	...	...

♦ – **NOTES** (LISTED BY TRAIN NUMBER)

10/1 – SAVA – [12] Beograd - Villach (**110/1**) - München and v.v.; ✕ Beograd - Jesenice and v.v.
10 – 🛌 1, 2 cl., 🛏 2 cl. and [2] Beograd - Zagreb - Ljubljana.
11 – 🛌 1, 2 cl., 🛏 2 cl. and [2] Ljubljana - Zagreb - Beograd; [2] (also 🍷 July 1 - Aug. 31) Banja Luka (**451**) - Vinkovci - Beograd.
12 – NIKOLA TESLA – [12] and ✕ Beograd - Zagreb; 🛏 2 cl. Beograd - Zagreb (**240**) - Venezia. Conveys June 20 - Aug. 29: [2] Vinkovci - Zagreb (**1984**) - Rijeka.
13 – NIKOLA TESLA – [12] and ✕ Zagreb - Beograd; 🛏 2 cl. Venezia (**241**) - Zagreb - Beograd. Conveys June 21 - Sept. 6 (from Split and Zadar, following day from Zagreb): [2] Split (**1822**) - Zagreb - Vinkovci; [2] Zadar (**1920**) - Knin (**1822**) - Zagreb - Vinkovci. Also conveys June 22 - Aug. 31 (from Rijeka and Zagreb): [2] Rijeka (**1901**) - Zagreb - Vinkovci.
14 – [2] Beograd - Schwarzach-St Veit (**464**) - Zürich; 🛌 1, 2 cl. and 🛏 2 cl. Zagreb - Schwarzach-St Veit - Zürich; [12] and ✕ Beograd - Ljubljana - Jesenice.
415 – [2] Zürich (**465**) - Schwarzach-St Veit - Beograd; 🛌 1, 2 cl. and 🛏 2 cl. Zürich (**465**) - Schwarzach-St Veit - Zagreb; [12] and ✕ Jesenice - Ljubljana - Beograd.
418 – [2] Beograd - Vinkovci; [2] (also 🍷 July 1 - Aug. 31) Beograd - Vinkovci (**450**) - Banja Luka; [2] Beograd - Vinkovci (**748**) - Zagreb (**296**) - Salzburg (**268**) - München.
419 – [2] Vinkovci - Beograd; [2] München (**269**) - Salzburg (**297**) - Zagreb (**741**) - Vinkovci - Beograd.
741 – [12] Zagreb - Vinkovci; [2] München (**269**) - Salzburg (**297**) - Zagreb - Vinkovci (**419**) - Beograd.
748 – [12] Vinkovci - Zagreb; [2] Beograd (**418**) - Vinkovci - Zagreb (**296**) - Salzburg (**268**) - München. Conveys June 20 - Sept. 5: [2] Vinkovci - Zagreb (**1823**) - Split; [2] Vinkovci - Zagreb (**1823**) - Knin (**1921**) - Zadar.

ZAGREB - BANJA LUKA - DOBOJ — 1325

HŽ, ŽRS 2nd class only except where shown

km	km							397					451	399
					Ⓐ⊗			Z	⊗	Ⓐ	⊗		L	S
0		**Zagreb 1343** d.	...	...	...	...	...	0857	...	...	...	...	...	2049
72		Sunja 1343 ⊡ d.	...	...	...	...	...	1022	...	...	...	...	...	2222
112	0	Novi Grad ⊡ d.	...	0512	...	...	...	1144	1155	1315	1715	1800	...	2351
	20	Blatna d.	...	0535	0540	...	...	|	1219	1338	1739	1823	...	|
	78	Bihać a.	...	...	0707	...	...	|	1346	━	1906	━	...	|
214		Banja Luka d.	0421	...	...	0730	0955	1315	...	1532	...	1930	2230	0124
324		**Doboj** a.	0637	...	...	1000	1212	1503	...	1749	...	2203	0014	0316
		Sarajevo 1350 a.	...	...	...	...	...	1805	...	...	...	...	|	0620
		Beograd 1320 a.	...	...	...	...	...	...	...	...	...	...	0623	...

								396			450	398
	Ⓐ⊗			⊗		Ⓐ	⊗	Z			L	S
Beograd 1320 d.	...	...	...	...	...	...	...	...	...	...	1320	...
Sarajevo 1350 d.	...	...	...	...	...	...	...	1027	...	...	|	2120
Doboj d.	...	0400	0720	...	1058	...	...	1329	1537	1920	2015	0032
Banja Luka d.	...	0619	0937	...	1330	...	...	1529	1803	2137	2159	0221
Bihać d.	0356	━	...	0944	...	...	1459	|	━	...	...	|
Blatna d.	0523	0617	...	1112	...	1400	1627	|	1832	...	...	|
Novi Grad ⊡ d.	...	0640	...	1135	...	1423	1650	1657	1855	...	...	0348
Sunja 1343 ⊡ d.	...	...	...	...	...	...	...	1823	...	...	...	0519
Zagreb 1343 a.	...	...	...	...	...	...	...	1947	...	...	...	0643

– [2] (also 🍷 July 1 - Aug. 31) Banja Luka - Vinkovci (**411/8**) - Beograd and v.v.

S – [2] and 🛏 2 cl. Zagreb - Sarajevo and v.v.
Z – [12] Zagreb - Sarajevo - Ploče and v.v.

⊗ – Not during heating season (nominally until Apr. 15).
⊡ – 🛃 at Volinja (Croatia) / Dobrljin (Bosnia-Herzegovina).

1330 ZAGREB - ZADAR and SPLIT (HŽ)

km			ICN 1521		ICN 1523		ICN 525		1823	1823	825	825
			ℝ 🍷		ℝ 🍷		ℝ 🍷		1921			5831
		2		2	w	2		2	A	♦	♦	2n
0	**Zagreb 1310** d.	...	0650	...	1100	...	1522	...	2145	2145	2255	2255
53	Karlovac **1310** d.	...	0723	...	1134	...	1556	...	2221	2221	2331	2331
109	**Ogulin 1310** d.	0350g	|	...	|	1548	|	...	2320	2320	0031	0031
177	Vrhovine d.	0514	|	...	|	1708	|	...	0057	0057	0207	0207
225	Gospić d.	...	0927	...	1341	▬	1759	...	0137	0137	0253	0253
269	Gračac d.	...	0958	...	|	...	1831	...	0217	0217	0328	0328
333	Knin a.	...	1048	...	1501	2	1921	...	0327	0327	0438	0438
333	Knin § d.	...	1049	...	1502	1549	1922	1948	0342	0339	0440	0440
	Zadar ⊡ § a.	...	|	...	|	|	|	|	0536	|	|	|
387	Perković § a.	...	1132	...	1544	1708	2005	2051	...	0443	0543	0543
387	Perković § d.	...	1133	1135	1552	1709	2006	2052	...	0445	0554	0559
	Šibenik ⊡ § a.	...	|	1202	|	1737	|	2120	...	|	|	0627
435	**Split** ⊡ § a.	...	1217	...	1642	...	2048	...	...	0554	0657	...

		ICN 520		ICN 1522			ICN 524	1920	1822	5828	824
		ℝ 🍷		ℝ 🍷			ℝ 🍷	1822		824	
	2		2	w	2	2		B	♦	2h	♦
Split ⊡ § d.	...	0737	...	1047	...	...	1506	...	2100	...	2222
Šibenik ⊡ § d.	0740	|	1027	|	...	1515	|	...	|	2255	|
Perković § a.	0812	0819	1058	1129	...	1546	1550	...	2211	2325	2333
Perković § d.	▬	0820	...	1134	...	...	1551	...	2212	2344	2344
Zadar ⊡ § d.	...	|	...	|	...	...	|	2100	|	|	|
Knin § a.	...	0903	...	12186	...	...	1634	2257	2316	0047	0047
Knin d.	...	0904	...	1218	...	...	1635	2331	2331	0048	0048
Gračac d.	...	0959	...	|	...	...	1726	0058	0058	0215	0215
Gospić d.	2	1030	...	1340	...	...	1758	0147	0147	0250	0250
Vrhovine d.	0530	|	...	|	1758	...	|	0242	0242	0336	0336
Ogulin 1310 d.	0648	|	...	|	1916	...	|	0408	0408	0501	0501
Karlovac **1310** d.	...	1233	...	1541	...	...	2000	0500	0500	0555	0555
Zagreb 1310 a.	...	1307	...	1623	...	...	2033	0536	0536	0631	0631

KNIN - ZADAR and v.v.:

km		A				Ⓐ	
0	Knin d.	0342	0423	0528	1058	1308	1640
57	Benkovac d.	|	0538	0643	1218	1423	1755
95	Zadar a.	0536	0629	0740	1309	1521	1846

				Ⓐ	z	B	y
Zadar d.	0639	1000	1420	1536	2008	2100	2130
Benkovac d.	0731	1052	1514	1628	2100	|	2222
Knin a.	0845	1206	1628	1747	2214	2257	2336

KNIN - PERKOVIĆ - ŠIBENIK and v.v. (additional services):

km			x				Ⓐv			x
0	Knin d.	0407	...	...	0714	...	...	...	1948	...
54	Perković d.	0508	0548	0704	0816	1316	1442	...	2052	2335
76	Šibenik a.	...	0616	0732	0844	1344	1506	...	2120	2359

		x					Ⓐv			
Šibenik d.	0433	0626	...	0740	1235	...	1405	...	2009	2255
Perković d.	0512q	0657	...	0832t	1306	...	1434	1636	2054r	2325
Knin a.	0619	...	...	0934	...	...	...	1738	2157	...

PERKOVIĆ - SPLIT and v.v.:

km				Ⓑ		y	z
0	Perković d.	0532	0823	1229	1720	2101	2123
48	Split a.	0632	0923	1330	1820	2201	2228

			Ⓑ				
Split d.	0405	0705	1003	...	1532	1939	...
Perković a.	0505	0805	1104	...	1633	2045	...

1335 ZAGREB - VARAŽDIN - NAGYKANIZSA

2nd class only except where shown — HŽ, MÁV

km		7600			205				7602					992	790		IC 590			7604					
					♦							Ⓐ	Ⓐ		Ⓑ		ℝZ								⚒
0	**Zagreb** d.	...	0455	...	0720	0740	...	...	0934	...	1123	...	1259	1416	1515	...	1626	...	1524	...	...	1759	1904	2053	2223
38	Zabok d.	...	0552	...	0805	0834	...	...	1033	...	1217	...	1415	1513	1602	...	k	...	1630	...	...	1911	2009	2205	2316
104	**Varaždin** ▲ d.	0537	0743	...	0922	1005	1026	...	1220	1311	1422f	1517	1556	1635	1716	...	1814	...	1855e	...	1955	2038	2214p	2330	0041
115	Čakovec **1313** d.	0550	0755	...	0934	...	1037	...	...	1323	1438	1536	...	1647	1731	...	1824	...	1907	...	2019	2048	2225	...	0051
145	Kotoriba 🏛 d.	0625	0827b	...	1005	...	1108	...	...	1400	1511	1609	...	1720	1800	...	...	...	1940	2000	2052	...	2255	...	...
151	Murakeresztúr 🏛 d.	0632	...	...	1035	...	...	...	...	1407	...	...	...	...	...	...	...	...	...	2007	...	...	...	...	...
165	**Nagykanizsa** a.	*0653*	...	...	1045	...	...	...	...	...	...	...	...	...	...	...	...	...	...	*2028*	...	...	...	...	...
	Budapest K **1220** a.	...	...	...	1458	...	...	...	...	...	...	...	...	...	...	...	...	...	...	...	...	...	...	...	...

				991	IC 591			791	7601								7603		995		204			
			Ⓑ		ℝZ		Ⓑ	Ⓑ		Ⓑ		Ⓐ			Ⓐ		Ⓑ		K		♦			
Budapest K **1220** d.	...	...	...	...	...	...	...	...	...	...	...	...	...	...	...	...	...	...	...	...	...	1500	...	...	...
Nagykanizsa d.	...	...	...	...	...	...	...	...	*0657*	...	...	...	...	...	...	...	...	...	...	...	...	1904	1942	...	...
Murakeresztúr 🏛 d.	...	...	...	...	...	...	...	...	0726	...	...	...	...	...	...	...	...	1435	...	...	...	1935	1957	*2035*	...
Kotoriba 🏛 d.	...	...	...	0443	...	0553	0649	...	0739	...	...	1111	1159	1244	...	...	1404a	1444	...	1653	1807a	1944	...	2100	2210
Čakovec **1313** d.	...	...	...	0520	0549	0635	0723	0726	0816	1005	...	1151	1234	1324	1407	...	1437	1529	...	1735	1843	2012	...	2132	2246
Varaždin ▲ d.	0301	0353	0431	0535	0601	0648	...	0741	0826	1015	1042	1204	1244	1334	1417	1421	1447	1539	1542	1751	1904	2024	...	2142	2256
Zabok d.	0430	0519	0625	0655	k	0836	...	0901	...	...	1218	1348	...	...	...	1604	...	...	1728	1910	2039	2138	...	...	...
Zagreb a.	0524	0613	0724	0745	0748	0929	...	0948	...	...	1311	1442	...	...	...	1700	...	...	1823	1959	2131	2222	...	...	...

▲ – **VARAŽDIN - KOPRIVNICA and v.v.** 2nd class only except where shown:

km			Z				Ⓑ			⑦Q		
0	Varaždin d.	0440	0601	0650	...	1036	1253	1424	1602	1653	1907	2215
42	Koprivnica a.	0526	0633	0733	...	1120	1337	1511	1646	1740	1951	2258

	Ⓑ					Ⓐ			Z	⑦Q			
Koprivnica d.	0446	0554	0831	1150	1252	1424	1534	1659	1740	1808	1909	2014	2151
Varaždin a.	0533	0642	0915	1234	1341	1511	1627	1742	1812	1850	1953	2056	2241

1340 ZAGREB - KOPRIVNICA - NAGYKANIZSA and OSIJEK (HŽ, MÁV)

km		EN 241	1201	783	703	981	IC 201		IC 590	IC 581	971	995
		V	♦	♦		2	♦		ℝZ	ℝ 🍷	2	K
	Rijeka **1310** d.	...	...	0020d	0545	...	...	...	...	...	...	...
0	**Zagreb** d.	0456	0640	0640	1000	1245	1546	...	1626	1705	1825	2012
57	Križevci d.	0537	0736	0736	1042	1337	1627	...	1703	1742	1915	2110
88	Koprivnica **1335** d.	0611	0812	0821	1126	1425	1701	...	1732	1820	1954	2144
103	Gyékényes 🏛 d.	0647	0845	|	|	|	1735	...	...	|	...	...
132	**Nagykanizsa** a.	0710	0909	|	|	|	1758	...	...	|	...	...
	Budapest K **1220** a.	1058	...	|	|	|	2153	...	...	|	...	...
153	Virovitica d.	...	...	0924	1226	1543	...	...	...	1917	...	...
225	Našice d.	...	...	1050	1353	1734	...	...	...	2039	...	...
275	**Osijek 1345/50** a.	...	...	1132	1435	1826	...	...	...	2119	...	...

	980	IC 591	IC 580	IC 200		702	782	1200	EN 240	1984
	2	ℝZ	ℝ 🍷	♦			♦	♦	V	♦
Osijek 1345/50 d.	0000	...	0515	...	...	1205	1605	...	...	1936
Našice d.	0048	...	0558	...	...	1250	1650	...	...	2043
Virovitica d.	0220	...	0724	...	...	1425	1819	...	...	2232
Budapest K **1220** d.	|	...	|	0605	...	|	|	...	1700	|
Nagykanizsa d.	|	...	|	0950	...	|	|	1858	2051	|
Gyékényes 🏛 d.	|	...	|	1030	...	|	|	1941	2134	|
Koprivnica **1335** d.	0333	0641	0828	1050	...	1530	1941	1958	2153	2340
Križevci d.	0410	0711	0858	1120	...	1600	2011	2034	2223	0016
Zagreb a.	0505	0748	0936	1201	...	1648	2055	2123	2305	0058
Rijeka **1310** a.	...	...	...	...	...	2111	...	...	...	0516

♦ – **NOTES FOR TABLES 1330/35/40** (LISTED BY TRAIN NUMBER)

200/1 – KVARNER – [12] Budapest - Zagreb and v.v.

204/5 – MAESTRAL – [12] Budapest (**855/6**) - Murakeresztúr - Zagreb and v.v. Conveys June 6 - Sept. 12 (from Budapest, one day later from Split): 🛏 1, 2 cl. and [2] (also ▬ 2 cl. on ⑤ from Budapest, ⑥ from Split) Budapest - Zagreb (**824/5**) - Split and v.v. Conveys June 20 - Aug. 29 (from Budapest, two days later from Rijeka): ▬ 1, 2 cl. and [2] Budapest - Zagreb (**1901/84**) - Rijeka and v.v. Conveys on dates in Table **97**: 🛏 1, 2 cl. Moskva / Kyïv - Budapest - Zagreb and v.v.

782 – [12] Osijek - Zagreb. Conveys June 20 - Sept. 5: [2] Osijek - Zagreb (**1823**) - Split.

783 – [12] Zagreb - Osijek. Conveys June 21 - Sept. 6 (from Split, one day later from Zagreb): [2] Split (**1822**) - Zagreb - Osijek; 🛏 1, 2 cl., ▬ 2 cl. and [2] Split (**1822**) - Zagreb - Koprivnica (**1201**) - Bratislava - Praha. Conveys June 22 - Aug. 31 (from Rijeka): [2] Rijeka (**1901**) - Zagreb - Osijek.

824 – 🛏 1, 2 cl. and [2] Split - Zagreb. Conveys June 7 - Sept. 13: 🛏 1, 2 cl. and [2] (also ▬ 2 cl. on ⑥) Split - Zagreb (**205**) - Murakeresztur (**855**) - Budapest. Conveys on ⑦ June 15 - Aug. 24: ▬ 2 cl. Split - Zagreb (**158**) - Wien.

825 – 🛏 1, 2 cl. and [2] Zagreb - Split. Conveys June 6 - Sept. 12: 🛏 1, 2 cl. and [2] (also ▬ 2 cl. on ⑤) Budapest (**856**) - Murakeresztur (**204**) - Zagreb - Split. Conveys on ⑥ June 14 - Aug. 23 (from Wien): ▬ 2 cl. Wien (**159**) - Zagreb - Split.

1200 – JADRAN – June 20 - Sept. 5 (from Praha): 🛏 1, 2 cl., ▬ 2 cl. and [2] Praha - Bratislava - Zagreb (**1823**) - Split.

1201 – JADRAN – June 21 - Sept. 6 (from Split, one day later from Zagreb): 🛏 1, 2 cl., ▬ 2 cl. and [2] Split (**1822**) - Zagreb (**783**) - Koprivnica - Bratislava - Praha.

1822 – June 21 - Sept. 6: 🛏 1, 2 cl. and [2] Split - Zagreb; [2] Split - Zagreb (**413**) - Vinkovci; [2] Split - Zagreb (**783**) - Osijek; 🛏 1, 2 cl., ▬ 2 cl. and [2] Split - Zagreb - Koprivnica (**1201**) - Bratislava - Praha.

1823 – June 20 - Sept. 5: 🛏 1, 2 cl. and [2] Zagreb - Split; [2] Vinkovci (**748**) - Zagreb - Split; [2] Osijek (**782**) - Zagreb - Split; 🛏 1, 2 cl., ▬ 2 cl. and [2] Praha (**1200**) - Bratislava - Zagreb - Split.

1984 – June 20 - Aug. 29: [2] Osijek - Zagreb - Rijeka.

A – June 20 - Sept. 5 (from Vinkovci and Zagreb, one day later from Knin): [2] Vinkovci (**748**) - Zagreb (**1823**) - Knin (**1921**) - Zadar.

B – June 21 - Sept. 6: [2] Zadar (**1920**) - Knin (**1822**) - Zagreb (**413**) - Vinkovci.

K – [2] Kotoriba - Zagreb - Koprivnica.

Q – Also Mar. 24; not Mar. 23.

V – VENEZIA – For days of running and composition – see Table **1305**.

Z – Ⓐ: [12] and 🍷 Čakovec - Zagreb and v.v. ℝ.

§ – Additional local services operate – see separate panels.

⊡ – Frequent 🚌 services operate Zadar - Šibenik - Split and v.v.; some continue to Ploče and Dubrovnik. Bus station locations: Zadar, Split and Ploče are adjacent to rail station, Šibenik approximately 10 minutes walk.

a – Ⓐ only.
b – Ⓑ only.
d – June 22 - Aug. 31.
e – Arrive 1805.
f – Arrive 1344.
g – Depart 0328 June 22 - Sept. 7.
h – June 7 - Sept. 13.
k – Via Koprivnica.
n – June 6 - Sept. 13.
p – Arrive 2150.
q – Arrive 0503.
r – Arrive 2041.
t – Arrive 0812.
v – Not June 21 - Aug. 31.
w – June 13 - Sept. 14.
x – Not June 7 - Sept. 13.
y – Not June 21 - Sept. 6.
z – June 21 - Sept. 6.

1343 LOCAL SERVICES in Croatia

2nd class only — HŽ

ZAGREB - SISAK CAPRAG and v.v.: Journey 60–75 minutes. All services call at Sisak (6 minutes from Sisak Caprag).
From Zagreb: 0545, 0648, 0748Ⓐ, 1049, 1149Ⓐ, 1349, 1448Ⓐ, 1549, 1649Ⓐ, 1749Ⓐ, 1849, 1949, 2249.
From Sisak Caprag: 0408Ⓑ, 0512, 0617, 0719, 0819Ⓐ, 1019Ⓐ, 1219, 1419Ⓐ, 1519, 1619Ⓐ, 1719, 1819Ⓐ, 1919, 2119.

SISAK CAPRAG - SUNJA and v.v.: Journey 25 minutes.
From Sisak Caprag: 0342, 0805, 1220, 1459, 1659, 1920Ⓐ, 1959.
From Sunja: 0448, 0553, 1155, 1255, 1632, 1855, 2055, 2132Ⓐ.

SUNJA - NOVSKA and v.v.: Journey 70 minutes.
From Sunja: 0839, 1246Ⓐ**q**, 1533, 2033.
From Novska: 0428, 0520, 1031, 1406Ⓐ**q**, 1730.

q – Not June 21 - Aug. 31.

PÉCS - OSIJEK 1345

HŽ ; MÁV 2nd class only except where shown

km			8110					259			8116			
		Ⓐ					Ⓑ	B						
	Budapest K **1200** d.	...	...	...	...	...	...	0925	...	...	...	...	...	...
0	**Pécs** d.	...	0455	...	...	...	...	1240	...	...	1642	...	...	...
43	Magyarbóly 🏛 d.	...	0627	...	...	...	...	1340	...	...	1805	...	...	...
54	Beli Manastir 🏛 d.	0545	0640	0707	0830	1055	1224	1422	1439	1607	1818	1845	2006	2225
82	**Osijek 1340/50** a.	0617	...	0739	0902	1127	1256	1450	1511	1640	...	1918	2039	2257

				8117			258				8111		
	Ⓐ					Ⓑ	B						
Osijek 1340/50 d.	0505	0627	0749	...	0954	1144	1315	1344	1522	1802	...	1924	2145
Beli Manastir 🏛 d.	0537	0659	0821	0848	1026	1216	1410	1416	1555	1835	1927	1956	2217
Magyarbóly 🏛 d.	...	...	...	0920	...	...	1438	...	...	...	2010	...	...
Pécs a.	...	...	...	1016	...	...	1518	...	...	...	2108	...	...
Budapest K **1200** a.	...	...	...	...	...	...	1858	...	...	...	...	...	...

B – (2) Budapest (**802/3**) - Pécs (**812/3**) - Magyarbóly - Sarajevo and v.v.

OSIJEK - DOBOJ - SARAJEVO 1350

HŽ, ŽFBH, ŽRS Most services 2nd class only

km								397			259		450	399
								Z			B		L	S
	Zagreb **1325** d.	...	...	...	...	...	...	0857	...	...	...	...	...	2049
	Beograd **1320** d.	...	...	...	...	...	...	|	...	...	...	...	1320	|
	Vinkovci **1320** d.	...	...	...	...	...	...	|	...	...	...	...	1740	|
0	**Osijek 1340/5** d.	...	...	...	...	...	...	|	...	...	1454	...	|	|
48	Strizivojna-Vrpolje d.	...	...	...	...	...	...	|	...	...	1546	...	1802	|
68	Slavonski Šamac 🏛 d.	...	...	...	...	...	...	b	...	...	1621	...	1833	b
72	Šamac 🏛 d.	...	...	...	...	0454	1016	|	...	...	1648	...	1854	|
144	**Doboj** d.	...	...	...	...	0625j	1154	1503	...	...	1800	...	2006	0316
144	**Doboj** d.	...	...	0423	0725	▬	▬	1512	1541	...	1814	1925	...	0326
167	Maglaj d.	...	0500	0450	0801	0940	...	1539	1617	*1700*	1842	2001	...	0354
190	Zavidovici d.	...	0528	▬	▬	1008	...	1600	...	*1728*	1903	...	...	0415
239	Zenica d.	0445	0626	0730	1116	1106j	1532	1647	...	1935	1951	...	...	0502
267	Kakanj d.	0524	...	0809	1155	...	1611	1713	...	2014	2017	...	...	0528
285	Visoko d.	0553	...	0832	1218	...	1747	1730	...	2037	2034	...	...	0545
292	Podlugovi d.	0604	...	0843	1229	...	1758	1737	...	2054	2041	...	...	0552
316	**Sarajevo 1355** a.	0642	...	0921	1307	...	1836	1805	...	2132	2109	...	...	0620

			258		396						451	398
			B		Z						L	S
Sarajevo 1355 d.	0431	...	0714	0715	1027	1125	...	1550	...	1920	...	2120
Podlugovi d.	0516	...	0743	0754	1056	1204	...	1629	...	1959	...	2149
Visoko d.	0527	...	0750	0805	1103	1221	...	1650	...	2010	...	2156
Kakanj d.	0550	...	0807	0834	1120	1244	...	1737	...	2041	...	2213
Zenica d.	0628	0732	0834	0912	1147	1322	1522	1815	1917	2118	...	2240
Zavidovici d.	▬	0831	0920	▬	1233	...	1621	▬	2016	▬	...	2326
Maglaj d.	0554	0858	0941	1128	1254	...	1648	1734	2043	2050	...	2347
Doboj a.	0630	▬	1007	1204	1320	...	...	1810	▬	2126	...	0013
Doboj d.	...	0732	1017	...	1329	...	...	...	1942	...	0023	0032
Šamac 🏛 d.	...	0903	1144	...	|	...	...	...	2122	...	0150	|
Slavonski Šamac 🏛 d.	...	...	1209	...	b	...	...	...	...	...	0214	b
Strizivojna-Vrpolje d.	...	...	1227	...	|	...	...	...	...	...	0231	|
Osijek 1340/5 a.	...	...	1313	...	|	...	...	...	...	...	|	|
Vinkovci **1320** a.	...	...	...	...	|	...	...	...	...	...	0251	|
Beograd **1320** a.	...	...	...	...	|	...	...	...	...	...	0623	|
Zagreb **1325** a.	...	...	...	...	1947	...	...	...	...	...	...	0643

B – (2) Budapest (**802/3**) - Pécs (**812/3**) - Magyarbóly - Sarajevo and v.v.
L – (2) (also 🍷 July 1 - Aug. 31) Banja Luka - Vinkovci (**411/8**) - Beograd and v.v.
S – (2) and ▬ 2 cl. Zagreb - Sarajevo and v.v.
Z – (12) Zagreb - Sarajevo - Ploče and v.v.

b – Via Banja Luka (see Table **1325**).
j – Connects with train in previous column.

SARAJEVO - PLOČE 1355

HŽ, ŽFBH Most services 2nd class only

km				391						397	
		⚒		P						Z	
	Zagreb **1325** d.	...	...	...	...	...	...	...	...	0857	...
0	**Sarajevo 1350** d.	...	...	0645	0718	...	1511	...	...	1818	1924
67	Konjic d.	...	...	0758	0906	...	1653	...	...	1931	2112
129	Mostar d.	...	...	0906	...	...	...	...	...	2043	...
149	Žitomislići d.	...	...	0926	...	...	...	...	...	2103	...
163	Čapljina 🏛 d.	...	...	0957	...	...	...	...	...	2134	...
173	Metković d.	0520	0715	1022	...	1325	...	1727	1850	2157	...
194	**Ploče** a.	0543	0738	1041	...	1348	...	1750	1913	2216	...

		396						390		
		Z						P		
Ploče d.	...	0605	0615	1247	...	1410	...	1700	...	1810
Metković d.	...	0635	0638	1310	...	1433	...	1734	...	1833
Čapljina 🏛 d.	...	0700	...	...	...	...	...	1802	...	...
Žitomislići d.	...	0717	...	...	...	...	...	1819	...	...
Mostar d.	...	0738	...	...	...	...	...	1840	...	...
Konjic d.	0502	0850	...	...	1115	...	1703	1947	...	...
Sarajevo 1352 a.	0653	1002	...	...	1258	...	1855	2059	...	...
Zagreb **1325** a.	...	1947	...	...	...	...	...	...	...	...

P – (12) (also 🍷 June 14 - Sept. 7) Ploče - Sarajevo and v.v.

Z – (12) Zagreb - Sarajevo - Ploče and v.v.

LOCAL SERVICES in Bosnia 1358

HŽ, ŽFBH, ŽRS 2nd class only

VINKOVCI - TUZLA and v.v. :

km				⊗		⊗	Ⓑ
0	Vinkovci d.	0401	0920	...	1455	...	2000
46	Drenovci 🏛 d.	0456	1016	1050	1551	...	2055
55	Brčko d.	...	...	1118	...	1730	...
127	Tuzla a.	...	...	1325	...	1935	...

		⊗			⊗	Ⓑ
Tuzla d.	...	0722	...	...	1514	...
Brčko d.	...	0941	...	...	1719	...
Drenovci 🏛 d.	0524	0954	1041	1617	...	2117
Vinkovci a.	0619	...	1136	1711	...	2212

Additional services on Ⓑ: Vinkovci d. 1212, Drenovci a. 1307; Drenovci d. 1326, Vinkovci a. 1420.

TUZLA - DOBOJ and v.v. :

km				⚒		
0	Tuzla d.	...	1036	...	1709	...
32	Petrovo Novo d.	0540	1120	1402	1753	2100
60	Doboj a.	0628	1208	1450	1841	2148

			⚒		
Doboj d.	0442	0728	1305	1528	1930
Petrovo Novo d.	0530	0817	1353	1617	2018
Tuzla a.	...	0900	...	1700	...

⊗ – Not during heating season (nominally until Apr. 15).

SERBIA, MONTENEGRO and MACEDONIA

MAP PAGE 492

Operators: **ŽS**: Železnice Srbije (Железнице Србије). **ŽCG**: Železnice Crne Gore (Железнице Црне Горе). **MŽ**: Makedonski Železnici (Македонски Железници). Services in Kosovo are overseen by the United Nations Interim Administration Mission in Kosovo (UNMIK), operating as **KŽ** Kosovske Železnice.

Services: All trains convey first- and second-class seating, except where shown otherwise in footnotes, by a '2' in the train column, or where the footnote shows that the train conveys sleeping- (🛏) and/or couchette (▬) cars only. Descriptions of sleeping- and couchette cars are given on page 10.

Timings: Valid from **December 9, 2007**. *However, readers should note that only partial information was available at press date and services are subject to alteration. Services may be amended or cancelled at short notice and passengers are strongly advised to check locally before travelling.*

Tickets: A supplement is payable for travel by internal express trains. Reservation of seats is possible on most express trains.

Visas: Most nationals do not require a visa to enter Serbia and Montenegro, but must obtain an entry stamp in their passport, sight of which will be required by officials on leaving the country. These must be obtained at an authorised border point recognised by the government - this excludes Kosovo's external borders with Macedonia and Albania. Note that the authorities in Serbia and Montenegro do not consider the designated crossing points from Kosovo to be official border crossing points. Visas are not required for entry into Macedonia for most nationals.

Currency: Visitors to Macedonia must declare all foreign currency on arrival. In Serbia and Montenegro this applies only to large amounts (currently €2000). A certificate issued by the customs officer must be presented on departure, otherwise any funds held may be confiscated.

Security: Caution is advised, particularly in the northern and western border regions of Macedonia.

(BUDAPEST -) KELEBIA - SUBOTICA - BEOGRAD 1360

ŽS

km			541		331	543		345		437		341
		2		2	2		2	⚡	2	🍷	2	◐
					N			A		P		B
	Budapest K **1295** d.	...	...	...	0700	...	...	1320	...	...	...	2325
0	**Kelebia** 🏛 d.	...	...	...	1030	...	...	1650	1818	...	...	0240
10	**Subotica 1362** 🏛 a.	...	...	...	1041	...	...	1701	1828	...	...	0251
10	**Subotica** ⊖ d.	...	0605	0714	1056	1353	1454	1726	▬	1910	1953	0316
108	Novi Sad **1362** ⊖ a.	...	0756	0918	1248	1541	1701	1919	2	2106	2206	0514
108	Novi Sad d.	0612	0803	0943	...	1547	1707	1919	2014	2130	2227	0514
181	Novi Beograd a.	0737	0919	1112	...	1703	1838	2033	2138	2247	|	0627
186	**Beograd** a.	0746	0928	1121	...	1712	1847	2043	2147	...	0009	0639

	436		344	540		330			542		340
	🍷	2	⚡		2	2	2	2		2	◐
	P		A			N					B
Beograd d.	...	0440	0645	1005	1100	...	1315	1505	1825	2005	2200
Novi Beograd d.	0339	0450	|	1016	1110	...	1325	1515	1835	2015	|
Novi Sad **1362** a.	0525	0631	0810	1133	1238	...	1456	1648	1956	2147	2328
Novi Sad ⊖ d.	0530	...	0810	1136	...	1358	1507	1657	2011	2214	2328
Subotica 1362 ⊖ a.	0737	...	1000	1324	...	1549	1712	1904	2208	0012	0119
Subotica 🏛 d.	...	...	1044	...	...	1614	*1847*	...	...	...	0144
Kelebia 🏛 a.	...	...	1055	...	...	1625	*1857*	...	...	...	0155
Budapest K **1295** a.	...	...	1409	...	...	1953	...	...	...	...	0503

A – AVALA – (12) and ✕ Wien - Budapest - Beograd and v.v. Conveys June 5 - Sept. 20 (from Praha), June 7 - Sept. 22 (from Thessaloníki): ▬ 2 cl. Praha - Budapest - Beograd (**334/5**) - Thessaloníki and v.v. Conveys ②⑥ June 7 - Sept. 20 (from Praha), ④⑦ June 5 - Sept. 18 (from Bar): ▬ 2 cl. Praha - Budapest - Subotica (**436/7**) - Bar and v.v. Conveys 🛏 2 cl. Moskva/Kyïv - Budapest - Beograd and v.v. (see Table **97**). Train numbers *IC* **793/4** in Hungary.
B – BEOGRAD – (2) Budapest - Beograd and v.v.; 🛏 1, 2 cl. and ▬ 2 cl. Wien - Budapest - Beograd and v.v.; 🛏 1, 2 cl. Wien - Beograd (**490/1**) - Sofija and v.v. Train numbers **790/9** in Hungary.
N – BAČKA – (2) Budapest - Novi Sad and v.v. Train numbers **791/2** in Hungary.
P – PANONIJA – 🛏 1, 2 cl., ▬ 1, 2 cl., (12) and 🍷 Subotica - Novi Beograd - Bar and v.v. Conveys ②⑥ June 7 - Sept. 20 (from Praha), ④⑦ June 5 - Sept. 18 (from Bar): ▬ 2 cl. Praha - Budapest (**344/5**) - Subotica - Bar and v.v.

⊖ – Additional local services operate – see panel below.

SUBOTICA - NOVI SAD (additional services) : 2nd class only

Subotica d.	0410	1807	2218	...
Novi Sad a.	0640	2010	0027	...

Novi Sad d.	0425	0723	1020	1912
Subotica a.	0632	0931	1222	2125

◐ – Supplement payable for travel in Serbia.
⚡ – Supplement payable for travel in Hungary and Serbia.

1362 SUBOTICA - KIKINDA, ZRENJANIN, NOVI SAD and PANČEVO

2nd class only ŽS

km											
	Subotica 1360 d.	0244	...	...	0730	...	1312	...	...	1605	2133
	Senta d.	0359	...	...	0845	...	1417	1425	...	1720	2238
	Banatsko Miloševo a.	0437	...	...	0933	...	▬	1513	...	1815	▬
0	**Kikinda 1377** d.	▬	0426	0815	0950	1020	...	1530	1754	1832	...
19	Banatsko Miloševo d.	...	0449	0845	▬	1038	...	▬	1812	...	...
71	**Zrenjanin** d.	...	0640	1024	1050	1217	1510	...	1954	...	2028
96	Orlovat stajalište d.	0436	0729	...	1144	...	1600	1654	...	...	2120
	Novi Sad **1360** a.	0628	|	...	1340	...	|	1847	...	...	|
145	**Pančevo** glavna **1365** a.	...	0832	...	...	...	1701	...	...	...	2221

Pančevo glavna **1365** d.	...	...	...	...	...	1245	...	1740	...	...	2255
Novi Sad **1360** d.	...	...	0712	...	...	|	1450	|	...	1920	|
Orlovat stajalište d.	0544	...	0910	...	...	1347	1642	1842	...	2125	2357
Zrenjanin d.	0633	0700	0959	1047	...	1440	▬	1931	2025	2214	0046
Banatsko Miloševo a.	▬	0840	▬	1228	...	1620	...	...	2205	▬	...
Kikinda 1377 a.	...	0857	1001	|	...	1637	1850	...	2222	...	...
Banatsko Miloševo d.	0457	...	1030	1228	...	...	1917	...	...	...	...
Senta d.	0545	...	1122	1317	1429	...	2005	...	...	2251	...
Subotica 1360 a.	0651	...	1228	...	1535	...	2111	...	...	2357	...

1365 BEOGRAD - VRŠAC - TIMIŞOARA

2nd class only except where shown ŽS, CFR

km								361				
								B				
0	**Beograd** d.	...	...	...	...	...	...	1555	...	...	...	...
	Beograd centar ▶ d.	0556	...	0956	...	1456	...	|	1756	...	2156	...
19	Pančevo glavna **1362** ▶ d.	0625	0715	1025	1115	1525	1535	1634	1825	1910	2225	2235
87	Vršac a.	...	0840	...	1230	...	1650	1751	...	2025	...	2350
87	Vršac 🛃 d.	...	...	...	...	...	...	1816	...	...	...	...
107	Stamora Moravița 🛃 § a.	...	...	...	...	...	...	1938	...	...	...	...
107	Stamora Moravița § d.	...	...	...	...	...	...	2000	...	...	...	...
163	**Timişoara** Nord § a.	...	...	...	...	...	...	2118	...	...	...	...
	Bucureşti N **1600** a.	...	...	...	...	...	...	0539	...	...	...	...

			360								
			B								
Bucureşti N **1600** d.	...	...	2145	...	...	...	...	...	...	...	...
Timişoara Nord § d.	...	...	0603	...	...	...	...	...	...	...	...
Stamora Moravița § a.	...	...	0658	...	...	...	...	...	...	...	...
Stamora Moravița 🛃 § d.	...	...	0720	...	...	...	...	...	...	...	...
Vršac 🛃 a.	...	...	0642	...	...	...	...	...	...	...	...
Vršac d.	0430	...	0702	0905	...	1340	...	1710	...	2055	...
Pančevo glavna **1362** ▷ d.	0546	0608	0817	1020	1108	1455	1508	1838	1908	2211	2306
Beograd centar ▷ a.	...	0640	|	...	1140	...	1540	...	1940	...	2334
Beograd a.	...	...	0853	...	...	...	...	...	...	...	...

B – BUCUREŞTI – 🛏 1, 2 cl., ▬ 2 cl. and [12] Beograd - Timişoara - Bucureşti and v.v.

▶ – Beograd centar - Pančevo glavna: 0356, 0456 and hourly until 2156.
▷ – Pančevo glavna - Beograd centar: 0508 and hourly until 2208, 2306.

§ – Romanian (East European) time.

1370 BEOGRAD - PODGORICA - BAR

ŽCG, ŽS

km		1141										433		431		781	513		1139		435		437		1343
			2	2	2	2	2	2	2	2	2	✕		✕	2					2	🍷		🍷		
		N										T				R			G		L		P		
0	**Beograd** d.	...	...	...	0315	...	0715	...	...	...	1130	1010	...	1310	...	1515	1715	...	2030n	...	2210	...	2249n	...	2310
93	Valjevo d.	...	...	...	0532	...	0919	...	...	...	1332	1137	...	1437	...	1658	1848	...	2152	...	2337	...	0022	...	|
	Kraljevo **1372/5** d.	0135	...	...	|	...	|	...	...	...	|	|	...	|	...	|	|	...	|	...	|	...	|	...	|
159	Požega **1372** d.	|	...	...	0646	...	1023	...	...	...	1439	1238	...	1545	1757	1810	1948	...	2252	...	0041	...	0146	...	0156
185	Užice d.	0320	...	...	0723	...	1105	...	...	...	1528	1312	...	1612	1933	...	2018	...	2325	...	0115	...	0230	...	0244
288	Prijepolje d.	0504	...	...	0901	...	1249	...	...	...	1715	1445	...	1729	2111	...	2138	...	0057	...	0239	...	0358	...	|
338	Bijelo Polje d.	0618	0630	...	0949	...	...	...	...	1737	1802	1600	...	1841	...	...	...	...	0230	...	0400	...	0510	...	0556
468	**Podgorica** d.	0842	0900	1015	...	1300	...	1454	1640	2002	...	1830	...	2101	...	...	...	...	0440	0505	0640	...	0800	...	0818
524	**Bar** a.	0935	0956	1114	...	1404	...	1553	1743	2057	...	1921	...	2159	...	...	...	...	0535	0559	0740	...	0900	...	0920

	512		780								432		430				436		1140	1138			434		1342
		2		2	2	2	2	2	2	2	✕		✕	2	2	2	🍷	2				2	🍷		
			R								T						P		N	G			L		
Bar d.	...	...	...	...	0537	0635	...	1020	...	1130	1010	...	1230	1500	...	1650	1750	1815	1900	2000	...	...	2100	...	2200
Podgorica d.	...	...	...	...	0641	0730	...	1118	...	1226	1100	...	1330	1600	...	1749	1855	1918	2000	2100	...	...	2205	...	2300
Bijelo Polje d.	...	...	...	0645	0859	...	1135	...	...	...	1335	...	1615	...	1900	2022	2150	...	2240	2340	...	...	0040	...	0128
Prijepolje d.	0305	0327	...	0734	...	...	1223	...	1525	...	1424	...	1702	...	1948	...	2237	...	2327	0027	...	...	0135	...	|
Užice d.	0450	0522	...	0930	...	...	1430	...	1724	...	1555	...	1836	...	2143	...	0000	...	0052	0213	...	0305	0307	...	0400
Požega **1372** d.	0515	0549	0653	1000	...	...	1500	...	1751	...	1628	...	1901	...	...	...	0055	...	|	0235	...	0333	0340	...	0427
Kraljevo **1372/5** a.	|	...	|	|	...	...	|	...	|	...	|	...	|	...	...	...	|	...	0248	|	...	|	|	...	|
Valjevo d.	0614	...	0752	1108	...	...	1610	...	1903	...	1729	...	2001	...	...	...	0204	...	...	0332	...	0440	0444	...	|
Beograd a.	0749	...	0934	1307	...	...	1822	...	2116	...	1857	...	2126	...	...	...	0337n	...	...	0447n	...	0634	0609	...	0636

G – June 13 - Sept. 6 (from Novi Sad (d. 1910, a. 0615) and Novi Beograd, one day later from Bar): 🛏 1, 2 cl., ▬ 1, 2 cl. and [12] Novi Sad - Bar and v.v.

L – LOVĆEN – 🛏 1, 2 cl., ▬ 1, 2 cl., [12] and 🍷 Beograd - Bar and v.v.

N – NIŠAVA – 🛏 1, 2 cl., ▬ 1, 2 cl. and [12] Niš - Bar and v.v. Conveys June 27 - Aug. 30 (from Skopje, one day later from Bar): 🛏 1, 2 cl. Skopje (**392/3**) - Niš - Bar and v.v.

P – PANONIJA – 🛏 1, 2 cl., ▬ 1, 2 cl., [12] and 🍷 Subotica - Novi Beograd - Bar and v.v. Conveys ②⑥ June 7 - Sept. 20 (from Praha), ④⑦ June 5 - Sept. 18 (from Bar): ▬ 2 cl. Praha - Budapest (**344/5**) - Subotica - Bar and v.v.

R – [12] Beograd - Kraljevo - Raška and v.v.

T – TARA – [12] and ✕ Beograd - Bar and v.v. Also conveys motorcars.

n – **Novi Beograd**.

1372 POŽEGA - KRALJEVO

2nd class only except where shown ŽS

tariff km		1140							781		
		♦							♦		
0	**Požega 1370** d.	...	...	0525	...	...	1630	...	1825	...	...
45	Čačak d.	0220	...	0612	0805	1350	1707	...	1853	2014	2205
83	**Kraljevo 1370/5** ◧ d.	0305	...	0656	0849	1434	1751	...	1919	2058	2249
	Lapovo **1375/80** a.	0457	...	...	...	...	...	...	...	...	...
	Niš **1373/80** a.	0746	...	...	...	...	...	...	...	...	...

		780							1141	
		♦							♦	
Niš **1373/80** d.	...	...	...	...	...	...	...	...	2050	...
Lapovo **1375/80** d.	...	...	...	...	...	...	...	...	2340	...
Kraljevo 1370/5 ◧ d.	0350	0535	0635	1255	1445	1922	2108	...	0135	...
Čačak d.	0436	0605	0729	1339	1531	2006	2152	...	0204	...
Požega 1370 a.	0513	0638	...	...	1608	...	...	...	...	...

♦ – For days of running and composition – see Table **1370**.

◧ – Kraljevo - Stalać is currently suspended.

1373 BEOGRAD - ZAJEČAR - NIŠ

2nd class only except where shown ŽS

tariff km													991
													Z
0	**Beograd** d.	...	...	...	...	...	...	0730	...	...	...	...	1600
98	Požarevac d.	...	...	...	...	...	...	0933	...	...	...	...	1842
199	Majdanpek d.	...	0415	...	...	0938	...	...	...	1603	...	...	2120
★	Prahovo d.	...	|	0423	0936	|	...	...	...	|	1638	2051	|
296	**Zaječar** d.	0356	0618	0624	1113	1143	1152	...	1440	1802	1830	2225	2314
343	Knjaževac d.	0453	...	0721	...	...	1249	...	1537	...	1928	...	...
420	**Niš 1372/80** a.	0627	...	0855	...	...	1423	...	1713	...	2102	...	...

		970										
		Z										
Niš 1372/80 d.	...	...	0315	...	0705	1110	...	...	1520	...	1910	...
Knjaževac d.	...	...	0449	...	0845	1254	...	...	1702	...	2053	...
Zaječar d.	...	0210	0630j	0645	0940	1349	1400	1430	1840r	1825	2148	2340
Prahovo a.	...	|	0806	|	...	▬	|	1606	2016	|	...	0116
Majdanpek d.	...	0420	...	0852	...	...	1600	...	...	2034	...	...
Požarevac d.	0425	0654	...	...	...	1635	...	...	...	...	...	...
Beograd a.	0618	0829	...	...	...	1831	...	...	...	...	...	...

Z – [12] Beograd - Zaječar and v.v.

j – Arrive 0554.

r – Arrive 1757.

★ – Prahovo - Zaječar: *81 km*.

1375 LAPOVO and PRIŠTINA - KOSOVO POLJE - DENERAL JANKOVIĆ

2nd class only except where shown ŽS, KŽ

km				891	881							781		
				⊠	◇	⊠				⊠		R		
	Beograd **1380** d.	...	...	...	...	...	...	...	...	...	...	1515	...	...
	Lapovo 1380 d.	0425	...	...	0842	...	1005	1200	...	...	1655	|	...	2244
0	**Kragujevac** d.	0516	...	...	0918	...	1050	1240	...	...	1744	|	...	2324
54	Kraljevo **1370/2** d.	0632	0705	...	1045	...	1206	1356	1430	...	1900	1935	2205	0040
135	Raška d.	...	0843	...	1202	...	▬	▬	1616	...	▬	2055	2340	...
152	Lešak d.	...	0909	...	▬	0955	...	...	1642	1650	...	...	▬	...
182	Zvečan d.	...	▬	...	...	1052	**893**	**761**	...	1747	...	...	...	...
186	Kosovska Mitrovica d.	...	...	...	⊠	1058	⊠	⊠	...	1753	...	...	⊠	...
	Priština d.	...	⊠	0624	0740	|	1250	1730	...	|	⊠	...	1905	...
219	**Kosovo Polje** d.	...	0425	0636	0751	1159	1302	1739	...	1854	1900	...	1915	...
	Peć a.	...	|	|	0940	...	|	1906	...	...	|	...	...	...
248	Uroševac d.	...	0802	0709	...	...	1344	...	...	...	1946	...	...	...
276	**Deneral Janković** a.	...	0540	0747	...	...	1425	...	...	...	2027	...	...	...
	Skopje a.	...	...	0901	...	...	...	...	...	...	...	...	...	...

		780	760			890			880		892	
	⊠	R	⊠	⊠	⊠	⊠	⊠	⊠	◇		⊠	⊠
Skopje d.	...	...	...	...	...	...	...	...	...	...	1613	...
Deneral Janković d.	...	...	...	0557	...	1047	...	...	...	...	1730	2045
Uroševac d.	...	...	...	0643	...	1135	...	...	...	...	1814	2129
Peć d.	...	...	0550	|	...	|	1120	...	...	...	|	|
Kosovo Polje d.	0558	...	0722	0730	0735	1217	1321	1415	...	...	1857	2209
Priština a.	0608	...	0730	▬	|	1227	1330	|	...	...	1908	...
Kosovska Mitrovica d.	...	...	▬	...	0837	▬	▬	1517	...	...	▬	...
Zvečan d.	...	...	...	...	0844	...	...	1524	...	...	...	...
Lešak d.	...	...	...	...	0940	1025	...	1620	...	1705	...	...
Raška d.	...	0355	0450	...	▬	1054	...	...	1355	1734	...	...
Kraljevo **1370/2** d.	...	0535	0600	0642	0917	1236	1425	...	1525	1910	1940	...
Kragujevac d.	...	|	...	0801	1048	...	1551	...	1637	...	2106	...
Lapovo 1380 a.	...	|	...	0838	1126	...	1629	...	1712	...	2144	...
Beograd **1380** a.	...	0934	...	...	...	...	...	...	...	...	...	...

R – [12] Beograd - Požega - Kraljevo - Raška and v.v.

◇ – Service liable to late running awaiting connection from / to Beograd.

⊠ – Service operated by KŽ (see country heading).

MINOR BORDER CROSSINGS 1377

ŽS, MÁV, CFR

SUBOTICA - SZEGED and v.v. : 2nd class only

km								
0	Subotica ... d.	0845	1018	*1435*	Szeged ...... d.	0647	1225	1431
24	Horgoš d.	0947	1120	1537	Röszke . d.	0716	1255	1401
31	Röszke d.	1018	1151	1608	Horgoš.. d.	0747	1326	1517
43	Szeged .... a.	1033	1206	1623	Subotica .... a.	0835	1414	*1736*

KIKINDA - TIMIŞOARA and v.v. : 2nd class only

km																
0	Kikinda 1362 d.	...	0600	...	...	1545	...	...	Timişoara .. § d.	0701	...	1315	1610	...	1925	2330
19	Jimbolia § d.	0530	0718	0812	1430	1703	1730	1952	Jimbolia § d.	0746	0835	1403	1656	1820	2031	0024
58	Timişoara .. § a.	0617	...	0902	1520	...	1816	2056	Kikinda 1362 a.	...	0753	...	...	1738	...	...

§ – East European time, one hour ahead of Central European time.

BEOGRAD - NIŠ - SOFIYA, SKOPJE and THESSALONÍKI 1380

ŽS, MŽ, BDŽ

km							1140	393				491							391		591			293	335
		2	2	2		2	N	S	2		2	F		2	2	2	2	2	🍷	2		2	2	Z	H
0	**Beograd 1375** d.	...	...	...	...	...	...	...	0330	...	0740	0840	...	...	...	...	...	...	1405	1530	1650	...	1935	2110	2220
110	Lapovo **1372/5** d.	0340	...	...	...	...	0525	...	0640	...	1040	1041	...	...	...	...	1530	...	1559	1825	1852	...	2228	2314	0024
135	Jagodina d.	0406	...	...	...	...	0545	...	0706	...	1106	1101	...	...	...	...	1556	...	1621	1852	1916	...	2258	2335	0045
155	Paraćin d.	0428	...	...	...	...	0607	...	0730	...	1128	1122	...	...	...	...	1620	...	1642	1919	1938	...	2320	2357	0107
176	Stalać **1372** d.	0456	...	...	...	...	0627	...	0753	...	1156	1141	...	...	...	...	1643	...	1702	1941	1958	...	2342	0017	0127
244	**Niš 1372/3** a.	0615	...	...	...	...	0746	...	0920	...	1330	1236	...	...	...	...	1817	...	1759	2109	2058	...	0106	0133	0224
244	**Niš** d.	...	...	0720	...	0730	0830	0830	...	...	...	1320	...	1510	1528	...	...	...	1810	...	...	...	...	0205	0240
	Dimitrovgrad d.	...	...	|	...	0940	|	|	...	...	...	1554	...	|	1800	...	...	...	|	...	...	...	...	0435	|
	Kalotina Zapad § d.	...	...	|	...	...	|	|	...	...	...	1704	...	|	...	...	...	...	|	...	...	...	...	0545	|
	Dragoman § d.	...	...	|	...	...	|	|	...	...	...	1731	...	|	...	...	...	...	|	...	...	...	...	0612	|
	Sofiya § a.	...	...	|	...	...	|	|	...	...	...	1815	...	|	...	...	...	...	|	...	...	...	...	0755	|
288	Leskovac d.	...	...	0817	...	...	0909	0909	...	...	...	...	...	1610	...	...	...	...	1846	...	...	...	...	...	0319
392	Preševo d.	...	...	1035	...	...	1154	1154	...	...	...	...	...	1836	...	...	...	...	2110	...	...	...	...	...	0603
401	Tabanovci d.	...	0732	...	...	...	1224	1224	...	...	...	...	...	...	...	...	...	1934	2210	...	...	0505	...	...	0641
462	**Skopje** a.	...	0827	...	...	...	1317	1317	...	...	...	...	...	...	...	...	...	2032	2254	...	...	0600	...	...	0729
462	**Skopje 1385** d.	...	...	...	...	...	...	...	...	...	...	...	...	...	...	1625	...	...	...	...	...	0615	...	...	0800
524	Veles **1385** d.	...	...	...	...	...	...	...	...	...	...	...	...	...	...	1716	...	...	...	...	...	0707	...	...	0842
651	Gevgelija a.	...	...	...	...	...	...	...	...	...	...	...	...	...	...	1911	...	...	...	...	...	0900	...	...	1015
651	Gevgelija d.	...	...	...	...	...	...	...	...	...	...	...	...	...	...	...	...	...	...	...	...	...	...	...	1040
654	Idoméni a.	...	...	...	...	...	...	...	...	...	...	...	...	...	...	...	...	...	...	...	...	...	...	...	1145
654	Idoméni d.	...	...	...	...	...	...	...	...	...	...	...	...	...	...	...	...	...	...	...	...	...	...	...	1215
730	**Thessaloníki 1400** ... § a.	...	...	...	...	...	...	...	...	...	...	...	...	...	...	...	...	...	...	...	...	...	...	...	1307

km					590			390					490					392	1141				334		292
		2	2	2		2	2	🍷	2	2	2	2	F		2		2	S	N	2	2	2	H		Z
	Thessaloníki 1400 ... § d.	...	...	...	...	...	...	...	...	...	...	...	...	...	...	...	...	...	...	...	...	...	1615	...	...
	Idoméni a.	...	...	...	...	...	...	...	...	...	...	...	...	...	...	...	...	...	...	...	...	...	1707	...	...
	Idoméni d.	...	...	...	...	...	...	...	...	...	...	...	...	...	...	...	...	...	...	...	...	...	1740	...	...
	Gevgelija a.	...	...	...	...	...	...	...	...	...	...	...	...	...	...	...	...	...	...	...	...	...	1645	...	...
	Gevgelija d.	...	...	...	...	...	...	...	0509	...	...	...	...	...	...	...	...	...	...	...	...	1520	1715	...	...
	Veles **1385** d.	...	...	...	...	...	...	...	0706	...	...	...	...	...	...	...	...	...	...	...	...	1717	1857	...	...
	Skopje 1385 a.	...	...	...	...	...	...	...	0753	...	...	...	...	...	...	...	...	...	...	...	...	1807	1939	...	...
	Skopje d.	...	...	...	...	0350	...	0612	...	...	...	...	...	...	...	...	...	1520	1520	...	...	1820	2006	...	...
	Tabanovci a.	...	...	...	...	0444	...	0707	...	...	...	...	...	...	...	...	...	1614	1614	...	...	1914	2050	...	...
	Preševo d.	...	0230	...	...	...	...	0805	...	...	1120	...	...	...	...	...	...	1716	1716	...	...	...	2159	...	...
	Leskovac d.	...	0447	...	...	...	...	1009	...	...	1343	...	...	...	1710	...	...	1939	1939	...	...	...	0016	...	...
0	**Sofiya** § d.	...	|	...	...	...	...	|	...	...	|	...	1235	...	|	...	...	|	|	...	...	...	|	...	2220
42	Dragoman § d.	...	|	...	...	...	...	|	...	...	|	...	1326	...	|	...	...	|	|	...	...	...	|	...	2311
54	Kalotina Zapad § d.	...	|	...	...	...	...	|	...	...	|	...	1346	...	|	...	...	|	|	...	...	...	|	...	2331
63	Dimitrovgrad d.	...	|	0415	...	...	...	|	...	1130	|	...	1315	...	|	...	...	|	|	1845	...	...	|	...	2259
161	**Niš 1372/3** a.	...	0548	0622	...	...	...	1044	...	1341	1438	...	1523	...	1804	...	...	2016	2016	2053	...	...	0054	...	0100
	Niš d.	0345	...	...	0635	...	0727	1058	...	...	...	1525	1605	...	...	...	1935	...	2050	...	2315	...	0105	...	0130
	Stalać **1372** d.	0517	...	...	0736	...	0853	1155	...	...	...	1657	1724	...	...	...	2101	...	2212	...	0047	...	0215	...	0240
	Paraćin d.	0538	...	...	0755	...	0919	1214	...	...	...	1718	1746	...	...	...	2122	...	2233	...	0108	...	0237	...	0302
	Jagodina d.	0602	...	...	0817	...	0942	1237	...	...	...	1742	1820	...	...	...	2147	...	2257	...	0131	...	0303	...	0328
	Lapovo **1372/5** d.	0645	...	...	0841	...	1020	1259	...	...	...	1820	1834	...	...	...	2230	...	2317	...	0156	...	0325	...	0350
	Beograd 1375 a.	0950	...	...	1043	...	1252	1459	...	...	...	2106	2030	...	...	...	0100	...	...	...	...	...	0506	...	0545

F – BALKAN – Beograd - Sofiya and v.v.; 1, 2 cl. Beograd - Sofiya - İstanbul and v.v.; 1, 2 cl. Wien - Budapest - Beograd - Sofiya and v.v.

H – HELLAS EXPRESS – 1, 2 cl., 2 cl. and Beograd - Skopje - Thessaloníki and v.v. Conveys June 5 - Sept. 20 (from Praha, one day later from Budapest), June 7 - Sept. 22 (from Thessaloníki): 2 cl. Praha - Budapest (**344/5**) - Beograd - Thessaloníki and v.v. Conveys on dates in Table **97**: 1, 2 cl. Moskva / Kyïv - Budapest - Beograd - Thessaloníki and v.v.

N – NIŠAVA – 1, 2 cl., 1, 2 cl. and Niš - Bar and v.v. Conveys June 27 - Aug. 30 (from Skopje, one day later from Bar): 1, 2 cl. Skopje (**392/3**) - Niš - Bar and v.v.

S – Skopje - Niš and v.v. Conveys June 27 - Aug. 30 (from Skopje, one day later from Bar): 1, 2 cl. Skopje - Niš (**1140/1**) - Bar and v.v.

Z – 1, 2 cl., 2 cl. and Beograd - Sofiya and v.v.

♦ – For days of running and composition – see Table **1370**.

* – Estimated time.

§ – East European time, one hour ahead of Central European time.

LOCAL SERVICES in Macedonia 1385

MŽ

SKOPJE - KOČANI and BITOLA and v.v. : 2nd class only

km												
0	Skopje **1380** d.	0312	0705	1430	1525	1946	Bitola d.	0509	...	1339	...	1849
62	Veles **1380** d.	0359	0759	1524	1614	2042	Prilep d.	0550	...	1427	...	1937
★	Kočani a.	0551	|	|	1806	|	Kočani d.	|	0602	|	1827	|
170	Prilep d.	...	0955	1734	...	2237	Veles **1380** d.	0734	0800	1616	2019	2129
228	Bitola a.	...	1044	1820	...	2315	Skopje **1380** a.	0832	0853	1713	2108	2223

SKOPJE - KIČEVO and v.v. : 2nd class only

km								
0	Skopje d.	0310	0620	1530	Kičevo d.	0540	1305	1757
86	Tetovo d.	0407	0725	1635	Tetovo d.	0643	1409	1858
163	Kičevo a.	0505	0826	1737	Skopje a.	0756	1512	1958

★ – Veles - Kočani : *110 km.*

ALBANIA

SEE MAP PAGE 492

Operator: **HSH** : Hekurudhë e Shqipërisë.

Timings: last updated **September 2007**.

Services: Trains convey one class of accommodation only. Tickets are not sold in advance, only for the next available departure.

Security: Most visits to Albania are now reported to be trouble free, but travellers are advised to avoid the north-east of the country unless on essential business.

ALBANIAN RAILWAYS 1390

HSH One class only

Times for Milot, Vorë, Rrogozhinë, Lushnjë and Fier are subject to minor variation

km												
0	Shkodër a.	...	...	0640	...	...	...	1215	...	...	...	...
47	Milot d.	...	...	0816	...	...	...	1350	...	...	...	...
	Tiranë d.	0555	0630	|	0930	1155	1420	|	1455	1615	2005	...
82	Vorë a.	0617	0652	0930	0952	1217	1437	1505	1517	1638	2027	...
82	Vorë d.	0619	0655	0955	0954	1219	1439	1522	1519	1640	2029	...
98	**Tiranë** a.	|	|	1018	|	|	|	1545	|	|	|	...
102	**Durrës** a.	0658	0730	...	1036	1254	1518	...	1555	1715	2106	...
102	**Durrës** d.	0713	0745	...	...	1320	1530	...	1610	...	...	...
	Durrës Plazh a.	|	|	...	...	|	|	...	|	...	...	...
138	Rrogozhinë d.	0826	0900	...	...	1434	1648	...	1722	...	...	...
179	Elbasan a.	0945	|	...	...	1551	1805	...	|	...	...	...
255	Pogradec a.	1240	|	...	...	1857	...	...	|	...	...	...
155	Lushnjë a.	...	0933	...	...	...	...	...	1752	...	...	...
187	Fier a.	...	1028	...	...	...	...	...	1843	...	...	...
221	Vlorë a.	...	1137	...	...	...	...	...	1954	...	...	...

Vlorë d.	...	...	...	...	0550	...	...	...	1155	...	...
Fier d.	...	...	...	...	0700	...	...	...	1307	...	...
Lushnjë d.	...	...	...	...	0754	...	...	...	1400	...	...
Pogradec d.	...	...	...	...	|	0450	...	...	|	1305	...
Elbasan d.	...	...	0535	...	|	0746	...	...	|	1605	...
Rrogozhinë d.	...	...	0648	...	0827	0859	...	...	1433	1721	...
Durrës Plazh d.	...	...	|	...	|	|	...	...	|	|	...
Durrës a.	...	...	0756	...	0933	1007	...	...	1542	1828	...
Durrës d.	0610	0645	0815	...	0950	1025	1305	...	1600	1845	...
Tiranë d.	|	|	|	0820	|	|	|	1318	|	|	...
Vorë a.	0651	0722	0850	0842	1025	1059	1341	1340	1635	1920	...
Vorë d.	0653	0724	0852	0857	1027	1101	1343	1405	1637	1922	...
Tiranë a.	0715	0747	0915	|	1050	1124	1405	|	1700	1945	...
Milot d.	...	...	...	1012	...	...	...	1523	...	...	...
Shkodër a.	...	...	...	1153	...	...	...	1705	...	...	...

GREECE

SEE MAP PAGE 492

Operator: Οργανισμος Σιδηροδρομων Ελλαδας - Organismós Sidiródromon Elládas / Hellenic Railways Organisation (ΟΣΕ - OSE). Some suburban services are operated by Proastiakos.

Services: All trains convey first and second class seating except where shown otherwise in footnotes or by '2' in the train column, or where the footnote shows sleeping and/or couchette cars only. Descriptions of sleeping (🛏) and couchette (▬) cars appear on page 10. Services that convey catering may vary from day to day.

Timings: Timings have been compiled from the latest information received. However, readers should be aware that a substantial amount of engineering work is taking place throughout the country and timetable amendments may come into effect at short notice.

Tickets: Reservation of seats is possible (and recommended) on most express trains. *IC* trains carry a supplement which varies depending upon distance travelled. Break of journey is only permitted when tickets are so endorsed before travel with the station quoted.

1400 ATHÍNA - LÁRISA - THESSALONÍKI - ALEXANDRÚPOLI - SVILENGRAD

km		1630	IC90	604	571	883	IC70	IC50	884	1592	614	500	IC52	1520	IC54	IC92	1594	444	502	IC40	IC48	602	1522	IC56	IC74	504
		2	🍴⚡	🍷▮	590	592	🍴⚡	🍴◇		2	🍷	🍷	🍴⚡	2	🍴⚡	🍴⚡	2	Ⓡ	🍷▮	🍷⚡	🍷⚡	🍷▮	2	🍴◇	🍴⚡	Ⓡ
				◆	V	K												◆				◆				◆
0	**Athína** Lárisa **1402** ... d.	...	...	2351	...	...	0650	0754	0821	...	...	0921	1051	1220	1321	...	...	...	1453	1553	1553	1651	1751	1929	2039	2255
61	Inói ... d.	...	...	0046	...	...	0734	|	0912	...	...	1010	1135	1317	1405	...	...	...	1542	1637	1637	1745	1846	|	2123	2350
89	Thíva ... d.	...	...	0107	...	...	0750	|	0929	...	...	1028	1151	1337	1422	...	...	...	1602	1654	1654	1803	1907	|	2140	0012
129	Levadiá ... d.	...	...	0133	...	...	0808	|	0950	...	...	1053	1209	1403	1440	...	...	...	1626	1714	1714	1828	1932	|	2159	|
154	Tithoréa ... d.	...	...	0148x	...	...	|	|	1001x	...	...	1106	|	1421	1451x	...	...	...	1642x	1725x	1725x	1847	1951	|	|	|
169	Amfíklia ... d.	...	...	|	...	...	|	|	1017	...	...	|	|	1433x	|	...	...	...	1654x	|	|	1859x	2003x	|	|	|
182	Brálos ... d.	...	...	|	...	...	|	|	1027x	...	...	|	|	1443x	|	...	...	...	1708x	|	|	1910x	2023x	|	|	|
210	Lianokládi ... d.	...	...	0250	...	...	0902	0948	1059	...	...	1157	1304	1515	1536	...	...	...	1739	1813	1813	1939	2055	2123	2256	0147
	Stilída ... a.	...	...	|	...	...	|	|	|	...	...	|	|	1556	|	...	...	...	|	|	|	|	2137	|	|	|
291	Paleofársalos **1408** ... d.	...	...	0421	...	0836	1009	|	1213	...	...	1308	1407	▬	1639	...	...	...	1854	1921	1923	2100	...	|	|	|
	Kalambáka **1408** ... a.	...	...	|	...	|	|	|	1300	...	...	|	|	...	|	...	...	...	|	|	2010	|	...	|	|	|
333	**Lárisa 1405** ... d.	...	...	0450	0649	0857	1030	1100	▬	1203	...	1330	1428	...	1700	...	1755	...	1918	1941	...	2126	...	2235	0020	0347
	Vólos **1405** ... a.	...	...	|	|	|	|	|	...	|	...	|	|	...	|	...	|	...	|	2025	...	|	...	|	|	|
417	Kateríni ... △ d.	...	...	0546	0742	0948	1108	|	...	1302	...	1419	1506	...	1738	...	1854	...	2008	...	...	2219	...	|	0058	0437
465	Platí **1410** ... △ d.	...	...	0617	0807	1013	1128	|	**1632**	1333	...	1441	1526	**1634**	1758	...	1925	...	2032	...	...	2250	...	|	|	0504
502	**Thessaloníki 1410** △ a.	...	...	0640	0830	1039	1148	1209	2	1359	...	1503	1546	2	1818	...	1951	...	2055	...	...	2313	...	2344	0138	0529
502	**Thessaloníki** ... d.	0625	0730	0748	...	▬	1221	▬	1302	...	1417	...	...	1636	...	1825	▬	2035	...	...	...	2344	...	...	0201	...
544	Kilkís ... d.	0708	0756	0822	...	...	1250	...	1336	...	1446	...	...	1710	...	1850	...	2101	...	...	...	0016	...	...	0227	...
599	Rodópoli ... d.	0750	0827	0902	...	...	1322	...	1423	...	1524	...	...	1800	...	1923	...	|	...	...	...	0058	...	...	0259	...
632	Strimón ... d.	0819	|	0931	...	...	|	...	1454	...	1548	...	...	1830	...	|	...	|	...	...	...	0127	...	...	|	...
664	Sérres ... d.	0841	0905	0958	...	...	1400	...	1516	...	1610	...	...	1852	...	2001	...	2205	...	...	...	0151	...	...	0337	...
734	Dráma ... d.	...	0953	1048	...	...	1444	...	...	...	1701	...	...	...	...	2051	...	2249	...	...	...	0242	...	...	0421	...
829	Xánthi ... d.	...	1106	1210	...	...	1557	...	...	...	1821	...	...	...	...	2212	...	2358	...	...	...	0410	...	...	0535	...
876	Komotiní ... d.	...	1133	1243	...	**1684**	1624	**1680**	...	...	1850	...	...	...	...	2239	...	0025	...	...	...	0444	...	...	0602	...
944	Alexandrúpoli ... a.	...	1219	1336	...	2	1710	2	...	...	1941	...	...	...	...	2325	...	0114	...	...	...	0538	...	...	0647	...
945	**Alexandrúpoli Port** .. d.	...	1230	1350	...	1507	1716	1756	...	...	2036	...	...	...	...	2331	...	|	...	...	...	0550	...	...	0658	...
1058	Píthio ... d.	...	1406	1539	...	1649	...	1941	...	...	2229	...	...	...	...	...	...	0305	...	...	...	0743	...	...	0835	...
	İstanbul Sirkeci **1550** a.	...	*2127*	|	...	|	...	|	...	...	|	...	...	...	...	...	**1690**	0805	...	...	...	|	...	...	|	...
1076	Néa Orestiáda ... d.	...	1421	1609	...	1711	...	2003	...	...	2252	...	...	...	...	...	2	...	...	...	...	0807	...	...	0850	...
1113	**Díkea** ... d.	...	1455	1646	...	1745	...	2039	...	...	2328	...	...	...	...	...	0545	...	...	...	...	0850	...	...	0922	...
1120	Orménio ... a.	...	1505	1656	...	...	...	2048	...	...	...	...	...	...	...	...	0555	...	...	...	...	0900	...	...	...	...
1129	Svilengrad ⊞ **1550** ... a.	...	...	...	...	...	...	...	...	...	...	...	...	...	...	...	...	...	...	...	...	0940	...	...	...	...

km		IC53	1681	IC71	501	IC55	613	1593	885	503	1683	591	IC93	IC57	1691	605	1635	IC91	1693	IC75	1521	IC41	IC47	1591	1695	603	445
		🍴⚡	2	🍴⚡	🍷▮	🍴⚡	🍷	2		🍷	2	886	🍴⚡	🍴◇	2	🍷▮	2	🍴⚡	2	🍴⚡	2	🍷⚡	🍷⚡	2	2	🍷▮	Ⓡ
												K				◆										◆	◆
	Svilengrad ⊞ **1550** ... d.	...	...	...	...	...	...	...	...	...	...	...	...	...	1025	...	...	...	...	...	...	...	...	...	...	...	...
	Orménio ... d.	...	...	...	...	...	0600	...	...	...	...	...	...	...	1050	...	...	1515	1705	...	...	...	...	...	2100	...	...
	Díkea ... d.	...	0409	...	...	...	0611	...	...	...	0935	...	...	...	1100	1237	...	1530	1715	1801	...	...	...	...	2110	2128	...
	Néa Orestiáda ... d.	...	0444	...	...	...	0646	...	...	...	1009	...	...	...	▬	1313	...	1603	▬	1834	...	...	...	...	▬	2204	...
0	*İstanbul Sirkeci* **1550** ... d.	...	|	...	...	...	|	...	...	...	|	...	...	...	...	|	...	*0830*	...	|	...	...	...	...	...	|	2000
268	Píthio ... d.	...	0459	...	...	...	0710	...	...	...	1033	...	...	...	...	1336	...	1618	...	1849	...	...	...	...	...	2228	0131
—	**Alexandrúpoli Port** ... d.	...	0641	0642	...	...	0934	...	...	...	1218	...	1342	...	...	1522	...	1755	...	2032	...	...	...	...	...	0029	|
	Alexandrúpoli ... d.	...	▬	0648	...	...	0940	...	...	...	▬	...	1347	...	...	1528	...	1801	...	2038	...	...	...	...	...	0035	0255
	Komotiní ... d.	...	...	0735	...	...	1034	...	...	...	...	...	1434	...	...	1625	...	1849	...	2125	...	...	...	...	...	0132	0342
	Xánthi ... d.	...	**1631**	0803	...	...	1107	...	...	...	**1633**	...	1502	...	...	1701	...	1917	...	2153	...	...	...	...	...	0207	0409
	Dráma ... d.	...	2	0913	...	...	1229	...	...	...	2	...	1620	...	...	1828	...	2031	...	2313	...	...	...	...	...	0336	0519
	Sérres ... d.	...	0907	0957	...	...	1318	...	...	...	1524	...	1704	...	...	1919	2012	2116	...	2358	...	...	...	...	...	0436	0603
	Strimón ... d.	...	0932	|	...	...	1341	...	...	...	1549	...	|	...	...	1942	2035	|	...	|	...	...	...	...	...	0500	|
	Rodópoli ... d.	...	1003	1033	...	...	1406	...	...	...	1622	...	1741	...	**595**	2007	2107	2158	**505**	0034	...	...	...	...	*IC***51**	0529	|
	Kilkís ... d.	...	1047	1105	...	...	1447	...	...	...	1711	...	1815	...	**578**	2044	2151	2230	Ⓡ	0107	...	...	...	...	🍴◇	0610	0707
	Thessaloníki ... a.	...	1119	1130	...	...	1518	...	...	...	1743	...	1843	...	**V**	2119	2222	2255	◆	0132	...	...	...	...		0648	0732
	Thessaloníki 1410 .. △ d.	1020	...	1138	1243	1454	▬	1525	...	1646	...	1759	...	1901	2102	2235	...	...	2339	0151	...	...	...	0551	0724	0735	...
	Platí **1410** ... △ d.	1041	...	1201	1306	1515	...	1554	...	1709	...	1824	...	|	2126	2302	...	...	0004	|	...	...	...	0618	|	0758	...
	Kateríni ... △ d.	1102	...	1222	1328	1536	...	1625	...	1735	...	1849	...	|	2151	2334	...	...	0032	0232	...	...	...	0649	|	0829	...
0	Vólos **1405** ... d.	|	...	|	|	|	...	|	...	|	...	|	...	|	|	|	...	...	|	|	...	0621	...	|	|	|	...
61	**Lárisa 1405** ... d.	1140	...	1300	1418	1614	...	1723	...	1827	...	1941	...	2011	2244	0032	...	...	0126	0311	...	0707	...	0747	0834	0924	...
—	Kalambáka **1408** ... d.	|	...	|	|	|	**1523**	...	1736	|	...	|	...	|	...	|	...	...	|	|	...	|	0633	...	|	|	...
	Paleofársalos **1408** ... d.	1201	...	1321	1439	1635	2	...	1824	1850	...	2001	...	|	...	0059	...	...	|	|	...	0730	0730	...	|	0951	...
0	Stilída ... d.	|	...	|	|	|	1753	...	|	|	...	...	...	|	...	|	...	...	|	|	0529	|	|	...	|	|	...
23	Lianokládi ... d.	1305	...	1430	1551	1738	1835	...	1940	2009	...	...	...	2124	...	0223	...	...	0324	0434	0611	0838	0838	...	0947	1120	...
—	Brálos ... d.	|	...	|	|	|	1911	...	2008x	2038x	...	...	...	|	...	|	...	...	|	|	0642x	0912x	0912x	...	|	1151x	...
	Amfíklia ... d.	|	...	|	|	|	1922x	...	2019x	2053	...	...	...	|	...	|	...	...	|	|	0653x	0924x	0924x	...	|	1202x	...
	Tithoréa ... d.	1350x	...	|	1638	|	1934	...	2031x	2105x	...	...	...	|	...	0318x	...	...	|	|	0705	0936x	0936x	...	|	1214	...
	Levadiá ... d.	1402	...	1528	1651	1832	1954	...	2042	2118	...	...	...	|	...	0335	...	...	|	0528	0724	0951	0951	...	|	1233	...
	Thíva ... d.	1421	...	1546	1714	1850	2020	...	2102	2141	...	...	...	|	...	0403	...	...	0456	0546	0751	1011	1011	...	|	1258	...
	Inói ... d.	1437	...	1602	1730	1906	2042	...	2118	2158	...	...	...	|	...	0424	...	...	0518	0602	0811	1032	1032	...	|	1318	...
	Athína Lárisa **1402** ... a.	1520	...	1645	1818	1949	2138	...	2208	2246	...	...	...	2316	...	0519	...	...	0612	0645	0907	1115	1115	...	1139	1410	...

◆ – **NOTES** (LISTED BY TRAIN NUMBER)

444/5 – FILÍA - DOSTLUK EXPRESS – 🛏 1, 2 cl. Thessaloníki - İstanbul and v.v.
504/5 – 🛏 1, 2 cl. Athína - Thessaloníki and v.v.; 🛏 1, 2 cl. Athína - Thessaloníki (**360/3**) - Sofiya and v.v.
602 – [12] and 🍷 Athína - Thessaloníki - Díkea; [2] Athína - Thessaloníki - Svilengrad; ▬ 2 cl. Thessaloníki - Díkea.
603 – [12] and 🍷 Díkea - Thessaloníki - Athína; ▬ 2 cl. Díkea - Thessaloníki.
604 – [12] and 🍷 Athína - Thessaloníki - Orménio; ▬ 2 cl. Athína - Thessaloníki.
605 – [12] and 🍷 Díkea - Thessaloníki - Athína; ▬ 2 cl. Thessaloníki - Athína.

K – From / to Kalambáka.
V – From / to Vólos.

x – Stops on request.
⚡ – Ⓡ with supplement payable. *Icity* train.
◇ – Ⓡ with supplement payable. *IcityE* train.
▮ – Reservation recommended.

△ – Additional services operate **Thessaloníki - Platí - Kateríni - Litóhoro** (for Mount Ólimbos) **and v.v.**: Journey ± 55 minutes.
From **Thessaloníki**: 0457, 0600, 0653, 0812, 0902, 1047, 1205, 1311, 1416, 1520, 1615, 1736, 1832, 1950, 2043, 2207.
From **Litóhoro**: 0609, 0702, 0820, 0911, 1025, 1213, 1319, 1426, 1527, 1624, 1745, 1840, 1943, 2052, 2142, 2325.

1402 ATHÍNA - INÓI - HALKÍDA

Local rail service. 2nd class. *83 km*. Journey: 70 – 90 minutes.
All trains call at Inói (± 60 minutes from Athína).

From **Athína** Lárisa: 0432Ⓐ, 0516, 0616, 0721, 0851, 0951Ⓐ, 1023, 1124Ⓐ, 1251, 1351Ⓐ, 1421, 1521, 1625, 1725Ⓐ, 1823, 1951, 2051Ⓐ, 2154, 2321.
From **Inói**: 0536Ⓐ, 0620, 0645Ⓐ, 0720, 0745Ⓐ, 0846, 0952, 1116Ⓐ, 1215, 1246Ⓐ, 1352, 1452, 1522, 1622Ⓐ, 1646, 1746, 1916Ⓐ, 2016, 2139, 2246Ⓐ, 2341, 0030.

Service currently suspended Inói - Halkída and v.v. owing to engineering work; an hourly replacement 🚌 *service will operate* (0600 - 2200).

1405 LÁRISA - VÓLOS

Local rail service. Journey: ± 60 minutes.
See Table **1400** for *IC* services from / to Athína.

From **Lárisa**: 0455, 0555Ⓐ, 0706, 0802Ⓐ, 0930, 1106Ⓐ, 1207, 1340Ⓐ, 1443, 1621Ⓐ, 1705, 1841Ⓐ, 2025, 2140Ⓐ, 2247.
From **Vólos**: 0553, 0704Ⓐ, 0822, 0928Ⓐ, 1039, 1227Ⓐ, 1313, 1503Ⓐ, 1554, 1725Ⓐ, 1901, 1951Ⓐ, 2128Ⓐ, 2303.

LÁRISA - PALEOFÁRSALOS - KALAMBÁKA 1408

km						884				*IC* 48	886
		2	2	2	2		2⊖	2	2⊖	🍷✗	
	Thessaloníki **1400** ... d.	...	...	...	...	...	...	...	...	...	1759
	Athína **1400** ... d.	...	...	...	...	0821	...	...	...	1553	|
	Lárisa 1400 ... d.	0500	0626	0725	...	|	...	...	...	|	1941
0	Paleofársalos **1400** ... d.	0522	0650	0756	1017	1213	1343	1444	1642	1923	2004
31	Kardítsa ... d.	0538x	0706	0815	1036	1229	1404	1500	1701	1939	2020
60	Tríkala ... d.	0554	0722	0833	1054	1246	1422	1516	1719	1955	2036
82	**Kalambáka 1400** ... a.	0609	0737	0849	1110	1300	1438	1531	1735	2010	2051

	IC 47	883					885			
	🍷✗		2	2	2	2⊖		2⊖	2	
Kalambáka 1400 ... d.	0633	0742	0853	1153	1331	1532	1736	1903	2100	...
Tríkala ... d.	0648	0757	0909	1209	1346	1548	1751	1919	2115	...
Kardítsa ... d.	0707	0816	0928	1230	1403	1607	1808	1940	2132	...
Paleofársalos **1400** ... a.	0722	0832	0946	1248	1418	1625	1823	1958	2147	...
Lárisa 1400 ... a.	|	0856	...	...	...	...	|	2030	2211	...
Athína **1400** ... a.	1115	|	...	...	...	...	2208	...	...	...
Thessaloníki **1400** a.	...	1039	...	...	...	...	...	...	...	...

x – Stops on request. ⊖ – Days and dates of running are subject to confirmation. ✗ – [R] with supplement payable.

THESSALONÍKI - ÉDESSA - KOZÁNI and FLÓRINA 1410

km		Ⓐ					Ⓐ⊖	Ⓐ						Ⓐ				Ⓐ				⊖	Ⓐ		
0	**Thessaloníki 1400** ... d.	0428	0618	0618	...	0657	0835	0835	...	0954	1109	1109	...	1231	1400	1510	1510	1629	1739	...	1908	1908	2014	2215	...
38	Platí **1400** ... d.	0452	0644	0644	...	0728	0905	0905	...	1025	1139	1139	...	1259	1428	1537	1537	1656	1816	...	1939	1939	2045	2243	...
69	Véria ... d.	0517	0716	0716	...	0803	0936	0936	...	1054	1212	1212	...	1330	1500	1610	1610	1729	1847	...	2010	2010	2118	2316	...
97	Skídra ... d.	0536	0738	0738	...	0824	0957	0957	...	1116	1234	1234	...	1352	1523	1632	1632	1751	1909	...	2031	2031	2139	2337	...
112	**Édessa** ... d.	0548	0751	0751	...	0836	1010	1010	...	1128	1247	1247	...	1404	1535	1645	1645	1803	1921	...	2045	2045	2151	2349	...
162	Amíndeo ... d.	...	0838	0839	...	...	1058	1059	...	...	1336	1337	...	...	...	1733	1734	...	...	...	2133	2134	...	...	...
	Kozáni ... a.	...	0920	|	...	...	1141	|	...	...	1419	|	...	...	...	|	1817	...	...	...	|	2217	...	...	...
196	**Flórina** ... a.	...	...	0904	...	...	...	1124	...	...	...	1402	...	...	...	1758	...	...	...	...	2158	...	...	...	...

km			Ⓐ	⊖								Ⓐ⊖	Ⓐ		Ⓐ					Ⓐ					Ⓐ
	Flórina ... d.	...	...	...	0608	...	...	...	0941	...	...	...	1219	...	...	...	1501	...	...	...	...	...	1926	...	...
0	Kozáni ... d.	...	...	0548	|	...	...	0926	|	...	...	1155	|	...	...	1438	|	...	...	...	...	1903	|	...	...
60	Amíndeo ... d.	...	...	0638	0638	...	...	1011	1011	...	...	1249	1249	...	...	1531	1531	...	...	...	...	1956	1956	...	...
	Édessa ... d.	0440	0640	0725	0725	...	0917	1100	1100	...	1152	1337	1337	...	1444	1617	1617	...	1710	1830	1935	2044	2044	...	2156
	Skídra ... d.	0453	0653	0739	0739	...	0930	1114	1114	...	1205	1351	1351	...	1457	1631	1631	...	1723	1843	1948	2057	2057	...	2209
	Véria ... d.	0515	0715	0802	0802	...	0953	1133	1133	...	1228	1412	1412	...	1519	1650	1650	...	1745	1906	2011	2118	2118	...	2230
	Platí **1400** ... d.	0546	0746	0833	0833	...	1026	1202	1202	...	1307	1445	1445	...	1555	1714	1714	...	1825	1938	2044	2149	2149	...	2302
	Thessaloníki 1400 ... a.	0615	0815	0901	0901	...	1058	1228	1228	...	1333	1515	1515	...	1621	1740	1740	...	1851	2004	2110	2215	2215	...	2328

⊖ – Days and dates of running are subject to confirmation.

ATHÍNA AIRPORT- NERATZIÓTISSA 1430

2nd class, journey 20 minutes

From **Athína Airport**: 0552, 0612, 0626, 0648, 0712, 0726, 0748, and at the same minutes past each hour until 1248, then 1316, 1326, 1348, 1412, 1426, 1448, 1512, 1526, 1548, 1612, 1626, 1648, 1716, 1726, 1748, 1812, 1826, 1848, and at the same minutes past each hour until 2148, then 2226, 2248, 2312.

From **Neratziótissa**: 0623, 0638, 0651, 0723, 0738, 0751, and at the same minutes past each hour until 1251, then 1323, 1341, 1351, 1423, 1438, 1451, 1523, 1539, 1551, 1623, 1638, 1651, 1723, 1742, 1752, 1823, 1838, 1851, and at the same minutes past each hour until 2151, then 2223, 2254, 2323, 2338.

ATHÍNA - KÓRINTHOS - KIÁTO 1440

2nd class

km													
	Pireás ... ▲ d.	0545	0614	0645	0708	0738	and	1908	1938	2038	2138	2208	2238
0	**Athína** Lárisa ... ▲ d.	0606	0636	0706	0736	0806	in the	1936	2006	2106	2206	2236	2306
	Neratziótissa **1430** ... d.	0621	0649	0721	0749	0821	same	1949	2021	2121	2221	2249	2321
80	**Kórinthos** (new station) d.	0725	...	0825	...	0925	pattern	...	2125	2225	2325	...	0025
101	**Kiáto 1450** ... a.	0739	...	0839	...	0939	until	...	2139	2239	2339	...	0039

Kiáto 1450 ... d.	0522	...	0622	and	...	1922	2022	2122	...	2222
Kórinthos (new station) d.	0538	...	0638	in the	...	1938	2038	2138	...	2238
Neratziótissa **1430** ... d.	0644	0714	0744	same	2014	2044	2144	2244	2314	2344
Athína Lárisa ... ▲ d.	0708	0738	0808	pattern	2038	2108	2208	2308	2338	0003
Pireás ... ▲ a.	0726	0756	0826	until	2056	2126	2226	2326	2356	0021

▲ – Attiko Metro operates frequent services between Athína Lárisa (for **Athína** mainline station) and Omónia [Line 2], with connections to **Pireás** [Line 1] (journey time: ± 30 minutes).

Allow sufficient time for connecting shipping services at Pireás as the port is very large.

KIÁTO - PÁTRA - KALAMÁTA 1450

Narrow gauge. 2nd class only (except *IC* trains)

km		308		*IC* 20	300		*IC* 22		302	304	*IC* 24	306	*IC* 12
				✗			✗				✗		✗
0	**Kiáto 1440** ... d.	0052	...	0747	0955	...	1247	...	1353	1453	1647	1951	2147
13	Xilókastro ... d.	0106	...	0759	1009	...	1259	...	1410	1507	1659	2008	2159
56	Diakoftó ... d.	0152	...	0837	1055	...	1337	...	1456	1555	1737	2057	2237
109	**Pátra** ... a.	0249	...	0927	1154	...	1427	...	1555	1652	1830	2154	2327
		|	**1350**	|	**1352**	**1354**	|	**350**	|	**1356**	|	**1358**	
109	**Pátra** ... d.	0301	0617	0930	1200	...	1433	...	1558	1706	1834	...	...
175	Kavásila ... d.	0416x	0733x	1037	1316x	...	1539	...	1713x	1821x	1942	...	...
209	**Pírgos** ... d.	0457	0814	1108	1401	1422	1608	1610	1758	1903	2013	...	...
266	Kaloneró ... d.	0601	0920	1203	...	1528	...	1705	1904	...	2107	...	...
272	Kiparissía ... ◧ a.	0608	*0929*	*1212*	...	*1537*	...	*1714*	*1915*	...	*2116*	2154	...
339	**Kalamáta 1452** ... a.	0752	1042	1319	...	1657	...	1821	2023	...	2227	2330	...

	1351	1353	*IC* 21	1357	1355	351	*IC* 23	305		*IC* 25	1359	309
			✗				✗					
Kalamáta 1452 d.	0559	...	0643	...	0928	1044	...	1236	...	1546	1738	2212
Kiparissía ◧ d.	0736	...	*0750*	0952	1103	*1151*	...	*1349*	...	1653	*1852*	2353
Kaloneró ... d.	...	...	0800	1000	...	1202	...	1359	...	1704	1906	0001
Pírgos ... d.	...	0611	0855	1110	...	1255	1257	1504	...	1759	2012	0106
Kavásila ... d.	...	0651x	0925	1150x	...	...	1327	1546x	...	1829	2052x	0146x
Pátra ... d.	...	0806	1031	1305	...	...	1432	1702	...	1934	2206	0300
	IC **11** ✗	**301**	|		**303**		|	|	**307**	|		|
Pátra ... d.	0530	0710	1034	...	1210	...	1435	1707	1806	1937	...	0312
Diakoftó ... d.	0621	0808	1125	...	1308	...	1526	1807	1907	2028	...	0410
Xilókastro ... d.	0659	0857	1203	...	1357	...	1604	1854	1954	2106	...	0457
Kiáto 1440 ... a.	0710	0910	1214	...	1413	...	1615	1907	2010	2117	...	0510

x – Stops on request. ✗ – [R] with supplement payable, 🍷. ◧ – Kiparissía passengers are required to change train at Kaloneró where times are shown in *italics*.

KÓRINTHOS - ÁRGOS - KALAMÁTA 1452

Service by 🚌 during reconstruction of the narrow gauge line. Árgos - Náfplio is currently suspended. For connections Athína - Kórinthos see Table **1440**

			🚌			🚌			
Kórinthos (new) 1440 ... d.	...	...	0930	...	...	1540	...	...	...
Árgos ... d.	...	...	|	...	...	|	...	...	...
Náfplio ... a.	...	...	|	...	...	|	...	...	...
Trípoli ... d.	...	...	1031	...	...	1630	...	...	...
Kalamáta 1450 ... a.	...	...	1230	...	...	...	...	...	...

			🚌			🚌			
Kalamáta 1450 ... d.	...	...	...	...	...	1233	...	...	...
Trípoli ... d.	...	...	0825	...	...	1433	...	...	...
Náfplio ... d.	...	...	|	...	...	|	...	...	...
Árgos ... d.	...	...	|	...	...	|	...	...	...
Kórinthos (new) 1440 ... a.	...	...	0925	...	...	1533	...	...	...

PELOPÓNNISOS narrow-gauge branches 1455

Athína – Lutráki *Service currently suspended* 2nd class only

km		⑥⑦	
0	**Athína** Ágii Anárgiri ◇ ... d.	0710	1600
79	Isthmós ... d.	0840	1730
85	**Lutráki** ... a.	0851	1741

	⑥⑦	
Lutráki ... d.	0909	1809
Isthmós ... d.	0921	1821
Athína Ágii Anárgiri ◇ ... a.	1050	1950

Diakoftó – Kalávrita *Service currently suspended* 2nd class only, rack railway

km			S		S	
0	**Diakoftó** ... d.	0653	0900	1058	1302	1458
23	**Kalávrita** ... a.	0800	1009	1207	1411	1607

		S		S	
Kalávrita d.	0926	1124	1328	1524	1730
Diakoftó a.	1035	1233	1437	1633	1837

Katákolo – Pírgos – Olimbía 2nd class only

km				⊖			⊖		⊖		⊖	
0	Katákolo ... d.	...	0836	0931	1013	1106	1200	1252	1353	1451	1547	1652
12	Pírgos ... a.	0655	0856	0951	1031	1126	1220	1312	1413	1511	1605	1710
33	Olimbía ... a.	0724	0917	1012	...	1152	1241	1341	1434	1538	...	...

		⊖				⊖		⊖		⊖	
Olimbía ... d.	0730	...	0922	...	...	1103	1157	1249	1346	1448	1542
Pírgos ... d.	0801	0858	0950	...	1043	1127	1221	1313	1414	1512	1612
Katákolo ... a.	0819	0916	1008	...	1101	1145	1239	1331	1432	1530	1630

S – Operates only when sufficient demand.
⊖ – Days and dates of running are subject to confirmation.
◇ – Ágii Anárgiri is situated 5 km north of Athína Lárisa station.

BULGARIA and TURKEY IN EUROPE

SEE MAP PAGE 492

Operator: Български Държавни Железници - Bâlgarski Dârzhavni Zheleznitsi (БДЖ - BDZh); Türkiye Cumhuryeti Devlet Demiryolları (TCDD).

Services: All trains convey first and second class seating, except where shown otherwise in footnotes or by '2' in the train column, or where the footnote shows sleeping and/or couchette cars only. Descriptions of sleeping (🛏) and couchette (▬) cars appear on page 10. Reservation of seats is possible on most express trains. Services covering Turkey in Asia and beyond are given in the **Thomas Cook Overseas Timetable**.

Timings: BDŽ schedules are valid **December 9, 2007 - December 13, 2008**. Timetable amendments are possible at short notice so please confirm timings locally before travelling. TCDD schedules are the latest available. Please refer to Tables **60**, **98** and **99** for international through cars to / from Burgas and Varna (summer only).

1500 BUCUREŞTI - RUSE - SOFIYA

km		4612		463	463 4643		383			
				®	®		®			
			...	R	T		B			
0	**Bucureşti** Nord d.	...	...	1253	1253	...	1953	...	...	...
114	Giurgiu Nord a.	...	...	1443	1443	...	2137	...	...	...
114	Giurgiu Nord 🛃 d.	...	...	1515	1515	...	2205	...	...	...
131	**Ruse** 🛃 a.	...	...	1540	1540	...	2230	...	...	...
131	**Ruse 1525** d.	0620	...	1600	1600	...	2330	...	...	...
242	Gorna Oryakhovitsa **1520/25** d.	0830	...	1805	1758	...	0140	...	...	...
342	Pleven **1520** d.	0949	...	1917	...	...	0258	...	...	...
448	Mezdra **1520** d.	1104	...	2026	...	...	0413	...	...	...
536	**Sofiya 1520** a.	1255	...	2212	...	...	0605	...	...	...

	4644 462	462		4613		382		4627	
	®	®				®			
	T	R				B		△	
Sofiya 1520 d.	...	0818	...	1515	...	1930	...	2230	...
Mezdra **1520** d.	...	0957	...	1655	...	2114	...	0038	...
Pleven **1520** d.	...	1108	...	1815	...	2236	...	0208	...
Gorna Oryakhovitsa **1520/25** d.	1227	1227	...	1943	...	2359	...	0328	...
Ruse 1525 a.	1425	1425	...	2144	...	0205	...	0530	...
Ruse 🛃 d.	1445	1445	...	...	...	0315	...	...	...
Giurgiu Nord 🛃 a.	1510	1510	...	...	...	0340	...	...	...
Giurgiu Nord d.	1525	1525	...	...	...	0423	...	...	...
Bucureşti Nord a.	1709	1709	...	...	...	0607	...	...	...

B – BULGARIA EXPRESS – 🛏 1, 2 cl. and [1,2] Bucureşti - Sofiya and v.v.; 🛏 1, 2 cl.* Moskva - Kyïv - Sofiya and v.v. Conveys on dates in Table **98**: 🛏 2 cl.* Minsk - Kyïv - Sofiya and v.v., 🛏 2 cl.* Lviv - Sofiya and v.v.

R – ROMANIA – [2] Bucureşti - Sofiya and v.v.; 🛏 1, 2 cl. and ▬ 1, 2 cl. Bucureşti - Sofiya - Thessaloníki and v.v.; 🛏 1, 2 cl. Bucureşti - Thessaloníki (**603/4**) - Athína and v.v.; 🛏 1, 2 cl. Budapest (**371/0**) - Bucureşti - Sofiya and v.v.;

T – BOSPHOR – 🛏 1, 2 cl. and ▬ 2 cl. Bucureşti - Svilengrad 🛃 - Kapıkule 🛃 - İstanbul and v.v.; [2] Bucureşti - Dimitrovgrad and v.v.

* – Only available for journeys from / to Russia, Belarus or Ukraine.

△ – Conveys ▬ 2 cl. and [2].

1510 SOFIYA - VIDIN - CALAFAT - CRAIOVA

km		70101	7621	1602	7623	7625	7631	70241
		2		P				2
0	**Sofiya 1520** d.	...	0705	0927	1215	1600	1900	...
88	Mezdra **1520** d.	0542	|	|	1409	1759	2059	...
106	Vratsa d.	0607	0910	1115	1429	1816	2119	...
182	Brusartsi ⊖ d.	0742	1034	...	1558	1941	2241	2245
204	Lom ⊖ a.	|	|	...	|	|	2312	|
269	**Vidin** 🛃 ★ a.	0936	1220	...	1746	2130	...	0038

	7630	7620	1601	7622	70102	7624
			P		2	
Vidin 🛃 ★ d.	...	0605	...	1240	1355	1615
Lom ⊖ d.	0535	|	...	|	|	|
Brusartsi ⊖ d.	0611	0740	...	1423	1554	1810
Vratsa d.	0737	0909	1320	1554	1727	1939
Mezdra **1520** a.	0800	|	|	1609	1747	|
Sofiya 1520 a.	1010	1111	1518	1813	2037	2145

km								
					▲			Ⓑ
0	**Calafat** 🛃 ★ d.	0335	0558	...	1150	...	1515	1928
107	**Craiova 1600** a.	0652	0915	...	1503	...	1842	2241

	⚒					
Craiova 1600 d.	0508	0801	...	1420	1650	1942
Calafat 🛃 ★ a.	0830	1120	...	1747	2018	2257

P – [1,2] Vratsa - Sofiya - Plovdiv and v.v.

⊖ – Additional journeys Brusartsi - Lom and v.v. Journey time: 28 – 37 minutes. **From Brusartsi** at 0650, 0745, 1042, 1425, 1605, 1816 and 1947. **From Lom** at 0655, 0822, 0957, 1340, 1518, 1725 and 1906.

▲ – During engineering work: Calafat 1324, Craiova 1642.

★ – An infrequent vehicle / passenger ⛴ service operates Vidin - Calafat and v.v. (the ferry terminal at Vidin is approx. 5 km north of the railway station). Only operates with a full load of vehicles so a long wait may be possible. Journey time: 20 minutes.

1520 SOFIYA - PLOVDIV - BURGAS and VARNA

km	km		2655				8605	8601	2601		3621	2611	8611	8611 8661	2613	8615	4613	4640	3601	8603	2607	2637	8637	3637	8627	2627
							⚡	⚡	⚡										⚡	⚡	⚡		△	▲	▲	▲
				⊙	⊙	⊙				⊙							R	A				B				
0	0	**Sofiya 1500 1510** ⊡ d.	...	...	...	...	...	0630	0650	...	0720	0950	1030	1030	1315	1330	1515	...	1555	1630	1725	2100	...	2200	2215	2325
	119	Pazardzhik ⊡ d.	...	...	...	...	...	0831	|	...	|	|	1246	1246	|	1544	|	...	|	1828	|	|	...	|	0031	|
	156	**Plovdiv** ⊡ a.	...	...	...	...	...	0853	|	...	|	|	1314	1314	|	1613	|	...	|	1854	|	|	...	|	0100	|
	156	**Plovdiv** d.	...	...	...	...	0650	0858	|	...	|	|	1320	1320	|	1620	|	...	|	1857	|	|	2255	|	0110	|
		Karlovo d.	...	...	...	...	|	|	|	0605	1002	|	|	|	|	|	|	...	1825	|	|	|	|	0042	|	|
		Tulovo d.	...	...	...	...	|	|	|	0800t	1118	|	|	|	|	|	|	...	1936	|	|	|	|	0158	|	|
		Sliven d.	...	0540	...	...	|	|	|	0929	1243	|	|	|	|	|	|	...	2043	|	|	|	|	0332	|	|
	262	Stara Zagora d.	...	|	...	...	0840	1040	|	▬	|	|	1522	1522	|	1810	|	...	|	2050	|	|	0052	|	0320	|
	340	Yambol d.	...	|	0655	0845	0950	1149	|	...	|	|	1633	1633	|	1930	|	...	|	2158	|	|	0205	|	0430	|
	389	Karnobat **1530** d.	...	0638	0810v	0937	1036	1227	|	...	1331	|	1723	1735	|	2016	|	...	2129	...	|	|	0250	0432	0516	|
	450	**Burgas 1530** a.	...	0757	0930	1053	|	1312	|	...	1420	|	|	1825	|	2105	|	...	2219	...	|	|	|	|	0605	|
88		Mezdra **1500 1510** d.	...	...	...	...	|	...	0830	...	...	1135	|	...	1507	...	1655	...	...	...	1904	2249	|	|	...	0111
194		Pleven **1500** d.	0650	...	...	...	|	...	0946	...	...	1301	|	...	1628	...	1815	...	...	...	2017	0016	|	|	...	0230
294		Gorna Oryakhovitsa **1500** a.	0803	...	...	...	|	...	1104	...	...	1418	|	...	1743	...	1930	...	...	...	2130	0131	|	|	...	0348
294		Gorna Oryakhovitsa d.	0808	...	...	...	|	...	1110	⊙	...	1428	|	...	1748	...	...	1948	...	...	...	0138	|	|	...	0403
435		Shumen **1530** d.	1003	...	...	...	|	...	1259	1307	...	1622	|	...	1940	...	...	2155	...	...	...	0331	|	|	...	0605
459		Kaspichan **1530** d.	|	...	...	...	|	...	|	1334	...	1640	|	...	1958	...	...	...	...	...	...	0348	|	|	...	0625
518		Povelyanovo **1530** d.	1107	...	...	...	|	...	|	1443	...	1729	1927	...	2046	...	...	...	...	...	...	...	0459	0644	...	0717
543	546	**Varna 1530** a.	1130	...	...	...	1305	...	1420	1517	...	1755	1950	...	2112	...	...	...	...	...	...	...	0525	0710	...	0744

km		2608	8604	3602	4641	4612	8610			2602	8660 8614	8614	2610	2612	3622	8602		8606	2654			8626	3636	2626	8636	2636
		⚡	⚡	⚡						⚡						⚡		⚡				▲	▲	▲	△	
					A	R		⊙	⊙								⊙			⊙	⊙					C
	Varna 1530 d.	...	...	...	...	...	...	...	0630	0755	...	0915	1055	1240	...	...	1405	1510	1720	...	1935	...	2140	2220	2304	...
	Povelyanovo **1530** d.	...	...	...	...	...	...	...	0702	0817	...	0939	|	1304	...	...	1438	1531	|	...	2010	...	2204	2244	2329	...
	Kaspichan **1530** d.	...	...	...	...	...	...	...	0810	0859	...	|	1204	1351	...	...	1545	|	1827	...	2116	...	|	2332	|	0034
	Shumen **1530** d.	...	...	...	0610	...	...	...	0838	0918	...	|	1224	1411	...	...	1612	|	1847	...	2142	...	|	2353	|	0054
	Gorna Oryakhovitsa a.	...	...	...	0818	...	...	...	▬	1106	...	|	1418	1602	...	...	▬	|	2039	...	▬	...	|	0148	|	0244
	Gorna Oryakhovitsa **1500** d.	0500	...	...	...	0830	...	...	...	1111	...	|	1428	1612	...	...	...	|	2044	...	...	...	|	0156	|	0250
	Pleven **1500** d.	0617	...	...	...	0949	...	...	...	1228	...	|	1548	1730	...	...	...	|	2159	...	...	...	|	0320	|	0409
	Mezdra **1500 1510** d.	0737	...	...	...	1104	...	...	...	1341	...	|	1719	1856	...	...	...	|	...	...	⊙	...	|	0441	|	0539
0	**Burgas 1530** d.	|	...	0530	...	|	0650	0705	...	|	1040	|	|	|	1420	1540	...	|	...	1810	1942	2155	|	|	|	|
61	Karnobat **1530** d.	|	...	0618	...	|	0742	0824	...	|	1150	1150	|	|	1510	1625	...	1728	...	1930	2107	2250	0013	|	0130	|
	Yambol d.	|	0500	|	...	|	0828	|	...	|	1236	1236	|	|	|	1704	...	1808	...	|	2158	2334	|	|	0220	|
	Stara Zagora d.	|	0612	|	...	|	0952	|	...	|	1349	1349	|	|	|	1817	⊙	1920	...	|	...	0047	|	|	0346t	|
119	Sliven d.	|	|	0703	...	|	|	0925	⊙	|	|	|	|	|	1557	|	1740	|	...	2028	...	|	0109	|	|	|
195	Tulovo d.	|	|	0808	...	|	|	*1109*	1136	|	|	|	|	|	1724t	|	1947z	|	...	...	...	|	0237t	|	|	|
269	Karlovo d.	|	|	0921	...	|	|	...	1313	|	|	|	|	|	1845	|	2120	|	...	...	...	|	0355	|	|	|
	Plovdiv a.	|	0754	|	...	|	1151	...	...	|	1539	1539	|	|	|	2001	...	2105	...	...	...	0231	|	|	0535	|
	Plovdiv ⊡ d.	|	0800	|	...	|	1200	...	...	|	1550	1550	|	|	|	2008	...	...	...	...	...	0240	|	|	...	|
	Pazardzhik ⊡ d.	|	0827	|	...	|	1232	...	...	|	1623	1623	|	|	|	2038	...	...	...	...	...	0313	|	|	...	|
418	**Sofiya 1500 1510** ⊡ a.	0925	1030	1145	...	1255	1445	...	...	1530	1832	1832	1914	2050	2120	2237	...	...	...	...	...	0535	0635	0635	...	0736

	8601	1621	8611	8615		1601	8603	1623	1651	8627	
	⚡				⊙	⚡F	⚡		D		
Sofiya d.	0630	0830	1030	1330	1405	1530	1630	1730	1815	2215	...
Pazardzhik d.	0831	1039	1246	1544	1642	1726	1828	1939	2029	0031	...
Plovdiv a.	0853	1106	1314	1613	1722	1750	1854	2006	2100	0100	...

	8626	1650	1602	8604	8610		1620		8614	1622	8602
		D	⚡F	⚡		⊙		⊙			⚡
Plovdiv d.	0240	0600	0700	0800	1200	1210	1300	1400	1550	1800	2008
Pazardzhik d.	0313	0632	0729	0827	1232	1255	1332	1445	1623	1834	2038
Sofiya a.	0535	0843	0922	1030	1445	1532	1541	1728	1832	2040	2237

A – [1,2] Plovdiv - Veliko Târnovo - Shumen and v.v. (Table **1525**).

B – 🛏 1, 2 cl. and [1,2] Sofiya - Dobrich - Kardam (Table **1540**). Conveys 🛏 1, 2 cl. and [2] Sofiya - Kaspichan (**9636**) - Samuil - Silistra (Table **1530**).

C – 🛏 1, 2 cl. and [1,2] Kardam - Dobrich - Sofiya (Table **1540**). Conveys 🛏 1, 2 cl. and [2] Silistra (**9637**) - Samuil - Kaspichan (**2636**) - Sofiya (Table **1530**).

D – To / from Dimitrovgrad (Table **1550**).

F – [1,2] Vratsa - Sofiya - Plovdiv and v.v.

R – To / from Ruse (Table **1500**).

t – Arrives 15 – 18 minutes earlier.

v – Arrives 0745.

z – Arrives 1913.

⊙ – Local stopping train. 2nd class only.

▲ – Conveys 🛏 1, 2 cl., ▬ 2 cl. and [1,2].

△ – Conveys 🛏 1, 2 cl. and [1,2].

⚡ – Express Train. Higher fare payable. ®.

⊡ – See panel below main table for complete service Sofia - Plovdiv and v.v.

RUSE - STARA ZAGORA - PLOVDIV 1525

km					4641				463 4643	4647	4647 8636
		⊙	⊙	⊙	S	⊙	⊙	⊙	🄡 B		
0	**Ruse 1500** d.	...	...	...	*0620*	*0745*	1131	1308	1600	2155	2155
111	Gorna Oryakhovitsa **1500** a.	...	...	...	*0823*	*1025*	1412	1545	1758	2356	2356
111	Gorna Oryakhovitsa d.	...	...	0505	0835	1120	1432	1627	1824	0002	0002
125	Veliko Târnovo d.	...	...	0526	0854	1140	1453	1652	1841	0019	0019
226	Tulovo d.	...	...	0819	1130	...	1721	1948**v**	2052	0236	0236
253	Stara Zagora a.	...	...	0859	1205	...	1800	2025	2126	0313	0313
253	Stara Zagora **1520** d.	0455	...	...	1210	...	...	...	2128	0333	0346
310	Dimitrovgrad **1550** a.	0632	0740	...	|	...	...	...	2245	0451	|
411	Momchilgrad **1550** a.	...	1032	...	|	...	...	...	...	*0820*	|
359	**Plovdiv 1520** a.	...	...	...	1352	...	...	...	...	...	0535

			4644 462		4640			8637 4646	4646
	⊙	⊙	🄡 B	⊙	S	⊙	⊙		
Plovdiv 1520 d.	...	...	...	...	1415	...	...	2255	...
Momchilgrad **1550** d.	...	...	...	...	|	...	*1650*	|	*1940*
Dimitrovgrad **1550** d.	...	...	0650	...	|	...	1958	|	2305
Stara Zagora **1520** a.	...	...	0808	...	1605	...	2127	0040	0027
Stara Zagora d.	...	0705	0814	1050	1615	1830	...	0057	0057
Tulovo d.	...	0748	0857	1129	1658	1915	...	0208**t**	0208**t**
Veliko Târnovo d.	0634	1027	1112	1354	1919	2215	...	0426	0426
Gorna Oryakhovitsa a.	0655	1048	1138	1412	1938	2235	...	0443	0443
Gorna Oryakhovitsa **1500** d.	0724	1118	1227	1440	*1943*	...	...	0451	0451
Ruse 1500 a.	1004	1338	1425	1710	*2144*	...	...	0710	0710

B – BOSPHOR – 🛏 1,2 cl. and ▬ 2 cl. Bucureşti - Ruse - İstanbul and v.v.; [2] Bucureşti - Dimitrovgrad and v.v.

S – To / from Shumen (Table **1520**).

t – Arrives 0135.

v – Arrives 1942.

⊙ – Local stopping train. 2nd class only.

RUSE - SILISTRA, VARNA and BURGAS 1530

km		9636	9621	3660*				9623			9637
		K		2	⊙	⊙	⊙	2	⊙	⊙	L
0	**Ruse** d.	...	0610	0610	0730	...	...	1620	1730	...	...
71	Razgrad d.	...	0735	0735	0906	...	...	1739	1919	...	...
93	Samuil d.	0508	0756	0756	0929	0935	...	1759	1940	2025	2319
206	**Silistra** a.	0725	|	|	|	1158	...	|	...	2301	|
142	Kaspichan a.	...	0853	0853	1036	▬	...	1902	...	...	0021
142	Kaspichan **1520** d.	...	0900	0915	*1204*	⊙	...	1903	...	...	...
166	Shumen **1520** d.	...	|	0938	*1222*	1355	...	|	...	...	...
216	Komunari d.	...	|	1044	...	1510**r**	1518	|	...	...	...
299	Karnobat **1520** a.	...	|	1200	...	|	1700	|	...	...	...
360	**Burgas 1520** a.	...	|	1303	...	|	*1825*	|	...	...	...
201	Povelyanovo **1520** d.	...	|	...	...	1622	...	1952	...	...	...
226	**Varna 1520** a.	...	1015	...	...	1656	...	2017	...	...	...

	9636				9620	8605				9622	3661	9637
	K	⊙	⊙	⊙	2	✗	⊙	⊙	⊙		2	L
Varna 1520 d.	...	...	...	...	0850	...	...	...	...	1730	...	...
Povelyanovo **1520** d.	...	...	...	...	0915	...	...	...	...	1755	...	...
Burgas 1520 d.	...	...	...	...	|	*0855*	...	...	...	|	1500	...
Karnobat **1520** d.	...	...	...	...	|	1036	...	...	...	|	1606	...
Komunari d.	...	...	...	...	|	1159	1210	...	...	|	1730	...
Shumen **1520** d.	...	...	...	*0605*	|	...	1325	...	*1622*	|	1836	...
Kaspichan **1520** a.	...	...	...	*0623*	0959	...	▬	...	*1639*	1852	1854	...
Kaspichan d.	0358	...	...	0708	1000	...	...	...	1650	1904	1904	...
Silistra d.	|	...	0510	|	|	...	⊙	1505	|	|	|	2050
Samuil d.	0458	0525	0743	0818	1056	...	1555	1730	1802	2007	2007	2309
Razgrad d.	...	0546	...	0841	1117	...	1618	...	1825	2027	2027	...
Ruse a.	...	0728	...	1010	1235	...	1802	...	1958	2146	2146	...

K – 🛏 1,2 cl. and [2] Sofiya (**2637**) - Kaspichan (**9636**) - Samuil - Silistra.

L – 🛏 1,2 cl. and [2] Silistra - Samuil - Kaspichan (**2636**) - Sofiya.

r – Arrival time. Departs 1524.

* – Train **9621** Ruse - Kaspichan.

⊙ – Local stopping train. 2nd class only.

✗ – Express Train. Higher fare payable. 🄡.

VARNA and SOFIYA - DOBRICH - KARDAM 1540

km		2637	2627						2613	
		△	▲	2		2	2			2
0	**Varna 1520 1530** d.	...	...	0700	...	1105	1430	...	...	2025
	Sofiya 1520 d.	2100	2325	|	...	|	|	...	1315	|
25	Povelyanovo **1520 1530** a.	|	0715	0732	...	1136	1501	...	2045	2056
25	Povelyanovo d.	|	...	0733	...	1137	1502	...	...	2057
93	**Dobrich** a.	0623	...	0911	...	1308	1625	...	...	2228
131	Kardam a.	0740	...	1020	...	...	1731	...	...	...

		2602			2612					2636
	2	✗		2		2		2		△
Kardam d.	...	...	...	1028	...	...	...	1736	...	2040
Dobrich d.	0638	...	...	1135	...	1355	...	1842	...	2205
Povelyanovo a.	0803	...	...	1259	...	1525	...	2005	...	|
Povelyanovo **1520 1530** d.	0804	0817	...	1305	1304	1532	...	2011	...	|
Sofiya 1520 a.	|	1530	...	|	2050	|	...	|	...	0736
Varna 1520 1530 a.	0838	...	...	1338	...	1604	...	2042	...	...

△ – Conveys 🛏 1,2 cl. and [12].

▲ – Conveys 🛏 1,2 cl., ▬ 2 cl. and [12].

✗ – Express Train. Higher fare payable. 🄡.

PLOVDIV - İSTANBUL 1550

BDŽ; TCDD

km	*Bulgarian/Greek train number*					1641	1651	491	463	444
	Turkish train number			81721				81031	81031	81021
		2	2		2	2		🄡 R	🄡 B	🄡 T
	Bucureşti **1500** d.	...	...	...	...	...	...	...	1253	...
	Beograd **1380** d.	...	...	...	...	...	...	0840	|	...
0	*Sofiya* **1540** d.	...	*1030*	...	*1330*	*1630*	1815	1915	|	...
156	**Plovdiv** d.	0500	1405	...	1705	1910	2115	2155	|	...
234	Dimitrovgrad **1525** d.	0718	1613	...	1910	2047	2251	2324	2324	...
	Momchilgrad **1525** a.	|	|	...	|	2306	▬	|	|	...
299	Svilengrad a.	0837	1741	...	2035	▬	...	0025	0025	...
299	Svilengrad 🏛 d.	▬	▬	...	▬	**81731**	...	0100*	0100*	...
318	Kapıkule 🏛 a.	...	...	...	...		...	0125*	0125*	...
318	Kapıkule d.	...	...	0700	**82901**	1535	...	0300*	0300*	...
338	Edirne d.	...	...	0735	2	1605	...	0322*	0322*	...
	Thessaloníki **1400** d.	...	**82861**	|	*0730*	|	**81711**	|	|	2035
	Píthio 🏛 d.	...	2	|	1530	|		|	|	0305
	Uzunköprü 🏛 d.	...	0745	|	1556	|	1640	|	|	0359
385	Pehlivanköy d.	**81601**	0812	0829	...	1659	1704	|	|	0422
406	Alpullu d.		0836	0853	...	1718	1733	0429*	0429*	0450
506	Çerkezköy d.	0700	...	1033	...	...	1916	0550*	0550*	0608
593	Halkalı d.	0836	...	1215	...	...	2059	0711*	0711*	0728
621	**İstanbul** Sirkeci a.	0915	...	1255	...	...	2131	0800*	0800*	0805

km	*Turkish train number*	81732	81712	82902	81722	82864	81602	81022	81032	81032
	Bulgarian/Greek train number							445	490	462
				2		2		🄡 T	🄡 R	🄡 B
0	**İstanbul** Sirkeci d.	*0830*	0830	...	1550	...	1800	2000	2200	2200
28	Halkalı d.	*0916*	0916	...	1636	...	1839	2036	2242	2242
115	Çerkezköy d.	*1056*	1056	...	1819	...	2014	2156	0006	0006
215	Alpullu d.	1240	1244	...	2001	2010	▬	2323	0130	0130
237	Pehlivanköy d.	1301	1305	...	2022	2036	...	2342	|	|
258	Uzunköprü 🏛 d.	|	1327	1410	|	2101	...	0034	|	|
268	Píthio 🏛 a.	|	▬	1436	|	...	...	0058	|	|
	Thessaloníki **1400** a.	|	...	*2255*	|	...	...	0732	|	|
	Edirne d.	1355	...	▬	2117	...	...	▬	0234	0234
	Kapıkule a.	1423	...	...	2145	...	...	...	0255	0255
	Kapıkule 🏛 d.	▬	...	...	▬	...	...	...	0405	0405
	Svilengrad 🏛 a.	2	2	2	2	...	...	**1640**	0430	0430
	Svilengrad d.	0540	1140	1532	1830	...	**1650**	2	0505	0505
	Momchilgrad **1525** d.	|	|	|	|	...		0350	|	|
	Dimitrovgrad **1525** d.	0733**v**	1306	1652	1949	...	0410	0615	0640	0650
	Plovdiv a.	0940	1449	1832	2136	...	0546	0743	0801	|
	Sofiya **1540** a.	...	*1832*	...	...	...	0843	*1030*	1050	|
	Beograd **1380** a.	...	...	...	...	...	...	...	2012	|
	Bucureşti **1500** a.	...	...	...	...	...	...	...	...	1709

B – BOSPHOR – 🛏 1,2 cl. and ▬ 2 cl. Bucureşti - İstanbul and v.v.

R – BALKAN EXPRESS – 🛏 1,2 cl. Beograd - İstanbul and v.v. Conveys June 1 - Oct. 29 from Sofiya, June 2 - Oct. 30 from İstanbul ▬ 2 cl. Sofiya - İstanbul and v.v.

T – FILIA - DOSTLUK EXPRESS – 🛏 1,2 cl. Thessaloníki - İstanbul and v.v.

v – Arrives 0655.

* – Timings are subject to confirmation.

BOSPHORUS FERRIES 1555

IDO

Ferry service **İstanbul Karaköy - Haydarpaşa** (for Asian rail services) and v.v. *2 km*

Journey time: 20 - 35 minutes

Operator: IDO – İstanbul Deniz Otobüsleri.

From İstanbul Karaköy: On ⚒ at 0630, 0700, 0730, 0750 and every 20 minutes until 1930, then 2000, 2030, 2100, 2130, 2200, 2230, 2300. On † at 0630 and every 30 minutes until 2300.

From Haydarpaşa: On ⚒ at 0635, 0705, 0725, 0750, 0810 and every 20 minutes until 1950, then 2005, 2035, 2105, 2135, 2205, 2235, 2305. On † at 0635, 0705, 0735, 0850, 0920 and every 30 minutes until 2320.

SOFIYA - KULATA - THESSALONÍKI 1560

BDŽ, OSE

km		361*	5621	6621	5611	6623	5623	363*	363*	6625	5625	463
									V 🄡			T 🄡
0	**Sofiya** d.	0655	0735	0805	1130	1405	1550	1700	1700	1710	1950	2242
33	Pernik d.	|	0834	0903	1227	1458	1651	|	|	1817	2053	2327
48	Radomir d.	|	0857	0926	1249	1521	1714	|	|	1845	2117	|
102	**Kyustendil** a.	|	|	1045	|	1644	|	|	|	2008	|	|
91	Dupnitsa d.	|	0951	...	1343	...	1811	|	|	...	2218	0037
123	**Blagoevgrad** d.	0911	1029	...	1415	...	1848	1917	1917	...	2257	0106
186	Sandanski d.	1013	1143	...	1525	...	2005	2020	2020	...	...	0209
210	Kulata a.	1035	1220	...	1605	...	2120	2042	2042	...	...	0233
210	Kulata 🏛 d.	1055	...	...	...	...	...	2102	2102	...	...	0300*
211	Promahónas 🏛 a.	1100	...	...	...	...	...	2107	2107	...	...	0305*
211	Promahónas d.	1120	...	...	...	...	...	2127	2127	...	...	0345*
225	Strimón **1420** d.	1143	...	...	...	...	...	2150	2150	...	...	0408*
354	**Thessaloníki 1420** a.	1259	...	...	...	...	...	2306	2306	...	...	0541*
	Athína **1400** a.	...	...	...	...	...	...	...	0645	...	...	1410*

	462	5620	6620	5622	360*	360*	6622	5624	6624	5610	362*
	T 🄡				Z 🄡						
Athína **1400** d.	1651*	...	...	...	2255	...	...	...	...	...	...
Thessaloníki 1420 d.	0004*	...	...	...	0630	0630	...	...	...	...	1750
Strimón **1420** d.	0146*	...	...	...	0758	0758	...	...	...	...	1918
Promahónas a.	0158*	...	...	...	0810	0810	...	...	...	...	1930
Promahónas 🏛 d.	0310*	...	...	...	0830	0830	...	...	...	...	1950
Kulata 🏛 a.	0315*	...	...	...	0835	0835	...	...	...	...	1955
Kulata d.	0340	...	...	0530	0855	0855	...	1340	...	1650	2015
Sandanski d.	0405	...	...	0612	0919	0919	...	1421	...	1731	2045
Blagoevgrad d.	0512	0550	...	0733	1028	1028	...	1542	...	1850	2148
Dupnitsa d.	0542	0633	...	0806	|	|	...	1613	...	1929	|
Kyustendil d.	|	|	0707	|	|	|	1109	|	1715	|	|
Radomir d.	0635	0736	0839	0918	|	|	1234	1712	1844	2022	|
Pernik d.	0654	0757	0902	0937	|	|	1258	1739	1911	2041	|
Sofiya a.	0748	0902	0950	1034	1240	1240	1345	1841	2005	2130	2355

T – ROMANIA – 🛏 1,2 cl. Bucureşti - Thessaloníki - Athína (**603/2**) and v.v.; 🛏 1,2 cl. and ▬ 1,2 cl. Bucureşti - Sofiya - Thessaloníki and v.v.; 🛏 1,2 cl. and [2] Sofiya - Thessaloniki and v.v.;

V – 🛏 1,2 cl. Sofiya - Thessaloníki (**75**) - Athína.

Z – 🛏 1,2 cl. Athína (**504**) - Thessaloníki - Sofiya.

* – Timings are subject to confirmation.

ROMANIA

SEE MAP PAGE 492

Operator: **CFR** – Compania Naţională de Căi Ferate (www.cfr.ro).

Services: Trains convey 1st- and 2nd-class seating accommodation unless otherwise indicated. Sleeping- (🛏) and couchette (▬) cars are described on page **10**. Russian-type sleeping-cars, as used in trains to and from destinations in Belarus, Moldova, Russia and Ukraine, are described on page **512**; these cars are not accessible to passengers making journeys wholly within Romania or between Romania and Bulgaria. Services marked ⊗ are subject to cancellation or alteration during periods of planned maintenance work.

Timings: Valid from **December 9, 2007**.

Tickets: Reservation is obligatory for travel by all services for which a train number is shown in the tables, and passengers boarding without a prior reservation are surcharged. Supplements are payable for travel by **Intercity** (*IC*) and most other fast trains. Trains shown without numbers are slow stopping-services calling at all, or most, stations.

1600 BUCUREŞTI - CRAIOVA - TIMIŞOARA

km		1762		*IC* 591	791	1891	1789	797	1791	*RM* 821	*IC* 595	1893	693	1793	1725	1795	*IC* 593	1823	1895	795	1797	1821		1799	360	695	1691
		S	2	✕				⑤ⓒ		M	✕				J		✕	C				A	2		B	V	
0	**Bucureşti** Nord d.	...	...	0545	0645	0520	0720	0845	0920	0945	1045	1120	1245	1320	1445	1520	1545	1645	1720	1745	1920	1945	...	2120	2145	2245	2345
51	Videle d.	...	...	|	0729	|	|	0933	|	1028	1128	|	|	|	1529	|	|	1729	|	1830	|	2029	...	|	|	|	0029
100	Roşiori Nord d.	...	...	0705	0809	|	|	1017	|	1105	1208	|	1409	|	1610	|	1702	1810	|	1910	|	2110	...	|	2305	|	0109
155	Caracal d.	...	...	|	0852	|	|	1100	|	1145	1307	|	1452	|	1657	|	|	1859	|	1952	|	2158	...	|	2348	|	0156
108	Piteşti d.	...	...	|	|	0714	0900	|	1100	...	|	1307	|	1500	|	1700	|	|	1914	|	2100	|	...	2300	|	|	|
189	Slatina d.	...	...	|	|	0827	...	|	▬	...	|	1420	|	...	|	▬	|	|	2027	|	...	|	...	...	|	|	|
206	Piatra Olt **1602** d.	...	...	|	|	0847	...	|	...	...	|	1440	|	...	|	...	|	|	2047	|	...	|	...	...	|	|	|
209	**Craiova 1602** a.	...	...	0824	0932	0932	...	1150	...	...	1347	1525	1532	...	1737	...	1820	1940	2132	2032	...	2238	...	...	0028	0118	0236
209	**Craiova 1605** d.	...	0350	0830	0936	...	...	▬	1220	...	1354	...	1540	...	1745	...	1826	1950	...	...	...	2248	2300	...	0036	0130	0245
245	Filiaşi **1605** d.	...	0427	|	1004	...	...	...	1316	...	1422	...	1608	...	1811	...	|	2016	...	...	...	2316	2352	...	0103	|	0313
	Deva **1605** a.	...	|	|	|	...	...	...	|	...	|	...	|	...	...	...	|	...	...	...	...	0348	|	...	|	|	|
323	Drobeta Turnu Severin d.	...	0631	1017	1127	...	...	⊗	1526	...	1538	...	1734	...	...	1815	2003	...	...	...	...	|	0154	...	0220	0307	0440
347	Orşova d.	...	0710	|	...	...	...	1307	...	...	1605	...	1802	...	...	1858	|	...	...	...	...	|	0227	...	0248	|	0508
364	Băile Herculane d.	...	...	1102	...	...	...	1331	...	...	1626	...	1823	...	...	1922	2048	...	...	...	...	|	|	...	0308	0351	0529
435	Caransebeş d.	0805	...	1226	...	...	...	1552	...	...	1756	...	1954	...	...	2122	2212	...	...	...	...	|	0450	...	0432	0523	0654
474	Lugoj **1620** d.	0829	...	1255	...	...	...	1644	...	...	1825	...	2023	...	...	2202	2241	...	...	...	...	|	0534	...	0500	0552	0727
533	**Timişoara** Nord **1620** a.	0911	...	1337	...	...	...	1804	...	...	1907	...	2105	...	...	2308	2323	...	...	...	...	|	0701	...	0543	0641	0809
	Arad **1625** a.	...	...	...	...	...	...	...	...	...	...	...	...	...	...	...	...	...	...	...	...	0556	...	...	|	...	...
	Budapest Keleti **1280** a.	...	...	...	...	...	...	...	...	...	...	...	...	...	...	...	...	...	...	...	...	...	...	...	|	...	...
	Beograd **1365** a.	...	...	...	...	...	...	...	...	...	...	...	...	...	...	...	...	...	...	...	...	...	...	...	0853	...	...

	1788	794	1892	1724		1790	1792	*IC* 592	1794	*IC* 596	1894	798	*RM* 822	1796	792	1896	1824	694		1798	*IC* 594		1764	1692	361	1822	696
				J	2			✕		✕		⑤ⓒ	M				C	✕	2		✕	2	S		B	A	V
Beograd **1365** d.	...	...	...	...	...	...	...	...	...	...	...	...	...	...	...	...	...	...	...	...	...	...	...	...	1555	...	...
Budapest Keleti **1280** d.	...	...	...	...	...	...	...	...	...	...	...	...	...	...	...	...	...	...	...	...	...	...	...	...	|	...	...
Arad **1625** d.	...	...	...	...	...	...	...	...	...	...	...	...	...	...	...	...	...	...	...	...	...	...	...	...	|	1956	...
Timişoara Nord **1620** d.	...	...	...	...	2227	...	...	0600	...	0644	...	...	...	...	...	...	...	1345	...	...	1600	...	1640	2022	2118	|	2252
Lugoj **1620** d.	...	...	...	...	2358	...	...	0644	...	0729	...	...	...	...	...	...	...	1429	...	...	1643	...	1724	2113	2202	|	2342
Caransebeş d.	...	...	...	...	0047	...	...	0713	...	0758	...	...	...	...	...	...	...	1458	...	...	1712	...	1749	2142	2233	|	0020
Băile Herculane d.	...	...	...	...	0248	...	...	0837	...	0922	...	...	...	...	...	...	...	1627	...	...	1836	1822	...	2315	2357	|	0144
Orşova d.	...	...	...	...	0333	...	...	|	...	0945	...	...	...	...	...	...	...	1651	1620	...	|	1850	...	2339	0021	|	|
Drobeta Turnu Severin d.	...	...	...	...	0411	...	...	0925	...	1015	...	...	...	...	1420	...	...	1720	1658	...	1924	1936	...	0005	0050	|	0247
Deva **1605** d.	...	...	...	...	|	...	...	|	...	|	...	...	...	...	|	...	...	|	|	...	|	|	...	|	|	2157	|
Filiaşi **1605** d.	...	...	...	0644	0620	...	...	|	...	1134	...	...	...	...	1550	...	1735	1840	1920	...	|	2138	...	0127	0216	0245	|
Craiova 1605 a.	...	...	...	0710	0722	...	...	1104	...	1201	...	...	...	...	1617	...	1800	1907	2015	...	2110	2215	...	0154	0243	0313	0440
Craiova 1602 d.	...	0500	0445	0715	...	...	...	1110	...	1208	1245	1430	...	...	1620	1645	1810	1915	...	...	2118	...	...	0204	0255	0324	0450
Piatra Olt **1602** d.	...	|	0532	|	...	...	...	|	...	|	1330	|	...	...	|	1732	|	|	...	...	|	...	...	|	|	|	|
Slatina d.	...	|	0550	|	...	...	...	|	...	|	1348	|	...	...	|	1750	|	|	...	...	|	...	...	|	|	|	|
Piteşti d.	0515	|	0715	|	...	0915	1115	|	1315	|	1515	|	...	1715	|	1915	|	|	...	2115	|	...	...	|	|	|	|
Caracal d.	|	0540	|	0755	...	|	|	|	|	1248	|	1510	1608	|	1700	|	1850	1955	...	|	|	...	...	0243	0335	0404	|
Roşiori Nord d.	|	0625	|	0843	...	|	|	1230	|	1334	|	1554	1653	|	1745	|	1936	2040	...	|	2240	...	...	0328	0419	0452	|
Videle d.	|	0706	|	0924	...	|	|	|	|	1422	|	1634	1734	|	1826	|	2017	|	...	|	|	...	...	0409	|	0533	|
Bucureşti Nord a.	0657	0750	0857	1012	...	1103	1303	1347	1457	1505	1657	1715	1815	1857	1908	2057	2100	2203	...	2257	2359	...	...	0451	0539	0615	0726

CARANSEBEŞ - REŞIŢA: (Journey: ± 65 minutes) From Caransebeş: 0455, 0543 **R**, 0802, 1248, 1555, 1754 **S**, 1901, 2144.
From Reşiţa Sud: 0441, 0623, 0705 **S**, 1245, 1524, 1734, 2028, 2304 **R**.

Local trains also operate 4–5 times daily **Reşiţa** Sud - **Timişoara** Nord and v.v. (journey ± 2 hrs 55 mins).

A – 🛏 1, 2 cl., ▬ 2 cl. and (12) Bucureşti - Târgu Jiu - Arad and v.v.
B – BUCUREŞTI – 🛏 1, 2 cl., ▬ 2 cl. and (12) Bucureşti - Beograd and v.v.
C – (12) Bucureşti - Târgu Jiu - Cluj and v.v.
J – (12) Bucureşti - Târgu Jiu and v.v.
M – To / from Râmnicu Vâlcea (Table **1602**).
R – 🛏 1, 2 cl. and (12) Ⓡ Bucureşti - Reşiţa and v.v.
S – (12) Reşiţa - Timişoara and v.v.
V – VALAHIA – 🛏 1, 2 cl., ▬ 2 cl. and (12) Bucureşti - Timişoara and v.v.; 🛏 1, 2 cl. and (12) Bucureşti - Caransebeş - Reşiţa and v.v.

1602 BRAŞOV / SIBIU - RÂMNICU VÂLCEA - CRAIOVA

km		1828			*RM* 804		*RM* 822			*RM* 805	*RM* 884
			2	2	⊗	2	B	2⊗	2		
	Braşov 1620 d.	...	...	...	...	...	...	...	...	1628	...
	Făgăraş 1620 a.	...	...	...	...	...	...	...	...	1754	...
0	**Sibiu** 1620 d.	0255	0315	...	0730	0800	...	1222	1547	|	1815
22	Podu Olt 1620 d.	0321	0352	...	|	0839	...	1258	1624	1855	1855
83	Călimănesti d.	0439	0540	...	|	1047	...	1447	1835	|	|
99	**Râmnicu Vâlcea** d.	0500	0610	...	0928	1114	1428	1515	1915	2045	2045
186	Piatra Olt 1600 d.	0613	0831	0833	1035	...	1540	1751	2130	2154	2154
219	Caracal a.	0640	|	0915	|	...	1605	1835	|	|	|
230	**Craiova** 1600 a.	...	0958	...	1120	...	...	...	2256	2238	2238

		RM 802	*RM* 802		*RM* 821				*RM* 806	1827	
	2			2	B	2	2	2	⊗		2
Craiova 1600 d.	...	0712	0712	0505	...	...	1213	...	1440	...	*1930*
Caracal d.	...	|	|	|	1150	1215	|	1412	|	1725	|
Piatra Olt 1600 d.	0400	0800	0800	0620	1218	1258	1322	1455	1539	1752	2050
Râmnicu Vâlcea d.	0638	0913	0913	0846	1327	...	1545	...	1655	1912	2323
Călimănesti d.	0703	|	|	0941	...	...	1611	...	|	1933	...
Podu Olt 1620 a.	0920	1052	1057	1202	...	...	1800	...	|	2124	...
Sibiu 1620 a.	1000	1115	|	1244	...	...	1839	...	1853	2148	...
Făgăraş 1620 a.	...	...	1149	...	...	...	...	...	...	...	...
Braşov 1620 a.	...	...	1257	...	...	...	...	...	...	...	...

B – (12) Râmnicu Vâlcea - Bucureşti and v.v.

1605 CRAIOVA - TÂRGU JIU - DEVA

km		*RM* 839			1829				1823		1821
			2	2		2	2	2		2	A
	Bucureşti Nord **1600** d.	...	...	...	...	...	...	...	1645	...	1945
0	**Craiova 1600** d.	...	0550	...	0835	1405	...	1550	1950	1953	2248
36	Filiaşi **1600** d.	...	0643	...	0900	1505	...	1643	2018	2045	2316
107	**Târgu Jiu** d.	...	0827	...	1012	1650	...	1836	2130	2218	0025
157	Petroşani d.	0330	...	1114	...	1825	1845	2013	2245	...	0144
237	Simeria **1620** ▲ d.	0548j	...	1401	...	...	2127	...	0048	...	0340
246	**Deva 1620** a.	0534	...	1411	...	...	2136	...	0056	...	0348
	Cluj Napoca **1620** a.	0853	...	...	...	...	...	...	0423	...	|
	Arad **1620** a.	...	...	...	...	...	...	...	...	...	0556

			1820		1824				*RM* 838	1822
				2			2			A
Arad **1620** d.	...	...	...	...	...	...	...	1502	...	1956
Cluj Napoca **1620** d.	...	...	...	...	0919	...	...	|	1600	|
Deva 1620 d.	...	...	...	...	1301	1539	...	1710	1913	2157
Simeria **1620** ▲ d.	...	0750	...	...	1232j	1611	...	1723	1900j	2208
Petroşani d.	0750	1034	...	1135	1509	1834	1910	1934	2104	0014
Târgu Jiu d.	0930	...	1320	1325	1625	...	2058	2118	...	0133
Filiaşi **1600** a.	1114	...	1430	1504	1733	...	2248	...	...	0243
Craiova 1600 a.	1210	...	1500	1557	1800	...	2342	...	...	0313
Bucureşti Nord **1600** a.	...	...	...	...	2100	...	...	...	...	0615

▲ – Service **Simeria** - **Hunedoara** and v.v.: From Simeria: 0053, 0412, 0535, 0712 ①–⑤, 1015 ⊗, 1405, 1610, 1955, 2220. Journey time: ± 28 minutes
From Hunedoara: 0140, 0500, 0625, 0755 ①–⑤, 1103 ⊗, 1530, 1720, 2050, 2310.

A – 🛏 1, 2 cl., ▬ 2 cl. and (12) Bucureşti - Arad and v.v.

j – Via Deva.

BUCUREŞTI - BRAŞOV - SIBIU - ARAD 1620

For Bucureşti - Timişoara and v.v. via Craiova, see Table **1600**

km		RM 811	1837 J	354 T	625 354 A	2		1825 L	2⊗	374 P	RM 825	1621		RM 837 R	1973 G	RM 815	IC 531 V	RM 805	RM 827	346 D		1941 S	EN 370 Y	1765 N	1821 C
0	**Bucureşti** Nord **1630** d.	...	...	...	2358	...	...	...	...	0630	...	0942	...	...	...	...	1300	...	1530	1645	...	...	1850	...	1945
59	Ploieşti Vest **1630** d.	...	...	...	0044	...	...	...	...	0713	...	1023	...	...	...	...	1342	...	1612	1727	...	...	1930	...	|
121	Sinaia **1630** d.	...	...	...	0145	...	...	...	...	0815	...	1140	...	...	...	...	1438	...	1720	1822	...	...	2026	...	|
140	Predeal **1630** d.	...	...	...	0216	...	...	...	...	0851	...	1224	...	...	...	...	1508	...	1753	1852	...	...	2056	...	|
166	**Braşov 1630** a.	...	...	...	0246	...	...	...	...	0922	...	1254	...	...	...	...	1539	...	1824	1922	...	...	2127	...	|
166	**Braşov 1630** d.	...	...	...	0304	...	0606	...	...	0937	0945	1307	1410	...	...	...	1550	1628	1836	1930	1955	...	2135	...	|
	Sighişoara **1630** d.	...	...	...	|	...	|	...	...	1129	|	|	|	...	...	...	1741	|	|	2120	|	...	2326	...	|
231	Făgăraş d.	...	...	...	0425	...	0745	...	...	|	1053	1420	1552	...	...	...	|	1754	1946	|	2130	...	|	...	▽
293	Podu Olt **1602** d.	...	...	...	|	...	0914	...	...	|	|	|	1744	...	...	...	|	1850	|	|	2250	...	|	...	|
315	**Sibiu 1602 1635** a.	...	...	...	0543	...	0951	...	...	|	1225	1545	1821	...	...	...	|	1913	2101	|	2324	...	|	...	|
315	**Sibiu 1635** d.	0500	...	...	0552	0738	▬	...	1029	|	▬	1556	...	...	...	1735	|	...	...	|	...	...	|	...	|
389	Sebeş Alba **1635** d.	0620	...	...	0719	0935	...	...	1225	|	...	1726	...	...	...	1859	|	...	...	|	...	...	|	...	|
397	Vinţu de Jos **1635** a.	0628	...	...	0728	0946	...	...	1236	|	...	1735	...	...	...	1907	|	...	...	|	...	...	|	...	|
	Cluj Napoca **1635** d.	|	0509	...	|	...	...	0919	...	|	...	|	...	1600	...	|	|	...	...	|	...	2220	|	2354	|
	Alba Iulia 1630 1635 d.	|	0723	0732	|	...	...	1133	...	1316	...	|	...	1805	1815	|	1946	...	...	2303	...	0031	0126	0206	|
397	Vinţu de Jos **1635** d.	0632	0735	0802	0802	...	...	1144	...	|	...	1736	...	1820	1827	1913	1957	...	...	|	...	0042	|	0217	|
441	Simeria **1605** d.	0709	0832	0843	0843	...	1215	1232	...	1410	1538	1820	...	1900	1911	1951	2037	...	...	2356	...	0130	|	0303	0340
450	Deva **1605** d.	0718	0843	0852	0852	...	1225	1240	...	1419	1550	1831	...	1908	1921	2001	2047	...	...	0006	...	0140	|	0313	0350
474	Ilia d.	|	0908	|	|	...	1301	...	...	|	1625	1853	...	...	1944	|	|	...	...	|	...	0204	|	0337	0414
564	Radna d.	|	|	|	|	...	1457	...	...	|	1810	|	...	...	2052	|	|	...	...	|	...	0314	|	0444	0522
599	**Arad 1625** a.	|	|	1048	1048	...	1545	...	...	1616	1856	|	...	...	2127	|	2245	...	...	0203	...	0348	0414	0528n	0556
557	Lugoj **1600** d.	0906	1104	|	|	...	...	...	...	|	...	2031	...	...	|	2149	...	...	...	|	...	|	|	|	...
616	**Timişoara** Nord **1600 1625** a.	1012	1215	|	|	...	...	...	...	|	...	2142	...	...	2224	2255	...	...	...	|	...	0446	|	0632	...
	Budapest Keleti **1280** a.	...	...	1417	1417	...	...	...	...	1917	...	...	...	...	...	...	...	...	...	0517	...	...	0717	...	...

		RM 826	RM 830 R	2	347 D	2	RM 802 ⊗	RM 813	1971 G		1629	IC 526 V	375 P	RM 828	2	K	1767 N	RM 817	355 T	355 626 B	1839 J	1822 C	EN 371 Y	1826 L	1943 S
Budapest Keleti **1280** d.	...	...	...	...	2325	...	...	...	...	...	...	...	0745	...	...	...	...	...	1245	1245	...	...	1745	...	...
Timişoara Nord **1600 1625** d.	...	...	...	...	|	...	...	0519	0615	...	0820	...	|	...	...	1345	1510	1555	|	|	1803	...	|	...	2310
Lugoj **1600** d.	...	...	...	...	|	...	...	0628	|	...	0946	...	|	...	...	|	|	1703	|	|	1916	...	|	...	|
Arad 1625 d.	...	...	...	...	0427	...	...	|	0715	...	|	1220	1322	...	...	1502	1557n	|	1826	1826	|	1956	2249	...	0015
Radna d.	...	...	...	...	|	...	...	|	0743	...	|	|	|	...	...	1530	1631	|	|	|	|	2023	|	...	0043
Ilia d.	...	...	...	0527	|	...	...	|	0857	...	1125	|	|	...	...	1650	1746	|	|	|	2129	2137	|	...	0158
Deva **1605** d.	...	...	0539	0557	0618	...	...	0826	0918	...	1147	1412	1514	...	...	1710	1806	1848	2018	2018	2152	2157	|	0115	0219
Simeria **1605** d.	...	...	0551	0612	0638	...	...	0841	0929	...	1158	1422	1535	...	...	1720	1819	1858	2030	2030	2221	2208	|	0128	0236
Vinţu de Jos **1635** a.	...	...	0631	...	|	...	...	0918	1011	...	1241	1459	|	...	...	▬	1902	1943	2108	2108	2304	|	|	0211	0319
Alba Iulia 1630 1635 d.	...	...	0653	...	0724	...	...	|	1022	...	|	1510	1620	...	...	...	1913	|	2128	|	2316	|	0132	0222	0330
Cluj Napoca **1635** a.	...	...	0853	...	|	...	...	|	...	...	|	|	|	...	...	...	2112	|	...	|	0120	|	|	0423	0534
Vinţu de Jos **1635** d.	...	...	...	...	|	0704	...	0919	...	...	1242	|	|	...	1635	...	...	1944	...	2138	...	|	|	...	...
Sebeş Alba **1635** d.	...	...	...	...	|	0716	...	0928	...	...	1254	|	|	...	1648	...	...	1953	...	2150	...	|	|	...	...
Sibiu 1635 a.	...	...	...	...	|	0908	...	1047	...	...	1422	|	|	...	1854	...	...	2112	...	2315	...	|	|	...	...
Sibiu 1602 1635 d.	0337	0625	...	...	|	...	1020	...	...	1215	1431	|	|	1740	...	1915	...	...	...	2332	...	|	|	...	...
Podu Olt **1602** d.	0404	|	...	...	|	...	1057	...	...	1251	|	|	|	|	...	1953	...	...	...	|	...	▽	|	...	...
Făgăraş d.	0554	0744	...	...	|	...	1152	...	...	1421	1554	|	|	1910	...	2129	...	...	...	0100	...	|	|	...	...
Sighişoara **1630** d.	|	|	...	...	0918	...	|	...	...	|	|	1734	1814	|	...	|	...	...	...	|	...	|	0346	...	...
Braşov 1630 a.	0729	0852	...	...	1114	...	1257	...	...	1554	1703	1923	2003	2034	...	2259	...	...	...	0210	...	|	0535	...	...
Braşov 1630 d.	...	0904	...	...	1125	...	...	...	...	...	1715	1935	2015	...	...	...	...	...	...	0226	...	|	0547	...	...
Predeal **1630** d.	...	0947	...	...	1157	...	...	...	...	...	1748	2014	2054	...	...	...	...	...	...	0259	...	|	0628	...	...
Sinaia **1630** d.	...	1016	...	...	1225	...	...	...	...	...	1821	2052	2123	...	...	...	...	...	...	0328	...	|	0656	...	...
Ploieşti Vest **1630** d.	...	1123	...	...	1324	...	...	...	...	...	1946	2150	2235	...	...	...	...	...	...	0432	...	|	0802	...	...
Bucureşti Nord **1630** a.	...	1212	...	...	1402	...	...	...	...	...	2025	2232	2316	...	...	...	...	...	...	0515	...	0615	0843	...	...

A – MUREŞ – [12] Bucureşti (**625**) - Vinţu de Joş (**354**) - Arad; 1, 2 cl. (also [2] on ①②④⑤⑦) Bucureşti - Budapest (**240**) - Venezia.
B – MUREŞ – [12] Arad (**355**) - Vinţu de Joş (**626**) - Bucureşti; 1, 2 cl. (also [2] on ②③④⑥⑦) Venezia (**240**) - Budapest - Bucureşti.
C – 1, 2 cl., 2 cl. and [12] Bucureşti - Arad and v.v.
D – DACIA – [12] and ✕ Bucureşti - Curtici and v.v.; [2] Bucureşti - Budapest and v.v.; 1, 2 cl., 2 cl. and [2] Bucureşti - Budapest - Wien and v.v.
G – [12] Galaţi - Timişoara and v.v.
J – 2 cl. and [12] Iaşi - Timişoara and v.v.
K – [12] Timişoara - Arad - Târgu Jiu.
L – [12] Cluj - Târgu Jiu - Bucureşti and v.v. (Table **1605**).
N – [12] Iaşi - Timişoara and v.v.
P – PANNONIA – [12] and ✕ Bucureşti - Budapest and v.v.; [2] Bucureşti - Praha and v.v. (also 1, 2 cl. on dates in Table **60**).
R – [12] Cluj - Deva - Petrosani and v.v. (Table **1605**).
S – [12] Sighetu - Timişoara and v.v.
T – [12] Târgu Mures - Lökosháza (**734/5**) - Budapest and v.v.
V – AUREL VLAICU – [12] and ✕ Bucureşti (*IC* **531/2**) - Teius (*IÇ* **525/6**) - Arad and v.v.
Y – ISTER – 1, 2 cl., 2 cl., [2] and ✕ Bucureşti - Budapest and v.v.; 1, 2 cl. Sofiya - Bucureşti - Budapest and v.v. Supplement payable.
n – Aradu Nou.
▽ – Via Craiova (Table **1600**).

TIMIŞOARA - ARAD - ORADEA 1625

km		IC 78 C	233 2	1835 J			1743 B	74 T	IC 235 2		1943 A
0	**Timişoara** Nord **1620** ▲ d.	0530	0600	0654	...	1249	1614	1600	1735	1752	2310
33	Vinga d.	|	|	|	...	1327	|	|	|	1829	|
57	**Arad 1620** ▲ a.	0616	0646	0742	...	1354	1702	1646	1821	1856	2357
57	**Arad** d.	...	0651	0756	0730	1356	1704	...	1824	1900	0015
139	Salonta d.	...	0809	0929	1005	1543	1832	...	1942	2052	|
178	**Oradea** a.	...	0834	0958	1047	1626	1857	...	2008	2129	|
	Cluj Napoca **1630** a.	...	1059	1237	...	...	...	...	2234	...	0534

	1944 A	1744 B	2		IC 234 2	75 T		1836 J	79 C	IC 236 2
Cluj Napoca **1630** d.	2220	...	...	...	0620	...	...	1458	...	1720
Oradea d.	|	0436	0457	0729	0843	...	1550	1741	...	1953
Salonta d.	|	0503	0534	0810	0909	...	1636	1811	...	2026
Arad a.	0348	0622	0739	0955	1024	...	1831	1943	...	2140
Arad 1620 ▲ d.	0359	0624	0749	...	1027	1448	1903	1953	2048	2147
Vinga d.	|	|	0816	...	|	|	1930	|	|	|
Timişoara Nord **1620** ▲ a.	0446	0735	0856	...	1113	1534	2010	2040	2134	2233

km		2	2	2
0	Békéscsaba **1280** d.	0644	1344	1644
16	Gyula **1280** d.	0702	1402	1702
36	Kötegyán HU a.	0727	1427	1727
50	Salonta RO a.	0903	1607	1907
89	Oradea a.	...	...	...

	2	2	2
Oradea d.	...	...	...
Salonta RO d.	0950	1650	2055
Kötegyán HU d.	0931	1631	2031
Gyula **1280** d.	1001	1701	2101
Békéscsaba **1280** a.	1017	1717	2117

▲ – Additional trains:
Timişoara Nord - **Arad**: 0551, 0748, 1345, 1603 Ⓑ, 1950, 2341.
Arad - **Timişoara** Nord: 0448, 0558, 1300, 1426, 1618, 1743 Ⓑ, 2137, 2337.

HU – Hungary (Central European Time).
RO – Romania (East European Time).

A – [12] Timişoara - Sighetu and v.v. Via Alba Iulia (Tables **1620** and **1635**).
B – [12] Timişoara - Baia Mare and v.v.
C – CRIŞ – [12] and ✕ Timişoara - Budapest and v.v.
J – [12] Timişoara - Iaşi and v.v.
T – TRAIANUS – [12] and ✕ Timişoara - Budapest - Wien and v.v. See Table **1280**.

DEBRECEN and ORADEA - SATU MARE - BAIA MARE 1627

km			1741 B		2		2		369 K	1743 T	
	Budapest Keleti **1270** d.	...	...	...	...	...	...	...	1215	...	...
0	**Debrecen** d.	...	...	...	0712	...	1359	...	1530	...	...
30	Nyirábrány HU a.	...	...	...	0751	...	1444	...	1605	...	...
**	**Oradea** d.	0326	0703	0745	|	...	|	1538	|	1903	1955
39	Valea lui Mihai RO d.	0455	0806	0902	0925	1216	1620	1655	1805	2000	2112
70	Carei **1630** d.	0531	0834	...	...	1253	...	1737	1832	2026	2148
106	**Satu Mare 1630** ▲ a.	0612	0903	...	...	1335	...	1818	1901	2054	2229
165	Baia Mare **1630** ▲ a.	...	...	...	...	...	...	...	2120	2253	...

	1744 T		368 L		2			1742 B	2	
Baia Mare **1630** ▲ d.	0125	...	0349	...	...	...	...	...	...	...
Satu Mare 1630 ▲ d.	0243	0340	0526	0745	...	1440	1535	1705	...	1939
Carei **1630** d.	0313	0419	0612	0838	...	1518	1617	1735	...	2028
Valea lui Mihai RO d.	0336	0452	0658	0930	1135	...	1700	1802	1833	2116
Oradea a.	0433	0615	|	1055	|	...	1821	1902	|	2237
Nyirábrány HU d.	...	...	0633	...	1116	...	...	...	1809	...
Debrecen a.	...	...	0705	...	1201	...	...	...	1848	...
Budapest Keleti **1270** a.	...	...	1017	...	...	...	...	...	...	...

▲ – Other local trains **Satu Mare - Baia Mare** at 0350, 0801, 1118 ⚒, 1615, 1933; **Baia Mare - Satu Mare** at 0414, 0725, 1224 ⚒, 1550, 1938. Journey time: ±1 h. 45 m.

B – 1, 2 cl., 2 cl. and [12] Bucureşti - Satu Mare and v.v.
K – SOMEŞ – [12] Budapest (**684**) - Debrecen (**369**) - Satu Mare - Baia Mare.
L – SOMEŞ – [12] Baia Mare (**368**) - Satu Mare - Debrecen (**689**) - Budapest.
T – [12] Timişoara - Baia Mare and v.v.
** – Oradea - Valea lui Mihai: *66 km.*
HU – Hungary (Central European Time).
RO – Romania (East European Time).

1630 BUCUREŞTI - BRAŞOV - SIGHIŞOARA - CLUJ - ORADEA and SATU MARE

km								IC	RM		IC							370					RM	IC	
		633	374	1935	1833	1745	831	237	848	1937	531		406	735	346	1643	370	741	1741	635	1641	364	844	231	631
			P		J			T			✕		C		D	H	Y	M	V	W	V	Z		T	F
0	**Bucureşti** Nord **1620**...d.	...	0630	...	...	0730	0830	...	...	...	1300	...	...	1620	1645	1730	1850	1850	1930	2035	2130	...	...	...	2324
59	Ploieşti Vest **1620**........d.	...	0713	...	...	0811	0918	...	...	...	1342	...	...	1705	1727	1814	1930	1930	2019	2118	2215	...	...	...	0008
121	Sinaia **1620**.................d.	...	0815	...	...	0915	1015	...	...	...	1438	...	...	...	1822	1914	2026	2026	2133	2224	2319	...	...	...	0107
140	Predeal **1620**..............d.	...	0851	...	...	0948	1053	...	...	...	1508	...	...	...	1852	1948	2056	2056	2205	2259	2348	...	...	...	0138
166	**Braşov 1620**...............a.	...	0922	...	...	1019	1124	...	...	...	1539	...	...	...	1922	2019	2127	2127	2236	2329	0019	...	...	...	0209
166	**Braşov 1620**...............d.	0430	0937	...	...	1032	▬	...	...	...	1550	...	1912	...	1930	▬	2135	2135	2246	...	0032	...	...	...	0217
294	Sighişoara **1620**..........d.	0619	1129	...	...	1236	...	...	...	...	1741	...	|	...	2120	...	2326	2326	0039	...	|	...	...	...	0408
333	Mediaş.........................d.	0649	1200	...	...	1311	...	...	...	...	1811	...	|	...	2151	...	|	|	0113	...	|	...	...	...	0439
344	Copşa Mică.............¶ d.	0702	|	...	...	1325	...	...	...	...	|	...	|	...	|	...	|	|	0126	...	|	...	...	...	|
374	Blaj..............................d.	0728	1240	...	...	1352	...	...	...	...	1851	...	|	...	2230	...	|	|	0153	...	|	...	...	...	0518
407	**Alba Iulia 1620**.........a.	|	1316	...	...	|	...	...	...	...	|	...	|	...	2303	...	0126v	|	|	...	|	...	...	...	|
395	Teiuş **1635**.................d.	0749	...	...	...	1413	...	...	...	...	1920	...	◐	...	...	...	0045	0055	0215	...	◐	...	...	...	0539
408	Aiud **1635**...................d.	0800	...	...	...	1424	...	...	...	...	1932	...	|	...	...	...	...	|	0226	...	|	...	...	...	0550
429	Războieni **1635**....... ▼ d.	0821	...	...	...	1445	...	...	...	...	1953	...	|	...	...	...	...	|	0247	...	|	...	...	...	|
	Târgu Mureş .... ▼ a.	|	...	...	...	|	...	...	...	...	|	...	|	...	...	...	...	|	|	...	|	...	...	...	|
446	Câmpia Turzii **1635**......d.	0837	...	...	...	1502	...	...	...	...	2009	...	|	...	...	...	...	|	0304	...	|	...	...	...	0625
497	**Cluj Napoca 1635**.......a.	0929	...	...	...	1554	...	...	...	...	2101	...	0210	...	...	...	...	|	0356	...	|	...	...	...	0719
497	**Cluj Napoca**...............d.	...	...	1400	1458	1610	...	1720	1830	1936	2118	...	0222	...	...	...	...	|	0414	...	|	0548	0607	0620	0736
547	Huedin ....d.	...	...	1453	1555	|	...	1810	|	2029	2211	...	|	...	...	...	...	|	0511	...	|	0639	|	0711	0828
650	**Oradea** ....a.	...	...	1631	1737	|	...	1948	|	2221	2346	...	0447	...	...	...	...	|	0658	...	|	0819	|	0839	1014
	Budapest Nyu. **1275**...a.	...	...	...	...	|	...	...	|	...	...	...	0817	...	...	...	...	|	|	...	|	1147	|	...	...
556	Dej Călători....................d.	...	...	...	...	1728	...	...	1927	...	...	...	...	...	...	...	...	0303	|	...	0716	...	0656	...	...
632	Jibou **1627**...................d.	...	...	...	...	1906	1901	...	2050	...	...	...	...	...	...	0330	...	0415	⊡	...	0849	...	0826	...	...
655	Zalău Nord **1627**........d.	...	...	...	...	|	1930	...	|	...	...	...	...	...	...	0410	...	|	|	...	|	...	|	...	...
743	Carei **1627**...................a.	...	...	...	...	|	2117	...	|	...	...	...	...	...	...	0556	...	|	0832	...	|	...	|	...	...
690	**Baia Mare 1627**...........a.	...	...	...	...	2011	|	...	2135	...	...	...	...	...	...	|	...	0504	|	...	0953	...	0924	...	...
749	**Satu Mare 1627**..........a.	...	...	...	...	2222	2202	...	2255	...	...	...	...	...	...	0700	...	0635	0903	...	...	...	1040	...	...

							IC	RM		IC								RM	IC						
	736	347	1936	832		1747	232	847	1834	532	375	634			1642	365	1742	843	238	632	636	743	371	407	
		D					T		J	✕	P				V	Z	V		T	F	W	M	Y	C	
Satu Mare 1627..........d.	...	...	...	...	0318	0507	...	0735	...	...	...	...	...	1440	...	...	1705	1756	...	...	...	2023	...	...	...
Baia Mare 1627...........d.	...	...	...	...	|	0645	...	0853	...	...	...	...	...	|	1700	...	|	1914	...	...	...	2144	...	...	...
Carei **1627**...................d.	...	...	...	...	0405	|	...	|	...	...	...	...	...	1533	|	...	1735	|	...	...	...	|	...	...	...
Zalău Nord **1627**........d.	...	...	...	...	0618	|	...	|	...	...	...	...	...	1720	|	...	|	|	...	...	...	|	...	...	...
Jibou **1627**...................d.	...	...	...	...	0657	0740	...	0954	...	...	...	...	...	1802	1811	...	⊡	2003	...	...	...	2235	...	...	...
Dej Călători....................d.	...	...	...	...	...	0904	...	1102	...	...	...	...	...	...	1937	...	|	2113	...	...	...	2353	...	...	...
Budapest Nyu. **1275**...d.	...	...	...	...	...	|	...	|	...	...	...	...	...	...	|	1315	|	|	...	...	...	|	...	1715	...
Oradea ....d.	...	...	0604	...	...	|	0840	|	1002	1105	...	...	1536	...	|	1850	1907	|	2014	2042	...	|	...	2245	...
Huedin ....d.	...	...	0756	...	...	|	1011	|	1143	1245	...	...	1826	...	|	2037	2053	|	2146	2222	...	|	...	|	...
Cluj Napoca...............a.	...	...	0848	...	...	0954	1059	1150	1237	1336	...	...	1942	...	|	2128	2147	2201	2234	2312	...	|	...	0117	...
Cluj Napoca 1635.......d.	...	...	...	...	...	1006	...	...	...	1348	...	1712	...	...	|	...	2203	▬	...	2327	...	|	...	0129	...
Câmpia Turzii **1635**......d.	...	...	...	...	...	1103	...	...	...	1446	...	1810	...	...	|	...	2300	...	...	0024	...	|	...	|	...
Târgu Mureş........ ▲ d.	...	...	...	...	...	|	...	...	...	|	...	|	...	...	|	...	|	...	...	|	...	|	...	|	...
Războieni **1635**....... ▲ d.	...	...	...	...	...	1122	...	...	...	1503	...	1828	...	...	|	...	2317	...	...	|	...	|	...	|	...
Aiud **1635**...................d.	...	...	...	...	...	1140	...	...	...	|	...	1846	...	...	|	...	2335	...	...	0057	...	|	...	|	...
Teiuş **1635**..................d.	...	...	...	...	...	1158	...	...	...	1551	...	1910	...	...	◐	...	2353	...	...	0115	...	0212	0212	◐	...
Alba Iulia 1620.........d.	...	0724	...	...	...	|	...	...	...	|	1620	|	...	...	|	...	|	...	...	|	...	|	0132v	|	...
Blaj..............................d.	...	0802	...	...	...	1223	...	...	...	1616	1657	1935	...	...	|	...	0017	...	...	0139	...	|	|	|	...
Copşa Mică ....¶ d.	...	|	...	...	...	1252	...	...	...	|	|	2002	...	...	|	...	0045	...	...	|	...	|	|	|	...
Mediaş............................d.	...	0837	...	...	...	1308	...	...	...	1653	1733	2014	...	...	|	...	0058	...	...	0215	...	|	|	|	...
Sighişoara **1620**..........d.	...	0918	...	...	...	1351	...	...	...	1734	1814	2055	...	...	|	...	0141	**1644**	...	0256	...	0346	0346	|	...
Braşov 1620...............a.	...	1114	...	...	...	1545	...	...	...	1923	2003	2245	...	...	0241	...	0332	**H**	...	0445	...	0535	0535	0822	...
Braşov 1620...............d.	...	1125	...	1405	...	1600	...	...	...	1935	2015	...	...	...	0253	...	0344	0415	...	0457	0515	0547	0547	...	...
Predeal **1620**..............d.	...	1157	...	1437	...	1632	...	...	...	2014	2054	...	...	...	0331	...	0423	0454	...	0536	0548	0628	0628	...	...
Sinaia **1620**.................d.	...	1225	...	1514	...	1705	...	...	...	2052	2123	...	...	...	0359	...	0453	0532	...	0604	0628	0656	0656	...	...
Ploieşti Vest **1620**........d.	1247	1324	...	1613	...	1810	...	...	...	2150	2235	...	...	...	0500	...	0601	0635	...	0714	0729	0802	0802	...	...
Bucureşti Nord **1620**...a.	1332	1402	...	1652	...	1853	...	...	...	2232	2316	...	...	...	0542	...	0644	0719	...	0801	0835	0843	0843	...	...

km	▼					1974					355
			2			G		2Ⓐ	2		E
0	Războieni ....d.	0348	0446	0725	...	1128	1146	1510	1715	2006	2230
19	Luduş ....d.	0415	0526	0754	...	1148	1213	1539	1740	2053	2251
59	**Târgu Mureş**............a.	0520	0638	0909	...	1230	1316	1654	1842	2152	2330

▲		354					1973			
		E	⊗		2Ⓐ	2	G		2	
Târgu Mureş ....d.	0345	0523	0734	...	1243	1430	1602	1620	1915	2213
Luduş.........................d.	0454	0604	0838	...	1355	1541	1644	1742	2019	2330
Războieni ....a.	0521	0624	0904	...	1422	1608	1704	1810	2046	2357

¶ – **COPŞA MICĂ - SIBIU** and v.v. ❖ : **From Copşa Mică**: 0450, 0757, 1300, 1622, 1812, 2140. **From Sibiu**: 0501, 0725, 1303, 1551, 1930, 2335. Journey time: ± 75 minutes.

C – CORONA – [sleeper] 1,2 cl., [couchette] 1,2 cl. and [12] Budapest - Cluj Napoca - Deda - Braşov and v.v.; [couchette] 2 cl. and [2] Budapest - Deda - Târgu Mureş and v.v.
D – DACIA – [12] and ✕ Bucureşti - Curtici and v.v.; [2] Bucureşti - Budapest and v.v.; [sleeper] 1,2 cl., [couchette] 2 cl. and [2] Bucureşti - Budapest - Wien and v.v.
E – MUREŞ – [12] Târgu Mureş - Arad - Budapest and v.v. See Table **1620**.
F – TRANSILVANIA – [sleeper] 1,2 cl., [couchette] 2 cl. and [12] Bucureşti - Oradea and v.v.
G – [12] Timişoara - Galaţi and v.v.
H – [sleeper] 1,2 cl., [couchette] 2 cl. and [12] Bucureşti - Sighetu M. and v.v.
J – [12] Iaşi - Timişoara and v.v.
M – MARAMUREŞ – [sleeper] 1,2 cl. and [couchette] 2 cl. Bucureşti -Satu Mare and v.v..
P – PANNONIA – [12] and ✕ Bucureşti - Budapest and v.v.; [2] Bucureşti - Budapest - Praha and v.v. (also [sleeper] 1,2 cl. on dates in Table **60**).

T – [2] Cluj - Oradea - Timişoara (Table **1625**).
V – Conveys [sleeper] 1,2 cl., [couchette] 2 cl. and [12]
W – [12] Constanţa - Bucureşti - Braşov and v.v.
Y – ISTER – [sleeper] 1,2 cl., [couchette] 2 cl., [2] and ✕ Bucureşti - Budapest and v.v.; [sleeper] 1,2 cl. Sofiya - Bucureşti - Budapest and v.v. Supplement payable.
Z – ADY ENDRE – [12] amd ✕ Cluj - Budapest and v.v.

v – Via Teiuş.

◐ – Via Miercurea Ciuc (Table **1640**).
⊡ – Via Valea lui Vihai (Table **1627**).
❖ – Timings subject to confirmation.

1635 SIBIU - ALBA IULIA - CLUJ

km				RM						
		1826	1942	811		1974			1766	1838
		B	S	830 *		G				C
0	**Sibiu 1620** ....d.	...	...	0500	...	...	...	1602	...	...
74	Sebeş Alba **1620** ....d.	...	...	0620	...	...	...	1759	...	...
	Timişoara N. **1620**...........d.	...	2310	|	...	0615	...	|	1510	1803
82	Vinţu de Jos **1620**.............d.	0212	0320	0644	...	1012	1548	1828	1903	2306
92	**Alba Iulia 1620** ....d.	0222	0330	0653	...	1022	1558	1837	1913	2316
111	Teiuş **1630** ....d.	0243	0351	0714	0850	1043	1628	1907	1933	2337
124	Aiud **1630**...........................d.	0254	0402	0725	0903	1054	1642	1920	1944	2349
145	Războieni **1630**....................d.	0315	0424	0744	0935	1128	1708	2006	2004	0011
	Târgu Mureş **1630**.............a.	|	|	|	|	1230	|	2152	|	|
162	Câmpia Turzii **1630**.............d.	0331	0442	0801	0955	...	1727	...	2020	0028
213	**Cluj Napoca 1630**..............a.	0423	0534	0853	1112	...	1842	...	2112	0120
	Iaşi **1650**..........................a.	...	...	...	...	...	...	...	0607	1008

				RM				
		1830	1824		838	1972		1944	1768
		C	B		834 *	G		S	
Iaşi **1650** ....d.	...	2021	...	...	...	...	...	...	1500
Cluj Napoca 1630 ....d.	...	0509	0919	1206	1600	...	1948	2220	2354
Câmpia Turzii **1630**.............d.	...	0607	1016	1318	1656	...	2101	2317	0052
Târgu Mureş **1630** ....d.	0345	|	|	|	|	1602	|	|	|
Războieni **1630**....................d.	0522	0626	1033	1339	1713	1719	2122	2335	0110
Aiud **1630** ....d.	0547	0644	1055	1401	1729	1737	2145	2353	0128
Teiuş **1630**...........................d.	0605	0702	1113	1420	1745	1755	2200	0011	0146
Alba Iulia 1620..................d.	0636	0723	1133	1448	1805	1815	...	0031	0206
Vinţu de Jos **1620**..............d.	0704	0735	1143	1458	1823	1827	...	0042	0217
Timişoara N. **1620** ....a.	|	1215	...	...	|	2224	...	0446	0632
Sebeş Alba **1620** ....d.	0716	...	...	...	1833	...	...	...	...
Sibiu 1620..........................a.	0908	...	...	...	1952	...	...	...	...

B – [12] and ✕ Bucureşti - Târgu Jiu - Cluj and v.v. (Table **1605**).
C – [couchette] 2 cl. and [12] Timişoara - Iaşi and v.v.
G – [12] Timişoara - Târgu Mureş - Galaţi and v.v.

S – [12] Timişoara - Cluj - Sighetu Marmaţiei and v.v.
* – Train number from Vinţu.

BRAŞOV - DEDA - DEJ - CLUJ 1640

km		1641		1973			641		406	406	1643	
		Y	⊗	T					C	D	S	
	Bucureşti **1630** d.	2130	...	...	...	...	...	...	...	...	1730	...
0	**Braşov 1645** d.	0032	0403	...	1108	...	1552	1602	1912	...	2033	...
32	Sfântu Gheorghe **1645** d.	0108	0445	...	1151	...	1624	1644	1945	...	2108	...
	Galaţi **1645** d.	|	|	0540	|	...	|	|	|	...	|	...
95	**Miercurea Ciuc 1645** d.	0217	0623	1149	1317	1542	1732	1825	2051	...	2218	...
103	Siculeni **1645** d.	0228	0638	1159	1330	1552	1743	1837	2103	...	2229	...
150	Gheorghieni d.	0319	0753	1250	1443	1718	1832	2006	2149	...	2320	...
184	Topliţa d.	0354	0834	1325	1529	1759	1914	2048	2223	...	2356	...
	Târgu Mureş d.	|	|	|	|	|	|	|	|	2205	|	...
228	Deda a.	0505	0946	1428	1649	1922	2014	2212	2325	2321	0109	...
228	Deda ▼ d.	0515	...	1440	1711	1934	2032	2224	2342	2342	0112	...
	Târgu Mureş ▼ a.	0632	...	1553	1825	2056	2141	2346	|	|	|	...
275	Sărăţel ▷ d.	0621	...	...	...	...	...	...	0034	0034	0202	...
300	Beclean pe Someş ▷ d.	0645	...	...	...	...	...	...	0056	0056	0221	...
324	Dej Călători ▷ d.	0716	...	...	...	...	...	...	0119	0119	...	...
	Baia Mare **1630** a.	0953	...	...	...	...	...	...	|	|	...	...
383	**Cluj Napoca** ▷ a.	...	...	...	...	...	...	...	0210	0210	...	...
	Budapest Keleti **1275** a.	...	...	...	...	...	...	...	0817	0817	...	...

		2		1974	640			1642	1644	407	407
			⑥⑦	⊗	T				Y	S	C	D
Budapest Keleti **1275** d.	...	...	...	...	...	...	...	...	...	1715	1715
Cluj Napoca ▷ d.	...	...	...	...	...	...	...	...	...	0129	0129
Baia Mare **1630** d.	...	...	...	...	...	...	...	1700	...	|	|
Dej Călători ▷ d.	...	...	...	...	...	...	...	1937	...	0221	0221
Beclean pe Someş ▷ d.	...	...	...	...	...	...	...	1958	2211	0242	0242
Sărăţel ▷ d.	...	...	...	...	...	...	...	2036	2233	0304	0304
Târgu Mureş ▲ d.	0325	0730	1037	1240	1334	1420	1533	2015	|	|	|
Deda ▲ a.	0454	0851	1154	1345	1438	1539	1709	2127	2320	0355	0355
Deda d.	0522	0910	1206	1359	1451	1611	1721	2142	2326	0406	0432
Târgu Mureş a.	|	|	|	|	|	|	|	|	|	|	0550
Topliţa d.	0645	1033	1327	1509	1600	1736	1833	2256	0029	0515	...
Gheorghieni d.	0729	1116	1419	1546	1633	1834	1916	2342	0107	0551	...
Siculeni **1645** d.	0850	...	1526	1644	1721	1945	2024	0034	0201	0637	...
Miercurea Ciuc 1645 d.	0900	...	1537	1705	1731	1956	2033	0045	0219	0648	...
Galaţi **1645** a.	...	...	|	2255	|	|	...	|	|	|	...
Sfântu Gheorghe **1645** d.	...	...	1713	...	1837	2130	...	0209	0329	0754	...
Braşov 1645 a.	...	...	1753	...	1907	2208	...	0241	0401	0822	...
Bucureşti **1630** a.	...	...	...	...	...	...	...	0542	0719	...	...

km	▼		1843				1973				641	
		2	b		⑥⑦	①–⑤	T	2			d	
0	**Deda** d.	0432	0526	0611	0958	1156	1440	1610	1711	1934	2032	2224
22	Reghin d.	0500	0548	0637	1023	1224	1510	1637	1737	1959	2057	2256
54	**Târgu Mureş** a.	0550	0632	0727	1122	1322	1553	1727	1825	2056	2141	2346

▲			1974	640					1844	
	2	⊗	T	d				2	b	
Târgu Mureş d.	0325	0730	1037	1240	1334	1420	1533	...	1905	2015	2205
Reghin d.	0414	0820	1125	1322	1414	1508	1639	...	2001	2059	2254
Deda a.	0454	0851	1154	1345	1438	1539	1709	...	2030	2123	2321

C – CORONA – 1, 2 cl., 1, 2 cl. and (12) Braşov - Cluj Napoca - Budapest and v.v.
D – 2 cl. and (2) Târgu Mureş - Budapest and v.v.
S – 1, 2 cl., 2 cl. and (12) Bucureşti - Sighetu and v.v.
T – (12) Galaţi - Târgu Mureş - Timişoara and v.v.
Y – 1, 2 cl., 2 cl. and (12) Bucureşti - Baia Mare and v.v. Conveys (12) Bucureşti - Deda - Târgu Mureş and v.v., (12) Bucureşti - Sărăţel - Bistriţa and v.v.
b – From / to Bucureşti (see note **N**).
d – From / to Braşov (see table above).
▷ – See also Tables **1630 / 50 / 55**.

BRAŞOV- CICEU - ADJUD - GALAŢI 1645

km		*IC* 550							1974		1751
		B							G		b
0	**Braşov 1640** d.	...	...	0403	...	...	...	...	...	...	2323
32	Sfântu Gheorghe **1640** d.	...	...	0445	...	...	...	...	...	...	0006
	Târgu Mureş **1640** d.	...	...	|	...	...	...	...	1240	...	|
	Siculeni d.	...	...	|	...	...	...	...	1644	...	|
95	**Miercurea Ciuc 1640** d.	...	...	0623	0715	...	...	...	1705	1929	0113
103	Siculeni **1640** d.	...	0431	0632	0731	...	...	...	|	1944	0124
144	Ghimeş d.	...	0551	...	0841	...	...	1637	1812	2052	0221
179	Comăneşti d.	0319	0640	...	0943	1258	...	1733	1848	2138	0257
216	Oneşti d.	0408	0742	...	▬	1355	...	1834	1935	2329	0344
254	**Adjud 1670** d.	0448	0839	...	...	1452	...	1938	2021	0032	0439
	Suceava Nord **1670** a.	...	|	...	Ⓑ	|	...	|	|	|	0736
279	Mărăşeşti **1670** d.	...	0911	...	1049	1526	1550	2012	2050	0112	...
298	Tecuci **1670** a.	...	...	...	1119	...	1620	...	2123	...	...
383	**Galaţi 1670** a.	...	...	...	1336	...	1840	...	2255	...	...

	1972			1753				*IC* 559		
	G			b				B	Ⓐ	
Galaţi 1670 d.	0540	0750	...	...	...	...	...	...	1526	...
Tecuci **1670** d.	0727	1014	...	...	...	...	...	...	1749	...
Mărăşeşti **1670** d.	0754	1041	1234	...	1410	...	1705	...	1815	1909
Suceava Nord **1670** d.	|	...	|	1110	|	...	|	...	...	|
Adjud 1670 d.	0829	...	1310	1424	1506	...	1755	1855	...	1945
Oneşti d.	0904	...	1400	1500	1556	...	1845	1936	...	2035
Comăneşti d.	0952	...	1516	1548	1654	...	1948	2024	...	2140
Ghimeş d.	1030	...	1604	1626	1742	...	2054	...	...	2228
Siculeni **1640** d.	1128	...	...	1742	1859	1945	2201	...	...	...
Miercurea Ciuc 1640 d.	1149	...	...	1755	1908	1956	...	...	...	...
Siculeni a.	1158	...	...	|	...	|	...	...	...	...
Târgu Mureş **1640** a.	1553	...	...	|	...	|	...	...	...	...
Sfântu Gheorghe **1640** d.	...	...	...	1907	...	2130	...	...	...	...
Braşov 1640 a.	...	...	...	1948	...	2208	...	...	...	...

B – (12) Comăneşti - Bucureşti and v.v.
G – (12) Timişoara - Galaţi and v.v.
b – Also conveys (12) Braşov - Adjud - Iaşi and v.v. (a. 0824 / d. 1014).

IAŞI - SUCEAVA - DEJ - CLUJ 1650

km		1653		1833	857	1931	1944	1644	1765	1837
		B				G		A		J
0	**Iaşi** d.	...	...	0612	0748	1055	...	...	1500	2021
76	Paşcani **1670** d.	0250	...	0724	0853	1206	...	...	1611	2134
122	Vereşti **1670** d.	0324	...	0757	|	1239	...	...	1644	2206
137	**Suceava 1670** d.	0349	...	0825	0937	1301	...	...	1657	2230
140	Suceava Nord **1670** a.	|	...	|	|	|	...		1707	|
140	Suceava Nord d.	|	...	|	|	|	...	...	1727	|
187	Gura Humorului Oraş d.	0437	...	0912	1022	1348	...	...	1814	2319
219	Câmpulung Moldovenesc d.	0523	...	0959	1104	1440	...	...	1903	0014
257	Vatra Dornei Băi d.	0625	...	1101	1158	1542	...	...	2006	0116
351	Năsăud d.	...	...	1259	...	1736	...	...	2158	0305
	Sighetu Marmaţiei d.	...	0125	|	...	|	1624	1741	|	|
	Vişeu de Jos d.	...	0325	|	...	|	1811	1930	|	|
357	Salva d.	...	0535	1308	...	1747	2030	2128	2207	0318
379	Beclean pe Someş **1640** d.	...	0559	1332	...	1812	2056	2151	2231	0343
402	Dej Călători **1640** ▲ d.	...	0738	1354	...	1834	2118	...	2253	0406
460	**Cluj Napoca 1640** ▲ a.	...	...	1444	...	1922	2208	...	2342	0455
	Oradea **1630** a.	...	...	1737	...	...	|	...	|	|
	Timişoara Nord **1620 / 35** a.	...	...	2041	...	...	0446	...	0632	1215

	1646	1838	1942	1932	858	1834	1654		1766
	A	J		G			B		
Timişoara Nord **1620 / 35** d.	...	1803	2310	...	...	0654	...	...	1510
Oradea **1630** d.	...	|	|	...	...	1002	...	...	|
Cluj Napoca 1640 ▲ d.	...	0135	0554	0910	...	1252	...	1548	2132
Dej Călători **1640** ▲ d.	...	0231	0647	1003	...	1352	...	1705	2223
Beclean pe Someş **1640** d.	0243	0255	0709	1026	...	1413	...	1728	2244
Salva d.	0332	0317	0748	1048	...	1435	...	1808	2306
Vişeu de Jos d.	0522	|	0937	|	...	|	...	2033	|
Sighetu Marmaţiei a.	0706	|	1121	|	...	|	...	2230	|
Năsăud d.	...	0325	...	1057	...	1444	...	...	2313
Vatra Dornei Băi d.	...	0518	...	1252	1609	1646	2155	...	0102
Câmpulung Moldovenesc d.	...	0623	...	1355	1704	1751	2258	...	0213
Gura Humorului Oraş d.	...	0707	...	1439	1741	1838	2345	...	0257
Suceava Nord a.	...	|	...	|	|	|	|	...	0347
Suceava Nord **1670** d.	...	|	...	|	|	|	|	...	0402
Suceava 1670 d.	...	0811	...	1537	1836	1937	0042	...	0409
Vereşti **1670** d.	...	0823	...	1549	|	1949	0054	...	0422
Paşcani **1670** d.	...	0903	...	1629	1919	2029	0131	...	0502
Iaşi a.	...	1008	...	1734	2020	2134	...	...	0607

A – 1, 2 cl., 2 cl. and (12) Sighetu - Bucureşti and v.v.
B – 1, 2 cl., 2 cl. and (12) Bucureşti - Vatra Dornei Băi and v.v.
G – (12) Galaţi - Cluj and v.v.
J – 2 cl. and (12) Iaşi - Timişoara and v.v.
▲ – See also Tables **1630** and **1655**.

BISTRIŢA - DEJ - CLUJ 1655

km											1845
			Ⓐ								A
0	**Bistriţa** Nord d.	0420	0525	0724	0729	1236	1523	1550	1922	1930	2010
11	Sărăţel ‡ d.	0437	0540	0741	0800	1250	1556	1605	1940	2000	2022
58	Deda **1640** a.	|	|	|	0907	|	1701	|	|	2108	...
36	Beclean pe Someş ‡ d.	0511	0604	0824	...	1325	...	1640	2014	...	...
60	Dej Călători ‡ d.	0550	0646	0912	...	...	...	1717	2048	...	...
119	**Cluj Napoca** ‡ a.	0709	0738	1030	...	...	...	1836	*2201*	...	...

			1846							
			B				Ⓐ			
Cluj Napoca ‡ d.	...	...	...	...	...	1200	1548	...	...	1957
Dej Călători ‡ d.	...	0508	...	...	...	1315	1649	1721	...	2120
Beclean pe Someş ‡ d.	...	0543	...	0839	...	1351	1715	1756	...	2155
Deda **1640** d.	0444	|	...	|	1238	|	|	|	1717	|
Sărăţel ‡ d.	0612	0619	0630	0907	1400	1422	1730	1829	1842	2227
Bistriţa Nord a.	0629	0637	0641	0927	1419	1441	1749	1845	1858	2245

A – (12) Bistriţa - Sărăţel (**1642**) - Bucureşti.
B – (12) Bucureşti (**1641**) - Sărăţel - Bistriţa.
‡ – See also Tables **1630 / 40 / 50**.

BUCUREŞTI - GALAŢI 1660

km			*IC* 575		871	1673		1871	*IC* 571	732	875
			2					J	2		
0	**Bucureşti** Nord **1670** d.	...	0700	...	0940	1330	...	...	1545	...	1900
	Ploieşti Sud **1670** d.	...	0744	...	|	|	...	...	|	...	1945
**	Buzău **1670** d.	0425	0850	...	|	|	1517	...	|	1940	2051
	Constanţa **1680** d.	|	|	...	|	|	|	1311	|	|	|
138	Făurei d.	0535	0948	...	1205	1556	1632	1655	1757	2037	2149
	Constanţa **1680** a.	|	|	...	|	|	2016	|	|	|	|
198	Brăila d.	0639	1027	...	1247	1640	...	1735	1837	2115	2230
229	**Galaţi** a.	0725	1100	...	1320	1716	...	1812	1910	2148	2304

	1872	*IC* 572	734	1674	876			*IC* 576	872	
	J	2						2		
Galaţi d.	0220	0515	0640	0655	0930	...	...	1340	1750	1942
Brăila d.	0256	0550	0716	0732	1006	...	...	1415	1825	2032
Constanţa **1680** d.	|	|	|	|	|	0742	...	|	|	|
Făurei d.	0415	0631	0757	0825	1048	1134	...	1455	1905	2140
Constanţa **1680** a.	0740	|	|	|	|	|	...	|	|	|
Buzău **1670** d.	...	|	0852	|	1146	1245	...	1553	|	2252
Ploieşti Sud **1670** d.	...	|	...	|	1302	...	...	1656	|	...
Bucureşti Nord **1670** a.	...	0840	...	1037	1345	...	...	1737	2116	...

J – ①⑤⑥⑦ (daily June 21 - Sept. 8).
** – Buzău - Făurei: *40 km.*

1670 BUCUREŞTI - BUZĂU - BACĂU - IAŞI and SUCEAVA

km		1751	1956	1665	1854	IC 551	1934	382		751	661	651	RM 868	1861	IC 557	1661	IC 553	IC 561		402	1653		663	753
		V		b	H	✕	U	A	2			F	⊗	S	T		✕	2		D	N	2	cd	d
0	**Bucureşti** Nord **1660** d.	...	...	...	...	0600	...	0638	...	1103	1200	1400	...	...	1500	1600	1700	1800	...	2000	2100	...	2300	2350
59	Ploieşti Sud **1660** d.	...	...	...	...	0642	...	0733	...	1147	1244	1444	...	...	1543	1646	1743	1843	...	2053	2146	...	2344	0034
128	**Buzău 1660** d.	...	...	...	0343	0746	...	0838	...	1252	1349	1549	...	...	1647	1754	1848	1947	...	2207	2258	...	0049	0139
161	Râmnicu Sărat d.	...	...	...	0413	|	...	|	...	1322	1418	|	...	...	|	1824	|	|	...	|	2327	...	|	|
199	Focşani d.	...	...	...	0451	0845	...	0941	...	1358	1452	1651	...	...	1747	1900	1948	2047	...	2310	0002	...	0151	0241
219	Mărăşeşti **1645** d.	...	...	0500	0522	|	...	|	...	1430	|	|	...	...	|	|	|	|	...	|	0032	...	|	|
244	Adjud **1645** d.	0452	...	|	0547	0934	...	|	...	1456	|	1746	...	...	1838	|	|	|	...	|	0056	...	|	0333
303	**Bacău** ◧ d.	0538	0556	|	0627	1013	...	1117	...	1536	|	1836	...	...	1917	|	2114	|	...	0046	0136	...	|	0414
346	Roman d.	0608	0625	|	0657	1043	...	|	...	1606	|	1906	...	...	...	|	2144	|	...	0120	0206	...	|	0445
	Galaţi 1645 d.	|	|	|	|	|	0600	|	...	|	|	|	1652	...	...	|	|	|	...	|	|	...	|	|
	Tecuci **1645** d.	|	|	0526n	|	|	0748	|	...	|	1550	|	1823	1840	...	1959	|	2130n	...	|	|	...	0250	|
	Bârlad d.	|	|	0614	|	|	0833	|	...	|	1634	|	1859	1931	...	2043	|	2203	...	|	|	...	0334	|
	Vaslui d.	|	|	0712	|	|	0926	|	...	|	1724	|	1947	2025	...	2138	|	2249	...	|	|	...	0427	|
	Iaşi a.	|	0800	0824	|	|	1038	|	...	|	1833	|	2045	2145	...	2249	|	2347	...	0259	|	...	0536	|
	Iaşi 1650 ‡ RO d.	|	...	...	|	|	1055	|	1300	|	...	|	...	...	...	...	|	...	...	0304	|	0447	...	|
	Ungheni **1730** 🏛 MD a.	|	...	...	|	|	|	|	1450	|	...	|	...	...	...	...	|	...	...	0524	|	0638	...	|
	Chişinău 1730 a.	|	...	...	|	|	|	|	...	|	...	|	...	...	...	...	|	...	...	0858	|	...	...	|
387	Paşcani **1650** ▼ d.	0641	...	...	0731	1120	1206	1233	...	1648	...	1941	...	...	...	...	2221	...	...	...	0250	...	...	0527
432	Vereşti **1650** ★ a.	0714	...	...	0804	|	1239	|	...	1722	...	2014	...	...	...	...	|	...	...	...	0324	...	...	0617
476	Botoşani ★ a.	|	...	...	|	|	|	|	...	1843	...	|	...	...	...	...	|	...	...	...	|	...	...	0718
448	**Suceava** a.	0725	...	...	0820	1157	1254	1317	...	1739p	...	2025	...	...	...	...	2258	...	...	...	0339	...	...	0619p
450	**Suceava** Nord **1650** § RO a.	0736	...	...	0831	1208	...	|	...	1748p	...	2036	...	...	...	...	2309	...	...	...	...	...	...	0627p
539	Chernivtsi § UA a.	...	...	...	...	...	...	1816	...	...	...	...	...	...	...	...	...	...	...	...	...	...	...	...

km		1654	IC 558		IC 562	IC 552	1662	RM 866	652		1664	1752	383	754	662	1932		IC 554	1955	1852	1862	664	752	105
		N	T		2	✕		⊗	G	2	b	V	B			U	2	✕		H	S	cd	d	E
	Chernivtsi § UA d.	...	...	...	...	...	...	...	...	...	...	...	0704	...	...	...	...	...	...	...	...	...	...	...
	Suceava Nord **1650** § RO d.	...	...	...	...	0515	...	...	0757	...	...	1110	|	1308q	...	...	...	1635	...	2139	...	...	2304q	...
	Suceava d.	0042	...	...	...	0521	...	...	0804	...	...	1117	1230	1315q	...	1537	...	1642	...	2146	...	...	2311q	...
	Botoşani ★ d.	|	...	...	...	|	...	...	|	...	...	|	|	1227	...	|	...	|	...	|	...	...	2220	...
	Vereşti **1650** ★ d.	0054	...	...	...	|	...	...	0815	...	...	1129	|	1345	...	1549	...	|	...	2200	...	...	2338	...
	Paşcani **1650** ▼ d.	0145	...	...	...	0606	...	...	0856	...	...	1209	1329	1433	...	1629	...	1741	...	2242	...	...	0025	...
0	**Chişinău 1730** d.	|	...	...	...	|	...	...	|	...	...	|	|	|	...	|	...	|	...	|	...	...	|	1710
107	Ungheni **1730** 🏛 MD d.	|	...	...	...	|	...	...	|	0755	...	|	|	|	...	|	1740	|	...	|	...	...	|	2110
128	**Iaşi 1650** ‡ RO a.	|	...	...	...	|	...	...	|	0925	...	|	|	|	...	1734	1912	|	...	|	...	...	|	2325
128	**Iaşi** d.	|	...	...	0532	|	0552	0705	|	...	1014	|	|	|	1508	1750	...	|	1811	|	2244	2320	|	2328
196	Vaslui d.	|	...	...	0629	|	0711	0804	|	...	1131	|	|	|	1621	1905	...	|	|	|	0011	0033	|	|
248	Bârlad d.	|	...	...	0710	|	0759	0846	|	...	1224	|	|	|	1705	1953	...	|	|	|	0102	0120	|	|
297	Tecuci **1645** d.	|	...	...	0742n	|	0902	0920	|	...	1303n	|	|	|	1759	2045	...	|	|	|	0145	0213	|	|
382	**Galaţi 1645** a.	|	...	...	|	|	|	1045	|	...	|	|	|	|	|	2217	...	|	|	|	...	|	|	|
	Roman d.	0215	...	...	|	0632	|	...	0924	...	|	1237	|	1503	|	...	...	1807	1950	2312	...	|	0055	0107
	Bacău ◧ d.	0250	0411	...	|	0708	|	...	1011	...	|	1316	1434	1538	|	...	...	1842	2022	2348	...	|	0130	0147
	Adjud **1645** d.	0334	0502	...	|	0750	|	...	1058	...	|	1358	|	1623	|	...	...	|	...	0032	...	|	0215	|
	Mărăşeşti **1645** d.	0359	|	...	|	|	|	...	|	...	1325	...	|	|	|	...	...	|	...	0056	...	|	0242	|
	Focşani d.	0430	0550	...	0827	0839	0954	...	1151	...	...	...	1617	1717	1846	...	...	2015	...	0126	...	0302	0313	0328
	Râmnicu Sărat d.	0505	|	...	|	|	1030	...	|	...	...	...	|	1752	1919	...	...	|	...	0200	...	|	|	|
	Buzău 1660 d.	0536	0650	...	0927	0942	1102	...	1254	...	...	...	1719	1823	1950	...	...	2124	...	0228	...	0404	0415	0438
	Ploieşti Sud **1660** d.	0643	0754	...	1028	1042	1215	...	1403	...	...	...	1821	1925	2052	...	...	2226	...	...	...	0508	0518	0541
	Bucureşti Nord **1660** a.	0727	0835	...	1109	1123	1309	...	1444	...	...	...	1913	2008	2133	...	...	2307	...	...	...	0551	0600	0632

km	◧		①–⑤				J	IC 557	1955		
0	**Bacău** d.	0415	0609	0915	1408	1659	1857	1925	2027	2230	...
60	Piatra Neamţ a.	0558	0741	1054	1540	1847	2005	2033	2133	0002	...
86	**Bicaz** a.	0643	...	...	1626	1934	...	2112	2204	...	...

◧	IC 558	1956			K	①–⑤				
Bicaz d.	0230	0417	...	0706	...	...	...	1649	2000	...
Piatra Neamţ d.	0302	0445	0510	0747	0844	1420	1613	1729	2048	...
Bacău a.	0409	0551	0649	0914	0951	1555	1741	1856	2223	...

▼ – **PAŞCANI - TÂRGU NEAMT**: From Paşcani: 0320, 0733, 1658, 2035. (Journey: ± 45 minutes) From Târgu Neamt: 0047, 0455, 0953, 1818.

★ – **VEREŞTI - BOTOŞANI**: From Vereşti: 0515 [R], 0611 [R], 0833, 1624, 1740 [R], 2131. (Journey: ± 65 minutes) From Botoşani: 0540, 1000, 1236 [R], 1514 [R], 1800, 2216 [R].

A – BULGARIA EXPRES – 🛏 1,2 cl. Sofiya (**9647**) - Ruse (**382**) - Vadul Siret (**60**) - Kyïv - Moskva; 🛏 2 cl. Sofiya - Kyïv; ✕ Sofiya - Vadul Siret. ◇
B – BULGARIA EXPRES – 🛏 1,2 cl. Moskva (**59**) - Kyïv - Vadul Siret (**383**) - Ruse (**9646**) - Sofiya; 🛏 2 cl. Kyïv - Sofiya; ✕ Vadul Siret - Sofiya. ◇.
D – PRIETENIA – 🛏 2 cl. Bucureşti - Ungheni (**106**) - Chişinău. ◇.
E – PRIETENIA – 🛏 2 cl. Chişinău - Ungheni (**401**) - Bucureşti. ◇.
F – Conveys (12) Bucureşti - Bacău (**657**) - Piatra Neamţ.
G – Conveys (12) Piatra Neamţ (**658**) - Bacău - Bucureşti.
H – (12) Constanţa - Suceava and v.v.
J – (12) Bucureşti (**651**) - Bacău (**657**) - Piatra Neamţ.
K – (12) Piatra Neamţ (**658**) - Bacău (**652**) - Bucureşti.
N – 🛏 1,2 cl., ▬ 2 cl. and (12) Bucureşti - Vatra Dornei Băi and v.v.
S – (12) Constanţa - Iaşi and v.v.

T – (12) Bucureşti - Bicaz / Comăneşti and v.v.
U – (12) Galaţi - Cluj and v.v.
V – (12) Braşov - Suceava and v.v.

b – (12) Iaşi - Brasov and v.v. (Table **1645**).
c – Also conveys ▬ 2 cl.
d – Also conveys 🛏 1,2 cl.
n – Tecuci Nord.
p – Portion detached from main train at Vereşti.
q – Portion attached to main train at Vereşti.

◇ – See also Table **98**.

‡ – 🏛 : Nicolina (RO).
§ – 🏛 : Vicşani (RO) / Vadul Siret (UA).

MD – Moldova.
RO – Romania.
UA – Ukraine.

Other train names:

551/4 MIHAI EMINESCU
552/3 STEFAN CEL MARE
651/2 ALEXANDRU CEL BUN
661/4 DIMITRIE CANTEMIR
662/3 TREI IERARHI
751/2 NICOLAE IORGA
753/4 PETRU RAREŞ

Local services to Târgu Neamt and Botoşani are subject to confirmation.

1680 BUCUREŞTI - CONSTANŢA - MANGALIA

km			1853	1862			1681	1681			687	681				689	889						683	685	
		2	S	Jz	2	2		2	2		✕	b	2	2	2	✕		2			2	G			2
0	**Bucureşti** Nord d.	...	...	...	...	...	0537r	0537r	...	...	0712	0835	...	...	...	1353	...	...	1320r	...	...	...	1812r	1842	...
	Buzău d.	...	0252	...	...	...	|	|	...	0655	|	|	...	...	...	|	...	...	|	1517	...	...	|	|	...
	Făurei d.	...	0350	0415	...	...	|	|	...	0817	|	|	...	...	...	|	...	...	|	1632	...	1907	|	|	...
146	Feteşti d.	...	0510	0545	...	...	0815	0815	...	0956	1037	1147	...	...	...	1703	...	...	1714	1812	...	2044	2103	2156	...
190	Medgidia d.	...	0604	0646	...	0811	0930	0933	...	...	|	1238	...	1604	...	1804	1812	...	1835	1918	...	...	2200	2249	2310
334	**Tulcea** Oraş a.	...	|	|	...	1118	|	1214	...	...	|	|	...	1933	...	|	2056	...	|	|	...	...	|	|	0153
225	**Constanţa** a.	...	0650	0740	...	...	1016	...	...	...	1208	1324	...	...	...	1850	...	...	1933	2016	...	...	2246	2335	...
225	**Constanţa** d.	0554	...	...	0800	...	...	...	1040	...	...	...	1418	...	1622	...	...	1910	...	...	2031	...	...	...	...
239	Eforie Nord d.	0619	...	...	0827	...	...	...	1102	...	...	...	1440	...	1644	...	...	1937	...	...	2054	...	...	...	...
268	**Mangalia** a.	0710	...	...	0919	...	...	...	1156	...	...	...	1533	...	1738	...	...	2030	...	...	2144	...	...	...	...

km			680			886	686						682	1864	684			688		1682	1982				1854
				H	2		✕		2	2		2		Jz	b		2	✕	2		2	2	2	2	S
0	**Mangalia** d.	...	...	...	0523	...	...	...	0813	...	...	1100	...	...	...	...	1426	...	1610	...	...	...	1815	2125	...
29	Eforie Nord d.	...	...	...	0622	...	...	...	0914	...	...	1150	...	...	...	...	1527	...	1701	...	...	...	1909	2223	...
43	**Constanţa** a.	...	...	...	0647	...	...	...	0941	...	...	1213	...	...	...	...	1554	...	1724	...	...	...	1936	2246	...
43	**Constanţa** d.	...	0445	...	...	...	0703	0742	...	...	1056	...	1227	1311	1432	...	...	1643	...	1812	...	...	...	...	2258
	Tulcea Oraş d.	0220	|	...	...	0500	|	|	...	0804	|	...	|	|	|	...	...	|	...	|	1600	1723	...	...	|
78	Medgidia d.	0512	0530	...	...	0745	0800	0837	...	1135	1154	...	1315	1357	1519	...	...	|	...	1922	1922	2054	...	...	2352
122	Feteşti d.	...	0625	0630	...	...	0856	0947	...	...	1308	...	1412	1453	1615	1720	...	1821	...	2018	2018	...	...	...	0052
211	Făurei d.	...	|	0838	...	...	|	1134	...	...	|	...	|	1624	|	1911	...	|	...	|	|	...	...	...	0225
251	Buzău a.	...	|	...	...	...	|	1245	...	...	|	...	|	...	|	2023	...	|	...	|	|	...	...	...	0320
268	**Bucureşti** Nord a.	...	0949	...	...	...	1223	...	...	...	1641r	...	1655r	...	1949	...	...	2144	...	2308r	2308r	...	...	...	...

G – From Galaţi (depart 1640).
H – To Galaţi (arrive 1030).
J – From / to Iaşi.

S – From / to Suceava.
b – To / from Braşov (train **635/6**, Table **1630**).
r – Bucureşti Obor.

z – On ①⑤⑥⑦ conveys (12) Galaţi - Constanţa and v.v. (Table **1660**).

Engineering work may affect these services

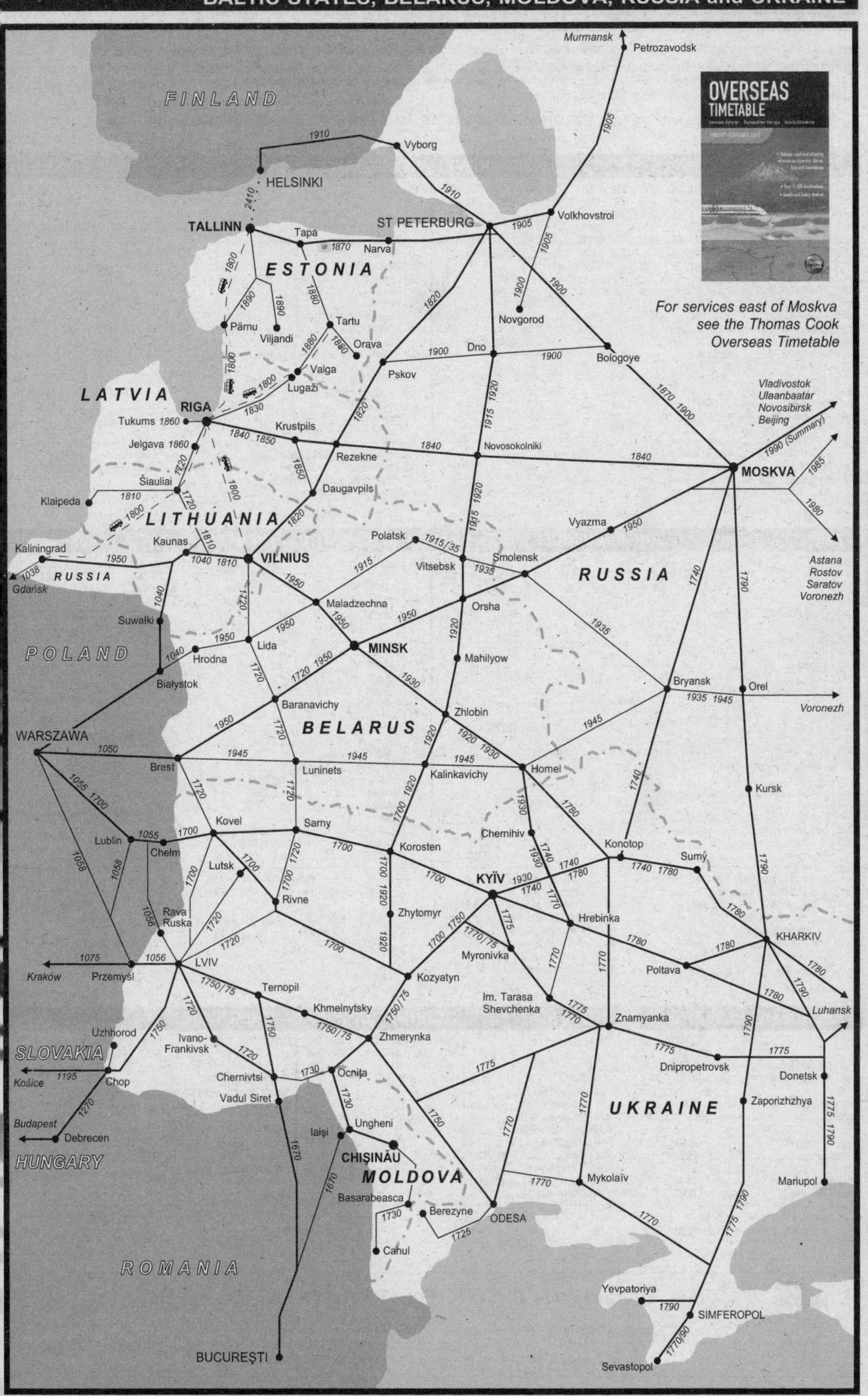

For International Time Zones see page 2

UKRAINE and MOLDOVA

SEE MAP PAGE 509

Operators: UZ: Ukrzaliznytsya (УЗ: Укрзалізниця). **CFM**: Calea Ferată din Moldova. Other operators as indicated in the table headings and notes.

Timings: Valid to **May 31, 2008**. Timings of international services to and from non-CIS countries should be verified from the international tables at the front of this book. Local time is used throughout: i.e. East European Time for Ukraine and Moldova – for other countries, see the time comparison chart on page **2**.

Tickets: Prior reservation is necessary except for travel by purely local trains.

SEE ALSO THE PANEL ***RAIL TRAVEL IN RUSSIA, BELARUS, UKRAINE, and MOLDOVA*** ON PAGE 515

1700 KYÏV - KOVEL - WARSZAWA (UZ, PKP)

km		Sko 111 H	Fir 77	Sko 29 A	Sko 55		Sko 67 K	Pas 659	Fir 43 F	Fir 363
	Moskva Kiyevskaya **1740** d.	...	1638	...	1908	...	...	...	...	...
0	**Kyïv 1750** d.	0427	0544	0800	0800	...	1241	1604	1916	2120
156	Korosten **1920** d.	0645	|	1023	1120	...	|	1900	2132	|
241	Zhytomyr **1920** a.	|	|	|	1320	...	|	|	|	|
311	Sarny **1720** d.	|	|	1254	...	...	|	2315	|	|
159	Kozyatyn **1750** d.	|	0834	|	...	...	|	|	|	2356
383	Rivne **1720** d.	|	1330	|	...	...	1853	|	|	0457
469	Lutsk **1720** d.	|	1510	|	...	...	|	|	|	0648
453	**Kovel 1720** d.	|	1708	1542	...	...	2128	0220	|	0858
652	Lviv **1720 1750** a.	1448	...	|	...	...	|	0641	0357	...
512	Yahodyn 🏛 UA d.	...	...	1833	...	...	0030	...	...	...
520	Dorohusk 🏛 PL a.	...	...	1743	...	...	0011	...	...	...
541	Chełm **1055** a.	...	...	1922	...	...	0150	...	...	...
615	Lublin **1055** a.	...	...	2014	...	...	0245	...	...	...
785	Warszawa Wschodnia **1055** a.	...	...	2231	...	...	0636	...	...	...
790	**Warszawa** Centralna **1055** a.	...	...	2321	...	...	0645	...	...	...
	Berlin Lichtenberg **1001** a.	...	...	0714	...	...	...	...	...	...

km		Sko 112 H	Fir 364	Fir 44 F	Pas 660		Sko 68 K	Fir 78	Sko 642	Sko 345 B
	Berlin Lichtenberg **1001** d.	...	...	...	...	...	...	...	...	2138
0	**Warszawa** Centralna **1055** d.	...	...	...	...	...	2135	...	...	0608
5	Warszawa Wschodnia **1055** d.	...	...	...	...	...	2147	...	...	0646
175	Lublin **1055** d.	...	...	...	...	...	0040	...	...	0920
249	Chełm **1055** d.	...	...	...	...	...	0132	...	...	1014
270	Dorohusk 🏛 PL d.	...	...	...	...	...	0247	...	...	1125
278	Yahodyn 🏛 UA d.	...	...	...	...	...	0614	...	...	1442
	Lviv **1720 1750** d.	1701	...	2125	1943	...	|	...	...	|
337	**Kovel 1720** d.	|	1723	|	0046	...	0738	0928	...	1557
421	Lutsk **1720** d.	|	1950	|	|	...	|	1146	...	|
473	Rivne **1720** d.	|	2132	|	|	...	1022	1311	...	|
705	Kozyatyn **1750** d.	|	0320	|	|	...	|	1754	...	|
	Sarny **1720** d.	|	|	|	0351	...	|	|	...	1800
	Zhytomyr **1920** d.	|	|	|	|	...	|	|	1802	|
	Korosten **1920** d.	0038	|	0355	0758	...	|	|	2044	2044
	Kyïv 1750 a.	0254	0536	0622	1034	...	1626	2007	2252	2252
	Moskva Kiyevskaya **1740** a.	...	...	...	...	...	...	1130	1434	...

A – KASHTAN – 🛏 2 cl. Kyïv - Dorohusk (**344**) - Berlin. Conveys on ②⑤ from Kharkiv (next day from Kyïv): 🛏 2 cl. Kharkiv (**343**) - Kyïv - Berlin.
B – KASHTAN – 🛏 2 cl. Berlin - Yahodyn (**30**) - Kyïv. Conveys on ④⑦: 🛏 2 cl. Berlin - Kyïv (**320**) - Kharkiv.
F – To / from Ivano-Frankivsk (Table **1720**).
H – From / to Kharkiv (Table **1780**).
K – KYÏV EKSPRES / KIEV EXPRESS – 🛏 1, 2 cl. Kyïv - Warszawa and v.v.
PL – Poland (Central European Time).
UA – Ukraine (East European Time).

1720 RIGA, VILNIUS, MINSK and BREST - LVIV - CHERNIVTSI (LDZ, LG, BCh, UZ)

km		Fir 43 K	Pas 357 AY	Pas 371 T		Sko 141 M	Pas 47 J	181 CS	Sko 76 P	Pas 604
0	**Riga** d.	...	0740	...	...	...	...	1830	...	...
43	Jelgava ◧ LV d.	...	0824	...	...	...	...	1908	...	...
136	Šiauliai ◧ LT d.	...	1009	...	...	...	...	2043	...	...
156	Radviliškis d.	...	1027	...	...	...	...	2103	...	...
348	**Vilnius** a.	...	1235	...	...	...	...	2333	...	...
348	**Vilnius** § LT d.	...	1250	...	...	...	...	2353	...	...
443	Lida § BY d.	...	1532	...	...	...	...	0256	...	...
	St Peterburg Vit. **1920** d.	...	|	...	...	...	1242	|	...	...
	Minsk d.	...	|	1547	...	...	0224	|	...	...
548	Baranavichy Polesskiye d.	...	1819	1819	...	...	0430	0450	...	...
664	Luninets **1700** ‡ BY d.	...	2019	2019	...	...	0620	0703	...	...
770	Sarny **1700** ‡ UA d.	...	2331	2331	...	...	0947	1019	...	...
857	Rivne **1700** d.	...	0114	0114	...	...	1131	...	...	...
	Brest Tsentralny ¶ BY d.	...	|	|	...	...	|	...	...	...
	Kovel ¶ UA d.	...	|	|	...	...	|	...	...	...
	Lutsk d.	...	|	|	...	...	|	...	...	...
1064	**Lviv** a.	...	0510	0510	...	...	1529	...	...	...
1064	**Lviv** d.	0417	...	...	...	1036	...	...	2246	2144
1205	Ivano-Frankivsk d.	0702	...	...	...	1334	...	...	0122	0508
1260	Kolomyya d.	...	...	...	...	1446	...	...	0232	0641
1331	**Chernivtsi** a.	...	...	...	...	1625	...	...	0350	0844

km		182 DS	Sko 76 P	Pas 372 U	Pas 372 BZ	Fir 44 K	Sko 48 H		Pas 604	Sko 142 M
0	**Chernivtsi** d.	...	0810	...	...	...	...	...	2030	2230
71	Kolomyya d.	...	0947	...	...	...	...	...	2240	2359
126	Ivano-Frankivsk d.	...	1055	...	...	1815	...	...	0040	0132
267	**Lviv** a.	...	1330	...	...	2105	...	...	0805	0412
267	**Lviv** d.	...	...	1859	1859	...	2307	...	...	...
443	Lutsk d.	...	...	|	|	...	|	...	...	...
527	Kovel ¶ UA d.	...	...	|	|	...	|	...	...	...
651	**Brest** Tsentralny ¶ BY a.	...	...	|	|	...	|	...	...	...
474	Rivne **1700** d.	...	...	2306	2306	...	0303	...	...	...
561	Sarny **1700** ‡ UA d.	2005	...	0050	0050	...	0450	...	...	...
667	Luninets **1700** ‡ BY d.	2342	...	0418	0418	...	0834	...	...	...
783	Baranavichy Polesskiye d.	0146	...	0703	0705	...	1049	...	...	...
923	**Minsk** a.	|	...	0900	|	...	1240	...	...	...
	St Peterburg Vit. **1920** a.	|	...	...	|	...	0532	...	...	...
	Lida § BY d.	0343	...	...	0910	...	...	...	...	...
	Vilnius § LT a.	0647	...	...	1156	...	...	...	...	...
	Vilnius d.	0707	...	...	1211	...	...	...	...	...
	Radviliškis d.	0927	...	...	1422	...	...	...	...	...
	Šiaullai ◧ LT d.	0946	...	...	1442	...	...	...	...	...
	Jelgava ◧ LV a.	1125	...	...	1621	...	...	...	...	...
	Riga a.	1205	...	...	1700	...	...	...	...	...

A – On the 2nd, 6th, 10th, 14th, 18th, 22nd and 26th of each month.
B – On the 3rd, 7th, 11th, 15th, 19th, 23rd and 27th of each month.
C – Uneven dates [... *31, 3* ...].
D – Uneven dates [... *31, 2, 5* ...] (next day from Sarny).
H – Even dates.
J – Even dates [... *30, 1, 4* ...].
K – From / to Kyïv.
M – From / to Moskva (Table **1750**).
P – 🛏 2 cl. and 🛏 3 cl. from / to Przemyśl.
S – To / from Simferopol.
T – Even dates.
U – Uneven dates [... *31, 3* ...].
Y – Riga - Baranavichy (**371**) - Lviv.
Z – Lviv - Baranavichy (**358**) - Riga.
BY – Belarus.
LT – Lithuania.
LV – Latvia.
UA – Ukraine.
◧ – 🏛 : Joniškis (LT) / Meitene (LV).
§ – 🏛 : Benyakoni (BY) / Stasylos (LT).
‡ – 🏛 : Horyn (BY) / Udrytsk (UA).
¶ – 🏛 : Khatsislav (BY) / Zabolottya (UA).

1725 ODESA - BEREZYNE (UZ)

km		Pas 686	
0	**Odesa** Holovna d.	1545	...
84	Bilhorod-Dnistrovsky d.	1812	...
174	Artsyz d.	2034	...
209	**Berezyne** a.	2302	...

		Pas 686	
Berezyne d.	...	2327	...
Artsyz d.	...	0239	...
Bilhorod-Dnistrovsky d.	...	0441	...
Odesa Holovna a.	...	0637	...

M – To / from Moskva (Table **1750**).
S – To / from St Peterburg (Table **1750**).

1730 CAHUL - CHIŞINĂU - CHERNIVTSI (UZ, CFM)

km		Pas 645 d	Pas 609 d	Sko 47 M		Sko 61 S	Sko 341 M
0	**Cahul** d.	1616	...	...	...	...	...
136	Basarabeasca a.	0227	...	...	...	...	...
136	Basarabeasca d.	0313	...	...	...	...	...
331	**Chişinău 1670** d.	0715	...	1140	...	1920	1957
438	Ungheni **1670** d.	...	...	|	...	2216	2251
516	Bălţi Oraş d.	...	...	1508	...	2359	0042
614	Ocniţa 🏛 MD d.	...	1425	1705	...	0252	0353
768	**Zhmerynka** ‡ UA a.	...	|	2200	...	0747	0912
729	Mamalyha 🏛 UA a.	...	1804	...	...	...	...
787	**Chernivtsi** a.	...	1942	...	...	...	...

	Pas 646 d	Sko 342 M	Pas 610 d	Sko 48 M		Sko 62 S
Chernivtsi d.	...	...	0848	...	...	...
Mamalyha 🏛 UA d.	...	...	1030	...	...	...
Zhmerynka ‡ UA d.	...	0650	|	1308	...	1911
Ocniţa 🏛 MD d.	...	1228	1400	1810	...	0047
Bălţi Oraş d.	...	1509	...	1956	...	0322
Ungheni **1670** d.	...	1729	...	|	...	0529
Chişinău 1670 d.	1905	2031	...	2308	...	0748
Basarabeasca a.	0331	...	...	...	...	...
Basarabeasca d.	0516	...	...	...	...	...
Cahul a.	1139	...	...	...	...	...

d – ④ only.
MD – Moldova.
UA – Ukraine.
‡ – 🏛 : Mohyliv-Podilski (UA).

RZhD, UZ — MOSKVA - BRYANSK - SUMY, CHERNIHIV and KYÏV — 1740

km		Sko 59 Ac	Sko 33 F	Sko 141	Sko 341	Sko 89 Z	Sko 73	Sko 41	Fir 77 K	Sko 55 LX	Sko 117	Sko 57	Sko 47	Fir 5	Fir 23	Sko 15 S	Fir 1	Fir 3	Fir 3 Ad	Sko 21
0	**Moskva** Kiyevskaya d.	0025	1048	1235	1243	1346	1552	1624	1638	1908	1801	1916	1937	2023	2120	2131	2323	2139	2139	2300
387	Bryansk Orlovski d.	0642	1705	1900	1919	1948	2204	2312	2326	0114	0025	0128	0216	0252	0323	0342	|	0357	0357	0507
504	Suzemka RU d.	|	|	|	|	2146	|	|	0125	|	0240	0332	|	|	|	|	0457	0556	0556	|
519	Zernove UA d.	|	|	2016	|	|	2318	|	|	|	0228	|	0337	|	|	|	|	|	|	0610
651	Konotop **1780** d.	0946	1956	2223	2240	2302	0121	0200	0258	0343	0500	0528	0557	0550	0604	0642	|	0738	0738	0758
780	**Sumy 1780** d.	|	|	|	|	|	|	|	|	|	0805	|	|	|	|	|	|	|	|	|
829	**Chernihiv** a.	|	|	|	|	|	|	|	|	|	...	0832	|	|	|	|	|	|	|	|
872	**Kyïv** a.	1308	|	0104	0140	0123	0406	0502	0529	0620	...	...	0838	0823	0850	0926	0800	1018	1018	1105
	Odesa Holovna **1750 1770** a.	|	1155	|	|	...	|	...	...	...	...	...	|	...	1910	|	...	...	|	...
	Chişinău **1750** a.	|	...	|	2031	...	|	...	...	...	...	...	2308	...	...	|	...	...	|	...
	Lviv **1750** a.	|	...	1010	...	...	1439	...	...	...	...	...	...	...	...	2001	...	...	|	...
	Chernivtsi **1750** a.	0620	...	1625	...	...	...	...	...	...	...	...	...	...	...	...	...	...	0620	...

	Sko 56 LY	Fir 24	Sko 48	Sko 34 G	Sko 60 Bu	Sko 58	Sko 142	Sko 342	Sko 42	Sko 42 Bv	Sko 22	Fir 2	Fir 6	Sko 74	Sko 117	Sko 90 Z	Sko 16 T	Fir 78 K	Fir 4
Chernivtsi **1750** d.	...	...	...	...	1856	...	2230	...	...	1856	...	...	...	...	...	...	...	...	...
Lviv **1750** d.	...	...	...	...	|	...	0430	...	...	|	...	...	...	0811	...	...	0925	...	...
Chişinău **1750** d.	...	...	1140	...	|	...	|	1957	...	|	...	...	...	|	...	...	|	...	...
Odesa Holovna **1750 1770** d.	...	1510	|	1744	|	...	|	|	...	|	...	...	...	|	...	...	|	...	...
Kyïv d.	0024	0124	0219	|	0958	...	1347	1341	1430	1430	1703	2009	1845	1851	...	2015	2035	2041	2117
Chernihiv d.	|	|	|	|	|	1320	|	|	|	|	|	|	|	|	...	|	|	|	|
Sumy 1780 d.	|	|	|	|	|	|	|	|	|	|	|	|	|	|	1845	|	|	|	|
Konotop **1780** d.	0308	0359	0505	1009	1250	1620	1648	1656	1810	1810	2004	|	2143	2123	2219	2304	2330	2338	0010
Zernove UA d.	|	|	|	|	|	1854	1919	|	|	|	|	|	|	|	0105	|	|	0154	|
Suzemka RU d.	0628	0723	|	|	1617	|	2103	|	|	|	|	0135	|	|	|	0237	|	0338	|
Bryansk Orlovski d.	0815	0910	1044	1507	1735‡	2205	2247	2306	2337	2337	0047	|	0233	0256	0410	|	0424	0521	0445
Moskva Kiyevskaya a.	1434	1515	1623	2118	2236	0420	0452	0518	0533	0533	0619	0639	0900	0908	0952	0933	1000	1130	1058

FOR NOTES, SEE TABLE **1750** BELOW.

UZ, CFM — KYÏV - ODESA, CHERNIVTSI and LVIV / ODESA - CHERNIVTSI and LVIV — 1750

km		Sko 141	Sko 89	Sko 341	Sko 73	Sko 111	Sko 55	Sko 47	Fir 23	Sko 15	Sko 15 S	Sko 15 D	Sko 59 A	Sko 61	Sko 115	Fir 43 N	Fir 108 R	Fir 26	Sko 51 P	Sko 13	Fir 105	Fir 91	Sko 9	Sko 19 H	Sko 7 E
	Moskva Kiyevskaya **1740** d.	1235	1346	1243	1552	...	1908	1937	2120	2131	2131	2131	2139e	...	...	...	...	...	...	...	...	...	...	...	...
	Kharkiv **1780** d.	|	|	|	|	1724	|	|	|	|	|	|	|	...	0712	...	...	...	...	1045	...	...	...	...	...
0	**Kyïv 1700** d.	0119	0143	0155	0421	0427	0641	0853	0910	0953	0953	0953	1404	...	1711	1916	...	...	2041	2114	2200	2220	2259	...	2356
	St Peterburg Vitebski **1920** d.	|	|	|	|	|	|	|	|	|	|	|	|	1618r	|	|	...	...	|	|	|	|	|	2340q	|
159	Kozyatyn **1700** d.	|	0422	0430	0636	|	0858	1101	1126	1207	1207	1207	1622	1707	1941	|	...	...	2307	|	2349	|	0116	0201	0217
221	Vinnytsya d.	|	0518	0534	0734	|	0953	1152	1220	1301	1301	1301	1748	1802	2039	|	...	...	0002	|	0036	|	0215	0256	0315
	Odesa Holovna d.	|	|	|	|	|	|	|	|	|	|	|	|	|	|	|	1700	1802	|	|	|	|	|	|	|
268	Zhmerynka **1775** d.	|	0605	0650	0844	|	|	1308	1327	|	|	|	|	1911	2148	|	2311	2358	0118	|	0127	|	0318	0414	|
654	**Odesa** Holovna a.	|	...	|	|	◧	|	|	1910	|	|	|	|	|	|	◧	|	|	|	|	0610	|	0848	1019	|
	Chişinău **1730** a.	|	...	2031	|	|	|	2308	...	|	|	|	|	0748	|	|	|	|	|	|	...	|	...	...	|
367	Khmelnytsky **1775** d.	|	...	...	1017	|	1155	...	...	1511	1511	1511	2023	...	2343	|	0044	0131	0250	|	...	|	...	...	0528
486	Ternopil **1775** d.	|	...	...	1217	|	...	...	...	1734	1734	1734	2336	...	0144	|	0239	0326	0439	|	...	|	...	...	0723
594	**Chernivtsi** a.	1625j	...	...	|	|	...	...	...	|	|	|	0620	...	|	|	|	|	|	|	...	|	...	...	|
	Bucureşti Nord **1670** a.	...	...	...	|	|	...	...	...	|	|	|	1913	...	|	|	|	|	|	|	...	|	...	...	|
	Sofiya **1500** a.	...	...	...	|	|	...	...	...	|	|	|	0605	...	|	|	|	|	|	|	...	|	...	...	|
627	**Lviv 1775** a.	1010	...	...	1439	1448	...	...	...	2001	2001	2001	...	...	0410	0357	0500	0542	0650	0709	...	0634	...	...	0934
627	**Lviv** d.	...	...	...	...	...	...	...	...	2030	2030	2030	...	...	...	...	0526	...	...	0735	...	...	...	...	1000
852	Mukacheve d.	...	...	...	...	...	...	...	...	0136	0136	0136	...	...	...	...	1020	...	...	1212	...	...	...	...	1507
893	**Chop** a.	...	...	...	...	...	...	...	...	0234	0234	0234	...	...	...	...	1122	...	...	1333	...	...	...	...	1615
	Košice **1195** a.	...	...	...	...	...	...	...	...	|	|	0640	...	...	...	...	|	...	...	|	...	...	...	...	2200
	Budapest Keleti **1270** a.	...	...	...	...	...	...	...	...	|	0947	...	...	...	...	...	|	...	...	|	...	...	...	...	...
915	**Uzhhorod** a.	...	...	...	...	...	...	...	...	0348	...	...	...	...	...	...	1215	...	...	1407	...	...	...	...	...

	Sko 52 Q	Fir 107 R	Sko 61	Sko 142	Sko 341	Sko 74	Sko 13	Sko 90	Sko 15	Sko 16 T	Sko 16 DE	Sko 116	Sko 56	Fir 24	Sko 47	Sko 112	Sko 20 J	Fir 26	Sko 8	Fir 44 N	Fir 92	Fir 106	Sko 10	Sko 60 B
Uzhhorod d.	...	1635	...	...	...	...	0123	...	0102	...	...	...	...	...	...	...	...	...	...	...	...	...	...	...
Budapest Keleti **1270** d.	...	|	...	...	...	...	|	...	|	1815	...	...	...	...	...	...	...	...	...	...	...	...	...	...
Košice **1195** d.	...	|	...	...	...	...	|	...	|	|	2007	...	...	...	...	...	...	...	...	...	...	...	...	...
Chop d.	...	1727	...	...	...	...	0210	...	0256	0256	0256	...	...	...	...	...	...	...	1510	...	...	...	...	...
Mukacheve d.	...	1835	...	...	...	...	0326	...	0359	0359	0359	...	...	...	...	...	...	...	1616	...	...	...	...	...
Lviv a.	...	2335	...	...	...	...	0825	...	0859	0859	0859	...	...	...	...	...	...	...	2051	...	...	...	...	...
Lviv 1775 d.	0008	0024	...	0430	...	0811	0854	...	0925	0925	0925	1223	...	...	...	1701	...	1952	2111	2125	2247	...	...	...
Sofiya **1500** d.	|	|	...	|	...	|	|	...	|	|	|	|	...	...	...	|	...	|	|	|	|	...	...	1930
Bucureşti Nord **1670** d.	|	|	...	|	...	|	|	...	|	|	|	|	...	...	...	|	...	|	|	|	|	...	...	0638
Chernivtsi d.	|	|	...	2230j	...	|	|	...	|	|	|	|	...	...	...	|	...	|	|	|	|	...	...	1856
Ternopil **1775** d.	0228	0245	...	|	...	1033	|	...	1143	1143	1143	1441	...	...	...	|	...	2213	|	|	|	...	...	0155
Khmelnytsky **1775** d.	0427	0446	...	|	...	1238	|	...	1422	1422	1422	1710	1906	...	...	|	...	0030	|	|	|	...	...	0359
Chişinău **1730** d.	|	|	1920	|	1957	|	|	...	|	|	|	|	|	...	1140	|	...	|	|	|	|	...	...	|
Odesa Holovna d.	|	|	|	|	|	|	|	|	|	|	|	|	|	1510	|	◧	1825	|	|	◧	|	2300	2308	|
Zhmerynka **1775** d.	0630	0629	0812	|	0931	1423	|	1526	|	|	|	1920	|	2119	2222	|	0047	0218	|	|	|	0358	0437	|
Odesa Holovna a.	|	1212	|	|	|	|	|	|	|	|	|	|	|	|	|	|	|	0805	|	|	|	|	|	|
Vinnytsya d.	0717	...	0900	|	1018	1511	|	1621	1646	1646	1646	2018	2106	2206	2307	|	0133	...	...	|	...	0438	0523	0613
Kozyatyn **1700** d.	0812	...	1013	|	1114	1611	|	1733	1748	1748	1748	2142	2200	2301	0002	|	0247	...	...	|	...	0526	0617	0712
St Peterburg Vitebski **1920** a.	|	...	1207z	|	|	|	|	|	|	|	|	|	|	|	|	|	0618z	...	...	|	...	|	|	|
Kyïv 1700 a.	1024	...	...	1332	1326	1826	1937	1950	2001	2001	2001	0012	0004	0107	0204	0254	...	...	0716	0622	0723	0736	0833	0926
Kharkiv **1780** a.	...	...	...	|	|	|	0417	|	|	|	|	1022	|	|	|	1333	...	...	...	...	...	...	...	|
Moskva Kiyevskaya **1740** a.	...	...	...	0452	0518	0908	...	0933	1000	1000	1000	...	1434	1515	1623	...	...	...	...	...	...	...	...	0533f

A – BOLGARIYA EKSPRESS – 🛏 1, 2 cl. Moskva - Kyïv - Vadul Siret (**383**) - Ruse - Sofiya. Conveys on ⑥ (also ② in summer) 🛏 2 cl. Minsk (**86**) - Kyïv - Sofiya. Conveys on dates shown in Table **98** 🛏 2 cl. Moskva - Ruse - Varna and 🛏 2 cl. Moskva - Ruse - Burgas.

B – BOLGARIYA EKSPRES – 🛏 1, 2 cl. Sofiya (**382**) - Ruse - Vadul Siret - Kyïv - Moskva. Conveys on ② (also ⑤ in summer) 🛏 2 cl. Sofiya - Kyïv - Minsk. Conveys on dates shown in Table **98** 🛏 2 cl. Varna - Ruse - Moskva and 🛏 2 cl. Burgas - Ruse - Moskva.

D – 🛏 1, 2 cl. Moskva - Chop - Košice and v.v. (extended to / from Žilina on dates shown in Table **1180**).

E – Conveys on dates shown in Table **96** 🛏 1, 2 cl. Kyïv / Lvov - Chop - Bratislava - Wien and v.v.

F – Uneven dates (daily from early June).

G – Even dates (daily from early June).

H – From St Peterburg ①②③⑤ (daily May 27 - Sept. 26).

J – ③④⑤⑦ (daily May 30 - Sept. 28).

K – To / from Kovel (Table **1700**).

L – To / from Khmelnytsky (Table **1750**).

N – To / from Ivano-Frankivsk (Table **1720**).

P – To Przemyśl (Table **1056**). Conveys 🛏 1, 2 cl. Kyïv - Praha; on ①②③⑤⑦ 🛏 2 cl. Kyïv - Wrocław. See Table **96**.

Q – From Przemyśl (Table **1056**). Conveys 🛏 1, 2 cl. Praha - Kyïv; on ①②④⑥⑦ 🛏 2 cl. Wrocław - Kyïv. See Table **96**.

R – Conveys 🛏 2 cl. Odesa - Lviv - Przemyśl - Warszawa and v.v. See Table **1056**.

S – TISSA – 🛏 2 cl. Moskva - Kyïv - Záhony (**629**) - Budapest (**794**) - Kelebia (**345**) - Beograd. Conveys on dates shown in Table **97** 🛏 1, 2 cl. Moskva - Budapest - Zagreb / Venezia; 🛏 2 cl. Kyïv - Budapest - Zagreb.

T – TISSA – 🛏 2 cl. Beograd (**344**) - Kelebia (**793**) - Budapest (**628**) - Záhony - Kyïv - Moskva. Conveys on dates shown in Table **97** 🛏 1, 2 cl. Venezia / Zagreb (**205**) - Budapest - Moskva; 🛏 2 cl. Zagreb - Budapest - Kyïv.

X – Conveys 🛏 2 cl. Moskva - Kyïv (**29**) - Korosten (**642**) - Zhytomyr. See Table **1700**.

Y – Conveys 🛏 2 cl. Zhytomyr (**642**) - Korosten (**30**) - Kyïv - Moskva. See Table **1700**.

Z – To / from Zhmerynka (Table **1750**).

c – June 5 - Sept. 3.

d – Not June 4 - Sept. 2.

e – Train **3**. June 5 - Sept. 3 depart Moskva 0025 in Train **59**.

f – Train **42**. June 6 - Sept. 4 arrive Moskva 2236 in Train **60**.

j – Via Lviv.

q – Two days earlier.

r – Previous day.

u – June 4 - Sept. 2 (next day from Chernivtsi).

v – Until June 3 and from Sept. 3 (next day from Chernivtsi).

z – Next day.

RU – Russia (Moskva Time).

UA – Ukraine (East European Time).

◧ – Via Korosten (Table **1700**).

‡ – Bryansk Lgovski.

1770 KYÏV and ODESA - SEVASTOPOL UZ

km		Fir	Fir	Fir	Sko	Fir	Fir	Fir	Pas	Sko
		23	40	650	250	12	28	121	382	33
		Z		A	E	S			Q	C
	Moskva Kiyevskaya **1740** d.	2120	...	...	...	...	...	...	...	1048
0	Konotop d.	0604	...	...	...	...	...	...	...	1956
414	Znamyanka d.	|	...	...	...	...	...	...	...	0503
	Kyïv 1775 d.	0910	1251	...	...	1751	2021	1903	...	|
	Myronivka **1775** d.	|	1425	...	...	|	|	2209	...	|
	Minsk **1930** d.	|	|	...	...	|	|	|	0910	|
	Chernihiv d.	|	|	...	1208	|	|	|	1826	|
	Hrebinka d.	|	|	...	1555	|	|	|	2340	|
	Cherkasy d.	|	|	...	1742	|	|	|	0111	|
	Im. T. Shevchenka **1775** d.	|	1607	...	1854	2055	2317	0001	0219	|
826	**Odesa** Holovna a.	1910	|	1944	|	|	|	|	|	1155
	Mykolaïv d.	...	**d**	0047	0114	**d**	0448	0555	**d**	...
	Kherson d.	...	|	0206	0223	|	0551	...	|	...
	Simferopol **1775 1790** a.	...	0417	0801	0741	0845	1101	...	1543	...
	Sevastopol 1775 1790 a.	...	0616	...	...	...	1306	...	...	...

km		Sko	Fir	Fir	Fir	Fir	Fir	Fir	Pas	Sko
		250	122	12	40	28	650	24	382	34
		F		S			A	Z	P	D
0	**Sevastopol 1775 1790** d.	...	...	...	1324	1452	...	...	...	...
78	Simferopol **1775 1790** d.	1014	...	1433	1530	1711	1700	...	2152	...
360	Kherson d.	1531	...	|	|	2220	2306	...	|	...
415	Mykolaïv d.	1646	1923	**d**	**d**	2342	0117	...	**d**	...
	Odesa Holovna d.	|	|	|	|	|	0543	1510	|	1744
726	Im. T. Shevchenka **1775** d.	2227	0123	0250	0433	0524	...	|	1301	|
756	Cherkasy d.	2319	|	|	|	|	...	|	1356	|
848	Hrebinka d.	0134	|	|	|	|	...	|	1552	|
1054	**Chernihiv** a.	0535	|	|	|	|	...	|	1945	|
	Minsk **1930** a.	...	|	|	|	|	...	|	0529	|
835	Myronivka **1775** d.	...	0301	|	|	|	...	|	...	|
942	**Kyïv 1775** a.	...	0530	0542	0708	0844	...	0107	...	|
	Znamyanka d.	...	...	...	...	...	...	|	...	0034
	Konotop a.	...	...	...	...	...	...	0339	...	0936
	Moskva Kiyevskaya **1740** a.	...	...	...	...	...	...	1515	...	2118

A – Even dates in Feb., Mar., Aug., Nov., Dec. Uneven dates in Jan., Apr., May, June, July, Sept., Oct.
C – Uneven dates (daily from June 1).
D – Even dates (daily from June 1).
E – Even dates June 2 - Aug. 30.
F – Uneven dates June 3 - Aug. 31 (not Aug. 1).
P – Even dates.
Q – Even dates [... *30, 1, 4* ...].
S – SLAVUTICH.
Z – Via Zhmerynka (Table **1750**).
d – Via Dnipropetrovsk (Table **1775**).

1775 LVIV and KYÏV - MARIUPOL and SEVASTOPOL UZ

km		Fir	Fir	Fir	Sko	Fir	Fir	Fir	Sko	Sko
		40	84	12	86	38	72	80	22	70
				S		D		N	T	E
0	**Lviv 1750** d.	...	...	...	0945	...	...	...	1606	1739
141	Ternopil **1750** d.	...	...	...	1204	...	...	...	1825	2005
260	Khmelnytsky **1750** d.	...	...	...	1402	...	...	...	2042	2220
359	Zhmerynka **1750** d.	...	...	...	1547	...	...	...	2230	0008
468	Kozyatyn **1750** d.	...	...	...	1740	...	...	...	|	0202
	Kyïv 1770 d.	1251	1504	1751	|	1921	2027	2312	|	|
663	Myronivka **1770** d.	1425	1631	|	2019	|	2149	0028	|	0449
772	Im. T. Shevchenka **1770** d.	1607	1820	2055	2156	2220	2336	0200	|	0639
864	Znamyanka d.	1724	1945	2209	2314	2335	0050	0316	0801	0801
973	Pyatykhatky d.	|	2141	|	0107	|	0246	0510	0959	0959
1052	Dniprodzerzhynsk d.	|	2246	|	0210	|	0353	0615	1114	1114
1088	**Dnipropetrovsk** Holovny d.	2107	0014	0143	0259	0306	0447	0705	1215	1215
1357	Donetsk a.	|	0503	|	|	0710	|	...	1650	1650
1489	**Mariupol** a.	|	0804	|	|	...	|	...	...	1957
1214	Zaporizhzhya **I 1790** d.	2313	...	0350	0453	...	0642	...	...	...
1326	Melitopol **1790** d.	0103	...	0532	0637	...	...	...	...	...
1570	Simferopol **1770 1790** a.	0417	...	0845	0950	...	...	...	...	...
1648	**Sevastopol 1770 1790** a.	0616	...	...	...	...	...	...	...	...

	Sko	Sko	Sko	Fir	Fir	Fir	Fir	Fir	Fir
	70	21	86	12	72	79	37	40	83
	U	E		S		N	D		
Sevastopol 1770 1790 d.	...	...	...	...	...	...	...	1324	...
Simferopol **1770 1790** d.	...	...	1312	1433	...	...	...	1530	...
Melitopol **1790** d.	...	...	1644	1748	...	...	...	1858	...
Zaporizhzhya **I 1790** d.	...	...	1814	1918	1925	...	...	2030	...
Mariupol d.	1018	...	|	|	|	...	...	|	1655
Donetsk d.	1349	1349	|	|	|	...	1910	|	2003
Dnipropetrovsk Holovny d.	1830	1830	2026	2150	2159	2245	2322	2330	0041
Dniprodzerzhynsk d.	1906	1906	2104	|	2236	2324	|	|	0120
Pyatykhatky d.	2018	2018	2210	|	2348	0038	|	|	0235
Znamyanka d.	2216	2244	0009	0126	0142	0240	0255	0310	0438
Im. T. Shevchenka **1770** d.	2352	|	0137	0250	0305	0408	0419	0433	0649
Myronivka **1770** d.	0129	|	0311	|	0440	0536	|	|	0838
Kyïv 1770 a.	|	|	|	0542	0600	0654	0701	0708	1003
Kozyatyn **1750** d.	0443	|	0600	...	...	...	...	...	...
Zhmerynka **1750** d.	0658	0821	0807	...	...	...	...	...	...
Khmelnytsky **1750** d.	0834	1003	0941	...	...	...	...	...	...
Ternopil **1750** d.	1042	1206	1137	...	...	...	...	...	...
Lviv 1750 a.	1315	1426	1357	...	...	...	...	...	...

D – DONBAS.
E – Even dates.
N – DNIPRO.
S – SLAVUTICH.
T – Uneven dates [... *31, 3* ...].
U – Uneven dates [... *29, 1* ...].
‡ – Dnipropetrovsk Pivdenny.

1780 KYÏV and HOMEL - KHARKIV and LUHANSK BCh, UZ

km **		Sko	Sko	Fir	Pas	Fir	Pas	Sko	Sko	Fir	Pas
		116	112	164	312	20	606	100	14	64	344
		J		S	E			R			
	Uzhhorod **1750** d.	...	...	...	...	...	...	...	0123	...	...
	Lviv **1750** d.	1223	1701	...	...	...	...	...	0854	...	...
0	**Kyïv** d.	0042	0319	0633	...	1839	...	...	2000	2225	2235
148	Hrebinka d.	|	|	|	...	2035	...	...	2210	0030	|
333	**Poltava** Kyïvska d.	|	|	1035	...	2343	...	...	0133	0342	|
	Kaliningrad **1950** d.	|	|	|	1404	|	...	...	|	|	|
	Minsk **1930** d.	|	|	|	0053	|	...	0825	|	|	|
	Homel § BY d.	|	|	|	0618	|	...	1404	|	|	|
	Konotop **1740** § UA d.	0348	0637	|	1236	|	...	1932	|	|	0202
	Sumy **1740** d.	0631	0955	|	1536	|	1650	2211	|	|	0506
491	**Kharkiv** a.	1022	1333	1228	1921	|	2120	0121	0417	0625	0938
	Simferopol **1790** a.	...	...	...	...	|	|	1035	...	...	...
814	**Luhansk** a.	...	...	...	...	0957	1008	...	...	...	...

	Fir	Pas	Pas	Sko	Sko	Fir	Sko	Pas	Fir	Sko
	20	311	606	115	13	163	111	343	63	99
		U				S		K		Q
Luhansk d.	1635	...	1747	...	...	...	...	...	...	...
Simferopol **1790** d.	|	...	|	...	...	...	...	...	...	1335
Kharkiv d.	|	0038	0636	0712	1045	1627	1724	1835	2255	2314
Sumy **1740** d.	|	0437	1200	1059	1435	|	2120	2320	|	0232
Konotop **1740** § UA d.	|	0743	...	1358	1725	|	0059	0247	|	0518
Homel § BY a.	|	1339	...	|	|	|	|	|	|	1038
Minsk **1930** a.	|	1917	...	|	|	|	|	|	|	1614
Kaliningrad **1950** a.	|	0822	...	|	|	|	|	|	|	...
Poltava Kyïvska d.	0327	...	...	|	|	1840	|	|	0145	...
Hrebinka d.	0620	...	...	|	|	|	|	|	0455	...
Kyïv a.	0806	...	...	1650	2054	2217	0400	0613	0714	...
Lviv **1750** a.	...	...	...	0410	0709	...	1448	...	...	...
Uzhhorod **1750** a.	...	...	...	...	1407	...	...	...	...	...

E – Even dates.
J – On ④⑦ from Berlin conveys 🛏 2 cl. Berlin (**345**) - Yahodyn (**30**) - Kyïv - Kharkiv.
K – On ②⑤ conveys 🛏 2 cl. Kharkiv - Kyïv (**29**) - Berlin.
Q – Even dates (daily June 2 - Oct. 2).
R – Uneven dates [... *29, 1* ...] (daily June 1 - Oct. 1).
S – STOLICHNY EKSPRES.
U – Uneven dates [... *29, 1* ...].
§ – 🏛 : Terekowka (BY) / Khorobychi (UA).
BY – Belarus.
UA – Ukraine.
** – Homel - Konotop: *222 km*. Sumy - Kharkiv: *195 km*. Kharkiv - Luhansk: *439 km*.

1790 MOSKVA - KHARKIV - MARIUPOL and SEVASTOPOL RZhD, UZ

km		Sko	Sko	Fir	Sko	Sko	Sko	Fir	Sko	Sko
		7	25	29	17	99	9	15	67	77
		S				R			K	
0	**Moskva** Kurskaya d.	0430	0819	0934	1021	...	1442	1447	1520	1638
194	Tula **I** d.	0732	1128	1231	1318	...	1729	1737	1845	1950
383	Orel d.	1004	1424	1506	1558	...	2010	2025	2119	2300
537	Kursk d.	1214	1635	1725	1825	...	2230	2240	2320	0100
697	Belgorod § RU d.	1525	2015	2039	2144	...	0143	0151	0237	0410
	Kyïv **1780** d.	|	|	|	|	...	|	|	|	|
	Minsk **1780** d.	|	|	|	|	0825	|	|	|	|
781	**Kharkiv** § UA a.	1621	2042	2152	2244	0121	0204	0249	0300	0509
781	**Kharkiv** d.	1653	2117	2212	2309	0141	0244	0314	0335	0530
1098	Donetsk a.	|	|	|	|	|	0831	|	|	1218
1230	**Mariupol** a.	|	|	|	|	|	...	|	|	1500
1081	Dnipropetrovsk Holovny a.	|	|	|	|	|	...	0738	|	...
1108	Zaporizhzhya **I 1775** d.	2139	0137	0220	0334	0606	...	...	0801	...
1220	Melitopol **1775** d.	2325	0302	0348	0517	0733	...	...	0950	...
1464	Simferopol **1770 1775** a.	0225	|	0645	0836	1035	...	...	1250	...
1543	Yevpatoriya a.	|	0711	...	|	...	...	...	...	...
1542	**Sevastopol 1770 1775** a.	0428	...	...	1041	...	...	...	...	...

	Fir	Sko	Sko	Sko	Sko	Fir	Sko	Sko	Sko
	16	10	78	68	100	30	18	26	8
				K	Q				S
Sevastopol 1770 1775 d.	...	...	...	...	...	...	1705	...	2243
Yevpatoriya d.	...	...	...	...	...	...	|	1929	|
Simferopol **1770 1775** d.	...	...	...	1212	1335	1441	1929	|	0100
Melitopol **1775** d.	...	...	...	1526	1652	1741	2257	2347	0419
Zaporizhzhya **I 1775** d.	...	...	...	1704	1833	1911	0028	0117	0604
Dnipropetrovsk Holovny d.	1415	...	...	|	|	|	|	|	|
Mariupol d.	|	...	1050	|	|	|	|	|	|
Donetsk d.	|	1447	1335	|	|	|	|	|	|
Kharkiv a.	1842	2043	2049	2130	2254	2355	0456	0550	1028
Kharkiv § UA d.	1920	2115	2109	2205	2314	0036	0516	0605	1101
Minsk **1780** a.	|	|	|	|	1614	|	|	|	|
Kyïv **1780** a.	|	|	|	|	...	|	|	|	|
Belgorod § RU d.	2223	0011	0037	0100	...	0330	0847	0938	1356
Kursk d.	0114	0255	0335	0345	...	0623	1145	1230	1652
Orel d.	0320	0500	0537	0548	...	0825	1400	1445	1925
Tula **I** d.	0542	0733	0807	0817	...	1105	1638	1728	2203
Moskva Kurskaya a.	0912	1031	1111	1117	...	1420	1942	2029	0100

K – KRYM.
Q – Even dates (daily June 2 - Oct. 2).
R – Uneven dates [... *29, 1* ...] (daily June 1 - Oct. 1).
S – From / to St Peterburg (Table **1900**).
RU – Russia (Moskva Time).
UA – Ukraine (East European Time).
§ – 🏛 : Krasny Khutor (RU) / Kozacha Lopan (UA).
☛ For services Moskva - Kharkiv - Rostov and beyond, see the *Thomas Cook Overseas Timetable*.

LITHUANIA, LATVIA and ESTONIA

SEE MAP PAGE 509

Operators: Lithuania: **LG** (Lietuvos Geležinkeliai). Latvia: **LDz** (Latvijas Dzelzceļš). Estonia: **Edelaraudtee** (except for international trains, which are operated by **GoRail**).

Services: Trains convey first- and second-class seating unless indicated otherwise. International trains to and from CIS countries (Belarus, Russia, Ukraine) are composed of Russian-style sleeping-cars (for details of train types and classes of travel in the CIS, see the panel on page **515**).

Timings: The schedules shown are those most recently received from the operators. Timings are expressed in local time at the station concerned (time comparison chart: page **2**).

Reservations: Reservation is compulsory for travel by long-distance and international services – *i.e.* all those for which a train number is shown.

🚌 KALININGRAD and VILNIUS - RIGA - TARTU and TALLINN — 1800

For (summer only) rail service **Vilnius** - **Riga** and v.v., see Table **1720**

Operators:	E	N	E	E	T	E	E	T	E	T	E	E
Kaliningrad d.	2100	...	...	...	...	...	...	...	...	...	...	...
Vilnius d.	|	...	...	0730	1000	...	...	1330	...	1800	...	2100
Riga d.	0615	0720	0830	1200	1450	1530	1700	1820	1900	2230	2340	0140
Valga d.	|	|	|	|	...	|	|	...	2200	...	|	|
Tartu a.	|	|	|	|	...	|	|	...	2320	...	|	|
Pärnu d.	0915	1040	1125	|	...	1830	2000	...	...	...	0305	0430
Tallinn harbour *term. A* a.	|	1235	|	1630	...	|	|	...	...	...	0500	0640
Tallinn harbour *term. D* a.	|	1240	|	1640	...	|	|	...	...	...	0505	0635
Tallinn bus station a.	1100	1250	1335	1650	...	2015	2150	...	...	...	0510	0625

Operators:	T	E	E	T	E	E	E	N	E	E
Tallinn bus station d.	...	0600	...	...	1000	1200	1315	1525	1700	2100
Tallinn harbour *term. D* d.	...	|	...	...	1010	1210	1325	1535	|	|
Tallinn harbour *term. A* d.	...	|	...	...	1015	1220	1330	1545	|	|
Pärnu d.	...	0745	...	...	1215	|	1530	1745	1855	2255
Tartu d.	...	|	0645	...	|	|	|	|	|	|
Valga d.	...	|	0810	...	|	|	|	|	|	|
Riga d.	0800	1045	1105	1315	1535	1700	1850	2055	2210	0150
Vilnius a.	1215	...	...	1745	...	2130	...	...	|	0625
Kaliningrad a.	...	...	...	...	...	...	...	...	0710	...

E – Mootor Reisi (www.eurolines.ee). N – Nordeka (www.nordeka.lv). T – TOKS or BAL (www.eurolines.lt). ☛ Also (**T**): Riga - Vilnius at 1600.

LG, LDz — VILNIUS - KLAIPEDA — 1810

km		c	c	17 🍷	d	c	c	c	c	19 🍷	c
0	**Vilnius 1040** ¶ d.	...	0635	0645	0813	0942	1405	...	1620	1700	2020
‡	Kaunas **1040** ¶ d.	...	0747	|	|	1101	1546	...	1816	|	2155
192	Radviliškis d.	0610	...	0906	1120	...	...	1617	...	1921	...
212	Šiauliai d.	0633	...	0929	1156	...	...	1649	...	1944	...
376	**Klaipeda** a.	0938	...	1136	...	...	...	1953	...	2151	...

	c	18 🍷	c	c	c	c	d	c	c	20 🍷
Klaipeda d.	...	0645	0700	...	...	...	...	1443	...	1700
Šiauliai d.	...	0858	0951	...	...	...	1530	1744	...	1913
Radviliškis d.	...	0918	1020	...	...	...	1606	1820	...	1933
Kaunas **1040** ¶ d.	0800	|	...	1045	1455	1642	|	...	1945	|
Vilnius 1040 ¶ a.	0944	1143	...	1225	1621	1828	1914	...	2117	2158

c – 3rd class only.
d – ⑤⑦. 3rd class only.
¶ – ± 13 local trains operate daily Vilnius - Kaunas and v.v.
‡ – Vilnius - Kaunas *104 km*, Kaunas - Radviliškis *138 km*.

LG, LDz, RZhD — VILNIUS - ST PETERBURG — 1820

km		c	c	c	c Ⓐ	*Pas* 392 A	c	*Fir* 38 B
0	**Vilnius** d.	0511	0822	1210	1452	1810	1838	...
147	Turmantas 🏛 LT a.	0741	1101	1449	1732	2003	2128	...
173	Daugavpils 🏛 LV a.	...	...	...	...	2027	...	...
173	Daugavpils d.	...	...	...	...	2057	...	...
	Riga **1840** d.	...	...	...	...	|	...	1930
260	Rezekne **I** d.	...	...	...	...	2215	...	2300r
304	Karsava 🏛 LV d.	...	...	...	...	2321	...	0018
337	Pytalovo 🏛 RU d.	...	...	...	...	0145	...	0240
431	Pskov d.	...	...	...	...	0335	...	0419
715	**St Peterburg** Vitebski a.	...	...	...	...	0820	...	0850

	c	*Pas* 391 N	c	*Fir* 37 B	c	c	c Ⓐ
St Peterburg Vitebski d.	...	2002	...	2208	...	...	...
Pskov d.	...	0103	...	0258	...	...	...
Pytalovo 🏛 RU d.	...	0334	...	0518	...	...	...
Karsava 🏛 LV d.	...	0352	...	0535	...	...	...
Rezekne **I** d.	...	0432	...	0639r	...	...	...
Riga **1840** a.	...	|	...	0940	...	...	...
Daugavpils a.	...	0541	...	...	...	...	...
Daugavpils 🏛 LV d.	...	0602	...	...	...	...	...
Turmantas 🏛 LT d.	0439	0655	0800	...	1136	1511	1754
Vilnius a.	0711	0852	1023	...	1416	1751	2045

A – Even dates.
B – BALTIYA – 🛏 1, 2 cl., ▬ 3 cl. and [4].
N – Uneven dates [... *31*, *3* ...].
c – 3rd class only.
r – Rezekne II.
LT – Lithuania.
LV – Latvia (East European Time).
RU – Russia (Moskva Time).

LDz — RIGA - CESIS - LUGAŽI — 1830

km												①–⑤	
0	**Riga** d.	0558	0635	0747	...	1002	1151	1402	1540	1724	1801	1900	2100
53	Sigulda d.	0712	0739	0901	...	1111	1305	1510	1654	1838	1854	2014	2211
93	Cesis d.	...	0821	...	...	1155	...	1554	...	...	1938	...	2252
121	Valmiera d.	...	0852	...	...	...	...	1625	...	...	2009	...	2323
164	**Lugaži** a.	...	0938	...	...	...	...	1711	...	...	2055	...	...

	①–⑤									①–⑤		
Lugaži d.	...	...	0536	...	...	0954	...	...	...	...	1735	...
Valmiera d.	...	0525	0621	...	...	1039	...	...	...	...	1821	...
Cesis d.	...	0552	0652	...	...	1110	...	1506	...	...	1852	...
Sigulda d.	0558	0630	0733	0811	0958	1154	1351	1550	1728	1854	1934	2132
Riga a.	0704	0740	0840	0923	1110	1300	1503	1702	1840	2006	2036	2244

LDz, RZhD — RIGA - REZEKNE - MOSKVA — 1840

km			*Pas* 662 N			*Fir* 2 L		*Fir* 4 P	*Fir* 38 B
0	**Riga 1850** d.	0808	...	1114	...	1620	1650	1810	1930
129	Krustpils (Jekabpils) **1850** d.	1009	...	1259	...	1810	1900	2003	2116
224	**Rezekne** II d.	1152	...	1417	...	1938	2050	2129	2300
	St Peterburg Vitebski **1820** a.	|	...	...	...	|	|	|	0850
279	Zilupe 🏛 LV d.	1252	...	...	...	2113	2150	2304	...
305	Sebezh 🏛 RU d.	...	1530	...	...	2335	...	0122	...
416	Novosokolniki d.	...	1816	...	...	|	...	|	...
445	**Velikiye Luki** a.	...	1927	...	...	0139	...	0340	...
445	**Velikiye Luki** d.	...	2040	...	...	0200	...	0400	...
686	Rzhev d.	...	0213	...	...	0536	...	0753	...
921	**Moskva** Rizhskaya a.	...	0642	...	...	0941	...	1216	...

		Fir 37 B	*Fir* 1 L	*Fir* 3 P	*Pas* 661 N			
Moskva Rizhskaya d.	...	...	1911	2102	2009	...	...	...
Rzhev d.	...	...	2303	0100	0039	...	...	...
Velikiye Luki a.	...	...	0227	0425	0650	...	...	...
Velikiye Luki d.	...	...	0252	0450	0840	...	...	...
Novosokolniki d.	...	...	|	|	1002	...	...	...
Sebezh 🏛 RU d.	...	...	0555	0804	1230	...	...	...
Zilupe 🏛 LV d.	0340	...	0610	0820	...	...	...	1755
St Peterburg Vitebski **1820** d.	|	2208	|	|	...	...	...	|
Rezekne II d.	0444	0639	0705	0915	...	1447	...	1902
Krustpils (Jekabpils) **1850** d.	0621	0757	0824	1040	...	1604	...	2050
Riga 1850 a.	0830	0940	1005	1220	...	1746	...	2244

B – BALTIJA – 🛏 1, 2 cl. and ▬ 3 cl.
L – LATVIJAS EKSPRESIS – 🛏 1, 2 cl.
N – 🛏 2 cl. and ▬ 3 cl.
P – JURMALA – 🛏 1, 2 cl.
LV – Latvia (East European Time).
RU – Russia (Moskva Time)

LDz, BCh — RIGA - DAUGAVPILS - POLATSK — 1850

km							D		
0	**Riga 1840** d.	0710	0909	...	1300	1525	1605	1725	2052
129	Krustpils (Jekabpils) **1840** d.	0931	1134	...	1504	1746	1754	1944	2314
218	Daugavpils § LV d.	1057	...	...	1638	...	1900	2110	...
379	**Polatsk** § BY a.	...	...	...	...	...	...	...	...

		D						
Polatsk § BY d.	...	...	...	...	...	...	...	...
Daugavpils § LV d.	...	0615	0723	...	1315	...	...	1745
Krustpils (Jekabpils) **1840** d.	0502	0723	0851	1155	1441	...	1819	1922
Riga 1840 a.	0729	0901	1102	1415	1650	...	2039	2147

D – DINABURGA express service: special fares payable. BY – Belarus. LV – Latvia. § – 🏛: Indra (LV) / Bihosava (BY).

LDz — RIGA AREA local trains — 1860

RIGA - JELGAVA and v.v. *43 km*
1–2 trains per hour. Journey ± 49 mins.

RIGA - LIELVARDE and v.v. *51 km*
1–2 trains per hour. Journey ± 60 mins. Certain of these trains continue to / start from **Aizkraukle** *82 km* ± 86 mins.

RIGA - SAULKRASTI and v.v. *48 km*
1–2 trains per hour. Journey ± 60 mins. Certain of these trains continue to / start from **Skulte** *56 km* ± 70 mins.

RIGA - SLOKA (JURMALA) and v.v. *35 km*
1–2 trains per hour. Journey ± 52 mins. Certain of these trains continue to / start from **Tukums** *65 km* ± 84 mins.

1870 TALLINN - ST PETERBURG and MOSKVA

Edelaraudtee, GoRail, RZhD

km		bus	bus	bus	34 A	B	B	bus	650 R	bus
0	**Tallinn 1880** d.	0700	1100	1430	1710	1724	1810	2300	2224	2359
77	**Tapa 1880** d.	|	|	|	1826	1848	1943	|	2342	|
104	Rakvere d.	|	1230	|	|	1911	2006	|	0007	0130
163	Jõhvi d.	0920	1350	1650	1933	2009	...	|	0057	0240
209	Narva EE d.	1020	1455	1750	2053	2058	...	0200	0223	0335
380	**St Peterburg** Baltiski RU a.	1530	2010	2305	|	...	...	0700	0726v	0830
633	Bologoye **1900** RU a.	...	...	...	0553	...	...	...	...	...
797	Tver **1900** a.	...	...	...	0731	...	...	...	...	...
964	**Moskva** Oktyabrskaya **1900** a.	...	...	...	0920	...	...	...	...	...

	649 R	bus	B	34 A	B	bus	bus	bus	bus
Moskva Oktyabrskaya **1900** d.	...	...	...	1810	...	...	...	...	...
Tver **1900** d.	...	...	...	2037	...	...	...	...	...
Bologoye **1900** RU d.	...	...	...	2224	...	...	...	...	...
St Peterburg Baltiski RU d.	2150v	2345	...	|	...	0715	1115	1400	1645
Narva EE d.	0310	0255	...	0510	0630	1025	1425	1710	1955
Jõhvi d.	0400	0355	...	0604	0719	1120	1525	1805	2050
Rakvere d.	0456	0515	0552	|	0818	|	1645	|	|
Tapa 1880 d.	0523	|	0616	0720	0841	|	|	|	|
Tallinn 1880 a.	0628	0640	0741	0827	1002	1335	1810	2020	2305

A – *Firmenny.* 1, 2 cl. R.
B – (*tavaklassi*; general class).
v – St Peterburg Vitebski.
EE – Estonia (East European Time).
RU – Russia (Moskva Time).
bus – Operated by Eurolines Estonia (www.eurolines.ee). Timings apply to bus, not rail, stations.

1880 TALLINN - TARTU - ORAVA and VALGA

Edelaraudtee

km				K	①–⑤ ◇		W ◇		⑧		◇	⑤⑦ ◇
0	**Tallinn 1870** d.	...	0640	...	0746	...	1355	1442	...	...	1650	1959
77	Tapa **1870** d.	...	0810	...	0854	...	1503	1612	...	...	1758	2107
142	Jõgeva d.	...	0913	...	0938	...	1552	1713	...	...	1846	2149
190	**Tartu** a.	...	0954	...	1009	...	1625	1758	...	...	1917	2222
190	**Tartu** d.	0510	1010	1003	...	1326	...	...	1813	1858	...	...
233	Põlva d.	|	|	1106	...	|	...	...	1917	|	...	...
262	**Orava** a.	|	|	1146	...	|	...	...	1957	|	...	...
215	Elva d.	0554	1048	...	...	1408	...	...	...	1943	...	...
273	**Valga** a.	0722	1219	...	...	1536	...	...	...	2111	...	...

	①–⑥ ◇		①–⑥			W ◇	K	⑧ ◇			⑤⑦ ◇
Valga d.	...	0510	...	...	0739	...	...	...	1551	1719	...
Elva d.	...	0638	...	...	0907	...	...	...	1719	1847	...
Orava d.	...	|	0550	...	|	...	1513	...	|	|	...
Põlva d.	...	|	0630	...	|	...	1553	...	|	|	...
Tartu a.	...	0721	0734	...	0950	...	1657	...	1802	1930	...
Tartu d.	0640	...	...	0735	...	1420	...	1724	1804	...	1940
Jõgeva d.	0712	...	...	0817	...	1451	...	1755	1846	...	2012
Tapa **1870** d.	0754	...	...	0924	...	1533	...	1839	1947	...	2054
Tallinn 1870 a.	0850	...	...	1047	...	1629	...	1935	2110	...	2150

K – Until Sept. 30, 2007.
W – ⑤⑦ from Aug. 3, 2007.
◇ – Conveys 12 (and in 1st class). All other trains convey (*tavaklass*; general class).
Express bus services operate Tallinn - Tartu and v.v. 20+ times daily (journey: 2½ hrs).

1890 TALLINN - PÄRNU and VILJANDI

Edelaraudtee

km							⑤⑥⑦					
0	**Tallinn** d.	0658	0750	0836	1035	1338	1435	1630	1735	1815	1938	2125
54	Rapla d.	0811	0845	0950	1146	1447	1529	1738	1849	1906	2048	2234
72	Lelle d.	0830	0857	...	...	1504	1543	1754	...	1919	2103	2249
136	**Pärnu** a.	0939	|	...	...	...	|	1901	...	|	|	|
98	Türi d.	...	0922	...	...	...	1606	...	...	1943	2127	2312
151	**Viljandi** a.	...	1016	...	...	...	1701	...	...	2042	...	...

	①–⑤				⑥⑦			⑤⑥⑦			
Viljandi d.	...	...	0642	...	...	...	...	1427	...	...	1730
Türi d.	0528	0620	0736	...	0925	...	...	1520	...	...	1824
Pärnu d.	|	|	|	0718	|	...	...	|	...	1642	|
Lelle d.	0552	0645	0758	0829	0949	...	...	1542	1618	1753	1853
Rapla d.	0607	0700	0811	0844	1003	1040	1222	1556	1633	1808	1905
Tallinn a.	0716	0807	0905	0952	1105	1150	1330	1649	1752	1922	1956

All trains convey (*tavaklass*; general class).

RUSSIA and BELARUS

SEE MAP PAGE 509

Operators: **RZhD**: Rossiskiye Zheleznye Dorogi (РЖД: Российские Железные Дороги). **BCh**: Belaruskaya Chyhunka (БЧ: Беларуская Чыгунка).

Timings: Valid to **May 31, 2008**. Moskva Time is used for all Russian stations (including Kaliningrad, where local time is one hour behind Moskva Time). The timings of international services to and from non-CIS countries should be verified from the international tables at the front of this book.

Tickets: Except for travel by purely local trains, prior reservation is necessary and passports and visas must be presented when purchasing tickets.

SEE ALSO THE PANEL ***RAIL TRAVEL IN RUSSIA, BELARUS, UKRAINE, and MOLDOVA*** ON THE FACING PAGE

1900 MOSKVA - ST PETERBURG

RZhD

km		*Fir* 38	*Sko* 16	*Sko* 30 A	*Sko* 8	*Sko* 802		*Fir* 24 △		*Sko* 814	*Fir* 160 △	*Sko* 18	*Fir* 10	*Sko* 56	*Fir* 28 D	*Sko* 66 F	*Sko* 42	*Fir* 32	*Fir* 26	*Fir* 6 B	*Sko* 54	*Fir* 2	*Fir* 4
	Sevastopol **1790** d.	...	...	...	2243	...	...	...	...	...	...	...	...	...	...	...	...	...	...	...	...	...	...
0	**Moskva** Oktyabrskaya § **1870** d.	0030	0050	0105	0134k	...	...	1230	...	1530	1630	1825	1928	2018	2130	2130	2150	2250	2300	2330	2340	2355	2359
167	Tver **1870** d.	0231	0246	0310	0338	...	...	1413	...	1722	1752	2044	2158	2300	2338	2338	0010	0057	0122	|	|	|	|
331	Bologoye **1870** d.	0416	0432	0508	0528	...	...	1557	...	1928	1909	2240	0040	0123	0150	0150	0208	|	0301	|	|	|	|
588	Dno d.	|	|	|	|	...	...	|	...	|	|	|	0544	|	|	|	|	|	|	|	|	|	|
687	**Pskov** a.	|	|	|	|	...	...	|	...	|	|	|	0735	|	|	|	|	|	|	|	|	|	|
606	Novgorod na Volkhove d.	|	|	|	|	0805	...	|	...	|	|	|	...	|	|	|	0550	|	|	|	|	|	|
650	**St Peterburg** Glavny ‡ a.	0848	0839a	0937	1008	1125	...	1951	...	2306	2200	|	...	0500	0528	0528	...	0604a	0650	0740	0835	0755	0800
	Helsinki **1910** a.	...	|	...	...	...	...	...	...	...	...	|	...	...	...	...	...	1137	...	...	...	...	...
	Petrozavodsk **1905** a.	...	1623	...	...	...	...	...	...	...	...	0850	...	...	...	...	...	...	...	...	...	...	...
	Murmansk **1905** a.	...	1241	...	...	...	...	...	...	...	...	...	...	...	...	...	...	...	...	...	...	...	...

km		*Fir* 31	*Sko* 17	*Sko* 55		*Fir* 23 △		*Fir* 159 △	*Sko* 813	*Sko* 801	*Sko* 7	*Sko* 42	*Sko* 29 B	*Fir* 37	*Fir* 27 E	*Sko* 65 D	*Fir* 10	*Sko* 15	*Fir* 25	*Fir* 5 B	*Sko* 53	*Fir* 1	*Fir* 3
	Murmansk **1905** d.	...	...	...	...	...	...	...	...	...	...	...	...	...	...	...	...	1855	...	...	...	...	...
	Petrozavodsk **1905** d.	...	1900	...	...	...	...	...	...	...	...	...	...	...	...	...	...	1448	...	...	...	...	...
	Helsinki **1910** d.	1823	|	...	...	...	...	...	...	...	...	...	...	...	...	...	...	|	...	...	...	...	...
0	**St Peterburg** Glavny ‡ d.	0151a	|	0040	...	1305	...	1600	1505	1718	2000	...	2200	2220	2230	2230	...	|	2300	2330	2340	2355	2359
192	Novgorod na Volkhove d.	|	|	|	...	|	...	|	|	2033	|	2120	|	|	|	|	...	|	|	|	|	|	|
	Pskov d.	|	|	|	...	|	...	|	|	...	|	|	|	|	|	|	1800	|	|	|	|	|	|
	Dno d.	|	|	|	...	|	...	|	|	...	|	|	|	|	|	|	2017	|	|	|	|	|	|
319	Bologoye **1870** d.	|	0442	0507	...	1713	...	1838	1843	...	0014	0137	0200	0213	0224	0224	0206	0304	0310	|	|	|	|
483	Tver **1870** d.	0625	0651	0706	...	1856	...	1950	2032	...	0152	0333	0341	0349	0358	0358	0418	0443	0450	|	|	|	|
650	**Moskva** Oktyabrskaya § **1870** a.	0825	0857	0953	...	2055	...	2130	2213	...	0400k	0532	0550	0602	0556	0556	0625	0654	0700	0710	0835	0755	0800
	Sevastopol **1790** a.	...	...	...	...	...	...	...	...	...	0428	...	...	...	...	...	...	...	...	...	...	...	...

A – Daily until Sept. 8, 2007; then ①–⑥.
B – Daily until Sept. 7, 2007; then ⑧.
D – Uneven dates [... *31, 3* ...].
E – Even dates.
F – Even dates [... *30, 1, 4* ...].

a – St Peterburg Ladozhski.
k – Moskva Kurskaya.
△ – Conveys (Sd) seating.

§ – Also known as *Leningradski vokzal*.
‡ – Also known as *Moskovski vokzal*.

Named trains:

1/2	KRASNAYA STRELA
3/4	EKSPRESS
5/6	NIKOLAYEVSKI EKSPRESS
7/8	NEVA
17/18	KARELIYA
25/26	SMENA
31/32	LEV TOLSTOI
37/38	AFANASI NIKITIN
42	ILMEN
159/160	AVRORA

1905 (MOSKVA and) ST PETERBURG - PETROZAVODSK - MURMANSK

RZhD

km		*Sko* 18 K		*Sko* 212 A	*Sko* 16	*Sko* 12	*Sko* 22		*Pas* 658
	Moskva Oktyabrskaya **1900** d.	1825	...	0117	0050	...	...	...	...
0	**St Peterburg** Ladozhski d.	|	...	|	|	0931	1720	...	2202
121	Volkhovstroi I d.	0343	...	1007d	1118	1145	1947	...	0015
401	**Petrozavodsk** d.	0850	...	1539	1643	1704	0120	...	0650
780	Belomorsk d.	...	...	2312	0003	0025	0845	...	...
1168	Kandalaksha d.	...	...	0612	0659	0737	1605	...	...
1445	**Murmansk** a.	...	...	1120	1241	1306	2127	...	...

	Sko 21		*Sko* 11	*Sko* 211 B	*Sko* 15		*Sko* 17 K	*Pas* 657
Murmansk d.	0840	...	1630	1700	1855	...	...	...
Kandalaksha d.	1415	...	2205	2252	0046	...	...	...
Belomorsk d.	2105	...	0526	0600	0721	...	...	...
Petrozavodsk d.	0448	...	1310	1356	1448	...	1900	2300
Volkhovstroi I d.	1006	...	1819	1859d	2017	...	0030	0505
St Peterburg Ladozhski a.	1211	...	2028	|	|	...	|	0707
Moskva Oktyabrskaya **1900** a.	...	...	...	0418	0654	...	0857	...

A – Until Sept. 2, 2007.
B – May 28 - Sept. 3, 2007.
K – KARELIYA.
d – Volkhovstroi II.

RZhD, VR — ST PETERBURG - HELSINKI — 1910

km		Fir 32 T	Fir 33 R	Sko 35 S△		Sko 36 S	Fir 34 R	Fir 32 T
	Moskva Okt. **1900**.. d.	2250	...	...	**Helsinki 797** .... d.	0723	1523	1823
***	**St Peterburg** Lad. ◧ d.	0609	...	...	Pasila **797** .... d.	0729	1529	1829
0	**St Peterburg** Finl. § a.	|	0727	1540	Tikkurila **797** .... d.	0739	1540	1840
129	Vyborg .... ▦ RU d.	0839	0952	1815	Lahti **797** .... d.	0825	1633	1933
160	Vainikkala ..... ▦ FI a.	0825	0932	1755	**Kouvola 797** .... d.	0900	1714	2015
160	Vainikkala .... d.	0845	0952	1815	Vainikkala .... a.	0951	1811	2114
251	**Kouvola 797** .... a.	0944	1047	1907	Vainikkala ..... ▦ FI d.	1011	1834	2134
313	Lahti **797** .... a.	1026	1125	1943	Vyborg .... ▦ RU a.	1150	2013	2317
401	Tikkurila **797** .... a.	1120	1218	2032	**St Peterburg** Finl. § a.	1405	2228	|
414	Pasila **797** .... a.	1131	1229	2042	**St Peterburg** Lad. ◧ a.	...	...	0140
417	**Helsinki 797** .... a.	1137	1235	2048	*Moskva Okt.* **1900**.. a.	...	...	0825

RZhD, BCh — ST PETERBURG - MALADZECHNA — 1915

km		Sko 79 A			Sko 80 B	
0	**St Peterburg** Vit. **1920**.. d.	1816	...	*Kaliningrad* **1950** .... d.	0949	...
245	Dno **1920** .... d.	2222	...	*Vilnius* **1950** .... d.	1549	...
421	Novosokolniki **1920** ‡ RU d.	0149	...	*Homel* **1930** .... d.	|	...
568	Vitsebsk **1920** .... d.	0356	...	*Minsk Pass.* **1950** ...... d.	|	...
669	Polatsk .... ‡ BY d.	0552	...	**Maladzechna** .... d.	1913	...
867	**Maladzechna** .... a.	0859	...	Polatsk .... ‡ BY d.	2253	...
	Minsk Pass. **1950** ...... a.	|	...	Vitsebsk **1920** .... d.	0050	...
	Homel **1930** .... a.	|	...	Novosokolniki **1920** ‡ RU d.	0438	...
	Vilnius **1950** .... a.	1242	...	Dno **1920** .... d.	0730	...
	Kaliningrad **1950** .... a.	2026	...	**St Peterburg** Vit. **1920**.. a.	1110	...

NOTES FOR TABLES **1910** and **1915**:

A – Even dates (daily June 6 - Sept. 6).
B – Uneven dates [... *29, 1* ...] (daily June 5 - Sept. 5).
R – REPIN – 🛏 1 cl. and [2] [R].
S – SIBELIUS – [12] [R].
T – LEV TOLSTOI – 🛏 1, 2 cl.
§ – Finlyandski vokzal.
◧ – Ladozhski vokzal.
BY – Belarus (East European Time).
FI – Finland (East European Time).
RU – Russia (Moskva Time).
*** *142 km* St Peterburg Ladozhski - Vyborg.
‡ – ▦ : Yezyaryshcha (BY) / Zaverezhye (RU).
△ – Runs 70 minutes later May 25 - 31.

RZhD, BCh, UZ — ST PETERBURG - HOMEL and KOZYATYN — 1920

km		Sko 47 D	Sko 49 A	Sko 61	Fir 55	Sko 83 C	Fir 51	Sko 53 ◧	Sko 19 BG
0	**St Peterburg** Vitebski **1915** ...... d.	1242	1500	1618	...	1747	1908	2120	2340
245	Dno **1915** .... d.	1637	1900	2006	...	2136	2311	0106	0353
421	Novosokolniki **1915** .... § RU d.	1940	2154	2337	...	0047	0243	0434	0724
568	Vitsebsk .... § BY d.	2133	2344	0125	...	0305	0428	0616	0917
	Moskva Belorusskaya **1950** .... d.	|	|	|	2109	|	|	|	|
651	**Orsha** Tsentralnaya .... a.	2300	0104	0245	0325	0425	0600	0742	1046
651	**Orsha** Tsentralnaya .... d.	2318	0123	0300	0344	0441	0620	0759	1111
	Minsk Passazhirski **1950** .... a.	0158	0354	|	|	|	0917	|	|
	Lviv **1720** .... a.	1529	|	|	|	|	...	|	|
	Brest Tsentralny **1950** .... a.	...	0826	|	|	|	...	|	|
729	Mahilyow **I** .... d.	...	...	0436	0548	0625	...	0950	1253
856	Zhlobin **1930** .... d.	...	...	0709	0805	0857	...	1208	1608
	Homel 1930 .... a.	...	...	|	0932	1027	...	1328	|
	Kyïv Passazhirski **1930** .... a.	...	...	|	...	...	...	2007	|
957	Kalinkavichy **1700** .... ‡ BY d.	...	...	0850	...	...	...	...	1811
1110	Korosten **1700** .... ‡ UA d.	...	...	1318	...	...	...	...	2214
1192	Zhytomyr **1700** .... d.	...	...	1506	...	...	...	...	2359
1268	**Kozyatyn** .... a.	...	...	1647	...	...	...	...	0140
	Odesa Holovna **1750** .... a.	...	...	|	...	...	...	...	1019
	Chişinău **1750** .... a.	...	...	0748	...	...	...	...	...

	Sko 48 E	Sko 20 BH	Fir 52	Sko 50	Sko 54 ◧	Sko 62 A	Sko 84 F	Fir 56
Chişinău **1750** .... d.	...	...	...	...	...	1920	...	...
Odesa Holovna **1750** .... d.	...	1825	...	...	...	|	...	...
Kozyatyn .... d.	...	0247	...	...	...	1013	...	...
Zhytomyr **1700** .... d.	...	0430	...	...	...	1200	...	...
Korosten **1700** .... ‡ UA d.	...	0626	...	...	...	1352	...	...
Kalinkavichy **1700** .... ‡ BY d.	...	1025	...	...	...	1745	...	...
Kyïv Passazhirski **1930** ...... d.	...	|	...	...	0935	|	...	...
Homel 1930 .... d.	...	|	...	...	1633	|	1850	1918
Zhlobin **1930** .... d.	...	1209	...	...	1755	1935	2010	2056
Mahilyow **I** .... d.	...	1448	...	...	2035	2201	2242	2347
Brest Tsentralny **1950** .... d.	...	|	...	1410	|	|	|	|
Lviv **1720** .... d.	2307	|	...	|	|	|	|	|
Minsk Passazhirski **1950** .... d.	1257	|	1740	1848	|	|	|	|
Orsha Tsentralnaya .... a.	1548	1611	2013	2119	2202	2327	0005	0114
Orsha Tsentralnaya .... d.	1608	1637	2030	2135	2220	2358	0022	0134
Moskva Belorusskaya **1950** .... a.	|	|	|	|	|	|	|	0955
Vitsebsk .... § BY d.	1758	1832	2215	2308	2359	0141	0205	...
Novosokolniki **1915** .... § RU d.	2158	2249	0217	0305	0410	0528	0617	...
Dno **1915** .... d.	0143	0218	0515	0557	0702	0810	0907	...
St Peterburg Vitebski **1915** ...... a.	0532	0618	0903	0938	1044	1207	1243	...

A – Conveys (on dates shown in Table **95**) 🛏 2 cl. St Peterburg - Brest - Praha and v.v.
B – Conveys (on dates shown in Table **56**) 🛏 1, 2 cl. St Peterburg - Orsha - Berlin and v.v.
C – Uneven dates [... *31, 3* ...].
D – Daily until Sept. 8; then even dates [... *30, 1, 4* ...].
E – Daily until Sept. 6; then even dates.
F – Even dates.
G – ①②③⑤ (daily May 28 - Sept. 26).
H – ③④⑤⑦ (daily May 30 - Sept. 28).
BY – Belarus (East European Time).
RU – Russia (Moskva Time).
UA – Ukraine.
§ – ▦ : Yezyaryshcha (BY) / Zaverezhye (RU).
‡ – ▦ : Slovechno (BY) / Berezhest (UA).

Named trains: **51/52** ZVYAZDA; **53/54** LYBID; **55/56** SOZH

BCh, UZ — MINSK - HOMEL - KYÏV — 1930

km		Pas 312 P	Pas 386 N	Sko 53 L	Sko 100 R	Pas 382 K	Sko 94 B		Sko 86 A
	Kaliningrad **1950** .... d.	1404	2006	...	...	...	...	...	...
	Vilnius **1950** .... d.	2000	0203	...	...	...	...	...	...
0	**Minsk** Passazhirski .... d.	0053	0648	...	0825	0910	1132	...	2050
	St Peterburg Vitebski **1920** .... d.	|	|	2120	|	|	|	...	|
214	Zhlobin **1920** .... d.	0425	1016	1208	1217	1304	1513	...	0036
300	**Homel 1920** .... a.	0553	1144	1328	1344	1426	1636	...	0156
300	**Homel** .... ‡ BY d.	0618	...	1348	1404	1449	1701	...	0221
	Kharkiv Passazhirski **1780** ..... a.	1921	...	|	0121	|	|	...	|
411	Chernihiv .... ‡ UA d.	...	...	1725	|	1826	2048	...	0606
	Simferopol **1775 1790** .... a.	...	...	|	1035	1543	|	...	|
620	**Kyïv** Passazhirski **1700 1720** .... a.	...	...	2007	...	...	0001	...	0856
	Odesa **1750** .... a.	...	...	...	...	...	1039	...	...

	Sko 94 C	Sko 99 S	Pas 311 Q	Sko 54 L	Pas 385 P		Pas 382 P	Sko 86 A
Odesa **1750** .... d.	1430	...	...	...	...	...	...	...
Kyïv Passazhirski **1700 1720** .... d.	0054	...	...	0935	...	...	...	1818
Simferopol **1775 1790** .... d.	|	1335	...	|	...	...	2152	|
Chernihiv .... ‡ UA d.	0412	|	...	1247	...	...	2005	2130
Kharkiv Passazhirski **1780** ..... d.	|	2314	0038	|	...	...	|	|
Homel .... ‡ BY a.	0743	1038	1339	1602	...	...	2337	0051
Homel 1920 .... d.	0807	1111	1402	1633	1658	...	2358	0115
Zhlobin **1920** .... d.	0932	1238	1543	1755	1826	...	0145	0239
St Peterburg Vitebski **1920** .... a.	|	|	|	1044	|	...	|	|
Minsk Passazhirski .... a.	1255	1614	1917	...	2206	...	0529	0601
Vilnius **1950** .... a.	...	...	0049	...	0254	...	...	...
Kaliningrad **1950** .... a.	...	...	0822	...	1028	...	...	...

A – Conveys (on dates shown in Table **98**) 🛏 2 cl. Minsk - Kyïv - Sofiya and v.v.
B – ①⑤ (daily June 11 - Sept. 30).
C – ②⑥ (daily June 12 - Oct. 1).
K – Even dates [... *30, 1, 4* ...].
L – LYBID.
N – Uneven dates [... *31, 3* ...].
P – Even dates.
Q – Uneven dates [... *29, 1* ...].
R – Daily June 1 - Oct. 1; then uneven dates [... *29, 1* ...].
S – Daily June 2 - Sept. 30; then even dates.
‡ – ▦ : Teryukha (BY) / Hornostayivka (UA).
BY – Belarus. UA – Ukraine.

RAIL TRAVEL IN RUSSIA, BELARUS, UKRAINE, and MOLDOVA

CARRIAGE TYPES

As trains generally operate over very long distances, most accommodation is designed for overnight as well as day use. Carriage types (with their Russian names) are:

Spálny vagón СВ (🛏 1 cl. in the tables) – 2-berth compartments (9 per carriage)

Kupéiny К (🛏 2 cl. in the tables) – 4-berth compartments (9 per carriage)

Platskártny ПЛ (▬ 3 cl. in the tables) – Dormitory-style carriage with 54 bunks

Óbshchi О ([4] in the tables) – 4th-class hard seating (81 places per carriage) ★

★ Not recommended for long-distance travel and not normally indicated in the tables.

A few day trains convey more comfortable *Sidyáchi* (seating) accommodation with 54–62 places per carriage (shown as [Sd] in the tables).

TRAIN TYPES

Ordinary long-distance trains are classified *Passazhírsky* (shown as *Pas* in the tables): they normally convey at least ▬ 3 cl. and 🛏 2 cl.

Faster long-distance trains are classified *Skóry* (shown as *Sko* in the tables): they normally convey at least ▬ 3 cl. and 🛏 2 cl. and often also 🛏 1 cl.

The top grade of fast long-distance trains are classified *Firménny* (shown as *Fir* in the tables). They are composed of higher-quality carriages dedicated to a particular, and usually named, service. They normally convey 🛏 2 cl. and 🛏 1 cl. carriages.

International services to, from and via Poland, Slovakia, Hungary and Romania convey through sleeping cars of the normal European ('RIC') types, with single and double compartments in first class, and 3- or 4-berth compartments in second class. The railways of the former Soviet Union being of broad gauge (1520mm), the bogies (trucks) of these through cars are changed at the frontier with these countries.

DAYS OF RUNNING

Many trains run on alternate days only: even dates or uneven dates. The examples below illustrate the system used to indicate exceptions to the pattern of even or uneven dates at the end of a month with 31 days and at the beginning of the month following:

e.g. "Uneven dates [... *29, 1* ...]" means that the train does not run on the 31st of a month with 31 days.

e.g. "Even dates [... *30, 1, 4* ...]" means that the train, **following a month with 31 days**, runs exceptionally on the 1st, but not the 2nd, of the month.

1935 VORONEZH - POLATSK RZhD, BCh

km		Pas 468 A	Fir 40 D
0	**Voronezh** d.	0243	...
246	Kursk d.	1110	...
324	Lgov d.	1300	...
541	Bryansk Orlovski a.	1823	...
541	Bryansk Orlovski d.	1853	...
	Moskva Beloruss. **1950** d.	|	2119
796	Smolensk a.	0145	0314
796	Smolensk d.	...	0354
937	Vitsebsk § RU d.	...	0556
1039	**Polatsk** § BY a.	...	0745

	Pas 467 B	Fir 39 D
Polatsk § BY d.	...	1752
Vitsebsk § RU d.	...	1959
Smolensk a.	...	2322
Smolensk d.	0727	2352
Moskva Beloruss. **1950** a.	|	0551
Bryansk Orlovski a.	1306	...
Bryansk Orlovski d.	1336	...
Lgov a.	1755	...
Kursk a.	1943	...
Voronezh a.	0150	...

1945 VORONEZH - HOMEL - BREST RZhD, BCh

km		Sko 75	Pas 376 Y	Pas 663
0	**Voronezh** d.	...	1828	...
**	Moskva Beloruss. d.	1554	|	...
548	Bryansk Orlovski d.	0045	0738	...
776	Zlynka 🏛 RU d.	0505	1218	...
802	Dobrush 🏛 BY d.	0436	1145	...
827	**Homel** a.	0502	1212	...
827	**Homel** d.	0522	...	2100
956	Kalinkavichy **1700** d.	0753	...	2340
1133	Luninets **1700** d.	1118	...	0325
1361	**Brest** Tsentr. **1700** a.	1544	...	0735

	Pas 376 Z	Sko 76	Pas 664
Brest Tsentr. **1700** d.	...	1013	1940
Luninets **1700** d.	...	1429	0008
Kalinkavichy **1700** d.	...	1740	0409
Homel a.	...	1941	0626
Homel d.	1739	2010	...
Dobrush 🏛 BY d.	1810	2044	...
Zlynka 🏛 RU d.	1935	2211	...
Bryansk Orlovski a.	0009	0240	...
Moskva Beloruss. a.	|	1204	...
Voronezh a.	1150	...	...

NOTES FOR TABLES **1935** and **1945**:

A – June 4 - Sept. 28. Even dates [... *30, 1, 4* ...].
B – June 1 - Sept. 25. Uneven dates [... *29, 1* ...].
D – DVINA.
Y – Even dates [... *30, 1, 3, 6* ...].
Z – Uneven dates [... *31, 3* ...].
§ – 🏛 : Zavolsha (BY) / Rudnya (RU).
** – Moskva - Bryansk: *485 km*.
BY – Belarus (East European Time).
RU – Russia (Moskva Time).

1950 MOSKVA - MINSK, VILNIUS, KALININGRAD and BREST RZhD, BCh, LG

km		Fir 105	Sko 69 S	Sko 19 B	Sko 13 M		Pas 301 N	Pas 311 K	Sko 25	Sko 103		Pas 385 Ge	Fir 29		Sko 27	Sko 47 E	Fir 77	Sko 5	Sko 9 P	Sko 49 J	Sko 147 U	Pas 395	Fir 3 e	Fir 55 Z
0	**Moskva** Belorusskaya d.	...	...	...	0800	...	...	...	1023	...	...	...	1406	...	1542	...	1654	1820	1920	...	1855	1937	2059	2106
243	Vyazma d.	...	0732	...	|	...	...	...	1359	...	...	...	1738	...	1910	...	2046	2143	|	...	2253	2349	0023	0047
419	Smolensk § RU d.	...	1122	...	1223	...	...	...	1620	...	...	...	2000	...	2135	...	2316	2359	2359	...	0116	0238	0230	0300
	St Peterburg Vitebski ▲ d.	...	|	2340	|	...	...	...	|	...	...	...	|	...	|	1242	|	|	|	1500	|	|	|	|
538	Orsha Tsentralnaya § BY a.	...	1204	1046	1235	...	...	...	1653	...	...	...	2029	...	2208	2300	2344	0020	0040	0104	0145	0309	0257	0325
538	Orsha Tsentralnaya d.	...	1217	1250	1250	...	...	...	1707	...	...	...	2044	...	2221	2318	2359	0033	0050	0123	0200	0323	0311	...
750	**Minsk** a.	...	1442	1510	1510	...	...	...	2006	...	...	...	2321	...	0059	0158	0234	0259	0313	0354	0456	0615	0606	...
750	**Minsk** d.	1352	1503	1526	1526	...	1816	1937	...	2040	...	2226	2343	...	0118	0224	0300	0318	0323	0408	0515	0630	...	...
828	Maladzechna ‡ BY d.	|	|	|	|	...	1924	2117	...	|	...	2345	0103	...	|	|	0419	0430	|	|	0644	|	...	...
956	Lida d.	|	|	|	|	...	|	|	...	|	...	|	|	...	|	|	0703	|	|	|	|	|	...	...
1101	Hrodna a.	|	|	|	|	...	|	|	...	|	...	|	|	...	|	|	0929	|	|	|	|	|	...	...
944	**Vilnius** ‡ LT a.	|	|	|	|	...	2200	0049	...	|	...	0254	0418	...	|	|	...	0746	|	|	1013	|	...	...
944	**Vilnius** ¶ LT d.	|	|	|	|	...	...	0109	...	|	...	0314	0438	...	|	|	...	...	|	|	1033	|	...	...
1286	**Kaliningrad** ¶ Ka a.	|	|	|	|	...	...	0822	...	|	...	1028	1206	...	|	|	...	...	|	|	1814	|	...	...
898	Baranavichy Tsentralnye d.	1540	1651	1707	1707	...	...	...	...	2224	...	...	...	...	0305	0430p	...	...	|	0558	...	0915p	...	...
	Lviv **1720** a.	|	|	|	|	...	...	...	...	|	...	...	...	...	|	1529	...	...	|	|	...	|	...	...
1100	**Brest** Tsentralny a.	1810	1855	1855	1855	...	...	...	...	0029	...	...	...	...	0535	...	...	...	0642	0826	...	1228	...	...
	Warszawa Wschodnia **1050** a.	...	0033	0033	0033	...	...	...	...	0614	...	...	...	...	...	...	...	...	1133	...	...	...	...	...

	Fir 7 F	Pas 305 ③⑥⑦	Sko 11 A	Fir 40 D	Fir 1	Sko 131	Sko 21 V	Sko 79 Y	Fir 51
Moskva Belorusskaya d.	2335	...	2109	2119	2225	2255	2344	...	...
Vyazma d.	|	...	0034	0056	0201	0233	0304	...	...
Smolensk § RU d.	|	...	0300	0314	|	0452	0508	...	...
St Peterburg Vitebski ▲ d.	|	...	|	...	|	|	|	1816	1908
Orsha Tsentralnaya § BY a.	0342	...	0325	...	0443	0514	0528	|	0600
Orsha Tsentralnaya d.	0352	...	0338	...	0456	0527	0542	|	0620
Minsk a.	0606	...	0615	...	0729	0817	0808	|	0917
Minsk d.	...	0630	0643	...	...	0832	0824	|	...
Maladzechna ‡ BY d.	...	0754	|	...	...	|	|	0915	...
Lida d.	...	|	|	...	...	|	|	|	...
Hrodna a.	...	|	|	...	...	|	|	|	...
Vilnius ‡ LT a.	...	1100	|	...	...	|	|	1242	...
Vilnius ¶ LT d.	...	...	|	...	...	|	|	1302	...
Kaliningrad ¶ Ka a.	...	...	|	...	...	|	|	2026	...
Baranavichy Tsentralnye d.	...	...	0828	...	...	1023	1009	...	...
Lviv **1720** a.	...	...	|	...	...	|	|	...	...
Brest Tsentralny a.	...	...	1030	...	...	1241	1215	...	...
Warszawa Wschodnia **1050** a.	...	...	1611	...	...	...	...	...	...

	Sko 104	Sko 132		Pas 302 N	Fir 106	Sko 14 M	Sko 14 Q	Sko 70 T	Sko 48 C
Warszawa Wschodnia **1050** d.	2050	...	...	...	...	2358	2358	2358	...
Brest Tsentralny d.	0424	0434	...	...	0624	0720	0720	0720	...
Lviv **1720** d.	|	|	...	...	|	|	|	|	2307
Baranavichy Tsentralnye d.	0632	0658	...	...	0855	0910	0910	0928	1049p
Kaliningrad ¶ Ka d.	|	|	...	...	|	|	|	|	|
Vilnius 1850 ¶ LT a.	|	|	...	...	|	|	|	|	|
Vilnius ‡ LT d.	|	|	...	0642	|	|	|	|	|
Hrodna d.	|	|	...	|	|	|	|	|	|
Lida d.	|	|	...	|	|	|	|	|	|
Maladzechna ‡ BY d.	|	|	...	0920	|	|	|	|	|
Minsk a.	0814	0837	...	1034	1037	1046	1046	1114	1240
Minsk d.	...	0851	...	...	...	1105	1105	1136	1257
Orsha Tsentralnaya a.	...	1136	...	...	...	1330	1330	1408	1548
Orsha Tsentralnaya § BY d.	...	1150	...	...	...	1348	1637	1426	1608
St Peterburg Vitebski ▲ a.	...	|	...	...	...	|	0618	|	0532
Smolensk § RU d.	...	1413	...	...	...	1611	...	1702	...
Vyazma d.	...	1643	...	...	...	|	...	1909	...
Moskva Belorusskaya a.	...	1954	...	...	...	2035	...	...	...

	Fir 52	Fir 39 D	Sko 50	Sko 26	Fir 4 F	Pas 306 ③⑥⑦	Sko 80 R	Sko 22 V	Sko 22 Jd	Fir 8 e	Fir 2	Sko 6	Fir 30	Fir 56 Z	Fir 78	Sko 12 A		Pas 312 K		Sko 10 P	Sko 148 Y	Pas 396		Pas 386 Gn
Warszawa Wschodnia **1050** d.	...	...	...	...	...	...	...	...	...	...	...	...	...	...	...	1208	...	...	...	1635	...	...	...	...
Brest Tsentralny d.	...	...	1410	...	...	...	...	1641	1641	...	...	...	...	...	...	1945	...	...	...	2326	...	2155	...	...
Lviv **1720** d.	...	...	|	...	...	...	...	|	|	...	...	...	...	...	...	|	...	...	...	|	...	|	...	...
Baranavichy Tsentralnye d.	...	...	1642	...	...	...	...	1853	1853	...	...	...	...	...	...	2153	...	...	...	|	...	0116p	...	...
Kaliningrad ¶ Ka d.	...	...	|	...	...	...	0949	|	|	...	...	...	1144	...	...	|	...	1404	...	|	1630	|	...	2006
Vilnius 1850 ¶ LT a.	...	...	|	...	...	...	1529	|	|	...	...	...	1728	...	...	|	...	1940	...	|	2220	|	...	0143
Vilnius ‡ LT d.	...	...	|	...	...	1420	1549	|	|	...	...	1707	1748	...	...	|	...	2000	...	|	2240	|	...	0203
Hrodna d.	...	...	|	...	...	|	|	|	|	...	...	|	|	...	1717	|	...	|	...	|	|	|	...	|
Lida d.	...	...	|	...	...	|	|	|	|	...	...	|	|	...	1932	|	...	|	...	|	|	|	...	|
Maladzechna ‡ BY d.	...	...	|	...	...	1728	1913	|	|	...	...	2012	2057	...	2157	|	...	2313	...	|	0145	|	...	0515
Minsk a.	...	...	1831	...	...	1846	|	2034	2034	...	...	2140	2216	...	2312	2333	...	0053	...	0251	0258	0326	...	0648
Minsk d.	1740	...	1848	1812	1930	...	|	2052	2052	2147	2155	2203	2237	...	2332	2356	...	...	...	0301	0324	0341	...	...
Orsha Tsentralnaya a.	2013	...	2119	2131	2203	...	|	2318	2318	0002	0012	0036	0103	...	0206	0220	...	...	...	0514	0608	0634	...	...
Orsha Tsentralnaya § BY d.	2030	...	2135	2145	2216	...	|	2332	2358	0014	0036	0050	0119	0134	0221	0233	...	...	...	0525	0623	0646	...	...
St Peterburg Vitebski ▲ a.	0903	...	0938	|	|	...	1110	|	1207	|	|	|	|	|	|	|	...	...	...	|	|	|	...	...
Smolensk § RU d.	...	2352	...	0010	0036	...	...	0152	...	|	|	0313	0342	0357	0446	0501	...	...	...	0738	0856	0930	...	...
Vyazma d.	...	0233	...	0242	0307	...	...	0410	...	|	0522	0530	0603	0620	0717	0728	...	...	...	|	1151	1232	...	...
Moskva Belorusskaya a.	...	0551	...	0600	0623	...	...	0720	...	0623	0846	0905	0927	0955	1026	1059	...	...	...	1210	1548	1623	...	...

A – VOSTOK-ZAPAD EKSPRESS – 🛏 1, 2 cl. Moskva - Warszawa - Amsterdam, Basel and München and v.v. See Table **24**.
B – 🛏 2 cl. St Peterburg - Orsha (**13**) - Berlin. For days of running, see Table **56**.
C – Daily until Sept. 6, 2007; then even dates.
D – DVINA – to / from Polatsk (Table **1935**).
E – Daily until Sept. 8, 2007; then even dates [... *30, 1, 4* ...].
F – Uneven dates [... *29, 1* ...].
G – 🛏 2 cl. and 🛌 3 cl. Homel - Kaliningrad and v.v.
J – Conveys (on dates in Table **95**) 🛏 2 cl. St Peterburg - Praha and v.v. See Table **95**.
K – Uneven dates [... *29, 1* ...] from Kharkiv; even dates from Kaliningrad. 🛏 2 cl., 🛌 3 cl. Kharkiv - Kaliningrad and v.v.
M – MOSKVA EKSPRESS – 🛏 1, 2 cl. Moskva - Berlin and v.v. For days of running, see Table **56**. Conveys on dates shown in Table **24** 🛏 1, 2 cl. Moskva - Paris and v.v.
N – 🛏 2 cl. and 🚃 (LG) Minsk - Vilnius and v.v.
P – POLONEZ – 🛏 1, 2 cl. Moskva - Warszawa and v.v.
Q – 🛏 2 cl. Berlin - Orsha (**20**) - St Peterburg. For days of running, see Table **56**.
R – Uneven dates [... *29, 1* ...] (daily June 5 - Sept. 5, 2007).
S – ④ from Saratov (⑤ from Vyazma). 🛏 1, 2 cl. Saratov - Vyazma - Berlin; 🛏 2 cl. Novosibirsk (**113**) - Brest - Berlin. For other cars see Tables **1980** amd **1985**.
T – ⑥ from Berlin and Warszawa. 🛏 1, 2 cl. Berlin - Vyazma - Saratov; 🛏 2 cl. Berlin - Minsk (**64**) - Novosibirsk. For other cars see Tables **1980** amd **1985**.
U – Uneven dates [... *31, 3* ...] (daily June 7 - Sept. 7, 2007).
V – VLTAVA – 🛏 1, 2 cl. Moskva - Praha, Budapest and Cheb and v.v. See Table **95**. Conveys (on dates in Table **95**) 🛏 1, 2 cl. Moskva / Minsk - Wien and v.v.
Y – Even dates (daily June 6 - Sept. 6, 2007).
Z – SOZH – to / from Homel (Table **1920**).
d – Train **61** from Orsha.
e – Even dates.
n – Uneven dates [... *31, 3* ...].
p – Baranavichy Polesskiye.
▲ – See Tables **1915** and **1920**.
§ – 🏛 : Osinovka (BY) / Krasnoye (RU).
‡ – 🏛 : Hudahai (BY) / Kena (LT).
¶ – 🏛 : Kybartai (LT) / Nesterov (Ka).
BY – Belarus (East European Time).
Ka – Kaliningrad region of Russia (Moskva Time).
LT – Lithuania (East European Time).
RU – Russia (Moskva Time).

Other named trains:

1/2 BELORUSSIYA / BELARUS
3/4 MINSK
7/8 SLAVYANSKI EKSPRESS
29/30 YANTAR
77/78 NEMAN / NYOMAN
103/104 SUZORYE
105/106 BUH

RZhD, KTZh — VYAZMA - ROSTOV and A[...]

km		Sko 70 B	Sko 70 C	Sko 108 A
	Berlin Hbf **56** .... d.	1522	1522	...
	Warszawa W. **1050** d.	2358	2358	2147
	Brest Tsentr. **1950**.. d.	0720	0720	|
	Minsk **1950**............ d.	1136	1136	|
0	**Vyazma**.................... d.	1932	1932	|
472	Ryazan...................... d.	0332	0332	|
682	Michurinsk .... a.	0630	0630	|
682	Michurinsk .... d.	0707	0723	|
1060	Rossosh.................. a.	|	1337	|
1500	**Rostov na Donu**... a.	|	2237	|
755	Tambov .... d.	0824	...	|
1135	**Saratov** .... a.	1519	...	2253
1135	**Saratov** .... d.	...	...	2338
3353	**Astana** (Aqmola) ....‡ a.	...	...	2322

	F		
Astana (Aqmola)... ‡ d.	1025	...	
Saratov .... a.	0556	...	
Saratov .... d.	0635	...	1129
Tambov .... d.	|	...	1804
Rostov na Donu .. d.	|	0251	|
Rossosh.................. d.	|	0925	|
Michurinsk .... a.	|	1443	1917
Michurinsk .... d.	|	1952	1952
Ryazan...................... d.	|	2316	2316
Vyazma.................... a.	|	0709	0709
Minsk **1950** .... a.	|	1442	1442
Brest Tsentr. **1950**.. a.	|	1855	1855
Warszawa W. **1050** a.	0636	0033	0033
Berlin Hbf **56** .... a.	...	0901	0901

[...]OSIBIRSK — 1985

km		
21[...]		
331	Sm[...]	[...]
507	Vyazma **1950** .... d.	0025 ①
1346	Sergach .... a.	1532 :
1615	**Kazan** .... a.	1941 :
1919	Agryz .... a.	0112 ②
2265	Krasnoufimsk .... a.	0719 :
2490	**Yekaterinburg** (Sverdlovsk) a.	1143 :
3388	Omsk .... a.	0206 ③
4015	**Novosibirsk**...................... a.	1053 :

	Sko 113 P
.... d.	1956 ②
.... d.	0353 ③
	1745 :
Kazan .... d.	0903 :
Sergach .... d.	1346 :
Vyazma **1950** .... a.	0512 ⑤
Smolensk **1950** .... § RU a.	0752 :
Orsha **1950** .... § BY a.	0824 :
Minsk 1950.......................a.	1201 :
Brest Tsentr. **1950** ....a.	1722 :
Warszawa W. **1050**.........a.	0033 ⑥
Berlin Hbf **56**...................a.	0901 :

INTERNATIONAL SHIPPING

RUSSIA

NOTES FOR TABLES **1980** and **1985**:

A – ⑥ from Warszawa. 🛏 2 cl. Warszawa (**68**) - Kyïv (**108**) - Astana. Arrives Saratov ① (journey: 2 nights), Astana ③ (journey 4 nights).

B – ⑥ from Berlin. 🛏 2 cl. Berlin (**1249**) - Brest - Saratov. Arrives Saratov ①.

C – ⑥ from Berlin. 🛏 1, 2 cl. Berlin (**1249**) - Brest - Michurinsk (**87**) - Rostov. Arrives Voronezh and Rostov ①. To Adler (arrive on ②).

D – ④ from Rostov. 🛏 1, 2 cl. Rostov - Michurinsk (**69**) - Brest (**1248**) - Berlin. Arrives Minsk ⑤, Berlin ⑥. Starts from Adler (depart on ③).

E – ④ from Saratov. 🛏 2 cl. Saratov - Brest (**1248**) - Berlin. Arrives Minsk ⑤, Berlin ⑥.

F – ② from Astana, ④ from Saratov. 🛏 2 cl. Astana - Kyïv (**67**) - Warszawa. Arrives Warszawa ⑥ (journey: 4 nights).

N – 🛏 2 cl. Berlin (**1249**) - Terespol - Orsha (**64**) - Novosibirsk.

P – 🛏 2 cl. Novosibirsk - Brest (**69**) - Terespol (**1248**) - Berlin.

‡ – Kazak Eastern Time (= Moskva Time + 3 hrs).

§ – 🏛 : Osinovka (BY) / Krasnoye (RU).

BY – Belarus (East European Time).

RU – Russia (Moskva Time).

RZhD, MTZ, CR — TRANS-SIBERIAN RAILWAY (Summary Table) — 1990

For full details of this and other services east of Moskva, see the Thomas Cook Overseas Timetable in the blue cover

km	*All timings in Russia are in Moskva Time*	Sko 4 ②		Fir 2 Ra		Sko 20 ⑤	
0	**Moskva** Yaroslavskaya..........d.	2135	*1st day*	2125	*1st day*	2355	*1st day*
461	Nizhni-Novgorod (Gorki).........d.	0355	*2nd day*	0345	*2nd day*	0621	*2nd day*
917	Vyatka (Kirov).......................d.	1008	*2nd day*	0958	*2nd day*	1232	*2nd day*
1397	Perm ....d.	1750	*2nd day*	1740	*2nd day*	2021	*2nd day*
1778	**Yekaterinburg** (Sverdlovsk) ..d.	2338	*2nd day*	2345	*2nd day*	0209	*3rd day*
2676	Omsk.....................................d.	1142	*3rd day*	1154	*3rd day*	1433	*3rd day*
3303	**Novosibirsk** ....d.	1928	*3rd day*	1957	*3rd day*	2217	*3rd day*
4065	Krasnoyarsk...........................d.	0713	*4th day*	0813	*4th day*	1018	*4th day*
5153	**Irkutsk** ....d.	0043	*5th day*	0220	*5th day*	0403	*5th day*
5609	Ulan-Ude ....d.	0830	*5th day*	0939	*5th day*	1114	*5th day*
6266	Ulaanbaatar....................‡ a.	0730	*6th day*	|	|	|	|
6166	Chita......................................d.	|	|	1930	*5th day*	2101	*5th day*
7573	**Harbin** ....§ a.	|	|	|	|	1250	*7th day*
8120	Shenyang........................§ a.	|	|	|	|	1918	*7th day*
****	**Beijing**............................§ a.	1404	*7th day*	|	|	0531	*8th day*
8493	Khabarovsk ....a.	...	...	1208	*7th day*	...	...
9259	**Vladivostok** ....a.	...	...	0103	*8th day*	...	...

All timings in Russia are in Moskva Time	Sko 3 ③		Fir 1 Rb		Sko 19 ⑥	
Vladivostok .... d.	...	...	1435	*1st day*	...	...
Khabarovsk .... d.	...	...	0325	*2nd day*	...	...
Beijing ....§ d.	0745	*1st day*	|	|	2256	*1st day*
Shenyang ....§ d.	|	|	|	|	0850	*2nd day*
Harbin ....§ d.	|	|	|	|	1505	*2nd day*
Chita .... d.	|	|	2005	*3rd day*	2116	*3rd day*
Ulaanbaatar .... ‡ d.	1350	*2nd day*	|	|	|	|
Ulan-Ude............................... d.	0335	*3rd day*	0522	*4th day*	0636	*4th day*
Irkutsk................................ d.	1048	*3rd day*	1240	*4th day*	1355	*4th day*
Krasnoyarsk .... d.	0412	*4th day*	0656	*5th day*	0746	*5th day*
Novosibirsk.......................... d.	1610	*4th day*	1914	*5th day*	2024	*5th day*
Omsk .... d.	2354	*4th day*	0306	*6th day*	0343	*6th day*
Yekaterinburg (Sverdlovsk) .. d.	1205	*5th day*	1553	*6th day*	1601	*6th day*
Perm .... d.	1747	*5th day*	2137	*6th day*	2147	*6th day*
Vyatka (Kirov)........................ d.	0102	*6th day*	0453	*7th day*	0503	*7th day*
Nizhni-Novgorod (Gorki) .... d.	0654	*6th day*	1047	*7th day*	1057	*7th day*
Moskva Yaroslavskaya .... a.	1428	*6th day*	1743	*7th day*	1757	*7th day*

R – ROSSIYA – 🛏 1, 2 cl. and 🛏 3 cl. Moskva - Vladivostok and v.v.
a – From Moskva on uneven dates (except the 31st).
b – From Vladivostok on even dates (however, on the 1st, 3rd and 5th – not the 2nd, 4th or 6th – of Jan., Feb., Apr., June, Aug., Sept., Nov.).

**** *7622 km* via Ulaanbaatar (Trans-Mongolian Railway); *8961 km* via Harbin (Trans-Manchurian Railway).

‡ – Mongolian time. § – Chinese time.

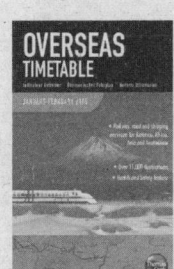

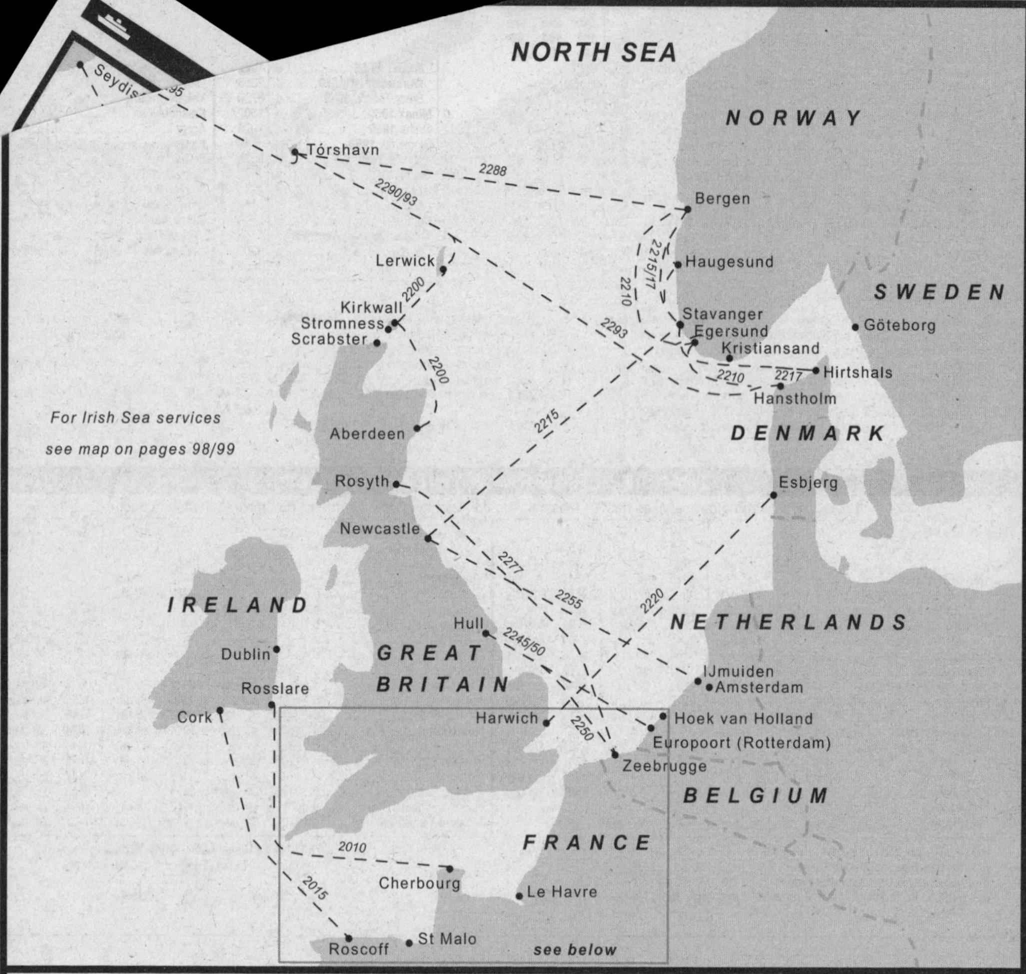

NORTH SEA

NORWAY

SWEDEN

DENMARK

NETHERLANDS

BELGIUM

FRANCE

IRELAND

GREAT BRITAIN

Seydis... 95

Tórshavn

2288

2290/93

Bergen

Haugesund

2215/17

2210

Stavanger

Egersund

Kristiansand

Göteborg

Hirtshals

2210

2217

Hanstholm

2293

Lerwick

2200

Kirkwall

Stromness

Scrabster

2200

Aberdeen

2215

For Irish Sea services see map on pages 98/99

Rosyth

Esbjerg

Newcastle

2277

2255

2220

Hull

2245/50

Dublin

Rosslare

Cork

IJmuiden

Amsterdam

Harwich

Hoek van Holland

2250

Europoort (Rotterdam)

Zeebrugge

2010

2015

Cherbourg

Le Havre

Roscoff

St Malo

see below

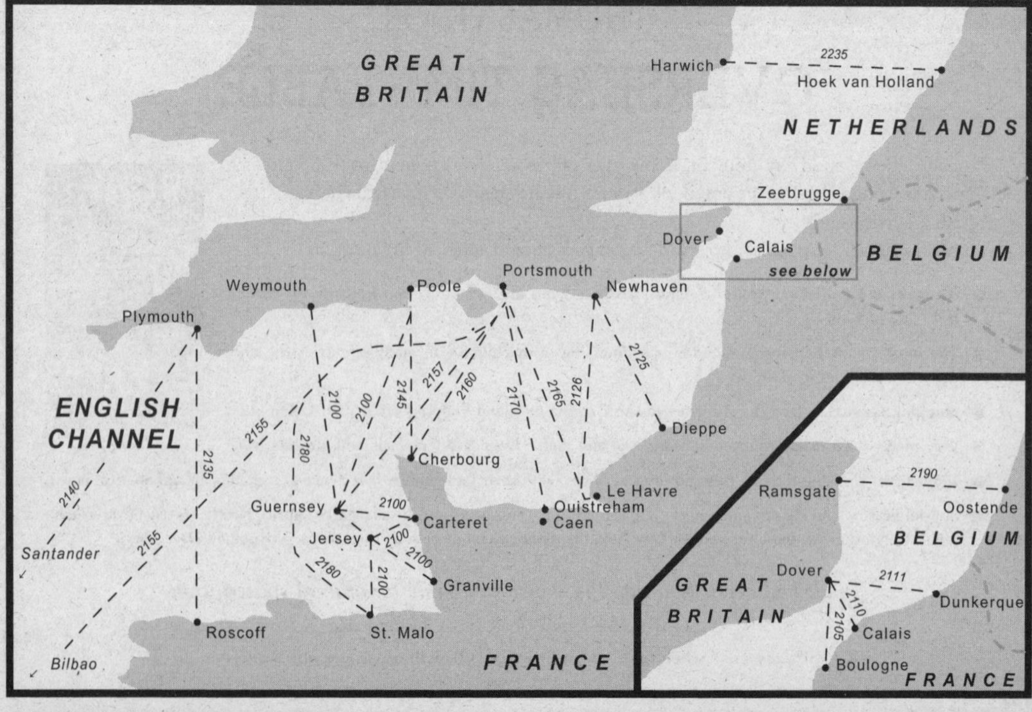

GREAT BRITAIN

Harwich

2235

Hoek van Holland

NETHERLANDS

Zeebrugge

Dover

Calais

see below

BELGIUM

Weymouth

Poole

Portsmouth

Newhaven

Plymouth

ENGLISH CHANNEL

2100

2100

2145

2157

2160

2170

2165

2126

2125

Dieppe

2155

2180

2135

2140

Cherbourg

Le Havre

Ouistreham

Caen

Guernsey

2100

Carteret

Jersey

2100

2100

Santander

2155

2180

2100

Granville

Roscoff

St. Malo

Bilbao

FRANCE

Ramsgate

2190

Oostende

BELGIUM

GREAT BRITAIN

Dover

2111

2110

2105

Dunkerque

Calais

Boulogne

FRANCE

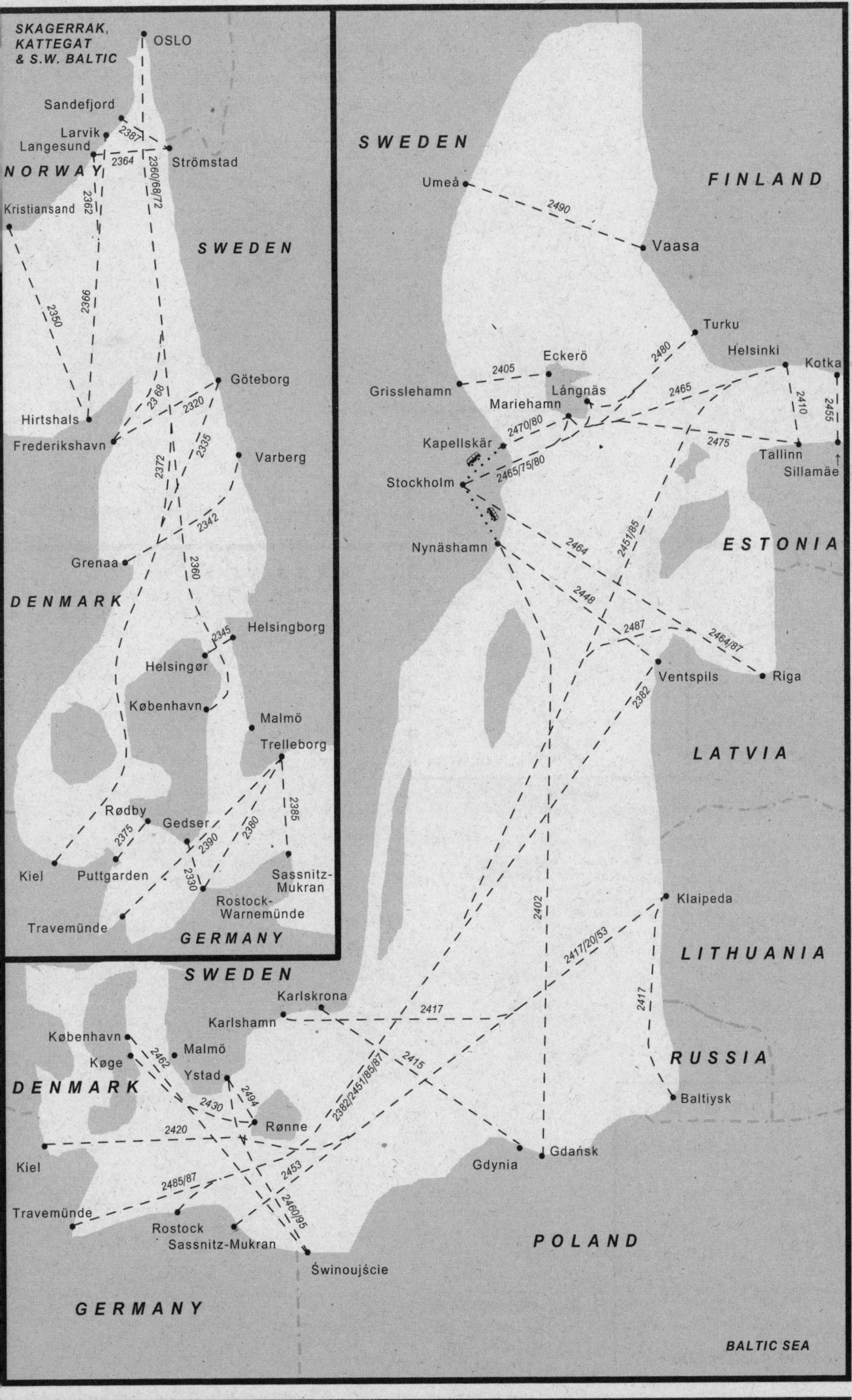

SKAGERRAK,
KATTEGAT
& S.W. BALTIC

OSLO
Sandefjord
Larvik
Langesund
2387
2364
Strömstad
2360/68/72
NORWAY
Kristiansand
2362
SWEDEN
2366
2350
Hirtshals
Göteborg
2368
2320
Frederikshavn
2335
Varberg
2372
2342
Grenaa
2360
DENMARK
2345
Helsingborg
Helsingør
København
Malmö
Trelleborg
2385
Rødby
Gedser
2375
2390
2380
Kiel
Puttgarden
2330
Sassnitz-
Mukran
Rostock-
Warnemünde
Travemünde
GERMANY

SWEDEN
FINLAND
Umeå
2490
Vaasa
Turku
2480
Eckerö
Helsinki
Kotka
2405
Grisslehamn
Långnäs
2465
Mariehamn
2410
2455
2470/80
Kapellskär
2475
Tallinn
Sillamäe
2465/75/80
Stockholm
Nynäshamn
2464
2451/85
ESTONIA
2448
2487
2464/87
Ventspils
Riga
2382
LATVIA
Klaipeda
2402
LITHUANIA
2417/20/53
SWEDEN
Karlskrona
2417
Karlshamn
2417
København
Malmö
Køge
2462
RUSSIA
Ystad
2415
DENMARK
2382/2451/85/87
2494
Baltiysk
2430
Rønne
2420
Kiel
Gdańsk
Gdynia
2453
2485/87
Travemünde
Rostock
2460/95
Sassnitz-Mukran
POLAND
Świnoujście
GERMANY
BALTIC SEA

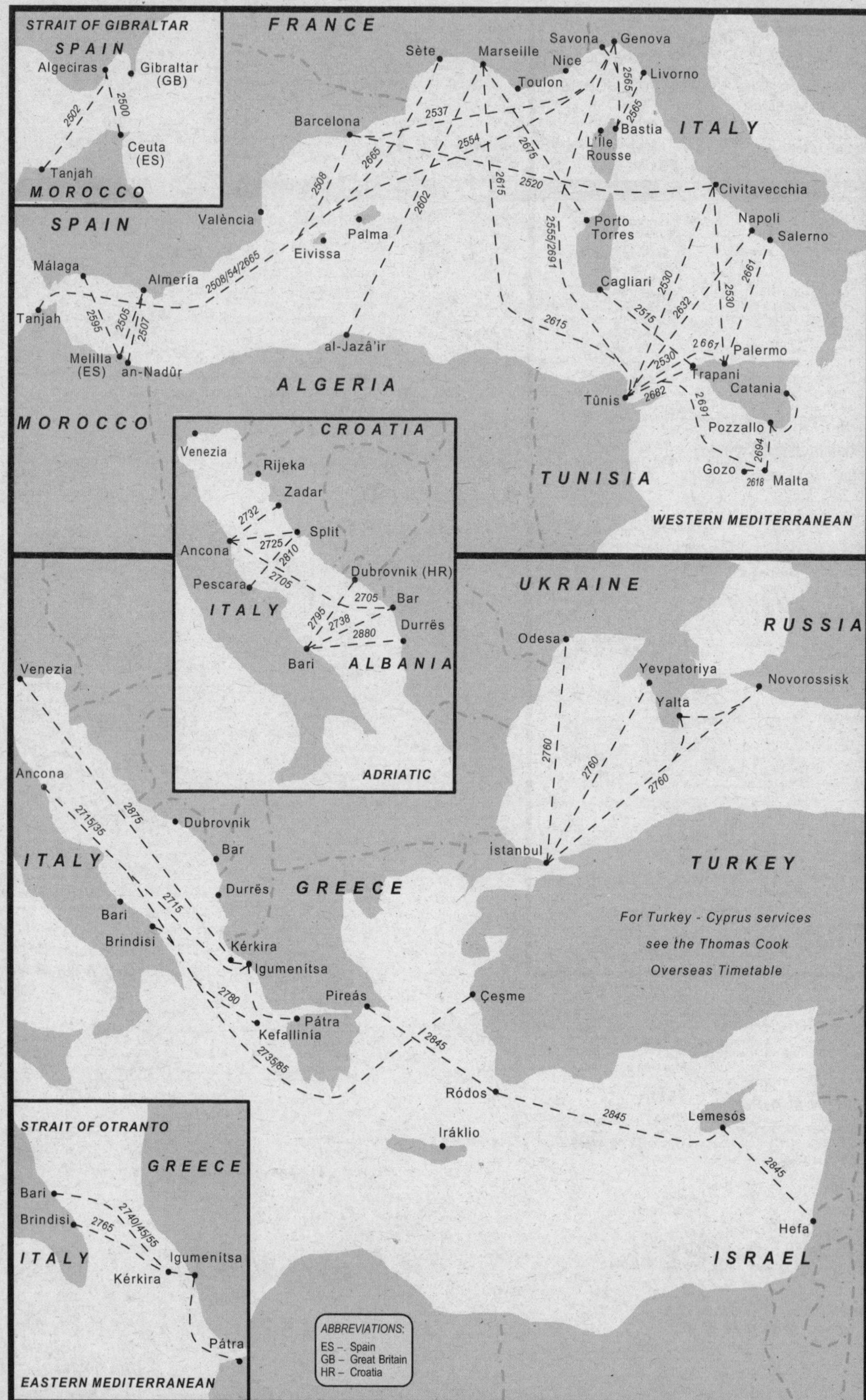

For domestic shipping routes please see relevant country maps

SHIPPING CONTENTS

SHIPPING OPERATORS

A G EMS: Postfach 11 54, 26691 Emden-Außenhafen.
✆ +49 (0)1805 180 182, fax +49 21 / 89 07 405.

ALILAURO: Via Caracciolo 11, 80122 Napoli.
✆ +39 081 76 14 909, fax +39 081 76 14 250.

ANEK LINES: 32 Akti Possidonos, 185 31 Pireás.
✆ +30 210 4118611, fax +30 210 4115465.
UK agent: Viamare Travel, Graphic House, 2 Sumatra Road, West Hampstead, London NW6 1PU. ✆ 08704 10 60 40, fax 020 7431 5456.

ARKADIA LINES: Kifissias Ave 215, 15124 Maroussi, Greece.
✆ +30 210 6123402, fax +30 210 6126206.
UK agent: Viamare Travel (see Anek Lines) ✆ 08704 10 60 40, fax 020 7431 5456.

AZZURRA LINE: Old Bakery Street, Valletta, Malta.
Italy agent: Pier Paola Santelia, Stazione marittima, Bari ✆ +39 080 52 31 824, fax +39 080 52 30 287.
Croatia agent: Elite Shipping Agency, Gruska obala 1, 20000 Dubrovnik, Croatia.
✆ +385 (20) 31 31 78, fax +385 (20) 31 31 80.

BALEÀRIA (EUROLÍNIES MARÍTIMES): Estació Marítima, 03700 Dénia.
✆ +34 902 160 180, fax +34 (96) 578 76 06.

BLUE STAR FERRIES: 26, Akti Posidonos, 185 31 Pireás.
✆ +30 210 422 5000, fax +30 210 422 5265.
UK agent: Viamare Travel (see Anek Lines) ✆ 08704 10 60 40, fax 020 7431 5456.

BORNHOLMSTRAFIKKEN: Havnen, 3700 Rønne.
✆ +45 56 95 18 66, fax +45 56 91 07 66.

BRITTANY FERRIES: Millbay, Plymouth, PL1 3EW. ✆ 08709 076 103.
Wharf Road, Portsmouth, PO2 8RU. ✆ 0990 360 360, fax 023 9289 2204.
42 Grand Parade, Cork. ✆ +353 (0)21 277801, fax +353 (0)21 277262.
Gare Maritime, Port du Bloscon, 29688 Roscoff. ✆ +33 825 828 828.
Estación Maritima, 39002 Santander. ✆ +34 942 36 06 11.

BUMERANG SHIPPING COMPANY TOURISM TRAVEL & TRADE S.A.: Rihtim Cad. Veli Alemdar Han Kat. 6, 80030 Karaköy - Istanbul.
✆ +90 (0)212 251 7373, fax +90 (0)212 251 1472.

CAREMAR: Campania Regionale Marittima S.p.A., Molo Beverello, 80133 Napoli.
✆ +39 081 58 05 111, fax +39 081 55 14 551.

COLOR LINE: Postboks 1422 Vika, 0115 Oslo.
✆ +47 810 00 811, fax +47 22 83 07 76.

COMARIT: 7 Rue du Mexique, Tanjah (Tangiers), Morocco.
✆ + 212 (0)9 32 00 32, fax + 212 (0)9 32 59 00.

COMPAGNIE MAROCAINE DE NAVIGATION (COMANAV):
7 Boulevard de la Résistance, Casablanca 05.
✆ +212 (0)2 30 30 12, fax +212 (0)2 30 84 55.
U.K. Agent: Southern Ferries, London. ✆ 020 7491 4968, fax 020 7491 3502.

COMPAGNIE TUNISIENNE DE NAVIGATION: Dag Hammarskjoeld Avenue 5, Tûnis.
✆ +216 (1) 341777, fax +216 (1) 335714.
UK agent: Southern Ferries, London. ✆ 020 7491 4968, fax 020 7491 3502.
France agent: SNCM, Marseille. ✆ +33 (0)4 91 56 30 10, fax +33 (0)4 91 56 31 00.

CONDOR FERRIES LTD.: New Harbour Rd. South, Hamworthy, Poole, BH15 4AJ.
✆ 01202 207 216.
The Quay, Weymouth, Dorset DT4 8DX. ✆ 01305 761 551, fax 01305 760 776.
Jersey: ✆ 01534 872 240. Guernsey 12023 (local calls only).
Reservations: ✆ 0870 243 5140.

CORSICA FERRIES: (including SARDINIA FERRIES), 5 bis, Rue Chanoine Leschi, 20296 Bastia. ✆ +33 (0)4 95 32 95 95, fax +33 (0)4 95 32 14 71.

DESTINATION GOTLAND: PO Box 1234, 621 23 Visby, Gotland, Sweden.
✆ +46 (0)498 20 10 20, fax +46 (0)498 20 18 90.

DFDS LISCO: Ostuferhafen 15, 24149, Kiel.
✆ +49 (0)431 20976 420, fax +49 (0)431 20976 102.
Reservations: ✆ +370 46 393616.

DFDS SEAWAYS: Scandinavia House, Parkeston Quay, Harwich CO12 4QG.
✆ 0871 522 9955; Reservations: ✆ 08702 520 524.
International Ferry Terminal, Royal Quays, North Shields, NE29 6EE.
Axelborg Vesterbrogade 4A, 1620 København V. ✆ +45 33 156341, fax +45 33 936330.
Skandiahamnen, P.O. Box 8895, 402 72 Göteborg. ✆ +46 (0)31 65 06 00, fax +46 (0)31 54 3925.
Van-den-Smissen Strasse 4, 2000 Hamburg 50. ✆ +49 (0)40 389 0371, fax +49 (0)40 389 03120.
P.O. Box 548, 1970 BA, IJmuiden. ✆ +31 (0)255 534 546, fax +31 (0)255 535 349.

ECKERÖ LINJEN: Keskuskatu 1, 00100 Helsinki.
✆ +358 (0)9 22 88 544, fax (0)9 22 88 5222.
Torggatan 2, Box 158, 22101 Mariehamn.
✆ +358 (0)18 28 000, fax +358 (0)18 28 380.
Grisslehamn: ✆ +46 (0)175 30 920, fax +46 (0)175 30 820.
Eckerö: ✆ +358 (0)18 28 300, fax +358 (0)18 38 230.

EIMSKIP: Iceland Steamship Company Ltd, P.O. Box 220, 121 Reykjavík.
✆ +354 525 7000, fax +354 525 7179.

FERRIMAROC: Muelle de Ribera s/n, 04002 Almeria.
✆ +34 (50) 27 48 00, fax +34 (50) 27 63 66.
UK agent: Wasteels London. ✆ 020 7834 7066, fax 020 7630 7628.

FERRYS RAPIDOS DEL SUR (FRS): C/ Alcade Juan Núñez 10, Edificio Santa Catalina, Bloque 2, Bajo A, 11380 Tarifa - Cádiz. ✆ +34 956 68 18 30, fax +34 956 62 71 80.

FINNLINES DEUTSCHLAND AG: Finnlines Passagierdienst, Einsiedelstrasse 45, 23554 Lübeck. ✆ +49 (0)451 1507 443, fax +49 (0)451 1507 444.
Finland agent: Nordic Ferry Center, Itämerenkatu 21, 5th floor, 00180 Helsinki.
✆ +358 (0)9 2510 200, fax +358 (0)9 2510 2022.
Finnlines UK Ltd., 8 Heron Quay, London. ✆ (0)207 519 7300, fax (0)207 536 0255.

FJORD LINE: Rosenkrantzgt 3, Postboks 4008 Dreggen, 5023 Bergen.
✆ +47 55 323 770, fax +47 55 323 815.

FLAGGRUTEN: Partrederiet Flagruten ANS, Postboks 2005 Nordnes, 5024 Bergen.
✆ +47 55 23 87 00, +47 952 61 507.

FÖRDE REEDEREI SEETOURISTIK: Postfach 2626, 24916 Flensburg.
✆ +49 461 864 602, fax +49 461 864 30.

GOZO CHANNEL: Hay Wharf, Sa Maison, Malta.
✆ +356 21 243964.

GRANDI NAVI VELOCI: Via Fieschi 17, 16121 Genova.
✆ +39 010 58 93 31, fax +39 010 55 09 225.
UK agent: Viamare Travel (see Anek Lines) ✆ 08704 10 60 40, fax 020 7431 5456.

GRIMALDI FERRIES: Via M. Campodisola 13, Napoli.
✆ +39 081 496 444, fax +39 081 551 7716.
UK agent: Viamare Travel (see Anek Lines) ✆ 08704 10 60 40, fax 020 7431 5456.

HELLENIC MEDITERRANEAN LINES: 4 Loudovikou Sq., P.O. Box 80057, 185 10 Pireás.
✆ +30 210 4225 341-4, fax +30 210 4225 317.

HURTIGRUTEN (NORWEGIAN COASTAL VOYAGE):
TFDS, Postboks 548, 9001 Tromsø. ✆ +47 77 68 60 88, fax +47 77 68 87 10.
OVDS, Postboks 43, 8501 Narvik. ✆ +47 76 92 37 00, fax +47 76 92 37 25.
OVDS, Postboks 1064, 8001 Bodø. ✆ +47 75 52 10 20, fax +47 75 52 08 35.
UK agent: 3 Shortlands, London W6 8NE. ✆ 020 8846 2666, fax 020 8846 2678.

INTERNATIONAL MARITIME TRANSPORT CORPORATION (I M T C): 122 Bd Anfa, Casablanca. ✆ +212 (0)2 299 209, fax +212 (0)2 299 202.
Spain agent: Vapores Suardiaz Andalucia S.A. (VS), Avda. Del Puerto 1-6, 11006 Cádiz. ✆ +34 956 282 111, fax +34 956 282 846.

IRISH FERRIES: 2-4 Merrion Row, Dublin 2. ✆ +353 (0)1 890 31 31 31.
Corn Exchange Building, Ground Floor, Brunswick Street, Liverpool L2 7TP.
✆ 08705 17 17 17, fax 0151 236 0562.

ISLE OF MAN STEAM PACKET CO.: Imperial Buildings, Douglas, Isle of Man IM1 2BY.
✆ 08705 523 523, fax 01624 645697.

ISLES OF SCILLY STEAMSHIP CO.: The Weighbridge, Quay Street, Penzance, Cornwall, TR18 4BZ. ✆ 0845 710 5555, fax 01736 51223.

ITALIAN RAILWAYS: Piazza della Croce Rossa, 00161 Roma.
✆ +39 06 884 0724, fax +39 06 883 1108.

JADROLINIJA: Riva 16, 51000 Rijeka, Croatia.
✆ +385 (51) 66 61 11, fax +385 (51) 21 31 16.
UK agent: Viamare Travel (see Anek Lines) ✆ 08704 10 60 40, fax 020 7431 5456.

KYSTLINK: Kongshavn 8, 3970 Langesund, Norway.
✆ +47 35 96 68 00, fax +47 35 96 68 01.
Denmark: ✆ +45 96 56 00 68, fax +45 96 56 00 69.
Sweden: ✆ +46 526 14 000, fax +46 526 14 125.

L D LINES: Continental Ferry Port, Wharf Road, Portsmouth, PO2 8QW.
✆ 0870 428 4335, fax 01235 84 56 08.
Terminal de la Citadelle, BP 90746, F-76060 Le Havre. +33 2 35 19 78 78, fax +33 (0)2 35 19 78 82..

LINDA LINE OY: Makasiiniterminaali, 00140 Helsinki.
✆ +358 (0)9 668 9700, fax +358 (0)9 668 97070.
Tallinn: ✆ +372 -6 412 412.

LINEAS FRED. OLSEN: Polígono Industrial de Añaza, 38109 Santa Cruz de Tenerife.
✆ +34 (902) 10 01 07, fax +34 (922) 62 82 32.

MANCHE ÎLES EXPRESS: Albert Quay, St Helier, Jersey.
✆ 01534 880 756, fax 01534 880 314.
Terminal Building, New Jetty, White Rock, St Peter Port, Guernsey
✆ 01481 701 316, fax 01481 701 319.

MARMARA LINES:
Germany agent: RECA Handels GmbH, Neckarstrasse 37, 71065 Sindelfingen.
✆ +49 (0)7031 86 60 10, fax +49 (0)7031 87 65 68.

MED LINK LINES: 49 Corso Garibaldi Str., 72100 Brindisi.
✆ +39 0831 52 76 67, fax +39 0831 56 40 70.

MEDMAR LINEE LAURO: Piazza Municipo 88, 80133 Napoli. ✆ +39 081 551 33 52, fax +39 081 552 43 29.
UK agent: Viamare Travel (see Anek Lines) ✆ 08704 10 60 40, fax 020 7431 5456.

MINOAN LINES: 2 Vassileos Konstantinou Ave. (Stadion), 116 35 Athína.
✆ +30 210 7512356, fax +30 210 7520540.
UK agent: Magnum Travel, 747 Green Lanes, Winchmore Hill, London N21 3SA.
✆ 020 8360 5353, fax 020 8360 1056.

MOBY LINES: Via Ninci 1, 57037 Portoferraio, Italy.
✆ +39 0565 91 81 01, fax +39 0565 91 67 58.
UK agent: SMS, London. ✆ 020 7244 8422, fax 020 7244 9829.

MOLS-LINIEN: Færgehavnen, 8400 Ebeltoft.
✆ +45 89 52 52 52, fax +45 89 52 52 92.

MONTENEGRO LINES: Barska Plovidba, Obala 13 jula bb, 85000 Bar.
✆ +381 85 312-366/312-809/311-465, fax +381 85 311-652.

NARVA LINE: Kohtu 1, 93812 Kuressaare, Estonia.
✆ +372 45 24 376, fax +372 45 24 373.

NAUTAS FERRY:
✆ +34 902 161 181, fax +34 (96) 578 76 06.

NAVIERA ARMAS: Juan Rejón 32-5y6, 35008 Las Palmas de Gran Canaria, España. ✆ +34 (928) 22 72 82, fax +34 (928) 46 99 91.

NAVIGAZIONE LIBERA del GOLFO: Molo Beverello, 80133 Napoli. ✆ +39 081 55 20 763, fax +39 081 55 25 589.

NORDIC JET LINE: Kanavaterminaali, 00161 Helsinki. ✆ +358 (0)9 681 770, fax +358 (0)9 681 77 111.

NORDLANDSEKSPRESSEN: OVDS, Bodø. ✆ +47 75 52 10 20, fax +47 75 52 08 35.

NORFOLK LINE: Reservations: ✆ 0870 870 1020.

NORFOLK LINE IRISH SEA FERRIES: 12 Quays Terminal, Tower Road, Birkenhead, CH41 1FE. ✆ 0151 906 2700, fax 0151 906 2718.
Victoria Business Park, 9 West Bank Road, Belfast, BT3 9JL. ✆ 028 9077 9090.
Reservations: UK ✆ 0870 600 4321, Republic of Ireland ✆ +353 (0)1 819 2999.

NORTHLINK FERRIES: Kiln Corner, Ayre Road, Kirkwall, Orkney KW15 1QX. ✆ 01856 851 144, fax 01856 851 155.
Reservations: ✆ 0845 6000 449.

P & O FERRIES:

United Kingdom:	Channel House, Channel View Road, Dover, CT17 9TJ. King George Dock, Hedon Road, Hull HU9 5QA. Peninsular House, Wharf Road, Portsmouth PO2 8TA. ✆ 08705 980 333.
Belgium:	Leopold II Dam 13, Kaaien 106-108, 8380, Zeebrugge. ✆ +32 070 70 77 71.
France:	41 Place d'Armes, BP 888, 62225, Calais. Gare Maritime Transmanche, BP 46, 50652, Cherbourg. Terminal de la Citadelle, BP 439, 76057, Le Havre. ✆ +33 0825 12 01 56.
Netherlands:	Europoort Beneluxhaven, Havennummer 5805, Rotterdam/ Europoort, Postbus 1123, 3180 AC, Rozenburg. ✆ +31 020 200 8333.
Spain:	Cosme Echevarrieta 1, 48009, Bilbao. ✆ +34 902 02 04 61.

P & O IRISH SEA: Larne Harbour, Larne BT40 1AQ. ✆ 0870 24 24 777.

POLFERRIES: Polish Baltic Shipping Co., ul. Portowa 41, 78 100 Kolobrzeg. ✆ +48 (0)965 252 11, fax +48 (0)965 266 12.

POSEIDON LINES: 32 Alkyonidon Avenue, 166 73 Voula, Athína. ✆ +30 210 965 8300, fax +30 210 965 8310.
UK agent: Viamare Travel (see Anek Lines) ✆ 08704 10 60 40, fax 020 7431 5456.

REEDEREI CASSEN EILS: Bei der Alten Liebe 12, 27472 Cuxhaven. ✆ +49 (0)4721 35082, fax +49 (0)4721 31161.

RG LINE: Satamaterminaali, Vaskiluoto, 65170 Vaasa. ✆ +358 (0)6 3200 300.

SALAMIS LINES: 28th October Avenue, P.O. Box 531, Limassol, Cyprus. ✆ +357 (0)5 35 55 55, fax +357 (0)5 36 44 10.
Greece agent: Salamis Lines (Hellas), 9 Filellinon Str., 18536 Pireás. ✆ +30 210 429 4325, fax +30 210 429 4557.

SAMSØ LINIEN: Sælvig Havn, 8305 Samsø, Denmark. ✆ +45 87 92 17 66 or +45 87 92 17 44, fax +45 87 92 17 10.

SARDINIA FERRIES: see Corsica Ferries.

SCANDLINES: DSB Kunde, Vester Farimagsgade 3, København. ✆ +45 33 151515, fax +45 33 151020.
Gedser: ✆ +45 54 160 055, fax +45 54 160 0533.
Helsingborg: ✆ +46 (0)42 186 100, fax +46 (0)42 187 410.
Helsingør: ✆ +45 49 258 892, fax +45 49 258 895.
Rødby: ✆ +45 54 605 166, fax +45 54 605 834.
Rønne: ✆ +45 56 951 069, fax +45 56 958 910.
Trelleborg: ✆ +46 410 65000, fax +46 410 13386.

SCANDLINES DEUTSCHLAND GmbH: Am Warnowkai 8, 18147 Rostock Seehafen. ✆ +49 (0)381 673 12 92, fax +49 (0)381 673 12 99.
Puttgarden: ✆ +49 (0)4371 86 51 61, fax +49 (0)4371 86 51 62.
Sassnitz: ✆ +49 (0)38392 644 20, fax +49 (0)38392 644 29.
Klaipeda: ✆ +370 6 314 376, fax +370 6 311 121.

SCANDLINES EUROSEABRIDGE: Uberseehafen, 18147 Rostock. ✆ +49 (0)381 458 4448, fax +49 (0)381 458 4442.

SEA CONTAINERS FINLAND: ✆ +358 9 180 4678, fax ✆ +358 9 180 4699.
Bookings: ✆ +372 610 0000.

SEAFRANCE: Eastern Docks, Dover, Kent CT16 1JA. ✆ 0871 663 2546.

SEAWIND: SeaWind Line Oy Ab, Linnankatu 84, 20100 Turku. ✆ +358 (0)2 210 28 00, fax +358 (0)2 210 28 10. Stockholm: ✆ +46 (0)8 795 331.

SEM MARITIME COMPANY: SEM Marina, Gat Sv. Duje, Split, Croatia. ✆ +385 21 33 82 92, fax +385 21 33 82 91.

SILJA LINE: Mannerheimintie 2, 00100 Helsinki. ✆ +358 (0)9 180 4422, fax +358 (0)9 180 4279.
Reservations: ✆ +358 600 174 552.

SIREMAR: Sicilia Regionale Marittima, Via Principe di Belmonte 1/c, 90139 Palermo. ✆ +39 091 58 26 88, fax +39 091 58 22 67.

SMYRIL LINE: Jonas Broncksgøta 37, Postboks 370, 110 Tórshavn. ✆ +298 315 900, fax +298 315 707.

SNAV FERRIES: Via Giordano Bruno 84, 80122 Napoli. ✆ +39 081 428 5555, fax +39 081 428 5259.
UK agent: Viamare Travel (see Anek Lines) ✆ 08704 10 60 40, fax 020 7431 5456.

SNCM: Société Nationale Maritime Corse Mediterranée, 61, Boulevard des Dames, 13002 Marseille. ✆ +33 (0)4 91 56 30 10, fax +33 (0)4 91 56 31 00.
UK agent: Southern Ferries, 179 Piccadilly, London W1V 9DB. ✆ 020 7491 4968, fax 020 7491 3502.

SPEEDFERRIES: Hoverport, Western Docks, Dover, CT17 9TG. ✆ 0870 22 00 570, fax 01304 20 8000.
Place de la République, F-62200 Boulogne-sur-Mer. ✆ +33 (0) 3 21 10 50 00, fax +33 (0)3 21 10 21 59.

STENA LINE: Stena House, Station Approach, Holyhead, LL65 1DQ. ✆ 08705 70 70 70.
Prince's Dock, 14 Clarendon Road, Belfast, BT1 3GB. ✆ 08705 204 204.
The Ferry Terminal, Dun Laoghaire, Co. Dublin. ✆ 01 204 7777.
Masthuggskajen, 405 19 Göteborg. ✆ +46 (0)31 704 00 00, fax +46 (0)31 85 85 95.
Trafikhavn, 9900 Frederikshavn. ✆ +45 98 424366, fax +45 98 422750.
Box 94, 432 22, Varberg. ✆ +46 (0)340 690 900, fax +46 (0)340 851 25.
Box 150 8500, Grenaa. ✆ +45 87 58 75 00, fax +45 86 32 01 18.
Box 104 371 22, Karlskrona. ✆ +46 (0)455 665 50, fax +46 (0)455 220 99.

SUPERFAST FERRIES: 157 C. Karamanli Av., 166 73 Voula, Athína. ✆ +30 210 969 1100, fax +30 210 969 1190.
Reservations: ✆ +30 210 89 19 130, fax +30 210 89 19 139.
United Kingdom: The Terminal Building, Port of Rosyth, Fife, KY11 2XP. ✆ 0870 234 0870, fax 0138 360 8020.
UK agent: Viamare Travel (see Anek Lines) ✆ 08704 10 60 40, fax 020 8343 5839.
Germany: ✆ +49 451 88 00 61 66, fax +49 451 88 00 61 29.

SWANSEA CORK FERRIES: 52 South Mall, Cork, Ireland. ✆ +353 (0)21 271166, fax +353 (0)21 275061.
Swansea: ✆ 01792 456116, fax 01792 644356.

TALLINK: Erottajankatu 19, 00130 Helsinki. ✆ +358 (0)9 2282 1211, fax +358 (0)9 635311.

TIRRENIA: Rione Sirignano 2, Casella Postale 438, 80121 Napoli. ✆ +39 081 720 11 11, fax +39 081 720 14 41.
UK agent: S.M.S. Travel & Tourism, 40/42 Kenway Road, London SW5 0RA. ✆ 020 7373 6548, fax 020 7244 9829.

TOREMAR: Via Calafati 6, Casella Postale 482, 57123 Livorno. ✆ +39 0586 22 45 11, fax +39 0586 22 46 24.

TRANSMANCHE FERRIES: Harbour, Newhaven, BN9 0BG. ✆ 0800 917 12 01.
Quai Gaston Lalitte, 76200 Dieppe. ✆ +33 (0)800 650 100, fax +33 (0)2 32 14 52 00.

TRASMEDITERRANEA: Obenque 4, Alameda de Osuna, 28042 Madrid. ✆ +34 (91) 322 91 00, fax +34 (91) 322 91 10.
U.K. agent: Southern Ferries (see SNCM) ✆ 020 7491 4968, fax 020 7491 3502.

TT-LINE: Mattentwiete 8, 20457 Hamburg. ✆ +49 (0)40 3601 442 446, fax +49 (0)40 3601 407.

UKRFERRY SHIPPING COMPANY: 4a Sabanskiy lane, Odesa, 65014, Ukraine. ✆ +380 (482) 344 059, fax +380 (482) 348 297, 348 108.

UNITY LINE: Plac Rodła 8, 70419, Szczecin, Poland. ✆ +48 (0)91 35 95 592, fax +48 (0)91 35 95 673.
Sweden agent: Pol-Line AB, Färjeterminalen, 27139 Ystad. ✆ +46 (0)411 55 69 00, fax +46 (0)411 55 69 53.

USTICA LINES: Via A. Staita 23, 91100 Trapani, Sicily. ✆ +39 092 322 200, fax + 39 092 323 289.
Reservations: ✆ +39 0923 873 813, fax +39 0923 593 200.

VENTOURIS FERRIES: 91 Pireos Avenue, 185 41 Pireás. ✆ +30 210 4825815, fax +30 210 4832919.

VIKING LINE: P.O. Box 35, 22101 Mariehamn. ✆ +358 (0)18 26011, fax +358 (0)18 15811.
UK agent: Emagine UK Ltd, Leigh, WN7 1AZ. ✆ 01942 262662, fax 01942 606500.

VIRTU FERRIES LTD: Sea Passenger Terminal, Pinto Road, Valletta, Malta. Reservations: ✆ +356 21 228777, fax +356 21 235435.

CAIRNRYAN - LARNE 2005

P & O Irish Sea by ship — Journey 1 hour 45 minutes — Service to January 8, 2008

February 1 - March 15 and October 2 - January 8

Depart Cairnryan: 0415①②③④⑤⑥, 0730, 1030①②③④⑤⑥, 1300⑦, 1330①②③④⑤⑥, 1630, 2000, 2300⑦, 2359①②③④⑤.
Depart Larne: 0415①②③④⑤⑥, 0730, 1030①②③④⑤⑥, 1330⑦, 1630, 2000, 2300⑦, 2359①②③④⑤.

March 16 - October 1

Depart Cairnryan: 0415①②③④⑤⑥, 0730, 1030, 1300⑦, 1330①②③④⑤⑥, 1630, 2000, 2300⑦, 2359①②③④⑤.
Depart Larne: 0415①②③④⑤⑥, 0730, 1030①②③④⑤⑥, 1300⑦, 1330①②③④⑤⑥, 1630, 2000, 2300⑦, 2359①②③④⑤.

Subject to alteration July 8 - 22 and during Xmas/New Year period.

Cairnryan - Glasgow Buchanan Street (operated by Stagecoach Express).

P & O Irish Sea by fast ferry — March 16 - October 1, 2007 (No winter service)

Cairnryan		Larne	Larne		Cairnryan
1500	→	1600	1255	→	1355

Cairnryan - Glasgow Buchanan Street (operated by Stagecoach Express).

CHERBOURG - ROSSLARE 2010

Irish Ferries — 2007 service

Cherbourg		Rosslare	
1800	→	1130	Even dates Mar. 4-30; uneven dates Apr. 1-29 (not Apr. 27); May 1, 3, 7, 9, 13, 15, 17, 21, 23, 29; June 4, 6, 12, 18, 20, 26; July 2, 4, 8, 10, 16, 18, 22, 24, 30; Aug. 1, 5, 7, 11, 13, 15, 19, 21, 23, 27, 29; Sept. 2, 4, 6, 10, 12, 18, 20, 25, 27; Oct. 2, 4, 6, 9, 11, 13, 16, 18, 20, 23, 25, 27, 30; Nov. 1, 3, 6, 8, 10, 13, 15, 17, 20, 20, 22, 24, 27, 29; Dec. 1, 4, 6, 8, 11, 13, 15, 18, 20, 22.
2100	→	1500	②④⑥ Feb. 6 - Mar. 1.
Rosslare		**Cherbourg**	
1600	→	1130	Uneven dates Mar. 3-31; even dates Apr. 2-30 (not Apr. 26); May 2, 6, 8, 12, 14, 16, 20, 22, 28; June 3, 5, 11, 17, 19, 25; July 1, 3, 7, 9, 15, 17, 21, 23, 29, 31; Aug. 4, 6, 10, 12, 14, 18, 20, 22, 26, 28; Sept. 1, 3, 5, 9, 11, 16, 19, 23, 26, 30; Oct. 3, 5, 7, 10, 12, 14, 17, 19, 21, 24, 26, 28, 31; Nov. 2, 4, 7, 9, 11, 14, 16, 18, 21, 23, 25, 28, 30; Dec. 2, 5, 7, 9, 12, 14, 16, 19, 21.
1700	→	1300	⑦ Feb. 4-25.
2300	→	1900	③⑤ Feb. 7-28.

Cherbourg Port - Cherbourg station (operated by Zéphir).

CORK - ROSCOFF 2015

Brittany Ferries — Service to October 31, 2008 (No winter service)

Sailings from Cork (Ringaskiddy) and Roscoff.

Cork		Roscoff	
1600	→	0700	⑥ until Nov. 3, Mar. 15 - Oct. 25.
Roscoff		**Cork**	
2130	→	1030	⑤ until Nov. 2, Mar. 14 - Oct. 24.

Departure times may vary owing to tidal conditions.

DOUGLAS - BELFAST 2020

Isle Of Man Steam Packet Co. by SEACAT catamaran — 2007 service (No winter service)

Sailings from Belfast Donegall Quay.

Douglas		Belfast		Belfast		Douglas	
0700	→	0945	See note E.	0200	→		July 13 only.
0930	→		See note F.	1045	→	1330	See note E.
1400	→		July 26, 30 only.	1330	→		See note H.
1500	→	1745	③ Sept. 5-26.	1745	→		July 26, 30 only.
1530	→		See note G.	1900	→	2145	③ Sept. 5-26.
2200	→		July 12 only.	1915	→		See note J.

E – ⑦ Aug. 19 - Sept. 30 (also July 22).
F – ⑥ June 16 - Aug. 18 (also June 21, July 20; not July 21).
G – ① June 18 - July 16; ①④ Aug. 2-16 (also June 28, July 18, Aug. 21, 28).
H – ⑥ June 16 - Aug. 18 (also July 20; not July 21).
J – ①④ June 18 - July 2, Aug. 2-16 (also July 9, 16, 18, Aug. 21, 28).

A special service will operate during the TT Race period (May 23 - June 14)

DOUGLAS - DUBLIN 2025

Isle Of Man Steam Packet Co. by SEACAT catamaran — 2007 service (No winter service)

Sailings from Dublin North Wall.

Douglas		Dublin		Dublin		Douglas	
0700	→	0950	July 8 only.	1045	→	1335	July 8 only.
0930	→	1220	See note A.	1330	→	1620	See note C.
1400	→	1650	July 27 only.	1745	→	2035	July 27 only.
1530	→	1820	See note B.	1915	→	2205	See note D.

A – ⑤ June 15 - Aug. 17 (also July 21, Aug. 12; not July 20, 27).
B – ⑦ June 17 - Aug. 5 (also July 19, 23, Aug. 22, 24, 29, Sept. 1; not July 8).
C – ⑤ June 22 - Aug. 17 (also July 21; not July 20, 27).
D – ⑦ June 17 - Aug. 12 (also July 15, 19, 23, Aug. 22, 24, 29, Sept. 1; not July 8, 22).

A special service will operate during the TT Race period (May 23 - June 14)

FISHGUARD - ROSSLARE 2030

Stena Line by ship — 2007 service (No service Dec. 25, 26)

Fishguard		Rosslare		Rosslare		Fishguard	
0245	→	0615		0900	→	1230	
1430	→	1800	Not Dec. 24.	2115	→	0045	Not Dec. 24.

Stena Line by *LYNX* catamaran — May 2 - September 23, 2007 (No winter service)

Fishguard		Rosslare	Rosslare		Fishguard
1130	→	1330	0800	→	1000
1830	→	2030	1500	→	1700

HEYSHAM - DOUGLAS 2035

Isle Of Man Steam Packet Co. by ship — Service to January 8, 2008 (No service Dec. 25)

Heysham		Douglas	
0215	→	0545	Not June 24, July 15, Sept. 9, Oct. 7, Nov. 11, Dec. 9, 24, 26, 30, Jan. 1).
1415	→	1745	
Douglas		**Heysham**	
0845	→	1215	
1945	→	2315	①②③④⑤⑦ (not Dec. 23, 24, 31).
2000	→	2330	⑥ (not June 23, July 14, Sept. 8, Oct. 6, Nov. 10, Dec. 8, 29).

A special service will operate during the TT Race period (May 23 - June 14)

HOLYHEAD - DUBLIN 2040

Irish Ferries by ship — 2007 service (No service Dec. 25, 26)

Sailings from Holyhead and Dublin Ferryport.

Holyhead		Dublin	Dublin		Holyhead
0240	→	0555	0805	→	1130
1410	→	1725	2055	→	0020

Sailing times may vary owing to tidal conditions.

Dublin Ferryport - Dublin Busaras (Central Bus Station).

Irish Ferries by fast ferry — Journey 1 hour 50 minutes — 2007 service (No service Dec. 25, 26)

Sailings from Holyhead and Dublin Ferryport.

Depart Holyhead: 1200, 1715. Depart Dublin: 0845, 1430.

Dublin Ferryport - Dublin Busaras (Central Bus Station).

Stena Line *Conveys passengers with vehicles only* — 2007 service (No service Dec. 25, 26)

Sailings from Holyhead and Dublin Ferryport.

Holyhead		Dublin		Dublin		Holyhead	
0230	→	0545		0830	→	1145	
1430	→	1745	Not Dec. 24.	2115	→	0030	Not Dec. 24.

Subject to alteration during Xmas/New Year period

HOLYHEAD - DUN LAOGHAIRE 2045

Stena Line by *HSS* fast ferry — 2007 service (No service Jan. 1 - Mar. 1, Dec. 25, 26)

Sailings from Holyhead and Dun Laoghaire.

Service from March 2

Holyhead		Dun Laoghaire	Dun Laoghaire		Holyhead
0855	→	1035	1110	→	1250
1530	→	1710	1800	→	1940

Dun Laoghaire - Dublin Busaras (Central Bus Station).

BIRKENHEAD (LIVERPOOL) - DUBLIN 2049

Norfolk Line Irish Sea Ferries — Service to December 31, 2007

Sailings from Birkenhead Twelve Quays Terminal and Dublin Port Passenger Terminal.

Birkenhead		Dublin		Dublin		Birkenhead	
1000	→	1700	②③④⑤⑥	1000	→	1700	②③④⑤⑥
2200	→	0500		2200	→	0515	

BIRKENHEAD (LIVERPOOL) - BELFAST 2050

Norfolk Line Irish Sea Ferries — Service to December 31, 2007

Sailings from Birkenhead Twelve Quays Terminal and Belfast.

Birkenhead		Belfast		Belfast		Birkenhead	
1030	→	1830	②③④⑤⑥⑦	1030	→	1830	②③④⑤⑥⑦
2200	→	0600	①	2200	→	0600	①
2230	→	0630	②③④⑤⑥⑦	2230	→	0630	②③④⑤⑥⑦

LIVERPOOL - DUBLIN 2052

P & O Irish Sea — 2007 service

Conveys passengers with vehicles only

Liverpool		Dublin		Dublin		Liverpool	
1000	→	1800	②③④⑤⑥	1000	→	1800	②③④⑤⑥
2200	→	0600		2200	→	0600	

Subject to alteration during holiday periods

LIVERPOOL - DOUGLAS 2053

Isle Of Man Steam Packet Co. by *SeaCat* — Service to January 8, 2008

Liverpool		Douglas	
1045	→	1315	Aug. 24, 25 only.
1115	→	1345	Daily June 15 - Aug. 23; ①②③④⑤⑥ Aug. 27 - Sept. 29 (not June 17, July 8, 22).
1200	→	1430	①②③④⑤ Oct. 1 - Nov. 1; ⑤ Nov. 9 - Dec. 14 (also Dec. 24, 28, 29, 31, Jan. 4; not Oct. 26).
1230	→	1500	Dec. 23 only.
1900	→	2130	①②③⑤⑥⑦ June 15 - Aug. 15; daily Aug. 17 - Sept. 4; ①②④⑤⑥⑦ Sept. 6-30; ⑥⑦ Oct. 6 - Jan. 6 (also July 12, Oct. 26, Nov. 2, Dec. 21; not July 13, Dec. 23, 29, 30).
2115	→	2345	④ June 21 - Aug. 16 (also July 8, 13, 22; not July 12).
2215	→	0045	Aug. 23, 25-27, 30, 31.
Douglas		**Liverpool**	
0600	→	0830	Aug. 24, 25 only.
0730	→	1000	Daily June 15 - Aug. 23; ①②③④⑤⑥ Aug. 27 - Sept. 29 (not June 17, July 8, 22).
0800	→	1030	①②③④⑤ Oct. 1 - Nov. 1; ⑤ Nov. 9 - Dec. 14 (also Dec. 24, 28, 29, 31, Jan. 4; not Oct. 26).
0900	→	1130	⑥ Oct. 6 - Jan. 5 (also Dec. 23; not Oct. 27, Nov. 3, Dec. 22, 29).
1000	→	1230	Oct. 27, Nov. 3, Dec. 22 only.
1345	→	1615	Jan. 6 only.
1415	→	1645	Aug. 24, 25 only.
1500	→	1730	①②③⑤⑥⑦ June 15 - Aug. 15; daily Aug. 17 - Sept. 4; ①②④⑤⑥⑦ Sept. 6-30 (also July 12; not July 13, Aug. 24, 25).
1530	→	1800	⑦ Oct. 7 - Dec. 16 (also Oct. 26, Nov. 2, Dec. 21).
1745	→	2015	④ June 21 - Aug. 30 (also July 8, 13, 22, Aug. 25-27, 31, Sept. 2; not July 12).

A special service will operate during the TT Race period (May 23 - June 14)

2055 PEMBROKE - ROSSLARE

Irish Ferries **2007 service (No service Dec. 25, 26)**

Pembroke		Rosslare	Rosslare		Pembroke
0245	→	0630	0845	→	1230
1430	→	1815	2100	→	0045

Sailing times may vary owing to tidal conditions.

2065 ROSSLARE - ROSCOFF

Irish Ferries **2007 service (No winter service)**

Rosslare		Roscoff	
1700	→	1100	Apr. 26; May 4, 10, 18, 24, 26, 30; June 1, 7, 9, 13, 15, 21, 23, 27, 29; July 5, 11, 13, 19, 25, 27; Aug. 2, 8, 16, 24, 30; Sept. 7, 14, 21, 28.

Roscoff		Rosslare	
1830	→	1100	Apr. 27; May 5, 11, 19, 25, 27, 31; June 2, 8, 10, 14, 16, 22, 24, 28, 30; July 6, 12, 14, 20, 26, 28; Aug. 3, 9, 17, 25, 31; Sept. 8, 15, 22, 29.

2070 STRANRAER - BELFAST

Stena Line by *HSS* fast ferry **2007 service**
Sailings from Stranraer and Belfast. **(No service Dec. 25, 26)**

Stranraer		Belfast		Belfast		Stranraer	
0030	→	0215	⑥⑦	0250	→	0435	⑥⑦
0455	→	0640		0735	→	0920	
0955	→	1140		1220	→	1405	
1450	→	1635		1720	→	1905	
1950	→	2135		2210	→	2355	

Subject to alteration during Xmas / New Year period

Stena Line by ship **2007 service**
Sailings from Stranraer and Belfast. **(No service Dec. 25, 26)**

Stranraer		Belfast		Belfast		Stranraer	
0715§	→	1030	②③④⑤⑥	0315§	→	0630	②③④⑤⑥
1515§	→	1830	③⑤	1100§	→	1415	③⑤
1550	→	1905	⑥⑦	1150	→	1505	⑥⑦
2300§	→	0215	①②③④⑤	1900§	→	2215	①②③④⑤
2350	→	0305	⑥⑦	2000	→	2315	⑥⑦

§ – No foot passengers conveyed.

Subject to alteration during Xmas / New Year period

2075 SWANSEA - CORK

Swansea Cork Ferries Journey 10 hours **2007 service**
Sailings from Swansea and Cork (Ringaskiddy). **(No winter service)**
Departure times vary.

NO SAILINGS IN 2007

2080 TROON - LARNE

P & O Irish Sea by fast ferry **March 16 - October 1, 2007**
(No winter service)

Troon		Larne	Larne		Troon
1005	→	1155	0715	→	0905
2020	→	2210	1730	→	1920

ENGLISH CHANNEL

2100 CHANNEL ISLAND SERVICES

POOLE and WEYMOUTH - GUERNSEY - JERSEY by fast ferry
Condor Ferries **2007 service**
Sailings from St Helier Elizabeth Terminal and St Peter Port.

Weymouth - Guernsey: Jan. 1 - Dec. 31; journey time 2 hours 10 minutes.
Weymouth - Jersey (via Guernsey): Jan. 1 - Dec. 31; journey time 3 hours 25 minutes.
Poole - Guernsey: Apr. 2 - Oct. 29; journey time 2 hours 30 minutes.
Poole - Jersey (most services via Guernsey): Apr. 2 - Oct. 29; journey time from 3 hours.

Departure times vary owing to tidal conditions.

POOLE and WEYMOUTH - GUERNSEY - JERSEY - ST MALO by fast ferry
Condor Ferries **2007 service**
Sailings by catamaran from St Helier Elizabeth Terminal or Albert Quay, St Malo Gare Maritime de la Bourse and St Peter Port.

Weymouth - St Malo: Jan. 1 - Dec. 31; journey 5 hours 15 minutes. A change of vessel is necessary in either Guernsey or Jersey May 22 - Sept. 30 (extended journey time).
Poole - St Malo (via Guernsey or Jersey): May 22 - Sept. 30; journey 4 hours 35 minutes.

OTHER SERVICES:

Manche Iles Express operate catamaran services in summer from Jersey to Carteret, Granville, Sark and Guernsey, and from Alderney to Diélette and Guernsey.

2105 DOVER - BOULOGNE

SpeedFerries by catamaran **Service to June 30, 2008**
Conveys passengers with vehicles only Journey 50 minutes **(No service Dec. 25)**

November 1 - March 13▲
Depart Dover: 0800, 1200, 1600. Depart Boulogne: 1100, 1500, 1845.
March 14 - June 30
Depart Dover: 0700, 1045, 1420, 1800, 2135 **S**.
Depart Boulogne: 1000, 1330, 1710, 2050, 2355 **S**.

▲ – No sailings Jan. 8 - 31. **S** – Not daily.

2110 DOVER - CALAIS

P & O Ferries Journey 75-90 minutes **2007 service**
Sailings from Dover Eastern Docks and Calais Maritime. **(No service Dec. 25)**
Conveys passengers with vehicles only on night services.

April 16 - May 11, December 26 - 31
Depart Dover: 0245, 0415, 0540, 0635, 0825, 0915, 1005, 1055, 1240, 1330, 1420, 1515, 1700, 1750. 1840, 1935, 2120, 2210, 2300, 2359.
Depart Calais: 0045, 0155, 0315, 0435, 0700, 0800, 0850, 0945, 1130, 1220, 1310, 1405, 1550, 1640, 1730, 1825, 2010, 2100, 2150, 2245.
May 12 - December 24
Depart Dover: 0210, 0320, 0430, 0530, 0625, 0740①⑤⑦, 0755②③④⑥, 0840, 0925, 1005, 1050, 1215, 1300, 1345, 1425, 1510, 1635, 1720, 1805, 1845, 1930, 2055, 2140, 2225, 2310, 2359.
Depart Calais: 0015, 0100, 0210, 0310, 0410, 0630, 0720, 0805, 0850, 0935, 1050①⑤⑦, 1105②③④⑥, 1150, 1235, 1315, 1400, 1525, 1610, 1655, 1735, 1820, 1945, 2030, 2115, 2155, 2240.

A reduced service will operate on Dec. 24, 26 (no service Dec. 25)

🚌 connections:
Dover Eastern Docks - Dover Priory station: from Dover Eastern Docks 0700 – 2100 on arrival of ship; from Dover Priory station 0715 – 1930.
Calais Port - Calais (Place d'Armes) - Calais Ville station - Calais Port 1000 – 1915.

SeaFrance Journey 70 - 90 minutes **2007 service**
Sailings from Dover Eastern Docks and Calais Maritime.
Conveys passengers with vehicles only on night services.

Depart Dover: 0200, 0445, 0700, 0815, 0930, 1100, 1215, 1345, 1515, 1630, 1800, 1930, 2045, 2230, 2345.
Depart Calais: 0015, 0300, 0530, 0645, 0830, 1000, 1115, 1245, 1415, 1530, 1700, 1830, 1930, 2100, 2245.

🚌 connections: Dover Eastern Docks - Dover Priory station.
Calais Port - Calais (Place d'Armes) - Calais Ville station - Calais Port 1000 – 1915.

2111 DOVER - DUNKERQUE

Norfolk Line by ship *Conveys passengers with vehicles only*
Service to December 31, 2007
Sailings from Dover Eastern Docks and Dunkerque. Journey 2 hours

Depart Dover: 0200①②③④⑤⑥, 0405①②③④⑤⑥, 0800, 1000, 1200, 1400, 1600, 1800, 2000①②③④⑤⑦, 2200, 2359①②③④⑤⑦.
Depart Dunkerque: 0200①②③④⑤⑥, 0600, 0800, 1000, 1200, 1400, 1600, 1800①②③④⑤⑦, 2000, 2200①②③④⑤⑦, 2359①②③④⑤⑦.

2125 NEWHAVEN - DIEPPE

Transmanche Ferries by ship **Service to March 31, 2008**
Sailings from Newhaven and Dieppe. **(No service Dec. 25)**

Newhaven		Dieppe		Dieppe		Newhaven	
April 1 - September 30							
0130	→	0630		0030	→	0330	
0700	→	1200		0800	→	1100	
1800	→	2300		1330	→	1630	
October 1 - March 31							
0700	→	1200	⑥⑦	0300	→	0600	①
1700	→	2200	①②③④⑤	0800	→	1100	⑥⑦
1900	→	2400	⑦	1800	→	2100	①②③④⑤
2200	→	0300	⑥	2000	→	2300	⑥
2300	→	0400	①②③④⑤	2359	→	0300	①②③④⑤

2126 NEWHAVEN - LE HAVRE

L D Lines by ship **May 1 - September 30, 2007**
Sailings from Newhaven and Le Havre. **(No winter service)**

Newhaven		Le Havre	Le Havre		Newhaven
1230	→	1830	2000	→	2359

2130 PENZANCE - ST. MARY'S

Isles Of Scilly Steamship Co. **2007 service**
Sailings from Penzance Lighthouse Pier and St Mary's. **(No winter service)**

Penzance		St Mary's		St Mary's		Penzance	
0630	→	0910	⑥ May 21 - June 2.	0945	→	1225	⑥ May 21 - June 2.
0800	→	1040	③ July 2 - Sept. 1.	1500	→	1740	⑥ July 23 - Sept. 1.
0915	→	1155	See note **A**.	1630	→	1910	See note **B**.
1100	→	1340	⑥ July 23 - Sept. 1.	1700	→	1940	⑥ May 21 - June 2.
1345	→	1625	⑥ May 21 - June 2.				

A – ①③⑤ Mar. 26 - 31; ①③⑤⑥ Apr. 2 - 7; ①②③④⑤⑥ Apr. 9 - May 19; ①②③④⑤ May 21 - June 2; ①②③④⑤⑥ June 4 - 30; ①②④⑤⑥ July 2 - 21; ①②④⑤ July 23 - Sept. 1; ①②③④⑤⑥ Sept. 3 - Oct. 20; ①③⑤⑥ Oct. 22 - Nov. 3.
B – ①③⑤ Mar. 26 - 31; ①③⑤⑥ Apr. 2 - 7; ①②③④⑤⑥ Apr. 9 - May 19; ①②③④⑤ May 21 - June 2; ①②③④⑤⑥ June 4 - July 21; ①②③④⑤ July 23 - Sept. 1; ①②③④⑤⑥ Sept. 3 - Oct. 20; ①③⑤⑥ Oct. 22 - Nov. 3.

Departure times may vary owing to tidal conditions.

PLYMOUTH - ROSCOFF 2135

Brittany Ferries — November 1, 2007 - October 31, 2008

Sailings from Plymouth Millbay, Roscoff and St Malo Terminal Ferry du Naye.

Plymouth		Roscoff		Roscoff		Plymouth	
November 1 - 17							
1230	→	1900	Nov. 2 only.	0915	→	1330	Nov. 4 only.
2200	→	0800	See note **D**.	1430	→	1930	See note **J**.
2300	→	0800	Nov. 1, 2, 4.				
2300	→	1000	Nov. 3.	1530	→	2030	Nov. 1 - 4.
				2200	→	0700	Nov. 9, 10.
				2200	→	0800	Nov. 17 only.
November 18 - October 31							
0745	→	1500	See note **B**.	0815	→	1330	See note **E**.
1030	→	1800	See note **C**.	0915	→	1330	⑦ Mar. 16 - Oct. 26.
1200	→	1900	Jan. 1 only.	1000	→	1530	Dec. 30 only.
1230	→	1900	②⑤ Mar. 14 - Oct. 28.	1300	→	1830	See note **M**.
1500	→	2200	See note **E**.	1500	→	2030	See note **K**.
2200	→	0800	See note **A**.	1600	→	2130	See note **N**.
2200	→	1000	See note **F**.	1630	→	2130	See note **B**.
2300	→	0645	See note **G**.	2200	→	0800	See note **L**.
2300	→	0700	See note **H**.	2330	→	0615	See note **E**.

- **A** – Daily Nov. 18 - Dec. 23, Dec. 26 - 29; ⑤ Feb. 1 - Mar. 7; ①②③④⑤⑦ Mar. 31 - May 23, June 9 - July 9, Sept. 1 - Oct. 31 (also Jan. 4; not Feb. 8).
- **B** – ⑤⑦ Mar. 14 - 30, May 25 - June 8, July 11 - Aug. 31.
- **C** – ①②③④⑦ Feb. 3 - Mar. 10 (also Jan. 2, 3, 6 - 10).
- **D** – Nov. 5 - 17 (not Nov. 16).
- **E** – ④⑥ Mar. 13 - 29, May 24 - June 7, July 10 - Aug. 30.
- **F** – ⑥ Apr. 5 - May 17, June 14 - July 5, Sept. 6 - Oct. 25.
- **G** – ③⑤ Mar. 12 - 28, May 28 - June 6, July 11 - Aug. 29.
- **H** – ①②⑦ Mar. 11 - 30, May 25 - June 8, July 13 - Aug. 26.
- **J** – ①②③④⑦ Nov. 5 - 15.
- **K** – ①②③④⑦ Nov. 18 - Dec. 20; daily Mar. 31 - May 23, June 9 - July 9, Sept. 1 - Oct. 30 (also Dec. 23, 26 - 29).
- **L** – ⑤⑥ Nov. 23 - Dec. 22; daily Jan. 1 - 3, 5 - 9; ①②③④⑥⑦ Feb. 2 - Mar. 11; ② Mar. 18 - Oct. 28 (also Oct. 31).
- **M** – ② Mar. 18 - 25, May 27 - June 3, July 15 - Aug. 26.
- **N** – ①③ Mar. 12 - 26, May 26 - June 4, July 14 - Aug. 27.

PLYMOUTH - SANTANDER 2140

Brittany Ferries — November 1, 2007 - October 31, 2008 (No service Jan., Feb.)

Sailings from Plymouth Millbay or Santander.

Plymouth		Santander	
1200	→	0900	③ Mar. 12 - Oct. 29.
1200	→	1200	Nov. 7, 11, 14 only.
1200	→	1300	③⑦ Nov. 18 - Dec. 19.
1600	→	1230	⑦ Mar. 16 - Oct. 26 (also Nov. 4).
Santander		**Plymouth**	
1500	→	0930	④ Mar. 13 - Oct. 23 (also Nov. 1).
1600	→	1000	① Mar. 17 - Oct. 27.
1900	→	1700	①④ Nov. 5 - 15 (also Oct. 30).
1900	→	1800	①④ Nov. 19 - Dec. 20.

POOLE - CHERBOURG 2145

Brittany Ferries by ship — November 1, 2007 - October 31, 2008

Poole		Cherbourg		Cherbourg		Poole	
0830	→	1400	See note **S**.	0800	→	1115	See note **T**.
1230	→	1745	See note **T**.	0930	→	1300	②④ Nov. 1 - 15.
1600	→	2130	②④ Nov. 1 - 15.	0930	→	1330	See note **Y**.
1600	→	2200	See note **V**.	1830	→	2215	See note **Z**.
2345	→	0630	See note **W**.	1900	→	2215	See note **R**.
2345	→	0730	See note **X**.	2345	→	0600	See note **Q**.

- **Q** – ②④ Nov. 1 - May 15, Sept. 30 - Oct. 30 (not Dec. 25, Jan. 1).
- **R** – ①③⑤⑥⑦ Nov. 2 - 18; ⑥⑦ Nov. 24 - May 11; daily May 17 - Sept. 28; ⑥⑦ Oct. 4 - 26.
- **S** – ③⑤ Nov. 2 - May 16, Oct. 1 - 31 (not Dec. 26, Jan. 2).
- **T** – ⑥⑦ Nov. 3 - May 18; ②③④⑤⑥⑦ May 20 - Sept. 28; ⑥⑦ Oct. 4 - 26.
- **V** – ②④ Dec. 4 - May 15, Sept. 30 - Oct. 30 (not Dec. 25, Jan. 1).
- **W** – ⑤⑥ Nov. 2 - May 10; daily May 16 - Sept. 27; ⑤⑥ Oct. 3 - Nov. 8 (also Dec. 23, 30).
- **X** – ①③⑦ Nov. 4 - May 14, Sept. 28 - Nov. 9 (not Dec. 23, 24, 30, 31).
- **Y** – ②④ Nov. 20 - May 15, Sept. 30 - Oct. 30 (not Dec. 25, Jan. 1).
- **Z** – ①③⑤ Nov. 19 - May 16, Sept. 29 - Oct. 31 (not Dec. 24, 31).

🚘 Cherbourg Port - Cherbourg station (operated by Zéphir).

Brittany Ferries by fast ferry — May 19 - September 28, 2008 (No winter service)

Poole		Cherbourg	Cherbourg		Poole
0730	→	1045	1130	→	1245

PORTSMOUTH - BILBAO 2155

P & O Ferries — Service to January 4, 2008

Sailings from Portsmouth Continental Ferry Port and Bilbao (Santurtzi).
Santurtzi is located approximately 13 km to the north west of Bilbao city centre.

Portsmouth		Bilbao		Bilbao		Portsmouth	
2115	→	0800 §	See note **P**.	1315	→	1715 ¶	See note **S**.
2115	→	0930 §	Dec. 22 only.	1615	→	1715 §	Dec. 24 only.

- **P** – **May** 2, 5, 8, 11, 14, 17, 20, 23, 26, 29; **June** 1, 4, 7, 10, 13, 16, 19, 22, 25, 28; **July** 1, 4, 7, 10, 13, 16, 19, 22, 25, 28, 30; **Aug.** 3, 6, 9, 12, 15, 18, 21, 24, 27, 30; **Sept.** 2, 5, 8, 11, 14, 17, 20, 23, 26, 29; **Oct.** 2, 5, 8, 11, 14, 17, 20, 23, 26, 29; **Nov.** 1, 4, 8, 11, 15, 18, 22, 25, 29; **Dec.** 2, 6, 9, 12, 15, 18, 26, 30; **Jan.** 2.
- **S** – **May** 1, 4, 7, 10, 13, 16, 19, 22, 25, 28, 31; **June** 3, 6, 9, 12, 15, 18, 21, 24, 27, 30; **July** 3, 6, 9, 12, 15, 18, 21, 24, 27, 30; **Aug.** 2, 5, 8, 11, 14, 17, 20, 23, 26, 29; **Sept.** 1, 4, 7, 10, 13, 16, 19, 22, 25, 28, 31; **Oct.** 1, 4, 7, 10, 13, 16, 19, 22, 25, 28, 31; **Nov.** 3, 6, 10, 13, 17, 20, 24, 27; **Dec.** 1, 4, 8, 11, 14, 17, 20, 28; **Jan.** 1, 4.

§ – Approximate time (two days later). ¶ – Approximate time (following day).

PORTSMOUTH - CHANNEL ISLANDS 2157

Condor Ferries — 2007 service (No service Dec. 25, 26, Jan. 1, 2)

Sailings from Portsmouth Continental Ferry Port, St Helier and St Peter Port.

Portsmouth		St Peter Port		St Peter Port		St Helier		St Helier		Portsmouth
0900 **A**	→	1600 **A**	→	1730 **A**	→	1930 **A**	→	2130 **A**	→	0630 **B**

A – ①②③④⑤⑥. **B** – ②③④⑤⑥⑦.

Departure times may vary owing to tidal conditions.

PORTSMOUTH - CHERBOURG 2160

Brittany Ferries by fast ferry — March 1 - October 31, 2008 (No winter service)

Sailings from Portsmouth Continental Ferry Port and Cherbourg.

Portsmouth		Cherbourg		Cherbourg		Portsmouth	
0800	→	1145	See note **B**.	1245	→	1445	See note **B**.
0815	→	1200	See note **C**.	1730	→	1915	See note **C**.
1545	→	1930	See note **A**.	2015	→	2200	See note **A**.

- **A** – Daily Mar. 13 - 30; ⑤⑥⑦ Apr. 4 - May 18; daily May 22 - Aug. 31; ⑤⑥⑦ Sept. 5 - Oct. 26.
- **B** – ①②③④ Mar. 13 - 27, May 22 - Aug. 28.
- **C** – ①②③④ Mar. 31 - May 21, Sept. 1 - Oct. 23.

🚘 Cherbourg Port - Cherbourg station (operated by Zéphir).

Condor Ferries by ship — 2007 service (No winter service)

Sailings from Portsmouth Continental Ferry Port and Cherbourg.

Portsmouth		Cherbourg		Cherbourg		Portsmouth	
0930	→	1600	⑦ July 15 - Sept. 9.	1700	→	2100	⑦ July 15 - Sept. 9.

PORTSMOUTH - LE HAVRE 2165

L D Lines — 2007 service

Sailings from Portsmouth Continental Ferry Port and Le Havre Quai de Southampton.

Portsmouth		Le Havre	Le Havre		Portsmouth
2300	→	0730	1700	→	2130

PORTSMOUTH - OUISTREHAM (CAEN) 2170

Brittany Ferries by ship — November 1, 2007 - October 31, 2008 (No service Dec. 25, Jan. 1)

Sailings from Portsmouth Continental Ferry Port and Ouistreham.

Portsmouth		Ouistreham		Ouistreham		Portsmouth	
0845	→	1530	See note **P**.	0900	→	1345	See note **P**.
0845	→	1545	See note **Q**.	0900	→	1400	See note **T**.
1515	→	2200	Nov. 1 - 16.	1700	→	2145	Nov. 1 - 16.
1530	→	2230	See note **R**.	1715	→	2215	See note **N**.
1515	→	2200	Not Feb. 1 - 28.	2300	→	0700	Dec. 29 only.
2315	→	0715	Nov. 1 - 16.	2330	→	0700	Nov. 1 - 16.
2345	→	0730	See note **S**.	2359	→	0700	See note **M**.

- **M** – Nov. 17 - Oct. 31 (not Dec. 24, 29, 31).
- **N** – Nov. 17 - Oct. 31 (not Dec. 24, 26, 31).
- **P** – ①②③④⑥⑦ Nov. 1 - 15.
- **Q** – ①②③④⑥⑦ Nov. 17 - Mar. 11; ①②④⑤⑥⑦ Mar. 13 - Oct. 30 (not Dec. 24, 26, Jan. 2).
- **R** – Nov. 17 - Oct. 31 (not Dec. 31).
- **S** – Nov. 17 - Oct. 31 (not Dec. 24, 31).
- **T** – ①②③④⑥⑦ Nov. 17 - Mar. 11; ①②④⑤⑥⑦ Mar. 13 - Oct. 30 (not Jan. 1, 2).

🚘 Ouistreham - Caen station (journey 45 minutes) to connect with most sailings.

Brittany Ferries by fast ferry — March 14 - October 26, 2008 (No winter service)

Sailings from Portsmouth Continental Ferry Port and Ouistreham.

Portsmouth		Ouistreham		Ouistreham		Portsmouth	
0700	→	1130	⑤⑥⑦	1230	→	1500	⑤⑥⑦

PORTSMOUTH - ST MALO 2180

Brittany Ferries — November 1, 2007 - October 31, 2008

Sailings from Portsmouth Continental Ferry Port and St. Malo Terminal Ferry du Naye.

Portsmouth		St. Malo		St. Malo		Portsmouth	
1030	→	1930	Dec. 23 only.	1045	→	1830	See note **B**.
2030	→	0815	See note **A**.	2200	→	0800	See note **C**.

- **A** – ①②③④⑤⑦ Nov. 1 - Dec. 21, Jan. 1 - Mar. 7; daily Mar. 9 - Oct. 31 (also Dec. 27, 28).
- **B** – ①②③④⑤ Nov. 1 - Dec. 21, Jan. 3 - Mar. 7; daily Mar. 10 - Oct. 31 (also Dec. 29).
- **C** – ⑥ Nov. 3 - Mar. 8 (also Dec. 23, 28, Jan. 2; not Dec. 29).

Departure times may vary owing to tidal conditions.

RAMSGATE - OOSTENDE 2190

Transeuropa Ferries — 2007 service

Conveys passengers with vehicles only

Ramsgate		Oostende		Oostende		Ramsgate	
0700	→	1200		0100	→	0400	Summer only.
1200	→	1700	⑥⑦	0700	→	1000	
1330	→	1830	①②③④⑤	1330	→	1630	
1830	→	2330		1800	→	2100	
2230	→	0330	Summer only.				

2200 ABERDEEN - KIRKWALL - LERWICK

NorthLink Ferries — 2007 service

Aberdeen	Kirkwall	Kirkwall	Lerwick	
1700②④⑥⑦	2300②④⑥⑦	2345②④⑥⑦	0730③⑤⑦①	See note **B**.
1900①③⑤	→	→	0730②④⑥	See note **A**.
Lerwick	**Kirkwall**	**Kirkwall**	**Aberdeen**	
1730①③⑤	2300①③⑤	2345①③⑤	0700②④⑥	See note **D**.
1900②④⑥⑦	→	→	0700③⑤⑦①	See note **C**.

A – Also ② Jan. 1 - Mar. 31 and Nov. 1 - Dec. 31.
B – Not ② Jan. 1 - Mar. 31 and Nov. 1 - Dec. 31.
C – Also ① Jan. 1 - Mar. 31 and Nov. 1 - Dec. 31.
D – Not ① Jan. 1 - Mar. 31 and Nov. 1 - Dec. 31.

A 🚐 transfer service is available Kirkwall - Stromness and v.v. in conjunction with evening sailings.

2210 BERGEN - EGERSUND - HANSTHOLM

Fjord Line — Service to June 14, 2008 ▲

Bergen	Egersund	Hanstholm	Hanstholm	Egersund	Bergen
August 28 - December 23					
1500②	0130③	1000③	1800③	0200④	1200④
1500④	0130⑤	1000⑤	1800⑤	0200⑥	1200⑥
1500⑥	0130⑦	1000⑦	1400⑦	2130⑦	0730①
January 1 - June 14					
1400②	0030③	0900③	1830①	0230②	1230②
1500④	0130⑤	0900⑤	1800③	0200④	1200④
1030⑥	2100⑥	0900⑦	1500⑤	2300⑤	0900⑥

▲ – *Subject to alteration during Xmas/New Year period*

Additional services operate Egersund - Hanstholm and v.v. in summer.

A connecting bus service operates between Egersund and Stavanger.

2215 BERGEN - STAVANGER - NEWCASTLE

DFDS Seaways — Service to April 30, 2008

Sailings from Bergen Skoltegrunnskaien, Stavanger Strandkaien and Newcastle International Ferry Terminal, North Shields.

Bergen	Haugesund	Stavanger	Newcastle	
September 27 - December 23				
1100①	1530①	1800①	1300②	
1700④	2130④	2355④	1900⑤	
December 26 - 29				
1700③	2130③	2355③	1900④	
January 1 - April 30				
1000①	1430①	1800①	1330②	Not Jan. 21, 28.
1100④	1530④	1900④	1500⑤	Not Jan. 17, 24, 31.
1700④	2130④	0100⑤	2000⑤	Jan. 31 only.
Newcastle	**Stavanger**	**Haugesund**	**Bergen**	
September 27 - December 23				
1900②⑥	1500③⑦	1730③⑦	2200③⑦	
December 26 - 29				
1900⑤	1500⑥	1730⑥	2200⑥	
January 1 - April 30				
1830②⑥	1500③⑦	1800③⑦	2300③⑦	Not Jan. 19 - 29.

2217 BERGEN - STAVANGER - HIRTSHALS

Color Line — 2007 service (No service Apr. 10 - 24)

Bergen	Stavanger	Hirtshals	Hirtshals	Stavanger	Bergen
January 3 - June 14 and August 13 - December 30					
1300①③⑤	2015①③⑤	0730②④⑥	1100②④	2130②④	0800③⑤
			1800⑥	0615⑦	1230⑦
June 15 - August 12					
1300①③⑤	2015①③⑤	0730②④⑥	0900⑥	1945⑥	...
...	2115⑥	0730⑦	1030②④⑦	2130②④⑦	0800③⑤①

2220 HARWICH - ESBJERG

DFDS Seaways — Service to April 30, 2008

Sailings from Harwich International Port and Esbjerg Englandskajen.

Harwich	Esbjerg	
1800	1300	③⑤⑦ Dec. 2 - Apr. 30 (not Dec. 26, Jan. 2, Apr. 2 - 11).
Esbjerg	**Harwich**	
1845	1200	②④⑥ Dec. 1 - Apr. 29 (not Dec. 25, Jan. 1, Apr. 1 - 10).

For rail services from/to London – see Table **204**

2235 HARWICH - HOEK VAN HOLLAND

Stena Line by ship — Service to April 30, 2008 (No service Dec. 24, 25)

Sailings from Harwich International Port and Hoek van Holland.

Harwich	Hoek		Hoek	Harwich	
November 5 - December 23					
0900	1615		1430	2000	
2330	0730		2200	0630	
December 24 - January 6					
0900	1615	Not Dec. 26, Jan. 1.	1445	2015	Not Dec. 26.
1100	1815	Jan. 1 only.	2200	0630	Not Dec. 31.
2330	0730	Not Dec. 31.			
January 7 - April 30					
0900	1615	Not Mar. 7 - 13.	1430	2000	Not Mar. 15.
2345	0745	Not Mar. 15.	2200	0630	Not Mar. 6 - 12.

See Table **15a** for connecting rail services London - Harwich and v.v. and Hoek van Holland - Amsterdam and v.v.

Subject to alteration during Xmas/New Year period

2240 NORWEGIAN COASTAL SERVICES

Flaggruten — 2007 service

BERGEN - HAUGESUND - KOPERVIK - STAVANGER

Sailings from Bergen Strandkaiterminalen, Haugesund Hurtigbåtterminalen, Kopervik and Stavanger Hurtigbåtterminalen.

Bergen	Haugesund	Kopervik	Stavanger	
...	0640	0700	0800	①②③④⑤
...	0830	0855	0950	⑥
0950	1300	1320	1420	①②③④⑤
1010	1325	1350	1445	⑥
...	1500	1520	1620	①②③④⑤
1245	1535	1600	1655	⑦
1615	1920	1940	2040	①②③④⑤
1630	1920	1945	2040	⑦
Stavanger	**Kopervik**	**Haugesund**	**Bergen**	
0720	0815	0835	...	①②③④⑤
0930	1025	1050	1350	①②③④⑤
0950	1045	1110	1410	⑥
1200	1255	1320	1605	⑦
1645	1740	1805	2110	①②③④⑤
1715	1810	1835	2120	⑦
2045	2140	2210	...	①②③④⑤
2050	2145	2215	...	⑦

Hurtigruten

BERGEN - TRONDHEIM - TROMSØ - KIRKENES

SUMMER SERVICE – **April 15 - September 14, 2007**

NORTHBOUND	*arrive*	*depart*	*day*	SOUTHBOUND	*arrive*	*depart*	*day*
Bergen ♣	...	2000	A	Kirkenes	...	1245	A
Florø		0215	B	Vadsø		|	A
Måløy		0430	B	Vardø	1600	1700	A
Ålesund	0845	0930	B	Honningsvåg		0615	B
Geiranger ▲		1330	B	Hammerfest	1115	1245	B
Ålesund		1845	B	Tromsø	2345	0130	B/C
Molde		2200	B	Finnsnes		0445	C
Kristiansund		0145	C	Harstad	0800	0830	C
Trondheim	0815	1200	C	Stokmarknes		1515	C
Rørvik		2115	C	Svolvaer	1830	1930	C
Brønnøysund		0100	D	Stamsund		2130	C
Sandnessjøen		0415	D	Bodø	0130	0400	D
Bodø	1230	1500	D	Sandnessjøen		1330	D
Stamsund		1930	D	Brønnøysund		1700	D
Svolvaer	2100	2200	D	Rørvik		2130	D
Stokmarknes		0100	E	Trondheim	0630	1000	E
Harstad	0645	0800	E	Kristiansund		1700	E
Finnsnes		1145	E	Molde		2130	E
Tromsø	1430	1830	E	Ålesund		|	E
Hammerfest	0515	0645	F	Geiranger		|	E
Honningsvåg	1145	1515	F	Ålesund	2359	0045	E/F
Vardø	0400	0415	G	Måløy		0545	F
Vadsø		0815	G	Florø		0815	F
Kirkenes	1000	...	G	Bergen ♣	1430	...	F

WINTER SERVICE – **September 15 - December 31, 2007**

NORTHBOUND	*arrive*	*depart*	*day*	SOUTHBOUND	*arrive*	*depart*	*day*
Bergen ♣	...	2230	A	Kirkenes	...	1245	A
Florø		0445	B	Vadsø		|	A
Måløy		0730	B	Vardø	1600	1700	A
Ålesund	1200	1500	B	Honningsvåg		0615	B
Molde		1830	B	Hammerfest	1115	1245	B
Kristiansund		2300	B	Tromsø	2345	0130	B/C
Trondheim	0600	1200	C	Finnsnes		0445	C
Rørvik		2115	C	Harstad	0800	0830	C
Brønnøysund		0100	D	Stokmarknes		1515	C
Sandnessjøen		0415	D	Svolvaer	1830	1930	C
Bodø	1230	1500	D	Stamsund		2130	C
Stamsund		1930	D	Bodø	0130	0400	D
Svolvaer	2100	2200	D	Sandnessjøen		1330	D
Stokmarknes		0100	E	Brønnøysund		1700	D
Harstad	0645	0800	E	Rørvik		2130	D
Finnsnes		1145	E	Trondheim	0630	1000	E
Tromsø	1430	1830	E	Kristiansund		1700	E
Hammerfest	0515	0645	F	Molde		2130	E
Honningsvåg	1145	1515	F	Ålesund	2359	0045	E/F
Vardø	0400	0415	G	Måløy		0545	F
Vadsø		0815	G	Florø		0815	F
Kirkenes	1000	...	G	Bergen ♣	1430	...	F

A – 1st day .... **G** – 7th day.
♣ – Sailings from Bergen Frilenesset.
▲ – Embarkation and disembarkation take place by tender - passengers are required to be at the quay 30 minutes before departure.

Other ports served: Torvik, Nesna, Ørnes, Sortland, Risøyhamn, Skjervøy, Øksfjord, Havøysund, Kjøllefjord, Mehamn, Berlevåg, Båtsfjord.

Nordlandsekspressen — Service to March 24, 2008

BODØ - SVOLVÆR

Bodø	Svolvær		Svolvær	Bodø	
April 17 - August 21					
0730	1000	②	0630	1000	①②③④⑤⑥
1030	1250	④	1515	1750	②④
1715	2050	①②③④⑥	1600	1930	⑦
1800	2135	⑤			
2030	2330	⑦			
August 22 - March 24					
1715	2050	①②③④⑥	0630	1000	①②③④⑤⑥
1800	2135	⑤	1600	1930	⑦
2030	2330	⑦			

HELGOLAND (Germany) services 2242

The following services operate:

Route:		Operator:
BREMERHAVEN - HELGOLAND		Förde Reederei Seetouristik
BÜSUM - HELGOLAND	Summer only	Reederei Cassen Eils
CUXHAVEN - HELGOLAND	Summer service	Förde Reederei Seetouristik
	Winter service	Reederei Cassen Eils
WILHELMSHAVEN - HELGOLAND	Summer only	A G Ems

HULL - ROTTERDAM 2245

P & O Ferries — Service to December 30, 2007 (No service Jan. 1, Dec. 25, 26)

Sailings from Hull King George Dock and Rotterdam Europoort.

Hull		Rotterdam	Rotterdam		Hull
2100	→	0800	2100	→	0800

🚌 connections (reservation recommended):
Hull railway station (depart 1715) - King George Dock and v.v.
Rotterdam Centraal Station (depart 1700) - Europoort and v.v.
Amsterdam Centraal Station (depart 1700) - Europoort and v.v.

HULL - ZEEBRUGGE 2250

P & O Ferries — Service to December 29, 2007 (No service Jan. 1, Dec. 24, 25)

Sailings from Hull King George Dock and Zeebrugge Leopold II Dam.

Hull		Zeebrugge	Zeebrugge		Hull
1900	→	0830	1900	→	0800

🚌 connections (reservation recommended):
Hull railway station (depart 1715) - King George Dock and v.v.
Brugge Station (depart 1730) - Zeebrugge and v.v.

NEWCASTLE - IJMUIDEN (AMSTERDAM) 2255

DFDS Seaways — Service to April 30, 2008

Sailings from Newcastle International Ferry Terminal, Royal Quays and IJmuiden Felison Terminal.

Newcastle		IJmuiden		IJmuiden		Newcastle	
1730	→	0930▲	See note **N**.	1800	→	0900◆	See note **P**.

N – Not Dec. 24, 25, 31, Jan. 8, 10, 12, 14, 16, 18, 20, 22, 24, 26, 28.
P – Not Dec. 24, 25, 30, Jan. 7, 9, 11, 13, 15, 17, 19, 21, 23, 25, 27.
▲ – 1030 on even dates Dec. 2 - 30. ◆ – 1100 on Jan. 1.

🚌 connections:
Newcastle rail station - International Ferry Terminal (North Shields) and v.v.
Depart Newcastle station 2½ and 1¼ hours before sailing; depart Ferry Terminal following arrival of ship).
Victoria Hotel Amsterdam (near Centraal station) - IJmuiden and v.v.
Depart hotel every 10 minutes 1530 - 1630; depart Ferry Terminal following arrival of ship).

ROSYTH - ZEEBRUGGE 2277

Superfast Ferries — 2008 service

Rosyth		Zeebrugge		Zeebrugge		Rosyth	
1700	→	1200	②④⑥	1800	→	1100	①③⑤

🚌 services operate from Rosyth to Edinburgh and Dunfermline and v.v.

SCRABSTER - STROMNESS 2280

NorthLink Ferries — 2007 service

Scrabster		Stromness		Stromness		Scrabster	
0845	→	1015	See note **A**.	0630	→	0800	See note **A**.
1200	→	1330	See note **B**.	0900	→	1030	See note **B**.
1315	→	1445	See note **A**.	1100	→	1230	See note **A**.
1900	→	2030	Daily.	1645	→	1815	Daily.

A – ①②③④⑤ (also ⑥ June 9 - Aug. 18).
B – ⑦ (also ⑥ until June 2 and from Aug. 25).

TÓRSHAVN - BERGEN 2288

Smyril Line — Service to March 16, 2008

Tórshavn		Bergen		Bergen		Tórshavn	
May 20 - December 31							
0830①	→	0600②	June 11 - Aug. 27.	0600⑦	→	0600①	See note **T**.
1700④	→	0500⑦	See note **Y**.	0900②	→	1530④	See note **V**.
1800④	→	1700⑤	Oct. 4 - Dec. 27.	0900⑦	→	0600①	Sept. 30 - Dec. 30.
January 1 - March 16							
1700④	→	1600⑤		1000⑦	→	0600①	

T – May 20 - June 10, Sept. 2 - 23. V – June 12, 26, July 10, 24, Aug. 7, 21.
Y – May 24 - June 14, Sept. 6 - 27.

TÓRSHAVN - LERWICK 2290

Smyril Line — 2007 service (No winter service)

Tórshavn		Lerwick		Lerwick		Tórshavn	
0830⑤	→	1600⑦	Aug. 10, 24.	1630⑦	→	0600①	Aug. 12, 26.
0830⑤	→	2100⑤	Aug. 3, 17, 31.	2130⑤	→	0600①	Aug. 3, 17, 31.
1700④	→	0500⑤	Sept. 6 - 27.	0530⑤	→	0600①	Sept. 7 - 28.

TÓRSHAVN - HANSTHOLM 2293

Smyril Line — Service to March 16, 2008

Tórshavn		Hanstholm		Hanstholm		Tórshavn	
May 20 - December 31							
0830⑤	→	1700⑥	June 22 - Aug. 31.	1400⑥	→	0600①	See note **Z**.
1700④	→	0900⑥	See note **Y**.	1700⑥	→	0600①	Sept. 29 - Dec. 29.
1800④	→	1200⑥	Oct. 4 - Dec. 27.	2100⑥	→	0600①	June 23 - Sept. 1.
January 1 - March 16							
1700④	→	1200⑥		1700⑥	→	0600①	

Y – May 24 - June 14, Sept. 6 - 27. Z – May 19 - June 16, Sept. 8 - 29.

TÓRSHAVN - SEYDISFJÖRDUR (Iceland) 2295

Smyril Line — Service to March 16, 2008 (No service Jan. 1 - Mar. 16)

Tórshavn		Seydisfjördur		Seydisfjördur		Tórshavn	
May 20 - December 31							
1700①	→	0900②	See note **A**.	1300④	→	0600⑤	June 21 - Aug. 30.
1800③	→	0900④	June 13 - Aug. 29.	1700③	→	1100④	Oct. 3 - Dec. 26.
				1800③	→	1100④	See note **B**.

A – May 21 - June 11, Sept. 3 - Dec. 31. B – May 23 - June 13, Sept. 5 - 26.

SKAGERRAK, KATTEGAT & SOUTH WEST BALTIC

ÅRHUS - KALUNDBORG 2300

Mols-Linien by ship — Journey 2 hours 40 minutes — 2007 service

August 13 - 26
Depart Århus: 0300①②③④⑤, 0700②③④⑤, 0900⑥, 1000⑦, 1100①②③④⑤, 1230⑥, 1400⑦, 1500①②③④⑤, 1900①②③④⑤⑦, 2300①②③④⑤⑦.
Depart Kalundborg: 0300②③④⑤, 0700①②③④⑤, 0900⑥, 1000⑦, 1100①②③④⑤, 1230⑥, 1400⑦, 1500①②③④⑤, 1900①②③④⑤⑦, 2300①②③④⑤⑦.
August 27 - October 14
Depart Århus: 0300①②③④⑤, 0700②③④⑤, 0900⑥, 1000⑦, 1100①②③④⑤, 1400⑦, 1500①②③④⑤, 1900①②③④⑤⑦, 2300①②③④⑤⑦.
Depart Kalundborg: 0300②③④⑤, 0700①②③④⑤, 1000⑦, 1100①②③④⑤, 1230⑥, 1400⑦, 1500①②③④⑤, 1900①②③④⑤⑦, 2300①②③④⑤⑦.
October 15 - December 21
Depart Århus: 0115①, 0300②③④⑤, 0700②③④⑤, 0900⑥, 1000⑦, 1100①②③④⑤, 1500①②③④⑤, 1745⑦, 1900①②③④⑤, 2300①②③④⑤.
Depart Kalundborg: 0300②③④⑤, 0500①, 0700②③④⑤, 1100①②③④⑤, 1230⑥, 1400⑦, 1500①②③④⑤, 1900①②③④⑤, 2130⑦, 2300①②③④⑤.

Subject to alteration during holiday periods

BØJDEN - FYNSHAV 2304

Scandlines — Journey 50 minutes — 2007 service

Depart Bøjden: 0700**A**, 0900, 1100, 1300, 1500, 1700, 1900, 2100**B**.
Depart Fynshav: 0800**A**, 1000, 1200, 1400, 1600, 1800, 2000, 2200**B**.
A – ①②③④⑤ (also ⑦ Mar. 4 - Oct. 21).
B – ①②③④⑤ (also ⑦ May 29 - Aug. 31; not Apr. 5, 6, 8, May 4, 17).

Subject to alteration on and around holidays

EBELTOFT - SJÆLLANDS ODDE 2310

Mols-Linien by catamaran — Journey 65 minutes — 2007 service

Ebeltoft - Sjællands Odde and v.v.: 10 - 15 sailings daily in summer; 5 - 9 in winter.

Subject to alteration during holiday periods

ESBJERG - FANØ 2312

Scandlines — Journey 12 minutes — 2007 service

Departures every 40 minutes 0540 - 1950, then hourly to 0010.

Subject to alteration on and around holidays

FREDERIKSHAVN - GÖTEBORG 2320

Stena Line by ship — Service to December 9, 2007

Sailings from Frederikshavn Trafikhavn and Göteborg.

Frederikshavn		Göteborg		Göteborg		Frederikshavn	
January 1 - April 1							
0545	→	0900	⑦ Jan. 7 - Feb. 25.	0210	→	0515	⑦ Jan. 7 - Feb. 25.
1150	→	1515	②③④⑤⑥⑦	0800	→	1115	②③④⑤⑥⑦
1430	→	1755		0930	→	1245	
2000	→	2315		1600	→	1915	
2245	→	0215		1845	→	2200	
April 2 - July 5							
0345	→	0715	June 22 - July 5.	0800	→	1115	⑥⑦
1150	→	1515	②③④⑤⑥⑦	0930	→	1245	
1430	→	1755		1600	→	1915	
2000	→	2315		1845	→	2200	①②③④⑤⑦
2245	→	0215	①②③④⑤⑦	2355	→	0315	June 22 - July 5.
July 6 - August 12							
0345	→	0715		0800	→	1115	
1150	→	1515		0930	→	1245	
1430	→	1755		1600	→	1915	
2000	→	2315		1845	→	2200	
2245	→	0215		2355	→	0315	
August 13 - December 9							
1150	→	1515	②③④⑤⑥⑦	0800	→	1115	⑥⑦
1430	→	1755		0930	→	1245	
2000	→	2315		1600	→	1915	
2245	→	0215	①②③④⑤⑦	1845	→	2200	①②③④⑤⑦

Stena Line by *HSS* fast ferry — Journey 2 hours — 2007 service

Sailings from Frederikshavn Trafikhavn and Göteborg.

March 16 - April 1
Depart Frederikshavn: 1000⑤⑥⑦, 1530. Depart Göteborg: 0730⑤⑥⑦, 1245.
April 2 - July 5
Depart Frederikshavn: 1000①②③④⑤⑥, 1530, 1730.
Depart Göteborg: 0730①②③④⑤⑥, 1245, 1500.
July 6 - August 12
Depart Frederikshavn: 0945, 1515, 2045. Depart Göteborg: 0700, 1230, 1800.
August 13 - December 9
Depart Frederikshavn: 1000①②③④⑤⑥, 1730⑤⑥⑦.
Depart Göteborg: 0730①②③④⑤⑥, 1500⑤⑥⑦.

2330 GEDSER - ROSTOCK

Scandlines Deutschland **2007 service**

Sailings from Rostock Überseehafen and Gedser. **(No service Dec. 24, 25, 31)**

Journey 1 hour 45 minutes

Depart Gedser: 0200 **A**, 0230 **D**, 0345 **A**, 0700, 0900, 1100, 1300, 1500, 1700, 1900, 2100, 2345 **E**.

Depart Rostock: 0200 **A**, 0230 **B**, 0415 **A**, 0600, 0900, 1100, 1300, 1500, 1700, 1900, 2100, 2345 **C**.

A – ① (also Apr. 10, May 29; not Apr. 9, May 28).
B – ②④⑤⑥ (not Apr. 7).
C – ①②③④⑤⑦ (also ⑥ June 30 - Aug. 11; not Apr. 6, 8, May 27).
D – ②③④⑤⑥ (also ⑦ July 1 - Aug. 12; not Apr. 7, 10, May 29).
E – ①③④⑤⑦ (not Apr. 6, 8, May 27).

Subject to alteration on and around holidays

2335 GÖTEBORG - KIEL

Stena Line **2007 service (No service Dec. 24, 25)**

Sailings from Kiel Schwedenkai and Göteborg.

Göteborg		Kiel	Kiel		Göteborg
1930▲	→	0900	1930♦	→	0900

▲ – Depart 1900 on Dec. 31. ♦ – Depart 1900 on Dec. 30, 31.

No departure from Göteborg uneven dates Jan. 9 - 31; from Kiel even dates Jan. 10 - 30, Feb. 1 owing to ship maintenance.

2342 GRENAA - VARBERG

Stena Line Journey 4 - 5½ hours **2007 service**

Grenaa		Varberg		Varberg		Grenaa	
January 12 - April 1 and September 24 - December 21							
0100	→	0615	See note **A**.	0900	→	1315	See note **B**.
1430	→	1845	①②③④⑤⑦	1955	→	0010	①②③④⑤⑦
April 2 - June 28 and August 13 - September 23							
0100	→	0615	See note **D**.	0900	→	1315	Not June 7.
1430	→	1845	Not June 7.	1955	→	0010	See note **C**.
June 29 - August 12							
0100	→	0615	June 29 only.	0800	→	1215	
1315	→	1730		1830	→	2245	
2345	→	0415					

A – ①②③④⑤ (also Mar. 31; not Jan. 12).
B – ①②③④⑤ (also Apr. 1).
C – Not Apr. 6, 7, 14, 21, 28, May 5, 12, Sept. 22.
D – Not Apr. 7, 8, 15, 22, 29, May 6, 13, Aug. 13, Sept. 23).

2345 HELSINGØR - HELSINGBORG

Scandlines Journey 20 minutes **2007 service**

From Helsingør and Helsingborg: Sailings every 20 minutes 0640 - 2140 (every 30 minutes at other times).

Subject to alteration on and around holidays

2350 HIRTSHALS - KRISTIANSAND

Color Line **by ship** **Service to April 30, 2008**

Hirtshals		Kristiansand		Kristiansand		Hirtshals	
August 13 - December 9							
0115	→	0700		0815	→	1245	②③④⑤⑥⑦
1345	→	1815	②③④⑤⑥⑦	1915	→	2345	
December 10 - April 30 ▲							
0100	→	0700	②③④	0800	→	1115	
1215	→	1530	See note **H**.	1630	→	1945	See note **H**.
1430	→	1745	①②③ (not Dec. 31).	2000	→	2315	①②③ (not Dec. 31).
2045	→	2359	See note **H**.				

H – ④⑤⑥⑦ (also Dec. 31).

▲ – No sailings Jan. 1 - 6, 14, Feb. 11, Mar. 10, Apr. 7.

Color Line **by fast ferry** **2007 service (no winter service)**

Hirtshals		Kristiansand		Kristiansand		Hirtshals	
1230	→	1500	See note **A**.	0900	→	1130	See note **A**.
1645	→	1915	See note **C**.	1200	→	1430	See note **D**.
1730	→	2000	See note **B**.	1700	→	1930	See note **A**.
2030	→	2300	See note **A**.				

A – Mar. 30 - Apr. 9, May 18 - Sept. 2.
B – ①②③④⑤⑦ Apr. 10 - May 17; ④⑤⑦ Sept. 3 - Oct. 7.
C – ⑥ Apr. 10 - May 17, Sept. 3 - Oct. 7.
D – Daily Apr. 10 - May 17; ④⑤⑥⑦ Sept. 3 - Oct. 7.

2355 KALUNDBORG - SAMSØ

Samsø Linien Journey 1 hour 50 minutes **Service to April 24, 2008**

August 27 - September 30

Depart Kalundborg: 0855⑦, 0955①②③④⑤⑥, 1325⑦, 1430⑤, 1800①②③④⑥⑦, 1900⑤, 2225⑦.

Depart Kolby Kås (Samsø): 0640⑦, 0740①②③④⑤⑥, 1110⑦, 1215⑤, 1540①②③④⑥⑦, 1645⑤, 2015⑦.

October 1 - 28 and March 28 - April 24

Depart Kalundborg: 0955, 1430⑤⑦, 1800①②③④⑥, 1900⑤⑦.

Depart Kolby Kås (Samsø): 0740, 1215⑤⑦, 1540①②③④⑥, 1645⑤⑦.

October 29 - March 27

Depart Kalundborg: 0955①②③④⑤⑥, 1035⑦, 1800.

Depart Kolby Kås (Samsø): 0740①②③④⑤⑥, 0820⑦, 1540.

Subject to alteration during holiday periods

2360 KØBENHAVN - OSLO

DFDS Seaways **Service to April 30, 2008**

Sailings from København Dampfærgevej and Oslo Vippetangen (Utstikker 2).

København		Oslo		Oslo		København	
1700	→	0930♦	Not Dec. 24.	1700	→	0930♦	Not Dec. 25.

♦ – 1100 on Jan. 1.

2362 LANGESUND - HIRTSHALS

Kystlink **Service to June 12, 2008**

Langesund		Hirtshals	Hirtshals		Langesund	
1900	→	2400	0130	→	0800	Not Jan. 1.
			1300	→	1800	Jan. 1 only.

2364 LANGESUND - STRÖMSTAD

Kystlink **Service to June 12, 2008**

Langesund		Strömstad		Strömstad		Langesund	
1030	→	1345	②③④⑤⑥⑦	1430	→	1730	②③④⑤⑥⑦

2366 LARVIK - HIRTSHALS

Color Line **Service to April 30, 2008**

Larvik		Hirtshals		Hirtshals		Larvik	
December 1 - 31 and March 17 - April 15							
1900	→	0800	Not Dec. 23, 24.	1000	→	1515	Dec. 31 only.
				1215	→	1800	Mar. 17 - Apr. 15.
				1245	→	1800	Not Dec. 1 - 23, 26 - 31
January 1 - March 16							
0830	→	1415	⑤⑦	0830	→	1415	⑥
1515	→	2045	⑥	1245	→	1800	①②③
1900	→	0800	①②③	1515	→	2045	⑤⑦
2145	→	0700	⑤	2030	→	0730	④
2145	→	0800	⑦	2145	→	0730	⑥
April 16 - 30							
0800	→	1145		1245	→	1630	①②③④⑤⑦
1730	→	2115	①②③④⑤⑦	1900	→	2245	⑥
				2215	→	0200	①②③④⑤⑦

2368 OSLO - FREDERIKSHAVN

Color Line **Service to April 30, 2008**

Sailings from Oslo Color Line Terminalen, Hjortneskaia and Frederikshavn.

Oslo		Frederikshavn	
2000	→	0800	②③④⑤⑥⑦ (not Apr. 1 - 3).

Frederikshavn		Oslo	
1030	→	1900	③④⑤⑥⑦ (not Mar. 31, Apr. 1 - 3).
1800	→	0800	① Jan. 1 - Apr. 30.
2000	→	0800	① Sept. 1 - Dec. 31.

Subject to alteration Dec. 23 - 31

Stena Line **2007 service**

Sailings from Oslo Vippetangen and Frederikshavn.

Oslo		Frederikshavn		Frederikshavn		Oslo	
1930	→	0730	See note **F**.	1000	→	1830	See note **G**.
				1830	→	0730	See note **H**.

F – ②③④⑤⑥⑦ Jan. 1 - June 17; daily June 18 - Aug. 26; ②③④⑤⑥⑦ Aug. 28 - Dec. 31.
G – ③④⑤⑥⑦ Jan. 2 - June 17; daily June 18 - Aug. 26; ③④⑤⑥⑦ Aug. 27 - Dec. 31.
H – ① Jan. 8 - June 11, Aug. 27 - Dec. 31.

Subject to alteration Dec. 24 - 31

2372 OSLO - KIEL

Color Line **Service to April 30, 2008**

Sailings from Oslo Color Line Terminalen, Hjortnes and Kiel Oslo-Kai.

Oslo		Kiel		Kiel		Oslo	
1400	→	0930	See note **K**.	1400	→	0930	See note **L**.

K – Not Dec. 24, 31, Mar. 24, 26, 28, 30, Apr. 1.
L – Not Dec. 24, 31, Mar. 25, 27, 29, 31, Apr. 2.

🚌 Oslo Color Line Terminal - Oslo Sentral rail station.
Kiel Oslo-Kai - Hamburg ZOB (Central Bus Station).

2375 PUTTGARDEN - RØDBY

Scandlines Deutschland Journey 45 minutes **2007 service**

Departures every 30 minutes (40 minutes 2215⑥⑦ - 0615⑦①).

Subject to alteration on and around holidays

2380 ROSTOCK - TRELLEBORG

Scandlines Deutschland **2007 service**

Sailings from Rostock Überseehafen and Trelleborg.

Journey 5 hours 45 minutes (§ – 7½ hours)

Depart Rostock: 0745②③④⑤⑥⑦, 1515, 2245§.

Depart Trelleborg: 0800②③④⑤⑥⑦, 1515, 2245§.

Subject to alteration on and around holidays

TT Line **by ship** **2007 service**

Sailings from Rostock Überseehafen and Trelleborg.

Rostock		Trelleborg		Trelleborg		Rostock	
0800	→	1330		0800	→	1330	②③④⑤⑥⑦
1530	→	2100	②③④⑤⑥⑦	1530	→	2100	
2300	→	0600		2300	→	0630	

Subject to alteration during holiday periods

For international shipping maps – see pages 518 - 520

SKAGERRAK, KATTEGAT & SOUTH WEST BALTIC continued

ROSTOCK - VENTSPILS 2382

:andlines Deutschland **2007 service**

ailings from Rostock Überseehafen and Ventspils.

ourney 26 hours

)epart Rostock: 1800②③⑤⑥. Depart Ventspils: 0400②④⑤⑦.

Subject to alteration on and around holidays

SASSNITZ-MUKRAN - TRELLEBORG 2385

:andlines Deutschland Journey 3 hours 45 minutes **2007 service**

ailings from Trelleborg and Fährhafen Sassnitz-Mukran.

part Sassnitz-Mukran: 0300 **A**, 0800, 1245, 1745, 2215.

part Trelleborg: 0300 **A**, 0815, 1245, 1730, 2215.

– ①③④⑤⑥⑦ (daily May 9 - Sept. 3).

Subject to alteration on and around holidays

STRÖMSTAD - SANDEFJORD 2387

Color Line Journey 2½ hours **2007 service**

January 1 - February 1

Depart Strømstad: 1300 (not Jan. 1), 1630 (Jan. 1 only), 1930 (not Jan 1).

Depart Sandefjord: 1000 (not Jan. 1), 1300 (Jan. 1 only), 1630 (not Jan. 1).

February 2 - June 21 and August 13 - December 23

Depart Strømstad: 1000, 1300, 1630, 1930, 2230②③④⑤⑥⑦.

Depart Sandefjord: 0700, 1000, 1300, 1630, 1930②③④⑤⑥⑦.

June 22 - August 12

Depart Strømstad: 0630 (not June 22), 1000, 1330, 1700, 2000, 2300.

Depart Sandefjord: 0700, 1000, 1330, 1700, 2000, 2300 (not Aug. 12).

Subject to alteration on Mar. 26, 27, Apr. 10, 11 – contact operator for details.

TRAVEMÜNDE - TRELLEBORG 2390

TT Line **2007 service**

Sailings from Travemünde Skandinavienkai and Trelleborg.

Travemünde		Trelleborg		Trelleborg		Travemünde	
0300	→	1000	②③④⑤⑥	0230	→	1000	②③④⑤⑥
0400	→	1100	①	1000	→	1715	
1000	→	1715		1330	→	2100	⑥
1715	→	0015	①②③④⑤	1715	→	0015	①②③④⑤⑦
2200	→	0730		2200	→	0730	
2300	→	0630	⑥				

Subject to alteration during holiday periods

connection available Trelleborg - Malmö railway station and v.v. for certain sailings.

BALTIC SEA

GDAŃSK - NYNÄSHAMN 2402

ɔlferries **Service to April 30, 2008**

Gdańsk		Nynäshamn		Nynäshamn		Gdańsk	
1800	→	1200	See note **A**.	1800	→	1200	See note **B**.

A – Jan. 2-11, 13-18, 20, 22, 24, 27, 29, 31; Feb. 2, 4-8, 10-15, 17-22, 24-29; Mar. 2-7, 9-14, 16-21, 25-28, 30, 31; Apr. 1-4, 6-11, 13-18, 20-25, 27-30.

B – Jan. 3-11, 13-18, 21, 23, 25, 28, 30; Feb. 1, 3-8, 10-15, 17-22, 24-29; Mar. 2-7, 9-14, 16-21, 25-28, 30, 31; Apr. 1-4, 6-11, 13-18, 20-25, 27-30.

GRISSLEHAMN - ECKERÖ 2405

:kerö Linjen Journey 2 hours **2007 service**
(No service Dec. 24,25)

January 1 - March 22 and September 24 - December 31

)epart Grisslehamn: 1000, 1500, 2000④⑤⑥⑦.

)epart Eckerö: 0830①⑤⑥⑦, 1330, 1830.

March 23 - June 14 and August 20 - September 23

)epart Grisslehamn: 1000, 1500, 2000.

)epart Eckerö: 0830, 1330, 1830.

June 15 - August 19

)epart Grisslehamn: 1000, 1130, 1500, 1700, 2000.

)epart Eckerö: 0830, 1330, 1530, 1830, 2015.

connections: Stockholm (Tekniska Högskolan T-banan station) - Grisslehamn and v.v. (departing 2 hours before ship departure).
Eckerö - Mariehamn and v.v. (departing 1 hour before ship departure).

HELSINKI - TALLINN 2410

ckerö Line by ship **Service to June 30, 2008**
(No service Dec. 24, 25, 31)

ailings from Helsinki Länsiterminaali and Tallinn A-terminal.

Helsinki		Tallinn		Tallinn		Helsinki	
Until December 31							
0800	→	1130	①②③④⑤⑥	1600	→	1930	⑦
1030	→	1400	⑦	1800	→	2130	①②③④⑤⑥
January 1 - June 30							
0800	→	1100	①②③④⑤ (not Jan. 1).	1600	→	1930	⑦ (also Jan. 1).
0800	→	1130	⑥	1700	→	2030	①②③④⑤⑥ (not Jan. 1).
1030	→	1330	⑦ (also Jan. 1).				

inda Line Oy by hydrofoil **April 4 - September 30, 2007** △

nda Line Express Journey 1 hour 30 minutes

ailings from Helsinki Makasiiniterminaali and Tallinn Linnahalli.

epart Helsinki: 0800, 1000, 1200, 1400, 1600⑤⑦, 1800, 2000, 2200⑤⑦.

epart Tallinn: 0800①⑥, 1000, 1200, 1400⑤⑦, 1600, 1800, 2000, 2200.

ordic Jet Line by catamaran Journey 100 minutes **2007 service** △
(No service Jan. 1 - Apr. 4)

ailings from Helsinki Kanavaterminaali and Tallinn C-terminal.

)epart Helsinki: 0800①②③④⑤⑥, 1005, 1225, 1500, 1710, 1930, 2135⑦.

)epart Tallinn: 0800①②③④⑤⑥, 1015, 1255, 1500, 1725, 1930, 2135⑦.

ea Containers Finland by SUPERSEACAT **Service to January 6, 2008** △

ailings from Helsinki Makasiini Terminal and Tallinn A-terminal.

Journey 100 minutes

May 4 - June 17 and August 20 - October 28

Depart Helsinki: 0800①②③④⑤⑥, 1030, 1240, 1640, 1850.

Depart Tallinn: 0745①②③④⑤⑥, 1020, 1400, 1615, 1930.

June 18 - August 19

Depart Helsinki: 0800, 1030, 1240, 1640, 1850, 2140 (from June 25).

Depart Tallinn: 0745, 1020, 1400, 1615, 1930, 2140 (from June 25).

October 29 - January 6

Depart Helsinki: 0800①②③④⑤⑥, 1030⑤⑥⑦, 1240⑤⑦, 1530⑤⑥⑦, 1720.

Depart Tallinn: 1020①②③④⑤⑥, 1300⑤⑥⑦, 1500⑤⑦, 1750⑤⑥⑦, 1940.

continued

Tallink by ship **Service to March 31, 2008 (not Dec. 24, 25)**

Sailings from Helsinki Länsiterminaali and Tallinn D-terminal.

Helsinki		Tallinn	Notes	Tallinn		Helsinki	Notes
0830	→	1100	See note **S**.	0700	→	0900	See note **T**.
1030	→	1230	①②③④⑤⑥	0730	→	0930	See note **V**.
1045	→	1245	⑦	1330	→	1645	
1700	→	1900		1400	→	1600	
1830	→	2200		1615§	→	1845§	Not May 30.
2355	→	0200	See note **W**.	2030	→	2230	

S – Not June 2, Dec. 27, 28.
T – ①②③④⑤⑥ until Dec. 23.
V – ①②③④⑤⑥ Dec. 27 - Mar. 31.
W – ①②③④⑤⑦ (not Dec. 23).
§ – 15 minutes earlier from Dec. 27.

Other variations: Dec. 24 sailings from Helsinki at 0830, 1030, 1600; from Tallinn at 1100. Dec. 25 sailings from Helsinki at 0830; from Tallinn at 1600.

Tallink by catamaran Journey 100 minutes *Tallink Express* **2007 service** △

Sailings from Helsinki Länsiterminaali and Tallinn D-terminal.

SERVICE SUSPENDED

Viking Line by ship Journey 3 hours **Service to June 15, 2008**
(No service Dec. 23-26)

Sailings from Helsinki Katajanokka terminal and Tallinn A-terminal.

Depart Helsinki: 1230, 2100. Depart Tallinn: 0815, 1645.

△ – These services operate during the ice-free period only (generally from mid-April to November/December)

KARLSKRONA - GDYNIA 2415

Stena Line **2007 service**

Karlskrona		Gdynia		Gdynia		Karlskrona	
January 9 - June 24 and September 3 - December 16							
0900	→	1930	②③④⑥⑦	0900	→	1930	②③④⑥⑦
1930	→	0730	⑤	1930	→	0730	①⑤
2100	→	0730	①②③⑥	2100	→	0730	②③⑥⑦
2100	→	0900	④⑦	2100	→	0900	④
June 25 - September 2							
0900	→	1900		0900	→	1900	
2100	→	0700		2100	→	0700	

KARLSHAMN - KLAIPEDA - BALTISK 2417

DFDS Lisco **Service to December 20, 2007**

Sailings from Karlshamn Ferry Terminal, Klaipeda International Ferry Port and Baltisk Ferry Terminal.

Karlshamn		Klaipeda		Baltisk	Baltisk		Klaipeda		Karlshamn
1800①	→	0900②		...	...		1900①	→	0900②
1800②	→	1000③		...	...		1900②	→	0830③
1800③	→	0900④		...	...		2000③	→	1000④
1800④	→	1000⑤		...	...		1900④	→	0830⑤
1800⑤	→	0900/1300⑥	→	2000⑥	...		2100⑤	→	1100⑥
1600⑥	→	0900⑦		...	2300⑥	→	1000/1800⑦	→	0800①

KIEL - KLAIPEDA 2420

DFDS Lisco **Service to December 20, 2007**

Sailings from Kiel Ostuferhafen and Klaipeda International Ferry Port.

Kiel		Klaipeda	Klaipeda		Kiel
1400①	→	1200②	1500①	→	1100②
1600②	→	1400③	1700②	→	1300③
1800③	→	1600④	1900③	→	1500④
2000④	→	1800⑤	2100④	→	1700⑤
2200⑤	→	2000⑥	2300⑤	→	1900⑥
2300⑥	→	2100⑦	0100⑦	→	2100⑦

2430 KØGE - RØNNE

BornholmsTrafikken — Service to January 6, 2008

Køge		Rønne		Rønne		Køge	
0800	→	1345	See note **K**.	1430	→	2030	See note **K**.
2330	→	0600	Daily.	2330	→	0600	Daily.

K – ④ Apr. 5 - May 31; ⑥⑦ July 7 - Aug. 12; ① Aug. 13 - Sept. 10 (also Apr. 4, May 16, June 18, 25; not Apr. 5, May 17).

2445 NYNÄSHAMN - VISBY

Destination Gotland — 2007 service

Nynäshamn		Visby		Visby		Nynäshamn	
June 29 - August 14							
0450	→	0805	See note **W**.	0050	→	0405	See note **S**.
0730	→	1045	See note **X**.	0055	→	0410	④
1030	→	1320		0330	→	0645	See note **R**.
1250	→	1605		0705	→	0955	
1720	→	2010		0850	→	1205	
2330	→	0245		1355	→	1645	
				1910	→	2225	
August 15 - October 14							
1100	→	1415	See note **Y**.	0705	→	1020	①②③④⑤⑥
1200	→	1515	⑦	0805	→	1120	⑦
1620	→	1910	See note **Z**.	1255	→	1545	See note **Z**.
2005	→	2320	⑤⑥⑦	1600	→	1915	⑤⑥⑦ (not Oct. 13).
2105	→	0020	①②③④	1645	→	2000	①②③④
2310	→	0200	See note **V**.	1945	→	2235	See note **V**.
October 15 - December 31							
1100	→	1415	See note **T**.	0705	→	1020	①②③④⑤⑥
1200	→	1515	⑦	0805	→	1120	⑦
2005	→	2320	See note **U**.	1600	→	1915	⑤⑦ (not Nov. 4).
2105	→	0020	①②③④	1645	→	2000	①②③④ (also Nov. 4).

R – ①⑥⑦ (not June 29 - July 2).
S – ①②③⑤⑥⑦ (not June 29, July 17, Aug. 14).
T – ①②③④⑤ (also Nov. 3, Dec. 15).
U – ⑤⑥⑦ (not Nov. 3, Dec. 15).
V – Aug. 17, 19, 26, Sept. 2; ⑦ Sept. 9 - Oct. 7.
W – ①⑥⑦ (not June 29 - July 2).
X – June 30 - July 2 - Aug. 13 (not July 17).
Y – ①②③④⑤⑥ (not Oct. 13).
Z – Daily Aug. 15 - 21, 25, 26, Sept. 2; ⑤⑦ Sept. 3 - Oct. 14.

Subject to alteration during Xmas / New Year period

🚌 service Stockholm Cityterminalen - Nynäshamn connects with most sailings.

2448 NYNÄSHAMN - VENTSPILS

Scandlines — 2007 service

Journey 11 hours

Depart Nynäshamn: 0900⑦, 1000①, 1930②, 2200③⑤.
Depart Ventspils: 0900③, 1900⑥, 2100④, 2200⑦, 2359①.

2450 OSKARSHAMN - VISBY

Destination Gotland — 2007 service (No service Dec. 24, 25)

Oskarshamn		Visby		Visby		Oskarshamn	
February 1 - June 14 and September 3 - December 30							
1055	→	1350	See note **A**.	0720	→	1015	See note **A**.
2110	→	0005	See note **C**.	1705	→	2000	See note **C**.
2115	→	0010	③				
June 15 - 28							
1055	→	1350	Daily.	0720	→	1015	Daily.
2110	→	0005	①②④⑤⑦	1705	→	2000	①②③④⑤⑦
2115	→	0010	③				
June 29 - August 14							
1510	→	1805	Daily.	1130	→	1425	Daily.
2110	→	0005	①②④⑤⑥⑦	1705	→	2000	Daily.
2115	→	0010	③				
August 15 - September 2							
1055	→	1350	See note **B**.	0720	→	1015	See note **B**.
2110	→	0005	①②④⑤⑦	1705	→	2000	①②③④⑤⑦
2115	→	0010	③				

A – ③ Feb. 28 - Mar. 21; ③⑥ Mar. 24 - June 13; ③⑥ Sept. 5 - Nov. 3 (also Apr. 6, Dec. 22; not May 16, June 6).
B – ③④⑤⑥⑦ (not Aug. 30, 31, Sept. 2).
C – ①②③④⑤⑦ (not Apr. 6).

Subject to alteration Feb. 1 - 13, May 20, June 21 - 25, Aug. 30 - Sept. 2 and during Xmas / New Year period

2451 ROSTOCK - HELSINKI

Tallink — Service to October 31, 2008

Sailings from Rostock Überseehafen and Helsinki Länsiterminaali. Journey 23 - 24 hours

Rostock		Helsinki	Helsinki		Rostock
0500①-⑥	→	0600②-⑦	2200	→	2130
0430⑦	→	0530①			

Variations: no sailings from Rostock June 1, Dec. 26, 27; from Helsinki May 30, Dec. 24, 25.

2453 SASSNITZ-MUKRAN - KLAIPEDA

DFDS Lisco — 2007 service

Sailings from Sassnitz Fahrhafen and Klaipeda International Ferry Port.

Sassnitz-Mukran		Klaipeda	Klaipeda		Sassnitz-Mukran
1600②④⑥	→	1100③⑤⑦	1600③⑤⑦	→	1000④⑥①

2455 SILLAMÄE - KOTKA

Narva Line — 2007 service (No service Dec. 23 - 26, 31, Jan. 1)

Sillamäe	Kotka	Kotka	Sillamäe

SERVICE SUSPENDED

2460 ŚWINOUJŚCIE - RØNNE

Polferries — June 28 - August 30, 200 (No winter servic

Świnoujście		Rønne		Rønne		Świnoujście	
1000	→	1515	⑥	1730	→	2245	⑥

2462 ŚWINOUJŚCIE - KØBENHAVN

Polferries — Service to April 30, 200 (No service Dec. 23, 3

Świnoujście		København	København		Świnoujście
2200②④⑥⑦	→	0830③⑤⑦①	1030⑦	→	1930⑦
			2000①③⑤	→	0800②④⑥

No departure from Świnoujście Mar. 22; from København Mar. 23.

2464 STOCKHOLM - RIGA

Tallink — Service to October 31, 200

Sailings from Stockholm Frihamnterminalen and Riga passenger port.

Stockholm		Riga		Riga		Stockholm	
1700	→	1100	Not Dec. 30, 31, Jan. 1 - 8.	1730	→	0930	Not Dec. 29 - 31, Jan. 1

2465 STOCKHOLM - MARIEHAMN - HELSINKI

Silja Line — Service to October 31, 200

Sailings from Stockholm Värtahamnen and Helsinki Olympiaterminaali.

Stockholm		Mariehamn		Helsinki		Helsinki		Mariehamn		Stockholm
1700	→	2355	→	0955	Note **C**.	1700	→	0425	→	0930
2100	→	0400	→	1330	June 9.					

C – Not June 9.

Subject to alteration Dec. 24.

🚌 Stockholm Värtahamnen - Ropsten metro station (for Stockholm Centralen).

Viking Line — Service to June 15, 200 (No service Dec. 24, 2

Sailings from Stockholm Stadsgården and Helsinki Katajanokka.

Stockholm		Mariehamn		Helsinki		Helsinki		Mariehamn		Stockholm
1645	→	2345	→	0955	Note **B**.	1730	→	0435	→	0940
2030	→	0330	→	1400	Note **A**.					

A – June 9, 10, 2007. B – Not June 9, 10, 2007.

Connections:
🚌 Stockholm Cityterminalen (near Central station) - Slussen metro station - Viking Line terminal. Tram no. 4T runs daily from Helsinki city centre to the Viking Line Terminal.

2470 (STOCKHOLM -) KAPELLSKÄR - MARIEHAMN

Viking Line Sailings from Kapellskär and Mariehamn. — Service to January 6, 200

Stockholm (*by* 🚌)		Kapellskär		Mariehamn		Mariehamn		Kapellskär		Stockholm (*by* 🚌)	
March 17 - June 10 and August 13 - January 6▲											
0720♦	→	0900	→	1230	⑤⑥	0700	→	0830	→	*1000*♦	⑤⑥
1020♦	→	1200	→	1530	①②③④	0800	→	0930	→	*1100*♦	①②③④
1320♦	→	1500	→	1830	⑤⑥⑦	1300	→	1430	→	*1600*♦	⑤⑥⑦
1720♦	→	1900	→	2230	①②③④	1600	→	1730	→	*1900*♦	①②③④
1850♦	→	2030	→	0005	⑤⑥⑦	1900	→	2015	→	*2145*♦	⑤⑥⑦
June 11 - August 12											
0720♦	→	0900	→	1230		0700	→	0830	→	*1000*♦	
1320♦	→	1500	→	1830		1300	→	1430	→	*1600*♦	
1850♦	→	2030	→	0005		1900	→	2015	→	*2145*♦	

▲ – Variations: no service Dec. 24, 25; a ⑦ service will operate on Dec. 23, 26.
♦ – Connecting 🚌 service from / to Stockholm Cityterminalen (near Central station).

2475 STOCKHOLM - TALLINN

Tallink — Service to December 31, 200

Sailings from Stockholm Frihamnterminalen and Tallinn D-terminal.

Stockholm		Mariehamn		Tallinn	Tallinn		Mariehamn		Stockholm
1800	→	0105	→	1000	1800	→	0500	→	1000

For international shipping maps – see pages 518 - 520

STOCKHOLM - TURKU via Mariehamn / Långnäs — 2480

Seawind — **Service to March 31, 2008 ▲**

Sailings from Stockholm Värtahamnen and Turku. *Conveys passengers with vehicles only.*

Stockholm		Långnäs		Turku	Turku		Långnäs		Stockholm
Until December 31									
0845	→	1600	→	2030	2145	→	0210	→	0730
January 1 - March 31									
0815②–⑤	→	1525②–⑤	→	2000②–⑤	0915⑦	→	1340⑦	→	1900⑦
2015⑥⑦	→	0325⑦①	→	0800⑦①	2115①–⑤	→	0135②–⑥	→	0700②–⑥

▲ – *No sailings from Stockholm Dec. 25, 26; from Turku Dec. 24, 25.*

Silja Line — **Service to October 31, 2008**

Sailings from Stockholm Värtahamnen and Turku.

Until December 19

Stockholm	Kapellskär	Mariehamn	Långnäs §	Turku	
▲	0730	1100	→	1700	Not Dec. 8, 9.
1915	→	0150	→	0800	

Turku	Långnäs §	Mariehamn	Kapellskär	Stockholm	
0900	1305	→	→	1815	
1830	2330	→	0600	▲	Not Dec. 7, 8, 19.

From December 20

Stockholm	Mariehamn	Långnäs §	Turku	
0710	1345	→	1915	See note **A**.
1915	→	0245	0700	See note **B**.

Turku	Långnäs §	Mariehamn	Stockholm	
0800	→	1345	1815	See note **C**.
2015	0050	→	0610	See note **D**.

A – Not Dec. 20, 24-26, 31, Jan. 1-3, 11, 12, 25-27, Feb. 7, 8, 10, 12, 14, 15, Mar. 2, 3, Apr. 19.
B – Not Dec. 23-25, 31, Jan. 1, 2, 10, 11, 24-26, Feb. 6, 7, 9, 11, 13, 14, Mar. 1, 2, Apr. 18.
C – Not Dec. 20, 24-26. **D** – Not Dec. 23-25, 31, Jan. 1.

§ – Långnäs is 28km from Mariehamn.
▲ – 🚌 connection available – contact operator for details.

🚌 Stockholm Värtahamnen - Ropsten metro station (for Stockholm Centralen).

Viking Line — **Service to June 15, 2008** **(No service Dec. 24, 25)**

Sailings from Stockholm Stadsgården and Turku Linnansatama.

Stockholm	Mariehamn	Långnäs §	Turku	
0745	1425	→	1950	Not Sept. 4-19.
2010	→	0330	0735	Not Sept. 4-6.

Turku	Långnäs §	Mariehamn	Stockholm	
0845	→	1425	1855	Not Sept. 4-6.
2100	0110	→	0630	Not Sept. 3-18.

§ – Långnäs is 28km from Mariehamn.

🚌 connections: Stockholm Cityterminalen (near Central station) - Slussen metro station - Viking Line terminal; Turku city centre - harbour - airport (bus no. 1).

TRAVEMÜNDE - HELSINKI — 2485

Finnlines Deutschland — **Service from December 1, 2007**

Sailings from Travemünde Skandinavienkai and Helsinki Hansaterminaali.

Travemünde		Helsinki	Helsinki		Travemünde
0300②③④⑤⑦	→	0645③④⑤⑥①	1800①②③④⑤⑥	→	2000②③④⑤⑥⑦
0300⑥	→	0700⑦	2200②⑤	→	0700④⑦
1900③	→	0645⑤	1500⑦	→	0700②
1900⑤	→	0700⑦			
1500⑦	→	0645②			

TRAVEMÜNDE - RIGA — 2487

DFDS Lisco — **2007 service**

Sailings from Travemünde Skandinavienkai and Riga Vecmilgravis.

Travemünde		Riga	Riga		Travemünde
1400②	→	2359④	0800②	→	2100③
0100④	→	1600⑤	0600④	→	1400⑤
2200⑤	→	0800⑦	2000⑤	→	0900⑦
1300⑦	→	0400②	1500⑦	→	2300①

VAASA - UMEÅ (HOLMSUND) — 2490

RG Line — **Service to April 30, 2008** **(No service Dec. 23-25, 29)**

Vaasa		Umeå		Umeå		Vaasa	
0900	→	1230	See note **V**.	0800	→	1330	③
1500	→	1830	③	0900	→	1430	①②
2000	→	2330	①②	1400	→	1930	See note **W**.
2100	→	0030	⑦	1800	→	2330	④⑤
				2000	→	0130	③

Subject to alteration Dec. 22 - Jan. 2, Mar. 21-23

V – ④⑤⑦ (also Feb. 23, Mar. 1). **W** – ⑦ (also Feb. 23, Mar. 1).

YSTAD - RØNNE — 2494

BornholmsTrafikken by fast ferry — **2007 service**

Up to 5 sailings daily, journey 75 minutes.

See Table **727** for rail connections Ystad - København and v.v.

BornholmsTrafikken by ship — **2007 service**

Up to 3 sailings daily, journey 2 hours 30 minutes.

See Table **727** for rail connections Ystad - København and v.v.

YSTAD - ŚWINOUJŚCIE — 2495

Polferries — **Service to April 30, 2008** **(No service Dec. 24, 25, 31, Jan. 1, Mar. 22)**

Ystad		Świnoujście		Świnoujście		Ystad	
1400	→	2030	See note **A**.	2330	→	0630	See note **B**.

A – Not Dec. 26, Jan. 2, Mar. 23. **B** – Not Dec. 23, 30, Mar. 21.

Unity Line — **2007 service**

Ystad		Świnoujście	Świnoujście		Ystad
2200	→	0700	1300	→	1945

A connecting 🚌 service operates Świnoujście terminal - Szczecin Hotel Radisson SAS and v.v.: Świnoujście depart 0730, Szczecin arrive 0900. Return journey Szczecin depart 1000, Świnoujście arrive 1130.

WESTERN MEDITERRANEAN

ALGECIRAS - CEUTA — 2500

Baleària (Eurolínies Marítimes) by fast ferry — **Service from September 1, 2007**

Journey 30 minutes

Depart Algeciras: 0530, 0700, 0730, 0830, 1000, 1030, 1130, 1300, 1330, 1430, 1600, 1630, 1730, 1900, 1930, 2030, 2200, 2245.

Depart Ceuta: 0700, 0830, 0900, 1000, 1130, 1200, 1300, 1430, 1500, 1600, 1730, 1800, 1900, 2030, 2100, 2200, 2330, 0015.

Trasmediterranea by fast ferry Journey 45 mins. — **2007 service**

Subject to alteration at Easter and Christmas

Depart Algeciras: 0800, 1100, 1400, 1700, 2000.

Depart Ceuta: 0930, 1230, 1530, 1830, 2130.

Additional services operate in summer.

ALGECIRAS - TANJAH (TANGIERS) — 2502

Nautas Ferry — **June 16 - September 10, 2007**

Algeciras		Tanjah		Tanjah		Algeciras	
2359	→	2330	July 20 - Sept. 10.	0030	→	0400	July 20 - Sept. 10.
0900	→	0830		0930	→	1300	
1400	→	1330		1430	→	1800	
1900	→	1830		1930	→	2300	

Trasmediterranea (& associated operators) Journey 2½ hours — **2007 service**

From Algeciras and Tanjah: Up to 4 departures daily in winter (additional services in summer).

Also sailings by hydrofoil: Algeciras depart 0600, 1000; Tanjah depart 0600, 1430 (journey 1½ hours).

ALMERÍA - MELILLA — 2505

Trasmediterranea Journey 6-8 hours — **2007 service**

July 1 - August 5 and September 6 - December 17

Depart Almería: 1730①, 2359②③④⑤⑥⑦. Depart Melilla: 1000①, 1430②③④⑤⑥⑦.

August 6 - September 5

Depart Almería: 1600③④⑤⑥, 1730①, 1800②, 2359⑦.
Depart Melilla: 0200③④⑤⑥⑦, 1000①②.

ALMERÍA - AN-NADÛR (NADOR) — 2507

Ferrimaroc / Trasmediterranea Journey 5-10 hours — **2007 service**

From Almería and an-Nadûr: 1–3 sailings daily, departure times vary.

BARCELONA - TANJAH (TANGIERS) — 2508

Grandi Navi Veloci — **2007 service**

Barcelona		Tanjah		Tanjah		Barcelona	
1900⑦	→	1900①	Not Apr. 22, 29.	1100②	→	1400③	Not Apr. 24, May 1.

BALEARIC ISLANDS (see map page 321) — 2510

Trasmediterranea — **Service to June 15, 2008**

BARCELONA - EIVISSA (IBIZA) by catamaran Journey 4½ - 7 hours
Depart Barcelona: **Dec. 5 - Jan. 9 and Mar. 1 - June 15**: 1600 (via Palma).
Depart Eivissa: **Dec. 5 - Jan. 9 and Mar. 1 - June 15**: 0700 (via Palma).

BARCELONA - EIVISSA (IBIZA) by ship Journey 9-14 hours
Depart Barcelona: **Sept. 17 - June 15**: 2130②④, 2300⑥ (via Palma).
Depart Eivissa: **Sept. 17 - June 15**: 1000③⑤, 1900⑦ (via Palma).

BARCELONA - MAÓ (MAHÓN) by ship Journey 8-9 hours
Depart Barcelona: **Sept. 17 - June 15**: 2200①③⑤.
Depart Maó: **Sept. 17 - June 15**: 1030②④, 2200⑥.

BARCELONA - MAÓ (MAHÓN) by catamaran Journey 4½ hours
Depart Barcelona: **June 19 - 30**: 1500②④⑥; **July 1 - Sept. 5**: 1500①②④⑥.
Depart Maó: **June 19 - 30**: 0800③⑤⑦; **July 1 - Sept. 5**: 0800②③⑤⑦.

BARCELONA - PALMA by ship Journey 6½ - 8½ hours
Depart Barcelona: **Sept. 17 - June 15**: 2300.
Depart Palma: **Sept. 17 - June 15**: 1300①②③④⑤⑥, 2330⑦.

BARCELONA - PALMA by catamaran Journey 3½-4 hours
Depart Barcelona: **Dec. 5 - Jan. 9 and Mar. 1 - June 15**: 1600.
Depart Palma: **Dec. 5 - Jan. 9 and Mar. 1 - June 15**: 1000.

PALMA - EIVISSA (IBIZA) by ship Journey 3½-4 hours
Depart Palma: **Sept. 17 - June 15**: 0900⑦.
Depart Eivissa: **Sept. 17 - June 15**: 1900⑦.

PALMA - EIVISSA (IBIZA) by catamaran Journey 2-2½ hours
Depart Palma: **Dec. 5-13**: 2045; **Dec. 14 - Jan. 9**: 0730①②④⑤⑥⑦, 2045; **Jan. 10-13**: 0730①②④⑤⑥⑦; **Mar. 1-13**: 2045; **Mar. 14 - June 15**: 0730①②④⑤⑥⑦, 2045.
Depart Eivissa: **Dec. 5-13**: 0700; **Dec. 14 - Jan. 9**: 0700, 1945①②④⑤⑥⑦; **Jan. 10-13**: 1945①②④⑤⑥⑦; **Mar. 1-13**: 0700; **Mar. 14 - June 15**: 0700, 1945①②④⑤⑥⑦.

continued

PALMA - MAÓ (MAHÓN) by ship Journey 5½ hours
Depart Palma: **Sept. 19 - June 15**: 0800⑦.
Depart Maó: **Sept. 19 - June 15**: 1730⑦.

VALÈNCIA - EIVISSA (IBIZA) by catamaran Journey 3-3½ hours
Depart València: **Dec. 14 - Jan. 13 and Mar. 14 - June 15**: 1600①②④⑤⑥⑦.
Depart Eivissa: **Dec. 14 - Jan. 13 and Mar. 14 - June 15**: 1030①②④⑤⑥⑦.

VALÈNCIA - MAÓ (MAHÓN) via Palma by ship Journey 15 hours
Depart València: **Sept. 17 - June 15**: 2300⑥.
Depart Maó: **Sept. 17 - June 15** 1700⑦.

VALÈNCIA - PALMA by ship Journey 7¼-8½ hours
Depart València: **Sept. 17 - June 15**: 2300①②③④⑤⑥.
Depart Palma: **Sept. 17 - June 15**: 1145②③④⑤⑥, 2359⑦.

VALÈNCIA - PALMA by catamaran Journey 4-6½ hours
Depart Valencia: **Dec. 14 - Jan. 13 and Mar. 14 - June 15**: 1600①②④⑤⑥⑦.
Depart Palma: **Dec. 14 - Jan. 13 and Mar. 14 - June 15**: 0730①②④⑤⑥⑦.

Baleària (Eurolínies Marítimes) **March 1 - October 31, 2007**

DÉNIA - EIVISSA (IBIZA) - PALMA by fast ferry

Dénia		Eivissa		Palma	Palma		Eivissa		Dénia
1700	→	1900/2000	→	2200	0800	→	1000/1100	→	1300

OTHER SERVICES:
Dénia - Sant Antoni and v.v.: 1–2 sailings daily, journey 4 hours.
València - Palma and v.v.: 1 sailing daily except ②, journey 6½ hours by fast ferry (some services via Eivissa).

2512 CANARY ISLANDS

Lineas Fred. Olsen **2007 services** (subject to confirmation)

CORRALEJO (FUERTEVENTURA) - PLAYA BLANCA (LANZAROTE) Journey 30 mins.
Depart Corralejo: 0745①②③④⑤, 0900, 1100, 1330①②③④⑤, 1500, 1700, 1900.
Depart Playa Blanca: 0710①②③④⑤, 0830, 1000, 1230①②③④⑤, 1400, 1600, 1800.

LOS CRISTIANOS (TENERIFE) - SANTA CRUZ (PALMA) Journey 5 hours
Depart Los Cristianos: 2000. Depart Santa Cruz: 0630.

LOS CRISTIANOS (TENERIFE) - VALVERDE (EL HIERRO)
Depart Los Cristianos: 1530. Depart Valverde: 1800.

SAN SEBASTIÁN (GOMERA) - LOS CRISTIANOS (TENERIFE) Journey 30 mins.
Depart San Sebastián: 0730, 1030, 1300, 1630, 1830.
Depart Los Cristianos: 0830, 0930, 1330, 1730, 2030.

SANTA CRUZ (TENERIFE) - AGAETE (GRAN CANARIA) Journey 60 minutes
Departures from Santa Cruz and Agaete: 0630①②③④⑤, 0800, 0930, 1100①②③④⑤, 1400, 1700, 1900, 2030.

Naviera Armas **2007 services** (subject to confirmation)

Corralejo (Fuerteventura) - Playa Blanca (Lanzarote) and v.v.	5-7 sailings daily.
Las Palmas (Gran Canaria) - Arrecife (Lanzarote) and v.v.	3 sailings per week.
Las Palmas (Gran Canaria) - Morro Jable (Fuerteventura) and v.v.	1 sailing daily.
Las Palmas (G. Canaria) - Puerto del Rosario (Fuerteventura) and v.v.	2 sailings per week.
Las Palmas (Gran Canaria) - Santa Cruz (Tenerife) and v.v.	1-2 sailings daily.
Los Cristianos - San Sebastián Gomera and v.v.	1-2 sailings daily.
Los Cristianos - Valverde and v.v.	6 sailings per week.
San Sebastián Gomera - Valverde and v.v.	6 sailings per week.
Santa Cruz (La Palma) - Arrecife (Lanzarote) and v.v.	1 sailing per week.
Santa Cruz (La Palma) - Puerto del Rosario (Fuerteventura) and v.v.	1 sailing per week.
Santa Cruz (Tenerife) - Arrecife (Lanzarote) and v.v.	1 sailing per week.
Santa Cruz (Tenerife) - Puerto del Rosario (Fuerteventura) and v.v.	1 sailing per week.
Santa Cruz (Tenerife) - Santa Cruz (La Palma) and v.v.	3 sailings per week.

Trasmediterranea **2007 service**

CÁDIZ - LAS PALMAS - SANTA CRUZ TENERIFE

Cádiz		Las Palmas		Tenerife	Tenerife		Las Palmas		Cádiz
0100⑦	→		→	0800①	1500①	→		→	0900③
1800③	→	0030⑤		...	...		0800⑤	→	1900⑥

OTHER SUMMER SERVICES:

Las Palmas - Morro Jable and v.v.	2-7 sailings per week by hydrofoil.
Santa Cruz Tenerife - Morro Jable and v.v.	2-7 sailings per week by hydrofoil.
San Sebastián Gomera - Los Cristianos and v.v.	3-4 sailings daily by hydrofoil, 1-2 sailings daily by ferry.
Valverde - Los Cristianos and v.v.	1-6 sailings per week.
Santa Cruz Tenerife - Las Palmas and v.v.	up to 3 sailings daily.
Santa Cruz Tenerife - Santa Cruz Palma and v.v.	1 sailing per week.

2520 CIVITAVECCHIA - BARCELONA

Grimaldi Lines **2007 service**

Civitavecchia		Barcelona		Civitavecchia	
1800	→	1300/1800	→	1300	① Feb. 5 - Dec. 24
1900	→	1400/1900	→	1400	See note **X**.

X – ①②③④⑥ Feb. 1 - July 21; ①②③④⑥⑦ July 23 - Sept. 8; ①②③④⑥ Sept. 11 - Dec. 29.

2530 CIVITAVECCHIA - PALERMO - TÛNIS

Grandi Navi Veloci **2007 service (No service Dec. 31)**

Civitavecchia		Palermo		Tûnis		Palermo		Civitavecchia
1900**V**	→	0800**W**		...		1830⑦	→	0630①
2000①③	→	0800②④		...		1900**X**	→	0800**Y**
2000⑤	→	0800/1000⑥	→	1930/2300⑥	→	0900/1830⑦	→	0630①
2350⑦**S**	→	1250①**T**		...		2000②④	→	0800③⑤

S – ⑦ July 29 - Aug. 26.
T – ① July 30 - Aug. 27.
V – ②④⑥ Apr. 5 - Sept. 29.
W – ③⑤⑦ Apr. 6 - Sept. 30.
X – ①③⑤ Apr. 6 - Sept. 28.
Y – ②④⑥ Apr. 7 - Sept. 29.

Grimaldi Ferries **2007 service**

Civitavecchia		Tûnis	Tûnis		Civitavecchia
2300③	→	1600④	2330②	→	1800③

2537 GENOVA - BARCELONA

Grandi Navi Veloci **April 1 - December 31, 2007**

Genova		Barcelona		Barcelona		Genova	
2000	→	1400	Apr. 6, 27 only.	0200	→	2000	⑦ (not Apr. 8, 29).
2100	→	1500	See note **G**.	2100	→	1500	See note **J**.
2130	→	1530	See note **H**.	2130	→	1530	See note **K**.

G – ④⑥ (not Apr. 19, 21, 26, 28, May 3).
H – ①③⑤ (also Apr. 19, 21, 24, 26, 28, May 3; not Apr. 6, 27, Dec. 31).
J – ③⑤ (not Apr. 20, 25, 27, May 2, 4).
K – ②④ (also Apr. 20, 23, 25, 27, 30, May 2, 4).

2547 GENOVA - PALERMO

Grandi Navi Veloci **2007 service**

Genova		Palermo	
2100	→	1700	June 25 - Sept. 9 (not Aug. 15).
2200	→	1800	①②③④⑤⑥ Apr. 1 - June 23, Sept. 10 - Dec. 29 (not Apr. 7).
Palermo		**Genova**	
2100	→	1700	June 25 - Sept. 9 (not Aug. 15).
2200	→	1800	①②③④⑤⑥ Apr. 1 - June 23, Sept. 10 - Dec. 29 (not Apr. 7).

2554 GENOVA - TANJAH (TANGIERS)

Cie. Marocaine de Navigation (Comanav) **2007 service**

Depart 1300 from Genova and Tanjah. Sailings arrive 2 days later.
Departures from Genova: ⑥ Mar. 3 - June 30; July 6, 12, 18, 24, 30, Aug. 5, 11, 17, 23, 29, Sept. 4, 10, 16, 22, 28; ⑥ Oct. 6 - Dec. 30.
Departures from Tanjah: ③ Feb. 28 - June 27; July 3, 9, 15, 21, 27, Aug. 2, 8, 14, 20, 26, Sept. 1, 7, 13, 19, 25, Oct. 1; ③ Oct. 10 - Dec. 27.

Grandi Naví Veloci **2007 service**

Genova		Tanjah		Tanjah		Genova	
2100⑥	→	1900①	Not Apr. 21, 28.	1100②	→	1500④	Not Apr. 24, May 1.

2555 GENOVA - TÛNIS

Compagnie Tunisienne de Navigation / S N C M **2007 service**

Departure times vary. Journey 22-24 hours
From Genova: ⑥ Feb. 3 - June 16; June 18, 21, 23, 27, 30, July 2, 5, 7, 9, 10, 12, 14, 15, 18, 19, 21, 22, 25, 28, 30, Aug. 1, 4, 6, 7, 9, 11, 14, 18, 22, 25, 27, 29, Sept. 1, 6, 7, 9, 12, 13, 15, 16, 17, 20, 22, 26, 29, Oct. 2, 5, 6, 9, 13, 20, 22, 27, Nov. 3, 10, 17, 24, Dec. 1, 8, 15, 17, 22, 24, 27, 29.
From Tûnis: ⑤ Feb. 4 - June 15; June 17, 20, 22, 25, 29, July 1, 6, 9, 11, 13, 18, 20, 24, 27, 29, Aug. 3, 5, 8, 10, 13, 16, 17, 18, 21, 23, 24, 26, 28, 31, Sept. 2, 5, 6, 8, 11, 12, 14, 15, 16, 17, 19, 21, 25, 28, Oct. 1, 4, 5, 8, 12, 19, 21, 26, Nov. 2, 9, 16, 23, 30, Dec. 7, 13, 14, 16, 20, 21, 23, 26, 28.

Grandi Navi Veloci **2007 service**

Departure times vary. Journey 24 hours
From Genova: ③⑥ Apr. 4 - July 14; ①③⑥ July 16 - Aug. 11; ②⑤⑦ Aug. 14 - Sept. 9; ③⑥ Sept. 12 - Dec. 29.
From Tûnis: ④⑦ Apr. 1 - July 15; ②④⑦ July 17 - Aug. 12; ①③⑥ Aug. 15 - Sept. 10; ④⑦ Sept. 13 - Dec. 30.

2560 GULF OF NAPOLI (including Gulf of Salerno and Ponziane Islands)

Alilauro **2007 services** (subject to confirmation)

Napoli Mergellina or Beverello - Capri: 5-11 sailings daily.
Napoli Mergellina - Forio: 6 sailings daily (summer only).
Napoli Beverello - Ischia: 2-6 sailings daily by ship, 4-8 sailings daily by catamaran.
Napoli Mergellina - Ischia: 4-10 sailings daily.
Napoli Mergellina or Beverello - Sorrento: 5-9 sailings daily.
Napoli - Sorrento - Positano - Amalfi: summer only, infrequent sailings.
Pozzuoli - Ischia: frequent service by ship.
Sorrento - Capri: 7-16 sailings daily by catamaran, also 1-6 sailings by ship.
Salerno - Amalfi - Positano - Capri: summer only, infrequent sailings by catamaran.
Additional infrequent services to Capri operate (summer only) from Ischia, Castellammare di Stábia, Torre Annunziata, Positano and Amalfi.

Caremar **2007 services** (subject to confirmation)

Napoli - Capri: 6 sailings daily by catamaran, 3 sailings by ship.
Napoli - Ischia: 9 sailings daily by catamaran, 5 sailings by ship.
Napoli - Procida: 8 sailings daily by catamaran, 5 sailings by ship.
Pozzuoli - Procida - Ischia: 2 sailings daily by catamaran, 2 sailings by ship.
Sorrento - Capri: 4 sailings daily by catamaran.
Additional infrequent services operate between Procida and Ischia, Formia and Ventotene, Formia and Ponza, Anzio and Ponza.

Nav. Libera del Golfo by *Linea Jet* **2007 services** (subject to confirmation)

Napoli (Molo Beverello) - Capri: 4-12 sailings daily. Journey 40 minutes.
Sorrento - Capri: 7-16 sailings daily. Journey 25 minutes.
Additional services operate (summer only) between Castellammare di Stábia and Capri.

SNAV Journey 40 minutes **2007 service**

Napoli (Mergellina) - Capri: 0710⚒, 0930, 1135, 1440, 1735.
Capri - Napoli (Mergellina): 0815⚒, 1035, 1335, 1630, 1835.

For international shipping maps – see pages 518 - 520

CORSICA 2565

Sailings from mainland FRANCE

ARSEILLE - AJACCIO

N C M October 1 - December 31, 2007
eparture times vary. Journey 9 - 12 hours
rom Marseille:
day sailings: Oct. 14, 21, 28, Nov. 4.
night sailings: Oct. 1 - 12, 14 - 19, 21 - 26, 28 - 31, Nov. 1, 2, 4 - 30, Dec. 1 - 31.
rom Ajaccio:
day sailings: Oct. 6.
night sailings: Oct. 1 - 31, Nov. 1 - 30, Dec. 1 - 31.

ARSEILLE - BASTIA

N C M October 1 - December 31, 2007
eparture times vary. Journey 10 - 13 hours
rom Marseille:
day sailings: no sailings.
night sailings: Oct. 1 - 31, Nov. 1 - 30, Dec. 1 - 31.
rom Bastia:
day sailings: Dec. 22, 29.
night sailings: Oct. 1 - 31, Nov. 1 - 30, Dec. 1 - 31.

ARSEILLE - L'ÎLE ROUSSE

N C M October 1 - December 31, 2007
eparture times vary (all sailings overnight). Journey 8 - 11½ hours
rom Marseille: Oct. 1, 3, 5, 8, 10, 12, 15, 17, 19, 22, 24, 26, 29, 31, Nov. 2, 5, 9, 12, 16, 19, 23, 26, 30, Dec. 3, 5, 7, 10, 12, 14, 17, 19, 21, 24, 26, 28, 31.
rom L'Île Rousse: Oct. 2, 4, 7, 9, 11, 14, 16, 18, 21, 23, 25, 28, 30, Nov. 1, 4, 6, 11, 13, 18, 20, 25, 27, Dec. 2, 4, 6, 9, 11, 13, 16, 18, 20, 23, 25, 27, 30.

ARSEILLE - PORTO VECCHIO

N C M October 1 - December 31, 2007
eparture times vary (all sailings overnight). Journey 13½ hours
rom Marseille: Oct. 1, 3, 5, 8, 10, 12, 15, 17, 19, 22, 24, 26, 29, 31, Nov. 2, 5, 7, 9, 12, 14, 16, 19, 21, 23, 26, 28, 30, Dec. 3, 5, 7, 10, 12, 14, 17, 19, 21, 24, 26, 28, 31.
rom Porto Vecchio: Oct. 2, 4, 6, 9, 11, 13, 16, 18, 20, 23, 25, 27, 30, Nov. 1, 3, 6, 8, 10, 13, 15, 17, 20, 22, 24, 27, 29, Dec. 1, 4, 6, 8, 11, 13, 15, 18, 20, 22, 25, 27, 29.

ARSEILLE - PROPRIANO

N C M October 1 - December 31, 2007
eparture times vary. Journey 9½ - 11 hours.
rom Marseille:
day sailings: no sailings.
night sailings: Oct. 1, 3, 5, 6, 8, 11, 13, 15, 17, 19, 20, 22, 24, 26, 27, 29, 31, Nov. 2, 3, 5, 7, 9, 12, 14, 16, 19, 21, 23, 26, 28, 30, Dec. 3, 5, 7, 10, 12, 14, 17, 19, 21, 24, 26, 28, 31.
rom Propriano:
day sailings: no sailings.
night sailings: Oct. 2, 4, 6, 7, 9, 10, 12, 14, 16, 18, 20, 21, 23, 25, 27, 28, 30, Nov. 1, 3, 4, 6, 8, 10, 13, 15, 17, 20, 22, 24, 27, 29, Dec. 1, 4, 6, 8, 11, 13, 15, 18, 20, 22, 25, 27, 29.

CE - AJACCIO

orsica Ferries October 1 - December 31, 2007
eparture times vary. Journey 4½ - 9 hours
om Nice:
day sailings: Oct. 3, 6, 10, 13, 17, 20, 24, 27, 29, 31, Nov. 5, 7, 10, 18, 25, Dec. 2, 9, 16.
night sailings: Oct. 5, 12, 19, 26, Nov. 2, 9, Dec. 23.
om Ajaccio:
day sailings: Oct. 3, 6, 10, 13, 17, 20, 24, 27, 29, 31, Nov. 3, 5, 7, 10, 12, 17, 24, Dec. 1, 8, 15.
night sailings: Oct. 6, 13, 20, 27, Nov. 10, Dec. 25.

N C M 2007 service (No winter service)
eparture times vary (all day sailings). Journey 4 - 5½ hours
om Nice and Ajaccio: Apr. 14, 16, 21, 23, 28 - 30, May 1, 5, 7, 8, 12, 16, 17, 19 - 21, 26 - 28, June 2, 4, 9, 11, 15 - 18, 22 - 25, 29, 30, July 1, 2, 6 - 9, 13 - 16, 20 - 22, 27 - 30, Aug. 3 - 6, 10 - 13, 17 - 20, 24 - 27, 31, Sept. 1 - 3, 8, 10, 15, 17, 22, 24, 29, Oct. 1.

CE - BASTIA

orsica Ferries October 1 - December 31, 2007
eparture times vary. Journey 5 - 10 hours
rom Nice:
day sailings: Oct. 1, 4 - 8, 11 - 15, 18 - 22, 25 - 29, Nov. 1 - 5, 7 - 13, 18, 20, 25, 27, Dec. 2, 4, 9, 11, 16, 18, 21 - 23, 25 - 30.
night sailings: Oct. 7, Nov. 17, 24, Dec. 1, 8, 15, 26.
rom Bastia:
day sailings: Oct. 1, 4 - 8, 11 - 15, 18 - 22, 25 - 29, Nov. 1 - 5, 7 - 11, 13, 17, 18, 20, 24, 25, 27, Dec. 1, 2, 4, 8, 9, 11, 15, 16, 18, 21 - 24, 26 - 30.
night sailings: Oct. 4, Dec. 22.

CE - CALVI

orsica Ferries October 1 - December 31, 2007
eparture times vary. Journey 3 - 6 hours
rom Nice:
day sailings: Nov. 3, 17, 24, Dec. 1, 8, 15, 23, 26.
night sailings: no sailings.
rom Calvi:
day sailings: Dec. 23, 26.
night sailings: Nov. 17, 24, Dec. 1, 8, 15.

N C M 2007 service (No winter service)
eparture times vary. Journey 3 - 4 hours
rom Nice: Apr. 15, 22, May 6, 13, June 3, 10, 20, 27, July 3, 4, 10, 11, 17, 18, 22 - 26, 30, 31, Aug. 1, 2, 6 - 9, 13 - 16, 20 - 23, 27 - 30, Sept. 2, 8, 9, 15, 16, 22, 23, 29, 30.
rom Calvi: Apr. 15, 22, May 6, 13, June 3, 10, 20, 27, July 3, 4, 6, 8 - 11, 15 - 18, 22 - 26, 29 - 31, Aug. 1, 2, 6 - 9, 13 - 16, 20 - 23, 27 - 30, Sept. 2, 9, 16, 23, 30.

NICE - L'ÎLE ROUSSE

Corsica Ferries October 1 - December 31, 2007
Departure times vary. Journey 4 - 5½ hours
From Nice:
day sailings: Oct. 7, 14, 21, 28, Nov. 11.
night sailings: no sailings.
From L'Île Rousse:
day sailings: Oct. 5, 12, 19, 26, Nov. 2, 9.
night sailings: no sailings.

S N C M October 1 - December 31, 2007
Departure times vary. Journey 3 - 6½ hours (night = 12 hours)
From Nice:
day sailings: no sailings.
night sailings: Oct. 6, 13, 20, 27, Nov. 3, 10, 17, 24, Dec. 1, 8, 15, 22, 29.
From L'Île Rousse:
day sailings: Oct. 6, 13, 20, 27, Nov. 3, 10, 17, 24, Dec. 1, 8, 15, 22, 29.
night sailings: no sailings.

TOULON - AJACCIO

Corsica Ferries October 1 - December 31, 2007
Departure times vary. Journey 6 - 10 hours
From Toulon:
day sailings: Oct. 1, 2, 4 - 9, 11 - 16, 18 - 23, 25 - 29, 31, Nov. 1 - 4, 6 - 11, 16, 17, 19, 23, 24, 26, 30, Dec. 1, 3, 7, 8, 10, 14, 15, 17, 21 - 24, 26, 28 - 31.
night sailings: Oct. 2, 7, 9, 16, 21, 23, 28, 30, Nov. 4, 6, 11.
From Ajaccio:
day sailings: Oct. 1, 2, 5 - 9, 12, 13, 16, 19 - 23, 26 - 29, 31, Nov. 2 - 4, 6, 7, 9 - 11, 16, 18, 19, 23, 25, 26, 30, Dec. 2, 3, 7, 9, 10, 14, 16, 17, 21 - 23, 25, 26, 28 - 30.
night sailings: Oct. 1, 3, 4, 8, 10, 11, 14, 15, 17, 18, 22, 24, 25, 29, 31, Nov. 1, 5, 7, 8.

TOULON - BASTIA

Corsica Ferries October 1 - December 31, 2007
Departure times vary. Journey 8½ - 10 hours
From Toulon:
day sailings: no sailings.
night sailings: Oct. 1 - 31, Nov. 1 - 16, 18 - 23, 25 - 30, Dec. 2 - 7, 9 - 14, 16 - 23, 25 - 30.
From Bastia:
day sailings: no sailings.
night sailings: Oct. 1 - 31, Nov. 1 - 16, 18 - 23, 25 - 30, Dec. 2 - 7, 9 - 14, 16 - 23, 25 - 30.

TOULON - L'ÎLE ROUSSE

Corsica Ferries October 1 - December 31, 2007
Departure times vary. Journey 6 hours
From Toulon:
day sailings: Oct. 3, 5, 10, 12, 17, 19, 24, 26, 30, Nov. 2, 5, 9.
night sailings: no sailings.
From L'Île Rousse:
day sailings: Oct. 3, 7, 10, 14, 17, 21, 24, 28, 30, Nov. 5, 11.
night sailings: no sailings.

Sailings from ITALY

GENOVA - BASTIA

Moby Lines 2007 service (No winter service)

Genova		Bastia	Bastia		Genova	
0900	→	1345	1445	→	1930	Daily May 24 - Sept. 9; ⑥⑦ Sept. 15 - 30.

LIVORNO - BASTIA

Corsica Ferries October 1 - December 31, 2007
Departure times vary. Journey 3 - 4 hours
From Livorno:
day sailings: Oct. 1 - 20, 22 - 27, 29 - 31, Nov. 1 - 10, 13 - 17, 19, 21 - 24, 26, 28 - 30, Dec. 1, 3, 5 - 10, 12 - 15, 17, 19 - 22, 26 - 29, 31.
night sailings: no sailings.
From Bastia:
day sailings: Oct. 1 - 20, 22 - 27, 29 - 31, Nov. 1 - 10, 12 - 17, 19 - 24, 26 - 30, Dec. 1, 3 - 15, 17 - 22, 26 - 29, 31.
night sailings: Oct. 6.

Moby Lines 2007 service (No winter service)

Livorno		Bastia		Bastia		Livorno	
0900	→	1300	See note **R**.	0130	→	0630	①⑥⑦ July 7 - Aug. 27.
2030	→	0030	⑤⑥⑦ July 6 - Aug. 26.	1500	→	1900	See note **R**.

R – Apr. 5 - 10, 12 - 16, 19 - 30, May 1, 3 - 7, 10 - 14, May 17 - Sept. 23.

SAVONA - BASTIA

Corsica Ferries October 1 - December 31, 2007
Departure times vary. Journey 6 - 10 hours
From Savona:
day sailings: Oct. 6, 13, Nov. 16, 23, 30, Dec. 7, 14, 20.
night sailings: Oct. 2, 3, 5, 7, 9, 10, 12, 14, 16, 17, 19, 21, 23, 24, 26, 28, 30, 31, Nov. 2, 4, 6, 7, 9, 19, 26, Dec. 3, 10, 17, 21, 28.
From Bastia:
day sailings: Oct. 3, 6, 10, 13, 17, 21, 24, 28, 31, Nov. 4, 7, 11, 16, 19, 23, 26, 30, Dec. 3, 7, 10, 14, 17, 29.
night sailings: Oct. 1, 4, 6, 8, 11, 13, 15, 18, 22, 25, 29, Nov. 1, 5, 8, Dec. 20, 27.

CORSICA - SARDINIA

BONIFACIO - SANTA TERESA DI GALLURA

Moby Lines 2007 services
4 sailings daily (Apr. 5 - Sept. 23 only), journey 1 hour.

Saremar 2007 service (subject to confirmation)
Up to 3 sailings per day Apr. - Oct., journey 1 hour.

2570 ITALIAN COASTAL SERVICES (including Egadi and Eolian Islands)

Siremar 2007 services

NAPOLI - MILAZZO via Stromboli, Ginostra, Panarea, Lipari and Vulcano.
Also serves Rinella and S.M. Salina on certain days. Journey 16 - 20 hours.
Sailings from Napoli: 2100②⑤. Sailings from Milazzo: 1430①④.

See Table 2621 for faster sailings Napoli - Milazzo and v.v. (summer only).

OTHER SERVICES by ship:
Milazzo - Vulcano - Lipari: 2–3 sailings per day; journey 2 hours.
Milazzo - Vulcano - Lipari - Panarea - Ginostra - Stromboli: 1–3 sailings per week; journey 6 hours.
Milazzo - Vulcano - Lipari - S. M. Salina - Filicudi - Alicudi: 4–5 sailings per week; journey 6 hours.
Trapani - Favignana - Levanzo - Marettimo: 6–7 sailings per week; journey 3 hours.
Palermo - Ustica: 5–7 sailings per week; journey 2½ hours.
Trapani - Pantelleria: 6–7 sailings per week; journey 4½ - 5½ hours.
Porto Empedocle (Agrigento) - Linosa - Lampedusa: 6–7 sailings per week; journey 8 hours.

OTHER SERVICES by hydrofoil 2–6 sailings per day:
Lipari - Panarea - Ginostra - Stromboli
Lipari - S. M. Salina - Rinella
Milazzo - Vulcano - Lipari
Milazzo - Vulcano - Lipari - Rinella - Filicudi - Alicudi
Milazzo - Vulcano - Lipari - S. M. Salina
Palermo - Ustica
Trapani - Levanzo - Favignana - Marettimo

Ustica Lines **by hydrofoil** 2007 services

EGADI & EOLIAN ISLANDS
Napoli, and the Sicilian ports of Cefalù, Messina, Milazzo, Palermo and Trapani are linked by island-hopping services serving Alicudi, Favignana, Filicudi, Levanzo, Lipari, Marettimo, Panarea, Salina Rinella, Salina S. M., Stromboli, Ustica and Vulcano.
Services operate to differing frequencies (additional sailings June 15 - Sept. 30).

LAMPEDUSA - LINOSA **by hydrofoil** Journey 1 hour
Depart Lampedusa: 0730①③④⑤⑥⑦ May 1 - Oct. 31▲; 0900 Apr. 1 - 30, Sept. 16 - Oct. 31; 0930 May 1 - Sept. 15; 1315③⑥ Jan. 1 - Apr. 30, Nov. 1 - Dec. 31▲; 1635 Apr. 1 - 30, Sept. 16 - Oct. 31; 1715 May 1 - Sept. 15.
Depart Linosa: 1015 Apr. 1 - 30, Sept. 16 - Nov. 4; 1045 May 1 - Sept. 15; 1115③⑥ Jan. 1 - Apr. 30, Nov. 1 - Dec. 31▲; 1735①③④⑤⑥⑦ Sept. 16 - Oct. 31▲; 1740 Apr. 1 - 30, Sept. 16 - Nov. 4; 1815①③④⑤⑥⑦ May 1 - Sept. 15; 1830 May 1 - Sept. 15.
▲ – From / to Porto Empedocle (for Agrigento); additional journey time 3 – 3¼ hours.

MILAZZO - VULCANO **by hydrofoil** Journey 45 minutes
Jan. 1 - May 31, Sept. 17 - Dec. 31: 6–7 departures daily; June 1 - Sept. 16: 8 daily.

PALERMO - MILAZZO - CEFALÙ - PALERMO **by hydrofoil**

Palermo		Milazzo		Cefalù		Palermo	
...		0630	→	1110§	→	1220	①⑤⑦ Jan. 1 - June 14, Oct 1 - Dec. 31.
0655	→	1245		...		...	June 1 - Sept. 16.
1400	→	1920	→	2010	→	2105	June 1 - Sept. 16.
1400	→	2000		...		...	①⑤⑦ Jan. 1 - June 14, Oct 1 - Dec. 31.

§ – Jan. 1 - May 31, Sept. 17 - Dec. 31.

TRAPANI - PANTELLERIA **by hydrofoil** **June 10 - Oct. 10 only** Journey 2½ hours
Depart Trapani: 1800. Depart Pantelleria: 0830.

2595 MÁLAGA - MELILLA

Trasmediterranea Journey time 7 - 8 hours 2007 service
Depart Málaga: 1400②③④⑤⑥, 2300①⑦. Depart Melilla: 0900①, 2359①②③④⑤⑥.
Also daily sailings by fast ferry in summer (journey 4 hours)

2602 MARSEILLE - AL-JAZÂ'IR (ALGIERS)

S N C M Journey 20 hours **Service to December 31, 2007**
Departures from Marseille: **Apr.** 3, 4, 7, 9 - 12, 14, 16, 17, 21, 24, 25, 28; **May** 1 - 3, 5, 7 - 10, 12, 14, 15, 19, 21 - 24, 26, 29, 30; **June** 2, 4 - 7, 9, 11, 12, 16, 18, 19, 21, 23 - 30; **July** 1 - 8, 10 - 19, 21 - 30; **Aug.** 1 - 9, 11, 12, 14, 15, 17 - 31; **Sept.** 1 - 5, 7 - 12, 15, 17 - 20, 22, 24 - 26, 29; **Oct.** 1, 2, 4, 6, 9, 10, 15 - 18, 20, 22 - 24, 27, 30, 31; **Nov.** 3, 6, 10, 13, 14, 17, 19, 20, 24, 27, 28; **Dec.** 1, 4, 8, 11, 12, 15, 17, 18, 20, 22, 25, 26, 29.
Departures from al-Jazâ'ir: **Apr.** 2, 4, 7, 9, 10 - 13, 16, 18, 21, 23, 25, 28, 30; **May** 2 - 4, 7, 9 - 12, 14, 16, 21, 23 - 26, 28, 30, 31; **June** 4, 6 - 9, 11, 13, 18, 20, 22 - 24, 25 - 27, 29, 30; **July** 1 - 9, 11, 13, - 20, 22, 23, 25 - 31; **Aug.** 2 - 5, 7 - 13, 15 - 20, 22 - 31; **Sept.** 1 - 5, 7 - 9, 11 - 13, 15, 17, 19 - 22, 24, 26, 27, 29; **Oct.** 1, 3, 5, 6, 8, 10, 15, 17 - 20, 22, 24, 25, 27, 29, 31; **Nov.** 1, 5, 7, 12, 14, 15, 19, 21, 24, 26, 28, 29; **Dec.** 3, 5, 10, 12, 13, 17, 19, 21, 22, 24, 26, 27, 31.
Departure times vary
Other services operate from Marseille to Annâbah, Bijâyah, Sakîkdah, Wâhran (Oran) and v.v.

2615 MARSEILLE - TÛNIS

Compagnie Tunisienne de Navigation / S N C M 2007 servic
Departure times vary. Journey time 22 - 24 hours
Departures from Marseille: May 3, 5, 10, 12, 17, 19, 24, 26, 31, June 2, 7, 9, 14, 16, 21, 23 - 26, 29, 30, July 3 - 6, 8 - 14, 17 - 24, 26, 29 - 31, Aug. 1, 2, 4 - 6, 8, 9, 11 - 16, 18, 20 - 22, 24, 26 - 29, 31, Sept. 1, 2, 4, 5, 7 - 9, 11, 15, 17, 19, 22, 27 - 29, Oct. 4, 6, 11, 13, 18, 20, 25, 27, Nov. 1, 3, 8, 1 0, 15, 17, 22, 24, 29, Dec. 1, 6, 8, 12, 13, 15, 17, 20, 22, 25, 27, 29, 30.
Departures from Tûnis: May 2, 6, 9, 13, 16, 20, 23, 27, 30, June 3, 6, 10, 13, 17, 20, 24 - 28, July 1, 3, 6 - 8, 10 - 13, 15 - 20, 22 - 25, 29 - 31, Aug. 1, 3, 5 - 9, 12 - 15, 17 - 20, Sept. 6 - 11, 14, 16, 18, 22, 23, 26, 27, 30, Oct. 3, 7, 10, 14, 17, 21, 24, 28, 31, Nov. 4, 7, 11, 14, 18, 21, 25, 28, Dec. 2, 5, 9, 11, 12, 16, 19, 23, 24, 26, 29, 30.

2618 MGARR (Gozo) - CIRKEWWA (Malta)

Gozo Channel Co. Journey 25 minutes 2007 servic
Departures from Mgarr and Cirkewwa: every 30 - 45 minutes 0600 - 1930 (less frequent a other times).

2621 NAPOLI - MILAZZO

Ustica Lines **by hydrofoil** **June 1 - September 16, 200**

Napoli		Milazzo	Milazzo		Napoli
0800	→	1450	1200	→	2100

See Table 2570 for alternative sailings Napoli - Milazzo and v.v. (all year).

2625 NAPOLI - PALERMO

Tirrenia 2007 servic

Napoli		Palermo		Napoli	
1000	→	1800 / 1000	→	1800	⑥⑦ July 28 - Sept. 2.
2015	→	0630 / 2015	→	0630	Jan. 1 - July 31, Sept. 1 - Dec. 31.
2045	→	0630 / 2045	→	0630	Aug. 1 - 31.

SNAV **2007 service (No service Dec. 24, 25, 31**

Napoli		Palermo		Palermo		Napoli	
0930⑥	→	1930⑥	July 28 - Sept. 1.	2000	→	0630	Daily.
2000	→	0630	Daily.	2230⑥	→	0830⑦	July 28 - Sept. 1.

2630 NAPOLI - TRAPANI

Ustica Lines **by hydrofoil** **June 1 - September 30, 200** **(No winter service**
①④⑥▲: Napoli 1500 → Ustica 1915 → Favignana 2130 → Trapani 2205.
①④⑥▲: Trapani 0630 → Favignana 0655 → Ustica 0915 → Napoli 1315.
▲ – Also ⑤ July 1 - Aug. 31.

2632 NAPOLI - TÛNIS

Medmar 2007 servic
SERVICE SUSPENDED

2660 REGGIO DI CALABRIA - MESSINA

Italian Railways **by catamaran** Journey 25 minutes **Service to December 8, 200**
From Reggio di Calabria: 0650Ⓐ, 0720Ⓐ, 0825, 0855Ⓐ, 0955, 1025Ⓐ, 1125, 1250Ⓐ, 1355, 1530Ⓐ, 1705, 1830, 2000.
From Messina: 0600Ⓐ, 0630Ⓐ, 0735, 0805Ⓐ, 0910, 0940Ⓐ, 1040, 1200Ⓐ, 1310, 1415Ⓐ, 1620, 1750, 1915Ⓐ.

Ustica Lines **by hydrofoil** Journey 15 minutes 2007 servic
From Reggio di Calabria and Messina: 3 sailings in summer, 2 in winter.

2661 SALERNO - PALERMO - TÛNIS

Grimaldi Ferries 2007 servic

Salerno		Palermo		Tûnis		Palermo		Salerno
1900①	→	0600② / 1000②	→	2030② / 2100④	→	0800⑤ / 1200⑤	→	2100⑤
2359⑤	→	1100⑥ / 2000⑥	→	0830⑦ / 1100⑦	→	2200⑦ / 2359⑦	→	0900①

2665 SÈTE - TANJAH (TANGIERS)

Cie. Marocaine de Navigation (Comanav) 2007 servic
Depart 1900 from Sète, 1800 from Tanjah. Sailings arrive 2 days later.
Departures from Sète: Apr. 3, 7, 11, 15, 19, 23, 27, May 1, 5, 9, 13, 17, 21, 25, 29, June 3, 7, 12, 16, 20, 24, 28, July 2, 6, 10, 14, 18, 22, 26, 30, Aug. 3, 7, 11, 15, 19, 23, 27, 31, Sept. 4, 8, 12, 16, 20, 24, 28, Oct. 2, 6, 10, 14, 18, 22, 26, 30, Nov. 3, 7, 11, 15, 19, 23, 27, Dec. 1, 5, 9, 13, 17, 21, 25, 29.
Departures from Tanjah: Apr. 1, 5, 9, 13, 17, 21, 25, 29, May 3, 7, 11, 15, 19, 23, 27, June 1, 5, 10, 14, 18, 22, 26, 30, July 4, 8, 12, 16, 20, 24, 28, Aug. 1, 5, 9, 13, 17, 21, 25, 29, Sept. 2, 6, 10, 14, 18, 22, 26, 30, Oct. 4, 8, 12, 16, 20, 24, 28, Nov. 1, 5, 9, 13, 17, 21, 25, 29, Dec. 3, 7, 11, 15, 19, 23, 27, 31.
Comanav also operate Sète - an-Nadûr (Nador) in summer only.

SARDINIA 2675

Sailings from FRANCE

ARSEILLE - PORTO TORRES

S N C M — Service to December 31, 2007

eparture times vary. Journey 16 - 19 hours. T – from / to Toulon

rom Marseille: Apr. 2, 4, 7, 9, 11, 14, 16, 18, 20, 23, 25, 27, 29, 30, May 2, 5, 7, 9, 12, 14, 16, 18, 21, 23, 26, 28, 30, June 2, 4, 6, 9, 11, 13, 16, 18, 20, 22, 25, 27, July 2 - 4, 8 - 11, 16 - 18, 22 - 25, 29, 30, Aug. 1, 6, 8, 10, 12, 13, 15, 20 - 22, 25, 27, 29, Sept. 2, 3, 5, 7, 10, 12, 14, 17, 19, 21, 24, 26, 28, Oct. 1, 3, 6, 8, 12, 15, 17, 19, 22, 24, 26, 29, 31, Nov. 6, 14, 20, 28, Dec. 3, 5, 10, 12, 17, 19, 26, 31.

rom Porto Torres: Apr. 3, 5, 8, 10, 12, 15, 17, 19, 21, 24, 26, 28, 30, May 1, 3, 6, 8, 10, 13, 15, 17, 19, 22, 24, 27, 29, 31, June 3, 5, 7, 10, 11T*, 12, 14, 17, 18T*, 19, 21, 23, 25T*, 26, 28, July 3 - 5, 9, 10, 12, 17, 19, 23, 24, 26, 30, 31, Aug. 2, 7, 9, 11, 13, 14, 16, 21 - 23, 26, 28, 30, Sept. 3, 4, 6, 8, 11, 13, 15, 18, 20, 22, 25, 27, 29, Oct. 2, 4, 7, 9, 13, 16, 18, 20, 23, 25, 27, 30, Nov. 1, 7, 15, 21, 29, Dec. 4, 6, 11, 13, 18, 20, 27.

All sailings are overnight except those marked *.

Sailings from mainland ITALY

VITAVECCHIA - ARBATAX

Tirrenia — 2007 service

vitavecchia		Arbatax	
1830	→	0500	③⑤ Jan. 3 - June 29; ⑤⑦ July 1 - Sept. 23; ③⑤ Sept. 26 - Dec. 28.
Arbatax		**Civitavecchia**	
2359	→	1030	③⑦ Jan. 3 - June 27; ⑤⑦ July 1 - Sept. 23; ③⑦ Sept. 26 - Dec. 30.

VITAVECCHIA - CAGLIARI

Tirrenia — 2007 service

vitavecchia		Cagliari	
1830	→	0900	Daily **except** when service below sails. 2 hours later on Apr. 28.
1830	→	1115	③⑤ Jan. 3 - June 29; ⑤⑦ July 1 - Sept. 23; ③⑤ Sept. 26 - Dec. 28 (via Arbatax).
Cagliari		**Civitavecchia**	
1800	→	0830	Daily **except** when service below sails.
1800	→	1030	③⑦ Jan. 3 - June 27; ⑤⑦ July 1 - Sept. 23; ③⑦ Sept. 26 - Dec. 30 (via Arbatax).

VITAVECCHIA - GOLFO ARANCI

Sardinia Ferries — Service to September 30, 2007

vitavecchia		Golfo Aranci		Golfo Aranci		Civitavecchia	
0815	→	1515	See note **A**.	0815	→	1300	See note **B**.
1415	→	1900	See note **B**.	1630	→	2330	May 26 - Sept. 23.
				2100	→	0700	May 1 only.

A – May 26 - Sept. 23 (also May 1).
B – ①②④⑤⑥⑦ June 8 - Aug. 21; ①②③⑤⑥⑦ Aug. 22 - Sept. 24 (also Sept. 28 - 30).

VITAVECCHIA - OLBIA

Moby Lines — 2007 service (No winter service)

vitavecchia		Olbia		Olbia		Civitavecchia	
0900	→	1530	Aug. 16 - Sept. 30.	0900	→	1345	See note **C**.
1500	→	1945	See note **C**.	1200	→	1900	May 25 - Aug. 14.
2200	→	0800	May 24 - Aug. 14.	2200	→	0700	Aug. 15 - Sept. 30.

C – ①⑤⑥⑦ Mar. 30 - May 21; daily May 24 - Sept. 30 (also Mar. 29, Apr. 5, 10, 19, 24 - 26, May 1).

Tirrenia — 2007 service

vitavecchia		Olbia	
0830	→	1330	June 1 - Sept. 9.
1500	→	2000	⑥ July 7 - 21; daily July 27 - Sept. 2 (also Sept. 8).
2300	→	0600	June 1 - Sept. 11.
2300	→	0630	Jan. 1 - May 31, Sept. 12 - Dec. 31.
Olbia		**Civitavecchia**	
0830	→	1330	⑥ July 7 - 21; daily July 27 - Sept. 2 (also Sept. 8).
1200	→	1700	Daily June 1 - 30; ①②③④⑤⑦ July 1 - 26, Sept. 3 - 9.
1500	→	2000	⑥ July 7 - 21; daily July 27 - Sept. 2 (also Sept. 8).
2300	→	0600	June 1 - Sept. 11.
2300	→	0630	Jan. 1 - May 31, Sept. 12 - Dec. 31.

ENOVA - ARBATAX

Tirrenia — 2007 service

Genova		Arbatax	
1800	→	1300	①⑤ Jan. 1 - Apr. 13.
1930	→	1400	①⑤ Apr. 16 - June 18, Sept. 10 - Dec. 31.
2130	→	1330	①⑥ June 23 - Aug. 13; ①⑤ Aug. 17 - Sept. 7.
Arbatax		**Genova**	
1400	→	0715	②⑥ Apr. 17 - June 16, Sept. 11 - Dec. 29.
1400	→	1000	②⑥ Jan. Apr. 14.
1500	→	0715	②⑦ June 19 - Aug. 14; ②⑥ Aug. 18 - Sept. 8.

ENOVA - OLBIA

Grandi Navi Veloci — 2007 service (No winter service)

Genova		Olbia		Olbia		Genova	
0930	→	1830	Aug. 16 - Sept. 23.	0930	→	1830	May 25 - Aug. 15.
2100	→	0700	May 24 - Aug. 14.	2100	→	0700	Aug. 16 - Sept. 23.

Moby Lines — 2007 service (No winter service)

Genova		Olbia		Olbia		Genova	
2200	→	0730	May 23 - Oct. 7.	2200	→	0730	May 23 - Oct. 7.

Tirrenia — 2007 service

Genova		Olbia	
0900	→	1900	③④⑦ Aug. 15 - Sept. 9.
1800	→	0715	①③⑤ Jan. 1 - Apr. 13.
1930	→	0715	①③⑤ Apr. 16 - June 18, Sept. 10 - Dec. 31.
2130	→	0715	①③④⑤⑥ June 20 - Aug. 11; ①⑤ Aug. 13 - Sept. 7.
Olbia		**Genova**	
0900	→	1900	④⑤⑥ June 21 - Aug. 11.
2030	→	0715	②④⑥ Apr. 17 - June 16, Sept. 11 - Dec. 29.
2030	→	1000	②④⑥ Jan. 2 Apr. 14.
2130	→	0715	②⑦ June 19 - Aug. 7; ②③④⑥⑦ Aug. 12 - Sept. 9.

GENOVA - PORTO TORRES

Grandi Navi Veloci — 2007 service (No service Dec. 31)

Genova		Porto Torres		Porto Torres		Genova	
0930	→	2030	See note **A**.	0930	→	2030	See note **A**.
2000	→	0700	See note **B**.	2000	→	0700	See note **B**.
2030	→	0730	See note **G**.	2030	→	0730	See note **G**.
2130	→	0830	July 20 - Sept. 2.	2130	→	0830	July 20 - Sept. 2.

A – July 28, 30, Aug. 2, 4, 6, 11, 18, 23, 25, 27, 30, Sept. 1.
B – Apr. 1 - July 19, Sept. 3 - Dec. 30.
G – July 27, 29, Aug. 1, 3, 5, 10, 17, 22, 24, 26, 29, 31.

Tirrenia — 2007 service

Genova		P. Torres		P. Torres		Genova	
0900	→	1700		0900	→	1700	⑥⑦ July 28 - Sept. 8 (also Aug. 24).
2030	→	0630		2030	→	0630	Jan. 1 - July 31, Sept. 1 - Dec. 31.
2100	→	0630		2100	→	0630	Aug. 1 - 31.

LIVORNO - GOLFO ARANCI

Sardinia Ferries by fast ferry — Service to November 11, 2007

Livorno		Golfo Aranci		Golfo Aranci		Livorno	
0815	→	1430	See note **A**.	0815	→	1430	See note **F**.
1530	→	2145	See note **B**.	1200	→	1815	See note **G**.
2100	→	0700	Oct. 1 - Nov. 11.	1530	→	2145	See note **H**.
				2100	→	0700	Oct. 1 - Nov. 11.

A – ⑤⑦ May 4 - 20; daily May 28 - Sept. 29 (not June 2, 4, 27).
B – ⑥ May 5 - 19 (also May 25, 27, June 2, 4).
F – ⑥ May 5 - 19; ③ June 13 - Aug. 15; ④ Aug. 23 - Sept. 27 (also May 25, 27, June 2, 4).
G – ①②③ May 1 - 23 (also May 24).
H – ⑤⑦ May 4 - 20; ①②④⑤⑥⑦ June 8 - Aug. 21; ①②③⑤⑥⑦ Aug. 22 - Sept. 29 (also May 26, June 1, 3; not June 28).

Additional sailings available by ship, journey 8 - 10 hours.

LIVORNO - OLBIA

Moby Lines — 2007 service

Sailings from Livorno Marittima, Varco Galvani and Olbia. (No service Dec. 24, 25, 31)

Jan. - Mar.: 1 sailing per day; Apr. - May: 1 - 2 sailings per day; June - Sept.: 2 - 4 sailings per day; Oct. - Dec. 1 - 2 sailings per day. Departure times vary.

LIVORNO - PIOMBINO

Sardinia Ferries by fast ferry — Service to September 30, 2007

Piombino		Golfo Aranci		Golfo Aranci		Piombino	
0900	→	1300	See note **J**.	0900	→	1300	See note **K**.
1330	→	1730	See note **K**.	1330	→	1730	See note **J**.
1800	→	2200	See note **L**.	1800	→	2200	See note **K**.

J – ①⑤⑥⑦ June 29 - July 23; daily July 26 - Sept. 3 (also June 28, Sept. 7 - 9; not July 29, Aug. 5, 7, 12, 14, 26, Sept. 2).
K – July 1, 29, Aug. 5, 12, 26, Sept. 2.
L – June 30, July 28, Aug. 4, 11, 25, Sept. 1.

NAPOLI - CAGLIARI

Tirrenia — 2007 service

Napoli		Cagliari	
1915	→	1130	④ Jan. 4 - July 19; ②④ July 24 - Sept. 6; ④ Sept. 13 - Dec. 27.
Cagliari		**Napoli**	
1830	→	1045	③ Jan. 3 - July 18; ①③ July 23 - Sept. 5; ③ Sept. 12 - Dec. 26.

Sailings from SICILY

PALERMO - CAGLIARI

Tirrenia — 2007 service

Palermo		Cagliari		Cagliari		Palermo	
1700⑥	→	0630⑦	July 14 - Sept. 1.	1900⑤	→	0830⑥	Feb. 2 - Dec. 28.
1900⑥	→	0930⑦	Feb. 3 - July 7, Sept. 8 - Dec. 29.				

TRAPANI - CAGLIARI

Tirrenia — 2007 service

Cagliari		Trapani	
1000	→	2000	⑦ July 22 - Sept. 2.
1900	→	0600	① Jan. 8 - July 16, Sept. 10 - Dec. 31.
Trapani		**Cagliari**	
2100	→	0830	② Jan. 9 - July 17, Sept. 11 - Dec. 25.
2359	→	1000	⑦ July 22 - Sept. 2.

TRAPANI - TÛNIS 2682

Ustica Lines — 2007 service

Trapani		Tûnis	Tûnis		Trapani
1030①③⑤	→	1930①③⑤	2230①③⑤	→	0800②④⑥

VALLETTA - CATANIA 2690

Virtu Ferries by catamaran — November 1 - December 31, 2007

Valletta		Catania	Catania		Valletta
0500⑥	→	0800⑥	1930⑥	→	2230⑥

VALLETTA - GENOVA 2691

Grandi Navi Veloci — 2007 service

Valletta		Genova		Genova		Valletta	
1500①	→	2030②	Apr. 1 - July 9, Sept. 16 - Dec. 30.	1800⑥	→	0830①	Apr. 7 - July 7, Oct. 20 - Dec. 29.
				1900⑥	→	0930①	Sept. 15 - Oct. 13.

2694 VALLETTA - POZZALLO

Virtu Ferries **by catamaran** Journey 1½ hours **March 1 - December 31, 2007**

Valletta		Pozzallo		Pozallo		Valletta	
0645	→	0815	See note **C**.	0915	→	1045	See note **E**.
0700	→	0830	See note **A**.	1530	→	1700	See note **D**.
1300	→	1430	⑦ July 10 - Sept. 10.	1600	→	1730	Dec. 31 only.
1600	→	1730	⑤ Nov. 1 - Dec. 31.	1930	→	2100	See note **G**.
1830	→	2000	See note **D**.	2130	→	2300	See note **F**.
1845	→	2015	See note **B**.				

A – ①③④⑦ Apr. 1 - May 31; ①③⑤⑦ June 1 - July 9; ③⑤ July 10 - Sept. 10; ①③⑤⑦ Sept. 11 - Oct. 4; ①③④⑦ Oct. 5 - 31; ①④⑤⑦ Nov. 1 - Dec. 31.
B – ④ Apr. 1 - July 9; ①④ July 10 - Sept. 10; ④ Sept. 11 - Oct. 31.
C – ④ June 1 - July 9; ①④⑦ July 10 - Sept. 10; ④ Sept. 11 - Oct. 4.
D – ⑤⑦ June 1 - July 9; ③⑤ July 10 - Aug. 31; ⑤ Sept. 1 - 10; ⑤⑦ Sept. 11 - Oct. 4.
E – ④ Apr. 1 - July 9; ①④⑦ July 10 - Sept. 10; ④ Sept. 11 - Oct. 31; ⑤ Nov. 1 - Dec. 31.
F – ①③④⑦ Apr. 1 - May 31; ①③④⑤⑦ June 1 - Oct. 4; ①③④⑦ Oct. 5 - 31.
G – ①④⑤⑦ Nov. 1 - Dec. 31.

2695 VILLA S. GIOVANNI - MESSINA

Italian Railways Journey 35 minutes **Service to December 8, 200**

From Villa S.G.: 0055, 0140, 0215, 0335, 0420, 0455, 0625, 0700, 0735, 0900, 0935, 1005, 1140, 1215, 1250, 1425, 1510, 1530, 1655, 1750, 1825, 1935, 2030, 2105, 2215, 2300, 2340.

From Messina: 0020, 0055, 0215, 0300, 0335, 0455, 0540, 0615, 0740, 0820, 0850, 1020, 1055, 1130, 1300, 1350, 1410, 1540, 1630, 1650, 1815, 1910, 1945, 2055, 2145, 2225, 2335.

2699 OTHER SERVICES

Moby Lines **2007 service**

Piombino - Portoferraio (Elba): 7 sailings daily in winter, 13 - 16 sailings in summer, journey 1 hour (no service on Dec. 25).

Tirrenia **2007 service**

Fiumicino - Arbatax: by fast ferry: ①③ July 30 - Sept. 3 only, journey 4 - 5½ hours.
Fiumicino - Golfo Aranci: by fast ferry: 1 sailing daily July 20 - Sept. 9, journey 4½ hours.

Toremar **2007 service**

Piombino - Portoferraio: by ship: 8 – 15 sailings daily, journey 1 hour. By hydrofoil: 2 – 4 sailings daily (also serving Cavo), journey 30 – 40 minutes.
Piombino - Isola Pianosa, journey 3 hours.
Piombino - Rio Marina - Porto Azzurro: 2 – 3 sailings daily, journey 60 – 85 minutes.
Livorno - Capraia: 1 – 2 sailings daily, journey 2½ – 3½ hours.
Porto Santo Stefano - Isola del Giglio: 2 – 5 sailings per day, journey 1 hour.

ADRIATIC / EASTERN MEDITERRANEAN / BLACK SEA

2705 ANCONA - BAR

Montenegro Lines **July 1 - September 10, 2007** **(No winter service)**

Ancona		Bar	Bar		Ancona
1600④⑥	→	0700⑤⑦	1600③⑤	→	0700④⑥

2715 ANCONA - PÁTRA via Igumenítsa

Anek Lines **Service to January 7, 2008**

Ancona		Igumenítsa		Pátra	Pátra		Igumenítsa		Ancona
January 9 - March 18 and October 30 - January 6 (from Pátra, following day from Ancona)									
1600 **C**	→	0830 **D**	→	1400 **D**	1700 **E**	→	2230 **E**	→	1300 **F**
March 20 - October 28 (from Pátra, following day from Ancona)									
1600	→	0800	→	1330	1700	→	2230	→	1230

C – ①③④⑤⑥⑦ **D** – ②④⑤⑥⑦①
E – ②③④⑤⑥⑦ **F** – ③④⑤⑥⑦①

▲ – No sailings from Pátra (folowing day from Ancona): Mar. 26, Apr. 9, 23, May 7, 21, June 4, 18, July 2, 30, Sept. 17, Oct. 1, 15.

connection Pátra - Pireás - Athína and v.v. operates most days in summer.

Minoan Lines **2007 service**

Ancona		Igumenítsa		Pátra	Pátra		Igumenítsa		Ancona
February 6 - May 20									
1600⑥	→	0900⑦	→	1430⑦	1600⑤	→	2200⑤	→	1300⑥
1700②⑤⑦	→	0900③⑥①	→	1500③⑥①	1730⑦	→	2330⑦	→	1430①
1700①	→	1000②	→	1530②	1800①④⑥	→	2330①④⑥	→	1400②⑤⑦
1800③	→	1100④	→	1630④	1830②	→	2359②	→	1530③
May 21 - December 31									
1700	→	0900	→	1500	1800	→	2330	→	1400

No sailings from Pátra May 23, 30, June 13, 27, July 18, Aug. 15, Sept. 5, 19, Oct. 3, 10, 17, 24, 31, Nov. 7, 14, 21, 28, Dec. 5, 12, 19, 25, 26, 31 (one day later from Ancona).

Superfast Ferries **Service to June 22, 2008**

Ancona		Igumenítsa		Pátra	
1330	→	0530	→	1130	
1900	→	→	→	1600	②④⑥

Pátra		Igumenítsa		Ancona	
1430	→	2000	→	1030	
2000	→	→	→	1500	①③⑤

Subject to alteration during ship maintenance periods

connection Pátra - Pireás - Athína and v.v.
Tickets available on-board ship and from 30 Amalías av., Síndagma, Athína.

2725 ANCONA - SPLIT

Jadrolinija **Service to May 31, 200**

Ancona		Split		Split		Ancona	
July 13 - September 6							
1130	→	1915	⑦	0930	→	1845	⑥
2100	→	0600	①③⑤	2100	→	0700	③
2100	→	0700	④	2200	→	0700	②④
2100	→	0830	⑥	2200	→	0900	⑥⑦
September 7 - 30							
2100	→	0700	①③⑤⑦	2100	→	0700	②④⑥⑦
October 1 - May 31							
2100	→	0700	①③⑤ (not Dec. 26).	1000	→	1730	Dec. 24, 31 only.
				2100	→	0700	②④⑦ (not Dec. 24, 25, 31).

S E M Maritime Company Journey 9 hours **2007 servic**

April 1 - July 19
Depart Ancona: 2100①②③④⑤⑥. Depart Split: 2100①②③④⑤⑦.
July 20 - September 2
Depart Ancona: 1100①⑥⑦, 2100. Depart Split: 1100①⑥⑦, 2100.
September 3 - December 28
Depart Ancona: 2100①③⑤. Depart Split: 2100②④⑦.

SNAV **by catamaran** *Croazia Jet* **June 9 - September 16, 200**
Journey 4½ hours **(No winter service**

Ancona		Split	Split		Ancona
1100	→	1530	1700	→	2130

2732 ANCONA - ZADAR

Jadrolinija **Service to May 31, 200**

Ancona		Zadar		Zadar		Ancona	
July 20 - September 4							
1100	→	1700	⑦	0800	→	1400	⑥
1600	→	2200	⑥	1100	→	1700	②③④⑤
2200	→	0530	⑤	2200	→	0700	⑦
2200	→	0600	①②③④	2359	→	0700	⑥
September 5 - 30							
2200	→	0700	②④⑤⑥	1100	→	1700	⑤⑥
				2200	→	0700	①③
October 1 - May 31							
2200	→	0700	②④⑥ (not Dec. 25, Jan. 1).	2200	→	0700	①③⑤ (not Dec. 24, 31).

2735 ANCONA - ÇEŞME

Marmara Lines **2007 service (No winter service**

Ancona		Çeşme	
2230⑥	→	0700②	Mar. 24 - June 16, Sept. 15 - Nov. 11.
2230⑥	→	1845①	June 23 - Sept. 8.

Çeşme		Ancona	
1000④	→	1800⑥	Mar. 29 - June 21, Sept. 20 - Nov. 1.
2330④	→	1800⑥	June 28 - Sept. 13.

2738 BARI - BAR

Montenegro Lines **2007 servic**

Bari		Bar		Bar		Bari	
1200	→	1900	See note **B**.	1200	→	1900	See note **C**.
1700	→	0700	⑦ Aug. 10 - Sept. 10.	1700	→	0700	⑦ Aug. 10 - Sept. 10
2200	→	0700	See note **A**.	2200	→	0700	See note **D**.

A – ①③⑤ Jan. 1 - July 1; ①②③⑥ July 1 - 30; ②③⑤⑥⑦ July 30 - Aug. 10; ②③ Aug. 10 - Sept. 10; ①③⑤ Sept. 10 - Dec. 31.
B – ⑤ July 1 - 30; ⑤⑥⑦ Aug. 10 - Sept. 10.
C – ⑥ July 1 - 30; ④⑥⑦ July 30 - Aug. 10.
D – ②④⑦ Jan. 1 - July 1; ①②④⑦ July 1 - 30; ①⑦ July 30 - Aug. 10; ①④⑤⑥⑦ Aug. 10 - Sept. 10; ②④⑦ Sept. 10 - Dec. 31.

For international shipping maps – see pages 518 - 520

BARI - KÉRKIRA (CORFU) 2740

Ventouris Ferries — Service to September 30, 2007

Bari		Kérkira	
1800	→	0500	⑤ July 27 - Aug. 10.
1900	→	0600	③④ Apr. 4 - May 31; ①②③④ June 4 - July 12; ③④ Sept. 12 - 27 (also July 16, 18, 19, 23, 24, 28, 29).
2000	→	0700	July 26, 30, Aug. 1, 2, 6 - 9, 13, 15, 16, 21 - 23, 26, 28 - 30, Sept. 2, 4 - 6.
2200	→	0900	⑥ July 7 - Sept. 8 (also July 25, 29, Aug. 5, 12, 14).
Kérkira		**Bari**	
2030	→	0530	⑤ Apr. 13 - July 20; ⑤ Aug. 17 - Sept. 28.
2230	→	0730	① Apr. 2 - May 28; ①③④ June 4 - 28; ① Sept. 10 - 24 (also Apr. 3 - 6, 10, 11, July 1, 2, 4, 5, 8, 9, 11, 12, 15, 16, 18, 23).
2230	→	0830	July 19, 22, 26, 27, 29 - 31, Aug. 1 - 3, 5 - 10, 12, 13, 15, 16, 20 - 23, 26 - 30, Sept. 2 - 6, 9.
0030	→	0930	⑦ Aug. 19 - Sept. 9.

BARI - IGUMENÍTSA 2745

Ventouris Ferries — Journey 12½ hours — Service to September 30, 2007

From Bari and Igumenítsa: Daily sailings (1 - 2 per day in summer). Departure times vary.

BARI - PÁTRA via Kérkira and Igumenítsa 2755

Blue Star Ferries / Superfast Ferries — Service to June 22, 2008

Bari		Kérkira		Igumenítsa		Pátra
1200⑦	→	→	→	2230⑦	→	0600①
2000①-⑥	→	→	→	0630②-⑦	→	1230②-⑦
Pátra		**Igumenítsa**		**Kérkira**		**Bari**
1800	→	2359	→	→	→	0830

Subject to alteration during ship maintenance periods

🚌 connection Pátra - Pireás - Athína and v.v.

Tickets available on-board ship and from 30 Amalías av., Síndagma, Athína.

BLACK SEA services 2760

Bumerang Shipping Company Tourism Travel & Trade S.A.

İSTANBUL - YALTA - NOVOROSSISK Irregular sailings, journey 30 hours

İSTANBUL - YEVPATORIYA Journey 24 hours

Ukrferry — 2007 service

İSTANBUL - ODESA

İstanbul		Odesa	Odesa		İstanbul
1200⑤	→	1300⑥	1500①	→	1530②
2359②	→	1200④	2000⑥	→	0900①

BRINDISI - KÉRKIRA (CORFU) - IGUMENÍTSA - PÁTRA 2765

Fragline — 2007 service (No winter service)

Brindisi		Kérkira		Igumenítsa		Kérkira	
2100	→	0600	→	0700		...	May 22, 28, June 5, 12, 19, 26, July 3, 10, 17, 24, 27 - 31, Aug. 1 - 31, Sept. 1 - 8, 12, 17.
2100	→	→	→	0615	→	0830	May 21, 24 - 27, 30, 31, June 1 - 4, 7 - 11, 14 - 18, 21 - 25, 28 - 30, July 1, 2, 4 - 9, 11 - 16, 18 - 23, 25, 26, Sept. 9 - 11, 14 - 16.
Kérkira		**Igumenítsa**		**Kérkira**		**Brindisi**	
...		0730	→	0915	→	1615	May 21, 22, 24 - 28, 30, 31, June 1 - 5, 7 - 12, 14 - 19, 21 - 26, 28 - 30, July 1 - 3, 5 - 10, 12 - 17, 19 - 24, 26, Sept. 9 - 11, 14 - 17.
...		0930	→	1130	→	1715	July 27 - 31, Aug. 1 - 31, Sept. 1 - 8.
...		1030	→	1200	→	1800	July 4, 11, 18, 25, Sept. 12.

Hellenic Mediterranean Lines — 2007 service

Brindisi		Kérkira		Igumenítsa		Kérkira		Pátra	
1400	→	→	→	2200	→	→	→	0600	⑦ Nov. 4 - Dec. 30.
1700	→	→	→	0100	→	→	→	0900	See note **B**.
1900	→	→	→	0300	→	→	→	1030	See note **A**.
1900	→	→	→	→	→	→	→	1130	See note **C**.
Pátra		**Kérkira**		**Igumenítsa**		**Kérkira**		**Brindisi**	
1730	→	→	→	0030	→	→	→	0830	See note **S**.
1730	→	→	→	0200	→	→	→	0930	See note **T**.

A – May 1 - 5, 7 - 12, 14 - 19, 21 - 26, 28 - 31, June 4, 5, 7, 11, 12, 14, 18, 19, 21, 24 - 26, 28, July 2, 3, 5, 9, 10, 12, Aug. 28, 30, Sept. 3 - 15, 17 - 22, 24 - 29, Oct. 1 - 6, 8 - 13, 15 - 20, 22 - 31, Nov. 2, 3, 5 - 10, 12 - 17, 19 - 24, 26 - 30, Dec. 1, 3 - 8, 10 - 15, 17 - 22, 27 - 29.

B – ⑦ May 6 - June 17, Sept. 16 - Oct. 21.

C – June 1, 2, 6, 8, 9, 13, 15, 16, 20, 22, 23, 27, 29, 30, July 1, 4, 6 - 8, 11, 13 - 31, Aug. 1 - 27, 29, 31, Sept. 1, 2.

S – May 3 - 31, June 1 - 9, 11 - 16, 18 - 20, 22, 23, 25 - 27, 29, 30, July 2 - 4, 6, 9 - 11, 13, 16 - 18, Sept. 11 - 30, Oct. 1 - Dec. 22, 26 - 29.

T – June 10, 17, 21, 24, 28, July 1, 5, 7, 8, 12, 14, 15, 19 - 31, Aug. 1 - Sept. 10.

🚌 service (subject to confirmation) operates June 1 - Sept. 30 to/from Athína (28 Amalías Avenue). Also departs from Pireás Harbour (ISAP Station) 30 minutes later.

BRINDISI - SÁMI (Kefallinía) 2780

Hellenic Mediterranean Lines — 2007 service (No winter service)

From Brindisi and Sámi: infrequent sailings operate June - September.

Sailings also operate from Brindisi to Zákinthos (Zante); mid June - early September.

BRINDISI - ÇEŞME 2785

Marmara Lines — 2007 service (No winter service)

Brindisi		Çeşme		Çeşme		Brindisi	
1130③	→	1815④	June 27 - Sept. 12.	2345①	→	0645③	June 25 - Sept. 10.

DUBROVNIK - BARI 2795

Azzurra Line — 2007 service (No winter service)

Dubrovnik		Bari	
1200	→	2000	June 10, 17, July 1, 8, Aug. 1, 4, 5, 8, 15, 18, 19, 22, 25, 26, 29, Sept. 2, 9, 16, 23.
1300	→	2100	June 23, 24, July 15, 22, 28, 29, Aug. 10, 11, 12, 23, 24.
2300	→	0800	June 29 only.
Bari		**Dubrovnik**	
2300	→	0800	June 9, 16, 28, 30, July 31, Aug. 3, 4, 7, 14, 17, 18, 21, 25, 28, Sept. 1, 8, 15, 22.
2350	→	0900	June 22, 23, July 7, 14, 21, 27, 28, Aug. 9, 10, 11, 22, 23, 24.

Jadrolinija — Service to May 31, 2008

Dubrovnik		Bari		Dubrovnik	
June 1 - September 30					
1600⑥	→	2200⑥ / 2359⑥	→	0700⑦	
2300②	→	0800③ / 2200③	→	0700④	
October 1 - May 31					
1530⑥	→	2130⑥ / 2230⑥	→	0700⑦	Not Nov. 3 - Mar. 15.
2300②	→	0800③ / 2200③	→	0700④	

GREEK ISLANDS 2800

Summary table of regular ⛴ services to the Greek Islands.

Each route is operated by various shipping companies to differing schedules.
Further details are given in the **Thomas Cook Guide to Greek Island Hopping**.
Additional inter-island routes are operated at less regular intervals.

Pireás to Égina, Póros, Ídra, Spétses, Kíthira, Andikíthira.
Pireás to Sérifos, Sífnos, Mílos, Folégandros.
Pireás to Páros, Íos, Thíra (Santoríni), Iráklio.
Pireás to Náxos, Amorgós, Astipálea.
Pireás to Pátmos, Léros, Kálimnos, Kos, Nísiros, Tílos, Sími, Ródos, Kárpathos, Kásos.
Pireás to Ikaría, Sámos, Híos, Lésvos.
Pireás and **Rafína** to Síros, Dílos, Míkonos, Tínos, Ándros.
Pátra to Zákinthos (Zante), Kefallinía, Itháki, Kérkira (Corfu), Igumenítsa.
Vólos, **Ágios Konstantínos** and **Kími** to Skíathos, Skópelos, Alónissos, Skíros.
Kavála to Thásos, Samothráki, Límnos.

PESCARA - SPLIT 2810

Jadrolinija — Service to September 30, 2007 (No winter service)

Pescara		Split		Split		Pescara	
June 4 - July 12 and September 10 - 27							
2100	→	0700	②④	2100	→	0700	①③
July 13 - September 3							
2100	→	0700	①	0900	→	1900	⑤
2100	→	0800	⑤	2100	→	0700	⑦

SNAV by catamaran *Croazia Jet* — June 16 - September 9, 2007 (No winter service)

Journey 4½ hours

Pescara		Split	Split		Pescara
1030	→	1615	1700	→	2300

PIREÁS - LEMESÓS (LIMASSOL) - HEFA 2845

Poseidon Lines

SERVICE SUSPENDED

Salamis Lines

SERVICE SUSPENDED

RIJEKA - SPLIT - DUBROVNIK 2855

Jadrolinija — Service to May 31, 2008

Rijeka		Split		Stari Grad		Korčula		Dubrovnik	
June 1 - September 29									
2000①	→	0700②	→	0900②	→	1300②	→	1615②	
2000⑤	→	0630⑥	→	0820⑥	→	1140⑥	→	1440⑥	
Dubrovnik		**Korčula**		**Stari Grad**		**Split**		**Rijeka**	
1000④	→	1330④	→	1700④	→	2000④	→	0700⑤	
1000⑦	→	1330⑦	→	1700⑦	→	2000⑦	→	0700①	
October 1 - May 31									
Rijeka		**Split**		**Stari Grad**		**Korčula**		**Dubrovnik**	
1900①▲	→	0700②	→	0900②	→	1300②	→	1615②	
1900⑤	→	0700⑥	→	0900⑥	→	1300⑥	→	1615⑥	Nov. 2 - Mar. 14.
2000⑤	→	0630⑥	→	0815⑥	→	1130⑥	→	1430⑥	See note **R**.
Dubrovnik		**Korčula**		**Stari Grad**		**Split**		**Rijeka**	
0900④	→	1235④	→	1630④	→	1930④	→	0700⑤	
0900⑦	→	1235⑦	→	1630⑦	→	1930⑦	→	0700①	

R – Not Nov. 2 - Mar. 14.
▲ – Oct. 1 - 29 and Mar. 24 - May 26 Rijeka depart 2000.

2875 VENEZIA - PÁTRA via Igumenítsa and Kérkira (Corfu)

Anek Lines — **Service to January 7, 2008**

Venezia	Igumenítsa	Kérkira	Pátra	Pátra	Kérkira	Igumenítsa	Venezia
June 9 - September 26 (from Pátra, 2 days later from Venezia)							
1900② →	2030③ →	2230③ →	0600④	2359① →	0630② →	0830② →	0730③
1900③ →	2030④ →	2230④ →	0600⑤	2300④ →	0600⑤ →	0830⑤ →	0730⑥
1200⑥ →	1300⑦ →	1430⑦ →	2100⑦	2359⑤ →	0630⑥ →	0830⑥ →	0730⑦
1200⑦ →	1400① →	1430① →	2100①	2359⑦ →	0630① →	0830① →	0730②
September 27 - October 22 (from Pátra, 2 days later from Venezia)							
1800① →	2100② →	2300② →	0600③	2359① →	0630② →	0830② →	0730③
1900② →	2030③ →	2230③ →	0600④	2300③ →	0600④ →	0800④ →	0830⑤
1900③ →	2030④ →	2230④ →	0600⑤	2300④ →	0600⑤ →	0830⑤ →	0730⑥
1200⑤ →	1400⑥ →	1630⑥ →	2100⑥	2359⑤ →	0630⑥ →	0830⑥ →	0730⑦
1200⑥ →	1300⑦ →	1430⑦ →	2100⑦	2359⑥ →	0700⑦ →	0900⑦ →	0900①
1200⑦ →	1300① →	1430① →	2100①	2359⑦ →	0630① →	0830① →	0730②
October 25 - January 7 (from Pátra, 2 days later from Venezia)							
1900② →	2100③ →	2300③ →	0600④	2359① →	0630② →	0830② →	0730③
1900③ →	2100④ →	→	→ 0600⑤	2300④ →	0600⑤ →	0800⑤ →	0730⑥
1300⑥ →	1400⑦ →	→	→ 2100⑦	2359⑤ →	→	→ 0800⑥ →	0730⑦
1300⑦ →	1400① →	→	→ 2100①	2359⑦ →	→	→ 0830① →	0730②

Minoan Lines — **2007 service**

Venezia	Kérkira	Igumenítsa	Pátra	Pátra	Kérkira	Igumenítsa	Venezia
October 31 - November 5 (from Pátra, 2 days later from Venezia)							
1400① →	1115② →	1230② →	1930②	2359③ →	0700④ →	1000④ →	0700⑤
1400⑤ →	1200⑥ →	1330⑥ →	2000⑥	2359⑥ →	→	→ 0930⑦ →	0700①
November 6 - 30 (from Pátra, 2 days later from Venezia)							
1400④ →	1115⑤ →	1230⑤ →	1930⑤	2359② →	0700③ →	0930③ →	0700④
1400⑦ →	1115① →	1230① →	1930①	2359⑤ →	0700⑥ →	0930⑥ →	0700⑦
December 1 - 31 (from Pátra, 2 days later from Venezia)							
1400① →	1115② →	1230② →	1930②	2359① →	0700② →	0930② →	0700③
1400③ →	1115④ →	1230④ →	1930④	2359③ →	0700④ →	0930④ →	0700⑤
1400⑤ →	→	→ 1230⑥ →	1930⑥	2359④ →	0700⑤ →	0930⑤ →	0700⑥
1400⑥ →	1115⑦ →	1230⑦ →	1930⑦	2359⑥ →	→	→ 0930⑦ →	0700①

Subject to alteration during Xmas / New Year period.

2880 BARI - DURRËS

Azzurra Line — **2007 service (No winter service)**

Bari		Durrës	
1100	→	2000	Aug. 31 only.
2300	→	0800	②④ June 5 - July 26, Sept. 4 - 20 (also June 3, Aug. 29; not June 28).
2350	→	0900	July 13, 20 only.
Durrës		**Bari**	
1100	→	2000	July 13, 20 only.
1200	→	2100	June 22, July 14, 21, 27.
2300	→	0800	③⑤ June 6 - July 6; ③ July 11 - 25; ③⑤ Aug. 31 - Sept. 21 (also June 2, 4, Aug. 30; not June 22, 29).

Tirrenia — **2007 service**

Bari		Durrës	Durrës		Bari	
1200	→	1900	1200	→	1900	See note **B**.
2300	→	0800	2300	→	0800	

B – ⑥ July 14 - 21; ②④⑥ July 26 - Sept. 1 (also Aug. 6, Sept. 3, Dec. 20, 22, 24; not Aug. 7, 14, 16).

Ventouris Ferries Journey 10 hours — **2007 service**

March 1 - May 31 and October 1 - November 30
From Bari and Durrës: 4 – 5 sailings per week.
June 1 - September 30
From Bari and Durrës: 1 – 2 sailings per day (most departures overnight).

§ – Sailings depart Durrës at 2300 on some dates.

2899 OTHER SERVICES

Jadrolinija — **2007 services**

Many local services operate to the Islands along the Croatian coast.

S E M Maritime Company — **2007 services**

Operate many local Island services from Split.

Venezia Lines — **2007 services** (subject to confirmation)

Operate summer services from Venezia to Mali Lošinj, Piran, Poreč, Pula, Rabac, Rovinj and Umag, from Rimini to Poreč and Pula, and from Ravenna to Poreč.

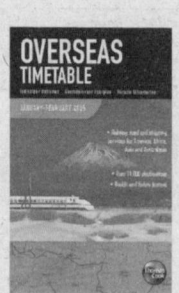

SCENIC RAIL ROUTES OF EUROPE

The following is a list of some of the most scenic rail routes of Europe, detailed timings for most of which can be found within the timetable. Routes marked * are the Editor's personal choice. This list does not include specialised mountain and tourist railways.

Many more scenic lines are clearly marked on the Thomas Cook New Rail Map of Europe - see the back of this book for details.

Types of scenery : C-Coastline, F-Forest, G-Gorge, L-Lake, M-Mountain, R-River.

ALBANIA

Route	Scenery
Elbasan - Pogradec	ML G R

AUSTRIA

Route	Scenery
Bruck an der Mur - Villach	R
Gmunden - Stainach Irdning*	ML
Innsbruck - Brennero	M
Innsbruck - Garmisch Partenkirchen*	M
Innsbruck - Schwarzach-St Veit	M G
Klagenfurt - Unzmarkt	M
Landeck - Bludenz*	M
Linz - Krems	R
St Pölten - Mariazell*	M
Salzburg - Villach*	M G
Selzthal - Hieflau - Steyr	M G R
Wiener Neustadt - Semmering - Graz	M

BELGIUM and LUXEMBOURG

Route	Scenery
Liège - Luxembourg*	R
Liège - Marloie	R
Namur - Dinant	R

BULGARIA

Route	Scenery
Septemvri - Dobriniste	M
Sofija - Burgas	M
Tulova - Gorna Orjahovitza	M

CROATIA and BOSNIA

Route	Scenery
Rijeka - Ogulin	M
Ogulin - Split	M
Sarajevo - Ploče	M G R

CZECH REPUBLIC

Route	Scenery
Karlovy Vary - Mariánské Lázně	R F
Karlovy Vary - Chomutov	R
Praha - Děčín	R

DENMARK

Route	Scenery
Struer - Thisted	C

FINLAND

Route	Scenery
Kouvola - Joensuu	L F

Many other lines run through scenic areas.

FRANCE

Route	Scenery
Aurillac - Neussargues	M G
Bastia - Ajaccio	M
Chambéry - Bourg St Maurice	M
Chambéry - Modane	ML
Chamonix - Martigny*	M G
Clermont Ferrand - Béziers	M G
Clermont Ferrand - Nîmes*	M G R
Gap - Briançon	ML
Genève - Aix les Bains	M R
Grenoble - Veynes - Marseille	M
Marseille - Ventimiglia	C
Mouchard - Besançon - Montbéliard	R
Nice - Digne	M
Nice / Ventimiglia - Cuneo*	M G
Perpignan - Latour de Carol*	M G
Portbou - Perpignan	C
Sarlat - Bergerac	R
Toulouse - Latour de Carol	M
Valence - Veynes	M

GERMANY

Route	Scenery
Arnstadt - Meiningen	M
Bonn - Siegen	R
Dresden - Děčín	G R
Freiburg - Donaueschingen	G F
Garmisch Partenkirchen - Kempten	M
Heidelberg - Neckarelz	R
Koblenz - Mainz*	G R
München - Lindau	M
Murnau - Oberammergau	ML
Naumburg - Saalfeld	R

GERMANY - continued

Route	Scenery
Niebüll - Westerland	C
Nürnberg - Pegnitz	G R
Offenburg - Konstanz	M F
Pforzheim - Nagold / Wildbad	F
Plattling - Bayerisch Eisenstein	F
Rosenheim - Freilassing - Berchtesgaden	ML
Rosenheim - Wörgl	M
Stuttgart - Singen	F
Titisee - Seebrugg	L F
Trier - Koblenz - Giessen	R
Ulm - Göppingen	M
Ulm - Tuttlingen	R

GREAT BRITAIN and IRELAND

Route	Scenery
Alnmouth - Dunbar	C
Barrow in Furness - Maryport	C
Coleraine - Londonderry	C
Dun Laoghaire - Wicklow	C
Edinburgh - Aberdeen	C
Exeter - Newton Abbot	C
Glasgow - Oban / Mallaig*	ML
Inverness - Kyle of Lochalsh*	M C
Liskeard - Looe	R
Llanelli - Craven Arms	M
Machynlleth - Pwllheli	M C
Perth - Inverness	M
Plymouth - Gunnislake	R
Rosslare - Waterford	C
St Erth - St Ives	C
Sheffield - New Mills	M
Shrewsbury - Aberystwyth	M R
Skipton - Carlisle	M R

GREECE

Route	Scenery
Korinthos - Patras	C
Diakoptó - Kalávrita	M G

HUNGARY

Route	Scenery
Budapest - Szob	R
Eger - Szilvásvárad	M
Székesfehérvár - Balatonszentgyörgy	L
Székesfehérvár - Tapolca	L

ITALY

Route	Scenery
Bologna - Pistoia	M
Bolzano - Merano	M
Brennero - Verona*	M
Brig - Arona	ML
Domodossola - Locarno*	M G
Firenze - Viareggio	M
Fortezza - San Candido	M
Genova - Pisa	C
Genova - Ventimiglia	C
Lecco - Tirano	ML
Messina - Palermo	C
Napoli - Sorrento	C
Roma - Pescara	M
Salerno - Reggio Calabria	C
Taranto - Reggio Calabria	C
Torino - Aosta	M

NORWAY

Route	Scenery
Bergen - Oslo*	ML
Bodø - Trondheim	ML
Dombås - Åndalsnes	M
Drammen - Larvik	C
Lillestrom - Kongsvinger	R
Myrdal - Flåm*	M C
Oslo / Røros - Trondheim	ML
Stavanger - Kristiansand	M

POLAND

Route	Scenery
Jelenia Góra - Walbrzych	M
Kraków - Zakopane	M
Olsztyn - Elk	L
Olsztyn - Morag	L
Tarnów - Krynica	M

PORTUGAL

Route	Scenery
Guarda - Entroncamento	M R
Pampilhosa - Guarda	M
Porto - Coimbra	C R
Porto - Pocinho*	R
Porto - Valença	M C
Regua - Vila Real	M G
Tua - Mirandela*	M G R

ROMANIA

Route	Scenery
Braşov - Ploeşti	M
Caransebeş - Craiova	M G R
Feteşti - Constanţa	R
Oradea - Cluj Napoca	R

SERBIA and MONTENEGRO

Route	Scenery
Priboj - Bar	ML

SLOVAKIA

Route	Scenery
Banská Bystrica - Brezno - Košice	M
Žilina - Poprad Tatry	M

SLOVENIA

Route	Scenery
Jesenice - Sežana	M R
Maribor - Zidani Most	M
Trieste - Ljubljana - Zagreb	G R

SPAIN

Route	Scenery
Algeciras - Ronda	M R
Barcelona - Latour de Carol	M
Bilbao - San Sebastián	M
Bilbao - Santander	M
Ferrol - Gijón*	C
Granada - Almería	M
Huesca - Canfranc	M G R
León - Monforte de Lemos	M
León - Oviedo	M
Lleida - La Pobla de Segur	ML
Madrid - Aranda - Burgos	ML
Málaga - Bobadilla	G
Santander - Oviedo	M C
Zaragoza - València	M R

SWEDEN

Route	Scenery
Bollnäs - Ånge - Sundsvall	ML
Borlänge - Mora	ML F
Borlänge - Ludvika - Frövi	ML F
Narvik - Kiruna	M F
Östersund - Storlien	L F

Many other lines run through scenic areas.

SWITZERLAND

Route	Scenery
Andermatt - Göschenen	G
Basel - Delémont - Moutier	M R
Chur - Arosa	M G
Chur - Brig - Zermatt*	M
Chur - St Moritz*	M G
Davos - Filisur	M G
Davos - Landquart	M
Interlaken Ost - Jungfraujoch*	M
Interlaken Ost - Luzern	ML
Interlaken West - Spiez	L
Lausanne - Brig	ML R
Lausanne - Neuchâtel - Biel	ML
Montreux - Zweisimmen - Lenk	ML G
Rorschach - Kreuzlingen	L
St Moritz - Scuol Tarasp	M
St Moritz - Tirano*	M
Spiez - Zweisimmen	G
Thun - Brig*	ML
Zürich / Luzern - Chiasso	ML
Zürich - Chur	ML

Many other lines run through scenic areas.

New high-speed services from December 23, 24

The latest additions to Spain's high-speed rail network are due to be inaugurated on December 23 and 24, 2007. They are the first stage, as far as Valladolid, of the new northwestern high-speed line from Madrid, and the final section, south of Antequera-Santa Ana station, of the high-speed route from Madrid to Málaga.

Opening of the northwestern route will not only permit *Alta Velocidad Española (AVE)* trains to reach Valladolid, but will mean the acceleration of all long-distance trains between the capital and Asturias, Cantabria, and the Basque Country, as these services will in future be provided by high-speed *Alvia* units, which can run on both the new international-gauge line and the 'classic' Iberian-gauge lines north of Valladolid. As a result, journey times to Gijón, Santander, and Bilbao will be cut by at least an hour.

In Andalucía too, gauge-changing trains, in this case known as *Altaria*, are able to use the high-speed network for most of their journeys to Algeciras and Granada – and completion of the high-speed line to Málaga will enable faster *AVE* services to run direct to Málaga, cutting the fastest journey time from 3 h. 47 to 2 h. 30.

A third opening – of the final stretch of the high-speed line between Tarragona and Barcelona – was also due to take place just before Christmas. However, geological problems encountered on the approaches to Spain's second city have put back the completion of tunnelling work and this section is not now expected to open before the end of February at the earliest.

From Dec. 23 MADRID - GIJÓN, SANTANDER, BILBAO and IRÚN — Via Valladolid high-speed line

	AVE 4069 ①–⑤	*Alvia* 4071 ①–⑥	*Alta* 601	*Alvia* 4073 ①–⑥	*Alvia* 4085	*AVE* 4089	*AVE* 4119	*Alvia* 4133	*Alvia* 4141	*AVE* 4159 Ⓑ	*Alvia* 4167	*Talgo* 533 U	*Alvia* 4183 Ⓑ	*Alvia* 4181 Ⓑ	*AVE* 4209
Alacant Terminal d.	...	...	...	...	...	...	...	...	1035	...	...	...	1405	...	...
Madrid Atocha Cercanías d.	...	...	0715p	...	...	...	...	...	1415	...	...	...	1734	...	...
Madrid Chamartín d.	0635	0650	|	0740	0800	0830	1120	1330	1440	1515	1610	...	1805	1820	2040
Segovia Alta Velocidad d.	|	|	|	|	0833	0902	|	|	1516	|	1643	...	1841	|	2112
Valladolid Campo Grande d.	0737	0803	|	0853	0919	0937	1222	1443	1601	1611	1734	...	1926	1937	2147
Palencia a.	...	0834	|	0924	|	...	...	1514	1632	...	|	...	1957	2004	...
León a.	...	0936	|	|	|	...	...	|	1737	...	|	...	|	2108	...
Pola de Lena a.	...	|	|	|	|	...	...	|	1857	...	|	...	|	|	...
Oviedo a.	...	1126	|	|	|	...	...	|	1930	...	|	...	|	2300	...
Gijón Cercanías a.	...	1155	|	|	|	...	...	|	2002	...	|	...	|	2329	...
Aguilar de Campoo a.	...	...	▲	1026	|	...	...	|	...	...	|	...	2100	...	...
Reinosa a.	...	...	|	1051	|	...	...	|	...	...	|	...	2126	...	...
Torrelavega a.	...	...	|	1140	|	...	...	1729	...	...	|	...	2216	...	...
Santander a.	...	...	|	1207	|	...	...	1755	...	...	|	...	2242	...	...
Burgos a.	...	...	|	...	1020	...	...	...	...	...	1835	...	...	...	...
Miranda de Ebro a.	...	...	|	...	|	...	...	...	...	...	1929	1951	...	...	...
Bibao Abando a.	...	...	|	...	1246	...	...	...	...	...	|	2142	...	...	...
Vitoria / Gasteiz a.	...	...	|	...	...	...	...	...	...	...	1951	...	...	...	...
San Sebastián / Donostia a.	...	...	1234	...	...	...	...	...	...	...	2130	...	...	...	...
Irún a.	...	...	1252	...	...	...	...	...	...	...	2154	...	...	...	...
Hendaye a.	...	...	1257	...	...	...	...	...	...	...	2200	...	...	...	...

	AVE 4068 ①–⑤	*AVE* 4088	*Alvia* 4072 ①–⑥	*Alvia* 4070 ①–⑥	*Alvia* 4086	*AVE* 4138 Ⓑ	*AVE* 4158 Ⓑ	*Alvia* 4142	*Alvia* 4140	*AVE* 4198	*Alvia* 4174	*Alta* 610	*Alvia* 4180 Ⓑ	*Alvia* 4182 Ⓑ
Irún d.	...	...	...	...	0815	...	...	...	...	...	...	1705	...	...
San Sebastián / Donostia d.	...	...	...	...	0832	...	...	...	...	...	...	1721	...	...
Vitoria / Gasteiz d.	...	...	...	...	1009	...	...	...	...	...	...	|	...	...
Bilbao Abando d.	...	...	...	...	|	...	...	...	...	...	1710	|	...	...
Miranda de Ebro d.	...	...	...	...	1030	...	...	...	...	...	|	|	...	...
Burgos d.	...	...	...	...	1125	...	...	...	...	...	1931	|	...	...
Santander d.	...	...	0705	...	|	...	...	1405	...	...	|	|	...	1920
Torrelavega d.	...	...	0730	...	|	...	...	1430	...	...	|	|	...	1945
Reinosa d.	...	...	0819	...	|	...	...	|	...	...	|	|	...	2034
Aguilar de Campoo d.	...	...	0843	...	|	...	...	|	...	...	|	▲	...	2058
Gijón Cercanías d.	...	...	|	0715	|	...	...	|	1400	...	|	|	1815	|
Oviedo d.	...	...	|	0743	|	...	...	|	1428	...	|	|	1843	|
Pola de Lena d.	...	...	|	|	|	...	...	|	1500	...	|	|	|	|
León d.	...	...	|	0937	|	...	...	|	1624	...	|	|	2035	|
Palencia d.	...	...	0947	1040	|	...	...	1644	1727	...	|	|	2136	2203
Valladolid Campo Grande d.	0650	0830	1021	1114	1233	1330	1515	1718	1801	1935	2039	|	2210	2237
Segovia Alta Velocidad a.	|	0903	1104	|	1316	|	|	|	1844	2008	2122	|	|	|
Madrid Chamartín a.	0752	0937	1143	1229	1353	1432	1611	1833	1923	2042	2159	|	2325	2352
Madrid Atocha Cercanías a.	...	...	1218	...	...	...	...	...	1958	...	...	2244p	...	...
Alacant terminal a.	...	...	1550	...	...	...	...	...	2330	...	...	...	...	...

U – MIGUEL DE UNAMUNO – From Barcelona. *Subject to confirmation.*

p – Madrid Puerta de Atocha.

▲ – Via Pamplona (Table **687**).

From Dec. 24 MADRID - GRANADA, MÁLAGA and ALGECIRAS — High-speed services

	AVE 2062 ①–⑤	*AVE* 2072	*Alta* 9214 ①–⑥	*Alta* 9366	*AVE* 2092	*AVE* 2102	*Alta* 9222 ⑦	*AVE* 2122	*AVE* 2142	*Alta* 9330	*AVE* 2152 ⑤⑦	*AVE* 2162	*Alta* 9234 ⑤	*AVE* 2172 Ⓑ	*AVE* 2182	*Alta* 9238 R	*AVE* 2192 ⑤⑦	*AVE* 2202	*AVE* 2212
Madrid Puerta de Atocha d.	0635	0735	0740	0840	0935	1035	1135	1235	1435	1505	1535	1635	1705	1735	1835	1905	1935	2035	2135
Ciudad Real d.	|	|	0842	0940	1026	|	|	1326	|	|	|	|	|	1826	|	|	|	|	2226
Puertollano d.	|	|	0858	0957	1044	|	|	1342	|	|	|	|	|	1844	|	|	|	|	2242
Córdoba d.	0825	|	0950	1043	1127	1219	|	1427	1619	1706	|	1819	1907	1927	1819	2106	2119	|	2327
Puente Genil - Herrera ¶ a.	0848	|	|	|	|	|	|	1448	|	|	|	|	|	|	|	|	|	|	2348
Antequera - Santa Ana § a.	0901	|	1029	1122	|	|	1444a	1501	|	|	|	|	|	|	|	2214	|	|	0001
Granada a.	|	|	1216	|	|	|	1613	|	|	|	|	|	2134	|	|	2336	|	|	|
Málaga a.	0930	1014	...	|	1223	1315	...	1530	1715	|	1810	1915	...	2023	2110	...	2215	2305	0030
Ronda a.	...	...	...	1227	...	...	...	...	...	1901	...	...	...	...	...	...	...	...	...
Algeciras a.	...	...	...	1405	...	...	...	...	...	2033	...	...	...	...	...	...	...	...	...

	AVE 2263 ①–⑤	*AVE* 2073	*AVE* 2083 ①–⑤	*Alta* 9213 ①–⑥	*AVE* 2093	*AVE* 2113	*Alta* 9367	*Alta* 9221 ⑦	*AVE* 2143	*AVE* 2153	*AVE* 2163 ⑤⑦	*AVE* 2173	*AVE* 2183	*Alta* 9331	*AVE* 2193 ⑤⑦	*AVE* 2203	*Alta* 9237	*AVE* 2213
Algeciras d.	...	...	...	...	...	...	0830	...	...	...	...	...	...	1515	...	...	...	...
Ronda d.	...	...	...	...	...	...	1000	...	...	...	...	...	...	1646	...	...	...	...
Málaga d.	0635	0710	0800	...	0900	1100	|	...	1400	1500	1600	1700	1805	|	1900	2000	...	2100
Granada d.	|	|	|	0642	|	|	|	1022	|	|	|	|	|	|	|	|	1800	|
Antequera - Santa Ana § d.	0701	|	|	0803	|	|	|	1145a	|	1526	|	|	|	1749	|	|	1952	2126
Puente Genil - Herrera ¶ d.	0714	|	|	|	|	|	|	|	|	1539	|	|	|	|	|	|	|	2139
Córdoba d.	0739	|	0856	0909	0956	1156	1144	|	1456	1604	|	1756	|	1834	2002	|	2031	2204
Puertollano a.	0820	|	|	|	1037	|	|	|	|	1645	|	|	|	1921	|	|	2118	2247
Ciudad Real a.	0836	|	|	|	1053	|	|	|	|	1701	|	|	|	1938	|	|	2137	2303
Madrid Puerta de Atocha a.	0932	0940	1040	1121	1147	1340	1357	1456	1640	1755	1840	1940	2040	2050	2145	2235	2248	2355

R – Not ⑤.

a – Antequera (not Antequera - Santa Ana)

¶ – ± *8 km* from Puente Genil.

§ – ± *17 km* from Antequera.

DUBLIN - SLIGO

IÉ — 236

Service from January 21. *For service to January 20 see page 168*

km	From January 21		Ⓐ 🍷	⚒ 🍷	⚒ 🍷	⚒ 🍷	⚒ 🍷	⚒ 🍷	⚒ 🍷	Ⓐ	Ⓐ	⑥	⚒ 🍷	⑦ 🍷	⑦ 🍷	⑦ 🍷	⑦ 🍷	⑦ 🍷	⑦ 🍷
0	**Dublin Connolly**	d.	0705	0905	1105	1305	1505	1600	1705	1715	1818	1818	1905	0905	1305	1505	1600	1705	1905
26	Maynooth	d.	0732	0934	1133	1332	1533	1627	|	1757	1901	1901	1937	0932	1333	1533	1626	|	1933
83	Mullingar	d.	0815	1012	1212	1413	1612	1712	1810	1843	1950	1950	2017	1012	1412	1612	1712	1810	2015
125	**Longford**	d.	0844	1041	1241	1441	1641	1741	1840	1923	2020	...	2046	1041	1441	1641	1741	1841	2044
143	Dromod	d.	0858	1055	1255	1455	1655	1800	1855	...	...	...	2100	1055	1455	1655	1800	1855	2058
159	Carrick on Shannon	d.	0914	1111	1311	1511	1711	1816	1911	...	...	...	2117	1112	1511	1711	1816	1911	2115
173	Boyle	d.	0933	1145	1333	1533	1733	1827	1933	...	...	...	2130	1133	1533	1733	1827	1933	2128
219	**Sligo**	a.	1010	1210	1410	1610	1810	1910	2010	...	...	...	2208	1210	1610	1810	1910	2010	2205

From January 21		Ⓐ	Ⓐ 🍷	⚒ 🍷	⚒ 🍷	⚒ 🍷	⚒ 🍷	⚒ 🍷	⚒ 🍷	⚒ 🍷	Ⓐ		⑦ 🍷	⑦ 🍷	⑦ 🍷	⑦ 🍷	⑦ 🍷	⑦ 🍷	
ligo	d.	...	0545	0700	0900	1100	1300	1500	1700	1900	...	...	0900	1100	1300	1500	1700	1900	...
oyle	d.	...	0616	0732	0932	1132	1332	1532	1732	1932	...	...	0932	1132	1332	1532	1732	1932	...
arrick on Shannon	d.	...	0627	0744	0944	1144	1344	1544	1744	1944	...	...	0944	1144	1344	1544	1744	1944	...
romod	d.	...	0642	0758	0958	1158	1358	1558	1758	1958	...	...	0958	1158	1358	1558	1758	1958	...
ongford	d.	0615	0657	0814	1014	1214	1414	1614	1814	2022	2050	...	1014	1214	1414	1614	1816	2014	...
ullingar	d.	0648	0726	0853	1051	1250	1451	1650	1850	2056	2122	...	1051	1245	1451	1651	1851	2054	...
aynooth	d.	0730	0810	0933	1128	1327	1528	1727	1934	2133	2201	...	1130	1322	1528	1728	1928	2131	...
ublin Connolly	a.	0820	0847	1003	1158	1359	1559	1800	2006	2205	2230	...	1203	1354	1559	1805	2005	2208	...

EUROPEAN RAIL PASSES

THIS IS AN EXTRACT FROM THE RAIL PASSES FEATURE WHICH APPEARS IN OUR MAY EDITION AND ALSO OUR INDEPENDENT TRAVELLER'S EDITIONS (available from bookshops and our website, and based on the June and December monthly editions)

Rail passes represent excellent value for train travellers who are touring around Europe (or parts of it) or making a number of journeys within a short period. They can offer substantial savings over point-to-point tickets, as well as greater flexibility.

Passes may cover most of Europe (e.g. InterRail or Eurail), a specific group of countries, single countries, or just a certain area. InterRail passes are only available to European residents, whereas Eurail passes are only for non-European residents. Most passes cannot be used in your country of residence.

Passes either cover a specified number of consecutive days, or are of the *flexi* type where you get so many 'travel days' within a specified period (you write each date of use in a box on the pass). Free travel will mean the use of a travel day, whereas discounted travel may not. Many passes are available from appointed agents or their websites, whereas some may be purchased from principal railway stations. Your passport may be required for identification, also one or two passport-size photos.

Passes generally cover the ordinary services of the national rail companies, but supplements often have to be paid for travel on express and high-speed services and on 'global price' trains. 'Private' railways may not accept passes but may give discounts to passholders. Extra charges always apply for travel in sleeping cars or couchettes.

In this feature USD = US dollars, € = euros, £ = pounds sterling.

InterRail

InterRail Global Pass

Area of validity

The *InterRail Global Pass* is valid for unlimited travel on the national railways of 30 European countries, namely Austria, Belgium, Bosnia-Herzegovina, Bulgaria, Croatia, Czech Republic, Denmark, Finland, France, Germany, Great Britain, Greece, Hungary, Republic of Ireland, Italy, Luxembourg, Republic of Macedonia, Montenegro, the Netherlands, Norway, Poland, Portugal, Romania, Serbia, Slovakia, Slovenia, Spain, Sweden, Switzerland and Turkey, also on ferry services between Italy and Greece operated by Attica (i.e. SuperFast Ferries and Blue Star Ferries). Passes are **not** valid in the purchaser's country of residence. Note that passes are no longer valid in Morocco or Northern Ireland.

Who can buy the pass?

The pass can be purchased by anyone who has lived for at least six months in one of the European countries where the pass is valid, or is a national of that country and holds a valid passport. Those resident for at least six months in other European countries (including Russia) are also entitled to purchase the pass, and can do so in any of the participating countries - others have to buy it in their country of residence. Passes can be purchased up to three months before travel begins.

Periods of validity and prices

- Any 5 days within 10 days (flexi): adult 1st class €329/£241, adult 2nd class €249/£182, youth 2nd class €159/£117.
- Any 10 days within 22 days (flexi): adult 1st class €489/£357, adult 2nd class €359/£263, youth 2nd class €239/£175.
- 22 days (continuous): adult 1st class €629/£460, adult 2nd class €469/£343, youth 2nd class €309/£226.
- 1 month (continuous): adult 1st class €809/£591, adult 2nd class €599/£438, youth 2nd class €399/£292.

Youth prices are available to those aged 25 or under on the first day for which the pass is valid. Child fares for ages 4 to 11 are available at approximately half the price of the adult pass.

Note that under the new scheme there are no 'zonal' InterRail passes.

Supplements payable

Supplements are payable for certain types of express or high-speed train, including: *Alaris, Altaria, Arco, AVE, Euromed, Talgo* (Spain), *Alfa Pendular* (Portugal), *ES* (Eurostar Italia), *S220* (Finnish Pendolino), *TGV*, *Téoz* (France), *X2000 (Sweden), Cisalpino* (Switzerland - Italy), also *Icity* and *IcityE* trains in Greece. Discounted 'passholder' fares apply on *Eurostar* and *Thalys* trains, also on *Elipsos* (night trains France/Italy - Spain), Artesia (France - Italy), Lyria (*TGV* service France - Switzerland) and on certain other 'global price' routes. Passholders now travel free on German *ICE* services. The official website www.interrailnet.com gives further details.

Sleeping car and couchette supplements are not included. Seat reservation fees are also excluded - these can sometimes be compulsory, for example on all main-line trains in Spain (€6 in tourist class, €10 on *AVE* and *Talgo 200* trains), on German *Nachtzüge* night trains, French *TGV* trains and express trains in Norway and Sweden.

Note that on the Greece - Italy ferry services (SuperFast and Blue Star), you will need to pay port taxes, also fuel and high-season surcharges. Upgrades to cabin accommodation or reclining seats are extra.

Discount in country of residence

Although the pass is not valid in the country of residence, passholders can obtain a reduction for one return ticket to the border of 25% - 50%, except in Great Britain, Poland or Romania (children pay half this reduced fare).

Validity on other railways

InterRail passes are valid on the principal railway companies in each country but may not be valid on 'private' or locally run railways (some give discounts) Selected details are as follows (some require reservations): **Denmark**: 50% discount on Hjørring - Hirtshals and Frederikshavn - Skagen. **France**: 25% discount on CP (Nice - Digne), 50% on railways in Corsica. **Hungary** GySEV services are included. **Norway**: the Myrdal - Flåm line is treated as a 'private' line and gives 30% discount. **Spain**: FGC railways give 50% discount. **Sweden**: the Arlanda Express and Inlandsbanan are included, as are services operated by Veolia, which includes the night trains to the north. **Switzerland**: free travel on certain railways including BLS, FART/SSIF MOB, RhB, SOB, THURBO. Many others offer 50% discount, including CJ LSE, Rigibahnen, Pilatusbahn. The MGB (Disentis - Brig - Zermatt and Göschenen - Andermatt) and Gornergratbahn offer 50% to under-26s only No discounts are available on the BRB or the narrow gauge railways in the Jungfrau area (BOB, JB, WAB). Information is subject to change and it's best to check before travelling.

Discounts on other ferry services

Reductions of between 20% and 50% are available on various ferry services many of which are shown below (details are subject to alteration). Ferry discounts usually exclude cabin accommodation, and other restrictions (such as compulsory reservation) may apply:

Color Line day sailings 50%; DFDS 25% on certain services; Fjord Line special prices; Flaggruten 50%; Fylkesbaatane 40%; Grimaldi 20%; Hellenic Mediterranean 50% (summer); Irish Ferries 50%; Iscomar 30% (not high summer); Minoan Lines special prices; Sea France 50%; Silja Line 50% (restrictions apply); Stena 30% (25% on *Lynx* Fishguard - Rosslare), Superfast Rosyth - Zeebrugge 25%; Tallink Rostock - Helsinki special prices; Viking Line 50%. No discount on SNCM to Corsica.

Note that passes are valid on Austrian lake services operated by ÖBB, and discounts are available on certain Swiss lake steamers. For further details of discounts see the InterRail website www.interrailnet.com.

Other discounts

DDSG offer 20% on Melk - Krems river cruises. Certain bus services in Norway offer a 50% discount. Some railway museums offer free or discounted entry and a limited number of tourist attractions, hotels, hostels and cycle hire outlets offer discounts.

InterRail One Country Pass

This new pass replaced the EuroDomino scheme from April 1, 2007.

Area of validity

The *InterRail One Country Pass* is valid for travel in any **one** of the participating countries above, with the exception of Bosnia- Herzegovina and Montenegro. It is **not** available for travel in the purchaser's country of residence. Note that Benelux (Belgium, Luxembourg and the Netherlands) counts as one country. There are two passes for Greece - the *Greece Plus* variant includes ferry services between Italy and Greece operated by Attica (i.e. SuperFast Ferries and Blue Star Ferries).

Periods of validity and prices

All passes are flexi passes, valid for 3, 4, 6 or 8 days within 1 month. Prices shown are for adult 1st class, adult 2nd class and youth (under 26) respectively, and are in euros (for approx £ prices multiply by 0.73). Eligibility/supplements/discounts are as for the *InterRail Global Pass*.

- Price level 1 - France, Germany, Great Britain, Norway, Sweden: 3 days €255/189/125, 4 days €285/209/139, 6 days €363/269/175, 8 days €404/299/194.
- Price level 2 - Austria, Benelux, Finland, Greece 'Plus', Republic of Ireland, Italy, Spain, Switzerland: 3 days €147/109/71, 4 days €188/139/90, 6 days €255/189/123, 8 days €309/229/149.
- Price level 3 - Croatia, Denmark, Greece, Hungary, Poland, Portugal, Romania: 3 days €93/69/45, 4 days €120/89/58, 6 days €161/119/77, 8 days €188/139/90.
- Price level 4 - Bulgaria, Czech Republic, Republic of Macedonia, Serbia, Slovakia, Slovenia, Turkey: 3 days €66/49/32, 4 days €93/69/45, 6 days €134/99/64, 8 days €161/119/77.

PUBLICATIONS LIST AND ORDER FORM

To view our full range of titles visit our website: www.thomascookpublishing.com

To order publications please tick the boxes for the titles required, note the prices in the shaded columns and fill in the reverse of this form. Please add postage and packing overleaf.

TIMETABLES AND RAIL MAPS

£

☐ **EUROPEAN RAIL TIMETABLE** • Published monthly, this timetable has guided generations of travellers throughout Europe. Ideal as a planning aid and for easy en route reference. *Edition required* . . . .

Price: £13.50 *excluding postage and packing*

☐ **Independent Travellers Edition** • Available through bookshops, this special edition of the European Rail Timetable contains an additional section of country by country travel information. Editions: Summer (June) and Winter (December).

Price: £15.99 *excluding postage and packing*

EUROPEAN RAIL TIMETABLE SUBSCRIPTION
Annual subscription (12 issues) including post and packing to:
☐ UK £150 ☐ Europe £174 ☐ Rest of World £192
HELD AT 2007 PRICES *Starting issue* . . . .

☐ **OVERSEAS TIMETABLE** • For world (and armchair) travellers, the only rail and public transport timetable to cover the whole world outside Europe. Published every two months at the beginning of January, March, May, July, September and November. *Edition required* . . . .

Price: £13.50 *excluding postage and packing*

☐ **Independent Travellers Edition** • Published twice a year in May (Summer) and November (Winter), this special edition of the Overseas Timetable contains a host of additional travel tips and essential country by country information. Also available from bookshops.

Price: £15.99 *excluding postage and packing*

OVERSEAS TIMETABLE SUBSCRIPTION
Annual subscription (6 issues) including post and packing to:
☐ UK £75 ☐ Europe £87 ☐ Rest of World £96
HELD AT 2007 PRICES *Starting issue* . . . .

☐ **RAIL MAP OF EUROPE** • 16th edition. Covers all of Europe, with central Europe enlarged on the reverse. Scenic routes are highlighted.

Price: £8.99 *excluding postage and packing*

☐ **RAIL MAP OF BRITAIN & IRELAND** • 5th edition. Lines colour-coded to show operating companies. Includes tourist information guide.

Price: £8.99 *excluding postage and packing*

PHRASEGUIDES

PhraseGuides are designed to make the languages of major holiday destinations accessible to all travellers. Each guide includes a two-way dictionary and sections on greetings, eating out, shopping, getting around and accommodation.

☐ Arabic ☐ Croatian ☐ French ☐ German
☐ Greek ☐ Italian ☐ Latin American Spanish
☐ Portuguese ☐ Spanish ☐ Turkish

Price: £3.99 *excluding postage and packing*

PHRASEBOOKS

☐ **EUROPEAN 12-Language Phrasebook** • French, German, Italian, Spanish, Portuguese, Polish, Czech, Hungarian, Romanian, Bulgarian, Greek and Turkish.

Price: £4.99 *excluding postage and packing*

☐ **EASTERN EUROPEAN 12-Language Phrasebook** • Bulgarian, Croatian, Czech, Estonian, Hungarian, Latvian, Lithuanian, Polish, Romanian, Russian, Slovenian, Ukrainian.

Price: £4.99 *excluding postage and packing*

☐ **SOUTH-EAST ASIAN 9 Language Phrasebook** • Contains Burmese, Indonesian, Malaysian, Chinese (Mandarin), Filipino, Cambodian, Laotian, Thai and Vietnamese.

Price: £5.99 *excluding postage and packing*

INDEPENDENT TRAVELLERS

£

☐ **EUROPE BY RAIL** • Features over 300 cities, towns and villages. Detailed city and journey maps. Cross- referenced to the European Rail Timetable table numbers.

☐ **GREEK ISLAND HOPPING 2008** • The only guide to include details of all the island ferry services as well as advice on exploring this fascinating region, finding accommodation, and sightseeing.

Price: £14.99 *per title, excluding postage and packing*

TRAVELLERS

A range of popular, compact guidebooks perfect for planning all sorts of holidays - whether long-haul, short-haul, regional tours or city breaks. Full of useful information on walks and tours, eating out, shopping options and top travel tips. All you need for your holiday right at your fingertips.

☐ Algarve and Southern Portugal	☐ Amsterdam
☐ Andalucia inc Seville	☐ Argentina
☐ Austria	☐ Bali & Lombok
☐ Barcelona	☐ Bavaria
☐ Belgium	☐ Berlin*
☐ Bosnia, Serbia & Montenegro	☐ Boston
☐ Brazil	☐ Brittany
☐ Budapest	☐ Bulgaria
☐ California*	☐ Caribbean Cruising inc Miami*
☐ Cape Town	☐ Catalonia
☐ Chile	☐ China - Beijing
☐ China - Shanghai	☐ Costa Rica
☐ Crete	☐ Croatia
☐ Cuba*	☐ Cyprus
☐ Delhi, Agra & Rajasthan	☐ Denmark
☐ Dominican Republic	☐ Dubai
☐ Dublin*	☐ Egypt
☐ Estonia	☐ Finland
☐ Florence & Tuscany	☐ Gambia
☐ Goa*	☐ Gran Canaria & Tenerife
☐ Greek Islands	☐ Greece (Mainland) inc Athens*
☐ Hawaii	☐ Ibiza
☐ Iceland	☐ Ireland
☐ Italian Lakes	☐ Jamaica
☐ Japan*	☐ Jordan
☐ Kenya*	☐ Kerala & Southern India*
☐ Krakow	☐ Lanzarote & Fuerteventura
☐ Las Vegas*	☐ Latvia
☐ Lisbon & Porto*	☐ Lithuania
☐ Loire Valley*	☐ London
☐ Madeira	☐ Madrid
☐ Maldives	☐ Mallorca
☐ Malta & Gozo	☐ Mauritius
☐ Menorca	☐ Mexico
☐ Morocco	☐ Moscow & St. Petersburg
☐ Naples & the Amalfi Coast	☐ New York
☐ New Zealand*	☐ Normandy
☐ Norway	☐ Oman
☐ Ontario & Quebec	☐ Orlando*
☐ Paris	☐ Peru
☐ Poland	☐ Prague
☐ Provence	☐ Puglia
☐ Romania	☐ Rome
☐ San Francisco*	☐ Sardinia
☐ Seychelles	☐ Sicily
☐ Singapore & Malaysia*	☐ South Africa
☐ Sri Lanka	☐ Sweden
☐ Switzerland	☐ Tanzania
☐ Thailand*	☐ Tunisia
☐ Turkey	☐ Vancouver & British Columbia
☐ Venice	☐ Vietnam
☐ Warsaw	

Titles marked with an asterisk are £8.99 each.

Price: £ 9.99 *per title, excluding postage and packing*

PUBLICATIONS LIST AND ORDER FORM

To view our full range of titles visit our website: www.thomascookpublishing.com

To order publications please tick the boxes for the titles required, note the prices in the shaded columns and fill in the reverse of this form. Please add postage and packing below.

HOTSPOTS

Pocket guides covering main resorts and excursion destinations. Includes maps, eating out, shopping, sightseeing, useful phrases and menu decoders.

☐ Algarve ☐ Bali ☐ Bulgaria - Black Sea Resorts
☐ Corfu ☐ Corsica ☐ Costa Blanca
☐ Costa del Sol & Almeria ☐ Costa Brava & Costa Dorada
☐ Cote d'Azur ☐ Crete ☐ Croatia - Dalmatian Coast
☐ Cuba ☐ Cyprus ☐ Dominican Republic
☐ Egypt Red Sea Resorts ☐ Fuerteventura ☐ Gibraltar
☐ Goa ☐ Gran Canaria ☐ Greek Islands ☐ Guernsey
☐ Ibiza ☐ Ionian Islands ☐ Lanzarote ☐ Jamaica
☐ Jersey ☐ Madeira ☐ Mallorca ☐ Malta
☐ Menorca ☐ Mexico ☐ Morocco
☐ Neopolitan Riviera ☐ Orlando ☐ Rhodes & Kos
☐ Santorini ☐ Sicily ☐ Sri Lanka ☐ Tenerife
☐ Thailand ☐ Tunisia ☐ Turkey - Aegean Coast
☐ Turkey - Lycian Coast ☐ Turkey - Mediterranean Coast

Price: £4.99 *per title excluding postage and packing*

DRIVE AROUND

These unique guidebooks for driving holidays include road safety information, full colour detailed maps, descriptive introductions to routes, and a glossary of road signs appropriate to the destination.

☐ Andalucia & the Costa del Sol ☐ Australia
☐ Bavaria & the Austrian Tyrol ☐ Brittany & Normandy
☐ Burgundy & the Rhône Valley ☐ California
☐ Canadian Rockies ☐ Catalonia & Spanish Pyrenees
☐ Dordogne & Western France ☐ England & Wales
☐ Florida ☐ Ireland
☐ Italian Lakes & Mountains ☐ Languedoc & Southwest France
☐ Loire Valley ☐ New England
☐ Portugal ☐ Provence & the Côte d'Azur
☐ New Zealand ☐ Scotland
☐ Tuscany & Umbria ☐ Vancouver & British Columbia
☐ Washington D.C.

Price: £15.99 *per title excluding postage and packing*

To view the entire range of Thomas Cook Publishing titles go to:
www.thomascookpublishing.com

CITYSPOTS

New from Thomas Cook Publishing. Perfect for pleasure-seeking city breakers wanting to quickly pinpoint the city's most entertaining highlights and decide what to see and do in a limited time with essential advice on shopping, sightseeing, eating and drinking, plus great entertainment ideas too.

New and revised editions:

☐ Aarhus ☐ Hamburg ☐ Helsinki ☐ Kiev
☐ Marrakech ☐ Marseille ☐ Nice ☐ Palma
☐ Riga ☐ Rotterdam ☐ Toulouse ☐ Tallinn
☐ Valencia

Price: £6.99 *per title excluding postage and packing*

Still available:

☐ Amsterdam ☐ Antwerp ☐ Athens ☐ Bangkok
☐ Barcelona ☐ Belfast ☐ Belgrade ☐ Berlin
☐ Bilbao ☐ Bologna ☐ Bratislava ☐ Bruges
☐ Brussels ☐ Bucharest ☐ Budapest ☐ Cardiff
☐ Cologne ☐ Copenhagen ☐ Cork ☐ Dubai
☐ Dublin ☐ Dubrovnik ☐ Dusseldorf ☐ Edinburgh
☐ Florence ☐ Frankfurt ☐ Gdansk ☐ Geneva
☐ Genoa ☐ Glasgow ☐ Gothenburg ☐ Granada
☐ Hannover ☐ Hong Kong ☐ Istanbul ☐ Krakow
☐ Kuala Lumpur ☐ Leipzig ☐ Lille ☐ Lisbon
☐ Ljubljana ☐ London ☐ Los Angeles ☐ Lyon
☐ Madrid ☐ Milan ☐ Monte Carlo ☐ Munich
☐ Naples ☐ New York ☐ Oslo ☐ Palermo
☐ Paris ☐ Porto ☐ Prague ☐ Reykjavik
☐ Rome ☐ Salzburg ☐ Sarajevo ☐ Seville
☐ Singapore ☐ Sofia ☐ Stockholm ☐ St. Petersburg
☐ Strasbourg ☐ Tokyo ☐ Turin ☐ Venice
☐ Verona ☐ Vienna ☐ Vilnius ☐ Warsaw
☐ Zagreb ☐ Zurich

Price: £5.99 *per title excluding postage and packing*

BED & BREAKFAST FRANCE

☐ **BED AND BREAKFAST FRANCE 2008** • Describes over 650 selected quality properties in all regions of France, with details of rates, rooms, facilities and locations. Also features maps showing where you can enjoy the best in local cuisine, and where to buy local specialities.

Price: £14.99 *excluding postage and packing*

WAYS TO PAY

- £ Sterling cheque drawn on UK bank.
- Bank transfer to HSBC Bank plc., City of London Corporate Office, PO Box 125, 27-32 Poultry, LONDON, EC2P 2BX, UK. Account name Thomas Cook Tour Operations Ltd., Account no. 31212508, sort code 40-02-50.
- Credit card: Mastercard, Visa or American Express.
- Switch / Maestro / Delta / Solo.
- *Any bank or similar charges incurred to be paid by remitter.*

VAT Registration No. GB 239 3841 42

* If you order more than three items you only pay postage for three

VAT / TVA / IVA
If you are registered for VAT or equivalent please enter your registration number:

SUB TOTAL FROM ALL COLUMNS £

ADD POSTAGE AND PACKING:

TO UK - £1.50 per item * £

TO EUROPE - £3.50 per item * £

REST OF WORLD - £5.00 per item * £

TOTAL ENCLOSED £

Please complete the following and send form to Thomas Cook Publishing, Unit 18, Coningsby Road, Peterborough PE3 8SB, United Kingdom.
✆ +44 (0)1733 416477 fax +44 (0)1733 416688
publishing-sales@thomascook.com

FOR CREDIT CARD PAYMENTS – please complete:

☐ Mastercard ☐ Visa ☐ American Express ☐ Switch / Delta

Cardholders name ____________

Signature ____________

Card number |_|_|_|_| |_|_|_|_| |_|_|_|_| |_|_|_|_|

Card expiry date ________ Card issue number ________

Card security number (Last 3 digits) ________

Address ____________

Postcode ____________

Daytime Telephone No. ____________

Delivery details (if different from above):

Name ____________

Address ____________

____________ Postcode ________